A

Cross-Cultural

Summary

Compiled by
Robert B. Textor

HRAF PRESS
New Haven, Connecticut

Library of Congress Catalog Card Number: 67–18560
Printed in the United States of America
Production of this volume has been financed in part
by grant GN 416 from the National Science Foundation.

This book is dedicated to my father,

Clinton Kenney Textor

Foreword

IT IS perhaps paradoxical that an anthropologist who has never done any cross-cultural research, who has never used the HRAF files, nor the **Ethnographic Atlas,** should write the foreword to **A Cross-Cultural Summary.** By persuasion as well as nature (perhaps these preferences run deep in one's personal world view) I am one of those who prefer configurated uniqueness to isolable uniformity. It is the differences between human societies and their cultures that fascinate me, not the similarities. It is the particularistic statement that arouses my interest, not the generalized or the abstract. Whether researching or teaching, I want to treat culture cases as holistic systems comparable as such rather than as collections of classifiable parts whose associations (or lack of them) cross-culturally can be tested.

Precisely because of this bias I can argue a certain objectivity in my view of the **Summary.** After thoughtful examination of it, and the rationale for it furnished by Robert Textor, I am convinced that this mammoth, largely computer-written volume will be a significant and influential resource for our discipline, and in fact for all the social sciences. (I have been aided to an understanding of the volume and its significance by André Köbben of the University of Amsterdam and Ernest Boesch of the University of the Saar, with whom I have recently consulted.)

This volume contains statements, in sentences in English, of some 20,000 statistically significant correlations that tell us what classes of cultures co-occur or overlap with other classes. The classes of cultures are arranged dichotomously (e.g. slavery present, slavery absent), and utilize, selectively, all available sources of coded cross-cultural data (38 all told) for the 400-culture sample developed by George Peter Murdock in the **Ethnographic Atlas.** The computer has winnowed out all "uninteresting" (nonsignificant) associations, and Textor has winnowed out the tautological and redundant ones. The 20,000 remaining are arranged in an order congenial to anthropologists, e.g. location, linguistic affiliation, natural environment, settlement pattern, diet, subsistence base, technology, etc. The result makes interesting, if aesthetically unsatisfying, reading.

It is possible, using this volume, for an individual scholar to test out, in at least preliminary fashion, a very wide variety of hypotheses. Often what should be a hypothesis has become a fixed idea, based upon a single case or a few cases, but accepted as applicable on a wide scale without testing. The hypothesis based upon the single case may not only be lacking in general applicability because the functional relationships observed in the single case are more or less unique but also because the hypothesis may be based upon a fortuitous, not functional, relationship. The literature abounds with statements of this sort. When a scholar makes a statement intended to have general applicability he should be sure it does. Heretofore checks of applicability have been very time-consuming and, on any substantial scale, costly. Textor's volume permits a scholar to check many of his hypotheses with impressive ease. There will no longer be any excuse for loose statements about the association (or lack of it) between, for instance, structural complexity and independence training, premarital sexual freedom and centralized political authority, slavery and economic surplus, matrilineality and frequency of divorce, social integration and openness to technological change, or the hundreds of other possible co-occurrences about which hypotheses may be advanced.

It is also possible for a scholar to **generate** hypotheses through examination of the sections relevant to his interests in this volume. Most hypotheses formulated by anthropologists to date have been generated in the study of single cases. In my opinion there will never be a substitute for immersion in depth in single cases as a source of generalized insight as well as specific hypotheses. The contextual, intricate, convolutional richness of the single culture cannot be duplicated. But the parameters of this volume are different. Another kind of rich complexity is created by the 20,000 correlations it contains. New insights and hunches emerge as one reads through the correlational statements that would be unlikely in the reading of a single case, simply because only a fraction of the associations could occur in the single case. Further, the very lack of unique context and of qualitative or aesthetic features in the computer-written statements reveals in stark outline the possible associations (or lack of them) upon which hypotheses may be based.

There are, to be sure, problems in the collation, presentation, and use of the **Summary.** The usual objections that we configurationalists raise about cross-cultural collations can be raised about this volume. Perhaps the most significant one is that the integrity of the cultural system is violated by the classification of the culture in terms of isolable dichotomous variables. The context as well as the internal articulation and the textural quality of any single aspect of social life, such as the settlement of disputes, the working of residence rules, the values covering sex roles, may make what appears to be similar or convergent in any two or more societies actually quite different. Durkheim, Mauss, Lowie, Benedict, Levi-Strauss, Mead, and Leach, to name only a few of the more prominent, have all made their objections in this general respect very clear.

There is probably no way of mollifying the intransigence of some of our colleagues concerning cross-cultural collations. There is indeed, in my opinion, no completely adequate answer to their objections. But we must always try to avoid certain major threats to validity that are inherent in our data. The errors of applicability produced by inference and generalization from single cases are not inherently less damaging than the errors produced by generalization from correlation of decontextualized variables. They are of a different order. If we know what we are doing—if our procedures are explicit enough—we can build our generalizations, and our theories, more adequately by using both approaches and using one to check and control the other.

One of the very strong features of **A Cross-Cultural Summary** is the care with which Robert Textor has made all procedures explicit. The conditions of the 400-culture sample and its rationale, and the samples of each of the 38 studies from which codings were taken, the possible sources of bias in ethnographic reporting due to nationality of ethnographer and period of reporting, the statistical procedures and criteria applied, the winnowing process, and particularly the coding rules and the sources of these rules, are described in forthright operational language in the chapters written by Textor. His careful statements and modest claims should be appreciated particularly by those who feel cross-cultural methodology to be incompatible or who perceive it as potentially misleading. Perhaps with the help of this volume the chasm between configurationalists and structuralists at the one extreme, and the cross-cultural comparativists at the other, will be bridged. In any event, the greater mass of social scientists who are not firmly committed to either position will find the **Summary** very useful, for the reasons already mentioned.

George D. Spindler
Beutelsbach bei Stuttgart, Germany
February 1967

Acknowledgments

THE HISTORY of this book began in 1958, when I returned to Cornell University after five years of ethnographic field work in Thailand. Much of this field work focused on Thai supernatural belief and behavior. This domain of inquiry had proven to be a complex one indeed, a domain populated by a large number of variegated and improbable supernaturals. Optimistically, I made the not-uncommon anthropological assumption that however complex this domain might appear to the outside observer—or indeed to the Thai participant—it must nonetheless possess an underlying structure, a covert patterning. Under the guidance of Lauriston Sharp, my mentor for many years, I set about to discover this patterning. Because of the quantity and complexity of the data, it was not long before I found myself deeply involved with punched cards and data processing equipment.

Work on this project continued during the period 1959–61 at Yale University, where I enjoyed the support of the Southeast Asia Studies program and its director, Karl J. Pelzer. The faculty of the Department of Anthropology, particularly George Peter Murdock, provided guidance and encouragement. It was during this period that it first occurred to me that perhaps the computer could somehow be programed to provide output suggestive of covert patterning not only in the form of numerical tables but also in the form of English sentences coordinated with such tables.

In 1962 I was appointed a Research Fellow in Statistics at Harvard University, where I had ready access to advice from many statisticians and to the wise and kind guidance of Frederick Mosteller. Others who helped me during this period included William G. Cochran, Miles Davis, and Robert M. Elashoff. The latter two were then graduate students and are currently on the faculties of Johns Hopkins University and the University of California Medical Center at San Francisco, respectively. Miles Davis also did much of the early computer programing.

In 1962 it was finally possible to produce computer output containing both two-by-two contingency tables and coordinated English-language sentences stating the manifest content of these tables. This "Pattern Search and Table Translation Technique," as it was called, was then applied to the analysis of Thai supernaturals. Publication of the results is planned for the near future.

The Pattern Search and Table Translation Technique was next applied to cross-national analysis in comparative politics. This led to the publication, in collaboration with Arthur S. Banks, of **A Cross-Polity Survey** by the M.I.T. Press in 1963.

In early 1962, the journal **Ethnology** began publication, under the editorship of George Peter Murdock. Included in this journal were installments of Murdock's **Ethnographic Atlas.** In August of that year I decided to apply the Pattern Search and Table Translation Technique to selected variables from the **Atlas.** After viewing preliminary output, Murdock encouraged me to broaden the scope of my inquiry by incorporating selected variables from virtually all other available sources of coded cross-cultural materials. The result, after several successive computer runs and many interruptions, is the present work. George Peter Murdock has been the principal advisor throughout. While I cannot hold him responsible for the shortcomings of this book, I do owe him a great debt of gratitude. Indeed, without his support and guidance, it is doubtful that this work would have appeared at all.

Besides those already mentioned, many other scholars have offered valuable assistance and support. First of all, I am indebted to the staff of the Human Relations Area Files for their assistance at every step, and in particular to George R. Bedell, Robert O. Lagacé, Frank M. LeBar, Timothy J. O'Leary, and Elizabeth P. Swift. I am also obliged to all of the scholars whose codings are employed in this book. Wherever appropriate and practicable, I consulted them on problems of adapting their coded data for treatment by the Pattern Search and Table Translation Technique. The following contributors, in particular, provided valuable consultation: Charles Ackerman, Herbert Barry, III, Irvin S. Child, William M. Evan, C. S. Ford, John K. Harley, Frank W. Moore, John M. Roberts, Philip E. Slater, Stanley H. Udy, Jr., and Marjorie Grant Whiting.

Besides those already listed, a number of social scientist colleagues have provided help of one kind or another. These include David F. Aberle, Edward M. Bruner, Roy G. D'Andrade, Melvin Ember, David B. Eyde, Karl Heider, William W. Howells, the late Clyde Kluckhohn, Floyd Lounsbury, Margaret Mead, Leo Meltzer, Raoul Naroll, George D. Spindler, Melford E. Spiro, and Wayne E. Thompson.

For advice on methodology I am indebted to J. E. Morton and James N. Mosél.

For a critical reading of all or part of the text manuscript of this

Summary, thanks are due to Arthur S. Banks, Harold E. Driver, Robert M. Elashoff, and Joan E. Sieber.

Thanks are also due to the staffs of the computation centers at Harvard University, the Massachusetts Institute of Technology, and Stanford University. For programing assistance I am indebted to Byron A. Marshall, Jr., and Michaèl L. Burton.

For their unflagging assistance in preparing the coded data for processing during 1963–64, I am much indebted to Hugh and Betsy Root Blackmer. Subsequently, I received valued help on the manuscript from Margaret Rose Comstock, David and Judy Kronenfeld, Dennis C. Sims, and Lora Simms.

The Pattern Search and Table Translation Technique was developed with financing received from the National Institute of Mental Health under Public Health Service Grant No. MO5478. Valuable financial assistance was also received from the Wenner-Gren Foundation for Anthropological Research, from the Procter and Gamble Fund of the Stanford University School of Education, and from the Faculty Research Fund of the Stanford University Graduate School. Production of this volume has been supported in part by National Science Foundation Grant No. GN416. All of these sources of support are hereby gratefully acknowledged.

While I am in all these ways indebted to so many for so much, it goes without saying that I alone am responsible for all errors and shortcomings in this **Summary.**

R. B. T.

Stanford University
Stanford, California
September 23, 1966

Contents

Contents

List of Charts

List of Appendices

1. Introduction

THE PURPOSE OF THIS BOOK

THIS BOOK is intended as a research and reference tool in the field of cross-cultural statistical inquiry. It attempts to summarize, selectively, a large amount of information on cross-cultural phenomena drawn from virtually the entire existing body of coded cross-cultural materials. More specifically, the purpose of this **Summary** is to provide two interrelated services to social scientists and social thinkers who wish to search for, and analyze, regularities in man's behavior as viewed cross-culturally. The first of these functions is heuristic and the second is precautionary. They may be summarized as follows:

1. The book attempts to serve a heuristic function by providing cross-cultural information in a form that will stimulate the development of more general, more powerful, and more rigorous insights, hypotheses, and theories about (a) the nature and extent of interlinkages among various environmental, cultural, social, and psychological phenomena in the cross-cultural domain, and (b) the mode of causation, sequential process, or functional significance of such interlinkages.

2. The book attempts to serve a precautionary function by providing cross-cultural information in a form intended to facilitate the prompt and rigorous checking of "hunches," conjectures, and a priori hypotheses concerning such interlinkages.

A HISTORICAL NOTE

Cross-cultural statistical research has a long history. Indeed, it is remarkable that Sir Edward Burnett Tylor, who is often regarded as the father of modern cultural anthropology, can also be regarded as the father of cross-cultural statistical analysis. He inaugurated this form of analysis in a classic paper delivered to the Royal Anthropological Institute of Great Britain and Ireland in 1888 (see Moore 1966:1–25).* Tylor wrote in this paper:

> For years past it has become evident that the great need of anthropology is that its methods should be strengthened and systematized. . . . It is my aim to show that the development of institutions may be investigated on a basis of tabulation and classification. For this end I have taken up a subject of the utmost real as well as theoretical interest, the formation of laws of marriage and descent, as to which during many years I have been collecting the evidence found among between three and four hundred peoples, ranging from insignificant savage hordes to great cultured nations. The particular rules have been scheduled out into tables, so as to ascertain what may be called the "adhesions" of each custom, showing which peoples have the same custom, and what other customs accompany it or lie apart from it. From the recurrence or absence of these customs it will be our business to infer their dependence on causes acting over the whole range of mankind.

It was Tylor's opinion, which he shared with the German anthropologist Bastian, that "in statistical investigation the future of anthropology lies" (Moore 1966:1, 22).

Before long, Tylor was emulated by the Dutch sociologist-anthropologist Steinmetz and his students, and in 1915 by Hobhouse, Wheeler, and Ginsburg in Great Britain (Moore 1966:26–39). During the late 1930s, another period of activity began, epitomized by the publication in 1949 of George Peter Murdock's monumental **Social Structure.** The 1950s and 1960s have witnessed a steady expansion in the United States of scholarly output in cross-cultural research, accompanied by indications of gradually increasing interest on the part of anthropologists and other social scientists in other countries. For a critical history of the cross-cultural statistical method from its inception until the early 1950s, see the valuable article by André J. Köbben (Moore 1966:166–92).

In 1954, John W. M. Whiting, a leading cross-cultural scholar, wrote an article emphasizing the value of cooperation among researchers in this field. Since it is an arduous task to classify, or "code," an adequately large sample of the world's cultures in terms of variables relevant to a particular theoretical problem, Whiting pointed out the great advantage to be gained when researchers share their codings based on the same or overlapping samples (Whiting 1954:530). Whiting then mentioned five published sources of cross-cultural codings which could be shared by other researchers. It is a striking fact that within ten years of

*This work by Tylor, as well as many other important contributions to the methodology of cross-cultural research, have been conveniently reprinted in Frank W. Moore, ed., **Readings in Cross-Cultural Methodology** (first printing, 1961; second printing, reset, 1966). Readers planning to make serious use of this **Summary** are urged to read the Moore volume first. Whenever reference is made here to papers reprinted in the Moore volume, page citations will refer to the 1966 printing, and not to the original sources. For page citations to the original sources, see the Bibliography, page 189.

the time Whiting wrote, the number of such sources available for sharing had grown at least seven-fold. The present **Summary** can be regarded as one kind of response to Whiting's call for collaboration among cross-cultural scholars. With the aid of computer technology, this book draws together the most promising materials from the entire corpus of available cross-cultural codings,* and by utilizing the Pattern Search and Table Translation Technique (page 7), it attempts to present in summary form the most salient, strategically promising conclusions or propositions about cross-cultural phenomena that can be reached by the sharing of codings and for which there is at least prima facie statistical support.

THE CROSS-CULTURAL STATISTICAL APPROACH

Techniques of comparison are of the essence in cultural anthropology. There are many such techniques, and these have been usefully summarized by Oscar Lewis (Moore 1966:50–85). The cross-cultural statistical technique is but one of these. It has been described in its most rigorous form by such scholars as Murdock (Moore 1966:40–49) and Köbben (1967).

As the quotation from Tylor indicates, the cross-cultural statistical technique is based on procedures of classification and tabulation. The analyst first defines his problem as clearly as possible, specifying his theoretical orientation and interests, his assumptions, and his expectations or hypotheses. He then establishes **variables** (referred to in this book as "raw characteristics") which he considers valid to these interests and hypotheses. For each such variable he then formulates two or more **categories** (referred to in this book as "raw attribute" categories), which he subsumes under that variable. He then establishes rules in accordance with which each culture in his sample can be validly and reliably assigned to one—and only one—raw attribute category for each raw characteristic. He or his coding assistants then proceed to apply these rules to each culture in the sample—that is, to "code" each culture by assigning it to the appropriate raw attribute category. When these coding assignments have been completed, the analyst then cross-tabulates the codings for one characteristic against those for another appropriate characteristic. The resulting table will tell him whether there is a significant, interesting, or meaningful "adhesion," "co-occurrence," or "correlation" between one type of custom and another, viewed broadly across cultures.

Tylor's paper provides an illustrative example of cross-cultural re-

*"Available cross-cultural codings" are those that appeared in the professional literature by early 1964 or, if unpublished, were specifically authorized for use in this **Summary.**

search procedure. He coded his sample of cultures on the basis of the customary place of residence of husband and wife after marriage. He also coded these cultures on the basis of whether a husband customarily avoids interacting with his wife's kinfolk, or a wife with her husband's kinfolk. Examining the results, Tylor found that: "there is a well-marked preponderance indicating that ceremonial avoidance by the husband of the wife's family is in some way connected with his living with them; and vice versa as to the wife and the husband's family." Tylor's presentation of data is brief and incomplete, but Chart 1 represents one plausible tabulation that can be derived from his data (Moore 1966:2).

CHART 1: Marital Residence by Avoidance of Spouse's Kinfolk, Using Data from Tylor

	Cultures where the husband avoids his wife's kinfolk	Cultures where the wife avoids her husband's kinfolk	TOTALS
Cultures where the married couple resides with the husband's kinfolk	9	8	17
Cultures where the married couple resides with the wife's kinfolk	14	0	14
TOTALS	23	8	31

Chi-square = 6.59
Fisher Exact Test Probability = 0.0035
Phi Coefficient = 0.461

Most readers would probably agree that the table in Chart 1 does indeed suggest an impressive "adhesion" in the data—a decided divergence from what would be the "expected," or proportionate, distribution of the numbers in the four cells. Of course, the table does not tell us **why** there is such an "adhesion"—nor even whether the adhesion makes sense in any way at all. Interpretation of such a table is solely the responsibility of the analyst—and indeed Tylor proceeded immediately to supply an interpretation that seemed plausible to him. Other important questions that must be raised are: (1) whether Tylor defined his units (cultures) appropriately and (2) whether he coded them by valid rules and by reliable procedures. Questions of this sort must always be raised in assessing the results of any cross-cultural statistical study, and they will be discussed in greater detail later (pages 11 and 42).

Working as he did before the development of modern statistics, Tylor could not, of course, tell us how strong his adhesion was or how significant. Measures of strength of association, such as the phi coefficient, had yet to be developed, and the same is true of measures of significance of association, such as the chi-square test and the Fisher Exact Test. In Chart 1, the values of these three statistics are supplied.

Some seventy years elapsed between the time Tylor did his work and the time the electronic computer became generally available to social scientists. Even if statistical measures such as the three mentioned above had been available to Tylor, their calculation for large numbers of tables would have been extremely arduous. By contrast, the tens of thousands of such calculations appearing in this **Summary** were calculated and printed by the computer in just a few hours.

Tylor must also have spent much time in the routine drudgery of what might be called "flat analysis" of his tables—i.e. putting into English words the manifest content or message contained in each table. (See, for example, Moore 1966:2.) The present **Summary** performs this labor for the reader by means of the computer and the Pattern Search and Table Translation Technique. Each of the thousands of two-by-two tables in this volume is accompanied by a "statement"—consisting of two contrasting sentences—which states the manifest content of that table. For example, if the Pattern Search and Table Translation Technique were applied to the Tylor table in Chart 1, the computer would print out this statement: "Cultures where the husband avoids his wife's kinfolk lean toward being those where the married couple resides with the wife's kinfolk"; whereas, by contrast, "Cultures where the wife avoids her husband's kinfolk in all available cases are those where the married couple resides with the husband's kinfolk." The use of "table translation," by removing much of the drudgery from the cross-cultural statistical approach, may make this approach more attractive to a variety of creative social scientists and social thinkers who have previously found it laborious or forbidding.

SOURCES OF CODINGS

Listed below are the authors of each published, or authorized unpublished, source from which this **Summary** has derived codings—together with the principal subject with which the contributor deals. Full bibliographical information is given in the Bibliography, page 189. Detailed discussion of these sources appears in Chapter 4, page 64.

Charles Ackerman: Divorce
Albert S. Anthony: Male initiation rites
Dorrian Apple: Grandparenthood
Barbara C. Ayres: Pregnancy
Bacon, Barry, and Child: Child rearing; personal crime
Herbert Barry, III: Art
Judith K. Brown: Female initiation rites
Roy G. D'Andrade: Dreams
Ethnographic Atlas (George Peter Murdock): Numerous subjects
William M. Evan: Law
Clellan S. Ford: Sex and reproduction
Ford and Beach: Sex
Freeman and Winch: Societal complexity
Joan Friendly Goodman: Mourning behavior
John K. Harley: Adolescent peer groups
John M. Hickman: Folk-urban continuum
Donald Horton: Alcoholism
Merrill Jackson: Criminal law and medicine
Lambert, Triandis, and Wolf: Supernatural beings
James R. Leary: Food taboos
David C. McClelland: Achievement motivation
Frank W. Moore: Natural environment
George Peter Murdock ("World Ethnographic Sample"): Level of political integration
Moni Nag: Fertility
Raoul Naroll: Societal complexity
Roberts, Arth, and Bush: Games
Shirley and Romney: Love magic
Leo W. Simmons: Treatment of the aged
Philip E. Slater: Narcissism
William N. Stephens: Oedipus complex
Guy E. Swanson: Gods
Stanley H. Udy, Jr.: Work organization
Joseph Veroff: Achievement motivation as revealed in folk tales
John T. Westbrook: Premarital sexual behavior
Beatrice B. Whiting: Sorcery
Whiting and Child: Child training and personality
Whiting and D'Andrade: Mother-child households
Whiting, Kluckhohn, and Anthony: Male initiation ceremonies
Marjorie Grant Whiting: Diet

THE PATTERN SEARCH AND TABLE TRANSLATION TECHNIQUE

The pattern Search and Table Translation Technique, which is the basic computer technique used in this book, should perhaps be summarized at this point. When the computer is programed for this technique, it performs the following operations:

1. It receives, as input on punched data cards, codings about each culture in a sample of 400 cultures. These codings are in the form of dichotomous variables (page 21).
2. It crosses each dichotomous variable with every other such variable, thereby generating a very large number of two-by-two contingency tables (page 27).
3. It "winnows out" each of the resulting contingency tables where the "significance" level of the association between the two variables is not satisfactory (page 34).
4. It retains each "significant" table. It then "translates" each such table into a proposition or "statement"—consisting of a pair of contrasting English sentences—which states the manifest content of the table. In performing the translation, it uses syntactical and grammatical rules that are explicit, simple, and uniform (page 34).
5. The computer automatically prints out each of these English-language statements, as well as its supporting table and associated statistical measures. The statements in the printout are ordered and grouped into paragraphs, and the paragraphs into sections. This printout constitutes the bulk of this **Summary.**

THE CONCEPT OF "PATTERN"

A basic concept used in this book is that of "pattern." This concept is widely used in cultural anthropology, especially by ethnographers, who frequently refer to the "patterns" they perceive in the particular culture in which they have done field research. The selected cross-cultural materials in this **Summary** are organized and presented in a manner designed to assist the reader in discerning patterns that apply **across** cultures. For purposes of this **Summary,** a pattern is defined simply as a "concatenation of co-occurrences among attributes considered important by the researcher."*

To be of value to the cross-cultural researcher, a pattern must state, or at least imply, some kind of **contrast** between classes of cultures. To

*This **Summary** uses dichotomous (two-attribute) variables and performs two-way cross-classifications. It would, of course, be possible to use polychotomous variables and to perform cross-classifications that are more than two-way.

take a nonsense example, it would be of no analytical value to point out that all cultures in our sample that are located in North America are characterized by the presence of some kind of marriage—because the same is also true of all cultures that are located outside of North America. By the same token, it would be of little value from most analytical points of view to learn that in all of our North American cultures marriage is nonpolyandrous, because the same is also true of almost all of the non-American cultures in our sample (page 124).

A hypothetical illustration of a pattern is the following excerpt from an imaginary lecture by a political anthropologist on the subject of "Statehood Organization."

> As we look about the world and its various cultures, we find in every major geographical region actual or historical examples of statehood organization—which can be defined roughly as political integration in independent units of at least 1,500 population. The development of statehood has been particularly marked in the Circum-Mediterranean and East Eurasian areas. Cultures attaining at least a minimum level of state organization generally have depended upon agriculture as their subsistence base—although there have been some exceptions. Social stratification is generally present, and tends to be based on hereditary aristocracy rather than on wealth or occupational status. Nonetheless, life in these states has tended to place relatively strong emphasis on the invidious display of wealth. Castes and slavery have generally been present. In statehood-organized cultures, the contribution of females to subsistence is limited, and property rights in women are likely to be present. States are strongly marked by the presence of warfare, with attendant emphasis on military glory and bellicosity. As far as religion is concerned, cultures with statehood are likely to have high gods; and if so, the gods are likely to be active; and if active, the gods are likely to intervene in supporting human morality.

This cross-cultural pattern might or might not seem reasonable to the reader. Based on the sample of 400 cultures used in this **Summary,** however, it is quite reasonable. Indeed, it is directly derived from Paragraph 86 of the printout, which contrasts cultures coded by Murdock as being politically integrated at the level of the large state, the little state, or the minimal state versus cultures where the highest level of political integration is the autonomous community or the family.* It should be noted that the sample of 400 cultures used in this book is deliberately selected so as to de-emphasize postindustrial and European cultures (page 13). Needless to add, another political anthropologist reviewing the same paragraph of printout might have perceived and presented quite a dif-

*Paragraph 86 is identified in the printout by the number 86 in the upper left corner of the page. The statements in Paragraph 86, on which this illustrative pattern is based, are identified by the following numbers, proceeding in the order of presentation used by the hypothetical political anthropologist: 4, 5; 51, 53, 54, 55; 102, 106, 107, 108, 137; 109, 110; 127, 278; 417, 419, 420; 426, 427, 428. All of these statements are based on 2-by-2 tables for which the probability level is lower than 5 per cent. For an explanation of the background of Paragraph 86, see page 82.

ferent "pattern" as far as cultures possessing statehood organization are concerned. Depending on his interests and training he might, for example, have assembled a pattern giving emphasis to kinship and local community organization, or to child-rearing practices, and so forth. The function of the printout is simply to present the data in convenient form, so that the analyst can choose for himself those statements and tables he thinks are important. In other words, the tables, statements, and paragraphs in the printout are designed to facilitate the **search** for patterns or other types of regularity among cross-cultural phenomena that might not otherwise be apparent to the researcher. It should be emphasized, however, that this is all that the printout does. Responsibility for selecting and formulating these patterns belongs to the individual researcher.

The use of the printout in searching for patterns across cultures is in a sense simply an extension of more traditional methods. A more conventional approach would be to steep oneself in ethnographies and hope that one's creative intellect would succeed in generating hypotheses or perceiving patterns. While it is furthest from the intentions of this **Summary** to discourage the reading of ethnographies, nonetheless the claim can perhaps be made that use of the printout is for many purposes a more efficient and rigorous procedure. Indeed, Tylor's resort to classification and tabulation strategies as long ago as the 1880s was evidently born of an impatience with sheer resort to ethnographic reading and impressionistic cross-cultural thinking. In a sense, this book simply carries the long tradition started by Tylor one step further, by bringing together the work of many scholars in one place and in a relatively convenient form.

COMBINING THE "HOLISTIC" AND "ATOMISTIC" APPROACHES

Some social scientists feel quite at home with the kind of pattern-seeking, "holistic," or inductive approach just described. Others are by training or temperament inclined to a relatively more "atomistic" or deductive approach, which concentrates attention on a small number of variables derived from theory and considered to be crucial to the solution of a problem and on a small number of tabulations involving just those variables. Of course, the same analyst will often employ differing approaches to different problems, letting the problem of the moment determine the "mix" between the holistic and the atomistic emphasis. At one moment, for example, an analyst might use this **Summary** in a manner that is primarily holistic and heuristic—as when he is just breaking into a subject and is reading primarily for background and "leads." At another moment, the same analyst might wish to use another part of the printout in a manner that is primarily "atomistic"—as when he wishes to check a specific hypothesis involving just one or a few tables.

A deliberate attempt has been made in designing this **Summary** to facilitate **both** the holistic and the atomistic approaches, while assisting the reader to avoid the disadvantages likely to stem from undue emphasis on either approach at the expense of the other. Thus, the data have been ordered and "translated," to make it as easy as possible for the analyst pursuing a holistic approach to discern over-all patterns. At the same time, however, he is encouraged to tie his patterns to statistical tables, and is hence discouraged from forming unsupportable conclusions. These statistical tables are also, of course, of benefit to the analyst pursuing a more atomistic approach. At the same time, however, the **Summary** encourages this latter type of analyst to "look at all the evidence" by providing him with a considerable context of other statements and tables which he can examine for the presence of intervening or interpretive variables, or alternative or supplementary "efficient causes." (For a systematic discussion, see Köbben 1967.) He is thus discouraged from arriving at unduly narrow conclusions based on co-occurrences among too limited a range of variables, and encouraged to consider ways of reformulating his analytical categories and hypotheses so as to broaden their scope and heighten their analytical and predictive power. Whether this effort at accommodating both the holistic and atomistic approaches has been successful is, of course, a matter for each reader to judge.

2. Universe, Units, Sample, and Statistical Measures

UNIVERSE AND UNITS

THE IDEAL goal of a book of this type would be to provide statements or propositions that could be generalized, without too many exceptions, to the entire "known ethnographic universe" of cultures. Ideally, this book should be based on a proper sample of all cultures, extant or defunct, for which ethnographically adequate description is available.

In pursuing this ideal, however, we immediately confront a serious problem—one that has been common to all cross-cultural research since Tylor. This is the problem of the "unit"—i.e. of properly defining each unit to be classified, cross-classified, counted, and tabulated. For the statistical approach to be fully and unquestionably valid, it is necessary that each unit, each culture, be fully independent—uniquely and unambiguously defined. Unfortunately, the actual situation often falls considerably short of this ideal. There are, for example, geographical areas where one expert might perceive the existence of two distinct "cultures," A and B. A second expert might define B as a subculture of A. A third might regard both A and B as subcultures of another culture, C. And so on. As Edmund Leach, for example, has been making clear since at least as long ago as 1950, these are serious problems deserving honest and hard-headed attention (Leach 1950:108).

Where it is obvious that two "cultures" are closely related historically, it is also obvious that it would be improper to include both of them in the same sample. As historical relationship becomes more distant, however, a point is gradually reached where experts would disagree whether only one or both of the two "cultures" could properly be included. And as historical relationship becomes even more attenuated, another point is reached where experts would agree that both cultures could legitimately be included. Discerning precisely where these points of disagreement are located is not always an easy task, and resolving the disagreements themselves is even more difficult. In this connection,

Murdock's comments are instructive. He has made it clear that the "mere fact of historical relatedness" does not disturb him, because:

> the evidence now seems clear that societies borrow from one another, much as they invent for themselves, cultural elements for which they have a need and which are at least reasonably consistent with preexisting usages, and that borrowed like invented and traditional elements undergo a continual process of integrative modification leading to the emergence of new independent configurations. Diffusion negates the independence of two cultures only if it has occurred too recently for the integrative process to have run its course.*

In the **Ethnographic Atlas** Murdock and his colleagues have devised the concept of "cultural type" as a means of coming to closer grips with the problem of defining units. Murdock defines a "cultural type" as "either a single unquestionably distinctive culture or a group of cultures which differ from one another to a degree not significantly greater than the local variations to be expected of any homogeneous society of substantial geographical extent." They have also introduced the term, "known cultural type." This is defined as "any type of which at least one component culture has been described—by ethnographers, historians, or others—sufficiently fully so that at least the main features of its subsistence economy and its social organization are unambiguously apparent to any competent anthropologist" (**EA** 1963:249).†

In line with the above definitions, we may now redefine the goal of this **Summary** as follows: to provide statements or propositions that can be generalized, without too many exceptions, to a universe consisting of all "known cultural types."

SAMPLE

Ideally, when a sample is drawn to represent the universe of known cultural types, each known cultural type in the universe should have an equal—or known—chance of falling into the sample. Moreover, each known culture belonging to a particular known cultural type that does fall into the sample should have an equal chance of being chosen to represent its type. This ideal cannot be attained, however, unless and until there is a complete, systematic, and reliable enumeration of all ethnographically known cultural types in the universe and of all known cultures belonging to each known cultural type. Unfortunately, no such enumeration existed in 1964 when the design for the present **Summary** was made final. Indeed, even as this book went to press in 1966, Mur-

*Moore 1966:198. Murdock made this comment in 1957 in the course of introducing his "World Ethnographic Sample." That sample has since been superseded by his **Ethnographic Atlas** sample of 400 cultures, which is the one used in this **Summary**.

†The **Ethnographic Atlas** will hereafter be abbreviated **EA**. The **EA** appears serially in the journal **Ethnology**; hence, year and page citations refer to **Ethnology**.

dock was far from finished with his attempt at complete enumeration (Murdock 1966:97–114), although an impressive beginning had been made.

Since it was impossible for this **Summary** to draw its sample on the basis of random-stratified procedures, it was decided to use a judgmental sample as the best available alternative. The sample of 400 cultures recommended by the **Ethnographic Atlas** was adopted as a "representative sample of the world's known cultures." This sample reflects Murdock's judgment—acquired over more than thirty years of cross-cultural research experience—as to what ought to comprise a balanced sample of known cultural types. For sampling purposes, the **EA** divides the entire world into six geographical regions, each containing a considerable number of cultural types. Of the 400 cultures, 80 are taken from Africa, 45 from the Circum-Mediterranean region, 70 from East Eurasia, 70 from the Insular Pacific, 70 from North America, and 65 from South America. The **EA** sample includes nearly all of the South American cultures with reasonably adequate documentation, since cultures in that region are relatively underreported in the literature. In other regions, however, there are well-described cultures that have not been included, since, in Murdock's opinion, any further expansion of the sample would "distort the geographical distribution." Thus, "additions from the Circum-Mediterranean region would in most cases involve overrepresentation of essentially similar cultures" (**EA** 1963:109).

It should be made clear that this sample consists of 400 cultures, as distinct from societies. In establishing the sample, Murdock was:

> concerned with cultures, not with populations or societies. Reference to two large land areas of approximately equal size—China (exclusive of Tibet and Mongolia) and Australia—should make the distinction very clear. China is, and has long been, essentially a single society, but N. B. Tindale . . . has listed, with names and locations, no fewer than 573 distinct societies which occupied the Australian continent on the aboriginal level. On the other hand, there have never been more than a few tens of thousands of Australian aborigines, whereas China has a population of many hundreds of millions. In a random sample of societies, therefore, aboriginal Australia would be represented more than 500 times as heavily as China, whereas in a random sample of equivalent populations it would have less than one representative for every 10,000 from China. Either would grossly misrepresent cultural realities for, despite their differences in other respects, the two areas contain approximately the same number of distinct cultural types. Any comparative study of cultural phenomena should, therefore, be so structured that China and aboriginal Australia have roughly an equal chance of being comparably represented in a world sample [**EA** 1963:249–50].

Appendix One is an alphabetical list of the 400 cultures in the **EA** sample. Names bearing asterisks are the regular culture names as given in the **EA.** Many of these cultures, however, also have one or more alternative names. Such alternative names also appear in Appendix One, but they are indented and are without asterisks. It is thus possible for the reader to look up the name of any culture he chooses and to determine whether or not it is included in this sample of 400 cultures and under what name.

Appendix Two presents the 400 cultures by regular name, listed by geographical region and subregion. This list should prove useful to readers who wish to draw special subsamples based on location (page 48).

Appendices Three and Four are concerned with the "time level," or date of the "ethnographic present," for each of the 400 cultures. The date appearing after each culture name indicates the approximate time level to which the **EA** ethnographic codings apply.* Appendix Three lists the cultures in alphabetical order, and Appendix Four lists them in chronological order.†

STATISTICAL MEASURES USED

The Chi-Square and Fisher Exact Test

Three statistical measures appear below each table in the printout. From top to bottom, these are: (1) the chi-square value, abbreviated as "XSQ" (2) the phi coefficient of strength of association, indicated by "PHI," and (3) the probability value, indicated by "XP" or "EP." The first and third of these measures is discussed here; the phi coefficient will be discussed in the next subsection.

The chi-square value is printed out for purposes of completeness and as a means of checking other calculations. This value, as such, has no other importance in the functioning of the Pattern Search and Table Translation Technique that governs the content of the printout, except as indicated in the next paragraph.

The probability value is the basic measure used in this **Summary.** Where the total number of cultures in a table is greater than 40, the computer determines and prints out the probability value appropriate to the table's chi-square value, for one degree of freedom.‡ Where the number of cultures in the table is forty or less, the exact probability value

*A note of caution should be sounded here. There is some danger that a contributor other than the **EA** may have coded a particular culture as of a time level different from that used by the **EA.** However, because of the general tendency for cross-cultural researchers to use the same sources, this danger is probably not serious. Nonetheless, it must be borne in mind.

†The remaining Appendices, Five through Nine, are explained on pages 184, 47, and 41.

‡This value is an approximation to the true probability value. The chi-square calculation on which it is based includes the correction for continuity (Siegel 1956:107).

is calculated by the Fisher Exact Test.* Where the probability value is based on the chi-square value, it is indicated in the printout by "XP"; where determined by the Fisher Exact Test, by "EP." Both tests are two tailed.†

Whichever of the two ways it is calculated, the probability value is a measure of how probable it is that the mere process of chance could produce cell values as extreme as, or more extreme than, the values that actually appear in the table. Thus, in Tylor's table in Chart 1 (page 4), the probability value of .0035 indicates that there are fewer than 4 chances out of 1,000 that a table that extreme, or more extreme, could occur by chance. A way to check this would be to devise a roulette wheel with just 4 pockets, one for each of the 4 cells in Tylor's table. We would spin the wheel 31 times—31 being the number of cultures in Tylor's table —noting each time whether the ball fell into the pocket for the upper-left, upper-right, lower-left, or lower-right cell. Then we would repeat this entire 31-spin operation 999 additional times. The statistical expectation is that in only about 3 or 4 out of these 1,000 cases would the distribution be as extreme or more extreme than that in Tylor's table. If this 1,000-case experiment were repeated a large number of times, the mean number of resulting tables with cell values as extreme or more extreme than in Tylor's table would be 3½.

In two respects the probability value is essential to the functioning of the Pattern Search and Table Translation Technique.

1. The probability value determines whether a particular table will appear in the printout or whether it will be "winnowed out" (page 34). Where the probability value of a table is .100 or greater, the table is winnowed out. Where the cell values in the table are such that there are fewer than 100 out of 1,000 chances of obtaining a table that extreme or more extreme by roulette wheel, the computer retains the table and proceeds to translate it into a pair of English sentences.

2. The probability value is also essential to the process of translating the tables that are retained. In this process the computer must decide, among other things, which of several verbs to use. In most cases, the choice of verb is determined by how low the probability value is—i.e. how "improbable" or "unusual" the table is (page 35).

*The Fisher Exact Test is especially appropriate where N is small and where expected cell frequencies are small (Siegel 1956:110). The probability values calculated by the Fisher Test are in accord with P. Armsen's definition D-3 (Armsen 1955).

†If a researcher feels that it is appropriate to use a particular table to test on a priori directional hypothesis, and if this hypothesis is confirmed in the direction predicted (by means of rejecting the null hypothesis), then, in the opinion of some statisticians, it is permissible to divide the probability value in half (Siegel 1956:108–10).

The Phi Coefficient

The phi coefficient was chosen for use in this **Summary** because several anthropological colleagues had expressed a wish to see some measure of strength of association included, as well as a preference for this particular measure over other measures that might have been used. The phi value and the chi-square value of a two-by-two table are related by the following formula:

$$\phi = \sqrt{\frac{\chi^2}{N}}$$

The phi coefficient is a form of the Pearson product-moment coefficient of correlation, and hence offers advantages in the event that a reader wishes to apply more advanced techniques, such as factor analysis. For such reasons, Harold E. Driver, a leader in the field of cross-cultural statistical methodology, is of the opinion that "Phi and chi-square make a better combination for most purposes than the Q and chi-square" (Moore 1966:326).

The phi value can vary from minus 1 to plus 1. However, these extreme values occur only under rare conditions, namely where there are two diagonally-opposed zero cells, **and** where the two row marginal frequencies are equal to each other, **and** where the two column marginal frequencies are equal to each other. When a table has widely differing row or column marginal frequencies, the effect will sometimes be intuitively displeasing to some readers, who may feel that such an "obviously strong" table really ought to have a higher phi value. For technical discussions of the phi coefficient, see Goodman and Kruskal (1954:732–64; 1959:123–63) and Guilford (1956:311–15).

The printout also indicates whether the phi value is "positive" or "negative." The sign of the phi is related to the syntax of table translation (page 38). Otherwise, the phi value has no relation to the functioning of the Pattern Search and Table Translation procedure.

DISCUSSION

Before concluding this chapter it is appropriate to look once again at some of the problems arising from the fact that the 400-culture sample used in this **Summary** is nonrandom. The following discussion will also apply more or less closely to every other cross-cultural statistical study to date, since none of these studies has been based on a random sample (Naroll 1962:42). The nonrandomness of the sample means that the use of probability values in this **Summary** is technically unwarranted. Each reader who makes use of the printout must therefore decide for himself how he will regard the probability values: as measures or indicators of significance, of unusualness, of remarkability, of strength of association, and so forth. Whatever position he takes, he is likely to confront some opposition, for there are a variety of statistical "faiths," and it is often difficult to reconcile all of them where data and design are imperfect. As a nonstatistician, I can at least claim the advantage of lacking partisan devotion to any one such "faith." It is my intention in producing this **Summary** to use, but not abuse, the statistical approach. The sampling problem is certainly serious enough to warrant caution on the part of all readers in interpreting the tables and statements appearing in the printout. However, if such caution is properly used, I believe the statements and tables can serve many useful purposes—especially purposes of a heuristic nature. The following six observations are relevant to this position:

1. For most research purposes, the 400-culture **Ethnographic Atlas** sample would seem to be reasonably adequate. To my knowledge, no better general-purpose sample has yet been devised.

2. The **Ethnographic Atlas** sample is a very large one. For many variables, it represents well over half the total number of cultural types or cultures for which relevant information is available. In this connection we can take some comfort from the words of Driver, who has long been professionally concerned with sampling problems in cross-cultural research: "Generally speaking the larger the sample, the greater is the probability of its being representative, but when the sample is not randomly chosen, increase in size may not improve it. On the other hand, if the researcher can demonstrate his own lack of bias in choosing his sample, the larger it is the more likely it is to be representative of a larger universe" (Moore 1966:330). In offering pragmatic advice on how to draw a sample of cultures, Driver adds: "choose as large a sample as possible. If you collect over half of the data in existence on your problem, it will push the next researcher pretty hard to find enough additional information to significantly alter your conclusions" (Moore 1966: 332–33). If in the future parts of this **Summary** are replicated, using other appropriate samples, I doubt that such restudies will upset many of the statements or tables in the present **Summary** where the probability is .001 or perhaps .01—and such low probability levels appear frequently in the printout (page 54). And if such upsets should occur, a satisfactory explanation might well be found in substantially different sample design or coding rules. A similar opinion has been expressed by Melvin Ember, who has devoted several years to cross-cultural research (Ember 1963a and 1963b, Ember and Baldwin 1965, 1966, and 1967):

> The only protection against biased or unrepresentative sample results is replication by other investigators, who use similar definitions of variables. So, for ex-

ample, Spiro [1965] found substantially the same relationship between economic and political development that I found [Ember 1963a].

> In my opinion, most cross-cultural studies will be found, in replication, to be reliable. My reason for expecting few upsets of earlier findings is that most investigators either use random samples or acquire their samples in some other automatic way, thus eliminating the possibility that sample cases have been deliberately or unconsciously selected to support a particular hypothesis [Ember, personal communication, 1966].

3. Also relevant to the sampling problem is the fact that probability-based thinking pervades all social science, regardless of whether or not a random sampling design is utilized. In this sense, the present **Summary** is similar to a great many social science books and lectures—except for the incidental fact that it makes explicit use of precise probability measures.* Stanley H. Udy, Jr., has summed up this point:

> the methodological problems of observational independence and sample bias are in no way related to the use of statistical procedures, but are common to all studies of this type whether statistical procedures are used or not. Implicit in the statement of any general relationship reached through the examination of a number of cases by whatever method is the contention that the relationship observed did not occur by chance. The use of statistical procedures does nothing more than make this contention explicit and in itself introduces no additional problems or assumptions provided appropriate techniques are employed [Moore 1966:307].

4. Another scholar who has dealt with the problem of nonrandom samples and probability measures is Raoul Naroll. The following quotation seems quite convincing, especially in view of Naroll's position as an eminent contributor to the development of rigorous cross-cultural methodology:

> Some statistical purists would prefer us to restrict the use of statistical inference to inference about universes made from rigorously random samples. But investigators whose chief interest is social science rather than mathematics are often interested in the likelihood of a similar result occurring through chance from a random sample from a universe in which no relationship of the sort investigated exists, even when they know well that the data in question are not a random sample, or even a sample at all! They want to know if this is the sort of thing you would expect to get by chance. . . . [The probability value] specifies a probability of the investigator being deceived by a freak sample [Naroll 1962:25–26].

5. There is another, quite different approach which also permits productive and fruitful use of the printout. This is to regard the 400 cul-

*The same statement would hold for all other cross-cultural statistical studies, including, of course, those from which this **Summary** has derived its codings. Problems concerning the samples used in these various studies are discussed on page 180.

tures simply as an interesting subuniverse, and not as a sample of any larger universe. One could regard this subuniverse as "interesting" because the selection of its 400 cultures reflects expert judgment and because 400 cultures is a rather large proportion of the total ethnographic universe, however that might be defined. This volume can then be regarded simply as a summary of statistically suggestive statements about co-occurrences among variables as these variables apply to the 400 cultures themselves.* The propositions would be "statistically suggestive" in the sense that the probability value is regarded as a kind of inverse index of strength of association.†

6. However a particular reader might choose to regard the statements and tables in the printout, I am hopeful that this **Summary** will serve as a spur to further methodological research on the problem of definition of units and the problem of sampling (page 11). I hope that various replication studies will be carried out on other types of samples, so that the degree of correspondence of results can be noted and measured. By such replications we will gradually be able to narrow the range of disagreement on methodological issues. This will free more of our energies for an attack on substantive problems—to the benefit of everyone concerned. The ultimate and most desirable replication will be based, of course, on a random-stratified sample drawn from a complete enumeration of the entire universe of known cultural types. The day when such an enumeration is available and consensually accepted by the profession will be a welcome one.

*More precisely, this volume would be regarded as summarizing such co-occurrences as they apply to those cultures, out of the 400, for which unambiguous, relevant codings are available (page 25).

†For a technical discussion, see Banks and Textor (1963:29–30).

3. Methodology

THIS CHAPTER will describe the methodology of the Pattern Search and Table Translation Technique as it was used to produce the printout in this book. As indicated earlier, this **Summary** is the second book to be produced by means of this technique. The first was **A Cross-Polity Survey** (Banks and Textor 1963), which classified, cross-classified, and tabulated a "total sample" of the world's independent polities in terms of concepts relevant to theories in the domain of comparative politics. Readers interested in more detailed description of the Pattern Search and Table Translation Technique are referred to Chapter 2 of that book, which is hereafter abbreviated **CPS.**

OUTLINE OF PROCEDURE

Definition of Terms

The following four terms are used throughout this book:

RAW CHARACTERISTIC: A raw characteristic is any variable derived from the **Ethnographic Atlas** or any of the other 38 sources of codings used in this **Summary.** An example would be "Level of Political Integration," full details of which appear on page 82.

RAW ATTRIBUTE: Subsumed under each raw characteristic are two or more raw attributes. Under the raw characteristic "Level of Political Integration," for example, there are several raw attributes, including "Large State," "Little State," "Minimal State," "Autonomous Community," and "Family."

FINISHED CHARACTERISTIC: A finished characteristic is always a dichotomous, or two-attribute, characteristic. Frequently a characteristic is dichotomous in its original form, in which case the "raw characteristic" and the "finished characteristic" are identical. In other instances, the raw characteristic is polychotomous. Where this is so, several finished characteristics might be constructed by dichotomization of the same raw characteristic in a variety of ways that seem strategically promising. Thus, for example, the "Level of Political Integration" raw characteristic is variously dichotomized to yield four finished characteristics, Numbers 84, 85, 86, and 87.

FINISHED ATTRIBUTE: The two attributes subsumed under each finished characteristic are referred to as its "finished attributes."

Initial Selection of the Raw Characteristics

The first step in selecting raw characteristics for use in this **Summary** was to examine the entire available coded cross-cultural literature.* It was then necessary to decide whether the codings on a particular variable were of sufficient general and theoretical interest to social scientists to warrant inclusion in the corpus of raw characteristics. It was decided, for example, that the codings in the **Ethnographic Atlas** on "Primary House Type" were not of sufficiently wide interest—even though there might be some readers interested in that variable. In making my initial selection, I was advised by Murdock and other cross-cultural scholars.

Construction of the Finished Characteristics

The Pattern Search and Table Translation Technique deals only with dichotomous characteristics. Characteristics that are polychotomous in raw form must therefore be dichotomized before they can be used. While dichotomization has certain disadvantages, it has two very substantial advantages when used with data of the type with which we are here concerned. First, dichotomization simplifies the analysis. Anyone who has had experience poring through large numbers of "M-by-N" contingency tables (tables with more than two columns and more than two rows) will readily appreciate the advantages to be gained by selective collapsing or selective eliminating of certain columns and rows. Dichotomization is simply one form of such selection and elimination. The second advantage is that dichotomization makes possible the simple, direct, and meaningful translation of tables into sentences.†

An example of a case where a raw characteristic was dichotomous to begin with, and hence identical with a finished characteristic, is the

*"Coded" cross-cultural literature refers to that portion of the total literature involving comparative studies in which the author has formally coded a sample of cultures. Most such sources had been published at the time I selected them for use in this **Summary**. A few were as yet unpublished, and in each such case explicit permission to use the codings was obtained from the author.

†Additional statistical techniques designed to compensate for the disadvantages of dichotomization are discussed on pages 50 and 53.

Whiting, Kluckhohn, and Anthony characteristic that distinguishes between cultures where male initiation ceremonies at puberty are present and cultures where such ceremonies are absent. Without further change, this raw characteristic became Finished Characteristic (FC) 373.*

In the many instances where the raw characteristic was polychotomous in form, decisions were required as to how to dichotomize. There are a number of types of dichotomization. With some oversimplification for the sake of clarity, these types are summarized below as "simple" and "complex," and as involving "nominal" and "ordinal" data.

"Nominal" data deal with essentially "qualitative" subjects. An example is the nature of a culture's kin group—whether "patrilineal," "matrilineal," "cognatic," or the like. "Ordinal" data deal with classes of cultures that have been measured or ranked along a continuum that is quantitative or quasi-quantitative in nature. FCs 10 through 16, for example, classify cultures according to the latitude at which they are located (page 66). In this case, the underlying continuum is of a fairly precise quantitative and "interval" nature, namely degrees of latitude. FCs 84 through 87, dealing with "Level of Political Integration," are based on a more "quasi"-quantitative continuum, namely size of the population unit at which political integration is present—ranging from large state, through little state, minimal state, and autonomous community, down to family (page 82).

A "simple" FC is one in which each of the two finished attributes is constructed from a single raw attribute and both raw attributes come from the same raw characteristic. A "complex" FC is one in which one or both of the finished attributes are constructed from a plurality of raw attributes, which raw attributes might in turn come from one, two, or more raw characteristics. The examples that follow will make these distinctions clear.

SIMPLE DICHOTOMIZATION WITH ONE POSITIVE ATTRIBUTE: This is the simplest form of dichotomization. Attention is focused on cultures possessing a certain positive attribute, and these cultures are contrasted with those that lack this attribute. In the printout, the positive attribute is always the left attribute and the other attribute is always the right attribute. In the tables in the printout, cultures characterized by the positive attribute always appear in the left column, while cultures characterized by the other attribute always appear in the right. And in the portion of the printout where the tables are translated into English, the positive subject is the left subject, and the other subject is the right (page

*Details on FC 373 are found on page 150. This FC provides the pair of subjects in Paragraph 373. To find this paragraph, refer to the paragraph identification numbers in the upper left corner of each page of the printout.

30, Chart 2, Arrows G and H). Simple dichotomizations with one positive attribute are of two principal subtypes, as follows:

(1) The first subtype is "positive" versus "negative," and deals with features that are present in some cultures and absent in others. An example is that already mentioned, in which cultures were classified according to whether male initiation ceremonies at puberty were "present" or "absent."

(2) The second subtype is "positive" versus "all other." This subtype deals with a feature that is present in all cultures, but which varies in its form. Thus all cultures have a kin group of some kind, but the form of this kin group varies considerably. FC 186, for example, contrasts the 150 cultures in the sample where "the kin group is exclusively patrilineal" with the 250 cultures where "the kin group is other than exclusively patrilineal" (page 108).

SIMPLE DICHOTOMIZATION WITH TWO POSITIVE ATTRIBUTES: This type of dichotomization involves a positive attribute in both the left and right columns. The assignment of one attribute to the left column and the other to the right column is essentially arbitrary, since both attributes are equally "positive." An example of this positive-positive contrast is FC 190, which contrasts "cultures where the kin group is patrilineal or double-descent, rather than matrilineal" versus "cultures where the kin group is matrilineal, rather than patrilineal or double-descent" (page 110). In the syntax of table translation, the phrase "rather than" always indicates that the FC is contrasting two positive attributes. In such a "rather than" contrast there will invariably be a "residue" of additional cultures that are irrelevant to the particular contrast being made, which must therefore be excluded from the computer's consideration. In this case, the residue consists of those cultures where the kin group is cognatic. These "residual" coding assignments will be discussed in the next subsection (page 25).

COMPLEX DICHOTOMIZATION WITH ONE POSITIVE ATTRIBUTE: This type of dichotomization contrasts a complex "positive" attribute with a "negative" or an "all other" attribute. The positive attribute is complex in the sense that it combines two or more raw attributes derived from one, two, or more raw characteristics. Such combinations may be "additive" or "alternative."*

An extreme example of the "additive" type is FC 246, which contrasts "cultures where the family is independent and marriage is commonly polygynous and preferentially sororal and co-wives dwell to-

*In the syntax of table translation, "or" is the "inclusive or," meaning "and/or." See **CPS**, page 24.

gether," versus "all others." In order to be assigned to the positive attribute category, a culture must meet every one of the conditions stated. If it fails to meet any one of them, it is assigned to the "all other" category (page 124).

An example of the "alternative" type is FC 175, which contrasts "cultures where the community is 'kin-homogeneous,' i.e. a clan community or a deme," versus "cultures where the community is 'kin-heterogeneous,' i.e. other than a clan community or a deme" (page 105).

COMPLEX DICHOTOMIZATION WITH TWO POSITIVE ATTRIBUTES: An example of this type of dichotomization is FC 250, which "controls" for kin group and then contrasts cultures that are polygynous with those that are monogamous. As in all cases where both attributes are positive, the phrase "rather than" appears. Thus the contrast is: "Cultures where, with the patrilineal kin group present, marriage is commonly or occasionally polygynous, rather than monogamous" versus "cultures where, with the patrilineal kin group present, marriage is monogamous, rather than commonly or occasionally polygynous" (page 126). This FC illustrates how the Pattern Search and Table Translation Technique can be used to focus on a particular and precise contrast. The assignment of cultures to the left or right attribute category of this FC or to the residue will be discussed in the next subsection, "Assignments to the Residue."

ORDINAL FINISHED CHARACTERISTICS: In shifting the discussion from nominal to ordinal characteristics, it must first be observed that the distinction between these two kinds of characteristics is sometimes difficult to draw. There are a number of characteristics which appear to be essentially nominal in nature, but which nonetheless possess, or might possess, ordinal coloration. An example is FC 417, which is based on Leo W. Simmons' distinction between cultures where warfare is "prevalent" and those where it is "not prevalent" (page 160). In a somewhat more explicitly ordinal manner, FC 418, derived from dichotomous codings by Donald Horton, separates cultures where warfare is "common or chronic" from those where it is "rare or infrequent" (page 160). An explicitly ordinal finished characteristic is FC 419, based on Philip E. Slater's trichotomous raw characteristic, which classified cultures in terms of whether military glory is "strongly," "moderately," or "negligibly" emphasized (page 160).

Where an ordinal or quasi-ordinal raw characteristic is dichotomous, it is, of course, identical with its finished characteristic. Where it is trichotomous, it is often simply dichotomized, with the middle raw attribute being assigned to the high or low side, whichever serves best to balance the frequencies of the left and right attribute categories. Thus

FC 419 contrasts "cultures where military glory is strongly or moderately emphasized" with those where it is "negligibly" emphasized.

A trichotomous raw characteristic is sometimes first dichotomized by dropping the middle raw attribute and contrasting the two extremes. Then additional FCs are constructed by moving the cutting point. An example is James R. Leary's raw characteristic: "observation of food taboos," under which are three raw attributes, "high," "medium," and "low." FC 448 contrasts the 25 cultures coded as "high" versus the 26 coded as "low." The 35 cultures coded as "medium" drop out into the residue as irrelevant. FC 449 contrasts "high" versus "medium or low." FC 450 contrasts "high or medium" versus "low." Thus the printout will indicate those attributes that correlate with the extremes and those attributes that vary concomitantly with observation of food taboos (page 167).*

The Pattern Search and Table Translation Technique does not handle "metric" or "interval" characteristics, but instead converts them into ordinal form. This ordinalization often consists simply in the contrasting of cultures coded above the median on a metric scale versus those coded below. Uniformly, the adjective "high" means "above the median," and "low" means "below the median." For a large number of such FC's, the number of cultures coded was so small that no more than a dichotomous break was feasible. In some cases, deeper analysis of selected results will entail a return to the original source of the codings and the use of these codings in their original interval form.

Regardless of the mode of dichotomization, the positive, strong, or high attribute will always be on the left.

Assignments to the "Residue"

For most finished characteristics there is a "residue" of cultures that are excluded from both finished attribute categories, do not enter the tables for that FC, and are not reflected in the statements into which those tables are translated. There are three reasons why a culture may be excluded and assigned to the residue of a particular FC:

(1) It may be **"unascertained,"** i.e. not coded for this particular characteristic because ethnographic information is lacking or because the coder did not code it.

(2) Though ascertained, the culture may be **"irrelevant"** to the particular FC. In FC 250, for example, a matrilineal culture is irrelevant because membership in both the right and left attribute categories is conditional upon a culture's having patrilineal kin groups (page 126).

*FC 448 is run as "subject only," while FCs 449 and 450 are run as "predicate only." This matter is discussed on page 29.

(3) Finally, though ascertained and relevant, a culture may be **"ambiguous"** with respect to a particular FC. If a culture is not classifiable, on a mutually exclusive basis, as belonging in either the left or the right attribute category, it must be assigned to the residue on grounds of ambiguity.

At the top of each paragraph in the printout are the "culture listings" (page 29). These listings specify the number of cultures assigned to the residue and the grounds for such assignment—whether "ambiguous," "irrelevant," or "unascertained." For each FC, the rationale for assigning cultures to the residue is given in Chapter 4.

FC 250 illustrates the three categories of residue. These will be briefly summarized here; further details are given on page 126. This FC contrasts "cultures where, with the patrilineal kin group present, marriage is commonly or occasionally polygynous" with "cultures where, with the patrilineal kin group present, marriage is monogamous." Assignments of cultures to the residue were determined as follows:

(1) Unascertained: Two cultures were indicated by the **Ethnographic Atlas** to be unascertained for either their type of kin group or for whether their marriage system was polygynous or monogamous or for both. This left 398 cultures to consider.

(2) Irrelevant: Of the remaining 398 cultures, three were excluded as irrelevant because their marriage system is polyandrous—and hence neither polygynous nor monogamous. Of the remaining 395 cultures, 227 were excluded as irrelevant because their kin group was primarily of a type other than patrilineal—i.e. matrilineal, cognatic, and so forth. This left 168 cultures to consider.

(3) Ambiguous: Of the remaining 168 cultures, one was excluded because its kin group was ambiguous; it could not be satisfactorily classified as primarily patrilineal or primarily nonpatrilineal. This left 167 cultures.

Of the remaining 167 cultures, 146 were assigned to the left attribute category as being patrilineal and polygynous. The remaining 21 were assigned to the right category as being patrilineal and monogamous. Thus no table appearing under Paragraph 250 will be found to contain more than 167 cultures.*

A further discussion of the "residue" is found in **CPS,** pages 20–22 and 26–27.†

*Often the number will be smaller, because of residues associated with the row FC with which this column FC is crossed.

†"Reassignment of the residue," as discussed in **CPS** on pages 26–27, was not performed in preparing the present printout. In general, I believe that there is considerably less need for it than in the case of **CPS.** Furthermore, since I did not do the coding for this **Summary,** reassignment of the residue would have been practically impossible in that it would have required the cooperation of numerous contributors to this volume, for each of whom the process would have been time-consuming, expensive, and arduous.

Ordering the Finished Characteristics

Once all of the finished characteristics were constructed, the next step was to group them together meaningfully and arrange them in a satisfactory order. Generally, FCs derived from the same raw characteristic are grouped together in the same section or subsection. Often a section will contain FCs derived from several related raw characteristics. The sections are then ordered in more or less the same manner in which an ethnographer would order the chapters of his ethnography, as will be clear from a glance at the Table of Contents.

Within a particular section or subsection, FCs usually follow an order in which categories containing larger numbers of cultures are first contrasted, after which smaller categories, involving somewhat narrower contrasts, are presented. In the section on "Lineality of Kin Group," for example, the order is "patrilineal" versus "all other"; followed by "matrilineal" versus "all other"; followed by "cognatic" versus "all other"; and so on (FCs 186–89). Thereafter the focus narrows, as "patrilineal or double-descent" is contrasted with "matrilineal"—with the cognatic cultures dropping into the residue (FC 190, page 110).

For a discussion of the mechanical details of constructing the actual deck of FC punched cards, see **CPS,** pages 25–26.

The Pattern Search Procedure

When the Finished Characteristic deck was finally ready, the next step was the administration of the Pattern Search procedure. The computer takes each FC in turn, and cross-tabulates it with each other FC. For example, it takes FC 1 and crosses it with FCs 2 through 536. Then it takes FC 2 and crosses it with FC 1 and with FCs 3 through 536, and so forth. As output, the computer produces a very large number of two-by-two tables, for each of which it calculates the chi-square value, the probability value, and the phi coefficient. Each table whose probability value is .10 or higher is automatically disregarded, that is, "winnowed out." (See **CPS,** pages 27–28.)*

The Table Translation Procedure

The output from the Pattern Search procedure became the input to the Table Translation procedure. This procedure produced output in the form of the printout used in this book. Each table whose probability value was lower than .10 was translated into a statement consisting of two English sentences.† Each sentence contains the following parts of

*It need hardly be pointed out that the probability value applies to the four-cell table as a whole. It does not follow from this, of course, that a particular column or row taken from a significant 2-by-2 table and regarded as a 2-by-1 table would necessarily be significant.

†Languages other than English can also be used in table translation. To date, the procedure has been used experimentally with French, German, Russian, and romanized Thai.

speech: subject lead, subject clause, verb, and predicate clause. In some cases there is also an adverb. The precise grammatical rules for building these sentences are given on page 34.

Progressive Selection of Finished Characteristics

The printout appearing in this **Summary** is the result of four successive computer runs using the Pattern Search and Table Translation Technique. After each of the first three runs, the printout was inspected, and decisions were made about those characteristics that should be dropped, simplified, elaborated, or redefined. While every finished characteristic was retained if judged likely to contribute in some reasonable measure to the development of cross-cultural studies, nonetheless considerable stringency was also exercised in the interest of brevity.*

THE FORMAT OF THE PRINTOUT

The format of the printout contains three principal elements: the subject listings, the culture listings, and the predicate listings. These three elements and their respective subelements are illustrated in Chart 2, which presents two specimen pages from Paragraph 86 of the printout.† Various features of the printout are identified on the chart by means of arrows, each of which bears an identifying letter.

The Subject Listings

Like all paragraphs in the printout, Paragraph 86 contains two contrasting subjects. These are indicated by Arrow A: "Cultures where the level of political integration is the large state, the little state, or the minimal state"—versus "Cultures where the level of political integration is the autonomous community, or the family." These two subjects were, of course, derived from the raw characteristic: "Level of Political Integration." As indicated by Arrow D, "GPM" or George Peter Murdock is the source for the original codings for the subject characteristic. The "Background Page Reference" (Arrow E) indicates the page in Chapter 4, "Coding Background," to which the reader may turn for further information about the codings, including the citation of source. For the further convenience of the reader, the upper corner of each page in Chapter 4 indicates the number of the finished characteristic described on that page.

At the end of each subject clause is a figure indicating the number of cultures, out of the total sample of 400, coded as belonging in that

*Decisions were also made between runs as to which FCs could best be run as subject only or predicate only (page 29), and which statements should be hand-winnowed (page 39). By such means the length of the printout was reduced from about 4,000 to about 2,400 pages.

†The first page of the chart is an exact reproduction of the first page of Paragraph 86. The second page consists of nine predicate-pairs chosen to illustrate various points.

finished attribute category (Arrow C). Thus in Paragraph 86 there are 148 cultures that have been coded by Murdock as being integrated politically at the level of a minimal state or higher, and 156 cultures coded as being integrated at lower levels.*

The Culture Listings

Immediately beneath the subject listings are the culture listings. The computer specifies the number of cultures in each listing; this acts as a check to insure that its count and my own earlier count are identical. Note that these two counts found the same numbers of cultures in the left and right columns, respectively: 148 and 156.

The sum of 148 and 156 is 304. This leaves 96 additional cultures to be accounted for, out of the total sample of 400. As Arrow I indicates, these 96 cultures have been assigned to the "residue," and the grounds for such assignment are specified. The sum of the computer's count of the number of cultures in the left column, right column, and residue should always equal 400.

The cultures in the left and right subject categories are listed alphabetically, ten across.† The purpose of these listings is to make it convenient for the reader to know how each culture was coded and to satisfy himself as to the adequacy or inadequacy of the coding. (For further discussion, see page 42.) Readers who possess specialized knowledge of particular cultures and who discover errors in coding, are urged to report their objections and corrections to the **Ethnographic Atlas** or to the Human Relations Area Files, where they will be carefully considered as part of a continuous process of upgrading the data.

In some circumstances the culture listings also serve a heuristic function. Especially where the codings are of a highly judgmental nature, the culture listings may help the reader by indicating which cultures exemplify a particular attribute category.

Subject-only and Predicate-only Characteristics

In the typical case, a table appears twice in the printout. The computer has found, for example, that the table resulting from the crossing of FCs 86 and 426 possesses a sufficiently low probability value to warrant retention. This table therefore appears twice, once as Table 86/426

*Similar figures appear at the end of each predicate clause (Arrow V), serving to remind the reader of the proportion of the total sample included in that particular finished attribute category. Where this proportion is small and the proportion in the other predicate attribute is also small, the reader should exercise particular caution in reaching conclusions. FC 86 also occurs as a predicate-pair in many other paragraphs, so that the numbers 148 and 156 also appear, for example, in Statement 426/86.

†Because of space limitations, cultures assigned to the residue are often not listed. In a further effort to conserve space, listings for one paragraph are sometimes indicated by reference to the appropriate listings for another paragraph. Examples are found in Paragraphs 483 and 458.

CHART 2: Specimen Printout

CHART 2 : SPECIMEN PRINTOUT

86 CULTURES
WHERE THE LEVEL OF POLITICAL INTEGRATION
IS THE LARGE STATE, THE LITTLE STATE,
OR THE MINIMAL STATE (148) GPM

86 CULTURES
WHERE THE LEVEL OF POLITICAL INTEGRATION
IS THE AUTONOMOUS COMMUNITY, OR
THE FAMILY (156) GPM

(A) LEFT AND RIGHT SUBJECTS

(B) PARAGRAPH NUMBER

(C) 148 CULTURES OUT OF 400 WERE CODED AS HAVING SOME KIND OF STATE

(D) INITIALS INDICATING SOURCE OF CODINGS FOR SUBJECT FC

BACKGROUND ON PAGE 82

BOTH SUBJECT AND PREDICATE

(E) BACKGROUND PAGE REFERENCE

(F) HOW FC 86 IS RUN

148 IN LEFT COLUMN

AJIE	ALBANIANS	AMERICANS	ARYANS	ASHANTI	AZANDE	AZTEC	BABWA	BALINESE	BEJA
BELU	BEMBA	BOERS	BULGARIANS	BURMESE	BURUSHO	BURYAT	CADUVEO	CAMBODIANS	CHAGGA
CHAMACOCO	CHERKESS	CHEROKEE	CHEYENNE	CHIBCHA	CHIRIGUANO	COORG	CREEK	CROW	CUNA
CZECHS	DARD	DILLING	DUSUN	DUTCH	EGYPTIANS	ELLICE	FON	FOX	FUTAJALONKE
GANDA	GARO	GOND	GROS VENTRE	HASINAI	HAWAIIANS	HAZARA	HEBREWS	HEHE	HO
HURON	ICELANDERS	INCA	IRISH	JAPANESE	JAVANESE	JUKUN	KABYLE	KACHIN	KALMYK
KAZAK	KERALA	KHALKA	KHASI	KIOW-APACHE	KISSI	KONSO	OREANS	KUBA	LAKHER
LAMBA	LAU	LIFU	LOZI	LUBA	MACASSARESE	MAGUZAWA	LAYS	MANDAN	MANGAIANS
MAORI	MARGI	MARICOPA	MARQUESANS	MAYA	NDU	MENDE	INA	MIAMI	MISKITO
MONGO	MONGUOR	MOSSI	MZAB	NAMA	N HEZ	NGONI	N	NYAKYUSA	NYANEKA
NYORO	OMAHA	ORAON	PAEZ	PALAUANS	PA	PENOBSCOT	PO EANS	RIFFIANS	ROMANS
ROTINESE	ROTUMANS	RWALA	SAMOANS	SANTAL	SARA A	SARSI	SE G	SERBS	SHERENTE
SHILLUK	SHLUH	SINHALESE	SIWANS	SOMALI	SONGHA	SOTHO	TAL CA	TANALA	TENDA
THAI	THONGA	TIBETANS	TIMUCUA	TIV	TOKELAU	TOTONAC	TRUR ND	TURKMEN	VIETNAMESE
WICHITA	WINNEBAGO	WOLOF	WUTE	YAKUT	YAO	PESE	YORUB		

156 IN RIGHT COLUMN

ABIPON	ABOR	AKHA	ALACALUF	ALORESE	ANDAMANESE	APINA	ARANDA	ARAPESH	ARAUCANIANS
ATAYAL	ATSUGEWI	AWEIKOMA	BACAIRI	BANDA	BARI	BATAK	BAYA	ERGDAMA	BETE
BIRIFOR	BORORO	BOTOCUDO	BOZO	BUDUMA	CAGABA	CALLINAGO	AMAYURA	RAJA	CARIB
CAYAPA	CHENCHU	CHIR-APACHE	CHOROTI	CHUKCHEE	COCHITI	CREE	AWARE	GUENO	DIERI
DOBUANS	DOGON	DOROBO	FANG	GILBERTESE	GILYAK	GOAJIRO	IBO	G D	GURE
HAIDA	HANUNOO	HAVASUPAI	HERERO	HUKUNDIKA	IBAN	IFUGAO	IL	IN SANA	IRAQW
JEMEZ	JIVARO	KAREN	KARIERA	KASKA	KERAKI	KET	KIKU	KOR	KPE
KUNG	KURTATCHI	KUTENAI	LAKALAI	LAMET	LANGO	LAPPS	LESU	LOLO	LUO
MANIHIKI	MANUS	MATACO	MATAKAM	MBUGWE	MBUTI	MENTAWEI	MINANGK	MIWOK	MOTA
MOTILON	MUNDURUCU	MURNGIN	NAMBICUARA	NASKAPI	NAVAHO	NICOBARESE	NOMLAKI	NIVA	OJIBWA
ONA	ONTONG-JAVA	PALIKUR	PAPAGO	PUKAPUKA	RAROIANS	SAMOYED	SANDAWE	UNG	SEMANO
SERI	SIRIONO	SIUAI	BANUN	TALLENSI	TANIMBARESE	TAOS	TAPIRAPE	UMA	TEHUELCHE
TENETEHARA	TERENA	TIKOP	MBIRA	TIWI	TODA	TOLOWA	TORAJA	TRU SE	TRUMAI
TUBATULABAL	TUCANO	TUC	TUPINAMBA	TURKANA	TZELTAL	ULAWANS	UTE	VEDDA	WAICA
WAPISHANA	WAROPEN	WA	WASHO	WITOTO	WOGEO	WOLEAIANS	YAGUA	YAHGAN	YAKO
YARURO	YOKUTS	YU R	YUKI	YUROK	ZUNI				

(G) LEFT SUBJECT KEYED TO LEFT COLUMN OF EACH TABLE

(H) RIGHT SUBJECT KEYED TO RIGHT COLUMN OF EACH TABLE

(I) RESIDUE

33 EXCLUDED BECAUSE IRRELEVANT

63 EXCLUDED BECAUSE UNASCERTAINED

```
102  TEND TO BE THOSE                  0.72 OF 142   102  TEND TO BE THOSE                  0.68 OF 155     102   49
     WHERE CLASS STRATIFICATION IS                        WHERE CLASS STRATIFICATION IS                     40  106
     PRESENT  (203)                                       ABSENT  (180)                               XSQ=   46.37
                                                                                                      PHI=   0.395
                                                                                                      XP =   0.

109  TEND LESS TO BE THOSE             0.78 OF 133   109  TEND MORE TO BE THOSE             0.97 OF 152      29    5
     WHERE CASTES ARE ABSENT  (317)                       WHERE CASTES ARE ABSENT  (317)                   104  147
                                                                                                      XSQ=   21.42
                                                                                                      PHI=   0.274
                                                                                                      XP =   0.0000

116  LEAN TOWARD BEING THOSE           0.63 OF  24   116  LEAN TOWARD BEING THOSE           0.85 OF  26      15    4
     WHERE OCCUPATIONAL SPECIALIZATION IS                 WHERE OCCUPATIONAL SPECIALIZATION IS               9   22
     FULL-TIME, WHETHER OR NOT FOR                        PART-TIME ONLY  (34) JMH                    XSQ=    9.84
     SURPLUS PRODUCTION  (20) JMH                                                                     PHI=   0.444
                                                                                                      XP =   0.0017

127  TILT TOWARD BEING THOSE           0.65 OF  26   127  TILT TOWARD BEING THOSE           0.65 OF  31       9   20
     WHERE THE FEMALES' CONTRIBUTION                      WHERE THE FEMALES' CONTRIBUTION                   17   11
     TO SUBSISTENCE                                       TO SUBSISTENCE                              XSQ=    3.93
     IS LOW  (32) JKB                                     IS HIGH  (33) JKB                           PHI=  -0.263
                                                                                                      XP =   0.0474

360  DRIFT TOWARD BEING THOSE          0.53 OF  15   360  DRIFT TOWARD BEING THOSE          0.81 OF  16       8    3
     WHERE ADOLESCENT PEER GROUPS ARE PRESENT             WHERE ADOLESCENT PEER GROUPS ARE PRESENT           7   13
     IN A SETTING OF WORK AND PUBLIC GATHERINGS           ONLY IN A SETTING OF LEISURE, OR ELSE       XSQ=    2.68
     AND LEISURE, OR AT LEAST OF                          ARE ABSENT  (23) JKH                        PHI=   0.294
     PUBLIC GATHERINGS AND LEISURE  (14) JKH                                                          EP =   0.0659

417  IN ALL CASES ARE THOSE            1.00 OF  17   417  TILT LESS TOWARD BEING THOSE      0.65 OF  23      17   15
     WHERE WARFARE IS                                     WHERE WARFARE IS                                   0    8
     PREVALENT  (34) LWS                                  PREVALENT  (34) LWS                         XSQ=    5.38
                                                                                                      PHI=   0.367
                                                                                                      EP =   0.0125

426  TEND TO BE THOSE                  0.75 OF  93   426  TEND TO BE THOSE                  0.57 OF 109      70   47
     WHERE A HIGH GOD IS                                  WHERE A HIGH GOD IS                               23   62
     PRESENT  (156) GES,EA                                ABSENT  (104) GES,EA                        XSQ=   19.98
                                                                                                      PHI=   0.315
                                                                                                      XP =   0.0000

427  TILT TOWARD BEING THOSE           0.63 OF  70   427  TILT TOWARD BEING THOSE           0.62 OF  47      44   18
     WHERE A HIGH GOD, IF PRESENT, IS                     WHERE A HIGH GOD, IF PRESENT, IS                  26   29
     ACTIVE, RATHER THAN                                  INACTIVE, RATHER THAN                       XSQ=    5.86
     INACTIVE  (87) GES,EA                                ACTIVE  (69) GES,EA                         PHI=   0.224
                                                                                                      XP =   0.0155

428  LEAN TOWARD BEING THOSE           0.80 OF  44   428  LEAN TOWARD BEING THOSE           0.61 OF  18      35    7
     WHERE A HIGH GOD, IF PRESENT AND ACTIVE,             WHERE A HIGH GOD, IF PRESENT AND ACTIVE,           9   11
     SUPPORTS HUMAN MORALITY, RATHER THAN                 DOES NOT SUPPORT HUMAN MORALITY,            XSQ=    7.89
     NOT SUPPORTING IT  (61) GES,EA                       RATHER THAN SUPPORTING IT  (26) GES,EA      PHI=   0.357
                                                                                                      XP =   0.0050
```

(J) STRONGEST VERB $P < .001$

(K) ADVERBS

(L) SECOND STRONGEST VERB $.001 < P < .01$

(M) LEFT MAJORITY CELL IS 78% OF LEFT COLUMN TOTAL

(N) RIGHT MAJORITY CELL IS 97% OF RIGHT COLUMN TOTAL

(O) THIRD STRONGEST VERB $.01 < P < .05$

(P) PHI COEFFICIENT WITH POSITIVE SIGN

(Q) WEAKEST VERB $.05 < P < .10$

(R) PHI COEFFICIENT WITH NEGATIVE SIGN

(S) SPECIAL VERB-PHRASE INDICATING NO DEVIANT CASES IN LEFT COLUMN OF THE TABLE

(T) INDICATES STATEMENT 86/426

(U) EXACT PROBABILITY VALUE FROM FISHER TEST

(V) 156 CULTURES OUT OF 400 CODED AS HAVING A HIGH GOD

(W) CHI-SQUARE VALUE

(X) INITIALS INDICATING SOURCE OF CODINGS FOR THIS FC

(Y) CHI-SQUARE-BASED APPROXIMATE PROBABILITY VALUE

and once as Table 426/86. In the former case, FC 86 is the subject characteristic and FC 426 the predicate characteristic (Arrow T). In the latter case, the table is "turned over," and FC 426 provides the two subjects, while FC 86 provides the two predicates. In a number of instances, however, it was decided to run a particular FC as "subject only" or as "predicate only," in order to reduce the printout to manageable size and make it easier to read. Each subject listing indicates the way in which a particular FC is run (Arrow F). There are four possibilities: "both subject and predicate," "subject only," "predicate only," and "neither subject nor predicate."* The rationale for deciding which FCs to run both ways and which to run only one way is summarized below. For further details, see **CPS,** pages 34–36.

SUBJECT-ONLY CHARACTERISTICS: The decision to run a particular FC as "subject only" was often based on the judgment that the FC was of limited interest to social scientists in general, even though it might be of special interest to a limited number. It was considered important not to clutter the paragraphs with large numbers of statements dealing with matters of such limited interest.

A second, and often converging, reason why an FC was run as "subject only" had to do with imbalanced marginal frequencies. FC 35, for example, contrasts a mere 11 cultures where the natural environment is "tundra" against 389 cultures where it is "other than tundra." If this FC had been run as a predicate, the result would have been a number of irksome statements such as potential Statement 86/35 (which does not, of course, appear in the printout): "Cultures where the level of political integration is the large state, the little state, or the minimal state drift more toward being those where the natural environment is other than tundra—while cultures where the level of political integration is the autonomous community or the family drift less toward being those where the natural environment is other than tundra." In other words, virtually all of the statements would express "more" or "less" of an inclination toward the "other than tundra" attribute category, because of that category's overwhelming statistical weight. Furthermore, most such statements would be of little help because the category "other than

*There are 536 finished characteristics in this **Summary.** Of these, the first 480 are substantive and the remaining 56 are of a purely methodological nature (page 176). Of the 480 substantive FCs, 259 were run as "both subject and predicate," 150 as "subject only," 19 as "predicate only," and 52 as "neither subject nor predicate." FCs of the "neither subject nor predicate" type were totally removed from the Pattern Search procedure because earlier test runs made it clear that the information provided by these FCs was of limited interest to social scientists. Nonetheless, the subject and culture listings have been retained in the printout, and the codings have been retained in the FC data decks (page 47), in order to accommodate the occasional specialist who might wish to make use of them. There are three exceptional cases where such FCs were totally excised from the printout in order to prevent possible confusion: FCs 218, 381, and 384. In the Methodological Section, FC 521 was similarly excised.

tundra" is so internally heterogeneous that it would have relatively little meaning in most analytical situations (pages 36 and 69).

PREDICATE-ONLY CHARACTERISTICS: FCs run as "predicate only" are usually derived from raw characteristics of an ordinal rather than a nominal nature. For details, see **CPS,** pages 35–36.

Although a "predicate-only" characteristic is not run as a subject, the printout includes culture listings for each such characteristic, to enable the reader to check the coding assignments. After the culture listing, the printout proceeds immediately to the next paragraph, since there are no predicates to appear.

It is important to emphasize that running a finished characteristic as predicate only or as subject only often does not mean that any information is thrown away. It means simply that the information is presented only once, rather than twice.*

Predicate Listings, Sentences, and Statements

Each pair of subjects has its own paragraph identification number, which is, of course, the same as the identification number of the finished characteristic from which it is derived (page 30, Chart 2, Arrow B). The same is true of each pair of predicates. Thus Left Subject 86, when joined with Left Predicate 426, becomes Left Sentence 86/426. Left sentences will always provide some kind of contrast with corresponding right sentences. Left Sentence 86/426, when read together with Right Sentence 86/426, forms a compound sentence, referred to as Statement 86/426 (Arrow T). A literal reading of this statement is: "Cultures where the level of political integration is the large state, the little state, or the minimal state tend to be those where a high god is present; [whereas, by contrast,] cultures where the level of political integration is the autonomous community or the family tend to be those where a high god is absent."† A more comfortable reading would be something like: "Cultures with states tend to have high gods, while cultures without states tend not to."

*There is one exception to this, which is discussed on page 45.

†Even this literal reading is a kind of shorthand, in the sense that it communicates a kind of finality about the codings that is not intended in this **Summary.** A more precise reading of Statement 86/426 would be: "Cultures coded by Murdock as being those where the level of political integration is the large state, the little state, or the minimal state tend to be those coded by Swanson and the **Ethnographic Atlas** as being those where a high god is present—whereas, by contrast: cultures coded by Murdock as being those where the level of political integration is the autonomous community or the family tend to be those coded by Swanson and the **Ethnographic Atlas** as being those where a high god is absent." What this unwieldy reading brings out is that the codings in this **Summary**—or at least those of a more highly judgmental nature—are not necessarily to be regarded as reflecting "facts" in any unchanging or final sense. Rather, the codings reflect the rules and decisions of a particular scholar, pursuing particular interests at a particular point in the development of social science, using data available to him at that time.

Computer-winnowed Statements

In the actual Paragraph 86 in the printout (as distinct from the specimen in Chart 2), the first statement to appear is 86/4. There is no Statement 86/1, because FC 1 is run as subject only and hence cannot appear as a predicate in any paragraph. There is no Statement 86/2, because FC 2 is "neither subject nor predicate." FC 3, however, **could** have appeared in Paragraph 86, because it was run as "both subject and predicate." The reader may therefore assume that there is only one reason why potential Statement 86/3 does not appear in the printout, namely that this statement has been winnowed out. The winnowing might have been a hand-winnowing, or it might have been a computer-winnowing. In this case, a moment's investigation will reveal that it was a computer-winnowing.* The computer winnowed out this potential statement because the probability value of potential Table 86/3 proved to be higher than the winnowing level of .10. By this automatic winnowing process, the reader has been spared the chore of poring through thousands of such "weak" or "less supportable" statements as 86/3 and 3/86—statements that are of little or no importance. It should be emphasized, however, that under some circumstances the **non**appearance of a potential statement can be highly important, depending on the analyst's purposes, theoretical interests, expectations, and hypotheses. The nonconfirmation of a particular relationship is often as scientifically important as the confirmation of another. This point will be discussed in greater detail on page 44.

The Grammar of the Sentences

The sentences produced by the computer are in every case grammatical. The subject invariably contains a "subject lead" and a "subject clause." The predicate invariably contains a "verb" and a "predicate clause." In addition, some predicates also contain "adverbs." The computer is programed to look for, select, and print the subject lead, subject clause, verb, and predicate clause. It is also programed to decide whether an adverb is necessary and, if so, to select and print it. These operations will be illustrated with reference to Statement 86/102, the first statement in the specimen printout in Chart 2, page 30.

THE SUBJECT LEAD: The subject lead appears at the beginning of every sentence and specifies what it is that is being discussed—by means of classification, cross-classification, and tabulation. The subject lead of every sentence is, of course, "Cultures . . . "

*For an explanation of hand-winnowing, see page 39. Potential Statement 86/3 could not have been winnowed by hand, however, because FC 3 does not belong to a set of two or more ordinally-based FCs. In any case, one may easily check whether potential Statement 86/3 was hand-winnowed by turning to Appendix Nine: "Checklist of Hand-Winnowed Quasi-Redundant Statements."

THE SUBJECT CLAUSE: The subject clause is next retrieved from the computer's memory. This clause modifies the subject lead by defining the finished attribute category involved. For example, in Chart 2 the computer has joined the subject lead to the left subject clause and printed out Left Subject 86: "Cultures where the level of political integration is the large state, the little state, or the minimal state" (Arrow A).

THE PREDICATE CLAUSE: The next task of the computer is to select the predicate clause to be appended to the left subject, in order to begin to form a particular left sentence. For example, in Chart 2 the first left sentence is Left Sentence 86/102, which is based on Table 86/102. The left column of the table is keyed to the left subject, and the right column to the right subject (Arrows G and H). This table reads as follows:

	State Present	State Absent
Stratification Present	102	49
Stratification Absent	40	106
	142	155

The computer notes that a majority of 102 out of 142 of the cultures that possess states also possess stratification. In deciding what to "predicate" about state-possessing cultures, the computer takes its cue from the "majority" cell and decides to regard the 40 cultures in the "minority" cell as being, in a sense, deviant cases that can be disregarded for purposes of translation. The computer now searches its memory for the clause appropriate to the majority cell, which in this case is the cell in the top row.*

The computer chooses the predicate clause for Right Predicate 86/102 in a like manner. It notices that a majority of 106 out of 155 cultures in the right column are those with stratification absent, and it therefore chooses and prints that predicate clause.†

THE FOUR VERBS: The computer must next select and print a verb that will join each of the two subjects to its appropriate predicate clause in

*The top row of a finished characteristic in predicate position is the same as the left column of that FC in subject position—and the bottom row is the same as the right column. Thus, if the reader were to turn to Paragraph 102, he would find that the left subject is "Cultures where class stratification is present" and that the right subject is "Cultures where class stratification is absent."

†It sometimes happens that the top and bottom cell in a particular column are equal. In such cases, the computer is programed to "break the tie" by choosing the predicate appropriate to the cell in the row **opposite** that from which the other predicate was taken. The computer thus slightly "forces" a contrast. For example, suppose that in the right column of Table 86/102 the same number of cultures possessed stratification as did not possess it. The computer would have broken the tie by printing the "stratification absent" predicate. For an example, see Left Sentence 84/182 in the printout.

order to form two meaningful sentences. The verb is chosen by reference to the table that provides the basis for the two sentences. For the most part, the computer chooses the verb from among four alternatives, and the choice depends on how "significant," "strong," "improbable," or "interesting" the table is—in other words, on how low the table's probability value is (page 15). If the probability value indicates that the distribution of the cultures among the four cells is such that this distribution (or one more extreme) could occur by chance less than once out of a thousand times, the computer prints out its strongest verb, **"tend."** In the case of Statement 86/102 the probability value is indeed considerably lower than one out of a thousand, and the verb "tend" is chosen (Arrow J).

The remaining three verbs have been chosen to suggest progressively less "significance," "strength," "improbability," or "interest." The second strongest verb is **"lean,"** keyed to a probability value beyond .01 but not beyond .001 (Arrow L). The third strongest verb is **"tilt,"** keyed to a probability value beyond .05 but not .01 (Arrow O). The weakest verb is **"drift,"** keyed to a probability value beyond .10 but not .05 (Arrow Q). If the probability value of a table is .10 or greater, that table is, of course, winnowed out (page 34).

THE TWO ADVERBS: None of the statements cited to exemplify the verbs "tend," "lean," "tilt," or "drift" contains an adverb. In none of these statements was an adverb necessary, because in every case the "state present" cultures were inclined one way and the "state absent" cultures the other way. Thus the "state present" cultures were inclined toward stratification, full-time occupational specialization, low female subsistence contribution, and a certain type of adolescent peer group. By contrast, the "state absent" cultures were inclined to lack stratification, to possess only part-time occupational specialization, to be those where female contribution to subsistence is high, and to have a different kind of adolescent peer group (Arrows J, L, O, and Q).

There are numerous other cases, however, where both the left and the right subjects are inclined the **same** way—the difference being that one is inclined that way "more" and the other "less." An example is seen in Statement 86/109 (Arrow K). Here, both the "state present" and the "state absent" cultures tend to be those where castes are absent. That is, they both take their predicates from majority cells in the same row—the "castes absent" row. Note however, that only 78 per cent of the 133 "state present" cultures lack castes, whereas 97 per cent of the 152 "state absent" cultures lack them (Arrows M and N). The "state absent" cultures, in short, tend **more** in that direction, while the "state present" cultures tend **less** to be that way. Since this is the case, the computer has added the adverbs "more" and "less" to these two sentences, respectively.

The adverbs "more" and "less" can be added to any predicate where the verb is "tend," "lean," "tilt," or "drift."

THE SPECIAL VERB-PHRASE, "IN ALL CASES ARE": Before completing this discussion of the grammar of table translation it is necessary to deal with one more type of situation, that in which there are no deviant cases —i.e. where one cell in the table is a zero cell. Left Sentence 86/417 provides an example (Arrow S). Table 86/417 contains a zero cell, which indicates that in 100 per cent of the 17 cases where a state is present, warfare is prevalent. Accordingly, the computer selects and prints as the left verb the special verb-phrase, "in all cases are those . . . " This should be read cautiously to mean "in all **available** cases are those where warfare is prevalent," for there might be other cultures among the 148 coded by Murdock as possessing states which Leo W. Simmons **would** have coded as being "warfare not prevalent" **if** he had coded them at all. Note that Right Sentence 86/417 takes the verb "tilt," which is appropriate to a probability value beyond .05 but not .01. And since the tilting is **also** in the direction of "warfare prevalent," the computer has added the adverb "less." If the tilting had been in the opposite direction—toward "warfare not prevalent"—the computer would not have printed any adverb.

Now and then it happens that there will be a zero cell in both columns, one in each of the two rows. If this occurs, and if the probability value is lower than .10, the computer will print the verb-phrase: "in all cases are those . . . " in both the right and left sentences. An example is Statement 187/210 in the printout.

Syntax and Usage

A number of standard features have been built into the syntax and usage of table translation to maximize clarity and minimize the reading burden. The more important of these are described below.

TERMINOLOGY OF CONTRAST: In formulating the syntax of table translation, every effort has been made to simplify and standardize terminology and thus reduce the likelihood of the reader's drawing inappropriate conclusions from the statements in the printout. One such syntactic practice is the use of the term "rather than," which has already been introduced on page 23. Wherever the left subject clause includes this term, the right subject clause will also include it in a converse manner. For example, Left Subject 190 is "Cultures where the kin group is patrilineal or double-descent, rather than matrilineal," and

Right Subject 190 is "Cultures where the kin group is matrilineal, rather than patrilineal or double-descent." The presence of the term "rather than" reminds the reader that the contrast is **restricted**—i.e. that some substantively coded cultures have been excluded from both the left and right attribute categories and assigned to the residue as irrelevant. In this case, the excluded cultures are those where the kin group is cognatic. On the other hand, the absence of the term "rather than" reminds the reader that the contrast is **unrestricted**—i.e. that the cultures in the left attribute category are being contrasted against **all** other substantively coded cultures in the sample of 400 and that no cultures are irrelevant to the contrast. For example, Left Subject 186 is "Cultures where the kin group is exclusively patrilineal," which makes it clear that Right Subject 186 refers to all other substantively coded cultures in the sample.*

SYNTAX AND THE PHI COEFFICIENT: The phi coefficient has already been described (page 16). Its value tends to be high and its sign positive when the frequencies of the upper left and/or lower right cells are relatively large. Its value tends to be high and its sign negative when the frequencies in the upper right and/or lower left cells are relatively large.

The phi coefficient is relevant to the syntax of table translation in that its sign indicates whether the left sentence is essentially positive, negative, or what might be called "double-negative." In Chart 2, Arrow P indicates a positive phi coefficient.† The positive coefficient indicates that the left sentence is stating a relationship that is positive in content, namely that cultures possessing states are inclined also to possess full-time occupational specialization.‡

*The use of the term "rather than" is important primarily with respect to clauses appearing in predicate position. As suggested on page 29, Left Subject Clause 190, for example, is identical with Top Row Predicate Clause 190, and Right Subject Clause 190 is identical with Bottom Row Predicate Clause 190. As explained on page 36, it often occurs that both the left and the right sentences will include the same predicate clause, with one sentence containing the adverb "more" and the other the adverb "less." In such a case it is not possible for the reader to compare predicates and decide what category of cultures is being compared with what other category. It is thus essential that the internal phrasing of each predicate clause specify the restrictedness of the contrast by means of the term "rather than," or else denote its unrestrictedness by the absence of that term. For examples, see Statements 85/186 and 85/190 in the printout.

†Where the phi cofficient is positive, the computer does not print any sign before it. Where it is negative, the computer prints a minus sign.

‡The left, or positive, subject attribute class is associated with the "more positive" predicate attribute class—which is the attribute class in the top row. Accordingly, the upper left and lower right cells of Table 86/116 have larger frequencies. It should be borne in mind, however, that in some FCs the left attribute class (which is the top-row attribute class in predicate position) is no more "positive," in a substantive sense, than the right attribute class (which is the bottom-row attribute class in predicate position). Where this is the case, the sign of the resulting phi coefficient has no meaning as far as a substantively "positive" or "negative" relationship is concerned. An example of an FC

Arrow R indicates a case in which the phi coefficient is negative. Here, the left sentence states a relationship that is essentially negative in content, namely that cultures where states are present are inclined to be those where the contribution of females to subsistence is low.

The "double-negative" nature of the syntax is best understood by reference to Paragraph 86 in the printout itself, as distinct from the specimen in Chart 2. On the first page of this paragraph, look first at Left Sentences 86/6 and 86/9. Both have negative phi coefficients because in both, the state-possessing cultures are "more" inclined in an essentially negative direction—namely an "outside of" or "other than" direction. Left Sentence 86/4 is different, however. While it reveals that state-possessing cultures are also inclined in an essentially negative direction, the inclination is **less** in this direction than in the case of cultures where states are absent. In a sense, there is a "double-negative" aspect to this sentence, which makes it almost positive in implication. The fact that state-possessing cultures are **less** inclined to be located **outside** of the Circum-Mediterranean region suggests a kind of indirect positive relationship between a culture's possessing states and its being located in the Circum-Mediterranean. This "indirect positive" relationship is indicated by the fact that the phi coefficient for Table 86/4 is positive. The phi coefficient uniformly behaves this way.

FACILITATION OF QUICK READING: It is recommended that in first reading a paragraph the reader devote primary attention to the left sentences, with occasional glances when necessary at the right sentences and the tables. This will afford a quick overview of the entire "terrain" of the paragraph. The syntax of table translation should facilitate this overview, being designed in such a way that after a brief period of practice the reader, as his eye moves down the left sentences, will usually know what is contained in the corresponding right sentences without having to look at them. Chart 3 gives the relevant syntactic rules.

Hand-winnowed Statements

There are only two means by which statements can be winnowed out of the printout. The first, described on page 34, is computer-winnowing. The second is hand-winnowing. Hand-winnowing is not an automatic process, though it does follow fixed rules. In brief, the next-to-last printout is inspected to decide what statements are redundant. The computer is then given appropriate instructions, and these redundant statements are eliminated from the final printout. The purpose of hand-

where left and right attribute categories are equally "positive" is FC 20, where the left attribute category is "Cultures where the linguistic affiliation is Niger-Congo" and the right attribute category is "Cultures where the linguistic affiliation is Afro-Asiatic."

CHART 3: Syntactic Rules

If the left verb line is:	The right verb line will be:
Tend Lean Tilt Drift	Tend—in the opposite direction—or In all cases—in the opposite direction Lean—in the opposite direction—or In all cases—in the opposite direction Tilt—in the opposite direction—or In all cases—in the opposite direction Drift—in the opposite direction—or In all cases—in the opposite direction
Tend more Lean more Tilt more Drift more	Tend less—in the same direction Lean less—in the same direction Tilt less—in the same direction Drift less—in the same direction
Tend less Lean less Tilt less Drift less	Tend more—in the same direction—or In all cases—in the same direction Lean more—in the same direction—or In all cases—in the same direction Tilt more—in the same direction—or In all cases—in the same direction Drift more—in the same direction—or In all cases—in the same direction
In all cases	[There are many possibilities. It is best to examine the right predicate rather than attempt to guess.]

winnowing is to minimize the reading burden without sacrificing information and, in some cases, to eliminate confusion that might otherwise result.

Redundant statements take two principal forms: the "pure" redundant and the "quasi-redundant." Pure redundant statements result from tables where both the subject FC and the predicate FC derive from the same raw characteristic. For example, both FCs 35 and 33 derive from the raw characteristic: "Type of Natural Environment." Unless it had been hand-winnowed, Statement 35/33 would have appeared in the printout, saying: "Cultures where the natural environment is tundra in all cases are those where the natural environment is 'very harsh,' i.e. desert, desert grasses and shrubs, tundra, or high plateau steppe." All such tautologies have been systematically removed by hand-winnowing.

Quasi-redundant statements are more complex, and are explained in detail in **CPS,** pages 40–41. In brief, they are eliminated by removing the appropriate predicate-pairs from a series of predicate-pairs, where two conditions prevail: (1) all predicate-pairs in the series derive from the same raw characteristic, and (2) there is some kind of ordinal aspect to that raw characteristic. Appendix Nine lists the identification numbers of all statements removed for reasons of quasi-redundance, so that the reader can check whether the nonappearance of a particular predicate-pair and table is explainable on this ground.*

This policy on the hand-winnowing of quasi-redundant statements means that in some cases only one statement remains which derives from a particular ordinal raw characteristic. Therefore, if the reader finds even one such statement, and it deals with a subject that interests him, he might do well to assemble the two raw characteristics concerned into a 2-by-N or M-by-N table, as described on page 49.†

It should be mentioned, finally, that all hand-winnowing was conservatively carried out. In any case where there was any real doubt as to the propriety of removing a statement, it was left in the printout.

HOW TO USE THE PRINTOUT

At this point it should be emphasized once again that the printout simply tells us what classes of cultures significantly co-occur or overlap with what other classes. The computer is utterly incapable of telling us **why** these overlaps occur. The computer, as used to produce this **Summary,** can perform only those operations that it has been explicitly instructed to perform. And while many of these tasks are highly complex, they are all wholly mechanical. The proper interpretation of the printout must, then, come from the creative intellect of the researcher himself. The following recommendations for using the printout are intended primarily for the reader who is unfamiliar with cross-cultural statistical research. The recommendations assume that the reader is pursuing a mixed "holistic" and "atomistic" approach (page 9).

Selection of Relevant Paragraphs

It is suggested that the reader select first a section that covers a subject with which he is familiar. It would also be well to examine the commentary dealing with that section and its finished characteristics which appears in Chapter 4, "Coding Background."

*In hand-winnowing these quasi-redundant statements, I was particularly on the alert **not** to remove any statements where ordinal predicates suggested a curvilineal or bimodal distribution of cultures along a continuum. Despite this caution, not a single such instance was detected.

†Before doing so, he should refer to Appendix Nine to ascertain just which related additional statements were hand-winnowed.

Evaluation of Sources and Codings

Before turning to the printout and to a paragraph embodying a finished characteristic related to his chosen topic, the reader may wish first to examine the culture listings for that paragraph, to determine whether he would have coded certain cultures differently. In doing so, he will naturally find himself looking first to see how a culture with which he is personally familiar has been coded.* For example, my own specialty is Thai culture, which I studied in the field for five years. As an experiment, I checked all of the culture listings to see whether I agreed with the manner in which the Thai culture had been coded. I was reassured to find myself generally satisfied by these codings. There were, however, two kinds of exceptions. The first type of exception occurred two or three times. An example is the coding for slavery. In Paragraph 110 the dichotomy is simply "slavery present" versus "slavery absent." I found Thai culture listed among those with slavery present. In checking the "time level" for Thai culture (Appendix Three), I noted that it is 1940. My doubts gathered when I recalled that the Thai government abolished slavery in the first decade of this century—although, of course, certain informal vestiges remained and were evident to the field ethnographer working, as I did, during the 1950s. In checking the actual coding categories and rules used, however, my doubts were dispelled (page 90). The **Ethnographic Atlas** coding for the Thai is "Hf," meaning: "hereditary slavery present—formerly." Since the period between legal abolition of slavery and the "time level" was hardly more than a generation, it seemed reasonable for the **EA** to have coded the Thai as "Hf." By contrast, the **EA** coded the "Americans" as "O," meaning "slavery absent." Again upon reflection this seemed reasonable, since the corresponding period for the Americans was 1863 to 1920—a significantly longer period from the standpoint of cultural change.†

The second kind of exception occurred only once. In the culture listings for Paragraph 272, I noted that the Thai are coded as having a "low" rather than "high" divorce rate. As a field ethnographer, I had always felt that the Thai divorce rate was definitely "high"—relative, that is, to the rate in my own and other cultures. Against these doubts, however, stood two important facts. First of all, Charles Ackerman, the

*As an alternative to checking the culture listings, he may turn to Appendices Seven and Eight, which indicate how each of the 400 cultures has been coded for all finished characteristics and almost all raw characteristics. For details, see page 47.

†I have described this example as if I were a typical reader of the printout. Actually, as the compiler of this **Summary,** in constructing FC 110 I made the decision to include in the left attribute category ("Cultures where slavery is present") **both** cultures coded by the **Atlas** as having some kind of slavery present **and** cultures coded as formerly having had some kind of slavery present. This decision was somewhat arbitrary and might be challenged on some grounds, but the question of whether it was appropriate is irrelevant to this example, in which we are concentrating simply on the manner in which the reader can check a particular coding assignment to a particular FC category.

contributor of these codings, is a careful social scientist who was relying for this study on the best ethnographic sources he could find. And second, when I looked at the names of the other cultures that had been coded for divorce rate, it was clear that I knew little or nothing about most of them in this respect. Unless I were prepared to carry out something like the same kind of coding operation that Ackerman carried out, I could never be sure that the Thai divorce rate was not, **relatively speaking,** a low one. And such an operation would not be easy. Ackerman has put the problem this way:

> The author must admit that the data used in the research have many faults. For the most part, ethnographers have stated only that divorce is "low," "common," "infrequent," etc. Rarely has any ethnographer justified his assessment of the rate by any statement of the actual incidence of divorce. . . . since the ethnographers have not necessarily had reference to a common baseline, it is impossible to assert with confidence that one society's "low" is exactly equivalent to another society's "low" rate. There is no way of dealing with these faults. The researcher can only use the data as given—or stop his research. This [study] is built on the hope that the ethnographic data are neither wholly meaningless nor wholly incomparable [Ackerman 1963:15].

The question now arises: To what extent can the reader disagree with the codings found in a particular paragraph* and still be justified in regarding its statements as being reasonably valid? The answer depends on the extent and distribution of the cases involved. If the reader disagrees with a substantial proportion of the codings listed at the top of a particular paragraph, obviously there would be little point in proceeding to read the paragraph. However, if the reader disagrees with only a small proportion of the codings, and especially if one questionable coding would seem to cancel out another, he can proceed to read the paragraph with a measure of confidence. Of crucial importance is the extent to which the **proportions** of a particular column or row may thus be affected. If, for example, the left column has a relatively small marginal total to begin with, a considerable disturbance could result from the shift of two or three cultures from the left to the right column or from the top to the bottom cell within the left column. It should be borne in mind, however, that the result might be either a weakening **or** a strengthening of the association between the two finished characteristics, depending on the nature of the shift. For such reasons, it would be wise to regard tables with a small "N" more cautiously than tables with a large "N." For further discussion and examples, see **CPS,** pages 42–44.

*The codings with which the reader might disagree include both the "column" codings for the subject FC, which are specified in the culture listings of that paragraph, and the "row" codings for a predicate FC, which are specified in the culture listings for that FC at the point in the printout where that FC is the subject of its own paragraph.

Quick Reading

Assuming that questions of coding reliability and validity present no unduly difficult problems, the next recommended step in utilizing the printout is to obtain a quick over-all picture of the "general terrain" of the section. The reader will thus gain a holistic contextual "feel" for the data before embarking on a more atomistic search for crucial relationships.

Detailed Reading

The reader may now wish to return to the beginning of the section and read the paragraphs more thoroughly. Attention should be paid to the tables on which the statements are based, and to the distribution of the cultures among the four cells of these tables.

Checking Statements That Fail to Appear

When the reader has a sharply focused interest in a particular analytical problem, it is important to check the printout for "missing" predicate-pairs, i.e. for statements that "ought" to print out but do not. In some analytical situations, it is often more important that a particular statement has **failed** to print out because it did not survive the winnowing test at the 10 per cent level than that certain other statements did pass the test and did therefore appear in the printout.

The mere fact that a statement is missing from the printout of a particular paragraph does not mean, however, that it has failed to pass the winnowing test. Rather, in some cases the reason will be simply that the predicate-pair of that statement did not print out because that particular finished characteristic was run as "subject-only" and hence was not eligible to appear as a predicate-pair. Indications of whether a particular FC was run so as to be eligible to appear as a predicate-pair are given in Chapter 4, "Coding Background," where a large dot placed before a particular FC listing indicates that it is **not** so eligible (page 64). Where this is so, the reader should turn to the place in the printout where the particular FC is in subject position to its own paragraph, and examine that paragraph to determine whether the other FC in question appears there as a predicate-pair. For example, there is a strong relationship between a culture's being located in Africa (FC 3) and its possessing a Niger-Congo linguistic affiliation (FC 17). Yet in examining Paragraph 3 on Africa, one notes that Statement 3/17 fails to appear. Turning to Paragraph 17 on Niger-Congo languages, however, we note in Statement 17/3 that cultures with Niger-Congo linguistic affiliation "tend to be located in Africa." The reason, of course, is that the Niger-Congo language FC (like all of the FCs dealing with linguistic affiliation) was run as "subject only."

If the paragraph the reader is examining is itself a subject-only paragraph, and if the "missing" predicate-pair also stems from an FC run as "subject only," there is unfortunately no way to detect from the printout whether a statistically supportable relationship exists between the two FCs. Thus, if the "Africa" and the "Niger-Congo" FCs had **both** been run as "subject only," it would then have been necessary to resort to the original finished characteristic data decks of punched cards in order to assemble the relevant table and thus be in a position to compute that table's probability level. However, it is not anticipated that this problem will occur very often.*

Draft of Preliminary Conclusions

The reader might wish at this point to prepare a draft compilation of the major conclusions that seem to emerge from the section, perhaps annotated with statement numbers from which these conclusions derive. In reaching such conclusions, it is recommended that the reader place primary weight on the "tend" and "lean" statements—which, in my view, are not likely to be upset by future restudies of the same subject. Moderate weight may be placed on the "tilt" statements, whereas the "drift" statements are perhaps of value primarily insofar as they "pattern with" the stronger types of statements. Statements containing the verb-phrase, "in all cases are those . . ." should be evaluated more individually, but certainly the probability level is a relevant consideration in their cases as well. Occasionally the reader may reach a conclusion from a single isolated statement—and such conclusions can deal with quite crucial relationships—but experience suggests that a conclusion of value will more frequently assume the form of a pattern based on a concatenation of interrelated statements.

Cross-checking

One of the advantages of the Pattern Search procedure is that tables are "turned over" so that an interesting predicate-pair can be examined in another paragraph where it becomes the subject-pair.† By reading this other paragraph, the analyst can obtain a considerably fuller contextual view of the new subject characteristic. This can be valuable both for identifying important intervening variables and for suggesting new research leads involving variables not included in this **Summary.**

An example may help to illustrate this advantage. Suppose that the

*Unfortunately, there was no practicable way to avoid this inconvenience. If all FCs had been run so as to make them eligible to print out as predicates, the result would have been to clutter the **Summary** with too many statements of unduly limited interest.

†There are 19 FCs run as "predicate only," and in these cases—a small minority of the total—such examination is not possible.

reader is examining Paragraph 187 and his interest is aroused by Statement 187/390 that cultures coded as matrilineal in no case severely punish premarital sex relations. He may decide that he would like to know more about the other significant attributes of cultures where premarital sex relations are not (or are) severely punished. He therefore turns to Paragraph 390, which contrasts "cultures where premarital sex relations are strongly punished and in fact rare" versus cultures that are more permissive. Here he finds, among others, Statements 390/86, 87, which clearly suggest a strong relationship between severe punishment for premarital sex relations and a higher level of political integration.

Cross-checking may also produce negative results, which can be as important as positive results. If the reader has previously suspected, for example, that strength of desire for children is more a function of subsistence base than a function of form of social organization, his attention may be arrested in reading Paragraph 190 by Statements 190/282, 295. These tell him that cultures which are patrilineal (or double-descent) are characterized by a "high" desire for children and a high punishment for abortion—while matrilineal cultures, by contrast, are characterized by a "low or absent" coding on both counts. The reader also notes Statements 190/51, 55, 62, 63, which reassure him by revealing positive associations between patrilineal (or double-descent) cultures and more complex forms of subsistence. Pressing his analysis further, he turns to Paragraphs 282 and 295. Here he discovers that in both paragraphs, potential Statements 51 through 70 (those dealing with subsistence base) fail in every case to appear in the printout. At this point, perhaps the only permissible conclusion is that the patrilineality-matrilineality distinction has a more important bearing on strength of desire for children than does type of subsistence base. The conclusion must, however, remain tentative because of the small "N"s of Tables 282/190 and 295/190.

Examples of Use of the Printout

Prior to publication of this **Summary,** two contributors utilized the printout in conjunction with the analysis of cross-cultural problem areas. Each of the resulting articles will serve as an instructive example of the manner in which the printout can serve a researcher. One article deals with maternal ambivalence and narcissism (Slater and Slater 1965) and the other with games of chance (Roberts and Sutton-Smith 1966).

TECHNIQUES FOR FURTHER ANALYSIS

The use of the procedures suggested in the foregoing sections might be adequate for the reasonably satisfactory resolution of some analytical problems. For other problems, however, further analysis will be needed. Such analysis requires that the reader obtain the original data decks and either (1) build additional contingency tables of new or wider scope or (2) utilize more sophisticated techniques. In this section only the former type of further analysis will be described. The building of additional contingency tables is simple and easy to learn, even for an analyst without previous experience. Only the simplest of punched-card processing equipment is required: the sorter, the tabulator, and the reproducer. These machines are easily learned even by an unskilled student assistant.

The original data decks are available from the publisher at cost plus postage. These decks are of two kinds. First is the set of two decks of 400 cards each—one card for each of the 400 cultures—on which are punched the code symbols for all of the data columns in the **Ethnographic Atlas,** plus a few additional raw characteristics. (See Appendix Seven.) Second, there is the set of eleven Finished Characteristic decks —each deck, again, containing 400 cards. (See Appendix Eight.)*

In general, each of the two **EA** data decks and the eleven FC data decks includes data codes punched in Columns 1 through 50. Columns 51 through 63 are invariably blank. Columns 64 through 74 carry the name of the culture, for convenient identification. Column 75 is blank. Columns 76 and 77 carry the identification symbol for the deck. Columns 78, 79, and 80 carry the identification numbers of the cultures, alphabetically arranged from 001, which is Abipon, to 400, which is Zuni. The format of these data decks is slightly different from that of the two relevant appendices. Appendix Seven (for the **EA** data decks) and Appendix Eight (for the FC data decks) generally carry 100 columns of data codes per page, in order to conserve space. Moreover, certain other obvious changes have been made to improve clarity of presentation. As far as data entries are concerned, however, the columns and codes in the Appendices and in the corresponding data decks are identical.

As will be noted in Appendix Seven, there are three double entries of special data, labeled respectively "EX," "LP," and "NE." In the **second** of the **EA** data decks, the two "EX" entries are punched in Columns 41 and 42; the two "LP" entries in Columns 45 and 46, and the two "NE" entries in Columns 49 and 50. Each of these special pairs of entries requires brief explanation.

The "EX" entries are "Extra" data from the **Ethnographic Atlas.** It

*To obtain these decks, write to "Summary Decks," Human Relations Area Files, Inc., 2054 Yale Station, New Haven, Connecticut 06520. Explanation sheets will be shipped with each batch of cards. In addition, further developments in the updating, expanding, and correcting of the data decks will be announced from time to time in the quarterly journal, **Behavior Science Notes,** published by the Human Relations Area Files.

is necessary to punch them in Columns 41 and 42 of the second **EA** data deck because, inadvertently, the original columnization of the **EA** did not allow space in which to punch these two columns. Entries in Column 41 are the lower-case postposited code symbols from the **EA**'s "Column 19" (1962: 118–19), and are explained in more detail on page 105, footnote. Entries in Column 42 are the lower-case postposited code symbols from the **EA**'s "Column 24" (1962: 119), and are explained in more detail on page 109, footnote.

The "LP" entries are "Level of Political Integration" data from the "World Ethnographic Sample" (Murdock 1957a: 674). Entries in Column 45 are the capital-letter code symbols from Murdock's "Column 15," and entries in Column 46 are his lower-case code symbols from the same Column 15. Further explanation is found on page 82.

The "NE" entries are "Natural Environment" data from unpublished codings by Frank W. Moore (1962). Entries in Column 49 are the primary environment type, and entries in Column 50 are the secondary environment type, if any. If there is no secondary environment type, then the code is "Z." Further explanation is found on page 69.

In Appendix Seven and in the **EA** data deck, the substantive codes are usually alphabetical. The numerical code "5" means "unascertained." In Appendix Eight and in the Finished Characteristic data deck, all codes are numerical. Code "1" (punch "1") means "left column" or "left attribute category." Code "2" means "right column." The three residual codes are "3," meaning "excluded because ambiguous"; "4," meaning "excluded because irrelevant"; and "5," meaning "excluded because unascertained."

Checking Relationships on Special Subsamples

This is perhaps the simplest of all follow-up techniques. If the reader discovers in the printout a relationship that is crucial to his hypothesis or theory, he will often want to check this relationship on special subsamples. He can thereby explore and perhaps confirm the generality of the relationship. For example, if the relationship he has discovered in the total sample of cultures used in this **Summary** is found **also** to hold within each of six subsamples representing the six regions, then a very strong case will have been made for the contention that the relationship is functional rather than historical-diffusional.* By the same token, if a relationship is to be regarded as general, one would expect it to hold for cultures regardless of subsistence base. Perhaps the simplest test of

*The six subsamples can easily be constructed by sorting the first **EA** data deck on Column 1. If the relationship to be checked involves a Finished Characteristic data deck, then Column 1 of the **EA** data deck should first be transferred to the relevant FC deck, using the reproducer. On each FC deck, Columns 51 through 63 have been left blank in order to accommodate such column transfers.

this would be to draw two subsamples, one of food producing cultures and the other of gathering cultures.*

Construction of New Contingency Tables

This technique is related to the one just described, and is also relatively simple. It can be helpful in instances where the printout suggests relationships of interest to the reader that can only be searched adequately by construction of new contingency tables which cross raw attributes not crossed in any tables appearing in the printout. These new tables might involve raw attributes not selected at all for use as finished attributes in the present **Summary.** Or they might involve some raw attributes already used, but not yet crossed with particular other raw attributes. Or, finally, they might involve complex recombination of raw attributes in various additive or alternative ways (page 23) appropriate to the particular interests of the analyst. Such new contingency tables might be 2-by-2, 2-by-N, or M-by-N. Examples are given later (page 51).

The extent to which an analyst should engage in the construction of formal a priori hypotheses, which he can then proceed to test, is a question about which scholars may differ on the basis of their background and training and also, of course, on the basis of the problem that is being researched. Regardless of what position one takes, however, one point seems clear: the analyst who proceeds to formulate such hypotheses and test them with recombined or refined variables, and who demonstrates the ability to predict nonobvious relationships of substantive importance, will normally be better justified in regarding himself as having mastered his subject-matter area than will the analyst who confines his efforts to post hoc explanations of relationships that he did not predict but which emerged in the printout. Such attempts to predict from hypotheses and theory are to be encouraged. Not only this, but it is my hope that one of the main advantages of this **Summary** will prove to be its efficacy in stimulating the generation of new and fruitful hypotheses.

A valuable resource for constructing additional contingency tables is the publication, **Cross-Tabulations of Murdock's World Ethnographic Sample** (Coult and Habenstein 1965). As its title page indicates, this book is a "reference handbook containing a complete set of all possible two-dimensional cross-tabulations of Murdock's World Ethnographic Sample, presented in 528 tables accompanied by paired tables showing the level of significance and coefficient of association for the relationship between each pair of variables." The "World Ethnographic Sam-

*This can be done by sorting on Column 1 of FC Deck 2—i.e. on FC 51. All cards representing food-producing cultures will drop into the "1" pocket, and all cards representing gathering cultures into the "2" pocket.

ple" (Murdock 1957a) contains 565 cultures and overlaps substantially with the **EA** sample used in this **Summary,** which superseded it. Coult and Habenstein's "level of significance" is calculated by the Fisher Exact Test. This is used regardless of the size of the table, and is a one-tailed test—as distinct from the two-tailed test used in this **Summary.** The "coefficient of association" is the phi coefficient. Consultation of the Coult-Habenstein book will prove more convenient than use of the sorter and tabulator, provided that both variables (raw characteristics) concerned are included in the codings of the "World Ethnographic Sample." In interpreting the results, however, it would be well to bear in mind that the 1957 sample is judged by Murdock to be less satisfactory than his present **Ethnographic Atlas** sample (**EA** 1963: 109). Moreover, this latter sample incorporates numerous coding addenda and corrigenda not found in the 1957 sample.*

Concomitant Variation with Ordinal Variables

This type of follow-up analysis is simply a special case of the construction of new contingency tables. As will be recalled, quite a large number of the raw characteristics in this **Summary** are ordinal in nature, and have been dichotomized into finished characteristics by means of a moving cutting point (page 24). When paragraphs or predicate-pairs derived from such FCs suggest concomitant variation between one raw characteristic and another, it is often useful to reassemble one or both raw characteristics into a single table. An example is found in the raw characteristic, "Level of Political Integration." FCs 84 through 87 result in Paragraphs 84 through 87, which embrace the continuum from Large State to Little State to Minimal State to Autonomous Community to Family, with each FC representing the dichotomy that results from moving the cutting point. Reading through these four paragraphs, an analyst's interest might be stimulated by the fact that several statements appear, all suggesting a concomitant relationship between higher levels of political integration and the presence of high gods, especially active gods that support human morality. In order to assess the relationship more precisely, he might wish to assemble 2-by-N or M-by-N tables, as illustrated in Charts 4 and 5, below.

If one is looking for evidence of concomitant variation, it will sometimes be appropriate to collapse certain columns or rows in order to achieve a kind of "staircasing" of cell frequencies. (See **CPS,** pages 45–47.) In the present example, it was discovered that unless the "large" and "little" states were combined into a single column, the staircasing

*The Coult-Habenstein volume, being based on the earlier Murdock work, does not include a number of variables found in the **EA**, nor does it include codings from any of the numerous other studies in the literature. It is to be hoped that the Coult-Habenstein approach will before long be applied to some of the variables in this wider range of data.

CHART 4: Level of Political Integration, by Type of High God: Five 2-by-3 Tables

	Large or Little State	Minimal State	No State (Autonomous Community or Family)
Some kind of high god present	38	32	47
All others	8	15	62

	Large or Little State	Minimal State	No State (Autonomous Community or Family)
High god present and active	25	19	18
All others	21	28	91

	Large or Little State	Minimal State	No State (Autonomous Community or Family)
High god present and active and supportive of human morality	21	14	7
All others	15	33	102

	Large or Little State	Minimal State	No State (Autonomous Community or Family)
High god present and active	25	19	18
High god present, but not active	13	13	29

	Large or Little State	Minimal State	No State (Autonomous Community or Family)
High god present and active and supportive of human morality	20	14	7
High god present and active, but not supportive of human morality	5	5	11

CHART 5: Level of Political Integration, by Type of High God: 3-by-3 Table

	Large or Little State	Minimal State	No State (Autonomous Community or Family)	
High god present and supportive of human morality	21 = 10%	14 = 7%	7 = 4%	42 = 21%
High god present, but not supportive of human morality	17 = 8%	18 = 9%	40 = 20%	75 = 37%
High god absent	8 = 4%	15 = 7%	62 = 31%	85 = 42%
	46 = 22%	47 = 23%	109 = 55%	202 = 100%

would be considerably impaired. Staircasing was further improved by collapsing into one column those cultures where the level of political integration is the autonomous community and those where it is the family.*

Chart 4 presents five 2-by-3 tables dealing with the relationship between level of political integration and type of high god present, if any. These tables suggest rather strongly that the evolution or emergence of higher levels of political integration is accompanied by the evolution or emergence of high gods that are active and morality-supporting.

Chart 5 presents more or less the same data, but with additional collapsing of the "high god" raw attribute categories. Percentage figures indicate the ratio between the number of cultures in each cell and the total "N" of the table. Once again, the concomitant relationship between level of political integration and the "high god" raw attribute seems clear.

*Whether it is legitimate to collapse columns in this manner depends on whether the analyst holds to a theoretical position which necessitates that the relevant raw attribute categories be kept distinct—large state from little state, for example—or whether he is simply treating the entire set of categories as a continuum. If the former is the case, then it would be an improper procedure to collapse certain columns simply for the purpose of "making the results come out nicely." In the present instance, the entire set is simply being treated as a continuum.

Matrices and the Analysis of Deviant Cases

Each card in the original data decks is punched with the name of the culture it represents. It is therefore a simple matter to produce a matrix which includes in each cell the names of the cultures that belong there.* A matrix for Chart 5, for example, would identify those cultures that constitute the more extreme deviant cases—namely, the seven cultures in the upper right corner, and the eight cultures in the lower left corner. Once these cultures are identified, the analyst will perhaps be stimulated to see beyond the attribute categories immediately involved, and to perceive the possible relevance of outside factors not included among the characteristics employed in the present **Summary.** Skillful analysis of deviant cases can also lead to other fruitful discoveries, such as (1) the existence of coding errors (2) the need for a refinement of coding rules, or (3) the need for redefinition of coding categories.† For an example, see **CPS,** pages 13–17. For further discussion, see Köbben 1967.

REVIEW OF THE LITERATURE AND CONSTRUCTION OF NEW CODINGS

It cannot be stressed too strongly that before an analyst utilizes any of the tables or statements from this **Summary** in preparation of a serious publication or lecture, he must understand the codings that underlie these tables and statements. This will often require close study of the source of the codings to ascertain the precise coding rules used, the theoretical and research interests that prompted the establishment of such rules, the manner in which borderline cases were decided, and the reliability checks, if any, that were made on coding assignments. It would also be advisable for the analyst actually to examine at least a

*A complete example is given in **CPS,** page 48.

†The seven deviant cases in the upper right corner are: Bozo, Lapps, Mbuti, Papago, Tarahumara, Warrau, and Yahgan. Swanson, in doing a similar deviant case analysis on the Yahgan, speculates on the possible existence of ethnographer bias in this instance (1960:71–72). Turnbull has similar suspicions about certain reporting on the Mbuti (1965:241, 248). In analyzing these deviant cases it would also be well to bear in mind the "time level" of each culture (page 14). For all of them except the Yahgan, this time level is 1930 or later—i.e. recent enough so that the effects of religious acculturation might well be worth investigating. The Bozo, for example, are evidently well acculturated to Islam (Murdock 1958:2053). Acculturation to Christianity is perhaps the explanation in the case of the Lapps (Minn 1965:71); the Papago (Underhill 1946:14; Joseph, Spicer, and Chesky 1949:72); and the Tarahumara (Lumholtz 1902:295). Kirchhoff raises a generally similar question about the Warrau (1948:879).

The eight deviant cases in the lower left corner are: Coorg, Dard, Fon, Hawaiians, Koreans, Romans, Sotho, and Thai. Of the Romans, the **EA** says that there were "variable beliefs" during the period around 100 A.D., which is the "time level" for that culture (1962:541). The Dards are a mixed population with some Muslims (**EA** 1963:262). It is perhaps also worth noting that although the Thai and Korean cultures lack high gods, they do partake of religions that are generally regarded as highly developed in a philosophical and morality-regulating sense: Buddhism and Confucianism-Buddhism, respectively.

reasonable sampling of the original ethnographies—or Human Relations Area Files data slips—from which the codings were derived. The degree of care to be exercised by the analyst will depend in part on the inherent difficulty of coding the subject matter concerned. It is, for example, considerably easier to code "subsistence base" (page 72), than to code some of the psychological characteristics found in this **Summary** (page 137).

Close examination of the source of the codings for a particular raw characteristic will often reveal a gap between the coding categories and rules used by the coder and the categories and rules that would be ideally appropriate to the reader's interests. Where this gap is very great, the resulting statements and tables will have little or no validity to the reader's interests. Where the gap is not too great, the relevant statements and tables will perhaps be of some suggestive value to the reader, but not of conclusive importance. In the latter case, it is to be hoped that the analyst will feel encouraged to proceed to do his own coding of a sample of cultures in accordance with his own interests. In such manner, all of social science will benefit, especially if the analyst later shares his codings with his colleagues.

A PARTIAL TEST OF THE MEANINGFULNESS OF THE PARAGRAPHS

At this point we must squarely face the question: How meaningful are the statements in the printout and the tables on which they are based? To what extent can they be taken seriously and to what extent should they be regarded as simply the consequence of chance? I personally regard most of the paragraphs as being reasonably meaningful, primarily because I perceive in them a reassuringly high degree of internal consistency and patterning among statements.

The nagging question still arises, however: How do we know that the processes of sheer chance could not produce statements among which a reasonable reader would perceive an equal degree of internal consistency and patterning? And, to move from a qualitative to a quantitative question: How do we know that sheer chance would not produce an equal or greater number of such statements?

To answer these questions, at least partially, a test was devised.* Ten nonsense FCs were established, which appear in the printout as Paragraphs 527–36. These are the "whiskers" characteristics, which straight-facedly tell us what color whiskers are worn, or are not worn, by particular cultures. Paragraph 527 contrasts the 200 cultures "that belong to the 50 per cent that have purple whiskers" versus the 200 that do not. To determine which 50 per cent were to be regarded as sporting purple whiskers, a table of random numbers was consulted.

*A similar test is described in **CPS,** pages 51–53.

Partial Test of Meaningfulness of Paragraphs

Since the "N" of a paragraph might possibly bear a general relationship to the number of statements that survive the winnowing test, Paragraph 528 reduces this N. Here, half of the cultures wearing purple whiskers and half not wearing them are dropped into the residue. Again, a table of random numbers was used in determining which cultures to drop. In succeeding paragraphs, the N is progressively reduced: to 100, to 50, and finally to 25 in Paragraph 531.

The remaining whiskers paragraphs keep the N at 400, but vary the frequencies of the left and right attributes. Thus in Paragraph 532 the 40 per cent of the cultures having blue whiskers are contrasted against "all others." In the next paragraph, the 30 per cent that have green whiskers are contrasted against "all others." Then there are the 20 per cent that have pink whiskers, the 10 per cent that have yellow whiskers, and finally, in Paragraph 536, the 5 per cent that have white whiskers.

The reader may turn to the whiskers paragraphs and judge for himself whether they reveal as much internal consistency or patterning as is generally true in the substantively coded paragraphs. Such judgments are, of course, somewhat subjective. Nonetheless, it seems likely that most readers would agree that the whiskers paragraphs generally are characterized by considerably less internal consistency than are most of the substantive paragraphs. One relatively objective indication of this lack of patterning is the fact that in all of the ten whiskers paragraphs there was only one statement that had to be hand-winnowed because of quasi-redundancy, while such hand-winnowings in the substantive paragraphs are much more common.*

The next question to be asked is whether processes of sheer chance would have yielded as great a number of statements per paragraph as actually appear in the substantive paragraphs of the printout. In attempting to answer this question, the first step was to tally the number of tend, lean, tilt, and drift statements in each of the ten whiskers paragraphs.†

The same operation was then performed on a one-in-ten sample of all substantive paragraphs.‡ Chart 6 summarizes the results and

*"Quasi-redundancy" is defined on page 40. The reader might also wish to check Appendix Nine, "Checklist of Hand-Winnowed Quasi-Redundant Statements."

†Statements where both predicates bore the verb-phrase "in all cases are those" were tallied as tends, leans, tilts, or drifts in accordance with the probability value of the associated table. Thus, for example, Statement 530/444 was tallied as a "tilt."

‡Paragraphs 481 and beyond, being methodological rather than substantive in content, were not included in the tally. Among the first 480 paragraphs, there are 259 run as "both subject and predicate"; 150 run as "subject only"; 19 run as "predicate only"; and 52 that were "neither subject nor predicate." The one-in-ten sample was drawn from the paragraphs that **could** take a predicate-pair—i.e. the first two categories just mentioned. Thus the population of paragraphs was 259 plus 150, or 409. Moving from a random start with the eighth eligible paragraph, I took the eighteenth, twenty-eighth, and so forth. The total number of paragraphs tallied was 41. The use of such a sample for tallying, rather than the entire corpus of 409 paragraphs, was made necessary by the size of the undertaking and the fact that the tally had to be done by hand.

CHART 6: Distribution of Statements in "Whiskers" and Substantive Paragraphs

	"WHISKERS" PARAGRAPHS					SUBSTANTIVE PARAGRAPHS				
	All Statements	Tend Statements	Lean Statements	Tilt Statements	Drift Statements	All Statements	Tend Statements	Lean Statements	Tilt Statements	Drift Statements
A. Total Actual	126	1	7	60	58	1548	286	243	505	514
B. Mean Actual	12.6	0.1	0.7	6	5.8	37.8	7.0	5.9	12.3	12.5
C. Total Expected	250	2.5	22.5	100	125	1025	10.25	92.25	410	512.5
D. Total Actual over Total Expected	.50	.40	.31	.60	.46	1.5	27.9	2.6	1.2	1.0
E. Maximum Actual	21	1	4	11	14	104	33	17	31	26
F. Median Actual	14	0	0	6	4	33	4	5	11	12
G. Minimum Actual	4	0	0	1	0	10	0	0	1	3
H. Expected Level Per Paragraph	25	.25	2.25	10	12.5	25	.25	2.25	10	12.5
I. Number of Paragraphs Meeting Expected Level	0	1	2	1	1	29	32	31	24	15
J. Number of Paragraphs Meeting Expected Level over Total Number of Paragraphs	.00	.10	.20	.10	.10	.71	.78	.76	.59	.37

makes it possible to compare the whiskers paragraphs with the substantive paragraphs in terms of the quantity of each kind of statement. The theoretical maximum number of statements that could appear in a particular paragraph is about 250.* Since the winnowing level is 10 per cent, the statistical expectation is that, through the operation of sheer chance, a typical paragraph ought to contain about 25 statements. Since the whiskers paragraphs were established by chance processes, the mean number of statements in the whiskers paragraphs ought to be about 25. However, as Row E of Chart 6 shows, not a single whiskers paragraph meets this level of expectation. The maximum is 21 and, as Row F indicates, the median is 14. A plausible explanation for this "conservative" discrepancy has to do with the procedures used to calculate the probability levels. In tables where N is greater than 40 and the probability level is based on the chi-square value, this value is calculated by a formula that includes the correction for continuity, which has a "conservative" effect on the results (page 14). Where N is 40 or smaller, the Fisher Test for "Exact Probability" is used, and this is calculated in accord with a procedure suggested by Armsen, which results in a significance level smaller than the nominal level (page 15).

The theoretical maximum number of statements that could appear in the sample of 41 substantive paragraphs is 41 x 250 = 10,250. Ten per cent of this figure is 1,025. As Row D of the chart indicates, this level of expectation is exceeded by the substantive paragraphs (taken together) by a factor of 1.5.†

Rows C and A indicate the expected and actual numbers of statements by type of verb. The expected numbers of such statements for the ten whiskers paragraphs, taken together, are as follows:

Tends:	.001 x 2,500 =	2.5
Leans:	.009 x 2,500 =	22.5
Tilts:	.04 x 2,500 =	100.0
Drifts:	.05 x 2,500 =	125.0
Total:	.10 x 2,500 =	250.0

As will be seen in Row A, none of these types of statements meets the expected level.

*There are 259 substantive FCs run as "both subject and predicate" and 19 run as "predicate only." There are therefore 278 possible predicates. I have reduced this to 250 to allow, perhaps conservatively, for the effects of hand-winnowing of redundant and quasi-redundant statements in the typical theoretical-maximum case. For example, if in a typical case predicate-pairs 84, 85, 86, and 87 were all to appear, it is likely that at least two or three of them would be hand-winnowed on grounds of quasi-redundancy (page 40). Likewise, in many cases there would be some loss through pure redundancy (page 40).

†The corresponding factor was considerably greater in the cross-polity research project, suggesting that there is more patterning in the "cross-polity universe" (given the finished characteristics used in that study) than there is in the present sample of 400 cultures (given the FCs used in this **Summary**). See **CPS**, pages 51–53.

For the substantive paragraphs, the expected numbers of such statements are:

Tends:	.001 x 10,250 =	10.25
Leans:	.009 x 10,250 =	92.25
Tilts:	.04 x 10,250 =	410.00
Drifts:	.05 x 10,250 =	512.50
Total:	=	1,025.00

Row A of the chart indicates that the expectation for every type of statement is exceeded.

Row D of the chart provides what is perhaps the most important result of this partial test. Note first the figures on the "whiskers" side. For each of the various types of statement, the number that actually print out is somewhere between 30 and 60 per cent of the number expected for that type of statement—with no particular pattern among the percentages. Then note the patterning on the "substantive" side. The number of actual "tend" statements is more than 27 times greater than would be expected by chance, and then there is a patterned decrease until the number of "drifts" is almost exactly equal to the number that would be expected by chance. I interpret this as cogent support for the notion that the cross-cultural domain is indeed a patterned one. To be sure, a certain proportion of these "tend" statements are "truistic" or "quasi-truistic"—such as Statement 17/3, which says that cultures whose linguistic affiliation is Niger-Congo tend to be located in Africa. The reader must judge for himself whether the proportion of such truisms and quasi-truisms is so great that the 27-to-1 ratio of actual "tend" statements to expected "tend" statements loses cogency. In making such a judgment, it would be well to bear in mind that all "pure redundant" and "quasi-redundant" statements were removed prior to the tally.*

This analysis has so far compared the 10 whiskers paragraphs and the 41 substantive paragraphs as two **classes** of paragraphs. It is also instructive to look at the internal variation and distribution within each class and to compare these distributions. This internal variation is demonstrated in Chart 6 in Rows E, F, G, I, and J. Note in Rows G and E, for example, that the variation on the whiskers side for "all Statements" extends from a minimum of 4 to a maximum of 21. By contrast, the corresponding figures for the substantive paragraphs are 10 and 104. Simi-

*To digress slightly, it might well be pointed out that the appearance in the printout of truistic and quasi-truistic statements at least has the value of providing reassurance that the methods employed are functioning correctly. To digress somewhat further, it might be observed that the reader who fundamentally challenges the validity of the cross-cultural statistical approach might appropriately hesitate to dismiss its product as "truistic"—for if the approach is fundamentally invalid, then it is difficult to see how it should be able to produce "truistic" results.

larly impressive differences are also found for each "verb-type" of statement. Row J shows that on the whiskers side the number of paragraphs meeting the expected level is never more than 20 per cent. On the substantive side the percentages are higher and reveal a pattern congruent with that just discussed for Row D: again, the ratio is highest for the "tend" statements, followed by progressive decreases for the "leans," "tilts," and "drifts."

Further informal inspection of the results of the test suggests a very definite positive correlation between the size of the "N" and the number of statements in a paragraph where the "whiskers" paragraphs are concerned, but no such pronounced relationship where the substantive paragraphs are concerned. In other words, where actual substance determines the content of an FC, this substance will probably have a more important bearing on that FC's productivity of statements than will the size of that FC's N.*

One further comment is relevant to the mean or median number of statements in the substantive paragraphs. During the preliminary runs, the decision as to whether to retain or discard a particular paragraph in the final printout was by no means made exclusively, or even primarily, on the basis of the number of statements that paragraph contained. Rather, the decision was governed by whether the paragraph contained information likely to be interesting to social scientists.

It is possible to conclude this section on an additional note of optimism. It has already been mentioned that the probability measures used in this book were calculated in a "conservative" manner, which should increase confidence in the meaningfulness of the statements that appear in the printout (page 57). There is another factor, not previously mentioned, that ought also to increase this confidence. This has to do with random error. In making this point I am following Naroll (1962), who shows how random error can be introduced by the informant in the field, by the ethnographer in the field, or by the cross-cultural researcher who does the coding of a particular culture for a particular raw characteristic. If the reader believes he is warranted in assuming the presence of random error of one or more of these three types, then he is perhaps also warranted in assuming that certain statements that ought to appear in the printout have thusly been prevented from appearing, and that other statements that ought to contain a strong verb have thusly appeared with a weaker verb. Naroll explains how random errors can produce such results:

> The great danger from random errors is that they may prevent the investigator from confirming the existence of relationships which do in fact exist. For exam-

*These results are consistent with the experience in running the Harley finished characteristics on adolescent peer groups. See page 149.

> ple, if the true correlation is high, random errors will most likely tend to lower the correlation in the observations. Consider the typical four-fold test of association between, say, matrilineal descent and matrilocal residence rules. Assume that in fact these two are highly correlated but that in the course of collecting data on them, random errors are made by informants, field workers, and the investigator in a cross-cultural survey. Since the two variables are highly correlated, there are many more favorable cases than unfavorable; consequently, informants, field workers, and comparativists are more likely through random error to change a favorable case to an unfavorable one than vice versa [Naroll 1962:18].

RECAPITULATION

In recapitulating, it would be well to sound again a note of caution about the entire cross-cultural statistical approach. Any investigator who has ever made serious use of this approach is likely to be vividly aware of its limitations—and of how far we have yet to go in placing this type of comparative analysis on a truly satisfactory scientific footing. There are problems, often serious ones, at every step: problems of informant and ethnographer bias, of bias and unreliability on the part of coders, of invalid coding categories or improper use of codings, and problems of sampling and of statistical analysis. Readers intending to make serious use of this **Summary** are therefore urged to familiarize themselves with the literature on the inadequacies of the cross-cultural statistical approach, as a precaution against placing undue faith in this approach, or reaching unwarranted conclusions. In particular, readers are urged to consult Naroll (1962), and the 1952 article by Köbben (Moore 1966:166–92). It would also be advisable to consult some of the more basic critiques of the validity of the formal statistical approach in cross-cultural analysis. An example is the book by E. E. Evans-Pritchard, which takes the position that "the method of statistical correlation can only pose questions, it cannot give us the answers to them" (1963:14).

This **Summary** is intended both for scholars positively committed to the cross-cultural statistical approach, and for scholars who are skeptical in varying degrees: both for those who take the position that under some circumstances statistical tables can give the answers to questions and for those who believe that such tables may properly be used only to pose questions. There is no reason why scholars of the latter type should not feel free to regard the "statements" in this **Summary** as "questions." Rodney Needham unknowingly summed up a good part of the spirit of this book in an article published two years after work on it began, in which he said: "Professor Murdock's 'World Ethnographic Sample' has a permanent place on my own desk; and, far from wishing to decry its usefulness, I only wish there were a vaster thing of the kind, an electronic device, for example, into which ethnographic information could be fed and which would rapidly retrieve it in any desired combination of features" (1964:238). While this **Summary** certainly does not offer the degree of flexibility of inquiry called for by Dr. Needham, perhaps it can be considered a step in that direction.

Below are recapitulated the principal ways in which, it is hoped, this **Summary** will be of utility. If the reader, in pursuing a particular problem, realizes significant benefit in even a few of the ways listed below, this will constitute sufficient reward for the effort of producing this book.

(1) This **Summary** attempts to encompass the relevant literature in a comprehensive manner. Virtually the entire available body of coded cross-cultural literature was canvassed in selecting finished characteristics.

(2) Finished characteristics appearing in this book have been selected on the basis of their apparent potential yield in terms of theory-building.

(3) All tabular information is included in the printout, as well as the principal types of statistical information customarily preferred by scholars in the cross-cultural field.

(4) This **Summary** attempts to enhance the heuristic value of this tabular and statistical material by "translating" it into linguistic form, on the assumption that the typical reader is more likely to be "word-minded" than "number-minded."

(5) Various techniques have been employed to minimize reading burden while maximizing information (pages 29 and 37).

(6) Since all eligible significant statements appear in the printout, and since these statements appear in a uniform order, it is hoped that the reader will be assisted in developing a sense of holistic context and pattern, which in turn can give rise to the development of more explicit insights and hypotheses about trend, process, and cause.

(7) Cross-checking is made easy (page 45).

(8) The logical-conventional ordering of the finished characteristics is intended to stimulate the perception of previously unsuspected relationships among quite different domains of data.

(9) If the reader examines the entirety of a paragraph on a subject of interest to him, he forces himself, in effect, to confront all of the relevant statistically supportable information, perhaps including some that is contrary to his expectations or biases.

(10) The reader, in studying the entirety of a paragraph, will perhaps be enabled to discover some **other** variable, rather than the one under consideration, which might explain a particular phenomenon more adequately.

(11) The failure of a potential statement to appear in the printout can mean, or suggest, that a previously suspected relationship does not hold (page 44).

(12) By use of composite characteristics, this book controls for a variety of intervening or interpretive variables and focuses on particular contrasts believed to be of crucial interest (page 23).

(13) The structure and ordering of the finished characteristics is intended to facilitate explorations by researchers with various cultural evolutionary approaches. An example is seen in FCs 84–87 (page 82).

(14) If the reader wishes to test a directional **a priori** hypothesis, the printout enables him to do so conveniently (page 9).

(15) Experience indicates that the printout readily suggests to the trained analyst what further analytical techniques are needed.

(16) By listing each culture in its appropriate coding category at the beginning of each paragraph, the printout facilitates the checking of coding assignments and the detection of errors (page 29).

(17) The "contributors' sample" paragraphs are intended to make maximally visible whatever biases or inadequacies might inhere in the samples used by various contributors, as well as in the **Ethnographic Atlas** sample itself.*

(18) The paragraphs on the dates of the principal ethnographies are intended to help the reader develop a feel for over-all patterns in the development of ethnology as a science, and in the development of ethnographic techniques.†

(19) The paragraphs on nationality of the principal ethnographers might stimulate insights of a "sociology of knowledge" nature.‡

(20) This book can be used to avoid "false starts." It makes possible the preliminary investigation of a hypothesis or interest to see whether there are enough promising statements on relevant or partially relevant topics to warrant the expenditure of substantial time and money on a further, full-fledged investigation involving new theoretical formulations and new coding operations.

(21) As a tool for the field researcher to carry with him into the field, this **Summary** is intended to serve as a stimulus to more creative inquiry, or at least as a prod upon the field worker to obtain more complete descriptive coverage of the variables that have heretofore been used in cross-cultural studies.

(22) The printout might prove useful to a teacher preparing a lecture.

(23) Experience suggests that the printout can serve usefully as collateral and reference reading assignments for students, especially

*These are Paragraphs 489–526, explained on page 180.
†These are Paragraphs 486–88, explained on page 178.
‡These are Paragraphs 481–85, explained on page 177.

when supplemented with research problems involving the use of the data decks for further exploration of relationships and further tests of hypotheses.

(24) Finally, this **Summary** attempts to provide a quick, convenient, and relatively objective means by which social scientists who are wary of the cross-cultural statistical approach can enter into dispassionate and meaningful dialogues with social scientists who are committed to such methods.

4. Coding Background

IT HAS already been emphasized that the reader cannot obtain full benefit from reading the paragraphs in this **Summary** unless he adequately understands the theoretical orientation and assumptions, the purposes, and the operational problems of the contributor who did the original coding. Indeed, failure to understand such background could even produce misleading and destructive research results. This is especially true, of course, where coding categories are highly abstract or reflect a theoretical point of view unfamiliar to the reader. The purpose of this chapter is to provide a certain minimum of background to the codings. It is hoped that this background will be sufficient to enable the reader to decide confidently whether, for his **particular** purposes, he needs to consult the original source. It should be made clear, however, that the burden of making that decision must be borne by the reader himself. When in doubt, it is always best to consult the source.

The coding background for this **Summary's** 536 finished characteristics is organized into sections and subsections. The identification number of an FC is the same as the identification number of the paragraph for which that FC provides the two subjects. The numbers in parentheses following the title of each section and subsection indicate the FCs contained therein. The format for presenting the coding background for a particular FC is similar to the format of the corresponding paragraph in the printout—i.e. background is first given on the left and right finished attribute categories and then on the three "residual" categories: ambiguous, irrelevant, and unascertained. For explanations of these categories, see page 25.

As has been explained on page 29, some FCs are run as "subject only" and others as "neither subject nor predicate." Such FCs are ineligible to appear in predicate position even if they are significantly associated with the subject FC at the .10 level or better. In this chapter, as each such ineligible FC is introduced, it will be indicated by a large dot. This dot should be regarded as a kind of warning sign, indicating that there may or may not be a significant association between this FC and a given subject FC—and that failure of this FC to appear in predicate position in a given paragraph does not necessarily betoken a lack of significant association between it and the subject FC. The reader must probe further in order to determine whether such significant association exists. The procedure for probing is described on page 44.

LOCATION (1–16)

Regional Identification (1–9)

Column 1 of the **EA** (1962:114) assigns each of the 400 cultures to one of six major ethnographic regions, as follows:

A: "Africa, exclusive of Madagascar and the northern and northeastern portions of the continent." 80 cultures.

C: "Circum-Mediterranean, including Europe, Turkey and the Caucasus, the Semitic Near East, and northern and northeastern Africa." 45 cultures.

E: "East Eurasia, excluding Formosa, the Philippines, Indonesia, and the area assigned to the Circum-Mediterranean, but including Madagascar and other islands in the Indian Ocean." 70 cultures.

I: "Insular Pacific, embracing all of Oceania as well as areas like Australia, Indonesia, Formosa, and the Philippines that are not always included therewith." 70 cultures.

N: "North America, including the indigenous societies of this continent as far south as the Isthmus of Tehuantepec." 70 cultures.

S: "South America, including the Antilles, Yucatan, and Central America as well as the continent itself." 65 cultures.

● FC 1. Left: 265 cultures located in the Old World (Code A C E or I).
Right: 135 cultures located in the New World (Code N or S).

● FC 2. Left: 115 cultures located in the Circum-Mediterranean or East Eurasian area (Code C or E). This area corresponds roughly to the "Ancient Oikoumene," of which Kroeber says: "The old name Oikoumene, with a partial shift of meaning from the 'range of mankind' to 'range of man's most developed cultures,' thus remains a convenient designation for an interwoven set of happenings and products which are significant equally for the culture historian and for the theoretical anthropologist" (1952:379–80).
Right: 285 remaining cultures. (Code A I N or S).

FC 3. Left: 80 cultures located in Africa (Code A).
Right: 320 remaining cultures (Code C E I N or S).

FC 4. Left: 45 cultures located in the Circum-Mediterranean (Code C).
Right: 355 remaining cultures (Code A E I N or S).

FC 5. Left: 70 cultures located in East Eurasia (Code E).
Right: 330 remaining cultures (Code A C I N or S).

FC 6. Left: 70 cultures located in the Insular Pacific (Code I).
Right: 330 remaining cultures (Code A C E N or S).

● FC 7. Left: 32 cultures located in Southeast Asia. The **EA** gives precise latitude and longitude locations for each culture (1962:113). This left category includes all cultures indicated as falling within the modern political boundaries of Burma, Thailand, Laos, Cambodia, North Vietnam, South Vietnam, Malaysia, Singapore, Indonesia, and the Philippines. The island of New Guinea is excluded, despite Indonesia's assumption of political control over West Irian. The Atayal and Paiwan of Formosa are excluded, despite their Malayo-Polynesian linguistic affiliation. The Andamanese and Nicobarese are included, despite the fact that they are under the political control of India. These definitions are admittedly quite arbitrary. Moreover, some borderline cases cause difficulty. For example, there are Miao living within the political boundaries of Southeast Asia; nonetheless, the Miao are excluded here since the **EA** codings refer especially to the Magpie Miao, who are located in China.
Right: 368 remaining cultures.

FC 8. Left: 70 cultures located in North America (Code N).
Right: 330 remaining cultures (Code A C E I or S).

FC 9. Left: 65 cultures located in South America (Code S).
Right: 335 remaining cultures (Code A C E I or N).

Latitude (10-16)

The source of codings for this subsection is the **EA** latitude listing for each culture (1962:113). FC 10 is run as subject-only. FC 11 is run as both subject and predicate. FCs 12 through 16 are run as predicate-only.

● FC 10. Left: 251 cultures located in the tropics, i.e. within 23½ degrees of the equator.
Right: 149 cultures located outside of the tropics.

FC 11. Left: 15 cultures where the latitude is 60 degrees or greater.

Right: 385 cultures where the latitude is less than 60 degrees.

FC 12. Left: 33 cultures where the latitude is 50 degrees or greater.
Right: 367 cultures where the latitude is less than 50 degrees.

FC 13. Left: 71 cultures where the latitude is 40 degrees or greater.
Right: 329 cultures where the latitude is less than 40 degrees.

FC 14. Left: 119 cultures where the latitude is 30 degrees or greater.
Right: 281 cultures where the latitude is less than 30 degrees.

FC 15. Left: 183 cultures where the latitude is 20 degrees or greater.
Right: 217 cultures where the latitude is less than 20 degrees.

FC 16. Left: 277 cultures where the latitude is 10 degrees or greater.
Right: 123 cultures where the latitude is less than 10 degrees.

LINGUISTIC AFFILIATION (17–32)

The source for this section is **EA** Column 64 (1963:111–14). The rationale for including linguistic affiliation in this **Summary** is the same as that stated in the source, namely that "genetic relationships in culture and past historical connections among societies are commonly revealed or suggested by the degree of relationship exhibited among the languages spoken by the peoples in question." This section deals with all linguistic stocks or families which are represented by at least 8 cultures out of the total sample of 400. For details as to families and subfamilies, see the source.

● FC 17. Left: 61 cultures whose linguistic affiliation is Niger-Congo (Code Nc).
Right: 339 remaining cultures.

● FC 18. Left: 14 cultures whose linguistic affiliation is Chari-Nile (Code Cn).
Right: 386 remaining cultures.

● FC 19. Left: 21 cultures whose linguistic affiliation is Afro-Asiatic (Code Aa).
Right: 379 remaining cultures.

- FC 20. Left: 61 cultures whose linguistic affiliation is Niger-Congo (Code Nc).
  Right: 21 cultures whose linguistic affiliation is Afro-Asiatic (Code Aa).
  Irrelevant: 318 remaining cultures.
- FC 21. Left: 28 cultures whose linguistic affiliation is Indo-European (Code Ie).
  Right: 372 remaining cultures.
- FC 22. Left: 28 cultures whose linguistic affiliation is Indo-European (Code Ie).
  Right: 21 cultures whose linguistic affiliation is Afro-Asiatic (Code Aa).
  Irrelevant: 351 remaining cultures.
- FC 23. Left: 11 cultures whose linguistic affiliation is Altaic (Code Al).
  Right: 389 remaining cultures.
- FC 24. Left: 60 cultures whose linguistic affiliation is Malayo-Polynesian (Code Mp).
  Right: 340 remaining cultures.
- FC 25. Left: 12 cultures whose linguistic affiliation is Tibeto-Burman (Tb).
  Right: 388 remaining cultures.
- FC 26. Left: 10 cultures whose linguistic affiliation is Mon-Khmer (Code Mk).
  Right: 390 remaining cultures.
- FC 27. Left: 60 cultures whose linguistic affiliation is Malayo-Polynesian (Code Mp).
  Right: 12 cultures whose linguistic affiliation is Tibeto-Burman (Code Tb).
  Irrelevant: 328 remaining cultures.
- FC 28. Left: 60 cultures whose linguistic affiliation is Malayo-Polynesian (Code Mp).
  Right: 10 cultures whose linguistic affiliation is Mon-Khmer (Code Mk).
  Irrelevant: 330 remaining cultures.
- FC 29. Left: 12 cultures whose linguistic affiliation is Tibeto-Burman (Code Tb).
  Right: 10 cultures whose linguistic affiliation is Mon-Khmer (Code Mk).
  Irrelevant: 378 remaining cultures.
- FC 30. Left: 8 cultures whose linguistic affiliation is Athabaskan (Code At).
  Right: 392 remaining cultures.

- ● FC 31. Left: 9 cultures whose linguistic affiliation is Algonkian (Code Ag).
  Right: 391 remaining cultures.
- ● FC 32. Left: 8 cultures whose linguistic affiliation is Cariban (Code Ca).
  Right: 392 remaining cultures.

NATURAL ENVIRONMENT (33–43)

FCs in this section are derived from Frank W. Moore, unpublished codings (1962). Moore's coding categories are taken or derived from those used in the Philips' Series Comparative Wall Atlases, on which his coding assignments are also based. The determination of coding assignments was in many cases made difficult by the fact that people belonging to a particular culture inhabit an area which the atlases place in more than one natural environmental zone. In an attempt to cope partially with this problem, Moore assigned each culture a primary code and where necessary, a secondary code. (For further information on both codes, see page 48.) This **Summary,** however, uses only Moore's primary codes. These are as follows:

S: "Tropical Grassland (including Savanna with tall and low grasses)." 64 cultures.

G: "Temperate Grassland (including Bushveld, Seasonal Grassland, Scrub, and Fern Heath), Temperate Steppe." 25 cultures.

E: "Desert Grasses and Shrubs (Semi-Desert, Arid regions)." 37 cultures.

D:"Desert (little or no vegetation, including arctic areas)." 3 cultures.

T: "Tropical Rain Forest (including mangrove swamp forest)." 115 cultures.

O: "Monsoon Forest (Tropical and Semi-Tropical areas with pronounced seasons)." 14 cultures.

R: "Sub-Tropical Rain Forest (including Tropical Mountain Rain Forest, High areas of little seasonal change)." 27 cultures.

M: "Mediterranean (Dry Deciduous and Evergreen Forests)." 11 cultures.

B: "Sub-Tropical Bush (including Forest and Bush, Tropical Dry Forest, Open Jungle, Scrub and Thorn, Chaco)." 24 cultures.

V: "Oases and Valley (including Oases, certain restricted river valleys)." 5 cultures.

U: "Tundra (Northern tundra areas)." 11 cultures.

C: "Northern Coniferous Forest (Evergreens, seasonal cold, including Northern part of Cordilleran and Pacific Coniferous)." 21 cultures.

H: "High Plateau Steppe (including Andean Plateau Scrub)." 8 cultures.

L: "Temperate Woodland (Forest and Meadow Land, Broad-leaved deciduous, Upland Broad-leaved Forest, Temperate Evergreen Forest and Shrubs, Dry Woodland)." 16 cultures.

F: "Temperate Forest (mostly mountainous regions, including Southern part of Cordilleran and Pacific Coniferous Forest)." 19 cultures.

FC 33. Left: 59 cultures where the natural environment is "very harsh," i.e. desert, desert grasses and shrubs, tundra, or high plateau steppe (Code D E U or H).
Right: 341 remaining cultures.

● FC 34. Left: 40 cultures where the natural environment is desert or desert grasses and shrubs (Code D or E).
Right: 360 remaining cultures.

● FC 35. Left: 11 cultures where the natural environment is tundra (Code U).
Right: 389 remaining cultures.

FC 36. Left: 108 cultures where the natural environment is "very harsh" (as defined in FC 33), or subtropical bush, or temperate grassland (Code D E U H B or G).
Right: 292 remaining cultures.

● FC 37. Left: 24 cultures where the natural environment is subtropical bush (Code B).
Right: 376 remaining cultures.

● FC 38. Left: 25 cultures where the natural environment is temperate grassland (Code G).
Right: 375 remaining cultures.

● FC 39. Left: 21 cultures where the natural environment is northern coniferous forest (Code C).
Right: 379 remaining cultures.

● FC 40. Left: 35 cultures where the natural environment is temperate woodland or temperate forest (Code L or F).
Right: 365 remaining cultures.

● FC 41. Left: 64 cultures where the natural environment is tropical grassland (Code S).
Right: 336 remaining cultures.

FC 42. Left: 156 cultures where the natural environment is tropical or subtropical rain forest, or monsoon forest (Code T R or O).
Right: 244 remaining cultures.

● FC 43. Left: 115 cultures where the natural environment is tropical rain forest (Code T).
Right: 285 remaining cultures.

SETTLEMENT PATTERN (44–47)

FCs in this section are derived from **EA** Column 30 (1962:268). This source codes all but 68 of the 400 cultures according to "prevailing patterns of settlement," as follows:

B: "Fully migratory or nomadic bands." 36 cultures.

H: "Separated hamlets where several such form a more or less permanent single community." 33 cultures.

N: "Neighborhoods of dispersed family homesteads." 40 cultures.

S: "Seminomadic communities whose members wander in bands for at least half of the year but occupy a fixed settlement at some season or seasons, e.g., recurrently occupied winter quarters." 36 cultures.

T: "Semisedentary communities whose members shift from one to another fixed settlement at different seasons or who occupy more or less permanently a single settlement from which, however, a substantial proportion of the population departs seasonally to occupy shifting camps, e.g., during transhumance." 28 cultures.

V: "Compact and relatively permanent settlements, i.e., nucleated villages or towns." 140 cultures.

W: "Compact but impermanent settlements, i.e., villages whose location is shifted every few years." 10 cultures.

X: "Complex settlements consisting of a nucleated village or town with outlying homesteads or satellite hamlets. Urban aggregations of population will not be separately indicated since Column 31 [of the **EA**] deals with community size." 9 cultures.

Unascertained: 68 cultures.

FC 44. Left: 222 cultures where settlements are fixed (Code X V H or N).

Right: 110 cultures where settlements are nonfixed (Code W T S or B).

Unascertained: 68 cultures.

FC 45. Left: 149 cultures where settlements, if fixed, are compact (Code X or V).

Right: 73 cultures where settlements, if fixed, are noncompact (Code H or N).

Irrelevant: 110 cultures where settlements are nonfixed (Code B S T or W).

Unascertained: 68 cultures.

FC 46. Left: 72 cultures where settlements are nonfixed **and** where movement is nomadic (Code S or B).

Right: 260 remaining substantively coded cultures (Code H N T V W or X).

Unascertained: 68 cultures.

FC 47. Left: 72 cultures where, if settlements are nonfixed, movement is nomadic (Code S or B).
Right: 38 cultures where, if settlements are nonfixed, movement is nonnomadic (Code W or T).
Irrelevant: 222 cultures where settlements are fixed (Code H N V or X).
Unascertained: 68 cultures.

DIET (48–50)

FCs in this section are based on Marjorie Grant Whiting's Table V (1958).

FC 48. Left: 38 cultures where the food supply is secure, i.e. where food shortages are rare or occasional (Column 7, Code "Rare" or "Occasional").
Right: 41 cultures where the food supply is not secure, i.e. where food shortages are frequent or annual (same, Code "Frequent" or "Annual").
Unascertained: 321 cultures.

● FC 49. Left: 32 cultures where the quantity of food is plentiful (Column 6, Code "Plentiful").
Right: 48 cultures where the quantity of food is less than plentiful (same, Code "Adequate," "Subsistence," or "Minimal").
Unascertained: 320 cultures.

● FC 50. Left: 43 cultures where the daily protein intake is 90 grams or higher (Column 2, Code 90 or any higher number).
Right: 39 cultures where the daily protein intake is 80 grams or lower (same, Code 80 or any lower number).
Unascertained: 318 cultures.

SUBSISTENCE (51–70)

Finished characteristics in this section derive from a number of columns in the **EA.** The most important of these codings have to do with "subsistence economy." These appear in the **EA**'s Column 7, which is a five-digit entry (1962:115). Each of these digits indicates "the relative dependence of the society on each of the five major types of subsistence activity. The first digit refers to the gathering of wild plants and small land fauna; the second, to hunting, including trapping and fowling; the third, to fishing, including shellfishing and the pursuit of large aquatic animals; the fourth, to animal husbandry, embracing the consumption of such products as meat, milk, and eggs; the fifth, to agriculture." Codes for each of these subsistence-type columns are as follows:

0: Zero to 5 per cent dependence.
1: Six to 15 per cent dependence.
2: 16 to 25 per cent dependence.
3: 26 to 35 per cent dependence.
4: 36 to 45 per cent dependence.
5: 46 to 55 per cent dependence.
6: 56 to 65 per cent dependence.
7: 66 to 75 per cent dependence.
8: 76 to 85 per cent dependence.
9: 86 to 100 per cent dependence.

Thus, for example, a code entry of "3" in the third of the five columns would indicate that members of that culture were estimated to be dependent on fishing to the extent of 26 to 35 per cent. The **EA** adds this precautionary note: "Since ethnographies rarely present exact data on percentages of the diet derived from each type of subsistence activity, the entries usually represent inferences from descriptions of foods or economic pursuits, and are doubtless often inexact."

On Murdock's advice (personal communication, 1962), the above five-digit code has been used to build the following typology of cultures on the basis of their sources of subsistence:

CATEGORY A: FOOD PRODUCTION: Cultures so coded are those that derive more than half of their total subsistence from agriculture or animal husbandry or a combination of the two. For each such culture, the last two digits total six or more.

Subcategory A–1: Agriculture: Within Category A, cultures coded in this subcategory derive at least as much of their subsistence from agriculture as from animal husbandry. The fifth digit is equal to, or greater than, the fourth.

Subcategory A–2: Animal Husbandry: Within Category A, cultures coded in this subcategory derive more of their subsistence from animal husbandry than from agriculture. The fourth digit is greater than the fifth.

CATEGORY B: GATHERING: Cultures so coded are those that derive half or more of their subsistence from hunting, fishing, collecting, or any combination of these three techniques. For each such culture, the first three digits total five or more.

Subcategory B–1: Incipient Food Production: Within Category B, cultures coded in this subcategory are those which, while primarily subsisting by gathering, nonetheless derive more of their subsistence from agriculture and animal husbandry than from any single one of the three gathering techniques. The sum of the last two digits is greater than the first or the second or the third digit.

Subcategory B–2: Hunting: Within Category B, cultures coded in this subcategory derive at least as much of their subsistence from hunting as from fishing, collecting, or food production. The second digit is equal to or greater than the first digit, the third digit, or the sum of the fourth and fifth digits.

Subcategory B–3: Fishing: Within Category B, cultures coded in this subcategory derive more of their subsistence from fishing than from hunting and at least as much from fishing as from collecting or food production. The third digit is greater than the second digit and equal to, or greater than, the first digit or the sum of the fourth and fifth digits.

Subcategory B–4: Collecting: Within Category B, cultures coded in this subcategory derive more of their subsistence from collecting than from hunting or fishing and at least as much as from food producing. The first digit is greater than the second and third digits and equal to or greater than the sum of the fourth and fifth digits.

Food Production (51–56)

FC 51. Left: 253 cultures where subsistence is primarily by food production (Category A).
Right: 147 cultures where subsistence is primarily by food gathering (Category B).

● FC 52. Left: 237 cultures where subsistence is primarily by agriculture (Subcategory A–1).
Right: 163 cultures where subsistence is primarily by means other than agriculture (Subcategory A–2 or Category B).

Intensivity of Agriculture and Food Production (53–56)

This subsection deals with intensive agriculture, simple agriculture, and incipient food production. The last of these three coding categories has already been defined above, as Subcategory B–1. The first two of these categories are defined in **EA** Column 28 (1962:267–68).

Cultures coded as possessing intensive agriculture are indicated by the symbol I or J in Column 28:

I: "Intensive agriculture on permanent fields, utilizing fertilization by compost or animal manure, crop rotation, or other techniques so that fallowing is either unnecessary or is confined to relatively short periods."

J: "Intensive agriculture where it is largely dependent on irrigation."

Cultures coded as possessing simple agriculture are indicated by the symbol E or H in Column 28.

E: "Extensive or shifting agriculture, i.e., where new fields are cleared annually, cultivated for a year or two, and then allowed to revert to forest or brush for a long fallow period."

H: "Horticulture, i.e., semi-intensive agriculture limited mainly to small vegetable gardens or groves of fruit trees rather than to the cultivation of field crops."

FC 53. Left: 91 cultures where food production is by intensive agriculture (Column 28, Code I or J).

Right: 147 cultures where food production is by simple agriculture (Column 28, Code E or H) or by incipient food production (Subcategory B–1).

Irrelevant: 117 cultures, including: 16 cultures where food production is by animal husbandry (Subcategory A–2). 101 cultures where subsistence is by hunting, fishing, or collecting (Subcategories B–2, B–3, or B–4).

Unascertained: 45 cultures.

FC 54. Left: 192 cultures where food production is by intensive or simple agriculture (Column 28, Code I J E or H).

Right: 46 cultures where subsistence is by incipient food production (Subcategory B–1).

Irrelevant: 117 cultures, including: 16 cultures where food production is by animal husbandry (Subcategory A–2). 101 cultures where subsistence is by hunting, fishing, or collecting (Subcategories B–2, B–3, or B–4).

Unascertained: 45 cultures.

FC 55. Left: 91 cultures where food production is by intensive agriculture (Column 28, Code I or J).

Right: 101 cultures where food production is by simple agriculture (Column 28, Code E or H).

Irrelevant: 163 cultures, including: 16 cultures where food production is by animal husbandry (Subcategory A–2). 147 cultures where subsistence is by gathering (Category B).

Unascertained: 45 cultures.

FC 56. Left: 101 cultures where food production is by simple agriculture (Column 28, Code E or H).
Right: 46 cultures where subsistence is by incipient food production (Subcategory B–1).
Irrelevant: 208 cultures, including: 16 cultures where food production is by animal husbandry (Subcategory A–2). 91 cultures where food production is by intensive agriculture (Column 28, Code I or J). 101 cultures where subsistence is by hunting, fishing, or collecting (Subcategories B–2, B–3, or B–4).
Unascertained: 45 cultures.

Types of Agriculture (57–60)

● FC 57. Left: 121 cultures where subsistence is primarily by shifting agriculture (Column 28, Code E).
Right: 213 cultures where subsistence is primarily by means other than shifting agriculture (Column 28, all other substantive codes).
Unascertained: 66 cultures.

● FC 58. Left: 26 cultures where subsistence is primarily by horticulture (Column 28, Code H).
Right: 308 cultures where subsistence is primarily by means other than horticulture (Column 28, all other substantive codes).
Unascertained: 66 cultures.

The next FC is based on **EA** Column 28, lower-case codes (1962: 268). Only two of these codes concern us:

c: "Cereal grains, e.g., maize, millet, rice, or wheat, the principal food crops or at least as important as any other type of crop."

r: "Roots or tubers, e.g., manioc, potato, taro, or yam, the principal food crops or at least as important as tree crops or vegetables and more important than cereal grains."

● FC 59: Left: 168 cultures where crops are mainly cereal (Column 28, Code c).
Right: 66 cultures where crops are mainly root (same, Code r).
Irrelevant: 112 remaining substantively coded cultures.
Unascertained: 54 cultures.

The next FC combines the capital-letter and lower-case codes of **EA** Column 28.

● FC 60: Left: 45 cultures where crops are mainly cereal **and** where cultivation is intensive-irrigated (Column 28, Code Jc).
Right: 46 cultures where crops are mainly cereal **and**

where crops are mainly intensive-dry (same, Code Ic).

Irrelevant: 243 remaining cultures bearing substantive capital-letter and lower-case codes in Column 28.

Unascertained: 66 cultures.

Subsistence by Animal Husbandry (61)

The FC in this subsection is based on the typology explained on page 73.

● FC 61. Left: 16 cultures where subsistence is primarily by animal husbandry (Subcategory A–2).

Right: 384 remaining cultures (Subcategory A–1 or Category B).

Types of Animal Husbandry (62–67)

This subsection deals with types of animal husbandry, whether or not husbandry constitutes the principal source of subsistence for a particular culture. While only 16 of the 400 cultures are coded as deriving subsistence primarily from animal husbandry, 226 of them are coded as having some kind of husbandry present.

Finished characteristics in this subsection are based on **EA** Column 39 (1962:271–72). In this column, the capital-letter codes indicate the "predominant type of domestic animals kept in the particular society. The smaller animals, e.g., pigs and sheep, will be indicated only when larger animals are absent or unimportant in the economy." The codes are:

B: "Bovine animals, e.g., cattle, mithun, water buffaloes, yaks." 120 cultures.

C: "Camels or other animals of related genera, e.g., alpacas, llamas." 7 cultures.

D: "Deer, e.g., reindeer." 3 cultures.

E: "Equine animals, e.g., horses, donkeys." 22 cultures.

O: "Absence or near absence of domestic animals other than bees, cats, dogs, fowl, guinea pigs, or the like." 174 cultures.

P: "Pigs the only domestic animals of consequence." 46 cultures.

S: "Sheep and/or goats in the absence of important larger domestic animals." 28 cultures.

FC 62. Left: 228 cultures where husbandry of some kind is present (Code B C D E P or S).*

Right: 172 cultures where husbandry of any kind is absent.

*The sum of the frequencies for these codes is 226. In this left attribute category, however, two additional cultures have been included: the Buryat and the Kalmyk. These two cultures belong to Subcategory B-2; i.e. they derive subsistence primarily from animal husbandry. Due to a clerical error in Column 39, however, they are coded as "husbandry absent."

FC 63. Left: 152 cultures where husbandry, if present, is in bovine, equine, camel-like or deerlike animals (Code B E C or D).
Right: 74 cultures where husbandry, if present, is in pigs, sheep, or goats (Code P or S).
Irrelevant: 174 cultures where husbandry is absent (Code O).

● FC 64. Left: 120 cultures where husbandry in bovine animals, as the principal form of husbandry, is present (Code B).
Right: 280 cultures where such husbandry, as the principal form of husbandry, is absent (Code C D E O P or S).

The next FC is based in part on **EA** Column 39, lower-case code (1962:271). "A postposited lower-case m indicates that domestic animals are milked other than sporadically; a lower-case o indicates the absence or near absence of milking."

● FC 65. Left: 79 cultures where bovine animals, if present, are milked (Code Bm).
Right: 41 cultures where bovine animals, if present, are not milked (Code Bo).
Irrelevant: All 280 other substantively coded cultures.

● FC 66. Left: 46 cultures where husbandry in pigs, as the principal form of husbandry, is present (Code P).
Right: 354 cultures where such husbandry, as the principal form of husbandry, is absent (Code B C D E O or S).

● FC 67. Left: 28 cultures where husbandry in sheep or goats, as the principal form of husbandry, is present (Code S).
Right: 372 cultures where such husbandry, as the principal form of husbandry, is absent (Code B C D E O or P).

Subsistence by Gathering (68–70)

FCs in this subsection are based on the typology explained on page 73.

● FC 68. Left: 26 cultures where subsistence is primarily by hunting (Subcategory B–2).
Right: 374 remaining cultures (Category A, or Subcategories B–1, B–3, and B–4).

● FC 69. Left: 44 cultures where subsistence is primarily by fishing (Subcategory B–3).

Right: 356 remaining cultures (Category A, or Subcategories B–1, B–2, and B–4).

● FC 70. Left: 31 cultures where subsistence is primarily by collecting (Subcategory B–4).
Right: 369 remaining cultures (Category A, or Subcategories B–1, B–2, and B–3).

TECHNOLOGY (71–76)

Each of the six FCs in this section consists of a simple "present-absent" contrast. All six are derived from **EA.** Five of the six are based on rather complex codes which specify sex roles and division of labor. These codes will not be listed here, as they are irrelevant to a simple "present-absent" contrast. The sex role codes are listed on page 95 of this **Summary.**

FC 71 is based on **EA** Column 42 (1962:389–90), and deals with metal working. "Only such arts as smelting, casting, and forging, which involve the application of fire, will be indicated." The coding ignores "other processes, such as cold hammering of native or imported metals."

FC 71. Left: 98 cultures where metal working is present (Code D E F G I M N or P).
Right: 153 cultures where metal working is absent or unimportant (Code O).
Unascertained: 149 cultures.

FC 72 is based on **EA** Column 39 (1962:271). "A preposited lower-case p indicates that animals were employed in plow cultivation prior to the contact period; a lower-case q indicates that plow cultivation, though not aboriginal, was well established at the period of observation."

● FC 72. Left: 61 cultures where the plow is present (Code: preposited p or q).
Right: 339 cultures where the plow is absent (Code: absence of preposited p or q).

FC 73 is based on **EA** Column 44 (1962:390) and deals with weaving. "Only the manufacture of true cloth on a loom or frame will be indicated—not the manufacture of nets, baskets, mats, or nonwoven fabrics like barkcloth or felt."

FC 73. Left: 118 cultures where weaving is present (Code D E F G I M N or P).
Right: 130 cultures where weaving is absent or unimportant (Code O).
Unascertained: 152 cultures.

FC 74 is based on **EA** Column 48 (1962:390) and deals with pottery. "Only the manufacture of earthenware utensils will be indicated."

FC 74. Left: 145 cultures where the manufacture of pottery is present (Code D E F G I M N or P).
Right: 93 cultures where the manufacture of pottery is absent or unimportant (Code O).
Unascertained: 162 cultures.

FC 75 is based on **EA** Column 46 (1962:390) and deals with leather working. "Only the dressing of skins, e.g., by tanning, will be indicated, not the manufacture of artifacts from raw hides or undressed skins."

● FC 75. Left: 123 cultures where leather working is present (Code D E F G I M N or P).
Right: 53 cultures where leather working is absent or unimportant (Code O).
Unascertained: 224 cultures.

FC 76 is based on **EA** Column 50 (1962:390) and deals with boat building. "Only the construction of true water craft will be indicated, not the making of simple floats or the like."

● FC 76. Left: 142 cultures where boat building is present (Code D E F G I M N or P).
Right: 63 cultures where boat building is absent or unimportant (Code O).
Unascertained: 195 cultures.

WRITING SYSTEM (77–78)

FCs in this section are based on John M. Hickman, Table 2, Column III (1962:215–16). The codes are:

1: "No mnemonic aids." 18 cultures.
2: "Mnemonic aids." 21 cultures.
3: "Mixed alphabetic and phonetic." 15 cultures.
Unascertained: 346 cultures.

FC 77. Left: 15 cultures where the writing system is alphabetic or phonetic (Code 3).
Right: 39 cultures where the writing system is mnemonic or absent (Code 2 or 1).
Unascertained: 346 cultures.

FC 78. Left: 36 cultures where the writing system is either alphabetic-or-phonetic or mnemonic (Code 3 or 2).
Right: 18 cultures where a writing system is absent (Code 1).
Unascertained: 346 cultures.

DEMOGRAPHY (79–83)

FCs in this section are derived from **EA** Column 31, "Mean Size of Local Communities" (1962:268–69). These codings were "inspired by an early unpublished study by W. H. Goodenough undertaken at the instigation of the late W. F. Ogburn. The average population of local communities, whatever the pattern of settlement, is computed from census data or other evidence, and is ranked in one of the following categories":

1: Fewer than 50 persons. 46 cultures.

2: From 50 to 99 persons. 43 cultures.

3: From 100 to 199 persons. 46 cultures.

4: From 200 to 399 persons. 21 cultures.

5: From 400 to 1,000 persons. 24 cultures.

6: More than 1,000 persons in the absence of any indigenous urban aggregation of more than 5,000. 5 cultures.

7: One or more indigenous towns of more than 5,000 inhabitants but none of more than 50,000. 16 cultures.

8: One or more indigenous cities with more than 50,000 inhabitants. 23 cultures.

Unascertained: 176 cultures.

The first four of the five FCs in this section are designed to form an ordinal continuum.

FC 79. Left: 23 cultures where a city is present (Code 8).
Right: 201 cultures where no city is present (Code 7 6 5 4 3 2 or 1).
Unascertained: 176 cultures.

FC 80. Left: 39 cultures where a city or town is present (Code 8 or 7).
Right: 185 cultures where no city or town is present (Code 6 5 4 3 2 or 1).
Unascertained: 176 cultures.

FC 81. Left: 89 cultures where the average community size is 200 or greater (Code 8 7 6 5 or 4).
Right: 135 cultures where the average community size is smaller than 200 (Code 3 2 or 1).
Unascertained: 176 cultures.

FC 82. Left: 178 cultures where the average community size is 50 or greater (Code 8 7 6 5 4 3 or 2).
Right: 46 cultures where the average community size is smaller than 50 (Code 1).
Unascertained: 176 cultures.

FC 83. Left: 45 cultures where, with no city and no town

present, the average community size is between 200 and 999 (Code 4 or 5).

Right: 135 cultures where, with no city and no town present, the average community size is smaller than 200 (Code 1 2 or 3).

Irrelevant: 44 cultures where the average community size is greater than 1,000 or where a town or city is present (Code 6 7 or 8).

Unascertained: 176 cultures.

POLITICAL ORGANIZATION (84–90)

Level of Political Integration (84–87)

The background of these four FCs has already been partly described in Chapter 3, page 48. The source is George Peter Murdock, "World Ethnographic Sample," Column 15, capital-letter code only (1957a: 674). These four FCs have been constructed so as to form an ordinal series. In doing so, the last two codes, as listed below, have been dropped from consideration because they do not fit into an ordinal continuum. The codes are:

S: "States, i.e., political integration in large independent units averaging at least 100,000 in population." 42 cultures.

L: "Little states, i.e., political integration in independent units averaging between 10,000 and 100,000 in population." 28 cultures.

M: "Minimal states, i.e., political integration in independent units averaging between 1,500 and 10,000 in population." 78 cultures.

A: "Autonomous local communities, i.e., politically independent local groups which do not exceed 1,500 in average population." 133 cultures.

0: "Absence of any political integration even at the local level, e.g., where family heads acknowledge no higher political authority." 23 cultures.

D: "Dependent societies lacking any political organization of their own, e.g., those forming an integral part of some larger political system and those governed exclusively and directly by agents of another and politically dominant society. Colonial governments operating through indirect rule are ignored." 24 cultures.

P: "Peace groups transcending the local community where the basis of unity is other than political, e.g., derived from reciprocal trade relations, defensive military agreements, or a common cult or age-grade organization." 9 cultures.

Unascertained: 63 cultures.

FC 84. Left: 42 cultures where the level of political integra-

tion is the large state (Code S).
Right: 262 cultures where the level of political integration is lower (Code L M A or O).
Irrelevant: 33 cultures not fitting the ordinal continuum (Code D or P).
Unascertained: 63 cultures.

FC 85. Left: 70 cultures where the level of political integration is the large state or the little state (Code S or L).
Right: 234 cultures where the level of political integration is lower (Code M A or O).
Irrelevant: 33 cultures not fitting the ordinal continuum (Code D or P).
Unascertained: 63 cultures.

FC 86. Left: 148 cultures where the level of political integration is the large state, the little state, or the minimal state (Code S L or M).
Right: 156 cultures where the level of political integration is lower (Code A or O).
Irrelevant: 33 cultures not fitting the ordinal continuum (Code D or P).
Unascertained: 63 cultures.

FC 87. Left: 281 cultures where the level of political integration is the large state, the little state, the minimal state, or the autonomous community (Code S L M or A).
Right: 23 cultures where the level of political integration is lower (Code O).
Irrelevant: 33 cultures not fitting the ordinal continuum (Code D or P).
Unascertained: 63 cultures.

Succession to Headmanship (88–90)

FCs in this subsection derive from **EA** Column 73, "Succession to the Office of Local Headman" (1963:115). "Without reference to rules of succession prevailing on higher levels of political integration, those applying to the office of local headman (or a close equivalent such as clan chief) are indicated by the following symbols":

A: "Nonhereditary succession through appointment by some higher political authority." 12 cultures.

C: "Nonhereditary succession through informal consensus." 23 cultures.

E: "Nonhereditary succession through election or some other method of formal consensus." 40 cultures.

I: "Nonhereditary succession through influence, e.g., of wealth or social status." 18 cultures.

M: "Hereditary succession by a sister's son." 13 cultures.

N: "Hereditary succession by a matrilineal heir who takes precedence over a sister's son, e.g. a younger brother." 25 cultures.

O: "Absence of any office resembling that of a local headman." 39 cultures.

P: "Hereditary succession by a son." 99 cultures.

Q: "Hereditary succession by a patrilineal heir who takes precedence over a son, e.g. a younger brother." 28 cultures.

S: "Nonhereditary succession on the basis primarily of seniority or age." 13 cultures.

Unascertained: 90 cultures.

FC 88. Left: 106 cultures where, if a headmanship is present, succession is nonhereditary (Code A C E I or S).

Right: 165 cultures where, if a headmanship is present, succession is hereditary (Code M N P or Q).

Irrelevant: 39 cultures lacking any office resembling that of local headman (Code O).

Unascertained: 90 cultures.

FC 89. Left: 63 cultures where, if a nonhereditary headmanship is present, succession is by consensus (Code C or E).*

Right: 43 cultures where, if a nonhereditary headmanship is present, succession is by means other than consensus (Code A I or S).

Irrelevant: 204 cultures, including: 39 cultures lacking any office resembling that of local headman (Code O). 165 cultures where succession to the headmanship is hereditary (Code M N P or Q).

Unascertained: 90 cultures.

FC 90. Left: 127 cultures where, if a hereditary headmanship is present, succession is patrilineal (Code P or Q).

Right: 38 cultures where, if a hereditary headmanship is present, succession is matrilineal (Code M or N).

Irrelevant: 145 cultures, including: 39 cultures lacking any office resembling that of local headman (Code O). 106 cultures where succession to the headmanship is nonhereditary (Code A C E I or S).

Unascertained: 90 cultures.

*The Zuni belong here but were inadvertently placed in the right attribute category. This error was discovered too late for correction. So far as is known, this is the only punching error in the printout.

SOCIETAL COMPLEXITY (91–101)

This section includes a variety of indicators of societal complexity, drawn from a variety of sources.

FC 91 is derived from Linton C. Freeman and Robert F. Winch, Table 3 (1957:465). Freeman and Winch established a Guttman Scale of societal complexity, with a coefficient of reproducibility of .97, using items relating to the following six areas: written language, government, education, religion, punishment, and economy. This permitted them to array their societies from the most complex to the least complex. FC 91 divides this array at the median, resulting in a "high" and a "low" category.

FC 91. Left: 18 cultures where societal complexity is high (Table 3, Vietnamese down through Mbundu).
Right: 22 cultures where societal complexity is low (Table 3, Cayapa down through Yaruro).
Unascertained: 360 cultures.

FC 92 is based on Raoul Naroll's Table 3, Index column (1956:705). Using an indexing technique too complex to summarize here, Naroll arrives at composite indices of social development for a number of cultures. The Aztecs receive the highest index score of 58, and the Yahgan the lowest of 12. FC 92 divides this array at the median, resulting in a "high" and a "low" category.

● FC 92. Left: 10 cultures where the index of social development is high (Table 3, Aztec down through Crow).
Right: 10 cultures where the index of social development is low (Table 3, Lepcha down through Yahgan).
Unascertained: 380 cultures.

FC 93 is based on a composite index of social structural complexity devised by Merrill Jackson and appearing in his Table 10, First Column (1962:178). Jackson employs two indices of societal differentiation, namely the number and the permanence of societal "parts" (pages 88–92). These two indices serve "double duty," since they are also indices of societal integration. In addition, three other indices of integration are used: "leadership of all kinds, persistence of leadership, and power of leadership" (page 96). For full detail, see pages 88–97.

● FC 93. Left: 10 cultures where over-all social structural complexity is high (Table 10, First Column, above the median in rank order).
Right: 10 cultures where over-all social structural complexity is low (Table 10, First Column, below the median in rank order).
Unascertained: 380 cultures.

FCs 94 through 100 are based on codings by Guy E. Swanson for use in his book, **The Birth of the Gods** (1960). These codings have been modified by the **EA,** where they appear in a two-digit code in Column 32, "Jurisdictional Hierarchy" (1962:269). The **EA** explains:

> Our definition of jurisdictional levels coincides closely with his definition of organizations characterized by sovereignty, i.e., by original and definitive jurisdiction over some sphere of social life in which the organization has the legitimate right to make decisions having a significant effect on its members, e.g., distribution of food, allocation of productive resources, punishment of delicts, assignment or conscription of labor, levying of taxes, initiation of war or peace. Like Swanson, we exclude organizations that are merely agents of others and those not held to be legitimate (including colonial regimes and others imposed by force), and we always include the nuclear family and the local community in default of explicit evidence that they lack sovereignty in the defined sense. We differ from him mainly in insisting that such organizations fall into a single hierarchical order; we would, for example, count a lineage and its localized equivalent or clan as only a single jurisdictional level, not as two organizations. The number of jurisdictional levels of each society is shown by a pair of digits, of which the first indicates the number of levels up to and including the local community and the second beyond the local community. Thus 44 would represent a situation close to the theoretical maximum, e.g., with nuclear family, extended family, clan-barrio, village, parish, district, province, and nation-state, whereas 20 would approximate the theoretical minimum, e.g., nuclear family and nomadic band. The second digit, incidentally, provides a measure of the degree of political complexity, ranging from 0 for stateless societies to 3 or 4 for those organized in large states.

The first-digit code in Column 32 refers to the number of levels of local jurisdiction, which can range from 2 to 4. The distribution is:

2: 93 cultures.
3: 180 cultures.
4: 58 cultures.
Unascertained: 69 cultures.

The second-digit code in Column 32 refers to the number of levels of national jurisdiction, which can range from 0 to 4. The distribution is:

0: 156 cultures.
1: 98 cultures.
2: 42 cultures.
3: 26 cultures.
4: 8 cultures.
Unascertained: 70 cultures.

FC 94. Left: 34 cultures where the hierarchy of national jurisdiction has 4 or 3 levels (second-digit Code 4 or 3).

Right: 296 cultures where the hierarchy of national jurisdiction has 2, 1, or no levels (second-digit Code 2 1 or 0).

Unascertained: 70 cultures.

FC 95. Left: 76 cultures where the hierarchy of national jurisdiction has 4, 3, or 2 levels (second-digit Code 4 3 or 2).

Right: 254 cultures where the hierarchy of national jurisdiction has 1 or no levels (second-digit Code 1 or 0).

Unascertained: 70 cultures.

FC 96. Left: 174 cultures where the hierarchy of national jurisdiction has 4, 3, 2, or 1 level (second-digit Code 4 3 2 or 1).

Right: 156 cultures where the hierarchy of national jurisdiction has no levels (second-digit Code 0).

Unascertained: 70 cultures.

FC 97. Left: 58 cultures where the hierarchy of local jurisdiction has 4 levels (first-digit Code 4).

Right: 273 cultures where the hierarchy of local jurisdiction has 3 or 2 levels (first-digit Code 3 or 2).

Unascertained: 69 cultures.

FC 98. Left: 238 cultures where the hierarchy of local jurisdiction has 4 or 3 levels (first-digit Code 4 or 3).

Right: 93 cultures where the hierarchy of local jurisdiction has 2 levels (first-digit Code 2).

Unascertained: 69 cultures.

FC 99. Left: 93 cultures where, with national hierarchy absent, the hierarchy of local jurisdiction has 4 or 3 levels (first-digit Code 4 or 3 and second-digit Code 0).

Right: 63 cultures where, with a national hierarchy absent, the hierarchy of local jurisdiction has 2 levels (first-digit Code 2 and second-digit Code 0).

Irrelevant: 174 cultures where a national hierarchy is present (second-digit Code 4 3 2 or 1).

Unascertained: 70 cultures.

FC 100. Left: 267 cultures where hierarchies are more complex than the "simplest," i.e. more complex than two local levels with no national levels (all first- and second-digit substantive codes except those that apply to the right category).

Right: 63 cultures where hierarchies are the "simplest," i.e. where there are only two local levels with no national levels (first-digit Code 2 and second-digit Code 0).

Unascertained: 70 cultures.

FC 101 derives its codings from Guy E. Swanson directly, without modification by the **EA.** Swanson (1960:202) defines "specialties in communal activities" as "behaviors which conform to the following stipulations:

(a) They are performed only by persons who meet some customary criteria of competence (ascribed or achieved).

(b) Those criteria are not obtained through normal socialization for an age or sex role or a role in the nuclear family.

(c) The behaviors concerned are directed primarily toward meeting the needs of some sovereign or nonsovereign organization rather than the needs of particular individuals as such."

Swanson adds that "such specialties will almost always include any political offices, magical or religious roles, many educational and socializing roles, and slaves."

● FC 101. Left: 17 cultures where the number of communal activities is above the median, that is, 5 or more.

Right: 20 cultures where the number of communal specialties is below the median, that is, 4 or fewer.

Unascertained: 363 cultures.

STRATIFICATION (102–10)

FCs 102–08 deal with class stratification and are based on **EA** Column 67 (1963:114). "The degree and type of class differentiation, excluding purely political and religious statuses, is indicated by the following symbols":

C: "Complex stratification into social classes correlated in large measure with extensive differentiation of occupational statuses." 43 cultures.

D: "Dual stratification into a hereditary aristocracy and a lower class of ordinary commoners or freemen, where traditionally ascribed noble status is at least as decisive as the control over scarce resources and may even determine the latter." 74 cultures.

E: "Elite stratification, in which an elite class derives its superior status from, and perpetuates it through, control over scarce resources, particularly land, and is thereby differentiated from a propertyless proletariat or serf class." 9 cultures.

O: "Absence of significant class distinctions among freemen . . . ignoring variations in individual repute achieved through skill, valor, piety, or wisdom." 180 cultures. (The variable of slavery is treated separately in FC 110.)

W: "Wealth distinctions, based on the possession or distribution of property, present and socially important but not crystallized into distinct and hereditary social classes." 77 cultures.

Unascertained: 17 cultures.

FC 102. Left: 203 cultures where class stratification is present (Code C D E or W).
Right: 180 cultures where class stratification is absent (Code O).
Unascertained: 17 cultures.

● FC 103. Left: 126 cultures where class stratification is present and based on criteria other than wealth (Code C D or E).
Right: 257 cultures where class stratification is present and based on wealth, or else is absent (Code W or O).
Unascertained: 17 cultures.

● FC 104. Left: 120 cultures where class stratification is based on wealth or occupational status (Code W or C).
Right: 263 cultures where class stratification based on wealth or occupational status is absent (Code D E or O).
Unascertained: 17 cultures.

● FC 105. Left: 43 cultures where class stratification based on occupational status is present (Code C).
Right: 340 cultures where class stratification based on occupational status is absent (Code D E W or O).
Unascertained: 17 cultures.

FC 106. Left: 77 cultures where class stratification, if present, is based on wealth (Code W).
Right: 126 cultures where class stratification, if present, is based on something other than wealth (Code C D or E).
Irrelevant: 180 cultures where class stratification is absent (Code O).
Unascertained: 17 cultures.

FC 107. Left: 43 cultures where class stratification, if present, is based on occupational status (Code C).
Right: 160 cultures where class stratification, if present, is based on something other than occupational status (Code D E or W).
Irrelevant: 180 cultures where class stratification is absent (Code O).
Unascertained: 17 cultures.

FC 108. Left: 74 cultures where class stratification, if present, is based on a hereditary aristocracy (Code D).

Right: 129 cultures where class stratification, if present, is based on something other than a hereditary aristocracy (Code C E or W).

Irrelevant: 180 cultures where class stratification is absent (Code O).

Unascertained: 17 cultures.

FC 109 concerns caste stratification and derives from **EA** Column 69 (1963:114). "The degree and type of caste differentiation is indicated by the following symbols":

C: "Complex caste stratification in which occupational differentiation emphasizes hereditary ascription and endogamy to the near exclusion of achievable class statuses." 16 cultures.

D: "One or more despised occupational groups, e.g., smiths or leather workers, distinguished from the general population, regarded as outcastes by the latter, and characterized by strict endogamy." 25 cultures.

E: "Ethnic stratification, in which a superordinate caste withholds privileges from and refuses to intermarry with a subordinate caste (or castes) which it stigmatizes as ethnically alien, e.g., as descended from a conquered and culturally inferior indigenous population, from former slaves, or from foreign immigrants of different race and/or culture." 10 cultures.

O: "Caste distinctions absent or insignificant." 317 cultures.

Unascertained: 32 cultures.

"The use of two symbols, a capital followed by a lower-case letter, indicates a combination or mixture of two of the types defined above." The lower-case codes are ignored here. Because of the relatively small marginal frequencies associated with Codes C, D, and E, only one FC has been constructed on this subject.

FC 109. Left: 51 cultures where castes are present (Code C D or E).

Right: 317 cultures where castes are absent (Code O).

Unascertained: 32 cultures.

FC 110 deals with slavery, and derives its codings from **EA** Column 71 (1963:114–15). "Slave status is here treated entirely independently of both class and caste status. Its forms and prevalence are indicated by the following symbols":

H: "Hereditary slavery present and of at least modest social significance. Hf if formerly present but abolished before the date indicated under 'Notes' as the time of observation." 64 cultures.

I: "Incipient or nonhereditary slavery, i.e., where slave status is temporary and is not transmitted to the children of slaves. If if formerly present." 61 cultures.

O: "Absence or near absence of slavery." 218 cultures.

S: "Slavery reported but not identified as hereditary or nonhereditary. Sf if formerly present." 38 cultures.

Unascertained: 19 cultures.

These codes are discussed briefly on page 42 of this **Summary.**

FC 110. Left: 163 cultures where slavery is present (Code H Hf I If S or Sf).

Right: 218 cultures where slavery is absent (Code O).

Unascertained: 19 cultures.

WORK ORGANIZATION (111–14)

FCs in this section are derived from Stanley H. Udy, Jr.'s study of the organization of work (1959a). Udy coded a rather large number of cultures for the various types of work organizations that each of them possessed. As will be noted in the culture listings for Paragraphs 111–14, it often happens that a culture will possess more than one type of work organization. Codings for these four FCs are taken from Udy's Summary Table, pages 143ff., Column H, first digit. It should be noted that some entries in this column are composite entries. Code 2, for example, is "custodial-contractual." Cultures so coded were regarded as possessing "custodial" aspects in FC 113 and as possessing "contractual" aspects in FC 112.*

● FC 111. Left: 34 cultures where work organizations having a voluntary aspect are reported. According to Udy (1959a:58): "**Voluntary** recruitment is defined as determination of membership on the basis of self-defined self-interest, with no purely social sanctions attached to nonparticipation. This does not mean that severe personal deprivations cannot result from failure to participate, but only that no social mechanism is present which is expected to compel membership" (Column H, first-digit Code 9).

Right: 71 cultures where work organizations having a voluntary aspect are not reported (same, absence of first-digit Code 9).

Unascertained: 295 cultures.

● FC 112. Left: 50 cultures where work organizations having a contractual aspect are reported. Udy (1959a:57) explains that: "**Contractual** recruitment, as the name implies, is defined as determination of organiza-

*In more recent work, Udy has somewhat altered his taxonomy. For details, see Udy, forthcoming.

tional membership by the conclusion, at some point, of a voluntary contract between two or more parties; i.e., an agreement to behave in a specified way for a specified time in the future. . . . Once the contract has been concluded, participation in accordance with its terms is generally considered compulsory . . ." (Column H, first-digit Code 2 4 7 or 8).

Right: 55 cultures where work organizations having a contractual aspect are not reported (same, abscence of first-digit Code 2 4 7 or 8).

Unascertained: 295 cultures.

● FC 113. Left: 46 cultures where work organizations having a custodial aspect are reported (Udy 1959a:56): "In **custodial** recruitment, the obligation to participate is based on differential ascribed power, with kinship status secondary, if operative at all. Personnel are drawn from some group defined in predominantly political terms. Membership is compulsory in that participation may be legitimately compelled by force, if necessary, or sanctioned by severe punishment" (Column H, first-digit Code 1 or 2).

Right: 59 cultures where work organizations having a custodial aspect are not reported (same, absence of first-digit Code 1 or 2).

Unascertained: 295 cultures.

● FC 114. Left: 87 cultures where work organizations having a familial aspect are reported (Udy 1959a:56): "Recruitment is **familial,** if the obligation to participate is based on ascribed kinship status. Personnel are drawn from some kind of kinship group, which may range in size from a nuclear family to a ramified set of extended kin relations. Membership is compulsory in the sense that sanctions of whatever sort relative to the maintenance of kinship solidarity are operative. Other institutional content may operate to reinforce kinship obligations, but need not consistently do so, and may be highly variable" (Column H, first-digit Code 3 4 5 or 6).

Right: 18 cultures where work organizations having a familial aspect are not reported (same, absence of first-digit Code 3 4 5 or 6).

Unascertained: 295 cultures.

OCCUPATIONAL SPECIALIZATION (115–31)

Degree of Occupational Specialization (115–24)

FCs 115–16 are based on codings from John M. Hickman's Table 2, Column IV (1962:216), dealing with "Division of Labor." Hickman's codes are:

1. "Part-time specialization." 34 cultures.
2. "Full-time specialization." 13 cultures.
3. "Full-time specialization for surplus production." 7 cultures.

Unascertained: 346 cultures.

● FC 115. Left: 7 cultures where occupational specialization is full-time and for surplus production (Code 3).
Right: 47 cultures where occupational specialization is full-time, but not for surplus production, or part-time only (Code 2 or 1).
Unascertained: 346 cultures.

FC 116. Left: 20 cultures where occupational specialization is full-time, whether or not for surplus production (Code 3 or 2).
Right: 34 cultures where occupational specialization is part-time only (Code 1).
Unascertained: 346 cultures.

FCs 117–26 are based, in whole or in part, on codings by William M. Evan (1963). Unfortunately, all available copies of Evan's coding guide were destroyed in an accident, so that explicit definitions of coding categories cannot be presented here. The wording of these FCs is similar to that used uniformly in this **Summary:** A "high-low" contrast indicates a division at the median of an underlying ordinal scale, and a "high-medium-low" series indicates a division into terciles. FCs 121–24 are complex FCs in which the Evan codings have been composited with those of George Peter Murdock on level of political integration, and with those of the **EA** on stratification.

● FC 117. Left: 19 cultures where the percentage of occupations that are specialized is high.
Right: 30 cultures where the percentage of occupations that are specialized is medium or low.
Unascertained: 351 cultures.

FC 118. Left: 24 cultures where the percentage of occupations that are specialized is high or medium.
Right: 25 cultures where the percentage of occupations that are specialized is low.
Unascertained: 351 cultures.

● FC 119. Left: 16 cultures where the craft specialization score is high.

Right: 37 cultures where the craft specialization score is medium or low.
Unascertained: 347 cultures.

FC 120. Left: 36 cultures where the craft specialization score is high or medium.
Right: 17 cultures where the craft specialization score is low.
Unascertained: 347 cultures.

● FC 121. Left: 21 cultures where, with a state present, the craft specialization score is high or medium.
Right: 6 cultures where, with a state present, the craft specialization score is low.
Irrelevant: 29 remaining cultures substantively coded for craft specialization score, where a state is not present (page 82 of this **Summary,** Code A O D or P).
Unascertained: 344 cultures.

● FC 122. Left: 13 cultures where, without a state present, the craft specialization score is high or medium.
Right: 8 cultures where, without a state present, the craft specialization score is low.
Irrelevant: 38 cultures where a state is present (page 82 of this **Summary,** Code S L or M).
Unascertained: 341 cultures.

● FC 123. Left: 25 cultures where, with stratification present, the craft specialization score is high or medium.
Right: 8 cultures where, with stratification present, the craft specialization score is low.
Irrelevant: 24 remaining cultures substantively coded for craft specialization score, where stratification is absent (page 88 of this **Summary,** Code O).
Unascertained: 343 cultures.

● FC 124. Left: 11 cultures where, without stratification present, the craft specialization score is high or medium.
Right: 9 cultures where, without stratification present, the craft specialization score is low.
Irrelevant: 37 cultures where stratification is present (page 88 of this **Summary,** Code C D E or W).
Unascertained: 343 cultures.

Occupational Specialization by Sex (125–31)

The first two FCs in this subsection continue to utilize the Evan codings.

● FC 125. Left: 15 cultures where the ratio of male to female occupational specialization is high.
Right: 32 cultures where the ratio of male to female occupational specialization is medium or low.
Unascertained: 353 cultures.

● FC 126. Left: 22 cultures where the ratio of male to female occupational specialization is high or medium.
Right: 25 cultures where the ratio of male to female occupational specialization is low.
Unascertained: 353 cultures.

FC 127 is based on Judith K. Brown's codings for females' contribution to subsistence, appearing in her Table 5 (1963:848). For Brown's explanation of her detailed coding rationale, see pages 849 and 851–52.

FC 127. Left: 33 cultures where females' contribution to subsistence is above the median (Table 5, Left Column).
Right: 32 cultures where females' contributions to subsistence is below the median (same, Right Column).
Unascertained: 335 cultures.

FCs 128–31 are based on **EA** Columns 62, 44, 46, and 52, respectively. All of these columns have to do with occupational specialization by sex. The codes used here are:

D: "Differentiation of specific tasks by sex but approximately equal participation by both sexes in the total activity."

E: "Equal participation in the activity by both sexes without marked or reported differentiation in specific tasks."

F: "Females alone perform the activity, male participation being negligible or absent."

G: "Both sexes participate, but females do appreciably more than males."

I: "Sex participation irrelevant, especially where production is industrialized."

M: "Males alone perform the activity, female participation being negligible or absent."

N: "Both sexes participate, but males do appreciably more than females."

O: "The activity is absent or unimportant in the particular society."

P: "The activity is present, but sex participation is unspecified in the sources consulted."*

FC 128. Left: 40 cultures where, if subsistence is primarily by

*The postposited lower-case codes used with the above categories were not used in constructing FCs 128–31.

agriculture, the work is mainly done by males (**EA** Column 62, Code M or N).

Right: 37 cultures where, if subsistence is primarily by agriculture, the work is mainly done by females (same, Code F or G).

Irrelevant: 214 cultures. This category includes cultures where the agricultural work is not mainly performed by either sex (Code D or E). It also includes cultures where sex participation is irrelevant (Code I). Further, it includes cultures where agriculture is absent or unimportant (Code O). Finally, it includes cultures where subsistence is primarily by means other than agriculture (Subcategory A–2 and Category B, as explained on page 73 of this **Summary**).

Unascertained: 109 cultures.

FCs 129–31 simply inquire into sexual specialization, regardless of how important the productive activity is to the particular culture.

FC 129. Left: 31 cultures where weaving is mainly done by males (**EA** Column 44, Code M or N).

Right: 73 cultures where weaving is mainly done by females (same, Code F or G).

Ambiguous: 3 cultures where weaving is present but not mainly done by either sex (Code D).

Irrelevant: 136 cultures (Code I or O).

Unascertained: 157 cultures.

FC 130. Left: 39 cultures where leather working is mainly done by males (**EA** Column 46, Code M or N).

Right: 45 cultures where leather working is mainly done by females (same, Code F or G).

Irrelevant: 56 cultures (Code I or O).

Unascertained: 260 cultures.

FC 131. Left: 136 cultures where the construction of permanent houses or the erection of temporary dwellings is mainly done by males (**EA** Column 52, Code M or N).

Right: 21 cultures where such work is mainly done by females (same, Code F or G).

Ambiguous: 29 cultures (Code D or E).

Unascertained: 214 cultures.

ECONOMICS (132–37)

FC 132 is derived from John M. Hickman's Table 2, Column C (1962: 215). Hickman's codes for economic exchange are:

1: "Local exchange."
2: "Trade (Barter)."
3: "Trade (Money)."

FC 132. Left: 37 cultures where economic exchange involves the use of money (Code 3).
Right: 17 cultures where economic exchange does not involve the use of money (Code 1 or 2).
Unascertained: 346 cultures.

FC 133, dealing with contracted debts, is based on Guy E. Swanson's Column 7 (1960:200). Swanson's classification "records the presence and size of loans which individuals or groups are obliged to repay. The loans may consist of goods or services. It excludes loans when the obligations for repayment are determined by rules of kinship or such ritual relations as blood brotherhood. The intent of this exclusion is to eliminate the less formal and contractual kinds of borrowing which frequently occur and which, presumably, do not reflect the degree of impersonality and specialization of relationship related to other kinds of debts."

0: "None—the ethnographer denies that such debt relations exist or fails to mention them."

1: "Moderate—some debt relations exist, but there is no indication that they are frequent or that they are of a size that debtors find difficult to repay."

2: "Considerable—debt relations exist and the ethnographer mentions that some debtors find it difficult to repay the loan."

FC 133. Left: 17 cultures where contracted debts are significantly present (Code 2).
Right: 17 cultures where contracted debts are moderately present or absent (Code 1 or 0).
Unascertained: 366 cultures.

The codings for FC 134 were made by Joseph Veroff, and appear in David C. McClelland's Table 3.1, Fourth Column (McClelland 1961: 66–67). Veroff coded a sample of cultures for "percentage of income-producing property which is individually owned." Commenting on Veroff's coding operation, McClelland observes: "The ownership estimates are . . . very rough, because of the difficulty of deciding where the 'individual' left off and the 'community' began. It seemed unwise to hold too rigidly to a criterion of individual ownership, since frequently items were the property of a family or household, but then the problem arose of how extended did a household have to be before it became the 'community.' "

● FC 134. Left: 16 cultures where income-producing property is 100 per cent individually owned (Code 100).
Right: 18 cultures where income-producing property

is less than 100 per cent individually owned (Code: any number lower than 100).

Unascertained: 366 cultures.

FC 135 is based on Guy E. Swanson's Column 6 (1960:199–200), concerning "individually owned property."

> An individual owns property if he has the legitimate right to determine the way the property shall be employed, or to determine the distribution of benefits realized from the property, or to dispose of the property or some part of it. His rights in these respects need not be held by him exclusively, but he should have larger powers of determination concerning the property than other persons who share ownership in that property. Individual rights to property do not exist, however, when some person (such as a headman or elder) is given wealth with the tacit or explicit understanding that it is his to distribute to the population according to customary criteria. In this classification, property refers to anything which is important in the production of the society's more significant means of sustenance. Such means of sustenance include sources of food which are important, though not among the staples. Property important in the production of such means of sustenance may take many forms. Among them are land, tools, domestic animals, seed, or magical techniques employed to ensure success in production.

Swanson's categories are:

0: "Individuals do not own economically significant property."

1: "Individuals own property which is used in producing what the ethnographer designates as forms of sustenance, but not those which he calls the most important forms of wealth or the staple foods."

2: "Individuals **can** own property employed in producing what the ethnographer designates as the most important forms of wealth or the staple foods."

FC 135. Left: 24 cultures where individual ownership of economically significant property is present (Code 2).

Right: 14 cultures where individual ownership of economically significant property is negligible or absent (Code 1 or 0).

Unascertained: 362 cultures.

FC 136, like FC 134, is based on codings done by Joseph Veroff for David C. McClelland, and appears in the latter's Table 3.1, Second Column (1961:65–67). Veroff coded a sample of cultures and tried to "decide what percentage of the adult males were engaged in 'full time' entrepreneurial activity. An entrepreneur was defined as 'someone who exercises some control over the means of production and produces more than he can consume in order to sell (or exchange) it for individual (or household) income.' . . . a full-time entrepreneur was defined as someone who received 75 per cent or more of his income from entrepreneurial activities." FC 136 dichotomizes simply between cultures where **some** percentage of the adult males are full-time entrepreneurs, and where this percentage is zero.

FC 136. Left: 18 cultures where full-time entrepreneurs are present (Code: any number other than zero).

Right: 14 cultures where full-time entrepreneurs are absent (Code: zero).

Unascertained: 368 cultures.

FC 137 derives from Philip E. Slater's codings for invidious display of wealth (Slater 1964:5–6). Slater's code is:

2. "Present":

(1) "When ethnographer states explicitly that one of the central values attached to wealth in the society is its use in display, or if he refers to the importance of 'conspicuous consumption,' or if he states that ambition, social mobility, and competitiveness are focused upon the ability to display wealth or the symbols of wealth. Or,

(2) "When prestige, rank, and power in the society are dependent upon displayed wealth, or displayed wealth is said to be a major goal in the society. Or,

(3) "When gift-giving and hospitality in the society are essentially invidious (e.g., the potlatch). That is, liberality is not conceived as an obligation or a kindness but as an act of self-aggrandizement and ostentation.

"(Displayed wealth includes subsistence goods, currency, luxuries, servants or retainers, or anything which symbolizes the ability of the individual to command wealth)."

1. "Absent: When none of the above are conspicuous and:

(1) "Ethnographer states that gradations of wealth are unimportant, static, or minimized by those who possess it. Or,

(2) "Wealthy persons have no prestige in the society or are regarded as immoral. Or,

(3) "There is a norm that surplus wealth must be shared, and that the accumulation of wealth confers prestige upon the group rather than the individual. Or,

(4) "The value of wealth is seen as residing altogether in the security it provides or the power to procure goods and services. Or,

(5) "Ethnographer says that ostentatious approach to wealth is frowned upon or looked down on. Or,

(6) "Gift-giving is closely regulated on the basis of reciprocity and obligation.

"Note: Since invidiousness is virtually universal, one should be cautious about making a positive rating on the basis of scanty support."

FC 137. Left: 37 cultures where invidious display of wealth is strongly emphasized (Code 2).

Right: 52 cultures where invidious display of wealth

is moderately, little, or negatively emphasized (Code 1 or X, the latter symbol meaning that there is conflicting information).

Unascertained: 311 cultures.

JUSTICE AND LAW (138–49)

FC 138 is based on codings by Beatrice Blyth Whiting concerning superordinate justice (1950:84–85). Cultures where murder cases are referred to a delegated authority were coded as possessing "superordinate" justice. Cultures where murder cases are settled by retaliation were coded as possessing "coordinate" justice.

FC 138. Left: 22 cultures where superordinate justice is present (Table I, Right Column).

Right: 18 cultures where superordinate justice is absent (Table I, Left Column).

Unascertained: 360 cultures.

FC 139, concerning the concept of superordinate punishment, also derives from Beatrice Blyth Whiting (1950:86–87). Whiting distinguishes between superordinate justice and superordinate punishment as follows: "If the members of a group avenged the murder of one of its members without securing permission from an individual or group of individuals, the society was listed as having coordinate control; if the group secured permission before it took action, the society was listed as having superordinate justice but no superordinate punishment; if the group presented its case to a chief or court and depended on them to punish the murderer, the society was listed as having both superordinate justice and punishment."

FC 139. Left: 15 cultures where superordinate punishment is present (Table II, Right Column).

Right: 25 cultures where superordinate punishment is absent (same, Left Column).

Unascertained: 360 cultures.

FCs 140–42 concern three levels of public sanction; codings are from John M. Hickman's Table 1, Column V (1962:215). Hickman's categories are:

1: "Private settlement." 16 cultures.

2. "Public property sanctions." 10 cultures.

3: "Public corporeal sanctions." 28 cultures.

Unascertained: 346 cultures.

● FC 140. Left: 28 cultures where the level of social sanction is the public corporeal sanction (Code 3).

Right: 16 cultures where the level of social sanction is the private settlement (Code 1).

Irrelevant: 10 cultures where the level of social sanction is the public property sanction (Code 2).

Unascertained: 346 cultures.

FC 141. Left: 28 cultures where the level of social sanction is the public corporeal sanction (Code 3).

Right: 26 cultures where the level of social sanction is the public property sanction or private settlement (Code 2 or 1).

Unascertained: 346 cultures.

FC 142. Left: 38 cultures where the level of social sanction is the public corporeal sanction or public property sanction (Code 3 or 2).

Right: 16 cultures where the level of social sanction is the private settlement (Code 1).

Unascertained: 346 cultures.

FCs 143–46 derive from William M. Evan (1963). Because Evan's records were destroyed, as mentioned earlier, precise coding category descriptions cannot be given here.

FC 143. Left: 20 cultures where the ratio of restitutive to repressive sanctions is high.

Right: 32 cultures where the ratio of restitutive to repressive sanctions is medium or low.

Unascertained: 348 cultures.

FC 144. Left: 27 cultures where the ratio of restitutive to repressive sanctions is high or medium.

Right: 25 cultures where the ratio of restitutive to repressive sanctions is low.

Unascertained: 348 cultures.

● FC 145. Left: 28 cultures where the legal role differentiation is high.

Right: 21 cultures where the legal role differentiation is medium or low.

Unascertained: 351 cultures.

● FC 146. Left: 36 cultures where the legal role differentiation is high or medium.

Right: 13 cultures where the legal role differentiation is low.

Unascertained: 351 cultures.

FC 147, dealing with codified law, is derived from Leo W. Simmons' Code Chart, Column 38 (1945).

FC 147. Left: 20 cultures where codified laws are present (Code Plus or Equals).

Right: 13 cultures where codified laws are unimportant or absent (Code Minus or Zero).

Unascertained: 367 cultures.

FCs 148 and 149, concerning the incidence of personal crime and of theft, respectively, derive from codings described by Bacon, Child, and Barry (1963).

FC 148. Left: 12 cultures where the incidence of personal crime is above the median.
Right: 21 cultures where the incidence of personal crime is below the median.
Unascertained: 367 cultures.

FC 149. Left: 18 cultures where the incidence of theft is above the median.
Right: 19 cultures where the incidence of theft is below the median.
Unascertained: 363 cultures.

JURISPRUDENCE AND MEDICINE (150–74)

All codings in this section are based on Merrill Jackson (1962). Jackson's coding rules are unusually clear and detailed, and for reasons of space will be simply cited here rather than quoted in full. All FCs in this section are simple "high-low" dichotomies based on Jackson's having rank-ordered his cultures from highest to lowest on each variable. Coding column references are to Jackson's serially ordered columns appearing in Tables 10, 11, and 12, on pages 178–80.

● FC 150. Left: 10 cultures where the differentiation of the juridical agency from all other agencies in the society is high (Column 1A and page 148).
Right: 10 cultures where this differentiation is low.
Unascertained: 380 cultures.

● FC 151. Left: 10 cultures where the differentiation of the medical agency from all other agencies in the society is high (Column 1B and page 159).
Right: 10 cultures where this differentiation is low.
Unascertained: 380 cultures.

FC 152. Left: 10 cultures where the differentiation of the juridical agency from the medical agency is high (Column 2 and page 149).
Right: 10 cultures where this differentiation is low.
Unascertained: 380 cultures.

● FC 153. Left: 10 cultures where the division of labor among juridical specialists and subunits is high (Column 3A and page 149).
Right: 10 cultures where this division of labor is low.
Unascertained: 380 cultures.

- FC 154. Left: 10 cultures where the division of labor among medical specialists and subunits is high (Column 3B and page 160).
  Right: 10 cultures where this division of labor is low.
  Unascertained: 380 cultures.
- FC 155. Left: 9 cultures where the extent of training of juridical specialists is high (Column 4A and page 150).
  Right: 11 cultures where this extent of training is low.
  Unascertained: 380 cultures.
- FC 156. Left: 9 cultures where the extent of training of medical specialists is high (Column 4B and page 161).
  Right: 8 cultures where this extent of training is low.
  Unascertained: 383 cultures.
- FC 157. Left: 9 cultures where the extent of hierarchization of the juridical agency is high (Column 5A and page 151).
  Right: 11 cultures where this extent is low.
  Unascertained: 380 cultures.
- FC 158. Left: 11 cultures where the extent of development of medical subsystems is high (Column 5B and page 162).
  Right: 9 cultures where this extent of development is low.
  Unascertained: 380 cultures.
- FC 159. Left: 10 cultures where the degree of localization of juridical activity is high (Column 6A and page 152).
  Right: 10 cultures where this degree of localization is low.
  Unascertained: 380 cultures.
- FC 160. Left: 10 cultures where the degree of localization of medical activity is high (Column 6B and page 163).
  Right: 10 cultures where this degree of localization is low.
  Unascertained: 380 cultures.
- FC 161. Left: 10 cultures where the degree of control over clients by the juridical agency is high (Column 7A and page 152).
  Right : 10 cultures where this degree of control is low.
  Unascertained: 380 cultures.
- FC 162. Left: 10 cultures where the degree of control over clients by the medical agency is high (Column 7B and page 163).
  Right: 10 cultures where this degree of control is low.

Unascertained: 380 cultures.

FC 163. Left: 7 cultures where the emphasis on individual volition as the cause of crime is high (Column 8A and page 153).
Right: 10 cultures where this emphasis is low.
Unascertained: 383 cultures.

FC 164. Left: 9 cultures where the emphasis on individual volition as the cause or source of illness is high (Column 8B and page 164).
Right: 9 cultures where this emphasis is low.
Unascertained: 382 cultures.

● FC 165. Left: 7 cultures where the juridical client's comments are disregarded or used against him to a high extent (Column 9A and page 153).
Right: 9 cultures where the juridical client's comments are disregarded or used against him to a low extent.
Unascertained: 384 cultures.

● FC 166. Left: 10 cultures where the medical client's comments are regarded as relevant in diagnosis and cure to a high extent (Column 9B and page 165).
Right: 10 cultures where the medical client's comments are so regarded to a low extent.
Unascertained: 380 cultures.

● FC 167. Left: 9 cultures where juridical solution is based on the client's actions to a high extent (Column 10A and page 154).
Right: 7 cultures where juridical solution is so based to a low extent.
Unascertained: 384 cultures.

● FC 168. Left: 9 cultures where diagnosis and cure are based on the client's moral and social actions to a high extent (Column 10B and page 165).
Right: 10 cultures where diagnosis and cure are so based to a low extent.
Unascertained: 381 cultures.

● FC 169. Left: 10 cultures where the degree of manipulation of the client in juridical matters is high (Column 11A and pages 154–55).
Right: 10 cultures where this degree of manipulation is low.
Unascertained: 380 cultures.

● FC 170. Left: 10 cultures where the degree of manipulation of the client in medical matters is high (Column 11B and page 166).

Right: 10 cultures where the degree of this manipulation is low.
Unascertained: 380 cultures.

● FC 171. Left: 10 cultures where the juridical client is hampered from returning to normal social roles as a consequence of crime to a high extent (Column 12A and pages 156–57).
Right: 10 cultures where the juridical client is so hampered to a low extent.
Unascertained: 380 cultures.

● FC 172. Left: 9 cultures where the medical client is hampered from returning to normal social roles as a consequence of illness to a high extent (Column 12B and pages 166–67).
Right: 11 cultures where the medical client is so hampered to a low extent.
Unascertained: 380 cultures.

● FC 173. Left: 10 cultures where the social and emotional support given to the juridical client during judgment and punishment is high (Column 13A and page 157).
Right: 10 cultures where such support is low.
Unascertained: 380 cultures.

● FC 174. Left: 9 cultures where the social and emotional support given to the medical client during diagnosis and treatment is high (Column 13B and page 167).
Right: 11 cultures where such support is low.
Unascertained: 380 cultures.

COMMUNITY ORGANIZATION (175–82)

This entire section is based on **EA** Column 19 (1962:118–19). "The prevalence of local endogamy, agamy, and exogamy, together with the presence or absence of localized kin groups, is indicated by the following symbols:

A: "Agamous communities without localized clans or any marked tendency toward either local exogamy or local endogamy." 126 cultures.

C: "Clan-communities, each consisting essentially of a single localized exogamous kin group or clan. Cs* if also segmented into clan-barrios." 77 cultures.

*The **EA** columnization inadvertently neglected to provide a column in which the postposited lower-case symbol can be punched. If the reader wishes to carry out further analysis using these postposited codes, he may do so by sorting on Column 41 of the second **EA** data deck. In Appendix Seven, this column is identified by the symbol "EX" and is the left-hand of the two columns thusly identified. For further explanation, see page 47.

D: "Demes, i.e., communities revealing a marked tendency toward local endogamy but not segmented into clan-barrios." 45 cultures.

E: "Exogamous communities, i.e., those revealing a marked tendency toward local exogamy without having the specific structure of clans." 42 cultures.

S: "Segmented communities, i.e., those divided into barrios, wards, or hamlets, each of which is essentially a localized kin group or clan, in the absence of any indication of local exogamy. Large extended families, indicated by E in Column 14, are here treated as clan-barrios if they are integrated by a rule of ambilineal, matrilineal, or patrilineal descent, but are ignored if descent is bilateral." 87 cultures.

T: "Segmented communities where a marked tendency toward local exogamy is also specifically reported." 5 cultures.

Unascertained: 18 cultures.

FC 175. Left: 122 cultures where the community is "kin-homogeneous," i.e. a clan-community or a deme (Code C or D).

Right: 260 cultures where the community is "kin-heterogeneous," i.e. other than a clan-community or a deme (Code A E S or T).

Unascertained: 18 cultures.

FC 176. Left: 169 cultures where the community is a clan-community or a community structured or segmented on a clan basis (Code C S or T).

Right: 213 remaining substantively coded cultures (Code A D or E).

Unascertained: 18 cultures.

FC 177. Left: 77 cultures where the community is a single clan-community and exogamous (Code C).

Right: 305 remaining substantively coded cultures (Code A D E S or T).

Unascertained: 18 cultures.

FC 178. Left: 87 cultures where the community is segmented on a clan basis and nonexogamous (Code S).

Right: 295 remaining substantively coded cultures (Code A C D E or T).

Unascertained: 18 cultures.

FC 179. Left: 42 cultures where the community is structured on a nonclan basis and commonly exogamous (Code E).

Right: 340 remaining substantively coded cultures (Code A C D S or T).

Unascertained: 18 cultures.

FC 180. Left: 124 cultures where the community is commonly

exogamous (Code C E or T).
Right: 258 cultures where the community is commonly nonexogamous (Code A D or S).
Unascertained: 18 cultures.

FC 181. Left: 45 cultures where the community is a deme (Code D).
Right: 337 remaining substantively coded cultures (Code A C E S or T).
Unascertained: 18 cultures.

FC 182. Left: 126 cultures where the community is structured on a nonclan basis and agamous (Code A).
Right: 256 remaining substantively coded cultures (Code C D E S or T).
Unascertained: 18 cultures.

LARGEST NONCOGNATIC KIN GROUP (183–85)

This section is derived from codings appearing in **EA** Columns 20 and 22 (1962:119). Column 20 deals with patrilineal kin groups, Column 22 with matrilineal. Otherwise, the codes used are identical. This section is concerned only with capital-letter codes, which indicate "the largest type of kin group reported for the particular society." The coding categories listed below follow from the **EA,** but have been reordered and amalgamated somewhat in order to clarify their relevance to the FCs in this section.

M: "Moieties (patrilineal or matrilineal), i.e., maximal lineages when there are only two such in the society." 34 cultures.

P: "Phratries (patrilineal or matrilineal), maximal lineages when there are more than two and when sibs are also present." 43 cultures.

S: "Sibs (patrilineal or matrilineal)—or 'clans' in British usage—i.e., lineages whose core membership normally comprises residents of more than one community." 117 cultures.

L: "Lineages (patrilineal or matrilineal) of modest size, i.e., kin groups whose core membership is normally confined to a single community or part thereof." 58 cultures.

Irrelevant: 148 cultures where the kin group is exclusively cognatic. (These cultures are further examined on page 109.)

Construction of the three FCs in this section is based on the underlying ordinal continuum of size of largest kin group—from moiety to phratry to sib to lineage.

FC 183. Left: 34 cultures where the largest noncognatic kin group is the moiety (Code M).
Right: 218 cultures where the largest noncognatic kin group is phratry, sib, or lineage (Code P S or L).

Irrelevant: 148 cultures where the kin group is exclusively cognatic.

FC 184. Left: 77 cultures where the largest noncognatic kin group is the moiety or phratry (Code M or P).

Right: 175 cultures where the largest noncognatic kin group is the sib or lineage (Code S or L).

Irrelevant: 148 cultures where the kin group is exclusively cognatic.

FC 185. Left: 194 cultures where the largest noncognatic kin group is the moiety or phratry or sib (Code M P or S).

Right: 58 cultures where the largest noncognatic kin group is the lineage (Code L).

Irrelevant: 148 cultures where the kin group is exclusively cognatic.

LINEALITY OF KIN GROUP (186–95)

This section is derived from **EA** Columns 20, 22, and 24, which deal respectively with patrilineal, matrilineal, and cognatic kin groups (1962: 119). Because more than one of these three basic types are often found in the same culture, FCs in this section have been constructed by sorting for various codes on all three columns. The relevant codes for Columns 20 and 22 have been listed just above. For Column 24, "the presence or probable absence, and the typology, of ambilineal and bilateral kin groups are indicated by the following symbols":

A: "Ambilineal descent as inferred from the presence of ambilocal extended families, true ramages being absent or unreported."

B: "Bilateral descent as inferred from the absence of reported ambilineal, matrilineal, or patrilineal kin groups, kindreds being absent or unreported."

K: "Kindreds, i.e., Ego-oriented bilateral kin groups, specifically reported."

O: "Absence of cognatic kin groups as inferred from the presence of unilineal descent."

Q: "Quasi-lineages, i.e., cognatic groups approximating the structure of lineages but based on filiation rather than on unilineal or ambilineal descent."

R: "Ramages, i.e., ancestor-oriented ambilineal kin groups comparable to lineages under patrilineal or matrilineal descent, specifically reported, if they are agamous, endogamous, or not specifically stated to be exogamous."

S: "Exogamous ramages specifically reported."

"When both kindreds and ramages are reported for the same society, they are indicated by a capital followed by a lower-case letter, the former designating the group of the greater functional importance."*

The following typology and frequency distribution of kin group types should serve to make clear the basis for FCs 186–91.

1. "Exclusively Patrilineal": In these cultures, a patrilineal kin group is present, while matrilineal and cognatic kin groups are absent. 150 cultures.

2. "Exclusively Matrilineal": A matrilineal kin group is present, while patrilineal and cognatic kin groups are absent. 55 cultures.

3. "Ambiguous": A patrilineal kin group is present while cognatic kin groups are absent. Matrilineal exogamy is present in the absence of a matrilineal kin group. 3 cultures, the Merina, Tallensi, and Tanala.

4. "Unascertained": A matrilineal kin group is present, while cognatic kin groups are absent. It is unascertained whether a patrilineal kin group is present. 1 culture, the Ainu.

5. "Double-Descent": A patrilineal and a matrilineal kin group are present, while cognatic kin groups are absent. 20 cultures.

6. "Patrilineal-Cognatic": A patrilineal and a cognatic kin group are present, while matrilineal kin groups are absent. 16 cultures.

7. "Matrilineal-Cognatic": A matrilineal and a cognatic kin group are present, while patrilineal kin groups are absent. 6 cultures.

8. "Patrilineal-Matrilineal-Cognatic": A patrilineal, a matrilineal, and a cognatic kin group are present. 1 culture, the Pukapuka.

9. "Exclusively Cognatic": A cognatic kin group is present, while patrilineal and matrilineal kin groups are absent. 148 cultures.

FC 186. Left: 150 cultures where the kin group is exclusively patrilineal. These are cultures which, according to **EA** Column 20, possess a patrilineal kin group and, according to Columns 22 and 24, do not possess a matrilineal or cognatic kin group.

Right: 250 remaining cultures.

FC 187. Left: 55 cultures where the kin group is exclusively matrilineal. These are cultures which, according to **EA** Column 22, possess a matrilineal kin group and, according to Columns 20 and 24, do not possess a patrilineal or cognatic kin group.

Right: 344 remaining substantively coded cultures.

Unascertained: 1 culture. (The **EA** indicates uncertainty as to whether this culture possesses a patrilineal kin group.)

*The **EA** columnization inadvertently neglected to provide a column in which the postposited lower-case symbol can be punched. If the reader wishes to carry out further analysis using these postposited codes, he may do so by sorting on Column 42 of the second **EA** data deck. In Appendix Seven, this column is identified by the symbol "EX" and is the right-hand of the two columns thusly identified. For further explanation, see page 47.

FC 188. Left: 148 cultures where the kin group is exclusively cognatic. These are cultures which, according to **EA** Column 24, possess a cognatic kin group and, according to **EA** Columns 20 and 22, do not possess a patrilineal or matrilineal kin group.

Right: 252 remaining cultures.

● FC 189. Left: 20 cultures where the kin group is double descent. These are cultures which, according to **EA** Columns 20 and 22, possess both a patrilineal and a matrilineal kin group and, according to Column 24, do not possess a cognatic kin group.

Right: 378 cultures where the kin group is other than double descent. These are cultures where the kin group is (1) exclusively patrilineal (2) exclusively matrilineal, or (3) exclusively cognatic; or where the kin groups are (4) patrilineal and cognatic or (5) matrilineal and cognatic.

Ambiguous: 1 culture which possesses a patrilineal, a matrilineal, and a cognatic kin group.

Unascertained: 1 culture, as in FC 187.

FC 190. Left: 186 cultures where the kin group is patrilineal or double descent. These include cultures where the kin group is (1) exclusively patrilineal; or where the kin groups are (2) patrilineal and matrilineal, or (3) patrilineal and cognatic.

Right: 61 cultures where the kin group is matrilineal. These include cultures where the kin group is (1) exclusively matrilineal; or where the kin groups are (2) matrilineal and cognatic.

Ambiguous: 4 cultures. These include the Pukapuka, where there is a patrilineal, a matrilineal, and a cognatic kin group. Also included are the Merina, Tallensi, and Tanala, each of which has a patrilineal kin group and matrilineal exogamy in the absence of a matrilineal kin group (**EA** Column 22, Code E).

Irrelevant: 148 cultures where the kin group is exclusively cognatic.

Unascertained: 1 culture, as in FC 187.

● FC 191. Left: 185 cultures where the kin group is the patrilineal or double-descent type. These include cultures where the kin group is (1) exclusively patrilineal; or where the kin groups are (2) patrilineal and matrilineal, or (3) patrilineal and cognatic

where the cognatic form is other than quasi-lineal.
Right: 14 cultures where the kin group is the quasi-lineage (Column 24, Code Q).
Ambiguous: 2 cultures. These are the Pukapuka, for reasons indicated in FC 190, and the Ojibwa, which are coded as possessing both patrilineages and quasi-lineages.
Irrelevant: 198 remaining substantively coded cultures.
Unascertained: 1 culture, as in FC 187.

FC 192. Left: 111 cultures where the only kin group present is a kindred or else bilateral descent is inferred (**EA** Column 24, Code B or K or postposited lower-case k—in the absence of substantive entries in Column 20 or 22).
Right: 289 remaining cultures.

● FC 193. Left: 68 cultures where the kindred is specifically reported present (**EA** Column 24, Code K or postposited lower-case k).
Right: 332 remaining cultures.

● FC 194. Left: 27 cultures where the ramage is present (**EA** Column 24, Code R or postposited lower-case r).
Right: 373 remaining cultures.

● FC 195. Left: 54 cultures where the kindred, rather than the ramage, is specifically reported present (**EA** Column 24, Code K in the absence of a postposited lower-case r; or postposited lower-case k in the absence of a preceding R).
Right: 13 cultures where the ramage, rather than the kindred, is specifically reported present (**EA** Column 24, Code R in the absence of a postposited lower-case k; or postposited lower-case r in the absence of a preceding K).
Ambiguous: 14 cultures where both the kindred and the ramage are present (Code K **and** postposited r; or Code R **and** postposited k).
Irrelevant: 319 remaining cultures.

INHERITANCE (196–200)

The FCs in this section are based on the capital-letter codes in Columns 74 and 76 of the **EA** (1963:115). Both columns use the same code symbols, with one exception to be noted for Code "O." The postposited lower-case symbols are not used in this section. "Inheritance of Real

Property" is described as "the basic rules governing the disposition or transmission of a man's property in land (exclusive of any dower right of his widow)." "Inheritance of Movable Property" has to do with "the rules governing the disposition or transmission of movable property (e.g., livestock, tools and other artifacts, accumulated food stores, money)." It is important to note that the **EA** cautions as follows: "In actual application, the codes for Columns 74 and 76 proved inadequate and in serious need of revision. The coded data for these columns should consequently be used only with circumspection." The symbols are:

C: "Inheritance by children of either sex or both."

D: "Inheritance by children of either sex or both, but with daughters receiving less than sons."

M: "Matrilineal inheritance by a sister's son or sons."

N: "Inheritance by matrilineal heirs who take precedence over sisters' sons, e.g., younger brothers."

O: "Absence of individual property rights . . . or of any rule of inheritance governing the transmission of such rights." (In the case of movable property, this category includes "the destruction, burial, or giving away of movable property.")

P: "Patrilineal inheritance by a son or sons."

Q: "Inheritance by patrilineal heirs who take precedence over sons, e.g., younger brothers."

For FCs 196–98, dealing with real property, the number of cultures assigned to each raw attribute category is as follows: C, 29; D, 16; M, 5; N, 16; O, 87; P, 108; Q, 20; Unascertained, 119.

FC 196. Left: 194 cultures where individual rights in real property and rules for inheritance are present (Column 74, Code C D M N P or Q).

Right: 87 cultures where individual rights in real property or rules for inheritance are absent (Column 74, Code O).

Unascertained: 119 cultures.

FC 197. Left: 165 cultures where rules for the inheritance of real property, if present, favor either the male heir or line or the female heir or line (Column 74, Code D M N P or Q).

Right: 29 cultures where such rules, if present, do not favor the male heir or line or the female heir or line (Column 74, Code C).

Irrelevant: 87 cultures where such rules are absent (Column 74, Code O).

Unascertained: 119 cultures.

FC 198. Left: 144 cultures where rules for the inheritance of real property, if present, favor the male heir or line (Column 74, Code D P or Q).

Right: 21 cultures where such rules, if present, favor the female heir or line (Column 74, Code M or N).

Irrelevant: 116 cultures, including: 29 cultures where such rules are present but favor neither male nor female heir or line (Column 74, Code C). 87 cultures where such rules are absent (Column 74, Code O).

Unascertained: 119 cultures.

For FCs 199–200, dealing with movable property, the number of cultures assigned to each raw attribute category is as follows: C, 46; D, 17; M, 13; N, 22; O, 32; P, 144; Q, 15; Unascertained, 111.

● FC 199. Left: 211 cultures where rules for the inheritance of movable property, if present, favor either the male heir or line or the female heir or line (Column 76, Code D M N P or Q).

Right: 46 cultures where such rules, if present, do not favor either the male heir or line or the female heir or line (Column 76, Code C).

Irrelevant: 32 cultures where such rules are absent (Column 76, Code O).

Unascertained: 111 cultures.

● FC 200. Left: 176 cultures where rules for the inheritance of movable property, if present, favor the male heir or line (Column 76, Code D P or Q).

Right: 35 cultures where such rules, if present, favor the female heir or line (Column 76, Code M or N).

Irrelevant: 78 cultures, including: 46 cultures where such rules are present but favor neither the male heir or line nor the female heir or line (Column 76, Code C). 32 cultures where such rules are absent (Column 76, Code O).

Unascertained: 111 cultures.

MARITAL RESIDENCE (201–12)

The FCs in this section are derived entirely from the capital-letter codes found in the **EA's** Column 16, "Profile of Marital Residence" (1962:117–18). In this column, the "primary objective is to indicate over-all societal profiles, especially as these relate to other categories of social organization, not to provide a means of identifying the residential alignment of individuals as, for example, in a household census. . . . We are not greatly concerned with distinguishing rules from practice in our definitions, since we assume that in integrated societies, for which our system is primarily designed, rules are ordinarily reasonably consistent with prevailing practice. We are quite aware of the importance of the degree of spatial removal demanded by different residence profiles in the context of particular structural situations. We prefer, however, not to complicate our definitions by introducing this dimension, especially since we believe that the most important facts about the extent of spatial removal in each society are implicit in the symbols in Column 19 indicating the relative prevalence of local endogamy and exogamy. It makes little difference whether the residence profile in an endogamous community involves a shift of a few yards or several rods, in comparison to the miles that one spouse may have to move where local exogamy is the rule. The following symbols represent the best compromise we can propose consistent with the above-stated objectives":

A: "Avunculocal, i.e., normal residence with or near the maternal uncle or other male matrilineal kinsmen of the husband." 18 cultures.

B: "Ambilocal, bilocal, or utrolocal, i.e., residence established optionally with or near the parents of the husband or of the wife, depending upon circumstances or personal choice, where neither alternative exceeds the other in actual frequency by a ratio greater than two to one. If the differential frequency is greater than this, the symbols Uv or Vu will be used to denote, respectively, a marked preponderance of uxorilocal or virilocal practice." (These postposited lower-case symbols were not used in constructing the FCs in this section.) 36 cultures.

C: "Ambilocal, where there is a similar option between uxorilocal and avunculocal residence. This symbol will also be frequently recorded for matrilocal societies characterized by preferential or prescriptive matrilateral cross-cousin marriage. Under these circumstances a man who marries his MoBrDa will be living in avunculocal as well as matrilocal residence. Such instances of a dual profile will be classed as avunculocal rather than matrilocal." 3 cultures.

D: "Ambilocal, where there is a similar option between patrilocal (or virilocal) and avunculocal residence." 2 cultures.

M: "Matrilocal, i.e., normal residence with or near the female matrilineal kinsmen of the wife. Cf. U Uxorilocal." 31 cultures.

N: "Neolocal, i.e., normal residence apart from the relatives of both spouses or at a place not determined by the kin ties of either." 23 cultures.

O: "Nonestablishment of a common household, e.g., where both spouses remain in their natal households (the "natolocal" residence of Barnes) or where men reside apart from their wives in special men's houses." 1 culture.

P: "Patrilocal, i.e., normal residence with or near the male patrilineal kinsmen of the husband. Cf. V Virilocal." 169 cultures.

U: "Uxorilocal. This term and symbol will be confined to instances where the place of residence is determined by the wife and her kinship affiliations but where female matrikin are not structurally aggregated in matrilocal and matrilineal kin groups." 33 cultures.

V: "Virilocal." This term is not to be confused with Avunculocal and Patrilocal, as defined above. The term "Virilocal" will be here confined to situations where neither of these two separate definitions applies, "particularly those in which male kinsmen are not structurally aggregated in localized unilineal kin groups, either patrilocal and patrilineal or avunculocal and matrilineal. Among such situations is that exemplified by the Lozi, where there is an option of establishing marital residence near either the father or some other relative of the husband. Another is where men have, and frequently exercise, the right to shift their place of residence from one group of kinsmen to another, as occurs not infrequently in societies organized in impermanent bands." 83 cultures.

Unascertained: 1 culture.

FC 201. Left: 334 cultures where marital residence is nonoptional (Code A M P U or V).
Right: 64 cultures where marital residence is ambilocal or neolocal (Code B C D or N).
Irrelevant: 1 culture where common marital residence is absent (Code O).
Unascertained: 1 culture.

● FC 202. Left: 41 cultures where marital residence is ambilocal (Code B C or D).
Right: 357 cultures where marital residence is other than ambilocal (Code A M N P U or V).
Irrelevant: 1 culture where common marital residence is absent (Code O).
Unascertained: 1 culture.

● FC 203. Left: 23 cultures where marital residence is neolocal (Code N).
Right: 375 cultures where marital residence is other than neolocal (Code A B C D M P U or V).
Irrelevant: 1 culture where common marital residence is absent (Code O).
Unascertained: 1 culture.

FC 204. Left: 270 cultures where marital residence is patrilocal, virilocal, or avunculocal (Code P V or A).
Right: 64 cultures where marital residence is ambilo-

cal or neolocal (Code B C D or N).
Irrelevant: 65 cultures where marital residence is matrilocal, uxorilocal, or absent (Code M U or O).
Unascertained: 1 culture.

● FC 205. Left: 169 cultures where marital residence is patrilocal (Code P).
Right: 229 cultures where marital residence is other than patrilocal (Code A B C D M N U or V).
Irrelevant: 1 culture where common marital residence is absent (Code O).
Unascertained: 1 culture.

● FC 206. Left: 18 cultures where marital residence is avunculocal (Code A).
Right: 380 cultures where marital residence is other than avunculocal (Code B C D M N P U or V).
Irrelevant: 1 culture where common marital residence is absent (Code O).
Unascertained: 1 culture.

FC 207. Left: 64 cultures where marital residence is matrilocal or uxorilocal (Code M or U).
Right: 64 cultures where marital residence is ambilocal or neolocal (Code B C D or N).
Irrelevant: 271 cultures where marital residence is patrilocal, virilocal, avunculocal, or absent (Code P V A or O).
Unascertained: 1 culture.

● FC 208. Left: 31 cultures where marital residence is matrilocal (Code M).
Right: 367 cultures where marital residence is other than matrilocal (Code A B C D N P U or V).
Irrelevant: 1 culture where common marital residence is absent (Code O).
Unascertained: 1 culture.

FC 209. Left: 270 cultures where marital residence is patrilocal, virilocal, or avunculocal (Code P V or A).
Right: 64 cultures where marital residence is matrilocal or uxorilocal (Code M or U).
Irrelevant: 65 cultures where marital residence is ambilocal, neolocal, or absent (Code B C D N or O).
Unascertained: 1 culture.

FC 210. Left: 169 cultures where marital residence is patrilocal (Code P).
Right: 31 cultures where marital residence is matrilocal (Code M).

Irrelevant: 199 cultures where marital residence is avunculocal, ambilocal, neolocal, uxorilocal, virilocal, or absent (Code A B C D N U V or O).
Unascertained: 1 culture.

● FC 211. Left: 83 cultures where marital residence is virilocal (Code V).
Right: 33 cultures where marital residence is uxorilocal (Code U).
Irrelevant: 283 cultures where marital residence is avunculocal, ambilocal, matrilocal, neolocal, patrilocal, or absent (Code A B C D M N P or O).
Unascertained: 1 culture.

● FC 212. Left: 18 cultures where marital residence is avunculocal (Code A).
Right: 31 cultures where marital residence is matrilocal (Code M).
Irrelevant: 350 cultures where marital residence is ambilocal, neolocal, uxorilocal, virilocal, or absent (Code B C D N P U V or O).
Unascertained: 1 culture.

COUSIN MARRIAGE (213–25)

The finished characteristics in this section derive from **EA** Column 25, "Cousin Marriage" (1962:119–20). For technical details, see the original. Column 25's capital-letter codes denote types of cousin marriage **permitted;** the postposited lower-case codes denote types of cousin marriage **preferred** or **prescribed.** The list below omits symbols which, as it turned out, did not apply to any of the 400 cultures in the sample (although they might well apply to other cultures listed in the **EA**).

C: "Duolateral cross-cousin marriage, i.e., marriage allowed with either cross-cousin but forbidden with a parallel cousin. A lower-case letter is appended to indicate preferential, as opposed to merely permitted unions, i.e., Cc, Cm, or Cp, respectively, for a symmetrical, matrilateral, or patrilateral preference." 80 cultures.

E: "Duolateral marriage with maternal cousins only. Em for preference for MoBrDa." 5 cultures.

M: "Matrilateral cross-cousin marriage, i.e., unilateral marriage with a MoBrDa only. Mm if preferred rather than merely permitted." 22 cultures.

N: "Nonlateral marriage, i.e., unions forbidden with any first or second cousin." 100 cultures.

O: "Nonlateral marriage when evidence is available only for first cousins, the rule or practice regarding second cousins being unreported." 63 cultures.

P: "Patrilateral cross-cousin marriage, i.e., unilateral marriage with a FaSiDa only. Pp if preferred rather than merely permitted." 6 cultures.

Q: "Quadrilateral marriage, i.e., marriage allowed with any first cousin. Qa for the Arabic or Islamic variant in which the FaBrDa is the preferred mate. Qc, Qm, and Qp for other preferences." 46 cultures.

R: "Nonlateral marriage in which all first cousins and some but not all second cousins are forbidden as spouses. Rr for the type of preferential marriage with particular second cross-cousins only, notably MoMoBrDaDa or FaMoBrSoDa, often characteristic of societies with subsection systems." 5 cultures.

S: "Nonlateral marriage in which unions are forbidden with any first cousin but are permitted with any second cousin (or at least any who is not a lineage mate). Ss if second-cousin is preferred rather than merely permitted." 30 cultures.

T: "Trilateral marriage, i.e., marriage allowed with any first cousin except an ortho-cousin or a lineage mate. Tc, Tm, and Tp, respectively, for preferences for a bilateral, matrilateral, or patrilateral cross-cousin." 13 cultures.

Unascertained: 30 cultures.

FC 213. Left: 172 cultures where cousin marriage is permitted (Code C E M P Q or T).

Right: 198 cultures where cousin marriage is not permitted (Code N O R or S).

Unascertained: 30 cultures.

FC 214. Left: 28 cultures where cousin marriage, if permitted, is unilateral (Code M or P).

Right: 144 cultures where cousin marriage, if permitted, is other than unilateral (Code C E Q or T).

Irrelevant: 198 cultures where cousin marriage is not permitted (Code N O R or S).

Unascertained: 30 cultures.

● FC 215. Left: 85 cultures where cousin marriage, if permitted, is duolateral (Code C or E).

Right: 87 cultures where cousin marriage, if permitted, is other than duolateral (Code M P Q or T).

Irrelevant: 198 cultures where cousin marriage is not permitted (Code N O R or S).

Unascertained: 30 cultures.

● FC 216. Left: 13 cultures where cousin marriage, if permitted, is trilateral (Code T).

Right: 159 cultures where cousin marriage, if permit-

ted, is other than trilateral (Code C E M P or Q).
Irrelevant: 198 cultures where cousin marriage is not permitted (Code N O R or S).
Unascertained: 30 cultures.

● FC 217. Left: 46 cultures where cousin marriage, if permitted, is quadrilateral (Code Q).
Right: 126 cultures where cousin marriage, if permitted, is other than quadrilateral (Code C E M P or T).
Irrelevant: 198 cultures where cousin marriage is not permitted (Code N O R or S).
Unascertained: 30 cultures.

FC 218 has been excised from the printout. It was identical in content (though not in wording) with FC 214, which is included as "both subject and predicate." Hence, no information has been lost.

● FC 219. Left: 85 cultures where cousin marriage, if permitted, is duolateral (Code C or E).
Right: 59 cultures where cousin marriage, if permitted, is tri- or quadrilateral (Code T or Q).
Irrelevant: 226 cultures, including: 28 cultures where cousin marriage is permitted but is unilateral (Code M or P). 198 cultures where cousin marriage is not permitted (Code N O R or S).
Unascertained: 30 cultures.

FC 220. Left: 97 cultures where cousin marriage in some form or other is prescribed or preferred (Postposited Code a c m p r or s).
Right: 273 remaining substantively coded cultures.
Unascertained: 30 cultures.

FC 221. Left: 35 cultures where matrilateral cross-cousin marriage is prescribed or preferred (Postposited Code m).
Right: 335 remaining substantively coded cultures.
Unascertained: 30 cultures.

● FC 222. Left: 23 cultures where, with the kin group patrilineal, matrilateral cross-cousin marriage is prescribed or preferred (Postposited Code m and patrilineal or patrilineal-cognatic kin groups present, as explained on page 109).
Right: 137 cultures where, with the kin group patrilineal, matrilateral cross-cousin marriage is not prescribed or preferred (Postposited Code other than m and patrilineal or patrilineal-cognatic kin groups present).

Ambiguous: 1 culture where patrilineal, matrilineal, and cognatic kin groups are present.

Irrelevant: 208 cultures where the kin group is matrilineal, matrilineal-cognatic, cognatic, or double descent.

Unascertained: 31 cultures, including: 1 culture where the existence of a patrilineal kin group is unascertained. 30 cultures where the type of cousin marriage is unascertained.

● FC 223. Left: 9 cultures where, with the kin group matrilineal, matrilateral cross-cousin marriage is prescribed or preferred (Postposited Code m and kin group matrilineal or matrilineal-cognatic, as explained on page 109).

Right: 50 cultures where, with the kin group matrilineal, matrilateral cross-cousin marriage is not prescribed or preferred (Postposited Code other than m and kin group matrilineal or matrilineal-cognatic).

Ambiguous: 1 culture where patrilineal, matrilineal, and cognatic kin groups are present.

Irrelevant: 310 cultures where the kin group is patrilineal, patrilineal-cognatic, cognatic, or double descent.

Unascertained: 30 cultures where the type of cousin marriage is unascertained.

FC 224. Left: 66 cultures where cousin marriage is preferentially or permissively either patri- or matrilateral (Code Cm Cp E M Mm P Pp Qa Qm Qp Tm or Tp).

Right: 106 cultures where cousin marriage is preferentially or permissively symmetrical (Code C Cc Q Qc T or Tc).

Irrelevant: 198 remaining substantively coded cultures (Code N O R Rr or S).

Unascertained: 30 cultures.

FC 225. Left: 23 cultures where cousin marriage is preferentially or permissively patrilateral (Code Cp P Pp Qa Qp or Tp).

Right: 43 cultures where cousin marriage is preferentially or permissively matrilateral (Code Cm E M Mm Qm or Tm).

Irrelevant: 304 remaining substantively coded cultures (Code C Cc N O Q Qc R Rr S T or Tc).

Unascertained: 30 cultures.

COUSIN TERMINOLOGY (226–35)

FCs in this section are based on **EA** Column 27 (1962:121). "The prevailing pattern of kinship terminology employed for first cousins is indicated by the following symbols":

C: "Crow, i.e., FaSiCh equated with Fa or FaSi and/or MoBrCh with Ch or BrCh (w.s.)." 28 cultures.

D: "Descriptive or derivative, rather than elementary, terms employed for all cousins." 30 cultures.

E: "Eskimo, i.e., FaBrCh, FaSiCh, MoBrCh, and MoSiCh equated with each other but differentiated from siblings." 47 cultures.

H: "Hawaiian, i.e., all cousins equated with siblings or called by terms clearly derivative from those for siblings." 123 cultures.

I: "Iroquois, i.e., FaSiCh equated with MoBrCh but differentiated from both siblings and parallel cousins." 93 cultures.

O: "Omaha, i.e., MoBrCh equated with MoBr or M and/or FaSiCh with SiCh (m.s.) or Ch." 31 cultures.

S: "Sudanese, i.e., FaSiCh and MoBrCh distinguished alike from siblings, parallel cousins, and one another but without conforming to either the Crow, the descriptive, or the Omaha patterns." 7 cultures.

Z: "Mixed or deviant patterns not adequately represented by any of the foregoing symbols." These are specifically described in the **EA**'s "Notes." 5 cultures.

Unascertained: 36 cultures.

- FC 226. Left: 152 cultures where the cousin terminology is of Crow, Omaha, or Iroquois type (Code C O or I).
  Right: 212 remaining substantively coded cultures (Code D E H S or Z).
  Unascertained: 36 cultures.
- FC 227. Left: 59 cultures where the cousin terminology is of Crow or Omaha type (Code C or O).
  Right: 305 remaining substantively coded cultures (Code D E H I S or Z).
  Unascertained: 36 cultures.
- FC 228. Left: 28 cultures where cousin terminology is of Crow type (Code C).
  Right: 336 remaining substantively coded cultures (Code D E H I O S or Z).
  Unascertained: 36 cultures.
- FC 229. Left: 31 cultures where cousin terminology is of Omaha type (Code O).
  Right: 333 remaining substantively coded cultures (Code C D E H I S or Z).
  Unascertained: 36 cultures.

- ● FC 230. Left: 93 cultures where the cousin terminology is of Iroquois type (Code I).
  Right: 271 remaining substantively coded cultures (Code C D E H O S or Z).
  Unascertained: 36 cultures.
- ● FC 231. Left: 170 cultures where the cousin terminology is of Eskimo or Hawaiian type (Code E or H).
  Right: 194 remaining substantively coded cultures (Code C D I O S or Z).
  Unascertained: 36 cultures.
- ● FC 232. Left: 47 cultures where the cousin terminology is of Eskimo type (Code E).
  Right: 317 remaining substantively coded cultures (Code C D H I O S or Z).
  Unascertained: 36 cultures.
- ● FC 233. Left: 123 cultures where the cousin terminology is of Hawaiian type (Code H).
  Right: 241 remaining substantively coded cultures (Code C D E I O S or Z).
  Unascertained: 36 cultures.
- FC 234. Left: 152 cultures where the cousin terminology is of Crow, Omaha, or Iroquois type (Code C O or I).
  Right: 170 cultures where the cousin terminology is of Eskimo or Hawaiian type (Code E or H).
  Irrelevant: 42 cultures where the cousin terminology is of Descriptive, Sudanese, or Mixed type (Code D S or Z).
  Unascertained: 36 cultures.
- ● FC 235. Left: 30 cultures where the cousin terminology is of Descriptive type (Code D).
  Right: 334 remaining substantively coded cultures (Code C E H I O S or Z).
  Unascertained: 36 cultures.

FAMILY ORGANIZATION (236–41)

FCs in this section are based on **EA** Column 14 (1962:116). "The prevailing form of domestic or familial organization is characterized by the following symbols:

E: "Large extended families, i.e., corporate aggregations of smaller family units occupying a single dwelling or a number of adjacent dwellings and normally embracing the families of procreation of at least two siblings or cousins in each of at least two adjacent generations." 78 cultures.

F: "Small extended families, i.e., those normally embracing the families of procreation of only one individual in the senior generation but of at least two individuals in the next generation. Families of this type usually dissolve on the death of the head." 109 cultures.

G: "Minimal extended or 'stem' families, i.e., those consisting of only two related families of procreation (disregarding polygamous unions), particularly of adjacent generations." 26 cultures.

M: "Independent nuclear families with monogamy." 39 cultures.

N: "Independent nuclear families with occasional or limited polygyny." 72 cultures.

O: "Independent polyandrous families." 1 culture.

P: "Independent polygynous families, where polygyny is general and not reported to be preferentially sororal, and where co-wives are not reported to occupy separate dwellings or apartments." 19 cultures.

Q: "Independent polygynous families, where polygyny is general and not specified as preferentially sororal, and where co-wives typically occupy separate dwellings or apartments." 34 cultures.

R: "Independent polygynous families, where polygyny is common and preferentially sororal, and where co-wives are not reported to occupy separate dwellings." 15 cultures.

S: "Independent polygynous families, where polygyny is common and preferentially sororal, and where co-wives normally occupy separate dwellings." 5 cultures.

Unascertained: 2 cultures.

"Lower-case letters from m to s, following E, F, or G, suggest the marital composition of the component familial units in extended families, e.g., Gm for stem families with monogamy."

FC 236. Left: 213 cultures where the family is of an extended type (Code E F or G).
Right: 185 cultures where the family is of an independent type (Code M N O P Q R or S).
Unascertained: 2 cultures.

● FC 237. Left: 78 cultures where the family is of the large extended type (Code E).
Right: 320 remaining substantively coded cultures (Code F G M N O P Q R or S).
Unascertained: 2 cultures.

● FC 238. Left: 109 cultures where the family is of the small extended type (Code F).
Right: 289 remaining substantively coded cultures (Code E G M N O P Q R or S).
Unascertained: 2 cultures.

● FC 239. Left: 26 cultures where the family is of the stem extended type (Code G).

Right: 372 remaining substantively coded cultures (Code E F M N O P Q R or S).

Unascertained: 2 cultures.

FC 240. Left: 78 cultures where the family, if extended, is large (Code E).

Right: 135 cultures where the family, if extended, is small or stem (Code F or G).

Irrelevant: 185 cultures where the family is independent rather than extended (Code M N O P Q R or S).

Unascertained: 2 cultures.

FC 241. Left: 187 cultures where the family, if extended, is large or small (Code E or F).

Right: 26 cultures where the family, if extended, is stem (Code G).

Irrelevant: 185 cultures where the family is independent rather than extended (Code M N O P Q R or S).

Unascertained: 2 cultures.

POLYGYNY (242–53)

Most of the FCs in this section derive from **EA** Column 14, which is summarized at the beginning of the foregoing section.

FC 242. Left: 314 cultures where marriage is commonly or occasionally polygynous (Code N P Q R or S, also E F or G if followed by n p q r or s).

Right: 81 cultures where marriage is monogamous (Code M, also E F or G if followed by m).

Irrelevant: 3 cultures where marriage is polyandrous (Code O, also E F or G if followed by o).

Unascertained: 2 cultures.

FC 243, alone among the FCs in the section, departs from the **EA** and takes its codings from a study by John W. M. Whiting and Roy G. D'Andrade, as modified by William N. Stephens and appearing in the latter's Table 45 (1962:244–45).

FC 243. Left: 24 cultures where polygyny, if present, has a high incidence—with "40 per cent or more wives . . . estimated to be polygynous" (Table 45, first column).

Right: 36 cultures where polygyny, if present, has a low incidence—less than 40 per cent (same, second column from left).

Unascertained: 340 cultures.

- FC 244. Left: 44 cultures where marriage, if commonly polygynous, is preferentially sororal (**EA** Column 14, Code R S r or s).
  Right: 108 cultures where marriage, if commonly polygynous, is not preferentially sororal (Code P Q p or q).
  Irrelevant: 246 remaining substantively coded cultures (Code E F or G if not followed by p q r or s, also M N or O).
  Unascertained: 2 cultures.
- FC 245. Left: 71 cultures where marriage, if commonly polygynous, is the type where co-wives dwell together (Code P R p or r).
  Right: 81 cultures where marriage, if commonly polygynous, is the type where co-wives dwell separately (Code Q S q or s).
  Irrelevant: 246 remaining substantively coded cultures (Code E F or G if not followed by p q r or s, also M N or O).
  Unascertained: 2 cultures.
- FC 246. Left: 15 cultures where the family is independent and marriage is commonly polygynous and preferentially sororal and co-wives dwell together (Code R).
  Right: 383 remaining substantively coded cultures (Code E F G M N O P Q or S).
  Unascertained: 2 cultures.
- FC 247. Left: 34 cultures where the family is independent and marriage is commonly polygynous and not preferentially sororal and co-wives dwell separately (Code Q).
  Right: 364 remaining substantively coded cultures (Code E F G M N O P R or S).
  Unascertained: 2 cultures.
- FC 248. Left: 170 cultures where, with the extended family present, marriage is commonly or occasionally polygynous (Code E F or G, if followed by n p q r or s).
  Right: 42 cultures where, with the extended family present, marriage is monogamous (Code E F or G, if followed by m).
  Irrelevant: 186 remaining substantively coded cultures (Code M N O P Q R or S, also Postposited Code o).
  Unascertained: 2 cultures.

- FC 249. Left: 144 cultures where, with the independent family present, marriage is commonly or occasionally polygynous (Code N P Q R or S).
  Right: 39 cultures where, with the independent family present, marriage is monogamous (Code M).
  Irrelevant: 215 remaining substantively coded cultures (Code E F G or O, also Postposited Code o).
  Unascertained: 2 cultures.
- FC 250. Left: 146 cultures where, with the patrilineal kin group present, marriage is commonly or occasionally polygynous (Code E F or G if followed by n p q r or s, also N P Q R or S—but all cultures included in this category must also be those where the kin group is patrilineal, or patrilineal and cognatic, as explained on page 109).
  Right: 21 cultures where, with the patrilineal kin group present, marriage is monogamous (Code E F or G if followed by m, also M—but all cultures included in this category must also be those where the kin group is patrilineal, or patrilineal and cognatic).
  Ambiguous: 1 culture where the kin group is patrilineal, matrilineal, and cognatic.
  Irrelevant: 230 remaining substantively coded cultures.
  Unascertained: 2 cultures.
- FC 251. Left: 43 cultures where, with the matrilineal kin group present, marriage is commonly or occasionally polygynous (Code E F or G if followed by n p q r or s, also N P Q R or S—but all cultures included in this category must also be those where the kin group is matrilineal, or matrilineal and cognatic, as explained on page 109).
  Right: 18 cultures where, with the matrilineal kin group present, marriage is monogamous (Code E F or G if followed by m, also M—but all cultures included in this category must also be those where the kin group is matrilineal or matrilineal and cognatic).
  Ambiguous: 1 culture where the kin group is patrilineal, matrilineal, and cognatic.
  Irrelevant: 337 remaining substantively coded cultures.
  Unascertained: 1 culture.
- FC 252. Left: 107 cultures where, with the exclusively cognatic kin group present, marriage is commonly or occasionally polygynous (Code E F or G if followed

by n p q r or s, also N P Q R or S—but all cultures included in this category must also be those where the kin group is exclusively cognatic, as explained on page 109).

Right: 39 cultures where, with the exclusively cognatic kin group present, marriage is monogamous (Code E F or G if followed by m, also M—but all cultures in this category must also be those where the kin group is exclusively cognatic).

Ambiguous: 1 culture where the kin group is patrilineal, matrilineal, and cognatic.

Irrelevant: 252 remaining substantively coded cultures.

Unascertained: 1 culture.

● FC 253. Left: 39 cultures where the family is independent and marriage is monogamous (Code M).

Right: 359 remaining substantively coded cultures (Code E F G N O P Q R or S).

Unascertained: 2 cultures.

AUTHORITY WITHIN THE FAMILY (254–56)

FCs in this section derive from Dorrian Apple's Tables 1 and 2 (1956:659, 661).

FC 254. Left: 9 cultures where household authority is on the father's side (Table 2, top row).

Right: 6 cultures where household authority is on the mother's side (same, bottom row).

Unascertained: 385 cultures.

FC 255. Left: 7 cultures where grandparental authority over parents is present (Table 1, left column).

Right: 26 cultures where grandparental authority over parents is absent (same, right column).

Unascertained: 367 cultures.

FC 256. Left: 25 cultures where grandparent and grandchild are friendly equals (Table 1, bottom row).

Right: 8 cultures where grandparent and grandchild are not friendly equals (same, top row).

Unascertained: 367 cultures.

AVOIDANCES (257–59)

FCs in this section are based on codings by William N. Stephens, which appear in his Table 41 (1962:146 ff., 222–24).

FC 257. Left: 10 cultures where the severity of sister avoidance is high (right column, Code 3 or 4).

Right: 17 cultures where the severity of sister avoidance is low (same, Code 2 or 1).

Unascertained: 373 cultures.

FC 258. Left: 15 cultures where the severity of son's wife avoidance is high (middle column, Code 2 3 4 or 5).

Right: 16 cultures where the severity of son's wife avoidance is low (same, Code 1).

Unascertained: 369 cultures.

FC 259. Left: 26 cultures where the severity of mother-in-law avoidance is high (left column, Code 3 4 or 5).

Right: 20 cultures where the severity of mother-in-law avoidance is low (same, Code 2 or 1).

Unascertained: 354 cultures.

MODE OF MARRIAGE (260–71)

FC 260 is based on John K. Harley's Appendix B, Second List, Column M (1963).

FC 260. Left: 38 cultures where the age of males at marriage is less than 20 (Code 1 2 or 3).

Right: 17 cultures where the age of males at marriage is 20 or over (Code 4).

Unascertained: 345 cultures.

FC 261 is derived from John T. Westbrook's codings, as modified by the **EA**, and appears in **EA** Column 78 (1963:116). A complete listing of the codes for this source appears on page 154.

● FC 261. Left: 19 cultures where female marriage occurs at or before puberty (Code E).

Right: 183 remaining substantively coded cultures (Code A F P T or V).

Unascertained: 198 cultures.

All remaining FCs in this section derive from the capital-letter codes in **EA** Column 12, "Mode of Marriage" (1962:115–16). "The prevailing mode of obtaining a wife is characterized by the following symbols":

B: "Bride-price or bride-wealth, i.e., transfer of a substantial consideration in the form of livestock, goods, or money from the groom or his relatives to the kinsmen of the bride." 163 cultures.

D: "Dowry, i.e., transfer of a substantial amount of property from the bride's relatives to the bride, the groom, or the kinsmen of the latter." 15 cultures.

G: "Gift exchange, i.e., reciprocal exchange of gifts of substantial value between the relatives of the bride and groom, or a continuing exchange of goods and services in approximately equal amounts between the groom or his kinsmen and the bride's relatives. . . ." 26 cultures.

O: "Absence of any significant consideration, or bridal gifts only." 90 cultures.

S: "Bride-service, i.e., a substantial material consideration in which the principal element consists of labor or other service rendered by the groom to the bride's kinsmen. Matrilocal or uxorilocal residence, as indicated in Column 16, commonly entails bride-service, but is not indicated by S unless the sources specifically mention the rendering of service." 54 cultures.

T: "Token bride-price, i.e., a small or symbolic payment only." 31 cultures.

X: "Exchange, i.e., transfer of a sister or other female relative of the groom in exchange for the bride." 16 cultures.

Unascertained: 5 cultures.

FC 262. Left: 305 cultures where wives are obtained by means involving the presence of some consideration (Code B D G S T or X).

Right: 90 cultures where wives are obtained by means involving the absence of any consideration (Code O).

Unascertained: 5 cultures.

FC 263. Left: 233 cultures where wives are obtained by relatively difficult means, namely by bride-price, bride-service, or exchanging a female relative (Code B S or X).

Right: 162 cultures where wives are obtained by relatively easy means, namely by token bride-price, gift exchange, absence of any consideration, or receipt of dowry (Code T G O or D).

Unascertained: 5 cultures.

● FC 264. Left: 163 cultures where wives are obtained by bride-price (Code B).

Right: 232 remaining substantively coded cultures (Code D G O S T or X).

Unascertained: 5 cultures.

● FC 265. Left: 54 cultures where wives are obtained by bride-service (Code S).

Right: 341 remaining substantively coded cultures (Code B D G O T or X).

Unascertained: 5 cultures.

● FC 266. Left: 163 cultures where wives are obtained by bride-price (Code B).

Right: 54 cultures where wives are obtained by bride-service (Code S).

Irrelevant: 178 cultures where wives are obtained by other means (Code D G O T or X).

Unascertained: 5 cultures.

● FC 267. Left: 31 cultures where wives are obtained by token bride-price (Code T).

Right: 364 remaining substantively coded cultures (Code B D G O S or X).

Unascertained: 5 cultures.

● FC 268. Left: 163 cultures where wives are obtained by bride-price (Code B).

Right: 31 cultures where wives are obtained by token bride-price (Code T).

Irrelevant: 201 cultures where wives are obtained by other means (Code D G O S or X).

Unascertained: 5 cultures.

● FC 269. Left: 16 cultures where wives are obtained by exchanging a female relative (Code X).

Right: 379 remaining substantively coded cultures (Code B D G O S or T).

Unascertained: 5 cultures.

● FC 270. Left: 26 cultures where wives are obtained by gift exchange (Code G).

Right: 369 remaining substantively coded cultures (Code B D O S T or X).

Unascertained: 5 cultures.

● FC 271. Left: 15 cultures where wives are obtained by means involving receipt of dowry (Code D).

Right: 380 remaining substantively coded cultures (Code B G O S T or X).

Unascertained: 5 cultures.

DIVORCE (272–76)

FCs in this section are based on Charles Ackerman's codings on divorce rate (1963:15–18). For a comment by Ackerman on the difficulty of making such coding decisions, see this **Summary**, page 43. FCs 273–76 are, in addition, derived partially from **EA** codings on kin groups.

FC 272. Left: 29 cultures where the divorce rate is high (Table 1, right column or Table 3, right column).

Right: 28 cultures where the divorce rate is low (Table 1, left column or Table 3, left column).

Unascertained: 343 cultures.

In FC 273 both left and right attribute categories concern only cultures where the kin group is other than exclusively cognatic, as explained on page 109. To check this, note that none of the 33 cultures listed in the left or the right attribute category is listed in the left category of FC 188, and that all of the cultures listed as irrelevant in this FC are listed in the left category of FC 188.

● FC 273. Left: 16 cultures where, with the kin group noncognatic, the divorce rate is high (Table 1 or 3, right column and kin group other than exclusively cognatic).

Right: 17 cultures where, with the kin group noncognatic, the divorce rate is low (Table 1 or 3, left column and kin group other than exclusively cognatic).

Irrelevant: 24 cultures for which codings on divorce rate are available, but where the kin group is exclusively cognatic.

Unascertained: 343 cultures.

In FC 274 both left and right attribute categories concern only cultures where the kin group is patrilineal or patrilineal-cognatic, as explained on page 109. To check this, note that all of the 21 cultures listed in the left or the right attribute category are also listed in the left attribute category of FC 190 and also that all of them are missing from the left category of FC 189. Note also that all of the 36 cultures listed in the irrelevant category are missing from the left attribute category of FC 190.*

● FC 274. Left: 9 cultures where, with the kin group patrilineal, the divorce rate is high (Table 1 or 3, right column and kin group patrilineal or patrilineal-cognatic).

Right: 12 cultures where, with the kin group patrilineal, the divorce rate is low (Table 1 or 3, left column and kin group patrilineal or patrilineal-cognatic).

Irrelevant: 36 cultures for which codings on divorce rate are available, but where the kin group is other than patrilineal or patrilineal-cognatic.

Unascertained: 343 cultures.

In FC 275 both left and right attribute categories concern only cultures where the kin group is exclusively cognatic, as explained on page 109. To check this, note that all 24 cultures in the left or the right attri-

*There are three exceptions: Ila, Mbundu, and Toda. These three are listed in the left attribute category of FC 190 because they are coded as possessing double-descent kin groups—as distinct from patrilineal or patrilineal-cognatic. This can be checked by noting that these three cultures are listed in the left attribute category of FC 189.

bute category are also listed in the left attribute category of FC 188. Note also that all of the 33 cultures listed in the irrelevant category are missing from the left category of FC 188.

● FC 275. Left: 13 cultures where, with the kin group exclusively cognatic, the divorce rate is high (Table 1 or 3, right column and kin group exclusively cognatic).

Right: 11 cultures where, with the kin group exclusively cognatic, the divorce rate is low (Table 1 or 3, left column and kin group exclusively cognatic).

Irrelevant: 33 cultures for which codings on divorce rate are available, but where the kin group is other than exclusively cognatic.

Unascertained: 343 cultures.

In FC 276 both the left and right attribute categories concern only cultures where the only kin group present is the kindred or where bilateral descent is inferred, as explained on page 111. To check this, note that all of the 18 cultures listed in the left or the right attribute category are also listed in the left category of FC 192. Note also that all of the 39 cultures listed in the irrelevant category are missing from the left category of FC 192.

● FC 276. Left: 9 cultures where, with the kindred the only kin group present or with bilateral descent inferred, the divorce rate is high (Table 1 or 3, right column and kin group as specified).

Right: 9 cultures where, with the kindred the only kin group present or with bilateral descent inferred, the divorce rate is low (Table 1 or 3, left column and kin group as specified).

Irrelevant: 39 cultures for which codings on divorce rate are available, but where the kin group is other than as specified.

Unascertained: 343 cultures.

STATUS OF WOMEN (277–79)

All three of the FCs in this section derive from Leo W. Simmons' Code Chart (1945).

FC 277. Left: 14 cultures where the status of women is inferior or subjected (Column 74, Code Equal or Plus).

Right: 22 cultures where the status of women is not strongly inferior or subjected (same, Code Minus or Zero).

Unascertained: 364 cultures.

FC 278. Left: 8 cultures where property rights in women are present (Column 80, Code Plus or Equal).
Right: 14 cultures where property rights in women are unimportant or absent (same, Code Minus or Zero).
Unascertained: 378 cultures.

FC 279. Left: 10 cultures where wife-lending or wife-exchange is present (Column 68, Code Plus or Equal).
Right: 19 cultures where wife-lending and wife-exchange are unimportant or absent (same, Code Minus or Zero).
Unascertained: 371 cultures.

FERTILITY (280–81)

The two finished characteristics in this section are taken from Moni Nag (1962).

Codings for FC 280 are taken from Nag's Table 8, pp. 177–78. These codings refer to a culture's "composite fertility level," which Nag derives from somewhat complex calculations and judgments, explained on pages 16–18.

FC 280. Left: 13 cultures where the composite fertility level is high (Table 8, "High" Column).
Right: 12 cultures where the composite fertility level is low (same, "Low" and "Very Low" Columns).
Unascertained: 375 cultures.

FC 281 is based on Nag's codings for incidence of sterility. These codings appear in his Table 62, pages 208–10. Explanation of the coding rationale is found on pages 120–22, while particular coding decisions are explained in the table itself.

● FC 281. Left: 10 cultures where the incidence of sterility is high (Table 62, Code H).
Right: 5 cultures where the incidence of sterility is low (same, Code L).
Unascertained: 385 cultures.

PREGNANCY AND CHILDBIRTH (282–301)

FCs 282 and 283 are based on Barbara Chartier Ayres' Appendix II, Columns 2 and 4, respectively (1954:112–14).

FC 282. Left: 16 cultures where the strength of desire for children is high (Column 2, Code 5 or higher).
Right: 20 cultures where the strength of desire for children is low or absent (same, Code 4 or lower).
Unascertained: 364 cultures.

● FC 283. Left: 14 cultures where the severity of penalties for barrenness is high (Column 4, Code 4 or higher).
Right: 17 cultures where the severity of penalties for barrenness is low or absent (same, Code 3 or lower).
Unascertained: 369 cultures.

FC 284 is based on C. S. Ford's study of human reproduction, and deals with the presence or absence of methods of contraception, other than abstinence from sexual intercourse (1945:101).

FC 284. Left: 10 cultures where contraception is practiced (Code "Present").
Right: 7 cultures where contraception is not practiced (Code "Absent").
Unascertained: 383 cultures.

FCs 285 and 286 are based on Barbara Chartier Ayres, Appendix, Columns 1 and 6, respectively (1954:112–14).

FC 285. Left: 14 cultures where the sex taboo during pregnancy is present (Column 1, Code 2 or higher).
Right: 17 cultures where the sex taboo during pregnancy is absent or inferred absent (same, Code 1 or Minus).
Unascertained: 369 cultures.

FC 286. Left: 20 cultures where the number of food taboos during pregnancy is high (Column 6, Code 3 or higher).
Right: 14 cultures where the number of food taboos during pregnancy is low or absent (same, Code 2 1 or Minus).
Unascertained: 366 cultures.

FCs 287 to 291 are taken from C. S. Ford (1945).

● FC 287. Left: 16 cultures where the isolation of women in childbirth is practiced (page 102, Code "Present").
Right: 20 cultures where the isolation of women in childbirth is not practiced (same, Code "Absent").
Unascertained: 364 cultures.

● FC 288. Left: 17 cultures where the delivery of a child may be attended by the husband (page 103, Code "Present").
Right: 11 cultures where the delivery of a child may not be attended by the husband (same, Code "Probably absent").
Unascertained: 372 cultures.

● FC 289. Left: 12 cultures where the delivery of a child may be attended by a male doctor (page 103, Code "Present").

Right: 9 cultures where the delivery of a child may not be attended by a male doctor (same, Code "Probably absent").
Unascertained: 379 cultures.

● FC 290. Left: 12 cultures where women after delivery are isolated in a special shelter (page 103, Code "Present" or "Probably present").
Right: 21 cultures where women are not so isolated (same, Code "Absent").
Unascertained: 367 cultures.

● FC 291. Left: 20 cultures where women after delivery are confined to the dwelling (page 103, Code "Present").
Right: 12 cultures where women are not so confined (same, Code "Absent").
Unascertained: 368 cultures.

Codings forming the basis for FCs 292–96 all are taken from the Appendix to Barbara Chartier Ayres' work (1954:112–14).

● FC 292. Left: 16 cultures where practices to beautify the newborn child are present (Column 8, Code 2 or higher).
Right: 16 cultures where such practices are absent or inferred absent (same, Code 1 or Minus).
Unascertained: 368 cultures.

● FC 293. Left: 20 cultures where the importance of practices to bring good luck to the newborn child is high (Column 9, Code 3 or higher).
Right: 14 cultures where the importance of such practices is low or absent (same, Code 2 or Minus).*
Unascertained: 366 cultures.

● FC 294. Left: 16 cultures where practices to protect the newborn child from harmful influences are present (Column 10, Code 2 or higher).
Right: 18 cultures where such practices are absent or inferred absent (same, Code 1 or Minus).
Unascertained: 366 cultures.

FC 295. Left: 11 cultures where the severity of punishment for abortion is high (Column 3, Code 3 or higher).
Right: 12 cultures where the severity of punishment for abortion is low or absent (same, Code 2 1 or Minus).
Unascertained: 377 cultures.

FC 296. Left: 18 cultures where infanticide is present (Col-

*Code "Minus" means "inferred absent." Code 1 means "Absent"; in this case no cultures were so coded.

umn 7, Code 2 or higher).

Right: 15 cultures where infanticide is absent or inferred absent (same, Code 1 or Minus).

Unascertained: 367 cultures.

FC 297 is taken from C. S. Ford (1945:104).

● FC 297. Left: 13 cultures where twins are unwelcome and one or both killed (Code "Present").

Right: 9 cultures where twins are not unwelcome and not killed (Code "Absent" or "Probably absent").

Unascertained: 378 cultures.

Codings for FCs 298–301 derive from **EA** Column 36, "Post-Partum Sex Taboos" (1962:270). The code is:

0: "No taboo, especially where the husband is expected to have intercourse with his wife as soon as possible after childbirth for the alleged benefit of the child." 1 culture.

1: "Short post-partum sex taboo, lasting not more than one month." 28 cultures.

2: "Duration of from one month to six months." 45 cultures.

3: "Duration of from more than six months to one year." 16 cultures.

4: "Duration of from more than one year to two years." 20 cultures.

5: "Duration of more than two years." 15 cultures.

Unascertained: 275 cultures.

● FC 298. Left: 35 cultures where the postpartum sex taboo lasts longer than one year (Code 4 or 5).

Right: 28 cultures where this taboo lasts one month or less (Code 1).

Irrelevant: 62 cultures (Code 2 3 or 0).*

Unascertained: 275 cultures.

FC 299. Left: 35 cultures where the postpartum sex taboo is longer than one year (Code 4 or 5).

Right: 89 cultures where this taboo lasts one year or less (Code 3 2 or 1).

Irrelevant: 1 culture (Code 0).

Unascertained: 275 cultures.

FC 300. Left: 51 cultures where the postpartum sex taboo lasts longer than six months (Code 3 4 or 5).

Right: 73 cultures where this taboo lasts six months or less (Code 2 or 1).

Irrelevant: 1 culture (Code 0).

Unascertained: 275 cultures.

FC 301. Left: 96 cultures where the postpartum sex taboo lasts longer than one month (Code 2 3 4 or 5).

*In FCs 298–301, the one culture coded "0" will be regarded as "irrelevant."

Right: 28 cultures where this taboo lasts one month or less (Code 1).
Irrelevant: 1 culture (Code 0).
Unascertained: 275 cultures.

INFANCY AND CHILDHOOD (302–55)

Early Satisfaction Potential (302–07)

These FCs derive from the Appendix to Whiting and Child (1953: 341–46). Since this book is widely available, quotations from it in this **Summary** will be held to a minimum. The authors' explanation of their concept of early satisfaction potential appears on pages 50–52 and is summarized on page 52:

> The measure of initial satisfaction is . . . a measure of the custom potential of an internal response in the children of a society, the response of deriving acquired reward from performing the responses of a particular system of behavior. The initial satisfaction of oral behavior is a measure, for example, of the extent to which oral responses in children of a given society are predicted to have an acquired reward value above and beyond their basic biological reward value.

The FCs in this subsection are based on both plain type and italic codes, as explained on pages 338–39.

FC 302 in a sense summarizes the five FCs to follow, as it is based on the mean scores for those five.

FC 302. Left: 23 cultures where the average early satisfaction potential is high (Column F, Code 13 or higher).
Right: 17 cultures where this potential is low (same, Code 12 or lower).
Unascertained: 360 cultures.

FC 303. Left: 32 cultures where the early oral satisfaction potential is high (Column A, Code 15 or higher).
Right: 25 cultures where this potential is low (same, Code 14 or lower).
Unascertained: 343 cultures.

FC 304. Left: 19 cultures where the early anal satisfaction potential is high (Column B, Code 13 or higher).
Right: 22 cultures where this potential is low (same, Code 12 or lower).
Unascertained: 359 cultures.

FC 305. Left: 27 cultures where the early sexual satisfaction potential is high (Column C, Code 12 or higher).
Right: 24 cultures where this potential is low (same, Code 11 or lower).
Unascertained: 349 cultures.

FC 306. Left: 28 cultures where the early dependence satisfaction potential is high (Column D, Code 15 or higher).
Right: 24 cultures where this potential is low (same, Code 14 or lower).
Unascertained: 348 cultures.

FC 307. Left: 33 cultures where the early aggression satisfaction potential is high (Column E, Code 11 or higher).
Right: 19 cultures where this potential is low (same, Code 10 or lower).
Unascertained: 348 cultures.

Socialization Anxiety (308–13)

FCs in this subsection also derive from the Appendix in Whiting and Child (1953:341–46). The authors explain their concept of socialization anxiety on pages 52–55. On page 54 they say:

> As with initial satisfaction, this judgment was intended primarily as a measure of the custom potential of certain internal responses in the children of a society but also may be used as an approximate measure of certain aspects of the overt behavior of the parents. As a measure of custom potential of internal responses in the children it is a measure of the strength of the kind of custom which we have defined as a motive; it measures the custom potential of the tendency for responses and impulses of a given system of behavior to arouse the drive of anxiety in the typical child of a society. As a measure of the behavior of the parents it may be called a measure of **severity of socialization,** for it reflects the extent to which the child training practices of the parents are severe in the sense of being likely to produce anxiety in their children.

The FCs in this subsection are based on both plain type and italic codes, as explained on pages 338–39.

FC 308 in a sense summarizes the five FCs to follow, as it is based on the mean scores for those five.

FC 308. Left: 22 cultures where average socialization anxiety is high (Column L, Code 12 or higher).
Right: 18 cultures where this anxiety is low (same, Code 11 or lower).
Unascertained: 360 cultures.

FC 309. Left: 26 cultures where oral socialization anxiety is high (Column G, Code 11 or higher).
Right: 27 cultures where this anxiety is low (same, Code 10 or lower).
Unascertained: 347 cultures.

FC 310. Left: 22 cultures where anal socialization anxiety is high (Column H, Code 11 or higher).
Right: 19 cultures where this anxiety is low (same, Code 10 or lower).

Unascertained: 359 cultures.

FC 311. Left: 28 cultures where sexual socialization anxiety is high (Column I, Code 12 or higher).
Right: 23 cultures where this anxiety is low (same, Code 11 or lower).
Unascertained: 349 cultures.

FC 312. Left: 24 cultures where dependence socialization anxiety is high (Column J, Code 13 or higher).
Right: 23 cultures where this anxiety is low (same, Code 12 or lower).
Unascertained: 353 cultures.

FC 313. Left: 26 cultures where aggression socialization anxiety is high (Column K, Code 13 or higher).
Right: 28 cultures where this anxiety is low (same, Code 12 or lower).
Unascertained: 346 cultures.

Mother-Child Arrangements (314–16)

FC 314 employs codings by Whiting and D'Andrade, as utilized by William N. Stephens and appearing in the latter's Table 45 (1962:245). On pages 244 and 246, Stephens defines a mother-child household as one where the father sleeps outside the house at least half the time. The percentage of mother-child households is rated "high" in cultures where at least 40 per cent of all households are estimated to be mother-child; otherwise the rating is "low."

FC 314. Left: 19 cultures where the incidence of mother-child households is high (Column 1, Code X).
Right: 61 cultures where this incidence is low (same, Code Minus).
Unascertained: 320 cultures.

FC 315 also employs codings from Whiting and D'Andrade, as utilized by Stephens and listed in his Table 1 (1962:9–10).

FC 315. Left: 37 cultures where mother and nursing child customarily sleep in the same bed (Table 1, left column).
Right: 14 cultures where mother and nursing child customarily sleep in different beds (same, right column).
Unascertained: 349 cultures.

FC 316 uses codings appearing in Whiting, Kluckhohn, and Anthony's Table 1 (1958:365).

FC 316. Left: 19 cultures where exclusive mother-son sleeping arrangements last one year or longer (Table 1, above mid-line).

Right: 25 cultures where these arrangements last less than one year (same, below mid-line).
Unascertained: 356 cultures.

Treatment of the Infant (317–26)

All FCs in this subsection are derived from the codings of Barry, Bacon, and Child (1967). This subsection applies to the initial period of life, defined as "approximately the first year . . . and as long thereafter as the treatment of the infant remains approximately constant, but if there is any change it is the first year that is to be dealt with" in making coding assignments. "If there is a change in treatment at the end of the **neonatal** period, the treatment characteristic of the rest of infancy is what will be dealt with here, not the treatment of the neonate. . . . Separate judgments for boys and girls were rarely made. When they were, the entry for boys has been used here. This arbitrary choice cannot have much influence, since the few discrepancies between the sexes here were mostly very small." All codes were used, even those where underscoring indicated less confidence.

FC 317. Left: 39 cultures where display of affection toward the infant—fondling, caressing, playing with him—is high (Column 1, Code 11 or higher).
Right: 29 cultures where such display is low (same, Code 10 or lower).
Unascertained: 332 cultures.

FC 318 is a composite judgmental coding based on codings appearing in FCs 317 and 319–24.

FC 318. Left: 40 cultures where the over-all indulgence of the infant is high (Column 8, Code 11 or higher).
Right: 31 cultures where such indulgence is low (same, Code 10 or lower).
Unascertained: 329 cultures.

FC 319. Left: 35 cultures where the protection of the infant from environmental discomforts is high (Column 2, Code 9 or higher).
Right: 30 cultures where such protection is low (same, Code 8 or lower).
Unascertained: 335 cultures.

FC 320. Left: 45 cultures where the degree of drive reduction—considering particularly hunger, thirst, and unidentified discomforts—is high (Column 3, Code 12 or higher).
Right: 24 cultures where such degree is low (same, Code 11 or lower).
Unascertained: 331 cultures.

FC 321. Left: 35 cultures where the immediacy—i.e. the speed —of reduction of the infant's drives is high (Column 4, Code 12 or higher).
Right: 25 cultures where such immediacy is low (same, Code 11 or lower).
Unascertained: 340 cultures.

FC 322. Left: 27 cultures where the consistency of reduction of the infant's drives is high (Column 5, Code 12 or higher).
Right: 32 cultures where such consistency is low (same, Code 11 or lower).
Unascertained: 341 cultures.

FC 323. Left: 29 cultures where the constancy of presence of the infant's nurturant agent—the mother or a mother-substitute if there is one—is high (Column 6, Code 13 or higher).
Right: 45 cultures where such constancy is low (same, Code 12 or lower).
Unascertained: 326 cultures.

FC 324. Left: 32 cultures where the pain inflicted on the infant by the nurturant agent is high (Column 7, Code 10 or higher).
Right: 34 cultures where such pain is low or negligible (same, Code 9 or lower).
Unascertained: 334 cultures.

FC 325. Left: 42 cultures where the degree of diffusion among the infant's nurturant agents—i.e. the degree to which the nurturance of the infant is shared by other people—is high (Column 9, Code 8 or higher).
Right: 32 cultures where such degree is low (same, Code 7 or lower).
Unascertained: 326 cultures.

FC 326. Left: 32 cultures where the inferred transition anxiety between infancy and childhood is high (Column 13, Code 8 or higher).
Right: 35 cultures where such inferred anxiety is low (same, Code 7 or lower).
Unascertained: 333 cultures.

Transitional Ages (327–33)

Each FC in this subsection deals with the typical or customary age at which a transition in the early part of the life cycle occurs. The left and right attribute categories are based on a break at the median point, as stated in the text of each FC. Sources for these FCs are either Barry, Bacon, and Child (1967) or Whiting and Child (1953:338–46).

FC 327. Left: 28 cultures where the age of the infant at time of reduced contact with the mother is higher than two years (Barry, Bacon, and Child 1967, Column 11, Code higher than 2,0).
Right: 27 cultures where this age is two years or lower (same, Code 2,0 or lower).
Unascertained: 345 cultures.

FC 328. Left: 21 cultures where the age of the infant at the onset of serious socialization, other than weaning, is higher than two years (Barry, Bacon, and Child 1967, Column 12, Code higher than 2,0).
Right: 20 cultures where this age is two years or lower (same, Code 2,0 or lower).
Unascertained: 359 cultures.

FC 329. Left: 10 cultures where the age at toilet training is two years or higher (Whiting and Child 1953, Column N, Code 2.0 or higher).
Right: 11 cultures where this age is lower than two years (same, Code lower than 2.0).
Unascertained: 379 cultures.

FC 330. Left: 34 cultures where the age of the infant at the time of weaning is 2.5 years or higher (Barry, Bacon, and Child 1967, Column 10, Code 2,6 or higher).
Right: 36 cultures where this age is lower than 2.5 years (same, Code lower than 2,6).
Unascertained: 330 cultures.

FC 331. Left: 16 cultures where the age at beginning of independence training is 3.8 years or higher (Whiting and Child 1953, Column Q, Code 3.8 or higher).
Right: 21 cultures where this age is lower than 3.8 years (same, Code lower than 3.8).
Unascertained: 363 cultures.

FC 332. Left: 9 cultures where the age at beginning of modesty training is six years or higher (Whiting and Child 1953, Column O, Code 6.0 or higher).
Right: 8 cultures where this age is lower than six years (same, Code lower than 6.0).
Unascertained: 383 cultures.

FC 333. Left: 8 cultures where the age at beginning of training in heterosexual play inhibition is eight years or higher (Whiting and Child 1953, Column P, Code 8.0 or higher).

Right: 8 cultures where this age is lower than eight years (same, Code lower than 8.0).
Unascertained: 384 cultures.

Treatment of the Child (334–55)

The first FC in this subsection deals with the over-all indulgence of the child, and derives from Barry, Bacon, and Child (1967), Column 14.

FC 334. Left: 40 cultures where the indulgence of the child is high (Code 10 or higher).
Right: 38 cultures where this indulgence is low (Code 9 or lower).
Unascertained: 322 cultures.

FC 335 is taken from William N. Stephens' Table 2, and assesses "how much a young child's dependent demands are indulged and rewarded" (1962:11).

FC 335. Left: 20 cultures where initial indulgence of dependency is high (left column).
Right: 18 cultures where this indulgence is low (right column).
Unascertained: 362 cultures.

FCs 336 through 355 are based exclusively on Barry, Bacon, and Child (1967). These columns indicate coding decisions with respect to the treatment of boy children in the various cultures coded. Five types of behavior, or the lack of it, are encompassed in these codings: responsible, nurturant, self-reliant, achieving, and obeying behavior. Responsible behavior refers to the "performance of tasks, duties, or routines which are demanded by the culture." Nurturant behavior includes such activities as "to give sympathy and gratify the needs of a helpless one." Self-reliant behavior includes "learning to take care of oneself, learning to be independent of the assistance of other people, in supplying one's needs and wishes." Achievement means, among other things, "to accomplish something difficult. To master, manipulate or organize physical objects, human beings, or ideas. To do this as rapidly and independently as possible." Obedience behavior requires little definition.

Barry, Bacon, and Child examine each of these areas of behavior in terms of four rubrics. They examine (1) the total positive pressure on the child to develop the type of behavior in question. They also reach inferences as to the child's (2) anxiety over nonperformance of that type of behavior; such anxiety is "a function of severity and frequency of punishment for non-performance." They also infer the degree of the child's anxiety over (3) performance of that type of behavior—which is "a function of the severity and frequency of punishment for it." And finally, they code each culture for the child's (4) inferred conflict with regard to that type of behavior—which is a "function of the extent to which the positive learning (together with anxiety about non-performance) on the one hand, and anxiety about performance on the other hand, are both strong and [approximately equal]." The coding rules used by these three scholars are of considerable complexity and have been inadequately summarized here. For a more technical understanding of these coding categories, the reader should obtain a copy of the 1967 publication. The twenty FCs that follow will indicate the column on the source code sheet from which the data were taken. In every case "high" and "low" categories are determined by the position of the median; these median cutting points will not, however, be given.

FC 336. Left: 43 cultures where the total positive pressure toward developing responsible behavior in the child is high (Column 16).
Right: 32 cultures where such pressure is low (Column 16).
Unascertained: 325 cultures.

FC 337. Left: 38 cultures where the child's inferred anxiety over nonperformance of responsible behavior is high (Column 17).
Right: 35 cultures where such anxiety is low (Column 17).
Unascertained: 327 cultures.

FC 338. Left: 44 cultures where the child's inferred anxiety over performance of responsible behavior is high (Column 18).
Right: 29 cultures where such anxiety is low (Column 18).
Unascertained: 327 cultures.

FC 339. Left: 31 cultures where the child's inferred conflict regarding responsible behavior is high (Column 19).
Right: 42 cultures where such conflict is low (Column 19).
Unascertained: 327 cultures.

FC 340. Left: 28 cultures where the total positive pressure toward developing nurturant behavior in the child is high (Column 21).
Right: 20 cultures where such pressure is low (Column 21).
Unascertained: 352 cultures.

FC 341. Left: 30 cultures where the child's inferred anxiety over nonperformance of nurturant behavior is high (Column 22).
Right: 16 cultures where such anxiety is low (Column 22).

Unascertained: 354 cultures.

FC 342. Left: 18 cultures where the child's inferred anxiety over performance of nurturant behavior is high (Column 23).

Right: 28 cultures where such anxiety is low (Column 23).

Unascertained: 354 cultures.

FC 343. Left: 29 cultures where the child's inferred conflict regarding nurturant behavior is high (Column 24).

Right: 18 cultures where such conflict is low (Column 24).

Unascertained: 353 cultures.

FC 344. Left: 36 cultures where the total positive pressure toward developing self-reliant behavior in the child is high (Column 26).

Right: 40 cultures where such pressure is low (Column 26).

Unascertained: 324 cultures.

FC 345. Left: 37 cultures where the child's inferred anxiety over nonperformance of self-reliant behavior is high (Column 27).

Right: 39 cultures where such anxiety is low (Column 27).

Unascertained: 324 cultures.

FC 346. Left: 37 cultures where the child's inferred anxiety over performance of self-reliant behavior is high (Column 28).

Right: 39 cultures where such anxiety is low (Column 28).

Unascertained: 324 cultures.

FC 347. Left: 37 cultures where the child's inferred conflict regarding self-reliant behavior is high (Column 29).

Right: 39 cultures where such conflict is low (Column 29).

Unascertained: 324 cultures.

FC 348. Left: 32 cultures where the total positive pressure toward developing achievement behavior in the child is high (Column 31).

Right: 31 cultures where such pressure is low (Column 31).

Unascertained: 337 cultures.

FC 349. Left: 34 cultures where the child's inferred anxiety over nonperformance of achievement behavior is high (Column 32).

Right: 28 cultures where such anxiety is low (Column 32).
Unascertained: 338 cultures.

FC 350. Left: 34 cultures where the child's inferred anxiety over performance of achievement behavior is high (Column 33).
Right: 26 cultures where such anxiety is low (Column 33).
Unascertained: 340 cultures.

FC 351. Left: 26 cultures where the child's inferred conflict regarding achievement behavior is high (Column 34).
Right: 34 cultures where such conflict is low (Column 34).
Unascertained: 340 cultures.

FC 352. Left: 44 cultures where the total positive pressure toward developing obedient behavior in the child is high (Column 36).
Right: 28 cultures where such pressure is low (Column 36).
Unascertained: 328 cultures.

FC 353. Left: 42 cultures where the child's inferred anxiety over nonperformance of obedient behavior is high (Column 37).
Right: 32 cultures where such anxiety is low (Column 37).
Unascertained: 326 cultures.

FC 354. Left: 36 cultures where the child's inferred anxiety over performance of obedient behavior is high (Column 38).
Right: 37 cultures where such anxiety is low (Column 38).
Unascertained: 327 cultures.

FC 355. Left: 35 cultures where the child's inferred conflict regarding obedient behavior is high (Column 39).
Right: 38 cultures where such conflict is low (Column 39).
Unascertained: 327 cultures.

ADOLESCENCE (356–84)

Adolescent Peer Groups (356–65)

All FCs in this subsection are based on codings appearing in Appendix B of John K. Harley (1963). Harley has coded a sample of cultures in terms of whether adolescent peer groups are present and, if present, whether they function in various types of "settings." The first type of setting that will be presented here is that of courtship. After that, in FCs 358–63, three settings will be examined: work, public gatherings, and leisure. In performing his coding operation, Harley discovered that his cultures could be arrayed along a near-perfect Guttman Scale, in the sense that if a culture possesses adolescent peer groups in a work setting, it will almost invariably possess them also in a public gathering and leisure setting. Similarly, if a culture possesses them in a public gathering setting, it will also possess them in a leisure setting. Finally, there are cultures that possess adolescent peer groups only in a setting of leisure. This implicit Guttman Scale has been taken into account in formulating FCs 358–60.

FC 356. Left: 29 cultures where adolescent peer groups or pairs are present in a setting of courtship (First List, Column C, Code g or p).

Right: 22 cultures where adolescent peer groups and pairs are absent in a setting of courtship (same, Code a l or x).

Unascertained: 349 cultures.

● FC 357. Left: 23 cultures where adolescent peer groups are present in a setting of courtship (First List, Column C, Code g).

Right: 28 cultures where these groups are absent in a setting of courtship (same, Code a l p or x).

Unascertained: 349 cultures.

FC 358. Left: 41 cultures where adolescent peer groups are present in a setting of work and public gatherings and leisure, or of public gatherings and leisure, or of leisure only (First List, Columns W G and L, substantive entry in at least one column).

Right: 11 cultures where adolescent peer groups are absent in a setting of work, and of public gatherings, and of leisure (same, lack of substantive entry in any column).

Unascertained: 348 cultures.

● FC 359. Left: 20 cultures where adolescent peer groups are present in a setting of work and public gatherings and leisure, or at least of public gatherings and leisure—with some doubtful codings included (First List, Columns W G and L, substantive entry in all three columns or at least in Columns G and L).

Right: 32 cultures where adolescent peer groups are present only in a setting of leisure, or else are absent —with some doubtful codings included (same, substantive entry in Column L only, or else no substantive entry).

Unascertained: 348 cultures.

FC 360. Left: 14 cultures (same as left attribute category for FC 359, except that doubtful codings are omitted).

Right: 23 cultures (same as right attribute category for FC 359, except that doubtful codings have been omitted).

Unascertained: 363 cultures (including 15 treated as substantively coded in FC 359).

● FC 361. Left: 11 cultures where adolescent peer groups in a work setting are present (Column W, substantive entry).

Right: 40 cultures where adolescent peer groups in a work setting are absent (same, no substantive entry).

Unascertained: 349 cultures.

● FC 362. Left: 21 cultures where adolescent peer groups in a setting of public gatherings are present (Column G, substantive entry).

Right: 30 cultures where adolescent peer groups in a setting of public gatherings are absent (same, no substantive entry).

Unascertained: 349 cultures.

● FC 363. Left: 44 cultures where adolescent peer groups in a leisure setting are present (Column L, substantive entry).

Right: 11 cultures where adolescent peer groups in a leisure setting are absent (same, no substantive entry).

Unascertained: 345 cultures.

● FC 364. Left: 22 cultures where time spent in adolescent peer group activity is high (Second List, Column T, Code 6 5 or 4).

Right: 6 cultures where time spent in adolescent peer group activity is low (same, Code 1 or 0).

Ambiguous: 17 cultures where the time spent in adolescent peer group activity is high-medium or low-medium (same, Code 3 or 2).

Unascertained: 355 cultures.

FC 365. Left: 30 cultures where the time spent in adolescent peer group activity is high or high-medium (Second List, Column T, Code 6 5 4 or 3).

Right: 15 cultures where time spent in adolescent peer

group activity is low-medium or low (same, Code 2 1 or 0).

Unascertained: 355 cultures.

Dissociation of the Sexes at Adolescence (366–71)

Some of the FCs in this subsection, like all of those in the previous subsection, derive from the work of John K. Harley (1963). In formulating all such FCs, I was in touch with Harley and attempted to adhere as closely as possible to the contrasts he wanted run on the computer. In the process of successive computer runs, one instructive methodological lesson was learned. As will be noted, FCs 367 and 368 are identical, except that in the former are included 20 codings regarded by Harley as "doubtful," while in the latter these 20 doubtful cultures are dropped into the residue as "unascertained." The result is, of course, a much smaller "N" for Paragraph 368. Nonetheless, there are 43 predicate-pairs in Paragraph 368, compared with only 26 in Paragraph 367.* This is a cogent demonstration of the positive relationship between reliable and valid codings, and number of resulting significant tables and predicate-pairs. For further discussion, see the section on "The Meaningfulness of the Paragraphs," page 59.

FC 366. Left: 16 cultures where dissociation of the sexes at adolescence is high (Harley's Appendix B, First List, Column T, Code 5 4 or 3).

Right: 41 cultures where such dissociation is medium or low (same, Code 2 1 or 0).

Unascertained: 343 cultures.

● FC 367. Left: 28 cultures where dissociation of the sexes at adolescence is high or medium—with some doubtful codings included (Harley's Appendix B, First List, Column T, Code 5 4 3 or 2).

Right: 29 cultures where such dissociation is low—with some doubtful codings included (same, Code 1 or 0).

Unascertained: 343 cultures.

FC 368. Left: 16 cultures (same as left attribute category for FC 367, except that doubtful codings are omitted).

Right: 21 cultures (same as right attribute category for FC 367, except that doubtful codings are omitted).

Unascertained: 363 cultures (including 20 treated as substantively coded in FC 367).

FC 369. Left: 42 cultures where either high dissociation of the sexes at adolescence or customs of initiation at

*For this reason, and because of the need to conserve space, in the final run of the printout Paragraph 367 was run as "Neither Subject Nor Predicate."

adolescence are present (Harley's Appendix B, First List, Column T, Code 2 3 4 or 5; or Second List, Column I, Code 1 2 or 3).

Right: 15 cultures where both high dissociation of the sexes at adolescence and customs of initiation at adolescence are absent (Harley's Appendix B, First List, Column T, Code 0 or 1; and Second List, Column I, Code Minus).

Unascertained: 343 cultures.

FCs 370 and 371 are derived from **EA** Column 38, "Segregation of Adolescent Boys" (1962:271). The coding refers to "whether or not boys at or approaching puberty are segregated from their primary female relatives—their mothers and sisters . . ." The code is:

A: "Absence of segregation, adolescent boys residing and sleeping in the same dwelling as their mothers and sisters." 148 cultures.

P: "Partial segregation, adolescent boys residing or eating with their natal families but sleeping apart from them, e.g., in a special hut or in a cattle shed." 34 cultures.

R: "Complete segregation, in which adolescent boys go to live as individuals with relatives outside the nuclear family, e.g., with grandparents or with a maternal or paternal uncle." 15 cultures.

S: "Complete segregation, in which adolescent boys go to live as individuals with nonrelatives, e.g., as retainers to a chief or as apprentices to specialists." 5 cultures.

T: "Complete segregation, in which adolescent boys reside with a group of their own peers, e.g., in bachelor dormitories, military regiments, or age-villages." 41 cultures.

Unascertained: 157 cultures.

The segregation of females at menarche is dealt with in FC 380, page 153.

FC 370. Left: 95 cultures where segregation of adolescent boys is complete or partial (Code P R S or T).

Right: 148 cultures where such segregation is absent (Code A).

Unascertained: 157 cultures.

● FC 371. Left: 41 cultures where adolescent boys are segregated and reside with a group of peers (Code T).

Right: 202 remaining substantively coded cultures (Code A P R or S).

Unascertained: 157 cultures.

Male Initiation Rites and Genital Mutilation (372–79)

FC 372. Left: 48 cultures where male initiation rites are present (Albert S. Anthony 1955, Appendix IV, Column 1, Code P).

Right: 63 cultures where such rites are absent (same, Code A).

Unascertained: 289 cultures.

FC 373. Left: 17 cultures where male initiation ceremonies at puberty are present (Whiting, Kluckhohn, and Anthony 1958:365, Table 1, "Present" Column).

Right: 27 cultures where such ceremonies are absent (same, "Absent" Column).

Unascertained: 356 cultures.

● FC 374. Left: 43 cultures where male puberty rites are present. (Ford and Beach 1951:177).

Right: 18 cultures where such rites are absent (C. S. Ford, personal communication, 1963).

Unascertained: 339 cultures.

● FC 375. Left: 12 cultures where important secrets associated with male initiation rites are present (Albert S. Anthony 1955: Appendix III, Column 4, Code 2 3 4 5 6 or 7).

Right: 11 cultures where such secrets are absent (same, Code 1 or 1A—meaning "stated absence" or "no information—assumed absence").

Irrelevant: 26 cultures where male initiation rites are coded as absent (same, "Absence of rites" or "Female rites only").

Unascertained: 351 cultures.

● FC 376. Left: 9 cultures where ordeals of considerable severity associated with male initiation rites are present (Albert S. Anthony 1955: Appendix III, Column 1, Code 2 3 4 5 6 or 7).

Right: 13 cultures where such ordeals are absent (same, Code 1 or 1A—meaning "stated absence" or "no information—assumed absence").

Irrelevant: 26 cultures where male initiation rites are coded as absent (same, "Absence of rites" or "Female rites only").

Unascertained: 352 cultures.

FCs 377 and 378 derive from **EA** Column 37, "Male Genital Mutilations" (1962:270–71). The **EA** records genital mutilations "only when they are culturally normative for all males. Such drastic forms as subincision and the excision of a testicle will be specially indicated under 'Notes.' Otherwise, circumcision or one of its variants such as Polynesian 'superincision' is implied. The following symbols refer to the presence or absence of circumcision and to the age at which it is normally performed."

0: "Absent or not generally practiced." 242 cultures.

1: "Performed shortly after birth, i.e., within the first two months." 4 cultures.

2: "Performed during infancy, i.e., from two months to two years of age." 4 cultures.

3: "Performed during early childhood, i.e., from two to five years of age." 7 cultures.

4: "Performed during late childhood, i.e., from six to ten years of age." 23 cultures.

5: "Performed during adolescence, i.e., from eleven to fifteen years of age." 21 cultures.

6: "Performed during early adulthood, i.e., from sixteen to 25 years of age." 7 cultures.

7: "Performed during maturity, i.e., from 25 to 50 years of age." 1 culture.

8: "Performed in old age, i.e., after 50 years of age." No culture.

9: "Circumcision customary, but the normal age unspecified or unclear." 16 cultures.

Unascertained: 75 cultures.

FC 377. Left: 83 cultures where male genital mutilation is present (Code 1 2 3 4 5 6 7 or 9).

Right: 242 cultures where male genital mutilation is absent (Code 0).

Unascertained: 75 cultures.

● FC 378. Left: 38 cultures where male genital mutilation, if present, occurs in late childhood or earlier (Code 4 3 2 or 1).

Right: 29 cultures where male genital mutilation, if present, occurs in adolescence or later (Code 5 6 or 7).

Ambiguous: 16 cultures where male genital mutilation is present, but where the normal age is unspecified or unclear (Code 9).

Irrelevant: 242 cultures where male genital mutilation is absent (Code 0).

Unascertained: 75 cultures.

● FC 379. Left: 14 cultures where severe genital operations associated with male initiation rites are present (Albert S. Anthony 1955, Appendix III, Column 7, Code 2 3 4 5 6 or 7).

Right: 9 cultures where such operations are absent

(same, Code 1 or 1A, meaning "stated absence" or "no information—assumed absence").

Irrelevant: 26 cultures where male initiation rites are coded as absent (same, "Absence of rites" or "Female rites only").

Unascertained: 351 cultures.

Female Initiation Rites (380–84)

In the next-to-last computer run it was decided to run Paragraphs 381 and 384 as "neither subject nor predicate" because of inadequate yields of predicate-pairs. It was then discovered that the source of codings for these two paragraphs contained ambiguous information, and that mistakes in constructing these two FCs had probably been made. To prevent confusion, therefore, the subject and culture listings for these two paragraphs have been removed from the printout.

FC 380. Left: 35 cultures where segregation of girls at menarche is present (Ford and Beach 1951:174; and C. S. Ford, personal communication, 1963).

Right: 20 cultures where such segregation is absent (same).

Unascertained: 345 cultures.

FCs 382 and 383 are taken from Judith K. Brown's Table 3 (1963: 844–45). Brown defines female initiation rites as consisting of "one or more prescribed ceremonial events, mandatory for all girls of a given society, and celebrated between their eighth and twentieth years. The rite may be a cultural elaboration of menarche, but it should not include betrothal or marriage customs" (838).

FC 382. Left: 38 cultures where female initiation rites are present (Table 3, right and middle columns).

Right: 27 cultures where such rites are absent (same, left column).

Unascertained: 335 cultures.

● FC 383. Left: 9 cultures where female initiation rites, if present, are painful (Table 3, right column).

Right: 29 cultures where such rites, if present, are not painful (same, middle column).

Irrelevant: 27 cultures where such rites are absent (same, left column).

Unascertained: 335 cultures.

SEXUAL BEHAVIOR (385–401)

FC 385. Left: 22 cultures where sexual expression by the young is restricted (Ford and Beach 1951:180–82).

Right: 64 cultures where such expression is semi-restricted or permitted (same, 187–90).

Unascertained: 314 cultures.

FC 386. Left: 46 cultures where sexual expression by the young is restricted or semi-restricted (Ford and Beach 1951:180–82, 187).

Right: 40 cultures where sexual expression by the young is permitted (same, 188–90).

Unascertained: 314 cultures.

● FC 387. Left: 19 cultures where premarital coitus is forbidden (C. S. Ford 1945:100).

Right: 17 cultures where premarital coitus is not forbidden (same).

Unascertained: 364 cultures.

● FC 388. Left: 24 cultures where premarital coitus is present (C. S. Ford 1945:100).

Right: 8 cultures where premarital coitus is absent or rare (same).

Unascertained: 368 cultures.

FCs 389–92 are based on **EA** Column 78, "Norms of Premarital Sex Behavior" (1963:116). "This code was suggested and worked out by John T. Westbrook, who is also responsible for much of the codified material. The following symbols define the standards of sex behavior prevailing for unmarried females." These four FCs are designed to span an ordinal continuum; in order to accomplish this it was necessary in every instance to treat codes E and T below as "irrelevant." The code is:

V: "Insistence on virginity; premarital sex relations prohibited, strongly sanctioned, and in fact rare." 47 cultures.

P: "Premarital sex relations prohibited but weakly sanctioned and not infrequent in fact." 42 cultures.

A: "Premarital sex relations allowed and not sanctioned unless pregnancy results." 23 cultures.

F: "Premarital sex relations freely permitted and not sanctioned even if pregnancy results." 67 cultures.

E: "Early marriage of females, i.e., at or before puberty, precluding the possibility of premarital sex relations as defined." 19 cultures.

T: "Trial marriage; monogamous premarital sex relations permitted with the expectation of marriage if pregnancy results, promiscuous relations being prohibited and sanctioned." 4 cultures.

Unascertained: 198 cultures.

● FC 389. Left: 47 cultures where premarital sex relations are strongly punished and in fact rare (Code V).

Right: 67 cultures where such relations are freely permitted (Code F).

Irrelevant: 88 remaining substantively coded cultures (Code P A E or T).

Unascertained: 198 cultures.

FC 390. Left: 47 cultures where premarital sex relations are strongly punished and in fact rare (Code V).

Right: 132 cultures where such relations are weakly punished and in fact not rare, or punished only if pregnancy results, or freely permitted (Code P A or F).

Irrelevant: 23 remaining substantively coded cultures (Code E or T).

Unascertained: 198 cultures.

FC 391. Left: 89 cultures where premarital sex relations are strongly punished and in fact rare, or weakly punished and in fact not rare (Code V or P).

Right: 90 cultures where such relations are punished only if pregnancy results, or freely permitted (Code A or F).

Irrelevant: 23 remaining substantively coded cultures (Code E or T).

Unascertained: 198 cultures.

FC 392. Left: 112 cultures where premarital sex relations are strongly punished and in fact rare, or weakly punished and in fact not rare, or punished only if pregnancy results (Code V P or A).

Right: 67 cultures where such relations are freely permitted (Code F).

Irrelevant: 23 remaining substantively coded cultures (Code E or T).

Unascertained: 198 cultures.

FC 393. Left: 43 cultures where extramarital coitus is punished (Ford and Beach 1951:116, footnote 4; also C. S. Ford, personal communication, 1963).

Right: 41 cultures where extramarital coitus is permitted (C. S. Ford, personal communication, 1963).

Unascertained: 316 cultures.

● FC 394. Left: 16 cultures where extramarital coitus is present (C. S. Ford 1945:101).

Right: 8 cultures where extramarital coitus is absent (same).

Unascertained: 376 cultures.

FC 395. Left: 18 cultures where belief in the uncleanness of women is present (Leo W. Simmons 1945: Code Chart, Column 75, Code Plus or Equals).

Right: 15 cultures where such belief is absent (same, Code Minus or Zero).
Unascertained: 367 cultures.

FC 396. Left: 18 cultures where the strength of menstrual taboos is high (William N. Stephens 1962:85–97, 174; and Table 39, page 211, Code 5 or 4).
Right: 35 cultures where such strength is low (same, Code 3 2 or 1).
Unascertained: 347 cultures.

FC 397. Left: 14 cultures where sex disability is present (John K. Harley 1963: Appendix B, Second List, Column SD, Code Plus).
Right: 42 cultures where sex disability is absent (same, Code Minus).
Unascertained: 344 cultures.

FC 398. Left: 16 cultures where the intensity of sex anxiety is high (William N. Stephens 1962:80–81 and Table 6 on page 82, Code: all positive numbers and zero).
Right: 16 cultures where such intensity is low (same, Code: all minus numbers).
Unascertained: 368 cultures.

FC 399. Left: 23 cultures where the intensity of castration anxiety is high (William N. Stephens 1962:112–13 and Table 19 on page 115, Code: all positive numbers and zero).
Right: 22 cultures where such intensity is low (same, Code: all minus numbers).
Unascertained: 355 cultures.

FC 400. Left: 22 cultures where homosexual activity on the part of either sex is prohibited (Ford and Beach 1951:129).
Right: 36 cultures where homosexual activity on the part of one or both sexes is permitted (same, page 130).
Unascertained: 342 cultures.

● FC 401. Left: 10 cultures where the incidence of venereal disease is high (Moni Nag 1962:122–25 and Table 65 on pages 211–12, Code H).
Right: 9 cultures where such incidence is low (same, Code L).
Unascertained: 381 cultures.

ILLNESS AND THERAPY (402–15)

The 14 FCs in this section all derive from Whiting and Child (1953: 344–46). All entries are either "present" (Code Plus) or "absent" (Code Zero). Since the coding categories are derived from relatively complex theoretical formulations, and since the Whiting and Child book is widely available, this **Summary** will not attempt to summarize the authors' coding rules in any depth.

This section is divided into three subsections, dealing with explanations of illness, performance therapies, and avoidance therapies. Within each subsection, FCs focus on five systems of behavior: oral, anal, sexual, dependence, and aggression.*

Explanations of Illness (402–06)

Whiting and Child devised the codings used in the FCs in this subsection in order to pursue a general hypothesis, which they express in terms of individual behavior as follows: "In any system of behavior [e.g. oral, anal, sexual, dependence, or aggression] variations in severity of socialization will give rise to variations in the degree of anxiety associated with that system, and through continuation of this anxiety into adult life will give rise to variations in the extent to which that system of behavior is a focus of worry or concern in the adult." In the specific form in which the authors attempt to test their general hypothesis cross-culturally, it is expressed as follows: "In any society, the greater the custom potential of socialization anxiety for a system of behavior, the greater will be the custom potential of explanations of illness which attribute illness to events associated with that system" (page 149). FCs in this subsection are derived from Columns a through e respectively, on pages 344–46.

FC 402. Left: 31 cultures where explanations of illness of an oral nature are present. Examples: oral ingestion of various materials, "verbal spells and incantations performed by other people" (page 150).
Right: 30 cultures where such explanations are absent.
Unascertained: 339 cultures.

FC 403. Left: 23 cultures where explanations of illness of an anal nature are present. Examples: defecation, feces, urine, or their odors; carelessness with one's exuviae; the use of charms, curses, spells, or incantations in ritual; failure on the part of the patient to perform some ritual (pages 150–51).

*There is one exception. There is no FC dealing with cultures where sexual performance therapy is present, for only two cultures could so qualify (page 196).

Right: 38 cultures where such explanations are absent.
Unascertained: 339 cultures.

FC 404. Left: 19 cultures where explanations of illness of a sexual nature are present. Examples: sexual behavior, or sexual excretions or menstrual blood (page 152).
Right: 42 cultures where such explanations are absent.
Unascertained: 339 cultures.

FC 405. Left: 34 cultures where explanations of illness of a dependence nature are present. Examples: soul loss; spirit possession (page 152).
Right: 27 cultures where such explanations are absent.
Unascertained: 339 cultures.

FC 406. Left: 28 cultures where explanations of illness of an aggression nature are present. Examples: aggression or disobedience to spirits; magical weapons introjected into, or brought into contact with, the patient (page 153).
Right: 33 cultures where such explanations are absent.
Unascertained: 339 cultures.

Performance Therapies (407–10)

Whiting and Child devised the codings used in the FCs in this subsection in order to pursue a general hypothesis which they express with reference to individual behavior as follows: "In any system of behavior, variations in its initial indulgence in the young child will give rise to variations in the acquired reward potential of that system and, through continuation of this reward potential into adult life, will give rise to variations in the extent to which performance of responses in that system is a source of security in the adult." The hypothesis is stated for cross-cultural testing as follows: "In any society, the greater the custom potential of initial satisfaction in any system of behavior, the greater will be the custom potential of therapeutic practices which involve the performance of responses in that system" (page 192). FCs in this subsection are derived from Columns f, g, i, and j, respectively, on pages 344–46.

● FC 407. Left: 37 cultures where performance therapies of an oral nature are present. Example: swallowing something (page 194).
Right: 17 cultures where such therapies are absent.
Unascertained: 346 cultures.

- FC 408. Left: 22 cultures where performance therapies of an anal nature are present. Examples: defecation; urination (page 195).
  Right: 32 cultures where such therapies are absent.
  Unascertained: 346 cultures.
- FC 409. Left: 28 cultures where performance therapies of a dependence nature are present. Example: prayer (page 196).
  Right: 26 cultures where such therapies are absent.
  Unascertained: 346 cultures.
- FC 410. Left: 31 cultures where performance therapies of an aggression nature are present. Example: destruction of the agent (person or spirit) believed responsible for the illness (page 197).
  Right: 23 cultures where such therapies are absent.
  Unascertained: 346 cultures.

Avoidance Therapies (411–15)

Avoidance therapy, in contrast to performance therapy, involves "the avoidance or the undoing of responses" in a given system. "It would appear that severe anxiety about a given system of behavior might, when coupled with the added anxiety of illness, lead a person to attempt such avoidance or undoing as a means of reducing anxiety" (page 209). FCs in this subsection are derived from Columns k through o, respectively.

- FC 411. Left: 36 cultures where avoidance therapies of an oral nature are present. Examples: spitting; vomiting; adherence to food taboos (page 209).
  Right: 18 cultures where such therapies are absent.
  Unascertained: 346 cultures.
- FC 412. Left: 31 cultures where avoidance therapies of an anal nature are present. Examples: retention of feces; washing or cleansing; adherence to cleanliness taboos (page 209).
  Right: 23 cultures where such therapies are absent.
  Unascertained: 346 cultures.
- FC 413. Left: 13 cultures where avoidance therapies of a sexual nature are present. Examples: general sexual abstention; adherence to specific sexual taboos (page 209).
  Right: 41 cultures where such therapies are absent.
  Unascertained: 346 cultures.
- FC 414. Left: 23 cultures where avoidance therapies of a de-

pendence nature are present. Examples: isolating a patient; removing him from his home for the duration of his illness (page 209).

Right: 31 cultures where such therapies are absent.

Unascertained: 346 cultures.

● FC 415. Left: 25 cultures where avoidance therapies of an aggression nature are present. Examples: the sacrifice of property; attempting to placate the agent responsible for the illness (pages 209–10).

Right: 29 cultures where such therapies are absent.

Unascertained: 346 cultures.

AGGRESSION AND WARFARE (416–22)

● FC 416. Left: 10 cultures where the threat of armed attack by alien societies is considerable (Guy E. Swanson 1960, 197–98, Column 3, Code 2).

Right: 26 cultures where such threat is limited or negligible (same, Code 1 or 0).

Unascertained: 364 cultures.

FC 417. Left: 34 cultures where warfare is prevalent (Leo W. Simmons 1945, Code Chart, Column 36, Code Plus or Equals).

Right: 9 cultures where warfare is not prevalent (same, Code Minus or Zero).

Unascertained: 357 cultures.

● FC 418. Left: 8 cultures where warfare is common or chronic (Donald Horton 1943: 270–72, 307–09, and Table 20, Column 4, Code C).

Right: 24 cultures where warfare is rare or infrequent (same, Code R).

Unascertained: 368 cultures.

FC 419 is based on Philip E. Slater (1964:6–7), whose code for "Pursuit of Military Glory" is as follows:

3: "High: When the ethnographer says that members of the tribe seek death in battle, or regard it as preferable to defeat and behave accordingly, or see it as the principal road to earthly or other-worldly glory. Or,

"When war is said to be considered by the tribe as glorious, the primary source of status and prestige, or to be waged principally for the purpose of obtaining rank, honor, or fame. Or,

"When military virtues, such as valor, recklessness, fighting skill, etc., are said to be the most important ones in the society. Or,

"When military trophies are said to be the principal source of rank or prestige in the society."

1: "Low: When none of the above are present and:

"Ethnographer says military virtues are not valued. Or,

"Some indication is given that saving one's own life in battle is considered normal and appropriate behavior. Or,

"War is regarded as abhorrent."

2: "Moderate: When none of the above are present but:

"**Defensive** virtues are said to be valued—military resistance, endurance, fortitude, etc. Or,

"Values other than military ones predominate, though the latter are important.

"Contests of bravery, skill or endurance (e.g. ability to withstand pain) are an important feature of masculine relationships.

"Raids, etc., are frequent, but conducted primarily for economic reasons."

FC 419. Left: 55 cultures where military glory is strongly or moderately emphasized (Code 3 or 2).
Right: 31 cultures where military glory is negligibly emphasized (Code 1).
Unascertained: 314 cultures.

FC 420 is based on Philip E. Slater (1964:7–8), whose code for "Bellicosity" is as follows:

2: "High: When ethnographer describes tribe explicitly as currently belligerent or warlike. Or,

"When the majority of adult males are said to spend most of their daily life engaged in or preparing for war, raids, or homicidal vendettas. Or,

"When ethnographer says the tribe is feared by surrounding tribes as an aggressor."

1: "Low: When none of the above are present and:

"War is said to be defined as waged primarily in revenge, or defensively, in response to the presence of warlike neighbors. Or,

"When tribe is described as peaceful, meek, friendly, non-aggressive, etc. Or,

"War, raids, vendettas, etc., are said to be absent."

FC 420. Left: 41 cultures where bellicosity is extreme (Code 2).
Right: 46 cultures where bellicosity is moderate or negligible (Code 1).
Unascertained: 313 cultures.

FC 421 is also based on Slater (1964:8–9), whose code for "Killing, Torturing, or Mutilating the Enemy" is as follows:

3: "High: When members of the tribe habitually take prisoners in warfare or raids for the explicit purpose of torturing them. Or,

"When prolonged or elaborate torture of captives is mentioned as a common phenomenon. Or,

"When prisoners are regularly sacrificed under conditions that approximate torture (slow, painful death, dismemberment while still alive, eaten alive, etc.). Or,

"When particularly large numbers of prisoners are slaughtered in ways that produce a rapid but especially painful or terrifying death."

2: "Medium: When none of the above are present but:

"Warriors are said never to take prisoners in battles or raids but have a policy of killing all their enemies on the spot. Or,

"Headhunting or scalp-collecting is said to be practiced on a wide scale, and provides a major source of prestige and status. Or,

"Killing is a prerequisite of manhood."

1: "Low: When none of the above are present and:

"The tribe is described as peaceful, gentle, kindly, etc. Or,

"Prisoners are taken and kept as slaves, or otherwise incorporated into the society. Or,

"There is no consistent policy regarding prisoners. Or,

"Prisoners are not taken but battles or raids are typically concluded before everyone is killed, i.e., when some objective is obtained or when ritual expression of defeat is rendered by the enemy. Or,

"Wars and raiding are rare."

FC 421. Left: 37 cultures where killing, torturing, or mutilating of the enemy is strongly or moderately emphasized (Code 3 or 2).

Right: 47 cultures where killing, torturing, or mutilating of the enemy is negligibly emphasized (Code 1).

Unascertained: 316 cultures.

● FC 422. Left: 6 cultures where cannibalism is present (Leo W. Simmons 1945: Code Chart, Column 90, Code Plus or Equals).

Right: 21 cultures where cannibalism is unimportant or absent (same, Code Minus or Zero).

Unascertained: 373 cultures.

RELIGION, MAGIC, AND ESCHATOLOGY (423–56)

● FC 423. Left: 13 cultures where an organized priesthood is present (Leo W. Simmons 1945: Code Chart, Column 81, Code Plus or Equals).

Right: 21 cultures where an organized priesthood is unimportant or absent (same, Code Minus or Zero).

Unascertained: 366 cultures.

FC 424. Left: 21 cultures where religious specialists are full time (John M. Hickman 1962: 216, Table 2, Column F, Code 2).
Right: 33 cultures where religious specialists are part time (same, Code 1).
Unascertained: 346 cultures.

FC 425. Left: 16 cultures where supernaturals are mainly benevolent (Lambert, Triandis, and Wolf 1959, 163–64, Table 2, bottom row).
Right: 20 cultures where supernaturals are mainly aggressive (same, top row).
Unascertained: 364 cultures.

FCs 426–28 are based on original codings appearing in Guy E. Swanson 1960, and modified by the **Ethnographic Atlas.** Codings used here are from **EA** column 34, "High Gods" (1962:269–70). "This code is taken directly from Swanson (1960), and we accept his judgments wherever we include the same societies unless we have utilized different and, in our opinion, superior sources. By a high god is meant a spiritual being who is believed to have created all reality and/or to be its ultimate governor, even if his sole act was to create other spirits who, in turn, created or control the natural world. The symbols employed are the following:

A: "A high god present but otiose or not concerned with human affairs." 69 cultures.

B: "A high god present and active in human affairs but not offering positive support to human morality." 26 cultures.

C: "A high god present, active, and specifically supportive of human morality." 61 cultures.

O: "A high god absent or not reported in substantial descriptions of religious beliefs." 104 cultures.

Unascertained: 140 cultures.

For further discussion of this raw characteristic, see page 50.

FC 426. Left: 156 cultures where a high god is present (Code A B or C).
Right: 104 cultures where a high god is absent (Code O).
Unascertained: 140 cultures.

FC 427. Left: 87 cultures where a high god, if present, is active (Code B or C).
Right: 69 cultures where a high god, if present, is inactive (Code A).
Irrelevant: 104 cultures where a high god is absent (Code O).
Unascertained: 140 cultures.

FC 428. Left: 61 cultures where a high god, if present and active, supports human morality (Code C).
Right: 26 cultures where a high god, if present and active, does not support human morality (Code B).
Irrelevant: 173 cultures, including: 69 cultures where a high god is present but not active (Code A). 104 cultures where a high god is absent (Code O).
Unascertained: 140 cultures.

FC 429. Left: 28 cultures where supernatural sanctions for morality are present (Guy E. Swanson 1960: 212–17, Table C, Column 37, Code 1; **or** Column 38, Code 1; **or** Column 39, Code 1).
Right: 9 cultures where such sanctions are absent or unreported (same, Column 37, Code O; **and** Column 38, Code O; **and** Column 39, Code O).
Unascertained: 363 cultures.

FC 430. Left: 16 cultures where supernatural sanctions for morality, having an effect on an individual's health, are present (Guy E. Swanson 1960:212–17, Table C, Column 37, Code 1).
Right: 22 cultures where such sanctions are absent or unreported (same, Code O).
Unascertained: 362 cultures.

FC 431. Left: 10 cultures where supernatural sanctions for morality, having an effect on an individual's afterlife, are present (Guy E. Swanson 1960:212–17, Table C, Column 38, Code 1).
Right: 25 cultures where such sanctions are absent or unreported (same, Code O).
Unascertained: 365 cultures.

FC 432. Left: 27 cultures where an attractive afterlife is believed in (Leo W. Simmons 1945: Code Chart, Column 98, Code Plus or Equals).
Right: 11 cultures where an attractive afterlife is not believed in (same, Code Minus or Zero).
Unascertained: 362 cultures.

FC 433. Left: 10 cultures where belief in reincarnation is present (Guy E. Swanson 1960:211, 214–17, Table C, Column 30, Code 1 or 2).
Right: 28 cultures where belief in reincarnation is absent (same, Code O).
Unascertained: 362 cultures.

FC 434. Left: 37 cultures where asceticism in mourning behavior is high (Joan Friendly Goodman 1956: Table I on pages 95–97, Column 20, Code 4 or higher).

Right: 30 cultures where such asceticism is low (same, Code 3 or lower).

Unascertained: 333 cultures.

FC 435. Left: 12 cultures where abandonment of the house of the dead is practiced (Leo W. Simmons 1945: Code Chart, Column 94, Code Plus or Equals).

Right: 19 cultures where such abandonment is not practiced (same, Code Minus or Zero).

Unascertained: 369 cultures.

FC 436. Left: 27 cultures where active ancestral spirits are present (Guy E. Swanson 1960:210–11 and Table C on pages 214–17, Column 29, Code 1 2 or 3).

Right: 11 cultures where active ancestral spirits are absent (same, Code O).

Unascertained: 362 cultures.

FCs 437–43 are based on codings in Whiting and Child 1953:344–46, Columns p through t, which concern various kinds of fears which the authors define on pages 263–65 and 286. The first two FCs in this group are taken from Joan Friendly Goodman 1956. Goodman has combined the Whiting and Child scores in various ways. The distinction between "spirits" and "ghosts" is that the latter refer specifically to spirits of dead persons (Whiting and Child 1953:286).

FC 437. Left: 21 cultures where fear of ghosts, spirits, humans, or animals is high (Whiting and Child 1953, with scores combined by Joan Friendly Goodman 1956, appearing in Table VII, page 72, top half).

Right: 23 cultures where such fear is low (same, bottom half).

Unascertained: 356 cultures.

FC 438. Left: 27 cultures where other-worldly fears of ghosts or spirits are greater than this-worldly fears of humans or animals (Whiting and Child 1953, with scores combined by Joan Friendly Goodman 1956, and appearing in the Appendix, page 100, Table 4, top half.

Right: 17 cultures where this-worldly fears of humans or animals are greater than other-worldly fears of ghosts or spirits (same, bottom half).

Unascertained: 356 cultures.

FC 439. Left: 30 cultures where fear of ghosts is high (Whiting and Child 1953:344–46, Column s, Code 7 or higher).

Right: 31 cultures where fear of ghosts is low (same, Code 6 or lower).

Unascertained: 339 cultures.

FC 440. Left: 32 cultures where fear of spirits is high (Whiting and Child 1953:344–46, Column q, Code 9 or higher).

Right: 29 cultures where fear of spirits is low (same, Code 8 or lower).

Unascertained: 339 cultures.

FC 441. Left: 29 cultures where fear of human beings is high (Whiting and Child 1953:344–46, Column p, Code 8 or higher).

Right: 32 cultures where fear of human beings is low (same, Code 7 or lower).

Unascertained: 339 cultures.

FC 442. Left: 28 cultures where fear of animal spirits is high (Whiting and Child 1953:344–46, Column t, Code any positive number).

Right: 33 cultures where fear of animal spirits is low (same, Code zero).

Unascertained: 339 cultures.

FC 443. Left: 31 cultures where over-all fear of others is high (Whiting and Child 1953:344–46, Column r, Code 16 or higher).

Right: 30 cultures where over-all fear of others is low (same, Code 15 or lower).

Unascertained: 339 cultures.

FC 444. Left: 28 cultures where the use of dreams to seek and control supernatural powers is high (Roy G. D'Andrade 1961: 323, Table 1, top half).

Right: 27 cultures where such use is low (same, bottom half).

Unascertained: 345 cultures.

FC 445 is based on Beatrice Blyth Whiting's Yale University doctoral dissertation of 1942, which was later published (1950). Donald Horton used her codings and extended them to other cultures in his sample (Horton 1943:273).

FC 445. Left: 26 cultures where sorcery is important (Horton 1943: 307–09, Table 20, Column 7, Code I.

Right: 23 cultures where sorcery is unimportant (same, Code U).

Unascertained: 351 cultures.

FC 446. Left: 14 cultures where witchcraft is significantly present (Guy E. Swanson 1960:211, Table C on pages 214–17, Column 36, Code 2).

Right: 24 cultures where witchcraft is moderately present or absent (same, Code 1 or 0).

Unascertained: 362 cultures.

FC 447. Left: 20 cultures where love magic is present (Shirley and Romney 1962:1030, Table 2, right column).

Right: 13 cultures where love magic is absent (same, left column).

Unascertained: 367 cultures.

FCs 448 to 450 are based on codings in James R. Leary (1961: Appendix A, Table 6). These codings concern the frequency of observation of food taboos in a sample of cultures. For purposes of this **Summary,** Leary's sample of cultures was divided into terciles, from which three FCs were constructed. Cutting points between terciles occur between scores of 9 and 8, and between 5 and 4.

● FC 448. Left: 25 cultures where the observation of food taboos is high (top tercile).

Right: 26 cultures in which such observation is low (bottom tercile).

Irrelevant: 35 remaining substantively coded cultures (middle tercile).

Unascertained: 314 cultures.

FC 449. Left: 25 cultures where the observation of food taboos is high (top tercile).

Right: 61 cultures where such observation is medium or low (middle or bottom tercile).

Unascertained: 314 cultures.

FC 450. Left: 60 cultures where the observation of food taboos is high or medium (top or middle tercile).

Right: 26 cultures where such observation is low (bottom tercile).

Unascertained: 314 cultures.

FC 451. Left: 15 cultures where totemism is present (Leo W. Simmons 1945: Column 88, Code Plus or Equals).

Right: 12 cultures where totemism is unimportant or absent (same, Code Minus or Zero).

Unascertained: 373 cultures.

FC 452. Left: 19 cultures where totemism with food taboos is present (William N. Stephens 1962: Table 29 on page 165, Code Present). This attribute refers specifically to taboos on the eating of one's totem. "For instance, if one is a raccoon (i.e., a member of a kin-group that traces its descent from a raccoon), one is not allowed to eat (or kill) raccoons" (page 160).

Right: 24 cultures where totemism with food taboos is absent (same, Code Absent).

Unascertained: 357 cultures.

FCs 453–56 derive from David C. McClelland (1961:488–89 and Table D on page 491). All concern McClelland's interest in the "need to achieve." The left and right attributes of each of these FCs are based on a simple high-low dichotomy, determined by the medians in Columns II, III, I, and IV of Table D. No attempt will be made here to summarize McClelland's scoring system, since it is somewhat complex and is clearly presented in his book.

FC 453. Left: 13 cultures where the role of religious experts is conducive to the development of the individual's need to achieve (Table D, Column II, Code 1.67 or higher).

Right: 23 cultures where this role is not conducive to such development (same, Code 1.50 or lower).

Unascertained: 364 cultures.

FC 454. Left: 18 cultures where the objective of the individual's contact with the divine is conducive to the development of the individual's need to achieve (Table D, Column III, Code 1.50 or higher).

Right: 18 cultures where this objective is not conducive to such development (same, Code 1.33 or lower).

Unascertained: 364 cultures.

FC 455. Left: 17 cultures where the mode of the individual's contact with the divine is conducive to the development of the individual's need to achieve (Table D, Column I, Code 2.01 or higher).

Right: 19 cultures where this mode is not conducive to such development (same, Code 2.00 or lower).

Unascertained: 364 cultures.

FC 456. Left: 19 cultures where the internalization of the individual's contact with the divine is conducive to the development of the individual's need to achieve (Table D, Column IV, Code 1.83 or higher).

Right: 17 cultures where this internalization is not conducive to such development (same, Code 1.67 or lower).

Unascertained: 364 cultures.

GAMES (457–66)

All of the FCs in this section derive from the codings of Roberts, Arth, and Bush (1959), as modified by the **Ethnographic Atlas** and appearing in Column 35 (1962:270). The **EA** uses the Roberts, Arth, and Bush codings "wherever we deal with the same societies unless we have reason to suspect that we have had access to more recent and/or more exhaustive source materials. Following them, we classify games into three types and define them in identical fashion, but we are concerned only with the presence or absence of the types, not with the number of games they include. The following symbols are employed:

O: "No games of any of the three types." 18 cultures.

A: "Games of physical skill only, whether or not they may also involve incidental elements of chance or strategy, e.g., foot racing, wrestling, the hoop-and-pole game." 67 cultures.

B: "Games of chance only, with no significant element of either physical skill or strategy involved, e.g., dice games." 1 culture.

C: "Games of physical skill and of chance both present." 51 cultures.

P: "Games of strategy only, involving no significant element of physical skill, e.g., chess, go, poker. Whether or not an element of chance is also involved is considered irrelevant." 3 cultures.

Q: "Games of physical skill and of strategy present, but not games of chance." 19 cultures.

R: "Games of chance and of strategy present, but not games of physical skill." No culture.

S: "Games of all three types present." 30 cultures.

Unascertained: 211 cultures.

● FC 457. Left: 171 cultures where games of some kind are present (Code A B C P Q or S).
Right: 18 cultures where no games of any kind are present (Code O).
Unascertained: 211 cultures.

FC 458. Left: 52 cultures where games, if present, include games of strategy (Code P Q or S).
Right: 119 cultures where games, if present, do not include games of strategy (Code A B or C).
Irrelevant: 18 cultures where no games of any kind are present (Code O).
Unascertained: 211 cultures.

FC 459. Left: 82 cultures where games, if present, include games of chance (Code B C or S).
Right: 89 cultures where games, if present, do not include games of chance (Code A P or Q).

Irrelevant: 18 cultures where no games of any kind are present (Code O).

Unascertained: 211 cultures.

FC 460. Left: 67 cultures where games, if present, are limited to games of skill only (Code A).

Right: 104 cultures where games, if present, are not limited to games of skill only (Code B C P Q or S).

Irrelevant: 18 cultures where no games of any kind are present (Code O).

Unascertained: 211 cultures.

● FC 461. Left: 22 cultures where games of strategy, rather than chance, are present (Code P or Q).

Right: 52 cultures where games of chance, rather than strategy, are present (Code B or C).

Ambiguous: 30 cultures where both games of strategy and games of chance are present (Code S).

Irrelevant: 85 cultures, including: 67 cultures where games of neither strategy nor chance are present (Code A). 18 cultures where no games of any kind are present (Code O).

Unascertained: 211 cultures.

● FC 462. Left: 30 cultures where games of strategy, chance, and skill—rather than skill only—are present (Code S).

Right: 67 cultures where games of skill only—rather than strategy, chance, and skill—are present (Code A).

Irrelevant: 92 remaining substantively coded cultures (Code O B C P or Q).

Unascertained: 211 cultures.

● FC 463. Left: 30 cultures where games of strategy, chance, and skill—rather than strategy and skill only—are present (Code S).

Right: 19 cultures where games of strategy and skill only—rather than strategy, chance, and skill—are present (Code Q).

Irrelevant: 140 remaining substantively coded cultures (Code O A B C or P).

Unascertained: 211 cultures.

● FC 464. Left: 30 cultures where games of strategy, chance, and skill—rather than chance and skill only—are present (Code S).

Right: 51 cultures where games of chance and skill

only—rather than strategy, chance, and skill—are present (Code C).

Irrelevant: 108 remaining substantively coded cultures (Code O A B P or Q).

Unascertained: 211 cultures.

● FC 465. Left: 30 cultures where games of strategy, chance, and skill—rather than no games at all—are present (Code S).

Right: 18 cultures where no games at all—rather than games of strategy, chance, and skill—are present (Code O).

Irrelevant: 141 remaining substantively coded cultures (Code A B C P or Q).

Unascertained: 211 cultures.

● FC 466. Left: 51 cultures where, if games are present but games of strategy absent, games include those of both chance and skill, rather than skill only (Code C).

Right: 67 cultures where, if games are present but games of strategy absent, games include those of skill only, rather than both chance and skill (Code A).

Irrelevant: 71 remaining substantively coded cultures (Code O B P Q or S).

Unascertained: 211 cultures.

CULTURE CONTACT AND CULTURE CHANGE (467–70)

All FCs in this section are based on John M. Hickman (1962:215–16). Paragraphs in this section raise the question of the "time level"—discussed on page 14—more pointedly than do most other FCs. That is, since most of the cultures in our sample of 400 have undergone marked change as the result of culture contact, it is important to specify the point in time as of when the coding assignment for a particular culture is considered valid. Hickman has been unable to do this in his article, for reasons of space. Nonetheless, it seemed desirable to include these FCs based on his codings, on the assumption that he used more or less the same ethnographic sources as did the **EA,** and as did most of the other contributors to this **Summary.** The source is Hickman's Table 2, Column E, "Isolation from Other Cultures." The code is:

1: "Irregular culture contact." 11 cultures.

2: "Regular culture contact." 26 cultures.

3: "Frequent culture contact." 17 cultures.

Unascertained: 346 cultures.

● FC 467. Left: 17 cultures where contact with other cultures is frequent (Code 3).

Right: 11 cultures where such contact is irregular (Code 1).

Irrelevant: 26 cultures where such contact is regular (Code 2).

Unascertained: 346 cultures.

FC 468. Left: 17 cultures where contact with other cultures is frequent (Code 3).

Right: 37 cultures where such contact is regular or irregular (Code 2 or 1).

Unascertained: 346 cultures.

FC 469. Left: 43 cultures where contact with other cultures is frequent or regular (Code 3 or 2).

Right: 11 cultures where such contact is irregular (Code 1).

Unascertained: 346 cultures.

FC 470. Left: 21 cultures where innovations are generally accepted (John M. Hickman 1962:216, Table 2, Column VI, Code 2).

Right: 33 cultures where innovations are accepted only selectively (same, Code 1).

Unascertained: 346 cultures.

MISCELLANEOUS (471–80)

Included in this section are ten FCs that are not readily classifiable elsewhere. Their inclusion here is not to suggest that they are less useful than the other FCs. On the contrary, I believe that some of them will prove highly useful.

FC 471. Left: 9 cultures where secret societies are present (Leo W. Simmons 1945: Code Chart, Column 35, Code Plus or Equals).

Right: 14 cultures where secret societies are unimportant or absent (same, Code Minus or Zero).

Unascertained: 377 cultures.

FC 472 is based on Philip E. Slater's "composite narcissism index," an index derived from five narcissism measures used in his study, all of which also appear in this **Summary:** FC 137, "Invidious Display of Wealth," page 99; FC 419, "Military Glory," page 160; FC 473, "Sensitivity to Insult," page 173; FC 474, "Boastfulness," page 174; and FC 475, "Exhibitionistic Dancing," page 174. To be scored "high" on this composite narcissism index, a culture must fulfill both of the following requirements (Philip E. Slater 1964: personal communication):

1. It must be scored "high" on at least two of the five above-mentioned raw characteristics. "High" means a score of 2 for "Invidious Display of Wealth" and for "Boastfulness"; a score of 2 or 3 for "Military Glory"; and a score of 3 for "Sensitivity to Insult" and "Exhibitionistic Dancing." And:

2. It must achieve a total score of at least 9 on the above five raw characteristics.*

FC 472. Left: 47 cultures where the composite narcissism index is high.
Right: 43 cultures where this index is low.
Unascertained: 310 cultures.

FC 473, which deals with "Sensitivity to Insult," is also based on Philip E. Slater (1964:3–5). The code is:

3: "High" if:

"Public humiliation **frequently** leads to suicide or some other violent response. Or,

"Interpersonal insults, slights, snubs frequently lead to suicide, homicide, vendetta, permanent estrangement, or demand for heavy remuneration (because of narcissistic wounds, not because of malediction, etc.). Or,

"Ethnographer says explicitly they are acutely sensitive to narcissistic wounds, easily take offense, etc.; (**not** if says merely 'easily hurt' —must be some indication that pride is wounded, or vanity, **not** merely that they feel rejected, unloved, or deprived). Or,

"Abnormally elaborate etiquette precautions designed to avoid giving offense are present, (not limited to specific groups or relationships)."

1: "Low" if none of the above are present **and:**

"Ridicule and shame are specifically excluded as important public sanctions. Or,

"Incidents are specifically mentioned (as typical) by ethnographer in which insults, scorn, etc., are received without marked reaction. Offenses can be erased with small gifts, etc. Or,

"Ethnographer specifically describes them as phlegmatic, serene, easygoing, not easily offended, quick to forgive slights, etc."

2: "Moderate" if none of the above are present but:

"Ridicule and shame are nevertheless important public sanctions. Or,

*In figuring this total score, ratings of "0" and "X" are treated as 1 on 2-point scales, and as 2 on 3-point scales. "0" means "No information"; "X" means that information is available which supports making ratings at both extremes of a variable. In composing the above-mentioned five FCs, these two ratings were utilized in only two instances: In FC 474, "0" is treated as "low"; in FC 137, "X" is treated as "low."

"Insults, slights, snubs, etc., are explicitly mentioned as giving rise to sulking, tears, or anger of brief duration. Or,

"There is mention of mild etiquette precautions for face-saving. Or,

"Ridicule may yield suicide **attempts,** but actual suicide is rare. Or,

"Ethnographer characterizes culture as 'shame culture.' "

FC 473. Left: 32 cultures where sensitivity to insult is extreme (Code 3).

Right: 56 cultures where sensitivity to insult is moderate or negligible (Code 2 or 1).

Unascertained: 312 cultures.

FC 474, dealing with "Boastfulness," is also based on Philip E. Slater (1964:10). Slater's code is:

2: "Present":

"When ethnographer refers to tribe as generally boastful. Or,

"When ethnographer says boasting is typical at certain times (feasts, bragging after battles, crowing over achievements, etc.), or describes instances in which this is general and accepted behavior. Or,

"When ethnographer describes, as typical, instances of boasting-by-contrast, i.e., the speaker scorns, taunts, or ridicules others for not possessing attributes, achievements, or goods which the speaker possesses."

1: "Absent": When none of the above are present and:

"Ethnographer refers to tribe as modest, unassuming, humble etc. Or,

"Ethnographer explicitly says they do not boast over triumphs, achievements, etc., or describes incidents, **in detail,** of triumph, achievement, etc., following which the speaker speaks modestly, etc. Or,

"Ethnographer says boasting or scorning is negatively sanctioned."

FC 474. Left: 41 cultures where boastfulness is extreme (Code 2).

Right: 48 cultures where boastfulness is moderate, negligible, or unreported (Code 1 or 0, the latter symbol meaning that information is lacking).

Unascertained: 311 cultures.

FC 475 deals with "exhibitionistic dancing," and is also based on codings by Philip E. Slater (1964:11). His code is:

3: "High":

"When ethnographer reports that most dancing is performed individually, with an audience present. Or,

"When there is strong emphasis on being a good performer, with prestige or material rewards going to the best individual dancer. Or,

"When there is considerable competitiveness with regard to costume among dancers."

1: "Low":

"When dancing is primarily social—men and women dancing together with no attention paid to individual skill. Or,

"When dancing is primarily ritual and ceremonial, with no audience and most members participating. Or,

"When emphasis is placed primarily on ritual exactitude rather than skill."

2: "Medium":

"When social-ceremonial and exhibitionistic elements seem to be about equal."

FC 475. Left: 48 cultures where exhibitionistic dancing is strongly or moderately emphasized (Code 3 or 2).
Right: 38 cultures where exhibitionistic dancing is negligibly emphasized (Code 1).
Unascertained: 314 cultures.

FC 476 is taken from Donald Horton's "Scale of Drinking Behavior" (1943:265–66). The code is:

S: "Strong Insobriety"—" 'Excessive' drinking; drinking bouts may last for many hours or days. Drinking to unconsciousness is a regular occurrence."

M: "Moderate Insobriety"—"Drinking usually ends in intoxication but does not continue for days. Unconsciousness not regular or frequent."

Sl: "Slight Insobriety"—"Liquor is rarely taken or, when used, is used with restraint."

FC 476. Left: 31 cultures where the degree of insobriety is strong (Table 20 on pages 308–09, Column 1, Code S).
Right: 18 cultures where the degree of insobriety is moderate or slight (same, Code M or Sl).
Unascertained: 351 cultures.

FC 477 is taken from Donald Horton's "Measure for Drunken Aggression" (1943:284–85). The code is:

S: "Strong"

"Armed assault is frequent; homicide, common. Or,

"Homicide is very frequent."

M: "Moderate"

"Verbal conflict is very frequent; simple assault, common; all other forms of aggression, rare. Or,

"Simple assault is very frequent; assault with weapons, common; homicide, rare."

Sl: "Slight"

"All types of [drunken] aggression are rare. Or,

"Verbal conflict is common; all other aggression, rare."

FC 477. Left: 15 cultures where alcoholic aggression is strong

(Table 20 on pages 308–09, Column 10, Code S).

Right: 19 cultures where alcoholic aggression is moderate or slight (same, Code M or Sl).

Unascertained: 366 cultures.

FC 478. Left: 12 cultures where the abandonment or killing of old people is present (Leo W. Simmons 1945: Columns 217, 218, 219, and 220; Code Plus or Equals in at least one of the four columns).

Right: 12 cultures where such abandonment or killing is unimportant or absent (same, Code Minus or Zero on **all** four columns).

Unascertained: 376 cultures.

FC 479 is based on codings done by Joseph Veroff and appearing in David C. McClelland 1961:64–67). Veroff is concerned with the "need to achieve," as inferred from folk tales.

FC 479. Left: 18 cultures where the need to achieve, as inferred from folk tales, is high (McClelland 1961: Table 3.1 on page 66, Code "Above the median in need for achievement").

Right: 18 cultures where this need is low (same, Code "Below the median in need for achievement").

Unascertained: 364 cultures.

FC 480. Left: 14 cultures where the complexity of artistic design is high (Herbert Barry, III 1952: Table III, Code 3.11 or higher).

Right: 15 cultures where such complexity is low (same, Code 3.10 or lower).

Unascertained: 371 cultures.

METHODOLOGICAL SECTION (481–536)

The remaining paragraphs in the printout concern methodological rather than substantive matters. These paragraphs deal with the nationality of the principal ethnographers, the dates of the principal ethnographies, the samples used by the various contributors, and the "whiskers" characteristics. A few of the FCs in this section are run as "subject only," and are hence indicated by a large dot (page 64). The others, however, are run as "subject plus limited eligibility as predicate," and are indicated by a large half-dot. "Limited eligibility" means that an FC is not eligible to appear as a predicate in a paragraph in any of the substantive sections of the printout—i.e. in any of the paragraphs from 1 through 480.*

*For a precise statement of the eligibility of each such FC to appear as a predicate, see the subject listing, as explained on page 29 and as indicated in Chart 2, page 30, Arrow F.

Methodological Section (481–536)

Nationality of Principal Ethnographers (481–85)

All FCs in this subsection derive from the raw characteristic, "Nationality of Principal Ethnographers." A "principal ethnographer" of a culture is an ethnographer listed as a source on that culture by the **EA.** Often there is just one such ethnographer for a culture, often two or three, occasionally more.*

The "nationality" of an ethnographer is determined by two considerations: first, the nation in which he received his professional training, if any, and second, the nation in which he was enculturated. For example, an ethnographer is classified as "French" if he was trained **and** enculturated in France. If he received no professional training but was enculturated in France, he is still classified as French. A **culture** is coded as one whose "principal ethnographers are French" only when **all** of its principal ethnographers (including all co-authors of an ethnography) are French.

Since the **EA** does not provide data on nationality of principal ethnographers, FCs in this section required independent research. Coding assignments were determined either from personal knowledge or from a search of published materials, biographical records, obituaries, etc., available in the library of the Peabody Museum of Archaeology and Ethnology at Harvard University.† The raw attribute code is as follows:

"American": Includes cultures where every principal ethnographer was trained and enculturated in the United States or Canada. 113 cultures.

"British": Includes cultures where every principal ethnographer was trained and enculturated in Great Britain, Australia, New Zealand, or the Union of South Africa. 52 cultures.

"German": Includes cultures where every principal ethnographer was trained and enculturated in Germany, Austria, or the German-speaking portion of Switzerland. 18 cultures.

"French": Includes cultures where every principal ethnographer was trained and enculturated in France or the French-speaking portion of Switzerland. 12 cultures.

"Other": Includes cultures where every principal ethnographer was trained and enculturated in some country other than those listed above. The number of cultures assigned to such countries was invariably so small as not to justify statistical treatment in this **Summary.**‡ This cate-

*Principal ethnographers included here are those listed in the **EA** up to and including vol. 2, No. 1 of **Ethnology** (1963). The actual citations are not included in this **Summary,** as they may be identified by reference to the consolidated version of the **EA** which appears as vol. 6, No. 2 of **Ethnology** (1967:109).

†I am indebted to Hugh A. Blackmer for carrying out the details of this research. However, I am solely responsible for any errors.

‡These were: 5 cultures: Dutch; 4 cultures: Russian; 2 cultures: Belgian, Finnish, Indian, Norwegian; 1 culture: Italian, Japanese, Swedish.

gory also includes "mixed" cases, i.e. where one ethnographer was trained and enculturated in one country, while another ethnographer was trained and enculturated in another. It also includes "mixed" cases in another sense, i.e. where one ethnographer was trained in one country but enculturated in another. 207 cultures.

Unascertained: 12 cultures.

It is hoped that the paragraphs in this subsection will throw some light on the peculiarities of cultures that ethnographers of the principal nationalities have chosen for study. This in turn may assist the reader in arriving at tentative insights of a "sociology of knowledge" character. Paragraph 483, which prints out the significant contrasts between the cultures that have been chosen by American ethnographers versus those chosen by British ethnographers, will perhaps be of particular interest. Some of the statements in this paragraph are relatively obvious, such as Statements 483/8, 15. Others, however, are perhaps sufficiently lacking in obviousness to merit consideration, as for example Statements 483/51, 55, 190, 370, 428.*

◖ FC 481. Left: 113 cultures where the principal ethnographers have been American.
Right: 275 remaining ascertained cultures.
Unascertained: 12 cultures.

◖ FC 482. Left: 52 cultures where the principal ethnographers have been British.
Right: 336 remaining ascertained cultures.
Unascertained: 12 cultures.

◖ FC 483. Left: 113 cultures where the principal ethnographers have been American.
Right: 52 cultures where the principal ethnographers have been British.
Irrelevant: 223 remaining ascertained cultures.
Unascertained: 12 cultures.

● FC 484. Left: 18 cultures where the principal ethnographers have been German.
Right: 370 remaining ascertained cultures.
Unascertained: 12 cultures.

● FC 485. Left: 12 cultures where the principal ethnographers have been French.
Right: 376 remaining ascertained cultures.
Unascertained: 12 cultures.

Date of Principal Ethnographies (486–88)

FCs in this subsection concern the date of publication of each princi-

*Note that FCs 481–83 are run as "subject plus limited eligibility as predicate," as explained on page 176.

pal ethnography, as defined above. These dates are taken from the **EA.** With due reference to marginal frequencies, it was decided to distribute these dates into three raw attribute categories: (1) the period prior to 1930, when anthropology was, so to speak, "coming of age" (2) an intermediate and war-torn period of 1930–49, and (3) the period since 1950. The raw attribute code is as follows:

C: Dates of all principal ethnographies prior to 1930. 32 cultures.

D: Dates of all principal ethnographies between 1930 and 1949. 89 cultures.

E: Dates of all principal ethnographies 1950 or later. 72 cultures.

F: At least one principal ethnography dated prior to 1930 and at least one dated 1930–49; with none dated 1950 or later. 64 cultures.

G: At least one principal ethnography dated 1930–49 and at least one dated 1950 or later; with none dated prior to 1930. 66 cultures.

I: At least one principal ethnography dated prior to 1930 and at least one dated 1950 or later. This category includes some cases with at least one principal ethnography in each of the three periods. 65 cultures.

Unascertained: 12 cultures.

It is hoped that the three paragraphs in this subsection will provide insights into the development of ethnology and ethnography as disciplines. These paragraphs may also provide some safeguard against reporting bias, as ethnographers in the earlier periods are hardly likely to have reported thoroughly on some subjects that only became important later, as theory developed.*

● FC 486. Left: 32 cultures about which the principal ethnographies were published before 1930 (Code C).
Right: 72 cultures about which the principal ethnographies were published in 1950 or after (Code E).
Irrelevant: 284 remaining ascertained cultures (Code D F G or I).
Unascertained: 12 cultures.

◖ FC 487. Left: 32 cultures about which the principal ethnographies were published before 1930 (Code C).
Right: 227 cultures about which the principal ethnographies were published in 1930 or after (Code D E or G).
Irrelevant: 129 remaining ascertained cultures (Code F or I).
Unascertained: 12 cultures.

◖ FC 488. Left: 185 cultures about which the principal ethnog-

*Note that FCs 487 and 488 are run as "subject plus limited eligibility as predicate," as explained on page 176.

raphies were published before 1950 (Code C D or F).

Right: 72 cultures about which the principal ethnographies were published in 1950 or after (Code E).

Irrelevant: 131 remaining ascertained cultures (Code G or I).

Unascertained: 12 cultures.

Contributors' Samples (489–526)

FCs in this subsection in each case consist of a left attribute category that includes every culture in a particular contributor's sample—out of the 400 used in this **Summary.** The right attribute category always includes all other cultures in the 400. As will be made clear in the next chapter (page 188), all but 6 of the 38 contributors' samples as given in this section are smaller than in their original form, due to the loss of some cultures that did not belong to the **EA** sample of 400 cultures. Thus Charles Ackerman's original sample was 62 cultures; of these, 5 did not belong to the 400, so that only 57 were retained. In similar fashion, Albert S. Anthony's original sample of 194 cultures was reduced by 81 cultures—yielding a retention ratio of only 58 per cent. Complete information on these "retention ratios" is given in the next chapter (page 187), permitting the reader to judge in each case whether the ratio is seriously low.

Paragraphs 489–524 inform the reader of the significant attributes of each contributor's sample, when considered vis-à-vis the other cultures in the total culture of 400. Whether these significant attributes constitute serious "biases" is in each case a question for the reader to determine.

In each of the paragraphs through Paragraph 524, predicate-pairs numbered 489 through 524 indicate whether there was a significant overlap between the sample used by one contributor and that used by another—after both samples had been reduced to fit the **EA** total sample of 400. While in most cases the overlap is sufficient to print out as a significant table, it will nonetheless be important in some cases to examine the extent of the overlap. This is indicated by the upper left cell. For example, Table 489/490 indicates that Charles Ackerman's sample on divorce overlaps with Albert S. Anthony's sample on male initiation ceremonies by 25 cultures. No table involving a crossing of an Ackerman FC and an Anthony FC, therefore, could have an N of greater than 25—and often it will be lower because of residual codings in either or both FCs. Where the potential N is low, the reader would do well to bear this in mind in assessing the failure of a potential table to appear in the printout.

Where a contributor has used varying numbers of cultures in coding various items in his study, the phrasing of the appropriate FC in this section will make clear which item's sample is being used. This comment applies to FCs 490, 499, 511, 515, 516, and 517.

If the reader wishes to check which FCs have been constructed from a particular contributor's codings, he may turn to the Bibliography, page 189.

FCs 489 through 524 are indicated by a large half-dot, signifying that their eligibility to appear as predicate-pairs is limited to Paragraphs 489 through 526.

◖ FC 489. Left: 57 cultures included in Charles Ackerman's 1963 study of divorce.
Right: 343 cultures not so included.

◖ FC 490. Left: 113 cultures included in Albert S. Anthony's 1959 sample on male initiation rites.
Right: 287 cultures not so included.

◖ FC 491. Left: 48 cultures included in Dorrian Apple's 1956 study of grandparenthood.
Right: 352 cultures not so included.

◖ FC 492. Left: 39 cultures included in Barbara Chartier Ayres' 1954 study of pregnancy.
Right: 361 cultures not so included.

◖ FC 493. Left: 78 cultures included in Barry, Bacon, and Child's 1967 study of childrearing.
Right: 322 cultures not so included.

◖ FC 494. Left: 29 cultures included in Herbert Barry, III's 1952 study of art.
Right: 371 cultures not so included.

◖ FC 495. Left: 65 cultures included in Judith K. Brown's 1963 study of female initiation rites.
Right: 335 cultures not so included.

◖ FC 496. Left: 55 cultures included in Roy G. D'Andrade's 1961 study of dreams.
Right: 345 cultures not so included.

◖ FC 497. Left: 61 cultures included in William M. Evan's 1963 study of law.
Right: 339 cultures not so included.

◖ FC 498. Left: 51 cultures included in C. S. Ford's 1945 study of sex.
Right: 349 cultures not so included.

◖ FC 499. Left: 86 cultures included in Ford and Beach's 1951 sample on sexual expression by the young.
Right: 314 cultures not so included.

◖ FC 500. Left: 40 cultures included in Freeman and Winch's 1957 study of societal complexity.

Right: 360 cultures not so included.

◖ FC 501. Left: 67 cultures included in Joan Friendly Goodman's 1956 study of ascetic mourning behavior.
Right: 333 cultures not so included.

◖ FC 502. Left: 57 cultures included in John K. Harley's 1963 study of adolescent peer groups.
Right: 343 cultures not so included.

◖ FC 503. Left: 54 cultures included in John M. Hickman's 1962 study of the folk-urban continuum.
Right: 346 cultures not so included.

◖ FC 504. Left: 49 cultures included in Donald Horton's 1943 study of alcoholism.
Right: 351 cultures not so included.

◖ FC 505. Left: 20 cultures included in Merrill Jackson's 1962 study of criminal law and medicine.
Right: 380 cultures not so included.

◖ FC 506. Left: 36 cultures included in Lambert, Triandis, and Wolf's 1959 study of supernatural beings.
Right: 364 cultures not so included.

◖ FC 507. Left: 86 cultures included in James R. Leary's 1961 study of food taboos.
Right: 314 cultures not so included.

◖ FC 508. Left: 40 cultures included in David C. McClelland's 1961 study of achievement motivation.
Right: 360 cultures not so included.

◖ FC 509. Left: 25 cultures included in Moni Nag's 1962 study of fertility.
Right: 375 cultures not so included.

◖ FC 510. Left: 20 cultures included in Raoul Naroll's 1956 study of societal complexity.
Right: 380 cultures not so included.

◖ FC 511. Left: 189 cultures included in Roberts, Arth, and Bush's 1959 sample on games, as modified by the **EA.**
Right: 211 cultures not so included.

◖ FC 512. Left: 33 cultures included in Shirley and Romney's 1962 study of love magic.
Right: 367 cultures not so included.

◖ FC 513. Left: 43 cultures included in Leo W. Simmons' 1945 study of the treatment of the aged.
Right: 357 cultures not so included.

◖ FC 514. Left: 90 cultures included in Philip E. Slater's 1964 study of narcissism.
Right: 310 cultures not so included.

◖ FC 515. Left: 52 cultures included in William N. Stephens' 1962 sample on avoidance relationships. (To be so coded, a culture must be substantively coded in FC 257, 258, or 259.)
Right: 348 cultures not so included.

◖ FC 516. Left: 331 cultures included in Guy E. Swanson's 1960 sample on local jurisdiction, as modified by the **EA.**
Right: 69 cultures not so included.

◖ FC 517. Left: 260 cultures included in Guy E. Swanson's 1960 sample on high gods, as modified by the **EA.**
Right: 140 cultures not so included.

◖ FC 518. Left: 105 cultures included in Stanley H. Udy, Jr.'s 1959a study of work organization.
Right: 295 cultures not so included.

◖ FC 519. Left: 36 cultures included in Joseph Veroff's 1961 study of achievement motivation as revealed in folk tales.
Right: 364 cultures not so included.

◖ FC 520. Left: 40 cultures included in Beatrice Blyth Whiting's 1950 study of sorcery.
Right: 360 cultures not so included.

FC 521 has been excised from the printout, as it represents a contributor's sample used in a preliminary computer run but not in the final run.

◖ FC 522. Left: 82 cultures included in Marjorie Grant Whiting's 1958 study of diet.
Right: 318 cultures not so included.

◖ FC 523. Left: 61 cultures included in Whiting and Child's 1953 study of child training and personality.
Right: 339 cultures not so included.

◖ FC 524. Left: 44 cultures included in Whiting, Kluckhohn, and Anthony's 1958 study of male initiation ceremonies.
Right: 356 cultures not so included.

FCs 525 and 526 attempt to summarize the information in the foregoing paragraphs. FC 525 essentially asks the question: What significant differences distinguish cultures included in at least one contributor's sample from cultures used only in the **EA** sample but not in the sample of any contributor? It will be noted that this is a relatively short paragraph. One reason for its brevity is that cultures in the right attribute category have not been coded for any finished attributes other than those appearing in the **EA**, so that the only predicate-pairs that print out are those derived from the **EA.***

*These include finished attributes derived from contributors' samples that have been expanded by the **EA**, as note in Statements 525/99, 100, 428, 458, and 459. They also include finished attributes derived from George Peter Murdock's "World Ethnographic Sample," as note in Statement 525/84

FC 526 essentially asks the question: What significant differences distinguish cultures included in a rather large number of contributors' samples from cultures used in a smaller number of contributors' samples? "Rather large" here means above the median of 5.5 cultures and "smaller" means below the median. Note that the 155 cultures not used in any contributor's sample have been excluded as irrelevant.

Appendix Five lists the 400 cultures alphabetically, indicating the number of contributors' samples in which each culture appears. Appendix Six lists the cultures in numerical order. It will be noted that this number ranges from a maximum of 27 to a minimum of 1.

- FC 525. Left: 245 cultures included in at least one contributor's sample.
  Right: 155 cultures not included in any contributor's sample.
- FC 526. Left: 108 cultures included in between 6 and 27 contributors' samples.
  Right: 137 cultures included in between 1 and 5 contributors' samples.
  Irrelevant: 155 cultures included in the **EA** sample of 400 but not in any contributor's sample.

"Whiskers" Characteristics (527–36)

FCs 527 through 536 are the "Whiskers" FCs, explained in the section on "A Partial Test of the Meaningfulness of the Findings," page 54. All of the "Whiskers" FCs are run as "subject only," and none of them takes a predicate-pair of a methodological nature—i.e. any predicate-pair numbered from 481 through 536.

and 85. If a potential predicate-pair is derived from some other source, it will not print out, because both cells in its table's right column would contain zeros. The same is true of potential predicate-pairs 489 through 526.

5. Contributors, Sources, and Bibliography

THE PURPOSE of this chapter is to provide a reasonably complete bibliography of sources relevant to cross-cultural statistical research and to provide certain additional information needed to interpret more fully the tables and statements in the printout resulting from use of the codings of the 38 contributors.

IDENTIFYING INITIALS OF CONTRIBUTORS

The phrasing of the clauses for each substantive FC always includes at the end a set of identifying initials to show which contributor—out of the 38—supplied the codings on which that FC is based (Chart 2, page 30, Arrows D and X). There is, however, one exception: If the **Ethnographic Atlas** is the "contributor," then no initials are used. Thus, if a subject-pair or a predicate-pair bears no initials, the reader is safe in assuming that the sole source is the **EA.***

The form taken by a set of initials is governed by four rules:

1. Initials without punctuation indicate the full name of a single contributor. For example "BBW" indicates Beatrice Blyth Whiting.

2. Initials separated by hyphens indicate surnames of joint contributors. For example "R-A-B" indicates Roberts, Arth, and Bush.

3. Initials separated by a comma indicate that one contributor's codings have been modified by another contributor or by the **Ethnographic Atlas.** "Modification" can mean changing the earlier coder's coding of particular cultures, or it can mean applying the earlier coder's categories to additional cultures, or both. For example in FC 457, "R-A-B,

*This rule applies to the substantive FCs only—i.e. FCs 1 through 480. FCs 481 through 536 are of a methodological rather than a substantive nature, and do not require identifying initials.

EA" indicates that Roberts, Arth, and Bush's codings have been modified by the **EA** (page 169).

4. Initials separated by a slash indicate a composite finished characteristic deriving from the codings of two contributors. For example in FC 273, "EA/CA" indicates that codings from both the **EA** and Charles Ackerman have been used (page 131).

Below, in alphabetical order, are listed the initials of all contributors, followed by full identification.

ASA	Albert S. Anthony 1955
B-B-C	Bacon, Barry, and Child 1963 and Barry, Bacon, and Child 1967
BBW	Beatrice Blyth Whiting 1950
BCA	Barbara Chartier Ayres 1954
CA	Charles Ackerman 1963
CSF	C. S. Ford 1945
DA	Dorrian Apple 1956
DCM	David C. McClelland 1961
DH	Donald Horton 1943
F-B	Ford and Beach 1951
F-W	Freeman and Winch 1957
FWM	Frank W. Moore 1963
GES	Guy E. Swanson 1960
GPM	George Peter Murdock 1957a ("World Ethnographic Sample")
HB	Herbert Barry, III 1952
JFG	Joan Friendly Goodman 1956
JKB	Judith K. Brown 1963
JKH	John K. Harley 1963
JMH	John M. Hickman 1962
JRL	James R. Leary 1961
JTW	John T. Westbrook 1963
JV	Joseph Veroff in David C. McClelland 1961
L-T-W	Lambert, Triandis, and Wolf 1959
LWS	Leo W. Simmons 1937 and 1945
MGW	Marjorie Grant Whiting 1958
MJ	Merrill Jackson 1962
MN	Moni Nag 1962
PES	Philip E. Slater 1964
R-A-B	Roberts, Arth, and Bush 1959
RGD	Roy G. D'Andrade 1961
RN	Raoul Naroll 1956
SHU	Stanley H. Udy, Jr. 1959a
S-R	Shirley and Romney 1962
W-C	Whiting and Child 1953

W-D	Whiting and D'Andrade 1962
W-K-A	Whiting, Kluckhohn, and Anthony 1958
WME	William M. Evan 1963
WNS	William N. Stephens 1962

RETENTION RATIOS OF CONTRIBUTORS' SAMPLES

Chart 7 presents the "retention ratio" for each contributor's sample. The retention ratio is simply the percentage of a contributor's original sample of cultures that has been retained for use in this **Summary.** If all of the cultures in a contributor's sample are also included among the **EA**'s sample of 400 cultures, the retention ratio is 100 per cent. As Chart 7 makes clear, the retention ratios range from 100 down to 41 per cent. The semi-interquartile range is from 86 down to 71 per cent. The median is 80 per cent.* Where a contributor's retention ratio is low, the reader would do well to exercise special care in relating statements in the print-out based on that contributor's codings, to conclusions reached by that contributor in his original monograph or article.†

Chart 7 includes six columns. Column 1 lists the contributors in alphabetical order. Column 2 indicates each contributor's identifying initials. Column 3 gives the paragraph in the methodological section to which the reader may turn in order to examine the significant attributes (or biases) of a contributor's sample when contrasted with the rest of the 400 cultures in the **EA** sample.‡ Column 4 indicates the number of cultures in the contributor's original sample. Column 5 indicates how many of those cultures were retained in this **Summary** because they were also included in the **EA** sample of 400 cultures. The figure in Column 6 is the retention ratio, which is obtained by dividing the figure in Column 5 by the figure in Column 4.

*Cultures retained include every culture listed in a contributor's original sample by either its "regular" name or an acceptable "alternative" name, as indicated in the **Ethnographic Atlas,** and as explained on page 13. Somewhat arbitrarily, it was decided to regard the "Hausa" as "Maguzawa," or "Pagan Hausa" (**EA** 1962:126), even though it is recognized that the pagan Hausa are but a small part of the total, largely-Muslim, Hausa population. Since the "Muria" are not listed in the **EA** as an acceptable alternative for the "Gond," the "Muria" were excluded from the four contributors' samples where they appeared. By the same token, the "Twi" were not regarded as Ashanti; nor the "Montagnais" as Naskapi; nor the "Ngonde" as Nyakyusa. The "Twi" appeared in two contributors' samples; the others in one each.

The following clerical errors were detected just prior to going to press, and should be regarded as errata: "Yaghan" (Yahgan) was omitted from the Anthony sample; "Fiji, Lau Islands" (Lau) from Apple; "Siwa" (Siwans) from Ford; "Bunyoro" (Nyoro) from Jackson; "Hausa" (Maguzawa) from Leary; "Suyemura" (Japanese) and "Vetseamites" (Naskapi) from Marjorie Grant Whiting; "Chippewa" (Ojibwa) from Simmons; and "Nyoro" from Udy.

†It need hardly be added that a "low" retention ratio is in no sense necessarily related to the quality of the original study. There are many legitimate reasons why the original study might be based on a sample of cultures that overlaps with the **EA** sample only to a limited degree.

‡These significant attributes apply only to those cultures in the contributor's "**retained** sample," i.e. those cultures retained for use in this **Summary** because included in the **EA** sample of 400 cultures.

CHART 7: Retention Ratios of Contributors' Samples

1. Contributor	2. Initials	3. Paragraph in which sample examined	4. Number of cultures in original sample	5. Number of cultures retained in this **Summary**	6. Retention ratio
Charles Ackerman	CA	489	62	57	.92
Albert S. Anthony	ASA	490	194	113	.58
Dorrian Apple	DA	491	75	48	.64
Barbara Chartier Avres	BCA	492	46	39	.85
Bacon, Barry, and Child	B-B-C	493	110	78	.71
Herbert Barry, III	HB	494	31	29	.93
Judith K. Brown	JKB	495	75	65	.87
Roy G. D'Andrade	RGD	496	57	55	.96
William M. Evan	WME	497	61	61	1.00
C. S. Ford	CSF	498	64	51	.80
Freeman and Winch	F-W	500	48	40	.84
Joan Friendly Goodman	JFG	501	86	67	.78
John K. Harley	JKH	502	71	57	.80
John M. Hickman	JMH	503	70	54	.77
Donald Horton	DH	504	57	49	.86
Merrill Jackson	MJ	505	24	20	.83
Lambert, Triandis, and Wolf	L-T-W	506	43	36	.84
James R. Leary	JRL	507	100	86	.86
David C. McClelland	DCM	508	52	40	.77
Moni Nag	MN	509	61	25	.41
Raoul Naroll	RN	510	30	20	.67
Shirley and Romney	S-R	512	38	33	.87
Leo W. Simmons	LWS	513	71	43	.61
Philip E. Slater	PES	514	90	90	1.00
William N. Stephens	WNS	515	71	52	.73
Stanley H. Udy, Jr.	SHU	518	150	105	.61
Joseph Veroff	JV	519	45	36	.80
Beatrice Blyth Whiting	BBW	520	50	40	.80
Marjorie Grant Whiting	MGW	522	118	82	.69
Whiting and Child	W-C	523	74	61	.82
Whiting, Kluckhohn, and Anthony	W-K-A	524	56	44	.79

There are six contributors' samples that require special discussion. The first two are those of William M. Evan and Philip E. Slater. These two samples were drawn in conjunction with the preparation of this **Summary,** and for this reason have "retention ratios" of 100 per cent—i.e. these two contributors chose for inclusion in their samples only cultures that belonged to the **EA**'s 400. Three additional contributors' samples actually gained in number—i.e. they have retention ratios of greater than 100 per cent. These are the Roberts, Arth, and Bush sample on games and the Swanson samples on local jurisdiction **and** on high gods. All three of these samples were expanded by the **EA**, as indicated on pages 169, 86, and 163, respectively. Finally, there is the Ford and Beach sample on sex (page 155). This sample also gained; cultures that do not appear in the Ford and Beach book were added to it by means of a personal communication from C. S. Ford. None of these latter four cases of "gain" is included in Chart 7. They are, however, included in the Methodological Section of the printout in Paragraphs 511, 515, 516, and 499.*

BIBLIOGRAPHY

In the bibliographical list below, the names of the 38 contributors of codings to this **Summary**, with their initials, are indicated by asterisks. Each such entry also includes the numbers of all FCs derived in whole or in part from that contributor's codings. Also included, where available, are citations of various reviews or commentaries written about the source, which the reader intending to make serious use of statements deriving from a particular contributor's codings may wish to consult. The bibliography also includes a listing of other sources relevant to content and method in the field of cross-cultural statistical research. A more complete cross-cultural bibliography, prepared by Timothy J. O'Leary of the Human Relations Area Files, will be published by HRAF Press in the near future.

Aberle, David F.
1961 Matrilineal descent in cross-cultural perspective. **In** Matrilineal Kinship, David M. Schneider and Kathleen Gough, eds. Berkeley, University of California Press. Pp. 655–727.

Ackerknecht, Erwin H.
1954 On the comparative method in anthropology. **In** Method and Perspective in Anthropology, Robert F. Spencer, ed. Minneapolis, University of Minnesota Press. Pp. 117–25.

* Ackerman, Charles (CA)
1963 Affiliations: structural determinants of differential divorce rates. American Journal of Sociology 69:13–20. Codings used in constructing FCs 272–76, 489.

* Anthony, Albert S. (ASA)
1955 A cross-cultural study of male initiation. Unpublished doctoral dissertation.

*For a variety of technical reasons, Chart 7 does not include retention ratios for Frank W. Moore's sample on natural environment, George Peter Murdock's sample on level of political integration, the John T. Westbrook/**Ethnographic Atlas** sample on premarital sex relations, or the Whiting and D'Andrade sample appearing in William N. Stephens 1962.

Cambridge, Harvard University, Graduate School of Education. Codings used in constructing FCs 372, 375, 376, 379, 490.

* Apple, Dorrian (DA)
1956 The social structure of grandparenthood. American Anthropologist 58: 656–63. Codings used in constructing FCs 254, 256, 491. See also: Sweetser, Dorrian Apple.

Armsen, P.
1955 Tables for significance tests of 2 x 2 contingency tables. Biometrika 42: 494–511.

* Ayres, Barbara Chartier (BCA)
1954 A cross-cultural study of factors relating to pregnancy taboos. Unpublished doctoral dissertation. Cambridge, Radcliffe College. Codings used in constructing FCs 282, 283, 285, 286, 292–96, 492.

Bacon, Margaret K., Herbert Barry, III, and Irvin L. Child
1965 A cross-cultural study of drinking: II. relations to other features of the culture. Quarterly Journal of Studies on Alcohol, Supplement 3:29–48.

Bacon, Margaret K., Herbert Barry, III, Irvin L. Child, and Charles R. Snyder
1965 A cross-cultural study of drinking: V. detailed definitions and data. Quarterly Journal of Studies on Alcohol, Supplement 3:78–111.

* Bacon, Margaret K., Irvin L. Child, and Herbert Barry, III (B-B-C)
1963 A cross-cultural study of correlates of crime. Journal of Abnormal and Social Psychology 66:241–300. Used in constructing FCs 148 and 149. This article describes the codings but does not state coding assignments. Codings and explanatory materials for these FCs can be obtained from Prof. Herbert Barry, III, Department of Pharmacology, School of Pharmacy, University of Pittsburgh, Pittsburgh, Pa. See also: Barry, Bacon, and Child, 1967.

Banks, Arthur S. and Phillip M. Gregg
1965 Grouping political systems: Q-factor analysis of **A Cross-Polity Survey.** American Behavioral Scientist 9:3–6.

Banks, Arthur S. and Robert B. Textor
1963 A cross-polity survey. Cambridge, Mass. The M.I.T. Press. For reviews, see: Philip E. Converse 1964; Phillips Cutright 1964; Harold Guetzkow 1965; and Michael Haas 1966.

* Barry, Herbert, III (HB)
1952 Influence of socialization on the graphic arts: a cross-cultural study. Unpublished honors thesis. Cambridge, Harvard College, Department of Social Relations. Codings used in constructing FCs 480 and 494.

Barry, Herbert, III
1957 Relationships between child training and the pictorial arts. Journal of Abnormal and Social Psychology 54:380–83.

* Barry, Herbert, III, Margaret K. Bacon, and Irvin L. Child (B-B-C)
1967 Definitions, ratings, and bibliographic sources for child-training practices of 110 cultures. In Cross-Cultural Approaches, Clellan S. Ford, ed. New Haven, HRAF Press. Pp. 293–331. Previously unpublished codings used in constructing FCs 317–28, 330, 334, 336–55, 493.

Barry, Herbert, III, Margaret K. Bacon, and Irvin L. Child

1957 A cross-cultural survey of some sex differences in socialization. Journal of Abnormal and Social Psychology 55:327–32.

Barry, Herbert, III, Charles Buchwald, Irvin L. Child, and Margaret K. Bacon

1965 A cross-cultural study of drinking: IV. comparisons with Horton ratings. Quarterly Journal of Studies on Alcohol, Supplement 3:62–77.

Barry, Herbert, III, Irvin L. Child, and Margaret K. Bacon

1959 Relation of child training to subsistence economy. American Anthropologist 61:51–63.

Bayley, Nancy

1954 Review of Whiting and Child 1953. Psychological Bulletin 51:313–15.

Beals, Alan R.

1964 Food is to eat: the nature of subsistence activity. American Anthropologist 66:134–36.

Befu, Harumi

1966 Political complexity and village community: test of an hypothesis. Anthropological Quarterly 39:43–52.

Bennett, Wendell C.

1953 Area archeology. American Anthropologist 55:5–16.

Berry, Brewton

1946 Review of Leo W. Simmons 1945. American Sociological Review 11:768–69.

Beshers, James M.

1964 Review of Raoul Naroll 1962. American Journal of Sociology 70:131.

Blalock, Hubert M., Jr.

1960 Correlational analysis and causal inferences. American Anthropologist 62:624–31.

Boas, Franz

1896 The limitations of the comparative method in anthropology. Science, N.S. 4:901–08.

1927 Anthropology and statistics. In The Social Sciences and their Interrelations, W. F. Ogburn and A. Goldenweiser, eds. Boston, Houghton Mifflin. Pp. 114–21.

Bohannan, Laura M.

1951 A comparative study of social differentiation in primitive society. Unpublished doctoral dissertation. Oxford, University of Oxford.

* Brown, Judith K. (JKB)

1963 A cross-cultural study of female initiation rites. American Anthropologist 65:837–53. Codings used in constructing FCs 127, 382, 383, 495.

Buchler, I. R.

1964a A formal account of the Hawaiian- and Eskimo-type kinship terminologies. Southwestern Journal of Anthropology 20:286–318.

1964b Measuring the development of kinship terminologies: scalogram and transformational accounts of Crow-type systems. American Anthropologist 66:765–88.

Burton, Michael L.

1965 Cluster analysis of data from the **Cross-Cultural Summary.** Mimeographed Master's essay. Stanford, Calif., Stanford University.

Burton, Roger V. and John W. M. Whiting
1961 The absent father and cross-sex identity. Merrill-Palmer Quarterly of Behavior and Development 7:85–95.
Carneiro, Robert L.
1962 Scale analysis as an instrument for the study of cultural evolution. Southwestern Journal of Anthropology 18:149–69.
1968 Scaling levels of civilization. **In** Naroll and Cohen 1968.
Child, Irvin L.
1954 Socialization. **In** Handbook of Social Psychology, vol. 2, Gardner Lindzey, ed. Cambridge, Addison-Wesley Publishing Company, Inc. Pp. 655–92.
Child, Irvin L., Margaret K. Bacon, and Herbert Barry, III
1965 A cross-cultural study of drinking: I. descriptive measurements of drinking customs. Quarterly Journal of Studies on Alcohol, Supplement 3:1–28.
Child, Irvin L., Herbert Barry, III, and Margaret K. Bacon
1965 A cross-cultural study of drinking: III. sex differences. Quarterly Journal of Studies on Alcohol, Supplement 3:49–61.
Clements, Forrest E.
1931 Plains Indian tribal correlations with sun dance data. American Anthropologist, N.S. 33:216–27.
1954 The use of cluster analysis with anthropological data. American Anthropologist 56:180–99.
Clignet, Remi
1968 Concomitant variation studies: a critical review. **In** Naroll and Cohen 1968.
Cohen, Yehudi A.
1961a Food and its vicissitudes: a cross-cultural study of sharing and non-sharing. **In** Social Structure and Personality: A Casebook, Yehudi A. Cohen, ed. New York, Holt, Rinehart, and Winston. Pp. 312–50.
1961b Patterns of friendship. **In** Social Structure and Personality: A Casebook, Yehudi A. Cohen, ed. New York, Holt, Rinehart, and Winston. Pp. 351–86.
1964a The transition from childhood to adolescence: cross-cultural studies of initiation ceremonies, legal systems, and incest taboos. Chicago, Aldine Publishing Company. For review, see: Melvin Ember 1965.
1964b The establishment of identity in a social nexus: the special case of initiation ceremonies and their relation to value and legal systems. American Anthropologist 66:529–52.
Converse, Philip E.
1964 Review of Banks and Textor 1963. American Political Science Review 58: 679–80.
Coult, Allan D. and Robert W. Habenstein
1965 Cross-tabulations of Murdock's **World Ethnographic Sample.** Columbia, Mo., University of Missouri Press.
CPS See Banks and Textor 1963.
Crockett, Harry J.
1962 Review of David C. McClelland 1961. Social Forces 41:208–09.
Cutright, Phillips
1964 Review of Banks and Textor 1963. American Sociological Review 29:635–36.

1965 Political structure, economic development, and national social security programs. American Journal of Sociology 70:537–50.

* D'Andrade, Roy G. (RGD)

1961 Anthropological studies of dreams. In Psychological Anthropology: Approaches to Culture and Personality, Francis L. K. Hsu, ed. Homewood, Ill., Dorsey Press. Pp. 296–332. Codings used in constructing FCs 444, 496.

D'Andrade, Roy G.

1962 See William N. Stephens 1962.

1966 Sex differences and cultural institutions. In The Development of Sex Differences, Eleanor Maccoby, ed. Stanford, Calif., Stanford University Press. Pp. 174–204.

Davie, Maurice Rea

1929 The evolution of war: a study of its role in early societies. New Haven, Yale University Press.

Davis, Kingsley

1950 Review of George Peter Murdock 1949. American Sociological Review 15: 138–40.

Devereux, George

1955 A study of abortion in primitive societies. New York, Julian Press.

DeVos, George

1963 Review of William N. Stephens 1962. Contemporary Psychology 8:434–38.

Dole, Gertrude E.

1965 The lineage pattern of kinship nomenclature: its significance and development. Southwestern Journal of Anthropology 21:36–62.

Driver, Edwin D.

1964 Review of Moni Nag 1962. American Journal of Sociology 69:669.

Driver, Harold E.

1939 Culture element distributions: X, northwest California. University of California Anthropological Records 1:297–433.

1941 Girls' puberty rites in western North America. University of California Anthropological Records 6:21–90.

1953 Statistics in anthropology. American Anthropologist 55:42–59.

1956 An integration of functional, evolutionary, and historical theory by means of correlations. Indiana University Publications in Anthropology and Linguistics, Memoir 12:1–36.

1961 Indians of North America. Chicago, University of Chicago Press.

1966 Geographical-historical versus psycho-functional explanations of kin avoidances. Current Anthropology 7:131–60, 176–82.

1968 Statistical trait distribution studies. In Naroll and Cohen 1968.

Driver, Harold E. and Alfred L. Kroeber

1932 Quantitative expression of cultural relationships. University of California Publications in American Archaeology and Ethnology 31:211–56.

Driver, Harold E. and William C. Massey

1957 Comparative studies of North American Indians. Transactions of the American Philosophical Society 47:165–460.

Driver, Harold E. and Peggy R. Sanday

1966 Factors and clusters of kin avoidances and related variables. Current Anthropology 7:169–76.

Driver, Harold E. and Karl F. Schuessler

1957 Factor analysis of ethnographic data. American Anthropologist 59:655–63.

EA See Ethnographic Atlas.

Eggan, Fred

1954 Social anthropology and the method of controlled comparison. American Anthropologist 56:743–63.

1965 Some reflections on comparative method in anthropology. **In** Context and Meaning in Cultural Anthropology, Melford E. Spiro, ed. New York, The Free Press of Glencoe. Pp. 357–72.

Eisenstadt, S. N.

1956 From generation to generation: age-groups and social structure. London, Routledge and Kegan Paul.

Elashoff, Robert M.

1963 Multivariate two-sample problems with discrete and continuous variables. Unpublished doctoral dissertation. Cambridge, Harvard University.

Ellegard, Alvar

1959 Statistical measurement of linguistic relationship. Language 35:131–56.

Ellis, Robert A.

1963 Review of William N. Stephens 1962. American Journal of Sociology 69: 211.

Ember, Melvin

1963a The relationship between economic and political development in non-industrialized societies. Ethnology 2:228–48.

1963b A new interpretation of the extension of incest taboos. Manuscript.

1965 Review of Yehudi A. Cohen 1964. American Anthropologist 67:1039–40.

Ember, Melvin and Carol R. Baldwin

1965 The conditions that favor matrilocal and patrilocal residence. American Anthropological Association Abstracts, 64th Annual Meetings: 18.

1966 The conditions that favor bilocal residence. American Anthropological Association Abstracts, 65th Annual Meeting: 17.

1967 Patterns of marital residence. Forthcoming book.

Erasmus, Charles John

1950 Patolli, pachisi, and the limitation of possibilities. Southwestern Journal of Anthropology 6:369–87.

1962 Review of David C. McClelland 1961. American Anthropologist 64:622–25.

Ethnographic Atlas (Abbreviated "**EA**")

1962ff. Appears in installments in the quarterly journal, **Ethnology,** edited by Prof. George Peter Murdock. In this **Summary,** citations will be to **EA,** followed by the year and page number.

* Evan, William M. (WME)

1963 Unpublished codings on law. Codings used in constructing FCs 117–26, 143–46, 497.

Evans-Pritchard, Edward Evan

1963 The comparative method in social anthropology. London University, King's College, L. T. Hobhouse Memorial Trust Lectures 33.

Field, Peter B.
1962 A new cross-cultural study of drunkenness. In Society, Culture, and Drinking Patterns, D. J. Pittman and C. R. Snyder, eds. New York, John Wiley. Pp. 48–74.
Fischer, John L.
1961 Art styles as cultural cognitive maps. American Anthropologist 63:79–93.
* Ford, Clellan S. (CSF)
1945 A comparative study of human reproduction. Yale University Publications in Anthropology 32. Codings used in constructing FCs 284, 287–91, 297, 387, 388, 394, 498. For review, see: H. Scudder Mekeel 1946.
Ford, Clellan S.
1939 Society, culture, and the human organism. Journal of General Psychology 20:135–79.
* Ford, Clellan S. and Frank A. Beach (F-B)
1951 Patterns of sexual behavior. New York: Harper & Brothers. Codings used in constructing FCs 374, 380, 385, 386, 393, 400, 499. For reviews, see: Allan R. Holmberg 1951; Margaret Mead 1952; and Eliot Stellar 1952.
* Freeman, Linton D. and Robert F. Winch (F-W)
1957 Societal complexity: an empirical test of a typology of societies. American Journal of Sociology 62:461–66. Codings used in constructing FCs 91, 500.
Friedman, G. A.
1950 A cross-cultural study of the relationship between independence training and achievement as revealed by mythology. Unpublished honors thesis. Cambridge, Harvard University.
Friendly, Joan P.
See Goodman, Joan Friendly.
Gamson, William A.
1962 Review of Guy E. Swanson 1960. Contemporary Psychology 7:23–24.
Gayton, Anna H.
1946 Review of Leo W. Simmons 1945. American Anthropologist, N.S. 48:649–50.
Gebhard, Paul H.
1963 Review of Moni Nag 1962. American Anthropologist 65:970–71.
Gladwin, Thomas
1954 Review of Whiting and Child 1953. American Anthropologist 56:893–97.
*Goodman, Joan Friendly (JFG)
1956 A cross-cultural study of ascetic mourning behavior. Unpublished honors thesis. Cambridge, Radcliffe College. Codings used in constructing FCs 434, 437, 438, 501.
Goodman, Leo A. and William H. Kruskal
1954 Measures of association for cross classifications. Journal of the American Statistical Association 49:732–64.
1959 Measures of association for cross classifications. II: further discussion and references. Journal of the American Statistical Association 54:123–63.
Gouldner, Alvin W. and Richard A. Peterson.
1962 Notes on technology and the moral order. Indianapolis: Bobbs-Merrill Co. For review, see: Arthur L. Stinchcombe 1964.
Gregg, Phillip M. and Arthur S. Banks

1965 Dimensions of political systems: factor analysis of **A Cross-Polity Survey.** American Political Science Review 59:602–14.
Gross, Llewellyn
1950 Review of George Peter Murdock 1949. American Journal of Sociology 55:498–500.
Guetzkow, Harold
1965 Review of Banks and Textor 1963. American Anthropologist 67: 137–39.
Guilford, Joy Paul
1956 Fundamental statistics in psychology and education. 3d ed. New York, McGraw-Hill.
Haas, Michael
1966 Aggregate analysis. World Politics 19: 106–21. Review article on Banks and Textor 1963, and two other books.
*Harley, John K. (JKH)
1963 Adolescent youths in peer groups: a cross-cultural study. Unpublished doctoral dissertation. Cambridge, Harvard University. Codings used in constructing FCs 260, 356–69, 397, 502.
Heath, Dwight B.
1958 Sexual division of labor and cross-cultural research. Social Forces 37: 77–79.
Heinicke, Christoph and Beatrice Blyth Whiting
1953 Bibliographies on personality and social development of the child. Social Science Research Council Pamphlet 10.
Herskovits, Melville J.
1954 Some problems of method in ethnography. **In** Method and Perspective in Anthropology, Robert F. Spencer, ed. Minneapolis, University of Minnesota Press. Pp. 3–24.
*Hickman, John M. (JMH)
1962 Dimensions of a complex concept: a method exemplified. Human Organization 21:214–18. Codings used in constructing FCs 77, 78, 115, 116, 132, 140–42, 424, 467–70, 503.
Hobhouse, L. T., G. C. Wheeler, and M. Ginsberg
1965 The Material Culture and Social Institutions of the Simpler Peoples: An Essay in Correlation, L. T. Hobhouse, G. C. Wheeler and M. Ginsberg. London, Routledge and Kegan Paul. Pp. 1–15. Also **in** Readings in Cross-Cultural Methodology, Frank W. Moore, ed. New Haven, HRAF Press, 1966. Pp. 26–39.
Höltker, Georg
1949 Review of Leo W. Simmons 1945. Anthropos 41–44: 959–60.
Hollingshead, August B.
1953 Review of Whiting and Child 1953. Rural Sociology 18: 388–89.
Holmberg, Allan R.
1951 Review of Ford and Beach 1951. American Sociological Review 16:578–79.
Homans, George C. and David M. Schneider
1955 Marriage, authority and final causes: a study of unilateral cross-cousin marriage. Glencoe, The Free Press.
Honigmann, John J.

1961 Review of Guy E. Swanson 1960. Social Forces 39:356–57.

*Horton, Donald (DH)

1943 The functions of alcohol in primitive societies: a cross-cultural study. Quarterly Journal of Studies on Alcohol 4:199–320. Codings used in constructing FCs 418, 445, 476, 477, 504.

Hoselitz, Bert F.

1962 Review of David C. McClelland 1961. American Journal of Sociology 68: 129–30.

Hsu, Francis L. K.

1961 Psychological anthropology: approaches to culture and personality. Homewood, Ill., Dorsey Press.

Human Relations Area Files

1965 Guide to the use of the Human Relations Area Files. New Haven, Human Relations Area Files.

Hymes, Dell H.

1960 Lexicostatistics so far. Current Anthropology 1:3–44.

Hymes, Dell H., ed.

1965 The use of computers in anthropology. Studies in General Anthropology 2. The Hague, Mouton & Co.

*Jackson, Merrill (MJ)

1962 A study of the evolution of social control: the organization, theory and practice of jurisprudence and medicine. Ann Arbor, Mich., Mental Health Research Institute, University of Michigan. For limited circulation. Codings used in constructing FCs 93, 150–174, 505.

Jorgensen, Joseph J. G.

1966 Geographical clusterings and functional explanations of in-law avoidances: an analysis of comparative method. Current Anthropology 7:161–69.

Joseph, Alice, Rosamond B. Spicer, and Jane Chesky

1949 The desert people: a study of the Papago Indians. Chicago, University of Chicago Press. Page 72: ". . . the native religion is still important in varying degree to all the Papago except the strictest Presbyterians. However, even some of the most ardent followers of the old religion are also Sonora or Roman Catholics."

Kalleberg, Arthur L.

1966 The logic of comparison: a methodological note on the comparative structure of political systems. World Politics 19:69–82.

Karsten, Rafael

1955 The religion of the Samek: ancient beliefs and cults of the Scandinavian and Finnish Lapps. Leiden, E. J. Brill.

Kay, Brian R.

1957 The reliability of HRAF coding procedures. American Anthropologist 59: 524–27.

Kimball, Solon T.

1946 Review of Leo W. Simmons 1945. American Journal of Sociology 52:287.

Kirchhoff, Paul

1948 The Warrau. Bulletin of the Bureau of American Ethnology 143, volume 3:869–81. Washington, Smithsonian Institution. Page 879: "A belief in a supreme being has been reported. Competent students doubt whether this is an original Warrau belief, but no details are known."

Klimek, Stanislaw
1935 The structure of California Indian culture. University of California Publications in American Archaeology and Ethnology 37:1–70.

Kluckhohn, Clyde
1939 On certain recent applications of association coefficients to ethnological data. American Anthropologist, N.S. 41:345–77.
1953 Universal categories of culture. In Anthropology Today: An Encyclopedic Inventory. Alfred L. Kroeber, ed. Chicago, University of Chicago Press. Pp. 507–23.

Köbben, André J. F.
1952 New ways of presenting an old idea: the statistical method in social anthropology. Journal of the Royal Anthropological Institute of Great Britain and Ireland 82:129–46. Reprinted in Frank W. Moore 1966, pp. 166–92.
1965 The cross-cultural method. Paper presented to the Roundtable on Comparative Research, International Social Science Council, Paris, April 22–24. Unpublished.
1966 Comparativists and non-comparativists in anthropology. Paper given at the Symposium on Cross-Cultural Research Tools in Comparative Social Anthropology, Paris, 19–22 September 1966.
1967 Why exceptions? The logic of cross-cultural comparison. Current Anthropology 8:3–34.
1968 Taxonomy in comparative studies. In Naroll and Cohen 1968.

Kroeber, Alfred L.
1939 Cultural and natural areas of native North America. University of California Publications in American Archaeology and Ethnology 38.
1952 The ancient oikoumenê as a historic culture aggregate. In The Nature of Culture, by Alfred L. Kroeber. Chicago, University of Chicago Press. Pp. 379–95.
1954 Critical summary and commentary. In Method and Perspective in Anthropology, Robert F. Spencer, ed. Minneapolis, University of Minnesota Press. Pp. 273–99.
1960 Statistics, Indo-European, and taxonomy. Language 36:1–21.

Kroeber, Alfred L. and C. Douglas Chrétien
1937 Quantitative classification of Indo-European languages. Language 13: 83–103.

Lambert, William W.
1962 Review of Guy E. Swanson 1960. American Journal of Psychology 75: 704–05.

* Lambert, William W., Leigh Minturn Triandis, and Margery Wolf (L-T-W)
1959 Some correlates of beliefs in the malevolence and benevolence of supernatural beings—a cross-cultural study. Journal of Abnormal and Social Psychology 58:162–69. Codings used in constructing FCs 425, 506.

Landauer, Thomas K. and John W. M. Whiting
1964 Infantile stimulation and adult stature of human males. American Anthropologist 66:1007–28.

Landis, Judson T.
1946 Review of Leo W. Simmons 1945. Rural Sociology 11:69–70.
Leach, Edmund R.
1950 Review of George Peter Murdock 1949. Man 50:107–08.
1960 Review of Stanley H. Udy, Jr. 1959. American Sociological Review 25: 136–38. A number of Leach's indictments would appear to be general indictments of the cross-cultural statistical technique, rather than indictments limited just to the volume under review.
* Leary, James R. (JRL)
1961 Food taboos and level of culture: a cross-cultural study. New Haven, Human Relations Area Files. Mimeographed. Codings used in constructing FCs 448–50, 507.
LeBar, Frank M.
1968 Coding ethnographic data. **In** Naroll and Cohen 1968.
LeVine, Robert A.
1960 The role of the family in authority systems: a cross-cultural application of the stimulus-generalization theory. Behavioral Science 5:291–96.
LeVine, Robert A. and Donald T. Campbell
1961 A proposal for cooperative cross-cultural research on ethnocentrism. Journal of Conflict Resolution 5:82–108.
Levy, Marion J., Jr. and Lloyd A. Fallers
1959 The family: some comparative considerations. American Anthropologist 61:647–51.
Lewis, Don and C. J. Burke
1949 The use and misuse of the Chi-square test. Psychological Bulletin 46:433–89.
Lewis, Oscar
1956 Comparisons in cultural anthropology. **In** Current Anthropology: A Supplement to Anthropology Today, William L. Thomas, ed. Chicago, University of Chicago Press, Pp. 259–92. Also **in** Readings in Cross-Cultural Methodology, Frank W. Moore, ed. New Haven, HRAF Press, 1966. Pp. 50–85.
Lindstrom, D. E.
1965 Review of Meyer F. Nimkoff 1965. Rural Sociology 30:491–93.
Lindzey, Gardner
1961 Projective techniques and cross-cultural research. New York, Appleton-Century-Crofts.
Lumholtz, Carl
1902 Unknown Mexico. New York, Charles Scribners' Sons. Vol. 1, p. 295: "The pagans or **gentiles** in the barrancas say that they have two gods, but no devil. These gods are Father Sun (Nonorúgami) and Mother Moon (Yerúgami). . . . But the greater part of the Tarahumares are nominally Christians, . . . they have adapted the words **Tata** (Father) **Dios** (God) for their Father Sun."
* McClelland, David C. (DCM)
1961 The achieving society. Princeton, D. Van Nostrand. Codings used in constructing FCs 453–56, 508. Also contains codings credited to Joseph Veroff. For reviews, see: Harry J. Crockett 1962; Charles J. Erasmus 1962;

Bert F. Hoselitz 1962; Bernard Mausner 1963; and James N. Morgan 1963.

McClelland, David C. and G. A. Friedman
1952 A cross-cultural study of the relationship between child-training practices and achievement motivation appearing in folk-tales. In Readings in Social Psychology, Guy E. Swanson, Theodore M. Newcomb, and Eugene L. Hartley, eds. Rev. ed. New York, Henry Holt & Company. Pp. 243–49.

Madison, Peter
1964 Review of William N. Stephens 1962. American Journal of Psychology 77: 332–35.

Mausner, Bernard
1963 Review of David C. McClelland 1961. Contemporary Psychology 8:291–92.

Mead, Margaret
1952 Review of Ford and Beach 1951. American Anthropologist 54:75–76.

Mekeel, H. Scudder
1946 Review of Ford 1945. American Journal of Sociology 52:78–79.

Milke, Wilhelm
1949 The quantitative distribution of cultural similarities and their cartographic representation. American Anthropologist, N.S. 51:237–51.
1955 Theorie der kulterellen Ähnlichkeit. Mimeographed. Geseke (Westf.).

Minn, Eeva K.
1955 The Lapps. Bloomington, Ind., Subcontractor's Monograph HRAF-3, Indiana-6, prepared for the Human Relations Area Files. Page 71: "Although Christianity has been adopted by the Lapps in all areas, a number of pagan beliefs and practices have survived in distant regions until the present day." In 1876 the Finnish linguist, Arvid Benetz, was able to obtain a list of 16 major divinities; for details, see Karsten 1955.

* Moore, Frank W. (FWM)
1962 Unpublished codings on type of natural environment. New Haven, Human Relations Area Files. Codings used in constructing FCs 33–43.

Moore, Frank W.
1968 The Human Relations Area Files. In Naroll and Cohen 1968.

Moore, Frank W., ed.
1966 Readings in cross-cultural methodology. New Haven, HRAF Press. Distributed by Taplinger Publishing Co., New York. Original printing 1961, reset and reprinted in 1966.

Moore, Sally Falk
1964 Descent and symbolic filiation. American Anthropologist 66:1308–20.

Morant, Geoffrey McKay
1935 Cultural anthropology and statistics: a one-sided review of "Sex and Culture." Man 35:34–39.

Morgan, James N.
1963 Review of David C. McClelland 1961. Contemporary Psychology 8:289–91.

Mosteller, Frederick and Robert R. Bush
1954 Selected quantitative techniques. In Handbook of Social Psychology, vol.

1, Gardner Lindzey, ed. Cambridge, Addison-Wesley Publishing Company, Inc. Pp. 289–334.

Mueller, John H. and Karl F. Schuessler
1961 Statistical reasoning in sociology. Boston, Houghton Mifflin.

* Murdock, George Peter (GPM)
1957a World ethnographic sample. American Anthropologist 59:664–87. Codings used in constructing FCs 84–87. It should be noted that Murdock and his associates have also assembled the **Ethnographic Atlas** (**EA**), which is the principal source of codings for this **Summary.** For simplicity's sake, however, FCs derived solely from the **EA** bear no identifying initials, and it can be assumed that FCs bearing no initials derive solely from the **EA.** If, as explained on page 185, codings from the **EA** have been used in conjunction with codings from other contributors, then the initials "**EA**" will be included in the identification.

Murdock, George Peter
1937a Comparative data on division of labor by sex. Social Forces 15:551–53.
1937b Correlations of matrilineal and patrilineal institutions. **In** Studies in the Science of Society, George Peter Murdock, ed. New Haven, Yale University Press. Pp. 445–70.
1940 The cross-cultural survey. American Sociological Review 5:361–70.
1945 The common denominator of cultures. **In** The Science of Man in the World Crisis, Ralph Linton, ed. New York, Columbia University Press. Pp. 123–42.
1947 Bifurcate merging, a test of five theories. American Anthropologist, N.S. 49:56–68.
1949 Social structure. New York, Macmillan. For reviews, see: Kingsley Davis 1950; Llewellyn Gross 1950; E. R. Leach 1950; Morris Edward Opler 1950; and F. Steiner 1951.
1950 Family stability in non-European cultures. Annals of the American Academy of Political and Social Science 272:195–201.
1953 The processing of anthropological materials. **In** Anthropology Today: An Encyclopedic Inventory, Alfred L. Kroeber, ed. Chicago, University of Chicago Press. Pp. 476–87.
1957b Anthropology as a comparative science. Behavioral Science 2:249–54.
1958 African cultural summaries. New Haven, Human Relations Area Files. About the Bozo (MS6): "They have been Moslems since the 14th Century."
1962ff. See "Ethnographic Atlas."
1963 Outline of world cultures. 3rd edition, revised. New Haven, Human Relations Area Files.
1964 Cultural correlates of the regulation of premarital sex behavior. **In** Robert A. Manners, ed. Process and Pattern in Culture: Essays in Honor of Julian H. Steward. Chicago, Aldine Publishing Company. Pp. 399–410.
1966 Cross-cultural sampling. Ethnology 5:97–114.
1968 The cross-cultural survey—a historical review. **In** Naroll and Cohen 1968.

Murdock, George Peter et al.
1965 Outline of cultural materials. 4th revised edition, second printing with modifications. New Haven, Human Relations Area Files.

* Nag, Moni (MN)
1962 Factors affecting human fertility in nonindustrial societies: a cross-cultural study. Yale University Publications in Anthropology 66. Codings used in constructing FCs 280, 281, 401, 509. For reviews, see: Edwin D. Driver 1964; and Paul H. Gebhard 1963.
Naroll, Frada, Raoul Naroll, and Forrest H. Howard
1961 Position of women in childbirth. American Journal of Obstetrics and Gynecology 82:943–54.
* Naroll, Raoul (RN)
1956 A preliminary index of social development. American Anthropologist 58:687–715. Codings used in constructing FCs 92, 510.
Naroll, Raoul
1961 Two solutions to Galton's problem. Philosophy of Science 28:15–39.
1962 Data quality control. New York, The Free Press of Glencoe. For reviews, see: James M. Beshers 1964; and Albert C. Spaulding 1965.
1964a On ethnic unit classification. Current Anthropology 5:283–312.
1964b A fifth solution to Galton's problem. American Anthropologist 66: 863–67.
1968a Cross-cultural sampling—a general review. **In** Naroll and Cohen 1968.
1968b The cross-historical survey. **In** Naroll and Cohen 1968.
1968c Data quality control. **In** Naroll and Cohen 1968.
1968d Galton's problem. **In** Naroll and Cohen 1968.
1968e The societal unit of comparison. **In** Naroll and Cohen 1968.
Naroll, Raoul and Ronald Cohen, eds.
1968 A handbook of method in cultural anthropology. New York, Natural History Press. Forthcoming book.
Nash, Manning
1960 Review of Stanley H. Udy, Jr. 1959. American Anthropologist 62:161–62.
Needham, Rodney
1964 Descent, category, and alliance in Sirionó society. Southwestern Journal of Anthropology 20:229–40.
Nieboer, Herman Jeremias
1910 Slavery as an industrial system: ethnological researches. 2d revised edition. The Hague, M. Nijhoff.
Nimkoff, Meyer F.
1954 Review of Whiting and Child 1953. American Sociological Review 19: 364–66.
Nimkoff, Meyer F., ed.
1965 Comparative family systems. Boston, Houghton Mifflin. For review, see: D. E. Lindstrom 1965.
Nimkoff, Meyer F. and Russell Middleton
1960 Types of family and types of economy. American Journal of Sociology 66:215–25.
Norbeck, Edward, Donald E. Walker, and Mimi Cohen
1962 The interpretation of data: puberty rites. American Anthropologist 64: 463–86.
Opler, Morris Edward

1950 Review of George Peter Murdock 1949. American Anthropologist 52:77–80.

Osmond, Marie Withers
1964 Toward monogamy: a cross-cultural study of correlates of types of marriage. Unpublished Master's thesis. Tallahassee, Florida State University.

Otterbein, Keith F. and Charlotte Swanson Otterbein
1965 An eye for an eye, a tooth for a tooth: a cross-cultural study of feuding. American Anthropologist 67:1470–82.

Pilling, Arnold R.
1962 Statistics, sorcery, and justice. American Anthropologist 64:1057–59. A commentary on Beatrice Blyth Whiting 1950.

Radcliffe-Brown, A. R.
1951 The comparative method in social anthropology. Journal of the Royal Anthropological Institute of Great Britain and Ireland 81:15–22.

Rao, C. Radhakrishna
1952 Advanced statistical methods in biometric research. New York, John Wiley and Sons.

Riley, Matilda White, John W. Riley, Jr., and Jackson Toby
1954 Sociological studies in scale analysis. New Brunswick, Rutgers University Press.

Roberts, John M.
1965 Oaths, autonomic ordeals, and power. American Anthropologist 67, No. 6, Part 2:186–212.

* Roberts, John M., Malcolm J. Arth, and Robert R. Bush (R-A-B)
1959 Games in culture. American Anthropologist 61:597–605. Codings from this source have been used as modified by the **EA,** Column 35 (1962:270). Such codings, identified by the initials "R-A-B, EA," were used in constructing FCs 457–66, 511. For an article analyzing statements in these paragraphs, see Roberts and Sutton-Smith 1966.

Roberts, John M. and Brian Sutton-Smith
1962 Child training and game involvement. Ethnology 1:166–85.
1966 Cross-cultural correlates of games of chance. Behavior Science Notes 1:131–44. This article is based on a pre-publication version of Paragraphs 457–66 and 511 of this **Summary.**

Roberts, John M., Brian Sutton-Smith, and Adam Kendon
1963 Strategy in games and folk tales. Journal of Social Psychology 61: 185–99.

Romney, A. Kimball
1955 A structural analysis of preferential cross-cousin marriage. Unpublished doctoral dissertation. Cambridge, Harvard University.

Rose, Arnold M., ed.
1958 The institutions of advanced societies. Minneapolis, University of Minnesota Press.

Rose, Edward and Gary Willoughby
1958 Culture profiles and emphases. American Journal of Sociology 63: 476–90.

Rosenblatt, Paul C.

1966 A cross-cultural study of child rearing and romantic love. Journal of Personality and Social Psychology 4:336–38.

Sawyer, Jack and Robert A. LeVine
1966 Cultural dimensions: a factor analysis of the **World Ethnographic Sample.** American Anthropologist 68:708–31.

Schapera, Isaac
1953 Some comments on comparative method in social anthropology. American Anthropologist 55:353–61.

Schwartz, Richard D. and James C. Miller
1964 Legal evolution and societal complexity. American Journal of Sociology 70:159–69.

Segall, Marshall, Donald T. Campbell, and Melville J. Herskovits
1963 Cultural differences in the perception of geometric illusions. Science 139:769–71.

*Shirley, Robert W. and A. Kimball Romney (S-R)
1962 Love magic and socialization anxiety: a cross-cultural study. American Anthropologist 64:1028–31. Codings used in constructing FCs 447, 512.

Siegel, Bernard J.
1945 Some methodological considerations for a comparative study of slavery. American Anthropologist, N.S. 47:357–92.

Siegel, Sidney
1956 Nonparametric statistics for the behavioral sciences. New York, McGraw-Hill.

* Simmons, Leo W. (LWS)
1945 The role of the aged in primitive society. New Haven, Yale University Press. Codings used in constructing FCs 147, 277–79, 395, 417, 422, 423, 432, 435, 451, 471, 478, 513. Codings for data columns 1–110 are also found in Simmons 1937. For reviews, see: Brewton Berry 1946; Anna H. Gayton 1946; Georg Höltker 1949; Solon T. Kimball 1946; and Judson T. Landis 1946.

Simmons, Leo W.
1937 Statistical correlations in the science of society. **In** Studies in the Science of Society, George Peter Murdock, ed. New Haven, Yale University Press. Pp. 495–517. Also **in** Cross-Cultural Approaches, Clellan S. Ford, ed. New Haven, HRAF Press, 1967. Pp. 221–45.

Singer, Milton B.
1953 Summary of comments and discussion/of Schapera 1953/. American Anthropologist 55:362–66.

* Slater, Philip E. (PES)
1964 Unpublished coding guide for the cross-cultural study of narcissism. Waltham, Mass., Brandeis University. Codings produced by this study were made available by Slater. These were used in constructing FCs 137, 419–21, 472–75, 514. For an article analyzing statements in these paragraphs, see Slater and Slater 1965.

Slater, Philip E.
1965 Culture, sexuality, and narcissism: a cross-cultural study. Mimeographed typescript. Waltham, Mass., Brandeis University.

Slater, Philip E. and Dori A. Slater

1965 Maternal ambivalence and narcissism: a cross-cultural study. Merrill-Palmer Quarterly of Behavior and Development 11:241–59. This article is based on a prepublication version of Paragraphs 137, 419–21, 472–75, and 514 of this **Summary.**

Spaulding, Albert C.
1965 Review of Raoul Naroll 1962. American Anthropologist 67:1041–42.

Spencer, Robert F., ed.
1954 Method and perspective in anthropology. Minneapolis, University of Minnesota Press.

Spiro, Melford E.
1954 Human nature in its psychological dimensions. American Anthropologist 56:19–30.
1959 Cultural heritage, personal tensions, and mental illness in a South Sea culture. **In** Culture and Mental Health: Cross-Cultural Studies, Marvin K. Opler, ed. New York, Macmillan. Pp. 141–71.
1963 Review of William N. Stephens 1962. American Anthropologist 65:764–66.
1965 A typology of social structure and the patterning of social institutions: a cross-cultural study. American Anthropologist 67:1097–119.

Spiro, Melford E. and Roy G. D'Andrade
1958 A cross-cultural study of some supernatural beliefs. American Anthropologist 60:456–66.

Steiner, F.
1951 Review of Murdock 1949. British Journal of Sociology 2:366–68.

Steinmetz, Sebald Rudolf
1898/9 Classification des types sociaux et catalogue des peuples. Année Sociologique 3:43–147.

Stellar, Eliot
1952 Review of Ford and Beach 1951. Psychological Bulletin 49:75–78.

* Stephens, William N. (WNS)
1962 The Oedipus complex: cross-cultural evidence. With a chapter on kin avoidances written in collaboration with Roy G. D'Andrade. New York, Free Press of Glencoe. Used in constructing FCs 257–59, 335, 396, 398, 399, 452, 515. This source also contains codings made by John W. M. Whiting and Roy G. D'Andrade which Stephens has utilized or modified for his particular purposes. Such codings, identified by "W-D,S," were used in constructing FCs 243, 314, 315. For reviews, see: George DeVos 1963; Robert A. Ellis 1963; Peter Madison 1964; and Melford E. Spiro 1963.

Stephens, William N.
1961 A cross-cultural study of menstrual taboos. Genetic Psychology Monographs 64:385–416. Also **in** Cross-Cultural Approaches, Clellan S. Ford, ed. New Haven, HRAF Press, 1967. Pp. 67–94.
1963 The family in cross-cultural perspective. New York, Holt, Rinehart and Winston, Inc.

Stewart, Omer C.
1951 Review of Beatrice Blyth Whiting 1950. American Anthropologist 53: 385–86.

Stinchcombe, Arthur L.

1964 Review of Gouldner and Peterson 1962. American Journal of Sociology 69:549–51.

Strodtbeck, Fred L.

1964 Considerations of meta-method in cross-cultural studies. American Anthropologist 66, No. 3, Part 2: 223–29.

* Swanson, Guy E. (GES)

1960 The birth of the gods: the origin of primitive beliefs. Ann Arbor, University of Michigan Press. Codings from this source were used, without modification, in constructing FCs 101, 133, 135, 416, 429–31, 433, 436, 446. Other codings from this source have been used as modified by the **EA,** Column 32 (1962:269). Such codings, identified by the initials "GES, EA," were used in constructing FCs 94–100, 516. Still other codings from this source have been used as modified by the **EA,** Column 34 (1962:269–70). Such codings, also identified by the initials "GES, EA," were used in constructing FCs 426–28, 517. For reviews of the Swanson book, see: William A. Gamson 1962; John J. Honigmann 1961; and W. W. Lambert 1962.

Sweetser, Dorrian A.

1966 Avoidance, social affiliation, and the incest taboo. Ethnology 5:304–16. See also Apple, Dorrian.

Tanter, Raymond

1968 Testing political development theories. **In** Naroll and Cohen 1968.

Tatje, Terrence A. and Raoul Naroll

1968 Two complexity measures. **In** Naroll and Cohen 1968.

Thoden van Velzen, H. U. E. and W. van Wetering

1960 Residence, power groups and intra-societal aggression. International Archives of Ethnography 49:169–200.

Tijm, Jan

1933 Die Stellung der Frau bei den Indianern der vereinigten Staaten und Canada's. Zutphen, W. J. Thieme & Cie.

Triandis, Leigh Minturn and William W. Lambert

1961 Sources of frustration and targets of aggression: a cross-cultural study. Journal of Abnormal and Social Psychology 62:640–48.

Turnbull, Colin M.

1965 The Mbuti pygmies: an ethnographic survey. Anthropological Papers of the American Museum of Natural History 50, Part 3. For evidence of possible ethnographer bias, see pages 241 and 248.

Tylor, Edward B.

1889 On a method of investigating the development of institutions; applied to laws of marriage and descent. Journal of the Anthropological Institute of Great Britain and Ireland 18:245–72. Also **in** Readings in Cross-Cultural Metholology, Frank W. Moore, ed. New Haven, HRAF Press, 1966. Pp. 1–25.

* Udy, Stanley H., Jr. (SHU)

1959a Organization of work: a comparative analysis of production among nonindustrial peoples. New Haven, HRAF Press. Codings used in constructing FCs 111–14, 518. For reviews, see: E. R. Leach 1960; and Manning Nash 1960.

Udy, Stanley H., Jr.
1958 "Bureaucratic" elements in organizations: some research findings. American Sociological Review 23:415–18.
1959b "Bureaucracy" and "rationality" in Weber's organization theory: an empirical study. American Sociological Review 24:791–95.
1959c The structure of authority in non-industrial production organizations. American Journal of Sociology 64:582–84.
1962 Administrative rationality, social setting, and organizational development. American Journal of Sociology 68:299–308.
1965 Dynamic inferences from static data. American Journal of Sociology 70: 625–28. Includes comment by Richard D. Schwartz.
n.d. Work in traditional and modern society. Englewood Cliffs, N.J., Prentice-Hall. Forthcoming book.

Underhill, Ruth
1946 Papago Indian religion. Columbia University Contributions to Anthropology 33. New York. Page 14: "The influence of Christianity has had its effect in raising I'itoi's status as the supreme supernatural, and many now speak of him as 'the Papago Christ.' "

* Veroff, Joseph (JV)
1961 Contributor of codings to David C. McClelland 1961, which see. The Veroff codings were used in constructing FCs 134, 136, 479, 519.

Wallis, Wilson D.
1928 Probability and the diffusion of culture traits. American Anthropologist, N.S. 30:94–106.

Walsh, John E.
1962 Handbook of nonparametric statistics. Princeton, N.J., D. Van Nostrand.

* Westbrook, John T. (JTW, EA)
1963 Unpublished codings modified by the **Ethnographic Atlas** and appearing in **EA** Column 78 (1963:116). These codings, as modified, were used in constructing FCs 261, 389–92.

* Whiting, Beatrice Blyth (BBW)
1950 Paiute sorcery. Viking Fund Publications in Anthropology 15. Codings used in constructing FCs 138, 139, 445, 520. For a review, see: Omer C. Stewart 1951. For a commentary, see: Arnold R. Pilling 1962.

Whiting, John W. M.
1941 Becoming a Kwoma. New Haven, Yale University Press.
1954 The cross-cultural method. **In** Handbook of Social Psychology, vol. 1, Gardner Lindzey, ed. Cambridge, Addison-Wesley Publishing Company, Inc. Pp. 523–31.
1959 Sorcery, sin, and the superego: a cross-cultural study of some mechanisms of social control. **In** Nebraska Symposium on Motivation, Marshall R. Jones, ed. Lincoln, University of Nebraska Press. Pp. 174–95.
1961 Socialization process and personality. **In** Psychological Anthropology: Approaches to Culture and Personality, Francis L. K. Hsu, ed. Homewood, Ill., Dorsey Press, Inc. Pp. 355–80.
1964 The effects of climate on certain cultural practices. **In** Explorations in Cultural Anthropology: Essays in Honor of George Peter Murdock, Ward H.

Goodenough, ed. New York, McGraw-Hill. Pp. 511–44.
* Whiting, John W. M. and Irvin L. Child (W-C)
1953 Child training and personality: a cross-cultural study. New Haven, Yale University Press. Codings used in constructing FCs 302–13, 329, 331–33, 402–15, 437–43, 523. For reviews, see: Nancy Bayley 1954; Thomas Gladwin 1954; August B. Hollingshead 1953; and M. F. Nimkoff 1954.
*Whiting, John W. M. and Roy G. D'Andrade (W-D,S)
1962 Contributors of codings to William N. Stephens 1962, which see. These codings were used in constructing FCs 243, 314, 315.
Whiting, John W. M. et al.
1953 Field manual for the cross cultural study of child rearing. New York, Social Science Research Council.
1954 Field guide for a study of socialization in five societies. New York, Social Science Research Council.
* Whiting, John W. M., Richard Kluckhohn, and Albert S. Anthony (W-K-A)
1958 The function of male initiation ceremonies at puberty. **In** Readings in Social Psychology, Eleanor E. Maccoby, Theodore M. Newcomb, and Eugene L. Hartley, eds., 3d edition. New York, Holt, Rinehart, and Winston. Pp. 359–70. Codings used in constructing FCs 316, 373, 524. For a commentary, see Frank W. Young 1962.
* Whiting, Marjorie Grant (MGW)
1958 A cross-cultural nutrition survey of 118 societies representing the major cultural and geographic areas of the world. Unpublished D. Sc. thesis. Cambridge, Harvard School of Public Health. Codings used in constructing FCs 48–50, 522.
Wilson, Thurlow R.
1952 Randomness of the distribution of social organization forms: a note on Murdock's **Social Structure.** American Anthropologist 54:134.
Wright, George O.
1952 Projection and displacement: a cross-cultural study of the expression of aggression in myths. Unpublished doctoral dissertation. Cambridge, Harvard University.
1954 Projection and displacement: a cross-cultural study of folk-tale aggression. Journal of Abnormal and Social Psychology 49:523–28.
Young, Frank W.
1962 The function of male initiation ceremonies: a cross-cultural test of an alternative hypothesis. American Journal of Sociology 67:379–96. A commentary on Whiting, Kluckhohn, and Anthony 1958. This entry includes a rejoinder by John W. M. Whiting.
1965 Initiation ceremonies: a cross-cultural study of status dramatization. Indianapolis, Bobbs-Merrill.
Young, Frank W. and Ruth C. Young
1962 The sequence and direction of community growth: a cross-cultural generalization. Rural Sociology 27:374–86.
Yule, G. Udny and M. G. Kendall
1950 An introduction to the theory of statistics. 14th ed. New York, Hafner.

Appendices

APPENDIX ONE/ 1 -- CULTURES IN THIS SUMMARY,
LISTED BY REGULAR AND ALTERNATIVE NAMES

EXPLANATION ON PAGE 13   ASTERISKS INDICATE REGULAR NAMES.

ABABWA, SEE *BABWA
*ABIPON
*ABOR = ADI
ACHAWA, SEE *YAO
ADI, SEE *ABOR
AFRIKANDERS, SEE *BOERS
AIMORE, SEE *BOTOCUDO
*AINU
*AJIE = HUAILU
AKAR-BALE, SEE *ANDAMANESE
*AKHA
AKIKUYU, SEE *KIKUYU
*ALACALUF
*ALBANIANS = GHEG
*ALORESE
*AMBA = AWAMBA
= BAAMBA
= BAMBA
AMASWAZI, SEE *SWAZI
*AMERICANS
*ANDAMANESE = AKAR-BALE
ANDEMBU, SEE *NDEMBU
ANDOROBO, SEE *DOROBO
ANGONI, SEE *NGONI
ANNAMESE, SEE *VIETNAMESE
ANTIMERINA, SEE *MERINA
*APINAYE
*ARANDA = ARUNTA
*ARAPESH
*ARAUCANIANS = MAPUCHE
ARCHER RIVER GROUP, SEE *WIKMUNKAN
ARUNTA, SEE *ARANDA
*ARYANS = INDO-ARYANS
*ASHANTI
*ATAYAL = TAYAL
ATSINA, SEE *GROS VENTRE
*ATSUGEWI
ATTAWAPISKAT SWAMPY CREE, SEE *CREE
AWAMBA, SEE *AMBA
*AWEIKOMA = SANTA CATARINA CAINGANG
AWEMBA, SEE *BEMBA
AWUNLEN, SEE *TENDA
*AYMARA
*AZANDE = NIAM-NIAM
= ZANDE
*AZTEC = TENOCHCA
BAAMBA, SEE *AMBA
BABEMBA, SEE *BEMBA
*BABWA = ABABWA
= BOBUA
*BACAIRI
BAFUTE, SEE *WUTE
BAGANDA, SEE *GANDA
BAGESU, SEE *GISU
BAGIUNI, SEE *BAJUN
BAJA, SEE *BAYA
BAILA, SEE *ILA
*BAJUN = BAGIUNI
= BARJUN
= WAGUNYA
BAKUBA, SEE *KUBA
BAKWEDI, SEE *KPE
BAKWIRI, SEE *KPE
BALAMBA, SEE *LAMBA
*BALINESE
BALOLO, SEE *MONGO
BALUBA, SEE *LUBA
BAMBA, SEE *AMBA
*BAMBARA = BANMANA
BAMBUTI, SEE *MBUTI
*BAMILEKE
BAMONGO, SEE *MONGO
BANANO, SEE *MBUNDU
*BANDA
BANIANEKA, SEE *NYANEKA
BANKS ISLANDERS, SEE *MOTA
BANKUNDU, SEE *MONGO
BANMANA, SEE *BAMBARA
BANYORO, SEE *NYORO
BAPENDE, SEE *PENDE
*BARABRA = NILE NUBIANS
BARAMA RIVER CARIB, SEE *CARIB
*BARI
BARJUN, SEE *BAJUN
BAROTSE, SEE *LOZI
BARUNDI, SEE *RUNDI
*BASQUES
*BASSERI
BASUTO, SEE *SOTHO
*BATAK = TOBA BATAK
BATESO, SEE *TESO
BATHONGA, SEE *THONGA
BAVENDA, SEE *VENDA
BAWENDA, SEE *VENDA
*BAYA = BAJA
= GBAYA
BAYOMBE, SEE *YOMBE
*BEJA = BISHARIN
*BELU
*BEMBA = AWEMBA
= BABEMBA
= WABEMBA
BENA KALUNDWE, SEE *LUBA
*BENGALI
BENI MZAB, SEE *MZAB
*BERGDAMA = HAUKOIN
= MOUNTAIN DAMARA
*BETE
*BHIL
*BHUIYA = HILL BHUIYA
= PAURI
BIRIFON, SEE *BIRIFOR
BISHARIN, SEE *BEJA
*BIRIFOR = BIRIFON
*BLACK CARIB = GARIF
BOBUA, SEE *BABWA
*BOERS = AFRIKANDERS
*BORORO

BORUN, SEE *BOTOCUDO
BOTAHA, SEE *DAGUR
*BOTOCUDO = AIMORE
= BORUN
*BOZO
*BRAZILIANS
BRIBRI, SEE *TALAMANCA
*BUDUMA = YEDINA
BUKA, SEE *KURTATCHI
*BULGARIANS
*BUNLAP = PENTECOST ISLANDERS
*BURMESE
*BURUSHO
*BURYAT
BUSH NEGROES, SEE *SARAMACCA
BUTE, SEE *WUTE
CACHAMA, SEE *CARINYA
CADDO, SEE *HASINAI
*CADUVEO
*CAGABA = KAGABA
= KOGI
*CALLINAGO = ISLAND CARIB
*CAMAYURA
*CAMBA
*CAMBODIANS = KHMER
*CARAJA
*CARIB = BARAMA RIVER CARIB
*CARINYA = CACHAMA
*CAYAPA
CENTRAL WINTUN, SEE *NOMLAKI
*CHAGGA = DSCHAGGA
= WACHAGGA
*CHAMACOCO
*CHENCHU
*CHEREMIS = MARI
CHERENTE, SEE *SHERENTE
*CHERKESS = CIRCASSIANS
*CHEROKEE
CHEVSUR, SEE *KHEVSUR
*CHEYENNE

*CHIBCHA = MUISCA
*CHINANTEC = IJITLAN
CHIPPEWA, SEE *OJIBWA
*CHIR-APACHE = CHIRICAHUA APACHE
CHIRICAHUA APACHE, SEE
*CHIR-APACHE
*CHIRIGUANO
CHIWARO, SEE *JIVARO
CHLEUCH, SEE *SHLUH
*CHOCO
*CHOROTI = ZOLOTA
*CHORTI
*CHUKCHEE = REINDEER CHUKCHEE
CIRCASSIANS, SEE *CHERKESS
*COCHITI
*COMANCHE
CONIAGUI, SEE *TENDA
CONSO, SEE *KONSO
*COORG
COPPER ESKIMO, SEE *COPR ESKIMO
*COPR ESKIMO = COPPER ESKIMO
*CREE = ATTAWAPISKAT SWAMPY CREE
*CREEK
*CROW
CUBEO, SEE *TUCANO
*CUNA = SAN BLAS
*CZECHS
DAGOM, SEE *DOGON
DAGOR, SEE *DAGUR
*DAGUR = BOTAHA
= DAGOR
DAHOMEANS, SEE *FON
DAMARA, SEE *HERERO
DANGER ISLANDERS, SEE *PUKAPUKA
*DARD = SHINA
*DELAWARE = LENAPE
= MUNSEE
*DIEGUENO
*DIERI
*DILLING

*DOBUANS
*DOGON = DAGOM
= HABBE
= KADO
= TOMBO
*DOROBO = ANDOROBO
= OKIEK
= WANDOROBBO
DSCHAGGA, SEE *CHAGGA
*DUSUN
*DUTCH
EDDYSTONE ISLANDERS, SEE
*SIMBOESE
*EGYPTIANS = SILWA
ELGUME, SEE *TURKANA
*ELLICE = TUVALU
*ENGA = MAE
ENGASSANA, SEE *INGASSANA
EROKH, SEE *IRAQW
*EYAK = IGGIAK
FAN, SEE *FANG
*FANG = FAN
= PAHOUIN
= PANGWE
*FON = DAHOMEANS
FOUTADJALLONKE, SEE *FUTAJALONKE
*FOX
*FUTAJALONKE = FOUTADJALLONKE
*GANDA = BAGANDA
GARIF, SEE *BLACK CARIB
*GARO
GBAYA, SEE *BAYA
GHEG, SEE *ALBANIANS
GHIZI, SEE *KISSI
GIGUYU, SEE *KIKUYU
*GILBERTESE
*GILYAK
GISHU, SEE *GISU
*GISU = BAGESU
= GISHU

APPENDIX ONE/ 3 -- CULTURES IN THIS SUMMARY, LISTED BY REGULAR AND ALTERNATIVE NAMES

*GOAJIRO
*GOND = HILL MARIA
*GROS VENTRE = ATSINA
*GUAHIBO
  GUAIKA, SEE *WAICA
  GUARAUNO, SEE *WARRAU
*GUATO
*GURE
  HABBE, SEE *DOGON
*HAIDA = MASSET
*HANO = HOPI-TEWA
*HASINAI = CADDO
  = TEXAS
*HANUNOO
*HASANIA = HASSANYEH
  HASSANYEH, SEE *HASANIA
  HAUKOIN, SEE *BERGDAMA
*HAVASUPAI
*HAWAIIANS
*HAZARA = URAZGANI
*HEBREWS = ISRAELITES
*HEHE = IRINGA
  = WAHEHE
*HERERO = DAMARA
  = OVAHERERO
  HIBARO, SEE *JIVARO
  HILL BHUIYA, SEE *BHUIYA
  HILL MARIA, SEE *GOND
*HO
  HOPI-TEWA, SEE *HANO
  HOTTENTOT, SEE *NAMA
  HOVA, SEE *MERINA
  HUAILU, SEE *AJIE
  HUCUL, SEE *HUTSUL
*HUICHOL
*HUKUNDIKA
*HURON
*HUTSUL = HUCUL
  = HUZUL
  HUZUL, SEE *HUTSUL

  IBADAN, SEE *YORUBA
*IBAN = SEA DYAK
*ICELANDERS
  IFALUK, SEE *WOLEAIANS
*IFUGAO
  IGGIAK, SEE *EYAK
  IJITLAN, SEE *CHINANTEC
*ILA = BAILA
  IMERINA, SEE *MERINA
*INCA
  INDO-ARYANS, SEE *ARYANS
*INGALIK
*INGASSANA = ENGASSANA
  = METABE
  = TABI
*IRAQW = EROKH
  = MBULU
  = WAMBULU
  IRINGA, SEE *HEHE
*IRISH
  IROKA, SEE *MOTILON
  ISLAND CARIB, SEE *CALLINAGO
  ISRAELITES, SEE *HEBREWS
  ITESO, SEE *TESO
  JALUO, SEE *LUO
*JAPANESE
*JAVANESE
  JEHAI, SEE *SEMANG
*JEMEZ
  JINGHPAW, SEE *KACHIN
*JIVARO = CHIWARO
  = HIBARO
  = ZIBARO
  JOLOF, SEE *WOLOF
  JUKO, SEE *JUKUN
*JUKUN = JUKO
*KABYLE
*KACHIN = JINGHPAW
  KADO, SEE *DOGON
  KAFIRS, SEE *NURI

  KAGABA, SEE *CAGABA
  KALMUCK, SEE *KALMYK
*KALMYK = KALMUCK
*KAPAUKU
*KAREN
*KARIERA
*KASKA = NAHANI
*KATAB
  KAYAKENT, SEE *KUMYK
*KAZAK
  KEDI, SEE *TESO
*KERAKI
*KERALA = NAYAR
*KET = YENISEI OSTYAK
  = YENISEIANS
*KHALKA = KHALKA MONGOLS
  KHALKA MONGOLS, SEE *KHALKA
*KHASI
*KHEVSUR = CHEVSUR
  KHMER, SEE *CAMBODIANS
*KIKUYU = AKIKUYU
  = GIGUYU
  = WAKIKUYU
  KILBA, SEE *MARGI
*KIOW-APACHE = KIOWA APACHE
  KIOWA APACHE, SEE *KIOW-APACHE
*KISSI = GHIZI
  KITARA, SEE *NYORO
  KOGI, SEE *CAGABA
*KOHISTANI = KOHISTEI
  = MAYAN
  KOHISTEI, SEE *KOHISTANI
*KOL
  KONIAGI, SEE *TENDA
*KONSO = CONSO
*KOREANS
*KORYAK
  KOSSA, SEE *MENDE
*KPE = BAKWEDI
  = BAKWIRI

= KPELI
= KWIRI
KPELI, SEE *KPE
*KUBA = BAKUBA
KUMUK, SEE *KUMYK
*KUMYK = KAYAKENT
= KUMUK
KUNDU, SEE *MONGO
*KUNG = KUNG BUSHMEN
KUNG BUSHMEN, SEE *KUNG
*KURTATCHI = BUKA
*KUTENAI
*KWAKIUTL
KWIRI, SEE *KPE
*LAKALAI = WESTERN NAKANAI
*LAKHER = MARA
= SHENDU
*LAMBA = BALAMBA
= WALAMBA
*LAMET
*LANGO = UMIRO
*LAPPS
*LAU
LENAPE, SEE *DELAWARE
*LEPCHA
*LESU
LEUENEUWA, SEE *ONTONG-JAVA
*LHOTA NAGA
*LIFU = LOYALTY ISLANDERS
*LOLO
LORD HOWE'S ISLANDERS, SEE *ONTONG-JAVA
LOYALTY ISLANDERS, SEE *LIFU
*LOZI = BAROTSE
= MARUTSE
= ROZI
*LUBA = BALUBA
= BENA KALUNDWE
*LUO = JALUO
= LUWO
= NILOTIC KAVIRONDO
= NYIFWA
LUWO, SEE *LUO
*MACASSARESE
MAE, SEE *ENGA
MAGPIE MIAO, SEE *MIAO
*MAGUZAWA = PAGAN HAUSA
*MALAYS
MALEKULANS, SEE *SENIANG
*MAM
*MAMBILA = TORBI
*MAMVU = MOMVU
*MANCHU
*MANDAN
*MANGAIANS
*MANIHIKI
*MANUS
*MAORI
MAPUCHE, SEE *ARAUCANIANS
MARA, SEE *LAKHER
MARGHI, SEE *MARGI
*MARGI = KILBA
= MARGHI
MARI, SEE *CHEREMIS
*MARICOPA
*MARQUESANS
*MARSHALLESE
MARUTSE, SEE *LOZI
*MASAI
MASSET, SEE *HAIDA
*MATACO = NOCTEN
*MATAKAM
MAWKEN, SEE *SELUNG
*MAYA
MAYAN, SEE *KOHISTANI
MAYOMBE, SEE *YOMBE
*MAZATECO
MBARI, SEE *MBUNDU
*MBUGWE = WAMBUGWE
MBULU, SEE *IRAQW
*MBUNDU = BANANO
= MBARI
= NANO
= OVIMBUNDU
*MBUTI = BAMBUTI
= WAMBUTI
MENABE, SEE *TANALA
*MENDE = KOSSA
= MENDI
MENDI, SEE *MENDE
*MENTAWEI
*MERINA = ANTIMERINA
= HOVA
= IMERINA
METABE, SEE *INGASSANA
MFUTE, SEE *WUTE
*MIAMI = OUMAMI
*MIAO = MAGPIE MIAO
= YACHIO MIAO
*MIN CHINESE
*MINANGKABAU
*MINCHIA
*MISKITO = MOSQUITO
*MIWOK
*MNONG GAR
MOMVU, SEE *MAMVU
*MONGO = BALOLO
= BAMONGO
= BANKUNDU
= KUNDU
= NKUNDO
*MONGUOR
MOSHI, SEE *MOSSI
MOSQUITO, SEE *MISKITO
*MOSSI = MOSHI
*MOTA = BANKS ISLANDERS
*MOTILON = IROKA
= YUKO
MOTUNA, SEE *SIUAI
MOUNTAIN DAMARA, SEE *BERGDAMA

APPENDIX ONE/ 5 -- CULTURES IN THIS SUMMARY, LISTED BY REGULAR AND ALTERNATIVE NAMES

MOWATAVIWATSIU, SEE *UTE
MOWATCI, SEE *UTE
MOZABITES, SEE *MZAB
MPEZENI, SEE *NGONI
MUISCA, SEE *CHIBCHA
*MUNDURUCU
MUNSEE, SEE *DELAWARE
MUNSHI, SEE *TIV
MUNYANEKA, SEE *NYANEKA
*MURINBATA
*MURNGIN = WULAMBA
*MZAB = BENI MZAB
= MOZABITES
*NABESNA = UPPER TANANA INDIANS
NAHANI, SEE *KASKA
*NAMA = HOTTENTOT
= NAMA HOTTENTOT
= NAMAN
= NAMAQUA
NAMA HOTTENTOT, SEE *NAMA
NAMAN, SEE *NAMA
NAMAQUA, SEE *NAMA
*NAMBICUARA
*NANDI
NANO, SEE *MBUNDU
*NASKAPI
*NATCHEZ
*NAVAHO
NAYAR, SEE *KERALA
*NDEMBU = ANDEMBU
= SOUTHERN LUNDA
NENETS, SEE *SAMOYED
*NGONI = ANGONI
= MPEZENI
NIAM-NIAM, SEE *AZANDE
*NICOBARESE
NILE NUBIANS, SEE *BARABRA
NILOTIC KAVIRONDO, SEE *LUO
NKUNDO, SEE *MONGO
NOCTEN, SEE *MATACO

*NOMLAKI = CENTRAL WINTUN
*NUER
*NUNIVAK
*NUPE
*NURI = KAFIRS
*NYAKYUSA = SOKILE
*NYANEKA = BANIANEKA
= MUNYANEKA
= OVANYANEKA
= VANYANEKA
*NYARO
NYIFWA, SEE *LUO
*NYORO = BANYORO
= KITARA
*OJIBWA = CHIPPEWA
= PEKANGEKUM
OKIEK, SEE *DOROBO
*OKINAWANS
*OMAHA
*ONA = SHELKNAM
ONOTO, SEE *PARAUJANO
*ONTONG-JAVA = LEUENEUWA
= LORD HOWE'S ISLANDERS
*ORAON
OUALOF, SEE *WOLOF
OUITOTO, SEE *WITOTO
OUMAMI, SEE *MIAMI
OVAHERERO, SEE *HERERO
OVANYANEKA, SEE *NYANEKA
OVIMBUNDU, SEE *MBUNDU
OYO, SEE *YORUBA
*PAEZ
PAGAN HAUSA, SEE *MAGUZAWA
PAHOUIN, SEE *FANG
*PAIWAN
*PALAUANS
*PALIKUR = WASA
PANGWE, SEE *FANG
*PAPAGO

*PARAUJANO = ONOTO
PATAGONIANS, SEE *TEHUELCHE
*PATHAN = PUKHTUN
*PAWNEE = SKIDI
PAURI, SEE *BHUIYA
PEKANGEKUM, SEE *OJIBWA
*PENDE = BAPENDE
*PENOBSCOT
PENTECOST ISLANDERS, SEE *BUNLAP
POINT BARROW ESKIMO, SEE *TAREUMIUT
*PONAPEANS
*POPOLUCA
*PORTUGUESE
*PUKAPUKA = DANGER ISLANDERS
PUKHTUN, SEE *PATHAN
*PURARI
*PURUM
RAMCOCA MECRA, SEE *TIMBIRA
*RAROIANS
*REGEIBAT = RGIBAT
REINDEER CHUKCHEE, SEE *CHUKCHEE
RGIBAT, SEE *REGEIBAT
RIF, SEE *RIFFIANS
*RIFFIANS = RIF
*ROMANS
*ROTINESE
*ROTUMANS
ROZI, SEE *LOZI
*RUNDI = BARUNDI
= WARUNDI
*RWALA = RWALA BEDOUINS
RWALA BEDOUINS, SEE *RWALA
*SAGADA
SALON, SEE *SELUNG
*SAMOANS
*SAMOYED = NENETS
= TUNDRA SAMOYED
= YURAK
SAN BLAS, SEE *CUNA

APPENDIX ONE/ 6 -- CULTURES IN THIS SUMMARY, LISTED BY REGULAR AND ALTERNATIVE NAMES

*SANDAWE = WASSANDAUI
*SANPOIL
  SANTA CATARINA CAINGANG, SEE *AWEIKOMA
*SANTAL
*SARAMACCA = BUSH NEGROES
  SARSEE, SEE *SARSI
*SARSI = SARSEE
  SEA DAYAK, SEE *IBAN
  SEA GYPSIES, SEE *SELUNG
*SELUNG = MAWKEN
  = SALON
  = SEA GYPSIES
*SEMANG = JEHAI
*SEMINOLE
*SENIANG = MALEKULANS
*SERBS
*SERI
  SHANGANA-TONGA, SEE *THONGA
  SHELKNAM, SEE *ONA
  SHENDU, SEE *LAKHER
*SHERENTE = CHERENTE
*SHILLUK
  SHINA, SEE *DARD
*SHLUH = CHLEUCH
  SILWA, SEE *EGYPTIANS
*SIMBOESE = EDDYSTONE ISLANDERS
*SINDHI
*SINHALESE
*SIRIONO
*SIUAI = MOTUNA
*SIWANS
  SKIDI, SEE *PAWNEE
  SOKILE, SEE *NYAKYUSA
*SOMALI
*SONGHAI = SONRAI
  SONRAI, SEE *SONGHAI
*SOTHO = BASUTO
  SOUTHERN LUNDA, SEE *NDEMBU
*SUBANUN

*SWAZI = AMASWAZI
*SYRIANS
  TABI, SEE *INGASSANA
*TAGBANUA
*TALAMANCA = BRIBRI
*TALLENSI
*TAMIL
*TANALA = MENABE
*TANIMBARESE
*TAOS
*TAPIRAPE
*TARAHUMARA
*TAREUMIUT = POINT BARROW ESKIMO
  TAYAL, SEE *ATAYAL
  TEBU, SEE *TEDA
*TEDA = TEBU
  = TIBESTI
  = TIBBOU
  = TUBBU
*TEHUELCHE = PATAGONIANS
*TENDA = AWUNLEN
  = CONIAGUI
  = KONIAGI
*TENETEHARA
*TENINO = WARM SPRINGS SAHAPTIN
  TENOCHCA, SEE *AZTEC
*TERA
*TERENA
*TESO = BATESO
  = ITESO
  = KEDI
*TETON
  TEXAS, SEE *HASINAI
*THAI
*THONGA = BATHONGA
  = SHANGANA-TONGA
  TIBBOU, SEE *TEDA
  TIBESTI, SEE *TEDA
*TIBETANS
*TIGRINYA

*TIKOPIA
  TIKUNA, SEE *TUCUNA
*TIMBIRA = RAMCOCA MECRA
*TIMUCUA
*TIV = MUNSHI
*TIWI
  TOBA BATAK, SEE *BATAK
*TODA
*TOKELAU
*TOLOWA
  TOMBO, SEE *DOGON
*TORAJA
  TORBI, SEE *MAMBILA
*TOTONAC
*TRISTAN
*TROBRIAND
*TRUKESE
*TRUMAI
*TSIMSHIAN
*TUBATULABAL
  TUBBU, SEE *TEDA
*TUCANO = CUBEO
*TUCUNA = TIKUNA
*TUNEBO
  TUNDRA SAMOYED, SEE *SAMOYED
*TUPINAMBA
*TURKANA = ELGUME
*TURKMEN
  TUVALU, SEE *ELLICE
*TWANA
*TZELTAL
*ULAWANS
  UPPER TANANA INDIANS, SEE *NABESNA
  UITOTO, SEE *WITOTO
  UMIRO, SEE *LANGO
  UMOR, SEE *YAKO
  URAZGANI, SEE *HAZARA
*UTE = MOWATAVIWATSIU
  = MOWATCI

= WIMONUNTCI
VANYANEKA, SEE *NYANEKA
*VEDDA
*VENDA = BAVENDA
= BAWENDA
*VIETNAMESE = ANNAMESE
WABEMBA, SEE *BEMBA
WACHAGGA, SEE *CHAGGA
WAGUNYA, SEE *BAJUN
WAHEHE, SEE *HEHE
*WAICA = GUAIKA
WAKIKUYU, SEE *KIKUYU
WALAMBA, SEE *LAMBA
*WALLOONS
WAMBUGWE, SEE *MBUGWE
WAMBULU, SEE *IRAQW
WAMBUTI, SEE *MBUTI
WANDOROBBO, SEE *DOROBO
*WANTOAT
*WAPISHANA
WARAO, SEE *WARRAU
WARM SPRINGS SAHAPTIN, SEE *TENINO
*WAROPEN
*WARRAU = GUARAUNO
= WARAO
= WINIKINA
WARUNDI, SEE *RUNDI
WASA, SEE *PALIKUR
*WASHO
WASSANDAUI, SEE *SANDAWE
WAYAO, SEE *YAO
WESTERN NAKANAI, SEE *LAKALAI
*WICHITA
*WIKMUNKAN = ARCHER RIVER GROUP
WIMONUNTCI, SEE *UTE
WINIKINA, SEE *WARRAU
*WINNEBAGO
*WITOTO = OUITOTO
= UITOTO
*WOGEO
*WOLEAIANS = IFALUK
*WOLOF = JOLOF
= OUALOF
= YOLOF
WULAMBA, SEE *MURNGIN
*WUTE = BAFUTE
= BUTE
= MFUTE
*YABARANA
YACHIO MIAO, SEE *MIAO
*YAGUA
*YAHGAN = YAMANA
*YAKO = UMOR
*YAKUT
YAMANA, SEE *YAHGAN
*YAO = ACHAWA
= WAYAO
*YAPESE
*YARURO
YEDINA, SEE *BUDUMA
YENISEI OSTYAK, SEE *KET
YENISEIANS, SEE *KET
*YOKUTS
YOLOF, SEE *WOLOF
*YOMBE = BAYOMBE
= MAYOMBE
*YORUBA = IBADAN
= OYO
*YUKAGHIR
*YUKI
YUKO, SEE *MOTILON
YURAK, SEE *SAMOYED
*YUROK
ZANDE, SEE *AZANDE
ZIBARO, SEE *JIVARO
ZOLOTA, SEE *CHOROTI
*ZUNI

APPENDIX TWO/ 1 -- CULTURES IN THIS SUMMARY,
LISTED BY ETHNOGRAPHIC REGION AND SUB-REGION

EXPLANATION ON PAGE 14

AFRICAN REGION

AA01 KUNG
AA02 DOROBO
AA03 NAMA
AA04 BERGDAMA
AA05 MBUTI
AA06 SANDAWE

AB01 HERERO
AB02 SWAZI
AB03 LOZI
AB04 THONGA
AB05 MBUNDU
AB06 VENDA
AB07 NYANEKA
AB08 SOTHO

AC01 ILA
AC02 PENDE
AC03 BEMBA
AC04 KUBA
AC05 LAMBA
AC06 NDEMBU
AC07 YAO
AC08 YOMBE
AC09 NGONI

AD01 BAJUN
AD02 NYORO
AD03 CHAGGA
AD04 KIKUYU
AD05 MBUGWE
AD06 NYAKYUSA
AD07 GANDA
AD08 HEHE
AD09 GISU

AE01 AMBA
AE02 KPE
AE03 FANG
AE04 MONGO
AE05 BAMILEKE
AE06 LUBA
AE07 BABWA
AE08 RUNDI

AF01 FON
AF02 KISSI
AF03 ASHANTI
AF04 YAKO
AF05 MENDE
AF06 YORUBA
AF07 BETE
AF08 NUPE

AG01 BAMBARA
AG02 MOSSI
AG03 DOGON
AG04 TALLENSI
AG05 BIRIFOR
AG06 FUTAJALONKE
AG07 BOZO
AG08 TENDA

AH01 KATAB
AH02 JUKUN
AH03 TIV
AH04 MAMBILA
AH05 MARGI
AH06 GURE
AH07 MATAKAM
AH08 WUTE

AI01 BANDA
AI02 NYARO
AI03 AZANDE
AI04 INGASSANA
AI05 MAMVU
AI06 SHILLUK
AI07 BAYA
AI08 DILLING

AJ01 TESO
AJ02 MASAI
AJ03 NUER
AJ04 LANGO
AJ05 TURKANA
AJ06 LUO
AJ07 NANDI
AJ08 BARI

CIRCUM-
MEDITERRANEAN
REGION

CA01 KONSO
CA02 SOMALI
CA03 TIGRINYA
CA04 IRAQW
CA05 BEJA

CB01 MAGUZAWA
CB02 WOLOF
CB03 SONGHAI
CB04 HASANIA
CB05 BUDUMA
CB06 TERA

CC01 REGEIBAT
CC02 TEDA
CC03 SIWANS
CC04 MZAB

CD01 BARABRA
CD02 EGYPTIANS
CD03 RIFFIANS
CD04 KABYLE
CD05 SHLUH

CE01 ALBANIANS
CE02 PORTUGUESE
CE03 ROMANS
CE04 BASQUES

CF01 AMERICANS
CF02 BOERS
CF03 TRISTAN
CF04 BRAZILIANS

CG01 DUTCH
CG02 ICELANDERS
CG03 IRISH
CG04 LAPPS
CG05 WALLOONS

CH01 SERBS
CH02 HUTSUL
CH03 CZECHS
CH04 CHEREMIS
CH05 BULGARIANS

CI01 KALMYK
CI02 KHEVSUR
CI03 KUMYK
CI04 CHERKESS

CJ01 SYRIANS
CJ02 RWALA
CJ03 HEBREWS

EAST EURASIAN
REGION

EA01 SINDHI
EA02 PATHAN
EA03 HAZARA
EA04 KOHISTANI
EA05 NURI
EA06 BASSERI

EB01 KAZAK
EB02 MONGUOR
EB03 KHALKA
EB04 DAGUR
EB05 TURKMEN
EB06 BURYAT

EC01 GILYAK
EC02 YAKUT
EC03 CHUKCHEE
EC04 SAMOYED
EC05 KORYAK
EC06 YUKAGHIR
EC07 AINU
EC08 KET

ED01 KOREANS
ED02 LOLO
ED03 MANCHU
ED04 MIAO
ED05 JAPANESE
ED06 MIN CHINESE
ED07 OKINAWANS
ED08 MINCHIA

EE01 ABOR
EE02 BURUSHO
EE03 LEPCHA
EE04 TIBETANS
EE05 DARD

EF01 SANTAL
EF02 BENGALI
EF03 ARYANS
EF04 HO
EF05 BHIL
EF06 ORAON

EG01 CHENCHU
EG02 TAMIL
EG03 GOND
EG04 TODA
EG05 COORG
EG06 KERALA
EG07 BHUIYA
EG08 KOL

EH01 ANDAMANESE
EH02 MERINA
EH03 TANALA
EH04 VEDDA
EH05 NICOBARESE
EH06 SINHALESE

EI01 GARO
EI02 LHOTA NAGA
EI03 BURMESE
EI04 LAKHER
EI05 KACHIN
EI06 PURUM
EI07 KAREN
EI08 KHASI

EJ01 LAMET
EJ02 MNONG GAR
EJ03 SEMANG
EJ04 VIETNAMESE
EJ05 CAMBODIANS
EJ06 SELUNG
EJ07 AKHA
EJ08 MALAYS
EJ09 THAI

APPENDIX TWO/ 2 -- CULTURES IN THIS SUMMARY,
LISTED BY ETHNOGRAPHIC REGION AND SUB-REGION

INSULAR PACIFIC REGION

IA01 ATAYAL
IA02 SAGADA
IA03 IFUGAO
IA04 SUBANUN
IA05 HANUNOO
IA06 PAIWAN
IA07 TAGBANUA

IB01 IBAN
IB02 JAVANESE
IB03 BALINESE
IB04 BATAK
IB05 DUSUN
IB06 MINANGKABAU
IB07 MENTAWEI

IC01 MACASSARESE
IC02 ALORESE
IC03 BELU
IC04 ROTINESE
IC05 TORAJA
IC06 TANIMBARESE

ID01 ARANDA
ID02 MURNGIN
ID03 TIWI
ID04 DIERI
ID05 KARIERA
ID06 WIKMUNKAN
ID07 MURINBATA

IE01 KAPAUKU
IE02 WANTOAT
IE03 ARAPESH
IE04 WOGEO
IE05 KERAKI
IE06 WAROPEN
IE07 ENGA
IE08 PURARI

IF01 PALAUANS
IF02 TRUKESE
IF03 MARSHALLESE
IF04 WOLEAIANS
IF05 PONAPEANS
IF06 YAPESE
IF07 GILBERTESE

IG01 SIUAI
IG02 TROBRIAND
IG03 KURTATCHI
IG04 LESU
IG05 DOBUANS
IG06 ULAWANS
IG07 LAKALAI
IG08 SIMBOESE
IG09 MANUS

IH01 MOTA
IH02 SENIANG
IH03 BUNLAP
IH04 LAU
IH05 AJIE
IH06 ROTUMANS
IH07 LIFU

II01 SAMOANS
II02 TIKOPIA
II03 PUKAPUKA
II04 ELLICE
II05 ONTONG-JAVA
II06 TOKELAU

IJ01 MANGAIANS
IJ02 MAORI
IJ03 MARQUESANS
IJ04 MANIHIKI
IJ05 RAROIANS
IJ06 HAWAIIANS

NORTH AMERICAN REGION

NA01 NABESNA
NA02 TAREUMIUT
NA03 COPPER ESK
NA04 KASKA
NA05 NASKAPI
NA06 NUNIVAK
NA07 CREE
NA08 INGALIK

NB01 HAIDA
NB02 TWANA
NB03 KWAKIUTL
NB04 YUROK
NB05 EYAK
NB06 TOLOWA
NB07 TSHIMSHIAN

NC01 NOMLAKI
NC02 TUBATULABAL
NC03 YOKUTS
NC04 ATSUGEWI
NC05 MIWOK
NC06 DIEGUENO
NC07 YUKI

ND01 TENINO
ND02 UTE
ND03 HAVASUPAI
ND04 SANPOIL
ND05 HUKUNDIKA
ND06 WASHO
ND07 KUTENAI

NE01 GROS VENTRE
NE02 KIOW-APACHE
NE03 COMANCHE
NE04 CROW
NE05 CHEYENNE
NE06 MANDAN
NE07 SARSI
NE08 TETON

NF01 OJIBWA
NF02 WINNEBAGO
NF03 OMAHA
NF04 MIAMI
NF05 WICHITA
NF06 PAWNEE
NF07 FOX
NF08 HASINAI

NG01 HURON
NG02 SEMINOLE
NG03 CREEK
NG04 PENOBSCOT
NG05 CHEROKEE
NG06 DELAWARE
NG07 NATCHEZ
NG08 TIMUCUA

NH01 CHIR-APACHE
NH02 HANO
NH03 NAVAHO
NH04 ZUNI
NH05 MARICOPA
NH06 TAOS
NH07 COCHITI
NH08 JEMEZ

NI01 TARAHUMARA
NI02 PAPAGO
NI03 HUICHOL
NI04 SERI

NJ01 CHINANTEC
NJ02 AZTEC
NJ03 POPOLUCA
NJ04 TOTONAC
NJ05 MAZATECO

SOUTH AMERICAN REGION

SA01 CUNA
SA02 TZELTAL
SA03 CHORTI
SA04 CHOCO
SA05 TALAMANCA
SA06 MAYA
SA07 BLACK CARIB
SA08 MAM
SA09 MISKITO

SB01 CALLINAGO
SB02 CAGABA
SB03 MOTILON
SB04 CARINYA
SB05 PARAUJANO
SB06 GOAJIRO

SC01 WARRAU
SC02 YARURO
SC03 CARIB
SC04 GUAHIBO
SC05 WAPISHANA
SC06 SARAMACCA
SC07 YABARANA

SD01 MUNDURUCU
SD02 TAPIRAPE
SD03 PALIKUR
SD04 WAICA

SE01 SIRIONO
SE02 TUCUNA
SE03 JIVARO
SE04 YAGUA
SE05 TUCANO
SE06 WITOTO
SE07 CAMBA

SF01 INCA
SF02 AYMARA
SF03 CAYAPA
SF04 TUNEBO
SF05 PAEZ
SF06 CHIBCHA

SG01 YAHGAN
SG02 ARAUCANIANS
SG03 ONA
SG04 TEHUELCHE
SG05 ALACALUF

SH01 MATACO
SH02 TERENA
SH03 ABIPON
SH04 CADUVEO
SH05 CHOROTI
SH06 CHAMACOCO
SH07 CHIRIGUANO

SI01 BORORO
SI02 TRUMAI
SI03 BACAIRI
SI04 NAMBICUARA
SI05 CAMAYURA
SI06 GUATO

SJ01 CARAJA
SJ02 SHERENTE
SJ03 AWEIKOMA
SJ04 TIMBIRA
SJ05 BOTOCUDO
SJ06 TENETEHARA
SJ07 APINAYE
SJ08 TUPINAMBA

APPENDIX THREE/ 1 -- CULTURES IN THIS SUMMARY BY TIME LEVEL, LISTED ALPHABETICALLY

EXPLANATION ON PAGE 14

ABIPON	1800	BERGDAMA	1920	CHORTI	1930	GURE	1920	KERAKI	1930	MAMBILA	1920
ABOR	1940	BETE	1940	CHUKCHEE	1900	HAIDA	1890	KERALA	1800	MAMVU	1920
AINU	1900	BHIL	1900	COCHITI	1900	HANO	1950	KET	1900	MANCHU	1920
AJIE	1860	BHUIYA	1930	COMANCHE	1870	HANUNOO	1950	KHALKA	1940	MANDAN	1830
AKHA	1950	BIRIFOR	1930	COORG	1930	HASANIA	1920	KHASI	1900	MANGAIANS	1820
ALACALUF	1900	BLACK CARIB	1940	COPR ESKIMO	1920	HASINAI	1770	KHEVSUR	1930	MANIHIKI	1850
ALBANIANS	1900	BOERS	1850	CREE	1900	HAVASUPAI	1880	KIKUYU	1930	MANUS	1920
ALORESE	1940	BORORO	1920	CREEK	1750	HAWAIIANS	1800	KIOW-APACHE	1870	MAORI	1820
AMBA	1950	BOTOCUDO	1880	CROW	1870	HAZARA	1930	KISSI	1950	MARGI	1930
AMERICANS	1920	BOZO	1930	CUNA	1940	HEBREWS	800BC	KOHISTANI	1950	MARICOPA	1850
ANDAMANESE	1870	BRAZILIANS	1940	CZECHS	1940	HEHE	1910	KOL	1940	MARQUESANS	1900
APINAYE	1920	BUDUMA	1910	DAGUR	1940	HERERO	1900	KONSO	1930	MARSHALLESE	1940
ARANDA	1900	BULGARIANS	1940	DARD	1870	HO	1920	KOREANS	1950	MASAI	1900
ARAPESH	1930	BUNLAP	1950	DELAWARE	1700	HUICHOL	1900	KORYAK	1900	MATACO	1860
ARAUCANIANS	1880	BURMESE	1950	DIEGUENO	1850	HUKUNDIKA	1870	KPE	1950	MATAKAM	1940
ARYANS	800BC	BURUSHO	1930	DIERI	1900	HURON	1640	KUBA	1910	MAYA	1520
ASHANTI	1900	BURYAT	1900	DILLING	1930	HUTSUL	1890	KUMYK	1900	MAZATECO	1940
ATAYAL	1930	CADUVEO	1940	DOBUANS	1920	IBAN	1950	KUNG	1950	MBUGWE	1940
ATSUGEWI	1860	CAGABA	1940	DOGON	1930	ICELANDERS	1100	KURTATCHI	1930	MBUNDU	1930
AWEIKOMA	1910	CALLINAGO	1650	DOROBO	1920	IFUGAO	1920	KUTENAI	1880	MBUTI	1930
AYMARA	1940	CAMAYURA	1940	DUSUN	1920	ILA	1920	KWAKIUTL	1890	MENDE	1930
AZANDE	1920	CAMBA	1950	DUTCH	1950	INCA	1520	LAKALAI	1950	MENTAWEI	1920
AZTEC	1520	CAMBODIANS	1950	EGYPTIANS	1950	INGALIK	1880	LAKHER	1930	MERINA	1900
BABWA	1910	CARAJA	1950	ELLICE	1890	INGASSANA	1920	LAMBA	1920	MIAMI	1720
BACAIRI	1940	CARIB	1930	ENGA	1950	IRAQW	1950	LAMET	1940	MIAO	1940
BAJUN	1950	CARINYA	1950	EYAK	1890	IRISH	1930	LANGO	1920	MIN CHINESE	1920
BALINESE	1950	CAYAPA	1910	FANG	1910	JAPANESE	1950	LAPPS	1950	MINANGKABAU	1920
BAMBARA	1920	CHAGGA	1910	FON	1890	JAVANESE	1950	LAU	N.D.	MINCHIA	1930
BAMILEKE	1910	CHAMACOCO	1890	FOX	1830	JEMEZ	1920	LEPCHA	1930	MISKITO	1920
BANDA	1920	CHENCHU	1940	FUTAJALONKE	1890	JIVARO	1930	LESU	1930	MIWOK	1850
BARABRA	1920	CHEREMIS	1900	GANDA	1880	JUKUN	1920	LHOTA NAGA	1920	MNONG GAR	1940
BARI	1920	CHERKESS	1920	GARO	1900	KABYLE	1890	LIFU	1910	MONGO	1930
BASQUES	1930	CHEROKEE	1750	GILBERTESE	1940	KACHIN	1940	LOLO	1940	MONGUOR	1920
BASSERI	1950	CHEYENNE	1860	GILYAK	1920	KALMYK	1920	LOZI	1890	MOSSI	1950
BATAK	1930	CHIBCHA	1540	GISU	1900	KAPAUKU	1950	LUBA	1930	MOTA	1890
BAYA	1910	CHINANTEC	1940	GOAJIRO	1940	KAREN	1910	LUO	1940	MOTILON	1940
BEJA	1930	CHIR-APACHE	1880	GOND	1930	KARIERA	1910	MACASSARESE	1940	MUNDURUCU	1950
BELU	1950	CHIRIGUANO	1900	GROS VENTRE	1880	KASKA	1920	MAGUZAWA	1940	MURINBATA	1940
BEMBA	1900	CHOCO	1960	GUAHIBO	1950	KATAB	1930	MALAYS	1940	MURNGIN	1930
BENGALI	1940	CHOROTI	1910	GUATO	1900	KAZAK	1910	MAM	1930	MZAB	1920

APPENDIX THREE/ 2 -- CULTURES IN THIS SUMMARY BY TIME LEVEL, LISTED ALPHABETICALLY

NABESNA	1930	PALAUANS	1940	SANTAL	1940	TAMIL	1880	TOLOWA	1870	WAROPEN	1930
NAMA	1850	PALIKUR	1920	SARAMACCA	1920	TANALA	1930	TORAJA	1910	WARRAU	1950
NAMBICUARA	1940	PAPAGO	1930	SARSI	1880	TANIMBARESE	1930	TOTONAC	1940	WASHO	1850
NANDI	1910	PARAUJANO	1950	SELUNG	1920	TAOS	1830	TRISTAN	1930	WICHITA	1860
NASKAPI	1890	PATHAN	1950	SEMANG	1920	TAPIRAPE	1930	TROBRIAND	1910	WIKMUNKAN	1920
NATCHEZ	1700	PAWNEE	1860	SEMINOLE	1940	TARAHUMARA	1930	TRUKESE	1940	WINNEBAGO	1850
NAVAHO	1930	PENDE	1920	SENIANG	1930	TAREUMIUT	1880	TRUMAI	1930	WITOTO	1910
NDEMBU	1930	PENOBSCOT	1900	SERBS	1950	TEDA	1950	TSIMSHIAN	1880	WOGEO	1930
NGONI	1940	PONAPEANS	1910	SERI	1900	TEHUELCHE	1870	TUBATULABAL	1850	WOLEAIANS	1940
NICOBARESE	1890	POPOLUCA	1940	SHERENTE	1850	TENDA	1910	TUCANO	1940	WOLOF	1950
NOMLAKI	1850	PORTUGUESE	1950	SHILLUK	1900	TENETEHARA	1930	TUCUNA	N.D.	WUTE	1910
NUER	1930	PUKAPUKA	1930	SHLUH	1920	TENINO	1850	TUNEBO	1950	YABARANA	1950
NUNIVAK	1930	PURARI	1910	SIMBOESE	1910	TERA	1920	TUPINAMBA	1600	YAGUA	1940
NUPE	1930	PURUM	1930	SINDHI	1950	TERENA	1850	TURKANA	1920	YAHGAN	1870
NURI	1890	RAROIANS	1900	SINHALESE	1950	TESO	1950	TURKMEN	1910	YAKO	1930
NYAKYUSA	1930	REGEIBAT	1950	SIRIONO	1940	TETON	1870	TWANA	1850	YAKUT	1900
NYANEKA	1920	RIFFIANS	1920	SIUAI	1940	THAI	1940	TZELTAL	1940	YAO	1920
NYARO	1940	ROMANS	100AD	SIWANS	1920	THONGA	1920	ULAWANS	1900	YAPESE	1910
NYORO	1950	ROTINESE	1920	SOMALI	1950	TIBETANS	1920	UTE	1850	YARURO	1950
OJIBWA	1940	ROTUMANS	1890	SONGHAI	1940	TIGRINYA	1950	VEDDA	1900	YOKUTS	1850
OKINAWANS	1950	RUNDI	1910	SOTHO	1860	TIKOPIA	1930	VENDA	1900	YOMBE	1930
OMAHA	1850	RWALA	1920	SUBANUN	1950	TIMBIRA	1930	VIETNAMESE	1950	YORUBA	1950
ONA	1880	SAGADA	1950	SWAZI	1880	TIMUCUA	1560	WAICA	1950	YUKAGHIR	1900
ONTONG-JAVA	1920	SAMOANS	1920	SYRIANS	1950	TIV	1920	WALLOONS	1950	YUKI	1850
ORAON	1940	SAMOYED	1900	TAGBANUA	1950	TIWI	1920	WANTOAT	1920	YUROK	1850
PAEZ	1900	SANDAWE	1920	TALAMANCA	1950	TODA	1900	WAPISHANA	1900	ZUNI	1910
PAIWAN	1930	SANPOIL	1870	TALLENSI	1930	TOKELAU	1900				

APPENDIX FOUR/ 1 -- CULTURES IN THIS SUMMARY BY TIME LEVEL, LISTED CHRONOLOGICALLY

EXPLANATION ON PAGE 14

ARYANS 800BC
HEBREWS 800BC

ROMANS 100AD

ICELANDERS 1100

AZTEC 1520
INCA 1520
MAYA 1520

CHIBCHA 1540

TIMUCUA 1560

TUPINAMBA 1600

HURON 1640

CALLINAGO 1650

DELAWARE 1700
NATCHEZ 1700

MIAMI 1720

CHEROKEE 1750
CREEK 1750

HASINAI 1770

ABIPON 1800
HAWAIIANS 1800
KERALA 1800

MANGAIANS 1820
MAORI 1820

FOX 1830
MANDAN 1830

BOERS 1850
DIEGUENO 1850
MANIHIKI 1850
MARICOPA 1850
MIWOK 1850
NAMA 1850
NOMLAKI 1850
OMAHA 1850
SHERENTE 1850
TENINO 1850
TERENA 1850
TUBATULABAL 1850
TWANA 1850
UTE 1850
WASHO 1850
WINNEBAGO 1850
YOKUTS 1850
YUKI 1850
YUROK 1850

AJIE 1860
ATSUGEWI 1860
CHEYENNE 1860
MATACO 1860
PAWNEE 1860
SOTHO 1860
WICHITA 1860

ANDAMANESE 1870
COMANCHE 1870
CROW 1870
DARD 1870
HUKUNDIKA 1870
KIOW-APACHE 1870
SANPOIL 1870
TEHUELCHE 1870
TETON 1870
TOLOWA 1870
YAHGAN 1870

ARAUCANIANS 1880
BOTOCUDO 1880
CHIR-APACHE 1880
GANDA 1880
GROS VENTRE 1880
HAVASUPAI 1880
INGALIK 1880
KUTENAI 1880
ONA 1880
SARSI 1880
SWAZI 1880
TAMIL 1880
TAREUMIUT 1880
TSIMSHIAN 1880

CHAMACOCO 1890
ELLICE 1890
EYAK 1890
FON 1890
FUTAJALONKE 1890
HAIDA 1890
HUTSUL 1890
KABYLE 1890
KWAKIUTL 1890
LOZI 1890
MOTA 1890
NASKAPI 1890
NICOBARESE 1890
NURI 1890
ROTUMANS 1890
TAOS 1890

AINU 1900
ALACALUF 1900
ALBANIANS 1900
ARANDA 1900
ASHANTI 1900
BEMBA 1900
BHIL 1900
BURYAT 1900
CHEREMIS 1900
CHIRIGUANO 1900
CHUKCHEE 1900
COCHITI 1900
CREE 1900
DIERI 1900
GARO 1900
GISU 1900
GUATO 1900
HERERO 1900
HUICHOL 1900
KET 1900
KHASI 1900
KORYAK 1900
KUMYK 1900
MARQUESANS 1900
MASAI 1900
MERINA 1900
PAEZ 1900
PENOBSCOT 1900
RAROIANS 1900
SAMOYED 1900
SERI 1900
SHILLUK 1900
TODA 1900
TOKELAU 1900
ULAWANS 1900
VEDDA 1900
VENDA 1900
WAPISHANA 1900
YAKUT 1900
YUKAGHIR 1900

AWEIKOMA 1910
BABWA 1910
BAMILEKE 1910
BAYA 1910
BUDUMA 1910
CAYAPA 1910
CHAGGA 1910
CHOROTI 1910
FANG 1910
HEHE 1910
KAREN 1910
KARIERA 1910
KAZAK 1910
KUBA 1910
LIFU 1910
NANDI 1910
PONAPEANS 1910
PURARI 1910
RUNDI 1910
SIMBOESE 1910
TENDA 1910
TORAJA 1910
TROBRIAND 1910
TURKMEN 1910
WITOTO 1910
WUTE 1910
YAPESE 1910
ZUNI 1910

AMERICANS 1920
APINAYE 1920
AZANDE 1920
BAMBARA 1920
BANDA 1920
BARABRA 1920
BARI 1920
BERGDAMA 1920
BORORO 1920
CHERKESS 1920
COPR ESKIMO 1920
DOBUANS 1920
DOROBO 1920
DUSUN 1920
GILYAK 1920
GURE 1920
HASANIA 1920
HO 1920
IFUGAO 1920
ILA 1920
INGASSANA 1920
JEMEZ 1920
JUKUN 1920
KALMYK 1920
KASKA 1920
LAMBA 1920
LANGO 1920
LHOTA NAGA 1920
MAMBILA 1920
MAMVU 1920
MANCHU 1920
MANUS 1920
MENTAWEI 1920
MIN CHINESE 1920
MINANGKABAU 1920
MISKITO 1920
MONGUOR 1920
MZAB 1920
NYANEKA 1920
ONTONG-JAVA 1920
PALIKUR 1920
PENDE 1920
RIFFIANS 1920
ROTINESE 1920
RWALA 1920
SAMOANS 1920
SANDAWE 1920
SARAMACCA 1920
SELUNG 1920
SEMANG 1920
SHLUH 1920
SIWANS 1920
TERA 1920
THONGA 1920
TIBETANS 1920
TIV 1920
TIWI 1920

APPENDIX FOUR/ 2 -- CULTURES IN THIS SUMMARY BY TIME LEVEL, LISTED CHRONOLOGICALLY

TURKANA	1920
WANTOAT	1920
WIKMUNKAN	1920
YAO	1920
ARAPESH	1930
ATAYAL	1930
BASQUES	1930
BATAK	1930
BEJA	1930
BHUIYA	1930
BIRIFOR	1930
BOZO	1930
BURUSHO	1930
CARIB	1930
CHORTI	1930
COORG	1930
DILLING	1930
DOGON	1930
GOND	1930
HAZARA	1930
IRISH	1930
JIVARO	1930
KATAB	1930
KERAKI	1930
KHEVSUR	1930
KIKUYU	1930
KONSO	1930
KURTATCHI	1930
LAKHER	1930
LEPCHA	1930
LESU	1930
LUBA	1930
MAM	1930
MARGI	1930
MBUNDU	1930
MBUTI	1930
MENDE	1930
MINCHIA	1930
MONGO	1930
MURNGIN	1930
NABESNA	1930
NAVAHO	1930
NDEMBU	1930
NUER	1930
NUNIVAK	1930
NUPE	1930
NYAKYUSA	1930
PAIWAN	1930
PAPAGO	1930
PUKAPUKA	1930
PURUM	1930
SENIANG	1930
TALLENSI	1930
TANALA	1930
TANIMBARESE	1930
TAPIRAPE	1930
TARAHUMARA	1930
TENETEHARA	1930
TIKOPIA	1930
TIMBIRA	1930
TRISTAN	1930
TRUMAI	1930
WAROPEN	1930
WOGEO	1930
YAKO	1930
YOMBE	1930
ABOR	1940
ALORESE	1940
AYMARA	1940
BACAIRI	1940
BENGALI	1940
BETE	1940
BLACK CARIB	1940
BRAZILIANS	1940
BULGARIANS	1940
CADUVEO	1940
CAGABA	1940
CAMAYURA	1940
CHENCHU	1940
CHINANTEC	1940
CUNA	1940
CZECHS	1940
DAGUR	1940
GILBERTESE	1940
GOAJIRO	1940
KACHIN	1940
KHALKA	1940
KOL	1940
LAMET	1940
LOLO	1940
LUO	1940
MACASSARESE	1940
MAGUZAWA	1940
MALAYS	1940
MARSHALLESE	1940
MATAKAM	1940
MAZATECO	1940
MBUGWE	1940
MIAO	1940
MNONG GAR	1940
MOTILON	1940
MURINBATA	1940
NAMBICUARA	1940
NGONI	1940
NYARO	1940
OJIBWA	1940
ORAON	1940
PALAUANS	1940
POPOLUCA	1940
SANTAL	1940
SEMINOLE	1940
SIRIONO	1940
SIUAI	1940
SONGHAI	1940
THAI	1940
TOTONAC	1940
TRUKESE	1940
TUCANO	1940
TZELTAL	1940
WOLEAIANS	1940
YAGUA	1940
AKHA	1950
AMBA	1950
BAJUN	1950
BALINESE	1950
BASSERI	1950
BELU	1950
BUNLAP	1950
BURMESE	1950
CAMBA	1950
CAMBODIANS	1950
CARAJA	1950
CARINYA	1950
DUTCH	1950
EGYPTIANS	1950
ENGA	1950
GUAHIBO	1950
HANO	1950
HANUNOO	1950
IBAN	1950
IRAQW	1950
JAPANESE	1950
JAVANESE	1950
KAPAUKU	1950
KISSI	1950
KOHISTANI	1950
KOREANS	1950
KPE	1950
KUNG	1950
LAKALAI	1950
LAPPS	1950
MOSSI	1950
MUNDURUCU	1950
NYORO	1950
OKINAWANS	1950
PARAUJANO	1950
PATHAN	1950
PORTUGUESE	1950
REGEIBAT	1950
SAGADA	1950
SERBS	1950
SINDHI	1950
SINHALESE	1950
SOMALI	1950
SUBANUN	1950
SYRIANS	1950
TAGBANUA	1950
TALAMANCA	1950
TEDA	1950
TESO	1950
TIGRINYA	1950
TUNEBO	1950
VIETNAMESE	1950
WAICA	1950
WALLOONS	1950
WARRAU	1950
WOLOF	1950
YABARANA	1950
YARURO	1950
YORUBA	1950
CHOCO	1960
LAU	N.D.
TUCUNA	N.D.

APPENDIX FIVE/ 1 -- CULTURES IN THIS SUMMARY,
BY NUMBER OF CONTRIBUTORS' SAMPLES IN WHICH USED, LISTED ALPHABETICALLY

EXPLANATION ON PAGE 184

ABIPON	08	BERGDAMA	00	CHORTI	00	GURE	00	KERAKI	01	MAMBILA	00
ABOR	00	BETE	00	CHUKCHEE	18	HAIDA	05	KERALA	01	MAMVU	00
AINU	16	BHIL	06	COCHITI	01	HANO	22	KET	00	MANCHU	00
AJIE	00	BHUIYA	02	COMANCHE	17	HANUNOO	00	KHALKA	01	MANDAN	07
AKHA	00	BIRIFOR	00	COORG	01	HASANIA	00	KHASI	05	MANGAIANS	01
ALACALUF	00	BLACK CARIB	00	COPR ESKIMO	17	HASINAI	00	KHEVSUR	00	MANIHIKI	00
ALBANIANS	03	BOERS	00	CREE	01	HAVASUPAI	05	KIKUYU	07	MANUS	09
ALORESE	18	BORORO	00	CREEK	10	HAWAIIANS	00	KIOW-APACHE	03	MAORI	21
AMBA	00	BOTOCUDO	00	CROW	18	HAZARA	01	KISSI	00	MARGI	01
AMERICANS	04	BOZO	00	CUNA	19	HEBREWS	03	KOHISTANI	00	MARICOPA	05
ANDAMANESE	23	BRAZILIANS	00	CZECHS	04	HEHE	01	KOL	00	MARQUESANS	14
APINAYE	05	BUDUMA	00	DAGUR	00	HERERO	00	KONSO	00	MARSHALLESE	09
ARANDA	18	BULGARIANS	02	DARD	04	HO	01	KOREANS	07	MASAI	16
ARAPESH	14	BUNLAP	01	DELAWARE	01	HUICHOL	02	KORYAK	07	MATACO	06
ARAUCANIANS	16	BURMESE	07	DIEGUENO	00	HUKUNDIKA	00	KPE	00	MATAKAM	00
ARYANS	00	BURUSHO	03	DIERI	04	HURON	00	KUBA	00	MAYA	00
ASHANTI	25	BURYAT	00	DILLING	02	HUTSUL	01	KUMYK	00	MAZATECO	00
ATAYAL	02	CADUVEO	00	DOBUANS	09	IBAN	09	KUNG	02	MBUGWE	00
ATSUGEWI	02	CAGABA	05	DOGON	01	ICELANDERS	00	KURTATCHI	24	MBUNDU	17
AWEIKOMA	04	CALLINAGO	05	DOROBO	01	IFUGAO	21	KUTENAI	06	MBUTI	00
AYMARA	13	CAMAYURA	05	DUSUN	05	ILA	05	KWAKIUTL	17	MENDE	05
AZANDE	26	CAMBA	00	DUTCH	00	INCA	06	LAKALAI	00	MENTAWEI	00
AZTEC	06	CAMBODIANS	02	EGYPTIANS	04	INGALIK	00	LAKHER	14	MERINA	00
BABWA	00	CARAJA	00	ELLICE	00	INGASSANA	01	LAMBA	15	MIAMI	00
BACAIRI	00	CARIB	10	ENGA	00	IRAQW	00	LAMET	00	MIAO	03
BAJUN	00	CARINYA	00	EYAK	01	IRISH	02	LANGO	10	MIN CHINESE	01
BALINESE	17	CAYAPA	09	FANG	05	JAPANESE	05	LAPPS	11	MINANGKABAU	00
BAMBARA	01	CHAGGA	20	FON	19	JAVANESE	01	LAU	10	MINCHIA	02
BAMILEKE	00	CHAMACOCO	01	FOX	02	JEMEZ	00	LEPCHA	25	MISKITO	02
BANDA	00	CHENCHU	13	FUTAJALONKE	00	JIVARO	21	LESU	20	MIWOK	00
BARABRA	00	CHEREMIS	00	GANDA	14	JUKUN	06	LHOTA NAGA	01	MNONG GAR	00
BARI	01	CHERKESS	00	GARO	00	KABYLE	01	LIFU	00	MONGO	02
BASQUES	00	CHEROKEE	02	GILBERTESE	00	KACHIN	02	LOLO	03	MONGUOR	00
BASSERI	00	CHEYENNE	15	GILYAK	03	KALMYK	00	LOZI	02	MOSSI	03
BATAK	01	CHIBCHA	00	GISU	01	KAPAUKU	04	LUBA	00	MOTA	02
BAYA	00	CHINANTEC	00	GOAJIRO	04	KAREN	03	LUO	01	MOTILON	00
BEJA	00	CHIR-APACHE	18	GOND	11	KARIERA	01	MACASSARESE	03	MUNDURUCU	06
BELU	01	CHIRIGUANO	00	GROS VENTRE	02	KASKA	12	MAGUZAWA	04	MURINBATA	00
BEMBA	09	CHOCO	00	GUAHIBO	00	KATAB	02	MALAYS	02	MURNGIN	16
BENGALI	00	CHOROTI	05	GUATO	00	KAZAK	15	MAM	01	MZAB	01

APPENDIX FIVE/ 2 -- CULTURES IN THIS SUMMARY,
BY NUMBER OF CONTRIBUTORS' SAMPLES IN WHICH USED, LISTED ALPHABETICALLY

NABESNA	00	PALAUANS	02	SANTAL	00	TAMIL	00	TOLOWA	00	WAROPEN	00
NAMA	18	PALIKUR	00	SARAMACCA	01	TANALA	18	TORAJA	00	WARRAU	06
NAMBICUARA	07	PAPAGO	25	SARSI	00	TANIMBARESE	00	TOTONAC	00	WASHO	00
NANDI	02	PARAUJANO	00	SELUNG	01	TAOS	05	TRISTAN	00	WICHITA	03
NASKAPI	05	PATHAN	00	SEMANG	07	TAPIRAPE	01	TROBRIAND	22	WIKMUNKAN	00
NATCHEZ	01	PAWNEE	01	SEMINOLE	02	TARAHUMARA	08	TRUKESE	08	WINNEBAGO	08
NAVAHO	24	PENDE	00	SENIANG	08	TAREUMIUT	00	TRUMAI	02	WITOTO	06
NDEMBU	00	PENOBSCOT	02	SERBS	02	TEDA	01	TSIMSHIAN	00	WOGEO	11
NGONI	01	PONAPEANS	01	SERI	01	TEHUELCHE	04	TUBATULABAL	06	WOLEAIANS	12
NICOBARESE	00	POPOLUCA	01	SHERENTE	03	TENDA	00	TUCANO	00	WOLOF	07
NOMLAKI	00	PORTUGUESE	00	SHILLUK	03	TENETEHARA	07	TUCUNA	03	WUTE	00
NUER	12	PUKAPUKA	20	SHLUH	00	TENINO	02	TUNEBO	00	YABARANA	00
NUNIVAK	00	PURARI	02	SIMBOESE	00	TERA	00	TUPINAMBA	14	YAGUA	14
NUPE	05	PURUM	00	SINDHI	00	TERENA	02	TURKANA	03	YAHGAN	05
NURI	00	RAROIANS	00	SINHALESE	01	TESO	00	TURKMEN	00	YAKO	02
NYAKYUSA	10	REGEIBAT	00	SIRIONO	19	TETON	09	TWANA	00	YAKUT	12
NYANEKA	00	RIFFIANS	12	SIUAI	01	THAI	06	TZELTAL	00	YAO	05
NYARO	00	ROMANS	02	SIWANS	04	THONGA	27	ULAWANS	00	YAPESE	05
NYORO	02	ROTINESE	00	SOMALI	07	TIBETANS	02	UTE	00	YARURO	04
OJIBWA	20	ROTUMANS	00	SONGHAI	01	TIGRINYA	00	VEDDA	03	YOKUTS	03
OKINAWANS	00	RUNDI	01	SOTHO	04	TIKOPIA	20	VENDA	19	YOMBE	00
OMAHA	15	RWALA	10	SUBANUN	01	TIMBIRA	16	VIETNAMESE	06	YORUBA	07
ONA	05	SAGADA	00	SWAZI	04	TIMUCUA	00	WAICA	00	YUKAGHIR	05
ONTONG-JAVA	11	SAMOANS	22	SYRIANS	00	TIV	17	WALLOONS	00	YUKI	00
ORAON	01	SAMOYED	05	TAGBANUA	00	TIWI	00	WANTOAT	00	YUROK	08
PAEZ	00	SANDAWE	00	TALAMANCA	00	TODA	13	WAPISHANA	05	ZUNI	13
PAIWAN	00	SANPOIL	16	TALLENSI	16	TOKELAU	04				

APPENDIX SIX/ 1 -- CULTURES IN THIS SUMMARY,
BY NUMBER OF CONTRIBUTORS' SAMPLES IN WHICH USED, LISTED NUMERICALLY

EXPLANATION ON PAGE 184

THONGA	27
AZANDE	26
ASHANTI	25
LEPCHA	25
PAPAGO	25
KURTATCHI	24
NAVAHO	24
ANDAMANESE	23
HANO	22
SAMOANS	22
TROBRIAND	22
IFUGAO	21
JIVARO	21
MAORI	21
CHAGGA	20
LESU	20
OJIBWA	20
PUKAPUKA	20
TIKOPIA	20
CUNA	19
FON	19
SIRIONO	19
VENDA	19
ALORESE	18
ARANDA	18
CHIR-APACHE	18
CHUKCHEE	18
CROW	18
NAMA	18
TANALA	18
BALINESE	17
COMANCHE	17
COPR ESKIMO	17
KWAKIUTL	17
MBUNDU	17
TIV	17
AINU	16
ARAUCANIANS	16
MASAI	16
MURNGIN	16
SANPOIL	16
TALLENSI	16
TIMBIRA	16
CHEYENNE	15
KAZAK	15
LAMBA	15
OMAHA	15
ARAPESH	14
GANDA	14
LAKHER	14
MARQUESANS	14
TUPINAMBA	14
YAGUA	14
AYMARA	13
CHENCHU	13
TODA	13
ZUNI	13
KASKA	12
NUER	12
RIFFIANS	12
WOLEAIANS	12
YAKUT	12
GOND	11
LAPPS	11
ONTONG-JAVA	11
WOGEO	11
CARIB	10
CREEK	10
LANGO	10
LAU	10
NYAKYUSA	10
RWALA	10
BEMBA	09
CAYAPA	09
DOBUANS	09
IBAN	09
MANUS	09
MARSHALLESE	09
TETON	09
ABIPON	08
SENIANG	08
TARAHUMARA	08
TRUKESE	08
WINNEBAGO	08
YUROK	08
BURMESE	07
KIKUYU	07
KOREANS	07
KORYAK	07
MANDAN	07
NAMBICUARA	07
SEMANG	07
SOMALI	07
TENETEHARA	07
WOLOF	07
YORUBA	07
AZTEC	06
BHIL	06
INCA	06
JUKUN	06
KUTENAI	06
MATACO	06
MUNDURUCU	06
THAI	06
TUBATULABAL	06
VIETNAMESE	06
WARRAU	06
WITOTO	06
APINAYE	05
CAGABA	05
CALLINAGO	05
CAMAYURA	05
CHOROTI	05
DUSUN	05
FANG	05
HAIDA	05
HAVASUPAI	05
ILA	05
JAPANESE	05
KHASI	05
MARICOPA	05
MENDE	05
NASKAPI	05
NUPE	05
ONA	05
SAMOYED	05
TAOS	05
WAPISHANA	05
YAHGAN	05
YAO	05
YAPESE	05
YUKAGHIR	05
AMERICANS	04
AWEIKOMA	04
CZECHS	04
DARD	04
DIERI	04
EGYPTIANS	04
GOAJIRO	04
KAPAUKU	04
MAGUZAWA	04
SIWANS	04
SOTHO	04
SWAZI	04
TEHUELCHE	04
TOKELAU	04
YARURO	04
ALBANIANS	03
BURUSHO	03
GILYAK	03
HEBREWS	03
KAREN	03
KIOW-APACHE	03
LOLO	03
MACASSARESE	03
MIAO	03
MOSSI	03
SHERENTE	03
SHILLUK	03
TUCUNA	03
TURKANA	03
VEDDA	03
WICHITA	03
YOKUTS	03
ATAYAL	02
ATSUGEWI	02
BHUIYA	02
BULGARIANS	02
CAMBODIANS	02
CHEROKEE	02
DILLING	02
FOX	02
GROS VENTRE	02
HUICHOL	02
IRISH	02
KACHIN	02
KATAB	02
KUNG	02
LOZI	02
MALAYS	02
MINCHIA	02
MISKITO	02
MONGO	02
MOTA	02
NANDI	02
NYORO	02
PALAUANS	02
PENOBSCOT	02
PURARI	02
ROMANS	02
SEMINOLE	02
SERBS	02
TENINO	02
TERENA	02
TIBETANS	02
TRUMAI	02
YAKO	02
BAMBARA	01
BARI	01
BATAK	01
BELU	01
BUNLAP	01
CHAMACOCO	01
COCHITI	01
COORG	01
CREE	01
DELAWARE	01
DOGON	01
DOROBO	01
EYAK	01
GISU	01
HAZARA	01
HEHE	01
HO	01

APPENDIX SIX/ 2 -- CULTURES IN THIS SUMMARY,
BY NUMBER OF CONTRIBUTORS' SAMPLES IN WHICH USED, LISTED NUMERICALLY

HUTSUL	01	KERALA	01	MARGI	01	PAWNEE	01	SERI	01	TAPIRAPE	01
INGASSANA	01	KHALKA	01	MIN CHINESE	01	PONAPEANS	01	SINHALESE	01	TEDA	01
JAVANESE	01	LHOTA NAGA	01	MZAB	01	POPOLUCA	01	SIUAI	01		
KABYLE	01	LUO	01	NATCHEZ	01	RUNDI	01	SONGHAI	01	ALL OTHERS	00
KARIERA	01	MAM	01	NGONI	01	SARAMACCA	01	SUBANUN	01		
KERAKI	01	MANGAIANS	01	ORAON	01	SELUNG	01				

APPENDIX SEVEN/ 1 -- ETHNOGRAPHIC ATLAS CODE SHEET

Note: Due to technical difficulties discovered too late for correction certain letters in this table are indistinct. See Ethnology, Vol. 6, No. 2. 1967.

EXPLANATICN CN PAGE 47

'EX' IN COLUMNS 91-92 = 'EXTRA' CODINGS IN ETHNOGRAPHIC ATLAS. PAGES 47-48

'LP' IN COLUMNS 95-96 = 'LEVEL OF POLITICAL INTEGRATION' CODINGS BY MURDCCK. SEE PAGE PAGES 47-48

'NE' IN COLUMNS 99-100 = 'NATURAL ENVIRONMENT' CODINGS BY MOORE. SEE PAGES 47-48

	10	20	30	40	50	60	70	80	90	EX	LP	NE
ABIPON	SH03XX2611	0BONOUNOA0	000BNOE00B	5200A5050E	000F0F0F0M	050GXX0M0E	00XGL0D000	HOP0055VXR	GRSMVVVVV	00	AS	BZ
ABOR	EE01XX0222	4BSNOOVNAM	SOOCMC5ECV	3300A50T0B	CMCF050P05	0505XX0E05	0NXTBOW000	HOOPUPEFXR	PWGGVVVVV	00	AE	RZ
AINU	EC07XX2340	100FNOVUC5	OLOOTOSECV	5310A20A00	000F0P000P	000FXX0N00	0FXXX00000	COP50PEFXR	GGGGVVVVV	00	DP	LZ
AJIE	IH05XX0031	6X0500POCP	SOOOCCI505	5555555500	0505050505	0505XX0505	05XMP00000	COP50555XC	EBCGRGGGG	00	MS	TE
AKHA	EJ07XX1211	500NOOPOAL	000000IECV	320555050B	0505050505	0505XX0505	05XTB0000C	CCQPPPEFXR	PWHGVVVVV	00	AB	TZ
ALACALUF	SG05XX1270	000NOUBNA0	000BQC500B	1200010500	00000C000M	0MC5XX0D00	00XXX000C0	C0000555XC	GRDHVVVVV	00	00	FZ
ALBANIANS	CE01XX0004	6BOFPOPOES	000KCMEICN	432CQ50APB	MMCFCMCFOP	050FXX0C0D	0EXIEA005C	CCPPEPEVXR	EWGWRESGT	00	MS	CZ
ALORESE	IC02XX2001	7BDNOOVUES	000KNOHECX	332A530A0P	0500050000	5M5GXX0C0M	0GXMPOW0C0	IF55C55PXR	555555555	00	A5	TZ
AMBA	AE01XX1111	6XBQ0OPACS	000CNC0ETH	3300550A0S	0500050P05	0M05XX0M0M	0GXNCB00EC	CCOPPPEFXC	GRBGRGP5G	00	55	SZ
AMERICANS	CF01XX0014	500MOONVA0	000KQCEICX	823CS10APB	MMCIIIIIIM	CMC0XX0MCM	0MXIEGC000	COECECEPXR	EWGWVVVVV	00	SE	LZ
ANDAMANESE	EH01XX424C	000M00B0A0	000B0CH00S	1200A50T00	0000000F0M	0G0GXX0D00	00XXY00000	C0C0055FXR	GOSGVVVVV	00	00	TZ
APINAYE	SJ07XX2210	5TOEMOMOSO	0M000CCCERV	230AA50A00	000005000M	050FXX0N00	0EXGECC0CC	CCN5055EXR	GGGGVVVVV	00	AM	TZ
ARANDA	ID01XX6400	0XCR00POCM	CM00RRI05B	1200A15P00	0000000000	5F5FXX0C00	00XAU000C0	CCPOCPPEXR	GRSGVVVVV	00	AS	EZ
ARAPESH	IE03XX2101	600P00POSM	L0000C0ERH	520053050P	0505050505	5555XX0505	05XPAC00C0	COOPEPEEXR	E5GGVVVVV	00	00	TZ
ARAUCANIANS	SG02XX1012	6BOFQOPNSL	0000MMOICH	240BC30A0P	CM0F0G0F0M	0N0FXX0M0N	0NXAC0W000	IFPPEPEAXR	GMHGRGPGG	00	AP	FM
ARYANS	EF03XX0103	6BOEPOPOSS	LOOKNOH505	5555555500	0505050505	0505XX0505	05XIEI50C0	5C5PEPE5X5	555555555	00	SP	BZ
ASHANTI	AF03XX0120	7BOFQOAVAS	LSOCCCDERV	742AQ10R0S	0MCMCP0F00	0500XX0M05	0DXNCKD000	IFENPNPVXQ	GAGGVVVVV	00	SE	TZ
ATAYAL	IA01XX0211	6BOGMOVUAL	000RNOHECV	331055050P	0505050505	0505XX0505	05XMP00000	IFEPUPU5XR	GWGGVVVVV	00	AP	TZ
ATSUGEWI	NC04XX4330	0GBFRUVOEO	000BNCE00S	2200C10A00	00000M000M	0MCFXX0M00	00XH0SW000	CCPPPPEVXR	SRHECSRCE	00	AS	FZ
AWEIKOMA	SJ03XX4600	000P00B0C0	000BQCH00B	1200550500	0000050F00	0G0GXX0C00	0EXCG000C0	C000005FXR	GRRGVVVVV	00	00	RZ
AYMARA	SF02XX0013	600EMOPODL	00000CHIRV	535CC50AQC	0M0D0M0N0M	0MC0XX0M0G	0EXKE0WCC0	C05PEPEAXR	GEGGVVVVV	00	D0	HZ
AZANDE	AI03XX1210	6BSQOOVNAS	0C0C0C0ECN	332BS44P00	0MCM000F0M	0M05XX0G00	0GXNCED0C0	IFQQPQPAXC	GACGVVVVV	00	LS	ST
AZTEC	NJ02XX0120	7TONOOVOSO	000R0CHJCV	832BS50500	CMCFCMCMCP	0MC0XX0MC0	0NXNA5C000	IOPPPPPPXR	EAFGQGSF5	00	SS	FZ
BABWA	AE07XX0210	7BOFQOPOCL	000050HETH	5425550P00	0505050505	0505XX0505	05XNCB00C0	IC5PPPP5XC	G5CGRG5GG	SO	MS	TZ
BACAIRI	SI03XX0230	500FNUVND0	000QC0IERV	1400A50500	0000050E0M	0M05XX0M00	0DXCA00000	C0C50555XE	GRHGVVVVV	00	AI	TS
BAJUN	AD01XX0141	4BOMOUNUAL	0C00QAD555	5555555500	000500C0005	0500XX0M0N	0EXNCB00D0	HFPCECE5XR	GWGGCG5CG	00	55	EZ
BALINESE	IB03XX0013	6TOFNOVUC0	000RQAH555	5555555500	0505050505	0505XX0505	05XMP0D0C0	HFQ50555XQ	5PGGVVVVV	00	SI	TZ
BAMBARA	AG01XX2012	5BSEQOPOSS	L000CMIICV	741B525A0B	MMCMCMCFCP	0N0GXX0N0D	0NXNCMD0D0	HFQQPQP5XQ	GAFECGACG	00	55	SZ
BAMILEKE	AE05XX0101	8B0Q00POSL	0000N05ECN	533A54550S	0M0MC50F05	0MC0XX0005	0GXNCBD0C0	HFPPCPQ5XR	GACGVVVVV	00	55	TZ
BANDA	AI01XX0201	7XBS00POCL	000C0C0ECN	530555550S	0505050505	0505XX0505	05XNCE000C	ICQPPQE5XC	GACGVVVVV	00	AP	TS
BARABRA	CC01XX0013	6BONOUPOAS	0000QADJTV	230C554APB	M505050505	0505XX0505	05XCNNW050	H05DEDE5XQ	GAFECGSCM	00	D0	DE
BARI	AJ08XX0104	5BSQOUPNCS	000CNC0ECN	520A550P0B	MMC0050P05	0500XXCMCN	0DXCNEW0DE	COPPEPEPXC	GPCGVVVVV	00	AS	TZ
BASQUES	CE04XX0023	5D0GM0BNA0	000850E555	5555555500	0505050505	0505XX0505	05XXX5C0CC	CC5CPCE5XR	555555555	00	DE	MZ
BASSERI	EA06XX0108	1BSNOOPNCP	CCCCQA5CCB	521CS52A0S	MMCF0P0000	0E0FXX000N	05XIEPW0D0	CCPOCPEVXR	GFFFRGFGF	00	55	EZ
BATAK	IB04XX0003	7BOFNOPUAS	0000MMS555	5555555500	0505050505	0505XX0505	05XMP000CC	SFPPEPEFXR	P5GGVVVVV	00	AP	RZ
BAYA	AI07XX1111	6B0Q00POCL	000CNC5ERV	430555450S	0505050505	0505XX0505	05XNCE00C0	HCPPPPPPXC	GACGCGRDG	00	AS	TS
BEJA	CA05XX0008	2BONOUPOCP	CCCCQADJCS	531C55450C	M505050505	0505XX0505	05XAAC005C	CC05CPE5XR	GMGMVVVVV	00	MP	EZ
BELU	IC03XX0003	7BOEPOMOSO	OLOCMMH555	5555555500	0505050505	5555XX0505	05XMP0D0E0	HFN50555XR	GWGGVVVVV	00	MM	RT
BEMBA	AC03XX1110	7STSOUCVA0	0SOKCCIECW	332B520R0S	CMC00P0F05	0D0GXX0NC5	0GXNCBD0C0	IFNNPNQEXC	GPCGVVVVV	00	SY	SZ
BENGALI	EF02XX0022	6BOENOPOTS	LCOKNCH505	5555555500	0505050505	0505XX0505	05XIEIC0C0	C055C555X5	555555555	00	D5	TZ

	10	20	30	40	50	60	70	80	90	EX	LP	NE
BERGDAMA	AA04XX4312	OSOSOUVUEO	OOOBQCO555	5555555500	0505050505	0505XX0505	05XKHOOOOO	ICPOCPE5XC	GRBGVVVVV	OO	A5	EZ
BETE	AF07XX0111	7BOFQOPOCL	OOOOOO5555	5555555500	0505050505	0505XX0505	05XNCKOOOO	COSOOQE5XR	GP5GVVVVV	SO	AP	TZ
BHIL	EF05XX1122	4BOFNOPOES	OOOONOCICN	231BA50APB	MMCOOPOPOP	OMOGXXOEON	ONXIEICOCC	CCPPEPEPXR	GPGWCGRBG	OO	CS	OZ
BHUIYA	EG07XX1112	5BOMOOPOCS	OOOCCCHERW	221AA50TOB	0505050505	0505XX0505	05XMKM5050	COP5OPEFXR	GWGGVVVVV	CO	55	OZ
BIRIFOR	AG05XX1111	6BSEQOPACS	OMLOCPCECN	340A550AOB	OMOMOPOFO5	OOOFXXOEOM	ONXNCGOO5C	IF5QPNP5XQ	GAFEVVVVV	OO	AP	SZ
BLACK CARIB	SA07XX0130	600NOONOAO	OOOBCOIHRV	620C520A00	OOOOOCOOOM	OMC5XXOOCO	OGXCA5OOCC	COA5O555XR	GGGGVVVVV	OO	DA	TZ
BOERS	CF02XX0108	1DOFMOVNAO	OOOB5OEICN	532C550APB	M505050505	0505XX0505	05XIEGEOEC	IO55C555XR	GAGGVVVVV	OO	LE	SZ
BORORO	SI01XX4510	OOOFNOMOSO	OMOOCOCOOS	5410A50500	OOOOO5OFOO	OMOFXXO500	OOXBOOOOOO	CON5055FXR	GGGGCGRCG	OO	AM	RT
BOTOCUDO	SJ05XX5410	OOOERO5OEO	OCOBQOHOOB	2205550500	OOOOO5OOOO	O5OFXXOMOO	OOXXYOOOCO	CCCOO55EXC	GRDGRFRSG	OO	AI	RZ
BOZO	AG07XX1060	3BSEPOPO5L	OOOCQC5JCT	541C555TOO	0505050505	0505XX0505	05XNCMOOCO	SF5QPPE5XQ	GAFECGRDG	OO	AP	SZ
BRAZILIANS	CF04XX0112	600MOONVAO	OOOBOOEICV	824C550APB	MIIIIMOFO5	OMO5XXOMON	ONXIERCOEO	HFECECEPXR	GAGTVVVVV	OO	D5	TS
BUDUMA	CB05XX0044	2BOPOOPO5L	OOOOQCI555	5555555500	0505050505	Q505XX0505	05XAADOOOC	SF55OPP5XC	GRBGVVVVV	OO	A5	SZ
BULGARIANS	CH05XX0002	800FMOVNAO	OOOB5CDICV	833C555APB	M5OFO50505	OMOOXXOMOE	OEXIESCOOO	CO5DECE5XR	GAHTVVVVV	OO	S5	LZ
BUNLAP	IH03XX1011	7XBNOOPOSS	OMOONOIERV	1300A43TOP	0505050505	0505XX05C5	05XMPO5050	55550555X5	555555555	OO	55	TZ
BURMESE	EI03XX0022	6DOMOOUNCO	OOOKQOH555	5555555500	0505050505	0505XX0505	05XTBOCO5C	SFACECE5XR	PWGGVVVVV	OO	SA	OZ
BURUSHO	EE02XX0004	6TDFNOPOAS	OOOOOOHJCV	441CQ59APB	MMCMCPOPOO	ONOOXXOOOM	OEXXXOCODO	5055055VXR	GSFEVVVVV	OO	L5	HZ
BURYAT	EB06XX0207	1BOENOPOCS	OOOOEOZ505	5555555505	0505050505	0505XX0505	05XALMDO5O	SF550555XC	GFCFRGWFE	OO	MP	CD
CADUVEO	SH04XX0431	2OOFNOUO5O	OOOB5OHERB	5315A5050E	0505050505	0505XX0505	05XGUOOOOC	CO55C555XR	GPGGVVVVV	OO	M5	SZ
CAGABA	SB02XX0002	8SONOOUOAO	OOOBSOHERV	530A05050P	OOOMO5OMOM	ONOFXXOEO5	OEXCH5WOOO	COPPEPE5XC	GMCGCGACG	OO	A5	RT
CALLINAGO	SB01XX0150	4SOENCMOSO	OLOOPPIIRH	530A520TOO	OOOFO5OFOM	OMCOXXODOO	OGXCA5OOCC	HCC5C55TXR	GWGGVVVVV	OO	AI	TZ
CAMAYURA	SI05XX2130	4SOENUVOAO	OOOQCCIERW	330AA50POO	OOOFC5OOOM	OMOFXXOMOO	ONXTGOOOOO	COPOOO55XR	GRHGVVVVV	OO	AP	TS
CAMBA	SE07XX0111	700MOONBAC	OOOBOOE505	5555555500	0505050505	0505XX0505	C5XIEREOCC	COA5OPP5X5	555555555	OO	55	BZ
CAMBODIANS	EJ05XX0022	6BONOUNOAO	OOOBQOEJCV	8235550APB	0505050505	0505XX0505	05XMKCCDCO	SFCPECEVXR	PWGGVVVVV	OO	SI	TZ
CARAJA	SJ01XX2240	2OOFNOUNCO	OCOKQCH505	5555555500	0505050505	0505XX0505	05XXXOOOCC	ICQ5C555XR	GRHGVVVVV	OO	AP	TZ
CARIB	SC03XX222C	4SONOUBNAO	OOOBCCIERN	120AA10AOO	OOOFOOOFOM	OMO5XXONOO	ODXCA5OOOO	COC5055FXR	GOGGVVVVV	OO	AI	TZ
CARINYA	SB04XX2110	65ONOUNBDO	OOOBOOE505	5555555500	0505050505	0505XX0505	05XCA5505O	5055O555X5	555555555	OO	55	SZ
CAYAPA	SF03XX1121	5OOFMOVUAO	OOOBNOEHTN	5300050AOP	OOOFO5OFOM	O5OFXXOMO5	OGXCHCOOCC	COP5C555XR	POHGVVVVV	OO	AS	TZ
CHAGGA	AD03XX0103	6BOQOOPNCS	OOOCNCOJCN	5210S2550B	M505050505	0505XX0505	05XNCBDOCC	COPPPPPPXC	GMCGVVVVV	CO	MA	BZ
CHAMACOCO	SH06XX6400	OSOMOOUVAO	OOOB5C5CNB	521B540500	OOOPOFOPOO	O5OEXXO500	OFXZMODOOO	SO55O555XR	GRSMVVVVV	OO	M5	BZ
CHENCHU	EG01XX8101	OBOMOOBOEP	OOOOCMICCT	1300010AOB	MOOOOOOOO5	ONOEXXOMON	OOXDROOOOO	COCPEPEFXC	GMCGCGRCG	OO	AI	BZ
CHEREMIS	CH04XX0023	5DCMOONOAC	OOOBNO5555	5555555500	0505050505	0505XX0505	05XURFEOOC	CC5CUCU5XR	GWGGVVVVV	OO	D5	LZ
CHERKESS	CI04XX0104	5BOPFOPNAS	OOCC5CEICH	531C559SPB	M505050505	0505XX0505	05XAK5DOOO	SFPDEDE5XR	GP5GVVVVV	OO	MP	FZ
CHEROKEE	NG05XX1220	5OOFNOMOSO	OSOCSOCECV	4325C50AOO	OOO5O5OFOM	O5OFXXOMOO	OGXIR5OOCO	CO55C555XR	GPGWCGRCE	OO	LM	LZ
CHEYENNE	NE05XX2701	OTOEROUVEO	OOOKNCHCCB	5310C50AOE	OOOOOFOFO5	OFOFXXOCOM	OFXAGOOOOO	CCOOCO5VXC	GRCHVVVVV	OO	MI	GZ
CHIBCHA	SF06XX0110	8BOPOOVO5C	OOOB5CEJRV	7325550500	0505050505	0505XX0505	05XCHCDCCC	SOMPEPEFXR	PPGGCPPCG	OO	LN	HR
CHINANTEC	NJ01XX0002	800GMOVODO	OOOBNOH505	5555555500	0505050505	0505XX0505	05XXX55OOO	COEPUPU5XR	GAGGVVVVV	OO	DE	BZ
CHIR-APACHE	NH01XX6400	OOOFROUVAO	OOOBNCHCCB	5300C50AOE	OOOOOFOFOM	OFOFXXOCOM	OEXATSOOOO	CCCOCO5VXC	GRDGVVVVV	OO	AI	EZ
CHIRIGUANO	SH07XX1121	5SOFNUVNAO	OOOBQC5ECV	5315C50500	OOOFOMOFOO	CMC5XXOOOE	ONXTGO5OOO	5OPPE555XR	GPGGVVVVV	OO	MP	BR
CHOCO	SA04XX1210	600MOUNVCO	OOOKSOHETN	220A550AOO	OOOOO5OFAM	0505XXOMOO	OEXXY5OOCC	CO5PP555XC	POCGVVVVV	OO	55	TZ
CHOROTI	SH05XX4320	1SONOOUOEO	OOOBOOECVW	1200C50AOO	OOOFOFOFOO	OEOGXXOMOG	ODXMMCOOOO	CO5OCO5FXC	GRCGVVVVV	OO	A5	BZ

	10	20	30	40	50	60	70	80	90	EX	LP	NE
CHORTI	SA03XX0112	6SOFMCBOEC	CCCBSCHECX	541A050AOP	000FOMOG05	OMOGXXONCD	OMXMA500CC	CCECECE5XR	EGGGVVVVV	00	CA	TZ
CHUKCHEE	EC03XX0235	OSOGQUVUAC	OCOBQCECOB	130BC10AOC	CMCOCFOP05	OCOFXXOMON	OOXLUOWCCO	IFIOOPEFXC	GHCHCGRCH	00	AI	UZ
COCHITI	NH07XX0210	7OOFMCMNCC	OSOONCHJCV	5300510A00	0505050505	0505XX05C5	C5XKR5OCCC	CCE5CCE5XR	GAFEVVVVV	00	AI	EZ
COMANCHE	NE03XX1801	OOOEROBOCC	OCOAOCH505	5555555500	00000F0000	C50FXXOCOM	OOXSSCOOCO	IFCOC055XC	GRCGVVVVV	00	PP	GZ
COORG	EG05XX0112	6CCFMCPOTS	OOOOCCIICH	3420A20APB	MMC5C50500	CMCCXXOMC5	CMXDRCCCCC	HFPPEPEVXR	GSHGVVVVV	00	SP	OZ
COPPER ESK	NA03XX046C	OSOMCONBCC	OOOBSCEC0S	1200C50AOC	COOOCFOCOM	OMCFXXONCO	COXESCOOCC	CCOOCCETXC	GRDIEGRGH	CO	55	UZ
CREE	NA07XX1360	OSONCUVUAC	OCCCCCI005	2300C50A00	00000FOOCM	OOOFXXONOO	CCXAGCOOCC	CCCPEPE5XC	SRCECGRCB	00	AI	CZ
CREEK	NG03XX222C	4TOENCMOAO	OMSCNCCECV	541AC20500	OMOFCFOFCM	CMCFXXONCO	OGXNM5CCCC	CCN5CPEEXR	GPGBCGPCG	00	LI	ML
CROW	NE04XX2701	OTCRCCVCEC	OPCCOOCCNS	5210C1050E	00000F0000	OFOFXXOCOM	O5XSXOOOCC	CCIOCNE5XC	GRCHVVVVV	00	MI	GZ
CUNA	SA01XX013C	6SOENCUODC	OCOBSCHECV	231C050AOP	OOOF050GCM	CMONXXOMO5	OMXCH5WCOO	SFE5C55VXR	GWGGVVVVV	CO	ME	TZ
CZECHS	CH03XXC003	7COGMOVNAC	OOCKSCEICV	823CS50APB	MMCIIIIII5	OMCOXXCCOF	CEXIESCOCC	CC5PEPE5XR	555555555	CO	SE	LZ
DAGUR	EB04XX0103	6BOFMCPOCP	OOOOOCIJCV	543C559500	0505050505	05C5XX05C5	O5XALMCCCC	CCCPEPE5XR	EA5GVVVVV	00	DO	GL
DARD	EE05XX0103	6BCEPCPOAS	CCCCOCHJCT	5320S105PB	MMCMOPOOOM	OMCOXXOCCN	OGXIEIDOCC	5C5PEPE5XR	5SF555555	00	L5	EZ
DELAWARE	NG06XX222C	4COENCMVSC	OSOC5CHECT	430B550A00	00050FOPCM	CMCGXXOMCO	OGXAG500CC	CCNNC55FXC	GRDBRGB5B	CO	AN	LZ
DIEGUENC	NC06XX640C	OCOSCOPOCL	CCCCNCIOOS	5200C30A00	OOOGCMCPOP	C50FXXOCCO	COXHCYOOCC	CCPOCC55XC	GRDEVVVVV	00	AS	EZ
DIERI	IC04XX7300	OXORCOVOEO	OMOCRRIO5B	1200A54POO	0000050005	555FXXCMCO	COXAUCOOCC	CC55C555X5	555555555	00	AP	EZ
DILLING	AI08XX1103	5BSQCUPNSP	OCCCCCCICH	5315555POB	M505050505	0505XX0505	05XCNNCOCO	HF5PUPE5XC	GACGVVVVV	CC	MP	SZ
DOBUANS	IG05XX0031	6GOMCOCOCC	OSOCOCI555	5555555500	0505050505	5555XX0505	05XMPCOCCC	CCOMCM5FXR	PMGGVVVVV	00	CO	TZ
DOGON	AG03XX2002	6STENCPOTL	OCCCOCIICV	341555550B	CMC5CMC505	050EXXOCOM	CNXNCGWCDC	HFCQPPP5XQ	GAFEVVVVV	CC	AB	SZ
DORCBC	AA02XX460C	OBOMCOPOCS	OCOCOCCO5B	1200526500	0505050505	05C5XX05C5	C5XCNEOOCC	CCCPPCE5XC	GRDGVVVVV	00	AC	RZ
DUSUN	IB05XX0122	5BOMOOVUCC	OOOKNCE555	5555555500	0505050505	05C5XX0505	05XMPOWOCC	CC5CECE5XR	PWGGVVVVV	OR	MS	RZ
DUTCH	CG01XXCC13	6CCFMCBNAC	CCCKQCEICV	833C550APB	MMCIIIIIII	IMCCXXOMCN	CNXIEGCOCC	CC5CECETXR	ESGTVVVVV	00	SC	LZ
EGYPTIANS	CC02XXCC13	6BOFNUPOCP	OCCCQACJCV	843CS23APB	MMCMCMCMCP	C5COXXOMCN	ONXAASCECO	SFEDEDEVXR	GSFEVVVVV	CO	SE	VZ
ELLICE	II04XX0051	4GOFNOVUSC	OOOSOCHHTV	5315A55TOP	00000COOCM	CNCOXXOCC5	CNXMPCCOCC	CC5QPPEFXR	EMGGVVVVV	CO	M5	TZ
ENGA	IE07XX0102	7BONCOPUCP	SCCCOCIERN	4405550POP	0000050005	555OXXOCOF	OGXPACOOOC	CCOPEPEVXR	55GGVVVVV	SO	55	RT
EYAK	NB05XX2350	OSOPFUAOAO	CMCCCCIOOV	1310C50RCO	00000FOOOM	OMOFXXOMCO	COXXYCWOCC	IFN5CNE5XR	GWGBVVVVV	CC	5Y	CZ
FANG	AE03XX1121	5BOFQOPOCS	OOOCNCCERV	230AA45AOS	CMCOC50FOP	C5CGXXONOM	OGXNCBWCEC	CCPOCPPFXR	GBGGVVVVV	SO	AS	TZ
FON	AF01XX0212	5BSQOOPUSP	OCOCTCDERV	7330S36POS	OMCMCPOFCP	0500XXOMCE	CGXNCKDCCC	HCPPPPPVXR	GAHGVVVVV	00	SP	TS
FOX	NF07XX1311	4SOERUBOAS	OCOKNCOECS	541C550AOE	COOOCF05CM	C505XX050M	OFXAG5CCCC	SFP5CC55XR	GB5BCGRDM	00	MS	CL
FUTAJALCNKE	AG06XX0005	5BSQ50POSL	OCCCQCIECX	542C555POB	M505050505	0505XX0505	05XNCADOCC	SF5CPPEFXC	GACGCGRBG	CC	SP	SZ
GANCA	AC07XX0111	7BOQOOVNES	OOOOOCIITN	723AQ40POB	MMCOCMCMCM	CMCOXXOMCM	OGXNCBCOCC	HFAPCPQPXC	GRBGVVVVV	00	SA	TZ
GARO	EI01XXC011	8COGNCMAAC	CMOCCMIECV	331A05CPOB	OOOFOCOFOC	OMCEXXOCCD	ODXTBCWOCC	SFMCCMOAXR	PMGGVVVVV	00	MM	TZ
GILBERTESE	IF07XX1050	4BCNCCVUSO	OOORNCH555	5555555500	COOCCCCOCM	555EXXOCCO	OEXMPCWOCC	IFEDECEVXR	EMGGVVVVV	OK	AC	BZ
GILYAK	EC01XX2350	OBONOOPOSS	OCOCMMICOS	220A550A00	OPOOOFOOOP	OMCFXXOMCO	COXXXOOOCC	CCQCCPEPXR	SWFERPWGG	CO	CO	CZ
GISU	AC09XX0112	6BOQCOPNCS	LCCCNCHECN	531A556POB	MMCCOPOGOC	C5CCXX050N	CGXNCBWCCC	IFCPEPEAXC	GPCGVVVVV	00	55	SZ
GOAJIRO	SB06XX0117	1BOQOUAOAC	OSLCTCCCCB	120BA2050B	MOOFCMOPOC	CMCFXXOMCD	OFXAR5WCCC	HCM5CMEPXR	GRGGVVVVV	CO	AN	EZ
GOND	EG03XX2102	5BCEROPCCP	OCOOCCIECV	231B510TOP	00000500CM	ODCGXXOMCN	CDXDRCWC5C	CCPCCC5FXR	GPGGVVVVV	00	MP	BZ
GROS VENTRE	NE01XX280C	CBOROCVUEC	OCCBNCHCOB	521CC2050E	00000FOFOO	OFOFXXOCOM	OOXAGCOOCC	CCIOCO5EXC	GRCHVVVVV	OC	MI	GZ
GUAHIBO	SC04XX343C	OSOFNCMOSC	OLCCCCICOB	1305550A00	0505050505	05C5XX05C5	05XXX5CCCC	CCPCC555XR	GRSGVVVVV	00	AS	SZ
GUATO	SIC6XX423C	15CROONC5C	OCCB5CICTS	5205550500	OOOFC50FCM	C5CNXXOMOO	C5XXXOOOCC	CCP5C555XR	GRGGVVVVV	OC	AP	RZ

	10	20	30	40	50	60	70	80	90	EX	LP	NE
GURE	AHC6XX1202	6TCENOAOSC	OSLCNCHECH	540A559ROS	0505050505	05C5XX0505	C5XNCBCOCC	SF55C555XC	GACGVVVVV	CC	CC	SZ
HAIDA	NB01XX2260	OSOENUAOCC	CMCCCPCCOV	5300C50ROO	OOOFOFOOOM	OMCFXXOMCO	OOXXYOOOCC	FFNNPNPAXR	SWGWVVVVV	OO	AY	CZ
HANO	NF02XX0003	7OOFMCMOSC	OLOCNCCJCV	5405550AOB	0505050505	C5C5XX0505	05XTAEOOCO	CO5NC55AXR	GAFEVVVVV	OC	5C	EZ
HANUNCO	IA05XX1011	7SOFNOUVAC	OOOKNCEECH	3205550AOB	0505050505	05C5XX05C5	C5XMPCCCCC	CCCCCCE5XR	EWHGVVVVV	OO	OO	TZ
HASANIA	CB04XX0005	5BOPOUPOAP	COCCQAC555	5555555500	0505050505	0505XX0505	05XAASWO5O	SC5OEDE5XR	GFGFVVVVV	OO	55	EZ
HASINAI	NF08XX131C	5COENOUVAC	CCOBNCHECH	532CC50AOC	COOOOGOF05	OMOFXXO500	CGXCD5DOCC	ICP5C555XC	GRBGVVVVV	CO	MS	ML
HAVASUPAI	NC03XX320C	5TOENUVOCC	OCOQNCIJCT	4305550500	0505C5C505	C5C5XXC505	05XHCYOOCC	CCQPEO55XC	GRDGVVVVV	OC	AP	EV
HAWAIIANS	IJ06XX1040	4OOENOBOSC	OCORSCHJRV	5320S5550P	OOOOOCOOOM	CMC5XXONC5	CMXMPCDECC	FFPCPCPFXR	EGGGRESHG	OK	LS	BS
HAZARA	EA03XXC005	5BCFNCPCCP	OCCCQACJCT	331C559APB	M505050505	05C5XX05C5	C5XALMWC5C	SCPPPPPVXQ	EAFECESFG	OO	MS	EZ
HEBREWS	CJ03XX0113	6BOFPOPO5P	CCCCQCEJCV	532C5595PB	M505050505	0505XX05C5	C5XAASWOCC	IC55CPEVX5	555555555	CO	S5	ME
HEHE	AC08XX0103	6BCFPCPNCS	OOOOCMI555	5555555500	0505050505	05C5XXC5C5	C5XNCBCCCC	FF55CDE5XR	G5FEVVVVV	OO	LP	BS
HERERC	AB01XX1306	CBOFQCVAEP	SSCCCPIC5B	5305559POB	M505050505	0505XX0505	C5XNCBWOCC	FFQOCNP5XC	GRBPVVVVV	OO	AB	EZ
HC	EF04XX0112	6BCPCCPOCS	OCCCMCI5O5	5555555500	0505C50505	05C5XX05C5	05XMKMCC5C	5CAPEPE5XR	GAGGREAGT	OO	SA	OZ
HUICHOL	NI03XX1211	5COFNUBCCC	CCCKQCHECH	5305050AOB	M5OFOPOFO5	OMCNXXOMCD	ONXNA5WCCC	CCEQPCE5XR	GSHGVVVVV	CC	DE	EZ
HUKUNDIKA	NCO5XX532C	CCCFROBOCC	OOOBNCHCOS	5200C505CC	COOOC5000C	C5CEXXO5OO	COXSSCOOCC	CCPCCPE5XC	GRCGCGRDG	CO	AS	EZ
HURON	NG01XX113C	5COEMCMOSC	OSCCOCIECV	531AC50500	OOOOOFOFCM	OMCFXXOMCO	CFXIR5WCCC	CON5C555XR	GBRBVVVVV	OO	MN	CL
HUTSUL	CH02XX0114	4DCMCVNCCC	OOOK5CEICN	755CB50APB	MMCFCMOP05	OMCOXXO5OD	CNXIESWCCC	CC5PEPEFXR	GPHGVVVVV	OO	CO	FZ
IBAN	IBC1XXC022	6CCGMCBOAC	OCCKNCEECV	5300A50AOP	OPOFO505CM	OMCEXXONO5	CDXMPOOOCC	FF5CECEPXR	PGGGVVVVV	OC	AI	TZ
ICELANDERS	CG02XX0234	1OOFMCVNAC	OOCK5CD555	5555555500	0505C50505	C5C5XX0505	C5XIEGEWCC	FC5PEPE5XR	555555555	OO	LP	UF
IFUGAC	IA03XX0211	6BOMOOBOAC	OCCKNCHJCH	3300550SOP	0505C50505	C5O5XX05C5	05XMPOWCCC	FF55C55FXR	PMHGVVVVV	CR	CO	RZ
ILA	AC01XX1003	6BCFQCVAAL	OSOCPPIECT	431AQ50POB	MMCOCGOFCM	OOCFXXOMCM	OGXNCBWCCC	FFMCCNCFXC	GPCGVVVVV	OO	AM	SZ
INCA	SF01XX0102	7CCMCOVNCC	OCCBQCHJCV	724AS50AOC	CMCFCCOFOC	CMCOXXOCOM	ONXKECCOCC	CC5OCPEVXR	GSGGRGAHG	CC	SS	HZ
INGALIK	NA08XX145C	CCONCCUVAC	CCCBSCHCOS	520AA50500	COOOCFOFON	ONOFXXONCO	COXATNWCCC	CCCCCPEPXR	SWDERGBGB	OO	55	CZ
INGASSANA	AI04XX0103	6STFMUBACO	OCOANCHICN	5305559ROB	M505050505	05C5XXC5C5	05XCNEOOOC	COP5C555X5	555555555	CK	AS	SZ
IRAQW	CA04XX0005	5BCNOOPN5S	OLOC5CCICN	331555950B	M505C50505	05C5XX05C5	C5XAACWC5C	5COPEPE5XC	GPCGRSWFE	OO	AP	SZ
IRISH	CG03XX0104	5COGMCVNAC	OCCKNCEIRN	822CS50APB	M505050505	05C5XX05C5	O5XIECCCCC	CC5PCPQVXR	GSGGVVVVV	CO	SE	LZ
JAPANESE	ED05XXCC21	7COGMCVNAC	CCCKQCEJCX	8345S20APB	MIIII5OIIP	OMCOXXOMCM	OEXJROCODC	CCEPPPPVXR	EWHGREWHT	CC	SE	RL
JAVANESE	IB02XX0012	7TOGNUUVAO	OOOKQCEJCV	824C525APB	CMCFCCCECC	CNCEXXCECE	OGXMPCCCCC	CCECECEVXR	GMGGRGMHT	OR	SE	TZ
JEMEZ	NH08XX120C	7COMCBNOCC	OLOCNCEJCV	5305C50AOE	OOOMO5OPCO	O5OEXXOCO5	CMXTACOOCC	CCE5CQE5XR	GAFEVVVVV	OO	AM	EZ
JIVARC	SE03XX112C	6SCEPUVUCC	OCOQTC5ERH	520AO50AOP	COOMC5OFCM	CMCFXXONCF	OGXXXCCCCC	CCI5C55FXE	GWHGVVVVV	CO	OO	HR
JUKUN	AH02XXC112	6BOENODOAC	OCORSCHECV	5405Q5050S	0505C50505	0505XX0505	O5XNCBDOCC	IFQ5C555XC	GACGVVVVV	CC	LP	SZ
KABYLE	CC04XX0003	7BOFNCPOSS	OCOOQC5ICV	543C559APB	M505050505	05C5XXC5C5	05XAABOC5C	IFEPEDE5XR	5PGTVVVVV	OO	LC	EZ
KACHIN	EI05XX1102	6BOFNOPNSS	LCOCMMIECV	341B550AOB	OMC5C50PO5	CMCFXXOCOG	CNXTBCDOCC	SFPPLPUAXR	EMGGVVVVV	OO	MS	FZ
KALMYK	CI01XX0117	1BOENCPNCP	SOCCNCO555	5555555505	0505C50505	05C5XXC5C5	05XALMCCCC	5CPCCPE5XC	GFDFVVVVV	SO	LP	EZ
KAPAUKU	IE01XXC112	6BCFPCPOCP	SCCCSSIERV	231A510ROP	OOOOOCOOOM	5M5FXXOFOG	ODXPACWCCC	CCI5C55AXR	GWGGVVVVV	CC	PI	TS
KAREN	EI07XX0121	6OOMCCMOAC	CLCC5CE555	5555555500	0505C5C5C5	C5C5XX05C5	C5XXYOWOCC	IFP5C555XR	PWGWVVVVV	OO	AS	TZ
KARIERA	IC05XX352C	CXOROOPOCM	OMOCCCI05B	1205550POO	COOOO5OOO5	555FXXOMCO	COXAUCCOCC	CC55C555X5	555555555	OO	AP	EZ
KASKA	NA04XX1450	OSCEMCMOSC	CMOOMMCOOS	2200C20500	OOOOOFOCO5	OMCFXXOECO	COXATNCOCC	CCC5CPEFXC	GRCERGRGG	OO	CO	CU
KATAB	AHC1XX2111	5TCFQCPACL	OCCCNCHICV	440BC50POS	OOOOO5OOOC	OMC5XXO5OE	BNXNCBOOCC	SFSPEPE5XC	GACGVVVVV	SC	55	SZ
KAZAK	EB01XX0108	1BCFPOPOCP	SCOCNCCCOS	233CS54POE	MMCFCPCOOC	OFCCXXCCCN	CEXALTCCCC	FF5CCPUPXC	GFDFQGAFE	OO	SP	GZ

	10	20	30	40	50	60	70	80	90	EX	LP	NE
KERAKI	IE05XX0111	7XCPOOPOCM	OCOCCCIERT	2200A30TOP	00000C000M	5M5CXXODCF	OEXPACOOCC	CCQQPPEEXE	GBGBRGOGB	CC	AB	SZ
KERALA	EG06XX0013	6COENCABAC	OSOCCMIJCN	8425550RPB	M505050505	05C5XX05C5	C5XDRCCOCC	CCN5C555X5	555555555	OO	SM	RZ
KET	EC08XX0361	CBCMOCVN5S	OCCC5C5505	5555555500	0505050505	0505XX0505	05XXXOOOCC	CC5OCPU5XR	SFFECGRCB	CC	CC	CZ
KHALKA	EB03XX0108	1BCGMOPNAS	LOCKNCCCOS	13355505PE	MMCCCM05CC	CMCCXXOCOD	OMXALMCO5C	HFPPEPE5XC	GFCFVVVVV	OO	LS	EZ
KHASI	EI08XX1112	5COEMOMOSC	OSLCCCIECV	241AA50TOB	OMCFOPOFCP	OMCFXXOECN	CGXMKKCO5C	COMNCN55XE	EWGGVVVVV	OO	MY	RZ
KHEVSUR	CI02XX0113	5BDNOCPCCS	CCCCOC5555	5555555500	0505050505	0505XX0505	05XGR500CC	CCCPEPEVXR	555555555	CC	55	GZ
KIKUYU	AC04XXC003	7BOQOOPOCS	OCOCNCCICV	430BQ26TOB	MMCOCMOFCO	OCCOXXOOOM	OGXNCBWOCO	CCOPEPEVXC	GPCGVVVVV	CO	AC	SZ
KIOW-APACHE	NE02XX2800	OGOEROUVAC	OOOKNCH505	5555555500	0000CF0005	OFCFXXOCCM	COXATSCOCC	CC5CCO5PXC	GRCHVVVVV	OO	MI	GZ
KISSI	AF02XX0001	9BSEQOPOTS	LCCCMMHECV	3415555POB	0505050505	C505XX0505	C5XNCAOOCC	HF5PEPE5XC	EACGVVVVV	OC	MP	SZ
KOHISTANI	EA04XX1104	4BONOCPOSP	OOOC5CCJCT	531C553APB	MMCMC5OMC5	OMCEXXOCCD	CDXIEIECCC	5CCOECE5XR	GSFEVVVVV	OC	55	FZ
KOL	EG08XX1002	7BCFNCPOEC	OCOBOCHICV	5315550APB	0505050505	0505XX0505	05XMKM50CC	CCCPEPE5XR	GAGGVVVVV	CO	CI	CZ
KONSO	CA01XXC004	6CCGCCPNEM	SCOCMC0555	5555555500	0505C50505	05C5XX0505	05XAACOOCC	CCPPP555XC	GWCGCSSFE	CO	MP	GS
KOREANS	EC01XX0022	6OOGMOPNES	OOOCOCEJCV	8320S50APB	CMCFCPOMOP	CMCCXXONOM	CEXXXCSOCO	HFSPPPPPXR	EWHGQEWHG	OO	SI	LZ
KORYAK	EC05XX1153	OSCENUVUAC	COOBSCEOOT	230BA50AOP	CMCOCFOOCM	O5OFXXCNCM	COXLUCWCCC	IFSP5PEVXP	SWFECSRCW	OO	AI	UC
KPE	AE02XX0113	5BCQOCPASS	LLCCNC5ERV	230A54450B	0005050P05	05CNXXOFOM	OGXNCBWCOO	IFPOCPP5XR	GMGGVVVVV	CC	AS	TZ
KUBA	AC04XX0121	6BOFNVAOSC	OSCCNCHECW	332AS21POS	OMCMOPCO05	05COXXONOO	CGXNCBDOEC	HCSOCNP5XR	GGGGVVVVV	OC	LM	TS
KUMYK	CI03XXC003	7BCNOCNOCC	OCOK5CE555	5555555500	0505C50505	C5C5XXC5C5	C5XALT505C	5C55C555XR	555555555	CO	55	FZ
KUNG	AA01XX8200	OSCFNUBOEC	OCCKNCEO5B	130BA20POO	OOOOCMOOCC	OFCGXXOCOO	COXKHCOOCC	CCPCCQ5EXC	GRDGSGREG	OO	AS	EZ
KURTATCHI	IG03XX1121	5BOSOCBOEC	OSCKNCIERH	3300A40TOP	COOOCCOFCM	5M5GXXCNOF	OGXMPCDWCC	CCM5C55AXR	GRRGRPWGG	CO	AN	TZ
KUTENAI	NC07XX334C	CCCNCUBOAC	OCOBNCHCOS	5210C50AOE	OOOOOFOPOM	ODCFXXOMCM	COXXXCCOCC	IFICECEPXR	SRGMCGRCM	OC	AI	CZ
KWAKIUTL	NB03XX3250	OGBFNOVUEC	OOORSSHOOV	5315C30500	050FC5050M	OMCFXXCNC5	C5XWACCCCC	HFP5CPPVXR	SWGWVVVVV	OK	55	CZ
LAKALAI	IG07XX2121	4BXFRVCNSC	OPCKCCI555	5555555500	0505050505	5555XX0505	05XMPCWOCC	CCO5C555X5	555555555	OO	OO	TZ
LAKHER	EI04XX0211	6BCNOCPCAS	OCOCEMCECV	531CQ50SOB	CMCFCCOF05	CMCOXXCMCD	OEXTBCCCCC	HCPPPPPAXR	PMGGVVVVV	OC	MS	OZ
LAMBA	AC05XXC22C	6STNCUCUAC	OSCCCMIECV	522AQ1050C	OMC5050FCM	0500XXONOO	OEXNCBOCCC	SCM5CNP5XC	GPCGVVVVV	CO	MM	SZ
LAMET	EJ01XX1202	5BSNOUPOSS	OOOCMMCECV	2305550TOB	OOOOC5CCO5	CNCFXXOMCD	OEXMKKWCCC	CCP5C55FXR	PW5WVVVVV	CO	AS	OZ
LANGO	AJ04XXC104	5BCGCCPOAS	OCCCOCCECV	330B550TOB	M505050505	C5C5XX0505	C5XCNEWOCC	IFPPPPP5XC	GPDGCP55G	CO	AS	SZ
LAPPS	CG04XX0226	OCOMCCVUEC	CCOKSCECOB	120CA2050C	M505050505	0505XX05C5	C5XURFWCCC	CC5PLCEAXR	GFGFR5W55	CO	AS	UZ
LAU	IH04XX0041	5GOFRCPUCP	SCOCCCIHRV	2320A45TOP	COOOCCOFOM	OMCGXXODOM	ONXMPCWOCC	COQ5CPEAXR	GGGGVVVVV	OO	MB	TZ
LEPCHA	EE03XX0103	6BSFNCPOES	OOOCNCHICN	330BACOAPB	MOOFC5OOOC	CMCFXXOCCE	CEXTBCWC5C	HFPPEPEFXR	GMGGRPMGG	CO	CS	FZ
LESU	IG04XX0141	4BONOCMOSC	CMCCSCIHRH	4300A44TOP	OOOOOCOOCM	5M50XXONOF	OGXMPCCOCC	CCI5CME5XR	GWGGVVVVV	CO	AI	TZ
LHOTA NAGA	EI02XX1112	5BSPCUPNSP	SCCCMMCECV	5300A50TOB	OMCFOCOF05	OMCCXXOMCM	CNXTBCWCCC	HFCPEPE5XR	EWGGVVVVV	CC	55	RZ
LIFU	IH07XX1031	5BSEQOPOCL	OCCCNCH505	5555555500	C505050505	C5C5XX0505	05XMPCDCCC	SFPPEPE5XC	GRBGVVVVV	CO	MS	TZ
LOLO	EC02XX0103	6BONOCPOCP	OCOCCMCICV	3300550APB	OMCPCP0505	CMCOXXOCCE	SEXTBCCO5C	HCPPEPEFXR	G55W55555	OO	AS	FZ
LOZI	AB03XX1212	4TSQOVVAEO	CCORNCHICT	223A5505QB	MMCOCMOFOP	CDCGXXCNCM	CGXNCBCCCC	HCPPCPQ5XC	GPCGRG5GG	CK	SP	SZ
LUBA	AE06XX1221	4BCQCCPCAL	OOOOOC5555	5555555500	0505C50505	05C5XX05C5	C5XNCBDOCC	HFCCFCPEXR	G55GVVVVV	OO	LA	SZ
LUO	AJ06XX0112	6BOFSOPNCS	OOOONODICN	331AQ20POB	MMCOCPOFOC	C5CCXXOCCM	OEXCNEWCCC	CCPPPPPVXC	SPCGVVVVV	SO	AS	SZ
MACASSARESE	IC01XX0022	6BCNOOBNSC	CCCRQCEJCN	333CA245PB	CMCFO5OPOP	5M50XXOMON	CNXMPCDCCC	HFP5C55PXR	PG5GVVVVV	OO	LP	TZ
MAGUZAWA	CB01XX0012	7BOEQOPOAS	OOOCCMH555	5555555500	0505050505	C5C5XX05C5	C5XAACCCCC	IFAQEPEFXC	GACGVVVVV	CO	SA	SZ
MALAYS	EJ08XX0022	6BCFNUVNAC	CCCKQCHJCN	532C559APB	0505050505	0505XX0505	C5XMPCCO5C	IF5PEPE5XR	PMGGVVVVV	OO	SP	TZ
MAM	SA08XX0001	9TCFMCPOSL	OCCCNCHECV	640C550AOE	0505050505	C505XX0505	05XMA5WCCC	CCAPEPEVXR	GAGGRGAGT	CC	55	FZ

APPENDIX SEVEN/ 6 -- ETHNOGRAPHIC ATLAS CODE SHEET

	10	20	30	40	50	60	70	80	90	EX	LP	NE
MAMBILA	AH04XX0002	8XBENOVASC	OCORNCHICH	5405555AOS	0505050505	05C5XX05C5	C5XNCBCCCC	SFN5CPE5XC	GMCGVVVVV	CK	55	GZ
MAMVU	AI05XX1101	7BCQCOPOCL	CCCC5CHETV	220A55550S	OMCOOPOPOO	0505XXOC05	OGXCNCOOCC	SF55C55VXC	GGCGVVVVV	00	55	TZ
MANCHU	EC03XX0012	7BOEMOPOCS	OOOCCCI505	5555555500	0505050505	0505XX0505	05XALGWCCC	IFEPUPU5XR	5A5GVVVVV	CO	CE	GZ
MANDAN	NE06XX0221	5COFRCMV5C	CMSCMCCICT	5315550AOE	0000C50P05	0500XXOMCM	OFXSXOOOCC	CC5NCM55XC	5RDECGRCH	CO	ME	LZ
MANGAIANS	IJ01XX004C	6COFRCVUEC	OCOSNCHHRN	5410A56A00	00000COCCM	CMCOXXONCO	CFXMPOCOOC	COQ5C55PXR	GWGGVVVVV	00	MB	TZ
MANIHIKI	IJ04XX0050	5CCFNOVU5C	CCCBQCHHTV	5310A50500	00000C00CM	050CXX0000	05XMPODOCC	CCP5C55FXR	GMGGVVVVV	00	AS	TZ
MANUS	IG09XX2071	OGCNOOPNSL	CLOCRRZCTV	3300A50ROP	0005050PCM	555FXXONC5	OOXMPCWCCC	CCCOCC5VXR	P5GGVVVVV	CO	AP	TZ
MAORI	IJ02XX222C	4GOEPOBOSC	OCORSCHERV	541AA50500	000P05CCOM	OMCNXXONOO	ONXMPODOCC	IFPPP55FXR	GWGBRGGGG	CK	MS	GF
MARGI	AH05XX0112	6BSFQOPASL	OOOONCHICH	5415550AOB	0505C50505	C5C5XXC5C5	C5XAACOOCC	SFEPPPP5XC	GACGVVVVV	00	LP	SZ
MARICOPA	NH05XX4120	3CONOOPOAS	OCOCNCIJCV	2310C50A00	000MAMOFOP	OMCFXXCMCO	CNXHCYOOCC	CC5CEC55XC	GRDERGAFE	00	MP	EZ
MARQUESANS	IJ03XX0041	5GCOCCVNAC	CCCKCCHHTN	2310A17AOP	00000C000M	CMCOXXONCF	OMXMPCDOCC	CCPCPCPFXR	EGGGVVVVV	OC	MS	TZ
MARSHALLESE	IF03XX0041	5COEMOBOSC	OSCKCCIHTV	5310A10AOP	C000CCCOOM	5M5CXXON05	ONXMPCDOCO	CON5CPEFXR	GGGGRPWGG	00	DO	TZ
MASAI	AJ02XX0109	OBOQCCPNAS	OOOCNCOO5B	1225Q35TOB	MMCOCPOCOO	O5COXXOCOD	BOXCNECOCC	CCCPEPEFXE	GRRPVVVVV	00	PC	EZ
MATACO	SH01XX2241	1SOFNUUVEC	OCOBOCHCVS	2200C30AOS	OOOFOFOFOC	OFOGXXOMCF	OGXMMCOOCC	CC5OCO5FXC	GRBGVVVVV	00	A5	BZ
MATAKAM	AH07XX0001	9BCENCPOCS	OOOOCOOICH	540A550AOS	CMCOOPOFCO	OMCOXXOCO5	ODXAACOOCC	5CQ5C555XC	GACGVVVVV	SO	AP	SZ
MAYA	SA06XX012C	7STMCUVNAL	OCOOMCHECX	7315C50TOC	CPOFC50POP	C5COXXOMCO	CMXMA5COCC	HO5QEQE5XR	G5GGVVVVV	00	MS	TZ
MAZATECO	NJ05XX0002	8CCNCCVOAC	OCOBNCH505	5555555500	0505050505	05C5XX05C5	C5XOM5505C	5C55C555X5	555555555	00	C5	BZ
MBUGWE	AC05XX0204	4BOFMCPCAL	OSLCOCC555	5555555500	0505C50505	C5C5XX0505	C5XNCBWOCC	CCNPPPP5XR	G5FEVVVVV	CO	AC	MS
MBUNDU	AB05XX1112	5BCQCCPACL	OLCCCMIECV	432AQ50POB	OMCOOPOFOM	OMCFXXONOM	CGXNCBDOCC	HCPPCM55XC	GPCGVVVVV	SO	LP	SZ
MBUTI	AA05XX631C	CXBNOOPOCL	OCCCCC505B	120C550500	00000POOCO	OFOGXXOFOO	OOXNCBOOCC	CCCOC555XC	GRDGVVVVV	00	AS	TZ
MENDE	AF05XX1C11	7BTFQOPCSL	CCCCMMHECX	541AS55TOS	OMCMOPOFO5	C5CNXXOG05	CEXNCMDOCC	HFCCCQE5XC	GPCGRGPGG	OO	LP	TZ
MENTAWEI	IB07XX0121	6SCMOCVVSO	OOOSTC5555	5555555500	0000C5000P	O5CCXXONC5	CDXMPCCCCC	CCCNC55FXR	P55GVVVVV	00	00	TZ
MERINA	EH02XX0012	7TONOOVOAP	CECCTCHJCV	733555250B	0505050505	0505XX0505	C5XMPODOCC	HFACECEFXR	GMGGRGAGG	CC	SA	RZ
MIAMI	NF04XX231C	4GCROOPO5S	OOOCOCCECT	531BC50500	OOOFOFOPOP	C5CFXX05CO	CFXAGCOOCC	SFP5C555XR	GM5MVVVVV	00	MP	LZ
MIAO	EC04XX0112	6BCFNOPOSS	OCCKCCHJCH	5415550A0B	CMCFC50505	OMCOXXOMOF	CNXMYOOOCC	CCAPEPE5XR	EWGTVVVVV	00	55	OZ
MIN CHINESE	EC06XX0012	7BCFNOPOCS	LOOOEO5JCV	8345S50APB	0505050505	0505XX0505	C5XSICCC5C	IFAPEPE5XR	555555555	00	55	RZ
MINANGKABAU	IB06XX0012	7CCENCOMSC	OPSCCCH555	5555555500	0505050505	0505XX0505	05XMPOWCOC	CCNOCNE5XR	5WGCVVVVV	CC	AC	RZ
MINCHIA	EC08XXCC12	7BCFNCPOCL	OOCCQCCJCV	5415550APB	M505050505	05C5XX05C5	C5XTBCCO5C	CCEPEPEVXQ	ESGTRGSGG	00	CE	FZ
MISKITO	SA09XX3221	2TSENCUNAC	CCCQCCIERV	331CA10A0B	MCOFCPOFCM	CEOEXXON05	CFXMS500CC	CC55C55EXR	PMGGRGWGG	CC	ME	TZ
MIWOK	NC05XX631C	CCCROOVOCM	LCOOOCCOOT	5205C20500	0505C50505	C5C5XXC5C5	C5XPENCCCC	COPOCO55XC	SRDBVVVVV	CO	AS	FZ
MNONG GAR	EJ02XX1022	5GCNCCMOSC	OSOCMMCECW	3300550A0B	OMCFO5OF05	ONCFXXOEOE	OEXMKCWCCC	ICO5CCE5XE	GWGGVVVVV	CO	55	TZ
MONGO	AE04XX112C	6BCECCPACL	OCCCNCCERH	542A514POS	OMCMOCOFOM	OMCFXXONCO	CGXNCBOOEC	IFQQPQPFXR	GWGGVVVVV	SO	MB	TZ
MONGUOR	EB02XXC013	6BCFNCPOSS	OCCCCC5ICH	5315550APB	MMCMCP0505	C5CCXXOMOD	OEXALMD050	SCPPCPEAXR	GA5GVVVVV	CO	MS	HZ
MOSSI	AC02XX1002	7BCECCPOSS	OOOONCHICN	742AP34TOB	CMCMCMCFCC	ONOFXXCCCM	BEXNCGCCCC	HF5QPQP5XC	GACGVVVVV	00	SS	SZ
MOTA	IH01XX0031	6BCRCOAOSC	OMSCOCCHRV	5300A50TOP	000005000M	5550XXONON	05XMPCWOCO	COSMEME5XR	GWGGVVVVV	00	AI	TZ
MOTILON	SB03XX412C	3CCFPOUVAC	OOOQCCIERV	1305550500	0505050505	0505XX05C5	05XCA500CC	CC55C555X5	555555555	CO	A5	TZ
MUNDURUCU	SC01XX132C	4SOENOUOAM	OOCCCCZERW	2300550TOO	OOOFC50FOC	CNCEXXCNCO	ODXTGCOOCC	CCPOCO5TXR	GPGGRGOHG	OO	AP	TZ
MURINBATA	IC07XX7210	C5CPOOPACM	SCCCRRI05B	1200555500	0000050005	555FXXONCO	COXAUCCOCC	CC55C555X5	555555555	00	55	SZ
MURNGIN	IC02XX5320	OSCRCUPOCM	OMCCMMSC5B	1200014TOO	00000000OM	5G5GXXONCO	OOXAUCOOCC	COPOC55EXR	GRRBSGREB	00	AS	SZ
MZAB	CC04XX0001	9BCMCCPNSS	CCCC5C5JTV	730C553AOS	M505050505	0505XX05C5	O5XAABDOEC	SFC5C55VXQ	5SFEVVVVV	00	MC	VZ

	10	20	30	40	50	60	70	80	90	EX	LP	NE
NABESNA	NA01XX262C	OTSMCUUVAC	CPCCCCIOOS	1200C50500	00000F000P	OGC5XXOMCO	COXATNOOCC	CCCCCO5EXC	GRDHRGBFB	CC	55	CZ
NAMA	AA03XX1315	CGBNOUPOCS	OCCCCCIC5B	3210S20PCB	MMOOCGOFOO	OCOFXXOMOG	OOXKHCWCCC	CCPOCPPAXC	GRDMVVVVV	CO	MS	EZ
NAMBICUARA	SI04XX4310	2CONOCVUAC	OCOBCCIERS	1300520A00	OOOMC50CCC	CMCGXXOMCO	CNXXXOCCCC	CCC5055EXC	GRBGSGREG	OO	AI	SZ
NANDI	AJ07XX0005	5BCNOOPNAS	OCCKCCCICN	521A526TOB	MMCCCFOFCC	CDC5XXOCOD	CGXCNEOOCC	CCSPPPP5XC	GPCGVVVVV	OO	PC	SZ
NASKAPI	NA05XX1630	CXCNOOVUAO	OCOBCCI505	5555555500	0505050505	C5C5XX05C5	O5XAGCCCCC	CCSCC555XC	GRCHVVVVV	OO	AI	CZ
NATCHEZ	NG07XXC32C	5CCFRCVOAO	OOOBNCZECV	431AA505OC	OOOFOPOFOM	OMC5XXOMCO	OGXNM5EOCC	5CM5C55FXR	GPDGVVVVV	CO	MM	LZ
NAVAHC	NHC3XX2103	4TCFSCMVAC	OPSCNCIJCT	4300C20AOS	OMCFCMOFCC	CMCFXXOCOE	CNXATSOOCC	IFC5CMEPXC	GRDECSRCB	OO	AI	EZ
NDEMBU	AC06XX0211	6TCQOUAVCO	OSICCCIECW	1225555RCS	CMCOC5C5OP	C5COXXCNC5	CGXNCB5OOO	SFN5CN55XR	GP5GVVVVV	OO	55	SZ
NGONI	AC09XX0121	6TCQOOVUAC	OOOQCCI555	5555555500	0505050505	05C5XX05C5	O5XNCBOOCC	IFP5CPP5XC	G5CGVVVVV	OO	LS	SZ
NICOBARESE	EH05XX1121	5CCNOOUVAC	OCCBSCEHTH	5305A50AOP	OMCOO5OFCM	OMCFXXOMOF	ONXMKKOOOC	CCCOCCEFXC	PRBGRP5GG	OO	AI	TZ
NOMLAKI	NC01XX631C	CGCNCUPOCL	OCCCOCCCOV	320AC5050C	OOOOONCOCC	CNCFXXONOO	OOXPEWWCCC	CCP5CC5PXC	GRCGCS5CG	OO	AS	GZ
NUER	AJ03XX0015	4BCFQUVUCS	OOOCNCCECS	530C54CPOB	MOOOC5COOC	O5CFXXCNCN	CEXCNECOEC	CCOPEPE5XC	GPCGCGRDG	OO	PO	SZ
NUNIVAK	NA06XX136C	OCCFNUVNAC	CCOQQCIOOT	5300A5OPOO	OOOOOGOFOM	ONCFXXONCO	COXESCWOCC	CCCCCPE5XR	SWHEVVVVV	OO	AI	UZ
NUPE	AF08XX1011	7BCEQOPOSL	OCCCCCHECH	532C554POS	CMCMCMCFOP	CCCGXXO5OM	ONXNCKCDCC	HFSQPDEVXC	GACGVVVVV	CO	55	SZ
NURI	EAC5XXC103	6BCFCCPOAS	CCCOCOC5JCV	5315555APB	MMCMCMO505	O5O5XXOCCM	CGXIEIWCCC	HCPPEPE5XQ	5AFEVVVVV	OO	MS	EZ
NYAKYUSA	AC06XX0112	6BCQOCNUEL	OOOKNCIITV	322AQ50TOB	MMCPCCOPOM	OMCOXXONCM	CNXNCBCOCC	IFEQPQPEXC	GACGRGAGG	OO	MA	RZ
NYANEKA	AB07XX0114	4BCFQVAOCC	OSOCCCI555	5555555500	0505050505	05C5XX0505	O5XNCBDOCO	SFMMPMP5XC	GMCGVVVVV	CO	LN	SR
NYARO	AI02XX0102	7BSNCUPCSL	OLCCOC5555	5555555500	0505050505	05C5XX05C5	O5XKCCOCCC	IFCPEME5XC	GACGVVVVV	OC	55	SZ
NYORO	AC02XXC112	6BOQOOPOSS	CCCCOCCICN	523AQ50ACB	MMCOOMCMCM	COOOXXOMCN	OGXNCBDOCC	HFPPPPP5XC	GRBGVVVVV	CO	S5	SZ
OJIBWA	NF01XX1450	COCGNUVUCL	OOOQCCICOS	1315550AOO	OOOOCFCCCM	Ç5C5XXOMCO	ONXAGCOOCC	CC5PPPEFXR	GWGBCGRDB	OO	AI	CZ
OKINAWANS	EC07XX0022	6TCGMCPNAS	OOOKSCEIRV	8320S1OAPB	CMIGI5ONIM	CNCOXXOMCD	OEXJRCDCCC	CCEPPPCPXR	ZWHGRETDG	OO	MO	RZ
OMAHA	NF03XX1411	3GCNOUBCSM	SCCCNCCICT	2310C50AOE	OOOFOFOPOM	OOCFXXOECM	CGXSXCOOCC	IFIPEPEPXC	SWDECGRCH	CO	MI	GZ
ONA	SG03XX163C	CSOPCUVOEC	OCCBNCECOB	220AA5050C	COOOOF0005	O5OFXXONOO	OOXTHCOOOC	COCOCC5VXS	GREHCGRCG	OO	AI	UF
ONTONG-JAVA	II05XX0050	5COENCUVAC	OOOSNCHHTT	5400555AOO	OOOMCCOOCM	CDCOXXCMCO	CGXMPCWCCC	CCQ5C555XR	GMGGVVVVV	OO	A5	TZ
ORAON	EF06XX0002	8BOFNOPOES	OOOCOCHICV	5415550TPB	M505050505	0505XX0505	O5XDRC5OCC	IFEPEPE5XR	GPGGVVVVV	OO	ME	OZ
PAEZ	SF05XX1102	6CCPCONO5C	CCCB5C5IRN	5215051500	OPOFC5OFOC	OMO5XXOCOM	OEXCHC5OCC	CCECCPE5XR	GMHGRGSHG	CO	M5	HR
PAIWAN	IA06XXC211	6BOGNOVUCC	COORNCHECV	4310A50ROP	0505C50505	O5C5XX0505	O5XMPCOOCC	CCPCPCP5XR	GS5SVVVVV	CK	55	RT
PALAUANS	IF01XX0041	5BONOVAVSC	OPSSNCHHRV	5420C50AOP	OOOFC5OFCM	5M5CXXONC5	CGXMPCDWCC	CCNNPPEFXR	PGGGREWGG	EO	MY	TS
PALIKUR	SC03XXC23C	5COMCBVU5S	OCOC5C5505	555555550C	OOOPCCOPCM	CMC5XXCNCO	CEXARCCCCC	COE5O555XC	P55GVVVVV	OO	AI	TZ
PAPAGO	NI02XX320C	5CCFRCVOAO	OOOBNCHJCT	530CC50AOO	OOOMCMOFOC	O5OFXXOCCO	CNXPI5COCC	CCCPEO55XC	SG5ERGOFE	OO	AC	CE
PARAUJANO	SB05XX316C	OBCNCCBNCC	OOCBOCHCOV	521A550AOO	0505C50505	O5C5XX05C5	O5XAR5COCC	CC55C55FXR	PMGGVVVVV	OO	55	BE
PATHAN	EA02XX0003	7BONOOPOAP	OOCKQAHJCV	542C5535PB	M505050505	O5C5XX0505	O5XIEPCODO	SFIDEDE5XR	5SFEVVVVV	CO	55	BZ
PAWNEE	NF06XX1301	5COFRCMOCC	OLOCSSCECV	331555ORDE	0505C50505	C5C5XXC5C5	C5XCCCOCCC	IFPOCN55XC	5RDECGRCH	OO	MS	GZ
PENDE	AC02XX1012	6TCQCVAVCC	OSICPPC555	5555555500	0505050505	05C5XX0505	C5XNCBDOCC	SFM5CMP5XR	G5HGVVVVV	SO	55	SZ
PENOBSCOT	NG04XX242C	2SONOUBOAC	OOOBCCE505	5555555500	0505050505	C5C5XX05O5	O5XAG5OCCC	CC5PEPE5XR	G555CGRC5	CO	M5	CL
PONAPEANS	IF05XX0031	6OONOOMAAC	OSOCCCCHRN	132052050P	OOOFCCOOCM	C55CXXONC5	ONXMPOOOOO	CONNENEFXR	EMGGVVVVV	OO	MM	TZ
POPOLUCA	NJ03XX0211	6CORCOVO5C	OOOBOCH505	5555555500	0505050505	O5C5XXC5C5	C5XMZ5COCC	CCEPEPE5XR	GWHGVVVVV	OO	C5	TZ
PORTUGUESE	CE02XX0014	5COGMCVNCC	CCOBQCE555	5555555500	0505050505	O5C5XX0505	O5XIERCOCC	CCE5C555XR	ESGTVVVVV	CO	55	MZ
PUKAPUKA	II03XXC041	5GOMCCPCSS	OSLKNCHHTV	331AA10ACP	OOOOOCOOOM	OMCNXXOCCE	CFXMPCCCCC	CCP5C55FXR	G5GGVVVVV	CC	AS	TB
PURARI	IE08XX4121	2BCPOOPOSM	CCCCNCHHTV	5405550TOP	OOOOC5COOM	5M5DXXOGOF	CNXPAOOOCC	CCIPEPE5XR	PWGGVVVVV	CC	55	TZ

APPENDIX SEVEN/ 8 -- ETHNOGRAPHIC ATLAS CODE SHEET

	10	20	30	40	50	60	70	80	90	EX	LP	NE
PURUM	EI06XX0102	7SCGNUPOAS	LCOCMMSECV	2300520SPB	000F050005	0500XX0C0D	CNXTBCWOCC	5CCPUPUVXR	PWGGVVVVV	00	55	0Z
RARCIANS	IJ05XX1050	4CCENCBNAC	CCCR5CH505	5555555500	00000C000M	CMCEXXON00	ONXMPCCOCC	CCPCECEFXR	GCGGVVVVV	CK	AS	TZ
REGEIBAT	CC01XX0107	2BOFNCPOCP	CCCCQACJTS	543C5595PC	M505C50505	0505XX0505	C5XAASCECC	HCECECE5XR	GF5FVVVVV	00	55	CE
RIFFIANS	CC03XX0113	5BOENOPNCS	LCOCTC5JCV	731C521APB	MMCFCMCDCM	CMCOXXOMCD	OMXAABWOCE	CCOPEPEPXQ	GSF5VVVVV	CO	MC	MZ
ROMANS	CE03XX0022	6COMCONOAC	000BQCCICV	8550550APB	M505050505	0505XX05C5	O5XIERCCCC	HC5CECE5XR	555555555	00	SE	MZ
ROTINESE	IC04XX0012	7BCPOCPO5S	OCCCTCI555	5555555500	0505050505	5555XX05C5	O5XMPCDCCC	IF55C555X5	555555555	00	M5	TZ
ROTUMANS	IH06XXCC21	7COMCOMASC	OLOCSCH505	5555555500	0505050505	0505XX0505	O5XMPOOOCC	CCQ5C555X5	555555555	0C	M5	TZ
RUNCI	AE08XX0013	6TCQOOPNSS	OOOCCCIITN	533AQ20A0B	MMCOCPOMCM	CECCXXCMCM	CEXNCBCOEC	IFPPPPPVXC	GRBGVVVVV	00	55	GZ
RWALA	CJ02XX1108	0BCQOOPCCP	CCCKQACOOB	331CA23A0C	MMCFCF0500	OFCFXXOCCM	COXAASWCCC	HC5CCPEVXR	GFGFVVVVV	00	LP	EZ
SAGADA	IA02XX0003	7GCMOCBOAC	CCOKSCEJCV	6300A2CPPB	CMCFCCOOOC	CMCCXXOEON	BEXMPCWCCC	CCOCECEFXR	EWHGVVVVV	OR	55	TZ
SAMOANS	II01XX0031	6GOENOBOSO	OCCSNCHHRV	242AC44A0P	0000CCCCCM	OMCOXXOCOE	ODXMPODOCC	COP5C55FXE	EMGGVVVVV	00	MS	TZ
SAMCYED	EC04XX0334	0BCFNOPOEP	000CTM5COB	130B52050D	C000CFCC0P	CFCFXXOMCM	CCXURSWCCC	CC55C55EXC	GRCHVVVVV	00	A5	UZ
SANDAWE	AA06XX1112	5BONOBPOCL	CCCCMMZECN	521A554508	M505050505	0505XX0505	05XKHCOOCC	CC55CPE5XC	GRDGRGPFE	00	AP	BZ
SANPOIL	NC04XX3250	0TCGPCVOAC	CCO8NCHOOS	230BC10A00	0000C50FCM	05CFXXOMCO	COXSACCOCC	CCPCCQ5PXE	GRGMCGRCM	C0	55	GZ
SANTAL	EF01XXC111	7BCFNCPOES	CCCCCCCJCV	531A550APB	OMCMC50P05	ODOFXXOMON	OEXMKMOOCC	CCPPEPEVXQ	GAGGVVVVV	C0	MS	OZ
SARAMACCA	SC06XX1220	5BSQOOAUSC	CSLCTCH505	5555555500	0505C50505	05C5XX05C5	C5XIEROOCC	CCN5CNE5XR	GMGGVVVVV	00	MY	TZ
SARSI	NE07XX280C	CBOROOVNAC	OCCBOCHCOB	5215520AOE	COOOOF000P	CFCFXXOMCM	COXATNCCCC	CCICCCEVXC	GRCHVVVVV	00	MI	GZ
SELUNG	EJ06XX1180	OCCNOUNVAC	CCCB5CE05B	5205550A00	0505050505	0505XX0505	O5XMPCCOCC	CC55C555X5	5555VVVVV	00	00	TZ
SEMANG	EJ03XX433C	OCONCUVOEC	COCBCCHC5B	120BA50A00	0000050005	OFODXXOM00	OOXMKSOOCC	CCPOCCEPXR	GRSGVVVVV	0C	C0	OZ
SEMINCLE	NG02XX----	-OOMCCMOCC	OPSORCC505	5555555500	0505C50505	O5C5XX0505	O5XNM5CCCC	CC55C555XR	EOGGVVVVV	C0	55	TZ
SENIANG	IH02XX0131	5BOROCPOCP	OOOONCCHRV	5205A5CTOP	0000CC000M	555CXXONCN	CEXMPCWCCC	CCP5C555XR	GWGGVVVVV	00	MS	TZ
SERBS	CH01XX0004	6DCFMCPNSL	OCCC5CHICX	833CS50APB	MMCF050MC5	OMCOXXOCCG	CEXIESCOCC	CCE5C55VXQ	EPHTVVVVV	00	SC	LZ
SERI	NI04XX226C	CBOFMOVOAC	OCOBOCH505	5555555500	0505050505	C5C5XX0505	C5XXY5OCCC	CC5OC055XR	GRRGVVVVV	C0	A5	EZ
SHERENTE	SJ02XX2310	4CONCUPOSM	CCOCPCOERV	5300A50TOO	0505C505C5	C5C5XX05C5	O5XGECOOCC	CCP5C555XR	G5GGVVVVV	00	MP	TS
SHILLUK	AI06XX1112	5BSQOOPCSS	OCOCNCCECH	531A54CPOB	MMCOCPOFCM	CCCFXX05CM	CEXCNECCCO	HFEPPPPPXC	5ACGVVVVV	CC	SP	SZ
SHLUH	CD05XX1003	6BOFMCPOSL	OCCC5C5JCH	541C559APB	M505050505	0505XX0505	O5XAABOOCC	COEDEDEVXR	5SFEVVVVV	CO	MC	MZ
SIMBCESE	IG08XX0021	7BONOUBOSC	OOORNCH555	5555555500	0505050505	5555XX05C5	C5XMPC5C5C	5C55C555X5	555555555	CK	55	TZ
SINCHI	EA01XXC023	5DCFNOPOCL	CCCCQCC555	5555555500	0505050505	0505XX0505	O5XIEIEC5C	HCI5C555XR	555555555	CO	D5	BZ
SINHALESE	EH06XX0013	6CCMOOVVAC	OOOQCCIJCV	833555CAPB	M505C50505	05C5XXC5C5	O5XIEI50CC	CC5CECEFXR	GPGGRGAGT	00	S5	RZ
SIRICNO	SE01XX3510	1CCERCMOSC	OLCCMMCECS	130AA10A00	000FOCOFOC	OMCEXXOMCO	CEXTGCOOCC	CCPCCC5FXR	GRHGRGRSG	00	AS	ST
SIUAI	IG01XX2102	5BCNOVAUSC	OSCCCMHERH	530055050P	0505050505	5555XX0505	O5XPACWOCC	CCINCCEPXR	PGGGRGGGG	C0	AI	TZ
SIWANS	CC03XXC003	7BOFNOPODS	OCCCQCCJTX	640CP5450B	MOOFCMCFCC	O5COXXOOOM	OMXAABWC5C	HFODEDE5XR	5SFEVVVVV	00	MC	VZ
SOMALI	CA02XX0009	1BOFQOPOCP	LOOONCCICB	132CP24TOC	MMCMCMC000	OGCOXXSCCD	CIXAACWCCC	HFECECEPXC	GRDMCGACG	00	LE	EZ
SONGHAI	CB03XX0023	5BCNOOPNAL	OCCCQCIICV	733C55450B	MMCMCFCFCM	CDOOXXCMC5	CNXXXCCEDC	HFQDEDEPXE	GRRMQGAFE	CO	LP	SZ
SOTHC	AB08XX1103	5BCQCUPOAS	OCCCQCIICH	433055050B	M505050505	05C5XXC5C5	O5XNCBDCCC	CCPOCPP5XC	GPCGVVVVV	00	SS	GZ
SUBANUN	IA04XX0001	9BSNOUBNAC	OOCKQCHECN	1205550A0P	C505C50505	05C5XX0505	O5XMPCOOCC	CCOOCCE5XR	PGGGVVVVV	00	00	TZ
SWAZI	AB02XX1102	6BCESOPNCS	CCCCCCIECH	5330555PQB	MMCOCM0505	OECFXXOCCM	CGXNCBDOCC	CCPPPPP5XC	GRBGCGPCG	SO	55	BZ
SYRIANS	CJ01XX0004	6BOFNOPNAL	OCCCQACJCV	832CS52APB	MMCII50505	ONCOXXOCCN	CNXAASEC5C	CCE5C555XQ	EADFQEAGG	00	55	MZ
TAGBANUA	IA07XX0111	7STNCOUVCC	CCCKNCEECV	5205550A0B	0505050505	0505XX05C5	O5XMPCDOCC	IFCCECE5XR	5555VVVVV	00	PI	TZ
TALAMANCA	SA05XX012C	7SOENCMO5C	OMOCNCHECN	520B050A0P	000FOCOFOM	050GXXOM05	OEXCH5OOOO	CC5NP55AXC	G55GVVVVV	C0	MY	TZ

	10	20	30	40	50	60	70	80	90	EX	LP	NE
TALLENSI	AG04XX1002	7BSFQOPNCS	OECCNCHICN	5400C50A0B	MMCOCMOFOC	CDCFXXONCM	ONXNCGWOCC	IFSQPPEAXC	GACGCGAFE	00	AP	SZ
TAMIL	EG02XX0022	6TCGNCPVAL	0000CCI505	5555555500	0505050505	0505XX05C5	C5XDRCCCCC	CC55C555X5	555555555	00	C5	BZ
TANALA	EH03XX0022	6TOFQOPOSS	LECCCCIJCV	341AQ13P0B	MMCFCMCCOP	CMCOXXONOM	OEXMPCDOCO	HFEPECEFXR	EMGGVVVVV	CO	ME	RZ
TANIMBARESE	IC06XX1121	5BSFNUPOAL	OOOCCMH555	5555555500	0505050505	5555XX05C5	05XMPCDCCC	IFPPEPE5XR	50GGVVVVV	CO	AS	TZ
TAOS	NH06XXC201	7CCMOONOCC	OCCBNCEICV	5205C50AQE	0000050FOC	C5C5XXOCCN	ONXTAIOOCO	CCE5C55AXR	GAFEVVVVV	OC	AE	EZ
TAPIRAPE	SD02XX1130	5COEMOUCCC	OCOBOCHERV	3300A30T00	000FOCOFOO	OMCEXXONCO	CNXTGCOOCC	CC55C55EXR	GRRGVVVVV	00	A5	TZ
TARAHUMARA	NI01XX1103	5SCNOUNBCC	OOCKSCHICN	520CS1050B	050F050F05	CMCFXXOCOD	OMXTC5WCCC	CCECECEFXR	GWHWVVVVV	CC	A5	FZ
TAREUMIUT	NA02XX0370	OSCFNCBOAC	OCCKNCICOT	2300C10A00	COOCCFOFOM	OECOXXOCOO	COXESCWCCC	CCCOCPEFXC	SRDECGRDH	00	55	UZ
TEDA	CC02XX2003	5BCFQUPOES	LOOCNCIJTS	531C55550C	MMCCCMCPCC	C5CFXXOCCD	OEXKA550CO	IFSDEDEVXC	GSCGRGFRF	00	PP	VZ
TEHUELCHE	SG04XX2611	OGBFNOVOAO	0008QC5008	230AC30A0E	CMOFOFOPCC	OFCEXX05CM	COXTHCOOCC	ICPCC55PXS	GREHVVVVV	00	AS	EZ
TENCA	AG08XX2101	6STNOVAVAC	OSLCTC5ECV	231A544T0B	OMCDO50FOC	05OFXXCCCE	BDXNCACCCC	CCNNPNPFXC	GMCGVVVVV	00	MY	SZ
TENETEHARA	SJ06XX1211	5SOENOUOCC	OCCBOCHERV	5300020A0S	0505050505	0505XX0505	05XTGCOOCC	CCACCPE5XR	GGHGVVVVV	OC	A5	TS
TENINC	NC01XX3250	OGOGPOVUEO	OOOKNCHCOT	430CC50A0C	COOCCPCOCM	CMCGXXCNCO	OOXSHCWOCC	IFPOCO5VXE	SRHECGRCM	OO	PS	CE
TERA	CB06XX0111	7SEEQUPACL	OCOOCCIECV	5415554A0E	0505050505	05C5XXC5C5	C5XAACDCCC	SC5DEDE5XC	GACGVVVVV	00	55	SZ
TERENA	SH02XX2131	3COENUBNCC	OOOAOCHERS	540A550A0B	000FCM0505	CMCEXXOMC5	CNXARCDCCC	HCPCC55EXR	GRRGVVVVV	00	AP	RS
TESO	AJ01XX0103	6BOQOOPOSS	OCCCNCHECN	531A5505QB	M505050505	0505XX0505	05XCNEOOCO	IF5PPPP5XC	GRBGCG5CG	CO	55	SZ
TETCN	NE08XX1801	OBOROOVUEG	OGOKOOI505	5555555500	0505050505	05C5XX05C5	C5XSXCCOCC	CCICC555XC	GRCGVVVVV	00	PI	GZ
THAI	EJ09XX0C21	7TOGNOUNAC	CCCKQCHJCV	8340S50APB	0505050505	C5C5XX05C5	05XTKCCOCC	HFECECEVXR	P5GGRE5GT	OC	SE	TZ
THONGA	AB04XX0113	5BCESCPOCS	LCOCSCOECV	332AS26RQB	MMCOCCOFCM	OMCFXXOMCM	OGXNCBCCCC	CCCCCPEFXC	GPCGVVVVV	CO	LB	BG
TIBETANS	EE04XXC004	6DBGCOPOAS	CCCCTCE505	5555555500	OMCMCP050P	0500XXOMCD	OEXTBCC05C	SCEPCPC5XR	GSFEEGRHF	CC	SA	HZ
TIGRINYA	CA03XX0003	7DCMCOPOAL	OCCKNCCICV	732C5515PB	M505050505	05C5XXC5C5	C5XAASCDDC	HFAPEPE5XC	G5CGC55FE	CO	55	BZ
TIKOPIA	II02XX0050	5GOQOOPOAS	LCCKSCHHRH	5310A55A0C	000000000M	CMCOXXODOO	OGXMPCCCCC	CCPPE55AXR	GRGGVVVVV	CO	AP	TZ
TIMBIRA	SJ04XX2310	4SCFMCMOSC	CMOCOCCERV	3400A20P0P	00000C0C00	ONCGXXONCO	OGXGECOOCC	CC5CCN5PXR	GGHGVVVVV	00	00	SZ
TIMUCUA	NGC8XX2220	450ENCMOSO	OPCC5CCECT	5310550500	0000050MOP	0505XX0500	OGXNM5DOCO	5CMMFME5XC	G5CGRG55G	CO	M5	MZ
TIV	AH03XX1211	5XOEQCVACP	LOORSCHERN	441AQ44A0S	OMCMOPOFOP	CNCFXXONC5	ODXNCBOCCC	HFCCCPEAXC	GACGVVVVV	00	MP	SZ
TIWI	IC03XX5320	CBSFPOVUAO	OMSCPCS05B	330AA5CS00	00000500CM	555FXXODCO	COXAUCCCCC	CCPCC55EX5	5555VVVVV	00	A5	SZ
TODA	EG04XX1009	OTCOOOPCCS	CSCCCCIOOT	1310A10A0B	M000050000	OMCFXXOCOM	COXDRCOOCC	CCCOCPEFXR	GRRGVVVVV	00	AC	BZ
TOKELAU	II06XXCC6C	4CCENCUVCC	OCORNCCHTV	5315555TC0	0000000005	05CCXXOCOO	OMXMPCOOCC	CCP5CCEFXR	G5GGVVVVV	CK	MP	TZ
TOLOWA	NB06XX424C	CBCPOCPUCL	OCCCECICOT	5200C20A00	C0000PCOOM	05CGXXOMCO	OOXATPWOCC	ICPOCPEVXR	SWGWVVVVV	00	AI	FZ
TORAJA	IC05XXC202	6BOEMOUOAC	OCOBSCHECV	5315550A0B	0505050505	5555XXC5C5	C5XMPOWOCO	SFECECE5XR	G5GGRP5GG	OC	AE	TZ
TOTONAC	NJ04XX1111	6CO5OCVC5C	OCCBOCHECV	7315559A0E	COOF050F05	OMCFXXOMOD	ONXXX550CC	SF55C555XR	GWHGVVVVV	CC	SS	TZ
TRISTAN	CF03XX1032	4CCMCONOCC	COCK5CEERV	320C550APB	MMOOCMOOCM	OMCMXXOMCD	CNXIEGCCCC	CCOCECEPXR	ESGGVVVVV	OC	55	GZ
TROBRIAND	IG02XX1C31	5GONOOAVSC	OPCCPCCHRV	3210A40T0P	COOOCCOPCM	5N5FXXONOF	ODXMPCDOCC	CCMMEMEFXR	GWGGVVVVV	OO	MN	TZ
TRUKESE	IF02XX005C	5CCEMCMVSC	OSOCSCCHTH	3300C50T0P	COOFCCCOOM	5M5CXXOCCF	CNXMPCCOCC	CCNPEPEFXR	GGHGVVVVV	00	AM	RZ
TRUMAI	SI02XX2130	4TOENOVOAO	OOOCCCIERV	1300A50500	000F0500CM	OMCGXXOMCO	ODXXXOOOCC	IFPCC55FXE	GGGGVVVVV	00	AS	TZ
TSHIMSHIAN	NB07XX2260	OBCEPCACAC	OPCCCMICOT	5410550R00	000F0500OM	OMCFXXONOO	OOXXYODOCC	HFNNPNP5XR	SWGWVVVVV	CO	55	CZ
TUBATULABAL	NC02XX5320	CBCMCOVUAC	OCOBNCHCOS	12105205C0	COOOCMOFCM	ONOGXXONOO	OOXSSCOOOC	CCPOOO5PXC	SRDMRGGFG	CC	AS	EZ
TUCANC	SE05XX1130	5XCNOOPOCS	OOOCCCIERW	520A050A00	0000050FOP	OMCGXXOMCO	CGXBECCCCC	CC50C555XR	GWGGVVVVV	00	A5	TZ
TUCUNA	SE02XX114C	4XONOUPUCM	OCOCCCIERV	3200A30P00	OOOF050GCM	CMCEXXOMCO	OGXXYCOOCC	CC50CPEPXE	GGHGRPGGG	00	A5	TZ
TUNEBC	SF04XX1120	6TSPCUVUCC	COOBOCHECV	520A550A00	000FC50F05	C5CGXXOMCO	ODXCHCCCCC	5CC5C505XE	GWCGRGWGG	00	55	TZ

	10	20	30	40	50	60	70	80	90	EX	LP	NE
TUPINAMBA	SJ08XX2220	4SCEQUUVAO	OCCCCCIERV	431A050500	000FCCOFOM	OMOFXXOMOO	OGXTGOWOOO	ICP5C55FXR	GRRGVVVVV	00	AP	TZ
TURKANA	AJ05XX2103	4BOFQOPNES	OOOCNCCJCS	520B55050B	M505050505	05C5XX0505	05XCNE0000	COOPEPE5XC	GRDHSGREG	00	00	SZ
TURKMEN	EB05XX0004	6BOFNOPO5P	LOOOEMSJCV	543C5595PB	M505050505	0505XX0505	05XALTO050	SF55C555XR	GA55QGAFE	00	LS	VZ
TWANA	NB02XX136C	OGBENBVOEO	OCCKNCHCOS	2300C20A00	000FOGOOOM	CMOFXXONOO	OOXSAOWOOO	HFIOO55VXR	GWSWRGMGM	OC	55	CZ
TZELTAL	SA02XX0012	7STFNUPOAS	OOOOCMC505	5555555500	0505050505	05C5XX0505	05XMA55050	5O55C555XR	GPHGVVVVV	00	A5	FZ
ULAWANS	IG06XX0130	6BONOOVOSO	OOOROCHHRH	3300C50TOP	OOOOCCOOCM	CM5CXXCNCF	OEXMPOOOOO	CCOCECEVXR	GWGGVVVVV	00	AP	TZ
UTE	ND02XX3610	OCCFNUBOAO	OOOBNCHOOS	520AC4050E	OOOOOFOOOC	OFOFXXOMCM	COXSSCOOOO	OCCCCO5PXC	GRDBVVVVV	00	AS	EZ
VEDDA	EH04XX4330	OTOFMOMVCO	OSOCCPIO5S	1300010A00	OOOOOPOEO5	05COXXOMOO	OOXIEIOOOO	OC5PEPEPX5	5555RG5GG	OC	A5	OZ
VENDA	AB06XX1102	6BCESOPOSS	LLCOCMIICV	432BS50TOB	MOOOOPOFCO	OOOGXXOCOM	OGXNCBDOOC	IFPOCPPAXC	GPCGVVVVV	00	55	GZ
VIETNAMESE	EJ04XX0022	6TOFPOPOAS	OOOCOCHJCV	8345S555PB	0505050505	05C5XX0505	05XAMOCOCO	SFECECEVXQ	GPGGQGSGT	00	SE	TZ
WAICA	SD04XX233C	2CCNCOBOAO	OOOB5C5ETS	2205550500	0000050500	0505XXODOO	OGXCAOOOOO	OO55O555XR	GRSGVVVVV	00	A5	TZ
WALLOONS	CG05XX0013	6DOMCONOAO	OOOK5CEICV	824C550APB	M505050505	05C5XX05C5	05XIERCOOO	OO55C555XR	ESGTVVVVV	00	55	LZ
WANTOAT	IE02XXC201	7XOQOOPOCS	LCCKCCIHRV	520AA50TOP	000005C000	5550XXOCOF	ODXPAOOOOO	OCIPEPE5XR	GWGGVVVVV	00	55	RT
WAPISHANA	SC05XX2220	4SOPOUVOEO	OOOQCCIERV	5305A50500	0505C50505	C5C5XX0505	05XAROOOOO	OO55O555XE	GGHGRGPGG	00	A5	ST
WAROPEN	IE06XX3131	2GOENOPOSS	LCOCMMI555	5555555500	0505050505	5555XX0505	05XMPOOOOO	IFS5O555XR	P5HGVVVVV	00	00	TZ
WARRAU	SC01XX4320	1SCEROUODO	OOOB5CHCRT	230CA20A00	0505050505	0505XX05C5	05XXX50000	OOC5C555XR	POGGVVVVV	OO	AI	TZ
WASHO	ND06XX433C	COONOUBNAO	OOOBNCHCOS	1200C50ACC	COOOOMOOCM	OEOGXXOEOO	OOXXYOOOOO	OOPOOO55XC	GRCWCGRDG	00	AS	FZ
WICHITA	NF05XX1301	5SOFROUVAO	OOOKOOHECT	5315550AOE	0505050505	0505XX05C5	05XCCOOOCO	CCP5CO55XC	GRBGVVVVV	00	MI	GZ
WIKMUNKAN	IC06XX4420	OXOROOPOCM	OOOOMMIC5B	1205550500	0000050005	555FXXODOO	OOXAUOOOCO	CO55O555X5	555555555	00	55	SZ
WINNEBAGO	NF02XX2310	45CFNUPNSM	OOOOCCCJO5	5555555500	0505050505	0505XX05C5	05XSXOOOOO	CCP5C555XR	GBGBCGRDM	CO	MP	LZ
WITOTO	SE06XX222C	4SONOOPOCL	OOCCCC5ERV	520AA50AOC	COOOCCOFOM	OMCMXXOMOO	CGXWICOOOO	IOP5O55PXR	GGGGVVVVV	OC	AS	TZ
WOGEO	IE04XX2021	5GOPOOPOTL	CMCCSCIERV	2300A50TOP	OOOOOCOOCM	5M5GXXOMCO	ODXMPOOOOO	OOPPEPEAXR	GGGGVVVVV	00	00	TZ
WOLEAIANS	IF04XX0041	5OOEMOBOSO	OSOKNCHHTV	2310Q30AOP	COOFCCOOOM	CM5FXXONO5	CDXMPOOOOO	CCN5O55FXR	GWGGRGMGG	00	AC	TZ
WOLOF	CB02XX0013	6BCFQOPACL	OIOOCCHECW	332CS44AOB	MMCMCMCFCO	OMOGXXOMOM	ODXNCACDDO	HFQCECEPXC	GMCGVVVVV	00	S5	SZ
WUTE	AH08XX1111	6BOFQCPASP	LCCCOC5555	5555555500	0505050505	0505XX0505	05XNCBDOOO	HO5QPQP5XC	GPCGVVVVV	OC	MP	SZ
YABARANA	SC07XX1320	4SONOUUVEO	OCCQCCIERV	1200520500	OOOFCCOFCM	OMOFXXONCO	OGXCAOOOOO	OC55C55FXR	GOGGVVVVV	00	55	TZ
YAGUA	SE04XX0510	4SOMOUPOCL	OOOOOC5ERV	1200A30A00	OOOOCPOFAM	CNC5XXONCO	CGXPBOOOOO	OOEOOO5FXE	GRHGVVVVV	00	AE	TZ
YAHGAN	SG01XX1270	OSTNOOVOEO	OCOBNCECOB	120CA20500	OOOOOFOOCM	ODOFXXODOO	COXXXCOOOO	OCCCCC5PXC	SRDGCSRCG	00	00	UF
YAKO	AF04XX1101	7BCFQUPASL	OLOCCPIERV	740054050B	0505050505	C5C5XX0505	05XNCBOOCQ	IFNP5NE5XR	GWGGVVVVV	00	AM	TZ
YAKUT	EC02XX1224	1GSFQUPOCP	OCOCTCSCCS	232BS50AOB	MPOMCFOFOM	OMCFXXOMCN	OFXALTWOOO	SFEOPPEFXR	SRHECGRCB	00	LP	CZ
YAO	AC07XX0121	6COENCMASO	OSIOCCIECH	3310Q44500	OMCOCCOFOP	OMCOXXOMC5	CGXNCBOOOO	HFM5CNPAXC	G5CGRG55G	00	MN	SZ
YAPESE	IF06XX0041	5COFMOPASL	OSCCSCCHTN	5315530TOP	OOOFOOO5OM	C55CXXONOF	OGXMPOEOCO	CONQPPEFXR	EMGGVVVVV	00	M5	TZ
YARURO	SC02XX2211	4SOGNCUACO	OOOBCCHERV	520505050P	OOOOC5OFOM	OMCFXXOMOM	CNXXX5OOCO	CCQCEPE5XC	GRDGVVVVV	OC	AM	SZ
YOKUTS	NC03XX433C	CCCEQUPOSM	LCCCNCHOOS	5300C50500	COOOO5OFAP	O5OEXXONOO	COXPEYWOOO	CCQOCO55XC	GRDGCSRDE	OO	AB	GZ
YOMBE	AC08XX0221	5BOQOOAOCO	OSICOC5ECV	4315559ROS	0505050505	05C5XX05C5	C5XNCBDOOO	ICNNPNP5XR	GWGGVVVVV	00	55	TS
YORUBA	AF06XX0011	8BSECOPOSS	OOOKOCHERV	843A552AOS	CMCDOPOFOP	OMCOXXO5OF	ONXNCKCDOO	IFCQEQEPXQ	GAGGVVVVV	OO	SP	SZ
YUKAGHIR	EC06XX1540	OSOGNUUVEC	OCOBSC5OOS	1305550A00	0505050505	0505XX0505	05XXXOOOOO	IFSOCPU5XC	GRCGRGWHW	00	AI	UZ
YUKI	NC07XX433C	CGCNCUVNAO	OCOBNCHCOT	220AC20AOC	COOOC5OOOC	CMOFXXOMOO	OOXYUOWOOO	OOPOCO5PXC	SRCECGRCG	00	AS	GZ
YUROK	NB04XX4150	OBOFPOVUEO	OOOBNCHOOV	1300C50500	OOOOCNOOOM	OMCGXXCNCO	COXRICWOOO	IOI5CCE5XR	SWGWVVVVV	00	00	FZ
ZUNI	NH04XX110C	8SCEMOMOSO	OPLCOCCJCV	6400S50AOS	0505050505	0505XX0505	05XXX50000	OOENCCE5XR	GAFEVVVVV	CC	AC	EZ

APPENDIX EIGHT/ 1 -- FINISHED CHARACTERISTIC CODE SHEET

EXPLANATION ON PAGE 47

	FC 10	FC 20	FC 30	FC 40	FC 50	FC 60	FC 70	FC 80	FC 90	FC100
ABIPON	2222222212	2222112224	2422224442	2222211222	2222411555	2244442244	2112422122	2211115555	5552221241	5552222222
ABOR	1122122222	2222112224	2422122412	2222222222	2121124555	2222421214	2111222222	1211555522	2122221444	5552222111
AINU	1122122222	2211112224	2422224442	2222222221	2221124555	2244441214	2242422212	2212115555	5554444241	5252212141
AJIE	1222212221	2222112224	2421221142	2222222222	2115555555	1155555545	2242422222	5255555555	5552211241	5555555555
AKHA	1122121221	2222112224	2422122412	2222222222	2111124555	1121211214	2111222222	5255555522	2122221241	5552222222
ALACALUF	2222222212	2111112224	2422224442	2222222221	2222411555	2244442244	2242422212	2222215522	2222222444	5552222222
ALBANIANS	1121222222	2211112224	1122224442	2222222212	2221224555	1111142212	2111122222	1111115522	1112211241	5552112141
ALORESE	1222211221	2222222224	2421221142	2222222222	2111124222	1121211214	2122412222	5222525522	2122221555	5552112141
AMBA	1212222221	2222221221	2422224442	2222222222	1221224555	1121211244	2122421222	5221555522	2125555444	5552222111
AMERICANS	1121222222	2211112224	1122224442	2222222221	2221124555	1111142212	2111122222	1111115511	1141111114	5551112241
ANDAMANESE	1122121221	2222212224	2422224442	2222222222	2112411111	2244442244	2242422212	2221212122	2222222114	2522222222
APINAYE	2222222211	2222222224	2422224442	2222222222	2111124555	2222421224	2242422222	2222515522	2122221242	5552222111
ARANDA	1222212222	2222112224	2422224442	2211212222	2222411111	2244442254	2242422221	2222222122	2222221241	2552222222
ARAPESH	1222212221	2222222224	2422224442	2222222222	2111224122	1121211224	2122412222	5255555555	5552222444	5552222222
ARAUCANIANS	2222222212	2221112224	2422224442	2222222221	2221224222	1111142212	2122412222	1211111122	2122221241	5552221111
ARYANS	1122122222	2221112224	1122224442	2222211222	2225555555	1155555545	2242422222	5255555555	5551111555	5555555555
ASHANTI	1212222221	2222221221	2422224442	2222222222	2111124112	1121211224	2122421222	1211125521	1141111114	1552111141
ATAYAL	1222212222	2222112224	2421221142	2222222222	2111124555	1121211214	2122412222	5255555522	2122221114	5552212141
ATSUGEWI	2222222122	2211112224	2422224442	2222222221	2222411555	2244442244	2242422221	2222115522	2122221241	5552222222
AWEIKOMA	2222222212	2222112224	2422224442	2222222222	2122411555	2244442244	2242422122	2221525522	2222222444	5552222222
AYMARA	2222222211	2222212224	2422224442	2212212222	2221124221	1111142224	2112422222	1111115522	1114444555	5555552155
AZANDE	1212222221	2222221221	2422224442	2222222222	1221224222	1121211214	2242422222	1211212122	2122111241	2552112141
AZTEC	2222222121	2222212224	2422224442	2222222221	2221124555	1111142211	2242422222	1211111111	1141111241	5152112141
BABWA	1212222221	2222221221	2422224442	2222222222	2111224555	1121211244	2242422222	5255555555	5552211555	5552111141
BACAIRI	2222222211	2222212224	2422224442	2122222222	2111124555	2222421224	2242422222	2221515522	2222221114	5552221111
BAJUN	1212222221	2222221221	2422224442	2211212222	2225555555	2244445555	2242422212	2252255555	5555555241	5555555555
BALINESE	1222211221	2222222224	2421221142	2222222222	2115555122	1155555555	2242422222	5255555555	5551111241	1555555555
BAMBARA	1212222221	2222211221	2422224442	2222222222	1221124555	1111142212	2111122222	1211115521	1145555241	5552211141
BAMILEKE	1212222221	2222221221	2422224442	2222222222	2111224555	1121211214	2122421222	1211555555	5555555241	5551112141
BANDA	1212222221	2222221221	2422224442	2222222222	2111224555	1121211214	2122421222	5255555555	5552221241	5552222111
BARABRA	1121222221	2222112124	2422224442	2211212222	2221124555	1111142244	2111122222	5155555522	2124444555	5552222111
BARI	1212222221	2222222124	2422224442	2222222222	2111224555	1121211214	2111122222	1221555555	5552221241	5552222222
BASQUES	1121222222	2211112224	2422224442	2222222222	2225555555	1155555555	2242422222	5255555555	5554444555	5555555555
BASSERI	1122122222	2221112224	1122224442	2211212222	2222411555	1244442214	1122421222	1212125522	1115555241	5552212241
BATAK	1222211221	2222222224	2421221142	2222222222	2125555555	1155555555	2242422222	5255555555	5552221241	5555555555
BAYA	1212222221	2222221221	2422224442	2222222222	2111124555	1121211224	2122421222	5255555522	1112221241	5552222111
BEJA	1121222221	2222112212	2222224442	2211212222	2222411555	1244442211	1112422222	5255555555	5552211444	5552212141
BELU	1222211221	2222222224	2421221142	2222222222	2125555555	1155555555	2242422222	5255555555	5552211242	5555555555
BEMBA	1212222221	2222211221	2422224442	2222222222	1222422555	1121211214	2122421222	1221152122	2121111242	5512112141
BENGALI	1122122221	2222112224	1122224442	2222222222	2115555555	1155555545	2242422222	5255555555	5554444555	5555555555

	FC 10	FC 20	FC 30	FC 40	FC 50	FC 60	FC 70	FC 80	FC 90	FC100
BERGDAMA	1212222221	2222112224	2422224442	2211212222	2225555555	2244445555	2242422221	5255555555	5552221241	5555555555
BETE	1212222221	2222221221	2422224442	2222222222	2115555555	1155555555	2242422222	5255555555	5552221124	5555555555
BHIL	1122122221	2222112224	1122224442	2222222222	2121224555	2222422212	2111122222	1121115522	2124444241	5552212141
BHUIYA	1122122221	2222112224	2422214222	2222222222	2122422555	1121211224	2111222222	5255555522	2125555241	5552212241
BIRIFOR	1212222221	2222211221	2422224442	2222222222	1221224555	1121211214	2111222222	1211155522	2122221555	5552221111
BLACK CARIB	2222222211	2222212224	2422224442	2122222222	2111124555	1121212124	2242422222	2222215522	1144444124	5552222222
BOERS	1121222221	2222212224	1122224442	2222222222	1221224555	1244442212	1111122222	5155555555	5552111555	5552112141
BORORO	2222222211	2222212224	2422224442	2222222222	2122411555	2244442244	2242422122	2221525555	5552221242	5552211141
BOTOCUDO	2222222211	2222212224	2422224442	2222222222	2122411555	2244442244	2242422221	2222525522	2122221114	5552222222
BOZO	1212222221	2222211221	2422224442	2222222222	1222422555	2244442211	2242422212	5255555555	5552221555	5552211141
BRAZILIANS	1121222221	2222112224	1122224442	2222222222	2111124555	1111142212	2111122222	1111155511	1144444114	5551112241
BUDUMA	1121222221	2222212212	2222224442	2222222222	1225555555	2222425555	2242422222	5255555555	5552221555	5555555555
BULGARIANS	1121222222	2211112224	1122224442	2222222221	2221124555	1111142212	2111122222	5115551111	1141111555	5551112141
BUNLAP	1222212221	2222212224	2421221142	2222222222	2111124555	1121211224	2122412222	5255555522	2225555555	5552222111
BURMESE	1122121221	2222112224	2422122412	2222222222	2125555555	1155555555	2242422222	5255551155	5551111124	5515555555
BURUSHO	1122122222	2221112224	2422224442	2212212222	2221124555	1111142211	2111122222	1111122222	1112111555	5552211141
BURYAT	1122122222	2111112224	2412224442	2222222212	2225555555	1244445545	1142422222	5255555555	5552211555	5555555555
CADUVEO	2222222211	2222112224	2422224442	2222222222	1222411555	2244441224	2112422122	5255555555	5552211555	5552212141
CAGABA	2222222211	2222212224	2422224442	2222222222	2121124222	1121211224	2122412222	2211515555	5552221241	5552222111
CALLINAGO	2222222211	2222212224	2422224442	2122222222	2111224555	2244442224	2242422212	2211515555	5552221114	5552222111
CAMAYURA	2222222211	2222212224	2422224442	2222222222	2112422221	2222421224	2242422222	2212515522	2122221241	5552222111
CAMBA	2222222211	2222212224	1122224442	2222211222	2225555555	1155555545	2242422222	5255555555	5555555124	5555555555
CAMBODIANS	1122121221	2222212224	2422214222	2222222222	2111124555	1111142211	2111222222	5155551111	1141111114	5551112241
CARAJA	2222222211	2222212224	2422224442	2222222222	2115555555	2244445545	2242422212	5255555555	5552221241	5555555555
CARIB	2222222211	2222222224	2422224442	2122222222	2111224555	2222421224	2242422222	2211215522	2222221114	5552222222
CARINYA	2222222211	2222222224	2422224442	2122222222	1225555555	1155555545	2242422222	5255555555	5555555555	5555555555
CAYAPA	2222222211	2222222224	2422224442	2222222222	2111224555	1121212144	2122412222	2211512222	1112221241	2552222111
CHAGGA	1212222221	2222221221	2422224442	2222211222	2221224222	1111142211	2111122222	5255552122	1112211241	1552212241
CHAMACOCO	2222222211	2222112224	2422224442	2222211222	2222411555	2244442244	2242422221	2211125555	5552211555	5552212241
CHENCHU	1122122221	2222212224	2422224442	2222211222	2222422222	2244442214	2111122221	2222255522	2222221114	5552222111
CHEREMIS	1121222222	2211112224	2422224442	2222222221	2225555555	1155555555	2242422222	5255555555	5554444555	5555555555
CHERKESS	1121222222	2211112224	2422224442	2222222221	2221224555	1111142212	2111122222	5155555555	5552211241	5552212141
CHEROKEE	2222222122	2221112224	2422224442	2222222221	2221124555	2222421214	2242422222	2251515522	1112111555	5552112141
CHEYENNE	2222222122	2221112224	2422224442	1222212122	2222411211	2244442214	2112422122	2221155555	5552211444	5552212141
CHIBCHA	2222222211	2222222224	2422224442	2212212222	2221124555	1111142224	2242422222	5255555521	1142111242	5552112141
CHINANTEC	2222222121	2222212224	2422224442	2222211222	2225555555	1155555545	2242422222	5255555555	5554444114	5555555555
CHIR-APACHE	2222222122	2221112224	2422224441	2211212222	2222411211	2244442214	2112422221	2221115555	5552221114	5552222111
CHIRIGUANO	2222222211	2222112224	2422224442	2222211222	2221124555	1121211214	2242422222	2211125555	5552211241	5552212141
CHOCO	2222222211	2222222224	2422224442	2222222222	2111224555	1121211244	2242422222	2221515522	2125555555	5552222222
CHOROTI	2222222211	2222112224	2422224442	2222211222	2222422555	2244442244	2242422221	2211125522	2222221555	5552222222

APPENDIX EIGHT/ 3 -- FINISHED CHARACTERISTIC CODE SHEET

	FC 10	FC 20	FC 30	FC 40	FC 50	FC 60	FC 70	FC 80	FC 90	FC100
CHORTI	2222222211	2222212224	2422224442	2222222222	2111124555	1121211214	2122412222	2211155555	5554444114	5552211141
CHUKCHEE	1122122222	1111112224	2422224442	2212112222	2222411555	2222422244	2112422222	1221152222	2222221124	2552222111
COCHITI	2222222122	2221112224	2422224442	2211212222	2221124555	1111142211	2242422222	5255555522	1112221114	5552222111
COMANCHE	2222222122	2221112224	2422224442	2222212122	2225555555	2244445545	2242422122	2222125555	5554444114	5525555555
COORG	1122122221	2222212224	2422224442	2222222222	2121224555	1111142212	2111122222	1155525522	2121111241	5552111141
COPR ESKIMO	2222222122	1111112224	2422224442	2212112222	2222411111	2244442244	2242422212	2222112222	2225555444	2522222222
CREE	2222222122	2111112224	2422224442	1222222212	2225555555	2244442244	2242422212	2222115522	2122221114	5552222111
CREEK	2222222122	2221112224	2422224442	2222222222	2221124555	2222421214	2242422222	1211112122	1112111242	1552211141
CROW	2222222122	2211112224	2422224442	2222212122	2222411555	2244442244	2112422122	2222122255	5552211124	2152212241
CUNA	2222222211	2222222224	2422224442	2222222222	2111124111	1121211214	2122412222	2211512122	2122211114	1152212141
CZECHS	1121222222	2111112224	1122224442	2222222221	2221124555	1111142212	2111122222	1111155511	1141111555	1551112241
DAGUR	1122122222	2211112224	2412224442	2222212122	2221124555	1111142211	2242422222	5255555555	5554444114	5551111141
DARD	1122122222	2221112224	1122224442	2211212222	2222422555	1111142211	2111122222	1112112122	1112111555	5552112141
DELAWARE	2222222122	2211112224	2422224442	1222222221	2222422555	2222421214	2242422222	2251115522	1112221242	5552222111
DIEGUENO	2222222122	2221112224	2422224442	2211212222	2222411555	2244442244	2242422221	2211115555	5552221241	5552222222
DIERI	1222212222	2222112224	2422224442	2211212222	2222411555	2244442254	2242422221	2222555522	2222221555	5552222222
DILLING	1212222221	2222212124	2422224442	2222222222	1221224555	1111142212	2111122222	5255555555	5552211555	5552212141
DOBUANS	1222212221	2222212224	2421221142	2222222222	2115555555	1155555555	2242422222	5255555555	5552222444	5555555555
DOGON	1212222221	2222211221	2422224442	2222222222	1221124555	1111142212	2111222222	1255155522	2122221241	5552211141
DOROBO	1212222221	2222222124	2422224442	2222222222	2122411555	2244442254	2242422122	5255555522	2222221114	5552222222
DUSUN	1222211221	2222222224	2421221142	2222222222	2125555555	1155555555	2242422222	5255555555	5552211555	5555555555
DUTCH	1121222222	2111112224	1122224442	2222222221	2221124555	1111142212	2111122222	1111115511	1141111555	5551112141
EGYPTIANS	1121222222	2222112212	2222224442	2222222222	2221124222	1111142211	2111122222	1111115511	1141111114	5551111141
ELLICE	1222212221	2222222224	2421221142	2222222222	2111124555	2244442144	2122412212	2222215555	5552211555	5552212141
ENGA	1222212221	2222222224	2422224442	2222222222	2121224555	1121211224	2122412222	2222555522	1115555444	5552221111
EYAK	2222222122	1111112224	2422224442	2222222212	2221124555	2244442244	2242422212	2222115522	2225555242	5552212141
FANG	1212222221	2222221221	2422224442	2222222222	2111124555	1121211224	2122421222	1221515522	2122221241	5552222111
FON	1212222221	2222221221	2422224442	2222222222	2111124122	1121211224	2122421222	1211115521	1141111241	5151112141
FOX	2222222122	2211112224	2422224442	1222222212	2222411555	2222421214	2112422222	2225115555	5552211241	5552211141
FUTAJALONKE	1212222221	2222211221	2422224442	2222222222	1221124555	1121211214	2111122222	5255555555	5551111555	5552111141
GANDA	1212222221	2222221221	2422224442	2222222222	2111224212	1111142244	2111122222	1221115521	1141111124	5551112241
GARO	1122122222	2222112224	2422122412	2222222222	2111124555	1121211214	2111222222	2211225522	2122211242	5552212141
GILBERTESE	1222212221	2222222224	2421221142	2222211222	2225555555	2244445555	2242422212	2222215555	5552221114	5555555555
GILYAK	1122122222	2111112224	2422224442	2222222212	2222411555	2244442244	2242422212	1222112222	2122222241	5552222222
GISU	1212222221	2222221221	2422224442	2222222222	1221224555	1121211214	2111122222	1221125555	5555555241	5552212141
GOAJIRO	2222222211	2222212224	2422224442	2211212222	2222411555	1244442214	1111122222	2211125522	2222221242	5552222222
GOND	1122122221	2222112224	2422224442	2222211222	2221124555	1121211214	2122412222	2222515522	2122211241	5552212141
GROS VENTRE	2222222122	2211112224	2422224442	1222212122	2222411221	2244442244	2112422122	2221125555	5552211124	5552212241
GUAHIBO	2222222211	2222222224	2422224442	2222222222	1222411555	2244442244	2242422122	5255555522	2222221241	5552222111
GUATO	2222222211	2222212224	2422224442	2222222222	2122411555	2244442244	2242422221	2211515555	5552221241	5552222222

APPENDIX EIGHT/ 4 -- FINISHED CHARACTERISTIC CODE SHEET

	FC 10	FC 20	FC 30	FC 40	FC 50	FC 60	FC 70	FC 80	FC 90	FC100
GURE	1212222221	2222211221	2422224442	2222222222	1221224555	1121211214	2122421222	5255555555	5552222555	5552221111
HAIDA	2222222122	2111112224	2422224442	2222222212	2221124555	2244442244	2242422212	2212115555	5552221242	5552222111
HANO	2222222122	2221112224	2422224442	2211212222	2221124222	1111142211	2111222222	5255555522	1115555555	1152221111
HANUNOO	1222211221	2222212224	2421221142	2222222222	2111224555	1121211214	2111222222	5255555522	2122222444	5552222222
HASANIA	1121222221	2222212212	2222224442	2211212222	2225555555	1155555555	2242422222	5255555555	5555555555	5555555555
HASINAI	2222222122	2221112224	2422224442	2222222222	2221224555	2222421214	2242422222	2221155555	5552211241	5552112141
HAVASUPAI	2222222122	2221112224	2422224442	2211212222	2222422555	2222422211	2242422222	5255555522	1112221241	5552222111
HAWAIIANS	1222212221	2222112224	2421221142	2222211222	2221124555	2244442224	2122412212	2222215555	5552111241	5552112141
HAZARA	1122122222	2221112224	2412224442	2211212222	2222422555	1111142211	2111122222	5155555522	2122211241	5552212141
HEBREWS	1121222222	2221112212	2222224442	2222222222	2221124555	1111142211	2111122222	5155555555	5551111555	1552112141
HEHE	1212222221	2222221221	2422224442	2222211222	2225555555	1155555555	2242422222	5255555555	5552111555	5555555555
HERERO	1212222221	2222111221	2422224442	2211212222	2222411555	1244442254	1111122222	5255555555	5552221241	5552222111
HO	1122122221	2222112224	2422214222	2222222222	2125555555	1155555545	2242422222	5255555555	5551111124	5555555555
HUICHOL	2222222121	2222112224	2422224442	2211212222	2221224555	1121211214	2111122222	5211155522	1114444114	5552222111
HUKUNDIKA	2222222122	2211112224	2422224442	2211212222	2222411555	2244442244	2242422221	2222525555	5552221241	5552222222
HURON	2222222122	2211112224	2422224442	2222222212	2221124555	2222421214	2242422222	2221115555	5552211242	5552212141
HUTSUL	1121222222	2211112224	1122224442	2222222221	2221224555	1111142212	2111122222	1111155521	1144444555	5555555555
IBAN	1222211221	2222222224	2421221142	2222222222	2111124555	1121211214	2122412222	1215512155	5552221555	5552222111
ICELANDERS	1121222222	1111112224	1122224442	2212112222	2225555555	2222425555	2242422222	5255555555	5552111555	5555555555
IFUGAO	1222211221	2222212224	2421221142	2222222222	2121224555	1111142211	2122412222	5255555522	2122222555	2552222111
ILA	1212222221	2222211221	2422224442	2222222222	1222422555	1121211214	2111122222	1221115522	1112221242	5552212141
INCA	2222222211	2222212224	2422224442	2212212222	2221124555	1111142211	2112422222	1211225521	1141111555	5151112241
INGALIK	2222222122	1111112224	2422224441	2222222212	2222411555	2244442244	2242422212	2221115555	5555555444	5552222222
INGASSANA	1212222221	2222212124	2422224442	2222222222	1221224555	1111142212	2111122222	5255555555	5552221241	5552222111
IRAQW	1121222221	2222222212	2222224442	2222222222	1221224555	1111142212	2111122222	5255555522	2122221444	5552212141
IRISH	1121222222	2111112224	1122224442	2222222221	2221224555	1111142224	2111122222	5155555511	1141111555	5552112241
JAPANESE	1122122222	2221112224	2422224442	2222222222	2121124555	1111142211	2111122222	1111515511	1141111114	5551112141
JAVANESE	1222211221	2222222224	2421221142	2222222222	2111124555	1111142211	2111222222	1111225511	1141111114	5511112241
JEMEZ	2222222122	2221112224	2422224442	2211212222	2221124555	1111142211	2112422222	2211525522	1112221114	5552222111
JIVARO	2222222211	2222222224	2422224442	2212212222	2221224111	1121211224	2122412222	2211512155	5552222124	2522222222
JUKUN	1212222221	2222221221	2422224442	2222222222	1221124555	1121211214	2122421222	5255555555	5552111241	5552221111
KABYLE	1121222222	2221112212	2222224442	2211212222	2221124555	1111142212	2111122222	5155555522	1112111114	5551111141
KACHIN	1122121222	2222112224	2422122412	2222222221	2221124555	1121211214	2111222222	1251555522	2122211241	5552211141
KALMYK	1121222222	2211112224	2412224442	2211212222	2225555555	1244445555	1142422222	5255555555	5552111241	5555555555
KAPAUKU	1222212221	2222222224	2422224442	2222222222	2111124555	1121211224	2122412222	2222215522	2124444124	5552212141
KAREN	1122121221	2222212224	2422224442	2222222222	2115555555	1155555555	2242422222	5255552255	5552221241	5555555555
KARIERA	1222212221	2222112224	2422224442	2211212222	2222411555	2244442254	2242422122	2222555522	2222221555	5552222222
KASKA	2222222122	2111112224	2422224441	2222222212	2222411221	2244442244	2242422212	2222151122	2122222444	5552222222
KATAB	1212222221	2222211221	2422224442	2222222222	1221124555	1111142212	2122421222	2222525522	1115555124	5552221111
KAZAK	1122122222	2211112224	2412224442	2222212122	2222411211	1244442244	1112422222	1212125522	2121111555	2551112141

APPENDIX EIGHT/ 5 -- FINISHED CHARACTERISTIC CODE SHEET

	FC 10	FC 20	FC 30	FC 40	FC 50	FC 60	FC 70	FC 80	FC 90	FC100
KERAKI	1222212221	2222222224	2422224442	2222222222	1222422555	1121211224	2122412222	2222215522	2122221241	5552222222
KERALA	1122122221	2222212224	2422224442	2222222222	2121224555	1111142211	2111122222	5155555511	1141111242	5552111141
KET	1122122222	1111112224	2422224442	2222222212	2225555555	2244445545	2242422212	5255555555	5552222555	5555555555
KHALKA	1122122222	1111112224	2412224442	2211212222	2222411555	1244442244	1112422222	1125125522	2222111241	5551112141
KHASI	1122122222	2222112224	2422214222	2222222222	2121124555	1121211214	2111222222	1211112122	2122211242	5552211141
KHEVSUR	1121222222	2211112224	2422224442	2222212122	2225555555	1155555555	2242422222	5255555555	5555555444	5555555555
KIKUYU	1212222221	2222221221	2422224442	2222222222	1221124555	1111142212	2111122222	1221125522	1112221444	5512222111
KIOW-APACHE	2222222122	2221112224	2422224441	2222212122	2225555555	2244445545	2242422122	2222155555	5552211555	5555555555
KISSI	1212222221	2222221221	2422224442	2222222222	1221124555	1121211214	2111222222	5255555522	2122211555	5552211141
KOHISTANI	1122122222	2221112224	1122224442	2222222221	2222422555	1111142211	2111122222	1111555555	5555555444	5552212141
KOL	1122122222	2222112224	2422214222	2222222222	2121124555	1111142212	2111222222	5155555555	5554444114	5552212141
KONSO	1121222221	2222222212	2222224442	2222212122	2225555555	1155555555	2242422222	5255555555	5552211241	5555555555
KOREANS	1122122222	2221112224	2422224442	2222222221	2221124555	1111142211	2111222222	1111111111	1141111124	1552112141
KORYAK	1122122222	1111112224	2422224442	2212112222	2222422551	2244442244	2122412212	1222112122	2122221124	5552222111
KPE	1212222221	2222221221	2422224442	2222222222	2111124555	1121211224	2111222222	2251555522	2122221241	5552222111
KUBA	1212222221	2222221221	2422224442	2222222222	2112422555	1121211214	2122421222	1212155522	2122111124	5552112141
KUMYK	1121222222	2211112224	2412224442	2222222221	2225555555	1155555555	2242422222	5255555555	5555555555	5555555555
KUNG	1212222221	2222112224	2422224442	2211212222	2222411555	2244442254	2242422221	2222125522	2222221241	5522222111
KURTATCHI	1222212221	2222222224	2421221142	2222222222	2111224121	1121211224	2122412222	2221212122	2122221242	2552222111
KUTENAI	2222222122	2111112224	2422224442	2222222212	2222411555	2244442244	2112422212	2221115555	5552221124	5552212241
KWAKIUTL	2222222122	2111112224	2422224442	2222222212	2221124111	2244442244	2242422212	5215515555	5555555241	5552212141
LAKALAI	1222212221	2222222224	2421221142	2222222222	2115555555	2222425555	2242422222	5255555555	5552222444	5555555555
LAKHER	1122121221	2222112224	2422122412	2222222222	2121124112	1121211214	2111222222	1211255555	5552211241	2552212141
LAMBA	1212222221	2222211221	2422224442	2222222222	1221124222	1121211214	2242422222	1251515555	5552211242	5512112241
LAMET	1122121221	2222112224	2422214222	2222222222	2121124555	1121211214	2111222222	2222555522	2122221241	5552222111
LANGO	1212222221	2222222124	2422224442	2222222222	1221124221	1121211214	2111122222	5255555522	2122221241	5552222111
LAPPS	1121222222	1111112224	2422224442	2212112222	2222411111	1244442244	1112422222	5255555522	2222221555	1552222222
LAU	1222212221	2222212224	2421221142	2222222222	2111124122	1121212124	2122412222	2221215522	2122211241	5552112141
LEPCHA	1122122222	2222112224	2422122412	2222222221	2221224212	1111142212	2111122222	2112525522	2124444241	1252222111
LESU	1222212221	2222222224	2421221142	2222222222	2111224122	2222422124	2122412222	2222215522	1112221124	5252222111
LHOTA NAGA	1122122222	2222112224	2422122412	2222222222	2121124555	1121211214	2111222222	1211255555	5555555241	5552222111
LIFU	1222212221	2222112224	2421221142	2222222222	2115555555	1155555545	2242422222	5255555555	5552211241	5555555555
LOLO	1122122222	2222112224	2422122412	2222222221	2221124555	1111142212	2111222222	1115151122	2122221241	5552222111
LOZI	1212222221	2222211221	2422224442	2222222222	1222422555	2222422212	2111122222	1121115522	2121111241	5551112241
LUBA	1212222221	2222221221	2422224442	2222222222	1225555555	2222425555	2242422222	5255555555	5552111241	5555555555
LUO	1212222221	2222222124	2422224442	2222222222	1221224555	1111142212	2111122222	1221125522	2122221241	5552212141
MACASSARESE	1222211221	2222222224	2421221142	2222222222	2111224555	1111142211	2111222222	1111515522	2122111241	5551112141
MAGUZAWA	1121222221	2222212212	2222224442	2222222222	1225555112	1155555555	2242422222	5255555555	5551111124	5555555555
MALAYS	1122121221	2222222224	2421221142	2222222222	2111224555	1111142211	2111222222	5155555555	5551111555	5552112141
MAM	2222222211	2222212224	2422224442	2222222221	2221124555	1121211214	2112422222	5255555522	1145555124	5552221111

APPENDIX EIGHT/ 6 -- FINISHED CHARACTERISTIC CODE SHEET

	FC 10	FC 20	FC 30	FC 40	FC 50	FC 60	FC 70	FC 80	FC 90	FC100
MAMBILA	1212222221	2222221221	2422224442	2222212122	2221224555	1111142212	2122421222	5255555522	1115555242	5552221111
MAMVU	1212222221	2222222124	2422224442	2222222222	2111124555	1121211244	2122421222	1221125522	2125555555	5552222222
MANCHU	1122122222	2211112224	2412224442	2222212122	2225555555	1155555545	2242422222	5255555555	5554444114	5555555555
MANDAN	2222222122	2211112224	2422224442	2222222221	2222422555	1111142212	2112422222	2221552155	5552211555	5552212141
MANGAIANS	1222212221	2222112224	2421221142	2222222222	2111224555	1121212124	2242422222	2222215555	5552211241	5552211141
MANIHIKI	1222212221	2222212224	2421221142	2222222222	2111124555	2244442144	2242422212	2222215555	5552221241	5552212141
MANUS	1222212221	2222222224	2421221142	2222222222	2111124555	2244442244	2122412212	2251515522	2122221444	5552222111
MAORI	1222212222	2221112224	2421221142	2222212122	2221124112	2222421224	2242422222	2212515555	5552211241	1552211141
MARGI	1212222221	2222212212	2222224442	2222222222	1221224555	1111142212	2111222222	5255555522	1112111114	5552211141
MARICOPA	2222222122	2221112224	2422224442	2211212222	2221124555	2244442211	2242422221	2211115522	2122211555	5552212141
MARQUESANS	1222212221	2222222224	2421221142	2222222222	2111224555	1121212144	2122412222	2222215522	2122211241	5552212141
MARSHALLESE	1222212221	2222222224	2421221142	2222222222	2111124555	1121212144	2122412222	2222211155	5554444242	5552212141
MASAI	1212222221	2222222124	2422224442	2211212222	2222411211	1244442254	1111122222	1222125522	2224444444	5552112241
MATACO	2222222212	2222112224	2422224442	2222211222	2222411555	2244442244	2122421212	2211125522	2122221555	5552222222
MATAKAM	1212222221	2222212212	2222224442	2222222222	1221224555	1111142212	2122421222	1221125555	5552221241	5552221111
MAYA	2222222211	2222212224	2422224442	2222222222	2111124555	1121211214	2242422222	1211515521	1142211555	5552212141
MAZATECO	2222222121	2222212224	2422224442	2222211222	2225555555	1155555545	2242422222	5255555555	5554444555	5555555555
MBUGWE	1212222221	2222221221	2422224442	2222222222	2225555555	1155555555	2242422222	5255555555	5552221242	5555555555
MBUNDU	1212222221	2222211221	2422224442	2222222222	1221124122	1121211214	2111222222	1221112222	1112111241	1552112141
MBUTI	1212222221	2222221221	2422224442	2222222222	2112411555	2244442254	2242422221	2222125522	2222221114	5552222222
MENDE	1212222221	2222221221	2422224442	2222222222	2111124222	1121211214	2122421222	1211155522	1112111444	5552211141
MENTAWEI	1222211221	2222222224	2421221142	2222222222	2115555555	1155555555	2242422222	2222515555	5552222444	5555555555
MERINA	1122122221	2222212224	2421221142	2222222222	2121124555	1111142211	2111222222	5255555521	1141111124	5551112141
MIAMI	2222222122	2211112224	2422224442	1222222221	2222422555	2222421214	2242422222	2211115522	1112211241	5552212141
MIAO	1122122222	2222112224	2422224442	2222222222	2121224555	1111142211	2111222222	1215552255	5555555124	5552211141
MIN CHINESE	1122122222	2222112224	2422224442	2222222222	2121124555	1111142211	2111222222	5155555511	1145555124	5551112141
MINANGKABAU	1222211221	2222222224	2421221142	2222222222	2125555555	1155555555	2242422222	5255555555	5552221242	5555555555
MINCHIA	1122122222	2222112224	2422122412	2222222221	2221124122	1111142211	2111122222	5155555522	1114444114	5552211141
MISKITO	2222222211	2222212224	2422224442	2222222222	2111124555	2244441224	2111122221	2211115522	2122211555	5552212141
MIWOK	2222222122	2221112224	2422224442	2222222221	2222422555	2244442244	2242422221	5255555555	5552221241	5552222222
MNONG GAR	1122121221	2222212224	2422214222	2222222222	2112422555	1121211214	2111222222	1211555522	2125555444	5552222111
MONGO	1212222221	2222221221	2422224442	2222222222	2111224555	1121211224	2122421222	1211215555	5552211241	5552111141
MONGUOR	1122122222	2221112224	2412224442	2212212222	2221224555	1111142212	2111122222	1115155555	5552211241	5552212141
MOSSI	1212222221	2222211221	2422224442	2222222222	1221224555	1111142212	2111222222	1211125521	1141111555	5552111141
MOTA	1222212221	2222212224	2421221142	2222222222	2111124555	1121212124	2122412222	2222515555	5552221124	5552222111
MOTILON	2222222211	2222222224	2422224442	2122222222	2111124555	2244441224	2242422221	5255555522	2222221555	5552222111
MUNDURUCU	2222222211	2222222224	2422224442	2222222222	2112422555	2222421224	2242422222	2211525522	2122221241	5522222111
MURINBATA	1222212221	2222212224	2422224442	2222222222	1222411555	2244442254	2242422221	2222555522	2225555555	5552222222
MURNGIN	1222212221	2222212224	2422224442	2222222222	1222411555	2244442254	2242422221	2222215522	2222221241	5522222222
MZAB	1121222222	2221112212	2222224442	2222222222	2221124555	1111142244	2122421222	5255555521	1142211444	5552222111

APPENDIX EIGHT/ 7 -- FINISHED CHARACTERISTIC CODE SHEET

	FC 10	FC 20	FC 30	FC 40	FC 50	FC 60	FC 70	FC 80	FC 90	FC100
NABESNA	2222222122	1111112224	2422224441	2222222212	2222411555	2244442244	2242422122	2222115522	2225555114	5552222222
NAMA	1212222222	2222112224	2422224442	2211212222	2222411221	2222422254	2111122222	1221122122	2122211241	2222212241
NAMBICUARA	2222222211	2222212224	2422224442	2222222222	1222411221	2244441224	2242422221	2212525522	2222221114	5552222111
NANDI	1212222221	2222222124	2422224442	2222222222	1221224555	1111142212	2111122222	1221125555	5554444124	5552212241
NASKAPI	2222222122	2111112224	2422224442	1222222212	2225555555	2244445545	2242422122	5255555555	5552221124	5555555555
NATCHEZ	2222222122	2221112224	2422224442	2222222221	2221124555	2222421214	2242422222	2211115522	1112211242	5552212141
NAVAHO	2222222122	2221112224	2422224441	2211212222	2222422221	2222422211	2122421222	1211121122	1112221114	1522222111
NDEMBU	1212222221	2222211221	2422224442	2222222222	1222422555	1121211214	2122421222	1225515522	2225555242	5552112241
NGONI	1212222221	2222211221	2422224442	2222222222	1225555555	1155555555	2242422222	5255555555	5552111241	5555555555
NICOBARESE	1122121221	2222222224	2422214222	2222222222	2111224555	1121212144	2122412222	1221515555	5552221114	5552222111
NOMLAKI	2222222122	2221112224	2422224442	2222212122	2221124555	2244442244	2242422221	2222125522	2122221241	5552222222
NUER	1212222221	2222222124	2422224442	2222222222	1222411222	1244441214	1111122222	2222522255	5554444444	5152222111
NUNIVAK	2222222122	1111112224	2422224442	2212112222	2222422555	2244442244	2242422212	2221115555	5552221444	5552222111
NUPE	1212222221	2222221221	2422224442	2222222222	1221224555	1121211214	2122421222	1211115522	1115555124	5112112141
NURI	1122122222	2221112224	1122224442	2211212222	2221124555	1111142211	2111122222	1115155522	1112211241	5552212141
NYAKYUSA	1212222221	2222221221	2422224442	2222222222	2121124122	1111142244	2111122222	1211215522	2122211114	5552112241
NYANEKA	1212222221	2222211221	2422224442	2222222222	1225555555	1155555555	2242422222	5255555555	5552111242	5555555555
NYARO	1212222221	2222212224	2422224442	2222222222	1225555555	1155555555	2242422222	5255555555	5555555241	5555555555
NYORO	1212222221	2222221221	2422224442	2222222222	1221224555	1111142212	2111122222	1221115522	1111111241	5551112241
OJIBWA	2222222122	2111112224	2422224442	1222222212	2222411111	2244442244	2242422212	2222112122	2222221555	5552212141
OKINAWANS	1122122222	2222112224	2422224442	2222222222	2121124555	1111142224	2111222222	1111515511	1144444114	5552112141
OMAHA	2222222122	2211112224	2422224442	2222212122	2222422221	2244442212	2112422122	2211115522	2122211124	5552212141
ONA	2222222212	2111112224	2422224442	2212112222	2222411221	2244442244	2242422122	2222155522	2122221114	5252222222
ONTONG-JAVA	1222212221	2222222224	2421221142	2222222222	2112422111	2244442144	2242422212	2212215555	5552221241	5552221111
ORAON	1122122221	2222112224	2422224442	2222222222	2121124555	1111142212	2111122222	5155555555	5552211114	5552211141
PAEZ	2222222211	2222222224	2422224442	2212212222	2221224555	1111142224	2242422222	1211525555	5552211114	5552212241
PAIWAN	1222212221	2222112224	2421221142	2222222222	2121124555	1121211214	2122412222	5255555522	1115555241	5552212141
PALAUANS	1222212221	2222222224	2421221142	2222222222	2111124555	1121212124	2122412222	2211515555	5552211242	5552111141
PALIKUR	2222222211	2222222224	2422224442	2222222222	2115555555	2222425545	2242422222	2211215555	5552221114	5555555555
PAPAGO	2222222122	2221112224	2422224442	2211212222	2222422222	2222422211	2242422222	2211125555	5552221444	5552222111
PARAUJANO	2222222211	2222212224	2422224442	2222211222	2221124555	2244442244	2242422212	5255555555	5555555555	5552212241
PATHAN	1122122222	2221112224	1122224442	2222211222	2221124555	1111142211	2111122222	5155555522	1115555124	5552111141
PAWNEE	2222222122	2211112224	2422224442	2222212122	2221124555	1121211214	2112422222	5255555522	2122211241	5552212141
PENDE	1212222221	2222221221	2422224442	2222222222	1225555555	1155555555	2242422222	5255555555	5555555242	5555555555
PENOBSCOT	2222222122	2211112224	2422224442	1222222212	2225555555	2244445545	2242422122	5255555555	5552211555	5555555555
PONAPEANS	1222212221	2222222224	2421221142	2222222222	2111224555	1121212124	2122412222	2212215522	2222211242	5552112141
POPOLUCA	2222222121	2222212224	2422224442	2222222222	2115555555	1155555545	2242422222	5255555555	5554444114	5555555555
PORTUGUESE	1121222222	2211112224	1122224442	2222222222	2225555555	1155555555	2242422222	5255555555	5555555114	5555555555
PUKAPUKA	1222212221	2222212224	2421221142	2222222222	2111124122	1121212144	2122412222	2222212222	2122221241	5552212141
PURARI	1222212221	2222222224	2422224442	2222222222	2111124555	2244442144	2122412221	2222515555	5555555124	5552221111

APPENDIX EIGHT/ 8 -- FINISHED CHARACTERISTIC CODE SHEET

	FC 10	FC 20	FC 30	FC 40	FC 50	FC 60	FC 70	FC 80	FC 90	FC100
PURUM	1122122222	2222112224	2422122412	2222222222	2121124555	1121211214	2111222222	2112555522	2125555444	5552222111
RAROIANS	1222212221	2222212224	2421221142	2222222222	2115555555	2244445545	2242422212	2222215555	5552221241	5555555555
REGEIBAT	1121222221	2222112212	2222224442	2211212222	2222411555	1244442244	1112422222	5155555555	5555555114	5551111141
RIFFIANS	1121222222	2221112212	2222224442	2222222222	2221124555	1111142211	2111122222	1111115521	1142211444	1552212141
ROMANS	1121222222	2211112224	1122224442	2222222222	2221124555	1111142212	2111122222	5155555511	1141111555	1555555555
ROTINESE	1222211221	2222212224	2421221142	2222222222	2115555555	1155555555	2242422222	5255555555	5552211555	5555555555
ROTUMANS	1222212221	2222212224	2421221142	2222222222	2115555555	1155555545	2242422222	5255555555	5552211241	5555555555
RUNDI	1212222221	2222221221	2422224442	2222212122	2221224555	1111142244	2111122222	1221115555	5555555241	5551112141
RWALA	1121222222	2221112212	2222224442	2211212222	2222411555	1244442244	1112422222	1215121122	2122111555	5552212141
SAGADA	1222212221	2222212224	2421221142	2222222222	2111124555	1111142211	2111222222	1112225522	1145555444	5552222111
SAMOANS	1222212221	2222212224	2421221142	2222222222	2111124112	1121212124	2122412222	2222212122	2122211241	5112111141
SAMOYED	1122122222	1111112224	2422224442	2212112222	2222411555	2222422244	2112422222	2222111122	2222221555	5552222111
SANDAWE	1212222221	2222222224	2422224442	2222211222	2221224555	1121211214	2111122222	5255555555	5552221555	5552212241
SANPOIL	2222222122	2211112224	2422224442	2222212122	2222411221	2244442244	2242422212	2221515522	2125555241	2552222111
SANTAL	1122122222	2222112224	2422214222	2222222222	2121124555	1111142211	2111222222	1111555555	5552211241	5552212141
SARAMACCA	2222222211	2222222224	1122224442	2222222222	2115555555	2222425545	2242422222	5255555555	5552211242	5555555555
SARSI	2222222122	2111112224	2422224441	2222212122	2222411555	2244442244	2112422122	2222115555	5552211124	5552212241
SELUNG	1122121221	2222212224	2421221142	2222222222	2112411555	2244442254	2242422212	5255555555	5552222555	5252222222
SEMANG	1122121221	2222222224	2422214222	2222222222	2122411555	2244442254	2242422221	2222555522	2222222241	5552222222
SEMINOLE	2222222122	2222112224	2422224442	2222222222	2115555555	1155555545	2242422222	5255555555	5555555555	5555555555
SENIANG	1222212221	2222212224	2421221142	2222222222	2111124222	1121212124	2122412222	2222215555	5552211241	5552222222
SERBS	1121222222	2211112224	1122224442	2222222221	2221124555	1111142212	2111122222	1111555511	1141111114	5551112141
SERI	2222222122	2222112224	2422224442	2211212222	2225555555	2244445545	2242422212	5255555555	5552221555	5555555555
SHERENTE	2222222211	2222222224	2422224442	2222222222	2111124121	2222421224	2242422222	5255555555	5552211241	5552222111
SHILLUK	1212222221	2222212124	2422224442	2222222222	1221224555	1121211214	2111122222	1221115522	1111111114	5552212141
SHLUH	1121222221	2221112212	2222224442	2222222222	2221224555	1111142211	2111122222	5155555555	5552211114	5552211141
SIMBOESE	1222212221	2222222224	2421221142	2222222222	2115555555	1155555555	2242422222	5255555555	5555555555	5555555555
SINDHI	1122122222	2222112224	1122224442	2222211222	2225555555	1155555555	2242422222	5255555555	5554444124	5555555555
SINHALESE	1122122221	2222222224	1122224442	2222222222	2121124555	1111142211	2111122222	5155555511	1141111555	5551112141
SIRIONO	2222222211	2222212224	2422224442	2222222222	1222411221	2244441214	2242422122	2211222222	2222221241	2552222111
SIUAI	1222212221	2222222224	2422224442	2222222222	2111224555	1121211224	2122412222	5255555555	5552221124	5522222111
SIWANS	1121222222	2222112212	2222224442	2222222222	2221124555	1111142244	2111122222	2211125522	1142211444	2552221111
SOMALI	1121222221	2222222212	2222224442	2211212222	2222411555	1244442212	1112422222	1212125522	2222111114	5552112141
SONGHAI	1121222221	2222212224	2422224442	2222222222	1221124555	1111142212	2111122222	1211115521	1142111241	5551112141
SOTHO	1212222222	2222111221	2422224442	2222212122	2221224555	1111142212	2111122222	5155555522	1111111241	5551112141
SUBANUN	1222211221	2222222224	2421221142	2222222222	2111224555	1121211214	2122412222	5255555522	2222222444	5552222222
SWAZI	1212222222	2222111221	2422224442	2222211222	2221224555	1121211214	2111122222	1125155555	5555555241	5551112141
SYRIANS	1121222222	2221112212	2222224442	2222222222	2221124555	1111142211	2111122222	1115555511	1145555114	5552112141
TAGBANUA	1222211221	2222212224	2421221142	2222222222	2111124555	1121211214	2111222222	5255555555	5554444444	5552222222
TALAMANCA	2222222211	2222222224	2422224442	2222222222	2111224555	1121211214	2122412222	2211215555	5552211555	5552222222

	FC 10	FC 20	FC 30	FC 40	FC 50	FC 60	FC 70	FC 80	FC 90	FC100
TALLENSI	1212222221	2222211221	2422224442	2222222222	1221224222	1111142212	2111122222	1221122222	1112221124	5552221111
TAMIL	1122122221	2222212224	2422224442	2222211222	2225555555	1155555545	2242422222	5255555555	5554444555	5555555555
TANALA	1122122221	2222112224	2421221142	2222222222	2121124122	1111142211	2111122222	1212115522	2122211114	5552211141
TANIMBARESE	1222211221	2222222224	2421221142	2222222222	2115555555	1155555555	2242422222	5255555555	5552221241	5555555555
TAOS	2222222122	2221112224	2422224442	2211212222	2221124555	1111142212	2112422222	2121525522	1112221114	5552222222
TAPIRAPE	2222222211	2222212224	2422224442	2222222222	2111124555	2222421224	2242422222	2211225522	2122221555	5552222111
TARAHUMARA	2222222122	2222112224	2422224442	2222222221	2221124222	1111142212	2111222222	5211555555	5552221114	5552222222
TAREUMIUT	2222222122	1111112224	2422224442	2212112222	2222422555	2244442244	2242422212	2221115522	2125555444	5552222111
TEDA	1121222221	2222112224	2422224442	2222222222	2222411555	1111142244	2112422222	1221125555	5554444124	5552212141
TEHUELCHE	2222222212	2211112224	2422224442	2211212222	2222411555	2244442244	2112422122	1211122222	2122221241	5552222111
TENDA	1212222221	2222211221	2422224442	2222222222	1221124555	1121211214	2111222222	1211525522	2122211242	5552212141
TENETEHARA	2222222211	2222222224	2422224442	2222222222	2111124222	1121211224	2122421222	5255555555	5552221124	5552222111
TENINO	2222222122	2211112224	2422224442	2222222212	2222422111	2244442244	2242422212	2222115522	1114444241	5552222111
TERA	1121222221	2222212212	2222224442	2222222222	1221124555	1121211214	2112422222	5255555555	5555555555	5552211141
TERENA	2222222211	2222112224	2422224442	2222222222	2122411551	2222421224	2111222222	2215155555	5552221241	5552221111
TESO	1212222221	2222222124	2422224442	2222222222	1221224555	1121211214	2111122222	5155555555	5555555555	5552212141
TETON	2222222122	2211112224	2422224442	2222212122	2225555211	2244445545	2242422122	5255555555	5554444124	5555555555
THAI	1122121221	2222212224	2422224442	2222222222	2111124555	1111142211	2111222222	5155555511	1141111114	5511112141
THONGA	1212222222	2222111221	2422224442	2222211222	2221124212	1121211214	2111122222	1121212222	2122111241	2552112141
TIBETANS	1122122222	2221112224	2422122412	2212212222	2225555555	1155555545	2242422222	1215115555	5551111114	5555555555
TIGRINYA	1121222221	2222212212	2222224442	2222211222	2221124555	1111142212	2111122222	5155555521	1145555124	5552112141
TIKOPIA	1222212221	2222212224	2421221142	2222222222	2111224555	2244442124	2242422212	2222212222	1112221241	5152212141
TIMBIRA	2222222211	2222222224	2422224442	2222222222	1221124221	2222421224	2122412222	2222222222	2122222555	5252221111
TIMUCUA	2222222122	2222112224	2422224442	2222222222	2222422555	2222421214	2242422222	2221515555	5552211242	5552212141
TIV	1212222221	2222221221	2422224442	2222222222	1221224555	1121211224	2122421222	1211112122	1112211444	5552211141
TIWI	1222212221	2222212224	2422224442	2222222222	1222411555	2244442254	2242422221	2222515522	2122221241	5552222111
TODA	1122122221	2222212224	2422224442	2222211222	2222422555	1244442244	1111122222	2222522122	2222221114	5252212141
TOKELAU	1222212221	2222222224	2421221142	2222222222	2111124121	2244442144	2242422212	2222255555	5552211241	5552212141
TOLOWA	2222222122	2211112224	2422224441	2222222221	2222422555	2244442244	2242422212	2222115555	5552221241	5552222222
TORAJA	1222211221	2222222224	2421221142	2222222222	2111124555	1121211214	2111222222	5255555555	5552221114	5552212141
TOTONAC	2222222121	2222112224	2422224442	2222222222	2111124555	1121211214	2112422222	2211555521	1141111555	5552212141
TRISTAN	1121222222	2221112224	1122224442	2222212122	2221124555	2222421224	2111122222	1122115522	2125555444	5552222222
TROBRIAND	1222212221	2222222224	2421221142	2222222222	2111124112	1121212124	2122412222	2221212222	2122211242	5512212241
TRUKESE	1222212221	2222222224	2421221142	2222222222	2121224112	2244442144	2122412212	2212215522	2122221242	5552222111
TRUMAI	2222222211	2222212224	2422224442	2222222222	2111124555	2222421224	2242422222	2212515522	2222221241	5552222111
TSHIMSHIAN	2222222122	2111112224	2422224442	2222222212	2222422555	2244442244	2242422212	2212515555	5555555242	5552211141
TUBATULABAL	2222222122	2221112224	2422224442	2211212222	2222411555	2244442244	2242422221	2221115522	2222221241	5552212241
TUCANO	2222222211	2222222224	2422224442	2222222222	2112422555	2222421224	2242422222	2221515555	5552221555	5552222222
TUCUNA	2222222211	2222222224	2422224442	2222222222	2111124555	2244441224	2242422212	2211515522	2122221555	5552222222
TUNEBO	2222222211	2222222224	2422224442	2222222222	2111124555	1121211214	2242422222	2211555555	5555555114	5552222222

	FC 10	FC 20	FC 30	FC 40	FC 50	FC 60	FC 70	FC 80	FC 90	FC100
TUPINAMBA	2222222211	2222222224	2422224442	2222222222	2111124111	2222421224	2242422222	2211212122	1112221241	2552212141
TURKANA	1212222221	2222222124	2422224442	2222222222	1222411221	2222422211	2111122222	5255555555	5552222444	5552222222
TURKMEN	1122122222	2221112224	2412224442	2222222222	2221124555	1111142211	2111122222	5155555555	5552111555	5551111141
TWANA	2222222122	2211112224	2422224442	2222222212	2222411555	2244442244	2242422212	2212115522	2125555124	5552222111
TZELTAL	2222222211	2222212224	2422224442	2222222221	2225555555	1155555545	2242422222	5255555555	5552221555	5555555555
ULAWANS	1222212221	2222212224	2421221142	2222222222	2111224555	1121212124	2122412222	2222215522	2122221444	5552222111
UTE	2222222122	2221112224	2422224442	2211212222	2222411555	2244442244	2112422122	2222125555	5552221114	5552222222
VEDDA	1122122221	2222222224	1122224442	2222222222	2122411555	2244442254	2242422221	2221155522	2222221555	5552222111
VENDA	1212222221	2222111221	2422224442	2222212122	2221124211	1111142212	2111122222	2221125522	1115555241	1552112141
VIETNAMESE	1122121221	2222212224	2422224442	2222222222	2111124555	1111142211	2111222222	5155551111	1141111114	1511112141
WAICA	2222222211	2222222224	2422224442	2122222222	2112411555	2244441244	2242422122	2225525522	2122221555	5552222222
WALLOONS	1121222222	2111112224	1122224442	2222222221	2221124555	1111142212	2111122222	5155555511	1145555555	5551112241
WANTOAT	1222212221	2222222224	2422224442	2222222222	2121124555	1121212124	2122412222	2222525555	5555555124	5552222222
WAPISHANA	2222222211	2222222224	2422224442	2222222222	1221124221	2222421224	2242422222	5255555555	5552221555	5552222111
WAROPEN	1222212221	2222222224	2421221142	2222222222	2115555555	2244445555	2242422212	5255555555	5552222124	5555555555
WARRAU	2222222211	2222222224	2422224442	2222222222	2112422521	2244442224	2242422221	5255555522	2122221114	5552222111
WASHO	2222222122	2221112224	2422224442	2222222221	2222411555	2244442244	2242422221	2222115522	2222221241	5552222222
WICHITA	2222222122	2221112224	2422224442	2222212122	2222422555	1121211214	2112422222	5255555555	5552211241	5552212141
WIKMUNKAN	1222212221	2222212224	2422224442	2222222222	1222411555	2244442254	2242422122	2222555522	2225555555	5552222222
WINNEBAGO	2222222122	2211112224	2422224442	2222222221	2225555111	2222422244	2242422222	5255555555	5552211241	5555555555
WITOTO	2222222211	2222222224	2422224442	2222222222	2111124555	2222421224	2242422222	2221215555	5552221241	5552222222
WOGEO	1222212221	2222222224	2421221142	2222222222	2111124111	1121211224	2122412222	2222215522	2122222241	5552222111
WOLEAIANS	1222212221	2222222224	2421221142	2222222222	2111124112	1121212144	2122412222	2212211122	2122221242	2552212141
WOLOF	1121222221	2222211221	2422224442	2222222222	1222422555	1121211214	2111122222	1211125522	2121111241	5552112141
WUTE	1212222221	2222221221	2422224442	2222222222	1225555555	1155555555	2242422222	5255555555	5552211555	5555555555
YABARANA	2222222211	2222222224	2422224442	2122222222	2111124555	2222421224	2242422222	2211215522	2225555555	5552222222
YAGUA	2222222211	2222222224	2422224442	2222222222	2111124111	2244441224	2242422122	2221115522	2222221114	5252222222
YAHGAN	2222222212	2111112224	2422224442	2212112222	2222411555	2244442244	2242422212	2222115522	2222222444	5252222222
YAKO	1212222221	2222221221	2422224442	2222222222	2111124555	1121211224	2111222222	5255555521	1142221242	5552221111
YAKUT	1122122222	1111112224	2412224442	2222222212	2222411555	2222422214	2111122222	1211111122	2122111114	2552112141
YAD	1212222221	2222211221	2422224442	2222222222	1221224111	1121211214	2242422222	1221215522	2122211242	5552212141
YAPESE	1222212221	2222222224	2421221142	2222222222	2111224122	1121212144	2122412222	2215215555	5552211242	5552212141
YARURO	2222222211	2222222224	2422224442	2222222222	1221124555	2222421224	2122412222	2221515555	5552221241	2552222222
YOKUTS	2222222122	2221112224	2422224442	2222212122	2222411555	2244442244	2242422221	2221515555	5552221241	5552222111
YOMBE	1212222221	2222221221	2422224442	2222222222	2111124555	1121211214	2122421222	5255555522	1115555242	5552212141
YORUBA	1212222221	2222221221	2422224442	2222222222	1221124122	1121211224	2122421222	1211115511	1141111241	5551111141
YUKAGHIR	1122122222	1111112224	2422224442	2212112222	2222411221	2244442244	2242422122	5255555522	2222221124	5552222111
YUKI	2222222122	2211112224	2422224442	2222212122	2222422555	2244442244	2242422221	2222525522	2122221241	5552222222
YUROK	2222222122	2211112224	2422224442	2222222221	2221124555	2244442244	2242422212	2222112122	2222222124	2552222111
ZUNI	2222222122	2221112224	2422224442	2211212222	2221124555	1111142211	2122421222	5255555522	1142221124	5552221111

	FC110	FC120	FC130	FC140	FC150	FC160	FC170	FC180	FC190	FC200
ABIPON	5112222121	1222555555	5555555422	5555552555	5555552555	5555555555	5555555555	5555222222	2144422124	4122424455
ABOR	5121212221	5555555555	5555555425	5555555555	5555555555	5555555555	5555555555	5555222222	2111112221	1222411111
AINU	5222244422	5555555555	5555552425	3551522555	5555551555	5555555555	5555555555	5555122222	1222225255	5222455511
AJIE	5222244422	5555555555	5555555555	5555555555	5555555555	5555555555	5555555555	5555111221	2221112221	1222455555
AKHA	5222244422	5555555555	5555555555	5555555555	5555555555	5555555555	5555555555	5555222222	2122212221	1222411111
ALACALUF	5222244422	5555555555	5555555444	1555555555	5555555555	5555555555	5555555555	5555222222	2144422124	4122424455
ALBANIANS	5222244452	5555551111	1441225421	5555552555	5511551555	5555555555	5555555555	5555222211	2222122221	1212111111
ALORESE	5121212221	5555552222	4224221245	1555551555	5511115555	5555555555	5555555555	5555222211	2222122221	1212155555
AMBA	5222244412	5555555555	5555555245	1555555555	5555555555	5555555555	5555555555	5555111221	2222112221	1222411111
AMERICANS	5111121222	5555555555	5555552144	1555551555	5555555555	5555555555	5555555555	5555222222	2144422124	4112112424
ANDAMANESE	5222244422	1222225555	5555551444	2255552552	2255552222	2222252222	2222521121	2212222222	2144422124	4122424455
APINAYE	5222244422	5555555555	5555555445	5555555555	5555555555	5555555555	5555555555	5555212122	2211121222	4222455555
ARANDA	1222244422	1222222221	4141221444	2222252222	2222225555	5555555555	5555555555	5555111221	2211122211	1222424411
ARAPESH	2222244422	5555555555	5555555555	5511122555	5555555225	5555555555	5555555555	5555212122	2211112221	1222411111
ARAUCANIANS	5121212221	5555225555	5555552122	1152522551	1155551555	5555555555	5555555555	5555212122	2222212221	1222411111
ARYANS	5555555515	5555555555	5555555555	5555555555	5555555555	5555555555	5555555555	5555212122	2222122221	1212111111
ASHANTI	5112222121	2211551111	1414225415	5552511115	5522111115	5555555555	5555555555	5555222222	2122122211	1222411212
ATAYAL	5222244421	2111555555	5555555555	5555555555	5555555555	5555555555	5555555555	5555222222	2122222221	1221211111
ATSUGEWI	5121212222	5555555555	5555555441	1555555555	5555555555	5555555555	5555555555	5555222211	2244422124	4122411111
AWEIKOMA	5222244422	2221555555	5555555445	2555555555	5555555555	5555555555	5555555555	5555122222	1244422124	4122424444
AYMARA	1121212222	2111555555	5555551431	1555151555	5555555215	5555555555	5555555555	5555122222	1222212221	1222411111
AZANDE	1112222121	1212211111	1414111214	1211212121	1122115115	5555555555	5555555555	5555222222	2122112221	1222411111
AZTEC	1111121221	5555115555	5555555121	1115251551	1155551555	5555555555	5555555555	5555212122	2244422124	4221211111
BABWA	5222244421	5555555555	5555555555	5555555555	5555555555	5555555555	5555555555	5555111221	2222212221	1222411111
BACAIRI	5222244422	5555555555	5555555445	1555555555	5555555555	5555555555	5555555555	5555122222	1244422124	2222455555
BAJUN	5222244411	5555555555	5555555454	5555555555	5555555555	5555555555	5555555555	5555222222	2122212221	1222412424
BALINESE	5112222111	5555555555	5555552555	5555552115	5555555525	5555555555	5555555555	5555122222	1244422124	4221255555
BAMBARA	5112222111	5555555555	5555555111	1555555555	5555555555	5555555555	5555555555	5555212122	2222112221	1222411111
BAMILEKE	5112222121	5555555555	5555555215	1555555555	5555555555	5555555555	5555555555	5555212122	2222212221	1222411111
BANDA	5222244421	5555555555	5555555555	5555555555	5555555555	5555555555	5555555555	5555111221	2222212221	1222411111
BARABRA	5121212251	5555555555	5555555555	5555555555	5555555555	5555555555	5555555555	5555222222	2122112221	1222411111
BARI	5121212212	5555555555	5555555445	5555555555	5555555555	5555555555	5555555555	5555111221	2222112221	1222411111
BASQUES	5111121222	5555555555	5555555555	5555555555	5555555555	5555555555	5555555555	5555222222	2144422124	4122412424
BASSERI	5121212212	5555555555	5555555425	3555555555	5555555555	5555555555	5555555555	5555122222	1221112221	1222424411
BATAK	5222244421	5555555555	5555555555	5555555555	5555555555	5555555555	5555555555	5555222222	2122112221	1222411111
BAYA	5222244421	5555555555	5555555555	5555555555	5555555555	5555555555	5555555555	5555111221	2222212221	1222411111
BEJA	5222244452	5555555555	5555555455	5555555555	5555555555	5555555555	5555555555	5555111221	2221112221	1222455511
BELU	5112222111	2221555555	5555555555	5555555555	5555555555	5555555555	5555555555	5555212122	2222221222	4222455555
BEMBA	1112222121	1211225555	5555552245	3255151552	2255555551	1111111111	1122112211	1122222222	2122122222	4212111212
BENGALI	5111121212	5555555555	5555555555	5555555555	5555555555	5555555555	5555555555	5555212221	2222122221	1212155555

APPENDIX EIGHT/12 -- FINISHED CHARACTERISTIC CODE SHEET

	FC110	FC120	FC130	FC140	FC150	FC160	FC170	FC180	FC190	FC200
BERGDAMA	5222244421	5555555555	5555555455	5555555555	5555555555	5555555555	5555555555	5555222211	2244422124	4122424411
BETE	5222244422	5555555555	5555555555	5555555555	5555555555	5555555555	5555555555	5555111221	2222212221	1222424411
BHIL	5111121212	5555551111	4414221445	1555552555	5521555555	5555555555	5555555555	5555222211	2222112221	1222411111
BHUIYA	5555555552	5555555555	5555555555	5555555555	5555555555	5555555555	5555555555	5555111221	2222112221	1222455511
BIRIFOR	5222244451	5555555555	5555555115	3555555555	5555555555	5555555555	5555555555	5555111221	2211122211	1222411112
BLACK CARIB	5222244422	5555555555	5555555244	1555555555	5555555555	5555555555	5555555555	5555222222	2144422124	4122455555
BOERS	5112222211	5555555555	5555555455	5555555555	5555555555	5555555555	5555555555	5555222222	2144422124	4122455555
BORORO	5222244422	5555555555	5555555445	1555555555	5555555555	5555555555	5555555555	5555212122	2211121222	4222455555
BOTOCUDO	5222244422	5555555555	5555555445	5555555555	5555555555	5555555555	5555555555	5555222211	2244422124	4122424455
BOZO	5222244411	5555555555	5555555455	5555555555	5555555555	5555555555	5555555555	5555555555	5522212221	1222411111
BRAZILIANS	5111121211	5555555555	5555555141	1555555555	5555555555	5555555555	5555555555	5555222222	2144422124	4122412424
BUDUMA	5222244411	5555555555	5555555455	5555555555	5555555555	5555555555	5555555555	5555555555	5522212221	1222455511
BULGARIANS	5111121222	5555115555	5555551425	1155555554	2155555555	5555555555	5555555555	5555222222	2144422124	4122411124
BUNLAP	5555555555	5555555555	5555555555	5555555555	5555555555	5555555555	5555555555	5555212122	2211122211	1222455555
BURMESE	5111121251	2111115555	5555552555	5155555551	1155555551	1111111111	1112111212	1221122222	1244422124	4112112424
BURUSHO	5111121215	2111215555	5555555415	1155555551	1155555555	5555555555	5555555555	5555222222	2122112221	1222455555
BURYAT	5112222151	5555555555	5555555455	5555555555	5555555555	5555555555	5555555555	5555111221	2222112221	1222455555
CADUVEO	5222244422	5555555555	5555555455	5555555555	5555555555	5555555555	5555555555	5555555555	5544422124	4122455555
CAGABA	5121212222	2211555555	5555551415	1555555555	5555555555	5555555555	5555555555	5555222222	2144422124	4122411111
CALLINAGO	5222244421	5555555555	5555555425	1555555555	5555555555	5555555555	5555555555	5555212122	2222221222	4222455555
CAMAYURA	5222244422	2111555555	5555555425	1555555555	5555555555	5555555555	5555555555	5555222222	2144422124	2222424444
CAMBA	5112222222	5555555555	5555555555	5555555555	5555555555	5555555555	5555555555	5555222222	2144422124	4122455511
CAMBODIANS	5111121221	2111115555	5555555555	5155555551	1155555555	5555555555	5555555555	5555222222	2144422124	4122411124
CARAJA	5222244421	5555555555	5555555455	5555555555	5555555555	5555555555	5555555555	5555122222	1244422124	4112155555
CARIB	5222244422	1221552222	4242221424	1555555225	5522225555	5555555555	5555555555	5555222222	2144422124	4122455555
CARINYA	5555555555	5555555555	5555555555	5555555555	5555555555	5555555555	5555555555	5555122222	1244422124	4122455555
CAYAPA	5222244422	2221225555	5555551225	5155555111	1155555555	5555555555	5555555555	5555222222	2144422124	4122455555
CHAGGA	5112222122	2111222121	1414115555	5152521121	1111115115	5555555555	5555555555	5555111221	2222112221	1222411111
CHAMACOCO	5112222121	5555555555	5555551452	5555555555	5555555555	5555555555	5555555555	5555222222	2144422124	4122455555
CHENCHU	5222244422	5555555555	5555555444	1551522555	5555555225	5555555555	5555555555	5555222211	2221112221	1222411111
CHEREMIS	5112222222	5555555555	5555555555	5555555555	5555555555	5555555555	5555555555	5555222222	2144422124	4122412424
CHERKESS	5112222121	5555555555	5555555555	5555555555	5555555555	5555555555	5555555555	5555222222	2122112221	1222411111
CHEROKEE	5222244422	5555555555	5555555455	5555555555	5555555555	5555555555	5555555555	5555212122	2222121222	4222455555
CHEYENNE	5222244422	5555555555	5445552442	2555551115	5555555225	5555555555	5555555555	5555222211	2244422124	4112124444
CHIBCHA	5112222121	5555555555	5555555555	5555555555	5555555555	5555555555	5555555555	5555555555	5544422124	4122411111
CHINANTEC	5555555522	5555555555	5555555555	5555555555	5555555555	5555555555	5555555555	5555122222	1244422124	4122411111
CHIR-APACHE	5222244422	5555555555	5555551442	2551552555	5555555555	5555555555	5555555555	5555222222	2144422124	4122424444
CHIRIGUANO	5555555525	5555555555	5555555121	1555555555	5555555555	5555555555	5555555555	5555222222	2144422124	4122411155
CHOCO	5222244422	5555555555	5555555445	5555555555	5555555555	5555555555	5555555555	5555122222	1244422124	4112111155
CHOROTI	5222244422	5555555555	5555551422	3555555555	5555555555	5555555555	5555555555	5555222211	2244422124	4122424444

	FC110	FC120	FC130	FC140	FC150	FC160	FC170	FC180	FC190	FC200
CHORTI	5222244422	5555555555	5555555121	1555555555	5555555555	5555555555	5555555555	5555222211	2244422124	4122412424
CHUKCHEE	5121212221	2121225555	5555555442	3252512222	2255552115	5555555555	5555555555	5555222222	2144422124	4122424411
COCHITI	5222244422	5555555555	5555555555	5555555555	5555555555	5555555555	5555555555	5555122222	1222121222	4222455524
COMANCHE	5222244421	5555555555	5555555442	5551551555	5555555112	2222222221	2225122221	2212122222	1244422124	4222424444
COORG	5111121211	5555555511	1414555155	1555555555	5522215555	5555555555	5555555555	5555212221	2222112221	1222411111
COPR ESKIMO	2222244422	1221222222	4442112442	1225252221	1122225552	2222222222	2221521122	2212122222	1244422124	4122424424
CREE	5222244422	5555555555	5555555442	3555555555	5555555555	5555555555	5555555555	5555222222	2144422124	2222411111
CREEK	5222244422	5555225555	5555555422	1155552551	1155551555	5555555555	5555555555	5555222222	2111121222	4222455511
CROW	5222244422	2111225555	5555555442	2252511111	1155555555	5555555555	5555555555	5555222211	2221121222	4222424412
CUNA	1121212221	2111225555	5555552125	1112112551	1155555225	5555555555	5555555555	5555122222	1244422124	4122455555
CZECHS	5111121222	5555551111	1414555444	1555552555	5511115555	5555555555	5555555555	5555222222	2144422124	4112111111
DAGUR	5222244422	5555555555	5555555555	5555555555	5555555555	5555555555	5555555555	5555111221	2221112221	1222411111
DARD	5112222115	1222215555	5454555215	1155555551	1155115555	5555555555	5555555555	5555222222	2122112221	1222411111
DELAWARE	5222244422	5555555555	5555555452	1555555225	5555555555	5555555555	5555555555	5555212122	2222121222	4222411255
DIEGUENO	5222244422	5555555555	5555555421	5555555555	5555555555	5555555555	5555555555	5555111221	2222212221	1222424444
DIERI	5222244422	5555555555	5555555445	5555555225	5555551555	5555555555	5555555555	5555222211	2211121222	4222455555
DILLING	5222244421	5555555555	5555552555	5555555555	5555555555	5555555555	5555555555	5555212122	2221112221	1222411111
DOBUANS	2222244422	5555555555	5555555555	5515151225	5555555555	5555555555	5555555555	5555111221	2222121222	4222411212
DOGON	5121212211	1121555555	5555555151	5555555555	5555555555	5555555555	5555555555	5555212221	2222212221	1222411111
DOROBO	5222244422	5555555555	5555555455	5555555555	5555555555	5555555555	5555555555	5555111221	2222112221	1222411124
DUSUN	5121212222	5555555555	5555555555	5555555555	5555555555	5555555555	5555555555	5555122222	1244422124	4111312424
DUTCH	5111121222	5555555555	5555555144	1555555555	5555555555	5555555555	5555555555	5555222222	2144422124	4112112424
EGYPTIANS	5111121211	5555555555	5555552111	5555555555	5555555555	5555555555	5555555555	5555122222	1221112221	1222411111
ELLICE	5112222122	5555555555	5555555444	1555555555	5555555555	5555555555	5555555555	5555212122	2244422124	4221211111
ENGA	5222244422	5555555555	5555555245	5555555555	5555555555	5555555555	5555555555	5555111221	2221112221	1222411111
EYAK	5121212221	5555555555	5555555442	1555555555	5555555555	5555555555	5555555555	5555222222	2111121222	4222455512
FANG	5121212212	2122555555	5555555245	5555555555	5555552555	5555555555	5555555555	5555111221	2222112221	1222424411
FON	5112222121	2121555555	5555551215	5555551555	5555555215	5555555555	5555555555	5555212122	2221112221	1222411111
FOX	5222244421	5555555555	5555555442	5555555555	5555555555	5555555555	5555555555	5555222222	2122122221	1212155544
FUTAJALONKE	5112222111	5555555555	5555555555	5555555555	5555555555	5555555555	5555555555	5555212122	2222212221	1222411111
GANDA	1112222121	5555555555	5454551241	1515251555	5522115555	5555555555	5555555555	5555222211	2222112221	1222411111
GARO	5121212221	5555555555	5555555424	1555555555	5555555555	5555555555	5555555555	5555222222	2111121222	4222424412
GILBERTESE	5121212221	5555555555	5555555444	5555555555	5555555555	5555555555	5555555555	5555212122	2244422124	4211311124
GILYAK	5222244422	1121225555	5555555442	1255555554	2155555555	5555555555	5555555555	5555212122	2222112221	1222424411
GISU	5121212221	5555555555	5555555245	5555555555	5555555555	5555555555	5555555555	5555111221	2222112221	1222411111
GOAJIRO	5121212221	5555551111	4114211421	1555555555	5555555555	5555555555	5555555555	5555222222	2122121222	4222455512
GOND	5121212252	2211552222	2424115445	3555552125	5521115555	5555555555	5555555555	5555111221	2221112221	1222424444
GROS VENTRE	5222244422	5555555555	5555555442	2555555555	5555555555	5555555555	5555555555	5555222211	2244422124	4122424444
GUAHIBO	5222244422	5555555555	5555555455	5555555555	5555555555	5555555555	5555555555	5555212122	2222221222	4222424455
GUATO	5222244422	5555555555	5555555425	5555555555	5555555555	5555555555	5555555555	5555555555	5544422124	4122455555

	FC110	FC120	FC130	FC140	FC150	FC160	FC170	FC180	FC190	FC200
GURE	5222244421	5555555555	5555555555	5555555555	5555555555	5555555555	5555555555	5555212122	2222121222	4222455555
HAIDA	5112222121	2121555555	5555555422	1555551555	5555552555	5555555555	5555555555	5555111221	2211121222	4222411212
HANO	5222244422	2111555555	4445555555	5555552555	5555551225	5555555555	5555555555	5555212122	2222221222	4222411255
HANUNOO	5222244422	5555555555	5555555555	5555555555	5555555555	5555555555	5555555555	5555222222	2144422124	4112124424
HASANIA	5121212251	5555555555	5555555555	5555555555	5555555555	5555555555	5555555555	5555222222	2121112221	1222411111
HASINAI	5112222121	5555555555	5555555442	1555555555	5555555555	5555555555	5555555555	5555222222	2144422124	4122455555
HAVASUPAI	5222244422	1121552222	4242115455	5555555555	5522215555	5555555555	5555555555	5555122222	1244422124	2222411144
HAWAIIANS	5112222121	5555555555	5555555444	1555555555	5555555555	5555555555	5555555555	5555212122	2244422124	4211312424
HAZARA	5121212251	2221555555	5555555555	5555555555	5555555555	5555555555	5555555555	5555111221	2221112221	1222411111
HEBREWS	2121212221	5555555555	5555555555	5515151555	5555551555	5555555555	5555555555	5555555555	5521112221	1222455511
HEHE	5112222121	5555555555	5555555555	5555555555	5555555555	5555555555	5555555555	5555111221	2222112221	1222455511
HERERO	5121212221	5555555555	5555555455	5555555555	5555555555	5555555555	5555555555	5555222211	2221122211	1222424412
HO	5112222155	5555555555	5555555555	5555555555	5555555555	5555555555	5555555555	5555111221	2222112221	1222411111
HUICHOL	5121212222	5555555555	5555555125	1555555555	5555555555	5555555555	5555555555	5555122222	1244422124	4112111124
HUKUNDIKA	5222244422	5555555555	5555555445	5555555555	5555555555	5555555555	5555555555	5555122222	1244422124	4122424411
HURON	5121212222	5555555555	5555555442	1555555555	5555555555	5555555555	5555555555	5555212122	2222121222	4222455555
HUTSUL	5121212222	2121555555	5555555121	1555555555	5555555555	5555555555	5555555555	5555122222	1244422124	4112111111
IBAN	2222244421	1121222221	4141115425	1115151551	1111221555	5555555555	5555555555	5555222222	2144422124	4112112424
ICELANDERS	5112222221	5555555555	5555555455	5555555555	5555555555	5555555555	5555555555	5555222222	2144422124	4112111111
IFUGAO	2121212221	1121552221	4114225555	5515151225	5511225555	5555555555	5555555555	5555222222	2144422124	4111355555
ILA	5121212221	1221555555	5555555242	3555555555	5555555555	5555555555	5555555555	5555222222	2122122211	1222424412
INCA	5111121222	5555551111	1414225124	1555552555	5522111555	5555555555	5555555555	5555122222	1244422124	4122424411
INGALIK	5121212222	5555555555	5555555442	1555555555	5555555555	5555555555	5555555555	5555222222	2144422124	4122424411
INGASSANA	5222244422	5555555555	5555555555	5555555555	5555555555	5555555555	5555555555	5555122222	1244422124	4212155555
IRAQW	5121212255	5555555555	5555555555	5555555555	5555555555	5555555555	5555555555	5555555555	5522122211	1222411111
IRISH	5111121222	5555555555	5555555555	5555555555	5555555555	5555555555	5555555555	5555222222	2144422124	4112111111
JAPANESE	5111121212	5555555555	5555552445	1555555115	5555555555	5555555555	5555555555	5555222222	2144422124	4112111111
JAVANESE	5111121222	5555555555	5555555224	1555555555	5555555551	1111111111	1112111212	1221222222	2144422124	4111312424
JEMEZ	5222244422	5555555555	5555555115	5555555555	5555555555	5555555555	5555555555	5555122222	1222221222	4222455511
JIVARO	5222244422	1221222221	4141111215	1255555222	2222555122	2222222222	2222222121	2112122222	1244422124	2222455555
JUKUN	5112222121	1221555555	5555555555	5555555555	5555555555	5555555555	5555555555	5555222222	2144422124	4221255555
KABYLE	5222244451	2121555555	5555555555	5555555555	5555555555	5555555555	5555555555	5555212122	2222112221	1222411111
KACHIN	5112222121	5555552222	2424225155	1555555555	5511215555	5555555555	5555555555	5555212122	2222112221	1222411111
KALMYK	5222244425	5555555555	5555555455	5555555555	5555555555	5555555555	5555555555	5555111221	2221112221	1222424411
KAPAUKU	5121212222	5555552222	4424115444	1555555555	5555215555	5555555555	5555555555	5555111221	2221112221	1222455555
KAREN	2121212221	1121225555	5555555555	5155155554	2155555555	5555555555	5555555555	5555222222	2122221222	4222455555
KARIERA	5222244422	5555555555	5555555445	5555555555	5555555555	5555555555	5555555555	5555111221	2211122211	1222455555
KASKA	2222244422	5555225555	5555555442	1111121551	1155555215	5555555555	5555555555	5555212122	2211121222	4222455511
KATAB	5222244421	5555555555	5555555145	1555555555	5555555555	5555555555	5555555555	5555111221	2222212221	1222411111
KAZAK	5112222121	2221555511	1414551425	2555552125	5511111555	5555555555	5555555555	5555111221	2221112221	1222424411

	FC110	FC120	FC130	FC140	FC150	FC160	FC170	FC180	FC190	FC200
KERAKI	5222244422	5555555555	5555555444	1555555555	5555555555	5555555555	5555555555	5555111221	2211112221	1222411111
KERALA	5111121212	5555555555	5555555555	5555555555	5555555555	5555555555	5555555555	5555222222	2122121222	4222455555
KET	5222244422	5555555555	5555555455	5555555555	5555555555	5555555555	5555555555	5555555555	5522112221	1222424411
KHALKA	5112222151	5555555555	5555555441	1555555555	5555555555	5555555555	5555555555	5555222222	2122122221	1212111111
KHASI	5111121252	5555115555	5555552225	1155555554	2155555555	5555555555	5555555555	5555212122	2222121222	4222411212
KHEVSUR	5222244422	5555555555	5555555555	5555555555	5555555555	5555555555	5555555555	5555111221	2222112221	1222411111
KIKUYU	5121212222	2221555555	5555555241	3552515555	5555555552	2211111111	1121212111	1122111221	2222112221	1222411111
KIOW-APACHE	5222244422	5555555555	5555555442	2555555555	5555555555	5555555555	5555555555	5555222222	2144422124	4112124444
KISSI	5222244421	5555555555	5555555555	5555555555	5555555555	5555555555	5555555555	5555212221	2222112221	1222411111
KOHISTANI	5112222215	5555555555	5555555415	1555555555	5555555555	5555555555	5555555555	5555212122	2221112221	1222411111
KOL	5555555512	5555555555	5555555555	5555555555	5555555555	5555555555	5555555555	5555222211	2244422124	4122411111
KONSO	5222244412	5555555555	5555555555	5555555555	5555555555	5555555555	5555555555	5555222211	2211112221	1222411155
KOREANS	5111121211	5555111111	1414225425	1155551551	1122555555	5555555555	5555555555	5555222211	2222112221	1222411111
KORYAK	5121212221	5555225555	5555555442	5152515552	2255555555	5555555555	5555555555	5555222222	2144422124	4122411111
KPE	5121212221	5555555555	5555555255	5555555555	5555555555	5555555555	5555555555	5555212122	2222122211	1222424411
KUBA	5112222111	5555555555	5555555215	5555555555	5555555555	5555555555	5555555555	5555212122	2222121222	4222424412
KUMYK	5555555555	5555555555	5555555555	5555555555	5555555555	5555555555	5555555555	5555122222	1244422124	4112155555
KUNG	5222244422	5555555555	5555555441	2555555555	5555552552	2222222222	2221521121	2212222211	2244422124	4112124411
KURTATCHI	5112222122	1111225555	5555551244	1152522221	1155555115	5555555555	5555555555	5555222211	2222122222	4212155555
KUTENAI	5222244421	5555555555	5555555442	3555555555	5555555555	5555555555	5555555555	5555222222	2144422124	4122412424
KWAKIUTL	5112222121	2121555555	5555555425	1555551125	5555552115	5555555555	5555555555	5555222211	2244422124	4211355511
LAKALAI	5121212222	5555555555	5555555455	5555555555	5555555555	5555555555	5555555555	5555212122	2221122222	4212155555
LAKHER	5112222121	5555555555	5555555424	1555551555	5555555555	5555555555	5555555555	5555222222	2122112221	1222411111
LAMBA	5222244421	5555555555	5555552455	5555555115	5555555551	1111111111	1151215121	1122222222	2122121222	4222455512
LAMET	5121212222	5555555555	5555555445	1555555555	5555555555	5555555555	5555555555	5555212122	2222112221	1222455555
LANGO	5121212221	5555555555	5555555555	5555552225	5555551555	5555555555	5555555555	5555222222	2122112221	1222411111
LAPPS	5121212222	1121551111	4114212455	5555552555	5511111555	5555555555	5555555555	5555222211	2244422124	4112111124
LAU	5121212222	2211555555	5555555144	1555551555	5555555515	5555555555	5555555555	5555111221	2221112221	1222455511
LEPCHA	5121212251	5555551121	4414221425	1511122115	5511115225	5555555555	5555555555	5555222211	2222112221	1222411111
LESU	5222244422	5555555555	5555551444	1555551225	5555555225	5555555555	5555555555	5555212122	2211121222	4222455512
LHOTA NAGA	5121212221	5555555555	5555555124	1555555555	5555555555	5555555555	5555555555	5555212122	2221112221	1222411111
LIFU	5112222121	5555555555	5555555555	5555555555	5555555555	5555555555	5555555555	5555111221	2222212221	1222411111
LOLO	5112222151	5555225555	5555555455	1155555552	2255555555	5555555555	5555555555	5555111221	2221112221	1222411111
LOZI	1112222121	5555555555	5555555441	3525155555	5555555555	5555555555	5555555555	5555222211	2244422124	4211311111
LUBA	5112222121	5555555555	5555555455	5555555555	5555555555	5555555555	5555555555	5555222222	2122212221	1222411111
LUO	5121212222	5555555555	5555555445	5555555555	5555555555	5555555555	5555555555	5555111221	2222112221	1222411111
MACASSARESE	5112222121	2111555555	5555555125	1555555555	5555555555	5555555555	5555555555	5555212122	2244422124	4221255555
MAGUZAWA	5112222121	5555551111	1414112555	5555555555	5522115555	5555555555	5555555555	5555222222	2122112221	1222411111
MALAYS	5111121251	2112555555	5555555555	5555555555	5555555555	5555555555	5555555555	5555222222	2144422124	4112111111
MAM	5121212222	2121555555	5555555555	5555555555	5555555555	5555555555	5555555555	5555212122	2222212221	1222411111

	FC110	FC120	FC130	FC140	FC150	FC160	FC170	FC180	FC190	FC200
MAMBILA	5222244421	5555555555	5555555555	5555555555	5555555555	5555555555	5555555555	5555212122	2244422124	4211355511
MAMVU	5222244421	5555555555	5555555245	5555555555	5555555555	5555555555	5555555555	5555111221	2222212221	1222455555
MANCHU	5121212221	5555555555	5555555555	5555555555	5555555555	5555555555	5555555555	5555111221	2222112221	1222411111
MANDAN	5222244422	5555225555	5555555245	5251555552	2255555555	5555555555	5555555555	5555555555	5511121222	4222411212
MANGAIANS	5112222122	1211555555	5555555244	1555555555	5555555555	5555555555	5555555555	5555222211	2244422124	4221255555
MANIHIKI	5112222122	5555555555	5555555444	5555555555	5555555555	5555555555	5555555555	5555555555	5544422124	4122455555
MANUS	5121212222	5555555555	5555555455	5555551555	5555555125	5555555555	5555555555	5555212122	2222222211	1222424444
MAORI	5112222121	2111555555	5454555455	1555552225	5555555115	5555555555	5555555555	5555212122	2244422124	4211311155
MARGI	5222244411	5555555555	5555555555	5555555555	5555555555	5555555555	5555555555	5555212122	2222212221	1222411111
MARICOPA	5222244422	1221555555	5555555411	1555555555	5555555555	5555555555	5555555555	5555222222	2122112221	1222412444
MARQUESANS	1112222122	5555555555	5555555144	1511211555	5555555555	5555555555	5555555555	5555222222	2144422124	4112112424
MARSHALLESE	5112222122	2211215555	5555555144	1155555551	1155555555	5555555555	5555555555	5555212122	2222122222	4212155511
MASAI	5222244412	5555555555	5555555445	5552512125	5555555555	5555555555	5555555555	5555222222	2122112221	1222411111
MATACO	5222244422	5555552121	4141225422	2555555555	5522215555	5555555555	5555555555	5555222211	2244422124	4122424444
MATAKAM	5222244425	5555555555	5555555445	1555555555	5555555555	5555555555	5555555555	5555111221	2222112221	1222455555
MAYA	5111121221	5555555555	5555555125	5555555555	5555555555	5555555555	5555555555	5555222222	2122212221	1222411111
MAZATECO	5555555555	5555555555	5555555555	5555555555	5555555555	5555555555	5555555555	5555222222	2144422124	4122455555
MBUGWE	5121212222	5555555555	5555555555	5555555555	5555555555	5555555555	5555555555	5555222222	2122122211	1222411111
MBUNDU	5112222121	2211215555	5555555245	1151515551	1155555215	5555555555	5555555555	5555111221	2222222211	1222411112
MBUTI	5222244422	5555555555	5555555445	2555555555	5555555555	5555555555	5555555555	5555111221	2222212221	1222424455
MENDE	5112222121	5555555555	5555551415	5555555555	5555555555	5555555555	5555555555	5555212122	2222212221	1222424411
MENTAWEI	5222244422	5555555555	5555555445	5555555555	5555555555	5555555555	5555555555	5555212122	2244422124	4221211255
MERINA	5112222121	5555555555	5555555555	5555555555	5555555555	5555555555	5555555555	5555222222	2121112223	4222412424
MIAMI	5222244421	5555555555	5555555422	5555555555	5555555555	5555555555	5555555555	5555555555	5522112221	1222455555
MIAO	2222244422	5555225555	5555555125	1125155552	2255555555	5555555555	5555555555	5555212122	2222122221	1212111111
MIN CHINESE	5111121251	2111555555	5555555555	5555555555	5555555555	5555555555	5555555555	5555111221	2222112221	1222411111
MINANGKABAU	5121212222	5555555555	5555555555	5555555555	5555555555	5555555555	5555555555	5555212122	2221121222	4222424412
MINCHIA	5111121252	5555555555	5555555555	5555555555	5555555555	5555555555	5555555555	5555122222	1222212221	1222411111
MISKITO	5222244422	5555551121	1441225425	3555555555	5521215555	5555555555	5555555555	5555222222	2144422124	2222455555
MIWOK	5222244422	5555555555	5555555455	5555555555	5555555555	5555555555	5555555555	5555111221	2211112221	1222424444
MNONG GAR	5121212221	5555555555	5555555425	1555555555	5555555555	5555555555	5555555555	5555212122	2222121222	4222455524
MONGO	5222244411	5555555555	5555555214	1555555555	5555555555	5555555555	5555555555	5555111221	2222212221	1222411111
MONGUOR	5112222151	5555555555	5555555415	5555555555	5555555555	5555555555	5555555555	5555212122	2222112221	1222411111
MOSSI	5111121211	5555555555	5555552411	1555555555	5555555555	5555555555	5555555555	5555212122	2222112221	1222411111
MOTA	5121212222	5555555555	5555555545	5555555555	5555555555	5555555555	5555555555	5555212122	2211121222	4222411212
MOTILON	5222244422	5555555555	5555555455	5555555555	5555555555	5555555555	5555555555	5555222222	2144422124	2222455555
MUNDURUCU	5222244422	5555552222	4242222425	1555555555	5522555552	2222222222	2251222122	2211222222	2111112221	1222424444
MURINBATA	5222244422	5555555555	5555555445	5555555555	5555555555	5555555555	5555555555	5555111221	2211112221	1222455555
MURNGIN	5222244422	1221555555	5555555444	2555552225	5555555552	2222222222	2221521221	2112111221	2211122211	1222424455
MZAB	5112222111	2221555555	5555555555	5555555555	5555555555	5555555555	5555555555	5555212122	2222112221	1222455555

	FC110	FC120	FC130	FC140	FC150	FC160	FC170	FC180	FC190	FC200
NABESNA	5222244422	5555555555	5555555442	2555555555	5555555555	5555555555	5555555555	5555222222	2121121222	4222424444
NAMA	1121212222	1221221121	1414221442	3225152551	1122112551	2222222221	2122212111	1112111221	2222112221	1222424411
NAMBICUARA	5222244422	1221552222	4242111415	1555555555	5555215555	5555555555	5555555555	5555222222	2144422124	4122455555
NANDI	1222244422	5555555555	5555555242	3525255555	5555555555	5555555555	5555555555	5555222222	2122122221	1212111111
NASKAPI	5222244422	5555555555	5555551455	5555555555	5555555555	5555555555	5555555555	5555222222	2144422124	4122424455
NATCHEZ	5112222215	5555555555	5555555425	1555555555	5555555555	5555555555	5555555555	5555222222	2144422124	4122455555
NAVAHO	5222244421	1221115555	5555552421	1152512551	1155555112	1121212122	2221212111	2111222222	2121121222	4222455512
NDEMBU	5555555521	5555555555	5555555245	5555555555	5555555555	5555555555	5555555555	5555111221	2222121222	4222455512
NGONI	5112222121	5555555555	5555555555	5555555555	5555555555	5555555555	5555555555	5555222222	2144422124	2222455511
NICOBARESE	5222244422	5555555555	5555555145	1555555555	5555555555	5555555555	5555555555	5555222222	2144422124	4122424424
NOMLAKI	5121212222	5555555555	5555555441	1555555555	5555555555	5555555555	5555555555	5555111221	2222212221	1222455544
NUER	2222244412	2221225522	4442551445	5225152551	1111225555	5555555555	5555555555	5555111221	2222112221	1222411111
NUNIVAK	5121212222	5555555555	5555555442	1555555555	5555555555	5555555555	5555555555	5555222222	2144422124	2222424411
NUPE	5111121221	2111555555	5555555111	3555555555	5555555551	1111111111	1112115212	1221212122	2222212221	1222411111
NURI	5121212211	5555555555	5555555211	5555555555	5555555555	5555555555	5555555555	5555222222	2122112221	1222411111
NYAKYUSA	2222244421	5555552222	2442215154	1525151555	5522115555	5555555555	5555555555	5555222211	2222222221	1212111111
NYANEKA	5112222121	5555555555	5555555555	5555555555	5555555555	5555555555	5555555555	5555111221	2222121222	4222411212
NYARO	5222244421	5555555555	5555555555	5555555555	5555555555	5555555555	5555555555	5555212122	2222222211	1222411112
NYORO	5112222121	2122555555	5555555241	3555555555	5555555555	5555555555	5555555555	5555212122	2222112221	1222411111
OJIBWA	5222244422	2211222221	4141221442	5152511551	1122115555	5555555555	5555555555	5555111221	2222222221	3222411111
OKINAWANS	5112222122	5555555555	5555555425	1555555555	5555555555	5555555555	5555555555	5555222222	2122122221	1212111111
OMAHA	5222244421	5555555555	5555555422	3555555555	5555551555	5555555555	5555555555	5555212122	2211112221	1222411111
ONA	5222244422	1221555555	5555555442	5555555555	5555555555	5555555555	5555555555	5555222211	2244422124	4122424444
ONTONG-JAVA	5121212222	5555555555	5555555414	3555555115	5555555555	5555555555	5555555555	5555222222	2144422124	4221255555
ORAON	5555555511	5555555555	5555555555	5555555555	5555555555	5555555555	5555555555	5555222211	2222112221	1222411111
PAEZ	5555555522	5555555555	5555555425	1555555555	5555555555	5555555555	5555555555	5555555555	5544422124	4122424411
PAIWAN	5112222122	5555555555	5555555555	5555555555	5555555555	5555555555	5555555555	5555122222	1244422124	4211312424
PALAUANS	5112222122	5555555555	5555555225	1555555555	5555555555	5555555555	5555555555	5555212122	2221122222	4221211211
PALIKUR	5222244422	5555555555	5555555454	1555555555	5555555555	5555555555	5555555555	5555555555	5522112221	1222455555
PAPAGO	5222244422	2211552121	4141222411	5552512555	5522225225	5555555555	5555555555	5555222222	2144422124	4122411144
PARAUJANO	5222244422	5555555555	5555555455	5555555555	5555555555	5555555555	5555555555	5555122222	1244422124	4122455555
PATHAN	5111121211	5555555555	5555555555	5555555555	5555555555	5555555555	5555555555	5555222222	2121122221	1212111111
PAWNEE	5112222121	5555555555	5555555555	5555555555	5555555555	5555555555	5555555555	5555122222	1222221222	4222424412
PENDE	5112222121	5555555555	5555555555	5555555555	5555555555	5555555555	5555555555	5555111221	2222121222	4222455512
PENOBSCOT	5222244422	2111555555	5555555455	5555555555	5555555555	5555555555	5555555555	5555222222	2144422124	4122411111
PONAPEANS	5112222122	5555555555	5555555124	5555555555	5555555555	5555555555	5555555555	5555222222	2122121222	4222411212
POPOLUCA	5222244422	2221555555	5555555555	5555555555	5555555555	5555555555	5555555555	5555555555	5544422124	4122411111
PORTUGUESE	5111121222	5555555555	5555555555	5555555555	5555555555	5555555555	5555555555	5555122222	1244422124	4122455555
PUKAPUKA	5222244422	2111215555	5555551244	1152522552	2255555225	5555555555	5555555555	5555212122	2222122233	3212155555
PURARI	5222244422	5555555555	5555555445	1555555555	5555555555	5555555555	5555555555	5555212122	2211112221	1222411111

	FC110	FC120	FC130	FC140	FC150	FC160	FC170	FC180	FC190	FC200
PURUM	5121212225	5555555555	5555555125	5555555555	5555555555	5555555555	5555555555	5555222222	2122112221	1222411111
RAROIANS	5222244422	5555555555	5555555444	1555555555	5555555555	5555555555	5555555555	5555222222	2144422124	4211312424
REGEIBAT	5111121211	5555555555	5555555455	5555555555	5555555555	5555555555	5555555555	5555111221	2221112221	1222411111
RIFFIANS	5121212212	2222555521	1414555121	1555552115	5511115555	5555555555	5555555555	5555111221	2222112221	1222411111
ROMANS	1111121221	2112555555	5555555555	5515155555	5555555555	5555555555	5555555555	5555222222	2144422124	4122412424
ROTINESE	5112222121	5555555555	5555555555	5555555555	5555555555	5555555555	5555555555	5555555555	5522112221	1222455555
ROTUMANS	5222244422	5555555555	5555555555	5555555555	5555555555	5555555555	5555555555	5555212122	2222221222	4222455555
RUNDI	5111121211	5555555555	5555555445	3555555555	5555555555	5555555555	5555555555	5555212122	2222112221	1222411111
RWALA	5121212211	2112215555	5454552422	2155552552	2221551555	5555555555	5555555555	5555111221	2221122221	1212124411
SAGADA	5121212222	5555555555	5555555424	1555555555	5555555555	5555555555	5555555555	5555222222	2144422124	4111312424
SAMOANS	5112222122	2111215555	5555555444	1155551114	2155551211	1112151112	1211221212	1122212122	2244422124	4221255555
SAMOYED	2121212222	2221215555	5555552442	2155155551	1155555555	5555555555	5555555555	5555222211	2221112221	1222455555
SANDAWE	5222244422	5555555555	5555555555	5555555555	5555555555	5555555555	5555555555	5555111221	2222212221	1222455511
SANPOIL	5222244422	1122555555	5555552445	5555552115	5555555555	5555555555	5555555555	5555222222	2144422124	4122424411
SANTAL	5222244422	5555555555	5555555415	3555555555	5555555555	5555555555	5555555555	5555222211	2222112221	1222411111
SARAMACCA	5222244422	5555555555	5555555455	5555555555	5555555555	5555555555	5555555555	5555212122	2222121222	4222455512
SARSI	5222244422	5555555555	5555555442	2555555555	5555555555	5555555555	5555555555	5555222222	2144422124	4122424424
SELUNG	5222244422	5555555555	5555555455	5555555555	5555555555	5555555555	5555555555	5555222222	2144422124	4122455555
SEMANG	5222244422	1222555555	4545555445	2555555555	5511122555	5555555555	5555555555	5555222211	2244422124	4122424424
SEMINOLE	5222244422	5555555555	5555555555	5555555555	5555555555	5555555555	5555555555	5555111221	2221121222	4222455555
SENIANG	5121212222	2221552222	2424215444	5555555555	5522215555	5555555555	5555555555	5555111221	2221112221	1222455555
SERBS	5111121222	5555555555	5555555425	1555555555	5555555555	5555555555	5555555555	5555212122	2222212221	1222455555
SERI	5222244422	5555555555	5555555455	5555555555	5555552555	5555555555	5555555555	5555222222	2144422124	4122424444
SHERENTE	5222244422	5555555555	5555555455	5555555555	5555555555	5555555555	5555555555	5555212122	2211112221	1222455555
SHILLUK	5111121221	5555555555	5555555445	3555555555	5555551555	5555555555	5555555555	5555212122	2222112221	1222411111
SHLUH	5222244422	5555555555	5555555555	5555555555	5555555555	5555555555	5555555555	5555212122	2222212221	1222411111
SIMBOESE	5555555555	5555555555	5555555555	5555555555	5555555555	5555555555	5555555555	5555212122	2244422124	4211355555
SINDHI	5112222251	5555555555	5555555555	5555555555	5555555555	5555555555	5555555555	5555122222	1222212221	1222455555
SINHALESE	5555555512	5555555555	5555555555	5555555555	5555555555	5555555555	5555555555	5555222222	2144422124	2222412424
SIRIONO	5222244422	1221225555	5555555424	1255552552	2255555525	5555555555	5555555555	5555212122	2222221222	4222424444
SIUAI	5121212222	5555555555	5555555555	5555555555	5555555551	1122252212	1215225522	2221212122	2222121222	4222411224
SIWANS	5121212251	5555551121	1414225121	5555551555	5521115555	5555555555	5555555555	5555122222	1222112221	1222411111
SOMALI	5121212211	2111551111	1414222411	2555552555	5511555555	5555555555	5555555555	5555111221	2221112221	1222411111
SONGHAI	5111121211	2221555555	5555555112	3555555555	5555555555	5555555555	5555555555	5555222222	2122212221	1222411111
SOTHO	5112222122	2212555555	5555555555	5551515555	5555555555	5555555555	5555555555	5555222222	2122112221	1222424411
SUBANUN	5222244422	5555555555	5555555555	5555555555	5555555555	5555555555	5555555555	5555222222	2144422124	4112124424
SWAZI	5112222122	5555555555	5555555241	3555555555	5555555555	5555555555	5555555555	5555111221	2222112221	1222411111
SYRIANS	5112222252	5555555555	5555555145	1555555555	5555555555	5555555555	5555555555	5555222222	2122212221	1222455555
TAGBANUA	5112222121	5555555555	5555555555	5555555555	5555555555	5555555555	5555555555	5555122222	1244422124	4112112424
TALAMANCA	5222244422	5555555555	5555555424	5555555555	5555555555	5555555555	5555555555	5555555555	5511121222	4222411255

	FC110	FC120	FC130	FC140	FC150	FC160	FC170	FC180	FC190	FC200
TALLENSI	2121212221	2121222121	4114212141	3125152554	2111225555	5555555555	5555555555	5555111221	2222112223	4222411111
TAMIL	5111121212	5555555555	5555555555	5555555555	5555555555	5555555555	5555555555	5555222222	2122212221	1222455555
TANALA	1112222121	5555552221	1414112421	1525152115	5522115225	5555555555	5555555555	5555212122	2222112223	4222411124
TANIMBARESE	5112222121	5555555555	5555555555	5555555555	5555555555	5555555555	5555555555	5555222222	2122212221	1222411111
TAOS	5222244422	2211555555	5555555145	5555555555	5555555555	5555555555	5555555555	5555122222	1244422124	4122455555
TAPIRAPE	5222244422	5555555555	5555555424	1555551555	5555555555	5555555555	5555555555	5555122222	1244422124	4122455555
TARAHUMARA	5121212222	2121555555	5555555125	1555555555	5555555555	5555555555	5555555555	5555122222	1244422124	4112112424
TAREUMIUT	5121212222	5555555555	5555555442	3555555555	5555555555	5555555555	5555555555	5555222222	2144422124	4112124411
TEDA	5555555511	5555555555	5555552441	5555555555	5555555555	5555555555	5555555555	5555222211	2222112221	1222411111
TEHUELCHE	5222244421	5555225555	5555552422	2255555552	2255555555	5555555555	5555555555	5555222222	2144422124	4122424455
TENDA	5222244412	5555555555	5555555435	5555555555	5555555555	5555555555	5555555555	5555222222	2122121222	4222411212
TENETEHARA	5222244422	1221555555	5555555555	5552515555	5555555555	5555555555	5555555555	5555122222	1244422124	4122424411
TENINO	5121212221	5555555555	5555555445	1555555555	5555555555	5555555555	5555555555	5555222211	2244422124	4112124444
TERA	5112222121	5555555555	5555555555	5555555555	5555555555	5555555555	5555555555	5555122222	1222212221	1222411111
TERENA	5112222121	1221555555	5555555421	1555555555	5555555555	5555555555	5555555555	5555122222	1244422124	4222424455
TESO	5222244421	5555555555	5555555555	5555555555	5555555555	5555555555	5555555555	5555212122	2222112221	1222411111
TETON	5222244422	5555555555	5555555455	5551525555	5555555555	5555555555	5555555555	5555222211	2244422124	4112124455
THAI	5111121221	2111555555	5555552555	5555555555	5555555551	1111111111	1112111212	1221222222	2144422124	4112112424
THONGA	5112222122	2211222222	2424111244	1152511554	2121115215	5555555555	5555555555	5555111221	2222112221	1222424411
TIBETANS	5111121251	2111555555	5555555415	5555555555	5555555555	5555555555	5555555555	5555222222	2122112221	1222411111
TIGRINYA	5111121211	5555555555	5555555555	5555555555	5555555555	5555555555	5555555555	5555222222	2122222221	1212111111
TIKOPIA	5112222122	2221221121	4114215444	1255552111	1122115115	5555555555	5555555555	5555222222	2122122221	1212111155
TIMBIRA	1222244422	2121222222	4242221444	1225252552	2221215555	5555555555	5555555555	5555212122	2211121222	4222424412
TIMUCUA	5112222125	5555555555	5555555445	5555555555	5555555555	5555555555	5555555555	5555212122	2221121222	4222411212
TIV	2222244421	1111212211	1441225415	1115151124	2111225555	5555555555	5555555555	5555111221	2221122221	1221224411
TIWI	5222244422	5555555555	5555555445	5555555555	5555555555	5555555555	5555555555	5555222222	2111121222	4222424455
TODA	2222244422	5555212121	4141112445	1115152554	2111221555	5555555555	5555555555	5555111221	2222122211	1222424411
TOKELAU	5222244422	5555555555	5555555444	5555555555	5555555555	5555555555	5555555555	5555122222	1244422124	4211355524
TOLOWA	5121212221	5555555555	5555555445	5555555555	5555555555	5555555555	5555555555	5555111221	2222212221	1222424411
TORAJA	5121212221	5555555555	5555555555	5555555555	5555555555	5555555555	5555555555	5555222222	2144422124	4122412424
TOTONAC	5555555521	5555555555	5555555125	1555555555	5555555555	5555555555	5555555555	5555555555	5544422124	4122455555
TRISTAN	5222244422	5555555555	5555555441	1555555555	5555555555	5555555555	5555555555	5555122222	1244422124	4112112424
TROBRIAND	5112222122	2111222221	1414115444	1155551221	1122111222	2211222122	2151225222	2111212122	2221121222	4222411212
TRUKESE	5222244422	5555555555	4545555424	1555555555	5555555215	5555555555	5555555555	5555212122	2222121222	4222411111
TRUMAI	1222244421	1222555555	5555555425	1525252555	5555555555	5555555555	5555555555	5555222222	2144422124	2222424455
TSHIMSHIAN	5112222121	5555555555	5555555425	1555555555	5555555555	5555555555	5555555555	5555222222	2121121222	4222411212
TUBATULABAL	5222244422	1222555555	5555551441	1555555555	5555555555	5555555555	5555555555	5555222222	2144422124	4122424444
TUCANO	5222244422	5555555555	5555555445	1555555555	5555555555	5555555555	5555555555	5555111221	2222112221	1222424455
TUCUNA	5222244422	5555555555	5555555425	1555525555	5555555555	5555555555	5555555555	5555111221	2211112221	1222424411
TUNEBO	5222244425	5555555555	5555555425	5555555555	5555555555	5555555555	5555555555	5555122222	1244422124	4122455555

APPENDIX EIGHT/20 -- FINISHED CHARACTERISTIC CODE SHEET

	FC110	FC120	FC130	FC140	FC150	FC160	FC170	FC180	FC190	FC200
TUPINAMBA	5121212221	2221225555	5555551424	1255555552	2255555555	5555555555	5555555555	5555222222	2144422124	2222455555
TURKANA	5222244422	2121555555	5555555455	5555555555	5555555555	5555555555	5555555555	5555222211	2222112221	1222411111
TURKMEN	5112222151	5555555555	5555555555	5555555555	5555555555	5555555555	5555555555	5555555555	5521112221	1222455555
TWANA	5121212221	5555555555	5555555422	1555555555	5555555555	5555555555	5555555555	5555222211	2244422124	4112124455
TZELTAL	5555555555	5555555555	5555555555	5555555555	5555555555	5555555555	5555555555	5555222222	2122112221	1222455555
ULAWANS	5222244422	5555555555	5555555444	1555555555	5555555555	5555555555	5555555555	5555212122	2244422124	4221212424
UTE	5222244422	5555555555	5555555442	2555555555	5555555555	5555555555	5555555555	5555222222	2144422124	4122424444
VEDDA	5222244422	5555555555	5555555445	5555555555	5555552555	5555555555	5555555555	5555111221	2222121222	4222411111
VENDA	5112222121	5555555555	5555555245	3551522115	5555555555	5555555555	5555555555	5555212122	2222122211	1222424411
VIETNAMESE	5111121221	5555211111	1414555555	5155552551	1155115551	1111111111	1112111212	1221222222	2122112221	1222412424
WAICA	5222244422	5555555555	5555555445	5555555555	5555555555	5555555555	5555555555	5555222222	2144422124	4122455555
WALLOONS	5111121222	5555555555	5555555555	5555555555	5555555555	5555555555	5555555555	5555222222	2144422124	4112155555
WANTOAT	5222244422	5555555555	5555555445	5555555555	5555555555	5555555555	5555555555	5555111221	2222122221	1212111111
WAPISHANA	5222244422	2212555555	5555555455	5555555555	5555555555	5555555555	5555555555	5555222211	2244422124	2222455555
WAROPEN	5222244421	5555555555	5555555455	5555555555	5555555555	5555555555	5555555555	5555212122	2222112221	1222455555
WARRAU	5222244422	5555555555	5555555455	5555552555	5555555555	5555555555	5555555555	5555122222	1244422124	4122455555
WASHO	5222244422	5555555555	5555555441	3555555555	5555555555	5555555555	5555555555	5555222222	2144422124	4122424444
WICHITA	5222244422	5555555555	5555555555	5555525555	5555555555	5555555555	5555555555	5555222222	2144422124	4112155544
WIKMUNKAN	5222244422	5555555555	5555555445	5555555555	5555555555	5555555555	5555555555	5555111221	2211112221	1222455555
WINNEBAGO	2222244422	2212555555	5555555455	5521115555	5555555555	5555555555	5555555555	5555212122	2211112221	1222455555
WITOTO	5222244421	5555555555	5555555444	1555552225	5555552555	5555555555	5555555555	5555111221	2222212221	1222455555
WOGEO	5222244422	2211555555	5555555444	1555551555	5555555555	5555555555	5555555555	5555212221	2211122211	1222411111
WOLEAIANS	2222244422	2111225555	5555551424	1122222554	2155555525	5555555555	5555555555	5555212122	2222122222	4212155555
WOLOF	5111121211	2111551111	1414215411	1555551555	5522115555	5555555555	5555555555	5555111221	2222222211	1222411111
WUTE	5112222121	5555555555	5555555555	5555555555	5555555555	5555555555	5555555555	5555212122	2221112221	1222411111
YABARANA	5222244422	5555555555	5555555424	1555555555	5555555555	5555555555	5555555555	5555222211	2244422124	2222455555
YAGUA	2222244422	2221555555	5555552445	1525252555	5555555225	5555555555	5555555555	5555111221	2222212221	1222424444
YAHGAN	2222244422	5555552222	4242225442	3525252555	5522222555	5555555555	5555555555	5555222211	2244422124	4122424444
YAKO	5222244421	5555555555	5555555555	5555555555	5555555555	5555555555	5555555555	5555212122	2222222211	1222411112
YAKUT	5121212221	5555212222	2424225412	1155551551	1111115225	5555555555	5555555555	5555111221	2221112221	1222424411
YAO	5222244421	5555551121	1441225244	1555555555	5511115555	5555555555	5555555555	5555212122	2222121222	4222455512
YAPESE	5112222212	5555555555	5555555224	5555555555	5555555555	5555555555	5555555555	5555212122	2222122211	1222411111
YARURO	5222244422	5555555555	5555555445	1555555555	5555555555	5555555555	5555555555	5555122222	1244422124	4122412411
YOKUTS	1121212222	2211552222	4224115445	5525255555	5522115555	5555555555	5555555555	5555212122	2211112221	1222424444
YOMBE	5112222121	5555555555	5555555555	5555555555	5555555555	5555555555	5555555555	5555111221	2222121222	4222411212
YORUBA	5111121221	5555555555	5555555135	1551515555	5555555555	5555555555	5555555555	5555212122	2222122221	1212111111
YUKAGHIR	5222244421	5555555555	5555555455	5555555555	5555555555	5555555555	5555555555	5555222211	2244422124	4122424411
YUKI	5121212222	5555555555	5555555445	1555555555	5555555555	5555555555	5555555555	5555222222	2144422124	4122424444
YUROK	2121212221	5555222221	4114222441	1115151222	2211225555	5555555555	5555555555	5555222211	2244422124	4122455524
ZUNI	1222244422	2121555555	5555555555	5515252225	5555555555	5555555555	5555555555	5555212122	2221121222	4222411224

	FC210	FC220	FC230	FC240	FC250	FC260	FC270	FC280	FC290	FC300
ABIPON	2212222244	4424444442	2444422222	1122222224	4154422414	4125555552	2111212122	2144115555	5555555555	5555555111
ABOR	1221224214	1411222142	2241255555	5555522224	4154422411	4425555555	2111212122	2555555555	5555555555	5555555555
AINU	1221224214	1412212222	2522422222	2224212122	1154422145	5425555555	2222242422	2555551255	5122125155	5112211422
AJIE	1221124211	4412122211	2242412221	2221255555	5555555555	4455555555	5112242412	2555555555	5555555555	5555555555
AKHA	1221124211	4424444442	2244412221	2221222224	4154422411	4425555555	2222242422	2555555555	5555555555	5555555555
ALACALUF	2122222244	4412221222	2442455555	5555522224	4154422414	4125555555	5222242422	2555555555	5555555555	5555555222
ALBANIANS	1221124211	4412122211	1141222222	1122212122	1152122141	4425555555	2111212122	2555551155	5555555555	5555555555
ALORESE	1221224214	1424444442	2244422222	1212222224	4124422411	4425552221	2111212122	2111445551	5215125555	5221155421
AMBA	1221124211	4424444442	2244411212	2221222224	4152221411	4425555555	2112242412	2555555555	5555555555	5555555555
AMERICANS	2212222244	4412221222	2442422222	1122222224	4254422424	4215555555	2222242422	2555555555	5555555555	5555555222
ANDAMANESE	2122222244	4424444442	2444422222	1212222224	4254422424	4215555551	2222242422	2244222255	5555515155	5555525555
APINAYE	1224221122	4212122211	2422411122	2221211221	1254422244	2425555555	1122241222	2555555555	5551551222	1555555555
ARANDA	1221124211	4424444442	2444412221	2221222224	4111112414	4425555555	1112242412	2555551515	5552551225	5555551222
ARAPESH	1221124211	4424444442	2244411212	2221222224	4112122411	4425212555	1222242422	2555555555	5155115555	5211515421
ARAUCANIANS	1221124211	4411222141	1141211212	2221212122	1112222141	4425555112	2111212122	2555551155	5555555555	5555555421
ARYANS	1221124211	4424444442	2244422222	1212211221	1152122141	4425555555	5111212122	2555555555	5555555555	5555555555
ASHANTI	1221214214	4112122211	2442422222	2224112122	1122222144	4425122125	2111212122	2555552121	1115121221	5222122222
ATAYAL	1221224214	1424444442	2244422222	1212212212	2254422242	4425555555	5111212122	2222445555	5555555555	5555555555
ATSUGEWI	1221224214	1424444442	2444422222	1122212122	1151122144	4125125555	2122242421	2555555555	5555555555	5555555222
AWEIKOMA	2122222244	4412221222	2442422222	1212222224	4152122414	4125555555	2222242422	2244225555	5555555555	5555555555
AYMARA	1221124211	4424444442	2244422222	1212211221	1254422242	4425555551	2222242422	2555555555	5555555555	5555555555
AZANDE	1221224214	1424444442	2244422222	2224122224	4112221411	4425215552	2111212122	2222445555	5111225551	2211112111
AZTEC	1221224214	1424444442	2444422222	1212222224	4154422414	4125555555	2122241222	2244241125	5555555555	5555555555
BABWA	1221124211	4455555555	5555522222	1212212122	1152222141	4425555555	5111212122	2555555555	5555555555	5555555555
BACAIRI	1221224214	1412122212	2442412221	2221212122	1154422144	4125555555	5222242422	2555555555	5555555555	5555555555
BAJUN	2212222244	4412221221	2241122222	2224122224	4254422422	4415555555	5111212122	2555555555	5555555555	5555555555
BALINESE	1221224214	1412221221	2441122222	1212212122	1124422144	4125555551	5122241222	2555555555	5115555555	5511125555
BAMBARA	1221124211	4412122211	1141212221	2221211221	1152222141	4425555555	5111212122	2555555555	5555555555	5555555422
BAMILEKE	1221124211	4424444442	2244455555	5555522224	4152221411	4425555555	5111212122	2555555555	5555555555	5555555111
BANDA	1221124211	4424444442	2244411212	2221222224	4151222411	4425555555	5112242412	2555555555	5555555555	5555555555
BARABRA	1221124211	4412221221	2241122222	2224122224	4154422411	4425555555	5111212122	2555555555	5555555555	5555555555
BARI	1221124211	4424444442	2244411212	2221222224	4152221411	4425555555	2111212122	2555555555	5555555555	5555555555
BASQUES	2122222244	4455555555	5555522222	1122212212	2254422244	4225555555	5122242422	1555555555	5555555555	5555555555
BASSERI	1221124211	4412221221	2241155555	5555522224	4154422411	4425555555	2111212122	2555555555	5555555555	5555555555
BATAK	1221124211	4411222141	1141222222	2224212122	1154422141	4425555555	2111212122	2555555555	5555555555	5555555555
BAYA	1221124211	4424444442	2244455555	5555522224	4152221411	4425555555	2111212122	2555555555	5555555555	5555555555
BEJA	1221124211	4412221221	2241122222	2224122224	4154422411	4425555555	5111212122	2555555555	5555555555	5555555555
BELU	1224221122	4211222141	1411222222	1212211221	1152122144	1425555555	5111212122	2555555555	5555555555	5555555555
BEMBA	2122222244	4412122211	2422412221	2221222224	4111222414	1425555515	1112122422	2114445555	5555555555	5555555422
BENGALI	1221124211	4424444442	2244422222	1212211221	1154422141	4425555555	5111212122	2555555555	5555555555	5555555555

	FC210	FC220	FC230	FC240	FC250	FC260	FC270	FC280	FC290	FC300
BERGDAMA	1221224214	1412221222	2442422222	2224122224	4151222414	4125555555	5112122422	2555555555	5555555555	5555555555
BETE	1221124211	4424444442	2244455555	5555512122	1152222141	4425555555	5111212122	2555555555	5555555555	5555555555
BHIL	1221124211	4424444442	2244422222	2224112122	1114422141	4425555555	2111212122	2222445555	5555555555	5555555555
BHUIYA	1221124211	4412122212	2242422222	1212222224	4254422422	4415215555	2111212122	2555555555	5555555555	5555555555
BIRIFOR	1221124211	4412122211	2441111122	2221211221	1152222144	4425555555	5111212122	2555555555	5555555555	5555555111
BLACK CARIB	2212222244	4412122212	2442412221	2221222224	4154422414	4125555555	5222242422	2555555555	5555555555	5555555422
BOERS	1221224214	1455555555	5555522222	1122212122	1254422244	4225555555	5122242422	1555555555	5555555555	5555555555
BORORO	1224221122	4212122212	2422411122	2221212122	1154422144	1425555555	2222242422	2555555555	5555555555	5555555555
BOTOCUDO	5555555555	5512221222	2442422222	1212211221	1151122144	4125555555	1222242422	2555555555	5555555555	5555555555
BOZO	1221124211	4412221222	2242455555	5555511221	1152122141	4425555555	5111212122	2555555555	5555555555	5555555555
BRAZILIANS	2212222244	4424444442	2444422222	1122222224	4254422424	4215555555	2222242422	2555555555	5555555555	5555555555
BUDUMA	1221124211	4412221222	2242412221	2221222224	4152122411	4425555555	5111212122	2555555555	5555555555	5555555555
BULGARIANS	1221224214	1455555555	5555522222	2224112122	1254422244	4225555555	5222242422	2555555555	5555555555	5555555555
BUNLAP	1221124211	4424444442	2444412221	2221222224	4154422414	4425555555	5112242412	2555555555	5555555555	5555555111
BURMESE	1224221224	2412221222	2442422222	1212222224	4254422424	4215215555	5122242422	1244225555	5555555555	5555555555
BURUSHO	1221124211	4424444442	2244422222	1212212122	1154422141	4425555555	2122241222	2555555555	5555555555	5555555111
BURYAT	1221124211	4412122212	2241222222	2224211221	1154422141	4425555555	5111212122	2555555555	5555555555	5555555555
CADUVEO	1224221224	2455555555	5555522222	1212212122	1154422144	4125555555	5222242422	2555555555	5555555555	5555555555
CAGABA	1224221224	2424444442	2444422222	1212222224	4124422414	4125555551	5112122422	2555555555	5555555555	5555555555
CALLINAGO	1224221122	4211222141	2421112221	2221211221	1154422144	1425555115	2112122422	2224445555	5555555555	5555555422
CAMAYURA	1221224214	1412122211	2442412221	2221211221	1124422144	4125555551	5112122422	2555555555	5555555555	5555555555
CAMBA	2212222244	4424444442	2444422222	1122222224	4254422424	4215555555	5222242422	2555555555	5555555555	5555555555
CAMBODIANS	2212222244	4412221222	2442422222	1122222224	4154422414	4125555555	2111212122	2555555555	5555555555	5555555555
CARAJA	1224221224	2412221222	2442422222	1212212122	1154422144	4125555555	5222242422	2555555555	5555555555	5555555555
CARIB	2122222244	4412122211	2442412221	2221222224	4124422414	4125555551	2112122422	2555555555	5551552555	5555551222
CARINYA	2212222244	4424444442	2444422222	1122222224	4154422414	4125555555	5555555555	5555555555	5555555555	5555555555
CAYAPA	1221224214	1424444442	2444422222	1122212122	1254422244	4225555555	5222242422	2244225555	5555555555	5555555555
CHAGGA	1221124211	4424444442	2244411212	2221222224	4152221411	4425552155	2111212122	2555555555	5115115555	5111215422
CHAMACOCO	1224221224	2455555555	5555555555	5555522224	4254422424	4215555555	5112122422	2555555555	5555555555	5555555111
CHENCHU	2122222244	4412122211	1141212221	2221222224	4254422422	4415552225	2111212122	2555555555	5555555555	5555555222
CHEREMIS	2212222244	4424444442	2444455555	5555522224	4254422424	4215555555	5122242422	1555555555	5555555555	5555555555
CHERKESS	1221124211	4455555555	5555522222	1122222224	4152122411	4425555555	5111212122	2555555555	5555555555	5555555555
CHEROKEE	1224221122	4224444442	2424411122	2221212122	1154422144	1421555555	5222242422	2555555555	5555555555	5555555555
CHEYENNE	1224221224	2424444442	2444422222	1212211221	1151122144	4125211511	2122241222	2555555555	5555555555	5555555555
CHIBCHA	1221224214	1455555555	5555522222	1122222224	4152122414	4125555555	2111212122	2555555555	5555555555	5555555555
CHINANTEC	1221224214	1424444442	2444422222	1212212212	2254422244	4225555555	5222242422	2555555555	5555555555	5555555555
CHIR-APACHE	1224221224	2424444442	2444422222	1212212122	1121122144	4125211211	2222242422	2555555555	5215115555	5111115111
CHIRIGUANO	1221224214	1412221222	2442455555	5555512122	1154422144	4125555555	5112122422	2555555555	5555555555	5555555555
CHOCO	2212222244	4424444442	2444422222	1212222224	4254422424	4215555555	5222242422	2555555555	5555555555	5555555555
CHOROTI	1224221224	2424444442	2444422222	1122222224	4154422414	4125555555	2112122422	2555555555	5555555555	5555551555

	FC210	FC220	FC230	FC240	FC250	FC260	FC270	FC280	FC290	FC300
CHORTI	2122222244	4424444442	2444422222	1212212122	1254422244	4225555555	5112122422	2555555555	5555555555	5555555555
CHUKCHEE	1221224214	1412221222	2442422222	1122212212	2152222144	4125555551	2112122422	2144111215	5555552152	1555555222
COCHITI	1224221122	4224444442	2424422222	1212212122	1254422244	2425555555	5222242422	2555555555	5555555555	5555555222
COMANCHE	2122222244	4424444442	2444422222	1212211221	1121122144	4121552225	5222242422	2144145555	5255125555	5222555555
COORG	1221124211	4412122211	2242412221	2221212122	1254422242	4425555555	2222242422	2555555555	5555555555	5555555422
COPR ESKIMO	2212222244	4424444442	2444422222	1122222224	4224422424	4215555551	2112122422	2555555555	5555552112	1555551555
CREE	1221224214	1412122211	2442412221	2221222224	4154422414	4125555555	5112122422	2555555555	5555555555	5555555555
CREEK	1224221122	4224444442	2424411122	2221211221	1154422144	1425555551	1122241222	2555551555	5555551211	2555555422
CROW	1221224214	1424444442	2424411122	2221222224	4151112414	1425555515	5122241222	2555555555	5555551212	2555555222
CUNA	1224221224	2424444442	2444422222	1212211221	1154422144	4125555555	2112122422	2144115555	5555555555	5555555555
CZECHS	1221224214	1424444442	2444422222	1122212212	2254422244	4225555555	5122242422	1555555555	5555555555	5555555555
DAGUR	1221124211	4424444442	2244412221	2221212122	1254422242	4425555555	5111212122	2555555555	5555555555	5555555555
DARD	1221124211	4424444442	2244422222	1212211221	1152122141	4425555555	5111212122	2555555555	5555555555	5555555222
DELAWARE	1224221122	4255555555	5555522222	1212211221	1154422144	1425555555	2222242422	2555555555	5555555555	5555555555
DIEGUENO	1221124211	4424444442	2244412221	2221222224	4151222411	4425555555	5222242422	2555555555	5555555555	5555555421
DIERI	1221224214	1424444442	2424412221	2221222224	4151112414	1425555551	5112242412	2555555215	5555555555	5555555555
DILLING	1221124211	4412122212	2242422222	2224122224	4152221411	4425215555	5111212122	2555555555	5555555555	5555555555
DOBUANS	2122222244	4424444442	2424412221	2221222224	4254422424	2415555555	2122242421	2555555555	5225552552	1555211555
DOGON	1221124211	4424444442	2244412221	2221211221	1154422141	4425555555	5112122422	2555555555	5555555555	5555555555
DOROBO	1221124211	4424444442	2244411212	2221222224	4254422422	4415555555	5111212122	2555555555	5555555555	5555555422
DUSUN	1221224214	1424444442	2444422222	1122222224	4254422424	4215555555	5111212122	2555555552	1125515555	5551215555
DUTCH	2122222244	4412221222	2442422222	1122212122	1254422244	4225555555	2222242422	2555555555	5555555555	5555555555
EGYPTIANS	1221124211	4412221221	2241122222	2224112122	1124422141	4425555551	2111212122	2555555555	5555555555	5555555422
ELLICE	1221224214	1424444442	2444422222	1212212122	1154422144	4125555555	2122242421	2555555555	5555555555	5555555555
ENGA	1221124211	4424444442	2244412221	2221222224	4154422411	4425555555	2111212122	2555555555	5555555555	5555555555
EYAK	1221214214	4112122212	2422412221	2221222224	4152122414	1425555555	5112122422	2555555555	5555555555	5555555555
FANG	1221124211	4424444442	2244411212	2221212122	1152222141	4425555555	2111212122	2111441515	5555555555	5555555111
FON	1221124211	4412212222	2242422222	2224122224	4112221411	4421555221	2111212122	2555555515	5115125555	5212115421
FOX	2122222244	4424444442	2244411212	2221211221	1151122141	4425215555	5112122422	2555555555	5555555555	5555555555
FUTAJALONKE	1221124211	4412221221	2242412221	2221222224	4152221411	4425555555	2111212122	2555555555	5555555555	5555555555
GANDA	1221224214	1424444442	2244412221	2221222224	4112221411	4425555115	2111212122	2555555552	1555555555	5555555111
GARO	1224221122	4212122211	1411212221	2221212212	2154422144	1425555555	2222242422	2555555555	5555555555	5555555555
GILBERTESE	1221224214	1424444442	2444422222	1212222224	4154422414	4125555555	2111212122	2555555555	5555555555	5555555555
GILYAK	1221124211	4411222141	1141212221	2221222224	4124422411	4425555555	2111212122	2555555555	5555555555	5555555555
GISU	1221124211	4424444442	2244422222	1212222224	4152221411	4425555115	2111212122	2555555555	5555555555	5555555555
GOAJIRO	1221214214	4112212222	2422411122	2221222224	4152221414	1425555555	2111212122	2555555555	5555555555	5555555422
GOND	1221124211	4412122211	2242412221	2221211221	1151122141	4425555555	2111212122	2222445555	5555551221	2555555222
GROS VENTRE	1221224214	1424444442	2444422222	1212222224	4151112414	4125555515	1111212122	2555555555	5555555555	5555555422
GUAHIBO	1224221122	4212122211	2422412221	2221212122	1154422144	1425555555	5112122422	2555555555	5555555555	5555555555
GUATO	2212222244	4455555555	5555512221	2221222224	4151112414	4125555555	5555555555	5555555555	5555555555	5555555555

	FC210	FC220	FC230	FC240	FC250	FC260	FC270	FC280	FC290	FC300
GURE	1221214214	4124444442	2424422222	1212211221	1154422144	1425555555	5122241222	2555555555	5555555555	5555555555
HAIDA	1221214214	4112122211	2421111122	2221211221	1154422144	1422555555	2112122422	2555552515	5555555555	5555555111
HANO	1224221122	4224444442	2424411122	2221212122	1254422244	2422552225	2222242422	2555552555	5225222111	2112225555
HANUNOO	1224221224	2424444442	2444422222	1122212122	1154422144	4125555555	5112122422	2555555555	5555555555	5555555555
HASANIA	1221124211	4412221221	2241122222	2224122224	4152122411	4425555555	5111212122	2555555555	5555555555	5555555555
HASINAI	1224221224	2424444442	2444422222	1212211221	1154422144	4125555555	5222242422	2555555555	5555555555	5555555555
HAVASUPAI	1221224214	1424444442	2444412221	2221211221	1154422144	4125555555	5122241222	2555555551	2555555555	5555555555
HAWAIIANS	2122222244	4424444442	2444422222	1212211221	1154422144	4125555555	2222242422	2555555555	5555555555	5555555555
HAZARA	1221124211	4412221221	2241122222	2224112122	1154422141	4425555555	2111212122	2555555555	5555555555	5555555555
HEBREWS	1221124211	4412221222	2242422222	1122212122	1152122141	4425555555	2111212122	2555551125	5555555555	5555555555
HEHE	1221124211	4412122211	1141212221	2221212122	1152122141	4421555555	5111212122	2555555555	5555555555	5555555555
HERERO	1221224214	1412122211	2441112221	2221212122	1152222144	4425555555	5111212122	2555555555	5555555555	5555555555
HO	1221124211	4411222142	2241212221	2221222224	4152122411	4425555555	5111212122	2555555555	5555555555	5555555555
HUICHOL	2122222244	4412221222	2442422222	1212212122	1154422144	4125555555	5222242422	2555555555	5555555555	5555555555
HUKUNDIKA	2122222244	4424444442	2444422222	1212212122	1151122144	4125555555	5222242422	2555555555	5555555555	5555555555
HURON	1224221122	4224444442	2424412221	2221211221	1254422244	2425555555	5222242422	2555555555	5555555555	5555555555
HUTSUL	2212222244	4455555555	5555522222	1122222224	4254422424	4215555555	2122242422	1555555555	5555555555	5555555555
IBAN	2122222244	4424444442	2444422222	1122212212	2254422244	4225555525	2222242422	2244222225	5555555555	5555555555
ICELANDERS	1221224214	1455555555	5555522222	2224112122	1254422244	4225555555	5122242422	1555555555	5555555555	5555555555
IFUGAO	2122222244	4424444442	2444422222	1212222224	4254422424	4215552121	2111212122	2144145555	5112112152	1222525555
ILA	1221224214	1411222141	2441112221	2221212122	1152222144	4425555555	2111212122	2114445555	5555555555	5555555111
INCA	1221224214	1412221222	2442422222	1212222224	4254422424	4215555555	2222242422	2244225555	5555555555	5555555555
INGALIK	1224221224	2424444442	2444422222	1212222224	4154422414	4125555555	2222242422	2555555555	5555555555	5555555555
INGASSANA	2122222244	4424444442	2444422222	1212212122	1254422244	4225555555	5112122422	2555555555	5555555555	5555555555
IRAQW	1221124211	4455555555	5555511122	2221222224	4154422414	4425555555	5111212122	2555555555	5555555555	5555555555
IRISH	1221224214	1424444442	2444422222	1122212212	2254422244	4225555552	2122242422	1555555555	5555555555	5555555555
JAPANESE	1221224214	1412221222	2442422222	1122212212	2254422244	4225555552	2222242422	2555555555	5555555555	5555555422
JAVANESE	1224221224	2412221222	2442422222	1122212212	2154422144	4125555555	2122241222	2555555555	5555555555	5555555422
JEMEZ	2212222244	4424444442	2424422222	1122222224	4254422424	2415555555	5222242422	2555555555	5555555555	5555555555
JIVARO	1221224214	1412212222	2442455555	5555511221	1112122144	4125555551	2112122422	2555552515	5115211222	1111112111
JUKUN	2122222244	4424444442	2444422222	1212211221	1154422144	4125215551	5111212122	2555555555	5555555555	5555555555
KABYLE	1221124211	4412221222	2242455555	5555512122	1154422141	4425555555	5111212122	2555555555	5555555555	5555555555
KACHIN	1221124211	4411222141	1141212221	2221212122	1154422141	4425555555	2111212122	2555555555	5555555555	5555555555
KALMYK	1221124211	4424444442	2244411212	2221211221	1154422141	4425555555	5111212122	2555555555	5555555555	5555555555
KAPAUKU	1221124211	4424444442	2244412221	2221212122	1112122141	4425555555	2111212122	2555555552	1555555555	5555555222
KAREN	1224221122	4255555555	5555522222	1122222224	4254422424	2415555555	5222242422	2555555555	5555555555	5555555555
KARIERA	1221124211	4412122211	2442412221	2221222224	4151112414	4425555555	5112242412	2555555555	5555555555	5555555555
KASKA	1224221122	4211222141	1411211122	2221211221	1254422244	2425215555	2112122422	2555555555	5555555555	5555555422
KATAB	1221124211	4424444442	2244422222	1212212122	1152222141	4425215555	5122241222	2555555555	5555555555	5555555111
KAZAK	1221124211	4424444442	2244411212	2221212122	1122122141	4425555551	2111212122	2222442125	5555555555	5555555555

	FC210	FC220	FC230	FC240	FC250	FC260	FC270	FC280	FC290	FC300
KERAKI	1221124211	4412122212	2242412221	2221222224	4152122411	4425555555	1112242412	2555555555	5555555555	5555555421
KERALA	1221214214	4112122211	1411212221	2221211221	1154422144	1425555555	5222242422	2555555555	5555555555	5555555555
KET	1221224214	1455555555	5555555555	5555522224	4254422422	4415555555	5111212122	2555555555	5555555555	5555555555
KHALKA	1221124211	4424444442	2244411212	2221212212	2254422242	4425555555	5111212122	2555555555	5555555555	5555555555
KHASI	1224221122	4212122212	2422412221	2221211221	1254422244	2425555555	5222242422	2114445555	5555555555	5555555555
KHEVSUR	1221124211	4424444442	2244455555	5555522224	4154422411	4425555555	2111212122	2555555555	5555555555	5555555555
KIKUYU	1221124211	4424444442	2244411212	2221222224	4152221411	4425555555	2111212122	2222445555	5555555555	5555555422
KIOW-APACHE	1224221224	2424444442	2444422222	1212211221	1151122144	4125215555	2122242421	2555555555	5555555555	5555555555
KISSI	1221124211	4411222141	1141222222	1212211221	1152222141	4425555555	5111212122	2555555555	5555555555	5555555555
KOHISTANI	1221124211	4455555555	5555522222	2224122224	4154422411	4425555555	5111212122	2555555555	5555555555	5555555555
KOL	1221124211	4424444442	2444422222	1212212122	1154422144	4125555555	5111212122	2555555555	5555555555	5555555555
KONSO	1221124211	4411222142	2241211212	2221212212	2152222141	4425555555	5222242422	2555555555	5555555555	5555555555
KOREANS	1221124211	4424444442	2244422222	1122212212	2254422242	4425115555	2222242422	2555555551	5555555555	5555555555
KORYAK	1221224214	1424444442	2444422222	1122211221	1124422144	4125555555	2112122422	2244225555	5555555555	5555555555
KPE	1221124211	4424444442	2444455555	5555522224	4152221414	4425555555	5111212122	2555555555	5555555555	5555555111
KUBA	1221214214	4124444442	2424422222	1212212122	1154422144	1425555555	5111212122	2555555555	5555555555	5555555422
KUMYK	2212222244	4455555555	5555522222	1122222224	4154422414	4125555555	5111212122	2555555555	5555555555	5555555555
KUNG	2122222244	4424444442	2444422222	1122212122	1154422144	4125555555	1112122422	2555552225	5555555555	5555555422
KURTATCHI	2122222244	4424444442	2424412221	2221222224	4111222414	1421552211	2111212122	2555555555	5221212552	1121225111
KUTENAI	2122222244	4424444442	2444422222	1212222224	4124422414	4125555555	2222242422	2555551555	5225515555	5122555555
KWAKIUTL	1221224214	1424444442	2444422222	1212212122	1154422144	4125555551	2122242421	2555552525	5222211122	1111212421
LAKALAI	2122222244	4412122211	2422412221	2221212122	1151122144	1425555555	5111212122	2555555555	5555555555	5555555555
LAKHER	1221124211	4412122211	1141211212	2221222224	4154422411	4425225552	2111212122	2555555555	5225222152	1111525555
LAMBA	2122222244	4412122211	1411212221	2221222224	4124422414	1425555511	5112122422	2555555555	5555555555	5555555222
LAMET	1221124211	4411222141	1141211212	2221222224	4154422411	4425555555	2111212122	2555555555	5555555555	5555555555
LANGO	1221124211	4424444442	2244411212	2221212212	2152222141	4425555215	5111212122	2555552225	5555552551	2555552555
LAPPS	1221224214	1424444442	2444422222	1122222224	4254422424	4215555555	2222242422	2555552555	5555555555	5555555422
LAU	1221124211	4412122211	2242412221	2221212122	1121122141	4425551111	2122242421	2111445555	5555555555	5555555111
LEPCHA	1221124211	4424444442	2244422222	1212212122	1124422141	4425555521	2111212122	2222445555	5222212152	1222525444
LESU	1224221122	4224444442	2424412221	2221222224	4154422414	1425215512	5111212122	2555555552	1221112552	1212255111
LHOTA NAGA	1221124211	4411222141	1141211212	2221222224	4152122411	4425555555	5111212122	2555555555	5555555555	5555555555
LIFU	1221124211	4424444442	2244422222	1212211221	1152222141	4425555555	5111212122	2555555555	5555555555	5555555555
LOLO	1221124211	4412122211	1141222222	2224122224	4154422411	4425555555	2111212122	2222445555	5555555555	5555555555
LOZI	1221224214	1424444442	2444422222	1212222224	4152221414	4125215555	5122241222	2144145555	5555555555	5555555555
LUBA	1221124211	4424444442	2244455555	5555522224	4152221411	4425555555	1111212122	2555555555	5555555555	5555555555
LUO	1221124211	4424444442	2244422222	2224112122	1151222141	4425555555	2111212122	2555555555	5555555555	5555555422
MACASSARESE	2122222244	4412221222	2442422222	1122222224	4154422414	4125555555	2111212122	2244245555	5555555555	5555555422
MAGUZAWA	1221124211	4412122211	1141222222	1212211221	1152222141	4425555555	2111212122	2111445555	5555555555	5555555555
MALAYS	1221224214	1412221222	2442422222	1212212122	1154422144	4125555555	5111212122	2555555555	5555555555	5555555555
MAM	1221124211	4424444442	2244422222	1212212122	1254422242	4425555555	2122241222	2555555555	5555555555	5555555555

	FC210	FC220	FC230	FC240	FC250	FC260	FC270	FC280	FC290	FC300
MAMBILA	1221224214	1424444442	2444422222	1212211221	1154422144	4125555555	5112242412	2555555555	5555555555	5555555555
MAMVU	1221124211	4455555555	5555522222	1212222224	4152221411	4425555555	2111212122	2555555555	5555555555	5555555555
MANCHU	1221124211	4412122212	2242412221	2221211221	1254422242	4425555555	5111212122	2555555555	5555555555	5555555555
MANDAN	1224221122	4211222142	2421211122	2221212122	1151122144	1425555555	5222242422	2114445555	5555555555	5555555555
MANGAIANS	1221224214	1424444442	2444422222	1212212122	1151122144	4125555555	2222242422	2555555555	5555555555	5555555555
MANIHIKI	1221224214	1412221222	2442422222	1212212122	1154422144	4125555555	2222242422	2555555555	5555555555	5555555555
MANUS	1221124211	4424444442	2444422222	2224222224	4124422414	4422552115	2122242421	2555555555	5555555555	5555555555
MAORI	2122222244	4424444442	2444422222	1212211221	1122122144	4125555552	2122242421	2555551225	5121221121	2212515555
MARGI	1221124211	4424444442	2244422222	1212212122	1152222141	4425555555	5111212122	2555555555	5555555555	5555555555
MARICOPA	1221124211	4424444442	2244412221	2221222224	4154422411	4425555555	5222242422	2555555555	5555551111	2555555555
MARQUESANS	1221224214	1412122211	2442422222	1212222224	4454422444	4425555225	2122242421	2144115555	5555555555	5555555222
MARSHALLESE	2122222244	4412122212	2422412221	2221211221	1254422244	2422552225	2222242422	2555555555	5225225555	5211215222
MASAI	1221124211	4424444442	2244411212	2221222224	4152221411	4425555552	2111212122	2555555551	5111122115	5222112421
MATACO	1224221224	2424444442	2444422222	1212212122	1154422144	4125555555	2112122422	2555555555	5555555555	5555555421
MATAKAM	1221124211	4424444442	2244411212	2221211221	1154422141	4425555555	5111212122	2555555555	5555555555	5555555555
MAYA	1221224214	1411222142	2241222222	1212222224	4254422422	4415555555	5112122422	2555555555	5555555555	5555555555
MAZATECO	1221224214	1424444442	2444422222	1212222224	4154422414	4125555555	5222242422	2555555555	5555555555	5555555555
MBUGWE	1221124211	4424444442	2444411122	2221212122	1254422244	4425555555	5111212122	2555555555	5555555555	5555555555
MBUNDU	1221124211	4412122211	1441212221	2221222224	4152221414	4425555555	5111212122	2224445552	5555551555	5555552555
MBUTI	1221124211	4412122212	2242455555	5555522224	4154422411	4425555555	5112242412	2555555555	5555555555	5555555555
MENDE	1221124211	4411222141	1141222222	1212212122	1112222141	4425555555	5111212122	2555555552	5555555555	5555555111
MENTAWEI	1221224214	1412212222	2442455555	5555522224	4254422424	4215555555	2112122422	2555555555	5555555555	5555555555
MERINA	1221224214	1412212221	2242422222	1212222224	4154422411	4425555555	2122241222	2555555555	5555555555	5555555555
MIAMI	1221124211	4424444442	2244411212	2221222224	4151112411	4425555555	5122242421	2555555555	5555555555	5555555555
MIAO	1221124211	4412122211	2242422222	1212212122	1154422141	4425555551	5111212122	2555555555	5555555555	5555555555
MIN CHINESE	1221124211	4412122212	2241255555	5555512122	1154422141	4425555555	5111212122	2555555555	5555555555	5555555555
MINANGKABAU	4444444444	4412122211	2422422222	1212211221	1154422144	1425555555	5222242422	2555555555	5555555555	5555555555
MINCHIA	1221124211	4412221222	2242422222	2224112122	1154422141	4425555555	2111212122	2555555555	5555555555	5555555555
MISKITO	1224221224	2412122211	2442412221	2221211221	1154422144	4125555555	1122241222	2555555555	5555555555	5555555222
MIWOK	1221224214	1424444442	2244411212	2221222224	4151112411	4425555555	5222242422	2555555555	5555555555	5555555422
MNONG GAR	1224221122	4211222141	1411211122	2221222224	4154422414	1425555555	5122242421	2555555555	5555555555	5555555555
MONGO	1221124211	4424444442	2244411122	2221211221	1152222141	4425555555	2111212122	2555555552	1555555555	5555555222
MONGUOR	1221124211	4412122212	2242455555	5555512122	1154422141	4425555555	2111212122	2555555555	5555555555	5555555555
MOSSI	1221124211	4424444442	2244422222	1212211221	1152222141	4425555555	5111212122	2555555555	5555555555	5555555421
MOTA	1221214214	4124444442	2424411122	2221222224	4151112414	1425555555	5111212122	2555555515	5555555555	5555555555
MOTILON	1224221224	2412122211	2442412221	2221212122	1152122144	4125555555	5222242422	2555555555	5555555555	5555555555
MUNDURUCU	1224221224	2412122211	2242422222	2224211221	1124422141	4425555555	2112122422	2111445555	5555555555	5555555555
MURINBATA	1221124211	4424444442	2244412221	2221222224	4152122411	4425555555	5555555555	5555555555	5555555555	5555555555
MURNGIN	1221124211	4411222141	1441222222	2224222224	4111112414	4421551511	1112122422	2555555555	5555555555	5555551222
MZAB	1221124211	4455555555	5555555555	5555522224	4254422422	4415555555	2111212122	2555555555	5555555555	5555555555

	FC210	FC220	FC230	FC240	FC250	FC260	FC270	FC280	FC290	FC300
NABESNA	1224221224	2412122211	2422412221	2221222224	4254422424	2415555555	1122241222	2555555555	5555555555	5555555555
NAMA	1221124211	4412122212	2242412221	2221222224	4124422411	4425121515	2122242421	2555552155	5555552552	1555555422
NAMBICUARA	1221224214	1412122211	2442412221	2221222224	4114422414	4125555555	1222242422	2144115555	5555555555	5555555422
NANDI	1221124211	4424444442	2244411212	2221222224	4154422411	4425555555	5111212122	2555555555	5555555555	5555555422
NASKAPI	1221224214	1412122211	2442412221	2221222224	4154422414	4125555555	5112242412	2555555555	5555555555	5555555555
NATCHEZ	1221224214	1424444442	2444422222	2224212122	1151122144	4125555555	2222242422	2555555555	5555555555	5555555555
NAVAHO	1224221122	4224444442	2424412221	2221212122	1121222144	1422552115	2122241222	2555552551	1155225555	5111525422
NDEMBU	1221214214	4112122211	2422412221	2221222224	4152221414	1425555555	5122241222	2555555555	5555555555	5555555555
NGONI	1221224214	1412122212	2442412221	2221222224	4152221414	4125555555	5122241222	2555555551	5555555555	5555555555
NICOBARESE	1224221224	2424444442	2444422222	1122222224	4154422414	4125555555	2222242422	2555555555	5555555555	5555555555
NOMLAKI	1221124211	4424444442	2244411212	2221222224	4154422411	4425555555	2122242421	2555555555	5555555555	5555555555
NUER	1221224214	1424444442	2244422222	2224112122	1112222141	4425555512	5111212122	2555555555	5555555555	5555555111
NUNIVAK	1221224214	1412221222	2442412221	2221212122	1154422144	4125555555	5222242422	2555555555	5555555555	5555555555
NUPE	1221124211	4412122212	2242422222	1212211221	1152222141	4425555555	2111212122	2555555552	1555555555	5555555111
NURI	1221124211	4424444442	2244455555	5555512122	1152222141	4425555555	5111212122	2555555555	5555555555	5555555555
NYAKYUSA	2212222244	4424444442	2244412221	2221222224	4112221411	4425215152	1111212122	2222445555	5555555555	5555555555
NYANEKA	1221214214	4112122212	2422412221	2221212122	1152222144	1425555555	5111212122	2555555555	5555555555	5555555555
NYARO	1221124211	4424444442	2444455555	5555522224	4154422414	4425555555	5111212122	2555555555	5555555555	5555555555
NYORO	1221124211	4424444442	2244411212	2221222224	4152221411	4425555555	5111212122	2555555555	5555555555	5555555555
OJIBWA	1221224214	1412122212	2242412221	2221212212	2124422141	4425211115	2222242422	2111445551	2555555555	5555555555
OKINAWANS	1221124211	4424444442	2244422222	1122212212	2254422242	4425555555	2122241222	2555555555	5555555555	5555555222
OMAHA	2122222244	4424444442	2244411212	2221222224	4154422411	4425555115	2122242421	2111442525	5155551515	5525522555
ONA	1221224214	1424444442	2444422222	1122222224	4152122414	4125555555	2112122422	2555555555	5555555555	5555555555
ONTONG-JAVA	1224221224	2424444442	2444422222	1212211221	1154422144	4125211552	5222242422	2555555555	5555555555	5555555555
ORAON	1221124211	4424444442	2244422222	1212212122	1154422141	4425555551	5111212122	2555555555	5555555555	5555555555
PAEZ	2212222244	4455555555	5555555555	5555522224	4152122414	4125555555	5222242422	2555555555	5555555555	5555555555
PAIWAN	1221224214	1424444442	2444422222	1212212212	2154422144	4125555555	5111212122	2555555555	5555555555	5555555555
PALAUANS	1221214214	4124444442	2424422222	1212222224	4154422414	1425555555	2111212122	2555555555	5555555555	5555555555
PALIKUR	1221224214	1455555555	5555555555	5555522224	4254422422	4415555555	5222242422	2555555555	5555555555	5555555555
PAPAGO	1221224214	1424444442	2444422222	1212212122	1121122144	4125212221	5222242422	2144115555	5215225555	5555225555
PARAUJANO	2122222244	4424444442	2444422222	1212222224	4154422414	4125555555	2111212122	2555555555	5555555555	5555555555
PATHAN	1221124211	4412221221	2241122222	1212222224	4154422411	4425555555	5111212122	2555555555	5555555555	5555555555
PAWNEE	1224221122	4224444442	2424411122	2221212122	1151122144	1425555555	5222242422	2224445555	5555555555	5555555555
PENDE	1221214214	4111222141	2421111122	2221222224	4152221414	1425555555	5122241222	2555555555	5555555555	5555555555
PENOBSCOT	2122222244	4424444442	2444422222	1122222224	4154422414	4125555555	5112122422	2555555555	5555555555	5555555555
PONAPEANS	1224221122	4212122211	2422411122	2221222224	4154422414	1425555555	2222242422	2555555555	5555555555	5555555422
POPOLUCA	1221224214	1424444442	2444422222	1212222224	4151112414	4125555555	5222242422	2555555555	5555555555	5555555555
PORTUGUESE	1221224214	1412221222	2442422222	1122212212	2254422244	4225555555	5222242422	2555555555	5555555555	5555555555
PUKAPUKA	1221124211	4424444442	2334422222	1212222224	4254422423	3315551555	2122242421	2555555555	5225211215	5222225222
PURARI	1221124211	4424444442	2244422222	1212222224	4152122411	4425555555	5111212122	2555555552	5555555555	5555555555

	FC210	FC220	FC230	FC240	FC250	FC260	FC270	FC280	FC290	FC300
PURUM	1221124211	4411222141	1141222222	2224212212	2154422141	4425555555	2112122422	2555555555	5555555555	5555555422
RAROIANS	2122222244	4455555555	5555522222	1212211221	1154422144	4125555555	2222242422	2555555555	5555555555	5555555555
REGEIBAT	1221124211	4412221221	2241122222	2224112122	1154422141	4425555555	5111212122	2555555555	5555555555	5555555555
RIFFIANS	1221124211	4412212222	2242455555	5555511221	1114422141	4425555551	2111212122	2555555555	5555552551	2555552422
ROMANS	2212222244	4412221222	2442422222	2224122224	4254422424	4215555555	5122242422	1555555555	5555555555	5555555555
ROTINESE	1221124211	4412212221	2242412221	2221222224	4152122411	4425555555	5111212122	2555555555	5555555555	5555555555
ROTUMANS	1224221122	4224444442	2424422222	1212222224	4254422424	2415555555	5222242422	2555555555	5555555555	5555555555
RUNDI	1221124211	4412122211	2242412221	2221222224	4152221411	4425555555	2122241222	2555555555	5555555555	5555555422
RWALA	1221124211	4412221221	2241122222	2224122224	4152221411	4425555555	2111212122	2555551115	5555555555	5555555422
SAGADA	2122222244	4424444442	2444422222	1122222224	4254422424	4215555555	2122242421	2555555555	5555555555	5555555422
SAMOANS	2122222244	4424444442	2444422222	1212211221	1124422144	4125551521	2122242421	2144142525	5555555555	5555555111
SAMOYED	1221124211	4412212221	1141255555	5555512122	1154422141	4425555555	1111212122	2555555555	5555551225	5555555422
SANDAWE	1221124211	4411222141	1141222222	2224222224	4154422411	4425555555	5111212122	2555555555	5555555555	5555555555
SANPOIL	1221224214	1424444442	2444422222	1212212212	2152122144	4125215221	2122241222	2555555555	5551215512	1122115222
SANTAL	1221124211	4424444442	2244422222	2224112122	1154422141	4425555555	2111212122	2555555555	5555555555	5555555555
SARAMACCA	1221214214	4112212222	2422422222	1212222224	4152221414	1425215555	5111212122	2555555555	5555555555	5555555555
SARSI	1221224214	1424444442	2444422222	1212222224	4151112414	4125555555	2111212122	2555555555	5555555555	5555555422
SELUNG	2212222244	4455555555	5555522222	1122222224	4154422414	4125555555	5222242422	2555555555	5555555555	5555555555
SEMANG	1221224214	1424444442	2444422222	1212222224	4154422414	4125555115	2222242422	2144112225	5555555555	5555555555
SEMINOLE	1224221122	4224444442	2424411122	2221222224	4254422424	2415125555	5222242422	2555555555	5555555555	5555555555
SENIANG	1221124211	4424444442	2244411122	2221222224	4121112411	4425555555	5111212122	2555555555	5555552555	5555555555
SERBS	1221124211	4455555555	5555522222	1212212122	1254422242	4425555551	2122242422	1555555555	5555555555	5555555555
SERI	1221224214	1424444442	2444422222	1212212122	1254422244	4225555555	5111212122	2555552225	5555555555	5555555555
SHERENTE	1221124211	4411222142	2241111212	2221222224	4154422411	4425555555	5222242422	2555555555	5555555555	5555555555
SHILLUK	1221124211	4424444442	2244422222	2224122224	4152221411	4425225555	2111212122	2555552255	5555555555	5555555111
SHLUH	1221124211	4455555555	5555555555	5555512122	1254422242	4425555555	2111212122	2555555555	5555555555	5555555555
SIMBOESE	2122222244	4424444442	2444422222	1212222224	4154422414	4125555555	5111212122	2555555555	5555555555	5555555555
SINDHI	1221124211	4412221222	2242422222	2224112122	1154422141	4425555555	5122242422	1555555555	5555555555	5555555555
SINHALESE	1221224214	1412122211	2442412221	2221222224	4254422424	4215555555	2122242422	1555555551	5555555555	5555555555
SIRIONO	1224221122	4211222141	1411211122	2221211221	1111122144	1425552221	2222242422	2224445555	5515215555	5112525222
SIUAI	1221214214	4112122211	1411222222	1212222224	4124422414	1425555555	2111212122	2555555555	5555555555	5555555111
SIWANS	1221124211	4412221222	2242422222	2224112122	1154422141	4425555555	5111212122	2111445555	5555555555	5555555555
SOMALI	1221124211	4424444442	2244422222	2224112122	1152222141	4425555555	2111212122	2111445555	5555555555	5555555422
SONGHAI	1221124211	4412221222	2242412221	2221222224	4154422411	4425555555	2111212122	2555555555	5555555555	5555555555
SOTHO	1221124211	4412221221	2242412221	2221222224	4152221411	4425555555	5111212122	2555555555	5555555555	5555555555
SUBANUN	2122222244	4412221222	2442422222	1212222224	4154422414	4125552225	5111212122	2555555555	5555555555	5555555555
SWAZI	1221124211	4412122212	2242412221	2221211221	1151222141	4421555555	5111212122	2555555555	5555555555	5555555555
SYRIANS	1221124211	4412221221	2241122222	2224112122	1154422141	4425555555	5111212122	2555555555	5555555555	5555555555
TAGBANUA	1224221224	2424444442	2444422222	1122222224	4154422414	4125555555	5112122422	2555555555	5555555555	5555555555
TALAMANCA	1224221122	4224444442	2424422222	1212211221	1154422144	1425555555	2112122422	2555555555	5555555555	5555555555

	FC210	FC220	FC230	FC240	FC250	FC260	FC270	FC280	FC290	FC300
TALLENSI	1221124211	4424444442	2244422222	1212212122	1112222141	4425115222	2111212122	2555555551	2555555555	5555555111
TAMIL	1221124211	4412122211	2242412221	2221212212	2154422141	4425555555	5122241222	2555555555	5555555555	5555555555
TANALA	1221124211	4412122211	2242412221	2221212122	1112222141	4425125551	2122241222	2555555555	5215125552	1222515222
TANIMBARESE	1221124211	4412122211	1141222222	1212212122	1154422141	4425555555	5111212122	2555555555	5555555555	5555555555
TAOS	2212222244	4424444442	2444422222	1122222224	4254422424	4215555555	2222242422	2555555555	5555555555	5555555555
TAPIRAPE	1224221224	2424444442	2444422222	1212211221	1254422244	4225555555	1222242422	2555555555	5555555555	5555555421
TARAHUMARA	2212222244	4424444442	2444422222	1212222224	4124422414	4125212225	2112122422	2144115555	5552551252	1555555222
TAREUMIUT	2122222244	4424444442	2444412221	2221212122	1154422144	4125555555	2112122422	2555555555	5555555555	5555555222
TEDA	1221124211	4424444442	2244412221	2221212122	1152222141	4425555555	2111212122	2555555555	5555555555	5555555555
TEHUELCHE	1221224214	1412221222	2442455555	5555512122	1154422144	4125555555	2122242421	2555555555	5555555555	5555555421
TENDA	1221214214	4112212222	2422455555	5555522224	4154422414	1425555555	2112122422	2555555555	5555555555	5555555111
TENETEHARA	1224221224	2424444442	2444422222	1212211221	1154422144	4125555555	5112122422	2555555555	5555555555	5555555422
TENINO	1221224214	1424444442	2444422222	1212212212	2152122144	4125555555	2122242421	2555555555	5555555555	5555555555
TERA	1221124211	4412122212	2242412221	2221211221	1152222141	4425555555	5112122422	2555555555	5555555555	5555555555
TERENA	2122222244	4424444442	2444422222	1212211221	1154422144	4125555555	1222242422	2555555555	5555555555	5555555555
TESO	1221124211	4424444442	2244422222	1212222224	4152221411	4425555555	5111212122	2555555555	5555555555	5555555555
TETON	1221224214	1424444442	2444412221	2221222224	4151112414	4125555555	5111212122	2555555555	5555555555	5555555555
THAI	1224221224	2412221222	2442422222	1212212212	2124422144	4125555555	2122241222	2244225555	5555555555	5555555555
THONGA	1221124211	4424444442	2244411212	2221211221	1111222141	4421555512	2111212122	2555555551	5111215511	2112521422
TIBETANS	1221124211	4412212222	2242422222	1122212212	2454422444	4425555555	5122242422	1555555555	5555555555	5555555555
TIGRINYA	1221124211	4424444442	2244422222	2224122224	4254422422	4415555555	5122242422	1555555555	5555555555	5555555555
TIKOPIA	1221124211	4424444442	2244422222	1212222224	4122221411	4425215125	2122242421	2222445551	2225552555	5555211555
TIMBIRA	1224221122	4224444442	2424411122	2221212122	1254422244	2425225512	2112122422	2555555555	5555555555	5555555422
TIMUCUA	1224221122	4255555555	5555511122	2221211221	1154422144	1425555555	5555555555	5555555555	5555555555	5555555555
TIV	1221224214	1424444442	2244422222	1212211221	1112222141	4425555512	2112242412	2555555555	5255212552	1111555111
TIWI	1221224214	1411222142	2421122222	2224212122	1152122144	1425555555	1111212122	2555555555	5555555555	5555555555
TODA	1221124211	4412122211	2442412221	2221222224	4424421444	4425555555	2122241222	2114441512	1555552151	2555551222
TOKELAU	1224221224	2424444442	2444411212	2221211221	1154422144	4125555555	2222242422	2555555555	5555555555	5555555555
TOLOWA	1221124211	4412122212	2241212221	2221222224	4152122411	4425555555	2111212122	2555555555	5555555555	5555555422
TORAJA	1224221224	2424444442	2444422222	1212211221	1254422244	4225555555	5111212122	2555555555	5555555555	5555555555
TOTONAC	1221224214	1424444442	2444422222	1212255555	5555555554	4555555555	5222242422	2555555555	5555555555	5555555555
TRISTAN	2212222244	4455555555	5555522222	1122222224	4254422424	4215555555	2222242422	2555555555	5555555555	5555555555
TROBRIAND	1221214214	4111222142	2421111122	2221222224	4124422414	1425551522	2122242421	2555552525	5222112552	1121525111
TRUKESE	1224221122	4224444442	2424411122	2221211221	1224422244	2422552555	2222242422	2555555555	5555555555	5555555555
TRUMAI	1221224214	1412122211	2442412221	2221211221	1154422144	4125555555	2122241222	2555555555	5555555555	5555555555
TSHIMSHIAN	1221214214	4112122211	1411212221	2221211221	1152122144	1425555555	5111212122	2555555555	5555555555	5555555555
TUBATULABAL	1221224214	1424444442	2444422222	1212222224	4254422424	4215555555	2111212122	2244225555	5551555152	1555555422
TUCANO	1221124211	4412122211	2242412221	2221222224	4154422411	4425555555	5112242412	2555555555	5555555555	5555555555
TUCUNA	1221124211	4412122212	2242412221	2221222224	4154422411	4425555555	2112242412	2555555555	5555555555	5555555421
TUNEBO	1221224214	1424444442	2444422222	1212222224	4152122414	4125555555	5122241222	2555555555	5555555555	5555555555

APPENDIX EIGHT/30 -- FINISHED CHARACTERISTIC CODE SHEET

	FC210	FC220	FC230	FC240	FC250	FC260	FC270	FC280	FC290	FC300
TUPINAMBA	1224221224	2412122211	2442412221	2221211221	1152222144	4125555555	2112122422	2555555555	5555555155	5555555555
TURKANA	1221124211	4424444442	2244422222	2224112122	1122222141	4425555555	5111212122	2555555555	5555555555	5555555555
TURKMEN	1221124211	4412122211	1141222222	2224212122	1154422141	4425555555	5111212122	2555555555	5555555555	5555555555
TWANA	1221224214	1424444442	2444422222	1212211221	1154422144	4125555555	2122242421	2555555555	5555555555	5555555422
TZELTAL	1221124211	4412122211	1141211212	2221212122	1154422141	4425555555	5112122422	2555555555	5555555555	5555555555
ULAWANS	1221224214	1424444442	2444422222	1212222224	4154422414	4125555555	2111212122	2555555555	5555555555	5555555555
UTE	2122222244	4424444442	2444422222	1212212122	1154422144	4125555555	2222242422	2555555555	5555555555	5555555111
VEDDA	1224221122	4212122211	2421112221	2221212122	1254422244	2425555555	2122241222	2224442225	5555555555	5555555222
VENDA	1221124211	4412122211	1441212221	2221211221	1111222144	4421555551	2111212122	2555555555	5125212511	2111111555
VIETNAMESE	1221124211	4424444442	2244422222	1212212122	1152122141	4425555555	2122241222	2222445555	5555555555	5555555555
WAICA	2122222244	4455555555	5555555555	5555522224	4154422414	4125555555	5222242422	2555555555	5555555555	5555555555
WALLOONS	2212222244	4455555555	5555522222	1122222224	4254422424	4215555555	5122242422	1555555555	5555555555	5555555555
WANTOAT	1221124211	4412122211	2242412221	2221222224	4152221411	4425555555	5112242412	2555555555	5555555555	5555555555
WAPISHANA	1221224214	1412122211	2442412221	2221222224	4152122414	4125555555	5112122422	2555555555	5555555555	5555555555
WAROPEN	1221124211	4411222141	1141212221	2221211221	1154422141	4425555555	5122242421	2555555555	5555555555	5555555555
WARRAU	1224221224	2455555555	5555522222	1212211221	1151122144	4125555511	5112122422	2555555555	5555555555	5555555422
WASHO	2122222244	4424444442	2444422222	1212222224	4154422414	4125555555	5222242422	2555555555	5555555555	5555555555
WICHITA	1224221224	2424444442	2444422222	1212212122	1151122144	4125555555	5112122422	2555555555	5555555555	5555555111
WIKMUNKAN	1221124211	4411222141	1141212221	2221222224	4151112411	4425555555	5112242412	2555555555	5555555555	5555555555
WINNEBAGO	1221124211	4412122212	2242411212	2221212122	1154422141	4425555555	5555555555	5555555555	5555555555	5555555555
WITOTO	1221124211	4412122212	2242455555	5555522224	4154422411	4425555555	2112122422	2555552225	5555551225	5555551111
WOGEO	1221124211	4424444442	2444412221	2221222224	4112122414	4425555555	2122242421	2555555555	5255115555	5212115111
WOLEAIANS	2122222244	4424444442	2424422222	1212211221	1254422244	2425215555	2222242422	2555555555	5555555555	5555555421
WOLOF	1221124211	4412122211	2442422222	1212212122	1152222144	4425555555	2111212122	2555555555	5555555555	5555555111
WUTE	1221124211	4424444442	2244455555	5555512122	1152222141	4425555555	5111212122	2555555555	5555555555	5555555555
YABARANA	1224221224	2412122211	2442412221	2221222224	4154422414	4125555555	2112122422	2555555555	5555555555	5555555422
YAGUA	1221124211	4424444442	2244455555	5555522224	4224422422	4415555555	2112122422	2555555555	5225555555	5222555421
YAHGAN	1221224214	1424444442	2444422222	1122222224	4154422414	4125555555	2112122422	2555552525	5555555555	5555555422
YAKO	1221124211	4412122211	2441112221	2221212122	1152222144	4425555551	5111212122	2555555552	2555555555	5555555111
YAKUT	1221124211	4412212222	2242422222	2224212122	1152222141	4425555555	2122242421	2555551225	5555555112	1555555555
YAO	1224221122	4212122211	2422412221	2221211221	1154422144	1425555555	2222242422	2114445551	5555555555	5555555111
YAPESE	1221124211	4424444442	2444411122	2221212122	1254422244	4425555551	2222242422	2555555552	1555555555	5555555421
YARURO	1224221224	2412122211	2442422222	1212212212	2154422144	4125555555	5112122422	2555555555	5555555555	5555555555
YOKUTS	1221124211	4424444442	2244422222	1212211221	1152222141	4425555555	5222242422	2555555555	5555555555	5555555555
YOMBE	1221214214	4124444442	2424455555	5555522224	4152221414	1425555555	5111212122	2555555555	5555555555	5555555555
YORUBA	1221124211	4424444442	2244422222	1212211221	1152222141	4425555555	2111212122	2222445555	5555555555	5555555555
YUKAGHIR	1224221224	2424444442	2444455555	5555512212	2154422144	4125555555	5112122422	2555555525	5555555155	5555555555
YUKI	1221224214	1424444442	2444422222	1212222224	4154422414	4125555555	2122242421	2555555555	5555555555	5555555422
YUROK	1221224214	1424444442	2444422222	1212212122	1122122144	4125555555	5111212122	2144115555	5555555552	1555551555
ZUNI	1224221122	4224444442	2424411122	2221211221	1254422244	2425555555	5112122422	2114445555	5555555555	5555555555

APPENDIX EIGHT/31 -- FINISHED CHARACTERISTIC CODE SHEET

	FC310	FC320	FC330	FC340	FC350	FC360	FC370	FC380	FC390	FC400
ABIPON	1555225555	1525555555	5555555555	5555555555	5555555555	5555522222	2223111115	5555552452	5555555511	1115551555
ABOR	5555555555	5555555555	5555555555	5555555555	5555555555	5555555555	5555555551	1555552455	5555555522	2255555555
AINU	1221122222	2112252222	2221215251	1152211115	5552122222	2112255555	5555555552	2551552452	5245222522	2212525215
AJIE	5555555555	5555555555	5555555555	5555555555	5555555555	5555555555	5555555555	5555555555	5555555555	5555555555
AKHA	5555555555	5555555555	5555555555	5555555555	5555555555	5555555555	5555555555	5555552455	5555555522	2255555555
ALACALUF	2555555555	5555555555	5555555555	5555555555	5555555555	5555555555	5555555555	5555552455	5555555555	5555555555
ALBANIANS	5555555555	5555555555	5555555555	5555555555	5555555555	5555555555	5555555552	2555552455	5555555511	1155155555
ALORESE	1121121112	1112122222	2221112222	2222221112	1111111555	5211111125	2213222222	2221442442	2244215542	1115522111
AMBA	5555555555	5555555555	5555555555	5555555555	5555555555	5555555555	5555555552	2555552455	5555555522	2255555555
AMERICANS	2555555555	5555525555	5555555555	5555555555	5555555555	5555555555	5555555552	2225552455	2244555542	1155555555
ANDAMANESE	5515112525	2222151151	1112151551	5551155555	5555555555	5555522122	2213211111	1151222421	1121211122	2252252555
APINAYE	5555555555	5555555555	5555555555	5555555555	5555555555	5555555555	5555555552	2151552452	5555115544	4422555555
ARANDA	2555555555	5552552121	1111225551	5552522121	1111122111	1221155555	5555555551	2151551252	5115212144	4425155552
ARAPESH	1112112121	1211151121	1111111151	1221122221	1112222222	2555555555	5555555555	5155112415	2554555544	4455515115
ARAUCANIANS	1555555555	5552122112	5521125152	5552512125	5551211111	2222222115	2111122222	2225552455	2244555542	2155222525
ARYANS	5555555555	5555555555	5555555555	5555555555	5555555555	5555555555	5555555555	5555555555	5555555555	5555555555
ASHANTI	2222222111	1111112211	2222112252	5552211111	1112122111	1111155555	5555555551	2225442441	1554111211	1111115115
ATAYAL	5555555555	5555555555	5555555555	5555555555	5555555555	5555555555	5555555555	5555552455	5555555555	5555555555
ATSUGEWI	2555555555	5555555555	5555555555	5555555555	5555555555	5555555555	5555555552	2155552455	1552555511	1155555555
AWEIKOMA	5555555555	5555555555	5555555555	5555555555	5555555555	5555555555	5555555555	5255552455	2554555522	2255555555
AYMARA	5555555555	5552152222	2222212152	5552511111	1112111221	1111122115	2111122522	2255552455	2244225542	2115522512
AZANDE	1112211111	1111512222	2111225552	1552111115	5552211221	1111122555	2555522511	2111111115	5245215542	2115522112
AZTEC	5555555555	5555555555	5555555555	5555555555	5555555555	5555555555	5555555555	5555552455	5555555542	1155255555
BABWA	5555555555	5555555555	5555555555	5555555555	5555555555	5555555555	5555555551	2555552455	5555555555	5555555555
BACAIRI	5555555555	5555555555	5555555555	5555555555	5555555555	5555555555	5555555555	5555552455	5555555555	5555555555
BAJUN	5555555555	5555555555	5555555555	5555555555	5555555555	5555555555	5555555555	5555555555	5555555555	5555555555
BALINESE	5122121221	2122521212	2221112111	2511212221	2111111222	2221211115	2111122515	5121225522	1242225555	5555512221
BAMBARA	1555555555	5555555555	5555555555	5555555555	5555555555	5555555555	5555555552	2555551255	5555555555	5555555555
BAMILEKE	1555555555	5555555555	5555555555	5555555555	5555555555	5555555555	5555555555	5555551255	5555555555	5555555555
BANDA	5555555555	5555555555	5555555555	5555555555	5555555555	5555555555	5555555555	5555551255	5555555555	5555555555
BARABRA	5555555555	5555555555	5555555555	5555555555	5555555555	5555555555	5555555552	2555551155	5555555555	5555555555
BARI	5555555555	5555555555	5555555555	5555555555	5555555555	5555555555	5555555551	2155552455	1551555542	1155555555
BASQUES	5555555555	5555555555	5555555555	5555555555	5555555555	5555555555	5555555555	5555555555	5555555555	5555555555
BASSERI	5555555555	5555555555	5555555555	5555555555	5555555555	5555555555	5555555552	2555551155	5555555511	1155555555
BATAK	5555555555	5555555555	5555555555	5555555555	5555555555	5555555555	5555555555	5255555555	2554555522	2255555555
BAYA	5555555555	5555555555	5555555555	5555555555	5555555555	5555555555	5555555555	5555551155	5555555542	1155555555
BEJA	5555555555	5555555555	5555555555	5555555555	5555555555	5555555555	5555555555	5555551155	5555555555	5555555555
BELU	5555555555	5555555555	5555555555	5555555555	5555555555	5555555555	5555555555	5555555555	5555555555	5555555555
BEMBA	1555555555	5551555555	5555555555	5555555555	5555555555	5555555555	5555555551	2555552455	5125555544	4455555555
BENGALI	5555555555	5555555555	5555555555	5555555555	5555555555	5555555555	5555555555	5555555555	5555555555	5555555555

	FC310	FC320	FC330	FC340	FC350	FC360	FC370	FC380	FC390	FC400
BERGDAMA	5555555555	5555555555	5555555555	5555555555	5555555555	5555555555	5555555555	5555555555	5555555555	5555555555
BETE	5555555555	5555555555	5555555555	5555555555	5555555555	5555555555	5555555555	5555555555	5555555555	5555555555
BHIL	5555555555	5552155555	5555555555	5555555555	5555555555	5555555555	5555555552	2555552455	5245555542	1155555555
BHUIYA	5555555555	5555555555	5555555555	5555555555	5555555555	5555555555	5555555551	1255552455	2554555522	2255555555
BIRIFOR	1555555555	5555555555	5555555555	5555555555	5555555555	5555555555	5555555552	2555552455	5555555555	5555555555
BLACK CARIB	1555555555	5555555555	5555555555	5555555555	5555555555	5555555555	5555555552	2555552455	5555555555	5555555555
BOERS	5555555555	5555555555	5555555555	5555555555	5555555555	5555555555	5555555552	2555552455	5555555555	5555555555
BORORO	5555555555	5555555555	5555555555	5555555555	5555555555	5555555555	5555555555	5555552455	5555555522	2255555555
BOTOCUDO	5555555555	5555555555	5555555555	5555555555	5555555555	5555555555	5555555555	5555552455	5555555544	4455555555
BOZO	5555555555	5555555555	5555555555	5555555555	5555555555	5555555555	5555555551	1555551255	5555555555	5555555555
BRAZILIANS	5555555555	5555555555	5555555555	5555555555	5555555555	5555555555	5555555552	2555552455	5555555542	1155555555
BUDUMA	5555555555	5555555555	5555555555	5555555555	5555555555	5555555555	5555555555	5555555555	5555555555	5555555555
BULGARIANS	5555555555	5555555555	5555555555	5555555555	5555555555	5555555555	5555555552	2555555555	5245555555	5555555555
BUNLAP	1555555555	5555555555	5555555555	5555555555	5555555555	5555555555	5555555551	1555551155	5555555555	5555555555
BURMESE	5555555555	5555555555	5555555555	5555555555	5555555555	5555555555	5555555555	5555555555	5125555555	5555555555
BURUSHO	1555555555	5555555555	5555555555	5555555555	5555555555	5555555555	5555555552	2555551355	5555555511	1155555555
BURYAT	5555555555	5555555555	5555555555	5555555555	5555555555	5555555555	5555555555	5555555555	5555555555	5555555555
CADUVEO	5555555555	5555555555	5555555555	5555555555	5555555555	5555555555	5555555555	5555552455	5555555555	5555555555
CAGABA	5555555555	5552515555	5555555555	5555555555	5555555555	5555522222	2225522515	5515552455	5125555555	5555555555
CALLINAGO	1555555555	5555555555	5555555555	5555555555	5555555555	5555555555	5555555551	1155552455	5555555544	4455555555
CAMAYURA	5555555555	5552112111	1112221151	5551522221	1222211222	2222222222	2223221511	2515552455	5555555555	5555552555
CAMBA	5555555555	5555555555	5555555555	5555555555	5555555555	5555555555	5555555555	5555555555	5555555555	5555555555
CAMBODIANS	5555555555	5555555555	5555555555	5555555555	5555555555	5555555555	5555555552	2555552455	5555555511	1155555555
CARAJA	5555555555	5555555555	5555555555	5555555555	5555555555	5555555555	5555555555	5555555555	5555555555	5555555555
CARIB	2555555555	5552555555	5555555555	5555555555	5555555555	5555511125	2213211112	2252552451	1124222522	2255552555
CARINYA	5555555555	5555555555	5555555555	5555555555	5555555555	5555555555	5555555555	5555555555	5555555555	5555555555
CAYAPA	5555555555	5555555555	5555555555	5555555555	5555555555	5555555555	5555555552	2252552455	2244555555	5555555555
CHAGGA	1222111111	1225511212	2221212122	1512511112	1112111111	2111155555	5555555555	5511111211	5554115542	1115555155
CHAMACOCO	1555555555	5555555555	5555555555	5555555555	5555555555	5555555555	5555555555	5555552455	5115555555	5555555555
CHENCHU	2111111222	2222151121	1222212555	2551112215	5551222555	5122255555	5555555552	2255442445	2554555522	2225525225
CHEREMIS	5555555555	5555555555	5555555555	5555555555	5555555555	5555555555	5555555555	5555555555	5555555555	5555555555
CHERKESS	5555555555	5555555555	5555555555	5555555555	5555555555	5555555555	5555555551	2555551355	5555555555	5555555555
CHEROKEE	5555555555	5555555555	5555555555	5555555555	5555555555	5555555555	5555555552	2255552455	2554555555	5555555555
CHEYENNE	5555555555	5555511121	2222221551	5551512221	1211222111	2121122122	2211121112	2215552451	2124555511	1125511515
CHIBCHA	5555555555	5555555555	5555555555	5555555555	5555555555	5555555555	5555555555	5555552455	5555555522	2255555555
CHINANTEC	5555555555	5555555555	5555555555	5555555555	5555555555	5555555555	5555555555	5555555555	5555555555	5555555555
CHIR-APACHE	1222222121	1112511111	1122125552	1222511222	2221122111	1111122125	2213222212	2215442441	1124115511	1115521111
CHIRIGUANO	5555555555	5555555555	5555555555	5555555555	5555555555	5555555555	5555555555	5555552455	5555555555	5555555555
CHOCO	5555555555	5555555555	5555555555	5555555555	5555555555	5555555555	5555555552	2555552455	5555555555	5555555555
CHOROTI	5555555555	5555555555	5555555555	5555555555	5555555555	5555555555	5555555552	2555552452	5115115522	2225555555

	FC310	FC320	FC330	FC340	FC350	FC360	FC370	FC380	FC390	FC400
CHORTI	5555555555	5555555555	5555555555	5555555555	5555555555	5555555555	5555555552	2555552455	5555555555	5555555555
CHUKCHEE	2555555555	5555551111	5525255551	5551511115	5551122111	2122211111	2113122222	2555552455	5555115522	2225222512
COCHITI	2555555555	5555555555	5555555555	5555555555	5555555555	5555555555	5555555552	2555552455	5555555555	5555555555
COMANCHE	5111111222	2222252111	2222121225	2551122121	1211122112	2221255555	5555555555	5255445545	2554555555	5555555555
COORG	1555555555	5555555555	5555555555	5555555555	5555555555	5555555555	5555555552	2555552455	5555555511	1155555555
COPR ESKIMO	5515511525	5222125555	5555555555	5555155555	5555555555	5555555222	2222222222	2222442445	2244225544	4425522255
CREE	5555555555	5555555555	5555555555	5555555555	5555555555	5555555555	5555555552	2555552451	5555225555	5525555555
CREEK	1555555555	5555555555	5555555555	5555555555	5555555555	5555555222	2221122215	5251552455	2554211144	4415152552
CROW	2555555555	5555551111	2221112252	5551522221	2111111111	1111155555	5555555555	5255552455	2554211155	5512255552
CUNA	5555555555	5552251111	5521125551	5551512225	5551222222	2122255555	5555555552	2252552451	1124115511	1152555551
CZECHS	5555555555	5555555555	5555555555	5555555555	5555555555	5555555555	5555555552	2555552455	5555555555	5555555555
DAGUR	5555555555	5555555555	5555555555	5555555555	5555555555	5555555555	5555555555	5555551355	5555555555	5555555555
DARD	2555555555	5555555555	5555555555	5555555555	5555555555	5555555555	5555555555	5555552455	5555555555	5555555555
DELAWARE	5555555555	5555555555	5555555555	5555555555	5555555555	5555555555	5555555552	2551552455	5555555522	2255555555
DIEGUENO	1555555555	5555555555	5555555555	5555555555	5555555555	5555555555	5555555552	2555552455	5555555555	5555555555
DIERI	5555555555	5555555555	5555555555	5555555555	5555555555	5555511122	1211122211	2151551152	5555555555	5525252555
DILLING	5555555555	5555555555	5555555555	5555555555	5555555555	5555555555	5555555551	2555551255	5245555555	5555555555
DOBUANS	5222222111	1112155555	5555555555	1255255555	5555555555	5555555555	5555555555	5255445545	2554222122	2215555555
DOGON	5555555555	5555555555	5555555555	5555555555	5555555555	5555555555	5555555555	5555551255	5555555555	5555555555
DOROBO	1555555555	5555555555	5555555555	5555555555	5555555555	5555555555	5555555555	5155551255	5555555555	5555555555
DUSUN	5525511555	5125555555	5555555555	1155555555	5555555555	5555555555	5555555555	5551555552	5555215555	5525555555
DUTCH	5555555555	5555555555	5555555555	5555555555	5555555555	5555555555	5555555552	2555552455	5555555544	4455555555
EGYPTIANS	1555555555	5552125555	5555555555	5555555555	5555555555	5555522122	1211111512	2525551155	5245555511	1155551555
ELLICE	5555555555	5555555555	5555555555	5555555555	5555555555	5555555555	5555555551	1555555555	5555555522	2255555555
ENGA	5555555555	5555555555	5555555555	5555555555	5555555555	5555555555	5555555551	2555552455	5555555511	1155555555
EYAK	5555555555	5555555555	5555555555	5555555555	5555555555	5555555555	5555555551	2255552455	1554555555	5555555555
FANG	1555555555	5555555555	5555555555	5555555555	5555555555	5555555555	5555555552	2555551255	5555555522	2255555555
FON	1222212111	1211512222	2211212212	1112111115	5551122112	2555522125	1213122211	2111221211	1112115511	1115512112
FOX	5555555555	5555555555	5555555555	5555555555	5555555555	5555555555	5555555552	2255552451	1554555555	5555555555
FUTAJALONKE	5555555555	5555555555	5555555555	5555555555	5555555555	5555555555	5555555551	2555551255	5555555522	2255555555
GANDA	1555555555	5551212222	5511112252	5552511115	5551121111	1111111555	1515511511	2225552455	2124215542	1115511515
GARO	5555555555	5555555555	5555555555	5555555555	5555555555	5555555555	5555555551	2555552455	5555555542	2155555555
GILBERTESE	5555555555	5555555555	5555555555	5555555555	5555555555	5555555555	5555555555	5551555555	5555555511	1115555555
GILYAK	5555555555	5552255555	5555555555	5555555555	5555555555	5555555555	5555555552	2555552455	5555225542	1125555555
GISU	5555555555	5555555555	5555555555	5555555555	5555555555	5555555555	5555555551	2555551255	5555555542	2155555555
GOAJIRO	1555555555	5555555555	5555555555	5555555555	5555555555	5555555555	5555555555	5552552451	5125225542	1155555551
GOND	2555555555	5555555555	5555555555	5555555555	5555555555	5555555555	5555555551	1252552455	2554225522	2255515555
GROS VENTRE	1555555555	5555555555	5555555555	5555555555	5555555555	5555555555	5555555555	5555552455	5555555544	4455525555
GUAHIBO	5555555555	5555555555	5555555555	5555555555	5555555555	5555555555	5555555552	2555552455	5555555555	5555555555
GUATO	5555555555	5555555555	5555555555	5555555555	5555555555	5555555555	5555555555	5555552455	5555555555	5555555555

	FC310	FC320	FC330	FC340	FC350	FC360	FC370	FC380	FC390	FC400
GURE	5555555555	5555555555	5555555555	5555555555	5555555555	5555555555	5555555551	2555551355	5555555555	5555555555
HAIDA	1555555555	5555555555	5555555555	5555555555	5555555555	5555555555	5555555551	2255552455	1554555542	2155155555
HANO	5222222121	1212521111	1122112222	2521211112	5552211211	1112255555	5555555552	2111112421	5555225542	2125225222
HANUNOO	5555555555	5555555555	5555555555	5555555555	5555555555	5555555555	5555555552	2555552455	5555555555	5555555555
HASANIA	5555555555	5555555555	5555555555	5555555555	5555555555	5555555555	5555555555	5555555555	5555555555	5555555555
HASINAI	5555555555	5555555555	5555555555	5555555555	5555555555	5555555555	5555555552	2555552455	5555555555	5555555555
HAVASUPAI	5555555555	5555555555	5555555555	5555555555	5555555555	5555555555	5555555555	5255552451	1554215555	5555555555
HAWAIIANS	5555555555	5555555555	5555555555	5555555555	5555555555	5555555555	5555555555	5555555555	5555555522	2255555555
HAZARA	5555555555	5555555555	5555555555	5555555555	5555555555	5555555555	5555555552	2555551355	5555555511	1155555555
HEBREWS	5555555555	5555555555	5555555555	5555555555	5555555555	5555555555	5555555555	5555551355	5555555511	1155155555
HEHE	5555555555	5555555555	5555555555	5555555555	5555555555	5555555555	5555555555	5555555555	5555555555	5555555555
HERERO	5555555555	5555555555	5555555555	5555555555	5555555555	5555555555	5555555551	2555551355	5555555555	5555555555
HO	5555555555	5555555555	5555555555	5555555555	5555555555	5555555555	5555555555	5255555555	2554555555	5555555555
HUICHOL	5555555555	5555555555	5555555555	5555555555	5555555555	5555555555	5555555552	2552552455	5555215555	5555555555
HUKUNDIKA	5555555555	5555555555	5555555555	5555555555	5555555555	5555555555	5555555555	5555552455	5555555555	5555555555
HURON	5555555555	5555555555	5555555555	5555555555	5555555555	5555555555	5555555555	5555552455	5555555555	5555555555
HUTSUL	5555555555	5555555555	5555555555	5555555555	5555555555	5555555555	5555555552	2555552455	5555555522	2255555555
IBAN	5555555555	5552555555	5555555555	5555555555	5555555555	5555555555	5555555552	2555552455	5555555542	1155255555
ICELANDERS	5555555555	5555555555	5555555555	5555555555	5555555555	5555555555	5555555555	5555555555	5555555555	5555555555
IFUGAO	5515121525	2122155222	5525151552	1551211111	1111222555	5222211555	1515522221	2255442445	2554222122	2211552551
ILA	1555555555	5555555555	5555555555	5555555555	5555555555	5555555555	5555555551	2151552451	1552225522	2225555552
INCA	5555555555	5555555555	5555555555	5555555555	5555555555	5555555555	5555555552	2155552455	1552555511	1155555555
INGALIK	5555555555	5555555555	5555555555	5555555555	5555555555	5555555555	5555555555	5555552455	5555555542	1155555555
INGASSANA	5555555555	5555555555	5555555555	5555555555	5555555555	5555555555	5555555551	2155551355	1551555555	5555555555
IRAQW	5555555555	5555555555	5555555555	5555555555	5555555555	5555555555	5555555555	5555551355	5555555555	5555555555
IRISH	5555555555	5555555555	5555555555	5555555555	5555555555	5555511555	2153121212	2555552455	5555555511	1155551555
JAPANESE	1555555555	5555525555	5555555555	5555555555	5555555555	5555522111	1111122222	2525552455	5245555511	1155552555
JAVANESE	1555555555	5555555555	5555555555	5555555555	5555555555	5555555555	5555555552	2555551255	5555555511	1155555555
JEMEZ	5555555555	5555555555	5555555555	5555555555	5555555555	5555555555	5555555552	2555552455	5555555555	5555555555
JIVARO	1525552525	5512211115	5515221551	5551522125	5551122112	2212255222	2222221212	2511212425	5125555522	2212122215
JUKUN	5555555555	5555555555	5555555555	5555555555	5555555555	5555512111	2113121115	5151552455	5555115555	5515552555
KABYLE	5555555555	5555555555	5555555555	5555555555	5555555555	5555555555	5555555552	2555551355	5555555555	5555555555
KACHIN	5555555555	5555555555	5555555555	5555555555	5555555555	5555511125	5215522522	2555552455	5555555542	2155552555
KALMYK	5555555555	5555555555	5555555555	5555555555	5555555555	5555555555	5555555555	5555555555	5555555555	5555555555
KAPAUKU	2555555555	5551255555	5555555555	5555555555	5555555555	5555555555	5555555551	2555552455	5555555542	2155555555
KAREN	5555555555	5555555555	5555555555	5555555555	5555555555	5555555555	5555555555	5555555555	5555555555	5555555555
KARIERA	5555555555	5555555555	5555555555	5555555555	5555555555	5555555555	5555555551	2155552455	5555555555	5555555555
KASKA	1555555555	5552252112	1122212152	5552522111	1211111222	2212255555	5555555555	5255552455	2554555522	2255555555
KATAB	1555555555	5555555555	5555555555	5555555555	5555555555	5555555555	5555555551	2255552455	2554555555	5555555555
KAZAK	5555555555	5552555555	5555555555	5555555555	5555555555	5555511125	5515522211	2552551155	5245221542	1111222555

	FC310	FC320	FC330	FC340	FC350	FC360	FC370	FC380	FC390	FC400
KERAKI	1555555555	5555555555	5555555555	5555555555	5555555555	5555555555	5555555551	1151552455	5555555544	4425555552
KERALA	5555555555	5555555555	5555555555	5555555555	5555555555	5555555555	5555555551	2255552455	2554555555	5555555555
KET	5555555555	5555555555	5555555555	5555555555	5555555555	5555555555	5555555555	5555555555	5555555555	5555555555
KHALKA	5555555555	5555555555	5555555555	5555555555	5555555555	5555555555	5555555555	5555552455	5555555555	5555555555
KHASI	5555555555	5555555555	5555555555	5555555555	5555555555	5555555555	5555555551	1555552455	5245555555	5515555555
KHEVSUR	5555555555	5555555555	5555555555	5555555555	5555555555	5555555555	5555555555	5555555555	5555555511	1155555555
KIKUYU	1555555555	5555555225	5521122552	5551511222	2222211111	1112255555	5555555551	1555551255	5555555511	1155555555
KIOW-APACHE	5555555555	5555555555	5555555555	5555555555	5555555555	5555555555	5555555555	5252555552	2554215542	1125555555
KISSI	5555555555	5555555555	5555555555	5555555555	5555555555	5555555555	5555555551	2555551255	5555555555	5555555555
KOHISTANI	5555555555	5555555555	5555555555	5555555555	5555555555	5555555555	5555555552	2555551155	5555555555	5555555555
KOL	5555555555	5555555555	5555555555	5555555555	5555555555	5555555555	5555555552	2555552455	5555555555	5555555555
KONSO	5555555555	5555555555	5555555555	5555555555	5555555555	5555555555	5555555555	5555555555	5555555555	5555555555
KOREANS	5555555555	5555555555	5555555555	5555555555	5555555555	5555555555	5555555552	2555552455	5555555542	1155555555
KORYAK	5555555555	5552221222	5512521551	5551522215	5552222222	2522255555	5555555552	2525552455	5555555511	1155555552
KPE	1555555555	5555555555	5555555555	5555555555	5555555555	5555555555	5555555555	5555551155	5555555555	5555555555
KUBA	1555555555	5555555555	5555555555	5555555555	5555555555	5555555555	5555555551	2555551155	5555555555	5555555555
KUMYK	5555555555	5555555555	5555555555	5555555555	5555555555	5555555555	5555555555	5555555555	5555555555	5555555555
KUNG	1555555555	5555555555	5555555555	5555555555	5555555555	5555555555	5555555551	2555552455	5555555544	4455255555
KURTATCHI	1112111222	1221151121	1222122551	1512111115	2521111555	5221222122	2213121111	1151112425	5125211142	2151511111
KUTENAI	5211221111	1112555555	5555555555	2555255555	5555555555	5555555555	5555555552	2255442441	1554215542	1115555555
KWAKIUTL	1221222112	1112522211	1221111221	2552221112	1121122111	1111112111	5115521515	5515552451	5555221111	1151512111
LAKALAI	5555555555	5555555555	5555555555	5555555555	5555555555	5555555555	5555555555	5555555555	5555555555	5555555555
LAKHER	5112121221	2122525552	5555525551	5551255555	5555555555	5211111111	2111122221	2222442445	2554555542	2115522221
LAMBA	2525151515	2522525252	1125211552	5552525555	5551111555	5111155122	2213222225	5225442441	1124115555	5515511115
LAMET	5555555555	5555555555	5555555555	5555555555	5555555555	5555555555	5555555551	1555552455	5555555522	2255555555
LANGO	5555555555	5555555555	5555555555	5555555555	5555555555	5555555555	5555555551	1151552452	1551212155	5515155552
LAPPS	1515515515	5552225555	5555555555	5555155555	5555555555	5555555555	5555555555	5522552455	5245225542	2125155555
LAU	1555555555	5555551111	1112112252	5552511115	5552211115	5111155125	5213221511	1155551255	5555555542	2155552555
LEPCHA	4112122212	2212122111	1112111111	1112221111	1222212222	2212222222	2222222222	2222442445	2244222122	2221522221
LESU	1121112111	2125511152	2222121211	1511522221	1222222222	2112222125	2213111111	1111151115	5125222155	5521522125
LHOTA NAGA	5555555555	5555555555	5555555555	5555555555	5555555555	5555555555	5555555551	1255552455	2554555555	5525555555
LIFU	5555555555	5555555555	5555555555	5555555555	5555555555	5555555555	5555555555	5555555552	5555555555	5555555555
LOLO	5555555555	5555555555	5555555555	5555555555	5555555555	5555555555	5555555552	2555552455	5555555522	2255555555
LOZI	5555555555	5555555555	5555555555	5555555555	5555555555	5555555555	5555555555	5555552455	5555555555	5555555555
LUBA	5555555555	5555555555	5555555555	5555555555	5555555555	5555555555	5555555555	5555555555	5555555544	4455555555
LUO	1555555555	5555555555	5555555555	5555555555	5555555555	5555555555	5555555551	2555552455	5555555511	1155555555
MACASSARESE	1555555555	5555555555	5555555555	5555555555	5555555555	5555555555	5555555555	5555551155	5555555542	1155555555
MAGUZAWA	5555555555	5551155555	5555555555	5555555555	5555555555	5555555555	5555555555	5555555555	5245555522	2255555555
MALAYS	5555555555	5555555555	5555555555	5555555555	5555555555	5555555555	5555555552	2555551355	5555555555	5555555555
MAM	5555555555	5555555555	5555555555	5555555555	5555555555	5555555555	5555555552	2555552455	5555555511	1155555555

	FC310	FC320	FC330	FC340	FC350	FC360	FC370	FC380	FC390	FC400
MAMBILA	5555555555	5555555555	5555555555	5555555555	5555555555	5555555555	5555555552	2555555555	5555555555	5555555555
MAMVU	5555555555	5555555555	5555555555	5555555555	5555555555	5555555555	5555555555	5555551255	5555555511	1155555555
MANCHU	5555555555	5555555555	5555555555	5555555555	5555555555	5555555555	5555555555	5555555555	5555555555	5555555555
MANDAN	5555555555	5555555515	5525155555	5551511221	2222111111	1122255555	5555555552	2555552455	5555215555	5555555552
MANGAIANS	5555555555	5555555555	5555555555	5555555555	5555555555	5555555555	5555555552	2555551255	5555555542	1155555555
MANIHIKI	5555555555	5555555555	5555555555	5555555555	5555555555	5555555555	5555555555	5555552455	5555555522	2255555555
MANUS	5112221111	1222151122	1212222221	2521222222	2221122112	2222255555	5555555551	2155222421	1552115511	1155525111
MAORI	5121211112	2112521151	1221111512	2551122122	1111122111	2222211122	2213221115	5225442445	2554221122	2211122525
MARGI	5555555555	5555555555	5555555555	5555555555	5555555555	5555555555	5555555552	2155552455	1551555555	5555555555
MARICOPA	5555555555	5555555555	5555555555	5555555555	5555555555	5555555555	5555555552	2252552451	1554555555	5515555552
MARQUESANS	2221121212	2222552222	2221125522	1151222222	5551212555	5222255555	5555555552	2155221215	5555225522	2225525225
MARSHALLESE	2525121555	2225555555	5555555555	5555555555	5555555555	5555555555	5555555552	2251442441	1554225522	2225555551
MASAI	1525151515	2525552221	2221112552	5552511115	5551211111	2111111555	1515511511	1151221215	5555112122	2221522225
MATACO	1555555555	5555555555	5555555555	5555555555	5555555555	5555555555	5555555552	2255552451	1554115522	2215555555
MATAKAM	5555555555	5555555555	5555555555	5555555555	5555555555	5555555555	5555555552	2555552455	5555555555	5555555555
MAYA	5555555555	5555555555	5555555555	5555555555	5555555555	5555555555	5555555551	1555552455	5555555555	5555555555
MAZATECO	5555555555	5555555555	5555555555	5555555555	5555555555	5555555555	5555555555	5555555555	5555555555	5555555555
MBUGWE	5555555555	5555555555	5555555555	5555555555	5555555555	5555555555	5555555555	5555555555	5555555555	5555555555
MBUNDU	5555555555	5555552222	1221212151	5552521112	2222211221	1112255555	5555555551	2251552451	2554211255	5521555551
MBUTI	5555555555	5555555555	5555555555	5555555555	5555555555	5555555555	5555555555	5555552455	5555555555	5555555555
MENDE	1555555555	5551155555	5555555555	5555555555	5555555555	5555555555	5555555551	1155551255	1111555555	5555555555
MENTAWEI	5555555555	5555555555	5555555555	5555555555	5555555555	5555555555	5555555555	5555555555	5555555522	2255555555
MERINA	5555555555	5555555555	5555555555	5555555555	5555555555	5555555555	5555555555	5555551155	5555555522	2255555555
MIAMI	5555555555	5555555555	5555555555	5555555555	5555555555	5555555555	5555555555	5555552455	5555555555	5555555555
MIAO	5555555555	5555555555	5555555555	5555555555	5555555555	5555511111	1111122222	2555552455	5555555555	5555552555
MIN CHINESE	5555555555	5555555555	5555555555	5555555555	5555555555	5555555555	5555555552	2555552455	5555555555	5555555555
MINANGKABAU	5555555555	5555555555	5555555555	5555555555	5555555555	5555555555	5555555555	5555555555	5555555555	5555555555
MINCHIA	5555555555	5555555555	5555555555	5555555555	5555555555	5555555555	5555555552	2555552455	5555555511	1155555555
MISKITO	2555555555	5555555555	5555555555	5555555555	5555555555	5555555555	5555555552	2555552455	5555555544	4455555555
MIWOK	1555555555	5555555555	5555555555	5555555555	5555555555	5555555555	5555555555	5555552455	5555555555	5555555555
MNONG GAR	5555555555	5555555555	5555555555	5555555555	5555555555	5555555555	5555555552	2555552455	5555555555	5555555555
MONGO	2555555555	5555555555	5555555555	5555555555	5555555555	5555555555	5555555551	2555551155	5555555522	2255555555
MONGUOR	5555555555	5555555555	5555555555	5555555555	5555555555	5555555555	5555555552	2555552455	5555555542	2155555555
MOSSI	1555555555	5555555555	5555555555	5555555555	5555555555	5555555555	5555555551	1555551155	5115555555	5555555555
MOTA	5555555555	5555555555	5555555555	5555555555	5555555555	5555555555	5555555551	1255552455	1554555555	5555555555
...LON	5555555555	5555555555	5555555555	5555555555	5555555555	5555555555	5555555555	5555552455	5555555555	5555555555
...UCU	5555555555	5551555555	5555555555	5555555555	5555555555	5555555555	5555555551	1555552455	5115555544	4455555555
...A	5555555555	5555555555	5555555555	5555555555	5555555555	5555555555	5555555555	5555551255	5555555555	5555555555
[illegible]	2515111555	2522551555	5525155551	5551111115	5552211222	1222222222	5225511511	1155121115	5555111144	4421521225
[illegible]	5555555555	5555555555	5555555555	5555555555	5555555555	5555555555	5555555552	2555551155	5555555511	1155555555

FINISHED CHARACTERISTIC CODE SHEET

	FC310	FC320	FC330	FC340	FC350	FC360	FC370	FC380	FC390	FC400
NABESNA	5555555555	5555555555	5555555555	5555555555	5555555555	5555555555	5555555555	5555552455	5555555544	4455555555
NAMA	1555555555	5552555555	5555555555	5555555555	5555555555	5555555555	5555555551	2151552451	5125221242	2125115552
NAMBICUARA	1555555555	5552155555	5555555555	5555555555	5555555555	5555555555	5555555552	2155552455	1122555544	4455555555
NANDI	1555555555	5555555555	5555555555	5555555555	5555555555	5555555555	5555555551	1151551251	1551225555	5525555555
NASKAPI	5555555555	5555555555	5555555555	5555555555	5555555555	5555555555	5555555555	5552555555	5125225555	5525555552
NATCHEZ	5555555555	5555555555	5555555555	5555555555	5555555555	5555555555	5555555555	5555552455	5555225522	2225555552
NAVAHO	1111212111	1122122211	2211111211	2252111111	1212211111	1112155555	5555555552	2225442441	1124555542	1155225122
NDEMBU	5555555555	5555555555	5555555555	5555555555	5555555555	5555555555	5555555551	2555555555	5555555555	5555555555
NGONI	5555555555	5555555555	5555555555	5555555555	5555555555	5555555555	5555555555	5555555555	5555555555	5555555555
NICOBARESE	5555555555	5555555555	5555555555	5555555555	5555555555	5555555555	5555555552	2555552455	5555555522	2255555555
NOMLAKI	5555555555	5555555555	5555555555	5555555555	5555555555	5555555555	5555555555	5555552455	5555555542	1155555555
NUER	1555555555	5551511111	1121121551	5551511221	2212222222	2222211111	1111122511	2515552455	5245555555	5555552555
NUNIVAK	5555555555	5555555555	5555555555	5555555555	5555555555	5555555555	5555555551	2555552455	5555555555	5555555555
NUPE	1555555555	5555555555	5555555555	5555555555	5555555555	5555555555	5555555551	2555551155	5555555511	1155555555
NURI	5555555555	5555555555	5555555555	5555555555	5555555555	5555555555	5555555552	2555555555	5555555555	5555555555
NYAKYUSA	5555555555	5551515555	5555125551	5551511121	1211111111	1112211111	2111111111	1525552455	5555555544	4455521515
NYANEKA	5555555555	5555555555	5555555555	5555555555	5555555555	5555555555	5555555555	5555555555	5555555555	5555555555
NYARO	5555555555	5555555555	5555555555	5555555555	5555555555	5555555555	5555555555	5555555555	5555555555	5555555555
NYORO	5555555555	5555555555	5555555555	5555555555	5555555555	5555555555	5555555552	2155552455	1551555555	5555555555
OJIBWA	5555555555	5552222211	2221211151	5552511111	1221111111	1111155555	5555555552	2215552455	1124225522	2255515511
OKINAWANS	2555555555	5555555555	5555555555	5555555555	5555555555	5555555555	5555555552	2555552455	5555555542	1155555555
OMAHA	5525552515	5512251111	2122121551	5551522221	1211122111	1111155555	5555555552	2555552455	5555215542	1115155552
ONA	5555555555	5555551111	2221125152	5551522221	1212222222	2122255555	5555555555	5155552455	5555555511	1155555555
ONTONG-JAVA	5212211121	1225521151	1122221221	1151511225	5552222555	5212122122	2215522522	2225445545	2554555555	5555521525
ORAON	5555555555	5555555555	5555555555	5555555555	5555555555	5555511111	2111122211	1555552455	5555555555	5555552555
PAEZ	5555555555	5555555555	5555555555	5555555555	5555555555	5555555555	5555555555	5555551155	5555555555	5555555555
PAIWAN	5555555555	5555555555	5555555555	5555555555	5555555555	5555555555	5555555551	2555552455	5555555555	5555555555
PALAUANS	5555555555	5555555555	5555555555	5555555555	5555555555	5555555555	5555555552	2555552452	5555225522	2255555552
PALIKUR	5555555555	5555555555	5555555555	5555555555	5555555555	5555555555	5555555555	5555555555	5555555555	5555555555
PAPAGO	5111212222	1212121111	1112121122	2251112121	1212222111	1122222111	2111111112	2225442441	1124215555	5525512122
PARAUJANO	5555555555	5555555555	5555555555	5555555555	5555555555	5555555555	5555555552	2555552455	5555555522	2255555555
PATHAN	5555555555	5555555555	5555555555	5555555555	5555555555	5555555555	5555555555	5555551155	5555555555	5555555555
PAWNEE	5555555555	5555555555	5555555555	5555555555	5555555555	5555555555	5555555551	2555552455	5555555555	5555555555
PENDE	5555555555	5555555555	5555555555	5555555555	5555555555	5555555555	5555555555	5555555555	5555555555	5555555555
PENOBSCOT	5555555555	5555555555	5555555555	5555555555	5555555555	5555555555	5555555555	5555555555	5555115555	5515555555
PONAPEANS	1555555555	5555555555	5555555555	5555555555	5555555555	5555555555	5555555555	5551552455	5555225522	2225555555
POPOLUCA	5555555555	5555555555	5555555555	5555555555	5555555555	5555555555	5555555555	5555555555	5555555555	5555555555
PORTUGUESE	5555555555	5555555555	5555555555	5555555555	5555555555	5555555555	5555555555	5555555555	5555555555	5555555555
PUKAPUKA	2112111211	2122552212	2221112222	2552122222	2112222112	2211155555	5555555552	2151222422	1121222122	2225525522
PURARI	5555555555	5555555555	5555555555	5555555555	5555555555	5555555555	5555555551	1551552455	5555215555	5525555555

APPENDIX EIGHT/38 -- FINISHED CHARACTERISTIC CODE SHEET

	FC310	FC320	FC330	FC340	FC350	FC360	FC370	FC380	FC390	FC400
PURUM	1555555555	5555555555	5555555555	5555555555	5555555555	5555555555	5555555551	2555552455	5555555511	1155555555
RARDIANS	5555555555	5555555555	5555555555	5555555555	5555555555	5555555555	5555555555	5555555555	5555555522	2255555555
REGEIBAT	5555555555	5555555555	5555555555	5555555555	5555555555	5555555555	5555555555	5555551355	5555555555	5555555555
RIFFIANS	1555555555	1552155555	5555555555	5555555555	5555555555	5555555122	2212211512	2255441145	2554551242	1112551555
ROMANS	5555555555	5555555555	5555555555	5555555555	5555555555	5555555555	5555555552	2555552455	5555555555	5555555555
ROTINESE	5555555555	5555555555	5555555555	5555555555	5555555555	5555555555	5555555555	5555555555	5555555555	5555555555
ROTUMANS	5555555555	5555555555	5555555555	5555555555	5555555555	5555555555	5555555555	5555555555	5555555555	5555555555
RUNDI	1555555555	5555555555	5555555555	5555555555	5555555555	5555555555	5555555552	2555552455	5555555511	1155555555
RWALA	1221221111	1115555555	5555555555	5555555555	5555555555	5555555555	5555555552	2255441145	2244555511	1115225511
SAGADA	1555555555	5555555555	5555555555	5555555555	5555555555	5555555555	5555555551	2555552455	5555555522	2255555555
SAMOANS	1222221112	1112112151	1122121152	2111211111	1112212211	1111112111	1111121512	2115221112	5555225522	2255222522
SAMOYED	1555555555	5555555555	5555555555	5555555555	5555555555	5555555555	5555555555	5555552455	5245555544	4455555555
SANDAWE	5555555555	5555555555	5555555555	5555555555	5555555555	5555555555	5555555555	5555551155	5555555555	5555555555
SANPOIL	2212112111	1115555555	5555555555	5555555555	5555555555	5555522122	2213211112	2255442445	1124551142	1155511111
SANTAL	5555555555	5555555555	5555555555	5555555555	5555555555	5555555555	5555555552	2555552455	5555555511	1155555555
SARAMACCA	5555555555	5555555555	5555555555	5555555555	5555555555	5555555555	5555555555	5555555555	5555555555	5555555555
SARSI	1555555555	5555555555	5555555555	5555555555	5555555555	5555555555	5555555552	2555552455	5555555511	1155555555
SELUNG	5555555555	5555555555	5555555555	5555555555	5555555555	5555555555	5555555552	2555552455	5555555555	5555555555
SEMANG	5555555555	5552155555	5555555555	5555555555	5555555555	5555555555	5555555552	2555552455	5555555542	1115255555
SEMINOLE	5555555555	5555555555	5555555555	5555555555	5555555555	5555555555	5555555555	5551555555	5555215555	5555555552
SENIANG	5515225525	5152155555	5555555555	2555255555	5555555555	5555555555	5555555551	1151552452	5555115555	5511555555
SERBS	5555555555	5555525555	5555555555	5555555555	5555555555	5555511111	2111122222	2525552455	5555555511	1155552555
SERI	5555555555	5555555555	5555555555	5555555555	5555555555	5555555555	5555555555	5555555555	5555555555	5555555555
SHERENTE	5555555555	5555552555	5525255552	5552555555	5552222222	2111155555	5555555551	1251552455	2554555555	5555555555
SHILLUK	1555555555	5555555555	5555555555	5555555555	5555555555	5555555555	5555555551	2255552455	2554555542	1155555555
SHLUH	5555555555	5555555555	5555555555	5555555555	5555555555	5555555555	5555555552	2555551355	5555555511	1155555555
SIMBOESE	5555555555	5555555555	5555555555	5555555555	5555555555	5555555555	5555555555	5555555555	5555555555	5555555555
SINDHI	5555555555	5555555555	5555555555	5555555555	5555555555	5555555555	5555555555	5555555555	5555555555	5555555555
SINHALESE	5555555555	5555555555	5555555555	5555555555	5555555555	5555555555	5555555552	2555552455	5555555522	2255555555
SIRIONO	2111111222	2122111221	1211221111	2521125552	5121122225	5221222222	2222221112	2222442445	1554115522	2225522221
SIUAI	1555555555	5552155555	5555555555	5555555555	5555555555	5555555555	5555555555	5555552455	5555555542	1155555555
SIWANS	5555555555	5555555555	5555555555	5555555555	5555555555	5555555555	5555555555	5555551155	5555555555	5555555552
SOMALI	1555555555	5555555555	5555555555	5555555555	5555555555	5555555555	5555555551	1555551155	5245555542	1155555555
SONGHAI	5555555555	5555555555	5555555555	5555555555	5555555555	5555555555	5555555555	5555551155	5555555542	1155555555
SOTHO	5555555555	5555551121	1222212152	5552511111	1211121212	2111155555	5555555555	5555552455	5555555555	5555555555
ANUV	5555555555	5555555555	5555555555	5555555555	5555555555	5555555555	5555555552	2555552455	5555555555	5555555555
	5555555555	5555552222	2221211152	5552511112	1111111221	1111155555	5555555551	2151551251	5555115555	5515555555
	5555555555	5555555555	5555555555	5555555555	5555555555	5555555555	5555555552	2555551155	5555555555	5555555555
	5555555555	5555555555	5555555555	5555555555	5555555555	5555555555	5555555552	2555552455	5555555555	5555555555
	5555555555	5555555555	5555555555	5555555555	5555555555	5555555555	5555555552	2555552455	5555555542	2155555555

APPENDIX EIGHT/39

FINISHED CHARACTERISTIC CODE SHEET

	FC310	FC320	FC330	FC340	FC350	FC360	FC370	FC380	FC390	FC400
TALLENSI	1555555555	5551121221	1221121151	5551511221	1222212222	2112212222	2222211112	2225552455	2244555542	2155522525
TAMIL	5555555555	5555555555	5555555555	5555555555	5555555555	5555555555	5555555555	5555555555	5555555555	5555555555
TANALA	2212212121	1211122211	1111212222	2252122225	5552211221	2112222122	2213122221	2221441145	2244555522	2221522222
TANIMBARESE	5555555555	5555555555	5555555555	5555555555	5555555555	5555555555	5555555555	5555555555	5555555555	5555555555
TAOS	5525525515	5515555555	5555555555	5555555555	5555555555	5555555555	5555555552	2151122425	5555225542	2115555555
TAPIRAPE	1555555555	5555555555	5555555555	5555555555	5555555555	5555555555	5555555551	1555552455	5555555544	4455555555
TARAHUMARA	2555555555	5555155555	5555555555	5555555555	5555555555	5555555555	5555555555	5552552455	5555221122	2225525555
TAREUMIUT	2555555555	5555555555	5555555555	5555555555	5555555555	5555555555	5555555552	2555552455	5555555522	2255555555
TEDA	5555555555	5555555555	5555555555	5555555555	5555555555	5555555555	5555555555	5555551255	5125555511	1155555555
TEHUELCHE	1555555555	5555555555	5555555555	5555555555	5555555555	5555555555	5555555552	2552552451	5125555542	1115555555
TENDA	1555555555	5555555555	5555555555	5555555555	5555555555	5555555555	5555555551	1555551155	5555555522	2225555552
TENETEHARA	1555555555	5555552221	1111221152	5552522125	5552222555	5515555555	5555555552	2555552455	5555555555	5555555555
TENINO	5111211121	1115555555	5555555515	1125555555	5555555555	5555555555	5555555552	2555552455	5555555511	1125555555
TERA	5555555555	5555555555	5555555555	5555555555	5555555555	5555555555	5555555552	2555551155	5555555555	5555555555
TERENA	5555555555	5555555555	5555555555	5555555555	5555555555	5555555555	5555555552	2555552455	5555555544	4455555555
TESO	5555555555	5555555555	5555555555	5555555555	5555555555	5555555555	5555555555	5555552455	5555555555	5555555555
TETON	5111211222	1215551111	1112125511	2521512221	1222222111	1122255555	5555555555	5255445545	2554555555	5555555555
THAI	5555555555	5552255555	5555555555	5555555555	5555555555	5555555555	5555555552	2555552455	5125555511	1155555555
THONGA	1112221111	2121512222	2221111551	2552211112	2121111111	1111111125	2515511511	2111111211	5115112122	2212522212
TIBETANS	5555555555	5555555555	5555555555	5555555555	5555555555	5555555555	5555555555	5555555555	5555555555	5555555555
TIGRINYA	5555555555	5555555555	5555555555	5555555555	5555555555	5555555555	5555555555	5555551155	5555555555	5555555555
TIKOPIA	5221121222	2222551111	2122152555	2251212221	2222222555	5221155555	5555555552	2151221212	5555222142	2151555551
TIMBIRA	1555555555	5552521151	2115255552	5551522225	5552222122	2555512122	2211122211	2115552455	5245215542	1125522521
TIMUCUA	5555555555	5555555555	5555555555	5555555555	5555555555	5555555555	5555555555	5555552455	5555555555	5555555555
TIV	1555151555	1521115555	5555555555	5552522125	5551211111	1111112115	1111122512	2515221112	5555551242	2115511515
TIWI	5555555555	5555555555	5555555555	5555555555	5555555555	5555555555	5555555551	2555552455	5555555544	4455555555
TODA	2555555555	5555155555	5555555555	5555555555	5555555555	5555555555	5555555552	2555552452	5245222122	2251155555
TOKELAU	5555555555	5555555555	5555555555	5555555555	5555555555	5555555555	5555555551	1151551255	5555215522	2215555555
TOLOWA	1555555555	5555555555	5555555555	5555555555	5555555555	5555555555	5555555552	2555552451	5555555511	1115555555
TORAJA	5555555555	5555555555	5555555555	5555555555	5555555555	5555555555	5555555552	2555552455	5555555555	5555555555
TOTONAC	5555555555	5555555555	5555555555	5555555555	5555555555	5555555555	5555555552	2555551355	5555555555	5555555555
TRISTAN	5555555555	5555555555	5555555555	5555555555	5555555555	5555555555	5555555552	2555552455	5555555542	1155555555
TROBRIAND	1112111211	2122211111	1522125552	2511122125	5551222555	5222211115	2111121111	1225442441	2554222122	2225222221
TRUKESE	5555555555	5552522222	2222112152	5552522122	1111111222	2221155555	5555555551	1122552451	1551115522	2225555551
TRUMAI	5555555555	5555555555	5555555555	5555555555	5555555555	5555555555	5555555555	5555552455	5555555522	2255555555
TSHIMSHIAN	5555555555	5555555555	5555555555	5555555555	5555555555	5555555555	5555555551	2555552455	5555555555	5555555555
TUBATULABAL	1555555555	5552555555	5555555555	5555555555	5555555555	5555555555	5555555555	5555552455	5125551142	1155555552
TUCANO	5555555555	5555555555	5555555555	5555555555	5555555555	5555555555	5555555552	2555552455	5555555555	5555555555
TUCUNA	1555555555	5555555555	5555555555	5552511115	5552111555	5111155555	5555555551	2555552455	5555555542	1155555555
TUNEBO	5555555555	5555555555	5555555555	5555555555	5555555555	5555555555	5555555552	2555552455	5555555555	5555555555

	FC310	FC320	FC330	FC340	FC350	FC360	FC370	FC380	FC390	FC400
TUPINAMBA	5555555555	5552551121	5512225555	5551512225	5552222555	5122255555	5555555555	5255552455	1114112522	2215555552
TURKANA	5555555555	5555551111	1112222551	5552511115	5551111222	2222255555	5555555555	5555552455	5555555555	5555555555
TURKMEN	5555555555	5555555555	5555555555	5555555555	5555555555	5555555555	5555555555	5555551355	5555555555	5555555555
TWANA	1555555555	5555555555	5555555555	5555555555	5555555555	5555555555	5555555552	2555552455	5555555511	1155555555
TZELTAL	5555555555	5552155555	5555555555	5555555555	5555555555	5555555555	5555555555	5555555555	5555555555	5555555555
ULAWANS	5555555555	5555555555	5555555555	5555555555	5555555555	5555555555	5555555551	1555552455	5555555511	1155555555
UTE	1555555555	5555555555	5555555555	5555555555	5555555555	5555555555	5555555555	5555552455	5555555542	1155555555
VEDDA	2555555555	5555555555	5555555555	5555555555	5555555555	5555555555	5555555552	2255552455	2554555542	1115155555
VENDA	5112211222	1211555221	5521225251	5552111112	1221111111	1111111115	2111122511	1151112415	5555212142	2115552555
VIETNAMESE	5555555555	5555555555	5555555555	5555555555	5555555555	5555555555	5555555555	5555555555	5555555511	1155555555
WAICA	5555555555	5555555555	5555555555	5555555555	5555555555	5555555555	5555555555	5555552455	5555555555	5555555555
WALLOONS	5555555555	5555555555	5555555555	5555555555	5555555555	5555555555	5555555552	2555552455	5555555555	5555555555
WANTOAT	5555555555	5555555555	5555555555	5555555555	5555555555	5555555555	5555555551	1555552455	5555555555	5555555555
WAPISHANA	5515215555	1555555555	5555555555	5555555555	5555555555	5555555555	5555555555	5255442445	2554555555	5555555555
WAROPEN	5555555555	5555555555	5555555555	5555555555	5555555555	5555555555	5555555555	5555555555	5555555555	5555555555
WARRAU	1515555525	5555555555	5555555555	5555555555	5555555555	5555511222	5225522512	2555552452	5555555555	5555512555
WASHO	5555555555	5555555555	5555555555	5555555555	5555555555	5555555555	5555555552	2555552455	5555555555	5555555555
WICHITA	1555555555	5555552212	1212121252	5552511222	1212121211	2111155555	5555555552	2555552455	5555555555	5555555555
WIKMUNKAN	5555555555	5555555555	5555555555	5555555555	5555555555	5555555555	5555555555	5555552455	5555555555	5555555555
WINNEBAGO	5555555555	5555551111	1112212552	5552522121	2212111111	1222255555	5555555555	5255555555	1554555555	5555555555
WITOTO	1515225525	2252155555	5555555555	5555255555	5555555555	5555555555	5555555552	2555552455	5555551242	1115125152
WOGEO	1111111222	1225151111	1112222111	1151122222	1112222222	2222155555	5555555551	1151122411	5555225542	2155515522
WOLEAIANS	1555555555	5552151111	1111115151	5552521122	2212111255	5211155555	5555555552	2555552455	5125555522	2255515515
WOLOF	1555555555	5555555555	5555555555	5555555555	5555555555	5555555555	5555555552	2551551151	5555115542	1155555552
WUTE	5555555555	5555555555	5555555555	5555555555	5555555555	5555555555	5555555555	5555555555	5555555555	5555555555
YABARANA	1555555555	5555555555	5555555555	5555555555	5555555555	5555555555	5555555555	5555552455	5555555522	2255555555
YAGUA	1121111222	2222125125	5512222552	5551112221	2222222222	2122255555	5555555552	2225442445	1124215522	2255555255
YAHGAN	1555555555	5555551211	1211121552	5551522222	2212221122	2122255555	5555555555	5555552455	5555555542	1155155555
YAKO	1555555555	5555555555	5555555555	5555555555	5555555555	5555511111	2111111115	5555552455	5555555555	5555552555
YAKUT	5221122212	2215552222	2221215555	2552511115	5552211555	5111155555	5555555552	2555552455	5555221222	2251155552
YAO	1555555555	5555555555	5555555555	5555555555	5555555555	5555555555	5555555555	5155551155	5555555542	2155555555
YAPESE	1555555555	5555515555	5555555555	5555555555	5555555555	5555522111	2111111111	1525552451	5555225522	2255552555
YARURO	5555555555	5555555555	5555555555	5555555555	5555555555	5555555555	5555555555	5255552455	1554225555	5555555551
O-KUTS	5555555555	5555555555	5555555555	5555555555	5555555555	5555555555	5555555555	5555552455	5555555555	5555555555
YOMBE	5555555555	5555555555	5555555555	5555555555	5555555555	5555555555	5555555551	2555551355	5555555555	5555555555
YORUBA	5555555555	5555551121	1111251251	5551511125	5551122221	2122255555	5555555552	2555551155	5555555542	1155555555
YUKAGHIR	5512555522	5555555555	5555555555	5555555555	5555555555	5555555555	5555555552	2555552455	5555222155	5555155555
YUKI	1555555555	5555555555	5555555555	5555555555	5555555555	5555555555	5555555552	2555552455	5555555542	1155555555
YUROK	5555555555	5551555555	5555555555	5555555555	5555555555	5555555555	5555555555	5555552455	5125551255	5555555552
ZUNI	5555552555	5512551111	1112112252	5552522125	5552111221	1211155555	5555555552	2151112425	5555555555	5525555552

	FC410	FC420	FC430	FC440	FC450	FC460	FC470	FC480	FC490	FC500
ABIPON	5222221122	1122251111	1555524455	5151152222	1225155555	5555551221	4244425555	5111211555	2241211112	2222222222
ABOR	5555555555	5555555555	5555524455	5555555555	5555555555	5555551221	4244425555	5555555555	2242244422	2222222222
AINU	5112121111	1122152212	2225524455	5151251121	2115251555	1122221221	4244425555	2222212121	2242244422	2111122112
AJIE	5555555555	5555555555	5555555555	5555555555	5555555555	5555555555	5555555555	5555555555	2242142122	2222222222
AKHA	5555555555	5555555555	5555555555	5555555555	5555555555	5555555555	5555555555	5555555555	2241242122	2222222222
ALACALUF	5555555555	5555555555	5555524455	5555555555	5555555555	5555552444	4444245555	5555555555	2242244122	2222222222
ALBANIANS	5555555555	5555551511	1515511155	5555555555	5555555555	5555551122	1424445555	5111255555	2242244422	2222221222
ALORESE	2111112222	1121155522	1555212455	5552552111	2225551555	5255555555	5555555555	5212255551	2242242111	2111121212
AMBA	5555555555	5555555555	5555524455	5555555555	5555555555	5555555555	5555555555	5555555555	1212222222	2222222222
AMERICANS	5555555555	5555555522	2555511155	5555555555	5555555555	5555551112	3111145555	5222155555	1212222221	2222122222
ANDAMANESE	5122221121	1122252222	2252224455	5151151111	2221252111	5555551221	4244424212	5222215252	2122244111	2111112111
APINAYE	5555555555	5555555255	5555512455	5551555555	5555255555	5555551221	4244425555	5555512555	2242242421	2222222112
ARANDA	5555555555	5555522522	1112524422	2111115555	5555515421	1521121221	4244424212	2222155515	2122211121	2212121111
ARAPESH	5211222222	1222225522	2555124412	2525515512	1115521555	5122225555	5555555555	5222255521	1212242121	1111222222
ARAUCANIANS	5555555555	5555551511	1221511255	5152555555	5551555421	1522111212	2442414211	2121155115	2242242421	2212112222
ARYANS	5555555555	5555555555	5555555555	5555555555	5555555555	5555555555	5555555555	5555555555	2242222222	2222222222
ASHANTI	1212225555	5555551511	1215112455	5151252122	2222155555	5121221122	1424445555	1111122522	2122244421	1111211111
ATAYAL	5555555555	5555555555	5555524455	5555555555	5555555555	5555555555	5555555555	5555555555	2242255512	2222222222
ATSUGEWI	5555555555	5555555555	5555524455	5555555555	5555555555	5555551212	2442415555	5555555555	1212242421	1222222222
AWEIKOMA	5555555555	5555555555	5555524455	5555555555	5555555421	5555555555	5555555555	5555555555	1212242111	2222222222
AYMARA	5555555555	5555525522	1555211112	2521515555	5552515222	5255551212	2442415555	5222155555	1212242421	2212112212
AZANDE	5221111121	1121215511	1551511211	2512522222	1121111111	5111121112	3111144212	5111122515	2242244411	1112111111
AZTEC	5555555555	5555521511	1111511212	1125225555	5555525421	5555551112	3111141111	2111155255	2242242412	2222222222
BABWA	5555555555	5555555555	5555555555	5555555555	5555555555	5555555555	5555555555	5555555555	2242211122	2222222222
BACAIRI	5555555555	5555555555	5555524455	5555555555	5555555555	5555551221	4244425555	5555555555	1212242422	2222222222
BAJUN	5555555555	5555555555	5555555555	5555555555	5555555555	5555555555	5555555555	5555555555	2242222222	2222222222
BALINESE	5222121212	2121155222	2555555555	5552552121	2125252555	5255555555	5555555555	5112125551	2242242421	2111122211
BAMBARA	5555555555	5555555555	5555511255	5555555555	5555555222	5555555555	5555555555	5555555555	2242144422	2222222222
BAMILEKE	5555555555	5555555555	5555512455	5555555555	5555555555	5555555555	5555555555	5555555555	2242242422	2222222222
BANDA	5555555555	5555555555	5555555555	5555555555	5555555555	5555555555	5555555555	5555555555	2242142422	2222222222
BARABRA	5555555555	5555555555	5555511155	5555555555	5555555555	5555555555	5555555555	5555555555	2242244422	2222222222
BARI	5555555555	5555555555	5555512455	5555555555	5555555555	5555555555	5555555555	5555555555	2122244421	2222222222
BASQUES	5555555555	5555555555	5555555555	5555555555	5555555555	5555555555	5555555555	5555555555	2242144122	2222222222
BASSERI	5555555555	5555555555	5555511155	5555555555	5555555555	5555551112	3111145555	5555555555	2242222222	2222222222
BATAK	5555555555	5555555555	5555555555	5555555555	5555555555	5555555555	5555555555	5555555555	2242244421	2222222222
BAYA	5555555555	5555555555	5555555555	5555555555	5555555555	5555555555	5555555555	5555555555	2242244122	2222222222
BEJA	5555555555	5555555555	5555511155	5555555555	5555555555	5555555555	5555555555	5555555555	5555542122	2222222222
BELU	5555555555	5555555555	5555555555	5555555555	5555555555	5555555555	5555555555	5555555555	2242222222	2222222222
BEMBA	5555555555	5555525511	2552511222	2525515555	5551525421	5555555555	5555554211	5111155555	2122242412	2222112222
BENGALI	5555555555	5555555555	5555555555	5555555555	5555555555	5555555555	5555555555	5555555555	2242242422	2222222222

	FC410	FC420	FC430	FC440	FC450	FC460	FC470	FC480	FC490	FC500
BERGDAMA	5555555555	5555555555	5555555555	5555555555	5555555555	5555555555	5555555555	5555555555	2241242122	2222222222
BETE	5555555555	5555555555	5555555555	5555555555	5555555555	5555555555	5555555555	5555555555	2242242422	2222222222
BHIL	5555555555	5555555511	5555511255	5555555555	5552555421	5555551221	4244425555	5212255555	2242244412	2222111222
BHUIYA	5555555555	5555555555	5555512455	5555555555	5555555555	5555551221	4244425555	5555555555	2242242121	1222222222
BIRIFOR	5555555555	5555555555	5555512455	5555555555	5555555555	5555555555	5555555555	5555555555	2242242422	2222222222
BLACK CARIB	5555555555	5555555555	5555511155	5555555555	5555555555	5555555555	5555555555	5555555555	2242222222	2222222222
BOERS	5555555555	5555555555	5555511155	5555555555	5555555555	5555555555	5555555555	5555555555	2242244122	2222222222
BORORO	5555555555	5555555555	5555524455	5555555555	5555555555	5555551221	4244425555	5555555555	2242242422	2222222222
BOTOCUDO	5555555555	5555555555	5555555555	5555555555	5555555555	5555555555	5555555555	5555555555	2242244122	2222222222
BOZO	5555555555	5555555555	5555511155	5555555555	5555555555	5555555555	5555555555	5555555555	2242142122	2222222222
BRAZILIANS	5555555555	5555555555	5555511155	5555555555	5555555555	5555555555	5555555555	5555555555	1212222222	2222222222
BUDUMA	5555555555	5555555555	5555555555	5555555555	5555555555	5555555555	5555555555	5555555555	2242244122	2222222222
BULGARIANS	5555555555	5555555555	5551511155	5555555555	5555555555	5555555555	5555551112	5555555555	1212242122	2222122222
BUNLAP	5555555555	5555555555	5555524455	5555555555	5555555555	5555551221	4244425555	5555555555	2242244421	2222222222
BURMESE	5555555555	5555555555	5551555555	5555555555	5552555555	5555555555	5555551111	5555555555	2242244412	1222112222
BURUSHO	5555555555	5555555555	5551511155	5555555555	5555555222	5555551122	1424441111	5555555555	2122242122	2222222222
BURYAT	5555555555	5555555555	5555555555	5555555555	5555555555	5555555555	5555555555	5555555555	1212222222	2222222222
CADUVEO	5555555555	5555555555	5555555555	5555555555	5555555555	5555551221	4244425555	5555555555	1212242122	2222222222
CAGABA	5555555555	5555555555	5555512455	5555555555	5555555555	5155552444	4444245555	5555555555	2242242422	2222122222
CALLINAGO	5555555555	5555555555	5555512455	5555555555	5552555111	5555555555	5555555555	5555555555	2242242411	2222212222
CAMAYURA	5555555555	5555555555	5555512455	5555555555	5555555555	5555551221	4244425555	5555555555	1212222222	2212222222
CAMBA	5555555555	5555555555	5555555555	5555555555	5555555555	5555555555	5555555555	5555555555	1212222222	2222222222
CAMBODIANS	5555555555	5555555555	5551555555	5555555555	5555555555	5555555555	5555551111	5555555555	2242244422	2222222222
CARAJA	5555555555	5555555555	5555555555	5555555555	5555555555	5555555555	5555555555	5555555555	2242242422	2222222222
CARIB	5555555555	5555555255	5555512455	5555555555	5555155222	5555551221	4244425555	5555511555	1212242121	2222121112
CARINYA	5555555555	5555555555	5555555555	5555555555	5555555555	5555555555	5555555555	5555555555	2241222222	2222222222
CAYAPA	5555555555	5555555255	5551524455	5555555555	5555255222	5555552444	4444244211	5555511555	2242244111	2222122221
CHAGGA	5112221211	1122155515	2552224455	5551551111	1215151555	5121221112	3111144212	5112122525	2242244122	2112221211
CHAMACOCO	5555555555	5555555555	5555511255	5555555555	5555555555	5555555555	5555555555	5555555555	2242244122	2222122222
CHENCHU	5222121222	1222155522	2555124455	5552552112	2225552555	5555552444	4444245555	5222155522	2241242121	2211222222
CHEREMIS	5555555555	5555555555	5555555555	5555555555	5555555555	5555555555	5555555555	5555555555	2242244422	2222222222
CHERKESS	5555555555	5555555555	5555511155	5555555555	5555555555	5555555555	5555555555	5555555555	2242211122	2222222222
CHEROKEE	5555555555	5555555555	5555555555	5555555555	5555555555	5555551212	2442415555	5555555555	1212242121	1222222222
CHEYENNE	5555555555	5555555511	1555124455	5551555555	5555555555	5512121212	2442415555	5121155555	1212244421	1212121222
CHIBCHA	5555555555	5555555555	5555555555	5555555555	5555555555	5555555555	5555555555	5555555555	2242255522	2222222222
CHINANTEC	5555555555	5555555555	5555555555	5555555555	5555555555	5555555555	5555555555	5555555555	2242222222	2222222222
CHIR-APACHE	5111111111	1222255511	1555224455	5552551211	1115555555	5222111212	2442415555	5122155522	1212242121	1111122212
CHIRIGUANO	5555555555	5555555555	5555555555	5555555555	5555555555	5555551212	2442415555	5555555555	2242244122	2222222222
CHOCO	5555555555	5555555555	5555512455	5555555555	5555555555	5555555555	5555555555	5555555555	2242242422	2222222222
CHOROTI	5555555555	5555555255	5555524455	5551555555	5555155555	5555551212	2442415555	5555512555	2242244122	2222122112

	FC410	FC420	FC430	FC440	FC450	FC460	FC470	FC480	FC490	FC500
CHORTI	5555555555	5555555555	5555512455	5555555555	5555555555	5555552444	4444245555	5555555555	1212242122	2222222222
CHUKCHEE	5555555555	5555551212	2222511255	5152255555	5551155421	5521121212	2442414212	2122111115	2242211112	2212212111
COCHITI	5555555555	5555555555	5555524455	5555555555	5555555555	5555555555	5555555555	5555555555	2242244121	2222222222
COMANCHE	5122222221	2222255511	1555155555	5555555522	2121551421	5511115555	5555555555	5121255512	1212242111	1111212222
COORG	5555555555	5555555555	5555524455	5555555555	5555555555	5555551221	4244425555	5555555555	2242242422	2222221222
COPR ESKIMO	5222111221	1221125552	2552524411	2525515512	2221525421	5255551212	2442412222	5121155555	2242244121	2222111111
CREE	5555555555	5555555555	5555524455	5555555555	5555555555	5555551212	2442415555	5555555555	1212222222	2222222212
CREEK	5555555555	5555551111	1512512455	5155255555	5555155111	1555551212	2442414212	5121215255	1212244121	2222222111
CROW	5555555555	5555551511	1522524455	5151155555	5551555421	5512111212	2442414212	1121155515	2242244121	2212212111
CUNA	5555555555	5555525222	2552511112	1522525555	5551225222	5511112444	4444241111	5222212515	2242242111	2212112111
CZECHS	5555555555	5555555522	2555511155	5555555555	5555555222	5555551112	3111145555	5222255555	2242222222	2222221221
DAGUR	5555555555	5555555555	5555511155	5555555555	5555555555	5555555555	5555555555	5555555555	1212222222	2222222222
DARD	5555555555	5555555555	5551524455	5555555555	5555555222	5555551112	3111141111	5555555555	5555511122	2222221222
DELAWARE	5555555555	5555555555	5555511255	5555555555	5555555555	5555555555	5555555555	5555555555	1212244422	2222222222
DIEGUENO	5555555555	5555555555	5555524455	5555555555	5555555555	5555551212	2442415555	5555555555	1212244122	2222222222
DIERI	5555555555	5555551555	5125524455	5255155555	5555555555	1555551221	4244425555	1555555255	2122244421	2222222222
DILLING	5555555555	5555555555	5555555555	5555555555	5555555555	5555555555	5555555555	5555555555	5555542122	1222122222
DOBUANS	5112222222	2122225511	1555555512	2521511221	1115511555	5555555555	5555555555	5222255555	2122242121	2122222112
DOGON	5555555555	5555555555	5555555555	5555555555	5555555555	5555555555	5555555555	5555555555	2242144422	2222222222
DOROBO	5555555555	5555555555	5555524455	5555555555	5555555555	5555555555	5555555555	5555555555	2122242421	2222222222
DUSUN	1222121211	2121155555	5555555555	5555555511	2225255555	5555555555	5555555555	5555512555	2242255522	2122222212
DUTCH	5555555555	5555555555	5555511155	5555555555	5555555555	5555555555	5555555555	5555555555	1212242122	2222222222
EGYPTIANS	5555555555	5555555555	5555511155	5555555555	5555555555	5255551112	3111145555	5555555555	2242222222	2222122222
ELLICE	5555555555	5555555555	5555555555	5555555555	5555555555	5555551221	4244425555	5555555555	2122242122	2222222222
ENGA	5555555555	5555555555	5555555555	5555555555	5555555555	5555555555	5555555555	5555555555	2242222222	2222222222
EYAK	5555555555	5555555555	5555524455	5555555555	5555555555	5555551212	2442415555	5555555555	1212242121	2222222222
FANG	5555555555	5555551555	5155512455	5555255555	5551555111	1555551221	4244425555	1555555555	2242244412	2222212222
FON	5121221211	1112151511	1515224455	5551251112	2125555555	1155551112	3111145555	2121255551	2242244121	1111122212
FOX	5555555555	5555555555	5555511155	5555555555	5555555555	5555555555	5555555555	5555555555	1212242121	1222222222
FUTAJALONKE	5555555555	5555555555	5555511155	5555555555	5555555555	5555555555	5555555555	5555555555	2242144122	2222222222
GANDA	1555555555	5555525511	2555512412	1511515555	5552515555	5155551122	1424445555	5122155555	2242244421	2212111212
GARO	5555555555	5555555555	5555512455	5555555555	5555555555	5555552444	4444245555	5555555555	2242211122	2222222222
GILBERTESE	5555555555	5555555555	5555555555	5555555555	5555555555	5555555555	5555555555	5555555555	1212222222	2222222222
GILYAK	5555555555	5555555555	5552512455	5555555555	5555555555	5555555555	5555552222	5555555555	2242244122	2222222212
GISU	5555555555	5555555555	5555512455	5555555555	5555555555	5555555555	5555555555	5555555555	2122211122	2222222222
GOAJIRO	5555555555	5555555155	5555511255	5555555555	5555255555	5555551221	4244425555	5555511555	2242242422	2222121212
GOND	5555555555	5555555222	2555511255	5552555555	5555155421	5155555555	5555555555	5222122555	2122242111	2222221112
GROS VENTRE	5555555555	5555555555	5555511155	5555555555	5555555555	5555551212	2442415555	5555555555	1212244422	2222222222
GUAHIBO	5555555555	5555555555	5555555555	5555555555	5555555555	5555555555	5555555555	5555555555	2241222222	2222222222
GUATO	5555555555	5555555555	5555555555	5555555555	5555555555	5555555555	5555555555	5555555555	2241244122	2222222222

	FC410	FC420	FC430	FC440	FC450	FC460	FC470	FC480	FC490	FC500
GURE	5555555555	5555555555	5555512455	5555555555	5555555555	5555555555	5555555555	5555555555	2122242422	2222222222
HAIDA	5555555555	5555551511	1225524455	5255555555	5555555555	1555551212	2442415555	1111255555	1212244121	1222222222
HANO	5212211112	1112251222	2225155555	5552251221	1115155555	1155555555	5555555555	1222125551	1212222221	1111221111
HANUNOO	5555555555	5555555555	5555555555	5555555555	5555555555	5555555555	5555555555	5555555555	1212222222	2222222222
HASANIA	5555555555	5555555555	5555555555	5555555555	5555555555	5555555555	5555555555	5555555555	5555542122	2222222222
HASINAI	5555555555	5555555555	5555511155	5555555555	5555555555	5555551212	2442415555	5555555555	1212244422	2222222222
HAVASUPAI	2555555555	5555555555	5555555555	5555555555	5555555555	5555555555	5555555555	5555555555	1212211121	2222221212
HAWAIIANS	5555555555	5555555555	5555524455	5555555555	5555555555	5555551112	3111145555	5555555555	2242255522	2222222222
HAZARA	5555555555	5555555555	5555511155	5555555555	5555555555	5555555555	5555555555	5555555555	1212242422	2222222222
HEBREWS	5555555555	5555521511	1515511111	5125215555	5555525555	5555555555	5555555555	5111555255	2242244422	2222222221
HEHE	5555555555	5555555555	5555555555	5555555555	5555555555	5555555555	5555555555	5555555555	2242244122	1222222222
HERERO	5555555555	5555555555	5555555555	5555555555	5555555555	5555555555	5555555555	5555555555	2241211122	2222222222
HO	5555555555	5555555555	5555555555	5555555555	5555555555	5555555555	5555555555	5555555555	2242244121	2222222222
HUICHOL	5555555555	5555555255	5555555555	5555555555	5555155555	5555552444	4444245555	5555511555	2242244422	2222222212
HUKUNDIKA	5555555555	5555555555	5555524455	5555555555	5555555555	5555551212	2442415555	5555555555	1212242122	2222222222
HURON	5555555555	5555555555	5555512455	5555555555	5555555555	5555551212	2442415555	5555555555	1212242422	2222222222
HUTSUL	5555555555	5555555555	5555511155	5555555555	5555555555	5555551212	2444445555	5555555555	2242244122	2222222222
IBAN	5555555555	5555521511	1222524411	1125225555	5552525421	2555551221	4244422222	2121155255	2122244412	2222211222
ICELANDERS	5555555555	5555555555	5555555555	5555555555	5555555555	5555555555	5555555555	5555555555	2242244122	2222222222
IFUGAO	5122112212	2212115511	1555524411	2521511111	1211122111	5555555555	5555555555	5111211552	1212244111	2111211111
ILA	5555555555	5555555555	5555512455	5552555555	5555555555	5555551122	1424445555	5555555555	2242255511	2222222212
INCA	5555555555	5555551511	1515512455	5155555555	5555555555	5555551112	3111145555	5121255555	1212242111	2222221222
INGALIK	5555555555	5555555555	5555512455	5555555555	5555555555	5555551221	4244425555	5555555555	1212242422	2222222222
INGASSANA	5555555555	5555555555	5555555555	5555555555	5555555555	5555555555	5555555555	5555555555	2122244121	2222222222
IRAQW	5555555555	5555555555	5555555555	5555555555	5555555555	5555555555	5555555555	5555555555	2242222222	2222222222
IRISH	5555555555	5555555555	5555511155	5555555555	5555555222	5555551112	3111145555	5555555555	1212242122	2222222222
JAPANESE	5555555555	5555555555	5555555555	5555555555	5555555555	5555551112	3111145555	5555555551	1212242422	2221122222
JAVANESE	5555555555	5555555555	5555511155	5555555555	5555555555	5555555555	5555555555	5555555555	2242222222	2222222222
JEMEZ	5555555555	5555555555	5555555555	5555555555	5555555555	5555551212	2442415555	5555555555	1212244122	2222222222
JIVARO	5122211121	1111251111	1222512455	5151151221	1111155111	2255552444	4444242222	5111211555	2242242122	2112111121
JUKUN	5555555555	5555555555	5555555555	5551555555	5555555555	5555551122	1424445555	5555555555	2122242121	1222222212
KABYLE	5555555555	5555555555	5555511155	5555555555	5555555555	5555555555	5555555555	5555555555	2242144122	2222222222
KACHIN	5555555555	5555555555	5555511255	5555555555	5555555555	5555555555	5555555555	5555555555	2122242422	2222221222
KALMYK	5555555555	5555555555	5555555555	5555555555	5555555555	5555555555	5555555555	5555555555	1212255522	2222222222
KAPAUKU	2555555555	5555555555	5555512455	5555555555	5551555421	5555555555	5555555555	5555555555	2242222222	2222211222
KAREN	5555555555	5555515555	5552555512	1515515555	5552525555	5555555555	5555554212	5555555555	2242211122	2222212222
KARIERA	5555555555	5555555555	5555555555	5555555555	5555555555	5555555555	5555555555	5555555555	2242244421	2222222222
KASKA	5555555555	5555525512	1551524411	2511515555	5551525111	5521211212	2442414211	5222255525	1212242421	1212212222
KATAB	5555555555	5555555555	5555511255	5555555555	5555555555	5555552444	4444245555	5555555555	2122242421	1222222222
KAZAK	5555555555	5555551211	2525511155	5152552155	5555255222	5255551112	3111145555	5222525555	1212242112	2222121111

	FC410	FC420	FC430	FC440	FC450	FC460	FC470	FC480	FC490	FC500
KERAKI	5555555555	5555555555	5555524455	5555555555	5555555555	5555551221	4244425555	5555555555	2122242121	2222222222
KERALA	5555555555	5555555555	5555555555	5555555555	5555555555	5555555555	5555555555	5555555555	2122222221	2222222222
KET	5555555555	5555555555	5555555555	5555555555	5555555555	5555555555	5555555555	5555555555	2242242122	2222222222
KHALKA	5555555555	5555555255	5555555555	5555555555	5555255555	5555555555	5555555555	5555511555	1212222222	2222222222
KHASI	5555555555	5555555555	5551512455	5555555555	5555255222	5555551221	4244421112	5555515555	2242244112	2222122222
KHEVSUR	5555555555	5555555555	5555555555	5555555555	5555555555	5555555555	5555555555	5555555555	5555542122	2222222222
KIKUYU	5555555555	5555555555	5555511255	5555555555	5555555421	5521211122	1424445555	5555555525	2242242412	2212222222
KIOW-APACHE	5555555555	5555555555	5555555555	5555555555	5555555555	5555555555	5555555555	5555555555	1212242121	1222222212
KISSI	5555555555	5555555555	5555555555	5555555555	5555555555	5555555555	5555555555	5555555555	2242144422	2222222222
KOHISTANI	5555555555	5555555555	5555511155	5555555555	5555555555	5555555555	5555555555	5555555555	2242222222	2222222222
KOL	5555555555	5555555555	5555555555	5555555555	5555555555	5555555555	5555555555	5555555555	1212242122	2222222222
KONSO	5555555555	5555555555	5555555555	5555555555	5555555555	5555555555	5555555555	5555555555	2242255522	2222222222
KOREANS	5555555555	5555555522	2551524455	5555555555	5555555222	5555551112	3111141111	5111155555	1212222222	1222221221
KORYAK	5555555555	5555555555	5552511255	5555555555	5555555555	5221211221	4244424212	5555555515	2242211112	2212222222
KPE	5555555555	5555555555	5555512455	5555555555	5555555555	5555555555	5555555555	5555555555	2242244422	2222222222
KUBA	5555555555	5555555555	5555512455	5555555555	5555555555	5555551112	3111145555	5555555555	2242244422	2222222222
KUMYK	5555555555	5555555555	5555555555	5555555555	5555555555	5555555555	5555555555	5555555555	2242222222	2222222222
KUNG	5555555555	5555551555	5225511255	5255155555	5555555555	2555551221	4244425555	2555555155	2242242422	2222222222
KURTATCHI	5111221212	1222255511	1552224455	5551552122	1222551111	5112211221	4244424212	5222155525	2122242121	1112112111
KUTENAI	5222225555	5555551555	5555524455	5152552222	2225555555	2555551212	2442415555	2555555255	1212244121	2122222212
KWAKIUTL	5111111111	1121151512	2225255555	5151551112	1115551555	2555551212	2442415555	1111155551	2242242422	2111222112
LAKALAI	5555555555	5555555555	5555555555	5555555555	5555555555	5555555555	5555555555	5555555555	1212222222	2222222222
LAKHER	5222111222	1221155511	1555511155	5552551221	2115252555	5155551122	1424445555	5121112555	2242242421	1112222121
LAMBA	5111111221	1121155255	5555512455	5552552111	2225152555	5555551122	1424445555	5555525555	2122242421	2212122212
LAMET	5555555555	5555555555	5555555555	5555555555	5555555555	5555555555	5555555555	5555555555	2242222222	2222222222
LANGO	5555555555	5555551511	1225511255	5251155555	5555255555	5155555555	5555555555	5221221255	2122244121	2222222112
LAPPS	5222111111	1122152522	2555511155	5255555511	1111555555	2255551221	4244425555	5222255155	5555542422	2222111211
LAU	5555555555	5555555522	2555524455	5551555555	5555555111	5255551221	4244425555	5222155555	2242244111	2212222222
LEPCHA	5111111211	1122125222	2555211211	1511522222	2122225421	5221221221	4244425555	5222222525	2122242111	2112111111
LESU	1111221111	1111255522	2555224455	5552552222	1225551555	5555551221	4244425555	5122155555	1212242121	1112122112
LHOTA NAGA	5555555555	5555555555	5555524455	5555555555	5555555555	5555551221	4244425555	5555555555	2122211121	2222222222
LIFU	5555555555	5555555555	5555555555	5555555555	5555555555	5555555555	5555555555	5555555555	2122211122	2222222222
LOLO	5555555555	5555555555	5552524455	5555555555	5555555222	5555555555	5555551111	5555555555	2242222212	2222222222
LOZI	5555555555	5555525555	5555512422	2525515555	5555515555	5555555555	5555555555	5555555555	2122242412	1222222222
LUBA	5555555555	5555555555	5555555555	5555555555	5555555555	5555555555	5555555555	5555555555	2242242122	2222222222
LUO	5555555555	5555555555	5555512455	5555555555	5555555111	5555551122	1424445555	5555555555	2242244422	2222222222
MACASSARESE	5555555555	5555555555	5555511155	5555555555	5555555222	5555551221	4244425555	5555555555	2242222212	2222222222
MAGUZAWA	5555555555	5555555555	5555555555	5555555555	5555555555	5555555555	5555555555	5555555555	1212242112	2222121222
MALAYS	5555555555	5555555555	5555511155	5555555555	5555555222	5555555555	5555555555	5555555555	2242242422	2222222222
MAM	5555555555	5555555555	5555511155	5555555555	5555555555	5555555555	5555555555	5555555555	1212242122	2222222222

	FC410	FC420	FC430	FC440	FC450	FC460	FC470	FC480	FC490	FC500
MAMBILA	5555555555	5555555555	5555555555	5555555555	5555555555	5555555555	5555555555	5555555555	2242242422	2222222222
MAMVU	5555555555	5555555555	5555512455	5555555555	5555555555	5555555555	5555555555	5555555555	2242244422	2222222222
MANCHU	5555555555	5555555555	5555555555	5555555555	5555555555	5555555555	5555555555	5555555555	2242211122	2222222222
MANDAN	5555555555	5555555555	5552555555	5555555555	5555555421	5512115555	5555554212	5555555515	1212244412	2212222212
MANGAIANS	5555555555	5555555555	5555524455	5555555555	5555555555	5555551221	4244425555	5555555555	2122242122	2222222222
MANIHIKI	5555555555	5555555555	5555524455	5555555555	5555555555	5555551221	4244425555	5555555555	2122242122	2222222222
MANUS	5111122212	2112155515	5555224455	5555555511	2225555555	5255551221	4244425555	5121155555	2242242121	1212222212
MAORI	5121111111	1121251511	2115212455	5552251111	1115151555	5255551221	4244425555	5111215551	2242244121	2111221111
MARGI	5555555555	5555555555	5555555555	5555555555	5555555555	5555555555	5555555555	5555555555	2122242121	2222222222
MARICOPA	5555555555	5555555155	5555524455	5552555555	5555255555	5555551212	2442415555	5555522555	1212242121	2222222122
MARQUESANS	5122122222	2222215551	1555524412	1521511111	2212522111	5522221221	4244425555	5112155521	1212244111	2211212212
MARSHALLESE	5222121111	1111255555	5551524455	5555555511	2215555555	5555551221	4244424211	5555555552	1212242121	1121222212
MASAI	1112122122	1121255511	1555555555	5555555522	2225255555	5511221122	1424445555	5111215512	2242244121	2111222112
MATACO	5555555555	5555555555	5555524455	5551555555	5552555421	5555551212	2442415555	5555555555	2242244121	2222211212
MATAKAM	5555555555	5555555555	5555512455	5555555555	5555555555	5555555555	5555555555	5555555555	2242242422	2222222222
MAYA	5555555555	5555555555	5555555555	5555555555	5555555555	5555551212	2442415555	5555555555	2242244122	2222222222
MAZATECO	5555555555	5555555555	5555555555	5555555555	5555555555	5555555555	5555555555	5555555555	1212242122	2222222222
MBUGWE	5555555555	5555555555	5555555555	5555555555	5555555555	5555555555	5555555555	5555555555	1212255522	2222222222
MBUNDU	5555555555	5555555555	5551112455	5551555555	5555255421	5521211122	1424441112	5555525515	2122242411	2212222111
MBUTI	5555555555	5555555555	5555511155	5555555555	5555555555	5555555555	5555555555	5555555555	2242244422	2222222222
MENDE	5555555555	5555555555	5555512455	5555555555	5555555222	5255551112	3111145555	5555555555	2122242421	2222122222
MENTAWEI	5555555555	5555555555	5555555555	5555555555	5555555555	5555555555	5555555555	5555555555	2242244422	2222222222
MERINA	5555555555	5555555555	5555555555	5555555555	5555555555	5555555555	5555555555	5555555555	2242211122	2222222222
MIAMI	5555555555	5555555555	5555511255	5555555555	5555555555	5555551212	2442415555	5555555555	1212244122	2222222222
MIAO	5555555555	5555525555	5552555511	1515515555	5555525222	5555555555	5555551111	5555555555	2242222222	2222222222
MIN CHINESE	5555555555	5555555555	5555555555	5555555555	5555555555	5555551112	3111145555	5555555555	1212211122	2222222222
MINANGKABAU	5555555555	5555555555	5555555555	5555555555	5555555555	5555555555	5555555555	5555555555	2242244422	2222222222
MINCHIA	5555555555	5555555555	5555555555	5555555555	5552555555	5555555555	5555555555	5555555555	2122242122	2222212222
MISKITO	5555555555	5555555555	5555511155	5555555555	5555555421	5555551221	4244425555	5555555555	2242242122	2222221222
MIWOK	5555555555	5555555555	5555555555	5555555555	5555555555	5555551212	2442415555	5555555555	1212244122	2222222222
MNONG GAR	5555555555	5555555555	5555524455	5555555555	5555555555	5555555555	5555555555	5555555555	2242122222	2222222222
MONGO	1555555555	5555555555	5555512455	5555555555	5555555421	5555555555	5555555555	5555555555	2242242122	2222222222
MONGUOR	5555555555	5555555555	5555555555	5555555555	5555555555	5555555555	5555555555	5555555555	1212222222	2222222222
MOSSI	5555555555	5555555555	5555512455	5555555555	5552555421	5555551122	1444445555	5555555555	2242244422	2222112222
MOTA	5555555555	5555551555	5225524455	5255255555	5555555555	2555551221	4244425555	1555555155	2122211121	2222222222
MOTILON	5555555555	5555555555	5555555555	5555555555	5555555555	5555555555	5555555555	5555555555	2242242122	2222222222
MUNDURUCU	5555555555	5555555555	5555524455	5555555555	5551555222	5555555555	5555555555	5555555555	2242242412	2222111222
MURINBATA	5555555555	5555555555	5555524455	5555555555	5555555555	5555555555	5555555555	5555555555	2242222222	2222222222
MURNGIN	5212111121	1122255111	2555524455	5551551112	1215152555	5555552444	4444245555	5222111552	2242242421	1211222112
MZAB	5555555555	5555555555	5555511155	5555555555	5555555555	5555555555	5555555555	5555555555	2242111122	2222222222

	FC410	FC420	FC430	FC440	FC450	FC460	FC470	FC480	FC490	FC500
NABESNA	5555555555	5555555555	5555524455	5555555555	5555555555	5555551212	2442415555	5555555555	1212222222	2222222222
NAMA	5555555555	5555521511	5512524412	2125115555	5552115421	2255551112	3111142222	5222215155	2242244121	1222111111
NAMBICUARA	5555555555	5555555555	5555524455	5555555555	5555555421	5555555555	5555555555	5555555555	2242242411	2222121222
NANDI	5555555555	5555515555	5555512412	2515515555	5555525555	5555555555	5555555555	5555555555	5555544421	2222222212
NASKAPI	5555555555	5555555255	5555555555	5555555555	5551255421	5555555555	5555555555	5555512555	1212244122	2222112212
NATCHEZ	5555555555	5555555555	5555512455	5555555555	5555555555	5555551221	4244425555	5555555555	2242244122	2222222212
NAVAHO	2112212111	1111151512	1522224455	5151151111	2115551111	2222221212	2442414211	5222155512	1212244121	1111122221
NDEMBU	5555555555	5555555555	5555555555	5555555555	5555555555	5555555555	5555555555	5555555555	2242242422	2222222222
NGONI	1555555555	5555555555	5555555555	5555555555	5555555555	5555555555	5555555555	5555555555	2122222222	2222222222
NICOBARESE	5555555555	5555555555	5555555555	5555555555	5555555555	5555551221	4244425555	5555555555	2242211122	2222222222
NOMLAKI	5555555555	5555555555	5555512455	5555555555	5555555555	5555551212	2442415555	5555555555	1212222222	2222222222
NUER	5555555555	5555525511	2552511111	2525515555	5555525111	5555555555	5555552222	5112255555	2122242422	2212121222
NUNIVAK	5555555555	5555555555	5555524455	5555555555	5555555555	5555551221	4244425555	5555555555	1212242122	2222222222
NUPE	1555555555	5555555555	5555511155	5555555555	5555555222	5555555555	5555555555	5555555555	2242242422	2222222222
NURI	5555555555	5555555555	5555555555	5555555555	5555555555	5555555555	5555555555	5555555555	2242244422	2222222222
NYAKYUSA	5555555555	5555525511	2555512411	2525515555	5551515555	5255551122	1424445555	5115155555	2122242412	1212211222
NYANEKA	5555555555	5555555555	5555555555	5555555555	5555555555	5555555555	5555555555	5555555555	2242142122	2222222222
NYARO	5555555555	5555555555	5555555555	5555555555	5555555555	5555555555	5555555555	5555555555	2242222222	2222222222
NYORO	5555555555	5555555555	5555512455	5555555555	5555555555	5555551122	1424445555	5555555555	2122244421	2222222222
OJIBWA	2555555555	5555555512	1552255555	5555555555	5551555111	5512215555	5555554212	5111155525	2242222211	1212111212
OKINAWANS	5555555555	5555555555	5555524455	5555555555	5555555555	5555551112	3111145555	5555555555	2242222222	2222222222
OMAHA	5121211122	1121151555	5215524455	5152551112	1211255421	1555551212	2442415555	1555511252	1212211112	2111212112
ONA	5555555555	5555555555	5555512455	5555555555	5555555555	5555551221	4244425555	5555555555	2241242121	2212222222
ONTONG-JAVA	5222222211	2121255555	5555124455	5555555511	2215555555	5155555555	5555555555	5555555555	2122242121	1212222222
ORAON	5555555555	5555555555	5555555555	5555555555	5555555555	5555555555	5555555555	5555555555	2242222222	2222222222
PAEZ	5555555555	5555555555	5555555555	5555555555	5555555555	5555552444	4444245555	5555555555	2242244422	2222222222
PAIWAN	5555555555	5555555555	5555524455	5555555555	5555555555	5555551221	4244425555	5555555555	2242255522	2222222222
PALAUANS	5555555555	5555555555	5555524455	5552552255	5555555555	5555551212	2442415555	5555555555	1212222222	2222222212
PALIKUR	5555555555	5555555555	5555555555	5555555555	5555555555	5555555555	5555555555	5555555555	2241211122	2222222222
PAPAGO	5221211122	1222155122	2555111155	5552551111	2121151111	5522111212	2442415555	5222112512	1212242111	1111111212
PARAUJANO	5555555555	5555555555	5555512455	5555555555	5555555555	5555555555	5555555555	5555555555	2241244422	2222222222
PATHAN	5555555555	5555555555	5555511155	5555555555	5555555555	5555555555	5555555555	5555555555	2242222222	2222222222
PAWNEE	5555555555	5555555555	5555555555	5555555555	5555555555	5555555555	5555555555	5555555555	1212242412	2222222222
PENDE	5555555555	5555555555	5555555555	5555555555	5555555555	5555555555	5555555555	5555555555	2242244422	2222222222
PENOBSCOT	5555555555	5555555555	5555555555	5555555555	5555555555	5555555555	5555555555	5555555555	1212242122	2222222212
PONAPEANS	5555555555	5555555555	5555524455	5555555555	5555555555	5555555555	5555555555	5555555555	2242242122	2222222212
POPOLUCA	5555555555	5555555555	5555555555	5555555555	5555555555	5555555555	5555555555	5555555555	1212242122	2222222222
PORTUGUESE	5555555555	5555555555	5555555555	5555555555	5555555555	5555555555	5555555555	5555555555	2242222222	2222222222
PUKAPUKA	5121111111	1122255522	2551112455	5551552112	2221552421	5521221221	4244424211	5221155525	2242242121	2112112112
PURARI	2555555555	5555555555	5555555555	5555555555	5555555555	5555555555	5555555555	5555555555	2242244422	2222222212

	FC410	FC420	FC430	FC440	FC450	FC460	FC470	FC480	FC490	FC500
PURUM	5555555555	5555555555	5555524455	5555555555	5555555555	5555555555	5555555555	5555555555	2242242422	2222222222
RAROIANS	5555555555	5555555555	5555555555	5555555555	5555555555	5555555555	5555555555	5555555555	2242222222	2222222222
REGEIBAT	5555555555	5555555555	5555511155	5555555555	5555555555	5555555555	5555555555	5555555555	2242222222	2222222222
RIFFIANS	5111111221	2212255511	5555511155	5555555521	1112551421	5555555555	5555555555	5112155555	2242244121	2222211121
ROMANS	5555555555	5555525555	5555524411	5525525555	5555525555	5555555555	5555555555	5555555555	2242244122	2222222221
ROTINESE	5555555555	5555555555	5555555555	5555555555	5555555555	5555555555	5555555555	5555555555	2242211122	2222222222
ROTUMANS	5555555555	5555555555	5555555555	5555555555	5555555555	5555555555	5555555555	5555555555	5555544122	2222222222
RUNDI	5555555555	5555555555	5555512455	5555555555	5555555111	5555551122	1424445555	5555555555	2242244422	2222222222
RWALA	5211121111	2211151511	5551511155	5155555522	2221555222	5555551221	4244422222	5222555555	2242244121	2222111222
SAGADA	5555555555	5555555555	5555524455	5555555555	5555555555	5555551221	4244425555	5555555555	2242222222	2222222222
SAMOANS	5222215555	5555551552	2211112455	5255255512	2222552111	1155551212	2442414212	5112155151	2242242411	2211212212
SAMOYED	5555555555	5555525255	5552511212	5525525555	5555225555	5555555555	5555551111	5555512555	2242244422	2222122122
SANDAWE	5555555555	5555555555	5555512455	5555555555	5555555555	5555555555	5555555555	5555555555	2242255522	2222222222
SANPOIL	5222111121	1122255522	2555511255	5551551221	1115551421	5555551212	2442415555	5222255555	1212242121	1122122121
SANTAL	5555555555	5555555555	5555512455	5555555555	5555555555	5555555555	5555555555	5555555555	2242242422	2222222222
SARAMACCA	5555555555	5555555555	5555555555	5555555555	5555555555	5555555555	5555555555	5555555555	1212244122	1222222222
SARSI	5555555555	5555555555	5555555555	5555555555	5555555555	5555555555	5555555555	5555555555	2242242422	2222222222
SELUNG	5555555555	5555555555	5555555555	5555555555	5555555555	5555555555	5555555555	5555555555	5555511122	2222222222
SEMANG	5555555555	5555552555	5225511255	5155255555	5551555222	2555551221	4244425555	5555555255	2242244112	2222211222
SEMINOLE	5555555555	5555555555	5555555555	5555555555	5555555555	5555555555	5555555555	5555555555	1212242122	1222222212
SENIANG	5112212212	1212255555	5555555555	5551551112	1215555555	5555551221	4244425555	5555555555	2122242121	2222221112
SERBS	5555555555	5555555555	5555511155	5555555555	5555555555	5555551112	3111145555	5555555555	1212222222	2222222222
SERI	5555555555	5555551555	5555555555	5255555555	5555555555	1555555555	5555555555	2555555155	1212244422	2222222222
SHERENTE	5555555555	5555555555	5555524455	5555555555	5555555555	5555551221	4244425555	5555555555	2241242121	2212222222
SHILLUK	5555555555	5555551555	5525512455	5255255555	5555555555	1555555555	5555555555	5555555555	2242244421	1222222222
SHLUH	5555555555	5555555555	5555511155	5555555555	5555555555	5555555555	5555555555	5555555555	2242244122	2222222222
SIMBOESE	5555555555	5555555555	5555555555	5555555555	5555555555	5555555555	5555555555	5555555555	2242244422	2222222222
SINDHI	5555555555	5555555555	5555555555	5555555555	5555555555	5555555555	5555555555	5555555555	5555555522	2222222222
SINHALESE	2555555555	5555555555	5555555555	5555555555	5555555555	5555555555	5555555555	5555555555	2242244422	2222222222
SIRIONO	5122121221	2221255522	2552212455	5552552121	2122552421	5555551221	4244422222	5221255555	1212222211	2112212211
SIUAI	5555555555	5555555555	5555524455	5555555555	5555555555	5555555555	5555555555	5555555555	1212222222	2222222222
SIWANS	5555555555	5555555552	2555511155	5555555555	5555555555	5555551122	1444445555	5112155555	2242244112	2222221221
SOMALI	5555555555	5555555511	1555511155	5555555555	5552555222	5555551122	1444445555	5111255555	2242242412	2222111222
SONGHAI	5555555555	5555555555	5555511155	5555555555	5555555555	5555555555	5555555555	5555555555	2242242422	2222222222
SOTHO	5555555555	5555555555	5555524455	5555555555	5555555555	5522115555	5555555555	5555555525	2242244422	2212222222
SUBANUN	5555555555	5555555555	5555555555	5555555555	5555555555	5555555555	5555555555	5555555555	1212222222	2222222222
SWAZI	5555555555	5555555555	5555524455	5555555555	5555555555	5555555555	5555555555	5555555555	2122242421	1212222212
SYRIANS	5555555555	5555555555	5555511155	5555555555	5555555555	5555551112	3111145555	5555555555	1212222222	2222222222
TAGBANUA	5555555555	5555555555	5555555555	5555555555	5555555555	5555555555	5555555555	5555555555	1212222222	2222222222
TALAMANCA	5555555555	5555555555	5555511255	5555555555	5555555555	5555552444	4444245555	5555555555	1212211122	2222222222

	FC410	FC420	FC430	FC440	FC450	FC460	FC470	FC480	FC490	FC500
TALLENSI	2555555555	5555525522	2552124411	2525515555	5552525111	5155551212	2442414212	5221155555	2122242421	1212111222
TAMIL	5555555555	5555555555	5555555555	5555555555	5555555555	5555555555	5555555555	5555555555	2122222222	2222222222
TANALA	5212121221	2222115212	2555512411	1522511111	2212215421	5155551122	1424445555	5222522555	1212242121	1112111122
TANIMBARESE	5555555555	5555555555	5555555555	5555555555	5555555555	5555555555	5555555555	5555555555	2242242122	2222222222
TAOS	5222211211	1121155555	5555555555	5552552222	1115555555	5555551212	2442415555	5555555555	1212242121	2222222212
TAPIRAPE	5555555555	5555555512	2555524455	5555555555	5555555555	5555551221	4244425555	5221255555	2242242122	2222222222
TARAHUMARA	5555555555	5555555255	5555511155	5555555555	5555155555	5255551112	3111145555	5555512555	1212244112	1222222112
TAREUMIUT	5555555555	5555555555	5555524455	5555555555	5555555555	5555551212	2442415555	5555555555	1212222222	2222222222
TEDA	5555555555	5555555555	5555511155	5555555555	5555555555	5555555555	5555555555	5555555555	2242222222	2222122222
TEHUELCHE	5555555555	5555555255	5552512455	5555555555	5555155222	5555551212	2442414212	5555511555	2242244122	2222122222
TENDA	5555555555	5555555555	5555512455	5555555555	5555555555	5555555555	5555555555	5555555555	5555544422	2222222222
TENETEHARA	5555555555	5555555555	5555224455	5555555555	5555555555	5521212444	4444245555	5555555525	2242242122	2212222222
TENINO	5222121222	2222255555	5555511155	5555555522	1115555555	5555551212	2442415555	5555555555	1212242422	2222222222
TERA	5555555555	5555555555	5555555555	5555555555	5555555555	5555555555	5555555555	5555555555	2122255522	2222222222
TERENA	5555555555	5555555555	5555512455	5555555555	5555555555	5555555555	5555555555	5555555555	1212242122	2222222222
TESO	5555555555	5555555555	5555512455	5555555555	5555555555	5555555555	5555555555	5555555555	2122222222	2222222222
TETON	5221221212	2222155555	5555155555	5555555521	2225555555	5522125555	5555555555	5555555522	1212244121	2211222222
THAI	5555555555	5555555555	5555524455	5555555555	5552555222	5555551112	3111145555	5555555555	2242242412	2222112222
THONGA	5122121121	1112255511	1552212455	5551552122	2225151111	5512121112	3111141111	5121111522	2242211121	1111121111
TIBETANS	5555555555	5555555555	5555555555	5555555555	5555555222	5555555555	5555555555	5555555555	2242244422	2222222222
TIGRINYA	5555555555	5555555555	5555511155	5555555555	5555555555	5555555555	5555555555	5555555555	2242244422	2222222222
TIKOPIA	2222122211	2122155512	2551124455	5555555512	2125552111	5555551221	4244422222	5111155555	2122242111	1112221112
TIMBIRA	5555555555	5555515522	2552524422	2521515555	5555525111	5255551221	4244424212	5222155555	2241242121	1212121212
TIMUCUA	5555555555	5555555555	5555524455	5555555555	5555555555	5555555555	5555555555	5555555555	1212244122	2222222222
TIV	5111215555	5555515512	1552512411	2522512221	1112111111	5155551122	1424441111	5121125555	2242242422	2112211122
TIWI	5555555555	5555555555	5555512455	5555555555	5555555555	5555551221	4244425555	5555555555	2242242422	2222222222
TODA	1555555555	5555522222	2511524452	2111225555	5555125421	1555551221	4244421112	5222225555	2242244112	2222121112
TOKELAU	5555555555	5555555555	5555555555	5551555555	5555555555	5555555555	5555555555	5555555555	1212242121	2222222212
TOLOWA	5555555555	5555555555	5555524455	5555555555	5555555555	5555551212	2442415555	5555555555	1212242122	2222222222
TORAJA	5555555555	5555555555	5555555555	5555555555	5555555555	5555555555	5555555555	5555555555	2242211122	2222222222
TOTONAC	5555555555	5555555555	5555555555	5555555555	5555555555	5555555555	5555555555	5555555555	2242244422	2222222222
TRISTAN	5555555555	5555555555	5555511155	5555555555	5555555555	5555555555	5555555555	5555555555	2242242122	2222222222
TROBRIAND	5112222222	2222251511	2222524455	5151252121	1111551111	1155551221	4244424212	5111155251	2242244421	2111211112
TRUKESE	5555555555	5555555555	5555524455	5555555555	5555555555	5555551212	2442415555	5555555555	1212222221	1212221212
TRUMAI	5555555555	5555515522	2555524422	2525525555	5555525555	5555551221	4244425555	5251255555	1212222222	2222222222
TSHIMSHIAN	5555555555	5555555555	5555524455	5555555555	5555555555	5555555555	5555555555	5555555555	1212242422	2222222222
TUBATULABAL	5555555555	5555555555	5555524455	5555555555	5552555421	5555555555	5555555555	5555555555	1212244112	2222112122
TUCANO	5555555555	5555555555	5555512455	5555555555	5555555555	5555552444	4444245555	5555555555	1212242422	2222222222
TUCUNA	5555555555	5555555555	5555524455	5555555555	5555555555	5521221221	4244425555	5555555525	2241222222	2212222222
TUNEBO	5555555555	5555555555	5555512455	5555555555	5555555555	5555555555	5555555555	5555555555	2242244422	2222222222

	FC410	FC420	FC430	FC440	FC450	FC460	FC470	FC480	FC490	FC500
TUPINAMBA	5555555555	5555555155	5552512455	5552555555	5552255421	5555552444	4444242222	5555512555	2242244121	2212112111
TURKANA	5555555555	5555555555	5555511255	5555555555	5555555555	5255555555	5555555555	5555555555	5555544422	2212222222
TURKMEN	5555555555	5555555555	5555511155	5555555555	5555555555	5555555555	5555555555	5555555555	2242244422	2222222222
TWANA	5555555555	5555555555	5555524455	5555555555	5555555555	5555551212	2442415555	5555555555	1212242422	2222222222
TZELTAL	5555555555	5555555555	5555555555	5555555555	5555555555	5555555555	5555555555	5555555555	2242242122	2222222222
ULAWANS	5555555555	5555555555	5555524455	5555555555	5555555555	5555551212	2442415555	5555555555	2122211122	2222222222
UTE	5555555555	5555555555	5555512455	5555555555	5555555555	5555551212	2442415555	5555555555	1212242122	2222222222
VEDDA	5555555555	5555552555	5225524455	5155155555	5555555555	5555552444	4444245555	2555555255	2122211111	2222222222
VENDA	5222125555	5555555515	1555211255	5551551112	1115151555	5522221112	3111145555	5222122515	2242242121	1112222111
VIETNAMESE	5555555555	5555555522	2551555555	5555555555	5555555555	5555551112	3111141111	5222155555	2242242112	2222221221
WAICA	5555555555	5555555555	5555555555	5555555555	5555555555	5555555555	5555555555	5555555555	2242222222	2222222222
WALLOONS	5555555555	5555555555	5555511155	5555555555	5555555555	5555555555	5555555555	5555555555	1212222222	2222222222
WANTOAT	5555555555	5555555555	5555512455	5555555555	5555555555	5555551221	4244425555	5555555555	2241222222	2222222222
WAPISHANA	5122125555	5555555555	5555555555	5552552221	1215555555	5555551221	4244425555	5555555555	1212211121	2222222222
WAROPEN	5555555555	5555555555	5555555555	5555555555	5555555555	5555555555	5555555555	5555555555	2242242122	2222222222
WARRAU	5222212212	1221155511	1555511155	5552552122	2225555555	5555551221	4244425555	5111255555	2242244422	2222222222
WASHO	5555555555	5555555555	5555524455	5555555555	5555555555	5555551212	2442415555	5555555555	2242244422	2222222222
WICHITA	5555555555	5555555555	5555555555	5555555555	5555555555	5511115555	5555555555	5555555515	1212244422	2212222222
WIKMUNKAN	5555555555	5555555555	5555555555	5555555555	5555555555	5555555555	5555555555	5555555555	2122242422	2222222222
WINNEBAGO	5555555555	5555525555	5555155511	1515525555	5555525555	5512115555	5555555555	5555555515	2242244121	2212222222
WITOTO	5122121111	1211251511	1125512455	5155255511	1115551555	2555551221	4244425555	5221255155	2242244122	2222222122
WOGEO	5222222222	2222255522	2555224455	5555555512	1215555421	5555551221	4244425555	5121155555	2122242121	2112222212
WOLEAIANS	5555555555	5555525522	2552524422	2525515555	5552525111	5512211122	1424444212	5222255515	1212222222	1212112221
WOLOF	5555555555	5555555512	2555511155	5555555555	5551155222	5555551112	3111145555	5111111555	2242222222	2222211212
WUTE	5555555555	5555555555	5555555555	5555555555	5555555555	5555555555	5555555555	5555555555	2241211122	2222222222
YABARANA	5555555555	5555555555	5555524455	5555555555	5555555555	5555555555	5555555555	5555555555	2241222222	2222222222
YAGUA	5222212222	1222225522	2555224422	2522512222	1225515555	5255551221	4244425555	5222255552	2242242121	2111122212
YAHGAN	5555555555	5555552522	2255511111	2225115555	5555525555	2255551221	4244425555	2212255155	2241242122	2212221222
YAKO	5555555555	5555555555	5555524455	5555555555	5555555555	5555555555	5555555555	5555555555	2122242422	2222222222
YAKUT	5122112211	2221151211	5221511255	5255255521	2111252555	5555551112	3111144211	2252225151	2242242122	2211211111
YAO	5555555555	5555555555	5555524455	5555555555	5555555555	5555551122	1424445555	5555555555	2122244411	2222221222
YAPESE	1555555555	5555555555	5555555555	5555555555	5555555555	5555555555	5555555555	5555555555	2242244422	2222222212
YARURO	5555555555	5555555555	5555555555	5555555555	5551555555	5555552444	4444245555	5555555555	1212222221	2222212211
YOKUTS	5555555555	5555525555	5555524422	2525515555	5555515555	5555551212	2442415555	5555555555	1212244122	2222221222
YOMBE	5555555555	5555555555	5555555555	5555555555	5555555555	5555555555	5555555555	5555555555	2242244122	2222222222
YORUBA	5555555555	5555555555	5555512455	5555555555	5552555421	5521115555	5555555555	5555555515	2242222212	2212212222
YUKAGHIR	5222125555	5555552555	5255555555	5155555521	2225555555	5255555555	5555555555	2555555555	2242211122	2222222112
YUKI	5555555555	5555555555	5555512455	5555555555	5555555555	5555551212	2442415555	5555555555	1212242122	2222222222
YUROK	5555555555	5555515522	2552524422	2525525555	5555515555	5555551212	2442412222	5112155555	1212244412	2222121121
ZUNI	5222211212	1121255212	1555124412	2522512222	1225115555	5555551112	3111145555	5222225551	1212244411	2211222222

APPENDIX EIGHT/51 -- FINISHED CHARACTERISTIC CODE SHEET

	FC510	FC520	FC530	
ABIPON	1121222222	1211211122	2212112224	422222
ABOR	2222222222	1222211222	2222242444	212112
AINU	1221222121	1111211212	1212112244	411222
AJIE	2222222222	2222222222	2222242444	412122
AKHA	2222222222	2222212222	2222241114	122222
ALACALUF	2222222222	1222211222	2222242224	412222
ALBANIANS	2222222222	1211211222	2222122442	412222
ALORESE	1122212212	2121111222	2111111441	412222
AMBA	2222222222	2222211222	2222241144	412222
AMERICANS	2222222222	1221211222	2221122244	412222
ANDAMANESE	1111111222	1111211122	2112111444	412222
APINAYE	1221222222	1222211222	2222121114	422222
ARANDA	1212221122	1211211111	1122112442	422221
ARAPESH	2222212122	2121111212	1112111444	111222
ARAUCANIANS	1112221122	1211111212	1121111144	422212
ARYANS	2222222222	2222222222	2222241441	422222
ASHANTI	1221212112	1211111111	1111111111	412221
ATAYAL	2222222222	2222211122	2222122224	422222
ATSUGEWI	2222222222	1222211222	2222122444	412222
AWEIKOMA	2222221222	2222211122	2222122244	421222
AYMARA	1122211222	1221211122	1122112444	412221
AZANDE	1111221122	1121211111	1111112224	411122
AZTEC	2212221221	1211211222	2222111444	421222
BABWA	2222222222	2222212222	2222242442	422212
BACAIRI	2222222222	1222211222	2222242244	412222
BAJUN	2222222222	2222222222	2222242444	412222
BALINESE	1121222222	2121222221	1111111144	422221
BAMBARA	2222221222	2222211222	2222122224	421222
BAMILEKE	2222222222	2222211222	2222242444	421222
BANDA	2222222222	2222212222	2222242242	422212
BARABRA	2222222222	2222211222	2222242442	422112
BARI	2222222222	2222211222	2222121444	412222
BASQUES	2222222222	2222222222	2222241114	412222
BASSERI	2222222222	1222211222	2222241444	411222
BATAK	2222222222	2222222222	2222121144	421222
BAYA	2222222222	2222212222	2222241444	422222
BEJA	2222222222	2222211222	2222242222	411122
BELU	2222222222	2222222122	2222122444	412122
BEMBA	2212121222	2221111122	2222112244	422221
BENGALI	2222222222	2222222222	2222242444	412122

	FC510	FC520	FC530	
BERGDAMA	2222222222	2222222222	2222242224	412222
BETE	2222222222	2222222222	2222242442	422222
BHIL	2222221222	1221211222	2222111114	412222
BHUIYA	2222222222	1222211222	2222121444	411222
BIRIFOR	2222222222	2222211222	2222242244	421122
BLACK CARIB	2222222222	2222211222	2222242444	422212
BOERS	2222222222	2222211222	2222241144	412222
BORORO	2222222222	1222211222	2222242224	422122
BOTOCUDO	2222222222	2222212222	2222241441	422212
BOZO	2222222222	2222211222	2222242444	421122
BRAZILIANS	2222222222	2222211222	2222241114	422122
BUDUMA	2222222222	2222222222	2222242244	422222
BULGARIANS	2212222222	2222211222	2222122444	421122
BUNLAP	2222222222	1222211222	2222122224	411212
BURMESE	2212122222	2222222122	2222111444	422222
BURUSHO	2212221222	1222211122	2222121144	422222
BURYAT	2222222222	2222222222	2222242444	422122
CADUVEO	2222222222	1222212222	2222242244	422222
CAGABA	2122222222	1222211122	2121121444	421222
CALLINAGO	2222221222	2222111222	2222122444	412222
CAMAYURA	2122222222	1222211122	2121122224	222222
CAMBA	2222222222	2222222222	2222241114	412212
CAMBODIANS	2212222222	2222212122	2222121444	412112
CARAJA	2222222222	2222222222	2222241141	422222
CARIB	2121221222	1222211121	2222111444	412222
CARINYA	2222222222	2222222222	2222242444	421222
CAYAPA	2211221222	1222211121	2222112244	412222
CHAGGA	1211212122	1121111111	1111112444	421222
CHAMACOCO	2222222222	2222211222	2222122224	422222
CHENCHU	1222212122	1121111212	1112111114	421222
CHEREMIS	2222222222	2222222222	2222242444	421112
CHERKESS	2222222222	2222211222	2222242244	412212
CHEROKEE	2222222222	1222212222	2222122444	421212
CHEYENNE	1122212122	1221111221	1121111444	422222
CHIBCHA	2222222222	2222212222	2222241141	422222
CHINANTEC	2222222222	2222222222	2222242222	411122
CHIR-APACHE	1122212122	1221111212	1111111444	421222
CHIRIGUANO	2222222222	1222212222	2222241114	412222
CHOCO	2222222222	2222211222	2222241444	421221
CHOROTI	1221222222	1222211222	2222122444	421222

APPENDIX EIGHT/52 -- FINISHED CHARACTERISTIC CODE SHEET

	FC510	FC520	FC530	
CHORTI	2222222222	1222211222	2222241144	421222
CHUKCHEE	1111221122	1211211111	1222112244	422222
COCHITI	2222222222	2222211222	2222121444	422222
COMANCHE	2222111122	2121122212	1212111114	422222
COORG	2222222222	1222211222	2222121444	422122
COPR ESKIMO	2112121222	1221211121	2111111144	422121
CREE	2222222222	1222211222	2222121444	412222
CREEK	2111221222	1211211222	2222111114	421222
CROW	1212221121	1211111111	1222111444	421212
CUNA	1211221121	1221211112	1122111144	412222
CZECHS	2222221222	1221211222	2222122444	421222
DAGUR	2222222222	2222211222	2222241444	411222
DARD	2212221222	1222211122	2222121114	411222
DELAWARE	2222222222	2222211221	2222122224	422222
DIEGUENO	2222222222	1222211222	2222242444	412222
DIERI	2122222222	1212211221	2222121444	412222
DILLING	2222222222	2222212222	2222121144	122222
DOBUANS	1222222222	2121222221	2212111444	422222
DOGON	2222222222	2222212122	2222122244	422222
DOROBO	2222222222	2222211222	2222121114	412221
DUSUN	2221222212	2222222222	2212121444	412122
DUTCH	2222222222	2222211222	2222241144	421222
EGYPTIANS	2122222222	1222211222	2121121444	411222
ELLICE	2222222222	1222212222	2222242444	412222
ENGA	2222222222	2222212222	2222242224	422222
EYAK	2222222222	1222211222	2222121111	412222
FANG	2222221222	1212211122	2222121444	422222
FON	1122212221	1211111122	1111112444	422122
FOX	2222222222	2222211222	2222121141	422222
FUTAJALONKE	2222222222	2222211222	2222241444	412222
GANDA	1122222212	1221111222	1121112244	412222
GARO	2222222222	1222211222	2222242444	422222
GILBERTESE	2222222222	2222222222	2222241114	412222
GILYAK	2212222222	2222211122	2222121444	422122
GISU	2222222222	2222111222	2222122222	422122
GOAJIRO	2221222222	1222211222	2222122444	412222
GOND	1221221222	2221211121	2222111144	422222
GROS VENTRE	2222222222	1222111222	2122121444	422222
GUAHIBO	2222222222	2222212222	2222242244	421222
GUATO	2222222222	2222212222	2222241114	411222

	FC510	FC520	FC530	
GURE	2222222222	2222211222	2222241444	412122
HAIDA	2222222222	1211211122	2222122444	412222
HANO	1221212121	2211112122	1111112222	412222
HANUNOO	2222222222	2222212222	2222241144	112222
HASANIA	2222222222	2222222222	2222241444	411221
HASINAI	2222222222	1222211222	2222242444	412222
HAVASUPAI	2222222212	2222212122	2222122244	412122
HAWAIIANS	2222222222	1222211222	2222242444	412212
HAZARA	2222222222	2222211122	2222121114	412222
HEBREWS	2222222222	2211211222	2222121444	412222
HEHE	2222222222	2222222222	2222121144	111122
HERERO	2222222222	2222212222	2222242224	421122
HO	2222222222	2222222222	2222122444	422222
HUICHOL	2221222222	1222212222	2222121441	412222
HUKUNDIKA	2222222222	1222211222	2222242244	222222
HURON	2222222222	1222211222	2222241114	422222
HUTSUL	2222222222	1222221122	2222121444	422222
IBAN	2212221222	1211111122	2222112444	412222
ICELANDERS	2222222222	2222222222	2222242224	411222
IFUGAO	1121221222	2121111121	1212111144	422222
ILA	1222222222	1222211122	2222122444	411222
INCA	2222222221	1211211222	2222111444	422222
INGALIK	2222222222	1222211222	2222241111	412222
INGASSANA	2222222222	2222212222	2222121444	421122
IRAQW	2222222222	2222212222	2222241144	422222
IRISH	2122221222	1222211222	2222121444	422222
JAPANESE	2122222222	1222212221	2221121114	411222
JAVANESE	2222122222	2222211222	2222121444	411222
JEMEZ	2222222222	1222212222	2222241144	422222
JIVARO	1111121222	1211211121	1111111444	411222
JUKUN	1122222222	1222212122	2222111114	421222
KABYLE	2222222222	2222211122	2222121444	421222
KACHIN	2122222222	2222211222	2222121144	421222
KALMYK	2222222222	2222222222	2222241444	422212
KAPAUKU	2222221212	2222211222	2222122244	422222
KAREN	2212222222	2222222122	2222121111	421212
KARIERA	2222222222	2222212222	2222121441	411221
KASKA	1212221122	1221211212	1122112442	412212
KATAB	2222222222	1222211222	2222122224	422222
KAZAK	1121221222	1211211121	2122111141	421222

	FC510	FC520	FC530	
KERAKI	2222222222	1222211222	2222122444	421222
KERALA	2222222222	2222212222	2222121444	411222
KET	2222222222	2222222222	2222242244	412222
KHALKA	2221222222	2222212222	2222122444	412222
KHASI	2211221222	1222211222	2222122224	422222
KHEVSUR	2222222222	2222222222	2222242444	422212
KIKUYU	2222121122	1222211112	2222112244	412222
KIOW-APACHE	2222222222	2222222222	2222122444	422222
KISSI	2222222222	2222212222	2222242224	412222
KOHISTANI	2222222222	2222211222	2222242444	421222
KOL	2222222222	2222212222	2222242242	422222
KONSO	2222222222	2222222222	2222241114	421122
KOREANS	2212221212	1221211222	2222111444	412222
KORYAK	2212222122	1222211212	2121112444	421222
KPE	2222222222	2222211222	2222241144	412222
KUBA	2222222222	1222211222	2222242224	422212
KUMYK	2222222222	2222222222	2222241444	412222
KUNG	2222122222	1212211222	2222121114	422222
KURTATCHI	1112211122	1121111111	1112111444	422122
KUTENAI	1222222222	1212211222	2212112442	422222
KWAKIUTL	1122212122	1111212121	2111111144	412122
LAKALAI	2222222222	2222222222	2222241444	422222
LAKHER	1121222222	1121211222	2111111114	411222
LAMBA	1121122222	1122111221	1111111444	412222
LAMET	2222222222	2222212222	2222242244	421222
LANGO	1221222222	2211111221	2122112444	422222
LAPPS	2222222222	1211211122	2111112222	412222
LAU	1122221222	1221111122	2122112444	422222
LEPCHA	1121211121	1221111211	1111111144	422122
LESU	1122212211	1121111221	1111112244	412222
LHOTA NAGA	2222222222	1222211222	2222122444	421212
LIFU	2222222222	2222222222	2222241444	422122
LOLO	2212221222	2222211222	2222122224	411222
LOZI	2222222222	2222211222	2222122444	422122
LUBA	2222222222	2222222222	2222242244	422222
LUO	2222221222	1222211222	2222122444	412122
MACASSARESE	2222221222	1222211122	2222122224	412122
MAGUZAWA	2222222222	2222222222	2122122444	422222
MALAYS	2222221222	2222211122	2222121111	121222
MAM	2222222222	2222211122	2222121441	421222

	FC510	FC520	FC530	
MAMBILA	2222222222	2222212222	2222242242	422112
MAMVU	2222222222	2222211222	2222242444	421222
MANCHU	2222222222	2222222222	2222241144	421222
MANDAN	2212221122	2222212212	2222111444	422122
MANGAIANS	2222222222	1222211122	2222122224	222222
MANIHIKI	2222222222	1222211222	2222241114	412222
MANUS	2222212222	1221111222	1212111444	412212
MAORI	1121212222	1111211121	1111112444	222222
MARGI	2222222222	2222212222	2222121144	422222
MARICOPA	1221222222	1222211122	2222122244	421222
MARQUESANS	1222221122	1121111212	2212112444	411222
MARSHALLESE	2212222222	1222111122	2212111444	422222
MASAI	2121222112	1221212211	1112111114	422222
MATACO	1222221222	1222211222	2222112224	412122
MATAKAM	2222222222	2222211222	2222241444	421222
MAYA	2222222222	1222212222	2222242444	422222
MAZATECO	2222222222	2222222222	2222242244	422222
MBUGWE	2222222222	2222222222	2222241144	411222
MBUNDU	1211211112	1222211112	1122112444	422122
MBUTI	2222222222	2222211222	2222241444	421222
MENDE	2222221212	1222211222	2122122224	422222
MENTAWEI	2222222222	2222222222	2222241114	422222
MERINA	2222222222	2222212222	2222242444	411122
MIAMI	2222222222	1222211222	2222241444	122222
MIAO	2112221222	2222212222	2222121144	422122
MIN CHINESE	2222222222	1222212122	2222121444	422222
MINANGKABAU	2222222222	2222222222	2222241114	412122
MINCHIA	2222222222	2222212222	2122122244	412222
MISKITO	2222221222	1222211222	2222122444	411112
MIWOK	2222222222	1222212222	2222241444	411222
MNONG GAR	2222222222	2222211222	2222242224	412222
MONGO	2222221212	2222211222	2222122444	422222
MONGUOR	2222222222	2222212222	2222241144	422222
MOSSI	2222221222	1222211222	2222121444	422122
MOTA	2222222222	1212211222	2222122244	411222
MOTILON	2222222222	2222212222	2222242444	421222
MUNDURUCU	2222121222	2222211222	2222111114	412222
MURINBATA	2222222222	2222211222	2222241444	412222
MURNGIN	1121122222	1121111121	2212111144	421222
MZAB	2222222222	2222211122	2222121444	412222

	FC510	FC520	FC530	
NABESNA	2222222222	1222211222	2222242224	422222
NAMA	2211121221	1211111122	2122112444	422221
NAMBICUARA	2222221222	2222211122	2122112242	412222
NANDI	2222222222	2222211222	2222122444	422122
NASKAPI	2221221222	2222222222	2222121114	422122
NATCHEZ	2222222222	1222211222	2222121444	412222
NAVAHO	1212111112	1111111112	1111111144	411122
NDEMBU	2222222222	2222212222	2222242224	212221
NGONI	2222222212	2222222222	2222121444	412122
NICOBARESE	2222222222	1222212222	2222241114	422122
NOMLAKI	2222222222	1222211222	2222241441	412112
NUER	2112221221	2221111122	2121111144	411112
NUNIVAK	2222222222	1222211222	2222242444	422122
NUPE	2222121211	2222211122	2222122244	422212
NURI	2222222222	2222212222	2222242444	422122
NYAKYUSA	2122222222	1221111222	2121111444	421222
NYANEKA	2222222222	2222222222	2222242224	422212
NYARO	2222222222	2222222222	2222242444	411122
NYORO	2222222222	1222211122	2222122244	411212
OJIBWA	2212211112	2221112112	1121111114	422221
OKINAWANS	2222222222	1222211222	2222242444	411222
OMAHA	1221221222	1212111222	1112112224	421222
ONA	2222222221	1222211122	2122122442	411222
ONTONG-JAVA	2122212222	2222111221	1111111444	412222
ORAON	2122222222	2222212222	2222121141	422112
PAEZ	2222222222	1222212222	2222241444	422222
PAIWAN	2222222222	1222211222	2222241111	422222
PALAUANS	1222222222	1222211222	2222121444	422222
PALIKUR	2222222222	2222222222	2222242244	411222
PAPAGO	1121211122	1121111112	1111111144	422222
PARAUJANO	2222222222	2222211222	2222241444	412212
PATHAN	2222222222	2222211222	2222242444	422222
PAWNEE	2222222222	2222212222	2222122224	412222
PENDE	2222222222	2222222222	2222242444	421222
PENOBSCOT	2222222222	2222222122	2222122244	422122
PONAPEANS	2222222222	2222211222	2222122444	422222
POPOLUCA	2222222222	2222222122	2222121114	422222
PORTUGUESE	2222222222	2222222222	2222241441	412222
PUKAPUKA	1212211122	1121111112	1112112222	422222
PURARI	2222222212	2222212222	2222121144	422222

	FC510	FC520	FC530	
PURUM	2222222222	2222211222	2222242442	422222
RAROIANS	2222222222	2222222222	2222241444	422222
REGEIBAT	2222222222	2222211222	2222242244	422222
RIFFIANS	2122221222	2121211121	2212111114	422222
ROMANS	2222222222	2222221122	2222121444	422122
ROTINESE	2222222222	2222222222	2222241141	421222
ROTUMANS	2222222222	2222222222	2222241444	122222
RUNDI	2222221222	1222211222	2222121114	412222
RWALA	2212221222	1211211122	2212112444	412222
SAGADA	2222222222	1222211222	2222242224	222222
SAMOANS	2112111221	1111111121	1111112444	412222
SAMOYED	2211222222	2222211122	2222122244	411222
SANDAWE	2222222222	2222211222	2222242444	422221
SANPOIL	1122221222	1121111121	2112112222	411222
SANTAL	2222222222	2222211222	2222242444	421212
SARAMACCA	2222222222	2222222222	2222122244	412222
SARSI	2222222222	2222212222	2222241444	421222
SELUNG	2222222221	2222212222	2222122444	412222
SEMANG	2222221222	1212111122	2222111144	411222
SEMINOLE	2222222222	2222222222	2222122224	422122
SENIANG	1222222222	1222212122	2112112444	422222
SERBS	2122222222	1222211222	2221121444	421222
SERI	2222222222	2212222222	2222121114	421222
SHERENTE	2222222222	1222211222	2122121444	421222
SHILLUK	2222222222	2212211222	2222121144	122122
SHLUH	2222222222	2222211222	2222242244	421122
SIMBOESE	2222222222	2222222222	2222241444	421212
SINDHI	2222222222	2222222222	2222241114	122222
SINHALESE	2222222212	2222212222	2222122444	422222
SIRIONO	1112211222	1121111122	2111112224	422222
SIUAI	2222122222	2222211222	2222121444	422122
SIWANS	2222222222	1221211222	2222122442	422222
SOMALI	2222221222	1221211122	2222111141	422222
SONGHAI	2222222222	2222211122	2222122244	412222
SOTHO	2222222122	2222211112	2222121444	422222
SUBANUN	2222222222	2222112222	2222121114	412222
SWAZI	2222222222	2222211222	2222121444	422222
SYRIANS	2222222222	1222211222	2222242444	411222
TAGBANUA	2222222222	2222212222	2222242224	422222
TALAMANCA	2222222222	1222211222	2222242444	411222

	FC510	FC520	FC530	
TALLENSI	2112211212	1221111122	2121112244	422212
TAMIL	2222222222	2222222222	2222241144	422122
TANALA	1121221222	1221211221	1111111444	421222
TANIMBARESE	2222222222	2222222222	2222242442	211122
TAOS	1222222222	1222212122	2212122224	412222
TAPIRAPE	2222222222	1221211222	2222121114	422222
TARAHUMARA	2221222222	1222111122	2122111444	422122
TAREUMIUT	2222222222	1222211222	2222242444	421222
TEDA	2222222222	2222211222	2222121144	422122
TEHUELCHE	2211221222	1222211222	2222121444	422122
TENDA	2222222222	2222211222	2222241114	422222
TENETEHARA	2222212122	1222211112	1122112244	421122
TENINO	2222222222	1222211222	2112121441	421222
TERA	2222222222	2222212222	2222241144	422222
TERENA	2222222222	2222211122	2122122444	412222
TESO	2222222222	2222211222	2222241444	421122
TETON	2222212122	2222222212	1112112224	422222
THAI	2222121222	1222211122	2222112444	412221
THONGA	1111211112	1121111112	1111112244	422222
TIBETANS	2222221222	2222222122	2222122444	422222
TIGRINYA	2222222222	2222211222	2222241114	412122
TIKOPIA	2212211211	1121111121	1212112224	422222
TIMBIRA	1112221221	1221111122	2121111444	122122
TIMUCUA	2222222222	2222211222	2222242444	222221
TIV	1111221222	1121111121	2211111144	421222
TIWI	2222222222	1222211222	2222241444	412222
TODA	1211221211	1211211222	2222111114	122222
TOKELAU	1222222222	2222212222	2122121444	422222
TOLOWA	2222222222	1222211222	2222242244	412222
TORAJA	2222222222	2222212222	2222242442	422122
TOTONAC	2222222222	2222212222	2222242224	422222
TRISTAN	2222222222	2222211222	2222242444	412222
TROBRIAND	1112121222	1111111121	2111112244	412122
TRUKESE	2222222222	1222111222	2121112444	411122
TRUMAI	2222222222	1221211122	2222122224	421121
TSHIMSHIAN	2222222222	2222211222	2222241144	421122
TUBATULABAL	2222221222	2222211122	2222112444	422222
TUCANO	2222222222	1222211222	2222242244	411222
TUCUNA	2222222122	1222211212	2222121441	412222
TUNEBO	2222222222	2222211222	2222242444	421222

	FC510	FC520	FC530	
TUPINAMBA	1211221222	1222211122	1122111114	422222
TURKANA	2222222222	2222211122	2122121444	422222
TURKMEN	2222222222	2222211222	2222242224	421212
TWANA	2222222222	1222211222	2222241144	422222
TZELTAL	2222222222	2222222222	2222242444	422222
ULAWANS	2222222222	1222211222	2222241441	112212
UTE	2222222222	1222211222	2222242244	412221
VEDDA	2222222222	1212211222	2222122442	411222
VENDA	1121212122	1121211211	1112111114	412222
VIETNAMESE	2212122222	1221212222	2222112224	412212
WAICA	2222222222	2222212222	2222241444	412222
WALLOONS	2222222222	2222211222	2222242444	212222
WANTOAT	2222222222	1222211222	2222242244	422222
WAPISHANA	1222222222	1222212122	2112121144	422222
WAROPEN	2222222222	2222222222	2222242444	421211
WARRAU	1122222222	1221111222	2112111444	422222
WASHO	2222222222	1222211222	2222242222	422212
WICHITA	2222222122	2222212212	2222121114	411222
WIKMUNKAN	2222222222	2222212222	2222241444	411222
WINNEBAGO	2222212122	2222222112	1122111144	421222
WITOTO	2222222222	1111211221	2212111444	412222
WOGEO	2222211222	1221211122	1112112444	412222
WOLEAIANS	2212221122	1221211112	2122111111	422221
WOLOF	2221221222	1221211122	2222112244	421222
WUTE	2222222222	2222222222	2222241444	412222
YABARANA	2222222222	2222211222	2222242444	222122
YAGUA	1222212221	1221211122	2111112224	421222
YAHGAN	2222222221	1211211222	2222122444	422222
YAKO	2122222212	2222211222	2222121144	421212
YAKUT	2212222222	1111211222	2212112244	412222
YAO	2222222212	1222211222	2122122444	421122
YAPESE	2122222212	2222212222	2121121444	412222
YARURO	2222222222	1222212222	2222121114	412222
YOKUTS	2221222222	1222211122	2222121444	422122
YOMBE	2222222222	2222212222	2222242224	412122
YORUBA	2222221122	2222211212	2122111144	412222
YUKAGHIR	2222222222	2212212222	2112122444	222222
YUKI	2222222222	1222211222	2222242244	422222
YUROK	2212222222	1221211221	2222111444	421222
ZUNI	1221212122	1221211121	1212112444	422122

APPENDIX NINE/ 1 -- CHECKLIST OF HAND-WINNOWED QUASI-REDUNDANT STATEMENTS

EXPLANATION ON PAGE 41   DELETIONS FOR 'PURE' REDUNDANCY ARE NOT INDICATED.

001/012 013 014 016 053 084 085 094
001/095
003/011 012 013 095 299 301
004/013 016 079 084 094 392
005/011 016 084 085 094 095 300 449
006/012 014 084 085 087 183 390 450
007/013 015 033 144
008/011 012 183 392
009/013 014 016 053 084 085 094 095
010/054 299 390 392
017/012 013 082 084 085 095
019/080 085
021/013 016 094 096
022/015
024/012 014 390
033/011 012 016
034/016
035/013 014 015 016
036/011 013 016
038/013 016 392
039/011 014 015 016
040/079 080
041/012 013 016
042/011 012 014 085 392
043/011 012 013 085 392
044/011 012 013 014 016 053 079 082
044/084 085 094 095 183 185 299
045/014 015
046/011 012 013 014 016 079 084 085
046/087 094 095 097 183
047/081
050/012 014 084 085 095
051/011 012 013 014 016 053 054 056
051/079 082 084 085 087 094 095
052/012 013 014 016 053 054 056 079
052/082 084 085 094 095 183 299
053/013 014 016 079 080 084 299 390
053/392 449
054/079 082 084 085 094 095
055/013 014 079 080 084 086 390 392
055/449
056/011 013 014
057/011 013 014 016 299 390
058/013 033 036 390
059/013 014 082 084 085 094 095 183
062/084 085 094 095 390
063/013 014 079 080 084 085 087 094
063/095 392
064/011 012 013 016 054 079 080 082
064/084 085 087 094 095
066/013 014 085 087 183
067/015
068/012 013 083 183
069/011 012 085 087 095
070/080 083 084 097
071/054 080 082 084 087 095 392
072/014 016 079 082 094 392 449
073/080 082 084 085 087 094 095
074/079 084 085 094 095 183 299
075/012 013 390 450
077/079 084
079/013 046 085 086 096 100 392 460
080/046 390 392
081/054 084 094 095 142 390 392
082/053 085 087 094 095 097
083/085 142
084/054 392
084/100
085/054 082 390 392 449
086/016 080 082 142
086/095
087/095
088/054 079 080 390
090/391
091/079 082 084 142
092/084
093/033 085
094/054 082 096 392
094/086 100
095/054 082
096/080 082 085
097/082
098/085 087 095
099/081
100/079 081 087
100/084 094 095 096 097 098 099
101/084 085 087
102/016 080 082 085 087 094 095
103/054 080 082 084 094 142 469
104/011 016 054 079 080 082 390 392
105/054 100 392 449
106/080 082 084 087 469
107/054 392 449
108/390 392
109/012 054 080 082 084 095
110/084 085 087 094 095 299 301 392
111/082 084 085 095
113/084 085 087 095
115/080 085 086 094 106 108
116/078 079 084 469
118/085
120/054 183
127/299
128/015
130/011 012 015 080
137/095
138/391
140/085 087
147/084
150/079 084
151/079 084
152/079 084
163/033 046 079
164/079 084
165/079 086 096
166/084
175/095
176/011 012 013 014 016 299
178/012 013 014 016
179/013

APPENDIX NINE/ 2 -- CHECKLIST OF HAND-WINNOWED QUASI-REDUNDANT STATEMENTS

181/095
183/085 094
184/012 013 014
186/085 094 142
189/013 201
191/391
192/011 012 013 014 016 097
193/084 085
194/013 014 015
195/013
196/011 012 013 014 016 080 082 084
196/085 087 094 095
201/390
203/079 080
204/087 390
205/085 095
208/186 188 190 192
209/095
210/095
213/094 095 392
214/094
215/014
217/014 016 054 079 080 084 094 096
226/079 080 082 390 392
227/079 390
228/183
230/390
231/079 080
232/011 012 013 016 079 080 240
234/079 080 082 390 392
235/084 392
236/014 016 097
239/012 013
242/079 080
244/014 016 183
245/013 014 082 095 183
247/014 015 084
249/079 080
252/054 079 094 095
254/085

261/053
262/390
263/385
264/085 095 390 392
265/084 085 095
266/084 085 095
267/300
268/300
269/014
271/012 016 081 086 096
277/016
280/014
282/084
286/095
290/095
293/106
298/013 016
305/014
308/390
309/095
310/390
313/013
314/014 084
315/012
317/095
318/095 299
319/013
326/085 095
332/033
334/095
336/183
337/094 183
346/390
349/087
350/095
351/095
352/087 095
353/095
354/095
355/095

361/094
363/095
370/013 014 016
371/012 013 016
372/013 014 016
377/011 013 014 016 054 085 087 094
377/095
386/391
389/014 079 080 084 085
390/014 079 080 084 085
391/013 014 079 080 082 241 449
392/014 054 084 085
393/095
398/390
399/095
404/390
405/301
417/081 085 087
420/085 095
423/084
424/079 082 084 142
426/084 085 094 095 183 185 392
427/013 014 016 079 080 085 449
428/011 054 079 080 095
435/084
441/095 301
444/012 080 083
447/014
453/299
457/014
458/054 080 082 084 094 390 392
459/012 013 016 080 082 392
460/013 016 054 079 082 084 085 094
460/095 183 390
461/013 085
462/014 016 054 079 094 390
463/014
464/013 015 054
465/014 079 084 094
466/013 016

470/084
472/299
473/095
476/095
481/012 013 016
482/012
483/012 016
488/054
490/390
491/143 450

492/390
496/390
498/390
499/390
500/011 014
501/390 392
502/077 299
504/390
506/450
508/014

509/015
511/014
512/390
513/012 013 014
515/450
518/078
523/450
526/390
532/392

Computer Printout

1 CULTURES
LOCATED IN THE CLD WORLD (265)

1 CULTURES
LOCATED IN THE NEW WORLD (135)

BACKGROUND ON PAGE 65 — SUBJECT ONLY

265 IN LEFT COLUMN

135 IN RIGHT CCLUMN

ABIPON	ALACALUF	APINAYE	ARAUCANIANS	ATSUGEWI	AWEIKOMA	AYMARA	AZTEC	BACAIRI	BLACK CARIB
BORORO	BOTOCUDO	CADUVEO	CAGABA	CALLINAGO	CAMAYURA	CAMBA	CARAJA	CARIB	CARINYA
CAYAPA	CHAMACOCC	CHEROKEE	CHEYENNE	CHIBCHA	CHINANTEC	CHIR-APACHE	CHIRIGUANO	CHOCO	CHOROTI
CHORTI	COCHITI	COMANCHE	COPR ESKIMO	CREE	CREEK	CROW	CUNA	DELAWARE	DIEGUENO
EYAK	FOX	GOAJIRO	GROS VENTRE	GUAHIBO	GUATO	HAIDA	HANO	HASINAI	HAVASUPAI
HUICHOL	HUKUNDIKA	HURON	INCA	INGALIK	JEMEZ	JIVARO	KASKA	KIOW-APACHE	KUTENAI
KWAKIUTL	MAM	MANDAN	MARICOPA	MATACO	MAYA	MAZATECO	MIAMI	MISKITO	MIWOK
MUTILON	MUNDURUCU	NABESNA	NAMBICUARA	NASKAPI	NATCHEZ	NAVAHO	NOMLAKI	NUNIVAK	OJIBWA
OMAHA	ONA	PAEZ	PALIKUR	PAPAGO	PARAUJANO	PAWNEE	PENOBSCOT	POPOLUCA	SANPOIL
SARAMACCA	SARSI	SEMINOLE	SERI	SHERENTE	SIRIONO	TALAMANCA	TAOS	TAPIRAPE	TARAHUMARA
TAREUMIUT	TEHUELCHE	TENETEHARA	TENINO	TERENA	TETON	TIMBIRA	TIMUCUA	TOLOWA	TOTONAC
TRUMAI	TSHIMSHIAN	TUBATULABAL	TUCANO	TUCUNA	TUNEBO	TUPINAMBA	TWANA	TZELTAL	UTE
WAICA	WAPISHANA	WARRAU	WASHO	WICHITA	WINNEBAGO	WITOTO	YABARANA	YAGUA	YAHGAN
YARURO	YOKUTS	YUKI	YUROK	ZUNI					

	Left column (Old World)		Right column (New World)		Statistics
15	TEND TO BE THOSE WHERE THE LATITUDE IS LESS THAN TWENTY DEGREES (217) — 0.61 OF 265	15	TEND TO BE THOSE WHERE THE LATITUDE IS TWENTY DEGREES OR GREATER (183) — 0.59 OF 135		104 79 161 56 XSQ= 12.62 PHI= -0.178 XP = 0.0004
33	TILT MORE TOWARC BEING THOSE WHERE THE NATURAL ENVIRONMENT IS OTHER THAN 'VERY HARSH,' I.E., DESERT, DESERT GRASSES AND SHRUBS, TUNDRA, OR HIGH PLATEAU STEPPE (341) FWM — 0.88 OF 265	33	TILT LESS TOWARD BEING THOSE WHERE THE NATURAL ENVIRONMENT IS OTHER THAN 'VERY HARSH,' I.E., DESERT, DESERT GRASSES AND SHRUBS, TUNDRA, OR HIGH PLATEAU STEPPE (341) FWM — 0.79 OF 135		31 28 234 107 XSQ= 5.12 PHI= -0.113 XP = 0.0237
36	TEND MORE TO BE THOSE WHERE THE NATURAL ENVIRONMENT IS OTHER THAN 'VERY HARSH,' OR SUB-TROPICAL BUSH, OR TEMPERATE GRASSLAND (292) FWM — 0.78 OF 265	36	TEND LESS TO BE THOSE WHERE THE NATURAL ENVIRONMENT IS OTHER THAN 'VERY HARSH,' OR SUB-TROPICAL BUSH, OR TEMPERATE GRASSLAND (292) FWM — 0.62 OF 135		57 51 208 84 XSQ= 11.20 PHI= -0.167 XP = 0.0008
42	LEAN LESS TOWARD BEING THOSE WHERE THE NATURAL ENVIRONMENT IS OTHER THAN TROPICAL OR SUB-TRCPICAL RAIN FOREST, OR MONSOON FCREST (244) FWM — 0.56 OF 265	42	LEAN MORE TOWARD BEING THOSE WHERE THE NATURAL ENVIRONMENT IS OTHER THAN TROPICAL OR SUB-TROPICAL RAIN FOREST, OR MONSOON FOREST (244) FWM — 0.70 OF 135		116 40 149 95 XSQ= 6.94 PHI= 0.132 XP = 0.0084

1/

44	TEND TO BE THOSE WHERE SETTLEMENTS ARE FIXED (222)	0.77 OF 215	44	TEND TO BE THOSE WHERE SETTLEMENTS ARE NON-FIXED (110)	0.51 OF 117	165 57 50 60 XSQ= 25.61 PHI= 0.278 XP = 0.0000
45	TILT LESS TOWARD BEING THOSE WHERE SETTLEMENTS, IF FIXED, ARE COMPACT, RATHER THAN NON-COMPACT (149)	0.62 OF 165	45	TILT MORE TOWARD BEING THOSE WHERE SETTLEMENTS, IF FIXED, ARE COMPACT, RATHER THAN NON-COMPACT (149)	0.81 OF 57	103 46 62 11 XSQ= 5.61 PHI= -0.159 XP = 0.0178
46	TEND MORE TO BE THOSE OTHER THAN WHERE SETTLEMENTS ARE NON-FIXED AND MOVEMENT IS NOMADIC (260)	0.85 OF 215	46	TEND LESS TO BE THOSE OTHER THAN WHERE SETTLEMENTS ARE NON-FIXED AND MOVEMENT IS NOMADIC (260)	0.67 OF 117	33 39 182 78 XSQ= 13.39 PHI= -0.201 XP = 0.0003
48	TILT TOWARD BEING THOSE WHERE THE FOOD SUPPLY IS SECURE, AND FOOD SHORTAGES ARE RARE OR OCCASIONAL (38) MGW	0.58 OF 48	48	TILT TOWARD BEING THOSE WHERE THE FOOD SUPPLY IS NOT SECURE, AND FOOD SHORTAGES ARE FREQUENT OR ANNUAL (41) MGW	0.68 OF 31	28 10 20 21 XSQ= 4.14 PHI= 0.229 XP = 0.0419
51	TEND TO BE THOSE WHERE SUBSISTENCE IS PRIMARILY BY FOOD PRODUCTION -- I. E., AGRICULTURE OR HUSBANDRY -- RATHER THAN BY GATHERING (253)	0.81 OF 265	51	TEND TO BE THOSE WHERE SUBSISTENCE IS PRIMARILY BY FOOD GATHERING -- I. E., HUNTING, FISHING, OR COLLECTING -- RATHER THAN FOOD PRODUCTION (147)	0.72 OF 135	215 38 50 97 XSQ= 105.75 PHI= 0.514 XP = 0.
54	TEND TO BE THOSE WHERE FOOD PRODUCTION IS BY INTENSIVE OR SIMPLE AGRICULTURE, RATHER THAN BY INCIPIENT FOOD PRODUCTION (192)	0.92 OF 177	54	TEND TO BE THOSE WHERE FOOD PRODUCTION IS BY INCIPIENT FOOD PRODUCTION, RATHER THAN BY INTENSIVE OR SIMPLE AGRICULTURE (46)	0.51 OF 61	162 30 15 31 XSQ= 49.49 PHI= 0.456 XP = 0.
56	TEND TO BE THOSE WHERE FOOD PRODUCTION IS BY SIMPLE AGRICULTURE, RATHER THAN BY INCIPIENT FOOD PRODUCTION (101)	0.85 OF 99	56	TEND TO BE THOSE WHERE FOOD PRODUCTION IS BY INCIPIENT FOOD PRODUCTION, RATHER THAN BY SIMPLE AGRICULTURE (46)	0.65 OF 48	84 17 15 31 XSQ= 34.48 PHI= 0.484 XP = 0.
62	TEND TO BE THOSE WHERE HUSBANDRY OF SOME KIND IS PRESENT (228)	0.71 OF 265	62	TEND TO BE THOSE WHERE HUSBANDRY OF ANY KIND IS ABSENT (172)	0.70 OF 135	188 40 77 95 XSQ= 60.61 PHI= 0.389 XP = 0.
71	TEND TO BE THOSE WHERE METAL WORKING IS PRESENT (98)	0.59 OF 150	71	TEND TO BE THOSE WHERE METAL WORKING IS ABSENT (153)	0.91 OF 101	89 9 61 92 XSQ= 62.38 PHI= 0.499 XP = 0.

1/

74	DRIFT LESS TOWARD BEING THOSE 0.56 OF 138 WHERE POTTERY IS PRESENT (145)	74	DRIFT MORE TOWARD BEING THOSE 0.68 OF 100 WHERE POTTERY IS PRESENT (145)	77 68 61 32 XSQ= 3.13 PHI= -0.115 XP = 0.0768
79	LEAN LESS TOWARD BEING THOSE 0.86 OF 152 WHERE NO CITY IS PRESENT (201)	79	LEAN MORE TOWARD BEING THOSE 0.99 OF 72 WHERE NO CITY IS PRESENT (201)	22 1 130 71 XSQ= 7.71 PHI= 0.186 XP = 0.0055
80	LEAN LESS TOWARD BEING THOSE 0.78 OF 152 WHERE NO CITY OR TOWN IS PRESENT (185)	80	LEAN MORE TOWARD BEING THOSE 0.93 OF 72 WHERE NO CITY OR TOWN IS PRESENT (185)	34 5 118 67 XSQ= 7.05 PHI= 0.177 XP = 0.0079
82	TILT MORE TOWARD BEING THOSE 0.84 OF 152 WHERE A CITY OR TOWN IS PRESENT, OR THE AVERAGE COMMUNITY SIZE IS FIFTY OR GREATER (178)	82	TILT LESS TOWARD BEING THOSE 0.71 OF 72 WHERE A CITY OR TOWN IS PRESENT, OR THE AVERAGE COMMUNITY SIZE IS FIFTY OR GREATER (178)	127 51 25 21 XSQ= 4.10 PHI= 0.135 XP = 0.0430
86	TEND TO BE THOSE 0.58 OF 197 WHERE THE LEVEL OF POLITICAL INTEGRATION IS THE LARGE STATE, THE LITTLE STATE, OR THE MINIMAL STATE (148) GPM	86	TEND TO BE THOSE 0.68 OF 107 WHERE THE LEVEL OF POLITICAL INTEGRATION IS THE AUTONOMOUS COMMUNITY, OR THE FAMILY (156) GPM	114 34 83 73 XSQ= 17.87 PHI= 0.242 XP = 0.0000
96	TEND TO BE THOSE 0.64 OF 213 WHERE THE HIERARCHY OF NATIONAL JURISDICTION HAS FOUR, THREE, TWO OR ONE LEVEL (174) GES,EA	96	TEND TO BE THOSE 0.68 OF 117 WHERE THE HIERARCHY OF NATIONAL JURISDICTION HAS NO LEVELS (156) GES,EA	136 38 77 79 XSQ= 28.57 PHI= 0.294 XP = 0.0000
97	TILT LESS TOWARD BEING THOSE 0.78 OF 213 WHERE THE HIERARCHY OF LOCAL JURISDICTION HAS THREE OR TWO LEVELS (273) GES,EA	97	TILT MORE TOWARD BEING THOSE 0.90 OF 118 WHERE THE HIERARCHY OF LOCAL JURISDICTION HAS THREE OR TWO LEVELS (273) GES,EA	46 12 167 106 XSQ= 6.09 PHI= 0.136 XP = 0.0136
98	TEND MORE TO BE THOSE 0.78 OF 213 WHERE THE HIERARCHY OF LOCAL JURISDICTION HAS FOUR OR THREE LEVELS (238) GES,EA	98	TEND LESS TO BE THOSE 0.60 OF 118 WHERE THE HIERARCHY OF LOCAL JURISDICTION HAS FOUR OR THREE LEVELS (238) GES,EA	167 71 46 47 XSQ= 11.61 PHI= 0.187 XP = 0.0007
99	DRIFT MORE TOWARD BEING THOSE 0.68 OF 77 WHERE, WITH NATIONAL HIERARCHY ABSENT, THE HIERARCHY OF LOCAL JURISDICTION HAS FOUR OR THREE LEVELS (93) GES,EA	99	DRIFT LESS TOWARD BEING THOSE 0.52 OF 79 WHERE, WITH NATIONAL HIERARCHY ABSENT, THE HIERARCHY OF LOCAL JURISDICTION HAS FOUR OR THREE LEVELS (93) GES,EA	52 41 25 38 XSQ= 3.34 PHI= 0.146 XP = 0.0678

100	TEND MORE TO BE THOSE 0.88 OF 213 WHERE HIERARCHIES ARE MORE COMPLEX THAN THE 'SIMPLEST,' I. E., MORE COMPLEX THAN TWO LOCAL LEVELS WITH NO NATIONAL LEVELS (267) GES,EA	100	TEND LESS TO BE THOSE 0.68 OF 117 WHERE HIERARCHIES ARE MORE COMPLEX THAN THE 'SIMPLEST,' I. E., MORE COMPLEX THAN TWO LOCAL LEVELS WITH NO NATIONAL LEVELS (267) GES,EA	188 79 25 38 XSQ= 19.71 PHI= 0.244 XP = 0.0000
102	TEND TO BE THOSE 0.65 OF 255 WHERE CLASS STRATIFICATION IS PRESENT (203)	102	TEND TO BE THOSE 0.71 OF 128 WHERE CLASS STRATIFICATION IS ABSENT (180)	166 37 89 91 XSQ= 43.37 PHI= 0.337 XP = 0.
106	LEAN TOWARD BEING THOSE 0.67 OF 166 WHERE CLASS STRATIFICATION, IF PRESENT, IS BASED ON SOMETHING OTHER THAN WEALTH (126)	106	LEAN TOWARD BEING THOSE 0.59 OF 37 WHERE CLASS STRATIFICATION, IF PRESENT, IS BASED ON WEALTH (77)	55 22 111 15 XSQ= 7.82 PHI= -0.196 XP = 0.0052
107	DRIFT LESS TOWARD BEING THOSE 0.76 OF 166 WHERE CLASS STRATIFICATION, IF PRESENT, IS BASED ON SOMETHING OTHER THAN OCCUPATIONAL STATUS (160)	107	DRIFT MORE TOWARD BEING THOSE 0.92 OF 37 WHERE CLASS STRATIFICATION, IF PRESENT, IS BASED ON SOMETHING OTHER THAN OCCUPATIONAL STATUS (160)	40 3 126 34 XSQ= 3.72 PHI= 0.135 XP = 0.0536
109	TEND LESS TO BE THOSE 0.79 OF 236 WHERE CASTES ARE ABSENT (317)	109	TEND MORE TO BE THOSE 0.99 OF 132 WHERE CASTES ARE ABSENT (317)	50 1 186 131 XSQ= 27.91 PHI= 0.275 XP = 0.0000
110	TEND TO BE THOSE 0.52 OF 253 WHERE SLAVERY IS PRESENT (163)	110	TEND TO BE THOSE 0.75 OF 128 WHERE SLAVERY IS ABSENT (218)	131 32 122 96 XSQ= 23.82 PHI= 0.250 XP = 0.0000
116	TILT LESS TOWARD BEING THOSE 0.51 OF 37 WHERE OCCUPATIONAL SPECIALIZATION IS PART-TIME ONLY (34) JMH	116	TILT MORE TOWARD BEING THOSE 0.88 OF 17 WHERE OCCUPATIONAL SPECIALIZATION IS PART-TIME ONLY (34) JMH	18 2 19 15 XSQ= 5.31 PHI= 0.313 XP = 0.0213
128	DRIFT TOWARD BEING THOSE 0.54 OF 61 WHERE, IF SUBSISTENCE IS PRIMARILY BY AGRICULTURE, THE WORK IS MAINLY DONE BY FEMALES (37)	128	DRIFT TOWARD BEING THOSE 0.75 OF 16 WHERE, IF SUBSISTENCE IS PRIMARILY BY AGRICULTURE, THE WORK IS MAINLY DONE BY MALES (40)	28 12 33 4 XSQ= 3.21 PHI= -0.204 XP = 0.0731
129	TEND LESS TO BE THOSE 0.55 OF 56 WHERE WEAVING IS MAINLY DONE BY FEMALES (73)	129	TEND MORE TO BE THOSE 0.88 OF 48 WHERE WEAVING IS MAINLY DONE BY FEMALES (73)	25 6 31 42 XSQ= 11.27 PHI= 0.329 XP = 0.0008

1/ '

```
130  TEND TO BE THOSE                0.71 OF  34     130  TEND TO BE THOSE                0.70 OF  50         24   15
     WHERE LEATHER WORKING IS                             WHERE LEATHER WORKING IS                               10   35
     MAINLY DONE BY MALES  (39)                           MAINLY DONE BY FEMALES  (45)                      XSQ=   11.82
                                                                                                            PHI=   0.375
                                                                                                            XP =   0.0006

135  TILT TOWARD BEING THOSE         0.76 OF  25     135  TILT TOWARD BEING THOSE         0.62 OF  13         19    5
     WHERE INDIVIDUAL OWNERSHIP OF                        WHERE INDIVIDUAL OWNERSHIP OF                           6    8
     ECONOMICALLY SIGNIFICANT PROPERTY                    ECONOMICALLY SIGNIFICANT PROPERTY                 XSQ=    3.69
     IS PRESENT  (24) GES                                 IS NEGLIGIBLE OR ABSENT  (14) GES                 PHI=   0.312
                                                                                                            EP =   0.0353

143  TILT TOWARD BEING THOSE         0.50 OF  38     143  TILT TOWARD BEING THOSE         0.93 OF  14         19    1
     WHERE THE RATIO OF RESTITUTIVE                       WHERE THE RATIO OF RESTITUTIVE                         19   13
     TO REPRESSIVE SANCTIONS                              TO REPRESSIVE SANCTIONS                           XSQ=    6.23
     IS HIGH  (20) WME                                    IS MEDIUM OR LOW  (32) WME                        PHI=   0.346
                                                                                                            XP =   0.0125

144  TILT TOWARD BEING THOSE         0.63 OF  38     144  TILT TOWARD BEING THOSE         0.79 OF  14         24    3
     WHERE THE RATIO OF RESTITUTIVE                       WHERE THE RATIO OF RESTITUTIVE                         14   11
     TO REPRESSIVE SANCTIONS                              TO REPRESSIVE SANCTIONS                           XSQ=    5.56
     IS HIGH OR MEDIUM  (27) WME                          IS LOW  (25) WME                                  PHI=   0.327
                                                                                                            XP =   0.0183

176  TEND TO BE THOSE                0.53 OF 257     176  TEND TO BE THOSE                0.74 OF 125        137   32
     WHERE THE COMMUNITY IS                               WHERE THE COMMUNITY IS OTHER THAN                     120   93
     A CLAN-COMMUNITY OR A COMMUNITY                      A CLAN-COMMUNITY OR A COMMUNITY                   XSQ=   25.06
     STRUCTURED OR SEGMENTED                              STRUCTURED OR SEGMENTED                           PHI=   0.256
     ON A CLAN BASIS  (169)                               ON A CLAN BASIS  (213)                            XP =   0.0000

177  TEND LESS TO BE THOSE           0.74 OF 257     177  TEND MORE TO BE THOSE           0.91 OF 125         66   11
     WHERE THE COMMUNITY IS OTHER THAN                    WHERE THE COMMUNITY IS OTHER THAN                     191  114
     A SINGLE CLAN-COMMUNITY AND                          A SINGLE CLAN-COMMUNITY AND                       XSQ=   13.86
     EXOGAMOUS  (305)                                     EXOGAMOUS  (305)                                  PHI=   0.190
                                                                                                            XP =   0.0002

178  DRIFT LESS TOWARD BEING THOSE   0.74 OF 257     178  DRIFT MORE TOWARD BEING THOSE   0.83 OF 125         66   21
     WHERE THE COMMUNITY IS OTHER THAN                    WHERE THE COMMUNITY IS OTHER THAN                     191  104
     SEGMENTED ON A CLAN BASIS AND                        SEGMENTED ON A CLAN BASIS AND                     XSQ=    3.28
     NON-EXOGAMOUS  (295)                                 NON-EXOGAMOUS  (295)                              PHI=   0.093
                                                                                                            XP =   0.0700

180  LEAN LESS TOWARD BEING THOSE    0.63 OF 257     180  LEAN MORE TOWARD BEING THOSE    0.78 OF 125         96   28
     WHERE THE COMMUNITY IS                               WHERE THE COMMUNITY IS                                161   97
     COMMONLY NON-EXOGAMOUS, RATHER THAN                  COMMONLY NON-EXOGAMOUS, RATHER THAN               XSQ=    7.91
     EXOGAMOUS  (258)                                     EXOGAMOUS  (258)                                  PHI=   0.144
                                                                                                            XP =   0.0049

181  TEND MORE TO BE THOSE           0.93 OF 257     181  TEND LESS TO BE THOSE           0.78 OF 125         18   27
     WHERE THE COMMUNITY IS OTHER THAN                    WHERE THE COMMUNITY IS OTHER THAN                     239   98
     A DEME  (337)                                        A DEME  (337)                                     XSQ=   15.86
                                                                                                            PHI=  -0.204
                                                                                                            XP =   0.0001
```

182	DRIFT MORE TOWARD BEING THOSE 0.70 OF 257 OTHER THAN WHERE THE COMMUNITY IS STRUCTURED ON A NON-CLAN BASIS AND AGAMOUS (256)	182	DRIFT LESS TOWARD BEING THOSE 0.61 OF 125 OTHER THAN WHERE THE COMMUNITY IS STRUCTURED ON A NON-CLAN BASIS AND AGAMOUS (256)	77 49 180 76 XSQ= 2.84 PHI= -0.086 XP = 0.0918
183	TEND MORE TO BE THOSE 0.91 OF 201 WHERE THE LARGEST NON-COGNATIC KIN GROUP IS SMALLER THAN A MOEITY, I. E., A PHRATRY OR SIB OR LINEAGE (218)	183	TEND LESS TO BE THOSE 0.69 OF 51 WHERE THE LARGEST NON-COGNATIC KIN GROUP IS SMALLER THAN A MOEITY, I. E., A PHRATRY OR SIB OR LINEAGE (218)	18 16 183 35 XSQ= 15.65 PHI= -0.249 XP = 0.0001
184	TILT MORE TOWARD BEING THOSE 0.73 OF 201 WHERE THE LARGEST NON-COGNATIC KIN GROUP IS SMALLER THAN A PHRATRY, I. E. A SIB OR LINEAGE (175)	184	TILT LESS TOWARD BEING THOSE 0.55 OF 51 WHERE THE LARGEST NON-COGNATIC KIN GROUP IS SMALLER THAN A PHRATRY, I. E. A SIB OR LINEAGE (175)	54 23 147 28 XSQ= 5.54 PHI= -0.148 XP = 0.0186
186	TEND LESS TO BE THOSE 0.51 OF 265 WHERE THE KIN GROUP IS OTHER THAN EXCLUSIVELY PATRILINEAL (250)	186	TEND MORE TO BE THOSE 0.84 OF 135 WHERE THE KIN GROUP IS OTHER THAN EXCLUSIVELY PATRILINEAL (250)	129 21 136 114 XSQ= 40.47 PHI= 0.318 XP = 0.
187	LEAN MORE TOWARD BEING THOSE 0.90 OF 264 WHERE THE KIN GROUP IS OTHER THAN EXCLUSIVELY MATRILINEAL (344)	187	LEAN LESS TOWARD BEING THOSE 0.79 OF 135 WHERE THE KIN GROUP IS OTHER THAN EXCLUSIVELY MATRILINEAL (344)	27 28 237 107 XSQ= 7.45 PHI= -0.137 XP = 0.0064
188	TEND TO BE THOSE 0.76 OF 265 WHERE THE KIN GROUP IS OTHER THAN EXCLUSIVELY COGNATIC (252)	188	TEND TO BE THOSE 0.62 OF 135 WHERE THE KIN GROUP IS EXCLUSIVELY COGNATIC (148)	64 84 201 51 XSQ= 53.99 PHI= -0.367 XP = 0.
190	TEND TO BE THOSE 0.83 OF 196 WHERE THE KIN GROUP IS PATRILINEAL OR DOUBLE-DESCENT, RATHER THAN MATRILINEAL (186)	190	TEND TO BE THOSE 0.55 OF 51 WHERE THE KIN GROUP IS MATRILINEAL, RATHER THAN PATRILINEAL OR DOUBLE-DESCENT (61)	163 23 33 28 XSQ= 29.52 PHI= 0.346 XP = 0.0000
192	TEND TO BE THOSE 0.84 OF 265 OTHER THAN WHERE THE ONLY KIN GROUP PRESENT IS A KINDRED OR ELSE BILATERAL DESCENT IS INFERRED (289)	192	TEND TO BE THOSE 0.50 OF 135 WHERE THE ONLY KIN GROUP PRESENT IS A KINDRED OR ELSE BILATERAL DESCENT IS INFERRED (111)	43 68 222 67 XSQ= 50.32 PHI= -0.355 XP = 0.
196	TEND TO BE THOSE 0.81 OF 199 WHERE INDIVIDUAL RIGHTS IN REAL PROPERTY, AND RULES FOR INHERITANCE, ARE PRESENT (194)	196	TEND TO BE THOSE 0.61 OF 82 WHERE INDIVIDUAL RIGHTS IN REAL PROPERTY, OR RULES FOR INHERITANCE, ARE ABSENT (87)	162 32 37 50 XSQ= 46.84 PHI= 0.408 XP = 0.

1/

198	TILT MORE TOWARD BEING THOSE 0.91 OF 138 WHERE RULES FOR THE INHERITANCE OF REAL PROPERTY, IF PRESENT, FAVOR THE MALE HEIR OR LINE, RATHER THAN THE FEMALE (144)	198	TILT LESS TOWARD BEING THOSE 0.70 OF 27 WHERE RULES FOR THE INHERITANCE OF REAL PROPERTY, IF PRESENT, FAVOR THE MALE HEIR OR LINE, RATHER THAN THE FEMALE (144)	125 19 13 8 XSQ= 6.58 PHI= 0.200 XP = 0.0103
201	DRIFT MORE TOWARD BEING THOSE 0.86 OF 264 WHERE MARITAL RESIDENCE IS NON-OPTIONAL, RATHER THAN AMBILOCAL OR NEOLOCAL (334)	201	DRIFT LESS TOWARD BEING THOSE 0.79 OF 134 WHERE MARITAL RESIDENCE IS NON-OPTIONAL, RATHER THAN AMBILOCAL OR NEOLOCAL (334)	228 106 36 28 XSQ= 2.95 PHI= 0.086 XP = 0.0857
204	LEAN MORE TOWARD BEING THOSE 0.85 OF 243 WHERE MARITAL RESIDENCE IS PATRILOCAL, VIRILOCAL, OR AVUNCULOCAL, RATHER THAN AMBILOCAL OR NEOLOCAL (270)	204	LEAN LESS TOWARD BEING THOSE 0.69 OF 91 WHERE MARITAL RESIDENCE IS PATRILOCAL, VIRILOCAL, OR AVUNCULOCAL, RATHER THAN AMBILOCAL OR NEOLOCAL (270)	207 63 36 28 XSQ= 9.87 PHI= 0.172 XP = 0.0017
207	TILT TOWARD BEING THOSE 0.63 OF 57 WHERE MARITAL RESIDENCE IS AMBILOCAL OR NEOLOCAL, RATHER THAN MATRILOCAL OR UXORILOCAL (64)	207	TILT TOWARD BEING THOSE 0.61 OF 71 WHERE MARITAL RESIDENCE IS MATRILOCAL OR UXORILOCAL, RATHER THAN AMBILOCAL OR NEOLOCAL (64)	21 43 36 28 XSQ= 6.20 PHI= -0.220 XP = 0.0128
209	TEND MORE TO BE THOSE 0.91 OF 228 WHERE MARITAL RESIDENCE IS PATRILOCAL, VIRILOCAL, OR AVUNCULOCAL, RATHER THAN MATRILOCAL OR UXORILOCAL (270)	209	TEND LESS TO BE THOSE 0.59 OF 106 WHERE MARITAL RESIDENCE IS PATRILOCAL, VIRILOCAL, OR AVUNCULOCAL, RATHER THAN MATRILOCAL OR UXORILOCAL (270)	207 63 21 43 XSQ= 43.93 PHI= 0.363 XP = 0.
210	TEND TO BE THOSE 0.93 OF 164 WHERE MARITAL RESIDENCE IS PATRILOCAL, RATHER THAN MATRILOCAL (169)	210	TEND TO BE THOSE 0.56 OF 36 WHERE MARITAL RESIDENCE IS MATRILOCAL, RATHER THAN PATRILOCAL (31)	153 16 11 20 XSQ= 50.12 PHI= 0.501 XP = 0.
213	TILT TOWARD BEING THOSE 0.51 OF 245 WHERE FIRST COUSIN MARRIAGE IS PERMITTED (172)	213	TILT TOWARD BEING THOSE 0.62 OF 125 WHERE FIRST COUSIN MARRIAGE IS NOT PERMITTED (198)	124 48 121 77 XSQ= 4.48 PHI= 0.110 XP = 0.0342
220	TILT LESS TOWARD BEING THOSE 0.70 OF 245 WHERE FIRST COUSIN MARRIAGE IN SOME FORM OR OTHER IS NOT PRESCRIBED OR PREFERRED (273)	220	TILT MORE TOWARD BEING THOSE 0.81 OF 125 WHERE FIRST COUSIN MARRIAGE IN SOME FORM OR OTHER IS NOT PRESCRIBED OR PREFERRED (273)	73 24 172 101 XSQ= 4.27 PHI= 0.107 XP = 0.0387
	TILT LESS TOWARD BEING THOSE 0.88 OF 245 WHERE MATRILATERAL CROSS-COUSIN MARRIAGE S NOT PRESCRIBED OR PREFERRED (335)	221	TILT MORE TOWARD BEING THOSE 0.96 OF 125 WHERE MATRILATERAL CROSS-COUSIN MARRIAGE IS NOT PRESCRIBED OR PREFERRED (335)	30 5 215 120 XSQ= 5.64 PHI= 0.123 XP = 0.0175

1/

.24	TILT LESS TOWARD BEING THOSE 0.56 OF 124 WHERE COUSIN MARRIAGE IS PREFERENTIALLY OR PERMISSIVELY SYMMETRICAL, RATHER THAN EITHER PATRI- OR MATRILATERAL (106)	224	TILT MORE TOWARD BEING THOSE 0.77 OF 48 WHERE COUSIN MARRIAGE IS PREFERENTIALLY OR PERMISSIVELY SYMMETRICAL, RATHER THAN EITHER PATRI- OR MATRILATERAL (106)	55 11 69 37 XSQ= 5.85 PHI= 0.184 XP = 0.0156
240	DRIFT MORE TOWARD BEING THOSE 0.68 OF 140 WHERE THE FAMILY, IF EXTENDED, IS SMALL OR STEM, RATHER THAN LARGE (135)	240	DRIFT LESS TOWARD BEING THOSE 0.55 OF 73 WHERE THE FAMILY, IF EXTENDED, IS SMALL OR STEM, RATHER THAN LARGE (135)	45 33 95 40 XSQ= 2.99 PHI= -0.118 XP = 0.0839
262	TEND MORE TO BE THOSE 0.86 OF 264 WHERE WIVES ARE OBTAINED BY MEANS INVOLVING THE PRESENCE OF SOME CONSIDERATION (305)	262	TEND LESS TO BE THOSE 0.60 OF 131 WHERE WIVES ARE OBTAINED BY MEANS INVOLVING THE PRESENCE OF SOME CONSIDERATION (305)	227 78 37 53 XSQ= 33.31 PHI= 0.290 XP = 0.
263	TEND TO BE THOSE 0.67 OF 264 WHERE WIVES ARE OBTAINED BY RELATIVELY DIFFICULT MEANS, NAMELY BY BRIDE-PRICE, BRIDE-SERVICE, OR EXCHANGING A FEMALE RELATIVE (233)	263	TEND TO BE THOSE 0.58 OF 131 WHERE WIVES ARE OBTAINED BY RELATIVELY EASY MEANS, NAMELY BY TOKEN BRIDE-PRICE, GIFT EXCHANGE, ABSENCE OF ANY CONSIDERATION, OR RECEIPT OF DOWRY (162)	178 55 86 76 XSQ= 22.38 PHI= 0.238 XP = 0.0000
299	DRIFT LESS TOWARD BEING THOSE 0.66 OF 79 WHERE THE POST-PARTUM SEX TABOO LASTS ONE YEAR OR LESS (89)	299	DRIFT MORE TOWARD BEING THOSE 0.82 OF 45 WHERE THE POST-PARTUM SEX TABOO LASTS ONE YEAR OR LESS (89)	27 8 52 37 XSQ= 3.04 PHI= 0.157 XP = 0.0813
304	TILT TOWARD BEING THOSE 0.66 OF 29 WHERE THE EARLY ANAL SATISFACTION POTENTIAL IS LOW (22) W-C	304	TILT TOWARD BEING THOSE 0.75 OF 12 WHERE THE EARLY ANAL SATISFACTION POTENTIAL IS HIGH (19) W-C	10 9 19 3 XSQ= 4.09 PHI= -0.316 XP = 0.0431
305	TILT TOWARD BEING THOSE 0.64 OF 36 WHERE THE EARLY SEXUAL SATISFACTION POTENTIAL IS HIGH (27) W-C	305	TILT TOWARD BEING THOSE 0.73 OF 15 WHERE THE EARLY SEXUAL SATISFACTION POTENTIAL IS LOW (24) W-C	23 4 13 11 XSQ= 4.49 PHI= 0.297 XP = 0.0341
307	DRIFT TOWARD BEING THOSE 0.72 OF 36 WHERE THE EARLY AGGRESSION SATISFACTION POTENTIAL IS HIGH (33) W-C	307	DRIFT TOWARD BEING THOSE 0.56 OF 16 WHERE THE EARLY AGGRESSION SATISFACTION POTENTIAL IS LOW (19) W-C	26 7 10 9 XSQ= 2.74 PHI= 0.230 XP = 0.0977
314	TILT LESS TOWARD BEING THOSE 0.67 OF 51 WHERE THE INCIDENCE OF MOTHER-CHILD HOUSEHOLDS IS LOW (61) W-D,S	314	TILT MORE TOWARD BEING THOSE 0.93 OF 29 WHERE THE INCIDENCE OF MOTHER-CHILD HOUSEHOLDS IS LOW (61) W-D,S	17 2 34 27 XSQ= 5.75 PHI= 0.268 XP = 0.0165

1/

319	LEAN TOWARD BEING THOSE 0.63 OF 38 WHERE PROTECTION OF THE INFANT FROM ENVIRONMENTAL DISCOMFORTS IS LOW (30) B-B-C	319	LEAN TOWARD BEING THOSE 0.78 OF 27 WHERE PROTECTION OF THE INFANT FROM ENVIRONMENTAL DISCOMFORTS IS HIGH (35) B-B-C	14 21 24 6 XSQ= 9.06 PHI= -0.373 XP = 0.0026
320	TILT LESS TOWARD BEING THOSE 0.55 OF 44 WHERE THE DEGREE OF REDUCTION OF THE INFANT'S DRIVES IS HIGH (45) B-B-C	320	TILT MORE TOWARD BEING THOSE 0.84 OF 25 WHERE THE DEGREE OF REDUCTION OF THE INFANT'S DRIVES IS HIGH (45) B-B-C	24 21 20 4 XSQ= 4.87 PHI= -0.266 XP = 0.0274
333	TILT TOWARD BEING THOSE 0.73 OF 11 WHERE THE AGE AT BEGINNING OF TRAINING IN HETEROSEXUAL PLAY INHIBITION IS EIGHT YEARS OR HIGHER (8) W-C	333	IN ALL CASES ARE THOSE 1.00 OF 5 WHERE THE AGE AT BEGINNING OF TRAINING IN HETEROSEXUAL PLAY INHIBITION IS LOWER THAN EIGHT YEARS (8) W-C	8 0 3 5 XSQ= 4.65 PHI= 0.539 EP = 0.0256
337	TILT TOWARD BEING THOSE 0.64 OF 45 WHERE THE CHILD'S INFERRED ANXIETY OVER NON-PERFORMANCE OF RESPONSIBLE BEHAVIOR IS HIGH (38) B-B-C	337	TILT TOWARD BEING THOSE 0.68 OF 28 WHERE THE CHILD'S INFERRED ANXIETY OVER NON-PERFORMANCE OF RESPONSIBLE BEHAVIOR IS LOW (35) B-B-C	29 9 16 19 XSQ= 5.98 PHI= 0.286 XP = 0.0145
339	TILT TOWARD BEING THOSE 0.53 OF 45 WHERE THE CHILD'S INFERRED CONFLICT REGARDING RESPONSIBLE BEHAVIOR IS HIGH (31) B-B-C	339	TILT TOWARD BEING THOSE 0.75 OF 28 WHERE THE CHILD'S INFERRED CONFLICT REGARDING RESPONSIBLE BEHAVIOR IS LOW (42) B-B-C	24 7 21 21 XSQ= 4.57 PHI= 0.250 XP = 0.0325
342	TILT TOWARD BEING THOSE 0.54 OF 26 WHERE THE CHILD'S INFERRED ANXIETY OVER PERFORMANCE OF NURTURANT BEHAVIOR IS HIGH (18) B-B-C	342	TILT TOWARD BEING THOSE 0.80 OF 20 WHERE THE CHILD'S INFERRED ANXIETY OVER PERFORMANCE OF NURTURANT BEHAVIOR IS LOW (28) B-B-C	14 4 12 16 XSQ= 4.11 PHI= 0.299 XP = 0.0427
356	TILT TOWARD BEING THOSE 0.68 OF 37 WHERE ADOLESCENT PEER GROUPS OR PAIRS ARE PRESENT IN A SETTING OF COURTSHIP (29) JKH	356	TILT TOWARD BEING THOSE 0.71 OF 14 WHERE NEITHER ADOLESCENT PEER GROUPS NOR PAIRS ARE PRESENT IN A SETTING OF COURTSHIP (22) JKH	25 4 12 10 XSQ= 4.81 PHI= 0.307 XP = 0.0283
358	LEAN MORE TOWARD BEING THOSE 0.91 OF 35 WHERE ADOLESCENT PEER GROUPS ARE PRESENT IN A SETTING OF WORK AND PUBLIC GATHERINGS AND LEISURE, OR OF PUBLIC GATHERINGS AND LEISURE, OR OF LEISURE ONLY (41) JKH	358	LEAN LESS TOWARD BEING THOSE 0.53 OF 17 WHERE ADOLESCENT PEER GROUPS ARE PRESENT IN A SETTING OF WORK AND PUBLIC GATHERINGS AND LEISURE, OR OF PUBLIC GATHERINGS AND LEISURE, OR OF LEISURE ONLY (41) JKH	32 9 3 8 XSQ= 7.99 PHI= 0.392 XP = 0.0047
0	DRIFT TOWARD BEING THOSE 0.50 OF 24 WHERE ADOLESCENT PEER GROUPS ARE PRESENT IN A SETTING OF WORK AND PUBLIC GATHERINGS AND LEISURE, OR AT LEAST OF PUBLIC GATHERINGS AND LEISURE (14) JKH	360	DRIFT TOWARD BEING THOSE 0.85 OF 13 WHERE ADOLESCENT PEER GROUPS ARE PRESENT ONLY IN A SETTING OF LEISURE, OR ELSE ARE ABSENT (23) JKH	12 2 12 11 XSQ= 2.95 PHI= 0.282 EP = 0.0740

No.	Subject	Proportion	No.	Subject	Proportion	Statistics
370	TEND LESS TO BE THOSE WHERE THE SEGREGATION OF ADOLESCENT BOYS IS ABSENT (148)	0.51 OF 169	370	TEND MORE TO BE THOSE WHERE THE SEGREGATION OF ADOLESCENT BOYS IS ABSENT (148)	0.82 OF 74	82 13 87 61 XSQ= 19.43 PHI= 0.283 XP = 0.0000
372	TEND TO BE THOSE WHERE MALE INITIATION RITES ARE PRESENT (48) ASA	0.57 OF 67	372	TEND TO BE THOSE WHERE MALE INITIATION RITES ARE ABSENT (63) ASA	0.77 OF 44	38 10 29 34 XSQ= 11.15 PHI= 0.317 XP = 0.0008
373	DRIFT TOWARD BEING THOSE WHERE MALE INITIATION CEREMONIES AT PUBERTY ARE ABSENT (27) W-K-A	0.72 OF 29	373	DRIFT TOWARD BEING THOSE WHERE MALE INITIATION CEREMONIES AT PUBERTY ARE PRESENT (17) W-K-A	0.60 OF 15	8 9 21 6 XSQ= 3.12 PHI= -0.266 XP = 0.0773
377	TEND LESS TO BE THOSE WHERE MALE GENITAL MUTILATION IS ABSENT (242)	0.61 OF 207	377	TEND MORE TO BE THOSE WHERE MALE GENITAL MUTILATION IS ABSENT (242)	0.98 OF 118	81 2 126 116 XSQ= 53.44 PHI= 0.405 XP = 0.
382	LEAN TOWARD BEING THOSE WHERE FEMALE INITIATION RITES ARE ABSENT (27) JKB	0.56 OF 39	382	LEAN TOWARD BEING THOSE WHERE FEMALE INITIATION RITES ARE PRESENT (38) JKB	0.81 OF 26	17 21 22 5 XSQ= 7.41 PHI= -0.338 XP = 0.0065
403	DRIFT LESS TOWARD BEING THOSE WHERE EXPLANATICNS OF ILLNESS OF AN ANAL NATURE ARE ABSENT (38) W-C	0.52 OF 40	403	DRIFT MORE TOWARD BEING THOSE WHERE EXPLANATIONS OF ILLNESS OF AN ANAL NATURE ARE ABSENT (38) W-C	0.81 OF 21	19 4 21 17 XSQ= 3.61 PHI= 0.243 XP = 0.0574
405	DRIFT TOWARD BEING THOSE WHERE EXPLANATICNS OF ILLNESS OF A DEPENDENCE NATURE ARE PRESENT (34) W-C	0.65 OF 40	405	DRIFT TOWARD BEING THOSE WHERE EXPLANATIONS OF ILLNESS OF A DEPENDENCE NATURE ARE ABSENT (27) W-C	0.62 OF 21	26 8 14 13 XSQ= 3.02 PHI= 0.223 XP = 0.0821
421	DRIFT TOWARD BEING THOSE WHERE KILLING, TORTURING, OR MUTILATING OF THE ENEMY IS NEGLIGIBLY EMPHASIZED (47) PES	0.64 OF 53	421	DRIFT TOWARD BEING THOSE WHERE KILLING, TORTURING, OR MUTILATING OF THE ENEMY IS STRONGLY OR MODERATELY EMPHASIZED (37) PES	0.58 OF 31	19 18 34 13 XSQ= 3.07 PHI= -0.191 XP = 0.0799
426	TILT TOWARD BEING THOSE WHERE A HIGH GOD IS PRESENT (156) GES,EA	0.65 OF 168	426	TILT TOWARD BEING THOSE WHERE A HIGH GOD IS ABSENT (104) GES,EA	0.50 OF 92	110 46 58 46 XSQ= 5.31 PHI= 0.143 XP = 0.0213

No.	Statement		No.	Statement		Statistics
438	TILT TOWARD BEING THOSE 0.75 OF WHERE OTHER-WORLDLY FEARS OF GHOSTS OR SPIRITS ARE GREATER THAN THIS-WORLDLY FEARS OF HUMANS OR ANIMALS (27) W-C,JFG	28	438	TILT TOWARD BEING THOSE 0.63 OF WHERE THIS-WORLDLY FEARS OF HUMANS OR ANIMALS ARE GREATER THAN OTHER-WORLDLY FEARS OF GHOSTS OR SPIRITS (17) W-C,JFG	16	21 6 7 10 XSQ= 4.56 PHI= 0.322 XP = 0.0327
452	DRIFT TOWARD BEING THOSE 0.53 OF WHERE TOTEMISM WITH FOOD TABOOS IS PRESENT (19) WNS	32	452	DRIFT TOWARD BEING THOSE 0.82 OF WHERE TOTEMISM WITH FOOD TABOOS IS ABSENT (24) WNS	11	17 2 15 9 XSQ= 2.76 PHI= 0.253 XP = 0.0967
455	TILT TOWARD BEING THOSE 0.70 OF WHERE THE MODE OF THE INDIVIDUAL'S CONTACT WITH THE DIVINE IS NOT CONDUCIVE TO THE DEVELOPMENT OF THE INDIVIDUAL'S NEED TO ACHIEVE (19) DCM	20	455	TILT TOWARD BEING THOSE 0.69 OF WHERE THE MODE OF THE INDIVIDUAL'S CONTACT WITH THE DIVINE IS CONDUCIVE TO THE DEVELOPMENT OF THE INDIVIDUAL'S NEED TO ACHIEVE (17) DCM	16	6 11 14 5 XSQ= 3.91 PHI= -0.330 EP = 0.0425
456	TILT TOWARD BEING THOSE 0.65 OF WHERE THE INTERNALIZATION OF THE INDIVIDUAL'S CONTACT WITH THE DIVINE IS NOT CONDUCIVE TO THE DEVELOPMENT OF THE INDIVIDUAL'S NEED TO ACHIEVE (17) DCM	20	456	TILT TOWARD BEING THOSE 0.75 OF WHERE THE INTERNALIZATION OF THE INDIVIDUAL'S CONTACT WITH THE DIVINE IS CONDUCIVE TO THE DEVELOPMENT OF THE INDIVIDUAL'S NEED TO ACHIEVE (19) DCM	16	7 12 13 4 XSQ= 4.21 PHI= -0.342 EP = 0.0228
458	TEND LESS TO BE THOSE 0.51 OF WHERE GAMES, IF PRESENT, DO NOT INCLUDE GAMES OF STRATEGY (119) R-A-B,EA	98	458	TEND MORE TO BE THOSE 0.95 OF WHERE GAMES, IF PRESENT, DO NOT INCLUDE GAMES OF STRATEGY (119) R-A-B,EA	73	48 4 50 69 XSQ= 35.38 PHI= 0.455 XP = 0.
459	TEND TO BE THOSE 0.66 OF WHERE GAMES, IF PRESENT, DO NOT INCLUDE GAMES OF CHANCE (89) R-A-B,EA	98	459	TEND TO BE THOSE 0.67 OF WHERE GAMES, IF PRESENT, INCLUDE GAMES OF CHANCE (82) R-A-B,EA	73	33 49 65 24 XSQ= 17.44 PHI= -0.319 XP = 0.0000
468	DRIFT LESS TOWARD BEING THOSE 0.59 OF WHERE CONTACT WITH OTHER CULTURES IS REGULAR OR IRREGULAR, RATHER THAN FREQUENT (37) JMH	37	468	DRIFT MORE TOWARD BEING THOSE 0.88 OF WHERE CONTACT WITH OTHER CULTURES IS REGULAR OR IRREGULAR, RATHER THAN FREQUENT (37) JMH	17	15 2 22 15 XSQ= 3.24 PHI= 0.245 XP = 0.0720
476	TILT TOWARD BEING THOSE 0.50 OF WHERE THE DEGREE OF INSOBRIETY IS MODERATE OR SLIGHT (18) DH	30	476	TILT TOWARD BEING THOSE 0.84 OF WHERE THE DEGREE OF INSOBRIETY IS STRONG (31) DH	19	15 16 15 3 XSQ= 4.48 PHI= -0.302 XP = 0.0343

2 CULTURES
LOCATED IN THE CIRCUM-MEDITERRANEAN OR
EAST EURASIAN AREA (115)

2 CULTURES
LOCATED OUTSIDE OF
THE CIRCUM-MEDITERRANEAN OR
EAST EURASIAN AREA (285)

BACKGROUND ON PAGE 65

NEITHER SUBJECT NOR PREDICATE

115 IN LEFT COLUMN

ABOR	AINU	AKHA	ALBANIANS	AMERICANS	ANDAMANESE	ARYANS	BARABRA	BASQUES	BASSERI
BEJA	BENGALI	BHIL	BHUIYA	BOERS	BRAZILIANS	BUDUMA	BULGARIANS	BURMESE	BURUSHO
BURYAT	CAMBODIANS	CHENCHU	CHEREMIS	CHERKESS	CHUKCHEE	COORG	CZECHS	DAGUR	DARD
DUTCH	EGYPTIANS	GARO	GILYAK	GOND	HASANIA	HAZARA	HEBREWS	HO	HUTSUL
ICELANDERS	IRAQW	IRISH	JAPANESE	KABYLE	KACHIN	KALMYK	KAREN	KAZAK	KERALA
KET	KHALKA	KHASI	KHEVSUR	KOHISTANI	KOL	KONSO	KOREANS	KORYAK	KUMYK
LAKHER	LAMET	LAPPS	LEPCHA	LHOTA NAGA	LOLO	MAGUZAWA	MALAYS	MANCHU	MERINA
MIAO	MIN CHINESE	MINCHIA	MNONG GAR	MONGUOR	MZAB	NICOBARESE	NURI	OKINAWANS	ORAON
PATHAN	PORTUGUESE	PURUM	REGEIBAT	RIFFIANS	ROMANS	RWALA	SAMOYED	SANTAL	SELUNG
SEMANG	SERBS	SHLUH	SINDHI	SINHALESE	SIWANS	SOMALI	SONGHAI	SYRIANS	TAMIL
TANALA	TEDA	TERA	THAI	TIBETANS	TIGRINYA	TODA	TRISTAN	TURKMEN	VEDDA
VIETNAMESE	WALLOONS	WOLOF	YAKUT	YUKAGHIR					

285 IN RIGHT COLUMN

3 CULTURES LOCATED IN AFRICA (80)

3 CULTURES LOCATED OUTSIDE OF AFRICA (320)

BACKGROUND ON PAGE 65

BOTH SUBJECT AND PREDICATE

80 IN LEFT COLUMN

AMBA	ASHANTI	AZANDE	BABWA	BAJUN	BAMBARA	BAMILEKE	BANDA	BARI	BAYA
BEMBA	BERGDAMA	BETE	BIRIFOR	BOZO	CHAGGA	DILLING	DOGON	DOROBO	FANG
FON	FUTAJALONKE	GANDA	GISU	GURE	HEHE	HERERO	ILA	INGASSANA	JUKUN
KATAB	KIKUYU	KISSI	KPE	KUBA	KUNG	LAMBA	LANGO	LOZI	LUBA
LUO	MAMBILA	MAMVU	MARGI	MASAI	MATAKAM	MBUGWE	MBUNDU	MBUTI	MENDE
MONGO	MOSSI	NAMA	NANDI	NDEMBU	NGONI	NUER	NUPE	NYAKYUSA	NYANEKA
NYARO	NYORO	PENDE	RUNDI	SANDAWE	SHILLUK	SOTHO	SWAZI	TALLENSI	TENDA
TESO	THONGA	TIV	TURKANA	VENDA	WUTE	YAKO	YAO	YOMBE	YORUBA

320 IN RIGHT COLUMN

	Left column (80)			Right column (320)		
14	IN ALL CASES ARE THOSE WHERE THE LATITUDE IS LESS THAN THIRTY DEGREES (281)	1.00 OF 80	14	TEND LESS TO BE THOSE WHERE THE LATITUDE IS LESS THAN THIRTY DEGREES (281)	0.63 OF 320	0 119 80 201 XSQ= 40.59 PHI= -0.319 XP = 0.
15	TEND TO BE THOSE WHERE THE LATITUDE IS LESS THAN TWENTY DEGREES (217)	0.90 OF 80	15	TEND TO BE THOSE WHERE THE LATITUDE IS TWENTY DEGREES OR GREATER (183)	0.55 OF 320	8 175 72 145 XSQ= 49.71 PHI= -0.353 XP = 0.
16	TEND TO BE THOSE WHERE THE LATITUDE IS LESS THAN TEN DEGREES (123)	0.59 OF 80	16	TEND TO BE THOSE WHERE THE LATITUDE IS TEN DEGREES OR GREATER (277)	0.76 OF 320	33 244 47 76 XSQ= 35.19 PHI= -0.297 XP = 0.
33	DRIFT MORE TOWARD BEING THOSE WHERE THE NATURAL ENVIRONMENT IS OTHER THAN 'VERY HARSH,' I.E., DESERT, DESERT GRASSES AND SHRUBS, TUNDRA, OR HIGH PLATEAU STEPPE (341) FWM	0.92 OF 80	33	DRIFT LESS TOWARD BEING THOSE WHERE THE NATURAL ENVIRONMENT IS OTHER THAN 'VERY HARSH,' I.E., DESERT, DESERT GRASSES AND SHRUBS, TUNDRA, OR HIGH PLATEAU STEPPE (341) FWM	0.83 OF 320	6 53 74 267 XSQ= 3.49 PHI= -0.093 XP = 0.0617
36	DRIFT MORE TOWARD BEING THOSE WHERE THE NATURAL ENVIRONMENT IS OTHER THAN 'VERY HARSH,' OR SUB-TROPICAL BUSH, OR TEMPERATE GRASSLAND (292) FWM	0.81 OF 80	36	DRIFT LESS TOWARD BEING THOSE WHERE THE NATURAL ENVIRONMENT IS OTHER THAN 'VERY HARSH,' OR SUB-TROPICAL BUSH, OR TEMPERATE GRASSLAND (292) FWM	0.71 OF 320	15 93 65 227 XSQ= 2.95 PHI= -0.086 XP = 0.0859

42	LEAN MORE TOWARD BEING THOSE 0.75 OF 80 WHERE THE NATURAL ENVIRONMENT IS OTHER THAN TROPICAL OR SUB-TROPICAL RAIN FOREST, OR MONSOON FOREST (244) FWM	42	LEAN LESS TOWARD BEING THOSE 0.57 OF 320 WHERE THE NATURAL ENVIRONMENT IS OTHER THAN TROPICAL OR SUB-TROPICAL RAIN FOREST, OR MONSOON FOREST (244) FWM	20 136 60 184 XSQ= 7.52 PHI= -0.137 XP = 0.0061
44	TILT MORE TOWARD BEING THOSE 0.80 OF 69 WHERE SETTLEMENTS ARE FIXED (222)	44	TILT LESS TOWARD BEING THOSE 0.63 OF 263 WHERE SETTLEMENTS ARE FIXED (222)	55 167 14 96 XSQ= 5.77 PHI= 0.132 XP = 0.0163
45	TEND TO BE THOSE 0.56 OF 55 WHERE SETTLEMENTS, IF FIXED, ARE NON-COMPACT, RATHER THAN COMPACT (73)	45	TEND TO BE THOSE 0.75 OF 167 WHERE SETTLEMENTS, IF FIXED, ARE COMPACT, RATHER THAN NON-COMPACT (149)	24 125 31 42 XSQ= 16.88 PHI= -0.276 XP = 0.0000
46	TILT MORE TOWARD BEING THOSE 0.88 OF 69 OTHER THAN WHERE SETTLEMENTS ARE NON-FIXED AND MOVEMENT IS NOMADIC (260)	46	TILT LESS TOWARD BEING THOSE 0.76 OF 263 OTHER THAN WHERE SETTLEMENTS ARE NON-FIXED AND MOVEMENT IS NOMADIC (260)	8 64 61 199 XSQ= 4.50 PHI= -0.116 XP = 0.0339
51	TEND MORE TO BE THOSE 0.88 OF 80 WHERE SUBSISTENCE IS PRIMARILY BY FOOD PRODUCTION -- I. E., AGRICULTURE OR HUSBANDRY -- RATHER THAN BY GATHERING (253)	51	TEND LESS TO BE THOSE 0.57 OF 320 WHERE SUBSISTENCE IS PRIMARILY BY FOOD PRODUCTION -- I. E., AGRICULTURE OR HUSBANDRY -- RATHER THAN BY GATHERING (253)	70 183 10 137 XSQ= 24.01 PHI= 0.245 XP = 0.0000
54	LEAN MORE TOWARD BEING THOSE 0.94 OF 63 WHERE FOOD PRODUCTION IS BY INTENSIVE OR SIMPLE AGRICULTURE, RATHER THAN BY INCIPIENT FOOD PRODUCTION (192)	54	LEAN LESS TOWARD BEING THOSE 0.76 OF 175 WHERE FOOD PRODUCTION IS BY INTENSIVE OR SIMPLE AGRICULTURE, RATHER THAN BY INCIPIENT FOOD PRODUCTION (192)	59 133 4 42 XSQ= 8.16 PHI= 0.185 XP = 0.0043
55	TILT TOWARD BEING THOSE 0.66 OF 59 WHERE FOOD PRODUCTION IS BY SIMPLE AGRICULTURE, RATHER THAN BY INTENSIVE AGRICULTURE (101)	55	TILT TOWARD BEING THOSE 0.53 OF 133 WHERE FOOD PRODUCTION IS BY INTENSIVE AGRICULTURE, RATHER THAN BY SIMPLE AGRICULTURE (91)	20 71 39 62 XSQ= 5.47 PHI= -0.169 XP = 0.0194
56	TEND MORE TO BE THOSE 0.91 OF 43 WHERE FOOD PRODUCTION IS BY SIMPLE AGRICULTURE, RATHER THAN BY INCIPIENT FOOD PRODUCTION (101)	56	TEND LESS TO BE THOSE 0.60 OF 104 WHERE FOOD PRODUCTION IS BY SIMPLE AGRICULTURE, RATHER THAN BY INCIPIENT FOOD PRODUCTION (101)	39 62 4 42 XSQ= 12.26 PHI= 0.289 XP = 0.0005
62	TEND MORE TO BE THOSE 0.76 OF 80 WHERE HUSBANDRY OF SOME KIND IS PRESENT (228)	62	TEND LESS TO BE THOSE 0.52 OF 320 WHERE HUSBANDRY OF SOME KIND IS PRESENT (228)	61 167 19 153 XSQ= 14.15 PHI= 0.188 XP = 0.0002

71	TEND TO BE THOSE WHERE METAL WORKING IS PRESENT (98)	0.85 OF 47	71	TEND TO BE THOSE WHERE METAL WORKING IS ABSENT (153)	0.72 OF 204	40 58 7 146 XSQ= 49.20 PHI= 0.443 XP = 0.
73	DRIFT TOWARD BEING THOSE WHERE WEAVING IS ABSENT (130)	0.66 OF 44	73	DRIFT TOWARD BEING THOSE WHERE WEAVING IS PRESENT (118)	0.50 OF 204	15 103 29 101 XSQ= 3.27 PHI= -0.115 XP = 0.0704
74	TEND MORE TO BE THOSE WHERE POTTERY IS PRESENT (145)	0.84 OF 45	74	TEND LESS TO BE THOSE WHERE POTTERY IS PRESENT (145)	0.55 OF 193	38 107 7 86 XSQ= 11.71 PHI= 0.222 XP = 0.0006
79	DRIFT MORE TOWARD BEING THOSE WHERE NO CITY IS PRESENT (201)	0.98 OF 47	79	DRIFT LESS TOWARD BEING THOSE WHERE NO CITY IS PRESENT (201)	0.88 OF 177	1 22 46 155 XSQ= 3.23 PHI= -0.120 XP = 0.0722
82	DRIFT MORE TOWARD BEING THOSE WHERE A CITY OR TOWN IS PRESENT, OR THE AVERAGE COMMUNITY SIZE IS FIFTY OR GREATER (178)	0.89 OF 47	82	DRIFT LESS TOWARD BEING THOSE WHERE A CITY OR TOWN IS PRESENT, OR THE AVERAGE COMMUNITY SIZE IS FIFTY OR GREATER (178)	0.77 OF 177	42 136 5 41 XSQ= 2.84 PHI= 0.113 XP = 0.0917
83	LEAN LESS TOWARD BEING THOSE WHERE, WITH NO CITY AND NO TOWN PRESENT, THE AVERAGE COMMUNITY SIZE IS SMALLER THAN 200, RATHER THAN BETWEEN 200 AND 999 (135)	0.57 OF 40	83	LEAN MORE TOWARD BEING THOSE WHERE, WITH NO CITY AND NO TOWN PRESENT, THE AVERAGE COMMUNITY SIZE IS SMALLER THAN 200, RATHER THAN BETWEEN 200 AND 999 (135)	0.80 OF 140	17 28 23 112 XSQ= 7.24 PHI= 0.201 XP = 0.0071
85	LEAN LESS TOWARD BEING THOSE WHERE THE LEVEL OF POLITICAL INTEGRATION IS THE MINIMAL STATE, THE AUTONOMOUS COMMUNITY, OR THE FAMILY (234) GPM	0.63 OF 60	85	LEAN MORE TOWARD BEING THOSE WHERE THE LEVEL OF POLITICAL INTEGRATION IS THE MINIMAL STATE, THE AUTONOMOUS COMMUNITY, OR THE FAMILY (234) GPM	0.80 OF 244	22 48 38 196 XSQ= 6.92 PHI= 0.151 XP = 0.0085
88	LEAN MORE TOWARD BEING THOSE WHERE, IF A HEADMANSHIP IS PRESENT, SUCCESSION IS HEREDITARY (165)	0.78 OF 60	88	LEAN LESS TOWARD BEING THOSE WHERE, IF A HEADMANSHIP IS PRESENT, SUCCESSION IS HEREDITARY (165)	0.56 OF 211	13 93 47 118 XSQ= 8.93 PHI= -0.182 XP = 0.0028
96	TILT TOWARD BEING THOSE WHERE THE HIERARCHY OF NATIONAL JURISDICTION HAS FOUR, THREE, TWO OR ONE LEVEL (174) GES,EA	0.65 OF 69	96	TILT TOWARD BEING THOSE WHERE THE HIERARCHY OF NATIONAL JURISDICTION HAS NO LEVELS (156) GES,EA	0.51 OF 261	45 129 24 132 XSQ= 4.85 PHI= 0.121 XP = 0.0277

97	LEAN LESS TOWARD BEING THOSE 0.70 OF 69 WHERE THE HIERARCHY OF LOCAL JURISDICTION HAS THREE OR TWO LEVELS (273) GES,EA	97	LEAN MORE TOWARD BEING THOSE 0.86 OF 262 WHERE THE HIERARCHY OF LOCAL JURISDICTION HAS THREE OR TWO LEVELS (273) GES,EA		21 37 48 225 XSQ= 8.96 PHI= 0.165 XP = 0.0028
99	DRIFT MORE TOWARD BEING THOSE 0.79 OF 24 WHERE, WITH NATIONAL HIERARCHY ABSENT, THE HIERARCHY OF LOCAL JURISDICTION HAS FOUR OR THREE LEVELS (93) GES,EA	99	DRIFT LESS TOWARD BEING THOSE 0.56 OF 132 WHERE, WITH NATIONAL HIERARCHY ABSENT, THE HIERARCHY OF LOCAL JURISDICTION HAS FOUR OR THREE LEVELS (93) GES,EA		19 74 5 58 XSQ= 3.59 PHI= 0.152 XP = 0.0580
100	LEAN MORE TOWARD BEING THOSE 0.93 OF 69 WHERE HIERARCHIES ARE MORE COMPLEX THAN THE 'SIMPLEST,' I. E., MORE COMPLEX THAN TWO LOCAL LEVELS WITH NO NATIONAL LEVELS (267) GES,EA	100	LEAN LESS TOWARD BEING THOSE 0.78 OF 261 WHERE HIERARCHIES ARE MORE COMPLEX THAN THE 'SIMPLEST,' I. E., MORE COMPLEX THAN TWO LOCAL LEVELS WITH NO NATIONAL LEVELS (267) GES,EA		64 203 5 58 XSQ= 6.98 PHI= 0.145 XP = 0.0082
108	TEND TO BE THOSE 0.59 OF 44 WHERE CLASS STRATIFICATION, IF PRESENT, IS BASED ON A HEREDITARY ARISTOCRACY (74)	108	TEND TO BE THOSE 0.70 OF 159 WHERE CLASS STRATIFICATION, IF PRESENT, IS BASED ON SOMETHING OTHER THAN A HEREDITARY ARISTOCRACY (129)		26 48 18 111 XSQ= 11.21 PHI= 0.235 XP = 0.0008
109	DRIFT LESS TOWARD BEING THOSE 0.80 OF 79 WHERE CASTES ARE ABSENT (317)	109	DRIFT MORE TOWARD BEING THOSE 0.88 OF 289 WHERE CASTES ARE ABSENT (317)		16 35 63 254 XSQ= 2.80 PHI= 0.087 XP = 0.0944
110	TEND TO BE THOSE 0.72 OF 79 WHERE SLAVERY IS PRESENT (163)	110	TEND TO BE THOSE 0.65 OF 302 WHERE SLAVERY IS ABSENT (218)		57 106 22 196 XSQ= 33.62 PHI= 0.297 XP = 0.
128	TEND TO BE THOSE 0.73 OF 30 WHERE, IF SUBSISTENCE IS PRIMARILY BY AGRICULTURE, THE WORK IS MAINLY DONE BY FEMALES (37)	128	TEND TO BE THOSE 0.68 OF 47 WHERE, IF SUBSISTENCE IS PRIMARILY BY AGRICULTURE, THE WORK IS MAINLY DONE BY MALES (40)		8 32 22 15 XSQ= 10.98 PHI= -0.378 XP = 0.0009
129	IN ALL CASES ARE THOSE 1.00 OF 12 WHERE WEAVING IS MAINLY DONE BY MALES (31)	129	TEND TO BE THOSE 0.79 OF 92 WHERE WEAVING IS MAINLY DONE BY FEMALES (73)		12 19 0 73 XSQ= 28.26 PHI= 0.521 XP = 0.0000
130	TILT TOWARD BEING THOSE 0.79 OF 14 WHERE LEATHER WORKING IS MAINLY DONE BY MALES (39)	130	TILT TOWARD BEING THOSE 0.60 OF 70 WHERE LEATHER WORKING IS MAINLY DONE BY FEMALES (45)		11 28 3 42 XSQ= 5.51 PHI= 0.256 XP = 0.0189

138	DRIFT TOWARD BEING THOSE WHERE SUPERORDINATE JUSTICE IS PRESENT (22) BBW	0.88 OF 8	138	DRIFT TOWARD BEING THOSE WHERE SUPERORDINATE JUSTICE IS ABSENT (18) BBW	0.53 OF 32	7 15 1 17 XSQ= 2.78 PHI= 0.264 FP = 0.0537
149	IN ALL CASES ARE THOSE WHERE THE INCIDENCE OF THEFT IS HIGH (18) B-B-C	1.00 OF 6	149	LEAN TOWARD BEING THOSE WHERE THE INCIDENCE OF THEFT IS LOW (19) B-B-C	0.61 OF 31	6 12 0 19 XSQ= 5.30 PHI= 0.379 FP = 0.0080
175	DRIFT LESS TOWARD BEING THOSE WHERE THE COMMUNITY IS 'KIN-HETEROGENEOUS,' I. E. OTHER THAN A CLAN COMMUNITY OR A DEME (260)	0.59 OF 79	175	DRIFT MORE TOWARD BEING THOSE WHERE THE COMMUNITY IS 'KIN-HETEROGENEOUS,' I. E. OTHER THAN A CLAN COMMUNITY OR A DEME (260)	0.70 OF 303	32 90 47 213 XSQ= 2.89 PHI= 0.087 XP = 0.0894
176	TEND TO BE THOSE WHERE THE COMMUNITY IS A CLAN-COMMUNITY OR A COMMUNITY STRUCTURED OR SEGMENTED ON A CLAN BASIS (169)	0.71 OF 79	176	TEND TO BE THOSE WHERE THE COMMUNITY IS OTHER THAN A CLAN-COMMUNITY OR A COMMUNITY STRUCTURED OR SEGMENTED ON A CLAN BASIS (213)	0.63 OF 303	56 113 23 190 XSQ= 27.32 PHI= 0.267 XP = 0.0000
177	TEND LESS TO BE THOSE WHERE THE COMMUNITY IS OTHER THAN A SINGLE CLAN-COMMUNITY AND EXOGAMOUS (305)	0.61 OF 79	177	TEND MORE TO BE THOSE WHERE THE COMMUNITY IS OTHER THAN A SINGLE CLAN-COMMUNITY AND EXOGAMOUS (305)	0.85 OF 303	31 46 48 257 XSQ= 21.07 PHI= 0.235 XP = 0.0000
180	TEND TO BE THOSE WHERE THE COMMUNITY IS COMMONLY EXOGAMOUS, RATHER THAN NON-EXOGAMOUS (124)	0.51 OF 79	180	TEND TO BE THOSE WHERE THE COMMUNITY IS COMMONLY NON-EXOGAMOUS, RATHER THAN EXOGAMOUS (258)	0.72 OF 303	40 84 39 219 XSQ= 13.98 PHI= 0.191 XP = 0.0002
181	LEAN MORE TOWARD BEING THOSE WHERE THE COMMUNITY IS OTHER THAN A DEME (337)	0.99 OF 79	181	LEAN LESS TOWARD BEING THOSE WHERE THE COMMUNITY IS OTHER THAN A DEME (337)	0.85 OF 303	1 44 78 259 XSQ= 9.36 PHI= -0.157 XP = 0.0022
182	LEAN MORE TOWARD BEING THOSE OTHER THAN WHERE THE COMMUNITY IS STRUCTURED ON A NON-CLAN BASIS AND AGAMOUS (256)	0.81 OF 79	182	LEAN LESS TOWARD BEING THOSE OTHER THAN WHERE THE COMMUNITY IS STRUCTURED ON A NON-CLAN BASIS AND AGAMOUS (256)	0.63 OF 303	15 111 64 192 XSQ= 8.05 PHI= -0.145 XP = 0.0046
183	TEND MORE TO BE THOSE WHERE THE LARGEST NON-COGNATIC KIN GROUP IS SMALLER THAN A MOEITY, I. E., A PHRATRY OR SIB OR LINEAGE (218)	0.99 OF 73	183	TEND LESS TO BE THOSE WHERE THE LARGEST NON-COGNATIC KIN GROUP IS SMALLER THAN A MOEITY, I. E., A PHRATRY OR SIB OR LINEAGE (218)	0.82 OF 179	1 33 72 146 XSQ= 11.52 PHI= -0.214 XP = 0.0007

184	TEND MORE TO BE THOSE 0.92 OF 73 WHERE THE LARGEST NON-COGNATIC KIN GROUP IS SMALLER THAN A PHRATRY, I. E. A SIB OR LINEAGE (175)	184	TEND LESS TO BE THOSE 0.60 OF 179 WHERE THE LARGEST NON-COGNATIC KIN GROUP IS SMALLER THAN A PHRATRY, I. E. A SIB OR LINEAGE (175)	6 71 67 108 XSQ= 22.70 PHI= -0.300 XP = 0.0000
186	TEND TO BE THOSE 0.61 OF 80 WHERE THE KIN GROUP IS EXCLUSIVELY PATRILINEAL (150)	186	TEND TO BE THOSE 0.68 OF 320 WHERE THE KIN GROUP IS OTHER THAN EXCLUSIVELY PATRILINEAL (250)	49 101 31 219 XSQ= 22.82 PHI= 0.239 XP = 0.0000
188	TEND MORE TO BE THOSE 0.91 OF 80 WHERE THE KIN GROUP IS OTHER THAN EXCLUSIVELY COGNATIC (252)	188	TEND LESS TO BE THOSE 0.56 OF 320 WHERE THE KIN GROUP IS OTHER THAN EXCLUSIVELY COGNATIC (252)	7 141 73 179 XSQ= 32.74 PHI= -0.286 XP = 0.
190	TILT MORE TOWARD BEING THOSE 0.86 OF 72 WHERE THE KIN GROUP IS PATRILINEAL OR DOUBLE-DESCENT, RATHER THAN MATRILINEAL (186)	190	TILT LESS TOWARD BEING THOSE 0.71 OF 175 WHERE THE KIN GROUP IS PATRILINEAL OR DOUBLE-DESCENT, RATHER THAN MATRILINEAL (186)	62 124 10 51 XSQ= 5.59 PHI= 0.150 XP = 0.0181
192	TEND MORE TO BE THOSE 0.97 OF 80 OTHER THAN WHERE THE ONLY KIN GROUP PRESENT IS A KINDRED OR ELSE BILATERAL DESCENT IS INFERRED (289)	192	TEND LESS TO BE THOSE 0.66 OF 320 OTHER THAN WHERE THE ONLY KIN GROUP PRESENT IS A KINDRED OR ELSE BILATERAL DESCENT IS INFERRED (289)	2 109 78 211 XSQ= 30.24 PHI= -0.275 XP = 0.0000
197	LEAN MORE TOWARD BEING THOSE 0.98 OF 52 WHERE RULES FOR THE INHERITANCE OF REAL PROPERTY, IF PRESENT, FAVOR EITHER THE MALE HEIR OR LINE, OR THE FEMALE HEIR OR LINE (165)	197	LEAN LESS TOWARD BEING THOSE 0.80 OF 142 WHERE RULES FOR THE INHERITANCE OF REAL PROPERTY, IF PRESENT, FAVOR EITHER THE MALE HEIR OR LINE, OR THE FEMALE HEIR OR LINE (165)	51 114 1 28 XSQ= 8.13 PHI= 0.205 XP = 0.0043
201	DRIFT MORE TOWARD BEING THOSE 0.91 OF 80 WHERE MARITAL RESIDENCE IS NON-OPTIONAL, RATHER THAN AMBILOCAL OR NEOLOCAL (334)	201	DRIFT LESS TOWARD BEING THOSE 0.82 OF 318 WHERE MARITAL RESIDENCE IS NON-OPTIONAL, RATHER THAN AMBILOCAL OR NEOLOCAL (334)	73 261 7 57 XSQ= 3.34 PHI= 0.092 XP = 0.0678
204	TILT MORE TOWARD BEING THOSE 0.91 OF 79 WHERE MARITAL RESIDENCE IS PATRILOCAL, VIRILOCAL, OR AVUNCULOCAL, RATHER THAN AMBILOCAL OR NEOLOCAL (270)	204	TILT LESS TOWARD BEING THOSE 0.78 OF 255 WHERE MARITAL RESIDENCE IS PATRILOCAL, VIRILOCAL, OR AVUNCULOCAL, RATHER THAN AMBILOCAL OR NEOLOCAL (270)	72 198 7 57 XSQ= 6.24 PHI= 0.137 XP = 0.0125
207	DRIFT TOWARD BEING THOSE 0.88 OF 8 WHERE MARITAL RESIDENCE IS AMBILOCAL OR NEOLOCAL, RATHER THAN MATRILOCAL OR UXORILOCAL (64)	207	DRIFT TOWARD BEING THOSE 0.52 OF 120 WHERE MARITAL RESIDENCE IS MATRILOCAL OR UXORILOCAL, RATHER THAN AMBILOCAL OR NEOLOCAL (64)	1 63 7 57 XSQ= 3.33 PHI= -0.161 XP = 0.0679

209	TEND MORE TO BE THOSE WHERE MARITAL RESIDENCE IS PATRILOCAL, VIRILOCAL, OR AVUNCULOCAL, RATHER THAN MATRILOCAL OR UXORILOCAL (270)	0.99 OF 73	209	TEND LESS TO BE THOSE WHERE MARITAL RESIDENCE IS PATRILOCAL, VIRILOCAL, OR AVUNCULOCAL, RATHER THAN MATRILOCAL OR UXORILOCAL (270)	0.76 OF 261	72 198 1 63 XSQ= 17.65 PHI= 0.230 XP = 0.0000
210	LEAN MORE TOWARD BEING THOSE WHERE MARITAL RESIDENCE IS PATRILOCAL, RATHER THAN MATRILOCAL (169)	0.98 OF 55	210	LEAN LESS TOWARD BEING THOSE WHERE MARITAL RESIDENCE IS PATRILOCAL, RATHER THAN MATRILOCAL (169)	0.79 OF 145	54 115 1 30 XSQ= 9.45 PHI= 0.217 XP = 0.0021
234	LEAN TOWARD BEING THOSE WHERE THE COUSIN TERMINOLOGY IS OF CROW, OMAHA, OR IROQUOIS TYPE, RATHER THAN ESKIMO OR HAWAIIAN TYPE (152)	0.66 OF 58	234	LEAN TOWARD BEING THOSE WHERE THE COUSIN TERMINOLOGY IS OF ESKIMO OR HAWAIIAN TYPE, RATHER THAN CROW, OMAHA, OR IROQUOIS TYPE (170)	0.57 OF 264	38 114 20 150 XSQ= 8.64 PHI= 0.164 XP = 0.0033
241	DRIFT MORE TOWARD BEING THOSE WHERE THE FAMILY, IF EXTENDED, IS LARGE OR SMALL, RATHER THAN STEM (187)	0.97 OF 40	241	DRIFT LESS TOWARD BEING THOSE WHERE THE FAMILY, IF EXTENDED, IS LARGE OR SMALL, RATHER THAN STEM (187)	0.86 OF 173	39 148 1 25 XSQ= 3.29 PHI= 0.124 XP = 0.0699
242	TEND MORE TO BE THOSE WHERE MARRIAGE IS COMMONLY OR OCCASIONALLY POLYGYNOUS, RATHER THAN MONOGAMOUS (314)	0.95 OF 80	242	TEND LESS TO BE THOSE WHERE MARRIAGE IS COMMONLY OR OCCASIONALLY POLYGYNOUS, RATHER THAN MONOGAMOUS (314)	0.76 OF 315	76 238 4 77 XSQ= 13.63 PHI= 0.186 XP = 0.0002
243	LEAN TOWARD BEING THOSE WHERE POLYGYNY, IF PRESENT, HAS A HIGH INCIDENCE (24) W-D,S	0.73 OF 15	243	LEAN TOWARD BEING THOSE WHERE POLYGYNY, IF PRESENT, HAS A LOW INCIDENCE (36) W-D,S	0.71 OF 45	11 13 4 32 XSQ= 7.50 PHI= 0.354 XP = 0.0062
254	IN ALL CASES ARE THOSE WHERE HOUSEHOLD AUTHORITY IS ON THE FATHER'S SIDE, RATHER THAN THE MOTHER'S (9) DA	1.00 OF 5	254	TILT TOWARD BEING THOSE WHERE HOUSEHOLD AUTHORITY IS ON THE MOTHER'S SIDE, RATHER THAN THE FATHER'S (6) DA	0.60 OF 10	5 4 0 6 XSQ= 2.81 PHI= 0.433 EP = 0.0440
260	TILT TOWARD BEING THOSE WHERE THE AGE OF MALES AT MARRIAGE IS TWENTY OR OVER (17) JKH	0.58 OF 12	260	TILT TOWARD BEING THOSE WHERE THE AGE OF MALES AT MARRIAGE IS LESS THAN TWENTY (38) JKH	0.77 OF 43	5 33 7 10 XSQ= 3.89 PHI= -0.266 XP = 0.0486
262	TEND MORE TO BE THOSE WHERE WIVES ARE OBTAINED BY MEANS INVOLVING THE PRESENCE OF SOME CONSIDERATION (305)	0.99 OF 80	262	TEND LESS TO BE THOSE WHERE WIVES ARE OBTAINED BY MEANS INVOLVING THE PRESENCE OF SOME CONSIDERATION (305)	0.72 OF 315	79 226 1 89 XSQ= 24.93 PHI= 0.251 XP = 0.0000

263	TEND MORE TO BE THOSE 0.89 OF 80 WHERE WIVES ARE OBTAINED BY RELATIVELY DIFFICULT MEANS, NAMELY BY BRIDE-PRICE, BRIDE-SERVICE, OR EXCHANGING A FEMALE RELATIVE (233)	263	TEND LESS TO BE THOSE 0.51 OF 315 WHERE WIVES ARE OBTAINED BY RELATIVELY DIFFICULT MEANS, NAMELY BY BRIDE-PRICE, BRIDE-SERVICE, OR EXCHANGING A FEMALE RELATIVE (233)	71 162 9 153 XSQ= 35.21 PHI= 0.299 XP = 0.
282	TILT TOWARD BEING THOSE 0.88 OF 8 WHERE THE STRENGTH OF DESIRE FOR CHILDREN IS HIGH (16) BCA	282	TILT TOWARD BEING THOSE 0.68 OF 28 WHERE THE STRENGTH OF DESIRE FOR CHILDREN IS LOW OR ABSENT (20) BCA	7 9 1 19 XSQ= 5.64 PHI= 0.396 EP = 0.0121
295	DRIFT TOWARD BEING THOSE 0.83 OF 6 WHERE THE SEVERITY OF PUNISHMENT FOR ABORTION IS HIGH (11) BCA	295	DRIFT TOWARD BEING THOSE 0.65 OF 17 WHERE THE SEVERITY OF PUNISHMENT FOR ABORTION IS LOW OR ABSENT (12) BCA	5 6 1 11 XSQ= 2.40 PHI= 0.323 EP = 0.0686
300	TILT TOWARD BEING THOSE 0.57 OF 35 WHERE THE POST-PARTUM SEX TABOO LASTS LONGER THAN SIX MONTHS (51)	300	TILT TOWARD BEING THOSE 0.65 OF 89 WHERE THE POST-PARTUM SEX TABOO LASTS SIX MONTHS OR LESS (73)	20 31 15 58 XSQ= 4.28 PHI= 0.186 XP = 0.0385
304	IN ALL CASES ARE THOSE 1.00 OF 6 WHERE THE EARLY ANAL SATISFACTION POTENTIAL IS LOW (22) W-C	304	TILT TOWARD BEING THOSE 0.54 OF 35 WHERE THE EARLY ANAL SATISFACTION POTENTIAL IS HIGH (19) W-C	0 19 6 16 XSQ= 4.08 PHI= -0.316 XP = 0.0433
309	TILT TOWARD BEING THOSE 0.88 OF 8 WHERE ORAL SOCIALIZATION ANXIETY IS HIGH (26) W-C	309	TILT TOWARD BEING THOSE 0.58 OF 45 WHERE ORAL SOCIALIZATION ANXIETY IS LOW (27) W-C	7 19 1 26 XSQ= 3.91 PHI= 0.272 XP = 0.0481
314	TEND TO BE THOSE 0.86 OF 14 WHERE THE INCIDENCE OF MOTHER-CHILD HOUSEHOLDS IS HIGH (19) W-D,S	314	TEND TO BE THOSE 0.89 OF 66 WHERE THE INCIDENCE OF MOTHER-CHILD HOUSEHOLDS IS LOW (61) W-D,S	12 7 2 59 XSQ= 31.95 PHI= 0.632 XP = 0.
316	LEAN TOWARD BEING THOSE 0.82 OF 11 WHERE EXCLUSIVE MOTHER-SON SLEEPING ARRANGEMENTS LAST ONE YEAR OR LONGER (19) W-K-A	316	LEAN TOWARD BEING THOSE 0.70 OF 33 WHERE EXCLUSIVE MOTHER-SON SLEEPING ARRANGEMENTS LAST LESS THAN ONE YEAR (25) W-K-A	9 10 2 23 XSQ= 6.95 PHI= 0.397 XP = 0.0084
318	LEAN TOWARD BEING THOSE 0.76 OF 17 WHERE THE OVERALL INDULGENCE OF THE INFANT IS LOW (31) B-B-C	318	LEAN TOWARD BEING THOSE 0.67 OF 54 WHERE THE OVERALL INDULGENCE OF THE INFANT IS HIGH (40) B-B-C	4 36 13 18 XSQ= 8.11 PHI= -0.338 XP = 0.0044

```
319  TILT TOWARD BEING THOSE          0.75 OF  16    319  TILT TOWARD BEING THOSE            0.63 OF  49          4    31
     WHERE PROTECTION OF THE INFANT                       WHERE PROTECTION OF THE INFANT                         12    18
     FROM ENVIRONMENTAL DISCOMFORTS                       FROM ENVIRONMENTAL DISCOMFORTS                  XSQ=     5.65
     IS LOW  (30) B-B-C                                   IS HIGH  (35) B-B-C                             PHI=   -0.295
                                                                                                          XP =   0.0175

324  TILT TOWARD BEING THOSE          0.81 OF  16    324  TILT TOWARD BEING THOSE            0.58 OF  50         13    21
     WHERE THE PAIN INFLICTED                             WHERE THE PAIN INFLICTED                                3    29
     ON THE INFANT BY THE NURTURANT AGENT                 ON THE INFANT BY THE NURTURANT AGENT            XSQ=     5.99
     IS HIGH  (34) B-B-C                                  IS LOW OR NEGLIGIBLE  (32) B-B-C                PHI=    0.301
                                                                                                          XP =   0.0144

334  TILT TOWARD BEING THOSE          0.74 OF  19    334  TILT TOWARD BEING THOSE            0.59 OF  59          5    35
     WHERE THE INDULGENCE OF THE CHILD                    WHERE THE INDULGENCE OF THE CHILD                      14    24
     IS LOW  (38) B-B-C                                   IS HIGH  (40) B-B-C                             XSQ=     5.02
                                                                                                          PHI=   -0.254
                                                                                                          XP =   0.0251

336  TILT TOWARD BEING THOSE          0.84 OF  19    336  TILT TOWARD BEING THOSE            0.52 OF  56         16    27
     WHERE THE TOTAL POSITIVE PRESSURE TOWARD             WHERE THE TOTAL POSITIVE PRESSURE TOWARD                3    29
     DEVELOPING RESPONSIBLE BEHAVIOR                      DEVELOPING RESPONSIBLE BEHAVIOR                 XSQ=     6.12
     IN THE CHILD                                         IN THE CHILD                                    PHI=    0.286
     IS HIGH  (43) B-B-C                                  IS LOW  (32) B-B-C                              XP =   0.0134

337  TEND TO BE THOSE                 0.94 OF  18    337  TEND TO BE THOSE                   0.62 OF  55         17    21
     WHERE THE CHILD'S INFERRED ANXIETY OVER              WHERE THE CHILD'S INFERRED ANXIETY OVER                 1    34
     NON-PERFORMANCE OF RESPONSIBLE BEHAVIOR              NON-PERFORMANCE OF RESPONSIBLE BEHAVIOR         XSQ=    15.02
     IS HIGH  (38) B-B-C                                  IS LOW  (35) B-B-C                              PHI=    0.454
                                                                                                          XP =   0.0001

338  TILT MORE TOWARD BEING THOSE     0.83 OF  18    338  TILT LESS TOWARD BEING THOSE       0.53 OF  55         15    29
     WHERE THE CHILD'S INFERRED ANXIETY OVER              WHERE THE CHILD'S INFERRED ANXIETY OVER                 3    26
     PERFORMANCE OF RESPONSIBLE BEHAVIOR                  PERFORMANCE OF RESPONSIBLE BEHAVIOR             XSQ=     4.10
     IS HIGH  (44) B-B-C                                  IS HIGH  (44) B-B-C                             PHI=    0.237
                                                                                                          XP =   0.0428

339  TILT TOWARD BEING THOSE          0.67 OF  18    339  TILT TOWARD BEING THOSE            0.65 OF  55         12    19
     WHERE THE CHILD'S INFERRED CONFLICT                  WHERE THE CHILD'S INFERRED CONFLICT                     6    36
     REGARDING RESPONSIBLE BEHAVIOR                       REGARDING RESPONSIBLE BEHAVIOR                  XSQ=     4.49
     IS HIGH  (31) B-B-C                                  IS LOW  (42) B-B-C                              PHI=    0.248
                                                                                                          XP =   0.0341

346  DRIFT TOWARD BEING THOSE         0.68 OF  19    346  DRIFT TOWARD BEING THOSE           0.58 OF  57         13    24
     WHERE THE CHILD'S INFERRED ANXIETY OVER              WHERE THE CHILD'S INFERRED ANXIETY OVER                 6    33
     PERFORMANCE OF SELF-RELIANT BEHAVIOR                 PERFORMANCE OF SELF-RELIANT BEHAVIOR            XSQ=     2.97
     IS HIGH  (37) B-B-C                                  IS LOW  (39) B-B-C                              PHI=    0.198
                                                                                                          XP =   0.0850

347  TILT TOWARD BEING THOSE          0.74 OF  19    347  TILT TOWARD BEING THOSE            0.60 OF  57         14    23
     WHERE THE CHILD'S INFERRED CONFLICT                  WHERE THE CHILD'S INFERRED CONFLICT                     5    34
     REGARDING SELF-RELIANT BEHAVIOR                      REGARDING SELF-RELIANT BEHAVIOR                 XSQ=     5.07
     IS HIGH  (37) B-B-C                                  IS LOW  (39) B-B-C                              PHI=    0.258
                                                                                                          XP =   0.0243
```

352	TILT MORE TOWARD BEING THOSE 0.89 OF 18 WHERE THE TOTAL POSITIVE PRESSURE TOWARD DEVELOPING OBEDIENT BEHAVIOR IN THE CHILD IS HIGH (44) B-B-C	352	TILT LESS TOWARD BEING THOSE 0.52 OF 54 WHERE THE TOTAL POSITIVE PRESSURE TOWARD DEVELOPING OBEDIENT BEHAVIOR IN THE CHILD IS HIGH (44) B-B-C	16 28 2 26 XSQ= 6.31 PHI= 0.296 XP = 0.0120
353	TILT TOWARD BEING THOSE 0.83 OF 18 WHERE THE CHILD'S INFERRED ANXIETY OVER NON-PERFORMANCE OF OBEDIENT BEHAVIOR IS HIGH (42) B-B-C	353	TILT TOWARD BEING THOSE 0.52 OF 56 WHERE THE CHILD-S INFERRED ANXIETY OVER NON-PERFORMANCE OF OBEDIENT BEHAVIOR IS LOW (32) B-B-C	15 27 3 29 XSQ= 5.49 PHI= 0.272 XP = 0.0191
356	DRIFT TOWARD BEING THOSE 0.83 OF 12 WHERE ADOLESCENT PEER GROUPS OR PAIRS ARE PRESENT IN A SETTING OF COURTSHIP (29) JKH	356	DRIFT TOWARD BEING THOSE 0.51 OF 39 WHERE NEITHER ADOLESCENT PEER GROUPS NOR PAIRS ARE PRESENT IN A SETTING OF COURTSHIP (22) JKH	10 19 2 20 XSQ= 3.18 PHI= 0.250 XP = 0.0744
370	TEND TO BE THOSE 0.76 OF 51 WHERE THE SEGREGATION OF ADOLESCENT BOYS IS COMPLETE OR PARTIAL (95)	370	TEND TO BE THOSE 0.71 OF 192 WHERE THE SEGREGATION OF ADOLESCENT BOYS IS ABSENT (148)	39 56 12 136 XSQ= 35.91 PHI= 0.384 XP = 0.
372	LEAN TOWARD BEING THOSE 0.72 OF 25 WHERE MALE INITIATION RITES ARE PRESENT (48) ASA	372	LEAN TOWARD BEING THOSE 0.65 OF 86 WHERE MALE INITIATION RITES ARE ABSENT (63) ASA	18 30 7 56 XSQ= 9.41 PHI= 0.291 XP = 0.0022
377	TEND TO BE THOSE 0.54 OF 67 WHERE MALE GENITAL MUTILATION IS PRESENT (83)	377	TEND TO BE THOSE 0.82 OF 258 WHERE MALE GENITAL MUTILATION IS ABSENT (242)	36 47 31 211 XSQ= 33.43 PHI= 0.321 XP = 0.
385	TILT TOWARD BEING THOSE 0.50 OF 16 WHERE SEXUAL EXPRESSION BY THE YOUNG IS RESTRICTED (22) F-B	385	TILT TOWARD BEING THOSE 0.80 OF 70 WHERE SEXUAL EXPRESSION BY THE YOUNG IS SEMI-RESTRICTED OR PERMITTED (64) F-B	8 14 8 56 XSQ= 4.68 PHI= 0.233 XP = 0.0305
386	TILT TOWARD BEING THOSE 0.81 OF 16 WHERE SEXUAL EXPRESSION BY THE YOUNG IS RESTRICTED OR SEMI-RESTRICTED (46) F-B	386	TILT TOWARD BEING THOSE 0.53 OF 70 WHERE SEXUAL EXPRESSION BY THE YOUNG IS PERMITTED (40) F-B	13 33 3 37 XSQ= 4.80 PHI= 0.236 XP = 0.0285
399	DRIFT TOWARD BEING THOSE 0.80 OF 10 WHERE INTENSITY OF CASTRATION ANXIETY IS HIGH (23) WNS	399	DRIFT TOWARD BEING THOSE 0.57 OF 35 WHERE INTENSITY OF CASTRATION ANXIETY IS LOW (22) WNS	8 15 2 20 XSQ= 2.94 PHI= 0.255 XP = 0.0866

37 [handwritten]

No.	Statement	Ratio	No.	Statement	Ratio	Statistics
419	TILT MORE TOWARD BEING THOSE WHERE MILITARY GLORY IS STRONGLY OR MODERATELY EMPHASIZED (55) PES	0.93 OF 15	419	TILT LESS TOWARD BEING THOSE WHERE MILITARY GLORY IS STRONGLY OR MODERATELY EMPHASIZED (55) PES	0.58 OF 71	14 41 1 30 XSQ= 5.35 PHI= 0.249 XP = 0.0208
420	LEAN TOWARD BEING THOSE WHERE BELLICOSITY IS EXTREME (41) PES	0.85 OF 13	420	LEAN TOWARD BEING THOSE WHERE BELLICOSITY IS MODERATE OR NEGLIGIBLE (46) PES	0.59 OF 74	11 30 2 44 XSQ= 6.94 PHI= 0.282 XP = 0.0084
426	TEND MORE TO BE THOSE WHERE A HIGH GOD IS PRESENT (156) GES,EA	0.82 OF 55	426	TEND LESS TO BE THOSE WHERE A HIGH GOD IS PRESENT (156) GES,EA	0.54 OF 205	45 111 10 94 XSQ= 12.71 PHI= 0.221 XP = 0.0004
427	TEND TO BE THOSE WHERE A HIGH GOD, IF PRESENT, IS INACTIVE, RATHER THAN ACTIVE (69) GES,EA	0.69 OF 45	427	TEND TO BE THOSE WHERE A HIGH GOD, IF PRESENT, IS ACTIVE, RATHER THAN INACTIVE (87) GES,EA	0.66 OF 111	14 73 31 38 XSQ= 14.22 PHI= -0.302 XP = 0.0002
428	LEAN TOWARD BEING THOSE WHERE A HIGH GOD, IF PRESENT AND ACTIVE, DOES NOT SUPPORT HUMAN MORALITY, RATHER THAN SUPPORTING IT (26) GES,EA	0.64 OF 14	428	LEAN TOWARD BEING THOSE WHERE A HIGH GOD, IF PRESENT AND ACTIVE, SUPPORTS HUMAN MORALITY, RATHER THAN NOT SUPPORTING IT (61) GES,EA	0.77 OF 73	5 56 9 17 XSQ= 7.57 PHI= -0.295 XP = 0.0059
458	TEND TO BE THOSE WHERE GAMES, IF PRESENT, INCLUDE GAMES OF STRATEGY (52) R-A-B,EA	0.88 OF 26	458	TEND TO BE THOSE WHERE GAMES, IF PRESENT, DO NOT INCLUDE GAMES OF STRATEGY (119) R-A-B,EA	0.80 OF 145	23 29 3 116 XSQ= 45.65 PHI= 0.517 XP = 0.
460	TEND MORE TO BE THOSE WHERE GAMES, IF PRESENT, ARE NOT LIMITED TO GAMES OF SKILL ONLY (104) R-A-B,EA	0.92 OF 26	460	TEND LESS TO BE THOSE WHERE GAMES, IF PRESENT, ARE NOT LIMITED TO GAMES OF SKILL ONLY (104) R-A-B,EA	0.55 OF 145	2 65 24 80 XSQ= 11.25 PHI= -0.256 XP = 0.0008
476	TILT TOWARD BEING THOSE WHERE THE DEGREE OF INSOBRIETY IS MODERATE OR SLIGHT (18) CH	0.73 OF 11	476	TILT TOWARD BEING THOSE WHERE THE DEGREE OF INSOBRIETY IS STRONG (31) DH	0.74 OF 38	3 28 8 10 XSQ= 6.04 PHI= -0.351 XP = 0.0140

4 CULTURES
LOCATED IN THE CIRCUM-MEDITERRANEAN (45)

4 CULTURES
LOCATED OUTSIDE OF
THE CIRCUM-MEDITERRANEAN (355)

BACKGROUND ON PAGE 65

BOTH SUBJECT AND PREDICATE

45 IN LEFT COLUMN

ALBANIANS	AMERICANS	BARABRA	BASQUES	BEJA	BOERS	BRAZILIANS	BUDUMA	BULGARIANS	CHEREMIS
CHERKESS	CZECHS	DUTCH	EGYPTIANS	HASANIA	HEBREWS	HUTSUL	ICELANDERS	IRAQW	IRISH
KABYLE	KALMYK	KHEVSUR	KONSO	KUMYK	LAPPS	MAGUZAWA	MZAB	PORTUGUESE	REGEIBAT
RIFFIANS	ROMANS	RWALA	SERBS	SHLUH	SIWANS	SOMALI	SONGHAI	SYRIANS	TEDA
TERA	TIGRINYA	TRISTAN	WALLOONS	WOLOF					

355 IN RIGHT COLUMN

	Left column			Right column		
14	TEND TO BE THOSE WHERE THE LATITUDE IS THIRTY DEGREES OR GREATER (119)	0.60 OF 45	14	TEND TO BE THOSE WHERE THE LATITUDE IS LESS THAN THIRTY DEGREES (281)	0.74 OF 355	27 92 18 263 XSQ= 20.60 PHI= 0.227 XP = 0.0000
15	TEND TO BE THOSE WHERE THE LATITUDE IS TWENTY DEGREES OR GREATER (183)	0.76 OF 45	15	TEND TO BE THOSE WHERE THE LATITUDE IS LESS THAN TWENTY DEGREES (217)	0.58 OF 355	34 149 11 206 XSQ= 16.82 PHI= 0.205 XP = 0.0000
42	TEND MORE TO BE THOSE WHERE THE NATURAL ENVIRONMENT IS OTHER THAN TROPICAL OR SUB-TROPICAL RAIN FOREST, OR MONSOON FOREST (244) FWM	0.98 OF 45	42	TEND LESS TO BE THOSE WHERE THE NATURAL ENVIRONMENT IS OTHER THAN TROPICAL OR SUB-TROPICAL RAIN FOREST, OR MONSOON FOREST (244) FWM	0.56 OF 355	1 155 44 200 XSQ= 27.11 PHI= -0.260 XP = 0.0000
51	TEND MORE TO BE THOSE WHERE SUBSISTENCE IS PRIMARILY BY FOOD PRODUCTION -- I. E., AGRICULTURE OR HUSBANDRY -- RATHER THAN BY GATHERING (253)	0.93 OF 45	51	TEND LESS TO BE THOSE WHERE SUBSISTENCE IS PRIMARILY BY FOOD PRODUCTION -- I. E., AGRICULTURE OR HUSBANDRY -- RATHER THAN BY GATHERING (253)	0.59 OF 355	42 211 3 144 XSQ= 18.31 PHI= 0.214 XP = 0.0000
53	TEND TO BE THOSE WHERE FOOD PRODUCTION IS BY INTENSIVE AGRICULTURE, RATHER THAN BY SIMPLE AGRICULTURE OR INCIPIENT FOOD PRODUCTION (91)	0.83 OF 30	53	TEND TO BE THOSE WHERE FOOD PRODUCTION IS BY SIMPLE AGRICULTURE OR INCIPIENT FOOD PRODUCTION, RATHER THAN BY INTENSIVE AGRICULTURE (147)	0.68 OF 208	25 66 5 142 XSQ= 27.42 PHI= 0.339 XP = 0.0000

```
55  TEND TO BE THOSE                 0.93 OF  27    55  TEND TO BE THOSE                 0.60 OF 165         25   66
    WHERE FOOD PRODUCTION IS BY                           WHERE FOOD PRODUCTION IS BY                               2   99
    INTENSIVE AGRICULTURE, RATHER THAN BY                 SIMPLE AGRICULTURE, RATHER THAN BY                  XSQ=   23.68
    SIMPLE AGRICULTURE  (91)                              INTENSIVE AGRICULTURE  (101)                        PHI=   0.351
                                                                                                              XP =  0.0000

62  LEAN MORE TOWARD BEING THOSE     0.78 OF  45    62  LEAN LESS TOWARD BEING THOSE     0.54 OF 355         35  193
    WHERE HUSBANDRY OF SOME KIND                          WHERE HUSBANDRY OF SOME KIND                             10  162
    IS PRESENT  (228)                                     IS PRESENT  (228)                                   XSQ=    8.00
                                                                                                              PHI=   0.141
                                                                                                              XP =  0.0047

63  TEND MORE TO BE THOSE            0.97 OF  34    63  TEND LESS TO BE THOSE            0.62 OF 192         33  119
    WHERE HUSBANDRY, IF PRESENT,                          WHERE HUSBANDRY, IF PRESENT,                              1   73
    IS PRINCIPALLY IN THE FORM OF                         IS PRINCIPALLY IN THE FORM OF                       XSQ=   14.59
    BOVINE, EQUINE, CAMEL-LIKE, OR DEER-LIKE              BOVINE, EQUINE, CAMEL-LIKE, OR DEER-LIKE            PHI=   0.254
    ANIMALS, RATHER THAN                                  ANIMALS, RATHER THAN                                XP =  0.0001
    PIGS, SHEEP, OR GOATS  (152)                          PIGS, SHEEP, OR GOATS  (152)

71  TEND TO BE THOSE                 0.94 OF  17    71  TEND TO BE THOSE                 0.65 OF 234         16   82
    WHERE METAL WORKING IS                                WHERE METAL WORKING IS                                    1  152
    PRESENT  (98)                                         ABSENT  (153)                                       XSQ=   20.82
                                                                                                              PHI=   0.288
                                                                                                              XP =  0.0000

73  TEND TO BE THOSE                 0.89 OF  18    73  TEND TO BE THOSE                 0.56 OF 230         16  102
    WHERE WEAVING IS                                      WHERE WEAVING IS                                          2  128
    PRESENT  (118)                                        ABSENT  (130)                                       XSQ=   11.55
                                                                                                              PHI=   0.216
                                                                                                              XP =  0.0007

74  DRIFT MORE TOWARD BEING THOSE    0.87 OF  15    74  DRIFT LESS TOWARD BEING THOSE    0.59 OF 223         13  132
    WHERE POTTERY IS                                      WHERE POTTERY IS                                          2   91
    PRESENT  (145)                                        PRESENT  (145)                                      XSQ=    3.38
                                                                                                              PHI=   0.119
                                                                                                              XP =  0.0661

80  TEND TO BE THOSE                 0.62 OF  26    80  TEND TO BE THOSE                 0.88 OF 198         16   23
    WHERE A CITY OR TOWN IS PRESENT  (39)                 WHERE NO CITY OR TOWN IS PRESENT  (185)                  10  175
                                                                                                              XSQ=   36.44
                                                                                                              PHI=   0.403
                                                                                                              XP =  0.

81  TEND TO BE THOSE                 0.73 OF  26    81  TEND TO BE THOSE                 0.65 OF 198         19   70
    WHERE A CITY OR TOWN IS PRESENT, OR                   WHERE NO CITY OR TOWN IS PRESENT, AND                     7  128
    THE AVERAGE COMMUNITY SIZE IS                         THE AVERAGE COMMUNITY SIZE IS                       XSQ=   12.13
    200 OR GREATER  (89)                                  SMALLER THAN 200  (135)                             PHI=   0.233
                                                                                                              XP =  0.0005

85  TEND TO BE THOSE                 0.62 OF  29    85  TEND TO BE THOSE                 0.81 OF 275         18   52
    WHERE THE LEVEL OF POLITICAL INTEGRATION              WHERE THE LEVEL OF POLITICAL INTEGRATION                 11  223
    IS THE LARGE STATE, OR                                IS THE MINIMAL STATE,                               XSQ=   25.19
    THE LITTLE STATE  (70) GPM                            THE AUTONOMOUS COMMUNITY, OR                        PHI=   0.288
                                                          THE FAMILY  (234) GPM                               XP =  0.0000
```

	Left		Right	Statistics
86	TEND TO BE THOSE 0.90 OF 29 WHERE THE LEVEL OF POLITICAL INTEGRATION IS THE LARGE STATE, THE LITTLE STATE, OR THE MINIMAL STATE (148) GPM	86	TEND TO BE THOSE 0.56 OF 275 WHERE THE LEVEL OF POLITICAL INTEGRATION IS THE AUTONOMOUS COMMUNITY, OR THE FAMILY (156) GPM	26 122 3 153 XSQ= 19.77 PHI= 0.255 XP = 0.0000
88	TILT TOWARD BEING THOSE 0.68 OF 19 WHERE, IF A HEADMANSHIP IS PRESENT, SUCCESSION IS NON-HEREDITARY (106)	88	TILT TOWARD BEING THOSE 0.63 OF 252 WHERE, IF A HEADMANSHIP IS PRESENT, SUCCESSION IS HEREDITARY (165)	13 93 6 159 XSQ= 6.10 PHI= 0.150 XP = 0.0135
91	DRIFT TOWARD BEING THOSE 0.83 OF 6 WHERE SOCIETAL COMPLEXITY IS HIGH (18) F-W	91	DRIFT TOWARD BEING THOSE 0.62 OF 34 WHERE SOCIETAL COMPLEXITY IS LOW (22) F-W	5 13 1 21 XSQ= 2.57 PHI= 0.253 EP = 0.0734
95	TEND TO BE THOSE 0.59 OF 32 WHERE THE HIERARCHY OF NATIONAL JURISDICTION HAS FOUR, THREE, OR TWO LEVELS (76) GES,EA	95	TEND TO BE THOSE 0.81 OF 298 WHERE THE HIERARCHY OF NATIONAL JURISDICTION HAS ONE OR NO LEVELS (254) GES,EA	19 57 13 241 XSQ= 24.18 PHI= 0.271 XP = 0.0000
96	TEND TO BE THOSE 0.84 OF 32 WHERE THE HIERARCHY OF NATIONAL JURISDICTION HAS FOUR, THREE, TWO OR ONE LEVEL (174) GES,EA	96	TEND TO BE THOSE 0.51 OF 298 WHERE THE HIERARCHY OF NATIONAL JURISDICTION HAS NO LEVELS (156) GES,EA	27 147 5 151 XSQ= 12.87 PHI= 0.197 XP = 0.0003
100	DRIFT MORE TOWARD BEING THOSE 0.94 OF 32 WHERE HIERARCHIES ARE MORE COMPLEX THAN THE 'SIMPLEST,' I. E., MORE COMPLEX THAN TWO LOCAL LEVELS WITH NO NATIONAL LEVELS (267) GES,EA	100	DRIFT LESS TOWARD BEING THOSE 0.80 OF 298 WHERE HIERARCHIES ARE MORE COMPLEX THAN THE 'SIMPLEST,' I. E., MORE COMPLEX THAN TWO LOCAL LEVELS WITH NO NATIONAL LEVELS (267) GES,EA	30 237 2 61 XSQ= 2.92 PHI= 0.094 XP = 0.0876
102	TEND TO BE THOSE 0.79 OF 43 WHERE CLASS STRATIFICATION IS PRESENT (203)	102	TEND TO BE THOSE 0.50 OF 340 WHERE CLASS STRATIFICATION IS ABSENT (180)	34 169 9 171 XSQ= 12.06 PHI= 0.177 XP = 0.0005
107	TEND LESS TO BE THOSE 0.53 OF 34 WHERE CLASS STRATIFICATION, IF PRESENT, IS BASED ON SOMETHING OTHER THAN OCCUPATIONAL STATUS (160)	107	TEND MORE TO BE THOSE 0.84 OF 169 WHERE CLASS STRATIFICATION, IF PRESENT, IS BASED ON SOMETHING OTHER THAN OCCUPATIONAL STATUS (160)	16 27 18 142 XSQ= 14.57 PHI= 0.268 XP = 0.0001
108	LEAN MORE TOWARD BEING THOSE 0.88 OF 34 WHERE CLASS STRATIFICATION, IF PRESENT, IS BASED ON SOMETHING OTHER THAN A HEREDITARY ARISTOCRACY (129)	108	LEAN LESS TOWARD BEING THOSE 0.59 OF 169 WHERE CLASS STRATIFICATION, IF PRESENT, IS BASED ON SOMETHING OTHER THAN A HEREDITARY ARISTOCRACY (129)	4 70 30 99 XSQ= 9.50 PHI= -0.216 XP = 0.0021

109	TEND LESS TO BE THOSE WHERE CASTES ARE ABSENT (317)	0.61 OF 36	109	TEND MORE TO BE THOSE WHERE CASTES ARE ABSENT (317)	0.89 OF 332	14 37 22 295 XSQ= 18.68 PHI= 0.225 XP = 0.0000
118	IN ALL CASES ARE THOSE WHERE THE PERCENTAGE OF OCCUPATIONS THAT ARE SPECIALIZED IS HIGH OR MEDIUM (24) WME	1.00 OF 7	118	TILT TOWARD BEING THOSE WHERE THE PERCENTAGE OF OCCUPATIONS THAT ARE SPECIALIZED IS LOW (25) WME	0.60 OF 42	7 17 0 25 XSQ= 6.29 PHI= 0.358 XP = 0.0121
120	IN ALL CASES ARE THOSE WHERE THE CRAFT SPECIALIZATION SCORE IS HIGH OR MEDIUM (36) WME	1.00 OF 8	120	DRIFT LESS TOWARD BEING THOSE WHERE THE CRAFT SPECIALIZATION SCORE IS HIGH OR MEDIUM (36) WME	0.62 OF 45	8 28 0 17 XSQ= 2.88 PHI= 0.233 XP = 0.0894
127	DRIFT TOWARD BEING THOSE WHERE THE FEMALES' CONTRIBUTION TO SUBSISTENCE IS LOW (32) JKB	0.88 OF 8	127	DRIFT TOWARD BEING THOSE WHERE THE FEMALES' CONTRIBUTION TO SUBSISTENCE IS HIGH (33) JKB	0.56 OF 57	1 32 7 25 XSQ= 3.74 PHI= -0.240 XP = 0.0531
128	IN ALL CASES ARE THOSE WHERE, IF SUBSISTENCE IS PRIMARILY BY AGRICULTURE, THE WORK IS MAINLY DONE BY MALES (40)	1.00 OF 9	128	LEAN TOWARD BEING THOSE WHERE, IF SUBSISTENCE IS PRIMARILY BY AGRICULTURE, THE WORK IS MAINLY DONE BY FEMALES (37)	0.54 OF 68	9 31 0 37 XSQ= 7.37 PHI= 0.309 XP = 0.0066
130	TILT TOWARD BEING THOSE WHERE LEATHER WORKING IS MAINLY DONE BY MALES (39)	0.83 OF 12	130	TILT TOWARD BEING THOSE WHERE LEATHER WORKING IS MAINLY DONE BY FEMALES (45)	0.60 OF 72	10 29 2 43 XSQ= 6.03 PHI= 0.268 XP = 0.0140
176	TILT MORE TOWARD BEING THOSE WHERE THE COMMUNITY IS OTHER THAN A CLAN-COMMUNITY OR A COMMUNITY STRUCTURED OR SEGMENTED ON A CLAN BASIS (213)	0.71 OF 42	176	TILT LESS TOWARD BEING THOSE WHERE THE COMMUNITY IS OTHER THAN A CLAN-COMMUNITY OR A COMMUNITY STRUCTURED OR SEGMENTED ON A CLAN BASIS (213)	0.54 OF 340	12 157 30 183 XSQ= 4.01 PHI= -0.102 XP = 0.0452
178	TILT MORE TOWARD BEING THOSE WHERE THE COMMUNITY IS OTHER THAN SEGMENTED ON A CLAN BASIS AND NON-EXOGAMOUS (295)	0.90 OF 42	178	TILT LESS TOWARD BEING THOSE WHERE THE COMMUNITY IS OTHER THAN SEGMENTED ON A CLAN BASIS AND NON-EXOGAMOUS (295)	0.76 OF 340	4 83 38 257 XSQ= 3.90 PHI= -0.101 XP = 0.0482
186	DRIFT TOWARD BEING THOSE WHERE THE KIN GROUP IS EXCLUSIVELY PATRILINEAL (150)	0.51 OF 45	186	DRIFT TOWARD BEING THOSE WHERE THE KIN GROUP IS OTHER THAN EXCLUSIVELY PATRILINEAL (250)	0.64 OF 355	23 127 22 228 XSQ= 3.38 PHI= 0.092 XP = 0.0660

187	IN ALL CASES ARE THOSE WHERE THE KIN GROUP IS OTHER THAN EXCLUSIVELY MATRILINEAL (344)	1.00 OF 45	187	LEAN LESS TOWARD BEING THOSE WHERE THE KIN GROUP IS OTHER THAN EXCLUSIVELY MATRILINEAL (344)	0.84 OF 354	0 55 45 299 XSQ= 6.85 PHI= -0.131 XP = 0.0088
190	IN ALL CASES ARE THOSE WHERE THE KIN GROUP IS PATRILINEAL OR DOUBLE-DESCENT, RATHER THAN MATRILINEAL (186)	1.00 OF 28	190	LEAN LESS TOWARD BEING THOSE WHERE THE KIN GROUP IS PATRILINEAL OR DOUBLE-DESCENT, RATHER THAN MATRILINEAL (186)	0.72 OF 219	28 158 0 61 XSQ= 8.91 PHI= 0.190 XP = 0.0028
196	LEAN MORE TOWARD BEING THOSE WHERE INDIVIDUAL RIGHTS IN REAL PROPERTY, AND RULES FOR INHERITANCE, ARE PRESENT (194)	0.94 OF 35	196	LEAN LESS TOWARD BEING THOSE WHERE INDIVIDUAL RIGHTS IN REAL PROPERTY, AND RULES FOR INHERITANCE, ARE PRESENT (194)	0.65 OF 246	33 161 2 85 XSQ= 10.61 PHI= 0.194 XP = 0.0011
198	IN ALL CASES ARE THOSE WHERE RULES FOR THE INHERITANCE OF REAL PROPERTY, IF PRESENT, FAVOR THE MALE HEIR OR LINE, RATHER THAN THE FEMALE (144)	1.00 OF 26	198	DRIFT LESS TOWARD BEING THOSE WHERE RULES FOR THE INHERITANCE OF REAL PROPERTY, IF PRESENT, FAVOR THE MALE HEIR OR LINE, RATHER THAN THE FEMALE (144)	0.85 OF 139	26 118 0 21 XSQ= 3.24 PHI= 0.140 XP = 0.0717
207	IN ALL CASES ARE THOSE WHERE MARITAL RESIDENCE IS AMBILOCAL OR NEOLOCAL, RATHER THAN MATRILOCAL OR UXORILOCAL (64)	1.00 OF 10	207	LEAN TOWARD BEING THOSE WHERE MARITAL RESIDENCE IS MATRILOCAL OR UXORILOCAL, RATHER THAN AMBILOCAL OR NEOLOCAL (64)	0.54 OF 118	0 64 10 54 XSQ= 8.79 PHI= -0.262 XP = 0.0030
209	IN ALL CASES ARE THOSE WHERE MARITAL RESIDENCE IS PATRILOCAL, VIRILOCAL, OR AVUNCULOCAL, RATHER THAN MATRILOCAL OR UXORILOCAL (270)	1.00 OF 35	209	LEAN LESS TOWARD BEING THOSE WHERE MARITAL RESIDENCE IS PATRILOCAL, VIRILOCAL, OR AVUNCULOCAL, RATHER THAN MATRILOCAL OR UXORILOCAL (270)	0.79 OF 299	35 235 0 64 XSQ= 7.94 PHI= 0.154 XP = 0.0048
210	IN ALL CASES ARE THOSE WHERE MARITAL RESIDENCE IS PATRILOCAL, RATHER THAN MATRILOCAL (169)	1.00 OF 28	210	TILT LESS TOWARD BEING THOSE WHERE MARITAL RESIDENCE IS PATRILOCAL, RATHER THAN MATRILOCAL (169)	0.82 OF 172	28 141 0 31 XSQ= 4.68 PHI= 0.153 XP = 0.0306
213	TILT TOWARD BEING THOSE WHERE FIRST COUSIN MARRIAGE IS PERMITTED (172)	0.69 OF 32	213	TILT TOWARD BEING THOSE WHERE FIRST COUSIN MARRIAGE IS NOT PERMITTED (198)	0.56 OF 338	22 150 10 188 XSQ= 6.03 PHI= 0.128 XP = 0.0140
225	TILT TOWARD BEING THOSE WHERE COUSIN MARRIAGE IS PREFERENTIALLY OR PERMISSIVELY PATRILATERAL, RATHER THAN MATRILATERAL (23)	0.70 OF 10	225	TILT TOWARD BEING THOSE WHERE COUSIN MARRIAGE IS PREFERENTIALLY OR PERMISSIVELY MATRILATERAL, RATHER THAN PATRILATERAL (43)	0.71 OF 56	7 16 3 40 XSQ= 4.72 PHI= 0.267 XP = 0.0298

234	DRIFT MORE TOWARD BEING THOSE WHERE THE COUSIN TERMINOLOGY IS OF ESKIMO OR HAWAIIAN TYPE, RATHER THAN CROW, OMAHA, OR IROQUOIS TYPE (170)	0.73 OF 26	234	DRIFT LESS TOWARD BEING THOSE WHERE THE COUSIN TERMINOLOGY IS OF ESKIMO OR HAWAIIAN TYPE, RATHER THAN CROW, OMAHA, OR IROQUOIS TYPE (170)	0.51 OF 296	7 145 19 151 XSQ= 3.83 PHI= -0.109 XP = 0.0505
240	TILT MORE TOWARD BEING THOSE WHERE THE FAMILY, IF EXTENDED, IS SMALL OR STEM, RATHER THAN LARGE (135)	0.84 OF 25	240	TILT LESS TOWARD BEING THOSE WHERE THE FAMILY, IF EXTENDED, IS SMALL OR STEM, RATHER THAN LARGE (135)	0.61 OF 188	4 74 21 114 XSQ= 4.23 PHI= -0.141 XP = 0.0397
242	TEND LESS TO BE THOSE WHERE MARRIAGE IS COMMONLY OR OCCASIONALLY POLYGYNOUS, RATHER THAN MONOGAMOUS (314)	0.56 OF 45	242	TEND MORE TO BE THOSE WHERE MARRIAGE IS COMMONLY OR OCCASIONALLY POLYGYNOUS, RATHER THAN MONOGAMOUS (314)	0.83 OF 350	25 289 20 61 XSQ= 16.23 PHI= -0.203 XP = 0.0001
278	IN ALL CASES ARE THOSE WHERE PROPERTY RIGHTS IN WOMEN ARE PRESENT (8) LWS	1.00 OF 3	278	TILT TOWARD BEING THOSE WHERE PROPERTY RIGHTS IN WOMEN ARE UNIMPORTANT OR ABSENT (14) LWS	0.74 OF 19	3 5 0 14 XSQ= 3.31 PHI= 0.388 EP = 0.0364
370	LEAN MORE TOWARD BEING THOSE WHERE THE SEGREGATION OF ADOLESCENT BOYS IS ABSENT (148)	0.92 OF 25	370	LEAN LESS TOWARD BEING THOSE WHERE THE SEGREGATION OF ADOLESCENT BOYS IS ABSENT (148)	0.57 OF 218	2 93 23 125 XSQ= 9.91 PHI= -0.202 XP = 0.0016
377	TEND TO BE THOSE WHERE MALE GENITAL MUTILATION IS PRESENT (83)	0.61 OF 33	377	TEND TO BE THOSE WHERE MALE GENITAL MUTILATION IS ABSENT (242)	0.78 OF 292	20 63 13 229 XSQ= 21.74 PHI= 0.259 XP = 0.0000
382	TILT TOWARD BEING THOSE WHERE FEMALE INITIATION RITES ARE ABSENT (27) JKB	0.88 OF 8	382	TILT TOWARD BEING THOSE WHERE FEMALE INITIATION RITES ARE PRESENT (38) JKB	0.65 OF 57	1 37 7 20 XSQ= 5.92 PHI= -0.302 XP = 0.0149
390	TILT TOWARD BEING THOSE WHERE PREMARITAL SEX RELATIONS ARE STRONGLY PUNISHED AND IN FACT RARE (47) JTW,EA	0.50 OF 20	390	TILT TOWARD BEING THOSE WHERE PREMARITAL SEX RELATIONS ARE WEAKLY PUNISHED AND IN FACT NOT RARE OR PUNISHED ONLY IF PREGNANCY RESULTS, OR FREELY PERMITTED (132) JTW,EA	0.77 OF 159	10 37 10 122 XSQ= 5.25 PHI= 0.171 XP = 0.0220
391	LEAN TOWARD BEING THOSE WHERE PREMARITAL SEX RELATIONS ARE STRONGLY PUNISHED AND IN FACT RARE, OR WEAKLY PUNISHED AND IN FACT NOT RARE (89) JTW,EA	0.85 OF 20	391	LEAN TOWARD BEING THOSE WHERE PREMARITAL SEX RELATIONS ARE PUNISHED ONLY IF PREGNANCY RESULTS, OR FREELY PERMITTED (90) JTW,EA	0.55 OF 159	17 72 3 87 XSQ= 9.68 PHI= 0.233 XP = 0.0019

397	DRIFT TOWARD BEING THOSE WHERE SEX DISABILITY IS PRESENT (14) JKH	0.75 OF 4	397	DRIFT TOWARD BEING THOSE WHERE SEX DISABILITY IS ABSENT (42) JKH	0.79 OF 52	 XSQ= PHI= XP =	3 11 1 41 3.23 0.240 0.0723
426	TEND MORE TO BE THOSE WHERE A HIGH GOD IS PRESENT (156) GES,EA	0.97 OF 32	426	TEND LESS TO BE THOSE WHERE A HIGH GOD IS PRESENT (156) GES,EA	0.55 OF 228	 XSQ= PHI= XP =	31 125 1 103 18.96 0.270 0.0000
427	IN ALL CASES ARE THOSE WHERE A HIGH GOD, IF PRESENT, IS ACTIVE, RATHER THAN INACTIVE (87) GES,EA	1.00 OF 31	427	TEND TO BE THOSE WHERE A HIGH GOD, IF PRESENT, IS INACTIVE, RATHER THAN ACTIVE (69) GES,EA	0.55 OF 125	 XSQ= PHI= XP =	31 56 0 69 28.49 0.427 0.0000
428	IN ALL CASES ARE THOSE WHERE A HIGH GOD, IF PRESENT AND ACTIVE, SUPPORTS HUMAN MORALITY, RATHER THAN NOT SUPPORTING IT (61) GES,EA	1.00 OF 31	428	TEND LESS TO BE THOSE WHERE A HIGH GOD, IF PRESENT AND ACTIVE, SUPPORTS HUMAN MORALITY, RATHER THAN NOT SUPPORTING IT (61) GES,EA	0.54 OF 56	 XSQ= PHI= XP =	31 30 0 26 18.37 0.460 0.0000
450	TILT TOWARD BEING THOSE WHERE THE OBSERVATION OF FOOD TABOOS IS LOW, RATHER THAN HIGH OR MEDIUM (26) JRL	0.83 OF 6	450	TILT TOWARD BEING THOSE WHERE THE OBSERVATION OF FOOD TABOOS IS HIGH OR MEDIUM, RATHER THAN LOW (60) JRL	0.74 OF 80	 XSQ= PHI= XP =	1 59 5 21 6.13 -0.267 0.0133
458	TEND TO BE THOSE WHERE GAMES, IF PRESENT, INCLUDE GAMES OF STRATEGY (52) R-A-B,EA	0.77 OF 13	458	TEND TO BE THOSE WHERE GAMES, IF PRESENT, DO NOT INCLUDE GAMES OF STRATEGY (119) R-A-B,EA	0.73 OF 158	 XSQ= PHI= XP =	10 42 3 116 12.10 0.266 0.0005

5 CULTURES
LOCATED IN EAST EURASIA (70)

5 CULTURES
LOCATED OUTSIDE OF
EAST EURASIA (330)

BACKGROUND ON PAGE 65

BOTH SUBJECT AND PREDICATE

70 IN LEFT COLUMN

ABOR	AINU	AKHA	ANDAMANESE	ARYANS	BASSERI	BENGALI	BHIL	BHUIYA	BURMESE
BURUSHO	BURYAT	CAMBODIANS	CHENCHU	CHUKCHEE	COORG	DAGUR	DARD	GARO	GILYAK
GOND	HAZARA	HO	JAPANESE	KACHIN	KAREN	KAZAK	KERALA	KET	KHALKA
KHASI	KOHISTANI	KOL	KOREANS	KORYAK	LAKHER	LAMET	LEPCHA	LHOTA NAGA	LOLO
MALAYS	MANCHU	MERINA	MIAO	MIN CHINESE	MINCHIA	MNONG GAR	MONGUOR	NICOBARESE	NURI
OKINAWANS	ORAON	PATHAN	PURUM	SAMOYED	SANTAL	SELUNG	SEMANG	SINDHI	SINHALESE
TAMIL	TANALA	THAI	TIBETANS	TODA	TURKMEN	VEDDA	VIETNAMESE	YAKUT	YUKAGHIR

330 IN RIGHT COLUMN

	Left column (East Eurasia)			Right column (outside East Eurasia)		
15	TEND TO BE THOSE WHERE THE LATITUDE IS TWENTY DEGREES OR GREATER (183)	0.74 OF 70	15	TEND TO BE THOSE WHERE THE LATITUDE IS LESS THAN TWENTY DEGREES (217)	0.60 OF 330	52 131 18 199 XSQ= 26.46 PHI= 0.257 XP = 0.0000
42	TILT TOWARD BEING THOSE WHERE THE NATURAL ENVIRONMENT IS TROPICAL OR SUB-TROPICAL RAIN FOREST, OR MONSOON FOREST (156) FWM	0.51 OF 70	42	TILT TOWARD BEING THOSE WHERE THE NATURAL ENVIRONMENT IS OTHER THAN TROPICAL OR SUB-TROPICAL RAIN FOREST, OR MONSOON FOREST (244) FWM	0.64 OF 330	36 120 34 210 XSQ= 4.89 PHI= 0.111 XP = 0.0269
51	LEAN MORE TOWARD BEING THOSE WHERE SUBSISTENCE IS PRIMARILY BY FOOD PRODUCTION -- I. E., AGRICULTURE OR HUSBANDRY -- RATHER THAN BY GATHERING (253)	0.79 OF 70	51	LEAN LESS TOWARD BEING THOSE WHERE SUBSISTENCE IS PRIMARILY BY FOOD PRODUCTION -- I. E., AGRICULTURE OR HUSBANDRY -- RATHER THAN BY GATHERING (253)	0.60 OF 330	55 198 15 132 XSQ= 7.79 PHI= 0.140 XP = 0.0053
53	TEND TO BE THOSE WHERE FOOD PRODUCTION IS BY INTENSIVE AGRICULTURE, RATHER THAN BY SIMPLE AGRICULTURE OR INCIPIENT FOOD PRODUCTION (91)	0.63 OF 46	53	TEND TO BE THOSE WHERE FOOD PRODUCTION IS BY SIMPLE AGRICULTURE OR INCIPIENT FOOD PRODUCTION, RATHER THAN BY INTENSIVE AGRICULTURE (147)	0.68 OF 192	29 62 17 130 XSQ= 13.59 PHI= 0.239 XP = 0.0002
55	LEAN TOWARD BEING THOSE WHERE FOOD PRODUCTION IS BY INTENSIVE AGRICULTURE, RATHER THAN BY SIMPLE AGRICULTURE (91)	0.71 OF 41	55	LEAN TOWARD BEING THOSE WHERE FOOD PRODUCTION IS BY SIMPLE AGRICULTURE, RATHER THAN BY INTENSIVE AGRICULTURE (101)	0.59 OF 151	29 62 12 89 XSQ= 10.23 PHI= 0.231 XP = 0.0014

62	LEAN MORE TOWARD BEING THOSE WHERE HUSBANDRY OF SOME KIND IS PRESENT (228)	0.74 OF 70	62	LEAN LESS TOWARD BEING THOSE WHERE HUSBANDRY OF SOME KIND IS PRESENT (228)	0.53 OF 330	52 176 18 154 XSQ= 9.51 PHI= 0.154 XP = 0.0020
63	TEND MORE TO BE THOSE WHERE HUSBANDRY, IF PRESENT, IS PRINCIPALLY IN THE FORM OF BOVINE, EQUINE, CAMEL-LIKE, OR DEER-LIKE ANIMALS, RATHER THAN PIGS, SHEEP, OR GOATS (152)	0.92 OF 51	63	TEND LESS TO BE THOSE WHERE HUSBANDRY, IF PRESENT, IS PRINCIPALLY IN THE FORM OF BOVINE, EQUINE, CAMEL-LIKE, OR DEER-LIKE ANIMALS, RATHER THAN PIGS, SHEEP, OR GOATS (152)	0.60 OF 175	47 105 4 70 XSQ= 17.11 PHI= 0.275 XP = 0.0000
71	TEND TO BE THOSE WHERE METAL WORKING IS PRESENT (98)	0.71 OF 41	71	TEND TO BE THOSE WHERE METAL WORKING IS ABSENT (153)	0.67 OF 210	29 69 12 141 XSQ= 19.11 PHI= 0.276 XP = 0.0000
73	TILT TOWARD BEING THOSE WHERE WEAVING IS PRESENT (118)	0.64 OF 39	73	TILT TOWARD BEING THOSE WHERE WEAVING IS ABSENT (130)	0.56 OF 209	25 93 14 116 XSQ= 4.31 PHI= 0.132 XP = 0.0379
79	TILT LESS TOWARD BEING THOSE WHERE NO CITY IS PRESENT (201)	0.80 OF 45	79	TILT MORE TOWARD BEING THOSE WHERE NO CITY IS PRESENT (201)	0.92 OF 179	9 14 36 165 XSQ= 4.54 PHI= 0.142 XP = 0.0331
86	TILT TOWARD BEING THOSE WHERE THE LEVEL OF POLITICAL INTEGRATION IS THE LARGE STATE, THE LITTLE STATE, OR THE MINIMAL STATE (148) GPM	0.64 OF 50	86	TILT TOWARD BEING THOSE WHERE THE LEVEL OF POLITICAL INTEGRATION IS THE AUTONOMOUS COMMUNITY, OR THE FAMILY (156) GPM	0.54 OF 254	32 116 18 138 XSQ= 4.91 PHI= 0.127 XP = 0.0267
88	TILT TOWARD BEING THOSE WHERE, IF A HEADMANSHIP IS PRESENT, SUCCESSION IS NON-HEREDITARY (106)	0.54 OF 52	88	TILT TOWARD BEING THOSE WHERE, IF A HEADMANSHIP IS PRESENT, SUCCESSION IS HEREDITARY (165)	0.64 OF 219	28 78 24 141 XSQ= 5.12 PHI= 0.137 XP = 0.0236
96	TILT TOWARD BEING THOSE WHERE THE HIERARCHY OF NATIONAL JURISDICTION HAS FOUR, THREE, TWO OR ONE LEVEL (174) GES,EA	0.68 OF 59	96	TILT TOWARD BEING THOSE WHERE THE HIERARCHY OF NATIONAL JURISDICTION HAS NO LEVELS (156) GES,EA	0.51 OF 271	40 134 19 137 XSQ= 5.83 PHI= 0.133 XP = 0.0158
98	LEAN MORE TOWARD BEING THOSE WHERE THE HIERARCHY OF LOCAL JURISDICTION HAS FOUR OR THREE LEVELS (238) GES,EA	0.86 OF 59	98	LEAN LESS TOWARD BEING THOSE WHERE THE HIERARCHY OF LOCAL JURISDICTION HAS FOUR OR THREE LEVELS (238) GES,EA	0.69 OF 272	51 187 8 85 XSQ= 6.66 PHI= 0.142 XP = 0.0099

100	TILT MORE TOWARD BEING THOSE 0.92 OF 59 WHERE HIERARCHIES ARE MORE COMPLEX THAN THE 'SIMPLEST,' I. E., MORE COMPLEX THAN TWO LOCAL LEVELS WITH NO NATIONAL LEVELS (267) GES,EA	100	TILT LESS TOWARD BEING THOSE 0.79 OF 271 WHERE HIERARCHIES ARE MORE COMPLEX THAN THE 'SIMPLEST,' I. E., MORE COMPLEX THAN TWO LOCAL LEVELS WITH NO NATIONAL LEVELS (267) GES,EA	54 213 5 58 XSQ= 4.44 PHI= 0.116 XP = 0.0351
102	TEND TO BE THOSE 0.77 OF 65 WHERE CLASS STRATIFICATION IS PRESENT (203)	102	TEND TO BE THOSE 0.52 OF 318 WHERE CLASS STRATIFICATION IS ABSENT (180)	50 153 15 165 XSQ= 16.84 PHI= 0.210 XP = 0.0000
107	LEAN LESS TOWARD BEING THOSE 0.64 OF 50 WHERE CLASS STRATIFICATION, IF PRESENT, IS BASED ON SOMETHING OTHER THAN OCCUPATIONAL STATUS (160)	107	LEAN MORE TOWARD BEING THOSE 0.84 OF 153 WHERE CLASS STRATIFICATION, IF PRESENT, IS BASED ON SOMETHING OTHER THAN OCCUPATIONAL STATUS (160)	18 25 32 128 XSQ= 7.59 PHI= 0.193 XP = 0.0059
109	TEND LESS TO BE THOSE 0.68 OF 53 WHERE CASTES ARE ABSENT (317)	109	TEND MORE TO BE THOSE 0.89 OF 315 WHERE CASTES ARE ABSENT (317)	17 34 36 281 XSQ= 15.48 PHI= 0.205 XP = 0.0001
110	TILT TOWARD BEING THOSE 0.55 OF 64 WHERE SLAVERY IS PRESENT (163)	110	TILT TOWARD BEING THOSE 0.60 OF 317 WHERE SLAVERY IS ABSENT (218)	35 128 29 189 XSQ= 3.89 PHI= 0.101 XP = 0.0486
116	DRIFT TOWARD BEING THOSE 0.59 OF 17 WHERE OCCUPATIONAL SPECIALIZATION IS FULL-TIME, WHETHER OR NOT FOR SURPLUS PRODUCTION (20) JMH	116	DRIFT TOWARD BEING THOSE 0.73 OF 37 WHERE OCCUPATIONAL SPECIALIZATION IS PART-TIME ONLY (34) JMH	10 10 7 27 XSQ= 3.78 PHI= 0.265 XP = 0.0519
135	IN ALL CASES ARE THOSE 1.00 OF 6 WHERE INDIVIDUAL OWNERSHIP OF ECONOMICALLY SIGNIFICANT PROPERTY IS PRESENT (24) GES	135	DRIFT LESS TOWARD BEING THOSE 0.56 OF 32 WHERE INDIVIDUAL OWNERSHIP OF ECONOMICALLY SIGNIFICANT PROPERTY IS PRESENT (24) GES	6 18 0 14 XSQ= 2.49 PHI= 0.256 EP = 0.0672
164	IN ALL CASES ARE THOSE 1.00 OF 4 WHERE THE EMPHASIS ON INDIVIDUAL VOLITION AS THE CAUSE OR SOURCE OF ILLNESS IS LOW (9) MJ	164	DRIFT TOWARD BEING THOSE 0.64 OF 14 WHERE THE EMPHASIS ON INDIVIDUAL VOLITION AS THE CAUSE OR SOURCE OF ILLNESS IS HIGH (9) MJ	0 9 4 5 XSQ= 2.89 PHI= -0.401 EP = 0.0824
183	TILT MORE TOWARD BEING THOSE 0.96 OF 56 WHERE THE LARGEST NON-COGNATIC KIN GROUP IS SMALLER THAN A MOEITY, I. E., A PHRATRY OR SIB OR LINEAGE (218)	183	TILT LESS TOWARD BEING THOSE 0.84 OF 196 WHERE THE LARGEST NON-COGNATIC KIN GROUP IS SMALLER THAN A MOEITY, I. E., A PHRATRY OR SIB OR LINEAGE (218)	2 32 54 164 XSQ= 5.03 PHI= -0.141 XP = 0.0249

185	TILT MORE TOWARD BEING THOSE WHERE THE LARGEST NON-COGNATIC KIN GROUP IS THE MOEITY OR PHRATRY OR SIB (194)	0.89 OF 56	185	TILT LESS TOWARD BEING THOSE WHERE THE LARGEST NON-COGNATIC KIN GROUP IS THE MOEITY OR PHRATRY OR SIB (194)	0.73 OF 196	50 144 6 52 XSQ= 5.29 PHI= 0.145 XP = 0.0215
186	TEND TO BE THOSE WHERE THE KIN GROUP IS EXCLUSIVELY PATRILINEAL (150)	0.60 OF 70	186	TEND TO BE THOSE WHERE THE KIN GROUP IS OTHER THAN EXCLUSIVELY PATRILINEAL (250)	0.67 OF 330	42 108 28 222 XSQ= 17.18 PHI= 0.207 XP = 0.0000
188	LEAN MORE TOWARD BEING THOSE WHERE THE KIN GROUP IS OTHER THAN EXCLUSIVELY COGNATIC (252)	0.80 OF 70	188	LEAN LESS TOWARD BEING THOSE WHERE THE KIN GROUP IS OTHER THAN EXCLUSIVELY COGNATIC (252)	0.59 OF 330	14 134 56 196 XSQ= 9.65 PHI= -0.155 XP = 0.0019
190	TILT MORE TOWARD BEING THOSE WHERE THE KIN GROUP IS PATRILINEAL OR DOUBLE-DESCENT, RATHER THAN MATRILINEAL (186)	0.89 OF 53	190	TILT LESS TOWARD BEING THOSE WHERE THE KIN GROUP IS PATRILINEAL OR DOUBLE-DESCENT, RATHER THAN MATRILINEAL (186)	0.72 OF 194	47 139 6 55 XSQ= 5.61 PHI= 0.151 XP = 0.0179
192	DRIFT MORE TOWARD BEING THOSE OTHER THAN WHERE THE ONLY KIN GROUP PRESENT IS A KINDRED OR ELSE BILATERAL DESCENT IS INFERRED (289)	0.81 OF 70	192	DRIFT LESS TOWARD BEING THOSE OTHER THAN WHERE THE ONLY KIN GROUP PRESENT IS A KINDRED OR ELSE BILATERAL DESCENT IS INFERRED (289)	0.70 OF 330	13 98 57 232 XSQ= 3.03 PHI= -0.087 XP = 0.0816
198	DRIFT MORE TOWARD BEING THOSE WHERE RULES FOR THE INHERITANCE OF REAL PROPERTY, IF PRESENT, FAVOR THE MALE HEIR OR LINE, RATHER THAN THE FEMALE (144)	0.97 OF 38	198	DRIFT LESS TOWARD BEING THOSE WHERE RULES FOR THE INHERITANCE OF REAL PROPERTY, IF PRESENT, FAVOR THE MALE HEIR OR LINE, RATHER THAN THE FEMALE (144)	0.84 OF 127	37 107 1 20 XSQ= 3.43 PHI= 0.144 XP = 0.0642
201	TILT MORE TOWARD BEING THOSE WHERE MARITAL RESIDENCE IS NON-OPTIONAL, RATHER THAN AMBILOCAL OR NEOLOCAL (334)	0.94 OF 70	201	TILT LESS TOWARD BEING THOSE WHERE MARITAL RESIDENCE IS NON-OPTIONAL, RATHER THAN AMBILOCAL OR NEOLOCAL (334)	0.82 OF 328	66 268 4 60 XSQ= 5.86 PHI= 0.121 XP = 0.0155
204	LEAN MORE TOWARD BEING THOSE WHERE MARITAL RESIDENCE IS PATRILOCAL, VIRILOCAL, OR AVUNCULOCAL, RATHER THAN AMBILOCAL OR NEOLOCAL (270)	0.93 OF 61	204	LEAN LESS TOWARD BEING THOSE WHERE MARITAL RESIDENCE IS PATRILOCAL, VIRILOCAL, OR AVUNCULOCAL, RATHER THAN AMBILOCAL OR NEOLOCAL (270)	0.78 OF 273	57 213 4 60 XSQ= 6.69 PHI= 0.142 XP = 0.0097
213	TEND TO BE THOSE WHERE FIRST COUSIN MARRIAGE IS PERMITTED (172)	0.67 OF 66	213	TEND TO BE THOSE WHERE FIRST COUSIN MARRIAGE IS NOT PERMITTED (198)	0.58 OF 304	44 128 22 176 XSQ= 12.18 PHI= 0.181 XP = 0.0005

220	TILT LESS TOWARD BEING THOSE 0.62 OF 66 WHERE FIRST COUSIN MARRIAGE IN SOME FORM OR OTHER IS NOT PRESCRIBED OR PREFERRED (273)	220	TILT MORE TOWARD BEING THOSE 0.76 OF 304 WHERE FIRST COUSIN MARRIAGE IN SOME FORM OR OTHER IS NOT PRESCRIBED OR PREFERRED (273)	25 72 41 232 XSQ= 4.94 PHI= 0.116 XP = 0.0263
221	LEAN LESS TOWARD BEING THOSE 0.80 OF 66 WHERE MATRILATERAL CROSS-COUSIN MARRIAGE IS NOT PRESCRIBED OR PREFERRED (335)	221	LEAN MORE TOWARD BEING THOSE 0.93 OF 304 WHERE MATRILATERAL CROSS-COUSIN MARRIAGE IS NOT PRESCRIBED OR PREFERRED (335)	13 22 53 282 XSQ= 8.43 PHI= 0.151 XP = 0.0037
236	DRIFT MORE TOWARD BEING THOSE 0.64 OF 70 WHERE THE FAMILY IS OF AN EXTENDED TYPE, RATHER THAN AN INDEPENDENT TYPE (213)	236	DRIFT LESS TOWARD BEING THOSE 0.51 OF 328 WHERE THE FAMILY IS OF AN EXTENDED TYPE, RATHER THAN AN INDEPENDENT TYPE (213)	45 168 25 160 XSQ= 3.45 PHI= 0.093 XP = 0.0632
240	TILT MORE TOWARD BEING THOSE 0.80 OF 45 WHERE THE FAMILY, IF EXTENDED, IS SMALL OR STEM, RATHER THAN LARGE (135)	240	TILT LESS TOWARD BEING THOSE 0.59 OF 168 WHERE THE FAMILY, IF EXTENDED, IS SMALL OR STEM, RATHER THAN LARGE (135)	9 69 36 99 XSQ= 5.91 PHI= -0.167 XP = 0.0150
241	TILT LESS TOWARD BEING THOSE 0.76 OF 45 WHERE THE FAMILY, IF EXTENDED, IS LARGE OR SMALL, RATHER THAN STEM (187)	241	TILT MORE TOWARD BEING THOSE 0.91 OF 168 WHERE THE FAMILY, IF EXTENDED, IS LARGE OR SMALL, RATHER THAN STEM (187)	34 153 11 15 XSQ= 6.59 PHI= -0.176 XP = 0.0102
272	DRIFT TOWARD BEING THOSE 0.73 OF 15 WHERE THE DIVORCE RATE IS LOW (28) CA	272	DRIFT TOWARD BEING THOSE 0.60 OF 42 WHERE THE DIVORCE RATE IS HIGH (29) CA	4 25 11 17 XSQ= 3.55 PHI= -0.250 XP = 0.0595
301	LEAN TOWARD BEING THOSE 0.57 OF 14 WHERE THE POST-PARTUM SEX TABOO LASTS ONE MONTH OR LESS (28)	301	LEAN TOWARD BEING THOSE 0.82 OF 110 WHERE THE POST-PARTUM SEX TABOO LASTS LONGER THAN ONE MONTH (96)	6 90 8 20 XSQ= 8.67 PHI= -0.264 XP = 0.0032
308	DRIFT TOWARD BEING THOSE 0.83 OF 6 WHERE AVERAGE SOCIALIZATION ANXIETY IS LOW (18) W-C	308	DRIFT TOWARD BEING THOSE 0.62 OF 34 WHERE AVERAGE SOCIALIZATION ANXIETY IS HIGH (22) W-C	1 21 5 13 XSQ= 2.57 PHI= -0.253 EP = 0.0734
311	DRIFT TOWARD BEING THOSE 0.86 OF 7 WHERE SEXUAL SOCIALIZATION ANXIETY IS LOW (23) W-C	311	DRIFT TOWARD BEING THOSE 0.61 OF 44 WHERE SEXUAL SOCIALIZATION ANXIETY IS HIGH (28) W-C	1 27 6 17 XSQ= 3.67 PHI= -0.268 XP = 0.0553

330	DRIFT TOWARD BEING THOSE WHERE THE AGE OF THE INFANT AT TIME OF WEANING IS 2.5 YEARS OR HIGHER (34) B-B-C	0.86 OF 7	330	DRIFT TOWARD BEING THOSE WHERE THE AGE OF THE INFANT AT TIME OF WEANING IS LOWER THAN 2.5 YEARS (36) B-B-C	0.56 OF 63	6 28 1 35 XSQ= 2.80 PHI= 0.200 XP = 0.0941
339	TILT TOWARD BEING THOSE WHERE THE CHILD'S INFERRED CONFLICT REGARDING RESPONSIBLE BEHAVIOR IS HIGH (31) B-B-C	0.86 OF 7	339	TILT TOWARD BEING THOSE WHERE THE CHILD'S INFERRED CONFLICT REGARDING RESPONSIBLE BEHAVIOR IS LOW (42) B-B-C	0.62 OF 66	6 25 1 41 XSQ= 4.13 PHI= 0.238 XP = 0.0421
368	DRIFT TOWARD BEING THOSE WHERE DISSOCIATION OF THE SEXES AT ADOLESCENCE IS LOW (21) JKH	0.89 OF 9	368	DRIFT TOWARD BEING THOSE WHERE DISSOCIATION OF THE SEXES AT ADOLESCENCE IS HIGH OR MEDIUM (16) JKH	0.54 OF 28	1 15 8 13 XSQ= 3.42 PHI= -0.304 EP = 0.0501
369	LEAN TOWARD BEING THOSE WHERE BOTH DISSOCIATION OF THE SEXES AT ADOLESCENCE, AND CUSTOMS OF INITIATION AT ADOLESCENCE, ARE ABSENT (15) JKH	0.70 OF 10	369	LEAN TOWARD BEING THOSE WHERE DISSOCIATION OF THE SEXES AT ADOLESCENCE, OR CUSTOMS OF INITIATION AT ADOLESCENCE, ARE PRESENT (42) JKH	0.83 OF 47	3 39 7 8 XSQ= 9.36 PHI= -0.405 XP = 0.0022
372	TILT MORE TOWARD BEING THOSE WHERE MALE INITIATION RITES ARE ABSENT (63) ASA	0.91 OF 11	372	TILT LESS TOWARD BEING THOSE WHERE MALE INITIATION RITES ARE ABSENT (63) ASA	0.53 OF 100	1 47 10 53 XSQ= 4.36 PHI= -0.198 XP = 0.0368
382	TILT TOWARD BEING THOSE WHERE FEMALE INITIATION RITES ARE ABSENT (27) JKB	0.75 OF 12	382	TILT TOWARD BEING THOSE WHERE FEMALE INITIATION RITES ARE PRESENT (38) JKB	0.66 OF 53	3 35 9 18 XSQ= 5.20 PHI= -0.283 XP = 0.0226
386	DRIFT TOWARD BEING THOSE WHERE SEXUAL EXPRESSION BY THE YOUNG IS PERMITTED (40) F-B	0.80 OF 10	386	DRIFT TOWARD BEING THOSE WHERE SEXUAL EXPRESSION BY THE YOUNG IS RESTRICTED OR SEMI-RESTRICTED (46) F-B	0.58 OF 76	2 44 8 32 XSQ= 3.69 PHI= -0.207 XP = 0.0547
398	IN ALL CASES ARE THOSE WHERE THE INTENSITY OF SEX ANXIETY IS LOW (16) WNS	1.00 OF 5	398	TILT TOWARD BEING THOSE WHERE THE INTENSITY OF SEX ANXIETY IS HIGH (16) WNS	0.59 OF 27	0 16 5 11 XSQ= 3.79 PHI= -0.344 EP = 0.0434
417	TEND TO BE THOSE WHERE WARFARE IS NOT PREVALENT (9) LWS	0.67 OF 9	417	TEND TO BE THOSE WHERE WARFARE IS PREVALENT (34) LWS	0.91 OF 34	3 31 6 3 XSQ= 11.10 PHI= -0.508 XP = 0.0009

421	TILT TOWARD BEING THOSE WHERE KILLING, TORTURING, OR MUTILATING OF THE ENEMY IS NEGLIGIBLY EMPHASIZED (47) PES	0.92 OF 12	421	TILT TOWARD BEING THOSE WHERE KILLING, TORTURING, OR MUTILATING OF THE ENEMY IS STRONGLY OR MODERATELY EMPHASIZED (37) PES	0.50 OF 72	1 36 11 36 XSQ= 5.65 PHI= -0.259 XP = 0.0174
427	TILT MORE TOWARD BEING THOSE WHERE A HIGH GOD, IF PRESENT, IS ACTIVE, RATHER THAN INACTIVE (87) GES,EA	0.76 OF 25	427	TILT LESS TOWARD BEING THOSE WHERE A HIGH GOD, IF PRESENT, IS ACTIVE, RATHER THAN INACTIVE (87) GES,EA	0.52 OF 131	19 68 6 63 XSQ= 4.01 PHI= 0.160 XP = 0.0452
431	TILT TOWARD BEING THOSE WHERE SUPERNATURAL SANCTIONS FOR MORALITY, HAVING AN EFFECT ON AN INDIVIDUAL'S AFTER LIFE, ARE PRESENT (10) GES	0.80 OF 5	431	TILT TOWARD BEING THOSE WHERE SUPERNATURAL SANCTIONS FOR MORALITY, HAVING AN EFFECT ON AN INDIVIDUAL'S AFTERLIFE, ARE ABSENT OR UNREPORTED (25) GES	0.80 OF 30	4 6 1 24 XSQ= 4.91 PHI= 0.374 EP = 0.0169
433	TILT TOWARD BEING THOSE WHERE BELIEF IN REINCARNATION IS PRESENT (10) GES	0.67 OF 6	433	TILT TOWARD BEING THOSE WHERE BELIEF IN REINCARNATION IS ABSENT (28) GES	0.81 OF 32	4 6 2 26 XSQ= 3.77 PHI= 0.315 EP = 0.0314
441	IN ALL CASES ARE THOSE WHERE FEAR OF HUMAN BEINGS IS LOW (32) W-C	1.00 OF 8	441	TILT TOWARD BEING THOSE WHERE FEAR OF HUMAN BEINGS IS HIGH (29) W-C	0.55 OF 53	0 29 8 24 XSQ= 6.29 PHI= -0.321 XP = 0.0121
445	TILT TOWARD BEING THOSE WHERE SORCERY IS UNIMPORTANT (23) BBW,DH	0.77 OF 13	445	TILT TOWARD BEING THOSE WHERE SORCERY IS IMPORTANT (26) BBW,DH	0.64 OF 36	3 23 10 13 XSQ= 4.85 PHI= -0.315 XP = 0.0276
450	LEAN TOWARD BEING THOSE WHERE THE OBSERVATION OF FOOD TABOOS IS LOW, RATHER THAN HIGH OR MEDIUM (26) JRL	0.61 OF 18	450	LEAN TOWARD BEING THOSE WHERE THE OBSERVATION OF FOOD TABOOS IS HIGH OR MEDIUM, RATHER THAN LOW (60) JRL	0.78 OF 68	7 53 11 15 XSQ= 8.52 PHI= -0.315 XP = 0.0035
458	DRIFT LESS TOWARD BEING THOSE WHERE GAMES, IF PRESENT, DO NOT INCLUDE GAMES OF STRATEGY (119) R-A-B,EA	0.52 OF 27	458	DRIFT MORE TOWARD BEING THOSE WHERE GAMES, IF PRESENT, DO NOT INCLUDE GAMES OF STRATEGY (119) R-A-B,EA	0.73 OF 144	13 39 14 105 XSQ= 3.82 PHI= 0.150 XP = 0.0505
468	LEAN TOWARD BEING THOSE WHERE CONTACT WITH OTHER CULTURES IS FREQUENT, RATHER THAN REGULAR OR IRREGULAR (17) JMH	0.65 OF 17	468	LEAN TOWARD BEING THOSE WHERE CONTACT WITH OTHER CULTURES IS REGULAR OR IRREGULAR, RATHER THAN FREQUENT (37) JMH	0.84 OF 37	11 6 6 31 XSQ= 10.55 PHI= 0.442 XP = 0.0012

```
470  DRIFT TOWARD BEING THOSE          0.59 OF  17     470  DRIFT TOWARD BEING THOSE          0.70 OF  37          10     11
     WHERE INNCVATIONS ARE                                  WHERE INNOVATIONS ARE                                     7     26
     GENERALLY ACCEPTED  (21) JMH                           ACCEPTED ONLY SELECTIVELY  (33) JMH             XSQ=      3.01
                                                                                                           PHI=     0.236
                                                                                                           XP =    0.0825

472  TILT TOWARD BEING THOSE           0.79 OF  14     472  TILT TOWARD BEING THOSE           0.58 OF  76           3     44
     WHERE THE COMPOSITE NARCISSISM INCEX                   WHERE THE COMPOSITE NARCISSISM INDEX                     11     32
     IS LCW  (43) PES                                       IS HIGH  (47) PES                               XSQ=      4.92
                                                                                                           PHI=    -0.234
                                                                                                           XP =    0.0265

474  TILT TOWARD BEING THOSE           0.86 OF  14     474  TILT TOWARD BEING THOSE           0.52 OF  75           2     39
     WHERE BOASTFULNESS IS MODERATE,                        WHERE BOASTFULNESS IS EXTREME  (41) PES                  12     36
     NEGLIBIBLE, OR UNREPORTED  (48) PES                                                                    XSQ=      5.32
                                                                                                           PHI=    -0.245
                                                                                                           XP =    0.0211
```

6 CULTURES
LOCATED IN THE INSULAR PACIFIC (70)

6 CULTURES
LOCATED OUTSIDE OF
THE INSULAR PACIFIC (330)

BACKGROUND ON PAGE 65 — BOTH SUBJECT AND PREDICATE

70 IN LEFT COLUMN

AJIE	ALORESE	ARANDA	ARAPESH	ATAYAL	BALINESE	BATAK	BELU	BUNLAP	DIERI
DOBUANS	DUSUN	ELLICE	ENGA	GILBERTESE	HANUNOO	HAWAIIANS	IBAN	IFUGAO	JAVANESE
KAPAUKU	KARIERA	KERAKI	KURTATCHI	LAKALAI	LAU	LESU	LIFU	MACASSARESE	MANGAIANS
MANIHIKI	MANUS	MAORI	MARQUESANS	MARSHALLESE	MENTAWEI	MINANGKABAU	MOTA	MURINBATA	MURNGIN
ONTONG-JAVA	PAIWAN	PALAUANS	PONAPEANS	PUKAPUKA	PURARI	RAROIANS	ROTINESE	ROTUMANS	SAGADA
SAMOANS	SENIANG	SIMBOESE	SIUAI	SUBANUN	TAGBANUA	TANIMBARESE	TIKOPIA	TIWI	TOKELAU
TORAJA	TROBRIAND	TRUKESE	ULAWANS	WANTOAT	WAROPEN	WIKMUNKAN	WOGEO	WOLEAIANS	YAPESE

330 IN RIGHT COLUMN

	Left column (70)			Right column (330)		
13	IN ALL CASES ARE THOSE WHERE THE LATITUDE IS LESS THAN FORTY DEGREES (329)	1.00 OF 70	13	TEND LESS TO BE THOSE WHERE THE LATITUDE IS LESS THAN FORTY DEGREES (329)	0.78 OF 330	0 71 70 259 XSQ= 16.87 PHI= -0.205 XP = 0.0000
15	TEND TO BE THOSE WHERE THE LATITUDE IS LESS THAN TWENTY DEGREES (217)	0.86 OF 70	15	TEND TO BE THOSE WHERE THE LATITUDE IS TWENTY DEGREES OR GREATER (183)	0.52 OF 330	10 173 60 157 XSQ= 32.33 PHI= -0.284 XP = 0.
16	TEND TO BE THOSE WHERE THE LATITUDE IS LESS THAN TEN DEGREES (123)	0.56 OF 70	16	TEND TO BE THOSE WHERE THE LATITUDE IS TEN DEGREES OR GREATER (277)	0.75 OF 330	31 246 39 84 XSQ= 23.43 PHI= -0.242 XP = 0.0000
33	TILT MORE TOWARD BEING THOSE WHERE THE NATURAL ENVIRONMENT IS OTHER THAN 'VERY HARSH,' I.E., DESERT, DESERT GRASSES AND SHRUBS, TUNDRA, OR HIGH PLATEAU STEPPE (341) FWM	0.96 OF 70	33	TILT LESS TOWARD BEING THOSE WHERE THE NATURAL ENVIRONMENT IS OTHER THAN 'VERY HARSH,' I.E., DESERT, DESERT GRASSES AND SHRUBS, TUNDRA, OR HIGH PLATEAU STEPPE (341) FWM	0.83 OF 330	3 56 67 274 XSQ= 6.41 PHI= -0.127 XP = 0.0113
36	TEND MORE TO BE THOSE WHERE THE NATURAL ENVIRONMENT IS OTHER THAN 'VERY HARSH,' OR SUB-TROPICAL BUSH, OR TEMPERATE GRASSLAND (292) FWM	0.91 OF 70	36	TEND LESS TO BE THOSE WHERE THE NATURAL ENVIRONMENT IS OTHER THAN 'VERY HARSH,' OR SUB-TROPICAL BUSH, OR TEMPERATE GRASSLAND (292) FWM	0.69 OF 330	6 102 64 228 XSQ= 13.51 PHI= -0.184 XP = 0.0002

No.	Statement	Proportion	No.	Statement	Proportion	Statistics
42	TEND TO BE THOSE WHERE THE NATURAL ENVIRONMENT IS TROPICAL OR SUB-TROPICAL RAIN FOREST, OR MONSOON FOREST (156) FWM	0.84 OF 70	42	TEND TO BE THOSE WHERE THE NATURAL ENVIRONMENT IS OTHER THAN TROPICAL OR SUB-TROPICAL RAIN FOREST, OR MONSOON FOREST (244) FWM	0.71 OF 330	59 97 11 233 XSQ= 70.85 PHI= 0.421 XP = 0.
44	TILT MORE TOWARD BEING THOSE WHERE SETTLEMENTS ARE FIXED (222)	0.83 OF 53	44	TILT LESS TOWARD BEING THOSE WHERE SETTLEMENTS ARE FIXED (222)	0.64 OF 279	44 178 9 101 XSQ= 6.58 PHI= 0.141 XP = 0.0103
48	TEND TO BE THOSE WHERE THE FOOD SUPPLY IS SECURE, AND FOOD SHORTAGES ARE RARE OR OCCASIONAL (38) MGW	0.89 OF 18	48	TEND TO BE THOSE WHERE THE FOOD SUPPLY IS NOT SECURE, AND FOOD SHORTAGES ARE FREQUENT OR ANNUAL (41) MGW	0.64 OF 61	16 22 2 39 XSQ= 13.49 PHI= 0.413 XP = 0.0002
53	TEND MORE TO BE THOSE WHERE FOOD PRODUCTION IS BY SIMPLE AGRICULTURE OR INCIPIENT FOOD PRODUCTION, RATHER THAN BY INTENSIVE AGRICULTURE (147)	0.89 OF 38	53	TEND LESS TO BE THOSE WHERE FOOD PRODUCTION IS BY SIMPLE AGRICULTURE OR INCIPIENT FOOD PRODUCTION, RATHER THAN BY INTENSIVE AGRICULTURE (147)	0.56 OF 200	4 87 34 113 XSQ= 13.34 PHI= -0.237 XP = 0.0003
54	DRIFT MORE TOWARD BEING THOSE WHERE FOOD PRODUCTION IS BY INTENSIVE OR SIMPLE AGRICULTURE, RATHER THAN BY INCIPIENT FOOD PRODUCTION (192)	0.92 OF 38	54	DRIFT LESS TOWARD BEING THOSE WHERE FOOD PRODUCTION IS BY INTENSIVE OR SIMPLE AGRICULTURE, RATHER THAN BY INCIPIENT FOOD PRODUCTION (192)	0.78 OF 200	35 157 3 43 XSQ= 2.97 PHI= 0.112 XP = 0.0849
55	TEND TO BE THOSE WHERE FOOD PRODUCTION IS BY SIMPLE AGRICULTURE, RATHER THAN BY INTENSIVE AGRICULTURE (101)	0.89 OF 35	55	TEND TO BE THOSE WHERE FOOD PRODUCTION IS BY INTENSIVE AGRICULTURE, RATHER THAN BY SIMPLE AGRICULTURE (91)	0.55 OF 157	4 87 31 70 XSQ= 20.48 PHI= -0.327 XP = 0.0000
56	LEAN MORE TOWARD BEING THOSE WHERE FOOD PRODUCTION IS BY SIMPLE AGRICULTURE, RATHER THAN BY INCIPIENT FOOD PRODUCTION (101)	0.91 OF 34	56	LEAN LESS TOWARD BEING THOSE WHERE FOOD PRODUCTION IS BY SIMPLE AGRICULTURE, RATHER THAN BY INCIPIENT FOOD PRODUCTION (101)	0.62 OF 113	31 70 3 43 XSQ= 9.07 PHI= 0.248 XP = 0.0026
63	TEND TO BE THOSE WHERE HUSBANDRY, IF PRESENT, IS PRINCIPALLY IN THE FORM OF PIGS, SHEEP, OR GOATS, RATHER THAN BOVINE, EQUINE, CAMEL-LIKE, OR DEER-LIKE ANIMALS (74)	0.85 OF 40	63	TEND TO BE THOSE WHERE HUSBANDRY, IF PRESENT, IS PRINCIPALLY IN THE FORM OF BOVINE, EQUINE, CAMEL-LIKE, OR DEER-LIKE ANIMALS, RATHER THAN PIGS, SHEEP, OR GOATS (152)	0.78 OF 186	6 146 34 40 XSQ= 57.42 PHI= -0.504 XP = 0.
71	TEND MORE TO BE THOSE WHERE METAL WORKING IS ABSENT (153)	0.91 OF 45	71	TEND LESS TO BE THOSE WHERE METAL WORKING IS ABSENT (153)	0.54 OF 206	4 94 41 112 XSQ= 19.43 PHI= -0.278 XP = 0.0000

73	LEAN TOWARD BEING THOSE WHERE WEAVING IS ABSENT (130)	0.76 OF 45	73	LEAN TOWARD BEING THOSE WHERE WEAVING IS PRESENT (118)	0.53 OF 203	11 107 34 96 XSQ= 10.69 PHI= -0.208 XP = 0.0011
74	TEND TO BE THOSE WHERE POTTERY IS ABSENT (93)	0.84 OF 44	74	TEND TO BE THOSE WHERE POTTERY IS PRESENT (145)	0.71 OF 194	7 138 37 56 XSQ= 43.66 PHI= -0.428 XP = 0.
80	TILT MORE TOWARD BEING THOSE WHERE NO CITY OR TOWN IS PRESENT (185)	0.97 OF 34	80	TILT LESS TOWARD BEING THOSE WHERE NO CITY OR TOWN IS PRESENT (185)	0.80 OF 190	1 38 33 152 XSQ= 4.71 PHI= -0.145 XP = 0.0300
81	LEAN MORE TOWARD BEING THOSE WHERE NO CITY OR TOWN IS PRESENT, AND THE AVERAGE COMMUNITY SIZE IS SMALLER THAN 200 (135)	0.82 OF 34	81	LEAN LESS TOWARD BEING THOSE WHERE NO CITY OR TOWN IS PRESENT, AND THE AVERAGE COMMUNITY SIZE IS SMALLER THAN 200 (135)	0.56 OF 190	6 83 28 107 XSQ= 7.11 PHI= -0.178 XP = 0.0077
86	DRIFT TOWARD BEING THOSE WHERE THE LEVEL OF POLITICAL INTEGRATION IS THE AUTONOMOUS COMMUNITY, OR THE FAMILY (156) GPM	0.62 OF 58	86	DRIFT TOWARD BEING THOSE WHERE THE LEVEL OF POLITICAL INTEGRATION IS THE LARGE STATE, THE LITTLE STATE, OR THE MINIMAL STATE (148) GPM	0.51 OF 246	22 126 36 120 XSQ= 2.81 PHI= -0.096 XP = 0.0939
88	TILT MORE TOWARD BEING THOSE WHERE, IF A HEADMANSHIP IS PRESENT, SUCCESSION IS HEREDITARY (165)	0.77 OF 47	88	TILT LESS TOWARD BEING THOSE WHERE, IF A HEADMANSHIP IS PRESENT, SUCCESSION IS HEREDITARY (165)	0.58 OF 224	11 95 36 129 XSQ= 5.12 PHI= -0.137 XP = 0.0236
107	LEAN MORE TOWARD BEING THOSE WHERE CLASS STRATIFICATION, IF PRESENT, IS BASED ON SOMETHING OTHER THAN OCCUPATIONAL STATUS (160)	0.97 OF 38	107	LEAN LESS TOWARD BEING THOSE WHERE CLASS STRATIFICATION, IF PRESENT, IS BASED ON SOMETHING OTHER THAN OCCUPATIONAL STATUS (160)	0.75 OF 165	1 42 37 123 XSQ= 8.32 PHI= -0.202 XP = 0.0039
108	TILT TOWARD BEING THOSE WHERE CLASS STRATIFICATION, IF PRESENT, IS BASED ON A HEREDITARY ARISTOCRACY (74)	0.55 OF 38	108	TILT TOWARD BEING THOSE WHERE CLASS STRATIFICATION, IF PRESENT, IS BASED ON SOMETHING OTHER THAN A HEREDITARY ARISTOCRACY (129)	0.68 OF 165	21 53 17 112 XSQ= 6.18 PHI= 0.174 XP = 0.0129
109	TILT MORE TOWARD BEING THOSE WHERE CASTES ARE ABSENT (317)	0.96 OF 68	109	TILT LESS TOWARD BEING THOSE WHERE CASTES ARE ABSENT (317)	0.84 OF 300	3 48 65 252 XSQ= 5.30 PHI= -0.120 XP = 0.0213

110	LEAN MORE TOWARD BEING THOSE 0.75 OF 68 WHERE SLAVERY IS ABSENT (218)	110	LEAN LESS TOWARD BEING THOSE 0.53 OF 313 WHERE SLAVERY IS ABSENT (218)	17 146 51 167 XSQ= 9.83 PHI= -0.161 XP = 0.0017
118	DRIFT TOWARD BEING THOSE 0.88 OF 8 WHERE THE PERCENTAGE OF OCCUPATIONS THAT ARE SPECIALIZED IS LOW (25) WME	118	DRIFT TOWARD BEING THOSE 0.56 OF 41 WHERE THE PERCENTAGE OF OCCUPATIONS THAT ARE SPECIALIZED IS HIGH OR MEDIUM (24) WME	1 23 7 18 XSQ= 3.50 PHI= -0.267 XP = 0.0615
138	TILT TOWARD BEING THOSE 0.69 OF 13 WHERE SUPERORDINATE JUSTICE IS ABSENT (18) BBW	138	TILT TOWARD BEING THOSE 0.67 OF 27 WHERE SUPERORDINATE JUSTICE IS PRESENT (22) BBW	4 18 9 9 XSQ= 3.23 PHI= -0.284 EP = 0.0458
176	TEND TO BE THOSE 0.63 OF 68 WHERE THE COMMUNITY IS A CLAN-COMMUNITY OR A COMMUNITY STRUCTURED OR SEGMENTED ON A CLAN BASIS (169)	176	TEND TO BE THOSE 0.60 OF 314 WHERE THE COMMUNITY IS OTHER THAN A CLAN-COMMUNITY OR A COMMUNITY STRUCTURED OR SEGMENTED ON A CLAN BASIS (213)	43 126 25 188 XSQ= 11.18 PHI= 0.171 XP = 0.0008
178	TEND LESS TO BE THOSE 0.59 OF 68 WHERE THE COMMUNITY IS OTHER THAN SEGMENTED ON A CLAN BASIS AND NON-EXOGAMOUS (295)	178	TEND MORE TO BE THOSE 0.81 OF 314 WHERE THE COMMUNITY IS OTHER THAN SEGMENTED ON A CLAN BASIS AND NON-EXOGAMOUS (295)	28 59 40 255 XSQ= 14.68 PHI= 0.196 XP = 0.0001
182	DRIFT MORE TOWARD BEING THOSE 0.76 OF 68 OTHER THAN WHERE THE COMMUNITY IS STRUCTURED ON A NON-CLAN BASIS AND AGAMOUS (256)	182	DRIFT LESS TOWARD BEING THOSE 0.65 OF 314 OTHER THAN WHERE THE COMMUNITY IS STRUCTURED ON A NON-CLAN BASIS AND AGAMOUS (256)	16 110 52 204 XSQ= 2.85 PHI= -0.086 XP = 0.0916
184	LEAN TOWARD BEING THOSE 0.52 OF 44 WHERE THE LARGEST NON-COGNATIC KIN GROUP IS THE MOEITY OR PHRATRY (77)	184	LEAN TOWARD BEING THOSE 0.74 OF 208 WHERE THE LARGEST NON-COGNATIC KIN GROUP IS SMALLER THAN A PHRATRY, I. E. A SIB OR LINEAGE (175)	23 54 21 154 XSQ= 10.64 PHI= 0.205 XP = 0.0011
186	LEAN MORE TOWARD BEING THOSE 0.79 OF 70 WHERE THE KIN GROUP IS OTHER THAN EXCLUSIVELY PATRILINEAL (250)	186	LEAN LESS TOWARD BEING THOSE 0.59 OF 330 WHERE THE KIN GROUP IS OTHER THAN EXCLUSIVELY PATRILINEAL (250)	15 135 55 195 XSQ= 8.54 PHI= -0.146 XP = 0.0035
190	TILT LESS TOWARD BEING THOSE 0.60 OF 43 WHERE THE KIN GROUP IS PATRILINEAL OR DOUBLE-DESCENT, RATHER THAN MATRILINEAL (186)	190	TILT MORE TOWARD BEING THOSE 0.78 OF 204 WHERE THE KIN GROUP IS PATRILINEAL OR DOUBLE-DESCENT, RATHER THAN MATRILINEAL (186)	26 160 17 44 XSQ= 5.24 PHI= -0.146 XP = 0.0221

192	TILT MORE TOWARD BEING THOSE 0.84 OF 70 OTHER THAN WHERE THE ONLY KIN GROUP PRESENT IS A KINDRED OR ELSE BILATERAL DESCENT IS INFERRED (289)	192	TILT LESS TOWARD BEING THOSE 0.70 OF 330 OTHER THAN WHERE THE ONLY KIN GROUP PRESENT IS A KINDRED OR ELSE BILATERAL DESCENT IS INFERRED (289)	11 100 59 230 XSQ= 5.42 PHI= -0.116 XP = 0.0199
196	DRIFT MORE TOWARD BEING THOSE 0.83 OF 41 WHERE INDIVIDUAL RIGHTS IN REAL PROPERTY, AND RULES FOR INHERITANCE, ARE PRESENT (194)	196	DRIFT LESS TOWARD BEING THOSE 0.67 OF 240 WHERE INDIVIDUAL RIGHTS IN REAL PROPERTY, AND RULES FOR INHERITANCE, ARE PRESENT (194)	34 160 7 80 XSQ= 3.60 PHI= 0.113 XP = 0.0576
197	LEAN LESS TOWARD BEING THOSE 0.68 OF 34 WHERE RULES FOR THE INHERITANCE OF REAL PROPERTY, IF PRESENT, FAVOR EITHER THE MALE HEIR OR LINE, OR THE FEMALE HEIR OR LINE (165)	197	LEAN MORE TOWARD BEING THOSE 0.89 OF 160 WHERE RULES FOR THE INHERITANCE OF REAL PROPERTY, IF PRESENT, FAVOR EITHER THE MALE HEIR OR LINE, OR THE FEMALE HEIR OR LINE (165)	23 142 11 18 XSQ= 8.23 PHI= -0.206 XP = 0.0041
198	TILT LESS TOWARD BEING THOSE 0.70 OF 23 WHERE RULES FOR THE INHERITANCE OF REAL PROPERTY, IF PRESENT, FAVOR THE MALE HEIR OR LINE, RATHER THAN THE FEMALE (144)	198	TILT MORE TOWARD BEING THOSE 0.90 OF 142 WHERE RULES FOR THE INHERITANCE OF REAL PROPERTY, IF PRESENT, FAVOR THE MALE HEIR OR LINE, RATHER THAN THE FEMALE (144)	16 128 7 14 XSQ= 5.81 PHI= -0.188 XP = 0.0160
236	DRIFT TOWARD BEING THOSE 0.57 OF 69 WHERE THE FAMILY IS OF AN INDEPENDENT TYPE, RATHER THAN AN EXTENDED TYPE (185)	236	DRIFT TOWARD BEING THOSE 0.56 OF 329 WHERE THE FAMILY IS OF AN EXTENDED TYPE, RATHER THAN AN INDEPENDENT TYPE (213)	30 183 39 146 XSQ= 2.91 PHI= -0.086 XP = 0.0880
307	TILT MORE TOWARD BEING THOSE 0.84 OF 19 WHERE THE EARLY AGGRESSION SATISFACTION POTENTIAL IS HIGH (33) W-C	307	TILT LESS TOWARD BEING THOSE 0.52 OF 33 WHERE THE EARLY AGGRESSION SATISFACTION POTENTIAL IS HIGH (33) W-C	16 17 3 16 XSQ= 4.24 PHI= 0.285 XP = 0.0395
313	TILT TOWARD BEING THOSE 0.74 OF 19 WHERE AGGRESSION SOCIALIZATION ANXIETY IS LOW (28) W-C	313	TILT TOWARD BEING THOSE 0.60 OF 35 WHERE AGGRESSION SOCIALIZATION ANXIETY IS HIGH (26) W-C	5 21 14 14 XSQ= 4.33 PHI= -0.283 XP = 0.0375
325	TILT TOWARD BEING THOSE 0.80 OF 20 WHERE THE DEGREE OF DIFFUSION AMONG THE INFANT'S NURTURANT AGENTS IS HIGH (42) B-B-C	325	TILT TOWARD BEING THOSE 0.52 OF 54 WHERE THE DEGREE OF DIFFUSION AMONG THE INFANT'S NURTURANT AGENTS IS LOW (32) B-B-C	16 26 4 28 XSQ= 4.80 PHI= 0.255 XP = 0.0284
342	LEAN TOWARD BEING THOSE 0.71 OF 14 WHERE THE CHILD'S INFERRED ANXIETY OVER PERFORMANCE OF NURTURANT BEHAVIOR IS HIGH (18) B-B-C	342	LEAN TOWARD BEING THOSE 0.75 OF 32 WHERE THE CHILD'S INFERRED ANXIETY OVER PERFORMANCE OF NURTURANT BEHAVIOR IS LOW (28) B-B-C	10 8 4 24 XSQ= 6.97 PHI= 0.389 XP = 0.0083

350	DRIFT TOWARD BEING THOSE 0.73 OF 11 WHERE THE CHILD'S INFERRED ANXIETY OVER PERFORMANCE OF ACHIEVEMENT BEHAVIOR IS LOW (26) B-B-C	350	DRIFT TOWARD BEING THOSE 0.63 OF 49 WHERE THE CHILD'S INFERRED ANXIETY OVER PERFORMANCE OF ACHIEVEMENT BEHAVIOR IS HIGH (34) B-B-C	3 31 8 18 XSQ= 3.39 PHI= -0.238 XP = 0.0657
352	TEND TO BE THOSE 0.84 OF 19 WHERE THE TOTAL POSITIVE PRESSURE TOWARD DEVELOPING OBEDIENT BEHAVIOR IN THE CHILD IS LOW (28) B-B-C	352	TEND TO BE THOSE 0.77 OF 53 WHERE THE TOTAL POSITIVE PRESSURE TOWARD DEVELOPING OBEDIENT BEHAVIOR IN THE CHILD IS HIGH (44) B-B-C	3 41 16 12 XSQ= 19.79 PHI= -0.524 XP = 0.0000
353	DRIFT TOWARD BEING THOSE 0.63 OF 19 WHERE THE CHILD-S INFERRED ANXIETY OVER NON-PERFORMANCE OF OBEDIENT BEHAVIOR IS LOW (32) B-B-C	353	DRIFT TOWARD BEING THOSE 0.64 OF 55 WHERE THE CHILD'S INFERRED ANXIETY OVER NON-PERFORMANCE OF OBEDIENT BEHAVIOR IS HIGH (42) B-B-C	7 35 12 20 XSQ= 3.11 PHI= -0.205 XP = 0.0778
370	TEND TO BE THOSE 0.63 OF 43 WHERE THE SEGREGATION OF ADOLESCENT BOYS IS COMPLETE OR PARTIAL (95)	370	TEND TO BE THOSE 0.66 OF 200 WHERE THE SEGREGATION OF ADOLESCENT BOYS IS ABSENT (148)	27 68 16 132 XSQ= 11.14 PHI= 0.214 XP = 0.0008
372	LEAN TOWARD BEING THOSE 0.68 OF 28 WHERE MALE INITIATION RITES ARE PRESENT (48) ASA	372	LEAN TOWARD BEING THOSE 0.65 OF 83 WHERE MALE INITIATION RITES ARE ABSENT (63) ASA	19 29 9 54 XSQ= 7.95 PHI= 0.268 XP = 0.0048
380	LEAN TOWARD BEING THOSE 0.65 OF 17 WHERE SEGREGATION OF GIRLS AT MENARCHE IS ABSENT (20) F-B	380	LEAN TOWARD BEING THOSE 0.76 OF 38 WHERE SEGREGATION OF GIRLS AT MENARCHE IS PRESENT (35) F-B	6 29 11 9 XSQ= 6.86 PHI= -0.353 XP = 0.0088
391	LEAN TOWARD BEING THOSE 0.72 OF 36 WHERE PREMARITAL SEX RELATIONS ARE PUNISHED ONLY IF PREGNANCY RESULTS, OR FREELY PERMITTED (90) JTW,EA	391	LEAN TOWARD BEING THOSE 0.55 OF 143 WHERE PREMARITAL SEX RELATIONS ARE STRONGLY PUNISHED AND IN FACT RARE, OR WEAKLY PUNISHED AND IN FACT NOT RARE (89) JTW,EA	10 79 26 64 XSQ= 7.62 PHI= -0.206 XP = 0.0058
392	LEAN TOWARD BEING THOSE 0.58 OF 36 WHERE PREMARITAL SEX RELATIONS ARE FREELY PERMITTED (67) JTW,EA	392	LEAN TOWARD BEING THOSE 0.68 OF 143 WHERE PREMARITAL SEX RELATIONS ARE STRONGLY PUNISHED AND IN FACT RARE, OR WEAKLY PUNISHED AND IN FACT NOT RARE, OR PUNISHED ONLY IF PREGNANCY RESULTS (112) JTW,EA	15 97 21 46 XSQ= 7.33 PHI= -0.202 XP = 0.0068
400	DRIFT TOWARD BEING THOSE 0.60 OF 15 WHERE HOMOSEXUAL ACTIVITY IS PROHIBITED (22) F-B	400	DRIFT TOWARD BEING THOSE 0.70 OF 43 WHERE HOMOSEXUAL ACTIVITY IS PERMITTED (36) F-B	9 13 6 30 XSQ= 3.02 PHI= 0.228 XP = 0.0824

426	TEND TO BE THOSE WHERE A HIGH GOD IS ABSENT (104) GES,EA	0.78 OF 41	426	TEND TO BE THOSE WHERE A HIGH GOD IS PRESENT (156) GES,EA	0.67 OF 219	9 147 32 72 XSQ= 27.51 PHI= -0.325 XP = 0.0000
427	DRIFT TOWARD BEING THOSE WHERE A HIGH GOD, IF PRESENT, IS INACTIVE, RATHER THAN ACTIVE (69) GES,EA	0.78 OF 9	427	DRIFT TOWARD BEING THOSE WHERE A HIGH GOD, IF PRESENT, IS ACTIVE, RATHER THAN INACTIVE (87) GES,EA	0.58 OF 147	2 85 7 62 XSQ= 3.03 PHI= -0.139 XP = 0.0815
439	TILT TOWARD BEING THOSE WHERE FEAR OF GHOSTS IS HIGH (30) W-C	0.75 OF 20	439	TILT TOWARD BEING THOSE WHERE FEAR OF GHOSTS IS LOW (31) W-C	0.63 OF 41	15 15 5 26 XSQ= 6.47 PHI= 0.326 XP = 0.0109
449	TILT TOWARD BEING THOSE WHERE THE OBSERVATION OF FOOD TABOOS IS HIGH, RATHER THAN MEDIUM OR LOW (25) JRL	0.57 OF 14	449	TILT TOWARD BEING THOSE WHERE THE OBSERVATION OF FOOD TABOOS IS MEDIUM OR LOW, RATHER THAN HIGH (61) JRL	0.76 OF 72	8 17 6 55 XSQ= 4.87 PHI= 0.238 XP = 0.0273
458	LEAN MORE TOWARD BEING THOSE WHERE GAMES, IF PRESENT, DO NOT INCLUDE GAMES OF STRATEGY (119) R-A-B,EA	0.94 OF 32	458	LEAN LESS TOWARD BEING THOSE WHERE GAMES, IF PRESENT, DO NOT INCLUDE GAMES OF STRATEGY (119) R-A-B,EA	0.64 OF 139	2 50 30 89 XSQ= 9.50 PHI= -0.236 XP = 0.0021
459	TEND TO BE THOSE WHERE GAMES, IF PRESENT, DO NOT INCLUDE GAMES OF CHANCE (89) R-A-B,EA	0.84 OF 32	459	TEND TO BE THOSE WHERE GAMES, IF PRESENT, INCLUDE GAMES OF CHANCE (82) R-A-B,EA	0.55 OF 139	5 77 27 62 XSQ= 14.93 PHI= -0.295 XP = 0.0001
460	TEND TO BE THOSE WHERE GAMES, IF PRESENT, ARE LIMITED TO GAMES OF SKILL ONLY (67) R-A-B,EA	0.81 OF 32	460	TEND TO BE THOSE WHERE GAMES, IF PRESENT, ARE NOT LIMITED TO GAMES OF SKILL ONLY (104) R-A-B,EA	0.71 OF 139	26 41 6 98 XSQ= 27.11 PHI= 0.398 XP = 0.0000
468	IN ALL CASES ARE THOSE WHERE CONTACT WITH OTHER CULTURES IS REGULAR OR IRREGULAR, RATHER THAN FREQUENT (37) JMH	1.00 OF 9	468	DRIFT LESS TOWARD BEING THOSE WHERE CONTACT WITH OTHER CULTURES IS REGULAR OR IRREGULAR, RATHER THAN FREQUENT (37) JMH	0.62 OF 45	0 17 9 28 XSQ= 3.37 PHI= -0.250 XP = 0.0666

7 CULTURES
LOCATED IN SOUTHEAST ASIA (32)

7 CULTURES
LOCATED OUTSIDE OF
SOUTHEAST ASIA (368)

BACKGROUND ON PAGE 65

SUBJECT ONLY

32 IN LEFT COLUMN

AKHA	ALCRESE	ANDAMANESE	BALINESE	BATAK	BELU	BURMESE	CAMBODIANS	DUSUN	HANUNOO
IBAN	IFUGAO	JAVANESE	KACHIN	KAREN	LAKHER	LAMET	MACASSARESE	MALAYS	MENTAWEI
MINANGKABAU	MNONG GAR	NICOBARESE	ROTINESE	SELUNG	SEMANG	SUBANUN	TAGBANUA	TANIMBARESE	THAI
TORAJA	VIETNAMESE								

368 IN RIGHT COLUMN

	Left column (32)			Right column (368)		
14	IN ALL CASES ARE THOSE WHERE THE LATITUDE IS LESS THAN THIRTY DEGREES (281)	1.00 OF 32	14	TEND LESS TO BE THOSE WHERE THE LATITUDE IS LESS THAN THIRTY DEGREES (281)	0.68 OF 368	0 119 32 249 XSQ= 13.22 PHI= -0.182 XP = 0.0003
16	TILT TOWARD BEING THOSE WHERE THE LATITUDE IS LESS THAN TEN DEGREES (123)	0.50 OF 32	16	TILT TOWARD BEING THOSE WHERE THE LATITUDE IS TEN DEGREES OR GREATER (277)	0.71 OF 368	16 261 16 107 XSQ= 5.11 PHI= -0.113 XP = 0.0238
36	IN ALL CASES ARE THOSE WHERE THE NATURAL ENVIRONMENT IS OTHER THAN 'VERY HARSH,' OR SUB-TROPICAL BUSH, OR TEMPERATE GRASSLAND (292) FWM	1.00 OF 32	36	TEND LESS TO BE THOSE WHERE THE NATURAL ENVIRONMENT IS OTHER THAN 'VERY HARSH,' OR SUB-TROPICAL BUSH, OR TEMPERATE GRASSLAND (292) FWM	0.71 OF 368	0 108 32 260 XSQ= 11.42 PHI= -0.169 XP = 0.0007
42	TEND TO BE THOSE WHERE THE NATURAL ENVIRONMENT IS TROPICAL OR SUB-TROPICAL RAIN FOREST, OR MONSOON FOREST (156) FWM	0.97 OF 32	42	TEND TO BE THOSE WHERE THE NATURAL ENVIRONMENT IS OTHER THAN TROPICAL OR SUB-TROPICAL RAIN FOREST, OR MONSOON FOREST (244) FWM	0.66 OF 368	31 125 1 243 XSQ= 46.36 PHI= 0.340 XP = 0.
51	LEAN MORE TOWARD BEING THOSE WHERE SUBSISTENCE IS PRIMARILY BY FOOD PRODUCTION -- I. E., AGRICULTURE OR HUSBANDRY -- RATHER THAN BY GATHERING (253)	0.91 OF 32	51	LEAN LESS TOWARD BEING THOSE WHERE SUBSISTENCE IS PRIMARILY BY FOOD PRODUCTION -- I. E., AGRICULTURE OR HUSBANDRY -- RATHER THAN BY GATHERING (253)	0.61 OF 368	29 224 3 144 XSQ= 9.97 PHI= 0.158 XP = 0.0016

54	IN ALL CASES ARE THOSE 1.00 OF 19 WHERE FOOD PRODUCTION IS BY INTENSIVE OR SIMPLE AGRICULTURE, RATHER THAN BY INCIPIENT FOOD PRODUCTION (192)	54	DRIFT LESS TOWARD BEING THOSE 0.79 OF 219 WHERE FOOD PRODUCTION IS BY INTENSIVE OR SIMPLE AGRICULTURE, RATHER THAN BY INCIPIENT FOOD PRODUCTION (192)	19 173 0 46 XSQ= 3.69 PHI= 0.125 XP = 0.0547
56	IN ALL CASES ARE THOSE 1.00 OF 12 WHERE FOOD PRODUCTION IS BY SIMPLE AGRICULTURE, RATHER THAN BY INCIPIENT FOOD PRODUCTION (101)	56	TILT LESS TOWARD BEING THOSE 0.66 OF 135 WHERE FOOD PRODUCTION IS BY SIMPLE AGRICULTURE, RATHER THAN BY INCIPIENT FOOD PRODUCTION (101)	12 89 0 46 XSQ= 4.47 PHI= 0.174 XP = 0.0345
79	DRIFT LESS TOWARD BEING THOSE 0.73 OF 15 WHERE NO CITY IS PRESENT (201)	79	DRIFT MORE TOWARD BEING THOSE 0.91 OF 209 WHERE NO CITY IS PRESENT (201)	4 19 11 190 XSQ= 2.98 PHI= 0.115 XP = 0.0844
87	LEAN LESS TOWARD BEING THOSE 0.77 OF 30 WHERE THE LEVEL OF POLITICAL INTEGRATION IS THE LARGE STATE, THE LITTLE STATE, THE MINIMAL STATE, OR THE AUTONOMOUS COMMUNITY (281) GPM	87	LEAN MORE TOWARD BEING THOSE 0.94 OF 274 WHERE THE LEVEL OF POLITICAL INTEGRATION IS THE LARGE STATE, THE LITTLE STATE, THE MINIMAL STATE, OR THE AUTONOMOUS COMMUNITY (281) GPM	23 258 7 16 XSQ= 9.46 PHI= -0.176 XP = 0.0021
102	DRIFT MORE TOWARD BEING THOSE 0.69 OF 32 WHERE CLASS STRATIFICATION IS PRESENT (203)	102	DRIFT LESS TOWARD BEING THOSE 0.52 OF 351 WHERE CLASS STRATIFICATION IS PRESENT (203)	22 181 10 170 XSQ= 2.82 PHI= 0.086 XP = 0.0931
110	TILT TOWARD BEING THOSE 0.63 OF 32 WHERE SLAVERY IS PRESENT (163)	110	TILT TOWARD BEING THOSE 0.59 OF 349 WHERE SLAVERY IS ABSENT (218)	20 143 12 206 XSQ= 4.70 PHI= 0.111 XP = 0.0301
143	IN ALL CASES ARE THOSE 1.00 OF 5 WHERE THE RATIO OF RESTITUTIVE TO REPRESSIVE SANCTIONS IS HIGH (20) WME	143	TILT TOWARD BEING THOSE 0.68 OF 47 WHERE THE RATIO OF RESTITUTIVE TO REPRESSIVE SANCTIONS IS MEDIUM OR LOW (32) WME	5 15 0 32 XSQ= 6.21 PHI= 0.346 XP = 0.0127
164	IN ALL CASES ARE THOSE 1.00 OF 5 WHERE THE EMPHASIS ON INDIVIDUAL VOLITION AS THE CAUSE OR SOURCE OF ILLNESS IS LOW (9) MJ	164	TILT TOWARD BEING THOSE 0.69 OF 13 WHERE THE EMPHASIS ON INDIVIDUAL VOLITION AS THE CAUSE OR SOURCE OF ILLNESS IS HIGH (9) MJ	0 9 5 4 XSQ= 4.43 PHI= -0.496 EP = 0.0294
175	TILT MORE TOWARD BEING THOSE 0.87 OF 31 WHERE THE COMMUNITY IS 'KIN-HETEROGENEOUS,' I. E. OTHER THAN A CLAN COMMUNITY OR A DEME (260)	175	TILT LESS TOWARD BEING THOSE 0.66 OF 351 WHERE THE COMMUNITY IS 'KIN-HETEROGENEOUS,' I. E. OTHER THAN A CLAN COMMUNITY OR A DEME (260)	4 118 27 233 XSQ= 4.71 PHI= -0.111 XP = 0.0300

176	TILT MORE TOWARD BEING THOSE 0.77 OF 31 WHERE THE COMMUNITY IS OTHER THAN A CLAN-COMMUNITY OR A COMMUNITY STRUCTURED OR SEGMENTED ON A CLAN BASIS (213)	176	TILT LESS TOWARD BEING THOSE 0.54 OF 351 WHERE THE COMMUNITY IS OTHER THAN A CLAN-COMMUNITY OR A COMMUNITY STRUCTURED OR SEGMENTED ON A CLAN BASIS (213)	7 162 24 189 XSQ= 5.50 PHI= -0.120 XP = 0.0191
177	IN ALL CASES ARE THOSE 1.00 OF 31 WHERE THE COMMUNITY IS OTHER THAN A SINGLE CLAN-COMMUNITY AND EXOGAMOUS (305)	177	LEAN LESS TOWARD BEING THOSE 0.78 OF 351 WHERE THE COMMUNITY IS OTHER THAN A SINGLE CLAN-COMMUNITY AND EXOGAMOUS (305)	0 77 31 274 XSQ= 7.21 PHI= -0.137 XP = 0.0073
180	LEAN MORE TOWARD BEING THOSE 0.94 OF 31 WHERE THE COMMUNITY IS COMMONLY NON-EXOGAMOUS, RATHER THAN EXOGAMOUS (258)	180	LEAN LESS TOWARD BEING THOSE 0.65 OF 351 WHERE THE COMMUNITY IS COMMONLY NON-EXOGAMOUS, RATHER THAN EXOGAMOUS (258)	2 122 29 229 XSQ= 9.16 PHI= -0.155 XP = 0.0025
182	LEAN TOWARD BEING THOSE 0.58 OF 31 WHERE THE COMMUNITY IS STRUCTURED ON A NON-CLAN BASIS AND AGAMOUS (126)	182	LEAN TOWARD BEING THOSE 0.69 OF 351 OTHER THAN WHERE THE COMMUNITY IS STRUCTURED ON A NON-CLAN BASIS AND AGAMOUS (256)	18 108 13 243 XSQ= 8.41 PHI= 0.148 XP = 0.0037
188	TILT TOWARD BEING THOSE 0.59 OF 32 WHERE THE KIN GROUP IS EXCLUSIVELY COGNATIC (148)	188	TILT TOWARD BEING THOSE 0.65 OF 368 WHERE THE KIN GROUP IS OTHER THAN EXCLUSIVELY COGNATIC (252)	19 129 13 239 XSQ= 6.46 PHI= 0.127 XP = 0.0110
192	LEAN TOWARD BEING THOSE 0.50 OF 32 WHERE THE ONLY KIN GROUP PRESENT IS A KINDRED OR ELSE BILATERAL DESCENT IS INFERRED (111)	192	LEAN TOWARD BEING THOSE 0.74 OF 368 OTHER THAN WHERE THE ONLY KIN GROUP PRESENT IS A KINDRED OR ELSE BILATERAL DESCENT IS INFERRED (289)	16 95 16 273 XSQ= 7.42 PHI= 0.136 XP = 0.0064
197	TEND TO BE THOSE 0.50 OF 16 WHERE RULES FOR THE INHERITANCE OF REAL PROPERTY, IF PRESENT, DO NOT FAVOR EITHER THE MALE HEIR OR LINE, OR THE FEMALE HEIR OR LINE (29)	197	TEND TO BE THOSE 0.88 OF 178 WHERE RULES FOR THE INHERITANCE OF REAL PROPERTY, IF PRESENT, FAVOR EITHER THE MALE HEIR OR LINE, OR THE FEMALE HEIR OR LINE (165)	8 157 8 21 XSQ= 13.98 PHI= -0.268 XP = 0.0002
209	LEAN LESS TOWARD BEING THOSE 0.58 OF 24 WHERE MARITAL RESIDENCE IS PATRILOCAL, VIRILOCAL, OR AVUNCULOCAL, RATHER THAN MATRILOCAL OR UXORILOCAL (270)	209	LEAN MORE TOWARD BEING THOSE 0.83 OF 310 WHERE MARITAL RESIDENCE IS PATRILOCAL, VIRILOCAL, OR AVUNCULOCAL, RATHER THAN MATRILOCAL OR UXORILOCAL (270)	14 256 10 54 XSQ= 6.96 PHI= -0.144 XP = 0.0083
221	TILT LESS TOWARD BEING THOSE 0.77 OF 30 WHERE MATRILATERAL CROSS-COUSIN MARRIAGE IS NOT PRESCRIBED OR PREFERRED (335)	221	TILT MORE TOWARD BEING THOSE 0.92 OF 340 WHERE MATRILATERAL CROSS-COUSIN MARRIAGE IS NOT PRESCRIBED OR PREFERRED (335)	7 28 23 312 XSQ= 5.68 PHI= 0.124 XP = 0.0172

77

234	LEAN TOWARD BEING THOSE WHERE THE COUSIN TERMINOLOGY IS OF ESKIMO OR HAWAIIAN TYPE, RATHER THAN CROW, OMAHA, OR IROQUOIS TYPE (170)	0.80 OF 30	234	LEAN TOWARD BEING THOSE WHERE THE COUSIN TERMINOLOGY IS OF CROW, OMAHA, OR IROQUOIS TYPE, RATHER THAN ESKIMO OR HAWAIIAN TYPE (152)	0.50 OF 292	6 146 24 146 XSQ= 8.66 PHI= -0.164 XP = 0.0033
305	IN ALL CASES ARE THOSE WHERE THE EARLY SEXUAL SATISFACTION POTENTIAL IS HIGH (27) W-C	1.00 OF 5	305	DRIFT TOWARD BEING THOSE WHERE THE EARLY SEXUAL SATISFACTION POTENTIAL IS LOW (24) W-C	0.52 OF 46	5 22 0 24 XSQ= 3.06 PHI= 0.245 XP = 0.0804
320	DRIFT TOWARD BEING THOSE WHERE THE DEGREE OF REDUCTION OF THE INFANT'S DRIVES IS LOW (24) B-B-C	0.80 OF 5	320	DRIFT TOWARD BEING THOSE WHERE THE DEGREE OF REDUCTION OF THE INFANT'S DRIVES IS HIGH (45) B-B-C	0.69 OF 64	1 44 4 20 XSQ= 2.95 PHI= -0.207 XP = 0.0860
352	IN ALL CASES ARE THOSE WHERE THE TOTAL POSITIVE PRESSURE TOWARD DEVELOPING OBEDIENT BEHAVIOR IN THE CHILD IS LOW (28) B-B-C	1.00 OF 4	352	TILT TOWARD BEING THOSE WHERE THE TOTAL POSITIVE PRESSURE TOWARD DEVELOPING OBEDIENT BEHAVIOR IN THE CHILD IS HIGH (44) B-B-C	0.65 OF 68	0 44 4 24 XSQ= 4.21 PHI= -0.242 XP = 0.0402
369	DRIFT TOWARD BEING THOSE WHERE BOTH DISSOCIATION OF THE SEXES AT ADOLESCENCE, AND CUSTOMS OF INITIATION AT ADOLESCENCE, ARE ABSENT (15) JKH	0.67 OF 6	369	DRIFT TOWARD BEING THOSE WHERE DISSOCIATION OF THE SEXES AT ADOLESCENCE, OR CUSTOMS OF INITIATION AT ADOLESCENCE, ARE PRESENT (42) JKH	0.78 OF 51	2 40 4 11 XSQ= 3.55 PHI= -0.249 XP = 0.0597
395	IN ALL CASES ARE THOSE WHERE BELIEF IN THE UNCLEANNESS OF WOMEN IS UNIMPORTANT OR ABSENT (15) LWS	1.00 OF 3	395	DRIFT TOWARD BEING THOSE WHERE BELIEF IN THE UNCLEANNESS OF WOMEN IS PRESENT (18) LWS	0.60 OF 30	0 18 3 12 XSQ= 1.91 PHI= -0.241 EP = 0.0834
400	IN ALL CASES ARE THOSE WHERE HOMOSEXUAL ACTIVITY IS PROHIBITED (22) F-B	1.00 OF 4	400	TILT TOWARD BEING THOSE WHERE HOMOSEXUAL ACTIVITY IS PERMITTED (36) F-B	0.67 OF 54	4 18 0 36 XSQ= 4.48 PHI= 0.278 XP = 0.0342
440	IN ALL CASES ARE THOSE WHERE FEAR OF SPIRITS IS HIGH (32) W-C	1.00 OF 6	440	TILT TOWARD BEING THOSE WHERE FEAR OF SPIRITS IS LOW (29) W-C	0.53 OF 55	6 26 0 29 XSQ= 4.10 PHI= 0.259 XP = 0.0428

****

8	CULTURES LOCATED IN NORTH AMERICA (70)	8	CULTURES LOCATED OUTSIDE OF NORTH AMERICA (330)

BACKGROUND ON PAGE 65 BOTH SUBJECT AND PREDICATE

....

70 IN LEFT COLUMN

ATSUGEWI	AZTEC	CHEROKEE	CHEYENNE	CHINANTEC	CHIR-APACHE	COCHITI	COMANCHE	COPR ESKIMO	CREE
CREEK	CROW	DELAWARE	DIEGUENO	EYAK	FOX	GROS VENTRE	HAIDA	HANO	HASINAI
HAVASUPAI	HUICHOL	HUKUNDIKA	HURON	INGALIK	JEMEZ	KASKA	KIOW-APACHE	KUTENAI	KWAKIUTL
MANDAN	MARICOPA	MAZATECO	MIAMI	MIWOK	NABESNA	NASKAPI	NATCHEZ	NAVAHO	NOMLAKI
NUNIVAK	OJIBWA	OMAHA	PAPAGO	PAWNEE	PENOBSCOT	POPOLUCA	SANPOIL	SARSI	SEMINOLE
SERI	TAOS	TARAHUMARA	TAREUMIUT	TENINO	TETON	TIMUCUA	TOLOWA	TOTONAC	TSHIMSHIAN
TUBATULABAL	TWANA	UTE	WASHO	WICHITA	WINNEBAGO	YOKUTS	YUKI	YUROK	ZUNI

330 IN RIGHT COLUMN

13	TEND TO BE THOSE WHERE THE LATITUDE IS FORTY DEGREES OR GREATER (71)	0.50 OF 70	13	TEND TO BE THOSE WHERE THE LATITUDE IS LESS THAN FORTY DEGREES (329)	0.89 OF 330	35 36 35 294 XSQ= 57.80 PHI= 0.380 XP = 0.
14	TEND TO BE THOSE WHERE THE LATITUDE IS THIRTY DEGREES OR GREATER (119)	0.86 OF 70	14	TEND TO BE THOSE WHERE THE LATITUDE IS LESS THAN THIRTY DEGREES (281)	0.82 OF 330	60 59 10 271 XSQ= 123.93 PHI= 0.557 XP = 0.
15	TEND TO BE THOSE WHERE THE LATITUDE IS TWENTY DEGREES OR GREATER (183)	0.94 OF 70	15	TEND TO BE THOSE WHERE THE LATITUDE IS LESS THAN TWENTY DEGREES (217)	0.65 OF 330	66 117 4 213 XSQ= 78.18 PHI= 0.442 XP = 0.
16	IN ALL CASES ARE THOSE WHERE THE LATITUDE IS TEN DEGREES OR GREATER (277)	1.00 OF 70	16	TEND LESS TO BE THOSE WHERE THE LATITUDE IS TEN DEGREES OR GREATER (277)	0.63 OF 330	70 207 0 123 XSQ= 35.95 PHI= 0.300 XP = 0.
33	LEAN LESS TOWARD BEING THOSE WHERE THE NATURAL ENVIRONMENT IS OTHER THAN 'VERY HARSH,' I.E., DESERT, DESERT GRASSES AND SHRUBS, TUNDRA, OR HIGH PLATEAU STEPPE (341) FWM	0.73 OF 70	33	LEAN MORE TOWARD BEING THOSE WHERE THE NATURAL ENVIRONMENT IS OTHER THAN 'VERY HARSH,' I.E., DESERT, DESERT GRASSES AND SHRUBS, TUNDRA, OR HIGH PLATEAU STEPPE (341) FWM	0.88 OF 330	19 40 51 290 XSQ= 9.20 PHI= 0.152 XP = 0.0024

36	TEND TO BE THOSE WHERE THE NATURAL ENVIRONMENT IS 'VERY HARSH,' OR SUB-TROPICAL BUSH, OR TEMPERATE GRASSLAND (108) FWM	0.50 OF 70	36	TEND TO BE THOSE WHERE THE NATURAL ENVIRONMENT IS OTHER THAN 'VERY HARSH,' OR SUB-TROPICAL BUSH, OR TEMPERATE GRASSLAND (292) FWM	0.78 OF 330	35 73 35 257 XSQ= 21.38 PHI= 0.231 XP = 0.0000
42	TEND MORE TO BE THOSE WHERE THE NATURAL ENVIRONMENT IS OTHER THAN TROPICAL OR SUB-TROPICAL RAIN FOREST, OR MONSOON FOREST (244) FWM	0.96 OF 70	42	TEND LESS TO BE THOSE WHERE THE NATURAL ENVIRONMENT IS OTHER THAN TROPICAL OR SUB-TROPICAL RAIN FOREST, OR MONSOON FOREST (244) FWM	0.54 OF 330	3 153 67 177 XSQ= 41.23 PHI= -0.321 XP = 0.
44	TEND TO BE THOSE WHERE SETTLEMENTS ARE NON-FIXED (110)	0.64 OF 58	44	TEND TO BE THOSE WHERE SETTLEMENTS ARE FIXED (222)	0.73 OF 274	21 201 37 73 XSQ= 28.17 PHI= -0.291 XP = 0.0000
45	DRIFT MORE TOWARD BEING THOSE WHERE SETTLEMENTS, IF FIXED, ARE COMPACT, RATHER THAN NON-COMPACT (149)	0.86 OF 21	45	DRIFT LESS TOWARD BEING THOSE WHERE SETTLEMENTS, IF FIXED, ARE COMPACT, RATHER THAN NON-COMPACT (149)	0.65 OF 201	18 131 3 70 XSQ= 2.76 PHI= 0.112 XP = 0.0964
46	LEAN LESS TOWARD BEING THOSE OTHER THAN WHERE SETTLEMENTS ARE NON-FIXED AND MOVEMENT IS NOMADIC (260)	0.64 OF 58	46	LEAN MORE TOWARD BEING THOSE OTHER THAN WHERE SETTLEMENTS ARE NON-FIXED AND MOVEMENT IS NOMADIC (260)	0.81 OF 274	21 51 37 223 XSQ= 7.72 PHI= 0.152 XP = 0.0055
51	TEND TO BE THOSE WHERE SUBSISTENCE IS PRIMARILY BY FOOD GATHERING -- I. E., HUNTING, FISHING, OR COLLECTING -- RATHER THAN FOOD PRODUCTION (147)	0.77 OF 70	51	TEND TO BE THOSE WHERE SUBSISTENCE IS PRIMARILY BY FOOD PRODUCTION -- I. E., AGRICULTURE OR HUSBANDRY -- RATHER THAN BY GATHERING (253)	0.72 OF 330	16 237 54 93 XSQ= 57.47 PHI= -0.379 XP = 0.
54	TEND TO BE THOSE WHERE FOOD PRODUCTION IS BY INCIPIENT FOOD PRODUCTION, RATHER THAN BY INTENSIVE OR SIMPLE AGRICULTURE (46)	0.52 OF 25	54	TEND TO BE THOSE WHERE FOOD PRODUCTION IS BY INTENSIVE OR SIMPLE AGRICULTURE, RATHER THAN BY INCIPIENT FOOD PRODUCTION (192)	0.85 OF 213	12 180 13 33 XSQ= 16.85 PHI= -0.266 XP = 0.0000
56	TEND TO BE THOSE WHERE FOOD PRODUCTION IS BY INCIPIENT FOOD PRODUCTION, RATHER THAN BY SIMPLE AGRICULTURE (46)	0.76 OF 17	56	TEND TO BE THOSE WHERE FOOD PRODUCTION IS BY SIMPLE AGRICULTURE, RATHER THAN BY INCIPIENT FOOD PRODUCTION (101)	0.75 OF 130	4 97 13 33 XSQ= 15.95 PHI= -0.329 XP = 0.0001
62	TEND TO BE THOSE WHERE HUSBANDRY OF ANY KIND IS ABSENT (172)	0.71 OF 70	62	TEND TO BE THOSE WHERE HUSBANDRY OF SOME KIND IS PRESENT (228)	0.63 OF 330	20 208 50 122 XSQ= 26.59 PHI= -0.258 XP = 0.0000

63	TILT MORE TOWARD BEING THOSE WHERE HUSBANDRY, IF PRESENT, IS PRINCIPALLY IN THE FORM OF BOVINE, EQUINE, CAMEL-LIKE, OR DEER-LIKE ANIMALS, RATHER THAN PIGS, SHEEP, OR GOATS (152)	0.90 OF 20	63	TILT LESS TOWARD BEING THOSE WHERE HUSBANDRY, IF PRESENT, IS PRINCIPALLY IN THE FORM OF BOVINE, EQUINE, CAMEL-LIKE, OR DEER-LIKE ANIMALS, RATHER THAN PIGS, SHEEP, OR GOATS (152)	0.65 OF 206	18 134 2 72 XSQ= 4.08 PHI= 0.134 XP = 0.0433
71	TEND MORE TO BE THOSE WHERE METAL WORKING IS ABSENT (153)	0.94 OF 51	71	TEND LESS TO BE THOSE WHERE METAL WORKING IS ABSENT (153)	0.52 OF 200	3 95 48 105 XSQ= 27.85 PHI= -0.333 XP = 0.0000
73	TILT TOWARD BEING THOSE WHERE WEAVING IS ABSENT (130)	0.67 OF 52	73	TILT TOWARD BEING THOSE WHERE WEAVING IS PRESENT (118)	0.52 OF 196	17 101 35 95 XSQ= 5.12 PHI= -0.144 XP = 0.0237
80	DRIFT MORE TOWARD BEING THOSE WHERE NO CITY OR TOWN IS PRESENT (185)	0.94 OF 34	80	DRIFT LESS TOWARD BEING THOSE WHERE NO CITY OR TOWN IS PRESENT (185)	0.81 OF 190	2 37 32 153 XSQ= 2.82 PHI= -0.112 XP = 0.0931
83	TILT LESS TOWARD BEING THOSE WHERE, WITH NO CITY AND NO TOWN PRESENT, THE AVERAGE COMMUNITY SIZE IS SMALLER THAN 200, RATHER THAN BETWEEN 200 AND 999 (135)	0.58 OF 31	83	TILT MORE TOWARD BEING THOSE WHERE, WITH NO CITY AND NO TOWN PRESENT, THE AVERAGE COMMUNITY SIZE IS SMALLER THAN 200, RATHER THAN BETWEEN 200 AND 999 (135)	0.79 OF 149	13 32 18 117 XSQ= 4.69 PHI= 0.161 XP = 0.0304
84	TILT MORE TOWARD BEING THOSE WHERE THE LEVEL OF POLITICAL INTEGRATION IS THE LITTLE STATE, THE MINIMAL STATE, THE AUTONOMOUS COMMUNITY, OR THE FAMILY (262) GPM	0.96 OF 52	84	TILT LESS TOWARD BEING THOSE WHERE THE LEVEL OF POLITICAL INTEGRATION IS THE LITTLE STATE, THE MINIMAL STATE, THE AUTONOMOUS COMMUNITY, OR THE FAMILY (262) GPM	0.84 OF 252	2 40 50 212 XSQ= 4.28 PHI= -0.119 XP = 0.0387
85	LEAN MORE TOWARD BEING THOSE WHERE THE LEVEL OF POLITICAL INTEGRATION IS THE MINIMAL STATE, THE AUTONOMOUS COMMUNITY, OR THE FAMILY (234) GPM	0.92 OF 52	85	LEAN LESS TOWARD BEING THOSE WHERE THE LEVEL OF POLITICAL INTEGRATION IS THE MINIMAL STATE, THE AUTONOMOUS COMMUNITY, OR THE FAMILY (234) GPM	0.74 OF 252	4 66 48 186 XSQ= 7.31 PHI= -0.155 XP = 0.0069
94	IN ALL CASES ARE THOSE WHERE THE HIERARCHY OF NATIONAL JURISDICTION HAS TWO, ONE, OR NO LEVELS (296) GES,EA	1.00 OF 59	94	LEAN LESS TOWARD BEING THOSE WHERE THE HIERARCHY OF NATIONAL JURISDICTION HAS TWO, ONE, OR NO LEVELS (296) GES,EA	0.87 OF 271	0 34 59 237 XSQ= 6.95 PHI= -0.145 XP = 0.0084
95	TEND MORE TO BE THOSE WHERE THE HIERARCHY OF NATIONAL JURISDICTION HAS ONE OR NO LEVELS (254) GES,EA	0.95 OF 59	95	TEND LESS TO BE THOSE WHERE THE HIERARCHY OF NATIONAL JURISDICTION HAS ONE OR NO LEVELS (254) GES,EA	0.73 OF 271	3 73 56 198 XSQ= 11.85 PHI= -0.189 XP = 0.0006

97	DRIFT MORE TOWARD BEING THOSE 0.92 OF 59 WHERE THE HIERARCHY OF LOCAL JURISDICTION HAS THREE OR TWO LEVELS (273) GES,EA	97	DRIFT LESS TOWARD BEING THOSE 0.81 OF 272 WHERE THE HIERARCHY OF LOCAL JURISDICTION HAS THREE OR TWO LEVELS (273) GES,EA	5 53 54 219 XSQ= 3.34 PHI= -0.100 XP = 0.0676
102	LEAN TOWARD BEING THOSE 0.66 OF 67 WHERE CLASS STRATIFICATION IS ABSENT (180)	102	LEAN TOWARD BEING THOSE 0.57 OF 316 WHERE CLASS STRATIFICATION IS PRESENT (203)	23 180 44 136 XSQ= 10.48 PHI= -0.165 XP = 0.0012
106	LEAN TOWARD BEING THOSE 0.65 OF 23 WHERE CLASS STRATIFICATION, IF PRESENT, IS BASED ON WEALTH (77)	106	LEAN TOWARD BEING THOSE 0.66 OF 180 WHERE CLASS STRATIFICATION, IF PRESENT, IS BASED ON SOMETHING OTHER THAN WEALTH (126)	15 62 8 118 XSQ= 6.95 PHI= 0.185 XP = 0.0084
107	DRIFT MORE TOWARD BEING THOSE 0.96 OF 23 WHERE CLASS STRATIFICATION, IF PRESENT, IS BASED ON SOMETHING OTHER THAN OCCUPATIONAL STATUS (160)	107	DRIFT LESS TOWARD BEING THOSE 0.77 OF 180 WHERE CLASS STRATIFICATION, IF PRESENT, IS BASED ON SOMETHING OTHER THAN OCCUPATIONAL STATUS (160)	1 42 22 138 XSQ= 3.34 PHI= -0.128 XP = 0.0676
109	LEAN MORE TOWARD BEING THOSE 0.99 OF 69 WHERE CASTES ARE ABSENT (317)	109	LEAN LESS TOWARD BEING THOSE 0.83 OF 299 WHERE CASTES ARE ABSENT (317)	1 50 68 249 XSQ= 9.71 PHI= -0.162 XP = 0.0018
110	LEAN MORE TOWARD BEING THOSE 0.73 OF 67 WHERE SLAVERY IS ABSENT (218)	110	LEAN LESS TOWARD BEING THOSE 0.54 OF 314 WHERE SLAVERY IS ABSENT (218)	18 145 49 169 XSQ= 7.64 PHI= -0.142 XP = 0.0057
130	LEAN TOWARD BEING THOSE 0.73 OF 37 WHERE LEATHER WORKING IS MAINLY DONE BY FEMALES (45)	130	LEAN TOWARD BEING THOSE 0.62 OF 47 WHERE LEATHER WORKING IS MAINLY DONE BY MALES (39)	10 29 27 18 XSQ= 8.66 PHI= -0.321 XP = 0.0032
131	DRIFT LESS TOWARD BEING THOSE 0.76 OF 34 WHERE THE CONSTRUCTION OF PERMANENT HOUSES OR THE ERECTION OF TEMPORARY DWELLINGS IS MAINLY DONE BY MALES (136)	131	DRIFT MORE TOWARD BEING THOSE 0.89 OF 123 WHERE THE CONSTRUCTION OF PERMANENT HOUSES OR THE ERECTION OF TEMPORARY DWELLINGS IS MAINLY DONE BY MALES (136)	26 110 8 13 XSQ= 2.82 PHI= -0.134 XP = 0.0929
176	LEAN MORE TOWARD BEING THOSE 0.73 OF 66 WHERE THE COMMUNITY IS OTHER THAN A CLAN-COMMUNITY OR A COMMUNITY STRUCTURED OR SEGMENTED ON A CLAN BASIS (213)	176	LEAN LESS TOWARD BEING THOSE 0.52 OF 316 WHERE THE COMMUNITY IS OTHER THAN A CLAN-COMMUNITY OR A COMMUNITY STRUCTURED OR SEGMENTED ON A CLAN BASIS (213)	18 151 48 165 XSQ= 8.50 PHI= -0.149 XP = 0.0036

177	DRIFT MORE TOWARD BEING THOSE WHERE THE COMMUNITY IS OTHER THAN A SINGLE CLAN-COMMUNITY AND EXOGAMOUS (305)	0.89 OF 66	177	DRIFT LESS TOWARD BEING THOSE WHERE THE COMMUNITY IS OTHER THAN A SINGLE CLAN-COMMUNITY AND EXOGAMOUS (305)	0.78 OF 316	7 70 59 246 XSQ= 3.83 PHI= -0.100 XP = 0.0502
182	DRIFT LESS TOWARD BEING THOSE OTHER THAN WHERE THE COMMUNITY IS STRUCTURED ON A NON-CLAN BASIS AND AGAMOUS (256)	0.58 OF 66	182	DRIFT MORE TOWARD BEING THOSE OTHER THAN WHERE THE COMMUNITY IS STRUCTURED ON A NON-CLAN BASIS AND AGAMOUS (256)	0.69 OF 316	28 98 38 218 XSQ= 2.72 PHI= 0.084 XP = 0.0990
184	LEAN TOWARD BEING THOSE WHERE THE LARGEST NON-COGNATIC KIN GROUP IS THE MOEITY OR PHRATRY (77)	0.53 OF 30	184	LEAN TOWARD BEING THOSE WHERE THE LARGEST NON-COGNATIC KIN GROUP IS SMALLER THAN A PHRATRY, I. E. A SIB OR LINEAGE (175)	0.73 OF 222	16 61 14 161 XSQ= 7.15 PHI= 0.168 XP = 0.0075
186	TEND MORE TO BE THOSE WHERE THE KIN GROUP IS OTHER THAN EXCLUSIVELY PATRILINEAL (250)	0.87 OF 70	186	TEND LESS TO BE THOSE WHERE THE KIN GROUP IS OTHER THAN EXCLUSIVELY PATRILINEAL (250)	0.57 OF 330	9 141 61 189 XSQ= 20.73 PHI= -0.228 XP = 0.0000
187	TEND LESS TO BE THOSE WHERE THE KIN GROUP IS OTHER THAN EXCLUSIVELY MATRILINEAL (344)	0.73 OF 70	187	TEND MORE TO BE THOSE WHERE THE KIN GROUP IS OTHER THAN EXCLUSIVELY MATRILINEAL (344)	0.89 OF 329	19 36 51 293 XSQ= 11.42 PHI= 0.169 XP = 0.0007
188	TEND TO BE THOSE WHERE THE KIN GROUP IS EXCLUSIVELY COGNATIC (148)	0.57 OF 70	188	TEND TO BE THOSE WHERE THE KIN GROUP IS OTHER THAN EXCLUSIVELY COGNATIC (252)	0.67 OF 330	40 108 30 222 XSQ= 13.74 PHI= 0.185 XP = 0.0002
190	TEND TO BE THOSE WHERE THE KIN GROUP IS MATRILINEAL, RATHER THAN PATRILINEAL OR DOUBLE-DESCENT (61)	0.63 OF 30	190	TEND TO BE THOSE WHERE THE KIN GROUP IS PATRILINEAL OR DOUBLE-DESCENT, RATHER THAN MATRILINEAL (186)	0.81 OF 217	11 175 19 42 XSQ= 25.10 PHI= -0.319 XP = 0.0000
192	TEND LESS TO BE THOSE OTHER THAN WHERE THE ONLY KIN GROUP PRESENT IS A KINDRED OR ELSE BILATERAL DESCENT IS INFERRED (289)	0.51 OF 70	192	TEND MORE TO BE THOSE OTHER THAN WHERE THE ONLY KIN GROUP PRESENT IS A KINDRED OR ELSE BILATERAL DESCENT IS INFERRED (289)	0.77 OF 330	34 77 36 253 XSQ= 17.11 PHI= 0.207 XP = 0.0000
196	TEND TO BE THOSE WHERE INDIVIDUAL RIGHTS IN REAL PROPERTY, OR RULES FOR INHERITANCE, ARE ABSENT (87)	0.57 OF 49	196	TEND TO BE THOSE WHERE INDIVIDUAL RIGHTS IN REAL PROPERTY, AND RULES FOR INHERITANCE, ARE PRESENT (194)	0.75 OF 232	21 173 28 59 XSQ= 17.58 PHI= -0.250 XP = 0.0000

198	LEAN LESS TOWARD BEING THOSE 0.61 OF 18 WHERE RULES FOR THE INHERITANCE OF REAL PROPERTY, IF PRESENT, FAVOR THE MALE HEIR OR LINE, RATHER THAN THE FEMALE (144)	198	LEAN MORE TOWARD BEING THOSE 0.90 OF 147 WHERE RULES FOR THE INHERITANCE OF REAL PROPERTY, IF PRESENT, FAVOR THE MALE HEIR OR LINE, RATHER THAN THE FEMALE (144)	11 133 7 14 XSQ= 9.95 PHI= -0.246 XP = 0.0016
209	LEAN LESS TOWARD BEING THOSE 0.64 OF 56 WHERE MARITAL RESIDENCE IS PATRILOCAL, VIRILOCAL, OR AVUNCULOCAL, RATHER THAN MATRILOCAL OR UXORILOCAL (270)	209	LEAN MORE TOWARD BEING THOSE 0.84 OF 278 WHERE MARITAL RESIDENCE IS PATRILOCAL, VIRILOCAL, OR AVUNCULOCAL, RATHER THAN MATRILOCAL OR UXORILOCAL (270)	36 234 20 44 XSQ= 10.65 PHI= -0.179 XP = 0.0011
210	TEND TO BE THOSE 0.65 OF 20 WHERE MARITAL RESIDENCE IS MATRILOCAL, RATHER THAN PATRILOCAL (31)	210	TEND TO BE THOSE 0.90 OF 180 WHERE MARITAL RESIDENCE IS PATRILOCAL, RATHER THAN MATRILOCAL (169)	7 162 13 18 XSQ= 37.48 PHI= -0.433 XP = 0.
213	TEND TO BE THOSE 0.81 OF 68 WHERE FIRST COUSIN MARRIAGE IS NOT PERMITTED (198)	213	TEND TO BE THOSE 0.53 OF 302 WHERE FIRST COUSIN MARRIAGE IS PERMITTED (172)	13 159 55 143 XSQ= 23.76 PHI= -0.253 XP = 0.0000
220	TEND MORE TO BE THOSE 0.91 OF 68 WHERE FIRST COUSIN MARRIAGE IN SOME FORM OR OTHER IS NOT PRESCRIBED OR PREFERRED (273)	220	TEND LESS TO BE THOSE 0.70 OF 302 WHERE FIRST COUSIN MARRIAGE IN SOME FORM OR OTHER IS NOT PRESCRIBED OR PREFERRED (273)	6 91 62 211 XSQ= 11.95 PHI= -0.180 XP = 0.0005
221	DRIFT MORE TOWARD BEING THOSE 0.97 OF 68 WHERE MATRILATERAL CROSS-COUSIN MARRIAGE IS NOT PRESCRIBED OR PREFERRED (335)	221	DRIFT LESS TOWARD BEING THOSE 0.89 OF 302 WHERE MATRILATERAL CROSS-COUSIN MARRIAGE IS NOT PRESCRIBED OR PREFERRED (335)	2 33 66 269 XSQ= 3.25 PHI= -0.094 XP = 0.0713
243	IN ALL CASES ARE THOSE 1.00 OF 9 WHERE POLYGYNY, IF PRESENT, HAS A LOW INCIDENCE (36) W-D,S	243	TILT LESS TOWARD BEING THOSE 0.53 OF 51 WHERE POLYGYNY, IF PRESENT, HAS A LOW INCIDENCE (36) W-D,S	0 24 9 27 XSQ= 5.23 PHI= -0.295 XP = 0.0221
262	TEND LESS TO BE THOSE 0.54 OF 68 WHERE WIVES ARE OBTAINED BY MEANS INVOLVING THE PRESENCE OF SOME CONSIDERATION (305)	262	TEND MORE TO BE THOSE 0.82 OF 327 WHERE WIVES ARE OBTAINED BY MEANS INVOLVING THE PRESENCE OF SOME CONSIDERATION (305)	37 268 31 59 XSQ= 22.74 PHI= -0.240 XP = 0.0000
263	TEND TO BE THOSE 0.71 OF 68 WHERE WIVES ARE OBTAINED BY RELATIVELY EASY MEANS, NAMELY BY TOKEN BRIDE-PRICE, GIFT EXCHANGE, ABSENCE OF ANY CONSIDERATION, OR RECEIPT OF DOWRY (162)	263	TEND TO BE THOSE 0.65 OF 327 WHERE WIVES ARE OBTAINED BY RELATIVELY DIFFICULT MEANS, NAMELY BY BRIDE-PRICE, BRIDE-SERVICE, OR EXCHANGING A FEMALE RELATIVE (233)	20 213 48 114 XSQ= 28.24 PHI= -0.267 XP = 0.0000

```
305  TILT TOWARD BEING THOSE          0.80 OF  10    305  TILT TOWARD BEING THOSE          0.61 OF  41           2     25
     WHERE THE EARLY SEXUAL SATISFACTION                 WHERE THE EARLY SEXUAL SATISFACTION                    8     16
     POTENTIAL IS LOW  (24) W-C                          POTENTIAL IS HIGH  (27) W-C                      XSQ=      3.90
                                                                                                          PHI=    -0.276
                                                                                                          XP =    0.0483

307  DRIFT TOWARD BEING THOSE         0.62 OF  13    307  DRIFT TOWARD BEING THOSE         0.72 OF  39           5     28
     WHERE THE EARLY AGGRESSION SATISFACTION             WHERE THE EARLY AGGRESSION SATISFACTION                8     11
     POTENTIAL IS LOW  (19) W-C                          POTENTIAL IS HIGH  (33) W-C                      XSQ=      3.35
                                                                                                          PHI=    -0.254
                                                                                                          XP =    0.0674

311  TILT TOWARD BEING THOSE          0.90 OF  10    311  TILT TOWARD BEING THOSE          0.54 OF  41           9     19
     WHERE SEXUAL SOCIALIZATION ANXIETY                  WHERE SEXUAL SOCIALIZATION ANXIETY                     1     22
     IS HIGH  (28) W-C                                   IS LOW  (23) W-C                                 XSQ=      4.55
                                                                                                          PHI=     0.299
                                                                                                          XP =    0.0329

313  TILT TOWARD BEING THOSE          0.79 OF  14    313  TILT TOWARD BEING THOSE          0.63 OF  40          11     15
     WHERE AGGRESSION SOCIALIZATION ANXIETY              WHERE AGGRESSION SOCIALIZATION ANXIETY                 3     25
     IS HIGH  (26) W-C                                   IS LOW  (28) W-C                                 XSQ=      5.46
                                                                                                          PHI=     0.318
                                                                                                          XP =    0.0195

319  TEND TO BE THOSE                 0.94 OF  16    319  TEND TO BE THOSE                 0.59 OF  49          15     20
     WHERE PROTECTION OF THE INFANT                      WHERE PROTECTION OF THE INFANT                         1     29
     FROM ENVIRONMENTAL DISCOMFORTS                      FROM ENVIRONMENTAL DISCOMFORTS                   XSQ=     11.55
     IS HIGH  (35) B-B-C                                 IS LOW  (30) B-B-C                               PHI=     0.422
                                                                                                          XP =    0.0007

320  DRIFT MORE TOWARD BEING THOSE    0.87 OF  15    320  DRIFT LESS TOWARD BEING THOSE    0.59 OF  54          13     32
     WHERE THE DEGREE OF REDUCTION                       WHERE THE DEGREE OF REDUCTION                          2     22
     OF THE INFANT'S DRIVES                              OF THE INFANT'S DRIVES                           XSQ=      2.77
     IS HIGH  (45) B-B-C                                 IS HIGH  (45) B-B-C                              PHI=     0.200
                                                                                                          XP =    0.0959

324  DRIFT TOWARD BEING THOSE         0.73 OF  15    324  DRIFT TOWARD BEING THOSE         0.59 OF  51           4     30
     WHERE THE PAIN INFLICTED                            WHERE THE PAIN INFLICTED                              11     21
     ON THE INFANT BY THE NURTURANT AGENT                ON THE INFANT BY THE NURTURANT AGENT             XSQ=      3.60
     IS LOW OR NEGLIGIBLE  (32) B-B-C                    IS HIGH  (34) B-B-C                              PHI=    -0.233
                                                                                                          XP =    0.0579

333  IN ALL CASES ARE THOSE           1.00 OF   4    333  DRIFT TOWARD BEING THOSE         0.67 OF  12           0      8
     WHERE THE AGE AT BEGINNING                          WHERE THE AGE AT BEGINNING                             4      4
     OF TRAINING IN                                      OF TRAINING IN                                   XSQ=      3.00
     HETEROSEXUAL PLAY INHIBITION                        HETEROSEXUAL PLAY INHIBITION                     PHI=    -0.433
     IS LOWER THAN EIGHT YEARS  (8) W-C                  IS EIGHT YEARS OR HIGHER  (8) W-C                EP =    0.0769

342  DRIFT TOWARD BEING THOSE         0.86 OF  14    342  DRIFT TOWARD BEING THOSE         0.50 OF  32           2     16
     WHERE THE CHILD'S INFERRED ANXIETY OVER             WHERE THE CHILD'S INFERRED ANXIETY OVER               12     16
     PERFORMANCE OF NURTURANT BEHAVIOR                   PERFORMANCE OF NURTURANT BEHAVIOR                XSQ=      3.82
     IS LOW  (28) B-B-C                                  IS HIGH  (18) B-B-C                              PHI=    -0.288
                                                                                                          XP =    0.0505
```

348	DRIFT TOWARD BEING THOSE 0.75 OF 16 WHERE THE TOTAL POSITIVE PRESSURE TOWARD DEVELOPING ACHIEVEMENT BEHAVIOR IN THE CHILD IS HIGH (32) B-B-C	348 DRIFT TOWARD BEING THOSE 0.57 OF 47 WHERE THE TOTAL POSITIVE PRESSURE TOWARD DEVELOPING ACHIEVEMENT BEHAVIOR IN THE CHILD IS LOW (31) B-B-C	12 20 4 27 XSQ= 3.81 PHI= 0.246 XP = 0.0508
349	LEAN TOWARD BEING THOSE 0.88 OF 16 WHERE THE CHILD'S INFERRED ANXIETY OVER NON-PERFORMANCE OF ACHIEVEMENT BEHAVIOR IS HIGH (34) B-B-C	349 LEAN TOWARD BEING THOSE 0.57 OF 46 WHERE THE CHILD'S INFERRED ANXIETY OVER NON-PERFORMANCE OF ACHIEVEMENT BEHAVIOR IS LOW (28) B-B-C	14 20 2 26 XSQ= 7.60 PHI= 0.350 XP = 0.0058
350	LEAN TOWARD BEING THOSE 0.88 OF 16 WHERE THE CHILD'S INFERRED ANXIETY OVER PERFORMANCE OF ACHIEVEMENT BEHAVIOR IS HIGH (34) B-B-C	350 LEAN TOWARD BEING THOSE 0.55 OF 44 WHERE THE CHILD'S INFERRED ANXIETY OVER PERFORMANCE OF ACHIEVEMENT BEHAVIOR IS LOW (26) B-B-C	14 20 2 24 XSQ= 6.82 PHI= 0.337 XP = 0.0090
351	LEAN TOWARD BEING THOSE 0.75 OF 16 WHERE THE CHILD'S INFERRED CONFLICT REGARDING ACHIEVEMENT BEHAVIOR IS HIGH (26) B-B-C	351 LEAN TOWARD BEING THOSE 0.68 OF 44 WHERE THE CHILD'S INFERRED CONFLICT REGARDING ACHIEVEMENT BEHAVIOR IS LOW (34) B-B-C	12 14 4 30 XSQ= 7.24 PHI= 0.347 XP = 0.0071
370	TEND MORE TO BE THOSE 0.87 OF 38 WHERE THE SEGREGATION OF ADOLESCENT BOYS IS ABSENT (148)	370 TEND LESS TO BE THOSE 0.56 OF 205 WHERE THE SEGREGATION OF ADOLESCENT BOYS IS ABSENT (148)	5 90 33 115 XSQ= 11.47 PHI= -0.217 XP = 0.0007
372	LEAN TOWARD BEING THOSE 0.84 OF 25 WHERE MALE INITIATION RITES ARE ABSENT (63) ASA	372 LEAN TOWARD BEING THOSE 0.51 OF 86 WHERE MALE INITIATION RITES ARE PRESENT (48) ASA	4 44 21 42 XSQ= 8.38 PHI= -0.275 XP = 0.0038
377	TEND MORE TO BE THOSE 0.98 OF 59 WHERE MALE GENITAL MUTILATION IS ABSENT (242)	377 TEND LESS TO BE THOSE 0.69 OF 266 WHERE MALE GENITAL MUTILATION IS ABSENT (242)	1 82 58 184 XSQ= 20.05 PHI= -0.248 XP = 0.0000
380	TILT MORE TOWARD BEING THOSE 0.92 OF 13 WHERE SEGREGATION OF GIRLS AT MENARCHE IS PRESENT (35) F-B	380 TILT LESS TOWARD BEING THOSE 0.55 OF 42 WHERE SEGREGATION OF GIRLS AT MENARCHE IS PRESENT (35) F-B	12 23 1 19 XSQ= 4.53 PHI= 0.287 XP = 0.0332
382	DRIFT MORE TOWARD BEING THOSE 0.90 OF 10 WHERE FEMALE INITIATION RITES ARE PRESENT (38) JKB	382 DRIFT LESS TOWARD BEING THOSE 0.53 OF 55 WHERE FEMALE INITIATION RITES ARE PRESENT (38) JKB	9 29 1 26 XSQ= 3.43 PHI= 0.230 XP = 0.0641

385	DRIFT MORE TOWARD BEING THOSE 0.90 OF 21 WHERE SEXUAL EXPRESSION BY THE YOUNG IS SEMI-RESTRICTED OR PERMITTED (64) F-B	385	DRIFT LESS TOWARD BEING THOSE 0.69 OF 65 WHERE SEXUAL EXPRESSION BY THE YOUNG IS SEMI-RESTRICTED OR PERMITTED (64) F-B	2 20 19 45 XSQ= 2.73 PHI= -0.178 XP = 0.0985
391	DRIFT TOWARD BEING THOSE 0.68 OF 28 WHERE PREMARITAL SEX RELATIONS ARE STRONGLY PUNISHED AND IN FACT RARE, OR WEAKLY PUNISHED AND IN FACT NOT RARE (89) JTW,EA	391	DRIFT TOWARD BEING THOSE 0.54 OF 151 WHERE PREMARITAL SEX RELATIONS ARE PUNISHED ONLY IF PREGNANCY RESULTS, OR FREELY PERMITTED (90) JTW,EA	19 70 9 81 XSQ= 3.55 PHI= 0.141 XP = 0.0596
406	DRIFT TOWARD BEING THOSE 0.71 OF 14 WHERE EXPLANATIONS OF ILLNESS OF AN AGGRESSION NATURE ARE PRESENT (28) W-C	406	DRIFT TOWARD BEING THOSE 0.62 OF 47 WHERE EXPLANATIONS OF ILLNESS OF AN AGGRESSION NATURE ARE ABSENT (33) W-C	10 18 4 29 XSQ= 3.53 PHI= 0.240 XP = 0.0604
421	DRIFT TOWARD BEING THOSE 0.65 OF 17 WHERE KILLING, TORTURING, OR MUTILATING OF THE ENEMY IS STRONGLY OR MODERATELY EMPHASIZED (37) PES	421	DRIFT TOWARD BEING THOSE 0.61 OF 67 WHERE KILLING, TORTURING, OR MUTILATING OF THE ENEMY IS NEGLIGIBLY EMPHASIZED (47) PES	11 26 6 41 XSQ= 2.71 PHI= 0.180 XP = 0.0994
426	LEAN TOWARD BEING THOSE 0.62 OF 45 WHERE A HIGH GOD IS ABSENT (104) GES,EA	426	LEAN TOWARD BEING THOSE 0.65 OF 215 WHERE A HIGH GOD IS PRESENT (156) GES,EA	17 139 28 76 XSQ= 10.11 PHI= -0.197 XP = 0.0015
444	TILT TOWARD BEING THOSE 0.89 OF 9 WHERE THE USE OF DREAMS TO SEEK AND CONTROL SUPERNATURAL POWERS IS HIGH (28) RGD	444	TILT TOWARD BEING THOSE 0.57 OF 46 WHERE THE USE OF DREAMS TO SEEK AND CONTROL SUPERNATURAL POWERS IS LOW (27) RGD	8 20 1 26 XSQ= 4.53 PHI= 0.287 XP = 0.0334
447	IN ALL CASES ARE THOSE 1.00 OF 5 WHERE LOVE MAGIC IS PRESENT (20) S-R	447	DRIFT LESS TOWARD BEING THOSE 0.54 OF 28 WHERE LOVE MAGIC IS PRESENT (20) S-R	5 15 0 13 XSQ= 2.13 PHI= 0.254 EP = 0.0707
450	IN ALL CASES ARE THOSE 1.00 OF 14 WHERE THE OBSERVATION OF FOOD TABOOS IS HIGH OR MEDIUM, RATHER THAN LOW (60) JRL	450	TILT LESS TOWARD BEING THOSE 0.64 OF 72 WHERE THE OBSERVATION OF FOOD TABOOS IS HIGH OR MEDIUM, RATHER THAN LOW (60) JRL	14 46 0 26 XSQ= 5.64 PHI= 0.256 XP = 0.0176
453	DRIFT TOWARD BEING THOSE 0.58 OF 12 WHERE THE ROLE OF RELIGIOUS EXPERTS IS CONDUCIVE TO THE DEVELOPMENT OF THE INDIVIDUAL'S NEED TO ACHIEVE (13) DCM	453	DRIFT TOWARD BEING THOSE 0.75 OF 24 WHERE THE ROLE OF RELIGIOUS EXPERTS IS NOT CONDUCIVE TO THE DEVELOPMENT OF THE INDIVIDUAL'S NEED TO ACHIEVE (23) DCM	7 6 5 18 XSQ= 2.54 PHI= 0.266 EP = 0.0714

454	DRIFT TOWARD BEING THOSE WHERE THE OBJECTIVE OF THE INDIVIDUAL'S CONTACT WITH THE DIVINE IS NOT CONDUCIVE TO THE DEVELOPMENT OF THE INDIVIDUAL'S NEED TO ACHIEVE (18) DCM	0.75 OF 12	454	DRIFT TOWARD BEING THOSE WHERE THE OBJECTIVE OF THE INDIVIDUAL'S CONTACT WITH THE DIVINE IS CONDUCIVE TO THE DEVELOPMENT OF THE INDIVIDUAL'S NEED TO ACHIEVE (18) DCM	0.63 OF 24	3 15 9 9 XSQ= 3.12 PHI= -0.295 EP = 0.0750
455	TILT TOWARD BEING THOSE WHERE THE MODE OF THE INDIVIDUAL'S CONTACT WITH THE DIVINE IS CONDUCIVE TO THE DEVELOPMENT OF THE INDIVIDUAL'S NEED TO ACHIEVE (17) DCM	0.75 OF 12	455	TILT TOWARD BEING THOSE WHERE THE MODE OF THE INDIVIDUAL'S CONTACT WITH THE DIVINE IS NOT CONDUCIVE TO THE DEVELOPMENT OF THE INDIVIDUAL'S NEED TO ACHIEVE (19) DCM	0.67 OF 24	9 8 3 16 XSQ= 4.03 PHI= 0.334 EP = 0.0328
456	DRIFT TOWARD BEING THOSE WHERE THE INTERNALIZATION OF THE INDIVIDUAL'S CONTACT WITH THE DIVINE IS CONDUCIVE TO THE DEVELOPMENT OF THE INDIVIDUAL'S NEED TO ACHIEVE (19) DCM	0.75 OF 12	456	DRIFT TOWARD BEING THOSE WHERE THE INTERNALIZATION OF THE INDIVIDUAL'S CONTACT WITH THE DIVINE IS NOT CONDUCIVE TO THE DEVELOPMENT OF THE INDIVIDUAL'S NEED TO ACHIEVE (17) DCM	0.58 OF 24	9 10 3 14 XSQ= 2.35 PHI= 0.256 EP = 0.0830
458	TEND MORE TO BE THOSE WHERE GAMES, IF PRESENT, DO NOT INCLUDE GAMES OF STRATEGY (119) R-A-B,EA	0.93 OF 44	458	TEND LESS TO BE THOSE WHERE GAMES, IF PRESENT, DO NOT INCLUDE GAMES OF STRATEGY (119) R-A-B,EA	0.61 OF 127	3 49 41 78 XSQ= 14.12 PHI= -0.287 XP = 0.0002
459	TEND TO BE THOSE WHERE GAMES, IF PRESENT, INCLUDE GAMES OF CHANCE (82) R-A-B,EA	0.93 OF 44	459	TEND TO BE THOSE WHERE GAMES, IF PRESENT, DO NOT INCLUDE GAMES OF CHANCE (89) R-A-B,EA	0.68 OF 127	41 41 3 86 XSQ= 46.15 PHI= 0.519 XP = 0.
460	TEND TO BE THOSE WHERE GAMES, IF PRESENT, ARE NOT LIMITED TO GAMES OF SKILL ONLY (104) R-A-B,EA	0.93 OF 44	460	TEND TO BE THOSE WHERE GAMES, IF PRESENT, ARE LIMITED TO GAMES OF SKILL ONLY (67) R-A-B,EA	0.50 OF 127	3 64 41 63 XSQ= 24.24 PHI= -0.377 XP = 0.0000

9 CULTURES
LOCATED IN SOUTH AMERICA (65)

9 CULTURES
LOCATED OUTSIDE OF
SOUTH AMERICA (335)

BACKGROUND ON PAGE 65

BOTH SUBJECT AND PREDICATE

65 IN LEFT COLUMN

ABIPON	ALACALUF	APINAYE	ARAUCANIANS	AWEIKOMA	AYMARA	BACAIRI	BLACK CARIB	BORCRO	BOTOCUDO
CADUVEO	CAGABA	CALLINAGO	CAMAYURA	CAMBA	CARAJA	CARIB	CARINYA	CAYAPA	CHAMACOCO
CHIBCHA	CHIRIGUANO	CHOCO	CHOROTI	CHORTI	CUNA	GOAJIRO	GUAHIBO	GUATO	INCA
JIVARO	MAM	MATACO	MAYA	MISKITO	MOTILON	MUNDURUCU	NAMBICUARA	ONA	PAEZ
PALIKUR	PARAUJANC	SARAMACCA	SHERENTE	SIRIONO	TALAMANCA	TAPIRAPE	TEHUELCHE	TENETEHARA	TERENA
TIMBIRA	TRUMAI	TUCANO	TUCUNA	TUNEBO	TUPINAMBA	TZELTAL	WAICA	WAPISHANA	WARRAU
WITOTO	YABARANA	YAGUA	YAHGAN	YARURO					

335 IN RIGHT COLUMN

15	TEND TO BE THOSE WHERE THE LATITUDE IS LESS THAN TWENTY DEGREES (217)	0.80 OF 65	15	TEND TO BE THOSE WHERE THE LATITUDE IS TWENTY DEGREES OR GREATER (183)	0.51 OF 335	13 170 52 165 XSQ= 19.51 PHI= -0.221 XP = 0.0000
42	LEAN TOWARD BEING THOSE WHERE THE NATURAL ENVIRONMENT IS TROPICAL CR SUB-TRCPICAL RAIN FOREST, OR MONSOON FOREST (156) FWM	0.57 OF 65	42	LEAN TOWARD BEING THOSE WHERE THE NATURAL ENVIRONMENT IS OTHER THAN TROPICAL OR SUB-TROPICAL RAIN FOREST, OR MONSOON FOREST (244) FWM	0.64 OF 335	37 119 28 216 XSQ= 9.60 PHI= 0.155 XP = 0.0019
51	TEND TO BE THOSE WHERE SUBSISTENCE IS PRIMARILY BY FOOD GATHERING -- I. E., HUNTING, FISHING, OR COLLECTING -- RATHER THAN FOOD PRODUCTION (147)	0.66 OF 65	51	TEND TO BE THOSE WHERE SUBSISTENCE IS PRIMARILY BY FOOD PRODUCTION -- I. E., AGRICULTURE OR HUSBANDRY -- RATHER THAN BY GATHERING (253)	0.69 OF 335	22 231 43 104 XSQ= 27.38 PHI= -0.262 XP = 0.0000
54	TEND TO BE THOSE WHERE FOOD PRODUCTION IS BY INCIPIENT FOOD PRODUCTION, RATHER THAN BY INTENSIVE OR SIMPLE AGRICULTURE (46)	0.50 OF 36	54	TEND TO BE THOSE WHERE FOOD PRODUCTION IS BY INTENSIVE OR SIMPLE AGRICULTURE, RATHER THAN BY INCIPIENT FOOD PRODUCTION (192)	0.86 OF 202	18 174 18 28 XSQ= 23.33 PHI= -0.313 XP = 0.0000
56	TEND TO BE THOSE WHERE FOOD PRODUCTION IS BY INCIPIENT FOOD PRODUCTION, RATHER THAN BY SIMPLE AGRICULTURE (46)	0.58 OF 31	56	TEND TO BE THOSE WHERE FOOD PRODUCTION IS BY SIMPLE AGRICULTURE, RATHER THAN BY INCIPIENT FOOD PRODUCTION (101)	0.76 OF 116	13 88 18 28 XSQ= 11.57 PHI= -0.280 XP = 0.0007

62	TEND TO BE THOSE WHERE HUSBANDRY OF ANY KIND IS ABSENT (172)	0.69 OF 65	62	TEND TO BE THOSE WHERE HUSBANDRY OF SOME KIND IS PRESENT (228)	0.62 OF 335	20 208 45 127 XSQ= 20.53 PHI= -0.227 XP = 0.0000
63	TILT TOWARD BEING THOSE WHERE HUSBANDRY, IF PRESENT, IS PRINCIPALLY IN THE FORM OF PIGS, SHEEP, OR GOATS, RATHER THAN BOVINE, EQUINE, CAMEL-LIKE, OR DEER-LIKE ANIMALS (74)	0.55 OF 20	63	TILT TOWARD BEING THOSE WHERE HUSBANDRY, IF PRESENT, IS PRINCIPALLY IN THE FORM OF BOVINE, EQUINE, CAMEL-LIKE, OR DEER-LIKE ANIMALS, RATHER THAN PIGS, SHEEP, OR GOATS (152)	0.69 OF 206	9 143 11 63 XSQ= 3.89 PHI= -0.131 XP = 0.0486
71	TEND MORE TO BE THOSE WHERE METAL WORKING IS ABSENT (153)	0.88 OF 50	71	TEND LESS TO BE THOSE WHERE METAL WORKING IS ABSENT (153)	0.54 OF 201	6 92 44 109 XSQ= 17.79 PHI= -0.266 XP = 0.0000
73	LEAN TOWARD BEING THOSE WHERE WEAVING IS PRESENT (118)	0.68 OF 50	73	LEAN TOWARD BEING THOSE WHERE WEAVING IS ABSENT (130)	0.58 OF 198	34 84 16 114 XSQ= 9.47 PHI= 0.195 XP = 0.0021
74	LEAN MORE TOWARD BEING THOSE WHERE POTTERY IS PRESENT (145)	0.79 OF 48	74	LEAN LESS TOWARD BEING THOSE WHERE POTTERY IS PRESENT (145)	0.56 OF 190	38 107 10 83 XSQ= 7.47 PHI= 0.177 XP = 0.0063
79	IN ALL CASES ARE THOSE WHERE NO CITY IS PRESENT (201)	1.00 OF 38	79	TILT LESS TOWARD BEING THOSE WHERE NO CITY IS PRESENT (201)	0.88 OF 186	0 23 38 163 XSQ= 3.98 PHI= -0.133 XP = 0.0460
81	TILT MORE TOWARD BEING THOSE WHERE NO CITY OR TOWN IS PRESENT, AND THE AVERAGE COMMUNITY SIZE IS SMALLER THAN 200 (135)	0.79 OF 38	81	TILT LESS TOWARD BEING THOSE WHERE NO CITY OR TOWN IS PRESENT, AND THE AVERAGE COMMUNITY SIZE IS SMALLER THAN 200 (135)	0.56 OF 186	8 81 30 105 XSQ= 5.76 PHI= -0.160 XP = 0.0164
82	TILT LESS TOWARD BEING THOSE WHERE A CITY OR TOWN IS PRESENT, OR THE AVERAGE COMMUNITY SIZE IS FIFTY OR GREATER (178)	0.63 OF 38	82	TILT MORE TOWARD BEING THOSE WHERE A CITY OR TOWN IS PRESENT, OR THE AVERAGE COMMUNITY SIZE IS FIFTY OR GREATER (178)	0.83 OF 186	24 154 14 32 XSQ= 6.30 PHI= -0.168 XP = 0.0121
83	TILT MORE TOWARD BEING THOSE WHERE, WITH NO CITY AND NO TOWN PRESENT, THE AVERAGE COMMUNITY SIZE IS SMALLER THAN 200, RATHER THAN BETWEEN 200 AND 999 (135)	0.91 OF 33	83	TILT LESS TOWARD BEING THOSE WHERE, WITH NO CITY AND NO TOWN PRESENT, THE AVERAGE COMMUNITY SIZE IS SMALLER THAN 200, RATHER THAN BETWEEN 200 AND 999 (135)	0.71 OF 147	3 42 30 105 XSQ= 4.47 PHI= -0.157 XP = 0.0346

86	TEND TO BE THOSE WHERE THE LEVEL OF POLITICAL INTEGRATION IS THE AUTONOMOUS COMMUNITY, OR THE FAMILY (156) GPM	0.78 OF 55	86	TEND TO BE THOSE WHERE THE LEVEL OF POLITICAL INTEGRATION IS THE LARGE STATE, THE LITTLE STATE, OR THE MINIMAL STATE (148) GPM	0.55 OF 249	12 136 43 113 XSQ= 18.11 PHI= -0.244 XP = 0.0000
96	TEND TO BE THOSE WHERE THE HIERARCHY OF NATIONAL JURISDICTION HAS NO LEVELS (156) GES,EA	0.78 OF 58	96	TEND TO BE THOSE WHERE THE HIERARCHY OF NATIONAL JURISDICTION HAS FOUR, THREE, TWO OR ONE LEVEL (174) GES,EA	0.59 OF 272	13 161 45 111 XSQ= 24.49 PHI= -0.272 XP = 0.0000
98	LEAN LESS TOWARD BEING THOSE WHERE THE HIERARCHY OF LOCAL JURISDICTION HAS FOUR OR THREE LEVELS (238) GES,EA	0.54 OF 59	98	LEAN MORE TOWARD BEING THOSE WHERE THE HIERARCHY OF LOCAL JURISDICTION HAS FOUR OR THREE LEVELS (238) GES,EA	0.76 OF 272	32 206 27 66 XSQ= 10.05 PHI= -0.174 XP = 0.0015
100	TEND LESS TO BE THOSE WHERE HIERARCHIES ARE MORE COMPLEX THAN THE 'SIMPLEST,' I. E., MORE COMPLEX THAN TWO LOCAL LEVELS WITH NO NATIONAL LEVELS (267) GES,EA	0.60 OF 58	100	TEND MORE TO BE THOSE WHERE HIERARCHIES ARE MORE COMPLEX THAN THE 'SIMPLEST,' I. E., MORE COMPLEX THAN TWO LOCAL LEVELS WITH NO NATIONAL LEVELS (267) GES,EA	0.85 OF 272	35 232 23 40 XSQ= 17.68 PHI= -0.231 XP = 0.0000
102	TEND TO BE THOSE WHERE CLASS STRATIFICATION IS ABSENT (180)	0.77 OF 61	102	TEND TO BE THOSE WHERE CLASS STRATIFICATION IS PRESENT (203)	0.59 OF 322	14 189 47 133 XSQ= 24.89 PHI= -0.255 XP = 0.0000
109	IN ALL CASES ARE THOSE WHERE CASTES ARE ABSENT (317)	1.00 OF 63	109	TEND LESS TO BE THOSE WHERE CASTES ARE ABSENT (317)	0.83 OF 305	0 51 63 254 XSQ= 10.87 PHI= -0.172 XP = 0.0010
110	LEAN MORE TOWARD BEING THOSE WHERE SLAVERY IS ABSENT (218)	0.77 OF 61	110	LEAN LESS TOWARD BEING THOSE WHERE SLAVERY IS ABSENT (218)	0.53 OF 320	14 149 47 171 XSQ= 10.72 PHI= -0.168 XP = 0.0011
116	IN ALL CASES ARE THOSE WHERE OCCUPATIONAL SPECIALIZATION IS PART-TIME ONLY (34) JMH	1.00 OF 8	116	DRIFT LESS TOWARD BEING THOSE WHERE OCCUPATIONAL SPECIALIZATION IS PART-TIME ONLY (34) JMH	0.57 OF 46	0 20 8 26 XSQ= 3.82 PHI= -0.266 XP = 0.0507
129	LEAN MORE TOWARD BEING THOSE WHERE WEAVING IS MAINLY DONE BY FEMALES (73)	0.90 OF 31	129	LEAN LESS TOWARD BEING THOSE WHERE WEAVING IS MAINLY DONE BY FEMALES (73)	0.62 OF 73	3 28 28 45 XSQ= 7.24 PHI= -0.264 XP = 0.0071

137 DRIFT MORE TOWARD BEING THOSE 0.85 OF 13 WHERE INVIDIOUS DISPLAY OF WEALTH IS MODERATELY, LITTLE, OR NEGATIVELY EMPHASIZED (52) PES	137 DRIFT LESS TOWARD BEING THOSE 0.54 OF 76 WHERE INVIDIOUS DISPLAY OF WEALTH IS MODERATELY, LITTLE, OR NEGATIVELY EMPHASIZED (52) PES	2 35 11 41 XSQ= 3.13 PHI= -0.187 XP = 0.0769
142 DRIFT TOWARD BEING THOSE 0.63 OF 8 WHERE THE LEVEL OF SOCIAL SANCTION IS PRIVATE SETTLEMENT, RATHER THAN PUBLIC CORPOREAL SANCTION OR PUBLIC PROPERTY SETTLEMENT (16) JMH	142 DRIFT TOWARD BEING THOSE 0.76 OF 46 WHERE THE LEVEL OF SOCIAL SANCTION IS PUBLIC CORPOREAL SANCTION OR PUBLIC PROPERTY SANCTION, RATHER THAN PRIVATE SETTLEMENT (38) JMH	3 35 5 11 XSQ= 3.19 PHI= -0.243 XP = 0.0740
143 IN ALL CASES ARE THOSE 1.00 OF 8 WHERE THE RATIO OF RESTITUTIVE TO REPRESSIVE SANCTIONS IS MEDIUM OR LOW (32) WME	143 TILT LESS TOWARD BEING THOSE 0.55 OF 44 WHERE THE RATIO OF RESTITUTIVE TO REPRESSIVE SANCTIONS IS MEDIUM OR LOW (32) WME	0 20 8 24 XSQ= 4.14 PHI= -0.282 XP = 0.0418
176 TEND MORE TO BE THOSE 0.76 OF 59 WHERE THE COMMUNITY IS OTHER THAN A CLAN-COMMUNITY OR A COMMUNITY STRUCTURED OR SEGMENTED ON A CLAN BASIS (213)	176 TEND LESS TO BE THOSE 0.52 OF 323 WHERE THE COMMUNITY IS OTHER THAN A CLAN-COMMUNITY OR A COMMUNITY STRUCTURED OR SEGMENTED ON A CLAN BASIS (213)	14 155 45 168 XSQ= 10.94 PHI= -0.169 XP = 0.0009
177 LEAN MORE TOWARD BEING THOSE 0.93 OF 59 WHERE THE COMMUNITY IS OTHER THAN A SINGLE CLAN-COMMUNITY AND EXOGAMOUS (305)	177 LEAN LESS TOWARD BEING THOSE 0.77 OF 323 WHERE THE COMMUNITY IS OTHER THAN A SINGLE CLAN-COMMUNITY AND EXOGAMOUS (305)	4 73 55 250 XSQ= 6.81 PHI= -0.133 XP = 0.0091
180 TILT MORE TOWARD BEING THOSE 0.80 OF 59 WHERE THE COMMUNITY IS COMMONLY NON-EXOGAMOUS, RATHER THAN EXOGAMOUS (258)	180 TILT LESS TOWARD BEING THOSE 0.65 OF 323 WHERE THE COMMUNITY IS COMMONLY NON-EXOGAMOUS, RATHER THAN EXOGAMOUS (258)	12 112 47 211 XSQ= 4.05 PHI= -0.103 XP = 0.0443
181 TEND LESS TO BE THOSE 0.73 OF 59 WHERE THE COMMUNITY IS OTHER THAN A DEME (337)	181 TEND MORE TO BE THOSE 0.91 OF 323 WHERE THE COMMUNITY IS OTHER THAN A DEME (337)	16 29 43 294 XSQ= 14.10 PHI= 0.192 XP = 0.0002
183 TILT LESS TOWARD BEING THOSE 0.67 OF 21 WHERE THE LARGEST NON-COGNATIC KIN GROUP IS SMALLER THAN A MOEITY, I. E., A PHRATRY OR SIB OR LINEAGE (218)	183 TILT MORE TOWARD BEING THOSE 0.88 OF 231 WHERE THE LARGEST NON-COGNATIC KIN GROUP IS SMALLER THAN A MOEITY, I. E., A PHRATRY OR SIB OR LINEAGE (218)	7 27 14 204 XSQ= 5.98 PHI= 0.154 XP = 0.0144
185 TILT LESS TOWARD BEING THOSE 0.57 OF 21 WHERE THE LARGEST NON-COGNATIC KIN GROUP IS THE MOEITY OR PHRATRY OR SIB (194)	185 TILT MORE TOWARD BEING THOSE 0.79 OF 231 WHERE THE LARGEST NON-COGNATIC KIN GROUP IS THE MOEITY OR PHRATRY OR SIB (194)	12 182 9 49 XSQ= 3.94 PHI= -0.125 XP = 0.0471

186	TEND MORE TO BE THOSE WHERE THE KIN GROUP IS OTHER THAN EXCLUSIVELY PATRILINEAL (250)	0.82 OF 65	186	TEND LESS TO BE THOSE WHERE THE KIN GROUP IS OTHER THAN EXCLUSIVELY PATRILINEAL (250)	0.59 OF 335	12 138 53 197 XSQ= 11.05 PHI= -0.166 XP = 0.0009
188	TEND TO BE THOSE WHERE THE KIN GROUP IS EXCLUSIVELY COGNATIC (148)	0.68 OF 65	188	TEND TO BE THOSE WHERE THE KIN GROUP IS OTHER THAN EXCLUSIVELY COGNATIC (252)	0.69 OF 335	44 104 21 231 XSQ= 29.81 PHI= 0.273 XP = 0.0000
190	DRIFT LESS TOWARD BEING THOSE WHERE THE KIN GROUP IS PATRILINEAL OR DOUBLE-DESCENT, RATHER THAN MATRILINEAL (186)	0.57 OF 21	190	DRIFT MORE TOWARD BEING THOSE WHERE THE KIN GROUP IS PATRILINEAL OR DOUBLE-DESCENT, RATHER THAN MATRILINEAL (186)	0.77 OF 226	12 174 9 52 XSQ= 3.07 PHI= -0.112 XP = 0.0796
192	TEND TO BE THOSE WHERE THE ONLY KIN GROUP PRESENT IS A KINDRED OR ELSE BILATERAL DESCENT IS INFERRED (111)	0.52 OF 65	192	TEND TO BE THOSE OTHER THAN WHERE THE ONLY KIN GROUP PRESENT IS A KINDRED OR ELSE BILATERAL DESCENT IS INFERRED (289)	0.77 OF 335	34 77 31 258 XSQ= 21.91 PHI= 0.234 XP = 0.0000
196	TEND TO BE THOSE WHERE INDIVIDUAL RIGHTS IN REAL PROPERTY, OR RULES FOR INHERITANCE, ARE ABSENT (87)	0.67 OF 33	196	TEND TO BE THOSE WHERE INDIVIDUAL RIGHTS IN REAL PROPERTY, AND RULES FOR INHERITANCE, ARE PRESENT (194)	0.74 OF 248	11 183 22 65 XSQ= 20.45 PHI= -0.270 XP = 0.0000
204	TILT LESS TOWARD BEING THOSE WHERE MARITAL RESIDENCE IS PATRILOCAL, VIRILOCAL, OR AVUNCULOCAL, RATHER THAN AMBILOCAL OR NEOLOCAL (270)	0.66 OF 41	204	TILT MORE TOWARD BEING THOSE WHERE MARITAL RESIDENCE IS PATRILOCAL, VIRILOCAL, OR AVUNCULOCAL, RATHER THAN AMBILOCAL OR NEOLOCAL (270)	0.83 OF 293	27 243 14 50 XSQ= 5.72 PHI= -0.131 XP = 0.0168
209	TEND LESS TO BE THOSE WHERE MARITAL RESIDENCE IS PATRILOCAL, VIRILOCAL, OR AVUNCULOCAL, RATHER THAN MATRILOCAL OR UXORILOCAL (270)	0.54 OF 50	209	TEND MORE TO BE THOSE WHERE MARITAL RESIDENCE IS PATRILOCAL, VIRILOCAL, OR AVUNCULOCAL, RATHER THAN MATRILOCAL OR UXORILOCAL (270)	0.86 OF 284	27 243 23 41 XSQ= 25.34 PHI= -0.275 XP = 0.0000
210	LEAN LESS TOWARD BEING THOSE WHERE MARITAL RESIDENCE IS PATRILOCAL, RATHER THAN MATRILOCAL (169)	0.56 OF 16	210	LEAN MORE TOWARD BEING THOSE WHERE MARITAL RESIDENCE IS PATRILOCAL, RATHER THAN MATRILOCAL (169)	0.87 OF 184	9 160 7 24 XSQ= 8.38 PHI= -0.205 XP = 0.0038
213	TILT TOWARD BEING THOSE WHERE FIRST COUSIN MARRIAGE IS PERMITTED (172)	0.61 OF 57	213	TILT TOWARD BEING THOSE WHERE FIRST COUSIN MARRIAGE IS NOT PERMITTED (198)	0.56 OF 313	35 137 22 176 XSQ= 5.34 PHI= 0.120 XP = 0.0209

224	LEAN MORE TOWARD BEING THOSE WHERE COUSIN MARRIAGE IS PREFERENTIALLY OR PERMISSIVELY SYMMETRICAL, RATHER THAN EITHER PATRI- OR MATRILATERAL (106)	0.83 OF 35	224	LEAN LESS TOWARD BEING THOSE WHERE COUSIN MARRIAGE IS PREFERENTIALLY OR PERMISSIVELY SYMMETRICAL, RATHER THAN EITHER PATRI- OR MATRILATERAL (106)	0.56 OF 137	6 60 29 77 XSQ= 7.29 PHI= -0.206 XP = 0.0070
240	DRIFT TOWARD BEING THOSE WHERE THE FAMILY, IF EXTENDED, IS LARGE, RATHER THAN SMALL OR STEM (78)	0.52 OF 33	240	DRIFT TOWARD BEING THOSE WHERE THE FAMILY, IF EXTENDED, IS SMALL OR STEM, RATHER THAN LARGE (135)	0.66 OF 180	17 61 16 119 XSQ= 3.01 PHI= 0.119 XP = 0.0826
262	TILT LESS TOWARD BEING THOSE WHERE WIVES ARE OBTAINED BY MEANS INVOLVING THE PRESENCE OF SOME CONSIDERATION (305)	0.65 OF 63	262	TILT MORE TOWARD BEING THOSE WHERE WIVES ARE OBTAINED BY MEANS INVOLVING THE PRESENCE OF SOME CONSIDERATION (305)	0.80 OF 332	41 264 22 68 XSQ= 5.48 PHI= -0.118 XP = 0.0192
309	IN ALL CASES ARE THOSE WHERE ORAL SOCIALIZATION ANXIETY IS LOW (27) W-C	1.00 OF 5	309	DRIFT TOWARD BEING THOSE WHERE ORAL SOCIALIZATION ANXIETY IS HIGH (26) W-C	0.54 OF 48	0 26 5 22 XSQ= 3.37 PHI= -0.252 XP = 0.0664
325	DRIFT TOWARD BEING THOSE WHERE THE DEGREE OF DIFFUSION AMONG THE INFANT'S NURTURANT AGENTS IS LOW (32) B-B-C	0.69 OF 13	325	DRIFT TOWARD BEING THOSE WHERE THE DEGREE OF DIFFUSION AMONG THE INFANT'S NURTURANT AGENTS IS HIGH (42) B-B-C	0.62 OF 61	4 38 9 23 XSQ= 3.15 PHI= -0.206 XP = 0.0759
326	TILT TOWARD BEING THOSE WHERE THE INFERRED TRANSITION ANXIETY BETWEEN INFANCY AND CHILDHOOD IS LOW (35) B-B-C	0.91 OF 11	326	TILT TOWARD BEING THOSE WHERE THE INFERRED TRANSITION ANXIETY BETWEEN INFANCY AND CHILDHOOD IS HIGH (32) B-B-C	0.55 OF 56	1 31 10 25 XSQ= 6.14 PHI= -0.303 XP = 0.0132
328	IN ALL CASES ARE THOSE WHERE THE AGE OF THE INFANT AT THE ONSET OF SERIOUS SOCIALIZATION, OTHER THAN WEANING, IS HIGHER THAN TWO YEARS (21) B-B-C	1.00 OF 6	328	TILT TOWARD BEING THOSE WHERE THE AGE OF THE INFANT AT THE ONSET OF SERIOUS SOCIALIZATION, OTHER THAN WEANING, IS TWO YEARS OR LOWER (20) B-B-C	0.57 OF 35	6 15 0 20 XSQ= 4.60 PHI= 0.335 XP = 0.0319
337	TILT TOWARD BEING THOSE WHERE THE CHILD'S INFERRED ANXIETY OVER NON-PERFORMANCE OF RESPONSIBLE BEHAVIOR IS LOW (35) B-B-C	0.83 OF 12	337	TILT TOWARD BEING THOSE WHERE THE CHILD'S INFERRED ANXIETY OVER NON-PERFORMANCE OF RESPONSIBLE BEHAVIOR IS HIGH (38) B-B-C	0.59 OF 61	2 36 10 25 XSQ= 5.61 PHI= -0.277 XP = 0.0179
339	DRIFT MORE TOWARD BEING THOSE WHERE THE CHILD'S INFERRED CONFLICT REGARDING RESPONSIBLE BEHAVIOR IS LOW (42) B-B-C	0.83 OF 12	339	DRIFT LESS TOWARD BEING THOSE WHERE THE CHILD'S INFERRED CONFLICT REGARDING RESPONSIBLE BEHAVIOR IS LOW (42) B-B-C	0.52 OF 61	2 29 10 32 XSQ= 2.75 PHI= -0.194 XP = 0.0972

349	TILT TOWARD BEING THOSE 0.82 OF 11 WHERE THE CHILD'S INFERRED ANXIETY OVER NON-PERFORMANCE OF ACHIEVEMENT BEHAVIOR IS LOW (28) B-B-C	349	TILT TOWARD BEING THOSE 0.63 OF 51 WHERE THE CHILD'S INFERRED ANXIETY OVER NON-PERFORMANCE OF ACHIEVEMENT BEHAVIOR IS HIGH (34) B-B-C	2 32 9 19 XSQ= 5.57 PHI= -0.300 XP = 0.0183
350	TILT TOWARD BEING THOSE 0.80 OF 10 WHERE THE CHILD'S INFERRED ANXIETY OVER PERFORMANCE OF ACHIEVEMENT BEHAVIOR IS LOW (26) B-B-C	350	TILT TOWARD BEING THOSE 0.64 OF 50 WHERE THE CHILD'S INFERRED ANXIETY OVER PERFORMANCE OF ACHIEVEMENT BEHAVIOR IS HIGH (34) B-B-C	2 32 8 18 XSQ= 4.90 PHI= -0.286 XP = 0.0268
351	TILT TOWARD BEING THOSE 0.90 OF 10 WHERE THE CHILD'S INFERRED CONFLICT REGARDING ACHIEVEMENT BEHAVIOR IS LOW (34) B-B-C	351	TILT TOWARD BEING THOSE 0.50 OF 50 WHERE THE CHILD'S INFERRED CONFLICT REGARDING ACHIEVEMENT BEHAVIOR IS HIGH (26) B-B-C	1 25 9 25 XSQ= 3.92 PHI= -0.256 XP = 0.0476
358	LEAN TOWARD BEING THOSE 0.60 OF 10 WHERE ADOLESCENT PEER GROUPS ARE ABSENT IN A SETTING OF WORK, AND OF PUBLIC GATHERINGS, AND OF LEISURE (11) JKH	358	LEAN TOWARD BEING THOSE 0.88 OF 42 WHERE ADOLESCENT PEER GROUPS ARE PRESENT IN A SETTING OF WORK AND PUBLIC GATHERINGS AND LEISURE, OR OF PUBLIC GATHERINGS AND LEISURE, OR OF LEISURE ONLY (41) JKH	4 37 6 5 XSQ= 8.50 PHI= -0.404 XP = 0.0035
360	IN ALL CASES ARE THOSE 1.00 OF 7 WHERE ADOLESCENT PEER GROUPS ARE PRESENT ONLY IN A SETTING OF LEISURE, OR ELSE ARE ABSENT (23) JKH	360	TILT LESS TOWARD BEING THOSE 0.53 OF 30 WHERE ADOLESCENT PEER GROUPS ARE PRESENT ONLY IN A SETTING OF LEISURE, OR ELSE ARE ABSENT (23) JKH	0 14 7 16 XSQ= 3.46 PHI= -0.306 EP = 0.0309
370	TILT MORE TOWARD BEING THOSE 0.78 OF 36 WHERE THE SEGREGATION OF ADOLESCENT BOYS IS ABSENT (148)	370	TILT LESS TOWARD BEING THOSE 0.58 OF 207 WHERE THE SEGREGATION OF ADOLESCENT BOYS IS ABSENT (148)	8 87 28 120 XSQ= 4.26 PHI= -0.132 XP = 0.0391
377	TEND MORE TO BE THOSE 0.98 OF 59 WHERE MALE GENITAL MUTILATION IS ABSENT (242)	377	TEND LESS TO BE THOSE 0.69 OF 266 WHERE MALE GENITAL MUTILATION IS ABSENT (242)	1 82 58 184 XSQ= 20.05 PHI= -0.248 XP = 0.0000
385	DRIFT TOWARD BEING THOSE 0.50 OF 12 WHERE SEXUAL EXPRESSION BY THE YOUNG IS RESTRICTED (22) F-B	385	DRIFT TOWARD BEING THOSE 0.78 OF 74 WHERE SEXUAL EXPRESSION BY THE YOUNG IS SEMI-RESTRICTED OR PERMITTED (64) F-B	6 16 6 58 XSQ= 3.00 PHI= 0.187 XP = 0.0830
403	IN ALL CASES ARE THOSE 1.00 OF 7 WHERE EXPLANATICNS OF ILLNESS OF AN ANAL NATURE ARE ABSENT (38) W-C	403	DRIFT LESS TOWARD BEING THOSE 0.57 OF 54 WHERE EXPLANATIONS OF ILLNESS OF AN ANAL NATURE ARE ABSENT (38) W-C	0 23 7 31 XSQ= 3.14 PHI= -0.227 XP = 0.0762

```
427  DRIFT TOWARD BEING THOSE          0.62 OF  29    427  DRIFT TOWARD BEING THOSE          0.60 OF 127        11    76
     WHERE A HIGH GOD, IF PRESENT, IS                     WHERE A HIGH GOD, IF PRESENT, IS                     18    51
     INACTIVE, RATHER THAN                                ACTIVE, RATHER THAN                             XSQ=     3.75
     ACTIVE  (69) GES,EA                                  INACTIVE  (87) GES,EA                           PHI=   -0.155
                                                                                                          XP =   0.0528

458  LEAN MORE TOWARD BEING THOSE      0.97 OF  29    458  LEAN LESS TOWARD BEING THOSE      0.64 OF 142         1    51
     WHERE GAMES, IF PRESENT,                             WHERE GAMES, IF PRESENT,                             28    91
     DO NOT INCLUDE                                       DO NOT INCLUDE                                  XSQ=    10.51
     GAMES OF STRATEGY  (119) R-A-B,EA                    GAMES OF STRATEGY  (119) R-A-B,EA               PHI=   -0.248
                                                                                                          XP =   0.0012

459  TILT TOWARD BEING THOSE           0.72 OF  29    459  TILT TOWARD BEING THOSE           0.52 OF 142         8    74
     WHERE GAMES, IF PRESENT,                             WHERE GAMES, IF PRESENT,                             21    68
     DO NOT INCLUDE                                       INCLUDE GAMES OF CHANCE  (82) R-A-B,EA          XSQ=     4.86
     GAMES OF CHANCE  (89) R-A-B,EA                                                                       PHI=   -0.169
                                                                                                          XP =   0.0274

460  TEND TO BE THOSE                  0.72 OF  29    460  TEND TO BE THOSE                  0.68 OF 142        21    46
     WHERE GAMES, IF PRESENT,                             WHERE GAMES, IF PRESENT,                              8    96
     ARE LIMITED TO                                       ARE NOT LIMITED TO                              XSQ=    14.55
     GAMES OF SKILL CNLY  (67) R-A-B,EA                   GAMES OF SKILL ONLY  (104) R-A-B,EA             PHI=    0.292
                                                                                                          XP =   0.0001

475  TILT TOWARD BEING THOSE           0.79 OF  14    475  TILT TOWARD BEING THOSE           0.63 OF  72         3    45
     WHERE EXHIBITIONISTIC DANCING                        WHERE EXHIBITIONISTIC DANCING                        11    27
     IS NEGLIGIBLY EMPHASIZED  (38) PES                   IS STRONGLY OR MODERATELY                       XSQ=     6.44
                                                          EMPHASIZED  (48) PES                            PHI=   -0.274
                                                                                                          XP =   0.0112

476  IN ALL CASES ARE THOSE            1.00 OF  10    476  TILT LESS TOWARD BEING THOSE      0.54 OF  39        10    21
     WHERE THE DEGREE OF INSOBRIETY IS                    WHERE THE DEGREE OF INSOBRIETY IS                     0    18
     STRONG  (31) DH                                      STRONG  (31) DH                                 XSQ=     5.44
                                                                                                          PHI=    0.333
                                                                                                          XP =   0.0196
```

10 CULTURES
LOCATED IN THE TROPICS (251)

10 CULTURES
LOCATED OUTSIDE OF THE TROPICS (149)

BACKGROUND ON PAGE 66

SUBJECT ONLY

251 IN LEFT COLUMN

AJIE	AKHA	ALORESE	AMBA	ANDAMANESE	APINAYE	ARAPESH	ASHANTI	AYMARA	AZANDE
AZTEC	BABWA	BACAIRI	BAJUN	BALINESE	BAMBARA	BAMILEKE	BANDA	BARABRA	BARI
BATAK	BAYA	BEJA	BELU	BEMBA	BENGALI	BERGDAMA	BETE	BHIL	BHUIYA
BIRIFOR	BLACK CARIB	BOERS	BORORO	BOTOCUDO	BOZO	BRAZILIANS	BUDUMA	BUNLAP	BURMESE
CADUVEO	CAGABA	CALLINAGO	CAMAYURA	CAMBA	CAMBODIANS	CARAJA	CARIB	CARINYA	CAYAPA
CHAGGA	CHAMACOCO	CHENCHU	CHIBCHA	CHINANTEC	CHIRIGUANO	CHOCO	CHOROTI	CHORTI	COORG
CUNA	DILLING	DOBUANS	DOGON	DOROBO	DUSUN	ELLICE	ENGA	FANG	FON
FUTAJALONKE	GANDA	GILBERTESE	GISU	GOAJIRO	GOND	GUAHIBO	GUATO	GURE	HANUNOO
HASANIA	HAWAIIANS	HEHE	HERERO	HO	HUICHOL	IBAN	IFUGAO	ILA	INCA
INGASSANA	IRAQW	JAVANESE	JIVARO	JUKUN	KAPAUKU	KAREN	KARIERA	KATAB	KERAKI
KERALA	KIKUYU	KISSI	KONSO	KPE	KUBA	KUNG	KURTATCHI	LAKALAI	LAKHER
LAMBA	LAMET	LANGO	LAU	LESU	LIFU	LOZI	LUBA	LUO	MACASSARESE
MAGUZAWA	MALAYS	MAM	MAMBILA	MAMVU	MANGAIANS	MANIHIKI	MANUS	MARGI	MARQUESANS
MARSHALLESE	MASAI	MATAKAM	MAYA	MAZATECO	MBUGWE	MBUNDU	MBUTI	MENDE	MENTAWEI
MERINA	MINANGKABAU	MISKITO	MNONG GAR	MONGO	MOSSI	MOTA	MOTILON	MUNDURUCU	MURINBATA
MURNGIN	NAMBICUARA	NANDI	NDEMBU	NGONI	NICOBARESE	NUER	NUPE	NYAKYUSA	NYANEKA
NYARO	NYORO	ONTONG-JAVA	ORAON	PAEZ	PAIWAN	PALAUANS	PALIKUR	PARAUJANO	PENDE
PONAPEANS	POPOLUCA	PUKAPUKA	PURARI	RAROIANS	REGEIBAT	ROTINESE	ROTUMANS	RUNDI	SAGADA
SAMOANS	SANDAWE	SARAMACCA	SELUNG	SEMANG	SENIANG	SHERENTE	SHILLUK	SHLUH	SIMBOESE
SINHALESE	SIRIONO	SIUAI	SOMALI	SONGHAI	SUBANUN	TAGBANUA	TALAMANCA	TALLENSI	TAMIL
TANALA	TANIMBARESE	TAPIRAPE	TEDA	TENDA	TENETEHARA	TERA	TERENA	TESO	THAI
TIGRINYA	TIKOPIA	TIMBIRA	TIV	TIWI	TODA	TOKELAU	TORAJA	TOTONAC	TROBRIAND
TRUKESE	TRUMAI	TUCANO	TUCUNA	TUNEBO	TUPINAMBA	TURKANA	TZELTAL	ULAWANS	VEDDA
VENDA	VIETNAMESE	WAICA	WANTOAT	WAPISHANA	WAROPEN	WARRAU	WIKMUNKAN	WITOTO	WOGEO
WOLEAIANS	WOLOF	WUTE	YABARANA	YAGUA	YAKO	YAO	YAPESE	YARURO	YOMBE
YORUBA									

149 IN RIGHT COLUMN

3 TEND LESS TO BE THOSE LOCATED OUTSIDE OF AFRICA (320) — 0.70 OF 251

3 TEND MORE TO BE THOSE LOCATED OUTSIDE OF AFRICA (320) — 0.97 OF 149

76	4
175	145
XSQ=	42.79
PHI=	0.327
XP =	0.

4 TEND MORE TO BE THOSE LOCATED OUTSIDE OF THE CIRCUM-MEDITERRANEAN (355) — 0.93 OF 251

4 TEND LESS TO BE THOSE LOCATED OUTSIDE OF THE CIRCUM-MEDITERRANEAN (355) — 0.81 OF 149

17	28
234	121
XSQ=	12.35
PHI=	-0.176
XP =	0.0004

5	TEND MORE TO BE THOSE LOCATED OUTSIDE OF EAST EURASIA (330)	0.88 OF 251	5	TEND LESS TO BE THOSE LOCATED OUTSIDE OF EAST EURASIA (330)	0.72 OF 149	29 41 222 108 XSQ= 15.41 PHI= -0.196 XP = 0.0001
6	TEND LESS TO BE THOSE LOCATED OUTSIDE OF THE INSULAR PACIFIC (330)	0.74 OF 251	6	TEND MORE TO BE THOSE LOCATED OUTSIDE OF THE INSULAR PACIFIC (330)	0.97 OF 149	66 4 185 145 XSQ= 34.48 PHI= 0.294 XP = 0.
8	TEND MORE TO BE THOSE LOCATED OUTSIDE OF NORTH AMERICA (330)	0.98 OF 251	8	TEND LESS TO BE THOSE LOCATED OUTSIDE OF NORTH AMERICA (330)	0.57 OF 149	6 64 245 85 XSQ= 103.76 PHI= -0.509 XP = 0.
9	TEND LESS TO BE THOSE LOCATED OUTSIDE OF SOUTH AMERICA (335)	0.77 OF 251	9	TEND MORE TO BE THOSE LOCATED OUTSIDE OF SOUTH AMERICA (335)	0.95 OF 149	57 8 194 141 XSQ= 19.40 PHI= 0.220 XP = 0.0000
33	TEND MORE TO BE THOSE WHERE THE NATURAL ENVIRONMENT IS OTHER THAN 'VERY HARSH,' I.E., DESERT, DESERT GRASSES AND SHRUBS, TUNDRA, OR HIGH PLATEAU STEPPE (341) FWM	0.93 OF 251	33	TEND LESS TO BE THOSE WHERE THE NATURAL ENVIRONMENT IS OTHER THAN 'VERY HARSH,' I.E., DESERT, DESERT GRASSES AND SHRUBS, TUNDRA, OR HIGH PLATEAU STEPPE (341) FWM	0.72 OF 149	18 41 233 108 XSQ= 29.18 PHI= -0.270 XP = 0.0000
36	TEND MORE TO BE THOSE WHERE THE NATURAL ENVIRONMENT IS OTHER THAN 'VERY HARSH,' OR SUB-TROPICAL BUSH, OR TEMPERATE GRASSLAND (292) FWM	0.84 OF 251	36	TEND LESS TO BE THOSE WHERE THE NATURAL ENVIRONMENT IS OTHER THAN 'VERY HARSH,' OR SUB-TROPICAL BUSH, OR TEMPERATE GRASSLAND (292) FWM	0.54 OF 149	39 69 212 80 XSQ= 43.37 PHI= -0.329 XP = 0.
42	TEND TO BE THOSE WHERE THE NATURAL ENVIRONMENT IS TROPICAL OR SUB-TROPICAL RAIN FOREST, OR MONSOON FOREST (156) FWM	0.57 OF 251	42	TEND TO BE THOSE WHERE THE NATURAL ENVIRONMENT IS OTHER THAN TROPICAL OR SUB-TROPICAL RAIN FOREST, OR MONSOON FOREST (244) FWM	0.91 OF 149	142 14 109 135 XSQ= 85.50 PHI= 0.462 XP = 0.
44	TEND MORE TO BE THOSE WHERE SETTLEMENTS ARE FIXED (222)	0.76 OF 205	44	TEND LESS TO BE THOSE WHERE SETTLEMENTS ARE FIXED (222)	0.52 OF 127	156 66 49 61 XSQ= 19.53 PHI= 0.243 XP = 0.0000
45	LEAN LESS TOWARD BEING THOSE WHERE SETTLEMENTS, IF FIXED, ARE COMPACT, RATHER THAN NON-COMPACT (149)	0.61 OF 156	45	LEAN MORE TOWARD BEING THOSE WHERE SETTLEMENTS, IF FIXED, ARE COMPACT, RATHER THAN NON-COMPACT (149)	0.82 OF 66	95 54 61 12 XSQ= 8.27 PHI= -0.193 XP = 0.0040

46	TEND MORE TO BE THOSE 0.85 OF 205 OTHER THAN WHERE SETTLEMENTS ARE NON-FIXED AND MOVEMENT IS NOMADIC (260)	46	TEND LESS TO BE THOSE 0.68 OF 127 OTHER THAN WHERE SETTLEMENTS ARE NON-FIXED AND MOVEMENT IS NOMADIC (260)	31 41 174 86 XSQ= 12.61 PHI= -0.195 XP = 0.0004
48	DRIFT TOWARD BEING THOSE 0.57 OF 51 WHERE THE FOOD SUPPLY IS SECURE, AND FOOD SHORTAGES ARE RARE OR OCCASIONAL (38) MGW	48	DRIFT TOWARD BEING THOSE 0.68 OF 28 WHERE THE FOOD SUPPLY IS NOT SECURE, AND FOOD SHORTAGES ARE FREQUENT OR ANNUAL (41) MGW	29 9 22 19 XSQ= 3.49 PHI= 0.210 XP = 0.0617
51	TEND TO BE THOSE 0.72 OF 251 WHERE SUBSISTENCE IS PRIMARILY BY FOOD PRODUCTION -- I. E., AGRICULTURE OR HUSBANDRY -- RATHER THAN BY GATHERING (253)	51	TEND TO BE THOSE 0.51 OF 149 WHERE SUBSISTENCE IS PRIMARILY BY FOOD GATHERING -- I. E., HUNTING, FISHING, OR COLLECTING -- RATHER THAN FOOD PRODUCTION (147)	180 73 71 76 XSQ= 19.80 PHI= 0.222 XP = 0.0000
53	TEND TO BE THOSE 0.72 OF 161 WHERE FOOD PRODUCTION IS BY SIMPLE AGRICULTURE OR INCIPIENT FOOD PRODUCTION, RATHER THAN BY INTENSIVE AGRICULTURE (147)	53	TEND TO BE THOSE 0.60 OF 77 WHERE FOOD PRODUCTION IS BY INTENSIVE AGRICULTURE, RATHER THAN BY SIMPLE AGRICULTURE OR INCIPIENT FOOD PRODUCTION (91)	45 46 116 31 XSQ= 20.96 PHI= -0.297 XP = 0.0000
55	TEND TO BE THOSE 0.67 OF 136 WHERE FOOD PRODUCTION IS BY SIMPLE AGRICULTURE, RATHER THAN BY INTENSIVE AGRICULTURE (101)	55	TEND TO BE THOSE 0.82 OF 56 WHERE FOOD PRODUCTION IS BY INTENSIVE AGRICULTURE, RATHER THAN BY SIMPLE AGRICULTURE (91)	45 46 91 10 XSQ= 36.34 PHI= -0.435 XP = 0.
56	TEND TO BE THOSE 0.78 OF 116 WHERE FOOD PRODUCTION IS BY SIMPLE AGRICULTURE, RATHER THAN BY INCIPIENT FOOD PRODUCTION (101)	56	TEND TO BE THOSE 0.68 OF 31 WHERE FOOD PRODUCTION IS BY INCIPIENT FOOD PRODUCTION, RATHER THAN BY SIMPLE AGRICULTURE (46)	91 10 25 21 XSQ= 22.17 PHI= 0.388 XP = 0.0000
63	TEND LESS TO BE THOSE 0.55 OF 147 WHERE HUSBANDRY, IF PRESENT, IS PRINCIPALLY IN THE FORM OF BOVINE, EQUINE, CAMEL-LIKE, OR DEER-LIKE ANIMALS, RATHER THAN PIGS, SHEEP, OR GOATS (152)	63	TEND MORE TO BE THOSE 0.90 OF 79 WHERE HUSBANDRY, IF PRESENT, IS PRINCIPALLY IN THE FORM OF BOVINE, EQUINE, CAMEL-LIKE, OR DEER-LIKE ANIMALS, RATHER THAN PIGS, SHEEP, OR GOATS (152)	81 71 66 8 XSQ= 26.65 PHI= -0.343 XP = 0.0000
79	TILT MORE TOWARD BEING THOSE 0.93 OF 135 WHERE NO CITY IS PRESENT (201)	79	TILT LESS TOWARD BEING THOSE 0.84 OF 89 WHERE NO CITY IS PRESENT (201)	9 14 126 75 XSQ= 3.85 PHI= -0.131 XP = 0.0498
108	TILT LESS TOWARD BEING THOSE 0.57 OF 121 WHERE CLASS STRATIFICATION, IF PRESENT, IS BASED ON SOMETHING OTHER THAN A HEREDITARY ARISTOCRACY (129)	108	TILT MORE TOWARD BEING THOSE 0.73 OF 82 WHERE CLASS STRATIFICATION, IF PRESENT, IS BASED ON SOMETHING OTHER THAN A HEREDITARY ARISTOCRACY (129)	52 22 69 60 XSQ= 4.83 PHI= 0.154 XP = 0.0280

128	DRIFT TOWARD BEING THOSE 0.55 OF 56 WHERE, IF SUBSISTENCE IS PRIMARILY BY AGRICULTURE, THE WORK IS MAINLY DONE BY FEMALES (37)	128	DRIFT TOWARD BEING THOSE 0.71 OF 21 WHERE, IF SUBSISTENCE IS PRIMARILY BY AGRICULTURE, THE WORK IS MAINLY DONE BY MALES (40)	25 15 31 6 XSQ= 3.38 PHI= -0.210 XP = 0.0659
130	TEND TO BE THOSE 0.81 OF 26 WHERE LEATHER WORKING IS MAINLY DONE BY MALES (39)	130	TEND TO BE THOSE 0.69 OF 58 WHERE LEATHER WORKING IS MAINLY DONE BY FEMALES (45)	21 18 5 40 XSQ= 15.91 PHI= 0.435 XP = 0.0001
131	LEAN MORE TOWARD BEING THOSE 0.93 OF 90 WHERE THE CONSTRUCTION OF PERMANENT HOUSES OR THE ERECTION OF TEMPORARY DWELLINGS IS MAINLY DONE BY MALES (136)	131	LEAN LESS TOWARD BEING THOSE 0.78 OF 67 WHERE THE CONSTRUCTION OF PERMANENT HOUSES OR THE ERECTION OF TEMPORARY DWELLINGS IS MAINLY DONE BY MALES (136)	84 52 6 15 XSQ= 6.89 PHI= 0.210 XP = 0.0087
176	TEND TO BE THOSE 0.52 OF 238 WHERE THE COMMUNITY IS A CLAN-COMMUNITY OR A COMMUNITY STRUCTURED OR SEGMENTED ON A CLAN BASIS (169)	176	TEND TO BE THOSE 0.68 OF 144 WHERE THE COMMUNITY IS OTHER THAN A CLAN-COMMUNITY OR A COMMUNITY STRUCTURED OR SEGMENTED ON A CLAN BASIS (213)	123 46 115 98 XSQ= 13.38 PHI= 0.187 XP = 0.0003
178	TILT LESS TOWARD BEING THOSE 0.73 OF 238 WHERE THE COMMUNITY IS OTHER THAN SEGMENTED ON A CLAN BASIS AND NON-EXOGAMOUS (295)	178	TILT MORE TOWARD BEING THOSE 0.84 OF 144 WHERE THE COMMUNITY IS OTHER THAN SEGMENTED ON A CLAN BASIS AND NON-EXOGAMOUS (295)	64 23 174 121 XSQ= 5.48 PHI= 0.120 XP = 0.0193
182	TILT MORE TOWARD BEING THOSE 0.71 OF 238 OTHER THAN WHERE THE COMMUNITY IS STRUCTURED ON A NON-CLAN BASIS AND AGAMOUS (256)	182	TILT LESS TOWARD BEING THOSE 0.60 OF 144 OTHER THAN WHERE THE COMMUNITY IS STRUCTURED ON A NON-CLAN BASIS AND AGAMOUS (256)	69 57 169 87 XSQ= 4.09 PHI= -0.103 XP = 0.0432
184	TILT MORE TOWARD BEING THOSE 0.75 OF 165 WHERE THE LARGEST NON-COGNATIC KIN GROUP IS SMALLER THAN A PHRATRY, I. E. A SIB OR LINEAGE (175)	184	TILT LESS TOWARD BEING THOSE 0.60 OF 87 WHERE THE LARGEST NON-COGNATIC KIN GROUP IS SMALLER THAN A PHRATRY, I. E. A SIB OR LINEAGE (175)	42 35 123 52 XSQ= 5.19 PHI= -0.143 XP = 0.0228
185	DRIFT LESS TOWARD BEING THOSE 0.73 OF 165 WHERE THE LARGEST NON-COGNATIC KIN GROUP IS THE MOEITY OR PHRATRY OR SIB (194)	185	DRIFT MORE TOWARD BEING THOSE 0.84 OF 87 WHERE THE LARGEST NON-COGNATIC KIN GROUP IS THE MOEITY OR PHRATRY OR SIB (194)	121 73 44 14 XSQ= 3.02 PHI= -0.110 XP = 0.0821
192	LEAN MORE TOWARD BEING THOSE 0.78 OF 251 OTHER THAN WHERE THE ONLY KIN GROUP PRESENT IS A KINDRED OR ELSE BILATERAL DESCENT IS INFERRED (289)	192	LEAN LESS TOWARD BEING THOSE 0.62 OF 149 OTHER THAN WHERE THE ONLY KIN GROUP PRESENT IS A KINDRED OR ELSE BILATERAL DESCENT IS INFERRED (289)	55 56 196 93 XSQ= 10.68 PHI= -0.163 XP = 0.0011

196	TEND MORE TO BE THOSE 0.77 OF 165 WHERE INDIVIDUAL RIGHTS IN REAL PROPERTY, AND RULES FOR INHERITANCE, ARE PRESENT (194)	196	TEND LESS TO BE THOSE 0.58 OF 116 WHERE INDIVIDUAL RIGHTS IN REAL PROPERTY, AND RULES FOR INHERITANCE, ARE PRESENT (194)	127 67 38 49 XSQ= 10.88 PHI= 0.197 XP = 0.0010
220	LEAN LESS TOWARD BEING THOSE 0.69 OF 235 WHERE FIRST COUSIN MARRIAGE IN SOME FORM OR OTHER IS NOT PRESCRIBED OR PREFERRED (273)	220	LEAN MORE TOWARD BEING THOSE 0.82 OF 135 WHERE FIRST COUSIN MARRIAGE IN SOME FORM OR OTHER IS NOT PRESCRIBED OR PREFERRED (273)	73 24 162 111 XSQ= 7.15 PHI= 0.139 XP = 0.0075
236	LEAN TOWARD BEING THOSE 0.52 OF 249 WHERE THE FAMILY IS OF AN INDEPENDENT TYPE, RATHER THAN AN EXTENDED TYPE (185)	236	LEAN TOWARD BEING THOSE 0.63 OF 149 WHERE THE FAMILY IS OF AN EXTENDED TYPE, RATHER THAN AN INDEPENDENT TYPE (213)	119 94 130 55 XSQ= 8.16 PHI= -0.143 XP = 0.0043
240	TILT LESS TOWARD BEING THOSE 0.57 OF 119 WHERE THE FAMILY, IF EXTENDED, IS SMALL OR STEM, RATHER THAN LARGE (135)	240	TILT MORE TOWARD BEING THOSE 0.71 OF 94 WHERE THE FAMILY, IF EXTENDED, IS SMALL OR STEM, RATHER THAN LARGE (135)	51 27 68 67 XSQ= 3.93 PHI= 0.136 XP = 0.0474
241	TILT MORE TOWARD BEING THOSE 0.92 OF 119 WHERE THE FAMILY, IF EXTENDED, IS LARGE OR SMALL, RATHER THAN STEM (187)	241	TILT LESS TOWARD BEING THOSE 0.82 OF 94 WHERE THE FAMILY, IF EXTENDED, IS LARGE OR SMALL, RATHER THAN STEM (187)	110 77 9 17 XSQ= 4.49 PHI= 0.145 XP = 0.0341
243	DRIFT TOWARD BEING THOSE 0.50 OF 40 WHERE POLYGYNY, IF PRESENT, HAS A HIGH INCIDENCE (24) W-D,S	243	DRIFT TOWARD BEING THOSE 0.80 OF 20 WHERE POLYGYNY, IF PRESENT, HAS A LOW INCIDENCE (36) W-D,S	20 4 20 16 XSQ= 3.83 PHI= 0.253 XP = 0.0504
263	TILT MORE TOWARD BEING THOSE 0.64 OF 248 WHERE WIVES ARE OBTAINED BY RELATIVELY DIFFICULT MEANS, NAMELY BY BRIDE-PRICE, BRIDE-SERVICE, OR EXCHANGING A FEMALE RELATIVE (233)	263	TILT LESS TOWARD BEING THOSE 0.51 OF 147 WHERE WIVES ARE OBTAINED BY RELATIVELY DIFFICULT MEANS, NAMELY BY BRIDE-PRICE, BRIDE-SERVICE, OR EXCHANGING A FEMALE RELATIVE (233)	158 75 90 72 XSQ= 5.63 PHI= 0.119 XP = 0.0177
277	DRIFT TOWARD BEING THOSE 0.80 OF 15 WHERE THE STATUS OF WOMEN IS NOT STRONGLY INFERIOR OR SUBJECTED (22) LWS	277	DRIFT TOWARD BEING THOSE 0.52 OF 21 WHERE THE STATUS OF WOMEN IS INFERIOR OR SUBJECTED (14) LWS	3 11 12 10 XSQ= 2.62 PHI= -0.270 EP = 0.0833
280	TILT TOWARD BEING THOSE 0.60 OF 20 WHERE THE COMPOSITE FERTILITY LEVEL IS LOW (12) MN	280	IN ALL CASES ARE THOSE 1.00 OF 5 WHERE THE COMPOSITE FERTILITY LEVEL IS HIGH (13) MN	8 5 12 0 XSQ= 3.62 PHI= -0.380 EP = 0.0391

300	TILT TOWARD BEING THOSE WHERE THE POST-PARTUM SEX TABOO LASTS LONGER THAN SIX MONTHS (51)	0.50 OF 80	300	TILT TOWARD BEING THOSE WHERE THE POST-PARTUM SEX TABOO LASTS SIX MONTHS OR LESS (73)	0.75 OF 44	40 11 40 33 XSQ= 6.33 PHI= 0.226 XP = 0.0119
304	DRIFT TOWARD BEING THOSE WHERE THE EARLY ANAL SATISFACTION POTENTIAL IS LOW (22) W-C	0.67 OF 24	304	DRIFT TOWARD BEING THOSE WHERE THE EARLY ANAL SATISFACTION POTENTIAL IS HIGH (19) W-C	0.65 OF 17	8 11 16 6 XSQ= 2.78 PHI= -0.260 XP = 0.0956
305	TILT TOWARD BEING THOSE WHERE THE EARLY SEXUAL SATISFACTION POTENTIAL IS HIGH (27) W-C	0.65 OF 34	305	TILT TOWARD BEING THOSE WHERE THE EARLY SEXUAL SATISFACTION POTENTIAL IS LOW (24) W-C	0.71 OF 17	22 5 12 12 XSQ= 4.34 PHI= 0.292 XP = 0.0373
307	TILT TOWARD BEING THOSE WHERE THE EARLY AGGRESSION SATISFACTION POTENTIAL IS HIGH (33) W-C	0.76 OF 33	307	TILT TOWARD BEING THOSE WHERE THE EARLY AGGRESSION SATISFACTION POTENTIAL IS LOW (19) W-C	0.58 OF 19	25 8 8 11 XSQ= 4.53 PHI= 0.295 XP = 0.0334
313	LEAN TOWARD BEING THOSE WHERE AGGRESSION SOCIALIZATION ANXIETY IS LOW (28) W-C	0.70 OF 33	313	LEAN TOWARD BEING THOSE WHERE AGGRESSION SOCIALIZATION ANXIETY IS HIGH (26) W-C	0.76 OF 21	10 16 23 5 XSQ= 9.06 PHI= -0.410 XP = 0.0026
314	TILT LESS TOWARD BEING THOSE WHERE THE INCIDENCE OF MOTHER-CHILD HOUSEHOLDS IS LOW (61) W-D,S	0.68 OF 53	314	TILT MORE TOWARD BEING THOSE WHERE THE INCIDENCE OF MOTHER-CHILD HOUSEHOLDS IS LOW (61) W-D,S	0.93 OF 27	17 2 36 25 XSQ= 4.73 PHI= 0.243 XP = 0.0297
315	TILT TOWARD BEING THOSE WHERE MOTHER AND NURSING CHILD CUSTOMARILY SLEEP IN THE SAME BED (37) W-D,S	0.83 OF 35	315	TILT TOWARD BEING THOSE WHERE MOTHER AND NURSING CHILD CUSTOMARILY SLEEP IN DIFFERENT BEDS (14) W-D,S	0.50 OF 16	29 8 6 8 XSQ= 4.42 PHI= 0.294 XP = 0.0356
316	LEAN TOWARD BEING THOSE WHERE EXCLUSIVE MOTHER-SON SLEEPING ARRANGEMENTS LAST ONE YEAR OR LONGER (19) W-K-A	0.62 OF 26	316	LEAN TOWARD BEING THOSE WHERE EXCLUSIVE MOTHER-SON SLEEPING ARRANGEMENTS LAST LESS THAN ONE YEAR (25) W-K-A	0.83 OF 18	16 3 10 15 XSQ= 7.00 PHI= 0.399 XP = 0.0082
319	TILT TOWARD BEING THOSE WHERE PROTECTION OF THE INFANT FROM ENVIRONMENTAL DISCOMFORTS IS LOW (30) B-B-C	0.59 OF 37	319	TILT TOWARD BEING THOSE WHERE PROTECTION OF THE INFANT FROM ENVIRONMENTAL DISCOMFORTS IS HIGH (35) B-B-C	0.71 OF 28	15 20 22 8 XSQ= 4.94 PHI= -0.276 XP = 0.0263

327	DRIFT TOWARD BEING THOSE 0.60 OF 35 WHERE THE AGE OF THE INFANT AT TIME OF REDUCED CONTACT WITH MOTHER IS TWO YEARS OR LOWER (27) B-B-C	327	DRIFT TOWARD BEING THOSE 0.70 OF 20 WHERE THE AGE OF THE INFANT AT TIME OF REDUCED CONTACT WITH MOTHER IS HIGHER THAN TWO YEARS (28) B-B-C	14 14 21 6 XSQ= 3.46 PHI= -0.251 XP = 0.0628
348	DRIFT TOWARD BEING THOSE 0.60 OF 35 WHERE THE TOTAL POSITIVE PRESSURE TOWARD DEVELOPING ACHIEVEMENT BEHAVIOR IN THE CHILD IS LOW (31) B-B-C	348	DRIFT TOWARD BEING THOSE 0.64 OF 28 WHERE THE TOTAL POSITIVE PRESSURE TOWARD DEVELOPING ACHIEVEMENT BEHAVIOR IN THE CHILD IS HIGH (32) B-B-C	14 18 21 10 XSQ= 2.76 PHI= -0.209 XP = 0.0964
349	TILT TOWARD BEING THOSE 0.59 OF 34 WHERE THE CHILD'S INFERRED ANXIETY OVER NON-PERFORMANCE OF ACHIEVEMENT BEHAVIOR IS LOW (28) B-B-C	349	TILT TOWARD BEING THOSE 0.71 OF 28 WHERE THE CHILD'S INFERRED ANXIETY OVER NON-PERFORMANCE OF ACHIEVEMENT BEHAVIOR IS HIGH (34) B-B-C	14 20 20 8 XSQ= 4.52 PHI= -0.270 XP = 0.0335
350	DRIFT TOWARD BEING THOSE 0.56 OF 32 WHERE THE CHILD'S INFERRED ANXIETY OVER PERFORMANCE OF ACHIEVEMENT BEHAVIOR IS LOW (26) B-B-C	350	DRIFT TOWARD BEING THOSE 0.71 OF 28 WHERE THE CHILD'S INFERRED ANXIETY OVER PERFORMANCE OF ACHIEVEMENT BEHAVIOR IS HIGH (34) B-B-C	14 20 18 8 XSQ= 3.60 PHI= -0.245 XP = 0.0578
370	TEND TO BE THOSE 0.51 OF 152 WHERE THE SEGREGATION OF ADOLESCENT BOYS IS COMPLETE OR PARTIAL (95)	370	TEND TO BE THOSE 0.81 OF 91 WHERE THE SEGREGATION OF ADOLESCENT BOYS IS ABSENT (148)	78 17 74 74 XSQ= 24.11 PHI= 0.315 XP = 0.0000
372	LEAN TOWARD BEING THOSE 0.54 OF 71 WHERE MALE INITIATION RITES ARE PRESENT (48) ASA	372	LEAN TOWARD BEING THOSE 0.75 OF 40 WHERE MALE INITIATION RITES ARE ABSENT (63) ASA	38 10 33 30 XSQ= 7.36 PHI= 0.257 XP = 0.0067
377	LEAN LESS TOWARD BEING THOSE 0.69 OF 199 WHERE MALE GENITAL MUTILATION IS ABSENT (242)	377	LEAN MORE TOWARD BEING THOSE 0.83 OF 126 WHERE MALE GENITAL MUTILATION IS ABSENT (242)	62 21 137 105 XSQ= 7.77 PHI= 0.155 XP = 0.0053
391	LEAN TOWARD BEING THOSE 0.59 OF 108 WHERE PREMARITAL SEX RELATIONS ARE PUNISHED ONLY IF PREGNANCY RESULTS, OR FREELY PERMITTED (90) JTW,EA	391	LEAN TOWARD BEING THOSE 0.63 OF 71 WHERE PREMARITAL SEX RELATIONS ARE STRONGLY PUNISHED AND IN FACT RARE, OR WEAKLY PUNISHED AND IN FACT NOT RARE (89) JTW,EA	44 45 64 26 XSQ= 7.90 PHI= -0.210 XP = 0.0049
400	TILT TOWARD BEING THOSE 0.52 OF 31 WHERE HOMOSEXUAL ACTIVITY IS PROHIBITED (22) F-B	400	TILT TOWARD BEING THOSE 0.78 OF 27 WHERE HOMOSEXUAL ACTIVITY IS PERMITTED (36) F-B	16 6 15 21 XSQ= 4.12 PHI= 0.267 XP = 0.0424

406	DRIFT TOWARD BEING THOSE WHERE EXPLANATICNS OF ILLNESS OF AN AGGRESSION NATURE ARE ABSENT (33) W-C	0.65 OF 37	406	DRIFT TOWARD BEING THOSE WHERE EXPLANATIONS OF ILLNESS OF AN AGGRESSION NATURE ARE PRESENT (28) W-C	0.63 OF 24	13 15 24 9 XSQ= 3.36 PHI= -0.235 XP = 0.0669
427	TEND TO BE THOSE WHERE A HIGH GOD, IF PRESENT, IS INACTIVE, RATHER THAN ACTIVE (69) GES,EA	0.56 OF 96	427	TEND TO BE THOSE WHERE A HIGH GOD, IF PRESENT, IS ACTIVE, RATHER THAN INACTIVE (87) GES,EA	0.75 OF 60	42 45 54 15 XSQ= 13.38 PHI= -0.293 XP = 0.0003
439	DRIFT TOWARD BEING THOSE WHERE FEAR OF GHOSTS IS HIGH (30) W-C	0.59 OF 37	439	DRIFT TOWARD BEING THOSE WHERE FEAR OF GHOSTS IS LOW (31) W-C	0.67 OF 24	22 8 15 16 XSQ= 3.00 PHI= 0.222 XP = 0.0833
442	DRIFT TOWARD BEING THOSE WHERE FEAR OF ANIMAL SPIRITS IS LOW (33) W-C	0.65 OF 37	442	DRIFT TOWARD BEING THOSE WHERE FEAR OF ANIMAL SPIRITS IS HIGH (28) W-C	0.63 OF 24	13 15 24 9 XSQ= 3.36 PHI= -0.235 XP = 0.0669
447	TILT TOWARD BEING THOSE WHERE LOVE MAGIC IS ABSENT (13) S-R	0.52 OF 23	447	TILT TOWARD BEING THOSE WHERE LOVE MAGIC IS PRESENT (20) S-R	0.90 OF 10	11 9 12 1 XSQ= 3.58 PHI= -0.329 EP = 0.0495
452	LEAN TOWARD BEING THOSE WHERE TOTEMISM WITH FOOD TABOOS IS PRESENT (19) WNS	0.61 OF 28	452	LEAN TOWARD BEING THOSE WHERE TOTEMISM WITH FOOD TABOOS IS ABSENT (24) WNS	0.87 OF 15	17 2 11 13 XSQ= 7.07 PHI= 0.406 XP = 0.0078
454	DRIFT TOWARD BEING THOSE WHERE THE OBJECTIVE OF THE INDIVIDUAL'S CONTACT WITH THE DIVINE IS CONDUCIVE TO THE DEVELOPMENT OF THE INDIVIDUAL'S NEED TO ACHIEVE (18) DCM	0.69 OF 16	454	DRIFT TOWARD BEING THOSE WHERE THE OBJECTIVE OF THE INDIVIDUAL'S CONTACT WITH THE DIVINE IS NOT CONDUCIVE TO THE DEVELOPMENT OF THE INDIVIDUAL'S NEED TO ACHIEVE (18) DCM	0.65 OF 20	11 7 5 13 XSQ= 2.81 PHI= 0.280 EP = 0.0922
455	LEAN TOWARD BEING THOSE WHERE THE MODE OF THE INDIVIDUAL'S CONTACT WITH THE DIVINE IS NOT CONDUCIVE TO THE DEVELOPMENT OF THE INDIVIDUAL'S NEED TO ACHIEVE (19) DCM	0.81 OF 16	455	LEAN TOWARD BEING THOSE WHERE THE MODE OF THE INDIVIDUAL'S CONTACT WITH THE DIVINE IS CONDUCIVE TO THE DEVELOPMENT OF THE INDIVIDUAL'S NEED TO ACHIEVE (17) DCM	0.70 OF 20	3 14 13 6 XSQ= 7.42 PHI= -0.454 EP = 0.0031
459	TEND TO BE THOSE WHERE GAMES, IF PRESENT, DO NOT INCLUDE GAMES OF CHANCE (89) R-A-B,EA	0.77 OF 90	459	TEND TO BE THOSE WHERE GAMES, IF PRESENT, INCLUDE GAMES OF CHANCE (82) R-A-B,EA	0.75 OF 81	21 61 69 20 XSQ= 44.08 PHI= -0.508 XP = 0.

10/

```
460  TEND TO BE THOSE              0.56 OF  90      460  TEND TO BE THOSE              0.79 OF  81         50   17
     WHERE GAMES, IF PRESENT,                            WHERE GAMES, IF PRESENT,                          40   64
     ARE LIMITED TO                                      ARE NOT LIMITED TO                             XSQ=   19.95
     GAMES OF SKILL CNLY  (67) R-A-B,EA                  GAMES OF SKILL ONLY  (104) R-A-B,EA            PHI=   0.342
                                                                                                        XP =  0.0000
```

11 CULTURES
WHERE THE LATITUDE IS
SIXTY DEGREES OR GREATER (15)

11 CULTURES
WHERE THE LATITUDE IS
LESS THAN SIXTY DEGREES (385)

BACKGROUND ON PAGE 66

PREDICATE ONLY

15 IN LEFT COLUMN

385 IN RIGHT COLUMN

ABIPON	ABOR	AINU	AJIE	AKHA	ALACALUF	ALBANIANS	ALORESE	AMBA	AMERICANS
ANDAMANESE	APINAYE	ARANDA	ARAPESH	ARAUCANIANS	ARYANS	ASHANTI	ATAYAL	ATSUGEWI	AWEIKOMA
AYMARA	AZANDE	AZTEC	BABWA	BACAIRI	BAJUN	BALINESE	BAMBARA	BAMILEKE	BANDA
BARABRA	BARI	BASQUES	BASSERI	BATAK	BAYA	BEJA	BELU	BEMBA	BENGALI
BERGDAMA	BETE	BHIL	BHUIYA	BIRIFOR	BLACK CARIB	BOERS	BORORO	BOTOCUDO	BOZO
BRAZILIANS	BUDUMA	BULGARIANS	BUNLAP	BURMESE	BURUSHO	BURYAT	CADUVEO	CAGABA	CALLINAGO
CAMAYURA	CAMBA	CAMBODIANS	CARAJA	CARIB	CARINYA	CAYAPA	CHAGGA	CHAMACOCO	CHENCHU
CHEREMIS	CHERKESS	CHEROKEE	CHEYENNE	CHIBCHA	CHINANTEC	CHIR-APACHE	CHIRIGUANO	CHOCO	CHOROTI
CHORTI	COCHITI	COMANCHE	COORG	CREE	CREEK	CROW	CUNA	CZECHS	DAGUR
DARD	DELAWARE	DIEGUENO	DIERI	DILLING	DOBUANS	DOGON	DOROBO	DUSUN	DUTCH
EGYPTIANS	ELLICE	ENGA	FANG	FON	FOX	FUTAJALONKE	GANDA	GARO	GILBERTESE
GILYAK	GISU	GOAJIRO	GOND	GROS VENTRE	GUAHIBO	GUATO	GURE	HAIDA	HANO
HANUNOO	HASANIA	HASINAI	HAVASUPAI	HAWAIIANS	HAZARA	HEBREWS	HEHE	HERERO	HO
HUICHOL	HUKUNDIKA	HURON	HUTSUL	IBAN	IFUGAO	ILA	INCA	INGASSANA	IRAQW
IRISH	JAPANESE	JAVANESE	JEMEZ	JIVARO	JUKUN	KABYLE	KACHIN	KALMYK	KAPAUKU
KAREN	KARIERA	KASKA	KATAB	KAZAK	KERAKI	KERALA	KHASI	KHEVSUR	KIKUYU
KIOW-APACHE	KISSI	KOHISTANI	KOL	KONSO	KOREANS	KPE	KUBA	KUMYK	KUNG
KURTATCHI	KUTENAI	KWAKIUTL	LAKALAI	LAKHER	LAMBA	LAMET	LANGO	LAU	LEPCHA
LESU	LHOTA NAGA	LIFU	LOLO	LOZI	LUBA	LUO	MACASSARESE	MAGUZAWA	MALAYS
MAM	MAMBILA	MAMVU	MANCHU	MANDAN	MANGAIANS	MANIHIKI	MANUS	MAORI	MARGI
MARICOPA	MARQUESANS	MARSHALLESE	MASAI	MATACO	MATAKAM	MAYA	MAZATECO	MBUGWE	MBUNDU
MBUTI	MENDE	MENTAWEI	MERINA	MIAMI	MIAO	MIN CHINESE	MINANGKABAU	MINCHIA	MISKITO
MIWOK	MNONG GAR	MONGO	MONGUOR	MOSSI	MOTA	MOTILON	MUNDURUCU	MURINBATA	MURNGIN
MZAB	NAMA	NAMBICUARA	NANDI	NASKAPI	NATCHEZ	NAVAHO	NDEMBU	NGONI	NICOBARESE
NOMLAKI	NUER	NUPE	NURI	NYAKYUSA	NYANEKA	NYARO	NYORO	OJIBWA	OKINAWANS
OMAHA	ONA	ONTONG-JAVA	ORAON	PAEZ	PAIWAN	PALAUANS	PALIKUR	PAPAGO	PARAUJANO
PATHAN	PAWNEE	PENDE	PENOBSCOT	PONAPEANS	POPOLUCA	PORTUGUESE	PUKAPUKA	PURARI	PURUM
RAROIANS	REGEIBAT	RIFFIANS	ROMANS	ROTINESE	ROTUMANS	RUNDI	RWALA	SAGADA	SAMOANS
SANDAWE	SANPOIL	SANTAL	SARAMACCA	SARSI	SELUNG	SEMANG	SEMINOLE	SENIANG	SERBS
SERI	SHERENTE	SHILLUK	SHLUH	SIMBOESE	SINDHI	SINHALESE	SIRIONO	SIUAI	SIWANS
SOMALI	SONGHAI	SOTHO	SUBANUN	SWAZI	SYRIANS	TAGBANUA	TALAMANCA	TALLENSI	TAMIL
TANALA	TANIMBARESE	TAOS	TAPIRAPE	TARAHUMARA	TEDA	TEHUELCHE	TENDA	TENETEHARA	TENINO
TERA	TERENA	TESO	TETON	THAI	THONGA	TIBETANS	TIGRINYA	TIKOPIA	TIMBIRA
TIMUCUA	TIV	TIWI	TODA	TOKELAU	TOLOWA	TORAJA	TOTONAC	TRISTAN	TROBRIAND
TRUKESE	TRUMAI	TSHIMSHIAN	TUBATULABAL	TUCANO	TUCUNA	TUNEBO	TUPINAMBA	TURKANA	TURKMEN
TWANA	TZELTAL	ULAWANS	UTE	VEDDA	VENDA	VIETNAMESE	WAICA	WALLOONS	WANTOAT

11/

WAPISHANA WAROPEN WARRAU WASHO WICHITA WIKMUNKAN WINNEBAGO WITOTO WOGEO WOLEAIANS
WOLOF WUTE YABARANA YAGUA YAHGAN YAKO YAO YAPESE YARURO YOKUTS
YOMBE YORUBA YUKI YUROK ZUNI

---

12 CULTURES
WHERE THE LATITUDE IS
FIFTY DEGREES OR GREATER (33)

12 CULTURES
WHERE THE LATITUDE IS
LESS THAN FIFTY DEGREES (367)

BACKGROUND ON PAGE 66

PREDICATE ONLY

33 IN LEFT COLUMN

367 IN RIGHT COLUMN

ABIPON	ABOR	AINU	AJIE	AKHA	ALBANIANS	ALORESE	AMBA	AMERICANS	ANDAMANESE
APINAYE	ARANDA	ARAPESH	ARAUCANIANS	ARYANS	ASHANTI	ATAYAL	ATSUGEWI	AWEIKOMA	AYMARA
AZANDE	AZTEC	BABWA	BACAIRI	BAJUN	BALINESE	BAMBARA	BAMILEKE	BANDA	BARABRA
BARI	BASQUES	BASSERI	BATAK	BAYA	BEJA	BELU	BEMBA	BENGALI	BERGDAMA
BETE	BHIL	BHUIYA	BIRIFOR	BLACK CARIB	BOERS	BORORO	BOTOCUDO	BOZO	BRAZILIANS
BUDUMA	BULGARIANS	BUNLAP	BURMESE	BURUSHO	CADUVEO	CAGABA	CALLINAGO	CAMAYURA	CAMBA
CAMBODIANS	CARAJA	CARIB	CARINYA	CAYAPA	CHAGGA	CHAMACOCO	CHENCHU	CHEREMIS	CHERKESS
CHEROKEE	CHEYENNE	CHIBCHA	CHINANTEC	CHIR-APACHE	CHIRIGUANO	CHOCO	CHOROTI	CHORTI	COCHITI
COMANCHE	COORG	CREEK	CROW	CUNA	DAGUR	DARD	DELAWARE	DIEGUENO	DIERI
DILLING	DOBUANS	DOGON	DOROBO	DUSUN	EGYPTIANS	ELLICE	ENGA	FANG	FON
FOX	FUTAJALONKE	GANDA	GARO	GILBERTESE	GISU	GOAJIRO	GOND	GROS VENTRE	GUAHIBO
GUATO	GURE	HANO	HANUNOO	HASANIA	HASINAI	HAVASUPAI	HAWAIIANS	HAZARA	HEBREWS
HEHE	HERERO	HO	HUICHOL	HUKUNDIKA	HURON	HUTSUL	IBAN	IFUGAO	ILA
INCA	INGASSANA	IRAQW	JAPANESE	JAVANESE	JEMEZ	JIVARO	JUKUN	KABYLE	KACHIN
KALMYK	KAPAUKU	KAREN	KARIERA	KATAB	KAZAK	KERAKI	KERALA	KHASI	KHEVSUR
KIKUYU	KIOW-APACHE	KISSI	KOHISTANI	KOL	KONSO	KOREANS	KPE	KUBA	KUMYK
KUNG	KURTATCHI	LAKALAI	LAKHER	LAMBA	LAMET	LANGO	LAU	LEPCHA	LESU
LHOTA NAGA	LIFU	LOLO	LOZI	LUBA	LUO	MACASSARESE	MAGUZAWA	MALAYS	MAM
MAMBILA	MAMVU	MANCHU	MANDAN	MANGAIANS	MANIHIKI	MANUS	MAORI	MARGI	MARICOPA
MARQUESANS	MARSHALLESE	MASAI	MATACO	MATAKAM	MAYA	MAZATECO	MBUGWE	MBUNDU	MBUTI
MENDE	MENTAWEI	MERINA	MIAMI	MIAO	MIN CHINESE	MINANGKABAU	MINCHIA	MISKITO	MIWOK
MNONG GAR	MONGO	MONGUOR	MOSSI	MOTA	MOTILON	MUNDURUCU	MURINBATA	MURNGIN	MZAB
NAMA	NAMBICUARA	NANDI	NATCHEZ	NAVAHO	NDEMBU	NGONI	NICOBARESE	NOMLAKI	NUER
NUPE	NURI	NYAKYUSA	NYANEKA	NYARO	NYORO	OKINAWANS	OMAHA	ONTONG-JAVA	ORAON
PAEZ	PAIWAN	PALAUANS	PALIKUR	PAPAGO	PARAUJANO	PATHAN	PAWNEE	PENDE	PENOBSCOT
PONAPEANS	POPOLUCA	PORTUGUESE	PUKAPUKA	PURARI	PURUM	RAROIANS	REGEIBAT	RIFFIANS	ROMANS
ROTINESE	ROTUMANS	RUNDI	RWALA	SAGADA	SAMOANS	SANDAWE	SANPOIL	SANTAL	SARAMACCA
SELUNG	SEMANG	SEMINOLE	SENIANG	SERBS	SERI	SHERENTE	SHILLUK	SHLUH	SIMBOESE
SINDHI	SINHALESE	SIRIONO	SIUAI	SIWANS	SOMALI	SONGHAI	SOTHO	SUBANUN	SWAZI
SYRIANS	TAGBANUA	TALAMANCA	TALLENSI	TAMIL	TANALA	TANIMBARESE	TAOS	TAPIRAPE	TARAHUMARA
TEDA	TEHUELCHE	TENDA	TENETEHARA	TENINO	TERA	TERENA	TESO	TETON	THAI
THONGA	TIBETANS	TIGRINYA	TIKOPIA	TIMBIRA	TIMUCUA	TIV	TIWI	TODA	TOKELAU
TOLOWA	TORAJA	TOTONAC	TRISTAN	TROBRIAND	TRUKESE	TRUMAI	TUBATULABAL	TUCANO	TUCUNA
TUNEBO	TUPINAMBA	TURKANA	TURKMEN	TWANA	TZELTAL	ULAWANS	UTE	VEDDA	VENDA
VIETNAMESE	WAICA	WANTOAT	WAPISHANA	WAROPEN	WARRAU	WASHO	WICHITA	WIKMUNKAN	WINNEBAGO
WITOTO	WOGEO	WOLEAIANS	WOLOF	WUTE	YABARANA	YAGUA	YAKO	YAO	YAPESE

12/

YARURO	YOKUTS	YOMBE	YORUBA	YUKI	YUROK	ZUNI

13 CULTURES
WHERE THE LATITUDE IS
FORTY DEGREES OR GREATER (71)

13 CULTURES
WHERE THE LATITUDE IS
LESS THAN FORTY DEGREES (329)

BACKGROUND ON PAGE 66 | PREDICATE ONLY

71 IN LEFT COLUMN

329 IN RIGHT COLUMN

ABIPON	ABOR	AJIE	AKHA	ALORESE	AMBA	ANDAMANESE	APINAYE	ARANDA	ARAPESH
ARAUCANIANS	ARYANS	ASHANTI	ATAYAL	AWEIKOMA	AYMARA	AZANDE	AZTEC	BABWA	BACAIRI
BAJUN	BALINESE	BAMBARA	BAMILEKE	BANDA	BARABRA	BARI	BASSERI	BATAK	BAYA
BEJA	BELU	BEMBA	BENGALI	BERGDAMA	BETE	BHIL	BHUIYA	BIRIFOR	BLACK CARIB
BOERS	BORORO	BOTOCUDO	BOZO	BRAZILIANS	BUDUMA	BUNLAP	BURMESE	BURUSHO	CADUVEO
CAGABA	CALLINAGO	CAMAYURA	CAMBA	CAMBODIANS	CARAJA	CARIB	CARINYA	CAYAPA	CHAGGA
CHAMACOCO	CHENCHU	CHEROKEE	CHEYENNE	CHIBCHA	CHINANTEC	CHIR-APACHE	CHIRIGUANO	CHOCO	CHOROTI
CHORTI	COCHITI	COMANCHE	COORG	CREEK	CUNA	DARD	DIEGUENO	DIERI	DILLING
DOBUANS	DOGON	DOROBO	DUSUN	EGYPTIANS	ELLICE	ENGA	FANG	FON	FUTAJALONKE
GANDA	GARO	GILBERTESE	GISU	GOAJIRO	GOND	GUAHIBO	GUATO	GURE	HANO
HANUNOO	HASANIA	HASINAI	HAVASUPAI	HAWAIIANS	HAZARA	HEBREWS	HEHE	HERERO	HO
HUICHOL	IBAN	IFUGAO	ILA	INCA	INGASSANA	IRAQW	JAPANESE	JAVANESE	JEMEZ
JIVARO	JUKUN	KABYLE	KACHIN	KAPAUKU	KAREN	KARIERA	KATAB	KERAKI	KERALA
KHASI	KIKUYU	KIOW-APACHE	KISSI	KOHISTANI	KOL	KONSO	KOREANS	KPE	KUBA
KUNG	KURTATCHI	LAKALAI	LAKHER	LAMBA	LAMET	LANGO	LAU	LEPCHA	LESU
LHOTA NAGA	LIFU	LOLO	LOZI	LUBA	LUO	MACASSARESE	MAGUZAWA	MALAYS	MAM
MAMBILA	MAMVU	MANGAIANS	MANIHIKI	MANUS	MAORI	MARGI	MARICOPA	MARQUESANS	MARSHALLESE
MASAI	MATACO	MATAKAM	MAYA	MAZATECO	MBUGWE	MBUNDU	MBUTI	MENDE	MENTAWEI
MERINA	MIAO	MIN CHINESE	MINANGKABAU	MINCHIA	MISKITO	MIWOK	MNONG GAR	MONGO	MONGUOR
MOSSI	MOTA	MOTILON	MUNDURUCU	MURINBATA	MURNGIN	MZAB	NAMA	NAMBICUARA	NANDI
NATCHEZ	NAVAHO	NDEMBU	NGONI	NICOBARESE	NOMLAKI	NUER	NUPE	NURI	NYAKYUSA
NYANEKA	NYARO	NYCRO	OKINAWANS	ONTONG-JAVA	ORAON	PAEZ	PAIWAN	PALAUANS	PALIKUR
PAPAGO	PARAUJANO	PATHAN	PENDE	PONAPEANS	POPOLUCA	PUKAPUKA	PURARI	PURUM	RAROIANS
REGEIBAT	RIFFIANS	ROTINESE	ROTUMANS	RUNDI	RWALA	SAGADA	SAMOANS	SANDAWE	SANTAL
SARAMACCA	SELUNG	SEMANG	SEMINOLE	SENIANG	SERI	SHERENTE	SHILLUK	SHLUH	SIMBOESE
SINDHI	SINHALESE	SIRIONO	SIUAI	SIWANS	SOMALI	SONGHAI	SOTHO	SUBANUN	SWAZI
SYRIANS	TAGBANUA	TALAMANCA	TALLENSI	TAMIL	TANALA	TANIMBARESE	TAOS	TAPIRAPE	TARAHUMARA
TEDA	TENDA	TENETEHARA	TERA	TERENA	TESO	THAI	THONGA	TIBETANS	TIGRINYA
TIKOPIA	TIMBIRA	TIMUCUA	TIV	TIWI	TODA	TOKELAU	TORAJA	TOTONAC	TRISTAN
TROBRIAND	TRUKESE	TRUMAI	TUBATULABAL	TUCANO	TUCUNA	TUNEBO	TUPINAMBA	TURKANA	TURKMEN
TZELTAL	ULAWANS	UTE	VEDDA	VENDA	VIETNAMESE	WAICA	WANTOAT	WAPISHANA	WAROPEN
WARRAU	WASHO	WICHITA	WIKMUNKAN	WITOTO	WOGEO	WOLEAIANS	WOLOF	WUTE	YABARANA
YAGUA	YAKO	YAO	YAPESE	YARURO	YOKUTS	YOMBE	YORUBA	ZUNI	

****

14 CULTURES
WHERE THE LATITUDE IS
THIRTY DEGREES OR GREATER (119)

14 CULTURES
WHERE THE LATITUDE IS
LESS THAN THIRTY DEGREES (281)

BACKGROUND ON PAGE 66

PREDICATE ONLY

....

119 IN LEFT COLUMN

281 IN RIGHT COLUMN

ABIPON	ABOR	AJIE	AKHA	ALORESE	AMBA	ANDAMANESE	APINAYE	ARANDA	ARAPESH
ASHANTI	ATAYAL	AWEIKOMA	AYMARA	AZANDE	AZTEC	BABWA	BACAIRI	BAJUN	BALINESE
BAMBARA	BAMILEKE	BANDA	BARABRA	BARI	BATAK	BAYA	BEJA	BFLU	BEMBA
BENGALI	BERGDAMA	BETE	BHIL	BHUIYA	BIRIFOR	BLACK CARIB	BOERS	BORORO	BOTOCUDO
BOZO	BRAZILIANS	BUDUMA	BUNLAP	BURMESE	CADUVEO	CAGABA	CALLINAGO	CAMAYURA	CAMBA
CAMBODIANS	CARAJA	CARIB	CARINYA	CAYAPA	CHAGGA	CHAMACOCO	CHENCHU	CHIBCHA	CHINANTEC
CHIRIGUANO	CHOCO	CHOROTI	CHORTI	COORG	CUNA	DIERI	DILLING	DOBUANS	DOGON
DOROBO	DUSUN	EGYPTIANS	ELLICE	ENGA	FANG	FON	FUTAJALONKE	GANDA	GARO
GILBERTESE	GISU	GOAJIRC	GOND	GUAHIBO	GUATO	GURE	HANUNOO	HASANIA	HAWAIIANS
HEHE	HERERO	HO	HUICHOL	IBAN	IFUGAO	ILA	INCA	INGASSANA	IRAQW
JAVANESE	JIVARO	JUKUN	KACHIN	KAPAUKU	KAREN	KARIERA	KATAB	KERAKI	KERALA
KHASI	KIKUYU	KISSI	KOL	KONSO	KPE	KUBA	KUNG	KURTATCHI	LAKALAI
LAKHER	LAMBA	LAMET	LANGO	LAU	LEPCHA	LESU	LHOTA NAGA	LIFU	LOLO
LOZI	LUBA	LUO	MACASSARESE	MAGUZAWA	MALAYS	MAM	MAMBILA	MAMVU	MANGAIANS
MANIHIKI	MANUS	MARGI	MARQUESANS	MARSHALLESE	MASAI	MATACO	MATAKAM	MAYA	MAZATECO
MBUGWE	MBUNDU	MBUTI	MENDE	MENTAWEI	MERINA	MIAO	MIN CHINESE	MINANGKABAU	MINCHIA
MISKITO	MNONG GAR	MONGO	MOSSI	MOTA	MOTILON	MUNDURUCU	MURINBATA	MURNGIN	NAMA
NAMBICUARA	NANDI	NDEMBU	NGONI	NICOBARESE	NUER	NUPE	NYAKYUSA	NYANEKA	NYARO
NYORO	OKINAWANS	ONTONG-JAVA	ORAON	PAEZ	PAIWAN	PALAUANS	PALIKUR	PARAUJANO	PENDE
PONAPEANS	POPOLUCA	PUKAPUKA	PURARI	PURUM	RAROIANS	REGEIBAT	ROTINESE	ROTUMANS	RUNDI
SAGADA	SAMOANS	SANDAWE	SANTAL	SARAMACCA	SELUNG	SEMANG	SEMINOLE	SENIANG	SERI
SHERENTE	SHILLUK	SIMBOESE	SINDHI	SINHALESE	SIRIONO	SIUAI	SIWANS	SOMALI	SONGHAI
SOTHO	SUBANUN	SWAZI	TAGBANUA	TALAMANCA	TALLENSI	TAMIL	TANALA	TANIMBARESE	TAPIRAPE
TARAHUMARA	TEDA	TENDA	TENETEHARA	TERA	TERENA	TESO	THAI	THONGA	TIGRINYA
TIKOPIA	TIMBIRA	TIMUCUA	TIV	TIWI	TODA	TOKELAU	TORAJA	TOTONAC	TROBRIAND
TRUKESE	TRUMAI	TUCANO	TUCUNA	TUNEBO	TUPINAMBA	TURKANA	TZELTAL	ULAWANS	VEDDA
VENDA	VIETNAMESE	WAICA	WANTOAT	WAPISHANA	WAROPEN	WARRAU	WIKMUNKAN	WITOTO	WOGEO
WOLEAIANS	WOLOF	WUTE	YABARANA	YAGUA	YAKO	YAO	YAPESE	YARURO	YOMBE
YORUBA									

15	CULTURES WHERE THE LATITUDE IS TWENTY DEGREES CR GREATER (183)	15	CULTURES WHERE THE LATITUDE IS LESS THAN TWENTY DEGREES (217)

BACKGROUND ON PAGE 66 PREDICATE ONLY

183 IN LEFT COLUMN

217 IN RIGHT CCLUMN

ALORESE	AMBA	ANDAMANESE	APINAYE	ARAPESH	ASHANTI	AYMARA	AZANDE	AZTEC	BABWA
BACAIRI	BAJUN	BALINESE	BAMBARA	BAMILEKE	BANDA	BARI	BATAK	BAYA	BELU
BEMBA	BETE	BIRIFOR	BLACK CARIB	BOERS	BORORO	BOTOCUDO	BOZO	BUDUMA	BUNLAP
CAGABA	CALLINAGC	CAMAYURA	CAMBA	CAMBODIANS	CARAJA	CARIB	CARINYA	CAYAPA	CHAGGA
CHENCHU	CHIBCHA	CHINANTEC	CHOCO	CHORTI	COORG	CUNA	DILLING	DOBUANS	DOGON
DOROBO	DUSUN	ELLICE	ENGA	FANG	FON	FUTAJALONKE	GANDA	GILBERTESE	GISU
GOAJIRO	GUAHIBO	GUATO	GURE	HANUNOO	HASANIA	HEHE	IBAN	IFUGAO	ILA
INCA	INGASSANA	IRAQW	JAVANESE	JIVARO	JUKUN	KAPAUKU	KAREN	KATAB	KERAKI
KERALA	KIKUYU	KISSI	KONSO	KPE	KUBA	KURTATCHI	LAKALAI	LAMBA	LANGO
LAU	LESU	LOZI	LUBA	LUO	MACASSARESE	MAGUZAWA	MALAYS	MAM	MAMBILA
MAMVU	MANIHIKI	MANUS	MARGI	MARQUESANS	MARSHALLESE	MASAI	MATAKAM	MAYA	MAZATECO
MBUGWE	MBUNDU	MBUTI	MENDE	MENTAWEI	MERINA	MINANGKABAU	MISKITO	MNONG GAR	MONGO
MOSSI	MOTA	MOTILON	MUNDURUCU	MURINBATA	MURNGIN	NAMBICUARA	NANDI	NDEMBU	NGONI
NICOBARESE	NUER	NUPE	NYAKYUSA	NYANEKA	NYARO	NYORO	ONTONG-JAVA	PAEZ	PALAUANS
PALIKUR	PARAUJANO	PENDE	PONAPEANS	POPOLUCA	PUKAPUKA	PURARI	RAROIANS	ROTINESE	ROTUMANS
RUNDI	SAGADA	SAMOANS	SANDAWE	SARAMACCA	SELUNG	SEMANG	SENIANG	SHERENTE	SHILLUK
SIMBOESE	SINHALESE	SIRIONO	SIUAI	SOMALI	SONGHAI	SUBANUN	TAGBANUA	TALAMANCA	TALLENSI
TAMIL	TANIMBARESE	TAPIRAPE	TENDA	TENETEHARA	TERA	TESO	THAI	TIGRINYA	TIKOPIA
TIMBIRA	TIV	TIWI	TODA	TOKELAU	TORAJA	TROBRIAND	TRUKESE	TRUMAI	TUCANO
TUCUNA	TUNEBO	TUPINAMBA	TURKANA	TZELTAL	ULAWANS	VEDDA	VIETNAMESE	WAICA	WANTOAT
WAPISHANA	WAROPEN	WARRAU	WIKMUNKAN	WITOTO	WOGEO	WOLEAIANS	WOLOF	WUTE	YABARANA
YAGUA	YAKO	YAO	YAPESE	YARURO	YOMBE	YORUBA			

16 CULTURES WHERE THE LATITUDE IS TEN DEGREES OR GREATER (277)	16 CULTURES WHERE THE LATITUDE IS LESS THAN TEN DEGREES (123)

BACKGROUND ON PAGE 66

PREDICATE ONLY

277 IN LEFT COLUMN

123 IN RIGHT COLUMN

ALORESE	AMBA	APINAYE	ARAPESH	ASHANTI	AZANDE	BABWA	BAJUN	BALINESE	BAMILEKE
BANDA	BARI	BATAK	BAYA	BELU	BETE	CARIB	CARINYA	CAYAPA	CHAGGA
CHIBCHA	CHOCO	CUNA	DOROBO	DUSUN	ELLICE	ENGA	FANG	FON	GANDA
GILBERTESE	GISU	GUAHIBO	HEHE	IBAN	IRAQW	JAVANESE	JIVARO	JUKUN	KAPAUKU
KERAKI	KIKUYU	KISSI	KONSO	KPE	KUBA	KURTATCHI	LAKALAI	LANGO	LESU
LUBA	LUO	MACASSARESE	MALAYS	MAMBILA	MAMVU	MANUS	MARQUESANS	MARSHALLESE	MASAI
MBUGWE	MBUTI	MENDE	MENTAWEI	MINANGKABAU	MONGO	MOTILON	MUNDURUCU	NANDI	NICOBARESE
NUER	NUPE	NYAKYUSA	NYORO	ONTONG-JAVA	PAEZ	PALAUANS	PALIKUR	PENDE	PONAPEANS
PURARI	RUNDI	SANDAWE	SARAMACCA	SEMANG	SHERENTE	SIMBOESE	SINHALESE	SIUAI	SOMALI
SUBANUN	TALAMANCA	TANIMBARESE	TENETEHARA	TESO	TIMBIRA	TIV	TOKELAU	TORAJA	TROBRIAND
TRUKESE	TUCANO	TUCUNA	TUNEBO	TUPINAMBA	TURKANA	VEDDA	WAICA	WANTOAT	WAPISHANA
WAROPEN	WARRAU	WITOTO	WOGEO	WOLEAIANS	WUTE	YABARANA	YAGUA	YAKO	YAPESE
YARURO	YOMBE	YORUBA							

17 CULTURES WHOSE LINGUISTIC AFFILIATION IS NIGER-CONGO (61)	17 CULTURES WHOSE LINGUISTIC AFFILIATION IS OTHER THAN NIGER-CONGO (339)

BACKGROUND ON PAGE 67

SUBJECT ONLY

61 IN LEFT COLUMN

AMBA	ASHANTI	AZANDE	BABWA	BAJUN	BAMBARA	BAMILEKE	BANDA	BAYA	BEMBA
BETE	BIRIFOR	BOZO	CHAGGA	DOGON	FANG	FON	FUTAJALONKE	GANDA	GISU
GURE	HEHE	HERERO	ILA	JUKUN	KATAB	KIKUYU	KISSI	KPE	KUBA
LAMBA	LOZI	LUBA	MAMBILA	MBUGWE	MBUNDU	MBUTI	MENDE	MONGO	MOSSI
NDEMBU	NGONI	NUPE	NYAKYUSA	NYANEKA	NYORO	PENDE	RUNDI	SOTHO	SWAZI
TALLENSI	TENDA	THONGA	TIV	VENDA	WOLOF	WUTE	YAKO	YAO	YOMBE
YORUBA									

339 IN RIGHT COLUMN

3	TEND TO BE THOSE LOCATED IN AFRICA (80)	0.98 OF 61	3	TEND TO BE THOSE LOCATED OUTSIDE OF AFRICA (320)	0.94 OF 339	60 20 1 319 XSQ= 270.48 PHI= 0.822 XP = 0.
4	TILT MORE TOWARD BEING THOSE LOCATED OUTSIDE OF THE CIRCUM-MEDITERRANEAN (355)	0.98 OF 61	4	TILT LESS TOWARD BEING THOSE LOCATED OUTSIDE OF THE CIRCUM-MEDITERRANEAN (355)	0.87 OF 339	1 44 60 295 XSQ= 5.57 PHI= -0.118 XP = 0.0183
5	IN ALL CASES ARE THOSE LOCATED OUTSIDE OF EAST EURASIA (330)	1.00 OF 61	5	TEND LESS TO BE THOSE LOCATED OUTSIDE OF EAST EURASIA (330)	0.79 OF 339	0 70 61 269 XSQ= 13.87 PHI= -0.186 XP = 0.0002
6	IN ALL CASES ARE THOSE LOCATED OUTSIDE OF THE INSULAR PACIFIC (330)	1.00 OF 61	6	TEND LESS TO BE THOSE LOCATED OUTSIDE OF THE INSULAR PACIFIC (330)	0.79 OF 339	0 70 61 269 XSQ= 13.87 PHI= -0.186 XP = 0.0002
8	IN ALL CASES ARE THOSE LOCATED OUTSIDE OF NORTH AMERICA (330)	1.00 OF 61	8	TEND LESS TO BE THOSE LOCATED OUTSIDE OF NORTH AMERICA (330)	0.79 OF 339	0 70 61 269 XSQ= 13.87 PHI= -0.186 XP = 0.0002

9	IN ALL CASES ARE THOSE LOCATED OUTSIDE OF SOUTH AMERICA (335)	1.00 OF 61	9	TEND LESS TO BE THOSE LOCATED OUTSIDE OF SOUTH AMERICA (335)	0.81 OF 339	0 65 61 274 XSQ= 12.59 PHI= -0.177 XP = 0.0004
14	IN ALL CASES ARE THOSE WHERE THE LATITUDE IS LESS THAN THIRTY DEGREES (281)	1.00 OF 61	14	TEND LESS TO BE THOSE WHERE THE LATITUDE IS LESS THAN THIRTY DEGREES (281)	0.65 OF 339	0 119 61 220 XSQ= 28.82 PHI= -0.268 XP = 0.0000
15	TEND TO BE THOSE WHERE THE LATITUDE IS LESS THAN TWENTY DEGREES (217)	0.92 OF 61	15	TEND TO BE THOSE WHERE THE LATITUDE IS TWENTY DEGREES OR GREATER (183)	0.53 OF 339	5 178 56 161 XSQ= 39.13 PHI= -0.313 XP = 0.
16	TEND TO BE THOSE WHERE THE LATITUDE IS LESS THAN TEN DEGREES (123)	0.59 OF 61	16	TEND TO BE THOSE WHERE THE LATITUDE IS TEN DEGREES OR GREATER (277)	0.74 OF 339	25 252 36 87 XSQ= 25.46 PHI= -0.252 XP = 0.0000
33	TILT MORE TOWARD BEING THOSE WHERE THE NATURAL ENVIRONMENT IS OTHER THAN 'VERY HARSH,' I.E., DESERT, DESERT GRASSES AND SHRUBS, TUNDRA, OR HIGH PLATEAU STEPPE (341) FWM	0.97 OF 61	33	TILT LESS TOWARD BEING THOSE WHERE THE NATURAL ENVIRONMENT IS OTHER THAN 'VERY HARSH,' I.E., DESERT, DESERT GRASSES AND SHRUBS, TUNDRA, OR HIGH PLATEAU STEPPE (341) FWM	0.83 OF 339	2 57 59 282 XSQ= 6.49 PHI= -0.127 XP = 0.0108
36	DRIFT MORE TOWARD BEING THOSE WHERE THE NATURAL ENVIRONMENT IS OTHER THAN 'VERY HARSH,' OR SUB-TROPICAL BUSH, OR TEMPERATE GRASSLAND (292) FWM	0.84 OF 61	36	DRIFT LESS TOWARD BEING THOSE WHERE THE NATURAL ENVIRONMENT IS OTHER THAN 'VERY HARSH,' OR SUB-TROPICAL BUSH, OR TEMPERATE GRASSLAND (292) FWM	0.71 OF 339	10 98 51 241 XSQ= 3.50 PHI= -0.094 XP = 0.0615
42	DRIFT MORE TOWARD BEING THOSE WHERE THE NATURAL ENVIRONMENT IS OTHER THAN TROPICAL OR SUB-TROPICAL RAIN FOREST, OR MONSOON FOREST (244) FWM	0.72 OF 61	42	DRIFT LESS TOWARD BEING THOSE WHERE THE NATURAL ENVIRONMENT IS OTHER THAN TROPICAL OR SUB-TROPICAL RAIN FOREST, OR MONSOON FOREST (244) FWM	0.59 OF 339	17 139 44 200 XSQ= 3.22 PHI= -0.090 XP = 0.0729
44	TILT MORE TOWARD BEING THOSE WHERE SETTLEMENTS ARE FIXED (222)	0.83 OF 52	44	TILT LESS TOWARD BEING THOSE WHERE SETTLEMENTS ARE FIXED (222)	0.64 OF 280	43 179 9 101 XSQ= 6.15 PHI= 0.136 XP = 0.0132
45	TILT LESS TOWARD BEING THOSE WHERE SETTLEMENTS, IF FIXED, ARE COMPACT, RATHER THAN NON-COMPACT (149)	0.51 OF 43	45	TILT MORE TOWARD BEING THOSE WHERE SETTLEMENTS, IF FIXED, ARE COMPACT, RATHER THAN NON-COMPACT (149)	0.71 OF 179	22 127 21 52 XSQ= 5.29 PHI= -0.154 XP = 0.0215

```
46  LEAN MORE TOWARD BEING THOSE   0.96 OF  52     46  LEAN LESS TOWARD BEING THOSE   0.75 OF 280          2   70
    OTHER THAN WHERE SETTLEMENTS ARE                   OTHER THAN WHERE SETTLEMENTS ARE                    50  210
    NON-FIXED AND MOVEMENT IS                          NON-FIXED AND MOVEMENT IS                   XSQ=   10.34
    NOMADIC  (260)                                     NOMADIC  (260)                              PHI=  -0.177
                                                                                                   XP =   0.0013

47  TILT TOWARD BEING THOSE        0.78 OF   9     47  TILT TOWARD BEING THOSE        0.69 OF 101          2   70
    WHERE, IF SETTLEMENTS ARE NON-FIXED,               WHERE, IF SETTLEMENTS ARE NON-FIXED,                 7   31
    MOVEMENT IS NON-NOMADIC, RATHER THAN               MOVEMENT IS NOMADIC, RATHER THAN            XSQ=    6.15
    NOMADIC  (38)                                      NON-NOMADIC  (72)                           PHI=  -0.237
                                                                                                   XP =   0.0131

51  TEND MORE TO BE THOSE          0.92 OF  61     51  TEND LESS TO BE THOSE          0.58 OF 339         56  197
    WHERE SUBSISTENCE IS PRIMARILY BY                  WHERE SUBSISTENCE IS PRIMARILY BY                    5  142
    FOOD PRODUCTION -- I. E., AGRICULTURE              FOOD PRODUCTION -- I. E., AGRICULTURE       XSQ=   23.82
    OR HUSBANDRY -- RATHER THAN BY                     OR HUSBANDRY -- RATHER THAN BY              PHI=   0.244
    GATHERING  (253)                                   GATHERING  (253)                            XP =   0.0000

54  LEAN MORE TOWARD BEING THOSE   0.96 OF  50     54  LEAN LESS TOWARD BEING THOSE   0.77 OF 188         48  144
    WHERE FOOD PRODUCTION IS BY                        WHERE FOOD PRODUCTION IS BY                          2   44
    INTENSIVE OR SIMPLE                                INTENSIVE OR SIMPLE                         XSQ=    8.33
    AGRICULTURE, RATHER THAN BY                        AGRICULTURE, RATHER THAN BY                 PHI=   0.187
    INCIPIENT FOOD PRODUCTION  (192)                   INCIPIENT FOOD PRODUCTION  (192)            XP =   0.0039

55  LEAN TOWARD BEING THOSE        0.71 OF  48     55  LEAN TOWARD BEING THOSE        0.53 OF 144         14   77
    WHERE FOOD PRODUCTION IS BY                        WHERE FOOD PRODUCTION IS BY                         34   67
    SIMPLE AGRICULTURE, RATHER THAN BY                 INTENSIVE AGRICULTURE, RATHER THAN BY       XSQ=    7.58
    INTENSIVE AGRICULTURE  (101)                       SIMPLE AGRICULTURE  (91)                    PHI=  -0.199
                                                                                                   XP =   0.0059

56  TEND MORE TO BE THOSE          0.94 OF  36     56  TEND LESS TO BE THOSE          0.60 OF 111         34   67
    WHERE FOOD PRODUCTION IS BY                        WHERE FOOD PRODUCTION IS BY                          2   44
    SIMPLE AGRICULTURE, RATHER THAN BY                 SIMPLE AGRICULTURE, RATHER THAN BY          XSQ=   13.15
    INCIPIENT FOOD PRODUCTION  (101)                   INCIPIENT FOOD PRODUCTION  (101)            PHI=   0.299
                                                                                                   XP =   0.0003

62  LEAN MORE TOWARD BEING THOSE   0.75 OF  61     62  LEAN LESS TOWARD BEING THOSE   0.54 OF 339         46  182
    WHERE HUSBANDRY OF SOME KIND                       WHERE HUSBANDRY OF SOME KIND                        15  157
    IS PRESENT  (228)                                  IS PRESENT  (228)                           XSQ=    9.09
                                                                                                   PHI=   0.151
                                                                                                   XP =   0.0026

71  TEND TO BE THOSE               0.87 OF  38     71  TEND TO BE THOSE               0.69 OF 213         33   65
    WHERE METAL WORKING IS                             WHERE METAL WORKING IS                               5  148
    PRESENT  (98)                                      ABSENT  (153)                               XSQ=   40.65
                                                                                                   PHI=   0.402
                                                                                                   XP =   0.

74  TEND MORE TO BE THOSE          0.89 OF  36     74  TEND LESS TO BE THOSE          0.56 OF 202         32  113
    WHERE POTTERY IS                                   WHERE POTTERY IS                                     4   89
    PRESENT  (145)                                     PRESENT  (145)                              XSQ=   12.58
                                                                                                   PHI=   0.230
                                                                                                   XP =   0.0004
```

171

81	TILT TOWARD BEING THOSE 0.56 OF 39 WHERE A CITY OR TOWN IS PRESENT, OR THE AVERAGE COMMUNITY SIZE IS 200 OR GREATER (89)	81	TILT TOWARD BEING THOSE 0.64 OF 185 WHERE NO CITY OR TOWN IS PRESENT, AND THE AVERAGE COMMUNITY SIZE IS SMALLER THAN 200 (135)	22 67 17 118 XSQ= 4.67 PHI= 0.144 XP = 0.0306
83	LEAN LESS TOWARD BEING THOSE 0.53 OF 32 WHERE, WITH NO CITY AND NO TOWN PRESENT, THE AVERAGE COMMUNITY SIZE IS SMALLER THAN 200, RATHER THAN BETWEEN 200 AND 999 (135)	83	LEAN MORE TOWARD BEING THOSE 0.80 OF 148 WHERE, WITH NO CITY AND NO TOWN PRESENT, THE AVERAGE COMMUNITY SIZE IS SMALLER THAN 200, RATHER THAN BETWEEN 200 AND 999 (135)	15 30 17 118 XSQ= 8.56 PHI= 0.218 XP = 0.0034
86	TILT TOWARD BEING THOSE 0.66 OF 47 WHERE THE LEVEL OF POLITICAL INTEGRATION IS THE LARGE STATE, THE LITTLE STATE, OR THE MINIMAL STATE (148) GPM	86	TILT TOWARD BEING THOSE 0.54 OF 257 WHERE THE LEVEL OF POLITICAL INTEGRATION IS THE AUTONOMOUS COMMUNITY, OR THE FAMILY (156) GPM	31 117 16 140 XSQ= 5.85 PHI= 0.139 XP = 0.0156
88	LEAN MORE TOWARD BEING THOSE 0.81 OF 48 WHERE, IF A HEADMANSHIP IS PRESENT, SUCCESSION IS HEREDITARY (165)	88	LEAN LESS TOWARD BEING THOSE 0.57 OF 223 WHERE, IF A HEADMANSHIP IS PRESENT, SUCCESSION IS HEREDITARY (165)	9 97 39 126 XSQ= 9.15 PHI= -0.184 XP = 0.0025
96	LEAN TOWARD BEING THOSE 0.71 OF 52 WHERE THE HIERARCHY OF NATIONAL JURISDICTION HAS FOUR, THREE, TWO OR ONE LEVEL (174) GES,EA	96	LEAN TOWARD BEING THOSE 0.51 OF 278 WHERE THE HIERARCHY OF NATIONAL JURISDICTION HAS NO LEVELS (156) GES,EA	37 137 15 141 XSQ= 7.55 PHI= 0.151 XP = 0.0060
97	TEND LESS TO BE THOSE 0.63 OF 52 WHERE THE HIERARCHY OF LOCAL JURISDICTION HAS THREE OR TWO LEVELS (273) GES,EA	97	TEND MORE TO BE THOSE 0.86 OF 279 WHERE THE HIERARCHY OF LOCAL JURISDICTION HAS THREE OR TWO LEVELS (273) GES,EA	19 39 33 240 XSQ= 13.91 PHI= 0.205 XP = 0.0002
98	TILT MORE TOWARD BEING THOSE 0.85 OF 52 WHERE THE HIERARCHY OF LOCAL JURISDICTION HAS FOUR OR THREE LEVELS (238) GES,EA	98	TILT LESS TOWARD BEING THOSE 0.70 OF 279 WHERE THE HIERARCHY OF LOCAL JURISDICTION HAS FOUR OR THREE LEVELS (238) GES,EA	44 194 8 85 XSQ= 4.22 PHI= 0.113 XP = 0.0400
99	TILT MORE TOWARD BEING THOSE 0.93 OF 15 WHERE, WITH NATIONAL HIERARCHY ABSENT, THE HIERARCHY OF LOCAL JURISDICTION HAS FOUR OR THREE LEVELS (93) GES,EA	99	TILT LESS TOWARD BEING THOSE 0.56 OF 141 WHERE, WITH NATIONAL HIERARCHY ABSENT, THE HIERARCHY OF LOCAL JURISDICTION HAS FOUR OR THREE LEVELS (93) GES,EA	14 79 1 62 XSQ= 6.36 PHI= 0.202 XP = 0.0116
100	LEAN MORE TOWARD BEING THOSE 0.98 OF 52 WHERE HIERARCHIES ARE MORE COMPLEX THAN THE 'SIMPLEST,' I. E., MORE COMPLEX THAN TWO LOCAL LEVELS WITH NO NATIONAL LEVELS (267) GES,EA	100	LEAN LESS TOWARD BEING THOSE 0.78 OF 278 WHERE HIERARCHIES ARE MORE COMPLEX THAN THE 'SIMPLEST,' I. E., MORE COMPLEX THAN TWO LOCAL LEVELS WITH NO NATIONAL LEVELS (267) GES,EA	51 216 1 62 XSQ= 10.50 PHI= 0.178 XP = 0.0012

102	TILT MORE TOWARD BEING THOSE WHERE CLASS STRATIFICATION IS PRESENT (203)	0.67 OF 60	102	TILT LESS TOWARD BEING THOSE WHERE CLASS STRATIFICATION IS PRESENT (203)	0.50 OF 323	40 163 20 160 XSQ= 4.70 PHI= 0.111 XP = 0.0301
106	TILT MORE TOWARD BEING THOSE WHERE CLASS STRATIFICATION, IF PRESENT, IS BASED ON SOMETHING OTHER THAN WEALTH (126)	0.77 OF 40	106	TILT LESS TOWARD BEING THOSE WHERE CLASS STRATIFICATION, IF PRESENT, IS BASED ON SOMETHING OTHER THAN WEALTH (126)	0.58 OF 163	9 68 31 95 XSQ= 4.26 PHI= -0.145 XP = 0.0391
108	TEND TO BE THOSE WHERE CLASS STRATIFICATION, IF PRESENT, IS BASED ON A HEREDITARY ARISTOCRACY (74)	0.65 OF 40	108	TEND TO BE THOSE WHERE CLASS STRATIFICATION, IF PRESENT, IS BASED ON SOMETHING OTHER THAN A HEREDITARY ARISTOCRACY (129)	0.71 OF 163	26 48 14 115 XSQ= 16.02 PHI= 0.281 XP = 0.0001
109	DRIFT LESS TOWARD BEING THOSE WHERE CASTES ARE ABSENT (317)	0.78 OF 60	109	DRIFT MORE TOWARD BEING THOSE WHERE CASTES ARE ABSENT (317)	0.88 OF 308	13 38 47 270 XSQ= 2.92 PHI= 0.089 XP = 0.0874
110	TEND TO BE THOSE WHERE SLAVERY IS PRESENT' (163)	0.82 OF 61	110	TEND TO BE THOSE WHERE SLAVERY IS ABSENT (218)	0.65 OF 320	50 113 11 207 XSQ= 43.67 PHI= 0.339 XP = 0.
128	LEAN TOWARD BEING THOSE WHERE, IF SUBSISTENCE IS PRIMARILY BY AGRICULTURE, THE WORK IS MAINLY DONE BY FEMALES (37)	0.71 OF 28	128	LEAN TOWARD BEING THOSE WHERE, IF SUBSISTENCE IS PRIMARILY BY AGRICULTURE, THE WORK IS MAINLY DONE BY MALES (40)	0.65 OF 49	8 32 20 17 XSQ= 8.22 PHI= -0.327 XP = 0.0041
129	IN ALL CASES ARE THOSE WHERE WEAVING IS MAINLY DONE BY MALES (31)	1.00 OF 13	129	TEND TO BE THOSE WHERE WEAVING IS MAINLY DONE BY FEMALES (73)	0.80 OF 91	13 18 0 73 XSQ= 31.26 PHI= 0.548 XP = 0.
130	LEAN TOWARD BEING THOSE WHERE LEATHER WORKING IS MAINLY DONE BY MALES (39)	0.92 OF 12	130	LEAN TOWARD BEING THOSE WHERE LEATHER WORKING IS MAINLY DONE BY FEMALES (45)	0.61 OF 72	11 28 1 44 XSQ= 9.49 PHI= 0.336 XP = 0.0021
137	TILT TOWARD BEING THOSE WHERE INVIDIOUS DISPLAY OF WEALTH IS STRONGLY EMPHASIZED (37) PES	0.75 OF 12	137	TILT TOWARD BEING THOSE WHERE INVIDIOUS DISPLAY OF WEALTH IS MODERATELY, LITTLE, OR NEGATIVELY EMPHASIZED (52) PES	0.64 OF 77	9 28 3 49 XSQ= 4.89 PHI= 0.234 XP = 0.0270

138	IN ALL CASES ARE THOSE WHERE SUPERORDINATE JUSTICE IS PRESENT (22) BBW	1.00 OF 6	138	TILT TOWARD BEING THOSE WHERE SUPERORDINATE JUSTICE IS ABSENT (18) BBW	0.53 OF 34	6 16 0 18 XSQ= 3.83 PHI= 0.310 EP = 0.0243
149	IN ALL CASES ARE THOSE WHERE THE INCIDENCE OF THEFT IS HIGH (18) B-B-C	1.00 OF 6	149	LEAN TOWARD BEING THOSE WHERE THE INCIDENCE OF THEFT IS LOW (19) B-B-C	0.61 OF 31	6 12 0 19 XSQ= 5.30 PHI= 0.379 EP = 0.0080
176	TEND TO BE THOSE WHERE THE COMMUNITY IS A CLAN-COMMUNITY OR A COMMUNITY STRUCTURED OR SEGMENTED ON A CLAN BASIS (169)	0.73 OF 60	176	TEND TO BE THOSE WHERE THE COMMUNITY IS OTHER THAN A CLAN-COMMUNITY OR A COMMUNITY STRUCTURED OR SEGMENTED ON A CLAN BASIS (213)	0.61 OF 322	44 125 16 197 XSQ= 23.04 PHI= 0.246 XP = 0.0000
177	TEND LESS TO BE THOSE WHERE THE COMMUNITY IS OTHER THAN A SINGLE CLAN-COMMUNITY AND EXOGAMOUS (305)	0.60 OF 60	177	TEND MORE TO BE THOSE WHERE THE COMMUNITY IS OTHER THAN A SINGLE CLAN-COMMUNITY AND EXOGAMOUS (305)	0.84 OF 322	24 53 36 269 XSQ= 15.98 PHI= 0.205 XP = 0.0001
180	LEAN TOWARD BEING THOSE WHERE THE COMMUNITY IS COMMONLY EXOGAMOUS, RATHER THAN NON-EXOGAMOUS (124)	0.50 OF 60	180	LEAN TOWARD BEING THOSE WHERE THE COMMUNITY IS COMMONLY NON-EXOGAMOUS, RATHER THAN EXOGAMOUS (258)	0.71 OF 322	30 94 30 228 XSQ= 9.06 PHI= 0.154 XP = 0.0026
181	IN ALL CASES ARE THOSE WHERE THE COMMUNITY IS OTHER THAN A DEME (337)	1.00 OF 60	181	LEAN LESS TOWARD BEING THOSE WHERE THE COMMUNITY IS OTHER THAN A DEME (337)	0.86 OF 322	0 45 60 277 XSQ= 8.21 PHI= -0.147 XP = 0.0042
182	TILT MORE TOWARD BEING THOSE OTHER THAN WHERE THE COMMUNITY IS STRUCTURED ON A NON-CLAN BASIS AND AGAMOUS (256)	0.80 OF 60	182	TILT LESS TOWARD BEING THOSE OTHER THAN WHERE THE COMMUNITY IS STRUCTURED ON A NON-CLAN BASIS AND AGAMOUS (256)	0.65 OF 322	12 114 48 208 XSQ= 4.75 PHI= -0.112 XP = 0.0292
183	LEAN MORE TOWARD BEING THOSE WHERE THE LARGEST NON-COGNATIC KIN GROUP IS SMALLER THAN A MOEITY, I. E., A PHRATRY OR SIB OR LINEAGE (218)	0.98 OF 57	183	LEAN LESS TOWARD BEING THOSE WHERE THE LARGEST NON-COGNATIC KIN GROUP IS SMALLER THAN A MOEITY, I. E., A PHRATRY OR SIB OR LINEAGE (218)	0.83 OF 195	1 33 56 162 XSQ= 7.44 PHI= -0.172 XP = 0.0064
184	TEND MORE TO BE THOSE WHERE THE LARGEST NON-COGNATIC KIN GROUP IS SMALLER THAN A PHRATRY, I. E. A SIB OR LINEAGE (175)	0.91 OF 57	184	TEND LESS TO BE THOSE WHERE THE LARGEST NON-COGNATIC KIN GROUP IS SMALLER THAN A PHRATRY, I. E. A SIB OR LINEAGE (175)	0.63 OF 195	5 72 52 123 XSQ= 15.17 PHI= -0.245 XP = 0.0001

185	DRIFT LESS TOWARD BEING THOSE WHERE THE LARGEST NON-COGNATIC KIN GROUP IS THE MOEITY OR PHRATRY OR SIB (194)	0.67 OF 57	185	DRIFT MORE TOWARD BEING THOSE WHERE THE LARGEST NON-COGNATIC KIN GROUP IS THE MOEITY OR PHRATRY OR SIB (194)	0.80 OF 195	38 156 19 39 XSQ= 3.70 PHI= -0.121 XP = 0.0543
186	LEAN TOWARD BEING THOSE WHERE THE KIN GROUP IS EXCLUSIVELY PATRILINEAL (150)	0.56 OF 61	186	LEAN TOWARD BEING THOSE WHERE THE KIN GROUP IS OTHER THAN EXCLUSIVELY PATRILINEAL (250)	0.66 OF 339	34 116 27 223 XSQ= 9.32 PHI= 0.153 XP = 0.0023
188	TEND MORE TO BE THOSE WHERE THE KIN GROUP IS OTHER THAN EXCLUSIVELY COGNATIC (252)	0.93 OF 61	188	TEND LESS TO BE THOSE WHERE THE KIN GROUP IS OTHER THAN EXCLUSIVELY COGNATIC (252)	0.58 OF 339	4 144 57 195 XSQ= 27.10 PHI= -0.260 XP = 0.0000
192	IN ALL CASES ARE THOSE OTHER THAN WHERE THE ONLY KIN GROUP PRESENT IS A KINDRED OR ELSE BILATERAL DESCENT IS INFERRED (289)	1.00 OF 61	192	TEND LESS TO BE THOSE OTHER THAN WHERE THE ONLY KIN GROUP PRESENT IS A KINDRED OR ELSE BILATERAL DESCENT IS INFERRED (289)	0.67 OF 339	0 111 61 228 XSQ= 26.04 PHI= -0.255 XP = 0.0000
197	TILT MORE TOWARD BEING THOSE WHERE RULES FOR THE INHERITANCE OF REAL PROPERTY, IF PRESENT, FAVOR EITHER THE MALE HEIR OR LINE, OR THE FEMALE HEIR OR LINE (165)	0.97 OF 40	197	TILT LESS TOWARD BEING THOSE WHERE RULES FOR THE INHERITANCE OF REAL PROPERTY, IF PRESENT, FAVOR EITHER THE MALE HEIR OR LINE, OR THE FEMALE HEIR OR LINE (165)	0.82 OF 154	39 126 1 28 XSQ= 4.97 PHI= 0.160 XP = 0.0258
204	TILT MORE TOWARD BEING THOSE WHERE MARITAL RESIDENCE IS PATRILOCAL, VIRILOCAL, OR AVUNCULOCAL, RATHER THAN AMBILOCAL OR NEOLOCAL (270)	0.92 OF 60	204	TILT LESS TOWARD BEING THOSE WHERE MARITAL RESIDENCE IS PATRILOCAL, VIRILOCAL, OR AVUNCULOCAL, RATHER THAN AMBILOCAL OR NEOLOCAL (270)	0.78 OF 274	55 215 5 59 XSQ= 4.72 PHI= 0.119 XP = 0.0299
209	TEND MORE TO BE THOSE WHERE MARITAL RESIDENCE IS PATRILOCAL, VIRILOCAL, OR AVUNCULOCAL, RATHER THAN MATRILOCAL OR UXORILOCAL (270)	0.98 OF 56	209	TEND LESS TO BE THOSE WHERE MARITAL RESIDENCE IS PATRILOCAL, VIRILOCAL, OR AVUNCULOCAL, RATHER THAN MATRILOCAL OR UXORILOCAL (270)	0.77 OF 278	55 215 1 63 XSQ= 11.80 PHI= 0.188 XP = 0.0006
210	TILT MORE TOWARD BEING THOSE WHERE MARITAL RESIDENCE IS PATRILOCAL, RATHER THAN MATRILOCAL (169)	0.97 OF 40	210	TILT LESS TOWARD BEING THOSE WHERE MARITAL RESIDENCE IS PATRILOCAL, RATHER THAN MATRILOCAL (169)	0.81 OF 160	39 130 1 30 XSQ= 5.27 PHI= 0.162 XP = 0.0217
234	LEAN TOWARD BEING THOSE WHERE THE COUSIN TERMINOLOGY IS OF CROW, OMAHA, OR IROQUOIS TYPE, RATHER THAN ESKIMO OR HAWAIIAN TYPE (152)	0.66 OF 47	234	LEAN TOWARD BEING THOSE WHERE THE COUSIN TERMINOLOGY IS OF ESKIMO OR HAWAIIAN TYPE, RATHER THAN CROW, OMAHA, OR IROQUOIS TYPE (170)	0.56 OF 275	31 121 16 154 XSQ= 6.91 PHI= 0.146 XP = 0.0086

240	DRIFT TOWARD BEING THOSE 0.52 OF 33 WHERE THE FAMILY, IF EXTENDED, IS LARGE, RATHER THAN SMALL OR STEM (78)	240	DRIFT TOWARD BEING THOSE 0.66 OF 180 WHERE THE FAMILY, IF EXTENDED, IS SMALL OR STEM, RATHER THAN LARGE (135)	17 61 16 119 XSQ= 3.01 PHI= 0.119 XP = 0.0826
241	IN ALL CASES ARE THOSE 1.00 OF 33 WHERE THE FAMILY, IF EXTENDED, IS LARGE OR SMALL, RATHER THAN STEM (187)	241	TILT LESS TOWARD BEING THOSE 0.86 OF 180 WHERE THE FAMILY, IF EXTENDED, IS LARGE OR SMALL, RATHER THAN STEM (187)	33 154 0 26 XSQ= 4.17 PHI= 0.140 XP = 0.0413
242	TEND MORE TO BE THOSE 0.97 OF 61 WHERE MARRIAGE IS COMMONLY OR OCCASIONALLY POLYGYNOUS, RATHER THAN MONOGAMOUS (314)	242	TEND LESS TO BE THOSE 0.76 OF 334 WHERE MARRIAGE IS COMMONLY OR OCCASIONALLY POLYGYNOUS, RATHER THAN MONOGAMOUS (314)	59 255 2 79 XSQ= 11.91 PHI= 0.174 XP = 0.0006
243	LEAN TOWARD BEING THOSE 0.83 OF 12 WHERE POLYGYNY, IF PRESENT, HAS A HIGH INCIDENCE (24) W-D,S	243	LEAN TOWARD BEING THOSE 0.71 OF 48 WHERE POLYGYNY, IF PRESENT, HAS A LOW INCIDENCE (36) W-D,S	10 14 2 34 XSQ= 9.59 PHI= 0.400 XP = 0.0020
254	IN ALL CASES ARE THOSE 1.00 OF 5 WHERE HOUSEHOLD AUTHORITY IS ON THE FATHER'S SIDE, RATHER THAN THE MOTHER'S (9) DA	254	TILT TOWARD BEING THOSE 0.60 OF 10 WHERE HOUSEHOLD AUTHORITY IS ON THE MOTHER'S SIDE, RATHER THAN THE FATHER'S (6) DA	5 4 0 6 XSQ= 2.81 PHI= 0.433 EP = 0.0440
262	TEND MORE TO BE THOSE 0.98 OF 61 WHERE WIVES ARE OBTAINED BY MEANS INVOLVING THE PRESENCE OF SOME CONSIDERATION (305)	262	TEND LESS TO BE THOSE 0.73 OF 334 WHERE WIVES ARE OBTAINED BY MEANS INVOLVING THE PRESENCE OF SOME CONSIDERATION (305)	60 245 1 89 XSQ= 16.94 PHI= 0.207 XP = 0.0000
263	TEND MORE TO BE THOSE 0.87 OF 61 WHERE WIVES ARE OBTAINED BY RELATIVELY DIFFICULT MEANS, NAMELY BY BRIDE-PRICE, BRIDE-SERVICE, OR EXCHANGING A FEMALE RELATIVE (233)	263	TEND LESS TO BE THOSE 0.54 OF 334 WHERE WIVES ARE OBTAINED BY RELATIVELY DIFFICULT MEANS, NAMELY BY BRIDE-PRICE, BRIDE-SERVICE, OR EXCHANGING A FEMALE RELATIVE (233)	53 180 8 154 XSQ= 21.86 PHI= 0.235 XP = 0.0000
282	TILT TOWARD BEING THOSE 0.86 OF 7 WHERE THE STRENGTH OF DESIRE FOR CHILDREN IS HIGH (16) BCA	282	TILT TOWARD BEING THOSE 0.66 OF 29 WHERE THE STRENGTH OF DESIRE FOR CHILDREN IS LOW OR ABSENT (20) BCA	6 10 1 19 XSQ= 4.10 PHI= 0.337 EP = 0.0298
299	TEND TO BE THOSE 0.57 OF 28 WHERE THE POST-PARTUM SEX TABOO LASTS LONGER THAN ONE YEAR (35)	299	TEND TO BE THOSE 0.80 OF 96 WHERE THE POST-PARTUM SEX TABOO LASTS ONE YEAR OR LESS (89)	16 19 12 77 XSQ= 13.14 PHI= 0.326 XP = 0.0003

No.	Statement	Prop.	N	No.	Statement	Prop.	N	Statistics
300	LEAN TOWARD BEING THOSE WHERE THE POST-PARTUM SEX TABOO LASTS LONGER THAN SIX MONTHS (51)	0.64 OF	28	300	LEAN TOWARD BEING THOSE WHERE THE POST-PARTUM SEX TABOO LASTS SIX MONTHS OR LESS (73)	0.66 OF	96	18 33 10 63 XSQ= 6.82 PHI= 0.235 XP = 0.0090
304	IN ALL CASES ARE THOSE WHERE THE EARLY ANAL SATISFACTION POTENTIAL IS LOW (22) W-C	1.00 OF	6	304	TILT TOWARD BEING THOSE WHERE THE EARLY ANAL SATISFACTION POTENTIAL IS HIGH (19) W-C	0.54 OF	35	0 19 6 16 XSQ= 4.08 PHI= -0.316 XP = 0.0433
309	DRIFT TOWARD BEING THOSE WHERE ORAL SOCIALIZATION ANXIETY IS HIGH (26) W-C	0.86 OF	7	309	DRIFT TOWARD BEING THOSE WHERE ORAL SOCIALIZATION ANXIETY IS LOW (27) W-C	0.57 OF	46	6 20 1 26 XSQ= 2.81 PHI= 0.230 XP = 0.0936
314	TEND TO BE THOSE WHERE THE INCIDENCE OF MOTHER-CHILD HOUSEHOLDS IS HIGH (19) W-D,S	0.92 OF	12	314	TEND TO BE THOSE WHERE THE INCIDENCE OF MOTHER-CHILD HOUSEHOLDS IS LOW (61) W-D,S	0.88 OF	68	11 8 1 60 XSQ= 31.68 PHI= 0.629 XP = 0.
316	TILT TOWARD BEING THOSE WHERE EXCLUSIVE MOTHER-SON SLEEPING ARRANGEMENTS LAST ONE YEAR OR LONGER (19) W-K-A	0.80 OF	10	316	TILT TOWARD BEING THOSE WHERE EXCLUSIVE MOTHER-SON SLEEPING ARRANGEMENTS LAST LESS THAN ONE YEAR (25) W-K-A	0.68 OF	34	8 11 2 23 XSQ= 5.34 PHI= 0.348 XP = 0.0208
318	LEAN TOWARD BEING THOSE WHERE THE OVERALL INDULGENCE OF THE INFANT IS LOW (31) B-B-C	0.86 OF	14	318	LEAN TOWARD BEING THOSE WHERE THE OVERALL INDULGENCE OF THE INFANT IS HIGH (40) B-B-C	0.67 OF	57	2 38 12 19 XSQ= 10.50 PHI= -0.385 XP = 0.0012
319	LEAN TOWARD BEING THOSE WHERE PROTECTION OF THE INFANT FROM ENVIRONMENTAL DISCOMFORTS IS LOW (30) B-B-C	0.85 OF	13	319	LEAN TOWARD BEING THOSE WHERE PROTECTION OF THE INFANT FROM ENVIRONMENTAL DISCOMFORTS IS HIGH (35) B-B-C	0.63 OF	52	2 33 11 19 XSQ= 7.83 PHI= -0.347 XP = 0.0051
320	DRIFT TOWARD BEING THOSE WHERE THE DEGREE OF REDUCTION OF THE INFANT'S DRIVES IS LOW (24) B-B-C	0.62 OF	13	320	DRIFT TOWARD BEING THOSE WHERE THE DEGREE OF REDUCTION OF THE INFANT'S DRIVES IS HIGH (45) B-B-C	0.71 OF	56	5 40 8 16 XSQ= 3.71 PHI= -0.232 XP = 0.0542
324	TILT TOWARD BEING THOSE WHERE THE PAIN INFLICTED ON THE INFANT BY THE NURTURANT AGENT IS HIGH (34) B-B-C	0.85 OF	13	324	TILT TOWARD BEING THOSE WHERE THE PAIN INFLICTED ON THE INFANT BY THE NURTURANT AGENT IS LOW OR NEGLIGIBLE (32) B-B-C	0.57 OF	53	11 23 2 30 XSQ= 5.55 PHI= 0.290 XP = 0.0185

```
334  TILT TOWARD BEING THOSE           0.75 OF  16    334  TILT TOWARD BEING THOSE           0.58 OF  62             4     36
     WHERE THE INDULGENCE OF THE CHILD                     WHERE THE INDULGENCE OF THE CHILD                        12     26
     IS LOW   (38) B-B-C                                   IS HIGH   (40) B-B-C                               XSQ=      4.32
                                                                                                              PHI=    -0.235
                                                                                                              XP =    0.0377

336  DRIFT MORE TOWARD BEING THOSE  0.81 OF  16       336  DRIFT LESS TOWARD BEING THOSE  0.51 OF  59           13     30
     WHERE THE TOTAL POSITIVE PRESSURE TOWARD              WHERE THE TOTAL POSITIVE PRESSURE TOWARD                  3     29
     DEVELOPING RESPONSIBLE BEHAVIOR                       DEVELOPING RESPONSIBLE BEHAVIOR                XSQ=      3.59
     IN THE CHILD                                          IN THE CHILD                                   PHI=     0.219
     IS HIGH   (43) B-B-C                                  IS HIGH   (43) B-B-C                           XP =    0.0580

337  TEND TO BE THOSE                  0.93 OF  15    337  TEND TO BE THOSE                  0.59 OF  58            14     24
     WHERE THE CHILD'S INFERRED ANXIETY OVER               WHERE THE CHILD'S INFERRED ANXIETY OVER                   1     34
     NON-PERFORMANCE OF RESPONSIBLE BEHAVIOR               NON-PERFORMANCE OF RESPONSIBLE BEHAVIOR        XSQ=     10.89
     IS HIGH   (38) B-B-C                                  IS LOW   (35) B-B-C                            PHI=     0.386
                                                                                                          XP =    0.0010

338  TILT MORE TOWARD BEING THOSE   0.87 OF  15       338  TILT LESS TOWARD BEING THOSE   0.53 OF  58           13     31
     WHERE THE CHILD'S INFERRED ANXIETY OVER               WHERE THE CHILD'S INFERRED ANXIETY OVER                   2     27
     PERFORMANCE OF RESPONSIBLE BEHAVIOR                   PERFORMANCE OF RESPONSIBLE BEHAVIOR            XSQ=      4.19
     IS HIGH   (44) B-B-C                                  IS HIGH   (44) B-B-C                           PHI=     0.240
                                                                                                          XP =    0.0406

339  DRIFT TOWARD BEING THOSE          0.67 OF  15    339  DRIFT TOWARD BEING THOSE          0.64 OF  58            10     21
     WHERE THE CHILD'S INFERRED CONFLICT                   WHERE THE CHILD'S INFERRED CONFLICT                       5     37
     REGARDING RESPONSIBLE BEHAVIOR                        REGARDING RESPONSIBLE BEHAVIOR                 XSQ=      3.36
     IS HIGH   (31) B-B-C                                  IS LOW   (42) B-B-C                            PHI=     0.215
                                                                                                          XP =    0.0666

347  TILT TOWARD BEING THOSE           0.75 OF  16    347  TILT TOWARD BEING THOSE           0.58 OF  60            12     25
     WHERE THE CHILD'S INFERRED CONFLICT                   WHERE THE CHILD'S INFERRED CONFLICT                       4     35
     REGARDING SELF-RELIANT BEHAVIOR                       REGARDING SELF-RELIANT BEHAVIOR                XSQ=      4.36
     IS HIGH   (37) B-B-C                                  IS LOW   (39) B-B-C                            PHI=     0.240
                                                                                                          XP =    0.0367

350  DRIFT TOWARD BEING THOSE          0.80 OF  15    350  DRIFT TOWARD BEING THOSE          0.51 OF  45            12     22
     WHERE THE CHILD'S INFERRED ANXIETY OVER               WHERE THE CHILD'S INFERRED ANXIETY OVER                   3     23
     PERFORMANCE OF ACHIEVEMENT BEHAVIOR                   PERFORMANCE OF ACHIEVEMENT BEHAVIOR            XSQ=      3.26
     IS HIGH   (34) B-B-C                                  IS LOW   (26) B-B-C                            PHI=     0.233
                                                                                                          XP =    0.0711

351  DRIFT TOWARD BEING THOSE          0.67 OF  15    351  DRIFT TOWARD BEING THOSE          0.64 OF  45            10     16
     WHERE THE CHILD'S INFERRED CONFLICT                   WHERE THE CHILD'S INFERRED CONFLICT                       5     29
     REGARDING ACHIEVEMENT BEHAVIOR                        REGARDING ACHIEVEMENT BEHAVIOR                 XSQ=      3.26
     IS HIGH   (26) B-B-C                                  IS LOW   (34) B-B-C                            PHI=     0.233
                                                                                                          XP =    0.0711

352  IN ALL CASES ARE THOSE            1.00 OF  15    352  LEAN LESS TOWARD BEING THOSE   0.51 OF  57           15     29
     WHERE THE TOTAL POSITIVE PRESSURE TOWARD              WHERE THE TOTAL POSITIVE PRESSURE TOWARD                  0     28
     DEVELOPING OBEDIENT BEHAVIOR                          DEVELOPING OBEDIENT BEHAVIOR                   XSQ=     10.08
     IN THE CHILD                                          IN THE CHILD                                   PHI=     0.374
     IS HIGH   (44) B-B-C                                  IS HIGH   (44) B-B-C                           XP =    0.0015
```

353	LEAN TOWARD BEING THOSE 0.93 OF 15 WHERE THE CHILD'S INFERRED ANXIETY OVER NON-PERFORMANCE OF OBEDIENT BEHAVIOR IS HIGH (42) B-B-C	353	LEAN TOWARD BEING THOSE 0.53 OF 59 WHERE THE CHILD-S INFERRED ANXIETY OVER NON-PERFORMANCE OF OBEDIENT BEHAVIOR IS LOW (32) B-B-C	14 28 1 31 XSQ= 8.47 PHI= 0.338 XP = 0.0036
370	TEND TO BE THOSE 0.72 OF 39 WHERE THE SEGREGATION OF ADOLESCENT BOYS IS COMPLETE OR PARTIAL (95)	370	TEND TO BE THOSE 0.67 OF 204 WHERE THE SEGREGATION OF ADOLESCENT BOYS IS ABSENT (148)	28 67 11 137 XSQ= 19.26 PHI= 0.282 XP = 0.0000
377	TEND TO BE THOSE 0.60 OF 50 WHERE MALE GENITAL MUTILATION IS PRESENT (83)	377	TEND TO BE THOSE 0.81 OF 275 WHERE MALE GENITAL MUTILATION IS ABSENT (242)	30 53 20 222 XSQ= 34.79 PHI= 0.327 XP = 0.
385	LEAN TOWARD BEING THOSE 0.62 OF 13 WHERE SEXUAL EXPRESSION BY THE YOUNG IS RESTRICTED (22) F-B	385	LEAN TOWARD BEING THOSE 0.81 OF 73 WHERE SEXUAL EXPRESSION BY THE YOUNG IS SEMI-RESTRICTED OR PERMITTED (64) F-B	8 14 5 59 XSQ= 8.30 PHI= 0.311 XP = 0.0040
386	LEAN TOWARD BEING THOSE 0.92 OF 13 WHERE SEXUAL EXPRESSION BY THE YOUNG IS RESTRICTED OR SEMI-RESTRICTED (46) F-B	386	LEAN TOWARD BEING THOSE 0.53 OF 73 WHERE SEXUAL EXPRESSION BY THE YOUNG IS PERMITTED (40) F-B	12 34 1 39 XSQ= 7.53 PHI= 0.296 XP = 0.0061
393	DRIFT TOWARD BEING THOSE 0.79 OF 14 WHERE EXTRAMARITAL COITUS IS PUNISHED, RATHER THAN PERMITTED (43) F-B	393	DRIFT TOWARD BEING THOSE 0.54 OF 70 WHERE EXTRAMARITAL COITUS IS PERMITTED, RATHER THAN PUNISHED (41) F-B	11 32 3 38 XSQ= 3.81 PHI= 0.213 XP = 0.0509
399	TILT TOWARD BEING THOSE 0.89 OF 9 WHERE INTENSITY OF CASTRATION ANXIETY IS HIGH (23) WNS	399	TILT TOWARD BEING THOSE 0.58 OF 36 WHERE INTENSITY OF CASTRATION ANXIETY IS LOW (22) WNS	8 15 1 21 XSQ= 4.67 PHI= 0.322 XP = 0.0306
419	DRIFT MORE TOWARD BEING THOSE 0.92 OF 12 WHERE MILITARY GLORY IS STRONGLY OR MODERATELY EMPHASIZED (55) PES	419	DRIFT LESS TOWARD BEING THOSE 0.59 OF 74 WHERE MILITARY GLORY IS STRONGLY OR MODERATELY EMPHASIZED (55) PES	11 44 1 30 XSQ= 3.35 PHI= 0.197 XP = 0.0670
426	LEAN MORE TOWARD BEING THOSE 0.81 OF 42 WHERE A HIGH GOD IS PRESENT (156) GES,EA	426	LEAN LESS TOWARD BEING THOSE 0.56 OF 218 WHERE A HIGH GOD IS PRESENT (156) GES,EA	34 122 8 96 XSQ= 8.15 PHI= 0.177 XP = 0.0043

427	LEAN TOWARD BEING THOSE WHERE A HIGH GOD, IF PRESENT, IS INACTIVE, RATHER THAN ACTIVE (69) GES,EA	0.68 OF 34	427	LEAN TOWARD BEING THOSE WHERE A HIGH GOD, IF PRESENT, IS ACTIVE, RATHER THAN INACTIVE (87) GES,EA	0.62 OF 122	11 76 23 46 XSQ= 8.49 PHI= -0.233 XP = 0.0036
445	TILT TOWARD BEING THOSE WHERE SORCERY IS IMPORTANT (26) BBW,DH	0.89 OF 9	445	TILT TOWARD BEING THOSE WHERE SORCERY IS UNIMPORTANT (23) BBW,DH	0.55 OF 40	8 18 1 22 XSQ= 4.06 PHI= 0.288 XP = 0.0440
446	DRIFT TOWARD BEING THOSE WHERE WITCHCRAFT IS SIGNIFICANTLY PRESENT (14) GES	0.71 OF 7	446	DRIFT TOWARD BEING THOSE WHERE WITCHCRAFT IS MODERATELY PRESENT OR ABSENT (24) GES	0.71 OF 31	5 9 2 22 XSQ= 2.78 PHI= 0.270 EP = 0.0772
452	DRIFT TOWARD BEING THOSE WHERE TOTEMISM WITH FOOD TABOOS IS PRESENT (19) WNS	0.78 OF 9	452	DRIFT TOWARD BEING THOSE WHERE TOTEMISM WITH FOOD TABOOS IS ABSENT (24) WNS	0.65 OF 34	7 12 2 22 XSQ= 3.63 PHI= 0.290 XP = 0.0568
458	TEND TO BE THOSE WHERE GAMES, IF PRESENT, INCLUDE GAMES OF STRATEGY (52) R-A-B,EA	0.91 OF 23	458	TEND TO BE THOSE WHERE GAMES, IF PRESENT, DO NOT INCLUDE GAMES OF STRATEGY (119) R-A-B,EA	0.79 OF 148	21 31 2 117 XSQ= 43.30 PHI= 0.503 XP = 0.
460	TEND MORE TO BE THOSE WHERE GAMES, IF PRESENT, ARE NOT LIMITED TO GAMES OF SKILL ONLY (104) R-A-B,EA	0.96 OF 23	460	TEND LESS TO BE THOSE WHERE GAMES, IF PRESENT, ARE NOT LIMITED TO GAMES OF SKILL ONLY (104) R-A-B,EA	0.55 OF 148	1 66 22 82 XSQ= 11.90 PHI= -0.264 XP = 0.0006
472	TILT TOWARD BEING THOSE WHERE THE COMPOSITE NARCISSISM INDEX IS HIGH (47) PES	0.83 OF 12	472	TILT TOWARD BEING THOSE WHERE THE COMPOSITE NARCISSISM INDEX IS LOW (43) PES	0.53 OF 78	10 37 2 41 XSQ= 4.03 PHI= 0.212 XP = 0.0447
475	TILT TOWARD BEING THOSE WHERE EXHIBITIONISTIC DANCING IS STRONGLY OR MODERATELY EMPHASIZED (48) PES	0.92 OF 12	475	TILT TOWARD BEING THOSE WHERE EXHIBITIONISTIC DANCING IS NEGLIGIBLY EMPHASIZED (38) PES	0.50 OF 74	11 37 1 37 XSQ= 5.68 PHI= 0.257 XP = 0.0172
476	TILT TOWARD BEING THOSE WHERE THE DEGREE OF INSOBRIETY IS MODERATE OR SLIGHT (18) CH	0.78 OF 9	476	TILT TOWARD BEING THOSE WHERE THE DEGREE OF INSOBRIETY IS STRONG (31) DH	0.72 OF 40	2 29 7 11 XSQ= 5.97 PHI= -0.349 XP = 0.0145

18 CULTURES
WHOSE LINGUISTIC AFFILIATION IS
CHARI-NILE (14)

18 CULTURES
WHOSE LINGUISTIC AFFILIATION IS
OTHER THAN CHARI-NILE (386)

BACKGROUND ON PAGE 67

NEITHER SUBJECT NOR PREDICATE

14 IN LEFT COLUMN

BARABRA BARI DILLING DOROBO INGASSANA LANGO LUO MAMVU MASAI NANDI
NUER SHILLUK TESO TURKANA

386 IN RIGHT COLUMN

19 CULTURES:
WHOSE LINGUISTIC AFFILIATION IS
AFRO-ASIATIC (21)

19 CULTURES
WHOSE LINGUISTIC AFFILIATION IS
OTHER THAN AFRO-ASIATIC (379)

BACKGROUND ON PAGE 67

SUBJECT ONLY

21 IN LEFT COLUMN

BEJA	BUDUMA	EGYPTIANS	HASANIA	HEBREWS	IRAQW	KABYLE	KONSO	MAGUZAWA	MARGI
MATAKAM	MZAB	REGEIBAT	RIFFIANS	RWALA	SHLUH	SIWANS	SOMALI	SYRIANS	TERA
TIGRINYA									

379 IN RIGHT COLUMN

4	TEND TO BE THOSE LOCATED IN THE CIRCUM-MEDITERRANEAN (45)	0.90 OF 21	4	TEND TO BE THOSE LOCATED OUTSIDE OF THE CIRCUM-MEDITERRANEAN (355)	0.93 OF 379	19 26 2 353 XSQ= 131.09 PHI= 0.572 XP = 0.
5	IN ALL CASES ARE THOSE LOCATED OUTSIDE OF EAST EURASIA (330)	1.00 OF 21	5	DRIFT LESS TOWARD BEING THOSE LOCATED OUTSIDE OF EAST EURASIA (330)	0.82 OF 379	0 70 21 309 XSQ= 3.51 PHI= -0.094 XP = 0.0610
6	IN ALL CASES ARE THOSE LOCATED OUTSIDE OF THE INSULAR PACIFIC (330)	1.00 OF 21	6	DRIFT LESS TOWARD BEING THOSE LOCATED OUTSIDE OF THE INSULAR PACIFIC (330)	0.82 OF 379	0 70 21 309 XSQ= 3.51 PHI= -0.094 XP = 0.0610
8	IN ALL CASES ARE THOSE LOCATED OUTSIDE OF NORTH AMERICA (330)	1.00 OF 21	8	DRIFT LESS TOWARD BEING THOSE LOCATED OUTSIDE OF NORTH AMERICA (330)	0.82 OF 379	0 70 21 309 XSQ= 3.51 PHI= -0.094 XP = 0.0610
9	IN ALL CASES ARE THOSE LOCATED OUTSIDE OF SOUTH AMERICA (335)	1.00 OF 21	9	DRIFT LESS TOWARD BEING THOSE LOCATED OUTSIDE OF SOUTH AMERICA (335)	0.83 OF 379	0 65 21 314 XSQ= 3.13 PHI= -0.088 XP = 0.0767

13	IN ALL CASES ARE THOSE WHERE THE LATITUDE IS LESS THAN FORTY DEGREES (329)	1.00 OF 21	13	DRIFT LESS TOWARD BEING THOSE WHERE THE LATITUDE IS LESS THAN FORTY DEGREES (329)	0.81 OF 379	0 71 21 308 XSQ= 3.59 PHI= -0.095 XP = 0.0583
42	IN ALL CASES ARE THOSE WHERE THE NATURAL ENVIRONMENT IS OTHER THAN TROPICAL OR SUB-TROPICAL RAIN FOREST, OR MONSOON FOREST (244) FWM	1.00 OF 21	42	TEND LESS TO BE THOSE WHERE THE NATURAL ENVIRONMENT IS OTHER THAN TROPICAL OR SUB-TROPICAL RAIN FOREST, OR MONSOON FOREST (244) FWM	0.59 OF 379	0 156 21 223 XSQ= 12.49 PHI= -0.177 XP = 0.0004
51	LEAN MORE TOWARD BEING THOSE WHERE SUBSISTENCE IS PRIMARILY BY FOOD PRODUCTION -- I. E., AGRICULTURE OR HUSBANDRY -- RATHER THAN BY GATHERING (253)	0.95 OF 21	51	LEAN LESS TOWARD BEING THOSE WHERE SUBSISTENCE IS PRIMARILY BY FOOD PRODUCTION -- I. E., AGRICULTURE OR HUSBANDRY -- RATHER THAN BY GATHERING (253)	0.61 OF 379	20 233 1 146 XSQ= 8.36 PHI= 0.145 XP = 0.0038
53	TEND TO BE THOSE WHERE FOOD PRODUCTION IS BY INTENSIVE AGRICULTURE, RATHER THAN BY SIMPLE AGRICULTURE OR INCIPIENT FOOD PRODUCTION (91)	0.86 OF 14	53	TEND TO BE THOSE WHERE FOOD PRODUCTION IS BY SIMPLE AGRICULTURE OR INCIPIENT FOOD PRODUCTION, RATHER THAN BY INTENSIVE AGRICULTURE (147)	0.65 OF 224	12 79 2 145 XSQ= 12.14 PHI= 0.226 XP = 0.0005
55	LEAN TOWARD BEING THOSE WHERE FOOD PRODUCTION IS BY INTENSIVE AGRICULTURE, RATHER THAN BY SIMPLE AGRICULTURE (91)	0.92 OF 13	55	LEAN TOWARD BEING THOSE WHERE FOOD PRODUCTION IS BY SIMPLE AGRICULTURE, RATHER THAN BY INTENSIVE AGRICULTURE (101)	0.56 OF 179	12 79 1 100 XSQ= 9.43 PHI= 0.222 XP = 0.0021
62	TILT MORE TOWARD BEING THOSE WHERE HUSBANDRY OF SOME KIND IS PRESENT (228)	0.81 OF 21	62	TILT LESS TOWARD BEING THOSE WHERE HUSBANDRY OF SOME KIND IS PRESENT (228)	0.56 OF 379	17 211 4 168 XSQ= 4.21 PHI= 0.103 XP = 0.0402
63	DRIFT MORE TOWARD BEING THOSE WHERE HUSBANDRY, IF PRESENT, IS PRINCIPALLY IN THE FORM OF BOVINE, EQUINE, CAMEL-LIKE, OR DEER-LIKE ANIMALS, RATHER THAN PIGS, SHEEP, OR GOATS (152)	0.88 OF 17	63	DRIFT LESS TOWARD BEING THOSE WHERE HUSBANDRY, IF PRESENT, IS PRINCIPALLY IN THE FORM OF BOVINE, EQUINE, CAMEL-LIKE, OR DEER-LIKE ANIMALS, RATHER THAN PIGS, SHEEP, OR GOATS (152)	0.66 OF 209	15 137 2 72 XSQ= 2.72 PHI= 0.110 XP = 0.0994
71	TILT TOWARD BEING THOSE WHERE METAL WORKING IS PRESENT (98)	0.86 OF 7	71	TILT TOWARD BEING THOSE WHERE METAL WORKING IS ABSENT (153)	0.62 OF 244	6 92 1 152 XSQ= 4.73 PHI= 0.137 XP = 0.0297
73	DRIFT TOWARD BEING THOSE WHERE WEAVING IS PRESENT (118)	0.86 OF 7	73	DRIFT TOWARD BEING THOSE WHERE WEAVING IS ABSENT (130)	0.54 OF 241	6 112 1 129 XSQ= 2.77 PHI= 0.106 XP = 0.0958

81	TILT TOWARD BEING THOSE 0.73 OF 11 WHERE A CITY OR TOWN IS PRESENT, OR THE AVERAGE COMMUNITY SIZE IS 200 OR GREATER (89)	81	TILT TOWARD BEING THOSE 0.62 OF 213 WHERE NO CITY OR TOWN IS PRESENT, AND THE AVERAGE COMMUNITY SIZE IS SMALLER THAN 200 (135)	8 81 3 132 XSQ= 3.91 PHI= 0.132 XP = 0.0480
86	TILT TOWARD BEING THOSE 0.81 OF 16 WHERE THE LEVEL OF POLITICAL INTEGRATION IS THE LARGE STATE, THE LITTLE STATE, OR THE MINIMAL STATE (148) GPM	86	TILT TOWARD BEING THOSE 0.53 OF 288 WHERE THE LEVEL OF POLITICAL INTEGRATION IS THE AUTONOMOUS COMMUNITY, OR THE FAMILY (156) GPM	13 135 3 153 XSQ= 5.86 PHI= 0.139 XP = 0.0155
88	LEAN TOWARD BEING THOSE 0.82 OF 11 WHERE, IF A HEADMANSHIP IS PRESENT, SUCCESSION IS NCN-HEREDITARY (106)	88	LEAN TOWARD BEING THOSE 0.63 OF 260 WHERE, IF A HEADMANSHIP IS PRESENT, SUCCESSION IS HEREDITARY (165)	9 97 2 163 XSQ= 7.01 PHI= 0.161 XP = 0.0081
96	TILT MORE TOWARD BEING THOSE 0.82 OF 17 WHERE THE HIERARCHY OF NATIONAL JURISDICTION HAS FOUR, THREE, TWC OR ONE LEVEL (174) GES,EA	96	TILT LESS TOWARD BEING THOSE 0.51 OF 313 WHERE THE HIERARCHY OF NATIONAL JURISDICTION HAS FOUR, THREE, TWC OR ONE LEVEL (174) GES,EA	14 160 3 153 XSQ= 5.12 PHI= 0.125 XP = 0.0236
97	LEAN LESS TOWARD BEING THOSE 0.53 OF 17 WHERE THE HIERARCHY OF LOCAL JURISDICTION HAS THREE OR TWO LEVELS (273) GES,EA	97	LEAN MORE TOWARD BEING THOSE 0.84 OF 314 WHERE THE HIERARCHY OF LOCAL JURISDICTION HAS THREE OR TWO LEVELS (273) GES,EA	8 50 9 264 XSQ= 8.77 PHI= 0.163 XP = 0.0031
98	IN ALL CASES ARE THOSE 1.00 OF 17 WHERE THE HIERARCHY OF LOCAL JURISDICTION HAS FOUR OR THREE LEVELS (238) GES,EA	98	TILT LESS TOWARD BEING THOSE 0.70 OF 314 WHERE THE HIERARCHY OF LOCAL JURISDICTION HAS FOUR OR THREE LEVELS (238) GES,EA	17 221 0 93 XSQ= 5.61 PHI= 0.130 XP = 0.0178
100	IN ALL CASES ARE THOSE 1.00 OF 17 WHERE HIERARCHIES ARE MORE COMPLEX THAN THE 'SIMPLEST,' I. E., MORE COMPLEX THAN TWC LOCAL LEVELS WITH NO NATIONAL LEVELS (267) GES,EA	100	DRIFT LESS TOWARD BEING THOSE 0.80 OF 313 WHERE HIERARCHIES ARE MORE COMPLEX THAN THE 'SIMPLEST,' I. E., MORE COMPLEX THAN TWO LOCAL LEVELS WITH NO NATIONAL LEVELS (267) GES,EA	17 250 0 63 XSQ= 3.03 PHI= 0.096 XP = 0.0819
109	TEND TO BE THOSE 0.67 OF 15 WHERE CASTES ARE PRESENT (51)	109	TEND TO BE THOSE 0.88 OF 353 WHERE CASTES ARE ABSENT (317)	10 41 5 312 XSQ= 32.06 PHI= 0.295 XP = 0.
110	TILT TOWARD BEING THOSE 0.74 OF 19 WHERE SLAVERY IS PRESENT (163)	110	TILT TOWARD BEING THOSE 0.59 OF 362 WHERE SLAVERY IS ABSENT (218)	14 149 5 213 XSQ= 6.53 PHI= 0.131 XP = 0.0106

186	TEND TO BE THOSE WHERE THE KIN GROUP IS EXCLUSIVELY PATRILINEAL (150)	0.86 OF 21	186	TEND TO BE THOSE WHERE THE KIN GROUP IS OTHER THAN EXCLUSIVELY PATRILINEAL (250)	0.65 OF 379	18 132 3 247 XSQ= 19.87 PHI= 0.223 XP = 0.0000
188	IN ALL CASES ARE THOSE WHERE THE KIN GROUP IS OTHER THAN EXCLUSIVELY COGNATIC (252)	1.00 OF 21	188	TEND LESS TO BE THOSE WHERE THE KIN GROUP IS OTHER THAN EXCLUSIVELY COGNATIC (252)	0.61 CF 379	0 148 21 231 XSQ= 11.40 PHI= -0.169 XP = 0.0007
190	IN ALL CASES ARE THOSE WHERE THE KIN GROUP IS PATRILINEAL CR DOUBLE-CESCENT, RATHER THAN MATRILINEAL (186)	1.00 OF 21	190	TILT LESS TOWARD BEING THOSE WHERE THE KIN GROUP IS PATRILINEAL OR DOUBLE-DESCENT, RATHER THAN MATRILINEAL (186)	0.73 OF 226	21 165 0 61 XSQ= 6.15 PHI= 0.158 XP = 0.0132
192	IN ALL CASES ARE THOSE OTHER THAN WHERE THE CNLY KIN GROUP PRESENT IS A KINDRED OR ELSE BILATERAL DESCENT IS INFERRED (289)	1.00 OF 21	192	LEAN LESS TOWARD BEING THOSE OTHER THAN WHERE THE ONLY KIN GROUP PRESENT IS A KINDRED OR ELSE BILATERAL DESCENT IS INFERRED (289)	0.71 OF 379	0 111 21 268 XSQ= 7.11 PHI= -0.133 XP = 0.0076
196	DRIFT MORE TOWARD BEING THOSE WHERE INDIVIDUAL RIGHTS IN REAL PROPERTY, AND RULES FOR INHERITANCE, ARE PRESENT (194)	0.93 OF 15	196	DRIFT LESS TOWARD BEING THOSE WHERE INDIVIDUAL RIGHTS IN REAL PROPERTY, AND RULES FOR INHERITANCE, ARE PRESENT (194)	0.68 OF 266	14 180 1 86 XSQ= 3.26 PHI= 0.108 XP = 0.0711
201	IN ALL CASES ARE THOSE WHERE MARITAL RESICENCE IS NCN-OPTIONAL, RATHER THAN AMBILCCAL CR NECLOCAL (334)	1.00 OF 21	201	DRIFT LESS TOWARD BEING THOSE WHERE MARITAL RESIDENCE IS NON-OPTIONAL, RATHER THAN AMBILOCAL OR NEOLOCAL (334)	0.83 OF 377	21 313 0 64 XSQ= 3.08 PHI= 0.088 XP = 0.0791
204	IN ALL CASES ARE THOSE WHERE MARITAL RESICENCE IS PATRILOCAL, VIRILOCAL, OR AVUNCULOCAL, RATHER THAN AMBILOCAL OR NECLOCAL (270)	1.00 OF 21	204	TILT LESS TOWARD BEING THOSE WHERE MARITAL RESIDENCE IS PATRILOCAL, VIRILOCAL, OR AVUNCULOCAL, RATHER THAN AMBILOCAL OR NECLOCAL (270)	0.80 OF 313	21 249 0 64 XSQ= 4.07 PHI= 0.110 XP = 0.0436
209	IN ALL CASES ARE THOSE WHERE MARITAL RESICENCE IS PATRILOCAL, VIRILOCAL, OR AVUNCULOCAL, RATHER THAN MATRILOCAL OR UXCRILOCAL (270)	1.00 OF 21	209	TILT LESS TOWARD BEING THOSE WHERE MARITAL RESIDENCE IS PATRILOCAL, VIRILOCAL, OR AVUNCULOCAL, RATHER THAN MATRILOCAL OR UXORILOCAL (270)	0.80 CF 313	21 249 0 64 XSQ= 4.07 PHI= 0.110 XP = 0.0436
210	IN ALL CASES ARE THOSE WHERE MARITAL RESIDENCE IS PATRILOCAL, RATHER THAN MATRILOCAL (169)	1.00 OF 21	210	DRIFT LESS TOWARD BEING THOSE WHERE MARITAL RESIDENCE IS PATRILOCAL, RATHER THAN MATRILOCAL (169)	0.83 OF 179	21 148 0 31 XSQ= 3.08 PHI= 0.124 XP = 0.0791

	Subject	Proportion		Comparison	Proportion	Statistics
213	TILT TOWARD BEING THOSE WHERE FIRST COUSIN MARRIAGE IS PERMITTED (172)	0.78 OF 18	213	TILT TOWARD BEING THOSE WHERE FIRST COUSIN MARRIAGE IS NOT PERMITTED (198)	0.55 OF 352	14 158 4 194 XSQ= 6.18 PHI= 0.129 XP = 0.0129
225	TILT TOWARD BEING THOSE WHERE COUSIN MARRIAGE IS PREFERENTIALLY OR PERMISSIVELY PATRILATERAL, RATHER THAN MATRILATERAL (23)	0.75 OF 8	225	TILT TOWARD BEING THOSE WHERE COUSIN MARRIAGE IS PREFERENTIALLY OR PERMISSIVELY MATRILATERAL, RATHER THAN PATRILATERAL (43)	0.71 OF 58	6 17 2 41 XSQ= 4.61 PHI= 0.264 XP = 0.0318
262	DRIFT MORE TOWARD BEING THOSE WHERE WIVES ARE OBTAINED BY MEANS INVOLVING THE PRESENCE OF SOME CONSIDERATION (305)	0.95 OF 21	262	DRIFT LESS TOWARD BEING THOSE WHERE WIVES ARE OBTAINED BY MEANS INVOLVING THE PRESENCE OF SOME CONSIDERATION (305)	0.76 OF 374	20 285 1 89 XSQ= 3.08 PHI= 0.088 XP = 0.0790
263	LEAN MORE TOWARD BEING THOSE WHERE WIVES ARE OBTAINED BY RELATIVELY DIFFICULT MEANS, NAMELY BY BRIDE-PRICE, BRIDE-SERVICE, OR EXCHANGING A FEMALE RELATIVE (233)	0.90 OF 21	263	LEAN LESS TOWARD BEING THOSE WHERE WIVES ARE OBTAINED BY RELATIVELY DIFFICULT MEANS, NAMELY BY BRIDE-PRICE, BRIDE-SERVICE, OR EXCHANGING A FEMALE RELATIVE (233)	0.57 OF 374	19 214 2 160 XSQ= 7.77 PHI= 0.140 XP = 0.0053
370	DRIFT MORE TOWARD BEING THOSE WHERE THE SEGREGATION OF ADOLESCENT BOYS IS ABSENT (148)	0.91 OF 11	370	DRIFT LESS TOWARD BEING THOSE WHERE THE SEGREGATION OF ADOLESCENT BOYS IS ABSENT (148)	0.59 OF 232	1 94 10 138 XSQ= 3.14 PHI= -0.114 XP = 0.0766
377	TEND TO BE THOSE WHERE MALE GENITAL MUTILATION IS PRESENT (83)	0.88 OF 17	377	TEND TO BE THOSE WHERE MALE GENITAL MUTILATION IS ABSENT (242)	0.78 OF 308	15 68 2 240 XSQ= 33.68 PHI= 0.322 XP = 0.
382	IN ALL CASES ARE THOSE WHERE FEMALE INITIATION RITES ARE ABSENT (27) JKB	1.00 OF 4	382	DRIFT TOWARD BEING THOSE WHERE FEMALE INITIATION RITES ARE PRESENT (38) JKB	0.62 OF 61	0 38 4 23 XSQ= 3.71 PHI= -0.239 XP = 0.0542
390	TILT TOWARD BEING THOSE WHERE PREMARITAL SEX RELATIONS ARE STRONGLY PUNISHED AND IN FACT RARE (47) JTW,EA	0.63 OF 8	390	TILT TOWARD BEING THOSE WHERE PREMARITAL SEX RELATIONS ARE WEAKLY PUNISHED AND IN FACT NOT RARE OR PUNISHED ONLY IF PREGNANCY RESULTS, OR FREELY PERMITTED (132) JTW,EA	0.75 OF 171	5 42 3 129 XSQ= 3.89 PHI= 0.147 XP = 0.0486
391	DRIFT TOWARD BEING THOSE WHERE PREMARITAL SEX RELATIONS ARE STRONGLY PUNISHED AND IN FACT RARE, OR WEAKLY PUNISHED AND IN FACT NOT RARE (89) JTW,EA	0.88 OF 8	391	DRIFT TOWARD BEING THOSE WHERE PREMARITAL SEX RELATIONS ARE PUNISHED ONLY IF PREGNANCY RESULTS, OR FREELY PERMITTED (90) JTW,EA	0.52 OF 171	7 82 1 89 XSQ= 3.33 PHI= 0.136 XP = 0.0680

```
397  IN ALL CASES ARE THOSE           1.00 OF   2     397  DRIFT TOWARD BEING THOSE        0.78 OF  54          2   12
     WHERE SEX DISABILITY                                  WHERE SEX DISABILITY                                  0   42
     IS PRESENT  (14) JKH                                  IS ABSENT  (42) JKH                          XSQ=       2.77
                                                                                                       PHI=      0.222
                                                                                                       XP  =    0.0963

426  IN ALL CASES ARE THOSE           1.00 OF  14     426  LEAN LESS TOWARD BEING THOSE    0.58 OF 246         14  142
     WHERE A HIGH GOD IS                                   WHERE A HIGH GOD IS                                   0  104
     PRESENT  (156) GES,EA                                 PRESENT  (156) GES,EA                        XSQ=       8.18
                                                                                                       PHI=      0.177
                                                                                                       XP  =    0.0042

427  LEAN MORE TOWARD BEING THOSE     0.93 OF  14     427  LEAN LESS TOWARD BEING THOSE    0.52 OF 142         13   74
     WHERE A HIGH GOD, IF PRESENT, IS                      WHERE A HIGH GOD, IF PRESENT, IS                      1   68
     ACTIVE, RATHER THAN                                   ACTIVE, RATHER THAN                          XSQ=       7.00
     INACTIVE  (87) GES,EA                                 INACTIVE  (87) GES,EA                        PHI=      0.212
                                                                                                       XP  =    0.0081

428  IN ALL CASES ARE THOSE           1.00 OF  13     428  TILT LESS TOWARD BEING THOSE    0.65 OF  74         13   48
     WHERE A HIGH GOD, IF PRESENT AND ACTIVE,              WHERE A HIGH GOD, IF PRESENT AND ACTIVE,              0   26
     SUPPORTS HUMAN MORALITY, RATHER THAN                  SUPPORTS HUMAN MORALITY, RATHER THAN         XSQ=       4.95
     NOT SUPPORTING IT  (61) GES,EA                        NOT SUPPORTING IT  (61) GES,EA               PHI=      0.238
                                                                                                       XP  =    0.0262

458  DRIFT TOWARD BEING THOSE         0.80 OF   5     458  DRIFT TOWARD BEING THOSE        0.71 OF 166          4   48
     WHERE GAMES, IF PRESENT,                              WHERE GAMES, IF PRESENT,                              1  118
     INCLUDE GAMES OF STRATEGY  (52) R-A-B,EA              DO NOT INCLUDE                               XSQ=       3.81
                                                           GAMES OF STRATEGY  (119) R-A-B,EA            PHI=      0.149
                                                                                                       XP  =    0.0508
```

20	CULTURES WHERE THE LINGUISTIC AFFILIATION IS NIGER-CONGO, RATHER THAN AFRO-ASIATIC (61)	20	CULTURES WHERE THE LINGUISTIC AFFILIATION IS AFRO-ASIATIC, RATHER THAN NIGER-CONGO (21)

BACKGROUND ON PAGE 67 SUBJECT ONLY

61 IN LEFT COLUMN

AMBA	ASHANTI	AZANDE	BABWA	BAJUN	BAMBARA	BAMILEKE	BANDA	BAYA	BEMBA
BETE	BIRIFOR	BOZO	CHAGGA	DOGON	FANG	FON	FUTAJALONKE	GANDA	GISU
GURE	HEHE	HERERO	ILA	JUKUN	KATAB	KIKUYU	KISSI	KPE	KUBA
LAMBA	LOZI	LUBA	MAMBILA	MBUGWE	MBUNDU	MBUTI	MENDE	MONGO	MOSSI
NDEMBU	NGONI	NUPE	NYAKYUSA	NYANEKA	NYORO	PENDE	RUNDI	SOTHO	SWAZI
TALLENSI	TENDA	THONGA	TIV	VENDA	WOLOF	WUTE	YAKO	YAO	YOMBE
YORUBA									

21 IN RIGHT COLUMN

BEJA	BUDUMA	EGYPTIANS	HASANIA	HEBREWS	IRAQW	KABYLE	KONSO	MAGUZAWA	MARGI
MATAKAM	MZAB	REGEIBAT	RIFFIANS	RWALA	SHLUH	SIWANS	SOMALI	SYRIANS	TERA
TIGRINYA									

318 EXCLUDED BECAUSE IRRELEVANT

3	TEND TO BE THOSE LOCATED IN AFRICA (80)	0.98 OF 61	3	TEND TO BE THOSE LOCATED OUTSIDE OF AFRICA (320)	0.90 OF 21	60 2 1 19 XSQ= 62.12 PHI= 0.870 XP = 0.
4	TEND TO BE THOSE LOCATED OUTSIDE OF THE CIRCUM-MEDITERRANEAN (355)	0.98 OF 61	4	TEND TO BE THOSE LOCATED IN THE CIRCUM-MEDITERRANEAN (45)	0.90 OF 21	1 19 60 2 XSQ= 62.12 PHI= -0.870 XP = 0.
14	IN ALL CASES ARE THOSE WHERE THE LATITUDE IS LESS THAN THIRTY DEGREES (281)	1.00 OF 61	14	TEND LESS TO BE THOSE WHERE THE LATITUDE IS LESS THAN THIRTY DEGREES (281)	0.67 OF 21	0 7 61 14 XSQ= 18.17 PHI= -0.471 XP = 0.0000
15	TEND TO BE THOSE WHERE THE LATITUDE IS LESS THAN TWENTY DEGREES (217)	0.92 OF 61	15	TEND TO BE THOSE WHERE THE LATITUDE IS TWENTY DEGREES OR GREATER (183)	0.52 OF 21	5 11 56 10 XSQ= 16.71 PHI= -0.451 XP = 0.0000

16	LEAN TOWARD BEING THOSE 0.59 OF 61 WHERE THE LATITUDE IS LESS THAN TEN DEGREES (123)	16	LEAN TOWARD BEING THOSE 0.86 OF 21 WHERE THE LATITUDE IS TEN DEGREES OR GREATER (277)	25 18 36 3 XSQ= 10.80 PHI= -0.363 XP = 0.0010
33	LEAN MORE TOWARD BEING THOSE 0.97 OF 61 WHERE THE NATURAL ENVIRONMENT IS OTHER THAN 'VERY HARSH,' I.E., DESERT, DESERT GRASSES AND SHRUBS, TUNDRA, OR HIGH PLATEAU STEPPE (341) FWM	33	LEAN LESS TOWARD BEING THOSE 0.71 OF 21 WHERE THE NATURAL ENVIRONMENT IS OTHER THAN 'VERY HARSH,' I.E., DESERT, DESERT GRASSES AND SHRUBS, TUNDRA, OR HIGH PLATEAU STEPPE (341) FWM	2 6 59 15 XSQ= 8.66 PHI= -0.325 XP = 0.0033
36	DRIFT MORE TOWARD BEING THOSE 0.84 OF 61 WHERE THE NATURAL ENVIRONMENT IS OTHER THAN 'VERY HARSH,' OR SUB-TROPICAL BUSH, OR TEMPERATE GRASSLAND (292) FWM	36	DRIFT LESS TOWARD BEING THOSE 0.62 OF 21 WHERE THE NATURAL ENVIRONMENT IS OTHER THAN 'VERY HARSH,' OR SUB-TROPICAL BUSH, OR TEMPERATE GRASSLAND (292) FWM	10 8 51 13 XSQ= 3.12 PHI= -0.195 XP = 0.0773
42	TILT LESS TOWARD BEING THOSE 0.72 OF 61 WHERE THE NATURAL ENVIRONMENT IS OTHER THAN TROPICAL OR SUB-TROPICAL RAIN FOREST, OR MONSOON FOREST (244) FWM	42	IN ALL CASES ARE THOSE 1.00 OF 21 WHERE THE NATURAL ENVIRONMENT IS OTHER THAN TROPICAL OR SUB-TROPICAL RAIN FOREST, OR MONSOON FOREST (244) FWM	17 0 44 21 XSQ= 5.78 PHI= 0.266 XP = 0.0162
46	TILT MORE TOWARD BEING THOSE 0.96 OF 52 OTHER THAN WHERE SETTLEMENTS ARE NON-FIXED AND MOVEMENT IS NOMADIC (260)	46	TILT LESS TOWARD BEING THOSE 0.76 OF 17 OTHER THAN WHERE SETTLEMENTS ARE NON-FIXED AND MOVEMENT IS NOMADIC (260)	2 4 50 13 XSQ= 4.02 PHI= -0.241 XP = 0.0450
47	TILT TOWARD BEING THOSE 0.78 OF 9 WHERE, IF SETTLEMENTS ARE NON-FIXED, MOVEMENT IS NON-NOMADIC, RATHER THAN NOMADIC (38)	47	IN ALL CASES ARE THOSE 1.00 OF 4 WHERE, IF SETTLEMENTS ARE NON-FIXED, MOVEMENT IS NOMADIC, RATHER THAN NON-NOMADIC (72)	2 4 7 0 XSQ= 3.97 PHI= -0.553 EP = 0.0210
53	TEND TO BE THOSE 0.72 OF 50 WHERE FOOD PRODUCTION IS BY SIMPLE AGRICULTURE OR INCIPIENT FOOD PRODUCTION, RATHER THAN BY INTENSIVE AGRICULTURE (147)	53	TEND TO BE THOSE 0.86 OF 14 WHERE FOOD PRODUCTION IS BY INTENSIVE AGRICULTURE, RATHER THAN BY SIMPLE AGRICULTURE OR INCIPIENT FOOD PRODUCTION (91)	14 12 36 2 XSQ= 12.81 PHI= -0.447 XP = 0.0003
55	TEND TO BE THOSE 0.71 OF 48 WHERE FOOD PRODUCTION IS BY SIMPLE AGRICULTURE, RATHER THAN BY INTENSIVE AGRICULTURE (101)	55	TEND TO BE THOSE 0.92 OF 13 WHERE FOOD PRODUCTION IS BY INTENSIVE AGRICULTURE, RATHER THAN BY SIMPLE AGRICULTURE (91)	14 12 34 1 XSQ= 14.19 PHI= -0.482 XP = 0.0002
63	TILT LESS TOWARD BEING THOSE 0.57 OF 46 WHERE HUSBANDRY, IF PRESENT, IS PRINCIPALLY IN THE FORM OF BOVINE, EQUINE, CAMEL-LIKE, OR DEER-LIKE ANIMALS, RATHER THAN PIGS, SHEEP, OR GOATS (152)	63	TILT MORE TOWARD BEING THOSE 0.88 OF 17 WHERE HUSBANDRY, IF PRESENT, IS PRINCIPALLY IN THE FORM OF BOVINE, EQUINE, CAMEL-LIKE, OR DEER-LIKE ANIMALS, RATHER THAN PIGS, SHEEP, OR GOATS (152)	26 15 20 2 XSQ= 4.19 PHI= -0.258 XP = 0.0407

88	TEND TO BE THOSE WHERE, IF A HEADMANSHIP IS PRESENT, SUCCESSION IS HEREDITARY (165)	0.81 OF 48	88	TEND TO BE THOSE WHERE, IF A HEADMANSHIP IS PRESENT, SUCCESSION IS NON-HEREDITARY (106)	0.82 OF 11	9 9 39 2	XSQ= 13.95 PHI= -0.486 XP = 0.0002
108	TILT TOWARD BEING THOSE WHERE CLASS STRATIFICATION, IF PRESENT, IS BASED ON A HEREDITARY ARISTOCRACY (74)	0.65 OF 40	108	TILT TOWARD BEING THOSE WHERE CLASS STRATIFICATION, IF PRESENT, IS BASED ON SOMETHING OTHER THAN A HEREDITARY ARISTOCRACY (129)	0.79 OF 14	26 3 14 11	XSQ= 6.26 PHI= 0.341 XP = 0.0123
109	LEAN TOWARD BEING THOSE WHERE CASTES ARE ABSENT (317)	0.78 OF 60	109	LEAN TOWARD BEING THOSE WHERE CASTES ARE PRESENT (51)	0.67 OF 15	13 10 47 5	XSQ= 9.41 PHI= -0.354 XP = 0.0022
128	TILT TOWARD BEING THOSE WHERE, IF SUBSISTENCE IS PRIMARILY BY AGRICULTURE, THE WORK IS MAINLY DONE BY FEMALES (37)	0.71 OF 28	128	IN ALL CASES ARE THOSE WHERE, IF SUBSISTENCE IS PRIMARILY BY AGRICULTURE, THE WORK IS MAINLY DONE BY MALES (40)	1.00 OF 4	8 4 20 0	XSQ= 4.88 PHI= -0.390 EP = 0.0138
129	IN ALL CASES ARE THOSE WHERE WEAVING IS MAINLY DONE BY MALES (31)	1.00 OF 13	129	TILT TOWARD BEING THOSE WHERE WEAVING IS MAINLY DONE BY FEMALES (73)	0.60 OF 5	13 2 0 3	XSQ= 5.54 PHI= 0.555 EP = 0.0123
181	IN ALL CASES ARE THOSE WHERE THE COMMUNITY IS OTHER THAN A DEME (337)	1.00 OF 60	181	TILT LESS TOWARD BEING THOSE WHERE THE COMMUNITY IS OTHER THAN A DEME (337)	0.83 OF 18	0 3 60 15	XSQ= 6.38 PHI= -0.286 XP = 0.0115
184	LEAN MORE TOWARD BEING THOSE WHERE THE LARGEST NON-COGNATIC KIN GROUP IS SMALLER THAN A PHRATRY, I. E. A SIB OR LINEAGE (175)	0.91 OF 57	184	LEAN LESS TOWARD BEING THOSE WHERE THE LARGEST NON-COGNATIC KIN GROUP IS SMALLER THAN A PHRATRY, I. E. A SIB OR LINEAGE (175)	0.62 OF 21	5 8 52 13	XSQ= 7.51 PHI= -0.310 XP = 0.0061
186	TILT LESS TOWARD BEING THOSE WHERE THE KIN GROUP IS EXCLUSIVELY PATRILINEAL (150)	0.56 OF 61	186	TILT MORE TOWARD BEING THOSE WHERE THE KIN GROUP IS EXCLUSIVELY PATRILINEAL (150)	0.86 OF 21	34 18 27 3	XSQ= 4.83 PHI= -0.243 XP = 0.0280
190	DRIFT LESS TOWARD BEING THOSE WHERE THE KIN GROUP IS PATRILINEAL OR DOUBLE-DESCENT, RATHER THAN MATRILINEAL (186)	0.82 OF 56	190	IN ALL CASES ARE THOSE WHERE THE KIN GROUP IS PATRILINEAL OR DOUBLE-DESCENT, RATHER THAN MATRILINEAL (186)	1.00 OF 21	46 21 10 0	XSQ= 2.87 PHI= -0.193 XP = 0.0900

213	DRIFT TOWARD BEING THOSE 0.52 OF 60 WHERE FIRST COUSIN MARRIAGE IS NOT PERMITTED (198)	213	DRIFT TOWARD BEING THOSE 0.78 OF 18 WHERE FIRST COUSIN MARRIAGE IS PERMITTED (172)	29 14 31 4 XSQ= 3.74 PHI= -0.219 XP = 0.0533
300	TILT TOWARD BEING THOSE 0.64 OF 28 WHERE THE POST-PARTUM SEX TABOO LASTS LONGER THAN SIX MONTHS (51)	300	IN ALL CASES ARE THOSE 1.00 OF 4 WHERE THE POST-PARTUM SEX TABOO LASTS SIX MONTHS OR LESS (73)	18 0 10 4 XSQ= 3.56 PHI= 0.333 EP = 0.0278
314	DRIFT TOWARD BEING THOSE 0.92 OF 12 WHERE THE INCIDENCE OF MOTHER-CHILD HOUSEHOLDS IS HIGH (19) W-D,S	314	DRIFT TOWARD BEING THOSE 0.67 OF 3 WHERE THE INCIDENCE OF MOTHER-CHILD HOUSEHOLDS IS LOW (61) W-D,S	11 1 1 2 XSQ= 2.11 PHI= 0.375 EP = 0.0813
370	TEND TO BE THOSE 0.72 OF 39 WHERE THE SEGREGATION OF ADOLESCENT BOYS IS COMPLETE OR PARTIAL (95)	370	TEND TO BE THOSE 0.91 OF 11 WHERE THE SEGREGATION OF ADOLESCENT BOYS IS ABSENT (148)	28 1 11 10 XSQ= 11.39 PHI= 0.477 XP = 0.0007
377	DRIFT LESS TOWARD BEING THOSE 0.60 OF 50 WHERE MALE GENITAL MUTILATION IS PRESENT (83)	377	DRIFT MORE TOWARD BEING THOSE 0.88 OF 17 WHERE MALE GENITAL MUTILATION IS PRESENT (83)	30 15 20 2 XSQ= 3.40 PHI= -0.225 XP = 0.0654
382	TILT TOWARD BEING THOSE 0.78 OF 9 WHERE FEMALE INITIATION RITES ARE PRESENT (38) JKB	382	IN ALL CASES ARE THOSE 1.00 OF 4 WHERE FEMALE INITIATION RITES ARE ABSENT (27) JKB	7 0 2 4 XSQ= 3.97 PHI= 0.553 EP = 0.0210
390	DRIFT TOWARD BEING THOSE 0.78 OF 23 WHERE PREMARITAL SEX RELATIONS ARE WEAKLY PUNISHED AND IN FACT NOT RARE OR PUNISHED ONLY IF PREGNANCY RESULTS, OR FREELY PERMITTED (132) JTW,EA	390	DRIFT TOWARD BEING THOSE 0.63 OF 8 WHERE PREMARITAL SEX RELATIONS ARE STRONGLY PUNISHED AND IN FACT RARE (47) JTW,EA	5 5 18 3 XSQ= 2.84 PHI= -0.303 EP = 0.0742
391	TILT TOWARD BEING THOSE 0.57 OF 23 WHERE PREMARITAL SEX RELATIONS ARE PUNISHED ONLY IF PREGNANCY RESULTS, OR FREELY PERMITTED (90) JTW,EA	391	TILT TOWARD BEING THOSE 0.88 OF 8 WHERE PREMARITAL SEX RELATIONS ARE STRONGLY PUNISHED AND IN FACT RARE, OR WEAKLY PUNISHED AND IN FACT NOT RARE (89) JTW,EA	10 7 13 1 XSQ= 3.04 PHI= -0.313 EP = 0.0454
427	TEND TO BE THOSE 0.68 OF 34 WHERE A HIGH GOD, IF PRESENT, IS INACTIVE, RATHER THAN ACTIVE (69) GES,EA	427	TEND TO BE THOSE 0.93 OF 14 WHERE A HIGH GOD, IF PRESENT, IS ACTIVE, RATHER THAN INACTIVE (87) GES,EA	11 13 23 1 XSQ= 12.20 PHI= -0.504 XP = 0.0005

428	LEAN TOWARD BEING THOSE 0.55 OF 11 WHERE A HIGH GOD, IF PRESENT AND ACTIVE, DOES NOT SUPPORT HUMAN MORALITY, RATHER THAN SUPPORTING IT (26) GES,EA	428	IN ALL CASES ARE THOSE 1.00 OF 13 WHERE A HIGH GOD, IF PRESENT AND ACTIVE, SUPPORTS HUMAN MORALITY, RATHER THAN NOT SUPPORTING IT (61) GES,EA	5 13 6 0 XSQ= 6.77 PHI= -0.531 EP = 0.0034

****

21 CULTURES WHOSE LINGUISTIC AFFILIATICN IS INDO-EURCPEAN (28)	21 CULTURES WHOSE LINGUISTIC AFFILIATICN IS OTHER THAN INDO-EUROPEAN (372)

BACKGROUND ON PAGE 67 SUBJECT ONLY

....

28 IN LEFT COLUMN

ALBANIANS AMERICANS ARYANS BASSERI BENGALI BHIL BOERS BRAZILIANS BULGARIANS CAMBA
CZECHS DARD DUTCH HUTSUL ICELANDERS IRISH KOHISTANI NURI PATHAN PORTUGUESE
ROMANS SARAMACCA SERBS SINCHI SINHALESE TRISTAN VEDDA WALLOONS

372 IN RIGHT COLUMN

3	IN ALL CASES ARE THCSE LCCATED OUTSIDE CF AFRICA (320)	1.00 OF 28	3	TILT LESS TOWARD BEING THOSE LOCATED OUTSIDE OF AFRICA (320)	0.78 OF 372	0 80 28 292 XSQ= 6.24 PHI= -0.125 XP = 0.0125
4	TEND TC BE THCSE LOCATED IN THE CIRCUM-MEDITERRANEAN (45)	0.54 OF 28	4	TEND TO BE THOSE LOCATED OUTSIDE OF THE CIRCUM-MEDITERRANEAN (355)	0.92 OF 372	15 30 13 342 XSQ= 49.55 PHI= 0.352 XP = 0.
5	LEAN LESS TOWARD BEING THCSE LCCATED CUTSIDE CF EAST EURASIA (330)	0.61 OF 28	5	LEAN MORE TOWARD BEING THOSE LOCATED OUTSIDE OF EAST EURASIA (330)	0.84 OF 372	11 59 17 313 XSQ= 8.34 PHI= 0.144 XP = 0.0039
6	IN ALL CASES ARE THOSE LOCATED OUTSIDE OF THE INSULAR PACIFIC (330)	1.00 OF 28	6	TILT LESS TOWARD BEING THOSE LOCATED OUTSIDE OF THE INSULAR PACIFIC (330)	0.81 OF 372	0 70 28 302 XSQ= 5.15 PHI= -0.113 XP = 0.0233
8	IN ALL CASES ARE THOSE LOCATED CUTSIDE CF NORTH AMERICA (330)	1.00 OF 28	8	TILT LESS TOWARD BEING THCSE LOCATED OUTSIDE OF NORTH AMERICA (330)	0.81 OF 372	0 70 28 302 XSQ= 5.15 PHI= -0.113 XP = 0.0233

```
14  TEND TO BE THOSE                0.68 OF  28     14  TEND TO BE THOSE                0.73 OF 372          19  100
    WHERE THE LATITUDE IS                               WHERE THE LATITUDE IS                                 9  272
    THIRTY DEGREES OR GREATER  (119)                    LESS THAN THIRTY DEGREES  (281)             XSQ=    19.00
                                                                                                    PHI=    0.218
                                                                                                    XP =   0.0000

15  TEND TO BE THOSE                0.82 OF  28     15  TEND TO BE THOSE                0.57 OF 372          23  160
    WHERE THE LATITUDE IS                               WHERE THE LATITUDE IS                                 5  212
    TWENTY DEGREES OR GREATER  (183)                    LESS THAN TWENTY DEGREES  (217)             XSQ=    14.53
                                                                                                    PHI=    0.191
                                                                                                    XP =   0.0001

42  DRIFT MORE TOWARD BEING THOSE  0.79 OF  28     42  DRIFT LESS TOWARD BEING THOSE  0.60 OF 372            6  150
    WHERE THE NATURAL ENVIRONMENT IS                    WHERE THE NATURAL ENVIRONMENT IS                     22  222
    OTHER THAN                                          OTHER THAN                                  XSQ=     3.15
    TROPICAL OR SUB-TROPICAL RAIN FOREST, OR            TROPICAL OR SUB-TROPICAL RAIN FOREST, OR    PHI=   -0.089
    MONSOON FOREST  (244) FWM                           MONSOON FOREST  (244) FWM                   XP =   0.0758

51  DRIFT MORE TOWARD BEING THOSE  0.82 OF  28     51  DRIFT LESS TOWARD BEING THOSE  0.62 OF 372           23  230
    WHERE SUBSISTENCE IS PRIMARILY BY                   WHERE SUBSISTENCE IS PRIMARILY BY                     5  142
    FOOD PRODUCTION -- I. E., AGRICULTURE               FOOD PRODUCTION -- I. E., AGRICULTURE       XSQ=     3.79
    OR HUSBANDRY -- RATHER THAN BY                      OR HUSBANDRY -- RATHER THAN BY              PHI=    0.097
    GATHERING  (253)                                    GATHERING  (253)                            XP =   0.0515

53  TEND TO BE THOSE                0.80 OF  20     53  TEND TO BE THOSE                0.66 OF 218          16   75
    WHERE FOOD PRODUCTION IS BY                         WHERE FOOD PRODUCTION IS BY                           4  143
    INTENSIVE AGRICULTURE, RATHER THAN BY               SIMPLE AGRICULTURE OR                       XSQ=    14.25
    SIMPLE AGRICULTURE OR                               INCIPIENT FOOD PRODUCTION, RATHER THAN BY   PHI=    0.245
    INCIPIENT FOOD PRODUCTION  (91)                     INTENSIVE AGRICULTURE  (147)                XP =   0.0002

55  IN ALL CASES ARE THOSE          1.00 OF  16     55  TEND TO BE THOSE                0.57 OF 176          16   75
    WHERE FOOD PRODUCTION IS BY                         WHERE FOOD PRODUCTION IS BY                           0  101
    INTENSIVE AGRICULTURE, RATHER THAN BY               SIMPLE AGRICULTURE, RATHER THAN BY          XSQ=    17.14
    SIMPLE AGRICULTURE  (91)                            INTENSIVE AGRICULTURE  (101)                PHI=    0.299
                                                                                                    XP =   0.0000

56  IN ALL CASES ARE THOSE          1.00 OF   4     56  TILT TOWARD BEING THOSE         0.71 OF 143           0  101
    WHERE FOOD PRODUCTION IS BY                         WHERE FOOD PRODUCTION IS BY                           4   42
    INCIPIENT FOOD PRODUCTION, RATHER THAN BY           SIMPLE AGRICULTURE, RATHER THAN BY          XSQ=     6.04
    SIMPLE AGRICULTURE  (46)                            INCIPIENT FOOD PRODUCTION  (101)            PHI=   -0.203
                                                                                                    XP =   0.0140

63  TILT MORE TOWARD BEING THOSE   0.95 OF  20     63  TILT LESS TOWARD BEING THOSE   0.65 OF 206            19  133
    WHERE HUSBANDRY, IF PRESENT,                        WHERE HUSBANDRY, IF PRESENT,                          1   73
    IS PRINCIPALLY IN THE FORM OF                       IS PRINCIPALLY IN THE FORM OF               XSQ=     6.35
    BOVINE, EQUINE, CAMEL-LIKE, OR DEER-LIKE            BOVINE, EQUINE, CAMEL-LIKE, OR DEER-LIKE    PHI=    0.168
    ANIMALS, RATHER THAN                                ANIMALS, RATHER THAN                        XP =   0.0117
    PIGS, SHEEP, OR GOATS  (152)                        PIGS, SHEEP, OR GOATS  (152)

71  TEND TO BE THOSE                0.93 OF  14     71  TEND TO BE THOSE                0.64 OF 237          13   85
    WHERE METAL WORKING IS                              WHERE METAL WORKING IS                                1  152
    PRESENT  (98)                                       ABSENT  (153)                               XSQ=    15.73
                                                                                                    PHI=    0.250
                                                                                                    XP =   0.0001
```

73	TILT TCWARD BEING THOSE WHERE WEAVING IS PRESENT (118)	0.80 OF 15	73	TILT TOWARD BEING THOSE WHERE WEAVING IS ABSENT (130)	0.55 OF 233	12 106 3 127 XSQ= 5.42 PHI= 0.148 XP = 0.0200
79	TEND TC BE THCSE WHERE A CITY IS PRESENT (23)	0.53 OF 19	79	TEND TO BE THOSE WHERE NO CITY IS PRESENT (201)	0.94 CF 205	10 13 9 192 XSQ= 35.57 PHI= 0.398 XP = 0.
80	TEND TC BE THCSE WHERE A CITY CR TOWN IS PRESENT (39)	0.58 OF 19	80	TEND TO BE THOSE WHERE NO CITY OR TOWN IS PRESENT (185)	0.86 CF 205	11 28 8 177 XSQ= 20.69 PHI= 0.304 XP = 0.0000
81	TEND TC BE THCSE WHERE A CITY CR TOWN IS PRESENT, OR THE AVERAGE CCMMUNITY SIZE IS 200 CR GREATER (89)	0.84 OF 19	81	TEND TO BE THOSE WHERE NO CITY OR TOWN IS PRESENT, AND THE AVERAGE COMMUNITY SIZE IS SMALLER THAN 200 (135)	0.64 CF 205	16 73 3 132 XSQ= 15.18 PHI= 0.260 XP = 0.0001
83	TILT TOWARD BEING THOSE WHERE, WITH NC CITY ANC NC TOWN PRESENT, THE AVERAGE CCMMUNITY SIZE IS BETWEEN 200 AND 999, RATHER THAN SMALLER THAN 200 (45)	0.63 OF 8	83	TILT TOWARD BEING THOSE WHERE, WITH NO CITY AND NC TCWN PRESENT, THE AVERAGE COMMUNITY SIZE IS SMALLER THAN 200, RATHER THAN BETWEEN 200 AND 999 (135)	0.77 OF 172	5 40 3 132 XSQ= 4.36 PHI= 0.156 XP = 0.0368
84	TEND TC BE THCSE WHERE THE LEVEL OF POLITICAL INTEGRATION IS THE LARGE STATE (42) GPM	0.56 OF 16	84	TEND TO BE THOSE WHERE THE LEVEL OF POLITICAL INTEGRATION IS THE LITTLE STATE, THE MINIMAL STATE, THE AUTONOMOUS COMMUNITY, CR THE FAMILY (262) GPM	0.89 CF 288	9 33 7 255 XSQ= 21.92 PHI= 0.269 XP = 0.0000
85	TEND TC BE THCSE WHERE THE LEVEL CF PCLITICAL INTEGRATION IS THE LARGE STATE, CR THE LITTLE STATE (70) GPM	0.75 OF 16	85	TEND TO BE THOSE WHERE THE LEVEL OF PCLITICAL INTEGRATICN IS THE MINIMAL STATE, THE AUTONOMOUS COMMUNITY, CR THE FAMILY (234) GPM	0.80 OF 288	12 58 4 230 XSQ= 22.74 PHI= 0.273 XP = 0.0000
86	TEND TC BE THCSE WHERE THE LEVEL OF POLITICAL INTEGRATION IS THE LARGE STATE, THE LITTLE STATE, CR THE MINIMAL STATE (148) GPM	0.94 OF 16	86	TEND TO BE THOSE WHERE THE LEVEL OF POLITICAL INTEGRATION IS THE AUTONOMOUS COMMUNITY, OR THE FAMILY (156) GPM	0.54 CF 288	15 133 1 155 XSQ= 11.89 PHI= 0.198 XP = 0.0006
95	TEND TO BE THCSE WHERE THE HIERARCHY CF NATICNAL JURISDICTICN HAS FCUR, THREE, OR TWC LEVELS (76) GES,EA	0.68 OF 19	95	TEND TO BE THOSE WHERE THE HIERARCHY OF NATIONAL JURISDICTION HAS ONE OR NO LEVELS (254) GES,EA	0.80 CF 311	13 63 6 248 XSQ= 20.79 PHI= 0.251 XP = 0.0000

102	LEAN MORE TOWARD BEING THOSE WHERE CLASS STRATIFICATION IS PRESENT (203)	0.85 OF 26	102	LEAN LESS TOWARD BEING THOSE WHERE CLASS STRATIFICATION IS PRESENT (203)	0.51 OF 357	22 181 4 176 XSQ= 9.87 PHI= 0.161 XP = 0.0017
106	TILT MORE TOWARD BEING THOSE WHERE CLASS STRATIFICATION, IF PRESENT, IS BASED ON SOMETHING OTHER THAN WEALTH (126)	0.86 OF 22	106	TILT LESS TOWARD BEING THOSE WHERE CLASS STRATIFICATION, IF PRESENT, IS BASED ON SOMETHING OTHER THAN WEALTH (126)	0.59 OF 181	3 74 19 107 XSQ= 5.08 PHI= -0.158 XP = 0.0242
107	TEND TO BE THOSE WHERE CLASS STRATIFICATION, IF PRESENT, IS BASED ON OCCUPATIONAL STATUS (43)	0.59 OF 22	107	TEND TO BE THOSE WHERE CLASS STRATIFICATION, IF PRESENT, IS BASED ON SOMETHING OTHER THAN OCCUPATIONAL STATUS (160)	0.83 OF 181	13 30 9 151 XSQ= 18.77 PHI= 0.304 XP = 0.0000
108	LEAN MORE TOWARD BEING THOSE WHERE CLASS STRATIFICATION, IF PRESENT, IS BASED ON SOMETHING OTHER THAN A HEREDITARY ARISTOCRACY (129)	0.95 OF 22	108	LEAN LESS TOWARD BEING THOSE WHERE CLASS STRATIFICATION, IF PRESENT, IS BASED ON SOMETHING OTHER THAN A HEREDITARY ARISTOCRACY (129)	0.60 OF 181	1 73 21 108 XSQ= 9.35 PHI= -0.215 XP = 0.0022
109	TEND LESS TO BE THOSE WHERE CASTES ARE ABSENT (317)	0.58 OF 26	109	TEND MORE TO BE THOSE WHERE CASTES ARE ABSENT (317)	0.88 OF 342	11 40 15 302 XSQ= 16.49 PHI= 0.212 XP = 0.0000
130	IN ALL CASES ARE THOSE WHERE LEATHER WORKING IS MAINLY DONE BY MALES (39)	1.00 OF 5	130	TILT TOWARD BEING THOSE WHERE LEATHER WORKING IS MAINLY DONE BY FEMALES (45)	0.57 OF 79	5 34 0 45 XSQ= 4.06 PHI= 0.220 XP = 0.0440
176	TILT MORE TOWARD BEING THOSE WHERE THE COMMUNITY IS OTHER THAN A CLAN-COMMUNITY OR A COMMUNITY STRUCTURED OR SEGMENTED ON A CLAN BASIS (213)	0.79 OF 28	176	TILT LESS TOWARD BEING THOSE WHERE THE COMMUNITY IS OTHER THAN A CLAN-COMMUNITY OR A COMMUNITY STRUCTURED OR SEGMENTED ON A CLAN BASIS (213)	0.54 OF 354	6 163 22 191 XSQ= 5.42 PHI= -0.119 XP = 0.0200
177	TILT MORE TOWARD BEING THOSE WHERE THE COMMUNITY IS OTHER THAN A SINGLE CLAN-COMMUNITY AND EXOGAMOUS (305)	0.96 OF 28	177	TILT LESS TOWARD BEING THOSE WHERE THE COMMUNITY IS OTHER THAN A SINGLE CLAN-COMMUNITY AND EXOGAMOUS (305)	0.79 OF 354	1 76 27 278 XSQ= 4.11 PHI= -0.104 XP = 0.0426
180	DRIFT MORE TOWARD BEING THOSE WHERE THE COMMUNITY IS COMMONLY NON-EXOGAMOUS, RATHER THAN EXOGAMOUS (258)	0.86 OF 28	180	DRIFT LESS TOWARD BEING THOSE WHERE THE COMMUNITY IS COMMONLY NON-EXOGAMOUS, RATHER THAN EXOGAMOUS (258)	0.66 OF 354	4 120 24 234 XSQ= 3.70 PHI= -0.098 XP = 0.0544

182	TILT TOWARD BEING THOSE WHERE THE COMMUNITY IS STRUCTURED ON A NON-CLAN BASIS AND AGAMOUS (126)	0.54 OF 28	182	TILT TOWARD BEING THOSE OTHER THAN WHERE THE COMMUNITY IS STRUCTURED ON A NON-CLAN BASIS AND AGAMOUS (256)	0.69 OF 354	15 111 13 243 XSQ= 4.83 PHI= 0.112 XP = 0.0279
188	DRIFT TOWARD BEING THOSE WHERE THE KIN GROUP IS EXCLUSIVELY COGNATIC (148)	0.54 OF 28	188	DRIFT TOWARD BEING THOSE WHERE THE KIN GROUP IS OTHER THAN EXCLUSIVELY COGNATIC (252)	0.64 OF 372	15 133 13 239 XSQ= 2.82 PHI= 0.084 XP = 0.0929
192	TILT TOWARD BEING THOSE WHERE THE ONLY KIN GROUP PRESENT IS A KINDRED OR ELSE BILATERAL DESCENT IS INFERRED (111)	0.50 OF 28	192	TILT TOWARD BEING THOSE OTHER THAN WHERE THE ONLY KIN GROUP PRESENT IS A KINDRED OR ELSE BILATERAL DESCENT IS INFERRED (289)	0.74 OF 372	14 97 14 275 XSQ= 6.29 PHI= 0.125 XP = 0.0122
196	TILT MORE TOWARD BEING THOSE WHERE INDIVIDUAL RIGHTS IN REAL PROPERTY, AND RULES FOR INHERITANCE, ARE PRESENT (194)	0.95 OF 20	196	TILT LESS TOWARD BEING THOSE WHERE INDIVIDUAL RIGHTS IN REAL PROPERTY, AND RULES FOR INHERITANCE, ARE PRESENT (194)	0.67 OF 261	19 175 1 86 XSQ= 5.54 PHI= 0.140 XP = 0.0185
197	DRIFT LESS TOWARD BEING THOSE WHERE RULES FOR THE INHERITANCE OF REAL PROPERTY, IF PRESENT, FAVOR EITHER THE MALE HEIR OR LINE, OR THE FEMALE HEIR OR LINE (165)	0.68 OF 19	197	DRIFT MORE TOWARD BEING THOSE WHERE RULES FOR THE INHERITANCE OF REAL PROPERTY, IF PRESENT, FAVOR EITHER THE MALE HEIR OR LINE, OR THE FEMALE HEIR OR LINE (165)	0.87 OF 175	13 152 6 23 XSQ= 3.25 PHI= -0.129 XP = 0.0716
207	TILT TOWARD BEING THOSE WHERE MARITAL RESIDENCE IS AMBILOCAL OR NEOLOCAL, RATHER THAN MATRILOCAL OR UXORILOCAL (64)	0.89 OF 9	207	TILT TOWARD BEING THOSE WHERE MARITAL RESIDENCE IS MATRILOCAL OR UXORILOCAL, RATHER THAN AMBILOCAL OR NEOLOCAL (64)	0.53 OF 119	1 63 8 56 XSQ= 4.30 PHI= -0.183 XP = 0.0381
234	LEAN MORE TOWARD BEING THOSE WHERE THE COUSIN TERMINOLOGY IS OF ESKIMO OR HAWAIIAN TYPE, RATHER THAN CROW, OMAHA, OR IROQUOIS TYPE (170)	0.90 OF 20	234	LEAN LESS TOWARD BEING THOSE WHERE THE COUSIN TERMINOLOGY IS OF ESKIMO OR HAWAIIAN TYPE, RATHER THAN CROW, OMAHA, OR IROQUOIS TYPE (170)	0.50 OF 302	2 150 18 152 XSQ= 10.31 PHI= -0.179 XP = 0.0013
242	TEND TO BE THOSE WHERE MARRIAGE IS MONOGAMOUS, RATHER THAN COMMONLY OR OCCASIONALLY POLYGYNOUS (81)	0.61 OF 28	242	TEND TO BE THOSE WHERE MARRIAGE IS COMMONLY OR OCCASIONALLY POLYGYNOUS, RATHER THAN MONOGAMOUS (314)	0.83 OF 367	11 303 17 64 XSQ= 27.29 PHI= -0.263 XP = 0.0000
263	TILT TOWARD BEING THOSE WHERE WIVES ARE OBTAINED BY RELATIVELY EASY MEANS, NAMELY BY TOKEN BRIDE-PRICE, GIFT EXCHANGE, ABSENCE OF ANY CONSIDERATION, OR RECEIPT OF DOWRY (162)	0.64 OF 28	263	TILT TOWARD BEING THOSE WHERE WIVES ARE OBTAINED BY RELATIVELY DIFFICULT MEANS, NAMELY BY BRIDE-PRICE, BRIDE-SERVICE, OR EXCHANGING A FEMALE RELATIVE (233)	0.61 OF 367	10 223 18 144 XSQ= 5.75 PHI= -0.121 XP = 0.0165

301	IN ALL CASES ARE THOSE 1.00 OF 3 WHERE THE POST-PARTUM SEX TABOO LASTS ONE MONTH OR LESS (28)	301	TILT TOWARD BEING THOSE 0.79 OF 121 WHERE THE POST-PARTUM SEX TABOO LASTS LONGER THAN ONE MONTH (96)	0 96 3 25 XSQ= 6.49 PHI= -0.229 XP = 0.0108
370	IN ALL CASES ARE THOSE 1.00 OF 19 WHERE THE SEGREGATION OF ADOLESCENT BOYS IS ABSENT (148)	370	TEND LESS TO BE THOSE 0.58 OF 224 WHERE THE SEGREGATION OF ADOLESCENT BOYS IS ABSENT (148)	0 95 19 129 XSQ= 11.51 PHI= -0.218 XP = 0.0007
391	DRIFT TOWARD BEING THOSE 0.82 OF 11 WHERE PREMARITAL SEX RELATIONS ARE STRONGLY PUNISHED AND IN FACT RARE, OR WEAKLY PUNISHED AND IN FACT NOT RARE (89) JTW,EA	391	DRIFT TOWARD BEING THOSE 0.52 OF 168 WHERE PREMARITAL SEX RELATIONS ARE PUNISHED ONLY IF PREGNANCY RESULTS, OR FREELY PERMITTED (90) JTW,EA	9 80 2 88 XSQ= 3.56 PHI= 0.141 XP = 0.0592
426	TILT MORE TOWARD BEING THOSE 0.84 OF 19 WHERE A HIGH GOD IS PRESENT (156) GES,EA	426	TILT LESS TOWARD BEING THOSE 0.58 OF 241 WHERE A HIGH GOD IS PRESENT (156) GES,EA	16 140 3 101 XSQ= 3.98 PHI= 0.124 XP = 0.0461
427	IN ALL CASES ARE THOSE 1.00 OF 16 WHERE A HIGH GOD, IF PRESENT, IS ACTIVE, RATHER THAN INACTIVE (87) GES,EA	427	TEND LESS TO BE THOSE 0.51 OF 140 WHERE A HIGH GOD, IF PRESENT, IS ACTIVE, RATHER THAN INACTIVE (87) GES,EA	16 71 0 69 XSQ= 12.21 PHI= 0.280 XP = 0.0005
428	TILT MORE TOWARD BEING THOSE 0.94 OF 16 WHERE A HIGH GOD, IF PRESENT AND ACTIVE, SUPPORTS HUMAN MORALITY, RATHER THAN NOT SUPPORTING IT (61) GES,EA	428	TILT LESS TOWARD BEING THOSE 0.65 OF 71 WHERE A HIGH GOD, IF PRESENT AND ACTIVE, SUPPORTS HUMAN MORALITY, RATHER THAN NOT SUPPORTING IT (61) GES,EA	15 46 1 25 XSQ= 3.94 PHI= 0.213 XP = 0.0473
458	LEAN TOWARD BEING THOSE 0.78 OF 9 WHERE GAMES, IF PRESENT, INCLUDE GAMES OF STRATEGY (52) R-A-B,EA	458	LEAN TOWARD BEING THOSE 0.72 OF 162 WHERE GAMES, IF PRESENT, DO NOT INCLUDE GAMES OF STRATEGY (119) R-A-B,EA	7 45 2 117 XSQ= 7.85 PHI= 0.214 XP = 0.0051

****

22 CULTURES
WHERE THE LINGUISTIC AFFILIATION IS
INDO-EUROPEAN, RATHER THAN
AFRO-ASIATIC (28)

22 CULTURES
WHERE THE LINGUISTIC AFFILIATION IS
AFRO-ASIATIC, RATHER THAN
INDO-EUROPEAN (21)

BACKGROUND ON PAGE 67

SUBJECT ONLY

28 IN LEFT COLUMN

ALBANIANS	AMERICANS	ARYANS	BASSERI	BENGALI	BHIL	BOERS	BRAZILIANS	BULGARIANS	CAMBA
CZECHS	DARD	DUTCH	HUTSUL	ICELANDERS	IRISH	KOHISTANI	NURI	PATHAN	PORTUGUESE
ROMANS	SARAMACCA	SERBS	SINDHI	SINHALESE	TRISTAN	VEDDA	WALLOONS		

21 IN RIGHT COLUMN

BEJA	BUDUMA	EGYPTIANS	HASANIA	HEBREWS	IRAQW	KABYLE	KONSO	MAGUZAWA	MARGI
MATAKAM	MZAB	REGEIBAT	RIFFIANS	RWALA	SHLUH	SIWANS	SOMALI	SYRIANS	TERA
TIGRINYA									

351 EXCLUDED BECAUSE IRRELEVANT

4	TILT LESS TOWARD BEING THOSE LOCATED IN THE CIRCUM-MEDITERRANEAN (45)	0.54 OF 28	TILT MORE TOWARD BEING THOSE LOCATED IN THE CIRCUM-MEDITERRANEAN (45)	0.90 OF 21	15 19 13 2 XSQ= 6.05 PHI= -0.352 XP = 0.0139
5	LEAN LESS TOWARD BEING THOSE LOCATED OUTSIDE OF EAST EURASIA (330)	0.61 OF 28	IN ALL CASES ARE THOSE LOCATED OUTSIDE OF EAST EURASIA (330)	1.00 OF 21	11 0 17 21 XSQ= 8.50 PHI= 0.417 XP = 0.0035
13	LEAN LESS TOWARD BEING THOSE WHERE THE LATITUDE IS LESS THAN FORTY DEGREES (329)	0.57 OF 28	IN ALL CASES ARE THOSE WHERE THE LATITUDE IS LESS THAN FORTY DEGREES (329)	1.00 OF 21	12 0 16 21 XSQ= 9.71 PHI= 0.445 XP = 0.0018
14	TILT TOWARD BEING THOSE WHERE THE LATITUDE IS THIRTY DEGREES OR GREATER (119)	0.68 OF 28	TILT TOWARD BEING THOSE WHERE THE LATITUDE IS LESS THAN THIRTY DEGREES (281)	0.67 OF 21	19 7 9 14 XSQ= 4.44 PHI= 0.301 XP = 0.0351

42	DRIFT LESS TOWARD BEING THOSE 0.79 OF 28 WHERE THE NATURAL ENVIRONMENT IS OTHER THAN TROPICAL OR SUB-TROPICAL RAIN FOREST, OR MONSOON FOREST (244) FWM	42	IN ALL CASES ARE THOSE 1.00 OF 21 WHERE THE NATURAL ENVIRONMENT IS OTHER THAN TROPICAL OR SUB-TROPICAL RAIN FOREST, OR MONSOON FOREST (244) FWM	6 0 22 21 XSQ= 3.33 PHI= 0.261 XP = 0.0681
84	DRIFT TOWARD BEING THOSE 0.56 OF 16 WHERE THE LEVEL OF POLITICAL INTEGRATION IS THE LARGE STATE (42) GPM	84	DRIFT TOWARD BEING THOSE 0.81 OF 16 WHERE THE LEVEL OF POLITICAL INTEGRATION IS THE LITTLE STATE, THE MINIMAL STATE, THE AUTONOMOUS COMMUNITY, OR THE FAMILY (262) GPM	9 3 7 13 XSQ= 3.33 PHI= 0.323 EP = 0.0659
97	LEAN MORE TOWARD BEING THOSE 0.95 OF 19 WHERE THE HIERARCHY OF LOCAL JURISDICTION HAS THREE OR TWO LEVELS (273) GES,EA	97	LEAN LESS TOWARD BEING THOSE 0.53 OF 17 WHERE THE HIERARCHY OF LOCAL JURISDICTION HAS THREE OR TWO LEVELS (273) GES,EA	1 8 18 9 XSQ= 6.28 PHI= -0.418 EP = 0.0061
98	LEAN LESS TOWARD BEING THOSE 0.63 OF 19 WHERE THE HIERARCHY OF LOCAL JURISDICTION HAS FOUR OR THREE LEVELS (238) GES,EA	98	IN ALL CASES ARE THOSE 1.00 OF 17 WHERE THE HIERARCHY OF LOCAL JURISDICTION HAS FOUR OR THREE LEVELS (238) GES,EA	12 17 7 0 XSQ= 5.60 PHI= -0.394 EP = 0.0084
106	TILT TOWARD BEING THOSE 0.86 OF 22 WHERE CLASS STRATIFICATION, IF PRESENT, IS BASED ON SOMETHING OTHER THAN WEALTH (126)	106	TILT TOWARD BEING THOSE 0.50 OF 14 WHERE CLASS STRATIFICATION, IF PRESENT, IS BASED ON WEALTH (77)	3 7 19 7 XSQ= 3.97 PHI= -0.332 EP = 0.0262
107	TILT TOWARD BEING THOSE 0.59 OF 22 WHERE CLASS STRATIFICATION, IF PRESENT, IS BASED ON OCCUPATIONAL STATUS (43)	107	TILT TOWARD BEING THOSE 0.79 OF 14 WHERE CLASS STRATIFICATION, IF PRESENT, IS BASED ON SOMETHING OTHER THAN OCCUPATIONAL STATUS (160)	13 3 9 11 XSQ= 3.51 PHI= 0.312 EP = 0.0407
110	LEAN TOWARD BEING THOSE 0.72 OF 25 WHERE SLAVERY IS ABSENT (218)	110	LEAN TOWARD BEING THOSE 0.74 OF 19 WHERE SLAVERY IS PRESENT (163)	7 14 18 5 XSQ= 7.29 PHI= -0.407 XP = 0.0069
131	IN ALL CASES ARE THOSE 1.00 OF 11 WHERE THE CONSTRUCTION OF PERMANENT HOUSES OR THE ERECTION OF TEMPORARY DWELLINGS IS MAINLY DONE BY MALES (136)	131	DRIFT LESS TOWARD BEING THOSE 0.60 OF 5 WHERE THE CONSTRUCTION OF PERMANENT HOUSES OR THE ERECTION OF TEMPORARY DWELLINGS IS MAINLY DONE BY MALES (136)	11 3 0 2 XSQ= 2.04 PHI= 0.357 EP = 0.0833
175	DRIFT TOWARD BEING THOSE 0.79 OF 28 WHERE THE COMMUNITY IS 'KIN-HETEROGENEOUS,' I. E. OTHER THAN A CLAN COMMUNITY OR A DEME (260)	175	DRIFT TOWARD BEING THOSE 0.50 OF 18 WHERE THE COMMUNITY IS 'KIN-HOMOGENEOUS,' I. E. A CLAN COMMUNITY OR A DEME (122)	6 9 22 9 XSQ= 2.87 PHI= -0.250 XP = 0.0900

176	TILT TOWARD BEING THOSE WHERE THE COMMUNITY IS OTHER THAN A CLAN-COMMUNITY OR A COMMUNITY STRUCTURED OR SEGMENTED ON A CLAN BASIS (213)	0.79 OF	28	176	TILT TOWARD BEING THOSE WHERE THE COMMUNITY IS A CLAN-COMMUNITY OR A COMMUNITY STRUCTURED OR SEGMENTED ON A CLAN BASIS (169)	0.56 OF	18	6 10 22 8 XSQ= 4.22 PHI= -0.303 XP = 0.0399
177	TILT MORE TOWARD BEING THOSE WHERE THE COMMUNITY IS OTHER THAN A SINGLE CLAN-COMMUNITY AND EXOGAMOUS (305)	0.96 OF	28	177	TILT LESS TOWARD BEING THOSE WHERE THE COMMUNITY IS OTHER THAN A SINGLE CLAN-COMMUNITY AND EXOGAMOUS (305)	0.67 OF	18	1 6 27 12 XSQ= 5.39 PHI= -0.342 XP = 0.0202
182	DRIFT TOWARD BEING THOSE WHERE THE COMMUNITY IS STRUCTURED ON A NON-CLAN BASIS AND AGAMOUS (126)	0.54 OF	28	182	DRIFT TOWARD BEING THOSE OTHER THAN WHERE THE COMMUNITY IS STRUCTURED ON A NON-CLAN BASIS AND AGAMOUS (256)	0.78 OF	18	15 4 13 14 XSQ= 3.24 PHI= 0.265 XP = 0.0718
186	TEND TO BE THOSE WHERE THE KIN GROUP IS OTHER THAN EXCLUSIVELY PATRILINEAL (250)	0.75 OF	28	186	TEND TO BE THOSE WHERE THE KIN GROUP IS EXCLUSIVELY PATRILINEAL (150)	0.86 OF	21	7 18 21 3 XSQ= 15.36 PHI= -0.560 XP = 0.0001
188	TEND TO BE THOSE WHERE THE KIN GROUP IS EXCLUSIVELY COGNATIC (148)	0.54 OF	28	188	IN ALL CASES ARE THOSE WHERE THE KIN GROUP IS OTHER THAN EXCLUSIVELY COGNATIC (252)	1.00 OF	21	15 0 13 21 XSQ= 13.79 PHI= 0.530 XP = 0.0002
192	TEND TO BE THOSE WHERE THE ONLY KIN GROUP PRESENT IS A KINDRED OR ELSE BILATERAL DESCENT IS INFERRED (111)	0.50 OF	28	192	IN ALL CASES ARE THOSE OTHER THAN WHERE THE ONLY KIN GROUP PRESENT IS A KINDRED OR ELSE BILATERAL DESCENT IS INFERRED (289)	1.00 OF	21	14 0 14 21 XSQ= 12.35 PHI= 0.502 XP = 0.0004
197	TILT LESS TOWARD BEING THOSE WHERE RULES FOR THE INHERITANCE OF REAL PROPERTY, IF PRESENT, FAVOR EITHER THE MALE HEIR OR LINE, OR THE FEMALE HEIR OR LINE (165)	0.68 OF	19	197	IN ALL CASES ARE THOSE WHERE RULES FOR THE INHERITANCE OF REAL PROPERTY, IF PRESENT, FAVOR EITHER THE MALE HEIR OR LINE, OR THE FEMALE HEIR OR LINE (165)	1.00 OF	14	13 14 6 0 XSQ= 3.49 PHI= -0.325 EP = 0.0272
201	TILT LESS TOWARD BEING THOSE WHERE MARITAL RESIDENCE IS NON-OPTIONAL, RATHER THAN AMBILOCAL OR NEOLOCAL (334)	0.71 OF	28	201	IN ALL CASES ARE THOSE WHERE MARITAL RESIDENCE IS NON-OPTIONAL, RATHER THAN AMBILOCAL OR NEOLOCAL (334)	1.00 OF	21	20 21 8 0 XSQ= 5.23 PHI= -0.327 XP = 0.0222
204	TILT LESS TOWARD BEING THOSE WHERE MARITAL RESIDENCE IS PATRILOCAL, VIRILOCAL, OR AVUNCULOCAL, RATHER THAN AMBILOCAL OR NEOLOCAL (270)	0.70 OF	27	204	IN ALL CASES ARE THOSE WHERE MARITAL RESIDENCE IS PATRILOCAL, VIRILOCAL, OR AVUNCULOCAL, RATHER THAN AMBILOCAL OR NEOLOCAL (270)	1.00 OF	21	19 21 8 0 XSQ= 5.49 PHI= -0.338 XP = 0.0192

```
234  LEAN TOWARD BEING THOSE           0.90 OF  20     234  LEAN TOWARD BEING THOSE            0.63 OF   8          2    5
     WHERE THE COUSIN TERMINOLOGY IS                        WHERE THE COUSIN TERMINOLOGY IS                        18    3
     OF ESKIMO OR HAWAIIAN TYPE,                            OF CROW, OMAHA, OR IROQUOIS TYPE,               XSQ=     5.83
     RATHER THAN                                            RATHER THAN                                     PHI=   -0.456
     CROW, OMAHA, OR IROQUOIS TYPE  (170)                   ESKIMO OR HAWAIIAN TYPE  (152)                  EP =   0.0095

242  LEAN TOWARD BEING THOSE           0.61 OF  28     242  LEAN TOWARD BEING THOSE            0.86 OF  21         11   18
     WHERE MARRIAGE IS MONOGAMOUS,                          WHERE MARRIAGE IS                                      17    3
     RATHER THAN COMMONLY OR OCCASIONALLY                   COMMONLY OR OCCASIONALLY POLYGYNOUS,            XSQ=     8.87
     POLYGYNOUS  (81)                                       RATHER THAN MONOGAMOUS  (314)                   PHI=   -0.426
                                                                                                            XP =   0.0029

263  TEND TO BE THOSE                  0.64 OF  28     263  TEND TO BE THOSE                   0.90 OF  21         10   19
     WHERE WIVES ARE OBTAINED                               WHERE WIVES ARE OBTAINED BY                            18    2
     BY RELATIVELY EASY MEANS, NAMELY BY                    RELATIVELY DIFFICULT MEANS, NAMELY BY           XSQ=    12.72
     TOKEN BRIDE-PRICE, GIFT EXCHANGE,                      BRIDE-PRICE, BRIDE-SERVICE, OR                  PHI=   -0.509
     ABSENCE OF ANY CONSIDERATION, OR                       EXCHANGING A FEMALE RELATIVE  (233)             XP =   0.0004
     RECEIPT OF DOWRY  (162)

301  IN ALL CASES ARE THOSE            1.00 OF   3     301  IN ALL CASES ARE THOSE             1.00 OF   4          0    4
     WHERE THE POST-PARTUM SEX TABOO LASTS                  WHERE THE POST-PARTUM SEX TABOO LASTS                   3    0
     ONE MONTH OR LESS  (28)                                LONGER THAN ONE MONTH  (96)                     XSQ=     3.51
                                                                                                            PHI=   -0.708
                                                                                                            EP =   0.0286

377  TEND TO BE THOSE                  0.84 OF  19     377  TEND TO BE THOSE                   0.88 OF  17          3   15
     WHERE MALE GENITAL MUTILATION                          WHERE MALE GENITAL MUTILATION                          16    2
     IS ABSENT  (242)                                       IS PRESENT  (83)                                XSQ=    16.05
                                                                                                            PHI=   -0.668
                                                                                                            EP =   0.0000
```

23 CULTURES
WHOSE LINGUISTIC AFFILIATION IS
ALTAIC (11)

23 CULTURES
WHOSE LINGUISTIC AFFILIATION IS
OTHER THAN ALTAIC (389)

BACKGROUND ON PAGE 67

NEITHER SUBJECT NOR PREDICATE

11 IN LEFT COLUMN

BURYAT DAGUR HAZARA KALMYK KAZAK KHALKA KUMYK MANCHU MONGUOR TURKMEN
YAKUT

389 IN RIGHT COLUMN

24 CULTURES
WHOSE LINGUISTIC AFFILIATION IS
MALAYO-POLYNESIAN (60)

24 CULTURES
WHOSE LINGUISTIC AFFILIATION IS
OTHER THAN MALAYO-POLYNESIAN (340)

BACKGROUND ON PAGE 67

SUBJECT ONLY

60 IN LEFT COLUMN

AJIE	ALORESE	ATAYAL	BALINESE	BATAK	BELU	BUNLAP	DOBUANS	DUSUN	ELLICE
GILBERTESE	HANUNOO	HAWAIIANS	IBAN	IFUGAO	JAVANESE	KURTATCHI	LAKALAI	LAU	LESU
LIFU	MACASSARESE	MALAYS	MANGAIANS	MANIHIKI	MANUS	MAORI	MARQUESANS	MARSHALLESE	MENTAWEI
MERINA	MINANGKABAU	MOTA	ONTONG-JAVA	PAIWAN	PALAUANS	PONAPEANS	PUKAPUKA	RAROIANS	ROTINESE
ROTUMANS	SAGADA	SAMOANS	SELUNG	SENIANG	SIMBOESE	SUBANUN	TAGBANUA	TANALA	TANIMBARESE
TIKOPIA	TOKELAU	TORAJA	TROBRIAND	TRUKESE	ULAWANS	WAROPEN	WOGEO	WOLEAIANS	YAPESE

340 IN RIGHT COLUMN

	Malayo-Polynesian (60)			Other (340)		
3	IN ALL CASES ARE THOSE LOCATED OUTSIDE OF AFRICA (320)	1.00 OF 60	3	TEND LESS TO BE THOSE LOCATED OUTSIDE OF AFRICA (320)	0.76 OF 340	0 80 60 260 XSQ= 16.21 PHI= -0.201 XP = 0.0001
4	IN ALL CASES ARE THOSE LOCATED OUTSIDE OF THE CIRCUM-MEDITERRANEAN (355)	1.00 OF 60	4	LEAN LESS TOWARD BEING THOSE LOCATED OUTSIDE OF THE CIRCUM-MEDITERRANEAN (355)	0.87 OF 340	0 45 60 295 XSQ= 7.67 PHI= -0.138 XP = 0.0056
5	TILT MORE TOWARD BEING THOSE LOCATED OUTSIDE OF EAST EURASIA (330)	0.93 OF 60	5	TILT LESS TOWARD BEING THOSE LOCATED OUTSIDE OF EAST EURASIA (330)	0.81 OF 340	4 66 56 274 XSQ= 4.89 PHI= -0.111 XP = 0.0270
6	TEND TO BE THOSE LOCATED IN THE INSULAR PACIFIC (70)	0.93 OF 60	6	TEND TO BE THOSE LOCATED OUTSIDE OF THE INSULAR PACIFIC (330)	0.96 OF 340	56 14 4 326 XSQ= 275.02 PHI= 0.829 XP = 0.
8	IN ALL CASES ARE THOSE LOCATED OUTSIDE OF NORTH AMERICA (330)	1.00 OF 60	8	TEND LESS TO BE THOSE LOCATED OUTSIDE OF NORTH AMERICA (330)	0.79 OF 340	0 70 60 270 XSQ= 13.58 PHI= -0.184 XP = 0.0002

9	IN ALL CASES ARE THOSE LOCATED OUTSIDE OF SOUTH AMERICA (335)	1.00 OF 60	9	TEND LESS TO BE THOSE LOCATED OUTSIDE OF SOUTH AMERICA (335)	0.81 OF 340	0 65 60 275 XSQ= 12.33 PHI= -0.176 XP = 0.0004
13	IN ALL CASES ARE THOSE WHERE THE LATITUDE IS LESS THAN FORTY DEGREES (329)	1.00 OF 60	13	TEND LESS TO BE THOSE WHERE THE LATITUDE IS LESS THAN FORTY DEGREES (329)	0.79 OF 340	0 71 60 269 XSQ= 13.84 PHI= -0.186 XP = 0.0002
15	TEND TO BE THOSE WHERE THE LATITUDE IS LESS THAN TWENTY DEGREES (217)	0.87 OF 60	15	TEND TO BE THOSE WHERE THE LATITUDE IS TWENTY DEGREES OR GREATER (183)	0.51 OF 340	8 175 52 165 XSQ= 28.37 PHI= -0.266 XP = 0.0000
16	TEND TO BE THOSE WHERE THE LATITUDE IS LESS THAN TEN DEGREES (123)	0.55 OF 60	16	TEND TO BE THOSE WHERE THE LATITUDE IS TEN DEGREES OR GREATER (277)	0.74 OF 340	27 250 33 90 XSQ= 18.18 PHI= -0.213 XP = 0.0000
33	IN ALL CASES ARE THOSE WHERE THE NATURAL ENVIRONMENT IS OTHER THAN 'VERY HARSH,' I.E., DESERT, DESERT GRASSES AND SHRUBS, TUNDRA, OR HIGH PLATEAU STEPPE (341) FWM	1.00 OF 60	33	TEND LESS TO BE THOSE WHERE THE NATURAL ENVIRONMENT IS OTHER THAN 'VERY HARSH,' I.E., DESERT, DESERT GRASSES AND SHRUBS, TUNDRA, OR HIGH PLATEAU STEPPE (341) FWM	0.83 OF 340	0 59 60 281 XSQ= 10.87 PHI= -0.165 XP = 0.0010
36	TEND MORE TO BE THOSE WHERE THE NATURAL ENVIRONMENT IS OTHER THAN 'VERY HARSH,' OR SUB-TROPICAL BUSH, OR TEMPERATE GRASSLAND (292) FWM	0.95 OF 60	36	TEND LESS TO BE THOSE WHERE THE NATURAL ENVIRONMENT IS OTHER THAN 'VERY HARSH,' OR SUB-TROPICAL BUSH, OR TEMPERATE GRASSLAND (292) FWM	0.69 OF 340	3 105 57 235 XSQ= 16.05 PHI= -0.200 XP = 0.0001
42	TEND TO BE THOSE WHERE THE NATURAL ENVIRONMENT IS TROPICAL OR SUB-TROPICAL RAIN FOREST, OR MONSOON FOREST (156) FWM	0.95 OF 60	42	TEND TO BE THOSE WHERE THE NATURAL ENVIRONMENT IS OTHER THAN TROPICAL OR SUB-TROPICAL RAIN FOREST, OR MONSOON FOREST (244) FWM	0.71 OF 340	57 99 3 241 XSQ= 90.30 PHI= 0.475 XP = 0.
44	TEND MORE TO BE THOSE WHERE SETTLEMENTS ARE FIXED (222)	0.95 OF 43	44	TEND LESS TO BE THOSE WHERE SETTLEMENTS ARE FIXED (222)	0.63 OF 289	41 181 2 108 XSQ= 16.64 PHI= 0.224 XP = 0.0000
46	LEAN MORE TOWARD BEING THOSE OTHER THAN WHERE SETTLEMENTS ARE NON-FIXED AND MOVEMENT IS NOMADIC (260)	0.98 OF 43	46	LEAN LESS TOWARD BEING THOSE OTHER THAN WHERE SETTLEMENTS ARE NON-FIXED AND MOVEMENT IS NOMADIC (260)	0.75 OF 289	1 71 42 218 XSQ= 9.63 PHI= -0.170 XP = 0.0019

48	TEND TO BE THOSE WHERE THE FOOD SUPPLY IS SECURE, AND FOOD SHORTAGES ARE RARE OR OCCASIONAL (38) MGW	0.88 OF 17	48	TEND TO BE THOSE WHERE THE FOOD SUPPLY IS NOT SECURE, AND FOOD SHORTAGES ARE FREQUENT OR ANNUAL (41) MGW	0.63 OF 62	15 23 2 39 XSQ= 12.00 PHI= 0.390 XP = 0.0005
51	DRIFT MORE TOWARD BEING THOSE WHERE SUBSISTENCE IS PRIMARILY BY FOOD PRODUCTION -- I. E., AGRICULTURE OR HUSBANDRY -- RATHER THAN BY GATHERING (253)	0.75 OF 60	51	DRIFT LESS TOWARD BEING THOSE WHERE SUBSISTENCE IS PRIMARILY BY FOOD PRODUCTION -- I. E., AGRICULTURE OR HUSBANDRY -- RATHER THAN BY GATHERING (253)	0.61 OF 340	45 208 15 132 XSQ= 3.62 PHI= 0.095 XP = 0.0571
53	TILT MORE TOWARD BEING THOSE WHERE FOOD PRODUCTION IS BY SIMPLE AGRICULTURE OR INCIPIENT FOOD PRODUCTION, RATHER THAN BY INTENSIVE AGRICULTURE (147)	0.80 OF 35	53	TILT LESS TOWARD BEING THOSE WHERE FOOD PRODUCTION IS BY SIMPLE AGRICULTURE OR INCIPIENT FOOD PRODUCTION, RATHER THAN BY INTENSIVE AGRICULTURE (147)	0.59 OF 203	7 84 28 119 XSQ= 4.91 PHI= -0.144 XP = 0.0267
55	LEAN TOWARD BEING THOSE WHERE FOOD PRODUCTION IS BY SIMPLE AGRICULTURE, RATHER THAN BY INTENSIVE AGRICULTURE (101)	0.78 OF 32	55	LEAN TOWARD BEING THOSE WHERE FOOD PRODUCTION IS BY INTENSIVE AGRICULTURE, RATHER THAN BY SIMPLE AGRICULTURE (91)	0.52 OF 160	7 84 25 76 XSQ= 8.84 PHI= -0.215 XP = 0.0029
56	TILT MORE TOWARD BEING THOSE WHERE FOOD PRODUCTION IS BY SIMPLE AGRICULTURE, RATHER THAN BY INCIPIENT FOOD PRODUCTION (101)	0.89 OF 28	56	TILT LESS TOWARD BEING THOSE WHERE FOOD PRODUCTION IS BY SIMPLE AGRICULTURE, RATHER THAN BY INCIPIENT FOOD PRODUCTION (101)	0.64 OF 119	25 76 3 43 XSQ= 5.68 PHI= 0.197 XP = 0.0171
63	TEND TO BE THOSE WHERE HUSBANDRY, IF PRESENT, IS PRINCIPALLY IN THE FORM OF PIGS, SHEEP, OR GOATS, RATHER THAN BOVINE, EQUINE, CAMEL-LIKE, OR DEER-LIKE ANIMALS (74)	0.75 OF 36	63	TEND TO BE THOSE WHERE HUSBANDRY, IF PRESENT, IS PRINCIPALLY IN THE FORM OF BOVINE, EQUINE, CAMEL-LIKE, OR DEER-LIKE ANIMALS, RATHER THAN PIGS, SHEEP, OR GOATS (152)	0.75 OF 190	9 143 27 47 XSQ= 32.48 PHI= -0.379 XP = 0.
71	LEAN MORE TOWARD BEING THOSE WHERE METAL WORKING IS ABSENT (153)	0.85 OF 34	71	LEAN LESS TOWARD BEING THOSE WHERE METAL WORKING IS ABSENT (153)	0.57 OF 217	5 93 29 124 XSQ= 8.64 PHI= -0.186 XP = 0.0033
74	TEND TO BE THOSE WHERE POTTERY IS ABSENT (93)	0.79 OF 33	74	TEND TO BE THOSE WHERE POTTERY IS PRESENT (145)	0.67 OF 205	7 138 26 67 XSQ= 23.48 PHI= -0.314 XP = 0.0000
85	TILT MORE TOWARD BEING THOSE WHERE THE LEVEL OF POLITICAL INTEGRATION IS THE MINIMAL STATE, THE AUTONOMOUS COMMUNITY, OR THE FAMILY (234) GPM	0.89 OF 54	85	TILT LESS TOWARD BEING THOSE WHERE THE LEVEL OF POLITICAL INTEGRATION IS THE MINIMAL STATE, THE AUTONOMOUS COMMUNITY, OR THE FAMILY (234) GPM	0.74 OF 250	6 64 48 186 XSQ= 4.47 PHI= -0.121 XP = 0.0344

87	TILT LESS TOWARD BEING THOSE 0.83 OF 54 WHERE THE LEVEL OF POLITICAL INTEGRATION IS THE LARGE STATE, THE LITTLE STATE, THE MINIMAL STATE, OR THE AUTONOMOUS COMMUNITY (281) GPM	87	TILT MORE TOWARD BEING THOSE 0.94 OF 250 WHERE THE LEVEL OF POLITICAL INTEGRATION IS THE LARGE STATE, THE LITTLE STATE, THE MINIMAL STATE, OR THE AUTONOMOUS COMMUNITY (281) GPM	45 236 9 14 XSQ= 6.27 PHI= -0.144 XP = 0.0122
88	TILT MORE TOWARD BEING THOSE 0.78 OF 41 WHERE, IF A HEADMANSHIP IS PRESENT, SUCCESSION IS HEREDITARY (165)	88	TILT LESS TOWARD BEING THOSE 0.58 OF 230 WHERE, IF A HEADMANSHIP IS PRESENT, SUCCESSION IS HEREDITARY (165)	9 97 32 133 XSQ= 5.16 PHI= -0.138 XP = 0.0232
98	DRIFT MORE TOWARD BEING THOSE 0.84 OF 43 WHERE THE HIERARCHY OF LOCAL JURISDICTION HAS FOUR OR THREE LEVELS (238) GES,EA	98	DRIFT LESS TOWARD BEING THOSE 0.70 OF 288 WHERE THE HIERARCHY OF LOCAL JURISDICTION HAS FOUR OR THREE LEVELS (238) GES,EA	36 202 7 86 XSQ= 2.78 PHI= 0.092 XP = 0.0956
102	TILT MORE TOWARD BEING THOSE 0.67 OF 58 WHERE CLASS STRATIFICATION IS PRESENT (203)	102	TILT LESS TOWARD BEING THOSE 0.50 OF 325 WHERE CLASS STRATIFICATION IS PRESENT (203)	39 164 19 161 XSQ= 4.91 PHI= 0.113 XP = 0.0267
107	TILT MORE TOWARD BEING THOSE 0.95 OF 39 WHERE CLASS STRATIFICATION, IF PRESENT, IS BASED ON SOMETHING OTHER THAN OCCUPATIONAL STATUS (160)	107	TILT LESS TOWARD BEING THOSE 0.75 OF 164 WHERE CLASS STRATIFICATION, IF PRESENT, IS BASED ON SOMETHING OTHER THAN OCCUPATIONAL STATUS (160)	2 41 37 123 XSQ= 6.31 PHI= -0.176 XP = 0.0120
108	LEAN TOWARD BEING THOSE 0.59 OF 39 WHERE CLASS STRATIFICATION, IF PRESENT, IS BASED ON A HEREDITARY ARISTOCRACY (74)	108	LEAN TOWARD BEING THOSE 0.69 OF 164 WHERE CLASS STRATIFICATION, IF PRESENT, IS BASED ON SOMETHING OTHER THAN A HEREDITARY ARISTOCRACY (129)	23 51 16 113 XSQ= 9.40 PHI= 0.215 XP = 0.0022
109	DRIFT MORE TOWARD BEING THOSE 0.95 OF 57 WHERE CASTES ARE ABSENT (317)	109	DRIFT LESS TOWARD BEING THOSE 0.85 OF 311 WHERE CASTES ARE ABSENT (317)	3 48 54 263 XSQ= 3.37 PHI= -0.096 XP = 0.0666
131	IN ALL CASES ARE THOSE 1.00 OF 25 WHERE THE CONSTRUCTION OF PERMANENT HOUSES OR THE ERECTION OF TEMPORARY DWELLINGS IS MAINLY DONE BY MALES (136)	131	DRIFT LESS TOWARD BEING THOSE 0.84 OF 132 WHERE THE CONSTRUCTION OF PERMANENT HOUSES OR THE ERECTION OF TEMPORARY DWELLINGS IS MAINLY DONE BY MALES (136)	25 111 0 21 XSQ= 3.32 PHI= 0.145 XP = 0.0684
175	TILT MORE TOWARD BEING THOSE 0.83 OF 58 WHERE THE COMMUNITY IS 'KIN-HETEROGENEOUS,' I. E. OTHER THAN A CLAN COMMUNITY OR A DEME (260)	175	TILT LESS TOWARD BEING THOSE 0.65 OF 324 WHERE THE COMMUNITY IS 'KIN-HETEROGENEOUS,' I. E. OTHER THAN A CLAN COMMUNITY OR A DEME (260)	10 112 48 212 XSQ= 6.02 PHI= -0.126 XP = 0.0141

176	DRIFT TOWARD BEING THOSE WHERE THE COMMUNITY IS A CLAN-COMMUNITY OR A COMMUNITY STRUCTURED OR SEGMENTED ON A CLAN BASIS (169)	0.55 OF 58	176	DRIFT TOWARD BEING THOSE WHERE THE COMMUNITY IS OTHER THAN A CLAN-COMMUNITY OR A COMMUNITY STRUCTURED OR SEGMENTED ON A CLAN BASIS (213)	0.58 OF 324	32 137 26 187 XSQ= 2.81 PHI= 0.086 XP = 0.0936
177	TILT MORE TOWARD BEING THOSE WHERE THE COMMUNITY IS OTHER THAN A SINGLE CLAN-COMMUNITY AND EXOGAMOUS (305)	0.91 OF 58	177	TILT LESS TOWARD BEING THOSE WHERE THE COMMUNITY IS OTHER THAN A SINGLE CLAN-COMMUNITY AND EXOGAMOUS (305)	0.78 OF 324	5 72 53 252 XSQ= 4.84 PHI= -0.113 XP = 0.0278
178	TEND LESS TO BE THOSE WHERE THE COMMUNITY IS OTHER THAN SEGMENTED ON A CLAN BASIS AND NON-EXOGAMOUS (295)	0.55 OF 58	178	TEND MORE TO BE THOSE WHERE THE COMMUNITY IS OTHER THAN SEGMENTED ON A CLAN BASIS AND NON-EXOGAMOUS (295)	0.81 OF 324	26 61 32 263 XSQ= 17.46 PHI= 0.214 XP = 0.0000
180	LEAN MORE TOWARD BEING THOSE WHERE THE COMMUNITY IS COMMONLY NON-EXOGAMOUS, RATHER THAN EXOGAMOUS (258)	0.84 OF 58	180	LEAN LESS TOWARD BEING THOSE WHERE THE COMMUNITY IS COMMONLY NON-EXOGAMOUS, RATHER THAN EXOGAMOUS (258)	0.65 OF 324	9 115 49 209 XSQ= 8.07 PHI= -0.145 XP = 0.0045
186	TEND MORE TO BE THOSE WHERE THE KIN GROUP IS OTHER THAN EXCLUSIVELY PATRILINEAL (250)	0.83 OF 60	186	TEND LESS TO BE THOSE WHERE THE KIN GROUP IS OTHER THAN EXCLUSIVELY PATRILINEAL (250)	0.59 OF 340	10 140 50 200 XSQ= 12.05 PHI= -0.174 XP = 0.0005
190	LEAN LESS TOWARD BEING THOSE WHERE THE KIN GROUP IS PATRILINEAL OR DOUBLE-DESCENT, RATHER THAN MATRILINEAL (186)	0.52 OF 29	190	LEAN MORE TOWARD BEING THOSE WHERE THE KIN GROUP IS PATRILINEAL OR DOUBLE-DESCENT, RATHER THAN MATRILINEAL (186)	0.78 OF 218	15 171 14 47 XSQ= 8.44 PHI= -0.185 XP = 0.0037
196	TILT MORE TOWARD BEING THOSE WHERE INDIVIDUAL RIGHTS IN REAL PROPERTY, AND RULES FOR INHERITANCE, ARE PRESENT (194)	0.89 OF 35	196	TILT LESS TOWARD BEING THOSE WHERE INDIVIDUAL RIGHTS IN REAL PROPERTY, AND RULES FOR INHERITANCE, ARE PRESENT (194)	0.66 OF 246	31 163 4 83 XSQ= 6.13 PHI= 0.148 XP = 0.0133
197	TEND LESS TO BE THOSE WHERE RULES FOR THE INHERITANCE OF REAL PROPERTY, IF PRESENT, FAVOR EITHER THE MALE HEIR OR LINE, OR THE FEMALE HEIR OR LINE (165)	0.61 OF 31	197	TEND MORE TO BE THOSE WHERE RULES FOR THE INHERITANCE OF REAL PROPERTY, IF PRESENT, FAVOR EITHER THE MALE HEIR OR LINE, OR THE FEMALE HEIR OR LINE (165)	0.90 OF 163	19 146 12 17 XSQ= 14.24 PHI= -0.271 XP = 0.0002
198	TILT LESS TOWARD BEING THOSE WHERE RULES FOR THE INHERITANCE OF REAL PROPERTY, IF PRESENT, FAVOR THE MALE HEIR OR LINE, RATHER THAN THE FEMALE (144)	0.68 OF 19	198	TILT MORE TOWARD BEING THOSE WHERE RULES FOR THE INHERITANCE OF REAL PROPERTY, IF PRESENT, FAVOR THE MALE HEIR OR LINE, RATHER THAN THE FEMALE (144)	0.90 OF 146	13 131 6 15 XSQ= 5.09 PHI= -0.176 XP = 0.0241

201	TILT LESS TOWARD BEING THOSE 0.73 OF 59 WHERE MARITAL RESIDENCE IS NON-OPTIONAL, RATHER THAN AMBILOCAL OR NEOLOCAL (334)	201	TILT MORE TOWARD BEING THOSE 0.86 OF 339 WHERE MARITAL RESIDENCE IS NON-OPTIONAL, RATHER THAN AMBILOCAL OR NEOLOCAL (334)	43 291 16 48 XSQ= 5.33 PHI= -0.116 XP = 0.0210
204	TILT LESS TOWARD BEING THOSE 0.67 OF 48 WHERE MARITAL RESIDENCE IS PATRILOCAL, VIRILOCAL, OR AVUNCULOCAL, RATHER THAN AMBILOCAL OR NEOLOCAL (270)	204	TILT MORE TOWARD BEING THOSE 0.83 OF 286 WHERE MARITAL RESIDENCE IS PATRILOCAL, VIRILOCAL, OR AVUNCULOCAL, RATHER THAN AMBILOCAL OR NEOLOCAL (270)	32 238 16 48 XSQ= 6.24 PHI= -0.137 XP = 0.0125
234	TILT TOWARD BEING THOSE 0.67 OF 57 WHERE THE COUSIN TERMINOLOGY IS OF ESKIMO OR HAWAIIAN TYPE, RATHER THAN CROW, OMAHA, OR IROQUOIS TYPE (170)	234	TILT TOWARD BEING THOSE 0.50 OF 265 WHERE THE COUSIN TERMINOLOGY IS OF CROW, OMAHA, OR IROQUOIS TYPE, RATHER THAN ESKIMO OR HAWAIIAN TYPE (152)	19 133 38 132 XSQ= 4.69 PHI= -0.121 XP = 0.0303
259	DRIFT TOWARD BEING THOSE 0.69 OF 13 WHERE THE SEVERITY OF MOTHER-IN-LAW AVOIDANCE IS LOW (20) WNS	259	DRIFT TOWARD BEING THOSE 0.67 OF 33 WHERE THE SEVERITY OF MOTHER-IN-LAW AVOIDANCE IS HIGH (26) WNS	4 22 9 11 XSQ= 3.54 PHI= -0.277 XP = 0.0600
263	TILT TOWARD BEING THOSE 0.53 OF 60 WHERE WIVES ARE OBTAINED BY RELATIVELY EASY MEANS, NAMELY BY TOKEN BRIDE-PRICE, GIFT EXCHANGE, ABSENCE OF ANY CONSIDERATION, OR RECEIPT OF DOWRY (162)	263	TILT TOWARD BEING THOSE 0.61 OF 335 WHERE WIVES ARE OBTAINED BY RELATIVELY DIFFICULT MEANS, NAMELY BY BRIDE-PRICE, BRIDE-SERVICE, OR EXCHANGING A FEMALE RELATIVE (233)	28 205 32 130 XSQ= 3.86 PHI= -0.099 XP = 0.0495
307	DRIFT MORE TOWARD BEING THOSE 0.83 OF 18 WHERE THE EARLY AGGRESSION SATISFACTION POTENTIAL IS HIGH (33) W-C	307	DRIFT LESS TOWARD BEING THOSE 0.53 OF 34 WHERE THE EARLY AGGRESSION SATISFACTION POTENTIAL IS HIGH (33) W-C	15 18 3 16 XSQ= 3.47 PHI= 0.258 XP = 0.0625
313	DRIFT TOWARD BEING THOSE 0.72 OF 18 WHERE AGGRESSION SOCIALIZATION ANXIETY IS LOW (28) W-C	313	DRIFT TOWARD BEING THOSE 0.58 OF 36 WHERE AGGRESSION SOCIALIZATION ANXIETY IS HIGH (26) W-C	5 21 13 15 XSQ= 3.35 PHI= -0.249 XP = 0.0673
325	DRIFT TOWARD BEING THOSE 0.78 OF 18 WHERE THE DEGREE OF DIFFUSION AMONG THE INFANT'S NURTURANT AGENTS IS HIGH (42) B-B-C	325	DRIFT TOWARD BEING THOSE 0.50 OF 56 WHERE THE DEGREE OF DIFFUSION AMONG THE INFANT'S NURTURANT AGENTS IS LOW (32) B-B-C	14 28 4 28 XSQ= 3.23 PHI= 0.209 XP = 0.0725
342	DRIFT TOWARD BEING THOSE 0.67 OF 12 WHERE THE CHILD'S INFERRED ANXIETY OVER PERFORMANCE OF NURTURANT BEHAVIOR IS HIGH (18) B-B-C	342	DRIFT TOWARD BEING THOSE 0.71 OF 34 WHERE THE CHILD'S INFERRED ANXIETY OVER PERFORMANCE OF NURTURANT BEHAVIOR IS LOW (28) B-B-C	8 10 4 24 XSQ= 3.72 PHI= 0.284 XP = 0.0537

```
351  DRIFT MORE TOWARD BEING THOSE  0.89 OF    9   351  DRIFT LESS TOWARD BEING THOSE  0.51 OF   51          1   25
     WHERE THE CHILD'S INFERRED CONFLICT                WHERE THE CHILD'S INFERRED CONFLICT                    8   26
     REGARDING ACHIEVEMENT BEHAVIOR                     REGARDING ACHIEVEMENT BEHAVIOR               XSQ=     3.07
     IS LOW  (34) B-B-C                                 IS LOW  (34) B-B-C                           PHI=   -0.226
                                                                                                     XP =   0.0799

352  TEND TO BE THOSE                0.78 OF   18   352  TEND TO BE THOSE                0.74 OF   54          4   40
     WHERE THE TOTAL POSITIVE PRESSURE TOWARD           WHERE THE TOTAL POSITIVE PRESSURE TOWARD             14   14
     DEVELOPING OBEDIENT BEHAVIOR                       DEVELOPING OBEDIENT BEHAVIOR                 XSQ=    13.17
     IN THE CHILD                                       IN THE CHILD                                 PHI=   -0.428
     IS LOW  (28) B-B-C                                 IS HIGH  (44) B-B-C                          XP =   0.0003

380  DRIFT TOWARD BEING THOSE        0.60 OF   15   380  DRIFT TOWARD BEING THOSE        0.72 OF   40          6   29
     WHERE SEGREGATION OF GIRLS AT MENARCHE             WHERE SEGREGATION OF GIRLS AT MENARCHE                9   11
     IS ABSENT  (20) F-B                                IS PRESENT  (35) F-B                         XSQ=     3.67
                                                                                                     PHI=   -0.258
                                                                                                     XP =   0.0553

386  TILT TOWARD BEING THOSE         0.68 OF   22   386  TILT TOWARD BEING THOSE         0.61 OF   64          7   39
     WHERE SEXUAL EXPRESSION BY THE YOUNG               WHERE SEXUAL EXPRESSION BY THE YOUNG                 15   25
     IS PERMITTED  (40) F-B                             IS RESTRICTED OR                             XSQ=     4.47
                                                        SEMI-RESTRICTED  (46) F-B                    PHI=   -0.228
                                                                                                     XP =   0.0345

391  TEND TO BE THOSE                0.77 OF   35   391  TEND TO BE THOSE                0.56 OF  144          8   81
     WHERE PREMARITAL SEX RELATIONS ARE                 WHERE PREMARITAL SEX RELATIONS ARE                   27   63
     PUNISHED ONLY IF PREGNANCY RESULTS, OR             STRONGLY PUNISHED AND IN FACT RARE, OR       XSQ=    11.26
     FREELY PERMITTED  (90) JTW,EA                      WEAKLY PUNISHED AND                          PHI=   -0.251
                                                        IN FACT NOT RARE  (89) JTW,EA                XP =   0.0008

392  TEND TO BE THOSE                0.66 OF   35   392  TEND TO BE THOSE                0.69 OF  144         12  100
     WHERE PREMARITAL SEX RELATIONS ARE                 WHERE PREMARITAL SEX RELATIONS ARE                   23   44
     FREELY PERMITTED  (67) JTW,EA                      STRONGLY PUNISHED AND IN FACT RARE, OR       XSQ=    13.40
                                                        WEAKLY PUNISHED AND IN FACT NOT RARE, OR     PHI=   -0.274
                                                        PUNISHED ONLY IF                             XP =   0.0003
                                                        PREGNANCY RESULTS  (112) JTW,EA

399  DRIFT TOWARD BEING THOSE        0.71 OF   14   399  DRIFT TOWARD BEING THOSE        0.61 OF   31          4   19
     WHERE INTENSITY OF CASTRATION ANXIETY              WHERE INTENSITY OF CASTRATION ANXIETY                10   12
     IS LOW  (22) WNS                                   IS HIGH  (23) WNS                            XSQ=     2.93
                                                                                                     PHI=   -0.255
                                                                                                     XP =   0.0872

400  TILT TOWARD BEING THOSE         0.64 OF   14   400  TILT TOWARD BEING THOSE         0.70 OF   44          9   13
     WHERE HOMOSEXUAL ACTIVITY                          WHERE HOMOSEXUAL ACTIVITY                             5   31
     IS PROHIBITED  (22) F-B                            IS PERMITTED  (36) F-B                       XSQ=     4.07
                                                                                                     PHI=    0.265
                                                                                                     XP =   0.0437

426  TEND TO BE THOSE                0.76 OF   33   426  TEND TO BE THOSE                0.65 OF  227          8  148
     WHERE A HIGH GOD IS                                WHERE A HIGH GOD IS                                  25   79
     ABSENT  (104) GES,EA                               PRESENT  (156) GES,EA                        XSQ=    18.47
                                                                                                     PHI=   -0.267
                                                                                                     XP =   0.0000
```

439	TILT TOWARD BEING THOSE WHERE FEAR OF GHOSTS IS HIGH (30) W-C	0.74 OF 19	439	TILT TOWARD BEING THOSE WHERE FEAR OF GHOSTS IS LOW (31) W-C	0.62 OF 42	14 16 5 26 XSQ= 5.28 PHI= 0.294 XP = 0.0215
442	DRIFT TOWARD BEING THOSE WHERE FEAR OF ANIMAL SPIRITS IS LOW (33) W-C	0.74 OF 19	442	DRIFT TOWARD BEING THOSE WHERE FEAR OF ANIMAL SPIRITS IS HIGH (28) W-C	0.55 OF 42	5 23 14 19 XSQ= 3.19 PHI= -0.229 XP = 0.0739
449	TILT TOWARD BEING THOSE WHERE THE OBSERVATION OF FOOD TABOOS IS HIGH, RATHER THAN MEDIUM OR LOW (25) JRL	0.57 OF 14	449	TILT TOWARD BEING THOSE WHERE THE OBSERVATION OF FOOD TABOOS IS MEDIUM OR LOW, RATHER THAN HIGH (61) JRL	0.76 OF 72	8 17 6 55 XSQ= 4.87 PHI= 0.238 XP = 0.0273
458	TILT MORE TOWARD BEING THOSE WHERE GAMES, IF PRESENT, DO NOT INCLUDE GAMES OF STRATEGY (119) R-A-B,EA	0.89 OF 28	458	TILT LESS TOWARD BEING THOSE WHERE GAMES, IF PRESENT, DO NOT INCLUDE GAMES OF STRATEGY (119) R-A-B,EA	0.66 OF 143	3 49 25 94 XSQ= 5.07 PHI= -0.172 XP = 0.0243
459	LEAN TOWARD BEING THOSE WHERE GAMES, IF PRESENT, DO NOT INCLUDE GAMES OF CHANCE (89) R-A-B,EA	0.82 OF 28	459	LEAN TOWARD BEING THOSE WHERE GAMES, IF PRESENT, INCLUDE GAMES OF CHANCE (82) R-A-B,EA	0.54 OF 143	5 77 23 66 XSQ= 10.75 PHI= -0.251 XP = 0.0010
460	TEND TO BE THOSE WHERE GAMES, IF PRESENT, ARE LIMITED TO GAMES OF SKILL ONLY (67) R-A-B,EA	0.75 OF 28	460	TEND TO BE THOSE WHERE GAMES, IF PRESENT, ARE NOT LIMITED TO GAMES OF SKILL ONLY (104) R-A-B,EA	0.68 OF 143	21 46 7 97 XSQ= 16.27 PHI= 0.308 XP = 0.0001
468	IN ALL CASES ARE THOSE WHERE CONTACT WITH OTHER CULTURES IS REGULAR OR IRREGULAR, RATHER THAN FREQUENT (37) JMH	1.00 OF 8	468	DRIFT LESS TOWARD BEING THOSE WHERE CONTACT WITH OTHER CULTURES IS REGULAR OR IRREGULAR, RATHER THAN FREQUENT (37) JMH	0.63 OF 46	0 17 8 29 XSQ= 2.77 PHI= -0.227 XP = 0.0959

25 CULTURES
WHOSE LINGUISTIC AFFILIATION IS
TIBETO-BURMAN (12)

25 CULTURES
WHOSE LINGUISTIC AFFILIATION IS
OTHER THAN TIBETO-BURMAN (388)

BACKGROUND ON PAGE 67

NEITHER SUBJECT NOR PREDICATE

12 IN LEFT COLUMN

ABOR AKHA BURMESE GARO KACHIN LAKHER LEPCHA LHOTA NAGA LOLO MINCHIA
PURUM TIBETANS

388 IN RIGHT COLUMN

****

26 CULTURES WHOSE LINGUISTIC AFFILIATION IS MON-KHMER (10)	26 CULTURES WHOSE LINGUISTIC AFFILIATION IS OTHER THAN MON-KHMER (390)

BACKGROUND ON PAGE 67

NEITHER SUBJECT NOR PREDICATE

10 IN LEFT COLUMN

BHUIYA CAMBODIANS HO KHASI KOL LAMET MNONG GAR NICOBARESE SANTAL SEMANG

390 IN RIGHT COLUMN

27 CULTURES
WHERE THE LINGUISTIC AFFILIATION IS
MALAYO-POLYNESIAN, RATHER THAN
TIBETO-BURMAN (60)

27 CULTURES
WHERE THE LINGUISTIC AFFILIATION IS
TIBETO-BURMAN, RATHER THAN
MALAYO-POLYNESIAN (12)

BACKGROUND ON PAGE 67

NEITHER SUBJECT NOR PREDICATE

60 IN LEFT COLUMN

AJIE	ALCRESE	ATAYAL	BALINESE	BATAK	BELU	BUNLAP	DOBUANS	DUSUN	ELLICE
GILBERTESE	HANUNOO	HAWAIIANS	IBAN	IFUGAO	JAVANESE	KURTATCHI	LAKALAI	LAU	LESU
LIFU	MACASSARESE	MALAYS	MANGAIANS	MANIHIKI	MANUS	MAORI	MARQUESANS	MARSHALLESE	MENTAWEI
MERINA	MINANGKABAU	MOTA	ONTONG-JAVA	PAIWAN	PALAUANS	PONAPEANS	PUKAPUKA	RARCIANS	ROTINESE
ROTUMANS	SAGADA	SAMOANS	SELUNG	SENIANG	SIMBOESE	SUBANUN	TAGBANUA	TANALA	TANIMBARESE
TIKOPIA	TOKELAU	TORAJA	TROBRIAND	TRUKESE	ULAWANS	WAROPEN	WOGEO	WOLEAIANS	YAPESE

12 IN RIGHT COLUMN

ABOR	AKHA	BURMESE	GARO	KACHIN	LAKHER	LEPCHA	LHOTA NAGA	LOLO	MINCHIA
PURUM	TIBETANS								

328 EXCLUDED BECAUSE IRRELEVANT

28 CULTURES
WHERE THE LINGUISTIC AFFILIATION IS
MALAYC-PCLYNESIAN, RATHER THAN
MCN-KHMER (60)

28 CULTURES
WHERE THE LINGUISTIC AFFILIATION IS
MON-KHMER, RATHER THAN
MALAYO-POLYNESIAN (10)

BACKGROUND ON PAGE 67

NEITHER SUBJECT NOR PREDICATE

60 IN LEFT COLUMN

AJIE	ALCRESE	ATAYAL	BALINESE	BATAK	BELU	BUNLAP	DOBUANS	DUSUN	ELLICE
GILBERTESE	HANUNCO	HAWAIIANS	IBAN	IFUGAO	JAVANESE	KURTATCHI	LAKALAI	LAU	LESU
LIFU	MACASSARESE	MALAYS	MANGAIANS	MANIHIKI	MANUS	MAORI	MARQUESANS	MARSHALLESE	MENTAWEI
MERINA	MINANGKABAU	MOTA	ONTONG-JAVA	PAIWAN	PALAUANS	PONAPEANS	PUKAPUKA	RAROIANS	ROTINESE
ROTUMANS	SAGADA	SAMOANS	SELUNG	SENIANG	SIMBOESE	SUBANUN	TAGBANUA	TANALA	TANIMBARESE
TIKOPIA	TOKELAU	TORAJA	TROBRIAND	TRUKESE	ULAWANS	WAROPEN	WOGEO	WOLEAIANS	YAPESE

10 IN RIGHT CCLUMN

BHUIYA	CAMBODIANS	HC	KHASI	KOL	LAMET	MNONG GAR	NICOBARESE	SANTAL	SEMANG

330 EXCLUDED BECAUSE IRRELEVANT

29 CULTURES
WHERE THE LINGUISTIC AFFILIATION IS
TIBETC-BURMAN, RATHER THAN
MON-KHMER (12)

29 CULTURES
WHERE THE LINGUISTIC AFFILIATION IS
MON-KHMER, RATHER THAN
TIBETO-BURMAN (10)

BACKGROUND ON PAGE 67

NEITHER SUBJECT NOR PREDICATE

12 IN LEFT CCLUMN

ABOR AKHA BURMESE GARO KACHIN LAKHER LEPCHA LHOTA NAGA LOLC MINCHIA
PURUM TIBETANS

10 IN RIGHT CCLUMN

BHUIYA CAMBODIANS HO KHASI KOL LAMET MNONG GAR NICOBARESE SANTAL SEMANG

378 EXCLUDED BECAUSE IRRELEVANT

30 CULTURES
WHOSE LINGUISTIC AFFILIATION IS
ATHABASKAN (8)

30 CULTURES
WHOSE LINGUISTIC AFFILIATION IS
OTHER THAN ATHABASKAN (392)

BACKGROUND ON PAGE 67

NEITHER SUBJECT NOR PREDICATE

8 IN LEFT COLUMN

CHIR-APACHE INGALIK KASKA KIOW-APACHE NABESNA NAVAHO SARSI TOLOWA

392 IN RIGHT COLUMN

31 CULTURES WHOSE LINGUISTIC AFFILIATION IS ALGONKIAN (9)

31 CULTURES WHOSE LINGUISTIC AFFILIATICN IS OTHER THAN ALGONKIAN (391)

BACKGROUND ON PAGE 67

NEITHER SUBJECT NOR PREDICATE

9 IN LEFT CCLUMN

CHEYENNE   CREE   DELAWARE   FOX   GROS VENTRE   MIAMI   NASKAPI   OJIBWA   PENCBSCOT

391 IN RIGHT CCLUMN

32 CULTURES WHOSE LINGUISTIC AFFILIATION IS CARIBAN (8)	32 CULTURES WHOSE LINGUISTIC AFFILIATION IS OTHER THAN CARIBAN (392)

BACKGROUND ON PAGE 67

NEITHER SUBJECT NOR PREDICATE

8 IN LEFT COLUMN

BACAIRI BLACK CARIB CALLINAGO CARIB CARINYA MOTILON WAICA YABARANA

392 IN RIGHT COLUMN

33 CULTURES
WHERE THE NATURAL ENVIRONMENT IS
'VERY HARSH,' I.E., DESERT,
DESERT GRASSES AND SHRUBS, TUNDRA, OR
HIGH PLATEAU STEPPE (59) FWM

33 CULTURES
WHERE THE NATURAL ENVIRONMENT IS
OTHER THAN 'VERY HARSH,' I.E., DESERT,
DESERT GRASSES AND SHRUBS, TUNDRA, OR
HIGH PLATEAU STEPPE (341) FWM

BACKGROUND ON PAGE 69

BOTH SUBJECT AND PREDICATE

59 IN LEFT COLUMN

ARANDA	AYMARA	BAJUN	BARABRA	BASSERI	BEJA	BERGDAMA	BURUSHO	CHIBCHA	CHIR-APACHE
CHUKCHEE	COCHITI	COPR ESKIMO	DARC	DIEGUENO	DIERI	GOAJIRO	HANO	HASANIA	HAVASUPAI
HAZARA	HERERO	HUICHOL	HUKUNDIKA	ICELANDERS	INCA	JEMEZ	JIVARO	KABYLE	KALMYK
KARIERA	KHALKA	KORYAK	KUNG	LAPPS	MARICOPA	MASAI	MONGUOR	NAMA	NAVAHO
NUNIVAK	NURI	ONA	PAEZ	PAPAGO	REGEIBAT	RWALA	SAMOYED	SERI	SOMALI
TAOS	TAREUMIUT	TEHUELCHE	TIBETANS	TUBATULABAL	UTE	YAHGAN	YUKAGHIR	ZUNI	

341 IN RIGHT COLUMN

	Left column (59)			Right column (341)		
3	DRIFT MORE TOWARD BEING THOSE LOCATED OUTSIDE OF AFRICA (320)	0.90 OF 59	3	DRIFT LESS TOWARD BEING THOSE LOCATED OUTSIDE OF AFRICA (320)	0.78 OF 341	6 74 53 267 XSQ= 3.49 PHI= -0.093 XP = 0.0617
6	TILT MORE TOWARD BEING THOSE LOCATED OUTSIDE OF THE INSULAR PACIFIC (330)	0.95 OF 59	6	TILT LESS TOWARD BEING THOSE LOCATED OUTSIDE OF THE INSULAR PACIFIC (330)	0.80 OF 341	3 67 56 274 XSQ= 6.41 PHI= -0.127 XP = 0.0113
8	LEAN LESS TOWARD BEING THOSE LOCATED OUTSIDE OF NORTH AMERICA (330)	0.68 OF 59	8	LEAN MORE TOWARD BEING THOSE LOCATED OUTSIDE OF NORTH AMERICA (330)	0.85 OF 341	19 51 40 290 XSQ= 9.20 PHI= 0.152 XP = 0.0024
14	TEND TO BE THOSE WHERE THE LATITUDE IS THIRTY DEGREES OR GREATER (119)	0.63 OF 59	14	TEND TO BE THOSE WHERE THE LATITUDE IS LESS THAN THIRTY DEGREES (281)	0.76 OF 341	37 82 22 259 XSQ= 34.15 PHI= 0.292 XP = 0.
15	TEND TO BE THOSE WHERE THE LATITUDE IS TWENTY DEGREES OR GREATER (183)	0.83 OF 59	15	TEND TO BE THOSE WHERE THE LATITUDE IS LESS THAN TWENTY DEGREES (217)	0.61 OF 341	49 134 10 207 XSQ= 37.05 PHI= 0.304 XP = 0.

44	TEND TO BE THOSE WHERE SETTLEMENTS ARE NON-FIXED (110)	0.67 OF 52	44	TEND TO BE THOSE WHERE SETTLEMENTS ARE FIXED (222)	0.73 OF 280	17 205 35 75 XSQ= 30.70 PHI= -0.304 XP = 0.
46	TEND TO BE THOSE WHERE SETTLEMENTS ARE NON-FIXED AND MOVEMENT IS NOMADIC (72)	0.52 OF 52	46	TEND TO BE THOSE OTHER THAN WHERE SETTLEMENTS ARE NON-FIXED AND MOVEMENT IS NOMADIC (260)	0.84 OF 280	27 45 25 235 XSQ= 31.11 PHI= 0.306 XP = 0.
51	DRIFT LESS TOWARD BEING THOSE WHERE SUBSISTENCE IS PRIMARILY BY FOOD PRODUCTION -- I. E., AGRICULTURE OR HUSBANDRY -- RATHER THAN BY GATHERING (253)	0.53 OF 59	51	DRIFT MORE TOWARD BEING THOSE WHERE SUBSISTENCE IS PRIMARILY BY FOOD PRODUCTION -- I. E., AGRICULTURE OR HUSBANDRY -- RATHER THAN BY GATHERING (253)	0.65 OF 341	31 222 28 119 XSQ= 2.89 PHI= -0.085 XP = 0.0889
53	LEAN TOWARD BEING THOSE WHERE FOOD PRODUCTION IS BY INTENSIVE AGRICULTURE, RATHER THAN BY SIMPLE AGRICULTURE OR INCIPIENT FOOD PRODUCTION (91)	0.64 OF 25	53	LEAN TOWARD BEING THOSE WHERE FOOD PRODUCTION IS BY SIMPLE AGRICULTURE OR INCIPIENT FOOD PRODUCTION, RATHER THAN BY INTENSIVE AGRICULTURE (147)	0.65 OF 213	16 75 9 138 XSQ= 6.68 PHI= 0.168 XP = 0.0097
55	TEND TO BE THOSE WHERE FOOD PRODUCTION IS BY INTENSIVE AGRICULTURE, RATHER THAN BY SIMPLE AGRICULTURE (91)	0.89 OF 18	55	TEND TO BE THOSE WHERE FOOD PRODUCTION IS BY SIMPLE AGRICULTURE, RATHER THAN BY INTENSIVE AGRICULTURE (101)	0.57 OF 174	16 75 2 99 XSQ= 11.94 PHI= 0.249 XP = 0.0005
56	LEAN TOWARD BEING THOSE WHERE FOOD PRODUCTION IS BY INCIPIENT FOOD PRODUCTION, RATHER THAN BY SIMPLE AGRICULTURE (46)	0.78 OF 9	56	LEAN TOWARD BEING THOSE WHERE FOOD PRODUCTION IS BY SIMPLE AGRICULTURE, RATHER THAN BY INCIPIENT FOOD PRODUCTION (101)	0.72 OF 138	2 99 7 39 XSQ= 7.47 PHI= -0.225 XP = 0.0063
63	TILT MORE TOWARD BEING THOSE WHERE HUSBANDRY, IF PRESENT, IS PRINCIPALLY IN THE FORM OF BOVINE, EQUINE, CAMEL-LIKE, OR DEER-LIKE ANIMALS, RATHER THAN PIGS, SHEEP, OR GOATS (152)	0.85 OF 33	63	TILT LESS TOWARD BEING THOSE WHERE HUSBANDRY, IF PRESENT, IS PRINCIPALLY IN THE FORM OF BOVINE, EQUINE, CAMEL-LIKE, OR DEER-LIKE ANIMALS, RATHER THAN PIGS, SHEEP, OR GOATS (152)	0.64 OF 193	28 124 5 69 XSQ= 4.54 PHI= 0.142 XP = 0.0332
79	IN ALL CASES ARE THOSE WHERE NO CITY IS PRESENT (201)	1.00 OF 40	79	TILT LESS TOWARD BEING THOSE WHERE NO CITY IS PRESENT (201)	0.88 OF 184	0 23 40 161 XSQ= 4.30 PHI= -0.139 XP = 0.0382
80	TILT MORE TOWARD BEING THOSE WHERE NO CITY OR TOWN IS PRESENT (185)	0.95 OF 40	80	TILT LESS TOWARD BEING THOSE WHERE NO CITY OR TOWN IS PRESENT (185)	0.80 OF 184	2 37 38 147 XSQ= 4.22 PHI= -0.137 XP = 0.0400

82	LEAN LESS TOWARD BEING THOSE 0.63 OF 40 WHERE A CITY OR TOWN IS PRESENT, OR THE AVERAGE COMMUNITY SIZE IS FIFTY OR GREATER (178)	82	LEAN MORE TOWARD BEING THOSE 0.83 OF 184 WHERE A CITY OR TOWN IS PRESENT, OR THE AVERAGE COMMUNITY SIZE IS FIFTY OR GREATER (178)	 XSQ= PHI= XP =	25 153 15 31 7.37 -0.181 0.0066
84	DRIFT MORE TOWARD BEING THOSE 0.96 OF 48 WHERE THE LEVEL OF POLITICAL INTEGRATION IS THE LITTLE STATE, THE MINIMAL STATE, THE AUTONOMOUS COMMUNITY, OR THE FAMILY (262) GPM	84	DRIFT LESS TOWARD BEING THOSE 0.84 OF 256 WHERE THE LEVEL OF POLITICAL INTEGRATION IS THE LITTLE STATE, THE MINIMAL STATE, THE AUTONOMOUS COMMUNITY, OR THE FAMILY (262) GPM	 XSQ= PHI= XP =	2 40 46 216 3.55 -0.108 0.0597
96	TILT TOWARD BEING THOSE 0.63 OF 51 WHERE THE HIERARCHY OF NATIONAL JURISDICTION HAS NO LEVELS (156) GES,EA	96	TILT TOWARD BEING THOSE 0.56 OF 279 WHERE THE HIERARCHY OF NATIONAL JURISDICTION HAS FOUR, THREE, TWO OR ONE LEVEL (174) GES,EA	 XSQ= PHI= XP =	19 155 32 124 5.08 -0.124 0.0242
106	LEAN TOWARD BEING THOSE 0.67 OF 27 WHERE CLASS STRATIFICATION, IF PRESENT, IS BASED ON WEALTH (77)	106	LEAN TOWARD BEING THOSE 0.66 OF 176 WHERE CLASS STRATIFICATION, IF PRESENT, IS BASED ON SOMETHING OTHER THAN WEALTH (126)	 XSQ= PHI= XP =	18 59 9 117 9.56 0.217 0.0020
108	TILT MORE TOWARD BEING THOSE 0.85 OF 27 WHERE CLASS STRATIFICATION, IF PRESENT, IS BASED ON SOMETHING OTHER THAN A HEREDITARY ARISTOCRACY (129)	108	TILT LESS TOWARD BEING THOSE 0.60 OF 176 WHERE CLASS STRATIFICATION, IF PRESENT, IS BASED ON SOMETHING OTHER THAN A HEREDITARY ARISTOCRACY (129)	 XSQ= PHI= XP =	4 70 23 106 5.26 -0.161 0.0218
129	TILT TOWARD BEING THOSE 0.53 OF 19 WHERE WEAVING IS MAINLY DONE BY MALES (31)	129	TILT TOWARD BEING THOSE 0.75 OF 85 WHERE WEAVING IS MAINLY DONE BY FEMALES (73)	 XSQ= PHI= XP =	10 21 9 64 4.53 0.209 0.0333
131	LEAN LESS TOWARD BEING THOSE 0.64 OF 22 WHERE THE CONSTRUCTION OF PERMANENT HOUSES OR THE ERECTION OF TEMPORARY DWELLINGS IS MAINLY DONE BY MALES (136)	131	LEAN MORE TOWARD BEING THOSE 0.90 OF 135 WHERE THE CONSTRUCTION OF PERMANENT HOUSES OR THE ERECTION OF TEMPORARY DWELLINGS IS MAINLY DONE BY MALES (136)	 XSQ= PHI= XP =	14 122 8 13 9.48 -0.246 0.0021
136	IN ALL CASES ARE THOSE 1.00 OF 5 WHERE FULL-TIME ENTREPRENEURS ARE PRESENT (18) JV	136	DRIFT TOWARD BEING THOSE 0.52 OF 27 WHERE FULL-TIME ENTREPRENEURS ARE ABSENT (14) JV	 XSQ= PHI= EP =	5 13 0 14 2.74 0.293 0.0525
137	LEAN MORE TOWARD BEING THOSE 0.94 OF 16 WHERE INVIDIOUS DISPLAY OF WEALTH IS MODERATELY, LITTLE, OR NEGATIVELY EMPHASIZED (52) PES	137	LEAN LESS TOWARD BEING THOSE 0.51 OF 73 WHERE INVIDIOUS DISPLAY OF WEALTH IS MODERATELY, LITTLE, OR NEGATIVELY EMPHASIZED (52) PES	 XSQ= PHI= XP =	1 36 15 37 8.33 -0.306 0.0039

138	TILT TOWARD BEING THOSE 0.86 OF 7 WHERE SUPERORDINATE JUSTICE IS ABSENT (18) BBW	138	TILT TOWARD BEING THOSE 0.64 OF 33 WHERE SUPERORDINATE JUSTICE IS PRESENT (22) BBW	1 21 6 12 XSQ= 3.86 PHI= -0.311 EP = 0.0328
139	IN ALL CASES ARE THOSE 1.00 OF 7 WHERE SUPERORDINATE PUNISHMENT IS ABSENT (25) BBW	139	TILT LESS TOWARD BEING THOSE 0.55 OF 33 WHERE SUPERORDINATE PUNISHMENT IS ABSENT (25) BBW	0 15 7 18 XSQ= 3.34 PHI= -0.289 EP = 0.0328
163	IN ALL CASES ARE THOSE 1.00 OF 5 WHERE THE EMPHASIS ON INDIVIDUAL VOLITION AS THE CAUSE OF CRIME IS LOW (10) MJ	163	TILT TOWARD BEING THOSE 0.58 OF 12 WHERE THE EMPHASIS ON INDIVIDUAL VOLITION AS THE CAUSE OF CRIME IS HIGH (7) MJ	0 7 5 5 XSQ= 2.84 PHI= -0.409 EP = 0.0441
176	LEAN MORE TOWARD BEING THOSE 0.75 OF 57 WHERE THE COMMUNITY IS OTHER THAN A CLAN-COMMUNITY OR A COMMUNITY STRUCTURED OR SEGMENTED ON A CLAN BASIS (213)	176	LEAN LESS TOWARD BEING THOSE 0.52 OF 325 WHERE THE COMMUNITY IS OTHER THAN A CLAN-COMMUNITY OR A COMMUNITY STRUCTURED OR SEGMENTED ON A CLAN BASIS (213)	14 155 43 170 XSQ= 9.60 PHI= -0.159 XP = 0.0019
178	LEAN MORE TOWARD BEING THOSE 0.93 OF 57 WHERE THE COMMUNITY IS OTHER THAN SEGMENTED ON A CLAN BASIS AND NON-EXOGAMOUS (295)	178	LEAN LESS TOWARD BEING THOSE 0.74 OF 325 WHERE THE COMMUNITY IS OTHER THAN SEGMENTED ON A CLAN BASIS AND NON-EXOGAMOUS (295)	4 83 53 242 XSQ= 8.43 PHI= -0.149 XP = 0.0037
181	DRIFT LESS TOWARD BEING THOSE 0.81 OF 57 WHERE THE COMMUNITY IS OTHER THAN A DEME (337)	181	DRIFT MORE TOWARD BEING THOSE 0.90 OF 325 WHERE THE COMMUNITY IS OTHER THAN A DEME (337)	11 34 46 291 XSQ= 2.84 PHI= 0.086 XP = 0.0918
184	DRIFT LESS TOWARD BEING THOSE 0.55 OF 33 WHERE THE LARGEST NON-COGNATIC KIN GROUP IS SMALLER THAN A PHRATRY, I. E. A SIB OR LINEAGE (175)	184	DRIFT MORE TOWARD BEING THOSE 0.72 OF 219 WHERE THE LARGEST NON-COGNATIC KIN GROUP IS SMALLER THAN A PHRATRY, I. E. A SIB OR LINEAGE (175)	15 62 18 157 XSQ= 3.21 PHI= 0.113 XP = 0.0734
192	DRIFT LESS TOWARD BEING THOSE 0.61 OF 59 OTHER THAN WHERE THE ONLY KIN GROUP PRESENT IS A KINDRED OR ELSE BILATERAL DESCENT IS INFERRED (289)	192	DRIFT MORE TOWARD BEING THOSE 0.74 OF 341 OTHER THAN WHERE THE ONLY KIN GROUP PRESENT IS A KINDRED OR ELSE BILATERAL DESCENT IS INFERRED (289)	23 88 36 253 XSQ= 3.72 PHI= 0.096 XP = 0.0537
196	LEAN TOWARD BEING THOSE 0.50 OF 48 WHERE INDIVIDUAL RIGHTS IN REAL PROPERTY, OR RULES FOR INHERITANCE, ARE ABSENT (87)	196	LEAN TOWARD BEING THOSE 0.73 OF 233 WHERE INDIVIDUAL RIGHTS IN REAL PROPERTY, AND RULES FOR INHERITANCE, ARE PRESENT (194)	24 170 24 63 XSQ= 8.77 PHI= -0.177 XP = 0.0031

214	IN ALL CASES ARE THOSE 1.00 OF 23 WHERE FIRST COUSIN MARRIAGE, IF PERMITTED, IS OTHER THAN UNILATERAL (144)	214	TILT LESS TOWARD BEING THOSE 0.81 OF 149 WHERE FIRST COUSIN MARRIAGE, IF PERMITTED, IS OTHER THAN UNILATERAL (144)	0 28 23 121 XSQ= 3.88 PHI= -0.150 XP = 0.0490
221	DRIFT MORE TOWARD BEING THOSE 0.98 OF 56 WHERE MATRILATERAL CROSS-COUSIN MARRIAGE IS NOT PRESCRIBED OR PREFERRED (335)	221	DRIFT LESS TOWARD BEING THOSE 0.89 OF 314 WHERE MATRILATERAL CROSS-COUSIN MARRIAGE IS NOT PRESCRIBED OR PREFERRED (335)	1 34 55 280 XSQ= 3.54 PHI= -0.098 XP = 0.0598
225	TEND TO BE THOSE 0.90 OF 10 WHERE COUSIN MARRIAGE IS PREFERENTIALLY OR PERMISSIVELY PATRILATERAL, RATHER THAN MATRILATERAL (23)	225	TEND TO BE THOSE 0.75 OF 56 WHERE COUSIN MARRIAGE IS PREFERENTIALLY OR PERMISSIVELY MATRILATERAL, RATHER THAN PATRILATERAL (43)	9 14 1 42 XSQ= 13.06 PHI= 0.445 XP = 0.0003
240	DRIFT MORE TOWARD BEING THOSE 0.79 OF 34 WHERE THE FAMILY, IF EXTENDED, IS SMALL OR STEM, RATHER THAN LARGE (135)	240	DRIFT LESS TOWARD BEING THOSE 0.60 OF 179 WHERE THE FAMILY, IF EXTENDED, IS SMALL OR STEM, RATHER THAN LARGE (135)	7 71 27 108 XSQ= 3.70 PHI= -0.132 XP = 0.0545
307	DRIFT TOWARD BEING THOSE 0.67 OF 9 WHERE THE EARLY AGGRESSION SATISFACTION POTENTIAL IS LOW (19) W-C	307	DRIFT TOWARD BEING THOSE 0.70 OF 43 WHERE THE EARLY AGGRESSION SATISFACTION POTENTIAL IS HIGH (33) W-C	3 30 6 13 XSQ= 2.83 PHI= -0.233 XP = 0.0923
314	IN ALL CASES ARE THOSE 1.00 OF 13 WHERE THE INCIDENCE OF MOTHER-CHILD HOUSEHOLDS IS LOW (61) W-C,S	314	DRIFT LESS TOWARD BEING THOSE 0.72 OF 67 WHERE THE INCIDENCE OF MOTHER-CHILD HOUSEHOLDS IS LOW (61) W-D,S	0 19 13 48 XSQ= 3.40 PHI= -0.206 XP = 0.0654
332	IN ALL CASES ARE THOSE 1.00 OF 3 WHERE THE AGE AT BEGINNING OF MODESTY TRAINING IS LOWER THAN SIX YEARS (8) W-C	332	DRIFT TOWARD BEING THOSE 0.64 OF 14 WHERE THE AGE AT BEGINNING OF MODESTY TRAINING IS SIX YEARS OR HIGHER (9) W-C	0 9 3 5 XSQ= 1.92 PHI= -0.336 EP = 0.0824
370	DRIFT MORE TOWARD BEING THOSE 0.76 OF 37 WHERE THE SEGREGATION OF ADOLESCENT BOYS IS ABSENT (148)	370	DRIFT LESS TOWARD BEING THOSE 0.58 OF 206 WHERE THE SEGREGATION OF ADOLESCENT BOYS IS ABSENT (148)	9 86 28 120 XSQ= 3.30 PHI= -0.117 XP = 0.0693
392	DRIFT MORE TOWARD BEING THOSE 0.81 OF 26 WHERE PREMARITAL SEX RELATIONS ARE STRONGLY PUNISHED AND IN FACT RARE, OR WEAKLY PUNISHED AND IN FACT NOT RARE, OR PUNISHED ONLY IF PREGNANCY RESULTS (112) JTW,EA	392	DRIFT LESS TOWARD BEING THOSE 0.59 OF 153 WHERE PREMARITAL SEX RELATIONS ARE STRONGLY PUNISHED AND IN FACT RARE, OR WEAKLY PUNISHED AND IN FACT NOT RARE, OR PUNISHED ONLY IF PREGNANCY RESULTS (112) JTW,EA	21 91 5 62 XSQ= 3.44 PHI= 0.139 XP = 0.0636

406	DRIFT TOWARD BEING THOSE WHERE EXPLANATIONS OF ILLNESS OF AN AGGRESSION NATURE ARE PRESENT (28) W-C	0.75 OF 12	406	DRIFT TOWARD BEING THOSE WHERE EXPLANATIONS OF ILLNESS OF AN AGGRESSION NATURE ARE ABSENT (33) W-C	0.61 OF 49	9 19 3 30 XSQ= 3.74 PHI= 0.248 XP = 0.0531
427	TILT MORE TOWARD BEING THOSE WHERE A HIGH GOD, IF PRESENT, IS ACTIVE, RATHER THAN INACTIVE (87) GES,EA	0.78 OF 23	427	TILT LESS TOWARD BEING THOSE WHERE A HIGH GOD, IF PRESENT, IS ACTIVE, RATHER THAN INACTIVE (87) GES,EA	0.52 OF 133	18 69 5 64 XSQ= 4.51 PHI= 0.170 XP = 0.0336
435	TILT TOWARD BEING THOSE WHERE ABANDONMENT OF THE HOUSE OF THE DEAD IS PRACTICED (12) LWS	0.78 OF 9	435	TILT TOWARD BEING THOSE WHERE ABANDONMENT OF THE HOUSE OF THE DEAD IS NOT PRACTICED (19) LWS	0.77 OF 22	7 5 2 17 XSQ= 6.00 PHI= 0.440 EP = 0.0118
452	TILT TOWARD BEING THOSE WHERE TOTEMISM WITH FOOD TABOOS IS ABSENT (24) WNS	0.91 OF 11	452	TILT TOWARD BEING THOSE WHERE TOTEMISM WITH FOOD TABOOS IS PRESENT (19) WNS	0.56 OF 32	1 18 10 14 XSQ= 5.59 PHI= -0.361 XP = 0.0180
478	DRIFT TOWARD BEING THOSE WHERE THE ABANDONMENT OR KILLING OF OLD PEOPLE IS PRESENT (12) LWS	0.86 OF 7	478	DRIFT TOWARD BEING THOSE WHERE THE ABANDONMENT OR KILLING OF OLD PEOPLE IS UNIMPORTANT OR ABSENT (12) LWS	0.65 OF 17	6 6 1 11 XSQ= 3.23 PHI= 0.367 EP = 0.0686
479	DRIFT TOWARD BEING THOSE WHERE THE NEED TO ACHIEVE, AS INFERRED FROM FOLKTALES, IS HIGH (18) JV	0.86 OF 7	479	DRIFT TOWARD BEING THOSE WHERE THE NEED TO ACHIEVE, AS INFERRED FROM FOLKTALES, IS LOW (18) JV	0.59 OF 29	6 12 1 17 XSQ= 2.84 PHI= 0.281 EP = 0.0877

****

34 CULTURES WHERE THE NATURAL ENVIRONMENT IS DESERT CR DESERT GRASSES AND SHRUBS (40) FWM	34 CULTURES WHERE THE NATURAL ENVIRCNMENT IS OTHER THAN DESERT OR DESERT GRASSES AND SHRUBS (360) FWM

BACKGROUND ON PAGE 69

SUBJECT ONLY

....

40 IN LEFT COLUMN

ARANDA	BAJUN	BARABRA	BASSERI	BEJA	BERGDAMA	CHIR-APACHE	COCHITI	DARC	DIEGUENO
DIERI	GCAJIRC	HANC	HASANIA	HAVASUPAI	HAZARA	HERERO	HUICHCL	HUKUNDIKA	JEMEZ
KABYLE	KALMYK	KARIERA	KHALKA	KUNG	MARICOPA	MASAI	NAMA	NAVAHO	NURI
PAPAGO	REGEIBAT	RWALA	SERI	SOMALI	TAOS	TEHUELCHE	TUBATULABAL	UTE	ZUNI

360 IN RIGHT CCLUMN

8	TEND LESS TO BE THCSE LOCATED CUTSIDE CF NCRTH AMERICA (330)	0.60 OF 40	8	TEND MORE TO BE THOSE LOCATED OUTSIDE OF NORTH AMERICA (330)	0.85 OF 360	16 54 24 306 XSQ= 13.90 PHI= 0.186 XP = 0.0002
9	DRIFT MORE TCWARC BEING THCSE LCCATED CUTSIDE CF SCUTH AMERICA (335)	0.95 OF 40	9	DRIFT LESS TOWARD BEING THCSE LOCATED OUTSIDE OF SOUTH AMERICA (335)	0.82 CF 360	2 63 38 297 XSQ= 3.27 PHI= -0.09C XP = 0.0707
14	TEND TC BE THCSE WHERE THE LATITUCE IS THIRTY DEGREES CR GREATER (119)	0.57 OF 40	14	TEND TO BE THOSE WHERE THE LATITUDE IS LESS THAN THIRTY DEGREES (281)	0.73 OF 360	23 96 17 264 XSQ= 14.93 PHI= 0.193 XP = 0.0001
15	TEND TC BE THCSE WHERE THE LATITUDE IS TWENTY DEGREES CR GREATER (183)	0.88 OF 40	15	TEND TO BE THOSE WHERE THE LATITUDE IS LESS THAN TWENTY DEGREES (217)	0.59 CF 360	35 148 5 212 XSQ= 29.37 PHI= 0.271 XP = 0.0000
44	TEND TC BE THCSE WHERE SETTLEMENTS ARE NON-FIXEC (110)	0.71 OF 35	44	TEND TO BE THOSE WHERE SETTLEMENTS ARE FIXED (222)	0.71 OF 297	10 212 25 85 XSQ= 24.00 PHI= -0.269 XP = 0.0000

46	TEND TO BE THOSE 0.57 OF 35 WHERE SETTLEMENTS ARE NON-FIXED AND MOVEMENT IS NOMADIC (72)	46	TEND TO BE THOSE 0.82 OF 297 OTHER THAN WHERE SETTLEMENTS ARE NON-FIXED AND MOVEMENT IS NOMADIC (260)	20 52 15 245 XSQ= 26.67 PHI= 0.283 XP = 0.0000
53	TILT TOWARD BEING THOSE 0.67 OF 15 WHERE FOOD PRODUCTION IS BY INTENSIVE AGRICULTURE, RATHER THAN BY SIMPLE AGRICULTURE OR INCIPIENT FOOD PRODUCTION (91)	53	TILT TOWARD BEING THOSE 0.64 OF 223 WHERE FOOD PRODUCTION IS BY SIMPLE AGRICULTURE OR INCIPIENT FOOD PRODUCTION, RATHER THAN BY INTENSIVE AGRICULTURE (147)	10 81 5 142 XSQ= 4.27 PHI= 0.134 XP = 0.0388
55	LEAN TOWARD BEING THOSE 0.91 OF 11 WHERE FOOD PRODUCTION IS BY INTENSIVE AGRICULTURE, RATHER THAN BY SIMPLE AGRICULTURE (91)	55	LEAN TOWARD BEING THOSE 0.55 OF 181 WHERE FOOD PRODUCTION IS BY SIMPLE AGRICULTURE, RATHER THAN BY INTENSIVE AGRICULTURE (101)	10 81 1 100 XSQ= 7.11 PHI= 0.192 XP = 0.0077
56	DRIFT TOWARD BEING THOSE 0.80 OF 5 WHERE FOOD PRODUCTION IS BY INCIPIENT FOOD PRODUCTION, RATHER THAN BY SIMPLE AGRICULTURE (46)	56	DRIFT TOWARD BEING THOSE 0.70 OF 142 WHERE FOOD PRODUCTION IS BY SIMPLE AGRICULTURE, RATHER THAN BY INCIPIENT FOOD PRODUCTION (101)	1 100 4 42 XSQ= 3.61 PHI= -0.157 XP = 0.0575
63	TILT MORE TOWARD BEING THOSE 0.88 OF 24 WHERE HUSBANDRY, IF PRESENT, IS PRINCIPALLY IN THE FORM OF BOVINE, EQUINE, CAMEL-LIKE, OR DEER-LIKE ANIMALS, RATHER THAN PIGS, SHEEP, OR GOATS (152)	63	TILT LESS TOWARD BEING THOSE 0.65 OF 202 WHERE HUSBANDRY, IF PRESENT, IS PRINCIPALLY IN THE FORM OF BOVINE, EQUINE, CAMEL-LIKE, OR DEER-LIKE ANIMALS, RATHER THAN PIGS, SHEEP, OR GOATS (152)	21 131 3 71 XSQ= 4.02 PHI= 0.133 XP = 0.0449
80	IN ALL CASES ARE THOSE 1.00 OF 27 WHERE NO CITY OR TOWN IS PRESENT (185)	80	TILT LESS TOWARD BEING THOSE 0.80 OF 197 WHERE NO CITY OR TOWN IS PRESENT (185)	0 39 27 158 XSQ= 5.17 PHI= -0.152 XP = 0.0230
83	DRIFT LESS TOWARD BEING THOSE 0.58 OF 26 WHERE, WITH NO CITY AND NO TOWN PRESENT, THE AVERAGE COMMUNITY SIZE IS SMALLER THAN 200, RATHER THAN BETWEEN 200 AND 999 (135)	83	DRIFT MORE TOWARD BEING THOSE 0.78 OF 154 WHERE, WITH NO CITY AND NO TOWN PRESENT, THE AVERAGE COMMUNITY SIZE IS SMALLER THAN 200, RATHER THAN BETWEEN 200 AND 999 (135)	11 34 15 120 XSQ= 3.84 PHI= 0.146 XP = 0.0502
84	IN ALL CASES ARE THOSE 1.00 OF 32 WHERE THE LEVEL OF POLITICAL INTEGRATION IS THE LITTLE STATE, THE MINIMAL STATE, THE AUTONOMOUS COMMUNITY, OR THE FAMILY (262) GPM	84	TILT LESS TOWARD BEING THOSE 0.85 OF 272 WHERE THE LEVEL OF POLITICAL INTEGRATION IS THE LITTLE STATE, THE MINIMAL STATE, THE AUTONOMOUS COMMUNITY, OR THE FAMILY (262) GPM	0 42 32 230 XSQ= 4.51 PHI= -0.122 XP = 0.0337
89	DRIFT MORE TOWARD BEING THOSE 0.91 OF 11 WHERE, IF A NON-HEREDITARY HEADMANSHIP IS PRESENT, SUCCESSION IS BY CONSENSUS (63)	89	DRIFT LESS TOWARD BEING THOSE 0.56 OF 95 WHERE, IF A NON-HEREDITARY HEADMANSHIP IS PRESENT, SUCCESSION IS BY CONSENSUS (63)	10 53 1 42 XSQ= 3.69 PHI= 0.187 XP = 0.0547

102	TILT TOWARD BEING THOSE WHERE CLASS STRATIFICATION IS ABSENT (180)	0.65 OF 40	102	TILT TOWARD BEING THOSE WHERE CLASS STRATIFICATION IS PRESENT (203)	0.55 OF 343	14 189 26 154 XSQ= 5.03 PHI= -0.115 XP = 0.0249
106	LEAN TOWARD BEING THOSE WHERE CLASS STRATIFICATION, IF PRESENT, IS BASED ON WEALTH (77)	0.79 OF 14	106	LEAN TOWARD BEING THOSE WHERE CLASS STRATIFICATION, IF PRESENT, IS BASED ON SOMETHING OTHER THAN WEALTH (126)	0.65 OF 189	11 66 3 123 XSQ= 8.78 PHI= 0.208 XP = 0.0031
131	TEND TO BE THOSE WHERE THE CONSTRUCTION OF PERMANENT HOUSES OR THE ERECTION OF TEMPORARY DWELLINGS IS MAINLY DONE BY FEMALES (21)	0.50 OF 14	131	TEND TO BE THOSE WHERE THE CONSTRUCTION OF PERMANENT HOUSES OR THE ERECTION OF TEMPORARY DWELLINGS IS MAINLY DONE BY MALES (136)	0.90 OF 143	7 129 7 14 XSQ= 14.49 PHI= -0.304 XP = 0.0001
137	IN ALL CASES ARE THOSE WHERE INVIDIOUS DISPLAY OF WEALTH IS MODERATELY, LITTLE, OR NEGATIVELY EMPHASIZED (52) PES	1.00 OF 10	137	TILT LESS TOWARD BEING THOSE WHERE INVIDIOUS DISPLAY OF WEALTH IS MODERATELY, LITTLE, OR NEGATIVELY EMPHASIZED (52) PES	0.53 OF 79	0 37 10 42 XSQ= 6.20 PHI= -0.264 XP = 0.0127
178	TILT MORE TOWARD BEING THOSE WHERE THE COMMUNITY IS OTHER THAN SEGMENTED ON A CLAN BASIS AND NON-EXOGAMOUS (295)	0.92 OF 40	178	TILT LESS TOWARD BEING THOSE WHERE THE COMMUNITY IS OTHER THAN SEGMENTED ON A CLAN BASIS AND NON-EXOGAMOUS (295)	0.75 OF 342	3 84 37 258 XSQ= 5.00 PHI= -0.114 XP = 0.0254
184	TILT TOWARD BEING THOSE WHERE THE LARGEST NON-COGNATIC KIN GROUP IS THE MOEITY OR PHRATRY (77)	0.50 OF 28	184	TILT TOWARD BEING THOSE WHERE THE LARGEST NON-COGNATIC KIN GROUP IS SMALLER THAN A PHRATRY, I. E. A SIB OR LINEAGE (175)	0.72 OF 224	14 63 14 161 XSQ= 4.63 PHI= 0.136 XP = 0.0314
196	DRIFT LESS TOWARD BEING THOSE WHERE INDIVIDUAL RIGHTS IN REAL PROPERTY, AND RULES FOR INHERITANCE, ARE PRESENT (194)	0.53 OF 32	196	DRIFT MORE TOWARD BEING THOSE WHERE INDIVIDUAL RIGHTS IN REAL PROPERTY, AND RULES FOR INHERITANCE, ARE PRESENT (194)	0.71 OF 249	17 177 15 72 XSQ= 3.48 PHI= -0.111 XP = 0.0621
221	IN ALL CASES ARE THOSE WHERE MATRILATERAL CROSS-COUSIN MARRIAGE IS NOT PRESCRIBED OR PREFERRED (335)	1.00 OF 40	221	DRIFT LESS TOWARD BEING THOSE WHERE MATRILATERAL CROSS-COUSIN MARRIAGE IS NOT PRESCRIBED OR PREFERRED (335)	0.89 OF 330	0 35 40 295 XSQ= 3.53 PHI= -0.098 XP = 0.0603
225	IN ALL CASES ARE THOSE WHERE COUSIN MARRIAGE IS PREFERENTIALLY OR PERMISSIVELY PATRILATERAL, RATHER THAN MATRILATERAL (23)	1.00 OF 9	225	TEND TO BE THOSE WHERE COUSIN MARRIAGE IS PREFERENTIALLY OR PERMISSIVELY MATRILATERAL, RATHER THAN PATRILATERAL (43)	0.75 OF 57	9 14 0 43 XSQ= 16.30 PHI= 0.497 XP = 0.0001

240	DRIFT MORE TOWARD BEING THOSE 0.82 OF 22 WHERE THE FAMILY, IF EXTENDED, IS SMALL OR STEM, RATHER THAN LARGE (135)	240	DRIFT LESS TOWARD BEING THOSE 0.61 OF 191 WHERE THE FAMILY, IF EXTENDED, IS SMALL OR STEM, RATHER THAN LARGE (135)	4 74 18 117 XSQ= 2.76 PHI= -0.114 XP = 0.0965
332	IN ALL CASES ARE THOSE 1.00 OF 3 WHERE THE AGE AT BEGINNING OF MODESTY TRAINING IS LOWER THAN SIX YEARS (8) W-C	332	DRIFT TOWARD BEING THOSE 0.64 OF 14 WHERE THE AGE AT BEGINNING OF MODESTY TRAINING IS SIX YEARS OR HIGHER (9) W-C	0 9 3 5 XSQ= 1.92 PHI= -0.336 EP = 0.0824
350	IN ALL CASES ARE THOSE 1.00 OF 7 WHERE THE CHILD'S INFERRED ANXIETY OVER PERFORMANCE OF ACHIEVEMENT BEHAVIOR IS HIGH (34) B-B-C	350	TILT LESS TOWARD BEING THOSE 0.51 OF 53 WHERE THE CHILD'S INFERRED ANXIETY OVER PERFORMANCE OF ACHIEVEMENT BEHAVIOR IS HIGH (34) B-B-C	7 27 0 26 XSQ= 4.23 PHI= 0.265 XP = 0.0398
351	TILT TOWARD BEING THOSE 0.86 OF 7 WHERE THE CHILD'S INFERRED CONFLICT REGARDING ACHIEVEMENT BEHAVIOR IS HIGH (26) B-B-C	351	TILT TOWARD BEING THOSE 0.62 OF 53 WHERE THE CHILD'S INFERRED CONFLICT REGARDING ACHIEVEMENT BEHAVIOR IS LOW (34) B-B-C	6 20 1 33 XSQ= 4.01 PHI= 0.258 XP = 0.0453
392	TILT MORE TOWARD BEING THOSE 0.93 OF 14 WHERE PREMARITAL SEX RELATIONS ARE STRONGLY PUNISHED AND IN FACT RARE, OR WEAKLY PUNISHED AND IN FACT NOT RARE, OR PUNISHED ONLY IF PREGNANCY RESULTS (112) JTW,EA	392	TILT LESS TOWARD BEING THOSE 0.60 OF 165 WHERE PREMARITAL SEX RELATIONS ARE STRONGLY PUNISHED AND IN FACT RARE, OR WEAKLY PUNISHED AND IN FACT NOT RARE, OR PUNISHED ONLY IF PREGNANCY RESULTS (112) JTW,EA	13 99 1 66 XSQ= 4.63 PHI= 0.161 XP = 0.0314
427	DRIFT MORE TOWARD BEING THOSE 0.85 OF 13 WHERE A HIGH GOD, IF PRESENT, IS ACTIVE, RATHER THAN INACTIVE (87) GES,EA	427	DRIFT LESS TOWARD BEING THOSE 0.53 OF 143 WHERE A HIGH GOD, IF PRESENT, IS ACTIVE, RATHER THAN INACTIVE (87) GES,EA	11 76 2 67 XSQ= 3.59 PHI= 0.152 XP = 0.0580
435	TILT TOWARD BEING THOSE 0.83 OF 6 WHERE ABANDONMENT OF THE HOUSE OF THE DEAD IS PRACTICED (12) LWS	435	TILT TOWARD BEING THOSE 0.72 OF 25 WHERE ABANDONMENT OF THE HOUSE OF THE DEAD IS NOT PRACTICED (19) LWS	5 7 1 18 XSQ= 4.13 PHI= 0.365 EP = 0.0217
446	IN ALL CASES ARE THOSE 1.00 OF 3 WHERE WITCHCRAFT IS SIGNIFICANTLY PRESENT (14) GES	446	TILT TOWARD BEING THOSE 0.69 OF 35 WHERE WITCHCRAFT IS MODERATELY PRESENT OR ABSENT (24) GES	3 11 0 24 XSQ= 3.03 PHI= 0.282 EP = 0.0431

****

	Left column		Right column
35	CULTURES WHERE THE NATURAL ENVIRONMENT IS TUNDRA (11) FWM	35	CULTURES WHERE THE NATURAL ENVIRONMENT IS OTHER THAN TUNDRA (389) FWM

BACKGROUND ON PAGE 69 — SUBJECT ONLY

....

11 IN LEFT COLUMN

CHUKCHEE COPR ESKIMO ICELANDERS KORYAK LAPPS NUNIVAK ONA SAMOYED TAREUMIUT YAHGAN YUKAGHIR

389 IN RIGHT COLUMN

	Left column			Right column		Statistics
11	TEND TO BE THOSE WHERE THE LATITUDE IS SIXTY DEGREES OR GREATER (15)	0.82 OF 11	11	TEND TO BE THOSE WHERE THE LATITUDE IS LESS THAN SIXTY DEGREES (385)	0.98 OF 389	9 6 2 383 XSQ= 169.40 PHI= 0.651 XP = 0.
12	IN ALL CASES ARE THOSE WHERE THE LATITUDE IS FIFTY DEGREES OR GREATER (33)	1.00 OF 11	12	TEND TO BE THOSE WHERE THE LATITUDE IS LESS THAN FIFTY DEGREES (367)	0.94 OF 389	11 22 0 367 XSQ= 113.64 PHI= 0.533 XP = 0.
44	IN ALL CASES ARE THOSE WHERE SETTLEMENTS ARE NON-FIXED (110)	1.00 OF 10	44	TEND TO BE THOSE WHERE SETTLEMENTS ARE FIXED (222)	0.69 OF 322	0 222 10 100 XSQ= 17.81 PHI= -0.232 XP = 0.0000
46	TEND TO BE THOSE WHERE SETTLEMENTS ARE NON-FIXED AND MOVEMENT IS NOMADIC (72)	0.70 OF 10	46	TEND TO BE THOSE OTHER THAN WHERE SETTLEMENTS ARE NON-FIXED AND MOVEMENT IS NOMADIC (260)	0.80 OF 322	7 65 3 257 XSQ= 11.39 PHI= 0.185 XP = 0.0007
51	TEND TO BE THOSE WHERE SUBSISTENCE IS PRIMARILY BY FOOD GATHERING -- I. E., HUNTING, FISHING, OR COLLECTING -- RATHER THAN FOOD PRODUCTION (147)	0.91 OF 11	51	TEND TO BE THOSE WHERE SUBSISTENCE IS PRIMARILY BY FOOD PRODUCTION -- I. E., AGRICULTURE OR HUSBANDRY -- RATHER THAN BY GATHERING (253)	0.65 OF 389	1 252 10 137 XSQ= 11.98 PHI= -0.173 XP = 0.0005
54	IN ALL CASES ARE THOSE WHERE FOOD PRODUCTION IS BY INCIPIENT FOOD PRODUCTION, RATHER THAN BY INTENSIVE OR SIMPLE AGRICULTURE (46)	1.00 OF 3	54	LEAN TOWARD BEING THOSE WHERE FOOD PRODUCTION IS BY INTENSIVE OR SIMPLE AGRICULTURE, RATHER THAN BY INCIPIENT FOOD PRODUCTION (192)	0.82 OF 235	0 192 3 43 XSQ= 7.98 PHI= -0.183 XP = 0.0047

56	IN ALL CASES ARE THCSE WHERE FCOD PRODUCTICN IS BY INCIPIENT FCOD PRODUCTION, RATHER THAN BY SIMPLE AGRICULTURE (46)	1.00 OF 3	56	TILT TOWARD BEING THOSE WHERE FOOD PRODUCTION IS BY SIMPLE AGRICULTURE, RATHER THAN BY INCIPIENT FOOD PRODUCTION (101)	0.70 CF 144	0 101 3 43 XSQ= 3.86 PHI= -0.162 XP = 0.0495
73	IN ALL CASES ARE THCSE WHERE WEAVING IS ABSENT (130)	1.00 OF 8	73	TILT LESS TOWARD BEING THOSE WHERE WEAVING IS ABSENT (130)	0.51 OF 240	0 118 8 122 XSQ= 5.66 PHI= -0.151 XP = 0.0173
81	IN ALL CASES ARE THCSE WHERE NC CITY OR TCWN IS PRESENT, ANC THE AVERAGE COMMUNITY SIZE IS SMALLER THAN 200 (135)	1.00 OF 9	81	TILT LESS TOWARD BEING THOSE WHERE NO CITY OR TOWN IS PRESENT, AND THE AVERAGE COMMUNITY SIZE IS SMALLER THAN 200 (135)	0.59 CF 215	0 89 9 126 XSQ= 4.57 PHI= -0.143 XP = 0.0325
82	LEAN TOWARD BEING THOSE WHERE NC CITY CR TCWN IS PRESENT, AND THE AVERAGE COMMUNITY SIZE IS SMALLER THAN FIFTY (46)	0.67 OF 9	82	LEAN TOWARD BEING THOSE WHERE A CITY OR TOWN IS PRESENT, CR THE AVERAGE COMMUNITY SIZE IS FIFTY OR GREATER (178)	0.81 CF 215	3 175 6 40 XSQ= 9.46 PHI= -0.206 XP = 0.0021
86	DRIFT MORE TOWARD BEING THCSE WHERE THE LEVEL CF POLITICAL INTEGRATION IS THE AUTCNCMOUS COMMUNITY, OR THE FAMILY (156) GPM	0.89 OF 9	86	DRIFT LESS TOWARD BEING THCSE WHERE THE LEVEL OF POLITICAL INTEGRATION IS THE AUTONOMOUS COMMUNITY, OR THE FAMILY (156) GPM	0.50 CF 295	1 147 8 148 XSQ= 3.81 PHI= -0.112 XP = 0.0511
88	IN ALL CASES ARE THCSE WHERE, IF A HEACMANSHIP IS PRESENT, SUCCESSICN IS NCN-HEREDITARY (106)	1.00 OF 4	88	TILT TOWARD BEING THOSE WHERE, IF A HEADMANSHIP IS PRESENT, SUCCESSION IS HEREDITARY (165)	0.62 CF 267	4 102 0 165 XSQ= 3.99 PHI= 0.121 XP = 0.0457
96	IN ALL CASES ARE THCSE WHERE THE HIERARCHY OF NATIONAL JURISDICTION HAS NO LEVELS (156) GES,EA	1.00 OF 10	96	LEAN TOWARD BEING THOSE WHERE THE HIERARCHY OF NATIONAL JURISDICTION HAS FOUR, THREE, TWO OR ONE LEVEL (174) GES,EA	0.54 CF 320	0 174 10 146 XSQ= 9.42 PHI= -0.169 XP = 0.0021
106	TILT TOWARD BEING THOSE WHERE CLASS STRATIFICATICN, IF PRESENT, IS BASED CN WEALTH (77)	0.86 OF 7	106	TILT TOWARD BEING THOSE WHERE CLASS STRATIFICATION, IF PRESENT, IS BASED ON SOMETHING CTHER THAN WEALTH (126)	0.64 CF 196	6 71 1 125 XSQ= 5.09 PHI= 0.158 XP = 0.0241
130	IN ALL CASES ARE THCSE WHERE LEATHER WCRKING IS MAINLY DONE BY FEMALES (45)	1.00 OF 8	130	TILT TOWARD BEING THOSE WHERE LEATHER WORKING IS MAINLY DONE BY MALES (39)	0.51 CF 76	0 39 8 37 XSQ= 5.74 PHI= -0.261 XP = 0.0166

176	IN ALL CASES ARE THOSE 1.00 OF 11 WHERE THE COMMUNITY IS OTHER THAN A CLAN-COMMUNITY OR A COMMUNITY STRUCTURED OR SEGMENTED ON A CLAN BASIS (213)	176	LEAN LESS TOWARD BEING THOSE 0.54 OF 371 WHERE THE COMMUNITY IS OTHER THAN A CLAN-COMMUNITY OR A COMMUNITY STRUCTURED OR SEGMENTED ON A CLAN BASIS (213)	0 169 11 202 XSQ= 7.23 PHI= -0.138 XP = 0.0072
179	LEAN LESS TOWARD BEING THOSE 0.55 OF 11 WHERE THE COMMUNITY IS OTHER THAN STRUCTURED ON A NON-CLAN BASIS AND COMMONLY EXOGAMOUS (340)	179	LEAN MORE TOWARD BEING THOSE 0.90 OF 371 WHERE THE COMMUNITY IS OTHER THAN STRUCTURED ON A NON-CLAN BASIS AND COMMONLY EXOGAMOUS (340)	5 37 6 334 XSQ= 10.36 PHI= 0.165 XP = 0.0013
186	DRIFT MORE TOWARD BEING THOSE 0.91 OF 11 WHERE THE KIN GROUP IS OTHER THAN EXCLUSIVELY PATRILINEAL (250)	186	DRIFT LESS TOWARD BEING THOSE 0.62 OF 389 WHERE THE KIN GROUP IS OTHER THAN EXCLUSIVELY PATRILINEAL (250)	1 149 10 240 XSQ= 2.75 PHI= -0.083 XP = 0.0974
188	TEND TO BE THOSE 0.91 OF 11 WHERE THE KIN GROUP IS EXCLUSIVELY COGNATIC (148)	188	TEND TO BE THOSE 0.65 OF 389 WHERE THE KIN GROUP IS OTHER THAN EXCLUSIVELY COGNATIC (252)	10 138 1 251 XSQ= 11.82 PHI= 0.172 XP = 0.0006
192	TEND TO BE THOSE 0.82 OF 11 WHERE THE ONLY KIN GROUP PRESENT IS A KINDRED OR ELSE BILATERAL DESCENT IS INFERRED (111)	192	TEND TO BE THOSE 0.74 OF 389 OTHER THAN WHERE THE ONLY KIN GROUP PRESENT IS A KINDRED OR ELSE BILATERAL DESCENT IS INFERRED (289)	9 102 2 287 XSQ= 13.84 PHI= 0.186 XP = 0.0002
196	TILT TOWARD BEING THOSE 0.70 OF 10 WHERE INDIVIDUAL RIGHTS IN REAL PROPERTY, OR RULES FOR INHERITANCE, ARE ABSENT (87)	196	TILT TOWARD BEING THOSE 0.70 OF 271 WHERE INDIVIDUAL RIGHTS IN REAL PROPERTY, AND RULES FOR INHERITANCE, ARE PRESENT (194)	3 191 7 80 XSQ= 5.62 PHI= -0.141 XP = 0.0178
353	IN ALL CASES ARE THOSE 1.00 OF 4 WHERE THE CHILD-S INFERRED ANXIETY OVER NON-PERFORMANCE OF OBEDIENT BEHAVIOR IS LOW (32) B-B-C	353	DRIFT TOWARD BEING THOSE 0.60 OF 70 WHERE THE CHILD'S INFERRED ANXIETY OVER NON-PERFORMANCE OF OBEDIENT BEHAVIOR IS HIGH (42) B-B-C	0 42 4 28 XSQ= 3.37 PHI= -0.214 XP = 0.0662
417	TILT TOWARD BEING THOSE 0.75 OF 4 WHERE WARFARE IS NOT PREVALENT (9) LWS	417	TILT TOWARD BEING THOSE 0.85 OF 39 WHERE WARFARE IS PREVALENT (34) LWS	1 33 3 6 XSQ= 4.61 PHI= -0.327 XP = 0.0319

36 CULTURES
WHERE THE NATURAL ENVIRONMENT IS
'VERY HARSH,' OR SUB-TROPICAL BUSH, OR
TEMPERATE GRASSLAND (108) FWM

36 CULTURES
WHERE THE NATURAL ENVIRONMENT IS
OTHER THAN
'VERY HARSH,' OR SUB-TROPICAL BUSH, OR
TEMPERATE GRASSLAND (292) FWM

BACKGROUND ON PAGE 69

BOTH SUBJECT AND PREDICATE

108 IN LEFT COLUMN

ABIPON	ARANDA	ARYANS	AYMARA	BAJUN	BARABRA	BASSERI	BEJA	BERGDAMA	BURUSHO
CAMBA	CHAGGA	CHAMACOCO	CHENCHU	CHEYENNE	CHIBCHA	CHINANTEC	CHIR-APACHE	CHIRIGUANO	CHOROTI
CHUKCHEE	COCHITI	COMANCHE	COPR ESKIMO	CROW	DAGUR	DARD	DIEGUENO	DIERI	GILBERTESE
GOAJIRO	GOND	GROS VENTRE	HANO	HASANIA	HAVASUPAI	HAWAIIANS	HAZARA	HEHE	HERERO
HUICHOL	HUKUNDIKA	ICELANDERS	INCA	JEMEZ	JIVARO	KABYLE	KALMYK	KARIERA	KAZAK
KHALKA	KHEVSUR	KIOW-APACHE	KONSO	KORYAK	KUNG	LAPPS	MAMBILA	MANCHU	MAORI
MARICOPA	MASAI	MATACO	MAZATECO	MONGUOR	NAMA	NAVAHO	NOMLAKI	NUNIVAK	NURI
OMAHA	ONA	PAEZ	PAPAGO	PARAUJANO	PATHAN	PAWNEE	REGEIBAT	RUNDI	RWALA
SAMOYED	SANDAWE	SANPOIL	SARSI	SERI	SINDHI	SOMALI	SOTHO	SWAZI	TAMIL
TAOS	TAREUMIUT	TEHUELCHE	TETON	THONGA	TIBETANS	TIGRINYA	TODA	TRISTAN	TUBATULABAL
UTE	VENDA	WICHITA	YAHGAN	YOKUTS	YUKAGHIR	YUKI	ZUNI		

292 IN RIGHT COLUMN

	Left column			Right column		
3	DRIFT MORE TOWARD BEING THOSE LOCATED OUTSIDE OF AFRICA (320)	0.86 OF 108	3	DRIFT LESS TOWARD BEING THOSE LOCATED OUTSIDE OF AFRICA (320)	0.78 OF 292	15 65 93 227 XSQ= 2.95 PHI= -0.086 XP = 0.0859
6	TEND MORE TO BE THOSE LOCATED OUTSIDE OF THE INSULAR PACIFIC (330)	0.94 OF 108	6	TEND LESS TO BE THOSE LOCATED OUTSIDE OF THE INSULAR PACIFIC (330)	0.78 OF 292	6 64 102 228 XSQ= 13.51 PHI= -0.184 XP = 0.0002
8	TEND LESS TO BE THOSE LOCATED OUTSIDE OF NORTH AMERICA (330)	0.68 OF 108	8	TEND MORE TO BE THOSE LOCATED OUTSIDE OF NORTH AMERICA (330)	0.88 OF 292	35 35 73 257 XSQ= 21.38 PHI= 0.231 XP = 0.0000
14	TEND TO BE THOSE WHERE THE LATITUDE IS THIRTY DEGREES OR GREATER (119)	0.55 OF 108	14	TEND TO BE THOSE WHERE THE LATITUDE IS LESS THAN THIRTY DEGREES (281)	0.79 OF 292	59 60 49 232 XSQ= 42.20 PHI= 0.325 XP = 0.

15	TEND TO BE THOSE WHERE THE LATITUDE IS TWENTY DEGREES OR GREATER (183)	0.77 OF 108	15	TEND TO BE THOSE WHERE THE LATITUDE IS LESS THAN TWENTY DEGREES (217)	0.66 OF 292	83 100 25 192 XSQ= 55.96 PHI= 0.374 XP = 0.
44	TEND TO BE THOSE WHERE SETTLEMENTS ARE NON-FIXED (110)	0.59 OF 87	44	TEND TO BE THOSE WHERE SETTLEMENTS ARE FIXED (222)	0.76 OF 245	36 186 51 59 XSQ= 33.03 PHI= -0.315 XP = 0.
46	TEND LESS TO BE THOSE OTHER THAN WHERE SETTLEMENTS ARE NON-FIXED AND MOVEMENT IS NOMADIC (260)	0.57 OF 87	46	TEND MORE TO BE THOSE OTHER THAN WHERE SETTLEMENTS ARE NON-FIXED AND MOVEMENT IS NOMADIC (260)	0.86 OF 245	37 35 50 210 XSQ= 28.51 PHI= 0.293 XP = 0.0000
48	LEAN TOWARD BEING THOSE WHERE THE FOOD SUPPLY IS NOT SECURE, AND FOOD SHORTAGES ARE FREQUENT OR ANNUAL (41) MGW	0.79 OF 24	48	LEAN TOWARD BEING THOSE WHERE THE FOOD SUPPLY IS SECURE, AND FOOD SHORTAGES ARE RARE OR OCCASIONAL (38) MGW	0.60 OF 55	5 33 19 22 XSQ= 8.76 PHI= -0.333 XP = 0.0031
51	TILT LESS TOWARD BEING THOSE WHERE SUBSISTENCE IS PRIMARILY BY FOOD PRODUCTION -- I. E., AGRICULTURE OR HUSBANDRY -- RATHER THAN BY GATHERING (253)	0.54 OF 108	51	TILT MORE TOWARD BEING THOSE WHERE SUBSISTENCE IS PRIMARILY BY FOOD PRODUCTION -- I. E., AGRICULTURE OR HUSBANDRY -- RATHER THAN BY GATHERING (253)	0.67 OF 292	58 195 50 97 XSQ= 5.25 PHI= -0.115 XP = 0.0219
53	LEAN TOWARD BEING THOSE WHERE FOOD PRODUCTION IS BY INTENSIVE AGRICULTURE, RATHER THAN BY SIMPLE AGRICULTURE OR INCIPIENT FOOD PRODUCTION (91)	0.57 OF 42	53	LEAN TOWARD BEING THOSE WHERE FOOD PRODUCTION IS BY SIMPLE AGRICULTURE OR INCIPIENT FOOD PRODUCTION, RATHER THAN BY INTENSIVE AGRICULTURE (147)	0.66 OF 196	24 67 18 129 XSQ= 6.78 PHI= 0.169 XP = 0.0092
55	LEAN TOWARD BEING THOSE WHERE FOOD PRODUCTION IS BY INTENSIVE AGRICULTURE, RATHER THAN BY SIMPLE AGRICULTURE (91)	0.73 OF 33	55	LEAN TOWARD BEING THOSE WHERE FOOD PRODUCTION IS BY SIMPLE AGRICULTURE, RATHER THAN BY INTENSIVE AGRICULTURE (101)	0.58 OF 159	24 67 9 92 XSQ= 9.07 PHI= 0.217 XP = 0.0026
63	LEAN MORE TOWARD BEING THOSE WHERE HUSBANDRY, IF PRESENT, IS PRINCIPALLY IN THE FORM OF BOVINE, EQUINE, CAMEL-LIKE, OR DEER-LIKE ANIMALS, RATHER THAN PIGS, SHEEP, OR GOATS (152)	0.84 OF 58	63	LEAN LESS TOWARD BEING THOSE WHERE HUSBANDRY, IF PRESENT, IS PRINCIPALLY IN THE FORM OF BOVINE, EQUINE, CAMEL-LIKE, OR DEER-LIKE ANIMALS, RATHER THAN PIGS, SHEEP, OR GOATS (152)	0.61 OF 168	49 103 9 65 XSQ= 9.49 PHI= 0.205 XP = 0.0021
79	IN ALL CASES ARE THOSE WHERE NO CITY IS PRESENT (201)	1.00 OF 59	79	LEAN LESS TOWARD BEING THOSE WHERE NO CITY IS PRESENT (201)	0.86 OF 165	0 23 59 142 XSQ= 7.71 PHI= -0.186 XP = 0.0055

80	LEAN MORE TOWARD BEING THOSE 0.95 OF 59 WHERE NO CITY OR TOWN IS PRESENT (185)	80	LEAN LESS TOWARD BEING THOSE 0.78 OF 165 WHERE NO CITY OR TOWN IS PRESENT (185)	3 36 56 129 XSQ= 7.34 PHI= -0.181 XP = 0.0067
82	TILT LESS TOWARD BEING THOSE 0.69 OF 59 WHERE A CITY OR TOWN IS PRESENT, OR THE AVERAGE COMMUNITY SIZE IS FIFTY OR GREATER (178)	82	TILT MORE TOWARD BEING THOSE 0.83 OF 165 WHERE A CITY OR TOWN IS PRESENT, OR THE AVERAGE COMMUNITY SIZE IS FIFTY OR GREATER (178)	41 137 18 28 XSQ= 4.09 PHI= -0.135 XP = 0.0432
84	TILT MORE TOWARD BEING THOSE 0.94 OF 78 WHERE THE LEVEL OF POLITICAL INTEGRATION IS THE LITTLE STATE, THE MINIMAL STATE, THE AUTONOMOUS COMMUNITY, OR THE FAMILY (262) GPM	84	TILT LESS TOWARD BEING THOSE 0.84 OF 226 WHERE THE LEVEL OF POLITICAL INTEGRATION IS THE LITTLE STATE, THE MINIMAL STATE, THE AUTONOMOUS COMMUNITY, OR THE FAMILY (262) GPM	5 37 73 189 XSQ= 4.03 PHI= -0.115 XP = 0.0446
87	DRIFT MORE TOWARD BEING THOSE 0.97 OF 78 WHERE THE LEVEL OF POLITICAL INTEGRATION IS THE LARGE STATE, THE LITTLE STATE, THE MINIMAL STATE, OR THE AUTONOMOUS COMMUNITY (281) GPM	87	DRIFT LESS TOWARD BEING THOSE 0.91 OF 226 WHERE THE LEVEL OF POLITICAL INTEGRATION IS THE LARGE STATE, THE LITTLE STATE, THE MINIMAL STATE, OR THE AUTONOMOUS COMMUNITY (281) GPM	76 205 2 21 XSQ= 2.85 PHI= 0.097 XP = 0.0912
90	TILT MORE TOWARD BEING THOSE 0.92 OF 38 WHERE, IF A HEREDITARY HEADMANSHIP IS PRESENT, SUCCESSION IS PATRILINEAL, RATHER THAN MATRILINEAL (127)	90	TILT LESS TOWARD BEING THOSE 0.72 OF 127 WHERE, IF A HEREDITARY HEADMANSHIP IS PRESENT, SUCCESSION IS PATRILINEAL, RATHER THAN MATRILINEAL (127)	35 92 3 35 XSQ= 5.32 PHI= 0.180 XP = 0.0211
97	DRIFT MORE TOWARD BEING THOSE 0.90 OF 87 WHERE THE HIERARCHY OF LOCAL JURISDICTION HAS THREE OR TWO LEVELS (273) GES,EA	97	DRIFT LESS TOWARD BEING THOSE 0.80 OF 244 WHERE THE HIERARCHY OF LOCAL JURISDICTION HAS THREE OR TWO LEVELS (273) GES,EA	9 49 78 195 XSQ= 3.56 PHI= -0.104 XP = 0.0592
98	TILT LESS TOWARD BEING THOSE 0.63 OF 87 WHERE THE HIERARCHY OF LOCAL JURISDICTION HAS FOUR OR THREE LEVELS (238) GES,EA	98	TILT MORE TOWARD BEING THOSE 0.75 OF 244 WHERE THE HIERARCHY OF LOCAL JURISDICTION HAS FOUR OR THREE LEVELS (238) GES,EA	55 183 32 61 XSQ= 3.84 PHI= -0.108 XP = 0.0500
131	TEND LESS TO BE THOSE 0.61 OF 38 WHERE THE CONSTRUCTION OF PERMANENT HOUSES OR THE ERECTION OF TEMPORARY DWELLINGS IS MAINLY DONE BY MALES (136)	131	TEND MORE TO BE THOSE 0.95 OF 119 WHERE THE CONSTRUCTION OF PERMANENT HOUSES OR THE ERECTION OF TEMPORARY DWELLINGS IS MAINLY DONE BY MALES (136)	23 113 15 6 XSQ= 26.57 PHI= -0.411 XP = 0.0000
137	TILT TOWARD BEING THOSE 0.79 OF 29 WHERE INVIDIOUS DISPLAY OF WEALTH IS MODERATELY, LITTLE, OR NEGATIVELY EMPHASIZED (52) PES	137	TILT TOWARD BEING THOSE 0.52 OF 60 WHERE INVIDIOUS DISPLAY OF WEALTH IS STRONGLY EMPHASIZED (37) PES	6 31 23 29 XSQ= 6.50 PHI= -0.270 XP = 0.0108

163	IN ALL CASES ARE THOSE 1.00 OF 6 WHERE THE EMPHASIS ON INDIVIDUAL VOLITION AS THE CAUSE OF CRIME IS LOW (10) MJ	163	TILT TOWARD BEING THOSE 0.64 OF 11 WHERE THE EMPHASIS ON INDIVIDUAL VOLITICN AS THE CAUSE OF CRIME IS HIGH (7) MJ	0 7 6 4 XSQ= 4.13 PHI= -0.493 EP = 0.0175
176	LEAN MORE TOWARD BEING THOSE 0.67 OF 106 WHERE THE COMMUNITY IS OTHER THAN A CLAN-COMMUNITY OR A COMMUNITY STRUCTURED OR SEGMENTED ON A CLAN BASIS (213)	176	LEAN LESS TOWARD BEING THOSE 0.51 OF 276 WHERE THE COMMUNITY IS OTHER THAN A CLAN-COMMUNITY OR A COMMUNITY STRUCTURED OR SEGMENTED ON A CLAN BASIS (213)	35 134 71 142 XSQ= 6.87 PHI= -0.134 XP = 0.0087
178	LEAN MORE TOWARD BEING THOSE 0.88 OF 106 WHERE THE COMMUNITY IS OTHER THAN SEGMENTED ON A CLAN BASIS AND NON-EXOGAMOUS (295)	178	LEAN LESS TOWARD BEING THOSE 0.73 OF 276 WHERE THE COMMUNITY IS OTHER THAN SEGMENTED ON A CLAN BASIS AND NON-EXOGAMOUS (295)	13 74 93 202 XSQ= 8.41 PHI= -0.148 XP = 0.0037
179	DRIFT LESS TOWARD BEING THOSE 0.84 OF 106 WHERE THE COMMUNITY IS OTHER THAN STRUCTURED ON A NON-CLAN BASIS AND COMMONLY EXOGAMOUS (340)	179	DRIFT MORE TOWARD BEING THOSE 0.91 OF 276 WHERE THE COMMUNITY IS OTHER THAN STRUCTURED ON A NON-CLAN BASIS AND COMMONLY EXOGAMOUS (340)	17 25 89 251 XSQ= 3.13 PHI= 0.091 XP = 0.0767
184	DRIFT LESS TOWARD BEING THOSE 0.59 OF 59 WHERE THE LARGEST NON-COGNATIC KIN GROUP IS SMALLER THAN A PHRATRY, I. E. A SIB OR LINEAGE (175)	184	DRIFT MORE TOWARD BEING THOSE 0.73 OF 193 WHERE THE LARGEST NON-COGNATIC KIN GROUP IS SMALLER THAN A PHRATRY, I. E. A SIB OR LINEAGE (175)	24 53 35 140 XSQ= 3.12 PHI= 0.111 XP = 0.0772
187	DRIFT MORE TOWARD BEING THOSE 0.92 OF 108 WHERE THE KIN GROUP IS OTHER THAN EXCLUSIVELY MATRILINEAL (344)	187	DRIFT LESS TOWARD BEING THOSE 0.84 OF 291 WHERE THE KIN GROUP IS OTHER THAN EXCLUSIVELY MATRILINEAL (344)	9 46 99 245 XSQ= 3.10 PHI= -0.088 XP = 0.0783
188	TILT LESS TOWARD BEING THOSE 0.55 OF 108 WHERE THE KIN GROUP IS OTHER THAN EXCLUSIVELY COGNATIC (252)	188	TILT MORE TOWARD BEING THOSE 0.66 OF 292 WHERE THE KIN GROUP IS OTHER THAN EXCLUSIVELY COGNATIC (252)	49 99 59 193 XSQ= 3.97 PHI= 0.100 XP = 0.0464
190	DRIFT MORE TOWARD BEING THOSE 0.85 OF 59 WHERE THE KIN GROUP IS PATRILINEAL OR DOUBLE-DESCENT, RATHER THAN MATRILINEAL (186)	190	DRIFT LESS TOWARD BEING THOSE 0.72 OF 188 WHERE THE KIN GROUP IS PATRILINEAL OR DOUBLE-DESCENT, RATHER THAN MATRILINEAL (186)	50 136 9 52 XSQ= 3.08 PHI= 0.112 XP = 0.0793
192	LEAN LESS TOWARD BEING THOSE 0.62 OF 108 OTHER THAN WHERE THE ONLY KIN GROUP PRESENT IS A KINDRED OR ELSE BILATERAL DESCENT IS INFERRED (289)	192	LEAN MORE TOWARD BEING THOSE 0.76 OF 292 OTHER THAN WHERE THE ONLY KIN GROUP PRESENT IS A KINDRED OR ELSE BILATERAL DESCENT IS INFERRED (289)	41 70 67 222 XSQ= 7.01 PHI= 0.132 XP = 0.0081

Left	Right	Statistics
196 TEND TO BE THOSE 0.51 OF 86 WHERE INDIVIDUAL RIGHTS IN REAL PROPERTY, OR RULES FOR INHERITANCE, ARE ABSENT (87)	196 TEND TO BE THOSE 0.78 OF 195 WHERE INDIVIDUAL RIGHTS IN REAL PROPERTY, AND RULES FOR INHERITANCE, ARE PRESENT (194)	42 152 44 43 XSQ= 22.32 PHI= -0.282 XP = 0.0000
213 TILT TOWARD BEING THOSE 0.63 OF 103 WHERE FIRST COUSIN MARRIAGE IS NOT PERMITTED (198)	213 TILT TOWARD BEING THOSE 0.50 OF 267 WHERE FIRST COUSIN MARRIAGE IS PERMITTED (172)	38 134 65 133 XSQ= 4.76 PHI= -0.113 XP = 0.0291
214 DRIFT MORE TOWARD BEING THOSE 0.95 OF 38 WHERE FIRST COUSIN MARRIAGE, IF PERMITTED, IS OTHER THAN UNILATERAL (144)	214 DRIFT LESS TOWARD BEING THOSE 0.81 OF 134 WHERE FIRST COUSIN MARRIAGE, IF PERMITTED, IS OTHER THAN UNILATERAL (144)	2 26 36 108 XSQ= 3.37 PHI= -0.140 XP = 0.0665
221 DRIFT MORE TOWARD BEING THOSE 0.95 OF 103 WHERE MATRILATERAL CROSS-COUSIN MARRIAGE IS NOT PRESCRIBED OR PREFERRED (335)	221 DRIFT LESS TOWARD BEING THOSE 0.89 OF 267 WHERE MATRILATERAL CROSS-COUSIN MARRIAGE IS NOT PRESCRIBED OR PREFERRED (335)	5 30 98 237 XSQ= 2.83 PHI= -0.087 XP = 0.0926
225 TILT TOWARD BEING THOSE 0.63 OF 16 WHERE COUSIN MARRIAGE IS PREFERENTIALLY OR PERMISSIVELY PATRILATERAL, RATHER THAN MATRILATERAL (23)	225 TILT TOWARD BEING THOSE 0.74 OF 50 WHERE COUSIN MARRIAGE IS PREFERENTIALLY OR PERMISSIVELY MATRILATERAL, RATHER THAN PATRILATERAL (43)	10 13 6 37 XSQ= 5.60 PHI= 0.291 XP = 0.0180
282 DRIFT TOWARD BEING THOSE 0.67 OF 12 WHERE THE STRENGTH OF DESIRE FOR CHILDREN IS HIGH (16) BCA	282 DRIFT TOWARD BEING THOSE 0.67 OF 24 WHERE THE STRENGTH OF DESIRE FOR CHILDREN IS LOW OR ABSENT (20) BCA	8 8 4 16 XSQ= 2.38 PHI= 0.257 EP = 0.0815
332 IN ALL CASES ARE THOSE 1.00 OF 3 WHERE THE AGE AT BEGINNING OF MODESTY TRAINING IS LOWER THAN SIX YEARS (8) W-C	332 DRIFT TOWARD BEING THOSE 0.64 OF 14 WHERE THE AGE AT BEGINNING OF MODESTY TRAINING IS SIX YEARS OR HIGHER (9) W-C	0 9 3 5 XSQ= 1.92 PHI= -0.336 EP = 0.0824
335 DRIFT TOWARD BEING THOSE 0.80 OF 10 WHERE INITIAL INDULGENCE OF DEPENDENCY IS HIGH (20) WNS	335 DRIFT TOWARD BEING THOSE 0.57 OF 28 WHERE INITIAL INDULGENCE OF DEPENDENCY IS LOW (18) WNS	8 12 2 16 XSQ= 2.72 PHI= 0.268 EP = 0.0673
343 DRIFT TOWARD BEING THOSE 0.79 OF 19 WHERE THE CHILD'S INFERRED CONFLICT REGARDING NURTURANT BEHAVIOR IS HIGH (29) B-B-C	343 DRIFT TOWARD BEING THOSE 0.50 OF 28 WHERE THE CHILD'S INFERRED CONFLICT REGARDING NURTURANT BEHAVIOR IS LOW (18) B-B-C	15 14 4 14 XSQ= 2.88 PHI= 0.248 XP = 0.0896

348	DRIFT TOWARD BEING THOSE 0.68 OF 25 WHERE THE TOTAL POSITIVE PRESSURE TOWARD DEVELOPING ACHIEVEMENT BEHAVIOR IN THE CHILD IS HIGH (32) B-B-C	348	DRIFT TOWARD BEING THOSE 0.61 OF 38 WHERE THE TOTAL POSITIVE PRESSURE TOWARD DEVELOPING ACHIEVEMENT BEHAVIOR IN THE CHILD IS LOW (31) B-B-C	17 15 8 23 XSQ= 3.83 PHI= 0.247 XP = 0.0502
349	TILT TOWARD BEING THOSE 0.76 OF 25 WHERE THE CHILD'S INFERRED ANXIETY OVER NON-PERFORMANCE OF ACHIEVEMENT BEHAVIOR IS HIGH (34) B-B-C	349	TILT TOWARD BEING THOSE 0.59 OF 37 WHERE THE CHILD'S INFERRED ANXIETY OVER NON-PERFORMANCE OF ACHIEVEMENT BEHAVIOR IS LOW (28) B-B-C	19 15 6 22 XSQ= 6.21 PHI= 0.316 XP = 0.0127
350	TILT TOWARD BEING THOSE 0.76 OF 25 WHERE THE CHILD'S INFERRED ANXIETY OVER PERFORMANCE OF ACHIEVEMENT BEHAVIOR IS HIGH (34) B-B-C	350	TILT TOWARD BEING THOSE 0.57 OF 35 WHERE THE CHILD'S INFERRED ANXIETY OVER PERFORMANCE OF ACHIEVEMENT BEHAVIOR IS LOW (26) B-B-C	19 15 6 20 XSQ= 5.24 PHI= 0.296 XP = 0.0220
352	TILT MORE TOWARD BEING THOSE 0.80 OF 25 WHERE THE TOTAL POSITIVE PRESSURE TOWARD DEVELOPING OBEDIENT BEHAVIOR IN THE CHILD IS HIGH (44) B-B-C	352	TILT LESS TOWARD BEING THOSE 0.51 OF 47 WHERE THE TOTAL POSITIVE PRESSURE TOWARD DEVELOPING OBEDIENT BEHAVIOR IN THE CHILD IS HIGH (44) B-B-C	20 24 5 23 XSQ= 4.60 PHI= 0.253 XP = 0.0320
370	TILT MORE TOWARD BEING THOSE 0.74 OF 57 WHERE THE SEGREGATION OF ADOLESCENT BOYS IS ABSENT (148)	370	TILT LESS TOWARD BEING THOSE 0.57 OF 186 WHERE THE SEGREGATION OF ADOLESCENT BOYS IS ABSENT (148)	15 80 42 106 XSQ= 4.43 PHI= -0.135 XP = 0.0353
427	DRIFT MORE TOWARD BEING THOSE 0.70 OF 40 WHERE A HIGH GOD, IF PRESENT, IS ACTIVE, RATHER THAN INACTIVE (87) GES,EA	427	DRIFT LESS TOWARD BEING THOSE 0.51 OF 116 WHERE A HIGH GOD, IF PRESENT, IS ACTIVE, RATHER THAN INACTIVE (87) GES,EA	28 59 12 57 XSQ= 3.67 PHI= 0.153 XP = 0.0552
431	IN ALL CASES ARE THOSE 1.00 OF 8 WHERE SUPERNATURAL SANCTIONS FOR MORALITY, HAVING AN EFFECT ON AN INDIVIDUAL'S AFTERLIFE, ARE ABSENT OR UNREPORTED (25) GES	431	DRIFT LESS TOWARD BEING THOSE 0.63 OF 27 WHERE SUPERNATURAL SANCTIONS FOR MORALITY, HAVING AN EFFECT ON AN INDIVIDUAL'S AFTERLIFE, ARE ABSENT OR UNREPORTED (25) GES	0 10 8 17 XSQ= 2.53 PHI= -0.269 EP = 0.0734
435	LEAN TOWARD BEING THOSE 0.69 OF 13 WHERE ABANDONMENT OF THE HOUSE OF THE DEAD IS PRACTICED (12) LWS	435	LEAN TOWARD BEING THOSE 0.83 OF 18 WHERE ABANDONMENT OF THE HOUSE OF THE DEAD IS NOT PRACTICED (19) LWS	9 3 4 15 XSQ= 6.71 PHI= 0.465 EP = 0.0075
445	DRIFT TOWARD BEING THOSE 0.70 OF 23 WHERE SORCERY IS IMPORTANT (26) EBW,DH	445	DRIFT TOWARD BEING THOSE 0.62 OF 26 WHERE SORCERY IS UNIMPORTANT (23) BBW,DH	16 10 7 16 XSQ= 3.57 PHI= 0.270 XP = 0.0587

447	DRIFT TOWARD BEING THOSE WHERE LOVE MAGIC IS PRESENT (20) S-R	0.89 OF 9	447	DRIFT TOWARD BEING THOSE WHERE LOVE MAGIC IS ABSENT (13) S-R	0.50 OF 24		8 12 1 12 XSQ= 2.68 PHI= 0.285 EP = 0.0560
452	TILT TOWARD BEING THOSE WHERE TOTEMISM WITH FOOD TABOOS IS ABSENT (24) WNS	0.80 OF 15	452	TILT TOWARD BEING THOSE WHERE TOTEMISM WITH FOOD TABOOS IS PRESENT (19) WNS	0.57 OF 28		3 16 12 12 XSQ= 4.06 PHI= -0.307 XP = 0.0439
455	TILT TOWARD BEING THOSE WHERE THE MODE OF THE INDIVIDUAL'S CONTACT WITH THE DIVINE IS CONDUCIVE TO THE DEVELOPMENT OF THE INDIVIDUAL'S NEED TO ACHIEVE (17) DCM	0.69 OF 16	455	TILT TOWARD BEING THOSE WHERE THE MODE OF THE INDIVIDUAL'S CONTACT WITH THE DIVINE IS NOT CONDUCIVE TO THE DEVELOPMENT OF THE INDIVIDUAL'S NEED TO ACHIEVE (19) DCM	0.70 OF 20		11 6 5 14 XSQ= 3.91 PHI= 0.330 EP = 0.0425
459	LEAN TOWARD BEING THOSE WHERE GAMES, IF PRESENT, INCLUDE GAMES OF CHANCE (82) R-A-B,EA	0.67 OF 52	459	LEAN TOWARD BEING THOSE WHERE GAMES, IF PRESENT, DO NOT INCLUDE GAMES OF CHANCE (89) R-A-B,EA	0.61 OF 119		35 47 17 72 XSQ= 10.13 PHI= 0.243 XP = 0.0015
460	TILT MORE TOWARD BEING THOSE WHERE GAMES, IF PRESENT, ARE NOT LIMITED TO GAMES OF SKILL ONLY (104) R-A-B,EA	0.75 OF 52	460	TILT LESS TOWARD BEING THOSE WHERE GAMES, IF PRESENT, ARE NOT LIMITED TO GAMES OF SKILL ONLY (104) R-A-B,EA	0.55 OF 119		13 54 39 65 XSQ= 5.48 PHI= -0.179 XP = 0.0192
480	DRIFT TOWARD BEING THOSE WHERE COMPLEXITY OF ARTISTIC DESIGN IS LOW (15) HB	0.75 OF 12	480	DRIFT TOWARD BEING THOSE WHERE COMPLEXITY OF ARTISTIC DESIGN IS HIGH (14) HB	0.65 OF 17		3 11 9 6 XSQ= 2.99 PHI= -0.321 EP = 0.0604

```
37  CULTURES                                      37  CULTURES
    WHERE THE NATURAL ENVIRONMENT IS                  WHERE THE NATURAL ENVIRONMENT IS
    SUB-TROPICAL BUSH  (24) FWM                       OTHER THAN
                                                      SUB-TROPICAL BUSH  (376) FWM

BACKGROUND ON PAGE 69                                                                       SUBJECT ONLY

      24  IN LEFT COLUMN

ABIPON     ARYANS     CAMBA      CHAGGA     CHAMACOCO  CHENCHU    CHINANTEC  CHIRIGUANO  CHOROTI    GILBERTESE
GOND       HAWAIIANS  HEHE       MATACO     MAZATECO   PARAUJANO  PATHAN     SANDAWE     SINCHI     SWAZI
TAMIL      THONGA     TIGRINYA   TODA

      376  IN RIGHT COLUMN

------------------------------------------------------------------------------------------------------------
 13  IN ALL CASES ARE THOSE          1.00 OF  24      13  TILT LESS TOWARD BEING THOSE   0.81 OF 376         0   71
     WHERE THE LATITUDE IS                                WHERE THE LATITUDE IS                             24  305
     LESS THAN FORTY DEGREES  (329)                       LESS THAN FORTY DEGREES  (329)             XSQ=     4.29
                                                                                                     PHI=   -0.104
                                                                                                     XP =   0.0383

 14  TILT MORE TOWARD BEING THOSE    0.92 OF  24      14  TILT LESS TOWARD BEING THOSE   0.69 OF 376         2  117
     WHERE THE LATITUDE IS                                WHERE THE LATITUDE IS                             22  259
     LESS THAN THIRTY DEGREES  (281)                      LESS THAN THIRTY DEGREES  (281)            XSQ=     4.57
                                                                                                     PHI=   -0.107
                                                                                                     XP =   0.0326

187  IN ALL CASES ARE THOSE          1.00 OF  24     187  DRIFT LESS TOWARD BEING THOSE  0.85 OF 375         0   55
     WHERE THE KIN GROUP IS                               WHERE THE KIN GROUP IS                            24  320
     OTHER THAN                                           OTHER THAN                                 XSQ=     2.94
     EXCLUSIVELY MATRILINEAL  (344)                       EXCLUSIVELY MATRILINEAL  (344)             PHI=   -0.086
                                                                                                     XP =   0.0863

190  IN ALL CASES ARE THOSE          1.00 OF  13     190  DRIFT LESS TOWARD BEING THOSE  0.74 OF 234        13  173
     WHERE THE KIN GROUP IS                               WHERE THE KIN GROUP IS                             0   61
     PATRILINEAL OR DOUBLE-DESCENT,                       PATRILINEAL OR DOUBLE-DESCENT,             XSQ=     3.21
     RATHER THAN MATRILINEAL  (186)                       RATHER THAN MATRILINEAL  (186)             PHI=    0.114
                                                                                                     XP =   0.0733

339  IN ALL CASES ARE THOSE          1.00 OF   4     339  DRIFT TOWARD BEING THOSE       0.61 OF  69         4   27
     WHERE THE CHILD'S INFERRED CONFLICT                  WHERE THE CHILD'S INFERRED CONFLICT                0   42
     REGARDING RESPONSIBLE BEHAVIOR                       REGARDING RESPONSIBLE BEHAVIOR             XSQ=     3.51
     IS HIGH  (31) B-B-C                                  IS LOW  (42) B-B-C                         PHI=    0.219
                                                                                                     XP =   0.0609
```

385	TILT TOWARD BEING THOSE WHERE SEXUAL EXPRESSION BY THE YOUNG IS RESTRICTED (22) F-B	0.71 OF 7	385	TILT TOWARD BEING THOSE WHERE SEXUAL EXPRESSION BY THE YOUNG IS SEMI-RESTRICTED OR PERMITTED (64) F-B	0.78 OF 79	5 17 2 62 XSQ= 6.00 PHI= 0.264 XP = 0.0143
392	TILT TOWARD BEING THOSE WHERE PREMARITAL SEX RELATIONS ARE FREELY PERMITTED (67) JTW,EA	0.73 OF 11	392	TILT TOWARD BEING THOSE WHERE PREMARITAL SEX RELATIONS ARE STRONGLY PUNISHED AND IN FACT RARE, OR WEAKLY PUNISHED AND IN FACT NOT RARE, OR PUNISHED ONLY IF PREGNANCY RESULTS (112) JTW,EA	0.65 OF 168	3 109 8 59 XSQ= 4.73 PHI= -0.163 XP = 0.0296
445	IN ALL CASES ARE THOSE WHERE SORCERY IS IMPORTANT (26) EBW,DH	1.00 OF 6	445	TILT TOWARD BEING THOSE WHERE SORCERY IS UNIMPORTANT (23) BBW,DH	0.53 OF 43	6 20 0 23 XSQ= 4.09 PHI= 0.289 XP = 0.0431

```
************************************************************************************************************

38  CULTURES                                          38  CULTURES
    WHERE THE NATURAL ENVIRONMENT IS                      WHERE THE NATURAL ENVIRONMENT IS
    TEMPERATE GRASSLAND  (25) FWM                         OTHER THAN
                                                          TEMPERATE GRASSLAND  (375) FWM


BACKGROUND ON PAGE 69                                                                          SUBJECT ONLY
............................................................................................................

      25  IN LEFT COLUMN

CHEYENNE    COMANCHE    CROW        DAGUR       GROS VENTRE KAZAK       KHEVSUR     KIOW-APACHE KONSO       MAMBILA
MANCHU      MAORI       NOMLAKI     OMAHA       PAWNEE      RUNDI       SANPOIL     SARSI       SOTHO       TETON
TRISTAN     VENDA       WICHITA     YOKUTS      YUKI

     375  IN RIGHT COLUMN

------------------------------------------------------------------------------------------------------------
  8  TEND TO BE THOSE                0.56 OF  25      8  TEND TO BE THOSE               0.85 OF 375        14   56
     LOCATED IN NORTH AMERICA  (70)                      LOCATED OUTSIDE OF                                 11  319
                                                         NORTH AMERICA  (330)                         XSQ=   24.61
                                                                                                      PHI=   0.248
                                                                                                      XP =  0.0000

  9  IN ALL CASES ARE THOSE          1.00 OF  25      9  TILT LESS TOWARD BEING THOSE   0.83 OF 375         0   65
     LOCATED OUTSIDE OF                                  LOCATED OUTSIDE OF                                 25  310
     SOUTH AMERICA  (335)                                SOUTH AMERICA  (335)                         XSQ=    3.98
                                                                                                      PHI=  -0.100
                                                                                                      XP =  0.0461

 14  TEND TO BE THOSE                0.80 OF  25     14  TEND TO BE THOSE               0.74 OF 375        20   99
     WHERE THE LATITUDE IS                               WHERE THE LATITUDE IS                               5  276
     THIRTY DEGREES OR GREATER  (119)                    LESS THAN THIRTY DEGREES  (281)              XSQ=   29.71
                                                                                                      PHI=   0.273
                                                                                                      XP =  0.0000

 15  TEND TO BE THOSE                0.88 OF  25     15  TEND TO BE THOSE               0.57 OF 375        22  161
     WHERE THE LATITUDE IS                               WHERE THE LATITUDE IS                               3  214
     TWENTY DEGREES OR GREATER  (183)                    LESS THAN TWENTY DEGREES  (217)              XSQ=   17.41
                                                                                                      PHI=   0.209
                                                                                                      XP =  0.0000

 48  DRIFT TOWARD BEING THOSE        0.88 OF   8     48  DRIFT TOWARD BEING THOSE       0.52 OF  71         1   37
     WHERE THE FOOD SUPPLY IS NOT SECURE,                WHERE THE FOOD SUPPLY IS SECURE,                    7   34
     AND FOOD SHORTAGES ARE                              AND FOOD SHORTAGES ARE                       XSQ=    3.07
     FREQUENT OR ANNUAL  (41) MGW                        RARE OR OCCASIONAL  (38) MGW                 PHI=  -0.197
                                                                                                      XP =  0.0797
```

51	DRIFT TOWARD BEING THOSE 0.56 OF 25 WHERE SUBSISTENCE IS PRIMARILY BY FOOD GATHERING -- I. E., HUNTING, FISHING, OR COLLECTING -- RATHER THAN FOOD PRODUCTION (147)	51	DRIFT TOWARD BEING THOSE 0.65 OF 375 WHERE SUBSISTENCE IS PRIMARILY BY FOOD PRODUCTION -- I. E., AGRICULTURE OR HUSBANDRY -- RATHER THAN BY GATHERING (253)	11 242 14 133 XSQ= 3.41 PHI= -0.092 XP = 0.0647
63	DRIFT MORE TOWARD BEING THOSE 0.92 OF 13 WHERE HUSBANDRY, IF PRESENT, IS PRINCIPALLY IN THE FORM OF BOVINE, EQUINE, CAMEL-LIKE, OR DEER-LIKE ANIMALS, RATHER THAN PIGS, SHEEP, OR GOATS (152)	63	DRIFT LESS TOWARD BEING THOSE 0.66 OF 213 WHERE HUSBANDRY, IF PRESENT, IS PRINCIPALLY IN THE FORM OF BOVINE, EQUINE, CAMEL-LIKE, OR DEER-LIKE ANIMALS, RATHER THAN PIGS, SHEEP, OR GOATS (152)	12 140 1 73 XSQ= 2.82 PHI= 0.112 XP = 0.0933
73	TILT MORE TOWARD BEING THOSE 0.81 OF 16 WHERE WEAVING IS ABSENT (130)	73	TILT LESS TOWARD BEING THOSE 0.50 OF 232 WHERE WEAVING IS ABSENT (130)	3 115 13 117 XSQ= 4.53 PHI= -0.135 XP = 0.0333
86	TILT TOWARD BEING THOSE 0.80 OF 15 WHERE THE LEVEL OF POLITICAL INTEGRATION IS THE LARGE STATE, THE LITTLE STATE, OR THE MINIMAL STATE (148) GPM	86	TILT TOWARD BEING THOSE 0.53 OF 289 WHERE THE LEVEL OF POLITICAL INTEGRATION IS THE AUTONOMOUS COMMUNITY, OR THE FAMILY (156) GPM	12 136 3 153 XSQ= 4.95 PHI= 0.128 XP = 0.0262
131	TEND TO BE THOSE 0.60 OF 10 WHERE THE CONSTRUCTION OF PERMANENT HOUSES OR THE ERECTION OF TEMPORARY DWELLINGS IS MAINLY DONE BY FEMALES (21)	131	TEND TO BE THOSE 0.90 OF 147 WHERE THE CONSTRUCTION OF PERMANENT HOUSES OR THE ERECTION OF TEMPORARY DWELLINGS IS MAINLY DONE BY MALES (136)	4 132 6 15 XSQ= 15.97 PHI= -0.319 XP = 0.0001
196	LEAN TOWARD BEING THOSE 0.64 OF 22 WHERE INDIVIDUAL RIGHTS IN REAL PROPERTY, OR RULES FOR INHERITANCE, ARE ABSENT (87)	196	LEAN TOWARD BEING THOSE 0.72 OF 259 WHERE INDIVIDUAL RIGHTS IN REAL PROPERTY, AND RULES FOR INHERITANCE, ARE PRESENT (194)	8 186 14 73 XSQ= 10.32 PHI= -0.192 XP = 0.0013
213	TILT MORE TOWARD BEING THOSE 0.79 OF 24 WHERE FIRST COUSIN MARRIAGE IS NOT PERMITTED (198)	213	TILT LESS TOWARD BEING THOSE 0.52 OF 346 WHERE FIRST COUSIN MARRIAGE IS NOT PERMITTED (198)	5 167 19 179 XSQ= 5.73 PHI= -0.124 XP = 0.0167
306	IN ALL CASES ARE THOSE 1.00 OF 5 WHERE THE EARLY DEPENDENCE SATISFACTION POTENTIAL IS HIGH (28) W-C	306	DRIFT TOWARD BEING THOSE 0.51 OF 47 WHERE THE EARLY DEPENDENCE SATISFACTION POTENTIAL IS LOW (24) W-C	5 23 0 24 XSQ= 2.91 PHI= 0.237 XP = 0.0881
349	IN ALL CASES ARE THOSE 1.00 OF 9 WHERE THE CHILD'S INFERRED ANXIETY OVER NON-PERFORMANCE OF ACHIEVEMENT BEHAVIOR IS HIGH (34) B-B-C	349	LEAN TOWARD BEING THOSE 0.53 OF 53 WHERE THE CHILD'S INFERRED ANXIETY OVER NON-PERFORMANCE OF ACHIEVEMENT BEHAVIOR IS LOW (28) B-B-C	9 25 0 28 XSQ= 6.67 PHI= 0.328 XP = 0.0098

391	TILT TOWARD BEING THOSE 0.85 OF 13 WHERE PREMARITAL SEX RELATIONS ARE STRONGLY PUNISHED AND IN FACT RARE, OR WEAKLY PUNISHED AND IN FACT NCT RARE (89) JTW,EA	391	TILT TOWARD BEING THOSE 0.53 OF 166 WHERE PREMARITAL SEX RELATIONS ARE PUNISHED ONLY IF PREGNANCY RESULTS, OR FREELY PERMITTED (90) JTW,EA	11 78 2 88 XSQ= 5.41 PHI= 0.174 XP = 0.0201
455	TILT TOWARD BEING THOSE 0.86 OF 7 WHERE THE MODE CF THE INDIVIDUAL'S CONTACT WITH THE DIVINE IS CONDUCIVE TO THE DEVELOPMENT OF THE INDIVIDUAL'S NEED TO ACHIEVE (17) DCM	455	TILT TOWARD BEING THOSE 0.62 OF 29 WHERE THE MODE OF THE INDIVIDUAL'S CONTACT WITH THE DIVINE IS NOT CONDUCIVE TO THE DEVELOPMENT OF THE INDIVIDUAL'S NEED TO ACHIEVE (19) DCM	6 11 1 18 XSQ= 3.43 PHI= 0.309 EP = 0.0365
459	TILT TOWARD BEING THOSE 0.83 OF 12 WHERE GAMES, IF PRESENT, INCLUDE GAMES OF CHANCE (82) R-A-B,EA	459	TILT TOWARD BEING THOSE 0.55 OF 159 WHERE GAMES, IF PRESENT, DO NOT INCLUDE GAMES OF CHANCE (89) R-A-B,EA	10 72 2 87 XSQ= 5.04 PHI= 0.172 XP = 0.0248
460	TILT MORE TOWARD BEING THOSE 0.92 OF 12 WHERE GAMES, IF PRESENT, ARE NCT LIMITED TO GAMES OF SKILL CNLY (104) R-A-B,EA	460	TILT LESS TOWARD BEING THOSE 0.58 OF 159 WHERE GAMES, IF PRESENT, ARE NOT LIMITED TO GAMES OF SKILL ONLY (104) R-A-B,EA	1 66 11 93 XSQ= 3.86 PHI= -0.150 XP = 0.0496

39 CULTURES
WHERE THE NATURAL ENVIRONMENT IS
NORTHERN CONIFEROUS FOREST (21) FWM

39 CULTURES
WHERE THE NATURAL ENVIRONMENT IS
OTHER THAN
NORTHERN CONIFEROUS FOREST (379) FWM

BACKGROUND ON PAGE 69

SUBJECT ONLY

21 IN LEFT COLUMN

ALBANIANS, BURYAT, CREE, EYAK, FOX, GILYAK, HAIDA, HURON, INGALIK, KASKA, KET, KUTENAI, KWAKIUTL, NABESNA, NASKAPI, OJIBWA, PENOBSCOT, TENINO, TSHIMSHIAN, TWANA, YAKUT

379 IN RIGHT COLUMN

	Left column			Right column		
3	IN ALL CASES ARE THOSE LOCATED OUTSIDE OF AFRICA (320)	1.00 OF 21	3	TILT LESS TOWARD BEING THOSE LOCATED OUTSIDE OF AFRICA (320)	0.79 OF 379	0 80 21 299 XSQ= 4.30 PHI= -0.104 XP = 0.0381
6	IN ALL CASES ARE THOSE LOCATED OUTSIDE OF THE INSULAR PACIFIC (330)	1.00 OF 21	6	DRIFT LESS TOWARD BEING THOSE LOCATED OUTSIDE OF THE INSULAR PACIFIC (330)	0.82 OF 379	0 70 21 309 XSQ= 3.51 PHI= -0.094 XP = 0.0610
8	TEND TO BE THOSE LOCATED IN NORTH AMERICA (70)	0.76 OF 21	8	TEND TO BE THOSE LOCATED OUTSIDE OF NORTH AMERICA (330)	0.86 OF 379	16 54 5 325 XSQ= 48.68 PHI= 0.349 XP = 0.
9	IN ALL CASES ARE THOSE LOCATED OUTSIDE OF SOUTH AMERICA (335)	1.00 OF 21	9	DRIFT LESS TOWARD BEING THOSE LOCATED OUTSIDE OF SOUTH AMERICA (335)	0.83 OF 379	0 65 21 314 XSQ= 3.13 PHI= -0.088 XP = 0.0767
12	TEND TO BE THOSE WHERE THE LATITUDE IS FIFTY DEGREES OR GREATER (33)	0.71 OF 21	12	TEND TO BE THOSE WHERE THE LATITUDE IS LESS THAN FIFTY DEGREES (367)	0.95 OF 379	15 18 6 361 XSQ= 108.23 PHI= 0.520 XP = 0.

13	IN ALL CASES ARE THOSE WHERE THE LATITUDE IS FORTY DEGREES OR GREATER (71)	1.00 OF 21	13	TEND TO BE THOSE WHERE THE LATITUDE IS LESS THAN FORTY DEGREES (329)	0.87 OF 379	21 50 0 329 XSQ= 96.84 PHI= 0.492 XP = 0.
44	LEAN TOWARD BEING THOSE WHERE SETTLEMENTS ARE NON-FIXED (110)	0.69 OF 16	44	LEAN TOWARD BEING THOSE WHERE SETTLEMENTS ARE FIXED (222)	0.69 OF 316	5 217 11 99 XSQ= 8.01 PHI= -0.155 XP = 0.0047
46	LEAN TOWARD BEING THOSE WHERE SETTLEMENTS ARE NON-FIXED AND MOVEMENT IS NOMADIC (72)	0.56 OF 16	46	LEAN TOWARD BEING THOSE OTHER THAN WHERE SETTLEMENTS ARE NON-FIXED AND MOVEMENT IS NOMADIC (260)	0.80 OF 316	9 63 7 253 XSQ= 9.78 PHI= 0.172 XP = 0.0018
51	TEND TO BE THOSE WHERE SUBSISTENCE IS PRIMARILY BY FOOD GATHERING -- I. E., HUNTING, FISHING, OR COLLECTING -- RATHER THAN FOOD PRODUCTION (147)	0.90 OF 21	51	TEND TO BE THOSE WHERE SUBSISTENCE IS PRIMARILY BY FOOD PRODUCTION -- I. E., AGRICULTURE OR HUSBANDRY -- RATHER THAN BY GATHERING (253)	0.66 OF 379	2 251 19 128 XSQ= 25.14 PHI= -0.251 XP = 0.0000
54	TILT TOWARD BEING THOSE WHERE FOOD PRODUCTION IS BY INCIPIENT FOOD PRODUCTION, RATHER THAN BY INTENSIVE OR SIMPLE AGRICULTURE (46)	0.75 OF 4	54	TILT TOWARD BEING THOSE WHERE FOOD PRODUCTION IS BY INTENSIVE OR SIMPLE AGRICULTURE, RATHER THAN BY INCIPIENT FOOD PRODUCTION (192)	0.82 OF 234	1 191 3 43 XSQ= 4.86 PHI= -0.143 XP = 0.0274
56	IN ALL CASES ARE THOSE WHERE FOOD PRODUCTION IS BY INCIPIENT FOOD PRODUCTION, RATHER THAN BY SIMPLE AGRICULTURE (46)	1.00 OF 3	56	TILT TOWARD BEING THOSE WHERE FOOD PRODUCTION IS BY SIMPLE AGRICULTURE, RATHER THAN BY INCIPIENT FOOD PRODUCTION (101)	0.70 OF 144	0 101 3 43 XSQ= 3.86 PHI= -0.162 XP = 0.0495
62	LEAN TOWARD BEING THOSE WHERE HUSBANDRY OF ANY KIND IS ABSENT (172)	0.76 OF 21	62	LEAN TOWARD BEING THOSE WHERE HUSBANDRY OF SOME KIND IS PRESENT (228)	0.59 OF 379	5 223 16 156 XSQ= 8.58 PHI= -0.146 XP = 0.0034
74	TILT TOWARD BEING THOSE WHERE POTTERY IS ABSENT (93)	0.67 OF 15	74	TILT TOWARD BEING THOSE WHERE POTTERY IS PRESENT (145)	0.63 OF 223	5 140 10 83 XSQ= 3.96 PHI= -0.129 XP = 0.0467
130	LEAN TOWARD BEING THOSE WHERE LEATHER WORKING IS MAINLY DONE BY FEMALES (45)	0.93 OF 14	130	LEAN TOWARD BEING THOSE WHERE LEATHER WORKING IS MAINLY DONE BY MALES (39)	0.54 OF 70	1 38 13 32 XSQ= 8.62 PHI= -0.320 XP = 0.0033

137	DRIFT TOWARD BEING THOSE WHERE INVIDIOUS DISPLAY OF WEALTH IS STRONGLY EMPHASIZED (37) PES	0.83 OF	6	137	DRIFT TOWARD BEING THOSE WHERE INVIDIOUS DISPLAY OF WEALTH IS MODERATELY, LITTLE, OR NEGATIVELY EMPHASIZED (52) PES	0.61 OF	83	5 32 1 51 XSQ= 2.96 PHI= 0.182 XP = 0.0854
187	DRIFT LESS TOWARD BEING THOSE WHERE THE KIN GROUP IS OTHER THAN EXCLUSIVELY MATRILINEAL (344)	0.71 OF	21	187	DRIFT MORE TOWARD BEING THOSE WHERE THE KIN GROUP IS OTHER THAN EXCLUSIVELY MATRILINEAL (344)	0.87 OF	378	6 49 15 329 XSQ= 2.87 PHI= 0.085 XP = 0.0902
304	IN ALL CASES ARE THOSE WHERE THE EARLY ANAL SATISFACTION POTENTIAL IS HIGH (19) W-C	1.00 OF	4	304	DRIFT TOWARD BEING THOSE WHERE THE EARLY ANAL SATISFACTION POTENTIAL IS LOW (22) W-C	0.59 OF	37	4 15 0 22 XSQ= 3.02 PHI= 0.271 XP = 0.0823
315	IN ALL CASES ARE THOSE WHERE MOTHER AND NURSING CHILD CUSTOMARILY SLEEP IN DIFFERENT BEDS (14) W-C,S	1.00 OF	3	315	TILT TOWARD BEING THOSE WHERE MOTHER AND NURSING CHILD CUSTOMARILY SLEEP IN THE SAME BED (37) W-D,S	0.77 OF	48	0 37 3 11 XSQ= 5.00 PHI= -0.313 XP = 0.0254
317	IN ALL CASES ARE THOSE WHERE DISPLAY OF AFFECTION TOWARD THE INFANT IS LOW (29) B-B-C	1.00 OF	4	317	DRIFT TOWARD BEING THOSE WHERE DISPLAY OF AFFECTION TOWARD THE INFANT IS HIGH (39) B-B-C	0.61 OF	64	0 39 4 25 XSQ= 3.50 PHI= -0.227 XP = 0.0615
339	IN ALL CASES ARE THOSE WHERE THE CHILD'S INFERRED CONFLICT REGARDING RESPONSIBLE BEHAVIOR IS HIGH (31) B-B-C	1.00 OF	4	339	DRIFT TOWARD BEING THOSE WHERE THE CHILD'S INFERRED CONFLICT REGARDING RESPONSIBLE BEHAVIOR IS LOW (42) B-B-C	0.61 OF	69	4 27 0 42 XSQ= 3.51 PHI= 0.219 XP = 0.0609
372	IN ALL CASES ARE THOSE WHERE MALE INITIATION RITES ARE ABSENT (63) ASA	1.00 OF	6	372	DRIFT LESS TOWARD BEING THOSE WHERE MALE INITIATION RITES ARE ABSENT (63) ASA	0.54 OF	105	0 48 6 57 XSQ= 3.15 PHI= -0.168 XP = 0.0759
377	IN ALL CASES ARE THOSE WHERE MALE GENITAL MUTILATION IS ABSENT (242)	1.00 OF	17	377	TILT LESS TOWARD BEING THOSE WHERE MALE GENITAL MUTILATION IS ABSENT (242)	0.73 OF	308	0 83 17 225 XSQ= 4.82 PHI= -0.122 XP = 0.0282
459	TILT TOWARD BEING THOSE WHERE GAMES, IF PRESENT, INCLUDE GAMES OF CHANCE (82) R-A-B,EA	0.85 OF	13	459	TILT TOWARD BEING THOSE WHERE GAMES, IF PRESENT, DO NOT INCLUDE GAMES OF CHANCE (89) R-A-B,EA	0.55 OF	158	11 71 2 87 XSQ= 6.07 PHI= 0.188 XP = 0.0137

```
460  TILT MORE TOWARD BEING THCSE   0.92 OF  13      460  TILT LESS TOWARD BEING THOSE   0.58 OF 158          1   66
     WHERE GAMES, IF PRESENT,                              WHERE GAMES, IF PRESENT,                           12   92
     ARE NCT LIMITED TO                                    ARE NOT LIMITED TO                            XSQ=    4.51
     GAMES OF SKILL CNLY  (104) R-A-B,EA                   GAMES OF SKILL ONLY  (104) R-A-B,EA           PHI=  -0.162
                                                                                                         XP =  0.0337
```

40 CULTURES
WHERE THE NATURAL ENVIRONMENT IS
TEMPERATE WOODLAND OR FOREST (35) FWM

40 CULTURES
WHERE THE NATURAL ENVIRONMENT IS
OTHER THAN
TEMPERATE WOODLAND OR FOREST (365) FWM

BACKGROUND ON PAGE 69

SUBJECT ONLY

35 IN LEFT COLUMN

AINU	ALACALUF	AMERICANS	ARAUCANIANS	ATSUGEWI	AZTEC	BULGARIANS	CHEREMIS	CHERKESS	CHEROKEE
CZECHS	DELAWARE	DUTCH	HUTSUL	IRISH	KACHIN	KOHISTANI	KOREANS	KUMYK	LEPCHA
LOLO	MAM	MANDAN	MIAMI	MINCHIA	MIWOK	NATCHEZ	SERBS	TARAHUMARA	TOLOWA
TZELTAL	WALLOONS	WASHO	WINNEBAGO	YUROK					

365 IN RIGHT COLUMN

	Left column			Right column		Statistics
3	IN ALL CASES ARE THOSE LOCATED OUTSIDE OF AFRICA (320)	1.00 OF 35	3	LEAN LESS TOWARD BEING THOSE LOCATED OUTSIDE OF AFRICA (320)	0.78 OF 365	0 80 35 285 XSQ= 8.27 PHI= -0.144 XP = 0.0040
4	TEND LESS TO BE THOSE LOCATED OUTSIDE OF THE CIRCUM-MEDITERRANEAN (355)	0.69 OF 35	4	TEND MORE TO BE THOSE LOCATED OUTSIDE OF THE CIRCUM-MEDITERRANEAN (355)	0.91 OF 365	11 34 24 331 XSQ= 13.51 PHI= 0.184 XP = 0.0002
6	IN ALL CASES ARE THOSE LOCATED OUTSIDE OF THE INSULAR PACIFIC (330)	1.00 OF 35	6	LEAN LESS TOWARD BEING THOSE LOCATED OUTSIDE OF THE INSULAR PACIFIC (330)	0.81 OF 365	0 70 35 295 XSQ= 6.86 PHI= -0.131 XP = 0.0088
8	LEAN LESS TOWARD BEING THOSE LOCATED OUTSIDE OF NORTH AMERICA (330)	0.63 OF 35	8	LEAN MORE TOWARD BEING THOSE LOCATED OUTSIDE OF NORTH AMERICA (330)	0.84 OF 365	13 57 22 308 XSQ= 8.81 PHI= 0.148 XP = 0.0030
13	TEND TO BE THOSE WHERE THE LATITUDE IS FORTY DEGREES OR GREATER (71)	0.57 OF 35	13	TEND TO BE THOSE WHERE THE LATITUDE IS LESS THAN FORTY DEGREES (329)	0.86 OF 365	20 51 15 314 XSQ= 37.87 PHI= 0.308 XP = 0.

14	TEND TO BE THOSE WHERE THE LATITUDE IS THIRTY DEGREES OR GREATER (119)	0.77 OF 35	14	TEND TO BE THOSE WHERE THE LATITUDE IS LESS THAN THIRTY DEGREES (281)	0.75 OF 365	27 92 8 273 XSQ= 38.77 PHI= 0.311 XP = 0.
15	TEND TO BE THOSE WHERE THE LATITUDE IS TWENTY DEGREES OR GREATER (183)	0.91 OF 35	15	TEND TO BE THOSE WHERE THE LATITUDE IS LESS THAN TWENTY DEGREES (217)	0.59 OF 365	32 151 3 214 XSQ= 30.26 PHI= 0.275 XP = 0.
16	IN ALL CASES ARE THOSE WHERE THE LATITUDE IS TEN DEGREES OR GREATER (277)	1.00 OF 35	16	TEND LESS TO BE THOSE WHERE THE LATITUDE IS TEN DEGREES OR GREATER (277)	0.66 OF 365	35 242 0 123 XSQ= 15.49 PHI= 0.197 XP = 0.0001
47	DRIFT TOWARD BEING THOSE WHERE, IF SETTLEMENTS ARE NON-FIXED, MOVEMENT IS NON-NOMADIC, RATHER THAN NOMADIC (38)	0.67 OF 9	47	DRIFT TOWARD BEING THOSE WHERE, IF SETTLEMENTS ARE NON-FIXED, MOVEMENT IS NOMADIC, RATHER THAN NON-NOMADIC (72)	0.68 OF 101	3 69 6 32 XSQ= 3.06 PHI= -0.167 XP = 0.0803
53	TEND TO BE THOSE WHERE FOOD PRODUCTION IS BY INTENSIVE AGRICULTURE, RATHER THAN BY SIMPLE AGRICULTURE OR INCIPIENT FOOD PRODUCTION (91)	0.72 OF 25	53	TEND TO BE THOSE WHERE FOOD PRODUCTION IS BY SIMPLE AGRICULTURE OR INCIPIENT FOOD PRODUCTION, RATHER THAN BY INTENSIVE AGRICULTURE (147)	0.66 OF 213	18 73 7 140 XSQ= 11.93 PHI= 0.224 XP = 0.0006
55	TEND TO BE THOSE WHERE FOOD PRODUCTION IS BY INTENSIVE AGRICULTURE, RATHER THAN BY SIMPLE AGRICULTURE (91)	0.90 OF 20	55	TEND TO BE THOSE WHERE FOOD PRODUCTION IS BY SIMPLE AGRICULTURE, RATHER THAN BY INTENSIVE AGRICULTURE (101)	0.58 OF 172	18 73 2 99 XSQ= 14.40 PHI= 0.274 XP = 0.0001
56	DRIFT TOWARD BEING THOSE WHERE FOOD PRODUCTION IS BY INCIPIENT FOOD PRODUCTION, RATHER THAN BY SIMPLE AGRICULTURE (46)	0.71 OF 7	56	DRIFT TOWARD BEING THOSE WHERE FOOD PRODUCTION IS BY SIMPLE AGRICULTURE, RATHER THAN BY INCIPIENT FOOD PRODUCTION (101)	0.71 OF 140	2 99 5 41 XSQ= 3.72 PHI= -0.159 XP = 0.0537
63	TILT MORE TOWARD BEING THOSE WHERE HUSBANDRY, IF PRESENT, IS PRINCIPALLY IN THE FORM OF BOVINE, EQUINE, CAMEL-LIKE, OR DEER-LIKE ANIMALS, RATHER THAN PIGS, SHEEP, OR GOATS (152)	0.95 OF 19	63	TILT LESS TOWARD BEING THOSE WHERE HUSBANDRY, IF PRESENT, IS PRINCIPALLY IN THE FORM OF BOVINE, EQUINE, CAMEL-LIKE, OR DEER-LIKE ANIMALS, RATHER THAN PIGS, SHEEP, OR GOATS (152)	0.65 OF 207	18 134 1 73 XSQ= 5.82 PHI= 0.160 XP = 0.0159
73	TILT TOWARD BEING THOSE WHERE WEAVING IS PRESENT (118)	0.73 OF 22	73	TILT TOWARD BEING THOSE WHERE WEAVING IS ABSENT (130)	0.55 OF 226	16 102 6 124 XSQ= 5.06 PHI= 0.143 XP = 0.0244

77	TILT TOWARD BEING THOSE 0.71 OF 7 WHERE THE WRITING SYSTEM IS ALPHABETIC-OR-PHONETIC, RATHER THAN BEING MNEMONIC OR ABSENT (15) JMH	77	TILT TOWARD BEING THOSE 0.79 OF 47 WHERE THE WRITING SYSTEM IS MNEMONIC OR ABSENT, RATHER THAN BEING ALPHABETIC-OR-PHONETIC (39) JMH		5 10 2 37 XSQ= 5.34 PHI= 0.315 XP = 0.0208
81	LEAN TOWARD BEING THOSE 0.67 OF 24 WHERE A CITY OR TOWN IS PRESENT, OR THE AVERAGE COMMUNITY SIZE IS 200 OR GREATER (89)	81	LEAN TOWARD BEING THOSE 0.63 OF 200 WHERE NO CITY OR TOWN IS PRESENT, AND THE AVERAGE COMMUNITY SIZE IS SMALLER THAN 200 (135)		16 73 8 127 XSQ= 6.93 PHI= 0.176 XP = 0.0085
84	TILT LESS TOWARD BEING THOSE 0.69 OF 26 WHERE THE LEVEL OF POLITICAL INTEGRATION IS THE LITTLE STATE, THE MINIMAL STATE, THE AUTONOMOUS COMMUNITY, OR THE FAMILY (262) GPM	84	TILT MORE TOWARD BEING THOSE 0.88 OF 278 WHERE THE LEVEL OF POLITICAL INTEGRATION IS THE LITTLE STATE, THE MINIMAL STATE, THE AUTONOMOUS COMMUNITY, OR THE FAMILY (262) GPM		8 34 18 244 XSQ= 5.39 PHI= 0.133 XP = 0.0202
102	TILT MORE TOWARD BEING THOSE 0.73 OF 33 WHERE CLASS STRATIFICATION IS PRESENT (203)	102	TILT LESS TOWARD BEING THOSE 0.51 OF 350 WHERE CLASS STRATIFICATION IS PRESENT (203)		24 179 9 171 XSQ= 4.81 PHI= 0.112 XP = 0.0283
107	TILT LESS TOWARD BEING THOSE 0.58 OF 24 WHERE CLASS STRATIFICATION, IF PRESENT, IS BASED ON SOMETHING OTHER THAN OCCUPATIONAL STATUS (160)	107	TILT MORE TOWARD BEING THOSE 0.82 OF 179 WHERE CLASS STRATIFICATION, IF PRESENT, IS BASED ON SOMETHING OTHER THAN OCCUPATIONAL STATUS (160)		10 33 14 146 XSQ= 5.52 PHI= 0.165 XP = 0.0188
108	TILT MORE TOWARD BEING THOSE 0.88 OF 24 WHERE CLASS STRATIFICATION, IF PRESENT, IS BASED ON SOMETHING OTHER THAN A HEREDITARY ARISTOCRACY (129)	108	TILT LESS TOWARD BEING THOSE 0.60 OF 179 WHERE CLASS STRATIFICATION, IF PRESENT, IS BASED ON SOMETHING OTHER THAN A HEREDITARY ARISTOCRACY (129)		3 71 21 108 XSQ= 5.62 PHI= -0.166 XP = 0.0178
128	DRIFT TOWARD BEING THOSE 0.88 OF 8 WHERE, IF SUBSISTENCE IS PRIMARILY BY AGRICULTURE, THE WORK IS MAINLY DONE BY MALES (40)	128	DRIFT TOWARD BEING THOSE 0.52 OF 69 WHERE, IF SUBSISTENCE IS PRIMARILY BY AGRICULTURE, THE WORK IS MAINLY DONE BY FEMALES (37)		7 33 1 36 XSQ= 3.07 PHI= 0.200 XP = 0.0797
192	DRIFT LESS TOWARD BEING THOSE 0.57 OF 35 OTHER THAN WHERE THE ONLY KIN GROUP PRESENT IS A KINDRED OR ELSE BILATERAL DESCENT IS INFERRED (289)	192	DRIFT MORE TOWARD BEING THOSE 0.74 OF 365 OTHER THAN WHERE THE ONLY KIN GROUP PRESENT IS A KINDRED OR ELSE BILATERAL DESCENT IS INFERRED (289)		15 96 20 269 XSQ= 3.58 PHI= 0.095 XP = 0.0585
240	LEAN MORE TOWARD BEING THOSE 0.95 OF 20 WHERE THE FAMILY, IF EXTENDED, IS SMALL OR STEM, RATHER THAN LARGE (135)	240	LEAN LESS TOWARD BEING THOSE 0.60 OF 193 WHERE THE FAMILY, IF EXTENDED, IS SMALL OR STEM, RATHER THAN LARGE (135)		1 77 19 116 XSQ= 8.06 PHI= -0.195 XP = 0.0045

263	LEAN TOWARD BEING THOSE WHERE WIVES ARE OBTAINED BY RELATIVELY EASY MEANS, NAMELY BY TOKEN BRIDE-PRICE, GIFT EXCHANGE, ABSENCE OF ANY CONSIDERATION, OR RECEIPT OF DOWRY (162)	0.65 OF 34	263	LEAN TOWARD BEING THOSE WHERE WIVES ARE OBTAINED BY RELATIVELY DIFFICULT MEANS, NAMELY BY BRIDE-PRICE, BRIDE-SERVICE, OR EXCHANGING A FEMALE RELATIVE (233)	0.61 OF 361	12 221 22 140 XSQ= 7.59 PHI= -0.139 XP = 0.0059
277	IN ALL CASES ARE THOSE WHERE THE STATUS OF WOMEN IS INFERIOR OR SUBJECTED (14) LWS	1.00 OF 3	277	DRIFT TOWARD BEING THOSE WHERE THE STATUS OF WOMEN IS NOT STRONGLY INFERIOR OR SUBJECTED (22) LWS	0.67 OF 33	3 11 0 22 XSQ= 2.72 PHI= 0.275 EP = 0.0510
284	IN ALL CASES ARE THOSE WHERE CONTRACEPTION IS NOT PRACTICED (7) CSF	1.00 OF 3	284	DRIFT TOWARD BEING THOSE WHERE CONTRACEPTION IS PRACTICED (10) CSF	0.71 OF 14	0 10 3 4 XSQ= 2.67 PHI= -0.397 EP = 0.0515
354	IN ALL CASES ARE THOSE WHERE THE CHILD'S INFERRED ANXIETY OVER PERFORMANCE OF OBEDIENT BEHAVIOR IS LOW (37) B-B-C	1.00 OF 5	354	DRIFT TOWARD BEING THOSE WHERE THE CHILD'S INFERRED ANXIETY OVER PERFORMANCE OF OBEDIENT BEHAVIOR IS HIGH (36) B-B-C	0.53 OF 68	0 36 5 32 XSQ= 3.32 PHI= -0.213 XP = 0.0685
355	IN ALL CASES ARE THOSE WHERE THE CHILD'S INFERRED CONFLICT REGARDING OBEDIENT BEHAVIOR IS LOW (38) B-B-C	1.00 OF 5	355	DRIFT TOWARD BEING THOSE WHERE THE CHILD'S INFERRED CONFLICT REGARDING OBEDIENT BEHAVIOR IS HIGH (35) B-B-C	0.51 OF 68	0 35 5 33 XSQ= 3.10 PHI= -0.206 XP = 0.0785
369	TILT TOWARD BEING THOSE WHERE BOTH DISSOCIATION OF THE SEXES AT ADOLESCENCE, AND CUSTOMS OF INITIATION AT ADOLESCENCE, ARE ABSENT (15) JKH	0.80 OF 5	369	TILT TOWARD BEING THOSE WHERE DISSOCIATION OF THE SEXES AT ADOLESCENCE, OR CUSTOMS OF INITIATION AT ADOLESCENCE, ARE PRESENT (42) JKH	0.79 OF 52	1 41 4 11 XSQ= 5.39 PHI= -0.308 XP = 0.0202
370	TEND MORE TO BE THOSE WHERE THE SEGREGATION OF ADOLESCENT BOYS IS ABSENT (148)	0.96 OF 24	370	TEND LESS TO BE THOSE WHERE THE SEGREGATION OF ADOLESCENT BOYS IS ABSENT (148)	0.57 OF 219	1 94 23 125 XSQ= 12.07 PHI= -0.223 XP = 0.0005
377	TILT MORE TOWARD BEING THOSE WHERE MALE GENITAL MUTILATION IS ABSENT (242)	0.93 OF 30	377	TILT LESS TOWARD BEING THOSE WHERE MALE GENITAL MUTILATION IS ABSENT (242)	0.73 OF 295	2 81 28 214 XSQ= 5.14 PHI= -0.126 XP = 0.0233
382	DRIFT TOWARD BEING THOSE WHERE FEMALE INITIATION RITES ARE ABSENT (27) JKB	0.83 OF 6	382	DRIFT TOWARD BEING THOSE WHERE FEMALE INITIATION RITES ARE PRESENT (38) JKB	0.63 OF 59	1 37 5 22 XSQ= 3.05 PHI= -0.217 XP = 0.0808

427	TEND MORE TO BE THCSE WHERE A HIGH GCC, IF PRESENT, IS ACTIVE, RATHER THAN INACTIVE (87) GES,EA	0.95 OF 19	427	TEND LESS TO BE THOSE WHERE A HIGH GOD, IF PRESENT, IS ACTIVE, RATHER THAN INACTIVE (87) GES,EA	0.50 OF 137	18 69 1 68 XSQ= 11.58 PHI= 0.272 XP = 0.0007
431	DRIFT TCWARD BEING THCSE WHERE SUPERNATURAL SANCTICNS FOR MORALITY, HAVING AN EFFECT ON AN INDIVIDUAL'S AFTER LIFE, ARE PRESENT (10) GES	0.75 OF 4	431	DRIFT TOWARD BEING THOSE WHERE SUPERNATURAL SANCTIONS FOR MORALITY, HAVING AN EFFECT ON AN INDIVIDUAL'S AFTERLIFE, ARE ABSENT OR UNREPORTED (25) GES	0.77 OF 31	3 7 1 24 XSQ= 2.55 PHI= 0.270 EP = 0.0613
436	IN ALL CASES ARE THCSE WHERE ACTIVE ANCESTRAL SPIRITS ARE ABSENT (11) GES	1.00 OF 4	436	LEAN TOWARD BEING THOSE WHERE ACTIVE ANCESTRAL SPIRITS ARE PRESENT (27) GES	0.79 OF 34	0 27 4 7 XSQ= 7.45 PHI= -0.443 EP = 0.0045
459	LEAN TCWARD BEING THOSE WHERE GAMES, IF PRESENT, INCLUDE GAMES OF CHANCE (82) R-A-B,EA	0.84 OF 19	459	LEAN TOWARD BEING THOSE WHERE GAMES, IF PRESENT, DO NOT INCLUDE GAMES OF CHANCE (89) R-A-B,EA	0.57 OF 152	16 66 3 86 XSQ= 9.68 PHI= 0.238 XP = 0.0019
460	TILT MORE TOWARC BEING THOSE WHERE GAMES, IF PRESENT, ARE NCT LIMITED TO GAMES CF SKILL CNLY (104) R-A-B,EA	0.84 OF 19	460	TILT LESS TOWARD BEING THOSE WHERE GAMES, IF PRESENT, ARE NOT LIMITED TO GAMES OF SKILL ONLY (104) R-A-B,EA	0.58 OF 152	3 64 16 88 XSQ= 3.87 PHI= -0.150 XP = 0.0493

41 CULTURES
WHERE THE NATURAL ENVIRONMENT IS
TROPICAL GRASSLAND (64) FWM

41 CULTURES
WHERE THE NATURAL ENVIRONMENT IS
OTHER THAN
TROPICAL GRASSLAND (336) FWM

BACKGROUND ON PAGE 69

SUBJECT ONLY

64 IN LEFT COLUMN

AMBA	AZANDE	BAMBARA	BEMBA	BIRIFOR	BOERS	BOZO	BUDUMA	CADUVEO	CARINYA
DILLING	DOGON	FUTAJALONKE	GISU	GUAHIBO	GURE	ILA	INGASSANA	IRAQW	JUKUN
KATAB	KERAKI	KIKUYU	KISSI	LAMBA	LANGO	LOZI	LUBA	LUO	MAGUZAWA
MARGI	MATAKAM	MBUNDU	MOSSI	MURINBATA	MURNGIN	NAMBICUARA	NANDI	NDEMBU	NGONI
NUER	NUPE	NYANEKA	NYARO	NYORO	PENDE	SHILLUK	SIRIONO	SONGHAI	TALLENSI
TENDA	TERA	TESO	TIMBIRA	TIV	TIWI	TURKANA	WAPISHANA	WIKMUNKAN	WOLOF
WUTE	YAO	YARURO	YORUBA						

336 IN RIGHT COLUMN

3	TEND TO BE THOSE LOCATED IN AFRICA (80)	0.69 OF 64	TEND TO BE THOSE LOCATED OUTSIDE OF AFRICA (320)	0.89 OF 336	44 36 20 300 XSQ= 109.57 PHI= 0.523 XP = 0.
5	IN ALL CASES ARE THOSE LOCATED OUTSIDE OF EAST EURASIA (330)	1.00 OF 64	TEND LESS TO BE THOSE LOCATED OUTSIDE OF EAST EURASIA (330)	0.79 OF 336	0 70 64 266 XSQ= 14.75 PHI= -0.192 XP = 0.0001
6	TILT MORE TOWARD BEING THOSE LOCATED OUTSIDE OF THE INSULAR PACIFIC (330)	0.92 OF 64	TILT LESS TOWARD BEING THOSE LOCATED OUTSIDE OF THE INSULAR PACIFIC (330)	0.81 OF 336	5 65 59 271 XSQ= 4.19 PHI= -0.102 XP = 0.0408
8	IN ALL CASES ARE THOSE LOCATED OUTSIDE OF NORTH AMERICA (330)	1.00 OF 64	TEND LESS TO BE THOSE LOCATED OUTSIDE OF NORTH AMERICA (330)	0.79 OF 336	0 70 64 266 XSQ= 14.75 PHI= -0.192 XP = 0.0001
14	IN ALL CASES ARE THOSE WHERE THE LATITUDE IS LESS THAN THIRTY DEGREES (281)	1.00 OF 64	TEND LESS TO BE THOSE WHERE THE LATITUDE IS LESS THAN THIRTY DEGREES (281)	0.65 OF 336	0 119 64 217 XSQ= 30.59 PHI= -0.277 XP = 0.

```
15  TEND TO BE THOSE                  0.98 OF   64    15  TEND TO BE THOSE                  0.54 OF 336        1  182
    WHERE THE LATITUDE IS                                 WHERE THE LATITUDE IS                                   63  154
    LESS THAN TWENTY DEGREES  (217)                       TWENTY DEGREES OR GREATER  (183)                  XSQ=    57.84
                                                                                                            PHI=   -0.380
                                                                                                            XP =    0.

45  LEAN TOWARD BEING THOSE           0.55 OF   38    45  LEAN TOWARD BEING THOSE           0.72 OF 184       17  132
    WHERE SETTLEMENTS, IF FIXED, ARE                      WHERE SETTLEMENTS, IF FIXED, ARE                        21   52
    NON-COMPACT, RATHER THAN                              COMPACT, RATHER THAN                              XSQ=     9.22
    COMPACT  (73)                                         NON-COMPACT  (149)                                PHI=   -0.204
                                                                                                            XP =    0.0024

51  TILT MORE TOWARD BEING THOSE      0.75 OF   64    51  TILT LESS TOWARD BEING THOSE      0.61 OF 336       48  205
    WHERE SUBSISTENCE IS PRIMARILY BY                     WHERE SUBSISTENCE IS PRIMARILY BY                       16  131
    FOOD PRODUCTION -- I. E., AGRICULTURE                 FOOD PRODUCTION -- I. E., AGRICULTURE             XSQ=     3.94
    OR HUSBANDRY -- RATHER THAN BY                        OR HUSBANDRY -- RATHER THAN BY                    PHI=    0.099
    GATHERING  (253)                                      GATHERING  (253)                                  XP =    0.0470

62  DRIFT MORE TOWARD BEING THOSE     0.67 OF   64    62  DRIFT LESS TOWARD BEING THOSE     0.55 OF 336       43  185
    WHERE HUSBANDRY OF SOME KIND                          WHERE HUSBANDRY OF SOME KIND                            21  151
    IS PRESENT  (228)                                     IS PRESENT  (228)                                 XSQ=     2.75
                                                                                                            PHI=    0.083
                                                                                                            XP =    0.0972

71  TEND TO BE THOSE                  0.70 OF   37    71  TEND TO BE THOSE                  0.66 OF 214       26   72
    WHERE METAL WORKING IS                                WHERE METAL WORKING IS                                  11  142
    PRESENT  (98)                                         ABSENT  (153)                                     XSQ=    16.27
                                                                                                            PHI=    0.255
                                                                                                            XP =    0.0001

73  DRIFT TOWARD BEING THOSE          0.67 OF   36    73  DRIFT TOWARD BEING THOSE          0.50 OF 212       12  106
    WHERE WEAVING IS                                      WHERE WEAVING IS                                        24  106
    ABSENT  (130)                                         PRESENT  (118)                                    XSQ=     2.79
                                                                                                            PHI=   -0.106
                                                                                                            XP =    0.0948

74  DRIFT MORE TOWARD BEING THOSE     0.75 OF   36    74  DRIFT LESS TOWARD BEING THOSE     0.58 OF 202       27  118
    WHERE POTTERY IS                                      WHERE POTTERY IS                                         9   84
    PRESENT  (145)                                        PRESENT  (145)                                    XSQ=     2.87
                                                                                                            PHI=    0.110
                                                                                                            XP =    0.0904

85  TILT LESS TOWARD BEING THOSE      0.63 OF   49    85  TILT MORE TOWARD BEING THOSE      0.80 OF 255       18   52
    WHERE THE LEVEL OF POLITICAL INTEGRATION              WHERE THE LEVEL OF POLITICAL INTEGRATION                31  203
    IS THE MINIMAL STATE,                                 IS THE MINIMAL STATE,                             XSQ=     5.31
    THE AUTONOMOUS COMMUNITY, OR                          THE AUTONOMOUS COMMUNITY, OR                      PHI=    0.132
    THE FAMILY  (234) GPM                                 THE FAMILY  (234) GPM                             XP =    0.0213

88  TILT MORE TOWARD BEING THOSE      0.80 OF   40    88  TILT LESS TOWARD BEING THOSE      0.58 OF 231        8   98
    WHERE, IF A HEADMANSHIP IS PRESENT,                   WHERE, IF A HEADMANSHIP IS PRESENT,                     32  133
    SUCCESSION IS HEREDITARY  (165)                       SUCCESSION IS HEREDITARY  (165)                   XSQ=     6.29
                                                                                                            PHI=   -0.152
                                                                                                            XP =    0.0122
```

```
 97  LEAN LESS TOWARD BEING THOSE     0.69 OF  55     97  LEAN MORE TOWARD BEING THOSE     0.85 OF 276         17   41
     WHERE THE HIERARCHY                                  WHERE THE HIERARCHY                                  38  235
     OF LOCAL JURISDICTION HAS                            OF LOCAL JURISDICTION HAS                       XSQ=     7.11
     THREE OR TWO LEVELS  (273) GES,EA                    THREE OR TWO LEVELS  (273) GES,EA               PHI=    0.147
                                                                                                          XP =   0.0077

110  TEND TO BE THOSE                 0.67 OF  61    110  TEND TO BE THOSE                 0.62 OF 320         41  122
     WHERE SLAVERY IS PRESENT  (163)                      WHERE SLAVERY IS ABSENT  (218)                       20  198
                                                                                                          XSQ=    16.54
                                                                                                          PHI=    0.208
                                                                                                          XP =   0.0000

129  TEND TO BE THOSE                 0.90 OF  10    129  TEND TO BE THOSE                 0.77 OF  94          9   22
     WHERE WEAVING IS                                     WHERE WEAVING IS                                      1   72
     MAINLY DONE BY MALES  (31)                           MAINLY DONE BY FEMALES  (73)                    XSQ=    16.11
                                                                                                          PHI=    0.394
                                                                                                          XP =   0.0001

130  DRIFT TOWARD BEING THOSE         0.75 OF  12    130  DRIFT TOWARD BEING THOSE         0.58 OF  72          9   30
     WHERE LEATHER WORKING IS                             WHERE LEATHER WORKING IS                              3   42
     MAINLY DONE BY MALES  (39)                           MAINLY DONE BY FEMALES  (45)                    XSQ=     3.35
                                                                                                          PHI=    0.200
                                                                                                          XP =   0.0671

176  LEAN TOWARD BEING THOSE          0.63 OF  60    176  LEAN TOWARD BEING THOSE          0.59 OF 322         38  131
     WHERE THE COMMUNITY IS                               WHERE THE COMMUNITY IS OTHER THAN                    22  191
     A CLAN-COMMUNITY OR A COMMUNITY                      A CLAN-COMMUNITY OR A COMMUNITY                 XSQ=     9.62
     STRUCTURED OR SEGMENTED                              STRUCTURED OR SEGMENTED                         PHI=    0.159
     ON A CLAN BASIS  (169)                               ON A CLAN BASIS  (213)                          XP =   0.0019

177  TILT LESS TOWARD BEING THOSE     0.68 OF  60    177  TILT MORE TOWARD BEING THOSE     0.82 OF 322         19   58
     WHERE THE COMMUNITY IS OTHER THAN                    WHERE THE COMMUNITY IS OTHER THAN                    41  264
     A SINGLE CLAN-COMMUNITY AND                          A SINGLE CLAN-COMMUNITY AND                     XSQ=     5.04
     EXOGAMOUS  (305)                                     EXOGAMOUS  (305)                                PHI=    0.115
                                                                                                          XP =   0.0248

184  TILT MORE TOWARD BEING THOSE     0.81 OF  54    184  TILT LESS TOWARD BEING THOSE     0.66 OF 198         10   67
     WHERE THE LARGEST NON-COGNATIC KIN GROUP             WHERE THE LARGEST NON-COGNATIC KIN GROUP             44  131
     IS SMALLER THAN A PHRATRY, I. E.                     IS SMALLER THAN A PHRATRY, I. E.                XSQ=     4.00
     A SIB OR LINEAGE  (175)                              A SIB OR LINEAGE  (175)                         PHI=   -0.126
                                                                                                          XP =   0.0455

186  TILT TOWARD BEING THOSE          0.50 OF  64    186  TILT TOWARD BEING THOSE          0.65 OF 336         32  118
     WHERE THE KIN GROUP IS                               WHERE THE KIN GROUP IS                               32  218
     EXCLUSIVELY PATRILINEAL  (150)                       OTHER THAN                                      XSQ=     4.46
                                                          EXCLUSIVELY PATRILINEAL  (250)                  PHI=    0.106
                                                                                                          XP =   0.0346

188  TEND MORE TO BE THOSE            0.84 OF  64    188  TEND LESS TO BE THOSE            0.59 OF 336         10  138
     WHERE THE KIN GROUP IS                               WHERE THE KIN GROUP IS                               54  198
     OTHER THAN                                           OTHER THAN                                      XSQ=    13.86
     EXCLUSIVELY COGNATIC  (252)                          EXCLUSIVELY COGNATIC  (252)                     PHI=   -0.186
                                                                                                          XP =   0.0002
```

192	TEND MORE TO BE THOSE 0.92 OF 64 OTHER THAN WHERE THE ONLY KIN GROUP PRESENT IS A KINDRED OR ELSE BILATERAL DESCENT IS INFERRED (289)	TEND LESS TO BE THOSE 0.68 OF 336 OTHER THAN WHERE THE ONLY KIN GROUP PRESENT IS A KINDRED OR ELSE BILATERAL DESCENT IS INFERRED (289)	5 106 59 230 XSQ= 13.95 PHI= -0.187 XP = 0.0002
196	TILT MORE TOWARD BEING THOSE 0.85 OF 47 WHERE INDIVIDUAL RIGHTS IN REAL PROPERTY, AND RULES FOR INHERITANCE, ARE PRESENT (194)	TILT LESS TOWARD BEING THOSE 0.66 OF 234 WHERE INDIVIDUAL RIGHTS IN REAL PROPERTY, AND RULES FOR INHERITANCE, ARE PRESENT (194)	40 154 7 80 XSQ= 5.94 PHI= 0.145 XP = 0.0148
197	TILT MORE TOWARD BEING THOSE 0.97 OF 40 WHERE RULES FOR THE INHERITANCE OF REAL PROPERTY, IF PRESENT, FAVOR EITHER THE MALE HEIR OR LINE, OR THE FEMALE HEIR OR LINE (165)	TILT LESS TOWARD BEING THOSE 0.82 OF 154 WHERE RULES FOR THE INHERITANCE OF REAL PROPERTY, IF PRESENT, FAVOR EITHER THE MALE HEIR OR LINE, OR THE FEMALE HEIR OR LINE (165)	39 126 1 28 XSQ= 4.97 PHI= 0.160 XP = 0.0258
201	DRIFT MORE TOWARD BEING THOSE 0.92 OF 64 WHERE MARITAL RESIDENCE IS NON-OPTIONAL, RATHER THAN AMBILOCAL OR NEOLOCAL (334)	DRIFT LESS TOWARD BEING THOSE 0.82 OF 334 WHERE MARITAL RESIDENCE IS NON-OPTIONAL, RATHER THAN AMBILOCAL OR NEOLOCAL (334)	59 275 5 59 XSQ= 3.17 PHI= 0.089 XP = 0.0751
204	TILT MORE TOWARD BEING THOSE 0.91 OF 58 WHERE MARITAL RESIDENCE IS PATRILOCAL, VIRILOCAL, OR AVUNCULOCAL, RATHER THAN AMBILOCAL OR NEOLOCAL (270)	TILT LESS TOWARD BEING THOSE 0.79 OF 276 WHERE MARITAL RESIDENCE IS PATRILOCAL, VIRILOCAL, OR AVUNCULOCAL, RATHER THAN AMBILOCAL OR NEOLOCAL (270)	53 217 5 59 XSQ= 4.24 PHI= 0.113 XP = 0.0394
209	DRIFT MORE TOWARD BEING THOSE 0.90 OF 59 WHERE MARITAL RESIDENCE IS PATRILOCAL, VIRILOCAL, OR AVUNCULOCAL, RATHER THAN MATRILOCAL OR UXORILOCAL (270)	DRIFT LESS TOWARD BEING THOSE 0.79 OF 275 WHERE MARITAL RESIDENCE IS PATRILOCAL, VIRILOCAL, OR AVUNCULOCAL, RATHER THAN MATRILOCAL OR UXORILOCAL (270)	53 217 6 58 XSQ= 3.07 PHI= 0.096 XP = 0.0798
234	TILT TOWARD BEING THOSE 0.61 OF 51 WHERE THE COUSIN TERMINOLOGY IS OF CROW, OMAHA, OR IROQUOIS TYPE, RATHER THAN ESKIMO OR HAWAIIAN TYPE (152)	TILT TOWARD BEING THOSE 0.55 OF 271 WHERE THE COUSIN TERMINOLOGY IS OF ESKIMO OR HAWAIIAN TYPE, RATHER THAN CROW, OMAHA, OR IROQUOIS TYPE (170)	31 121 20 150 XSQ= 3.86 PHI= 0.109 XP = 0.0495
242	LEAN MORE TOWARD BEING THOSE 0.95 OF 64 WHERE MARRIAGE IS COMMONLY OR OCCASIONALLY POLYGYNOUS, RATHER THAN MONOGAMOUS (314)	LEAN LESS TOWARD BEING THOSE 0.76 OF 331 WHERE MARRIAGE IS COMMONLY OR OCCASIONALLY POLYGYNOUS, RATHER THAN MONOGAMOUS (314)	61 253 3 78 XSQ= 10.59 PHI= 0.164 XP = 0.0011
243	TILT TOWARD BEING THOSE 0.80 OF 10 WHERE POLYGYNY, IF PRESENT, HAS A HIGH INCIDENCE (24) W-D,S	TILT TOWARD BEING THOSE 0.68 OF 50 WHERE POLYGYNY, IF PRESENT, HAS A LOW INCIDENCE (36) W-D,S	8 16 2 34 XSQ= 6.12 PHI= 0.320 XP = 0.0133

262	LEAN MORE TOWARD BEING THOSE WHERE WIVES ARE OBTAINED BY MEANS INVOLVING THE PRESENCE OF SOME CONSIDERATION (305)	0.94 OF 62	262	LEAN LESS TOWARD BEING THOSE WHERE WIVES ARE OBTAINED BY MEANS INVOLVING THE PRESENCE OF SOME CONSIDERATION (305)	0.74 OF 333	58 247 4 86 XSQ= 10.08 PHI= 0.160 XP = 0.0015
263	TEND MORE TO BE THOSE WHERE WIVES ARE OBTAINED BY RELATIVELY DIFFICULT MEANS, NAMELY BY BRIDE-PRICE, BRIDE-SERVICE, OR EXCHANGING A FEMALE RELATIVE (233)	0.82 OF 62	263	TEND LESS TO BE THOSE WHERE WIVES ARE OBTAINED BY RELATIVELY DIFFICULT MEANS, NAMELY BY BRIDE-PRICE, BRIDE-SERVICE, OR EXCHANGING A FEMALE RELATIVE (233)	0.55 OF 333	51 182 11 151 XSQ= 15.34 PHI= 0.197 XP = 0.0001
299	TILT TOWARD BEING THOSE WHERE THE POST-PARTUM SEX TABOO LASTS LONGER THAN ONE YEAR (35)	0.50 OF 24	299	TILT TOWARD BEING THOSE WHERE THE POST-PARTUM SEX TABOO LASTS ONE YEAR OR LESS (89)	0.77 OF 100	12 23 12 77 XSQ= 5.70 PHI= 0.214 XP = 0.0170
300	DRIFT TOWARD BEING THOSE WHERE THE POST-PARTUM SEX TABOO LASTS LONGER THAN SIX MONTHS (51)	0.58 OF 24	300	DRIFT TOWARD BEING THOSE WHERE THE POST-PARTUM SEX TABOO LASTS SIX MONTHS OR LESS (73)	0.63 OF 100	14 37 10 63 XSQ= 2.81 PHI= 0.151 XP = 0.0937
314	TILT TOWARD BEING THOSE WHERE THE INCIDENCE OF MOTHER-CHILD HOUSEHOLDS IS HIGH (19) W-D,S	0.55 OF 11	314	TILT TOWARD BEING THOSE WHERE THE INCIDENCE OF MOTHER-CHILD HOUSEHOLDS IS LOW (61) W-D,S	0.81 OF 69	6 13 5 56 XSQ= 4.85 PHI= 0.246 XP = 0.0276
324	DRIFT TOWARD BEING THOSE WHERE THE PAIN INFLICTED ON THE INFANT BY THE NURTURANT AGENT IS HIGH (34) B-B-C	0.88 OF 8	324	DRIFT TOWARD BEING THOSE WHERE THE PAIN INFLICTED ON THE INFANT BY THE NURTURANT AGENT IS LOW OR NEGLIGIBLE (32) B-B-C	0.53 OF 58	7 27 1 31 XSQ= 3.22 PHI= 0.221 XP = 0.0726
349	TILT TOWARD BEING THOSE WHERE THE CHILD'S INFERRED ANXIETY OVER NON-PERFORMANCE OF ACHIEVEMENT BEHAVIOR IS LOW (28) B-B-C	0.82 OF 11	349	TILT TOWARD BEING THOSE WHERE THE CHILD'S INFERRED ANXIETY OVER NON-PERFORMANCE OF ACHIEVEMENT BEHAVIOR IS HIGH (34) B-B-C	0.63 OF 51	2 32 9 19 XSQ= 5.57 PHI= -0.300 XP = 0.0183
370	TEND TO BE THOSE WHERE THE SEGREGATION OF ADOLESCENT BOYS IS COMPLETE OR PARTIAL (95)	0.63 OF 41	370	TEND TO BE THOSE WHERE THE SEGREGATION OF ADOLESCENT BOYS IS ABSENT (148)	0.66 OF 202	26 69 15 133 XSQ= 11.05 PHI= 0.213 XP = 0.0009
372	DRIFT TOWARD BEING THOSE WHERE MALE INITIATION RITES ARE PRESENT (48) ASA	0.62 OF 21	372	DRIFT TOWARD BEING THOSE WHERE MALE INITIATION RITES ARE ABSENT (63) ASA	0.61 OF 90	13 35 8 55 XSQ= 2.80 PHI= 0.159 XP = 0.0944

No.	Left		No.	Right		Statistics
377	TEND LESS TO BE THOSE WHERE MALE GENITAL MUTILATION IS ABSENT (242)	0.56 OF 54	377	TEND MORE TO BE THOSE WHERE MALE GENITAL MUTILATION IS ABSENT (242)	0.78 OF 271	24 59 30 212 XSQ= 11.01 PHI= 0.184 XP = 0.0009
426	LEAN MORE TOWARD BEING THOSE WHERE A HIGH GOD IS PRESENT (156) GES,EA	0.80 OF 41	426	LEAN LESS TOWARD BEING THOSE WHERE A HIGH GOD IS PRESENT (156) GES,EA	0.56 OF 219	33 123 8 96 XSQ= 7.53 PHI= 0.170 XP = 0.0061
431	IN ALL CASES ARE THOSE WHERE SUPERNATURAL SANCTIONS FOR MORALITY, HAVING AN EFFECT ON AN INDIVIDUAL'S AFTERLIFE, ARE ABSENT OR UNREPORTED (25) GES	1.00 OF 8	431	DRIFT LESS TOWARD BEING THOSE WHERE SUPERNATURAL SANCTIONS FOR MORALITY, HAVING AN EFFECT ON AN INDIVIDUAL'S AFTERLIFE, ARE ABSENT OR UNREPORTED (25) GES	0.63 OF 27	0 10 8 17 XSQ= 2.53 PHI= -0.269 EP = 0.0734
432	IN ALL CASES ARE THOSE WHERE AN ATTRACTIVE AFTERLIFE IS NOT BELIEVED IN (11) LWS	1.00 OF 2	432	DRIFT TOWARD BEING THOSE WHERE AN ATTRACTIVE AFTERLIFE IS BELIEVED IN (27) LWS	0.75 OF 36	0 27 2 9 XSQ= 2.18 PHI= -0.239 EP = 0.0782
458	LEAN TOWARD BEING THOSE WHERE GAMES, IF PRESENT, INCLUDE GAMES OF STRATEGY (52) R-A-B,EA	0.63 OF 19	458	LEAN TOWARD BEING THOSE WHERE GAMES, IF PRESENT, DO NOT INCLUDE GAMES OF STRATEGY (119) R-A-B,EA	0.74 OF 152	12 40 7 112 XSQ= 9.16 PHI= 0.231 XP = 0.0025
459	LEAN TOWARD BEING THOSE WHERE GAMES, IF PRESENT, DO NOT INCLUDE GAMES OF CHANCE (89) R-A-B,EA	0.84 OF 19	459	LEAN TOWARD BEING THOSE WHERE GAMES, IF PRESENT, INCLUDE GAMES OF CHANCE (82) R-A-B,EA	0.52 OF 152	3 79 16 73 XSQ= 7.47 PHI= -0.209 XP = 0.0063

****

42 CULTURES
WHERE THE NATURAL ENVIRONMENT IS
TROPICAL OR SUB-TROPICAL RAIN FOREST, OR
MONSOON FOREST (156) FWM

42 CULTURES
WHERE THE NATURAL ENVIRONMENT IS
OTHER THAN
TROPICAL OR SUB-TROPICAL RAIN FOREST, OR
MONSOON FOREST (244) FWM

BACKGROUND ON PAGE 69

BOTH SUBJECT AND PREDICATE

....

156 IN LEFT COLUMN

ABOR	AJIE	AKHA	ALORESE	ANDAMANESE	APINAYE	ARAPESH	ASHANTI	ATAYAL	AWEIKOMA
BABWA	BACAIRI	BALINESE	BAMILEKE	BANDA	BARI	BATAK	BAYA	BELU	BENGALI
BETE	BHIL	BHUIYA	BLACK CARIB	BORORO	BOTOCUDO	BRAZILIANS	BUNLAP	BURMESE	CAGABA
CALLINAGO	CAMAYURA	CAMBODIANS	CARAJA	CARIB	CAYAPA	CHOCO	CHORTI	COORG	CUNA
DOBUANS	DORCBC	DUSUN	ELLICE	ENGA	FANG	FON	GANDA	GARC	GUATO
HANUNOO	HO	IBAN	IFUGAO	JAPANESE	JAVANESE	KAPAUKU	KAREN	KERALA	KHASI
KOL	KPE	KUBA	KURTATCHI	LAKALAI	LAKHER	LAMET	LAU	LESU	LHOTA NAGA
LIFU	MACASSARESE	MALAYS	MAMVU	MANGAIANS	MANIHIKI	MANUS	MARQUESANS	MARSHALLESE	MAYA
MBUTI	MENDE	MENTAWEI	MERINA	MIAO	MIN CHINESE	MINANGKABAU	MISKITO	MNONG GAR	MONGO
MOTA	MOTILON	MUNDURUCU	NICOBARESE	NYAKYUSA	OKINAWANS	ONTONG-JAVA	CRACN	PAIWAN	PALAUANS
PALIKUR	PONAPEANS	POPOLUCA	PUKAPUKA	PURARI	PURUM	RAROIANS	ROTINESE	ROTUMANS	SAGADA
SAMOANS	SANTAL	SARAMACCA	SELUNG	SEMANG	SEMINOLE	SENIANG	SHERENTE	SIMBOESE	SINHALESE
SIUAI	SUBANUN	TAGBANUA	TALAMANCA	TANALA	TANIMBARESE	TAPIRAPE	TENETEHARA	TERENA	THAI
TIKOPIA	TOKELAU	TORAJA	TOTONAC	TROBRIAND	TRUKESE	TRUMAI	TUCANO	TUCUNA	TUNEBO
TUPINAMBA	ULAWANS	VEDDA	VIETNAMESE	WAICA	WANTOAT	WAROPEN	WARRAU	WITOTO	WOGEO
WOLEAIANS	YABARANA	YAGUA	YAKO	YAPESE	YOMBE				

244 IN RIGHT COLUMN

	Left column			Right column		
3	LEAN MORE TOWARD BEING THOSE LOCATED OUTSIDE OF AFRICA (320)	0.87 OF 156	3	LEAN LESS TOWARD BEING THOSE LOCATED OUTSIDE OF AFRICA (320)	0.75 OF 244	20 60 136 184 XSQ= 7.52 PHI= -0.137 XP = 0.0061
4	TEND MORE TO BE THOSE LOCATED OUTSIDE OF THE CIRCUM-MEDITERRANEAN (355)	0.99 OF 156	4	TEND LESS TO BE THOSE LOCATED OUTSIDE OF THE CIRCUM-MEDITERRANEAN (355)	0.82 OF 244	1 44 155 200 XSQ= 27.11 PHI= -0.260 XP = 0.0000
5	TILT LESS TOWARD BEING THOSE LOCATED OUTSIDE OF EAST EURASIA (330)	0.77 OF 156	5	TILT MORE TOWARD BEING THOSE LOCATED OUTSIDE OF EAST EURASIA (330)	0.86 OF 244	36 34 120 210 XSQ= 4.89 PHI= 0.111 XP = 0.0269

6	TEND LESS TO BE THCSE LCCATED CUTSIDE OF THE INSULAR PACIFIC (330)	0.62 OF 156	6	TEND MORE TO BE THOSE LOCATED OUTSIDE OF THE INSULAR PACIFIC (330)	0.95 OF 244	59 11 97 233 XSQ= 70.85 PHI= 0.421 XP = 0.
8	TEND MORE TO BE THCSE LOCATED CUTSIDE CF NORTH AMERICA (330)	0.98 OF 156	8	TEND LESS TO BE THOSE LOCATED OUTSIDE OF NORTH AMERICA (330)	0.73 OF 244	3 67 153 177 XSQ= 41.23 PHI= -0.321 XP = 0.
9	LEAN LESS TOWARC BEING THOSE LOCATED CUTSIDE CF SOUTH AMERICA (335)	0.76 OF 156	9	LEAN MORE TOWARD BEING THOSE LOCATED OUTSIDE OF SOUTH AMERICA (335)	0.89 OF 244	37 28 119 216 XSQ= 9.60 PHI= 0.155 XP = 0.0019
13	IN ALL CASES ARE THCSE WHERE THE LATITUDE IS LESS THAN FORTY DEGREES (329)	1.00 OF 156	13	TEND LESS TO BE THOSE WHERE THE LATITUDE IS LESS THAN FORTY DEGREES (329)	0.71 CF 244	0 71 156 173 XSQ= 53.21 PHI= -0.365 XP = 0.
15	TEND TO BE THOSE WHERE THE LATITUDE IS LESS THAN TWENTY DEGREES (217)	0.80 OF 156	15	TEND TO BE THOSE WHERE THE LATITUDE IS TWENTY DEGREES OR GREATER (183)	0.62 CF 244	31 152 125 92 XSQ= 67.30 PHI= -0.410 XP = 0.
16	TEND TC BE THCSE WHERE THE LATITUDE IS LESS THAN TEN DEGREES (123)	0.53 OF 156	16	TEND TO BE THOSE WHERE THE LATITUDE IS TEN DEGREES OR GREATER (277)	0.84 CF 244	73 204 83 40 XSQ= 58.84 PHI= -0.384 XP = 0.
44	TEND MORE TO BE THCSE WHERE SETTLEMENTS ARE FIXEC (222)	0.85 OF 130	44	TEND LESS TO BE THOSE WHERE SETTLEMENTS ARE FIXED (222)	0.55 CF 202	110 112 20 90 XSQ= 29.08 PHI= 0.296 XP = 0.0000
46	TEND MCRE TC BE THCSE CTHER THAN WHERE SETTLEMENTS ARE NON-FIXED AND MCVEMENT IS NCMADIC (260)	0.91 OF 130	46	TEND LESS TO BE THOSE OTHER THAN WHERE SETTLEMENTS ARE NON-FIXED AND MOVEMENT IS NOMADIC (260)	0.70 CF 202	12 60 118 142 XSQ= 18.33 PHI= -0.235 XP = 0.0000
48	TEND TO BE THCSE WHERE THE FCCD SUPPLY IS SECURE, AND FCOD SHORTAGES ARE RARE CR OCCASIONAL (38) MGW	0.77 OF 31	48	TEND TO BE THOSE WHERE THE FOOD SUPPLY IS NCT SECURE, AND FOOD SHORTAGES ARE FREQUENT OR ANNUAL (41) MGW	0.71 OF 48	24 14 7 34 XSQ= 15.69 PHI= 0.446 XP = 0.0001

51	TILT MORE TOWARD BEING THOSE 0.70 OF 156 WHERE SUBSISTENCE IS PRIMARILY BY FOOD PRODUCTION -- I. E., AGRICULTURE OR HUSBANDRY -- RATHER THAN BY GATHERING (253)	51	TILT LESS TOWARD BEING THOSE 0.59 OF 244 WHERE SUBSISTENCE IS PRIMARILY BY FOOD PRODUCTION -- I. E., AGRICULTURE OR HUSBANDRY -- RATHER THAN BY GATHERING (253)	109 144 47 100	XSQ= 4.37 PHI= 0.105 XP = 0.0366
53	TEND TO BE THOSE 0.79 OF 108 WHERE FOOD PRODUCTION IS BY SIMPLE AGRICULTURE OR INCIPIENT FOOD PRODUCTION, RATHER THAN BY INTENSIVE AGRICULTURE (147)	53	TEND TO BE THOSE 0.52 OF 130 WHERE FOOD PRODUCTION IS BY INTENSIVE AGRICULTURE, RATHER THAN BY SIMPLE AGRICULTURE OR INCIPIENT FOOD PRODUCTION (91)	23 68 85 62	XSQ= 22.73 PHI= -0.309 XP = 0.0000
55	TEND TO BE THOSE 0.74 OF 89 WHERE FOOD PRODUCTION IS BY SIMPLE AGRICULTURE, RATHER THAN BY INTENSIVE AGRICULTURE (101)	55	TEND TO BE THOSE 0.66 OF 103 WHERE FOOD PRODUCTION IS BY INTENSIVE AGRICULTURE, RATHER THAN BY SIMPLE AGRICULTURE (91)	23 68 66 35	XSQ= 29.32 PHI= -0.391 XP = 0.0000
56	TILT MORE TOWARD BEING THOSE 0.78 OF 85 WHERE FOOD PRODUCTION IS BY SIMPLE AGRICULTURE, RATHER THAN BY INCIPIENT FOOD PRODUCTION (101)	56	TILT LESS TOWARD BEING THOSE 0.56 OF 62 WHERE FOOD PRODUCTION IS BY SIMPLE AGRICULTURE, RATHER THAN BY INCIPIENT FOOD PRODUCTION (101)	66 35 19 27	XSQ= 6.54 PHI= 0.211 XP = 0.0106
63	TEND TO BE THOSE 0.54 OF 92 WHERE HUSBANDRY, IF PRESENT, IS PRINCIPALLY IN THE FORM OF PIGS, SHEEP, OR GOATS, RATHER THAN BOVINE, EQUINE, CAMEL-LIKE, OR DEER-LIKE ANIMALS (74)	63	TEND TO BE THOSE 0.82 OF 134 WHERE HUSBANDRY, IF PRESENT, IS PRINCIPALLY IN THE FORM OF BOVINE, EQUINE, CAMEL-LIKE, OR DEER-LIKE ANIMALS, RATHER THAN PIGS, SHEEP, OR GOATS (152)	42 110 50 24	XSQ= 31.25 PHI= -0.372 XP = 0.
71	TILT MORE TOWARD BEING THOSE 0.70 OF 99 WHERE METAL WORKING IS ABSENT (153)	71	TILT LESS TOWARD BEING THOSE 0.55 OF 152 WHERE METAL WORKING IS ABSENT (153)	30 68 69 84	XSQ= 4.66 PHI= -0.136 XP = 0.0309
81	DRIFT MORE TOWARD BEING THOSE 0.68 OF 87 WHERE NO CITY OR TOWN IS PRESENT, AND THE AVERAGE COMMUNITY SIZE IS SMALLER THAN 200 (135)	81	DRIFT LESS TOWARD BEING THOSE 0.55 OF 137 WHERE NO CITY OR TOWN IS PRESENT, AND THE AVERAGE COMMUNITY SIZE IS SMALLER THAN 200 (135)	28 61 59 76	XSQ= 2.89 PHI= -0.114 XP = 0.0892
83	LEAN MORE TOWARD BEING THOSE 0.87 OF 68 WHERE, WITH NO CITY AND NO TOWN PRESENT, THE AVERAGE COMMUNITY SIZE IS SMALLER THAN 200, RATHER THAN BETWEEN 200 AND 999 (135)	83	LEAN LESS TOWARD BEING THOSE 0.68 OF 112 WHERE, WITH NO CITY AND NO TOWN PRESENT, THE AVERAGE COMMUNITY SIZE IS SMALLER THAN 200, RATHER THAN BETWEEN 200 AND 999 (135)	9 36 59 76	XSQ= 7.09 PHI= -0.198 XP = 0.0078
86	DRIFT TOWARD BEING THOSE 0.58 OF 125 WHERE THE LEVEL OF POLITICAL INTEGRATION IS THE AUTONOMOUS COMMUNITY, OR THE FAMILY (156) GPM	86	DRIFT TOWARD BEING THOSE 0.54 OF 179 WHERE THE LEVEL OF POLITICAL INTEGRATION IS THE LARGE STATE, THE LITTLE STATE, OR THE MINIMAL STATE (148) GPM	52 96 73 83	XSQ= 3.80 PHI= -0.112 XP = 0.0514

110	DRIFT MORE TOWARD BEING THOSE 0.64 OF 151 WHERE SLAVERY IS ABSENT (218)	110	DRIFT LESS TOWARD BEING THOSE 0.53 OF 230 WHERE SLAVERY IS ABSENT (218)	55 108 96 122 XSQ= 3.71 PHI= -0.099 XP = 0.0540
129	DRIFT MORE TOWARD BEING THOSE 0.81 OF 47 WHERE WEAVING IS MAINLY DONE BY FEMALES (73)	129	DRIFT LESS TOWARD BEING THOSE 0.61 OF 57 WHERE WEAVING IS MAINLY DONE BY FEMALES (73)	9 22 38 35 XSQ= 3.77 PHI= -0.190 XP = 0.0521
130	IN ALL CASES ARE THOSE 1.00 OF 5 WHERE LEATHER WORKING IS MAINLY DONE BY MALES (39)	130	TILT TOWARD BEING THOSE 0.57 OF 79 WHERE LEATHER WORKING IS MAINLY DONE BY FEMALES (45)	5 34 0 45 XSQ= 4.06 PHI= 0.220 XP = 0.0440
131	TILT MORE TOWARD BEING THOSE 0.94 OF 67 WHERE THE CONSTRUCTION OF PERMANENT HOUSES OR THE ERECTION OF TEMPORARY DWELLINGS IS MAINLY DONE BY MALES (136)	131	TILT LESS TOWARD BEING THOSE 0.81 OF 90 WHERE THE CONSTRUCTION OF PERMANENT HOUSES OR THE ERECTION OF TEMPORARY DWELLINGS IS MAINLY DONE BY MALES (136)	63 73 4 17 XSQ= 4.47 PHI= 0.169 XP = 0.0344
163	LEAN TOWARD BEING THOSE 0.86 OF 7 WHERE THE EMPHASIS ON INDIVIDUAL VOLITION AS THE CAUSE OF CRIME IS HIGH (7) MJ	163	LEAN TOWARD BEING THOSE 0.90 OF 10 WHERE THE EMPHASIS ON INDIVIDUAL VOLITION AS THE CAUSE OF CRIME IS LOW (10) MJ	6 1 1 9 XSQ= 6.87 PHI= 0.636 EP = 0.0037
178	DRIFT LESS TOWARD BEING THOSE 0.72 OF 149 WHERE THE COMMUNITY IS OTHER THAN SEGMENTED ON A CLAN BASIS AND NON-EXOGAMOUS (295)	178	DRIFT MORE TOWARD BEING THOSE 0.81 OF 233 WHERE THE COMMUNITY IS OTHER THAN SEGMENTED ON A CLAN BASIS AND NON-EXOGAMOUS (295)	42 45 107 188 XSQ= 3.58 PHI= 0.097 XP = 0.0585
186	DRIFT MORE TOWARD BEING THOSE 0.68 OF 156 WHERE THE KIN GROUP IS OTHER THAN EXCLUSIVELY PATRILINEAL (250)	186	DRIFT LESS TOWARD BEING THOSE 0.59 OF 244 WHERE THE KIN GROUP IS OTHER THAN EXCLUSIVELY PATRILINEAL (250)	50 100 106 144 XSQ= 2.87 PHI= -0.085 XP = 0.0903
190	DRIFT LESS TOWARD BEING THOSE 0.68 OF 92 WHERE THE KIN GROUP IS PATRILINEAL OR DOUBLE-DESCENT, RATHER THAN MATRILINEAL (186)	190	DRIFT MORE TOWARD BEING THOSE 0.79 OF 155 WHERE THE KIN GROUP IS PATRILINEAL OR DOUBLE-DESCENT, RATHER THAN MATRILINEAL (186)	63 123 29 32 XSQ= 3.11 PHI= -0.112 XP = 0.0778
196	DRIFT MORE TOWARD BEING THOSE 0.76 OF 99 WHERE INDIVIDUAL RIGHTS IN REAL PROPERTY, AND RULES FOR INHERITANCE, ARE PRESENT (194)	196	DRIFT LESS TOWARD BEING THOSE 0.65 OF 182 WHERE INDIVIDUAL RIGHTS IN REAL PROPERTY, AND RULES FOR INHERITANCE, ARE PRESENT (194)	75 119 24 63 XSQ= 2.76 PHI= 0.099 XP = 0.0966

No.	Statement	Proportion	No.	Statement	Proportion	Statistics
197	TILT LESS TOWARD BEING THOSE WHERE RULES FOR THE INHERITANCE OF REAL PROPERTY, IF PRESENT, FAVOR EITHER THE MALE HEIR OR LINE, OR THE FEMALE HEIR CR LINE (165)	0.77 OF 75	197	TILT MORE TOWARD BEING THOSE WHERE RULES FOR THE INHERITANCE CF REAL PROPERTY, IF PRESENT, FAVOR EITHER THE MALE HEIR OR LINE, OR THE FEMALE HEIR OR LINE (165)	0.90 OF 119	58 107 17 12 XSQ= 4.78 PHI= -0.157 XP = 0.0288
209	LEAN LESS TOWARC BEING THOSE WHERE MARITAL RESICENCE IS PATRILOCAL, VIRILOCAL, OR AVUNCULOCAL, RATHER THAN MATRILOCAL OR UXCRILOCAL (270)	0.73 OF 128	209	LEAN MORE TOWARD BEING THOSE WHERE MARITAL RESIDENCE IS PATRILOCAL, VIRILOCAL, OR AVUNCULOCAL, RATHER THAN MATRILOCAL OR UXORILOCAL (270)	0.86 OF 206	93 177 35 29 XSQ= 8.13 PHI= -0.156 XP = 0.0043
262	DRIFT LESS TCWARD BEING THOSE WHERE WIVES ARE CBTAINEC BY MEANS INVCLVING THE PRESENCE OF SOME CCNSIDERATION (305)	0.72 OF 155	262	DRIFT MORE TOWARD BEING THOSE WHERE WIVES ARE OBTAINED BY MEANS INVOLVING THE PRESENCE OF SOME CONSIDERATION (305)	0.80 OF 240	112 193 43 47 XSQ= 3.11 PHI= -0.089 XP = 0.0776
277	DRIFT MORE TCWARD BEING THOSE WHERE THE STATUS OF WOMEN IS NOT STRONGLY INFERIOR OR SUBJECTED (22) LWS	0.89 OF 9	277	DRIFT LESS TOWARD BEING THOSE WHERE THE STATUS OF WOMEN IS NOT STRONGLY INFERIOR OR SUBJECTED (22) LWS	0.52 OF 27	1 13 8 14 XSQ= 2.49 PHI= -0.263 EP = 0.0620
280	TILT TOWARD BEING THOSE WHERE THE COMPOSITE FERTILITY LEVEL IS LOW (12) MN	0.69 OF 13	280	TILT TOWARD BEING THOSE WHERE THE COMPOSITE FERTILITY LEVEL IS HIGH (13) MN	0.75 OF 12	4 9 9 3 XSQ= 3.28 PHI= -0.362 EP = 0.0472
285	TILT TOWARD BEING THOSE WHERE THE SEX TABOC DURING PREGNANCY IS PRESENT (14) BCA	0.69 OF 13	285	TILT TOWARD BEING THOSE WHERE THE SEX TABOO DURING PREGNANCY IS ABSENT OR INFERRED ABSENT (17) BCA	0.72 OF 18	9 5 4 13 XSQ= 3.70 PHI= 0.345 EP = 0.0325
313	TILT TOWARD BEING THOSE WHERE AGGRESSION SCCIALIZATION ANXIETY IS LOW (28) W-C	0.70 OF 23	313	TILT TOWARD BEING THOSE WHERE AGGRESSION SOCIALIZATION ANXIETY IS HIGH (26) W-C	0.61 OF 31	7 19 16 12 XSQ= 3.88 PHI= -0.268 XP = 0.0490
350	TILT TCWARD BEING THOSE WHERE THE CHILD'S INFERREC ANXIETY OVER PERFORMANCE CF ACHIEVEMENT BEHAVIOR IS LOW (26) B-B-C	0.71 OF 17	350	TILT TOWARD BEING THOSE WHERE THE CHILD'S INFERRED ANXIETY OVER PERFORMANCE OF ACHIEVEMENT BEHAVIOR IS HIGH (34) B-B-C	0.67 OF 43	5 29 12 14 XSQ= 5.71 PHI= -0.309 XP = 0.0169
351	DRIFT TOWARD BEING THOSE WHERE THE CHILD'S INFERREC CONFLICT REGARDING ACHIEVEMENT BEHAVIOR IS LOW (34) B-B-C	0.76 OF 17	351	DRIFT TOWARD BEING THOSE WHERE THE CHILD'S INFERRED CONFLICT REGARDING ACHIEVEMENT BEHAVIOR IS HIGH (26) B-B-C	0.51 OF 43	4 22 13 21 XSQ= 2.75 PHI= -0.214 XP = 0.0974

352 TILT TOWARD BEING THOSE 0.56 OF 27 WHERE THE TOTAL POSITIVE PRESSURE TOWARD DEVELOPING OBEDIENT BEHAVIOR IN THE CHILD IS LOW (28) B-B-C	352 TILT TOWARD BEING THOSE 0.71 OF 45 WHERE THE TOTAL POSITIVE PRESSURE TOWARD DEVELOPING OBEDIENT BEHAVIOR IN THE CHILD IS HIGH (44) B-B-C	12 32 15 13 XSQ= 3.99 PHI= -0.235 XP = 0.0458
370 TILT LESS TOWARD BEING THOSE 0.51 OF 102 WHERE THE SEGREGATION OF ADOLESCENT BOYS IS ABSENT (148)	370 TILT MORE TOWARD BEING THOSE 0.68 OF 141 WHERE THE SEGREGATION OF ADOLESCENT BOYS IS ABSENT (148)	50 45 52 96 XSQ= 6.57 PHI= 0.164 XP = 0.0104
391 TILT TOWARD BEING THOSE 0.60 OF 75 WHERE PREMARITAL SEX RELATIONS ARE PUNISHED ONLY IF PREGNANCY RESULTS, OR FREELY PERMITTED (90) JTW,EA	391 TILT TOWARD BEING THOSE 0.57 OF 104 WHERE PREMARITAL SEX RELATIONS ARE STRONGLY PUNISHED AND IN FACT RARE, OR WEAKLY PUNISHED AND IN FACT NOT RARE (89) JTW,EA	30 59 45 45 XSQ= 4.23 PHI= -0.154 XP = 0.0396
400 DRIFT TOWARD BEING THOSE 0.55 OF 20 WHERE HOMOSEXUAL ACTIVITY IS PROHIBITED (22) F-B	400 DRIFT TOWARD BEING THOSE 0.71 OF 38 WHERE HOMOSEXUAL ACTIVITY IS PERMITTED (36) F-B	11 11 9 27 XSQ= 2.75 PHI= 0.218 XP = 0.0971
406 DRIFT TOWARD BEING THOSE 0.69 OF 26 WHERE EXPLANATIONS OF ILLNESS OF AN AGGRESSION NATURE ARE ABSENT (33) W-C	406 DRIFT TOWARD BEING THOSE 0.57 OF 35 WHERE EXPLANATIONS OF ILLNESS OF AN AGGRESSION NATURE ARE PRESENT (28) W-C	8 20 18 15 XSQ= 3.18 PHI= -0.228 XP = 0.0744
426 LEAN TOWARD BEING THOSE 0.52 OF 96 WHERE A HIGH GOD IS ABSENT (104) GES,EA	426 LEAN TOWARD BEING THOSE 0.67 OF 164 WHERE A HIGH GOD IS PRESENT (156) GES,EA	46 110 50 54 XSQ= 8.48 PHI= -0.181 XP = 0.0036
427 TEND TO BE THOSE 0.72 OF 46 WHERE A HIGH GOD, IF PRESENT, IS INACTIVE, RATHER THAN ACTIVE (69) GES,EA	427 TEND TO BE THOSE 0.67 OF 110 WHERE A HIGH GOD, IF PRESENT, IS ACTIVE, RATHER THAN INACTIVE (87) GES,EA	13 74 33 36 XSQ= 18.46 PHI= -0.344 XP = 0.0000
431 DRIFT TOWARD BEING THOSE 0.50 OF 14 WHERE SUPERNATURAL SANCTIONS FOR MORALITY, HAVING AN EFFECT ON AN INDIVIDUAL'S AFTER LIFE, ARE PRESENT (10) GES	431 DRIFT TOWARD BEING THOSE 0.86 OF 21 WHERE SUPERNATURAL SANCTIONS FOR MORALITY, HAVING AN EFFECT ON AN INDIVIDUAL'S AFTERLIFE, ARE ABSENT OR UNREPORTED (25) GES	7 3 7 18 XSQ= 3.65 PHI= 0.323 EP = 0.0529
439 DRIFT TOWARD BEING THOSE 0.65 OF 26 WHERE FEAR OF GHOSTS IS HIGH (30) W-C	439 DRIFT TOWARD BEING THOSE 0.63 OF 35 WHERE FEAR OF GHOSTS IS LOW (31) W-C	17 13 9 22 XSQ= 3.70 PHI= 0.246 XP = 0.0545

442	DRIFT TOWARD BEING THCSE WHERE FEAR OF ANIMAL SPIRITS IS LCW (33) W-C	0.69 OF 26	442	DRIFT TOWARD BEING THOSE WHERE FEAR OF ANIMAL SPIRITS IS HIGH (28) W-C	0.57 CF 35	8 20 18 15 XSQ= 3.18 PHI= -0.228 XP = 0.0744
445	TILT TOWARD BEING THOSE WHERE SCRCERY IS UNIMPCRTANT (23) BBW,CH	0.77 OF 13	445	TILT TOWARD BEING THOSE WHERE SORCERY IS IMPORTANT (26) BBW,DH	0.64 CF 36	3 23 10 13 XSQ= 4.85 PHI= -0.315 XP = 0.0276
455	TILT TCWARD BEING THOSE WHERE THE MODE CF THE INDIVIDUAL'S CCNTACT WITH THE DIVINE IS NCT CCNDUCIVE TC THE CEVELOPMENT OF THE INDIVIDUAL'S NEED TC ACHIEVE (19) DCM	0.89 OF 9	455	TILT TOWARD BEING THOSE WHERE THE MODE OF THE INDIVIDUAL'S CONTACT WITH THE DIVINE IS CONDUCIVE TO THE DEVELOPMENT OF THE INDIVIDUAL'S NEED TO ACHIEVE (17) DCM	0.59 CF 27	1 16 8 11 XSQ= 4.50 PHI= -0.353 EP = 0.0198
459	TEND TO BE THCSE WHERE GAMES, IF PRESENT, DC NCT INCLUDE GAMES CF CHANCE (89) R-A-B,EA	0.79 OF 63	459	TEND TO BE THOSE WHERE GAMES, IF PRESENT, INCLUDE GAMES OF CHANCE (82) R-A-B,EA	0.64 CF 108	13 69 50 39 XSQ= 28.12 PHI= -0.406 XP = 0.0000
460	TEND TC BE THCSE WHERE GAMES, IF PRESENT, ARE LIMITED TC GAMES OF SKILL CNLY (67) R-A-B,EA	0.70 OF 63	460	TEND TO BE THOSE WHERE GAMES, IF PRESENT, ARE NOT LIMITED TC GAMES OF SKILL ONLY (104) R-A-B,EA	0.79 CF 108	44 23 19 85 XSQ= 37.34 PHI= 0.467 XP = 0.

43 CULTURES
WHERE THE NATURAL ENVIRONMENT IS
TROPICAL RAIN FOREST (115) FWM

43 CULTURES
WHERE THE NATURAL ENVIRONMENT IS
OTHER THAN
TROPICAL RAIN FOREST (285) FWM

BACKGROUND ON PAGE 69

SUBJECT ONLY

115 IN LEFT COLUMN

AJIE	AKHA	ALORESE	ANDAMANESE	APINAYE	ARAPESH	ASHANTI	ATAYAL	BABWA	BACAIRI
BALINESE	BAMILEKE	BANDA	BARI	BAYA	BENGALI	BETE	BLACK CARIB	BRAZILIANS	BUNLAP
CALLINAGO	CAMAYURA	CAMBODIANS	CARAJA	CARIB	CAYAPA	CHOCO	CHORTI	CUNA	DOBUANS
ELLICE	FANG	FON	GANDA	GARO	HANUNOO	IBAN	JAVANESE	KAPAUKU	KAREN
KPE	KUBA	KURTATCHI	LAKALAI	LAU	LESU	LIFU	MACASSARESE	MALAYS	MAMVU
MANGAIANS	MANIHIKI	MANUS	MARQUESANS	MARSHALLESE	MAYA	MBUTI	MENDE	MENTAWEI	MISKITO
MNONG GAR	MONGO	MOTA	MOTILON	MUNDURUCU	NICOBARESE	ONTONG-JAVA	PALAUANS	PALIKUR	PONAPEANS
POPOLUCA	PUKAPUKA	PURARI	RAROIANS	ROTINESE	ROTUMANS	SAGADA	SAMOANS	SARAMACCA	SELUNG
SEMINOLE	SENIANG	SHERENTE	SIMBOESE	SIUAI	SUBANUN	TAGBANUA	TALAMANCA	TANIMBARESE	TAPIRAPE
TENETEHARA	THAI	TIKOPIA	TOKELAU	TORAJA	TOTONAC	TROBRIAND	TRUMAI	TUCANO	TUCUNA
TUNEBO	TUPINAMBA	ULAWANS	VIETNAMESE	WAICA	WAROPEN	WARRAU	WITOTO	WOGEO	WOLEAIANS
YABARANA	YAGUA	YAKO	YAPESE	YOMBE					

285 IN RIGHT COLUMN

4	TEND MORE TO BE THOSE LOCATED OUTSIDE OF THE CIRCUM-MEDITERRANEAN (355)	0.99 OF 115	4	TEND LESS TO BE THOSE LOCATED OUTSIDE OF THE CIRCUM-MEDITERRANEAN (355)	0.85 OF 285	1 44 114 241 XSQ= 15.99 PHI= -0.200 XP = 0.0001
5	TILT MORE TOWARD BEING THOSE LOCATED OUTSIDE OF EAST EURASIA (330)	0.90 OF 115	5	TILT LESS TOWARD BEING THOSE LOCATED OUTSIDE OF EAST EURASIA (330)	0.80 OF 285	12 58 103 227 XSQ= 4.91 PHI= -0.111 XP = 0.0266
6	TEND LESS TO BE THOSE LOCATED OUTSIDE OF THE INSULAR PACIFIC (330)	0.57 OF 115	6	TEND MORE TO BE THOSE LOCATED OUTSIDE OF THE INSULAR PACIFIC (330)	0.93 OF 285	50 20 65 265 XSQ= 72.94 PHI= 0.427 XP = 0.
8	TEND MORE TO BE THOSE LOCATED OUTSIDE OF NORTH AMERICA (330)	0.97 OF 115	8	TEND LESS TO BE THOSE LOCATED OUTSIDE OF NORTH AMERICA (330)	0.76 OF 285	3 67 112 218 XSQ= 23.36 PHI= -0.242 XP = 0.0000

9	TEND LESS TO BE THOSE LOCATED OUTSIDE OF SOUTH AMERICA (335)	0.73 OF 115	9	TEND MORE TO BE THOSE LOCATED OUTSIDE OF SOUTH AMERICA (335)	0.88 OF 285	31 34 84 251 XSQ= 12.51 PHI= 0.177 XP = 0.0004
14	IN ALL CASES ARE THOSE WHERE THE LATITUDE IS LESS THAN THIRTY DEGREES (281)	1.00 OF 115	14	TEND LESS TO BE THOSE WHERE THE LATITUDE IS LESS THAN THIRTY DEGREES (281)	0.58 OF 285	0 119 115 166 XSQ= 66.37 PHI= -0.407 XP = 0.
15	TEND TO BE THOSE WHERE THE LATITUDE IS LESS THAN TWENTY DEGREES (217)	0.91 OF 115	15	TEND TO BE THOSE WHERE THE LATITUDE IS TWENTY DEGREES OR GREATER (183)	0.61 OF 285	10 173 105 112 XSQ= 87.21 PHI= -0.467 XP = 0.
16	TEND TO BE THOSE WHERE THE LATITUDE IS LESS THAN TEN DEGREES (123)	0.62 OF 115	16	TEND TO BE THOSE WHERE THE LATITUDE IS TEN DEGREES OR GREATER (277)	0.82 OF 285	44 233 71 52 XSQ= 70.76 PHI= -0.421 XP = 0.
44	TEND MORE TO BE THOSE WHERE SETTLEMENTS ARE FIXED (222)	0.88 OF 95	44	TEND LESS TO BE THOSE WHERE SETTLEMENTS ARE FIXED (222)	0.58 OF 237	84 138 11 99 XSQ= 26.56 PHI= 0.283 XP = 0.0000
46	TEND MORE TO BE THOSE OTHER THAN WHERE SETTLEMENTS ARE NON-FIXED AND MOVEMENT IS NOMADIC (260)	0.96 OF 95	46	TEND LESS TO BE THOSE OTHER THAN WHERE SETTLEMENTS ARE NON-FIXED AND MOVEMENT IS NOMADIC (260)	0.71 OF 237	4 68 91 169 XSQ= 22.51 PHI= -0.260 XP = 0.0000
47	DRIFT TOWARD BEING THOSE WHERE, IF SETTLEMENTS ARE NON-FIXED, MOVEMENT IS NON-NOMADIC, RATHER THAN NOMADIC (38)	0.64 OF 11	47	DRIFT TOWARD BEING THOSE WHERE, IF SETTLEMENTS ARE NON-FIXED, MOVEMENT IS NOMADIC, RATHER THAN NON-NOMADIC (72)	0.69 OF 99	4 68 7 31 XSQ= 3.26 PHI= -0.172 XP = 0.0711
48	TEND TO BE THOSE WHERE THE FOOD SUPPLY IS SECURE, AND FOOD SHORTAGES ARE RARE OR OCCASIONAL (38) MGW	0.77 OF 26	48	TEND TO BE THOSE WHERE THE FOOD SUPPLY IS NOT SECURE, AND FOOD SHORTAGES ARE FREQUENT OR ANNUAL (41) MGW	0.66 OF 53	20 18 6 35 XSQ= 11.23 PHI= 0.377 XP = 0.0008
53	TEND TO BE THOSE WHERE FOOD PRODUCTION IS BY SIMPLE AGRICULTURE OR INCIPIENT FOOD PRODUCTION, RATHER THAN BY INTENSIVE AGRICULTURE (147)	0.89 OF 81	53	TEND TO BE THOSE WHERE FOOD PRODUCTION IS BY INTENSIVE AGRICULTURE, RATHER THAN BY SIMPLE AGRICULTURE OR INCIPIENT FOOD PRODUCTION (91)	0.52 OF 157	9 82 72 75 XSQ= 36.53 PHI= -0.392 XP = 0.

55	TEND TO BE THOSE WHERE FOOD PRODUCTION IS BY SIMPLE AGRICULTURE, RATHER THAN BY INTENSIVE AGRICULTURE (101)	0.86 OF 65	55	TEND TO BE THOSE WHERE FOOD PRODUCTION IS BY INTENSIVE AGRICULTURE, RATHER THAN BY SIMPLE AGRICULTURE (91)	0.65 OF 127	9 82 56 45 XSQ= 42.35 PHI= -0.470 XP = 0.
56	TILT MORE TOWARD BEING THOSE WHERE FOOD PRODUCTION IS BY SIMPLE AGRICULTURE, RATHER THAN BY INCIPIENT FOOD PRODUCTION (101)	0.78 OF 72	56	TILT LESS TOWARD BEING THOSE WHERE FOOD PRODUCTION IS BY SIMPLE AGRICULTURE, RATHER THAN BY INCIPIENT FOOD PRODUCTION (101)	0.60 OF 75	56 45 16 30 XSQ= 4.60 PHI= 0.177 XP = 0.0319
63	TEND TO BE THOSE WHERE HUSBANDRY, IF PRESENT, IS PRINCIPALLY IN THE FORM OF PIGS, SHEEP, OR GOATS, RATHER THAN BOVINE, EQUINE, CAMEL-LIKE, OR DEER-LIKE ANIMALS (74)	0.69 OF 64	63	TEND TO BE THOSE WHERE HUSBANDRY, IF PRESENT, IS PRINCIPALLY IN THE FORM OF BOVINE, EQUINE, CAMEL-LIKE, OR DEER-LIKE ANIMALS, RATHER THAN PIGS, SHEEP, OR GOATS (152)	0.81 OF 162	20 132 44 30 XSQ= 50.31 PHI= -0.472 XP = 0.
71	LEAN MORE TOWARD BEING THOSE WHERE METAL WORKING IS ABSENT (153)	0.76 OF 74	71	LEAN LESS TOWARD BEING THOSE WHERE METAL WORKING IS ABSENT (153)	0.55 OF 177	18 80 56 97 XSQ= 8.70 PHI= -0.186 XP = 0.0032
83	DRIFT MORE TOWARD BEING THOSE WHERE, WITH NO CITY AND NO TOWN PRESENT, THE AVERAGE COMMUNITY SIZE IS SMALLER THAN 200, RATHER THAN BETWEEN 200 AND 999 (135)	0.86 OF 50	83	DRIFT LESS TOWARD BEING THOSE WHERE, WITH NO CITY AND NO TOWN PRESENT, THE AVERAGE COMMUNITY SIZE IS SMALLER THAN 200, RATHER THAN BETWEEN 200 AND 999 (135)	0.71 OF 130	7 38 43 92 XSQ= 3.69 PHI= -0.143 XP = 0.0547
86	TILT TOWARD BEING THOSE WHERE THE LEVEL OF POLITICAL INTEGRATION IS THE AUTONOMOUS COMMUNITY, OR THE FAMILY (156) GPM	0.61 OF 95	86	TILT TOWARD BEING THOSE WHERE THE LEVEL OF POLITICAL INTEGRATION IS THE LARGE STATE, THE LITTLE STATE, OR THE MINIMAL STATE (148) GPM	0.53 OF 209	37 111 58 98 XSQ= 4.69 PHI= -0.124 XP = 0.0303
96	DRIFT TOWARD BEING THOSE WHERE THE HIERARCHY OF NATIONAL JURISDICTION HAS NO LEVELS (156) GES,EA	0.56 OF 95	96	DRIFT TOWARD BEING THOSE WHERE THE HIERARCHY OF NATIONAL JURISDICTION HAS FOUR, THREE, TWO OR ONE LEVEL (174) GES,EA	0.56 OF 235	42 132 53 103 XSQ= 3.42 PHI= -0.102 XP = 0.0645
109	TILT MORE TOWARD BEING THOSE WHERE CASTES ARE ABSENT (317)	0.93 OF 112	109	TILT LESS TOWARD BEING THOSE WHERE CASTES ARE ABSENT (317)	0.83 OF 256	8 43 104 213 XSQ= 5.30 PHI= -0.120 XP = 0.0213
131	TILT MORE TOWARD BEING THOSE WHERE THE CONSTRUCTION OF PERMANENT HOUSES OR THE ERECTION OF TEMPORARY DWELLINGS IS MAINLY DONE BY MALES (136)	0.96 OF 50	131	TILT LESS TOWARD BEING THOSE WHERE THE CONSTRUCTION OF PERMANENT HOUSES OR THE ERECTION OF TEMPORARY DWELLINGS IS MAINLY DONE BY MALES (136)	0.82 OF 107	48 88 2 19 XSQ= 4.44 PHI= 0.168 XP = 0.0351

163	TILT TOWARD BEING THOSE 0.83 OF 6 WHERE THE EMPHASIS ON INDIVIDUAL VOLITION AS THE CAUSE OF CRIME IS HIGH (7) MJ	163	TILT TOWARD BEING THOSE 0.82 OF 11 WHERE THE EMPHASIS ON INDIVIDUAL VOLITION AS THE CAUSE OF CRIME IS LOW (10) MJ	5 2 1 9 XSQ= 4.38 PHI= 0.508 EP = 0.0345
176	DRIFT TOWARD BEING THOSE 0.51 OF 109 WHERE THE COMMUNITY IS A CLAN-COMMUNITY OR A COMMUNITY STRUCTURED OR SEGMENTED ON A CLAN BASIS (169)	176	DRIFT TOWARD BEING THOSE 0.59 OF 273 WHERE THE COMMUNITY IS OTHER THAN A CLAN-COMMUNITY OR A COMMUNITY STRUCTURED OR SEGMENTED ON A CLAN BASIS (213)	56 113 53 160 XSQ= 2.76 PHI= 0.085 XP = 0.0969
178	TILT LESS TOWARD BEING THOSE 0.70 OF 109 WHERE THE COMMUNITY IS OTHER THAN SEGMENTED ON A CLAN BASIS AND NON-EXOGAMOUS (295)	178	TILT MORE TOWARD BEING THOSE 0.80 OF 273 WHERE THE COMMUNITY IS OTHER THAN SEGMENTED ON A CLAN BASIS AND NON-EXOGAMOUS (295)	33 54 76 219 XSQ= 4.30 PHI= 0.106 XP = 0.0381
179	TILT MORE TOWARD BEING THOSE 0.94 OF 109 WHERE THE COMMUNITY IS OTHER THAN STRUCTURED ON A NON-CLAN BASIS AND COMMONLY EXOGAMOUS (340)	179	TILT LESS TOWARD BEING THOSE 0.87 OF 273 WHERE THE COMMUNITY IS OTHER THAN STRUCTURED ON A NON-CLAN BASIS AND COMMONLY EXOGAMOUS (340)	6 36 103 237 XSQ= 3.95 PHI= -0.102 XP = 0.0470
185	DRIFT LESS TOWARD BEING THOSE 0.69 OF 67 WHERE THE LARGEST NON-COGNATIC KIN GROUP IS THE MOEITY OR PHRATRY OR SIB (194)	185	DRIFT MORE TOWARD BEING THOSE 0.80 OF 185 WHERE THE LARGEST NON-COGNATIC KIN GROUP IS THE MOEITY OR PHRATRY OR SIB (194)	46 148 21 37 XSQ= 2.96 PHI= -0.108 XP = 0.0853
186	TILT MORE TOWARD BEING THOSE 0.71 OF 115 WHERE THE KIN GROUP IS OTHER THAN EXCLUSIVELY PATRILINEAL (250)	186	TILT LESS TOWARD BEING THOSE 0.59 OF 285 WHERE THE KIN GROUP IS OTHER THAN EXCLUSIVELY PATRILINEAL (250)	33 117 82 168 XSQ= 4.82 PHI= -0.110 XP = 0.0281
190	DRIFT LESS TOWARD BEING THOSE 0.67 OF 66 WHERE THE KIN GROUP IS PATRILINEAL OR DOUBLE-DESCENT, RATHER THAN MATRILINEAL (186)	190	DRIFT MORE TOWARD BEING THOSE 0.78 OF 181 WHERE THE KIN GROUP IS PATRILINEAL OR DOUBLE-DESCENT, RATHER THAN MATRILINEAL (186)	44 142 22 39 XSQ= 3.01 PHI= -0.110 XP = 0.0829
197	TILT LESS TOWARD BEING THOSE 0.74 OF 46 WHERE RULES FOR THE INHERITANCE OF REAL PROPERTY, IF PRESENT, FAVOR EITHER THE MALE HEIR OR LINE, OR THE FEMALE HEIR OR LINE (165)	197	TILT MORE TOWARD BEING THOSE 0.89 OF 148 WHERE RULES FOR THE INHERITANCE OF REAL PROPERTY, IF PRESENT, FAVOR EITHER THE MALE HEIR OR LINE, OR THE FEMALE HEIR OR LINE (165)	34 131 12 17 XSQ= 4.79 PHI= -0.157 XP = 0.0286
198	LEAN LESS TOWARD BEING THOSE 0.71 OF 34 WHERE RULES FOR THE INHERITANCE OF REAL PROPERTY, IF PRESENT, FAVOR THE MALE HEIR OR LINE, RATHER THAN THE FEMALE (144)	198	LEAN MORE TOWARD BEING THOSE 0.92 OF 131 WHERE RULES FOR THE INHERITANCE OF REAL PROPERTY, IF PRESENT, FAVOR THE MALE HEIR OR LINE, RATHER THAN THE FEMALE (144)	24 120 10 11 XSQ= 8.92 PHI= -0.233 XP = 0.0028

209	LEAN LESS TOWARD BEING THOSE 0.70 OF 94 WHERE MARITAL RESIDENCE IS PATRILOCAL, VIRILOCAL, OR AVUNCULOCAL, RATHER THAN MATRILOCAL OR UXORILOCAL (270)	209	LEAN MORE TOWARD BEING THOSE 0.85 OF 240 WHERE MARITAL RESIDENCE IS PATRILOCAL, VIRILOCAL, OR AVUNCULOCAL, RATHER THAN MATRILOCAL OR UXORILOCAL (270)	66 204 28 36 XSQ= 8.60 PHI= -0.161 XP = 0.0034
224	DRIFT MORE TOWARD BEING THOSE 0.74 OF 46 WHERE COUSIN MARRIAGE IS PREFERENTIALLY OR PERMISSIVELY SYMMETRICAL, RATHER THAN EITHER PATRI- OR MATRILATERAL (106)	224	DRIFT LESS TOWARD BEING THOSE 0.57 OF 126 WHERE COUSIN MARRIAGE IS PREFERENTIALLY OR PERMISSIVELY SYMMETRICAL, RATHER THAN EITHER PATRI- OR MATRILATERAL (106)	12 54 34 72 XSQ= 3.33 PHI= -0.139 XP = 0.0680
236	DRIFT TOWARD BEING THOSE 0.54 OF 113 WHERE THE FAMILY IS OF AN INDEPENDENT TYPE, RATHER THAN AN EXTENDED TYPE (185)	236	DRIFT TOWARD BEING THOSE 0.56 OF 285 WHERE THE FAMILY IS OF AN EXTENDED TYPE, RATHER THAN AN INDEPENDENT TYPE (213)	52 161 61 124 XSQ= 3.16 PHI= -0.089 XP = 0.0755
280	TILT TOWARD BEING THOSE 0.73 OF 11 WHERE THE COMPOSITE FERTILITY LEVEL IS LOW (12) MN	280	TILT TOWARD BEING THOSE 0.71 OF 14 WHERE THE COMPOSITE FERTILITY LEVEL IS HIGH (13) MN	3 10 8 4 XSQ= 3.21 PHI= -0.358 EP = 0.0472
300	TILT TOWARD BEING THOSE 0.56 OF 41 WHERE THE POST-PARTUM SEX TABOO LASTS LONGER THAN SIX MONTHS (51)	300	TILT TOWARD BEING THOSE 0.66 OF 83 WHERE THE POST-PARTUM SEX TABOO LASTS SIX MONTHS OR LESS (73)	23 28 18 55 XSQ= 4.78 PHI= 0.196 XP = 0.0288
347	DRIFT TOWARD BEING THOSE 0.68 OF 25 WHERE THE CHILD'S INFERRED CONFLICT REGARDING SELF-RELIANT BEHAVIOR IS LOW (39) B-B-C	347	DRIFT TOWARD BEING THOSE 0.57 OF 51 WHERE THE CHILD'S INFERRED CONFLICT REGARDING SELF-RELIANT BEHAVIOR IS HIGH (37) B-B-C	8 29 17 22 XSQ= 3.22 PHI= -0.206 XP = 0.0729
350	LEAN TOWARD BEING THOSE 0.79 OF 14 WHERE THE CHILD'S INFERRED ANXIETY OVER PERFORMANCE OF ACHIEVEMENT BEHAVIOR IS LOW (26) B-B-C	350	LEAN TOWARD BEING THOSE 0.67 OF 46 WHERE THE CHILD'S INFERRED ANXIETY OVER PERFORMANCE OF ACHIEVEMENT BEHAVIOR IS HIGH (34) B-B-C	3 31 11 15 XSQ= 7.46 PHI= -0.353 XP = 0.0063
368	TILT TOWARD BEING THOSE 0.78 OF 9 WHERE DISSOCIATION OF THE SEXES AT ADOLESCENCE IS HIGH OR MEDIUM (16) JKH	368	TILT TOWARD BEING THOSE 0.68 OF 28 WHERE DISSOCIATION OF THE SEXES AT ADOLESCENCE IS LOW (21) JKH	7 9 2 19 XSQ= 4.07 PHI= 0.332 EP = 0.0239
372	DRIFT TOWARD BEING THOSE 0.58 OF 33 WHERE MALE INITIATION RITES ARE PRESENT (48) ASA	372	DRIFT TOWARD BEING THOSE 0.63 OF 78 WHERE MALE INITIATION RITES ARE ABSENT (63) ASA	19 29 14 49 XSQ= 3.14 PHI= 0.168 XP = 0.0762

382	TILT TOWARD BEING THOSE WHERE FEMALE INITIATION RITES ARE PRESENT (38) JKB	0.82 OF 17	382	TILT TOWARD BEING THOSE WHERE FEMALE INITIATION RITES ARE ABSENT (27) JKB	0.50 OF 48	14 24 3 24 XSQ= 4.16 PHI= 0.253 XP = 0.0414
391	DRIFT TOWARD BEING THOSE WHERE PREMARITAL SEX RELATIONS ARE PUNISHED ONLY IF PREGNANCY RESULTS, OR FREELY PERMITTED (90) JTW,EA	0.61 OF 54	391	DRIFT TOWARD BEING THOSE WHERE PREMARITAL SEX RELATIONS ARE STRONGLY PUNISHED AND IN FACT RARE, OR WEAKLY PUNISHED AND IN FACT NOT RARE (89) JTW,EA	0.54 OF 125	21 68 33 57 XSQ= 3.04 PHI= -0.130 XP = 0.0815
405	TILT TOWARD BEING THOSE WHERE EXPLANATIONS OF ILLNESS OF A DEPENDENCE NATURE ARE ABSENT (27) W-C	0.64 OF 22	405	TILT TOWARD BEING THOSE WHERE EXPLANATIONS OF ILLNESS OF A DEPENDENCE NATURE ARE PRESENT (34) W-C	0.67 OF 39	8 26 14 13 XSQ= 4.08 PHI= -0.259 XP = 0.0434
406	DRIFT TOWARD BEING THOSE WHERE EXPLANATIONS OF ILLNESS OF AN AGGRESSION NATURE ARE ABSENT (33) W-C	0.73 OF 22	406	DRIFT TOWARD BEING THOSE WHERE EXPLANATIONS OF ILLNESS OF AN AGGRESSION NATURE ARE PRESENT (28) W-C	0.56 OF 39	6 22 16 17 XSQ= 3.71 PHI= -0.247 XP = 0.0542
419	DRIFT TOWARD BEING THOSE WHERE MILITARY GLORY IS NEGLIGIBLY EMPHASIZED (31) PES	0.52 OF 25	419	DRIFT TOWARD BEING THOSE WHERE MILITARY GLORY IS STRONGLY OR MODERATELY EMPHASIZED (55) PES	0.70 OF 61	12 43 13 18 XSQ= 2.98 PHI= -0.186 XP = 0.0845
426	TILT TOWARD BEING THOSE WHERE A HIGH GOD IS ABSENT (104) GES,EA	0.52 OF 73	426	TILT TOWARD BEING THOSE WHERE A HIGH GOD IS PRESENT (156) GES,EA	0.65 OF 187	35 121 38 66 XSQ= 5.47 PHI= -0.145 XP = 0.0194
427	TEND TO BE THOSE WHERE A HIGH GOD, IF PRESENT, IS INACTIVE, RATHER THAN ACTIVE (69) GES,EA	0.71 OF 35	427	TEND TO BE THOSE WHERE A HIGH GOD, IF PRESENT, IS ACTIVE, RATHER THAN INACTIVE (87) GES,EA	0.64 OF 121	10 77 25 44 XSQ= 12.15 PHI= -0.279 XP = 0.0005
430	TILT TOWARD BEING THOSE WHERE SUPERNATURAL SANCTIONS FOR MORALITY, HAVING AN EFFECT ON AN INDIVIDUAL'S HEALTH, ARE ABSENT OR UNREPORTED (22) GES	0.90 OF 10	430	TILT TOWARD BEING THOSE WHERE SUPERNATURAL SANCTIONS FOR MORALITY, HAVING AN EFFECT ON AN INDIVIDUAL'S HEALTH, ARE PRESENT (16) GES	0.54 OF 28	1 15 9 13 XSQ= 4.09 PHI= -0.328 EP = 0.0250
435	DRIFT TOWARD BEING THOSE WHERE ABANDONMENT OF THE HOUSE OF THE DEAD IS NOT PRACTICED (19) LWS	0.89 OF 9	435	DRIFT TOWARD BEING THOSE WHERE ABANDONMENT OF THE HOUSE OF THE DEAD IS PRACTICED (12) LWS	0.50 OF 22	1 11 8 11 XSQ= 2.60 PHI= -0.289 EP = 0.0568

```
455  TILT TOWARD BEING THOSE            0.89 OF   9    455  TILT TOWARD BEING THOSE            0.59 OF  27          1   16
     WHERE THE MODE OF THE INDIVIDUAL'S                     WHERE THE MODE OF THE INDIVIDUAL'S                     8   11
     CONTACT WITH THE DIVINE                                CONTACT WITH THE DIVINE                          XSQ=      4.50
     IS NOT CONDUCIVE TO THE DEVELOPMENT OF THE             IS CONDUCIVE TO THE DEVELOPMENT OF THE           PHI=    -0.353
     INDIVIDUAL'S NEED TO ACHIEVE  (19) DCM                 INDIVIDUAL'S NEED TO ACHIEVE  (17) DCM           EP =    0.0198

458  TILT MORE TOWARD BEING THOSE       0.83 OF  46    458  TILT LESS TOWARD BEING THOSE       0.65 OF 125          8   44
     WHERE GAMES, IF PRESENT,                               WHERE GAMES, IF PRESENT,                              38   81
     DO NOT INCLUDE                                         DO NOT INCLUDE                                   XSQ=      4.23
     GAMES OF STRATEGY  (119) R-A-B,EA                      GAMES OF STRATEGY  (119) R-A-B,EA                PHI=    -0.157
                                                                                                             XP =    0.0396

459  TEND TO BE THOSE                   0.80 OF  46    459  TEND TO BE THOSE                   0.58 OF 125          9   73
     WHERE GAMES, IF PRESENT,                               WHERE GAMES, IF PRESENT,                              37   52
     DO NOT INCLUDE                                         INCLUDE GAMES OF CHANCE  (82) R-A-B,EA           XSQ=     18.79
     GAMES OF CHANCE  (89) R-A-B,EA                                                                          PHI=    -0.332
                                                                                                             XP =    0.0000

460  TEND TO BE THOSE                   0.74 OF  46    460  TEND TO BE THOSE                   0.74 OF 125         34   33
     WHERE GAMES, IF PRESENT,                               WHERE GAMES, IF PRESENT,                              12   92
     ARE LIMITED TO                                         ARE NOT LIMITED TO                               XSQ=     29.89
     GAMES OF SKILL ONLY  (67) R-A-B,EA                     GAMES OF SKILL ONLY  (104) R-A-B,EA              PHI=     0.418
                                                                                                             XP =    0.0000
```

44 CULTURES
WHERE SETTLEMENTS ARE FIXED (222)

44 CULTURES
WHERE SETTLEMENTS ARE NON-FIXED (110)

BACKGROUND ON PAGE 71

BOTH SUBJECT AND PREDICATE

222 IN LEFT COLUMN

ABOR	AINU	AKHA	ALBANIANS	ALORESE	AMBA	AMERICANS	APINAYE	ARAPESH	ARAUCANIANS
ASHANTI	ATAYAL	AYMARA	AZANDE	AZTEC	BABWA	BACAIRI	BAMBARA	BAMILEKE	BANDA
BARABRA	BARI	BAYA	BHIL	BIRIFOR	BLACK CARIB	BOERS	BRAZILIANS	BULGARIANS	BUNLAP
BURUSHO	CAGABA	CALLINAGO	CAMBODIANS	CARIB	CAYAPA	CHAGGA	CHERKESS	CHEROKEE	CHIBCHA
CHIRIGUANO	CHOCO	CHORTI	COCHITI	COORG	CREEK	CUNA	CZECHS	DAGUR	DILLING
DOGON	DUTCH	EGYPTIANS	ELLICE	ENGA	EYAK	FANG	FON	FUTAJALONKE	GANDA
GARO	GISU	GOND	GURE	HAIDA	HANO	HANUNOO	HASINAI	HAWAIIANS	HEBREWS
HUICHOL	HURON	HUTSUL	IBAN	IFUGAO	INCA	INGASSANA	IRAQW	IRISH	JAPANESE
JAVANESE	JEMEZ	JIVARO	JUKUN	KABYLE	KACHIN	KAPAUKU	KATAB	KERALA	KHASI
KIKUYU	KISSI	KOL	KOREANS	KPE	KURTATCHI	KWAKIUTL	LAKHER	LAMBA	LAMET
LANGO	LAU	LEPCHA	LESU	LHOTA NAGA	LOLO	LUO	MACASSARESE	MALAYS	MAM
MAMBILA	MAMVU	MANGAIANS	MANIHIKI	MANUS	MAORI	MARGI	MARICOPA	MARQUESANS	MARSHALLESE
MATAKAM	MAYA	MBUNDU	MENDE	MERINA	MIAO	MIN CHINESE	MINCHIA	MISKITO	MONGO
MONGUOR	MOSSI	MOTA	MOTILON	MZAB	NANDI	NATCHEZ	NICOBARESE	NOMLAKI	NUPE
NURI	NYAKYUSA	NYORO	OKINAWANS	ORAON	PAEZ	PAIWAN	PALAUANS	PARAUJANO	PATHAN
PAWNEE	PONAPEANS	PUKAPUKA	PURARI	PURUM	RIFFIANS	ROMANS	RUNDI	SAGADA	SAMOANS
SANDAWE	SANTAL	SENIANG	SERBS	SHERENTE	SHILLUK	SHLUH	SINHALESE	SIUAI	SIWANS
SONGHAI	SOTHO	SUBANUN	SWAZI	SYRIANS	TAGBANUA	TALAMANCA	TALLENSI	TANALA	TAOS
TAPIRAPE	TARAHUMARA	TENDA	TENETEHARA	TERA	TESO	THAI	THONGA	TIGRINYA	TIKOPIA
TIMBIRA	TIV	TOKELAU	TORAJA	TOTONAC	TRISTAN	TROBRIAND	TRUKESE	TRUMAI	TUCUNA
TUNEBO	TUPINAMBA	TURKMEN	ULAWANS	VENDA	VIETNAMESE	WALLOONS	WANTOAT	WAPISHANA	WITOTO
WOGEO	WOLEAIANS	YABARANA	YAGUA	YAKO	YAO	YAPESE	YARURO	YOMBE	YORUBA
YUROK	ZUNI								

110 IN RIGHT COLUMN

ABIPON	ALACALUF	ANDAMANESE	ARANDA	ATSUGEWI	AWEIKOMA	BASSERI	BEJA	BEMBA	BHUIYA
BORORO	BOTOCUDO	BOZO	CADUVEO	CAMAYURA	CHAMACOCO	CHENCHU	CHEYENNE	CHIR-APACHE	CHOROTI
CHUKCHEE	COPR ESKIMO	CROW	DARD	DELAWARE	DIEGUENO	DIERI	DOROBO	FOX	GILYAK
GOAJIRO	GROS VENTRE	GUAHIBO	GUATO	HAVASUPAI	HAZARA	HERERO	HUKUNDIKA	ILA	INGALIK
KARIERA	KASKA	KAZAK	KERAKI	KHALKA	KOHISTANI	KORYAK	KUBA	KUNG	KUTENAI
LAPPS	LOZI	MANDAN	MASAI	MATACO	MBUTI	MIAMI	MIWOK	MNONG GAR	MUNDURUCU
MURINBATA	MURNGIN	NABESNA	NAMA	NAMBICUARA	NAVAHO	NDEMBU	NUER	NUNIVAK	OJIBWA
OMAHA	ONA	ONTONG-JAVA	PAPAGO	REGEIBAT	RWALA	SAMOYED	SANPOIL	SARSI	SELUNG
SEMANG	SIRIONO	SOMALI	TAREUMIUT	TEDA	TEHUELCHE	TENINO	TERENA	TIMUCUA	TIWI
TODA	TOLOWA	TSHIMSHIAN	TUBATULABAL	TUCANO	TURKANA	TWANA	UTE	VEDDA	WAICA
WARRAU	WASHO	WICHITA	WIKMUNKAN	WOLOF	YAHGAN	YAKUT	YOKUTS	YUKAGHIR	YUKI

68 EXCLUDED BECAUSE UNASCERTAINED

3	TILT LESS TOWARD BEING THOSE LOCATED OUTSIDE OF AFRICA (320)	0.75 OF 222	3	TILT MORE TOWARD BEING THOSE LOCATED OUTSIDE OF AFRICA (320)	0.87 OF 110	55 14 167 96 XSQ= 5.77 PHI= 0.132 XP = 0.0163
6	TILT LESS TOWARD BEING THOSE LOCATED OUTSIDE OF THE INSULAR PACIFIC (330)	0.80 OF 222	6	TILT MORE TOWARD BEING THOSE LOCATED OUTSIDE OF THE INSULAR PACIFIC (330)	0.92 OF 110	44 9 178 101 XSQ= 6.58 PHI= 0.141 XP = 0.0103
8	TEND MORE TO BE THOSE LOCATED OUTSIDE OF NORTH AMERICA (330)	0.91 OF 222	8	TEND LESS TO BE THOSE LOCATED OUTSIDE OF NORTH AMERICA (330)	0.66 OF 110	21 37 201 73 XSQ= 28.17 PHI= -0.291 XP = 0.0000
15	TEND TO BE THOSE WHERE THE LATITUDE IS LESS THAN TWENTY DEGREES (217)	0.63 OF 222	15	TEND TO BE THOSE WHERE THE LATITUDE IS TWENTY DEGREES OR GREATER (183)	0.65 OF 110	83 72 139 38 XSQ= 22.17 PHI= -0.258 XP = 0.0000
33	TEND MORE TO BE THOSE WHERE THE NATURAL ENVIRONMENT IS OTHER THAN 'VERY HARSH,' I.E., DESERT, DESERT GRASSES AND SHRUBS, TUNDRA, OR HIGH PLATEAU STEPPE (341) FWM	0.92 OF 222	33	TEND LESS TO BE THOSE WHERE THE NATURAL ENVIRONMENT IS OTHER THAN 'VERY HARSH,' I.E., DESERT, DESERT GRASSES AND SHRUBS, TUNDRA, OR HIGH PLATEAU STEPPE (341) FWM	0.68 OF 110	17 35 205 75 XSQ= 30.70 PHI= -0.304 XP = 0.
36	TEND MORE TO BE THOSE WHERE THE NATURAL ENVIRONMENT IS OTHER THAN 'VERY HARSH,' OR SUB-TROPICAL BUSH, OR TEMPERATE GRASSLAND (292) FWM	0.84 OF 222	36	TEND LESS TO BE THOSE WHERE THE NATURAL ENVIRONMENT IS OTHER THAN 'VERY HARSH,' OR SUB-TROPICAL BUSH, OR TEMPERATE GRASSLAND (292) FWM	0.54 OF 110	36 51 186 59 XSQ= 33.03 PHI= -0.315 XP = 0.
42	TEND LESS TO BE THOSE WHERE THE NATURAL ENVIRONMENT IS OTHER THAN TROPICAL OR SUB-TROPICAL RAIN FOREST, OR MONSOON FOREST (244) FWM	0.50 OF 222	42	TEND MORE TO BE THOSE WHERE THE NATURAL ENVIRONMENT IS OTHER THAN TROPICAL OR SUB-TROPICAL RAIN FOREST, OR MONSOON FOREST (244) FWM	0.82 OF 110	110 20 112 90 XSQ= 29.08 PHI= 0.296 XP = 0.0000
48	TILT TOWARD BEING THOSE WHERE THE FOOD SUPPLY IS SECURE, AND FOOD SHORTAGES ARE RARE OR OCCASIONAL (38) MGW	0.57 OF 49	48	TILT TOWARD BEING THOSE WHERE THE FOOD SUPPLY IS NOT SECURE, AND FOOD SHORTAGES ARE FREQUENT OR ANNUAL (41) MGW	0.73 OF 26	28 7 21 19 XSQ= 5.08 PHI= 0.260 XP = 0.0242
51	TEND TO BE THOSE WHERE SUBSISTENCE IS PRIMARILY BY FOOD PRODUCTION -- I. E., AGRICULTURE OR HUSBANDRY -- RATHER THAN BY GATHERING (253)	0.81 OF 222	51	TEND TO BE THOSE WHERE SUBSISTENCE IS PRIMARILY BY FOOD GATHERING -- I. E., HUNTING, FISHING, OR COLLECTING -- RATHER THAN FOOD PRODUCTION (147)	0.75 OF 110	179 27 43 83 XSQ= 95.88 PHI= 0.537 XP = 0.

54	TEND TO BE THOSE WHERE FOOD PRODUCTION IS BY INTENSIVE OR SIMPLE AGRICULTURE, RATHER THAN BY INCIPIENT FOOD PRODUCTION (192)	0.89 OF 200	54	TEND TO BE THOSE WHERE FOOD PRODUCTION IS BY INCIPIENT FOOD PRODUCTION, RATHER THAN BY INTENSIVE OR SIMPLE AGRICULTURE (46)	0.55 OF 31	178 14 22 17 XSQ= 33.70 PHI= 0.382 XP = 0.
56	TEND TO BE THOSE WHERE FOOD PRODUCTION IS BY SIMPLE AGRICULTURE, RATHER THAN BY INCIPIENT FOOD PRODUCTION (101)	0.81 OF 114	56	TEND TO BE THOSE WHERE FOOD PRODUCTION IS BY INCIPIENT FOOD PRODUCTION, RATHER THAN BY SIMPLE AGRICULTURE (46)	0.65 OF 26	92 9 22 17 XSQ= 20.14 PHI= 0.379 XP = 0.0000
62	TEND TO BE THOSE WHERE HUSBANDRY OF SOME KIND IS PRESENT (228)	0.79 OF 222	62	TEND TO BE THOSE WHERE HUSBANDRY OF ANY KIND IS ABSENT (172)	0.55 OF 110	176 50 46 60 XSQ= 37.18 PHI= 0.335 XP = 0.
63	LEAN LESS TOWARD BEING THOSE WHERE HUSBANDRY, IF PRESENT, IS PRINCIPALLY IN THE FORM OF BOVINE, EQUINE, CAMEL-LIKE, OR DEER-LIKE ANIMALS, RATHER THAN PIGS, SHEEP, OR GOATS (152)	0.63 OF 176	63	LEAN MORE TOWARD BEING THOSE WHERE HUSBANDRY, IF PRESENT, IS PRINCIPALLY IN THE FORM OF BOVINE, EQUINE, CAMEL-LIKE, OR DEER-LIKE ANIMALS, RATHER THAN PIGS, SHEEP, OR GOATS (152)	0.84 OF 50	110 42 66 8 XSQ= 7.23 PHI= -0.179 XP = 0.0072
71	TEND LESS TO BE THOSE WHERE METAL WORKING IS ABSENT (153)	0.50 OF 149	71	TEND MORE TO BE THOSE WHERE METAL WORKING IS ABSENT (153)	0.75 OF 93	74 23 75 70 XSQ= 13.80 PHI= 0.239 XP = 0.0002
73	TEND TO BE THOSE WHERE WEAVING IS PRESENT (118)	0.58 OF 148	73	TEND TO BE THOSE WHERE WEAVING IS ABSENT (130)	0.67 OF 92	86 30 62 62 XSQ= 13.77 PHI= 0.240 XP = 0.0002
74	TEND TO BE THOSE WHERE POTTERY IS PRESENT (145)	0.71 OF 143	74	TEND TO BE THOSE WHERE POTTERY IS ABSENT (93)	0.52 OF 87	102 42 41 45 XSQ= 11.31 PHI= 0.222 XP = 0.0008
80	TEND LESS TO BE THOSE WHERE NO CITY OR TOWN IS PRESENT (185)	0.74 OF 150	80	IN ALL CASES ARE THOSE WHERE NO CITY OR TOWN IS PRESENT (185)	1.00 OF 73	39 0 111 73 XSQ= 21.24 PHI= 0.309 XP = 0.0000
81	TEND TO BE THOSE WHERE A CITY OR TOWN IS PRESENT, OR THE AVERAGE COMMUNITY SIZE IS 200 OR GREATER (89)	0.54 OF 150	81	TEND TO BE THOSE WHERE NO CITY OR TOWN IS PRESENT, AND THE AVERAGE COMMUNITY SIZE IS SMALLER THAN 200 (135)	0.89 OF 73	81 8 69 65 XSQ= 36.16 PHI= 0.403 XP = 0.

83	TEND LESS TO BE THOSE WHERE, WITH NO CITY AND NO TOWN PRESENT, THE AVERAGE COMMUNITY SIZE IS SMALLER THAN 200, RATHER THAN BETWEEN 200 AND 999 (135)	0.65 OF 106	83	TEND MORE TO BE THOSE WHERE, WITH NO CITY AND NO TOWN PRESENT, THE AVERAGE COMMUNITY SIZE IS SMALLER THAN 200, RATHER THAN BETWEEN 200 AND 999 (135)	0.89 OF 73	37 8 69 65 XSQ= 11.93 PHI= 0.258 XP = 0.0006
86	TEND TO BE THOSE WHERE THE LEVEL OF POLITICAL INTEGRATION IS THE LARGE STATE, THE LITTLE STATE, OR THE MINIMAL STATE (148) GPM	0.59 OF 167	86	TEND TO BE THOSE WHERE THE LEVEL OF POLITICAL INTEGRATION IS THE AUTONOMOUS COMMUNITY, OR THE FAMILY (156) GPM	0.73 OF 91	98 25 69 66 XSQ= 21.77 PHI= 0.290 XP = 0.0000
91	TILT TOWARD BEING THOSE WHERE SOCIETAL COMPLEXITY IS HIGH (18) F-W	0.56 OF 27	91	TILT TOWARD BEING THOSE WHERE SOCIETAL COMPLEXITY IS LOW (22) F-W	0.83 OF 12	15 2 12 10 XSQ= 3.65 PHI= 0.306 EP = 0.0365
96	TEND TO BE THOSE WHERE THE HIERARCHY OF NATIONAL JURISDICTION HAS FOUR, THREE, TWO OR ONE LEVEL (174) GES,EA	0.61 OF 219	96	TEND TO BE THOSE WHERE THE HIERARCHY OF NATIONAL JURISDICTION HAS NO LEVELS (156) GES,EA	0.64 OF 110	134 40 85 70 XSQ= 17.13 PHI= 0.228 XP = 0.0000
97	TEND LESS TO BE THOSE WHERE THE HIERARCHY OF LOCAL JURISDICTION HAS THREE OR TWO LEVELS (273) GES,EA	0.77 OF 220	97	TEND MORE TO BE THOSE WHERE THE HIERARCHY OF LOCAL JURISDICTION HAS THREE OR TWO LEVELS (273) GES,EA	0.94 OF 110	51 7 169 103 XSQ= 13.18 PHI= 0.200 XP = 0.0003
98	TEND MORE TO BE THOSE WHERE THE HIERARCHY OF LOCAL JURISDICTION HAS FOUR OR THREE LEVELS (238) GES,EA	0.81 OF 220	98	TEND LESS TO BE THOSE WHERE THE HIERARCHY OF LOCAL JURISDICTION HAS FOUR OR THREE LEVELS (238) GES,EA	0.54 OF 110	178 59 42 51 XSQ= 25.62 PHI= 0.279 XP = 0.0000
99	TEND TO BE THOSE WHERE, WITH NATIONAL HIERARCHY ABSENT, THE HIERARCHY OF LOCAL JURISDICTION HAS FOUR OR THREE LEVELS (93) GES,EA	0.72 OF 85	99	TEND TO BE THOSE WHERE, WITH NATIONAL HIERARCHY ABSENT, THE HIERARCHY OF LOCAL JURISDICTION HAS TWO LEVELS (63) GES,EA	0.56 OF 70	61 31 24 39 XSQ= 10.90 PHI= 0.265 XP = 0.0010
100	TEND MORE TO BE THOSE WHERE HIERARCHIES ARE MORE COMPLEX THAN THE 'SIMPLEST,' I. E., MORE COMPLEX THAN TWO LOCAL LEVELS WITH NO NATIONAL LEVELS (267) GES,EA	0.89 OF 219	100	TEND LESS TO BE THOSE WHERE HIERARCHIES ARE MORE COMPLEX THAN THE 'SIMPLEST,' I. E., MORE COMPLEX THAN TWO LOCAL LEVELS WITH NO NATIONAL LEVELS (267) GES,EA	0.65 OF 110	195 71 24 39 XSQ= 26.82 PHI= 0.286 XP = 0.0000
102	TEND TO BE THOSE WHERE CLASS STRATIFICATION IS PRESENT (203)	0.62 OF 215	102	TEND TO BE THOSE WHERE CLASS STRATIFICATION IS ABSENT (180)	0.64 OF 107	133 38 82 69 XSQ= 18.87 PHI= 0.242 XP = 0.0000

106	LEAN TOWARD BEING THOSE 0.66 OF 133 WHERE CLASS STRATIFICATION, IF PRESENT, IS BASED ON SOMETHING OTHER THAN WEALTH (126)	106	LEAN TOWARD BEING THOSE 0.63 OF 38 WHERE CLASS STRATIFICATION, IF PRESENT, IS BASED ON WEALTH (77)	45 24 88 14 XSQ= 9.38 PHI= -0.234 XP = 0.0022
107	TILT LESS TOWARD BEING THOSE 0.74 OF 133 WHERE CLASS STRATIFICATION, IF PRESENT, IS BASED ON SOMETHING OTHER THAN OCCUPATIONAL STATUS (160)	107	TILT MORE TOWARD BEING THOSE 0.95 OF 38 WHERE CLASS STRATIFICATION, IF PRESENT, IS BASED ON SOMETHING OTHER THAN OCCUPATIONAL STATUS (160)	35 2 98 36 XSQ= 6.53 PHI= 0.195 XP = 0.0106
110	TILT LESS TOWARD BEING THOSE 0.53 OF 214 WHERE SLAVERY IS ABSENT (218)	110	TILT MORE TOWARD BEING THOSE 0.68 OF 107 WHERE SLAVERY IS ABSENT (218)	100 34 114 73 XSQ= 5.96 PHI= 0.136 XP = 0.0146
128	TILT TOWARD BEING THOSE 0.56 OF 71 WHERE, IF SUBSISTENCE IS PRIMARILY BY AGRICULTURE, THE WORK IS MAINLY DONE BY MALES (40)	128	IN ALL CASES ARE THOSE 1.00 OF 6 WHERE, IF SUBSISTENCE IS PRIMARILY BY AGRICULTURE, THE WORK IS MAINLY DONE BY FEMALES (37)	40 0 31 6 XSQ= 4.96 PHI= 0.254 XP = 0.0260
130	TEND TO BE THOSE 0.76 OF 33 WHERE LEATHER WORKING IS MAINLY DONE BY MALES (39)	130	TEND TO BE THOSE 0.71 OF 48 WHERE LEATHER WORKING IS MAINLY DONE BY FEMALES (45)	25 14 8 34 XSQ= 15.19 PHI= 0.433 XP = 0.0001
131	IN ALL CASES ARE THOSE 1.00 OF 103 WHERE THE CONSTRUCTION OF PERMANENT HOUSES OR THE ERECTION OF TEMPORARY DWELLINGS IS MAINLY DONE BY MALES (136)	131	TEND LESS TO BE THOSE 0.61 OF 51 WHERE THE CONSTRUCTION OF PERMANENT HOUSES OR THE ERECTION OF TEMPORARY DWELLINGS IS MAINLY DONE BY MALES (136)	103 31 0 20 XSQ= 43.02 PHI= 0.529 XP = 0.
132	LEAN TOWARD BEING THOSE 0.84 OF 31 WHERE ECONOMIC EXCHANGE INVOLVES THE USE OF MONEY (37) JMH	132	LEAN TOWARD BEING THOSE 0.57 OF 21 WHERE ECONOMIC EXCHANGE DOES NOT INVOLVE THE USE OF MONEY (17) JMH	26 9 5 12 XSQ= 7.80 PHI= 0.387 XP = 0.0052
137	TILT LESS TOWARD BEING THOSE 0.51 OF 57 WHERE INVIDIOUS DISPLAY OF WEALTH IS MODERATELY, LITTLE, OR NEGATIVELY EMPHASIZED (52) PES	137	TILT MORE TOWARD BEING THOSE 0.76 OF 29 WHERE INVIDIOUS DISPLAY OF WEALTH IS MODERATELY, LITTLE, OR NEGATIVELY EMPHASIZED (52) PES	28 7 29 22 XSQ= 3.99 PHI= 0.215 XP = 0.0458
147	DRIFT TOWARD BEING THOSE 0.78 OF 18 WHERE CODIFIED LAWS ARE PRESENT (20) LWS	147	DRIFT TOWARD BEING THOSE 0.57 OF 14 WHERE CODIFIED LAWS ARE UNIMPORTANT OR ABSENT (13) LWS	14 6 4 8 XSQ= 2.74 PHI= 0.293 EP = 0.0683

163	LEAN TOWARD BEING THOSE 0.75 OF 8 WHERE THE EMPHASIS ON INDIVIDUAL VOLITION AS THE CAUSE OF CRIME IS HIGH (7) MJ	163	IN ALL CASES ARE THOSE 1.00 OF 7 WHERE THE EMPHASIS ON INDIVIDUAL VOLITION AS THE CAUSE OF CRIME IS LOW (10) MJ	6 0 2 7 XSQ= 5.90 PHI= 0.627 EP = 0.0070
176	DRIFT LESS TOWARD BEING THOSE 0.52 OF 214 WHERE THE COMMUNITY IS OTHER THAN A CLAN-COMMUNITY OR A COMMUNITY STRUCTURED OR SEGMENTED ON A CLAN BASIS (213)	176	DRIFT MORE TOWARD BEING THOSE 0.63 OF 105 WHERE THE COMMUNITY IS OTHER THAN A CLAN-COMMUNITY OR A COMMUNITY STRUCTURED OR SEGMENTED ON A CLAN BASIS (213)	103 39 111 66 XSQ= 3.01 PHI= 0.097 XP = 0.0826
178	TEND LESS TO BE THOSE 0.71 OF 214 WHERE THE COMMUNITY IS OTHER THAN SEGMENTED ON A CLAN BASIS AND NON-EXOGAMOUS (295)	178	TEND MORE TO BE THOSE 0.89 OF 105 WHERE THE COMMUNITY IS OTHER THAN SEGMENTED ON A CLAN BASIS AND NON-EXOGAMOUS (295)	62 12 152 93 XSQ= 11.20 PHI= 0.187 XP = 0.0008
179	LEAN MORE TOWARD BEING THOSE 0.92 OF 214 WHERE THE COMMUNITY IS OTHER THAN STRUCTURED ON A NON-CLAN BASIS AND COMMONLY EXOGAMOUS (340)	179	LEAN LESS TOWARD BEING THOSE 0.79 OF 105 WHERE THE COMMUNITY IS OTHER THAN STRUCTURED ON A NON-CLAN BASIS AND COMMONLY EXOGAMOUS (340)	17 22 197 83 XSQ= 9.93 PHI= -0.176 XP = 0.0016
180	TEND MORE TO BE THOSE 0.73 OF 214 WHERE THE COMMUNITY IS COMMONLY NON-EXOGAMOUS, RATHER THAN EXOGAMOUS (258)	180	TEND LESS TO BE THOSE 0.53 OF 105 WHERE THE COMMUNITY IS COMMONLY NON-EXOGAMOUS, RATHER THAN EXOGAMOUS (258)	58 49 156 56 XSQ= 11.23 PHI= -0.188 XP = 0.0008
184	TEND TO BE THOSE 0.76 OF 149 WHERE THE LARGEST NON-COGNATIC KIN GROUP IS SMALLER THAN A PHRATRY, I. E. A SIB OR LINEAGE (175)	184	TEND TO BE THOSE 0.52 OF 62 WHERE THE LARGEST NON-COGNATIC KIN GROUP IS THE MOEITY OR PHRATRY (77)	36 32 113 30 XSQ= 13.88 PHI= -0.256 XP = 0.0002
186	TILT LESS TOWARD BEING THOSE 0.59 OF 222 WHERE THE KIN GROUP IS OTHER THAN EXCLUSIVELY PATRILINEAL (250)	186	TILT MORE TOWARD BEING THOSE 0.71 OF 110 WHERE THE KIN GROUP IS OTHER THAN EXCLUSIVELY PATRILINEAL (250)	91 32 131 78 XSQ= 3.97 PHI= 0.109 XP = 0.0463
188	DRIFT MORE TOWARD BEING THOSE 0.67 OF 222 WHERE THE KIN GROUP IS OTHER THAN EXCLUSIVELY COGNATIC (252)	188	DRIFT LESS TOWARD BEING THOSE 0.56 OF 110 WHERE THE KIN GROUP IS OTHER THAN EXCLUSIVELY COGNATIC (252)	73 48 149 62 XSQ= 3.22 PHI= -0.099 XP = 0.0726
192	LEAN MORE TOWARD BEING THOSE 0.77 OF 222 OTHER THAN WHERE THE ONLY KIN GROUP PRESENT IS A KINDRED OR ELSE BILATERAL DESCENT IS INFERRED (289)	192	LEAN LESS TOWARD BEING THOSE 0.62 OF 110 OTHER THAN WHERE THE ONLY KIN GROUP PRESENT IS A KINDRED OR ELSE BILATERAL DESCENT IS INFERRED (289)	50 42 172 68 XSQ= 8.24 PHI= -0.158 XP = 0.0041

196	TEND TO BE THOSE 0.86 OF 155 WHERE INDIVIDUAL RIGHTS IN REAL PROPERTY, AND RULES FOR INHERITANCE, ARE PRESENT (194)	196	TEND TO BE THOSE 0.65 OF 86 WHERE INDIVIDUAL RIGHTS IN REAL PROPERTY, OR RULES FOR INHERITANCE, ARE ABSENT (87)	134 30 21 56 XSQ= 65.30 PHI= 0.521 XP = 0.
242	TILT LESS TOWARD BEING THOSE 0.77 OF 220 WHERE MARRIAGE IS COMMONLY OR OCCASIONALLY POLYGYNOUS, RATHER THAN MONOGAMOUS (314)	242	TILT MORE TOWARD BEING THOSE 0.89 OF 109 WHERE MARRIAGE IS COMMONLY OR OCCASIONALLY POLYGYNOUS, RATHER THAN MONOGAMOUS (314)	170 97 50 12 XSQ= 5.80 PHI= -0.133 XP = 0.0160
259	DRIFT TOWARD BEING THOSE 0.54 OF 28 WHERE THE SEVERITY OF MOTHER-IN-LAW AVOIDANCE IS LOW (20) WNS	259	DRIFT TOWARD BEING THOSE 0.76 OF 17 WHERE THE SEVERITY OF MOTHER-IN-LAW AVOIDANCE IS HIGH (26) WNS	13 13 15 4 XSQ= 2.78 PHI= -0.248 XP = 0.0955
272	DRIFT TOWARD BEING THOSE 0.61 OF 33 WHERE THE DIVORCE RATE IS LOW (28) CA	272	DRIFT TOWARD BEING THOSE 0.67 OF 21 WHERE THE DIVORCE RATE IS HIGH (29) CA	13 14 20 7 XSQ= 2.81 PHI= -0.228 XP = 0.0940
300	TILT TOWARD BEING THOSE 0.50 OF 76 WHERE THE POST-PARTUM SEX TABOO LASTS LONGER THAN SIX MONTHS (51)	300	TILT TOWARD BEING THOSE 0.73 OF 48 WHERE THE POST-PARTUM SEX TABOO LASTS SIX MONTHS OR LESS (73)	38 13 38 35 XSQ= 5.47 PHI= 0.210 XP = 0.0194
319	DRIFT TOWARD BEING THOSE 0.59 OF 39 WHERE PROTECTION OF THE INFANT FROM ENVIRONMENTAL DISCOMFORTS IS LOW (30) B-B-C	319	DRIFT TOWARD BEING THOSE 0.68 OF 22 WHERE PROTECTION OF THE INFANT FROM ENVIRONMENTAL DISCOMFORTS IS HIGH (35) B-B-C	16 15 23 7 XSQ= 3.13 PHI= -0.227 XP = 0.0766
320	TILT LESS TOWARD BEING THOSE 0.55 OF 42 WHERE THE DEGREE OF REDUCTION OF THE INFANT'S DRIVES IS HIGH (45) B-B-C	320	TILT MORE TOWARD BEING THOSE 0.83 OF 23 WHERE THE DEGREE OF REDUCTION OF THE INFANT'S DRIVES IS HIGH (45) B-B-C	23 19 19 4 XSQ= 3.90 PHI= -0.245 XP = 0.0484
327	DRIFT TOWARD BEING THOSE 0.59 OF 34 WHERE THE AGE OF THE INFANT AT TIME OF REDUCED CONTACT WITH MOTHER IS TWO YEARS OR LOWER (27) B-B-C	327	DRIFT TOWARD BEING THOSE 0.72 OF 18 WHERE THE AGE OF THE INFANT AT TIME OF REDUCED CONTACT WITH MOTHER IS HIGHER THAN TWO YEARS (28) B-B-C	14 13 20 5 XSQ= 3.39 PHI= -0.255 XP = 0.0658
335	TILT TOWARD BEING THOSE 0.58 OF 26 WHERE INITIAL INDULGENCE OF DEPENDENCY IS LOW (18) WNS	335	TILT TOWARD BEING THOSE 0.89 OF 9 WHERE INITIAL INDULGENCE OF DEPENDENCY IS HIGH (20) WNS	11 8 15 1 XSQ= 4.12 PHI= -0.343 EP = 0.0221

```
338  DRIFT TOWARD BEING THOSE         0.70 OF  46     338  DRIFT TOWARD BEING THOSE         0.57 OF  23         32    10
     WHERE THE CHILD'S INFERRED ANXIETY OVER               WHERE THE CHILD'S INFERRED ANXIETY OVER               14    13
     PERFORMANCE OF RESPONSIBLE BEHAVIOR                   PERFORMANCE OF RESPONSIBLE BEHAVIOR              XSQ=      3.35
     IS HIGH  (44) B-B-C                                   IS LOW  (29) B-B-C                               PHI=     0.220
                                                                                                            XP =    0.0670

340  DRIFT TOWARD BEING THOSE         0.57 OF  28     34C  DRIFT TOWARD BEING THOSE         0.75 OF  16         12    12
     WHERE THE TOTAL POSITIVE PRESSURE TOWARD              WHERE THE TOTAL POSITIVE PRESSURE TOWARD              16     4
     DEVELOPING NURTURANT BEHAVIOR                         DEVELOPING NURTURANT BEHAVIOR                    XSQ=      3.05
     IN THE CHILD                                          IN THE CHILD                                     PHI=    -0.263
     IS LOW  (20) B-B-C                                    IS HIGH  (28) B-B-C                              XP =    0.0810

342  DRIFT TOWARD BEING THOSE         0.54 OF  26     342  DRIFT TOWARD BEING THOSE         0.81 OF  16         14     3
     WHERE THE CHILD'S INFERRED ANXIETY OVER               WHERE THE CHILD'S INFERRED ANXIETY OVER               12    13
     PERFORMANCE OF NURTURANT BEHAVIOR                     PERFORMANCE OF NURTURANT BEHAVIOR                XSQ=      3.71
     IS HIGH  (18) B-B-C                                   IS LOW  (28) B-B-C                               PHI=     0.297
                                                                                                            XP =    0.0540

353  TILT TOWARD BEING THOSE          0.70 OF  46     353  TILT TOWARD BEING THOSE          0.58 OF  24         32    10
     WHERE THE CHILD'S INFERRED ANXIETY OVER               WHERE THE CHILD-S INFERRED ANXIETY OVER               14    14
     NON-PERFORMANCE OF OBEDIENT BEHAVIOR                  NON-PERFORMANCE OF OBEDIENT BEHAVIOR             XSQ=      4.02
     IS HIGH  (42) B-B-C                                   IS LOW  (32) B-B-C                               PHI=     0.240
                                                                                                            XP =    0.0450

377  TILT LESS TOWARD BEING THOSE     0.70 OF 216     377  TILT MORE TOWARD BEING THOSE     0.82 OF 108         64    19
     WHERE MALE GENITAL MUTILATION                         WHERE MALE GENITAL MUTILATION                        152    89
     IS ABSENT  (242)                                      IS ABSENT  (242)                                 XSQ=      4.86
                                                                                                            PHI=     0.122
                                                                                                            XP =    0.0275

391  DRIFT TOWARD BEING THOSE         0.55 OF 121     391  DRIFT TOWARD BEING THOSE         0.62 OF  50         55    31
     WHERE PREMARITAL SEX RELATIONS ARE                    WHERE PREMARITAL SEX RELATIONS ARE                    66    19
     PUNISHED ONLY IF PREGNANCY RESULTS, OR                STRONGLY PUNISHED AND IN FACT RARE, OR           XSQ=      3.24
     FREELY PERMITTED  (90) JTW,EA                         WEAKLY PUNISHED AND                              PHI=    -0.138
                                                           IN FACT NOT RARE  (89) JTW,EA                    XP =    0.0718

417  TILT MORE TOWARD BEING THOSE     0.95 OF  22     417  TILT LESS TOWARD BEING THOSE     0.60 OF  20         21    12
     WHERE WARFARE IS                                      WHERE WARFARE IS                                       1     8
     PREVALENT  (34) LWS                                   PREVALENT  (34) LWS                              XSQ=      5.86
                                                                                                            PHI=     0.373
                                                                                                            XP =    0.0155

426  DRIFT MORE TOWARD BEING THOSE    0.64 OF 168     426  DRIFT LESS TOWARD BEING THOSE    0.53 OF  91        108    48
     WHERE A HIGH GOD IS                                   WHERE A HIGH GOD IS                                   60    43
     PRESENT  (156) GES,EA                                 PRESENT  (156) GES,EA                            XSQ=      2.82
                                                                                                            PHI=     0.104
                                                                                                            XP =    0.0933

427  TILT TOWARD BEING THOSE          0.50 OF 108     427  TILT TOWARD BEING THOSE          0.69 OF  48         54    33
     WHERE A HIGH GOD, IF PRESENT, IS                      WHERE A HIGH GOD, IF PRESENT, IS                      54    15
     INACTIVE, RATHER THAN                                 ACTIVE, RATHER THAN                              XSQ=      4.01
     ACTIVE  (69) GES,EA                                   INACTIVE  (87) GES,EA                            PHI=    -0.160
                                                                                                            XP =    0.0453
```

431	TILT LESS TOWARD BEING THOSE 0.64 OF 22 WHERE SUPERNATURAL SANCTIONS FOR MORALITY, HAVING AN EFFECT ON AN INDIVIDUAL'S AFTERLIFE, ARE ABSENT OR UNREPORTED (25) GES	431	IN ALL CASES ARE THOSE 1.00 OF 10 WHERE SUPERNATURAL SANCTIONS FOR MORALITY, HAVING AN EFFECT ON AN INDIVIDUAL'S AFTERLIFE, ARE ABSENT OR UNREPORTED (25) GES	8 0 14 10 XSQ= 3.10 PHI= 0.311 EP = 0.0353
435	LEAN TOWARD BEING THOSE 0.88 OF 17 WHERE ABANDONMENT OF THE HOUSE OF THE DEAD IS NOT PRACTICED (19) LWS	435	LEAN TOWARD BEING THOSE 0.71 OF 14 WHERE ABANDONMENT OF THE HOUSE OF THE DEAD IS PRACTICED (12) LWS	2 10 15 4 XSQ= 9.14 PHI= -0.543 EP = 0.0011
444	TILT TOWARD BEING THOSE 0.65 OF 31 WHERE THE USE OF DREAMS TO SEEK AND CONTROL SUPERNATURAL POWERS IS LOW (27) RGD	444	TILT TOWARD BEING THOSE 0.75 OF 20 WHERE THE USE OF DREAMS TO SEEK AND CONTROL SUPERNATURAL POWERS IS HIGH (28) RGD	11 15 20 5 XSQ= 6.10 PHI= -0.346 XP = 0.0135
452	TILT TOWARD BEING THOSE 0.58 OF 31 WHERE TOTEMISM WITH FOOD TABOOS IS PRESENT (19) WNS	452	TILT TOWARD BEING THOSE 0.91 OF 11 WHERE TOTEMISM WITH FOOD TABOOS IS ABSENT (24) WNS	18 1 13 10 XSQ= 6.01 PHI= 0.378 XP = 0.0142
458	LEAN LESS TOWARD BEING THOSE 0.61 OF 108 WHERE GAMES, IF PRESENT, DO NOT INCLUDE GAMES OF STRATEGY (119) R-A-B,EA	458	LEAN MORE TOWARD BEING THOSE 0.84 OF 62 WHERE GAMES, IF PRESENT, DO NOT INCLUDE GAMES OF STRATEGY (119) R-A-B,EA	42 10 66 52 XSQ= 8.57 PHI= 0.224 XP = 0.0034
459	DRIFT TOWARD BEING THOSE 0.58 OF 108 WHERE GAMES, IF PRESENT, DO NOT INCLUDE GAMES OF CHANCE (89) R-A-B,EA	459	DRIFT TOWARD BEING THOSE 0.58 OF 62 WHERE GAMES, IF PRESENT, INCLUDE GAMES OF CHANCE (82) R-A-B,EA	45 36 63 26 XSQ= 3.61 PHI= -0.146 XP = 0.0573
468	DRIFT LESS TOWARD BEING THOSE 0.58 OF 31 WHERE CONTACT WITH OTHER CULTURES IS REGULAR OR IRREGULAR, RATHER THAN FREQUENT (37) JMH	468	DRIFT MORE TOWARD BEING THOSE 0.86 OF 21 WHERE CONTACT WITH OTHER CULTURES IS REGULAR OR IRREGULAR, RATHER THAN FREQUENT (37) JMH	13 3 18 18 XSQ= 3.29 PHI= 0.251 XP = 0.0698
476	DRIFT LESS TOWARD BEING THOSE 0.52 OF 29 WHERE THE DEGREE OF INSOBRIETY IS STRONG (31) DH	476	DRIFT MORE TOWARD BEING THOSE 0.82 OF 17 WHERE THE DEGREE OF INSOBRIETY IS STRONG (31) DH	15 14 14 3 XSQ= 3.10 PHI= -0.260 XP = 0.0783
477	DRIFT TOWARD BEING THOSE 0.67 OF 21 WHERE ALCOHOLIC AGGRESSION IS MODERATE OR SLIGHT (19) DH	477	DRIFT TOWARD BEING THOSE 0.73 OF 11 WHERE ALCOHOLIC AGGRESSION IS STRONG (15) DH	7 8 14 3 XSQ= 3.06 PHI= -0.309 EP = 0.0617

479	DRIFT TOWARD BEING THOSE WHERE THE NEED TO ACHIEVE, AS INFERRED FROM FOLKTALES, IS LOW (18) JV	0.65 OF 20	479	DRIFT TOWARD BEING THOSE WHERE THE NEED TO ACHIEVE, AS INFERRED FROM FOLKTALES, IS HIGH (18) JV	0.69 OF 13	7 9 13 4 XSQ= 2.45 PHI= -0.273 EP = 0.0799
480	TILT TOWARD BEING THOSE WHERE COMPLEXITY OF ARTISTIC DESIGN IS HIGH (14) HB	0.71 OF 17	480	TILT TOWARD BEING THOSE WHERE COMPLEXITY OF ARTISTIC DESIGN IS LOW (15) HB	0.89 OF 9	12 1 5 8 XSQ= 6.12 PHI= 0.485 EP = 0.0112

****

45 CULTURES WHERE SETTLEMENTS, IF FIXED, ARE COMPACT, RATHER THAN NON-COMPACT (149)	45 CULTURES WHERE SETTLEMENTS, IF FIXED, ARE NON-COMPACT, RATHER THAN COMPACT (73)

BACKGROUND ON PAGE 71

BOTH SUBJECT AND PREDICATE

....

149 IN LEFT COLUMN

ABOR	AINU	AKHA	ALORESE	AMERICANS	APINAYE	ASHANTI	ATAYAL	AYMARA	AZTEC
BACAIRI	BAMBARA	BARABRA	BAYA	BLACK CARIB	BRAZILIANS	BULGARIANS	BUNLAP	BURUSHO	CAGABA
CAMBODIANS	CHEROKEE	CHIBCHA	CHIRIGUANO	CHORTI	COCHITI	CREEK	CUNA	CZECHS	DAGUR
DOGON	DUTCH	EGYPTIANS	ELLICE	EYAK	FANG	FON	FUTAJALONKE	GARO	GOND
HAIDA	HANO	HAWAIIANS	HEBREWS	HURON	IBAN	INCA	JAPANESE	JAVANESE	JEMEZ
JUKUN	KABYLE	KACHIN	KAPAUKU	KATAB	KHASI	KIKUYU	KISSI	KOL	KOREANS
KPE	KWAKIUTL	LAKHER	LAMBA	LAMET	LANGO	LAU	LHOTA NAGA	LOLO	MAM
MAMVU	MANIHIKI	MANUS	MAORI	MARICOPA	MARSHALLESE	MAYA	MBUNDU	MENDE	MERINA
MIN CHINESE	MINCHIA	MISKITO	MOTA	MOTILON	MZAB	NATCHEZ	NOMLAKI	NURI	NYAKYUSA
OKINAWANS	ORAON	PAIWAN	PALAUANS	PARAUJANO	PATHAN	PAWNEE	PUKAPUKA	PURARI	PURUM
RIFFIANS	ROMANS	SAGADA	SAMOANS	SANTAL	SENIANG	SERBS	SHERENTE	SINHALESE	SIWANS
SONGHAI	SYRIANS	TAGBANUA	TANALA	TAOS	TAPIRAPE	TENDA	TENETEHARA	TERA	THAI
THONGA	TIGRINYA	TIMBIRA	TOKELAU	TORAJA	TOTONAC	TRISTAN	TROBRIAND	TRUMAI	TUCUNA
TUNEBO	TUPINAMBA	TURKMEN	VENDA	VIETNAMESE	WALLOONS	WANTOAT	WAPISHANA	WITOTO	WOGEO
WOLEAIANS	YABARANA	YAGUA	YAKO	YARURO	YOMBE	YORUBA	YUROK	ZUNI	

73 IN RIGHT COLUMN

ALBANIANS	AMBA	ARAPESH	ARAUCANIANS	AZANDE	BABWA	BAMILEKE	BANDA	BARI	BHIL
BIRIFOR	BOERS	CALLINAGO	CARIB	CAYAPA	CHAGGA	CHERKESS	CHOCO	COORG	DILLING
ENGA	GANDA	GISU	GURE	HANUNOO	HASINAI	HUICHOL	HUTSUL	IFUGAO	INGASSANA
IRAQW	IRISH	JIVARO	KERALA	KURTATCHI	LEPCHA	LESU	LUO	MACASSARESE	MALAYS
MAMBILA	MANGAIANS	MARGI	MARQUESANS	MATAKAM	MIAO	MONGO	MONGUOR	MOSSI	NANDI
NICOBARESE	NUPE	NYORO	PAEZ	PONAPEANS	RUNDI	SANDAWE	SHILLUK	SHLUH	SIUAI
SOTHO	SUBANUN	SWAZI	TALAMANCA	TALLENSI	TARAHUMARA	TESO	TIKOPIA	TIV	TRUKESE
ULAWANS	YAO	YAPESE							

110 EXCLUDED BECAUSE IRRELEVANT (SEE RIGHT COLUMN, PARAGRAPH 44)

68 EXCLUDED BECAUSE UNASCERTAINED

----

3 TEND MORE TO BE THOSE LOCATED OUTSIDE OF AFRICA (320)	0.84 OF 149	3 TEND LESS TO BE THOSE LOCATED OUTSIDE OF AFRICA (320)	0.58 OF 73

24	31
125	42
XSQ=	16.88
PHI=	-0.276
XP =	0.0000

8 DRIFT LESS TOWARD BEING THOSE 0.88 OF 149 LOCATED OUTSIDE OF NORTH AMERICA (330)	8 DRIFT MORE TOWARD BEING THOSE 0.96 OF 73 LOCATED OUTSIDE OF NORTH AMERICA (330)	18 3 131 70 XSQ= 2.76 PHI= 0.112 XP = 0.0964
16 LEAN TOWARD BEING THOSE 0.69 OF 149 WHERE THE LATITUDE IS TEN DEGREES OR GREATER (277)	16 LEAN TOWARD BEING THOSE 0.53 OF 73 WHERE THE LATITUDE IS LESS THAN TEN DEGREES (123)	103 34 46 39 XSQ= 9.61 PHI= 0.208 XP = 0.0019
51 TILT LESS TOWARD BEING THOSE 0.76 OF 149 WHERE SUBSISTENCE IS PRIMARILY BY FOOD PRODUCTION -- I. E., AGRICULTURE OR HUSBANDRY -- RATHER THAN BY GATHERING (253)	51 TILT MORE TOWARD BEING THOSE 0.90 OF 73 WHERE SUBSISTENCE IS PRIMARILY BY FOOD PRODUCTION -- I. E., AGRICULTURE OR HUSBANDRY -- RATHER THAN BY GATHERING (253)	113 66 36 7 XSQ= 5.76 PHI= -0.161 XP = 0.0164
71 DRIFT TOWARD BEING THOSE 0.56 OF 102 WHERE METAL WORKING IS ABSENT (153)	71 DRIFT TOWARD BEING THOSE 0.62 OF 47 WHERE METAL WORKING IS PRESENT (98)	45 29 57 18 XSQ= 3.31 PHI= -0.149 XP = 0.0690
79 DRIFT LESS TOWARD BEING THOSE 0.81 OF 109 WHERE NO CITY IS PRESENT (201)	79 DRIFT MORE TOWARD BEING THOSE 0.95 OF 41 WHERE NO CITY IS PRESENT (201)	21 2 88 39 XSQ= 3.71 PHI= 0.157 XP = 0.0542
80 TILT LESS TOWARD BEING THOSE 0.69 OF 109 WHERE NO CITY OR TOWN IS PRESENT (185)	80 TILT MORE TOWARD BEING THOSE 0.88 OF 41 WHERE NO CITY OR TOWN IS PRESENT (185)	34 5 75 36 XSQ= 4.64 PHI= 0.176 XP = 0.0311
87 DRIFT MORE TOWARD BEING THOSE 0.97 OF 110 WHERE THE LEVEL OF POLITICAL INTEGRATION IS THE LARGE STATE, THE LITTLE STATE, THE MINIMAL STATE, OR THE AUTONOMOUS COMMUNITY (281) GPM	87 DRIFT LESS TOWARD BEING THOSE 0.89 OF 57 WHERE THE LEVEL OF POLITICAL INTEGRATION IS THE LARGE STATE, THE LITTLE STATE, THE MINIMAL STATE, OR THE AUTONOMOUS COMMUNITY (281) GPM	107 51 3 6 XSQ= 3.08 PHI= 0.136 XP = 0.0793
120 DRIFT LESS TOWARD BEING THOSE 0.60 OF 20 WHERE THE CRAFT SPECIALIZATION SCORE IS HIGH OR MEDIUM (36) WME	120 DRIFT MORE TOWARD BEING THOSE 0.92 OF 13 WHERE THE CRAFT SPECIALIZATION SCORE IS HIGH OR MEDIUM (36) WME	12 12 8 1 XSQ= 2.68 PHI= -0.285 EP = 0.0560
176 DRIFT TOWARD BEING THOSE 0.56 OF 144 WHERE THE COMMUNITY IS OTHER THAN A CLAN-COMMUNITY OR A COMMUNITY STRUCTURED OR SEGMENTED ON A CLAN BASIS (213)	176 DRIFT TOWARD BEING THOSE 0.57 OF 70 WHERE THE COMMUNITY IS A CLAN-COMMUNITY OR A COMMUNITY STRUCTURED OR SEGMENTED ON A CLAN BASIS (169)	63 40 81 30 XSQ= 2.87 PHI= -0.116 XP = 0.0903

184	DRIFT LESS TOWARD BEING THOSE 0.70 OF 98 WHERE THE LARGEST NON-COGNATIC KIN GROUP IS SMALLER THAN A PHRATRY, I. E. A SIB OR LINEAGE (175)	184 DRIFT MORE TOWARD BEING THOSE 0.86 OF 51 WHERE THE LARGEST NON-COGNATIC KIN GROUP IS SMALLER THAN A PHRATRY, I. E. A SIB OR LINEAGE (175)	29 7 69 44 XSQ= 3.78 PHI= 0.159 XP = 0.0518
197	TILT LESS TOWARD BEING THOSE 0.78 OF 85 WHERE RULES FOR THE INHERITANCE OF REAL PROPERTY, IF PRESENT, FAVOR EITHER THE MALE HEIR OR LINE, OR THE FEMALE HEIR OR LINE (165)	197 TILT MORE TOWARD BEING THOSE 0.94 OF 49 WHERE RULES FOR THE INHERITANCE OF REAL PROPERTY, IF PRESENT, FAVOR EITHER THE MALE HEIR OR LINE, OR THE FEMALE HEIR OR LINE (165)	66 46 19 3 XSQ= 4.84 PHI= -0.190 XP = 0.0278
241	DRIFT LESS TOWARD BEING THOSE 0.85 OF 86 WHERE THE FAMILY, IF EXTENDED, IS LARGE OR SMALL, RATHER THAN STEM (187)	241 DRIFT MORE TOWARD BEING THOSE 0.97 OF 37 WHERE THE FAMILY, IF EXTENDED, IS LARGE OR SMALL, RATHER THAN STEM (187)	73 36 13 1 XSQ= 2.82 PHI= -0.151 XP = 0.0932
242	DRIFT LESS TOWARD BEING THOSE 0.74 OF 148 WHERE MARRIAGE IS COMMONLY OR OCCASIONALLY POLYGYNOUS, RATHER THAN MONOGAMOUS (314)	242 DRIFT MORE TOWARD BEING THOSE 0.85 OF 72 WHERE MARRIAGE IS COMMONLY OR OCCASIONALLY POLYGYNOUS, RATHER THAN MONOGAMOUS (314)	109 61 39 11 XSQ= 2.78 PHI= -0.112 XP = 0.0954
257	DRIFT LESS TOWARD BEING THOSE 0.56 OF 9 WHERE THE SEVERITY OF SISTER AVOIDANCE IS LOW (17) WNS	257 IN ALL CASES ARE THOSE 1.00 OF 7 WHERE THE SEVERITY OF SISTER AVOIDANCE IS LOW (17) WNS	4 0 5 7 XSQ= 2.12 PHI= 0.364 EP = 0.0885
263	TILT LESS TOWARD BEING THOSE 0.56 OF 149 WHERE WIVES ARE OBTAINED BY RELATIVELY DIFFICULT MEANS, NAMELY BY BRIDE-PRICE, BRIDE-SERVICE, OR EXCHANGING A FEMALE RELATIVE (233)	263 TILT MORE TOWARD BEING THOSE 0.71 OF 73 WHERE WIVES ARE OBTAINED BY RELATIVELY DIFFICULT MEANS, NAMELY BY BRIDE-PRICE, BRIDE-SERVICE, OR EXCHANGING A FEMALE RELATIVE (233)	83 52 66 21 XSQ= 4.33 PHI= -0.140 XP = 0.0375
286	TILT TOWARD BEING THOSE 0.60 OF 15 WHERE THE NUMBER OF FOOD TABOOS DURING PREGNANCY IS LOW OR ABSENT (14) BCA	286 TILT TOWARD BEING THOSE 0.89 OF 9 WHERE THE NUMBER OF FOOD TABOOS DURING PREGNANCY IS HIGH (20) BCA	6 8 9 1 XSQ= 3.70 PHI= -0.393 EP = 0.0333
305	TILT TOWARD BEING THOSE 0.59 OF 22 WHERE THE EARLY SEXUAL SATISFACTION POTENTIAL IS LOW (24) W-C	305 TILT TOWARD BEING THOSE 0.90 OF 10 WHERE THE EARLY SEXUAL SATISFACTION POTENTIAL IS HIGH (27) W-C	9 9 13 1 XSQ= 4.89 PHI= -0.391 EP = 0.0189
328	TILT TOWARD BEING THOSE 0.68 OF 19 WHERE THE AGE OF THE INFANT AT THE ONSET OF SERIOUS SOCIALIZATION, OTHER THAN WEANING, IS TWO YEARS OR LOWER (20) B-B-C	328 TILT TOWARD BEING THOSE 0.80 OF 10 WHERE THE AGE OF THE INFANT AT THE ONSET OF SERIOUS SOCIALIZATION, OTHER THAN WEANING, IS HIGHER THAN TWO YEARS (21) B-B-C	6 8 13 2 XSQ= 4.37 PHI= -0.388 EP = 0.0209

```
331  LEAN TOWARD BEING THOSE          0.79 OF  14     331  LEAN TOWARD BEING THOSE          0.89 OF   9           3     8
     WHERE THE AGE AT BEGINNING                           WHERE THE AGE AT BEGINNING                             11     1
     OF INDEPENDENCE TRAINING                             OF INDEPENDENCE TRAINING                       XSQ=     7.47
     IS LOWER THAN 3.8 YEARS  (21) W-C                    IS 3.8 YEARS OR HIGHER  (16) W-C               PHI=   -0.570
                                                                                                         EP =   0.0028

400  DRIFT TOWARD BEING THOSE         0.66 OF  29     400  DRIFT TOWARD BEING THOSE         0.83 OF   6          10     5
     WHERE HOMOSEXUAL ACTIVITY                            WHERE HOMOSEXUAL ACTIVITY                              19     1
     IS PERMITTED  (36) F-B                               IS PROHIBITED  (22) F-B                        XSQ=     3.05
                                                                                                         PHI=   -0.295
                                                                                                         EP =   0.0640

429  DRIFT LESS TOWARD BEING THOSE  0.64 OF  14       429  IN ALL CASES ARE THOSE           1.00 OF  10           9    10
     WHERE SUPERNATURAL SANCTIONS FOR MORALITY            WHERE SUPERNATURAL SANCTIONS FOR MORALITY               5     0
     ARE PRESENT  (28) GES                                ARE PRESENT  (28) GES                          XSQ=     2.61
                                                                                                         PHI=   -0.330
                                                                                                         EP =   0.0530

433  IN ALL CASES ARE THOSE           1.00 OF  14     433  LEAN TOWARD BEING THOSE          0.50 OF  10           0     5
     WHERE BELIEF IN REINCARNATION                        WHERE BELIEF IN REINCARNATION                          14     5
     IS ABSENT  (28) GES                                  IS PRESENT  (10) GES                           XSQ=     6.07
                                                                                                         PHI=   -0.503
                                                                                                         EP =   0.0059
```

46 CULTURES
WHERE SETTLEMENTS ARE
NCN-FIXED AND MCVEMENT IS
NOMADIC (72)

46 CULTURES
OTHER THAN WHERE SETTLEMENTS ARE
NON-FIXED AND MOVEMENT IS
NOMADIC (260)

BACKGROUND ON PAGE 71

BCTH SUBJECT AND PREDICATE

72 IN LEFT CCLUMN

ABIPCN	ALACALUF	ANCAMANESE	ARANCA	ATSUGEWI	AWEIKOMA	BASSERI	BEJA	BORCRO	BOTOCUDO
CADUVEO	CHAMACCCC	CHEYENNE	CHIR-APACHE	CHUKCHEE	COPR ESKIMO	CROW	DIEGUENO	DIERI	COROBO
FOX	GILYAK	GOAJIRC	GROS VENTRE	GUAHIBO	GUATO	HERERO	HUKUNDIKA	INGALIK	KARIERA
KASKA	KAZAK	KHALKA	KUNG	KUTENAI	LAPPS	MASAI	MATACC	MBUTI	MURINBATA
MURNGIN	NABESNA	NAMA	NAMBICUARA	NUER	OJIBWA	ONA	REGEIBAT	RWALA	SAMOYED
SANPOIL	SARSI	SELUNG	SEMANG	SIRIONO	SOMALI	TEDA	TEHUELCHE	TERENA	TIWI
TUBATULABAL	TURKANA	TWANA	UTE	VEDDA	WAICA	WASHO	WIKMUNKAN	YAHGAN	YAKUT
YOKUTS	YUKAGHIR								

260 IN RIGHT CCLUMN

ABOR	AINU	AKHA	ALBANIANS	ALORESE	AMBA	AMERICANS	APINAYE	ARAPESH	ARAUCANIANS
ASHANTI	ATAYAL	AYMARA	AZANCE	AZTEC	BABWA	BACAIRI	BAMBARA	BAMILEKE	BANDA
BARABRA	BARI	BAYA	BEMBA	BHIL	BHUIYA	BIRIFOR	BLACK CARIB	BOERS	BOZO
BRAZILIANS	BULGARIANS	BUNLAP	BURUSHO	CAGABA	CALLINAGO	CAMAYURA	CAMBODIANS	CARIB	CAYAPA
CHAGGA	CHENCHU	CHERKESS	CHEROKEE	CHIBCHA	CHIRIGUANO	CHCCO	CHCROTI	CHORTI	COCHITI
CCORG	CREEK	CUNA	CZECHS	DAGUR	DARD	DELAWARE	DILLING	DOGCN	DUTCH
EGYPTIANS	ELLICE	ENGA	EYAK	FANG	FON	FUTAJALONKE	GANDA	GARC	GISU
GOND	GURE	HAICA	HANO	HANUNOO	HASINAI	HAVASUPAI	HAWAIIANS	HAZARA	HEBREWS
HUICHOL	HURCN	HUTSUL	IBAN	IFUGAO	ILA	INCA	INGASSANA	IRACW	IRISH
JAPANESE	JAVANESE	JEMEZ	JIVARC	JUKUN	KABYLE	KACHIN	KAPAUKU	KATAB	KERAKI
KERALA	KHASI	KIKUYU	KISSI	KOHISTANI	KOL	KOREANS	KORYAK	KPE	KUBA
KURTATCHI	KWAKIUTL	LAKHER	LAMBA	LAMET	LANGO	LAU	LEPCHA	LESU	LHOTA NAGA
LOLO	LCZI	LUC	MACASSARESE	MALAYS	MAM	MAMBILA	MAMVU	MANCAN	MANGAIANS
MANIHIKI	MANUS	MACRI	MARGI	MARICOPA	MARQUESANS	MARSHALLESE	MATAKAM	MAYA	MBUNCU
MENDE	MERINA	MIAMI	MIAO	MIN CHINESE	MINCHIA	MISKITO	MIWOK	MNONG GAR	MONGO
MONGUOR	MOSSI	MCTA	MOTILON	MUNDURUCU	MZAB	NANDI	NATCHEZ	NAVAHO	NCEMBU
NICOBARESE	NOMLAKI	NUNIVAK	NUPE	NURI	NYAKYUSA	NYORO	OKINAWANS	OMAHA	ONTONG-JAVA
ORACN	PAEZ	PAIWAN	PALAUANS	PAPAGO	PARAUJANO	PATHAN	PAWNEE	PONAPEANS	PUKAPUKA
PURARI	PURUM	RIFFIANS	ROMANS	RUNDI	SAGADA	SAMOANS	SANDAWE	SANTAL	SENIANG
SERBS	SHERENTE	SHILLUK	SHLUH	SINHALESE	SIUAI	SIWANS	SONGHAI	SOTHO	SUBANUN
SWAZI	SYRIANS	TAGBANUA	TALAMANCA	TALLENSI	TANALA	TAOS	TAPIRAPE	TARAHUMARA	TAREUMIUT
TENDA	TENETEHARA	TENINO	TERA	TESO	THAI	THONGA	TIGRINYA	TIKCPIA	TIMBIRA
TIMUCUA	TIV	TOCA	TOKELAU	TOLOWA	TORAJA	TOTONAC	TRISTAN	TROBRIAND	TRUKESE
TRUMAI	TSHIMSHIAN	TUCANO	TUCUNA	TUNEBO	TUPINAMBA	TURKMEN	ULAWANS	VENCA	VIETNAMESE
WALLOONS	WANTOAT	WAPISHANA	WARRAU	WICHITA	WITOTO	WOGEO	WOLEAIANS	WOLOF	YABARANA
YAGUA	YAKC	YAC	YAPESE	YARURO	YOMBE	YORUBA	YUKI	YURCK	ZUNI

68 EXCLUDED BECAUSE UNASCERTAINEC

3	TILT MORE TOWARD BEING THOSE 0.89 OF 72 LOCATED OUTSIDE OF AFRICA (320)	3	TILT LESS TOWARD BEING THOSE 0.77 OF 260 LOCATED OUTSIDE OF AFRICA (320)	8 61 64 199 XSQ= 4.50 PHI= -0.116 XP = 0.0339
8	LEAN LESS TOWARD BEING THOSE 0.71 OF 72 LOCATED OUTSIDE OF NORTH AMERICA (330)	8	LEAN MORE TOWARD BEING THOSE 0.86 OF 260 LOCATED OUTSIDE OF NORTH AMERICA (330)	21 37 51 223 XSQ= 7.72 PHI= 0.152 XP = 0.0055
15	TEND TO BE THOSE 0.69 OF 72 WHERE THE LATITUDE IS TWENTY DEGREES OR GREATER (183)	15	TEND TO BE THOSE 0.60 OF 260 WHERE THE LATITUDE IS LESS THAN TWENTY DEGREES (217)	50 105 22 155 XSQ= 17.98 PHI= 0.233 XP = 0.0000
33	TEND LESS TO BE THOSE 0.63 OF 72 WHERE THE NATURAL ENVIRONMENT IS OTHER THAN 'VERY HARSH,' I.E., DESERT, DESERT GRASSES AND SHRUBS, TUNDRA, OR HIGH PLATEAU STEPPE (341) FWM	33	TEND MORE TO BE THOSE 0.90 OF 260 WHERE THE NATURAL ENVIRONMENT IS OTHER THAN 'VERY HARSH,' I.E., DESERT, DESERT GRASSES AND SHRUBS, TUNDRA, OR HIGH PLATEAU STEPPE (341) FWM	27 25 45 235 XSQ= 31.11 PHI= 0.306 XP = 0.
36	TEND TO BE THOSE 0.51 OF 72 WHERE THE NATURAL ENVIRONMENT IS 'VERY HARSH,' OR SUB-TROPICAL BUSH, OR TEMPERATE GRASSLAND (108) FWM	36	TEND TO BE THOSE 0.81 OF 260 WHERE THE NATURAL ENVIRONMENT IS OTHER THAN 'VERY HARSH,' OR SUB-TROPICAL BUSH, OR TEMPERATE GRASSLAND (292) FWM	37 50 35 210 XSQ= 28.51 PHI= 0.293 XP = 0.0000
42	TEND MORE TO BE THOSE 0.83 OF 72 WHERE THE NATURAL ENVIRONMENT IS OTHER THAN TROPICAL OR SUB-TROPICAL RAIN FOREST, OR MONSOON FOREST (244) FWM	42	TEND LESS TO BE THOSE 0.55 OF 260 WHERE THE NATURAL ENVIRONMENT IS OTHER THAN TROPICAL OR SUB-TROPICAL RAIN FOREST, OR MONSOON FOREST (244) FWM	12 118 60 142 XSQ= 18.33 PHI= -0.235 XP = 0.0000
48	DRIFT TOWARD BEING THOSE 0.74 OF 19 WHERE THE FOOD SUPPLY IS NOT SECURE, AND FOOD SHORTAGES ARE FREQUENT OR ANNUAL (41) MGW	48	DRIFT TOWARD BEING THOSE 0.54 OF 56 WHERE THE FOOD SUPPLY IS SECURE, AND FOOD SHORTAGES ARE RARE OR OCCASIONAL (38) MGW	5 30 14 26 XSQ= 3.21 PHI= -0.207 XP = 0.0732
51	TEND TO BE THOSE 0.82 OF 72 WHERE SUBSISTENCE IS PRIMARILY BY FOOD GATHERING -- I. E., HUNTING, FISHING, OR COLLECTING -- RATHER THAN FOOD PRODUCTION (147)	51	TEND TO BE THOSE 0.74 OF 260 WHERE SUBSISTENCE IS PRIMARILY BY FOOD PRODUCTION -- I. E., AGRICULTURE OR HUSBANDRY -- RATHER THAN BY GATHERING (253)	13 193 59 67 XSQ= 73.19 PHI= -0.470 XP = 0.
54	TEND TO BE THOSE 0.88 OF 8 WHERE FOOD PRODUCTION IS BY INCIPIENT FOOD PRODUCTION, RATHER THAN BY INTENSIVE OR SIMPLE AGRICULTURE (46)	54	TEND TO BE THOSE 0.86 OF 223 WHERE FOOD PRODUCTION IS BY INTENSIVE OR SIMPLE AGRICULTURE, RATHER THAN BY INCIPIENT FOOD PRODUCTION (192)	1 191 7 32 XSQ= 24.47 PHI= -0.325 XP = 0.0000

56	IN ALL CASES ARE THOSE WHERE FOOD PRODUCTION IS BY INCIPIENT FOOD PRODUCTION, RATHER THAN BY SIMPLE AGRICULTURE (46)	1.00 OF 7	56	TEND TO BE THOSE WHERE FOOD PRODUCTION IS BY SIMPLE AGRICULTURE, RATHER THAN BY INCIPIENT FOOD PRODUCTION (101)	0.76 OF 133	0 101 7 32 XSQ= 15.49 PHI= -0.333 XP = 0.0001
62	TEND TO BE THOSE WHERE HUSBANDRY OF ANY KIND IS ABSENT (172)	0.57 OF 72	62	TEND TO BE THOSE WHERE HUSBANDRY OF SOME KIND IS PRESENT (228)	0.75 OF 260	31 195 41 65 XSQ= 25.02 PHI= -0.275 XP = 0.0000
63	LEAN MORE TOWARD BEING THOSE WHERE HUSBANDRY, IF PRESENT, IS PRINCIPALLY IN THE FORM OF BOVINE, EQUINE, CAMEL-LIKE, OR DEER-LIKE ANIMALS, RATHER THAN PIGS, SHEEP, OR GOATS (152)	0.94 OF 31	63	LEAN LESS TOWARD BEING THOSE WHERE HUSBANDRY, IF PRESENT, IS PRINCIPALLY IN THE FORM OF BOVINE, EQUINE, CAMEL-LIKE, OR DEER-LIKE ANIMALS, RATHER THAN PIGS, SHEEP, OR GOATS (152)	0.63 OF 195	29 123 2 72 XSQ= 9.94 PHI= 0.210 XP = 0.0016
71	TEND MORE TO BE THOSE WHERE METAL WORKING IS ABSENT (153)	0.81 OF 62	71	TEND LESS TO BE THOSE WHERE METAL WORKING IS ABSENT (153)	0.53 OF 180	12 85 50 95 XSQ= 13.77 PHI= -0.239 XP = 0.0002
73	TEND TO BE THOSE WHERE WEAVING IS ABSENT (130)	0.74 OF 62	73	TEND TO BE THOSE WHERE WEAVING IS PRESENT (118)	0.56 OF 178	16 100 46 78 XSQ= 15.79 PHI= -0.257 XP = 0.0001
74	TEND TO BE THOSE WHERE POTTERY IS ABSENT (93)	0.58 OF 57	74	TEND TO BE THOSE WHERE POTTERY IS PRESENT (145)	0.69 OF 173	24 120 33 53 XSQ= 12.47 PHI= -0.233 XP = 0.0004
80	IN ALL CASES ARE THOSE WHERE NO CITY OR TOWN IS PRESENT (185)	1.00 OF 47	80	TEND LESS TO BE THOSE WHERE NO CITY OR TOWN IS PRESENT (185)	0.78 OF 176	0 39 47 137 XSQ= 11.13 PHI= -0.223 XP = 0.0008
81	TEND TO BE THOSE WHERE NO CITY OR TOWN IS PRESENT, AND THE AVERAGE COMMUNITY SIZE IS SMALLER THAN 200 (135)	0.98 OF 47	81	TEND TO BE THOSE WHERE A CITY OR TOWN IS PRESENT, OR THE AVERAGE COMMUNITY SIZE IS 200 OR GREATER (89)	0.50 OF 176	1 88 46 88 XSQ= 33.48 PHI= -0.387 XP = 0.
82	TEND TO BE THOSE WHERE NO CITY OR TOWN IS PRESENT, AND THE AVERAGE COMMUNITY SIZE IS SMALLER THAN FIFTY (46)	0.66 OF 47	82	TEND TO BE THOSE WHERE A CITY OR TOWN IS PRESENT, OR THE AVERAGE COMMUNITY SIZE IS FIFTY OR GREATER (178)	0.91 OF 176	16 161 31 15 XSQ= 71.27 PHI= -0.565 XP = 0.

83	TEND MORE TO BE THOSE 0.98 OF 47 WHERE, WITH NO CITY AND NO TOWN PRESENT, THE AVERAGE COMMUNITY SIZE IS SMALLER THAN 200, RATHER THAN BETWEEN 200 AND 999 (135)	83	TEND LESS TO BE THOSE 0.67 OF 132 WHERE, WITH NO CITY AND NO TOWN PRESENT, THE AVERAGE COMMUNITY SIZE IS SMALLER THAN 200, RATHER THAN BETWEEN 200 AND 999 (135)	1 44 46 88 XSQ= 16.31 PHI= -0.302 XP = 0.0001
86	TEND TO BE THOSE 0.77 OF 60 WHERE THE LEVEL OF POLITICAL INTEGRATION IS THE AUTONOMOUS COMMUNITY, OR THE FAMILY (156) GPM	86	TEND TO BE THOSE 0.55 OF 198 WHERE THE LEVEL OF POLITICAL INTEGRATION IS THE LARGE STATE, THE LITTLE STATE, OR THE MINIMAL STATE (148) GPM	14 109 46 89 XSQ= 17.32 PHI= -0.259 XP = 0.0000
90	DRIFT MORE TOWARD BEING THOSE 0.92 OF 26 WHERE, IF A HEREDITARY HEADMANSHIP IS PRESENT, SUCCESSION IS PATRILINEAL, RATHER THAN MATRILINEAL (127)	90	DRIFT LESS TOWARD BEING THOSE 0.74 OF 116 WHERE, IF A HEREDITARY HEADMANSHIP IS PRESENT, SUCCESSION IS PATRILINEAL, RATHER THAN MATRILINEAL (127)	24 86 2 30 XSQ= 3.04 PHI= 0.146 XP = 0.0811
91	TILT TOWARD BEING THOSE 0.91 OF 11 WHERE SOCIETAL COMPLEXITY IS LOW (22) F-W	91	TILT TOWARD BEING THOSE 0.57 OF 28 WHERE SOCIETAL COMPLEXITY IS HIGH (18) F-W	1 16 10 12 XSQ= 5.59 PHI= -0.379 EP = 0.0106
96	TEND TO BE THOSE 0.69 OF 72 WHERE THE HIERARCHY OF NATIONAL JURISDICTION HAS NO LEVELS (156) GES,EA	96	TEND TO BE THOSE 0.59 OF 257 WHERE THE HIERARCHY OF NATIONAL JURISDICTION HAS FOUR, THREE, TWO OR ONE LEVEL (174) GES,EA	22 152 50 105 XSQ= 17.32 PHI= -0.229 XP = 0.0000
98	TEND TO BE THOSE 0.58 OF 72 WHERE THE HIERARCHY OF LOCAL JURISDICTION HAS TWO LEVELS (93) GES,EA	98	TEND TO BE THOSE 0.80 OF 258 WHERE THE HIERARCHY OF LOCAL JURISDICTION HAS FOUR OR THREE LEVELS (238) GES,EA	30 207 42 51 XSQ= 39.48 PHI= -0.346 XP = 0.
99	TEND TO BE THOSE 0.66 OF 50 WHERE, WITH NATIONAL HIERARCHY ABSENT, THE HIERARCHY OF LOCAL JURISDICTION HAS TWO LEVELS (63) GES,EA	99	TEND TO BE THOSE 0.71 OF 105 WHERE, WITH NATIONAL HIERARCHY ABSENT, THE HIERARCHY OF LOCAL JURISDICTION HAS FOUR OR THREE LEVELS (93) GES,EA	17 75 33 30 XSQ= 18.15 PHI= -0.342 XP = 0.0000
100	TEND LESS TO BE THOSE 0.54 OF 72 WHERE HIERARCHIES ARE MORE COMPLEX THAN THE 'SIMPLEST,' I. E., MORE COMPLEX THAN TWO LOCAL LEVELS WITH NO NATIONAL LEVELS (267) GES,EA	100	TEND MORE TO BE THOSE 0.88 OF 257 WHERE HIERARCHIES ARE MORE COMPLEX THAN THE 'SIMPLEST,' I. E., MORE COMPLEX THAN TWO LOCAL LEVELS WITH NO NATIONAL LEVELS (267) GES,EA	39 227 33 30 XSQ= 40.21 PHI= -0.350 XP = 0.
102	TEND TO BE THOSE 0.72 OF 71 WHERE CLASS STRATIFICATION IS ABSENT (180)	102	TEND TO BE THOSE 0.60 OF 251 WHERE CLASS STRATIFICATION IS PRESENT (203)	20 151 51 100 XSQ= 21.48 PHI= -0.258 XP = 0.0000

106	LEAN TOWARD BEING THOSE WHERE CLASS STRATIFICATION, IF PRESENT, IS BASED ON WEALTH (77)	0.70 OF 20	106	LEAN TOWARD BEING THOSE WHERE CLASS STRATIFICATION, IF PRESENT, IS BASED ON SOMETHING OTHER THAN WEALTH (126)	0.64 OF 151	14 55 6 96 XSQ= 6.94 PHI= 0.201 XP = 0.0084
110	LEAN MORE TOWARD BEING THOSE WHERE SLAVERY IS ABSENT (218)	0.75 OF 72	110	LEAN LESS TOWARD BEING THOSE WHERE SLAVERY IS ABSENT (218)	0.53 OF 249	18 116 54 133 XSQ= 9.83 PHI= -0.175 XP = 0.0017
130	LEAN TOWARD BEING THOSE WHERE LEATHER WORKING IS MAINLY DONE BY FEMALES (45)	0.72 OF 36	130	LEAN TOWARD BEING THOSE WHERE LEATHER WORKING IS MAINLY DONE BY MALES (39)	0.64 OF 45	10 29 26 16 XSQ= 9.35 PHI= -0.340 XP = 0.0022
131	TEND TO BE THOSE WHERE THE CONSTRUCTION OF PERMANENT HOUSES OR THE ERECTION OF TEMPORARY DWELLINGS IS MAINLY DONE BY FEMALES (21)	0.57 OF 35	131	IN ALL CASES ARE THOSE WHERE THE CONSTRUCTION OF PERMANENT HOUSES OR THE ERECTION OF TEMPORARY DWELLINGS IS MAINLY DONE BY MALES (136)	1.00 OF 119	15 119 20 0 XSQ= 73.17 PHI= -0.689 XP = 0.
132	LEAN TOWARD BEING THOSE WHERE ECONOMIC EXCHANGE DOES NOT INVOLVE THE USE OF MONEY (17) JMH	0.67 OF 15	132	LEAN TOWARD BEING THOSE WHERE ECONOMIC EXCHANGE INVOLVES THE USE OF MONEY (37) JMH	0.81 OF 37	5 30 10 7 XSQ= 8.99 PHI= -0.416 XP = 0.0027
133	DRIFT TOWARD BEING THOSE WHERE CONTRACTED DEBTS ARE MODERATELY PRESENT OR ABSENT (17) GES	0.86 OF 7	133	DRIFT TOWARD BEING THOSE WHERE CONTRACTED DEBTS ARE SIGNIFICANTLY PRESENT (17) GES	0.60 OF 25	1 15 6 10 XSQ= 2.93 PHI= -0.302 EP = 0.0829
137	DRIFT MORE TOWARD BEING THOSE WHERE INVIDIOUS DISPLAY OF WEALTH IS MODERATELY, LITTLE, OR NEGATIVELY EMPHASIZED (52) PES	0.77 OF 22	137	DRIFT LESS TOWARD BEING THOSE WHERE INVIDIOUS DISPLAY OF WEALTH IS MODERATELY, LITTLE, OR NEGATIVELY EMPHASIZED (52) PES	0.53 OF 64	5 30 17 34 XSQ= 3.02 PHI= -0.187 XP = 0.0823
147	TILT TOWARD BEING THOSE WHERE CODIFIED LAWS ARE UNIMPORTANT OR ABSENT (13) LWS	0.67 OF 12	147	TILT TOWARD BEING THOSE WHERE CODIFIED LAWS ARE PRESENT (20) LWS	0.80 OF 20	4 16 8 4 XSQ= 5.12 PHI= -0.400 EP = 0.0213
152	IN ALL CASES ARE THOSE WHERE THE DIFFERENTIATION OF THE JURIDICAL AGENCY FROM THE MEDICAL AGENCY IS LOW (10) MJ	1.00 OF 5	152	TILT TOWARD BEING THOSE WHERE THE DIFFERENTIATION OF THE JURIDICAL AGENCY FROM THE MEDICAL AGENCY IS HIGH (10) MJ	0.69 OF 13	0 9 5 4 XSQ= 4.43 PHI= -0.496 EP = 0.0294

163	IN ALL CASES ARE THOSE 1.00 OF 5 WHERE THE EMPHASIS ON INDIVIDUAL VOLITION AS THE CAUSE OF CRIME IS LOW (10) MJ	163	TILT TOWARD BEING THOSE 0.60 OF 10 WHERE THE EMPHASIS ON INDIVIDUAL VOLITION AS THE CAUSE OF CRIME IS HIGH (7) MJ	0 6 5 4 XSQ= 2.81 PHI= -0.433 EP = 0.0440
176	DRIFT MORE TOWARD BEING THOSE 0.66 OF 70 WHERE THE COMMUNITY IS OTHER THAN A CLAN-COMMUNITY OR A COMMUNITY STRUCTURED OR SEGMENTED ON A CLAN BASIS (213)	176	DRIFT LESS TOWARD BEING THOSE 0.53 OF 249 WHERE THE COMMUNITY IS OTHER THAN A CLAN-COMMUNITY OR A COMMUNITY STRUCTURED OR SEGMENTED ON A CLAN BASIS (213)	24 118 46 131 XSQ= 3.29 PHI= -0.102 XP = 0.0698
178	LEAN MORE TOWARD BEING THOSE 0.91 OF 70 WHERE THE COMMUNITY IS OTHER THAN SEGMENTED ON A CLAN BASIS AND NON-EXOGAMOUS (295)	178	LEAN LESS TOWARD BEING THOSE 0.73 OF 249 WHERE THE COMMUNITY IS OTHER THAN SEGMENTED ON A CLAN BASIS AND NON-EXOGAMOUS (295)	6 68 64 181 XSQ= 9.74 PHI= -0.175 XP = 0.0018
179	TEND LESS TO BE THOSE 0.74 OF 70 WHERE THE COMMUNITY IS OTHER THAN STRUCTURED ON A NON-CLAN BASIS AND COMMONLY EXOGAMOUS (340)	179	TEND MORE TO BE THOSE 0.92 OF 249 WHERE THE COMMUNITY IS OTHER THAN STRUCTURED ON A NON-CLAN BASIS AND COMMONLY EXOGAMOUS (340)	18 21 52 228 XSQ= 13.64 PHI= 0.207 XP = 0.0002
180	TEND TO BE THOSE 0.51 OF 70 WHERE THE COMMUNITY IS COMMONLY EXOGAMOUS, RATHER THAN NON-EXOGAMOUS (124)	180	TEND TO BE THOSE 0.71 OF 249 WHERE THE COMMUNITY IS COMMONLY NON-EXOGAMOUS, RATHER THAN EXOGAMOUS (258)	36 71 34 178 XSQ= 11.86 PHI= 0.193 XP = 0.0006
184	TEND TO BE THOSE 0.57 OF 37 WHERE THE LARGEST NON-COGNATIC KIN GROUP IS THE MOEITY OR PHRATRY (77)	184	TEND TO BE THOSE 0.73 OF 174 WHERE THE LARGEST NON-COGNATIC KIN GROUP IS SMALLER THAN A PHRATRY, I. E. A SIB OR LINEAGE (175)	21 47 16 127 XSQ= 11.04 PHI= 0.229 XP = 0.0009
186	TILT MORE TOWARD BEING THOSE 0.74 OF 72 WHERE THE KIN GROUP IS OTHER THAN EXCLUSIVELY PATRILINEAL (250)	186	TILT LESS TOWARD BEING THOSE 0.60 OF 260 WHERE THE KIN GROUP IS OTHER THAN EXCLUSIVELY PATRILINEAL (250)	19 104 53 156 XSQ= 3.91 PHI= -0.109 XP = 0.0479
188	TILT LESS TOWARD BEING THOSE 0.51 OF 72 WHERE THE KIN GROUP IS OTHER THAN EXCLUSIVELY COGNATIC (252)	188	TILT MORE TOWARD BEING THOSE 0.67 OF 260 WHERE THE KIN GROUP IS OTHER THAN EXCLUSIVELY COGNATIC (252)	35 86 37 174 XSQ= 5.22 PHI= 0.125 XP = 0.0223
192	TEND LESS TO BE THOSE 0.53 OF 72 OTHER THAN WHERE THE ONLY KIN GROUP PRESENT IS A KINDRED OR ELSE BILATERAL DESCENT IS INFERRED (289)	192	TEND MORE TO BE THOSE 0.78 OF 260 OTHER THAN WHERE THE ONLY KIN GROUP PRESENT IS A KINDRED OR ELSE BILATERAL DESCENT IS INFERRED (289)	34 58 38 202 XSQ= 16.25 PHI= 0.221 XP = 0.0001

196	TEND TO BE THOSE 0.77 OF 56 WHERE INDIVIDUAL RIGHTS IN REAL PROPERTY, OR RULES FOR INHERITANCE, ARE ABSENT (87)	196	TEND TO BE THOSE 0.82 OF 185 WHERE INDIVIDUAL RIGHTS IN REAL PROPERTY, AND RULES FOR INHERITANCE, ARE PRESENT (194)	13 151 43 34 XSQ= 64.79 PHI= -0.518 XP = 0.
257	TILT TOWARD BEING THOSE 0.83 OF 6 WHERE THE SEVERITY OF SISTER AVOIDANCE IS HIGH (10) WNS	257	TILT TOWARD BEING THOSE 0.75 OF 20 WHERE THE SEVERITY OF SISTER AVOIDANCE IS LOW (17) WNS	5 5 1 15 XSQ= 4.40 PHI= 0.411 EP = 0.0184
262	DRIFT LESS TOWARD BEING THOSE 0.69 OF 70 WHERE WIVES ARE OBTAINED BY MEANS INVOLVING THE PRESENCE OF SOME CONSIDERATION (305)	262	DRIFT MORE TOWARD BEING THOSE 0.79 OF 259 WHERE WIVES ARE OBTAINED BY MEANS INVOLVING THE PRESENCE OF SOME CONSIDERATION (305)	48 205 22 54 XSQ= 2.90 PHI= -0.094 XP = 0.0885
299	DRIFT MORE TOWARD BEING THOSE 0.85 OF 33 WHERE THE POST-PARTUM SEX TABOO LASTS ONE YEAR OR LESS (89)	299	DRIFT LESS TOWARD BEING THOSE 0.67 OF 91 WHERE THE POST-PARTUM SEX TABOO LASTS ONE YEAR OR LESS (89)	5 30 28 61 XSQ= 2.97 PHI= -0.155 XP = 0.0850
300	DRIFT MORE TOWARD BEING THOSE 0.73 OF 33 WHERE THE POST-PARTUM SEX TABOO LASTS SIX MONTHS OR LESS (73)	300	DRIFT LESS TOWARD BEING THOSE 0.54 OF 91 WHERE THE POST-PARTUM SEX TABOO LASTS SIX MONTHS OR LESS (73)	9 42 24 49 XSQ= 2.83 PHI= -0.151 XP = 0.0926
302	DRIFT TOWARD BEING THOSE 0.83 OF 6 WHERE THE AVERAGE EARLY SATISFACTION POTENTIAL IS LOW (17) W-C	302	DRIFT TOWARD BEING THOSE 0.63 OF 30 WHERE THE AVERAGE EARLY SATISFACTION POTENTIAL IS HIGH (23) W-C	1 19 5 11 XSQ= 2.72 PHI= -0.275 EP = 0.0689
314	DRIFT MORE TOWARD BEING THOSE 0.94 OF 17 WHERE THE INCIDENCE OF MOTHER-CHILD HOUSEHOLDS IS LOW (61) W-C,S	314	DRIFT LESS TOWARD BEING THOSE 0.71 OF 58 WHERE THE INCIDENCE OF MOTHER-CHILD HOUSEHOLDS IS LOW (61) W-D,S	1 17 16 41 XSQ= 2.78 PHI= -0.192 XP = 0.0957
320	DRIFT MORE TOWARD BEING THOSE 0.87 OF 15 WHERE THE DEGREE OF REDUCTION OF THE INFANT'S DRIVES IS HIGH (45) B-B-C	320	DRIFT LESS TOWARD BEING THOSE 0.58 OF 50 WHERE THE DEGREE OF REDUCTION OF THE INFANT'S DRIVES IS HIGH (45) B-B-C	13 29 2 21 XSQ= 2.99 PHI= 0.214 XP = 0.0839
391	DRIFT TOWARD BEING THOSE 0.66 OF 35 WHERE PREMARITAL SEX RELATIONS ARE STRONGLY PUNISHED AND IN FACT RARE, OR WEAKLY PUNISHED AND IN FACT NOT RARE (89) JTW,EA	391	DRIFT TOWARD BEING THOSE 0.54 OF 136 WHERE PREMARITAL SEX RELATIONS ARE PUNISHED ONLY IF PREGNANCY RESULTS, OR FREELY PERMITTED (90) JTW,EA	23 63 12 73 XSQ= 3.45 PHI= 0.142 XP = 0.0634

417	TILT LESS TOWARD BEING THOSE 0.59 OF 17 WHERE WARFARE IS PREVALENT (34) LWS	417	TILT MORE TOWARD BEING THOSE 0.92 OF 25 WHERE WARFARE IS PREVALENT (34) LWS	10 23 7 2 XSQ= 4.79 PHI= -0.338 XP = 0.0286
427	DRIFT MORE TOWARD BEING THOSE 0.73 OF 30 WHERE A HIGH GOD, IF PRESENT, IS ACTIVE, RATHER THAN INACTIVE (87) GES,EA	427	DRIFT LESS TOWARD BEING THOSE 0.52 OF 126 WHERE A HIGH GOD, IF PRESENT, IS ACTIVE, RATHER THAN INACTIVE (87) GES,EA	22 65 8 61 XSQ= 3.81 PHI= 0.156 XP = 0.0511
435	LEAN TOWARD BEING THOSE 0.75 OF 12 WHERE ABANDONMENT OF THE HOUSE OF THE DEAD IS PRACTICED (12) LWS	435	LEAN TOWARD BEING THOSE 0.84 OF 19 WHERE ABANDONMENT OF THE HOUSE OF THE DEAD IS NOT PRACTICED (19) LWS	9 3 3 16 XSQ= 8.52 PHI= 0.524 EP = 0.0019
451	DRIFT TOWARD BEING THOSE 0.75 OF 8 WHERE TOTEMISM IS UNIMPORTANT OR ABSENT (12) LWS	451	DRIFT TOWARD BEING THOSE 0.67 OF 18 WHERE TOTEMISM IS PRESENT (15) LWS	2 12 6 6 XSQ= 2.37 PHI= -0.302 EP = 0.0895
452	IN ALL CASES ARE THOSE 1.00 OF 8 WHERE TOTEMISM WITH FOOD TABOOS IS ABSENT (24) WNS	452	TILT TOWARD BEING THOSE 0.56 OF 34 WHERE TOTEMISM WITH FOOD TABOOS IS PRESENT (19) WNS	0 19 8 15 XSQ= 6.06 PHI= -0.380 XP = 0.0138
458	TILT MORE TOWARD BEING THOSE 0.85 OF 41 WHERE GAMES, IF PRESENT, DO NOT INCLUDE GAMES OF STRATEGY (119) R-A-B,EA	458	TILT LESS TOWARD BEING THOSE 0.64 OF 129 WHERE GAMES, IF PRESENT, DO NOT INCLUDE GAMES OF STRATEGY (119) R-A-B,EA	6 46 35 83 XSQ= 5.52 PHI= -0.180 XP = 0.0187
468	TILT MORE TOWARD BEING THOSE 0.93 OF 15 WHERE CONTACT WITH OTHER CULTURES IS REGULAR OR IRREGULAR, RATHER THAN FREQUENT (37) JMH	468	TILT LESS TOWARD BEING THOSE 0.59 OF 37 WHERE CONTACT WITH OTHER CULTURES IS REGULAR OR IRREGULAR, RATHER THAN FREQUENT (37) JMH	1 15 14 22 XSQ= 4.27 PHI= -0.287 XP = 0.0388
469	DRIFT LESS TOWARD BEING THOSE 0.60 OF 15 WHERE CONTACT WITH OTHER CULTURES IS FREQUENT OR REGULAR, RATHER THAN IRREGULAR (43) JMH	469	DRIFT MORE TOWARD BEING THOSE 0.86 OF 37 WHERE CONTACT WITH OTHER CULTURES IS FREQUENT OR REGULAR, RATHER THAN IRREGULAR (43) JMH	9 32 6 5 XSQ= 3.04 PHI= -0.242 XP = 0.0812
471	DRIFT TOWARD BEING THOSE 0.80 OF 10 WHERE SECRET SOCIETIES ARE UNIMPORTANT OR ABSENT (14) LWS	471	DRIFT TOWARD BEING THOSE 0.58 OF 12 WHERE SECRET SOCIETIES ARE PRESENT (9) LWS	2 7 8 5 XSQ= 1.92 PHI= -0.295 EP = 0.0991

477	TILT TOWARD BEING THOSE WHERE ALCCHOLIC AGGRESSION IS STRCNG (15) DH	0.86 OF 7	477	TILT TOWARD BEING THOSE WHERE ALCOHOLIC AGGRESSICN IS MODERATE OR SLIGHT (19) DH	0.64 OF 25	6 9 1 16 XSQ= 3.61 PHI= 0.336 EP = 0.0330

****

47 CULTURES
WHERE, IF SETTLEMENTS ARE NON-FIXED, MOVEMENT IS NOMADIC, RATHER THAN NON-NOMADIC (72)

47 CULTURES
WHERE, IF SETTLEMENTS ARE NON-FIXED, MOVEMENT IS NON-NOMADIC, RATHER THAN NOMADIC (38)

BACKGROUND ON PAGE 71

BOTH SUBJECT AND PREDICATE

....

72 IN LEFT COLUMN

ABIPON	ALACALUF	ANDAMANESE	ARANDA	ATSUGEWI	AWEIKOMA	BASSERI	BEJA	BORORO	BOTOCUDO
CADUVEO	CHAMACOCO	CHEYENNE	CHIR-APACHE	CHUKCHEE	COPR ESKIMO	CROW	DIEGUENO	DIERI	DOROBO
FOX	GILYAK	GOAJIRO	GROS VENTRE	GUAHIBO	GUATO	HERERO	HUKUNDIKA	INGALIK	KARIERA
KASKA	KAZAK	KHALKA	KUNG	KUTENAI	LAPPS	MASAI	MATACO	MBUTI	MURINBATA
MURNGIN	NABESNA	NAMA	NAMBICUARA	NUER	OJIBWA	ONA	REGEIBAT	RWALA	SAMOYED
SANPOIL	SARSI	SELUNG	SEMANG	SIRIONO	SOMALI	TEDA	TEHUELCHE	TERENA	TIWI
TUBATULABAL	TURKANA	TWANA	UTE	VEDDA	WAICA	WASHO	WIKMUNKAN	YAHGAN	YAKUT
YOKUTS	YUKAGHIR								

38 IN RIGHT COLUMN

BEMBA	BHUIYA	BOZO	CAMAYURA	CHENCHU	CHOROTI	DARD	DELAWARE	HAVASUPAI	HAZARA
ILA	KERAKI	KOHISTANI	KORYAK	KUBA	LOZI	MANDAN	MIAMI	MIWOK	MNONG GAR
MUNDURUCU	NAVAHO	NDEMBU	NUNIVAK	OMAHA	ONTONG-JAVA	PAPAGO	TAREUMIUT	TENINO	TIMUCUA
TODA	TOLOWA	TSHIMSHIAN	TUCANO	WARRAU	WICHITA	WOLOF	YUKI		

222 EXCLUDED BECAUSE IRRELEVANT (SEE LEFT COLUMN, PARAGRAPH 44)

68 EXCLUDED BECAUSE UNASCERTAINED

	Left column				Right column				
51	DRIFT MORE TOWARD BEING THOSE WHERE SUBSISTENCE IS PRIMARILY BY FOOD GATHERING -- I. E., HUNTING, FISHING, OR COLLECTING -- RATHER THAN FOOD PRODUCTION (147)	0.82 OF 72	51	DRIFT LESS TOWARD BEING THOSE WHERE SUBSISTENCE IS PRIMARILY BY FOOD GATHERING -- I. E., HUNTING, FISHING, OR COLLECTING -- RATHER THAN FOOD PRODUCTION (147)	0.63 OF 38	13 14 59 24	XSQ= 3.78 PHI= -0.185 XP = 0.0519
54	TILT TOWARD BEING THOSE WHERE FOOD PRODUCTION IS BY INCIPIENT FOOD PRODUCTION, RATHER THAN BY INTENSIVE OR SIMPLE AGRICULTURE (46)	0.88 OF 8	54	TILT TOWARD BEING THOSE WHERE FOOD PRODUCTION IS BY INTENSIVE OR SIMPLE AGRICULTURE, RATHER THAN BY INCIPIENT FOOD PRODUCTION (192)	0.57 OF 23	1 13 7 10	XSQ= 3.04 PHI= -0.313 EP = 0.0454
56	IN ALL CASES ARE THOSE WHERE FOOD PRODUCTION IS BY INCIPIENT FOOD PRODUCTION, RATHER THAN BY SIMPLE AGRICULTURE (46)	1.00 OF 7	56	DRIFT LESS TOWARD BEING THOSE WHERE FOOD PRODUCTION IS BY INCIPIENT FOOD PRODUCTION, RATHER THAN BY SIMPLE AGRICULTURE (46)	0.53 OF 19	0 9 7 10	XSQ= 3.19 PHI= -0.351 EP = 0.0578

63	DRIFT MORE TOWARD BEING THOSE 0.94 OF 31 WHERE HUSBANDRY, IF PRESENT, IS PRINCIPALLY IN THE FORM OF BOVINE, EQUINE, CAMEL-LIKE, OR DEER-LIKE ANIMALS, RATHER THAN PIGS, SHEEP, OR GOATS (152)	63	DRIFT LESS TOWARD BEING THOSE 0.68 OF 19 WHERE HUSBANDRY, IF PRESENT, IS PRINCIPALLY IN THE FORM OF BOVINE, EQUINE, CAMEL-LIKE, OR DEER-LIKE ANIMALS, RATHER THAN PIGS, SHEEP, OR GOATS (152)	29 13 2 6 XSQ= 3.82 PHI= 0.276 XP = 0.0506
73	DRIFT MORE TOWARD BEING THOSE 0.74 OF 62 WHERE WEAVING IS ABSENT (130)	73	DRIFT LESS TOWARD BEING THOSE 0.53 OF 30 WHERE WEAVING IS ABSENT (130)	16 14 46 16 XSQ= 3.11 PHI= -0.184 XP = 0.0778
78	DRIFT LESS TOWARD BEING THOSE 0.53 OF 15 WHERE THE WRITING SYSTEM IS ALPHABETIC-OR-PHONETIC, OR MNEMONIC, RATHER THAN BEING ABSENT (36) JMH	78	IN ALL CASES ARE THOSE 1.00 OF 6 WHERE THE WRITING SYSTEM IS ALPHABETIC-OR-PHONETIC, OR MNEMONIC, RATHER THAN BEING ABSENT (36) JMH	8 6 7 0 XSQ= 2.36 PHI= -0.335 EP = 0.0609
82	TEND TO BE THOSE 0.66 OF 47 WHERE NO CITY OR TOWN IS PRESENT, AND THE AVERAGE COMMUNITY SIZE IS SMALLER THAN FIFTY (46)	82	TEND TO BE THOSE 0.85 OF 26 WHERE A CITY OR TOWN IS PRESENT, OR THE AVERAGE COMMUNITY SIZE IS FIFTY OR GREATER (178)	16 22 31 4 XSQ= 15.19 PHI= -0.456 XP = 0.0001
83	LEAN MORE TOWARD BEING THOSE 0.98 OF 47 WHERE, WITH NO CITY AND NO TOWN PRESENT, THE AVERAGE COMMUNITY SIZE IS SMALLER THAN 200, RATHER THAN BETWEEN 200 AND 999 (135)	83	LEAN LESS TOWARD BEING THOSE 0.73 OF 26 WHERE, WITH NO CITY AND NO TOWN PRESENT, THE AVERAGE COMMUNITY SIZE IS SMALLER THAN 200, RATHER THAN BETWEEN 200 AND 999 (135)	1 7 46 19 XSQ= 8.16 PHI= -0.334 XP = 0.0043
87	DRIFT LESS TOWARD BEING THOSE 0.85 OF 60 WHERE THE LEVEL OF POLITICAL INTEGRATION IS THE LARGE STATE, THE LITTLE STATE, THE MINIMAL STATE, OR THE AUTONOMOUS COMMUNITY (281) GPM	87	IN ALL CASES ARE THOSE 1.00 OF 31 WHERE THE LEVEL OF POLITICAL INTEGRATION IS THE LARGE STATE, THE LITTLE STATE, THE MINIMAL STATE, OR THE AUTONOMOUS COMMUNITY (281) GPM	51 31 9 0 XSQ= 3.61 PHI= -0.199 XP = 0.0573
98	LEAN TOWARD BEING THOSE 0.58 OF 72 WHERE THE HIERARCHY OF LOCAL JURISDICTION HAS TWO LEVELS (93) GES,EA	98	LEAN TOWARD BEING THOSE 0.76 OF 38 WHERE THE HIERARCHY OF LOCAL JURISDICTION HAS FOUR OR THREE LEVELS (238) GES,EA	30 29 42 9 XSQ= 10.66 PHI= -0.311 XP = 0.0011
99	TILT TOWARD BEING THOSE 0.66 OF 50 WHERE, WITH NATIONAL HIERARCHY ABSENT, THE HIERARCHY OF LOCAL JURISDICTION HAS TWO LEVELS (63) GES,EA	99	TILT TOWARD BEING THOSE 0.70 OF 20 WHERE, WITH NATIONAL HIERARCHY ABSENT, THE HIERARCHY OF LOCAL JURISDICTION HAS FOUR OR THREE LEVELS (93) GES,EA	17 14 33 6 XSQ= 6.12 PHI= -0.296 XP = 0.0134
100	LEAN LESS TOWARD BEING THOSE 0.54 OF 72 WHERE HIERARCHIES ARE MORE COMPLEX THAN THE 'SIMPLEST,' I. E., MORE COMPLEX THAN TWO LOCAL LEVELS WITH NO NATIONAL LEVELS (267) GES,EA	100	LEAN MORE TOWARD BEING THOSE 0.84 OF 38 WHERE HIERARCHIES ARE MORE COMPLEX THAN THE 'SIMPLEST,' I. E., MORE COMPLEX THAN TWO LOCAL LEVELS WITH NO NATIONAL LEVELS (267) GES,EA	39 32 33 6 XSQ= 8.54 PHI= -0.279 XP = 0.0035

102	TILT TOWARD BEING THOSE WHERE CLASS STRATIFICATION IS ABSENT (180)	0.72 OF 71	102	TILT TOWARD BEING THOSE WHERE CLASS STRATIFICATION IS PRESENT (203)	0.50 OF 36	20 18 51 18 XSQ= 4.06 PHI= -0.195 XP = 0.0438
110	DRIFT MORE TOWARD BEING THOSE WHERE SLAVERY IS ABSENT (218)	0.75 OF 72	110	DRIFT LESS TOWARD BEING THOSE WHERE SLAVERY IS ABSENT (218)	0.54 OF 35	18 16 54 19 XSQ= 3.75 PHI= -0.187 XP = 0.0527
131	TEND TO BE THOSE WHERE THE CONSTRUCTION OF PERMANENT HOUSES OR THE ERECTION OF TEMPORARY DWELLINGS IS MAINLY DONE BY FEMALES (21)	0.57 OF 35	131	IN ALL CASES ARE THOSE WHERE THE CONSTRUCTION OF PERMANENT HOUSES OR THE ERECTION OF TEMPORARY DWELLINGS IS MAINLY DONE BY MALES (136)	1.00 OF 16	15 16 20 0 XSQ= 12.74 PHI= -0.500 XP = 0.0004
192	TILT LESS TOWARD BEING THOSE OTHER THAN WHERE THE ONLY KIN GROUP PRESENT IS A KINDRED OR ELSE BILATERAL DESCENT IS INFERRED (289)	0.53 OF 72	192	TILT MORE TOWARD BEING THOSE OTHER THAN WHERE THE ONLY KIN GROUP PRESENT IS A KINDRED OR ELSE BILATERAL DESCENT IS INFERRED (289)	0.79 OF 38	34 8 38 30 XSQ= 6.15 PHI= 0.236 XP = 0.0131
196	LEAN TOWARD BEING THOSE WHERE INDIVIDUAL RIGHTS IN REAL PROPERTY, OR RULES FOR INHERITANCE, ARE ABSENT (87)	0.77 OF 56	196	LEAN TOWARD BEING THOSE WHERE INDIVIDUAL RIGHTS IN REAL PROPERTY, AND RULES FOR INHERITANCE, ARE PRESENT (194)	0.57 OF 30	13 17 43 13 XSQ= 8.21 PHI= -0.309 XP = 0.0042
198	IN ALL CASES ARE THOSE WHERE RULES FOR THE INHERITANCE OF REAL PROPERTY, IF PRESENT, FAVOR THE MALE HEIR OR LINE, RATHER THAN THE FEMALE (144)	1.00 OF 12	198	DRIFT LESS TOWARD BEING THOSE WHERE RULES FOR THE INHERITANCE OF REAL PROPERTY, IF PRESENT, FAVOR THE MALE HEIR OR LINE, RATHER THAN THE FEMALE (144)	0.71 OF 17	12 12 0 5 XSQ= 2.45 PHI= 0.291 EP = 0.0588
240	DRIFT TOWARD BEING THOSE WHERE THE FAMILY, IF EXTENDED, IS SMALL OR STEM, RATHER THAN LARGE (135)	0.76 OF 34	240	DRIFT TOWARD BEING THOSE WHERE THE FAMILY, IF EXTENDED, IS LARGE, RATHER THAN SMALL OR STEM (78)	0.50 OF 22	8 11 26 11 XSQ= 3.08 PHI= -0.234 XP = 0.0794
272	DRIFT TOWARD BEING THOSE WHERE THE DIVORCE RATE IS LOW (28) CA	0.50 OF 12	272	DRIFT TOWARD BEING THOSE WHERE THE DIVORCE RATE IS HIGH (29) CA	0.89 OF 9	6 8 6 1 XSQ= 1.97 PHI= -0.306 EP = 0.0873
302	DRIFT TOWARD BEING THOSE WHERE THE AVERAGE EARLY SATISFACTION POTENTIAL IS LOW (17) W-C	0.83 OF 6	302	DRIFT TOWARD BEING THOSE WHERE THE AVERAGE EARLY SATISFACTION POTENTIAL IS HIGH (23) W-C	0.80 OF 5	1 4 5 1 XSQ= 2.23 PHI= -0.450 EP = 0.0801

324	TILT TCWARD BEING THOSE WHERE THE PAIN INFLICTEC ON THE INFANT BY THE NURTURANT AGENT IS HIGH (34) B-B-C	0.64 OF 14	324	TILT TOWARD BEING THOSE WHERE THE PAIN INFLICTED ON THE INFANT BY THE NURTURANT AGENT IS LOW OR NEGLIGIBLE (32) B-B-C	0.88 OF 8	9 1 5 7 XSQ= 3.62 PHI= 0.405 EP = 0.0310
344	DRIFT TCWARD BEING THOSE WHERE THE TOTAL PCSITIVE PRESSURE TOWARD DEVELCPING SELF-RELIANT BEHAVIOR IN THE CHILD IS HIGH (36) B-B-C	0.67 OF 15	344	DRIFT TOWARD BEING THOSE WHERE THE TOTAL POSITIVE PRESSURE TOWARC DEVELOPING SELF-RELIANT BEHAVICR IN THE CHILD IS LOW (40) B-B-C	0.78 CF 9	10 2 5 7 XSQ= 2.84 PHI= 0.344 EP = 0.0894
399	DRIFT TCWARD BEING THCSE WHERE INTENSITY CF CASTRATION ANXIETY IS HIGH (23) WNS	0.67 OF 9	399	IN ALL CASES ARE THOSE WHERE INTENSITY OF CASTRATICN ANXIETY IS LOW (22) WNS	1.00 OF 4	6 0 3 4 XSQ= 2.63 PHI= 0.450 EP = 0.0699
400	TILT TOWARD BEING THOSE WHERE HOMCSEXUAL ACTIVITY IS PRCHIBITED (22) F-B	0.50 OF 12	400	IN ALL CASES ARE THOSE WHERE HOMOSEXUAL ACTIVITY IS PERMITTED (36) F-B	1.00 OF 8	6 0 6 8 XSQ= 3.58 PHI= 0.423 EP = 0.0419
405	DRIFT TCWARD BEING THCSE WHERE EXPLANATICNS CF ILLNESS OF A DEPENDENCE NATURE ARE PRESENT (34) W-C	0.77 OF 13	405	DRIFT TOWARD BEING THOSE WHERE EXPLANATIONS OF ILLNESS OF A DEPENDENCE NATURE ARE ABSENT (27) W-C	0.71 OF 7	10 2 3 5 XSQ= 2.65 PHI= 0.364 EP = 0.0623

****

48 CULTURES WHERE THE FOOD SUPPLY IS SECURE, AND FOOD SHORTAGES ARE RARE OR OCCASIONAL (38) MGW	48 CULTURES WHERE THE FOOD SUPPLY IS NOT SECURE, AND FOOD SHORTAGES ARE FREQUENT OR ANNUAL (41) MGW

BACKGROUND ON PAGE 72 — BOTH SUBJECT AND PREDICATE

....

38 IN LEFT COLUMN

ANDAMANESE	ARANDA	ARAPESH	ASHANTI	BALINESE	COPR ESKIMO	CUNA	FON	JIVARO	KURTATCHI
KWAKIUTL	LAKHER	LAPPS	LAU	LESU	MAGUZAWA	MAORI	MBUNDU	MINCHIA	NYAKYUSA
OJIBWA	ONTONG-JAVA	PUKAPUKA	SAMOANS	SHERENTE	TANALA	TENINO	TOKELAU	TROBRIAND	TRUKESE
TUPINAMBA	WINNEBAGO	WOGEO	WOLEAIANS	YAGUA	YAO	YAPESE	YORUBA		

41 IN RIGHT COLUMN

ALORESE	ARAUCANIANS	AYMARA	AZANDE	CAGABA	CAMAYURA	CHAGGA	CHENCHU	CHEYENNE	CHIR-APACHE
EGYPTIANS	GANDA	GROS VENTRE	HANO	KASKA	KAZAK	LAMBA	LANGO	LEPCHA	MASAI
MENDE	NAMA	NAMBICUARA	NAVAHO	NUER	OMAHA	ONA	PAPAGO	SANPOIL	SENIANG
SIRIONO	TALLENSI	TARAHUMARA	TENETEHARA	TETON	THONGA	TIMBIRA	TURKANA	VENDA	WAPISHANA
YUKAGHIR									

321 EXCLUDED BECAUSE UNASCERTAINED

6	TEND LESS TO BE THOSE LOCATED OUTSIDE OF THE INSULAR PACIFIC (330)	0.58 OF 38	6	TEND MORE TO BE THOSE LOCATED OUTSIDE OF THE INSULAR PACIFIC (330)	0.95 OF 41	16 2 22 39 XSQ= 13.49 PHI= 0.413 XP = 0.0002
16	DRIFT TOWARD BEING THOSE WHERE THE LATITUDE IS LESS THAN TEN DEGREES (123)	0.53 OF 38	16	DRIFT TOWARD BEING THOSE WHERE THE LATITUDE IS TEN DEGREES OR GREATER (277)	0.71 OF 41	18 29 20 12 XSQ= 3.55 PHI= -0.212 XP = 0.0595
36	LEAN MORE TOWARD BEING THOSE WHERE THE NATURAL ENVIRONMENT IS OTHER THAN 'VERY HARSH,' OR SUB-TROPICAL BUSH, OR TEMPERATE GRASSLAND (292) FWM	0.87 OF 38	36	LEAN LESS TOWARD BEING THOSE WHERE THE NATURAL ENVIRONMENT IS OTHER THAN 'VERY HARSH,' OR SUB-TROPICAL BUSH, OR TEMPERATE GRASSLAND (292) FWM	0.54 OF 41	5 19 33 22 XSQ= 8.76 PHI= -0.333 XP = 0.0031
42	TEND TO BE THOSE WHERE THE NATURAL ENVIRONMENT IS TROPICAL OR SUB-TROPICAL RAIN FOREST, OR MONSOON FOREST (156) FWM	0.63 OF 38	42	TEND TO BE THOSE WHERE THE NATURAL ENVIRONMENT IS OTHER THAN TROPICAL OR SUB-TROPICAL RAIN FOREST, OR MONSOON FOREST (244) FWM	0.83 OF 41	24 7 14 34 XSQ= 15.69 PHI= 0.446 XP = 0.0001

44	TILT MORE TOWARD BEING THOSE 0.80 OF 35 WHERE SETTLEMENTS ARE FIXED (222)	44	TILT LESS TOWARD BEING THOSE 0.52 OF 40 WHERE SETTLEMENTS ARE FIXED (222)	28 21 7 19 XSQ= 5.08 PHI= 0.260 XP = 0.0242
46	DRIFT MORE TOWARD BEING THOSE 0.86 OF 35 OTHER THAN WHERE SETTLEMENTS ARE NON-FIXED AND MOVEMENT IS NOMADIC (260)	46	DRIFT LESS TOWARD BEING THOSE 0.65 OF 40 OTHER THAN WHERE SETTLEMENTS ARE NON-FIXED AND MOVEMENT IS NOMADIC (260)	5 14 30 26 XSQ= 3.21 PHI= -0.207 XP = 0.0732
53	DRIFT MORE TOWARD BEING THOSE 0.88 OF 25 WHERE FOOD PRODUCTION IS BY SIMPLE AGRICULTURE OR INCIPIENT FOOD PRODUCTION, RATHER THAN BY INTENSIVE AGRICULTURE (147)	53	DRIFT LESS TOWARD BEING THOSE 0.62 OF 26 WHERE FOOD PRODUCTION IS BY SIMPLE AGRICULTURE OR INCIPIENT FOOD PRODUCTION, RATHER THAN BY INTENSIVE AGRICULTURE (147)	3 10 22 16 XSQ= 3.41 PHI= -0.259 XP = 0.0648
55	TILT TOWARD BEING THOSE 0.85 OF 20 WHERE FOOD PRODUCTION IS BY SIMPLE AGRICULTURE, RATHER THAN BY INTENSIVE AGRICULTURE (101)	55	TILT TOWARD BEING THOSE 0.53 OF 19 WHERE FOOD PRODUCTION IS BY INTENSIVE AGRICULTURE, RATHER THAN BY SIMPLE AGRICULTURE (91)	3 10 17 9 XSQ= 4.63 PHI= -0.345 EP = 0.0187
63	LEAN TOWARD BEING THOSE 0.73 OF 22 WHERE HUSBANDRY, IF PRESENT, IS PRINCIPALLY IN THE FORM OF PIGS, SHEEP, OR GOATS, RATHER THAN BOVINE, EQUINE, CAMEL-LIKE, OR DEER-LIKE ANIMALS (74)	63	LEAN TOWARD BEING THOSE 0.72 OF 29 WHERE HUSBANDRY, IF PRESENT, IS PRINCIPALLY IN THE FORM OF BOVINE, EQUINE, CAMEL-LIKE, OR DEER-LIKE ANIMALS, RATHER THAN PIGS, SHEEP, OR GOATS (152)	6 21 16 8 XSQ= 8.50 PHI= -0.408 XP = 0.0036
99	DRIFT TOWARD BEING THOSE 0.50 OF 14 WHERE, WITH NATIONAL HIERARCHY ABSENT, THE HIERARCHY OF LOCAL JURISDICTION HAS TWO LEVELS (63) GES,EA	99	DRIFT TOWARD BEING THOSE 0.79 OF 24 WHERE, WITH NATIONAL HIERARCHY ABSENT, THE HIERARCHY OF LOCAL JURISDICTION HAS FOUR OR THREE LEVELS (93) GES,EA	7 19 7 5 XSQ= 2.26 PHI= -0.244 EP = 0.0812
138	DRIFT TOWARD BEING THOSE 0.54 OF 13 WHERE SUPERORDINATE JUSTICE IS ABSENT (18) BBW	138	DRIFT TOWARD BEING THOSE 0.90 OF 10 WHERE SUPERORDINATE JUSTICE IS PRESENT (22) BBW	6 9 7 1 XSQ= 3.05 PHI= -0.364 EP = 0.0743
144	TILT TOWARD BEING THOSE 0.82 OF 11 WHERE THE RATIO OF RESTITUTIVE TO REPRESSIVE SANCTIONS IS LOW (25) WME	144	TILT TOWARD BEING THOSE 0.62 OF 13 WHERE THE RATIO OF RESTITUTIVE TO REPRESSIVE SANCTIONS IS HIGH OR MEDIUM (27) WME	2 8 9 5 XSQ= 3.00 PHI= -0.353 EP = 0.0472
178	DRIFT LESS TOWARD BEING THOSE 0.61 OF 38 WHERE THE COMMUNITY IS OTHER THAN SEGMENTED ON A CLAN BASIS AND NON-EXOGAMOUS (295)	178	DRIFT MORE TOWARD BEING THOSE 0.80 OF 41 WHERE THE COMMUNITY IS OTHER THAN SEGMENTED ON A CLAN BASIS AND NON-EXOGAMOUS (295)	15 8 23 33 XSQ= 2.90 PHI= 0.192 XP = 0.0885

263	TILT TOWARD BEING THOSE WHERE WIVES ARE OBTAINED BY RELATIVELY EASY MEANS, NAMELY BY TOKEN BRIDE-PRICE, GIFT EXCHANGE, ABSENCE OF ANY CONSIDERATION, OR RECEIPT OF DOWRY (162)	0.57 OF 37	263	TILT TOWARD BEING THOSE WHERE WIVES ARE OBTAINED BY RELATIVELY DIFFICULT MEANS, NAMELY BY BRIDE-PRICE, BRIDE-SERVICE, OR EXCHANGING A FEMALE RELATIVE (233)	0.73 OF 41	16 30 21 11 XSQ= 6.02 PHI= -0.278 XP = 0.0142
300	TILT TOWARD BEING THOSE WHERE THE POST-PARTUM SEX TABOO LASTS LONGER THAN SIX MONTHS (51)	0.74 OF 19	300	TILT TOWARD BEING THOSE WHERE THE POST-PARTUM SEX TABOO LASTS SIX MONTHS OR LESS (73)	0.63 OF 24	14 9 5 15 XSQ= 4.22 PHI= 0.313 XP = 0.0399
342	DRIFT TOWARD BEING THOSE WHERE THE CHILD'S INFERRED ANXIETY OVER PERFORMANCE OF NURTURANT BEHAVIOR IS HIGH (18) B-B-C	0.59 OF 17	342	DRIFT TOWARD BEING THOSE WHERE THE CHILD'S INFERRED ANXIETY OVER PERFORMANCE OF NURTURANT BEHAVIOR IS LOW (28) B-B-C	0.72 OF 18	10 5 7 13 XSQ= 2.29 PHI= 0.256 EP = 0.0922
392	DRIFT TOWARD BEING THOSE WHERE PREMARITAL SEX RELATIONS ARE FREELY PERMITTED (67) JTW,EA	0.54 OF 28	392	DRIFT TOWARD BEING THOSE WHERE PREMARITAL SEX RELATIONS ARE STRONGLY PUNISHED AND IN FACT RARE, OR WEAKLY PUNISHED AND IN FACT NOT RARE, OR PUNISHED ONLY IF PREGNANCY RESULTS (112) JTW,EA	0.73 OF 26	13 19 15 7 XSQ= 2.94 PHI= -0.233 XP = 0.0865
427	DRIFT TOWARD BEING THOSE WHERE A HIGH GOD, IF PRESENT, IS INACTIVE, RATHER THAN ACTIVE (69) GES,EA	0.71 OF 14	427	DRIFT TOWARD BEING THOSE WHERE A HIGH GOD, IF PRESENT, IS ACTIVE, RATHER THAN INACTIVE (87) GES,EA	0.61 OF 23	4 14 10 9 XSQ= 2.46 PHI= -0.258 EP = 0.0911
459	LEAN TOWARD BEING THOSE WHERE GAMES, IF PRESENT, DO NOT INCLUDE GAMES OF CHANCE (89) R-A-B,EA	0.76 OF 25	459	LEAN TOWARD BEING THOSE WHERE GAMES, IF PRESENT, INCLUDE GAMES OF CHANCE (82) R-A-B,EA	0.67 OF 30	6 20 19 10 XSQ= 8.32 PHI= -0.389 XP = 0.0039
480	DRIFT TOWARD BEING THOSE WHERE COMPLEXITY OF ARTISTIC DESIGN IS HIGH (14) HB	0.70 OF 10	480	DRIFT TOWARD BEING THOSE WHERE COMPLEXITY OF ARTISTIC DESIGN IS LOW (15) HB	0.80 OF 10	7 2 3 8 XSQ= 3.23 PHI= 0.402 EP = 0.0698

49 CULTURES
WHERE THE QUANTITY CF FCOC
IS PLENTIFUL (32) MGW

49 CULTURES
WHERE THE QUANTITY OF FCCD IS
LESS THAN PLENTIFUL (48) MGW

BACKGROUND ON PAGE 72 SUBJECT ONLY

32 IN LEFT CCLUMN

ANDAMANESE	ARANDA	ASHANTI	CHEYENNE	CHIR-APACHE	COPR ESKIMO	CUNA	GANDA	JIVARO	KAZAK
KWAKIUTL	LAKHER	LAPPS	LEPCHA	MAGUZAWA	MAORI	MASAI	OJIBWA	ONTCNG-JAVA	SAMOANS
TENINO	TETCN	THCNGA	TROBRIAND	TRUKESE	TUPINAMBA	VENDA	WINNEBAGO	WOGEC	WOLEAIANS
YAGUA	YAC								

48 IN RIGHT CCLUMN

ALORESE	ARAPESH	ARAUCANIANS	AYMARA	AZANDE	BALINESE	CAGABA	CAMAYURA	CHAGGA	CHENCHU
EGYPTIANS	FCN	GRCS VENTRE	HANO	KASKA	KURTATCHI	LAMBA	LANGO	LAU	LESU
MBUNDU	MENDE	MINCHIA	NAMA	NAMBICUARA	NAVAHO	NUER	NYAKYUSA	OMAHA	ONA
PAPAGC	PUKAPUKA	SANPCIL	SENIANG	SHERENTE	SIRIONO	TALLENSI	TANALA	TARAHUMARA	TENETEHARA
TIMBIRA	TCKELAU	TURKANA	WAPISHANA	WARRAU	YAPESE	YORUBA	YUKAGHIR		

320 EXCLUDED BECAUSE UNASCERTAINEC

	Left column			Right column			Statistics	
48	LEAN TCWARD BEING THCSE WHERE THE FOOD SUPPLY IS SECURE, AND FCOD SHORTAGES ARE RARE CR OCCASIONAL (38) MGW	0.72 OF 32	48	LEAN TOWARD BEING THOSE WHERE THE FOOD SUPPLY IS NOT SECURE, AND FOOD SHORTAGES ARE FREQUENT OR ANNUAL (41) MGW	0.68 OF 47	23 15 9 32	XSQ= 10.63 PHI= 0.367 XP = 0.0011
240	DRIFT TOWARD BEING THCSE WHERE THE FAMILY, IF EXTENCEC, IS LARGE, RATHER THAN SMALL CR STEM (78)	0.62 OF 21	240	DRIFT TOWARD BEING THOSE WHERE THE FAMILY, IF EXTENDED, IS SMALL OR STEM, RATHER THAN LARGE (135)	0.69 OF 26	13 8 8 18	XSQ= 3.38 PHI= 0.268 XP = 0.0658
257	TILT TCWARD BEING THOSE WHERE THE SEVERITY CF SISTER AVCIDANCE IS HIGH (10) WNS	0.75 OF 8	257	TILT TOWARD BEING THOSE WHERE THE SEVERITY OF SISTER AVOIDANCE IS LOW (17) WNS	0.77 OF 13	6 3 2 10	XSQ= 3.54 PHI= 0.410 EP = 0.0318
300	DRIFT TCWARD BEING THCSE WHERE THE POST-PARTUM SEX TABOO LASTS LCNGER THAN SIX MONTHS (51)	0.73 OF 15	300	DRIFT TOWARD BEING THOSE WHERE THE POST-PARTUM SEX TABOC LASTS SIX MONTHS OR LESS (73)	0.59 OF 29	11 12 4 17	XSQ= 2.87 PHI= 0.255 XP = 0.0904

332	DRIFT TOWARD BEING THOSE 0.83 OF 6 WHERE THE AGE AT BEGINNING OF MODESTY TRAINING IS SIX YEARS OR HIGHER (9) W-C	332	DRIFT TOWARD BEING THOSE 0.83 OF 6 WHERE THE AGE AT BEGINNING OF MODESTY TRAINING IS LOWER THAN SIX YEARS (8) W-C	5 1 1 5 XSQ= 3.00 PHI= 0.500 EP = 0.0801
348	DRIFT TOWARD BEING THOSE 0.67 OF 21 WHERE THE TOTAL POSITIVE PRESSURE TOWARD DEVELOPING ACHIEVEMENT BEHAVIOR IN THE CHILD IS HIGH (32) B-B-C	348	DRIFT TOWARD BEING THOSE 0.63 OF 27 WHERE THE TOTAL POSITIVE PRESSURE TOWARD DEVELOPING ACHIEVEMENT BEHAVIOR IN THE CHILD IS LOW (31) B-B-C	14 10 7 17 XSQ= 3.05 PHI= 0.252 XP = 0.0809
349	TILT TOWARD BEING THOSE 0.75 OF 20 WHERE THE CHILD'S INFERRED ANXIETY OVER NON-PERFORMANCE OF ACHIEVEMENT BEHAVIOR IS HIGH (34) B-B-C	349	TILT TOWARD BEING THOSE 0.63 OF 27 WHERE THE CHILD'S INFERRED ANXIETY OVER NON-PERFORMANCE OF ACHIEVEMENT BEHAVIOR IS LOW (28) B-B-C	15 10 5 17 XSQ= 5.21 PHI= 0.333 XP = 0.0224
355	DRIFT TOWARD BEING THOSE 0.64 OF 25 WHERE THE CHILD'S INFERRED CONFLICT REGARDING OBEDIENT BEHAVIOR IS HIGH (35) B-B-C	355	DRIFT TOWARD BEING THOSE 0.64 OF 28 WHERE THE CHILD'S INFERRED CONFLICT REGARDING OBEDIENT BEHAVIOR IS LOW (38) B-B-C	16 10 9 18 XSQ= 3.17 PHI= 0.245 XP = 0.0749
356	DRIFT TOWARD BEING THOSE 0.67 OF 15 WHERE ADOLESCENT PEER GROUPS OR PAIRS ARE PRESENT IN A SETTING OF COURTSHIP (29) JKH	356	DRIFT TOWARD BEING THOSE 0.67 OF 21 WHERE NEITHER ADOLESCENT PEER GROUPS NOR PAIRS ARE PRESENT IN A SETTING OF COURTSHIP (22) JKH	10 7 5 14 XSQ= 2.68 PHI= 0.273 EP = 0.0895
398	DRIFT TOWARD BEING THOSE 0.73 OF 11 WHERE THE INTENSITY OF SEX ANXIETY IS LOW (16) WNS	398	DRIFT TOWARD BEING THOSE 0.69 OF 16 WHERE THE INTENSITY OF SEX ANXIETY IS HIGH (16) WNS	3 11 8 5 XSQ= 2.98 PHI= -0.332 EP = 0.0542
453	DRIFT TOWARD BEING THOSE 0.54 OF 13 WHERE THE ROLE OF RELIGIOUS EXPERTS IS CONDUCIVE TO THE DEVELOPMENT OF THE INDIVIDUAL'S NEED TO ACHIEVE (13) DCM	453	DRIFT TOWARD BEING THOSE 0.83 OF 12 WHERE THE ROLE OF RELIGIOUS EXPERTS IS NOT CONDUCIVE TO THE DEVELOPMENT OF THE INDIVIDUAL'S NEED TO ACHIEVE (23) DCM	7 2 6 10 XSQ= 2.30 PHI= 0.304 EP = 0.0968
472	DRIFT TOWARD BEING THOSE 0.63 OF 24 WHERE THE COMPOSITE NARCISSISM INDEX IS HIGH (47) PES	472	DRIFT TOWARD BEING THOSE 0.67 OF 27 WHERE THE COMPOSITE NARCISSISM INDEX IS LOW (43) PES	15 9 9 18 XSQ= 3.25 PHI= 0.252 XP = 0.0716

****

50 CULTURES WHERE THE DAILY PROTEIN INTAKE IS NINETY GRAMS OR HIGHER (43) MGW	50 CULTURES WHERE THE DAILY PROTEIN INTAKE IS EIGHTY GRAMS OR LOWER (39) MGW

BACKGROUND ON PAGE 72 SUBJECT ONLY

....

43 IN LEFT COLUMN

ANDAMANESE	ARANDA	AYMARA	CAMAYURA	CHEYENNE	CHIR-APACHE	COPR ESKIMO	CUNA	GROS VENTRE	JIVARO
KASKA	KAZAK	KORYAK	KURTATCHI	KWAKIUTL	LANGO	LAPPS	MASAI	NAMA	NAMBICUARA
NAVAHO	OJIBWA	OMAHA	ONA	ONTONG-JAVA	SANPOIL	SHERENTE	SIRIONO	TENINO	TERENA
TETON	TIMBIRA	TOKELAU	TUPINAMBA	TURKANA	VENDA	WAPISHANA	WARRAU	WINNEBAGO	WOGEO
YAGUA	YAO	YUKAGHIR							

39 IN RIGHT COLUMN

ALORESE	ARAPESH	ARAUCANIANS	ASHANTI	AZANDE	BALINESE	CAGABA	CHAGGA	CHENCHU	EGYPTIANS
FON	GANDA	HANO	LAKHER	LAMBA	LAU	LEPCHA	LESU	MAGUZAWA	MAORI
MBUNDU	MENDE	MINCHIA	NUER	NYAKYUSA	PAPAGO	PUKAPUKA	SAMOANS	SENIANG	TALLENSI
TANALA	TARAHUMARA	TENETEHARA	THONGA	TROBRIAND	TRUKESE	WOLEAIANS	YAPESE	YORUBA	

318 EXCLUDED BECAUSE UNASCERTAINED

3	DRIFT MORE TOWARD BEING THOSE LOCATED OUTSIDE OF AFRICA (320)	0.86 OF 43	3	DRIFT LESS TOWARD BEING THOSE LOCATED OUTSIDE OF AFRICA (320)	0.67 OF 39	6 13 37 26 XSQ= 3.29 PHI= -0.200 XP = 0.0695
6	TILT MORE TOWARD BEING THOSE LOCATED OUTSIDE OF THE INSULAR PACIFIC (330)	0.88 OF 43	6	TILT LESS TOWARD BEING THOSE LOCATED OUTSIDE OF THE INSULAR PACIFIC (330)	0.67 OF 39	5 13 38 26 XSQ= 4.43 PHI= -0.232 XP = 0.0353
8	TILT LESS TOWARD BEING THOSE LOCATED OUTSIDE OF NORTH AMERICA (330)	0.70 OF 43	8	TILT MORE TOWARD BEING THOSE LOCATED OUTSIDE OF NORTH AMERICA (330)	0.92 OF 39	13 3 30 36 XSQ= 5.26 PHI= 0.253 XP = 0.0218
9	TILT LESS TOWARD BEING THOSE LOCATED OUTSIDE OF SOUTH AMERICA (335)	0.67 OF 43	9	TILT MORE TOWARD BEING THOSE LOCATED OUTSIDE OF SOUTH AMERICA (335)	0.92 OF 39	14 3 29 36 XSQ= 6.26 PHI= 0.276 XP = 0.0124

13	TEND LESS TO BE THOSE WHERE THE LATITUDE IS LESS THAN FORTY DEGREES (329)	0.65 OF 43	13	IN ALL CASES ARE THOSE WHERE THE LATITUDE IS LESS THAN FORTY DEGREES (329)	1.00 OF 39	15 0 28 39 XSQ= 14.40 PHI= 0.419 XP = 0.0001
15	DRIFT TOWARD BEING THOSE WHERE THE LATITUDE IS TWENTY DEGREES OR GREATER (183)	0.51 OF 43	15	DRIFT TOWARD BEING THOSE WHERE THE LATITUDE IS LESS THAN TWENTY DEGREES (217)	0.72 OF 39	22 11 21 28 XSQ= 3.58 PHI= 0.209 XP = 0.0585
33	TILT LESS TOWARD BEING THOSE WHERE THE NATURAL ENVIRONMENT IS OTHER THAN 'VERY HARSH,' I.E., DESERT, DESERT GRASSES AND SHRUBS, TUNDRA, OR HIGH PLATEAU STEPPE (341) FWM	0.72 OF 43	33	TILT MORE TOWARD BEING THOSE WHERE THE NATURAL ENVIRONMENT IS OTHER THAN 'VERY HARSH,' I.E., DESERT, DESERT GRASSES AND SHRUBS, TUNDRA, OR HIGH PLATEAU STEPPE (341) FWM	0.95 OF 39	12 2 31 37 XSQ= 5.97 PHI= 0.270 XP = 0.0145
36	LEAN LESS TOWARD BEING THOSE WHERE THE NATURAL ENVIRONMENT IS OTHER THAN 'VERY HARSH,' OR SUB-TROPICAL BUSH, OR TEMPERATE GRASSLAND (292) FWM	0.56 OF 43	36	LEAN MORE TOWARD BEING THOSE WHERE THE NATURAL ENVIRONMENT IS OTHER THAN 'VERY HARSH,' OR SUB-TROPICAL BUSH, OR TEMPERATE GRASSLAND (292) FWM	0.85 OF 39	19 6 24 33 XSQ= 6.70 PHI= 0.286 XP = 0.0096
42	TILT TOWARD BEING THOSE WHERE THE NATURAL ENVIRONMENT IS OTHER THAN TROPICAL OR SUB-TROPICAL RAIN FOREST, OR MONSOON FOREST (244) FWM	0.72 OF 43	42	TILT TOWARD BEING THOSE WHERE THE NATURAL ENVIRONMENT IS TROPICAL OR SUB-TROPICAL RAIN FOREST, OR MONSOON FOREST (156) FWM	0.54 OF 39	12 21 31 18 XSQ= 4.69 PHI= -0.239 XP = 0.0303
44	TEND TO BE THOSE WHERE SETTLEMENTS ARE NON-FIXED (110)	0.63 OF 41	44	TEND TO BE THOSE WHERE SETTLEMENTS ARE FIXED (222)	0.92 OF 37	15 34 26 3 XSQ= 23.16 PHI= -0.545 XP = 0.0000
46	TEND LESS TO BE THOSE OTHER THAN WHERE SETTLEMENTS ARE NON-FIXED AND MOVEMENT IS NOMADIC (260)	0.54 OF 41	46	TEND MORE TO BE THOSE OTHER THAN WHERE SETTLEMENTS ARE NON-FIXED AND MOVEMENT IS NOMADIC (260)	0.97 OF 37	19 1 22 36 XSQ= 17.20 PHI= 0.470 XP = 0.0000
51	TEND TO BE THOSE WHERE SUBSISTENCE IS PRIMARILY BY FOOD GATHERING -- I. E., HUNTING, FISHING, OR COLLECTING -- RATHER THAN FOOD PRODUCTION (147)	0.74 OF 43	51	TEND TO BE THOSE WHERE SUBSISTENCE IS PRIMARILY BY FOOD PRODUCTION -- I. E., AGRICULTURE OR HUSBANDRY -- RATHER THAN BY GATHERING (253)	0.87 OF 39	11 34 32 5 XSQ= 28.90 PHI= -0.594 XP = 0.0000
54	TEND TO BE THOSE WHERE FOOD PRODUCTION IS BY INCIPIENT FOOD PRODUCTION, RATHER THAN BY INTENSIVE OR SIMPLE AGRICULTURE (46)	0.56 OF 18	54	TEND TO BE THOSE WHERE FOOD PRODUCTION IS BY INTENSIVE OR SIMPLE AGRICULTURE, RATHER THAN BY INCIPIENT FOOD PRODUCTION (192)	0.91 OF 34	8 31 10 3 XSQ= 11.33 PHI= -0.467 XP = 0.0008

56	LEAN TOWARD BEING THOSE WHERE FOOD PRODUCTION IS BY INCIPIENT FOOD PRODUCTION, RATHER THAN BY SIMPLE AGRICULTURE (46)	0.63 OF 16	56	LEAN TOWARD BEING THOSE WHERE FOOD PRODUCTION IS BY SIMPLE AGRICULTURE, RATHER THAN BY INCIPIENT FOOD PRODUCTION (101)	0.87 OF 23	6 20 10 3 XSQ= 8.28 PHI= -0.461 EP = 0.0020
62	TEND TO BE THOSE WHERE HUSBANDRY OF ANY KIND IS ABSENT (172)	0.53 OF 43	62	TEND TO BE THOSE WHERE HUSBANDRY OF SOME KIND IS PRESENT (228)	0.85 OF 39	20 33 23 6 XSQ= 11.38 PHI= -0.372 XP = 0.0007
71	TILT TOWARD BEING THOSE WHERE METAL WORKING IS ABSENT (153)	0.79 OF 33	71	TILT TOWARD BEING THOSE WHERE METAL WORKING IS PRESENT (98)	0.50 OF 30	7 15 26 15 XSQ= 4.53 PHI= -0.268 XP = 0.0332
80	IN ALL CASES ARE THOSE WHERE NO CITY OR TOWN IS PRESENT (185)	1.00 OF 30	80	TILT LESS TOWARD BEING THOSE WHERE NO CITY OR TOWN IS PRESENT (185)	0.81 OF 26	0 5 30 21 XSQ= 4.19 PHI= -0.274 XP = 0.0406
81	TILT MORE TOWARD BEING THOSE WHERE NO CITY OR TOWN IS PRESENT, AND THE AVERAGE COMMUNITY SIZE IS SMALLER THAN 200 (135)	0.83 OF 30	81	TILT LESS TOWARD BEING THOSE WHERE NO CITY OR TOWN IS PRESENT, AND THE AVERAGE COMMUNITY SIZE IS SMALLER THAN 200 (135)	0.54 OF 26	5 12 25 14 XSQ= 4.42 PHI= -0.281 XP = 0.0355
82	TILT LESS TOWARD BEING THOSE WHERE A CITY OR TOWN IS PRESENT, OR THE AVERAGE COMMUNITY SIZE IS FIFTY OR GREATER (178)	0.67 OF 30	82	TILT MORE TOWARD BEING THOSE WHERE A CITY OR TOWN IS PRESENT, OR THE AVERAGE COMMUNITY SIZE IS FIFTY OR GREATER (178)	0.96 OF 26	20 25 10 1 XSQ= 5.92 PHI= -0.325 XP = 0.0150
86	LEAN TOWARD BEING THOSE WHERE THE LEVEL OF POLITICAL INTEGRATION IS THE AUTONOMOUS COMMUNITY, OR THE FAMILY (156) GPM	0.71 OF 35	86	LEAN TOWARD BEING THOSE WHERE THE LEVEL OF POLITICAL INTEGRATION IS THE LARGE STATE, THE LITTLE STATE, OR THE MINIMAL STATE (148) GPM	0.63 OF 35	10 22 25 13 XSQ= 6.97 PHI= -0.315 XP = 0.0083
96	TILT TOWARD BEING THOSE WHERE THE HIERARCHY OF NATIONAL JURISDICTION HAS NO LEVELS (156) GES,EA	0.67 OF 40	96	TILT TOWARD BEING THOSE WHERE THE HIERARCHY OF NATIONAL JURISDICTION HAS FOUR, THREE, TWO OR ONE LEVEL (174) GES,EA	0.62 OF 37	13 23 27 14 XSQ= 5.65 PHI= -0.271 XP = 0.0174
97	TILT MORE TOWARD BEING THOSE WHERE THE HIERARCHY OF LOCAL JURISDICTION HAS THREE OR TWO LEVELS (273) GES,EA	0.93 OF 41	97	TILT LESS TOWARD BEING THOSE WHERE THE HIERARCHY OF LOCAL JURISDICTION HAS THREE OR TWO LEVELS (273) GES,EA	0.70 OF 37	3 11 38 26 XSQ= 5.20 PHI= -0.258 XP = 0.0226

102	LEAN TOWARD BEING THOSE 0.67 OF 43 WHERE CLASS STRATIFICATION IS ABSENT (180)	102	LEAN TOWARD BEING THOSE 0.69 OF 39 WHERE CLASS STRATIFICATION IS PRESENT (203)	14 27 29 12 XSQ= 9.58 PHI= -0.342 XP = 0.0020
106	DRIFT TOWARD BEING THOSE 0.64 OF 14 WHERE CLASS STRATIFICATION, IF PRESENT, IS BASED ON WEALTH (77)	106	DRIFT TOWARD BEING THOSE 0.70 OF 27 WHERE CLASS STRATIFICATION, IF PRESENT, IS BASED ON SOMETHING OTHER THAN WEALTH (126)	9 8 5 19 XSQ= 3.25 PHI= 0.281 XP = 0.0716
130	TILT TOWARD BEING THOSE 0.77 OF 13 WHERE LEATHER WORKING IS MAINLY DONE BY FEMALES (45)	130	TILT TOWARD BEING THOSE 0.83 OF 6 WHERE LEATHER WORKING IS MAINLY DONE BY MALES (39)	3 5 10 1 XSQ= 3.89 PHI= -0.453 EP = 0.0408
131	TILT LESS TOWARD BEING THOSE 0.75 OF 24 WHERE THE CONSTRUCTION OF PERMANENT HOUSES OR THE ERECTION OF TEMPORARY DWELLINGS IS MAINLY DONE BY MALES (136)	131	IN ALL CASES ARE THOSE 1.00 OF 22 WHERE THE CONSTRUCTION OF PERMANENT HOUSES OR THE ERECTION OF TEMPORARY DWELLINGS IS MAINLY DONE BY MALES (136)	18 22 6 0 XSQ= 4.31 PHI= -0.306 XP = 0.0378
132	DRIFT TOWARD BEING THOSE 0.57 OF 14 WHERE ECONOMIC EXCHANGE DOES NOT INVOLVE THE USE OF MONEY (17) JMH	132	DRIFT TOWARD BEING THOSE 0.82 OF 11 WHERE ECONOMIC EXCHANGE INVOLVES THE USE OF MONEY (37) JMH	6 9 8 2 XSQ= 2.44 PHI= -0.313 EP = 0.0992
142	TILT TOWARD BEING THOSE 0.50 OF 14 WHERE THE LEVEL OF SOCIAL SANCTION IS PRIVATE SETTLEMENT, RATHER THAN PUBLIC CORPOREAL SANCTION OR PUBLIC PROPERTY SETTLEMENT (16) JMH	142	TILT TOWARD BEING THOSE 0.91 OF 11 WHERE THE LEVEL OF SOCIAL SANCTION IS PUBLIC CORPOREAL SANCTION OR PUBLIC PROPERTY SANCTION, RATHER THAN PRIVATE SETTLEMENT (38) JMH	7 10 7 1 XSQ= 3.04 PHI= -0.349 EP = 0.0421
176	DRIFT TOWARD BEING THOSE 0.67 OF 43 WHERE THE COMMUNITY IS OTHER THAN A CLAN-COMMUNITY OR A COMMUNITY STRUCTURED OR SEGMENTED ON A CLAN BASIS (213)	176	DRIFT TOWARD BEING THOSE 0.56 OF 39 WHERE THE COMMUNITY IS A CLAN-COMMUNITY OR A COMMUNITY STRUCTURED OR SEGMENTED ON A CLAN BASIS (169)	14 22 29 17 XSQ= 3.81 PHI= -0.215 XP = 0.0511
178	DRIFT MORE TOWARD BEING THOSE 0.81 OF 43 WHERE THE COMMUNITY IS OTHER THAN SEGMENTED ON A CLAN BASIS AND NON-EXOGAMOUS (295)	178	DRIFT LESS TOWARD BEING THOSE 0.62 OF 39 WHERE THE COMMUNITY IS OTHER THAN SEGMENTED ON A CLAN BASIS AND NON-EXOGAMOUS (295)	8 15 35 24 XSQ= 3.07 PHI= -0.194 XP = 0.0796
183	TILT LESS TOWARD BEING THOSE 0.65 OF 20 WHERE THE LARGEST NON-COGNATIC KIN GROUP IS SMALLER THAN A MOEITY, I. E., A PHRATRY OR SIB OR LINEAGE (218)	183	TILT MORE TOWARD BEING THOSE 0.94 OF 32 WHERE THE LARGEST NON-COGNATIC KIN GROUP IS SMALLER THAN A MOEITY, I. E., A PHRATRY OR SIB OR LINEAGE (218)	7 2 13 30 XSQ= 5.24 PHI= 0.317 XP = 0.0221

186	TILT MORE TOWARD BEING THOSE 0.77 OF 43 WHERE THE KIN GROUP IS OTHER THAN EXCLUSIVELY PATRILINEAL (250)	186	TILT LESS TOWARD BEING THOSE 0.51 OF 39 WHERE THE KIN GROUP IS OTHER THAN EXCLUSIVELY PATRILINEAL (250)	10 19 33 20 XSQ= 4.74 PHI= -0.240 XP = 0.0295
188	LEAN TOWARD BEING THOSE 0.53 OF 43 WHERE THE KIN GROUP IS EXCLUSIVELY COGNATIC (148)	188	LEAN TOWARD BEING THOSE 0.82 OF 39 WHERE THE KIN GROUP IS OTHER THAN EXCLUSIVELY COGNATIC (252)	23 7 20 32 XSQ= 9.65 PHI= 0.343 XP = 0.0019
192	TILT LESS TOWARD BEING THOSE 0.65 OF 43 OTHER THAN WHERE THE ONLY KIN GROUP PRESENT IS A KINDRED OR ELSE BILATERAL DESCENT IS INFERRED (289)	192	TILT MORE TOWARD BEING THOSE 0.90 OF 39 OTHER THAN WHERE THE ONLY KIN GROUP PRESENT IS A KINDRED OR ELSE BILATERAL DESCENT IS INFERRED (289)	15 4 28 35 XSQ= 5.65 PHI= 0.263 XP = 0.0174
196	TEND TO BE THOSE 0.68 OF 28 WHERE INDIVIDUAL RIGHTS IN REAL PROPERTY, OR RULES FOR INHERITANCE, ARE ABSENT (87)	196	TEND TO BE THOSE 0.90 OF 30 WHERE INDIVIDUAL RIGHTS IN REAL PROPERTY, AND RULES FOR INHERITANCE, ARE PRESENT (194)	9 27 19 3 XSQ= 18.21 PHI= -0.560 XP = 0.0000
241	DRIFT LESS TOWARD BEING THOSE 0.81 OF 27 WHERE THE FAMILY, IF EXTENDED, IS LARGE OR SMALL, RATHER THAN STEM (187)	241	IN ALL CASES ARE THOSE 1.00 OF 22 WHERE THE FAMILY, IF EXTENDED, IS LARGE OR SMALL, RATHER THAN STEM (187)	22 22 5 0 XSQ= 2.74 PHI= -0.237 XP = 0.0978
259	TILT TOWARD BEING THOSE 0.85 OF 13 WHERE THE SEVERITY OF MOTHER-IN-LAW AVOIDANCE IS HIGH (26) WNS	259	TILT TOWARD BEING THOSE 0.61 OF 18 WHERE THE SEVERITY OF MOTHER-IN-LAW AVOIDANCE IS LOW (20) WNS	11 7 2 11 XSQ= 4.74 PHI= 0.391 EP = 0.0250
260	DRIFT MORE TOWARD BEING THOSE 0.82 OF 17 WHERE THE AGE OF MALES AT MARRIAGE IS LESS THAN TWENTY (38) JKH	260	DRIFT LESS TOWARD BEING THOSE 0.55 OF 22 WHERE THE AGE OF MALES AT MARRIAGE IS LESS THAN TWENTY (38) JKH	14 12 3 10 XSQ= 2.20 PHI= 0.238 EP = 0.0933
306	DRIFT MORE TOWARD BEING THOSE 0.88 OF 16 WHERE THE EARLY DEPENDENCE SATISFACTION POTENTIAL IS HIGH (28) W-C	306	DRIFT LESS TOWARD BEING THOSE 0.55 OF 20 WHERE THE EARLY DEPENDENCE SATISFACTION POTENTIAL IS HIGH (28) W-C	14 11 2 9 XSQ= 3.03 PHI= 0.290 EP = 0.0671
309	DRIFT TOWARD BEING THOSE 0.70 OF 20 WHERE ORAL SOCIALIZATION ANXIETY IS LOW (27) W-C	309	DRIFT TOWARD BEING THOSE 0.62 OF 21 WHERE ORAL SOCIALIZATION ANXIETY IS HIGH (26) W-C	6 13 14 8 XSQ= 3.01 PHI= -0.271 XP = 0.0828

314	TILT MORE TOWARD BEING THOSE 0.92 OF 24 WHERE THE INCIDENCE OF MOTHER-CHILD HOUSEHOLDS IS LOW (61) W-C,S	314	TILT LESS TOWARD BEING THOSE 0.60 OF 30 WHERE THE INCIDENCE OF MOTHER-CHILD HOUSEHOLDS IS LOW (61) W-D,S	2 12 22 18 XSQ= 5.41 PHI= -0.317 XP = 0.0200
315	DRIFT LESS TOWARD BEING THOSE 0.59 OF 17 WHERE MOTHER AND NURSING CHILD CUSTOMARILY SLEEP IN THE SAME BED (37) W-C,S	315	DRIFT MORE TOWARD BEING THOSE 0.89 OF 18 WHERE MOTHER AND NURSING CHILD CUSTOMARILY SLEEP IN THE SAME BED (37) W-D,S	10 16 7 2 XSQ= 2.71 PHI= -0.278 EP = 0.0599
320	TILT MORE TOWARD BEING THOSE 0.88 OF 25 WHERE THE DEGREE OF REDUCTION OF THE INFANT'S DRIVES IS HIGH (45) B-B-C	320	TILT LESS TOWARD BEING THOSE 0.53 OF 30 WHERE THE DEGREE OF REDUCTION OF THE INFANT'S DRIVES IS HIGH (45) B-B-C	22 16 3 14 XSQ= 6.14 PHI= 0.334 XP = 0.0132
324	DRIFT TOWARD BEING THOSE 0.64 OF 25 WHERE THE PAIN INFLICTED ON THE INFANT BY THE NURTURANT AGENT IS LOW OR NEGLIGIBLE (32) B-B-C	324	DRIFT TOWARD BEING THOSE 0.64 OF 28 WHERE THE PAIN INFLICTED ON THE INFANT BY THE NURTURANT AGENT IS HIGH (34) B-B-C	9 18 16 10 XSQ= 3.17 PHI= -0.245 XP = 0.0749
325	TILT TOWARD BEING THOSE 0.63 OF 27 WHERE THE DEGREE OF DIFFUSION AMONG THE INFANT'S NURTURANT AGENTS IS LOW (32) B-B-C	325	TILT TOWARD BEING THOSE 0.70 OF 30 WHERE THE DEGREE OF DIFFUSION AMONG THE INFANT'S NURTURANT AGENTS IS HIGH (42) B-B-C	10 21 17 9 XSQ= 4.97 PHI= -0.295 XP = 0.0258
326	TILT TOWARD BEING THOSE 0.72 OF 25 WHERE THE INFERRED TRANSITION ANXIETY BETWEEN INFANCY AND CHILDHOOD IS LOW (35) B-B-C	326	TILT TOWARD BEING THOSE 0.63 OF 30 WHERE THE INFERRED TRANSITION ANXIETY BETWEEN INFANCY AND CHILDHOOD IS HIGH (32) B-B-C	7 19 18 11 XSQ= 5.49 PHI= -0.316 XP = 0.0192
330	DRIFT TOWARD BEING THOSE 0.67 OF 27 WHERE THE AGE OF THE INFANT AT TIME OF WEANING IS 2.5 YEARS OR HIGHER (34) B-B-C	330	DRIFT TOWARD BEING THOSE 0.60 OF 30 WHERE THE AGE OF THE INFANT AT TIME OF WEANING IS LOWER THAN 2.5 YEARS (36) B-B-C	18 12 9 18 XSQ= 3.05 PHI= 0.231 XP = 0.0805
335	TILT TOWARD BEING THOSE 0.90 OF 10 WHERE INITIAL INDULGENCE OF DEPENDENCY IS HIGH (20) WNS	335	TILT TOWARD BEING THOSE 0.50 OF 18 WHERE INITIAL INDULGENCE OF DEPENDENCY IS LOW (18) WNS	9 9 1 9 XSQ= 2.91 PHI= 0.322 EP = 0.0484
360	DRIFT MORE TOWARD BEING THOSE 0.92 OF 12 WHERE ADOLESCENT PEER GROUPS ARE PRESENT ONLY IN A SETTING OF LEISURE, OR ELSE ARE ABSENT (23) JKH	360	DRIFT LESS TOWARD BEING THOSE 0.54 OF 13 WHERE ADOLESCENT PEER GROUPS ARE PRESENT ONLY IN A SETTING OF LEISURE, OR ELSE ARE ABSENT (23) JKH	1 6 11 7 XSQ= 2.75 PHI= -0.332 EP = 0.0730

421	DRIFT TOWARD BEING THOSE 0.54 OF 24 WHERE KILLING, TORTURING, OR MUTILATING OF THE ENEMY IS STRONGLY OR MODERATELY EMPHASIZED (37) PES	421	DRIFT TOWARD BEING THOSE 0.73 OF 26 WHERE KILLING, TORTURING, OR MUTILATING OF THE ENEMY IS NEGLIGIBLY EMPHASIZED (47) PES	13 7 11 19 XSQ= 2.81 PHI= 0.237 XP = 0.0938
424	DRIFT MORE TOWARD BEING THOSE 0.93 OF 14 WHERE RELIGIOUS SPECIALISTS ARE PART-TIME, RATHER THAN FULL-TIME (33) JMH	424	DRIFT LESS TOWARD BEING THOSE 0.55 OF 11 WHERE RELIGIOUS SPECIALISTS ARE PART-TIME, RATHER THAN FULL-TIME (33) JMH	1 5 13 6 XSQ= 3.08 PHI= -0.351 EP = 0.0561
435	IN ALL CASES ARE THOSE 1.00 OF 6 WHERE ABANDONMENT OF THE HOUSE OF THE DEAD IS PRACTICED (12) LWS	435	IN ALL CASES ARE THOSE 1.00 OF 6 WHERE ABANDONMENT OF THE HOUSE OF THE DEAD IS NOT PRACTICED (19) LWS	6 0 0 6 XSQ= 8.33 PHI= 0.833 EP = 0.0022
451	TILT TOWARD BEING THOSE 0.71 OF 7 WHERE TOTEMISM IS UNIMPORTANT OR ABSENT (12) LWS	451	IN ALL CASES ARE THOSE 1.00 OF 5 WHERE TOTEMISM IS PRESENT (15) LWS	2 5 5 0 XSQ= 3.54 PHI= -0.543 EP = 0.0278
452	TILT TOWARD BEING THOSE 0.81 OF 16 WHERE TOTEMISM WITH FOOD TABOOS IS ABSENT (24) WNS	452	TILT TOWARD BEING THOSE 0.59 OF 22 WHERE TOTEMISM WITH FOOD TABOOS IS PRESENT (19) WNS	3 13 13 9 XSQ= 4.64 PHI= -0.349 EP = 0.0202
458	LEAN TOWARD BEING THOSE 0.83 OF 30 WHERE GAMES, IF PRESENT, DO NOT INCLUDE GAMES OF STRATEGY (119) R-A-B,EA	458	LEAN TOWARD BEING THOSE 0.56 OF 27 WHERE GAMES, IF PRESENT, INCLUDE GAMES OF STRATEGY (52) R-A-B,EA	5 15 25 12 XSQ= 7.81 PHI= -0.370 XP = 0.0052
480	TILT TOWARD BEING THOSE 0.88 OF 8 WHERE COMPLEXITY OF ARTISTIC DESIGN IS LOW (15) HB	480	TILT TOWARD BEING THOSE 0.67 OF 12 WHERE COMPLEXITY OF ARTISTIC DESIGN IS HIGH (14) HB	1 8 7 4 XSQ= 3.71 PHI= -0.431 EP = 0.0281

51 CULTURES
WHERE SUBSISTENCE IS PRIMARILY BY
FOOD PRODUCTION -- I. E., AGRICULTURE
OR HUSBANDRY -- RATHER THAN BY
GATHERING (253)

51 CULTURES
WHERE SUBSISTENCE IS PRIMARILY BY
FOOD GATHERING -- I. E., HUNTING,
FISHING, OR COLLECTING -- RATHER THAN
FOOD PRODUCTION (147)

BACKGROUND ON PAGE 74

BOTH SUBJECT AND PREDICATE

253 IN LEFT COLUMN

AJIE	AKHA	ALBANIANS	ALORESE	AMBA	AMERICANS	ARAPESH	ARAUCANIANS	ARYANS	ASHANTI
ATAYAL	AYMARA	AZANDE	AZTEC	BABWA	BALINESE	BAMBARA	BAMILEKE	BANDA	BARABRA
BARI	BASQUES	BASSERI	BATAK	BAYA	BEJA	BELU	BEMBA	BENGALI	BETE
BHUIYA	BIRIFOR	BLACK CARIB	BOERS	BRAZILIANS	BULGARIANS	BUNLAP	BURMESE	BURUSHO	BURYAT
CAGABA	CAMBA	CAMBODIANS	CARINYA	CAYAPA	CHAGGA	CHEREMIS	CHERKESS	CHIBCHA	CHINANTEC
CHIRIGUANO	CHOCO	CHORTI	COCHITI	COORG	CUNA	CZECHS	DAGUR	DARD	DILLING
DOBUANS	DOGON	CUSUN	DUTCH	EGYPTIANS	ENGA	FANG	FON	FUTAJALONKE	GANDA
GARO	GISU	GOAJIRO	GOND	GURE	HANO	HANUNOO	HASANIA	HAZARA	HEBREWS
HEHE	HERERO	HO	HUICHOL	HUTSUL	IBAN	IFUGAO	ILA	INCA	INGASSANA
IRAQW	IRISH	JAPANESE	JAVANESE	JEMEZ	JIVARO	JUKUN	KABYLE	KACHIN	KALMYK
KAPAUKU	KAREN	KATAB	KAZAK	KERAKI	KERALA	KHALKA	KHASI	KHEVSUR	KIKUYU
KISSI	KOHISTANI	KOL	KONSO	KOREANS	KPE	KUBA	KUMYK	KURTATCHI	LAKHER
LAMBA	LAMET	LANGO	LAPPS	LAU	LEPCHA	LHOTA NAGA	LIFU	LOLO	LUO
MACASSARESE	MAGUZAWA	MALAYS	MAM	MAMBILA	MAMVU	MANCHU	MANDAN	MANGAIANS	MARGI
MARQUESANS	MARSHALLESE	MASAI	MATAKAM	MAYA	MAZATECO	MBUGWE	MBUNDU	MENDE	MENTAWEI
MERINA	MIAO	MIN CHINESE	MINANGKABAU	MINCHIA	MNONG GAR	MONGO	MONGUOR	MOSSI	MOTA
MZAB	NANDI	NDEMBU	NGONI	NICOBARESE	NUER	NUPE	NURI	NYAKYUSA	NYANEKA
NYARO	NYORO	OKINAWANS	ORAON	PAEZ	PAIWAN	PALAUANS	PATHAN	PAWNEE	PENDE
PONAPEANS	POPOLUCA	PORTUGUESE	PUKAPUKA	PURUM	REGEIBAT	RIFFIANS	ROMANS	ROTINESE	ROTUMANS
RUNDI	RWALA	SAGADA	SAMOANS	SANDAWE	SANTAL	SEMINOLE	SENIANG	SERBS	SHILLUK
SHLUH	SIMBOESE	SINCHI	SINHALESE	SIUAI	SIWANS	SOMALI	SONGHAI	SOTHO	SUBANUN
SWAZI	SYRIANS	TAGBANUA	TALAMANCA	TALLENSI	TAMIL	TANALA	TANIMBARESE	TAOS	TARAHUMARA
TEDA	TENDA	TENETEHARA	TERA	TESO	THAI	THONGA	TIBETANS	TIGRINYA	TIV
TODA	TORAJA	TOTONAC	TROBRIAND	TUNEBO	TURKMEN	TZELTAL	ULAWANS	VENDA	VIETNAMESE
WALLOONS	WANTOAT	WICHITA	WOGEO	WOLEAIANS	WOLOF	WUTE	YAKO	YAO	YAPESE
YOMBE	YORUBA	ZUNI							

147 IN RIGHT COLUMN

ABIPON	ABOR	AINU	ALACALUF	ANDAMANESE	APINAYE	ARANDA	ATSUGEWI	AWEIKOMA	BACAIRI
BAJUN	BERGDAMA	BHIL	BORORO	BOTOCUDO	BOZO	BUDUMA	CADUVEO	CALLINAGO	CAMAYURA
CARAJA	CARIB	CHAMACOCO	CHENCHU	CHEROKEE	CHEYENNE	CHIR-APACHE	CHOROTI	CHUKCHEE	COMANCHE
COPR ESKIMO	CREE	CREEK	CROW	DELAWARE	DIEGUENO	DIERI	DOROBO	ELLICE	EYAK
FOX	GILBERTESE	GILYAK	GROS VENTRE	GUAHIBO	GUATO	HAIDA	HASINAI	HAVASUPAI	HAWAIIANS
HUKUNDIKA	HURON	ICELANDERS	INGALIK	KARIERA	KASKA	KET	KIOW-APACHE	KORYAK	KUNG
KUTENAI	KWAKIUTL	LAKALAI	LESU	LOZI	LUBA	MANIHIKI	MANUS	MAORI	MARICOPA
MATACO	MBUTI	MIAMI	MISKITO	MIWOK	MOTILON	MUNDURUCU	MURINBATA	MURNGIN	NABESNA
NAMA	NAMBICUARA	NASKAPI	NATCHEZ	NAVAHO	NOMLAKI	NUNIVAK	OJIBWA	OMAHA	ONA
ONTONG-JAVA	PALIKUR	PAPAGO	PARAUJANO	PENOBSCOT	PURARI	RAROIANS	SAMOYED	SANPOIL	SARAMACCA

SARSI TERENA TRUMAI WAICA YAHGAN SELUNG TETCN TSHIMSHIAN WAPISHANA YAKUT SEMANG TIKOPIA TUBATULABAL WARCPEN YARURO SERI TIMBIRA TUCANO WARRAU YOKUTS SHERENTE TIMUCUA TUCUNA WASHO YUKAGHIR SIRIONO TIWI TUPINAMBA WIKMUNKAN YUKI TAPIRAPE TOKELAU TURKANA WINNEBAGO YUROK TAREUMIUT TOLOWA TWANA WITOTO TEHUELCHE TRISTAN UTE YABARANA TENINO TRUKESE VEDDA YAGUA

3	TEND LESS TO BE THCSE LOCATED CUTSIDE CF AFRICA (320)	0.72 OF 253	3	TEND MORE TO BE THOSE LOCATED OUTSIDE OF AFRICA (320)	0.93 OF 147	70 10 183 137	XSQ= 24.01 PHI= 0.245 XP = 0.0000
4	TEND LESS TO BE THCSE LOCATED OUTSIDE CF THE CIRCUM-MEDITERRANEAN (355)	0.83 OF 253	4	TEND MORE TO BE THOSE LOCATED OUTSIDE OF THE CIRCUM-MEDITERRANEAN (355)	0.98 OF 147	42 3 211 144	XSQ= 18.31 PHI= 0.214 XP = 0.0000
5	LEAN LESS TOWARC BEING THOSE LOCATED CUTSIDE OF EAST EURASIA (330)	0.78 OF 253	5	LEAN MORE TOWARD BEING THOSE LOCATED OUTSIDE OF EAST EURASIA (330)	0.90 OF 147	55 15 198 132	XSQ= 7.79 PHI= 0.140 XP = 0.0053
8	TEND MORE TO BE THCSE LOCATED OUTSIDE CF NORTH AMERICA (330)	0.94 OF 253	8	TEND LESS TO BE THOSE LOCATED OUTSIDE OF NORTH AMERICA (330)	0.63 OF 147	16 54 237 93	XSQ= 57.47 PHI= -0.379 XP = 0.
9	TEND MORE TO BE THCSE LOCATED CUTSIDE CF SOUTH AMERICA (335)	0.91 OF 253	9	TEND LESS TO BE THOSE LOCATED OUTSIDE OF SOUTH AMERICA (335)	0.71 OF 147	22 43 231 104	XSQ= 27.38 PHI= -0.262 XP = 0.0000
15	TEND TO BE THOSE WHERE THE LATITUDE IS LESS THAN TWENTY DEGREES (217)	0.61 OF 253	15	TEND TO BE THOSE WHERE THE LATITUDE IS TWENTY DEGREES OR GREATER (183)	0.58 OF 147	98 85 155 62	XSQ= 12.89 PHI= -0.180 XP = 0.0003
33	DRIFT MORE TOWARD BEING THOSE WHERE THE NATURAL ENVIRONMENT IS OTHER THAN 'VERY HARSH,' I.E., DESERT, DESERT GRASSES AND SHRUBS, TUNCRA, OR HIGH PLATEAU STEPPE (341) FWM	0.88 OF 253	33	DRIFT LESS TOWARD BEING THOSE WHERE THE NATURAL ENVIRONMENT IS OTHER THAN 'VERY HARSH,' I.E., DESERT, DESERT GRASSES AND SHRUBS, TUNDRA, OR HIGH PLATEAU STEPPE (341) FWM	0.81 OF 147	31 28 222 119	XSQ= 2.89 PHI= -0.085 XP = 0.0889
36	TILT MORE TOWARD BEING THOSE WHERE THE NATURAL ENVIRONMENT IS OTHER THAN 'VERY HARSH,' OR SUB-TROPICAL BUSH, OR TEMPERATE GRASSLAND (292) FWM	0.77 OF 253	36	TILT LESS TOWARD BEING THOSE WHERE THE NATURAL ENVIRONMENT IS OTHER THAN 'VERY HARSH,' OR SUB-TROPICAL BUSH, OR TEMPERATE GRASSLAND (292) FWM	0.66 OF 147	58 50 195 97	XSQ= 5.25 PHI= -0.115 XP = 0.0219

42	TILT LESS TOWARD BEING THOSE WHERE THE NATURAL ENVIRONMENT IS OTHER THAN TROPICAL OR SUB-TROPICAL RAIN FOREST, OR MONSOON FOREST (244) FWM	0.57 OF 253	TILT MORE TOWARD BEING THOSE WHERE THE NATURAL ENVIRONMENT IS OTHER THAN TROPICAL OR SUB-TROPICAL RAIN FOREST, OR MONSOON FOREST (244) FWM	0.68 OF 147	109 47 144 100 XSQ= 4.37 PHI= 0.105 XP = 0.0366
44	TEND TO BE THOSE WHERE SETTLEMENTS ARE FIXED (222)	0.87 OF 206	TEND TO BE THOSE WHERE SETTLEMENTS ARE NON-FIXED (110)	0.66 OF 126	179 43 27 83 XSQ= 95.88 PHI= 0.537 XP = 0.
45	TILT LESS TOWARD BEING THOSE WHERE SETTLEMENTS, IF FIXED, ARE COMPACT, RATHER THAN NON-COMPACT (149)	0.63 OF 179	TILT MORE TOWARD BEING THOSE WHERE SETTLEMENTS, IF FIXED, ARE COMPACT, RATHER THAN NON-COMPACT (149)	0.84 OF 43	113 36 66 7 XSQ= 5.76 PHI= -0.161 XP = 0.0164
46	TEND MORE TO BE THOSE OTHER THAN WHERE SETTLEMENTS ARE NON-FIXED AND MOVEMENT IS NOMADIC (260)	0.94 OF 206	TEND LESS TO BE THOSE OTHER THAN WHERE SETTLEMENTS ARE NON-FIXED AND MOVEMENT IS NOMADIC (260)	0.53 OF 126	13 59 193 67 XSQ= 73.19 PHI= -0.470 XP = 0.
47	DRIFT TOWARD BEING THOSE WHERE, IF SETTLEMENTS ARE NON-FIXED, MOVEMENT IS NON-NOMADIC, RATHER THAN NOMADIC (38)	0.52 OF 27	DRIFT TOWARD BEING THOSE WHERE, IF SETTLEMENTS ARE NON-FIXED, MOVEMENT IS NOMADIC, RATHER THAN NON-NOMADIC (72)	0.71 OF 83	13 59 14 24 XSQ= 3.78 PHI= -0.185 XP = 0.0519
62	TEND TO BE THOSE WHERE HUSBANDRY OF SOME KIND IS PRESENT (228)	0.76 OF 253	TEND TO BE THOSE WHERE HUSBANDRY OF ANY KIND IS ABSENT (172)	0.76 OF 147	193 35 60 112 XSQ= 102.33 PHI= 0.506 XP = 0.
71	TEND TO BE THOSE WHERE METAL WORKING IS PRESENT (98)	0.65 OF 133	TEND TO BE THOSE WHERE METAL WORKING IS ABSENT (153)	0.90 OF 118	86 12 47 106 XSQ= 75.74 PHI= 0.549 XP = 0.
73	TEND TO BE THOSE WHERE WEAVING IS PRESENT (118)	0.60 OF 133	TEND TO BE THOSE WHERE WEAVING IS ABSENT (130)	0.67 OF 115	80 38 53 77 XSQ= 17.10 PHI= 0.263 XP = 0.0000
74	TEND TO BE THOSE WHERE POTTERY IS PRESENT (145)	0.73 OF 123	TEND TO BE THOSE WHERE POTTERY IS ABSENT (93)	0.52 OF 115	90 55 33 60 XSQ= 14.99 PHI= 0.251 XP = 0.0001

80	TEND LESS TO BE THOSE WHERE NO CITY OR TOWN IS PRESENT (185)	0.73 OF 143	80	IN ALL CASES ARE THOSE WHERE NO CITY OR TOWN IS PRESENT (185)	1.00 OF 81	39 0 104 81 XSQ= 24.88 PHI= 0.333 XP = 0.0000
81	TEND TO BE THOSE WHERE A CITY OR TOWN IS PRESENT, OR THE AVERAGE COMMUNITY SIZE IS 200 OR GREATER (89)	0.55 OF 143	81	TEND TO BE THOSE WHERE NO CITY OR TOWN IS PRESENT, AND THE AVERAGE COMMUNITY SIZE IS SMALLER THAN 200 (135)	0.86 OF 81	78 11 65 70 XSQ= 34.55 PHI= 0.393 XP = 0.
83	LEAN LESS TOWARD BEING THOSE WHERE, WITH NO CITY AND NO TOWN PRESENT, THE AVERAGE COMMUNITY SIZE IS SMALLER THAN 200, RATHER THAN BETWEEN 200 AND 999 (135)	0.66 OF 99	83	LEAN MORE TOWARD BEING THOSE WHERE, WITH NO CITY AND NO TOWN PRESENT, THE AVERAGE COMMUNITY SIZE IS SMALLER THAN 200, RATHER THAN BETWEEN 200 AND 999 (135)	0.86 OF 81	34 11 65 70 XSQ= 9.17 PHI= 0.226 XP = 0.0025
86	TEND TO BE THOSE WHERE THE LEVEL OF POLITICAL INTEGRATION IS THE LARGE STATE, THE LITTLE STATE, OR THE MINIMAL STATE (148) GPM	0.66 OF 178	86	TEND TO BE THOSE WHERE THE LEVEL OF POLITICAL INTEGRATION IS THE AUTONOMOUS COMMUNITY, OR THE FAMILY (156) GPM	0.75 OF 126	117 31 61 95 XSQ= 48.32 PHI= 0.399 XP = 0.
91	TILT TOWARD BEING THOSE WHERE SOCIETAL COMPLEXITY IS HIGH (18) F-W	0.60 OF 25	91	TILT TOWARD BEING THOSE WHERE SOCIETAL COMPLEXITY IS LOW (22) F-W	0.80 OF 15	15 3 10 12 XSQ= 4.55 PHI= 0.337 EP = 0.0217
96	TEND TO BE THOSE WHERE THE HIERARCHY OF NATIONAL JURISDICTION HAS FOUR, THREE, TWO OR ONE LEVEL (174) GES,EA	0.67 OF 203	96	TEND TO BE THOSE WHERE THE HIERARCHY OF NATIONAL JURISDICTION HAS NO LEVELS (156) GES,EA	0.70 OF 127	136 38 67 89 XSQ= 41.61 PHI= 0.355 XP = 0.
97	LEAN LESS TOWARD BEING THOSE WHERE THE HIERARCHY OF LOCAL JURISDICTION HAS THREE OR TWO LEVELS (273) GES,EA	0.77 OF 204	97	LEAN MORE TOWARD BEING THOSE WHERE THE HIERARCHY OF LOCAL JURISDICTION HAS THREE OR TWO LEVELS (273) GES,EA	0.91 OF 127	47 11 157 116 XSQ= 10.22 PHI= 0.176 XP = 0.0014
98	TEND MORE TO BE THOSE WHERE THE HIERARCHY OF LOCAL JURISDICTION HAS FOUR OR THREE LEVELS (238) GES,EA	0.80 OF 204	98	TEND LESS TO BE THOSE WHERE THE HIERARCHY OF LOCAL JURISDICTION HAS FOUR OR THREE LEVELS (238) GES,EA	0.58 OF 127	164 74 40 53 XSQ= 17.89 PHI= 0.232 XP = 0.0000
99	TILT MORE TOWARD BEING THOSE WHERE, WITH NATIONAL HIERARCHY ABSENT, THE HIERARCHY OF LOCAL JURISDICTION HAS FOUR OR THREE LEVELS (93) GES,EA	0.72 OF 67	99	TILT LESS TOWARD BEING THOSE WHERE, WITH NATIONAL HIERARCHY ABSENT, THE HIERARCHY OF LOCAL JURISDICTION HAS FOUR OR THREE LEVELS (93) GES,EA	0.51 OF 89	48 45 19 44 XSQ= 6.21 PHI= 0.199 XP = 0.0127

100	TEND MORE TO BE THOSE WHERE HIERARCHIES ARE MORE COMPLEX THAN THE 'SIMPLEST,' I. E., MORE COMPLEX THAN TWO LOCAL LEVELS WITH NO NATIONAL LEVELS (267) GES,EA	0.91 OF 203	100	TEND LESS TO BE THOSE WHERE HIERARCHIES ARE MORE COMPLEX THAN THE 'SIMPLEST,' I. E., MORE COMPLEX THAN TWO LOCAL LEVELS WITH NO NATIONAL LEVELS (267) GES,EA	0.65 OF 127	184 83 19 44 XSQ= 30.72 PHI= 0.305 XP = 0.
102	TEND TO BE THOSE WHERE CLASS STRATIFICATION IS PRESENT (203)	0.68 OF 236	102	TEND TO BE THOSE WHERE CLASS STRATIFICATION IS ABSENT (180)	0.71 OF 147	161 42 75 105 XSQ= 55.58 PHI= 0.381 XP = 0.
106	LEAN TOWARD BEING THOSE WHERE CLASS STRATIFICATION, IF PRESENT, IS BASED ON SOMETHING OTHER THAN WEALTH (126)	0.67 OF 161	106	LEAN TOWARD BEING THOSE WHERE CLASS STRATIFICATION, IF PRESENT, IS BASED ON WEALTH (77)	0.57 OF 42	53 24 108 18 XSQ= 7.31 PHI= -0.190 XP = 0.0069
107	LEAN LESS TOWARD BEING THOSE WHERE CLASS STRATIFICATION, IF PRESENT, IS BASED ON SOMETHING OTHER THAN OCCUPATIONAL STATUS (160)	0.74 OF 161	107	LEAN MORE TOWARD BEING THOSE WHERE CLASS STRATIFICATION, IF PRESENT, IS BASED ON SOMETHING OTHER THAN OCCUPATIONAL STATUS (160)	0.98 OF 42	42 1 119 41 XSQ= 9.84 PHI= 0.220 XP = 0.0017
109	TEND LESS TO BE THOSE WHERE CASTES ARE ABSENT (317)	0.79 OF 221	109	TEND MORE TO BE THOSE WHERE CASTES ARE ABSENT (317)	0.97 OF 147	46 5 175 142 XSQ= 20.99 PHI= 0.239 XP = 0.0000
110	TEND TO BE THOSE WHERE SLAVERY IS PRESENT (163)	0.52 OF 236	110	TEND TO BE THOSE WHERE SLAVERY IS ABSENT (218)	0.72 OF 145	123 40 113 105 XSQ= 21.09 PHI= 0.235 XP = 0.0000
116	TILT TOWARD BEING THOSE WHERE OCCUPATIONAL SPECIALIZATION IS FULL-TIME, WHETHER OR NOT FOR SURPLUS PRODUCTION (20) JMH	0.50 OF 34	116	TILT TOWARD BEING THOSE WHERE OCCUPATIONAL SPECIALIZATION IS PART-TIME ONLY (34) JMH	0.85 OF 20	17 3 17 17 XSQ= 5.20 PHI= 0.310 XP = 0.0226
120	DRIFT TOWARD BEING THOSE WHERE THE CRAFT SPECIALIZATION SCORE IS HIGH OR MEDIUM (36) WME	0.77 OF 35	120	DRIFT TOWARD BEING THOSE WHERE THE CRAFT SPECIALIZATION SCORE IS LOW (17) WME	0.50 OF 18	27 9 8 9 XSQ= 2.87 PHI= 0.233 XP = 0.0902
129	TILT LESS TOWARD BEING THOSE WHERE WEAVING IS MAINLY DONE BY FEMALES (73)	0.62 OF 69	129	TILT MORE TOWARD BEING THOSE WHERE WEAVING IS MAINLY DONE BY FEMALES (73)	0.86 OF 35	26 5 43 30 XSQ= 5.01 PHI= 0.219 XP = 0.0252

130	TEND TO BE THOSE WHERE LEATHER WORKING IS MAINLY DONE BY MALES (39)	0.84 OF 31	130	TEND TO BE THOSE WHERE LEATHER WORKING IS MAINLY DONE BY FEMALES (45)	0.75 OF 53	26 13 5 40 XSQ= 25.36 PHI= 0.549 XP = 0.0000
131	TEND MORE TO BE THOSE WHERE THE CONSTRUCTION OF PERMANENT HOUSES OR THE ERECTION OF TEMPORARY DWELLINGS IS MAINLY DONE BY MALES (136)	0.96 OF 83	131	TEND LESS TO BE THOSE WHERE THE CONSTRUCTION OF PERMANENT HOUSES OR THE ERECTION OF TEMPORARY DWELLINGS IS MAINLY DONE BY MALES (136)	0.76 OF 74	80 56 3 18 XSQ= 12.75 PHI= 0.285 XP = 0.0004
132	LEAN TOWARD BEING THOSE WHERE ECONOMIC EXCHANGE INVOLVES THE USE OF MONEY (37) JMH	0.85 OF 34	132	LEAN TOWARD BEING THOSE WHERE ECONOMIC EXCHANGE DOES NOT INVOLVE THE USE OF MONEY (17) JMH	0.60 OF 20	29 8 5 12 XSQ= 9.97 PHI= 0.430 XP = 0.0016
133	TILT TOWARD BEING THOSE WHERE CONTRACTED DEBTS ARE SIGNIFICANTLY PRESENT (17) GES	0.68 OF 22	133	TILT TOWARD BEING THOSE WHERE CONTRACTED DEBTS ARE MODERATELY PRESENT OR ABSENT (17) GES	0.83 OF 12	15 2 7 10 XSQ= 6.31 PHI= 0.431 EP = 0.0104
138	DRIFT TOWARD BEING THOSE WHERE SUPERORDINATE JUSTICE IS PRESENT (22) BBW	0.70 OF 23	138	DRIFT TOWARD BEING THOSE WHERE SUPERORDINATE JUSTICE IS ABSENT (18) BBW	0.65 OF 17	16 6 7 11 XSQ= 3.36 PHI= 0.290 EP = 0.0534
143	TILT TOWARD BEING THOSE WHERE THE RATIO OF RESTITUTIVE TO REPRESSIVE SANCTIONS IS HIGH (20) WME	0.50 OF 34	143	TILT TOWARD BEING THOSE WHERE THE RATIO OF RESTITUTIVE TO REPRESSIVE SANCTIONS IS MEDIUM OR LOW (32) WME	0.83 OF 18	17 3 17 15 XSQ= 4.21 PHI= 0.284 XP = 0.0403
144	DRIFT TOWARD BEING THOSE WHERE THE RATIO OF RESTITUTIVE TO REPRESSIVE SANCTIONS IS HIGH OR MEDIUM (27) WME	0.62 OF 34	144	DRIFT TOWARD BEING THOSE WHERE THE RATIO OF RESTITUTIVE TO REPRESSIVE SANCTIONS IS LOW (25) WME	0.67 OF 18	21 6 13 12 XSQ= 2.76 PHI= 0.230 XP = 0.0968
147	TEND TO BE THOSE WHERE CODIFIED LAWS ARE PRESENT (20) LWS	0.94 OF 17	147	TEND TO BE THOSE WHERE CODIFIED LAWS ARE UNIMPORTANT OR ABSENT (13) LWS	0.75 OF 16	16 4 1 12 XSQ= 13.72 PHI= 0.645 EP = 0.0001
152	TILT TOWARD BEING THOSE WHERE THE DIFFERENTIATION OF THE JURIDICAL AGENCY FROM THE MEDICAL AGENCY IS HIGH (10) MJ	0.75 OF 12	152	TILT TOWARD BEING THOSE WHERE THE DIFFERENTIATION OF THE JURIDICAL AGENCY FROM THE MEDICAL AGENCY IS LOW (10) MJ	0.88 OF 8	9 1 3 7 XSQ= 5.21 PHI= 0.510 EP = 0.0198

163	LEAN TOWARD BEING THOSE WHERE THE EMPHASIS ON INDIVIDUAL VOLITION AS THE CAUSE OF CRIME IS HIGH (7) MJ	0.70 OF 10	163	IN ALL CASES ARE THOSE WHERE THE EMPHASIS ON INDIVIDUAL VOLITION AS THE CAUSE OF CRIME IS LOW (10) MJ	1.00 OF 7	7 0 3 7 XSQ= 5.69 PHI= 0.579 EP = 0.0098
175	TILT LESS TOWARD BEING THOSE WHERE THE COMMUNITY IS 'KIN-HETEROGENEOUS,' I. E. OTHER THAN A CLAN COMMUNITY OR A DEME (260)	0.64 OF 243	175	TILT MORE TOWARD BEING THOSE WHERE THE COMMUNITY IS 'KIN-HETEROGENEOUS,' I. E. OTHER THAN A CLAN COMMUNITY OR A DEME (260)	0.75 OF 139	87 35 156 104 XSQ= 4.11 PHI= 0.104 XP = 0.0425
176	LEAN TOWARD BEING THOSE WHERE THE COMMUNITY IS A CLAN-COMMUNITY OR A COMMUNITY STRUCTURED OR SEGMENTED ON A CLAN BASIS (169)	0.50 OF 243	176	LEAN TOWARD BEING THOSE WHERE THE COMMUNITY IS OTHER THAN A CLAN-COMMUNITY OR A COMMUNITY STRUCTURED OR SEGMENTED ON A CLAN BASIS (213)	0.66 OF 139	122 47 121 92 XSQ= 8.98 PHI= 0.153 XP = 0.0027
177	TILT LESS TOWARD BEING THOSE WHERE THE COMMUNITY IS OTHER THAN A SINGLE CLAN-COMMUNITY AND EXOGAMOUS (305)	0.77 OF 243	177	TILT MORE TOWARD BEING THOSE WHERE THE COMMUNITY IS OTHER THAN A SINGLE CLAN-COMMUNITY AND EXOGAMOUS (305)	0.86 OF 139	57 20 186 119 XSQ= 3.97 PHI= 0.102 XP = 0.0463
179	TEND MORE TO BE THOSE WHERE THE COMMUNITY IS OTHER THAN STRUCTURED ON A NON-CLAN BASIS AND COMMONLY EXOGAMOUS (340)	0.93 OF 243	179	TEND LESS TO BE THOSE WHERE THE COMMUNITY IS OTHER THAN STRUCTURED ON A NON-CLAN BASIS AND COMMONLY EXOGAMOUS (340)	0.81 OF 139	16 26 227 113 XSQ= 12.06 PHI= -0.178 XP = 0.0005
183	TEND MORE TO BE THOSE WHERE THE LARGEST NON-COGNATIC KIN GROUP IS SMALLER THAN A MOEITY, I. E., A PHRATRY OR SIB OR LINEAGE (218)	0.95 OF 184	183	TEND LESS TO BE THOSE WHERE THE LARGEST NON-COGNATIC KIN GROUP IS SMALLER THAN A MOEITY, I. E., A PHRATRY OR SIB OR LINEAGE (218)	0.65 OF 68	10 24 174 44 XSQ= 35.41 PHI= -0.375 XP = 0.
184	TEND MORE TO BE THOSE WHERE THE LARGEST NON-COGNATIC KIN GROUP IS SMALLER THAN A PHRATRY, I. E. A SIB OR LINEAGE (175)	0.76 OF 184	184	TEND LESS TO BE THOSE WHERE THE LARGEST NON-COGNATIC KIN GROUP IS SMALLER THAN A PHRATRY, I. E. A SIB OR LINEAGE (175)	0.51 OF 68	44 33 140 35 XSQ= 13.04 PHI= -0.228 XP = 0.0003
186	TEND LESS TO BE THOSE WHERE THE KIN GROUP IS OTHER THAN EXCLUSIVELY PATRILINEAL (250)	0.55 OF 253	186	TEND MORE TO BE THOSE WHERE THE KIN GROUP IS OTHER THAN EXCLUSIVELY PATRILINEAL (250)	0.76 OF 147	115 35 138 112 XSQ= 17.67 PHI= 0.210 XP = 0.0000
188	TEND TO BE THOSE WHERE THE KIN GROUP IS OTHER THAN EXCLUSIVELY COGNATIC (252)	0.73 OF 253	188	TEND TO BE THOSE WHERE THE KIN GROUP IS EXCLUSIVELY COGNATIC (148)	0.54 OF 147	69 79 184 68 XSQ= 26.82 PHI= -0.259 XP = 0.0000

190	LEAN MORE TOWARD BEING THOSE 0.80 OF 180 WHERE THE KIN GROUP IS PATRILINEAL OR DOUBLE-DESCENT, RATHER THAN MATRILINEAL (186)	190	LEAN LESS TOWARD BEING THOSE 0.63 OF 67 WHERE THE KIN GROUP IS PATRILINEAL OR DOUBLE-DESCENT, RATHER THAN MATRILINEAL (186)	144 42 36 25 XSQ= 6.97 PHI= 0.168 XP = 0.0083
192	TEND MORE TO BE THOSE 0.79 OF 253 OTHER THAN WHERE THE ONLY KIN GROUP PRESENT IS A KINDRED OR ELSE BILATERAL DESCENT IS INFERRED (289)	192	TEND LESS TO BE THOSE 0.61 OF 147 OTHER THAN WHERE THE ONLY KIN GROUP PRESENT IS A KINDRED OR ELSE BILATERAL DESCENT IS INFERRED (289)	54 57 199 90 XSQ= 13.24 PHI= -0.182 XP = 0.0003
196	TEND TO BE THOSE 0.86 OF 185 WHERE INDIVIDUAL RIGHTS IN REAL PROPERTY, AND RULES FOR INHERITANCE, ARE PRESENT (194)	196	TEND TO BE THOSE 0.64 OF 96 WHERE INDIVIDUAL RIGHTS IN REAL PROPERTY, OR RULES FOR INHERITANCE, ARE ABSENT (87)	159 35 26 61 XSQ= 70.12 PHI= 0.500 XP = 0.
204	TILT MORE TOWARD BEING THOSE 0.84 OF 226 WHERE MARITAL RESIDENCE IS PATRILOCAL, VIRILOCAL, OR AVUNCULOCAL, RATHER THAN AMBILOCAL OR NEOLOCAL (270)	204	TILT LESS TOWARD BEING THOSE 0.74 OF 108 WHERE MARITAL RESIDENCE IS PATRILOCAL, VIRILOCAL, OR AVUNCULOCAL, RATHER THAN AMBILOCAL OR NEOLOCAL (270)	190 80 36 28 XSQ= 4.09 PHI= 0.111 XP = 0.0431
209	TEND MORE TO BE THOSE 0.88 OF 216 WHERE MARITAL RESIDENCE IS PATRILOCAL, VIRILOCAL, OR AVUNCULOCAL, RATHER THAN MATRILOCAL OR UXORILOCAL (270)	209	TEND LESS TO BE THOSE 0.68 OF 118 WHERE MARITAL RESIDENCE IS PATRILOCAL, VIRILOCAL, OR AVUNCULOCAL, RATHER THAN MATRILOCAL OR UXORILOCAL (270)	190 80 26 38 XSQ= 18.75 PHI= 0.237 XP = 0.0000
210	TEND MORE TO BE THOSE 0.90 OF 152 WHERE MARITAL RESIDENCE IS PATRILOCAL, RATHER THAN MATRILOCAL (169)	210	TEND LESS TO BE THOSE 0.67 OF 48 WHERE MARITAL RESIDENCE IS PATRILOCAL, RATHER THAN MATRILOCAL (169)	137 32 15 16 XSQ= 13.60 PHI= 0.261 XP = 0.0002
224	DRIFT LESS TOWARD BEING THOSE 0.57 OF 113 WHERE COUSIN MARRIAGE IS PREFERENTIALLY OR PERMISSIVELY SYMMETRICAL, RATHER THAN EITHER PATRI- OR MATRILATERAL (106)	224	DRIFT MORE TOWARD BEING THOSE 0.71 OF 59 WHERE COUSIN MARRIAGE IS PREFERENTIALLY OR PERMISSIVELY SYMMETRICAL, RATHER THAN EITHER PATRI- OR MATRILATERAL (106)	49 17 64 42 XSQ= 2.88 PHI= 0.129 XP = 0.0896
240	TILT MORE TOWARD BEING THOSE 0.69 OF 136 WHERE THE FAMILY, IF EXTENDED, IS SMALL OR STEM, RATHER THAN LARGE (135)	240	TILT LESS TOWARD BEING THOSE 0.53 OF 77 WHERE THE FAMILY, IF EXTENDED, IS SMALL OR STEM, RATHER THAN LARGE (135)	42 36 94 41 XSQ= 4.67 PHI= -0.148 XP = 0.0306
242	TILT LESS TOWARD BEING THOSE 0.76 OF 248 WHERE MARRIAGE IS COMMONLY OR OCCASIONALLY POLYGYNOUS, RATHER THAN MONOGAMOUS (314)	242	TILT MORE TOWARD BEING THOSE 0.86 OF 147 WHERE MARRIAGE IS COMMONLY OR OCCASIONALLY POLYGYNOUS, RATHER THAN MONOGAMOUS (314)	188 126 60 21 XSQ= 4.97 PHI= -0.112 XP = 0.0258

243	TILT TOWARD BEING THOSE WHERE POLYGYNY, IF PRESENT, HAS A HIGH INCIDENCE (24) W-C,S	0.54 OF 35	243	TILT TOWARD BEING THOSE WHERE POLYGYNY, IF PRESENT, HAS A LOW INCIDENCE (36) W-D,S	0.80 OF 25	19 5 16 20 XSQ= 5.79 PHI= 0.311 XP = 0.0162
262	LEAN MORE TOWARD BEING THOSE WHERE WIVES ARE OBTAINED BY MEANS INVOLVING THE PRESENCE OF SOME CONSIDERATION (305)	0.82 OF 252	262	LEAN LESS TOWARD BEING THOSE WHERE WIVES ARE OBTAINED BY MEANS INVOLVING THE PRESENCE OF SOME CONSIDERATION (305)	0.69 OF 143	207 98 45 45 XSQ= 8.85 PHI= 0.150 XP = 0.0029
263	TEND TO BE THOSE WHERE WIVES ARE OBTAINED BY RELATIVELY DIFFICULT MEANS, NAMELY BY BRIDE-PRICE, BRIDE-SERVICE, OR EXCHANGING A FEMALE RELATIVE (233)	0.65 OF 252	263	TEND TO BE THOSE WHERE WIVES ARE OBTAINED BY RELATIVELY EASY MEANS, NAMELY BY TOKEN BRIDE-PRICE, GIFT EXCHANGE, ABSENCE OF ANY CONSIDERATION, OR RECEIPT OF DOWRY (162)	0.52 OF 143	165 68 87 75 XSQ= 11.39 PHI= 0.170 XP = 0.0007
278	LEAN TOWARD BEING THOSE WHERE PROPERTY RIGHTS IN WOMEN ARE PRESENT (8) LWS	0.70 OF 10	278	LEAN TOWARD BEING THOSE WHERE PROPERTY RIGHTS IN WOMEN ARE UNIMPORTANT OR ABSENT (14) LWS	0.92 OF 12	7 1 3 11 XSQ= 6.50 PHI= 0.543 EP = 0.0062
299	TILT LESS TOWARD BEING THOSE WHERE THE POST-PARTUM SEX TABOO LASTS ONE YEAR OR LESS (89)	0.63 OF 76	299	TILT MORE TOWARD BEING THOSE WHERE THE POST-PARTUM SEX TABOO LASTS ONE YEAR OR LESS (89)	0.85 OF 48	28 7 48 41 XSQ= 6.14 PHI= 0.222 XP = 0.0132
300	TILT LESS TOWARD BEING THOSE WHERE THE POST-PARTUM SEX TABOO LASTS SIX MONTHS OR LESS (73)	0.51 OF 76	300	TILT MORE TOWARD BEING THOSE WHERE THE POST-PARTUM SEX TABOO LASTS SIX MONTHS OR LESS (73)	0.71 OF 48	37 14 39 34 XSQ= 3.86 PHI= 0.176 XP = 0.0495
304	LEAN TOWARD BEING THOSE WHERE THE EARLY ANAL SATISFACTION POTENTIAL IS LOW (22) W-C	0.81 OF 21	304	LEAN TOWARD BEING THOSE WHERE THE EARLY ANAL SATISFACTION POTENTIAL IS HIGH (19) W-C	0.75 OF 20	4 15 17 5 XSQ= 10.75 PHI= -0.512 XP = 0.0010
314	LEAN LESS TOWARD BEING THOSE WHERE THE INCIDENCE OF MOTHER-CHILD HOUSEHOLDS IS LOW (61) W-C,S	0.62 OF 45	314	LEAN MORE TOWARD BEING THOSE WHERE THE INCIDENCE OF MOTHER-CHILD HOUSEHOLDS IS LOW (61) W-D,S	0.94 OF 35	17 2 28 33 XSQ= 9.48 PHI= 0.344 XP = 0.0021
318	TILT TOWARD BEING THOSE WHERE THE OVERALL INDULGENCE OF THE INFANT IS LOW (31) B-B-C	0.58 OF 38	318	TILT TOWARD BEING THOSE WHERE THE OVERALL INDULGENCE OF THE INFANT IS HIGH (40) B-B-C	0.73 OF 33	16 24 22 9 XSQ= 5.55 PHI= -0.279 XP = 0.0185

320	DRIFT LESS TOWARD BEING THOSE 0.54 OF 37 WHERE THE DEGREE OF REDUCTION OF THE INFANT'S DRIVES IS HIGH (45) B-B-C	320	DRIFT MORE TOWARD BEING THOSE 0.78 OF 32 WHERE THE DEGREE OF REDUCTION OF THE INFANT'S DRIVES IS HIGH (45) B-B-C	20 25 17 7 XSQ= 3.39 PHI= -0.222 XP = 0.0658
324	TILT TOWARD BEING THOSE 0.66 OF 35 WHERE THE PAIN INFLICTED ON THE INFANT BY THE NURTURANT AGENT IS HIGH (34) B-B-C	324	TILT TOWARD BEING THOSE 0.65 OF 31 WHERE THE PAIN INFLICTED ON THE INFANT BY THE NURTURANT AGENT IS LOW OR NEGLIGIBLE (32) B-B-C	23 11 12 20 XSQ= 4.87 PHI= 0.272 XP = 0.0274
334	DRIFT TOWARD BEING THOSE 0.60 OF 42 WHERE THE INDULGENCE OF THE CHILD IS LOW (38) B-B-C	334	DRIFT TOWARD BEING THOSE 0.64 OF 36 WHERE THE INDULGENCE OF THE CHILD IS HIGH (40) B-B-C	17 23 25 13 XSQ= 3.37 PHI= -0.208 XP = 0.0665
337	LEAN TOWARD BEING THOSE 0.67 OF 40 WHERE THE CHILD'S INFERRED ANXIETY OVER NON-PERFORMANCE OF RESPONSIBLE BEHAVIOR IS HIGH (38) B-B-C	337	LEAN TOWARD BEING THOSE 0.67 OF 33 WHERE THE CHILD'S INFERRED ANXIETY OVER NON-PERFORMANCE OF RESPONSIBLE BEHAVIOR IS LOW (35) B-B-C	27 11 13 22 XSQ= 7.14 PHI= 0.313 XP = 0.0075
346	TILT TOWARD BEING THOSE 0.63 OF 41 WHERE THE CHILD'S INFERRED ANXIETY OVER PERFORMANCE OF SELF-RELIANT BEHAVIOR IS HIGH (37) B-B-C	346	TILT TOWARD BEING THOSE 0.69 OF 35 WHERE THE CHILD'S INFERRED ANXIETY OVER PERFORMANCE OF SELF-RELIANT BEHAVIOR IS LOW (39) B-B-C	26 11 15 24 XSQ= 6.51 PHI= 0.293 XP = 0.0108
347	TILT TOWARD BEING THOSE 0.61 OF 41 WHERE THE CHILD'S INFERRED CONFLICT REGARDING SELF-RELIANT BEHAVIOR IS HIGH (37) B-B-C	347	TILT TOWARD BEING THOSE 0.66 OF 35 WHERE THE CHILD'S INFERRED CONFLICT REGARDING SELF-RELIANT BEHAVIOR IS LOW (39) B-B-C	25 12 16 23 XSQ= 4.37 PHI= 0.240 XP = 0.0366
353	LEAN TOWARD BEING THOSE 0.72 OF 40 WHERE THE CHILD'S INFERRED ANXIETY OVER NON-PERFORMANCE OF OBEDIENT BEHAVIOR IS HIGH (42) B-B-C	353	LEAN TOWARD BEING THOSE 0.62 OF 34 WHERE THE CHILD-S INFERRED ANXIETY OVER NON-PERFORMANCE OF OBEDIENT BEHAVIOR IS LOW (32) B-B-C	29 13 11 21 XSQ= 7.45 PHI= 0.317 XP = 0.0063
360	TILT TOWARD BEING THOSE 0.55 OF 20 WHERE ADOLESCENT PEER GROUPS ARE PRESENT IN A SETTING OF WORK AND PUBLIC GATHERINGS AND LEISURE, OR AT LEAST OF PUBLIC GATHERINGS AND LEISURE (14) JKH	360	TILT TOWARD BEING THOSE 0.82 OF 17 WHERE ADOLESCENT PEER GROUPS ARE PRESENT ONLY IN A SETTING OF LEISURE, OR ELSE ARE ABSENT (23) JKH	11 3 9 14 XSQ= 3.98 PHI= 0.328 EP = 0.0397
377	TEND LESS TO BE THOSE 0.63 OF 201 WHERE MALE GENITAL MUTILATION IS ABSENT (242)	377	TEND MORE TO BE THOSE 0.93 OF 124 WHERE MALE GENITAL MUTILATION IS ABSENT (242)	74 9 127 115 XSQ= 33.70 PHI= 0.322 XP = 0.

382	LEAN TOWARD BEING THOSE WHERE FEMALE INITIATION RITES ARE ABSENT (27) JKB	0.56 OF 39	382	LEAN TOWARD BEING THOSE WHERE FEMALE INITIATION RITES ARE PRESENT (38) JKB	0.81 OF 26	17 21 22 5 XSQ= 7.41 PHI= -0.338 XP = 0.0065
424	TILT TOWARD BEING THOSE WHERE RELIGIOUS SPECIALISTS ARE FULL-TIME, RATHER THAN PART-TIME (21) JMH	0.53 OF 34	424	TILT TOWARD BEING THOSE WHERE RELIGIOUS SPECIALISTS ARE PART-TIME, RATHER THAN FULL-TIME (33) JMH	0.85 OF 20	18 3 16 17 XSQ= 6.11 PHI= 0.337 XP = 0.0134
426	TEND TO BE THOSE WHERE A HIGH GOD IS PRESENT (156) GES,EA	0.71 OF 154	426	TEND TO BE THOSE WHERE A HIGH GOD IS ABSENT (104) GES,EA	0.57 OF 106	110 46 44 60 XSQ= 19.41 PHI= 0.273 XP = 0.0000
428	TILT TOWARD BEING THOSE WHERE A HIGH GOD, IF PRESENT AND ACTIVE, SUPPORTS HUMAN MORALITY, RATHER THAN NOT SUPPORTING IT (61) GES,EA	0.78 OF 64	428	TILT TOWARD BEING THOSE WHERE A HIGH GOD, IF PRESENT AND ACTIVE, DOES NOT SUPPORT HUMAN MORALITY, RATHER THAN SUPPORTING IT (26) GES,EA	0.52 OF 23	50 11 14 12 XSQ= 6.04 PHI= 0.263 XP = 0.0140
429	LEAN TOWARD BEING THOSE WHERE SUPERNATURAL SANCTIONS FOR MORALITY ARE PRESENT (28) GES	0.92 OF 24	429	LEAN TOWARD BEING THOSE WHERE SUPERNATURAL SANCTIONS FOR MORALITY ARE ABSENT OR UNREPORTED (9) GES	0.54 OF 13	22 6 2 7 XSQ= 7.18 PHI= 0.440 EP = 0.0041
435	TILT TOWARD BEING THOSE WHERE ABANDONMENT OF THE HOUSE OF THE DEAD IS NOT PRACTICED (19) LWS	0.86 OF 14	435	TILT TOWARD BEING THOSE WHERE ABANDONMENT OF THE HOUSE OF THE DEAD IS PRACTICED (12) LWS	0.59 OF 17	2 10 12 7 XSQ= 4.68 PHI= -0.389 EP = 0.0245
450	TILT LESS TOWARD BEING THOSE WHERE THE OBSERVATION OF FOOD TABOOS IS HIGH OR MEDIUM, RATHER THAN LOW (60) JRL	0.61 OF 56	450	TILT MORE TOWARD BEING THOSE WHERE THE OBSERVATION OF FOOD TABOOS IS HIGH OR MEDIUM, RATHER THAN LOW (60) JRL	0.87 OF 30	34 26 22 4 XSQ= 5.07 PHI= -0.243 XP = 0.0244
452	TILT TOWARD BEING THOSE WHERE TOTEMISM WITH FOOD TABOOS IS PRESENT (19) WNS	0.59 OF 29	452	TILT TOWARD BEING THOSE WHERE TOTEMISM WITH FOOD TABOOS IS ABSENT (24) WNS	0.86 OF 14	17 2 12 12 XSQ= 5.83 PHI= 0.368 XP = 0.0157
458	TEND TO BE THOSE WHERE GAMES, IF PRESENT, INCLUDE GAMES OF STRATEGY (52) R-A-B,EA	0.56 OF 88	458	TEND TO BE THOSE WHERE GAMES, IF PRESENT, DO NOT INCLUDE GAMES OF STRATEGY (119) R-A-B,EA	0.96 OF 83	49 3 39 80 XSQ= 52.29 PHI= 0.553 XP = 0.

460	DRIFT MORE TOWARD BEING THOSE 0.68 OF 88 WHERE GAMES, IF PRESENT, ARE NOT LIMITED TO GAMES OF SKILL ONLY (104) R-A-B,EA	460	DRIFT LESS TOWARD BEING THOSE 0.53 OF 83 WHERE GAMES, IF PRESENT, ARE NOT LIMITED TO GAMES OF SKILL ONLY (104) R-A-B,EA		28 60 XSQ= PHI= XP =	39 44 3.51 -0.143 0.0609
468	LEAN LESS TOWARD BEING THOSE 0.53 OF 34 WHERE CONTACT WITH OTHER CULTURES IS REGULAR OR IRREGULAR, RATHER THAN FREQUENT (37) JMH	468	LEAN MORE TOWARD BEING THOSE 0.95 OF 20 WHERE CONTACT WITH OTHER CULTURES IS REGULAR OR IRREGULAR, RATHER THAN FREQUENT (37) JMH		16 18 XSQ= PHI= XP =	1 19 8.47 0.396 0.0036
469	DRIFT MORE TOWARD BEING THOSE 0.88 OF 34 WHERE CONTACT WITH OTHER CULTURES IS FREQUENT OR REGULAR, RATHER THAN IRREGULAR (43) JMH	469	DRIFT LESS TOWARD BEING THOSE 0.65 OF 20 WHERE CONTACT WITH OTHER CULTURES IS FREQUENT OR REGULAR, RATHER THAN IRREGULAR (43) JMH		30 4 XSQ= PHI= XP =	13 7 2.88 0.231 0.0896
470	DRIFT TOWARD BEING THOSE 0.50 OF 34 WHERE INNOVATIONS ARE GENERALLY ACCEPTED (21) JMH	470	DRIFT TOWARD BEING THOSE 0.80 OF 20 WHERE INNOVATIONS ARE ACCEPTED ONLY SELECTIVELY (33) JMH		17 17 XSQ= PHI= XP =	4 16 3.59 0.258 0.0581
476	LEAN TOWARD BEING THOSE 0.53 OF 30 WHERE THE DEGREE OF INSOBRIETY IS MODERATE OR SLIGHT (18) DH	476	LEAN TOWARD BEING THOSE 0.89 OF 19 WHERE THE DEGREE OF INSOBRIETY IS STRONG (31) DH		14 16 XSQ= PHI= XP =	17 2 7.42 -0.389 0.0064
480	DRIFT TOWARD BEING THOSE 0.67 OF 15 WHERE COMPLEXITY OF ARTISTIC DESIGN IS HIGH (14) HB	480	DRIFT TOWARD BEING THOSE 0.71 OF 14 WHERE COMPLEXITY OF ARTISTIC DESIGN IS LOW (15) HB		10 5 XSQ= PHI= EP =	4 10 2.82 0.312 0.0656

****

52 CULTURES WHERE SUBSISTENCE IS PRIMARILY BY AGRICULTURE (237)	52 CULTURES WHERE SUBSISTENCE IS PRIMARILY BY MEANS OTHER THAN AGRICULTURE (163)

BACKGROUND ON PAGE 74

SUBJECT ONLY

....

237 IN LEFT COLUMN

AJIE	AKHA	ALBANIANS	ALORESE	AMBA	AMERICANS	ARAPESH	ARAUCANIANS	ARYANS	ASHANTI
ATAYAL	AYMARA	AZANDE	AZTEC	BABWA	BALINESE	BAMBARA	BAMILEKE	BANDA	BARABRA
BARI	BASQUES	BATAK	BAYA	BELU	BEMBA	BENGALI	BETE	BHUIYA	BIRIFOR
BLACK CARIB	BRAZILIANS	BULGARIANS	BUNLAP	BURMESE	BURUSHO	CAGABA	CAMBA	CAMBODIANS	CARINYA
CAYAPA	CHAGGA	CHEREMIS	CHERKESS	CHIBCHA	CHINANTEC	CHIRIGUANO	CHOCO	CHORTI	COCHITI
COORG	CUNA	CZECHS	DAGUR	DARD	DILLING	DOBUANS	DOGON	DUSUN	DUTCH
EGYPTIANS	ENGA	FANG	FON	FUTAJALONKE	GANDA	GARO	GISU	GOND	GURE
HANO	HANUNOO	HASANIA	HAZARA	HEBREWS	HEHE	HO	HUICHOL	HUTSUL	IBAN
IFUGAO	ILA	INCA	INGASSANA	IRAQW	IRISH	JAPANESE	JAVANESE	JEMEZ	JIVARO
JUKUN	KABYLE	KACHIN	KAPAUKU	KAREN	KATAB	KERAKI	KERALA	KHASI	KHEVSUR
KIKUYU	KISSI	KOHISTANI	KOL	KONSO	KOREANS	KPE	KUBA	KUMYK	KURTATCHI
LAKHER	LAMBA	LAMET	LANGO	LAU	LEPCHA	LHOTA NAGA	LIFU	LOLO	LUO
MACASSARESE	MAGUZAWA	MALAYS	MAM	MAMBILA	MAMVU	MANCHU	MANDAN	MANGAIANS	MARGI
MARQUESANS	MARSHALLESE	MATAKAM	MAYA	MAZATECO	MBUGWE	MBUNDU	MENDE	MENTAWEI	MERINA
MIAO	MIN CHINESE	MINANGKABAU	MINCHIA	MNONG GAR	MONGO	MONGUOR	MOSSI	MOTA	MZAB
NANDI	NDEMBU	NGONI	NICOBARESE	NUPE	NURI	NYAKYUSA	NYANEKA	NYARO	NYORO
OKINAWANS	ORAON	PAEZ	PAIWAN	PALAUANS	PATHAN	PAWNEE	PENDE	PONAPEANS	POPOLUCA
PORTUGUESE	PUKAPUKA	PURUM	RIFFIANS	ROMANS	ROTINESE	ROTUMANS	RUNDI	SAGADA	SAMOANS
SANDAWE	SANTAL	SEMINOLE	SENIANG	SERBS	SHILLUK	SHLUH	SIMBOESE	SINDHI	SINHALESE
SIUAI	SIWANS	SONGHAI	SOTHO	SUBANUN	SWAZI	SYRIANS	TAGBANUA	TALAMANCA	TALLENSI
TAMIL	TANALA	TANIMBARESE	TAOS	TARAHUMARA	TEDA	TENDA	TENETEHARA	TERA	TESO
THAI	THONGA	TIBETANS	TIGRINYA	TIV	TORAJA	TOTONAC	TROBRIAND	TUNEBO	TURKMEN
TZELTAL	ULAWANS	VENDA	VIETNAMESE	WALLOONS	WANTOAT	WICHITA	WOGEO	WOLEAIANS	WOLOF
WUTE	YAKO	YAO	YAPESE	YOMBE	YORUBA	ZUNI			

163 IN RIGHT COLUMN

3	TEND LESS TO BE THOSE LOCATED OUTSIDE OF AFRICA (320)	0.72 OF 237	3	TEND MORE TO BE THOSE LOCATED OUTSIDE OF AFRICA (320)	0.92 OF 163	67 13 170 150 XSQ= 23.61 PHI= 0.243 XP = 0.0000
4	TILT LESS TOWARD BEING THOSE LOCATED OUTSIDE OF THE CIRCUM-MEDITERRANEAN (355)	0.85 OF 237	4	TILT MORE TOWARD BEING THOSE LOCATED OUTSIDE OF THE CIRCUM-MEDITERRANEAN (355)	0.94 OF 163	35 10 202 153 XSQ= 6.37 PHI= 0.126 XP = 0.0116

5	TILT LESS TOWARD BEING THOSE LOCATED OUTSIDE OF EAST EURASIA (330)	0.79 OF 237	5	TILT MORE TOWARD BEING THOSE LOCATED OUTSIDE OF EAST EURASIA (330)	0.88 OF 163	50 20 187 143 XSQ= 4.62 PHI= 0.107 XP = 0.0316
8	TEND MORE TO BE THOSE LOCATED OUTSIDE OF NORTH AMERICA (330)	0.93 OF 237	8	TEND LESS TO BE THOSE LOCATED OUTSIDE OF NORTH AMERICA (330)	0.67 OF 163	16 54 221 109 XSQ= 44.73 PHI= -0.334 XP = 0.
9	TEND MORE TO BE THOSE LOCATED OUTSIDE OF SOUTH AMERICA (335)	0.91 OF 237	9	TEND LESS TO BE THOSE LOCATED OUTSIDE OF SOUTH AMERICA (335)	0.73 OF 163	21 44 216 119 XSQ= 22.02 PHI= -0.235 XP = 0.0000
11	IN ALL CASES ARE THOSE WHERE THE LATITUDE IS LESS THAN SIXTY DEGREES (385)	1.00 OF 237	11	TEND LESS TO BE THOSE WHERE THE LATITUDE IS LESS THAN SIXTY DEGREES (385)	0.91 OF 163	0 15 237 148 XSQ= 20.18 PHI= -0.225 XP = 0.0000
15	TEND TO BE THOSE WHERE THE LATITUDE IS LESS THAN TWENTY DEGREES (217)	0.63 OF 237	15	TEND TO BE THOSE WHERE THE LATITUDE IS TWENTY DEGREES OR GREATER (183)	0.58 OF 163	88 95 149 68 XSQ= 16.57 PHI= -0.204 XP = 0.0000
33	TEND MORE TO BE THOSE WHERE THE NATURAL ENVIRONMENT IS OTHER THAN 'VERY HARSH,' I.E., DESERT, DESERT GRASSES AND SHRUBS, TUNDRA, OR HIGH PLATEAU STEPPE (341) FWM	0.92 OF 237	33	TEND LESS TO BE THOSE WHERE THE NATURAL ENVIRONMENT IS OTHER THAN 'VERY HARSH,' I.E., DESERT, DESERT GRASSES AND SHRUBS, TUNDRA, OR HIGH PLATEAU STEPPE (341) FWM	0.76 OF 163	20 39 217 124 XSQ= 17.21 PHI= -0.207 XP = 0.0000
36	TEND MORE TO BE THOSE WHERE THE NATURAL ENVIRONMENT IS OTHER THAN 'VERY HARSH,' OR SUB-TROPICAL BUSH, OR TEMPERATE GRASSLAND (292) FWM	0.81 OF 237	36	TEND LESS TO BE THOSE WHERE THE NATURAL ENVIRONMENT IS OTHER THAN 'VERY HARSH,' OR SUB-TROPICAL BUSH, OR TEMPERATE GRASSLAND (292) FWM	0.61 OF 163	45 63 192 100 XSQ= 17.96 PHI= -0.212 XP = 0.0000
42	TEND LESS TO BE THOSE WHERE THE NATURAL ENVIRONMENT IS OTHER THAN TROPICAL OR SUB-TROPICAL RAIN FOREST, OR MONSOON FOREST (244) FWM	0.54 OF 237	42	TEND MORE TO BE THOSE WHERE THE NATURAL ENVIRONMENT IS OTHER THAN TROPICAL OR SUB-TROPICAL RAIN FOREST, OR MONSOON FOREST (244) FWM	0.71 OF 163	109 47 128 116 XSQ= 11.24 PHI= 0.168 XP = 0.0008
44	TEND TO BE THOSE WHERE SETTLEMENTS ARE FIXED (222)	0.93 OF 192	44	TEND TO BE THOSE WHERE SETTLEMENTS ARE NON-FIXED (110)	0.69 OF 140	178 44 14 96 XSQ= 134.48 PHI= 0.636 XP = 0.

45	TILT LESS TOWARD BEING THOSE WHERE SETTLEMENTS, IF FIXED, ARE COMPACT, RATHER THAN NON-COMPACT (149)	0.63 OF 178	45	TILT MORE TOWARD BEING THOSE WHERE SETTLEMENTS, IF FIXED, ARE COMPACT, RATHER THAN NON-COMPACT (149)	0.82 OF 44	113 36 65 8 XSQ= 4.58 PHI= -0.144 XP = 0.0324
46	TEND TO BE THOSE OTHER THAN WHERE SETTLEMENTS ARE NON-FIXED AND MOVEMENT IS NOMADIC (260)	0.99 OF 192	46	TEND TO BE THOSE WHERE SETTLEMENTS ARE NON-FIXED AND MOVEMENT IS NOMADIC (72)	0.51 OF 140	1 71 191 69 XSQ= 117.17 PHI= -0.594 XP = 0.
47	TEND TO BE THOSE WHERE, IF SETTLEMENTS ARE NON-FIXED, MOVEMENT IS NON-NOMADIC, RATHER THAN NOMADIC (38)	0.93 OF 14	47	TEND TO BE THOSE WHERE, IF SETTLEMENTS ARE NON-FIXED, MOVEMENT IS NOMADIC, RATHER THAN NON-NOMADIC (72)	0.74 OF 96	1 71 13 25 XSQ= 21.26 PHI= -0.440 XP = 0.0000
62	TEND TO BE THOSE WHERE HUSBANDRY OF SOME KIND IS PRESENT (228)	0.75 OF 237	62	TEND TO BE THOSE WHERE HUSBANDRY OF ANY KIND IS ABSENT (172)	0.69 OF 163	177 51 60 112 XSQ= 72.44 PHI= 0.426 XP = 0.
71	TEND TO BE THOSE WHERE METAL WORKING IS PRESENT (98)	0.65 OF 124	71	TEND TO BE THOSE WHERE METAL WORKING IS ABSENT (153)	0.86 OF 127	80 18 44 109 XSQ= 64.71 PHI= 0.508 XP = 0.
73	TEND TO BE THOSE WHERE WEAVING IS PRESENT (118)	0.60 OF 124	73	TEND TO BE THOSE WHERE WEAVING IS ABSENT (130)	0.65 OF 124	75 43 49 81 XSQ= 15.54 PHI= 0.250 XP = 0.0001
74	TEND TO BE THOSE WHERE POTTERY IS PRESENT (145)	0.77 OF 116	74	TEND TO BE THOSE WHERE POTTERY IS ABSENT (93)	0.54 OF 122	89 56 27 66 XSQ= 22.45 PHI= 0.307 XP = 0.0000
80	TEND LESS TO BE THOSE WHERE NO CITY OR TOWN IS PRESENT (185)	0.71 OF 134	80	IN ALL CASES ARE THOSE WHERE NO CITY OR TOWN IS PRESENT (185)	1.00 OF 90	39 0 95 90 XSQ= 29.72 PHI= 0.364 XP = 0.0000
81	TEND TO BE THOSE WHERE A CITY OR TOWN IS PRESENT, OR THE AVERAGE COMMUNITY SIZE IS 200 OR GREATER (89)	0.57 OF 134	81	TEND TO BE THOSE WHERE NO CITY OR TOWN IS PRESENT, AND THE AVERAGE COMMUNITY SIZE IS SMALLER THAN 200 (135)	0.87 OF 90	77 12 57 78 XSQ= 41.96 PHI= 0.433 XP = 0.

83	TEND LESS TC BE THCSE WHERE, WITH NC CITY ANC NC TOWN PRESENT, THE AVERAGE COMMUNITY SIZE IS SMALLER THAN 200, RATHER THAN BETWEEN 200 AND 999 (135)	0.63 OF 90	83	TEND MORE TO BE THOSE WHERE, WITH NO CITY AND NO TOWN PRESENT, THE AVERAGE COMMUNITY SIZE IS SMALLER THAN 200, RATHER THAN BETWEEN 200 AND 999 (135)	0.87 CF 90	33 12 57 78 XSQ= 11.85 PHI= 0.257 XP = 0.0006
86	TEND TO BE THCSE WHERE THE LEVEL CF POLITICAL INTEGRATICN IS THE LARGE STATE, THE LITTLE STATE, OR THE MINIMAL STATE (148) GPM	0.66 OF 166	86	TEND TO BE THOSE WHERE THE LEVEL OF POLITICAL INTEGRATION IS THE AUTONOMOUS COMMUNITY, OR THE FAMILY (156) GPM	0.72 OF 138	109 39 57 99 XSQ= 40.71 PHI= 0.366 XP = 0.
91	TILT TCWARD BEING THOSE WHERE SCCIETAL CCMPLEXITY IS HIGH (18) F-W	0.61 OF 23	91	TILT TOWARD BEING THOSE WHERE SOCIETAL COMPLEXITY IS LOW (22) F-W	0.76 OF 17	14 4 9 13 XSQ= 4.10 PHI= 0.320 EP = 0.0267
96	TEND TO BE THOSE WHERE THE HIERARCHY OF NATICNAL JURISDICTICN HAS FOUR, THREE, TWC OR ONE LEVEL (174) GES,EA	0.67 OF 189	96	TEND TO BE THOSE WHERE THE HIERARCHY OF NATIONAL JURISDICTION HAS NO LEVELS (156) GES,EA	0.66 OF 141	126 48 63 93 XSQ= 33.19 PHI= 0.317 XP = 0.
97	TEND LESS TO BE THCSE WHERE THE HIERARCHY OF LOCAL JURISDICTION HAS THREE OR TWO LEVELS (273) GES,EA	0.76 OF 190	97	TEND MORE TO BE THOSE WHERE THE HIERARCHY OF LOCAL JURISDICTION HAS THREE OR TWO LEVELS (273) GES,EA	0.91 OF 141	46 12 144 129 XSQ= 12.74 PHI= 0.196 XP = 0.0004
98	TEND MORE TO BE THCSE WHERE THE HIERARCHY OF LCCAL JURISDICTICN HAS FOUR CR THREE LEVELS (238) GES,EA	0.81 OF 190	98	TEND LESS TO BE THOSE WHERE THE HIERARCHY OF LOCAL JURISDICTICN HAS FOUR OR THREE LEVELS (238) GES,EA	0.60 OF 141	154 84 36 57 XSQ= 17.43 PHI= 0.229 XP = 0.0000
99	LEAN MCRE TCWARC BEING THCSE WHERE, WITH NATICNAL HIERARCHY ABSENT, THE HIERARCHY OF LCCAL JURISCICTION HAS FCUR CR THREE LEVELS (93) GES,EA	0.73 OF 63	99	LEAN LESS TOWARD BEING THOSE WHERE, WITH NATIONAL HIERARCHY ABSENT, THE HIERARCHY OF LOCAL JURISDICTION HAS FOUR OR THREE LEVELS (93) GES,EA	0.51 CF 93	46 47 17 46 XSQ= 6.98 PHI= 0.211 XP = 0.0083
100	TEND MCRE TO BE THCSE WHERE HIERARCHIES ARE MCRE COMPLEX THAN THE 'SIMPLEST,' I. E., MORE COMPLEX THAN TWC LCCAL LEVELS WITH NO NATIONAL LEVELS (267) GES,EA	0.91 OF 189	100	TEND LESS TO BE THOSE WHERE HIERARCHIES ARE MCRE CCMPLEX THAN THE 'SIMPLEST,' I. E., MORE CCMPLEX THAN TWO LOCAL LEVELS WITH NO NATIONAL LEVELS (267) GES,EA	0.67 OF 141	172 95 17 46 XSQ= 27.68 PHI= 0.290 XP = 0.0000
102	TEND TC BE THCSE WHERE CLASS STRATIFICATION IS PRESENT (203)	0.68 OF 220	102	TEND TO BE THOSE WHERE CLASS STRATIFICATICN IS ABSENT (180)	0.67 CF 163	150 53 70 110 XSQ= 46.39 PHI= 0.348 XP = 0.

```
106  LEAN TOWARD BEING THOSE          0.69 OF 150    106  LEAN TOWARD BEING THOSE          0.57 OF  53         47    30
     WHERE CLASS STRATIFICATION, IF PRESENT,              WHERE CLASS STRATIFICATION, IF PRESENT,              103    23
     IS BASED ON SOMETHING OTHER THAN                     IS BASED ON WEALTH  (77)                         XSQ=     9.58
     WEALTH  (126)                                                                                         PHI=   -0.217
                                                                                                           XP =   0.0020

107  TEND LESS TO BE THOSE            0.73 OF 150    107  TEND MORE TO BE THOSE            0.96 OF  53         41     2
     WHERE CLASS STRATIFICATION, IF PRESENT,              WHERE CLASS STRATIFICATION, IF PRESENT,              109    51
     IS BASED ON SOMETHING OTHER THAN                     IS BASED ON SOMETHING OTHER THAN                 XSQ=    11.65
     OCCUPATIONAL STATUS  (160)                           OCCUPATIONAL STATUS  (160)                       PHI=    0.240
                                                                                                           XP =   0.0006

109  LEAN LESS TOWARD BEING THOSE  0.81 OF 208    109  LEAN MORE TOWARD BEING THOSE  0.92 OF 160            39    12
     WHERE CASTES ARE ABSENT  (317)                       WHERE CASTES ARE ABSENT  (317)                      169   148
                                                                                                           XSQ=     8.67
                                                                                                           PHI=    0.153
                                                                                                           XP =   0.0032

110  TEND TO BE THOSE                 0.52 OF 221    110  TEND TO BE THOSE                 0.69 OF 160        114    49
     WHERE SLAVERY IS PRESENT  (163)                      WHERE SLAVERY IS ABSENT  (218)                      107   111
                                                                                                           XSQ=    15.81
                                                                                                           PHI=    0.204
                                                                                                           XP =   0.0001

116  DRIFT LESS TOWARD BEING THOSE  0.52 OF  31    116  DRIFT MORE TOWARD BEING THOSE  0.78 OF  23          15     5
     WHERE OCCUPATIONAL SPECIALIZATION IS                 WHERE OCCUPATIONAL SPECIALIZATION IS                 16    18
     PART-TIME ONLY  (34) JMH                             PART-TIME ONLY  (34) JMH                         XSQ=     2.96
                                                                                                           PHI=    0.234
                                                                                                           XP =   0.0854

129  TILT LESS TOWARD BEING THOSE   0.61 OF  64    129  TILT MORE TOWARD BEING THOSE   0.85 OF  40          25     6
     WHERE WEAVING IS                                     WHERE WEAVING IS                                     39    34
     MAINLY DONE BY FEMALES  (73)                         MAINLY DONE BY FEMALES  (73)                     XSQ=     5.71
                                                                                                           PHI=    0.234
                                                                                                           XP =   0.0169

130  TEND TO BE THOSE                 0.85 OF  27    130  TEND TO BE THOSE                 0.72 OF  57         23    16
     WHERE LEATHER WORKING IS                             WHERE LEATHER WORKING IS                              4    41
     MAINLY DONE BY MALES  (39)                           MAINLY DONE BY FEMALES  (45)                     XSQ=    21.79
                                                                                                           PHI=    0.509
                                                                                                           XP =   0.0000

131  IN ALL CASES ARE THOSE           1.00 OF  77    131  TEND LESS TO BE THOSE            0.74 OF  80         77    59
     WHERE THE CONSTRUCTION OF PERMANENT HOUSES           WHERE THE CONSTRUCTION OF PERMANENT HOUSES            0    21
     OR THE ERECTION OF TEMPORARY DWELLINGS               OR THE ERECTION OF TEMPORARY DWELLINGS           XSQ=    21.12
     IS MAINLY DONE BY MALES  (136)                       IS MAINLY DONE BY MALES  (136)                   PHI=    0.367
                                                                                                           XP =   0.0000

132  LEAN TOWARD BEING THOSE          0.87 OF  31    132  LEAN TOWARD BEING THOSE          0.57 OF  23         27    10
     WHERE ECONOMIC EXCHANGE                              WHERE ECONOMIC EXCHANGE                               4    13
     INVOLVES THE USE OF MONEY  (37) JMH                  DOES NOT INVOLVE                                 XSQ=     9.71
                                                          THE USE OF MONEY  (17) JMH                       PHI=    0.424
                                                                                                           XP =   0.0018
```

133	TILT TOWARD BEING THOSE 0.70 OF 20 WHERE CONTRACTED DEBTS ARE SIGNIFICANTLY PRESENT (17) GES	133	TILT TOWARD BEING THOSE 0.79 OF 14 WHERE CONTRACTED DEBTS ARE MODERATELY PRESENT OR ABSENT (17) GES	14 3 6 11 XSQ= 5.95 PHI= 0.418 EP = 0.0134
137	TILT TOWARD BEING THOSE 0.54 OF 46 WHERE INVIDIOUS DISPLAY OF WEALTH IS STRONGLY EMPHASIZED (37) PES	137	TILT TOWARD BEING THOSE 0.72 OF 43 WHERE INVIDIOUS DISPLAY OF WEALTH IS MODERATELY, LITTLE, OR NEGATIVELY EMPHASIZED (52) PES	25 12 21 31 XSQ= 5.35 PHI= 0.245 XP = 0.0207
147	LEAN TOWARD BEING THOSE 0.92 OF 13 WHERE CODIFIED LAWS ARE PRESENT (20) LWS	147	LEAN TOWARD BEING THOSE 0.60 OF 20 WHERE CODIFIED LAWS ARE UNIMPORTANT OR ABSENT (13) LWS	12 8 1 12 XSQ= 6.97 PHI= 0.460 EP = 0.0036
152	TILT TOWARD BEING THOSE 0.75 OF 12 WHERE THE DIFFERENTIATION OF THE JURIDICAL AGENCY FROM THE MEDICAL AGENCY IS HIGH (10) MJ	152	TILT TOWARD BEING THOSE 0.88 OF 8 WHERE THE DIFFERENTIATION OF THE JURIDICAL AGENCY FROM THE MEDICAL AGENCY IS LOW (10) MJ	9 1 3 7 XSQ= 5.21 PHI= 0.510 EP = 0.0198
163	LEAN TOWARD BEING THOSE 0.70 OF 10 WHERE THE EMPHASIS ON INDIVIDUAL VOLITION AS THE CAUSE OF CRIME IS HIGH (7) MJ	163	IN ALL CASES ARE THOSE 1.00 OF 7 WHERE THE EMPHASIS ON INDIVIDUAL VOLITION AS THE CAUSE OF CRIME IS LOW (10) MJ	7 0 3 7 XSQ= 5.69 PHI= 0.579 EP = 0.0098
176	TILT LESS TOWARD BEING THOSE 0.50 OF 227 WHERE THE COMMUNITY IS OTHER THAN A CLAN-COMMUNITY OR A COMMUNITY STRUCTURED OR SEGMENTED ON A CLAN BASIS (213)	176	TILT MORE TOWARD BEING THOSE 0.64 OF 155 WHERE THE COMMUNITY IS OTHER THAN A CLAN-COMMUNITY OR A COMMUNITY STRUCTURED OR SEGMENTED ON A CLAN BASIS (213)	113 56 114 99 XSQ= 6.42 PHI= 0.130 XP = 0.0113
178	DRIFT LESS TOWARD BEING THOSE 0.74 OF 227 WHERE THE COMMUNITY IS OTHER THAN SEGMENTED ON A CLAN BASIS AND NON-EXOGAMOUS (295)	178	DRIFT MORE TOWARD BEING THOSE 0.83 OF 155 WHERE THE COMMUNITY IS OTHER THAN SEGMENTED ON A CLAN BASIS AND NON-EXOGAMOUS (295)	60 27 167 128 XSQ= 3.76 PHI= 0.099 XP = 0.0526
179	TEND MORE TO BE THOSE 0.94 OF 227 WHERE THE COMMUNITY IS OTHER THAN STRUCTURED ON A NON-CLAN BASIS AND COMMONLY EXOGAMOUS (340)	179	TEND LESS TO BE THOSE 0.82 OF 155 WHERE THE COMMUNITY IS OTHER THAN STRUCTURED ON A NON-CLAN BASIS AND COMMONLY EXOGAMOUS (340)	14 28 213 127 XSQ= 12.13 PHI= -0.178 XP = 0.0005
184	TEND TO BE THOSE 0.79 OF 170 WHERE THE LARGEST NON-COGNATIC KIN GROUP IS SMALLER THAN A PHRATRY, I. E. A SIB OR LINEAGE (175)	184	TEND TO BE THOSE 0.50 OF 82 WHERE THE LARGEST NON-COGNATIC KIN GROUP IS THE MOEITY OR PHRATRY (77)	36 41 134 41 XSQ= 20.32 PHI= -0.284 XP = 0.0000

186	TEND LESS TO BE THOSE WHERE THE KIN GROUP IS OTHER THAN EXCLUSIVELY PATRILINEAL (250)	0.55 OF 237	186	TEND MORE TO BE THOSE WHERE THE KIN GROUP IS OTHER THAN EXCLUSIVELY PATRILINEAL (250)	0.73 OF 163	106 44 131 119 XSQ= 12.21 PHI= 0.175 XP = 0.0005
188	TEND MORE TO BE THOSE WHERE THE KIN GROUP IS OTHER THAN EXCLUSIVELY COGNATIC (252)	0.72 OF 237	188	TEND LESS TO BE THOSE WHERE THE KIN GROUP IS OTHER THAN EXCLUSIVELY COGNATIC (252)	0.50 OF 163	67 81 170 82 XSQ= 18.11 PHI= -0.213 XP = 0.0000
190	DRIFT MORE TOWARD BEING THOSE WHERE THE KIN GROUP IS PATRILINEAL OR DOUBLE-DESCENT, RATHER THAN MATRILINEAL (186)	0.79 OF 166	190	DRIFT LESS TOWARD BEING THOSE WHERE THE KIN GROUP IS PATRILINEAL OR DOUBLE-DESCENT, RATHER THAN MATRILINEAL (186)	0.68 OF 81	131 55 35 26 XSQ= 2.98 PHI= 0.110 XP = 0.0841
192	LEAN MORE TOWARD BEING THOSE OTHER THAN WHERE THE ONLY KIN GROUP PRESENT IS A KINDRED OR ELSE BILATERAL DESCENT IS INFERRED (289)	0.78 OF 237	192	LEAN LESS TOWARD BEING THOSE OTHER THAN WHERE THE ONLY KIN GROUP PRESENT IS A KINDRED OR ELSE BILATERAL DESCENT IS INFERRED (289)	0.64 OF 163	52 59 185 104 XSQ= 9.09 PHI= -0.151 XP = 0.0026
196	TEND TO BE THOSE WHERE INDIVIDUAL RIGHTS IN REAL PROPERTY, AND RULES FOR INHERITANCE, ARE PRESENT (194)	0.88 OF 173	196	TEND TO BE THOSE WHERE INDIVIDUAL RIGHTS IN REAL PROPERTY, OR RULES FOR INHERITANCE, ARE ABSENT (87)	0.62 OF 108	153 41 20 67 XSQ= 76.91 PHI= 0.523 XP = 0.
209	TEND MORE TO BE THOSE WHERE MARITAL RESIDENCE IS PATRILOCAL, VIRILOCAL, OR AVUNCULOCAL, RATHER THAN MATRILOCAL OR UXORILOCAL (270)	0.87 OF 200	209	TEND LESS TO BE THOSE WHERE MARITAL RESIDENCE IS PATRILOCAL, VIRILOCAL, OR AVUNCULOCAL, RATHER THAN MATRILOCAL OR UXORILOCAL (270)	0.72 OF 134	174 96 26 38 XSQ= 11.25 PHI= 0.184 XP = 0.0008
210	LEAN MORE TOWARD BEING THOSE WHERE MARITAL RESIDENCE IS PATRILOCAL, RATHER THAN MATRILOCAL (169)	0.89 OF 141	210	LEAN LESS TOWARD BEING THOSE WHERE MARITAL RESIDENCE IS PATRILOCAL, RATHER THAN MATRILOCAL (169)	0.73 OF 59	126 43 15 16 XSQ= 7.41 PHI= 0.193 XP = 0.0065
221	DRIFT LESS TOWARD BEING THOSE WHERE MATRILATERAL CROSS-COUSIN MARRIAGE IS NOT PRESCRIBED OR PREFERRED (335)	0.88 OF 221	221	DRIFT MORE TOWARD BEING THOSE WHERE MATRILATERAL CROSS-COUSIN MARRIAGE IS NOT PRESCRIBED OR PREFERRED (335)	0.94 OF 149	26 9 195 140 XSQ= 2.77 PHI= 0.087 XP = 0.0961
234	DRIFT TOWARD BEING THOSE WHERE THE COUSIN TERMINOLOGY IS OF ESKIMO OR HAWAIIAN TYPE, RATHER THAN CROW, OMAHA, OR IROQUOIS TYPE (170)	0.57 OF 192	234	DRIFT TOWARD BEING THOSE WHERE THE COUSIN TERMINOLOGY IS OF CROW, OMAHA, OR IROQUOIS TYPE, RATHER THAN ESKIMO OR HAWAIIAN TYPE (152)	0.54 OF 130	82 70 110 60 XSQ= 3.42 PHI= -0.103 XP = 0.0642

240	DRIFT MORE TOWARD BEING THOSE 0.69 OF 127 WHERE THE FAMILY, IF EXTENDED, IS SMALL OR STEM, RATHER THAN LARGE (135)	240	DRIFT LESS TOWARD BEING THOSE 0.56 OF 86 WHERE THE FAMILY, IF EXTENDED, IS SMALL OR STEM, RATHER THAN LARGE (135)	40 38 87 48 XSQ= 3.03 PHI= -0.119 XP = 0.0816
242	TILT LESS TOWARD BEING THOSE 0.76 OF 233 WHERE MARRIAGE IS COMMONLY OR OCCASIONALLY POLYGYNOUS, RATHER THAN MONOGAMOUS (314)	242	TILT MORE TOWARD BEING THOSE 0.85 OF 162 WHERE MARRIAGE IS COMMONLY OR OCCASIONALLY POLYGYNOUS, RATHER THAN MONOGAMOUS (314)	176 138 57 24 XSQ= 4.88 PHI= -0.111 XP = 0.0271
243	TILT TOWARD BEING THOSE 0.56 OF 32 WHERE POLYGYNY, IF PRESENT, HAS A HIGH INCIDENCE (24) W-C,S	243	TILT TOWARD BEING THOSE 0.79 OF 28 WHERE POLYGYNY, IF PRESENT, HAS A LOW INCIDENCE (36) W-D,S	18 6 14 22 XSQ= 6.16 PHI= 0.321 XP = 0.0130
259	DRIFT TOWARD BEING THOSE 0.58 OF 24 WHERE THE SEVERITY OF MOTHER-IN-LAW AVOIDANCE IS LOW (20) WNS	259	DRIFT TOWARD BEING THOSE 0.73 OF 22 WHERE THE SEVERITY OF MOTHER-IN-LAW AVOIDANCE IS HIGH (26) WNS	10 16 14 6 XSQ= 3.33 PHI= -0.269 XP = 0.0680
262	TILT MORE TOWARD BEING THOSE 0.81 OF 236 WHERE WIVES ARE OBTAINED BY MEANS INVOLVING THE PRESENCE OF SOME CONSIDERATION (305)	262	TILT LESS TOWARD BEING THOSE 0.71 OF 159 WHERE WIVES ARE OBTAINED BY MEANS INVOLVING THE PRESENCE OF SOME CONSIDERATION (305)	192 113 44 46 XSQ= 5.14 PHI= 0.114 XP = 0.0233
263	TILT MORE TOWARD BEING THOSE 0.64 OF 236 WHERE WIVES ARE OBTAINED BY RELATIVELY DIFFICULT MEANS, NAMELY BY BRIDE-PRICE, BRIDE-SERVICE, OR EXCHANGING A FEMALE RELATIVE (233)	263	TILT LESS TOWARD BEING THOSE 0.51 OF 159 WHERE WIVES ARE OBTAINED BY RELATIVELY DIFFICULT MEANS, NAMELY BY BRIDE-PRICE, BRIDE-SERVICE, OR EXCHANGING A FEMALE RELATIVE (233)	152 81 84 78 XSQ= 6.57 PHI= 0.129 XP = 0.0104
278	DRIFT TOWARD BEING THOSE 0.63 OF 8 WHERE PROPERTY RIGHTS IN WOMEN ARE PRESENT (8) LWS	278	DRIFT TOWARD BEING THOSE 0.79 OF 14 WHERE PROPERTY RIGHTS IN WOMEN ARE UNIMPORTANT OR ABSENT (14) LWS	5 3 3 11 XSQ= 2.15 PHI= 0.312 EP = 0.0815
300	TILT TOWARD BEING THOSE 0.51 OF 69 WHERE THE POST-PARTUM SEX TABOO LASTS LONGER THAN SIX MONTHS (51)	300	TILT TOWARD BEING THOSE 0.71 OF 55 WHERE THE POST-PARTUM SEX TABOO LASTS SIX MONTHS OR LESS (73)	35 16 34 39 XSQ= 5.06 PHI= 0.202 XP = 0.0245
304	TEND TO BE THOSE 0.85 OF 20 WHERE THE EARLY ANAL SATISFACTION POTENTIAL IS LOW (22) W-C	304	TEND TO BE THOSE 0.76 OF 21 WHERE THE EARLY ANAL SATISFACTION POTENTIAL IS HIGH (19) W-C	3 16 17 5 XSQ= 13.06 PHI= -0.564 XP = 0.0003

314	LEAN LESS TOWARD BEING THOSE 0.62 OF 42 WHERE THE INCIDENCE OF MOTHER-CHILD HOUSEHOLDS IS LOW (61) W-C,S	314	LEAN MORE TOWARD BEING THOSE 0.92 OF 38 WHERE THE INCIDENCE OF MOTHER-CHILD HOUSEHOLDS IS LOW (61) W-D,S	16 3 26 35 XSQ= 8.45 PHI= 0.325 XP = 0.0037
318	TILT TOWARD BEING THOSE 0.58 OF 36 WHERE THE OVERALL INDULGENCE OF THE INFANT IS LOW (31) B-B-C	318	TILT TOWARD BEING THOSE 0.71 OF 35 WHERE THE OVERALL INDULGENCE OF THE INFANT IS HIGH (40) B-B-C	15 25 21 10 XSQ= 5.24 PHI= -0.272 XP = 0.0221
320	TILT LESS TOWARD BEING THOSE 0.51 OF 35 WHERE THE DEGREE OF REDUCTION OF THE INFANT'S DRIVES IS HIGH (45) B-B-C	320	TILT MORE TOWARD BEING THOSE 0.79 OF 34 WHERE THE DEGREE OF REDUCTION OF THE INFANT'S DRIVES IS HIGH (45) B-B-C	18 27 17 7 XSQ= 4.78 PHI= -0.263 XP = 0.0287
324	DRIFT TOWARD BEING THOSE 0.64 OF 33 WHERE THE PAIN INFLICTED ON THE INFANT BY THE NURTURANT AGENT IS HIGH (34) B-B-C	324	DRIFT TOWARD BEING THOSE 0.61 OF 33 WHERE THE PAIN INFLICTED ON THE INFANT BY THE NURTURANT AGENT IS LOW OR NEGLIGIBLE (32) B-B-C	21 13 12 20 XSQ= 2.97 PHI= 0.212 XP = 0.0847
334	DRIFT TOWARD BEING THOSE 0.60 OF 40 WHERE THE INDULGENCE OF THE CHILD IS LOW (38) B-B-C	334	DRIFT TOWARD BEING THOSE 0.63 OF 38 WHERE THE INDULGENCE OF THE CHILD IS HIGH (40) B-B-C	16 24 24 14 XSQ= 3.31 PHI= -0.206 XP = 0.0690
337	TILT TOWARD BEING THOSE 0.66 OF 38 WHERE THE CHILD'S INFERRED ANXIETY OVER NON-PERFORMANCE OF RESPONSIBLE BEHAVIOR IS HIGH (38) B-B-C	337	TILT TOWARD BEING THOSE 0.63 OF 35 WHERE THE CHILD'S INFERRED ANXIETY OVER NON-PERFORMANCE OF RESPONSIBLE BEHAVIOR IS LOW (35) B-B-C	25 13 13 22 XSQ= 4.90 PHI= .0.259 XP = 0.0269
338	DRIFT TOWARD BEING THOSE 0.71 OF 38 WHERE THE CHILD'S INFERRED ANXIETY OVER PERFORMANCE OF RESPONSIBLE BEHAVIOR IS HIGH (44) B-B-C	338	DRIFT TOWARD BEING THOSE 0.51 OF 35 WHERE THE CHILD'S INFERRED ANXIETY OVER PERFORMANCE OF RESPONSIBLE BEHAVIOR IS LOW (29) B-B-C	27 17 11 18 XSQ= 2.96 PHI= 0.202 XP = 0.0851
342	DRIFT TOWARD BEING THOSE 0.55 OF 22 WHERE THE CHILD'S INFERRED ANXIETY OVER PERFORMANCE OF NURTURANT BEHAVIOR IS HIGH (18) B-B-C	342	DRIFT TOWARD BEING THOSE 0.75 OF 24 WHERE THE CHILD'S INFERRED ANXIETY OVER PERFORMANCE OF NURTURANT BEHAVIOR IS LOW (28) B-B-C	12 6 10 18 XSQ= 3.06 PHI= 0.258 XP = 0.0804
346	TILT TOWARD BEING THOSE 0.64 OF 39 WHERE THE CHILD'S INFERRED ANXIETY OVER PERFORMANCE OF SELF-RELIANT BEHAVIOR IS HIGH (37) B-B-C	346	TILT TOWARD BEING THOSE 0.68 OF 37 WHERE THE CHILD'S INFERRED ANXIETY OVER PERFORMANCE OF SELF-RELIANT BEHAVIOR IS LOW (39) B-B-C	25 12 14 25 XSQ= 6.41 PHI= 0.290 XP = 0.0114

347	TILT TOWARD BEING THOSE 0.62 OF 39 WHERE THE CHILD'S INFERRED CONFLICT REGARDING SELF-RELIANT BEHAVIOR IS HIGH (37) B-B-C	347	TILT TOWARD BEING THOSE 0.65 OF 37 WHERE THE CHILD'S INFERRED CONFLICT REGARDING SELF-RELIANT BEHAVIOR IS LOW (39) B-B-C	24 13 15 24 XSQ= 4.29 PHI= 0.238 XP = 0.0382
353	LEAN TOWARD BEING THOSE 0.74 OF 38 WHERE THE CHILD'S INFERRED ANXIETY OVER NON-PERFORMANCE OF OBEDIENT BEHAVIOR IS HIGH (42) B-B-C	353	LEAN TOWARD BEING THOSE 0.61 OF 36 WHERE THE CHILD-S INFERRED ANXIETY OVER NON-PERFORMANCE OF OBEDIENT BEHAVIOR IS LOW (32) B-B-C	28 14 10 22 XSQ= 7.76 PHI= 0.324 XP = 0.0054
360	DRIFT TOWARD BEING THOSE 0.53 OF 19 WHERE ADOLESCENT PEER GROUPS ARE PRESENT IN A SETTING OF WORK AND PUBLIC GATHERINGS AND LEISURE, OR AT LEAST OF PUBLIC GATHERINGS AND LEISURE (14) JKH	360	DRIFT TOWARD BEING THOSE 0.78 OF 18 WHERE ADOLESCENT PEER GROUPS ARE PRESENT ONLY IN A SETTING OF LEISURE, OR ELSE ARE ABSENT (23) JKH	10 4 9 14 XSQ= 2.46 PHI= 0.258 EP = 0.0911
377	TEND LESS TO BE THOSE 0.65 OF 187 WHERE MALE GENITAL MUTILATION IS ABSENT (242)	377	TEND MORE TO BE THOSE 0.88 OF 138 WHERE MALE GENITAL MUTILATION IS ABSENT (242)	66 17 121 121 XSQ= 20.85 PHI= 0.253 XP = 0.0000
417	IN ALL CASES ARE THOSE 1.00 OF 16 WHERE WARFARE IS PREVALENT (34) LWS	417	TILT LESS TOWARD BEING THOSE 0.67 OF 27 WHERE WARFARE IS PREVALENT (34) LWS	16 18 0 9 XSQ= 4.88 PHI= 0.337 XP = 0.0271
424	DRIFT TOWARD BEING THOSE 0.52 OF 31 WHERE RELIGIOUS SPECIALISTS ARE FULL-TIME, RATHER THAN PART-TIME (21) JMH	424	DRIFT TOWARD BEING THOSE 0.78 OF 23 WHERE RELIGIOUS SPECIALISTS ARE PART-TIME, RATHER THAN FULL-TIME (33) JMH	16 5 15 18 XSQ= 3.78 PHI= 0.265 XP = 0.0518
426	TEND TO BE THOSE 0.70 OF 143 WHERE A HIGH GOD IS PRESENT (156) GES,EA	426	TEND TO BE THOSE 0.52 OF 117 WHERE A HIGH GOD IS ABSENT (104) GES,EA	100 56 43 61 XSQ= 12.15 PHI= 0.216 XP = 0.0005
429	TILT TOWARD BEING THOSE 0.91 OF 23 WHERE SUPERNATURAL SANCTIONS FOR MORALITY ARE PRESENT (28) GES	429	TILT TOWARD BEING THOSE 0.50 OF 14 WHERE SUPERNATURAL SANCTIONS FOR MORALITY ARE ABSENT OR UNREPORTED (9) GES	21 7 2 7 XSQ= 5.98 PHI= 0.402 EP = 0.0141
431	TILT LESS TOWARD BEING THOSE 0.57 OF 21 WHERE SUPERNATURAL SANCTIONS FOR MORALITY, HAVING AN EFFECT ON AN INDIVIDUAL'S AFTERLIFE, ARE ABSENT OR UNREPORTED (25) GES	431	TILT MORE TOWARD BEING THOSE 0.93 OF 14 WHERE SUPERNATURAL SANCTIONS FOR MORALITY, HAVING AN EFFECT ON AN INDIVIDUAL'S AFTERLIFE, ARE ABSENT OR UNREPORTED (25) GES	9 1 12 13 XSQ= 3.65 PHI= 0.323 EP = 0.0280

435	TILT TOWARD BEING THOSE 0.85 OF 13 WHERE ABANDONMENT OF THE HOUSE OF THE DEAD IS NOT PRACTICED (19) LWS	435	TILT TOWARD BEING THOSE 0.56 OF 18 WHERE ABANDONMENT OF THE HOUSE OF THE DEAD IS PRACTICED (12) LWS	2 10 11 8 XSQ= 3.58 PHI= -0.340 EP = 0.0317
444	DRIFT TOWARD BEING THOSE 0.61 OF 31 WHERE THE USE OF DREAMS TO SEEK AND CONTROL SUPERNATURAL POWERS IS LOW (27) RGD	444	DRIFT TOWARD BEING THOSE 0.67 OF 24 WHERE THE USE OF DREAMS TO SEEK AND CONTROL SUPERNATURAL POWERS IS HIGH (28) RGD	12 16 19 8 XSQ= 3.19 PHI= -0.241 XP = 0.0743
452	LEAN TOWARD BEING THOSE 0.63 OF 27 WHERE TOTEMISM WITH FOOD TABOOS IS PRESENT (19) WNS	452	LEAN TOWARD BEING THOSE 0.88 OF 16 WHERE TOTEMISM WITH FOOD TABOOS IS ABSENT (24) WNS	17 2 10 14 XSQ= 8.43 PHI= 0.443 XP = 0.0037
458	TEND TO BE THOSE 0.56 OF 80 WHERE GAMES, IF PRESENT, INCLUDE GAMES OF STRATEGY (52) R-A-B,EA	458	TEND TO BE THOSE 0.92 OF 91 WHERE GAMES, IF PRESENT, DO NOT INCLUDE GAMES OF STRATEGY (119) R-A-B,EA	45 7 35 84 XSQ= 45.17 PHI= 0.514 XP = 0.
460	TILT MORE TOWARD BEING THOSE 0.70 OF 80 WHERE GAMES, IF PRESENT, ARE NOT LIMITED TO GAMES OF SKILL ONLY (104) R-A-B,EA	460	TILT LESS TOWARD BEING THOSE 0.53 OF 91 WHERE GAMES, IF PRESENT, ARE NOT LIMITED TO GAMES OF SKILL ONLY (104) R-A-B,EA	24 43 56 48 XSQ= 4.62 PHI= -0.164 XP = 0.0316
468	LEAN LESS TOWARD BEING THOSE 0.52 OF 31 WHERE CONTACT WITH OTHER CULTURES IS REGULAR OR IRREGULAR, RATHER THAN FREQUENT (37) JMH	468	LEAN MORE TOWARD BEING THOSE 0.91 OF 23 WHERE CONTACT WITH OTHER CULTURES IS REGULAR OR IRREGULAR, RATHER THAN FREQUENT (37) JMH	15 2 16 21 XSQ= 7.89 PHI= 0.382 XP = 0.0050
469	LEAN MORE TOWARD BEING THOSE 0.94 OF 31 WHERE CONTACT WITH OTHER CULTURES IS FREQUENT OR REGULAR, RATHER THAN IRREGULAR (43) JMH	469	LEAN LESS TOWARD BEING THOSE 0.61 OF 23 WHERE CONTACT WITH OTHER CULTURES IS FREQUENT OR REGULAR, RATHER THAN IRREGULAR (43) JMH	29 14 2 9 XSQ= 6.79 PHI= 0.355 XP = 0.0091
470	TILT TOWARD BEING THOSE 0.55 OF 31 WHERE INNOVATIONS ARE GENERALLY ACCEPTED (21) JMH	470	TILT TOWARD BEING THOSE 0.83 OF 23 WHERE INNOVATIONS ARE ACCEPTED ONLY SELECTIVELY (33) JMH	17 4 14 19 XSQ= 6.29 PHI= 0.341 XP = 0.0121
475	TILT TOWARD BEING THOSE 0.69 OF 45 WHERE EXHIBITIONISTIC DANCING IS STRONGLY OR MODERATELY EMPHASIZED (48) PES	475	TILT TOWARD BEING THOSE 0.59 OF 41 WHERE EXHIBITIONISTIC DANCING IS NEGLIGIBLY EMPHASIZED (38) PES	31 17 14 24 XSQ= 5.48 PHI= 0.252 XP = 0.0193

476	TILT TOWARD BEING THOSE WHERE THE DEGREE OF INSOBRIETY IS MODERATE OR SLIGHT (18) CH	0.56 OF 25	476	TILT TOWARD BEING THOSE WHERE THE DEGREE OF INSOBRIETY IS STRONG (31) DH	0.83 OF 24	11 20 14 4 XSQ= 6.55 PHI= -0.366 XP = 0.0105
480	TILT TOWARD BEING THOSE WHERE COMPLEXITY OF ARTISTIC DESIGN IS HIGH (14) HB	0.71 OF 14	480	TILT TOWARD BEING THOSE WHERE COMPLEXITY OF ARTISTIC DESIGN IS LOW (15) HB	0.73 OF 15	10 4 4 11 XSQ= 4.16 PHI= 0.379 EP = 0.0268

53 CULTURES
WHERE FOOD PRODUCTION IS BY
INTENSIVE AGRICULTURE, RATHER THAN BY
SIMPLE AGRICULTURE OR
INCIPIENT FOOD PRODUCTION (91)

53 CULTURES
WHERE FOOD PRODUCTION IS BY
SIMPLE AGRICULTURE OR
INCIPIENT FOOD PRODUCTION, RATHER THAN BY
INTENSIVE AGRICULTURE (147)

BACKGROUND ON PAGE 74

BOTH SUBJECT AND PREDICATE

91 IN LEFT COLUMN

ALBANIANS	AMERICANS	ARAUCANIANS	AYMARA	AZTEC	BAMBARA	BARABRA	BRAZILIANS	BULGARIANS	BURUSHO
CAMBODIANS	CHAGGA	CHERKESS	CHIBCHA	COCHITI	COORG	CZECHS	DAGUR	DARD	DILLING
DOGON	DUTCH	EGYPTIANS	GANDA	HANO	HAZARA	HEBREWS	HUTSUL	IFUGAO	INCA
INGASSANA	IRAQW	IRISH	JAPANESE	JAVANESE	JEMEZ	KABYLE	KATAB	KERALA	KIKUYU
KOHISTANI	KOL	KOREANS	LEPCHA	LOLO	LUO	MACASSARESE	MALAYS	MAMBILA	MANDAN
MARGI	MATAKAM	MERINA	MIAO	MIN CHINESE	MINCHIA	MONGUOR	MOSSI	MZAB	NANDI
NURI	NYAKYUSA	NYORO	OKINAWANS	ORAON	PAEZ	PATHAN	RIFFIANS	ROMANS	RUNDI
SAGADA	SANTAL	SERBS	SHLUH	SINHALESE	SIWANS	SONGHAI	SOTHO	SYRIANS	TALLENSI
TANALA	TAOS	TARAHUMARA	TEDA	THAI	TIGRINYA	TURKMEN	VENDA	VIETNAMESE	WALLOONS
ZUNI									

147 IN RIGHT COLUMN

ABOR	AKHA	ALORESE	AMBA	APINAYE	ARAPESH	ASHANTI	ATAYAL	AZANDE	BABWA
BACAIRI	BAMILEKE	BANDA	BARI	BAYA	BEMBA	BHIL	BHUIYA	BIRIFOR	BLACK CARIB
BUDUMA	BUNLAP	CAGABA	CAMAYURA	CARIB	CAYAPA	CHEROKEE	CHIRIGUANO	CHOCO	CHORTI
CHUKCHEE	CREEK	CUNA	DELAWARE	ENGA	FANG	FON	FOX	FUTAJALONKE	GARO
GISU	GOND	GURE	HANUNOO	HASINAI	HAVASUPAI	HUICHOL	HURON	IBAN	ICELANDERS
ILA	JIVARO	JUKUN	KACHIN	KAPAUKU	KERAKI	KHASI	KISSI	KPE	KUBA
KURTATCHI	LAKALAI	LAKHER	LAMBA	LAMET	LANGO	LAU	LESU	LHOTA NAGA	LOZI
LUBA	MAM	MAMVU	MANGAIANS	MAORI	MARQUESANS	MARSHALLESE	MAYA	MBUNDU	MENDE
MIAMI	MNONG GAR	MONGO	MOTA	MUNDURUCU	NAMA	NATCHEZ	NAVAHO	NDEMBU	NICOBARESE
NUPE	PAIWAN	PALAUANS	PALIKUR	PAPAGO	PAWNEE	PONAPEANS	PUKAPUKA	PURUM	SAMOANS
SAMOYED	SANDAWE	SARAMACCA	SENIANG	SHERENTE	SHILLUK	SIUAI	SUBANUN	SWAZI	TAGBANUA
TALAMANCA	TAPIRAPE	TENDA	TENETEHARA	TERA	TERENA	TESO	THONGA	TIMBIRA	TIMUCUA
TIV	TORAJA	TOTONAC	TRISTAN	TROBRIAND	TRUMAI	TUCANO	TUNEBO	TUPINAMBA	TURKANA
ULAWANS	WANTOAT	WAPISHANA	WICHITA	WINNEBAGO	WITOTO	WOGEO	WOLEAIANS	WOLOF	YABARANA
YAKO	YAKUT	YAO	YAPESE	YARURO	YOMBE	YORUBA			

117 EXCLUDED BECAUSE IRRELEVANT

ABIPON	AINU	ALACALUF	ANDAMANESE	ARANDA	ATSUGEWI	AWEIKOMA	BAJUN	BASSERI	BEJA
BERGDAMA	BOERS	BORORO	BOTOCUDO	BOZO	BURYAT	COPR ESKIMO	CADUVEO	CALLINAGO	CARAJA	CHAMACOCO
CHENCHU	CHEYENNE	CHIR-APACHE	CHOROTI	COMANCHE	COPR ESKIMO	CREE	CROW	DIEGUENO	DIERI
DOROBO	ELLICE	EYAK	GILBERTESE	GILYAK	GOAJIRO	GROS VENTRE	GUAHIBO	GUATO	HAIDA
HAWAIIANS	HERERO	HUKUNDIKA	INGALIK	KALMYK	KARIERA	KASKA	KAZAK	KET	KHALKA
KIOW-APACHE	KORYAK	KUNG	KUTENAI	KWAKIUTL	LAPPS	MANIHIKI	MANUS	MARICOPA	MASAI
MATACO	MBUTI	MISKITO	MIWOK	MOTILON	MURINBATA	MURNGIN	NABESNA	NAMBICUARA	NASKAPI
NOMLAKI	NUER	NUNIVAK	OJIBWA	OMAHA	ONA	ONTONG-JAVA	PARAUJANO	PENOBSCOT	PURARI

RAROIANS TAREUMIUT TSHIMSHIAN WIKMUNKAN REGEIBAT TEHUELCHE TUBATULABAL YAGUA RWALA TENINO TUCUNA YAHGAN SANPOIL TETON TWANA YOKUTS SARSI TIKOPIA UTE YUKAGHIR SELUNG TIWI VEDDA YUKI SEMANG TODA WAICA YUROK SERI TOKELAU WAROPEN SIRIONO TOLCWA WARRAU SOMALI TRUKESE WASHO

45 EXCLUDED BECAUSE UNASCERTAINED

4	TEND LESS TO BE THOSE LOCATED OUTSIDE OF THE CIRCUM-MEDITERRANEAN (355)	0.73 OF 91	4	TEND MORE TO BE THOSE LOCATED OUTSIDE OF THE CIRCUM-MEDITERRANEAN (355)	0.97 OF 147	25 5 66 142 XSQ= 27.42 PHI= 0.339 XP = 0.0000
5	TEND LESS TO BE THOSE LOCATED OUTSIDE OF EAST EURASIA (330)	0.68 OF 91	5	TEND MORE TO BE THOSE LOCATED OUTSIDE OF EAST EURASIA (330)	0.88 OF 147	29 17 62 130 XSQ= 13.59 PHI= 0.239 XP = 0.0002
6	TEND MORE TO BE THOSE LOCATED OUTSIDE OF THE INSULAR PACIFIC (330)	0.96 OF 91	6	TEND LESS TO BE THOSE LOCATED OUTSIDE OF THE INSULAR PACIFIC (330)	0.77 OF 147	4 34 87 113 XSQ= 13.34 PHI= -0.237 XP = 0.0003
9	LEAN MORE TOWARD BEING THOSE LOCATED OUTSIDE OF SOUTH AMERICA (335)	0.95 OF 91	9	LEAN LESS TOWARD BEING THOSE LOCATED OUTSIDE OF SOUTH AMERICA (335)	0.79 OF 147	5 31 86 116 XSQ= 9.47 PHI= -0.199 XP = 0.0021
15	TEND TO BE THOSE WHERE THE LATITUDE IS TWENTY DEGREES OR GREATER (183)	0.58 OF 91	15	TEND TO BE THOSE WHERE THE LATITUDE IS LESS THAN TWENTY DEGREES (217)	0.71 OF 147	53 43 38 104 XSQ= 18.44 PHI= 0.278 XP = 0.0000
33	LEAN LESS TOWARD BEING THOSE WHERE THE NATURAL ENVIRONMENT IS OTHER THAN 'VERY HARSH,' I.E., DESERT, DESERT GRASSES AND SHRUBS, TUNDRA, OR HIGH PLATEAU STEPPE (341) FWM	0.82 OF 91	33	LEAN MORE TOWARD BEING THOSE WHERE THE NATURAL ENVIRONMENT IS OTHER THAN 'VERY HARSH,' I.E., DESERT, DESERT GRASSES AND SHRUBS, TUNDRA, OR HIGH PLATEAU STEPPE (341) FWM	0.94 OF 147	16 9 75 138 XSQ= 6.68 PHI= 0.168 XP = 0.0097
36	LEAN LESS TOWARD BEING THOSE WHERE THE NATURAL ENVIRONMENT IS OTHER THAN 'VERY HARSH,' OR SUB-TROPICAL BUSH, OR TEMPERATE GRASSLAND (292) FWM	0.74 OF 91	36	LEAN MORE TOWARD BEING THOSE WHERE THE NATURAL ENVIRONMENT IS OTHER THAN 'VERY HARSH,' OR SUB-TROPICAL BUSH, OR TEMPERATE GRASSLAND (292) FWM	0.88 OF 147	24 18 67 129 XSQ= 6.78 PHI= 0.169 XP = 0.0092

42	TEND TO BE THOSE 0.75 OF 91 WHERE THE NATURAL ENVIRONMENT IS OTHER THAN TROPICAL OR SUB-TROPICAL RAIN FOREST, OR MONSOON FOREST (244) FWM	42	TEND TO BE THOSE 0.58 OF 147 WHERE THE NATURAL ENVIRONMENT IS TROPICAL OR SUB-TROPICAL RAIN FOREST, OR MONSOON FOREST (156) FWM	23 85 68 62 XSQ= 22.73 PHI= -0.309 XP = 0.0000
44	LEAN MORE TOWARD BEING THOSE 0.95 OF 91 WHERE SETTLEMENTS ARE FIXED (222)	44	LEAN LESS TOWARD BEING THOSE 0.81 OF 140 WHERE SETTLEMENTS ARE FIXED (222)	86 114 5 26 XSQ= 7.03 PHI= 0.174 XP = 0.0080
48	DRIFT TOWARD BEING THOSE 0.77 OF 13 WHERE THE FOOD SUPPLY IS NOT SECURE, AND FOOD SHORTAGES ARE FREQUENT OR ANNUAL (41) MGW	48	DRIFT TOWARD BEING THOSE 0.58 OF 38 WHERE THE FOOD SUPPLY IS SECURE, AND FOOD SHORTAGES ARE RARE OR OCCASIONAL (38) MGW	3 22 10 16 XSQ= 3.41 PHI= -0.259 XP = 0.0648
62	TEND MORE TO BE THOSE 0.95 OF 91 WHERE HUSBANDRY OF SOME KIND IS PRESENT (228)	62	TEND LESS TO BE THOSE 0.72 OF 147 WHERE HUSBANDRY OF SOME KIND IS PRESENT (228)	86 106 5 41 XSQ= 16.67 PHI= 0.265 XP = 0.0000
63	TEND TO BE THOSE 0.92 OF 86 WHERE HUSBANDRY, IF PRESENT, IS PRINCIPALLY IN THE FORM OF BOVINE, EQUINE, CAMEL-LIKE, OR DEER-LIKE ANIMALS, RATHER THAN PIGS, SHEEP, OR GOATS (152)	63	TEND TO BE THOSE 0.56 OF 106 WHERE HUSBANDRY, IF PRESENT, IS PRINCIPALLY IN THE FORM OF PIGS, SHEEP, OR GOATS, RATHER THAN BOVINE, EQUINE, CAMEL-LIKE, OR DEER-LIKE ANIMALS (74)	79 47 7 59 XSQ= 45.45 PHI= 0.487 XP = 0.
71	TEND TO BE THOSE 0.87 OF 52 WHERE METAL WORKING IS PRESENT (98)	71	TEND TO BE THOSE 0.59 OF 106 WHERE METAL WORKING IS ABSENT (153)	45 43 7 63 XSQ= 28.05 PHI= 0.421 XP = 0.0000
73	LEAN TOWARD BEING THOSE 0.75 OF 52 WHERE WEAVING IS PRESENT (118)	73	LEAN TOWARD BEING THOSE 0.50 OF 104 WHERE WEAVING IS ABSENT (130)	39 52 13 52 XSQ= 7.92 PHI= 0.225 XP = 0.0049
74	TILT MORE TOWARD BEING THOSE 0.89 OF 46 WHERE POTTERY IS PRESENT (145)	74	TILT LESS TOWARD BEING THOSE 0.72 OF 103 WHERE POTTERY IS PRESENT (145)	41 74 5 29 XSQ= 4.46 PHI= 0.173 XP = 0.0347
77	DRIFT TOWARD BEING THOSE 0.54 OF 13 WHERE THE WRITING SYSTEM IS ALPHABETIC-OR-PHONETIC, RATHER THAN BEING MNEMONIC OR ABSENT (15) JMH	77	DRIFT TOWARD BEING THOSE 0.79 OF 24 WHERE THE WRITING SYSTEM IS MNEMONIC OR ABSENT, RATHER THAN BEING ALPHABETIC-OR-PHONETIC (39) JMH	7 5 6 19 XSQ= 2.82 PHI= 0.276 EP = 0.0666

```
81  TEND TO BE THOSE                  0.81 OF  70     81  TEND TO BE THOSE                  0.68 OF  90           57   29
    WHERE A CITY OR TOWN IS PRESENT, OR                   WHERE NO CITY OR TOWN IS PRESENT, AND                 13   61
    THE AVERAGE COMMUNITY SIZE IS                         THE AVERAGE COMMUNITY SIZE IS                   XSQ=   36.40
    200 OR GREATER  (89)                                  SMALLER THAN 200  (135)                         PHI=   0.477
                                                                                                          XP =   0.

82  IN ALL CASES ARE THOSE            1.00 OF  70     82  TILT LESS TOWARD BEING THOSE      0.89 OF  90           70   80
    WHERE A CITY OR TOWN IS PRESENT, OR                   WHERE A CITY OR TOWN IS PRESENT, OR                    0   10
    THE AVERAGE COMMUNITY SIZE IS                         THE AVERAGE COMMUNITY SIZE IS                   XSQ=    6.51
    FIFTY OR GREATER  (178)                               FIFTY OR GREATER  (178)                         PHI=   0.202
                                                                                                          XP =   0.0107

83  TEND TO BE THOSE                  0.62 OF  34     83  TEND TO BE THOSE                  0.74 OF  82           21   21
    WHERE, WITH NO CITY AND NO TOWN PRESENT,              WHERE, WITH NO CITY AND NO TOWN PRESENT,              13   61
    THE AVERAGE COMMUNITY SIZE IS                         THE AVERAGE COMMUNITY SIZE IS                   XSQ=   12.08
    BETWEEN 200 AND 999, RATHER THAN                      SMALLER THAN 200, RATHER THAN                   PHI=   0.323
    SMALLER THAN 200  (45)                                BETWEEN 200 AND 999  (135)                      XP =   0.0005

85  TEND TO BE THOSE                  0.52 OF  66     85  TEND TO BE THOSE                  0.83 OF 117           34   20
    WHERE THE LEVEL OF POLITICAL INTEGRATION              WHERE THE LEVEL OF POLITICAL INTEGRATION              32   97
    IS THE LARGE STATE, OR                                IS THE MINIMAL STATE,                           XSQ=   22.41
    THE LITTLE STATE  (70) GPM                            THE AUTONOMOUS COMMUNITY, OR                    PHI=   0.350
                                                          THE FAMILY  (234) GPM                           XP =   0.0000

86  TEND TO BE THOSE                  0.77 OF  66     86  TEND TO BE THOSE                  0.50 OF 117           51   58
    WHERE THE LEVEL OF POLITICAL INTEGRATION              WHERE THE LEVEL OF POLITICAL INTEGRATION              15   59
    IS THE LARGE STATE, THE LITTLE STATE,                 IS THE AUTONOMOUS COMMUNITY, OR                 XSQ=   12.32
    OR THE MINIMAL STATE  (148) GPM                       THE FAMILY  (156) GPM                           PHI=   0.259
                                                                                                          XP =   0.0004

88  TEND TO BE THOSE                  0.59 OF  63     88  TEND TO BE THOSE                  0.75 OF 106           37   26
    WHERE, IF A HEADMANSHIP IS PRESENT,                   WHERE, IF A HEADMANSHIP IS PRESENT,                   26   80
    SUCCESSION IS NON-HEREDITARY  (106)                   SUCCESSION IS HEREDITARY  (165)                 XSQ=   18.33
                                                                                                          PHI=   0.329
                                                                                                          XP =   0.0000

91  TILT TOWARD BEING THOSE           0.83 OF  12     91  TILT TOWARD BEING THOSE           0.67 OF  18           10    6
    WHERE SOCIETAL COMPLEXITY                             WHERE SOCIETAL COMPLEXITY                              2   12
    IS HIGH  (18) F-W                                     IS LOW  (22) F-W                                XSQ=    5.36
                                                                                                          PHI=   0.423
                                                                                                          EP =   0.0106

94  TEND LESS TO BE THOSE             0.70 OF  88     94  TEND MORE TO BE THOSE             0.96 OF 140           26    5
    WHERE THE HIERARCHY                                   WHERE THE HIERARCHY                                   62  135
    OF NATIONAL JURISDICTION HAS                          OF NATIONAL JURISDICTION HAS                    XSQ=   28.86
    TWO, ONE, OR NO LEVELS  (296) GES,EA                  TWO, ONE, OR NO LEVELS  (296) GES,EA            PHI=   0.356
                                                                                                          XP =   0.0000

95  TEND LESS TO BE THOSE             0.51 OF  88     95  TEND MORE TO BE THOSE             0.81 OF 140           43   26
    WHERE THE HIERARCHY                                   WHERE THE HIERARCHY                                   45  114
    OF NATIONAL JURISDICTION HAS                          OF NATIONAL JURISDICTION HAS                    XSQ=   22.08
    ONE OR NO LEVELS  (254) GES,EA                        ONE OR NO LEVELS  (254) GES,EA                  PHI=   0.311
                                                                                                          XP =   0.0000
```

96	TEND MORE TO BE THOSE 0.77 OF 88 WHERE THE HIERARCHY OF NATIONAL JURISDICTION HAS FOUR, THREE, TWO OR ONE LEVEL (174) GES,EA	96	TEND LESS TO BE THOSE 0.51 OF 140 WHERE THE HIERARCHY OF NATIONAL JURISDICTION HAS FOUR, THREE, TWO OR ONE LEVEL (174) GES,EA	68 72 20 68 XSQ= 14.16 PHI= 0.249 XP = 0.0002
99	DRIFT MORE TOWARD BEING THOSE 0.90 OF 20 WHERE, WITH NATIONAL HIERARCHY ABSENT, THE HIERARCHY OF LOCAL JURISDICTION HAS FOUR OR THREE LEVELS (93) GES,EA	99	DRIFT LESS TOWARD BEING THOSE 0.68 OF 68 WHERE, WITH NATIONAL HIERARCHY ABSENT, THE HIERARCHY OF LOCAL JURISDICTION HAS FOUR OR THREE LEVELS (93) GES,EA	18 46 2 22 XSQ= 2.85 PHI= 0.180 XP = 0.0915
100	LEAN MORE TOWARD BEING THOSE 0.98 OF 88 WHERE HIERARCHIES ARE MORE COMPLEX THAN THE 'SIMPLEST,' I. E., MORE COMPLEX THAN TWO LOCAL LEVELS WITH NO NATIONAL LEVELS (267) GES,EA	100	LEAN LESS TOWARD BEING THOSE 0.84 OF 140 WHERE HIERARCHIES ARE MORE COMPLEX THAN THE 'SIMPLEST,' I. E., MORE COMPLEX THAN TWO LOCAL LEVELS WITH NO NATIONAL LEVELS (267) GES,EA	86 118 2 22 XSQ= 8.99 PHI= 0.199 XP = 0.0027
102	TEND MORE TO BE THOSE 0.77 OF 86 WHERE CLASS STRATIFICATION IS PRESENT (203)	102	TEND LESS TO BE THOSE 0.52 OF 142 WHERE CLASS STRATIFICATION IS PRESENT (203)	66 74 20 68 XSQ= 12.69 PHI= 0.236 XP = 0.0004
107	TEND LESS TO BE THOSE 0.56 OF 66 WHERE CLASS STRATIFICATION, IF PRESENT, IS BASED ON SOMETHING OTHER THAN OCCUPATIONAL STATUS (160)	107	TEND MORE TO BE THOSE 0.91 OF 74 WHERE CLASS STRATIFICATION, IF PRESENT, IS BASED ON SOMETHING OTHER THAN OCCUPATIONAL STATUS (160)	29 7 37 67 XSQ= 19.94 PHI= 0.377 XP = 0.0000
108	TILT MORE TOWARD BEING THOSE 0.74 OF 66 WHERE CLASS STRATIFICATION, IF PRESENT, IS BASED ON SOMETHING OTHER THAN A HEREDITARY ARISTOCRACY (129)	108	TILT LESS TOWARD BEING THOSE 0.55 OF 74 WHERE CLASS STRATIFICATION, IF PRESENT, IS BASED ON SOMETHING OTHER THAN A HEREDITARY ARISTOCRACY (129)	17 33 49 41 XSQ= 4.60 PHI= -0.181 XP = 0.0319
109	TEND LESS TO BE THOSE 0.69 OF 77 WHERE CASTES ARE ABSENT (317)	109	TEND MORE TO BE THOSE 0.92 OF 142 WHERE CASTES ARE ABSENT (317)	24 12 53 130 XSQ= 17.14 PHI= 0.280 XP = 0.0000
118	TILT TOWARD BEING THOSE 0.75 OF 12 WHERE THE PERCENTAGE OF OCCUPATIONS THAT ARE SPECIALIZED IS HIGH OR MEDIUM (24) WME	118	TILT TOWARD BEING THOSE 0.68 OF 22 WHERE THE PERCENTAGE OF OCCUPATIONS THAT ARE SPECIALIZED IS LOW (25) WME	9 7 3 15 XSQ= 4.21 PHI= 0.352 EP = 0.0299
120	TILT TOWARD BEING THOSE 0.93 OF 14 WHERE THE CRAFT SPECIALIZATION SCORE IS HIGH OR MEDIUM (36) WME	120	TILT TOWARD BEING THOSE 0.50 OF 22 WHERE THE CRAFT SPECIALIZATION SCORE IS LOW (17) WME	13 11 1 11 XSQ= 5.27 PHI= 0.383 EP = 0.0111

127	TILT TOWARD BEING THOSE 0.71 OF 14 WHERE THE FEMALES' CONTRIBUTION TO SUBSISTENCE IS LOW (32) JKB	127	TILT TOWARD BEING THOSE 0.68 OF 25 WHERE THE FEMALES' CONTRIBUTION TO SUBSISTENCE IS HIGH (33) JKB	4 17 10 8 XSQ= 4.14 PHI= -0.326 EP = 0.0237
128	LEAN TOWARD BEING THOSE 0.72 OF 32 WHERE, IF SUBSISTENCE IS PRIMARILY BY AGRICULTURE, THE WORK IS MAINLY DONE BY MALES (40)	128	LEAN TOWARD BEING THOSE 0.62 OF 45 WHERE, IF SUBSISTENCE IS PRIMARILY BY AGRICULTURE, THE WORK IS MAINLY DONE BY FEMALES (37)	23 17 9 28 XSQ= 7.40 PHI= 0.310 XP = 0.0065
130	TILT TOWARD BEING THOSE 0.86 OF 21 WHERE LEATHER WORKING IS MAINLY DONE BY MALES (39)	130	TILT TOWARD BEING THOSE 0.52 OF 21 WHERE LEATHER WORKING IS MAINLY DONE BY FEMALES (45)	18 10 3 11 XSQ= 5.25 PHI= 0.354 XP = 0.0219
139	DRIFT TOWARD BEING THOSE 0.63 OF 8 WHERE SUPERORDINATE PUNISHMENT IS PRESENT (15) BBW	139	DRIFT TOWARD BEING THOSE 0.76 OF 17 WHERE SUPERORDINATE PUNISHMENT IS ABSENT (25) BBW	5 4 3 13 XSQ= 2.09 PHI= 0.289 EP = 0.0870
176	DRIFT TOWARD BEING THOSE 0.60 OF 85 WHERE THE COMMUNITY IS OTHER THAN A CLAN-COMMUNITY OR A COMMUNITY STRUCTURED OR SEGMENTED ON A CLAN BASIS (213)	176	DRIFT TOWARD BEING THOSE 0.53 OF 142 WHERE THE COMMUNITY IS A CLAN-COMMUNITY OR A COMMUNITY STRUCTURED OR SEGMENTED ON A CLAN BASIS (169)	34 75 51 67 XSQ= 3.00 PHI= -0.115 XP = 0.0830
183	LEAN MORE TOWARD BEING THOSE 0.98 OF 64 WHERE THE LARGEST NON-COGNATIC KIN GROUP IS SMALLER THAN A MOEITY, I. E., A PHRATRY OR SIB OR LINEAGE (218)	183	LEAN LESS TOWARD BEING THOSE 0.84 OF 103 WHERE THE LARGEST NON-COGNATIC KIN GROUP IS SMALLER THAN A MOEITY, I. E., A PHRATRY OR SIB OR LINEAGE (218)	1 16 63 87 XSQ= 6.97 PHI= -0.204 XP = 0.0083
186	TILT TOWARD BEING THOSE 0.54 OF 91 WHERE THE KIN GROUP IS EXCLUSIVELY PATRILINEAL (150)	186	TILT TOWARD BEING THOSE 0.63 OF 147 WHERE THE KIN GROUP IS OTHER THAN EXCLUSIVELY PATRILINEAL (250)	49 54 42 93 XSQ= 6.03 PHI= 0.159 XP = 0.0141
187	TILT MORE TOWARD BEING THOSE 0.93 OF 91 WHERE THE KIN GROUP IS OTHER THAN EXCLUSIVELY MATRILINEAL (344)	187	TILT LESS TOWARD BEING THOSE 0.82 OF 147 WHERE THE KIN GROUP IS OTHER THAN EXCLUSIVELY MATRILINEAL (344)	6 26 85 121 XSQ= 5.03 PHI= -0.145 XP = 0.0249
190	LEAN MORE TOWARD BEING THOSE 0.90 OF 61 WHERE THE KIN GROUP IS PATRILINEAL OR DOUBLE-DESCENT, RATHER THAN MATRILINEAL (186)	190	LEAN LESS TOWARD BEING THOSE 0.69 OF 102 WHERE THE KIN GROUP IS PATRILINEAL OR DOUBLE-DESCENT, RATHER THAN MATRILINEAL (186)	55 70 6 32 XSQ= 8.74 PHI= 0.231 XP = 0.0031

196	LEAN MORE TOWARD BEING THCSE 0.95 OF 75 WHERE INDIVIDUAL RIGHTS IN REAL PROPERTY, AND RULES FOR INHERITANCE, ARE PRESENT (194)	196	LEAN LESS TOWARD BEING THOSE 0.76 CF 95 WHERE INDIVIDUAL RIGHTS IN REAL PRCPERTY, AND RULFS FOR INHERITANCE, ARE PRESENT (194)	71 72 4 23 XSQ= 9.81 PHI= 0.240 XP = 0.0017
198	TILT MORE TOWARD BEING THOSE 0.95 OF 60 WHERE RULES FOR THE INHERITANCE OF REAL PROPERTY, IF PRESENT, FAVOR THE MALE HEIR OR LINE, RATHER THAN THE FEMALE (144)	198	TILT LESS TOWARD BEING THCSE 0.79 OF 63 WHERE RULES FOR THE INHERITANCE CF REAL PROPERTY, IF PRESENT, FAVOR THE MALE HEIR OR LINE, RATHER THAN THE FEMALE (144)	57 50 3 13 XSQ= 5.33 PHI= 0.208 XP = 0.0210
207	TILT TOWARD BEING THOSE 0.73 OF 22 WHERE MARITAL RESICENCE IS AMBILOCAL OR NEOLOCAL, RATHER THAN MATRILOCAL OR UXORILOCAL (64)	207	TILT TOWARD BEING THOSE 0.61 CF 49 WHERE MARITAL RESIDENCE IS MATRILOCAL OR UXORILOCAL, RATHER THAN AMBILOCAL OR NEOLOCAL (64)	6 30 16 19 XSQ= 5.71 PHI= -0.284 XP = 0.0169
209	LEAN MORE TOWARD BEING THOSE 0.92 OF 75 WHERE MARITAL RESIDENCE IS PATRILOCAL, VIRILOCAL, CR AVUNCULOCAL, RATHER THAN MATRILOCAL OR UXORILOCAL (270)	209	LEAN LESS TOWARD BEING THOSE 0.77 OF 128 WHERE MARITAL RFSIDENCE IS PATRILOCAL, VIRILOCAL, CR AVUNCULOCAL, RATHER THAN MATRILOCAL OR UXORILOCAL (270)	69 98 6 30 XSQ= 6.70 PHI= 0.182 XP = 0.0096
210	TILT MORE TOWARD BEING THOSE 0.93 OF 60 WHERE MARITAL RESIDENCE IS PATRILOCAL, RATHER THAN MATRILOCAL (169)	210	TILT LESS TOWARD BEING THOSE 0.79 CF 76 WHERE MARITAL RESIDENCE IS PATRILOCAL, RATHER THAN MATRILOCAL (169)	56 60 4 16 XSQ= 4.44 PHI= 0.181 XP = 0.0350
214	DRIFT MORE TOWARD BEING THOSE 0.95 OF 39 WHERE FIRST COUSIN MARRIAGE, IF PERMITTED, IS OTHER THAN UNILATERAL (144)	214	DRIFT LESS TOWARD BEING THCSE 0.80 OF 65 WHERE FIRST COUSIN MARRIAGE, IF PERMITTED, IS OTHER THAN UNILATERAL (144)	2 13 37 52 XSQ= 3.25 PHI= -0.177 XP = 0.0716
234	TILT TOWARD BEING THOSE 0.65 OF 68 WHERE THE COUSIN TERMINOLOGY IS OF ESKIMO OR HAWAIIAN TYPE, RATHER THAN CROW, OMAHA, OR IROQUOIS TYPE (170)	234	TILT TOWARD BEING THOSE 0.55 CF 123 WHERE THE COUSIN TERMINCLOGY IS OF CROW, OMAHA, OR IROQUCIS TYPE, RATHER THAN ESKIMO OR HAWAIIAN TYPE (152)	24 68 44 55 XSQ= 6.23 PHI= -0.181 XP = 0.0126
240	LEAN MORE TOWARD BEING THOSE 0.80 OF 55 WHERE THE FAMILY, IF EXTENCED, IS SMALL OR STEM, RATHER THAN LARGE (135)	24C	LEAN LESS TOWARD BEING THOSE 0.53 OF 79 WHERE THE FAMILY, IF EXTENDED, IS SMALL OR STEM, RATHER THAN LARGE (135)	11 37 44 42 XSQ= 9.02 PHI= -0.259 XP = 0.0027
242	LEAN LESS TOWARD BEING THOSE 0.68 OF 91 WHERE MARRIAGE IS COMMONLY OR OCCASICNALLY POLYGYNOUS, RATHER THAN MONCGAMOUS (314)	242	LEAN MORE TOWARD BEING THOSE 0.86 CF 145 WHERE MARRIAGE IS COMMONLY OR OCCASIONALLY PCLYGYNOUS, RATHER THAN MONOGAMOUS (314)	62 124 29 21 XSQ= 9.11 PHI= -0.196 XP = 0.0025

278	IN ALL CASES ARE THCSE WHERE PROPERTY RIGHTS IN WOMEN ARE PRESENT (8) LWS	1.00 OF 4	278	TILT TOWARD BEING THOSE WHERE PROPERTY RIGHTS IN WOMEN ARE UNIMPORTANT OR ABSENT (14) LWS	0.78 OF 9	4 2 0 7 XSQ= 3.97 PHI= 0.553 EP = 0.0210
284	IN ALL CASES ARE THOSE WHERE CCNTRACEPTION IS NOT PRACTICED (7) CSF	1.00 OF 3	284	TILT TOWARD BEING THOSE WHERE CONTRACEPTION IS PRACTICED (10) CSF	0.88 OF 8	0 7 3 1 XSQ= 3.93 PHI= -0.598 EP = 0.0242
300	LEAN TCWARD BEING THCSE WHERE THE POST-PARTUM SEX TABCO LASTS SIX MCNTHS OR LESS (73)	0.76 OF 25	300	LEAN TOWARD BEING THOSE WHERE THE POST-PARTUM SEX TABOO LASTS LONGER THAN SIX MONTHS (51)	0.58 CF 55	6 32 19 23 XSQ= 6.74 PHI= -0.290 XP = 0.0094
316	DRIFT TOWARD BEING THCSE WHERE EXCLUSIVE MOTHER-SCN SLEEPING ARRANGEMENTS LAST LESS THAN ONE YEAR (25) W-K-A	0.75 OF 12	316	DRIFT TOWARD BEING THOSE WHERE EXCLUSIVE MOTHER-SON SLEEPING ARRANGEMENTS LAST ONE YEAR OR LONGER (19) W-K-A	0.63 OF 19	3 12 9 7 XSQ= 2.90 PHI= -0.306 EP = 0.0659
336	DRIFT TCWARD BEING THCSE WHERE THE TOTAL POSITIVE PRESSURE TOWARD DEVELCPING RESPCNSIBLE BEHAVIOR IN THE CHILD IS HIGH (43) B-B-C	0.80 OF 15	336	DRIFT TOWARD BEING THCSE WHERE THE TOTAL POSITIVE PRESSURE TOWARC DEVELOPING RESPONSIBLE BEHAVIOR IN THE CHILD IS LOW (32) B-B-C	0.50 CF 34	12 17 3 17 XSQ= 2.74 PHI= 0.236 XP = 0.0982
346	DRIFT TOWARD BEING THCSE WHERE THE CHILD'S INFERREC ANXIETY OVER PERFCRMANCE CF SELF-RELIANT BEHAVIOR IS HIGH (37) B-B-C	0.80 OF 15	346	DRIFT TOWARD BEING THOSE WHERE THE CHILD'S INFERRED ANXIETY OVER PERFORMANCE OF SELF-RELIANT BEHAVIOR IS LOW (39) B-B-C	0.51 OF 35	12 17 3 18 XSQ= 3.07 PHI= 0.248 XP = 0.0800
347	DRIFT TCWARD BEING THCSE WHERE THE CHILD'S INFERREC CONFLICT REGARDING SELF-RELIANT BEHAVIOR IS HIGH (37) B-B-C	0.80 OF 15	347	DRIFT TOWARD BEING THCSE WHERE THE CHILD'S INFERRED CONFLICT REGARDING SELF-RELIANT BEHAVIOR IS LOW (39) B-B-C	0.54 CF 35	12 16 3 19 XSQ= 3.71 PHI= 0.273 XP = 0.0539
369	DRIFT TOWARD BEING THCSE WHERE BCTH DISSCCIATICN CF THE SEXES AT ADCLESCENCE, ANC CUSTOMS CF INITIATICN AT ACOLESCENCE, ARE ABSENT (15) JKH	0.50 OF 16	369	DRIFT TOWARD BEING THOSE WHERE DISSOCIATION OF THE SEXES AT ADOLESCENCE, OR CUSTOMS OF INITIATION AT ADOLESCENCE, ARE PRESENT (42) JKH	0.80 OF 25	8 20 8 5 XSQ= 2.79 PHI= -0.261 XP = 0.0950
370	TEND TC BE THOSE WHERE THE SEGREGATION CF ACOLESCENT BOYS IS ABSENT (148)	0.77 OF 71	370	TEND TO BE THOSE WHERE THE SEGREGATION OF ADOLESCENT BOYS IS COMPLETE OR PARTIAL (95)	0.52 CF 106	16 55 55 51 XSQ= 14.05 PHI= -0.282 XP = 0.0002

373	DRIFT TOWARD BEING THOSE 0.83 OF 12 WHERE MALE INITIATION CEREMONIES AT PUBERTY ARE ABSENT (27) W-K-A	373	DRIFT TOWARD BEING THOSE 0.53 OF 19 WHERE MALE INITIATION CEREMONIES AT PUBERTY ARE PRESENT (17) W-K-A		2 10 10 9 XSQ= 2.64 PHI= -0.292 EP = 0.0652
377	TILT LESS TOWARD BEING THOSE 0.61 OF 87 WHERE MALE GENITAL MUTILATION IS ABSENT (242)	377	TILT MORE TOWARD BEING THOSE 0.76 OF 139 WHERE MALE GENITAL MUTILATION IS ABSENT (242)		34 33 53 106 XSQ= 5.32 PHI= 0.153 XP = 0.0210
382	TILT TOWARD BEING THOSE 0.71 OF 14 WHERE FEMALE INITIATION RITES ARE ABSENT (27) JKB	382	TILT TOWARD BEING THOSE 0.72 OF 25 WHERE FEMALE INITIATION RITES ARE PRESENT (38) JKB		4 18 10 7 XSQ= 5.23 PHI= -0.366 EP = 0.0172
391	LEAN TOWARD BEING THOSE 0.65 OF 49 WHERE PREMARITAL SEX RELATIONS ARE STRONGLY PUNISHED AND IN FACT RARE, OR WEAKLY PUNISHED AND IN FACT NOT RARE (89) JTW,EA	391	LEAN TOWARD BEING THOSE 0.66 OF 68 WHERE PREMARITAL SEX RELATIONS ARE PUNISHED ONLY IF PREGNANCY RESULTS, OR FREELY PERMITTED (90) JTW,EA		32 23 17 45 XSQ= 10.10 PHI= 0.294 XP = 0.0015
426	TILT MORE TOWARD BEING THOSE 0.79 OF 66 WHERE A HIGH GOD IS PRESENT (156) GES,EA	426	TILT LESS TOWARD BEING THOSE 0.63 OF 112 WHERE A HIGH GOD IS PRESENT (156) GES,EA		52 71 14 41 XSQ= 3.92 PHI= 0.148 XP = 0.0478
427	TEND TO BE THOSE 0.79 OF 52 WHERE A HIGH GOD, IF PRESENT, IS ACTIVE, RATHER THAN INACTIVE (87) GES,EA	427	TEND TO BE THOSE 0.66 OF 71 WHERE A HIGH GOD, IF PRESENT, IS INACTIVE, RATHER THAN ACTIVE (69) GES,EA		41 24 11 47 XSQ= 22.67 PHI= 0.429 XP = 0.0000
428	LEAN TOWARD BEING THOSE 0.83 OF 41 WHERE A HIGH GOD, IF PRESENT AND ACTIVE, SUPPORTS HUMAN MORALITY, RATHER THAN NOT SUPPORTING IT (61) GES,EA	428	LEAN TOWARD BEING THOSE 0.54 OF 24 WHERE A HIGH GOD, IF PRESENT AND ACTIVE, DOES NOT SUPPORT HUMAN MORALITY, RATHER THAN SUPPORTING IT (26) GES,EA		34 11 7 13 XSQ= 8.11 PHI= 0.353 XP = 0.0044
429	IN ALL CASES ARE THOSE 1.00 OF 13 WHERE SUPERNATURAL SANCTIONS FOR MORALITY ARE PRESENT (28) GES	429	TILT LESS TOWARD BEING THOSE 0.64 OF 14 WHERE SUPERNATURAL SANCTIONS FOR MORALITY ARE PRESENT (28) GES		13 9 0 5 XSQ= 3.58 PHI= 0.364 EP = 0.0407
444	DRIFT TOWARD BEING THOSE 0.75 OF 12 WHERE THE USE OF DREAMS TO SEEK AND CONTROL SUPERNATURAL POWERS IS LOW (27) RGD	444	DRIFT TOWARD BEING THOSE 0.56 OF 25 WHERE THE USE OF DREAMS TO SEEK AND CONTROL SUPERNATURAL POWERS IS HIGH (28) RGD		3 14 9 11 XSQ= 2.01 PHI= -0.233 EP = 0.0939

53/

450	DRIFT TOWARD BEING THOSE WHERE THE OBSERVATION OF FOOD TABOOS IS LOW, RATHER THAN HIGH OR MEDIUM (26) JRL	0.50 OF 24	450	DRIFT TOWARD BEING THOSE WHERE THE OBSERVATION OF FOOD TABOOS IS HIGH OR MEDIUM, RATHER THAN LOW (60) JRL	0.78 OF 36	12 28 12 8 XSQ= 3.83 PHI= -0.253 XP = 0.0504
458	TEND TO BE THOSE WHERE GAMES, IF PRESENT, INCLUDE GAMES OF STRATEGY (52) R-A-B,EA	0.75 OF 40	458	TEND TO BE THOSE WHERE GAMES, IF PRESENT, DO NOT INCLUDE GAMES OF STRATEGY (119) R-A-B,EA	0.74 OF 65	30 17 10 48 XSQ= 21.96 PHI= 0.457 XP = 0.0000
459	LEAN TOWARD BEING THOSE WHERE GAMES, IF PRESENT, INCLUDE GAMES OF CHANCE (82) R-A-B,EA	0.63 OF 40	459	LEAN TOWARD BEING THOSE WHERE GAMES, IF PRESENT, DO NOT INCLUDE GAMES OF CHANCE (89) R-A-B,EA	0.68 OF 65	25 21 15 44 XSQ= 7.98 PHI= 0.276 XP = 0.0047
460	TEND TO BE THOSE WHERE GAMES, IF PRESENT, ARE NOT LIMITED TO GAMES OF SKILL ONLY (104) R-A-B,EA	0.90 OF 40	460	TEND TO BE THOSE WHERE GAMES, IF PRESENT, ARE LIMITED TO GAMES OF SKILL ONLY (67) R-A-B,EA	0.54 OF 65	4 35 36 30 XSQ= 18.56 PHI= -0.420 XP = 0.0000
468	TILT TOWARD BEING THOSE WHERE CONTACT WITH OTHER CULTURES IS FREQUENT, RATHER THAN REGULAR OR IRREGULAR (17) JMH	0.69 OF 13	468	TILT TOWARD BEING THOSE WHERE CONTACT WITH OTHER CULTURES IS REGULAR OR IRREGULAR, RATHER THAN FREQUENT (37) JMH	0.75 OF 24	9 6 4 18 XSQ= 5.13 PHI= 0.372 EP = 0.0145
476	TILT TOWARD BEING THOSE WHERE THE DEGREE OF INSOBRIETY IS MODERATE OR SLIGHT (18) CH	0.75 OF 8	476	TILT TOWARD BEING THOSE WHERE THE DEGREE OF INSOBRIETY IS STRONG (31) DH	0.68 OF 25	2 17 6 8 XSQ= 3.00 PHI= -0.301 EP = 0.0473

****

54 CULTURES
WHERE FOOD PRODUCTION IS BY
INTENSIVE OR SIMPLE
AGRICULTURE, RATHER THAN BY
INCIPIENT FOOD PRODUCTION (192)

54 CULTURES
WHERE FOOD PRODUCTION IS BY
INCIPIENT FOOD PRODUCTION, RATHER THAN BY
INTENSIVE OR SIMPLE AGRICULTURE (46)

BACKGROUND ON PAGE 74

BOTH SUBJECT AND PREDICATE

....

192 IN LEFT COLUMN

AKHA	ALBANIANS	ALORESE	AMBA	AMERICANS	ARAPESH	ARAUCANIANS	ASHANTI	ATAYAL	AYMARA
AZANDE	AZTEC	BABWA	BAMBARA	BAMILEKE	BANDA	BARABRA	BARI	BAYA	BEMBA
BHUIYA	BIRIFOR	BLACK CARIB	BRAZILIANS	BULGARIANS	BUNLAP	BURUSHO	CAGABA	CAMBODIANS	CAYAPA
CHAGGA	CHERKESS	CHIBCHA	CHIRIGUANO	CHOCO	CHORTI	COCHITI	COORG	CUNA	CZECHS
DAGUR	DARD	DILLING	DOGON	DUTCH	EGYPTIANS	ENGA	FANG	FON	FUTAJALONKE
GANDA	GARO	GISU	GOND	GURE	HANO	HANUNOO	HAZARA	HEBREWS	HUICHOL
HUTSUL	IBAN	IFUGAO	ILA	INCA	INGASSANA	IRAQW	IRISH	JAPANESE	JAVANESE
JEMEZ	JIVARO	JUKUN	KABYLE	KACHIN	KAPAUKU	KATAB	KERAKI	KERALA	KHASI
KIKUYU	KISSI	KOHISTANI	KOL	KOREANS	KPE	KUBA	KURTATCHI	LAKHER	LAMBA
LAMET	LANGO	LAU	LEPCHA	LHOTA NAGA	LOLO	LUO	MACASSARESE	MALAYS	MAM
MAMBILA	MAMVU	MANDAN	MANGAIANS	MARGI	MARQUESANS	MARSHALLESE	MATAKAM	MAYA	MBUNDU
MENDE	MERINA	MIAO	MIN CHINESE	MINCHIA	MNONG GAR	MONGO	MONGUOR	MOSSI	MOTA
MZAB	NANDI	NDEMBU	NICOBARESE	NUPE	NURI	NYAKYUSA	NYORO	OKINAWANS	ORAON
PAEZ	PAIWAN	PALAUANS	PATHAN	PAWNEE	PONAPEANS	PUKAPUKA	PURUM	RIFFIANS	ROMANS
RUNDI	SAGADA	SAMOANS	SANDAWE	SANTAL	SENIANG	SERBS	SHILLUK	SHLUH	SINHALESE
SIUAI	SIWANS	SONGHAI	SOTHO	SUBANUN	SWAZI	SYRIANS	TAGBANUA	TALAMANCA	TALLENSI
TANALA	TAOS	TARAHUMARA	TEDA	TENDA	TENETEHARA	TERA	TESO	THAI	THONGA
TIGRINYA	TIV	TORAJA	TOTONAC	TROBRIAND	TUNEBO	TURKMEN	ULAWANS	VENDA	VIETNAMESE
WALLOONS	WANTOAT	WICHITA	WOGEO	WOLEAIANS	WOLOF	YAKO	YAO	YAPESE	YOMBE
YORUBA	ZUNI								

46 IN RIGHT COLUMN

ABOR	APINAYE	BACAIRI	BHIL	BUDUMA	CAMAYURA	CARIB	CHEROKEE	CHUKCHEE	CREEK
DELAWARE	FOX	HASINAI	HAVASUPAI	HURON	ICELANDERS	LAKALAI	LESU	LOZI	LUBA
MAORI	MIAMI	MUNDURUCU	NAMA	NATCHEZ	NAVAHO	PALIKUR	PAPAGO	SAMOYED	SARAMACCA
SHERENTE	TAPIRAPE	TERENA	TIMBIRA	TIMUCUA	TRISTAN	TRUMAI	TUCANO	TUPINAMBA	TURKANA
WAPISHANA	WINNEBAGO	WITOTO	YABARANA	YAKUT	YARURO				

117 EXCLUDED BECAUSE IRRELEVANT (SEE 'IRRELEVANT,' PARAGRAPH 53)

45 EXCLUDED BECAUSE UNASCERTAINED

----

3 LEAN LESS TOWARD BEING THOSE 0.69 OF 192
LOCATED OUTSIDE OF
AFRICA (320)

3 LEAN MORE TOWARD BEING THOSE 0.91 OF 46
LOCATED OUTSIDE OF
AFRICA (320)

59	4
133	42

XSQ= 8.16
PHI= 0.185
XP = 0.0043

6	DRIFT LESS TCWARC BEING THCSE LOCATED CUTSIDE CF THE INSULAR PACIFIC (330)	0.82 OF 192	6	DRIFT MORE TOWARD BEING THCSE LOCATED OUTSIDE OF THE INSULAR PACIFIC (330)	0.93 OF 46	35 3 157 43 XSQ= 2.97 PHI= 0.112 XP = 0.0849
8	TEND MCRE TC BE THCSE LOCATED OUTSIDE CF NORTH AMERICA (330)	0.94 OF 192	8	TEND LESS TO BE THOSE LOCATED OUTSIDE OF NORTH AMERICA (330)	0.72 OF 46	12 13 180 33 XSQ= 16.85 PHI= -0.266 XP = 0.0000
9	TEND MCRE TO BE THCSE LOCATED CUTSIDE CF SOUTH AMERICA (335)	0.91 OF 192	9	TEND LESS TO BE THOSE LOCATED OUTSIDE OF SOUTH AMERICA (335)	0.61 OF 46	18 18 174 28 XSQ= 23.33 PHI= -0.313 XP = 0.0000
11	IN ALL CASES ARE THOSE WHERE THE LATITUDE IS LESS THAN SIXTY DEGREES (385)	1.00 OF 192	11	TEND LESS TO BE THOSE WHERE THE LATITUDE IS LESS THAN SIXTY DEGREES (385)	0.91 OF 46	0 4 192 42 XSQ= 12.13 PHI= -0.226 XP = 0.0005
12	DRIFT MORE TCWARC BEING THCSE WHERE THE LATITUDE IS LESS THAN FIFTY DEGREES (367)	0.98 OF 192	12	DRIFT LESS TOWARD BEING THOSE WHERE THE LATITUDE IS LESS THAN FIFTY DEGREES (367)	0.91 OF 46	4 4 188 42 XSQ= 3.17 PHI= -0.115 XP = 0.0752
13	TILT MCRE TOWARC BEING THCSE WHERE THE LATITUDE IS LESS THAN FORTY DEGREES (329)	0.93 OF 192	13	TILT LESS TOWARD BEING THOSE WHERE THE LATITUDE IS LESS THAN FORTY DEGREES (329)	0.80 OF 46	14 9 178 37 XSQ= 5.07 PHI= -0.146 XP = 0.0243
14	LEAN MCRE TOWARC BEING THCSE WHERE THE LATITUDE IS LESS THAN THIRTY DEGREES (281)	0.81 OF 192	14	LEAN LESS TOWARD BEING THOSE WHERE THE LATITUDE IS LESS THAN THIRTY DEGREES (281)	0.61 OF 46	37 18 155 28 XSQ= 7.16 PHI= -0.173 XP = 0.0075
44	TEND MCRE TO BE THCSE WHERE SETTLEMENTS ARE FIXEC (222)	0.93 OF 192	44	TEND LESS TO BE THOSE WHERE SETTLEMENTS ARE FIXED (222)	0.56 OF 39	178 22 14 17 XSQ= 33.70 PHI= 0.382 XP = 0.
46	TEND MCRE TO BE THCSE OTHER THAN WHERE SETTLEMENTS ARE NON-FIXED AND MCVEMENT IS NOMADIC (260)	0.99 OF 192	46	TEND LESS TO BE THOSE OTHER THAN WHERE SETTLEMENTS ARE NON-FIXED AND MOVEMENT IS NOMADIC (260)	0.82 OF 39	1 7 191 32 XSQ= 24.47 PHI= -0.325 XP = 0.0000

47	TILT MORE TOWARD BEING THOSE 0.93 OF 14 WHERE, IF SETTLEMENTS ARE NON-FIXED, MOVEMENT IS NON-NOMADIC, RATHER THAN NOMADIC (38)	47	TILT LESS TOWARD BEING THOSE 0.59 OF 17 WHERE, IF SETTLEMENTS ARE NON-FIXED, MOVEMENT IS NON-NOMADIC, RATHER THAN NOMADIC (38)	1 7 13 10 XSQ= 3.04 PHI= -0.313 EP = 0.0454
62	TEND TO BE THOSE 0.92 OF 192 WHERE HUSBANDRY OF SOME KIND IS PRESENT (228)	62	TEND TO BE THOSE 0.67 OF 46 WHERE HUSBANDRY OF ANY KIND IS ABSENT (172)	177 15 15 31 XSQ= 80.70 PHI= 0.582 XP = 0.
71	TEND TO BE THOSE 0.65 OF 122 WHERE METAL WORKING IS PRESENT (98)	71	TEND TO BE THOSE 0.75 OF 36 WHERE METAL WORKING IS ABSENT (153)	79 9 43 27 XSQ= 16.23 PHI= 0.320 XP = 0.0001
80	LEAN LESS TOWARD BEING THOSE 0.71 OF 134 WHERE NO CITY OR TOWN IS PRESENT (185)	80	IN ALL CASES ARE THOSE 1.00 OF 26 WHERE NO CITY OR TOWN IS PRESENT (185)	39 0 95 26 XSQ= 8.49 PHI= 0.230 XP = 0.0036
81	DRIFT TOWARD BEING THOSE 0.57 OF 134 WHERE A CITY OR TOWN IS PRESENT, OR THE AVERAGE COMMUNITY SIZE IS 200 OR GREATER (89)	81	DRIFT TOWARD BEING THOSE 0.65 OF 26 WHERE NO CITY OR TOWN IS PRESENT, AND THE AVERAGE COMMUNITY SIZE IS SMALLER THAN 200 (135)	77 9 57 17 XSQ= 3.70 PHI= 0.152 XP = 0.0544
86	LEAN TOWARD BEING THOSE 0.66 OF 140 WHERE THE LEVEL OF POLITICAL INTEGRATION IS THE LARGE STATE, THE LITTLE STATE, OR THE MINIMAL STATE (148) GPM	86	LEAN TOWARD BEING THOSE 0.60 OF 43 WHERE THE LEVEL OF POLITICAL INTEGRATION IS THE AUTONOMOUS COMMUNITY, OR THE FAMILY (156) GPM	92 17 48 26 XSQ= 8.31 PHI= 0.213 XP = 0.0040
88	DRIFT LESS TOWARD BEING THOSE 0.59 OF 137 WHERE, IF A HEADMANSHIP IS PRESENT, SUCCESSION IS HEREDITARY (165)	88	DRIFT MORE TOWARD BEING THOSE 0.78 OF 32 WHERE, IF A HEADMANSHIP IS PRESENT, SUCCESSION IS HEREDITARY (165)	56 7 81 25 XSQ= 3.23 PHI= 0.138 XP = 0.0721
96	TEND TO BE THOSE 0.67 OF 189 WHERE THE HIERARCHY OF NATIONAL JURISDICTION HAS FOUR, THREE, TWO OR ONE LEVEL (174) GES,EA	96	TEND TO BE THOSE 0.64 OF 39 WHERE THE HIERARCHY OF NATIONAL JURISDICTION HAS NO LEVELS (156) GES,EA	126 14 63 25 XSQ= 11.65 PHI= 0.226 XP = 0.0006
102	TEND TO BE THOSE 0.68 OF 182 WHERE CLASS STRATIFICATION IS PRESENT (203)	102	TEND TO BE THOSE 0.63 OF 46 WHERE CLASS STRATIFICATION IS ABSENT (180)	123 17 59 29 XSQ= 13.27 PHI= 0.241 XP = 0.0003

107	DRIFT LESS TOWARD BEING THOSE 0.72 OF 123 WHERE CLASS STRATIFICATION, IF PRESENT, IS BASED ON SOMETHING OTHER THAN OCCUPATIONAL STATUS (160)	107	DRIFT MORE TOWARD BEING THOSE 0.94 OF 17 WHERE CLASS STRATIFICATION, IF PRESENT, IS BASED ON SOMETHING OTHER THAN OCCUPATIONAL STATUS (160)	35 1 88 16 XSQ= 2.89 PHI= 0.144 XP = 0.0891
109	DRIFT LESS TOWARD BEING THOSE 0.81 OF 173 WHERE CASTES ARE ABSENT (317)	109	DRIFT MORE TOWARD BEING THOSE 0.93 OF 46 WHERE CASTES ARE ABSENT (317)	33 3 140 43 XSQ= 3.31 PHI= 0.123 XP = 0.0691
110	DRIFT TOWARD BEING THOSE 0.52 OF 183 WHERE SLAVERY IS PRESENT (163)	110	DRIFT TOWARD BEING THOSE 0.64 OF 44 WHERE SLAVERY IS ABSENT (218)	95 16 88 28 XSQ= 2.84 PHI= 0.112 XP = 0.0921
120	DRIFT TOWARD BEING THOSE 0.75 OF 28 WHERE THE CRAFT SPECIALIZATION SCORE IS HIGH OR MEDIUM (36) WME	120	DRIFT TOWARD BEING THOSE 0.63 OF 8 WHERE THE CRAFT SPECIALIZATION SCORE IS LOW (17) WME	21 3 7 5 XSQ= 2.43 PHI= 0.260 EP = 0.0864
130	LEAN TOWARD BEING THOSE 0.85 OF 27 WHERE LEATHER WORKING IS MAINLY DONE BY MALES (39)	130	LEAN TOWARD BEING THOSE 0.67 OF 15 WHERE LEATHER WORKING IS MAINLY DONE BY FEMALES (45)	23 5 4 10 XSQ= 9.45 PHI= 0.474 XP = 0.0021
132	TILT TOWARD BEING THOSE 0.86 OF 29 WHERE ECONOMIC EXCHANGE INVOLVES THE USE OF MONEY (37) JMH	132	TILT TOWARD BEING THOSE 0.50 OF 8 WHERE ECONOMIC EXCHANGE DOES NOT INVOLVE THE USE OF MONEY (17) JMH	25 4 4 4 XSQ= 2.95 PHI= 0.282 EP = 0.0487
133	TILT TOWARD BEING THOSE 0.68 OF 19 WHERE CONTRACTED DEBTS ARE SIGNIFICANTLY PRESENT (17) GES	133	IN ALL CASES ARE THOSE 1.00 OF 5 WHERE CONTRACTED DEBTS ARE MODERATELY PRESENT OR ABSENT (17) GES	13 0 6 5 XSQ= 4.96 PHI= 0.455 EP = 0.0109
137	DRIFT TOWARD BEING THOSE 0.55 OF 44 WHERE INVIDIOUS DISPLAY OF WEALTH IS STRONGLY EMPHASIZED (37) PES	137	DRIFT TOWARD BEING THOSE 0.77 OF 13 WHERE INVIDIOUS DISPLAY OF WEALTH IS MODERATELY, LITTLE, OR NEGATIVELY EMPHASIZED (52) PES	24 3 20 10 XSQ= 2.82 PHI= 0.223 XP = 0.0929
138	LEAN TOWARD BEING THOSE 0.68 OF 19 WHERE SUPERORDINATE JUSTICE IS PRESENT (22) BBW	138	IN ALL CASES ARE THOSE 1.00 OF 6 WHERE SUPERORDINATE JUSTICE IS ABSENT (18) BBW	13 0 6 6 XSQ= 6.03 PHI= 0.491 EP = 0.0052

139	DRIFT LESS TOWARD BEING THOSE 0.53 OF 19 WHERE SUPERORDINATE PUNISHMENT IS ABSENT (25) BBW	139	IN ALL CASES ARE THOSE 1.00 OF 6 WHERE SUPERORDINATE PUNISHMENT IS ABSENT (25) BBW	9 0 10 6 XSQ= 2.62 PHI= 0.324 EP = 0.0571
147	TILT TOWARD BEING THOSE 0.92 OF 13 WHERE CODIFIED LAWS ARE PRESENT (20) LWS	147	TILT TOWARD BEING THOSE 0.75 OF 4 WHERE CODIFIED LAWS ARE UNIMPORTANT OR ABSENT (13) LWS	12 1 1 3 XSQ= 4.42 PHI= 0.510 EP = 0.0223
183	TEND MORE TO BE THOSE 0.94 OF 140 WHERE THE LARGEST NON-COGNATIC KIN GROUP IS SMALLER THAN A MOEITY, I. E., A PHRATRY OR SIB OR LINEAGE (218)	183	TEND LESS TO BE THOSE 0.70 OF 27 WHERE THE LARGEST NON-COGNATIC KIN GROUP IS SMALLER THAN A MOEITY, I. E., A PHRATRY OR SIB OR LINEAGE (218)	9 8 131 19 XSQ= 10.91 PHI= -0.256 XP = 0.0010
184	LEAN MORE TOWARD BEING THOSE 0.79 OF 140 WHERE THE LARGEST NON-COGNATIC KIN GROUP IS SMALLER THAN A PHRATRY, I. E. A SIB OR LINEAGE (175)	184	LEAN LESS TOWARD BEING THOSE 0.52 OF 27 WHERE THE LARGEST NON-COGNATIC KIN GROUP IS SMALLER THAN A PHRATRY, I. E. A SIB OR LINEAGE (175)	30 13 110 14 XSQ= 7.11 PHI= -0.206 XP = 0.0077
188	DRIFT MORE TOWARD BEING THOSE 0.73 OF 192 WHERE THE KIN GROUP IS OTHER THAN EXCLUSIVELY COGNATIC (252)	188	DRIFT LESS TOWARD BEING THOSE 0.59 OF 46 WHERE THE KIN GROUP IS OTHER THAN EXCLUSIVELY COGNATIC (252)	52 19 140 27 XSQ= 2.94 PHI= -0.111 XP = 0.0865
190	TILT MORE TOWARD BEING THOSE 0.80 OF 136 WHERE THE KIN GROUP IS PATRILINEAL OR DOUBLE-DESCENT, RATHER THAN MATRILINEAL (186)	190	TILT LESS TOWARD BEING THOSE 0.59 OF 27 WHERE THE KIN GROUP IS PATRILINEAL OR DOUBLE-DESCENT, RATHER THAN MATRILINEAL (186)	109 16 27 11 XSQ= 4.39 PHI= 0.164 XP = 0.0361
196	LEAN MORE TOWARD BEING THOSE 0.88 OF 148 WHERE INDIVIDUAL RIGHTS IN REAL PROPERTY, AND RULES FOR INHERITANCE, ARE PRESENT (194)	196	LEAN LESS TOWARD BEING THOSE 0.59 OF 22 WHERE INDIVIDUAL RIGHTS IN REAL PROPERTY, AND RULES FOR INHERITANCE, ARE PRESENT (194)	130 13 18 9 XSQ= 9.79 PHI= 0.240 XP = 0.0018
207	TILT TOWARD BEING THOSE 0.58 OF 50 WHERE MARITAL RESIDENCE IS AMBILOCAL OR NEOLOCAL, RATHER THAN MATRILOCAL OR UXORILOCAL (64)	207	TILT TOWARD BEING THOSE 0.71 OF 21 WHERE MARITAL RESIDENCE IS MATRILOCAL OR UXORILOCAL, RATHER THAN AMBILOCAL OR NEOLOCAL (64)	21 15 29 6 XSQ= 4.01 PHI= -0.238 XP = 0.0451
209	TEND MORE TO BE THOSE 0.87 OF 163 WHERE MARITAL RESIDENCE IS PATRILOCAL, VIRILOCAL, OR AVUNCULOCAL, RATHER THAN MATRILOCAL OR UXORILOCAL (270)	209	TEND LESS TO BE THOSE 0.63 OF 40 WHERE MARITAL RESIDENCE IS PATRILOCAL, VIRILOCAL, OR AVUNCULOCAL, RATHER THAN MATRILOCAL OR UXORILOCAL (270)	142 25 21 15 XSQ= 11.71 PHI= 0.240 XP = 0.0006

210	TEND MORE TO BE THOSE WHERE MARITAL RESIDENCE IS PATRILOCAL, RATHER THAN MATRILOCAL (169)	0.90 OF 115	210	TEND LESS TO BE THOSE WHERE MARITAL RESIDENCE IS PATRILOCAL, RATHER THAN MATRILOCAL (169)	0.57 OF 21	104 12 11 9 XSQ= 13.15 PHI= 0.311 XP = 0.0003
224	TILT LESS TOWARD BEING THOSE WHERE COUSIN MARRIAGE IS PREFERENTIALLY OR PERMISSIVELY SYMMETRICAL, RATHER THAN EITHER PATRI- OR MATRILATERAL (106)	0.61 OF 82	224	TILT MORE TOWARD BEING THOSE WHERE COUSIN MARRIAGE IS PREFERENTIALLY OR PERMISSIVELY SYMMETRICAL, RATHER THAN EITHER PATRI- OR MATRILATERAL (106)	0.86 OF 22	32 3 50 19 XSQ= 3.93 PHI= 0.195 XP = 0.0473
234	TILT TOWARD BEING THOSE WHERE THE COUSIN TERMINOLOGY IS OF ESKIMO OR HAWAIIAN TYPE, RATHER THAN CROW, OMAHA, OR IROQUOIS TYPE (170)	0.56 OF 156	234	TILT TOWARD BEING THOSE WHERE THE COUSIN TERMINOLOGY IS OF CROW, OMAHA, OR IROQUOIS TYPE, RATHER THAN ESKIMO OR HAWAIIAN TYPE (152)	0.69 OF 35	68 24 88 11 XSQ= 6.18 PHI= -0.180 XP = 0.0129
243	TILT TOWARD BEING THOSE WHERE POLYGYNY, IF PRESENT, HAS A HIGH INCIDENCE (24) W-C,S	0.58 OF 31	243	TILT TOWARD BEING THOSE WHERE POLYGYNY, IF PRESENT, HAS A LOW INCIDENCE (36) W-D,S	0.89 OF 9	18 1 13 8 XSQ= 4.43 PHI= 0.333 EP = 0.0214
263	TILT TOWARD BEING THOSE WHERE WIVES ARE OBTAINED BY RELATIVELY DIFFICULT MEANS, NAMELY BY BRIDE-PRICE, BRIDE-SERVICE, OR EXCHANGING A FEMALE RELATIVE (233)	0.67 OF 192	263	TILT TOWARD BEING THOSE WHERE WIVES ARE OBTAINED BY RELATIVELY EASY MEANS, NAMELY BY TOKEN BRIDE-PRICE, GIFT EXCHANGE, ABSENCE OF ANY CONSIDERATION, OR RECEIPT OF DOWRY (162)	0.52 OF 44	128 21 64 23 XSQ= 4.73 PHI= 0.142 XP = 0.0296
304	LEAN TOWARD BEING THOSE WHERE THE EARLY ANAL SATISFACTION POTENTIAL IS LOW (22) W-C	0.83 OF 18	304	IN ALL CASES ARE THOSE WHERE THE EARLY ANAL SATISFACTION POTENTIAL IS HIGH (19) W-C	1.00 OF 5	3 5 15 0 XSQ= 8.59 PHI= -0.611 EP = 0.0017
318	DRIFT TOWARD BEING THOSE WHERE THE OVERALL INDULGENCE OF THE INFANT IS LOW (31) B-B-C	0.57 OF 35	318	DRIFT TOWARD BEING THOSE WHERE THE OVERALL INDULGENCE OF THE INFANT IS HIGH (40) B-B-C	0.82 OF 11	15 9 20 2 XSQ= 3.65 PHI= -0.282 XP = 0.0561
353	TILT TOWARD BEING THOSE WHERE THE CHILD'S INFERRED ANXIETY OVER NON-PERFORMANCE OF OBEDIENT BEHAVIOR IS HIGH (42) B-B-C	0.76 OF 37	353	TILT TOWARD BEING THOSE WHERE THE CHILD-S INFERRED ANXIETY OVER NON-PERFORMANCE OF OBEDIENT BEHAVIOR IS LOW (32) B-B-C	0.64 OF 11	28 4 9 7 XSQ= 4.26 PHI= 0.298 XP = 0.0390
354	DRIFT TOWARD BEING THOSE WHERE THE CHILD'S INFERRED ANXIETY OVER PERFORMANCE OF OBEDIENT BEHAVIOR IS HIGH (36) B-B-C	0.56 OF 36	354	DRIFT TOWARD BEING THOSE WHERE THE CHILD'S INFERRED ANXIETY OVER PERFORMANCE OF OBEDIENT BEHAVIOR IS LOW (37) B-B-C	0.82 OF 11	20 2 16 9 XSQ= 3.34 PHI= 0.267 XP = 0.0674

372	DRIFT TOWARD BEING THOSE 0.53 OF 53 WHERE MALE INITIATION RITES ARE PRESENT (48) ASA	372	DRIFT TOWARD BEING THOSE 0.76 OF 17 WHERE MALE INITIATION RITES ARE ABSENT (63) ASA	28 4 25 13 XSQ= 3.35 PHI= 0.219 XP = 0.0672
377	TEND LESS TO BE THOSE 0.65 OF 187 WHERE MALE GENITAL MUTILATION IS ABSENT (242)	377	TEND MORE TO BE THOSE 0.97 OF 39 WHERE MALE GENITAL MUTILATION IS ABSENT (242)	66 1 121 38 XSQ= 15.04 PHI= 0.258 XP = 0.0001
390	TILT LESS TOWARD BEING THOSE 0.69 OF 101 WHERE PREMARITAL SEX RELATIONS ARE WEAKLY PUNISHED AND IN FACT NOT RARE OR PUNISHED ONLY IF PREGNANCY RESULTS, OR FREELY PERMITTED (132) JTW,EA	390	IN ALL CASES ARE THOSE 1.00 OF 16 WHERE PREMARITAL SEX RELATIONS ARE WEAKLY PUNISHED AND IN FACT NOT RARE OR PUNISHED ONLY IF PREGNANCY RESULTS, OR FREELY PERMITTED (132) JTW,EA	31 0 70 16 XSQ= 5.20 PHI= 0.211 XP = 0.0226
392	TILT TOWARD BEING THOSE 0.68 OF 101 WHERE PREMARITAL SEX RELATIONS ARE STRONGLY PUNISHED AND IN FACT RARE, OR WEAKLY PUNISHED AND IN FACT NOT RARE, OR PUNISHED ONLY IF PREGNANCY RESULTS (112) JTW,EA	392	TILT TOWARD BEING THOSE 0.63 OF 16 WHERE PREMARITAL SEX RELATIONS ARE FREELY PERMITTED (67) JTW,EA	69 6 32 10 XSQ= 4.44 PHI= 0.195 XP = 0.0351
428	TILT TOWARD BEING THOSE 0.76 OF 54 WHERE A HIGH GOD, IF PRESENT AND ACTIVE, SUPPORTS HUMAN MORALITY, RATHER THAN NOT SUPPORTING IT (61) GES,EA	428	TILT TOWARD BEING THOSE 0.64 OF 11 WHERE A HIGH GOD, IF PRESENT AND ACTIVE, DOES NOT SUPPORT HUMAN MORALITY, RATHER THAN SUPPORTING IT (26) GES,EA	41 4 13 7 XSQ= 4.99 PHI= 0.277 XP = 0.0256
429	DRIFT TOWARD BEING THOSE 0.90 OF 21 WHERE SUPERNATURAL SANCTIONS FOR MORALITY ARE PRESENT (28) GES	429	DRIFT TOWARD BEING THOSE 0.50 OF 6 WHERE SUPERNATURAL SANCTIONS FOR MORALITY ARE ABSENT OR UNREPORTED (9) GES	19 3 2 3 XSQ= 2.74 PHI= 0.319 EP = 0.0560
452	TILT TOWARD BEING THOSE 0.65 OF 26 WHERE TOTEMISM WITH FOOD TABOOS IS PRESENT (19) WNS	452	IN ALL CASES ARE THOSE 1.00 OF 5 WHERE TOTEMISM WITH FOOD TABOOS IS ABSENT (24) WNS	17 0 9 5 XSQ= 4.84 PHI= 0.395 EP = 0.0118
458	TEND TO BE THOSE 0.56 OF 80 WHERE GAMES, IF PRESENT, INCLUDE GAMES OF STRATEGY (52) R-A-B,EA	458	TEND TO BE THOSE 0.92 OF 25 WHERE GAMES, IF PRESENT, DO NOT INCLUDE GAMES OF STRATEGY (119) R-A-B,EA	45 2 35 23 XSQ= 16.04 PHI= 0.391 XP = 0.0001
460	TILT TOWARD BEING THOSE 0.70 OF 80 WHERE GAMES, IF PRESENT, ARE NOT LIMITED TO GAMES OF SKILL ONLY (104) R-A-B,EA	460	TILT TOWARD BEING THOSE 0.60 OF 25 WHERE GAMES, IF PRESENT, ARE LIMITED TO GAMES OF SKILL ONLY (67) R-A-B,EA	24 15 56 10 XSQ= 6.11 PHI= -0.241 XP = 0.0134

```
475  DRIFT TCWARD BEING THOSE          0.70 OF  43       475  DRIFT TOWARD BEING THOSE          0.62 OF  13          30     5
     WHERE EXHIBITICNISTIC CANCING                            WHERE EXHIBITIONISTIC DANCING                           13     8
     IS STRCNGLY OR MCDERATELY                                IS NEGLIGIBLY EMPHASIZED  (38)  PES              XSQ=     2.95
     EMPHASIZED  (48)  PES                                                                                     PHI=    0.229
                                                                                                               XP =   0.0861

476  TILT TCWARD BEING THOSE           0.57 OF  23       476  TILT TOWARD BEING THOSE           0.90 OF  10          10     9
     WHERE THE DEGREE OF INSCBRIETY IS                        WHERE THE DEGREE OF INSOBRIETY IS                       13     1
     MODERATE CR SLIGHT  (18)  CH                             STRONG  (31)  DH                                 XSQ=     4.42
                                                                                                               PHI=   -0.366
                                                                                                               EP =   0.0209

479  DRIFT TCWARD BEING THCSE          0.55 OF  20       479  IN ALL CASES ARE THOSE            1.00 OF   4           9     4
     WHERE THE NEED TC ACHIEVE,                               WHERE THE NEED TO ACHIEVE,                              11     0
     AS INFERRED FROM FCLKTALFS,                              AS INFERRED FROM FOLKTALES,                      XSQ=     2.15
     IS LCW  (18)  JV                                         IS HIGH  (18)  JV                                PHI=   -0.299
                                                                                                               EP =   0.0983
```

****

55 CULTURES WHERE FCOD PRODUCTICN IS BY INTENSIVE AGRICULTURE, RATFER THAN BY SIMPLE AGRICULTURE (91)	55 CULTURES WHERE FOOD PRODUCTION IS BY SIMPLE AGRICULTURE, RATHER THAN BY INTENSIVE AGRICULTURE (101)

BACKGROUND ON PAGE 74 BCTH SUBJECT AND PREDICATE

....

91 IN LEFT CCLUMN

ALBANIANS	AMERICANS	ARAUCANIANS	AYMARA	AZTEC	BAMBARA	BARABRA	BRAZILIANS	BULGARIANS	BURUSHO
CAMBODIANS	CHAGGA	CHERKESS	CHIBCHA	COCHITI	COORG	CZECHS	DAGUR	DARC	DILLING
DOGON	DUTCH	EGYPTIANS	GANCA	HANO	HAZARA	HEBREWS	HUTSUL	IFUGAO	INCA
INGASSANA	IRAQW	IRISH	JAPANESE	JAVANESE	JEMEZ	KABYLE	KATAB	KERALA	KIKUYU
KOHISTANI	KOL	KCREANS	LEPCHA	LOLO	LUO	MACASSARESE	MALAYS	MAMBILA	MANDAN
MARGI	MATAKAM	MERINA	MIAO	MIN CHINESE	MINCHIA	MONGUOR	MOSSI	MZAB	NANCI
NURI	NYAKYUSA	NYCRC	OKINAWANS	ORAON	PAEZ	PATHAN	RIFFIANS	ROMANS	RUNCI
SAGADA	SANTAL	SERBS	SHLUH	SINHALESE	SIWANS	SONGHAI	SCTHO	SYRIANS	TALLENSI
TANALA	TACS	TARAHUMARA	TECA	THAI	TIGRINYA	TURKMEN	VENDA	VIETNAMESE	WALLOONS
ZUNI									

101 IN RIGHT CCLUMN

AKHA	ALCRESE	AMBA	ARAPESH	ASHANTI	ATAYAL	AZANDE	BABWA	BAMILEKE	BANCA
BARI	BAYA	BEMBA	BHUIYA	BIRIFOR	BLACK CARIB	BUNLAP	CAGABA	CAYAPA	CHIRIGUANO
CHOCO	CHCRTI	CUNA	ENGA	FANG	FON	FUTAJALONKE	GARC	GISU	GOND
GURE	HANUNCO	HUICHCL	IBAN	ILA	JIVARO	JUKUN	KACHIN	KAPAUKU	KERAKI
KHASI	KISSI	KPE	KUBA	KURTATCHI	LAKHER	LAMBA	LAMET	LANGC	LAU
LHOTA NAGA	MAM	MAMVU	MANGAIANS	MARQUESANS	MARSHALLESE	MAYA	MBUNDU	MENCE	MNONG GAR
MONGO	MOTA	NDEMBU	NICOBARESE	NUPE	PAIWAN	PALAUANS	PAWNEE	PONAPEANS	PUKAPUKA
PURUM	SAMCANS	SANCAWE	SENIANG	SHILLUK	SIUAI	SUBANUN	SWAZI	TAGBANUA	TALAMANCA
TENDA	TENETEHARA	TERA	TESO	THONGA	TIV	TORAJA	TCTCNAC	TROBRIAND	TUNEBO
ULAWANS	WANTOAT	WICHITA	WOGEO	WOLEAIANS	WOLOF	YAKO	YAC	YAPESE	YOMBE
YORUBA									

163 EXCLUDED BECAUSE IRRELEVANT

45 EXCLUCED BECAUSE UNASCERTAINEC

----

3 TILT MORE TOWARC BEING THCSE 0.78 OF 91 LOCATED OUTSIDE CF AFRICA (320)	3 TILT LESS TOWARD BEING THOSE 0.61 CF 101 LOCATED OUTSIDE OF AFRICA (320)	20 39 71 62 XSQ= 5.47 PHI= -0.169 XP = 0.0194

4	TEND LESS TO BE THOSE LOCATED OUTSIDE OF THE CIRCUM-MEDITERRANEAN (355) 0.73 OF 91	4	TEND MORE TO BE THOSE LOCATED OUTSIDE OF THE CIRCUM-MEDITERRANEAN (355) 0.98 OF 101	25 2 66 99 XSQ= 23.68 PHI= 0.351 XP = 0.0000
5	LEAN LESS TOWARD BEING THOSE LOCATED OUTSIDE OF EAST EURASIA (330) 0.68 OF 91	5	LEAN MORE TOWARD BEING THOSE LOCATED OUTSIDE OF EAST EURASIA (330) 0.88 OF 101	29 12 62 89 XSQ= 10.23 PHI= 0.231 XP = 0.0014
6	TEND MORE TO BE THOSE LOCATED OUTSIDE OF THE INSULAR PACIFIC (330) 0.96 OF 91	6	TEND LESS TO BE THOSE LOCATED OUTSIDE OF THE INSULAR PACIFIC (330) 0.69 OF 101	4 31 87 70 XSQ= 20.48 PHI= -0.327 XP = 0.0000
15	TEND TO BE THOSE WHERE THE LATITUDE IS TWENTY DEGREES OR GREATER (183) 0.58 OF 91	15	TEND TO BE THOSE WHERE THE LATITUDE IS LESS THAN TWENTY DEGREES (217) 0.80 OF 101	53 20 38 81 XSQ= 28.41 PHI= 0.385 XP = 0.0000
16	TEND TO BE THOSE WHERE THE LATITUDE IS TEN DEGREES OR GREATER (277) 0.82 OF 91	16	TEND TO BE THOSE WHERE THE LATITUDE IS LESS THAN TEN DEGREES (123) 0.52 OF 101	75 48 16 53 XSQ= 23.82 PHI= 0.352 XP = 0.0000
33	TEND LESS TO BE THOSE WHERE THE NATURAL ENVIRONMENT IS OTHER THAN 'VERY HARSH,' I.E., DESERT, DESERT GRASSES AND SHRUBS, TUNDRA, OR HIGH PLATEAU STEPPE (341) FWM 0.82 OF 91	33	TEND MORE TO BE THOSE WHERE THE NATURAL ENVIRONMENT IS OTHER THAN 'VERY HARSH,' I.E., DESERT, DESERT GRASSES AND SHRUBS, TUNDRA, OR HIGH PLATEAU STEPPE (341) FWM 0.98 OF 101	16 2 75 99 XSQ= 11.94 PHI= 0.249 XP = 0.0005
36	LEAN LESS TOWARD BEING THOSE WHERE THE NATURAL ENVIRONMENT IS OTHER THAN 'VERY HARSH,' OR SUB-TROPICAL BUSH, OR TEMPERATE GRASSLAND (292) FWM 0.74 OF 91	36	LEAN MORE TOWARD BEING THOSE WHERE THE NATURAL ENVIRONMENT IS OTHER THAN 'VERY HARSH,' OR SUB-TROPICAL BUSH, OR TEMPERATE GRASSLAND (292) FWM 0.91 OF 101	24 9 67 92 XSQ= 9.07 PHI= 0.217 XP = 0.0026
42	TEND TO BE THOSE WHERE THE NATURAL ENVIRONMENT IS OTHER THAN TROPICAL OR SUB-TROPICAL RAIN FOREST, OR MONSOON FOREST (244) FWM 0.75 OF 91	42	TEND TO BE THOSE WHERE THE NATURAL ENVIRONMENT IS TROPICAL OR SUB-TROPICAL RAIN FOREST, OR MONSOON FOREST (156) FWM 0.65 OF 101	23 66 68 35 XSQ= 29.32 PHI= -0.391 XP = 0.0000
48	TILT TOWARD BEING THOSE WHERE THE FOOD SUPPLY IS NOT SECURE, AND FOOD SHORTAGES ARE FREQUENT OR ANNUAL (41) MGW 0.77 OF 13	48	TILT TOWARD BEING THOSE WHERE THE FOOD SUPPLY IS SECURE, AND FOOD SHORTAGES ARE RARE OR OCCASIONAL (38) MGW 0.65 OF 26	3 17 10 9 XSQ= 4.63 PHI= -0.345 EP = 0.0187

63	TEND TO BE THOSE WHERE HUSBANDRY, IF PRESENT, IS PRINCIPALLY IN THE FORM OF BOVINE, EQUINE, CAMEL-LIKE, OR DEER-LIKE ANIMALS, RATHER THAN PIGS, SHEEP, OR GOATS (152)	0.92 OF 86	63	TEND TO BE THOSE WHERE HUSBANDRY, IF PRESENT, IS PRINCIPALLY IN THE FORM OF PIGS, SHEEP, OR GOATS, RATHER THAN BOVINE, EQUINE, CAMEL-LIKE, OR DEER-LIKE ANIMALS (74)	0.60 OF 91	79 36 7 55 XSQ= 50.87 PHI= 0.536 XP = 0.
71	TEND TO BE THOSE WHERE METAL WORKING IS PRESENT (98)	0.87 OF 52	71	TEND TO BE THOSE WHERE METAL WORKING IS ABSENT (153)	0.51 OF 70	45 34 7 36 XSQ= 17.22 PHI= 0.376 XP = 0.0000
73	LEAN TOWARD BEING THOSE WHERE WEAVING IS PRESENT (118)	0.75 OF 52	73	LEAN TOWARD BEING THOSE WHERE WEAVING IS ABSENT (130)	0.50 OF 70	39 35 13 35 XSQ= 6.80 PHI= 0.236 XP = 0.0091
74	TILT MORE TOWARD BEING THOSE WHERE POTTERY IS PRESENT (145)	0.89 OF 46	74	TILT LESS TOWARD BEING THOSE WHERE POTTERY IS PRESENT (145)	0.70 OF 69	41 48 5 21 XSQ= 4.97 PHI= 0.208 XP = 0.0258
77	TILT TOWARD BEING THOSE WHERE THE WRITING SYSTEM IS ALPHABETIC-OR-PHONETIC, RATHER THAN BEING MNEMONIC OR ABSENT (15) JMH	0.54 OF 13	77	TILT TOWARD BEING THOSE WHERE THE WRITING SYSTEM IS MNEMONIC OR ABSENT, RATHER THAN BEING ALPHABETIC-OR-PHONETIC (39) JMH	0.88 OF 16	7 2 6 14 XSQ= 3.96 PHI= 0.370 EP = 0.0405
81	TEND TO BE THOSE WHERE A CITY OR TOWN IS PRESENT, OR THE AVERAGE COMMUNITY SIZE IS 200 OR GREATER (89)	0.81 OF 70	81	TEND TO BE THOSE WHERE NO CITY OR TOWN IS PRESENT, AND THE AVERAGE COMMUNITY SIZE IS SMALLER THAN 200 (135)	0.69 OF 64	57 20 13 44 XSQ= 32.42 PHI= 0.492 XP = 0.
83	TEND TO BE THOSE WHERE, WITH NO CITY AND NO TOWN PRESENT, THE AVERAGE COMMUNITY SIZE IS BETWEEN 200 AND 999, RATHER THAN SMALLER THAN 200 (45)	0.62 OF 34	83	TEND TO BE THOSE WHERE, WITH NO CITY AND NO TOWN PRESENT, THE AVERAGE COMMUNITY SIZE IS SMALLER THAN 200, RATHER THAN BETWEEN 200 AND 999 (135)	0.79 OF 56	21 12 13 44 XSQ= 13.14 PHI= 0.382 XP = 0.0003
85	TEND TO BE THOSE WHERE THE LEVEL OF POLITICAL INTEGRATION IS THE LARGE STATE, OR THE LITTLE STATE (70) GPM	0.52 OF 66	85	TEND TO BE THOSE WHERE THE LEVEL OF POLITICAL INTEGRATION IS THE MINIMAL STATE, THE AUTONOMOUS COMMUNITY, OR THE FAMILY (234) GPM	0.81 OF 74	34 14 32 60 XSQ= 15.04 PHI= 0.328 XP = 0.0001
88	TEND TO BE THOSE WHERE, IF A HEADMANSHIP IS PRESENT, SUCCESSION IS NON-HEREDITARY (106)	0.59 OF 63	88	TEND TO BE THOSE WHERE, IF A HEADMANSHIP IS PRESENT, SUCCESSION IS HEREDITARY (165)	0.74 OF 74	37 19 26 55 XSQ= 14.05 PHI= 0.320 XP = 0.0002

91	TILT TOWARD BEING THOSE WHERE SOCIETAL COMPLEXITY IS HIGH (18) F-W	0.83 OF 12	91	TILT TOWARD BEING THOSE WHERE SOCIETAL COMPLEXITY IS LOW (22) F-W	0.70 OF 10	10 3 2 7 XSQ= 4.40 PHI= 0.447 EP = 0.0274
94	TEND LESS TO BE THOSE WHERE THE HIERARCHY OF NATIONAL JURISDICTION HAS TWO, ONE, OR NO LEVELS (296) GES,EA	0.70 OF 88	94	TEND MORE TO BE THOSE WHERE THE HIERARCHY OF NATIONAL JURISDICTION HAS TWO, ONE, OR NO LEVELS (296) GES,EA	0.96 OF 101	26 4 62 97 XSQ= 21.18 PHI= 0.335 XP = 0.0000
95	TEND LESS TO BE THOSE WHERE THE HIERARCHY OF NATIONAL JURISDICTION HAS ONE OR NO LEVELS (254) GES,EA	0.51 OF 88	95	TEND MORE TO BE THOSE WHERE THE HIERARCHY OF NATIONAL JURISDICTION HAS ONE OR NO LEVELS (254) GES,EA	0.78 OF 101	43 22 45 79 XSQ= 14.11 PHI= 0.273 XP = 0.0002
96	LEAN MORE TOWARD BEING THOSE WHERE THE HIERARCHY OF NATIONAL JURISDICTION HAS FOUR, THREE, TWO OR ONE LEVEL (174) GES,EA	0.77 OF 88	96	LEAN LESS TOWARD BEING THOSE WHERE THE HIERARCHY OF NATIONAL JURISDICTION HAS FOUR, THREE, TWO OR ONE LEVEL (174) GES,EA	0.57 OF 101	68 58 20 43 XSQ= 7.47 PHI= 0.199 XP = 0.0063
99	DRIFT MORE TOWARD BEING THOSE WHERE, WITH NATIONAL HIERARCHY ABSENT, THE HIERARCHY OF LOCAL JURISDICTION HAS FOUR OR THREE LEVELS (93) GES,EA	0.90 OF 20	99	DRIFT LESS TOWARD BEING THOSE WHERE, WITH NATIONAL HIERARCHY ABSENT, THE HIERARCHY OF LOCAL JURISDICTION HAS FOUR OR THREE LEVELS (93) GES,EA	0.65 OF 43	18 28 2 15 XSQ= 3.12 PHI= 0.223 XP = 0.0773
100	LEAN MORE TOWARD BEING THOSE WHERE HIERARCHIES ARE MORE COMPLEX THAN THE 'SIMPLEST,' I. E., MORE COMPLEX THAN TWO LOCAL LEVELS WITH NO NATIONAL LEVELS (267) GES,EA	0.98 OF 88	100	LEAN LESS TOWARD BEING THOSE WHERE HIERARCHIES ARE MORE COMPLEX THAN THE 'SIMPLEST,' I. E., MORE COMPLEX THAN TWO LOCAL LEVELS WITH NO NATIONAL LEVELS (267) GES,EA	0.85 OF 101	86 86 2 15 XSQ= 7.62 PHI= 0.201 XP = 0.0058
102	TILT MORE TOWARD BEING THOSE WHERE CLASS STRATIFICATION IS PRESENT (203)	0.77 OF 86	102	TILT LESS TOWARD BEING THOSE WHERE CLASS STRATIFICATION IS PRESENT (203)	0.59 OF 96	66 57 20 39 XSQ= 5.48 PHI= 0.174 XP = 0.0192
107	TEND LESS TO BE THOSE WHERE CLASS STRATIFICATION, IF PRESENT, IS BASED ON SOMETHING OTHER THAN OCCUPATIONAL STATUS (160)	0.56 OF 66	107	TEND MORE TO BE THOSE WHERE CLASS STRATIFICATION, IF PRESENT, IS BASED ON SOMETHING OTHER THAN OCCUPATIONAL STATUS (160)	0.89 OF 57	29 6 37 51 XSQ= 15.17 PHI= 0.351 XP = 0.0001
108	TILT MORE TOWARD BEING THOSE WHERE CLASS STRATIFICATION, IF PRESENT, IS BASED ON SOMETHING OTHER THAN A HEREDITARY ARISTOCRACY (129)	0.74 OF 66	108	TILT LESS TOWARD BEING THOSE WHERE CLASS STRATIFICATION, IF PRESENT, IS BASED ON SOMETHING OTHER THAN A HEREDITARY ARISTOCRACY (129)	0.53 OF 57	17 27 49 30 XSQ= 5.31 PHI= -0.208 XP = 0.0212

No.		No.		
109	TEND LESS TO BE THOSE 0.69 OF 77 WHERE CASTES ARE ABSENT (317)	109	TEND MORE TO BE THOSE 0.91 OF 96 WHERE CASTES ARE ABSENT (317)	24 9 53 87 XSQ= 11.77 PHI= 0.261 XP = 0.0006
118	TILT TOWARD BEING THOSE 0.75 OF 12 WHERE THE PERCENTAGE OF OCCUPATIONS THAT ARE SPECIALIZED IS HIGH OR MEDIUM (24) WME	118	TILT TOWARD BEING THOSE 0.71 OF 14 WHERE THE PERCENTAGE OF OCCUPATIONS THAT ARE SPECIALIZED IS LOW (25) WME	9 4 3 10 XSQ= 3.87 PHI= 0.386 EP = 0.0472
120	DRIFT MORE TOWARD BEING THOSE 0.93 OF 14 WHERE THE CRAFT SPECIALIZATION SCORE IS HIGH OR MEDIUM (36) WME	120	DRIFT LESS TOWARD BEING THOSE 0.57 OF 14 WHERE THE CRAFT SPECIALIZATION SCORE IS HIGH OR MEDIUM (36) WME	13 8 1 6 XSQ= 3.05 PHI= 0.330 EP = 0.0768
127	TILT TOWARD BEING THOSE 0.71 OF 14 WHERE THE FEMALES' CONTRIBUTION TO SUBSISTENCE IS LOW (32) JKB	127	TILT TOWARD BEING THOSE 0.73 OF 15 WHERE THE FEMALES' CONTRIBUTION TO SUBSISTENCE IS HIGH (33) JKB	4 11 10 4 XSQ= 4.16 PHI= -0.379 EP = 0.0268
128	LEAN TOWARD BEING THOSE 0.72 OF 32 WHERE, IF SUBSISTENCE IS PRIMARILY BY AGRICULTURE, THE WORK IS MAINLY DONE BY MALES (40)	128	LEAN TOWARD BEING THOSE 0.62 OF 45 WHERE, IF SUBSISTENCE IS PRIMARILY BY AGRICULTURE, THE WORK IS MAINLY DONE BY FEMALES (37)	23 17 9 28 XSQ= 7.40 PHI= 0.310 XP = 0.0065
176	TILT TOWARD BEING THOSE 0.60 OF 85 WHERE THE COMMUNITY IS OTHER THAN A CLAN-COMMUNITY OR A COMMUNITY STRUCTURED OR SEGMENTED ON A CLAN BASIS (213)	176	TILT TOWARD BEING THOSE 0.60 OF 99 WHERE THE COMMUNITY IS A CLAN-COMMUNITY OR A COMMUNITY STRUCTURED OR SEGMENTED ON A CLAN BASIS (169)	34 59 51 40 XSQ= 6.26 PHI= -0.185 XP = 0.0123
177	TILT MORE TOWARD BEING THOSE 0.87 OF 85 WHERE THE COMMUNITY IS OTHER THAN A SINGLE CLAN-COMMUNITY AND EXOGAMOUS (305)	177	TILT LESS TOWARD BEING THOSE 0.74 OF 99 WHERE THE COMMUNITY IS OTHER THAN A SINGLE CLAN-COMMUNITY AND EXOGAMOUS (305)	11 26 74 73 XSQ= 4.26 PHI= -0.152 XP = 0.0391
183	DRIFT MORE TOWARD BEING THOSE 0.98 OF 64 WHERE THE LARGEST NON-COGNATIC KIN GROUP IS SMALLER THAN A MOEITY, I. E., A PHRATRY OR SIB OR LINEAGE (218)	183	DRIFT LESS TOWARD BEING THOSE 0.89 OF 76 WHERE THE LARGEST NON-COGNATIC KIN GROUP IS SMALLER THAN A MOEITY, I. E., A PHRATRY OR SIB OR LINEAGE (218)	1 8 63 68 XSQ= 3.27 PHI= -0.153 XP = 0.0705
186	TILT TOWARD BEING THOSE 0.54 OF 91 WHERE THE KIN GROUP IS EXCLUSIVELY PATRILINEAL (150)	186	TILT TOWARD BEING THOSE 0.61 OF 101 WHERE THE KIN GROUP IS OTHER THAN EXCLUSIVELY PATRILINEAL (250)	49 39 42 62 XSQ= 3.88 PHI= 0.142 XP = 0.0488

187	DRIFT MORE TOWARD BEING THOSE 0.93 OF 91 WHERE THE KIN GROUP IS OTHER THAN EXCLUSIVELY MATRILINEAL (344)	187	DRIFT LESS TOWARD BEING THOSE 0.84 OF 101 WHERE THE KIN GROUP IS OTHER THAN EXCLUSIVELY MATRILINEAL (344)	6 16 85 85 XSQ= 3.18 PHI= -0.129 XP = 0.0748
190	TILT MORE TOWARD BEING THOSE 0.90 OF 61 WHERE THE KIN GROUP IS PATRILINEAL OR DOUBLE-DESCENT, RATHER THAN MATRILINEAL (186)	190	TILT LESS TOWARD BEING THOSE 0.72 OF 75 WHERE THE KIN GROUP IS PATRILINEAL OR DOUBLE-DESCENT, RATHER THAN MATRILINEAL (186)	55 54 6 21 XSQ= 5.88 PHI= 0.208 XP = 0.0153
196	TILT MORE TOWARD BEING THOSE 0.95 OF 75 WHERE INDIVIDUAL RIGHTS IN REAL PROPERTY, AND RULES FOR INHERITANCE, ARE PRESENT (194)	196	TILT LESS TOWARD BEING THOSE 0.81 OF 73 WHERE INDIVIDUAL RIGHTS IN REAL PROPERTY, AND RULES FOR INHERITANCE, ARE PRESENT (194)	71 59 4 14 XSQ= 5.40 PHI= 0.191 XP = 0.0201
198	TILT MORE TOWARD BEING THOSE 0.95 OF 60 WHERE RULES FOR THE INHERITANCE OF REAL PROPERTY, IF PRESENT, FAVOR THE MALE HEIR OR LINE, RATHER THAN THE FEMALE (144)	198	TILT LESS TOWARD BEING THOSE 0.79 OF 52 WHERE RULES FOR THE INHERITANCE OF REAL PROPERTY, IF PRESENT, FAVOR THE MALE HEIR OR LINE, RATHER THAN THE FEMALE (144)	57 41 3 11 XSQ= 5.25 PHI= 0.217 XP = 0.0219
214	TILT MORE TOWARD BEING THOSE 0.95 OF 39 WHERE FIRST COUSIN MARRIAGE, IF PERMITTED, IS OTHER THAN UNILATERAL (144)	214	TILT LESS TOWARD BEING THOSE 0.74 OF 43 WHERE FIRST COUSIN MARRIAGE, IF PERMITTED, IS OTHER THAN UNILATERAL (144)	2 11 37 32 XSQ= 4.97 PHI= -0.246 XP = 0.0258
234	DRIFT TOWARD BEING THOSE 0.65 OF 68 WHERE THE COUSIN TERMINOLOGY IS OF ESKIMO OR HAWAIIAN TYPE, RATHER THAN CROW, OMAHA, OR IROQUOIS TYPE (170)	234	DRIFT TOWARD BEING THOSE 0.50 OF 88 WHERE THE COUSIN TERMINOLOGY IS OF CROW, OMAHA, OR IROQUOIS TYPE, RATHER THAN ESKIMO OR HAWAIIAN TYPE (152)	24 44 44 44 XSQ= 2.80 PHI= -0.134 XP = 0.0941
240	TILT MORE TOWARD BEING THOSE 0.80 OF 55 WHERE THE FAMILY, IF EXTENDED, IS SMALL OR STEM, RATHER THAN LARGE (135)	240	TILT LESS TOWARD BEING THOSE 0.55 OF 49 WHERE THE FAMILY, IF EXTENDED, IS SMALL OR STEM, RATHER THAN LARGE (135)	11 22 44 27 XSQ= 6.31 PHI= -0.246 XP = 0.0120
242	LEAN LESS TOWARD BEING THOSE 0.68 OF 91 WHERE MARRIAGE IS COMMONLY OR OCCASIONALLY POLYGYNOUS, RATHER THAN MONOGAMOUS (314)	242	LEAN MORE TOWARD BEING THOSE 0.86 OF 99 WHERE MARRIAGE IS COMMONLY OR OCCASIONALLY POLYGYNOUS, RATHER THAN MONOGAMOUS (314)	62 85 29 14 XSQ= 7.53 PHI= -0.199 XP = 0.0061
277	TILT TOWARD BEING THOSE 0.80 OF 5 WHERE THE STATUS OF WOMEN IS INFERIOR OR SUBJECTED (14) LWS	277	TILT TOWARD BEING THOSE 0.88 OF 8 WHERE THE STATUS OF WOMEN IS NOT STRONGLY INFERIOR OR SUBJECTED (22) LWS	4 1 1 7 XSQ= 3.41 PHI= 0.512 FP = 0.0319

299	LEAN TOWARD BEING THOSE 0.84 OF 25 WHERE THE POST-PARTUM SEX TABOO LASTS ONE YEAR OR LESS (89)	299	LEAN TOWARD BEING THOSE 0.52 OF 44 WHERE THE POST-PARTUM SEX TABOO LASTS LONGER THAN ONE YEAR (35)	4 23 21 21 XSQ= 7.35 PHI= -0.326 XP = 0.0067
300	LEAN TOWARD BEING THOSE 0.76 OF 25 WHERE THE POST-PARTUM SEX TABOO LASTS SIX MONTHS OR LESS (73)	300	LEAN TOWARD BEING THOSE 0.66 OF 44 WHERE THE POST-PARTUM SEX TABOO LASTS LONGER THAN SIX MONTHS (51)	6 29 19 15 XSQ= 9.59 PHI= -0.373 XP = 0.0020
316	TILT TOWARD BEING THOSE 0.75 OF 12 WHERE EXCLUSIVE MOTHER-SON SLEEPING ARRANGEMENTS LAST LESS THAN ONE YEAR (25) W-K-A	316	TILT TOWARD BEING THOSE 0.77 OF 13 WHERE EXCLUSIVE MOTHER-SON SLEEPING ARRANGEMENTS LAST ONE YEAR OR LONGER (19) W-K-A	3 10 9 3 XSQ= 4.82 PHI= -0.439 EP = 0.0169
336	DRIFT TOWARD BEING THOSE 0.80 OF 15 WHERE THE TOTAL POSITIVE PRESSURE TOWARD DEVELOPING RESPONSIBLE BEHAVIOR IN THE CHILD IS HIGH (43) B-B-C	336	DRIFT TOWARD BEING THOSE 0.52 OF 23 WHERE THE TOTAL POSITIVE PRESSURE TOWARD DEVELOPING RESPONSIBLE BEHAVIOR IN THE CHILD IS LOW (32) B-B-C	12 11 3 12 XSQ= 2.70 PHI= 0.267 EP = 0.0884
340	DRIFT TOWARD BEING THOSE 0.64 OF 11 WHERE THE TOTAL POSITIVE PRESSURE TOWARD DEVELOPING NURTURANT BEHAVIOR IN THE CHILD IS HIGH (28) B-B-C	340	DRIFT TOWARD BEING THOSE 0.75 OF 12 WHERE THE TOTAL POSITIVE PRESSURE TOWARD DEVELOPING NURTURANT BEHAVIOR IN THE CHILD IS LOW (20) B-B-C	7 3 4 9 XSQ= 2.09 PHI= 0.302 EP = 0.0995
342	DRIFT TOWARD BEING THOSE 0.70 OF 10 WHERE THE CHILD'S INFERRED ANXIETY OVER PERFORMANCE OF NURTURANT BEHAVIOR IS LOW (28) B-B-C	342	DRIFT TOWARD BEING THOSE 0.73 OF 11 WHERE THE CHILD'S INFERRED ANXIETY OVER PERFORMANCE OF NURTURANT BEHAVIOR IS HIGH (18) B-B-C	3 8 7 3 XSQ= 2.31 PHI= -0.332 EP = 0.0861
347	DRIFT TOWARD BEING THOSE 0.80 OF 15 WHERE THE CHILD'S INFERRED CONFLICT REGARDING SELF-RELIANT BEHAVIOR IS HIGH (37) B-B-C	347	DRIFT TOWARD BEING THOSE 0.52 OF 23 WHERE THE CHILD'S INFERRED CONFLICT REGARDING SELF-RELIANT BEHAVIOR IS LOW (39) B-B-C	12 11 3 12 XSQ= 2.70 PHI= 0.267 EP = 0.0884
370	TEND TO BE THOSE 0.77 OF 71 WHERE THE SEGREGATION OF ADOLESCENT BOYS IS ABSENT (148)	370	TEND TO BE THOSE 0.57 OF 83 WHERE THE SEGREGATION OF ADOLESCENT BOYS IS COMPLETE OR PARTIAL (95)	16 47 55 36 XSQ= 17.01 PHI= -0.332 XP = 0.0000
373	DRIFT TOWARD BEING THOSE 0.83 OF 12 WHERE MALE INITIATION CEREMONIES AT PUBERTY ARE ABSENT (27) W-K-A	373	DRIFT TOWARD BEING THOSE 0.54 OF 13 WHERE MALE INITIATION CEREMONIES AT PUBERTY ARE PRESENT (17) W-K-A	2 7 10 6 XSQ= 2.30 PHI= -0.304 EP = 0.0968

382	TILT TOWARD BEING THOSE WHERE FEMALE INITIATION RITES ARE ABSENT (27) JKB	0.71 OF 14	382	TILT TOWARD BEING THOSE WHERE FEMALE INITIATION RITES ARE PRESENT (38) JKB	0.73 OF 15	4 11 10 4 XSQ= 4.16 PHI= -0.379 EP = 0.0268
391	LEAN TOWARD BEING THOSE WHERE PREMARITAL SEX RELATIONS ARE STRONGLY PUNISHED AND IN FACT RARE, OR WEAKLY PUNISHED AND IN FACT NOT RARE (89) JTW,EA	0.65 OF 49	391	LEAN TOWARD BEING THOSE WHERE PREMARITAL SEX RELATIONS ARE PUNISHED ONLY IF PREGNANCY RESULTS, OR FREELY PERMITTED (90) JTW,EA	0.65 OF 52	32 18 17 34 XSQ= 8.32 PHI= 0.287 XP = 0.0039
396	DRIFT TOWARD BEING THOSE WHERE THE STRENGTH OF MENSTRUAL TABOOS IS LOW (35) WNS	0.89 OF 9	396	DRIFT TOWARD BEING THOSE WHERE THE STRENGTH OF MENSTRUAL TABOOS IS HIGH (18) WNS	0.50 OF 18	1 9 8 9 XSQ= 2.40 PHI= -0.298 EP = 0.0912
426	DRIFT MORE TOWARD BEING THOSE WHERE A HIGH GOD IS PRESENT (156) GES,EA	0.79 OF 66	426	DRIFT LESS TOWARD BEING THOSE WHERE A HIGH GOD IS PRESENT (156) GES,EA	0.62 OF 77	52 48 14 29 XSQ= 3.82 PHI= 0.164 XP = 0.0505
427	TEND TO BE THOSE WHERE A HIGH GOD, IF PRESENT, IS ACTIVE, RATHER THAN INACTIVE (87) GES,EA	0.79 OF 52	427	TEND TO BE THOSE WHERE A HIGH GOD, IF PRESENT, IS INACTIVE, RATHER THAN ACTIVE (69) GES,EA	0.73 OF 48	41 13 11 35 XSQ= 24.88 PHI= 0.499 XP = 0.0000
428	DRIFT MORE TOWARD BEING THOSE WHERE A HIGH GOD, IF PRESENT AND ACTIVE, SUPPORTS HUMAN MORALITY, RATHER THAN NOT SUPPORTING IT (61) GES,EA	0.83 OF 41	428	DRIFT LESS TOWARD BEING THOSE WHERE A HIGH GOD, IF PRESENT AND ACTIVE, SUPPORTS HUMAN MORALITY, RATHER THAN NOT SUPPORTING IT (61) GES,EA	0.54 OF 13	34 7 7 6 XSQ= 3.11 PHI= 0.240 XP = 0.0776
450	DRIFT TOWARD BEING THOSE WHERE THE OBSERVATION OF FOOD TABOOS IS LOW, RATHER THAN HIGH OR MEDIUM (26) JRL	0.50 OF 24	450	DRIFT TOWARD BEING THOSE WHERE THE OBSERVATION OF FOOD TABOOS IS HIGH OR MEDIUM, RATHER THAN LOW (60) JRL	0.77 OF 26	12 20 12 6 XSQ= 2.84 PHI= -0.239 XP = 0.0917
458	LEAN TOWARD BEING THOSE WHERE GAMES, IF PRESENT, INCLUDE GAMES OF STRATEGY (52) R-A-B,EA	0.75 OF 40	458	LEAN TOWARD BEING THOSE WHERE GAMES, IF PRESENT, DO NOT INCLUDE GAMES OF STRATEGY (119) R-A-B,EA	0.63 OF 40	30 15 10 25 XSQ= 9.96 PHI= 0.353 XP = 0.0016
459	LEAN TOWARD BEING THOSE WHERE GAMES, IF PRESENT, INCLUDE GAMES OF CHANCE (82) R-A-B,EA	0.63 OF 40	459	LEAN TOWARD BEING THOSE WHERE GAMES, IF PRESENT, DO NOT INCLUDE GAMES OF CHANCE (89) R-A-B,EA	0.72 OF 40	25 11 15 29 XSQ= 8.54 PHI= 0.327 XP = 0.0035

460	TEND TO BE THOSE WHERE GAMES, IF PRESENT, ARE NOT LIMITED TO GAMES OF SKILL ONLY (104) R-A-B,EA	0.90 OF 40	TEND TO BE THOSE WHERE GAMES, IF PRESENT, ARE LIMITED TO GAMES OF SKILL ONLY (67) R-A-B,EA	0.50 OF 40	4 20 36 20 XSQ= 13.39 PHI= -0.409 XP = 0.0003
468	DRIFT TOWARD BEING THOSE WHERE CONTACT WITH OTHER CULTURES IS FREQUENT, RATHER THAN REGULAR OR IRREGULAR (17) JMH	0.69 OF 13	DRIFT TOWARD BEING THOSE WHERE CONTACT WITH OTHER CULTURES IS REGULAR OR IRREGULAR, RATHER THAN FREQUENT (37) JMH	0.69 OF 16	9 5 4 11 XSQ= 2.76 PHI= 0.309 EP = 0.0656

56 CULTURES
WHERE FOOD PRODUCTION IS BY
SIMPLE AGRICULTURE, RATHER THAN BY
INCIPIENT FOOD PRODUCTION (101)

56 CULTURES
WHERE FOOD PRODUCTION IS BY
INCIPIENT FOOD PRODUCTION, RATHER THAN BY
SIMPLE AGRICULTURE (46)

BACKGROUND ON PAGE 74

BOTH SUBJECT AND PREDICATE

101 IN LEFT COLUMN

AKHA	ALORESE	AMBA	ARAPESH	ASHANTI	ATAYAL	AZANDE	BABWA	BAMILEKE	BANDA
BARI	BAYA	BEMBA	BHUIYA	BIRIFOR	BLACK CARIB	BUNLAP	CAGABA	CAYAPA	CHIRIGUANO
CHOCO	CHORTI	CUNA	ENGA	FANG	FON	FUTAJALONKE	GARO	GISU	GOND
GURE	HANUNOO	HUICHOL	IBAN	ILA	JIVARO	JUKUN	KACHIN	KAPAUKU	KERAKI
KHASI	KISSI	KPE	KUBA	KURTATCHI	LAKHER	LAMBA	LAMET	LANGO	LAU
LHOTA NAGA	MAM	MAMVU	MANGAIANS	MARQUESANS	MARSHALLESE	MAYA	MBUNDU	MENDE	MNONG GAR
MONGO	MOTA	NDEMBU	NICOBARESE	NUPE	PAIWAN	PALAUANS	PAWNEE	PONAPEANS	PUKAPUKA
PURUM	SAMOANS	SANDAWE	SENIANG	SHILLUK	SIUAI	SUBANUN	SWAZI	TAGBANUA	TALAMANCA
TENDA	TENETEHARA	TERA	TESO	THONGA	TIV	TORAJA	TOTONAC	TROBRIAND	TUNEBO
ULAWANS	WANTOAT	WICHITA	WOGEO	WOLEAIANS	WOLOF	YAKO	YAO	YAPESE	YOMBE
YORUBA									

46 IN RIGHT COLUMN

ABOR	APINAYE	BACAIRI	BHIL	BUDUMA	CAMAYURA	CARIB	CHEROKEE	CHUKCHEE	CREEK
DELAWARE	FOX	HASINAI	HAVASUPAI	HURON	ICELANDERS	LAKALAI	LESU	LOZI	LUBA
MAORI	MIAMI	MUNDURUCU	NAMA	NATCHEZ	NAVAHO	PALIKUR	PAPAGO	SAMOYED	SARAMACCA
SHERENTE	TAPIRAPE	TERENA	TIMBIRA	TIMUCUA	TRISTAN	TRUMAI	TUCANO	TUPINAMBA	TURKANA
WAPISHANA	WINNEBAGO	WITOTO	YABARANA	YAKUT	YARURO				

208 EXCLUDED BECAUSE IRRELEVANT

45 EXCLUDED BECAUSE UNASCERTAINED

3	TEND LESS TO BE THOSE LOCATED OUTSIDE OF AFRICA (320)	0.61 OF 101	3	TEND MORE TO BE THOSE LOCATED OUTSIDE OF AFRICA (320)	0.91 OF 46	39 4 62 42 XSQ= 12.26 PHI= 0.289 XP = 0.0005
6	LEAN LESS TOWARD BEING THOSE LOCATED OUTSIDE OF THE INSULAR PACIFIC (330)	0.69 OF 101	6	LEAN MORE TOWARD BEING THOSE LOCATED OUTSIDE OF THE INSULAR PACIFIC (330)	0.93 OF 46	31 3 70 43 XSQ= 9.07 PHI= 0.248 XP = 0.0026

8	TEND MORE TO BE THOSE LOCATED OUTSIDE OF NORTH AMERICA (330)	0.96 OF 101	8	TEND LESS TO BE THOSE LOCATED OUTSIDE OF NORTH AMERICA (330)	0.72 OF 46	4 13 97 33 XSQ= 15.95 PHI= -0.329 XP = 0.0001
9	TEND MORE TO BE THOSE LOCATED OUTSIDE OF SOUTH AMERICA (335)	0.87 OF 101	9	TEND LESS TO BE THOSE LOCATED OUTSIDE OF SOUTH AMERICA (335)	0.61 OF 46	13 18 88 28 XSQ= 11.57 PHI= -0.280 XP = 0.0007
12	IN ALL CASES ARE THOSE WHERE THE LATITUDE IS LESS THAN FIFTY DEGREES (367)	1.00 OF 101	12	TILT LESS TOWARD BEING THOSE WHERE THE LATITUDE IS LESS THAN FIFTY DEGREES (367)	0.91 OF 46	0 4 101 42 XSQ= 6.04 PHI= -0.203 XP = 0.0140
15	TEND TO BE THOSE WHERE THE LATITUDE IS LESS THAN TWENTY DEGREES (217)	0.80 OF 101	15	TEND TO BE THOSE WHERE THE LATITUDE IS TWENTY DEGREES OR GREATER (183)	0.50 OF 46	20 23 81 23 XSQ= 12.51 PHI= -0.292 XP = 0.0004
33	LEAN MORE TOWARD BEING THOSE WHERE THE NATURAL ENVIRONMENT IS OTHER THAN 'VERY HARSH,' I.E., DESERT, DESERT GRASSES AND SHRUBS, TUNDRA, OR HIGH PLATEAU STEPPE (341) FWM	0.98 OF 101	33	LEAN LESS TOWARD BEING THOSE WHERE THE NATURAL ENVIRONMENT IS OTHER THAN 'VERY HARSH,' I.E., DESERT, DESERT GRASSES AND SHRUBS, TUNDRA, OR HIGH PLATEAU STEPPE (341) FWM	0.85 OF 46	2 7 99 39 XSQ= 7.47 PHI= -0.225 XP = 0.0063
42	TILT TOWARD BEING THOSE WHERE THE NATURAL ENVIRONMENT IS TROPICAL OR SUB-TROPICAL RAIN FOREST, OR MONSOON FOREST (156) FWM	0.65 OF 101	42	TILT TOWARD BEING THOSE WHERE THE NATURAL ENVIRONMENT IS OTHER THAN TROPICAL OR SUB-TROPICAL RAIN FOREST, OR MONSOON FOREST (244) FWM	0.59 OF 46	66 19 35 27 XSQ= 6.54 PHI= 0.211 XP = 0.0106
44	TEND MORE TO BE THOSE WHERE SETTLEMENTS ARE FIXED (222)	0.91 OF 101	44	TEND LESS TO BE THOSE WHERE SETTLEMENTS ARE FIXED (222)	0.56 OF 39	92 22 9 17 XSQ= 20.14 PHI= 0.379 XP = 0.0000
46	IN ALL CASES ARE THOSE OTHER THAN WHERE SETTLEMENTS ARE NON-FIXED AND MOVEMENT IS NOMADIC (260)	1.00 OF 101	46	TEND LESS TO BE THOSE OTHER THAN WHERE SETTLEMENTS ARE NON-FIXED AND MOVEMENT IS NOMADIC (260)	0.82 OF 39	0 7 101 32 XSQ= 15.49 PHI= -0.333 XP = 0.0001
47	IN ALL CASES ARE THOSE WHERE, IF SETTLEMENTS ARE NON-FIXED, MOVEMENT IS NON-NOMADIC, RATHER THAN NOMADIC (38)	1.00 OF 9	47	DRIFT LESS TOWARD BEING THOSE WHERE, IF SETTLEMENTS ARE NON-FIXED, MOVEMENT IS NON-NOMADIC, RATHER THAN NOMADIC (38)	0.59 OF 17	0 7 9 10 XSQ= 3.19 PHI= -0.351 EP = 0.0578

62	TEND TO BE THOSE WHERE HUSBANDRY OF SOME KIND IS PRESENT (228)	0.90 OF 101	62	TEND TO BE THOSE WHERE HUSBANDRY OF ANY KIND IS ABSENT (172)	0.67 OF 46	91 15 10 31 XSQ= 49.12 PHI= 0.578 XP = 0.
63	TILT TOWARD BEING THOSE WHERE HUSBANDRY, IF PRESENT, IS PRINCIPALLY IN THE FORM OF PIGS, SHEEP, OR GOATS, RATHER THAN BOVINE, EQUINE, CAMEL-LIKE, OR DEER-LIKE ANIMALS (74)	0.60 OF 91	63	TILT TOWARD BEING THOSE WHERE HUSBANDRY, IF PRESENT, IS PRINCIPALLY IN THE FORM OF BOVINE, EQUINE, CAMEL-LIKE, OR DEER-LIKE ANIMALS, RATHER THAN PIGS, SHEEP, OR GOATS (152)	0.73 OF 15	36 11 55 4 XSQ= 4.66 PHI= -0.210 XP = 0.0308
71	TILT LESS TOWARD BEING THOSE WHERE METAL WORKING IS ABSENT (153)	0.51 OF 70	71	TILT MORE TOWARD BEING THOSE WHERE METAL WORKING IS ABSENT (153)	0.75 OF 36	34 9 36 27 XSQ= 4.54 PHI= 0.207 XP = 0.0330
82	DRIFT MORE TOWARD BEING THOSE WHERE A CITY OR TOWN IS PRESENT, OR THE AVERAGE COMMUNITY SIZE IS FIFTY OR GREATER (178)	0.94 OF 64	82	DRIFT LESS TOWARD BEING THOSE WHERE A CITY OR TOWN IS PRESENT, OR THE AVERAGE COMMUNITY SIZE IS FIFTY OR GREATER (178)	0.77 OF 26	60 20 4 6 XSQ= 3.73 PHI= 0.204 XP = 0.0533
96	TILT TOWARD BEING THOSE WHERE THE HIERARCHY OF NATIONAL JURISDICTION HAS FOUR, THREE, TWO OR ONE LEVEL (174) GES,EA	0.57 OF 101	96	TILT TOWARD BEING THOSE WHERE THE HIERARCHY OF NATIONAL JURISDICTION HAS NO LEVELS (156) GES,EA	0.64 OF 39	58 14 43 25 XSQ= 4.39 PHI= 0.177 XP = 0.0361
102	TILT TOWARD BEING THOSE WHERE CLASS STRATIFICATION IS PRESENT (203)	0.59 OF 96	102	TILT TOWARD BEING THOSE WHERE CLASS STRATIFICATION IS ABSENT (180)	0.63 OF 46	57 17 39 29 XSQ= 5.40 PHI= 0.195 XP = 0.0202
130	DRIFT TOWARD BEING THOSE WHERE LEATHER WORKING IS MAINLY DONE BY MALES (39)	0.83 OF 6	130	DRIFT TOWARD BEING THOSE WHERE LEATHER WORKING IS MAINLY DONE BY FEMALES (45)	0.67 OF 15	5 5 1 10 XSQ= 2.52 PHI= 0.347 EP = 0.0635
133	TILT TOWARD BEING THOSE WHERE CONTRACTED DEBTS ARE SIGNIFICANTLY PRESENT (17) GES	0.86 OF 7	133	IN ALL CASES ARE THOSE WHERE CONTRACTED DEBTS ARE MODERATELY PRESENT OR ABSENT (17) GES	1.00 OF 5	6 0 1 5 XSQ= 5.49 PHI= 0.676 EP = 0.0152
137	TILT TOWARD BEING THOSE WHERE INVIDIOUS DISPLAY OF WEALTH IS STRONGLY EMPHASIZED (37) PES	0.64 OF 22	137	TILT TOWARD BEING THOSE WHERE INVIDIOUS DISPLAY OF WEALTH IS MODERATELY, LITTLE, OR NEGATIVELY EMPHASIZED (52) PES	0.77 OF 13	14 3 8 10 XSQ= 3.88 PHI= 0.333 EP = 0.0354

138	TILT TOWARD BEING THOSE WHERE SUPERORDINATE JUSTICE IS PRESENT (22) BBW	0.64 OF 11	138	IN ALL CASES ARE THOSE WHERE SUPERORDINATE JUSTICE IS ABSENT (18) BBW	1.00 OF 6	7 0 4 6 XSQ= 4.13 PHI= 0.493 EP = 0.0175
147	DRIFT TOWARD BEING THOSE WHERE CODIFIED LAWS ARE PRESENT (20) LWS	0.86 OF 7	147	DRIFT TOWARD BEING THOSE WHERE CODIFIED LAWS ARE UNIMPORTANT OR ABSENT (13) LWS	0.75 OF 4	6 1 1 3 XSQ= 1.86 PHI= 0.411 EP = 0.0879
176	TILT TOWARD BEING THOSE WHERE THE COMMUNITY IS A CLAN-COMMUNITY OR A COMMUNITY STRUCTURED OR SEGMENTED ON A CLAN BASIS (169)	0.60 OF 99	176	TILT TOWARD BEING THOSE WHERE THE COMMUNITY IS OTHER THAN A CLAN-COMMUNITY OR A COMMUNITY STRUCTURED OR SEGMENTED ON A CLAN BASIS (213)	0.63 OF 43	59 16 40 27 XSQ= 5.16 PHI= 0.191 XP = 0.0231
177	TILT LESS TOWARD BEING THOSE WHERE THE COMMUNITY IS OTHER THAN A SINGLE CLAN-COMMUNITY AND EXOGAMOUS (305)	0.74 OF 99	177	TILT MORE TOWARD BEING THOSE WHERE THE COMMUNITY IS OTHER THAN A SINGLE CLAN-COMMUNITY AND EXOGAMOUS (305)	0.91 OF 43	26 4 73 39 XSQ= 4.21 PHI= 0.172 XP = 0.0402
179	DRIFT MORE TOWARD BEING THOSE WHERE THE COMMUNITY IS OTHER THAN STRUCTURED ON A NON-CLAN BASIS AND COMMONLY EXOGAMOUS (340)	0.96 OF 99	179	DRIFT LESS TOWARD BEING THOSE WHERE THE COMMUNITY IS OTHER THAN STRUCTURED ON A NON-CLAN BASIS AND COMMONLY EXOGAMOUS (340)	0.86 OF 43	4 6 95 37 XSQ= 3.11 PHI= -0.148 XP = 0.0777
183	TILT MORE TOWARD BEING THOSE WHERE THE LARGEST NON-COGNATIC KIN GROUP IS SMALLER THAN A MOEITY, I. E., A PHRATRY OR SIB OR LINEAGE (218)	0.89 OF 76	183	TILT LESS TOWARD BEING THOSE WHERE THE LARGEST NON-COGNATIC KIN GROUP IS SMALLER THAN A MOEITY, I. E., A PHRATRY OR SIB OR LINEAGE (218)	0.70 OF 27	8 8 68 19 XSQ= 4.18 PHI= -0.201 XP = 0.0409
184	TILT MORE TOWARD BEING THOSE WHERE THE LARGEST NON-COGNATIC KIN GROUP IS SMALLER THAN A PHRATRY, I. E. A SIB OR LINEAGE (175)	0.76 OF 76	184	TILT LESS TOWARD BEING THOSE WHERE THE LARGEST NON-COGNATIC KIN GROUP IS SMALLER THAN A PHRATRY, I. E. A SIB OR LINEAGE (175)	0.52 OF 27	18 13 58 14 XSQ= 4.56 PHI= -0.211 XP = 0.0326
188	DRIFT MORE TOWARD BEING THOSE WHERE THE KIN GROUP IS OTHER THAN EXCLUSIVELY COGNATIC (252)	0.75 OF 101	188	DRIFT LESS TOWARD BEING THOSE WHERE THE KIN GROUP IS OTHER THAN EXCLUSIVELY COGNATIC (252)	0.59 OF 46	25 19 76 27 XSQ= 3.38 PHI= -0.152 XP = 0.0661
196	DRIFT MORE TOWARD BEING THOSE WHERE INDIVIDUAL RIGHTS IN REAL PROPERTY, AND RULES FOR INHERITANCE, ARE PRESENT (194)	0.81 OF 73	196	DRIFT LESS TOWARD BEING THOSE WHERE INDIVIDUAL RIGHTS IN REAL PROPERTY, AND RULES FOR INHERITANCE, ARE PRESENT (194)	0.59 OF 22	59 13 14 9 XSQ= 3.25 PHI= 0.185 XP = 0.0716

209	TILT MORE TOWARD BEING THOSE 0.83 OF 88 WHERE MARITAL RESIDENCE IS PATRILOCAL, VIRILOCAL, OR AVUNCULOCAL, RATHER THAN MATRILOCAL OR UXORILOCAL (270)	209	TILT LESS TOWARD BEING THOSE 0.63 OF 40 WHERE MARITAL RESIDENCE IS PATRILOCAL, VIRILOCAL, OR AVUNCULOCAL, RATHER THAN MATRILOCAL OR UXORILOCAL (270)	73 25 15 15 XSQ= 5.32 PHI= 0.204 XP = 0.0211
210	TILT MORE TOWARD BEING THOSE 0.87 OF 55 WHERE MARITAL RESIDENCE IS PATRILOCAL, RATHER THAN MATRILOCAL (169)	210	TILT LESS TOWARD BEING THOSE 0.57 OF 21 WHERE MARITAL RESIDENCE IS PATRILOCAL, RATHER THAN MATRILOCAL (169)	48 12 7 9 XSQ= 6.59 PHI= 0.294 XP = 0.0103
224	TILT LESS TOWARD BEING THOSE 0.58 OF 43 WHERE COUSIN MARRIAGE IS PREFERENTIALLY OR PERMISSIVELY SYMMETRICAL, RATHER THAN EITHER PATRI- OR MATRILATERAL (106)	224	TILT MORE TOWARD BEING THOSE 0.86 OF 22 WHERE COUSIN MARRIAGE IS PREFERENTIALLY OR PERMISSIVELY SYMMETRICAL, RATHER THAN EITHER PATRI- OR MATRILATERAL (106)	18 3 25 19 XSQ= 4.09 PHI= 0.251 XP = 0.0432
234	DRIFT TOWARD BEING THOSE 0.50 OF 88 WHERE THE COUSIN TERMINOLOGY IS OF ESKIMO OR HAWAIIAN TYPE, RATHER THAN CROW, OMAHA, OR IROQUOIS TYPE (170)	234	DRIFT TOWARD BEING THOSE 0.69 OF 35 WHERE THE COUSIN TERMINOLOGY IS OF CROW, OMAHA, OR IROQUOIS TYPE, RATHER THAN ESKIMO OR HAWAIIAN TYPE (152)	44 24 44 11 XSQ= 2.78 PHI= -0.150 XP = 0.0953
236	DRIFT TOWARD BEING THOSE 0.51 OF 100 WHERE THE FAMILY IS OF AN INDEPENDENT TYPE, RATHER THAN AN EXTENDED TYPE (185)	236	DRIFT TOWARD BEING THOSE 0.65 OF 46 WHERE THE FAMILY IS OF AN EXTENDED TYPE, RATHER THAN AN INDEPENDENT TYPE (213)	49 30 51 16 XSQ= 2.72 PHI= -0.136 XP = 0.0993
243	TILT TOWARD BEING THOSE 0.55 OF 20 WHERE POLYGYNY, IF PRESENT, HAS A HIGH INCIDENCE (24) W-C,S	243	TILT TOWARD BEING THOSE 0.89 OF 9 WHERE POLYGYNY, IF PRESENT, HAS A LOW INCIDENCE (36) W-D,S	11 1 9 8 XSQ= 3.29 PHI= 0.337 EP = 0.0432
263	TILT TOWARD BEING THOSE 0.71 OF 101 WHERE WIVES ARE OBTAINED BY RELATIVELY DIFFICULT MEANS, NAMELY BY BRIDE-PRICE, BRIDE-SERVICE, OR EXCHANGING A FEMALE RELATIVE (233)	263	TILT TOWARD BEING THOSE 0.52 OF 44 WHERE WIVES ARE OBTAINED BY RELATIVELY EASY MEANS, NAMELY BY TOKEN BRIDE-PRICE, GIFT EXCHANGE, ABSENCE OF ANY CONSIDERATION, OR RECEIPT OF DOWRY (162)	72 21 29 23 XSQ= 6.41 PHI= 0.210 XP = 0.0114
299	DRIFT TOWARD BEING THOSE 0.52 OF 44 WHERE THE POST-PARTUM SEX TABOO LASTS LONGER THAN ONE YEAR (35)	299	DRIFT TOWARD BEING THOSE 0.82 OF 11 WHERE THE POST-PARTUM SEX TABOO LASTS ONE YEAR OR LESS (89)	23 2 21 9 XSQ= 2.86 PHI= 0.228 XP = 0.0905
300	TILT TOWARD BEING THOSE 0.66 OF 44 WHERE THE POST-PARTUM SEX TABOO LASTS LONGER THAN SIX MONTHS (51)	300	TILT TOWARD BEING THOSE 0.73 OF 11 WHERE THE POST-PARTUM SEX TABOO LASTS SIX MONTHS OR LESS (73)	29 3 15 8 XSQ= 3.93 PHI= 0.267 XP = 0.0475

```
304  LEAN TOWARD BEING THOSE          0.77 OF  13    304  IN ALL CASES ARE THOSE          1.00 OF   5           3    5
     WHERE THE EARLY ANAL SATISFACTION                   WHERE THE EARLY ANAL SATISFACTION                    10    0
     POTENTIAL IS LOW   (22) W-C                         POTENTIAL IS HIGH   (19) W-C                   XSQ=     5.82
                                                                                                        PHI=   -0.569
                                                                                                        EP  =  0.0065

307  TILT TOWARD BEING THOSE         0.76 OF  17    307  TILT TOWARD BEING THOSE         0.80 OF   5          13    1
     WHERE THE EARLY AGGRESSION SATISFACTION             WHERE THE EARLY AGGRESSION SATISFACTION               4    4
     POTENTIAL IS HIGH   (33) W-C                        POTENTIAL IS LOW   (19) W-C                    XSQ=     3.16
                                                                                                        PHI=    0.379
                                                                                                        EP  =  0.0393

318  DRIFT TOWARD BEING THOSE        0.55 OF  22    318  DRIFT TOWARD BEING THOSE        0.82 OF  11          10    9
     WHERE THE OVERALL INDULGENCE                        WHERE THE OVERALL INDULGENCE                         12    2
     OF THE INFANT                                       OF THE INFANT                                  XSQ=     2.62
     IS LOW   (31) B-B-C                                 IS HIGH   (40) B-B-C                           PHI=   -0.282
                                                                                                        EP  =  0.0674

340  TILT TOWARD BEING THOSE         0.75 OF  12    340  TILT TOWARD BEING THOSE         0.83 OF   6           3    5
     WHERE THE TOTAL POSITIVE PRESSURE TOWARD            WHERE THE TOTAL POSITIVE PRESSURE TOWARD              9    1
     DEVELOPING NURTURANT BEHAVIOR                       DEVELOPING NURTURANT BEHAVIOR                  XSQ=     3.40
     IN THE CHILD                                        IN THE CHILD                                   PHI=   -0.435
     IS LOW   (20) B-B-C                                 IS HIGH   (28) B-B-C                           EP  =  0.0430

342  TILT TOWARD BEING THOSE         0.73 OF  11    342  TILT TOWARD BEING THOSE         0.83 OF   6           8    1
     WHERE THE CHILD'S INFERRED ANXIETY OVER             WHERE THE CHILD'S INFERRED ANXIETY OVER               3    5
     PERFORMANCE OF NURTURANT BEHAVIOR                   PERFORMANCE OF NURTURANT BEHAVIOR              XSQ=     2.91
     IS HIGH   (18) B-B-C                                IS LOW   (28) B-B-C                            PHI=    0.413
                                                                                                        EP  =  0.0498

353  DRIFT TOWARD BEING THOSE        0.73 OF  22    353  DRIFT TOWARD BEING THOSE        0.64 OF  11          16    4
     WHERE THE CHILD'S INFERRED ANXIETY OVER             WHERE THE CHILD-S INFERRED ANXIETY OVER               6    7
     NON-PERFORMANCE OF OBEDIENT BEHAVIOR                NON-PERFORMANCE OF OBEDIENT BEHAVIOR           XSQ=     2.68
     IS HIGH   (42) B-B-C                                IS LOW   (32) B-B-C                            PHI=    0.285
                                                                                                        EP  =  0.0645

354  TILT TOWARD BEING THOSE         0.67 OF  21    354  TILT TOWARD BEING THOSE         0.82 OF  11          14    2
     WHERE THE CHILD'S INFERRED ANXIETY OVER             WHERE THE CHILD'S INFERRED ANXIETY OVER               7    9
     PERFORMANCE OF OBEDIENT BEHAVIOR                    PERFORMANCE OF OBEDIENT BEHAVIOR               XSQ=     4.99
     IS HIGH   (36) B-B-C                                IS LOW   (37) B-B-C                            PHI=    0.395
                                                                                                        EP  =  0.0233

355  DRIFT TOWARD BEING THOSE        0.67 OF  21    355  DRIFT TOWARD BEING THOSE        0.73 OF  11          14    3
     WHERE THE CHILD'S INFERRED CONFLICT                 WHERE THE CHILD'S INFERRED CONFLICT                   7    8
     REGARDING OBEDIENT BEHAVIOR                         REGARDING OBEDIENT BEHAVIOR                    XSQ=     3.06
     IS HIGH   (35) B-B-C                                IS LOW   (38) B-B-C                            PHI=    0.309
                                                                                                        EP  =  0.0617

372  TILT TOWARD BEING THOSE         0.58 OF  33    372  TILT TOWARD BEING THOSE         0.76 OF  17          19    4
     WHERE MALE INITIATION RITES ARE                     WHERE MALE INITIATION RITES ARE                      14   13
     PRESENT   (48) ASA                                  ABSENT   (63) ASA                              XSQ=     3.95
                                                                                                        PHI=    0.281
                                                                                                        XP  =  0.0467
```

```
377  TEND LESS TO BE THCSE              0.68 OF 100    377  TEND MORE TO BE THOSE              0.97 CF  39          32     1
     WHERE MALE GENITAL MUTILATION                          WHERE MALE GENITAL MUTILATICN                           68    38
     IS ABSENT   (242)                                      IS ABSENT   (242)                               XSQ=    11.85
                                                                                                            PHI=    0.292
                                                                                                            XP =    0.0006

399  DRIFT TCWARD BEING THCSE           0.65 OF  17    399  DRIFT TOWARD BEING THOSE           0.83 CF   6          11     1
     WHERE INTENSITY CF CASTRATION ANXIETY                  WHERE INTENSITY OF CASTRATION ANXIETY                    6     5
     IS HIGH   (23) WNS                                     IS LOW   (22) WNS                                   XSQ=     2.40
                                                                                                            PHI=    0.323
                                                                                                            EP =    0.0686

440  DRIFT TOWARD BEING THCSE           0.56 OF  18    440  DRIFT TOWARD BEING THOSE           0.86 OF   7           8     6
     WHERE FEAR CF SPIRITS                                  WHERE FEAR OF SPIRITS                                   10     1
     IS LCW   (29) W-C                                      IS HIGH   (32) W-C                                  XSQ=     2.01
                                                                                                            PHI=   -0.284
                                                                                                            EP =    0.0900

452  LEAN TCWARD BEING THCSE            0.75 OF  16    452  IN ALL CASES ARE THOSE             1.00 OF   5          12     0
     WHERE TCTEMISM WITH FCOC TABOCS                        WHERE TOTEMISM WITH FOOD TABOOS                          4     5
     IS PRESENT   (19) WNS                                  IS ABSENT   (24) WNS                                XSQ=     5.96
                                                                                                            PHI=    0.533
                                                                                                            EP =    0.0062

458  TILT LESS TOWARC BEING THCSE       0.63 OF  40    458  TILT MORE TOWARD BEING THOSE       0.92 CF  25          15     2
     WHERE GAMES, IF PRESENT,                               WHERE GAMES, IF PRESENT,                                25    23
     DO NCT INCLUDE                                         DO NOT INCLUDE                                  XSQ=     5.49
     GAMES OF STRATEGY   (119) R-A-B,EA                     GAMES OF STRATEGY   (119) R-A-B,EA              PHI=    0.291
                                                                                                            XP =    0.0191

475  DRIFT TCWARD BEING THCSE           0.70 OF  23    475  DRIFT TOWARD BEING THCSE           0.62 CF  13          16     5
     WHERE EXHIBITICNISTIC CANCING                          WHERE EXHIBITIONISTIC DANCING                            7     8
     IS STRCNGLY OR MODERATELY                              IS NEGLIGIBLY EMPHASIZED   (38) PES             XSQ=     2.15
     EMPHASIZED   (48) PES                                                                                  PHI=    0.244
                                                                                                            EP =    0.0895

476  DRIFT LESS TCWARD BEING THCSE      0.53 OF  15    476  DRIFT MORE TOWARD BEING THCSE      0.90 CF  10           8     9
     WHERE THE DEGREE OF INSCBRIETY IS                      WHERE THE DEGREE OF INSCBRIETY IS                        7     1
     STRCNG   (31) DH                                       STRONG   (31) DH                                XSQ=     2.21
                                                                                                            PHI=   -0.298
                                                                                                            EP =    0.0875
```

****

57 CULTURES WHERE SUBSISTENCE IS PRIMARILY BY SHIFTING AGRICULTURE (121)	57 CULTURES WHERE SUBSISTENCE IS PRIMARILY BY MEANS OTHER THAN SHIFTING AGRICULTURE (213)

BACKGROUND ON PAGE 76

SUBJECT ONLY

121 IN LEFT CCLUMN

ABOR	AINU	AKHA	ALORESE	AMBA	APINAYE	ARAPESH	ASHANTI	ATAYAL	AZANDE
BABWA	BACAIRI	BAMILEKE	BANCA	BARI	BAYA	BEMBA	BHUIYA	BIRIFOR	BUNLAP
CADUVEO	CAGABA	CAMAYURA	CARIB	CHEROKEE	CHIRIGUANO	CHOCO	CHORTI	CREEK	CUNA
DELAWARE	ENGA	FANG	FON	FOX	FUTAJALONKE	GARO	GISU	GOND	GURE
HANUNCO	HASINAI	HUICHOL	HURON	IBAN	ILA	JIVARO	JUKUN	KACHIN	KAPAUKU
KERAKI	KHASI	KISSI	KPE	KUBA	KURTATCHI	LAKHER	LAMBA	LAMET	LANGO
LHOTA NAGA	MAM	MAMVU	MAORI	MAYA	MBUNDU	MENDE	MIAMI	MISKITO	MNONG GAR
MONGO	MOTILON	MUNDURUCU	NAMBICUARA	NATCHEZ	NDEMBU	NUER	NUPE	PAIWAN	PAWNEE
PURUM	SANDAWE	SHERENTE	SHILLUK	SIRIONO	SIUAI	SUBANUN	SWAZI	TAGBANUA	TALAMANCA
TAPIRAPE	TENDA	TENETEHARA	TERA	TERENA	TESO	THONGA	TIMBIRA	TIMUCUA	TIV
TORAJA	TOTONAC	TRISTAN	TRUMAI	TUCANO	TUCUNA	TUNEBO	TUPINAMBA	WAICA	WAPISHANA
WICHITA	WITOTO	WOGEO	WOLOF	YABARANA	YAGUA	YAKO	YAO	YARURO	YOMBE
YORUBA									

213 IN RIGHT CCLUMN

66 EXCLUDED BECAUSE UNASCERTAINED

3	TEND LESS TO BE THOSE LOCATED OUTSIDE OF AFRICA (320)	0.67 OF 121	3	TEND MORE TO BE THOSE LOCATED OUTSIDE OF AFRICA (320)	0.86 OF 213	40 29 81 184 XSQ= 16.63 PHI= 0.223 XP = 0.0000
4	TEND MORE TO BE THOSE LOCATED OUTSIDE OF THE CIRCUM-MEDITERRANEAN (355)	0.98 OF 121	4	TEND LESS TO BE THOSE LOCATED OUTSIDE OF THE CIRCUM-MEDITERRANEAN (355)	0.85 OF 213	3 31 118 182 XSQ= 11.02 PHI= -0.182 XP = 0.0009
5	TILT MORE TOWARD BEING THOSE LOCATED OUTSIDE OF EAST EURASIA (330)	0.89 OF 121	5	TILT LESS TOWARD BEING THOSE LOCATED OUTSIDE OF EAST EURASIA (330)	0.78 OF 213	13 46 108 167 XSQ= 5.52 PHI= -0.129 XP = 0.0187

8	TILT MORE TOWARD BEING THOSE LOCATED OUTSIDE OF NORTH AMERICA (330)	0.89 OF 121	TILT LESS TOWARD BEING THOSE LOCATED OUTSIDE OF NORTH AMERICA (330)	0.78 OF 213	13 47 108 166 XSQ= 5.97 PHI= -0.134 XP = 0.0146
9	TEND LESS TO BE THOSE LOCATED OUTSIDE OF SOUTH AMERICA (335)	0.71 OF 121	TEND MORE TO BE THOSE LOCATED OUTSIDE OF SOUTH AMERICA (335)	0.89 OF 213	35 24 86 189 XSQ= 15.35 PHI= 0.214 XP = 0.0001
12	IN ALL CASES ARE THOSE WHERE THE LATITUDE IS LESS THAN FIFTY DEGREES (367)	1.00 OF 121	TEND LESS TO BE THOSE WHERE THE LATITUDE IS LESS THAN FIFTY DEGREES (367)	0.86 OF 213	0 29 121 184 XSQ= 16.36 PHI= -0.221 XP = 0.0001
15	TEND TO BE THOSE WHERE THE LATITUDE IS LESS THAN TWENTY DEGREES (217)	0.72 OF 121	TEND TO BE THOSE WHERE THE LATITUDE IS TWENTY DEGREES OR GREATER (183)	0.58 OF 213	34 123 87 90 XSQ= 26.05 PHI= -0.279 XP = 0.0000
33	TEND MORE TO BE THOSE WHERE THE NATURAL ENVIRONMENT IS OTHER THAN 'VERY HARSH,' I.E., DESERT, DESERT GRASSES AND SHRUBS, TUNDRA, OR HIGH PLATEAU STEPPE (341) FWM	0.98 OF 121	TEND LESS TO BE THOSE WHERE THE NATURAL ENVIRONMENT IS OTHER THAN 'VERY HARSH,' I.E., DESERT, DESERT GRASSES AND SHRUBS, TUNDRA, OR HIGH PLATEAU STEPPE (341) FWM	0.77 OF 213	2 50 119 163 XSQ= 26.32 PHI= -0.281 XP = 0.0000
36	TEND MORE TO BE THOSE WHERE THE NATURAL ENVIRONMENT IS OTHER THAN 'VERY HARSH,' OR SUB-TROPICAL BUSH, OR TEMPERATE GRASSLAND (292) FWM	0.91 OF 121	TEND LESS TO BE THOSE WHERE THE NATURAL ENVIRONMENT IS OTHER THAN 'VERY HARSH,' OR SUB-TROPICAL BUSH, OR TEMPERATE GRASSLAND (292) FWM	0.64 OF 213	11 76 110 137 XSQ= 26.96 PHI= -0.284 XP = 0.0000
42	TEND TO BE THOSE WHERE THE NATURAL ENVIRONMENT IS TROPICAL OR SUB-TROPICAL RAIN FOREST, OR MONSOON FOREST (156) FWM	0.55 OF 121	TEND TO BE THOSE WHERE THE NATURAL ENVIRONMENT IS OTHER THAN TROPICAL OR SUB-TROPICAL RAIN FOREST, OR MONSOON FOREST (244) FWM	0.70 OF 213	67 63 54 150 XSQ= 20.53 PHI= 0.248 XP = 0.0000
44	TEND MORE TO BE THOSE WHERE SETTLEMENTS ARE FIXED (222)	0.82 OF 121	TEND LESS TO BE THOSE WHERE SETTLEMENTS ARE FIXED (222)	0.58 OF 211	99 123 22 88 XSQ= 18.16 PHI= 0.234 XP = 0.0000
46	TEND MORE TO BE THOSE OTHER THAN WHERE SETTLEMENTS ARE NON-FIXED AND MOVEMENT IS NOMADIC (260)	0.94 OF 121	TEND LESS TO BE THOSE OTHER THAN WHERE SETTLEMENTS ARE NON-FIXED AND MOVEMENT IS NOMADIC (260)	0.69 OF 211	7 65 114 146 XSQ= 26.89 PHI= -0.285 XP = 0.0000

47	TEND TO BE THOSE WHERE, IF SETTLEMENTS ARE NON-FIXED, MOVEMENT IS NON-NOMADIC, RATHER THAN NOMADIC (38)	0.68 OF 22	47	TEND TO BE THOSE WHERE, IF SETTLEMENTS ARE NON-FIXED, MOVEMENT IS NOMADIC, RATHER THAN NON-NOMADIC (72)	0.74 OF 88	7 65 15 23 XSQ= 11.96 PHI= -0.330 XP = 0.0005
63	TEND LESS TO BE THOSE WHERE HUSBANDRY, IF PRESENT, IS PRINCIPALLY IN THE FORM OF BOVINE, EQUINE, CAMEL-LIKE, OR DEER-LIKE ANIMALS, RATHER THAN PIGS, SHEEP, OR GOATS (152)	0.51 OF 84	63	TEND MORE TO BE THOSE WHERE HUSBANDRY, IF PRESENT, IS PRINCIPALLY IN THE FORM OF BOVINE, EQUINE, CAMEL-LIKE, OR DEER-LIKE ANIMALS, RATHER THAN PIGS, SHEEP, OR GOATS (152)	0.77 OF 142	43 109 41 33 XSQ= 14.53 PHI= -0.254 XP = 0.0001
73	DRIFT TOWARD BEING THOSE WHERE WEAVING IS PRESENT (118)	0.57 OF 84	73	DRIFT TOWARD BEING THOSE WHERE WEAVING IS ABSENT (130)	0.57 OF 157	48 68 36 89 XSQ= 3.66 PHI= 0.123 XP = 0.0558
74	TEND MORE TO BE THOSE WHERE POTTERY IS PRESENT (145)	0.78 OF 83	74	TEND LESS TO BE THOSE WHERE POTTERY IS PRESENT (145)	0.53 OF 148	65 79 18 69 XSQ= 13.04 PHI= 0.238 XP = 0.0003
77	IN ALL CASES ARE THOSE WHERE THE WRITING SYSTEM IS MNEMONIC OR ABSENT, RATHER THAN BEING ALPHABETIC-OR-PHONETIC (39) JMH	1.00 OF 15	77	TILT LESS TOWARD BEING THOSE WHERE THE WRITING SYSTEM IS MNEMONIC OR ABSENT, RATHER THAN BEING ALPHABETIC-OR-PHONETIC (39) JMH	0.62 OF 37	0 14 15 23 XSQ= 5.96 PHI= -0.339 XP = 0.0146
79	LEAN MORE TOWARD BEING THOSE WHERE NO CITY IS PRESENT (201)	0.99 OF 78	79	LEAN LESS TOWARD BEING THOSE WHERE NO CITY IS PRESENT (201)	0.85 OF 146	1 22 77 124 XSQ= 9.04 PHI= -0.201 XP = 0.0026
80	LEAN MORE TOWARD BEING THOSE WHERE NO CITY OR TOWN IS PRESENT (185)	0.92 OF 78	80	LEAN LESS TOWARD BEING THOSE WHERE NO CITY OR TOWN IS PRESENT (185)	0.77 OF 146	6 33 72 113 XSQ= 6.86 PHI= -0.175 XP = 0.0088
81	DRIFT MORE TOWARD BEING THOSE WHERE NO CITY OR TOWN IS PRESENT, AND THE AVERAGE COMMUNITY SIZE IS SMALLER THAN 200 (135)	0.69 OF 78	81	DRIFT LESS TOWARD BEING THOSE WHERE NO CITY OR TOWN IS PRESENT, AND THE AVERAGE COMMUNITY SIZE IS SMALLER THAN 200 (135)	0.55 OF 146	24 65 54 81 XSQ= 3.46 PHI= -0.124 XP = 0.0628
88	LEAN MORE TOWARD BEING THOSE WHERE, IF A HEADMANSHIP IS PRESENT, SUCCESSION IS HEREDITARY (165)	0.77 OF 81	88	LEAN LESS TOWARD BEING THOSE WHERE, IF A HEADMANSHIP IS PRESENT, SUCCESSION IS HEREDITARY (165)	0.54 OF 151	19 70 62 81 XSQ= 10.74 PHI= -0.215 XP = 0.0010

94	LEAN MORE TOWARD BEING THOSE 0.97 OF 121 WHERE THE HIERARCHY OF NATIONAL JURISDICTION HAS TWO, ONE, OR NO LEVELS (296) GES,EA	94	LEAN LESS TOWARD BEING THOSE 0.86 OF 209 WHERE THE HIERARCHY OF NATIONAL JURISDICTION HAS TWO, ONE, OR NO LEVELS (296) GES,EA	4 30 117 179 XSQ= 8.96 PHI= -0.165 XP = 0.0028
95	TILT MORE TOWARD BEING THOSE 0.83 OF 121 WHERE THE HIERARCHY OF NATIONAL JURISDICTION HAS ONE OR NO LEVELS (254) GES,EA	95	TILT LESS TOWARD BEING THOSE 0.73 OF 209 WHERE THE HIERARCHY OF NATIONAL JURISDICTION HAS ONE OR NO LEVELS (254) GES,EA	20 56 101 153 XSQ= 3.99 PHI= -0.110 XP = 0.0456
98	TILT MORE TOWARD BEING THOSE 0.79 OF 121 WHERE THE HIERARCHY OF LOCAL JURISDICTION HAS FOUR OR THREE LEVELS (238) GES,EA	98	TILT LESS TOWARD BEING THOSE 0.68 OF 210 WHERE THE HIERARCHY OF LOCAL JURISDICTION HAS FOUR OR THREE LEVELS (238) GES,EA	96 142 25 68 XSQ= 4.66 PHI= 0.119 XP = 0.0310
107	TILT MORE TOWARD BEING THOSE 0.89 OF 54 WHERE CLASS STRATIFICATION, IF PRESENT, IS BASED ON SOMETHING OTHER THAN OCCUPATIONAL STATUS (160)	107	TILT LESS TOWARD BEING THOSE 0.74 OF 117 WHERE CLASS STRATIFICATION, IF PRESENT, IS BASED ON SOMETHING OTHER THAN OCCUPATIONAL STATUS (160)	6 31 48 86 XSQ= 4.29 PHI= -0.158 XP = 0.0383
109	DRIFT MORE TOWARD BEING THOSE 0.91 OF 116 WHERE CASTES ARE ABSENT (317)	109	DRIFT LESS TOWARD BEING THOSE 0.83 OF 197 WHERE CASTES ARE ABSENT (317)	10 33 106 164 XSQ= 3.42 PHI= -0.104 XP = 0.0646
110	TILT LESS TOWARD BEING THOSE 0.50 OF 115 WHERE SLAVERY IS ABSENT (218)	110	TILT MORE TOWARD BEING THOSE 0.63 OF 208 WHERE SLAVERY IS ABSENT (218)	57 77 58 131 XSQ= 4.30 PHI= 0.115 XP = 0.0381
120	TILT TOWARD BEING THOSE 0.56 OF 18 WHERE THE CRAFT SPECIALIZATION SCORE IS LOW (17) WME	120	TILT TOWARD BEING THOSE 0.79 OF 34 WHERE THE CRAFT SPECIALIZATION SCORE IS HIGH OR MEDIUM (36) WME	8 27 10 7 XSQ= 5.05 PHI= -0.312 XP = 0.0247
128	TILT TOWARD BEING THOSE 0.65 OF 34 WHERE, IF SUBSISTENCE IS PRIMARILY BY AGRICULTURE, THE WORK IS MAINLY DONE BY FEMALES (37)	128	TILT TOWARD BEING THOSE 0.65 OF 43 WHERE, IF SUBSISTENCE IS PRIMARILY BY AGRICULTURE, THE WORK IS MAINLY DONE BY MALES (40)	12 28 22 15 XSQ= 5.62 PHI= -0.270 XP = 0.0177
131	IN ALL CASES ARE THOSE 1.00 OF 54 WHERE THE CONSTRUCTION OF PERMANENT HOUSES OR THE ERECTION OF TEMPORARY DWELLINGS IS MAINLY DONE BY MALES (136)	131	LEAN LESS TOWARD BEING THOSE 0.80 OF 100 WHERE THE CONSTRUCTION OF PERMANENT HOUSES OR THE ERECTION OF TEMPORARY DWELLINGS IS MAINLY DONE BY MALES (136)	54 80 0 20 XSQ= 10.71 PHI= 0.264 XP = 0.0011

175	DRIFT LESS TOWARD BEING THOSE 0.62 OF 117 WHERE THE COMMUNITY IS 'KIN-HETEROGENEOUS,' I. E. OTHER THAN A CLAN COMMUNITY OR A DEME (260)	175	DRIFT MORE TOWARD BEING THOSE 0.73 OF 204 WHERE THE COMMUNITY IS 'KIN-HETEROGENEOUS,' I. E. OTHER THAN A CLAN COMMUNITY OR A DEME (260)	44 55 73 149 XSQ= 3.47 PHI= 0.104 XP = 0.0626
176	DRIFT TOWARD BEING THOSE 0.52 OF 117 WHERE THE COMMUNITY IS A CLAN-COMMUNITY OR A COMMUNITY STRUCTURED OR SEGMENTED ON A CLAN BASIS (169)	176	DRIFT TOWARD BEING THOSE 0.60 OF 204 WHERE THE COMMUNITY IS OTHER THAN A CLAN-COMMUNITY OR A COMMUNITY STRUCTURED OR SEGMENTED ON A CLAN BASIS (213)	61 82 56 122 XSQ= 3.82 PHI= 0.109 XP = 0.0506
179	LEAN MORE TOWARD BEING THOSE 0.96 OF 117 WHERE THE COMMUNITY IS OTHER THAN STRUCTURED ON A NON-CLAN BASIS AND COMMONLY EXOGAMOUS (340)	179	LEAN LESS TOWARD BEING THOSE 0.83 OF 204 WHERE THE COMMUNITY IS OTHER THAN STRUCTURED ON A NON-CLAN BASIS AND COMMONLY EXOGAMOUS (340)	5 34 112 170 XSQ= 9.57 PHI= -0.173 XP = 0.0020
184	DRIFT MORE TOWARD BEING THOSE 0.75 OF 84 WHERE THE LARGEST NON-COGNATIC KIN GROUP IS SMALLER THAN A PHRATRY, I. E. A SIB OR LINEAGE (175)	184	DRIFT LESS TOWARD BEING THOSE 0.63 OF 128 WHERE THE LARGEST NON-COGNATIC KIN GROUP IS SMALLER THAN A PHRATRY, I. E. A SIB OR LINEAGE (175)	21 48 63 80 XSQ= 3.06 PHI= -0.120 XP = 0.0801
192	TILT MORE TOWARD BEING THOSE 0.80 OF 121 OTHER THAN WHERE THE ONLY KIN GROUP PRESENT IS A KINDRED OR ELSE BILATERAL DESCENT IS INFERRED (289)	192	TILT LESS TOWARD BEING THOSE 0.68 OF 213 OTHER THAN WHERE THE ONLY KIN GROUP PRESENT IS A KINDRED OR ELSE BILATERAL DESCENT IS INFERRED (289)	24 68 97 145 XSQ= 5.06 PHI= -0.123 XP = 0.0245
207	TILT TOWARD BEING THOSE 0.67 OF 45 WHERE MARITAL RESIDENCE IS MATRILOCAL OR UXORILOCAL, RATHER THAN AMBILOCAL OR NEOLOCAL (64)	207	TILT TOWARD BEING THOSE 0.58 OF 64 WHERE MARITAL RESIDENCE IS AMBILOCAL OR NEOLOCAL, RATHER THAN MATRILOCAL OR UXORILOCAL (64)	30 27 15 37 XSQ= 5.40 PHI= 0.223 XP = 0.0201
209	TILT LESS TOWARD BEING THOSE 0.72 OF 106 WHERE MARITAL RESIDENCE IS PATRILOCAL, VIRILOCAL, OR AVUNCULOCAL, RATHER THAN MATRILOCAL OR UXORILOCAL (270)	209	TILT MORE TOWARD BEING THOSE 0.85 OF 175 WHERE MARITAL RESIDENCE IS PATRILOCAL, VIRILOCAL, OR AVUNCULOCAL, RATHER THAN MATRILOCAL OR UXORILOCAL (270)	76 148 30 27 XSQ= 5.99 PHI= -0.146 XP = 0.0144
214	DRIFT LESS TOWARD BEING THOSE 0.77 OF 56 WHERE FIRST COUSIN MARRIAGE, IF PERMITTED, IS OTHER THAN UNILATERAL (144)	214	DRIFT MORE TOWARD BEING THOSE 0.89 OF 84 WHERE FIRST COUSIN MARRIAGE, IF PERMITTED, IS OTHER THAN UNILATERAL (144)	13 9 43 75 XSQ= 3.08 PHI= 0.148 XP = 0.0794
220	DRIFT LESS TOWARD BEING THOSE 0.68 OF 114 WHERE FIRST COUSIN MARRIAGE IN SOME FORM OR OTHER IS NOT PRESCRIBED OR PREFERRED (273)	220	DRIFT MORE TOWARD BEING THOSE 0.78 OF 197 WHERE FIRST COUSIN MARRIAGE IN SOME FORM OR OTHER IS NOT PRESCRIBED OR PREFERRED (273)	37 43 77 154 XSQ= 3.73 PHI= 0.110 XP = 0.0534

225	DRIFT MORE TOWARD BEING THOSE WHERE COUSIN MARRIAGE IS PREFERENTIALLY OR PERMISSIVELY MATRILATERAL, RATHER THAN PATRILATERAL (43)	0.80 OF 20	225	DRIFT LESS TOWARD BEING THOSE WHERE COUSIN MARRIAGE IS PREFERENTIALLY OR PERMISSIVELY MATRILATERAL, RATHER THAN PATRILATERAL (43)	0.53 OF 32	4 15 16 17 XSQ= 2.76 PHI= -0.230 XP = 0.0965
234	TILT TOWARD BEING THOSE WHERE THE COUSIN TERMINOLOGY IS OF CROW, OMAHA, OR IROQUOIS TYPE, RATHER THAN ESKIMO OR HAWAIIAN TYPE (152)	0.57 OF 100	234	TILT TOWARD BEING THOSE WHERE THE COUSIN TERMINOLOGY IS OF ESKIMO OR HAWAIIAN TYPE, RATHER THAN CROW, OMAHA, OR IROQUOIS TYPE (170)	0.56 OF 172	57 75 43 97 XSQ= 4.02 PHI= 0.122 XP = 0.0449
240	TEND TO BE THOSE WHERE THE FAMILY, IF EXTENDED, IS LARGE, RATHER THAN SMALL OR STEM (78)	0.52 OF 67	240	TEND TO BE THOSE WHERE THE FAMILY, IF EXTENDED, IS SMALL OR STEM, RATHER THAN LARGE (135)	0.73 OF 113	35 30 32 83 XSQ= 10.94 PHI= 0.247 XP = 0.0009
242	TILT MORE TOWARD BEING THOSE WHERE MARRIAGE IS COMMONLY OR OCCASIONALLY POLYGYNOUS, RATHER THAN MONOGAMOUS (314)	0.88 OF 120	242	TILT LESS TOWARD BEING THOSE WHERE MARRIAGE IS COMMONLY OR OCCASIONALLY POLYGYNOUS, RATHER THAN MONOGAMOUS (314)	0.78 OF 211	105 164 15 47 XSQ= 4.18 PHI= 0.112 XP = 0.0409
243	DRIFT TOWARD BEING THOSE WHERE POLYGYNY, IF PRESENT, HAS A HIGH INCIDENCE (24) W-D,S	0.58 OF 24	243	DRIFT TOWARD BEING THOSE WHERE POLYGYNY, IF PRESENT, HAS A LOW INCIDENCE (36) W-D,S	0.71 OF 34	14 10 10 24 XSQ= 3.73 PHI= 0.254 XP = 0.0534
254	IN ALL CASES ARE THOSE WHERE HOUSEHOLD AUTHORITY IS ON THE FATHER'S SIDE, RATHER THAN THE MOTHER'S (9) DA	1.00 OF 5	254	TILT TOWARD BEING THOSE WHERE HOUSEHOLD AUTHORITY IS ON THE MOTHER'S SIDE, RATHER THAN THE FATHER'S (6) DA	0.75 OF 8	5 2 0 6 XSQ= 4.27 PHI= 0.573 EP = 0.0210
257	IN ALL CASES ARE THOSE WHERE THE SEVERITY OF SISTER AVOIDANCE IS LOW (17) WNS	1.00 OF 6	257	DRIFT TOWARD BEING THOSE WHERE THE SEVERITY OF SISTER AVOIDANCE IS HIGH (10) WNS	0.50 OF 20	0 10 6 10 XSQ= 2.99 PHI= -0.339 EP = 0.0532
263	TILT MORE TOWARD BEING THOSE WHERE WIVES ARE OBTAINED BY RELATIVELY DIFFICULT MEANS, NAMELY BY BRIDE-PRICE, BRIDE-SERVICE, OR EXCHANGING A FEMALE RELATIVE (233)	0.68 OF 120	263	TILT LESS TOWARD BEING THOSE WHERE WIVES ARE OBTAINED BY RELATIVELY DIFFICULT MEANS, NAMELY BY BRIDE-PRICE, BRIDE-SERVICE, OR EXCHANGING A FEMALE RELATIVE (233)	0.54 OF 210	82 113 38 97 XSQ= 6.08 PHI= 0.136 XP = 0.0137
300	TEND TO BE THOSE WHERE THE POST-PARTUM SEX TABOO LASTS LONGER THAN SIX MONTHS (51)	0.62 OF 47	300	TEND TO BE THOSE WHERE THE POST-PARTUM SEX TABOO LASTS SIX MONTHS OR LESS (73)	0.71 OF 77	29 22 18 55 XSQ= 11.90 PHI= 0.310 XP = 0.0006

302	DRIFT TOWARD BEING THOSE 0.77 OF 13 WHERE THE AVERAGE EARLY SATISFACTION POTENTIAL IS HIGH (23) W-C	302	DRIFT TOWARD BEING THOSE 0.57 OF 23 WHERE THE AVERAGE EARLY SATISFACTION POTENTIAL IS LOW (17) W-C	10 10 3 13 XSQ= 2.53 PHI= 0.265 EP = 0.0827
314	TILT LESS TOWARD BEING THOSE 0.60 OF 30 WHERE THE INCIDENCE OF MOTHER-CHILD HOUSEHOLDS IS LOW (61) W-C,S	314	TILT MORE TOWARD BEING THOSE 0.87 OF 45 WHERE THE INCIDENCE OF MOTHER-CHILD HOUSEHOLDS IS LOW (61) W-D,S	12 6 18 39 XSQ= 5.63 PHI= 0.274 XP = 0.0176
319	DRIFT TOWARD BEING THOSE 0.67 OF 21 WHERE PROTECTION OF THE INFANT FROM ENVIRONMENTAL DISCOMFORTS IS LOW (30) B-B-C	319	DRIFT TOWARD BEING THOSE 0.61 OF 41 WHERE PROTECTION OF THE INFANT FROM ENVIRONMENTAL DISCOMFORTS IS HIGH (35) B-B-C	7 25 14 16 XSQ= 3.21 PHI= -0.228 XP = 0.0730
325	TILT TOWARD BEING THOSE 0.64 OF 25 WHERE THE DEGREE OF DIFFUSION AMONG THE INFANT'S NURTURANT AGENTS IS LOW (32) B-B-C	325	TILT TOWARD BEING THOSE 0.65 OF 46 WHERE THE DEGREE OF DIFFUSION AMONG THE INFANT'S NURTURANT AGENTS IS HIGH (42) B-B-C	9 30 16 16 XSQ= 4.47 PHI= -0.251 XP = 0.0346
349	TILT TOWARD BEING THOSE 0.67 OF 21 WHERE THE CHILD'S INFERRED ANXIETY OVER NON-PERFORMANCE OF ACHIEVEMENT BEHAVIOR IS LOW (28) B-B-C	349	TILT TOWARD BEING THOSE 0.66 OF 38 WHERE THE CHILD'S INFERRED ANXIETY OVER NON-PERFORMANCE OF ACHIEVEMENT BEHAVIOR IS HIGH (34) B-B-C	7 25 14 13 XSQ= 4.51 PHI= -0.276 XP = 0.0338
370	TEND TO BE THOSE 0.54 OF 89 WHERE THE SEGREGATION OF ADOLESCENT BOYS IS COMPLETE OR PARTIAL (95)	370	TEND TO BE THOSE 0.69 OF 154 WHERE THE SEGREGATION OF ADOLESCENT BOYS IS ABSENT (148)	48 47 41 107 XSQ= 12.02 PHI= 0.222 XP = 0.0005
386	TILT TOWARD BEING THOSE 0.71 OF 28 WHERE SEXUAL EXPRESSION BY THE YOUNG IS RESTRICTED OR SEMI-RESTRICTED (46) F-B	386	TILT TOWARD BEING THOSE 0.57 OF 51 WHERE SEXUAL EXPRESSION BY THE YOUNG IS PERMITTED (40) F-B	20 22 8 29 XSQ= 4.73 PHI= 0.245 XP = 0.0296
391	TILT TOWARD BEING THOSE 0.63 OF 54 WHERE PREMARITAL SEX RELATIONS ARE PUNISHED ONLY IF PREGNANCY RESULTS, OR FREELY PERMITTED (90) JTW,EA	391	TILT TOWARD BEING THOSE 0.56 OF 117 WHERE PREMARITAL SEX RELATIONS ARE STRONGLY PUNISHED AND IN FACT RARE, OR WEAKLY PUNISHED AND IN FACT NOT RARE (89) JTW,EA	20 66 34 51 XSQ= 4.80 PHI= -0.168 XP = 0.0285
393	DRIFT TOWARD BEING THOSE 0.67 OF 27 WHERE EXTRAMARITAL COITUS IS PUNISHED, RATHER THAN PERMITTED (43) F-B	393	DRIFT TOWARD BEING THOSE 0.57 OF 51 WHERE EXTRAMARITAL COITUS IS PERMITTED, RATHER THAN PUNISHED (41) F-B	18 22 9 29 XSQ= 3.03 PHI= 0.197 XP = 0.0819

395	DRIFT TOWARD BEING THOSE WHERE BELIEF IN THE UNCLEANNESS OF WOMEN IS PRESENT (18) LWS	0.86 OF 7	395	DRIFT TOWARD BEING THOSE WHERE BELIEF IN THE UNCLEANNESS OF WOMEN IS UNIMPORTANT OR ABSENT (15) LWS	0.54 OF 26	6 12 1 14 XSQ= 2.07 PHI= 0.250 EP = 0.0952
427	TEND TO BE THOSE WHERE A HIGH GOD, IF PRESENT, IS INACTIVE, RATHER THAN ACTIVE (69) GES,EA	0.70 OF 63	427	TEND TO BE THOSE WHERE A HIGH GOD, IF PRESENT, IS ACTIVE, RATHER THAN INACTIVE (87) GES,EA	0.73 OF 93	19 68 44 25 XSQ= 26.38 PHI= -0.411 XP = 0.0000
452	DRIFT TOWARD BEING THOSE WHERE TOTEMISM WITH FOOD TABOOS IS PRESENT (19) WNS	0.65 OF 17	452	DRIFT TOWARD BEING THOSE WHERE TOTEMISM WITH FOOD TABOOS IS ABSENT (24) WNS	0.68 OF 25	11 8 6 17 XSQ= 3.15 PHI= 0.274 XP = 0.0760
459	TEND TO BE THOSE WHERE GAMES, IF PRESENT, DO NOT INCLUDE GAMES OF CHANCE (89) R-A-B,EA	0.74 OF 50	459	TEND TO BE THOSE WHERE GAMES, IF PRESENT, INCLUDE GAMES OF CHANCE (82) R-A-B,EA	0.57 OF 121	13 69 37 52 XSQ= 12.43 PHI= -0.270 XP = 0.0004
460	LEAN TOWARD BEING THOSE WHERE GAMES, IF PRESENT, ARE LIMITED TO GAMES OF SKILL ONLY (67) R-A-B,EA	0.58 OF 50	460	LEAN TOWARD BEING THOSE WHERE GAMES, IF PRESENT, ARE NOT LIMITED TO GAMES OF SKILL ONLY (104) R-A-B,EA	0.69 OF 121	29 38 21 83 XSQ= 9.41 PHI= 0.235 XP = 0.0022
474	TILT TOWARD BEING THOSE WHERE BOASTFULNESS IS EXTREME (41) PES	0.67 OF 27	474	TILT TOWARD BEING THOSE WHERE BOASTFULNESS IS MODERATE, NEGLIBIBLE, OR UNREPORTED (48) PES	0.63 OF 59	18 22 9 37 XSQ= 5.30 PHI= 0.248 XP = 0.0213

58 CULTURES
WHERE SUBSISTENCE IS PRIMARILY BY
HORTICULTURE (26)

58 CULTURES
WHERE SUBSISTENCE IS PRIMARILY BY
MEANS OTHER THAN
HORTICULTURE (308)

BACKGROUND ON PAGE 76

SUBJECT ONLY

26 IN LEFT COLUMN

BLACK CARIB	CAYAPA	ELLICE	LAU	LESU	MANGAIANS	MANIHIKI	MARQUESANS	MARSHALLESE	MOTA
NICOBARESE	ONTONG-JAVA	PALAUANS	PONAPEANS	PUKAPUKA	PURARI	SAMOANS	SENIANG	TIKOPIA	TOKELAU
TROBRIAND	TRUKESE	ULAWANS	WANTOAT	WOLEAIANS	YAPESE				

308 IN RIGHT COLUMN

66 EXCLUDED BECAUSE UNASCERTAINED

	Left column			Right column		
3	IN ALL CASES ARE THOSE LOCATED OUTSIDE OF AFRICA (320)	1.00 OF 26	3	TILT LESS TOWARD BEING THOSE LOCATED OUTSIDE OF AFRICA (320)	0.78 OF 308	0 69 26 239 XSQ= 6.04 PHI= -0.134 XP = 0.0140
5	DRIFT MORE TOWARD BEING THOSE LOCATED OUTSIDE OF EAST EURASIA (330)	0.96 OF 26	5	DRIFT LESS TOWARD BEING THOSE LOCATED OUTSIDE OF EAST EURASIA (330)	0.81 OF 308	1 58 25 250 XSQ= 2.74 PHI= -0.091 XP = 0.0977
6	TEND TO BE THOSE LOCATED IN THE INSULAR PACIFIC (70)	0.88 OF 26	6	TEND TO BE THOSE LOCATED OUTSIDE OF THE INSULAR PACIFIC (330)	0.90 OF 308	23 30 3 278 XSQ= 105.48 PHI= 0.562 XP = 0.
8	IN ALL CASES ARE THOSE LOCATED OUTSIDE OF NORTH AMERICA (330)	1.00 OF 26	8	TILT LESS TOWARD BEING THOSE LOCATED OUTSIDE OF NORTH AMERICA (330)	0.81 OF 308	0 60 26 248 XSQ= 4.92 PHI= -0.121 XP = 0.0265
14	IN ALL CASES ARE THOSE WHERE THE LATITUDE IS LESS THAN THIRTY DEGREES (281)	1.00 OF 26	14	TEND LESS TO BE THOSE WHERE THE LATITUDE IS LESS THAN THIRTY DEGREES (281)	0.67 OF 308	0 102 26 206 XSQ= 10.88 PHI= -0.181 XP = 0.0010

```
15  TEND TO BE THOSE                  0.96 OF  26     15  TEND TO BE THOSE                  0.51 OF 308          1  156
    WHERE THE LATITUDE IS                                 WHERE THE LATITUDE IS                                   25  152
    LESS THAN TWENTY DEGREES  (217)                       TWENTY DEGREES OR GREATER  (183)                  XSQ=   19.25
                                                                                                            PHI=  -0.240
                                                                                                            XP =  0.0000

16  TEND TO BE THOSE                  0.62 OF  26     16  TEND TO BE THOSE                  0.72 OF 308         10  223
    WHERE THE LATITUDE IS                                 WHERE THE LATITUDE IS                                   16   85
    LESS THAN TEN DEGREES  (123)                          TEN DEGREES OR GREATER  (277)                     XSQ=   11.53
                                                                                                            PHI=  -0.186
                                                                                                            XP =  0.0007

42  IN ALL CASES ARE THOSE            1.00 OF  26     42  TEND TO BE THOSE                  0.66 OF 308         26  104
    WHERE THE NATURAL ENVIRONMENT IS                      WHERE THE NATURAL ENVIRONMENT IS                         0  204
    TROPICAL OR SUB-TROPICAL RAIN FOREST, OR              OTHER THAN                                        XSQ=   41.50
    MONSOON FOREST  (156) FWM                             TROPICAL OR SUB-TROPICAL RAIN FOREST, OR          PHI=   0.353
                                                          MONSOON FOREST  (244) FWM                         XP =  0.

44  LEAN MORE TOWARD BEING THOSE      0.96 OF  26     44  LEAN LESS TOWARD BEING THOSE      0.64 OF 306         25  197
    WHERE SETTLEMENTS ARE FIXED  (222)                    WHERE SETTLEMENTS ARE FIXED  (222)                       1  109
                                                                                                            XSQ=    9.53
                                                                                                            PHI=   0.169
                                                                                                            XP =  0.0020

46  IN ALL CASES ARE THOSE            1.00 OF  26     46  TILT LESS TOWARD BEING THOSE      0.76 OF 306          0   72
    OTHER THAN WHERE SETTLEMENTS ARE                      OTHER THAN WHERE SETTLEMENTS ARE                        26  234
    NON-FIXED AND MOVEMENT IS                             NON-FIXED AND MOVEMENT IS                         XSQ=    6.49
    NOMADIC  (260)                                        NOMADIC  (260)                                    PHI=  -0.140
                                                                                                            XP =  0.0109

48  LEAN TOWARD BEING THOSE           0.91 OF  11     48  LEAN TOWARD BEING THOSE           0.60 OF  65         10   26
    WHERE THE FOOD SUPPLY IS SECURE,                      WHERE THE FOOD SUPPLY IS NOT SECURE,                     1   39
    AND FOOD SHORTAGES ARE                                AND FOOD SHORTAGES ARE                            XSQ=    7.84
    RARE OR OCCASIONAL  (38) MGW                          FREQUENT OR ANNUAL  (41) MGW                      PHI=   0.321
                                                                                                            XP =  0.0051

63  IN ALL CASES ARE THOSE            1.00 OF  20     63  TEND TO BE THOSE                  0.74 OF 206          0  152
    WHERE HUSBANDRY, IF PRESENT,                          WHERE HUSBANDRY, IF PRESENT,                            20   54
    IS PRINCIPALLY IN THE FORM OF                         IS PRINCIPALLY IN THE FORM OF                     XSQ=   41.78
    PIGS, SHEEP, OR GOATS, RATHER THAN                    BOVINE, EQUINE, CAMEL-LIKE, OR DEER-LIKE          PHI=  -0.430
    BOVINE, EQUINE, CAMEL-LIKE, OR DEER-LIKE              ANIMALS, RATHER THAN                              XP =  0.
    ANIMALS  (74)                                         PIGS, SHEEP, OR GOATS  (152)

71  TEND MORE TO BE THOSE             0.96 OF  26     71  TEND LESS TO BE THOSE             0.56 OF 217          1   96
    WHERE METAL WORKING IS                                WHERE METAL WORKING IS                                  25  121
    ABSENT  (153)                                         ABSENT  (153)                                     XSQ=   14.16
                                                                                                            PHI=  -0.241
                                                                                                            XP =  0.0002

73  TILT TOWARD BEING THOSE           0.73 OF  26     73  TILT TOWARD BEING THOSE           0.51 OF 215          7  109
    WHERE WEAVING IS                                      WHERE WEAVING IS                                        19  106
    ABSENT  (130)                                         PRESENT  (118)                                    XSQ=    4.34
                                                                                                            PHI=  -0.134
                                                                                                            XP =  0.0372
```

74	TEND TO BE THOSE WHERE POTTERY IS ABSENT (93)	0.80 OF 25	74	TEND TO BE THOSE WHERE POTTERY IS PRESENT (145)	0.67 OF 206	5 139 20 67 XSQ= 19.43 PHI= -0.290 XP = 0.0000
85	IN ALL CASES ARE THOSE WHERE THE LEVEL OF POLITICAL INTEGRATION IS THE MINIMAL STATE, THE AUTONOMOUS COMMUNITY, OR THE FAMILY (234) GPM	1.00 OF 22	85	TILT LESS TOWARD BEING THOSE WHERE THE LEVEL OF POLITICAL INTEGRATION IS THE MINIMAL STATE, THE AUTONOMOUS COMMUNITY, OR THE FAMILY (234) GPM	0.76 OF 238	0 58 22 180 XSQ= 5.57 PHI= -0.146 XP = 0.0183
89	DRIFT TOWARD BEING THOSE WHERE, IF A NON-HEREDITARY HEADMANSHIP IS PRESENT, SUCCESSION IS BY MEANS OTHER THAN CONSENSUS (43)	0.83 OF 6	89	DRIFT TOWARD BEING THOSE WHERE, IF A NON-HEREDITARY HEADMANSHIP IS PRESENT, SUCCESSION IS BY CONSENSUS (63)	0.65 OF 83	1 54 5 29 XSQ= 3.69 PHI= -0.204 XP = 0.0547
107	IN ALL CASES ARE THOSE WHERE CLASS STRATIFICATION, IF PRESENT, IS BASED ON SOMETHING OTHER THAN OCCUPATIONAL STATUS (160)	1.00 OF 15	107	DRIFT LESS TOWARD BEING THOSE WHERE CLASS STRATIFICATION, IF PRESENT, IS BASED ON SOMETHING OTHER THAN OCCUPATIONAL STATUS (160)	0.76 OF 156	0 37 15 119 XSQ= 3.25 PHI= -0.138 XP = 0.0715
108	TILT TOWARD BEING THOSE WHERE CLASS STRATIFICATION, IF PRESENT, IS BASED ON A HEREDITARY ARISTOCRACY (74)	0.67 OF 15	108	TILT TOWARD BEING THOSE WHERE CLASS STRATIFICATION, IF PRESENT, IS BASED ON SOMETHING OTHER THAN A HEREDITARY ARISTOCRACY (129)	0.68 OF 156	10 50 5 106 XSQ= 5.76 PHI= 0.184 XP = 0.0164
110	IN ALL CASES ARE THOSE WHERE SLAVERY IS ABSENT (218)	1.00 OF 26	110	TEND LESS TO BE THOSE WHERE SLAVERY IS ABSENT (218)	0.55 OF 297	0 134 26 163 XSQ= 18.23 PHI= -0.238 XP = 0.0000
176	DRIFT TOWARD BEING THOSE WHERE THE COMMUNITY IS A CLAN-COMMUNITY OR A COMMUNITY STRUCTURED OR SEGMENTED ON A CLAN BASIS (169)	0.64 OF 25	176	DRIFT TOWARD BEING THOSE WHERE THE COMMUNITY IS OTHER THAN A CLAN-COMMUNITY OR A COMMUNITY STRUCTURED OR SEGMENTED ON A CLAN BASIS (213)	0.57 OF 296	16 127 9 169 XSQ= 3.34 PHI= 0.102 XP = 0.0675
178	LEAN TOWARD BEING THOSE WHERE THE COMMUNITY IS SEGMENTED ON A CLAN BASIS AND NON-EXOGAMOUS (87)	0.52 OF 25	178	LEAN TOWARD BEING THOSE WHERE THE COMMUNITY IS OTHER THAN SEGMENTED ON A CLAN BASIS AND NON-EXOGAMOUS (295)	0.79 OF 296	13 62 12 234 XSQ= 10.74 PHI= 0.183 XP = 0.0010
180	DRIFT MORE TOWARD BEING THOSE WHERE THE COMMUNITY IS COMMONLY NON-EXOGAMOUS, RATHER THAN EXOGAMOUS (258)	0.84 OF 25	180	DRIFT LESS TOWARD BEING THOSE WHERE THE COMMUNITY IS COMMONLY NON-EXOGAMOUS, RATHER THAN EXOGAMOUS (258)	0.65 OF 296	4 103 21 193 XSQ= 2.87 PHI= -0.095 XP = 0.0903

185	IN ALL CASES ARE THOSE 1.00 OF 15 WHERE THE LARGEST NON-COGNATIC KIN GROUP IS THE MOEITY OR PHRATRY OR SIB (194)	185	DRIFT LESS TOWARD BEING THOSE 0.77 OF 197 WHERE THE LARGEST NON-COGNATIC KIN GROUP IS THE MOEITY OR PHRATRY OR SIB (194)	15 151 0 46 XSQ= 3.20 PHI= 0.123 XP = 0.0734
186	LEAN MORE TOWARD BEING THOSE 0.88 OF 26 WHERE THE KIN GROUP IS OTHER THAN EXCLUSIVELY PATRILINEAL (250)	186	LEAN LESS TOWARD BEING THOSE 0.61 OF 308 WHERE THE KIN GROUP IS OTHER THAN EXCLUSIVELY PATRILINEAL (250)	3 121 23 187 XSQ= 6.76 PHI= -0.142 XP = 0.0093
190	LEAN TOWARD BEING THOSE 0.57 OF 14 WHERE THE KIN GROUP IS MATRILINEAL, RATHER THAN PATRILINEAL OR DOUBLE-DESCENT (61)	190	LEAN TOWARD BEING THOSE 0.78 OF 193 WHERE THE KIN GROUP IS PATRILINEAL OR DOUBLE-DESCENT, RATHER THAN MATRILINEAL (186)	6 150 8 43 XSQ= 6.77 PHI= -0.181 XP = 0.0093
198	TILT LESS TOWARD BEING THOSE 0.60 OF 10 WHERE RULES FOR THE INHERITANCE OF REAL PROPERTY, IF PRESENT, FAVOR THE MALE HEIR OR LINE, RATHER THAN THE FEMALE (144)	198	TILT MORE TOWARD BEING THOSE 0.89 OF 132 WHERE RULES FOR THE INHERITANCE OF REAL PROPERTY, IF PRESENT, FAVOR THE MALE HEIR OR LINE, RATHER THAN THE FEMALE (144)	6 118 4 14 XSQ= 4.84 PHI= -0.185 XP = 0.0278
243	IN ALL CASES ARE THOSE 1.00 OF 6 WHERE POLYGYNY, IF PRESENT, HAS A LOW INCIDENCE (36) W-D,S	243	DRIFT LESS TOWARD BEING THOSE 0.54 OF 52 WHERE POLYGYNY, IF PRESENT, HAS A LOW INCIDENCE (36) W-D,S	0 24 6 28 XSQ= 3.01 PHI= -0.228 XP = 0.0826
257	DRIFT TOWARD BEING THOSE 0.71 OF 7 WHERE THE SEVERITY OF SISTER AVOIDANCE IS HIGH (10) WNS	257	DRIFT TOWARD BEING THOSE 0.74 OF 19 WHERE THE SEVERITY OF SISTER AVOIDANCE IS LOW (17) WNS	5 5 2 14 XSQ= 2.70 PHI= 0.322 EP = 0.0687
262	LEAN LESS TOWARD BEING THOSE 0.54 OF 26 WHERE WIVES ARE OBTAINED BY MEANS INVOLVING THE PRESENCE OF SOME CONSIDERATION (305)	262	LEAN MORE TOWARD BEING THOSE 0.79 OF 304 WHERE WIVES ARE OBTAINED BY MEANS INVOLVING THE PRESENCE OF SOME CONSIDERATION (305)	14 240 12 64 XSQ= 7.16 PHI= -0.147 XP = 0.0075
263	LEAN TOWARD BEING THOSE 0.73 OF 26 WHERE WIVES ARE OBTAINED BY RELATIVELY EASY MEANS, NAMELY BY TOKEN BRIDE-PRICE, GIFT EXCHANGE, ABSENCE OF ANY CONSIDERATION, OR RECEIPT OF DOWRY (162)	263	LEAN TOWARD BEING THOSE 0.62 OF 304 WHERE WIVES ARE OBTAINED BY RELATIVELY DIFFICULT MEANS, NAMELY BY BRIDE-PRICE, BRIDE-SERVICE, OR EXCHANGING A FEMALE RELATIVE (233)	7 188 19 116 XSQ= 10.68 PHI= -0.180 XP = 0.0011
282	IN ALL CASES ARE THOSE 1.00 OF 5 WHERE THE STRENGTH OF DESIRE FOR CHILDREN IS LOW OR ABSENT (20) BCA	282	DRIFT TOWARD BEING THOSE 0.52 OF 27 WHERE THE STRENGTH OF DESIRE FOR CHILDREN IS HIGH (16) BCA	0 14 5 13 XSQ= 2.74 PHI= -0.293 EP = 0.0525

295	IN ALL CASES ARE THOSE WHERE THE SEVERITY OF PUNISHMENT FOR ABORTION IS LOW OR ABSENT (12) BCA	1.00 OF 4	295	DRIFT TOWARD BEING THOSE WHERE THE SEVERITY OF PUNISHMENT FOR ABORTION IS HIGH (11) BCA	0.63 OF 16	0 10 4 6 XSQ= 2.81 PHI= -0.375 EP = 0.0867
313	DRIFT TOWARD BEING THOSE WHERE AGGRESSION SOCIALIZATION ANXIETY IS LOW (28) W-C	0.88 OF 8	313	DRIFT TOWARD BEING THOSE WHERE AGGRESSION SOCIALIZATION ANXIETY IS HIGH (26) W-C	0.56 OF 41	1 23 7 18 XSQ= 3.50 PHI= -0.267 XP = 0.0615
325	TILT TOWARD BEING THOSE WHERE THE DEGREE OF DIFFUSION AMONG THE INFANT'S NURTURANT AGENTS IS HIGH (42) B-B-C	0.90 OF 10	325	TILT TOWARD BEING THOSE WHERE THE DEGREE OF DIFFUSION AMONG THE INFANT'S NURTURANT AGENTS IS LOW (32) B-B-C	0.51 OF 61	9 30 1 31 XSQ= 4.25 PHI= 0.245 XP = 0.0392
352	DRIFT TOWARD BEING THOSE WHERE THE TOTAL POSITIVE PRESSURE TOWARD DEVELOPING OBEDIENT BEHAVIOR IN THE CHILD IS LOW (28) B-B-C	0.70 OF 10	352	DRIFT TOWARD BEING THOSE WHERE THE TOTAL POSITIVE PRESSURE TOWARD DEVELOPING OBEDIENT BEHAVIOR IN THE CHILD IS HIGH (44) B-B-C	0.68 OF 59	3 40 7 19 XSQ= 3.72 PHI= -0.232 XP = 0.0539
368	IN ALL CASES ARE THOSE WHERE DISSOCIATION OF THE SEXES AT ADOLESCENCE IS HIGH OR MEDIUM (16) JKH	1.00 OF 3	368	DRIFT TOWARD BEING THOSE WHERE DISSOCIATION OF THE SEXES AT ADOLESCENCE IS LOW (21) JKH	0.62 OF 34	3 13 0 21 XSQ= 2.14 PHI= 0.240 EP = 0.0721
386	DRIFT TOWARD BEING THOSE WHERE SEXUAL EXPRESSION BY THE YOUNG IS PERMITTED (40) F-B	0.71 OF 14	386	DRIFT TOWARD BEING THOSE WHERE SEXUAL EXPRESSION BY THE YOUNG IS RESTRICTED OR SEMI-RESTRICTED (46) F-B	0.58 OF 65	4 38 10 27 XSQ= 3.02 PHI= -0.196 XP = 0.0823
391	LEAN TOWARD BEING THOSE WHERE PREMARITAL SEX RELATIONS ARE PUNISHED ONLY IF PREGNANCY RESULTS, OR FREELY PERMITTED (90) JTW,EA	0.89 OF 18	391	LEAN TOWARD BEING THOSE WHERE PREMARITAL SEX RELATIONS ARE STRONGLY PUNISHED AND IN FACT RARE, OR WEAKLY PUNISHED AND IN FACT NOT RARE (89) JTW,EA	0.55 OF 153	2 84 16 69 XSQ= 10.66 PHI= -0.250 XP = 0.0011
392	TEND TO BE THOSE WHERE PREMARITAL SEX RELATIONS ARE FREELY PERMITTED (67) JTW,EA	0.78 OF 18	392	TEND TO BE THOSE WHERE PREMARITAL SEX RELATIONS ARE STRONGLY PUNISHED AND IN FACT RARE, OR WEAKLY PUNISHED AND IN FACT NOT RARE, OR PUNISHED ONLY IF PREGNANCY RESULTS (112) JTW,EA	0.69 OF 153	4 105 14 48 XSQ= 13.07 PHI= -0.276 XP = 0.0003
393	DRIFT TOWARD BEING THOSE WHERE EXTRAMARITAL COITUS IS PERMITTED, RATHER THAN PUNISHED (41) F-B	0.80 OF 10	393	DRIFT TOWARD BEING THOSE WHERE EXTRAMARITAL COITUS IS PUNISHED, RATHER THAN PERMITTED (43) F-B	0.56 OF 68	2 38 8 30 XSQ= 3.17 PHI= -0.202 XP = 0.0749

399	DRIFT TCWARD BEING THCSE WHERE INTENSITY CF CASTRATION ANXIETY IS LCW (22) WNS	0.86 OF 7	399	DRIFT TOWARD BEING THCSE WHERE INTENSITY OF CASTRATION ANXIETY IS HIGH (23) WNS	0.59 CF 37	 XSQ= PHI= XP =	1 22 6 15 3.17 -0.269 0.0748
426	TEND TO BE THOSE WHERE A HIGH GOC IS ABSENT (104) GES,EA	0.80 OF 20	426	TEND TO BE THOSE WHERE A HIGH GCD IS PRESENT (156) GES,EA	0.63 OF 240	 XSQ= PHI= XP =	4 152 16 88 12.70 -0.221 0.0004
449	TILT TCWARD BEING THCSE WHERE THE CBSERVATICN CF FCOD TABOOS IS HIGH, RATHER THAN MEDIUM CR LCW (25) JRL	0.75 OF 8	449	TILT TOWARD BEING THOSE WHERE THE OBSERVATION OF FCOD TABOOS IS MEDIUM OR LOW, RATHER THAN HIGH (61) JRL	0.75 OF 75	 XSQ= PHI= XP =	6 19 2 56 6.28 0.275 0.0122
458	TILT MORE TOWARC BEING THOSE WHERE GAMES, IF PRESENT, DC NCT INCLUDE GAMES OF STRATEGY (119) R-A-B,EA	0.95 OF 19	458	TILT LESS TOWARD BEING THOSE WHERE GAMES, IF PRESENT, DO NOT INCLUDE GAMES OF STRATEGY (119) R-A-B,EA	0.66 CF 152	 XSQ= PHI= XP =	1 51 18 101 5.12 -0.173 0.0237
459	TILT TCWARD BEING THOSE WHERE GAMES, IF PRESENT, DO NOT INCLUDE GAMES CF CHANCE (89) R-A-B,EA	0.79 OF 19	459	TILT TOWARD BEING THOSE WHERE GAMES, IF PRESENT, INCLUDE GAMES OF CHANCE (82) R-A-B,EA	0.51 CF 152	 XSQ= PHI= XP =	4 78 15 74 5.04 -0.172 0.0247
460	LEAN TCWARD BEING THOSE WHERE GAMES, IF PRESENT, ARE LIMITED TC GAMES OF SKILL CNLY (67) R-A-B,EA	0.74 OF 19	460	LEAN TOWARD BEING THOSE WHERE GAMES, IF PRESENT, ARE NOT LIMITED TO GAMES OF SKILL ONLY (104) R-A-B,EA	0.65 OF 152	 XSQ= PHI= XP =	14 53 5 99 9.11 0.231 0.0025

****

59 CULTURES WHERE CROPS ARE MAINLY CEREAL, RATHER THAN MAINLY ROOT (168)	59 CULTURES WHERE CROPS ARE MAINLY ROOT, RATHER THAN MAINLY CEREAL (66)

BACKGROUND ON PAGE 76 SUBJECT ONLY

....

168 IN LEFT COLUMN

ABOR	AINU	AKHA	ALBANIANS	ALORESE	AMERICANS	ARAUCANIANS	ATAYAL	AZANDE	AZTEC
BAMBARA	BAMILEKE	BANDA	BARI	BASSERI	BEJA	BEMBA	BHIL	BIRIFOR	BOERS
BOZO	BRAZILIANS	BULGARIANS	BURUSHO	CAMBODIANS	CHAGGA	CHENCHU	CHERKESS	CHEROKEE	CHEYENNE
CHIR-APACHE	CHIRIGUANO	CHORTI	COCHITI	COORG	CREEK	CUNA	CZECHS	DAGUR	DARD
DELAWARE	DILLING	DOGON	DUTCH	EGYPTIANS	FOX	FUTAJALONKE	GARO	GISU	GOAJIRO
GOND	GURE	HANO	HANUNOO	HASINAI	HAVASUPAI	HAZARA	HEBREWS	HUICHOL	HURON
HUTSUL	IBAN	IFUGAO	ILA	INCA	INGASSANA	IRAQW	JAPANESE	JAVANESE	JEMEZ
JUKUN	KABYLE	KACHIN	KATAB	KERALA	KHASI	KIKUYU	KISSI	KOHISTANI	KOL
KOREANS	KUBA	LAKHER	LAMBA	LAMET	LANGO	LEPCHA	LHOTA NAGA	LOLO	LOZI
LUO	MACASSARESE	MALAYS	MAM	MAMBILA	MANDAN	MARGI	MARICOPA	MATAKAM	MAYA
MBUNDU	MENDE	MERINA	MIAMI	MIAO	MIN CHINESE	MINCHIA	MNONG GAR	MONGUOR	MOSSI
NANDI	NATCHEZ	NAVAHO	NDEMBU	NUER	NUPE	NURI	NYORO	OMAHA	ORAON
PAIWAN	PAPAGO	PATHAN	PAWNEE	PURUM	RIFFIANS	ROMANS	SAGADA	SANDAWE	SANTAL
SERBS	SHILLUK	SHLUH	SINHALESE	SIRIONO	SOMALI	SONGHAI	SOTHO	SUBANUN	SWAZI
SYRIANS	TAGBANUA	TALAMANCA	TALLENSI	TANALA	TAOS	TARAHUMARA	TENDA	TERA	TESO
THAI	THONGA	TIGRINYA	TIMUCUA	TORAJA	TOTONAC	TUNEBO	TURKANA	TURKMEN	VENDA
VIETNAMESE	WALLOONS	WICHITA	WOLOF	YAKUT	YAO	YOMBE	ZUNI		

66 IN RIGHT COLUMN

APINAYE	ARAPESH	ASHANTI	AYMARA	BACAIRI	BAYA	BHUIYA	BLACK CARIB	BUNLAP	CADUVEO
CAGABA	CALLINAGO	CAMAYURA	CARIB	CHIBCHA	ENGA	FANG	FON	HAWAIIANS	IRISH
JIVARO	KAPAUKU	KERAKI	KPE	KURTATCHI	LAU	LESU	MANGAIANS	MAORI	MISKITO
MONGO	MOTA	MOTILON	MUNDURUCU	NAMBICUARA	OKINAWANS	PAEZ	PALAUANS	PONAPEANS	SAMOANS
SENIANG	SHERENTE	SIUAI	TAPIRAPE	TENETEHARA	TERENA	TIKOPIA	TIMBIRA	TIV	TRISTAN
TROBRIAND	TRUMAI	TUCANO	TUCUNA	TUPINAMBA	ULAWANS	WANTOAT	WAPISHANA	WARRAU	WITOTO
WOGEO	YABARANA	YAGUA	YAKO	YARURO	YORUBA				

112 EXCLUDED BECAUSE IRRELEVANT

ABIPON	AJIE	ALACALUF	AMBA	ANDAMANESE	ARYANS	ATSUGEWI	AWEIKOMA	BABWA	BARABRA
BENGALI	BORORO	BOTOCUDO	BURYAT	CAMBA	CARAJA	CARINYA	CAYAPA	CHAMACOCO	CHINANTEC
CHOCO	CHOROTI	CHUKCHEE	COMANCHE	COPR ESKIMO	CREE	CROW	DIEGUENO	ELLICE	EYAK
GANDA	GILYAK	GROS VENTRE	GUAHIBO	GUATO	HAIDA	HO	HUKUNDIKA	INGALIK	KASKA
KAZAK	KET	KHALKA	KIOW-APACHE	KORYAK	KUTENAI	KWAKIUTL	LAPPS	LIFU	MAMVU
MANCHU	MANIHIKI	MANUS	MARQUESANS	MARSHALLESE	MATACO	MAZATECO	MIWOK	MZAB	NABESNA
NASKAPI	NICOBARESE	NOMLAKI	NUNIVAK	NYAKYUSA	OJIBWA	ONA	ONTONG-JAVA	PALIKUR	PARAUJANO
PENOBSCOT	POPOLUCA	PUKAPUKA	PURARI	RAROIANS	REGEIBAT	ROTUMANS	RUNDI	RWALA	SAMOYED
SANPOIL	SARAMACCA	SARSI	SEMINOLE	SERI	SIWANS	TAMIL	TAREUMIUT	TEDA	TEHUELCHE

TENINO TETCN TIBETANS TODA TOKELAU TOLOWA TRUKESE TSHIMSHIAN TUBATULABAL TWANA
TZELTAL UTE WAICA WASHO WINNEBAGO WOLEAIANS YAHGAN YAPESE YOKUTS YUKAGHIR
YUKI YURCK

54 EXCLUDED BECAUSE UNASCERTAINEC

3	TILT LESS TOWARC BEING THCSE LOCATED OUTSIDE CF AFRICA (320)	0.71 OF 168	3	TILT MORE TOWARD BEING THOSE LOCATED OUTSIDE OF AFRICA (320)	0.86 OF 66	48 9 120 57 XSQ= 4.95 PHI= 0.146 XP = 0.0260
4	TILT LESS TOWARC BEING THCSE LOCATED CUTSIDE CF THE CIRCUM-MEDITERRANEAN (355)	0.85 OF 168	4	TILT MORE TOWARD BEING THOSE LOCATED OUTSIDE OF THE CIRCUM-MEDITERRANEAN (355)	0.97 OF 66	25 2 143 64 XSQ= 5.41 PHI= 0.152 XP = 0.0200
5	TEND LESS TO BE THCSE LOCATED CUTSIDE CF EAST EURASIA (330)	0.74 OF 168	5	TEND MORE TO BE THOSE LOCATED OUTSIDE OF EAST EURASIA (330)	0.97 OF 66	44 2 124 64 XSQ= 14.66 PHI= 0.250 XP = 0.0001
6	TEND MORE TO BE THCSE LOCATED CUTSIDE CF THE INSULAR PACIFIC (330)	0.93 OF 168	6	TEND LESS TO BE THOSE LOCATED OUTSIDE OF THE INSULAR PACIFIC (330)	0.67 OF 66	12 22 156 44 XSQ= 24.11 PHI= -0.321 XP = 0.0000
8	TEND LESS TO BE THCSE LOCATED OUTSIDE OF NORTH AMERICA (330)	0.83 OF 168	8	IN ALL CASES ARE THOSE LOCATED OUTSIDE OF NORTH AMERICA (330)	1.00 OF 66	28 0 140 66 XSQ= 10.96 PHI= 0.216 XP = 0.0009
9	TEND MORE TO BE THCSE LOCATED CUTSIDE CF SOUTH AMERICA (335)	0.93 OF 168	9	TEND LESS TO BE THOSE LOCATED OUTSIDE OF SOUTH AMERICA (335)	0.53 OF 66	11 31 157 35 XSQ= 49.86 PHI= -0.462 XP = 0.
15	TEND TO BE THCSE WHERE THE LATITUDE IS TWENTY DEGREES CR GREATER (183)	0.52 OF 168	15	TEND TO BE THOSE WHERE THE LATITUDE IS LESS THAN TWENTY DEGREES (217)	0.86 OF 66	87 9 81 57 XSQ= 26.95 PHI= 0.339 XP = 0.0000

16 TEND TO BE THOSE 0.79 OF 168 WHERE THE LATITUDE IS TEN DEGREES OR GREATER (277)	16 TEND TO BE THOSE 0.61 OF 66 WHERE THE LATITUDE IS LESS THAN TEN DEGREES (123)	133 26 35 40 XSQ= 32.62 PHI= 0.373 XP = 0.
36 TILT LESS TOWARD BEING THOSE 0.77 OF 168 WHERE THE NATURAL ENVIRONMENT IS OTHER THAN 'VERY HARSH,' OR SUB-TROPICAL BUSH, OR TEMPERATE GRASSLAND (292) FWM	36 TILT MORE TOWARD BEING THOSE 0.89 OF 66 WHERE THE NATURAL ENVIRONMENT IS OTHER THAN 'VERY HARSH,' OR SUB-TROPICAL BUSH, OR TEMPERATE GRASSLAND (292) FWM	39 7 129 59 XSQ= 4.00 PHI= 0.131 XP = 0.0454
42 TEND TO BE THOSE 0.70 OF 168 WHERE THE NATURAL ENVIRONMENT IS OTHER THAN TROPICAL OR SUB-TROPICAL RAIN FOREST, OR MONSOON FOREST (244) FWM	42 TEND TO BE THOSE 0.76 OF 66 WHERE THE NATURAL ENVIRONMENT IS TROPICAL OR SUB-TROPICAL RAIN FOREST, OR MONSOON FOREST (156) FWM	50 50 118 16 XSQ= 39.11 PHI= -0.409 XP = 0.
48 LEAN TOWARD BEING THOSE 0.79 OF 29 WHERE THE FOOD SUPPLY IS NOT SECURE, AND FOOD SHORTAGES ARE FREQUENT OR ANNUAL (41) MGW	48 LEAN TOWARD BEING THOSE 0.65 OF 23 WHERE THE FOOD SUPPLY IS SECURE, AND FOOD SHORTAGES ARE RARE OR OCCASIONAL (38) MGW	6 15 23 8 XSQ= 8.79 PHI= -0.411 XP = 0.0030
51 TEND MORE TO BE THOSE 0.85 OF 168 WHERE SUBSISTENCE IS PRIMARILY BY FOOD PRODUCTION -- I. E., AGRICULTURE OR HUSBANDRY -- RATHER THAN BY GATHERING (253)	51 TEND LESS TO BE THOSE 0.56 OF 66 WHERE SUBSISTENCE IS PRIMARILY BY FOOD PRODUCTION -- I. E., AGRICULTURE OR HUSBANDRY -- RATHER THAN BY GATHERING (253)	143 37 25 29 XSQ= 20.93 PHI= 0.299 XP = 0.0000
53 TEND TO BE THOSE 0.51 OF 154 WHERE FOOD PRODUCTION IS BY INTENSIVE AGRICULTURE, RATHER THAN BY SIMPLE AGRICULTURE OR INCIPIENT FOOD PRODUCTION (91)	53 TEND TO BE THOSE 0.91 OF 56 WHERE FOOD PRODUCTION IS BY SIMPLE AGRICULTURE OR INCIPIENT FOOD PRODUCTION, RATHER THAN BY INTENSIVE AGRICULTURE (147)	79 5 75 51 XSQ= 28.98 PHI= 0.371 XP = 0.0000
54 TEND MORE TO BE THOSE 0.89 OF 154 WHERE FOOD PRODUCTION IS BY INTENSIVE OR SIMPLE AGRICULTURE, RATHER THAN BY INCIPIENT FOOD PRODUCTION (192)	54 TEND LESS TO BE THOSE 0.66 OF 56 WHERE FOOD PRODUCTION IS BY INTENSIVE OR SIMPLE AGRICULTURE, RATHER THAN BY INCIPIENT FOOD PRODUCTION (192)	137 37 17 19 XSQ= 13.58 PHI= 0.254 XP = 0.0002
55 TEND TO BE THOSE 0.58 OF 137 WHERE FOOD PRODUCTION IS BY INTENSIVE AGRICULTURE, RATHER THAN BY SIMPLE AGRICULTURE (91)	55 TEND TO BE THOSE 0.86 OF 37 WHERE FOOD PRODUCTION IS BY SIMPLE AGRICULTURE, RATHER THAN BY INTENSIVE AGRICULTURE (101)	79 5 58 32 XSQ= 21.01 PHI= 0.347 XP = 0.0000
62 TEND MORE TO BE THOSE 0.86 OF 168 WHERE HUSBANDRY OF SOME KIND IS PRESENT (228)	62 TEND LESS TO BE THOSE 0.62 OF 66 WHERE HUSBANDRY OF SOME KIND IS PRESENT (228)	145 41 23 25 XSQ= 15.55 PHI= 0.258 XP = 0.0001

63	TEND TO BE THOSE WHERE HUSBANDRY, IF PRESENT, IS PRINCIPALLY IN THE FORM OF BOVINE, EQUINE, CAMEL-LIKE, OR DEER-LIKE ANIMALS, RATHER THAN PIGS, SHEEP, OR GOATS (152)	0.81 OF 145	TEND TO BE THOSE WHERE HUSBANDRY, IF PRESENT, IS PRINCIPALLY IN THE FORM OF PIGS, SHEEP, OR GOATS, RATHER THAN BOVINE, EQUINE, CAMEL-LIKE, OR DEER-LIKE ANIMALS (74)	0.76 OF 41	118 10 27 31 XSQ= 45.75 PHI= 0.496 XP = 0.
71	TEND TO BE THOSE WHERE METAL WORKING IS PRESENT (98)	0.68 OF 106	TEND TO BE THOSE WHERE METAL WORKING IS ABSENT (153)	0.81 OF 52	72 10 34 42 XSQ= 31.21 PHI= 0.444 XP = 0.
73	TILT TOWARD BEING THOSE WHERE WEAVING IS PRESENT (118)	0.68 OF 104	TILT TOWARD BEING THOSE WHERE WEAVING IS ABSENT (130)	0.51 OF 51	71 25 33 26 XSQ= 4.59 PHI= 0.172 XP = 0.0321
74	TEND MORE TO BE THOSE WHERE POTTERY IS PRESENT (145)	0.85 OF 98	TEND LESS TO BE THOSE WHERE POTTERY IS PRESENT (145)	0.57 OF 51	83 29 15 22 XSQ= 12.47 PHI= 0.289 XP = 0.0004
77	DRIFT LESS TOWARD BEING THOSE WHERE THE WRITING SYSTEM IS MNEMONIC OR ABSENT, RATHER THAN BEING ALPHABETIC-OR-PHONETIC (39) JMH	0.64 OF 25	IN ALL CASES ARE THOSE WHERE THE WRITING SYSTEM IS MNEMONIC OR ABSENT, RATHER THAN BEING ALPHABETIC-OR-PHONETIC (39) JMH	1.00 OF 8	9 0 16 8 XSQ= 2.35 PHI= 0.267 EP = 0.0731
81	LEAN TOWARD BEING THOSE WHERE A CITY OR TOWN IS PRESENT, OR THE AVERAGE COMMUNITY SIZE IS 200 OR GREATER (89)	0.60 OF 115	LEAN TOWARD BEING THOSE WHERE NO CITY OR TOWN IS PRESENT, AND THE AVERAGE COMMUNITY SIZE IS SMALLER THAN 200 (135)	0.66 OF 44	69 15 46 29 XSQ= 7.56 PHI= 0.218 XP = 0.0060
83	TILT LESS TOWARD BEING THOSE WHERE, WITH NO CITY AND NO TOWN PRESENT, THE AVERAGE COMMUNITY SIZE IS SMALLER THAN 200, RATHER THAN BETWEEN 200 AND 999 (135)	0.56 OF 82	TILT MORE TOWARD BEING THOSE WHERE, WITH NO CITY AND NO TOWN PRESENT, THE AVERAGE COMMUNITY SIZE IS SMALLER THAN 200, RATHER THAN BETWEEN 200 AND 999 (135)	0.81 OF 36	36 7 46 29 XSQ= 5.45 PHI= 0.215 XP = 0.0196
86	TEND TO BE THOSE WHERE THE LEVEL OF POLITICAL INTEGRATION IS THE LARGE STATE, THE LITTLE STATE, OR THE MINIMAL STATE (148) GPM	0.68 OF 127	TEND TO BE THOSE WHERE THE LEVEL OF POLITICAL INTEGRATION IS THE AUTONOMOUS COMMUNITY, OR THE FAMILY (156) GPM	0.64 OF 56	86 20 41 36 XSQ= 15.04 PHI= 0.287 XP = 0.0001
96	TEND TO BE THOSE WHERE THE HIERARCHY OF NATIONAL JURISDICTION HAS FOUR, THREE, TWO OR ONE LEVEL (174) GES,EA	0.72 OF 166	TEND TO BE THOSE WHERE THE HIERARCHY OF NATIONAL JURISDICTION HAS NO LEVELS (156) GES,EA	0.65 OF 65	119 23 47 42 XSQ= 24.48 PHI= 0.326 XP = 0.0000

98	DRIFT MORE TOWARD BEING THOSE 0.84 OF 166 WHERE THE HIERARCHY OF LOCAL JURISDICTION HAS FOUR OR THREE LEVELS (238) GES,EA	98	DRIFT LESS TOWARD BEING THOSE 0.73 OF 66 WHERE THE HIERARCHY OF LOCAL JURISDICTION HAS FOUR OR THREE LEVELS (238) GES,EA	140 48 26 18 XSQ= 3.42 PHI= 0.121 XP = 0.0644
100	LEAN MORE TOWARD BEING THOSE 0.93 OF 166 WHERE HIERARCHIES ARE MORE COMPLEX THAN THE 'SIMPLEST,' I. E., MORE COMPLEX THAN TWO LOCAL LEVELS WITH NO NATIONAL LEVELS (267) GES,EA	100	LEAN LESS TOWARD BEING THOSE 0.78 OF 65 WHERE HIERARCHIES ARE MORE COMPLEX THAN THE 'SIMPLEST,' I. E., MORE COMPLEX THAN TWO LOCAL LEVELS WITH NO NATIONAL LEVELS (267) GES,EA	155 51 11 14 XSQ= 9.27 PHI= 0.200 XP = 0.0023
102	LEAN TOWARD BEING THOSE 0.65 OF 162 WHERE CLASS STRATIFICATION IS PRESENT (203)	102	LEAN TOWARD BEING THOSE 0.59 OF 63 WHERE CLASS STRATIFICATION IS ABSENT (180)	106 26 56 37 XSQ= 9.95 PHI= 0.210 XP = 0.0016
107	TILT LESS TOWARD BEING THOSE 0.69 OF 106 WHERE CLASS STRATIFICATION, IF PRESENT, IS BASED ON SOMETHING OTHER THAN OCCUPATIONAL STATUS (160)	107	TILT MORE TOWARD BEING THOSE 0.92 OF 26 WHERE CLASS STRATIFICATION, IF PRESENT, IS BASED ON SOMETHING OTHER THAN OCCUPATIONAL STATUS (160)	33 2 73 24 XSQ= 4.75 PHI= 0.190 XP = 0.0294
108	DRIFT TOWARD BEING THOSE 0.69 OF 106 WHERE CLASS STRATIFICATION, IF PRESENT, IS BASED ON SOMETHING OTHER THAN A HEREDITARY ARISTOCRACY (129)	108	DRIFT TOWARD BEING THOSE 0.54 OF 26 WHERE CLASS STRATIFICATION, IF PRESENT, IS BASED ON A HEREDITARY ARISTOCRACY (74)	33 14 73 12 XSQ= 3.76 PHI= -0.169 XP = 0.0525
109	LEAN LESS TOWARD BEING THOSE 0.78 OF 152 WHERE CASTES ARE ABSENT (317)	109	LEAN MORE TOWARD BEING THOSE 0.97 OF 64 WHERE CASTES ARE ABSENT (317)	33 2 119 62 XSQ= 10.13 PHI= 0.217 XP = 0.0015
110	TEND TO BE THOSE 0.56 OF 158 WHERE SLAVERY IS PRESENT (163)	110	TEND TO BE THOSE 0.75 OF 65 WHERE SLAVERY IS ABSENT (218)	89 16 69 49 XSQ= 17.34 PHI= 0.279 XP = 0.0000
118	DRIFT TOWARD BEING THOSE 0.63 OF 24 WHERE THE PERCENTAGE OF OCCUPATIONS THAT ARE SPECIALIZED IS HIGH OR MEDIUM (24) WME	118	DRIFT TOWARD BEING THOSE 0.75 OF 12 WHERE THE PERCENTAGE OF OCCUPATIONS THAT ARE SPECIALIZED IS LOW (25) WME	15 3 9 9 XSQ= 3.12 PHI= 0.295 EP = 0.0750
127	TILT TOWARD BEING THOSE 0.64 OF 28 WHERE THE FEMALES' CONTRIBUTION TO SUBSISTENCE IS LOW (32) JKB	127	TILT TOWARD BEING THOSE 0.83 OF 12 WHERE THE FEMALES' CONTRIBUTION TO SUBSISTENCE IS HIGH (33) JKB	10 10 18 2 XSQ= 5.83 PHI= -0.382 EP = 0.0138

128	TILT TOWARD BEING THOSE WHERE, IF SUBSISTENCE IS PRIMARILY BY AGRICULTURE, THE WORK IS MAINLY DONE BY MALES (40)	0.60 OF 53	128	TILT TOWARD BEING THOSE WHERE, IF SUBSISTENCE IS PRIMARILY BY AGRICULTURE, THE WORK IS MAINLY DONE BY FEMALES (37)	0.77 OF 13	32 3 21 10 XSQ= 4.43 PHI= 0.259 XP = 0.0353
143	TILT TOWARD BEING THOSE WHERE THE RATIO OF RESTITUTIVE TO REPRESSIVE SANCTIONS IS HIGH (20) WME	0.56 OF 25	143	TILT TOWARD BEING THOSE WHERE THE RATIO OF RESTITUTIVE TO REPRESSIVE SANCTIONS IS MEDIUM OR LOW (32) WME	0.90 OF 10	14 1 11 9 XSQ= 4.44 PHI= 0.356 EP = 0.0220
144	DRIFT TOWARD BEING THOSE WHERE THE RATIO OF RESTITUTIVE TO REPRESSIVE SANCTIONS IS HIGH OR MEDIUM (27) WME	0.68 OF 25	144	DRIFT TOWARD BEING THOSE WHERE THE RATIO OF RESTITUTIVE TO REPRESSIVE SANCTIONS IS LOW (25) WME	0.70 OF 10	17 3 8 7 XSQ= 2.80 PHI= 0.283 EP = 0.0619
147	IN ALL CASES ARE THOSE WHERE CODIFIED LAWS ARE PRESENT (20) LWS	1.00 OF 12	147	DRIFT LESS TOWARD BEING THOSE WHERE CODIFIED LAWS ARE PRESENT (20) LWS	0.60 OF 5	12 3 0 2 XSQ= 2.27 PHI= 0.365 EP = 0.0735
184	LEAN TOWARD BEING THOSE WHERE THE LARGEST NON-COGNATIC KIN GROUP IS SMALLER THAN A PHRATRY, I. E. A SIB OR LINEAGE (175)	0.78 OF 122	184	LEAN TOWARD BEING THOSE WHERE THE LARGEST NON-COGNATIC KIN GROUP IS THE MOEITY OR PHRATRY (77)	0.50 OF 38	27 19 95 19 XSQ= 9.67 PHI= -0.246 XP = 0.0019
186	LEAN LESS TOWARD BEING THOSE WHERE THE KIN GROUP IS OTHER THAN EXCLUSIVELY PATRILINEAL (250)	0.52 OF 168	186	LEAN MORE TOWARD BEING THOSE WHERE THE KIN GROUP IS OTHER THAN EXCLUSIVELY PATRILINEAL (250)	0.73 OF 66	80 18 88 48 XSQ= 7.24 PHI= 0.176 XP = 0.0071
188	TILT MORE TOWARD BEING THOSE WHERE THE KIN GROUP IS OTHER THAN EXCLUSIVELY COGNATIC (252)	0.73 OF 168	188	TILT LESS TOWARD BEING THOSE WHERE THE KIN GROUP IS OTHER THAN EXCLUSIVELY COGNATIC (252)	0.58 OF 66	46 28 122 38 XSQ= 4.29 PHI= -0.135 XP = 0.0384
196	TILT MORE TOWARD BEING THOSE WHERE INDIVIDUAL RIGHTS IN REAL PROPERTY, AND RULES FOR INHERITANCE, ARE PRESENT (194)	0.87 OF 128	196	TILT LESS TOWARD BEING THOSE WHERE INDIVIDUAL RIGHTS IN REAL PROPERTY, AND RULES FOR INHERITANCE, ARE PRESENT (194)	0.67 OF 40	111 27 17 13 XSQ= 6.42 PHI= 0.195 XP = 0.0113
221	TILT LESS TOWARD BEING THOSE WHERE MATRILATERAL CROSS-COUSIN MARRIAGE IS NOT PRESCRIBED OR PREFERRED (335)	0.87 OF 157	221	TILT MORE TOWARD BEING THOSE WHERE MATRILATERAL CROSS-COUSIN MARRIAGE IS NOT PRESCRIBED OR PREFERRED (335)	0.98 OF 61	21 1 136 60 XSQ= 5.44 PHI= 0.158 XP = 0.0197

224	TILT LESS TOWARD BEING THOSE 0.55 OF 74 WHERE COUSIN MARRIAGE IS PREFERENTIALLY OR PERMISSIVELY SYMMETRICAL, RATHER THAN EITHER PATRI- OR MATRILATERAL (106)	224	TILT MORE TOWARD BEING THOSE 0.83 OF 30 WHERE COUSIN MARRIAGE IS PREFERENTIALLY OR PERMISSIVELY SYMMETRICAL, RATHER THAN EITHER PATRI- OR MATRILATERAL (106)	33 5 41 25 XSQ= 6.03 PHI= 0.241 XP = 0.0141
225	TILT TOWARD BEING THOSE 0.76 OF 33 WHERE COUSIN MARRIAGE IS PREFFRENTIALLY OR PERMISSIVELY MATRILATERAL, RATHER THAN PATRILATERAL (43)	225	TILT TOWARD BEING THOSE 0.80 OF 5 WHERE COUSIN MARRIAGE IS PREFERENTIALLY OR PERMISSIVELY PATRILATERAL, RATHER THAN MATRILATERAL (23)	8 4 25 1 XSQ= 3.93 PHI= -0.322 EP = 0.0272
234	DRIFT TOWARD BEING THOSE 0.56 OF 130 WHERE THE COUSIN TERMINOLOGY IS OF ESKIMO OR HAWAIIAN TYPE, RATHER THAN CROW, OMAHA, OR IROQUOIS TYPE (170)	234	DRIFT TOWARD BEING THOSE 0.60 OF 57 WHERE THE COUSIN TERMINOLOGY IS OF CROW, OMAHA, OR IROQUOIS TYPE, RATHER THAN ESKIMO OR HAWAIIAN TYPE (152)	57 34 73 23 XSQ= 3.35 PHI= -0.134 XP = 0.0670
236	DRIFT TOWARD BEING THOSE 0.62 OF 167 WHERE THE FAMILY IS OF AN EXTENDED TYPE, RATHER THAN AN INDEPENDENT TYPE (213)	236	DRIFT TOWARD BEING THOSE 0.52 OF 66 WHERE THE FAMILY IS OF AN INDEPENDENT TYPE, RATHER THAN AN EXTENDED TYPE (185)	104 32 63 34 XSQ= 3.16 PHI= 0.116 XP = 0.0756
240	TILT TOWARD BEING THOSE 0.67 OF 104 WHERE THE FAMILY, IF EXTENDED, IS SMALL OR STEM, RATHER THAN LARGE (135)	240	TILT TOWARD BEING THOSE 0.59 OF 32 WHERE THE FAMILY, IF EXTENDED, IS LARGE, RATHER THAN SMALL OR STEM (78)	34 19 70 13 XSQ= 6.25 PHI= -0.214 XP = 0.0124
316	TILT TOWARD BEING THOSE 0.67 OF 21 WHERE EXCLUSIVE MOTHER-SON SLEEPING ARRANGEMENTS LAST LESS THAN ONE YEAR (25) W-K-A	316	TILT TOWARD BEING THOSE 0.75 OF 12 WHERE EXCLUSIVE MOTHER-SON SLEEPING ARRANGEMENTS LAST ONE YEAR OR LONGER (19) W-K-A	7 9 14 3 XSQ= 3.77 PHI= -0.338 EP = 0.0324
318	TILT TOWARD BEING THOSE 0.57 OF 30 WHERE THE OVERALL INDULGENCE OF THE INFANT IS LOW (31) B-B-C	318	TILT TOWARD BEING THOSE 0.79 OF 19 WHERE THE OVERALL INDULGENCE OF THE INFANT IS HIGH (40) B-B-C	13 15 17 4 XSQ= 4.66 PHI= -0.308 XP = 0.0309
324	DRIFT TOWARD BEING THOSE 0.61 OF 28 WHERE THE PAIN INFLICTED ON THE INFANT BY THE NURTURANT AGENT IS HIGH (34) B-B-C	324	DRIFT TOWARD BEING THOSE 0.71 OF 17 WHERE THE PAIN INFLICTED ON THE INFANT BY THE NURTURANT AGENT IS LOW OR NEGLIGIBLE (32) B-B-C	17 5 11 12 XSQ= 2.99 PHI= 0.258 XP = 0.0838
329	DRIFT TOWARD BEING THOSE 0.63 OF 8 WHERE THE AGE AT TOILET TRAINING IS LOWER THAN TWO YEARS (11) W-C	329	IN ALL CASES ARE THOSE 1.00 OF 4 WHERE THE AGE AT TOILET TRAINING IS TWO YEARS OR HIGHER (10) W-C	3 4 5 0 XSQ= 2.10 PHI= -0.418 EP = 0.0808

337	TILT TOWARD BEING THOSE 0.72 OF 29 WHERE THE CHILD'S INFERRED ANXIETY OVER NON-PERFORMANCE OF RESPONSIBLE BEHAVIOR IS HIGH (38) B-B-C	337	TILT TOWARD BEING THOSE 0.62 OF 21 WHERE THE CHILD'S INFERRED ANXIETY OVER NON-PERFORMANCE OF RESPONSIBLE BEHAVIOR IS LOW (35) B-B-C	21 8 8 13 XSQ= 4.56 PHI= 0.302 XP = 0.0326
346	DRIFT TOWARD BEING THOSE 0.61 OF 31 WHERE THE CHILD'S INFERRED ANXIETY OVER PERFORMANCE OF SELF-RELIANT BEHAVIOR IS HIGH (37) B-B-C	346	DRIFT TOWARD BEING THOSE 0.68 OF 22 WHERE THE CHILD'S INFERRED ANXIETY OVER PERFORMANCE OF SELF-RELIANT BEHAVIOR IS LOW (39) B-B-C	19 7 12 15 XSQ= 3.37 PHI= 0.252 XP = 0.0664
347	TILT TOWARD BEING THOSE 0.61 OF 31 WHERE THE CHILD'S INFERRED CONFLICT REGARDING SELF-RELIANT BEHAVIOR IS HIGH (37) B-B-C	347	TILT TOWARD BEING THOSE 0.73 OF 22 WHERE THE CHILD'S INFERRED CONFLICT REGARDING SELF-RELIANT BEHAVIOR IS LOW (39) B-B-C	19 6 12 16 XSQ= 4.69 PHI= 0.297 XP = 0.0304
350	DRIFT TOWARD BEING THOSE 0.72 OF 25 WHERE THE CHILD'S INFERRED ANXIETY OVER PERFORMANCE OF ACHIEVEMENT BEHAVIOR IS HIGH (34) B-B-C	350	DRIFT TOWARD BEING THOSE 0.60 OF 15 WHERE THE CHILD'S INFERRED ANXIETY OVER PERFORMANCE OF ACHIEVEMENT BEHAVIOR IS LOW (26) B-B-C	18 6 7 9 XSQ= 2.78 PHI= 0.264 EP = 0.0939
369	TILT LESS TOWARD BEING THOSE 0.56 OF 25 WHERE DISSOCIATION OF THE SEXES AT ADOLESCENCE, OR CUSTOMS OF INITIATION AT ADOLESCENCE, ARE PRESENT (42) JKH	369	TILT MORE TOWARD BEING THOSE 0.94 OF 17 WHERE DISSOCIATION OF THE SEXES AT ADOLESCENCE, OR CUSTOMS OF INITIATION AT ADOLESCENCE, ARE PRESENT (42) JKH	14 16 11 1 XSQ= 5.46 PHI= -0.360 XP = 0.0195
370	DRIFT TOWARD BEING THOSE 0.64 OF 132 WHERE THE SEGREGATION OF ADOLESCENT BOYS IS ABSENT (148)	370	DRIFT TOWARD BEING THOSE 0.51 OF 47 WHERE THE SEGREGATION OF ADOLESCENT BOYS IS COMPLETE OR PARTIAL (95)	47 24 85 23 XSQ= 2.84 PHI= -0.126 XP = 0.0917
373	DRIFT TOWARD BEING THOSE 0.67 OF 21 WHERE MALE INITIATION CEREMONIES AT PUBERTY ARE ABSENT (27) W-K-A	373	DRIFT TOWARD BEING THOSE 0.67 OF 12 WHERE MALE INITIATION CEREMONIES AT PUBERTY ARE PRESENT (17) W-K-A	7 8 14 4 XSQ= 2.21 PHI= -0.259 EP = 0.0827
380	TILT TOWARD BEING THOSE 0.86 OF 21 WHERE SEGREGATION OF GIRLS AT MENARCHE IS PRESENT (35) F-B	380	TILT TOWARD BEING THOSE 0.58 OF 12 WHERE SEGREGATION OF GIRLS AT MENARCHE IS ABSENT (20) F-B	18 5 3 7 XSQ= 5.08 PHI= 0.393 EP = 0.0164
382	TILT TOWARD BEING THOSE 0.57 OF 28 WHERE FEMALE INITIATION RITES ARE ABSENT (27) JKB	382	TILT TOWARD BEING THOSE 0.83 OF 12 WHERE FEMALE INITIATION RITES ARE PRESENT (38) JKB	12 10 16 2 XSQ= 4.05 PHI= -0.318 EP = 0.0354

390	DRIFT LESS TOWARD BEING THOSE WHERE PREMARITAL SEX RELATIONS ARE WEAKLY PUNISHED AND IN FACT NOT RARE OR PUNISHED ONLY IF PREGNANCY RESULTS, OR FREELY PERMITTED (132) JTW,EA	0.68 OF 79	390	DRIFT MORE TOWARD BEING THOSE WHERE PREMARITAL SEX RELATIONS ARE WEAKLY PUNISHED AND IN FACT NOT RARE OR PUNISHED ONLY IF PREGNANCY RESULTS, OR FREELY PERMITTED (132) JTW,EA	0.86 OF 37	25 5 54 32 XSQ= 3.43 PHI= 0.172 XP = 0.0641
405	LEAN TOWARD BEING THOSE WHERE EXPLANATIONS OF ILLNESS OF A DEPENDENCE NATURE ARE PRESENT (34) W-C	0.68 OF 22	405	LEAN TOWARD BEING THOSE WHERE EXPLANATIONS OF ILLNESS OF A DEPENDENCE NATURE ARE ABSENT (27) W-C	0.76 OF 17	15 4 7 13 XSQ= 5.97 PHI= 0.391 EP = 0.0095
426	TEND TO BE THOSE WHERE A HIGH GOD IS PRESENT (156) GES,EA	0.76 OF 125	426	TEND TO BE THOSE WHERE A HIGH GOD IS ABSENT (104) GES,EA	0.53 OF 57	95 27 30 30 XSQ= 13.26 PHI= 0.270 XP = 0.0003
427	TEND TO BE THOSE WHERE A HIGH GOD, IF PRESENT, IS ACTIVE, RATHER THAN INACTIVE (87) GES,EA	0.65 OF 95	427	TEND TO BE THOSE WHERE A HIGH GOD, IF PRESENT, IS INACTIVE, RATHER THAN ACTIVE (69) GES,EA	0.78 OF 27	62 6 33 21 XSQ= 14.09 PHI= 0.340 XP = 0.0002
449	DRIFT MORE TOWARD BEING THOSE WHERE THE OBSERVATION OF FOOD TABOOS IS MEDIUM OR LOW, RATHER THAN HIGH (61) JRL	0.77 OF 40	449	DRIFT LESS TOWARD BEING THOSE WHERE THE OBSERVATION OF FOOD TABOOS IS MEDIUM OR LOW, RATHER THAN HIGH (61) JRL	0.52 OF 21	9 10 31 11 XSQ= 2.96 PHI= -0.220 XP = 0.0851
458	TEND TO BE THOSE WHERE GAMES, IF PRESENT, INCLUDE GAMES OF STRATEGY (52) R-A-B,EA	0.54 OF 70	458	TEND TO BE THOSE WHERE GAMES, IF PRESENT, DO NOT INCLUDE GAMES OF STRATEGY (119) R-A-B,EA	0.85 OF 40	38 6 32 34 XSQ= 14.77 PHI= 0.366 XP = 0.0001
459	TEND TO BE THOSE WHERE GAMES, IF PRESENT, INCLUDE GAMES OF CHANCE (82) R-A-B,EA	0.60 OF 70	459	TEND TO BE THOSE WHERE GAMES, IF PRESENT, DO NOT INCLUDE GAMES OF CHANCE (89) R-A-B,EA	0.80 OF 40	42 8 28 32 XSQ= 14.85 PHI= 0.367 XP = 0.0001
460	TEND TO BE THOSE WHERE GAMES, IF PRESENT, ARE NOT LIMITED TO GAMES OF SKILL ONLY (104) R-A-B,EA	0.80 OF 70	460	TEND TO BE THOSE WHERE GAMES, IF PRESENT, ARE LIMITED TO GAMES OF SKILL ONLY (67) R-A-B,EA	0.75 OF 40	14 30 56 10 XSQ= 29.83 PHI= -0.521 XP = 0.0000
468	DRIFT TOWARD BEING THOSE WHERE CONTACT WITH OTHER CULTURES IS FREQUENT, RATHER THAN REGULAR OR IRREGULAR (17) JMH	0.52 OF 25	468	DRIFT TOWARD BEING THOSE WHERE CONTACT WITH OTHER CULTURES IS REGULAR OR IRREGULAR, RATHER THAN FREQUENT (37) JMH	0.88 OF 8	13 1 12 7 XSQ= 2.42 PHI= 0.271 EP = 0.0982

470	TILT TOWARD BEING THOSE WHERE INNCVATIONS ARE GENERALLY ACCEPTED (21) JMH	0.56 OF 25	470	TILT TOWARD BEING THOSE WHERE INNOVATIONS ARE ACCEPTED ONLY SELECTIVELY (33) JMH	0.88 OF 8	14 1 11 7 XSQ= 3.04 PHI= 0.303 EP = 0.0463

60 CULTURES
WHERE, IF CROPS ARE MAINLY CEREAL,
CULTIVATION IS INTENSIVE-IRRIGATED,
RATHER THAN INTENSIVE-DRY (45)

60 CULTURES
WHERE, IF CROPS ARE MAINLY CEREAL,
CULTIVATION IS INTENSIVE-DRY, RATHER THAN
INTENSIVE-IRRIGATED (46)

BACKGROUND ON PAGE 76

SUBJECT ONLY

45 IN LEFT COLUMN

AZTEC	BEJA	BOZO	BURUSHO	CAMBODIANS	CHAGGA	COCHITI	DAGUR	DARD	EGYPTIANS
HANO	HAVASUPAI	HAZARA	HEBREWS	IFUGAO	INCA	JAPANESE	JAVANESE	JEMEZ	KERALA
KOHISTANI	KOREANS	MACASSARESE	MALAYS	MARICOPA	MERINA	MIAO	MIN CHINESE	MINCHIA	NAVAHO
NURI	PAPAGO	PATHAN	RIFFIANS	SAGADA	SANTAL	SHLUH	SINHALESE	SYRIANS	TANALA
THAI	TURKANA	TURKMEN	VIETNAMESE	ZUNI					

46 IN RIGHT COLUMN

ALBANIANS	AMERICANS	ARAUCANIANS	BAMBARA	BHIL	BOERS	BRAZILIANS	BULGARIANS	CHERKESS	COORG
CZECHS	DILLING	DOGON	DUTCH	HUTSUL	INGASSANA	IRAQW	KABYLE	KATAB	KIKUYU
KOL	LEPCHA	LOLO	LOZI	LUO	MAMBILA	MANDAN	MARGI	MATAKAM	MONGUOR
MOSSI	NANDI	NYORO	OMAHA	ORAON	ROMANS	SERBS	SOMALI	SONGHAI	SOTHO
TALLENSI	TAOS	TARAHUMARA	TIGRINYA	VENDA	WALLOONS				

243 EXCLUDED BECAUSE IRRELEVANT

66 EXCLUDED BECAUSE UNASCERTAINED

3	LEAN MORE TOWARD BEING THOSE LOCATED OUTSIDE OF AFRICA (320)	0.93 OF 45	3	LEAN LESS TOWARD BEING THOSE LOCATED OUTSIDE OF AFRICA (320)	0.63 OF 46	3 17 42 29 XSQ= 10.47 PHI= -0.339 XP = 0.0012
4	TILT MORE TOWARD BEING THOSE LOCATED OUTSIDE OF THE CIRCUM-MEDITERRANEAN (355)	0.87 OF 45	4	TILT LESS TOWARD BEING THOSE LOCATED OUTSIDE OF THE CIRCUM-MEDITERRANEAN (355)	0.63 OF 46	6 17 39 29 XSQ= 5.53 PHI= -0.246 XP = 0.0187
5	LEAN LESS TOWARD BEING THOSE LOCATED OUTSIDE OF EAST EURASIA (330)	0.51 OF 45	5	LEAN MORE TOWARD BEING THOSE LOCATED OUTSIDE OF EAST EURASIA (330)	0.85 OF 46	22 7 23 39 XSQ= 10.38 PHI= 0.338 XP = 0.0013

13	LEAN MORE TOWARD BEING THOSE WHERE THE LATITUDE IS LESS THAN FORTY DEGREES (329)	0.98 OF	45	13	LEAN LESS TOWARD BEING THOSE WHERE THE LATITUDE IS LESS THAN FORTY DEGREES (329)	0.74 OF	46	1 12 44 34 XSQ= 8.72 PHI= -0.310 XP = 0.0031
33	TILT LESS TOWARD BEING THOSE WHERE THE NATURAL ENVIRONMENT IS OTHER THAN 'VERY HARSH,' I.E., DESERT, DESERT GRASSES AND SHRUBS, TUNDRA, OR HIGH PLATEAU STEPPE (341) FWM	0.69 OF	45	33	TILT MORE TOWARD BEING THOSE WHERE THE NATURAL ENVIRONMENT IS OTHER THAN 'VERY HARSH,' I.E., DESERT, DESERT GRASSES AND SHRUBS, TUNDRA, OR HIGH PLATEAU STEPPE (341) FWM	0.91 OF	46	14 4 31 42 XSQ= 5.86 PHI= 0.254 XP = 0.0155
36	DRIFT LESS TOWARD BEING THOSE WHERE THE NATURAL ENVIRONMENT IS OTHER THAN 'VERY HARSH,' OR SUB-TROPICAL BUSH, OR TEMPERATE GRASSLAND (292) FWM	0.62 OF	45	36	DRIFT MORE TOWARD BEING THOSE WHERE THE NATURAL ENVIRONMENT IS OTHER THAN 'VERY HARSH,' OR SUB-TROPICAL BUSH, OR TEMPERATE GRASSLAND (292) FWM	0.80 OF	46	17 9 28 37 XSQ= 2.86 PHI= 0.177 XP = 0.0909
42	TILT LESS TOWARD BEING THOSE WHERE THE NATURAL ENVIRONMENT IS OTHER THAN TROPICAL OR SUB-TROPICAL RAIN FOREST, OR MONSOON FOREST (244) FWM	0.64 OF	45	42	TILT MORE TOWARD BEING THOSE WHERE THE NATURAL ENVIRONMENT IS OTHER THAN TROPICAL OR SUB-TROPICAL RAIN FOREST, OR MONSOON FOREST (244) FWM	0.89 OF	46	16 5 29 41 XSQ= 6.48 PHI= 0.267 XP = 0.0109
45	LEAN TOWARD BEING THOSE WHERE SETTLEMENTS, IF FIXED, ARE COMPACT, RATHER THAN NON-COMPACT (149)	0.81 OF	36	45	LEAN TOWARD BEING THOSE WHERE SETTLEMENTS, IF FIXED, ARE NON-COMPACT, RATHER THAN COMPACT (73)	0.52 OF	42	29 20 7 22 XSQ= 7.65 PHI= 0.313 XP = 0.0057
62	TILT LESS TOWARD BEING THOSE WHERE HUSBANDRY OF SOME KIND IS PRESENT (228)	0.84 OF	45	62	IN ALL CASES ARE THOSE WHERE HUSBANDRY OF SOME KIND IS PRESENT (228)	1.00 OF	46	38 46 7 0 XSQ= 5.72 PHI= -0.251 XP = 0.0168
73	IN ALL CASES ARE THOSE WHERE WEAVING IS PRESENT (118)	1.00 OF	21	73	LEAN LESS TOWARD BEING THOSE WHERE WEAVING IS PRESENT (118)	0.60 OF	30	21 18 0 12 XSQ= 8.87 PHI= 0.417 XP = 0.0029
88	DRIFT TOWARD BEING THOSE WHERE, IF A HEADMANSHIP IS PRESENT, SUCCESSION IS NON-HEREDITARY (106)	0.71 OF	28	88	DRIFT TOWARD BEING THOSE WHERE, IF A HEADMANSHIP IS PRESENT, SUCCESSION IS HEREDITARY (165)	0.56 OF	34	20 15 8 19 XSQ= 3.61 PHI= 0.241 XP = 0.0573
116	DRIFT TOWARD BEING THOSE WHERE OCCUPATIONAL SPECIALIZATION IS FULL-TIME, WHETHER OR NOT FOR SURPLUS PRODUCTION (20) JMH	0.78 OF	9	116	DRIFT TOWARD BEING THOSE WHERE OCCUPATIONAL SPECIALIZATION IS PART-TIME ONLY (34) JMH	0.80 OF	5	7 1 2 4 XSQ= 2.34 PHI= 0.409 EP = 0.0909

141	TILT TOWARD BEING THOSE WHERE THE LEVEL OF SOCIAL SANCTION IS PUBLIC CORPOREAL SANCTION, RATHER THAN PUBLIC PROPERTY SANCTION OR PRIVATE SETTLEMENT (28) JMH	0.89 OF	9	141	TILT TOWARD BEING THOSE WHERE THE LEVEL OF SOCIAL SANCTION IS PUBLIC PROPERTY SANCTION OR PRIVATE SETTLEMENT, RATHER THAN PUBLIC CORPOREAL SANCTION (26) JMH	0.80 OF	5	8 1 1 4 XSQ= 3.98 PHI= 0.533 EP = 0.0230
207	DRIFT TOWARD BEING THOSE WHERE MARITAL RESIDENCE IS MATRILOCAL OR UXORILOCAL, RATHER THAN AMBILOCAL OR NEOLOCAL (64)	0.55 OF	11	207	DRIFT TOWARD BEING THOSE WHERE MARITAL RESIDENCE IS AMBILOCAL OR NEOLOCAL, RATHER THAN MATRILOCAL OR UXORILOCAL (64)	0.91 OF	11	6 1 5 10 XSQ= 3.35 PHI= 0.390 EP = 0.0635
225	TILT TOWARD BEING THOSE WHERE COUSIN MARRIAGE IS PREFERENTIALLY OR PERMISSIVELY PATRILATERAL, RATHER THAN MATRILATERAL (23)	0.63 OF	8	225	IN ALL CASES ARE THOSE WHERE COUSIN MARRIAGE IS PREFERENTIALLY OR PERMISSIVELY MATRILATERAL, RATHER THAN PATRILATERAL (43)	1.00 OF	6	5 0 3 6 XSQ= 3.43 PHI= 0.495 EP = 0.0310
343	IN ALL CASES ARE THOSE WHERE THE CHILD'S INFERRED CONFLICT REGARDING NURTURANT BEHAVIOR IS HIGH (29) B-B-C	1.00 OF	4	343	DRIFT TOWARD BEING THOSE WHERE THE CHILD'S INFERRED CONFLICT REGARDING NURTURANT BEHAVIOR IS LOW (18) B-B-C	0.71 OF	7	4 2 0 5 XSQ= 2.75 PHI= 0.500 EP = 0.0606
440	TILT TOWARD BEING THOSE WHERE FEAR OF SPIRITS IS HIGH (32) W-C	0.88 OF	8	440	IN ALL CASES ARE THOSE WHERE FEAR OF SPIRITS IS LOW (29) W-C	1.00 OF	4	7 0 1 4 XSQ= 5.19 PHI= 0.657 EP = 0.0101
459	DRIFT MORE TOWARD BEING THOSE WHERE GAMES, IF PRESENT, INCLUDE GAMES OF CHANCE (82) R-A-B, EA	0.80 OF	20	459	DRIFT LESS TOWARD BEING THOSE WHERE GAMES, IF PRESENT, INCLUDE GAMES OF CHANCE (82) R-A-B, EA	0.53 OF	19	16 10 4 9 XSQ= 2.17 PHI= 0.236 EP = 0.0958
470	DRIFT TOWARD BEING THOSE WHERE INNOVATIONS ARE GENERALLY ACCEPTED (21) JMH	0.89 OF	9	470	DRIFT TOWARD BEING THOSE WHERE INNOVATIONS ARE ACCEPTED ONLY SELECTIVELY (33) JMH	0.60 OF	5	8 2 1 3 XSQ= 1.75 PHI= 0.354 EP = 0.0949

61	CULTURES WHERE SUBSISTENCE IS PRIMARILY BY ANIMAL HUSBANDRY (16)	61	CULTURES WHERE SUBSISTENCE IS PRIMARILY BY MEANS OTHER THAN ANIMAL HUSBANDRY (384)	

BACKGROUND ON PAGE 77

SUBJECT ONLY

16 IN LEFT COLUMN

BASSERI, MASAI, BEJA, NUER, BOERS, REGEIBAT, BURYAT, RWALA, GOAJIRO, SOMALI, HERERO, TODA, KALMYK, KAZAK, KHALKA, LAPPS

384 IN RIGHT COLUMN

4	TEND LESS TO BE THOSE LOCATED OUTSIDE OF THE CIRCUM-MEDITERRANEAN (355)	0.56 OF 16	4	TEND MORE TO BE THOSE LOCATED OUTSIDE OF THE CIRCUM-MEDITERRANEAN (355)	0.90 OF 384	7 38 9 346 XSQ= 14.40 PHI= 0.190 XP = 0.0001
33	TEND TO BE THOSE WHERE THE NATURAL ENVIRONMENT IS 'VERY HARSH,' I.E., DESERT, DESERT GRASSES AND SHRUBS, TUNDRA, OR HIGH PLATEAU STEPPE (59) FWM	0.69 OF 16	33	TEND TO BE THOSE WHERE THE NATURAL ENVIRONMENT IS OTHER THAN 'VERY HARSH,' I.E., DESERT, DESERT GRASSES AND SHRUBS, TUNDRA, OR HIGH PLATEAU STEPPE (341) FWM	0.88 OF 384	11 48 5 336 XSQ= 34.31 PHI= 0.293 XP = 0.
36	TEND TO BE THOSE WHERE THE NATURAL ENVIRONMENT IS 'VERY HARSH,' OR SUB-TROPICAL BUSH, OR TEMPERATE GRASSLAND (108) FWM	0.81 OF 16	36	TEND TO BE THOSE WHERE THE NATURAL ENVIRONMENT IS OTHER THAN 'VERY HARSH,' OR SUB-TROPICAL BUSH, OR TEMPERATE GRASSLAND (292) FWM	0.75 OF 384	13 95 3 289 XSQ= 22.10 PHI= 0.235 XP = 0.0000
42	IN ALL CASES ARE THOSE WHERE THE NATURAL ENVIRONMENT IS OTHER THAN TROPICAL OR SUB-TROPICAL RAIN FOREST, OR MONSOON FOREST (244) FWM	1.00 OF 16	42	LEAN LESS TOWARD BEING THOSE WHERE THE NATURAL ENVIRONMENT IS OTHER THAN TROPICAL OR SUB-TROPICAL RAIN FOREST, OR MONSOON FOREST (244) FWM	0.59 OF 384	0 156 16 228 XSQ= 9.02 PHI= -0.150 XP = 0.0027
44	TEND TO BE THOSE WHERE SETTLEMENTS ARE NON-FIXED (110)	0.93 OF 14	44	TEND TO BE THOSE WHERE SETTLEMENTS ARE FIXED (222)	0.69 OF 318	1 221 13 97 XSQ= 20.80 PHI= -0.250 XP = 0.0000
46	TEND TO BE THOSE WHERE SETTLEMENTS ARE NON-FIXED AND MOVEMENT IS NOMADIC (72)	0.86 OF 14	46	TEND TO BE THOSE OTHER THAN WHERE SETTLEMENTS ARE NON-FIXED AND MOVEMENT IS NOMADIC (260)	0.81 OF 318	12 60 2 258 XSQ= 31.46 PHI= 0.308 XP = 0.

47	DRIFT MORE TOWARD BEING THOSE 0.92 OF 13 WHERE, IF SETTLEMENTS ARE NON-FIXED, MOVEMENT IS NOMADIC, RATHER THAN NON-NOMADIC (72)	47	DRIFT LESS TOWARD BEING THOSE 0.62 OF 97 WHERE, IF SETTLEMENTS ARE NON-FIXED, MOVEMENT IS NOMADIC, RATHER THAN NON-NOMADIC (72)	12 60 1 37 XSQ= 3.45 PHI= 0.177 XP = 0.0632
62	IN ALL CASES ARE THOSE 1.00 OF 16 WHERE HUSBANDRY OF SOME KIND IS PRESENT (228)	62	LEAN LESS TOWARD BEING THOSE 0.55 OF 384 WHERE HUSBANDRY OF SOME KIND IS PRESENT (228)	16 212 0 172 XSQ= 10.81 PHI= 0.164 XP = 0.0010
63	DRIFT MORE TOWARD BEING THOSE 0.93 OF 14 WHERE HUSBANDRY, IF PRESENT, IS PRINCIPALLY IN THE FORM OF BOVINE, EQUINE, CAMEL-LIKE, OR DEER-LIKE ANIMALS, RATHER THAN PIGS, SHEEP, OR GOATS (152)	63	DRIFT LESS TOWARD BEING THOSE 0.66 OF 212 WHERE HUSBANDRY, IF PRESENT, IS PRINCIPALLY IN THE FORM OF BOVINE, EQUINE, CAMEL-LIKE, OR DEER-LIKE ANIMALS, RATHER THAN PIGS, SHEEP, OR GOATS (152)	13 139 1 73 XSQ= 3.29 PHI= 0.121 XP = 0.0698
74	TILT TOWARD BEING THOSE 0.86 OF 7 WHERE POTTERY IS ABSENT (93)	74	TILT TOWARD BEING THOSE 0.62 OF 231 WHERE POTTERY IS PRESENT (145)	1 144 6 87 XSQ= 4.73 PHI= -0.141 XP = 0.0297
82	LEAN TOWARD BEING THOSE 0.67 OF 9 WHERE NO CITY OR TOWN IS PRESENT, AND THE AVERAGE COMMUNITY SIZE IS SMALLER THAN FIFTY (46)	82	LEAN TOWARD BEING THOSE 0.81 OF 215 WHERE A CITY OR TOWN IS PRESENT, OR THE AVERAGE COMMUNITY SIZE IS FIFTY OR GREATER (178)	3 175 6 40 XSQ= 9.46 PHI= -0.206 XP = 0.0021
85	DRIFT TOWARD BEING THOSE 0.50 OF 12 WHERE THE LEVEL OF POLITICAL INTEGRATION IS THE LARGE STATE, OR THE LITTLE STATE (70) GPM	85	DRIFT TOWARD BEING THOSE 0.78 OF 292 WHERE THE LEVEL OF POLITICAL INTEGRATION IS THE MINIMAL STATE, THE AUTONOMOUS COMMUNITY, OR THE FAMILY (234) GPM	6 64 6 228 XSQ= 3.67 PHI= 0.110 XP = 0.0555
109	TEND TO BE THOSE 0.54 OF 13 WHERE CASTES ARE PRESENT (51)	109	TEND TO BE THOSE 0.88 OF 355 WHERE CASTES ARE ABSENT (317)	7 44 6 311 XSQ= 14.74 PHI= 0.200 XP = 0.0001
131	TILT TOWARD BEING THOSE 0.50 OF 6 WHERE THE CONSTRUCTION OF PERMANENT HOUSES OR THE ERECTION OF TEMPORARY DWELLINGS IS MAINLY DONE BY FEMALES (21)	131	TILT TOWARD BEING THOSE 0.88 OF 151 WHERE THE CONSTRUCTION OF PERMANENT HOUSES OR THE ERECTION OF TEMPORARY DWELLINGS IS MAINLY DONE BY MALES (136)	3 133 3 18 XSQ= 4.31 PHI= -0.166 XP = 0.0379
137	IN ALL CASES ARE THOSE 1.00 OF 7 WHERE INVIDIOUS DISPLAY OF WEALTH IS MODERATELY, LITTLE, OR NEGATIVELY EMPHASIZED (52) PES	137	DRIFT LESS TOWARD BEING THOSE 0.55 OF 82 WHERE INVIDIOUS DISPLAY OF WEALTH IS MODERATELY, LITTLE, OR NEGATIVELY EMPHASIZED (52) PES	0 37 7 45 XSQ= 3.71 PHI= -0.204 XP = 0.0542

143	DRIFT TOWARD BEING THOSE WHERE THE RATIO OF RESTITUTIVE TO REPRESSIVE SANCTIONS IS HIGH (20) WME	0.83 OF 6	143	DRIFT TOWARD BEING THOSE WHERE THE RATIO OF RESTITUTIVE TO REPRESSIVE SANCTIONS IS MEDIUM OR LOW (32) WME	0.67 OF 46	5 15 1 31 XSQ= 3.83 PHI= 0.271 XP = 0.0505
144	IN ALL CASES ARE THOSE WHERE THE RATIO OF RESTITUTIVE TO REPRESSIVE SANCTIONS IS HIGH OR MEDIUM (27) WME	1.00 OF 6	144	TILT TOWARD BEING THOSE WHERE THE RATIO OF RESTITUTIVE TO REPRESSIVE SANCTIONS IS LOW (25) WME	0.54 OF 46	6 21 0 25 XSQ= 4.29 PHI= 0.287 XP = 0.0383
175	TILT TOWARD BEING THOSE WHERE THE COMMUNITY IS 'KIN-HOMOGENEOUS,' I. E. A CLAN COMMUNITY OR A DEME (122)	0.63 OF 16	175	TILT TOWARD BEING THOSE WHERE THE COMMUNITY IS 'KIN-HETEROGENEOUS,' I. E. OTHER THAN A CLAN COMMUNITY OR A DEME (260)	0.69 OF 366	10 112 6 254 XSQ= 5.78 PHI= 0.123 XP = 0.0162
177	TEND TO BE THOSE WHERE THE COMMUNITY IS A SINGLE CLAN-COMMUNITY AND EXOGAMOUS (77)	0.56 OF 16	177	TEND TO BE THOSE WHERE THE COMMUNITY IS OTHER THAN A SINGLE CLAN-COMMUNITY AND EXOGAMOUS (305)	0.81 OF 366	9 68 7 298 XSQ= 11.28 PHI= 0.172 XP = 0.0008
178	IN ALL CASES ARE THOSE WHERE THE COMMUNITY IS OTHER THAN SEGMENTED ON A CLAN BASIS AND NON-EXOGAMOUS (295)	1.00 OF 16	178	DRIFT LESS TOWARD BEING THOSE WHERE THE COMMUNITY IS OTHER THAN SEGMENTED ON A CLAN BASIS AND NON-EXOGAMOUS (295)	0.76 OF 366	0 87 16 279 XSQ= 3.67 PHI= -0.098 XP = 0.0555
180	LEAN TOWARD BEING THOSE WHERE THE COMMUNITY IS COMMONLY EXOGAMOUS, RATHER THAN NON-EXOGAMOUS (124)	0.69 OF 16	180	LEAN TOWARD BEING THOSE WHERE THE COMMUNITY IS COMMONLY NON-EXOGAMOUS, RATHER THAN EXOGAMOUS (258)	0.69 OF 366	11 113 5 253 XSQ= 8.38 PHI= 0.148 XP = 0.0038
184	DRIFT TOWARD BEING THOSE WHERE THE LARGEST NON-COGNATIC KIN GROUP IS THE MOEITY OR PHRATRY (77)	0.57 OF 14	184	DRIFT TOWARD BEING THOSE WHERE THE LARGEST NON-COGNATIC KIN GROUP IS SMALLER THAN A PHRATRY, I. E. A SIB OR LINEAGE (175)	0.71 OF 238	8 69 6 169 XSQ= 3.70 PHI= 0.121 XP = 0.0544
185	IN ALL CASES ARE THOSE WHERE THE LARGEST NON-COGNATIC KIN GROUP IS THE MOEITY OR PHRATRY OR SIB (194)	1.00 OF 14	185	DRIFT LESS TOWARD BEING THOSE WHERE THE LARGEST NON-COGNATIC KIN GROUP IS THE MOEITY OR PHRATRY OR SIB (194)	0.76 OF 238	14 180 0 58 XSQ= 3.16 PHI= 0.112 XP = 0.0753
188	DRIFT MORE TOWARD BEING THOSE WHERE THE KIN GROUP IS OTHER THAN EXCLUSIVELY COGNATIC (252)	0.88 OF 16	188	DRIFT LESS TOWARD BEING THOSE WHERE THE KIN GROUP IS OTHER THAN EXCLUSIVELY COGNATIC (252)	0.62 OF 384	2 146 14 238 XSQ= 3.27 PHI= -0.090 XP = 0.0707

204	IN ALL CASES ARE THCSE WHERE MARITAL RESICENCE IS PATRILCCAL, VIRILOCAL, CR AVUNCULOCAL, RATHER THAN AMBILCCAL CR NECLOCAL (270)	1.00 OF 16	204	DRIFT LESS TOWARD BEING THCSE WHERE MARITAL RESIDENCE IS PATRILOCAL, VIRILOCAL, CR AVUNCULCCAL, RATHER THAN AMBILOCAL OR NEOLOCAL (270)	0.80 OF 318	16 254 0 64 XSQ= 2.79 PHI= 0.091 XP = 0.0948
209	IN ALL CASES ARE THCSE WHERE MARITAL RESICENCE IS PATRILCCAL, VIRILOCAL, CR AVUNCULOCAL, RATHER THAN MATRILCCAL OR UXCRILOCAL (270)	1.00 OF 16	209	DRIFT LESS TOWARD BEING THCSE WHERE MARITAL RESIDENCE IS PATRILOCAL, VIRILOCAL, OR AVUNCULOCAL, RATHER THAN MATRILOCAL OR UXORILOCAL (270)	0.80 OF 318	16 254 0 64 XSQ= 2.79 PHI= 0.091 XP = 0.0948
224	DRIFT TOWARD BEING THCSE WHERE CCUSIN MARRIAGE IS PREFERENTIALLY CR PERMISSIVELY EITHER PATRI- OR MATRILATERAL, RATHER THAN SYMMETRICAL (66)	0.75 OF 8	224	DRIFT TOWARD BEING THCSE WHERE COUSIN MARRIAGE IS PREFERENTIALLY CR PERMISSIVELY SYMMETRICAL, RATHER THAN EITHER PATRI- OR MATRILATERAL (106)	0.63 OF 164	6 60 2 104 XSQ= 3.27 PHI= 0.138 XP = 0.0704
225	TILT TOWARD BEING THOSE WHERE CCUSIN MARRIAGE IS PREFERENTIALLY CR PERMISSIVELY PATRILATERAL, RATHER THAN MATRILATERAL (23)	0.83 OF 6	225	TILT TOWARD BEING THOSE WHERE COUSIN MARRIAGE IS PREFERENTIALLY OR PERMISSIVELY MATRILATERAL, RATHER THAN PATRILATERAL (43)	0.70 OF 60	5 18 1 42 XSQ= 4.69 PHI= 0.266 XP = 0.0304
377	TILT TOWARD BEING THOSE WHERE MALE GENITAL MUTILATION IS PRESENT (83)	0.57 OF 14	377	TILT TOWARD BEING THCSE WHERE MALE GENITAL MUTILATICN IS ABSENT (242)	0.76 OF 311	8 75 6 236 XSQ= 6.05 PHI= 0.136 XP = 0.0139
382	TILT TOWARD BEING THOSE WHERE FEMALE INITIATICN RITES ARE ABSENT (27) JKB	0.86 OF 7	382	TILT TOWARD BEING THOSE WHERE FEMALE INITIATION RITES ARE PRESENT (38) JKB	0.64 OF 58	1 37 6 21 XSQ= 4.43 PHI= -0.261 XP = 0.0353
426	DRIFT MORE TOWARD BEING THOSE WHERE A HIGH GCC IS PRESENT (156) GES,EA	0.91 OF 11	426	DRIFT LESS TOWARD BEING THOSE WHERE A HIGH GOD IS PRESENT (156) GES,EA	0.59 OF 249	10 146 1 103 XSQ= 3.33 PHI= 0.113 XP = 0.0682
427	IN ALL CASES ARE THOSE WHERE A HIGH GOC, IF PRESENT, IS ACTIVE, RATHER THAN INACTIVE (87) GES,EA	1.00 OF 10	427	LEAN LESS TOWARD BEING THOSE WHERE A HIGH GCD, IF PRESENT, IS ACTIVE, RATHER THAN INACTIVE (87) GES,EA	0.53 OF 146	10 77 0 69 XSQ= 6.67 PHI= 0.207 XP = 0.0098
475	IN ALL CASES ARE THOSE WHERE EXHIBITIONISTIC DANCING IS NEGLIGIBLY EMPHASIZEC (38) PES	1.00 OF 5	475	TILT TOWARD BEING THOSE WHERE EXHIBITIONISTIC DANCING IS STRONGLY OR MODERATELY EMPHASIZED (48) PES	0.59 OF 81	0 48 5 33 XSQ= 4.52 PHI= -0.229 XP = 0.0335

62 CULTURES
WHERE HUSBANDRY CF SCME KIND
IS PRESENT (228)

62 CULTURES
WHERE HUSBANDRY OF ANY KIND
IS ABSENT (172)

BACKGROUND ON PAGE 77

BCTH SUBJECT AND PREDICATE

228 IN LEFT CCLUMN

ABIPON	ABCR	AKHA	ALBANIANS	ALORESE	AMBA	AMERICANS	ARAPESH	ARAUCANIANS	ASHANTI
ATAYAL	AYMARA	BAMBARA	BAMILEKE	BANDA	BARABRA	BARI	BASSERI	BAYA	BEJA
BEMBA	BHIL	BHUIYA	BIRIFOR	BOERS	BRAZILIANS	BULGARIANS	BUNLAP	BURUSHO	BURYAT
CADUVEO	CAGABA	CAMBODIANS	CAYAPA	CHAGGA	CHENCHU	CHERKESS	CHEYENNE	CHIR-APACHE	CHORTI
CHUKCHEE	COORG	CROW	CUNA	CZECHS	DARD	DILLING	DOGON	DUTCH	EGYPTIANS
ELLICE	ENGA	FANG	FON	FOX	FUTAJALONKE	GANDA	GARO	GISU	GOAJIRO
GOND	GRCS VENTRE	GURE	HANO	HANUNOO	HAWAIIANS	HAZARA	HEBREWS	HERERO	HUICHOL
HUTSUL	IBAN	IFUGAO	ILA	INCA	INGASSANA	IRAQW	IRISH	JAPANESE	JAVANESE
JEMEZ	JIVARO	JUKUN	KABYLE	KACHIN	KALMYK	KAPAUKU	KATAB	KAZAK	KERAKI
KERALA	KHALKA	KHASI	KIKUYU	KISSI	KOHISTANI	KOL	KOREANS	KORYAK	KPE
KUBA	KURTATCHI	KUTENAI	LAKHER	LAMET	LANGO	LAPPS	LAU	LEPCHA	LESU
LHOTA NAGA	LOLO	LOZI	LUO	MACASSARESE	MALAYS	MAM	MAMBILA	MAMVU	MANDAN
MANUS	MARGI	MARQUESANS	MARSHALLESE	MASAI	MATACO	MATAKAM	MBUNDU	MENDE	MERINA
MIAO	MIN CHINESE	MINCHIA	MISKITO	MNONG GAR	MONGO	MONGUOR	MOSSI	MOTA	MZAB
NAMA	NANDI	NAVAHO	NDEMBU	NICOBARESE	NUER	NUPE	NURI	NYAKYUSA	NYORO
OKINAWANS	OMAHA	ORAON	PAIWAN	PALAUANS	PATHAN	PAWNEE	PONAPEANS	PUKAPUKA	PURARI
PURUM	REGEIBAT	RIFFIANS	ROMANS	RUNDI	RWALA	SAGADA	SAMOANS	SAMOYED	SANDAWE
SANTAL	SARSI	SENIANG	SERBS	SHILLUK	SHLUH	SINHALESE	SIUAI	SIWANS	SOMALI
SONGHAI	SOTHO	SUBANUN	SWAZI	SYRIANS	TAGBANUA	TALAMANCA	TALLENSI	TANALA	TAOS
TARAHUMARA	TEDA	TEHUELCHE	TENDA	TENETEHARA	TERA	TERENA	TESO	THAI	THONGA
TIGRINYA	TIMBIRA	TIV	TOCA	TORAJA	TOTONAC	TRISTAN	TROBRIAND	TRUKESE	TURKANA
TURKMEN	ULAWANS	UTE	VENDA	VIETNAMESE	WALLOONS	WANTOAT	WICHITA	WOGEO	WOLEAIANS
WOLOF	YAKO	YAKUT	YAPESE	YARURO	YOMBE	YORUBA	ZUNI		

172 IN RIGHT CCLUMN

---

3 TEND LESS TO BE THCSE LOCATED OUTSIDE CF AFRICA (320) — 0.73 OF 228

3 TEND MORE TO BE THOSE LOCATED OUTSIDE OF AFRICA (320) — 0.89 OF 172

61 19
167 153
XSQ= 14.15
PHI= 0.188
XP = 0.0002

4 LEAN LESS TOWARD BEING THCSE LOCATED CUTSIDE CF THE CIRCUM-MEDITERRANEAN (355) — 0.85 OF 228

4 LEAN MORE TOWARD BEING THOSE LOCATED OUTSIDE OF THE CIRCUM-MEDITERRANEAN (355) — 0.94 OF 172

35 10
193 162
XSQ= 8.00
PHI= 0.141
XP = 0.0047

5	LEAN LESS TOWARC BEING THCSE LOCATED CUTSIDE OF EAST EURASIA (330)	0.77 OF 228	5	LEAN MORE TOWARD BEING THOSE LOCATED OUTSIDE OF EAST EURASIA (330)	0.90 OF 172	52 18 176 154 XSQ= 9.51 PHI= 0.154 XP = 0.0020
8	TEND MCRE TO BE THCSE LOCATED OUTSIDE CF NORTH AMERICA (330)	0.91 OF 228	8	TEND LESS TO BE THOSE LOCATED OUTSIDE OF NORTH AMERICA (330)	0.71 CF 172	20 50 208 122 XSQ= 26.59 PHI= -0.258 XP = 0.0000
9	TEND MORE TO BE THCSE LOCATED CUTSIDE OF SOUTH AMERICA (335)	0.91 OF 228	9	TEND LESS TO BE THOSE LOCATED OUTSIDE OF SOUTH AMERICA (335)	0.74 OF 172	20 45 208 127 XSQ= 20.53 PHI= -0.227 XP = 0.0000
12	DRIFT MCRE TCWARD BEING THOSE WHERE THE LATITUDE IS LESS THAN FIFTY DEGREES (367)	0.94 OF 228	12	DRIFT LESS TOWARD BEING THCSE WHERE THE LATITUDE IS LESS THAN FIFTY DEGREES (367)	0.88 CF 172	13 20 215 152 XSQ= 3.80 PHI= -0.097 XP = 0.0513
13	LEAN MORE TOWARC BEING THCSE WHERE THE LATITUDE IS LESS THAN FORTY CEGREES (329)	0.87 OF 228	13	LEAN LESS TOWARD BEING THOSE WHERE THE LATITUDE IS LESS THAN FORTY DEGREES (329)	0.76 OF 172	29 42 199 130 XSQ= 8.41 PHI= -0.145 XP = 0.0037
14	TILT MCRE TOWARC BEING THCSE WHERE THE LATITUDE IS LESS THAN THIRTY DEGREES (281)	0.75 OF 228	14	TILT LESS TOWARD BEING THOSE WHERE THE LATITUDE IS LESS THAN THIRTY DEGREES (281)	0.65 CF 172	58 61 170 111 XSQ= 4.25 PHI= -0.103 XP = 0.0393
44	TEND TO BE THOSE WHERE SETTLEMENTS ARE FIXEC (222)	0.78 OF 226	44	TEND TO BE THOSE WHERE SETTLEMENTS ARE NCN-FIXED (110)	0.57 CF 106	176 46 50 60 XSQ= 37.18 PHI= 0.335 XP = 0.
46	TEND MCRE TO BE THCSE OTHER THAN WHERE SETTLEMENTS ARE NON-FIXED AND MCVEMENT IS NCMADIC (260)	0.86 OF 226	46	TEND LESS TO BE THOSE OTHER THAN WHERE SETTLEMENTS ARE NON-FIXED AND MOVEMENT IS NOMADIC (260)	0.61 CF 106	31 41 195 65 XSQ= 25.02 PHI= -0.275 XP = 0.0000
51	TEND TO BE THCSE WHERE SUBSISTENCE IS PRIMARILY BY FOOD PRODUCTICN -- I. E., AGRICULTURE OR HUSBANDRY -- RATHER THAN BY GATHERING (253)	0.85 OF 228	51	TEND TO BE THOSE WHERE SUBSISTENCE IS PRIMARILY BY FOOD GATHERING -- I. E., HUNTING, FISHING, OR COLLECTING -- RATHER THAN FOOD PRODUCTION (147)	0.65 OF 172	193 60 35 112 XSQ= 102.33 PHI= 0.506 XP = 0.

54	TEND TC BE THCSE WHERE FOOD PRCDUCTION IS BY INTENSIVE CR SIMPLE AGRICULTURE, RATHER THAN BY INCIPIENT FOCD PROCUCTION (192)	0.92 OF 192	54	TEND TO BE THOSE WHERE FOOD PRODUCTION IS BY INCIPIENT FOOD PRODUCTICN, RATHER THAN BY INTENSIVE OR SIMPLE AGRICULTURE (46)	0.67 OF 46	177 15 15 31 XSQ= 80.70 PHI= 0.582 XP = 0.
56	TEND TC BE THCSE WHERE FCCD PRODUCTION IS BY SIMPLE AGRICULTURE, RATHER THAN BY INCIPIENT FOCD PROCUCTICN (101)	0.86 OF 106	56	TEND TO BE THOSE WHERE FOOD PRODUCTION IS BY INCIPIENT FOOD PRODUCTION, RATHER THAN BY SIMPLE AGRICULTURE (46)	0.76 OF 41	91 10 15 31 XSQ= 49.12 PHI= 0.578 XP = 0.
71	TEND TO BE THCSE WHERE METAL WORKING IS PRESENT (98)	0.58 OF 153	71	TEND TO BE THOSE WHERE METAL WORKING IS ABSENT (153)	0.91 OF 98	89 9 64 89 XSQ= 58.19 PHI= 0.481 XP = 0.
73	TILT TCWARD BEING THCSE WHERE WEAVING IS PRESENT (118)	0.54 OF 153	73	TILT TOWARD BEING THOSE WHERE WEAVING IS ABSENT (130)	0.63 OF 95	83 35 70 60 XSQ= 6.44 PHI= 0.161 XP = 0.0112
74	LEAN TCWARD BEING THCSE WHERE POTTERY IS PRESENT (145)	0.70 OF 142	74	LEAN TOWARD BEING THOSE WHERE POTTERY IS ABSENT (93)	0.52 OF 96	99 46 43 50 XSQ= 10.54 PHI= 0.210 XP = 0.0012
79	LEAN LESS TOWARD BEING THCSE WHERE NC CITY IS PRESENT (201)	0.86 OF 154	79	LEAN MORE TCWARD BEING THCSE WHERE NO CITY IS PRESENT (201)	0.99 OF 70	22 1 132 69 XSQ= 7.30 PHI= 0.180 XP = 0.0069
80	TEND LESS TO BE THCSE WHERE NC CITY CR TCWN IS PRESENT (185)	0.77 OF 154	80	TEND MORE TO BE THOSE WHERE NO CITY OR TOWN IS PRESENT (185)	0.96 OF 70	36 3 118 67 XSQ= 10.91 PHI= 0.221 XP = 0.0010
81	TEND LESS TO BE THCSE WHERE NC CITY OR TCWN IS PRESENT, AND THE AVERAGE COMMUNITY SIZE IS SMALLER THAN 200 (135)	0.51 OF 154	81	TEND MORE TO BE THOSE WHERE NO CITY OR TOWN IS PRESENT, AND THE AVERAGE COMMUNITY SIZE IS SMALLER THAN 200 (135)	0.80 OF 70	75 14 79 56 XSQ= 15.38 PHI= 0.262 XP = 0.0001
82	TEND MORE TO BE THCSE WHERE A CITY CR TOWN IS PRESENT, OR THE AVERAGE COMMUNITY SIZE IS FIFTY OR GREATER (178)	0.92 OF 154	82	TEND LESS TO BE THOSE WHERE A CITY OR TOWN IS PRESENT, OR THE AVERAGE COMMUNITY SIZE IS FIFTY OR GREATER (178)	0.53 OF 70	141 37 13 33 XSQ= 41.83 PHI= 0.432 XP = 0.

83	TILT LESS TOWARD BEING THOSE 0.69 OF 114 WHERE, WITH NO CITY AND NO TOWN PRESENT, THE AVERAGE COMMUNITY SIZE IS SMALLER THAN 200, RATHER THAN BETWEEN 200 AND 999 (135)	83	TILT MORE TOWARD BEING THOSE 0.85 OF 66 WHERE, WITH NO CITY AND NO TOWN PRESENT, THE AVERAGE COMMUNITY SIZE IS SMALLER THAN 200, RATHER THAN BETWEEN 200 AND 999 (135)	35 10 79 56 XSQ= 4.59 PHI= 0.160 XP = 0.0321
86	TEND TO BE THOSE 0.60 OF 173 WHERE THE LEVEL OF POLITICAL INTEGRATION IS THE LARGE STATE, THE LITTLE STATE, OR THE MINIMAL STATE (148) GPM	86	TEND TO BE THOSE 0.66 OF 131 WHERE THE LEVEL OF POLITICAL INTEGRATION IS THE AUTONOMOUS COMMUNITY, OR THE FAMILY (156) GPM	103 45 70 86 XSQ= 17.93 PHI= 0.243 XP = 0.0000
96	TEND TO BE THOSE 0.63 OF 223 WHERE THE HIERARCHY OF NATIONAL JURISDICTION HAS FOUR, THREE, TWO OR ONE LEVEL (174) GES,EA	96	TEND TO BE THOSE 0.68 OF 107 WHERE THE HIERARCHY OF NATIONAL JURISDICTION HAS NO LEVELS (156) GES,EA	140 34 83 73 XSQ= 26.66 PHI= 0.284 XP = 0.0000
97	TILT LESS TOWARD BEING THOSE 0.79 OF 224 WHERE THE HIERARCHY OF LOCAL JURISDICTION HAS THREE OR TWO LEVELS (273) GES,EA	97	TILT MORE TOWARD BEING THOSE 0.91 OF 107 WHERE THE HIERARCHY OF LOCAL JURISDICTION HAS THREE OR TWO LEVELS (273) GES,EA	48 10 176 97 XSQ= 6.50 PHI= 0.140 XP = 0.0108
98	TEND MORE TO BE THOSE 0.79 OF 224 WHERE THE HIERARCHY OF LOCAL JURISDICTION HAS FOUR OR THREE LEVELS (238) GES,EA	98	TEND LESS TO BE THOSE 0.57 OF 107 WHERE THE HIERARCHY OF LOCAL JURISDICTION HAS FOUR OR THREE LEVELS (238) GES,EA	177 61 47 46 XSQ= 16.29 PHI= 0.222 XP = 0.0001
99	TEND TO BE THOSE 0.73 OF 83 WHERE, WITH NATIONAL HIERARCHY ABSENT, THE HIERARCHY OF LOCAL JURISDICTION HAS FOUR OR THREE LEVELS (93) GES,EA	99	TEND TO BE THOSE 0.56 OF 73 WHERE, WITH NATIONAL HIERARCHY ABSENT, THE HIERARCHY OF LOCAL JURISDICTION HAS TWO LEVELS (63) GES,EA	61 32 22 41 XSQ= 12.99 PHI= 0.289 XP = 0.0003
100	TEND MORE TO BE THOSE 0.90 OF 223 WHERE HIERARCHIES ARE MORE COMPLEX THAN THE 'SIMPLEST,' I. E., MORE COMPLEX THAN TWO LOCAL LEVELS WITH NO NATIONAL LEVELS (267) GES,EA	100	TEND LESS TO BE THOSE 0.62 OF 107 WHERE HIERARCHIES ARE MORE COMPLEX THAN THE 'SIMPLEST,' I. E., MORE COMPLEX THAN TWO LOCAL LEVELS WITH NO NATIONAL LEVELS (267) GES,EA	201 66 22 41 XSQ= 36.08 PHI= 0.331 XP = 0.
102	TEND TO BE THOSE 0.65 OF 220 WHERE CLASS STRATIFICATION IS PRESENT (203)	102	TEND TO BE THOSE 0.63 OF 163 WHERE CLASS STRATIFICATION IS ABSENT (180)	142 61 78 102 XSQ= 26.57 PHI= 0.263 XP = 0.0000
107	DRIFT LESS TOWARD BEING THOSE 0.75 OF 142 WHERE CLASS STRATIFICATION, IF PRESENT, IS BASED ON SOMETHING OTHER THAN OCCUPATIONAL STATUS (160)	107	DRIFT MORE TOWARD BEING THOSE 0.87 OF 61 WHERE CLASS STRATIFICATION, IF PRESENT, IS BASED ON SOMETHING OTHER THAN OCCUPATIONAL STATUS (160)	35 8 107 53 XSQ= 2.74 PHI= 0.116 XP = 0.0976

109	TEND LESS TO BE THOSE WHERE CASTES ARE ABSENT (317)	0.80 OF 206	109	TEND MORE TO BE THOSE WHERE CASTES ARE ABSENT (317)	0.94 OF 162	41 10 165 152 XSQ= 13.19 PHI= 0.189 XP = 0.0003
110	LEAN TOWARD BEING THOSE WHERE SLAVERY IS PRESENT (163)	0.50 OF 220	110	LEAN TOWARD BEING THOSE WHERE SLAVERY IS ABSENT (218)	0.67 OF 161	110 53 110 108 XSQ= 10.39 PHI= 0.165 XP = 0.0013
130	DRIFT TOWARD BEING THOSE WHERE LEATHER WORKING IS MAINLY DONE BY MALES (39)	0.56 OF 50	130	DRIFT TOWARD BEING THOSE WHERE LEATHER WORKING IS MAINLY DONE BY FEMALES (45)	0.68 OF 34	28 11 22 23 XSQ= 3.65 PHI= 0.208 XP = 0.0561
132	DRIFT TOWARD BEING THOSE WHERE ECONOMIC EXCHANGE INVOLVES THE USE OF MONEY (37) JMH	0.77 OF 39	132	DRIFT TOWARD BEING THOSE WHERE ECONOMIC EXCHANGE DOES NOT INVOLVE THE USE OF MONEY (17) JMH	0.53 OF 15	30 7 9 8 XSQ= 3.30 PHI= 0.247 XP = 0.0692
135	TILT TOWARD BEING THOSE WHERE INDIVIDUAL OWNERSHIP OF ECONOMICALLY SIGNIFICANT PROPERTY IS PRESENT (24) GES	0.76 OF 25	135	TILT TOWARD BEING THOSE WHERE INDIVIDUAL OWNERSHIP OF ECONOMICALLY SIGNIFICANT PROPERTY IS NEGLIGIBLE OR ABSENT (14) GES	0.62 OF 13	19 5 6 8 XSQ= 3.69 PHI= 0.312 EP = 0.0353
144	LEAN TOWARD BEING THOSE WHERE THE RATIO OF RESTITUTIVE TO REPRESSIVE SANCTIONS IS HIGH OR MEDIUM (27) WME	0.65 OF 37	144	LEAN TOWARD BEING THOSE WHERE THE RATIO OF RESTITUTIVE TO REPRESSIVE SANCTIONS IS LOW (25) WME	0.80 OF 15	24 3 13 12 XSQ= 6.90 PHI= 0.364 XP = 0.0086
147	LEAN TOWARD BEING THOSE WHERE CODIFIED LAWS ARE PRESENT (20) LWS	0.80 OF 20	147	LEAN TOWARD BEING THOSE WHERE CODIFIED LAWS ARE UNIMPORTANT OR ABSENT (13) LWS	0.69 OF 13	16 4 4 9 XSQ= 6.07 PHI= 0.429 EP = 0.0096
176	TILT LESS TOWARD BEING THOSE WHERE THE COMMUNITY IS OTHER THAN A CLAN-COMMUNITY OR A COMMUNITY STRUCTURED OR SEGMENTED ON A CLAN BASIS (213)	0.51 OF 221	176	TILT MORE TOWARD BEING THOSE WHERE THE COMMUNITY IS OTHER THAN A CLAN-COMMUNITY OR A COMMUNITY STRUCTURED OR SEGMENTED ON A CLAN BASIS (213)	0.62 OF 161	108 61 113 100 XSQ= 4.12 PHI= 0.104 XP = 0.0424
178	DRIFT LESS TOWARD BEING THOSE WHERE THE COMMUNITY IS OTHER THAN SEGMENTED ON A CLAN BASIS AND NON-EXOGAMOUS (295)	0.74 OF 221	178	DRIFT MORE TOWARD BEING THOSE WHERE THE COMMUNITY IS OTHER THAN SEGMENTED ON A CLAN BASIS AND NON-EXOGAMOUS (295)	0.82 OF 161	58 29 163 132 XSQ= 3.14 PHI= 0.091 XP = 0.0766

183	LEAN MORE TOWARD BEING THOSE 0.91 OF 163 WHERE THE LARGEST NON-COGNATIC KIN GROUP IS SMALLER THAN A MOEITY, I. E., A PHRATRY OR SIB OR LINEAGE (218)	183	LEAN LESS TOWARD BEING THOSE 0.78 OF 89 WHERE THE LARGEST NON-COGNATIC KIN GROUP IS SMALLER THAN A MOEITY, I. E., A PHRATRY OR SIB OR LINEAGE (218)	14 20 149 69 XSQ= 8.35 PHI= -0.182 XP = 0.0038
186	TEND LESS TO BE THOSE 0.55 OF 228 WHERE THE KIN GROUP IS OTHER THAN EXCLUSIVELY PATRILINEAL (250)	186	TEND MORE TO BE THOSE 0.72 OF 172 WHERE THE KIN GROUP IS OTHER THAN EXCLUSIVELY PATRILINEAL (250)	102 48 126 124 XSQ= 11.14 PHI= 0.167 XP = 0.0008
187	DRIFT MORE TOWARD BEING THOSE 0.89 OF 228 WHERE THE KIN GROUP IS OTHER THAN EXCLUSIVELY MATRILINEAL (344)	187	DRIFT LESS TOWARD BEING THOSE 0.82 OF 171 WHERE THE KIN GROUP IS OTHER THAN EXCLUSIVELY MATRILINEAL (344)	25 30 203 141 XSQ= 3.03 PHI= -0.087 XP = 0.0819
188	TEND MORE TO BE THOSE 0.71 OF 228 WHERE THE KIN GROUP IS OTHER THAN EXCLUSIVELY COGNATIC (252)	188	TEND LESS TO BE THOSE 0.52 OF 172 WHERE THE KIN GROUP IS OTHER THAN EXCLUSIVELY COGNATIC (252)	65 83 163 89 XSQ= 15.56 PHI= -0.197 XP = 0.0001
190	LEAN MORE TOWARD BEING THOSE 0.81 OF 159 WHERE THE KIN GROUP IS PATRILINEAL OR DOUBLE-DESCENT, RATHER THAN MATRILINEAL (186)	190	LEAN LESS TOWARD BEING THOSE 0.65 OF 88 WHERE THE KIN GROUP IS PATRILINEAL OR DOUBLE-DESCENT, RATHER THAN MATRILINEAL (186)	129 57 30 31 XSQ= 7.30 PHI= 0.172 XP = 0.0069
192	LEAN MORE TOWARD BEING THOSE 0.78 OF 228 OTHER THAN WHERE THE ONLY KIN GROUP PRESENT IS A KINDRED OR ELSE BILATERAL DESCENT IS INFERRED (289)	192	LEAN LESS TOWARD BEING THOSE 0.65 OF 172 OTHER THAN WHERE THE ONLY KIN GROUP PRESENT IS A KINDRED OR ELSE BILATERAL DESCENT IS INFERRED (289)	51 60 177 112 XSQ= 7.05 PHI= -0.133 XP = 0.0079
196	TEND MORE TO BE THOSE 0.79 OF 180 WHERE INDIVIDUAL RIGHTS IN REAL PROPERTY, AND RULES FOR INHERITANCE, ARE PRESENT (194)	196	TEND LESS TO BE THOSE 0.51 OF 101 WHERE INDIVIDUAL RIGHTS IN REAL PROPERTY, AND RULES FOR INHERITANCE, ARE PRESENT (194)	142 52 38 49 XSQ= 21.47 PHI= 0.276 XP = 0.0000
209	TILT MORE TOWARD BEING THOSE 0.85 OF 194 WHERE MARITAL RESIDENCE IS PATRILOCAL, VIRILOCAL, OR AVUNCULOCAL, RATHER THAN MATRILOCAL OR UXORILOCAL (270)	209	TILT LESS TOWARD BEING THOSE 0.75 OF 140 WHERE MARITAL RESIDENCE IS PATRILOCAL, VIRILOCAL, OR AVUNCULOCAL, RATHER THAN MATRILOCAL OR UXORILOCAL (270)	165 105 29 35 XSQ= 4.67 PHI= 0.118 XP = 0.0306
210	LEAN MORE TOWARD BEING THOSE 0.90 OF 133 WHERE MARITAL RESIDENCE IS PATRILOCAL, RATHER THAN MATRILOCAL (169)	210	LEAN LESS TOWARD BEING THOSE 0.73 OF 67 WHERE MARITAL RESIDENCE IS PATRILOCAL, RATHER THAN MATRILOCAL (169)	120 49 13 18 XSQ= 8.67 PHI= 0.208 XP = 0.0032

262	TEND MORE TO BE THOSE 0.84 OF 228 WHERE WIVES ARE OBTAINED BY MEANS INVOLVING THE PRESENCE OF SOME CONSIDERATION (305)	262	TEND LESS TO BE THOSE 0.68 OF 167 WHERE WIVES ARE OBTAINED BY MEANS INVOLVING THE PRESENCE OF SOME CONSIDERATION (305)	191 114 37 53 XSQ= 12.31 PHI= 0.177 XP = 0.0005
263	LEAN TOWARD BEING THOSE 0.66 OF 228 WHERE WIVES ARE OBTAINED BY RELATIVELY DIFFICULT MEANS, NAMELY BY BRIDE-PRICE, BRIDE-SERVICE, OR EXCHANGING A FEMALE RELATIVE (233)	263	LEAN TOWARD BEING THOSE 0.50 OF 167 WHERE WIVES ARE OBTAINED BY RELATIVELY EASY MEANS, NAMELY BY TOKEN BRIDE-PRICE, GIFT EXCHANGE, ABSENCE OF ANY CONSIDERATION, OR RECEIPT OF DOWRY (162)	150 83 78 84 XSQ= 9.66 PHI= 0.156 XP = 0.0019
278	TILT TOWARD BEING THOSE 0.58 OF 12 WHERE PROPERTY RIGHTS IN WOMEN ARE PRESENT (8) LWS	278	TILT TOWARD BEING THOSE 0.90 OF 10 WHERE PROPERTY RIGHTS IN WOMEN ARE UNIMPORTANT OR ABSENT (14) LWS	7 1 5 9 XSQ= 3.62 PHI= 0.405 EP = 0.0310
299	TILT LESS TOWARD BEING THOSE 0.66 OF 87 WHERE THE POST-PARTUM SEX TABOO LASTS ONE YEAR OR LESS (89)	299	TILT MORE TOWARD BEING THOSE 0.86 OF 37 WHERE THE POST-PARTUM SEX TABOO LASTS ONE YEAR OR LESS (89)	30 5 57 32 XSQ= 4.65 PHI= 0.194 XP = 0.0311
300	DRIFT LESS TOWARD BEING THOSE 0.53 OF 87 WHERE THE POST-PARTUM SEX TABOO LASTS SIX MONTHS OR LESS (73)	300	DRIFT MORE TOWARD BEING THOSE 0.73 OF 37 WHERE THE POST-PARTUM SEX TABOO LASTS SIX MONTHS OR LESS (73)	41 10 46 27 XSQ= 3.54 PHI= 0.169 XP = 0.0599
306	DRIFT TOWARD BEING THOSE 0.58 OF 31 WHERE THE EARLY DEPENDENCE SATISFACTION POTENTIAL IS LOW (24) W-C	306	DRIFT TOWARD BEING THOSE 0.71 OF 21 WHERE THE EARLY DEPENDENCE SATISFACTION POTENTIAL IS HIGH (28) W-C	13 15 18 6 XSQ= 3.28 PHI= -0.251 XP = 0.0703
309	TILT TOWARD BEING THOSE 0.63 OF 32 WHERE ORAL SOCIALIZATION ANXIETY IS HIGH (26) W-C	309	TILT TOWARD BEING THOSE 0.71 OF 21 WHERE ORAL SOCIALIZATION ANXIETY IS LOW (27) W-C	20 6 12 15 XSQ= 4.56 PHI= 0.293 XP = 0.0327
337	DRIFT TOWARD BEING THOSE 0.60 OF 52 WHERE THE CHILD'S INFERRED ANXIETY OVER NON-PERFORMANCE OF RESPONSIBLE BEHAVIOR IS HIGH (38) B-B-C	337	DRIFT TOWARD BEING THOSE 0.67 OF 21 WHERE THE CHILD'S INFERRED ANXIETY OVER NON-PERFORMANCE OF RESPONSIBLE BEHAVIOR IS LOW (35) B-B-C	31 7 21 14 XSQ= 3.15 PHI= 0.208 XP = 0.0757
353	TILT TOWARD BEING THOSE 0.66 OF 50 WHERE THE CHILD'S INFERRED ANXIETY OVER NON-PERFORMANCE OF OBEDIENT BEHAVIOR IS HIGH (42) B-B-C	353	TILT TOWARD BEING THOSE 0.63 OF 24 WHERE THE CHILD-S INFERRED ANXIETY OVER NON-PERFORMANCE OF OBEDIENT BEHAVIOR IS LOW (32) B-B-C	33 9 17 15 XSQ= 4.27 PHI= 0.240 XP = 0.0388

360	TILT TOWARD BEING THOSE WHERE ADOLESCENT PEER GROUPS ARE PRESENT IN A SETTING OF WORK AND PUBLIC GATHERINGS AND LEISURE, OR AT LEAST OF PUBLIC GATHERINGS AND LEISURE (14) JKH	0.52 OF 23	360	TILT TOWARD BEING THOSE WHERE ADOLESCENT PEER GROUPS ARE PRESENT ONLY IN A SETTING OF LEISURE, OR ELSE ARE ABSENT (23) JKH	0.86 OF 14	12 2 11 12 XSQ= 3.82 PHI= 0.321 EP = 0.0355
365	TILT TOWARD BEING THOSE WHERE THE TIME SPENT IN ADOLESCENT PEER GROUP ACTIVITY IS HIGH OR HIGH-MEDIUM (30) JKH	0.79 OF 33	365	TILT TOWARD BEING THOSE WHERE THE TIME SPENT IN ADOLESCENT PEER GROUP ACTIVITY IS LOW-MEDIUM OR LOW (15) JKH	0.67 OF 12	26 4 7 8 XSQ= 6.26 PHI= 0.373 XP = 0.0123
377	TEND LESS TO BE THOSE WHERE MALE GENITAL MUTILATION IS ABSENT (242)	0.68 OF 219	377	TEND MORE TO BE THOSE WHERE MALE GENITAL MUTILATION IS ABSENT (242)	0.88 OF 106	70 13 149 93 XSQ= 13.56 PHI= 0.204 XP = 0.0002
380	DRIFT TOWARD BEING THOSE WHERE SEGREGATION OF GIRLS AT MENARCHE IS PRESENT (35) F-B	0.74 OF 35	380	DRIFT TOWARD BEING THOSE WHERE SEGREGATION OF GIRLS AT MENARCHE IS ABSENT (20) F-B	0.55 OF 20	26 9 9 11 XSQ= 3.54 PHI= 0.254 XP = 0.0600
382	DRIFT TOWARD BEING THOSE WHERE FEMALE INITIATION RITES ARE ABSENT (27) JKB	0.51 OF 43	382	DRIFT TOWARD BEING THOSE WHERE FEMALE INITIATION RITES ARE PRESENT (38) JKB	0.77 OF 22	21 17 22 5 XSQ= 3.75 PHI= -0.240 XP = 0.0529
392	TILT TOWARD BEING THOSE WHERE PREMARITAL SEX RELATIONS ARE STRONGLY PUNISHED AND IN FACT RARE, OR WEAKLY PUNISHED AND IN FACT NOT RARE, OR PUNISHED ONLY IF PREGNANCY RESULTS (112) JTW,EA	0.68 OF 127	392	TILT TOWARD BEING THOSE WHERE PREMARITAL SEX RELATIONS ARE FREELY PERMITTED (67) JTW,EA	0.50 OF 52	86 26 41 26 XSQ= 4.22 PHI= 0.153 XP = 0.0400
403	DRIFT LESS TOWARD BEING THOSE WHERE EXPLANATIONS OF ILLNESS OF AN ANAL NATURE ARE ABSENT (38) W-C	0.51 OF 37	403	DRIFT MORE TOWARD BEING THOSE WHERE EXPLANATIONS OF ILLNESS OF AN ANAL NATURE ARE ABSENT (38) W-C	0.79 OF 24	18 5 19 19 XSQ= 3.68 PHI= 0.246 XP = 0.0549
417	TILT MORE TOWARD BEING THOSE WHERE WARFARE IS PREVALENT (34) LWS	0.93 OF 27	417	TILT LESS TOWARD BEING THOSE WHERE WARFARE IS PREVALENT (34) LWS	0.56 OF 16	25 9 2 7 XSQ= 5.97 PHI= 0.373 XP = 0.0145
426	LEAN TOWARD BEING THOSE WHERE A HIGH GOD IS PRESENT (156) GES,EA	0.67 OF 174	426	LEAN TOWARD BEING THOSE WHERE A HIGH GOD IS ABSENT (104) GES,EA	0.55 OF 86	117 39 57 47 XSQ= 10.60 PHI= 0.202 XP = 0.0011

```
458  TEND LESS TO BE THOSE           0.55 OF 106   458  TEND MORE TO BE THOSE           0.94 OF  65        48     4
     WHERE GAMES, IF PRESENT,                           WHERE GAMES, IF PRESENT,                            58    61
     DO NOT INCLUDE                                     DO NOT INCLUDE                               XSQ=    27.33
     GAMES OF STRATEGY  (119) R-A-B,EA                  GAMES OF STRATEGY  (119) R-A-B,EA            PHI=    0.400
                                                                                                     XP =   0.0000

469  DRIFT MORE TOWARD BEING THOSE  0.87 OF  39    469  DRIFT LESS TOWARD BEING THOSE  0.60 OF  15         34     9
     WHERE CONTACT WITH OTHER CULTURES                  WHERE CONTACT WITH OTHER CULTURES                    5     6
     IS FREQUENT OR REGULAR, RATHER THAN                IS FREQUENT OR REGULAR, RATHER THAN          XSQ=     3.40
     IRREGULAR  (43) JMH                                IRREGULAR  (43) JMH                          PHI=    0.251
                                                                                                     XP =   0.0652

475  DRIFT TOWARD BEING THOSE        0.63 OF  59   475  DRIFT TOWARD BEING THOSE        0.59 OF  27        37    11
     WHERE EXHIBITIONISTIC DANCING                      WHERE EXHIBITIONISTIC DANCING                       22    16
     IS STRONGLY OR MODERATELY                          IS NEGLIGIBLY EMPHASIZED  (38) PES           XSQ=     2.79
     EMPHASIZED  (48) PES                                                                            PHI=    0.180
                                                                                                     XP =   0.0949

477  DRIFT TOWARD BEING THOSE        0.57 OF  23   477  DRIFT TOWARD BEING THOSE        0.82 OF  11        13     2
     WHERE ALCOHOLIC AGGRESSION IS                      WHERE ALCOHOLIC AGGRESSION IS                       10     9
     STRONG  (15) DH                                    MODERATE OR SLIGHT  (19) DH                  XSQ=     3.02
                                                                                                     PHI=    0.298
                                                                                                     EP =   0.0640
```

63 CULTURES
WHERE HUSBANDRY, IF PRESENT,
IS PRINCIPALLY IN THE FORM OF
BOVINE, EQUINE, CAMEL-LIKE, OR DEER-LIKE
ANIMALS, RATHER THAN
PIGS, SHEEP, OR GOATS (152)

63 CULTURES
WHERE HUSBANDRY, IF PRESENT,
IS PRINCIPALLY IN THE FORM OF
PIGS, SHEEP, OR GOATS, RATHER THAN
BOVINE, EQUINE, CAMEL-LIKE, OR DEER-LIKE
ANIMALS (74)

BACKGROUND ON PAGE 77

BOTH SUBJECT AND PREDICATE

152 IN LEFT COLUMN

ABIPON	ABOR	AKHA	ALBANIANS	AMERICANS	AYMARA	BAMBARA	BARABRA	BARI	BEJA
BHIL	BHUIYA	BIRIFOR	BOERS	BRAZILIANS	BULGARIANS	BURUSHO	CADUVEO	CAMBODIANS	CHAGGA
CHENCHU	CHERKESS	CHEYENNE	CHIR-APACHE	CHUKCHEE	COORG	CROW	CZECHS	DARD	DILLING
DOGON	DUTCH	EGYPTIANS	FOX	FUTAJALONKE	GANDA	GARO	GISU	GOAJIRO	GROS VENTRE
HANO	HANUNOO	HAZARA	HEBREWS	HERERO	HUICHOL	HUTSUL	ILA	INCA	INGASSANA
IRAQW	IRISH	JAPANESE	JAVANESE	JEMEZ	KABYLE	KACHIN	KAZAK	KERALA	KHALKA
KHASI	KIKUYU	KISSI	KOHISTANI	KOL	KOREANS	KPE	KUTENAI	LAKHER	LAMET
LANGO	LAPPS	LEPCHA	LHOTA NAGA	LOLO	LOZI	LUO	MACASSARESE	MALAYS	MAM
MANDAN	MARGI	MASAI	MBUNDU	MERINA	MIAO	MIN CHINESE	MINCHIA	MISKITO	MNONG GAR
MONGUOR	MOSSI	NAMA	NANDI	NUER	NURI	NYAKYUSA	NYORO	OKINAWANS	OMAHA
ORAON	PATHAN	PAWNEE	PURUM	REGEIBAT	RIFFIANS	ROMANS	RUNDI	RWALA	SAGADA
SAMOYED	SANDAWE	SANTAL	SARSI	SERBS	SHILLUK	SHLUH	SINHALESE	SIWANS	SOMALI
SONGHAI	SOTHO	SWAZI	SYRIANS	TAGBANUA	TALLENSI	TANALA	TAOS	TARAHUMARA	TEDA
TEHUELCHE	TENDA	TERA	TERENA	TESO	THAI	THONGA	TIGRINYA	TODA	TORAJA
TOTONAC	TRISTAN	TURKANA	TURKMEN	UTE	VENDA	VIETNAMESE	WALLOONS	WICHITA	WOLOF
YAKO	YAKUT								

74 IN RIGHT COLUMN

ALORESE	AMBA	ARAPESH	ARAUCANIANS	ASHANTI	ATAYAL	BAMILEKE	BANDA	BASSERI	BAYA
BEMBA	BUNLAP	CAGABA	CAYAPA	CHORTI	CUNA	ELLICE	ENGA	FANG	FON
GOND	GURE	HAWAIIANS	IBAN	IFUGAO	JIVARO	JUKUN	KAPAUKU	KATAB	KERAKI
KORYAK	KUBA	KURTATCHI	LAU	LESU	MAMBILA	MAMVU	MANUS	MARQUESANS	MARSHALLESE
MATACO	MATAKAM	MENDE	MONGO	MOTA	MZAB	NAVAHO	NDEMBU	NICOBARESE	NUPE
PAIWAN	PALAUANS	PONAPEANS	PUKAPUKA	PURARI	SAMOANS	SENIANG	SIUAI	SUBANUN	TALAMANCA
TENETEHARA	TIMBIRA	TIV	TROBRIAND	TRUKESE	ULAWANS	WANTOAT	WOGEO	WOLEAIANS	YAPESE
YARURO	YOMBE	YORUBA	ZUNI						

174 EXCLUDED BECAUSE IRRELEVANT

---

4 TEND LESS TO BE THOSE
LOCATED OUTSIDE OF
THE CIRCUM-MEDITERRANEAN (355)
0.78 OF 152

4 TEND MORE TO BE THOSE
LOCATED OUTSIDE OF
THE CIRCUM-MEDITERRANEAN (355)
0.99 OF 74

33	1
119	73

XSQ= 14.59
PHI= 0.254
XP = 0.0001

5	TEND LESS TO BE THOSE LOCATED OUTSIDE OF EAST EURASIA (330)	0.69 OF 152	5	TEND MORE TO BE THOSE LOCATED OUTSIDE OF EAST EURASIA (330)	0.95 OF 74	47 4 105 70 XSQ= 17.11 PHI= 0.275 XP = 0.0000
6	TEND MORE TO BE THOSE LOCATED OUTSIDE OF THE INSULAR PACIFIC (330)	0.96 OF 152	6	TEND LESS TO BE THOSE LOCATED OUTSIDE OF THE INSULAR PACIFIC (330)	0.54 OF 74	6 34 146 40 XSQ= 57.42 PHI= -0.504 XP = 0.
8	TILT LESS TOWARD BEING THOSE LOCATED OUTSIDE OF NORTH AMERICA (330)	0.88 OF 152	8	TILT MORE TOWARD BEING THOSE LOCATED OUTSIDE OF NORTH AMERICA (330)	0.97 OF 74	18 2 134 72 XSQ= 4.08 PHI= 0.134 XP = 0.0433
9	TILT MORE TOWARD BEING THOSE LOCATED OUTSIDE OF SOUTH AMERICA (335)	0.94 OF 152	9	TILT LESS TOWARD BEING THOSE LOCATED OUTSIDE OF SOUTH AMERICA (335)	0.85 OF 74	9 11 143 63 XSQ= 3.89 PHI= -0.131 XP = 0.0486
15	TEND TO BE THOSE WHERE THE LATITUDE IS TWENTY DEGREES OR GREATER (183)	0.59 OF 152	15	TEND TO BE THOSE WHERE THE LATITUDE IS LESS THAN TWENTY DEGREES (217)	0.85 OF 74	90 11 62 63 XSQ= 37.82 PHI= 0.409 XP = 0.
16	TEND TO BE THOSE WHERE THE LATITUDE IS TEN DEGREES OR GREATER (277)	0.83 OF 152	16	TEND TO BE THOSE WHERE THE LATITUDE IS LESS THAN TEN DEGREES (123)	0.65 OF 74	126 26 26 48 XSQ= 49.40 PHI= 0.468 XP = 0.
33	TILT LESS TOWARD BEING THOSE WHERE THE NATURAL ENVIRONMENT IS OTHER THAN 'VERY HARSH,' I.E., DESERT, DESERT GRASSES AND SHRUBS, TUNDRA, OR HIGH PLATEAU STEPPE (341) FWM	0.82 OF 152	33	TILT MORE TOWARD BEING THOSE WHERE THE NATURAL ENVIRONMENT IS OTHER THAN 'VERY HARSH,' I.E., DESERT, DESERT GRASSES AND SHRUBS, TUNDRA, OR HIGH PLATEAU STEPPE (341) FWM	0.93 OF 74	28 5 124 69 XSQ= 4.54 PHI= 0.142 XP = 0.0332
36	LEAN LESS TOWARD BEING THOSE WHERE THE NATURAL ENVIRONMENT IS OTHER THAN 'VERY HARSH,' OR SUB-TROPICAL BUSH, OR TEMPERATE GRASSLAND (292) FWM	0.68 OF 152	36	LEAN MORE TOWARD BEING THOSE WHERE THE NATURAL ENVIRONMENT IS OTHER THAN 'VERY HARSH,' OR SUB-TROPICAL BUSH, OR TEMPERATE GRASSLAND (292) FWM	0.88 OF 74	49 9 103 65 XSQ= 9.49 PHI= 0.205 XP = 0.0021
42	TEND TO BE THOSE WHERE THE NATURAL ENVIRONMENT IS OTHER THAN TROPICAL OR SUB-TROPICAL RAIN FOREST, OR MONSOON FOREST (244) FWM	0.72 OF 152	42	TEND TO BE THOSE WHERE THE NATURAL ENVIRONMENT IS TROPICAL OR SUB-TROPICAL RAIN FOREST, OR MONSOON FOREST (156) FWM	0.68 OF 74	42 50 110 24 XSQ= 31.25 PHI= -0.372 XP = 0.

44	LEAN LESS TOWARD BEING THOSE WHERE SETTLEMENTS ARE FIXED (222)	0.72 OF 152	44	LEAN MORE TOWARD BEING THOSE WHERE SETTLEMENTS ARE FIXED (222)	0.89 OF 74	110 66 42 8 XSQ= 7.23 PHI= -0.179 XP = 0.0072
46	LEAN LESS TOWARD BEING THOSE OTHER THAN WHERE SETTLEMENTS ARE NON-FIXED AND MOVEMENT IS NOMADIC (260)	0.81 OF 152	46	LEAN MORE TOWARD BEING THOSE OTHER THAN WHERE SETTLEMENTS ARE NON-FIXED AND MOVEMENT IS NOMADIC (260)	0.97 OF 74	29 2 123 72 XSQ= 9.94 PHI= 0.210 XP = 0.0016
47	DRIFT TOWARD BEING THOSE WHERE, IF SETTLEMENTS ARE NON-FIXED, MOVEMENT IS NOMADIC, RATHER THAN NON-NOMADIC (72)	0.69 OF 42	47	DRIFT TOWARD BEING THOSE WHERE, IF SETTLEMENTS ARE NON-FIXED, MOVEMENT IS NON-NOMADIC, RATHER THAN NOMADIC (38)	0.75 OF 8	29 2 13 6 XSQ= 3.82 PHI= 0.276 XP = 0.0506
48	LEAN TOWARD BEING THOSE WHERE THE FOOD SUPPLY IS NOT SECURE, AND FOOD SHORTAGES ARE FREQUENT OR ANNUAL (41) MGW	0.78 OF 27	48	LEAN TOWARD BEING THOSE WHERE THE FOOD SUPPLY IS SECURE, AND FOOD SHORTAGES ARE RARE OR OCCASIONAL (38) MGW	0.67 OF 24	6 16 21 8 XSQ= 8.50 PHI= -0.408 XP = 0.0036
53	TEND TO BE THOSE WHERE FOOD PRODUCTION IS BY INTENSIVE AGRICULTURE, RATHER THAN BY SIMPLE AGRICULTURE OR INCIPIENT FOOD PRODUCTION (91)	0.63 OF 126	53	TEND TO BE THOSE WHERE FOOD PRODUCTION IS BY SIMPLE AGRICULTURE OR INCIPIENT FOOD PRODUCTION, RATHER THAN BY INTENSIVE AGRICULTURE (147)	0.89 OF 66	79 7 47 59 XSQ= 45.45 PHI= 0.487 XP = 0.
55	TEND TO BE THOSE WHERE FOOD PRODUCTION IS BY INTENSIVE AGRICULTURE, RATHER THAN BY SIMPLE AGRICULTURE (91)	0.69 OF 115	55	TEND TO BE THOSE WHERE FOOD PRODUCTION IS BY SIMPLE AGRICULTURE, RATHER THAN BY INTENSIVE AGRICULTURE (101)	0.89 OF 62	79 7 36 55 XSQ= 50.87 PHI= 0.536 XP = 0.
56	TILT LESS TOWARD BEING THOSE WHERE FOOD PRODUCTION IS BY SIMPLE AGRICULTURE, RATHER THAN BY INCIPIENT FOOD PRODUCTION (101)	0.77 OF 47	56	TILT MORE TOWARD BEING THOSE WHERE FOOD PRODUCTION IS BY SIMPLE AGRICULTURE, RATHER THAN BY INCIPIENT FOOD PRODUCTION (101)	0.93 OF 59	36 55 11 4 XSQ= 4.66 PHI= -0.210 XP = 0.0308
71	TEND TO BE THOSE WHERE METAL WORKING IS PRESENT (98)	0.71 OF 97	71	TEND TO BE THOSE WHERE METAL WORKING IS ABSENT (153)	0.64 OF 56	69 20 28 36 XSQ= 16.88 PHI= 0.332 XP = 0.0000
73	DRIFT TOWARD BEING THOSE WHERE WEAVING IS PRESENT (118)	0.60 OF 96	73	DRIFT TOWARD BEING THOSE WHERE WEAVING IS ABSENT (130)	0.56 OF 57	58 25 38 32 XSQ= 3.31 PHI= 0.147 XP = 0.0688

74	TEND MORE TO BE THOSE WHERE POTTERY IS PRESENT (145)	0.80 OF 87	74	TEND LESS TO BE THOSE WHERE POTTERY IS PRESENT (145)	0.53 OF 55	70 29 17 26 XSQ= 11.00 PHI= 0.278 XP = 0.0009
81	DRIFT TOWARD BEING THOSE WHERE A CITY OR TOWN IS PRESENT, OR THE AVERAGE COMMUNITY SIZE IS 200 OR GREATER (89)	0.54 OF 105	81	DRIFT TOWARD BEING THOSE WHERE NO CITY OR TOWN IS PRESENT, AND THE AVERAGE COMMUNITY SIZE IS SMALLER THAN 200 (135)	0.63 OF 49	57 18 48 31 XSQ= 3.45 PHI= 0.150 XP = 0.0634
86	TEND TO BE THOSE WHERE THE LEVEL OF POLITICAL INTEGRATION IS THE LARGE STATE, THE LITTLE STATE, OR THE MINIMAL STATE (148) GPM	0.68 OF 114	86	TEND TO BE THOSE WHERE THE LEVEL OF POLITICAL INTEGRATION IS THE AUTONOMOUS COMMUNITY, OR THE FAMILY (156) GPM	0.60 OF 57	78 23 36 34 XSQ= 11.25 PHI= 0.256 XP = 0.0008
89	TILT TOWARD BEING THOSE WHERE, IF A NON-HEREDITARY HEADMANSHIP IS PRESENT, SUCCESSION IS BY CONSENSUS (63)	0.65 OF 49	89	TILT TOWARD BEING THOSE WHERE, IF A NON-HEREDITARY HEADMANSHIP IS PRESENT, SUCCESSION IS BY MEANS OTHER THAN CONSENSUS (43)	0.68 OF 19	32 6 17 13 XSQ= 5.02 PHI= 0.272 XP = 0.0250
90	TILT MORE TOWARD BEING THOSE WHERE, IF A HEREDITARY HEADMANSHIP IS PRESENT, SUCCESSION IS PATRILINEAL, RATHER THAN MATRILINEAL (127)	0.87 OF 52	90	TILT LESS TOWARD BEING THOSE WHERE, IF A HEREDITARY HEADMANSHIP IS PRESENT, SUCCESSION IS PATRILINEAL, RATHER THAN MATRILINEAL (127)	0.67 OF 36	45 24 7 12 XSQ= 3.86 PHI= 0.209 XP = 0.0495
96	TEND TO BE THOSE WHERE THE HIERARCHY OF NATIONAL JURISDICTION HAS FOUR, THREE, TWO OR ONE LEVEL (174) GES,EA	0.72 OF 149	96	TEND TO BE THOSE WHERE THE HIERARCHY OF NATIONAL JURISDICTION HAS NO LEVELS (156) GES,EA	0.57 OF 74	108 32 41 42 XSQ= 16.86 PHI= 0.275 XP = 0.0000
102	LEAN MORE TOWARD BEING THOSE WHERE CLASS STRATIFICATION IS PRESENT (203)	0.71 OF 146	102	LEAN LESS TOWARD BEING THOSE WHERE CLASS STRATIFICATION IS PRESENT (203)	0.51 OF 72	104 37 42 35 XSQ= 7.47 PHI= 0.185 XP = 0.0063
107	LEAN LESS TOWARD BEING THOSE WHERE CLASS STRATIFICATION, IF PRESENT, IS BASED ON SOMETHING OTHER THAN OCCUPATIONAL STATUS (160)	0.68 OF 104	107	LEAN MORE TOWARD BEING THOSE WHERE CLASS STRATIFICATION, IF PRESENT, IS BASED ON SOMETHING OTHER THAN OCCUPATIONAL STATUS (160)	0.95 OF 37	33 2 71 35 XSQ= 8.77 PHI= 0.249 XP = 0.0031
108	TILT TOWARD BEING THOSE WHERE CLASS STRATIFICATION, IF PRESENT, IS BASED ON SOMETHING OTHER THAN A HEREDITARY ARISTOCRACY (129)	0.72 OF 104	108	TILT TOWARD BEING THOSE WHERE CLASS STRATIFICATION, IF PRESENT, IS BASED ON A HEREDITARY ARISTOCRACY (74)	0.51 OF 37	29 19 75 18 XSQ= 5.69 PHI= -0.201 XP = 0.0171

109 TILT LESS TOWARD BEING THOSE 0.74 OF 133 WHERE CASTES ARE ABSENT (317)	109 TILT MORE TOWARD BEING THOSE 0.90 OF 72 WHERE CASTES ARE ABSENT (317)	34 7 99 65 XSQ= 6.37 PHI= 0.176 XP = 0.0116
110 DRIFT TOWARD BEING THOSE 0.54 OF 147 WHERE SLAVERY IS PRESENT (163)	110 DRIFT TOWARD BEING THOSE 0.60 OF 72 WHERE SLAVERY IS ABSENT (218)	80 29 67 43 XSQ= 3.32 PHI= 0.123 XP = 0.0683
118 LEAN TOWARD BEING THOSE 0.77 OF 22 WHERE THE PERCENTAGE OF OCCUPATIONS THAT ARE SPECIALIZED IS HIGH OR MEDIUM (24) WME	118 LEAN TOWARD BEING THOSE 0.83 OF 12 WHERE THE PERCENTAGE OF OCCUPATIONS THAT ARE SPECIALIZED IS LOW (25) WME	17 2 5 10 XSQ= 9.24 PHI= 0.521 EP = 0.0011
127 DRIFT TOWARD BEING THOSE 0.61 OF 28 WHERE THE FEMALES' CONTRIBUTION TO SUBSISTENCE IS LOW (32) JKB	127 DRIFT TOWARD BEING THOSE 0.73 OF 15 WHERE THE FEMALES' CONTRIBUTION TO SUBSISTENCE IS HIGH (33) JKB	11 11 17 4 XSQ= 3.27 PHI= -0.276 XP = 0.0705
131 DRIFT LESS TOWARD BEING THOSE 0.82 OF 61 WHERE THE CONSTRUCTION OF PERMANENT HOUSES OR THE ERECTION OF TEMPORARY DWELLINGS IS MAINLY DONE BY MALES (136)	131 DRIFT MORE TOWARD BEING THOSE 0.97 OF 37 WHERE THE CONSTRUCTION OF PERMANENT HOUSES OR THE ERECTION OF TEMPORARY DWELLINGS IS MAINLY DONE BY MALES (136)	50 36 11 1 XSQ= 3.71 PHI= -0.195 XP = 0.0540
133 DRIFT TOWARD BEING THOSE 0.62 OF 13 WHERE CONTRACTED DEBTS ARE MODERATELY PRESENT OR ABSENT (17) GES	133 DRIFT TOWARD BEING THOSE 0.78 OF 9 WHERE CONTRACTED DEBTS ARE SIGNIFICANTLY PRESENT (17) GES	5 7 8 2 XSQ= 1.92 PHI= -0.295 EP = 0.0991
138 DRIFT TOWARD BEING THOSE 0.83 OF 12 WHERE SUPERORDINATE JUSTICE IS PRESENT (22) BBW	138 DRIFT TOWARD BEING THOSE 0.55 OF 11 WHERE SUPERORDINATE JUSTICE IS ABSENT (18) BBW	10 5 2 6 XSQ= 2.15 PHI= 0.306 EP = 0.0894
176 TEND TO BE THOSE 0.61 OF 146 WHERE THE COMMUNITY IS OTHER THAN A CLAN-COMMUNITY OR A COMMUNITY STRUCTURED OR SEGMENTED ON A CLAN BASIS (213)	176 TEND TO BE THOSE 0.67 OF 73 WHERE THE COMMUNITY IS A CLAN-COMMUNITY OR A COMMUNITY STRUCTURED OR SEGMENTED ON A CLAN BASIS (169)	57 49 89 24 XSQ= 14.26 PHI= -0.255 XP = 0.0002
178 TEND MORE TO BE THOSE 0.81 OF 146 WHERE THE COMMUNITY IS OTHER THAN SEGMENTED ON A CLAN BASIS AND NON-EXOGAMOUS (295)	178 TEND LESS TO BE THOSE 0.59 OF 73 WHERE THE COMMUNITY IS OTHER THAN SEGMENTED ON A CLAN BASIS AND NON-EXOGAMOUS (295)	28 30 118 43 XSQ= 10.91 PHI= -0.223 XP = 0.0010

182	TILT LESS TOWARD BEING THOSE OTHER THAN WHERE THE COMMUNITY IS STRUCTURED ON A NON-CLAN BASIS AND AGAMOUS (256)	0.63 OF 146	182	TILT MORE TOWARD BEING THOSE OTHER THAN WHERE THE COMMUNITY IS STRUCTURED ON A NON-CLAN BASIS AND AGAMOUS (256)	0.81 OF 73	54 14 92 59 XSQ= 6.40 PHI= 0.171 XP = 0.0114
183	TILT MORE TOWARD BEING THOSE WHERE THE LARGEST NON-COGNATIC KIN GROUP IS SMALLER THAN A MOEITY, I. E., A PHRATRY OR SIB OR LINEAGE (218)	0.95 OF 108	183	TILT LESS TOWARD BEING THOSE WHERE THE LARGEST NON-COGNATIC KIN GROUP IS SMALLER THAN A MOEITY, I. E., A PHRATRY OR SIB OR LINEAGE (218)	0.83 OF 53	5 9 103 44 XSQ= 5.36 PHI= -0.183 XP = 0.0206
184	TILT MORE TOWARD BEING THOSE WHERE THE LARGEST NON-COGNATIC KIN GROUP IS SMALLER THAN A PHRATRY, I. E. A SIB OR LINEAGE (175)	0.77 OF 108	184	TILT LESS TOWARD BEING THOSE WHERE THE LARGEST NON-COGNATIC KIN GROUP IS SMALLER THAN A PHRATRY, I. E. A SIB OR LINEAGE (175)	0.60 OF 53	25 21 83 32 XSQ= 3.96 PHI= -0.157 XP = 0.0467
186	LEAN TOWARD BEING THOSE WHERE THE KIN GROUP IS EXCLUSIVELY PATRILINEAL (150)	0.51 OF 152	186	LEAN TOWARD BEING THOSE WHERE THE KIN GROUP IS OTHER THAN EXCLUSIVELY PATRILINEAL (250)	0.69 OF 74	77 23 75 51 XSQ= 6.96 PHI= 0.175 XP = 0.0083
187	TILT MORE TOWARD BEING THOSE WHERE THE KIN GROUP IS OTHER THAN EXCLUSIVELY MATRILINEAL (344)	0.93 OF 152	187	TILT LESS TOWARD BEING THOSE WHERE THE KIN GROUP IS OTHER THAN EXCLUSIVELY MATRILINEAL (344)	0.81 OF 74	11 14 141 60 XSQ= 5.77 PHI= -0.160 XP = 0.0163
190	TEND MORE TO BE THOSE WHERE THE KIN GROUP IS PATRILINEAL OR DOUBLE-DESCENT, RATHER THAN MATRILINEAL (186)	0.90 OF 105	190	TEND LESS TO BE THOSE WHERE THE KIN GROUP IS PATRILINEAL OR DOUBLE-DESCENT, RATHER THAN MATRILINEAL (186)	0.63 OF 52	94 33 11 19 XSQ= 13.64 PHI= 0.295 XP = 0.0002
198	TEND MORE TO BE THOSE WHERE RULES FOR THE INHERITANCE OF REAL PROPERTY, IF PRESENT, FAVOR THE MALE HEIR OR LINE, RATHER THAN THE FEMALE (144)	0.95 OF 88	198	TEND LESS TO BE THOSE WHERE RULES FOR THE INHERITANCE OF REAL PROPERTY, IF PRESENT, FAVOR THE MALE HEIR OR LINE, RATHER THAN THE FEMALE (144)	0.69 OF 32	84 22 4 10 XSQ= 13.75 PHI= 0.339 XP = 0.0002
210	DRIFT MORE TOWARD BEING THOSE WHERE MARITAL RESIDENCE IS PATRILOCAL, RATHER THAN MATRILOCAL (169)	0.94 OF 94	210	DRIFT LESS TOWARD BEING THOSE WHERE MARITAL RESIDENCE IS PATRILOCAL, RATHER THAN MATRILOCAL (169)	0.81 OF 37	88 30 6 7 XSQ= 3.37 PHI= 0.160 XP = 0.0664
213	LEAN TOWARD BEING THOSE WHERE FIRST COUSIN MARRIAGE IS PERMITTED (172)	0.52 OF 141	213	LEAN TOWARD BEING THOSE WHERE FIRST COUSIN MARRIAGE IS NOT PERMITTED (198)	0.72 OF 72	73 20 68 52 XSQ= 10.20 PHI= 0.219 XP = 0.0014

221	DRIFT LESS TOWARD BEING THOSE 0.87 OF 141 WHERE MATRILATERAL CROSS-COUSIN MARRIAGE IS NOT PRESCRIBED OR PREFERRED (335)	221	DRIFT MORE TOWARD BEING THOSE 0.96 OF 72 WHERE MATRILATERAL CROSS-COUSIN MARRIAGE IS NOT PRESCRIBED OR PREFERRED (335)	18 3 123 69 XSQ= 3.06 PHI= 0.120 XP = 0.0804
240	LEAN TOWARD BEING THOSE 0.78 OF 87 WHERE THE FAMILY, IF EXTENDED, IS SMALL OR STEM, RATHER THAN LARGE (135)	240	LEAN TOWARD BEING THOSE 0.51 OF 39 WHERE THE FAMILY, IF EXTENDED, IS LARGE, RATHER THAN SMALL OR STEM (78)	19 20 68 19 XSQ= 9.59 PHI= -0.276 XP = 0.0020
300	TILT TOWARD BEING THOSE 0.65 OF 51 WHERE THE POST-PARTUM SEX TABOO LASTS SIX MONTHS OR LESS (73)	300	TILT TOWARD BEING THOSE 0.64 OF 36 WHERE THE POST-PARTUM SEX TABOO LASTS LONGER THAN SIX MONTHS (51)	18 23 33 13 XSQ= 5.83 PHI= -0.259 XP = 0.0158
323	TILT TOWARD BEING THOSE 0.80 OF 25 WHERE THE CONSTANCY OF PRESENCE OF THE INFANT'S NURTURANT AGENT IS LOW (45) B-B-C	323	TILT TOWARD BEING THOSE 0.52 OF 25 WHERE THE CONSTANCY OF PRESENCE OF THE INFANT'S NURTURANT AGENT IS HIGH (29) B-B-C	5 13 20 12 XSQ= 4.25 PHI= -0.292 XP = 0.0392
336	LEAN TOWARD BEING THOSE 0.81 OF 26 WHERE THE TOTAL POSITIVE PRESSURE TOWARD DEVELOPING RESPONSIBLE BEHAVIOR IN THE CHILD IS HIGH (43) B-B-C	336	LEAN TOWARD BEING THOSE 0.62 OF 26 WHERE THE TOTAL POSITIVE PRESSURE TOWARD DEVELOPING RESPONSIBLE BEHAVIOR IN THE CHILD IS LOW (32) B-B-C	21 10 5 16 XSQ= 7.99 PHI= 0.392 XP = 0.0047
337	LEAN TOWARD BEING THOSE 0.81 OF 26 WHERE THE CHILD'S INFERRED ANXIETY OVER NON-PERFORMANCE OF RESPONSIBLE BEHAVIOR IS HIGH (38) B-B-C	337	LEAN TOWARD BEING THOSE 0.62 OF 26 WHERE THE CHILD'S INFERRED ANXIETY OVER NON-PERFORMANCE OF RESPONSIBLE BEHAVIOR IS LOW (35) B-B-C	21 10 5 16 XSQ= 7.99 PHI= 0.392 XP = 0.0047
342	DRIFT TOWARD BEING THOSE 0.72 OF 18 WHERE THE CHILD'S INFERRED ANXIETY OVER PERFORMANCE OF NURTURANT BEHAVIOR IS LOW (28) B-B-C	342	DRIFT TOWARD BEING THOSE 0.67 OF 12 WHERE THE CHILD'S INFERRED ANXIETY OVER PERFORMANCE OF NURTURANT BEHAVIOR IS HIGH (18) B-B-C	5 8 13 4 XSQ= 2.99 PHI= -0.316 EP = 0.0610
347	TILT TOWARD BEING THOSE 0.69 OF 26 WHERE THE CHILD'S INFERRED CONFLICT REGARDING SELF-RELIANT BEHAVIOR IS HIGH (37) B-B-C	347	TILT TOWARD BEING THOSE 0.65 OF 26 WHERE THE CHILD'S INFERRED CONFLICT REGARDING SELF-RELIANT BEHAVIOR IS LOW (39) B-B-C	18 9 8 17 XSQ= 4.93 PHI= 0.308 XP = 0.0264
350	TILT TOWARD BEING THOSE 0.79 OF 24 WHERE THE CHILD'S INFERRED ANXIETY OVER PERFORMANCE OF ACHIEVEMENT BEHAVIOR IS HIGH (34) B-B-C	350	TILT TOWARD BEING THOSE 0.61 OF 18 WHERE THE CHILD'S INFERRED ANXIETY OVER PERFORMANCE OF ACHIEVEMENT BEHAVIOR IS LOW (26) B-B-C	19 7 5 11 XSQ= 5.47 PHI= 0.361 XP = 0.0193

352	LEAN TOWARD BEING THOSE WHERE THE TOTAL POSITIVE PRESSURE TOWARD DEVELOPING OBEDIENT BEHAVIOR IN THE CHILD IS HIGH (44) B-B-C	0.85 OF 27	352	LEAN TOWARD BEING THOSE WHERE THE TOTAL POSITIVE PRESSURE TOWARD DEVELOPING OBEDIENT BEHAVIOR IN THE CHILD IS LOW (28) B-B-C	0.62 OF 21	23 8 4 13 XSQ= 9.49 PHI= 0.445 XP = 0.0021
370	TILT TOWARD BEING THOSE WHERE THE SEGREGATION OF ADOLESCENT BOYS IS ABSENT (148)	0.66 OF 118	370	TILT TOWARD BEING THOSE WHERE THE SEGREGATION OF ADOLESCENT BOYS IS COMPLETE OR PARTIAL (95)	0.53 OF 62	40 33 78 29 XSQ= 5.52 PHI= -0.175 XP = 0.0188
382	TILT TOWARD BEING THOSE WHERE FEMALE INITIATION RITES ARE ABSENT (27) JKB	0.64 OF 28	382	TILT TOWARD BEING THOSE WHERE FEMALE INITIATION RITES ARE PRESENT (38) JKB	0.73 OF 15	10 11 18 4 XSQ= 4.13 PHI= -0.310 XP = 0.0422
391	DRIFT TOWARD BEING THOSE WHERE PREMARITAL SEX RELATIONS ARE STRONGLY PUNISHED AND IN FACT RARE, OR WEAKLY PUNISHED AND IN FACT NOT RARE (89) JTW,EA	0.60 OF 82	391	DRIFT TOWARD BEING THOSE WHERE PREMARITAL SEX RELATIONS ARE PUNISHED ONLY IF PREGNANCY RESULTS, OR FREELY PERMITTED (90) JTW,EA	0.60 OF 45	49 18 33 27 XSQ= 3.79 PHI= 0.173 XP = 0.0515
398	DRIFT TOWARD BEING THOSE WHERE THE INTENSITY OF SEX ANXIETY IS LOW (16) WNS	0.78 OF 9	398	DRIFT TOWARD BEING THOSE WHERE THE INTENSITY OF SEX ANXIETY IS HIGH (16) WNS	0.73 OF 11	2 8 7 3 XSQ= 3.23 PHI= -0.402 EP = 0.0698
405	DRIFT TOWARD BEING THOSE WHERE EXPLANATIONS OF ILLNESS OF A DEPENDENCE NATURE ARE PRESENT (34) W-C	0.67 OF 18	405	DRIFT TOWARD BEING THOSE WHERE EXPLANATIONS OF ILLNESS OF A DEPENDENCE NATURE ARE ABSENT (27) W-C	0.68 OF 19	12 6 6 13 XSQ= 3.26 PHI= 0.297 EP = 0.0502
426	TEND TO BE THOSE WHERE A HIGH GOD IS PRESENT (156) GES,EA	0.77 OF 114	426	TEND TO BE THOSE WHERE A HIGH GOD IS ABSENT (104) GES,EA	0.52 OF 60	88 29 26 31 XSQ= 13.58 PHI= 0.279 XP = 0.0002
427	LEAN TOWARD BEING THOSE WHERE A HIGH GOD, IF PRESENT, IS ACTIVE, RATHER THAN INACTIVE (87) GES,EA	0.68 OF 88	427	LEAN TOWARD BEING THOSE WHERE A HIGH GOD, IF PRESENT, IS INACTIVE, RATHER THAN ACTIVE (69) GES,EA	0.66 OF 29	60 10 28 19 XSQ= 8.95 PHI= 0.277 XP = 0.0028
428	TILT TOWARD BEING THOSE WHERE A HIGH GOD, IF PRESENT AND ACTIVE, SUPPORTS HUMAN MORALITY, RATHER THAN NOT SUPPORTING IT (61) GES,EA	0.80 OF 60	428	TILT TOWARD BEING THOSE WHERE A HIGH GOD, IF PRESENT AND ACTIVE, DOES NOT SUPPORT HUMAN MORALITY, RATHER THAN SUPPORTING IT (26) GES,EA	0.60 OF 10	48 4 12 6 XSQ= 5.24 PHI= 0.274 XP = 0.0221

433	DRIFT LESS TOWARD BEING THOSE WHERE BELIEF IN REINCARNATION IS ABSENT (28) GES	0.67 OF 15	433	IN ALL CASES ARE THOSE WHERE BELIEF IN REINCARNATION IS ABSENT (28) GES	1.00 OF 10	5 0 10 10 XSQ= 2.34 PHI= 0.306 EP = 0.0613
449	LEAN MORE TOWARD BEING THOSE WHERE THE OBSERVATION OF FOOD TABOOS IS MEDIUM OR LOW, RATHER THAN HIGH (61) JRL	0.86 OF 37	449	LEAN LESS TOWARD BEING THOSE WHERE THE OBSERVATION OF FOOD TABOOS IS MEDIUM OR LOW, RATHER THAN HIGH (61) JRL	0.54 OF 26	5 12 32 14 XSQ= 6.68 PHI= -0.326 XP = 0.0097
450	TILT LESS TOWARD BEING THOSE WHERE THE OBSERVATION OF FOOD TABOOS IS HIGH OR MEDIUM, RATHER THAN LOW (60) JRL	0.51 OF 37	450	TILT MORE TOWARD BEING THOSE WHERE THE OBSERVATION OF FOOD TABOOS IS HIGH OR MEDIUM, RATHER THAN LOW (60) JRL	0.85 OF 26	19 22 18 4 XSQ= 6.04 PHI= -0.310 XP = 0.0140
458	LEAN TOWARD BEING THOSE WHERE GAMES, IF PRESENT, INCLUDE GAMES OF STRATEGY (52) R-A-B,EA	0.56 OF 68	458	LEAN TOWARD BEING THOSE WHERE GAMES, IF PRESENT, DO NOT INCLUDE GAMES OF STRATEGY (119) R-A-B,EA	0.74 OF 38	38 10 30 28 XSQ= 7.45 PHI= 0.265 XP = 0.0063
459	DRIFT TOWARD BEING THOSE WHERE GAMES, IF PRESENT, INCLUDE GAMES OF CHANCE (82) R-A-B,EA	0.53 OF 68	459	DRIFT TOWARD BEING THOSE WHERE GAMES, IF PRESENT, DO NOT INCLUDE GAMES OF CHANCE (89) R-A-B,EA	0.66 OF 38	36 13 32 25 XSQ= 2.73 PHI= 0.160 XP = 0.0986
460	LEAN TOWARD BEING THOSE WHERE GAMES, IF PRESENT, ARE NOT LIMITED TO GAMES OF SKILL ONLY (104) R-A-B,EA	0.76 OF 68	460	LEAN TOWARD BEING THOSE WHERE GAMES, IF PRESENT, ARE LIMITED TO GAMES OF SKILL ONLY (67) R-A-B,EA	0.55 OF 38	16 21 52 17 XSQ= 9.45 PHI= -0.299 XP = 0.0021
468	LEAN TOWARD BEING THOSE WHERE CONTACT WITH OTHER CULTURES IS FREQUENT, RATHER THAN REGULAR OR IRREGULAR (17) JMH	0.57 OF 23	468	LEAN TOWARD BEING THOSE WHERE CONTACT WITH OTHER CULTURES IS REGULAR OR IRREGULAR, RATHER THAN FREQUENT (37) JMH	0.88 OF 16	13 2 10 14 XSQ= 5.98 PHI= 0.392 EP = 0.0077

64 CULTURES WHERE HUSBANDRY IN BOVINE ANIMALS, AS THE PRINCIPAL FCRM OF FUSBANDRY, IS PRESENT (120)	64 CULTURES WHERE HUSBANDRY IN BOVINE ANIMALS, AS THE PRINCIPAL FORM OF HUSBANDRY, IS ABSENT (280)

BACKGROUND ON PAGE 77 — SUBJECT ONLY

120 IN LEFT CCLUMN

ABOR	AKHA	ALBANIANS	AMERICANS	BAMBARA	BARABRA	BARI	BHIL	BHUIYA	BIRIFOR
BOERS	BRAZILIANS	BULGARIANS	BURUSHO	CAMBODIANS	CHAGGA	CHENCHU	CHERKESS	COORG	CZECHS
DARD	DILLING	DOGON	DUTCH	EGYPTIANS	FUTAJALONKE	GANDA	GARO	GISU	GOAJIRO
HANO	HANUNCO	HAZARA	HEBREWS	HERERO	HUICHOL	HUTSUL	ILA	INGASSANA	IRAQW
IRISH	JAPANESE	JAVANESE	KABYLE	KACHIN	KERALA	KHASI	KIKUYU	KISSI	KOHISTANI
KOL	KOREANS	KPE	LAKHER	LAMET	LANGO	LEPCHA	LHCTA NAGA	LOLC	LOZI
LUO	MACASSARESE	MALAYS	MARGI	MASAI	MBUNDU	MERINA	MIAO	MIN CHINESE	MINCHIA
MISKITO	MNCNG GAR	MONGUOR	MOSSI	NAMA	NANDI	NUER	NURI	NYAKYUSA	NYORO
OKINAWANS	CRACN	PATHAN	PURUM	RIFFIANS	ROMANS	RUNDI	SAGADA	SANCAWE	SANTAL
SERBS	SHILLUK	SHLUH	SINHALESE	SIWANS	SONGHAI	SOTHO	SWAZI	SYRIANS	TAGBANUA
TALLENSI	TANALA	TARAHUMARA	TENCA	TERENA	TESO	THAI	THCNGA	TIGRINYA	TODA
TORAJA	TRISTAN	TURKANA	TURKMEN	VENDA	VIETNAMESE	WALLOONS	WOLOF	YAKO	YAKUT

280 IN RIGHT CCLUMN

	Present (120)		Absent (280)		
3	TEND LESS TC BE THCSE LOCATED CUTSIDE CF AFRICA (320)	0.67 OF 120	TEND MORE TO BE THOSE LOCATED OUTSIDE OF AFRICA (320)	0.85 OF 280	39 41 81 239 XSQ= 15.64 PHI= 0.198 XP = 0.0001
4	TEND LESS TO BE THCSE LOCATED OUTSIDE OF THE CIRCUM-MEDITERRANEAN (355)	0.78 OF 120	TEND MORE TO BE THOSE LOCATED OUTSIDE OF THE CIRCUM-MEDITERRANEAN (355)	0.93 CF 280	26 19 94 261 XSQ= 17.17 PHI= 0.207 XP = 0.0000
5	TEND LESS TO BE THCSE LOCATED CUTSIDE OF EAST EURASIA (330)	0.64 OF 120	TEND MORE TO BE THOSE LOCATED OUTSIDE OF EAST EURASIA (330)	0.90 OF 280	43 27 77 253 XSQ= 38.12 PHI= 0.309 XP = 0.
6	TEND MORE TO BE THCSE LOCATED OUTSIDE OF THE INSULAR PACIFIC (330)	0.95 OF 120	TEND LESS TO BE THOSE LOCATED OUTSIDE OF THE INSULAR PACIFIC (330)	0.77 CF 280	6 64 114 216 XSQ= 17.34 PHI= -0.208 XP = 0.0000

8	TEND MORE TO BE THOSE LOCATED OUTSIDE OF NORTH AMERICA (330)	0.97 OF 120	8	TEND LESS TO BE THOSE LOCATED OUTSIDE OF NORTH AMERICA (330)	0.76 OF 280	3 67 117 213 XSQ= 25.25 PHI= -0.251 XP = 0.0000
9	TEND MORE TO BE THOSE LOCATED OUTSIDE OF SOUTH AMERICA (335)	0.97 OF 120	9	TEND LESS TO BE THOSE LOCATED OUTSIDE OF SOUTH AMERICA (335)	0.78 OF 280	3 62 117 218 XSQ= 22.39 PHI= -0.237 XP = 0.0000
15	DRIFT TOWARD BEING THOSE WHERE THE LATITUDE IS TWENTY DEGREES OR GREATER (183)	0.52 OF 120	15	DRIFT TOWARD BEING THOSE WHERE THE LATITUDE IS LESS THAN TWENTY DEGREES (217)	0.57 OF 280	63 120 57 160 XSQ= 2.77 PHI= 0.083 XP = 0.0960
36	DRIFT MORE TOWARD BEING THOSE WHERE THE NATURAL ENVIRONMENT IS OTHER THAN 'VERY HARSH,' OR SUB-TROPICAL BUSH, OR TEMPERATE GRASSLAND (292) FWM	0.79 OF 120	36	DRIFT LESS TOWARD BEING THOSE WHERE THE NATURAL ENVIRONMENT IS OTHER THAN 'VERY HARSH,' OR SUB-TROPICAL BUSH, OR TEMPERATE GRASSLAND (292) FWM	0.70 OF 280	25 83 95 197 XSQ= 2.88 PHI= -0.085 XP = 0.0899
44	TEND MORE TO BE THOSE WHERE SETTLEMENTS ARE FIXED (222)	0.85 OF 120	44	TEND LESS TO BE THOSE WHERE SETTLEMENTS ARE FIXED (222)	0.57 OF 212	102 120 18 92 XSQ= 26.62 PHI= 0.283 XP = 0.0000
46	TEND MORE TO BE THOSE OTHER THAN WHERE SETTLEMENTS ARE NON-FIXED AND MOVEMENT IS NOMADIC (260)	0.93 OF 120	46	TEND LESS TO BE THOSE OTHER THAN WHERE SETTLEMENTS ARE NON-FIXED AND MOVEMENT IS NOMADIC (260)	0.70 OF 212	8 64 112 148 XSQ= 23.60 PHI= -0.267 XP = 0.0000
47	DRIFT TOWARD BEING THOSE WHERE, IF SETTLEMENTS ARE NON-FIXED, MOVEMENT IS NON-NOMADIC, RATHER THAN NOMADIC (38)	0.56 OF 18	47	DRIFT TOWARD BEING THOSE WHERE, IF SETTLEMENTS ARE NON-FIXED, MOVEMENT IS NOMADIC, RATHER THAN NON-NOMADIC (72)	0.70 OF 92	8 64 10 28 XSQ= 3.16 PHI= -0.170 XP = 0.0753
48	TILT TOWARD BEING THOSE WHERE THE FOOD SUPPLY IS NOT SECURE, AND FOOD SHORTAGES ARE FREQUENT OR ANNUAL (41) MGW	0.75 OF 20	48	TILT TOWARD BEING THOSE WHERE THE FOOD SUPPLY IS SECURE, AND FOOD SHORTAGES ARE RARE OR OCCASIONAL (38) MGW	0.56 OF 59	5 33 15 26 XSQ= 4.55 PHI= -0.240 XP = 0.0329
51	TEND MORE TO BE THOSE WHERE SUBSISTENCE IS PRIMARILY BY FOOD PRODUCTION -- I. E., AGRICULTURE OR HUSBANDRY -- RATHER THAN BY GATHERING (253)	0.92 OF 120	51	TEND LESS TO BE THOSE WHERE SUBSISTENCE IS PRIMARILY BY FOOD PRODUCTION -- I. E., AGRICULTURE OR HUSBANDRY -- RATHER THAN BY GATHERING (253)	0.51 OF 280	110 143 10 137 XSQ= 57.82 PHI= 0.380 XP = 0.

53	TEND TO BE THOSE WHERE FOOD PRODUCTION IS BY INTENSIVE AGRICULTURE, RATHER THAN BY SIMPLE AGRICULTURE OR INCIPIENT FOOD PRODUCTION (91)	0.65 OF 112	53	TEND TO BE THOSE WHERE FOOD PRODUCTION IS BY SIMPLE AGRICULTURE OR INCIPIENT FOOD PRODUCTION, RATHER THAN BY INTENSIVE AGRICULTURE (147)	0.86 OF 126	73 18 39 108 XSQ= 62.89 PHI= 0.514 XP = 0.
55	TEND TO BE THOSE WHERE FOOD PRODUCTION IS BY INTENSIVE AGRICULTURE, RATHER THAN BY SIMPLE AGRICULTURE (91)	0.70 OF 104	55	TEND TO BE THOSE WHERE FOOD PRODUCTION IS BY SIMPLE AGRICULTURE, RATHER THAN BY INTENSIVE AGRICULTURE (101)	0.80 OF 88	73 18 31 70 XSQ= 45.32 PHI= 0.486 XP = 0.
71	TEND TO BE THOSE WHERE METAL WORKING IS PRESENT (98)	0.82 OF 73	71	TEND TO BE THOSE WHERE METAL WORKING IS ABSENT (153)	0.79 OF 178	60 38 13 140 XSQ= 77.99 PHI= 0.557 XP = 0.
73	TEND TO BE THOSE WHERE WEAVING IS PRESENT (118)	0.67 OF 72	73	TEND TO BE THOSE WHERE WEAVING IS ABSENT (130)	0.60 OF 176	48 70 24 106 XSQ= 13.76 PHI= 0.236 XP = 0.0002
74	TEND MORE TO BE THOSE WHERE POTTERY IS PRESENT (145)	0.83 OF 66	74	TEND LESS TO BE THOSE WHERE POTTERY IS PRESENT (145)	0.52 OF 172	55 90 11 82 XSQ= 17.98 PHI= 0.275 XP = 0.0000
81	TEND TO BE THOSE WHERE A CITY OR TOWN IS PRESENT, OR THE AVERAGE COMMUNITY SIZE IS 200 OR GREATER (89)	0.57 OF 89	81	TEND TO BE THOSE WHERE NO CITY OR TOWN IS PRESENT, AND THE AVERAGE COMMUNITY SIZE IS SMALLER THAN 200 (135)	0.72 OF 135	51 38 38 97 XSQ= 17.84 PHI= 0.282 XP = 0.0000
86	TEND TO BE THOSE WHERE THE LEVEL OF POLITICAL INTEGRATION IS THE LARGE STATE, THE LITTLE STATE, OR THE MINIMAL STATE (148) GPM	0.70 OF 87	86	TEND TO BE THOSE WHERE THE LEVEL OF POLITICAL INTEGRATION IS THE AUTONOMOUS COMMUNITY, OR THE FAMILY (156) GPM	0.60 OF 217	61 87 26 130 XSQ= 21.22 PHI= 0.264 XP = 0.0000
89	TILT MORE TOWARD BEING THOSE WHERE, IF A NON-HEREDITARY HEADMANSHIP IS PRESENT, SUCCESSION IS BY CONSENSUS (63)	0.74 OF 35	89	TILT LESS TOWARD BEING THOSE WHERE, IF A NON-HEREDITARY HEADMANSHIP IS PRESENT, SUCCESSION IS BY CONSENSUS (63)	0.52 OF 71	26 37 9 34 XSQ= 3.91 PHI= 0.192 XP = 0.0481
91	TILT TOWARD BEING THOSE WHERE SOCIETAL COMPLEXITY IS HIGH (18) F-W	0.69 OF 16	91	TILT TOWARD BEING THOSE WHERE SOCIETAL COMPLEXITY IS LOW (22) F-W	0.71 OF 24	11 7 5 17 XSQ= 4.58 PHI= 0.339 EP = 0.0230

96	TEND TO BE THOSE 0.74 OF 118 WHERE THE HIERARCHY OF NATIONAL JURISDICTION HAS FOUR, THREE, TWO OR ONE LEVEL (174) GES,EA	96	TEND TO BE THOSE 0.59 OF 212 WHERE THE HIERARCHY OF NATIONAL JURISDICTION HAS NO LEVELS (156) GES,EA	87 87 31 125 XSQ= 31.20 PHI= 0.308 XP = 0.
98	DRIFT MORE TOWARD BEING THOSE 0.79 OF 118 WHERE THE HIERARCHY OF LOCAL JURISDICTION HAS FOUR OR THREE LEVELS (238) GES,EA	98	DRIFT LESS TOWARD BEING THOSE 0.68 OF 213 WHERE THE HIERARCHY OF LOCAL JURISDICTION HAS FOUR OR THREE LEVELS (238) GES,EA	93 145 25 68 XSQ= 3.82 PHI= 0.107 XP = 0.0507
100	TEND MORE TO BE THOSE 0.93 OF 118 WHERE HIERARCHIES ARE MORE COMPLEX THAN THE 'SIMPLEST,' I. E., MORE COMPLEX THAN TWO LOCAL LEVELS WITH NO NATIONAL LEVELS (267) GES,EA	100	TEND LESS TO BE THOSE 0.74 OF 212 WHERE HIERARCHIES ARE MORE COMPLEX THAN THE 'SIMPLEST,' I. E., MORE COMPLEX THAN TWO LOCAL LEVELS WITH NO NATIONAL LEVELS (267) GES,EA	110 157 8 55 XSQ= 16.80 PHI= 0.226 XP = 0.0000
102	TEND TO BE THOSE 0.78 OF 116 WHERE CLASS STRATIFICATION IS PRESENT (203)	102	TEND TO BE THOSE 0.58 OF 267 WHERE CLASS STRATIFICATION IS ABSENT (180)	90 113 26 154 XSQ= 38.97 PHI= 0.319 XP = 0.
107	TEND LESS TO BE THOSE 0.66 OF 90 WHERE CLASS STRATIFICATION, IF PRESENT, IS BASED ON SOMETHING OTHER THAN OCCUPATIONAL STATUS (160)	107	TEND MORE TO BE THOSE 0.89 OF 113 WHERE CLASS STRATIFICATION, IF PRESENT, IS BASED ON SOMETHING OTHER THAN OCCUPATIONAL STATUS (160)	31 12 59 101 XSQ= 15.64 PHI= 0.278 XP = 0.0001
108	TILT MORE TOWARD BEING THOSE 0.73 OF 90 WHERE CLASS STRATIFICATION, IF PRESENT, IS BASED ON SOMETHING OTHER THAN A HEREDITARY ARISTOCRACY (129)	108	TILT LESS TOWARD BEING THOSE 0.56 OF 113 WHERE CLASS STRATIFICATION, IF PRESENT, IS BASED ON SOMETHING OTHER THAN A HEREDITARY ARISTOCRACY (129)	24 50 66 63 XSQ= 5.95 PHI= -0.171 XP = 0.0147
109	TEND LESS TO BE THOSE 0.71 OF 103 WHERE CASTES ARE ABSENT (317)	109	TEND MORE TO BE THOSE 0.92 OF 265 WHERE CASTES ARE ABSENT (317)	30 21 73 244 XSQ= 26.18 PHI= 0.267 XP = 0.0000
110	TEND TO BE THOSE 0.57 OF 115 WHERE SLAVERY IS PRESENT (163)	110	TEND TO BE THOSE 0.63 OF 266 WHERE SLAVERY IS ABSENT (218)	65 98 50 168 XSQ= 11.91 PHI= 0.177 XP = 0.0006
116	DRIFT TOWARD BEING THOSE 0.59 OF 17 WHERE OCCUPATIONAL SPECIALIZATION IS FULL-TIME, WHETHER OR NOT FOR SURPLUS PRODUCTION (20) JMH	116	DRIFT TOWARD BEING THOSE 0.73 OF 37 WHERE OCCUPATIONAL SPECIALIZATION IS PART-TIME ONLY (34) JMH	10 10 7 27 XSQ= 3.78 PHI= 0.265 XP = 0.0519

118	TILT TOWARD BEING THOSE 0.74 OF 19 WHERE THE PERCENTAGE OF OCCUPATIONS THAT ARE SPECIALIZED IS HIGH OR MEDIUM (24) WME	118	TILT TOWARD BEING THOSE 0.67 OF 30 WHERE THE PERCENTAGE OF OCCUPATIONS THAT ARE SPECIALIZED IS LOW (25) WME	14 10 5 20 XSQ= 6.05 PHI= 0.351 XP = 0.0139
130	TEND TO BE THOSE 0.81 OF 26 WHERE LEATHER WORKING IS MAINLY DONE BY MALES (39)	130	TEND TO BE THOSE 0.69 OF 58 WHERE LEATHER WORKING IS MAINLY DONE BY FEMALES (45).	21 18 5 40 XSQ= 15.91 PHI= 0.435 XP = 0.0001
131	IN ALL CASES ARE THOSE 1.00 OF 46 WHERE THE CONSTRUCTION OF PERMANENT HOUSES OR THE ERECTION OF TEMPORARY DWELLINGS IS MAINLY DONE BY MALES (136)	131	LEAN LESS TOWARD BEING THOSE 0.81 OF 111 WHERE THE CONSTRUCTION OF PERMANENT HOUSES OR THE ERECTION OF TEMPORARY DWELLINGS IS MAINLY DONE BY MALES (136)	46 90 0 21 XSQ= 8.48 PHI= 0.232 XP = 0.0036
132	DRIFT MORE TOWARD BEING THOSE 0.88 OF 17 WHERE ECONOMIC EXCHANGE INVOLVES THE USE OF MONEY (37) JMH	132	DRIFT LESS TOWARD BEING THOSE 0.59 OF 37 WHERE ECONOMIC EXCHANGE INVOLVES THE USE OF MONEY (37) JMH	15 22 2 15 XSQ= 3.24 PHI= 0.245 XP = 0.0720
135	DRIFT MORE TOWARD BEING THOSE 0.85 OF 13 WHERE INDIVIDUAL OWNERSHIP OF ECONOMICALLY SIGNIFICANT PROPERTY IS PRESENT (24) GES	135	DRIFT LESS TOWARD BEING THOSE 0.52 OF 25 WHERE INDIVIDUAL OWNERSHIP OF ECONOMICALLY SIGNIFICANT PROPERTY IS PRESENT (24) GES	11 13 2 12 XSQ= 2.63 PHI= 0.263 EP = 0.0773
138	DRIFT TOWARD BEING THOSE 0.88 OF 8 WHERE SUPERORDINATE JUSTICE IS PRESENT (22) BBW	138	DRIFT TOWARD BEING THOSE 0.53 OF 32 WHERE SUPERORDINATE JUSTICE IS ABSENT (18) BBW	7 15 1 17 XSQ= 2.78 PHI= 0.264 EP = 0.0537
183	TEND MORE TO BE THOSE 0.97 OF 91 WHERE THE LARGEST NON-COGNATIC KIN GROUP IS SMALLER THAN A MOEITY, I. E., A PHRATRY OR SIB OR LINEAGE (218)	183	TEND LESS TO BE THOSE 0.81 OF 161 WHERE THE LARGEST NON-COGNATIC KIN GROUP IS SMALLER THAN A MOEITY, I. E., A PHRATRY OR SIB OR LINEAGE (218)	3 31 88 130 XSQ= 11.35 PHI= -0.212 XP = 0.0008
184	LEAN MORE TOWARD BEING THOSE 0.82 OF 91 WHERE THE LARGEST NON-COGNATIC KIN GROUP IS SMALLER THAN A PHRATRY, I. E. A SIB OR LINEAGE (175)	184	LEAN LESS TOWARD BEING THOSE 0.62 OF 161 WHERE THE LARGEST NON-COGNATIC KIN GROUP IS SMALLER THAN A PHRATRY, I. E. A SIB OR LINEAGE (175)	16 61 75 100 XSQ= 10.36 PHI= -0.203 XP = 0.0013
186	TEND TO BE THOSE 0.56 OF 120 WHERE THE KIN GROUP IS EXCLUSIVELY PATRILINEAL (150)	186	TEND TO BE THOSE 0.70 OF 280 WHERE THE KIN GROUP IS OTHER THAN EXCLUSIVELY PATRILINEAL (250)	67 83 53 197 XSQ= 23.48 PHI= 0.242 XP = 0.0000

187	LEAN MORE TOWARD BEING THOSE WHERE THE KIN GROUP IS OTHER THAN EXCLUSIVELY MATRILINEAL (344)	0.94 OF 120	187	LEAN LESS TOWARD BEING THOSE WHERE THE KIN GROUP IS OTHER THAN EXCLUSIVELY MATRILINEAL (344)	0.83 OF 279	7 48 113 231 XSQ= 8.20 PHI= -0.143 XP = 0.0042
188	TEND MORE TO BE THOSE WHERE THE KIN GROUP IS OTHER THAN EXCLUSIVELY COGNATIC (252)	0.76 OF 120	188	TEND LESS TO BE THOSE WHERE THE KIN GROUP IS OTHER THAN EXCLUSIVELY COGNATIC (252)	0.57 OF 280	29 119 91 161 XSQ= 11.34 PHI= -0.168 XP = 0.0008
190	TEND MORE TO BE THOSE WHERE THE KIN GROUP IS PATRILINEAL OR DOUBLE-DESCENT, RATHER THAN MATRILINEAL (186)	0.92 OF 88	190	TEND LESS TO BE THOSE WHERE THE KIN GROUP IS PATRILINEAL OR DOUBLE-DESCENT, RATHER THAN MATRILINEAL (186)	0.66 OF 159	81 105 7 54 XSQ= 19.23 PHI= 0.279 XP = 0.0000
192	TILT MORE TOWARD BEING THOSE OTHER THAN WHERE THE ONLY KIN GROUP PRESENT IS A KINDRED OR ELSE BILATERAL DESCENT IS INFERRED (289)	0.81 OF 120	192	TILT LESS TOWARD BEING THOSE OTHER THAN WHERE THE ONLY KIN GROUP PRESENT IS A KINDRED OR ELSE BILATERAL DESCENT IS INFERRED (289)	0.69 OF 280	23 88 97 192 XSQ= 5.70 PHI= -0.119 XP = 0.0169
196	TEND MORE TO BE THOSE WHERE INDIVIDUAL RIGHTS IN REAL PROPERTY, AND RULES FOR INHERITANCE, ARE PRESENT (194)	0.88 OF 104	196	TEND LESS TO BE THOSE WHERE INDIVIDUAL RIGHTS IN REAL PROPERTY, AND RULES FOR INHERITANCE, ARE PRESENT (194)	0.58 OF 177	92 102 12 75 XSQ= 27.71 PHI= 0.314 XP = 0.0000
198	LEAN MORE TOWARD BEING THOSE WHERE RULES FOR THE INHERITANCE OF REAL PROPERTY, IF PRESENT, FAVOR THE MALE HEIR OR LINE, RATHER THAN THE FEMALE (144)	0.96 OF 78	198	LEAN LESS TOWARD BEING THOSE WHERE RULES FOR THE INHERITANCE OF REAL PROPERTY, IF PRESENT, FAVOR THE MALE HEIR OR LINE, RATHER THAN THE FEMALE (144)	0.79 OF 87	75 69 3 18 XSQ= 9.04 PHI= 0.234 XP = 0.0026
209	LEAN MORE TOWARD BEING THOSE WHERE MARITAL RESIDENCE IS PATRILOCAL, VIRILOCAL, OR AVUNCULOCAL, RATHER THAN MATRILOCAL OR UXORILOCAL (270)	0.90 OF 104	209	LEAN LESS TOWARD BEING THOSE WHERE MARITAL RESIDENCE IS PATRILOCAL, VIRILOCAL, OR AVUNCULOCAL, RATHER THAN MATRILOCAL OR UXORILOCAL (270)	0.77 OF 230	94 176 10 54 XSQ= 8.01 PHI= 0.155 XP = 0.0046
210	LEAN MORE TOWARD BEING THOSE WHERE MARITAL RESIDENCE IS PATRILOCAL, RATHER THAN MATRILOCAL (169)	0.95 OF 81	210	LEAN LESS TOWARD BEING THOSE WHERE MARITAL RESIDENCE IS PATRILOCAL, RATHER THAN MATRILOCAL (169)	0.77 OF 119	77 92 4 27 XSQ= 10.28 PHI= 0.227 XP = 0.0013
213	LEAN TOWARD BEING THOSE WHERE FIRST COUSIN MARRIAGE IS PERMITTED (172)	0.58 OF 110	213	LEAN TOWARD BEING THOSE WHERE FIRST COUSIN MARRIAGE IS NOT PERMITTED (198)	0.58 OF 260	64 108 46 152 XSQ= 7.95 PHI= 0.147 XP = 0.0048

220	TILT LESS TOWARD BEING THOSE 0.66 OF 110 WHERE FIRST COUSIN MARRIAGE IN SOME FORM OR OTHER IS NOT PRESCRIBED OR PREFERRED (273)	220	TILT MORE TOWARD BEING THOSE 0.77 OF 260 WHERE FIRST COUSIN MARRIAGE IN SOME FORM OR OTHER IS NOT PRESCRIBED OR PREFERRED (273)	37 60 73 200 XSQ= 3.93 PHI= 0.103 XP = 0.0475
221	TILT LESS TOWARD BEING THOSE 0.85 OF 110 WHERE MATRILATERAL CROSS-COUSIN MARRIAGE IS NOT PRESCRIBED OR PREFERRED (335)	221	TILT MORE TOWARD BEING THOSE 0.93 OF 260 WHERE MATRILATERAL CROSS-COUSIN MARRIAGE IS NOT PRESCRIBED OR PREFERRED (335)	17 18 93 242 XSQ= 5.61 PHI= 0.123 XP = 0.0179
240	LEAN MORE TOWARD BEING THOSE 0.78 OF 68 WHERE THE FAMILY, IF EXTENDED, IS SMALL OR STEM, RATHER THAN LARGE (135)	240	LEAN LESS TOWARD BEING THOSE 0.57 OF 145 WHERE THE FAMILY, IF EXTENDED, IS SMALL OR STEM, RATHER THAN LARGE (135)	15 63 53 82 XSQ= 8.23 PHI= -0.197 XP = 0.0041
262	LEAN MORE TOWARD BEING THOSE 0.88 OF 120 WHERE WIVES ARE OBTAINED BY MEANS INVOLVING THE PRESENCE OF SOME CONSIDERATION (305)	262	LEAN LESS TOWARD BEING THOSE 0.73 OF 275 WHERE WIVES ARE OBTAINED BY MEANS INVOLVING THE PRESENCE OF SOME CONSIDERATION (305)	105 200 15 75 XSQ= 9.54 PHI= 0.155 XP = 0.0020
263	TILT MORE TOWARD BEING THOSE 0.67 OF 120 WHERE WIVES ARE OBTAINED BY RELATIVELY DIFFICULT MEANS, NAMELY BY BRIDE-PRICE, BRIDE-SERVICE, OR EXCHANGING A FEMALE RELATIVE (233)	263	TILT LESS TOWARD BEING THOSE 0.55 OF 275 WHERE WIVES ARE OBTAINED BY RELATIVELY DIFFICULT MEANS, NAMELY BY BRIDE-PRICE, BRIDE-SERVICE, OR EXCHANGING A FEMALE RELATIVE (233)	81 152 39 123 XSQ= 4.67 PHI= 0.109 XP = 0.0307
314	DRIFT LESS TOWARD BEING THOSE 0.56 OF 16 WHERE THE INCIDENCE OF MOTHER-CHILD HOUSEHOLDS IS LOW (61) W-D,S	314	DRIFT MORE TOWARD BEING THOSE 0.81 OF 64 WHERE THE INCIDENCE OF MOTHER-CHILD HOUSEHOLDS IS LOW (61) W-D,S	7 12 9 52 XSQ= 3.14 PHI= 0.198 XP = 0.0762
318	DRIFT TOWARD BEING THOSE 0.65 OF 17 WHERE THE OVERALL INDULGENCE OF THE INFANT IS LOW (31) B-B-C	318	DRIFT TOWARD BEING THOSE 0.63 OF 54 WHERE THE OVERALL INDULGENCE OF THE INFANT IS HIGH (40) B-B-C	6 34 11 20 XSQ= 2.98 PHI= -0.205 XP = 0.0844
336	TILT TOWARD BEING THOSE 0.83 OF 18 WHERE THE TOTAL POSITIVE PRESSURE TOWARD DEVELOPING RESPONSIBLE BEHAVIOR IN THE CHILD IS HIGH (43) B-B-C	336	TILT TOWARD BEING THOSE 0.51 OF 57 WHERE THE TOTAL POSITIVE PRESSURE TOWARD DEVELOPING RESPONSIBLE BEHAVIOR IN THE CHILD IS LOW (32) B-B-C	15 28 3 29 XSQ= 5.22 PHI= 0.264 XP = 0.0223
337	TEND TO BE THOSE 0.89 OF 18 WHERE THE CHILD'S INFERRED ANXIETY OVER NON-PERFORMANCE OF RESPONSIBLE BEHAVIOR IS HIGH (38) B-B-C	337	TEND TO BE THOSE 0.60 OF 55 WHERE THE CHILD'S INFERRED ANXIETY OVER NON-PERFORMANCE OF RESPONSIBLE BEHAVIOR IS LOW (35) B-B-C	16 22 2 33 XSQ= 11.10 PHI= 0.390 XP = 0.0009

339	LEAN TCWARC BEING THOSE WHERE THE CHILD'S INFERREC CONFLICT REGARDING RESPCNSIBLE BEHAVIOR IS HIGH (31) B-B-C	0.72 OF 18	339	LEAN TOWARD BEING THOSE WHERE THE CHILD'S INFERRED CONFLICT REGARDING RESPCNSIBLE BEHAVICR IS LOW (42) B-B-C	0.67 OF 55	13 18 5 37 XSQ= 7.12 PHI= 0.312 XP = 0.0076
346	TILT TCWARC BEING THCSE WHERE THE CHILD'S INFERREC ANXIETY OVER PERFCRMANCE CF SELF-RELIANT BEHAVIOR IS HIGH (37) B-B-C	0.78 OF 18	346	TILT TOWARD BEING THCSE WHERE THE CHILD'S INFERRED ANXIETY CVER PERFORMANCE OF SELF-RELIANT BEHAVICR IS LOW (39) B-B-C	0.60 CF 58	14 23 4 35 XSQ= 6.54 PHI= 0.293 XP = 0.0106
347	TILT TCWARC BEING THOSE WHERE THE CHILD'S INFERREC CONFLICT REGARDING SELF-RELIANT BEHAVICR IS HIGH (37) B-B-C	0.78 OF 18	347	TILT TOWARD BEING THOSE WHERE THE CHILD'S INFERRED CONFLICT REGARDING SELF-RELIANT BEHAVIOR IS LOW (39) B-B-C	0.60 OF 58	14 23 4 35 XSQ= 6.54 PHI= 0.293 XP = 0.0106
353	TILT TCWARC BEING THCSE WHERE THE CHILD'S INFERREC ANXIETY OVER NCN-PERFCRMANCE CF CBECIENT BEHAVIOR IS HIGH (42) B-B-C	0.84 OF 19	353	TILT TOWARD BEING THCSE WHERE THE CHILD-S INFERRED ANXIETY CVER NON-PERFORMANCE OF OBEDIENT BEHAVIOR IS LOW (32) B-B-C	0.53 OF 55	16 26 3 29 XSQ= 6.42 PHI= 0.294 XP = 0.0113
356	DRIFT TCWARD BEING THCSE WHERE ADCLESCENT PEER GROUPS CR PAIRS ARE PRESENT IN A SETTING CF CCURTSHIP (29) JKH	0.78 OF 18	356	DRIFT TOWARD BEING THOSE WHERE NEITHER ADOLESCENT PEER GRCUPS NOR PAIRS ARE PRESENT IN A SETTING OF COURTSHIP (22) JKH	0.55 CF 33	14 15 4 18 XSQ= 3.73 PHI= 0.270 XP = 0.0534
360	TILT TCWARC BEING THOSE WHERE ADCLESCENT PEER GRCUPS ARE PRESENT IN A SETTING CF WORK AND PUBLIC GATHERINGS AND LEISURE, CR AT LEAST CF PUBLIC GATHERINGS ANC LEISURE (14) JKH	0.62 OF 13	36C	TILT TOWARD BEING THOSE WHERE ADOLESCENT PEER GRCUPS ARE PRESENT ONLY IN A SETTING OF LEISURE, OR ELSE ARE ABSENT (23) JKH	0.75 CF 24	8 6 5 18 XSQ= 3.36 PHI= 0.301 EP = 0.0395
377	LEAN LESS TCWARC BEING THCSE WHERE MALE GENITAL MUTILATION IS ABSENT (242)	0.65 OF 117	377	LEAN MORE TOWARD BEING THOSE WHERE MALE GENITAL MUTILATICN IS ABSENT (242)	0.80 OF 208	41 42 76 166 XSQ= 7.92 PHI= 0.156 XP = 0.0049
382	TILT TCWARC BEING THCSE WHERE FEMALE INITIATICN RITES ARE ABSENT (27) JKB	0.67 OF 18	382	TILT TOWARD BEING THCSE WHERE FEMALE INITIATICN RITES ARE PRESENT (38) JKB	0.68 CF 47	6 32 12 15 XSQ= 5.12 PHI= -0.281 XP = 0.0236
395	DRIFT TCWARD BEING THCSE WHERE BELIEF IN THE UNCLEANNESS CF WOMEN IS PRESENT (18) LWS	0.86 OF 7	395	DRIFT TOWARD BEING THOSE WHERE BELIEF IN THE UNCLEANNESS OF WOMEN IS UNIMPORTANT OR ABSENT (15) LWS	0.54 OF 26	6 12 1 14 XSQ= 2.07 PHI= 0.250 EP = 0.0952

398	TILT TOWARD BEING THOSE 0.88 OF 8 WHERE THE INTENSITY OF SEX ANXIETY IS LOW (16) WNS	398	TILT TOWARD BEING THOSE 0.63 OF 24 WHERE THE INTENSITY OF SEX ANXIETY IS HIGH (16) WNS	1 15 7 9 XSQ= 4.17 PHI= -0.361 EP = 0.0373
424	DRIFT TOWARD BEING THOSE 0.59 OF 17 WHERE RELIGIOUS SPECIALISTS ARE FULL-TIME, RATHER THAN PART-TIME (21) JMH	424	DRIFT TOWARD BEING THOSE 0.70 OF 37 WHERE RELIGIOUS SPECIALISTS ARE PART-TIME, RATHER THAN FULL-TIME (33) JMH	10 11 7 26 XSQ= 3.01 PHI= 0.236 XP = 0.0825
426	TEND TO BE THOSE 0.78 OF 92 WHERE A HIGH GOD IS PRESENT (156) GES,EA	426	TEND TO BE THOSE 0.50 OF 168 WHERE A HIGH GOD IS ABSENT (104) GES,EA	72 84 20 84 XSQ= 18.62 PHI= 0.268 XP = 0.0000
427	TILT TOWARD BEING THOSE 0.65 OF 72 WHERE A HIGH GOD, IF PRESENT, IS ACTIVE, RATHER THAN INACTIVE (87) GES,EA	427	TILT TOWARD BEING THOSE 0.52 OF 84 WHERE A HIGH GOD, IF PRESENT, IS INACTIVE, RATHER THAN ACTIVE (69) GES,EA	47 40 25 44 XSQ= 4.21 PHI= 0.164 XP = 0.0402
428	DRIFT MORE TOWARD BEING THOSE 0.79 OF 47 WHERE A HIGH GOD, IF PRESENT AND ACTIVE, SUPPORTS HUMAN MORALITY, RATHER THAN NOT SUPPORTING IT (61) GES,EA	428	DRIFT LESS TOWARD BEING THOSE 0.60 OF 40 WHERE A HIGH GOD, IF PRESENT AND ACTIVE, SUPPORTS HUMAN MORALITY, RATHER THAN NOT SUPPORTING IT (61) GES,EA	37 24 10 16 XSQ= 2.78 PHI= 0.179 XP = 0.0956
430	DRIFT TOWARD BEING THOSE 0.62 OF 13 WHERE SUPERNATURAL SANCTIONS FOR MORALITY, HAVING AN EFFECT ON AN INDIVIDUAL'S HEALTH, ARE PRESENT (16) GES	430	DRIFT TOWARD BEING THOSE 0.68 OF 25 WHERE SUPERNATURAL SANCTIONS FOR MORALITY, HAVING AN EFFECT ON AN INDIVIDUAL'S HEALTH, ARE ABSENT OR UNREPORTED (22) GES	8 8 5 17 XSQ= 1.97 PHI= 0.228 EP = 0.0982
444	TILT TOWARD BEING THOSE 0.77 OF 13 WHERE THE USE OF DREAMS TO SEEK AND CONTROL SUPERNATURAL POWERS IS LOW (27) RGD	444	TILT TOWARD BEING THOSE 0.60 OF 42 WHERE THE USE OF DREAMS TO SEEK AND CONTROL SUPERNATURAL POWERS IS HIGH (28) RGD	3 25 10 17 XSQ= 3.92 PHI= -0.267 XP = 0.0477
450	TILT LESS TOWARD BEING THOSE 0.54 OF 28 WHERE THE OBSERVATION OF FOOD TABOOS IS HIGH OR MEDIUM, RATHER THAN LOW (60) JRL	450	TILT MORE TOWARD BEING THOSE 0.78 OF 58 WHERE THE OBSERVATION OF FOOD TABOOS IS HIGH OR MEDIUM, RATHER THAN LOW (60) JRL	15 45 13 13 XSQ= 4.09 PHI= -0.218 XP = 0.0432
458	TEND TO BE THOSE 0.71 OF 49 WHERE GAMES, IF PRESENT, INCLUDE GAMES OF STRATEGY (52) R-A-B,EA	458	TEND TO BE THOSE 0.86 OF 122 WHERE GAMES, IF PRESENT, DO NOT INCLUDE GAMES OF STRATEGY (119) R-A-B,EA	35 17 14 105 XSQ= 51.92 PHI= 0.551 XP = 0.

460	TILT MORE TOWARD BEING THOSE WHERE GAMES, IF PRESENT, ARE NOT LIMITED TO GAMES OF SKILL ONLY (104) R-A-B,EA	0.76 OF 49	460	TILT LESS TOWARD BEING THOSE WHERE GAMES, IF PRESENT, ARE NOT LIMITED TO GAMES OF SKILL ONLY (104) R-A-B,EA	0.55 OF 122	12 55 37 67 XSQ= 5.39 PHI= -0.177 XP = 0.0203
468	TEND TO BE THOSE WHERE CONTACT WITH OTHER CULTURES IS FREQUENT, RATHER THAN REGULAR OR IRREGULAR (17) JMH	0.71 OF 17	468	TEND TO BE THOSE WHERE CONTACT WITH OTHER CULTURES IS REGULAR OR IRREGULAR, RATHER THAN FREQUENT (37) JMH	0.86 OF 37	12 5 5 32 XSQ= 15.04 PHI= 0.528 XP = 0.0001

65 CULTURES WHERE BOVINE ANIMALS, IF PRESENT, ARE MILKED (79)

65 CULTURES WHERE BOVINE ANIMALS, IF PRESENT, ARE NOT MILKED (41)

BACKGROUND ON PAGE 77

SUBJECT ONLY

79 IN LEFT COLUMN

ALBANIANS	AMERICANS	BAMBARA	BARABRA	BARI	BHIL	BOERS	BRAZILIANS	BULGARIANS	BURUSHO
CHAGGA	CHENCHU	CHERKESS	COORG	CZECHS	DARD	DILLING	DUTCH	EGYPTIANS	FUTAJALONKE
GANDA	GISU	GOAJIRO	HAZARA	HEBREWS	HERERO	HUICHOL	HUTSUL	ILA	INGASSANA
IRAQW	IRISH	JAPANESE	KABYLE	KERALA	KIKUYU	KOHISTANI	LANGO	LEPCHA	LOZI
LUO	MASAI	MINCHIA	MISKITO	MONGUOR	NAMA	NANDI	NUER	NURI	NYAKYUSA
NYORO	ORACN	PATHAN	RIFFIANS	ROMANS	RUNDI	SANDAWE	SERBS	SHILLUK	SHLUH
SINHALESE	SIWANS	SONGHAI	SOTHO	SWAZI	SYRIANS	TALLENSI	TANALA	TESO	THONGA
TIGRINYA	TODA	TRISTAN	TURKANA	TURKMEN	VENDA	WALLOONS	WOLOF	YAKUT	

41 IN RIGHT COLUMN

ABOR	AKHA	BHUIYA	BIRIFOR	CAMBODIANS	DOGON	GARO	HANO	HANUNOO	JAVANESE
KACHIN	KHASI	KISSI	KOL	KOREANS	KPE	LAKHER	LAMET	LHOTA NAGA	LOLO
MACASSARESE	MALAYS	MARGI	MBUNDU	MERINA	MIAO	MIN CHINESE	MNONG GAR	MOSSI	OKINAWANS
PURUM	SAGADA	SANTAL	TAGBANUA	TARAHUMARA	TENDA	TERENA	THAI	TORAJA	VIETNAMESE
YAKO									

280 EXCLUDED BECAUSE IRRELEVANT (SEE RIGHT COLUMN, PARAGRAPH 64)

	Left column			Right column		Statistics
4	TEND LESS TO BE THOSE LOCATED OUTSIDE OF THE CIRCUM-MEDITERRANEAN (355)	0.67 OF 79	4	IN ALL CASES ARE THOSE LOCATED OUTSIDE OF THE CIRCUM-MEDITERRANEAN (355)	1.00 OF 41	26 0 53 41 XSQ= 15.34 PHI= 0.358 XP = 0.0001
5	LEAN TOWARD BEING THOSE LOCATED OUTSIDE OF EAST EURASIA (330)	0.75 OF 79	5	LEAN TOWARD BEING THOSE LOCATED IN EAST EURASIA (70)	0.56 OF 41	20 23 59 18 XSQ= 9.82 PHI= -0.286 XP = 0.0017
6	IN ALL CASES ARE THOSE LOCATED OUTSIDE OF THE INSULAR PACIFIC (330)	1.00 OF 79	6	LEAN LESS TOWARD BEING THOSE LOCATED OUTSIDE OF THE INSULAR PACIFIC (330)	0.85 OF 41	0 6 79 35 XSQ= 9.28 PHI= -0.278 XP = 0.0023

13	TILT LESS TOWARD BEING THOSE WHERE THE LATITUDE IS LESS THAN FORTY DEGREES (329)	0.85 OF 79	13	IN ALL CASES ARE THOSE WHERE THE LATITUDE IS LESS THAN FORTY DEGREES (329)	1.00 OF 41	12 0 67 41 XSQ= 5.33 PHI= 0.211 XP = 0.0209
14	TEND LESS TO BE THOSE WHERE THE LATITUDE IS LESS THAN THIRTY DEGREES (281)	0.66 OF 79	14	TEND MORE TO BE THOSE WHERE THE LATITUDE IS LESS THAN THIRTY DEGREES (281)	0.95 OF 41	27 2 52 39 XSQ= 11.10 PHI= 0.304 XP = 0.0009
33	DRIFT LESS TOWARD BEING THOSE WHERE THE NATURAL ENVIRONMENT IS OTHER THAN 'VERY HARSH,' I.E., DESERT, DESERT GRASSES AND SHRUBS, TUNDRA, OR HIGH PLATEAU STEPPE (341) FWM	0.85 OF 79	33	DRIFT MORE TOWARD BEING THOSE WHERE THE NATURAL ENVIRONMENT IS OTHER THAN 'VERY HARSH,' I.E., DESERT, DESERT GRASSES AND SHRUBS, TUNDRA, OR HIGH PLATEAU STEPPE (341) FWM	0.98 OF 41	12 1 67 40 XSQ= 3.32 PHI= 0.166 XP = 0.0685
36	TEND LESS TO BE THOSE WHERE THE NATURAL ENVIRONMENT IS OTHER THAN 'VERY HARSH,' OR SUB-TROPICAL BUSH, OR TEMPERATE GRASSLAND (292) FWM	0.70 OF 79	36	TEND MORE TO BE THOSE WHERE THE NATURAL ENVIRONMENT IS OTHER THAN 'VERY HARSH,' OR SUB-TROPICAL BUSH, OR TEMPERATE GRASSLAND (292) FWM	0.98 OF 41	24 1 55 40 XSQ= 11.14 PHI= 0.305 XP = 0.0008
42	TEND TO BE THOSE WHERE THE NATURAL ENVIRONMENT IS OTHER THAN TROPICAL OR SUB-TROPICAL RAIN FOREST, OR MONSOON FOREST (244) FWM	0.85 OF 79	42	TEND TO BE THOSE WHERE THE NATURAL ENVIRONMENT IS TROPICAL OR SUB-TROPICAL RAIN FOREST, OR MONSOON FOREST (156) FWM	0.71 OF 41	12 29 67 12 XSQ= 34.59 PHI= -0.537 XP = 0.
45	TILT LESS TOWARD BEING THOSE WHERE SETTLEMENTS, IF FIXED, ARE COMPACT, RATHER THAN NON-COMPACT (149)	0.55 OF 64	45	TILT MORE TOWARD BEING THOSE WHERE SETTLEMENTS, IF FIXED, ARE COMPACT, RATHER THAN NON-COMPACT (149)	0.79 OF 38	35 30 29 8 XSQ= 5.07 PHI= -0.223 XP = 0.0244
53	TILT TOWARD BEING THOSE WHERE FOOD PRODUCTION IS BY INTENSIVE AGRICULTURE, RATHER THAN BY SIMPLE AGRICULTURE OR INCIPIENT FOOD PRODUCTION (91)	0.75 OF 71	53	TILT TOWARD BEING THOSE WHERE FOOD PRODUCTION IS BY SIMPLE AGRICULTURE OR INCIPIENT FOOD PRODUCTION, RATHER THAN BY INTENSIVE AGRICULTURE (147)	0.51 OF 41	53 20 18 21 XSQ= 6.57 PHI= 0.242 XP = 0.0104
55	LEAN MORE TOWARD BEING THOSE WHERE FOOD PRODUCTION IS BY INTENSIVE AGRICULTURE, RATHER THAN BY SIMPLE AGRICULTURE (91)	0.82 OF 65	55	LEAN LESS TOWARD BEING THOSE WHERE FOOD PRODUCTION IS BY INTENSIVE AGRICULTURE, RATHER THAN BY SIMPLE AGRICULTURE (91)	0.51 OF 39	53 20 12 19 XSQ= 9.27 PHI= 0.299 XP = 0.0023
73	LEAN LESS TOWARD BEING THOSE WHERE WEAVING IS PRESENT (118)	0.56 OF 50	73	LEAN MORE TOWARD BEING THOSE WHERE WEAVING IS PRESENT (118)	0.91 OF 22	28 20 22 2 XSQ= 6.88 PHI= -0.309 XP = 0.0087

83	DRIFT LESS TOWARD BEING THOSE 0.57 OF 37 WHERE, WITH NO CITY AND NO TOWN PRESENT, THE AVERAGE COMMUNITY SIZE IS SMALLER THAN 200, RATHER THAN BETWEEN 200 AND 999 (135)	83	DRIFT MORE TOWARD BEING THOSE 0.85 OF 20 WHERE, WITH NO CITY AND NO TOWN PRESENT, THE AVERAGE COMMUNITY SIZE IS SMALLER THAN 200, RATHER THAN BETWEEN 200 AND 999 (135)	16 3 21 17 XSQ= 3.48 PHI= 0.247 XP = 0.0623
96	TILT MORE TOWARD BEING THOSE 0.81 OF 77 WHERE THE HIERARCHY OF NATIONAL JURISDICTION HAS FOUR, THREE, TWO OR ONE LEVEL (174) GES,EA	96	TILT LESS TOWARD BEING THOSE 0.61 OF 41 WHERE THE HIERARCHY OF NATIONAL JURISDICTION HAS FOUR, THREE, TWO OR ONE LEVEL (174) GES,EA	62 25 15 16 XSQ= 4.32 PHI= 0.191 XP = 0.0378
109	DRIFT LESS TOWARD BEING THOSE 0.65 OF 68 WHERE CASTES ARE ABSENT (317)	109	DRIFT MORE TOWARD BEING THOSE 0.83 OF 35 WHERE CASTES ARE ABSENT (317)	24 6 44 29 XSQ= 2.86 PHI= 0.167 XP = 0.0907
129	DRIFT LESS TOWARD BEING THOSE 0.52 OF 21 WHERE WEAVING IS MAINLY DONE BY FEMALES (73)	129	DRIFT MORE TOWARD BEING THOSE 0.83 OF 18 WHERE WEAVING IS MAINLY DONE BY FEMALES (73)	10 3 11 15 XSQ= 2.90 PHI= 0.273 EP = 0.0508
183	IN ALL CASES ARE THOSE 1.00 OF 62 WHERE THE LARGEST NON-COGNATIC KIN GROUP IS SMALLER THAN A MOEITY, I. E., A PHRATRY OR SIB OR LINEAGE (218)	183	DRIFT LESS TOWARD BEING THOSE 0.90 OF 29 WHERE THE LARGEST NON-COGNATIC KIN GROUP IS SMALLER THAN A MOEITY, I. E., A PHRATRY OR SIB OR LINEAGE (218)	0 3 62 26 XSQ= 3.78 PHI= -0.204 XP = 0.0517
186	DRIFT TOWARD BEING THOSE 0.62 OF 79 WHERE THE KIN GROUP IS EXCLUSIVELY PATRILINEAL (150)	186	DRIFT TOWARD BEING THOSE 0.56 OF 41 WHERE THE KIN GROUP IS OTHER THAN EXCLUSIVELY PATRILINEAL (250)	49 18 30 23 XSQ= 2.90 PHI= 0.155 XP = 0.0887
187	DRIFT MORE TOWARD BEING THOSE 0.97 OF 79 WHERE THE KIN GROUP IS OTHER THAN EXCLUSIVELY MATRILINEAL (344)	187	DRIFT LESS TOWARD BEING THOSE 0.88 OF 41 WHERE THE KIN GROUP IS OTHER THAN EXCLUSIVELY MATRILINEAL (344)	2 5 77 36 XSQ= 3.00 PHI= -0.158 XP = 0.0834
190	DRIFT MORE TOWARD BEING THOSE 0.97 OF 60 WHERE THE KIN GROUP IS PATRILINEAL OR DOUBLE-DESCENT, RATHER THAN MATRILINEAL (186)	190	DRIFT LESS TOWARD BEING THOSE 0.82 OF 28 WHERE THE KIN GROUP IS PATRILINEAL OR DOUBLE-DESCENT, RATHER THAN MATRILINEAL (186)	58 23 2 5 XSQ= 3.70 PHI= 0.205 XP = 0.0546
198	IN ALL CASES ARE THOSE 1.00 OF 53 WHERE RULES FOR THE INHERITANCE OF REAL PROPERTY, IF PRESENT, FAVOR THE MALE HEIR OR LINE, RATHER THAN THE FEMALE (144)	198	DRIFT LESS TOWARD BEING THOSE 0.88 OF 25 WHERE RULES FOR THE INHERITANCE OF REAL PROPERTY, IF PRESENT, FAVOR THE MALE HEIR OR LINE, RATHER THAN THE FEMALE (144)	53 22 0 3 XSQ= 3.77 PHI= 0.220 XP = 0.0523

207	LEAN TOWARD BEING THOSE 0.92 OF 12 WHERE MARITAL RESIDENCE IS AMBILOCAL OR NEOLOCAL, RATHER THAN MATRILOCAL OR UXORILOCAL (64)	207	LEAN TOWARD BEING THOSE 0.64 OF 14 WHERE MARITAL RESIDENCE IS MATRILOCAL OR UXORILOCAL, RATHER THAN AMBILOCAL OR NEOLOCAL (64)	1 9 11 5 XSQ= 6.35 PHI= -0.494 EP = 0.0053
209	TEND MORE TO BE THOSE 0.99 OF 68 WHERE MARITAL RESIDENCE IS PATRILOCAL, VIRILOCAL, OR AVUNCULOCAL, RATHER THAN MATRILOCAL OR UXORILOCAL (270)	209	TEND LESS TO BE THOSE 0.75 OF 36 WHERE MARITAL RESIDENCE IS PATRILOCAL, VIRILOCAL, OR AVUNCULOCAL, RATHER THAN MATRILOCAL OR UXORILOCAL (270)	67 27 1 9 XSQ= 12.41 PHI= 0.345 XP = 0.0004
210	IN ALL CASES ARE THOSE 1.00 OF 54 WHERE MARITAL RESIDENCE IS PATRILOCAL, RATHER THAN MATRILOCAL (169)	210	TILT LESS TOWARD BEING THOSE 0.85 OF 27 WHERE MARITAL RESIDENCE IS PATRILOCAL, RATHER THAN MATRILOCAL (169)	54 23 0 4 XSQ= 5.56 PHI= 0.262 XP = 0.0184
214	TILT MORE TOWARD BEING THOSE 0.95 OF 40 WHERE FIRST COUSIN MARRIAGE, IF PERMITTED, IS OTHER THAN UNILATERAL (144)	214	TILT LESS TOWARD BEING THOSE 0.71 OF 24 WHERE FIRST COUSIN MARRIAGE, IF PERMITTED, IS OTHER THAN UNILATERAL (144)	2 7 38 17 XSQ= 5.39 PHI= -0.290 XP = 0.0203
221	DRIFT MORE TOWARD BEING THOSE 0.90 OF 69 WHERE MATRILATERAL CROSS-COUSIN MARRIAGE IS NOT PRESCRIBED OR PREFERRED (335)	221	DRIFT LESS TOWARD BEING THOSE 0.76 OF 41 WHERE MATRILATERAL CROSS-COUSIN MARRIAGE IS NOT PRESCRIBED OR PREFERRED (335)	7 10 62 31 XSQ= 2.98 PHI= -0.165 XP = 0.0844
377	DRIFT LESS TOWARD BEING THOSE 0.58 OF 77 WHERE MALE GENITAL MUTILATION IS ABSENT (242)	377	DRIFT MORE TOWARD BEING THOSE 0.77 OF 40 WHERE MALE GENITAL MUTILATION IS ABSENT (242)	32 9 45 31 XSQ= 3.41 PHI= 0.171 XP = 0.0650
426	TILT MORE TOWARD BEING THOSE 0.85 OF 66 WHERE A HIGH GOD IS PRESENT (156) GES,EA	426	TILT LESS TOWARD BEING THOSE 0.62 OF 26 WHERE A HIGH GOD IS PRESENT (156) GES,EA	56 16 10 10 XSQ= 4.67 PHI= 0.225 XP = 0.0308
427	TILT TOWARD BEING THOSE 0.73 OF 56 WHERE A HIGH GOD, IF PRESENT, IS ACTIVE, RATHER THAN INACTIVE (87) GES,EA	427	TILT TOWARD BEING THOSE 0.63 OF 16 WHERE A HIGH GOD, IF PRESENT, IS INACTIVE, RATHER THAN ACTIVE (69) GES,EA	41 6 15 10 XSQ= 5.52 PHI= 0.277 XP = 0.0188
450	TILT TOWARD BEING THOSE 0.68 OF 19 WHERE THE OBSERVATION OF FOOD TABOOS IS HIGH OR MEDIUM, RATHER THAN LOW (60) JRL	450	TILT TOWARD BEING THOSE 0.78 OF 9 WHERE THE OBSERVATION OF FOOD TABOOS IS LOW, RATHER THAN HIGH OR MEDIUM (26) JRL	13 2 6 7 XSQ= 3.55 PHI= 0.356 EP = 0.0418

468 TILT TOWARD BEING THOSE 0.50 OF 10
WHERE CONTACT WITH OTHER CULTURES
IS REGULAR OR IRREGULAR, RATHER THAN
FREQUENT (37) JMH

468 IN ALL CASES ARE THOSE 1.00 OF 7
WHERE CONTACT WITH OTHER CULTURES
IS FREQUENT, RATHER THAN
REGULAR OR IRREGULAR (17) JMH

5 7
5 0
XSQ= 2.84
PHI= -0.409
EP = 0.0441

66 CULTURES
WHERE HUSBANDRY IN PIGS,
AS THE PRINCIPAL FORM OF HUSBANDRY,
IS PRESENT (46)

66 CULTURES
WHERE HUSBANDRY IN PIGS,
AS THE PRINCIPAL FORM OF HUSBANDRY,
IS ABSENT (354)

BACKGROUND ON PAGE 77

SUBJECT ONLY

46 IN LEFT COLUMN

ALORESE	ARAPESH	ARAUCANIANS	ATAYAL	BUNLAP	CAGABA	CAYAPA	CHORTI	CUNA	ELLICE
ENGA	GOND	HAWAIIANS	IBAN	IFUGAO	JIVARO	KAPAUKU	KERAKI	KORYAK	KURTATCHI
LAU	LESU	MANUS	MARQUESANS	MARSHALLESE	MOTA	NICOBARESE	PAIWAN	PALAUANS	PONAPEANS
PUKAPUKA	PURARI	SAMOANS	SENIANG	SIUAI	SUBANUN	TALAMANCA	TIMBIRA	TROBRIAND	TRUKESE
ULAWANS	WANTOAT	WOGEO	WOLEAIANS	YAPESE	YARURO				

354 IN RIGHT COLUMN

	Present (46)			Absent (354)		Statistics
3	IN ALL CASES ARE THOSE LOCATED OUTSIDE OF AFRICA (320)	1.00 OF 46	3	TEND LESS TO BE THOSE LOCATED OUTSIDE OF AFRICA (320)	0.77 OF 354	0 80 46 274 XSQ= 11.62 PHI= -0.170 XP = 0.0007
4	IN ALL CASES ARE THOSE LOCATED OUTSIDE OF THE CIRCUM-MEDITERRANEAN (355)	1.00 OF 46	4	TILT LESS TOWARD BEING THOSE LOCATED OUTSIDE OF THE CIRCUM-MEDITERRANEAN (355)	0.87 OF 354	0 45 46 309 XSQ= 5.38 PHI= -0.116 XP = 0.0204
5	DRIFT MORE TOWARD BEING THOSE LOCATED OUTSIDE OF EAST EURASIA (330)	0.93 OF 46	5	DRIFT LESS TOWARD BEING THOSE LOCATED OUTSIDE OF EAST EURASIA (330)	0.81 OF 354	3 67 43 287 XSQ= 3.52 PHI= -0.094 XP = 0.0605
6	TEND TO BE THOSE LOCATED IN THE INSULAR PACIFIC (70)	0.74 OF 46	6	TEND TO BE THOSE LOCATED OUTSIDE OF THE INSULAR PACIFIC (330)	0.90 OF 354	34 36 12 318 XSQ= 110.20 PHI= 0.525 XP = 0.
8	IN ALL CASES ARE THOSE LOCATED OUTSIDE OF NORTH AMERICA (330)	1.00 OF 46	8	LEAN LESS TOWARD BEING THOSE LOCATED OUTSIDE OF NORTH AMERICA (330)	0.80 OF 354	0 70 46 284 XSQ= 9.70 PHI= -0.156 XP = 0.0018

15	TEND TO BE THOSE WHERE THE LATITUDE IS LESS THAN TWENTY DEGREES (217)	0.87 OF 46	15	TEND TO BE THOSE WHERE THE LATITUDE IS TWENTY DEGREES OR GREATER (183)	0.50 OF 354	6 177 40 177 XSQ= 20.94 PHI= -0.229 XP = 0.0000
16	TEND TO BE THOSE WHERE THE LATITUDE IS LESS THAN TEN DEGREES (123)	0.65 OF 46	16	TEND TO BE THOSE WHERE THE LATITUDE IS TEN DEGREES OR GREATER (277)	0.74 OF 354	16 261 30 93 XSQ= 27.20 PHI= -0.261 XP = 0.0000
33	DRIFT MORE TOWARD BEING THOSE WHERE THE NATURAL ENVIRONMENT IS OTHER THAN 'VERY HARSH,' I.E., DESERT, DESERT GRASSES AND SHRUBS, TUNDRA, OR HIGH PLATEAU STEPPE (341) FWM	0.96 OF 46	33	DRIFT LESS TOWARD BEING THOSE WHERE THE NATURAL ENVIRONMENT IS OTHER THAN 'VERY HARSH,' I.E., DESERT, DESERT GRASSES AND SHRUBS, TUNDRA, OR HIGH PLATEAU STEPPE (341) FWM	0.84 OF 354	2 57 44 297 XSQ= 3.59 PHI= -0.095 XP = 0.0582
36	LEAN MORE TOWARD BEING THOSE WHERE THE NATURAL ENVIRONMENT IS OTHER THAN 'VERY HARSH,' OR SUB-TROPICAL BUSH, OR TEMPERATE GRASSLAND (292) FWM	0.91 OF 46	36	LEAN LESS TOWARD BEING THOSE WHERE THE NATURAL ENVIRONMENT IS OTHER THAN 'VERY HARSH,' OR SUB-TROPICAL BUSH, OR TEMPERATE GRASSLAND (292) FWM	0.71 OF 354	4 104 42 250 XSQ= 7.82 PHI= -0.140 XP = 0.0052
42	TEND TO BE THOSE WHERE THE NATURAL ENVIRONMENT IS TROPICAL OR SUB-TROPICAL RAIN FOREST, OR MONSOON FOREST (156) FWM	0.83 OF 46	42	TEND TO BE THOSE WHERE THE NATURAL ENVIRONMENT IS OTHER THAN TROPICAL OR SUB-TROPICAL RAIN FOREST, OR MONSOON FOREST (244) FWM	0.67 OF 354	38 118 8 236 XSQ= 39.50 PHI= 0.314 XP = 0.
44	TEND MORE TO BE THOSE WHERE SETTLEMENTS ARE FIXED (222)	0.96 OF 46	44	TEND LESS TO BE THOSE WHERE SETTLEMENTS ARE FIXED (222)	0.62 OF 286	44 178 2 108 XSQ= 18.49 PHI= 0.236 XP = 0.0000
46	IN ALL CASES ARE THOSE OTHER THAN WHERE SETTLEMENTS ARE NON-FIXED AND MOVEMENT IS NOMADIC (260)	1.00 OF 46	46	TEND LESS TO BE THOSE OTHER THAN WHERE SETTLEMENTS ARE NON-FIXED AND MOVEMENT IS NOMADIC (260)	0.75 OF 286	0 72 46 214 XSQ= 13.34 PHI= -0.200 XP = 0.0003
48	TILT TOWARD BEING THOSE WHERE THE FOOD SUPPLY IS SECURE, AND FOOD SHORTAGES ARE RARE OR OCCASIONAL (38) MGW	0.72 OF 18	48	TILT TOWARD BEING THOSE WHERE THE FOOD SUPPLY IS NOT SECURE, AND FOOD SHORTAGES ARE FREQUENT OR ANNUAL (41) MGW	0.59 OF 61	13 25 5 36 XSQ= 4.25 PHI= 0.232 XP = 0.0392
51	TILT MORE TOWARD BEING THOSE WHERE SUBSISTENCE IS PRIMARILY BY FOOD PRODUCTION -- I. E., AGRICULTURE OR HUSBANDRY -- RATHER THAN BY GATHERING (253)	0.80 OF 46	51	TILT LESS TOWARD BEING THOSE WHERE SUBSISTENCE IS PRIMARILY BY FOOD PRODUCTION -- I. E., AGRICULTURE OR HUSBANDRY -- RATHER THAN BY GATHERING (253)	0.61 OF 354	37 216 9 138 XSQ= 5.79 PHI= 0.120 XP = 0.0161

53	TEND MORE TO BE THOSE WHERE FOOD PRODUCTION IS BY SIMPLE AGRICULTURE OR INCIPIENT FOOD PRODUCTION, RATHER THAN BY INTENSIVE AGRICULTURE (147)	0.95 OF 40	53	TEND LESS TO BE THOSE WHERE FOOD PRODUCTION IS BY SIMPLE AGRICULTURE OR INCIPIENT FOOD PRODUCTION, RATHER THAN BY INTENSIVE AGRICULTURE (147)	0.55 OF 198	2 89 38 109 XSQ= 20.83 PHI= -0.296 XP = 0.0000
54	DRIFT MORE TOWARD BEING THOSE WHERE FOOD PRODUCTION IS BY INTENSIVE OR SIMPLE AGRICULTURE, RATHER THAN BY INCIPIENT FOOD PRODUCTION (192)	0.92 OF 40	54	DRIFT LESS TOWARD BEING THOSE WHERE FOOD PRODUCTION IS BY INTENSIVE OR SIMPLE AGRICULTURE, RATHER THAN BY INCIPIENT FOOD PRODUCTION (192)	0.78 OF 198	37 155 3 43 XSQ= 3.45 PHI= 0.120 XP = 0.0632
55	TEND TO BE THOSE WHERE FOOD PRODUCTION IS BY SIMPLE AGRICULTURE, RATHER THAN BY INTENSIVE AGRICULTURE (101)	0.95 OF 37	55	TEND TO BE THOSE WHERE FOOD PRODUCTION IS BY INTENSIVE AGRICULTURE, RATHER THAN BY SIMPLE AGRICULTURE (91)	0.57 OF 155	2 89 35 66 XSQ= 30.36 PHI= -0.398 XP = 0.
56	TEND MORE TO BE THOSE WHERE FOOD PRODUCTION IS BY SIMPLE AGRICULTURE, RATHER THAN BY INCIPIENT FOOD PRODUCTION (101)	0.92 OF 38	56	TEND LESS TO BE THOSE WHERE FOOD PRODUCTION IS BY SIMPLE AGRICULTURE, RATHER THAN BY INCIPIENT FOOD PRODUCTION (101)	0.61 OF 109	35 66 3 43 XSQ= 11.62 PHI= 0.281 XP = 0.0007
71	TEND MORE TO BE THOSE WHERE METAL WORKING IS ABSENT (153)	0.89 OF 38	71	TEND LESS TO BE THOSE WHERE METAL WORKING IS ABSENT (153)	0.56 OF 213	4 94 34 119 XSQ= 13.92 PHI= -0.236 XP = 0.0002
74	LEAN TOWARD BEING THOSE WHERE POTTERY IS ABSENT (93)	0.62 OF 37	74	LEAN TOWARD BEING THOSE WHERE POTTERY IS PRESENT (145)	0.65 OF 201	14 131 23 70 XSQ= 8.69 PHI= -0.191 XP = 0.0032
80	IN ALL CASES ARE THOSE WHERE NO CITY OR TOWN IS PRESENT (185)	1.00 OF 28	80	TILT LESS TOWARD BEING THOSE WHERE NO CITY OR TOWN IS PRESENT (185)	0.80 OF 196	0 39 28 157 XSQ= 5.43 PHI= -0.156 XP = 0.0198
81	LEAN MORE TOWARD BEING THOSE WHERE NO CITY OR TOWN IS PRESENT, AND THE AVERAGE COMMUNITY SIZE IS SMALLER THAN 200 (135)	0.86 OF 28	81	LEAN LESS TOWARD BEING THOSE WHERE NO CITY OR TOWN IS PRESENT, AND THE AVERAGE COMMUNITY SIZE IS SMALLER THAN 200 (135)	0.57 OF 196	4 85 24 111 XSQ= 7.48 PHI= -0.183 XP = 0.0062
84	IN ALL CASES ARE THOSE WHERE THE LEVEL OF POLITICAL INTEGRATION IS THE LITTLE STATE, THE MINIMAL STATE, THE AUTONOMOUS COMMUNITY, OR THE FAMILY (262) GPM	1.00 OF 38	84	TILT LESS TOWARD BEING THOSE WHERE THE LEVEL OF POLITICAL INTEGRATION IS THE LITTLE STATE, THE MINIMAL STATE, THE AUTONOMOUS COMMUNITY, OR THE FAMILY (262) GPM	0.84 OF 266	0 42 38 224 XSQ= 5.70 PHI= -0.137 XP = 0.0170

86	DRIFT TOWARD BEING THOSE 0.66 OF 38 WHERE THE LEVEL OF POLITICAL INTEGRATION IS THE AUTONOMOUS COMMUNITY, OR THE FAMILY (156) GPM	86	DRIFT TOWARD BEING THOSE 0.51 OF 266 WHERE THE LEVEL OF POLITICAL INTEGRATION IS THE LARGE STATE, THE LITTLE STATE, OR THE MINIMAL STATE (148) GPM	13 135 25 131 XSQ= 3.01 PHI= -0.099 XP = 0.0828
94	IN ALL CASES ARE THOSE 1.00 OF 46 WHERE THE HIERARCHY OF NATIONAL JURISDICTION HAS TWO, ONE, OR NO LEVELS (296) GES,EA	94	TILT LESS TOWARD BEING THOSE 0.88 OF 284 WHERE THE HIERARCHY OF NATIONAL JURISDICTION HAS TWO, ONE, OR NO LEVELS (296) GES,EA	0 34 46 250 XSQ= 4.91 PHI= -0.122 XP = 0.0267
107	IN ALL CASES ARE THOSE 1.00 OF 24 WHERE CLASS STRATIFICATION, IF PRESENT, IS BASED ON SOMETHING OTHER THAN OCCUPATIONAL STATUS (160)	107	TILT LESS TOWARD BEING THOSE 0.76 OF 179 WHERE CLASS STRATIFICATION, IF PRESENT, IS BASED ON SOMETHING OTHER THAN OCCUPATIONAL STATUS (160)	0 43 24 136 XSQ= 5.95 PHI= -0.171 XP = 0.0147
109	TILT MORE TOWARD BEING THOSE 0.98 OF 44 WHERE CASTES ARE ABSENT (317)	109	TILT LESS TOWARD BEING THOSE 0.85 OF 324 WHERE CASTES ARE ABSENT (317)	1 50 43 274 XSQ= 4.57 PHI= -0.111 XP = 0.0325
110	TEND MORE TO BE THOSE 0.82 OF 45 WHERE SLAVERY IS ABSENT (218)	110	TEND LESS TO BE THOSE 0.54 OF 336 WHERE SLAVERY IS ABSENT (218)	8 155 37 181 XSQ= 11.90 PHI= -0.177 XP = 0.0006
118	IN ALL CASES ARE THOSE 1.00 OF 9 WHERE THE PERCENTAGE OF OCCUPATIONS THAT ARE SPECIALIZED IS LOW (25) WME	118	LEAN TOWARD BEING THOSE 0.60 OF 40 WHERE THE PERCENTAGE OF OCCUPATIONS THAT ARE SPECIALIZED IS HIGH OR MEDIUM (24) WME	0 24 9 16 XSQ= 8.32 PHI= -0.412 XP = 0.0039
127	DRIFT TOWARD BEING THOSE 0.82 OF 11 WHERE THE FEMALES' CONTRIBUTION TO SUBSISTENCE IS HIGH (33) JKB	127	DRIFT TOWARD BEING THOSE 0.56 OF 54 WHERE THE FEMALES' CONTRIBUTION TO SUBSISTENCE IS LOW (32) JKB	9 24 2 30 XSQ= 3.72 PHI= 0.239 XP = 0.0537
131	IN ALL CASES ARE THOSE 1.00 OF 28 WHERE THE CONSTRUCTION OF PERMANENT HOUSES OR THE ERECTION OF TEMPORARY DWELLINGS IS MAINLY DONE BY MALES (136)	131	TILT LESS TOWARD BEING THOSE 0.84 OF 129 WHERE THE CONSTRUCTION OF PERMANENT HOUSES OR THE ERECTION OF TEMPORARY DWELLINGS IS MAINLY DONE BY MALES (136)	28 108 0 21 XSQ= 3.95 PHI= 0.159 XP = 0.0468
176	TILT TOWARD BEING THOSE 0.62 OF 45 WHERE THE COMMUNITY IS A CLAN-COMMUNITY OR A COMMUNITY STRUCTURED OR SEGMENTED ON A CLAN BASIS (169)	176	TILT TOWARD BEING THOSE 0.58 OF 337 WHERE THE COMMUNITY IS OTHER THAN A CLAN-COMMUNITY OR A COMMUNITY STRUCTURED OR SEGMENTED ON A CLAN BASIS (213)	28 141 17 196 XSQ= 5.89 PHI= 0.124 XP = 0.0153

178	TEND LESS TO BE THCSE 0.56 OF 45 WHERE THE COMMUNITY IS OTHER THAN SEGMENTED CN A CLAN BASIS AND NCN-EXOGAMCUS (295)	178	TEND MORE TO BE THOSE 0.80 OF 337 WHERE THE COMMUNITY IS OTHER THAN SEGMENTED ON A CLAN BASIS AND NON-EXOGAMOUS (295)	20 67 25 270 XSQ= 12.26 PHI= 0.179 XP = 0.0005
184	LEAN TOWARD BEING THOSE 0.55 OF 29 WHERE THE LARGEST NCN-CCGNATIC KIN GROUP IS THE MOEITY OR PHRATRY (77)	184	LEAN TOWARD BEING THOSE 0.73 CF 223 WHERE THE LARGEST NON-COGNATIC KIN GROUP IS SMALLER THAN A PHRATRY, I. E. A SIB OR LINEAGE (175)	16 61 13 162 XSQ= 8.09 PHI= 0.179 XP = 0.0044
186	TILT MORE TOWARC BEING THCSE 0.80 OF 46 WHERE THE KIN GRCUP IS OTHER THAN EXCLUSIVELY PATRILINEAL (250)	186	TILT LESS TOWARD BEING THOSE 0.60 CF 354 WHERE THE KIN GRCUP IS OTHER THAN EXCLUSIVELY PATRILINEAL (250)	9 141 37 213 XSQ= 6.29 PHI= -0.125 XP = 0.0121
190	TILT LESS TCWARC BEING THCSE 0.57 OF 28 WHERE THE KIN GRCUP IS PATRILINEAL CR CCUBLE-CESCENT, RATHER THAN MATRILINEAL (186)	19C	TILT MORE TOWARD BEING THOSE 0.78 OF 219 WHERE THE KIN GROUP IS PATRILINEAL OR DOUBLE-DESCENT, RATHER THAN MATRILINEAL (186)	16 170 12 49 XSQ= 4.55 PHI= -0.136 XP = 0.0329
196	DRIFT MORE TCWARC BEING THCSE 0.84 OF 31 WHERE INDIVIDUAL RIGHTS IN REAL PROPERTY, AND RULES FOR INHERITANCE, ARE PRESENT (194)	196	DRIFT LESS TOWARD BEING THOSE 0.67 CF 250 WHERE INDIVIDUAL RIGHTS IN REAL PRCPERTY, AND RULES FOR INHERITANCE, ARE PRESENT (194)	26 168 5 82 XSQ= 2.85 PHI= 0.101 XP = 0.0915
198	TILT LESS TCWARC BEING THCSE 0.68 OF 19 WHERE RULES FCR THE INHERITANCE OF REAL PROPERTY, IF PRESENT, FAVOR THE MALE HEIR OR LINE, RATHER THAN THE FEMALE (144)	198	TILT MORE TOWARD BEING THOSE 0.90 OF 146 WHERE RULES FOR THE INHERITANCE CF REAL PROPERTY, IF PRESENT, FAVOR THE MALE HEIR OR LINE, RATHER THAN THE FEMALE (144)	13 131 6 15 XSQ= 5.09 PHI= -0.176 XP = 0.0241
213	TILT MCRE TCWARC BEING THCSE 0.72 OF 46 WHERE FIRST CCUSIN MARRIACE IS NCT PERMITTED (198)	213	TILT LESS TOWARD BEING THOSE 0.51 OF 324 WHERE FIRST COUSIN MARRIAGE IS NOT PERMITTED (198)	13 159 33 165 XSQ= 6.20 PHI= -0.129 XP = 0.0128
300	LEAN TCWARC BEING THCSE 0.68 OF 22 WHERE THE POST-PARTUM SEX TABOO LASTS LCNGER THAN SIX MONTHS (51)	3CC	LEAN TOWARD BEING THOSE 0.65 OF 102 WHERE THE POST-PARTUM SEX TABOO LASTS SIX MONTHS OR LESS (73)	15 36 7 66 XSQ= 6.78 PHI= 0.234 XP = 0.0092
305	DRIFT TCWARD BEING THCSE 0.77 OF 13 WHERE THE EARLY SEXUAL SATISFACTION PCTENTIAL IS HIGH (27) W-C	305	DRIFT TOWARD BEING THOSE 0.55 CF 38 WHERE THE EARLY SEXUAL SATISFACTICN POTENTIAL IS LOW (24) W-C	10 17 3 21 XSQ= 2.84 PHI= 0.236 XP = 0.0920

325	DRIFT TOWARD BEING THOSE 0.78 OF 18 WHERE THE DEGREE OF DIFFUSION AMONG THE INFANT'S NURTURANT AGENTS IS HIGH (42) B-B-C	325	DRIFT TOWARD BEING THOSE 0.50 OF 56 WHERE THE DEGREE OF DIFFUSION AMONG THE INFANT'S NURTURANT AGENTS IS LOW (32) B-B-C	14 28 4 28 XSQ= 3.23 PHI= 0.209 XP = 0.0725
336	TILT TOWARD BEING THOSE 0.68 OF 19 WHERE THE TOTAL POSITIVE PRESSURE TOWARD DEVELOPING RESPONSIBLE BEHAVIOR IN THE CHILD IS LOW (32) B-B-C	336	TILT TOWARD BEING THOSE 0.66 OF 56 WHERE THE TOTAL POSITIVE PRESSURE TOWARD DEVELOPING RESPONSIBLE BEHAVIOR IN THE CHILD IS HIGH (43) B-B-C	6 37 13 19 XSQ= 5.56 PHI= -0.272 XP = 0.0184
337	DRIFT TOWARD BEING THOSE 0.68 OF 19 WHERE THE CHILD'S INFERRED ANXIETY OVER NON-PERFORMANCE OF RESPONSIBLE BEHAVIOR IS LOW (35) B-B-C	337	DRIFT TOWARD BEING THOSE 0.59 OF 54 WHERE THE CHILD'S INFERRED ANXIETY OVER NON-PERFORMANCE OF RESPONSIBLE BEHAVIOR IS HIGH (38) B-B-C	6 32 13 22 XSQ= 3.28 PHI= -0.212 XP = 0.0703
342	DRIFT TOWARD BEING THOSE 0.70 OF 10 WHERE THE CHILD'S INFERRED ANXIETY OVER PERFORMANCE OF NURTURANT BEHAVIOR IS HIGH (18) B-B-C	342	DRIFT TOWARD BEING THOSE 0.69 OF 36 WHERE THE CHILD'S INFERRED ANXIETY OVER PERFORMANCE OF NURTURANT BEHAVIOR IS LOW (28) B-B-C	7 11 3 25 XSQ= 3.59 PHI= 0.279 XP = 0.0581
350	LEAN TOWARD BEING THOSE 0.83 OF 12 WHERE THE CHILD'S INFERRED ANXIETY OVER PERFORMANCE OF ACHIEVEMENT BEHAVIOR IS LOW (26) B-B-C	350	LEAN TOWARD BEING THOSE 0.67 OF 48 WHERE THE CHILD'S INFERRED ANXIETY OVER PERFORMANCE OF ACHIEVEMENT BEHAVIOR IS HIGH (34) B-B-C	2 32 10 16 XSQ= 7.84 PHI= -0.362 XP = 0.0051
351	TILT TOWARD BEING THOSE 0.92 OF 12 WHERE THE CHILD'S INFERRED CONFLICT REGARDING ACHIEVEMENT BEHAVIOR IS LOW (34) B-B-C	351	TILT TOWARD BEING THOSE 0.52 OF 48 WHERE THE CHILD'S INFERRED CONFLICT REGARDING ACHIEVEMENT BEHAVIOR IS HIGH (26) B-B-C	1 25 11 23 XSQ= 5.81 PHI= -0.311 XP = 0.0160
352	LEAN TOWARD BEING THOSE 0.75 OF 16 WHERE THE TOTAL POSITIVE PRESSURE TOWARD DEVELOPING OBEDIENT BEHAVIOR IN THE CHILD IS LOW (28) B-B-C	352	LEAN TOWARD BEING THOSE 0.71 OF 56 WHERE THE TOTAL POSITIVE PRESSURE TOWARD DEVELOPING OBEDIENT BEHAVIOR IN THE CHILD IS HIGH (44) B-B-C	4 40 12 16 XSQ= 9.42 PHI= -0.362 XP = 0.0021
370	TILT TOWARD BEING THOSE 0.56 OF 39 WHERE THE SEGREGATION OF ADOLESCENT BOYS IS COMPLETE OR PARTIAL (95)	370	TILT TOWARD BEING THOSE 0.64 OF 204 WHERE THE SEGREGATION OF ADOLESCENT BOYS IS ABSENT (148)	22 73 17 131 XSQ= 5.02 PHI= 0.144 XP = 0.0251
377	TILT MORE TOWARD BEING THOSE 0.89 OF 44 WHERE MALE GENITAL MUTILATION IS ABSENT (242)	377	TILT LESS TOWARD BEING THOSE 0.72 OF 281 WHERE MALE GENITAL MUTILATION IS ABSENT (242)	5 78 39 203 XSQ= 4.55 PHI= -0.118 XP = 0.0329

391	TILT TOWARD BEING THOSE 0.71 OF 31 WHERE PREMARITAL SEX RELATIONS ARE PUNISHED ONLY IF PREGNANCY RESULTS, OR FREELY PERMITTED (90) JTW,EA	391	TILT TOWARD BEING THOSE 0.54 OF 148 WHERE PREMARITAL SEX RELATIONS ARE STRONGLY PUNISHED AND IN FACT RARE, OR WEAKLY PUNISHED AND IN FACT NOT RARE (89) JTW,EA	9 80 22 68 XSQ= 5.46 PHI= -0.175 XP = 0.0195
400	TILT TOWARD BEING THOSE 0.63 OF 16 WHERE HOMOSEXUAL ACTIVITY IS PROHIBITED (22) F-B	400	TILT TOWARD BEING THOSE 0.71 OF 42 WHERE HOMOSEXUAL ACTIVITY IS PERMITTED (36) F-B	10 12 6 30 XSQ= 4.32 PHI= 0.273 XP = 0.0378
419	DRIFT TOWARD BEING THOSE 0.59 OF 17 WHERE MILITARY GLORY IS NEGLIGIBLY EMPHASIZED (31) PES	419	DRIFT TOWARD BEING THOSE 0.70 OF 69 WHERE MILITARY GLORY IS STRONGLY OR MODERATELY EMPHASIZED (55) PES	7 48 10 21 XSQ= 3.62 PHI= -0.205 XP = 0.0572
426	TEND TO BE THOSE 0.66 OF 38 WHERE A HIGH GOD IS ABSENT (104) GES,EA	426	TEND TO BE THOSE 0.64 OF 222 WHERE A HIGH GOD IS PRESENT (156) GES,EA	13 143 25 79 XSQ= 11.11 PHI= -0.207 XP = 0.0009
428	TILT TOWARD BEING THOSE 0.80 OF 5 WHERE A HIGH GOD, IF PRESENT AND ACTIVE, DOES NOT SUPPORT HUMAN MORALITY, RATHER THAN SUPPORTING IT (26) GES,EA	428	TILT TOWARD BEING THOSE 0.73 OF 82 WHERE A HIGH GOD, IF PRESENT AND ACTIVE, SUPPORTS HUMAN MORALITY, RATHER THAN NOT SUPPORTING IT (61) GES,EA	1 60 4 22 XSQ= 4.07 PHI= -0.216 XP = 0.0435
442	DRIFT TOWARD BEING THOSE 0.79 OF 14 WHERE FEAR OF ANIMAL SPIRITS IS LOW (33) W-C	442	DRIFT TOWARD BEING THOSE 0.53 OF 47 WHERE FEAR OF ANIMAL SPIRITS IS HIGH (28) W-C	3 25 11 22 XSQ= 3.20 PHI= -0.229 XP = 0.0738
446	IN ALL CASES ARE THOSE 1.00 OF 7 WHERE WITCHCRAFT IS MODERATELY PRESENT OR ABSENT (24) GES	446	TILT LESS TOWARD BEING THOSE 0.55 OF 31 WHERE WITCHCRAFT IS MODERATELY PRESENT OR ABSENT (24) GES	0 14 7 17 XSQ= 3.25 PHI= -0.293 EP = 0.0334
449	TILT TOWARD BEING THOSE 0.53 OF 17 WHERE THE OBSERVATION OF FOOD TABOOS IS HIGH, RATHER THAN MEDIUM OR LOW (25) JRL	449	TILT TOWARD BEING THOSE 0.77 OF 69 WHERE THE OBSERVATION OF FOOD TABOOS IS MEDIUM OR LOW, RATHER THAN HIGH (61) JRL	9 16 8 53 XSQ= 4.50 PHI= 0.229 XP = 0.0339
458	LEAN MORE TOWARD BEING THOSE 0.93 OF 27 WHERE GAMES, IF PRESENT, DO NOT INCLUDE GAMES OF STRATEGY (119) R-A-B,EA	458	LEAN LESS TOWARD BEING THOSE 0.65 OF 144 WHERE GAMES, IF PRESENT, DO NOT INCLUDE GAMES OF STRATEGY (119) R-A-B,EA	2 50 25 94 XSQ= 6.78 PHI= -0.199 XP = 0.0092

459	LEAN TOWARD BEING THOSE WHERE GAMES, IF PRESENT, DO NOT INCLUDE GAMES OF CHANCE (89) R-A-B,EA	0.78 OF 27	459	LEAN TOWARD BEING THOSE WHERE GAMES, IF PRESENT, INCLUDE GAMES OF CHANCE (82) R-A-B,EA	0.53 OF 144	6 76 21 68 XSQ= 7.33 PHI= -0.207 XP = 0.0068
460	TEND TO BE THOSE WHERE GAMES, IF PRESENT, ARE LIMITED TO GAMES OF SKILL ONLY (67) R-A-B,EA	0.74 OF 27	460	TEND TO BE THOSE WHERE GAMES, IF PRESENT, ARE NOT LIMITED TO GAMES OF SKILL ONLY (104) R-A-B,EA	0.67 OF 144	20 47 7 97 XSQ= 14.69 PHI= 0.293 XP = 0.0001
468	DRIFT MORE TOWARD BEING THOSE WHERE CONTACT WITH OTHER CULTURES IS REGULAR OR IRREGULAR, RATHER THAN FREQUENT (37) JMH	0.92 OF 13	468	DRIFT LESS TOWARD BEING THOSE WHERE CONTACT WITH OTHER CULTURES IS REGULAR OR IRREGULAR, RATHER THAN FREQUENT (37) JMH	0.61 OF 41	1 16 12 25 XSQ= 3.16 PHI= -0.242 XP = 0.0756

67 CULTURES
WHERE HUSBANDRY IN SHEEP OR GOATS,
AS THE PRINCIPAL FORM OF HUSBANDRY,
IS PRESENT (28)

67 CULTURES
WHERE HUSBANDRY IN SHEEP OR GOATS,
AS THE PRINCIPAL FORM OF HUSBANDRY,
IS ABSENT (372)

BACKGROUND ON PAGE 77

SUBJECT ONLY

28 IN LEFT COLUMN

AMBA	ASHANTI	BAMILEKE	BANDA	BASSERI	BAYA	BEMBA	FANG	FON	GURE
JUKUN	KATAB	KUBA	MAMBILA	MAMVU	MATACO	MATAKAM	MENDE	MONGO	MZAB
NAVAHO	NDEMBU	NUPE	TENETEHARA	TIV	YOMBE	YORUBA	ZUNI		

372 IN RIGHT COLUMN

	Left column (28)			Right column (372)		Statistics
3	TEND TO BE THOSE LOCATED IN AFRICA (80)	0.79 OF 28	3	TEND TO BE THOSE LOCATED OUTSIDE OF AFRICA (320)	0.84 OF 372	22 58 6 314 XSQ= 60.68 PHI= 0.389 XP = 0.
5	DRIFT MORE TOWARD BEING THOSE LOCATED OUTSIDE OF EAST EURASIA (330)	0.96 OF 28	5	DRIFT LESS TOWARD BEING THOSE LOCATED OUTSIDE OF EAST EURASIA (330)	0.81 OF 372	1 69 27 303 XSQ= 3.07 PHI= -0.088 XP = 0.0795
6	IN ALL CASES ARE THOSE LOCATED OUTSIDE OF THE INSULAR PACIFIC (330)	1.00 OF 28	6	TILT LESS TOWARD BEING THOSE LOCATED OUTSIDE OF THE INSULAR PACIFIC (330)	0.81 OF 372	0 70 28 302 XSQ= 5.15 PHI= -0.113 XP = 0.0233
13	IN ALL CASES ARE THOSE WHERE THE LATITUDE IS LESS THAN FORTY DEGREES (329)	1.00 OF 28	13	TILT LESS TOWARD BEING THOSE WHERE THE LATITUDE IS LESS THAN FORTY DEGREES (329)	0.81 OF 372	0 71 28 301 XSQ= 5.26 PHI= -0.115 XP = 0.0219
16	TEND TO BE THOSE WHERE THE LATITUDE IS LESS THAN TEN DEGREES (123)	0.64 OF 28	16	TEND TO BE THOSE WHERE THE LATITUDE IS TEN DEGREES OR GREATER (277)	0.72 OF 372	10 267 18 105 XSQ= 14.25 PHI= -0.189 XP = 0.0002

46	DRIFT MORE TOWARD BEING THOSE 0.93 OF 28 OTHER THAN WHERE SETTLEMENTS ARE NON-FIXED AND MOVEMENT IS NOMADIC (260)	46	DRIFT LESS TOWARD BEING THOSE 0.77 OF 304 OTHER THAN WHERE SETTLEMENTS ARE NON-FIXED AND MOVEMENT IS NOMADIC (260)	2 70 26 234 XSQ= 2.93 PHI= -0.094 XP = 0.0869
51	LEAN MORE TOWARD BEING THOSE 0.93 OF 28 WHERE SUBSISTENCE IS PRIMARILY BY FOOD PRODUCTION -- I. E., AGRICULTURE OR HUSBANDRY -- RATHER THAN BY GATHERING (253)	51	LEAN LESS TOWARD BEING THOSE 0.61 OF 372 WHERE SUBSISTENCE IS PRIMARILY BY FOOD PRODUCTION -- I. E., AGRICULTURE OR HUSBANDRY -- RATHER THAN BY GATHERING (253)	26 227 2 145 XSQ= 10.03 PHI= 0.158 XP = 0.0015
53	DRIFT MORE TOWARD BEING THOSE 0.81 OF 26 WHERE FOOD PRODUCTION IS BY SIMPLE AGRICULTURE OR INCIPIENT FOOD PRODUCTION, RATHER THAN BY INTENSIVE AGRICULTURE (147)	53	DRIFT LESS TOWARD BEING THOSE 0.59 OF 212 WHERE FOOD PRODUCTION IS BY SIMPLE AGRICULTURE OR INCIPIENT FOOD PRODUCTION, RATHER THAN BY INTENSIVE AGRICULTURE (147)	5 86 21 126 XSQ= 3.61 PHI= -0.123 XP = 0.0576
54	DRIFT MORE TOWARD BEING THOSE 0.96 OF 26 WHERE FOOD PRODUCTION IS BY INTENSIVE OR SIMPLE AGRICULTURE, RATHER THAN BY INCIPIENT FOOD PRODUCTION (192)	54	DRIFT LESS TOWARD BEING THOSE 0.79 OF 212 WHERE FOOD PRODUCTION IS BY INTENSIVE OR SIMPLE AGRICULTURE, RATHER THAN BY INCIPIENT FOOD PRODUCTION (192)	25 167 1 45 XSQ= 3.44 PHI= 0.120 XP = 0.0636
55	LEAN TOWARD BEING THOSE 0.80 OF 25 WHERE FOOD PRODUCTION IS BY SIMPLE AGRICULTURE, RATHER THAN BY INTENSIVE AGRICULTURE (101)	55	LEAN TOWARD BEING THOSE 0.51 OF 167 WHERE FOOD PRODUCTION IS BY INTENSIVE AGRICULTURE, RATHER THAN BY SIMPLE AGRICULTURE (91)	5 86 20 81 XSQ= 7.44 PHI= -0.197 XP = 0.0064
56	LEAN MORE TOWARD BEING THOSE 0.95 OF 21 WHERE FOOD PRODUCTION IS BY SIMPLE AGRICULTURE, RATHER THAN BY INCIPIENT FOOD PRODUCTION (101)	56	LEAN LESS TOWARD BEING THOSE 0.64 OF 126 WHERE FOOD PRODUCTION IS BY SIMPLE AGRICULTURE, RATHER THAN BY INCIPIENT FOOD PRODUCTION (101)	20 81 1 45 XSQ= 6.65 PHI= 0.213 XP = 0.0099
71	TEND TO BE THOSE 0.89 OF 18 WHERE METAL WORKING IS PRESENT (98)	71	TEND TO BE THOSE 0.65 OF 233 WHERE METAL WORKING IS ABSENT (153)	16 82 2 151 XSQ= 18.05 PHI= 0.268 XP = 0.0000
74	DRIFT MORE TOWARD BEING THOSE 0.83 OF 18 WHERE POTTERY IS PRESENT (145)	74	DRIFT LESS TOWARD BEING THOSE 0.59 OF 220 WHERE POTTERY IS PRESENT (145)	15 130 3 90 XSQ= 3.15 PHI= 0.115 XP = 0.0758
81	TILT TOWARD BEING THOSE 0.67 OF 21 WHERE A CITY OR TOWN IS PRESENT, OR THE AVERAGE COMMUNITY SIZE IS 200 OR GREATER (89)	81	TILT TOWARD BEING THOSE 0.63 OF 203 WHERE NO CITY OR TOWN IS PRESENT, AND THE AVERAGE COMMUNITY SIZE IS SMALLER THAN 200 (135)	14 75 7 128 XSQ= 5.83 PHI= 0.161 XP = 0.0157

83	LEAN TOWARD BEING THOSE 0.56 OF 16 WHERE, WITH NO CITY AND NO TOWN PRESENT, THE AVERAGE COMMUNITY SIZE IS BETWEEN 200 AND 999, RATHER THAN SMALLER THAN 200 (45)	83	LEAN TOWARD BEING THOSE 0.78 OF 164 WHERE, WITH NO CITY AND NO TOWN PRESENT, THE AVERAGE COMMUNITY SIZE IS SMALLER THAN 200, RATHER THAN BETWEEN 200 AND 999 (135)	9 36 7 128 XSQ= 7.41 PHI= 0.203 XP = 0.0065
97	LEAN LESS TOWARD BEING THOSE 0.61 OF 28 WHERE THE HIERARCHY OF LOCAL JURISDICTION HAS THREE OR TWO LEVELS (273) GES,EA	97	LEAN MORE TOWARD BEING THOSE 0.84 OF 303 WHERE THE HIERARCHY OF LOCAL JURISDICTION HAS THREE OR TWO LEVELS (273) GES,EA	11 47 17 256 XSQ= 8.45 PHI= 0.160 XP = 0.0037
99	TILT MORE TOWARD BEING THOSE 0.87 OF 15 WHERE, WITH NATIONAL HIERARCHY ABSENT, THE HIERARCHY OF LOCAL JURISDICTION HAS FOUR OR THREE LEVELS (93) GES,EA	99	TILT LESS TOWARD BEING THOSE 0.57 OF 141 WHERE, WITH NATIONAL HIERARCHY ABSENT, THE HIERARCHY OF LOCAL JURISDICTION HAS FOUR OR THREE LEVELS (93) GES,EA	13 80 2 61 XSQ= 3.88 PHI= 0.158 XP = 0.0489
108	TILT TOWARD BEING THOSE 0.69 OF 13 WHERE CLASS STRATIFICATION, IF PRESENT, IS BASED ON A HEREDITARY ARISTOCRACY (74)	108	TILT TOWARD BEING THOSE 0.66 OF 190 WHERE CLASS STRATIFICATION, IF PRESENT, IS BASED ON SOMETHING OTHER THAN A HEREDITARY ARISTOCRACY (129)	9 65 4 125 XSQ= 5.02 PHI= 0.157 XP = 0.0251
110	TEND TO BE THOSE 0.78 OF 27 WHERE SLAVERY IS PRESENT (163)	110	TEND TO BE THOSE 0.60 OF 354 WHERE SLAVERY IS ABSENT (218)	21 142 6 212 XSQ= 13.04 PHI= 0.185 XP = 0.0003
128	DRIFT TOWARD BEING THOSE 0.75 OF 12 WHERE, IF SUBSISTENCE IS PRIMARILY BY AGRICULTURE, THE WORK IS MAINLY DONE BY FEMALES (37)	128	DRIFT TOWARD BEING THOSE 0.57 OF 65 WHERE, IF SUBSISTENCE IS PRIMARILY BY AGRICULTURE, THE WORK IS MAINLY DONE BY MALES (40)	3 37 9 28 XSQ= 2.96 PHI= -0.196 XP = 0.0856
129	LEAN TOWARD BEING THOSE 0.73 OF 11 WHERE WEAVING IS MAINLY DONE BY MALES (31)	129	LEAN TOWARD BEING THOSE 0.75 OF 93 WHERE WEAVING IS MAINLY DONE BY FEMALES (73)	8 23 3 70 XSQ= 8.66 PHI= 0.289 XP = 0.0033
176	LEAN TOWARD BEING THOSE 0.75 OF 28 WHERE THE COMMUNITY IS A CLAN-COMMUNITY OR A COMMUNITY STRUCTURED OR SEGMENTED ON A CLAN BASIS (169)	176	LEAN TOWARD BEING THOSE 0.58 OF 354 WHERE THE COMMUNITY IS OTHER THAN A CLAN-COMMUNITY OR A COMMUNITY STRUCTURED OR SEGMENTED ON A CLAN BASIS (213)	21 148 7 206 XSQ= 10.28 PHI= 0.164 XP = 0.0013
177	TILT LESS TOWARD BEING THOSE 0.61 OF 28 WHERE THE COMMUNITY IS OTHER THAN A SINGLE CLAN-COMMUNITY AND EXOGAMOUS (305)	177	TILT MORE TOWARD BEING THOSE 0.81 OF 354 WHERE THE COMMUNITY IS OTHER THAN A SINGLE CLAN-COMMUNITY AND EXOGAMOUS (305)	11 66 17 288 XSQ= 5.65 PHI= 0.122 XP = 0.0175

182	TILT MORE TOWARD BEING THOSE 0.86 OF 28 OTHER THAN WHERE THE COMMUNITY IS STRUCTURED ON A NON-CLAN BASIS AND AGAMOUS (256)	182	TILT LESS TOWARD BEING THOSE 0.66 OF 354 OTHER THAN WHERE THE COMMUNITY IS STRUCTURED ON A NON-CLAN BASIS AND AGAMOUS (256)	4 122 24 232 XSQ= 3.91 PHI= -0.101 XP = 0.0480
183	IN ALL CASES ARE THOSE 1.00 OF 24 WHERE THE LARGEST NON-COGNATIC KIN GROUP IS SMALLER THAN A MOEITY, I. E., A PHRATRY OR SIB OR LINEAGE (218)	183	DRIFT LESS TOWARD BEING THOSE 0.85 OF 228 WHERE THE LARGEST NON-COGNATIC KIN GROUP IS SMALLER THAN A MOEITY, I. E., A PHRATRY OR SIB OR LINEAGE (218)	0 34 24 194 XSQ= 2.96 PHI= -0.108 XP = 0.0854
188	TILT MORE TOWARD BEING THOSE 0.86 OF 28 WHERE THE KIN GROUP IS OTHER THAN EXCLUSIVELY COGNATIC (252)	188	TILT LESS TOWARD BEING THOSE 0.61 OF 372 WHERE THE KIN GROUP IS OTHER THAN EXCLUSIVELY COGNATIC (252)	4 144 24 228 XSQ= 5.66 PHI= -0.119 XP = 0.0174
192	TILT MORE TOWARD BEING THOSE 0.93 OF 28 OTHER THAN WHERE THE ONLY KIN GROUP PRESENT IS A KINDRED OR ELSE BILATERAL DESCENT IS INFERRED (289)	192	TILT LESS TOWARD BEING THOSE 0.71 OF 372 OTHER THAN WHERE THE ONLY KIN GROUP PRESENT IS A KINDRED OR ELSE BILATERAL DESCENT IS INFERRED (289)	2 109 26 263 XSQ= 5.32 PHI= -0.115 XP = 0.0211
213	DRIFT MORE TOWARD BEING THOSE 0.73 OF 26 WHERE FIRST COUSIN MARRIAGE IS NOT PERMITTED (198)	213	DRIFT LESS TOWARD BEING THOSE 0.52 OF 344 WHERE FIRST COUSIN MARRIAGE IS NOT PERMITTED (198)	7 165 19 179 XSQ= 3.50 PHI= -0.097 XP = 0.0614
240	DRIFT TOWARD BEING THOSE 0.59 OF 17 WHERE THE FAMILY, IF EXTENDED, IS LARGE, RATHER THAN SMALL OR STEM (78)	240	DRIFT TOWARD BEING THOSE 0.65 OF 196 WHERE THE FAMILY, IF EXTENDED, IS SMALL OR STEM, RATHER THAN LARGE (135)	10 68 7 128 XSQ= 2.95 PHI= 0.118 XP = 0.0857
262	IN ALL CASES ARE THOSE 1.00 OF 28 WHERE WIVES ARE OBTAINED BY MEANS INVOLVING THE PRESENCE OF SOME CONSIDERATION (305)	262	LEAN LESS TOWARD BEING THOSE 0.75 OF 367 WHERE WIVES ARE OBTAINED BY MEANS INVOLVING THE PRESENCE OF SOME CONSIDERATION (305)	28 277 0 90 XSQ= 7.55 PHI= 0.138 XP = 0.0060
263	LEAN MORE TOWARD BEING THOSE 0.86 OF 28 WHERE WIVES ARE OBTAINED BY RELATIVELY DIFFICULT MEANS, NAMELY BY BRIDE-PRICE, BRIDE-SERVICE, OR EXCHANGING A FEMALE RELATIVE (233)	263	LEAN LESS TOWARD BEING THOSE 0.57 OF 367 WHERE WIVES ARE OBTAINED BY RELATIVELY DIFFICULT MEANS, NAMELY BY BRIDE-PRICE, BRIDE-SERVICE, OR EXCHANGING A FEMALE RELATIVE (233)	24 209 4 158 XSQ= 7.75 PHI= 0.140 XP = 0.0054
314	LEAN TOWARD BEING THOSE 0.71 OF 7 WHERE THE INCIDENCE OF MOTHER-CHILD HOUSEHOLDS IS HIGH (19) W-D,S	314	LEAN TOWARD BEING THOSE 0.81 OF 73 WHERE THE INCIDENCE OF MOTHER-CHILD HOUSEHOLDS IS LOW (61) W-D,S	5 14 2 59 XSQ= 6.96 PHI= 0.295 XP = 0.0083

323	DRIFT TOWARD BEING THOSE WHERE THE CONSTANCY OF PRESENCE OF THE INFANT'S NURTURANT AGENT IS HIGH (29) B-B-C	0.83 OF 6	323	DRIFT TOWARD BEING THOSE WHERE THE CONSTANCY OF PRESENCE OF THE INFANT'S NURTURANT AGENT IS LOW (45) B-B-C	0.65 OF 68	5 24 1 44 XSQ= 3.51 PHI= 0.218 XP = 0.0609
334	DRIFT TOWARD BEING THOSE WHERE THE INDULGENCE OF THE CHILD IS LOW (38) B-B-C	0.86 OF 7	334	DRIFT TOWARD BEING THOSE WHERE THE INDULGENCE OF THE CHILD IS HIGH (40) B-B-C	0.55 OF 71	1 39 6 32 XSQ= 2.74 PHI= -0.188 XP = 0.0977
338	IN ALL CASES ARE THOSE WHERE THE CHILD'S INFERRED ANXIETY OVER PERFORMANCE OF RESPONSIBLE BEHAVIOR IS HIGH (44) B-B-C	1.00 OF 7	338	DRIFT LESS TOWARD BEING THOSE WHERE THE CHILD'S INFERRED ANXIETY OVER PERFORMANCE OF RESPONSIBLE BEHAVIOR IS HIGH (44) B-B-C	0.56 OF 66	7 37 0 29 XSQ= 3.43 PHI= 0.217 XP = 0.0639
377	TEND TO BE THOSE WHERE MALE GENITAL MUTILATION IS PRESENT (83)	0.62 OF 26	377	TEND TO BE THOSE WHERE MALE GENITAL MUTILATION IS ABSENT (242)	0.78 OF 299	16 67 10 232 XSQ= 17.26 PHI= 0.230 XP = 0.0000
385	IN ALL CASES ARE THOSE WHERE SEXUAL EXPRESSION BY THE YOUNG IS RESTRICTED (22) F-B	1.00 OF 4	385	LEAN TOWARD BEING THOSE WHERE SEXUAL EXPRESSION BY THE YOUNG IS SEMI-RESTRICTED OR PERMITTED (64) F-B	0.78 OF 82	4 18 0 64 XSQ= 8.45 PHI= 0.313 XP = 0.0037
405	IN ALL CASES ARE THOSE WHERE EXPLANATIONS OF ILLNESS OF A DEPENDENCE NATURE ARE ABSENT (27) W-C	1.00 OF 5	405	TILT TOWARD BEING THOSE WHERE EXPLANATIONS OF ILLNESS OF A DEPENDENCE NATURE ARE PRESENT (34) W-C	0.61 OF 56	0 34 5 22 XSQ= 4.62 PHI= -0.275 XP = 0.0316
427	DRIFT TOWARD BEING THOSE WHERE A HIGH GOD, IF PRESENT, IS INACTIVE, RATHER THAN ACTIVE (69) GES,EA	0.69 OF 16	427	DRIFT TOWARD BEING THOSE WHERE A HIGH GOD, IF PRESENT, IS ACTIVE, RATHER THAN INACTIVE (87) GES,EA	0.59 OF 140	5 82 11 58 XSQ= 3.31 PHI= -0.146 XP = 0.0689
458	LEAN TOWARD BEING THOSE WHERE GAMES, IF PRESENT, INCLUDE GAMES OF STRATEGY (52) R-A-B,EA	0.73 OF 11	458	LEAN TOWARD BEING THOSE WHERE GAMES, IF PRESENT, DO NOT INCLUDE GAMES OF STRATEGY (119) R-A-B,EA	0.72 OF 160	8 44 3 116 XSQ= 7.93 PHI= 0.215 XP = 0.0049
460	DRIFT MORE TOWARD BEING THOSE WHERE GAMES, IF PRESENT, ARE NOT LIMITED TO GAMES OF SKILL ONLY (104) R-A-B,EA	0.91 OF 11	460	DRIFT LESS TOWARD BEING THOSE WHERE GAMES, IF PRESENT, ARE NOT LIMITED TO GAMES OF SKILL ONLY (104) R-A-B,EA	0.59 OF 160	1 66 10 94 XSQ= 3.22 PHI= -0.137 XP = 0.0728

```
67/

476  IN ALL CASES ARE THCSE          1.00 OF   3        476  DRIFT TOWARD BEING THOSE       0.67 OF  46             0   31
     WHERE THE DEGREE OF INSCBRIETY IS                       WHERE THE DEGREE OF INSCBRIETY IS                         3   15
     MCDERATE CR SLIGHT  (18) CH                              STRONG  (31) DH                                    XSQ=     2.99
                                                                                                                 PHI=   -0.247
                                                                                                                 XP =   0.0840
```

```
68  CULTURES                                      68  CULTURES
    WHERE SUBSISTENCE IS PRIMARILY BY                  WHERE SUBSISTENCE IS PRIMARILY BY
    HUNTING  (26)                                      MEANS OTHER THAN
                                                       HUNTING  (374)

BACKGROUND ON PAGE 78                                                                      SUBJECT ONLY

      26  IN LEFT COLUMN

ABIPON     AWEIKOMA     BORORO    CADUVEO     CHEYENNE   COMANCHE   CROW        DOROBO   GROS VENTRE GUAHIBO
KARIERA    KIOW-APACHE  NABESNA   NASKAPI     OMAHA      ONA        PENOBSCOT   SARSI    SIRIONO     TEHUELCHE
TETON      UTE          WAICA     WIKMUNKAN   YAGUA      YUKAGHIR

     374  IN RIGHT COLUMN

--------------------------------------------------------------------------------------------------------------
 3  DRIFT MORE TOWARD BEING THOSE  0.96 OF  26     3  DRIFT LESS TOWARD BEING THOSE  0.79 OF 374          1   79
    LOCATED OUTSIDE OF                                LOCATED OUTSIDE OF                                  25  295
    AFRICA  (320)                                     AFRICA  (320)                               XSQ=     3.52
                                                                                                  PHI=   -0.094
                                                                                                  XP =   0.0606

 8  TEND LESS TO BE THOSE          0.54 OF  26     8  TEND MORE TO BE THOSE          0.84 OF 374         12   58
    LOCATED OUTSIDE OF                                LOCATED OUTSIDE OF                                  14  316
    NORTH AMERICA  (330)                              NORTH AMERICA  (330)                        XSQ=    13.76
                                                                                                  PHI=    0.185
                                                                                                  XP =   0.0002

 9  LEAN LESS TOWARD BEING THOSE   0.62 OF  26     9  LEAN MORE TOWARD BEING THOSE   0.85 OF 374         10   55
    LOCATED OUTSIDE OF                                LOCATED OUTSIDE OF                                  16  319
    SOUTH AMERICA  (335)                              SOUTH AMERICA  (335)                        XSQ=     8.41
                                                                                                  PHI=    0.145
                                                                                                  XP =   0.0037

14  LEAN TOWARD BEING THOSE        0.58 OF  26    14  LEAN TOWARD BEING THOSE        0.72 OF 374         15  104
    WHERE THE LATITUDE IS                             WHERE THE LATITUDE IS                               11  270
    THIRTY DEGREES OR GREATER  (119)                  LESS THAN THIRTY DEGREES  (281)             XSQ=     9.01
                                                                                                  PHI=    0.150
                                                                                                  XP =   0.0027

15  LEAN TOWARD BEING THOSE        0.73 OF  26    15  LEAN TOWARD BEING THOSE        0.56 OF 374         19  164
    WHERE THE LATITUDE IS                             WHERE THE LATITUDE IS                                7  210
    TWENTY DEGREES OR GREATER  (183)                  LESS THAN TWENTY DEGREES  (217)             XSQ=     7.23
                                                                                                  PHI=    0.134
                                                                                                  XP =   0.0072
```

36	LEAN TOWARD BEING THOSE WHERE THE NATURAL ENVIRONMENT IS 'VERY HARSH,' OR SUB-TROPICAL BUSH, OR TEMPERATE GRASSLAND (108) FWM	0.54 OF 26	36	LEAN TOWARD BEING THOSE WHERE THE NATURAL ENVIRONMENT IS OTHER THAN 'VERY HARSH,' OR SUB-TROPICAL BUSH, OR TEMPERATE GRASSLAND (292) FWM	0.75 OF 374	14 94 12 280 XSQ= 8.76 PHI= 0.148 XP = 0.0031
42	DRIFT MORE TOWARD BEING THOSE WHERE THE NATURAL ENVIRONMENT IS OTHER THAN TROPICAL OR SUB-TROPICAL RAIN FOREST, OR MONSOON FOREST (244) FWM	0.81 OF 26	42	DRIFT LESS TOWARD BEING THOSE WHERE THE NATURAL ENVIRONMENT IS OTHER THAN TROPICAL OR SUB-TROPICAL RAIN FOREST, OR MONSOON FOREST (244) FWM	0.60 OF 374	5 151 21 223 XSQ= 3.72 PHI= -0.096 XP = 0.0537
44	TEND TO BE THOSE WHERE SETTLEMENTS ARE NON-FIXED (110)	0.95 OF 21	44	TEND TO BE THOSE WHERE SETTLEMENTS ARE FIXED (222)	0.71 OF 311	1 221 20 90 XSQ= 36.09 PHI= -0.330 XP = 0.
46	TEND TO BE THOSE WHERE SETTLEMENTS ARE NON-FIXED AND MOVEMENT IS NOMADIC (72)	0.90 OF 21	46	TEND TO BE THOSE OTHER THAN WHERE SETTLEMENTS ARE NON-FIXED AND MOVEMENT IS NOMADIC (260)	0.83 OF 311	19 53 2 258 XSQ= 58.21 PHI= 0.419 XP = 0.
47	LEAN MORE TOWARD BEING THOSE WHERE, IF SETTLEMENTS ARE NON-FIXED, MOVEMENT IS NOMADIC, RATHER THAN NON-NOMADIC (72)	0.95 OF 20	47	LEAN LESS TOWARD BEING THOSE WHERE, IF SETTLEMENTS ARE NON-FIXED, MOVEMENT IS NOMADIC, RATHER THAN NON-NOMADIC (72)	0.59 OF 90	19 53 1 37 XSQ= 7.91 PHI= 0.268 XP = 0.0049
48	DRIFT TOWARD BEING THOSE WHERE THE FOOD SUPPLY IS NOT SECURE, AND FOOD SHORTAGES ARE FREQUENT OR ANNUAL (41) MGW	0.88 OF 8	48	DRIFT TOWARD BEING THOSE WHERE THE FOOD SUPPLY IS SECURE, AND FOOD SHORTAGES ARE RARE OR OCCASIONAL (38) MGW	0.52 OF 71	1 37 7 34 XSQ= 3.07 PHI= -0.197 XP = 0.0797
62	TILT TOWARD BEING THOSE WHERE HUSBANDRY OF ANY KIND IS ABSENT (172)	0.65 OF 26	62	TILT TOWARD BEING THOSE WHERE HUSBANDRY OF SOME KIND IS PRESENT (228)	0.59 OF 374	9 219 17 155 XSQ= 4.75 PHI= -0.109 XP = 0.0293
63	IN ALL CASES ARE THOSE WHERE HUSBANDRY, IF PRESENT, IS PRINCIPALLY IN THE FORM OF BOVINE, EQUINE, CAMEL-LIKE, OR DEER-LIKE ANIMALS, RATHER THAN PIGS, SHEEP, OR GOATS (152)	1.00 OF 9	63	DRIFT LESS TOWARD BEING THOSE WHERE HUSBANDRY, IF PRESENT, IS PRINCIPALLY IN THE FORM OF BOVINE, EQUINE, CAMEL-LIKE, OR DEER-LIKE ANIMALS, RATHER THAN PIGS, SHEEP, OR GOATS (152)	0.66 OF 217	9 143 0 74 XSQ= 3.15 PHI= 0.118 XP = 0.0761
71	LEAN MORE TOWARD BEING THOSE WHERE METAL WORKING IS ABSENT (153)	0.95 OF 19	71	LEAN LESS TOWARD BEING THOSE WHERE METAL WORKING IS ABSENT (153)	0.58 OF 232	1 97 18 135 XSQ= 8.38 PHI= -0.183 XP = 0.0038

```
73  TILT MORE TOWARD BEING THOSE      0.79 OF  19      73  TILT LESS TOWARD BEING THOSE    0.50 OF 229          4   114
    WHERE WEAVING IS                                       WHERE WEAVING IS                                       15   115
    ABSENT  (130)                                          ABSENT  (130)                                   XSQ=      4.71
                                                                                                          PHI=    -0.138
                                                                                                          XP =    0.0300

78  IN ALL CASES ARE THOSE            1.00 OF   3      78  DRIFT TOWARD BEING THOSE        0.71 OF  51           0    36
    WHERE A WRITING SYSTEM IS                              WHERE THE WRITING SYSTEM IS                             3    15
    ABSENT, RATHER THAN BEING PRESENT IN                   ALPHABETIC-OR-PHONETIC, OR MNEMONIC,            XSQ=      3.57
    EITHER ALPHABETIC-OR-PHONETIC FORM OR                  RATHER THAN BEING ABSENT  (36) JMH              PHI=    -0.257
    MNEMONIC FORM  (18) JMH                                                                               XP =    0.0587

81  IN ALL CASES ARE THOSE            1.00 OF  13      81  LEAN LESS TOWARD BEING THOSE    0.58 OF 211           0    89
    WHERE NO CITY OR TOWN IS PRESENT, AND                  WHERE NO CITY OR TOWN IS PRESENT, AND                  13   122
    THE AVERAGE COMMUNITY SIZE IS                          THE AVERAGE COMMUNITY SIZE IS                   XSQ=      7.42
    SMALLER THAN 200  (135)                                SMALLER THAN 200  (135)                         PHI=    -0.182
                                                                                                          XP =    0.0064

82  TEND TO BE THOSE                  0.69 OF  13      82  TEND TO BE THOSE                0.82 OF 211           4   174
    WHERE NO CITY OR TOWN IS PRESENT, AND                  WHERE A CITY OR TOWN IS PRESENT, OR                     9    37
    THE AVERAGE COMMUNITY SIZE IS                          THE AVERAGE COMMUNITY SIZE IS                   XSQ=     17.01
    SMALLER THAN FIFTY  (46)                               FIFTY OR GREATER  (178)                         PHI=    -0.276
                                                                                                          XP =    0.0000

85  IN ALL CASES ARE THOSE            1.00 OF  22      85  TILT LESS TOWARD BEING THOSE    0.75 OF 282           0    70
    WHERE THE LEVEL OF POLITICAL INTEGRATION               WHERE THE LEVEL OF POLITICAL INTEGRATION               22   212
    IS THE MINIMAL STATE,                                  IS THE MINIMAL STATE,                           XSQ=      5.76
    THE AUTONOMOUS COMMUNITY, OR                           THE AUTONOMOUS COMMUNITY, OR                    PHI=    -0.138
    THE FAMILY  (234) GPM                                  THE FAMILY  (234) GPM                           XP =    0.0164

88  LEAN TOWARD BEING THOSE           0.72 OF  18      88  LEAN TOWARD BEING THOSE         0.63 OF 253          13    93
    WHERE, IF A HEADMANSHIP IS PRESENT,                    WHERE, IF A HEADMANSHIP IS PRESENT,                     5   160
    SUCCESSION IS NON-HEREDITARY  (106)                    SUCCESSION IS HEREDITARY  (165)                 XSQ=      7.45
                                                                                                          PHI=     0.166
                                                                                                          XP =    0.0064

95  IN ALL CASES ARE THOSE            1.00 OF  21      95  TILT LESS TOWARD BEING THOSE    0.75 OF 309           0    76
    WHERE THE HIERARCHY                                    WHERE THE HIERARCHY                                    21   233
    OF NATIONAL JURISDICTION HAS                           OF NATIONAL JURISDICTION HAS                    XSQ=      5.39
    ONE OR NO LEVELS  (254) GES,EA                         ONE OR NO LEVELS  (254) GES,EA                  PHI=    -0.128
                                                                                                          XP =    0.0202

98  TEND TO BE THOSE                  0.62 OF  21      98  TEND TO BE THOSE                0.74 OF 310           8   230
    WHERE THE HIERARCHY                                    WHERE THE HIERARCHY                                    13    80
    OF LOCAL JURISDICTION HAS                              OF LOCAL JURISDICTION HAS                       XSQ=     10.96
    TWO LEVELS  (93) GES,EA                                FOUR OR THREE LEVELS  (238) GES,EA              PHI=    -0.182
                                                                                                          XP =    0.0009

99  TILT TOWARD BEING THOSE           0.71 OF  14      99  TILT TOWARD BEING THOSE         0.63 OF 142           4    89
    WHERE, WITH NATIONAL HIERARCHY ABSENT,                 WHERE, WITH NATIONAL HIERARCHY ABSENT,                 10    53
    THE HIERARCHY OF LOCAL JURISDICTION HAS                THE HIERARCHY OF LOCAL JURISDICTION HAS         XSQ=      4.82
    TWO LEVELS  (63) GES,EA                                FOUR OR THREE LEVELS  (93) GES,EA               PHI=    -0.176
                                                                                                          XP =    0.0281
```

100	LEAN LESS TOWARD BEING THOSE 0.52 OF 21 WHERE HIERARCHIES ARE MORE COMPLEX THAN THE 'SIMPLEST,' I. E., MORE COMPLEX THAN TWO LOCAL LEVELS WITH NO NATIONAL LEVELS (267) GES,EA	100	LEAN MORE TOWARD BEING THOSE 0.83 OF 309 WHERE HIERARCHIES ARE MORE COMPLEX THAN THE 'SIMPLEST,' I. E., MORE COMPLEX THAN TWO LOCAL LEVELS WITH NO NATIONAL LEVELS (267) GES,EA	11 256 10 53 XSQ= 9.93 PHI= -0.173 XP = 0.0016
102	TEND TO BE THOSE 0.96 OF 26 WHERE CLASS STRATIFICATION IS ABSENT (180)	102	TEND TO BE THOSE 0.57 OF 357 WHERE CLASS STRATIFICATION IS PRESENT (203)	1 202 25 155 XSQ= 24.98 PHI= -0.255 XP = 0.0000
109	IN ALL CASES ARE THOSE 1.00 OF 26 WHERE CASTES ARE ABSENT (317)	109	DRIFT LESS TOWARD BEING THOSE 0.85 OF 342 WHERE CASTES ARE ABSENT (317)	0 51 26 291 XSQ= 3.34 PHI= -0.095 XP = 0.0677
110	TILT MORE TOWARD BEING THOSE 0.81 OF 26 WHERE SLAVERY IS ABSENT (218)	110	TILT LESS TOWARD BEING THOSE 0.55 OF 355 WHERE SLAVERY IS ABSENT (218)	5 158 21 197 XSQ= 5.33 PHI= -0.118 XP = 0.0209
130	IN ALL CASES ARE THOSE 1.00 OF 12 WHERE LEATHER WORKING IS MAINLY DONE BY FEMALES (45)	130	LEAN TOWARD BEING THOSE 0.54 OF 72 WHERE LEATHER WORKING IS MAINLY DONE BY MALES (39)	0 39 12 33 XSQ= 10.05 PHI= -0.346 XP = 0.0015
131	TEND TO BE THOSE 0.75 OF 12 WHERE THE CONSTRUCTION OF PERMANENT HOUSES OR THE ERECTION OF TEMPORARY DWELLINGS IS MAINLY DONE BY FEMALES (21)	131	TEND TO BE THOSE 0.92 OF 145 WHERE THE CONSTRUCTION OF PERMANENT HOUSES OR THE ERECTION OF TEMPORARY DWELLINGS IS MAINLY DONE BY MALES (136)	3 133 9 12 XSQ= 37.02 PHI= -0.486 XP = 0.
132	IN ALL CASES ARE THOSE 1.00 OF 3 WHERE ECONOMIC EXCHANGE DOES NOT INVOLVE THE USE OF MONEY (17) JMH	132	TILT TOWARD BEING THOSE 0.73 OF 51 WHERE ECONOMIC EXCHANGE INVOLVES THE USE OF MONEY (37) JMH	0 37 3 14 XSQ= 3.96 PHI= -0.271 XP = 0.0466
179	DRIFT LESS TOWARD BEING THOSE 0.76 OF 25 WHERE THE COMMUNITY IS OTHER THAN STRUCTURED ON A NON-CLAN BASIS AND COMMONLY EXOGAMOUS (340)	179	DRIFT MORE TOWARD BEING THOSE 0.90 OF 357 WHERE THE COMMUNITY IS OTHER THAN STRUCTURED ON A NON-CLAN BASIS AND COMMONLY EXOGAMOUS (340)	6 36 19 321 XSQ= 3.31 PHI= 0.093 XP = 0.0688
184	DRIFT TOWARD BEING THOSE 0.60 OF 10 WHERE THE LARGEST NON-COGNATIC KIN GROUP IS THE MOEITY OR PHRATRY (77)	184	DRIFT TOWARD BEING THOSE 0.71 OF 242 WHERE THE LARGEST NON-COGNATIC KIN GROUP IS SMALLER THAN A PHRATRY, I. E. A SIB OR LINEAGE (175)	6 71 4 171 XSQ= 2.93 PHI= 0.108 XP = 0.0868

186	TILT MORE TOWARD BEING THOSE WHERE THE KIN GROUP IS OTHER THAN EXCLUSIVELY PATRILINEAL (250)	0.85 OF 26	186	TILT LESS TOWARD BEING THOSE WHERE THE KIN GROUP IS OTHER THAN EXCLUSIVELY PATRILINEAL (250)	0.61 OF 374	4 146 22 228 XSQ= 4.84 PHI= -0.110 XP = 0.0278
188	TILT TOWARD BEING THOSE WHERE THE KIN GROUP IS EXCLUSIVELY COGNATIC (148)	0.62 OF 26	188	TILT TOWARD BEING THOSE WHERE THE KIN GROUP IS OTHER THAN EXCLUSIVELY COGNATIC (252)	0.65 OF 374	16 132 10 242 XSQ= 6.10 PHI= 0.124 XP = 0.0135
192	TEND TO BE THOSE WHERE THE ONLY KIN GROUP PRESENT IS A KINDRED OR ELSE BILATERAL DESCENT IS INFERRED (111)	0.58 OF 26	192	TEND TO BE THOSE OTHER THAN WHERE THE ONLY KIN GROUP PRESENT IS A KINDRED OR ELSE BILATERAL DESCENT IS INFERRED (289)	0.74 OF 374	15 96 11 278 XSQ= 10.89 PHI= 0.165 XP = 0.0010
196	TEND TO BE THOSE WHERE INDIVIDUAL RIGHTS IN REAL PROPERTY, OR RULES FOR INHERITANCE, ARE ABSENT (87)	0.86 OF 21	196	TEND TO BE THOSE WHERE INDIVIDUAL RIGHTS IN REAL PROPERTY, AND RULES FOR INHERITANCE, ARE PRESENT (194)	0.73 OF 260	3 191 18 69 XSQ= 29.12 PHI= -0.322 XP = 0.0000
204	DRIFT LESS TOWARD BEING THOSE WHERE MARITAL RESIDENCE IS PATRILOCAL, VIRILOCAL, OR AVUNCULOCAL, RATHER THAN AMBILOCAL OR NEOLOCAL (270)	0.61 OF 18	204	DRIFT MORE TOWARD BEING THOSE WHERE MARITAL RESIDENCE IS PATRILOCAL, VIRILOCAL, OR AVUNCULOCAL, RATHER THAN AMBILOCAL OR NEOLOCAL (270)	0.82 OF 316	11 259 7 57 XSQ= 3.53 PHI= -0.103 XP = 0.0603
209	TILT LESS TOWARD BEING THOSE WHERE MARITAL RESIDENCE IS PATRILOCAL, VIRILOCAL, OR AVUNCULOCAL, RATHER THAN MATRILOCAL OR UXORILOCAL (270)	0.58 OF 19	209	TILT MORE TOWARD BEING THOSE WHERE MARITAL RESIDENCE IS PATRILOCAL, VIRILOCAL, OR AVUNCULOCAL, RATHER THAN MATRILOCAL OR UXORILOCAL (270)	0.82 OF 315	11 259 8 56 XSQ= 5.37 PHI= -0.127 XP = 0.0205
308	IN ALL CASES ARE THOSE WHERE AVERAGE SOCIALIZATION ANXIETY IS LOW (18) W-C	1.00 OF 4	308	TILT TOWARD BEING THOSE WHERE AVERAGE SOCIALIZATION ANXIETY IS HIGH (22) W-C	0.61 OF 36	0 22 4 14 XSQ= 3.24 PHI= -0.285 EP = 0.0335
310	IN ALL CASES ARE THOSE WHERE ANAL SOCIALIZATION ANXIETY IS LOW (19) W-C	1.00 OF 5	310	TILT TOWARD BEING THOSE WHERE ANAL SOCIALIZATION ANXIETY IS HIGH (22) W-C	0.61 OF 36	0 22 5 14 XSQ= 4.36 PHI= -0.326 XP = 0.0367
326	DRIFT TOWARD BEING THOSE WHERE THE INFERRED TRANSITION ANXIETY BETWEEN INFANCY AND CHILDHOOD IS LOW (35) B-B-C	0.88 OF 8	326	DRIFT TOWARD BEING THOSE WHERE THE INFERRED TRANSITION ANXIETY BETWEEN INFANCY AND CHILDHOOD IS HIGH (32) B-B-C	0.53 OF 59	1 31 7 28 XSQ= 3.06 PHI= -0.214 XP = 0.0800

```
334  IN ALL CASES ARE THCSE           1.00 OF    8    334  TILT TOWARD BEING THOSE          0.54 CF  70          8   32
     WHERE THE INDULGENCE CF THE CHILD                     WHERE THE INDULGENCE OF THE CHILD                     0   38
     IS HIGH  (40) B-B-C                                   IS LOW  (38) B-B-C                              XSQ=     6.44
                                                                                                           PHI=    0.287
                                                                                                           XP =   0.0112

337  IN ALL CASES ARE THOSE           1.00 OF    7    337  TILT TOWARD BEING THOSE          0.58 OF  66          0   38
     WHERE THE CHILD'S INFERREC ANXIETY OVER               WHERE THE CHILD'S INFERRED ANXIETY CVER               7   28
     NCN-PERFORMANCE OF RESPCNSIBLE BEHAVIOR               NON-PERFORMANCE OF RESPCNSIBLE BEHAVIOR         XSQ=     6.26
     IS LOW  (35) B-B-C                                    IS HIGH  (38) B-B-C                             PHI=   -0.293
                                                                                                           XP =   0.0124

338  TILT TCWARD BEING THCSE          0.86 OF    7    338  TILT TOWARD BEING THOSE          0.65 CF  66          1   43
     WHERE THE CHILD'S INFERREC ANXIETY OVER               WHERE THE CHILD'S INFERRED ANXIETY OVER               6   23
     PERFCRMANCE OF RESPCNSIBLE BEHAVIOR                   PERFORMANCE OF RESPONSIBLE BEHAVIOR             XSQ=     4.88
     IS LCW  (29) B-B-C                                    IS HIGH  (44) B-B-C                             PHI=   -0.259
                                                                                                           XP =   0.0272

339  IN ALL CASES ARE THCSE           1.00 OF    7    339  TILT LESS TOWARD BEING THOSE     0.53 OF  66          0   31
     WHERE THE CHILD'S INFERREC CONFLICT                   WHERE THE CHILD'S INFERRED CONFLICT                   7   35
     REGARDING RESPONSIBLE BEHAVIOR                        REGARDING RESPCNSIBLE BEHAVIOR                  XSQ=     3.95
     IS LCW  (42) B-B-C                                    IS LOW  (42) B-B-C                              PHI=   -0.233
                                                                                                           XP =   0.0468

346  DRIFT TCWARD BEING THCSE         0.88 OF    8    346  DRIFT TOWARD BEING THOSE         0.53 OF  68          1   36
     WHERE THE CHILD'S INFERREC ANXIETY OVER               WHERE THE CHILD'S INFERRED ANXIETY OVER               7   32
     PERFCRMANCE CF SELF-RELIANT BEHAVIOR                  PERFORMANCE OF SELF-RELIANT BEHAVIOR            XSQ=     3.21
     IS LCW  (39) B-B-C                                    IS HIGH  (37) B-B-C                             PHI=   -0.205
                                                                                                           XP =   0.0733

347  DRIFT TCWARD BEING THOSE         0.88 OF    8    347  DRIFT TOWARD BEING THOSE         0.53 OF  68          1   36
     WHERE THE CHILD'S INFERREC CONFLICT                   WHERE THE CHILD'S INFERRED CONFLICT                   7   32
     REGARDING SELF-RELIANT BEHAVICR                       REGARDING SELF-RELIANT BEHAVIOR                 XSQ=     3.21
     IS LCW  (39) B-B-C                                    IS HIGH  (37) B-B-C                             PHI=   -0.205
                                                                                                           XP =   0.0733

368  IN ALL CASES ARE THCSE           1.00 OF    3    368  DRIFT TOWARD BEING THOSE         0.62 CF  34          3   13
     WHERE DISSCCIATICN CF THE SEXES                       WHERE DISSOCIATION OF THE SEXES                       0   21
     AT ADCLESCENCE                                        AT ADOLESCENCE                                  XSQ=     2.14
     IS HIGH CR MEDIUM  (16) JKH                           IS LOW  (21) JKH                                PHI=    0.240
                                                                                                           EP =   0.0721

377  TILT MORE TOWARD BEING THCSE     0.95 OF   21    377  TILT LESS TOWARD BEING THOSE     0.73 OF 304          1   82
     WHERE MALE GENITAL MUTILATION                         WHERE MALE GENITAL MUTILATICN                        20  222
     IS ABSENT  (242)                                      IS ABSENT  (242)                                XSQ=     4.00
                                                                                                           PHI=   -0.111
                                                                                                           XP =   0.0456

403  IN ALL CASES ARE THCSE           1.00 OF    7    403  DRIFT LESS TOWARD BEING THCSE    0.57 CF  54          0   23
     WHERE EXPLANATICNS OF ILLNESS                         WHERE EXPLANATIONS OF ILLNESS                         7   31
     OF AN ANAL NATURE                                     OF AN ANAL NATURE                               XSQ=     3.14
     ARE ABSENT  (38) W-C                                  ARE ABSENT  (38) W-C                            PHI=   -0.227
                                                                                                           XP =   0.0762
```

443	DRIFT TOWARD BEING THOSE WHERE OVERALL FEAR OF OTHERS IS LOW (30) W-C	0.86 OF 7	443	DRIFT TOWARD BEING THOSE WHERE OVERALL FEAR OF OTHERS IS HIGH (31) W-C	0.56 OF 54	1 30 6 24 XSQ= 2.73 PHI= -0.212 XP = 0.0983
455	IN ALL CASES ARE THOSE WHERE THE MODE OF THE INDIVIDUAL'S CONTACT WITH THE DIVINE IS CONDUCIVE TO THE DEVELOPMENT OF THE INDIVIDUAL'S NEED TO ACHIEVE (17) DCM	1.00 OF 4	455	TILT TOWARD BEING THOSE WHERE THE MODE OF THE INDIVIDUAL'S CONTACT WITH THE DIVINE IS NOT CONDUCIVE TO THE DEVELOPMENT OF THE INDIVIDUAL'S NEED TO ACHIEVE (19) DCM	0.59 OF 32	4 13 0 19 XSQ= 2.93 PHI= 0.285 EP = 0.0404
458	IN ALL CASES ARE THOSE WHERE GAMES, IF PRESENT, DO NOT INCLUDE GAMES OF STRATEGY (119) R-A-B,EA	1.00 OF 13	458	TILT LESS TOWARD BEING THOSE WHERE GAMES, IF PRESENT, DO NOT INCLUDE GAMES OF STRATEGY (119) R-A-B,EA	0.67 OF 158	0 52 13 106 XSQ= 4.69 PHI= -0.166 XP = 0.0303
480	IN ALL CASES ARE THOSE WHERE COMPLEXITY OF ARTISTIC DESIGN IS LOW (15) HB	1.00 OF 4	480	DRIFT TOWARD BEING THOSE WHERE COMPLEXITY OF ARTISTIC DESIGN IS HIGH (14) HB	0.56 OF 25	0 14 4 11 XSQ= 2.38 PHI= -0.286 EP = 0.0996

69 CULTURES
WHERE SUBSISTENCE IS PRIMARILY BY
FISHING (44)

69 CULTURES
WHERE SUBSISTENCE IS PRIMARILY BY
MEANS OTHER THAN
FISHING (356)

BACKGROUND ON PAGE 78

SUBJECT ONLY

44 IN LEFT COLUMN

AINU	ALACALUF	ANDAMANESE	BAJUN	BOZO	CALLINAGO	CARAJA	COPR ESKIMO	CREE	ELLICE
EYAK	GILBERTESE	GILYAK	HAIDA	HAWAIIANS	INGALIK	KASKA	KET	KORYAK	KUTENAI
KWAKIUTL	MANIHIKI	MANUS	MATACO	NUNIVAK	OJIBWA	ONTONG-JAVA	PARAUJANO	RARCIANS	SANPOIL
SELUNG	SERI	TAREUMIUT	TENINO	TIKOPIA	TOKELAU	TOLOWA	TRUKESE	TSHIMSHIAN	TUCUNA
TWANA	WARCPEN	YAHGAN	YUROK						

356 IN RIGHT COLUMN

	Left column (44)			Right column (356)		
3	TILT MORE TOWARD BEING THOSE LOCATED OUTSIDE OF AFRICA (320)	0.95 OF 44	3	TILT LESS TOWARD BEING THOSE LOCATED OUTSIDE OF AFRICA (320)	0.78 OF 356	2 78 42 278 XSQ= 6.33 PHI= -0.126 XP = 0.0118
4	IN ALL CASES ARE THOSE LOCATED OUTSIDE OF THE CIRCUM-MEDITERRANEAN (355)	1.00 OF 44	4	TILT LESS TOWARD BEING THOSE LOCATED OUTSIDE OF THE CIRCUM-MEDITERRANEAN (355)	0.87 OF 356	0 45 44 311 XSQ= 5.06 PHI= -0.113 XP = 0.0244
8	TEND LESS TO BE THOSE LOCATED OUTSIDE OF NORTH AMERICA (330)	0.59 OF 44	8	TEND MORE TO BE THOSE LOCATED OUTSIDE OF NORTH AMERICA (330)	0.85 OF 356	18 52 26 304 XSQ= 16.99 PHI= 0.206 XP = 0.0000
13	TEND TO BE THOSE WHERE THE LATITUDE IS FORTY DEGREES OR GREATER (71)	0.52 OF 44	13	TEND TO BE THOSE WHERE THE LATITUDE IS LESS THAN FORTY DEGREES (329)	0.87 OF 356	23 48 21 308 XSQ= 37.75 PHI= 0.307 XP = 0.
14	LEAN TOWARD BEING THOSE WHERE THE LATITUDE IS THIRTY DEGREES OR GREATER (119)	0.52 OF 44	14	LEAN TOWARD BEING THOSE WHERE THE LATITUDE IS LESS THAN THIRTY DEGREES (281)	0.73 OF 356	23 96 21 260 XSQ= 10.82 PHI= 0.164 XP = 0.0010

15	DRIFT TCWARD BEING THCSE WHERE THE LATITUDE IS TWENTY DEGREES CR GREATER (183)	0.59 OF 44	15	DRIFT TOWARD BEING THOSE WHERE THE LATITUDE IS LESS THAN TWENTY DEGREES (217)	0.56 OF 356	26 157 18 199 XSQ= 2.97 PHI= 0.086 XP = 0.0850
44	LEAN TOWARC BEING THOSE WHERE SETTLEMENTS ARE NCN-FIXED (110)	0.58 OF 36	44	LEAN TOWARD BEING THOSE WHERE SETTLEMENTS ARE FIXED (222)	0.70 OF 296	15 207 21 89 XSQ= 10.33 PHI= -0.176 XP = 0.0013
46	TILT LESS TOWARC BEING THCSE OTHER THAN WHERE SETTLEMENTS ARE NCN-FIXED AND MCVEMENT IS NCMADIC (260)	0.64 OF 36	46	TILT MORE TOWARD BEING THCSE OTHER THAN WHERE SETTLEMENTS ARE NON-FIXED AND MOVEMENT IS NOMADIC (260)	0.80 OF 296	13 59 23 237 XSQ= 4.04 PHI= 0.110 XP = 0.0444
48	DRIFT TCWARD BEING THOSE WHERE THE FCCD SUPPLY IS SECURE, AND FCOD SHORTAGES ARE RARE CR CCCASICNAL (38) MCW	0.80 OF 10	48	DRIFT TOWARD BEING THOSE WHERE THE FOOD SUPPLY IS NCT SECURE, AND FOOD SHORTAGES ARE FREQUENT OR ANNUAL (41) MGW	0.57 OF 69	8 30 2 39 XSQ= 3.32 PHI= 0.205 XP = 0.0685
62	TEND TC BE THOSE WHERE HUSBANDRY CF ANY KINC IS ABSENT (172)	0.84 OF 44	62	TEND TO BE THOSE WHERE HUSBANDRY OF SOME KIND IS PRESENT (228)	0.62 OF 356	7 221 37 135 XSQ= 32.20 PHI= -0.284 XP = 0.
63	LEAN TOWARC BEING THOSE WHERE HUSBANDRY, IF PRESENT, IS PRINCIPALLY IN THE FCRM OF PIGS, SHEEP, CR GOATS, RATHER THAN BOVINE, EQUINE, CAMEL-LIKE, OR DEER-LIKE ANIMALS (74)	0.86 OF 7	63	LEAN TOWARD BEING THOSE WHERE HUSBANDRY, IF PRESENT, IS PRINCIPALLY IN THE FCRM CF BOVINE, EQUINE, CAMEL-LIKE, CR DEER-LIKE ANIMALS, RATHER THAN PIGS, SHEEP, OR GOATS (152)	0.69 OF 219	1 151 6 68 XSQ= 6.89 PHI= -0.175 XP = 0.0087
71	TEND MCRE TO BE THCSE WHERE METAL WORKING IS ABSENT (153)	0.94 OF 36	71	TEND LESS TO BE THOSE WHERE METAL WORKING IS ABSENT (153)	0.55 OF 215	2 96 34 119 XSQ= 18.20 PHI= -0.269 XP = 0.0000
73	TILT TCWARD BEING THOSE WHERE WEAVING IS ABSENT (130)	0.71 OF 35	73	TILT TOWARD BEING THOSE WHERE WEAVING IS PRESENT (118)	0.51 OF 213	10 108 25 105 XSQ= 5.05 PHI= -0.143 XP = 0.0246
74	TEND TC BE THCSE WHERE POTTERY IS ABSENT (93)	0.72 OF 36	74	TEND TO BE THOSE WHERE POTTERY IS PRESENT (145)	0.67 OF 202	10 135 26 67 XSQ= 17.97 PHI= -0.275 XP = 0.0000

80	IN ALL CASES ARE THCSE 1.00 OF 20 WHERE NC CITY OR TCWN IS PRESENT (185)	80	DRIFT LESS TOWARD BEING THCSE 0.81 OF 204 WHERE NO CITY OR TOWN IS PRESENT (185)	0 39 20 165 XSQ= 3.40 PHI= -0.123 XP = 0.0654
81	LEAN MORE TOWARC BEING THCSE 0.90 OF 20 WHERE NC CITY OR TCWN IS PRESENT, ANC THE AVERAGE COMMUNITY SIZE IS SMALLER THAN 200 (135)	81	LEAN LESS TOWARD BEING THOSE 0.57 CF 204 WHERE NO CITY OR TOWN IS PRESENT, AND THE AVERAGE COMMUNITY SIZE IS SMALLER THAN 200 (135)	2 87 18 117 XSQ= 6.80 PHI= -0.174 XP = 0.0091
84	IN ALL CASES ARE THCSE 1.00 OF 32 WHERE THE LEVEL CF POLITICAL INTEGRATION IS THE LITTLE STATE, THE MINIMAL STATE, THE AUTCNCMOUS COMMUNITY, CR THE FAMILY (262) GPM	84	TILT LESS TOWARD BEING THOSE 0.85 CF 272 WHERE THE LEVEL OF POLITICAL INTEGRATION IS THE LITTLE STATE, THE MINIMAL STATE, THE AUTONOMOUS COMMUNITY, CR THE FAMILY (262) GPM	0 42 32 230 XSQ= 4.51 PHI= -0.122 XP = 0.0337
86	TEND TO BE THCSE 0.91 OF 32 WHERE THE LEVEL OF POLITICAL INTEGRATION IS THE AUTCNOMOUS COMMUNITY, OR THE FAMILY (156) GPM	86	TEND TO BE THOSE 0.53 CF 272 WHERE THE LEVEL OF POLITICAL INTEGRATICN IS THE LARGE STATE, THE LITTLE STATE, OR THE MINIMAL STATE (148) GPM	3 145 29 127 XSQ= 20.40 PHI= -0.259 XP = 0.0000
94	IN ALL CASES ARE THCSE 1.00 OF 37 WHERE THE HIERARCHY OF NATICNAL JURISDICTION HAS TWO, CNE, CR NO LEVELS (296) GES,EA	94	DRIFT LESS TOWARD BEING THCSE 0.88 CF 293 WHERE THE HIERARCHY OF NATIONAL JURISDICTION HAS TWO, ONE, OR NO LEVELS (296) GES,EA	0 34 37 259 XSQ= 3.61 PHI= -0.105 XP = 0.0573
96	TILT TOWARD BEING THOSE 0.65 OF 37 WHERE THE HIERARCHY OF NATICNAL JURISDICTICN HAS NC LEVELS (156) GES,EA	96	TILT TOWARD BEING THOSE 0.55 CF 293 WHERE THE HIERARCHY OF NATIONAL JURISDICTION HAS FOUR, THREE, TWO OR ONE LEVEL (174) GES,EA	13 161 24 132 XSQ= 4.41 PHI= -0.116 XP = 0.0357
106	TILT TCWARD BEING THOSE 0.63 OF 19 WHERE CLASS STRATIFICATION, IF PRESENT, IS BASED CN WEALTH (77)	106	TILT TOWARD BEING THOSE 0.65 CF 184 WHERE CLASS STRATIFICATION, IF PRESENT, IS BASED ON SOMETHING OTHER THAN WEALTH (126)	12 65 7 119 XSQ= 4.55 PHI= 0.150 XP = 0.0330
107	IN ALL CASES ARE THCSE 1.00 OF 19 WHERE CLASS STRATIFICATION, IF PRESENT, IS BASED CN SCMETHING CTHER THAN OCCUPATICNAL STATUS (160)	107	TILT LESS TOWARD BEING THCSE 0.77 CF 184 WHERE CLASS STRATIFICATICN, IF PRESENT, IS BASED ON SOMETHING OTHER THAN OCCUPATIONAL STATUS (160)	0 43 19 141 XSQ= 4.32 PHI= -0.146 XP = 0.0377
109	DRIFT MORE TOWARC BEING THCSE 0.95 OF 44 WHERE CASTES ARE ABSENT (317)	109	DRIFT LESS TOWARD BEING THCSE 0.85 OF 324 WHERE CASTES ARE ABSENT (317)	2 49 42 275 XSQ= 2.80 PHI= -0.087 XP = 0.0943

116	IN ALL CASES ARE THOSE WHERE OCCUPATIONAL SPECIALIZATION IS PART-TIME ONLY (34) JMH	1.00 OF 8	116	DRIFT LESS TOWARD BEING THOSE WHERE OCCUPATIONAL SPECIALIZATION IS PART-TIME ONLY (34) JMH	0.57 OF 46	0 20 8 26 XSQ= 3.82 PHI= -0.266 XP = 0.0507
130	TEND TO BE THOSE WHERE LEATHER WORKING IS MAINLY DONE BY FEMALES (45)	0.94 OF 16	130	TEND TO BE THOSE WHERE LEATHER WORKING IS MAINLY DONE BY MALES (39)	0.56 OF 68	1 38 15 30 XSQ= 10.91 PHI= -0.360 XP = 0.0010
147	TILT TOWARD BEING THOSE WHERE CODIFIED LAWS ARE UNIMPORTANT OR ABSENT (13) LWS	0.83 OF 6	147	TILT TOWARD BEING THOSE WHERE CODIFIED LAWS ARE PRESENT (20) LWS	0.70 OF 27	1 19 5 8 XSQ= 3.89 PHI= -0.344 EP = 0.0248
186	LEAN MORE TOWARD BEING THOSE WHERE THE KIN GROUP IS OTHER THAN EXCLUSIVELY PATRILINEAL (250)	0.84 OF 44	186	LEAN LESS TOWARD BEING THOSE WHERE THE KIN GROUP IS OTHER THAN EXCLUSIVELY PATRILINEAL (250)	0.60 OF 356	7 143 37 213 XSQ= 8.83 PHI= -0.149 XP = 0.0030
188	TEND TO BE THOSE WHERE THE KIN GROUP IS EXCLUSIVELY COGNATIC (148)	0.61 OF 44	188	TEND TO BE THOSE WHERE THE KIN GROUP IS OTHER THAN EXCLUSIVELY COGNATIC (252)	0.66 OF 356	27 121 17 235 XSQ= 11.44 PHI= 0.169 XP = 0.0007
192	DRIFT LESS TOWARD BEING THOSE OTHER THAN WHERE THE ONLY KIN GROUP PRESENT IS A KINDRED OR ELSE BILATERAL DESCENT IS INFERRED (289)	0.59 OF 44	192	DRIFT MORE TOWARD BEING THOSE OTHER THAN WHERE THE ONLY KIN GROUP PRESENT IS A KINDRED OR ELSE BILATERAL DESCENT IS INFERRED (289)	0.74 OF 356	18 93 26 263 XSQ= 3.56 PHI= 0.094 XP = 0.0590
196	LEAN TOWARD BEING THOSE WHERE INDIVIDUAL RIGHTS IN REAL PROPERTY, OR RULES FOR INHERITANCE, ARE ABSENT (87)	0.55 OF 31	196	LEAN TOWARD BEING THOSE WHERE INDIVIDUAL RIGHTS IN REAL PROPERTY, AND RULES FOR INHERITANCE, ARE PRESENT (194)	0.72 OF 250	14 180 17 70 XSQ= 8.08 PHI= -0.170 XP = 0.0045
243	IN ALL CASES ARE THOSE WHERE POLYGYNY, IF PRESENT, HAS A LOW INCIDENCE (36) W-D,S	1.00 OF 9	243	TILT LESS TOWARD BEING THOSE WHERE POLYGYNY, IF PRESENT, HAS A LOW INCIDENCE (36) W-D,S	0.53 OF 51	0 24 9 27 XSQ= 5.23 PHI= -0.295 XP = 0.0221
254	IN ALL CASES ARE THOSE WHERE HOUSEHOLD AUTHORITY IS ON THE MOTHER'S SIDE, RATHER THAN THE FATHER'S (6) CA	1.00 OF 3	254	TILT TOWARD BEING THOSE WHERE HOUSEHOLD AUTHORITY IS ON THE FATHER'S SIDE, RATHER THAN THE MOTHER'S (9) DA	0.75 OF 12	0 9 3 3 XSQ= 2.93 PHI= -0.442 EP = 0.0440

262	DRIFT LESS TOWARD BEING THOSE WHERE WIVES ARE OBTAINED BY MEANS INVOLVING THE PRESENCE OF SOME CONSIDERATION (305)	0.66 OF 44	262	DRIFT MORE TOWARD BEING THOSE WHERE WIVES ARE OBTAINED BY MEANS INVOLVING THE PRESENCE OF SOME CONSIDERATION (305)	0.79 OF 351	29 276 15 75 XSQ= 2.91 PHI= -0.086 XP = 0.0880
302	DRIFT TOWARD BEING THOSE WHERE THE AVERAGE EARLY SATISFACTION POTENTIAL IS LOW (17) W-C	0.75 OF 8	302	DRIFT TOWARD BEING THOSE WHERE THE AVERAGE EARLY SATISFACTION POTENTIAL IS HIGH (23) W-C	0.66 OF 32	2 21 6 11 XSQ= 2.82 PHI= -0.266 EP = 0.0532
315	TILT TOWARD BEING THOSE WHERE MOTHER AND NURSING CHILD CUSTOMARILY SLEEP IN DIFFERENT BEDS (14) W-D,S	0.63 OF 8	315	TILT TOWARD BEING THOSE WHERE MOTHER AND NURSING CHILD CUSTOMARILY SLEEP IN THE SAME BED (37) W-D,S	0.79 OF 43	3 34 5 9 XSQ= 3.95 PHI= -0.278 XP = 0.0468
316	IN ALL CASES ARE THOSE WHERE EXCLUSIVE MOTHER-SON SLEEPING ARRANGEMENTS LAST LESS THAN ONE YEAR (25) W-K-A	1.00 OF 6	316	DRIFT TOWARD BEING THOSE WHERE EXCLUSIVE MOTHER-SON SLEEPING ARRANGEMENTS LAST ONE YEAR OR LONGER (19) W-K-A	0.50 OF 38	0 19 6 19 XSQ= 3.44 PHI= -0.280 XP = 0.0637
365	IN ALL CASES ARE THOSE WHERE THE TIME SPENT IN ADOLESCENT PEER GROUP ACTIVITY IS LOW-MEDIUM OR LOW (15) JKH	1.00 OF 3	365	DRIFT TOWARD BEING THOSE WHERE THE TIME SPENT IN ADOLESCENT PEER GROUP ACTIVITY IS HIGH OR HIGH-MEDIUM (30) JKH	0.71 OF 42	0 30 3 12 XSQ= 3.62 PHI= -0.283 XP = 0.0572
377	TILT MORE TOWARD BEING THOSE WHERE MALE GENITAL MUTILATION IS ABSENT (242)	0.91 OF 34	377	TILT LESS TOWARD BEING THOSE WHERE MALE GENITAL MUTILATION IS ABSENT (242)	0.73 OF 291	3 80 31 211 XSQ= 4.64 PHI= -0.119 XP = 0.0312
400	DRIFT TOWARD BEING THOSE WHERE HOMOSEXUAL ACTIVITY IS PROHIBITED (22) F-B	0.75 OF 8	400	DRIFT TOWARD BEING THOSE WHERE HOMOSEXUAL ACTIVITY IS PERMITTED (36) F-B	0.68 OF 50	6 16 2 34 XSQ= 3.74 PHI= 0.254 XP = 0.0530
420	TILT TOWARD BEING THOSE WHERE BELLICOSITY IS MODERATE OR NEGLIGIBLE (46) PES	0.91 OF 11	420	TILT TOWARD BEING THOSE WHERE BELLICOSITY IS EXTREME (41) PES	0.53 OF 76	1 40 10 36 XSQ= 5.67 PHI= -0.255 XP = 0.0173
426	TEND TO BE THOSE WHERE A HIGH GOD IS ABSENT (104) GES,EA	0.72 OF 32	426	TEND TO BE THOSE WHERE A HIGH GOD IS PRESENT (156) GES,EA	0.64 OF 228	9 147 23 81 XSQ= 13.97 PHI= -0.232 XP = 0.0002

449	DRIFT TCWARD BEING THCSE 0.63 OF 8 WHERE THE CBSERVATICN CF FCOC TABOOS IS HIGH, RATHER THAN MEDIUM CR LOW (25) JRL	449	DRIFT TOWARD BEING THOSE 0.74 OF 78 WHERE THE OBSERVATICN OF FCCD TABCCS IS MEDIUM OR LOW, RATHER THAN HIGH (61) JRL	5 20 3 58 XSQ= 3.16 PHI= 0.192 XP = 0.0754
455	IN ALL CASES ARE THCSE 1.00 OF 5 WHERE THE MODE CF THE INDIVICUAL'S CCNTACT WITH THE DIVINE IS NOT CONDUCIVE TC THE CEVELOPMENT OF THE INDIVIDUAL'S NEED TC ACHIEVE (19) DCM	455	TILT TOWARD BEING THOSE 0.55 CF 31 WHERE THE MODE OF THE INDIVIDUAL'S CONTACT WITH THE DIVINE IS CONDUCIVE TC THE DEVELCPMENT OF THE INDIVIDUAL'S NEED TO ACHIEVE (17) DCM	0 17 5 14 XSQ= 3.23 PHI= -0.299 EP = 0.0473
458	LEAN MORE TOWARC BEING THCSE 0.96 OF 27 WHERE GAMES, IF PRESENT, DC NCT INCLUDE GAMES OF STRATEGY (119) R-A-B,EA	458	LEAN LESS TOWARD BEING THOSE 0.65 CF 144 WHERE GAMES, IF PRESENT, DO NOT INCLUDE GAMES OF STRATEGY (119) R-A-B,EA	1 51 26 93 XSQ= 9.36 PHI= -0.234 XP = 0.0022
468	IN ALL CASES ARE THCSE 1.00 OF 8 WHERE CCNTACT WITH OTHER CULTURES IS REGULAR CR IRREGULAR, RATHER THAN FREQUENT (37) JMH	468	DRIFT LESS TOWARD BEING THCSE 0.63 CF 46 WHERE CONTACT WITH OTHER CULTURES IS REGULAR OR IRREGULAR, RATHER THAN FREQUENT (37) JMH	0 17 8 29 XSQ= 2.77 PHI= -0.227 XP = 0.0959
469	DRIFT TCWARD BEING THCSE 0.50 OF 8 WHERE CCNTACT WITH CTHER CULTURES IS IRREGULAR, RATHER THAN FREQUENT CR REGULAR (11) JMH	469	DRIFT TOWARD BEING THOSE 0.85 CF 46 WHERE CONTACT WITH OTHER CULTURES IS FREQUENT OR REGULAR, RATHER THAN IRREGULAR (43) JMH	4 39 4 7 XSQ= 3.16 PHI= -0.242 XP = 0.0752

70 CULTURES WHERE SUBSISTENCE IS PRIMARILY BY COLLECTING (31)

70 CULTURES WHERE SUBSISTENCE IS PRIMARILY BY MEANS OTHER THAN COLLECTING (369)

BACKGROUND ON PAGE 78

SUBJECT ONLY

31 IN LEFT COLUMN

ARANDA	ATSUGEWI	BERGDAMA	BOTOCUDO	CHAMACOCO	CHENCHU	CHIR-APACHE	CHOROTI	DIEGUENO	DIERI
GUATO	HUKUNDIKA	KUNG	MARICOPA	MBUTI	MISKITO	MIWOK	MOTILON	MURINBATA	MURNGIN
NAMBICUARA	NOMLAKI	PURARI	SEMANG	TIWI	TUBATULABAL	VEDDA	WARRAU	WASHO	YOKUTS
YUKI									

369 IN RIGHT COLUMN

	Left column (31)			Right column (369)		
4	IN ALL CASES ARE THOSE LOCATED OUTSIDE OF THE CIRCUM-MEDITERRANEAN (355)	1.00 OF 31	4	DRIFT LESS TOWARD BEING THOSE LOCATED OUTSIDE OF THE CIRCUM-MEDITERRANEAN (355)	0.88 OF 369	0 45 31 324 XSQ= 3.13 PHI= -0.088 XP = 0.0771
8	TILT LESS TOWARD BEING THOSE LOCATED OUTSIDE OF NORTH AMERICA (330)	0.65 OF 31	8	TILT MORE TOWARD BEING THOSE LOCATED OUTSIDE OF NORTH AMERICA (330)	0.84 OF 369	11 59 20 310 XSQ= 6.24 PHI= 0.125 XP = 0.0125
33	TILT LESS TOWARD BEING THOSE WHERE THE NATURAL ENVIRONMENT IS OTHER THAN 'VERY HARSH,' I.E., DESERT, DESERT GRASSES AND SHRUBS, TUNDRA, OR HIGH PLATEAU STEPPE (341) FWM	0.71 OF 31	33	TILT MORE TOWARD BEING THOSE WHERE THE NATURAL ENVIRONMENT IS OTHER THAN 'VERY HARSH,' I.E., DESERT, DESERT GRASSES AND SHRUBS, TUNDRA, OR HIGH PLATEAU STEPPE (341) FWM	0.86 OF 369	9 50 22 319 XSQ= 4.29 PHI= 0.104 XP = 0.0383
36	LEAN LESS TOWARD BEING THOSE WHERE THE NATURAL ENVIRONMENT IS OTHER THAN 'VERY HARSH,' OR SUB-TROPICAL BUSH, OR TEMPERATE GRASSLAND (292) FWM	0.52 OF 31	36	LEAN MORE TOWARD BEING THOSE WHERE THE NATURAL ENVIRONMENT IS OTHER THAN 'VERY HARSH,' OR SUB-TROPICAL BUSH, OR TEMPERATE GRASSLAND (292) FWM	0.75 OF 369	15 93 16 276 XSQ= 6.67 PHI= 0.129 XP = 0.0098
44	TEND TO BE THOSE WHERE SETTLEMENTS ARE NON-FIXED (110)	0.83 OF 30	44	TEND TO BE THOSE WHERE SETTLEMENTS ARE FIXED (222)	0.72 OF 302	5 217 25 85 XSQ= 35.07 PHI= -0.325 XP = 0.

46	TEND TO BE THOSE WHERE SETTLEMENTS ARE NON-FIXED AND MOVEMENT IS NOMADIC (72)	0.67 OF 30	46	TEND TO BE THOSE OTHER THAN WHERE SETTLEMENTS ARE NON-FIXED AND MOVEMENT IS NOMADIC (260)	0.83 OF 302	20 52 10 250 XSQ= 36.43 PHI= 0.331 XP = 0.
62	TEND TO BE THOSE WHERE HUSBANDRY OF ANY KIND IS ABSENT (172)	0.87 OF 31	62	TEND TO BE THOSE WHERE HUSBANDRY OF SOME KIND IS PRESENT (228)	0.61 OF 369	4 224 27 145 XSQ= 24.75 PHI= -0.249 XP = 0.0000
71	IN ALL CASES ARE THOSE WHERE METAL WORKING IS ABSENT (153)	1.00 OF 27	71	TEND LESS TO BE THOSE WHERE METAL WORKING IS ABSENT (153)	0.56 OF 224	0 98 27 126 XSQ= 17.58 PHI= -0.265 XP = 0.0000
73	TILT TOWARD BEING THOSE WHERE WEAVING IS ABSENT (130)	0.74 OF 27	73	TILT TOWARD BEING THOSE WHERE WEAVING IS PRESENT (118)	0.50 OF 221	7 111 20 110 XSQ= 4.76 PHI= -0.139 XP = 0.0291
74	TILT TOWARD BEING THOSE WHERE POTTERY IS ABSENT (93)	0.63 OF 27	74	TILT TOWARD BEING THOSE WHERE POTTERY IS PRESENT (145)	0.64 OF 211	10 135 17 76 XSQ= 6.21 PHI= -0.162 XP = 0.0127
81	IN ALL CASES ARE THOSE WHERE NO CITY OR TOWN IS PRESENT, AND THE AVERAGE COMMUNITY SIZE IS SMALLER THAN 200 (135)	1.00 OF 22	81	TEND LESS TO BE THOSE WHERE NO CITY OR TOWN IS PRESENT, AND THE AVERAGE COMMUNITY SIZE IS SMALLER THAN 200 (135)	0.56 OF 202	0 89 22 113 XSQ= 14.30 PHI= -0.253 XP = 0.0002
82	TEND TO BE THOSE WHERE NO CITY OR TOWN IS PRESENT, AND THE AVERAGE COMMUNITY SIZE IS SMALLER THAN FIFTY (46)	0.64 OF 22	82	TEND TO BE THOSE WHERE A CITY OR TOWN IS PRESENT, OR THE AVERAGE COMMUNITY SIZE IS FIFTY OR GREATER (178)	0.84 OF 202	8 170 14 32 XSQ= 24.92 PHI= -0.334 XP = 0.0000
85	IN ALL CASES ARE THOSE WHERE THE LEVEL OF POLITICAL INTEGRATION IS THE MINIMAL STATE, THE AUTONOMOUS COMMUNITY, OR THE FAMILY (234) GPM	1.00 OF 29	85	LEAN LESS TOWARD BEING THOSE WHERE THE LEVEL OF POLITICAL INTEGRATION IS THE MINIMAL STATE, THE AUTONOMOUS COMMUNITY, OR THE FAMILY (234) GPM	0.75 OF 275	0 70 29 205 XSQ= 8.21 PHI= -0.164 XP = 0.0042
86	TEND TO BE THOSE WHERE THE LEVEL OF POLITICAL INTEGRATION IS THE AUTONOMOUS COMMUNITY, OR THE FAMILY (156) GPM	0.90 OF 29	86	TEND TO BE THOSE WHERE THE LEVEL OF POLITICAL INTEGRATION IS THE LARGE STATE, THE LITTLE STATE, OR THE MINIMAL STATE (148) GPM	0.53 OF 275	3 145 26 130 XSQ= 17.20 PHI= -0.238 XP = 0.0000

90	IN ALL CASES ARE THOSE WHERE, IF A HEREDITARY HEADMANSHIP IS PRESENT, SUCCESSION IS PATRILINEAL, RATHER THAN MATRILINEAL (127)	1.00 OF 16	90	TILT LESS TOWARD BEING THOSE WHERE, IF A HEREDITARY HEADMANSHIP IS PRESENT, SUCCESSION IS PATRILINEAL, RATHER THAN MATRILINEAL (127)	0.74 OF 149	16 111 0 38 XSQ= 3.96 PHI= 0.155 XP = 0.0466
95	IN ALL CASES ARE THOSE WHERE THE HIERARCHY OF NATIONAL JURISDICTION HAS ONE OR NO LEVELS (254) GES,EA	1.00 OF 30	95	LEAN LESS TOWARD BEING THOSE WHERE THE HIERARCHY OF NATIONAL JURISDICTION HAS ONE OR NO LEVELS (254) GES,EA	0.75 OF 300	0 76 30 224 XSQ= 8.50 PHI= -0.160 XP = 0.0036
96	TEND TO BE THOSE WHERE THE HIERARCHY OF NATIONAL JURISDICTION HAS NO LEVELS (156) GES,EA	0.87 OF 30	96	TEND TO BE THOSE WHERE THE HIERARCHY OF NATIONAL JURISDICTION HAS FOUR, THREE, TWO OR ONE LEVEL (174) GES,EA	0.57 OF 300	4 170 26 130 XSQ= 18.84 PHI= -0.239 XP = 0.0000
98	TEND TO BE THOSE WHERE THE HIERARCHY OF LOCAL JURISDICTION HAS TWO LEVELS (93) GES,EA	0.60 OF 30	98	TEND TO BE THOSE WHERE THE HIERARCHY OF LOCAL JURISDICTION HAS FOUR OR THREE LEVELS (238) GES,EA	0.75 OF 301	12 226 18 75 XSQ= 14.93 PHI= -0.212 XP = 0.0001
99	TILT TOWARD BEING THOSE WHERE, WITH NATIONAL HIERARCHY ABSENT, THE HIERARCHY OF LOCAL JURISDICTION HAS TWO LEVELS (63) GES,EA	0.62 OF 26	99	TILT TOWARD BEING THOSE WHERE, WITH NATIONAL HIERARCHY ABSENT, THE HIERARCHY OF LOCAL JURISDICTION HAS FOUR OR THREE LEVELS (93) GES,EA	0.64 OF 130	10 83 16 47 XSQ= 4.79 PHI= -0.175 XP = 0.0286
100	TEND TO BE THOSE WHERE HIERARCHIES ARE THE 'SIMPLEST' I. E., WHERE THERE ARE ONLY TWO LOCAL LEVELS WITH NO NATIONAL LEVELS (63) GES,EA	0.53 OF 30	100	TEND TO BE THOSE WHERE HIERARCHIES ARE MORE COMPLEX THAN THE 'SIMPLEST,' I. E., MORE COMPLEX THAN TWO LOCAL LEVELS WITH NO NATIONAL LEVELS (267) GES,EA	0.84 OF 300	14 253 16 47 XSQ= 22.67 PHI= -0.262 XP = 0.0000
102	TEND TO BE THOSE WHERE CLASS STRATIFICATION IS ABSENT (180)	0.84 OF 31	102	TEND TO BE THOSE WHERE CLASS STRATIFICATION IS PRESENT (203)	0.56 OF 352	5 198 26 154 XSQ= 16.84 PHI= -0.210 XP = 0.0000
109	IN ALL CASES ARE THOSE WHERE CASTES ARE ABSENT (317)	1.00 OF 31	109	TILT LESS TOWARD BEING THOSE WHERE CASTES ARE ABSENT (317)	0.85 OF 337	0 51 31 286 XSQ= 4.25 PHI= -0.107 XP = 0.0392
110	TEND MORE TO BE THOSE WHERE SLAVERY IS ABSENT (218)	0.94 OF 31	110	TEND LESS TO BE THOSE WHERE SLAVERY IS ABSENT (218)	0.54 OF 350	2 161 29 189 XSQ= 16.62 PHI= -0.209 XP = 0.0000

127	IN ALL CASES ARE THOSE 1.00 OF 6 WHERE THE FEMALES' CONTRIBUTION TO SUBSISTENCE IS HIGH (33) JKB	127	TILT TOWARD BEING THOSE 0.54 OF 59 WHERE THE FEMALES' CONTRIBUTION TO SUBSISTENCE IS LOW (32) JKB	6 27 0 32 XSQ= 4.42 PHI= 0.261 XP = 0.0354
131	LEAN LESS TOWARD BEING THOSE 0.57 OF 14 WHERE THE CONSTRUCTION OF PERMANENT HOUSES OR THE ERECTION OF TEMPORARY DWELLINGS IS MAINLY DONE BY MALES (136)	131	LEAN MORE TOWARD BEING THOSE 0.90 OF 143 WHERE THE CONSTRUCTION OF PERMANENT HOUSES OR THE ERECTION OF TEMPORARY DWELLINGS IS MAINLY DONE BY MALES (136)	8 128 6 15 XSQ= 8.91 PHI= -0.238 XP = 0.0028
138	IN ALL CASES ARE THOSE 1.00 OF 3 WHERE SUPERORDINATE JUSTICE IS ABSENT (18) BBW	138	DRIFT TOWARD BEING THOSE 0.59 OF 37 WHERE SUPERORDINATE JUSTICE IS PRESENT (22) BBW	0 22 3 15 XSQ= 1.93 PHI= -0.219 EP = 0.0826
178	TILT MORE TOWARD BEING THOSE 0.93 OF 30 WHERE THE COMMUNITY IS OTHER THAN SEGMENTED ON A CLAN BASIS AND NON-EXOGAMOUS (295)	178	TILT LESS TOWARD BEING THOSE 0.76 OF 352 WHERE THE COMMUNITY IS OTHER THAN SEGMENTED ON A CLAN BASIS AND NON-EXOGAMOUS (295)	2 85 28 267 XSQ= 3.86 PHI= -0.101 XP = 0.0494
179	TILT LESS TOWARD BEING THOSE 0.73 OF 30 WHERE THE COMMUNITY IS OTHER THAN STRUCTURED ON A NON-CLAN BASIS AND COMMONLY EXOGAMOUS (340)	179	TILT MORE TOWARD BEING THOSE 0.90 OF 352 WHERE THE COMMUNITY IS OTHER THAN STRUCTURED ON A NON-CLAN BASIS AND COMMONLY EXOGAMOUS (340)	8 34 22 318 XSQ= 6.53 PHI= 0.131 XP = 0.0106
180	TILT TOWARD BEING THOSE 0.53 OF 30 WHERE THE COMMUNITY IS COMMONLY EXOGAMOUS, RATHER THAN NON-EXOGAMOUS (124)	180	TILT TOWARD BEING THOSE 0.69 OF 352 WHERE THE COMMUNITY IS COMMONLY NON-EXOGAMOUS, RATHER THAN EXOGAMOUS (258)	16 108 14 244 XSQ= 5.48 PHI= 0.120 XP = 0.0193
183	TEND TO BE THOSE 0.57 OF 14 WHERE THE LARGEST NON-COGNATIC KIN GROUP IS THE MOEITY (34)	183	TEND TO BE THOSE 0.89 OF 238 WHERE THE LARGEST NON-COGNATIC KIN GROUP IS SMALLER THAN A MOEITY, I. E., A PHRATRY OR SIB OR LINEAGE (218)	8 26 6 212 XSQ= 20.40 PHI= 0.285 XP = 0.0000
184	TILT TOWARD BEING THOSE 0.64 OF 14 WHERE THE LARGEST NON-COGNATIC KIN GROUP IS THE MOEITY OR PHRATRY (77)	184	TILT TOWARD BEING THOSE 0.71 OF 238 WHERE THE LARGEST NON-COGNATIC KIN GROUP IS SMALLER THAN A PHRATRY, I. E. A SIB OR LINEAGE (175)	9 68 5 170 XSQ= 6.35 PHI= 0.159 XP = 0.0117
188	DRIFT TOWARD BEING THOSE 0.55 OF 31 WHERE THE KIN GROUP IS EXCLUSIVELY COGNATIC (148)	188	DRIFT TOWARD BEING THOSE 0.64 OF 369 WHFRE THE KIN GROUP IS OTHER THAN EXCLUSIVELY COGNATIC (252)	17 131 14 238 XSQ= 3.80 PHI= 0.097 XP = 0.0514

```
192  TILT LESS TOWARD BEING THOSE    0.52 OF  31    192  TILT MORE TOWARD BEING THOSE   0.74 OF 369         15   96
     OTHER THAN WHERE THE ONLY KIN GROUP                 OTHER THAN WHERE THE ONLY KIN GROUP                 16  273
     PRESENT IS A KINDRED OR ELSE                        PRESENT IS A KINDRED OR ELSE                 XSQ=     6.07
     BILATERAL DESCENT IS INFERRED  (289)                BILATERAL DESCENT IS INFERRED  (289)         PHI=    0.123
                                                                                                      XP =   0.0138

196  TEND TO BE THOSE                0.77 OF  22    196  TEND TO BE THOSE               0.73 OF 259          5  189
     WHERE INDIVIDUAL RIGHTS IN REAL PROPERTY,           WHERE INDIVIDUAL RIGHTS IN REAL PROPERTY,          17   70
     OR RULES FOR INHERITANCE,                           AND RULES FOR INHERITANCE,                   XSQ=    21.66
     ARE ABSENT  (87)                                    ARE PRESENT  (194)                           PHI=   -0.278
                                                                                                      XP =   0.0000

236  DRIFT TOWARD BEING THOSE        0.65 OF  31    236  DRIFT TOWARD BEING THOSE       0.55 OF 367         11  202
     WHERE THE FAMILY IS                                 WHERE THE FAMILY IS                                 20  165
     OF AN INDEPENDENT TYPE, RATHER THAN                 OF AN EXTENDED TYPE, RATHER THAN             XSQ=     3.64
     AN EXTENDED TYPE  (185)                             AN INDEPENDENT TYPE  (213)                   PHI=   -0.096
                                                                                                      XP =   0.0563

262  DRIFT LESS TOWARD BEING THOSE   0.62 OF  29    262  DRIFT MORE TOWARD BEING THOSE  0.78 OF 366         18  287
     WHERE WIVES ARE OBTAINED BY                         WHERE WIVES ARE OBTAINED BY                         11   79
     MEANS INVOLVING THE PRESENCE                        MEANS INVOLVING THE PRESENCE                 XSQ=     3.20
     OF SOME CONSIDERATION  (305)                        OF SOME CONSIDERATION  (305)                 PHI=   -0.090
                                                                                                      XP =   0.0734

382  IN ALL CASES ARE THOSE          1.00 OF   6    382  DRIFT LESS TOWARD BEING THOSE  0.54 OF  59          6   32
     WHERE FEMALE INITIATION RITES                       WHERE FEMALE INITIATION RITES                        0   27
     ARE PRESENT  (38) JKB                               ARE PRESENT  (38) JKB                        XSQ=     3.00
                                                                                                      PHI=    0.215
                                                                                                      XP =   0.0832

386  IN ALL CASES ARE THOSE          1.00 OF   5    386  DRIFT LESS TOWARD BEING THOSE  0.51 OF  81          5   41
     WHERE SEXUAL EXPRESSION BY THE YOUNG                WHERE SEXUAL EXPRESSION BY THE YOUNG                 0   40
     IS RESTRICTED OR                                    IS RESTRICTED OR                             XSQ=     2.84
     SEMI-RESTRICTED  (46) F-B                           SEMI-RESTRICTED  (46) F-B                    PHI=    0.182
                                                                                                      XP =   0.0917

417  DRIFT TOWARD BEING THOSE        0.60 OF   5    417  DRIFT TOWARD BEING THOSE       0.84 OF  38          2   32
     WHERE WARFARE IS                                    WHERE WARFARE IS                                     3    6
     NOT PREVALENT  (9) LWS                              PREVALENT  (34) LWS                          XSQ=     2.89
                                                                                                      PHI=   -0.259
                                                                                                      XP =   0.0892

426  TILT TOWARD BEING THOSE         0.64 OF  25    426  TILT TOWARD BEING THOSE        0.63 OF 235          9  147
     WHERE A HIGH GOD IS                                 WHERE A HIGH GOD IS                                 16   88
     ABSENT  (104) GES,EA                                PRESENT  (156) GES,EA                        XSQ=     5.58
                                                                                                      PHI=   -0.146
                                                                                                      XP =   0.0182

429  IN ALL CASES ARE THOSE          1.00 OF   2    429  DRIFT TOWARD BEING THOSE       0.80 OF  35          0   28
     WHERE SUPERNATURAL SANCTIONS FOR MORALITY           WHERE SUPERNATURAL SANCTIONS FOR MORALITY            2    7
     ARE ABSENT OR UNREPORTED  (9) GES                   ARE PRESENT  (28) GES                        XSQ=     2.95
                                                                                                      PHI=   -0.282
                                                                                                      EP =   0.0541
```

435	DRIFT TOWARD BEING THOSE WHERE ABANDONMENT OF THE HOUSE OF THE DEAD IS PRACTICED (12) LWS	0.80 OF 5	435	DRIFT TOWARD BEING THOSE WHERE ABANDONMENT OF THE HOUSE OF THE DEAD IS NOT PRACTICED (19) LWS	0.69 OF 26	4 8 1 18 XSQ= 2.46 PHI= 0.282 EP = 0.0600
458	IN ALL CASES ARE THOSE WHERE GAMES, IF PRESENT, DO NOT INCLUDE GAMES OF STRATEGY (119) R-A-B,EA	1.00 OF 18	458	LEAN LESS TOWARD BEING THOSE WHERE GAMES, IF PRESENT, DO NOT INCLUDE GAMES OF STRATEGY (119) R-A-B,EA	0.66 OF 153	0 52 18 101 XSQ= 7.26 PHI= -0.206 XP = 0.0071

71 CULTURES
WHERE METAL WORKING IS
PRESENT (98)

71 CULTURES
WHERE METAL WORKING IS
ABSENT (153)

BACKGROUND ON PAGE 79 — BOTH SUBJECT AND PREDICATE

98 IN LEFT COLUMN

ABOR	ALBANIANS	AMERICANS	ARAUCANIANS	ASHANTI	AYMARA	AZANDE	AZTEC	BAMBARA	BAMILEKE
BARI	BASSERI	BEMBA	BHIL	BIRIFOR	BRAZILIANS	BURUSHO	CHUKCHEE	COORG	CREEK
CZECHS	DARD	DOGON	DUTCH	EGYPTIANS	FANG	FON	GANDA	GILYAK	GISU
HUTSUL	IBAN	ILA	INCA	JAPANESE	JAVANESE	KACHIN	KAZAK	KHALKA	KHASI
KIKUYU	KOHISTANI	KOREANS	KORYAK	KUBA	LAKHER	LAMBA	LHOTA NAGA	LOLO	LOZI
LUO	MACASSARESE	MAMVU	MASAI	MATAKAM	MAYA	MBUNDU	MENDE	MIAO	MNONG GAR
MONGO	MONGUOR	MOSSI	NAMA	NANDI	NAVAHO	NDEMBU	NICOBARESE	NUPE	NURI
NYAKYUSA	NYORO	OKINAWANS	PAEZ	RIFFIANS	RUNDI	RWALA	SAGADA	SANTAL	SERBS
SHILLUK	SOMALI	SONGHAI	SWAZI	SYRIANS	TALLENSI	TANALA	TEDA	TEHUELCHE	TENDA
THONGA	TIBETANS	TIV	TRISTAN	WOLOF	YAKUT	YAO	YORUBA		

153 IN RIGHT COLUMN

ABIPON	AINU	ALACALUF	ANDAMANESE	APINAYE	ARANDA	ATSUGEWI	AWEIKOMA	BACAIRI	BAJUN
BLACK CARIB	BORORO	BOTOCUDO	CAGABA	CALLINAGO	CAMAYURA	CARIB	CAYAPA	CHAMACOCO	CHENCHU
CHEROKEE	CHEYENNE	CHIR-APACHE	CHIRIGUANO	CHOCO	CHOROTI	CHORTI	COMANCHE	COPR ESKIMO	CREE
CROW	CUNA	DELAWARE	DIEGUENO	DIERI	ELLICE	ENGA	EYAK	FOX	GARO
GILBERTESE	GOAJIRO	GOND	GROS VENTRE	GUATO	HAIDA	HASINAI	HAWAIIANS	HUKUNDIKA	HURON
INGALIK	JEMEZ	JIVARO	KAPAUKU	KARIERA	KASKA	KATAB	KERAKI	KIOW-APACHE	KPE
KUNG	KURTATCHI	KUTENAI	LAMET	LAU	LEPCHA	LESU	MANDAN	MANGAIANS	MANIHIKI
MANUS	MACRI	MARICOPA	MARQUESANS	MARSHALLESE	MATACO	MBUTI	MENTAWEI	MIAMI	MISKITO
MOTA	MUNDURUCU	MURINBATA	MURNGIN	NABESNA	NAMBICUARA	NATCHEZ	NOMLAKI	NUER	NUNIVAK
OJIBWA	OMAHA	ONA	ONTONG-JAVA	PALAUANS	PALIKUR	PAPAGO	PONAPEANS	PUKAPUKA	PURARI
PURUM	RARCIANS	SAMOANS	SAMOYED	SANPOIL	SARSI	SEMANG	SENIANG	SIRIONO	SIWANS
TALAMANCA	TAOS	TAPIRAPE	TAREUMIUT	TENINO	TERENA	TIKOPIA	TIMBIRA	TIMUCUA	TIWI
TODA	TOKELAU	TOLOWA	TOTONAC	TROBRIAND	TRUKESE	TRUMAI	TSHIMSHIAN	TUBATULABAL	TUCANO
TUCUNA	TUNEBO	TUPINAMBA	TWANA	ULAWANS	UTE	VEDDA	VENDA	WAICA	WANTOAT
WASHO	WIKMUNKAN	WITOTO	WOGEO	WOLEAIANS	YABARANA	YAGUA	YAHGAN	YAPESE	YARURO
YOKUTS	YUKI	YUROK							

149 EXCLUDED BECAUSE UNASCERTAINED

---

3 TEND LESS TO BE THOSE LOCATED OUTSIDE OF AFRICA (320) — 0.59 OF 98

3 TEND MORE TO BE THOSE LOCATED OUTSIDE OF AFRICA (320) — 0.95 OF 153

40	7
58	146

XSQ= 49.20
PHI= 0.443
XP = 0.

```
 4  TEND LESS TO BE THOSE          0.84 OF  98     4  TEND MORE TO BE THOSE          0.99 OF 153        16    1
    LOCATED OUTSIDE OF                                LOCATED OUTSIDE OF                                82  152
    THE CIRCUM-MEDITERRANEAN  (355)                   THE CIRCUM-MEDITERRANEAN  (355)            XSQ=   20.82
                                                                                                 PHI=   0.288
                                                                                                 XP =  0.0000

 5  TEND LESS TO BE THOSE          0.70 OF  98     5  TEND MORE TO BE THOSE          0.92 OF 153        29   12
    LOCATED OUTSIDE OF                                LOCATED OUTSIDE OF                                69  141
    EAST EURASIA  (330)                               EAST EURASIA  (330)                        XSQ=   19.11
                                                                                                 PHI=   0.276
                                                                                                 XP =  0.0000

 6  TEND MORE TO BE THOSE          0.96 OF  98     6  TEND LESS TO BE THOSE          0.73 OF 153         4   41
    LOCATED OUTSIDE OF                                LOCATED OUTSIDE OF                                94  112
    THE INSULAR PACIFIC  (330)                        THE INSULAR PACIFIC  (330)                 XSQ=   19.43
                                                                                                 PHI=  -0.278
                                                                                                 XP =  0.0000

 8  TEND MORE TO BE THOSE          0.97 OF  98     8  TEND LESS TO BE THOSE          0.69 OF 153         3   48
    LOCATED OUTSIDE OF                                LOCATED OUTSIDE OF                                95  105
    NORTH AMERICA  (330)                              NORTH AMERICA  (330)                       XSQ=   27.85
                                                                                                 PHI=  -0.333
                                                                                                 XP =  0.0000

 9  TEND MORE TO BE THOSE          0.94 OF  98     9  TEND LESS TO BE THOSE          0.71 OF 153         6   44
    LOCATED OUTSIDE OF                                LOCATED OUTSIDE OF                                92  109
    SOUTH AMERICA  (335)                              SOUTH AMERICA  (335)                       XSQ=   17.79
                                                                                                 PHI=  -0.266
                                                                                                 XP =  0.0000

42  TILT MORE TOWARD BEING THOSE   0.69 OF  98    42  TILT LESS TOWARD BEING THOSE   0.55 OF 153        30   69
    WHERE THE NATURAL ENVIRONMENT IS                  WHERE THE NATURAL ENVIRONMENT IS                  68   84
    OTHER THAN                                        OTHER THAN                                 XSQ=    4.66
    TROPICAL OR SUB-TROPICAL RAIN FOREST, OR          TROPICAL OR SUB-TROPICAL RAIN FOREST, OR   PHI=  -0.136
    MONSOON FOREST  (244) FWM                         MONSOON FOREST  (244) FWM                  XP =  0.0309

44  TEND MORE TO BE THOSE          0.76 OF  97    44  TEND LESS TO BE THOSE          0.52 OF 145        74   75
    WHERE SETTLEMENTS ARE FIXED  (222)                WHERE SETTLEMENTS ARE FIXED  (222)                23   70
                                                                                                 XSQ=   13.80
                                                                                                 PHI=   0.239
                                                                                                 XP =  0.0002

45  DRIFT LESS TOWARD BEING THOSE  0.61 OF  74    45  DRIFT MORE TOWARD BEING THOSE  0.76 OF  75        45   57
    WHERE SETTLEMENTS, IF FIXED, ARE                  WHERE SETTLEMENTS, IF FIXED, ARE                  29   18
    COMPACT, RATHER THAN                              COMPACT, RATHER THAN                       XSQ=    3.31
    NON-COMPACT  (149)                                NON-COMPACT  (149)                         PHI=  -0.149
                                                                                                 XP =  0.0690

46  TEND MORE TO BE THOSE          0.88 OF  97    46  TEND LESS TO BE THOSE          0.66 OF 145        12   50
    OTHER THAN WHERE SETTLEMENTS ARE                  OTHER THAN WHERE SETTLEMENTS ARE                  85   95
    NON-FIXED AND MOVEMENT IS                         NON-FIXED AND MOVEMENT IS                  XSQ=   13.77
    NOMADIC  (260)                                    NOMADIC  (260)                             PHI=  -0.239
                                                                                                 XP =  0.0002
```

```
51  TEND TO BE THOSE               0.88 OF  98     51  TEND TO BE THOSE                 0.69 OF 153           86   47
    WHERE SUBSISTENCE IS PRIMARILY BY                  WHERE SUBSISTENCE IS PRIMARILY BY                      12  106
    FOOD PRODUCTION -- I. E., AGRICULTURE              FOOD GATHERING -- I. E., HUNTING,                XSQ=   75.74
    OR HUSBANDRY -- RATHER THAN BY                     FISHING, OR COLLECTING -- RATHER THAN            PHI=   0.549
    GATHERING  (253)                                   FOOD PRODUCTION  (147)                           XP =  0.

53  TEND TO BE THOSE               0.51 OF  88     53  TEND TO BE THOSE                 0.90 OF  70           45    7
    WHERE FOOD PRODUCTION IS BY                        WHERE FOOD PRODUCTION IS BY                            43   63
    INTENSIVE AGRICULTURE, RATHER THAN BY              SIMPLE AGRICULTURE OR                            XSQ=   28.05
    SIMPLE AGRICULTURE OR                              INCIPIENT FOOD PRODUCTION, RATHER THAN BY        PHI=   0.421
    INCIPIENT FOOD PRODUCTION  (91)                    INTENSIVE AGRICULTURE  (147)                     XP =  0.0000

55  TEND TO BE THOSE               0.57 OF  79     55  TEND TO BE THOSE                 0.84 OF  43           45    7
    WHERE FOOD PRODUCTION IS BY                        WHERE FOOD PRODUCTION IS BY                            34   36
    INTENSIVE AGRICULTURE, RATHER THAN BY              SIMPLE AGRICULTURE, RATHER THAN BY               XSQ=   17.22
    SIMPLE AGRICULTURE  (91)                           INTENSIVE AGRICULTURE  (101)                     PHI=   0.376
                                                                                                        XP =  0.0000

56  TILT MORE TOWARD BEING THOSE   0.79 OF  43     56  TILT LESS TOWARD BEING THOSE     0.57 OF  63           34   36
    WHERE FOOD PRODUCTION IS BY                        WHERE FOOD PRODUCTION IS BY                             9   27
    SIMPLE AGRICULTURE, RATHER THAN BY                 SIMPLE AGRICULTURE, RATHER THAN BY               XSQ=    4.54
    INCIPIENT FOOD PRODUCTION  (101)                   INCIPIENT FOOD PRODUCTION  (101)                 PHI=   0.207
                                                                                                        XP =  0.0330

62  TEND TO BE THOSE               0.91 OF  98     62  TEND TO BE THOSE                 0.58 OF 153           89   64
    WHERE HUSBANDRY OF SOME KIND                       WHERE HUSBANDRY OF ANY KIND                             9   89
    IS PRESENT  (228)                                  IS ABSENT  (172)                                 XSQ=   58.19
                                                                                                        PHI=   0.481
                                                                                                        XP =  0.

63  TEND TO BE THOSE               0.78 OF  89     63  TEND TO BE THOSE                 0.56 OF  64           69   28
    WHERE HUSBANDRY, IF PRESENT,                       WHERE HUSBANDRY, IF PRESENT,                           20   36
    IS PRINCIPALLY IN THE FORM OF                      IS PRINCIPALLY IN THE FORM OF                    XSQ=   16.88
    BOVINE, EQUINE, CAMEL-LIKE, OR DEER-LIKE           PIGS, SHEEP, OR GOATS, RATHER THAN               PHI=   0.332
    ANIMALS, RATHER THAN                               BOVINE, EQUINE, CAMEL-LIKE, OR DEER-LIKE         XP =  0.0000
    PIGS, SHEEP, OR GOATS  (152)                       ANIMALS  (74)

73  TEND TO BE THOSE               0.67 OF  94     73  TEND TO BE THOSE                 0.66 OF 148           63   51
    WHERE WEAVING IS                                   WHERE WEAVING IS                                       31   97
    PRESENT  (118)                                     ABSENT  (130)                                    XSQ=   23.17
                                                                                                        PHI=   0.309
                                                                                                        XP =  0.0000

74  TEND TO BE THOSE               0.87 OF  85     74  TEND TO BE THOSE                 0.54 OF 149           74   68
    WHERE POTTERY IS                                   WHERE POTTERY IS                                       11   81
    PRESENT  (145)                                     ABSENT  (93)                                     XSQ=   37.20
                                                                                                        PHI=   0.399
                                                                                                        XP =  0.

79  TEND LESS TO BE THOSE          0.83 OF  78     79  IN ALL CASES ARE THOSE           1.00 OF  94           13    0
    WHERE NO CITY IS PRESENT  (201)                    WHERE NO CITY IS PRESENT  (201)                        65   94
                                                                                                        XSQ=   14.65
                                                                                                        PHI=   0.292
                                                                                                        XP =  0.0001
```

81	TEND TO BE THOSE WHERE A CITY OR TOWN IS PRESENT, OR THE AVERAGE COMMUNITY SIZE IS 200 OR GREATER (89)	0.53 OF 78	81	TEND TO BE THOSE WHERE NO CITY OR TOWN IS PRESENT, AND THE AVERAGE COMMUNITY SIZE IS SMALLER THAN 200 (135)	0.82 OF 94	41 17 37 77 XSQ= 21.16 PHI= 0.351 XP = 0.0000
83	TILT LESS TOWARD BEING THOSE WHERE, WITH NO CITY AND NO TOWN PRESENT, THE AVERAGE COMMUNITY SIZE IS SMALLER THAN 200, RATHER THAN BETWEEN 200 AND 999 (135)	0.69 OF 54	83	TILT MORE TOWARD BEING THOSE WHERE, WITH NO CITY AND NO TOWN PRESENT, THE AVERAGE COMMUNITY SIZE IS SMALLER THAN 200, RATHER THAN BETWEEN 200 AND 999 (135)	0.85 OF 91	17 14 37 77 XSQ= 4.31 PHI= 0.172 XP = 0.0379
85	TEND TO BE THOSE WHERE THE LEVEL OF POLITICAL INTEGRATION IS THE LARGE STATE, OR THE LITTLE STATE (70) GPM	0.50 OF 74	85	TEND TO BE THOSE WHERE THE LEVEL OF POLITICAL INTEGRATION IS THE MINIMAL STATE, THE AUTONOMOUS COMMUNITY, OR THE FAMILY (234) GPM	0.98 OF 124	37 3 37 121 XSQ= 62.16 PHI= 0.560 XP = 0.
86	TEND TO BE THOSE WHERE THE LEVEL OF POLITICAL INTEGRATION IS THE LARGE STATE, THE LITTLE STATE, OR THE MINIMAL STATE (148) GPM	0.74 OF 74	86	TEND TO BE THOSE WHERE THE LEVEL OF POLITICAL INTEGRATION IS THE AUTONOMOUS COMMUNITY, OR THE FAMILY (156) GPM	0.70 OF 124	55 37 19 87 XSQ= 35.10 PHI= 0.421 XP = 0.
94	TEND LESS TO BE THOSE WHERE THE HIERARCHY OF NATIONAL JURISDICTION HAS TWO, ONE, OR NO LEVELS (296) GES,EA	0.78 OF 95	94	IN ALL CASES ARE THOSE WHERE THE HIERARCHY OF NATIONAL JURISDICTION HAS TWO, ONE, OR NO LEVELS (296) GES,EA	1.00 OF 146	21 0 74 146 XSQ= 32.63 PHI= 0.368 XP = 0.
96	TEND TO BE THOSE WHERE THE HIERARCHY OF NATIONAL JURISDICTION HAS FOUR, THREE, TWO OR ONE LEVEL (174) GES,EA	0.78 OF 95	96	TEND TO BE THOSE WHERE THE HIERARCHY OF NATIONAL JURISDICTION HAS NO LEVELS (156) GES,EA	0.66 OF 146	74 50 21 96 XSQ= 42.17 PHI= 0.418 XP = 0.
97	DRIFT LESS TOWARD BEING THOSE WHERE THE HIERARCHY OF LOCAL JURISDICTION HAS THREE OR TWO LEVELS (273) GES,EA	0.79 OF 96	97	DRIFT MORE TOWARD BEING THOSE WHERE THE HIERARCHY OF LOCAL JURISDICTION HAS THREE OR TWO LEVELS (273) GES,EA	0.89 OF 146	20 16 76 130 XSQ= 3.71 PHI= 0.124 XP = 0.0540
98	LEAN MORE TOWARD BEING THOSE WHERE THE HIERARCHY OF LOCAL JURISDICTION HAS FOUR OR THREE LEVELS (238) GES,EA	0.79 OF 96	98	LEAN LESS TOWARD BEING THOSE WHERE THE HIERARCHY OF LOCAL JURISDICTION HAS FOUR OR THREE LEVELS (238) GES,EA	0.62 OF 146	76 91 20 55 XSQ= 6.91 PHI= 0.169 XP = 0.0086
99	TILT TOWARD BEING THOSE WHERE, WITH NATIONAL HIERARCHY ABSENT, THE HIERARCHY OF LOCAL JURISDICTION HAS FOUR OR THREE LEVELS (93) GES,EA	0.81 OF 21	99	TILT TOWARD BEING THOSE WHERE, WITH NATIONAL HIERARCHY ABSENT, THE HIERARCHY OF LOCAL JURISDICTION HAS TWO LEVELS (63) GES,EA	0.50 OF 96	17 48 4 48 XSQ= 5.49 PHI= 0.217 XP = 0.0191

100	TEND MORE TO BE THOSE WHERE HIERARCHIES ARE MORE COMPLEX THAN THE 'SIMPLEST,' I. E., MORE COMPLEX THAN TWO LOCAL LEVELS WITH NO NATIONAL LEVELS (267) GES,EA	0.96 OF 95	100	TEND LESS TO BE THOSE WHERE HIERARCHIES ARE MORE COMPLEX THAN THE 'SIMPLEST,' I. E., MORE COMPLEX THAN TWO LOCAL LEVELS WITH NO NATIONAL LEVELS (267) GES,EA	0.67 OF 146	91 98 4 48 XSQ= 26.28 PHI= 0.330 XP = 0.0000
102	TEND TO BE THOSE WHERE CLASS STRATIFICATION IS PRESENT (203)	0.78 OF 95	102	TEND TO BE THOSE WHERE CLASS STRATIFICATION IS ABSENT (180)	0.64 OF 151	74 55 21 96 XSQ= 38.57 PHI= 0.396 XP = 0.
106	LEAN TOWARD BEING THOSE WHERE CLASS STRATIFICATION, IF PRESENT, IS BASED ON SOMETHING OTHER THAN WEALTH (126)	0.68 OF 74	106	LEAN TOWARD BEING THOSE WHERE CLASS STRATIFICATION, IF PRESENT, IS BASED ON WEALTH (77)	0.58 OF 55	24 32 50 23 XSQ= 7.50 PHI= -0.241 XP = 0.0062
107	TEND LESS TO BE THOSE WHERE CLASS STRATIFICATION, IF PRESENT, IS BASED ON SOMETHING OTHER THAN OCCUPATIONAL STATUS (160)	0.68 OF 74	107	IN ALL CASES ARE THOSE WHERE CLASS STRATIFICATION, IF PRESENT, IS BASED ON SOMETHING OTHER THAN OCCUPATIONAL STATUS (160)	1.00 OF 55	24 0 50 55 XSQ= 19.83 PHI= 0.392 XP = 0.0000
109	TEND LESS TO BE THOSE WHERE CASTES ARE ABSENT (317)	0.70 OF 90	109	TEND MORE TO BE THOSE WHERE CASTES ARE ABSENT (317)	0.97 OF 150	27 4 63 146 XSQ= 34.97 PHI= 0.382 XP = 0.
110	TEND TO BE THOSE WHERE SLAVERY IS PRESENT (163)	0.64 OF 94	110	TEND TO BE THOSE WHERE SLAVERY IS ABSENT (218)	0.78 OF 148	60 33 34 115 XSQ= 40.17 PHI= 0.407 XP = 0.
120	DRIFT MORE TOWARD BEING THOSE WHERE THE CRAFT SPECIALIZATION SCORE IS HIGH OR MEDIUM (36) WME	0.82 OF 22	120	DRIFT LESS TOWARD BEING THOSE WHERE THE CRAFT SPECIALIZATION SCORE IS HIGH OR MEDIUM (36) WME	0.54 OF 24	18 13 4 11 XSQ= 2.83 PHI= 0.248 XP = 0.0923
127	DRIFT TOWARD BEING THOSE WHERE THE FEMALES' CONTRIBUTION TO SUBSISTENCE IS LOW (32) JKB	0.63 OF 24	127	DRIFT TOWARD BEING THOSE WHERE THE FEMALES' CONTRIBUTION TO SUBSISTENCE IS HIGH (33) JKB	0.66 OF 32	9 21 15 11 XSQ= 3.30 PHI= -0.243 XP = 0.0691
129	LEAN LESS TOWARD BEING THOSE WHERE WEAVING IS MAINLY DONE BY FEMALES (73)	0.54 OF 52	129	LEAN MORE TOWARD BEING THOSE WHERE WEAVING IS MAINLY DONE BY FEMALES (73)	0.85 OF 48	24 7 28 41 XSQ= 10.20 PHI= 0.319 XP = 0.0014

130	LEAN TOWARD BEING THOSE WHERE LEATHER WORKING IS MAINLY DONE BY MALES (39)	0.68 OF 37	130	LEAN TOWARD BEING THOSE WHERE LEATHER WORKING IS MAINLY DONE BY FEMALES (45)	0.70 OF 47	25 14 12 33 XSQ= 10.41 PHI= 0.352 XP = 0.0013
131	DRIFT MORE TOWARD BEING THOSE WHERE THE CONSTRUCTION OF PERMANENT HOUSES OR THE ERECTION OF TEMPORARY DWELLINGS IS MAINLY DONE BY MALES (136)	0.93 OF 58	131	DRIFT LESS TOWARD BEING THOSE WHERE THE CONSTRUCTION OF PERMANENT HOUSES OR THE ERECTION OF TEMPORARY DWELLINGS IS MAINLY DONE BY MALES (136)	0.82 OF 93	54 76 4 17 XSQ= 2.97 PHI= 0.140 XP = 0.0846
136	TILT TOWARD BEING THOSE WHERE FULL-TIME ENTREPRENEURS ARE PRESENT (18) JV	0.91 OF 11	136	TILT TOWARD BEING THOSE WHERE FULL-TIME ENTREPRENEURS ARE ABSENT (14) JV	0.64 OF 14	10 5 1 9 XSQ= 5.69 PHI= 0.477 EP = 0.0119
138	TILT TOWARD BEING THOSE WHERE SUPERORDINATE JUSTICE IS PRESENT (22) BBW	0.90 OF 10	138	TILT TOWARD BEING THOSE WHERE SUPERORDINATE JUSTICE IS ABSENT (18) BBW	0.57 OF 23	9 10 1 13 XSQ= 4.42 PHI= 0.366 EP = 0.0209
149	DRIFT TOWARD BEING THOSE WHERE THE INCIDENCE OF THEFT IS HIGH (18) B-B-C	0.80 OF 10	149	DRIFT TOWARD BEING THOSE WHERE THE INCIDENCE OF THEFT IS LOW (19) B-B-C	0.64 OF 22	8 8 2 14 XSQ= 3.64 PHI= 0.337 EP = 0.0538
152	TILT TOWARD BEING THOSE WHERE THE DIFFERENTIATION OF THE JURIDICAL AGENCY FROM THE MEDICAL AGENCY IS HIGH (10) MJ	0.71 OF 7	152	TILT TOWARD BEING THOSE WHERE THE DIFFERENTIATION OF THE JURIDICAL AGENCY FROM THE MEDICAL AGENCY IS LOW (10) MJ	0.89 OF 9	5 1 2 8 XSQ= 3.81 PHI= 0.488 EP = 0.0350
183	TEND MORE TO BE THOSE WHERE THE LARGEST NON-COGNATIC KIN GROUP IS SMALLER THAN A MOEITY, I. E., A PHRATRY OR SIB OR LINEAGE (218)	0.96 OF 79	183	TEND LESS TO BE THOSE WHERE THE LARGEST NON-COGNATIC KIN GROUP IS SMALLER THAN A MOEITY, I. E., A PHRATRY OR SIB OR LINEAGE (218)	0.68 OF 79	3 25 76 54 XSQ= 19.14 PHI= -0.348 XP = 0.0000
184	TEND MORE TO BE THOSE WHERE THE LARGEST NON-COGNATIC KIN GROUP IS SMALLER THAN A PHRATRY, I. E. A SIB OR LINEAGE (175)	0.81 OF 79	184	TEND LESS TO BE THOSE WHERE THE LARGEST NON-COGNATIC KIN GROUP IS SMALLER THAN A PHRATRY, I. E. A SIB OR LINEAGE (175)	0.52 OF 79	15 38 64 41 XSQ= 13.74 PHI= -0.295 XP = 0.0002
186	TEND TO BE THOSE WHERE THE KIN GROUP IS EXCLUSIVELY PATRILINEAL (150)	0.56 OF 98	186	TEND TO BE THOSE WHERE THE KIN GROUP IS OTHER THAN EXCLUSIVELY PATRILINEAL (250)	0.79 OF 153	55 32 43 121 XSQ= 31.16 PHI= 0.352 XP = 0.

187	DRIFT MORE TOWARD BEING THOSE 0.91 OF 98 WHERE THE KIN GROUP IS OTHER THAN EXCLUSIVELY MATRILINEAL (344)	187	DRIFT LESS TOWARD BEING THOSE 0.82 OF 152 WHERE THE KIN GROUP IS OTHER THAN EXCLUSIVELY MATRILINEAL (344)	9 28 89 124 XSQ= 3.33 PHI= -0.115 XP = 0.0679
188	TEND MORE TO BE THOSE 0.81 OF 98 WHERE THE KIN GROUP IS OTHER THAN EXCLUSIVELY COGNATIC (252)	188	TEND LESS TO BE THOSE 0.52 OF 153 WHERE THE KIN GROUP IS OTHER THAN EXCLUSIVELY COGNATIC (252)	19 74 79 79 XSQ= 20.28 PHI= -0.284 XP = 0.0000
190	TEND MORE TO BE THOSE 0.87 OF 77 WHERE THE KIN GROUP IS PATRILINEAL OR DOUBLE-DESCENT, RATHER THAN MATRILINEAL (186)	190	TEND LESS TO BE THOSE 0.58 OF 77 WHERE THE KIN GROUP IS PATRILINEAL OR DOUBLE-DESCENT, RATHER THAN MATRILINEAL (186)	67 45 10 32 XSQ= 14.44 PHI= 0.306 XP = 0.0001
192	LEAN MORE TOWARD BEING THOSE 0.84 OF 98 OTHER THAN WHERE THE ONLY KIN GROUP PRESENT IS A KINDRED OR ELSE BILATERAL DESCENT IS INFERRED (289)	192	LEAN LESS TOWARD BEING THOSE 0.66 OF 153 OTHER THAN WHERE THE ONLY KIN GROUP PRESENT IS A KINDRED OR ELSE BILATERAL DESCENT IS INFERRED (289)	16 52 82 101 XSQ= 8.56 PHI= -0.185 XP = 0.0034
196	TEND TO BE THOSE 0.80 OF 86 WHERE INDIVIDUAL RIGHTS IN REAL PROPERTY, AND RULES FOR INHERITANCE, ARE PRESENT (194)	196	TEND TO BE THOSE 0.54 OF 99 WHERE INDIVIDUAL RIGHTS IN REAL PROPERTY, OR RULES FOR INHERITANCE, ARE ABSENT (87)	69 46 17 53 XSQ= 20.90 PHI= 0.336 XP = 0.0000
198	LEAN MORE TOWARD BEING THOSE 0.94 OF 62 WHERE RULES FOR THE INHERITANCE OF REAL PROPERTY, IF PRESENT, FAVOR THE MALE HEIR OR LINE, RATHER THAN THE FEMALE (144)	198	LEAN LESS TOWARD BEING THOSE 0.70 OF 37 WHERE RULES FOR THE INHERITANCE OF REAL PROPERTY, IF PRESENT, FAVOR THE MALE HEIR OR LINE, RATHER THAN THE FEMALE (144)	58 26 4 11 XSQ= 8.04 PHI= 0.285 XP = 0.0046
204	TILT MORE TOWARD BEING THOSE 0.87 OF 91 WHERE MARITAL RESIDENCE IS PATRILOCAL, VIRILOCAL, OR AVUNCULOCAL, RATHER THAN AMBILOCAL OR NEOLOCAL (270)	204	TILT LESS TOWARD BEING THOSE 0.72 OF 116 WHERE MARITAL RESIDENCE IS PATRILOCAL, VIRILOCAL, OR AVUNCULOCAL, RATHER THAN AMBILOCAL OR NEOLOCAL (270)	79 84 12 32 XSQ= 5.49 PHI= 0.163 XP = 0.0192
209	TEND MORE TO BE THOSE 0.92 OF 86 WHERE MARITAL RESIDENCE IS PATRILOCAL, VIRILOCAL, OR AVUNCULOCAL, RATHER THAN MATRILOCAL OR UXORILOCAL (270)	209	TEND LESS TO BE THOSE 0.70 OF 120 WHERE MARITAL RESIDENCE IS PATRILOCAL, VIRILOCAL, OR AVUNCULOCAL, RATHER THAN MATRILOCAL OR UXORILOCAL (270)	79 84 7 36 XSQ= 13.20 PHI= 0.253 XP = 0.0003
210	LEAN MORE TOWARD BEING THOSE 0.92 OF 66 WHERE MARITAL RESIDENCE IS PATRILOCAL, RATHER THAN MATRILOCAL (169)	210	LEAN LESS TOWARD BEING THOSE 0.69 OF 55 WHERE MARITAL RESIDENCE IS PATRILOCAL, RATHER THAN MATRILOCAL (169)	61 38 5 17 XSQ= 9.47 PHI= 0.280 XP = 0.0021

240 DRIFT MORE TOWARD BEING THOSE 0.68 OF 56 WHERE THE FAMILY, IF EXTENDED, IS SMALL OR STEM, RATHER THAN LARGE (135)	240 DRIFT LESS TOWARD BEING THOSE 0.51 OF 77 WHERE THE FAMILY, IF EXTENDED, IS SMALL OR STEM, RATHER THAN LARGE (135)	18 38 38 39 XSQ= 3.26 PHI= -0.157 XP = 0.0708
243 DRIFT TOWARD BEING THOSE 0.62 OF 21 WHERE POLYGYNY, IF PRESENT, HAS A HIGH INCIDENCE (24) W-D,S	243 DRIFT TOWARD BEING THOSE 0.69 OF 32 WHERE POLYGYNY, IF PRESENT, HAS A LOW INCIDENCE (36) W-D,S	13 10 8 22 XSQ= 3.68 PHI= 0.264 XP = 0.0550
255 TILT TOWARD BEING THOSE 0.50 OF 10 WHERE GRANDPARENTAL AUTHORITY OVER PARENTS IS PRESENT (7) DA	255 TILT TOWARD BEING THOSE 0.93 OF 15 WHERE GRANDPARENTAL AUTHORITY OVER PARENTS IS ABSENT (26) DA	5 1 5 14 XSQ= 4.03 PHI= 0.401 EP = 0.0225
256 DRIFT TOWARD BEING THOSE 0.50 OF 10 WHERE GRANDPARENT AND GRANDCHILD ARE NOT FRIENDLY EQUALS (8) DA	256 DRIFT TOWARD BEING THOSE 0.87 OF 15 WHERE GRANDPARENT AND GRANDCHILD ARE FRIENDLY EQUALS (25) DA	5 13 5 2 XSQ= 2.39 PHI= -0.309 EP = 0.0752
262 TEND MORE TO BE THOSE 0.86 OF 98 WHERE WIVES ARE OBTAINED BY MEANS INVOLVING THE PRESENCE OF SOME CONSIDERATION (305)	262 TEND LESS TO BE THOSE 0.66 OF 150 WHERE WIVES ARE OBTAINED BY MEANS INVOLVING THE PRESENCE OF SOME CONSIDERATION (305)	84 99 14 51 XSQ= 10.91 PHI= 0.210 XP = 0.0010
263 LEAN TOWARD BEING THOSE 0.66 OF 98 WHERE WIVES ARE OBTAINED BY RELATIVELY DIFFICULT MEANS, NAMELY BY BRIDE-PRICE, BRIDE-SERVICE, OR EXCHANGING A FEMALE RELATIVE (233)	263 LEAN TOWARD BEING THOSE 0.53 OF 150 WHERE WIVES ARE OBTAINED BY RELATIVELY EASY MEANS, NAMELY BY TOKEN BRIDE-PRICE, GIFT EXCHANGE, ABSENCE OF ANY CONSIDERATION, OR RECEIPT OF DOWRY (162)	65 70 33 80 XSQ= 8.46 PHI= 0.185 XP = 0.0036
278 TILT TOWARD BEING THOSE 0.64 OF 11 WHERE PROPERTY RIGHTS IN WOMEN ARE PRESENT (8) LWS	278 IN ALL CASES ARE THOSE 1.00 OF 8 WHERE PROPERTY RIGHTS IN WOMEN ARE UNIMPORTANT OR ABSENT (14) LWS	7 0 4 8 XSQ= 5.56 PHI= 0.541 EP = 0.0128
282 DRIFT TOWARD BEING THOSE 0.67 OF 9 WHERE THE STRENGTH OF DESIRE FOR CHILDREN IS HIGH (16) BCA	282 DRIFT TOWARD BEING THOSE 0.72 OF 18 WHERE THE STRENGTH OF DESIRE FOR CHILDREN IS LOW OR ABSENT (20) BCA	6 5 3 13 XSQ= 2.32 PHI= 0.293 EP = 0.0969
286 TILT TOWARD BEING THOSE 0.78 OF 9 WHERE THE NUMBER OF FOOD TABOOS DURING PREGNANCY IS LOW OR ABSENT (14) BCA	286 TILT TOWARD BEING THOSE 0.72 OF 18 WHERE THE NUMBER OF FOOD TABOOS DURING PREGNANCY IS HIGH (20) BCA	2 13 7 5 XSQ= 4.22 PHI= -0.395 EP = 0.0369

```
295  IN ALL CASES ARE THOSE           1.00 OF   4     295  DRIFT TOWARD BEING THOSE         0.58 OF  12           4     5
     WHERE THE SEVERITY CF PUNISHMENT                      WHERE THE SEVERITY OF PUNISHMENT                           0     7
     FCR ABCRTICN                                          FOR ABORTION                                        XSQ=     2.12
     IS HIGH   (11) BCA                                    IS LOW OR ABSENT   (12) BCA                         PHI=    0.364
                                                                                                               EP  =  0.0885

309  TILT TOWARD BEING THOSE          0.82 OF  11     309  TILT TOWARD BEING THOSE          0.60 OF  30           9    12
     WHERE ORAL SOCIALIZATICN ANXIETY                      WHERE ORAL SOCIALIZATION ANXIETY                           2    18
     IS HIGH   (26) W-C                                    IS LOW   (27) W-C                                   XSQ=     4.08
                                                                                                               PHI=    0.316
                                                                                                               XP  =  0.0433

310  TILT TOWARD BEING THOSE          0.89 OF   9     310  TILT TOWARD BEING THOSE          0.61 OF  23           8     9
     WHERE ANAL SOCIALIZATICN ANXIETY                      WHERE ANAL SOCIALIZATION ANXIETY                           1    14
     IS HIGH   (22) W-C                                    IS LOW   (19) W-C                                   XSQ=     4.59
                                                                                                               PHI=    0.379
                                                                                                               EP  =  0.0179

314  LEAN LESS TOWARD BEING THCSE     0.54 OF  24     314  LEAN MORE TOWARD BEING THOSE     0.86 OF  43          11     6
     WHERE THE INCIDENCE OF MOTHER-CHILD                   WHERE THE INCIDENCE OF MOTHER-CHILD                       13    37
     HOUSEHOLDS IS LCW   (61) W-C,S                        HOUSEHOLDS IS LOW   (61) W-D,S                      XSQ=     6.67
                                                                                                               PHI=    0.316
                                XP =   0.0098

317  LEAN TOWARD BEING THOSE          0.76 OF  17     317  LEAN TOWARD BEING THOSE          0.70 OF  37           4    26
     WHERE DISPLAY OF AFFECTICN TOWARD                     WHERE DISPLAY OF AFFECTICN TOWARD                         13    11
     THE INFANT IS LCW   (29) B-B-C                        THE INFANT IS HIGH   (39) B-B-C                     XSQ=     8.50
                                                                                                               PHI=   -0.397
                                                      XP =  0.0036

318  TEND TO BE THOSE                 0.84 OF  19     318  TEND TO BE THOSE                 0.79 CF  38           3    30
     WHERE THE OVERALL INDULGENCE                          WHERE THE OVERALL INDULGENCE                              16     8
     OF THE INFANT                                         OF THE INFANT                                       XSQ=    18.22
     IS LOW   (31) B-B-C                                   IS HIGH   (40) B-B-C                                PHI=   -0.565
                                                                                                               XP  =  0.0000

319  TILT TOWARD BEING THOSE          0.72 OF  18     319  TILT TOWARD BEING THOSE          0.64 OF  33           5    21
     WHERE PROTECTICN OF THE INFANT                        WHERE PROTECTION OF THE INFANT                            13    12
     FROM ENVIRCNMENTAL DISCOMFCRTS                        FROM ENVIRONMENTAL DISCOMFCRTS                      XSQ=     4.64
     IS LOW   (30) B-B-C                                   IS HIGH   (35) B-B-C                                PHI=   -0.302
                                                                                                               XP  =  0.0312

320  LEAN TOWARD BEING THOSE          0.63 OF  19     320  LEAN TOWARD BEING THOSE          0.81 CF  36           7    29
     WHERE THE DEGREE OF REDUCTION                         WHERE THE DEGREE OF REDUCTION                             12     7
     OF THE INFANT'S DRIVES                                OF THE INFANT'S DRIVES                              XSQ=     8.67
     IS LOW   (24) B-B-C                                   IS HIGH   (45) B-B-C                                PHI=   -0.397
                                                                                                               XP  =  0.0032

324  LEAN TOWARD BEING THOSE          0.82 OF  17     324  LEAN TOWARD BEING THOSE          0.61 OF  36          14    14
     WHERE THE PAIN INFLICTEC                              WHERE THE PAIN INFLICTED                                   3    22
     ON THE INFANT BY THE NURTURANT AGENT                  ON THE INFANT BY THE NURTURANT AGENT                XSQ=     7.10
     IS HIGH   (34) B-B-C                                  IS LOW OR NEGLIGIBLE   (32) B-B-C                   PHI=    0.366
                                                                                                               XP  =  0.0077
```

326	TILT TOWARD BEING THOSE 0.63 OF 19 WHERE THE INFERRED TRANSITION ANXIETY BETWEEN INFANCY AND CHILDHOOD IS HIGH (32) B-B-C	326	TILT TOWARD BEING THOSE 0.69 OF 35 WHERE THE INFERRED TRANSITION ANXIETY BETWEEN INFANCY AND CHILDHOOD IS LOW (35) B-B-C	12 11 7 24 XSQ= 3.86 PHI= 0.267 XP = 0.0496
334	TILT TOWARD BEING THOSE 0.68 OF 22 WHERE THE INDULGENCE OF THE CHILD IS LOW (38) B-B-C	334	TILT TOWARD BEING THOSE 0.68 OF 41 WHERE THE INDULGENCE OF THE CHILD IS HIGH (40) B-B-C	7 28 15 13 XSQ= 6.31 PHI= -0.316 XP = 0.0120
336	DRIFT TOWARD BEING THOSE 0.76 OF 21 WHERE THE TOTAL POSITIVE PRESSURE TOWARD DEVELOPING RESPONSIBLE BEHAVIOR IN THE CHILD IS HIGH (43) B-B-C	336	DRIFT TOWARD BEING THOSE 0.52 OF 40 WHERE THE TOTAL POSITIVE PRESSURE TOWARD DEVELOPING RESPONSIBLE BEHAVIOR IN THE CHILD IS LOW (32) B-B-C	16 19 5 21 XSQ= 3.54 PHI= 0.241 XP = 0.0600
337	LEAN TOWARD BEING THOSE 0.80 OF 20 WHERE THE CHILD'S INFERRED ANXIETY OVER NON-PERFORMANCE OF RESPONSIBLE BEHAVIOR IS HIGH (38) B-B-C	337	LEAN TOWARD BEING THOSE 0.64 OF 39 WHERE THE CHILD'S INFERRED ANXIETY OVER NON-PERFORMANCE OF RESPONSIBLE BEHAVIOR IS LOW (35) B-B-C	16 14 4 25 XSQ= 8.60 PHI= 0.382 XP = 0.0034
338	TILT TOWARD BEING THOSE 0.80 OF 20 WHERE THE CHILD'S INFERRED ANXIETY OVER PERFORMANCE OF RESPONSIBLE BEHAVIOR IS HIGH (44) B-B-C	338	TILT TOWARD BEING THOSE 0.54 OF 39 WHERE THE CHILD'S INFERRED ANXIETY OVER PERFORMANCE OF RESPONSIBLE BEHAVIOR IS LOW (29) B-B-C	16 18 4 21 XSQ= 4.89 PHI= 0.288 XP = 0.0270
339	TILT TOWARD BEING THOSE 0.65 OF 20 WHERE THE CHILD'S INFERRED CONFLICT REGARDING RESPONSIBLE BEHAVIOR IS HIGH (31) B-B-C	339	TILT TOWARD BEING THOSE 0.72 OF 39 WHERE THE CHILD'S INFERRED CONFLICT REGARDING RESPONSIBLE BEHAVIOR IS LOW (42) B-B-C	13 11 7 28 XSQ= 5.97 PHI= 0.318 XP = 0.0145
346	TILT TOWARD BEING THOSE 0.71 OF 21 WHERE THE CHILD'S INFERRED ANXIETY OVER PERFORMANCE OF SELF-RELIANT BEHAVIOR IS HIGH (37) B-B-C	346	TILT TOWARD BEING THOSE 0.63 OF 40 WHERE THE CHILD'S INFERRED ANXIETY OVER PERFORMANCE OF SELF-RELIANT BEHAVIOR IS LOW (39) B-B-C	15 15 6 25 XSQ= 5.06 PHI= 0.288 XP = 0.0245
347	LEAN TOWARD BEING THOSE 0.71 OF 21 WHERE THE CHILD'S INFERRED CONFLICT REGARDING SELF-RELIANT BEHAVIOR IS HIGH (37) B-B-C	347	LEAN TOWARD BEING THOSE 0.67 OF 40 WHERE THE CHILD'S INFERRED CONFLICT REGARDING SELF-RELIANT BEHAVIOR IS LOW (39) B-B-C	15 13 6 27 XSQ= 6.91 PHI= 0.337 XP = 0.0086
350	LEAN TOWARD BEING THOSE 0.84 OF 19 WHERE THE CHILD'S INFERRED ANXIETY OVER PERFORMANCE OF ACHIEVEMENT BEHAVIOR IS HIGH (34) B-B-C	350	LEAN TOWARD BEING THOSE 0.62 OF 29 WHERE THE CHILD'S INFERRED ANXIETY OVER PERFORMANCE OF ACHIEVEMENT BEHAVIOR IS LOW (26) B-B-C	16 11 3 18 XSQ= 8.20 PHI= 0.413 XP = 0.0042

352 LEAN TOWARC BEING THOSE 0.90 OF 20 WHERE THE TOTAL POSITIVE PRESSURE TOWARD DEVELCPING OBEDIENT BEHAVICR IN THE CHILD IS HIGH (44) B-B-C	352 LEAN TOWARD BEING THOSE 0.51 OF 39 WHERE THE TOTAL POSITIVE PRESSURE TOWARC DEVELOPING OBEDIENT BEHAVICR IN THE CHILD IS LOW (28) B-B-C	18 19 2 20 XSQ= 7.95 PHI= 0.367 XP = 0.0048
353 LEAN TCWARD BEING THCSE 0.81 OF 21 WHERE THE CHILD'S INFERREC ANXIETY OVER NCN-PERFORMANCE CF OBECIENT BEHAVIOR IS HIGH (42) B-B-C	353 LEAN TOWARD BEING THOSE 0.59 CF 39 WHERE THE CHILD-S INFERRED ANXIETY OVER NON-PERFORMANCE OF OBEDIENT BEHAVICR IS LOW (32) B-B-C	17 16 4 23 XSQ= 7.25 PHI= 0.348 XP = 0.0071
365 DRIFT MORE TCWARD BEING THCSE 0.81 OF 16 WHERE THE TIME SPENT IN ADCLESCENT PEER GRCUP ACTIVITY IS HIGH CR HIGH-MECIUM (30) JKH	365 DRIFT LESS TOWARD BEING THCSE 0.52 CF 23 WHERE THE TIME SPENT IN ADOLESCENT PEER GRCUP ACTIVITY IS HIGH OR HIGH-MEDIUM (30) JKH	13 12 3 11 XSQ= 2.32 PHI= 0.244 EP = 0.0930
368 LEAN TOWARD BEING THOSE 0.85 OF 13 WHERE DISSCCIATICN OF THE SEXES AT ADCLESCENCE IS LCW (21) JKH	368 LEAN TOWARD BEING THOSE 0.67 CF 18 WHERE DISSOCIATION OF THE SEXES AT ADOLESCENCE IS HIGH OR MEDIUM (16) JKH	2 12 11 6 XSQ= 6.08 PHI= -0.443 EP = 0.0094
369 TILT LESS TOWARC BEING THCSE 0.55 OF 22 WHERE DISSCCIATICN OF THE SEXES AT ADCLESCENCE, OR CUSTOMS OF INITIATICN AT ADOLESCENCE, ARE PRESENT (42) JKH	369 TILT MORE TOWARD BEING THOSE 0.88 CF 26 WHERE DISSOCIATION OF THE SEXES AT ADOLESCENCE, OR CUSTOMS OF INITIATION AT ADOLESCENCE, ARE PRESENT (42) JKH	12 23 10 3 XSQ= 5.33 PHI= -0.333 XP = 0.0210
377 TEND LESS TO BE THCSE 0.60 OF 95 WHERE MALE GENITAL MUTILATION IS ABSENT (242)	377 TEND MORE TO BE THOSE 0.90 OF 143 WHERE MALE GENITAL MUTILATION IS ABSENT (242)	38 14 57 129 XSQ= 28.76 PHI= 0.348 XP = 0.0000
380 DRIFT MORE TOWARD BEING THOSE 0.92 OF 13 WHERE SEGREGATICN CF GIRLS AT MENARCHE IS PRESENT (35) F-B	380 DRIFT LESS TOWARD BEING THCSE 0.59 OF 32 WHERE SEGREGATION OF GIRLS AT MENARCHE IS PRESENT (35) F-B	12 19 1 13 XSQ= 3.27 PHI= 0.269 XP = 0.0707
382 DRIFT TCWARD BEING THCSE 0.54 OF 24 WHERE FEMALE INITIATICN RITES ARE ABSENT (27) JKB	382 DRIFT TOWARD BEING THOSE 0.75 OF 32 WHERE FEMALE INITIATION RITES ARE PRESENT (38) JKB	11 24 13 8 XSQ= 3.81 PHI= -0.261 XP = 0.0509
391 LEAN TOWARD BEING THOSE 0.62 OF 66 WHERE PREMARITAL SEX RELATIONS ARE STRCNGLY PUNISHEC AND IN FACT RARE, OR WEAKLY PUNISHED AND IN FACT NCT RARE (89) JTW,EA	391 LEAN TOWARD BEING THOSE 0.61 OF 82 WHERE PREMARITAL SEX RELATICNS ARE PUNISHED ONLY IF PREGNANCY RESULTS, CR FREELY PERMITTED (90) JTW,EA	41 32 25 50 XSQ= 6.91 PHI= 0.216 XP = 0.0086

```
400  DRIFT MORE TOWARD BEING THOSE  0.82 OF  17     400  DRIFT LESS TOWARD BEING THOSE  0.53 OF  32          3   15
     WHERE HOMOSEXUAL ACTIVITY                          WHERE HOMOSEXUAL ACTIVITY                           14   17
     IS PERMITTED  (36) F-B                             IS PERMITTED  (36) F-B                       XSQ=      2.92
                                                                                                     PHI=    -0.244
                                                                                                     XP =    0.0875

403  DRIFT TOWARD BEING THOSE       0.62 OF  13     403  DRIFT TOWARD BEING THOSE       0.73 OF  33          8    9
     WHERE EXPLANATIONS OF ILLNESS                      WHERE EXPLANATIONS OF ILLNESS                        5   24
     OF AN ANAL NATURE                                  OF AN ANAL NATURE                            XSQ=      3.34
     ARE PRESENT  (23) W-C                              ARE ABSENT  (38) W-C                         PHI=     0.270
                                                                                                     XP =    0.0674

417  IN ALL CASES ARE THOSE         1.00 OF  16     417  TILT LESS TOWARD BEING THOSE   0.65 OF  20         16   13
     WHERE WARFARE IS                                   WHERE WARFARE IS                                     0    7
     PREVALENT  (34) LWS                                PREVALENT  (34) LWS                          XSQ=      4.90
                                                                                                     PHI=     0.369
                                                                                                     EP =    0.0107

419  LEAN TOWARD BEING THOSE        0.84 OF  32     419  LEAN TOWARD BEING THOSE        0.50 OF  40         27   20
     WHERE MILITARY GLORY                               WHERE MILITARY GLORY                                 5   20
     IS STRONGLY OR                                     IS NEGLIGIBLY EMPHASIZED  (31) P,ES          XSQ=      7.81
     MODERATELY EMPHASIZED  (55) PES                                                                 PHI=     0.329
                                                                                                     XP =    0.0052

420  LEAN TOWARD BEING THOSE        0.69 OF  32     420  LEAN TOWARD BEING THOSE        0.67 OF  42         22   14
     WHERE BELLICOSITY                                  WHERE BELLICOSITY                                   10   28
     IS EXTREME  (41) PES                               IS MODERATE OR NEGLIGIBLE  (46) PES          XSQ=      7.76
                                                                                                     PHI=     0.324
                                                                                                     XP =    0.0054

421  DRIFT TOWARD BEING THOSE       0.59 OF  27     421  DRIFT TOWARD BEING THOSE       0.67 OF  43         16   14
     WHERE KILLING, TORTURING, OR MUTILATING            WHERE KILLING, TORTURING, OR MUTILATING             11   29
     OF THE ENEMY                                       OF THE ENEMY                                 XSQ=      3.80
     IS STRONGLY OR MODERATELY                          IS NEGLIGIBLY EMPHASIZED  (47) PES           PHI=     0.233
     EMPHASIZED  (37) PES                                                                            XP =    0.0513

426  TEND TO BE THOSE               0.81 OF  86     426  TEND TO BE THOSE               0.57 OF 125         70   54
     WHERE A HIGH GOD IS                                WHERE A HIGH GOD IS                                 16   71
     PRESENT  (156) GES,EA                              ABSENT  (104) GES,EA                         XSQ=     29.12
                                                                                                     PHI=     0.371
                                                                                                     XP =    0.0000

450  LEAN LESS TOWARD BEING THOSE   0.56 OF  41     450  LEAN MORE TOWARD BEING THOSE   0.88 OF  40         23   35
     WHERE THE OBSERVATION OF FOOD TABOOS               WHERE THE OBSERVATION OF FOOD TABOOS                18    5
     IS HIGH OR MEDIUM, RATHER THAN                     IS HIGH OR MEDIUM, RATHER THAN               XSQ=      8.34
     LOW  (60) JRL                                      LOW  (60) JRL                                PHI=    -0.321
                                                                                                     XP =    0.0039

458  TEND TO BE THOSE               0.66 OF  61     458  TEND TO BE THOSE               0.96 OF  92         40    4
     WHERE GAMES, IF PRESENT,                           WHERE GAMES, IF PRESENT,                            21   88
     INCLUDE GAMES OF STRATEGY  (52) R-A-B,EA           DO NOT INCLUDE                               XSQ=     64.16
                                                        GAMES OF STRATEGY  (119) R-A-B,EA            PHI=     0.648
                                                                                                     XP =    0.
```

```
460  TEND TO BE THOSE               0.80 OF  61      460  TEND TO BE THOSE               0.51 OF  92          12    47
     WHERE GAMES, IF PRESENT,                             WHERE GAMES, IF PRESENT,                           49    45
     ARE NOT LIMITED TO                                   ARE LIMITED TO                             XSQ=   13.98
     GAMES OF SKILL ONLY  (104) R-A-B,EA                  GAMES OF SKILL ONLY  (67) R-A-B,EA         PHI=  -0.302
                                                                                                     XP =  0.0002

468  DRIFT LESS TOWARD BEING THOSE  0.58 OF  24      468  DRIFT MORE TOWARD BEING THOSE  0.88 OF  24          10     3
     WHERE CONTACT WITH OTHER CULTURES                    WHERE CONTACT WITH OTHER CULTURES                  14    21
     IS REGULAR OR IRREGULAR, RATHER THAN                 IS REGULAR OR IRREGULAR, RATHER THAN       XSQ=    3.80
     FREQUENT  (37) JMH                                   FREQUENT  (37) JMH                         PHI=   0.281
                                                                                                     XP =  0.0513
```

****

72 CULTURES
WHERE THE PLOW IS PRESENT (61)

72 CULTURES
WHERE THE PLOW IS ABSENT (339)

BACKGROUND ON PAGE 79

SUBJECT ONLY

....

61 IN LEFT CCLUMN

ALBANIANS	AMERICANS	AYMARA	BARABRA	BHIL	BOERS	BRAZILIANS	BULGARIANS	BURUSHO	CAMBODIANS
CHERKESS	CCORG	CZECHS	DARC	DUTCH	EGYPTIANS	HAZARA	HEBREWS	HUTSUL	IRISH
JAPANESE	JAVANESE	KABYLE	KERALA	KHALKA	KOHISTANI	KOL	KOREANS	LEPCHA	LOLO
LOZI	MACASSARESE	MALAYS	MIN CHINESE	MINCHIA	MONGUOR	NURI	OKINAWANS	ORACN	PATHAN
PURUM	REGEIBAT	RIFFIANS	ROMANS	SAGADA	SANTAL	SERBS	SHLUH	SINHALESE	SOTHO
SWAZI	SYRIANS	TAOS	TESO	THAI	THONGA	TIGRINYA	TRISTAN	TURKMEN	VIETNAMESE
WALLCONS									

339 IN RIGHT CCLUMN

	Plow present (61)			Plow absent (339)		
3	TILT MORE TOWARC BEING THCSE LCCATED CUTSIDE CF AFRICA (320)	0.92 OF 61	3	TILT LESS TOWARD BEING THOSE LOCATED OUTSIDE OF AFRICA (320)	0.78 OF 339	5 75 56 264 XSQ= 5.43 PHI= -0.116 XP = 0.0198
4	TEND LESS TO BE THCSE LOCATED OUTSIDE OF THE CIRCUM-MEDITERRANEAN (355)	0.62 OF 61	4	TEND MORE TO BE THOSE LOCATED OUTSIDE OF THE CIRCUM-MEDITERRANEAN (355)	0.94 OF 339	23 22 38 317 XSQ= 47.37 PHI= 0.344 XP = 0.
5	TEND LESS TO BE THCSE LOCATED OUTSIDE OF EAST EURASIA (330)	0.54 OF 61	5	TEND MORE TO BE THOSE LOCATED OUTSIDE OF EAST EURASIA (330)	0.88 OF 339	28 42 33 297 XSQ= 37.93 PHI= 0.308 XP = 0.
6	LEAN MORE TOWARC BEING THCSE LOCATED OUTSIDE OF THE INSULAR PACIFIC (330)	0.95 OF 61	6	LEAN LESS TOWARD BEING THOSE LOCATED OUTSIDE OF THE INSULAR PACIFIC (330)	0.80 OF 339	3 67 58 272 XSQ= 6.90 PHI= -0.131 XP = 0.0086
8	TEND MORE TO BE THCSE LCCATED CUTSIDE CF NORTH AMERICA (330)	0.98 OF 61	8	TEND LESS TO BE THOSE LOCATED OUTSIDE OF NORTH AMERICA (330)	0.80 OF 339	1 69 60 270 XSQ= 11.28 PHI= -0.168 XP = 0.0008

9	LEAN MORE TOWARD BEING THOSE LOCATED OUTSIDE OF SOUTH AMERICA (335)	0.98 OF 61	9	LEAN LESS TOWARD BEING THOSE LOCATED OUTSIDE OF SOUTH AMERICA (335)	0.81 OF 339	1 64 60 275 XSQ= 10.06 PHI= -0.159 XP = 0.0015
15	TEND TO BE THOSE WHERE THE LATITUDE IS TWENTY DEGREES OR GREATER (183)	0.75 OF 61	15	TEND TO BE THOSE WHERE THE LATITUDE IS LESS THAN TWENTY DEGREES (217)	0.60 OF 339	46 137 15 202 XSQ= 24.12 PHI= 0.246 XP = 0.0000
44	TEND MORE TO BE THOSE WHERE SETTLEMENTS ARE FIXED (222)	0.90 OF 61	44	TEND LESS TO BE THOSE WHERE SETTLEMENTS ARE FIXED (222)	0.62 OF 271	55 167 6 104 XSQ= 17.04 PHI= 0.227 XP = 0.0000
46	TEND MORE TO BE THOSE OTHER THAN WHERE SETTLEMENTS ARE NON-FIXED AND MOVEMENT IS NOMADIC (260)	0.97 OF 61	46	TEND LESS TO BE THOSE OTHER THAN WHERE SETTLEMENTS ARE NON-FIXED AND MOVEMENT IS NOMADIC (260)	0.74 OF 271	2 70 59 201 XSQ= 13.61 PHI= -0.202 XP = 0.0002
51	TEND MORE TO BE THOSE WHERE SUBSISTENCE IS PRIMARILY BY FOOD PRODUCTION -- I. E., AGRICULTURE OR HUSBANDRY -- RATHER THAN BY GATHERING (253)	0.95 OF 61	51	TEND LESS TO BE THOSE WHERE SUBSISTENCE IS PRIMARILY BY FOOD PRODUCTION -- I. E., AGRICULTURE OR HUSBANDRY -- RATHER THAN BY GATHERING (253)	0.58 OF 339	58 195 3 144 XSQ= 29.78 PHI= 0.273 XP = 0.0000
53	TEND TO BE THOSE WHERE FOOD PRODUCTION IS BY INTENSIVE AGRICULTURE, RATHER THAN BY SIMPLE AGRICULTURE OR INCIPIENT FOOD PRODUCTION (91)	0.88 OF 58	53	TEND TO BE THOSE WHERE FOOD PRODUCTION IS BY SIMPLE AGRICULTURE OR INCIPIENT FOOD PRODUCTION, RATHER THAN BY INTENSIVE AGRICULTURE (147)	0.78 OF 180	51 40 7 140 XSQ= 77.44 PHI= 0.570 XP = 0.
54	LEAN MORE TOWARD BEING THOSE WHERE FOOD PRODUCTION IS BY INTENSIVE OR SIMPLE AGRICULTURE, RATHER THAN BY INCIPIENT FOOD PRODUCTION (192)	0.95 OF 58	54	LEAN LESS TOWARD BEING THOSE WHERE FOOD PRODUCTION IS BY INTENSIVE OR SIMPLE AGRICULTURE, RATHER THAN BY INCIPIENT FOOD PRODUCTION (192)	0.76 OF 180	55 137 3 43 XSQ= 8.69 PHI= 0.191 XP = 0.0032
55	TEND TO BE THOSE WHERE FOOD PRODUCTION IS BY INTENSIVE AGRICULTURE, RATHER THAN BY SIMPLE AGRICULTURE (91)	0.93 OF 55	55	TEND TO BE THOSE WHERE FOOD PRODUCTION IS BY SIMPLE AGRICULTURE, RATHER THAN BY INTENSIVE AGRICULTURE (101)	0.71 OF 137	51 40 4 97 XSQ= 61.01 PHI= 0.564 XP = 0.
62	IN ALL CASES ARE THOSE WHERE HUSBANDRY OF SOME KIND IS PRESENT (228)	1.00 OF 61	62	TEND TO BE THOSE WHERE HUSBANDRY OF ANY KIND IS ABSENT (172)	0.51 OF 339	61 167 0 172 XSQ= 52.25 PHI= 0.361 XP = 0.

63	IN ALL CASES ARE THOSE 1.00 OF 61 WHERE HUSBANDRY, IF PRESENT, IS PRINCIPALLY IN THE FORM OF BOVINE, EQUINE, CAMEL-LIKE, OR DEER-LIKE ANIMALS, RATHER THAN PIGS, SHEEP, OR GOATS (152)	63	TEND LESS TO BE THOSE 0.55 OF 165 WHERE HUSBANDRY, IF PRESENT, IS PRINCIPALLY IN THE FORM OF BOVINE, EQUINE, CAMEL-LIKE, OR DEER-LIKE ANIMALS, RATHER THAN PIGS, SHEEP, OR GOATS (152)	61 91 0 74 XSQ= 38.67 PHI= 0.414 XP = 0.
71	TEND TO BE THOSE 0.91 OF 34 WHERE METAL WORKING IS PRESENT (98)	71	TEND TO BE THOSE 0.69 OF 217 WHERE METAL WORKING IS ABSENT (153)	31 67 3 150 XSQ= 42.41 PHI= 0.411 XP = 0.
73	TEND TO BE THOSE 0.79 OF 34 WHERE WEAVING IS PRESENT (118)	73	TEND TO BE THOSE 0.57 OF 214 WHERE WEAVING IS ABSENT (130)	27 91 7 123 XSQ= 14.56 PHI= 0.242 XP = 0.0001
74	TILT MORE TOWARD BEING THOSE 0.81 OF 27 WHERE POTTERY IS PRESENT (145)	74	TILT LESS TOWARD BEING THOSE 0.58 OF 211 WHERE POTTERY IS PRESENT (145)	22 123 5 88 XSQ= 4.48 PHI= 0.137 XP = 0.0344
77	DRIFT TOWARD BEING THOSE 0.63 OF 8 WHERE THE WRITING SYSTEM IS ALPHABETIC-OR-PHONETIC, RATHER THAN BEING MNEMONIC OR ABSENT (15) JMH	77	DRIFT TOWARD BEING THOSE 0.78 OF 46 WHERE THE WRITING SYSTEM IS MNEMONIC OR ABSENT, RATHER THAN BEING ALPHABETIC-OR-PHONETIC (39) JMH	5 10 3 36 XSQ= 3.79 PHI= 0.265 XP = 0.0514
80	TEND TO BE THOSE 0.51 OF 47 WHERE A CITY OR TOWN IS PRESENT (39)	80	TEND TO BE THOSE 0.92 OF 177 WHERE NO CITY OR TOWN IS PRESENT (185)	24 15 23 162 XSQ= 43.93 PHI= 0.443 XP = 0.
81	TEND TO BE THOSE 0.74 OF 47 WHERE A CITY OR TOWN IS PRESENT, OR THE AVERAGE COMMUNITY SIZE IS 200 OR GREATER (89)	81	TEND TO BE THOSE 0.69 OF 177 WHERE NO CITY OR TOWN IS PRESENT, AND THE AVERAGE COMMUNITY SIZE IS SMALLER THAN 200 (135)	35 54 12 123 XSQ= 28.16 PHI= 0.355 XP = 0.0000
83	TILT LESS TOWARD BEING THOSE 0.55 OF 22 WHERE, WITH NO CITY AND NO TOWN PRESENT, THE AVERAGE COMMUNITY SIZE IS SMALLER THAN 200, RATHER THAN BETWEEN 200 AND 999 (135)	83	TILT MORE TOWARD BEING THOSE 0.78 OF 158 WHERE, WITH NO CITY AND NO TOWN PRESENT, THE AVERAGE COMMUNITY SIZE IS SMALLER THAN 200, RATHER THAN BETWEEN 200 AND 999 (135)	10 35 12 123 XSQ= 4.42 PHI= 0.157 XP = 0.0355
84	TEND TO BE THOSE 0.52 OF 40 WHERE THE LEVEL OF POLITICAL INTEGRATION IS THE LARGE STATE (42) GPM	84	TEND TO BE THOSE 0.92 OF 264 WHERE THE LEVEL OF POLITICAL INTEGRATION IS THE LITTLE STATE, THE MINIMAL STATE, THE AUTONOMOUS COMMUNITY, OR THE FAMILY (262) GPM	21 21 19 243 XSQ= 54.21 PHI= 0.422 XP = 0.

85	TEND TO BE THOSE 0.72 OF 40 WHERE THE LEVEL OF POLITICAL INTEGRATION IS THE LARGE STATE, OR THE LITTLE STATE (70) GPM	85	TEND TO BE THOSE 0.84 OF 264 WHERE THE LEVEL OF POLITICAL INTEGRATION IS THE MINIMAL STATE, THE AUTONOMOUS COMMUNITY, OR THE FAMILY (234) GPM	29 41 11 223 XSQ= 60.43 PHI= 0.446 XP = 0.
86	TEND TO BE THOSE 0.95 OF 40 WHERE THE LEVEL OF POLITICAL INTEGRATION IS THE LARGE STATE, THE LITTLE STATE, OR THE MINIMAL STATE (148) GPM	86	TEND TO BE THOSE 0.58 OF 264 WHERE THE LEVEL OF POLITICAL INTEGRATION IS THE AUTONOMOUS COMMUNITY, OR THE FAMILY (156) GPM	38 110 2 154 XSQ= 37.44 PHI= 0.351 XP = 0.
88	TILT TOWARD BEING THOSE 0.56 OF 39 WHERE, IF A HEADMANSHIP IS PRESENT, SUCCESSION IS NON-HEREDITARY (106)	88	TILT TOWARD BEING THOSE 0.64 OF 232 WHERE, IF A HEADMANSHIP IS PRESENT, SUCCESSION IS HEREDITARY (165)	22 84 17 148 XSQ= 4.91 PHI= 0.135 XP = 0.0268
89	TILT MORE TOWARD BEING THOSE 0.82 OF 22 WHERE, IF A NON-HEREDITARY HEADMANSHIP IS PRESENT, SUCCESSION IS BY CONSENSUS (63)	89	TILT LESS TOWARD BEING THOSE 0.54 OF 84 WHERE, IF A NON-HEREDITARY HEADMANSHIP IS PRESENT, SUCCESSION IS BY CONSENSUS (63)	18 45 4 39 XSQ= 4.66 PHI= 0.210 XP = 0.0309
91	TILT TOWARD BEING THOSE 0.88 OF 8 WHERE SOCIETAL COMPLEXITY IS HIGH (18) F-W	91	TILT TOWARD BEING THOSE 0.66 OF 32 WHERE SOCIETAL COMPLEXITY IS LOW (22) F-W	7 11 1 21 XSQ= 5.31 PHI= 0.364 EP = 0.0138
95	TEND TO BE THOSE 0.64 OF 58 WHERE THE HIERARCHY OF NATIONAL JURISDICTION HAS FOUR, THREE, OR TWO LEVELS (76) GES,EA	95	TEND TO BE THOSE 0.86 OF 272 WHERE THE HIERARCHY OF NATIONAL JURISDICTION HAS ONE OR NO LEVELS (254) GES,EA	37 39 21 233 XSQ= 63.20 PHI= 0.438 XP = 0.
96	TEND TO BE THOSE 0.88 OF 58 WHERE THE HIERARCHY OF NATIONAL JURISDICTION HAS FOUR, THREE, TWO OR ONE LEVEL (174) GES,EA	96	TEND TO BE THOSE 0.55 OF 272 WHERE THE HIERARCHY OF NATIONAL JURISDICTION HAS NO LEVELS (156) GES,EA	51 123 7 149 XSQ= 33.29 PHI= 0.318 XP = 0.
98	DRIFT MORE TOWARD BEING THOSE 0.83 OF 59 WHERE THE HIERARCHY OF LOCAL JURISDICTION HAS FOUR OR THREE LEVELS (238) GES,EA	98	DRIFT LESS TOWARD BEING THOSE 0.69 OF 272 WHERE THE HIERARCHY OF LOCAL JURISDICTION HAS FOUR OR THREE LEVELS (238) GES,EA	49 189 10 83 XSQ= 3.77 PHI= 0.107 XP = 0.0522
100	LEAN MORE TOWARD BEING THOSE 0.97 OF 58 WHERE HIERARCHIES ARE MORE COMPLEX THAN THE 'SIMPLEST,' I. E., MORE COMPLEX THAN TWO LOCAL LEVELS WITH NO NATIONAL LEVELS (267) GES,EA	100	LEAN LESS TOWARD BEING THOSE 0.78 OF 272 WHERE HIERARCHIES ARE MORE COMPLEX THAN THE 'SIMPLEST,' I. E., MORE COMPLEX THAN TWO LOCAL LEVELS WITH NO NATIONAL LEVELS (267) GES,EA	56 211 2 61 XSQ= 9.95 PHI= 0.174 XP = 0.0016

102	TEND TO BE THOSE WHERE CLASS STRATIFICATION IS PRESENT (203)	0.88 OF 58	102	TEND TO BE THOSE WHERE CLASS STRATIFICATION IS ABSENT (180)	0.53 OF 325	51 152 7 173 XSQ= 31.84 PHI= 0.288 XP = 0.
106	LEAN MORE TOWARD BEING THOSE WHERE CLASS STRATIFICATION, IF PRESENT, IS BASED ON SOMETHING OTHER THAN WEALTH (126)	0.80 OF 51	106	LEAN LESS TOWARD BEING THOSE WHERE CLASS STRATIFICATION, IF PRESENT, IS BASED ON SOMETHING OTHER THAN WEALTH (126)	0.56 OF 152	10 67 41 85 XSQ= 8.70 PHI= -0.207 XP = 0.0032
107	TEND TO BE THOSE WHERE CLASS STRATIFICATION, IF PRESENT, IS BASED ON OCCUPATIONAL STATUS (43)	0.51 OF 51	107	TEND TO BE THOSE WHERE CLASS STRATIFICATION, IF PRESENT, IS BASED ON SOMETHING OTHER THAN OCCUPATIONAL STATUS (160)	0.89 OF 152	26 17 25 135 XSQ= 33.88 PHI= 0.409 XP = 0.
108	TILT MORE TOWARD BEING THOSE WHERE CLASS STRATIFICATION, IF PRESENT, IS BASED ON SOMETHING OTHER THAN A HEREDITARY ARISTOCRACY (129)	0.76 OF 51	108	TILT LESS TOWARD BEING THOSE WHERE CLASS STRATIFICATION, IF PRESENT, IS BASED ON SOMETHING OTHER THAN A HEREDITARY ARISTOCRACY (129)	0.59 OF 152	12 62 39 90 XSQ= 4.19 PHI= -0.144 XP = 0.0406
109	TEND LESS TO BE THOSE WHERE CASTES ARE ABSENT (317)	0.60 OF 48	109	TEND MORE TO BE THOSE WHERE CASTES ARE ABSENT (317)	0.90 OF 320	19 32 29 288 XSQ= 28.17 PHI= 0.277 XP = 0.0000
116	TILT TOWARD BEING THOSE WHERE OCCUPATIONAL SPECIALIZATION IS FULL-TIME, WHETHER OR NOT FOR SURPLUS PRODUCTION (20) JMH	0.75 OF 8	116	TILT TOWARD BEING THOSE WHERE OCCUPATIONAL SPECIALIZATION IS PART-TIME ONLY (34) JMH	0.70 OF 46	6 14 2 32 XSQ= 4.05 PHI= 0.274 XP = 0.0442
118	DRIFT TOWARD BEING THOSE WHERE THE PERCENTAGE OF OCCUPATIONS THAT ARE SPECIALIZED IS HIGH OR MEDIUM (24) WME	0.86 OF 7	118	DRIFT TOWARD BEING THOSE WHERE THE PERCENTAGE OF OCCUPATIONS THAT ARE SPECIALIZED IS LOW (25) WME	0.57 OF 42	6 18 1 24 XSQ= 2.86 PHI= 0.242 XP = 0.0907
130	IN ALL CASES ARE THOSE WHERE LEATHER WORKING IS MAINLY DONE BY MALES (39)	1.00 OF 11	130	TEND TO BE THOSE WHERE LEATHER WORKING IS MAINLY DONE BY FEMALES (45)	0.62 OF 73	11 28 0 45 XSQ= 12.23 PHI= 0.382 XP = 0.0005
131	IN ALL CASES ARE THOSE WHERE THE CONSTRUCTION OF PERMANENT HOUSES OR THE ERECTION OF TEMPORARY DWELLINGS IS MAINLY DONE BY MALES (136)	1.00 OF 26	131	DRIFT LESS TOWARD BEING THOSE WHERE THE CONSTRUCTION OF PERMANENT HOUSES OR THE ERECTION OF TEMPORARY DWELLINGS IS MAINLY DONE BY MALES (136)	0.84 OF 131	26 110 0 21 XSQ= 3.53 PHI= 0.150 XP = 0.0604

132	IN ALL CASES ARE THOSE WHERE ECONOMIC EXCHANGE INVOLVES THE USE OF MONEY (37) JMH	1.00 OF 8	132	DRIFT LESS TOWARD BEING THOSE WHERE ECONOMIC EXCHANGE INVOLVES THE USE OF MONEY (37) JMH	0.63 OF 46	8 29 0 17 XSQ= 2.77 PHI= 0.227 XP = 0.0959
139	IN ALL CASES ARE THOSE WHERE SUPERORDINATE PUNISHMENT IS PRESENT (15) BBW	1.00 OF 3	139	TILT TOWARD BEING THOSE WHERE SUPERORDINATE PUNISHMENT IS ABSENT (25) BBW	0.68 OF 37	3 12 0 25 XSQ= 2.91 PHI= 0.270 EP = 0.0461
163	IN ALL CASES ARE THOSE WHERE THE EMPHASIS ON INDIVIDUAL VOLITION AS THE CAUSE OF CRIME IS HIGH (7) MJ	1.00 OF 3	163	DRIFT TOWARD BEING THOSE WHERE THE EMPHASIS ON INDIVIDUAL VOLITION AS THE CAUSE OF CRIME IS LOW (10) MJ	0.71 OF 14	3 4 0 10 XSQ= 2.67 PHI= 0.397 EP = 0.0515
176	LEAN MORE TOWARD BEING THOSE WHERE THE COMMUNITY IS OTHER THAN A CLAN-COMMUNITY OR A COMMUNITY STRUCTURED OR SEGMENTED ON A CLAN BASIS (213)	0.75 OF 59	176	LEAN LESS TOWARD BEING THOSE WHERE THE COMMUNITY IS OTHER THAN A CLAN-COMMUNITY OR A COMMUNITY STRUCTURED OR SEGMENTED ON A CLAN BASIS (213)	0.52 OF 323	15 154 44 169 XSQ= 9.13 PHI= -0.155 XP = 0.0025
178	TILT MORE TOWARD BEING THOSE WHERE THE COMMUNITY IS OTHER THAN SEGMENTED ON A CLAN BASIS AND NON-EXOGAMOUS (295)	0.88 OF 59	178	TILT LESS TOWARD BEING THOSE WHERE THE COMMUNITY IS OTHER THAN SEGMENTED ON A CLAN BASIS AND NON-EXOGAMOUS (295)	0.75 OF 323	7 80 52 243 XSQ= 4.02 PHI= -0.103 XP = 0.0450
182	LEAN TOWARD BEING THOSE WHERE THE COMMUNITY IS STRUCTURED ON A NON-CLAN BASIS AND AGAMOUS (126)	0.51 OF 59	182	LEAN TOWARD BEING THOSE OTHER THAN WHERE THE COMMUNITY IS STRUCTURED ON A NON-CLAN BASIS AND AGAMOUS (256)	0.70 OF 323	30 96 29 227 XSQ= 9.14 PHI= 0.155 XP = 0.0025
183	IN ALL CASES ARE THOSE WHERE THE LARGEST NON-COGNATIC KIN GROUP IS SMALLER THAN A MOEITY, I. E., A PHRATRY OR SIB OR LINEAGE (218)	1.00 OF 39	183	TILT LESS TOWARD BEING THOSE WHERE THE LARGEST NON-COGNATIC KIN GROUP IS SMALLER THAN A MOEITY, I. E., A PHRATRY OR SIB OR LINEAGE (218)	0.84 OF 213	0 34 39 179 XSQ= 5.89 PHI= -0.153 XP = 0.0152
186	LEAN TOWARD BEING THOSE WHERE THE KIN GROUP IS EXCLUSIVELY PATRILINEAL (150)	0.54 OF 61	186	LEAN TOWARD BEING THOSE WHERE THE KIN GROUP IS OTHER THAN EXCLUSIVELY PATRILINEAL (250)	0.65 OF 339	33 117 28 222 XSQ= 7.65 PHI= 0.138 XP = 0.0057
187	LEAN MORE TOWARD BEING THOSE WHERE THE KIN GROUP IS OTHER THAN EXCLUSIVELY MATRILINEAL (344)	0.98 OF 61	187	LEAN LESS TOWARD BEING THOSE WHERE THE KIN GROUP IS OTHER THAN EXCLUSIVELY MATRILINEAL (344)	0.84 OF 338	1 54 60 284 XSQ= 7.77 PHI= -0.140 XP = 0.0053

190	LEAN MORE TOWARD BEING THOSE 0.97 OF 39 WHERE THE KIN GROUP IS PATRILINEAL OR DOUBLE-DESCENT, RATHER THAN MATRILINEAL (186)	190	LEAN LESS TOWARD BEING THOSE 0.71 OF 208 WHERE THE KIN GROUP IS PATRILINEAL OR DOUBLE-DESCENT, RATHER THAN MATRILINEAL (186)	38 148 1 60 XSQ= 10.83 PHI= 0.209 XP = 0.0010
196	TEND MORE TO BE THOSE 0.96 OF 51 WHERE INDIVIDUAL RIGHTS IN REAL PROPERTY, AND RULES FOR INHERITANCE, ARE PRESENT (194)	196	TEND LESS TO BE THOSE 0.63 OF 230 WHERE INDIVIDUAL RIGHTS IN REAL PROPERTY, AND RULES FOR INHERITANCE, ARE PRESENT (194)	49 145 2 85 XSQ= 19.79 PHI= 0.265 XP = 0.0000
198	IN ALL CASES ARE THOSE 1.00 OF 39 WHERE RULES FOR THE INHERITANCE OF REAL PROPERTY, IF PRESENT, FAVOR THE MALE HEIR OR LINE, RATHER THAN THE FEMALE (144)	198	TILT LESS TOWARD BEING THOSE 0.83 OF 126 WHERE RULES FOR THE INHERITANCE OF REAL PROPERTY, IF PRESENT, FAVOR THE MALE HEIR OR LINE, RATHER THAN THE FEMALE (144)	39 105 0 21 XSQ= 6.02 PHI= 0.191 XP = 0.0141
207	TILT TOWARD BEING THOSE 0.85 OF 13 WHERE MARITAL RESIDENCE IS AMBILOCAL OR NEOLOCAL, RATHER THAN MATRILOCAL OR UXORILOCAL (64)	207	TILT TOWARD BEING THOSE 0.54 OF 115 WHERE MARITAL RESIDENCE IS MATRILOCAL OR UXORILOCAL, RATHER THAN AMBILOCAL OR NEOLOCAL (64)	2 62 11 53 XSQ= 5.48 PHI= -0.207 XP = 0.0192
209	LEAN MORE TOWARD BEING THOSE 0.96 OF 50 WHERE MARITAL RESIDENCE IS PATRILOCAL, VIRILOCAL, OR AVUNCULOCAL, RATHER THAN MATRILOCAL OR UXORILOCAL (270)	209	LEAN LESS TOWARD BEING THOSE 0.78 OF 284 WHERE MARITAL RESIDENCE IS PATRILOCAL, VIRILOCAL, OR AVUNCULOCAL, RATHER THAN MATRILOCAL OR UXORILOCAL (270)	48 222 2 62 XSQ= 7.61 PHI= 0.151 XP = 0.0058
210	IN ALL CASES ARE THOSE 1.00 OF 39 WHERE MARITAL RESIDENCE IS PATRILOCAL, RATHER THAN MATRILOCAL (169)	210	LEAN LESS TOWARD BEING THOSE 0.81 OF 161 WHERE MARITAL RESIDENCE IS PATRILOCAL, RATHER THAN MATRILOCAL (169)	39 130 0 31 XSQ= 7.48 PHI= 0.193 XP = 0.0062
214	DRIFT MORE TOWARD BEING THOSE 0.97 OF 30 WHERE FIRST COUSIN MARRIAGE, IF PERMITTED, IS OTHER THAN UNILATERAL (144)	214	DRIFT LESS TOWARD BEING THOSE 0.81 OF 142 WHERE FIRST COUSIN MARRIAGE, IF PERMITTED, IS OTHER THAN UNILATERAL (144)	1 27 29 115 XSQ= 3.39 PHI= -0.140 XP = 0.0655
234	TEND TO BE THOSE 0.82 OF 40 WHERE THE COUSIN TERMINOLOGY IS OF ESKIMO OR HAWAIIAN TYPE, RATHER THAN CROW, OMAHA, OR IROQUOIS TYPE (170)	234	TEND TO BE THOSE 0.51 OF 282 WHERE THE COUSIN TERMINOLOGY IS OF CROW, OMAHA, OR IROQUOIS TYPE, RATHER THAN ESKIMO OR HAWAIIAN TYPE (152)	7 145 33 137 XSQ= 14.84 PHI= -0.215 XP = 0.0001
236	TILT MORE TOWARD BEING THOSE 0.67 OF 61 WHERE THE FAMILY IS OF AN EXTENDED TYPE, RATHER THAN AN INDEPENDENT TYPE (213)	236	TILT LESS TOWARD BEING THOSE 0.51 OF 337 WHERE THE FAMILY IS OF AN EXTENDED TYPE, RATHER THAN AN INDEPENDENT TYPE (213)	41 172 20 165 XSQ= 4.80 PHI= 0.110 XP = 0.0284

240	LEAN MORE TOWARD BEING THOSE 0.85 OF 41 WHERE THE FAMILY, IF EXTENDED, IS SMALL OR STEM, RATHER THAN LARGE (135)	240	LEAN LESS TOWARD BEING THOSE 0.58 OF 172 WHERE THE FAMILY, IF EXTENDED, IS SMALL OR STEM, RATHER THAN LARGE (135)	6 72 35 100 XSQ= 9.43 PHI= -0.210 XP = 0.0021
241	DRIFT LESS TOWARD BEING THOSE 0.78 OF 41 WHERE THE FAMILY, IF EXTENDED, IS LARGE OR SMALL, RATHER THAN STEM (187)	241	DRIFT MORE TOWARD BEING THOSE 0.90 OF 172 WHERE THE FAMILY, IF EXTENDED, IS LARGE OR SMALL, RATHER THAN STEM (187)	32 155 9 17 XSQ= 3.44 PHI= -0.127 XP = 0.0635
242	TEND LESS TO BE THOSE 0.62 OF 61 WHERE MARRIAGE IS COMMONLY OR OCCASIONALLY POLYGYNOUS, RATHER THAN MONOGAMOUS (314)	242	TEND MORE TO BE THOSE 0.83 OF 334 WHERE MARRIAGE IS COMMONLY OR OCCASIONALLY POLYGYNOUS, RATHER THAN MONOGAMOUS (314)	38 276 23 58 XSQ= 11.87 PHI= -0.173 XP = 0.0006
272	DRIFT TOWARD BEING THOSE 0.86 OF 7 WHERE THE DIVORCE RATE IS LOW (28) CA	272	DRIFT TOWARD BEING THOSE 0.56 OF 50 WHERE THE DIVORCE RATE IS HIGH (29) CA	1 28 6 22 XSQ= 2.77 PHI= -0.220 XP = 0.0961
300	TILT MORE TOWARD BEING THOSE 0.92 OF 13 WHERE THE POST-PARTUM SEX TABOO LASTS SIX MONTHS OR LESS (73)	300	TILT LESS TOWARD BEING THOSE 0.55 OF 111 WHERE THE POST-PARTUM SEX TABOO LASTS SIX MONTHS OR LESS (73)	1 50 12 61 XSQ= 5.25 PHI= -0.206 XP = 0.0219
326	IN ALL CASES ARE THOSE 1.00 OF 5 WHERE THE INFERRED TRANSITION ANXIETY BETWEEN INFANCY AND CHILDHOOD IS HIGH (32) B-B-C	326	TILT TOWARD BEING THOSE 0.56 OF 62 WHERE THE INFERRED TRANSITION ANXIETY BETWEEN INFANCY AND CHILDHOOD IS LOW (35) B-B-C	5 27 0 35 XSQ= 3.86 PHI= 0.240 XP = 0.0493
334	IN ALL CASES ARE THOSE 1.00 OF 5 WHERE THE INDULGENCE OF THE CHILD IS LOW (38) B-B-C	334	DRIFT TOWARD BEING THOSE 0.55 OF 73 WHERE THE INDULGENCE OF THE CHILD IS HIGH (40) B-B-C	0 40 5 33 XSQ= 3.64 PHI= -0.216 XP = 0.0563
337	IN ALL CASES ARE THOSE 1.00 OF 5 WHERE THE CHILD'S INFERRED ANXIETY OVER NON-PERFORMANCE OF RESPONSIBLE BEHAVIOR IS HIGH (38) B-B-C	337	DRIFT TOWARD BEING THOSE 0.51 OF 68 WHERE THE CHILD'S INFERRED ANXIETY OVER NON-PERFORMANCE OF RESPONSIBLE BEHAVIOR IS LOW (35) B-B-C	5 33 0 35 XSQ= 3.10 PHI= 0.206 XP = 0.0785
339	IN ALL CASES ARE THOSE 1.00 OF 5 WHERE THE CHILD'S INFERRED CONFLICT REGARDING RESPONSIBLE BEHAVIOR IS HIGH (31) B-B-C	339	TILT TOWARD BEING THOSE 0.62 OF 68 WHERE THE CHILD'S INFERRED CONFLICT REGARDING RESPONSIBLE BEHAVIOR IS LOW (42) B-B-C	5 26 0 42 XSQ= 4.96 PHI= 0.261 XP = 0.0259

368	IN ALL CASES ARE THOSE WHERE DISSOCIATION OF THE SEXES AT ADOLESCENCE IS LOW (21) JKH	1.00 OF 5	368	DRIFT TOWARD BEING THOSE WHERE DISSOCIATION OF THE SEXES AT ADOLESCENCE IS HIGH OR MEDIUM (16) JKH	0.50 OF 32	0 16 5 16 XSQ= 2.60 PHI= -0.265 EP = 0.0567
370	TEND MORE TO BE THOSE WHERE THE SEGREGATION OF ADOLESCENT BOYS IS ABSENT (148)	0.86 OF 49	370	TEND LESS TO BE THOSE WHERE THE SEGREGATION OF ADOLESCENT BOYS IS ABSENT (148)	0.55 OF 194	7 88 42 106 XSQ= 14.59 PHI= -0.245 XP = 0.0001
382	TILT TOWARD BEING THOSE WHERE FEMALE INITIATION RITES ARE ABSENT (27) JKB	0.78 OF 9	382	TILT TOWARD BEING THOSE WHERE FEMALE INITIATION RITES ARE PRESENT (38) JKB	0.64 OF 56	2 36 7 20 XSQ= 4.05 PHI= -0.250 XP = 0.0442
390	LEAN TOWARD BEING THOSE WHERE PREMARITAL SEX RELATIONS ARE STRONGLY PUNISHED AND IN FACT RARE (47) JTW,EA	0.50 OF 34	390	LEAN TOWARD BEING THOSE WHERE PREMARITAL SEX RELATIONS ARE WEAKLY PUNISHED AND IN FACT NOT RARE OR PUNISHED ONLY IF PREGNANCY RESULTS, OR FREELY PERMITTED (132) JTW,EA	0.79 OF 145	17 30 17 115 XSQ= 10.75 PHI= 0.245 XP = 0.0010
391	LEAN TOWARD BEING THOSE WHERE PREMARITAL SEX RELATIONS ARE STRONGLY PUNISHED AND IN FACT RARE, OR WEAKLY PUNISHED AND IN FACT NOT RARE (89) JTW,EA	0.74 OF 34	391	LEAN TOWARD BEING THOSE WHERE PREMARITAL SEX RELATIONS ARE PUNISHED ONLY IF PREGNANCY RESULTS, OR FREELY PERMITTED (90) JTW,EA	0.56 OF 145	25 64 9 81 XSQ= 8.38 PHI= 0.216 XP = 0.0038
424	DRIFT TOWARD BEING THOSE WHERE RELIGIOUS SPECIALISTS ARE FULL-TIME, RATHER THAN PART-TIME (21) JMH	0.75 OF 8	424	DRIFT TOWARD BEING THOSE WHERE RELIGIOUS SPECIALISTS ARE PART-TIME, RATHER THAN FULL-TIME (33) JMH	0.67 OF 46	6 15 2 31 XSQ= 3.52 PHI= 0.255 XP = 0.0605
426	TILT MORE TOWARD BEING THOSE WHERE A HIGH GOD IS PRESENT (156) GES,EA	0.77 OF 48	426	TILT LESS TOWARD BEING THOSE WHERE A HIGH GOD IS PRESENT (156) GES,EA	0.56 OF 212	37 119 11 93 XSQ= 6.31 PHI= 0.156 XP = 0.0120
427	TEND TO BE THOSE WHERE A HIGH GOD, IF PRESENT, IS ACTIVE, RATHER THAN INACTIVE (87) GES,EA	0.89 OF 37	427	TEND TO BE THOSE WHERE A HIGH GOD, IF PRESENT, IS INACTIVE, RATHER THAN ACTIVE (69) GES,EA	0.55 OF 119	33 54 4 65 XSQ= 20.22 PHI= 0.360 XP = 0.0000
428	TEND MORE TO BE THOSE WHERE A HIGH GOD, IF PRESENT AND ACTIVE, SUPPORTS HUMAN MORALITY, RATHER THAN NOT SUPPORTING IT (61) GES,EA	0.94 OF 33	428	TEND LESS TO BE THOSE WHERE A HIGH GOD, IF PRESENT AND ACTIVE, SUPPORTS HUMAN MORALITY, RATHER THAN NOT SUPPORTING IT (61) GES,EA	0.56 OF 54	31 30 2 24 XSQ= 12.63 PHI= 0.381 XP = 0.0004

444	IN ALL CASES ARE THOSE WHERE THE USE OF DREAMS TO SEEK AND CONTROL SUPERNATURAL POWERS IS LOW (27) RGD	1.00 OF 6	444	TILT TOWARD BEING THOSE WHERE THE USE OF DREAMS TO SEEK AND CONTROL SUPERNATURAL POWERS IS HIGH (28) RGD	0.57 OF 49	0 28 6 21 XSQ= 4.88 PHI= -0.298 XP = 0.0271
450	TEND TO BE THOSE WHERE THE OBSERVATION OF FOOD TABOOS IS LOW, RATHER THAN HIGH OR MEDIUM (26) JRL	0.71 OF 14	450	TEND TO BE THOSE WHERE THE OBSERVATION OF FOOD TABOOS IS HIGH OR MEDIUM, RATHER THAN LOW (60) JRL	0.78 OF 72	4 56 10 16 XSQ= 11.22 PHI= -0.361 XP = 0.0008
458	TEND TO BE THOSE WHERE GAMES, IF PRESENT, INCLUDE GAMES OF STRATEGY (52) R-A-B,EA	0.67 OF 24	458	TEND TO BE THOSE WHERE GAMES, IF PRESENT, DO NOT INCLUDE GAMES OF STRATEGY (119) R-A-B,EA	0.76 OF 147	16 36 8 111 XSQ= 15.41 PHI= 0.300 XP = 0.0001
459	TILT TOWARD BEING THOSE WHERE GAMES, IF PRESENT, INCLUDE GAMES OF CHANCE (82) R-A-B,EA	0.71 OF 24	459	TILT TOWARD BEING THOSE WHERE GAMES, IF PRESENT, DO NOT INCLUDE GAMES OF CHANCE (89) R-A-B,EA	0.56 OF 147	17 65 7 82 XSQ= 4.84 PHI= 0.168 XP = 0.0278
460	DRIFT MORE TOWARD BEING THOSE WHERE GAMES, IF PRESENT, ARE NOT LIMITED TO GAMES OF SKILL ONLY (104) R-A-B,EA	0.79 OF 24	460	DRIFT LESS TOWARD BEING THOSE WHERE GAMES, IF PRESENT, ARE NOT LIMITED TO GAMES OF SKILL ONLY (104) R-A-B,EA	0.58 OF 147	5 62 19 85 XSQ= 3.10 PHI= -0.135 XP = 0.0783
468	IN ALL CASES ARE THOSE WHERE CONTACT WITH OTHER CULTURES IS FREQUENT, RATHER THAN REGULAR OR IRREGULAR (17) JMH	1.00 OF 8	468	TEND TO BE THOSE WHERE CONTACT WITH OTHER CULTURES IS REGULAR OR IRREGULAR, RATHER THAN FREQUENT (37) JMH	0.80 OF 46	8 9 0 37 XSQ= 16.88 PHI= 0.559 XP = 0.0000
470	LEAN TOWARD BEING THOSE WHERE INNOVATIONS ARE GENERALLY ACCEPTED (21) JMH	0.88 OF 8	470	LEAN TOWARD BEING THOSE WHERE INNOVATIONS ARE ACCEPTED ONLY SELECTIVELY (33) JMH	0.70 OF 46	7 14 1 32 XSQ= 7.09 PHI= 0.362 XP = 0.0077

73 CULTURES WHERE WEAVING IS PRESENT (118)

73 CULTURES WHERE WEAVING IS ABSENT (130)

BACKGROUND ON PAGE 79

BOTH SUBJECT AND PREDICATE

118 IN LEFT COLUMN

ABIPON	ABOR	AINU	ALBANIANS	AMERICANS	ARAUCANIANS	ASHANTI	AYMARA	AZANDE	AZTEC
BAMBARA	BAMILEKE	BASSERI	BIRIFOR	BRAZILIANS	BULGARIANS	BURUSHO	CAGABA	CALLINAGO	CAMAYURA
CARIB	CAYAPA	CHAMACOCO	CHIRIGUANO	CHOROTI	CHORTI	CREEK	CUNA	CZECHS	DARD
DIEGUENO	DUTCH	EGYPTIANS	FON	GARO	GOAJIRO	GUATO	HAIDA	HUICHOL	HUTSUL
IBAN	INCA	JAPANESE	JAVANESE	JEMEZ	JIVARO	KAZAK	KHASI	KOHISTANI	KOREANS
KUBA	KWAKIUTL	LAKHER	LEPCHA	LHOTA NAGA	LOLO	MACASSARESE	MAORI	MARICOPA	MATACO
MAYA	MENDE	MIAMI	MIAO	MISKITO	MNONG GAR	MONGO	MONGUOR	MOSSI	MUNDURUCU
NAMBICUARA	NATCHEZ	NAVAHO	NUPE	NURI	NYAKYUSA	OKINAWANS	OMAHA	ONTONG-JAVA	PAEZ
PALAUANS	PALIKUR	PAPAGO	PONAPEANS	PURUM	RIFFIANS	RWALA	SAGADA	SANTAL	SERBS
SIRIONO	SIWANS	SOMALI	SONGHAI	SYRIANS	TALAMANCA	TANALA	TAPIRAPE	TARAHUMARA	TEHUELCHE
TENDA	TERENA	TIBETANS	TIV	TOTONAC	TRUKESE	TRUMAI	TSHIMSHIAN	TUCUNA	TUNEBO
TUPINAMBA	TWANA	WOLEAIANS	WOLOF	YABARANA	YAKUT	YAPESE	YORUBA		

130 IN RIGHT COLUMN

ALACALUF	ALORESE	AMBA	ANDAMANESE	APINAYE	ARANDA	ATSUGEWI	AWEIKOMA	BACAIRI	BARI
BEMBA	BHIL	BLACK CARIB	BORORO	BOTOCUDO	CHENCHU	CHEYENNE	CHIR-APACHE	CHOCO	CHUKCHEE
COMANCHE	COPR ESKIMO	CREE	CROW	DIERI	ELLICE	ENGA	EYAK	FANG	FOX
GANDA	GILBERTESE	GILYAK	GISU	GOND	GROS VENTRE	HASINAI	HAWAIIANS	HUKUNDIKA	HURON
ILA	INGALIK	KAPAUKU	KARIERA	KASKA	KATAB	KERAKI	KHALKA	KIKUYU	KIOW-APACHE
KORYAK	KUNG	KURTATCHI	KUTENAI	LAMET	LAU	LESU	LOZI	LUO	MAMVU
MANDAN	MANGAIANS	MANIHIKI	MARQUESANS	MARSHALLESE	MASAI	MATAKAM	MBUNDU	MBUTI	MENTAWEI
MOTA	MURINBATA	MURNGIN	NABESNA	NAMA	NANDI	NDEMBU	NICOBARESE	NOMLAKI	NUER
NUNIVAK	NYORO	OJIBWA	ONA	PUKAPUKA	PURARI	RAROIANS	RUNDI	SAMOANS	SAMOYED
SANPOIL	SARSI	SEMANG	SENIANG	SHILLUK	SWAZI	TALLENSI	TAOS	TAREUMIUT	TEDA
TENINO	THONGA	TIKOPIA	TIMBIRA	TIMUCUA	TIWI	TODA	TOKELAU	TOLOWA	TRISTAN
TROBRIAND	TUBATULABAL	TUCANO	ULAWANS	UTE	VEDDA	VENDA	WAICA	WANTOAT	WASHO
WIKMUNKAN	WITOTO	WOGEO	YAGUA	YAHGAN	YAO	YARURO	YOKUTS	YUKI	YUROK

152 EXCLUDED BECAUSE UNASCERTAINED

---

3 DRIFT MORE TOWARD BEING THOSE 0.87 OF 118 LOCATED OUTSIDE OF AFRICA (320)

3 DRIFT LESS TOWARD BEING THOSE 0.78 OF 130 LOCATED OUTSIDE OF AFRICA (320)

15	29
103	101
XSQ=	3.27
PHI=	-0.115
XP =	0.0704

```
 4  TEND LESS TO BE THOSE           0.86 OF 118    4  TEND MORE TO BE THOSE           0.98 OF 130        16    2
    LOCATED OUTSIDE OF                                LOCATED OUTSIDE OF                                102  128
    THE CIRCUM-MEDITERRANEAN  (355)                   THE CIRCUM-MEDITERRANEAN  (355)               XSQ=   11.55
                                                                                                     PHI=   0.216
                                                                                                     XP =  0.0007

 5  TILT LESS TOWARD BEING THOSE    0.79 OF 118    5  TILT MORE TOWARD BEING THOSE    0.89 OF 130        25   14
    LOCATED OUTSIDE OF                                LOCATED OUTSIDE OF                                 93  116
    EAST EURASIA  (330)                               EAST EURASIA  (330)                           XSQ=    4.31
                                                                                                     PHI=   0.132
                                                                                                     XP =  0.0379

 6  LEAN MORE TOWARD BEING THOSE    0.91 OF 118    6  LEAN LESS TOWARD BEING THOSE    0.74 OF 130        11   34
    LOCATED OUTSIDE OF                                LOCATED OUTSIDE OF                                107   96
    THE INSULAR PACIFIC  (330)                        THE INSULAR PACIFIC  (330)                    XSQ=   10.69
                                                                                                     PHI=  -0.208
                                                                                                     XP =  0.0011

 8  TILT MORE TOWARD BEING THOSE    0.86 OF 118    8  TILT LESS TOWARD BEING THOSE    0.73 OF 130        17   35
    LOCATED OUTSIDE OF                                LOCATED OUTSIDE OF                                101   95
    NORTH AMERICA  (330)                              NORTH AMERICA  (330)                          XSQ=    5.12
                                                                                                     PHI=  -0.144
                                                                                                     XP =  0.0237

 9  LEAN LESS TOWARD BEING THOSE    0.71 OF 118    9  LEAN MORE TOWARD BEING THOSE    0.88 OF 130        34   16
    LOCATED OUTSIDE OF                                LOCATED OUTSIDE OF                                 84  114
    SOUTH AMERICA  (335)                              SOUTH AMERICA  (335)                          XSQ=    9.47
                                                                                                     PHI=   0.195
                                                                                                     XP =  0.0021

11  TILT MORE TOWARD BEING THOSE    0.99 OF 118   11  TILT LESS TOWARD BEING THOSE    0.92 OF 130         1   10
    WHERE THE LATITUDE IS                             WHERE THE LATITUDE IS                             117  120
    LESS THAN SIXTY DEGREES  (385)                    LESS THAN SIXTY DEGREES  (385)                XSQ=    5.32
                                                                                                     PHI=  -0.146
                                                                                                     XP =  0.0211

12  TILT MORE TOWARD BEING THOSE    0.95 OF 118   12  TILT LESS TOWARD BEING THOSE    0.85 OF 130         6   19
    WHERE THE LATITUDE IS                             WHERE THE LATITUDE IS                             112  111
    LESS THAN FIFTY DEGREES  (367)                    LESS THAN FIFTY DEGREES  (367)                XSQ=    5.19
                                                                                                     PHI=  -0.145
                                                                                                     XP =  0.0227

13  DRIFT MORE TOWARD BEING THOSE   0.86 OF 118   13  DRIFT LESS TOWARD BEING THOSE   0.76 OF 130        17   31
    WHERE THE LATITUDE IS                             WHERE THE LATITUDE IS                             101   99
    LESS THAN FORTY DEGREES  (329)                    LESS THAN FORTY DEGREES  (329)                XSQ=    2.95
                                                                                                     PHI=  -0.109
                                                                                                     XP =  0.0858

44  TEND TO BE THOSE                0.74 OF 116   44  TEND TO BE THOSE                0.50 OF 124        86   62
    WHERE SETTLEMENTS ARE FIXED  (222)                WHERE SETTLEMENTS ARE NON-FIXED  (110)             30   62
                                                                                                     XSQ=   13.77
                                                                                                     PHI=   0.240
                                                                                                     XP =  0.0002
```

46	TEND MORE TO BE THOSE OTHER THAN WHERE SETTLEMENTS ARE NON-FIXED AND MOVEMENT IS NOMADIC (260)	0.86 OF 116	46	TEND LESS TO BE THOSE OTHER THAN WHERE SETTLEMENTS ARE NON-FIXED AND MOVEMENT IS NOMADIC (260)	0.63 OF 124	16 46 100 78 XSQ= 15.79 PHI= -0.257 XP = 0.0001
47	DRIFT LESS TOWARD BEING THOSE WHERE, IF SETTLEMENTS ARE NON-FIXED, MOVEMENT IS NOMADIC, RATHER THAN NON-NOMADIC (72)	0.53 OF 30	47	DRIFT MORE TOWARD BEING THOSE WHERE, IF SETTLEMENTS ARE NON-FIXED, MOVEMENT IS NOMADIC, RATHER THAN NON-NOMADIC (72)	0.74 OF 62	16 46 14 16 XSQ= 3.11 PHI= -0.184 XP = 0.0778
51	TEND TO BE THOSE WHERE SUBSISTENCE IS PRIMARILY BY FOOD PRODUCTION -- I. E., AGRICULTURE OR HUSBANDRY -- RATHER THAN BY GATHERING (253)	0.68 OF 118	51	TEND TO BE THOSE WHERE SUBSISTENCE IS PRIMARILY BY FOOD GATHERING -- I. E., HUNTING, FISHING, OR COLLECTING -- RATHER THAN FOOD PRODUCTION (147)	0.59 OF 130	80 53 38 77 XSQ= 17.10 PHI= 0.263 XP = 0.0000
53	LEAN LESS TOWARD BEING THOSE WHERE FOOD PRODUCTION IS BY SIMPLE AGRICULTURE OR INCIPIENT FOOD PRODUCTION, RATHER THAN BY INTENSIVE AGRICULTURE (147)	0.57 OF 91	53	LEAN MORE TOWARD BEING THOSE WHERE FOOD PRODUCTION IS BY SIMPLE AGRICULTURE OR INCIPIENT FOOD PRODUCTION, RATHER THAN BY INTENSIVE AGRICULTURE (147)	0.80 OF 65	39 13 52 52 XSQ= 7.92 PHI= 0.225 XP = 0.0049
55	LEAN TOWARD BEING THOSE WHERE FOOD PRODUCTION IS BY INTENSIVE AGRICULTURE, RATHER THAN BY SIMPLE AGRICULTURE (91)	0.53 OF 74	55	LEAN TOWARD BEING THOSE WHERE FOOD PRODUCTION IS BY SIMPLE AGRICULTURE, RATHER THAN BY INTENSIVE AGRICULTURE (101)	0.73 OF 48	39 13 35 35 XSQ= 6.80 PHI= 0.236 XP = 0.0091
62	TILT MORE TOWARD BEING THOSE WHERE HUSBANDRY OF SOME KIND IS PRESENT (228)	0.70 OF 118	62	TILT LESS TOWARD BEING THOSE WHERE HUSBANDRY OF SOME KIND IS PRESENT (228)	0.54 OF 130	83 70 35 60 XSQ= 6.44 PHI= 0.161 XP = 0.0112
63	DRIFT MORE TOWARD BEING THOSE WHERE HUSBANDRY, IF PRESENT, IS PRINCIPALLY IN THE FORM OF BOVINE, EQUINE, CAMEL-LIKE, OR DEER-LIKE ANIMALS, RATHER THAN PIGS, SHEEP, OR GOATS (152)	0.70 OF 83	63	DRIFT LESS TOWARD BEING THOSE WHERE HUSBANDRY, IF PRESENT, IS PRINCIPALLY IN THE FORM OF BOVINE, EQUINE, CAMEL-LIKE, OR DEER-LIKE ANIMALS, RATHER THAN PIGS, SHEEP, OR GOATS (152)	0.54 OF 70	58 38 25 32 XSQ= 3.31 PHI= 0.147 XP = 0.0688
71	TEND TO BE THOSE WHERE METAL WORKING IS PRESENT (98)	0.55 OF 114	71	TEND TO BE THOSE WHERE METAL WORKING IS ABSENT (153)	0.76 OF 128	63 31 51 97 XSQ= 23.17 PHI= 0.309 XP = 0.0000
74	TEND TO BE THOSE WHERE POTTERY IS PRESENT (145)	0.80 OF 106	74	TEND TO BE THOSE WHERE POTTERY IS ABSENT (93)	0.57 OF 125	85 54 21 71 XSQ= 31.22 PHI= 0.368 XP = 0.

77	DRIFT LESS TOWARD BEING THOSE 0.61 OF 23 WHERE THE WRITING SYSTEM IS MNEMONIC OR ABSENT, RATHER THAN BEING ALPHABETIC-OR-PHONETIC (39) JMH	77	DRIFT MORE TOWARD BEING THOSE 0.88 OF 26 WHERE THE WRITING SYSTEM IS MNEMONIC OR ABSENT, RATHER THAN BEING ALPHABETIC-OR-PHONETIC (39) JMH	9 3 14 23 XSQ= 3.64 PHI= 0.273 XP = 0.0563
79	TEND LESS TO BE THOSE 0.83 OF 84 WHERE NO CITY IS PRESENT (201)	79	IN ALL CASES ARE THOSE 1.00 OF 85 WHERE NO CITY IS PRESENT (201)	14 0 70 85 XSQ= 13.33 PHI= 0.281 XP = 0.0003
81	TEND TO BE THOSE 0.51 OF 84 WHERE A CITY OR TOWN IS PRESENT, OR THE AVERAGE COMMUNITY SIZE IS 200 OR GREATER (89)	81	TEND TO BE THOSE 0.82 OF 85 WHERE NO CITY OR TOWN IS PRESENT, AND THE AVERAGE COMMUNITY SIZE IS SMALLER THAN 200 (135)	43 15 41 70 XSQ= 19.63 PHI= 0.341 XP = 0.0000
83	DRIFT LESS TOWARD BEING THOSE 0.71 OF 58 WHERE, WITH NO CITY AND NO TOWN PRESENT, THE AVERAGE COMMUNITY SIZE IS SMALLER THAN 200, RATHER THAN BETWEEN 200 AND 999 (135)	83	DRIFT MORE TOWARD BEING THOSE 0.84 OF 83 WHERE, WITH NO CITY AND NO TOWN PRESENT, THE AVERAGE COMMUNITY SIZE IS SMALLER THAN 200, RATHER THAN BETWEEN 200 AND 999 (135)	17 13 41 70 XSQ= 3.03 PHI= 0.146 XP = 0.0820
86	TEND TO BE THOSE 0.63 OF 94 WHERE THE LEVEL OF POLITICAL INTEGRATION IS THE LARGE STATE, THE LITTLE STATE, OR THE MINIMAL STATE (148) GPM	86	TEND TO BE THOSE 0.70 OF 99 WHERE THE LEVEL OF POLITICAL INTEGRATION IS THE AUTONOMOUS COMMUNITY, OR THE FAMILY (156) GPM	59 30 35 69 XSQ= 19.16 PHI= 0.315 XP = 0.0000
89	TILT TOWARD BEING THOSE 0.79 OF 33 WHERE, IF A NON-HEREDITARY HEADMANSHIP IS PRESENT, SUCCESSION IS BY CONSENSUS (63)	89	TILT TOWARD BEING THOSE 0.51 OF 35 WHERE, IF A NON-HEREDITARY HEADMANSHIP IS PRESENT, SUCCESSION IS BY MEANS OTHER THAN CONSENSUS (43)	26 17 7 18 XSQ= 5.43 PHI= 0.283 XP = 0.0197
96	LEAN TOWARD BEING THOSE 0.62 OF 114 WHERE THE HIERARCHY OF NATIONAL JURISDICTION HAS FOUR, THREE, TWO OR ONE LEVEL (174) GES,EA	96	LEAN TOWARD BEING THOSE 0.59 OF 125 WHERE THE HIERARCHY OF NATIONAL JURISDICTION HAS NO LEVELS (156) GES,EA	71 51 43 74 XSQ= 10.17 PHI= 0.206 XP = 0.0014
97	TILT LESS TOWARD BEING THOSE 0.81 OF 115 WHERE THE HIERARCHY OF LOCAL JURISDICTION HAS THREE OR TWO LEVELS (273) GES,EA	97	TILT MORE TOWARD BEING THOSE 0.91 OF 125 WHERE THE HIERARCHY OF LOCAL JURISDICTION HAS THREE OR TWO LEVELS (273) GES,EA	22 11 93 114 XSQ= 4.55 PHI= 0.138 XP = 0.0328
98	TEND MORE TO BE THOSE 0.81 OF 115 WHERE THE HIERARCHY OF LOCAL JURISDICTION HAS FOUR OR THREE LEVELS (238) GES,EA	98	TEND LESS TO BE THOSE 0.58 OF 125 WHERE THE HIERARCHY OF LOCAL JURISDICTION HAS FOUR OR THREE LEVELS (238) GES,EA	93 72 22 53 XSQ= 14.03 PHI= 0.242 XP = 0.0002

99	TILT TOWARD BEING THOSE 0.70 OF 43 WHERE, WITH NATIONAL HIERARCHY ABSENT, THE HIERARCHY OF LOCAL JURISDICTION HAS FOUR OR THREE LEVELS (93) GES,EA	99	TILT TOWARD BEING THOSE 0.54 OF 74 WHERE, WITH NATIONAL HIERARCHY ABSENT, THE HIERARCHY OF LOCAL JURISDICTION HAS TWO LEVELS (63) GES,EA	30 34 13 40 XSQ= 5.30 PHI= 0.213 XP = 0.0213
100	TEND MORE TO BE THOSE 0.89 OF 114 WHERE HIERARCHIES ARE MORE COMPLEX THAN THE 'SIMPLEST,' I. E., MORE COMPLEX THAN TWO LOCAL LEVELS WITH NO NATIONAL LEVELS (267) GES,EA	100	TEND LESS TO BE THOSE 0.68 OF 125 WHERE HIERARCHIES ARE MORE COMPLEX THAN THE 'SIMPLEST,' I. E., MORE COMPLEX THAN TWO LOCAL LEVELS WITH NO NATIONAL LEVELS (267) GES,EA	101 85 13 40 XSQ= 13.49 PHI= 0.238 XP = 0.0002
102	LEAN TOWARD BEING THOSE 0.64 OF 115 WHERE CLASS STRATIFICATION IS PRESENT (203)	102	LEAN TOWARD BEING THOSE 0.57 OF 128 WHERE CLASS STRATIFICATION IS ABSENT (180)	74 55 41 73 XSQ= 10.28 PHI= 0.206 XP = 0.0013
106	TILT TOWARD BEING THOSE 0.66 OF 74 WHERE CLASS STRATIFICATION, IF PRESENT, IS BASED ON SOMETHING OTHER THAN WEALTH (126)	106	TILT TOWARD BEING THOSE 0.56 OF 55 WHERE CLASS STRATIFICATION, IF PRESENT, IS BASED ON WEALTH (77)	25 31 49 24 XSQ= 5.66 PHI= -0.209 XP = 0.0173
107	LEAN LESS TOWARD BEING THOSE 0.72 OF 74 WHERE CLASS STRATIFICATION, IF PRESENT, IS BASED ON SOMETHING OTHER THAN OCCUPATIONAL STATUS (160)	107	LEAN MORE TOWARD BEING THOSE 0.95 OF 55 WHERE CLASS STRATIFICATION, IF PRESENT, IS BASED ON SOMETHING OTHER THAN OCCUPATIONAL STATUS (160)	21 3 53 52 XSQ= 9.49 PHI= 0.271 XP = 0.0021
109	LEAN LESS TOWARD BEING THOSE 0.81 OF 109 WHERE CASTES ARE ABSENT (317)	109	LEAN MORE TOWARD BEING THOSE 0.94 OF 128 WHERE CASTES ARE ABSENT (317)	21 8 88 120 XSQ= 8.11 PHI= 0.185 XP = 0.0044
110	TEND TO BE THOSE 0.52 OF 111 WHERE SLAVERY IS PRESENT (163)	110	TEND TO BE THOSE 0.76 OF 128 WHERE SLAVERY IS ABSENT (218)	58 31 53 97 XSQ= 18.81 PHI= 0.281 XP = 0.0000
120	DRIFT TOWARD BEING THOSE 0.80 OF 25 WHERE THE CRAFT SPECIALIZATION SCORE IS HIGH OR MEDIUM (36) WME	120	DRIFT TOWARD BEING THOSE 0.50 OF 20 WHERE THE CRAFT SPECIALIZATION SCORE IS LOW (17) WME	20 10 5 10 XSQ= 3.25 PHI= 0.269 XP = 0.0714
128	TEND TO BE THOSE 0.70 OF 43 WHERE, IF SUBSISTENCE IS PRIMARILY BY AGRICULTURE, THE WORK IS MAINLY DONE BY MALES (40)	128	TEND TO BE THOSE 0.77 OF 30 WHERE, IF SUBSISTENCE IS PRIMARILY BY AGRICULTURE, THE WORK IS MAINLY DONE BY FEMALES (37)	30 7 13 23 XSQ= 13.44 PHI= 0.429 XP = 0.0002

130	TILT TOWARD BEING THOSE WHERE LEATHER WORKING IS MAINLY DONE BY MALES (39)	0.62 OF 37	130	TILT TOWARD BEING THOSE WHERE LEATHER WORKING IS MAINLY DONE BY FEMALES (45)	0.67 OF 45	23 15 14 30 XSQ= 5.68 PHI= 0.263 XP = 0.0172
131	LEAN MORE TOWARD BEING THOSE WHERE THE CONSTRUCTION OF PERMANENT HOUSES OR THE ERECTION OF TEMPORARY DWELLINGS IS MAINLY DONE BY MALES (136)	0.94 OF 82	131	LEAN LESS TOWARD BEING THOSE WHERE THE CONSTRUCTION OF PERMANENT HOUSES OR THE ERECTION OF TEMPORARY DWELLINGS IS MAINLY DONE BY MALES (136)	0.78 OF 72	77 56 5 16 XSQ= 7.15 PHI= 0.215 XP = 0.0075
138	DRIFT TOWARD BEING THOSE WHERE SUPERORDINATE JUSTICE IS PRESENT (22) BBW	0.79 OF 14	138	DRIFT TOWARD BEING THOSE WHERE SUPERORDINATE JUSTICE IS ABSENT (18) BBW	0.56 OF 18	11 8 3 10 XSQ= 2.52 PHI= 0.281 EP = 0.0751
147	DRIFT TOWARD BEING THOSE WHERE CODIFIED LAWS ARE PRESENT (20) LWS	0.79 OF 14	147	DRIFT TOWARD BEING THOSE WHERE CODIFIED LAWS ARE UNIMPORTANT OR ABSENT (13) LWS	0.64 OF 14	11 5 3 9 XSQ= 3.65 PHI= 0.361 EP = 0.0542
175	DRIFT MORE TOWARD BEING THOSE WHERE THE COMMUNITY IS 'KIN-HETEROGENEOUS,' I. E. OTHER THAN A CLAN COMMUNITY OR A DEME (260)	0.75 OF 112	175	DRIFT LESS TOWARD BEING THOSE WHERE THE COMMUNITY IS 'KIN-HETEROGENEOUS,' I. E. OTHER THAN A CLAN COMMUNITY OR A DEME (260)	0.63 OF 128	28 47 84 81 XSQ= 3.29 PHI= -0.117 XP = 0.0696
176	TILT TOWARD BEING THOSE WHERE THE COMMUNITY IS OTHER THAN A CLAN-COMMUNITY OR A COMMUNITY STRUCTURED OR SEGMENTED ON A CLAN BASIS (213)	0.64 OF 112	176	TILT TOWARD BEING THOSE WHERE THE COMMUNITY IS A CLAN-COMMUNITY OR A COMMUNITY STRUCTURED OR SEGMENTED ON A CLAN BASIS (169)	0.50 OF 128	40 64 72 64 XSQ= 4.40 PHI= -0.135 XP = 0.0359
177	LEAN MORE TOWARD BEING THOSE WHERE THE COMMUNITY IS OTHER THAN A SINGLE CLAN-COMMUNITY AND EXOGAMOUS (305)	0.88 OF 112	177	LEAN LESS TOWARD BEING THOSE WHERE THE COMMUNITY IS OTHER THAN A SINGLE CLAN-COMMUNITY AND EXOGAMOUS (305)	0.71 OF 128	13 37 99 91 XSQ= 9.81 PHI= -0.202 XP = 0.0017
180	TEND MORE TO BE THOSE WHERE THE COMMUNITY IS COMMONLY NON-EXOGAMOUS, RATHER THAN EXOGAMOUS (258)	0.79 OF 112	180	TEND LESS TO BE THOSE WHERE THE COMMUNITY IS COMMONLY NON-EXOGAMOUS, RATHER THAN EXOGAMOUS (258)	0.54 OF 128	24 59 88 69 XSQ= 14.99 PHI= -0.250 XP = 0.0001
182	TILT LESS TOWARD BEING THOSE OTHER THAN WHERE THE COMMUNITY IS STRUCTURED ON A NON-CLAN BASIS AND AGAMOUS (256)	0.59 OF 112	182	TILT MORE TOWARD BEING THOSE OTHER THAN WHERE THE COMMUNITY IS STRUCTURED ON A NON-CLAN BASIS AND AGAMOUS (256)	0.74 OF 128	46 33 66 95 XSQ= 5.65 PHI= 0.153 XP = 0.0174

183 DRIFT MORE TOWARD BEING THOSE 0.88 OF 73 WHERE THE LARGEST NON-COGNATIC KIN GROUP IS SMALLER THAN A MOEITY, I. E., A PHRATRY OR SIB OR LINEAGE (218)	183 DRIFT LESS TOWARD BEING THOSE 0.76 OF 78 WHERE THE LARGEST NON-COGNATIC KIN GROUP IS SMALLER THAN A MOEITY, I. E., A PHRATRY OR SIB OR LINEAGE (218)	9 19 64 59 XSQ= 2.86 PHI= -0.138 XP = 0.0908
185 DRIFT LESS TOWARD BEING THOSE 0.77 OF 73 WHERE THE LARGEST NON-COGNATIC KIN GROUP IS THE MOEITY OR PHRATRY OR SIB (194)	185 DRIFT MORE TOWARD BEING THOSE 0.88 OF 78 WHERE THE LARGEST NON-COGNATIC KIN GROUP IS THE MOEITY OR PHRATRY OR SIB (194)	56 69 17 9 XSQ= 2.87 PHI= -0.138 XP = 0.0900
196 LEAN MORE TOWARD BEING THOSE 0.75 OF 88 WHERE INDIVIDUAL RIGHTS IN REAL PROPERTY, AND RULES FOR INHERITANCE, ARE PRESENT (194)	196 LEAN LESS TOWARD BEING THOSE 0.51 OF 94 WHERE INDIVIDUAL RIGHTS IN REAL PROPERTY, AND RULES FOR INHERITANCE, ARE PRESENT (194)	66 48 22 46 XSQ= 10.13 PHI= 0.236 XP = 0.0015
213 DRIFT TOWARD BEING THOSE 0.52 OF 110 WHERE FIRST COUSIN MARRIAGE IS PERMITTED (172)	213 DRIFT TOWARD BEING THOSE 0.62 OF 125 WHERE FIRST COUSIN MARRIAGE IS NOT PERMITTED (198)	57 48 53 77 XSQ= 3.74 PHI= 0.126 XP = 0.0532
234 DRIFT TOWARD BEING THOSE 0.59 OF 88 WHERE THE COUSIN TERMINOLOGY IS OF ESKIMO OR HAWAIIAN TYPE, RATHER THAN CROW, OMAHA, OR IROQUOIS TYPE (170)	234 DRIFT TOWARD BEING THOSE 0.56 OF 117 WHERE THE COUSIN TERMINOLOGY IS OF CROW, OMAHA, OR IROQUOIS TYPE, RATHER THAN ESKIMO OR HAWAIIAN TYPE (152)	36 65 52 52 XSQ= 3.74 PHI= -0.135 XP = 0.0530
236 LEAN TOWARD BEING THOSE 0.63 OF 117 WHERE THE FAMILY IS OF AN EXTENDED TYPE, RATHER THAN AN INDEPENDENT TYPE (213)	236 LEAN TOWARD BEING THOSE 0.56 OF 130 WHERE THE FAMILY IS OF AN INDEPENDENT TYPE, RATHER THAN AN EXTENDED TYPE (185)	74 57 43 73 XSQ= 8.54 PHI= 0.186 XP = 0.0035
254 DRIFT TOWARD BEING THOSE 0.75 OF 4 WHERE HOUSEHOLD AUTHORITY IS ON THE MOTHER'S SIDE, RATHER THAN THE FATHER'S (6) CA	254 DRIFT TOWARD BEING THOSE 0.86 OF 7 WHERE HOUSEHOLD AUTHORITY IS ON THE FATHER'S SIDE, RATHER THAN THE MOTHER'S (9) DA	1 6 3 1 XSQ= 1.86 PHI= -0.411 EP = 0.0879
257 DRIFT TOWARD BEING THOSE 0.86 OF 7 WHERE THE SEVERITY OF SISTER AVOIDANCE IS LOW (17) WNS	257 DRIFT TOWARD BEING THOSE 0.64 OF 14 WHERE THE SEVERITY OF SISTER AVOIDANCE IS HIGH (10) WNS	1 9 6 5 XSQ= 2.89 PHI= -0.371 EP = 0.0635
278 DRIFT TOWARD BEING THOSE 0.60 OF 10 WHERE PROPERTY RIGHTS IN WOMEN ARE PRESENT (8) LWS	278 DRIFT TOWARD BEING THOSE 0.89 OF 9 WHERE PROPERTY RIGHTS IN WOMEN ARE UNIMPORTANT OR ABSENT (14) LWS	6 1 4 8 XSQ= 2.99 PHI= 0.397 EP = 0.0573

282 DRIFT TOWARD BEING THOSE 0.57 OF 14 WHERE THE STRENGTH OF DESIRE FOR CHILDREN IS HIGH (16) BCA	282 DRIFT TOWARD BEING THOSE 0.80 OF 15 WHERE THE STRENGTH OF DESIRE FOR CHILDREN IS LOW OR ABSENT (20) BCA	8 3 6 12 XSQ= 2.81 PHI= 0.311 EP = 0.0604
286 DRIFT TOWARD BEING THOSE 0.64 OF 14 WHERE THE NUMBER OF FOOD TABOOS DURING PREGNANCY IS LOW OR ABSENT (14) BCA	286 DRIFT TOWARD BEING THOSE 0.73 OF 15 WHERE THE NUMBER OF FOOD TABOOS DURING PREGNANCY IS HIGH (20) BCA	5 11 9 4 XSQ= 2.76 PHI= -0.309 EP = 0.0656
305 DRIFT TOWARD BEING THOSE 0.65 OF 17 WHERE THE EARLY SEXUAL SATISFACTION POTENTIAL IS LOW (24) W-C	305 DRIFT TOWARD BEING THOSE 0.67 OF 24 WHERE THE EARLY SEXUAL SATISFACTION POTENTIAL IS HIGH (27) W-C	6 16 11 8 XSQ= 2.78 PHI= -0.260 XP = 0.0956
307 TILT TOWARD BEING THOSE 0.61 OF 18 WHERE THE EARLY AGGRESSION SATISFACTION POTENTIAL IS LOW (19) W-C	307 TILT TOWARD BEING THOSE 0.83 OF 23 WHERE THE EARLY AGGRESSION SATISFACTION POTENTIAL IS HIGH (33) W-C	7 19 11 4 XSQ= 6.54 PHI= -0.399 XP = 0.0105
313 TILT TOWARD BEING THOSE 0.68 OF 19 WHERE AGGRESSION SOCIALIZATION ANXIETY IS HIGH (26) W-C	313 TILT TOWARD BEING THOSE 0.67 OF 24 WHERE AGGRESSION SOCIALIZATION ANXIETY IS LOW (28) W-C	13 8 6 16 XSQ= 3.92 PHI= 0.302 XP = 0.0478
323 DRIFT TOWARD BEING THOSE 0.52 OF 23 WHERE THE CONSTANCY OF PRESENCE OF THE INFANT'S NURTURANT AGENT IS HIGH (29) B-B-C	323 DRIFT TOWARD BEING THOSE 0.75 OF 36 WHERE THE CONSTANCY OF PRESENCE OF THE INFANT'S NURTURANT AGENT IS LOW (45) B-B-C	12 9 11 27 XSQ= 3.41 PHI= 0.241 XP = 0.0647
338 DRIFT TOWARD BEING THOSE 0.76 OF 25 WHERE THE CHILD'S INFERRED ANXIETY OVER PERFORMANCE OF RESPONSIBLE BEHAVIOR IS HIGH (44) B-B-C	338 DRIFT TOWARD BEING THOSE 0.51 OF 35 WHERE THE CHILD'S INFERRED ANXIETY OVER PERFORMANCE OF RESPONSIBLE BEHAVIOR IS LOW (29) B-B-C	19 17 6 18 XSQ= 3.50 PHI= 0.242 XP = 0.0614
341 TILT MORE TOWARD BEING THOSE 0.92 OF 12 WHERE THE CHILD'S INFERRED ANXIETY OVER NON-PERFORMANCE OF NURTURANT BEHAVIOR IS HIGH (30) B-B-C	341 TILT LESS TOWARD BEING THOSE 0.52 OF 25 WHERE THE CHILD'S INFERRED ANXIETY OVER NON-PERFORMANCE OF NURTURANT BEHAVIOR IS HIGH (30) B-B-C	11 13 1 12 XSQ= 3.99 PHI= 0.328 EP = 0.0272
370 TILT MORE TOWARD BEING THOSE 0.68 OF 93 WHERE THE SEGREGATION OF ADOLESCENT BOYS IS ABSENT (148)	370 TILT LESS TOWARD BEING THOSE 0.51 OF 92 WHERE THE SEGREGATION OF ADOLESCENT BOYS IS ABSENT (148)	30 45 63 47 XSQ= 4.65 PHI= -0.159 XP = 0.0310

No.	Subject	Ratio	No.	Subject	Ratio	Stats
372	TILT TOWARD BEING THOSE WHERE MALE INITIATION RITES ARE ABSENT (63) ASA	0.77 OF 30	372	TILT TOWARD BEING THOSE WHERE MALE INITIATION RITES ARE PRESENT (48) ASA	0.53 OF 58	7 31 / 23 27 / XSQ= 6.13 / PHI= -0.264 / XP = 0.0133
393	DRIFT TOWARD BEING THOSE WHERE EXTRAMARITAL COITUS IS PUNISHED, RATHER THAN PERMITTED (43) F-B	0.65 OF 31	393	DRIFT TOWARD BEING THOSE WHERE EXTRAMARITAL COITUS IS PERMITTED, RATHER THAN PUNISHED (41) F-B	0.61 OF 41	20 16 / 11 25 / XSQ= 3.63 / PHI= 0.224 / XP = 0.0569
404	DRIFT TOWARD BEING THOSE WHERE EXPLANATIONS OF ILLNESS OF A SEXUAL NATURE ARE PRESENT (19) W-C	0.50 OF 20	404	DRIFT TOWARD BEING THOSE WHERE EXPLANATIONS OF ILLNESS OF A SEXUAL NATURE ARE ABSENT (42) W-C	0.81 OF 26	10 5 / 10 21 / XSQ= 3.57 / PHI= 0.279 / XP = 0.0588
417	TILT MORE TOWARD BEING THOSE WHERE WARFARE IS PREVALENT (34) LWS	0.95 OF 19	417	TILT LESS TOWARD BEING THOSE WHERE WARFARE IS PREVALENT (34) LWS	0.67 OF 18	18 12 / 1 6 / XSQ= 3.09 / PHI= 0.289 / EP = 0.0422
426	TILT MORE TOWARD BEING THOSE WHERE A HIGH GOD IS PRESENT (156) GES,EA	0.67 OF 103	426	TILT LESS TOWARD BEING THOSE WHERE A HIGH GOD IS PRESENT (156) GES,EA	0.51 OF 106	69 54 / 34 52 / XSQ= 4.91 / PHI= 0.153 / XP = 0.0267
428	TILT TOWARD BEING THOSE WHERE A HIGH GOD, IF PRESENT AND ACTIVE, SUPPORTS HUMAN MORALITY, RATHER THAN NOT SUPPORTING IT (61) GES,EA	0.74 OF 39	428	TILT TOWARD BEING THOSE WHERE A HIGH GOD, IF PRESENT AND ACTIVE, DOES NOT SUPPORT HUMAN MORALITY, RATHER THAN SUPPORTING IT (26) GES,EA	0.55 OF 22	29 10 / 10 12 / XSQ= 3.92 / PHI= 0.253 / XP = 0.0477
431	TILT TOWARD BEING THOSE WHERE SUPERNATURAL SANCTIONS FOR MORALITY, HAVING AN EFFECT ON AN INDIVIDUAL'S AFTER LIFE, ARE PRESENT (10) GES	0.50 OF 12	431	TILT TOWARD BEING THOSE WHERE SUPERNATURAL SANCTIONS FOR MORALITY, HAVING AN EFFECT ON AN INDIVIDUAL'S AFTERLIFE, ARE ABSENT OR UNREPORTED (25) GES	0.88 OF 17	6 2 / 6 15 / XSQ= 3.41 / PHI= 0.343 / EP = 0.0382
440	DRIFT TOWARD BEING THOSE WHERE FEAR OF SPIRITS IS HIGH (32) W-C	0.60 OF 20	440	DRIFT TOWARD BEING THOSE WHERE FEAR OF SPIRITS IS LOW (29) W-C	0.69 OF 26	12 8 / 8 18 / XSQ= 2.83 / PHI= 0.248 / XP = 0.0925
442	TILT TOWARD BEING THOSE WHERE FEAR OF ANIMAL SPIRITS IS HIGH (28) W-C	0.70 OF 20	442	TILT TOWARD BEING THOSE WHERE FEAR OF ANIMAL SPIRITS IS LOW (33) W-C	0.65 OF 26	14 9 / 6 17 / XSQ= 4.33 / PHI= 0.307 / XP = 0.0373

No.		No.		
449	TILT MORE TOWARD BEING THOSE 0.82 OF 45 WHERE THE OBSERVATION OF FOOD TABOOS IS MEDIUM OR LOW, RATHER THAN HIGH (61) JRL	449	TILT LESS TOWARD BEING THOSE 0.56 OF 36 WHERE THE OBSERVATION OF FOOD TABOOS IS MEDIUM OR LOW, RATHER THAN HIGH (61) JRL	8 16 37 20 XSQ= 5.60 PHI= -0.263 XP = 0.0179
450	TEND LESS TO BE THOSE 0.51 OF 45 WHERE THE OBSERVATION OF FOOD TABOOS IS HIGH OR MEDIUM, RATHER THAN LOW (60) JRL	450	TEND MORE TO BE THOSE 0.97 OF 36 WHERE THE OBSERVATION OF FOOD TABOOS IS HIGH OR MEDIUM, RATHER THAN LOW (60) JRL	23 35 22 1 XSQ= 18.71 PHI= -0.481 XP = 0.0000
458	TEND LESS TO BE THOSE 0.57 OF 72 WHERE GAMES, IF PRESENT, DO NOT INCLUDE GAMES OF STRATEGY (119) R-A-B,EA	458	TEND MORE TO BE THOSE 0.84 OF 79 WHERE GAMES, IF PRESENT, DO NOT INCLUDE GAMES OF STRATEGY (119) R-A-B,EA	31 13 41 66 XSQ= 11.65 PHI= 0.278 XP = 0.0006
459	DRIFT TOWARD BEING THOSE 0.57 OF 72 WHERE GAMES, IF PRESENT, INCLUDE GAMES OF CHANCE (82) R-A-B,EA	459	DRIFT TOWARD BEING THOSE 0.58 OF 79 WHERE GAMES, IF PRESENT, DO NOT INCLUDE GAMES OF CHANCE (89) R-A-B,EA	41 33 31 46 XSQ= 2.89 PHI= 0.138 XP = 0.0892
460	TILT MORE TOWARD BEING THOSE 0.72 OF 72 WHERE GAMES, IF PRESENT, ARE NOT LIMITED TO GAMES OF SKILL ONLY (104) R-A-B,EA	460	TILT LESS TOWARD BEING THOSE 0.53 OF 79 WHERE GAMES, IF PRESENT, ARE NOT LIMITED TO GAMES OF SKILL ONLY (104) R-A-B,EA	20 37 52 42 XSQ= 5.04 PHI= -0.183 XP = 0.0248
468	DRIFT LESS TOWARD BEING THOSE 0.57 OF 23 WHERE CONTACT WITH OTHER CULTURES IS REGULAR OR IRREGULAR, RATHER THAN FREQUENT (37) JMH	468	DRIFT MORE TOWARD BEING THOSE 0.85 OF 26 WHERE CONTACT WITH OTHER CULTURES IS REGULAR OR IRREGULAR, RATHER THAN FREQUENT (37) JMH	10 4 13 22 XSQ= 3.44 PHI= 0.265 XP = 0.0635
470	DRIFT TOWARD BEING THOSE 0.52 OF 23 WHERE INNOVATIONS ARE GENERALLY ACCEPTED (21) JMH	470	DRIFT TOWARD BEING THOSE 0.77 OF 26 WHERE INNOVATIONS ARE ACCEPTED ONLY SELECTIVELY (33) JMH	12 6 11 20 XSQ= 3.28 PHI= 0.259 XP = 0.0700
474	DRIFT TOWARD BEING THOSE 0.59 OF 37 WHERE BOASTFULNESS IS EXTREME (41) PES	474	DRIFT TOWARD BEING THOSE 0.64 OF 39 WHERE BOASTFULNESS IS MODERATE, NEGLIBIBLE, OR UNREPORTED (48) PES	22 14 15 25 XSQ= 3.34 PHI= 0.210 XP = 0.0678

```
************************************************************************************************************

74  CULTURES                                             74  CULTURES
    WHERE PCTTERY IS                                         WHERE POTTERY IS
    PRESENT  (145)                                           ABSENT  (93)


BACKGROUND ON PAGE 79                                                              BOTH SUBJECT AND PREDICATE
............................................................................................................

     145  IN LEFT CCLUMN

ABIPON      ABCR        ALBANIANS   AMBA        AMERICANS   ANDAMANESE  ARAUCANIANS ASHANTI     AWEIKOMA    AYMARA
AZANDE      AZTEC       BACAIRI     BAMBARA     BAMILEKE    BARI        BEMBA       BHIL        BIRIFOR     BORORO
BRAZILIANS  BURUSHO     CAGABA      CALLINAGO   CARIB       CAYAPA      CHAMACOCO   CHEROKEE    CHEYENNE    CHIR-APACHE
CHIRIGUANO  CHCCO       CHCRCTI     CHORTI      CHUKCHEE    CREEK       CUNA        CZECHS      CELAWARE    DIEGUENO
DUTCH       EGYPTIANS   FANG        FON         GANDA       GARO        GISU        GOAJIRO     GROS VENTRE GUATO
HASINAI     HUICHOL     HURCN       HUTSUL      ILA         INCA        INGALIK     JAPANESE    JAVANESE    JEMEZ
JIVARO      KACHIN      KHASI       KIKUYU      KOHISTANI   KOREANS     KPE         KURTATCHI   KUTENAI     LAKHER
LAMBA       LAU         LHCTA NAGA  LOZI        LUO         MACASSARESE MAMVU       MANDAN      MANUS       MARICOPA
MATACO      MATAKAM     MAYA        MBUNDU      MENDE       MIAMI       MISKITO     MNCNG GAR   MONGO       MOSSI
MUNDURUCU   NAMA        NANCI       NATCHEZ     NAVAHO      NICOBARESE  NUNIVAK     NUPE        NYAKYUSA    NYORO
OKINAWANS   CMAHA       PAEZ        PALAUANS    PALIKUR     PAPAGO      RIFFIANS    RUNDI       SANPOIL     SANTAL
SERBS       SHILLUK     SIRICNC     SIWANS      SONGHAI     TALAMANCA   TALLENSI    TACS        TAPIRAPE    TARAHUMARA
TAREUMIUT   TEDA        TEHUELCHE   TENCA       THONGA      TIMUCUA     TIV         TOTONAC     TROBRIAND   TUBATULABAL
TUCANO      TUCUNA      TUNEBO      TUPINAMBA   VEDDA       VENDA       WITOTO      WOLOF       YABARANA    YAGUA
YAKUT       YAC         YARURC      YOKUTS      YORUBA

     93  IN RIGHT CCLUMN

AINU        ALACALUF    ALCRESE     APINAYE     ARANDA      ATSUGEWI    BAJUN       BASSERI     BLACK CARIB BOTOCUDO
CAMAYURA    CHENCHU     COMANCHE    COPR ESKIMO CREE        CROW        DARD        DIERI       ELLICE      ENGA
EYAK        GILBERTESE  GILYAK      GOND        HAIDA       HAWAIIANS   HUKUNDIKA   KAPAUKU     KARIERA     KASKA
KATAB       KAZAK       KERAKI      KICW-APACHE KORYAK      KUBA        KUNG        LAMET       LEPCHA      LESU
MANGAIANS   MANIHIKI    MACRI       MARQUESANS  MARSHALLESE MASAI       MBUTI       MENTAWEI    MOTA        MURINBATA
MURNGIN     NABESNA     NAMBICUARA  NOMLAKI     NUER        OJIBWA      ONA         ONTCNG-JAVA PONAPEANS   PUKAPUKA
PURARI      PURUM       RARCIANS    SACACA      SAMOANS     SAMOYED     SARSI       SEMANG      SENIANG     SOMALI
TANALA      TENINO      TIKOPIA     TIMBIRA     TIWI        TODA        TOKELAU     TOLOWA      TRISTAN     TRUKESE
TRUMAI      TSHIMSHIAN  TWANA       ULAWANS     UTE         WANTOAT     WASHO       WIKMUNKAN   WOGEO       WOLEAIANS
YAHGAN      YUKI        YURCK

     162  EXCLUDED BECAUSE UNASCERTAINEC

------------------------------------------------------------------------------------------------------------
HOSE          0.74 OF 145        3  TENC MORE TO BE THOSE        0.92 OF  93        38     7


     LCCATED CUTSIDE CF                          LOCATED OUTSIDE OF                                   107    86
     AFRICA  (320)                               AFRICA  (320)                                   XSQ=    11.71
                                                                                                 PHI=    0.222
                                                                                                 XP =   0.0006
```

4	DRIFT LESS TOWARD BEING THOSE LOCATED OUTSIDE OF THE CIRCUM-MEDITERRANEAN (355)	0.91 OF 145	4	DRIFT MORE TOWARD BEING THOSE LOCATED OUTSIDE OF THE CIRCUM-MEDITERRANEAN (355)	0.98 OF 93	13 2 132 91 XSQ= 3.38 PHI= 0.119 XP = 0.0661
6	TEND MORE TO BE THOSE LOCATED OUTSIDE OF THE INSULAR PACIFIC (330)	0.95 OF 145	6	TEND LESS TO BE THOSE LOCATED OUTSIDE OF THE INSULAR PACIFIC (330)	0.60 OF 93	7 37 138 56 XSQ= 43.66 PHI= -0.428 XP = 0.
9	LEAN LESS TOWARD BEING THOSE LOCATED OUTSIDE OF SOUTH AMERICA (335)	0.74 OF 145	9	LEAN MORE TOWARD BEING THOSE LOCATED OUTSIDE OF SOUTH AMERICA (335)	0.89 OF 93	38 10 107 83 XSQ= 7.47 PHI= 0.177 XP = 0.0063
12	TILT MORE TOWARD BEING THOSE WHERE THE LATITUDE IS LESS THAN FIFTY DEGREES (367)	0.94 OF 145	12	TILT LESS TOWARD BEING THOSE WHERE THE LATITUDE IS LESS THAN FIFTY DEGREES (367)	0.84 OF 93	8 15 137 78 XSQ= 6.14 PHI= -0.161 XP = 0.0132
13	TILT MORE TOWARD BEING THOSE WHERE THE LATITUDE IS LESS THAN FORTY DEGREES (329)	0.86 OF 145	13	TILT LESS TOWARD BEING THOSE WHERE THE LATITUDE IS LESS THAN FORTY DEGREES (329)	0.73 OF 93	20 25 125 68 XSQ= 5.51 PHI= -0.152 XP = 0.0190
44	TEND TO BE THOSE WHERE SETTLEMENTS ARE FIXED (222)	0.71 OF 144	44	TEND TO BE THOSE WHERE SETTLEMENTS ARE NON-FIXED (110)	0.52 OF 86	102 41 42 45 XSQ= 11.31 PHI= 0.222 XP = 0.0008
46	TEND MORE TO BE THOSE OTHER THAN WHERE SETTLEMENTS ARE NON-FIXED AND MOVEMENT IS NOMADIC (260)	0.83 OF 144	46	TEND LESS TO BE THOSE OTHER THAN WHERE SETTLEMENTS ARE NON-FIXED AND MOVEMENT IS NOMADIC (260)	0.62 OF 86	24 33 120 53 XSQ= 12.47 PHI= -0.233 XP = 0.0004
51	TEND TO BE THOSE WHERE SUBSISTENCE IS PRIMARILY BY FOOD PRODUCTION -- I. E., AGRICULTURE OR HUSBANDRY -- RATHER THAN BY GATHERING (253)	0.62 OF 145	51	TEND TO BE THOSE WHERE SUBSISTENCE IS PRIMARILY BY FOOD GATHERING -- I. E., HUNTING, FISHING, OR COLLECTING -- RATHER THAN FOOD PRODUCTION (147)	0.65 OF 93	90 33 55 60 XSQ= 14.99 PHI= 0.251 XP = 0.0001
53	TILT LESS TOWARD BEING THOSE WHERE FOOD PRODUCTION IS BY SIMPLE AGRICULTURE OR INCIPIENT FOOD PRODUCTION, RATHER THAN BY INTENSIVE AGRICULTURE (147)	0.64 OF 115	53	TILT MORE TOWARD BEING THOSE WHERE FOOD PRODUCTION IS BY SIMPLE AGRICULTURE OR INCIPIENT FOOD PRODUCTION, RATHER THAN BY INTENSIVE AGRICULTURE (147)	0.85 OF 34	41 5 74 29 XSQ= 4.46 PHI= 0.173 XP = 0.0347

55	TILT LESS TOWARD BEING THOSE WHERE FOOD PRODUCTION IS BY SIMPLE AGRICULTURE, RATHER THAN BY INTENSIVE AGRICULTURE (101)	0.54 OF 89	55	TILT MORE TOWARD BEING THOSE WHERE FOOD PRODUCTION IS BY SIMPLE AGRICULTURE, RATHER THAN BY INTENSIVE AGRICULTURE (101)	0.81 OF 26	41 5 48 21 XSQ= 4.97 PHI= 0.208 XP = 0.0258
62	LEAN TOWARD BEING THOSE WHERE HUSBANDRY OF SOME KIND IS PRESENT (228)	0.68 OF 145	62	LEAN TOWARD BEING THOSE WHERE HUSBANDRY OF ANY KIND IS ABSENT (172)	0.54 OF 93	99 43 46 50 XSQ= 10.54 PHI= 0.210 XP = 0.0012
63	TEND TO BE THOSE WHERE HUSBANDRY, IF PRESENT, IS PRINCIPALLY IN THE FORM OF BOVINE, EQUINE, CAMEL-LIKE, OR DEER-LIKE ANIMALS, RATHER THAN PIGS, SHEEP, OR GOATS (152)	0.71 OF 99	63	TEND TO BE THOSE WHERE HUSBANDRY, IF PRESENT, IS PRINCIPALLY IN THE FORM OF PIGS, SHEEP, OR GOATS, RATHER THAN BOVINE, EQUINE, CAMEL-LIKE, OR DEER-LIKE ANIMALS (74)	0.60 OF 43	70 17 29 26 XSQ= 11.00 PHI= 0.278 XP = 0.0009
71	TEND TO BE THOSE WHERE METAL WORKING IS PRESENT (98)	0.52 OF 142	71	TEND TO BE THOSE WHERE METAL WORKING IS ABSENT (153)	0.88 OF 92	74 11 68 81 XSQ= 37.20 PHI= 0.399 XP = 0.
73	TEND TO BE THOSE WHERE WEAVING IS PRESENT (118)	0.61 OF 139	73	TEND TO BE THOSE WHERE WEAVING IS ABSENT (130)	0.77 OF 92	85 21 54 71 XSQ= 31.22 PHI= 0.368 XP = 0.
80	TEND LESS TO BE THOSE WHERE NO CITY OR TOWN IS PRESENT (185)	0.77 OF 100	80	IN ALL CASES ARE THOSE WHERE NO CITY OR TOWN IS PRESENT (185)	1.00 OF 66	23 0 77 66 XSQ= 15.75 PHI= 0.308 XP = 0.0001
81	TEND LESS TO BE THOSE WHERE NO CITY OR TOWN IS PRESENT, AND THE AVERAGE COMMUNITY SIZE IS SMALLER THAN 200 (135)	0.52 OF 100	81	TEND MORE TO BE THOSE WHERE NO CITY OR TOWN IS PRESENT, AND THE AVERAGE COMMUNITY SIZE IS SMALLER THAN 200 (135)	0.86 OF 66	48 9 52 57 XSQ= 19.33 PHI= 0.341 XP = 0.0000
82	TEND MORE TO BE THOSE WHERE A CITY OR TOWN IS PRESENT, OR THE AVERAGE COMMUNITY SIZE IS FIFTY OR GREATER (178)	0.88 OF 100	82	TEND LESS TO BE THOSE WHERE A CITY OR TOWN IS PRESENT, OR THE AVERAGE COMMUNITY SIZE IS FIFTY OR GREATER (178)	0.62 OF 66	88 41 12 25 XSQ= 13.91 PHI= 0.290 XP = 0.0002
83	LEAN LESS TOWARD BEING THOSE WHERE, WITH NO CITY AND NO TOWN PRESENT, THE AVERAGE COMMUNITY SIZE IS SMALLER THAN 200, RATHER THAN BETWEEN 200 AND 999 (135)	0.68 OF 76	83	LEAN MORE TOWARD BEING THOSE WHERE, WITH NO CITY AND NO TOWN PRESENT, THE AVERAGE COMMUNITY SIZE IS SMALLER THAN 200, RATHER THAN BETWEEN 200 AND 999 (135)	0.89 OF 64	24 7 52 57 XSQ= 7.43 PHI= 0.230 XP = 0.0064

86	TEND TO BE THOSE 0.55 OF 119 WHERE THE LEVEL OF POLITICAL INTEGRATION IS THE LARGE STATE, THE LITTLE STATE, OR THE MINIMAL STATE (148) GPM	86	TEND TO BE THOSE 0.74 OF 68 WHERE THE LEVEL OF POLITICAL INTEGRATION IS THE AUTONOMOUS COMMUNITY, OR THE FAMILY (156) GPM	66 18 53 50 XSQ= 13.55 PHI= 0.269 XP = 0.0002
87	TILT MORE TOWARD BEING THOSE 0.97 OF 119 WHERE THE LEVEL OF POLITICAL INTEGRATION IS THE LARGE STATE, THE LITTLE STATE, THE MINIMAL STATE, OR THE AUTONOMOUS COMMUNITY (281) GPM	87	TILT LESS TOWARD BEING THOSE 0.87 OF 68 WHERE THE LEVEL OF POLITICAL INTEGRATION IS THE LARGE STATE, THE LITTLE STATE, THE MINIMAL STATE, OR THE AUTONOMOUS COMMUNITY (281) GPM	116 59 3 9 XSQ= 6.58 PHI= 0.188 XP = 0.0103
96	TEND TO BE THOSE 0.58 OF 142 WHERE THE HIERARCHY OF NATIONAL JURISDICTION HAS FOUR, THREE, TWO OR ONE LEVEL (174) GES,EA	96	TEND TO BE THOSE 0.66 OF 87 WHERE THE HIERARCHY OF NATIONAL JURISDICTION HAS NO LEVELS (156) GES,EA	83 30 59 57 XSQ= 11.46 PHI= 0.224 XP = 0.0007
100	TILT MORE TOWARD BEING THOSE 0.83 OF 142 WHERE HIERARCHIES ARE MORE COMPLEX THAN THE 'SIMPLEST,' I. E., MORE COMPLEX THAN TWO LOCAL LEVELS WITH NO NATIONAL LEVELS (267) GES,EA	100	TILT LESS TOWARD BEING THOSE 0.68 OF 87 WHERE HIERARCHIES ARE MORE COMPLEX THAN THE 'SIMPLEST,' I. E., MORE COMPLEX THAN TWO LOCAL LEVELS WITH NO NATIONAL LEVELS (267) GES,EA	118 59 24 28 XSQ= 6.33 PHI= 0.166 XP = 0.0118
102	TILT TOWARD BEING THOSE 0.57 OF 141 WHERE CLASS STRATIFICATION IS PRESENT (203)	102	TILT TOWARD BEING THOSE 0.58 OF 93 WHERE CLASS STRATIFICATION IS ABSENT (180)	81 39 60 54 XSQ= 4.79 PHI= 0.143 XP = 0.0286
106	DRIFT TOWARD BEING THOSE 0.59 OF 81 WHERE CLASS STRATIFICATION, IF PRESENT, IS BASED ON SOMETHING OTHER THAN WEALTH (126)	106	DRIFT TOWARD BEING THOSE 0.59 OF 39 WHERE CLASS STRATIFICATION, IF PRESENT, IS BASED ON WEALTH (77)	33 23 48 16 XSQ= 2.82 PHI= -0.153 XP = 0.0930
107	TEND LESS TO BE THOSE 0.73 OF 81 WHERE CLASS STRATIFICATION, IF PRESENT, IS BASED ON SOMETHING OTHER THAN OCCUPATIONAL STATUS (160)	107	IN ALL CASES ARE THOSE 1.00 OF 39 WHERE CLASS STRATIFICATION, IF PRESENT, IS BASED ON SOMETHING OTHER THAN OCCUPATIONAL STATUS (160)	22 0 59 39 XSQ= 11.22 PHI= 0.306 XP = 0.0008
110	LEAN LESS TOWARD BEING THOSE 0.56 OF 138 WHERE SLAVERY IS ABSENT (218)	110	LEAN MORE TOWARD BEING THOSE 0.77 OF 91 WHERE SLAVERY IS ABSENT (218)	61 21 77 70 XSQ= 9.75 PHI= 0.206 XP = 0.0018
118	TILT TOWARD BEING THOSE 0.62 OF 26 WHERE THE PERCENTAGE OF OCCUPATIONS THAT ARE SPECIALIZED IS HIGH OR MEDIUM (24) WME	118	TILT TOWARD BEING THOSE 0.75 OF 16 WHERE THE PERCENTAGE OF OCCUPATIONS THAT ARE SPECIALIZED IS LOW (25) WME	16 4 10 12 XSQ= 3.94 PHI= 0.306 XP = 0.0472

131	TILT MORE TOWARD BEING THOSE WHERE THE CONSTRUCTION OF PERMANENT HOUSES OR THE ERECTION OF TEMPORARY DWELLINGS IS MAINLY DONE BY MALES (136)	0.92 OF 88	131	TILT LESS TOWARD BEING THOSE WHERE THE CONSTRUCTION OF PERMANENT HOUSES OR THE ERECTION OF TEMPORARY DWELLINGS IS MAINLY DONE BY MALES (136)	0.78 OF 59	81 46 7 13 XSQ= 4.82 PHI= 0.181 XP = 0.0282
180	DRIFT MORE TOWARD BEING THOSE WHERE THE COMMUNITY IS COMMONLY NON-EXOGAMOUS, RATHER THAN EXOGAMOUS (258)	0.71 OF 138	180	DRIFT LESS TOWARD BEING THOSE WHERE THE COMMUNITY IS COMMONLY NON-EXOGAMOUS, RATHER THAN EXOGAMOUS (258)	0.59 OF 92	40 38 98 54 XSQ= 3.21 PHI= -0.118 XP = 0.0733
184	TEND TO BE THOSE WHERE THE LARGEST NON-COGNATIC KIN GROUP IS SMALLER THAN A PHRATRY, I. E. A SIB OR LINEAGE (175)	0.76 OF 92	184	TEND TO BE THOSE WHERE THE LARGEST NON-COGNATIC KIN GROUP IS THE MOEITY OR PHRATRY (77)	0.54 OF 54	22 29 70 25 XSQ= 12.01 PHI= -0.287 XP = 0.0005
196	DRIFT MORE TOWARD BEING THOSE WHERE INDIVIDUAL RIGHTS IN REAL PROPERTY, AND RULES FOR INHERITANCE, ARE PRESENT (194)	0.67 OF 108	196	DRIFT LESS TOWARD BEING THOSE WHERE INDIVIDUAL RIGHTS IN REAL PROPERTY, AND RULES FOR INHERITANCE, ARE PRESENT (194)	0.52 OF 67	72 35 36 32 XSQ= 3.04 PHI= 0.132 XP = 0.0812
207	DRIFT TOWARD BEING THOSE WHERE MARITAL RESIDENCE IS MATRILOCAL OR UXORILOCAL, RATHER THAN AMBILOCAL OR NEOLOCAL (64)	0.58 OF 57	207	DRIFT TOWARD BEING THOSE WHERE MARITAL RESIDENCE IS AMBILOCAL OR NEOLOCAL, RATHER THAN MATRILOCAL OR UXORILOCAL (64)	0.64 OF 28	33 10 24 18 XSQ= 2.86 PHI= 0.183 XP = 0.0907
209	TILT LESS TOWARD BEING THOSE WHERE MARITAL RESIDENCE IS PATRILOCAL, VIRILOCAL, OR AVUNCULOCAL, RATHER THAN MATRILOCAL OR UXORILOCAL (270)	0.73 OF 121	209	TILT MORE TOWARD BEING THOSE WHERE MARITAL RESIDENCE IS PATRILOCAL, VIRILOCAL, OR AVUNCULOCAL, RATHER THAN MATRILOCAL OR UXORILOCAL (270)	0.86 OF 74	88 64 33 10 XSQ= 4.29 PHI= -0.148 XP = 0.0384
296	DRIFT TOWARD BEING THOSE WHERE INFANTICIDE IS ABSENT OR INFERRED ABSENT (15) BCA	0.63 OF 16	296	DRIFT TOWARD BEING THOSE WHERE INFANTICIDE IS PRESENT (18) BCA	0.78 OF 9	6 7 10 2 XSQ= 2.30 PHI= -0.304 EP = 0.0968
300	TILT TOWARD BEING THOSE WHERE THE POST-PARTUM SEX TABOO LASTS LONGER THAN SIX MONTHS (51)	0.50 OF 66	300	TILT TOWARD BEING THOSE WHERE THE POST-PARTUM SEX TABOO LASTS SIX MONTHS OR LESS (73)	0.74 OF 42	33 11 33 31 XSQ= 5.08 PHI= 0.217 XP = 0.0242
304	DRIFT TOWARD BEING THOSE WHERE THE EARLY ANAL SATISFACTION POTENTIAL IS LOW (22) W-C	0.65 OF 17	304	DRIFT TOWARD BEING THOSE WHERE THE EARLY ANAL SATISFACTION POTENTIAL IS HIGH (19) W-C	0.67 OF 15	6 10 11 5 XSQ= 2.01 PHI= -0.250 EP = 0.0938

336	LEAN TCWARD BEING THOSE 0.76 OF 33 WHERE THE TOTAL POSITIVE PRESSURE TOWARD DEVELCPING RESPCNSIBLE BEHAVIOR IN THE CHILD IS HIGH (43) B-B-C	336	LEAN TOWARD BEING THOSE 0.68 OF 28 WHERE THE TOTAL POSITIVE PRESSURE TOWARD DEVELOPING RESPONSIBLE BEHAVIOR IN THE CHILD IS LOW (32) B-B-C	25 9 8 19 XSQ= 9.98 PHI= 0.404 XP = 0.0016
337	DRIFT TOWARD BEING THCSE 0.65 OF 31 WHERE THE CHILD'S INFERREC ANXIETY OVER NCN-PERFCRMANCE OF RESPONSIBLE BEHAVIOR IS HIGH (38) B-B-C	337	DRIFT TOWARD BEING THOSE 0.64 OF 28 WHERE THE CHILD'S INFERRED ANXIETY OVER NON-PERFORMANCE OF RESPCNSIBLE BEHAVIOR IS LOW (35) B-B-C	20 10 11 18 XSQ= 3.80 PHI= 0.254 XP = 0.0513
343	TILT TCWARD BEING THOSE 0.61 OF 18 WHERE THE CHILD'S INFERREC CONFLICT REGARDING NURTURANT BEHAVICR IS LOW (18) B-B-C	343	TILT TOWARD BEING THOSE 0.74 OF 19 WHERE THE CHILD'S INFERRED CCNFLICT REGARDING NURTURANT BEHAVICR IS HIGH (29) B-B-C	7 14 11 5 XSQ= 3.25 PHI= -0.296 EP = 0.0489
348	DRIFT TCWARD BEING THCSE 0.70 OF 27 WHERE THE TOTAL POSITIVE PRESSURE TOWARD DEVELCPING ACHIEVEMENT BEHAVIOR IN THE CHILD IS HIGH (32) B-B-C	348	DRIFT TOWARD BEING THOSE 0.61 OF 23 WHERE THE TOTAL POSITIVE PRESSURE TOWARC DEVELOPING ACHIEVEMENT BEHAVIOR IN THE CHILD IS LOW (31) B-B-C	19 9 8 14 XSQ= 3.73 PHI= 0.273 XP = 0.0533
349	TILT TCWARD BEING THCSE 0.70 OF 27 WHERE THE CHILD'S INFERREC ANXIETY OVER NCN-PERFCRMANCE OF ACHIEVEMENT BEHAVIOR IS HIGH (34) B-B-C	349	TILT TOWARD BEING THOSE 0.64 OF 22 WHERE THE CHILD'S INFERRED ANXIETY OVER NON-PERFORMANCE OF ACHIEVEMENT BEHAVIOR IS LOW (28) B-B-C	19 8 8 14 XSQ= 4.38 PHI= 0.299 XP = 0.0365
350	LEAN TCWARC BEING THOSE 0.76 OF 25 WHERE THE CHILD'S INFERREC ANXIETY OVER PERFCRMANCE OF ACHIEVEMENT BEHAVIOR IS HIGH (34) B-B-C	350	LEAN TOWARD BEING THOSE 0.68 OF 22 WHERE THE CHILD'S INFERRED ANXIETY CVER PERFORMANCE OF ACHIEVEMENT BEHAVIOR IS LOW (26) B-B-C	19 7 6 15 XSQ= 7.54 PHI= 0.401 XP = 0.0060
351	TILT TCWARC BEING THOSE 0.60 OF 25 WHERE THE CHILD'S INFERREC CONFLICT REGARDING ACHIEVEMENT BEHAVIOR IS HIGH (26) B-B-C	351	TILT TOWARD BEING THOSE 0.77 OF 22 WHERE THE CHILD'S INFERRED CONFLICT REGARDING ACHIEVEMENT BEHAVICR IS LOW (34) B-B-C	15 5 10 17 XSQ= 5.21 PHI= 0.333 XP = 0.0224
352	LEAN TOWARD BEING THOSE 0.79 OF 33 WHERE THE TCTAL POSITIVE PRESSURE TOWARD DEVELCPING OBEDIENT BEHAVICR IN THE CHILD IS HIGH (44) B-B-C	352	LEAN TOWARD BEING THOSE 0.62 CF 26 WHERE THE TOTAL POSITIVE PRESSURE TOWARC DEVELOPING OBEDIENT BEHAVICR IN THE CHILD IS LOW (28) B-B-C	26 10 7 16 XSQ= 8.32 PHI= 0.376 XP = 0.0039
370	TILT TCWARD BEING THOSE 0.65 OF 110 WHERE THE SEGREGATICN CF ACOLESCENT BOYS IS ABSENT (148)	370	TILT TOWARD BEING THOSE 0.53 OF 66 WHERE THE SEGREGATION OF ADOLESCENT BOYS IS COMPLETE OR PARTIAL (95)	38 35 72 31 XSQ= 5.07 PHI= -0.170 XP = 0.0243

380	LEAN TOWARD BEING THOSE WHERE SEGREGATION OF GIRLS AT MENARCHE IS PRESENT (35) F-B	0.85 OF 27	380	LEAN TOWARD BEING THOSE WHERE SEGREGATION OF GIRLS AT MENARCHE IS ABSENT (20) F-B	0.69 OF 16	23 5 4 11 XSQ= 10.60 PHI= 0.497 XP = 0.0011
382	TILT TOWARD BEING THOSE WHERE FEMALE INITIATION RITES ARE PRESENT (38) JKB	0.74 OF 38	382	TILT TOWARD BEING THOSE WHERE FEMALE INITIATION RITES ARE ABSENT (27) JKB	0.61 OF 18	28 7 10 11 XSQ= 4.91 PHI= 0.296 XP = 0.0267
386	TILT TOWARD BEING THOSE WHERE SEXUAL EXPRESSION BY THE YOUNG IS RESTRICTED OR SEMI-RESTRICTED (46) F-B	0.67 OF 39	386	TILT TOWARD BEING THOSE WHERE SEXUAL EXPRESSION BY THE YOUNG IS PERMITTED (40) F-B	0.60 OF 30	26 12 13 18 XSQ= 3.86 PHI= 0.236 XP = 0.0496
392	DRIFT MORE TOWARD BEING THOSE WHERE PREMARITAL SEX RELATIONS ARE STRONGLY PUNISHED AND IN FACT RARE, OR WEAKLY PUNISHED AND IN FACT NOT RARE, OR PUNISHED ONLY IF PREGNANCY RESULTS (112) JTW,EA	0.69 OF 90	392	DRIFT LESS TOWARD BEING THOSE WHERE PREMARITAL SEX RELATIONS ARE STRONGLY PUNISHED AND IN FACT RARE, OR WEAKLY PUNISHED AND IN FACT NOT RARE, OR PUNISHED ONLY IF PREGNANCY RESULTS (112) JTW,EA	0.53 OF 55	62 29 28 26 XSQ= 3.15 PHI= 0.148 XP = 0.0757
393	TILT TOWARD BEING THOSE WHERE EXTRAMARITAL COITUS IS PUNISHED, RATHER THAN PERMITTED (43) F-B	0.64 OF 39	393	TILT TOWARD BEING THOSE WHERE EXTRAMARITAL COITUS IS PERMITTED, RATHER THAN PUNISHED (41) F-B	0.69 OF 32	25 10 14 22 XSQ= 6.33 PHI= 0.299 XP = 0.0119
398	TILT TOWARD BEING THOSE WHERE THE INTENSITY OF SEX ANXIETY IS HIGH (16) WNS	0.65 OF 17	398	TILT TOWARD BEING THOSE WHERE THE INTENSITY OF SEX ANXIETY IS LOW (16) WNS	0.80 OF 10	11 2 6 8 XSQ= 3.41 PHI= 0.355 EP = 0.0461
399	LEAN TOWARD BEING THOSE WHERE INTENSITY OF CASTRATION ANXIETY IS HIGH (23) WNS	0.70 OF 23	399	LEAN TOWARD BEING THOSE WHERE INTENSITY OF CASTRATION ANXIETY IS LOW (22) WNS	0.76 OF 17	16 4 7 13 XSQ= 6.55 PHI= 0.405 EP = 0.0095
417	DRIFT MORE TOWARD BEING THOSE WHERE WARFARE IS PREVALENT (34) LWS	0.90 OF 21	417	DRIFT LESS TOWARD BEING THOSE WHERE WARFARE IS PREVALENT (34) LWS	0.62 OF 13	19 8 2 5 XSQ= 2.53 PHI= 0.273 EP = 0.0789
420	DRIFT TOWARD BEING THOSE WHERE BELLICOSITY IS EXTREME (41) PES	0.57 OF 42	420	DRIFT TOWARD BEING THOSE WHERE BELLICOSITY IS MODERATE OR NEGLIGIBLE (46) PES	0.68 OF 31	24 10 18 21 XSQ= 3.49 PHI= 0.219 XP = 0.0616

426	TEND TO BE THOSE WHERE A HIGH GOD IS PRESENT (156) GES,EA	0.69 OF 131	426	TEND TO BE THOSE WHERE A HIGH GOD IS ABSENT (104) GES,EA	0.57 OF 75	90 32 41 43 XSQ= 12.33 PHI= 0.245 XP = 0.0004
432	TILT TOWARD BEING THOSE WHERE AN ATTRACTIVE AFTERLIFE IS BELIEVED IN (27) LWS	0.89 OF 18	432	TILT TOWARD BEING THOSE WHERE AN ATTRACTIVE AFTERLIFE IS NOT BELIEVED IN (11) LWS	0.50 OF 12	16 6 2 6 XSQ= 3.76 PHI= 0.354 EP = 0.0342
439	DRIFT TOWARD BEING THOSE WHERE FEAR OF GHOSTS IS LOW (31) W-C	0.62 OF 26	439	DRIFT TOWARD BEING THOSE WHERE FEAR OF GHOSTS IS HIGH (30) W-C	0.70 OF 20	10 14 16 6 XSQ= 3.33 PHI= -0.269 XP = 0.0680
442	DRIFT TOWARD BEING THOSE WHERE FEAR OF ANIMAL SPIRITS IS HIGH (28) W-C	0.62 OF 26	442	DRIFT TOWARD BEING THOSE WHERE FEAR OF ANIMAL SPIRITS IS LOW (33) W-C	0.70 OF 20	16 6 10 14 XSQ= 3.33 PHI= 0.269 XP = 0.0680
446	DRIFT TOWARD BEING THOSE WHERE WITCHCRAFT IS SIGNIFICANTLY PRESENT (14) GES	0.64 OF 14	446	DRIFT TOWARD BEING THOSE WHERE WITCHCRAFT IS MODERATELY PRESENT OR ABSENT (24) GES	0.79 OF 14	9 3 5 11 XSQ= 3.65 PHI= 0.361 EP = 0.0542
458	LEAN LESS TOWARD BEING THOSE WHERE GAMES, IF PRESENT, DO NOT INCLUDE GAMES OF STRATEGY (119) R-A-B,EA	0.62 OF 91	458	LEAN MORE TOWARD BEING THOSE WHERE GAMES, IF PRESENT, DO NOT INCLUDE GAMES OF STRATEGY (119) R-A-B,EA	0.85 OF 59	35 9 56 50 XSQ= 8.21 PHI= 0.234 XP = 0.0042
460	LEAN TOWARD BEING THOSE WHERE GAMES, IF PRESENT, ARE NOT LIMITED TO GAMES OF SKILL ONLY (104) R-A-B,EA	0.71 OF 91	460	LEAN TOWARD BEING THOSE WHERE GAMES, IF PRESENT, ARE LIMITED TO GAMES OF SKILL ONLY (67) R-A-B,EA	0.51 OF 59	26 30 65 29 XSQ= 6.67 PHI= -0.211 XP = 0.0098

****

75 CULTURES WHERE LEATHER WCRKING IS PRESENT (123)	75 CULTURES WHERE LEATHER WORKING IS ABSENT (53)

BACKGROUND ON PAGE 79 SUBJECT ONLY

....

123 IN LEFT COLUMN

ABIPON	AINU	ALBANIANS	AMERICANS	ARAUCANIANS	ASHANTI	ATSUGEWI	AYMARA	AZTEC	BAMBARA
BASSERI	BEMBA	BHIL	BIRIFOR	BRAZILIANS	BURUSHO	CHAMACOCO	CHEYENNE	CHIR-APACHE	CHIRIGUANO
CHOROTI	CHCRTI	CHUKCHEE	COMANCHE	COPR ESKIMO	CREE	CREEK	CROW	CZECHS	DARD
DELAWARE	DIEGUENO	DOGCN	DUTCH	EGYPTIANS	EYAK	FON	FOX	GANDA	GILYAK
GISU	GOAJIRO	GRCS VENTRE	HAIDA	HASINAI	HUICHOL	HURON	HUTSUL	ILA	INGALIK
KASKA	KAZAK	KHALKA	KHASI	KIKUYU	KIOW-APACHE	KOREANS	KORYAK	KUBA	KUNG
KUTENAI	LOLC	LOZI	LUO	MAMVU	MARICOPA	MASAI	MATACO	MATAKAM	MBUNDU
MBUTI	MENDE	MIAMI	MISKITO	MONGUOR	MOSSI	NABESNA	NAMA	NANDI	NATCHEZ
NAVAHO	NCMLAKI	NUNIVAK	NUPE	NURI	NYORO	OJIBWA	OMAHA	CNA	PAPAGO
RIFFIANS	RUNDI	RWALA	SAMOYED	SARSI	SHILLUK	SIWANS	SOMALI	SONGHAI	SWAZI
TALLENSI	TANALA	TAREUMIUT	TEDA	TEHUELCHE	TENINO	TERENA	TIBETANS	TIV	TOLOWA
TRISTAN	TUBATULABAL	TWANA	UTE	VEDDA	VENDA	WASHO	WCLOF	YAGUA	YAHGAN
YAKUT	YCRUBA	YURCK							

53 IN RIGHT CCLUMN

ALACALUF	ANDAMANESE	ARANCA	AZANDE	BAJUN	BLACK CARIB	CARIB	CHENCHU	ELLICE	GARO
GILBERTESE	HAWAIIANS	INCA	JAVANESE	KAPAUKU	KERAKI	KURTATCHI	LAKHER	LAU	LESU
LHOTA NAGA	MANGAIANS	MANIHIKI	MARQUESANS	MARSHALLESE	MONGO	MURNGIN	NYAKYUSA	ONTONG-JAVA	PALIKUR
PONAPEANS	PUKAPUKA	RAROIANS	SAGADA	SAMOANS	SENIANG	SIRIONO	TALAMANCA	TAPIRAPE	THONGA
TIKOPIA	TIMBIRA	TOKELAU	TROBRIAND	TRUKESE	TUPINAMBA	ULAWANS	WITOTO	WOGEO	WOLEAIANS
YABARANA	YAC	YAPESE							

224 EXCLUDED BECAUSE UNASCERTAINEC

3	TILT LESS TOWARC BEING THCSE LOCATED OUTSIDE OF AFRICA (320)	0.74 OF 123	TILT MORE TOWARD BEING THOSE LOCATED OUTSIDE OF AFRICA (320)	0.89 OF 53	32 6 91 47 XSQ= 3.90 PHI= 0.149 XP = 0.0484
4	TILT LESS TOWARC BEING THCSE LOCATED CUTSIDE OF THE CIRCUM-MEDITERRANEAN (355)	0.88 OF 123	IN ALL CASES ARE THOSE LOCATED OUTSIDE OF THE CIRCUM-MEDITERRANEAN (355)	1.00 OF 53	15 0 108 53 XSQ= 5.59 PHI= 0.178 XP = 0.0181

6	IN ALL CASES ARE THCSE LOCATED CUTSIDE OF THE INSULAR PACIFIC (330)	1.00 OF 123	6	TEND TO BE THOSE LOCATED IN THE INSULAR PACIFIC (70)	0.57 OF 53	0 30 123 23 XSQ= 79.97 PHI= -0.674 XP = 0.
8	TEND LESS TO BE THCSE LOCATED CUTSIDE OF NORTH AMERICA (330)	0.67 OF 123	8	IN ALL CASES ARE THCSE LOCATED OUTSIDE OF NORTH AMERICA (330)	1.00 CF 53	41 0 82 53 XSQ= 21.20 PHI= 0.347 XP = 0.0000
11	DRIFT LESS TOWARD BEING THOSE WHERE THE LATITUDE IS LESS THAN SIXTY DEGREES (385)	0.91 OF 123	11	IN ALL CASES ARE THOSE WHERE THE LATITUDE IS LESS THAN SIXTY DEGREES (385)	1.00 OF 53	11 0 112 53 XSQ= 3.64 PHI= 0.144 XP = 0.0562
14	TEND TC BE THCSE WHERE THE LATITUDE IS THIRTY DEGREES CR GREATER (119)	0.54 OF 123	14	TEND TO BE THOSE WHERE THE LATITUDE IS LESS THAN THIRTY DEGREES (281)	0.98 CF 53	66 1 57 52 XSQ= 39.94 PHI= 0.476 XP = 0.
15	TEND TC BE THOSE WHERE THE LATITUDE IS TWENTY DEGREES CR GREATER (183)	0.69 OF 123	15	TEND TO BE THOSE WHERE THE LATITUDE IS LESS THAN TWENTY DEGREES (217)	0.85 OF 53	85 8 38 45 XSQ= 41.22 PHI= 0.484 XP = 0.
16	TEND TC BE THCSE WHERE THE LATITUDE IS TEN DEGREES OR GREATER (277)	0.84 OF 123	16	TEND TO BE THOSE WHERE THE LATITUDE IS LESS THAN TEN DEGREES (123)	0.53 CF 53	103 25 20 28 XSQ= 23.16 PHI= 0.363 XP = 0.0000
33	LEAN LESS TOWARD BEING THCSE WHERE THE NATURAL ENVIRONMENT IS OTHER THAN 'VERY HARSH,' I.E., DESERT, DESERT GRASSES AND SHRUBS, TUNDRA, OR HIGH PLATEAU STEPPE (341) FWM	0.75 OF 123	33	LEAN MORE TOWARD BEING THOSE WHERE THE NATURAL ENVIRCNMENT IS OTHER THAN 'VERY HARSH,' I.E., DESERT, DESERT GRASSES AND SHRUBS, TUNDRA, OR HIGH PLATEAU STEPPE (341) FWM	0.94 OF 53	31 3 92 50 XSQ= 7.87 PHI= 0.211 XP = 0.0050
36	TEND LESS TO BE THCSE WHERE THE NATURAL ENVIRONMENT IS OTHER THAN 'VERY HARSH,' OR SUB-TRCPICAL BUSH, OR TEMPERATE GRASSLANC (292) FWM	0.60 OF 123	36	TEND MORE TO BE THOSE WHERE THE NATURAL ENVIRCNMENT IS OTHER THAN 'VERY HARSH,' OR SUB-TROPICAL BUSH, OR TEMPERATE GRASSLAND (292) FWM	0.87 CF 53	49 7 74 46 XSQ= 10.91 PHI= 0.249 XP = 0.0010
42	TEND TC BE THCSE WHERE THE NATURAL ENVIRONMENT IS OTHER THAN TRCPICAL CR SUB-TRCPICAL RAIN FOREST, OR MONSCCN FCREST (244) FWM	0.87 OF 123	42	TEND TO BE THOSE WHERE THE NATURAL ENVIRCNMENT IS TROPICAL OR SUB-TROPICAL RAIN FOREST, OR MONSOON FOREST (156) FWM	0.74 CF 53	16 39 107 14 XSQ= 60.48 PHI= -0.586 XP = 0.

44	TEND LESS TO BE THCSE WHERE SETTLEMENTS ARE FIXEC (222)	0.51 OF 119	44	TEND MORE TO BE THOSE WHERE SETTLEMENTS ARE FIXED (222)	0.84 OF 49	61 41 58 8 XSQ= 13.96 PHI= -0.288 XP = 0.0002
46	LEAN LESS TOWARD BEING THCSE OTHER THAN WHERE SETTLEMENTS ARE NON-FIXED AND MCVEMENT IS NOMADIC (260)	0.66 OF 119	46	LEAN MORE TOWARD BEING THOSE OTHER THAN WHERE SETTLEMENTS ARE NON-FIXED AND MOVEMENT IS NOMADIC (260)	0.90 OF 49	41 5 78 44 XSQ= 9.08 PHI= 0.232 XP = 0.0026
48	LEAN TOWARD BEING THOSE WHERE THE FOOD SUPPLY IS NOT SECURE, AND FCOD SHORTAGES ARE FREQUENT CR ANNUAL (41) MGW	0.67 OF 27	48	LEAN TOWARD BEING THOSE WHERE THE FOOD SUPPLY IS SECURE, AND FOOD SHORTAGES ARE RARE OR OCCASIONAL (38) MGW	0.75 OF 24	9 18 18 6 XSQ= 7.26 PHI= -0.377 XP = 0.0070
53	TEND LESS TO BE THCSE WHERE FCOD PRODUCTION IS BY SIMPLE AGRICULTURE OR INCIPIENT FCOD PRODUCTION, RATHER THAN BY INTENSIVE AGRICULTURE (147)	0.53 OF 70	53	TEND MORE TO BE THOSE WHERE FOOD PRODUCTION IS BY SIMPLE AGRICULTURE OR INCIPIENT FOOD PRODUCTION, RATHER THAN BY INTENSIVE AGRICULTURE (147)	0.89 OF 37	33 4 37 33 XSQ= 12.56 PHI= 0.343 XP = 0.0004
55	TEND TO BE THOSE WHERE FCOD PRODUCTION IS BY INTENSIVE AGRICULTURE, RATHER THAN BY SIMPLE AGRICULTURE (91)	0.62 OF 53	55	TEND TO BE THOSE WHERE FOOD PRODUCTION IS BY SIMPLE AGRICULTURE, RATHER THAN BY INTENSIVE AGRICULTURE (101)	0.86 OF 29	33 4 20 25 XSQ= 15.88 PHI= 0.440 XP = 0.0001
63	TEND TO BE THOSE WHERE HUSBANDRY, IF PRESENT, IS PRINCIPALLY IN THE FORM OF BOVINE, EQUINE, CAMEL-LIKE, OR DEER-LIKE ANIMALS, RATHER THAN PIGS, SHEEP, CR GOATS (152)	0.80 OF 81	63	TEND TO BE THOSE WHERE HUSBANDRY, IF PRESENT, IS PRINCIPALLY IN THE FORM OF PIGS, SHEEP, OR GOATS, RATHER THAN BOVINE, EQUINE, CAMEL-LIKE, OR DEER-LIKE ANIMALS (74)	0.71 OF 31	65 9 16 22 XSQ= 24.00 PHI= 0.463 XP = 0.0000
71	TEND TO BE THOSE WHERE METAL WORKING IS PRESENT (98)	0.54 OF 122	71	TEND TO BE THOSE WHERE METAL WORKING IS ABSENT (153)	0.81 OF 53	66 10 56 43 XSQ= 17.26 PHI= 0.314 XP = 0.0000
74	LEAN TOWARD BEING THOSE WHERE POTTERY IS PRESENT (145)	0.69 OF 113	74	LEAN TOWARD BEING THOSE WHERE POTTERY IS ABSENT (93)	0.58 OF 52	78 22 35 30 XSQ= 9.56 PHI= 0.241 XP = 0.0020
81	TILT LESS TOWARD BEING THCSE WHERE NC CITY OR TCWN IS PRESENT, AND THE AVERAGE COMMUNITY SIZE IS SMALLER THAN 200 (135)	0.56 OF 91	81	TILT MORE TOWARD BEING THOSE WHERE NO CITY OR TOWN IS PRESENT, AND THE AVERAGE COMMUNITY SIZE IS SMALLER THAN 200 (135)	0.80 OF 35	40 7 51 28 XSQ= 5.22 PHI= 0.204 XP = 0.0223

83	TILT LESS TOWARD BEING THOSE 0.69 OF 74 WHERE, WITH NO CITY AND NO TOWN PRESENT, THE AVERAGE COMMUNITY SIZE IS SMALLER THAN 200, RATHER THAN BETWEEN 200 AND 999 (135)	83	TILT MORE TOWARD BEING THOSE 0.90 OF 31 WHERE, WITH NO CITY AND NO TOWN PRESENT, THE AVERAGE COMMUNITY SIZE IS SMALLER THAN 200, RATHER THAN BETWEEN 200 AND 999 (135)	23 3 51 28 XSQ= 4.28 PHI= 0.202 XP = 0.0385
84	TILT LESS TOWARD BEING THOSE 0.81 OF 96 WHERE THE LEVEL OF POLITICAL INTEGRATION IS THE LITTLE STATE, THE MINIMAL STATE, THE AUTONOMOUS COMMUNITY, OR THE FAMILY (262) GPM	84	TILT MORE TOWARD BEING THOSE 0.96 OF 46 WHERE THE LEVEL OF POLITICAL INTEGRATION IS THE LITTLE STATE, THE MINIMAL STATE, THE AUTONOMOUS COMMUNITY, OR THE FAMILY (262) GPM	18 2 78 44 XSQ= 4.21 PHI= 0.172 XP = 0.0403
85	TILT LESS TOWARD BEING THOSE 0.70 OF 96 WHERE THE LEVEL OF POLITICAL INTEGRATION IS THE MINIMAL STATE, THE AUTONOMOUS COMMUNITY, OR THE FAMILY (234) GPM	85	TILT MORE TOWARD BEING THOSE 0.89 OF 46 WHERE THE LEVEL OF POLITICAL INTEGRATION IS THE MINIMAL STATE, THE AUTONOMOUS COMMUNITY, OR THE FAMILY (234) GPM	29 5 67 41 XSQ= 5.37 PHI= 0.194 XP = 0.0205
88	DRIFT LESS TOWARD BEING THOSE 0.59 OF 88 WHERE, IF A HEADMANSHIP IS PRESENT, SUCCESSION IS HEREDITARY (165)	88	DRIFT MORE TOWARD BEING THOSE 0.77 OF 44 WHERE, IF A HEADMANSHIP IS PRESENT, SUCCESSION IS HEREDITARY (165)	36 10 52 34 XSQ= 3.51 PHI= 0.163 XP = 0.0611
91	TILT TOWARD BEING THOSE 0.50 OF 16 WHERE SOCIETAL COMPLEXITY IS HIGH (18) F-W	91	IN ALL CASES ARE THOSE 1.00 OF 9 WHERE SOCIETAL COMPLEXITY IS LOW (22) F-W	8 0 8 9 XSQ= 4.52 PHI= 0.425 EP = 0.0218
108	DRIFT TOWARD BEING THOSE 0.69 OF 75 WHERE CLASS STRATIFICATION, IF PRESENT, IS BASED ON SOMETHING OTHER THAN A HEREDITARY ARISTOCRACY (129)	108	DRIFT TOWARD BEING THOSE 0.54 OF 26 WHERE CLASS STRATIFICATION, IF PRESENT, IS BASED ON A HEREDITARY ARISTOCRACY (74)	23 14 52 12 XSQ= 3.53 PHI= -0.187 XP = 0.0604
109	DRIFT LESS TOWARD BEING THOSE 0.82 OF 115 WHERE CASTES ARE ABSENT (317)	109	DRIFT MORE TOWARD BEING THOSE 0.94 OF 53 WHERE CASTES ARE ABSENT (317)	21 3 94 50 XSQ= 3.73 PHI= 0.149 XP = 0.0534
110	TEND TO BE THOSE 0.53 OF 118 WHERE SLAVERY IS PRESENT (163)	110	TEND TO BE THOSE 0.77 OF 53 WHERE SLAVERY IS ABSENT (218)	62 12 56 41 XSQ= 12.13 PHI= 0.266 XP = 0.0005
118	DRIFT TOWARD BEING THOSE 0.67 OF 21 WHERE THE PERCENTAGE OF OCCUPATIONS THAT ARE SPECIALIZED IS HIGH OR MEDIUM (24) WME	118	DRIFT TOWARD BEING THOSE 0.67 OF 12 WHERE THE PERCENTAGE OF OCCUPATIONS THAT ARE SPECIALIZED IS LOW (25) WME	14 4 7 8 XSQ= 2.21 PHI= 0.259 EP = 0.0827

120	TILT TOWARD BEING THOSE 0.87 OF 23 WHERE THE CRAFT SPECIALIZATION SCORE IS HIGH OR MEDIUM (36) WME	120	TILT TOWARD BEING THOSE 0.50 OF 12 WHERE THE CRAFT SPECIALIZATION SCORE IS LOW (17) WME	20 6 3 6 XSQ= 3.87 PHI= 0.333 EP = 0.0378
127	LEAN TOWARD BEING THOSE 0.61 OF 33 WHERE THE FEMALES' CONTRIBUTION TO SUBSISTENCE IS LOW (32) JKB	127	IN ALL CASES ARE THOSE 1.00 OF 11 WHERE THE FEMALES' CONTRIBUTION TO SUBSISTENCE IS HIGH (33) JKB	13 11 20 0 XSQ= 9.90 PHI= -0.474 XP = 0.0017
129	DRIFT LESS TOWARD BEING THOSE 0.60 OF 52 WHERE WEAVING IS MAINLY DONE BY FEMALES (73)	129	DRIFT MORE TOWARD BEING THOSE 0.84 OF 19 WHERE WEAVING IS MAINLY DONE BY FEMALES (73)	21 3 31 16 XSQ= 2.74 PHI= 0.197 XP = 0.0977
131	TILT LESS TOWARD BEING THOSE 0.77 OF 69 WHERE THE CONSTRUCTION OF PERMANENT HOUSES OR THE ERECTION OF TEMPORARY DWELLINGS IS MAINLY DONE BY MALES (136)	131	TILT MORE TOWARD BEING THOSE 0.93 OF 44 WHERE THE CONSTRUCTION OF PERMANENT HOUSES OR THE ERECTION OF TEMPORARY DWELLINGS IS MAINLY DONE BY MALES (136)	53 41 16 3 XSQ= 4.04 PHI= -0.189 XP = 0.0443
178	DRIFT MORE TOWARD BEING THOSE 0.83 OF 122 WHERE THE COMMUNITY IS OTHER THAN SEGMENTED ON A CLAN BASIS AND NON-EXOGAMOUS (295)	178	DRIFT LESS TOWARD BEING THOSE 0.68 OF 50 WHERE THE COMMUNITY IS OTHER THAN SEGMENTED ON A CLAN BASIS AND NON-EXOGAMOUS (295)	21 16 101 34 XSQ= 3.76 PHI= -0.148 XP = 0.0525
183	TILT MORE TOWARD BEING THOSE 0.92 OF 78 WHERE THE LARGEST NON-COGNATIC KIN GROUP IS SMALLER THAN A MOEITY, I. E., A PHRATRY OR SIB OR LINEAGE (218)	183	TILT LESS TOWARD BEING THOSE 0.75 OF 32 WHERE THE LARGEST NON-COGNATIC KIN GROUP IS SMALLER THAN A MOEITY, I. E., A PHRATRY OR SIB OR LINEAGE (218)	6 8 72 24 XSQ= 4.66 PHI= -0.206 XP = 0.0309
184	DRIFT MORE TOWARD BEING THOSE 0.76 OF 78 WHERE THE LARGEST NON-COGNATIC KIN GROUP IS SMALLER THAN A PHRATRY, I. E. A SIB OR LINEAGE (175)	184	DRIFT LESS TOWARD BEING THOSE 0.56 OF 32 WHERE THE LARGEST NON-COGNATIC KIN GROUP IS SMALLER THAN A PHRATRY, I. E. A SIB OR LINEAGE (175)	19 14 59 18 XSQ= 3.19 PHI= -0.170 XP = 0.0740
186	DRIFT LESS TOWARD BEING THOSE 0.60 OF 123 WHERE THE KIN GROUP IS OTHER THAN EXCLUSIVELY PATRILINEAL (250)	186	DRIFT MORE TOWARD BEING THOSE 0.75 OF 53 WHERE THE KIN GROUP IS OTHER THAN EXCLUSIVELY PATRILINEAL (250)	49 13 74 40 XSQ= 3.16 PHI= 0.134 XP = 0.0753
190	DRIFT MORE TOWARD BEING THOSE 0.81 OF 75 WHERE THE KIN GROUP IS PATRILINEAL OR DOUBLE-DESCENT, RATHER THAN MATRILINEAL (186)	190	DRIFT LESS TOWARD BEING THOSE 0.61 OF 31 WHERE THE KIN GROUP IS PATRILINEAL OR DOUBLE-DESCENT, RATHER THAN MATRILINEAL (186)	61 19 14 12 XSQ= 3.74 PHI= 0.188 XP = 0.0532

197 DRIFT MORE TOWARD BEING THOSE 0.89 OF 63 WHERE RULES FOR THE INHERITANCE OF REAL PROPERTY, IF PRESENT, FAVOR EITHER THE MALE HEIR OR LINE, OR THE FEMALE HEIR OR LINE (165)	197 DRIFT LESS TOWARD BEING THOSE 0.70 OF 23 WHERE RULES FOR THE INHERITANCE OF REAL PROPERTY, IF PRESENT, FAVOR EITHER THE MALE HEIR OR LINE, OR THE FEMALE HEIR OR LINE (165)	56 16 7 7 XSQ= 3.31 PHI= 0.196 XP = 0.0690
204 TILT MORE TOWARD BEING THOSE 0.82 OF 106 WHERE MARITAL RESIDENCE IS PATRILOCAL, VIRILOCAL, OR AVUNCULOCAL, RATHER THAN AMBILOCAL OR NEOLOCAL (270)	204 TILT LESS TOWARD BEING THOSE 0.64 OF 39 WHERE MARITAL RESIDENCE IS PATRILOCAL, VIRILOCAL, OR AVUNCULOCAL, RATHER THAN AMBILOCAL OR NEOLOCAL (270)	87 25 19 14 XSQ= 4.27 PHI= 0.172 XP = 0.0389
209 TILT MORE TOWARD BEING THOSE 0.84 OF 104 WHERE MARITAL RESIDENCE IS PATRILOCAL, VIRILOCAL, OR AVUNCULOCAL, RATHER THAN MATRILOCAL OR UXORILOCAL (270)	209 TILT LESS TOWARD BEING THOSE 0.64 OF 39 WHERE MARITAL RESIDENCE IS PATRILOCAL, VIRILOCAL, OR AVUNCULOCAL, RATHER THAN MATRILOCAL OR UXORILOCAL (270)	87 25 17 14 XSQ= 5.29 PHI= 0.192 XP = 0.0215
210 TILT MORE TOWARD BEING THOSE 0.89 OF 63 WHERE MARITAL RESIDENCE IS PATRILOCAL, RATHER THAN MATRILOCAL (169)	210 TILT LESS TOWARD BEING THOSE 0.65 OF 23 WHERE MARITAL RESIDENCE IS PATRILOCAL, RATHER THAN MATRILOCAL (169)	56 15 7 8 XSQ= 5.02 PHI= 0.241 XP = 0.0251
236 DRIFT TOWARD BEING THOSE 0.60 OF 123 WHERE THE FAMILY IS OF AN EXTENDED TYPE, RATHER THAN AN INDEPENDENT TYPE (213)	236 DRIFT TOWARD BEING THOSE 0.55 OF 53 WHERE THE FAMILY IS OF AN INDEPENDENT TYPE, RATHER THAN AN EXTENDED TYPE (185)	74 24 49 29 XSQ= 2.75 PHI= 0.125 XP = 0.0974
240 DRIFT TOWARD BEING THOSE 0.62 OF 74 WHERE THE FAMILY, IF EXTENDED, IS SMALL OR STEM, RATHER THAN LARGE (135)	240 DRIFT TOWARD BEING THOSE 0.63 OF 24 WHERE THE FAMILY, IF EXTENDED, IS LARGE, RATHER THAN SMALL OR STEM (78)	28 15 46 9 XSQ= 3.53 PHI= -0.190 XP = 0.0602
255 DRIFT LESS TOWARD BEING THOSE 0.60 OF 15 WHERE GRANDPARENTAL AUTHORITY OVER PARENTS IS ABSENT (26) CA	255 IN ALL CASES ARE THOSE 1.00 OF 8 WHERE GRANDPARENTAL AUTHORITY OVER PARENTS IS ABSENT (26) DA	6 0 9 8 XSQ= 2.50 PHI= 0.330 EP = 0.0582
262 TILT MORE TOWARD BEING THOSE 0.80 OF 123 WHERE WIVES ARE OBTAINED BY MEANS INVOLVING THE PRESENCE OF SOME CONSIDERATION (305)	262 TILT LESS TOWARD BEING THOSE 0.62 OF 53 WHERE WIVES ARE OBTAINED BY MEANS INVOLVING THE PRESENCE OF SOME CONSIDERATION (305)	98 33 25 20 XSQ= 5.02 PHI= 0.169 XP = 0.0250
263 DRIFT TOWARD BEING THOSE 0.59 OF 123 WHERE WIVES ARE OBTAINED BY RELATIVELY DIFFICULT MEANS, NAMELY BY BRIDE-PRICE, BRIDE-SERVICE, OR EXCHANGING A FEMALE RELATIVE (233)	263 DRIFT TOWARD BEING THOSE 0.57 OF 53 WHERE WIVES ARE OBTAINED BY RELATIVELY EASY MEANS, NAMELY BY TOKEN BRIDE-PRICE, GIFT EXCHANGE, ABSENCE OF ANY CONSIDERATION, OR RECEIPT OF DOWRY (162)	73 23 50 30 XSQ= 3.19 PHI= 0.135 XP = 0.0743

```
286  DRIFT TOWARD BEING THCSE          0.67 OF  12     286  DRIFT TOWARD BEING THOSE          0.73 OF  11           4     8
     WHERE THE NUMBER OF FOCC TABOOS                        WHERE THE NUMBER OF FOOD TABOOS                         8     3
     DURING PREGNANCY                                       DURING PREGNANCY                                 XSQ=      2.17
     IS LOW OR ABSENT   (14) BCA                            IS HIGH   (20) BCA                               PHI=    -0.307
                                                                                                             EP =    0.0995

301  DRIFT MORE TCWARD BEING THCSE  0.83 OF  58        301  DRIFT LESS TOWARD BEING THCSE  0.65 OF  31          48    20
     WHERE THE POST-PARTUM SEX TABOO LASTS                  WHERE THE POST-PARTUM SEX TABOO LASTS                  10    11
     LONGER THAN CNE MONTH   (96)                           LONGER THAN ONE MONTH   (96)                     XSQ=      2.79
                                                                                                             PHI=     0.177
                                                                                                             XP =    0.0951

305  DRIFT TOWARD BEING THCSE          0.65 OF  17     305  DRIFT TOWARD BEING THOSE          0.68 OF  19           6    13
     WHERE THE EARLY SEXUAL SATISFACTION                    WHERE THE EARLY SEXUAL SATISFACTICN                    11     6
     POTENTIAL IS LOW   (24) W-C                            POTENTIAL IS HIGH   (27) W-C                     XSQ=      2.73
                                                                                                             PHI=    -0.276
                                                                                                             EP =    0.0933

307  TILT TOWARD BEING THCSE           0.50 OF  18     3C7  TILT TOWARD BEING THOSE           0.88 OF  17           9    15
     WHERE THE EARLY AGGRESSION SATISFACTION                WHERE THE EARLY AGGRESSICN SATISFACTION                 9     2
     POTENTIAL IS LOW   (19) W-C                            POTENTIAL IS HIGH   (33) W-C                     XSQ=      4.29
                                                                                                             PHI=    -0.350
                                                                                                             EP =    0.0275

311  TILT TOWARD BEING THOSE           0.72 OF  18     311  TILT TOWARD BEING THOSE           0.72 OF  18          13     5
     WHERE SEXUAL SOCIALIZATION ANXIETY                     WHERE SEXUAL SOCIALIZATION ANXIETY                      5    13
     IS HIGH   (28) W-C                                     IS LOW   (23) W-C                                XSQ=      5.44
                                                                                                             PHI=     0.389
                                                                                                             EP =    0.0184

313  LEAN TCWARD BEING THCSE           0.63 OF  19     313  LEAN TOWARD BEING THOSE           0.88 OF  17          12     2
     WHERE AGGRESSION SCCIALIZATION ANXIETY                 WHERE AGGRESSION SOCIALIZATION ANXIETY                  7    15
     IS HIGH   (26) W-C                                     IS LOW   (28) W-C                                XSQ=      7.93
                                                                                                             PHI=     0.469
                                                                                                             EP =    0.0022

318  DRIFT TCWARD BEING THCSE          0.59 OF  29     318  DRIFT TOWARD BEING THOSE          0.70 OF  20          12    14
     WHERE THE CVERALL INDULGENCE                           WHERE THE OVERALL INDULGENCE                           17     6
     OF THE INFANT                                          OF THE INFANT                                    XSQ=      2.83
     IS LCW   (31) B-B-C                                    IS HIGH   (40) B-B-C                             PHI=    -0.240
                                                                                                             XP =    0.0926

342  TILT TCWARD BEING THOSE           0.79 OF  19     342  TILT TOWARD BEING THOSE           0.64 OF  11           4     7
     WHERE THE CHILD'S INFERREC ANXIETY OVER                WHERE THE CHILD'S INFERRED ANXIETY OVER                15     4
     PERFORMANCE OF NURTURANT BEHAVIOR                      PERFORMANCE OF NURTURANT BEHAVIOR                XSQ=      3.76
     IS LOW   (28) B-B-C                                    IS HIGH   (18) B-B-C                             PHI=    -0.354
                                                                                                             EP =    0.0465

352  TEND TO BE THCSE                  0.89 OF  28     352  TEND TO BE THOSE                  0.62 OF  21          25     8
     WHERE THE TOTAL POSITIVE PRESSURE TOWARD               WHERE THE TOTAL POSITIVE PRESSURE TOWARD                3    13
     DEVELCPING OBEDIENT BEHAVICR                           DEVELOPING OBEDIENT BEHAVICR                     XSQ=     12.07
     IN THE CHILD                                           IN THE CHILD                                     PHI=     0.496
     IS HIGH   (44) B-B-C                                   IS LOW   (28) B-B-C                              XP =    0.0005
```

368	TILT TOWARD BEING THOSE 0.67 OF 12 WHERE DISSCCIATICN CF THE SEXES AT ADCLESCENCE IS LOW (21) JKH	368	TILT TOWARD BEING THCSE 0.80 OF 10 WHERE DISSOCIATION OF THE SEXES AT ADOLESCENCE IS HIGH OR MEDIUM (16) JKH	4 8 8 2 XSQ= 3.09 PHI= -0.375 EP = 0.0427
370	TEND TC BE THCSE 0.70 OF 90 WHERE THE SEGREGATION CF ACOLESCENT BOYS IS ABSENT (148)	370	TEND TO BE THOSE 0.62 OF 42 WHERE THE SEGREGATION OF ADCLESCENT BOYS IS COMPLETE OR PARTIAL (95)	27 26 63 16 XSQ= 10.84 PHI= -0.287 XP = 0.0010
372	LEAN TCWARD BEING THOSE 0.73 OF 41 WHERE MALE INITIATION RITES ARE ABSENT (63) ASA	372	LEAN TOWARD BEING THOSE 0.69 CF 29 WHERE MALE INITIATICN RITES ARE PRESENT (48) ASA	11 20 30 9 XSQ= 10.57 PHI= -0.389 XP = 0.0011
391	TEND TO BE THCSE 0.67 OF 75 WHERE PREMARITAL SEX RELATIONS ARE STRONGLY PUNISHED AND IN FACT RARE, OR WEAKLY PUNISHED AND IN FACT NCT RARE (89) JTW,EA	391	TEND TO BE THOSE 0.82 CF 40 WHERE PREMARITAL SEX RELATICNS ARE PUNISHED ONLY IF PREGNANCY RESULTS, CR FREELY PERMITTED (90) JTW,EA	50 7 25 33 XSQ= 23.30 PHI= 0.450 XP = 0.0000
392	TEND TC BE THCSE 0.79 OF 75 WHERE PREMARITAL SEX RELATIONS ARE STRCNGLY PUNISHEC AND IN FACT RARE, OR WEAKLY PUNISHED ANC IN FACT NOT RARE, OR PUNISHED CNLY IF PREGNANCY RESULTS (112) JTW,EA	392	TEND TO BE THOSE 0.57 CF 40 WHERE PREMARITAL SEX RELATICNS ARE FREELY PERMITTED (67) JTW,EA	59 17 16 23 XSQ= 13.65 PHI= 0.345 XP = 0.0002
399	DRIFT TCWARD BEING THCSE 0.65 OF 17 WHERE INTENSITY CF CASTRATION ANXIETY IS HIGH (23) WNS	399	DRIFT TOWARD BEING THOSE 0.71 OF 17 WHERE INTENSITY OF CASTRATICN ANXIETY IS LOW (22) WNS	11 5 6 12 XSQ= 2.95 PHI= 0.295 EP = 0.0844
419	DRIFT MORE TCWARD BEING THOSE 0.77 OF 40 WHERE MILITARY GLORY IS STRONGLY CR MODERATELY EMPHASIZED (55) PES	419	DRIFT LESS TOWARD BEING THCSE 0.52 CF 21 WHERE MILITARY GLORY IS STRONGLY OR MODERATELY EMPHASIZED (55) PES	31 11 9 10 XSQ= 2.96 PHI= 0.220 XP = 0.0851
426	TEND TO BE THOSE 0.68 OF 111 WHERE A HIGH GOC IS PRESENT (156) GES,EA	426	TEND TO BE THOSE 0.62 OF 45 WHERE A HIGH GOD IS ABSENT (104) GES,EA	76 17 35 28 XSQ= 11.28 PHI= 0.269 XP = 0.0008
427	DRIFT TCWARD BEING THCSE 0.58 OF 76 WHERE A HIGH GOC, IF PRESENT, IS ACTIVE, RATHER THAN INACTIVE (87) GES,EA	427	DRIFT TOWARD BEING THOSE 0.71 CF 17 WHERE A HIGH GOD, IF PRESENT, IS INACTIVE, RATHER THAN ACTIVE (69) GES,EA	44 5 32 12 XSQ= 3.45 PHI= 0.193 XP = 0.0632

447	DRIFT TOWARD BEING THOSE WHERE LOVE MAGIC IS PRESENT (20) S-R	0.88 OF 8	447	DRIFT TOWARD BEING THOSE WHERE LOVE MAGIC IS ABSENT (13) S-R	0.60 OF 15	7 6 1 9 XSQ= 3.05 PHI= 0.364 EP = 0.0743
449	LEAN TOWARD BEING THOSE WHERE THE OBSERVATION OF FOOD TABOOS IS MEDIUM OR LOW, RATHER THAN HIGH (61) JRL	0.80 OF 44	449	LEAN TOWARD BEING THOSE WHERE THE OBSERVATION OF FOOD TABOOS IS HIGH, RATHER THAN MEDIUM OR LOW (25) JRL	0.58 OF 19	9 11 35 8 XSQ= 6.94 PHI= -0.332 XP = 0.0084
459	TEND TO BE THOSE WHERE GAMES, IF PRESENT, INCLUDE GAMES OF CHANCE (82) R-A-B,EA	0.63 OF 84	459	TEND TO BE THOSE WHERE GAMES, IF PRESENT, DO NOT INCLUDE GAMES OF CHANCE (89) R-A-B,EA	0.79 OF 34	53 7 31 27 XSQ= 15.84 PHI= 0.366 XP = 0.0001
460	TEND TO BE THOSE WHERE GAMES, IF PRESENT, ARE NOT LIMITED TO GAMES OF SKILL ONLY (104) R-A-B,EA	0.82 OF 84	460	TEND TO BE THOSE WHERE GAMES, IF PRESENT, ARE LIMITED TO GAMES OF SKILL ONLY (67) R-A-B,EA	0.68 OF 34	15 23 69 11 XSQ= 25.25 PHI= -0.463 XP = 0.0000
468	DRIFT LESS TOWARD BEING THOSE WHERE CONTACT WITH OTHER CULTURES IS REGULAR OR IRREGULAR, RATHER THAN FREQUENT (37) JMH	0.65 OF 26	468	DRIFT MORE TOWARD BEING THOSE WHERE CONTACT WITH OTHER CULTURES IS REGULAR OR IRREGULAR, RATHER THAN FREQUENT (37) JMH	0.93 OF 14	9 1 17 13 XSQ= 2.34 PHI= 0.242 EP = 0.0696

76 CULTURES
WHERE BCAT BUILCING IS
PRESENT (142)

76 CULTURES
WHERE BOAT BUILDING IS
ABSENT (63)

BACKGROUND ON PAGE 79

SUBJECT ONLY

142 IN LEFT COLUMN

ABIPCN	AINU	ALACALUF	ALBANIANS	AMERICANS	ANDAMANESE	APINAYE	ARAUCANIANS	ATSUGEWI	AYMARA
AZANDE	AZTEC	BACAIRI	BAMBARA	BHIL	BLACK CARIB	CAGABA	CALLINAGO	CAMAYURA	CARIB
CAYAPA	CHEROKEE	CHIR-APACHE	CHOCO	COPR ESKIMO	CREE	CREEK	CUNA	CARD	DELAWARE
DIEGUENO	DUTCH	EGYPTIANS	ELLICE	EYAK	FANG	FON	FOX	GANCA	GILBERTESE
GILYAK	GCND	GUATC	HAICA	HAWAIIANS	HURON	IBAN	ILA	INGALIK	JAPANESE
JIVARO	KAPAUKU	KERAKI	KHASI	KOREANS	KORYAK	KURTATCHI	KUTENAI	KWAKIUTL	LAMBA
LAU	LESU	LCZI	MACASSARESE	MANGAIANS	MANIHIKI	MANUS	MACRI	MARICOPA	MARQUESANS
MARSHALLESE	MAYA	MBUNCU	MENTAWEI	MIAMI	MISKITO	MONGO	MOTA	MURNGIN	NABESNA
NATCHEZ	NDEMBU	NICOBARESE	NUNIVAK	NUPE	NYAKYUSA	NYORO	OJIBWA	OKINAWANS	OMAHA
ONTONG-JAVA	PALAUANS	PALIKUR	PONAPEANS	PUKAPUKA	PURARI	RAROIANS	RIFFIANS	RUNCI	SAMOANS
SAMOYED	SANPOIL	SARSI	SENIANG	SHILLUK	SONGHAI	TALAMANCA	TANALA	TAREUMIUT	TENINO
THONGA	TIBETANS	TIKOPIA	TIMUCUA	TIV	TIWI	TOLOWA	TRISTAN	TROBRIAND	TRUKESE
TRUMAI	TSHIMSHIAN	TUBATULABAL	TUCANO	TUCUNA	TUPINAMBA	TWANA	ULAWANS	WASHO	WITOTO
WOGEO	WCLEAIANS	YABARANA	YAGUA	YAHGAN	YAKUT	YAO	YAPESE	YARURO	YOKUTS
YORUBA	YURCK								

63 IN RIGHT CCLUMN

ALORESE	ARANDA	ASHANTI	AWEIKOMA	BASSERI	BORORO	BOTOCUDO	BURUSHO	CHAMACOCO	CHIRIGUANO
CHOROTI	CCMANCHE	CCCRG	CROW	GARO	GISU	GOAJIRO	GROS VENTRE	HUKUNDIKA	INCA
JAVANESE	JEMEZ	KATAB	KAZAK	KHALKA	KIKUYU	KUNG	LEPCHA	LUO	MAMVU
MASAI	MATACO	MATAKAM	MBUTI	MOSSI	MUNDURUCU	NAMA	NAMBICUARA	NANDI	NAVAHO
NOMLAKI	NUER	PAEZ	PAPAGO	RWALA	SAGADA	SIRIONO	SIWANS	SOMALI	TALLENSI
TAOS	TAPIRAPE	TECA	TEHUELCHE	TENDA	TIMBIRA	TODA	UTE	VENCA	WAICA
WANTOAT	WCLCF	YUKI							

195 EXCLUDED BECAUSE UNASCERTAINEC

3	TILT MORE TOWARC BEING THCSE LOCATED OUTSIDE CF AFRICA (320)	0.86 OF 142	3	TILT LESS TOWARD BEING THOSE LOCATED OUTSIDE OF AFRICA (320)	0.73 OF 63
					20 17 122 46 XSQ= 4.08 PHI= -0.141 XP = 0.0435
6	LEAN LESS TOWARC BEING THCSE LOCATED CUTSIDE OF THE INSULAR PACIFIC (330)	0.75 OF 142	6	LEAN MORE TOWARD BEING THOSE LOCATED OUTSIDE OF THE INSULAR PACIFIC (330)	0.92 CF 63
					35 5 107 58 XSQ= 6.73 PHI= 0.181 XP = 0.0095

12	TILT LESS TOWARD BEING THOSE 0.86 OF 142 WHERE THE LATITUDE IS LESS THAN FIFTY DEGREES (367)	12	TILT MORE TOWARD BEING THOSE 0.98 OF 63 WHERE THE LATITUDE IS LESS THAN FIFTY DEGREES (367)	20 1 122 62 XSQ= 6.12 PHI= 0.173 XP = 0.0134
13	DRIFT LESS TOWARD BEING THOSE 0.76 OF 142 WHERE THE LATITUDE IS LESS THAN FORTY DEGREES (329)	13	DRIFT MORE TOWARD BEING THOSE 0.89 OF 63 WHERE THE LATITUDE IS LESS THAN FORTY DEGREES (329)	34 7 108 56 XSQ= 3.73 PHI= 0.135 XP = 0.0536
33	TEND MORE TO BE THOSE 0.90 OF 142 WHERE THE NATURAL ENVIRONMENT IS OTHER THAN 'VERY HARSH,' I.E., DESERT, DESERT GRASSES AND SHRUBS, TUNDRA, OR HIGH PLATEAU STEPPE (341) FWM	33	TEND LESS TO BE THOSE 0.70 OF 63 WHERE THE NATURAL ENVIRONMENT IS OTHER THAN 'VERY HARSH,' I.E., DESERT, DESERT GRASSES AND SHRUBS, TUNDRA, OR HIGH PLATEAU STEPPE (341) FWM	14 19 128 44 XSQ= 11.85 PHI= -0.240 XP = 0.0006
36	TEND MORE TO BE THOSE 0.82 OF 142 WHERE THE NATURAL ENVIRONMENT IS OTHER THAN 'VERY HARSH,' OR SUB-TROPICAL BUSH, OR TEMPERATE GRASSLAND (292) FWM	36	TEND LESS TO BE THOSE 0.51 OF 63 WHERE THE NATURAL ENVIRONMENT IS OTHER THAN 'VERY HARSH,' OR SUB-TROPICAL BUSH, OR TEMPERATE GRASSLAND (292) FWM	26 31 116 32 XSQ= 19.24 PHI= -0.306 XP = 0.0000
42	LEAN LESS TOWARD BEING THOSE 0.56 OF 142 WHERE THE NATURAL ENVIRONMENT IS OTHER THAN TROPICAL OR SUB-TROPICAL RAIN FOREST, OR MONSOON FOREST (244) FWM	42	LEAN MORE TOWARD BEING THOSE 0.76 OF 63 WHERE THE NATURAL ENVIRONMENT IS OTHER THAN TROPICAL OR SUB-TROPICAL RAIN FOREST, OR MONSOON FOREST (244) FWM	63 15 79 48 XSQ= 6.98 PHI= 0.184 XP = 0.0083
44	LEAN TOWARD BEING THOSE 0.68 OF 136 WHERE SETTLEMENTS ARE FIXED (222)	44	LEAN TOWARD BEING THOSE 0.53 OF 62 WHERE SETTLEMENTS ARE NON-FIXED (110)	93 29 43 33 XSQ= 7.52 PHI= 0.195 XP = 0.0061
46	TEND MORE TO BE THOSE 0.82 OF 136 OTHER THAN WHERE SETTLEMENTS ARE NON-FIXED AND MOVEMENT IS NOMADIC (260)	46	TEND LESS TO BE THOSE 0.58 OF 62 OTHER THAN WHERE SETTLEMENTS ARE NON-FIXED AND MOVEMENT IS NOMADIC (260)	25 26 111 36 XSQ= 11.15 PHI= -0.237 XP = 0.0008
47	DRIFT LESS TOWARD BEING THOSE 0.58 OF 43 WHERE, IF SETTLEMENTS ARE NON-FIXED, MOVEMENT IS NOMADIC, RATHER THAN NON-NOMADIC (72)	47	DRIFT MORE TOWARD BEING THOSE 0.79 OF 33 WHERE, IF SETTLEMENTS ARE NON-FIXED, MOVEMENT IS NOMADIC, RATHER THAN NON-NOMADIC (72)	25 26 18 7 XSQ= 2.73 PHI= -0.190 XP = 0.0984
48	TEND TO BE THOSE 0.67 OF 40 WHERE THE FOOD SUPPLY IS SECURE, AND FOOD SHORTAGES ARE RARE OR OCCASIONAL (38) MGW	48	TEND TO BE THOSE 0.88 OF 16 WHERE THE FOOD SUPPLY IS NOT SECURE, AND FOOD SHORTAGES ARE FREQUENT OR ANNUAL (41) MGW	27 2 13 14 XSQ= 11.73 PHI= 0.458 XP = 0.0006

53	TEND TO BE THOSE 0.78 OF 90 WHERE FOOD PRODUCTION IS BY SIMPLE AGRICULTURE OR INCIPIENT FOOD PRODUCTION, RATHER THAN BY INTENSIVE AGRICULTURE (147)	53	TEND TO BE THOSE 0.56 OF 34 WHERE FOOD PRODUCTION IS BY INTENSIVE AGRICULTURE, RATHER THAN BY SIMPLE AGRICULTURE OR INCIPIENT FOOD PRODUCTION (91)	20 19 70 15 XSQ= 11.45 PHI= -0.304 XP = 0.0007
55	LEAN TOWARD BEING THOSE 0.69 OF 64 WHERE FOOD PRODUCTION IS BY SIMPLE AGRICULTURE, RATHER THAN BY INTENSIVE AGRICULTURE (101)	55	LEAN TOWARD BEING THOSE 0.68 OF 28 WHERE FOOD PRODUCTION IS BY INTENSIVE AGRICULTURE, RATHER THAN BY SIMPLE AGRICULTURE (91)	20 19 44 9 XSQ= 9.24 PHI= -0.317 XP = 0.0024
62	DRIFT LESS TOWARD BEING THOSE 0.54 OF 142 WHERE HUSBANDRY OF SOME KIND IS PRESENT (228)	62	DRIFT MORE TOWARD BEING THOSE 0.68 OF 63 WHERE HUSBANDRY OF SOME KIND IS PRESENT (228)	76 43 66 20 XSQ= 3.31 PHI= -0.127 XP = 0.0689
63	LEAN TOWARD BEING THOSE 0.54 OF 76 WHERE HUSBANDRY, IF PRESENT, IS PRINCIPALLY IN THE FORM OF PIGS, SHEEP, OR GOATS, RATHER THAN BOVINE, EQUINE, CAMEL-LIKE, OR DEER-LIKE ANIMALS (74)	63	LEAN TOWARD BEING THOSE 0.77 OF 43 WHERE HUSBANDRY, IF PRESENT, IS PRINCIPALLY IN THE FORM OF BOVINE, EQUINE, CAMEL-LIKE, OR DEER-LIKE ANIMALS, RATHER THAN PIGS, SHEEP, OR GOATS (152)	35 33 41 10 XSQ= 9.35 PHI= -0.280 XP = 0.0022
108	DRIFT LESS TOWARD BEING THOSE 0.61 OF 77 WHERE CLASS STRATIFICATION, IF PRESENT, IS BASED ON SOMETHING OTHER THAN A HEREDITARY ARISTOCRACY (129)	108	DRIFT MORE TOWARD BEING THOSE 0.81 OF 27 WHERE CLASS STRATIFICATION, IF PRESENT, IS BASED ON SOMETHING OTHER THAN A HEREDITARY ARISTOCRACY (129)	30 5 47 22 XSQ= 2.88 PHI= 0.166 XP = 0.0896
118	TILT TOWARD BEING THOSE 0.71 OF 24 WHERE THE PERCENTAGE OF OCCUPATIONS THAT ARE SPECIALIZED IS LOW (25) WME	118	TILT TOWARD BEING THOSE 0.71 OF 17 WHERE THE PERCENTAGE OF OCCUPATIONS THAT ARE SPECIALIZED IS HIGH OR MEDIUM (24) WME	7 12 17 5 XSQ= 5.30 PHI= -0.360 XP = 0.0213
131	TEND MORE TO BE THOSE 0.93 OF 92 WHERE THE CONSTRUCTION OF PERMANENT HOUSES OR THE ERECTION OF TEMPORARY DWELLINGS IS MAINLY DONE BY MALES (136)	131	TEND LESS TO BE THOSE 0.68 OF 38 WHERE THE CONSTRUCTION OF PERMANENT HOUSES OR THE ERECTION OF TEMPORARY DWELLINGS IS MAINLY DONE BY MALES (136)	86 26 6 12 XSQ= 12.13 PHI= 0.305 XP = 0.0005
132	DRIFT TOWARD BEING THOSE 0.77 OF 30 WHERE ECONOMIC EXCHANGE INVOLVES THE USE OF MONEY (37) JMH	132	DRIFT TOWARD BEING THOSE 0.58 OF 12 WHERE ECONOMIC EXCHANGE DOES NOT INVOLVE THE USE OF MONEY (17) JMH	23 5 7 7 XSQ= 3.28 PHI= 0.280 XP = 0.0701
175	LEAN MORE TOWARD BEING THOSE 0.77 OF 137 WHERE THE COMMUNITY IS 'KIN-HETEROGENEOUS,' I. E. OTHER THAN A CLAN COMMUNITY OR A DEME (260)	175	LEAN LESS TOWARD BEING THOSE 0.56 OF 62 WHERE THE COMMUNITY IS 'KIN-HETEROGENEOUS,' I. E. OTHER THAN A CLAN COMMUNITY OR A DEME (260)	32 27 105 35 XSQ= 7.40 PHI= -0.193 XP = 0.0065

177	DRIFT MORE TOWARD BEING THOSE 0.84 OF 137 WHERE THE COMMUNITY IS OTHER THAN A SINGLE CLAN-COMMUNITY AND EXOGAMOUS (305)	177	DRIFT LESS TOWARD BEING THOSE 0.71 OF 62 WHERE THE COMMUNITY IS OTHER THAN A SINGLE CLAN-COMMUNITY AND EXOGAMOUS (305)	22 18 115 44 XSQ= 3.70 PHI= -0.136 XP = 0.0543
178	LEAN LESS TOWARD BEING THOSE 0.71 OF 137 WHERE THE COMMUNITY IS OTHER THAN SEGMENTED ON A CLAN BASIS AND NON-EXOGAMOUS (295)	178	LEAN MORE TOWARD BEING THOSE 0.92 OF 62 WHERE THE COMMUNITY IS OTHER THAN SEGMENTED ON A CLAN BASIS AND NON-EXOGAMOUS (295)	40 5 97 57 XSQ= 9.72 PHI= 0.221 XP = 0.0018
180	TILT MORE TOWARD BEING THOSE 0.72 OF 137 WHERE THE COMMUNITY IS COMMONLY NON-EXOGAMOUS, RATHER THAN EXOGAMOUS (258)	180	TILT LESS TOWARD BEING THOSE 0.55 OF 62 WHERE THE COMMUNITY IS COMMONLY NON-EXOGAMOUS, RATHER THAN EXOGAMOUS (258)	39 28 98 34 XSQ= 4.61 PHI= -0.152 XP = 0.0319
196	TILT TOWARD BEING THOSE 0.65 OF 101 WHERE INDIVIDUAL RIGHTS IN REAL PROPERTY, AND RULES FOR INHERITANCE, ARE PRESENT (194)	196	TILT TOWARD BEING THOSE 0.53 OF 49 WHERE INDIVIDUAL RIGHTS IN REAL PROPERTY, OR RULES FOR INHERITANCE, ARE ABSENT (87)	66 23 35 26 XSQ= 3.90 PHI= 0.161 XP = 0.0482
240	TILT TOWARD BEING THOSE 0.51 OF 76 WHERE THE FAMILY, IF EXTENDED, IS LARGE, RATHER THAN SMALL OR STEM (78)	240	TILT TOWARD BEING THOSE 0.76 OF 34 WHERE THE FAMILY, IF EXTENDED, IS SMALL OR STEM, RATHER THAN LARGE (135)	39 8 37 26 XSQ= 6.32 PHI= 0.240 XP = 0.0119
257	DRIFT TOWARD BEING THOSE 0.67 OF 12 WHERE THE SEVERITY OF SISTER AVOIDANCE IS HIGH (10) WNS	257	DRIFT TOWARD BEING THOSE 0.86 OF 7 WHERE THE SEVERITY OF SISTER AVOIDANCE IS LOW (17) WNS	8 1 4 6 XSQ= 2.99 PHI= 0.397 EP = 0.0573
320	TILT LESS TOWARD BEING THOSE 0.56 OF 36 WHERE THE DEGREE OF REDUCTION OF THE INFANT'S DRIVES IS HIGH (45) B-B-C	320	TILT MORE TOWARD BEING THOSE 0.93 OF 14 WHERE THE DEGREE OF REDUCTION OF THE INFANT'S DRIVES IS HIGH (45) B-B-C	20 13 16 1 XSQ= 4.70 PHI= -0.307 XP = 0.0302
356	DRIFT TOWARD BEING THOSE 0.67 OF 27 WHERE NEITHER ADOLESCENT PEER GROUPS NOR PAIRS ARE PRESENT IN A SETTING OF COURTSHIP (22) JKH	356	DRIFT TOWARD BEING THOSE 0.70 OF 10 WHERE ADOLESCENT PEER GROUPS OR PAIRS ARE PRESENT IN A SETTING OF COURTSHIP (29) JKH	9 7 18 3 XSQ= 2.64 PHI= -0.267 EP = 0.0667
377	DRIFT MORE TOWARD BEING THOSE 0.83 OF 133 WHERE MALE GENITAL MUTILATION IS ABSENT (242)	377	DRIFT LESS TOWARD BEING THOSE 0.71 OF 62 WHERE MALE GENITAL MUTILATION IS ABSENT (242)	22 18 111 44 XSQ= 3.32 PHI= -0.130 XP = 0.0686

397	DRIFT LESS TOWARD BEING THOSE WHERE SEX DISABILITY IS ABSENT (42) JKH	0.63 OF 32	397	IN ALL CASES ARE THOSE WHERE SEX DISABILITY IS ABSENT (42) JKH	1.00 OF 10	12 0 20 10 XSQ= 3.57 PHI= 0.292 XP = 0.0587
426	DRIFT LESS TOWARD BEING THOSE WHERE A HIGH GOD IS PRESENT (156) GES,EA	0.53 OF 123	426	DRIFT MORE TOWARD BEING THOSE WHERE A HIGH GOD IS PRESENT (156) GES,EA	0.69 OF 54	65 37 58 17 XSQ= 3.16 PHI= -0.134 XP = 0.0754
433	TILT TOWARD BEING THOSE WHERE BELIEF IN REINCARNATION IS ABSENT (28) GES	0.89 OF 19	433	TILT TOWARD BEING THOSE WHERE BELIEF IN REINCARNATION IS PRESENT (10) GES	0.50 OF 8	2 4 17 4 XSQ= 3.05 PHI= -0.336 EP = 0.0441
435	DRIFT TOWARD BEING THOSE WHERE ABANDONMENT OF THE HOUSE OF THE DEAD IS NOT PRACTICED (19) LWS	0.76 OF 17	435	DRIFT TOWARD BEING THOSE WHERE ABANDONMENT OF THE HOUSE OF THE DEAD IS PRACTICED (12) LWS	0.71 OF 7	4 5 13 2 XSQ= 3.03 PHI= -0.355 EP = 0.0606
441	DRIFT TOWARD BEING THOSE WHERE FEAR OF HUMAN BEINGS IS HIGH (29) W-C	0.54 OF 35	441	DRIFT TOWARD BEING THOSE WHERE FEAR OF HUMAN BEINGS IS LOW (32) W-C	0.82 OF 11	19 2 16 9 XSQ= 3.06 PHI= 0.258 XP = 0.0801

77 CULTURES
WHERE THE WRITING SYSTEM IS
ALPHABETIC-OR-PHCNETIC, RATHER THAN BEING
MNEMCNIC CR ABSENT (15) JMH

77 CULTURES
WHERE THE WRITING SYSTEM IS
MNEMONIC OR ABSENT, RATHER THAN BEING
ALPHABETIC-OR-PHONETIC (39) JMH

BACKGROUND ON PAGE 80

BCTH SUBJECT AND PREDICATE

15 IN LEFT COLUMN

ARAUCANIANS AZTEC BULGARIANS BURMESE CAMBODIANS KASKA KOREANS LOLO MARSHALLESE NAVAHO
RWALA SAMCYED VIETNAMESE WOLEAIANS YAKUT

39 IN RIGHT CCLUMN

ANDAMANESE ARANDA AZANDE BEMBA BURUSHO CAYAPA CHAGGA CHUKCHEE COPR ESKIMO CREEK
CROW CUNA CARD GILYAK IBAN JIVARO KAREN KHASI KORYAK KURTATCHI
MANDAN MBUNDU MIAC NAMA NUER OJIBWA PUKAPUKA SAMOANS SIRIONO TALLENSI
TEHUELCHE THCNGA TIKOPIA TIMBIRA TIV TODA TROBRIAND TUPINAMBA YURCK

346 EXCLUDED BECAUSE UNASCERTAINEC

---

53 DRIFT TCWARD BEING THCSE WHERE FCCD PRODUCTION IS BY INTENSIVE AGRICULTURE, RATHER THAN BY SIMPLE AGRICULTURE OR INCIPIENT FCCD PRODUCTICN (91) — 0.58 OF 12

53 DRIFT TOWARD BEING THOSE WHERE FOOD PRODUCTION IS BY SIMPLE AGRICULTURE OR INCIPIENT FOOD PRODUCTION, RATHER THAN BY INTENSIVE AGRICULTURE (147) — 0.76 OF 25

7 6
5 19
XSQ= 2.82
PHI= 0.276
EP = 0.0666

55 TILT TOWARD BEING THOSE WHERE FCCD PRCDUCTION IS BY INTENSIVE AGRICULTURE, RATHER THAN BY SIMPLE AGRICULTURE (91) — 0.78 OF 9

55 TILT TOWARD BEING THOSE WHERE FOOD PRODUCTION IS BY SIMPLE AGRICULTURE, RATHER THAN BY INTENSIVE AGRICULTURE (101) — 0.70 OF 20

7 6
2 14
XSQ= 3.96
PHI= 0.370
EP = 0.0405

73 DRIFT TCWARD BEING THCSE WHERE WEAVING IS PRESENT (118) — 0.75 OF 12

73 DRIFT TOWARD BEING THOSE WHERE WEAVING IS ABSENT (130) — 0.62 OF 37

9 14
3 23
XSQ= 3.64
PHI= 0.273
XP = 0.0563

80 LEAN LESS TOWARD BEING THCSE WHERE NO CITY OR TCWN IS PRESENT (185) — 0.62 OF 13

80 IN ALL CASES ARE THOSE WHERE NO CITY OR TOWN IS PRESENT (185) — 1.00 OF 32

5 0
8 32
XSQ= 10.23
PHI= 0.477
XP = 0.0014

```
 85  TILT TOWARD BEING THOSE        0.57 OF  14     85  TILT TOWARD BEING THOSE        0.81 OF  36           8     7
     WHERE THE LEVEL OF POLITICAL INTEGRATION           WHERE THE LEVEL OF POLITICAL INTEGRATION              6    29
     IS THE LARGE STATE, OR                             IS THE MINIMAL STATE,                          XSQ=      5.14
     THE LITTLE STATE  (70) GPM                         THE AUTONOMOUS COMMUNITY, OR                   PHI=     0.321
                                                        THE FAMILY  (234) GPM                          XP =    0.0233

 94  TILT LESS TOWARD BEING THOSE   0.79 OF  14     94  IN ALL CASES ARE THOSE         1.00 OF  38           3     0
     WHERE THE HIERARCHY                                WHERE THE HIERARCHY                                  11    38
     OF NATIONAL JURISDICTION HAS                       OF NATIONAL JURISDICTION HAS                   XSQ=      5.15
     TWO, ONE, OR NO LEVELS  (296) GES,EA               TWO, ONE, OR NO LEVELS  (296) GES,EA           PHI=     0.315
                                                                                                       XP =    0.0233

 95  DRIFT LESS TOWARD BEING THOSE  0.57 OF  14     95  DRIFT MORE TOWARD BEING THOSE  0.84 OF  38           6     6
     WHERE THE HIERARCHY                                WHERE THE HIERARCHY                                   8    32
     OF NATIONAL JURISDICTION HAS                       OF NATIONAL JURISDICTION HAS                   XSQ=      2.84
     ONE OR NO LEVELS  (254) GES,EA                     ONE OR NO LEVELS  (254) GES,EA                 PHI=     0.234
                                                                                                       XP =    0.0922

107  TILT TOWARD BEING THOSE        0.50 OF  12    107  TILT TOWARD BEING THOSE        0.90 OF  20           6     2
     WHERE CLASS STRATIFICATION, IF PRESENT,            WHERE CLASS STRATIFICATION, IF PRESENT,               6    18
     IS BASED ON                                        IS BASED ON SOMETHING OTHER THAN               XSQ=      4.44
     OCCUPATIONAL STATUS  (43)                          OCCUPATIONAL STATUS  (160)                     PHI=     0.373
                                                                                                       EP =    0.0302

108  DRIFT TOWARD BEING THOSE       0.83 OF  12    108  DRIFT TOWARD BEING THOSE       0.50 OF  20           2    10
     WHERE CLASS STRATIFICATION, IF PRESENT,            WHERE CLASS STRATIFICATION, IF PRESENT,              10    10
     IS BASED ON SOMETHING OTHER THAN                   IS BASED ON                                    XSQ=      2.28
     A HEREDITARY ARISTOCRACY  (129)                    A HEREDITARY ARISTOCRACY  (74)                 PHI=    -0.267
                                                                                                       EP =    0.0753

110  DRIFT TOWARD BEING THOSE       0.67 OF  15    110  DRIFT TOWARD BEING THOSE       0.65 OF  37          10    13
     WHERE SLAVERY IS PRESENT  (163)                    WHERE SLAVERY IS ABSENT  (218)                        5    24
                                                                                                       XSQ=      3.12
                                                                                                       PHI=     0.245
                                                                                                       XP =    0.0774

116  LEAN TOWARD BEING THOSE        0.73 OF  15    116  LEAN TOWARD BEING THOSE        0.77 OF  39          11     9
     WHERE OCCUPATIONAL SPECIALIZATION IS               WHERE OCCUPATIONAL SPECIALIZATION IS                  4    30
     FULL-TIME, WHETHER OR NOT FOR                      PART-TIME ONLY  (34) JMH                       XSQ=      9.68
     SURPLUS PRODUCTION  (20) JMH                                                                      PHI=     0.423
                                                                                                       XP =    0.0019

128  IN ALL CASES ARE THOSE         1.00 OF   3    128  TILT TOWARD BEING THOSE        0.79 OF  14           3     3
     WHERE, IF SUBSISTENCE IS PRIMARILY BY              WHERE, IF SUBSISTENCE IS PRIMARILY BY                 0    11
     AGRICULTURE, THE WORK IS                           AGRICULTURE, THE WORK IS                       XSQ=      3.68
     MAINLY DONE BY MALES  (40)                         MAINLY DONE BY FEMALES  (37)                   PHI=     0.465
                                                                                                       EP =    0.0294

132  IN ALL CASES ARE THOSE         1.00 OF  15    132  LEAN LESS TOWARD BEING THOSE   0.56 OF  39          15    22
     WHERE ECONOMIC EXCHANGE                            WHERE ECONOMIC EXCHANGE                               0    17
     INVOLVES THE USE OF MONEY  (37) JMH                INVOLVES THE USE OF MONEY  (37) JMH            XSQ=      7.63
                                                                                                       PHI=     0.376
                                                                                                       XP =    0.0057
```

141	DRIFT TOWARD BEING THCSE 0.73 OF 15 WHERE THE LEVEL CF SOCIAL SANCTION IS PUBLIC CORPOREAL SANCTICN, RATHER THAN PUBLIC PRCPERTY SANCTICN CR PRIVATE SETTLEMENT (28) JMH	141	DRIFT TOWARD BEING THOSE 0.56 OF 39 WHERE THE LEVEL OF SOCIAL SANCTICN IS PUBLIC PROPERTY SANCTICN OR PRIVATE SETTLEMENT, RATHER THAN PUBLIC CORPOREAL SANCTICN (26) JMH	11 17 4 22 XSQ= 2.74 PHI= 0.225 XP = 0.0979
286	IN ALL CASES ARE THOSE 1.00 OF 2 WHERE THE NUMBER OF FCCC TABOOS DURING PREGNANCY IS LCW CR ABSENT (14) BCA	286	TILT TOWARD BEING THOSE 0.90 OF 10 WHERE THE NUMBER OF FCCD TABCOS DURING PREGNANCY IS HIGH (20) BCA	0 9 2 1 XSQ= 3.20 PHI= -0.516 EP = 0.0455
299	IN ALL CASES ARE THCSE 1.00 OF 7 WHERE THE PCST-PARTUM SEX TABCO LASTS CNE YEAR CR LESS (89)	299	DRIFT LESS TOWARD BEING THCSE 0.61 CF 23 WHERE THE POST-PARTUM SEX TABOO LASTS ONE YEAR OR LESS (89)	0 9 7 14 XSQ= 2.27 PHI= -0.275 EP = 0.0710
304	IN ALL CASES ARE THOSE 1.00 OF 3 WHERE THE EARLY ANAL SATISFACTION POTENTIAL IS HIGH (19) W-C	304	TILT TOWARD BEING THOSE 0.78 OF 9 WHERE THE EARLY ANAL SATISFACTICN POTENTIAL IS LOW (22) W-C	3 2 0 7 XSQ= 2.86 PHI= 0.488 EP = 0.0455
334	IN ALL CASES ARE THCSE 1.00 OF 5 WHERE THE INDULGENCE CF THE CHILC IS LCW (38) B-B-C	334	TILT TOWARD BEING THOSE 0.63 CF 24 WHERE THE INDULGENCE OF THE CHILD IS HIGH (4C) B-B-C	0 15 5 9 XSQ= 4.21 PHI= -0.381 EP = 0.0169
346	IN ALL CASES ARE THOSE 1.00 OF 5 WHERE THE CHILD'S INFERREC ANXIETY OVER PERFORMANCE CF SELF-RELIANT BEHAVIOR IS HIGH (37) B-B-C	346	DRIFT TOWARD BEING THOSE 0.52 OF 23 WHERE THE CHILD'S INFERRED ANXIETY OVER PERFORMANCE OF SELF-RELIANT BEHAVIOR IS LOW (39) B-B-C	5 11 0 12 XSQ= 2.68 PHI= 0.310 EP = 0.0525
347	IN ALL CASES ARE THCSE 1.00 OF 5 WHERE THE CHILD'S INFERREC CONFLICT REGARDING SELF-RELIANT BEHAVIOR IS HIGH (37) B-B-C	347	TILT TOWARD BEING THOSE 0.61 CF 23 WHERE THE CHILD'S INFERRED CONFLICT REGARDING SELF-RELIANT BEHAVIOR IS LOW (39) B-B-C	5 9 0 14 XSQ= 3.90 PHI= 0.373 EP = 0.0407
370	IN ALL CASES ARE THOSE 1.00 OF 10 WHERE THE SEGREGATION CF ACOLESCENT BOYS IS ABSENT (148)	37C	DRIFT LESS TOWARD BEING THCSE 0.63 OF 32 WHERE THE SEGREGATION OF ADOLESCENT BOYS IS ABSENT (148)	0 12 10 20 XSQ= 3.57 PHI= -0.292 XP = 0.0587
424	LEAN TOWARD BEING THCSE 0.73 OF 15 WHERE RELIGIOUS SPECIALISTS ARE FULL-TIME, RATHER THAN PART-TIME (21) JMH	424	LEAN TOWARD BEING THOSE 0.74 CF 39 WHERE RELIGIOUS SPECIALISTS ARE PART-TIME, RATHER THAN FULL-TIME (33) JMH	11 10 4 29 XSQ= 8.46 PHI= 0.396 XP = 0.0036

427	IN ALL CASES ARE THOSE WHERE A HIGH GOD, IF PRESENT, IS ACTIVE, RATHER THAN INACTIVE (87) GES,EA	1.00 OF 6	427	TILT TOWARD BEING THOSE WHERE A HIGH GOD, IF PRESENT, IS INACTIVE, RATHER THAN ACTIVE (69) GES,EA	0.63 OF 19	6 7 0 12 XSQ= 4.98 PHI= 0.446 EP = 0.0149
468	DRIFT TOWARD BEING THOSE WHERE CONTACT WITH OTHER CULTURES IS FREQUENT, RATHER THAN REGULAR OR IRREGULAR (17) JMH	0.53 OF 15	468	DRIFT TOWARD BEING THOSE WHERE CONTACT WITH OTHER CULTURES IS REGULAR OR IRREGULAR, RATHER THAN FREQUENT (37) JMH	0.77 OF 39	8 9 7 30 XSQ= 3.30 PHI= 0.247 XP = 0.0692
470	TEND TO BE THOSE WHERE INNOVATIONS ARE GENERALLY ACCEPTED (21) JMH	0.80 OF 15	470	TEND TO BE THOSE WHERE INNOVATIONS ARE ACCEPTED ONLY SELECTIVELY (33) JMH	0.77 OF 39	12 9 3 30 XSQ= 12.47 PHI= 0.481 XP = 0.0004

78 CULTURES
WHERE THE WRITING SYSTEM IS
ALPHABETIC-OR-PHONETIC, OR MNEMONIC,
RATHER THAN BEING ABSENT (36) JMH

78 CULTURES
WHERE A WRITING SYSTEM IS
ABSENT, RATHER THAN BEING PRESENT IN
EITHER ALPHABETIC-OR-PHONETIC FORM OR
MNEMONIC FORM (18) JMH

BACKGROUND ON PAGE 80

PREDICATE ONLY

36 IN LEFT COLUMN

ANDAMANESE	ARANDA	ARAUCANIANS	AZANDE	AZTEC	BEMBA	BULGARIANS	BURMESE	CAMBODIANS	CHAGGA
CREEK	CUNA	CARD	IBAN	JIVARO	KASKA	KHASI	KOREANS	KORYAK	KURTATCHI
LOLO	MANDAN	MARSHALLESE	NAMA	NAVAHO	OJIBWA	RWALA	SAMOANS	SAMOYED	TIV
TODA	TUPINAMBA	VIETNAMESE	WOLEAIANS	YAKUT	YUROK				

18 IN RIGHT COLUMN

BURUSHO	CAYAPA	CHUKCHEE	COPR ESKIMO	CROW	GILYAK	KAREN	MBUNDU	MIAO	NUER
PUKAPUKA	SIRIONO	TALLENSI	TEHUELCHE	THONGA	TIKOPIA	TIMBIRA	TROBRIAND		

346 EXCLUDED BECAUSE UNASCERTAINED

79 CULTURES
WHERE A CITY IS PRESENT (23)

79 CULTURES
WHERE NO CITY IS PRESENT (201)

BACKGROUND ON PAGE 81

BOTH SUBJECT AND PREDICATE

23 IN LEFT COLUMN

AMERICANS	AZTEC	BRAZILIANS	BULGARIANS	CAMBODIANS	CZECHS	DUTCH	EGYPTIANS	IRISH	JAPANESE
JAVANESE	KERALA	KOREANS	MIN CHINESE	OKINAWANS	ROMANS	SERBS	SINHALESE	SYRIANS	THAI
VIETNAMESE	WALLOONS	YORUBA							

201 IN RIGHT COLUMN

ABOR	AKHA	ALACALUF	ALBANIANS	ALORESE	AMBA	ANDAMANESE	APINAYE	ARANDA	ARAUCANIANS
ASHANTI	ATAYAL	ATSUGEWI	AWEIKOMA	AYMARA	AZANDE	BACAIRI	BAMBARA	BARABRA	BASSERI
BAYA	BEMBA	BHIL	BHUIYA	BIRIFOR	BLACK CARIB	BOTOCUDO	BUNLAP	BURUSHO	CAMAYURA
CARIB	CAYAPA	CHAGGA	CHENCHU	CHEROKEE	CHIBCHA	CHOCO	CHOROTI	CHUKCHEE	COCHITI
COORG	COPR ESKIMO	CREE	CREEK	CUNA	DARD	DELAWARE	DIERI	DOGON	DOROBO
ENGA	EYAK	FANG	FON	GANDA	GARO	GILYAK	GOAJIRO	GOND	GUAHIBO
HANO	HANUNOO	HAVASUPAI	HAZARA	HUICHOL	HUTSUL	IFUGAO	ILA	INCA	IRAQW
JEMEZ	KABYLE	KACHIN	KAPAUKU	KARIERA	KASKA	KATAB	KAZAK	KERAKI	KHALKA
KHASI	KIKUYU	KISSI	KORYAK	KPE	KUBA	KUNG	KURTATCHI	LAMET	LANGO
LAPPS	LAU	LEPCHA	LESU	LOLO	LOZI	LUO	MACASSARESE	MAM	MAMBILA
MAMVU	MANUS	MARGI	MARICOPA	MARQUESANS	MASAI	MATACO	MAYA	MBUNDU	MBUTI
MENDE	MERINA	MIAMI	MINCHIA	MISKITO	MNONG GAR	MOSSI	MOTILON	MUNDURUCU	MURINBATA
MURNGIN	MZAB	NABESNA	NAMA	NAMBICUARA	NATCHEZ	NAVAHO	NDEMBU	NOMLAKI	NUPE
NURI	NYAKYUSA	NYORO	OJIBWA	OMAHA	ONA	PAIWAN	PATHAN	PAWNEE	PONAPEANS
PUKAPUKA	PURUM	RIFFIANS	RWALA	SAGADA	SAMOANS	SAMOYED	SANPOIL	SEMANG	SHILLUK
SIRIONO	SIWANS	SOMALI	SONGHAI	SOTHO	SUBANUN	TALLENSI	TANALA	TAOS	TAPIRAPE
TAREUMIUT	TEHUELCHE	TENDA	TENINO	THONGA	TIGRINYA	TIKOPIA	TIMBIRA	TIV	TIWI
TODA	TOTONAC	TRISTAN	TROBRIAND	TRUKESE	TRUMAI	TUBATULABAL	TUCUNA	TUPINAMBA	TWANA
ULAWANS	VEDDA	VENDA	WAICA	WARRAU	WASHO	WIKMUNKAN	WOGEO	WOLEAIANS	WOLOF
YABARANA	YAGUA	YAHGAN	YAKO	YAKUT	YAO	YOMBE	YUKAGHIR	YUKI	YUROK
ZUNI									

176 EXCLUDED BECAUSE UNASCERTAINED

3 DRIFT MORE TOWARD BEING THOSE 0.96 OF 23
LOCATED OUTSIDE OF
AFRICA (320)

3 DRIFT LESS TOWARD BEING THOSE 0.77 OF 201
LOCATED OUTSIDE OF
AFRICA (320)

1	46
22	155
XSQ=	3.23
PHI=	-0.120
XP =	0.0722

4	TEND LESS TO BE THCSE LOCATED OUTSIDE OF THE CIRCUM-MEDITERRANEAN (355)	0.52 OF 23	4	TEND MORE TO BE THOSE LOCATED OUTSIDE OF THE CIRCUM-MEDITERRANEAN (355)	0.93 OF 201	11 15 12 186 XSQ= 28.96 PHI= 0.360 XP = 0.0000
5	TILT LESS TOWARC BEING THCSE LOCATED OUTSIDE OF EAST EURASIA (330)	0.61 OF 23	5	TILT MORE TOWARD BEING THOSE LOCATED OUTSIDE OF EAST EURASIA (330)	0.82 OF 201	9 36 14 165 XSQ= 4.54 PHI= 0.142 XP = 0.0331
9	IN ALL CASES ARE THCSE LOCATED OUTSIDE OF SOUTH AMERICA (335)	1.00 OF 23	9	TILT LESS TOWARD BEING THOSE LOCATED OUTSIDE OF SOUTH AMERICA (335)	0.81 OF 201	0 38 23 163 XSQ= 3.98 PHI= -0.133 XP = 0.0460
15	DRIFT TCWARD BEING THCSE WHERE THE LATITUDE IS TWENTY DEGREES CR GREATER (183)	0.65 OF 23	15	DRIFT TOWARD BEING THOSE WHERE THE LATITUDE IS LESS THAN TWENTY DEGREES (217)	0.56 OF 201	15 89 8 112 XSQ= 2.84 PHI= 0.113 XP = 0.0917
33	IN ALL CASES ARE THOSE WHERE THE NATURAL ENVIRONMENT IS OTHER THAN 'VERY HARSH,' I.E., DESERT, DESERT GRASSES AND SHRUBS, TUNCRA, OR HIGH PLATEAU STEPPE (341) FWM	1.00 OF 23	33	TILT LESS TOWARD BEING THOSE WHERE THE NATURAL ENVIRONMENT IS OTHER THAN 'VERY HARSH,' I.E., DESERT, DESERT GRASSES AND SHRUBS, TUNDRA, OR HIGH PLATEAU STEPPE (341) FWM	0.80 OF 201	0 40 23 161 XSQ= 4.30 PHI= -0.139 XP = 0.0382
36	IN ALL CASES ARE THCSE WHERE THE NATURAL ENVIRONMENT IS OTHER THAN 'VERY HARSH,' CR SUB-TROPICAL BUSH, OR TEMPERATE GRASSLANC (292) FWM	1.00 OF 23	36	LEAN LESS TOWARD BEING THOSE WHERE THE NATURAL ENVIRONMENT IS OTHER THAN 'VERY HARSH,' OR SUB-TROPICAL BUSH, OR TEMPERATE GRASSLAND (292) FWM	0.71 OF 201	0 59 23 142 XSQ= 7.71 PHI= -0.186 XP = 0.0055
44	IN ALL CASES ARE THCSE WHERE SETTLEMENTS ARE FIXEC (222)	1.00 OF 23	44	TEND LESS TO BE THOSE WHERE SETTLEMENTS ARE FIXED (222)	0.63 OF 200	23 127 0 73 XSQ= 10.88 PHI= 0.221 XP = 0.0010
45	DRIFT MORE TOWARD BEING THOSE WHERE SETTLEMENTS, IF FIXEC, ARE COMPACT, RATHER THAN NON-COMPACT (149)	0.91 OF 23	45	DRIFT LESS TOWARD BEING THCSE WHERE SETTLEMENTS, IF FIXED, ARE COMPACT, RATHER THAN NON-COMPACT (149)	0.69 OF 127	21 88 2 39 XSQ= 3.71 PHI= 0.157 XP = 0.0542
51	IN ALL CASES ARE THCSE WHERE SUBSISTENCE IS PRIMARILY BY FCCD PRCDUCTICN -- I. E., AGRICULTURE OR HUSBANDRY -- RATHER THAN BY GATHERING (253)	1.00 OF 23	51	TEND LESS TO BE THOSE WHERE SUBSISTENCE IS PRIMARILY BY FOOD PRODUCTION -- I. E., AGRICULTURE OR HUSBANDRY -- RATHER THAN BY GATHERING (253)	0.60 OF 201	23 120 0 81 XSQ= 12.83 PHI= 0.239 XP = 0.0003

53	TEND TO BE THOSE WHERE FOOD PRODUCTION IS BY INTENSIVE AGRICULTURE, RATHER THAN BY SIMPLE AGRICULTURE OR INCIPIENT FOOD PRODUCTION (91)	0.96 OF 23	53	TEND TO BE THOSE WHERE FOOD PRODUCTION IS BY SIMPLE AGRICULTURE OR INCIPIENT FOOD PRODUCTION, RATHER THAN BY INTENSIVE AGRICULTURE (147)	0.65 OF 137	22 48 1 89 XSQ= 26.99 PHI= 0.411 XP = 0.0000
54	IN ALL CASES ARE THOSE WHERE FOOD PRODUCTION IS BY INTENSIVE OR SIMPLE AGRICULTURE, RATHER THAN BY INCIPIENT FOOD PRODUCTION (192)	1.00 OF 23	54	TILT LESS TOWARD BEING THOSE WHERE FOOD PRODUCTION IS BY INTENSIVE OR SIMPLE AGRICULTURE, RATHER THAN BY INCIPIENT FOOD PRODUCTION (192)	0.81 OF 137	23 111 0 26 XSQ= 3.91 PHI= 0.156 XP = 0.0480
55	TEND TO BE THOSE WHERE FOOD PRODUCTION IS BY INTENSIVE AGRICULTURE, RATHER THAN BY SIMPLE AGRICULTURE (91)	0.96 OF 23	55	TEND TO BE THOSE WHERE FOOD PRODUCTION IS BY SIMPLE AGRICULTURE, RATHER THAN BY INTENSIVE AGRICULTURE (101)	0.57 OF 111	22 48 1 63 XSQ= 18.93 PHI= 0.376 XP = 0.0000
62	LEAN MORE TOWARD BEING THOSE WHERE HUSBANDRY OF SOME KIND IS PRESENT (228)	0.96 OF 23	62	LEAN LESS TOWARD BEING THOSE WHERE HUSBANDRY OF SOME KIND IS PRESENT (228)	0.66 OF 201	22 132 1 69 XSQ= 7.30 PHI= 0.180 XP = 0.0069
63	LEAN MORE TOWARD BEING THOSE WHERE HUSBANDRY, IF PRESENT, IS PRINCIPALLY IN THE FORM OF BOVINE, EQUINE, CAMEL-LIKE, OR DEER-LIKE ANIMALS, RATHER THAN PIGS, SHEEP, OR GOATS (152)	0.95 OF 22	63	LEAN LESS TOWARD BEING THOSE WHERE HUSBANDRY, IF PRESENT, IS PRINCIPALLY IN THE FORM OF BOVINE, EQUINE, CAMEL-LIKE, OR DEER-LIKE ANIMALS, RATHER THAN PIGS, SHEEP, OR GOATS (152)	0.64 OF 132	21 84 1 48 XSQ= 7.39 PHI= 0.219 XP = 0.0065
71	IN ALL CASES ARE THOSE WHERE METAL WORKING IS PRESENT (98)	1.00 OF 13	71	TEND TO BE THOSE WHERE METAL WORKING IS ABSENT (153)	0.59 OF 159	13 65 0 94 XSQ= 14.65 PHI= 0.292 XP = 0.0001
73	IN ALL CASES ARE THOSE WHERE WEAVING IS PRESENT (118)	1.00 OF 14	73	TEND TO BE THOSE WHERE WEAVING IS ABSENT (130)	0.55 OF 155	14 70 0 85 XSQ= 13.33 PHI= 0.281 XP = 0.0003
74	IN ALL CASES ARE THOSE WHERE POTTERY IS PRESENT (145)	1.00 OF 12	74	LEAN LESS TOWARD BEING THOSE WHERE POTTERY IS PRESENT (145)	0.57 OF 154	12 88 0 66 XSQ= 6.84 PHI= 0.203 XP = 0.0089
77	IN ALL CASES ARE THOSE WHERE THE WRITING SYSTEM IS ALPHABETIC-OR-PHONETIC, RATHER THAN BEING MNEMONIC OR ABSENT (15) JMH	1.00 OF 5	77	LEAN TOWARD BEING THOSE WHERE THE WRITING SYSTEM IS MNEMONIC OR ABSENT, RATHER THAN BEING ALPHABETIC-OR-PHONETIC (39) JMH	0.80 OF 40	5 8 0 32 XSQ= 10.23 PHI= 0.477 XP = 0.0014

No.		No.		
84	IN ALL CASES ARE THOSE 1.00 OF 18 WHERE THE LEVEL OF POLITICAL INTEGRATION IS THE LARGE STATE (42) GPM	84	TEND TO BE THOSE 0.91 OF 158 WHERE THE LEVEL OF POLITICAL INTEGRATION IS THE LITTLE STATE, THE MINIMAL STATE, THE AUTONOMOUS COMMUNITY, OR THE FAMILY (262) GPM	18 15 0 143 XSQ= 81.05 PHI= 0.679 XP = 0.
88	LEAN TOWARD BEING THOSE 0.81 OF 16 WHERE, IF A HEADMANSHIP IS PRESENT, SUCCESSION IS NON-HEREDITARY (106)	88	LEAN TOWARD BEING THOSE 0.64 OF 138 WHERE, IF A HEADMANSHIP IS PRESENT, SUCCESSION IS HEREDITARY (165)	13 49 3 89 XSQ= 10.64 PHI= 0.263 XP = 0.0011
91	IN ALL CASES ARE THOSE 1.00 OF 4 WHERE SOCIETAL COMPLEXITY IS HIGH (18) F-W	91	TILT TOWARD BEING THOSE 0.62 OF 29 WHERE SOCIETAL COMPLEXITY IS LOW (22) F-W	4 11 0 18 XSQ= 3.25 PHI= 0.314 EP = 0.0334
94	TEND TO BE THOSE 0.73 OF 22 WHERE THE HIERARCHY OF NATIONAL JURISDICTION HAS FOUR OR THREE LEVELS (34) GES,EA	94	TEND TO BE THOSE 0.94 OF 199 WHERE THE HIERARCHY OF NATIONAL JURISDICTION HAS TWO, ONE, OR NO LEVELS (296) GES,EA	16 12 6 187 XSQ= 73.73 PHI= 0.578 XP = 0.
95	IN ALL CASES ARE THOSE 1.00 OF 22 WHERE THE HIERARCHY OF NATIONAL JURISDICTION HAS FOUR, THREE, OR TWO LEVELS (76) GES,EA	95	TEND TO BE THOSE 0.81 OF 199 WHERE THE HIERARCHY OF NATIONAL JURISDICTION HAS ONE OR NO LEVELS (254) GES,EA	22 38 0 161 XSQ= 61.53 PHI= 0.528 XP = 0.
102	IN ALL CASES ARE THOSE 1.00 OF 22 WHERE CLASS STRATIFICATION IS PRESENT (203)	102	TEND LESS TO BE THOSE 0.51 OF 197 WHERE CLASS STRATIFICATION IS PRESENT (203)	22 101 0 96 XSQ= 17.16 PHI= 0.280 XP = 0.0000
106	IN ALL CASES ARE THOSE 1.00 OF 22 WHERE CLASS STRATIFICATION, IF PRESENT, IS BASED ON SOMETHING OTHER THAN WEALTH (126)	106	TEND TO BE THOSE 0.51 OF 101 WHERE CLASS STRATIFICATION, IF PRESENT, IS BASED ON WEALTH (77)	0 52 22 49 XSQ= 17.57 PHI= -0.378 XP = 0.0000
107	TEND TO BE THOSE 0.91 OF 22 WHERE CLASS STRATIFICATION, IF PRESENT, IS BASED ON OCCUPATIONAL STATUS (43)	107	TEND TO BE THOSE 0.86 OF 101 WHERE CLASS STRATIFICATION, IF PRESENT, IS BASED ON SOMETHING OTHER THAN OCCUPATIONAL STATUS (160)	20 14 2 87 XSQ= 49.83 PHI= 0.637 XP = 0.
108	TILT MORE TOWARD BEING THOSE 0.95 OF 22 WHERE CLASS STRATIFICATION, IF PRESENT, IS BASED ON SOMETHING OTHER THAN A HEREDITARY ARISTOCRACY (129)	108	TILT LESS TOWARD BEING THOSE 0.66 OF 101 WHERE CLASS STRATIFICATION, IF PRESENT, IS BASED ON SOMETHING OTHER THAN A HEREDITARY ARISTOCRACY. (129)	1 34 21 67 XSQ= 6.16 PHI= -0.224 XP = 0.0131

116	IN ALL CASES ARE THOSE 1.00 OF 5 WHERE OCCUPATIONAL SPECIALIZATION IS FULL-TIME, WHETHER OR NOT FOR SURPLUS PRODUCTION (20) JMH	116	TILT TOWARD BEING THOSE 0.67 OF 40 WHERE OCCUPATIONAL SPECIALIZATION IS PART-TIME ONLY (34) JMH	5 13 0 27 XSQ= 5.86 PHI= 0.361 XP = 0.0155
152	IN ALL CASES ARE THOSE 1.00 OF 3 WHERE THE DIFFERENTIATION OF THE JURIDICAL AGENCY FROM THE MEDICAL AGENCY IS HIGH (10) MJ	152	DRIFT TOWARD BEING THOSE 0.67 OF 12 WHERE THE DIFFERENTIATION OF THE JURIDICAL AGENCY FROM THE MEDICAL AGENCY IS LOW (10) MJ	3 4 0 8 XSQ= 2.03 PHI= 0.367 EP = 0.0769
163	IN ALL CASES ARE THOSE 1.00 OF 3 WHERE THE EMPHASIS ON INDIVIDUAL VOLITION AS THE CAUSE OF CRIME IS HIGH (7) MJ	163	TILT TOWARD BEING THOSE 0.80 OF 10 WHERE THE EMPHASIS ON INDIVIDUAL VOLITION AS THE CAUSE OF CRIME IS LOW (10) MJ	3 2 0 8 XSQ= 3.32 PHI= 0.505 EP = 0.0350
164	IN ALL CASES ARE THOSE 1.00 OF 3 WHERE THE EMPHASIS ON INDIVIDUAL VOLITION AS THE CAUSE OR SOURCE OF ILLNESS IS LOW (9) MJ	164	DRIFT TOWARD BEING THOSE 0.67 OF 12 WHERE THE EMPHASIS ON INDIVIDUAL VOLITION AS THE CAUSE OR SOURCE OF ILLNESS IS HIGH (9) MJ	0 8 3 4 XSQ= 2.03 PHI= -0.367 EP = 0.0769
175	TILT MORE TOWARD BEING THOSE 0.91 OF 23 WHERE THE COMMUNITY IS 'KIN-HETEROGENEOUS,' I. E. OTHER THAN A CLAN COMMUNITY OR A DEME (260)	175	TILT LESS TOWARD BEING THOSE 0.68 OF 197 WHERE THE COMMUNITY IS 'KIN-HETEROGENEOUS,' I. E. OTHER THAN A CLAN COMMUNITY OR A DEME (260)	2 64 21 133 XSQ= 4.48 PHI= -0.143 XP = 0.0344
176	TILT MORE TOWARD BEING THOSE 0.83 OF 23 WHERE THE COMMUNITY IS OTHER THAN A CLAN-COMMUNITY OR A COMMUNITY STRUCTURED OR SEGMENTED ON A CLAN BASIS (213)	176	TILT LESS TOWARD BEING THOSE 0.54 OF 197 WHERE THE COMMUNITY IS OTHER THAN A CLAN-COMMUNITY OR A COMMUNITY STRUCTURED OR SEGMENTED ON A CLAN BASIS (213)	4 91 19 106 XSQ= 5.84 PHI= -0.163 XP = 0.0157
177	DRIFT MORE TOWARD BEING THOSE 0.96 OF 23 WHERE THE COMMUNITY IS OTHER THAN A SINGLE CLAN-COMMUNITY AND EXOGAMOUS (305)	177	DRIFT LESS TOWARD BEING THOSE 0.78 OF 197 WHERE THE COMMUNITY IS OTHER THAN A SINGLE CLAN-COMMUNITY AND EXOGAMOUS (305)	1 43 22 154 XSQ= 2.92 PHI= -0.115 XP = 0.0877
180	TILT MORE TOWARD BEING THOSE 0.91 OF 23 WHERE THE COMMUNITY IS COMMONLY NON-EXOGAMOUS, RATHER THAN EXOGAMOUS (258)	180	TILT LESS TOWARD BEING THOSE 0.63 OF 197 WHERE THE COMMUNITY IS COMMONLY NON-EXOGAMOUS, RATHER THAN EXOGAMOUS (258)	2 72 21 125 XSQ= 5.96 PHI= -0.165 XP = 0.0146
182	TEND TO BE THOSE 0.74 OF 23 WHERE THE COMMUNITY IS STRUCTURED ON A NON-CLAN BASIS AND AGAMOUS (126)	182	TEND TO BE THOSE 0.70 OF 197 OTHER THAN WHERE THE COMMUNITY IS STRUCTURED ON A NON-CLAN BASIS AND AGAMOUS (256)	17 60 6 137 XSQ= 15.24 PHI= 0.263 XP = 0.0001

188	LEAN TOWARD BEING THOSE WHERE THE KIN GROUP IS EXCLUSIVELY COGNATIC (148)	0.61 OF 23	188	LEAN TOWARD BEING THOSE WHERE THE KIN GROUP IS OTHER THAN EXCLUSIVELY COGNATIC (252)	0.69 OF 201	14 62 9 139 XSQ= 7.01 PHI= 0.177 XP = 0.0081
192	LEAN TOWARD BEING THOSE WHERE THE ONLY KIN GROUP PRESENT IS A KINDRED OR ELSE BILATERAL DESCENT IS INFERRED (111)	0.52 OF 23	192	LEAN TOWARD BEING THOSE OTHER THAN WHERE THE ONLY KIN GROUP PRESENT IS A KINDRED OR ELSE BILATERAL DESCENT IS INFERRED (289)	0.77 OF 201	12 47 11 154 XSQ= 7.40 PHI= 0.182 XP = 0.0065
196	IN ALL CASES ARE THOSE WHERE INDIVIDUAL RIGHTS IN REAL PROPERTY, AND RULES FOR INHERITANCE, ARE PRESENT (194)	1.00 OF 19	196	LEAN LESS TOWARD BEING THOSE WHERE INDIVIDUAL RIGHTS IN REAL PROPERTY, AND RULES FOR INHERITANCE, ARE PRESENT (194)	0.61 OF 148	19 91 0 57 XSQ= 9.46 PHI= 0.238 XP = 0.0021
197	TEND LESS TO BE THOSE WHERE RULES FOR THE INHERITANCE OF REAL PROPERTY, IF PRESENT, FAVOR EITHER THE MALE HEIR OR LINE, OR THE FEMALE HEIR OR LINE (165)	0.58 OF 19	197	TEND MORE TO BE THOSE WHERE RULES FOR THE INHERITANCE OF REAL PROPERTY, IF PRESENT, FAVOR EITHER THE MALE HEIR OR LINE, OR THE FEMALE HEIR OR LINE (165)	0.92 OF 91	11 84 8 7 XSQ= 13.02 PHI= -0.344 XP = 0.0003
234	TEND TO BE THOSE WHERE THE COUSIN TERMINOLOGY IS OF ESKIMO OR HAWAIIAN TYPE, RATHER THAN CROW, OMAHA, OR IROQUOIS TYPE (170)	0.89 OF 18	234	TEND TO BE THOSE WHERE THE COUSIN TERMINOLOGY IS OF CROW, OMAHA, OR IROQUOIS TYPE, RATHER THAN ESKIMO OR HAWAIIAN TYPE (152)	0.55 OF 163	2 90 16 73 XSQ= 10.91 PHI= -0.246 XP = 0.0010
241	LEAN LESS TOWARD BEING THOSE WHERE THE FAMILY, IF EXTENDED, IS LARGE OR SMALL, RATHER THAN STEM (187)	0.56 OF 16	241	LEAN MORE TOWARD BEING THOSE WHERE THE FAMILY, IF EXTENDED, IS LARGE OR SMALL, RATHER THAN STEM (187)	0.89 OF 100	9 89 7 11 XSQ= 8.93 PHI= -0.277 XP = 0.0028
242	TEND TO BE THOSE WHERE MARRIAGE IS MONOGAMOUS, RATHER THAN COMMONLY OR OCCASIONALLY POLYGYNOUS (81)	0.57 OF 23	242	TEND TO BE THOSE WHERE MARRIAGE IS COMMONLY OR OCCASIONALLY POLYGYNOUS, RATHER THAN MONOGAMOUS (314)	0.81 OF 198	10 160 13 38 XSQ= 14.14 PHI= -0.253 XP = 0.0002
263	TEND TO BE THOSE WHERE WIVES ARE OBTAINED BY RELATIVELY EASY MEANS, NAMELY BY TOKEN BRIDE-PRICE, GIFT EXCHANGE, ABSENCE OF ANY CONSIDERATION, OR RECEIPT OF DOWRY (162)	0.78 OF 23	263	TEND TO BE THOSE WHERE WIVES ARE OBTAINED BY RELATIVELY DIFFICULT MEANS, NAMELY BY BRIDE-PRICE, BRIDE-SERVICE, OR EXCHANGING A FEMALE RELATIVE (233)	0.61 OF 200	5 122 18 78 XSQ= 11.42 PHI= -0.226 XP = 0.0007
370	LEAN MORE TOWARD BEING THOSE WHERE THE SEGREGATION OF ADOLESCENT BOYS IS ABSENT (148)	0.95 OF 21	370	LEAN LESS TOWARD BEING THOSE WHERE THE SEGREGATION OF ADOLESCENT BOYS IS ABSENT (148)	0.57 OF 152	1 65 20 87 XSQ= 9.74 PHI= -0.237 XP = 0.0018

390	TILT TOWARD BEING THOSE 0.53 OF 15 WHERE PREMARITAL SEX RELATIONS ARE STRONGLY PUNISHED AND IN FACT RARE (47) JTW,EA	390	TILT TOWARD BEING THOSE 0.78 OF 116 WHERE PREMARITAL SEX RELATIONS ARE WEAKLY PUNISHED AND IN FACT NOT RARE OR PUNISHED ONLY IF PREGNANCY RESULTS, OR FREELY PERMITTED (132) JTW,EA	8 26 7 90 XSQ= 5.10 PHI= 0.197 XP = 0.0240
391	LEAN TOWARD BEING THOSE 0.93 OF 15 WHERE PREMARITAL SEX RELATIONS ARE STRONGLY PUNISHED AND IN FACT RARE, OR WEAKLY PUNISHED AND IN FACT NOT RARE (89) JTW,EA	391	LEAN TOWARD BEING THOSE 0.54 OF 116 WHERE PREMARITAL SEX RELATIONS ARE PUNISHED ONLY IF PREGNANCY RESULTS, OR FREELY PERMITTED (90) JTW,EA	14 53 1 63 XSQ= 10.23 PHI= 0.280 XP = 0.0014
424	IN ALL CASES ARE THOSE 1.00 OF 5 WHERE RELIGIOUS SPECIALISTS ARE FULL-TIME, RATHER THAN PART-TIME (21) JMH	424	TILT TOWARD BEING THOSE 0.65 OF 40 WHERE RELIGIOUS SPECIALISTS ARE PART-TIME, RATHER THAN FULL-TIME (33) JMH	5 14 0 26 XSQ= 5.26 PHI= 0.342 XP = 0.0218
427	TILT MORE TOWARD BEING THOSE 0.92 OF 13 WHERE A HIGH GOD, IF PRESENT, IS ACTIVE, RATHER THAN INACTIVE (87) GES,EA	427	TILT LESS TOWARD BEING THOSE 0.55 OF 94 WHERE A HIGH GOD, IF PRESENT, IS ACTIVE, RATHER THAN INACTIVE (87) GES,EA	12 52 1 42 XSQ= 5.05 PHI= 0.217 XP = 0.0246
428	DRIFT MORE TOWARD BEING THOSE 0.92 OF 12 WHERE A HIGH GOD, IF PRESENT AND ACTIVE, SUPPORTS HUMAN MORALITY, RATHER THAN NOT SUPPORTING IT (61) GES,EA	428	DRIFT LESS TOWARD BEING THOSE 0.58 OF 52 WHERE A HIGH GOD, IF PRESENT AND ACTIVE, SUPPORTS HUMAN MORALITY, RATHER THAN NOT SUPPORTING IT (61) GES,EA	11 30 1 22 XSQ= 3.52 PHI= 0.235 XP = 0.0605
436	IN ALL CASES ARE THOSE 1.00 OF 2 WHERE ACTIVE ANCESTRAL SPIRITS ARE ABSENT (11) GES	436	DRIFT TOWARD BEING THOSE 0.73 OF 26 WHERE ACTIVE ANCESTRAL SPIRITS ARE PRESENT (27) GES	0 19 2 7 XSQ= 1.81 PHI= -0.255 EP = 0.0952
458	IN ALL CASES ARE THOSE 1.00 OF 13 WHERE GAMES, IF PRESENT, INCLUDE GAMES OF STRATEGY (52) R-A-B,EA	458	TEND TO BE THOSE 0.71 OF 114 WHERE GAMES, IF PRESENT, DO NOT INCLUDE GAMES OF STRATEGY (119) R-A-B,EA	13 33 0 81 XSQ= 22.52 PHI= 0.421 XP = 0.0000
459	IN ALL CASES ARE THOSE 1.00 OF 13 WHERE GAMES, IF PRESENT, INCLUDE GAMES OF CHANCE (82) R-A-B,EA	459	TEND TO BE THOSE 0.57 OF 114 WHERE GAMES, IF PRESENT, DO NOT INCLUDE GAMES OF CHANCE (89) R-A-B,EA	13 49 0 65 XSQ= 12.99 PHI= 0.320 XP = 0.0003
468	IN ALL CASES ARE THOSE 1.00 OF 5 WHERE CONTACT WITH OTHER CULTURES IS FREQUENT, RATHER THAN REGULAR OR IRREGULAR (17) JMH	468	LEAN TOWARD BEING THOSE 0.75 OF 40 WHERE CONTACT WITH OTHER CULTURES IS REGULAR OR IRREGULAR, RATHER THAN FREQUENT (37) JMH	5 10 0 30 XSQ= 8.13 PHI= 0.425 XP = 0.0044

80 CULTURES
WHERE A CITY OR TOWN IS PRESENT (39)

80 CULTURES
WHERE NO CITY OR TOWN IS PRESENT (185)

BACKGROUND ON PAGE 81

BOTH SUBJECT AND PREDICATE

39 IN LEFT COLUMN

AMERICANS	ASHANTI	AZTEC	BAMBARA	BRAZILIANS	BULGARIANS	CAMBODIANS	CHIBCHA	CZECHS	DUTCH
EGYPTIANS	FON	GANDA	HUTSUL	INCA	IRISH	JAPANESE	JAVANESE	KERALA	KOREANS
MAYA	MERINA	MIN CHINESE	MOSSI	MZAB	OKINAWANS	RIFFIANS	ROMANS	SERBS	SINHALESE
SONGHAI	SYRIANS	THAI	TIGRINYA	TOTONAC	VIETNAMESE	WALLOONS	YAKO	YORUBA	

185 IN RIGHT COLUMN

ABOR	AKHA	ALACALUF	ALBANIANS	ALORESE	AMBA	ANDAMANESE	APINAYE	ARANDA	ARAUCANIANS
ATAYAL	ATSUGEWI	AWEIKOMA	AYMARA	AZANDE	BACAIRI	BARABRA	BASSERI	BAYA	BEMBA
BHIL	BHUIYA	BIRIFOR	BLACK CARIB	BOTOCUDO	BUNLAP	BURUSHO	CAMAYURA	CARIB	CAYAPA
CHAGGA	CHENCHU	CHEROKEE	CHOCO	CHOROTI	CHUKCHEE	COCHITI	COORG	COPR ESKIMO	CREE
CREEK	CUNA	DARD	DELAWARE	DIERI	DOGON	DOROBO	ENGA	EYAK	FANG
GARO	GILYAK	GOAJIRO	GOND	GUAHIBO	HANO	HANUNOO	HAVASUPAI	HAZARA	HUICHOL
IFUGAO	ILA	IRAQW	JEMEZ	KABYLE	KACHIN	KAPAUKU	KARIERA	KASKA	KATAB
KAZAK	KERAKI	KHALKA	KHASI	KIKUYU	KISSI	KORYAK	KPE	KUBA	KUNG
KURTATCHI	LAMET	LANGO	LAPPS	LAU	LEPCHA	LESU	LOLO	LOZI	LUO
MACASSARESE	MAM	MAMBILA	MAMVU	MANUS	MARGI	MARICOPA	MARQUESANS	MASAI	MATACO
MBUNDU	MBUTI	MENDE	MIAMI	MINCHIA	MISKITO	MNONG GAR	MOTILON	MUNDURUCU	MURINBATA
MURNGIN	NABESNA	NAMA	NAMBICUARA	NATCHEZ	NAVAHO	NDEMBU	NOMLAKI	NUPE	NURI
NYAKYUSA	NYORO	OJIBWA	OMAHA	ONA	PAIWAN	PATHAN	PAWNEE	PONAPEANS	PUKAPUKA
PURUM	RWALA	SAGADA	SAMOANS	SAMOYED	SANPOIL	SEMANG	SHILLUK	SIRIONO	SIWANS
SOMALI	SOTHO	SUBANUN	TALLENSI	TANALA	TAOS	TAPIRAPE	TAREUMIUT	TEHUELCHE	TENDA
TENINO	THONGA	TIKOPIA	TIMBIRA	TIV	TIWI	TODA	TRISTAN	TROBRIAND	TRUKESE
TRUMAI	TUBATULABAL	TUCUNA	TUPINAMBA	TWANA	ULAWANS	VEDDA	VENDA	WAICA	WARRAU
WASHO	WIKMUNKAN	WOGEO	WOLEAIANS	WOLOF	YABARANA	YAGUA	YAHGAN	YAKUT	YAO
YOMBE	YUKAGHIR	YUKI	YUROK	ZUNI					

176 EXCLUDED BECAUSE UNASCERTAINED

---

4 TEND LESS TO BE THOSE LOCATED OUTSIDE OF THE CIRCUM-MEDITERRANEAN (355) 0.59 OF 39

4 TEND MORE TO BE THOSE LOCATED OUTSIDE OF THE CIRCUM-MEDITERRANEAN (355) 0.95 OF 185

16	10
23	175
XSQ=	36.44
PHI=	0.403
XP =	0.

6 TILT MORE TOWARD BEING THOSE LOCATED OUTSIDE OF THE INSULAR PACIFIC (330) 0.97 OF 39

6 TILT LESS TOWARD BEING THOSE LOCATED OUTSIDE OF THE INSULAR PACIFIC (330) 0.82 OF 185

1	33
38	152
XSQ=	4.71
PHI=	-0.145
XP =	0.0300

8	DRIFT MORE TOWARD BEING THOSE 0.95 OF 39 LOCATED OUTSIDE OF NORTH AMERICA (330)	8	DRIFT LESS TOWARD BEING THOSE 0.83 OF 185 LOCATED OUTSIDE OF NORTH AMERICA (330)	2 32 37 153 XSQ= 2.82 PHI= -0.112 XP = 0.0931
33	TILT MORE TOWARD BEING THOSE 0.95 OF 39 WHERE THE NATURAL ENVIRONMENT IS OTHER THAN 'VERY HARSH,' I.E., DESERT, DESERT GRASSES AND SHRUBS, TUNDRA, OR HIGH PLATEAU STEPPE (341) FWM	33	TILT LESS TOWARD BEING THOSE 0.79 OF 185 WHERE THE NATURAL ENVIRONMENT IS OTHER THAN 'VERY HARSH,' I.E., DESERT, DESERT GRASSES AND SHRUBS, TUNDRA, OR HIGH PLATEAU STEPPE (341) FWM	2 38 37 147 XSQ= 4.22 PHI= -0.137 XP = 0.0400
36	LEAN MORE TOWARD BEING THOSE 0.92 OF 39 WHERE THE NATURAL ENVIRONMENT IS OTHER THAN 'VERY HARSH,' OR SUB-TROPICAL BUSH, OR TEMPERATE GRASSLAND (292) FWM	36	LEAN LESS TOWARD BEING THOSE 0.70 OF 185 WHERE THE NATURAL ENVIRONMENT IS OTHER THAN 'VERY HARSH,' OR SUB-TROPICAL BUSH, OR TEMPERATE GRASSLAND (292) FWM	3 56 36 129 XSQ= 7.34 PHI= -0.181 XP = 0.0067
44	IN ALL CASES ARE THOSE 1.00 OF 39 WHERE SETTLEMENTS ARE FIXED (222)	44	TEND LESS TO BE THOSE 0.60 OF 184 WHERE SETTLEMENTS ARE FIXED (222)	39 111 0 73 XSQ= 21.24 PHI= 0.309 XP = 0.0000
45	TILT MORE TOWARD BEING THOSE 0.87 OF 39 WHERE SETTLEMENTS, IF FIXED, ARE COMPACT, RATHER THAN NON-COMPACT (149)	45	TILT LESS TOWARD BEING THOSE 0.68 OF 111 WHERE SETTLEMENTS, IF FIXED, ARE COMPACT, RATHER THAN NON-COMPACT (149)	34 75 5 36 XSQ= 4.64 PHI= 0.176 XP = 0.0311
51	IN ALL CASES ARE THOSE 1.00 OF 39 WHERE SUBSISTENCE IS PRIMARILY BY FOOD PRODUCTION -- I. E., AGRICULTURE OR HUSBANDRY -- RATHER THAN BY GATHERING (253)	51	TEND LESS TO BE THOSE 0.56 OF 185 WHERE SUBSISTENCE IS PRIMARILY BY FOOD PRODUCTION -- I. E., AGRICULTURE OR HUSBANDRY -- RATHER THAN BY GATHERING (253)	39 104 0 81 XSQ= 24.88 PHI= 0.333 XP = 0.0000
53	TEND TO BE THOSE 0.85 OF 39 WHERE FOOD PRODUCTION IS BY INTENSIVE AGRICULTURE, RATHER THAN BY SIMPLE AGRICULTURE OR INCIPIENT FOOD PRODUCTION (91)	53	TEND TO BE THOSE 0.69 OF 121 WHERE FOOD PRODUCTION IS BY SIMPLE AGRICULTURE OR INCIPIENT FOOD PRODUCTION, RATHER THAN BY INTENSIVE AGRICULTURE (147)	33 37 6 84 XSQ= 32.83 PHI= 0.453 XP = 0.
54	IN ALL CASES ARE THOSE 1.00 OF 39 WHERE FOOD PRODUCTION IS BY INTENSIVE OR SIMPLE AGRICULTURE, RATHER THAN BY INCIPIENT FOOD PRODUCTION (192)	54	LEAN LESS TOWARD BEING THOSE 0.79 OF 121 WHERE FOOD PRODUCTION IS BY INTENSIVE OR SIMPLE AGRICULTURE, RATHER THAN BY INCIPIENT FOOD PRODUCTION (192)	39 95 0 26 XSQ= 8.49 PHI= 0.230 XP = 0.0036
55	TEND TO BE THOSE 0.85 OF 39 WHERE FOOD PRODUCTION IS BY INTENSIVE AGRICULTURE, RATHER THAN BY SIMPLE AGRICULTURE (91)	55	TEND TO BE THOSE 0.61 OF 95 WHERE FOOD PRODUCTION IS BY SIMPLE AGRICULTURE, RATHER THAN BY INTENSIVE AGRICULTURE (101)	33 37 6 58 XSQ= 21.32 PHI= 0.399 XP = 0.0000

62	TEND MORE TO BE THCSE WHERE HUSBANDRY CF SOME KIND IS PRESENT (228)	0.92 OF 39	62	TEND LESS TO BE THOSE WHERE HUSBANDRY OF SOME KIND IS PRESENT (228)	0.64 OF 185	36 118 3 67 XSQ= 10.91 PHI= 0.221 XP = 0.0010
63	LEAN MORE TOWARC BEINC THCSE WHERE HUSBANDRY, IF PRESENT, IS PRINCIPALLY IN THE FORM OF BOVINE, EQUINE, CAMEL-LIKE, OR DEER-LIKE ANIMALS, RATHER THAN PIGS, SHEEP, CR GOATS (152)	0.89 OF 36	63	LEAN LESS TOWARD BEING THOSE WHERE HUSBANDRY, IF PRESENT, IS PRINCIPALLY IN THE FORM OF BOVINE, EQUINE, CAMEL-LIKE, CR DEER-LIKE ANIMALS, RATHER THAN PIGS, SHEEP, OR GOATS (152)	0.62 OF 118	32 73 4 45 XSQ= 8.08 PHI= 0.229 XP = 0.0045
71	TEND TO BE THCSE WHERE METAL WORKING IS PRESENT (98)	0.96 OF 24	71	TEND TO BE THOSE WHERE METAL WORKING IS ABSENT (153)	0.63 OF 148	23 55 1 93 XSQ= 26.36 PHI= 0.392 XP = 0.0000
73	TEND TC BE THOSE WHERE WEAVING IS PRESENT (118)	0.96 OF 25	73	TEND TO BE THOSE WHERE WEAVING IS ABSENT (130)	0.58 CF 144	24 60 1 84 XSQ= 23.03 PHI= 0.369 XP = 0.0000
74	IN ALL CASES ARE THOSE WHERE PCTTERY IS PRESENT (145)	1.00 OF 23	74	TEND LESS TO BE THOSE WHERE POTTERY IS PRESENT (145)	0.54 OF 143	23 77 0 66 XSQ= 15.75 PHI= 0.308 XP = 0.0001
77	IN ALL CASES ARE THCSE WHERE THE WRITING SYSTEM IS ALPHABETIC-OR-PHCNETIC, RATHER THAN BEING MNEMCNIC CR ABSENT (15) JMH	1.00 OF 5	77	LEAN TOWARD BEING THOSE WHERE THE WRITING SYSTEM IS MNEMONIC OR ABSENT, RATHER THAN BEING ALPHABETIC-OR-PHONETIC (39) JMH	0.80 CF 40	5 8 0 32 XSQ= 10.23 PHI= 0.477 XP = 0.0014
84	TEND TO BE THCSE WHERE THE LEVEL OF POLITICAL INTEGRATION IS THE LARGE STATE (42) GPM	0.81 OF 31	84	TEND TO BE THOSE WHERE THE LEVEL OF POLITICAL INTEGRATION IS THE LITTLE STATE, THE MINIMAL STATE, THE AUTONOMOUS COMMUNITY, CR THE FAMILY (262) GPM	0.94 OF 145	25 8 6 137 XSQ= 89.76 PHI= 0.714 XP = 0.
85	TEND TC BE THOSE WHERE THE LEVEL CF POLITICAL INTEGRATION IS THE LARGE STATE, CR THE LITTLE STATE (70) GPM	0.87 OF 31	85	TEND TO BE THOSE WHERE THE LEVEL OF POLITICAL INTEGRATION IS THE MINIMAL STATE, THE AUTONOMOUS COMMUNITY, CR THE FAMILY (234) GPM	0.83 CF 145	27 24 4 121 XSQ= 58.38 PHI= 0.576 XP = 0.
86	TEND TC BE THCSE WHERE THE LEVEL OF POLITICAL INTEGRATION IS THE LARGE STATE, THE LITTLE STATE, OR THE MINIMAL STATE (148) GPM	0.97 OF 31	86	TEND TO BE THOSE WHERE THE LEVEL OF POLITICAL INTEGRATION IS THE AUTONOMOUS COMMUNITY, OR THE FAMILY (156) GPM	0.64 OF 145	30 52 1 93 XSQ= 35.67 PHI= 0.450 XP = 0.

No.			No.			
88	LEAN TOWARD BEING THOSE WHERE, IF A HEADMANSHIP IS PRESENT, SUCCESSION IS NON-HEREDITARY (106)	0.68 OF 25	88	LEAN TOWARD BEING THOSE WHERE, IF A HEADMANSHIP IS PRESENT, SUCCESSION IS HEREDITARY (165)	0.65 OF 129	17 45 8 84 XSQ= 8.22 PHI= 0.231 XP = 0.0041
91	IN ALL CASES ARE THOSE WHERE SOCIETAL COMPLEXITY IS HIGH (18) F-W	1.00 OF 6	91	LEAN TOWARD BEING THOSE WHERE SOCIETAL COMPLEXITY IS LOW (22) F-W	0.67 OF 27	6 9 0 18 XSQ= 6.32 PHI= 0.438 EP = 0.0045
94	TEND TO BE THOSE WHERE THE HIERARCHY OF NATIONAL JURISDICTION HAS FOUR OR THREE LEVELS (34) GES,EA	0.57 OF 37	94	TEND TO BE THOSE WHERE THE HIERARCHY OF NATIONAL JURISDICTION HAS TWO, ONE, OR NO LEVELS (296) GES,EA	0.96 OF 184	21 7 16 177 XSQ= 73.35 PHI= 0.576 XP = 0.
95	TEND TO BE THOSE WHERE THE HIERARCHY OF NATIONAL JURISDICTION HAS FOUR, THREE, OR TWO LEVELS (76) GES,EA	0.84 OF 37	95	TEND TO BE THOSE WHERE THE HIERARCHY OF NATIONAL JURISDICTION HAS ONE OR NO LEVELS (254) GES,EA	0.84 OF 184	31 29 6 155 XSQ= 68.67 PHI= 0.557 XP = 0.
96	TEND TO BE THOSE WHERE THE HIERARCHY OF NATIONAL JURISDICTION HAS FOUR, THREE, TWO OR ONE LEVEL (174) GES,EA	0.95 OF 37	96	TEND TO BE THOSE WHERE THE HIERARCHY OF NATIONAL JURISDICTION HAS NO LEVELS (156) GES,EA	0.58 OF 184	35 77 2 107 XSQ= 32.21 PHI= 0.382 XP = 0.
100	IN ALL CASES ARE THOSE WHERE HIERARCHIES ARE MORE COMPLEX THAN THE 'SIMPLEST,' I. E., MORE COMPLEX THAN TWO LOCAL LEVELS WITH NO NATIONAL LEVELS (267) GES,EA	1.00 OF 37	100	LEAN LESS TOWARD BEING THOSE WHERE HIERARCHIES ARE MORE COMPLEX THAN THE 'SIMPLEST,' I. E., MORE COMPLEX THAN TWO LOCAL LEVELS WITH NO NATIONAL LEVELS (267) GES,EA	0.78 OF 184	37 143 0 41 XSQ= 8.70 PHI= 0.198 XP = 0.0032
102	TEND TO BE THOSE WHERE CLASS STRATIFICATION IS PRESENT (203)	0.97 OF 37	102	TEND TO BE THOSE WHERE CLASS STRATIFICATION IS ABSENT (180)	0.52 OF 182	36 87 1 95 XSQ= 28.62 PHI= 0.361 XP = 0.0000
106	TEND TO BE THOSE WHERE CLASS STRATIFICATION, IF PRESENT, IS BASED ON SOMETHING OTHER THAN WEALTH (126)	0.94 OF 36	106	TEND TO BE THOSE WHERE CLASS STRATIFICATION, IF PRESENT, IS BASED ON WEALTH (77)	0.57 OF 87	2 50 34 37 XSQ= 26.04 PHI= -0.460 XP = 0.0000
107	TEND TO BE THOSE WHERE CLASS STRATIFICATION, IF PRESENT, IS BASED ON OCCUPATIONAL STATUS (43)	0.69 OF 36	107	TEND TO BE THOSE WHERE CLASS STRATIFICATION, IF PRESENT, IS BASED ON SOMETHING OTHER THAN OCCUPATIONAL STATUS (160)	0.90 OF 87	25 9 11 78 XSQ= 41.56 PHI= 0.581 XP = 0.

109	LEAN LESS TOWARD BEING THOSE WHERE CASTES ARE ABSENT (317)	0.68 OF 37	109	LEAN MORE TOWARD BEING THOSE WHERE CASTES ARE ABSENT (317)	0.89 OF 170	12 18 25 152 XSQ= 10.00 PHI= 0.220 XP = 0.0016
110	TILT TOWARD BEING THOSE WHERE SLAVERY IS PRESENT (163)	0.59 OF 39	110	TILT TOWARD BEING THOSE WHERE SLAVERY IS ABSENT (218)	0.62 OF 179	23 68 16 111 XSQ= 4.97 PHI= 0.151 XP = 0.0258
116	IN ALL CASES ARE THOSE WHERE OCCUPATIONAL SPECIALIZATION IS FULL-TIME, WHETHER OR NOT FOR SURPLUS PRODUCTION (20) JMH	1.00 OF 5	116	TILT TOWARD BEING THOSE WHERE OCCUPATIONAL SPECIALIZATION IS PART-TIME ONLY (34) JMH	0.67 OF 40	5 13 0 27 XSQ= 5.86 PHI= 0.361 XP = 0.0155
118	IN ALL CASES ARE THOSE WHERE THE PERCENTAGE OF OCCUPATIONS THAT ARE SPECIALIZED IS HIGH OR MEDIUM (24) WME	1.00 OF 5	118	DRIFT TOWARD BEING THOSE WHERE THE PERCENTAGE OF OCCUPATIONS THAT ARE SPECIALIZED IS LOW (25) WME	0.55 OF 38	5 17 0 21 XSQ= 3.42 PHI= 0.282 XP = 0.0646
128	TILT TOWARD BEING THOSE WHERE, IF SUBSISTENCE IS PRIMARILY BY AGRICULTURE, THE WORK IS MAINLY DONE BY MALES (40)	0.82 OF 17	128	TILT TOWARD BEING THOSE WHERE, IF SUBSISTENCE IS PRIMARILY BY AGRICULTURE, THE WORK IS MAINLY DONE BY FEMALES (37)	0.56 OF 43	14 19 3 24 XSQ= 5.71 PHI= 0.309 XP = 0.0169
130	DRIFT TOWARD BEING THOSE WHERE LEATHER WORKING IS MAINLY DONE BY MALES (39)	0.89 OF 9	130	DRIFT TOWARD BEING THOSE WHERE LEATHER WORKING IS MAINLY DONE BY FEMALES (45)	0.52 OF 50	8 24 1 26 XSQ= 3.62 PHI= 0.248 XP = 0.0570
139	IN ALL CASES ARE THOSE WHERE SUPERORDINATE PUNISHMENT IS PRESENT (15) BBW	1.00 OF 3	139	TILT TOWARD BEING THOSE WHERE SUPERORDINATE PUNISHMENT IS ABSENT (25) BBW	0.74 OF 27	3 7 0 20 XSQ= 3.75 PHI= 0.354 EP = 0.0296
152	IN ALL CASES ARE THOSE WHERE THE DIFFERENTIATION OF THE JURIDICAL AGENCY FROM THE MEDICAL AGENCY IS HIGH (10) MJ	1.00 OF 3	152	DRIFT TOWARD BEING THOSE WHERE THE DIFFERENTIATION OF THE JURIDICAL AGENCY FROM THE MEDICAL AGENCY IS LOW (10) MJ	0.67 OF 12	3 4 0 8 XSQ= 2.03 PHI= 0.367 EP = 0.0769
163	IN ALL CASES ARE THOSE WHERE THE EMPHASIS ON INDIVIDUAL VOLITION AS THE CAUSE OF CRIME IS HIGH (7) MJ	1.00 OF 3	163	TILT TOWARD BEING THOSE WHERE THE EMPHASIS ON INDIVIDUAL VOLITION AS THE CAUSE OF CRIME IS LOW (10) MJ	0.80 OF 10	3 2 0 8 XSQ= 3.32 PHI= 0.505 EP = 0.0350

164	IN ALL CASES ARE THCSE 1.00 OF 3 WHERE THE EMPHASIS ON INCIVICUAL VOLITION AS THE CAUSE CR SOURCE CF ILLNESS IS LCW (9) MJ	164	DRIFT TOWARD BEING THOSE 0.67 CF 12 WHERE THE EMPHASIS ON INDIVIDUAL VCLITICN AS THE CAUSE OR SOURCE CF ILLNESS IS HIGH (9) MJ	0 8 3 4 XSQ= 2.03 PHI= -0.367 EP = 0.0769
175	TILT MORE TOWARC BEING THCSE 0.86 OF 37 WHERE THE COMMUNITY IS 'KIN-HETERCGENECUS,' I. E. CTHER THAN A CLAN CCMMUNITY CR A DEME (260)	175	TILT LESS TOWARD BEING THOSE 0.67 CF 183 WHERE THE COMMUNITY IS 'KIN-HETEROGENEOUS,' I. E. OTHER THAN A CLAN COMMUNITY OR A DEME (260)	5 61 32 122 XSQ= 4.85 PHI= -0.149 XP = 0.0276
176	TILT MORE TOWARC BEINC THCSE 0.73 OF 37 WHERE THE COMMUNITY IS OTHER THAN A CLAN-CCMMUNITY CR A COMMUNITY STRUCTURED OR SEGMENTEC CN A CLAN BASIS (213)	176	TILT LESS TOWARD BEING THOSE 0.54 OF 183 WHERE THE COMMUNITY IS CTHER THAN A CLAN-COMMUNITY OR A COMMUNITY STRUCTURED OR SEGMENTED ON A CLAN BASIS (213)	10 85 27 98 XSQ= 3.97 PHI= -0.134 XP = 0.0462
177	TILT MORE TOWARC BEING THCSE 0.95 OF 37 WHERE THE COMMUNITY IS CTHER THAN A SINGLE CLAN-CCMMUNITY ANC EXCGAMOUS (305)	177	TILT LESS TOWARD BEING THOSE 0.77 OF 183 WHERE THE COMMUNITY IS CTHER THAN A SINGLE CLAN-COMMUNITY AND EXOGAMOUS (305)	2 42 35 141 XSQ= 4.88 PHI= -0.149 XP = 0.0272
180	LEAN MORE TOWARC BEING THCSE 0.89 OF 37 WHERE THE COMMUNITY IS COMMCNLY NCN-EXCGAMOUS, RATHER THAN EXCGAMCUS (258)	180	LEAN LESS TOWARD BEING THOSE 0.62 OF 183 WHERE THE COMMUNITY IS COMMONLY NON-EXOGAMOUS, RATHER THAN EXOGAMOUS (258)	4 70 33 113 XSQ= 9.19 PHI= -0.204 XP = 0.0024
182	LEAN TOWARD BEING THOSE 0.59 OF 37 WHERE THE COMMUNITY IS STRUCTURED ON A NON-CLAN BASIS ANC AGAMOUS (126)	182	LEAN TOWARD BEING THOSE 0.70 OF 183 OTHER THAN WHERE THE COMMUNITY IS STRUCTURED ON A NON-CLAN BASIS AND AGAMOUS (256)	22 55 15 128 XSQ= 10.44 PHI= 0.218 XP = 0.0012
183	IN ALL CASES ARE THCSE 1.00 OF 21 WHERE THE LARGEST NCN-COGNATIC KIN GROUP IS SMALLER THAN A MCEITY, I. E., A PHRATRY CR SIB OR LINEACE (218)	183	DRIFT LESS TOWARD BEING THOSE 0.83 OF 127 WHERE THE LARGEST NON-COGNATIC KIN GROUP IS SMALLER THAN A MOEITY, I. E., A PHRATRY OR SIB OR LINEAGE (218)	0 22 21 105 XSQ= 3.01 PHI= -0.143 XP = 0.0826
187	TILT MCRE TOWARC BEING THCSE 0.97 OF 39 WHERE THE KIN GRCUP IS CTHER THAN EXCLUSIVELY MATRILINEAL (344)	187	TILT LESS TOWARD BEING THCSE 0.83 OF 185 WHERE THE KIN GROUP IS OTHER THAN EXCLUSIVELY MATRILINEAL (344)	1 32 38 153 XSQ= 4.45 PHI= -0.141 XP = 0.0348
190	DRIFT MORE TCWARC BEING THCSE 0.95 OF 2C WHERE THE KIN GRCUP IS PATRILINEAL CR DCUBLE-CESCENT, RATHER THAN MATRILINEAL (186)	190	DRIFT LESS TOWARD BEING THCSE 0.72 OF 124 WHERE THE KIN GROUP IS PATRILINEAL OR DOUBLE-DESCENT, RATHER THAN MATRILINEAL (186)	19 89 1 35 XSQ= 3.79 PHI= 0.162 XP = 0.0515

192	TILT LESS TOWARD BEING THOSE 0.59 OF 39 OTHER THAN WHERE THE ONLY KIN GROUP PRESENT IS A KINDRED OR ELSE BILATERAL DESCENT IS INFERRED (289)	192	TILT MORE TOWARD BEING THOSE 0.77 OF 185 OTHER THAN WHERE THE ONLY KIN GROUP PRESENT IS A KINDRED OR ELSE BILATERAL DESCENT IS INFERRED (289)	16 43 23 142 XSQ= 4.37 PHI= 0.140 XP = 0.0365
196	TEND MORE TO BE THOSE 0.97 OF 33 WHERE INDIVIDUAL RIGHTS IN REAL PROPERTY, AND RULES FOR INHERITANCE, ARE PRESENT (194)	196	TEND LESS TO BE THOSE 0.58 OF 134 WHERE INDIVIDUAL RIGHTS IN REAL PROPERTY, AND RULES FOR INHERITANCE, ARE PRESENT (194)	32 78 1 56 XSQ= 16.01 PHI= 0.310 XP = 0.0001
197	TILT LESS TOWARD BEING THOSE 0.72 OF 32 WHERE RULES FOR THE INHERITANCE OF REAL PROPERTY, IF PRESENT, FAVOR EITHER THE MALE HEIR OR LINE, OR THE FEMALE HEIR OR LINE (165)	197	TILT MORE TOWARD BEING THOSE 0.92 OF 78 WHERE RULES FOR THE INHERITANCE OF REAL PROPERTY, IF PRESENT, FAVOR EITHER THE MALE HEIR OR LINE, OR THE FEMALE HEIR OR LINE (165)	23 72 9 6 XSQ= 6.40 PHI= -0.241 XP = 0.0114
209	DRIFT MORE TOWARD BEING THOSE 0.94 OF 32 WHERE MARITAL RESIDENCE IS PATRILOCAL, VIRILOCAL, OR AVUNCULOCAL, RATHER THAN MATRILOCAL OR UXORILOCAL (270)	209	DRIFT LESS TOWARD BEING THOSE 0.78 OF 158 WHERE MARITAL RESIDENCE IS PATRILOCAL, VIRILOCAL, OR AVUNCULOCAL, RATHER THAN MATRILOCAL OR UXORILOCAL (270)	30 124 2 34 XSQ= 3.11 PHI= 0.128 XP = 0.0780
210	IN ALL CASES ARE THOSE 1.00 OF 16 WHERE MARITAL RESIDENCE IS PATRILOCAL, RATHER THAN MATRILOCAL (169)	210	DRIFT LESS TOWARD BEING THOSE 0.79 OF 102 WHERE MARITAL RESIDENCE IS PATRILOCAL, RATHER THAN MATRILOCAL (169)	16 81 0 21 XSQ= 2.72 PHI= 0.152 XP = 0.0989
213	DRIFT TOWARD BEING THOSE 0.64 OF 33 WHERE FIRST COUSIN MARRIAGE IS PERMITTED (172)	213	DRIFT TOWARD BEING THOSE 0.55 OF 179 WHERE FIRST COUSIN MARRIAGE IS NOT PERMITTED (198)	21 81 12 98 XSQ= 3.07 PHI= 0.120 XP = 0.0796
234	TEND TO BE THOSE 0.79 OF 29 WHERE THE COUSIN TERMINOLOGY IS OF ESKIMO OR HAWAIIAN TYPE, RATHER THAN CROW, OMAHA, OR IROQUOIS TYPE (170)	234	TEND TO BE THOSE 0.57 OF 152 WHERE THE COUSIN TERMINOLOGY IS OF CROW, OMAHA, OR IROQUOIS TYPE, RATHER THAN ESKIMO OR HAWAIIAN TYPE (152)	6 86 23 66 XSQ= 11.16 PHI= -0.248 XP = 0.0008
241	TILT LESS TOWARD BEING THOSE 0.67 OF 21 WHERE THE FAMILY, IF EXTENDED, IS LARGE OR SMALL, RATHER THAN STEM (187)	241	TILT MORE TOWARD BEING THOSE 0.88 OF 95 WHERE THE FAMILY, IF EXTENDED, IS LARGE OR SMALL, RATHER THAN STEM (187)	14 84 7 11 XSQ= 4.66 PHI= -0.200 XP = 0.0309
242	TEND LESS TO BE THOSE 0.53 OF 38 WHERE MARRIAGE IS COMMONLY OR OCCASIONALLY POLYGYNOUS, RATHER THAN MONOGAMOUS (314)	242	TEND MORE TO BE THOSE 0.82 OF 183 WHERE MARRIAGE IS COMMONLY OR OCCASIONALLY POLYGYNOUS, RATHER THAN MONOGAMOUS (314)	20 150 18 33 XSQ= 13.65 PHI= -0.248 XP = 0.0002

255	IN ALL CASES ARE THCSE WHERE GRANCPARENTAL AUTHORITY CVER PARENTS IS PRESENT (7) CA	1.00 OF 2	255	DRIFT TOWARD BEING THOSE WHERE GRANDPARENTAL AUTHCRITY OVER PARENTS IS ABSENT (26) DA	0.76 CF 17	2 4 0 13 XSQ= 1.95 PHI= 0.320 EP = 0.0877
263	TILT TOWARD BEING THOSE WHERE WIVES ARE CBTAINEC BY RELATIVELY EASY MEANS, NAMELY BY TOKEN BRIDE-PRICE, GIFT EXCHANGE, ABSENCE OF ANY CONSIDERATICN, OR RECEIPT OF DCWRY (162)	0.59 OF 39	263	TILT TOWARD BEING THOSE WHERE WIVES ARE OBTAINED BY RELATIVELY DIFFICULT MEANS, NAMELY BY BRIDE-PRICE, BRIDE-SERVICE, CR EXCHANGING A FEMALE RELATIVE (233)	0.60 OF 184	16 111 23 73 XSQ= 4.13 PHI= -0.136 XP = 0.0420
272	IN ALL CASES ARE THCSE WHERE THE DIVCRCE RATE IS LCW (28) CA	1.00 OF 5	272	DRIFT TOWARD BEING THOSE WHERE THE DIVORCE RATE IS HIGH (29) CA	0.53 CF 43	0 23 5 20 XSQ= 3.22 PHI= -0.259 XP = 0.0730
328	IN ALL CASES ARE THOSE WHERE THE AGE OF THE INFANT AT THE CNSET CF SERIOUS SOCIALIZATION, OTHER THAN WEANING, IS TWC YEARS OR LOWER (20) B-B-C	1.00 OF 4	328	TILT TOWARD BEING THOSE WHERE THE AGE OF THE INFANT AT THE ONSET OF SERIOUS SOCIALIZATION, OTHER THAN WEANING, IS HIGHER THAN TWO YEARS (21) B-B-C	0.62 OF 26	0 16 4 10 XSQ= 3.09 PHI= -0.321 EP = 0.0365
345	IN ALL CASES ARE THCSE WHERE THE CHILD'S INFERREC ANXIETY OVER NON-PERFORMANCE CF SELF-RELIANT BEHAVIOR IS HIGH (37) B-B-C	1.00 OF 4	345	DRIFT TOWARD BEING THOSE WHERE THE CHILD'S INFERRED ANXIETY OVER NON-PERFORMANCE OF SELF-RELIANT BEHAVIOR IS LOW (39) B-B-C	0.62 CF 50	4 19 0 31 XSQ= 3.56 PHI= 0.257 XP = 0.0591
346	IN ALL CASES ARE THOSE WHERE THE CHILD'S INFERREC ANXIETY OVER PERFORMANCE CF SELF-RELIANT BEHAVIOR IS LCW (39) B-B-C	1.00 OF 4	346	DRIFT TOWARD BEING THOSE WHERE THE CHILD'S INFERRED ANXIETY OVER PERFORMANCE OF SELF-RELIANT BEHAVIOR IS HIGH (37) B-B-C	0.60 OF 50	0 30 4 20 XSQ= 3.24 PHI= -0.245 XP = 0.0717
370	TILT MORE TOWARC BEING THCSE WHERE THE SEGREGATICN OF ADOLESCENT BOYS IS ABSENT (148)	0.81 OF 32	370	TILT LESS TOWARD BEING THOSE WHERE THE SEGREGATION OF ADOLESCENT BOYS IS ABSENT (148)	0.57 CF 141	6 60 26 81 XSQ= 5.29 PHI= -0.175 XP = 0.0214
391	TEND TO BE THOSE WHERE PREMARITAL SEX RELATIONS ARE STRONGLY PUNISHEC ANC IN FACT RARE, OR WEAKLY PUNISHED ANC IN FACT NCT RARE (89) JTW,EA	0.84 OF 25	391	TEND TO BE THOSE WHERE PREMARITAL SEX RELATIONS ARE PUNISHED ONLY IF PREGNANCY RESULTS, CR FREELY PERMITTED (90) JTW,EA	0.57 CF 106	21 46 4 60 XSQ= 11.77 PHI= 0.300 XP = 0.0006
393	IN ALL CASES ARE THCSE WHERE EXTRAMARITAL CCITUS IS PUNISHED, RATHER THAN PERMITTED (43) F-B	1.00 OF 4	393	DRIFT TOWARD BEING THOSE WHERE EXTRAMARITAL COITUS IS PERMITTED, RATHER THAN PUNISHED (41) F-B	0.60 CF 52	4 21 0 31 XSQ= 3.20 PHI= 0.239 XP = 0.0736

No.			No.			
396	IN ALL CASES ARE THOSE WHERE THE STRENGTH OF MENSTRUAL TABOOS IS HIGH (18) WNS	1.00 OF 3	396	TILT TOWARD BEING THOSE WHERE THE STRENGTH OF MENSTRUAL TABOOS IS LOW (35) WNS	0.74 OF 35	3 9 0 26 XSQ= 4.04 PHI= 0.326 EP = 0.0261
397	DRIFT TOWARD BEING THOSE WHERE SEX DISABILITY IS PRESENT (14) JKH	0.50 OF 8	397	DRIFT TOWARD BEING THOSE WHERE SEX DISABILITY IS ABSENT (42) JKH	0.84 OF 32	4 5 4 27 XSQ= 2.59 PHI= 0.254 EP = 0.0594
424	IN ALL CASES ARE THOSE WHERE RELIGIOUS SPECIALISTS ARE FULL-TIME, RATHER THAN PART-TIME (21) JMH	1.00 OF 5	424	TILT TOWARD BEING THOSE WHERE RELIGIOUS SPECIALISTS ARE PART-TIME, RATHER THAN FULL-TIME (33) JMH	0.65 OF 40	5 14 0 26 XSQ= 5.26 PHI= 0.342 XP = 0.0218
426	TILT MORE TOWARD BEING THOSE WHERE A HIGH GOD IS PRESENT (156) GES,EA	0.79 OF 29	426	TILT LESS TOWARD BEING THOSE WHERE A HIGH GOD IS PRESENT (156) GES,EA	0.55 OF 153	23 84 6 69 XSQ= 5.03 PHI= 0.166 XP = 0.0249
427	DRIFT MORE TOWARD BEING THOSE WHERE A HIGH GOD, IF PRESENT, IS ACTIVE, RATHER THAN INACTIVE (87) GES,EA	0.78 OF 23	427	DRIFT LESS TOWARD BEING THOSE WHERE A HIGH GOD, IF PRESENT, IS ACTIVE, RATHER THAN INACTIVE (87) GES,EA	0.55 OF 84	18 46 5 38 XSQ= 3.23 PHI= 0.174 XP = 0.0724
428	TILT MORE TOWARD BEING THOSE WHERE A HIGH GOD, IF PRESENT AND ACTIVE, SUPPORTS HUMAN MORALITY, RATHER THAN NOT SUPPORTING IT (61) GES,EA	0.89 OF 18	428	TILT LESS TOWARD BEING THOSE WHERE A HIGH GOD, IF PRESENT AND ACTIVE, SUPPORTS HUMAN MORALITY, RATHER THAN NOT SUPPORTING IT (61) GES,EA	0.54 OF 46	16 25 2 21 XSQ= 5.29 PHI= 0.287 XP = 0.0215
431	IN ALL CASES ARE THOSE WHERE SUPERNATURAL SANCTIONS FOR MORALITY, HAVING AN EFFECT ON AN INDIVIDUAL'S AFTER LIFE, ARE PRESENT (10) GES	1.00 OF 2	431	TILT TOWARD BEING THOSE WHERE SUPERNATURAL SANCTIONS FOR MORALITY, HAVING AN EFFECT ON AN INDIVIDUAL'S AFTERLIFE, ARE ABSENT OR UNREPORTED (25) GES	0.83 OF 24	2 4 0 20 XSQ= 3.29 PHI= 0.356 EP = 0.0462
444	IN ALL CASES ARE THOSE WHERE THE USE OF DREAMS TO SEEK AND CONTROL SUPERNATURAL POWERS IS LOW (27) RGD	1.00 OF 6	444	TILT TOWARD BEING THOSE WHERE THE USE OF DREAMS TO SEEK AND CONTROL SUPERNATURAL POWERS IS HIGH (28) RGD	0.56 OF 39	0 22 6 17 XSQ= 4.56 PHI= -0.318 XP = 0.0328
458	TEND TO BE THOSE WHERE GAMES, IF PRESENT, INCLUDE GAMES OF STRATEGY (52) R-A-B,EA	0.90 OF 20	458	TEND TO BE THOSE WHERE GAMES, IF PRESENT, DO NOT INCLUDE GAMES OF STRATEGY (119) R-A-B,EA	0.74 OF 107	18 28 2 79 XSQ= 27.02 PHI= 0.461 XP = 0.0000

```
459  LEAN TOWARD BEING THOSE         0.85 OF  20      459  LEAN TOWARD BEING THOSE         0.58 OF 107          17    45
     WHERE GAMES, IF PRESENT,                             WHERE GAMES, IF PRESENT,                              3    62
     INCLUDE GAMES OF CHANCE   (82) R-A-B,EA              DO NOT INCLUDE                               XSQ=    10.78
                                                          GAMES OF CHANCE   (89) R-A-B,EA              PHI=    0.291
                                                                                                       XP =   0.0010

460  IN ALL CASES ARE THOSE         1.00 OF  20      460  TEND LESS TO BE THOSE           0.56 OF 107           0    47
     WHERE GAMES, IF PRESENT,                             WHERE GAMES, IF PRESENT,                             20    60
     ARE NOT LIMITED TO                                   ARE NOT LIMITED TO                           XSQ=    12.13
     GAMES OF SKILL ONLY   (104) R-A-B,EA                 GAMES OF SKILL ONLY   (104) R-A-B,EA         PHI=   -0.309
                                                                                                       XP =   0.0005

468  IN ALL CASES ARE THOSE         1.00 OF   5      468  LEAN TOWARD BEING THOSE         0.75 OF  40           5    10
     WHERE CONTACT WITH OTHER CULTURES                    WHERE CONTACT WITH OTHER CULTURES                     0    30
     IS FREQUENT, RATHER THAN                             IS REGULAR OR IRREGULAR, RATHER THAN         XSQ=     8.13
     REGULAR OR IRREGULAR   (17) JMH                      FREQUENT   (37) JMH                          PHI=    0.425
                                                                                                       XP =   0.0044
```

```
81  CULTURES                                        81  CULTURES
    WHERE A CITY CR TOWN IS PRESENT, OR                 WHERE NO CITY OR TOWN IS PRESENT, AND
    THE AVERAGE COMMUNITY SIZE IS                       THE AVERAGE COMMUNITY SIZE IS
    200 CR GREATER  (89)                                SMALLER THAN 200  (135)

BACKGROUND ON PAGE 81                                             BOTH SUBJECT AND PREDICATE
.......................................................................................

     89  IN LEFT CCLUMN

ALBANIANS  AMERICANS    ASHANTI     AYMARA      AZTEC      BAMBARA     BASSERI     BAYA        BLACK CARIB BRAZILIANS
BULGARIANS BURUSHC      CAMBODIANS  CAYAPA      CHAGGA     CHEROKEE    CHIBCHA     COCHITI     CREEK       CZECHS
DARD       DELAWARE     DUTCH       EGYPTIANS   ENGA       FON         GANDA       HANC        HAVASUPAI   HUICHOL
HUTSUL     ILA          INCA        IRISH       JAPANESE   JAVANESE    JEMEZ       KABYLE      KATAB       KERALA
KIKUYU     KOREANS      LESU        MAM         MAMBILA    MARGI       MAYA        MBUNDU      MENDE       MERINA
MIAMI      MIN CHINESE  MINCHIA     MOSSI       MZAB       NATCHEZ     NAVAHO      NUPE        NURI        NYORO
OKINAWANS  PAIWAN       PATHAN      RIFFIANS    ROMANS     SAGADA      SERBS       SHILLUK     SINHALESE   SIWANS
SONGHAI    SOTHO        SYRIANS     TALLENSI    TAOS       TENINO      THAI        TIGRINYA    TIKOPIA     TIV
TOTONAC    TUPINAMBA    VENDA       VIETNAMESE  WALLOONS   YAKO        YOMBE       YORUBA      ZUNI

     135  IN RIGHT CCLUMN

ABOR       AKHA         ALACALUF    ALORESE     AMBA       ANDAMANESE  APINAYE     ARANDA      ARAUCANIANS ATAYAL
ATSUGEWI   AWEIKOMA     AZANDE      BACAIRI     BARABRA    BEMBA       BHIL        BHUIYA      BIRIFOR     BOTOCUDO
BUNLAP     CAMAYURA     CARIB       CHENCHU     CHOCO      CHOROTI     CHUKCHEE    COORG       COPR ESKIMO CREE
CUNA       DIERI        DOGON       DOROBO      EYAK       FANG        GARO        GILYAK      GOAJIRO     GOND
GUAHIBO    HANUNOC      HAZARA      IFUGAO      IRAQW      KACHIN      KAPAUKU     KARIERA     KASKA       KAZAK
KERAKI     KHALKA       KHASI       KISSI       KORYAK     KPE         KUBA        KUNG        KURTATCHI   LAMET
LANGO      LAPPS        LAU         LEPCHA      LOLO       LOZI        LUO         MACASSARESE MAMVU       MANUS
MARICOPA   MARQUESANS   MASAI       MATACO      MBUTI      MISKITO     MNONG GAR   MOTILON     MUNDURUCU   MURINBATA
MURNGIN    NABESNA      NAMA        NAMBICUARA  NDEMBU     NOMLAKI     NYAKYUSA    OJIBWA      OMAHA       ONA
PAWNEE     PONAPEANS    PUKAPUKA    PURUM       TAPIRAPE   SAMOANS     SAMOYED     SANPOIL     SEMANG      SIRIONO
SOMALI     SUBANUN      TANALA      TROBRIAND   TRUKESE    TAREUMIUT   TEHUELCHE   TENDA       THONGA      TIMBIRA     TIWI
TODA       TRISTAN      TRUMAI      TUBATULABAL TUCUNA     TWANA       ULAWANS     VEDDA
WAICA      WARRAU       WASHO       WIKMUNKAN   WOGEO      WOLEAIANS   WOLOF       YABARANA    YAGUA       YAHGAN
YAKUT      YAO          YUKAGHIR    YUKI        YUROK

     176  EXCLUDED BECAUSE UNASCERTAINED

---------------------------------------------------------------------------------------------------------
 4  TEND LESS TO BE THCSE          0.79 OF  89     4  TEND MORE TO BE THOSE          0.95 OF 135      19    7
    LOCATED CUTSIDE OF                                LOCATED OUTSIDE OF                              70  128
    THE CIRCUM-MEDITERRANEAN  (355)                   THE CIRCUM-MEDITERRANEAN  (355)          XSQ=   12.13
                                                                                               PHI=   0.233
                                                                                               XP =  0.0005

 6  LEAN MORE TOWARD BEING THCSE   0.93 OF  89     6  LEAN LESS TOWARD BEING THOSE   0.79 OF 135       6   28
    LOCATED OUTSIDE OF                                LOCATED OUTSIDE OF                              83  107
    THE INSULAR PACIFIC  (330)                        THE INSULAR PACIFIC  (330)               XSQ=    7.11
                                                                                               PHI=  -0.178
                                                                                               XP =  0.0077
```

9	TILT MORE TOWARD BEING THOSE 0.91 OF 89 LOCATED OUTSIDE OF SOUTH AMERICA (335)	9 TILT LESS TOWARD BEING THOSE 0.78 OF 135 LOCATED OUTSIDE OF SOUTH AMERICA (335)	8 30 81 105 XSQ= 5.76 PHI= -0.160 XP = 0.0164
11	IN ALL CASES ARE THOSE 1.00 OF 89 WHERE THE LATITUDE IS LESS THAN SIXTY DEGREES (385)	11 TILT LESS TOWARD BEING THOSE 0.92 OF 135 WHERE THE LATITUDE IS LESS THAN SIXTY DEGREES (385)	0 11 89 124 XSQ= 5.98 PHI= -0.163 XP = 0.0145
12	DRIFT MORE TOWARD BEING THOSE 0.96 OF 89 WHERE THE LATITUDE IS LESS THAN FIFTY DEGREES (367)	12 DRIFT LESS TOWARD BEING THOSE 0.87 OF 135 WHERE THE LATITUDE IS LESS THAN FIFTY DEGREES (367)	4 18 85 117 XSQ= 3.79 PHI= -0.130 XP = 0.0517
14	DRIFT LESS TOWARD BEING THOSE 0.62 OF 89 WHERE THE LATITUDE IS LESS THAN THIRTY DEGREES (281)	14 DRIFT MORE TOWARD BEING THOSE 0.74 OF 135 WHERE THE LATITUDE IS LESS THAN THIRTY DEGREES (281)	34 35 55 100 XSQ= 3.24 PHI= 0.120 XP = 0.0719
42	DRIFT MORE TOWARD BEING THOSE 0.69 OF 89 WHERE THE NATURAL ENVIRONMENT IS OTHER THAN TROPICAL OR SUB-TROPICAL RAIN FOREST, OR MONSOON FOREST (244) FWM	42 DRIFT LESS TOWARD BEING THOSE 0.56 OF 135 WHERE THE NATURAL ENVIRONMENT IS OTHER THAN TROPICAL OR SUB-TROPICAL RAIN FOREST, OR MONSOON FOREST (244) FWM	28 59 61 76 XSQ= 2.89 PHI= -0.114 XP = 0.0892
44	TEND MORE TO BE THOSE 0.91 OF 89 WHERE SETTLEMENTS ARE FIXED (222)	44 TEND LESS TO BE THOSE 0.51 OF 134 WHERE SETTLEMENTS ARE FIXED (222)	81 69 8 65 XSQ= 36.16 PHI= 0.403 XP = 0.
46	TEND MORE TO BE THOSE 0.99 OF 89 OTHER THAN WHERE SETTLEMENTS ARE NON-FIXED AND MOVEMENT IS NOMADIC (260)	46 TEND LESS TO BE THOSE 0.66 OF 134 OTHER THAN WHERE SETTLEMENTS ARE NON-FIXED AND MOVEMENT IS NOMADIC (260)	1 46 88 88 XSQ= 33.48 PHI= -0.387 XP = 0.
47	LEAN TOWARD BEING THOSE 0.88 OF 8 WHERE, IF SETTLEMENTS ARE NON-FIXED, MOVEMENT IS NON-NOMADIC, RATHER THAN NOMADIC (38)	47 LEAN TOWARD BEING THOSE 0.71 OF 65 WHERE, IF SETTLEMENTS ARE NON-FIXED, MOVEMENT IS NOMADIC, RATHER THAN NON-NOMADIC (72)	1 46 7 19 XSQ= 8.16 PHI= -0.334 XP = 0.0043
51	TEND TO BE THOSE 0.88 OF 89 WHERE SUBSISTENCE IS PRIMARILY BY FOOD PRODUCTION -- I. E., AGRICULTURE OR HUSBANDRY -- RATHER THAN BY GATHERING (253)	51 TEND TO BE THOSE 0.52 OF 135 WHERE SUBSISTENCE IS PRIMARILY BY FOOD GATHERING -- I. E., HUNTING, FISHING, OR COLLECTING -- RATHER THAN FOOD PRODUCTION (147)	78 65 11 70 XSQ= 34.55 PHI= 0.393 XP = 0.

53	TEND TO BE THOSE WHERE FOOD PRODUCTION IS BY INTENSIVE AGRICULTURE, RATHER THAN BY SIMPLE AGRICULTURE OR INCIPIENT FOOD PRODUCTION (91)	0.66 OF 86	53	TEND TO BE THOSE WHERE FOOD PRODUCTION IS BY SIMPLE AGRICULTURE OR INCIPIENT FOOD PRODUCTION, RATHER THAN BY INTENSIVE AGRICULTURE (147)	0.82 OF 74	57 13 29 61 XSQ= 36.40 PHI= 0.477 XP = 0.
55	TEND TO BE THOSE WHERE FOOD PRODUCTION IS BY INTENSIVE AGRICULTURE, RATHER THAN BY SIMPLE AGRICULTURE (91)	0.74 OF 77	55	TEND TO BE THOSE WHERE FOOD PRODUCTION IS BY SIMPLE AGRICULTURE, RATHER THAN BY INTENSIVE AGRICULTURE (101)	0.77 OF 57	57 13 20 44 XSQ= 32.42 PHI= 0.492 XP = 0.
62	TEND MORE TO BE THOSE WHERE HUSBANDRY OF SOME KIND IS PRESENT (228)	0.84 OF 89	62	TEND LESS TO BE THOSE WHERE HUSBANDRY OF SOME KIND IS PRESENT (228)	0.59 OF 135	75 79 14 56 XSQ= 15.38 PHI= 0.262 XP = 0.0001
63	DRIFT MORE TOWARD BEING THOSE WHERE HUSBANDRY, IF PRESENT, IS PRINCIPALLY IN THE FORM OF BOVINE, EQUINE, CAMEL-LIKE, OR DEER-LIKE ANIMALS, RATHER THAN PIGS, SHEEP, OR GOATS (152)	0.76 OF 75	63	DRIFT LESS TOWARD BEING THOSE WHERE HUSBANDRY, IF PRESENT, IS PRINCIPALLY IN THE FORM OF BOVINE, EQUINE, CAMEL-LIKE, OR DEER-LIKE ANIMALS, RATHER THAN PIGS, SHEEP, OR GOATS (152)	0.61 OF 79	57 48 18 31 XSQ= 3.45 PHI= 0.150 XP = 0.0634
71	TEND TO BE THOSE WHERE METAL WORKING IS PRESENT (98)	0.71 OF 58	71	TEND TO BE THOSE WHERE METAL WORKING IS ABSENT (153)	0.68 OF 114	41 37 17 77 XSQ= 21.16 PHI= 0.351 XP = 0.0000
73	TEND TO BE THOSE WHERE WEAVING IS PRESENT (118)	0.74 OF 58	73	TEND TO BE THOSE WHERE WEAVING IS ABSENT (130)	0.63 OF 111	43 41 15 70 XSQ= 19.63 PHI= 0.341 XP = 0.0000
74	TEND TO BE THOSE WHERE POTTERY IS PRESENT (145)	0.84 OF 57	74	TEND TO BE THOSE WHERE POTTERY IS ABSENT (93)	0.52 OF 109	48 52 9 57 XSQ= 19.33 PHI= 0.341 XP = 0.0000
85	TEND TO BE THOSE WHERE THE LEVEL OF POLITICAL INTEGRATION IS THE LARGE STATE, OR THE LITTLE STATE (70) GPM	0.59 OF 64	85	TEND TO BE THOSE WHERE THE LEVEL OF POLITICAL INTEGRATION IS THE MINIMAL STATE, THE AUTONOMOUS COMMUNITY, OR THE FAMILY (234) GPM	0.88 OF 112	38 13 26 99 XSQ= 42.86 PHI= 0.493 XP = 0.
86	TEND TO BE THOSE WHERE THE LEVEL OF POLITICAL INTEGRATION IS THE LARGE STATE, THE LITTLE STATE, OR THE MINIMAL STATE (148) GPM	0.75 OF 64	86	TEND TO BE THOSE WHERE THE LEVEL OF POLITICAL INTEGRATION IS THE AUTONOMOUS COMMUNITY, OR THE FAMILY (156) GPM	0.70 OF 112	48 34 16 78 XSQ= 30.85 PHI= 0.419 XP = 0.

87	IN ALL CASES ARE THOSE 1.00 OF 64 WHERE THE LEVEL OF POLITICAL INTEGRATION IS THE LARGE STATE, THE LITTLE STATE, THE MINIMAL STATE, OR THE AUTONOMOUS COMMUNITY (281) GPM	87	TILT LESS TOWARD BEING THOSE 0.88 OF 112 WHERE THE LEVEL OF POLITICAL INTEGRATION IS THE LARGE STATE, THE LITTLE STATE, THE MINIMAL STATE, OR THE AUTONOMOUS COMMUNITY (281) GPM	64 99 0 13 XSQ= 6.41 PHI= 0.191 XP = 0.0113
88	LEAN TOWARD BEING THOSE 0.53 OF 64 WHERE, IF A HEADMANSHIP IS PRESENT, SUCCESSION IS NON-HEREDITARY (106)	88	LEAN TOWARD BEING THOSE 0.69 OF 90 WHERE, IF A HEADMANSHIP IS PRESENT, SUCCESSION IS HEREDITARY (165)	34 28 30 62 XSQ= 6.65 PHI= 0.208 XP = 0.0099
91	TEND TO BE THOSE 0.80 OF 15 WHERE SOCIETAL COMPLEXITY IS HIGH (18) F-W	91	TEND TO BE THOSE 0.83 OF 18 WHERE SOCIETAL COMPLEXITY IS LOW (22) F-W	12 3 3 15 XSQ= 10.81 PHI= 0.572 EP = 0.0004
96	TEND TO BE THOSE 0.72 OF 86 WHERE THE HIERARCHY OF NATIONAL JURISDICTION HAS FOUR, THREE, TWO OR ONE LEVEL (174) GES,EA	96	TEND TO BE THOSE 0.63 OF 135 WHERE THE HIERARCHY OF NATIONAL JURISDICTION HAS NO LEVELS (156) GES,EA	62 50 24 85 XSQ= 24.45 PHI= 0.333 XP = 0.0000
97	TEND LESS TO BE THOSE 0.74 OF 87 WHERE THE HIERARCHY OF LOCAL JURISDICTION HAS THREE OR TWO LEVELS (273) GES,EA	97	TEND MORE TO BE THOSE 0.92 OF 135 WHERE THE HIERARCHY OF LOCAL JURISDICTION HAS THREE OR TWO LEVELS (273) GES,EA	23 11 64 124 XSQ= 12.27 PHI= 0.235 XP = 0.0005
98	LEAN MORE TOWARD BEING THOSE 0.84 OF 87 WHERE THE HIERARCHY OF LOCAL JURISDICTION HAS FOUR OR THREE LEVELS (238) GES,EA	98	LEAN LESS TOWARD BEING THOSE 0.65 OF 135 WHERE THE HIERARCHY OF LOCAL JURISDICTION HAS FOUR OR THREE LEVELS (238) GES,EA	73 88 14 47 XSQ= 8.39 PHI= 0.194 XP = 0.0038
99	LEAN MORE TOWARD BEING THOSE 0.92 OF 24 WHERE, WITH NATIONAL HIERARCHY ABSENT, THE HIERARCHY OF LOCAL JURISDICTION HAS FOUR OR THREE LEVELS (93) GES,EA	99	LEAN LESS TOWARD BEING THOSE 0.54 OF 85 WHERE, WITH NATIONAL HIERARCHY ABSENT, THE HIERARCHY OF LOCAL JURISDICTION HAS FOUR OR THREE LEVELS (93) GES,EA	22 46 2 39 XSQ= 9.70 PHI= 0.298 XP = 0.0018
100	TEND MORE TO BE THOSE 0.98 OF 86 WHERE HIERARCHIES ARE MORE COMPLEX THAN THE 'SIMPLEST,' I. E., MORE COMPLEX THAN TWO LOCAL LEVELS WITH NO NATIONAL LEVELS (267) GES,EA	100	TEND LESS TO BE THOSE 0.71 OF 135 WHERE HIERARCHIES ARE MORE COMPLEX THAN THE 'SIMPLEST,' I. E., MORE COMPLEX THAN TWO LOCAL LEVELS WITH NO NATIONAL LEVELS (267) GES,EA	84 96 2 39 XSQ= 22.81 PHI= 0.321 XP = 0.0000
102	TEND TO BE THOSE 0.74 OF 87 WHERE CLASS STRATIFICATION IS PRESENT (203)	102	TEND TO BE THOSE 0.55 OF 132 WHERE CLASS STRATIFICATION IS ABSENT (180)	64 59 23 73 XSQ= 16.59 PHI= 0.275 XP = 0.0000

106	TEND TO BE THOSE WHERE CLASS STRATIFICATION, IF PRESENT, IS BASED ON SOMETHING OTHER THAN WEALTH (126)	0.78 OF 64	106	TEND TO BE THOSE WHERE CLASS STRATIFICATION, IF PRESENT, IS BASED ON WEALTH (77)	0.64 OF 59	14 38 50 21 XSQ= 21.05 PHI= -0.414 XP = 0.0000
107	TEND LESS TO BE THOSE WHERE CLASS STRATIFICATION, IF PRESENT, IS BASED ON SOMETHING OTHER THAN OCCUPATIONAL STATUS (160)	0.53 OF 64	107	TEND MORE TO BE THOSE WHERE CLASS STRATIFICATION, IF PRESENT, IS BASED ON SOMETHING OTHER THAN OCCUPATIONAL STATUS (160)	0.93 OF 59	30 4 34 55 XSQ= 22.71 PHI= 0.430 XP = 0.0000
109	LEAN LESS TOWARD BEING THOSE WHERE CASTES ARE ABSENT (317)	0.77 OF 83	109	LEAN MORE TOWARD BEING THOSE WHERE CASTES ARE ABSENT (317)	0.91 OF 124	19 11 64 113 XSQ= 6.80 PHI= 0.181 XP = 0.0091
110	TILT TOWARD BEING THOSE WHERE SLAVERY IS PRESENT (163)	0.52 OF 86	110	TILT TOWARD BEING THOSE WHERE SLAVERY IS ABSENT (218)	0.65 OF 132	45 46 41 86 XSQ= 5.84 PHI= 0.164 XP = 0.0157
116	TILT TOWARD BEING THOSE WHERE OCCUPATIONAL SPECIALIZATION IS FULL-TIME, WHETHER OR NOT FOR SURPLUS PRODUCTION (20) JMH	0.63 OF 16	116	TILT TOWARD BEING THOSE WHERE OCCUPATIONAL SPECIALIZATION IS PART-TIME ONLY (34) JMH	0.72 OF 29	10 8 6 21 XSQ= 3.88 PHI= 0.294 XP = 0.0488
118	TILT TOWARD BEING THOSE WHERE THE PERCENTAGE OF OCCUPATIONS THAT ARE SPECIALIZED IS HIGH OR MEDIUM (24) WME	0.83 OF 12	118	TILT TOWARD BEING THOSE WHERE THE PERCENTAGE OF OCCUPATIONS THAT ARE SPECIALIZED IS LOW (25) WME	0.61 OF 31	10 12 2 19 XSQ= 5.22 PHI= 0.349 XP = 0.0223
120	DRIFT MORE TOWARD BEING THOSE WHERE THE CRAFT SPECIALIZATION SCORE IS HIGH OR MEDIUM (36) WME	0.92 OF 13	120	DRIFT LESS TOWARD BEING THOSE WHERE THE CRAFT SPECIALIZATION SCORE IS HIGH OR MEDIUM (36) WME	0.61 OF 33	12 20 1 13 XSQ= 3.06 PHI= 0.258 XP = 0.0804
130	TILT TOWARD BEING THOSE WHERE LEATHER WORKING IS MAINLY DONE BY MALES (39)	0.77 OF 22	130	TILT TOWARD BEING THOSE WHERE LEATHER WORKING IS MAINLY DONE BY FEMALES (45)	0.59 OF 37	17 15 5 22 XSQ= 6.09 PHI= 0.321 XP = 0.0136
131	IN ALL CASES ARE THOSE WHERE THE CONSTRUCTION OF PERMANENT HOUSES OR THE ERECTION OF TEMPORARY DWELLINGS IS MAINLY DONE BY MALES (136)	1.00 OF 37	131	TILT LESS TOWARD BEING THOSE WHERE THE CONSTRUCTION OF PERMANENT HOUSES OR THE ERECTION OF TEMPORARY DWELLINGS IS MAINLY DONE BY MALES (136)	0.82 OF 76	37 62 0 14 XSQ= 6.18 PHI= 0.234 XP = 0.0130

141	TILT TOWARD BEING THOSE 0.75 OF 16 WHERE THE LEVEL OF SOCIAL SANCTION IS PUBLIC CORPOREAL SANCTION, RATHER THAN PUBLIC PROPERTY SANCTION OR PRIVATE SETTLEMENT (28) JMH	141	TILT TOWARD BEING THOSE 0.62 OF 29 WHERE THE LEVEL OF SOCIAL SANCTION IS PUBLIC PROPERTY SANCTION OR PRIVATE SETTLEMENT, RATHER THAN PUBLIC CORPOREAL SANCTION (26) JMH	12 11 4 18 XSQ= 4.28 PHI= 0.309 XP = 0.0385
147	IN ALL CASES ARE THOSE 1.00 OF 7 WHERE CODIFIED LAWS ARE PRESENT (20) LWS	147	DRIFT LESS TOWARD BEING THOSE 0.56 OF 18 WHERE CODIFIED LAWS ARE PRESENT (20) LWS	7 10 0 8 XSQ= 2.76 PHI= 0.332 EP = 0.0573
152	TILT TOWARD BEING THOSE 0.83 OF 6 WHERE THE DIFFERENTIATION OF THE JURIDICAL AGENCY FROM THE MEDICAL AGENCY IS HIGH (10) MJ	152	TILT TOWARD BEING THOSE 0.78 OF 9 WHERE THE DIFFERENTIATION OF THE JURIDICAL AGENCY FROM THE MEDICAL AGENCY IS LOW (10) MJ	5 2 1 7 XSQ= 3.23 PHI= 0.464 EP = 0.0406
177	TILT MORE TOWARD BEING THOSE 0.87 OF 86 WHERE THE COMMUNITY IS OTHER THAN A SINGLE CLAN-COMMUNITY AND EXOGAMOUS (305)	177	TILT LESS TOWARD BEING THOSE 0.75 OF 134 WHERE THE COMMUNITY IS OTHER THAN A SINGLE CLAN-COMMUNITY AND EXOGAMOUS (305)	11 33 75 101 XSQ= 3.88 PHI= -0.133 XP = 0.0490
179	TILT MORE TOWARD BEING THOSE 0.95 OF 86 WHERE THE COMMUNITY IS OTHER THAN STRUCTURED ON A NON-CLAN BASIS AND COMMONLY EXOGAMOUS (340)	179	TILT LESS TOWARD BEING THOSE 0.84 OF 134 WHERE THE COMMUNITY IS OTHER THAN STRUCTURED ON A NON-CLAN BASIS AND COMMONLY EXOGAMOUS (340)	4 22 82 112 XSQ= 5.88 PHI= -0.163 XP = 0.0153
180	TEND MORE TO BE THOSE 0.83 OF 86 WHERE THE COMMUNITY IS COMMONLY NON-EXOGAMOUS, RATHER THAN EXOGAMOUS (258)	180	TEND LESS TO BE THOSE 0.56 OF 134 WHERE THE COMMUNITY IS COMMONLY NON-EXOGAMOUS, RATHER THAN EXOGAMOUS (258)	15 59 71 75 XSQ= 15.42 PHI= -0.265 XP = 0.0001
181	DRIFT LESS TOWARD BEING THOSE 0.85 OF 86 WHERE THE COMMUNITY IS OTHER THAN A DEME (337)	181	DRIFT MORE TOWARD BEING THOSE 0.93 OF 134 WHERE THE COMMUNITY IS OTHER THAN A DEME (337)	13 9 73 125 XSQ= 3.23 PHI= 0.121 XP = 0.0725
183	LEAN MORE TOWARD BEING THOSE 0.97 OF 60 WHERE THE LARGEST NON-COGNATIC KIN GROUP IS SMALLER THAN A MOEITY, I. E., A PHRATRY OR SIB OR LINEAGE (218)	183	LEAN LESS TOWARD BEING THOSE 0.77 OF 88 WHERE THE LARGEST NON-COGNATIC KIN GROUP IS SMALLER THAN A MOEITY, I. E., A PHRATRY OR SIB OR LINEAGE (218)	2 20 58 68 XSQ= 9.13 PHI= -0.248 XP = 0.0025
184	TILT MORE TOWARD BEING THOSE 0.82 OF 60 WHERE THE LARGEST NON-COGNATIC KIN GROUP IS SMALLER THAN A PHRATRY, I. E. A SIB OR LINEAGE (175)	184	TILT LESS TOWARD BEING THOSE 0.63 OF 88 WHERE THE LARGEST NON-COGNATIC KIN GROUP IS SMALLER THAN A PHRATRY, I. E. A SIB OR LINEAGE (175)	11 33 49 55 XSQ= 5.39 PHI= -0.191 XP = 0.0203

196	TEND TO BE THOSE 0.88 OF 69 WHERE INDIVIDUAL RIGHTS IN REAL PROPERTY, AND RULES FOR INHERITANCE, ARE PRESENT (194)	196	TEND TO BE THOSE 0.50 OF 98 WHERE INDIVIDUAL RIGHTS IN REAL PROPERTY, OR RULES FOR INHERITANCE, ARE ABSENT (87)	61 49 8 49 XSQ= 24.88 PHI= 0.386 XP = 0.0000
220	DRIFT MORE TOWARD BEING THOSE 0.79 OF 82 WHERE FIRST COUSIN MARRIAGE IN SOME FORM OR OTHER IS NOT PRESCRIBED OR PREFERRED (273)	220	DRIFT LESS TOWARD BEING THOSE 0.66 OF 130 WHERE FIRST COUSIN MARRIAGE IN SOME FORM OR OTHER IS NOT PRESCRIBED OR PREFERRED (273)	17 44 65 86 XSQ= 3.60 PHI= -0.130 XP = 0.0576
234	TEND TO BE THOSE 0.66 OF 70 WHERE THE COUSIN TERMINOLOGY IS OF ESKIMO OR HAWAIIAN TYPE, RATHER THAN CROW, OMAHA, OR IROQUOIS TYPE (170)	234	TEND TO BE THOSE 0.61 OF 111 WHERE THE COUSIN TERMINOLOGY IS OF CROW, OMAHA, OR IROQUOIS TYPE, RATHER THAN ESKIMO OR HAWAIIAN TYPE (152)	24 68 46 43 XSQ= 11.44 PHI= -0.251 XP = 0.0007
236	DRIFT TOWARD BEING THOSE 0.60 OF 88 WHERE THE FAMILY IS OF AN EXTENDED TYPE, RATHER THAN AN INDEPENDENT TYPE (213)	236	DRIFT TOWARD BEING THOSE 0.53 OF 135 WHERE THE FAMILY IS OF AN INDEPENDENT TYPE, RATHER THAN AN EXTENDED TYPE (185)	53 63 35 72 XSQ= 3.40 PHI= 0.123 XP = 0.0652
242	TILT LESS TOWARD BEING THOSE 0.69 OF 88 WHERE MARRIAGE IS COMMONLY OR OCCASIONALLY POLYGYNOUS, RATHER THAN MONOGAMOUS (314)	242	TILT MORE TOWARD BEING THOSE 0.82 OF 133 WHERE MARRIAGE IS COMMONLY OR OCCASIONALLY POLYGYNOUS, RATHER THAN MONOGAMOUS (314)	61 109 27 24 XSQ= 4.08 PHI= -0.136 XP = 0.0434
303	DRIFT TOWARD BEING THOSE 0.70 OF 10 WHERE THE EARLY ORAL SATISFACTION POTENTIAL IS LOW (25) W-C	303	DRIFT TOWARD BEING THOSE 0.70 OF 27 WHERE THE EARLY ORAL SATISFACTION POTENTIAL IS HIGH (32) W-C	3 19 7 8 XSQ= 3.40 PHI= -0.303 EP = 0.0563
311	TILT TOWARD BEING THOSE 0.82 OF 11 WHERE SEXUAL SOCIALIZATION ANXIETY IS HIGH (28) W-C	311	TILT TOWARD BEING THOSE 0.59 OF 22 WHERE SEXUAL SOCIALIZATION ANXIETY IS LOW (23) W-C	9 9 2 13 XSQ= 3.44 PHI= 0.323 EP = 0.0342
336	DRIFT TOWARD BEING THOSE 0.78 OF 18 WHERE THE TOTAL POSITIVE PRESSURE TOWARD DEVELOPING RESPONSIBLE BEHAVIOR IN THE CHILD IS HIGH (43) B-B-C	336	DRIFT TOWARD BEING THOSE 0.53 OF 36 WHERE THE TOTAL POSITIVE PRESSURE TOWARD DEVELOPING RESPONSIBLE BEHAVIOR IN THE CHILD IS LOW (32) B-B-C	14 17 4 19 XSQ= 3.42 PHI= 0.252 XP = 0.0645
352	TILT TOWARD BEING THOSE 0.88 OF 17 WHERE THE TOTAL POSITIVE PRESSURE TOWARD DEVELOPING OBEDIENT BEHAVIOR IN THE CHILD IS HIGH (44) B-B-C	352	TILT TOWARD BEING THOSE 0.50 OF 34 WHERE THE TOTAL POSITIVE PRESSURE TOWARD DEVELOPING OBEDIENT BEHAVIOR IN THE CHILD IS LOW (28) B-B-C	15 17 2 17 XSQ= 5.55 PHI= 0.330 XP = 0.0185

353	TILT TOWARD BEING THOSE 0.82 OF 17 WHERE THE CHILD'S INFERREC ANXIETY OVER NON-PERFORMANCE CF CBECIENT BEHAVIOR IS HIGH (42) B-B-C	353	TILT TOWARD BEING THOSE 0.54 OF 35 WHERE THE CHILD-S INFERRED ANXIETY OVER NON-PERFORMANCE OF OBEDIENT BEHAVIOR IS LOW (32) B-B-C	14 16 3 19 XSQ= 4.88 PHI= 0.306 XP = 0.0271
365	DRIFT TCWARD BEING THOSE 0.85 OF 13 WHERE THE TIME SPENT IN AUCLESCENT PEER GRCUP ACTIVITY IS HIGH CR HIGH-MEDIUM (30) JKH	365	DRIFT TOWARD BEING THOSE 0.50 OF 18 WHERE THE TIME SPENT IN ADOLESCENT PEER GROUP ACTIVITY IS LOW-MEDIUM OR LOW (15) JKH	11 9 2 9 XSQ= 2.58 PHI= 0.289 EP = 0.0656
370	TILT MORE TOWARC BEING THCSE 0.73 OF 71 WHERE THE SEGREGATION CF ACOLESCENT BOYS IS ABSENT (148)	370	TILT LESS TOWARD BEING THOSE 0.54 CF 102 WHERE THE SEGREGATION OF ADCLESCENT BOYS IS ABSENT (148)	19 47 52 55 XSQ= 5.83 PHI= -0.184 XP = 0.0158
391	LEAN TCWARD BEING THOSE 0.68 OF 50 WHERE PREMARITAL SEX RELATIONS ARE STRCNGLY PUNISHED ANC IN FACT RARE, OR WEAKLY PUNISHED ANC IN FACT NCT RARE (89) JTW,EA	391	LEAN TOWARD BEING THCSE 0.59 OF 81 WHERE PREMARITAL SEX RELATICNS ARE PUNISHED ONLY IF PREGNANCY RESULTS, OR FREELY PERMITTED (90) JTW,EA	34 33 16 48 XSQ= 8.14 PHI= 0.249 XP = 0.0043
398	DRIFT TCWARD BEING THOSE 0.83 OF 6 WHERE THE INTENSITY OF SEX ANXIETY IS HIGH (16) WNS	398	DRIFT TOWARD BEING THOSE 0.69 OF 16 WHERE THE INTENSITY CF SEX ANXIETY IS LOW (16) WNS	5 5 1 11 XSQ= 2.90 PHI= 0.363 EP = 0.0557
405	TILT TCWARD BEING THOSE 0.69 OF 13 WHERE EXPLANATICNS OF ILLNESS OF A DEPENDENCE NATURE ARE ABSENT (27) W-C	405	TILT TOWARD BEING THOSE 0.70 OF 27 WHERE EXPLANATIONS OF ILLNESS OF A DEPENDENCE NATURE ARE PRESENT (34) W-C	4 19 9 8 XSQ= 4.13 PHI= -0.321 EP = 0.0383
417	IN ALL CASES ARE THCSE 1.00 OF 9 WHERE WARFARE IS PREVALENT (34) LWS	417	DRIFT LESS TOWARD BEING THCSE 0.62 OF 21 WHERE WARFARE IS PREVALENT (34) LWS	9 13 0 8 XSQ= 2.93 PHI= 0.313 EP = 0.0665
424	DRIFT TCWARD BEING THOSE 0.63 OF 16 WHERE RELIGIOUS SPECIALISTS ARE FULL-TIME, RATHER THAN PART-TIME (21) JMH	424	DRIFT TOWARD BEING THOSE 0.69 OF 29 WHERE RELIGIOUS SPECIALISTS ARE PART-TIME, RATHER THAN FULL-TIME (33) JMH	10 9 6 20 XSQ= 2.99 PHI= 0.258 XP = 0.0836
426	LEAN MORE TOWARC BEING THCSE 0.73 OF 66 WHERE A HIGH GOC IS PRESENT (156) GES,EA	426	LEAN LESS TOWARD BEING THOSE 0.51 OF 116 WHERE A HIGH GOD IS PRESENT (156) GES,EA	48 59 18 57 XSQ= 7.42 PHI= 0.202 XP = 0.0064

427	DRIFT MORE TCWARC BEING THCSE 0.71 OF 48 WHERE A HIGH GCC, IF PRESENT, IS ACTIVE, RATHER THAN INACTIVE (87) GES,EA	427	DRIFT LESS TOWARD BEING THCSE 0.51 OF 59 WHERE A HIGH GCD, IF PRESENT, IS ACTIVE, RATHER THAN INACTIVE (87) GES,EA	34 30 14 29 XSQ= 3.61 PHI= 0.184 XP = 0.0576
428	TILT TCWARD BEING THCSE 0.79 OF 34 WHERE A HIGH GCC, IF PRESENT AND ACTIVE, SUPPORTS HUMAN MORALITY, RATHER THAN NOT SUPPORTING IT (61) GES,EA	428	TILT TOWARD BEING THOSE 0.53 CF 30 WHERE A HIGH GOD, IF PRESENT AND ACTIVE, DOES NOT SUPPORT HUMAN MORALITY, RATHER THAN SUPPORTING IT (26) GES,EA	27 14 7 16 XSQ= 6.07 PHI= 0.308 XP = 0.0138
429	IN ALL CASES ARE THOSE 1.00 OF 7 WHERE SUPERNATURAL SANCTICNS FOR MORALITY ARE PRESENT (28) GES	429	DRIFT LESS TOWARD BEING THCSE 0.60 OF 20 WHERE SUPERNATURAL SANCTICNS FCR MCRALITY ARE PRESENT (28) GES	7 12 0 8 XSQ= 2.29 PHI= 0.291 EP = 0.0681
441	DRIFT TCWARD BEING THCSE 0.69 OF 13 WHERE FEAR OF HUMAN BEINGS IS HIGH (29) W-C	441	DRIFT TOWARD BEING THCSE 0.63 CF 27 WHERE FEAR OF HUMAN BEINGS IS LOW (32) W-C	9 10 4 17 XSQ= 2.47 PHI= 0.249 EP = 0.0915
442	TILT TOWARD BEING THOSE 0.69 OF 13 WHERE FEAR OF ANIMAL SPIRITS IS HIGH (28) W-C	442	TILT TOWARD BEING THOSE 0.74 OF 27 WHERE FEAR OF ANIMAL SPIRITS IS LOW (33) W-C	9 7 4 20 XSQ= 5.17 PHI= 0.360 EP = 0.0154
444	IN ALL CASES ARE THCSE 1.00 OF 11 WHERE THE USE OF DREAMS TO SEEK AND CONTROL SUPERNATURAL POWERS IS LOW (27) RGC	444	TEND TO BE THOSE 0.65 CF 34 WHERE THE USE OF DREAMS TO SEEK AND CONTROL SUPERNATURAL PCWERS IS HIGH (28) RGD	0 22 11 12 XSQ= 11.46 PHI= -0.505 XP = 0.0007
447	DRIFT TCWARD BEING THCSE 0.86 OF 7 WHERE LOVE MAGIC IS PRESENT (20) S-R	447	DRIFT TOWARD BEING THOSE 0.60 OF 15 WHERE LOVE MAGIC IS ABSENT (13) S-R	6 6 1 9 XSQ= 2.39 PHI= 0.330 EP = 0.0743
450	DRIFT LESS TCWARD BEING THCSE 0.52 OF 23 WHERE THE CBSERVATICN CF FCOD TABOOS IS HIGH OR MEDIUM, RATHER THAN LOW (60) JRL	450	DRIFT MORE TOWARD BEING THCSE 0.76 CF 49 WHERE THE OBSERVATION OF FCOD TABOOS IS HIGH OR MEDIUM, RATHER THAN LOW (60) JRL	12 37 11 12 XSQ= 2.92 PHI= -0.201 XP = 0.0874
453	IN ALL CASES ARE THOSE 1.00 OF 8 WHERE THE ROLE CF RELIGIOUS EXPERTS IS NCT CONDUCIVE TC THE DEVELOPMENT OF THE INDIVIDUAL'S NEED TC ACHIEVE (23) DCM	453	DRIFT LESS TOWARD BEING THCSE 0.56 OF 16 WHERE THE ROLE OF RELIGICUS EXPERTS IS NOT CONDUCIVE TO THE DEVELOPMENT CF THE INDIVIDUAL'S NEED TO ACHIEVE (23) DCM	0 7 8 9 XSQ= 3.05 PHI= -0.357 EP = 0.0538

```
458  TEND TO BE THOSE                  0.67 OF  48      458  TEND TO BE THOSE                 0.82 OF  79          32    14
     WHERE GAMES, IF PRESENT,                                WHERE GAMES, IF PRESENT,                              16    65
     INCLUDE GAMES OF STRATEGY  (52) R-A-B,EA                DO NOT INCLUDE                                 XSQ=    28.88
                                                             GAMES OF STRATEGY  (119) R-A-B,EA              PHI=    0.477
                                                                                                            XP =   0.0000

459  LEAN TOWARD BEING THOSE           0.67 OF  48      459  LEAN TOWARD BEING THOSE          0.62 OF  79          32    30
     WHERE GAMES, IF PRESENT,                                WHERE GAMES, IF PRESENT,                              16    49
     INCLUDE GAMES OF CHANCE  (82) R-A-B,EA                  DO NOT INCLUDE                                 XSQ=     8.72
                                                             GAMES OF CHANCE  (89) R-A-B,EA                 PHI=    0.262
                                                                                                            XP =   0.0031

460  TEND TO BE THOSE                  0.90 OF  48      460  TEND TO BE THOSE                 0.53 OF  79           5    42
     WHERE GAMES, IF PRESENT,                                WHERE GAMES, IF PRESENT,                              43    37
     ARE NOT LIMITED TO                                      ARE LIMITED TO                                 XSQ=    21.61
     GAMES OF SKILL ONLY  (104) R-A-B,EA                     GAMES OF SKILL ONLY  (67) R-A-B,EA             PHI=   -0.412
                                                                                                            XP =   0.0000

468  TILT TOWARD BEING THOSE           0.56 OF  16      468  TILT TOWARD BEING THOSE          0.79 OF  29           9     6
     WHERE CONTACT WITH OTHER CULTURES                       WHERE CONTACT WITH OTHER CULTURES                      7    23
     IS FREQUENT, RATHER THAN                                IS REGULAR OR IRREGULAR, RATHER THAN           XSQ=     4.38
     REGULAR OR IRREGULAR  (17) JMH                          FREQUENT  (37) JMH                             PHI=    0.312
                                                                                                            XP =   0.0364
```

82 CULTURES
WHERE A CITY OR TOWN IS PRESENT, OR
THE AVERAGE COMMUNITY SIZE IS
FIFTY OR GREATER (178)

82 CULTURES
WHERE NO CITY OR TOWN IS PRESENT, AND
THE AVERAGE COMMUNITY SIZE IS
SMALLER THAN FIFTY (46)

BACKGROUND ON PAGE 81

BOTH SUBJECT AND PREDICATE

178 IN LEFT COLUMN

ABOR	AKHA	ALBANIANS	ALORESE	AMBA	AMERICANS	APINAYE	ARAUCANIANS	ASHANTI	ATAYAL
ATSUGEWI	AYMARA	AZANDE	AZTEC	BAMBARA	BARABRA	BASSERI	BAYA	BEMBA	BHIL
BHUIYA	BIRIFOR	BLACK CARIB	BOTOCUDO	BRAZILIANS	BULGARIANS	BURUSHO	CAMAYURA	CAMBODIANS	CAYAPA
CHAGGA	CHEROKEE	CHIBCHA	CHOCO	COCHITI	COORG	CREE	CREEK	CUNA	CZECHS
DARD	DELAWARE	DOGON	DUTCH	EGYPTIANS	ENGA	FANG	FON	GANDA	GARO
GILYAK	GOND	HANO	HANUNOO	HAVASUPAI	HAZARA	HUICHOL	HUTSUL	IFUGAO	ILA
INCA	IRAQW	IRISH	JAPANESE	JAVANESE	JEMEZ	KABYLE	KACHIN	KAPAUKU	KASKA
KATAB	KAZAK	KERAKI	KERALA	KHASI	KIKUYU	KISSI	KOREANS	KORYAK	KPE
KUBA	KURTATCHI	LAMET	LANGO	LAU	LEPCHA	LESU	LOLO	LOZI	LUO
MACASSARESE	MAM	MAMBILA	MAMVU	MANUS	MARGI	MARICOPA	MARQUESANS	MATACO	MAYA
MBUNDU	MENDE	MERINA	MIAMI	MIN CHINESE	MINCHIA	MISKITO	MNONG GAR	MOSSI	MUNDURUCU
MZAB	NAMA	NATCHEZ	NAVAHO	NOMLAKI	NUPE	NURI	NYAKYUSA	NYORO	OKINAWANS
OMAHA	ONA	PAIWAN	PATHAN	PAWNEE	PUKAPUKA	PURUM	RIFFIANS	ROMANS	RWALA
SAGADA	SAMOANS	SANPOIL	SERBS	SHILLUK	SINHALESE	SIWANS	SONGHAI	SOTHO	SYRIANS
TALLENSI	TANALA	TAOS	TAPIRAPE	TAREUMIUT	TEHUELCHE	TENDA	TENINO	TROBRIAND	THAI	THONGA
TIGRINYA	TIKOPIA	TIMBIRA	TIV	TIWI	TOTONAC	TRISTAN	WARRAU	TRUKESE	TUCUNA
TUPINAMBA	TWANA	ULAWANS	VENDA	VIETNAMESE	WAICA	WALLOONS	ZUNI	WOGEO	WOLEAIANS
WOLOF	YAKO	YAKUT	YAO	YOMBE	YORUBA	YUKI			

46 IN RIGHT COLUMN

ALACALUF	ANDAMANESE	ARANDA	AWEIKOMA	BACAIRI	BUNLAP	CARIB	CHENCHU	CHOROTI	CHUKCHEE
COPR ESKIMO	DIERI	DOROBO	EYAK	GOAJIRO	GUAHIBO	KARIERA	KHALKA	KUNG	LAPPS
MASAI	MBUTI	MOTILON	MURINBATA	MURNGIN	NABESNA	NAMBICUARA	NDEMBU	OJIBWA	PONAPEANS
SAMOYED	SEMANG	SIRIONO	SOMALI	SUBANUN	TODA	TRUMAI	TUBATULABAL	VEDDA	WASHO
WIKMUNKAN	YABARANA	YAGUA	YAHGAN	YUKAGHIR	YUROK				

176 EXCLUDED BECAUSE UNASCERTAINED

---

3 DRIFT LESS TOWARD BEING THOSE 0.76 OF 178
LOCATED OUTSIDE OF
AFRICA (320)

3 DRIFT MORE TOWARD BEING THOSE 0.89 OF 46
LOCATED OUTSIDE OF
AFRICA (320)

42	5
136	41
XSQ=	2.84
PHI=	0.113
XP =	0.0917

9 TILT MORE TOWARD BEING THOSE 0.87 OF 178
LOCATED OUTSIDE OF
SOUTH AMERICA (335)

9 TILT LESS TOWARD BEING THOSE 0.70 OF 46
LOCATED OUTSIDE OF
SOUTH AMERICA (335)

24	14
154	32
XSQ=	6.30
PHI=	-0.168
XP =	0.0121

11	TEND MORE TO BE THOSE WHERE THE LATITUDE IS LESS THAN SIXTY DEGREES (385)	0.98 OF 178	11	TEND LESS TO BE THOSE WHERE THE LATITUDE IS LESS THAN SIXTY DEGREES (385)	0.83 OF 46	3 8 175 38 XSQ= 16.09 PHI= -0.268 XP = 0.0001
12	TEND MORE TO BE THOSE WHERE THE LATITUDE IS LESS THAN FIFTY DEGREES (367)	0.94 OF 178	12	TEND LESS TO BE THOSE WHERE THE LATITUDE IS LESS THAN FIFTY DEGREES (367)	0.76 OF 46	11 11 167 35 XSQ= 11.05 PHI= -0.222 XP = 0.0009
33	LEAN MORE TOWARD BEING THOSE WHERE THE NATURAL ENVIRONMENT IS OTHER THAN 'VERY HARSH,' I.E., DESERT, DESERT GRASSES AND SHRUBS, TUNDRA, OR HIGH PLATEAU STEPPE (341) FWM	0.86 OF 178	33	LEAN LESS TOWARD BEING THOSE WHERE THE NATURAL ENVIRONMENT IS OTHER THAN 'VERY HARSH,' I.E., DESERT, DESERT GRASSES AND SHRUBS, TUNDRA, OR HIGH PLATEAU STEPPE (341) FWM	0.67 OF 46	25 15 153 31 XSQ= 7.37 PHI= -0.181 XP = 0.0066
36	TILT MORE TOWARD BEING THOSE WHERE THE NATURAL ENVIRONMENT IS OTHER THAN 'VERY HARSH,' OR SUB-TROPICAL BUSH, OR TEMPERATE GRASSLAND (292) FWM	0.77 OF 178	36	TILT LESS TOWARD BEING THOSE WHERE THE NATURAL ENVIRONMENT IS OTHER THAN 'VERY HARSH,' OR SUB-TROPICAL BUSH, OR TEMPERATE GRASSLAND (292) FWM	0.61 OF 46	41 18 137 28 XSQ= 4.09 PHI= -0.135 XP = 0.0432
44	TEND TO BE THOSE WHERE SETTLEMENTS ARE FIXED (222)	0.79 OF 177	44	TEND TO BE THOSE WHERE SETTLEMENTS ARE NON-FIXED (110)	0.76 OF 46	139 11 38 35 XSQ= 47.02 PHI= 0.459 XP = 0.
46	TEND TO BE THOSE OTHER THAN WHERE SETTLEMENTS ARE NON-FIXED AND MOVEMENT IS NOMADIC (260)	0.91 OF 177	46	TEND TO BE THOSE WHERE SETTLEMENTS ARE NON-FIXED AND MOVEMENT IS NOMADIC (72)	0.67 OF 46	16 31 161 15 XSQ= 71.27 PHI= -0.565 XP = 0.
47	TEND TO BE THOSE WHERE, IF SETTLEMENTS ARE NON-FIXED, MOVEMENT IS NON-NOMADIC, RATHER THAN NOMADIC (38)	0.58 OF 38	47	TEND TO BE THOSE WHERE, IF SETTLEMENTS ARE NON-FIXED, MOVEMENT IS NOMADIC, RATHER THAN NON-NOMADIC (72)	0.89 OF 35	16 31 22 4 XSQ= 15.19 PHI= -0.456 XP = 0.0001
51	TEND TO BE THOSE WHERE SUBSISTENCE IS PRIMARILY BY FOOD PRODUCTION -- I. E., AGRICULTURE OR HUSBANDRY -- RATHER THAN BY GATHERING (253)	0.75 OF 178	51	TEND TO BE THOSE WHERE SUBSISTENCE IS PRIMARILY BY FOOD GATHERING -- I. E., HUNTING, FISHING, OR COLLECTING -- RATHER THAN FOOD PRODUCTION (147)	0.78 OF 46	133 10 45 36 XSQ= 42.18 PHI= 0.434 XP = 0.
54	TEND TO BE THOSE WHERE FOOD PRODUCTION IS BY INTENSIVE OR SIMPLE AGRICULTURE, RATHER THAN BY INCIPIENT FOOD PRODUCTION (192)	0.87 OF 150	54	TEND TO BE THOSE WHERE FOOD PRODUCTION IS BY INCIPIENT FOOD PRODUCTION, RATHER THAN BY INTENSIVE OR SIMPLE AGRICULTURE (46)	0.60 OF 10	130 4 20 6 XSQ= 11.77 PHI= 0.271 XP = 0.0006

56	DRIFT TCWARD BEING THCSE WHERE FCCD PRCDUCTION IS BY SIMPLE AGRICULTURE, RATHER THAN BY INCIPIENT FOCD PRCCUCTICN (101)	0.75 OF 80	56	DRIFT TOWARD BEING THOSE WHERE FOOD PRODUCTION IS BY INCIPIENT FOOD PRODUCTICN, RATHER THAN BY SIMPLE AGRICULTURE (46)	0.60 CF 10	60 4 20 6 XSQ= 3.73 PHI= 0.204 XP = 0.0533
62	TEND TC BE THCSE WHERE HUSBANDRY CF SOME KIND IS PRESENT (228)	0.79 OF 178	62	TEND TO BE THOSE WHERE HUSBANDRY OF ANY KIND IS ABSENT (172)	0.72 CF 46	141 13 37 33 XSQ= 41.83 PHI= 0.432 XP = 0.
71	TEND TC BE THCSE WHERE METAL WCRKING IS PRESENT (98)	0.55 OF 133	71	TEND TO BE THOSE WHERE METAL WORKING IS ABSENT (153)	0.87 CF 39	73 5 60 34 XSQ= 19.87 PHI= 0.340 XP = 0.0000
73	TEND TC BE THOSE WHERE WEAVING IS PRESENT (118)	0.58 OF 130	73	TEND TO BE THOSE WHERE WEAVING IS ABSENT (130)	0.77 CF 39	75 9 55 30 XSQ= 13.03 PHI= 0.278 XP = 0.0003
74	TEND TC BE THCSE WHERE PCTTERY IS PRESENT (145)	0.68 OF 129	74	TEND TO BE THOSE WHERE POTTERY IS ABSENT (93)	0.68 CF 37	88 12 41 25 XSQ= 13.91 PHI= 0.290 XP = 0.0002
84	LEAN LESS TOWARC BEING THCSE WHERE THE LEVEL CF POLITICAL INTEGRATION IS THE LITTLE STATE, THE MINIMAL STATE, THE AUTCNCMOUS CCMMUNITY, CR THE FAMILY (262) GPM	0.76 OF 139	84	IN ALL CASES ARE THOSE WHERE THE LEVEL OF POLITICAL INTEGRATION IS THE LITTLE STATE, THE MINIMAL STATE, THE AUTONOMOUS COMMUNITY, CR THE FAMILY (262) GPM	1.00 CF 37	33 0 106 37 XSQ= 9.31 PHI= 0.230 XP = 0.0023
86	TEND TO BE THCSE WHERE THE LEVEL CF PCLITICAL INTEGRATION IS THE LARGE STATE, THE LITTLE STATE, OR THE MINIMAL STATE (148) GPM	0.57 OF 139	86	TEND TO BE THOSE WHERE THE LEVEL OF POLITICAL INTEGRATION IS THE AUTONOMOUS COMMUNITY, OR THE FAMILY (156) GPM	0.92 CF 37	79 3 60 34 XSQ= 25.96 PHI= 0.384 XP = 0.0000
91	DRIFT TOWARD BEING THCSE WHERE SCCIETAL CCMPLEXITY IS HIGH (18) F-W	0.54 OF 26	91	DRIFT TOWARD BEING THOSE WHERE SOCIETAL COMPLEXITY IS LOW (22) F-W	0.86 CF 7	14 1 12 6 XSQ= 2.07 PHI= 0.250 EP = 0.0952
96	TEND TO BE THCSE WHERE THE HIERARCHY OF NATICNAL JURISDICTICN HAS FCUR, THREE, TWC OR CNE LEVEL (174) GES,EA	0.59 OF 175	96	TEND TO BE THOSE WHERE THE HIERARCHY OF NATIONAL JURISDICTION HAS NO LEVELS (156) GES,EA	0.80 CF 46	103 9 72 37 XSQ= 20.95 PHI= 0.308 XP = 0.0000

No.			No.			
98	TEND TO BE THOSE WHERE THE HIERARCHY OF LOCAL JURISDICTION HAS FOUR OR THREE LEVELS (238) GES,EA	0.80 OF 176	98	TEND TO BE THOSE WHERE THE HIERARCHY OF LOCAL JURISDICTION HAS TWO LEVELS (93) GES,EA	0.57 OF 46	141 20 35 26 XSQ= 22.76 PHI= 0.320 XP = 0.0000
99	TEND TO BE THOSE WHERE, WITH NATIONAL HIERARCHY ABSENT, THE HIERARCHY OF LOCAL JURISDICTION HAS FOUR OR THREE LEVELS (93) GES,EA	0.75 OF 72	99	TEND TO BE THOSE WHERE, WITH NATIONAL HIERARCHY ABSENT, THE HIERARCHY OF LOCAL JURISDICTION HAS TWO LEVELS (63) GES,EA	0.62 OF 37	54 14 18 23 XSQ= 12.84 PHI= 0.343 XP = 0.0003
100	TEND TO BE THOSE WHERE HIERARCHIES ARE MORE COMPLEX THAN THE 'SIMPLEST,' I. E., MORE COMPLEX THAN TWO LOCAL LEVELS WITH NO NATIONAL LEVELS (267) GES,EA	0.90 OF 175	100	TEND TO BE THOSE WHERE HIERARCHIES ARE THE 'SIMPLEST' I. E., WHERE THERE ARE ONLY TWO LOCAL LEVELS WITH NO NATIONAL LEVELS (63) GES,EA	0.50 OF 46	157 23 18 23 XSQ= 35.44 PHI= 0.400 XP = 0.
102	TEND TO BE THOSE WHERE CLASS STRATIFICATION IS PRESENT (203)	0.65 OF 175	102	TEND TO BE THOSE WHERE CLASS STRATIFICATION IS ABSENT (180)	0.80 OF 44	114 9 61 35 XSQ= 26.73 PHI= 0.349 XP = 0.0000
106	DRIFT TOWARD BEING THOSE WHERE CLASS STRATIFICATION, IF PRESENT, IS BASED ON SOMETHING OTHER THAN WEALTH (126)	0.61 OF 114	106	DRIFT TOWARD BEING THOSE WHERE CLASS STRATIFICATION, IF PRESENT, IS BASED ON WEALTH (77)	0.78 OF 9	45 7 69 2 XSQ= 3.57 PHI= -0.170 XP = 0.0589
109	DRIFT LESS TOWARD BEING THOSE WHERE CASTES ARE ABSENT (317)	0.83 OF 163	109	DRIFT MORE TOWARD BEING THOSE WHERE CASTES ARE ABSENT (317)	0.95 OF 44	28 2 135 42 XSQ= 3.50 PHI= 0.130 XP = 0.0614
110	LEAN LESS TOWARD BEING THOSE WHERE SLAVERY IS ABSENT (218)	0.53 OF 173	110	LEAN MORE TOWARD BEING THOSE WHERE SLAVERY IS ABSENT (218)	0.80 OF 45	82 9 91 36 XSQ= 9.93 PHI= 0.213 XP = 0.0016
131	TEND MORE TO BE THOSE WHERE THE CONSTRUCTION OF PERMANENT HOUSES OR THE ERECTION OF TEMPORARY DWELLINGS IS MAINLY DONE BY MALES (136)	0.95 OF 87	131	TEND LESS TO BE THOSE WHERE THE CONSTRUCTION OF PERMANENT HOUSES OR THE ERECTION OF TEMPORARY DWELLINGS IS MAINLY DONE BY MALES (136)	0.62 OF 26	83 16 4 10 XSQ= 18.14 PHI= 0.401 XP = 0.0000
137	TILT LESS TOWARD BEING THOSE WHERE INVIDIOUS DISPLAY OF WEALTH IS MODERATELY, LITTLE, OR NEGATIVELY EMPHASIZED (52) PES	0.53 OF 55	137	TILT MORE TOWARD BEING THOSE WHERE INVIDIOUS DISPLAY OF WEALTH IS MODERATELY, LITTLE, OR NEGATIVELY EMPHASIZED (52) PES	0.88 OF 16	26 2 29 14 XSQ= 4.90 PHI= 0.263 XP = 0.0268

138	TILT TOWARD BEING THOSE 0.68 OF 22 WHERE SUPERORDINATE JUSTICE IS PRESENT (22) BBW	138	TILT TOWARD BEING THOSE 0.88 OF 8 WHERE SUPERORDINATE JUSTICE IS ABSENT (18) BBW	15 1 7 7 XSQ= 5.24 PHI= 0.418 EP = 0.0121
139	TILT LESS TOWARD BEING THOSE 0.55 OF 22 WHERE SUPERORDINATE PUNISHMENT IS ABSENT (25) BBW	139	IN ALL CASES ARE THOSE 1.00 OF 8 WHERE SUPERORDINATE PUNISHMENT IS ABSENT (25) BBW	10 0 12 8 XSQ= 3.60 PHI= 0.346 EP = 0.0288
147	LEAN TOWARD BEING THOSE 0.88 OF 16 WHERE CODIFIED LAWS ARE PRESENT (20) LWS	147	LEAN TOWARD BEING THOSE 0.67 OF 9 WHERE CODIFIED LAWS ARE UNIMPORTANT OR ABSENT (13) LWS	14 3 2 6 XSQ= 5.48 PHI= 0.468 EP = 0.0099
152	DRIFT TOWARD BEING THOSE 0.64 OF 11 WHERE THE DIFFERENTIATION OF THE JURIDICAL AGENCY FROM THE MEDICAL AGENCY IS HIGH (10) MJ	152	IN ALL CASES ARE THOSE 1.00 OF 4 WHERE THE DIFFERENTIATION OF THE JURIDICAL AGENCY FROM THE MEDICAL AGENCY IS LOW (10) MJ	7 0 4 4 XSQ= 2.56 PHI= 0.413 EP = 0.0769
178	TILT LESS TOWARD BEING THOSE 0.75 OF 174 WHERE THE COMMUNITY IS OTHER THAN SEGMENTED ON A CLAN BASIS AND NON-EXOGAMOUS (295)	178	TILT MORE TOWARD BEING THOSE 0.93 OF 46 WHERE THE COMMUNITY IS OTHER THAN SEGMENTED ON A CLAN BASIS AND NON-EXOGAMOUS (295)	44 3 130 43 XSQ= 6.55 PHI= 0.173 XP = 0.0105
179	LEAN MORE TOWARD BEING THOSE 0.91 OF 174 WHERE THE COMMUNITY IS OTHER THAN STRUCTURED ON A NON-CLAN BASIS AND COMMONLY EXOGAMOUS (340)	179	LEAN LESS TOWARD BEING THOSE 0.76 OF 46 WHERE THE COMMUNITY IS OTHER THAN STRUCTURED ON A NON-CLAN BASIS AND COMMONLY EXOGAMOUS (340)	15 11 159 35 XSQ= 6.76 PHI= -0.175 XP = 0.0093
180	LEAN TOWARD BEING THOSE 0.71 OF 174 WHERE THE COMMUNITY IS COMMONLY NON-EXOGAMOUS, RATHER THAN EXOGAMOUS (258)	180	LEAN TOWARD BEING THOSE 0.52 OF 46 WHERE THE COMMUNITY IS COMMONLY EXOGAMOUS, RATHER THAN NON-EXOGAMOUS (124)	50 24 124 22 XSQ= 7.93 PHI= -0.190 XP = 0.0049
183	TILT MORE TOWARD BEING THOSE 0.89 OF 123 WHERE THE LARGEST NON-COGNATIC KIN GROUP IS SMALLER THAN A MOEITY, I. E., A PHRATRY OR SIB OR LINEAGE (218)	183	TILT LESS TOWARD BEING THOSE 0.68 OF 25 WHERE THE LARGEST NON-COGNATIC KIN GROUP IS SMALLER THAN A MOEITY, I. E., A PHRATRY OR SIB OR LINEAGE (218)	14 8 109 17 XSQ= 5.45 PHI= -0.192 XP = 0.0196
184	DRIFT MORE TOWARD BEING THOSE 0.74 OF 123 WHERE THE LARGEST NON-COGNATIC KIN GROUP IS SMALLER THAN A PHRATRY, I. E. A SIB OR LINEAGE (175)	184	DRIFT LESS TOWARD BEING THOSE 0.52 OF 25 WHERE THE LARGEST NON-COGNATIC KIN GROUP IS SMALLER THAN A PHRATRY, I. E. A SIB OR LINEAGE (175)	32 12 91 13 XSQ= 3.81 PHI= -0.160 XP = 0.0509

186	TILT LESS TOWARD BEING THOSE 0.59 OF 178 WHERE THE KIN GROUP IS OTHER THAN EXCLUSIVELY PATRILINEAL (250)	186	TILT MORE TOWARD BEING THOSE 0.80 OF 46 WHERE THE KIN GROUP IS OTHER THAN EXCLUSIVELY PATRILINEAL (250)	73 9 105 37 XSQ= 6.35 PHI= 0.168 XP = 0.0117
188	DRIFT MORE TOWARD BEING THOSE 0.69 OF 178 WHERE THE KIN GROUP IS OTHER THAN EXCLUSIVELY COGNATIC (252)	188	DRIFT LESS TOWARD BEING THOSE 0.54 OF 46 WHERE THE KIN GROUP IS OTHER THAN EXCLUSIVELY COGNATIC (252)	55 21 123 25 XSQ= 2.92 PHI= -0.114 XP = 0.0874
192	DRIFT MORE TOWARD BEING THOSE 0.76 OF 178 OTHER THAN WHERE THE ONLY KIN GROUP PRESENT IS A KINDRED OR ELSE BILATERAL DESCENT IS INFERRED (289)	192	DRIFT LESS TOWARD BEING THOSE 0.63 OF 46 OTHER THAN WHERE THE ONLY KIN GROUP PRESENT IS A KINDRED OR ELSE BILATERAL DESCENT IS INFERRED (289)	42 17 136 29 XSQ= 2.71 PHI= -0.110 XP = 0.0997
196	TEND TO BE THOSE 0.74 OF 136 WHERE INDIVIDUAL RIGHTS IN REAL PROPERTY, AND RULES FOR INHERITANCE, ARE PRESENT (194)	196	TEND TO BE THOSE 0.71 OF 31 WHERE INDIVIDUAL RIGHTS IN REAL PROPERTY, OR RULES FOR INHERITANCE, ARE ABSENT (87)	101 9 35 22 XSQ= 21.01 PHI= 0.355 XP = 0.0000
234	TILT TOWARD BEING THOSE 0.54 OF 142 WHERE THE COUSIN TERMINOLOGY IS OF ESKIMO OR HAWAIIAN TYPE, RATHER THAN CROW, OMAHA, OR IROQUOIS TYPE (170)	234	TILT TOWARD BEING THOSE 0.67 OF 39 WHERE THE COUSIN TERMINOLOGY IS OF CROW, OMAHA, OR IROQUOIS TYPE, RATHER THAN ESKIMO OR HAWAIIAN TYPE (152)	66 26 76 13 XSQ= 4.21 PHI= -0.153 XP = 0.0401
236	LEAN TOWARD BEING THOSE 0.58 OF 177 WHERE THE FAMILY IS OF AN EXTENDED TYPE, RATHER THAN AN INDEPENDENT TYPE (213)	236	LEAN TOWARD BEING THOSE 0.70 OF 46 WHERE THE FAMILY IS OF AN INDEPENDENT TYPE, RATHER THAN AN EXTENDED TYPE (185)	102 14 75 32 XSQ= 9.75 PHI= 0.209 XP = 0.0018
278	TILT TOWARD BEING THOSE 0.70 OF 10 WHERE PROPERTY RIGHTS IN WOMEN ARE PRESENT (8) LWS	278	IN ALL CASES ARE THOSE 1.00 OF 6 WHERE PROPERTY RIGHTS IN WOMEN ARE UNIMPORTANT OR ABSENT (14) LWS	7 0 3 6 XSQ= 4.89 PHI= 0.553 EP = 0.0114
299	TILT LESS TOWARD BEING THOSE 0.68 OF 72 WHERE THE POST-PARTUM SEX TABOO LASTS ONE YEAR OR LESS (89)	299	TILT MORE TOWARD BEING THOSE 0.96 OF 23 WHERE THE POST-PARTUM SEX TABOO LASTS ONE YEAR OR LESS (89)	23 1 49 22 XSQ= 5.65 PHI= 0.244 XP = 0.0175
300	TILT LESS TOWARD BEING THOSE 0.54 OF 72 WHERE THE POST-PARTUM SEX TABOO LASTS SIX MONTHS OR LESS (73)	300	TILT MORE TOWARD BEING THOSE 0.87 OF 23 WHERE THE POST-PARTUM SEX TABOO LASTS SIX MONTHS OR LESS (73)	33 3 39 20 XSQ= 6.63 PHI= 0.264 XP = 0.0100

305	DRIFT LESS TOWARD BEING THOSE WHERE THE EARLY SEXUAL SATISFACTION POTENTIAL IS HIGH (27) W-C	0.54 OF	26	305	IN ALL CASES ARE THOSE WHERE THE EARLY SEXUAL SATISFACTION POTENTIAL IS HIGH (27) W-C	1.00 OF	6	14 6 12 0 XSQ= 2.68 PHI= -0.289 EP = 0.0613
306	TILT TOWARD BEING THOSE WHERE THE EARLY DEPENDENCE SATISFACTION POTENTIAL IS LOW (24) W-C	0.50 OF	26	306	IN ALL CASES ARE THOSE WHERE THE EARLY DEPENDENCE SATISFACTION POTENTIAL IS HIGH (28) W-C	1.00 OF	7	13 7 13 0 XSQ= 3.87 PHI= -0.342 EP = 0.0266
308	DRIFT TOWARD BEING THOSE WHERE AVERAGE SOCIALIZATION ANXIETY IS HIGH (22) W-C	0.63 OF	24	308	IN ALL CASES ARE THOSE WHERE AVERAGE SOCIALIZATION ANXIETY IS LOW (18) W-C	1.00 OF	3	15 0 9 3 XSQ= 2.07 PHI= 0.277 EP = 0.0752
309	TILT TOWARD BEING THOSE WHERE ORAL SOCIALIZATION ANXIETY IS HIGH (26) W-C	0.68 OF	28	309	TILT TOWARD BEING THOSE WHERE ORAL SOCIALIZATION ANXIETY IS LOW (27) W-C	0.75 OF	8	19 2 9 6 XSQ= 3.10 PHI= 0.294 EP = 0.0461
310	TILT TOWARD BEING THOSE WHERE ANAL SOCIALIZATION ANXIETY IS HIGH (22) W-C	0.63 OF	24	310	IN ALL CASES ARE THOSE WHERE ANAL SOCIALIZATION ANXIETY IS LOW (19) W-C	1.00 OF	4	15 0 9 4 XSQ= 3.16 PHI= 0.336 EP = 0.0349
311	LEAN TOWARD BEING THOSE WHERE SEXUAL SOCIALIZATION ANXIETY IS HIGH (28) W-C	0.67 OF	27	311	IN ALL CASES ARE THOSE WHERE SEXUAL SOCIALIZATION ANXIETY IS LOW (23) W-C	1.00 OF	6	18 0 9 6 XSQ= 6.32 PHI= 0.438 EP = 0.0045
313	TILT TOWARD BEING THOSE WHERE AGGRESSION SOCIALIZATION ANXIETY IS HIGH (26) W-C	0.55 OF	29	313	IN ALL CASES ARE THOSE WHERE AGGRESSION SOCIALIZATION ANXIETY IS LOW (28) W-C	1.00 OF	7	16 0 13 7 XSQ= 4.90 PHI= 0.369 EP = 0.0107
320	DRIFT LESS TOWARD BEING THOSE WHERE THE DEGREE OF REDUCTION OF THE INFANT'S DRIVES IS HIGH (45) B-B-C	0.56 OF	41	320	IN ALL CASES ARE THOSE WHERE THE DEGREE OF REDUCTION OF THE INFANT'S DRIVES IS HIGH (45) B-B-C	1.00 OF	8	23 8 18 0 XSQ= 3.82 PHI= -0.279 XP = 0.0505
335	TILT TOWARD BEING THOSE WHERE INITIAL INDULGENCE OF DEPENDENCY IS LOW (18) WNS	0.53 OF	19	335	IN ALL CASES ARE THOSE WHERE INITIAL INDULGENCE OF DEPENDENCY IS HIGH (20) WNS	1.00 OF	7	9 7 10 0 XSQ= 3.97 PHI= -0.391 EP = 0.0227

353	TILT TOWARD BEING THOSE WHERE THE CHILD'S INFERRED ANXIETY OVER NON-PERFORMANCE OF OBEDIENT BEHAVIOR IS HIGH (42) B-B-C	0.65 OF 43	353	TILT TOWARD BEING THOSE WHERE THE CHILD-S INFERRED ANXIETY OVER NON-PERFORMANCE OF OBEDIENT BEHAVIOR IS LOW (32) B-B-C	0.78 OF 9	28 2 15 7 XSQ= 3.99 PHI= 0.277 XP = 0.0458
390	LEAN LESS TOWARD BEING THOSE WHERE PREMARITAL SEX RELATIONS ARE WEAKLY PUNISHED AND IN FACT NOT RARE OR PUNISHED ONLY IF PREGNANCY RESULTS, OR FREELY PERMITTED (132) JTW,EA	0.69 OF 110	390	IN ALL CASES ARE THOSE WHERE PREMARITAL SEX RELATIONS ARE WEAKLY PUNISHED AND IN FACT NOT RARE OR PUNISHED ONLY IF PREGNANCY RESULTS, OR FREELY PERMITTED (132) JTW,EA	1.00 OF 21	34 0 76 21 XSQ= 7.23 PHI= 0.235 XP = 0.0072
391	TILT TOWARD BEING THOSE WHERE PREMARITAL SEX RELATIONS ARE STRONGLY PUNISHED AND IN FACT RARE, OR WEAKLY PUNISHED AND IN FACT NOT RARE (89) JTW,EA	0.55 OF 110	391	TILT TOWARD BEING THOSE WHERE PREMARITAL SEX RELATIONS ARE PUNISHED ONLY IF PREGNANCY RESULTS, OR FREELY PERMITTED (90) JTW,EA	0.71 OF 21	61 6 49 15 XSQ= 4.08 PHI= 0.177 XP = 0.0434
392	LEAN TOWARD BEING THOSE WHERE PREMARITAL SEX RELATIONS ARE STRONGLY PUNISHED AND IN FACT RARE, OR WEAKLY PUNISHED AND IN FACT NOT RARE, OR PUNISHED ONLY IF PREGNANCY RESULTS (112) JTW,EA	0.71 OF 110	392	LEAN TOWARD BEING THOSE WHERE PREMARITAL SEX RELATIONS ARE FREELY PERMITTED (67) JTW,EA	0.67 OF 21	78 7 32 14 XSQ= 9.34 PHI= 0.267 XP = 0.0022
393	TILT TOWARD BEING THOSE WHERE EXTRAMARITAL COITUS IS PUNISHED, RATHER THAN PERMITTED (43) F-B	0.53 OF 43	393	TILT TOWARD BEING THOSE WHERE EXTRAMARITAL COITUS IS PERMITTED, RATHER THAN PUNISHED (41) F-B	0.85 OF 13	23 2 20 11 XSQ= 4.42 PHI= 0.281 XP = 0.0354
398	TILT TOWARD BEING THOSE WHERE THE INTENSITY OF SEX ANXIETY IS HIGH (16) WNS	0.63 OF 16	398	IN ALL CASES ARE THOSE WHERE THE INTENSITY OF SEX ANXIETY IS LOW (16) WNS	1.00 OF 6	10 0 6 6 XSQ= 4.59 PHI= 0.457 EP = 0.0152
404	TILT LESS TOWARD BEING THOSE WHERE EXPLANATIONS OF ILLNESS OF A SEXUAL NATURE ARE ABSENT (42) W-C	0.61 OF 31	404	IN ALL CASES ARE THOSE WHERE EXPLANATIONS OF ILLNESS OF A SEXUAL NATURE ARE ABSENT (42) W-C	1.00 OF 9	12 0 19 9 XSQ= 3.30 PHI= 0.287 EP = 0.0375
417	IN ALL CASES ARE THOSE WHERE WARFARE IS PREVALENT (34) LWS	1.00 OF 19	417	TEND TO BE THOSE WHERE WARFARE IS NOT PREVALENT (9) LWS	0.73 OF 11	19 3 0 8 XSQ= 15.31 PHI= 0.714 EP = 0.0000
419	DRIFT TOWARD BEING THOSE WHERE MILITARY GLORY IS STRONGLY OR MODERATELY EMPHASIZED (55) PES	0.65 OF 52	419	DRIFT TOWARD BEING THOSE WHERE MILITARY GLORY IS NEGLIGIBLY EMPHASIZED (31) PES	0.67 OF 15	34 5 18 10 XSQ= 3.69 PHI= 0.235 XP = 0.0548

420 DRIFT LESS TOWARD BEING THOSE 0.54 OF 52 WHERE BELLICOSITY IS MODERATE OR NEGLIGIBLE (46) PES	420 DRIFT MORE TOWARD BEING THOSE 0.81 OF 16 WHERE BELLICOSITY IS MODERATE OR NEGLIGIBLE (46) PES	24 3 28 13 XSQ= 2.78 PHI= 0.202 XP = 0.0955
424 DRIFT TOWARD BEING THOSE 0.50 OF 36 WHERE RELIGIOUS SPECIALISTS ARE FULL-TIME, RATHER THAN PART-TIME (21) JMH	424 DRIFT TOWARD BEING THOSE 0.89 OF 9 WHERE RELIGIOUS SPECIALISTS ARE PART-TIME, RATHER THAN FULL-TIME (33) JMH	18 1 18 8 XSQ= 3.01 PHI= 0.259 XP = 0.0827
426 TEND TO BE THOSE 0.66 OF 146 WHERE A HIGH GOD IS PRESENT (156) GES,EA	426 TEND TO BE THOSE 0.69 OF 36 WHERE A HIGH GOD IS ABSENT (104) GES,EA	96 11 50 25 XSQ= 13.35 PHI= 0.271 XP = 0.0003
435 DRIFT TOWARD BEING THOSE 0.77 OF 13 WHERE ABANDONMENT OF THE HOUSE OF THE DEAD IS NOT PRACTICED (19) LWS	435 DRIFT TOWARD BEING THOSE 0.67 OF 9 WHERE ABANDONMENT OF THE HOUSE OF THE DEAD IS PRACTICED (12) LWS	3 6 10 3 XSQ= 2.57 PHI= -0.342 EP = 0.0789
447 TILT TOWARD BEING THOSE 0.67 OF 18 WHERE LOVE MAGIC IS PRESENT (20) S-R	447 IN ALL CASES ARE THOSE 1.00 OF 4 WHERE LOVE MAGIC IS ABSENT (13) S-R	12 0 6 4 XSQ= 3.49 PHI= 0.398 EP = 0.0287
452 DRIFT TOWARD BEING THOSE 0.52 OF 27 WHERE TOTEMISM WITH FOOD TABOOS IS PRESENT (19) WNS	452 IN ALL CASES ARE THOSE 1.00 OF 5 WHERE TOTEMISM WITH FOOD TABOOS IS ABSENT (24) WNS	14 0 13 5 XSQ= 2.74 PHI= 0.293 EP = 0.0525
458 LEAN LESS TOWARD BEING THOSE 0.57 OF 103 WHERE GAMES, IF PRESENT, DO NOT INCLUDE GAMES OF STRATEGY (119) R-A-B,EA	458 LEAN MORE TOWARD BEING THOSE 0.92 OF 24 WHERE GAMES, IF PRESENT, DO NOT INCLUDE GAMES OF STRATEGY (119) R-A-B,EA	44 2 59 22 XSQ= 8.53 PHI= 0.259 XP = 0.0035
459 DRIFT TOWARD BEING THOSE 0.53 OF 103 WHERE GAMES, IF PRESENT, INCLUDE GAMES OF CHANCE (82) R-A-B,EA	459 DRIFT TOWARD BEING THOSE 0.71 OF 24 WHERE GAMES, IF PRESENT, DO NOT INCLUDE GAMES OF CHANCE (89) R-A-B,EA	55 7 48 17 XSQ= 3.66 PHI= 0.170 XP = 0.0559
460 LEAN TOWARD BEING THOSE 0.69 OF 103 WHERE GAMES, IF PRESENT, ARE NOT LIMITED TO GAMES OF SKILL ONLY (104) R-A-B,EA	460 LEAN TOWARD BEING THOSE 0.63 OF 24 WHERE GAMES, IF PRESENT, ARE LIMITED TO GAMES OF SKILL ONLY (67) R-A-B,EA	32 15 71 9 XSQ= 6.96 PHI= -0.234 XP = 0.0084

```
476  TILT TOWARD BEING THOSE         0.54 OF  28     476  TILT TOWARD BEING THOSE         0.90 OF  10           13     9
     WHERE THE DEGREE OF INSOBRIETY IS                    WHERE THE DEGREE OF INSOBRIETY IS                     15     1
     MODERATE OR SLIGHT  (18) CH                          STRONG  (31) DH                                 XSQ=     4.09
                                                                                                          PHI=   -0.328
                                                                                                          EP =   0.0250

480  TILT TOWARD BEING THOSE         0.64 OF  14     480  IN ALL CASES ARE THOSE          1.00 OF   5            9     0
     WHERE COMPLEXITY OF ARTISTIC DESIGN                  WHERE COMPLEXITY OF ARTISTIC DESIGN                    5     5
     IS HIGH  (14) HB                                     IS LOW  (15) HB                                 XSQ=     3.80
                                                                                                          PHI=    0.447
                                                                                                          EP =   0.0325
```

83 CULTURES
WHERE, WITH NC CITY ANC NC TOWN PRESENT,
THE AVERAGE COMMUNITY SIZE IS
BETWEEN 200 AND 999, RATHER THAN
SMALLER THAN 200 (45)

83 CULTURES
WHERE, WITH NO CITY AND NO TOWN PRESENT,
THE AVERAGE COMMUNITY SIZE IS
SMALLER THAN 200, RATHER THAN
BETWEEN 200 AND 999 (135)

BACKGROUND ON PAGE 81 BOTH SUBJECT AND PREDICATE

45 IN LEFT COLUMN

ALBANIANS AYMARA BASSERI BAYA BURUSHO CAYAPA CHAGGA CHEROKEE COCHITI CREEK
DARD DELAWARE ENGA HANO HAVASUPAI HUICHOL ILA JEMEZ KABYLE KATAB
KIKUYU LESU MAMBILA MARGI MBUNDU MENDE MIAMI MINCHIA NATCHEZ NAVAHO
NUPE NURI NYCRO PAIWAN PATHAN SHILLUK SOTHO TALLENSI TAOS TENINO
TIKOPIA TIV TUPINAMBA VENDA YOMBE

135 IN RIGHT COLUMN

ABOR AKHA ALACALUF ALORESE AMBA ANDAMANESE APINAYE ARANDA ARAUCANIANS ATAYAL
ATSUGEWI AWEIKOMA AZANDE BACAIRI BARABRA BEMBA BHIL BHUIYA BIRIFOR BOTOCUDO
BUNLAP CAMAYURA CARIB CHENCHU CHOCO CHOROTI CHUKCHEE CCCRG COPR ESKIMO CREE
CUNA DIERI DOGON DOROBO EYAK FANG GARO GILYAK GOAJIRO GOND
GUAHIBO HANUNCO HAZARA IFUGAO IRAQW KACHIN KAPAUKU KARIERA KASKA KAZAK
KERAKI KHALKA KHASI KISSI KORYAK KPE KUBA KUNG KURTATCHI LAMET
LANGO LAPPS LAU LEPCHA LOLO LOZI LUO MACASSARESE MAMVU MANUS
MARICOPA MARQUESANS MASAI MATACO MBUTI MISKITO MNONG GAR MOTILON MUNCURUCU MURINBATA
MURNGIN NABESNA NAMA NAMBICUARA NDEMBU NOMLAKI NYAKYUSA OJIBWA OMAHA ONA
PAWNEE PONAPEANS PUKAPUKA PURUM RWALA SAMOANS SAMOYED SANPOIL SEMANG SIRIONO
SOMALI SUBANUN TANALA TAPIRAPE TAREUMIUT TEHUELCHE TENDA THONGA TIMBIRA TIWI
TODA TRISTAN TROBRIAND TRUKESE TRUMAI TUBATULABAL TUCUNA TWANA ULAWANS VEDDA
WAICA WARRAU WASHO WIKMUNKAN WOGEO WOLEAIANS WOLOF YABARANA YAGUA YAHGAN
YAKUT YAC YUKAGHIR YUKI YUROK

44 EXCLUDED BECAUSE IRRELEVANT

AMERICANS ASHANTI AZTEC BAMBARA BLACK CARIB BRAZILIANS BULGARIANS CAMBODIANS CHIBCHA CZECHS
DUTCH EGYPTIANS FON GANDA HUTSUL INCA IRISH JAPANESE JAVANESE KERALA
KOREANS MAM MAYA MERINA MIN CHINESE MOSSI MZAB OKINAWANS RIFFIANS ROMANS
SAGADA SERBS SINHALESE SIWANS SONGHAI SYRIANS THAI TIGRINYA TOTONAC VIETNAMESE
WALLOONS YAKO YORUBA ZUNI

176 EXCLUDED BECAUSE UNASCERTAINED

---

3 LEAN LESS TOWARD BEING THOSE 0.62 OF 45
LOCATED OUTSIDE OF
AFRICA (320)

3 LEAN MORE TOWARD BEING THOSE 0.83 OF 135
LOCATED OUTSIDE OF
AFRICA (320)

17	23
28	112
XSQ=	7.24
PHI=	0.201
XP =	0.0071

8	TILT LESS TOWARD BEING THCSE LOCATED CUTSIDE OF NORTH AMERICA (330)	0.71 OF 45	8	TILT MORE TOWARD BEING THOSE LOCATED OUTSIDE OF NORTH AMERICA (330)	0.87 OF 135	13 18 32 117 XSQ= 4.69 PHI= 0.161 XP = 0.0304
9	TILT MORE TOWARD BEING THCSE LOCATED OUTSIDE CF SOUTH AMERICA (335)	0.93 OF 45	9	TILT LESS TOWARD BEING THCSE LOCATED OUTSIDE OF SOUTH AMERICA (335)	0.78 CF 135	3 30 42 105 XSQ= 4.47 PHI= -0.157 XP = 0.0346
12	IN ALL CASES ARE THOSE WHERE THE LATITUDE IS LESS THAN FIFTY DEGREES (367)	1.00 OF 45	12	TILT LESS TOWARD BEING THOSE WHERE THE LATITUDE IS LESS THAN FIFTY DEGREES (367)	0.87 CF 135	0 18 45 117 XSQ= 5.27 PHI= -0.171 XP = 0.0217
14	DRIFT LESS TCWARD BEING THOSE WHERE THE LATITUDE IS LESS THAN THIRTY DEGREES (281)	0.58 OF 45	14	DRIFT MORE TOWARD BEING THCSE WHERE THE LATITUDE IS LESS THAN THIRTY DEGREES (281)	0.74 CF 135	19 35 26 100 XSQ= 3.53 PHI= 0.140 XP = 0.0604
42	LEAN MORE TOWARD BEING THCSE WHERE THE NATURAL ENVIRONMENT IS OTHER THAN TROPICAL CR SUB-TRCPICAL RAIN FOREST, OR MONSCCN FCREST (244) FWM	0.80 OF 45	42	LEAN LESS TOWARD BEING THOSE WHERE THE NATURAL ENVIRONMENT IS OTHER THAN TROPICAL OR SUB-TROPICAL RAIN FOREST, OR MONSOON FOREST (244) FWM	0.56 CF 135	9 59 36 76 XSQ= 7.09 PHI= -0.198 XP = 0.0078
44	TEND MCRE TO BE THCSE WHERE SETTLEMENTS ARE FIXEC (222)	0.82 OF 45	44	TEND LESS TO BE THOSE WHERE SETTLEMENTS ARE FIXED (222)	0.51 CF 134	37 69 8 65 XSQ= 11.93 PHI= 0.258 XP = 0.0006
46	TEND MORE TO BE THCSE OTHER THAN WHERE SETTLEMENTS ARE NON-FIXED AND MCVEMENT IS NOMADIC (260)	0.98 OF 45	46	TEND LESS TO BE THOSE OTHER THAN WHERE SETTLEMENTS ARE NON-FIXED AND MOVEMENT IS NOMADIC (260)	0.66 CF 134	1 46 44 88 XSQ= 16.31 PHI= -0.302 XP = 0.0001
47	LEAN TOWARD BEING THCSE WHERE, IF SETTLEMENTS ARE NON-FIXEC, MOVEMENT IS NCN-NOMADIC, RATHER THAN NOMADIC (38)	0.88 OF 8	47	LEAN TOWARD BEING THOSE WHERE, IF SETTLEMENTS ARE NON-FIXED, MOVEMENT IS NOMADIC, RATHER THAN NON-NOMADIC (72)	0.71 CF 65	1 46 7 19 XSQ= 8.16 PHI= -0.334 XP = 0.0043
51	LEAN TOWARD BEING THOSE WHERE SUBSISTENCE IS PRIMARILY BY FCCD PRCDUCTION -- I. E., AGRICULTURE OR HUSBANDRY -- RATHER THAN BY GATHERING (253)	0.76 OF 45	51	LEAN TOWARD BEING THOSE WHERE SUBSISTENCE IS PRIMARILY BY FOOD GATHERING -- I. E., HUNTING, FISHING, OR COLLECTING -- RATHER THAN FOOD PRODUCTION (147)	0.52 OF 135	34 65 11 70 XSQ= 9.17 PHI= 0.226 XP = 0.0025

53	TEND TO BE THOSE WHERE FOOD PRODUCTION IS BY INTENSIVE AGRICULTURE, RATHER THAN BY SIMPLE AGRICULTURE OR INCIPIENT FOOD PRODUCTION (91)	0.50 OF 42	53	TEND TO BE THOSE WHERE FOOD PRODUCTION IS BY SIMPLE AGRICULTURE OR INCIPIENT FOOD PRODUCTION, RATHER THAN BY INTENSIVE AGRICULTURE (147)	0.82 OF 74	21 13 21 61 XSQ= 12.08 PHI= 0.323 XP = 0.0005
55	TEND TO BE THOSE WHERE FOOD PRODUCTION IS BY INTENSIVE AGRICULTURE, RATHER THAN BY SIMPLE AGRICULTURE (91)	0.64 OF 33	55	TEND TO BE THOSE WHERE FOOD PRODUCTION IS BY SIMPLE AGRICULTURE, RATHER THAN BY INTENSIVE AGRICULTURE (101)	0.77 OF 57	21 13 12 44 XSQ= 13.14 PHI= 0.382 XP = 0.0003
62	TILT MORE TOWARD BEING THOSE WHERE HUSBANDRY OF SOME KIND IS PRESENT (228)	0.78 OF 45	62	TILT LESS TOWARD BEING THOSE WHERE HUSBANDRY OF SOME KIND IS PRESENT (228)	0.59 OF 135	35 79 10 56 XSQ= 4.59 PHI= 0.160 XP = 0.0321
71	TILT TOWARD BEING THOSE WHERE METAL WORKING IS PRESENT (98)	0.55 OF 31	71	TILT TOWARD BEING THOSE WHERE METAL WORKING IS ABSENT (153)	0.68 OF 114	17 37 14 77 XSQ= 4.31 PHI= 0.172 XP = 0.0379
73	DRIFT TOWARD BEING THOSE WHERE WEAVING IS PRESENT (118)	0.57 OF 30	73	DRIFT TOWARD BEING THOSE WHERE WEAVING IS ABSENT (130)	0.63 OF 111	17 41 13 70 XSQ= 3.03 PHI= 0.146 XP = 0.0820
74	LEAN TOWARD BEING THOSE WHERE POTTERY IS PRESENT (145)	0.77 OF 31	74	LEAN TOWARD BEING THOSE WHERE POTTERY IS ABSENT (93)	0.52 OF 109	24 52 7 57 XSQ= 7.43 PHI= 0.230 XP = 0.0064
86	TILT TOWARD BEING THOSE WHERE THE LEVEL OF POLITICAL INTEGRATION IS THE LARGE STATE, THE LITTLE STATE, OR THE MINIMAL STATE (148) GPM	0.55 OF 31	86	TILT TOWARD BEING THOSE WHERE THE LEVEL OF POLITICAL INTEGRATION IS THE AUTONOMOUS COMMUNITY, OR THE FAMILY (156) GPM	0.70 OF 112	17 34 14 78 XSQ= 5.32 PHI= 0.193 XP = 0.0211
91	LEAN TOWARD BEING THOSE WHERE SOCIETAL COMPLEXITY IS HIGH (18) F-W	0.75 OF 8	91	LEAN TOWARD BEING THOSE WHERE SOCIETAL COM LEXITY IS LOW (22) F-	0.83 OF 18	6 3 2 15 XSQ= 5.95 PHI= 0.478 EP = 0.0077
96	LEAN TOWARD BEING THOSE WHERE THE HIERARCHY OF NATIONAL JURISDICTION HAS FOUR, THREE, TWO OR ONE LEVEL (174) GES,EA	0.61 OF 44	96	LEAN TOWARD BEING THOSE WHERE THE HIERARCHY OF NATIONAL JURISDICTION HAS NO LEVELS (156) GES,EA	0.63 OF 135	27 50 17 85 XSQ= 7.05 PHI= 0.198 XP = 0.0079

97	TEND LESS TO BE THOSE WHERE THE HIERARCHY OF LOCAL JURISDICTION HAS THREE OR TWO LEVELS (273) GES,EA	0.71 OF 45	97	TEND MORE TO BE THOSE WHERE THE HIERARCHY OF LOCAL JURISDICTION HAS THREE OR TWO LEVELS (273) GES,EA	0.92 OF 135	13 11 32 124 XSQ= 10.83 PHI= 0.245 XP = 0.0010
98	LEAN MORE TOWARD BEING THOSE WHERE THE HIERARCHY OF LOCAL JURISDICTION HAS FOUR OR THREE LEVELS (238) GES,EA	0.91 OF 45	98	LEAN LESS TOWARD BEING THOSE WHERE THE HIERARCHY OF LOCAL JURISDICTION HAS FOUR OR THREE LEVELS (238) GES,EA	0.65 OF 135	41 88 4 47 XSQ= 9.93 PHI= 0.235 XP = 0.0016
99	LEAN MORE TOWARD BEING THOSE WHERE, WITH NATIONAL HIERARCHY ABSENT, THE HIERARCHY OF LOCAL JURISDICTION HAS FOUR OR THREE LEVELS (93) GES,EA	0.94 OF 17	99	LEAN LESS TOWARD BEING THOSE WHERE, WITH NATIONAL HIERARCHY ABSENT, THE HIERARCHY OF LOCAL JURISDICTION HAS FOUR OR THREE LEVELS (93) GES,EA	0.54 OF 85	16 46 1 39 XSQ= 7.90 PHI= 0.278 XP = 0.0049
100	TEND MORE TO BE THOSE WHERE HIERARCHIES ARE MORE COMPLEX THAN THE 'SIMPLEST,' I. E., MORE COMPLEX THAN TWO LOCAL LEVELS WITH NO NATIONAL LEVELS (267) GES,EA	0.98 OF 44	100	TEND LESS TO BE THOSE WHERE HIERARCHIES ARE MORE COMPLEX THAN THE 'SIMPLEST,' I. E., MORE COMPLEX THAN TWO LOCAL LEVELS WITH NO NATIONAL LEVELS (267) GES,EA	0.71 OF 135	43 96 1 39 XSQ= 12.06 PHI= 0.260 XP = 0.0005
106	TILT TOWARD BEING THOSE WHERE CLASS STRATIFICATION, IF PRESENT, IS BASED ON SOMETHING OTHER THAN WEALTH (126)	0.64 OF 25	106	TILT TOWARD BEING THOSE WHERE CLASS STRATIFICATION, IF PRESENT, IS BASED ON WEALTH (77)	0.64 OF 59	9 38 16 21 XSQ= 4.65 PHI= -0.235 XP = 0.0310
141	DRIFT TOWARD BEING THOSE WHERE THE LEVEL OF SOCIAL SANCTION IS PUBLIC CORPOREAL SANCTION, RATHER THAN PUBLIC PROPERTY SANCTION OR PRIVATE SETTLEMENT (28) JMH	0.73 OF 11	141	DRIFT TOWARD BEING THOSE WHERE THE LEVEL OF SOCIAL SANCTION IS PUBLIC PROPERTY SANCTION OR PRIVATE SETTLEMENT, RATHER THAN PUBLIC CORPOREAL SANCTION (26) JMH	0.62 OF 29	8 11 3 18 XSQ= 2.60 PHI= 0.255 EP = 0.0775
179	DRIFT MORE TOWARD BEING THOSE WHERE THE COMMUNITY IS OTHER THAN STRUCTURED ON A NON-CLAN BASIS AND COMMONLY EXOGAMOUS (340)	0.95 OF 44	179	DRIFT LESS TOWARD BEING THOSE WHERE THE COMMUNITY IS OTHER THAN STRUCTURED ON A NON-CLAN BASIS AND COMMONLY EXOGAMOUS (340)	0.84 OF 134	2 22 42 112 XSQ= 3.05 PHI= -0.131 XP = 0.0808
180	TILT MORE TOWARD BEING THOSE WHERE THE COMMUNITY IS COMMONLY NON-EXOGAMOUS, RATHER THAN EXOGAMOUS (258)	0.75 OF 44	180	TILT LESS TOWARD BEING THOSE WHERE THE COMMUNITY IS COMMONLY NON-EXOGAMOUS, RATHER THAN EXOGAMOUS (258)	0.56 OF 134	11 59 33 75 XSQ= 4.26 PHI= -0.155 XP = 0.0390
181	TILT LESS TOWARD BEING THOSE WHERE THE COMMUNITY IS OTHER THAN A DEME (337)	0.80 OF 44	181	TILT MORE TOWARD BEING THOSE WHERE THE COMMUNITY IS OTHER THAN A DEME (337)	0.93 OF 134	9 9 35 125 XSQ= 5.45 PHI= 0.175 XP = 0.0196

183	TILT MORE TOWARD BEING THCSE 0.94 OF 36 WHERE THE LARGEST NCN-COGNATIC KIN GROUP IS SMALLER THAN A MOEITY, I. E., A PHRATRY CR SIB OR LINEAGE (218)	183	TILT LESS TOWARD BEING THOSE 0.77 CF 88 WHERE THE LARGEST NON-COGNATIC KIN GROUP IS SMALLER THAN A MOEITY, I. E., A PHRATRY OR SIB OR LINEAGE (218)	2 20 34 68 XSQ= 4.05 PHI= -0.181 XP = 0.0441
184	DRIFT MORE TOWARD BEING THOSE 0.81 OF 36 WHERE THE LARGEST NON-COGNATIC KIN GROUP IS SMALLER THAN A PHRATRY, I. E. A SIB OR LINEAGE (175)	184	DRIFT LESS TOWARD BEING THCSE 0.63 OF 88 WHERE THE LARGEST NON-COGNATIC KIN GROUP IS SMALLER THAN A PHRATRY, I. E. A SIB OR LINEAGE (175)	7 33 29 55 XSQ= 3.03 PHI= -0.156 XP = 0.0817
188	DRIFT MORE TOWARD BEING THOSE 0.80 OF 45 WHERE THE KIN GRCUP IS OTHER THAN EXCLUSIVELY COGNATIC (252)	188	DRIFT LESS TOWARD BEING THCSE 0.65 CF 135 WHERE THE KIN GROUP IS OTHER THAN EXCLUSIVELY COGNATIC (252)	9 47 36 88 XSQ= 2.80 PHI= -0.125 XP = 0.0943
192	DRIFT MORE TOWARD BEING THOSE 0.89 OF 45 OTHER THAN WHERE THE ONLY KIN GROUP PRESENT IS A KINDRED CR ELSE BILATERAL DESCENT IS INFERRED (289)	192	DRIFT LESS TOWARD BEING THCSE 0.73 OF 135 OTHER THAN WHERE THE ONLY KIN GRCUP PRESENT IS A KINDRED OR ELSE BILATERAL DESCENT IS INFERRED (289)	5 36 40 99 XSQ= 3.80 PHI= -0.145 XP = 0.0512
196	LEAN TOWARD BEING THCSE 0.78 OF 32 WHERE INDIVIDUAL RIGHTS IN REAL PROPERTY, AND RULES FOR INHERITANCE, ARE PRESENT (194)	196	LEAN TOWARD BEING THOSE 0.50 CF 98 WHERE INDIVIDUAL RIGHTS IN REAL PROPERTY, OR RULES FOR INHERITANCE, ARE ABSENT (87)	25 49 7 49 XSQ= 6.68 PHI= 0.227 XP = 0.0098
213	TILT TOWARD BEING THOSE 0.70 OF 44 WHERE FIRST CCUSIN MARRIAGE IS NOT PERMITTED (198)	213	TILT TOWARD BEING THOSE 0.51 OF 130 WHERE FIRST COUSIN MARRIAGE IS PERMITTED (172)	13 66 31 64 XSQ= 5.15 PHI= -0.172 XP = 0.0233
234	DRIFT TOWARD BEING THCSE 0.57 OF 37 WHERE THE COUSIN TERMINCLOGY IS OF ESKIMO CR HAWAIIAN TYPE, RATHER THAN CROW, OMAHA, OR IRCQUCIS TYPE (170)	234	DRIFT TOWARD BEING THOSE 0.61 CF 111 WHERE THE COUSIN TERMINOLOGY IS OF CROW, OMAHA, OR IROQUOIS TYPE, RATHER THAN ESKIMO OR HAWAIIAN TYPE (152)	16 68 21 43 XSQ= 2.97 PHI= -0.142 XP = 0.0847
236	DRIFT TOWARD BEING THOSE 0.64 OF 45 WHERE THE FAMILY IS OF AN EXTENDED TYPE, RATHER THAN AN INDEPENDENT TYPE (213)	236	DRIFT TOWARD BEING THOSE 0.53 OF 135 WHERE THE FAMILY IS OF AN INDEPENDENT TYPE, RATHER THAN AN EXTENDED TYPE (185)	29 63 16 72 XSQ= 3.59 PHI= 0.141 XP = 0.0582
299	LEAN TOWARD BEING THOSE 0.60 OF 15 WHERE THE POST-PARTUM SEX TABOO LASTS LONGER THAN ONE YEAR (35)	299	LEAN TOWARD BEING THOSE 0.80 CF 66 WHERE THE POST-PARTUM SEX TABOO LASTS ONE YEAR OR LESS (89)	9 13 6 53 XSQ= 8.10 PHI= 0.316 XP = 0.0044

352 TILT TOWARD BEING THOSE 0.92 OF 13 WHERE THE TOTAL POSITIVE PRESSURE TOWARD DEVELOPING OBEDIENT BEHAVIOR IN THE CHILD IS HIGH (44) B-B-C	352 TILT TOWARD BEING THOSE 0.50 OF 34 WHERE THE TOTAL POSITIVE PRESSURE TOWARD DEVELOPING OBEDIENT BEHAVIOR IN THE CHILD IS LOW (28) B-B-C	12 17 1 17 XSQ= 5.45 PHI= 0.340 XP = 0.0196
353 TILT TOWARD BEING THOSE 0.85 OF 13 WHERE THE CHILD'S INFERRED ANXIETY OVER NON-PERFORMANCE OF OBEDIENT BEHAVIOR IS HIGH (42) B-B-C	353 TILT TOWARD BEING THOSE 0.54 OF 35 WHERE THE CHILD-S INFERRED ANXIETY OVER NON-PERFORMANCE OF OBEDIENT BEHAVIOR IS LOW (32) B-B-C	11 16 2 19 XSQ= 4.36 PHI= 0.301 XP = 0.0369
390 DRIFT LESS TOWARD BEING THOSE 0.65 OF 23 WHERE PREMARITAL SEX RELATIONS ARE WEAKLY PUNISHED AND IN FACT NOT RARE OR PUNISHED ONLY IF PREGNANCY RESULTS, OR FREELY PERMITTED (132) JTW,EA	390 DRIFT MORE TOWARD BEING THOSE 0.84 OF 81 WHERE PREMARITAL SEX RELATIONS ARE WEAKLY PUNISHED AND IN FACT NOT RARE OR PUNISHED ONLY IF PREGNANCY RESULTS, OR FREELY PERMITTED (132) JTW,EA	8 13 15 68 XSQ= 2.83 PHI= 0.165 XP = 0.0928
392 TILT MORE TOWARD BEING THOSE 0.83 OF 23 WHERE PREMARITAL SEX RELATIONS ARE STRONGLY PUNISHED AND IN FACT RARE, OR WEAKLY PUNISHED AND IN FACT NOT RARE, OR PUNISHED ONLY IF PREGNANCY RESULTS (112) JTW,EA	392 TILT LESS TOWARD BEING THOSE 0.54 OF 81 WHERE PREMARITAL SEX RELATIONS ARE STRONGLY PUNISHED AND IN FACT RARE, OR WEAKLY PUNISHED AND IN FACT NOT RARE, OR PUNISHED ONLY IF PREGNANCY RESULTS (112) JTW,EA	19 44 4 37 XSQ= 4.88 PHI= 0.217 XP = 0.0272
441 DRIFT TOWARD BEING THOSE 0.78 OF 9 WHERE FEAR OF HUMAN BEINGS IS HIGH (29) W-C	441 DRIFT TOWARD BEING THOSE 0.63 OF 27 WHERE FEAR OF HUMAN BEINGS IS LOW (32) W-C	7 10 2 17 XSQ= 3.01 PHI= 0.289 EP = 0.0551
442 TILT TOWARD BEING THOSE 0.78 OF 9 WHERE FEAR OF ANIMAL SPIRITS IS HIGH (28) W-C	442 TILT TOWARD BEING THOSE 0.74 OF 27 WHERE FEAR OF ANIMAL SPIRITS IS LOW (33) W-C	7 7 2 20 XSQ= 5.61 PHI= 0.395 EP = 0.0144
443 DRIFT TOWARD BEING THOSE 0.78 OF 9 WHERE OVERALL FEAR OF OTHERS IS HIGH (31) W-C	443 DRIFT TOWARD BEING THOSE 0.63 OF 27 WHERE OVERALL FEAR OF OTHERS IS LOW (30) W-C	7 10 2 17 XSQ= 3.01 PHI= 0.289 EP = 0.0551
444 IN ALL CASES ARE THOSE 1.00 OF 5 WHERE THE USE OF DREAMS TO SEEK AND CONTROL SUPERNATURAL POWERS IS LOW (27) RGD	444 TILT TOWARD BEING THOSE 0.65 OF 34 WHERE THE USE OF DREAMS TO SEEK AND CONTROL SUPERNATURAL POWERS IS HIGH (28) RGD	0 22 5 12 XSQ= 5.02 PHI= -0.359 EP = 0.0107
458 LEAN LESS TOWARD BEING THOSE 0.52 OF 25 WHERE GAMES, IF PRESENT, DO NOT INCLUDE GAMES OF STRATEGY (119) R-A-B,EA	458 LEAN MORE TOWARD BEING THOSE 0.82 OF 79 WHERE GAMES, IF PRESENT, DO NOT INCLUDE GAMES OF STRATEGY (119) R-A-B,EA	12 14 13 65 XSQ= 7.74 PHI= 0.273 XP = 0.0054

83/

```
460  LEAN TOWARD BEING THOSE          0.84 OF  25      460  LEAN TOWARD BEING THOSE          0.53 OF  79          4    42
     WHERE GAMES, IF PRESENT,                               WHERE GAMES, IF PRESENT,                              21    37
     ARE NOT LIMITED TO                                     ARE LIMITED TO                                  XSQ=     9.18
     GAMES OF SKILL ONLY  (104) R-A-B,EA                    GAMES OF SKILL ONLY  (67) R-A-B,EA              PHI=   -0.297
                                                                                                             XP =   0.0024
```

84 CULTURES
WHERE THE LEVEL OF POLITICAL INTEGRATION
IS THE LARGE STATE (42) GPM

84 CULTURES
WHERE THE LEVEL OF POLITICAL INTEGRATION
IS THE LITTLE STATE, THE MINIMAL STATE,
THE AUTONOMOUS COMMUNITY, OR
THE FAMILY (262) GPM

BACKGROUND ON PAGE 82

BOTH SUBJECT AND PREDICATE

42 IN LEFT COLUMN

AMERICANS	ARYANS	ASHANTI	AZTEC	BALINESE	BEMBA	BULGARIANS	BURMESE	CAMBODIANS	COORG
CZECHS	DUTCH	EGYPTIANS	FON	FUTAJALONKE	GANDA	HEBREWS	HO	INCA	IRISH
JAPANESE	JAVANESE	KAZAK	KERALA	KOREANS	LOZI	MAGUZAWA	MALAYS	MERINA	MOSSI
NYORO	ROMANS	SERBS	SHILLUK	SINHALESE	SOTHO	THAI	TIBETANS	TOTONAC	VIETNAMESE
WOLOF	YORUBA								

262 IN RIGHT COLUMN

ABIPON	ABOR	AJIE	AKHA	ALACALUF	ALBANIANS	ALORESE	ANDAMANESE	APINAYE	ARANDA
ARAPESH	ARAUCANIANS	ATAYAL	ATSUGEWI	AWEIKOMA	AZANDE	BABWA	BACAIRI	BANDA	BARI
BATAK	BAYA	BEJA	BELU	BERGDAMA	BETE	BIRIFOR	BOERS	BORORO	BOTOCUDO
BOZO	BUDUMA	BURUSHO	BURYAT	CADUVEO	CAGABA	CALLINAGO	CAMAYURA	CARAJA	CARIB
CAYAPA	CHAGGA	CHAMACOCO	CHENCHU	CHERKESS	CHEROKEE	CHEYENNE	CHIBCHA	CHIR-APACHE	CHIRIGUANO
CHOROTI	CHUKCHEE	COCHITI	CREE	CREEK	CROW	CUNA	DARD	DELAWARE	DIEGUENO
DIERI	DILLING	DOBUANS	DOGON	DOROBO	DUSUN	ELLICE	FANG	FOX	GARO
GILBERTESE	GILYAK	GOAJIRO	GOND	GROS VENTRE	GUAHIBO	GUATO	GURE	HAIDA	HANUNOO
HASINAI	HAVASUPAI	HAWAIIANS	HAZARA	HEHE	HERERO	HUKUNDIKA	HURON	IBAN	ICELANDERS
IFUGAO	ILA	INGASSANA	IRAQW	JEMEZ	JIVARO	JUKUN	KABYLE	KACHIN	KALMYK
KAREN	KARIERA	KASKA	KERAKI	KET	KHALKA	KHASI	KIKUYU	KIOW-APACHE	KISSI
KONSO	KORYAK	KPE	KUBA	KUNG	KURTATCHI	KUTENAI	LAKALAI	LAKHER	LAMBA
LAMET	LANGO	LAPPS	LAU	LESU	LIFU	LOLO	LUBA	LUO	MACASSARESE
MANDAN	MANGAIANS	MANIHIKI	MANUS	MAORI	MARGI	MARICOPA	MARQUESANS	MATACO	MATAKAM
MAYA	MBUGWE	MBUNDU	MBUTI	MENDE	MENTAWEI	MIAMI	MINANGKABAU	MISKITO	MIWOK
MONGO	MONGUOR	MOTA	MOTILON	MUNDURUCU	MURNGIN	MZAB	NAMA	NAMBICUARA	NASKAPI
NATCHEZ	NAVAHO	NGONI	NICOBARESE	NOMLAKI	NUNIVAK	NURI	NYAKYUSA	NYANEKA	OJIBWA
OMAHA	ONA	ONTONG-JAVA	ORAON	PAEZ	PALAUANS	PALIKUR	PAPAGO	PAWNEE	PENOBSCOT
PONAPEANS	PUKAPUKA	RARCIANS	RIFFIANS	ROTINESE	ROTUMANS	RWALA	SAMOANS	SAMOYED	SANDAWE
SANTAL	SARAMACCA	SARSI	SELUNG	SEMANG	SENIANG	SERI	SHERENTE	SHLUH	SIRIONO
SIUAI	SIWANS	SOMALI	SONGHAI	SUBANUN	TALAMANCA	TALLENSI	TANALA	TANIMBARESE	TAOS
TAPIRAPE	TARAHUMARA	TEHUELCHE	TENDA	TENETEHARA	TERENA	THONGA	TIKOPIA	TIMBIRA	TIMUCUA
TIV	TIWI	TOBA	TOKELAU	TOLOWA	TORAJA	TROBRIAND	TRUKESE	TRUMAI	TUBATULABAL
TUCANO	TUCUNA	TUPINAMBA	TURKANA	TURKMEN	TZELTAL	ULAWANS	UTE	VEDDA	WAICA
WAPISHANA	WAROPEN	WARRAU	WASHO	WICHITA	WINNEBAGO	WITOTO	WOGEO	WOLEAIANS	WUTE
YAGUA	YAHGAN	YAKO	YAKUT	YAO	YAPESE	YARURO	YOKUTS	YUKAGHIR	YUKI
YUROK	ZUNI								

33 EXCLUDED BECAUSE IRRELEVANT

AINU	AYMARA	BARABRA	BASQUES	BENGALI	BHIL	BLACK CARIB	BRAZILIANS	CHEREMIS	CHINANTEC

CHORTI, COMANCHE, DAGUR, HUICHOL, HUTSUL, KAPAUKU, KOL, LEPCHA, MANCHU, MARSHALLESE, MASAI, MAZATECO, MINCHIA, NANDI, NUER, OKINAWANS, POPOLUCA, SINDHI, TAGBANUA, TAMIL, TEDA, TENINO, TETON

63 EXCLUDED BECAUSE UNASCERTAINED

4	TEND LESS TO BE THOSE LOCATED OUTSIDE OF THE CIRCUM-MEDITERRANEAN (355)	0.74 OF 42	4	TEND MORE TO BE THOSE LOCATED OUTSIDE OF THE CIRCUM-MEDITERRANEAN (355)	0.93 OF 262	11 18 31 244 XSQ= 13.50 PHI= 0.211 XP = 0.0002
5	TEND LESS TO BE THOSE LOCATED OUTSIDE OF EAST EURASIA (330)	0.64 OF 42	5	TEND MORE TO BE THOSE LOCATED OUTSIDE OF EAST EURASIA (330)	0.87 OF 262	15 35 27 227 XSQ= 11.59 PHI= 0.195 XP = 0.0007
6	TILT MORE TOWARD BEING THOSE LOCATED OUTSIDE OF THE INSULAR PACIFIC (330)	0.95 OF 42	6	TILT LESS TOWARD BEING THOSE LOCATED OUTSIDE OF THE INSULAR PACIFIC (330)	0.79 OF 262	2 56 40 206 XSQ= 5.44 PHI= -0.134 XP = 0.0197
8	TILT MORE TOWARD BEING THOSE LOCATED OUTSIDE OF NORTH AMERICA (330)	0.95 OF 42	8	TILT LESS TOWARD BEING THOSE LOCATED OUTSIDE OF NORTH AMERICA (330)	0.81 OF 262	2 50 40 212 XSQ= 4.28 PHI= -0.119 XP = 0.0387
9	LEAN MORE TOWARD BEING THOSE LOCATED OUTSIDE OF SOUTH AMERICA (335)	0.98 OF 42	9	LEAN LESS TOWARD BEING THOSE LOCATED OUTSIDE OF SOUTH AMERICA (335)	0.79 OF 262	1 54 41 208 XSQ= 6.93 PHI= -0.151 XP = 0.0085
33	DRIFT MORE TOWARD BEING THOSE WHERE THE NATURAL ENVIRONMENT IS OTHER THAN 'VERY HARSH,' I.E., DESERT, DESERT GRASSES AND SHRUBS, TUNDRA, OR HIGH PLATEAU STEPPE (341) FWM	0.95 OF 42	33	DRIFT LESS TOWARD BEING THOSE WHERE THE NATURAL ENVIRONMENT IS OTHER THAN 'VERY HARSH,' I.E., DESERT, DESERT GRASSES AND SHRUBS, TUNDRA, OR HIGH PLATEAU STEPPE (341) FWM	0.82 OF 262	2 46 40 216 XSQ= 3.55 PHI= -0.108 XP = 0.0597
36	TILT MORE TOWARD BEING THOSE WHERE THE NATURAL ENVIRONMENT IS OTHER THAN 'VERY HARSH,' OR SUB-TROPICAL BUSH, OR TEMPERATE GRASSLAND (292) FWM	0.88 OF 42	36	TILT LESS TOWARD BEING THOSE WHERE THE NATURAL ENVIRONMENT IS OTHER THAN 'VERY HARSH,' OR SUB-TROPICAL BUSH, OR TEMPERATE GRASSLAND (292) FWM	0.72 OF 262	5 73 37 189 XSQ= 4.03 PHI= -0.115 XP = 0.0446

44	LEAN MORE TOWARD BEING THOSE WHERE SETTLEMENTS ARE FIXED (222)	0.89 OF 36	44	LEAN LESS TOWARD BEING THOSE WHERE SETTLEMENTS ARE FIXED (222)	0.61 OF 222	32 135 4 87 XSQ= 9.50 PHI= 0.192 XP = 0.0021
46	LEAN MORE TOWARD BEING THOSE OTHER THAN WHERE SETTLEMENTS ARE NON-FIXED AND MOVEMENT IS NOMADIC (260)	0.97 OF 36	46	LEAN LESS TOWARD BEING THOSE OTHER THAN WHERE SETTLEMENTS ARE NON-FIXED AND MOVEMENT IS NOMADIC (260)	0.73 OF 222	1 59 35 163 XSQ= 8.54 PHI= -0.182 XP = 0.0035
51	TEND MORE TO BE THOSE WHERE SUBSISTENCE IS PRIMARILY BY FOOD PRODUCTION -- I. E., AGRICULTURE OR HUSBANDRY -- RATHER THAN BY GATHERING (253)	0.98 OF 42	51	TEND LESS TO BE THOSE WHERE SUBSISTENCE IS PRIMARILY BY FOOD PRODUCTION -- I. E., AGRICULTURE OR HUSBANDRY -- RATHER THAN BY GATHERING (253)	0.52 OF 262	41 137 1 125 XSQ= 28.81 PHI= 0.308 XP = 0.0000
53	TEND TO BE THOSE WHERE FOOD PRODUCTION IS BY INTENSIVE AGRICULTURE, RATHER THAN BY SIMPLE AGRICULTURE OR INCIPIENT FOOD PRODUCTION (91)	0.74 OF 35	53	TEND TO BE THOSE WHERE FOOD PRODUCTION IS BY SIMPLE AGRICULTURE OR INCIPIENT FOOD PRODUCTION, RATHER THAN BY INTENSIVE AGRICULTURE (147)	0.73 OF 148	26 40 9 108 XSQ= 25.41 PHI= 0.373 XP = 0.0000
55	TEND TO BE THOSE WHERE FOOD PRODUCTION IS BY INTENSIVE AGRICULTURE, RATHER THAN BY SIMPLE AGRICULTURE (91)	0.76 OF 34	55	TEND TO BE THOSE WHERE FOOD PRODUCTION IS BY SIMPLE AGRICULTURE, RATHER THAN BY INTENSIVE AGRICULTURE (101)	0.62 OF 106	26 40 8 66 XSQ= 13.98 PHI= 0.316 XP = 0.0002
62	TEND MORE TO BE THOSE WHERE HUSBANDRY OF SOME KIND IS PRESENT (228)	0.83 OF 42	62	TEND LESS TO BE THOSE WHERE HUSBANDRY OF SOME KIND IS PRESENT (228)	0.53 OF 262	35 138 7 124 XSQ= 12.65 PHI= 0.204 XP = 0.0004
63	LEAN MORE TOWARD BEING THOSE WHERE HUSBANDRY, IF PRESENT, IS PRINCIPALLY IN THE FORM OF BOVINE, EQUINE, CAMEL-LIKE, OR DEER-LIKE ANIMALS, RATHER THAN PIGS, SHEEP, OR GOATS (152)	0.89 OF 35	63	LEAN LESS TOWARD BEING THOSE WHERE HUSBANDRY, IF PRESENT, IS PRINCIPALLY IN THE FORM OF BOVINE, EQUINE, CAMEL-LIKE, OR DEER-LIKE ANIMALS, RATHER THAN PIGS, SHEEP, OR GOATS (152)	0.61 OF 136	31 83 4 53 XSQ= 8.30 PHI= 0.220 XP = 0.0040
71	TEND TO BE THOSE WHERE METAL WORKING IS PRESENT (98)	0.96 OF 24	71	TEND TO BE THOSE WHERE METAL WORKING IS ABSENT (153)	0.71 OF 174	23 51 1 123 XSQ= 37.08 PHI= 0.433 XP = 0.
73	LEAN TOWARD BEING THOSE WHERE WEAVING IS PRESENT (118)	0.79 OF 24	73	LEAN TOWARD BEING THOSE WHERE WEAVING IS ABSENT (130)	0.56 OF 169	19 75 5 94 XSQ= 8.84 PHI= 0.214 XP = 0.0030

74	LEAN MORE TOWARD BEING THOSE WHERE POTTERY IS PRESENT (145)	0.95 OF 22	74	LEAN LESS TOWARD BEING THOSE WHERE POTTERY IS PRESENT (145)	0.59 OF 165	21 98 1 67 XSQ= 9.41 PHI= 0.224 XP = 0.0022
77	LEAN TOWARD BEING THOSE WHERE THE WRITING SYSTEM IS ALPHABETIC-OR-PHONETIC, RATHER THAN BEING MNEMONIC OR ABSENT (15) JMH	0.86 OF 7	77	LEAN TOWARD BEING THOSE WHERE THE WRITING SYSTEM IS MNEMONIC OR ABSENT, RATHER THAN BEING ALPHABETIC-OR-PHONETIC (39) JMH	0.81 OF 43	6 8 1 35 XSQ= 10.33 PHI= 0.454 XP = 0.0013
79	TEND TO BE THOSE WHERE A CITY IS PRESENT (23)	0.55 OF 33	79	IN ALL CASES ARE THOSE WHERE NO CITY IS PRESENT (201)	1.00 OF 143	18 0 15 143 XSQ= 81.05 PHI= 0.679 XP = 0.
80	TEND TO BE THOSE WHERE A CITY OR TOWN IS PRESENT (39)	0.76 OF 33	80	TEND TO BE THOSE WHERE NO CITY OR TOWN IS PRESENT (185)	0.96 OF 143	25 6 8 137 XSQ= 89.76 PHI= 0.714 XP = 0.
81	TEND TO BE THOSE WHERE A CITY OR TOWN IS PRESENT, OR THE AVERAGE COMMUNITY SIZE IS 200 OR GREATER (89)	0.85 OF 33	81	TEND TO BE THOSE WHERE NO CITY OR TOWN IS PRESENT, AND THE AVERAGE COMMUNITY SIZE IS SMALLER THAN 200 (135)	0.75 OF 143	28 36 5 107 XSQ= 38.72 PHI= 0.469 XP = 0.
82	IN ALL CASES ARE THOSE WHERE A CITY OR TOWN IS PRESENT, OR THE AVERAGE COMMUNITY SIZE IS FIFTY OR GREATER (178)	1.00 OF 33	82	LEAN LESS TOWARD BEING THOSE WHERE A CITY OR TOWN IS PRESENT, OR THE AVERAGE COMMUNITY SIZE IS FIFTY OR GREATER (178)	0.74 OF 143	33 106 0 37 XSQ= 9.31 PHI= 0.230 XP = 0.0023
88	LEAN TOWARD BEING THOSE WHERE, IF A HEADMANSHIP IS PRESENT, SUCCESSION IS NON-HEREDITARY (106)	0.61 OF 28	88	LEAN TOWARD BEING THOSE WHERE, IF A HEADMANSHIP IS PRESENT, SUCCESSION IS HEREDITARY (165)	0.70 OF 185	17 56 11 129 XSQ= 8.70 PHI= 0.202 XP = 0.0032
91	TILT TOWARD BEING THOSE WHERE SOCIETAL COMPLEXITY IS HIGH (18) F-W	0.88 OF 8	91	TILT TOWARD BEING THOSE WHERE SOCIETAL COMPLEXITY IS LOW (22) F-W	0.70 OF 27	7 8 1 19 XSQ= 6.24 PHI= 0.422 EP = 0.0111
94	TEND TO BE THOSE WHERE THE HIERARCHY OF NATIONAL JURISDICTION HAS FOUR OR THREE LEVELS (34) GES,EA	0.60 OF 35	94	TEND TO BE THOSE WHERE THE HIERARCHY OF NATIONAL JURISDICTION HAS TWO, ONE, OR NO LEVELS (296) GES,EA	0.98 OF 223	21 5 14 218 XSQ= 105.08 PHI= 0.638 XP = 0.

95	TEND TO BE THCSE 0.94 OF 35 WHERE THE HIERARCHY CF NATICNAL JURISDICTICN HAS FOUR, THREE, CR TWC LEVELS (76) GES,EA	95	TEND TO BE THOSE 0.88 OF 223 WHERE THE HIERARCHY OF NATIONAL JURISDICTION HAS ONE OR NO LEVELS (254) GES,EA	33 27 2 196 XSQ= 109.91 PHI= 0.653 XP = 0.
96	IN ALL CASES ARE THCSE 1.00 OF 35 WHERE THE HIERARCHY OF NATICNAL JURISDICTICN HAS FOUR, THREE, TWC OR ONE LEVEL (174) GES,EA	96	TEND TO BE THOSE 0.55 CF 223 WHERE THE HIERARCHY OF NATIONAL JURISDICTION HAS NO LEVELS (156) GES,EA	35 100 0 123 XSQ= 34.72 PHI= 0.367 XP = 0.
102	IN ALL CASES ARE THOSE 1.00 OF 39 WHERE CLASS STRATIFICATICN IS PRESENT (203)	102	TEND TO BE THOSE 0.57 OF 258 WHERE CLASS STRATIFICATICN IS ABSENT (180)	39 112 0 146 XSQ= 41.17 PHI= 0.372 XP = 0.
106	TEND TC BE THCSE 0.97 OF 39 WHERE CLASS STRATIFICATION, IF PRESENT, IS BASED CN SCMETHING CTHER THAN WEALTH (126)	106	TEND TO BE THOSE 0.50 CF 112 WHERE CLASS STRATIFICATION, IF PRESENT, IS BASED ON WEALTH (77)	1 56 38 56 XSQ= 25.72 PHI= -0.413 XP = 0.0000
107	TEND TO BE THCSE 0.64 OF 39 WHERE CLASS STRATIFICATION, IF PRESENT, IS BASED CN OCCUPATICNAL STATUS (43)	107	TEND TO BE THOSE 0.96 CF 112 WHERE CLASS STRATIFICATION, IF PRESENT, IS BASED ON SOMETHING OTHER THAN OCCUPATIONAL STATUS (160)	25 4 14 108 XSQ= 64.46 PHI= 0.653 XP = 0.
109	LEAN LESS TOWARC BEING THCSE 0.71 OF 38 WHERE CASTES ARE ABSENT (317)	109	LEAN MORE TOWARD BEING THOSE 0.91 CF 247 WHERE CASTES ARE ABSENT (317)	11 23 27 224 XSQ= 10.29 PHI= 0.190 XP = 0.0013
110	TEND TO BE THCSE 0.70 OF 40 WHERE SLAVERY IS PRESENT (163)	110	TEND TO BE THOSE 0.61 OF 253 WHERE SLAVERY IS ABSENT (218)	28 99 12 154 XSQ= 12.18 PHI= 0.204 XP = 0.0005
116	TILT TOWARD BEING THCSE 0.86 OF 7 WHERE OCCUPATICNAL SPECIALIZATION IS FULL-TIME, WHETHER OR NOT FOR SURPLUS PRODUCTICN (20) JMH	116	TILT TOWARD BEING THOSE 0.70 OF 43 WHERE OCCUPATIONAL SPECIALIZATION IS PART-TIME ONLY (34) JMH	6 13 1 30 XSQ= 5.69 PHI= 0.337 XP = 0.0171
118	IN ALL CASES ARE THOSE 1.00 OF 7 WHERE THE PERCENTAGE CF CCCUPATIONS THAT ARE SPECIALIZED IS HIGH OR MEDIUM (24) WME	118	TILT TOWARD BEING THOSE 0.61 OF 38 WHERE THE PERCENTAGE OF CCCUPATICNS THAT ARE SPECIALIZED IS LOW (25) WME	7 15 0 23 XSQ= 6.41 PHI= 0.378 XP = 0.0113

120	IN ALL CASES ARE THOSE WHERE THE CRAFT SPECIALIZATION SCORE IS HIGH OR MEDIUM (36) WME	1.00 OF 9	120	DRIFT LESS TOWARD BEING THOSE WHERE THE CRAFT SPECIALIZATION SCORE IS HIGH OR MEDIUM (36) WME	0.64 OF 39	9 25 0 14 XSQ= 2.99 PHI= 0.250 XP = 0.0838
130	IN ALL CASES ARE THOSE WHERE LEATHER WORKING IS MAINLY DONE BY MALES (39)	1.00 OF 7	130	LEAN TOWARD BEING THOSE WHERE LEATHER WORKING IS MAINLY DONE BY FEMALES (45)	0.62 OF 60	7 23 0 37 XSQ= 7.31 PHI= 0.330 XP = 0.0069
147	IN ALL CASES ARE THOSE WHERE CODIFIED LAWS ARE PRESENT (20) LWS	1.00 OF 6	147	DRIFT TOWARD BEING THOSE WHERE CODIFIED LAWS ARE UNIMPORTANT OR ABSENT (13) LWS	0.50 OF 24	6 12 0 12 XSQ= 3.13 PHI= 0.323 EP = 0.0568
152	IN ALL CASES ARE THOSE WHERE THE DIFFERENTIATION OF THE JURIDICAL AGENCY FROM THE MEDICAL AGENCY IS HIGH (10) MJ	1.00 OF 5	152	TILT TOWARD BEING THOSE WHERE THE DIFFERENTIATION OF THE JURIDICAL AGENCY FROM THE MEDICAL AGENCY IS LOW (10) MJ	0.67 OF 12	5 4 0 8 XSQ= 3.90 PHI= 0.479 EP = 0.0294
163	DRIFT TOWARD BEING THOSE WHERE THE EMPHASIS ON INDIVIDUAL VOLITION AS THE CAUSE OF CRIME IS HIGH (7) MJ	0.80 OF 5	163	DRIFT TOWARD BEING THOSE WHERE THE EMPHASIS ON INDIVIDUAL VOLITION AS THE CAUSE OF CRIME IS LOW (10) MJ	0.78 OF 9	4 2 1 7 XSQ= 2.34 PHI= 0.409 EP = 0.0909
164	IN ALL CASES ARE THOSE WHERE THE EMPHASIS ON INDIVIDUAL VOLITION AS THE CAUSE OR SOURCE OF ILLNESS IS LOW (9) MJ	1.00 OF 5	164	TILT TOWARD BEING THOSE WHERE THE EMPHASIS ON INDIVIDUAL VOLITION AS THE CAUSE OR SOURCE OF ILLNESS IS HIGH (9) MJ	0.73 OF 11	0 8 5 3 XSQ= 4.65 PHI= -0.539 EP = 0.0256
177	DRIFT MORE TOWARD BEING THOSE WHERE THE COMMUNITY IS OTHER THAN A SINGLE CLAN-COMMUNITY AND EXOGAMOUS (305)	0.92 OF 40	177	DRIFT LESS TOWARD BEING THOSE WHERE THE COMMUNITY IS OTHER THAN A SINGLE CLAN-COMMUNITY AND EXOGAMOUS (305)	0.79 OF 247	3 53 37 194 XSQ= 3.43 PHI= -0.109 XP = 0.0641
180	DRIFT MORE TOWARD BEING THOSE WHERE THE COMMUNITY IS COMMONLY NON-EXOGAMOUS, RATHER THAN EXOGAMOUS (258)	0.82 OF 40	180	DRIFT LESS TOWARD BEING THOSE WHERE THE COMMUNITY IS COMMONLY NON-EXOGAMOUS, RATHER THAN EXOGAMOUS (258)	0.66 OF 247	7 85 33 162 XSQ= 3.78 PHI= -0.115 XP = 0.0519
182	DRIFT TOWARD BEING THOSE WHERE THE COMMUNITY IS STRUCTURED ON A NON-CLAN BASIS AND AGAMOUS (126)	0.50 OF 40	182	DRIFT TOWARD BEING THOSE OTHER THAN WHERE THE COMMUNITY IS STRUCTURED ON A NON-CLAN BASIS AND AGAMOUS (256)	0.67 OF 247	20 81 20 166 XSQ= 3.75 PHI= 0.114 XP = 0.0529

183	IN ALL CASES ARE THOSE 1.00 OF 24 WHERE THE LARGEST NON-COGNATIC KIN GROUP IS SMALLER THAN A MOEITY, I. E., A PHRATRY OR SIB OR LINEAGE (218)	183	DRIFT LESS TOWARD BEING THOSE 0.83 OF 167 WHERE THE LARGEST NON-COGNATIC KIN GROUP IS SMALLER THAN A MOEITY, I. E., A PHRATRY OR SIB OR LINEAGE (218)	0 29 24 138 XSQ= 3.66 PHI= -0.138 XP = 0.0558
187	TILT MORE TOWARD BEING THOSE 0.98 OF 42 WHERE THE KIN GROUP IS OTHER THAN EXCLUSIVELY MATRILINEAL (344)	187	TILT LESS TOWARD BEING THOSE 0.83 OF 262 WHERE THE KIN GROUP IS OTHER THAN EXCLUSIVELY MATRILINEAL (344)	1 45 41 217 XSQ= 5.07 PHI= -0.129 XP = 0.0243
190	DRIFT MORE TOWARD BEING THOSE 0.91 OF 23 WHERE THE KIN GROUP IS PATRILINEAL OR DOUBLE-DESCENT, RATHER THAN MATRILINEAL (186)	190	DRIFT LESS TOWARD BEING THOSE 0.70 OF 164 WHERE THE KIN GROUP IS PATRILINEAL OR DOUBLE-DESCENT, RATHER THAN MATRILINEAL (186)	21 115 2 49 XSQ= 3.56 PHI= 0.138 XP = 0.0593
196	TEND MORE TO BE THOSE 0.92 OF 37 WHERE INDIVIDUAL RIGHTS IN REAL PROPERTY, AND RULES FOR INHERITANCE, ARE PRESENT (194)	196	TEND LESS TO BE THOSE 0.59 OF 178 WHERE INDIVIDUAL RIGHTS IN REAL PROPERTY, AND RULES FOR INHERITANCE, ARE PRESENT (194)	34 105 3 73 XSQ= 13.11 PHI= 0.247 XP = 0.0003
197	TILT LESS TOWARD BEING THOSE 0.74 OF 34 WHERE RULES FOR THE INHERITANCE OF REAL PROPERTY, IF PRESENT, FAVOR EITHER THE MALE HEIR OR LINE, OR THE FEMALE HEIR OR LINE (165)	197	TILT MORE TOWARD BEING THOSE 0.90 OF 105 WHERE RULES FOR THE INHERITANCE OF REAL PROPERTY, IF PRESENT, FAVOR EITHER THE MALE HEIR OR LINE, OR THE FEMALE HEIR OR LINE (165)	25 94 9 11 XSQ= 4.11 PHI= -0.172 XP = 0.0425
209	TILT MORE TOWARD BEING THOSE 0.92 OF 37 WHERE MARITAL RESIDENCE IS PATRILOCAL, VIRILOCAL, OR AVUNCULOCAL, RATHER THAN MATRILOCAL OR UXORILOCAL (270)	209	TILT LESS TOWARD BEING THOSE 0.76 OF 222 WHERE MARITAL RESIDENCE IS PATRILOCAL, VIRILOCAL, OR AVUNCULOCAL, RATHER THAN MATRILOCAL OR UXORILOCAL (270)	34 168 3 54 XSQ= 3.96 PHI= 0.124 XP = 0.0466
210	IN ALL CASES ARE THOSE 1.00 OF 19 WHERE MARITAL RESIDENCE IS PATRILOCAL, RATHER THAN MATRILOCAL (169)	210	DRIFT LESS TOWARD BEING THOSE 0.78 OF 129 WHERE MARITAL RESIDENCE IS PATRILOCAL, RATHER THAN MATRILOCAL (169)	19 101 0 28 XSQ= 3.77 PHI= 0.160 XP = 0.0522
213	TILT TOWARD BEING THOSE 0.65 OF 40 WHERE FIRST COUSIN MARRIAGE IS PERMITTED (172)	213	TILT TOWARD BEING THOSE 0.54 OF 241 WHERE FIRST COUSIN MARRIAGE IS NOT PERMITTED (198)	26 110 14 131 XSQ= 4.40 PHI= 0.125 XP = 0.0359
214	DRIFT MORE TOWARD BEING THOSE 0.96 OF 26 WHERE FIRST COUSIN MARRIAGE, IF PERMITTED, IS OTHER THAN UNILATERAL (144)	214	DRIFT LESS TOWARD BEING THOSE 0.80 OF 110 WHERE FIRST COUSIN MARRIAGE, IF PERMITTED, IS OTHER THAN UNILATERAL (144)	1 22 25 88 XSQ= 2.84 PHI= -0.145 XP = 0.0919

224	DRIFT MORE TOWARD BEING THOSE 0.81 OF 26 WHERE COUSIN MARRIAGE IS PREFERENTIALLY OR PERMISSIVELY SYMMETRICAL, RATHER THAN EITHER PATRI- OR MATRILATERAL (106)	224	DRIFT LESS TOWARD BEING THOSE 0.59 OF 110 WHERE COUSIN MARRIAGE IS PREFERENTIALLY OR PERMISSIVELY SYMMETRICAL, RATHER THAN EITHER PATRI- OR MATRILATERAL (106)	5 45 21 65 XSQ= 3.37 PHI= -0.157 XP = 0.0664
234	TILT TOWARD BEING THOSE 0.72 OF 36 WHERE THE COUSIN TERMINOLOGY IS OF ESKIMO OR HAWAIIAN TYPE, RATHER THAN CROW, OMAHA, OR IROQUOIS TYPE (170)	234	TILT TOWARD BEING THOSE 0.52 OF 210 WHERE THE COUSIN TERMINOLOGY IS OF CROW, OMAHA, OR IROQUOIS TYPE, RATHER THAN ESKIMO OR HAWAIIAN TYPE (152)	10 110 26 100 XSQ= 6.49 PHI= -0.162 XP = 0.0108
240	DRIFT MORE TOWARD BEING THOSE 0.79 OF 24 WHERE THE FAMILY, IF EXTENDED, IS SMALL OR STEM, RATHER THAN LARGE (135)	240	DRIFT LESS TOWARD BEING THOSE 0.59 OF 146 WHERE THE FAMILY, IF EXTENDED, IS SMALL OR STEM, RATHER THAN LARGE (135)	5 60 19 86 XSQ= 2.78 PHI= -0.128 XP = 0.0956
241	LEAN LESS TOWARD BEING THOSE 0.71 OF 24 WHERE THE FAMILY, IF EXTENDED, IS LARGE OR SMALL, RATHER THAN STEM (187)	241	LEAN MORE TOWARD BEING THOSE 0.93 OF 146 WHERE THE FAMILY, IF EXTENDED, IS LARGE OR SMALL, RATHER THAN STEM (187)	17 136 7 10 XSQ= 9.06 PHI= -0.231 XP = 0.0026
242	TILT LESS TOWARD BEING THOSE 0.67 OF 40 WHERE MARRIAGE IS COMMONLY OR OCCASIONALLY POLYGYNOUS, RATHER THAN MONOGAMOUS (314)	242	TILT MORE TOWARD BEING THOSE 0.83 OF 259 WHERE MARRIAGE IS COMMONLY OR OCCASIONALLY POLYGYNOUS, RATHER THAN MONOGAMOUS (314)	27 216 13 43 XSQ= 4.76 PHI= -0.126 XP = 0.0292
263	DRIFT TOWARD BEING THOSE 0.55 OF 42 WHERE WIVES ARE OBTAINED BY RELATIVELY EASY MEANS, NAMELY BY TOKEN BRIDE-PRICE, GIFT EXCHANGE, ABSENCE OF ANY CONSIDERATION, OR RECEIPT OF DOWRY (162)	263	DRIFT TOWARD BEING THOSE 0.61 OF 259 WHERE WIVES ARE OBTAINED BY RELATIVELY DIFFICULT MEANS, NAMELY BY BRIDE-PRICE, BRIDE-SERVICE, OR EXCHANGING A FEMALE RELATIVE (233)	19 158 23 101 XSQ= 3.09 PHI= -0.101 XP = 0.0790
278	TILT TOWARD BEING THOSE 0.80 OF 5 WHERE PROPERTY RIGHTS IN WOMEN ARE PRESENT (8) LWS	278	TILT TOWARD BEING THOSE 0.75 OF 16 WHERE PROPERTY RIGHTS IN WOMEN ARE UNIMPORTANT OR ABSENT (14) LWS	4 4 1 12 XSQ= 2.83 PHI= 0.367 EP = 0.0475
282	IN ALL CASES ARE THOSE 1.00 OF 3 WHERE THE STRENGTH OF DESIRE FOR CHILDREN IS HIGH (16) BCA	282	DRIFT TOWARD BEING THOSE 0.60 OF 25 WHERE THE STRENGTH OF DESIRE FOR CHILDREN IS LOW OR ABSENT (20) BCA	3 10 0 15 XSQ= 1.84 PHI= 0.256 EP = 0.0873
314	TILT TOWARD BEING THOSE 0.56 OF 9 WHERE THE INCIDENCE OF MOTHER-CHILD HOUSEHOLDS IS HIGH (19) W-D,S	314	TILT TOWARD BEING THOSE 0.82 OF 60 WHERE THE INCIDENCE OF MOTHER-CHILD HOUSEHOLDS IS LOW (61) W-D,S	5 11 4 49 XSQ= 4.18 PHI= 0.246 XP = 0.0410

```
326  IN ALL CASES ARE THCSE            1.00 OF    5     326  TILT TOWARD BEING THOSE          0.61 CF  51             5    20
     WHERE THE INFERRED TRANSITION ANXIETY                   WHERE THE INFERRED TRANSITICN ANXIETY                  0    31
     BETWEEN INFANCY ANC CHILCFCOC                           BETWEEN INFANCY AND CHILDHCOD                    XSQ=     4.57
     IS HIGH   (32) B-B-C                                    IS LOW   (35) B-B-C                              PHI=    0.286
                                                                                                              XP =   0.0325

336  IN ALL CASES ARE THCSE            1.00 OF    6     336  DRIFT TOWARD BEING THOSE         0.50 OF  58             6    29
     WHERE THE TOTAL PCSITIVE PRESSURE TOWARD                WHERE THE TOTAL POSITIVE PRESSURE TOWARC               0    29
     DEVELCPING RESPCNSIBLE BEFAVICR                         DEVELOPING RESPONSIBLE BEHAVIOR                  XSQ=     3.65
     IN THE CHILD                                            IN THE CHILD                                     PHI=    0.239
     IS HIGH   (43) B-B-C                                    IS LOW   (32) B-B-C                              XP =   0.0560

345  IN ALL CASES ARE THCSE            1.00 OF    6     345  TILT TOWARD BEING THOSE          0.58 CF  59             6    25
     WHERE THE CHILD'S INFERREC ANXIETY OVER                 WHERE THE CHILD'S INFERRED ANXIETY OVER                0    34
     NCN-PERFORMANCE CF SELF-RELIANT BEFAVIOR                NON-PERFORMANCE OF SELF-RELIANT BEHAVIOR         XSQ=     5.12
     IS HIGH   (37) B-B-C                                    IS LOW   (39) B-B-C                              PHI=    0.281
                                                                                                              XP =   0.0236

368  IN ALL CASES ARE THCSE            1.00 OF    5     368  TILT TOWARD BEING THOSE          0.54 OF  28             0    15
     WHERE DISSCCIATICN CF THE SEXES                         WHERE DISSOCIATION OF THE SEXES                        5    13
     AT ADCLESCENCE                                          AT ADOLESCENCE                                   XSQ=     2.99
     IS LOW   (21) JKH                                       IS HIGH OR MEDIUM   (16) JKH                     PHI=   -0.301
                                                                                                              EP =   0.0488

390  TEND TO BE THCSE                  0.52 OF   25     390  TEND TO BE THOSE                 0.82 OF 119            13    21
     WHERE PREMARITAL SEX RELATIONS ARE                      WHERE PREMARITAL SEX RELATICNS ARE                    12    98
     STRCNGLY PUNISHED AND                                   WEAKLY PUNISHED AND IN FACT NOT RARE OR          XSQ=    11.68
     IN FACT RARE   (47) JTW,EA                              PUNISHED ONLY IF PREGNANCY RESULTS, CR           PHI=    0.285
                                                             FREELY PERMITTED   (132) JTW,EA                  XP =   0.0006

391  TEND TC BE THOSE                  0.84 OF   25     391  TEND TO BE THOSE                 0.59 CF 119            21    49
     WHERE PREMARITAL SEX RELATIONS ARE                      WHERE PREMARITAL SEX RELATICNS ARE                     4    70
     STRCNGLY PUNISHEC AND IN FACT RARE, OR                  PUNISHED ONLY IF PREGNANCY RESULTS, CR           XSQ=    13.50
     WEAKLY PUNISHED ANC                                     FREELY PERMITTED   (90) JTW,EA                   PHI=    0.306
     IN FACT NCT RARE   (89) JTW,EA                                                                           XP =   0.0002

396  DRIFT TOWARD BEING THCSE          0.80 OF    5     396  DRIFT TOWARD BEING THOSE         0.70 CF  40             4    12
     WHERE THE STRENGTH OF MENSTRUAL TABOOS                  WHERE THE STRENGTH OF MENSTRUAL TABOOS                 1    28
     IS HIGH   (18) WNS                                      IS LOW   (35) WNS                                XSQ=     2.91
                                                                                                              PHI=    0.254
                                                                                                              XP =   0.0879

424  TILT TCWARD BEING THCSE           0.86 OF    7     424  TILT TOWARD BEING THOSE          0.67 CF  43             6    14
     WHERE RELIGICUS SPECIALISTS ARE                         WHERE RELIGIOUS SPECIALISTS ARE                        1    29
     FULL-TIME, RATHER THAN                                  PART-TIME, RATHER THAN                           XSQ=     5.05
     PART-TIME   (21) JMH                                    FULL-TIME   (33) JMH                             PHI=    0.318
                                                                                                              XP =   0.0247

426  TILT MORE TOWARC BEING THCSE      0.79 OF   29     426  TILT LESS TOWARD BEING THOSE     0.54 CF 173            23    94
     WHERE A HIGH GCC IS                                     WHERE A HIGH GOD IS                                    6    79
     PRESENT   (156) GES,EA                                  PRESENT   (156) GES,EA                           XSQ=     5.37
                                                                                                              PHI=    0.163
                                                                                                              XP =   0.0205
```

No.		No.		
435	IN ALL CASES ARE THOSE 1.00 OF 5 WHERE ABANDONMENT OF THE HOUSE OF THE DEAD IS NOT PRACTICED (19) LWS	435	DRIFT TOWARD BEING THOSE 0.50 OF 24 WHERE ABANDONMENT OF THE HOUSE OF THE DEAD IS PRACTICED (12) LWS	0 12 5 12 XSQ= 2.45 PHI= -0.291 EP = 0.0588
449	IN ALL CASES ARE THOSE 1.00 OF 12 WHERE THE OBSERVATION OF FOOD TABOOS IS MEDIUM OR LOW, RATHER THAN HIGH (61) JRL	449	TILT LESS TOWARD BEING THOSE 0.63 OF 62 WHERE THE OBSERVATION OF FOOD TABOOS IS MEDIUM OR LOW, RATHER THAN HIGH (61) JRL	0 23 12 39 XSQ= 4.84 PHI= -0.256 XP = 0.0278
450	LEAN TOWARD BEING THOSE 0.67 OF 12 WHERE THE OBSERVATION OF FOOD TABOOS IS LOW, RATHER THAN HIGH OR MEDIUM (26) JRL	450	LEAN TOWARD BEING THOSE 0.77 OF 62 WHERE THE OBSERVATION OF FOOD TABOOS IS HIGH OR MEDIUM, RATHER THAN LOW (60) JRL	4 48 8 14 XSQ= 7.36 PHI= -0.315 XP = 0.0067
458	TEND TO BE THOSE 0.95 OF 19 WHERE GAMES, IF PRESENT, INCLUDE GAMES OF STRATEGY (52) R-A-B,EA	458	TEND TO BE THOSE 0.78 OF 124 WHERE GAMES, IF PRESENT, DO NOT INCLUDE GAMES OF STRATEGY (119) R-A-B,EA	18 27 1 97 XSQ= 37.36 PHI= 0.511 XP = 0.
459	TILT TOWARD BEING THOSE 0.74 OF 19 WHERE GAMES, IF PRESENT, INCLUDE GAMES OF CHANCE (82) R-A-B,EA	459	TILT TOWARD BEING THOSE 0.57 OF 124 WHERE GAMES, IF PRESENT, DO NOT INCLUDE GAMES OF CHANCE (89) R-A-B,EA	14 53 5 71 XSQ= 5.15 PHI= 0.190 XP = 0.0232
460	LEAN MORE TOWARD BEING THOSE 0.95 OF 19 WHERE GAMES, IF PRESENT, ARE NOT LIMITED TO GAMES OF SKILL ONLY (104) R-A-B,EA	460	LEAN LESS TOWARD BEING THOSE 0.56 OF 124 WHERE GAMES, IF PRESENT, ARE NOT LIMITED TO GAMES OF SKILL ONLY (104) R-A-B,EA	1 55 18 69 XSQ= 8.99 PHI= -0.251 XP = 0.0027
468	LEAN TOWARD BEING THOSE 0.86 OF 7 WHERE CONTACT WITH OTHER CULTURES IS FREQUENT, RATHER THAN REGULAR OR IRREGULAR (17) JMH	468	LEAN TOWARD BEING THOSE 0.77 OF 43 WHERE CONTACT WITH OTHER CULTURES IS REGULAR OR IRREGULAR, RATHER THAN FREQUENT (37) JMH	6 10 1 33 XSQ= 8.11 PHI= 0.403 XP = 0.0044
470	TILT TOWARD BEING THOSE 0.86 OF 7 WHERE INNOVATIONS ARE GENERALLY ACCEPTED (21) JMH	470	TILT TOWARD BEING THOSE 0.70 OF 43 WHERE INNOVATIONS ARE ACCEPTED ONLY SELECTIVELY (33) JMH	6 13 1 30 XSQ= 5.69 PHI= 0.337 XP = 0.0171

85 CULTURES
WHERE THE LEVEL OF POLITICAL INTEGRATICN
IS THE LARGE STATE, CR
THE LITTLE STATE (70) GPM

85 CULTURES
WHERE THE LEVEL OF POLITICAL INTEGRATION
IS THE MINIMAL STATE,
THE AUTONOMOUS COMMUNITY, CR
THE FAMILY (234) GPM

BACKGROUND ON PAGE 82

BCTH SUBJECT AND PREDICATE

70 IN LEFT COLUMN

AMERICANS	ARYANS	ASHANTI	AZANDE	AZTEC	BALINESE	BEMBA	BOERS	BULGARIANS	BURMESE
BURUSHO	CAMBODIANS	CHEROKEE	CHIBCHA	COORG	CREEK	CZECHS	DARD	DUTCH	EGYPTIANS
FON	FUTAJALONKE	GANDA	HAWAIIANS	HEBREWS	HEHE	HO	ICELANDERS	INCA	IRISH
JAPANESE	JAVANESE	JUKUN	KABYLE	KALMYK	KAZAK	KERALA	KHALKA	KOREANS	KUBA
LOZI	LUBA	MACASSARESE	MAGUZAWA	MALAYS	MARGI	MBUNDU	MENDE	MERINA	MOSSI
NGONI	NYANEKA	NYCRC	ROMANS	RWALA	SERBS	SHILLUK	SINHALESE	SOMALI	SONGHAI
SOTHO	THAI	THCNGA	TIBETANS	TOTONAC	TURKMEN	VIETNAMESE	WCLOF	YAKUT	YORUBA

234 IN RIGHT CCLUMN

ABIPCN	ABCR	AJIE	AKHA	ALACALUF	ALBANIANS	ALORESE	ANDAMANESE	APINAYE	ARANDA
ARAPESH	ARAUCANIANS	ATAYAL	ATSUGEWI	AWEIKOMA	BABWA	BACAIRI	BANDA	BARI	BATAK
BAYA	BEJA	BELU	BERGDAMA	BETE	BIRIFOR	BORCRO	BOTCCUDO	BOZC	BUDUMA
BURYAT	CADUVEC	CAGABA	CALLINAGO	CAMAYURA	CARAJA	CARIB	CAYAPA	CHAGGA	CHAMACOCO
CHENCHU	CHERKESS	CHEYENNE	CHIR-APACHE	CHIRIGUANO	CHOROTI	CHUKCHEE	COCHITI	CREE	CROW
CUNA	DELAWARE	DIEGUENC	DIERI	DILLING	DOBUANS	DOGON	DORCBO	DUSUN	ELLICE
FANG	FCX	GARC	GILBERTESE	GILYAK	GOAJIRO	GOND	GRCS VENTRE	GUAHIBC	GUATO
GURE	HAIDA	HANUNCC	HASINAI	HAVASUPAI	HAZARA	HERERO	HUKUNDIKA	HURCN	IBAN
IFUGAO	ILA	INGASSANA	IRAQW	JEMEZ	JIVARO	KACHIN	KAREN	KARIERA	KASKA
KERAKI	KET	KHASI	KIKUYU	KIOW-APACHE	KISSI	KONSO	KORYAK	KPE	KUNG
KURTATCHI	KUTENAI	LAKALAI	LAKHER	LAMBA	LAMET	LANGO	LAPPS	LAU	LESU
LIFU	LCLC	LUC	MANDAN	MANGAIANS	MANIHIKI	MANUS	MACRI	MARICOPA	MARQUESANS
MATACO	MATAKAM	MAYA	MBUGWE	MBUTI	MENTAWEI	MIAMI	MINANGKABAU	MISKITO	MIWOK
MONGO	MONGUCR	MOTA	MOTILON	MUNDURUCU	MURNGIN	MZAB	NAMA	NAMBICUARA	NASKAPI
NATCHEZ	NAVAHC	NICCBARESE	NOMLAKI	NUNIVAK	NURI	NYAKYUSA	OJIBWA	OMAHA	ONA
ONTONG-JAVA	CRACN	PAEZ	PALAUANS	PALIKUR	PAPAGO	PAWNEE	PENCBSCOT	PONAPEANS	PUKAPUKA
RAROIANS	RIFFIANS	ROTINESE	ROTUMANS	SAMOANS	SAMOYED	SANDAWE	SANTAL	SARAMACCA	SARSI
SELUNG	SEMANG	SENIANG	SERI	SHERENTE	SHLUH	SIRIONC	SIUAI	SIWANS	SUBANUN
TALAMANCA	TALLENSI	TANALA	TANIMBARESE	TAOS	TAPIRAPE	TARAHUMARA	TEHUELCHE	TENDA	TENETEHARA
TERENA	TIKCPIA	TIMBIRA	TIMUCUA	TIV	TIWI	TODA	TOKELAU	TOLCWA	TORAJA
TROBRIAND	TRUKESE	TRUMAI	TUBATULABAL	TUCANO	TUCUNA	TUPINAMBA	TURKANA	TZELTAL	ULAWANS
UTE	VEDDA	WAICA	WAPISHANA	WAROPEN	WARRAU	WASHO	WICHITA	WINNEBAGO	WITOTO
WOGEO	WCLEAIANS	WUTE	YAGUA	YAHGAN	YAKO	YAO	YAPESE	YARURO	YOKUTS
YUKAGHIR	YUKI	YURCK	ZUNI						

33 EXCLUDED BECAUSE IRRELEVANT (SEE 'IRRELEVANT,' PARAGRAPH 84)

63 EXCLUDED BECAUSE UNASCERTAINED

3	LEAN LESS TOWARD BEING THOSE LOCATED OUTSIDE OF AFRICA (320)	0.69 OF 70	3	LEAN MORE TOWARD BEING THOSE LOCATED OUTSIDE OF AFRICA (320)	0.84 OF 234	22 38 48 196 XSQ= 6.92 PHI= 0.151 XP = 0.0085
4	TEND LESS TO BE THOSE LOCATED OUTSIDE OF THE CIRCUM-MEDITERRANEAN (355)	0.74 OF 70	4	TEND MORE TO BE THOSE LOCATED OUTSIDE OF THE CIRCUM-MEDITERRANEAN (355)	0.95 OF 234	18 11 52 223 XSQ= 25.19 PHI= 0.288 XP = 0.0000
5	LEAN LESS TOWARD BEING THOSE LOCATED OUTSIDE OF EAST EURASIA (330)	0.71 OF 70	5	LEAN MORE TOWARD BEING THOSE LOCATED OUTSIDE OF EAST EURASIA (330)	0.87 OF 234	20 30 50 204 XSQ= 8.61 PHI= 0.168 XP = 0.0033
6	LEAN MORE TOWARD BEING THOSE LOCATED OUTSIDE OF THE INSULAR PACIFIC (330)	0.94 OF 70	6	LEAN LESS TOWARD BEING THOSE LOCATED OUTSIDE OF THE INSULAR PACIFIC (330)	0.77 OF 234	4 54 66 180 XSQ= 9.43 PHI= -0.176 XP = 0.0021
8	LEAN MORE TOWARD BEING THOSE LOCATED OUTSIDE OF NORTH AMERICA (330)	0.94 OF 70	8	LEAN LESS TOWARD BEING THOSE LOCATED OUTSIDE OF NORTH AMERICA (330)	0.79 OF 234	4 48 66 186 XSQ= 7.31 PHI= -0.155 XP = 0.0069
9	TEND MORE TO BE THOSE LOCATED OUTSIDE OF SOUTH AMERICA (335)	0.97 OF 70	9	TEND LESS TO BE THOSE LOCATED OUTSIDE OF SOUTH AMERICA (335)	0.77 OF 234	2 53 68 181 XSQ= 12.94 PHI= -0.206 XP = 0.0003
42	TILT MORE TOWARD BEING THOSE WHERE THE NATURAL ENVIRONMENT IS OTHER THAN TROPICAL OR SUB-TROPICAL RAIN FOREST, OR MONSOON FOREST (244) FWM	0.71 OF 70	42	TILT LESS TOWARD BEING THOSE WHERE THE NATURAL ENVIRONMENT IS OTHER THAN TROPICAL OR SUB-TROPICAL RAIN FOREST, OR MONSOON FOREST (244) FWM	0.55 OF 234	20 105 50 129 XSQ= 5.26 PHI= -0.132 XP = 0.0218
44	LEAN MORE TOWARD BEING THOSE WHERE SETTLEMENTS ARE FIXED (222)	0.83 OF 58	44	LEAN LESS TOWARD BEING THOSE WHERE SETTLEMENTS ARE FIXED (222)	0.59 OF 200	48 119 10 81 XSQ= 9.66 PHI= 0.193 XP = 0.0019
46	LEAN MORE TOWARD BEING THOSE OTHER THAN WHERE SETTLEMENTS ARE NON-FIXED AND MOVEMENT IS NOMADIC (260)	0.91 OF 58	46	LEAN LESS TOWARD BEING THOSE OTHER THAN WHERE SETTLEMENTS ARE NON-FIXED AND MOVEMENT IS NOMADIC (260)	0.72 OF 200	5 55 53 145 XSQ= 7.95 PHI= -0.176 XP = 0.0048

51	TEND TC BE THCSE WHERE SUBSISTENCE IS PRIMARILY BY FCCD FRODUCTICN -- I. E., AGRICULTURE OR HUSBANDRY -- RATHER THAN BY GATHERING (253)	0.90 OF 70	51	TEND TO BE THOSE WHERE SUBSISTENCE IS PRIMARILY BY FOOD GATHERING -- I. E., HUNTING, FISHING, OR COLLECTING -- RATHER THAN FOOD PRODUCTION (147)	0.51 CF 234	63 115 7 119 XSQ= 35.39 PHI= 0.341 XP = 0.
53	TEND TO BE THOSE WHERE FCCD PRCDUCTICN IS BY INTENSIVE AGRICULTURE, RATFER THAN BY SIMPLE AGRICULTURE CR INCIPIENT FOCD PROCUCTICN (91)	0.63 OF 54	53	TEND TO BE THOSE WHERE FOOD PRODUCTION IS BY SIMPLE AGRICULTURE OR INCIPIENT FOOD PRODUCTICN, RATHER THAN BY INTENSIVE AGRICULTURE (147)	0.75 CF 129	34 32 20 97 XSQ= 22.41 PHI= 0.350 XP = 0.0000
55	TEND TC BE THCSE WHERE FCCD PRODUCTICN IS BY INTENSIVE AGRICULTURE, RATHER THAN BY SIMPLE AGRICULTURE (91)	0.71 OF 48	55	TEND TO BE THOSE WHERE FOOD PRODUCTION IS BY SIMPLE AGRICULTURE, RATHER THAN BY INTENSIVE AGRICULTURE (101)	0.65 CF 92	34 32 14 60 XSQ= 15.04 PHI= 0.328 XP = 0.0001
62	TEND MORE TO BE THCSE WHERE HUSBANDRY CF SOME KIND IS PRESENT (228)	0.77 OF 7C	62	TEND LESS TO BE THOSE WHERE HUSBANDRY OF SOME KIND IS PRESENT (228)	0.51 CF 234	54 119 16 115 XSQ= 14.13 PHI= 0.216 XP = 0.0002
63	LEAN MORE TOWARC BEING THCSE WHERE HUSBANDRY, IF PRESENT, IS PRINCIPALLY IN THE FORM OF BOVINE, ECUINE, CAMEL-LIKE, OR DEER-LIKE ANIMALS, RATHER THAN PIGS, SHEEP, CR GOATS (152)	0.85 OF 53	63	LEAN LESS TOWARD BEING THOSE WHERE HUSBANDRY, IF PRESENT, IS PRINCIPALLY IN THE FORM OF BOVINE, EQUINE, CAMEL-LIKE, CR DEER-LIKE ANIMALS, RATHER THAN PIGS, SHEEP, OR GOATS (152)	0.58 CF 118	45 69 8 49 XSQ= 10.34 PHI= 0.246 XP = 0.0013
71	TEND TC BE THCSE WHERE METAL WCRKING IS PRESENT (98)	0.92 OF 40	71	TEND TO BE THOSE WHERE METAL WORKING IS ABSENT (153)	0.77 OF 158	37 37 3 121 XSQ= 62.16 PHI= 0.560 XP = 0.
73	TEND TC BE THOSE WHERE WEAVING IS PRESENT (118)	0.77 OF 39	73	TEND TO BE THOSE WHERE WEAVING IS ABSENT (130)	0.58 OF 154	30 64 9 90 XSQ= 14.19 PHI= 0.271 XP = 0.0002
74	LEAN MORE TOWARC BEING THCSE WHERE PCTTERY IS PRESENT (145)	0.86 OF 36	74	LEAN LESS TOWARD BEING THOSE WHERE POTTERY IS PRESENT (145)	0.58 OF 151	31 88 5 63 XSQ= 8.57 PHI= 0.214 XP = 0.0034
77	TILT TCWARD BEING THOSE WHERE THE WRITING SYSTEM IS ALPHABETIC-OR-PHCNETIC, RATHER THAN BEING MNEMCNIC CR ABSENT (15) JMH	0.53 OF 15	77	TILT TOWARD BEING THOSE WHERE THE WRITING SYSTEM IS MNEMONIC OR ABSENT, RATHER THAN BEING ALPHABETIC-OR-PHONETIC (39) JMH	0.83 CF 35	8 6 7 29 XSQ= 5.14 PHI= 0.321 XP = 0.0233

```
79  TEND LESS TC BE THCSE              0.65 OF  51     79  IN ALL CASES ARE THOSE          1.00 OF 125          18    0
    WHERE NC CITY IS PRESENT   (201)                       WHERE NO CITY IS PRESENT   (201)                     33  125
                                                                                                           XSQ=     45.37
                                                                                                           PHI=     0.508
                                                                                                           XP =  0.

80  TEND TC BE THCSE                   0.53 OF  51     8C  TEND TO BE THOSE                0.97 OF 125          27    4
    WHERE A CITY CR TOWN IS PRESENT   (39)                 WHERE NO CITY OR TOWN IS PRESENT   (185)             24  121
                                                                                                           XSQ=     58.38
                                                                                                           PHI=     0.576
                                                                                                           XP =  0.

81  TEND TC BE THCSE                   0.75 OF  51     81  TEND TO BE THOSE                0.79 OF 125          38   26
    WHERE A CITY CR TOWN IS PRESENT, CR                    WHERE NO CITY OR TOWN IS PRESENT, AND               13   99
    THE AVERAGE COMMUNITY SIZE IS                          THE AVERAGE COMMUNITY SIZE IS                   XSQ=     42.86
    200 OR GREATER   (89)                                  SMALLER THAN 2C0   (135)                        PHI=     0.493
                                                                                                           XP =  0.

83  LEAN LESS TOWARC BEING THCSE   0.54 OF  24         83  LEAN MORE TOWARD BEING THOSE   0.83 OF 119           11   20
    WHERE, WITH NC CITY ANC NC TOWN PRESENT,               WHERE, WITH NO CITY AND NC TOWN PRESENT,            13   99
    THE AVERAGE COMMUNITY SIZE IS                          THE AVERAGE COMMUNITY SIZE IS                   XSQ=      8.27
    SMALLER THAN 200, RATHER THAN                          SMALLER THAN 200, RATHER THAN                   PHI=     0.241
    BETWEEN 200 AND 999   (135)                            BETWEEN 200 AND 999   (135)                     XP =  0.0040

88  DRIFT LESS TOWARD BEING THCSE  0.53 OF  47         88  DRIFT MORE TOWARD BEING THCSE  0.69 OF 166           22   51
    WHERE, IF A HEACMANSHIP IS PRESENT,                    WHERE, IF A HEADMANSHIP IS PRESENT,                 25  115
    SUCCESSICN IS HEREDITARY   (165)                       SUCCESSION IS HEREDITARY   (165)                XSQ=      3.52
                                                                                                           PHI=     0.129
                                                                                                           XP =  0.0605

91  TILT TOWARD BEING THCSE            0.69 OF  13     91  TILT TOWARD BEING THOSE         0.73 OF  22           9    6
    WHERE SOCIETAL CCMPLEXITY                              WHERE SOCIETAL COMPLEXITY                            4   16
    IS HIGH   (18) F-W                                     IS LOW   (22) F-W                               XSQ=      4.29
                                                                                                           PHI=     0.350
                                                                                                           EP =  0.0322

94  TEND LESS TO BE THCSE              0.54 OF  57     94  IN ALL CASES ARE THOSE          1.00 OF 201          26    0
    WHERE THE HIERARCHY                                    WHERE THE HIERARCHY                                 31  201
    OF NATIONAL JURISDICTION HAS                           OF NATIONAL JURISDICTION HAS                    XSQ=     96.99
    TWO, CNE, CR NO LEVELS   (296) GES,EA                  TWO, ONE, OR NO LEVELS   (296) GES,EA           PHI=     0.613
                                                                                                           XP =  0.

95  TEND TC BE THCSE                   0.86 OF  57     95  TEND TO BE THOSE                0.95 OF 201          49   11
    WHERE THE HIERARCHY                                    WHERE THE HIERARCHY                                  8  190
    CF NATICNAL JURISDICTION HAS                           OF NATIONAL JURISDICTION HAS                    XSQ=    156.73
    FOUR, THREE, OR TWC LEVELS   (76) GES,EA               ONE OR NO LEVELS   (254) GES,EA                 PHI=     0.779
                                                                                                           XP =  0.

96  TEND TC BE THCSE                   0.98 OF  57     96  TEND TO BE THOSE                0.61 OF 201          56   79
    WHERE THE HIERARCHY                                    WHERE THE HIERARCHY                                  1  122
    OF NATICNAL JURISDICTICN HAS                           OF NATIONAL JURISDICTION HAS                    XSQ=     59.50
    FOUR, THREE, TWC OR                                    NO LEVELS   (156) GES,EA                        PHI=     0.480
    ONE LEVEL   (174) GES,EA                                                                               XP =  0.
```

98	TILT MORE TOWARD BEING THOSE 0.84 OF 57 WHERE THE HIERARCHY OF LOCAL JURISDICTION HAS FOUR OR THREE LEVELS (238) GES,EA	98	TILT LESS TOWARD BEING THOSE 0.69 OF 201 WHERE THE HIERARCHY OF LOCAL JURISDICTION HAS FOUR OR THREE LEVELS (238) GES,EA	 XSQ= PHI= XP =	48 138 9 63 4.59 0.133 0.0321
100	IN ALL CASES ARE THOSE 1.00 OF 57 WHERE HIERARCHIES ARE MORE COMPLEX THAN THE 'SIMPLEST,' I. E., MORE COMPLEX THAN TWO LOCAL LEVELS WITH NO NATIONAL LEVELS (267) GES,EA	100	TEND LESS TO BE THOSE 0.75 OF 201 WHERE HIERARCHIES ARE MORE COMPLEX THAN THE 'SIMPLEST,' I. E., MORE COMPLEX THAN TWO LOCAL LEVELS WITH NO NATIONAL LEVELS (267) GES,EA	 XSQ= PHI= XP =	57 151 0 50 16.03 0.249 0.0001
102	TEND TO BE THOSE 0.93 OF 67 WHERE CLASS STRATIFICATION IS PRESENT (203)	102	TEND TO BE THOSE 0.61 OF 230 WHERE CLASS STRATIFICATION IS ABSENT (180)	 XSQ= PHI= XP =	62 89 5 141 58.05 0.442 0.
106	TEND TO BE THOSE 0.94 OF 62 WHERE CLASS STRATIFICATION, IF PRESENT, IS BASED ON SOMETHING OTHER THAN WEALTH (126)	106	TEND TO BE THOSE 0.60 OF 89 WHERE CLASS STRATIFICATION, IF PRESENT, IS BASED ON WEALTH (77)	 XSQ= PHI= XP =	4 53 58 36 41.62 -0.525 0.
107	TEND LESS TO BE THOSE 0.56 OF 62 WHERE CLASS STRATIFICATION, IF PRESENT, IS BASED ON SOMETHING OTHER THAN OCCUPATIONAL STATUS (160)	107	TEND MORE TO BE THOSE 0.98 OF 89 WHERE CLASS STRATIFICATION, IF PRESENT, IS BASED ON SOMETHING OTHER THAN OCCUPATIONAL STATUS (160)	 XSQ= PHI= XP =	27 2 35 87 37.55 0.499 0.
109	TEND LESS TO BE THOSE 0.70 OF 63 WHERE CASTES ARE ABSENT (317)	109	TEND MORE TO BE THOSE 0.93 OF 222 WHERE CASTES ARE ABSENT (317)	 XSQ= PHI= XP =	19 15 44 207 23.40 0.287 0.0000
110	TEND TO BE THOSE 0.77 OF 65 WHERE SLAVERY IS PRESENT (163)	110	TEND TO BE THOSE 0.66 OF 228 WHERE SLAVERY IS ABSENT (218)	 XSQ= PHI= XP =	50 77 15 151 36.62 0.354 0.
116	TEND TO BE THOSE 0.80 OF 15 WHERE OCCUPATIONAL SPECIALIZATION IS FULL-TIME, WHETHER OR NOT FOR SURPLUS PRODUCTION (20) JMH	116	TEND TO BE THOSE 0.80 OF 35 WHERE OCCUPATIONAL SPECIALIZATION IS PART-TIME ONLY (34) JMH	 XSQ= PHI= XP =	12 7 3 28 13.60 0.522 0.0002
118	TILT TOWARD BEING THOSE 0.82 OF 11 WHERE THE PERCENTAGE OF OCCUPATIONS THAT ARE SPECIALIZED IS HIGH OR MEDIUM (24) WME	118	TILT TOWARD BEING THOSE 0.62 OF 34 WHERE THE PERCENTAGE OF OCCUPATIONS THAT ARE SPECIALIZED IS LOW (25) WME	 XSQ= PHI= XP =	9 13 2 21 4.69 0.323 0.0303

129	LEAN TOWARD BEING THOSE WHERE WEAVING IS MAINLY DONE BY MALES (31)	0.56 OF 25	129	LEAN TOWARD BEING THOSE WHERE WEAVING IS MAINLY DONE BY FEMALES (73)	0.78 OF 58	14 13 11 45 XSQ= 7.51 PHI= 0.301 XP = 0.0061
130	DRIFT TOWARD BEING THOSE WHERE LEATHER WORKING IS MAINLY DONE BY MALES (39)	0.69 OF 13	130	DRIFT TOWARD BEING THOSE WHERE LEATHER WORKING IS MAINLY DONE BY FEMALES (45)	0.61 OF 54	9 21 4 33 XSQ= 2.77 PHI= 0.203 XP = 0.0960
136	IN ALL CASES ARE THOSE WHERE FULL-TIME ENTREPRENEURS ARE PRESENT (18) JV	1.00 OF 6	136	DRIFT LESS TOWARD BEING THOSE WHERE FULL-TIME ENTREPRENEURS ARE PRESENT (18) JV	0.52 OF 21	6 11 0 10 XSQ= 2.73 PHI= 0.318 EP = 0.0570
138	IN ALL CASES ARE THOSE WHERE SUPERORDINATE JUSTICE IS PRESENT (22) BBW	1.00 OF 5	138	TILT TOWARD BEING THOSE WHERE SUPERORDINATE JUSTICE IS ABSENT (18) BBW	0.59 OF 29	5 12 0 17 XSQ= 3.75 PHI= 0.332 EP = 0.0445
141	DRIFT TOWARD BEING THOSE WHERE THE LEVEL OF SOCIAL SANCTION IS PUBLIC CORPOREAL SANCTION, RATHER THAN PUBLIC PROPERTY SANCTION OR PRIVATE SETTLEMENT (28) JMH	0.73 OF 15	141	DRIFT TOWARD BEING THOSE WHERE THE LEVEL OF SOCIAL SANCTION IS PUBLIC PROPERTY SANCTION OR PRIVATE SETTLEMENT, RATHER THAN PUBLIC CORPOREAL SANCTION (26) JMH	0.60 OF 35	11 14 4 21 XSQ= 3.43 PHI= 0.262 XP = 0.0641
147	IN ALL CASES ARE THOSE WHERE CODIFIED LAWS ARE PRESENT (20) LWS	1.00 OF 8	147	LEAN TOWARD BEING THOSE WHERE CODIFIED LAWS ARE UNIMPORTANT OR ABSENT (13) LWS	0.55 OF 22	8 10 0 12 XSQ= 5.18 PHI= 0.415 EP = 0.0100
152	IN ALL CASES ARE THOSE WHERE THE DIFFERENTIATION OF THE JURIDICAL AGENCY FROM THE MEDICAL AGENCY IS HIGH (10) MJ	1.00 OF 5	152	TILT TOWARD BEING THOSE WHERE THE DIFFERENTIATION OF THE JURIDICAL AGENCY FROM THE MEDICAL AGENCY IS LOW (10) MJ	0.67 OF 12	5 4 0 8 XSQ= 3.90 PHI= 0.479 EP = 0.0294
163	DRIFT TOWARD BEING THOSE WHERE THE EMPHASIS ON INDIVIDUAL VOLITION AS THE CAUSE OF CRIME IS HIGH (7) MJ	0.80 OF 5	163	DRIFT TOWARD BEING THOSE WHERE THE EMPHASIS ON INDIVIDUAL VOLITION AS THE CAUSE OF CRIME IS LOW (10) MJ	0.78 OF 9	4 2 1 7 XSQ= 2.34 PHI= 0.409 EP = 0.0909
164	IN ALL CASES ARE THOSE WHERE THE EMPHASIS ON INDIVIDUAL VOLITION AS THE CAUSE OR SOURCE OF ILLNESS IS LOW (9) MJ	1.00 OF 5	164	TILT TOWARD BEING THOSE WHERE THE EMPHASIS ON INDIVIDUAL VOLITION AS THE CAUSE OR SOURCE OF ILLNESS IS HIGH (9) MJ	0.73 OF 11	0 8 5 3 XSQ= 4.65 PHI= -0.539 EP = 0.0256

179	DRIFT MORE TCWARC BEING THCSE 0.95 OF 66 WHERE THE COMMUNITY IS CTHER THAN STRUCTURED ON A NON-CLAN BASIS ANC COMMCNLY EXOGAMCUS (340)	179	DRIFT LESS TOWARD BEING THCSE 0.87 OF 221 WHERE THE COMMUNITY IS CTHER THAN STRUCTURED ON A NON-CLAN BASIS AND COMMONLY EXOGAMOUS (340)	3 29 63 192 XSQ= 2.96 PHI= -0.102 XP = 0.0855
180	DRIFT MCRE TCWARC BEING THOSE 0.77 OF 66 WHERE THE COMMUNITY IS COMMCNLY NCN-EXCGAMCUS, RATHER THAN EXCGAMOUS (258)	180	DRIFT LESS TOWARD BEING THCSE 0.65 CF 221 WHERE THE COMMUNITY IS COMMONLY NON-EXCGAMOUS, RATHER THAN EXOGAMOUS (258)	15 77 51 144 XSQ= 2.89 PHI= -0.100 XP = 0.0891
182	TILT LESS TOWARC BEING THCSE 0.53 OF 66 CTHER THAN WHERE THE COMMUNITY IS STRUCTURED CN A NON-CLAN BASIS ANC AGAMCUS (256)	182	TILT MORE TOWARD BEING THOSE 0.68 CF 221 OTHER THAN WHERE THE COMMUNITY IS STRUCTURED ON A NON-CLAN BASIS AND AGAMOUS (256)	31 70 35 151 XSQ= 4.56 PHI= 0.126 XP = 0.0326
183	TILT MCRE TOWARC BEING THCSE 0.98 OF 45 WHERE THE LARGEST NCN-COGNATIC KIN GROUP IS SMALLER THAN A MOEITY, I. E., A PHRATRY CR SIB OR LINEACE (218)	183	TILT LESS TOWARD BEING THCSE 0.81 CF 146 WHERE THE LARGEST NON-COGNATIC KIN GROUP IS SMALLER THAN A MOEITY, I. E., A PHRATRY OR SIB CR LINEAGE (218)	1 28 44 118 XSQ= 6.42 PHI= -0.183 XP = 0.0113
186	DRIFT LESS TCWARC BEING THOSE 0.54 OF 70 WHERE THE KIN GRCUP IS OTHER THAN EXCLUSIVELY PATRILINEAL (250)	186	DRIFT MORE TOWARD BEING THCSE 0.67 CF 234 WHERE THE KIN GROUP IS OTHER THAN EXCLUSIVELY PATRILINEAL (250)	32 78 38 156 XSQ= 3.06 PHI= 0.100 XP = 0.0802
187	DRIFT MCRE TCWARC BEING THCSE 0.93 OF 70 WHERE THE KIN GRCUP IS OTHER THAN EXCLUSIVELY MATRILINEAL (344)	187	DRIFT LESS TOWARD BEING THCSE 0.82 CF 234 WHERE THE KIN GROUP IS OTHER THAN EXCLUSIVELY MATRILINEAL (344)	5 41 65 193 XSQ= 3.75 PHI= -0.111 XP = 0.0529
190	TILT MORE TOWARC BEING THCSE 0.86 OF 44 WHERE THE KIN GRCUP IS PATRILINEAL CR CCUBLE-CESCENT, RATHER THAN MATRILINEAL (186)	190	TILT LESS TOWARD BEING THOSE 0.69 OF 143 WHERE THE KIN GROUP IS PATRILINEAL OR DOUBLE-DESCENT, RATHER THAN MATRILINEAL (186)	38 98 6 45 XSQ= 4.53 PHI= 0.156 XP = 0.0333
196	TEND MCRE TO BE THCSE 0.84 OF 56 WHERE INDIVIDUAL RIGHTS IN REAL PROPERTY, AND RULES FOR INHERITANCE, ARE PRESENT (194)	196	TEND LESS TO BE THOSE 0.58 CF 159 WHERE INDIVIDUAL RIGHTS IN REAL PROPERTY, AND RULES FOR INHERITANCE, ARE PRESENT (194)	47 92 9 67 XSQ= 11.20 PHI= 0.228 XP = 0.0008
209	LEAN MCRE TOWARC BEING THCSE 0.92 OF 62 WHERE MARITAL RESICENCE IS PATRILCCAL, VIRILCCAL, CR AVUNCULOCAL, RATHER THAN MATRILOCAL OR UXCRILOCAL (270)	209	LEAN LESS TOWARD BEING THOSE 0.74 OF 197 WHERE MARITAL RESIDENCE IS PATRILOCAL, VIRILOCAL, CR AVUNCULCCAL, RATHER THAN MATRILOCAL OR UXORILOCAL (270)	57 145 5 52 XSQ= 8.20 PHI= 0.178 XP = 0.0042

210	TILT MORE TOWARD BEING THOSE WHERE MARITAL RESIDENCE IS PATRILOCAL, RATHER THAN MATRILOCAL (169)	0.95 OF 37	210	TILT LESS TOWARD BEING THOSE WHERE MARITAL RESIDENCE IS PATRILOCAL, RATHER THAN MATRILOCAL (169)	0.77 OF 111	35 85 2 26 XSQ= 4.76 PHI= 0.179 XP = 0.0292
214	DRIFT MORE TOWARD BEING THOSE WHERE FIRST COUSIN MARRIAGE, IF PERMITTED, IS OTHER THAN UNILATERAL (144)	0.95 OF 37	214	DRIFT LESS TOWARD BEING THOSE WHERE FIRST COUSIN MARRIAGE, IF PERMITTED, IS OTHER THAN UNILATERAL (144)	0.79 OF 99	2 21 35 78 XSQ= 3.73 PHI= -0.166 XP = 0.0534
234	TILT TOWARD BEING THOSE WHERE THE COUSIN TERMINOLOGY IS OF ESKIMO OR HAWAIIAN TYPE, RATHER THAN CROW, OMAHA, OR IROQUOIS TYPE (170)	0.64 OF 56	234	TILT TOWARD BEING THOSE WHERE THE COUSIN TERMINOLOGY IS OF CROW, OMAHA, OR IROQUOIS TYPE, RATHER THAN ESKIMO OR HAWAIIAN TYPE (152)	0.53 OF 190	20 100 36 90 XSQ= 4.30 PHI= -0.132 XP = 0.0381
240	DRIFT MORE TOWARD BEING THOSE WHERE THE FAMILY, IF EXTENDED, IS SMALL OR STEM, RATHER THAN LARGE (135)	0.75 OF 44	240	DRIFT LESS TOWARD BEING THOSE WHERE THE FAMILY, IF EXTENDED, IS SMALL OR STEM, RATHER THAN LARGE (135)	0.57 OF 126	11 54 33 72 XSQ= 3.68 PHI= -0.147 XP = 0.0551
241	DRIFT LESS TOWARD BEING THOSE WHERE THE FAMILY, IF EXTENDED, IS LARGE OR SMALL, RATHER THAN STEM (187)	0.82 OF 44	241	DRIFT MORE TOWARD BEING THOSE WHERE THE FAMILY, IF EXTENDED, IS LARGE OR SMALL, RATHER THAN STEM (187)	0.93 OF 126	36 117 8 9 XSQ= 3.27 PHI= -0.139 XP = 0.0704
254	IN ALL CASES ARE THOSE WHERE HOUSEHOLD AUTHORITY IS ON THE FATHER'S SIDE, RATHER THAN THE MOTHER'S (9) CA	1.00 OF 4	254	DRIFT TOWARD BEING THOSE WHERE HOUSEHOLD AUTHORITY IS ON THE MOTHER'S SIDE, RATHER THAN THE FATHER'S (6) DA	0.67 OF 6	4 2 0 4 XSQ= 2.10 PHI= 0.458 EP = 0.0762
262	DRIFT MORE TOWARD BEING THOSE WHERE WIVES ARE OBTAINED BY MEANS INVOLVING THE PRESENCE OF SOME CONSIDERATION (305)	0.84 OF 70	262	DRIFT LESS TOWARD BEING THOSE WHERE WIVES ARE OBTAINED BY MEANS INVOLVING THE PRESENCE OF SOME CONSIDERATION (305)	0.73 OF 231	59 169 11 62 XSQ= 3.04 PHI= 0.100 XP = 0.0813
272	DRIFT TOWARD BEING THOSE WHERE THE DIVORCE RATE IS LOW (28) CA	0.71 OF 14	272	DRIFT TOWARD BEING THOSE WHERE THE DIVORCE RATE IS HIGH (29) CA	0.60 OF 40	4 24 10 16 XSQ= 2.94 PHI= -0.233 XP = 0.0864
278	DRIFT TOWARD BEING THOSE WHERE PROPERTY RIGHTS IN WOMEN ARE PRESENT (8) LWS	0.71 OF 7	278	DRIFT TOWARD BEING THOSE WHERE PROPERTY RIGHTS IN WOMEN ARE UNIMPORTANT OR ABSENT (14) LWS	0.79 OF 14	5 3 2 11 XSQ= 3.05 PHI= 0.381 EP = 0.0555

282	IN ALL CASES ARE THOSE WHERE THE STRENGTH OF DESIRE FOR CHILDREN IS HIGH (16) BCA	1.00 OF 5	282	TILT TOWARD BEING THOSE WHERE THE STRENGTH OF DESIRE FOR CHILDREN IS LOW OR ABSENT (20) BCA	0.65 OF 23	5 8 0 15 XSQ= 4.65 PHI= 0.407 EP = 0.0131
295	IN ALL CASES ARE THOSE WHERE THE SEVERITY OF PUNISHMENT FOR ABORTION IS HIGH (11) BCA	1.00 OF 4	295	DRIFT TOWARD BEING THOSE WHERE THE SEVERITY OF PUNISHMENT FOR ABORTION IS LOW OR ABSENT (12) BCA	0.67 OF 12	4 4 0 8 XSQ= 3.00 PHI= 0.433 EP = 0.0769
314	TEND TO BE THOSE WHERE THE INCIDENCE OF MOTHER-CHILD HOUSEHOLDS IS HIGH (19) W-D,S	0.67 OF 12	314	TEND TO BE THOSE WHERE THE INCIDENCE OF MOTHER-CHILD HOUSEHOLDS IS LOW (61) W-D,S	0.86 OF 57	8 8 4 49 XSQ= 12.60 PHI= 0.427 XP = 0.0004
317	DRIFT TOWARD BEING THOSE WHERE DISPLAY OF AFFECTION TOWARD THE INFANT IS LOW (29) B-B-C	0.70 OF 10	317	DRIFT TOWARD BEING THOSE WHERE DISPLAY OF AFFECTION TOWARD THE INFANT IS HIGH (39) B-B-C	0.69 OF 48	3 33 7 15 XSQ= 3.76 PHI= -0.255 XP = 0.0525
318	TILT TOWARD BEING THOSE WHERE THE OVERALL INDULGENCE OF THE INFANT IS LOW (31) B-B-C	0.80 OF 10	318	TILT TOWARD BEING THOSE WHERE THE OVERALL INDULGENCE OF THE INFANT IS HIGH (40) B-B-C	0.66 OF 50	2 33 8 17 XSQ= 5.49 PHI= -0.302 XP = 0.0192
319	TILT TOWARD BEING THOSE WHERE PROTECTION OF THE INFANT FROM ENVIRONMENTAL DISCOMFORTS IS LOW (30) B-B-C	0.80 OF 10	319	TILT TOWARD BEING THOSE WHERE PROTECTION OF THE INFANT FROM ENVIRONMENTAL DISCOMFORTS IS HIGH (35) B-B-C	0.61 OF 44	2 27 8 17 XSQ= 4.07 PHI= -0.274 XP = 0.0437
320	TILT TOWARD BEING THOSE WHERE THE DEGREE OF REDUCTION OF THE INFANT'S DRIVES IS LOW (24) B-B-C	0.70 OF 10	320	TILT TOWARD BEING THOSE WHERE THE DEGREE OF REDUCTION OF THE INFANT'S DRIVES IS HIGH (45) B-B-C	0.71 OF 48	3 34 7 14 XSQ= 4.34 PHI= -0.273 XP = 0.0373
324	DRIFT TOWARD BEING THOSE WHERE THE PAIN INFLICTED ON THE INFANT BY THE NURTURANT AGENT IS HIGH (34) B-B-C	0.80 OF 10	324	DRIFT TOWARD BEING THOSE WHERE THE PAIN INFLICTED ON THE INFANT BY THE NURTURANT AGENT IS LOW OR NEGLIGIBLE (32) B-B-C	0.56 OF 45	8 20 2 25 XSQ= 2.84 PHI= 0.227 XP = 0.0920
326	TILT TOWARD BEING THOSE WHERE THE INFERRED TRANSITION ANXIETY BETWEEN INFANCY AND CHILDHOOD IS HIGH (32) B-B-C	0.89 OF 9	326	TILT TOWARD BEING THOSE WHERE THE INFERRED TRANSITION ANXIETY BETWEEN INFANCY AND CHILDHOOD IS LOW (35) B-B-C	0.64 OF 47	8 17 1 30 XSQ= 6.50 PHI= 0.341 XP = 0.0108

334	TILT TOWARD BEING THOSE WHERE THE INDULGENCE OF THE CHILD IS LOW (38) B-B-C	0.80 OF 10	334	TILT TOWARD BEING THOSE WHERE THE INDULGENCE OF THE CHILD IS HIGH (40) B-B-C	0.60 OF 57	2 34 8 23 XSQ= 3.90 PHI= -0.241 XP = 0.0482
336	TILT TOWARD BEING THOSE WHERE THE TOTAL POSITIVE PRESSURE TOWARD DEVELOPING RESPONSIBLE BEHAVIOR IN THE CHILD IS HIGH (43) B-B-C	0.90 OF 10	336	TILT TOWARD BEING THOSE WHERE THE TOTAL POSITIVE PRESSURE TOWARD DEVELOPING RESPONSIBLE BEHAVIOR IN THE CHILD IS LOW (32) B-B-C	0.52 OF 54	9 26 1 28 XSQ= 4.39 PHI= 0.262 XP = 0.0361
337	LEAN TOWARD BEING THOSE WHERE THE CHILD'S INFERRED ANXIETY OVER NON-PERFORMANCE OF RESPONSIBLE BEHAVIOR IS HIGH (38) B-B-C	0.90 OF 10	337	LEAN TOWARD BEING THOSE WHERE THE CHILD'S INFERRED ANXIETY OVER NON-PERFORMANCE OF RESPONSIBLE BEHAVIOR IS LOW (35) B-B-C	0.62 OF 52	9 20 1 32 XSQ= 7.00 PHI= 0.336 XP = 0.0082
338	TILT TOWARD BEING THOSE WHERE THE CHILD'S INFERRED ANXIETY OVER PERFORMANCE OF RESPONSIBLE BEHAVIOR IS HIGH (44) B-B-C	0.90 OF 10	338	TILT TOWARD BEING THOSE WHERE THE CHILD'S INFERRED ANXIETY OVER PERFORMANCE OF RESPONSIBLE BEHAVIOR IS LOW (29) B-B-C	0.50 OF 52	9 26 1 26 XSQ= 3.95 PHI= 0.252 XP = 0.0468
339	LEAN TOWARD BEING THOSE WHERE THE CHILD'S INFERRED CONFLICT REGARDING RESPONSIBLE BEHAVIOR IS HIGH (31) B-B-C	0.80 OF 10	339	LEAN TOWARD BEING THOSE WHERE THE CHILD'S INFERRED CONFLICT REGARDING RESPONSIBLE BEHAVIOR IS LOW (42) B-B-C	0.71 OF 52	8 15 2 37 XSQ= 7.34 PHI= 0.344 XP = 0.0067
365	IN ALL CASES ARE THOSE WHERE THE TIME SPENT IN ADOLESCENT PEER GROUP ACTIVITY IS HIGH OR HIGH-MEDIUM (30) JKH	1.00 OF 8	365	TILT LESS TOWARD BEING THOSE WHERE THE TIME SPENT IN ADOLESCENT PEER GROUP ACTIVITY IS HIGH OR HIGH-MEDIUM (30) JKH	0.60 OF 30	8 18 0 12 XSQ= 3.01 PHI= 0.281 EP = 0.0385
368	DRIFT TOWARD BEING THOSE WHERE DISSOCIATION OF THE SEXES AT ADOLESCENCE IS LOW (21) JKH	0.86 OF 7	368	DRIFT TOWARD BEING THOSE WHERE DISSOCIATION OF THE SEXES AT ADOLESCENCE IS HIGH OR MEDIUM (16) JKH	0.54 OF 26	1 14 6 12 XSQ= 2.07 PHI= -0.250 EP = 0.0952
377	LEAN LESS TOWARD BEING THOSE WHERE MALE GENITAL MUTILATION IS ABSENT (242)	0.58 OF 55	377	LEAN MORE TOWARD BEING THOSE WHERE MALE GENITAL MUTILATION IS ABSENT (242)	0.80 OF 198	23 39 32 159 XSQ= 10.22 PHI= 0.201 XP = 0.0014
382	DRIFT TOWARD BEING THOSE WHERE FEMALE INITIATION RITES ARE ABSENT (27) JKB	0.56 OF 18	382	DRIFT TOWARD BEING THOSE WHERE FEMALE INITIATION RITES ARE PRESENT (38) JKB	0.72 OF 39	8 28 10 11 XSQ= 2.87 PHI= -0.224 XP = 0.0902

391	TEND TO BE THOSE WHERE PREMARITAL SEX RELATIONS ARE STRONGLY PUNISHED AND IN FACT RARE, OR WEAKLY PUNISHED AND IN FACT NOT RARE (89) JTW,EA	0.74 OF 35	391	TEND TO BE THOSE WHERE PREMARITAL SEX RELATIONS ARE PUNISHED ONLY IF PREGNANCY RESULTS, OR FREELY PERMITTED (90) JTW,EA	0.60 OF 109	26 44 9 65 XSQ= 10.88 PHI= 0.275 XP = 0.0010
393	TILT TOWARD BEING THOSE WHERE EXTRAMARITAL COITUS IS PUNISHED, RATHER THAN PERMITTED (43) F-B	0.90 OF 10	393	TILT TOWARD BEING THOSE WHERE EXTRAMARITAL COITUS IS PERMITTED, RATHER THAN PUNISHED (41) F-B	0.51 OF 61	9 30 1 31 XSQ= 4.25 PHI= 0.245 XP = 0.0392
399	DRIFT TOWARD BEING THOSE WHERE INTENSITY OF CASTRATION ANXIETY IS HIGH (23) WNS	0.86 OF 7	399	DRIFT TOWARD BEING THOSE WHERE INTENSITY OF CASTRATION ANXIETY IS LOW (22) WNS	0.58 OF 31	6 13 1 18 XSQ= 2.80 PHI= 0.272 EP = 0.0897
417	IN ALL CASES ARE THOSE WHERE WARFARE IS PREVALENT (34) LWS	1.00 OF 10	417	DRIFT LESS TOWARD BEING THOSE WHERE WARFARE IS PREVALENT (34) LWS	0.73 OF 30	10 22 0 8 XSQ= 1.88 PHI= 0.217 EP = 0.0906
420	TILT TOWARD BEING THOSE WHERE BELLICOSITY IS EXTREME (41) PES	0.70 OF 20	420	TILT TOWARD BEING THOSE WHERE BELLICOSITY IS MODERATE OR NEGLIGIBLE (46) PES	0.59 OF 56	14 23 6 33 XSQ= 3.85 PHI= 0.225 XP = 0.0499
424	TEND TO BE THOSE WHERE RELIGIOUS SPECIALISTS ARE FULL-TIME, RATHER THAN PART-TIME (21) JMH	0.80 OF 15	424	TEND TO BE THOSE WHERE RELIGIOUS SPECIALISTS ARE PART-TIME, RATHER THAN FULL-TIME (33) JMH	0.77 OF 35	12 8 3 27 XSQ= 12.00 PHI= 0.490 XP = 0.0005
426	TEND MORE TO BE THOSE WHERE A HIGH GOD IS PRESENT (156) GES,EA	0.83 OF 46	426	TEND LESS TO BE THOSE WHERE A HIGH GOD IS PRESENT (156) GES,EA	0.51 OF 156	38 79 8 77 XSQ= 13.61 PHI= 0.260 XP = 0.0002
427	DRIFT TOWARD BEING THOSE WHERE A HIGH GOD, IF PRESENT, IS ACTIVE, RATHER THAN INACTIVE (87) GES,EA	0.66 OF 38	427	DRIFT TOWARD BEING THOSE WHERE A HIGH GOD, IF PRESENT, IS INACTIVE, RATHER THAN ACTIVE (69) GES,EA	0.53 OF 79	25 37 13 42 XSQ= 2.98 PHI= 0.160 XP = 0.0844
428	TILT MORE TOWARD BEING THOSE WHERE A HIGH GOD, IF PRESENT AND ACTIVE, SUPPORTS HUMAN MORALITY, RATHER THAN NOT SUPPORTING IT (61) GES,EA	0.84 OF 25	428	TILT LESS TOWARD BEING THOSE WHERE A HIGH GOD, IF PRESENT AND ACTIVE, SUPPORTS HUMAN MORALITY, RATHER THAN NOT SUPPORTING IT (61) GES,EA	0.57 OF 37	21 21 4 16 XSQ= 3.90 PHI= 0.251 XP = 0.0484

435	IN ALL CASES ARE THOSE WHERE ABANDONMENT OF THE HOUSE OF THE DEAD IS NOT PRACTICED (19) LWS	1.00 OF 7	435	TILT TOWARD BEING THOSE WHERE ABANDONMENT OF THE HOUSE OF THE DEAD IS PRACTICED (12) LWS	0.55 OF 22	0 12 7 10 XSQ= 4.46 PHI= -0.392 EP = 0.0230
439	DRIFT TOWARD BEING THOSE WHERE FEAR OF GHOSTS IS LOW (31) W-C	0.86 OF 7	439	DRIFT TOWARD BEING THOSE WHERE FEAR OF GHOSTS IS HIGH (30) W-C	0.60 OF 42	1 25 6 17 XSQ= 3.28 PHI= -0.259 XP = 0.0701
450	TEND TO BE THOSE WHERE THE OBSERVATION OF FOOD TABOOS IS LOW, RATHER THAN HIGH OR MEDIUM (26) JRL	0.64 OF 22	450	TEND TO BE THOSE WHERE THE OBSERVATION OF FOOD TABOOS IS HIGH OR MEDIUM, RATHER THAN LOW (60) JRL	0.85 OF 52	8 44 14 8 XSQ= 15.00 PHI= -0.450 XP = 0.0001
458	TEND TO BE THOSE WHERE GAMES, IF PRESENT, INCLUDE GAMES OF STRATEGY (52) R-A-B,EA	0.85 OF 34	458	TEND TO BE THOSE WHERE GAMES, IF PRESENT, DO NOT INCLUDE GAMES OF STRATEGY (119) R-A-B,EA	0.85 OF 109	29 16 5 93 XSQ= 56.69 PHI= 0.630 XP = 0.
459	LEAN TOWARD BEING THOSE WHERE GAMES, IF PRESENT, INCLUDE GAMES OF CHANCE (82) R-A-B,EA	0.68 OF 34	459	LEAN TOWARD BEING THOSE WHERE GAMES, IF PRESENT, DO NOT INCLUDE GAMES OF CHANCE (89) R-A-B,EA	0.60 OF 109	23 44 11 65 XSQ= 6.69 PHI= 0.216 XP = 0.0097
460	TEND MORE TO BE THOSE WHERE GAMES, IF PRESENT, ARE NOT LIMITED TO GAMES OF SKILL ONLY (104) R-A-B,EA	0.91 OF 34	460	TEND LESS TO BE THOSE WHERE GAMES, IF PRESENT, ARE NOT LIMITED TO GAMES OF SKILL ONLY (104) R-A-B,EA	0.51 OF 109	3 53 31 56 XSQ= 15.60 PHI= -0.330 XP = 0.0001
468	LEAN TOWARD BEING THOSE WHERE CONTACT WITH OTHER CULTURES IS FREQUENT, RATHER THAN REGULAR OR IRREGULAR (17) JMH	0.67 OF 15	468	LEAN TOWARD BEING THOSE WHERE CONTACT WITH OTHER CULTURES IS REGULAR OR IRREGULAR, RATHER THAN FREQUENT (37) JMH	0.83 OF 35	10 6 5 29 XSQ= 9.67 PHI= 0.440 XP = 0.0019
470	TILT TOWARD BEING THOSE WHERE INNOVATIONS ARE GENERALLY ACCEPTED (21) JMH	0.67 OF 15	470	TILT TOWARD BEING THOSE WHERE INNOVATIONS ARE ACCEPTED ONLY SELECTIVELY (33) JMH	0.74 OF 35	10 9 5 26 XSQ= 5.84 PHI= 0.342 XP = 0.0157

86 CULTURES
WHERE THE LEVEL OF POLITICAL INTEGRATION
IS THE LARGE STATE, THE LITTLE STATE,
OR THE MINIMAL STATE (148) GPM

86 CULTURES
WHERE THE LEVEL OF POLITICAL INTEGRATION
IS THE AUTONOMOUS COMMUNITY, OR
THE FAMILY (156) GPM

BACKGROUND ON PAGE 82

BOTH SUBJECT AND PREDICATE

148 IN LEFT COLUMN

AJIE	ALBANIANS	AMERICANS	ARYANS	ASHANTI	AZANDE	AZTEC	BABWA	BALINESE	BEJA
BELU	BEMBA	BOERS	BULGARIANS	BURMESE	BURUSHO	BURYAT	CADUVEO	CAMBODIANS	CHAGGA
CHAMACOCO	CHERKESS	CHEROKEE	CHEYENNE	CHIBCHA	CHIRIGUANO	COORG	CREEK	CROW	CUNA
CZECHS	DARD	DILLING	DUSUN	DUTCH	EGYPTIANS	ELLICE	FON	FOX	FUTAJALONKE
GANDA	GARO	GOND	GROS VENTRE	HASINAI	HAWAIIANS	HAZARA	HEBREWS	HEHE	HO
HURON	ICELANDERS	INCA	IRISH	JAPANESE	JAVANESE	JUKUN	KABYLE	KACHIN	KALMYK
KAZAK	KERALA	KHALKA	KHASI	KIOW-APACHE	KISSI	KONSO	KOREANS	KUBA	LAKHER
LAMBA	LAU	LIFU	LOZI	LUBA	MACASSARESE	MAGUZAWA	MALAYS	MANDAN	MANGAIANS
MAORI	MARGI	MARICOPA	MARQUESANS	MAYA	MBUNDU	MENDE	MERINA	MIAMI	MISKITO
MONGO	MONGUOR	OMAHA	MZAB	NAMA	NATCHEZ	NGONI	NURI	NYAKYUSA	NYANEKA
NYORO	OMAHA	CRAON	PAEZ	PALAUANS	PAWNEE	PENOBSCOT	PONAPEANS	RIFFIANS	ROMANS
ROTINESE	ROTUMANS	RWALA	SAMOANS	SANTAL	SARAMACCA	SARSI	SENIANG	SERBS	SHERENTE
SHILLUK	SHLUH	SINHALESE	SIWANS	SOMALI	SONGHAI	SOTHO	TALAMANCA	TANALA	TENDA
THAI	THONGA	TIBETANS	TIMUCUA	TIV	TOKELAU	TOTONAC	TROBRIAND	TURKMEN	VIETNAMESE
WICHITA	WINNEBAGO	WOLOF	WUTE	YAKUT	YAO	YAPESE	YORUBA		

156 IN RIGHT COLUMN

ABIPON	ABOR	AKHA	ALACALUF	ALORESE	ANDAMANESE	APINAYE	ARANDA	ARAPESH	ARAUCANIANS
ATAYAL	ATSUGEWI	AWEIKOMA	BACAIRI	BANDA	BARI	BATAK	BAYA	BERGDAMA	BETE
BIRIFOR	BORORO	BOTOCUDO	BOZO	BUDUMA	CAGABA	CALLINAGO	CAMAYURA	CARAJA	CARIB
CAYAPA	CHENCHU	CHIR-APACHE	CHOROTI	CHUKCHEE	COCHITI	CREE	DELAWARE	DIEGUENO	DIERI
DOBUANS	DOGON	DOROBO	FANG	GILBERTESE	GILYAK	GOAJIRO	GUAHIBO	GUATO	GURE
HAIDA	HANUNOO	HAVASUPAI	HERERO	HUKUNDIKA	IBAN	IFUGAO	ILA	INGASSANA	IRAQW
JEMEZ	JIVARO	KAREN	KARIERA	KASKA	KERAKI	KET	KIKUYU	KORYAK	KPE
KUNG	KURTATCHI	KUTENAI	LAKALAI	LAMET	LANGO	LAPPS	LESU	LOLO	LUO
MANIHIKI	MANUS	MATACO	MATAKAM	MBUGWE	MBUTI	MENTAWEI	MINANGKABAU	MIWOK	MOTA
MOTILON	MUNDURUCU	MURNGIN	NAMBICUARA	NASKAPI	NAVAHO	NICOBARESE	NOMLAKI	NUNIVAK	OJIBWA
ONA	ONTONG-JAVA	PALIKUR	PAPAGO	PUKAPUKA	RAROIANS	SAMOYED	SANDAWE	SELUNG	SEMANG
SERI	SIRIONO	SIUAI	SUBANUN	TALLENSI	TANIMBARESE	TAOS	TAPIRAPE	TARAHUMARA	TEHUELCHE
TENETEHARA	TERENA	TIKOPIA	TIMBIRA	TIWI	TODA	TOLOWA	TORAJA	TRUKESE	TRUMAI
TUBATULABAL	TUCANO	TUCUNA	TUPINAMBA	TURKANA	TZELTAL	ULAWANS	UTE	VEDDA	WAICA
WAPISHANA	WARRAU	WARRAU	WASHO	WITOTO	WOGEO	WOLEAIANS	YAGUA	YAHGAN	YAKO
YARURO	YOKUTS	YUKAGHIR	YUKI	YUROK	ZUNI				

33 EXCLUDED BECAUSE IRRELEVANT (SEE 'IRRELEVANT,' PARAGRAPH 84)

63 EXCLUDED BECAUSE UNASCERTAINED

4	TEND LESS TO BE THOSE LOCATED OUTSIDE OF THE CIRCUM-MEDITERRANEAN (355)	0.82 OF 148	4	TEND MORE TO BE THOSE LOCATED OUTSIDE OF THE CIRCUM-MEDITERRANEAN (355)	0.98 OF 156	26 3 122 153 XSQ= 19.77 PHI= 0.255 XP = 0.0000
5	TILT LESS TOWARD BEING THOSE LOCATED OUTSIDE OF EAST EURASIA (330)	0.78 OF 148	5	TILT MORE TOWARD BEING THOSE LOCATED OUTSIDE OF EAST EURASIA (330)	0.88 OF 156	32 18 116 138 XSQ= 4.91 PHI= 0.127 XP = 0.0267
6	DRIFT MORE TOWARD BEING THOSE LOCATED OUTSIDE OF THE INSULAR PACIFIC (330)	0.85 OF 148	6	DRIFT LESS TOWARD BEING THOSE LOCATED OUTSIDE OF THE INSULAR PACIFIC (330)	0.77 OF 156	22 36 126 120 XSQ= 2.81 PHI= -0.096 XP = 0.0939
9	TEND MORE TO BE THOSE LOCATED OUTSIDE OF SOUTH AMERICA (335)	0.92 OF 148	9	TEND LESS TO BE THOSE LOCATED OUTSIDE OF SOUTH AMERICA (335)	0.72 OF 156	12 43 136 113 XSQ= 18.11 PHI= -0.244 XP = 0.0000
15	TILT TOWARD BEING THOSE WHERE THE LATITUDE IS TWENTY DEGREES OR GREATER (183)	0.51 OF 148	15	TILT TOWARD BEING THOSE WHERE THE LATITUDE IS LESS THAN TWENTY DEGREES (217)	0.63 OF 156	76 58 72 98 XSQ= 5.63 PHI= 0.136 XP = 0.0177
42	DRIFT MORE TOWARD BEING THOSE WHERE THE NATURAL ENVIRONMENT IS OTHER THAN TROPICAL OR SUB-TROPICAL RAIN FOREST, OR MONSOON FOREST (244) FWM	0.65 OF 148	42	DRIFT LESS TOWARD BEING THOSE WHERE THE NATURAL ENVIRONMENT IS OTHER THAN TROPICAL OR SUB-TROPICAL RAIN FOREST, OR MONSOON FOREST (244) FWM	0.53 OF 156	52 73 96 83 XSQ= 3.80 PHI= -0.112 XP = 0.0514
44	TEND MORE TO BE THOSE WHERE SETTLEMENTS ARE FIXED (222)	0.80 OF 123	44	TEND LESS TO BE THOSE WHERE SETTLEMENTS ARE FIXED (222)	0.51 OF 135	98 69 25 66 XSQ= 21.77 PHI= 0.290 XP = 0.0000
46	TEND MORE TO BE THOSE OTHER THAN WHERE SETTLEMENTS ARE NON-FIXED AND MOVEMENT IS NOMADIC (260)	0.89 OF 123	46	TEND LESS TO BE THOSE OTHER THAN WHERE SETTLEMENTS ARE NON-FIXED AND MOVEMENT IS NOMADIC (260)	0.66 OF 135	14 46 109 89 XSQ= 17.32 PHI= -0.259 XP = 0.0000
51	TEND TO BE THOSE WHERE SUBSISTENCE IS PRIMARILY BY FOOD PRODUCTION -- I. E., AGRICULTURE OR HUSBANDRY -- RATHER THAN BY GATHERING (253)	0.79 OF 148	51	TEND TO BE THOSE WHERE SUBSISTENCE IS PRIMARILY BY FOOD GATHERING -- I. E., HUNTING, FISHING, OR COLLECTING -- RATHER THAN FOOD PRODUCTION (147)	0.61 OF 156	117 61 31 95 XSQ= 48.32 PHI= 0.399 XP = 0.

53	TEND LESS TO BE THOSE WHERE FOOD PRODUCTION IS BY SIMPLE AGRICULTURE OR INCIPIENT FOOD PRODUCTION, RATHER THAN BY INTENSIVE AGRICULTURE (147)	0.53 OF 109	53	TEND MORE TO BE THOSE WHERE FOOD PRODUCTION IS BY SIMPLE AGRICULTURE OR INCIPIENT FOOD PRODUCTION, RATHER THAN BY INTENSIVE AGRICULTURE (147)	0.80 OF 74	51 15 58 59 XSQ= 12.32 PHI= 0.259 XP = 0.0004
54	LEAN MORE TOWARD BEING THOSE WHERE FOOD PRODUCTION IS BY INTENSIVE OR SIMPLE AGRICULTURE, RATHER THAN BY INCIPIENT FOOD PRODUCTION (192)	0.84 OF 109	54	LEAN LESS TOWARD BEING THOSE WHERE FOOD PRODUCTION IS BY INTENSIVE OR SIMPLE AGRICULTURE, RATHER THAN BY INCIPIENT FOOD PRODUCTION (192)	0.65 OF 74	92 48 17 26 XSQ= 8.31 PHI= 0.213 XP = 0.0040
55	TILT TOWARD BEING THOSE WHERE FOOD PRODUCTION IS BY INTENSIVE AGRICULTURE, RATHER THAN BY SIMPLE AGRICULTURE (91)	0.55 OF 92	55	TILT TOWARD BEING THOSE WHERE FOOD PRODUCTION IS BY SIMPLE AGRICULTURE, RATHER THAN BY INTENSIVE AGRICULTURE (101)	0.69 OF 48	51 15 41 33 XSQ= 6.47 PHI= 0.215 XP = 0.0110
62	TEND TO BE THOSE WHERE HUSBANDRY OF SOME KIND IS PRESENT (228)	0.70 OF 148	62	TEND TO BE THOSE WHERE HUSBANDRY OF ANY KIND IS ABSENT (172)	0.55 OF 156	103 70 45 86 XSQ= 17.93 PHI= 0.243 XP = 0.0000
63	TEND MORE TO BE THOSE WHERE HUSBANDRY, IF PRESENT, IS PRINCIPALLY IN THE FORM OF BOVINE, EQUINE, CAMEL-LIKE, OR DEER-LIKE ANIMALS, RATHER THAN PIGS, SHEEP, OR GOATS (152)	0.77 OF 101	63	TEND LESS TO BE THOSE WHERE HUSBANDRY, IF PRESENT, IS PRINCIPALLY IN THE FORM OF BOVINE, EQUINE, CAMEL-LIKE, OR DEER-LIKE ANIMALS, RATHER THAN PIGS, SHEEP, OR GOATS (152)	0.51 OF 70	78 36 23 34 XSQ= 11.25 PHI= 0.256 XP = 0.0008
71	TEND TO BE THOSE WHERE METAL WORKING IS PRESENT (98)	0.60 OF 92	71	TEND TO BE THOSE WHERE METAL WORKING IS ABSENT (153)	0.82 OF 106	55 19 37 87 XSQ= 35.10 PHI= 0.421 XP = 0.
73	TEND TO BE THOSE WHERE WEAVING IS PRESENT (118)	0.66 OF 89	73	TEND TO BE THOSE WHERE WEAVING IS ABSENT (130)	0.66 OF 104	59 35 30 69 XSQ= 19.16 PHI= 0.315 XP = 0.0000
74	TEND MORE TO BE THOSE WHERE POTTERY IS PRESENT (145)	0.79 OF 84	74	TEND LESS TO BE THOSE WHERE POTTERY IS PRESENT (145)	0.51 OF 103	66 53 18 50 XSQ= 13.55 PHI= 0.269 XP = 0.0002
79	TEND LESS TO BE THOSE WHERE NO CITY IS PRESENT (201)	0.78 OF 82	79	IN ALL CASES ARE THOSE WHERE NO CITY IS PRESENT (201)	1.00 OF 94	18 0 64 94 XSQ= 20.66 PHI= 0.343 XP = 0.0000

81	TEND TO BE THOSE WHERE A CITY OR TOWN IS PRESENT, OR THE AVERAGE COMMUNITY SIZE IS 200 OR GREATER (89)	0.59 OF 82	81	TEND TO BE THOSE WHERE NO CITY OR TOWN IS PRESENT, AND THE AVERAGE COMMUNITY SIZE IS SMALLER THAN 200 (135)	0.83 OF 94	48 16 34 78 XSQ= 30.85 PHI= 0.419 XP = 0.
83	TILT LESS TOWARD BEING THOSE WHERE, WITH NO CITY AND NO TOWN PRESENT, THE AVERAGE COMMUNITY SIZE IS SMALLER THAN 200, RATHER THAN BETWEEN 200 AND 999 (135)	0.67 OF 51	83	TILT MORE TOWARD BEING THOSE WHERE, WITH NO CITY AND NO TOWN PRESENT, THE AVERAGE COMMUNITY SIZE IS SMALLER THAN 200, RATHER THAN BETWEEN 200 AND 999 (135)	0.85 OF 92	17 14 34 78 XSQ= 5.32 PHI= 0.193 XP = 0.0211
91	LEAN TOWARD BEING THOSE WHERE SOCIETAL COMPLEXITY IS HIGH (18) F-W	0.62 OF 21	91	LEAN TOWARD BEING THOSE WHERE SOCIETAL COMPLEXITY IS LOW (22) F-W	0.86 OF 14	13 2 8 12 XSQ= 5.95 PHI= 0.412 EP = 0.0069
94	TEND LESS TO BE THOSE WHERE THE HIERARCHY OF NATIONAL JURISDICTION HAS TWO, ONE, OR NO LEVELS (296) GES,EA	0.79 OF 122	94	IN ALL CASES ARE THOSE WHERE THE HIERARCHY OF NATIONAL JURISDICTION HAS TWO, ONE, OR NO LEVELS (296) GES,EA	1.00 OF 136	26 0 96 136 XSQ= 29.92 PHI= 0.341 XP = 0.0000
96	TEND TO BE THOSE WHERE THE HIERARCHY OF NATIONAL JURISDICTION HAS FOUR, THREE, TWO OR ONE LEVEL (174) GES,EA	0.95 OF 122	96	TEND TO BE THOSE WHERE THE HIERARCHY OF NATIONAL JURISDICTION HAS NO LEVELS (156) GES,EA	0.86 OF 136	116 19 6 117 XSQ= 166.37 PHI= 0.803 XP = 0.
97	LEAN LESS TOWARD BEING THOSE WHERE THE HIERARCHY OF LOCAL JURISDICTION HAS THREE OR TWO LEVELS (273) GES,EA	0.76 OF 122	97	LEAN MORE TOWARD BEING THOSE WHERE THE HIERARCHY OF LOCAL JURISDICTION HAS THREE OR TWO LEVELS (273) GES,EA	0.90 OF 136	29 14 93 122 XSQ= 7.47 PHI= 0.170 XP = 0.0063
98	TEND MORE TO BE THOSE WHERE THE HIERARCHY OF LOCAL JURISDICTION HAS FOUR OR THREE LEVELS (238) GES,EA	0.83 OF 122	98	TEND LESS TO BE THOSE WHERE THE HIERARCHY OF LOCAL JURISDICTION HAS FOUR OR THREE LEVELS (238) GES,EA	0.63 OF 136	101 85 21 51 XSQ= 12.17 PHI= 0.217 XP = 0.0005
100	TEND MORE TO BE THOSE WHERE HIERARCHIES ARE MORE COMPLEX THAN THE 'SIMPLEST,' I. E., MORE COMPLEX THAN TWO LOCAL LEVELS WITH NO NATIONAL LEVELS (267) GES,EA	0.98 OF 122	100	TEND LESS TO BE THOSE WHERE HIERARCHIES ARE MORE COMPLEX THAN THE 'SIMPLEST,' I. E., MORE COMPLEX THAN TWO LOCAL LEVELS WITH NO NATIONAL LEVELS (267) GES,EA	0.65 OF 136	120 88 2 48 XSQ= 44.49 PHI= 0.415 XP = 0.
102	TEND TO BE THOSE WHERE CLASS STRATIFICATION IS PRESENT (203)	0.72 OF 142	102	TEND TO BE THOSE WHERE CLASS STRATIFICATION IS ABSENT (180)	0.68 OF 155	102 49 40 106 XSQ= 46.37 PHI= 0.395 XP = 0.

106	TEND TO BE THCSE 0.84 OF 102 WHERE CLASS STRATIFICATICN, IF PRESENT, IS BASED CN SOMETHING CTHER THAN WEALTH (126)	106	TEND TO BE THOSE 0.84 CF 49 WHERE CLASS STRATIFICATION, IF PRESENT, IS BASED ON WEALTH (77)	16 41 86 8 XSQ= 62.25 PHI= -0.642 XP = 0.
107	TEND LESS TO BE THCSE 0.72 OF 102 WHERE CLASS STRATIFICATION, IF PRESENT, IS BASED CN SOMETHING OTHER THAN OCCUPATICNAL STATUS (160)	107	IN ALL CASES ARE THOSE 1.00 CF 49 WHERE CLASS STRATIFICATION, IF PRESENT, IS BASED ON SOMETHING OTHER THAN OCCUPATIONAL STATUS (160)	29 0 73 49 XSQ= 15.46 PHI= 0.320 XP = 0.0001
108	TEND TO BE THOSE 0.52 OF 102 WHERE CLASS STRATIFICATICN, IF PRESENT, IS BASED CN A HEREDITARY ARISTCCRACY (74)	108	TEND TO BE THOSE 0.84 CF 49 WHERE CLASS STRATIFICATION, IF PRESENT, IS BASED ON SOMETHING OTHER THAN A HEREDITARY ARISTOCRACY (129)	53 8 49 41 XSQ= 16.01 PHI= 0.326 XP = 0.0001
109	TEND LESS TO BE THCSE 0.78 OF 133 WHERE CASTES ARE ABSENT (317)	109	TEND MORE TO BE THOSE 0.97 CF 152 WHERE CASTES ARE ABSENT (317)	29 5 104 147 XSQ= 21.42 PHI= 0.274 XP = 0.0000
110	TEND TO BE THCSE 0.59 OF 140 WHERE SLAVERY IS PRESENT (163)	110	TEND TO BE THOSE 0.71 CF 153 WHERE SLAVERY IS ABSENT (218)	83 44 57 109 XSQ= 26.51 PHI= 0.301 XP = 0.0000
116	LEAN TCWARD BEING THOSE 0.63 OF 24 WHERE OCCUPATIONAL SPECIALIZATION IS FULL-TIME, WHETHER CR NOT FOR SURPLUS PRODUCTION (20) JMH	116	LEAN TOWARD BEING THOSE 0.85 CF 26 WHERE OCCUPATIONAL SPECIALIZATION IS PART-TIME ONLY (34) JMH	15 4 9 22 XSQ= 9.84 PHI= 0.444 XP = 0.0017
118	DRIFT TOWARD BEING THCSE 0.63 OF 24 WHERE THE PERCENTAGE CF OCCUPATIONS THAT ARE SPECIALIZED IS HIGH CR MEDIUM (24) WME	118	DRIFT TOWARD BEING THOSE 0.67 CF 21 WHERE THE PERCENTAGE OF OCCUPATICNS THAT ARE SPECIALIZED IS LOW (25) WME	15 7 9 14 XSQ= 2.74 PHI= 0.247 XP = 0.0982
127	TILT TOWARD BEING THCSE 0.65 OF 26 WHERE THE FEMALES' CONTRIBUTION TO SUBSISTENCE IS LOW (32) JKB	127	TILT TOWARD BEING THOSE 0.65 OF 31 WHERE THE FEMALES' CONTRIBUTION TO SUBSISTENCE IS HIGH (33) JKB	9 20 17 11 XSQ= 3.93 PHI= -0.263 XP = 0.0474
137	TILT TOWARD BEING THOSE 0.58 OF 38 WHERE INVIDIOUS DISPLAY OF WEALTH IS STRONGLY EMPHASIZED (37) PES	137	TILT TOWARD BEING THOSE 0.69 CF 39 WHERE INVIDIOUS DISPLAY CF WEALTH IS MODERATELY, LITTLE, OR NEGATIVELY EMPHASIZED (52) PES	22 12 16 27 XSQ= 4.70 PHI= 0.247 XP = 0.0302

138	TEND TO BE THOSE WHERE SUPERORDINATE JUSTICE IS PRESENT (22) BBW	0.88 OF 16	138	TEND TO BE THOSE WHERE SUPERORDINATE JUSTICE IS ABSENT (18) BBW	0.83 OF 18	 XSQ= PHI= EP =	14 3 2 15 14.28 0.648 0.0001
139	TILT TOWARD BEING THOSE WHERE SUPERORDINATE PUNISHMENT IS PRESENT (15) BBW	0.56 OF 16	139	TILT TOWARD BEING THOSE WHERE SUPERORDINATE PUNISHMENT IS ABSENT (25) BBW	0.83 OF 18	 XSQ= PHI= EP =	9 3 7 15 4.21 0.352 0.0299
141	TILT TOWARD BEING THOSE WHERE THE LEVEL OF SOCIAL SANCTION IS PUBLIC CORPOREAL SANCTION, RATHER THAN PUBLIC PROPERTY SANCTION OR PRIVATE SETTLEMENT (28) JMH	0.67 OF 24	141	TILT TOWARD BEING THOSE WHERE THE LEVEL OF SOCIAL SANCTION IS PUBLIC PROPERTY SANCTION OR PRIVATE SETTLEMENT, RATHER THAN PUBLIC CORPOREAL SANCTION (26) JMH	0.65 OF 26	 XSQ= PHI= XP =	16 9 8 17 3.93 0.280 0.0475
147	LEAN TOWARD BEING THOSE WHERE CODIFIED LAWS ARE PRESENT (20) LWS	0.92 OF 13	147	LEAN TOWARD BEING THOSE WHERE CODIFIED LAWS ARE UNIMPORTANT OR ABSENT (13) LWS	0.65 OF 17	 XSQ= PHI= EP =	12 6 1 11 7.74 0.508 0.0024
152	DRIFT TOWARD BEING THOSE WHERE THE DIFFERENTIATION OF THE JURIDICAL AGENCY FROM THE MEDICAL AGENCY IS HIGH (10) MJ	0.78 OF 9	152	DRIFT TOWARD BEING THOSE WHERE THE DIFFERENTIATION OF THE JURIDICAL AGENCY FROM THE MEDICAL AGENCY IS LOW (10) MJ	0.75 OF 8	 XSQ= PHI= EP =	7 2 2 6 2.85 0.410 0.0567
183	LEAN MORE TOWARD BEING THOSE WHERE THE LARGEST NON-COGNATIC KIN GROUP IS SMALLER THAN A MOEITY, I. E., A PHRATRY OR SIB OR LINEAGE (218)	0.92 OF 102	183	LEAN LESS TOWARD BEING THOSE WHERE THE LARGEST NON-COGNATIC KIN GROUP IS SMALLER THAN A MOEITY, I. E., A PHRATRY OR SIB OR LINEAGE (218)	0.76 OF 89	 XSQ= PHI= XP =	8 21 94 68 7.98 -0.204 0.0047
185	DRIFT MORE TOWARD BEING THOSE WHERE THE LARGEST NON-COGNATIC KIN GROUP IS THE MOEITY OR PHRATRY OR SIB (194)	0.83 OF 102	185	DRIFT LESS TOWARD BEING THOSE WHERE THE LARGEST NON-COGNATIC KIN GROUP IS THE MOEITY OR PHRATRY OR SIB (194)	0.72 OF 89	 XSQ= PHI= XP =	85 64 17 25 2.98 0.125 0.0843
186	LEAN LESS TOWARD BEING THOSE WHERE THE KIN GROUP IS OTHER THAN EXCLUSIVELY PATRILINEAL (250)	0.55 OF 148	186	LEAN MORE TOWARD BEING THOSE WHERE THE KIN GROUP IS OTHER THAN EXCLUSIVELY PATRILINEAL (250)	0.72 OF 156	 XSQ= PHI= XP =	67 43 81 113 9.56 0.177 0.0020
188	TILT MORE TOWARD BEING THOSE WHERE THE KIN GROUP IS OTHER THAN EXCLUSIVELY COGNATIC (252)	0.69 OF 148	188	TILT LESS TOWARD BEING THOSE WHERE THE KIN GROUP IS OTHER THAN EXCLUSIVELY COGNATIC (252)	0.57 OF 156	 XSQ= PHI= XP =	46 67 102 89 4.09 -0.116 0.0432

192	DRIFT MORE TOWARD BEING THOSE 0.78 OF 148 OTHER THAN WHERE THE ONLY KIN GROUP PRESENT IS A KINDRED OR ELSE BILATERAL DESCENT IS INFERRED (289)	192	DRIFT LESS TOWARD BEING THOSE 0.68 OF 156 OTHER THAN WHERE THE ONLY KIN GROUP PRESENT IS A KINDRED OR ELSE BILATERAL DESCENT IS INFERRED (289)	32 50 116 106 XSQ= 3.68 PHI= -0.110 XP = 0.0550
196	TEND TO BE THOSE 0.81 OF 107 WHERE INDIVIDUAL RIGHTS IN REAL PROPERTY, AND RULES FOR INHERITANCE, ARE PRESENT (194)	196	TEND TO BE THOSE 0.52 OF 108 WHERE INDIVIDUAL RIGHTS IN REAL PROPERTY, OR RULES FOR INHERITANCE, ARE ABSENT (87)	87 52 20 56 XSQ= 24.43 PHI= 0.337 XP = 0.0000
204	DRIFT MORE TOWARD BEING THOSE 0.87 OF 123 WHERE MARITAL RESIDENCE IS PATRILOCAL, VIRILOCAL, OR AVUNCULOCAL, RATHER THAN AMBILOCAL OR NEOLOCAL (270)	204	DRIFT LESS TOWARD BEING THOSE 0.78 OF 122 WHERE MARITAL RESIDENCE IS PATRILOCAL, VIRILOCAL, OR AVUNCULOCAL, RATHER THAN AMBILOCAL OR NEOLOCAL (270)	107 95 16 27 XSQ= 2.92 PHI= 0.109 XP = 0.0875
236	DRIFT MORE TOWARD BEING THOSE 0.62 OF 146 WHERE THE FAMILY IS OF AN EXTENDED TYPE, RATHER THAN AN INDEPENDENT TYPE (213)	236	DRIFT LESS TOWARD BEING THOSE 0.51 OF 156 WHERE THE FAMILY IS OF AN EXTENDED TYPE, RATHER THAN AN INDEPENDENT TYPE (213)	91 79 55 77 XSQ= 3.73 PHI= 0.111 XP = 0.0536
254	IN ALL CASES ARE THOSE 1.00 OF 4 WHERE HOUSEHOLD AUTHORITY IS ON THE FATHER'S SIDE, RATHER THAN THE MOTHER'S (9) CA	254	DRIFT TOWARD BEING THOSE 0.67 OF 6 WHERE HOUSEHOLD AUTHORITY IS ON THE MOTHER'S SIDE, RATHER THAN THE FATHER'S (6) DA	4 2 0 4 XSQ= 2.10 PHI= 0.458 EP = 0.0762
257	DRIFT TOWARD BEING THOSE 0.71 OF 7 WHERE THE SEVERITY OF SISTER AVOIDANCE IS HIGH (10) WNS	257	DRIFT TOWARD BEING THOSE 0.71 OF 17 WHERE THE SEVERITY OF SISTER AVOIDANCE IS LOW (17) WNS	5 5 2 12 XSQ= 2.08 PHI= 0.294 EP = 0.0850
278	LEAN TOWARD BEING THOSE 0.70 OF 10 WHERE PROPERTY RIGHTS IN WOMEN ARE PRESENT (8) LWS	278	LEAN TOWARD BEING THOSE 0.91 OF 11 WHERE PROPERTY RIGHTS IN WOMEN ARE UNIMPORTANT OR ABSENT (14) LWS	7 1 3 10 XSQ= 5.86 PHI= 0.528 EP = 0.0075
282	DRIFT TOWARD BEING THOSE 0.69 OF 13 WHERE THE STRENGTH OF DESIRE FOR CHILDREN IS HIGH (16) BCA	282	DRIFT TOWARD BEING THOSE 0.73 OF 15 WHERE THE STRENGTH OF DESIRE FOR CHILDREN IS LOW OR ABSENT (20) BCA	9 4 4 11 XSQ= 3.51 PHI= 0.354 EP = 0.0557
303	TILT TOWARD BEING THOSE 0.67 OF 18 WHERE THE EARLY ORAL SATISFACTION POTENTIAL IS LOW (25) W-C	303	TILT TOWARD BEING THOSE 0.70 OF 27 WHERE THE EARLY ORAL SATISFACTION POTENTIAL IS HIGH (32) W-C	6 19 12 8 XSQ= 4.59 PHI= -0.320 XP = 0.0321

309	TILT TOWARD BEING THOSE 0.76 OF 17 WHERE ORAL SOCIALIZATION ANXIETY IS HIGH (26) W-C	309	TILT TOWARD BEING THOSE 0.64 OF 25 WHERE ORAL SOCIALIZATION ANXIETY IS LOW (27) W-C	13 9 4 16 XSQ= 5.12 PHI= 0.349 XP = 0.0236
314	LEAN LESS TOWARD BEING THOSE 0.58 OF 26 WHERE THE INCIDENCE OF MOTHER-CHILD HOUSEHOLDS IS LOW (61) W-D,S	314	LEAN MORE TOWARD BEING THOSE 0.88 OF 43 WHERE THE INCIDENCE OF MOTHER-CHILD HOUSEHOLDS IS LOW (61) W-D,S	11 5 15 38 XSQ= 6.93 PHI= 0.317 XP = 0.0085
326	DRIFT TOWARD BEING THOSE 0.60 OF 25 WHERE THE INFERRED TRANSITION ANXIETY BETWEEN INFANCY AND CHILDHOOD IS HIGH (32) B-B-C	326	DRIFT TOWARD BEING THOSE 0.68 OF 31 WHERE THE INFERRED TRANSITION ANXIETY BETWEEN INFANCY AND CHILDHOOD IS LOW (35) B-B-C	15 10 10 21 XSQ= 3.26 PHI= 0.241 XP = 0.0710
332	DRIFT TOWARD BEING THOSE 0.80 OF 5 WHERE THE AGE AT BEGINNING OF MODESTY TRAINING IS SIX YEARS OR HIGHER (9) W-C	332	DRIFT TOWARD BEING THOSE 0.78 OF 9 WHERE THE AGE AT BEGINNING OF MODESTY TRAINING IS LOWER THAN SIX YEARS (8) W-C	4 2 1 7 XSQ= 2.34 PHI= 0.409 EP = 0.0909
333	IN ALL CASES ARE THOSE 1.00 OF 5 WHERE THE AGE AT BEGINNING OF TRAINING IN HETEROSEXUAL PLAY INHIBITION IS EIGHT YEARS OR HIGHER (8) W-C	333	TILT TOWARD BEING THOSE 0.71 OF 7 WHERE THE AGE AT BEGINNING OF TRAINING IN HETEROSEXUAL PLAY INHIBITION IS LOWER THAN EIGHT YEARS (8) W-C	5 2 0 5 XSQ= 3.54 PHI= 0.543 EP = 0.0278
349	DRIFT TOWARD BEING THOSE 0.71 OF 24 WHERE THE CHILD'S INFERRED ANXIETY OVER NON-PERFORMANCE OF ACHIEVEMENT BEHAVIOR IS HIGH (34) B-B-C	349	DRIFT TOWARD BEING THOSE 0.59 OF 27 WHERE THE CHILD'S INFERRED ANXIETY OVER NON-PERFORMANCE OF ACHIEVEMENT BEHAVIOR IS LOW (28) B-B-C	17 11 7 16 XSQ= 3.51 PHI= 0.262 XP = 0.0610
350	LEAN TOWARD BEING THOSE 0.78 OF 23 WHERE THE CHILD'S INFERRED ANXIETY OVER PERFORMANCE OF ACHIEVEMENT BEHAVIOR IS HIGH (34) B-B-C	350	LEAN TOWARD BEING THOSE 0.65 OF 26 WHERE THE CHILD'S INFERRED ANXIETY OVER PERFORMANCE OF ACHIEVEMENT BEHAVIOR IS LOW (26) B-B-C	18 9 5 17 XSQ= 7.72 PHI= 0.397 XP = 0.0055
352	LEAN TOWARD BEING THOSE 0.79 OF 28 WHERE THE TOTAL POSITIVE PRESSURE TOWARD DEVELOPING OBEDIENT BEHAVIOR IN THE CHILD IS HIGH (44) B-B-C	352	LEAN TOWARD BEING THOSE 0.58 OF 33 WHERE THE TOTAL POSITIVE PRESSURE TOWARD DEVELOPING OBEDIENT BEHAVIOR IN THE CHILD IS LOW (28) B-B-C	22 14 6 19 XSQ= 6.76 PHI= 0.333 XP = 0.0093
353	DRIFT TOWARD BEING THOSE 0.68 OF 28 WHERE THE CHILD'S INFERRED ANXIETY OVER NON-PERFORMANCE OF OBEDIENT BEHAVIOR IS HIGH (42) B-B-C	353	DRIFT TOWARD BEING THOSE 0.57 OF 35 WHERE THE CHILD-S INFERRED ANXIETY OVER NON-PERFORMANCE OF OBEDIENT BEHAVIOR IS LOW (32) B-B-C	19 15 9 20 XSQ= 2.97 PHI= 0.217 XP = 0.0847

354	TILT TOWARD BEING THOSE 0.64 OF 28 WHERE THE CHILD'S INFERRED ANXIETY OVER PERFORMANCE OF OBEDIENT BEHAVIOR IS HIGH (36) B-B-C	354	TILT TOWARD BEING THOSE 0.65 OF 34 WHERE THE CHILD'S INFERRED ANXIETY OVER PERFORMANCE OF OBEDIENT BEHAVIOR IS LOW (37) B-B-C	18 12 10 22 XSQ= 4.07 PHI= 0.256 XP = 0.0436
358	TILT MORE TOWARD BEING THOSE 0.96 OF 23 WHERE ADOLESCENT PEER GROUPS ARE PRESENT IN A SETTING OF WORK AND PUBLIC GATHERINGS AND LEISURE, OR OF PUBLIC GATHERINGS AND LEISURE, OR OF LEISURE ONLY (41) JKH	358	TILT LESS TOWARD BEING THOSE 0.62 OF 21 WHERE ADOLESCENT PEER GROUPS ARE PRESENT IN A SETTING OF WORK AND PUBLIC GATHERINGS AND LEISURE, OR OF PUBLIC GATHERINGS AND LEISURE, OR OF LEISURE ONLY (41) JKH	22 13 1 8 XSQ= 5.75 PHI= 0.361 XP = 0.0165
360	DRIFT TOWARD BEING THOSE 0.53 OF 15 WHERE ADOLESCENT PEER GROUPS ARE PRESENT IN A SETTING OF WORK AND PUBLIC GATHERINGS AND LEISURE, OR AT LEAST OF PUBLIC GATHERINGS AND LEISURE (14) JKH	360	DRIFT TOWARD BEING THOSE 0.81 OF 16 WHERE ADOLESCENT PEER GROUPS ARE PRESENT ONLY IN A SETTING OF LEISURE, OR ELSE ARE ABSENT (23) JKH	8 3 7 13 XSQ= 2.68 PHI= 0.294 EP = 0.0659
365	DRIFT MORE TOWARD BEING THOSE 0.81 OF 21 WHERE THE TIME SPENT IN ADOLESCENT PEER GROUP ACTIVITY IS HIGH OR HIGH-MEDIUM (30) JKH	365	DRIFT LESS TOWARD BEING THOSE 0.53 OF 17 WHERE THE TIME SPENT IN ADOLESCENT PEER GROUP ACTIVITY IS HIGH OR HIGH-MEDIUM (30) JKH	17 9 4 8 XSQ= 2.24 PHI= 0.243 EP = 0.0873
377	TEND LESS TO BE THOSE 0.63 OF 118 WHERE MALE GENITAL MUTILATION IS ABSENT (242)	377	TEND MORE TO BE THOSE 0.87 OF 135 WHERE MALE GENITAL MUTILATION IS ABSENT (242)	44 18 74 117 XSQ= 18.26 PHI= 0.269 XP = 0.0000
390	TILT LESS TOWARD BEING THOSE 0.68 OF 71 WHERE PREMARITAL SEX RELATIONS ARE WEAKLY PUNISHED AND IN FACT NOT RARE OR PUNISHED ONLY IF PREGNANCY RESULTS, OR FREELY PERMITTED (132) JTW,EA	390	TILT MORE TOWARD BEING THOSE 0.85 OF 73 WHERE PREMARITAL SEX RELATIONS ARE WEAKLY PUNISHED AND IN FACT NOT RARE OR PUNISHED ONLY IF PREGNANCY RESULTS, OR FREELY PERMITTED (132) JTW,EA	23 11 48 62 XSQ= 5.07 PHI= 0.188 XP = 0.0244
392	DRIFT MORE TOWARD BEING THOSE 0.69 OF 71 WHERE PREMARITAL SEX RELATIONS ARE STRONGLY PUNISHED AND IN FACT RARE, OR WEAKLY PUNISHED AND IN FACT NOT RARE, OR PUNISHED ONLY IF PREGNANCY RESULTS (112) JTW,EA	392	DRIFT LESS TOWARD BEING THOSE 0.53 OF 73 WHERE PREMARITAL SEX RELATIONS ARE STRONGLY PUNISHED AND IN FACT RARE, OR WEAKLY PUNISHED AND IN FACT NOT RARE, OR PUNISHED ONLY IF PREGNANCY RESULTS (112) JTW,EA	49 39 22 34 XSQ= 3.05 PHI= 0.146 XP = 0.0805
417	IN ALL CASES ARE THOSE 1.00 OF 17 WHERE WARFARE IS PREVALENT (34) LWS	417	TILT LESS TOWARD BEING THOSE 0.65 OF 23 WHERE WARFARE IS PREVALENT (34) LWS	17 15 0 8 XSQ= 5.38 PHI= 0.367 EP = 0.0125

No.			No.		
419	TILT MORE TOWARD BEING THOSE WHERE MILITARY GLORY IS STRONGLY OR MODERATELY EMPHASIZED (55) PES	0.77 OF 35	419	TILT LESS TOWARD BEING THOSE WHERE MILITARY GLORY IS STRONGLY OR MODERATELY EMPHASIZED (55) PES	0.52 OF 40	27 21 8 19 XSQ= 3.91 PHI= 0.228 XP = 0.0480
420	TILT TOWARD BEING THOSE WHERE BELLICOSITY IS EXTREME (41) PES	0.65 OF 37	420	TILT TOWARD BEING THOSE WHERE BELLICOSITY IS MODERATE OR NEGLIGIBLE (46) PES	0.67 OF 39	24 13 13 26 XSQ= 6.35 PHI= 0.289 XP = 0.0118
424	TILT TOWARD BEING THOSE WHERE RELIGIOUS SPECIALISTS ARE FULL-TIME, RATHER THAN PART-TIME (21) JMH	0.58 OF 24	424	TILT TOWARD BEING THOSE WHERE RELIGIOUS SPECIALISTS ARE PART-TIME, RATHER THAN FULL-TIME (33) JMH	0.77 OF 26	14 6 10 20 XSQ= 5.08 PHI= 0.319 XP = 0.0242
426	TEND TO BE THOSE WHERE A HIGH GOD IS PRESENT (156) GES,EA	0.75 OF 93	426	TEND TO BE THOSE WHERE A HIGH GOD IS ABSENT (104) GES,EA	0.57 OF 109	70 47 23 62 XSQ= 19.98 PHI= 0.315 XP = 0.0000
427	TILT TOWARD BEING THOSE WHERE A HIGH GOD, IF PRESENT, IS ACTIVE, RATHER THAN INACTIVE (87) GES,EA	0.63 OF 70	427	TILT TOWARD BEING THOSE WHERE A HIGH GOD, IF PRESENT, IS INACTIVE, RATHER THAN ACTIVE (69) GES,EA	0.62 OF 47	44 18 26 29 XSQ= 5.86 PHI= 0.224 XP = 0.0155
428	LEAN TOWARD BEING THOSE WHERE A HIGH GOD, IF PRESENT AND ACTIVE, SUPPORTS HUMAN MORALITY, RATHER THAN NOT SUPPORTING IT (61) GES,EA	0.80 OF 44	428	LEAN TOWARD BEING THOSE WHERE A HIGH GOD, IF PRESENT AND ACTIVE, DOES NOT SUPPORT HUMAN MORALITY, RATHER THAN SUPPORTING IT (26) GES,EA	0.61 OF 18	35 7 9 11 XSQ= 7.89 PHI= 0.357 XP = 0.0050
431	TILT TOWARD BEING THOSE WHERE SUPERNATURAL SANCTIONS FOR MORALITY, HAVING AN EFFECT ON AN INDIVIDUAL'S AFTER LIFE, ARE PRESENT (10) GES	0.50 OF 12	431	TILT TOWARD BEING THOSE WHERE SUPERNATURAL SANCTIONS FOR MORALITY, HAVING AN EFFECT ON AN INDIVIDUAL'S AFTERLIFE, ARE ABSENT OR UNREPORTED (25) GES	0.88 OF 17	6 2 6 15 XSQ= 3.41 PHI= 0.343 EP = 0.0382
435	DRIFT TOWARD BEING THOSE WHERE ABANDONMENT OF THE HOUSE OF THE DEAD IS NOT PRACTICED (19) LWS	0.83 OF 12	435	DRIFT TOWARD BEING THOSE WHERE ABANDONMENT OF THE HOUSE OF THE DEAD IS PRACTICED (12) LWS	0.59 OF 17	2 10 10 7 XSQ= 3.56 PHI= -0.350 EP = 0.0535
449	DRIFT MORE TOWARD BEING THOSE WHERE THE OBSERVATION OF FOOD TABOOS IS MEDIUM OR LOW, RATHER THAN HIGH (61) JRL	0.79 OF 38	449	DRIFT LESS TOWARD BEING THOSE WHERE THE OBSERVATION OF FOOD TABOOS IS MEDIUM OR LOW, RATHER THAN HIGH (61) JRL	0.58 OF 36	8 15 30 21 XSQ= 2.77 PHI= -0.193 XP = 0.0962

450	TILT LESS TOWARD BEING THOSE 0.58 OF 38 WHERE THE OBSERVATION OF FOOD TABOOS IS HIGH OR MEDIUM, RATHER THAN LOW (60) JRL	450	TILT MORE TOWARD BEING THOSE 0.83 OF 36 WHERE THE OBSERVATION OF FOOD TABOOS IS HIGH OR MEDIUM, RATHER THAN LOW (60) JRL	22 30 16 6 XSQ= 4.57 PHI= -0.249 XP = 0.0325
451	DRIFT TOWARD BEING THOSE 0.86 OF 7 WHERE TOTEMISM IS PRESENT (15) LWS	451	DRIFT TOWARD BEING THOSE 0.59 OF 17 WHERE TOTEMISM IS UNIMPORTANT OR ABSENT (12) LWS	6 7 1 10 XSQ= 2.37 PHI= 0.314 EP = 0.0778
453	DRIFT TOWARD BEING THOSE 0.57 OF 14 WHERE THE ROLE OF RELIGIOUS EXPERTS IS CONDUCIVE TO THE DEVELOPMENT OF THE INDIVIDUAL'S NEED TO ACHIEVE (13) DCM	453	DRIFT TOWARD BEING THOSE 0.81 OF 16 WHERE THE ROLE OF RELIGIOUS EXPERTS IS NOT CONDUCIVE TO THE DEVELOPMENT OF THE INDIVIDUAL'S NEED TO ACHIEVE (23) DCM	8 3 6 13 XSQ= 3.23 PHI= 0.328 EP = 0.0567
455	DRIFT TOWARD BEING THOSE 0.71 OF 14 WHERE THE MODE OF THE INDIVIDUAL'S CONTACT WITH THE DIVINE IS CONDUCIVE TO THE DEVELOPMENT OF THE INDIVIDUAL'S NEED TO ACHIEVE (17) DCM	455	DRIFT TOWARD BEING THOSE 0.69 OF 16 WHERE THE MODE OF THE INDIVIDUAL'S CONTACT WITH THE DIVINE IS NOT CONDUCIVE TO THE DEVELOPMENT OF THE INDIVIDUAL'S NEED TO ACHIEVE (19) DCM	10 5 4 11 XSQ= 3.35 PHI= 0.334 EP = 0.0656
458	TEND TO BE THOSE 0.57 OF 68 WHERE GAMES, IF PRESENT, INCLUDE GAMES OF STRATEGY (52) R-A-B,EA	458	TEND TO BE THOSE 0.92 OF 75 WHERE GAMES, IF PRESENT, DO NOT INCLUDE GAMES OF STRATEGY (119) R-A-B,EA	39 6 29 69 XSQ= 38.02 PHI= 0.516 XP = 0.
460	TEND TO BE THOSE 0.78 OF 68 WHERE GAMES, IF PRESENT, ARE NOT LIMITED TO GAMES OF SKILL ONLY (104) R-A-B,EA	460	TEND TO BE THOSE 0.55 OF 75 WHERE GAMES, IF PRESENT, ARE LIMITED TO GAMES OF SKILL ONLY (67) R-A-B,EA	15 41 53 34 XSQ= 14.58 PHI= -0.319 XP = 0.0001
468	LEAN TOWARD BEING THOSE 0.54 OF 24 WHERE CONTACT WITH OTHER CULTURES IS FREQUENT, RATHER THAN REGULAR OR IRREGULAR (17) JMH	468	LEAN TOWARD BEING THOSE 0.88 OF 26 WHERE CONTACT WITH OTHER CULTURES IS REGULAR OR IRREGULAR, RATHER THAN FREQUENT (37) JMH	13 3 11 23 XSQ= 8.56 PHI= 0.414 XP = 0.0034
472	LEAN TOWARD BEING THOSE 0.71 OF 38 WHERE THE COMPOSITE NARCISSISM INDEX IS HIGH (47) PES	472	LEAN TOWARD BEING THOSE 0.63 OF 40 WHERE THE COMPOSITE NARCISSISM INDEX IS LOW (43) PES	27 15 11 25 XSQ= 7.53 PHI= 0.311 XP = 0.0061
473	DRIFT LESS TOWARD BEING THOSE 0.51 OF 37 WHERE SENSITIVITY TO INSULT IS MODERATE OR NEGLIGIBLE (56) PES	473	DRIFT MORE TOWARD BEING THOSE 0.74 OF 39 WHERE SENSITIVITY TO INSULT IS MODERATE OR NEGLIGIBLE (56) PES	18 10 19 29 XSQ= 3.39 PHI= 0.211 XP = 0.0657

```
475  DRIFT TCWARD BEING THCSE         0.71 OF  34     475  DRIFT TOWARD BEING THOSE         0.52 OF  40          24    19
     WHERE EXHIBITIONISTIC CANCING                        WHERE EXHIBITICNISTIC DANCING                          10    21
     IS STRCNGLY CR MCDERATELY                            IS NEGLIGIBLY EMPHASIZED  (38)  PES             XSQ=     3.13
     EMPHASIZED  (48) PES                                                                                 PHI=    0.206
                                                                                                          XP =   0.0768

476  TILT TCWARD BEING THCSE          0.52 OF  23     476  TILT TOWARD BEING THCSE          0.85 OF  20          11    17
     WHERE THE DEGREE OF INSOBRIETY IS                    WHERE THE DEGREE OF INSOBRIETY IS                      12     3
     MCDERATE CR SLIGHT  (18) CH                          STRONG  (31) DH                                 XSQ=     4.97
                                                                                                          PHI=   -0.340
                                                                                                          XP =   0.0257

480  DRIFT TCWARD BEING THCSE         0.73 OF  11     48C  DRIFT TOWARD BEING THOSE         0.73 OF  11           8     3
     WHERE COMPLEXITY CF ARTISTIC CESIGN                  WHERE COMPLEXITY OF ARTISTIC DESIGN                     3     8
     IS HIGH  (14) HB                                     IS LOW  (15) HB                                 XSQ=     2.91
                                                                                                          PHI=    0.364
                                                                                                          EP =   0.0861
```

****

87 CULTURES:
WHERE THE LEVEL OF POLITICAL INTEGRATION
IS THE LARGE STATE, THE LITTLE STATE,
THE MINIMAL STATE, CR
THE AUTONCMOUS CCMMUNITY (281) GPM

87 CULTURES
WHERE THE LEVEL OF POLITICAL INTEGRATION
IS THE FAMILY (23) GPM

BACKGROUND ON PAGE 82

BOTH SUBJECT AND PREDICATE

....

281 IN LEFT CCLUMN

ABIPON	ABCR	AJIE	AKHA	ALBANIANS	ALORESE	AMERICANS	APINAYE	ARANDA	ARAUCANIANS
ARYANS	ASHANTI	ATAYAL	ATSUGEWI	AZANDE	AZTEC	BABWA	BACAIRI	BALINESE	BANDA
BARI	BATAK	BAYA	BEJA	BELU	BEMBA	BERGDAMA	BETE	BIRIFOR	BOERS
BORORO	BOTOCUDO	BOZO	BUDUMA	BULGARIANS	BURMESE	BURUSHO	BURYAT	CADUVEO	CAGABA
CALLINAGO	CAMAYURA	CAMBODIANS	CARAJA	CARIB	CAYAPA	CHAGGA	CHAMACOCO	CHENCHU	CHERKESS
CHEROKEE	CHEYENNE	CHIBCHA	CHIR-APACHE	CHIRIGUANO	CHOROTI	CHUKCHEE	COCHITI	COORG	CREE
CREEK	CROW	CUNA	CZECHS	DARD	DELAWARE	DIEGUENO	DIERI	DILLING	DOGON
DOROBO	DUSUN	DUTCH	EGYPTIANS	ELLICE	FANG	FON	FOX	FUTAJALONKE	GANDA
GARO	GILBERTESE	GOAJIRO	GOND	GROS VENTRE	GUAHIBO	GUATO	HAIDA	HASINAI	HAVASUPAI
HAWAIIANS	HAZARA	HEBREWS	HEHE	HERERO	HO	HUKUNDIKA	HURON	IBAN	ICELANDERS
ILA	INCA	INGASSANA	IRAQW	IRISH	JAPANESE	JAVANESE	JEMEZ	JUKUN	KABYLE
KACHIN	KALMYK	KAREN	KARIERA	KAZAK	KERAKI	KERALA	KHALKA	KHASI	KIKUYU
KIOW-APACHE	KISSI	KONSO	KOREANS	KORYAK	KPE	KUBA	KUNG	KURTATCHI	KUTENAI
LAKHER	LAMBA	LAMET	LANGO	LAPPS	LAU	LESU	LIFU	LOLO	LOZI
LUBA	LUO	MACASSARESE	MAGUZAWA	MALAYS	MANDAN	MANGAIANS	MANIHIKI	MANUS	MAORI
MARGI	MARICOPA	MARQUESANS	MATACO	MATAKAM	MAYA	MBUGWE	MBUNDU	MBUTI	MENDE
MERINA	MIAMI	MINANGKABAU	MISKITO	MIWOK	MONGO	MONGUOR	MOSSI	MOTA	MOTILON
MUNDURUCU	MURNGIN	MZAB	NAMA	NAMBICUARA	NASKAPI	NATCHEZ	NAVAHO	NGONI	NICOBARESE
NOMLAKI	NUNIVAK	NURI	NYAKYUSA	NYANEKA	NYORO	OJIBWA	OMAHA	ONA	ONTONG-JAVA
ORAON	PAEZ	PALAUANS	PALIKUR	PAPAGO	PAWNEE	PENOBSCOT	PONAPEANS	PUKAPUKA	RAROIANS
RIFFIANS	ROMANS	ROTINESE	ROTUMANS	RWALA	SAMOANS	SAMOYED	SANDAWE	SANTAL	SARAMACCA
SARSI	SENIANG	SERBS	SERI	SHERENTE	SHILLUK	SHLUH	SINHALESE	SIRIONO	SIUAI
SIWANS	SOMALI	SONGHAI	SOTHO	TALAMANCA	TALLENSI	TANALA	TANIMBARESE	TAOS	TAPIRAPE
TARAHUMARA	TEHUELCHE	TENDA	TENETEHARA	TERENA	THAI	THONGA	TIBETANS	TIKOPIA	TIMUCUA
TIV	TIWI	TODA	TOKELAU	TOLOWA	TORAJA	TOTONAC	TROBRIAND	TRUKESE	TRUMAI
TUBATULABAL	TUCANO	TUCUNA	TUPINAMBA	TURKMEN	TZELTAL	ULAWANS	UTE	VEDDA	VIETNAMESE
WAICA	WAPISHANA	WARRAU	WASHO	WICHITA	WINNEBAGO	WITOTO	WOLEAIANS	WOLOF	WUTE
YAGUA	YAKO	YAKUT	YAO	YAPESE	YARURO	YOKUTS	YORUBA	YUKAGHIR	YUKI
ZUNI									

23 IN RIGHT CCLUMN

ALACALUF	ANDAMANESE	ARAPESH	AWEIKOMA	DOBUANS	GILYAK	GURE	HANUNOO	IFUGAO	JIVARO
KASKA	KET	LAKALAI	MENTAWEI	SELUNG	SEMANG	SUBANUN	TIMBIRA	TURKANA	WAROPEN
WOGEO	YAHGAN	YURCK							

33 EXCLUDED BECAUSE IRRELEVANT (SEE 'IRRELEVANT,' PARAGRAPH 84)

63 EXCLUDED BECAUSE UNASCERTAINED

6	TILT MORE TOWARD BEING THOSE 0.83 OF 281 LOCATED OUTSIDE OF THE INSULAR PACIFIC (330)	6	TILT LESS TOWARD BEING THOSE 0.61 OF 23 LOCATED OUTSIDE OF THE INSULAR PACIFIC (330)	49 9 232 14 XSQ= 5.15 PHI= -0.130 XP = 0.0232
12	TILT MORE TOWARD BEING THOSE 0.93 OF 281 WHERE THE LATITUDE IS LESS THAN FIFTY DEGREES (367)	12	TILT LESS TOWARD BEING THOSE 0.78 OF 23 WHERE THE LATITUDE IS LESS THAN FIFTY DEGREES (367)	20 5 261 18 XSQ= 4.24 PHI= -0.118 XP = 0.0395
36	DRIFT LESS TOWARD BEING THOSE 0.73 OF 281 WHERE THE NATURAL ENVIRONMENT IS OTHER THAN 'VERY HARSH,' OR SUB-TROPICAL BUSH, OR TEMPERATE GRASSLAND (292) FWM	36	DRIFT MORE TOWARD BEING THOSE 0.91 OF 23 WHERE THE NATURAL ENVIRONMENT IS OTHER THAN 'VERY HARSH,' OR SUB-TROPICAL BUSH, OR TEMPERATE GRASSLAND (292) FWM	76 2 205 21 XSQ= 2.85 PHI= 0.097 XP = 0.0912
45	DRIFT TOWARD BEING THOSE 0.68 OF 158 WHERE SETTLEMENTS, IF FIXED, ARE COMPACT, RATHER THAN NON-COMPACT (149)	45	DRIFT TOWARD BEING THOSE 0.67 OF 9 WHERE SETTLEMENTS, IF FIXED, ARE NON-COMPACT, RATHER THAN COMPACT (73)	107 3 51 6 XSQ= 3.08 PHI= 0.136 XP = 0.0793
46	TILT TOWARD BEING THOSE 0.79 OF 240 OTHER THAN WHERE SETTLEMENTS ARE NON-FIXED AND MOVEMENT IS NOMADIC (260)	46	TILT TOWARD BEING THOSE 0.50 OF 18 WHERE SETTLEMENTS ARE NON-FIXED AND MOVEMENT IS NOMADIC (72)	51 9 189 9 XSQ= 6.23 PHI= -0.155 XP = 0.0126
47	DRIFT LESS TOWARD BEING THOSE 0.62 OF 82 WHERE, IF SETTLEMENTS ARE NON-FIXED, MOVEMENT IS NOMADIC, RATHER THAN NON-NOMADIC (72)	47	IN ALL CASES ARE THOSE 1.00 OF 9 WHERE, IF SETTLEMENTS ARE NON-FIXED, MOVEMENT IS NOMADIC, RATHER THAN NON-NOMADIC (72)	51 9 31 0 XSQ= 3.61 PHI= -0.199 XP = 0.0573
51	DRIFT TOWARD BEING THOSE 0.60 OF 281 WHERE SUBSISTENCE IS PRIMARILY BY FOOD PRODUCTION -- I. E., AGRICULTURE OR HUSBANDRY -- RATHER THAN BY GATHERING (253)	51	DRIFT TOWARD BEING THOSE 0.61 OF 23 WHERE SUBSISTENCE IS PRIMARILY BY FOOD GATHERING -- I. E., HUNTING, FISHING, OR COLLECTING -- RATHER THAN FOOD PRODUCTION (147)	169 9 112 14 XSQ= 3.05 PHI= 0.100 XP = 0.0807
63	TILT TOWARD BEING THOSE 0.69 OF 162 WHERE HUSBANDRY, IF PRESENT, IS PRINCIPALLY IN THE FORM OF BOVINE, EQUINE, CAMEL-LIKE, OR DEER-LIKE ANIMALS, RATHER THAN PIGS, SHEEP, OR GOATS (152)	63	TILT TOWARD BEING THOSE 0.78 OF 9 WHERE HUSBANDRY, IF PRESENT, IS PRINCIPALLY IN THE FORM OF PIGS, SHEEP, OR GOATS, RATHER THAN BOVINE, EQUINE, CAMEL-LIKE, OR DEER-LIKE ANIMALS (74)	112 2 50 7 XSQ= 6.47 PHI= 0.194 XP = 0.0110
71	DRIFT LESS TOWARD BEING THOSE 0.61 OF 186 WHERE METAL WORKING IS ABSENT (153)	71	DRIFT MORE TOWARD BEING THOSE 0.92 OF 12 WHERE METAL WORKING IS ABSENT (153)	73 1 113 11 XSQ= 3.38 PHI= 0.131 XP = 0.0661

73	LEAN TOWARD BEING THOSE WHERE WEAVING IS PRESENT (118)	0.51 OF 181	73	LEAN TOWARD BEING THOSE WHERE WEAVING IS ABSENT (130)	0.92 OF 12	93 1 88 11 XSQ= 6.71 PHI= 0.187 XP = 0.0096
74	TILT TOWARD BEING THOSE WHERE POTTERY IS PRESENT (145)	0.66 OF 175	74	TILT TOWARD BEING THOSE WHERE POTTERY IS ABSENT (93)	0.75 OF 12	116 3 59 9 XSQ= 6.58 PHI= 0.188 XP = 0.0103
81	TILT LESS TOWARD BEING THOSE WHERE NO CITY OR TOWN IS PRESENT, AND THE AVERAGE COMMUNITY SIZE IS SMALLER THAN 200 (135)	0.61 OF 163	81	IN ALL CASES ARE THOSE WHERE NO CITY OR TOWN IS PRESENT, AND THE AVERAGE COMMUNITY SIZE IS SMALLER THAN 200 (135)	1.00 OF 13	64 0 99 13 XSQ= 6.41 PHI= 0.191 XP = 0.0113
82	LEAN TOWARD BEING THOSE WHERE A CITY OR TOWN IS PRESENT, OR THE AVERAGE COMMUNITY SIZE IS FIFTY OR GREATER (178)	0.82 OF 163	82	LEAN TOWARD BEING THOSE WHERE NO CITY OR TOWN IS PRESENT, AND THE AVERAGE COMMUNITY SIZE IS SMALLER THAN FIFTY (46)	0.54 OF 13	133 6 30 7 XSQ= 7.10 PHI= 0.201 XP = 0.0077
96	TEND TO BE THOSE WHERE THE HIERARCHY OF NATIONAL JURISDICTION HAS FOUR, THREE, TWO OR ONE LEVEL (174) GES,EA	0.56 OF 240	96	IN ALL CASES ARE THOSE WHERE THE HIERARCHY OF NATIONAL JURISDICTION HAS NO LEVELS (156) GES,EA	1.00 OF 18	135 0 105 18 XSQ= 19.04 PHI= 0.272 XP = 0.0000
98	TEND TO BE THOSE WHERE THE HIERARCHY OF LOCAL JURISDICTION HAS FOUR OR THREE LEVELS (238) GES,EA	0.75 OF 240	98	TEND TO BE THOSE WHERE THE HIERARCHY OF LOCAL JURISDICTION HAS TWO LEVELS (93) GES,EA	0.72 OF 18	181 5 59 13 XSQ= 16.59 PHI= 0.254 XP = 0.0000
99	LEAN TOWARD BEING THOSE WHERE, WITH NATIONAL HIERARCHY ABSENT, THE HIERARCHY OF LOCAL JURISDICTION HAS FOUR OR THREE LEVELS (93) GES,EA	0.65 OF 105	99	LEAN TOWARD BEING THOSE WHERE, WITH NATIONAL HIERARCHY ABSENT, THE HIERARCHY OF LOCAL JURISDICTION HAS TWO LEVELS (63) GES,EA	0.72 OF 18	68 5 37 13 XSQ= 7.25 PHI= 0.243 XP = 0.0071
100	TEND TO BE THOSE WHERE HIERARCHIES ARE MORE COMPLEX THAN THE 'SIMPLEST,' I. E., MORE COMPLEX THAN TWO LOCAL LEVELS WITH NO NATIONAL LEVELS (267) GES,EA	0.85 OF 240	100	TEND TO BE THOSE WHERE HIERARCHIES ARE THE 'SIMPLEST' I. E., WHERE THERE ARE ONLY TWO LOCAL LEVELS WITH NO NATIONAL LEVELS (63) GES,EA	0.72 OF 18	203 5 37 13 XSQ= 31.04 PHI= 0.347 XP = 0.
102	TEND TO BE THOSE WHERE CLASS STRATIFICATION IS PRESENT (203)	0.54 OF 274	102	TEND TO BE THOSE WHERE CLASS STRATIFICATION IS ABSENT (180)	0.87 OF 23	148 3 126 20 XSQ= 12.66 PHI= 0.206 XP = 0.0004

106	DRIFT TOWARD BEING THOSE 0.64 OF 148 WHERE CLASS STRATIFICATION, IF PRESENT, IS BASED ON SOMETHING OTHER THAN WEALTH (126)	106	IN ALL CASES ARE THOSE 1.00 OF 3 WHERE CLASS STRATIFICATION, IF PRESENT, IS BASED ON WEALTH (77)	54 3 94 0 XSQ= 2.71 PHI= -0.134 XP = 0.0999
110	TILT LESS TOWARD BEING THOSE 0.54 OF 270 WHERE SLAVERY IS ABSENT (218)	110	TILT MORE TOWARD BEING THOSE 0.83 OF 23 WHERE SLAVERY IS ABSENT (218)	123 4 147 19 XSQ= 5.75 PHI= 0.140 XP = 0.0165
118	DRIFT TOWARD BEING THOSE 0.55 OF 40 WHERE THE PERCENTAGE OF OCCUPATIONS THAT ARE SPECIALIZED IS HIGH OR MEDIUM (24) WME	118	IN ALL CASES ARE THOSE 1.00 OF 5 WHERE THE PERCENTAGE OF OCCUPATIONS THAT ARE SPECIALIZED IS LOW (25) WME	22 0 18 5 XSQ= 3.40 PHI= 0.275 XP = 0.0650
147	DRIFT TOWARD BEING THOSE 0.67 OF 27 WHERE CODIFIED LAWS ARE PRESENT (20) LWS	147	IN ALL CASES ARE THOSE 1.00 OF 3 WHERE CODIFIED LAWS ARE UNIMPORTANT OR ABSENT (13) LWS	18 0 9 3 XSQ= 2.61 PHI= 0.295 EP = 0.0542
196	TILT TOWARD BEING THOSE 0.67 OF 200 WHERE INDIVIDUAL RIGHTS IN REAL PROPERTY, AND RULES FOR INHERITANCE, ARE PRESENT (194)	196	TILT TOWARD BEING THOSE 0.67 OF 15 WHERE INDIVIDUAL RIGHTS IN REAL PROPERTY, OR RULES FOR INHERITANCE, ARE ABSENT (87)	134 5 66 10 XSQ= 5.53 PHI= 0.160 XP = 0.0187
201	LEAN MORE TOWARD BEING THOSE 0.87 OF 279 WHERE MARITAL RESIDENCE IS NON-OPTIONAL, RATHER THAN AMBILOCAL OR NEOLOCAL (334)	201	LEAN LESS TOWARD BEING THOSE 0.65 OF 23 WHERE MARITAL RESIDENCE IS NON-OPTIONAL, RATHER THAN AMBILOCAL OR NEOLOCAL (334)	244 15 35 8 XSQ= 6.88 PHI= 0.151 XP = 0.0087
204	TILT MORE TOWARD BEING THOSE 0.84 OF 225 WHERE MARITAL RESIDENCE IS PATRILOCAL, VIRILOCAL, OR AVUNCULOCAL, RATHER THAN AMBILOCAL OR NEOLOCAL (270)	204	TILT LESS TOWARD BEING THOSE 0.60 OF 20 WHERE MARITAL RESIDENCE IS PATRILOCAL, VIRILOCAL, OR AVUNCULOCAL, RATHER THAN AMBILOCAL OR NEOLOCAL (270)	190 12 35 8 XSQ= 5.99 PHI= 0.156 XP = 0.0144
207	DRIFT TOWARD BEING THOSE 0.61 OF 89 WHERE MARITAL RESIDENCE IS MATRILOCAL OR UXORILOCAL, RATHER THAN AMBILOCAL OR NEOLOCAL (64)	207	DRIFT TOWARD BEING THOSE 0.73 OF 11 WHERE MARITAL RESIDENCE IS AMBILOCAL OR NEOLOCAL, RATHER THAN MATRILOCAL OR UXORILOCAL (64)	54 3 35 8 XSQ= 3.20 PHI= 0.179 XP = 0.0737
322	DRIFT TOWARD BEING THOSE 0.60 OF 42 WHERE THE CONSISTENCY OF REDUCTION OF THE INFANT'S DRIVES IS LOW (32) B-B-C	322	DRIFT TOWARD BEING THOSE 0.86 OF 7 WHERE THE CONSISTENCY OF REDUCTION OF THE INFANT'S DRIVES IS HIGH (27) B-B-C	17 6 25 1 XSQ= 3.28 PHI= -0.259 XP = 0.0701

323	DRIFT TOWARD BEING THOSE 0.63 OF 54 WHERE THE CONSTANCY OF PRESENCE OF THE INFANT'S NURTURANT AGENT IS LOW (45) B-B-C	323	DRIFT TOWARD BEING THOSE 0.78 OF 9 WHERE THE CONSTANCY OF PRESENCE OF THE INFANT'S NURTURANT AGENT IS HIGH (29) B-B-C	20 7 34 2 XSQ= 3.70 PHI= -0.242 XP = 0.0545
331	TILT TOWARD BEING THOSE 0.65 OF 26 WHERE THE AGE AT BEGINNING OF INDEPENDENCE TRAINING IS LOWER THAN 3.8 YEARS (21) W-C	331	IN ALL CASES ARE THOSE 1.00 OF 4 WHERE THE AGE AT BEGINNING OF INDEPENDENCE TRAINING IS 3.8 YEARS OR HIGHER (16) W-C	9 4 17 0 XSQ= 3.67 PHI= -0.350 EP = 0.0261
349	DRIFT TOWARD BEING THOSE 0.61 OF 44 WHERE THE CHILD'S INFERRED ANXIETY OVER NON-PERFORMANCE OF ACHIEVEMENT BEHAVIOR IS HIGH (34) B-B-C	349	DRIFT TOWARD BEING THOSE 0.86 OF 7 WHERE THE CHILD'S INFERRED ANXIETY OVER NON-PERFORMANCE OF ACHIEVEMENT BEHAVIOR IS LOW (28) B-B-C	27 1 17 6 XSQ= 3.67 PHI= 0.268 XP = 0.0553
350	LEAN TOWARD BEING THOSE 0.64 OF 42 WHERE THE CHILD'S INFERRED ANXIETY OVER PERFORMANCE OF ACHIEVEMENT BEHAVIOR IS HIGH (34) B-B-C	350	IN ALL CASES ARE THOSE 1.00 OF 7 WHERE THE CHILD'S INFERRED ANXIETY OVER PERFORMANCE OF ACHIEVEMENT BEHAVIOR IS LOW (26) B-B-C	27 0 15 7 XSQ= 7.59 PHI= 0.394 XP = 0.0059
351	DRIFT LESS TOWARD BEING THOSE 0.52 OF 42 WHERE THE CHILD'S INFERRED CONFLICT REGARDING ACHIEVEMENT BEHAVIOR IS LOW (34) B-B-C	351	IN ALL CASES ARE THOSE 1.00 OF 7 WHERE THE CHILD'S INFERRED CONFLICT REGARDING ACHIEVEMENT BEHAVIOR IS LOW (34) B-B-C	20 0 22 7 XSQ= 3.83 PHI= 0.280 XP = 0.0502
352	DRIFT TOWARD BEING THOSE 0.64 OF 55 WHERE THE TOTAL POSITIVE PRESSURE TOWARD DEVELOPING OBEDIENT BEHAVIOR IN THE CHILD IS HIGH (44) B-B-C	352	DRIFT TOWARD BEING THOSE 0.83 OF 6 WHERE THE TOTAL POSITIVE PRESSURE TOWARD DEVELOPING OBEDIENT BEHAVIOR IN THE CHILD IS LOW (28) B-B-C	35 1 20 5 XSQ= 3.18 PHI= 0.228 XP = 0.0744
354	TILT TOWARD BEING THOSE 0.54 OF 56 WHERE THE CHILD'S INFERRED ANXIETY OVER PERFORMANCE OF OBEDIENT BEHAVIOR IS HIGH (36) B-B-C	354	IN ALL CASES ARE THOSE 1.00 OF 6 WHERE THE CHILD'S INFERRED ANXIETY OVER PERFORMANCE OF OBEDIENT BEHAVIOR IS LOW (37) B-B-C	30 0 26 6 XSQ= 4.27 PHI= 0.262 XP = 0.0389
377	DRIFT LESS TOWARD BEING THOSE 0.74 OF 235 WHERE MALE GENITAL MUTILATION IS ABSENT (242)	377	DRIFT MORE TOWARD BEING THOSE 0.94 OF 18 WHERE MALE GENITAL MUTILATION IS ABSENT (242)	61 1 174 17 XSQ= 2.74 PHI= 0.104 XP = 0.0979
390	DRIFT LESS TOWARD BEING THOSE 0.74 OF 132 WHERE PREMARITAL SEX RELATIONS ARE WEAKLY PUNISHED AND IN FACT NOT RARE OR PUNISHED ONLY IF PREGNANCY RESULTS, OR FREELY PERMITTED (132) JTW,EA	390	IN ALL CASES ARE THOSE 1.00 OF 12 WHERE PREMARITAL SEX RELATIONS ARE WEAKLY PUNISHED AND IN FACT NOT RARE OR PUNISHED ONLY IF PREGNANCY RESULTS, OR FREELY PERMITTED (132) JTW,EA	34 0 98 12 XSQ= 2.74 PHI= 0.138 XP = 0.0976

```
417  TILT TOWARD BEING THOSE          0.86 OF  36     417  TILT TOWARD BEING THOSE          0.75 OF   4          31     1
     WHERE WARFARE IS                                      WHERE WARFARE IS                                          5     3
     PREVALENT  (34) LWS                                   NOT PREVALENT  (9) LWS                          XSQ=      5.02
                                                                                                           PHI=     0.354
                                                                                                           EP =    0.0204

434  TILT TOWARD BEING THOSE          0.54 OF  54     434  IN ALL CASES ARE THOSE           1.00 OF   6          25     6
     WHERE ASCETICISM IN MOURNING BEHAVIOR                 WHERE ASCETICISM IN MOURNING BEHAVIOR                29     0
     IS LOW  (30) JFG                                      IS HIGH  (37) JFG                               XSQ=      4.27
                                                                                                           PHI=    -0.267
                                                                                                           XP =    0.0388

437  TILT TOWARD BEING THOSE          0.65 OF  34     437  IN ALL CASES ARE THOSE           1.00 OF   4          12     4
     WHERE FEAR OF GHOSTS, SPIRITS,                        WHERE FEAR OF GHOSTS, SPIRITS,                       22     0
     HUMANS OR ANIMALS                                     HUMANS OR ANIMALS                               XSQ=      3.78
     IS LOW  (23) W-C,JFG                                  IS HIGH  (21) W-C,JFG                           PHI=    -0.315
                                                                                                           EP =    0.0247

444  DRIFT TOWARD BEING THOSE         0.53 OF  43     444  IN ALL CASES ARE THOSE           1.00 OF   5          20     5
     WHERE THE USE OF DREAMS                               WHERE THE USE OF DREAMS                              23     0
     TO SEEK AND CONTROL SUPERNATURAL POWERS               TO SEEK AND CONTROL SUPERNATURAL POWERS         XSQ=      3.22
     IS LOW  (27) RGD                                      IS HIGH  (28) RGD                               PHI=    -0.259
                                                                                                           XP =    0.0730

451  DRIFT TOWARD BEING THOSE         0.62 OF  21     451  IN ALL CASES ARE THOSE           1.00 OF   3          13     0
     WHERE TOTEMISM IS                                     WHERE TOTEMISM IS                                     8     3
     PRESENT  (15) LWS                                     UNIMPORTANT OR ABSENT  (12) LWS                 XSQ=      1.94
                                                                                                           PHI=     0.284
                                                                                                           EP =    0.0815
```

****

88 CULTURES
WHERE, IF A HEADMANSHIP IS PRESENT,
SUCCESSION IS NON-HEREDITARY (106)

88 CULTURES
WHERE, IF A HEADMANSHIP IS PRESENT,
SUCCESSION IS HEREDITARY (165)

BACKGROUND ON PAGE 83

BOTH SUBJECT AND PREDICATE

....

106 IN LEFT COLUMN

AMERICANS	ANDAMANESE	ASHANTI	ATAYAL	BACAIRI	BETE	BLACK CARIB	BOTOCUDO	BRAZILIANS	BURMESE
CALLINAGO	CAMBA	CAMBODIANS	CARIB	CHENCHU	CHINANTEC	CHIR-APACHE	CHORTI	CHUKCHEE	COCHITI
COMANCHE	CREE	CROW	CUNA	DAGUR	DOROBO	EGYPTIANS	GANDA	GILBERTESE	GROS VENTRE
HO	HUICHOL	JAPANESE	JAVANESE	JEMEZ	JIVARO	KABYLE	KAPAUKU	KATAB	KOL
KOREANS	KORYAK	KUBA	KUTENAI	LESU	MAGUZAWA	MAM	MANCHU	MARGI	MBUTI
MERINA	MIAO	MIN CHINESE	MINCHIA	MOTA	NABESNA	NAMBICUARA	NANDI	NASKAPI	NAVAHO
NICOBARESE	NUPE	NYAKYUSA	OKINAWANS	OMAHA	ONA	ORAON	PAEZ	PALIKUR	PATHAN
POPOLUCA	PORTUGUESE	PURARI	REGEIBAT	SARSI	SERBS	SHILLUK	SHLUH	SINCHI	SIUAI
SOMALI	SYRIANS	TALLENSI	TANALA	TAOS	TARAHUMARA	TEDA	TENETEHARA	TETON	THAI
TIBETANS	TIGRINYA	TODA	TORAJA	TUNEBO	TWANA	UTE	VIETNAMESE	WANTOAT	WAROPEN
WARRAU	YAGUA	YAKUT	YUKAGHIR	YUROK	ZUNI				

165 IN RIGHT COLUMN

ABIPON	AINU	AJIE	AKHA	ALBANIANS	APINAYE	ARANDA	ARAUCANIANS	ATSUGEWI	AZANDE
AZTEC	BAJUN	BALINESE	BAMBARA	BAMILEKE	BANDA	BARI	BASSERI	BATAK	BAYA
BELU	BEMBA	BERGDAMA	BHIL	BHUIYA	BORORO	CAGABA	CAMAYURA	CARAJA	CAYAPA
CHAGGA	CHERKESS	CHIBCHA	CHIRIGUANO	COORG	CREEK	DELAWARE	DIEGUENO	DOGON	EYAK
FANG	FON	FOX	GARO	GILYAK	GISU	GOAJIRO	GOND	GUAHIBO	GUATO
HAIDA	HASINAI	HAVASUPAI	HAWAIIANS	HAZARA	HERERO	HUKUNDIKA	HURON	ILA	INGASSANA
JUKUN	KACHIN	KALMYK	KAREN	KERAKI	KERALA	KHALKA	KHASI	KONSO	KPE
KUNG	KURTATCHI	KWAKIUTL	LAKHER	LAMBA	LAMET	LANGO	LAU	LEPCHA	LHOTA NAGA
LIFU	LOLO	LOZI	LUBA	LUO	MACASSARESE	MAMBILA	MANGAIANS	MANIHIKI	MAORI
MARQUESANS	MARSHALLESE	MATAKAM	MBUGWE	MBUNDU	MIAMI	MINANGKABAU	MIWOK	MONGO	MONGUOR
MUNDURUCU	MURNGIN	NAMA	NATCHEZ	NDEMBU	NGONI	NOMLAKI	NURI	NYANEKA	NYARO
NYORO	ONTONG-JAVA	PAIWAN	PALAUANS	PAWNEE	PENDE	PONAPEANS	PUKAPUKA	RAROIANS	ROTUMANS
RUNDI	SAMOANS	SANPOIL	SANTAL	SARAMACCA	SEMANG	SENIANG	SHERENTE	SIRIONO	SONGHAI
SOTHO	SWAZI	TANIMBARESE	TEHUELCHE	TENDA	TENINO	TERENA	THONGA	TIKOPIA	TIMUCUA
TIWI	TOKELAU	TOLOWA	TROBRIAND	TRUKESE	TRUMAI	TSHIMSHIAN	TUBATULABAL	TUPINAMBA	VENDA
WASHO	WICHITA	WINNEBAGO	WITOTO	WOGEO	WOLEAIANS	WOLOF	YAKO	YAO	YAPESE
YARURO	YOKUTS	YOMBE	YORUBA	YUKI					

39 EXCLUDED BECAUSE IRRELEVANT

ABOR	ALACALUF	AMBA	ARAPESH	AWEIKOMA	BEJA	CHEYENNE	COPR ESKIMO	DOBUANS	ENGA
HANUNOO	INGALIK	IRAQW	KASKA	KHEVSUR	KIKUYU	KOHISTANI	LAKALAI	MANUS	MASAI
MENDE	MENTAWEI	MNONG GAR	MZAB	NUER	NUNIVAK	PAPAGO	PURUM	RIFFIANS	SAGADA
SIWANS	SUBANUN	TAGBANUA	TAREUMIUT	TIV	TRISTAN	TURKANA	ULAWANS	YAHGAN	

90 EXCLUDED BECAUSE UNASCERTAINED

3	LEAN MORE TOWARD BEING THOSE LOCATED OUTSIDE OF AFRICA (320)	0.88 OF 106	LEAN LESS TOWARD BEING THOSE LOCATED OUTSIDE OF AFRICA (320)	0.72 OF 165	13 47 93 118 XSQ= 8.93 PHI= -0.182 XP = 0.0028
4	TILT LESS TOWARD BEING THOSE LOCATED OUTSIDE OF THE CIRCUM-MEDITERRANEAN (355)	0.88 OF 106	TILT MORE TOWARD BEING THOSE LOCATED OUTSIDE OF THE CIRCUM-MEDITERRANEAN (355)	0.96 OF 165	13 6 93 159 XSQ= 6.10 PHI= 0.150 XP = 0.0135
5	TILT LESS TOWARD BEING THOSE LOCATED OUTSIDE OF EAST EURASIA (330)	0.74 OF 106	TILT MORE TOWARD BEING THOSE LOCATED OUTSIDE OF EAST EURASIA (330)	0.85 OF 165	28 24 78 141 XSQ= 5.12 PHI= 0.137 XP = 0.0236
6	TILT MORE TOWARD BEING THOSE LOCATED OUTSIDE OF THE INSULAR PACIFIC (330)	0.90 OF 106	TILT LESS TOWARD BEING THOSE LOCATED OUTSIDE OF THE INSULAR PACIFIC (330)	0.78 OF 165	11 36 95 129 XSQ= 5.12 PHI= -0.137 XP = 0.0236
12	DRIFT LESS TOWARD BEING THOSE WHERE THE LATITUDE IS LESS THAN FIFTY DEGREES (367)	0.91 OF 106	DRIFT MORE TOWARD BEING THOSE WHERE THE LATITUDE IS LESS THAN FIFTY DEGREES (367)	0.96 OF 165	10 6 96 159 XSQ= 2.93 PHI= 0.104 XP = 0.0869
53	TEND TO BE THOSE WHERE FOOD PRODUCTION IS BY INTENSIVE AGRICULTURE, RATHER THAN BY SIMPLE AGRICULTURE OR INCIPIENT FOOD PRODUCTION (91)	0.59 OF 63	TEND TO BE THOSE WHERE FOOD PRODUCTION IS BY SIMPLE AGRICULTURE OR INCIPIENT FOOD PRODUCTION, RATHER THAN BY INTENSIVE AGRICULTURE (147)	0.75 OF 106	37 26 26 80 XSQ= 18.33 PHI= 0.329 XP = 0.0000
55	TEND TO BE THOSE WHERE FOOD PRODUCTION IS BY INTENSIVE AGRICULTURE, RATHER THAN BY SIMPLE AGRICULTURE (91)	0.66 OF 56	TEND TO BE THOSE WHERE FOOD PRODUCTION IS BY SIMPLE AGRICULTURE, RATHER THAN BY INTENSIVE AGRICULTURE (101)	0.68 OF 81	37 26 19 55 XSQ= 14.05 PHI= 0.320 XP = 0.0002
81	LEAN TOWARD BEING THOSE WHERE A CITY OR TOWN IS PRESENT, OR THE AVERAGE COMMUNITY SIZE IS 200 OR GREATER (89)	0.55 OF 62	LEAN TOWARD BEING THOSE WHERE NO CITY OR TOWN IS PRESENT, AND THE AVERAGE COMMUNITY SIZE IS SMALLER THAN 200 (135)	0.67 OF 92	34 30 28 62 XSQ= 6.65 PHI= 0.208 XP = 0.0099
84	LEAN LESS TOWARD BEING THOSE WHERE THE LEVEL OF POLITICAL INTEGRATION IS THE LITTLE STATE, THE MINIMAL STATE, THE AUTONOMOUS COMMUNITY, OR THE FAMILY (262) GPM	0.77 OF 73	LEAN MORE TOWARD BEING THOSE WHERE THE LEVEL OF POLITICAL INTEGRATION IS THE LITTLE STATE, THE MINIMAL STATE, THE AUTONOMOUS COMMUNITY, OR THE FAMILY (262) GPM	0.92 OF 140	17 11 56 129 XSQ= 8.70 PHI= 0.202 XP = 0.0032

85 DRIFT LESS TOWARD BEING THOSE 0.70 OF 73 WHERE THE LEVEL OF POLITICAL INTEGRATION IS THE MINIMAL STATE, THE AUTONOMOUS COMMUNITY, OR THE FAMILY (234) GPM	85 DRIFT MORE TOWARD BEING THOSE 0.82 OF 140 WHERE THE LEVEL OF POLITICAL INTEGRATION IS THE MINIMAL STATE, THE AUTONOMOUS COMMUNITY, OR THE FAMILY (234) GPM	22 25 51 115 XSQ= 3.52 PHI= 0.129 XP = 0.0605
94 DRIFT LESS TOWARD BEING THOSE 0.83 OF 89 WHERE THE HIERARCHY OF NATIONAL JURISDICTION HAS TWO, ONE, OR NO LEVELS (296) GES,EA	94 DRIFT MORE TOWARD BEING THOSE 0.92 OF 142 WHERE THE HIERARCHY OF NATIONAL JURISDICTION HAS TWO, ONE, OR NO LEVELS (296) GES,EA	15 11 74 131 XSQ= 3.68 PHI= 0.126 XP = 0.0552
102 TILT TOWARD BEING THOSE 0.52 OF 101 WHERE CLASS STRATIFICATION IS ABSENT (180)	102 TILT TOWARD BEING THOSE 0.61 OF 162 WHERE CLASS STRATIFICATION IS PRESENT (203)	48 99 53 63 XSQ= 4.12 PHI= -0.125 XP = 0.0423
107 TEND LESS TO BE THOSE 0.58 OF 48 WHERE CLASS STRATIFICATION, IF PRESENT, IS BASED ON SOMETHING OTHER THAN OCCUPATIONAL STATUS (160)	107 TEND MORE TO BE THOSE 0.91 OF 99 WHERE CLASS STRATIFICATION, IF PRESENT, IS BASED ON SOMETHING OTHER THAN OCCUPATIONAL STATUS (160)	20 9 28 90 XSQ= 19.65 PHI= 0.366 XP = 0.0000
108 TEND TO BE THOSE 0.83 OF 48 WHERE CLASS STRATIFICATION, IF PRESENT, IS BASED ON SOMETHING OTHER THAN A HEREDITARY ARISTOCRACY (129)	108 TEND TO BE THOSE 0.53 OF 99 WHERE CLASS STRATIFICATION, IF PRESENT, IS BASED ON A HEREDITARY ARISTOCRACY (74)	8 52 40 47 XSQ= 15.75 PHI= -0.327 XP = 0.0001
128 TILT TOWARD BEING THOSE 0.73 OF 22 WHERE, IF SUBSISTENCE IS PRIMARILY BY AGRICULTURE, THE WORK IS MAINLY DONE BY MALES (40)	128 TILT TOWARD BEING THOSE 0.62 OF 39 WHERE, IF SUBSISTENCE IS PRIMARILY BY AGRICULTURE, THE WORK IS MAINLY DONE BY FEMALES (37)	16 15 6 24 XSQ= 5.31 PHI= 0.295 XP = 0.0212
131 DRIFT LESS TOWARD BEING THOSE 0.80 OF 45 WHERE THE CONSTRUCTION OF PERMANENT HOUSES OR THE ERECTION OF TEMPORARY DWELLINGS IS MAINLY DONE BY MALES (136)	131 DRIFT MORE TOWARD BEING THOSE 0.93 OF 73 WHERE THE CONSTRUCTION OF PERMANENT HOUSES OR THE ERECTION OF TEMPORARY DWELLINGS IS MAINLY DONE BY MALES (136)	36 68 9 5 XSQ= 3.43 PHI= -0.171 XP = 0.0639
164 TILT TOWARD BEING THOSE 0.88 OF 8 WHERE THE EMPHASIS ON INDIVIDUAL VOLITION AS THE CAUSE OR SOURCE OF ILLNESS IS LOW (9) MJ	164 TILT TOWARD BEING THOSE 0.75 OF 8 WHERE THE EMPHASIS ON INDIVIDUAL VOLITION AS THE CAUSE OR SOURCE OF ILLNESS IS HIGH (9) MJ	1 6 7 2 XSQ= 4.06 PHI= -0.504 EP = 0.0406
176 LEAN TOWARD BEING THOSE 0.66 OF 103 WHERE THE COMMUNITY IS OTHER THAN A CLAN-COMMUNITY OR A COMMUNITY STRUCTURED OR SEGMENTED ON A CLAN BASIS (213)	176 LEAN TOWARD BEING THOSE 0.52 OF 161 WHERE THE COMMUNITY IS A CLAN-COMMUNITY OR A COMMUNITY STRUCTURED OR SEGMENTED ON A CLAN BASIS (169)	35 84 68 77 XSQ= 7.68 PHI= -0.171 XP = 0.0056

181	TILT LESS TOWARD BEING THOSE 0.83 OF 103 WHERE THE COMMUNITY IS OTHER THAN A DEME (337)	181	TILT MORE TOWARD BEING THOSE 0.93 OF 161 WHERE THE COMMUNITY IS OTHER THAN A DEME (337)	18 12 85 149 XSQ= 5.31 PHI= 0.142 XP = 0.0212
187	DRIFT MORE TOWARD BEING THOSE 0.90 OF 106 WHERE THE KIN GROUP IS OTHER THAN EXCLUSIVELY MATRILINEAL (344)	187	DRIFT LESS TOWARD BEING THOSE 0.80 OF 164 WHERE THE KIN GROUP IS OTHER THAN EXCLUSIVELY MATRILINEAL (344)	11 32 95 132 XSQ= 3.36 PHI= -0.112 XP = 0.0668
188	TILT LESS TOWARD BEING THOSE 0.57 OF 106 WHERE THE KIN GROUP IS OTHER THAN EXCLUSIVELY COGNATIC (252)	188	TILT MORE TOWARD BEING THOSE 0.72 OF 165 WHERE THE KIN GROUP IS OTHER THAN EXCLUSIVELY COGNATIC (252)	46 46 60 119 XSQ= 6.26 PHI= 0.152 XP = 0.0124
192	TEND LESS TO BE THOSE 0.61 OF 106 OTHER THAN WHERE THE ONLY KIN GROUP PRESENT IS A KINDRED OR ELSE BILATERAL DESCENT IS INFERRED (289)	192	TEND MORE TO BE THOSE 0.85 OF 165 OTHER THAN WHERE THE ONLY KIN GROUP PRESENT IS A KINDRED OR ELSE BILATERAL DESCENT IS INFERRED (289)	41 24 65 141 XSQ= 19.31 PHI= 0.267 XP = 0.0000
220	DRIFT MORE TOWARD BEING THOSE 0.80 OF 101 WHERE FIRST COUSIN MARRIAGE IN SOME FORM OR OTHER IS NOT PRESCRIBED OR PREFERRED (273)	220	DRIFT LESS TOWARD BEING THOSE 0.69 OF 158 WHERE FIRST COUSIN MARRIAGE IN SOME FORM OR OTHER IS NOT PRESCRIBED OR PREFERRED (273)	20 49 81 109 XSQ= 3.41 PHI= -0.115 XP = 0.0648
221	TILT MORE TOWARD BEING THOSE 0.96 OF 101 WHERE MATRILATERAL CROSS-COUSIN MARRIAGE IS NOT PRESCRIBED OR PREFERRED (335)	221	TILT LESS TOWARD BEING THOSE 0.87 OF 158 WHERE MATRILATERAL CROSS-COUSIN MARRIAGE IS NOT PRESCRIBED OR PREFERRED (335)	4 20 97 138 XSQ= 4.56 PHI= -0.133 XP = 0.0328
224	DRIFT MORE TOWARD BEING THOSE 0.74 OF 43 WHERE COUSIN MARRIAGE IS PREFERENTIALLY OR PERMISSIVELY SYMMETRICAL, RATHER THAN EITHER PATRI- OR MATRILATERAL (106)	224	DRIFT LESS TOWARD BEING THOSE 0.57 OF 79 WHERE COUSIN MARRIAGE IS PREFERENTIALLY OR PERMISSIVELY SYMMETRICAL, RATHER THAN EITHER PATRI- OR MATRILATERAL (106)	11 34 32 45 XSQ= 2.93 PHI= -0.155 XP = 0.0868
234	TEND TO BE THOSE 0.66 OF 86 WHERE THE COUSIN TERMINOLOGY IS OF ESKIMO OR HAWAIIAN TYPE, RATHER THAN CROW, OMAHA, OR IROQUOIS TYPE (170)	234	TEND TO BE THOSE 0.60 OF 137 WHERE THE COUSIN TERMINOLOGY IS OF CROW, OMAHA, OR IROQUOIS TYPE, RATHER THAN ESKIMO OR HAWAIIAN TYPE (152)	29 82 57 55 XSQ= 13.41 PHI= -0.245 XP = 0.0003
240	TILT MORE TOWARD BEING THOSE 0.75 OF 60 WHERE THE FAMILY, IF EXTENDED, IS SMALL OR STEM, RATHER THAN LARGE (135)	240	TILT LESS TOWARD BEING THOSE 0.53 OF 94 WHERE THE FAMILY, IF EXTENDED, IS SMALL OR STEM, RATHER THAN LARGE (135)	15 44 45 50 XSQ= 6.48 PHI= -0.205 XP = 0.0109

242	LEAN LESS TOWARD BEING THOSE 0.73 OF 104 WHERE MARRIAGE IS COMMONLY OR OCCASIONALLY POLYGYNOUS, RATHER THAN MONOGAMOUS (314)	242	LEAN MORE TOWARD BEING THOSE 0.89 OF 163 WHERE MARRIAGE IS COMMONLY OR OCCASIONALLY POLYGYNOUS, RATHER THAN MONOGAMOUS (314)	76 145 28 18 XSQ= 10.14 PHI= -0.195 XP = 0.0014
285	DRIFT TOWARD BEING THOSE 0.71 OF 7 WHERE THE SEX TABOO DURING PREGNANCY IS PRESENT (14) BCA	285	DRIFT TOWARD BEING THOSE 0.71 OF 17 WHERE THE SEX TABOO DURING PREGNANCY IS ABSENT OR INFERRED ABSENT (17) BCA	5 5 2 12 XSQ= 2.08 PHI= 0.294 EP = 0.0850
300	DRIFT MORE TOWARD BEING THOSE 0.72 OF 39 WHERE THE POST-PARTUM SEX TABOO LASTS SIX MONTHS OR LESS (73)	300	DRIFT LESS TOWARD BEING THOSE 0.53 OF 55 WHERE THE POST-PARTUM SEX TABOO LASTS SIX MONTHS OR LESS (73)	11 26 28 29 XSQ= 2.72 PHI= -0.170 XP = 0.0989
307	LEAN TOWARD BEING THOSE 0.67 OF 15 WHERE THE EARLY AGGRESSION SATISFACTION POTENTIAL IS LOW (19) W-C	307	LEAN TOWARD BEING THOSE 0.80 OF 25 WHERE THE EARLY AGGRESSION SATISFACTION POTENTIAL IS HIGH (33) W-C	5 20 10 5 XSQ= 6.83 PHI= -0.413 EP = 0.0062
332	IN ALL CASES ARE THOSE 1.00 OF 3 WHERE THE AGE AT BEGINNING OF MODESTY TRAINING IS LOWER THAN SIX YEARS (8) W-C	332	TILT TOWARD BEING THOSE 0.89 OF 9 WHERE THE AGE AT BEGINNING OF MODESTY TRAINING IS SIX YEARS OR HIGHER (9) W-C	0 8 3 1 XSQ= 4.50 PHI= -0.612 EP = 0.0182
334	DRIFT TOWARD BEING THOSE 0.65 OF 23 WHERE THE INDULGENCE OF THE CHILD IS HIGH (40) B-B-C	334	DRIFT TOWARD BEING THOSE 0.61 OF 36 WHERE THE INDULGENCE OF THE CHILD IS LOW (38) B-B-C	15 14 8 22 XSQ= 2.91 PHI= 0.222 XP = 0.0880
338	DRIFT TOWARD BEING THOSE 0.55 OF 22 WHERE THE CHILD'S INFERRED ANXIETY OVER PERFORMANCE OF RESPONSIBLE BEHAVIOR IS LOW (29) B-B-C	338	DRIFT TOWARD BEING THOSE 0.72 OF 32 WHERE THE CHILD'S INFERRED ANXIETY OVER PERFORMANCE OF RESPONSIBLE BEHAVIOR IS HIGH (44) B-B-C	10 23 12 9 XSQ= 2.80 PHI= -0.228 XP = 0.0944
340	LEAN TOWARD BEING THOSE 0.92 OF 12 WHERE THE TOTAL POSITIVE PRESSURE TOWARD DEVELOPING NURTURANT BEHAVIOR IN THE CHILD IS HIGH (28) B-B-C	340	LEAN TOWARD BEING THOSE 0.64 OF 22 WHERE THE TOTAL POSITIVE PRESSURE TOWARD DEVELOPING NURTURANT BEHAVIOR IN THE CHILD IS LOW (20) B-B-C	11 8 1 14 XSQ= 7.52 PHI= 0.470 EP = 0.0031
342	TILT TOWARD BEING THOSE 0.83 OF 12 WHERE THE CHILD'S INFERRED ANXIETY OVER PERFORMANCE OF NURTURANT BEHAVIOR IS LOW (28) B-B-C	342	TILT TOWARD BEING THOSE 0.57 OF 21 WHERE THE CHILD'S INFERRED ANXIETY OVER PERFORMANCE OF NURTURANT BEHAVIOR IS HIGH (18) B-B-C	2 12 10 9 XSQ= 3.60 PHI= -0.330 EP = 0.0328

352	TILT TCWARD BEING THOSE 0.85 OF 20 WHERE THE TOTAL POSITIVE PRESSURE TOWARD DEVELCPING OBEDIENT BEHAVICR IN THE CHILD IS HIGH (44) B-B-C	352	TILT TOWARD BEING THOSE 0.54 OF 35 WHERE THE TOTAL POSITIVE PRESSURE TOWARD DEVELOPING OBEDIENT BEHAVICR IN THE CHILD IS LOW (28) B-B-C	17 16 3 19 XSQ= 6.63 PHI= 0.347 XP = 0.0100
370	LEAN MCRE TCWARC BEING THCSE 0.74 OF 68 WHERE THE SEGREGATICN CF ACOLESCENT BOYS IS ABSENT (148)	370	LEAN LESS TOWARD BEING THCSE 0.51 OF 99 WHERE THE SEGREGATICN OF ADCLESCENT BOYS IS ABSENT (148)	18 49 50 50 XSQ= 7.96 PHI= -0.218 XP = 0.0048
391	LEAN TCWARD BEING THOSE 0.67 OF 48 WHERE PREMARITAL SEX RELATIONS ARE STRCNGLY PUNISHED AND IN FACT RARE, OR WEAKLY PUNISHED ANC IN FACT NCT RARE (89) JTW,EA	391	LEAN TOWARD BEING THOSE 0.61 OF 82 WHERE PREMARITAL SEX RELATICNS ARE PUNISHED ONLY IF PREGNANCY RESULTS, OR FREELY PERMITTED (90) JTW,EA	32 32 16 50 XSQ= 8.18 PHI= 0.251 XP = 0.0042
405	TILT TCWARD BEING THCSE 0.72 OF 18 WHERE EXPLANATICNS CF ILLNESS OF A DEPENDENCE NATURE ARE ABSENT (27) W-C	405	TILT TOWARD BEING THOSE 0.68 OF 28 WHERE EXPLANATICNS OF ILLNESS OF A DEPENDENCE NATURE ARE PRESENT (34) W-C	5 19 13 9 XSQ= 5.54 PHI= -0.347 XP = 0.0186
427	DRIFT TOWARD BEING THCSE 0.62 OF 42 WHERE A HIGH GOC, IF PRESENT, IS ACTIVE, RATHER THAN INACTIVE (87) GES,EA	427	DRIFT TOWARD BEING THOSE 0.58 OF 67 WHERE A HIGH GCD, IF PRESENT, IS INACTIVE, RATHER THAN ACTIVE (69) GES,EA	26 28 16 39 XSQ= 3.41 PHI= 0.177 XP = 0.0647
428	LEAN TCWARD BEING THOSE 0.85 OF 26 WHERE A HIGH GOC, IF PRESENT AND ACTIVE, SUPPORTS HUMAN MCRALITY, RATHER THAN NCT SUPPORTING IT (61) GES,EA	428	LEAN TOWARD BEING THOSE 0.61 CF 28 WHERE A HIGH GOD, IF PRESENT AND ACTIVE, DOES NOT SUPPORT HUMAN MORALITY, RATHER THAN SUPPORTING IT (26) GES,EA	22 11 4 17 XSQ= 9.83 PHI= 0.427 XP = 0.0017
434	DRIFT TCWARD BEING THCSE 0.63 OF 19 WHERE ASCETICISM IN MOURNING BEHAVIOR IS LCW (30) JFG	434	DRIFT TOWARD BEING THOSE 0.67 OF 33 WHERE ASCETICISM IN MOURNING BEHAVIOR IS HIGH (37) JFG	7 22 12 11 XSQ= 3.22 PHI= -0.249 XP = 0.0726
452	DRIFT TCWARD BEING THCSE 0.69 OF 13 WHERE TCTEMISM WITH FCCC TABOCS IS ABSENT (24) WNS	452	DRIFT TOWARD BEING THOSE 0.71 OF 17 WHERE TOTEMISM WITH FCOD TABCOS IS PRESENT (19) WNS	4 12 9 5 XSQ= 3.23 PHI= -0.328 EP = 0.0634
459	TILT TOWARD BEING THOSE 0.63 OF 46 WHERE GAMES, IF PRESENT, INCLUDE GAMES OF CHANCE (82) R-A-B,EA	459	TILT TOWARD BEING THOSE 0.59 OF 82 WHERE GAMES, IF PRESENT, DO NOT INCLUDE GAMES OF CHANCE (89) R-A-B,EA	29 34 17 48 XSQ= 4.66 PHI= 0.191 XP = 0.0308

```
460  DRIFT MORE TOWARD BEING THOSE  0.74 OF  46      460  DRIFT LESS TOWARD BEING THOSE  0.55 OF  82           12    37
     WHERE GAMES, IF PRESENT,                              WHERE GAMES, IF PRESENT,                                34    45
     ARE NOT LIMITED TO                                    ARE NOT LIMITED TO                                XSQ=      3.75
     GAMES OF SKILL ONLY  (104) R-A-B,EA                   GAMES OF SKILL ONLY  (104) R-A-B,EA               PHI=    -0.171
                                                                                                             XP =    0.0528

480  TILT TOWARD BEING THOSE         0.75 OF  12      480  TILT TOWARD BEING THOSE         0.73 OF  11            3     8
     WHERE COMPLEXITY OF ARTISTIC DESIGN                   WHERE COMPLEXITY OF ARTISTIC DESIGN                  9     3
     IS LOW  (15) HB                                       IS HIGH  (14) HB                                  XSQ=      3.50
                                                                                                             PHI=    -0.390
                                                                                                             EP =    0.0391
```

89 CULTURES
WHERE, IF A NON-HEREDITARY HEADMANSHIP
IS PRESENT, SUCCESSION IS
BY CONSENSUS (63)

89 CULTURES
WHERE, IF A NON-HEREDITARY HEADMANSHIP
IS PRESENT, SUCCESSION IS BY MEANS
OTHER THAN CONSENSUS (43)

BACKGROUND ON PAGE 83

BOTH SUBJECT AND PREDICATE

63 IN LEFT COLUMN

AMERICANS	ANDAMANESE	ASHANTI	ATAYAL	BACAIRI	BOTOCUDO	BRAZILIANS	CALLINAGO	CAMBODIANS	CARIB
CHENCHU	CHINANTEC	CHIR-APACHE	CHORTI	COCHITI	COMANCHE	CREE	CUNA	DAGUR	DOROBO
EGYPTIANS	GILBERTESE	HUICHOL	JAPANESE	JAVANESE	JEMEZ	KABYLE	KOL	MANCHU	MARGI
MBUTI	MINCHIA	NABESNA	NAMBICUARA	NAVAHO	NICOBARESE	NYAKYUSA	OKINAWANS	ONA	ORAON
PAEZ	PALIKUR	POPOLUCA	PORTUGUESE	REGEIBAT	SERBS	SHILLUK	SHLUH	SOMALI	SYRIANS
TANALA	TAOS	TARAHUMARA	THAI	TIBETANS	TODA	TORAJA	TUNEBO	UTE	VIETNAMESE
WARRAU	YAGUA	YAKUT							

43 IN RIGHT COLUMN

BETE	BLACK CARIB	BURMESE	CAMBA	CHUKCHEE	CROW	GANDA	GROS VENTRE	HO	JIVARO
KAPAUKU	KATAB	KOREANS	KORYAK	KUBA	KUTENAI	LESU	MAGUZAWA	MAM	MERINA
MIAO	MIN CHINESE	MOTA	NANDI	NASKAPI	NUPE	OMAHA	PATHAN	PURARI	SARSI
SINDHI	SIUAI	TALLENSI	TECA	TENETEHARA	TETON	TIGRINYA	TWANA	WANTOAT	WAROPEN
YUKAGHIR	YUROK	ZUNI							

204 EXCLUDED BECAUSE IRRELEVANT

90 EXCLUDED BECAUSE UNASCERTAINED

---

63 TILT MORE TOWARD BEING THOSE 0.84 OF 38
WHERE HUSBANDRY, IF PRESENT,
IS PRINCIPALLY IN THE FORM OF
BOVINE, EQUINE, CAMEL-LIKE, OR DEER-LIKE
ANIMALS, RATHER THAN
PIGS, SHEEP, OR GOATS (152)

63 TILT LESS TOWARD BEING THOSE 0.57 OF 30
WHERE HUSBANDRY, IF PRESENT,
IS PRINCIPALLY IN THE FORM OF
BOVINE, EQUINE, CAMEL-LIKE, OR DEER-LIKE
ANIMALS, RATHER THAN
PIGS, SHEEP, OR GOATS (152)

32 17
6 13
XSQ= 5.02
PHI= 0.272
XP = 0.0250

73 TILT TOWARD BEING THOSE 0.60 OF 43
WHERE WEAVING IS
PRESENT (118)

73 TILT TOWARD BEING THOSE 0.72 OF 25
WHERE WEAVING IS
ABSENT (130)

26 7
17 18
XSQ= 5.43
PHI= 0.283
XP = 0.0197

78 IN ALL CASES ARE THOSE 1.00 OF 7
WHERE THE WRITING SYSTEM IS
ALPHABETIC-OR-PHONETIC, OR MNEMONIC,
RATHER THAN BEING ABSENT (36) JMH

78 DRIFT LESS TOWARD BEING THOSE 0.56 OF 9
WHERE THE WRITING SYSTEM IS
ALPHABETIC-OR-PHONETIC, OR MNEMONIC,
RATHER THAN BEING ABSENT (36) JMH

7 5
0 4
XSQ= 2.12
PHI= 0.364
EP = 0.0885

99	DRIFT TOWARD BEING THOSE 0.50 OF 24 WHERE, WITH NATIONAL HIERARCHY ABSENT, THE HIERARCHY OF LOCAL JURISDICTION HAS TWO LEVELS (63) GES,EA	99	DRIFT TOWARD BEING THOSE 0.82 OF 17 WHERE, WITH NATIONAL HIERARCHY ABSENT, THE HIERARCHY OF LOCAL JURISDICTION HAS FOUR OR THREE LEVELS (93) GES,EA	12 14 12 3 XSQ= 3.20 PHI= -0.280 XP = 0.0735
128	TILT TOWARD BEING THOSE 0.92 OF 13 WHERE, IF SUBSISTENCE IS PRIMARILY BY AGRICULTURE, THE WORK IS MAINLY DONE BY MALES (40)	128	TILT TOWARD BEING THOSE 0.56 OF 9 WHERE, IF SUBSISTENCE IS PRIMARILY BY AGRICULTURE, THE WORK IS MAINLY DONE BY FEMALES (37)	12 4 1 5 XSQ= 3.97 PHI= 0.425 EP = 0.0461
183	IN ALL CASES ARE THOSE 1.00 OF 32 WHERE THE LARGEST NON-COGNATIC KIN GROUP IS SMALLER THAN A MOEITY, I. E., A PHRATRY OR SIB OR LINEAGE (218)	183	DRIFT LESS TOWARD BEING THOSE 0.86 OF 28 WHERE THE LARGEST NON-COGNATIC KIN GROUP IS SMALLER THAN A MOEITY, I. E., A PHRATRY OR SIB OR LINEAGE (218)	0 4 32 24 XSQ= 2.87 PHI= -0.219 XP = 0.0902
201	DRIFT LESS TOWARD BEING THOSE 0.76 OF 62 WHERE MARITAL RESIDENCE IS NON-OPTIONAL, RATHER THAN AMBILOCAL OR NEOLOCAL (334)	201	DRIFT MORE TOWARD BEING THOSE 0.91 OF 43 WHERE MARITAL RESIDENCE IS NON-OPTIONAL, RATHER THAN AMBILOCAL OR NEOLOCAL (334)	47 39 15 4 XSQ= 2.86 PHI= -0.165 XP = 0.0908
204	DRIFT LESS TOWARD BEING THOSE 0.71 OF 51 WHERE MARITAL RESIDENCE IS PATRILOCAL, VIRILOCAL, OR AVUNCULOCAL, RATHER THAN AMBILOCAL OR NEOLOCAL (270)	204	DRIFT MORE TOWARD BEING THOSE 0.89 OF 38 WHERE MARITAL RESIDENCE IS PATRILOCAL, VIRILOCAL, OR AVUNCULOCAL, RATHER THAN AMBILOCAL OR NEOLOCAL (270)	36 34 15 4 XSQ= 3.57 PHI= -0.200 XP = 0.0589
225	DRIFT TOWARD BEING THOSE 0.80 OF 5 WHERE COUSIN MARRIAGE IS PREFERENTIALLY OR PERMISSIVELY PATRILATERAL, RATHER THAN MATRILATERAL (23)	225	DRIFT TOWARD BEING THOSE 0.83 OF 6 WHERE COUSIN MARRIAGE IS PREFERENTIALLY OR PERMISSIVELY MATRILATERAL, RATHER THAN PATRILATERAL (43)	4 1 1 5 XSQ= 2.23 PHI= 0.450 EP = 0.0801
242	TILT LESS TOWARD BEING THOSE 0.64 OF 61 WHERE MARRIAGE IS COMMONLY OR OCCASIONALLY POLYGYNOUS, RATHER THAN MONOGAMOUS (314)	242	TILT MORE TOWARD BEING THOSE 0.86 OF 43 WHERE MARRIAGE IS COMMONLY OR OCCASIONALLY POLYGYNOUS, RATHER THAN MONOGAMOUS (314)	39 37 22 6 XSQ= 5.19 PHI= -0.223 XP = 0.0227
262	TILT LESS TOWARD BEING THOSE 0.68 OF 63 WHERE WIVES ARE OBTAINED BY MEANS INVOLVING THE PRESENCE OF SOME CONSIDERATION (305)	262	TILT MORE TOWARD BEING THOSE 0.91 OF 43 WHERE WIVES ARE OBTAINED BY MEANS INVOLVING THE PRESENCE OF SOME CONSIDERATION (305)	43 39 20 4 XSQ= 6.12 PHI= -0.240 XP = 0.0133
263	DRIFT TOWARD BEING THOSE 0.51 OF 63 WHERE WIVES ARE OBTAINED BY RELATIVELY EASY MEANS, NAMELY BY TOKEN BRIDE-PRICE, GIFT EXCHANGE, ABSENCE OF ANY CONSIDERATION, OR RECEIPT OF DOWRY (162)	263	DRIFT TOWARD BEING THOSE 0.67 OF 43 WHERE WIVES ARE OBTAINED BY RELATIVELY DIFFICULT MEANS, NAMELY BY BRIDE-PRICE, BRIDE-SERVICE, OR EXCHANGING A FEMALE RELATIVE (233)	31 29 32 14 XSQ= 2.76 PHI= -0.161 XP = 0.0968

89/

299	DRIFT MORE TOWARD BEING THOSE WHERE THE POST-PARTUM SEX TABOO LASTS ONE YEAR OR LESS (89)	0.86 OF 22	299	DRIFT LESS TOWARD BEING THOSE WHERE THE POST-PARTUM SEX TABOO LASTS ONE YEAR OR LESS (89)	0.59 OF 17		3 7 19 10
						XSQ=	2.51
						PHI=	-0.254
						EP =	0.0711
472	DRIFT TOWARD BEING THOSE WHERE THE COMPOSITE NARCISSISM INDEX IS LOW (43) PES	0.63 OF 16	472	DRIFT TOWARD BEING THOSE WHERE THE COMPOSITE NARCISSISM INDEX IS HIGH (47) PES	0.78 OF 9		6 7 10 2
						XSQ=	2.30
						PHI=	-0.304
						EP =	0.0968

90 CULTURES
WHERE, IF A HEREDITARY HEADMANSHIP
IS PRESENT, SUCCESSION IS
PATRILINEAL, RATHER THAN
MATRILINEAL (127)

90 CULTURES
WHERE, IF A HEREDITARY HEADMANSHIP
IS PRESENT, SUCCESSION IS
MATRILINEAL, RATHER THAN
PATRILINEAL (38)

BACKGROUND ON PAGE 83

BOTH SUBJECT AND PREDICATE

127 IN LEFT COLUMN

ABIPON	AINU	AJIE	AKHA	ALBANIANS	ARANDA	ARAUCANIANS	ATSUGEWI	AZANDE	AZTEC
BAJUN	BALINESE	BAMBARA	BAMILEKE	BANDA	BARI	BASSERI	BATAK	BAYA	BERGDAMA
BHIL	BHUIYA	CAGABA	CAMAYURA	CARAJA	CAYAPA	CHAGGA	CHERKESS	CHIRIGUANO	COORG
DIEGUENO	DOGON	FANG	FON	FOX	GILYAK	GISU	GOND	GUAHIBO	GUATO
HASINAI	HAVASUPAI	HAWAIIANS	HAZARA	HERERO	HUKUNDIKA	INGASSANA	JUKUN	KACHIN	KALMYK
KAREN	KERAKI	KHALKA	KONSO	KPE	KUNG	KWAKIUTL	LAKHER	LAMET	LANGO
LAU	LEPCHA	LHOTA NAGA	LIFU	LOLO	LOZI	LUBA	LUC	MACASSARESE	MANGAIANS
MANIHIKI	MAORI	MARQUESANS	MATAKAM	MBUNDU	MIAMI	MIWOK	MONGO	MONGUOR	MUNDURUCU
MURNGIN	NAMA	NGONI	NOMLAKI	NURI	NYARO	NYORO	ONTONG-JAVA	PAIWAN	PAWNEE
PUKAPUKA	RARCIANS	ROTUMANS	RUNDI	SAMOANS	SANPOIL	SANTAL	SEMANG	SENIANG	SHERENTE
SIRIONO	SONGHAI	SOTHO	SWAZI	TANIMBARESE	TEHUELCHE	TENINO	TERENA	THONGA	TIKOPIA
TIWI	TOKELAU	TOLOWA	TRUMAI	TUBATULABAL	TUPINAMBA	VENDA	WASHO	WICHITA	WINNEBAGO
WITOTO	WOGEO	WOLOF	YARURO	YOKUTS	YORUBA	YUKI			

38 IN RIGHT COLUMN

APINAYE	BELU	BEMBA	BORORO	CHIBCHA	CREEK	DELAWARE	EYAK	GARO	GOAJIRO
HAIDA	HURON	ILA	KERALA	KHASI	KURTATCHI	LAMBA	MAMBILA	MARSHALLESE	MBUGWE
MINANGKABAU	NATCHEZ	NDEMBU	NYANEKA	PALAUANS	PENDE	PONAPEANS	SARAMACCA	TENDA	TIMUCUA
TROBRIAND	TRUKESE	TSHIMSHIAN	WOLEAIANS	YAKO	YAO	YAPESE	YOMBE		

145 EXCLUDED BECAUSE IRRELEVANT

90 EXCLUDED BECAUSE UNASCERTAINED

15 TILT LESS TOWARD BEING THOSE 0.52 OF 127
WHERE THE LATITUDE IS
LESS THAN TWENTY DEGREES (217)

15 TILT MORE TOWARD BEING THOSE 0.74 OF 38
WHERE THE LATITUDE IS
LESS THAN TWENTY DEGREES (217)

61	10
66	28
XSQ=	4.78
PHI=	0.170
XP =	0.0289

16 DRIFT MORE TOWARD BEING THOSE 0.71 OF 127
WHERE THE LATITUDE IS
TEN DEGREES OR GREATER (277)

16 DRIFT LESS TOWARD BEING THOSE 0.53 OF 38
WHERE THE LATITUDE IS
TEN DEGREES OR GREATER (277)

90	20
37	18
XSQ=	3.59
PHI=	0.148
XP =	0.0580

36	TILT LESS TOWARC BEING THCSE 0.72 OF 127 WHERE THE NATURAL ENVIRCNMENT IS OTHER THAN 'VERY HARSH,' OR SUB-TROPICAL BUSH, OR TEMPERATE GRASSLANC (292) FWM	36	TILT MORE TOWARD BEING THOSE 0.92 OF 38 WHERE THE NATURAL ENVIRCNMENT IS OTHER THAN 'VERY HARSH,' OR SUB-TROPICAL BUSH, OR TEMPERATE GRASSLAND (292) FWM	35 3 92 35 XSQ= 5.32 PHI= 0.180 XP = 0.0211
46	DRIFT LESS TCWARC BEING THCSE 0.78 OF 110 OTHER THAN WHERE SETTLEMENTS ARE NON-FIXED AND MCVEMENT IS NOMADIC (260)	46	DRIFT MORE TOWARD BEING THCSE 0.94 CF 32 OTHER THAN WHERE SETTLEMENTS ARE NON-FIXED AND MOVEMENT IS NOMADIC (260)	24 2 86 30 XSQ= 3.04 PHI= 0.146 XP = 0.0811
63	TILT TOWARD BEING THOSE 0.65 OF 69 WHERE HUSBANDRY, IF PRESENT, IS PRINCIPALLY IN THE FORM OF BOVINE, EQUINE, CAMEL-LIKE, OR DEER-LIKE ANIMALS, RATHER THAN PIGS, SHEEP, CR GOATS (152)	63	TILT TOWARD BEING THOSE 0.63 OF 19 WHERE HUSBANDRY, IF PRESENT, IS PRINCIPALLY IN THE FORM OF PIGS, SHEEP, OR GOATS, RATHER THAN BOVINE, EQUINE, CAMEL-LIKE, CR DEER-LIKE ANIMALS (74)	45 7 24 12 XSQ= 3.86 PHI= 0.209 XP = 0.0495
96	TILT LESS TOWARC BEING THCSE 0.53 OF 110 WHERE THE HIERARCHY OF NATICNAL JURISDICTICN HAS FOUR, THREE, TWC OR CNE LEVEL (174) GES,EA	96	TILT MORE TOWARD BEING THOSE 0.75 CF 32 WHERE THE HIERARCHY OF NATIONAL JURISDICTICN HAS FOUR, THREE, TWO OR ONE LEVEL (174) GES,EA	58 24 52 8 XSQ= 4.17 PHI= -0.171 XP = 0.0412
100	DRIFT LESS TCWARD BEING THCSE 0.82 OF 110 WHERE HIERARCHIES ARE MORE COMPLEX THAN THE 'SIMPLEST,' I. E., MORE COMPLEX THAN TWO LCCAL LEVELS WITH NO NATICNAL LEVELS (267) GES,EA	100	DRIFT MORE TOWARD BEING THCSE 0.97 CF 32 WHERE HIERARCHIES ARE MCRE COMPLEX THAN THE 'SIMPLEST,' I. E., MORE COMPLEX THAN TWO LOCAL LEVELS WITH NO NATIONAL LEVELS (267) GES,EA	90 31 20 1 XSQ= 3.34 PHI= -0.153 XP = 0.0674
129	TILT LESS TOWARC BEING THCSE 0.66 OF 35 WHERE WEAVING IS MAINLY DCNE BY FEMALES (73)	129	IN ALL CASES ARE THOSE 1.00 CF 12 WHERE WEAVING IS MAINLY DONE BY FEMALES (73)	12 0 23 12 XSQ= 3.87 PHI= 0.287 XP = 0.0492
130	TILT TCWARD BEING THOSE 0.67 OF 27 WHERE LEATHER WCRKING IS MAINLY DCNE BY MALES (39)	130	TILT TOWARD BEING THOSE 0.86 OF 7 WHERE LEATHER WORKING IS MAINLY DONE BY FEMALES (45)	18 1 9 6 XSQ= 4.24 PHI= 0.353 EP = 0.0282
175	TILT LESS TOWARC BEING THOSE 0.65 OF 124 WHERE THE COMMUNITY IS 'KIN-HETERCGENECUS,' I. E. OTHER THAN A CLAN COMMUNITY OR A DEME (260)	175	TILT MORE TOWARD BEING THOSE 0.86 CF 37 WHERE THE COMMUNITY IS 'KIN-HETEROGENEOUS,' I. E. OTHER THAN A CLAN COMMUNITY OR A DEME (260)	43 5 81 32 XSQ= 5.13 PHI= 0.179 XP = 0.0235
178	LEAN MORE TOWARC BEING THCSE 0.78 OF 124 WHERE THE COMMUNITY IS OTHER THAN SEGMENTED CN A CLAN BASIS AND NCN-EXOGAMCUS (295)	178	LEAN LESS TOWARD BEING THOSE 0.51 OF 37 WHERE THE COMMUNITY IS OTHER THAN SEGMENTED ON A CLAN BASIS AND NON-EXOGAMOUS (295)	27 18 97 19 XSQ= 8.93 PHI= -0.236 XP = 0.0028

180	TILT LESS TOWARD BEING THOSE WHERE THE COMMUNITY IS COMMONLY NON-EXOGAMOUS, RATHER THAN EXOGAMOUS (258)	0.61 OF 124	180	TILT MORE TOWARD BEING THOSE WHERE THE COMMUNITY IS COMMONLY NON-EXOGAMOUS, RATHER THAN EXOGAMOUS (258)	0.84 OF 37	48 6 76 31 XSQ= 5.50 PHI= 0.185 XP = 0.0190
185	LEAN LESS TOWARD BEING THOSE WHERE THE LARGEST NON-COGNATIC KIN GROUP IS THE MOEITY OR PHRATRY OR SIB (194)	0.70 OF 84	185	LEAN MORE TOWARD BEING THOSE WHERE THE LARGEST NON-COGNATIC KIN GROUP IS THE MOEITY OR PHRATRY OR SIB (194)	0.94 OF 35	59 33 25 2 XSQ= 6.83 PHI= -0.240 XP = 0.0090
186	TEND LESS TO BE THOSE WHERE THE KIN GROUP IS OTHER THAN EXCLUSIVELY PATRILINEAL (250)	0.51 OF 127	186	IN ALL CASES ARE THOSE WHERE THE KIN GROUP IS OTHER THAN EXCLUSIVELY PATRILINEAL (250)	1.00 OF 38	62 0 65 38 XSQ= 27.67 PHI= 0.410 XP = 0.0000
187	TEND TO BE THOSE WHERE THE KIN GROUP IS OTHER THAN EXCLUSIVELY MATRILINEAL (344)	0.95 OF 126	187	TEND TO BE THOSE WHERE THE KIN GROUP IS EXCLUSIVELY MATRILINEAL (55)	0.68 OF 38	6 26 120 12 XSQ= 71.34 PHI= -0.660 XP = 0.
188	LEAN LESS TOWARD BEING THOSE WHERE THE KIN GROUP IS OTHER THAN EXCLUSIVELY COGNATIC (252)	0.66 OF 127	188	LEAN MORE TOWARD BEING THOSE WHERE THE KIN GROUP IS OTHER THAN EXCLUSIVELY COGNATIC (252)	0.92 OF 38	43 3 84 35 XSQ= 8.56 PHI= 0.228 XP = 0.0034
190	TEND TO BE THOSE WHERE THE KIN GROUP IS PATRILINEAL OR DOUBLE-DESCENT, RATHER THAN MATRILINEAL (186)	0.93 OF 82	190	TEND TO BE THOSE WHERE THE KIN GROUP IS MATRILINEAL, RATHER THAN PATRILINEAL OR DOUBLE-DESCENT (61)	0.89 OF 35	76 4 6 31 XSQ= 71.19 PHI= 0.780 XP = 0.
196	DRIFT LESS TOWARD BEING THOSE WHERE INDIVIDUAL RIGHTS IN REAL PROPERTY, AND RULES FOR INHERITANCE, ARE PRESENT (194)	0.62 OF 94	196	DRIFT MORE TOWARD BEING THOSE WHERE INDIVIDUAL RIGHTS IN REAL PROPERTY, AND RULES FOR INHERITANCE, ARE PRESENT (194)	0.85 OF 20	58 17 36 3 XSQ= 3.01 PHI= -0.162 XP = 0.0828
198	IN ALL CASES ARE THOSE WHERE RULES FOR THE INHERITANCE OF REAL PROPERTY, IF PRESENT, FAVOR THE MALE HEIR OR LINE, RATHER THAN THE FEMALE (144)	1.00 OF 52	198	TEND TO BE THOSE WHERE RULES FOR THE INHERITANCE OF REAL PROPERTY, IF PRESENT, FAVOR THE FEMALE HEIR OR LINE, RATHER THAN THE MALE (21)	0.71 OF 17	52 5 0 12 XSQ= 39.66 PHI= 0.758 XP = 0.
209	LEAN MORE TOWARD BEING THOSE WHERE MARITAL RESIDENCE IS PATRILOCAL, VIRILOCAL, OR AVUNCULOCAL, RATHER THAN MATRILOCAL OR UXORILOCAL (270)	0.88 OF 112	209	LEAN LESS TOWARD BEING THOSE WHERE MARITAL RESIDENCE IS PATRILOCAL, VIRILOCAL, OR AVUNCULOCAL, RATHER THAN MATRILOCAL OR UXORILOCAL (270)	0.63 OF 32	98 20 14 12 XSQ= 8.89 PHI= 0.248 XP = 0.0029

210	TEND TO BE THOSE 0.93 OF 76 WHERE MARITAL RESIDENCE IS PATRILOCAL, RATHER THAN MATRILOCAL (169)	210	TEND TO BE THOSE 0.80 OF 15 WHERE MARITAL RESIDENCE IS MATRILOCAL, RATHER THAN PATRILOCAL (31)	71 3 5 12 XSQ= 39.75 PHI= 0.661 XP = 0.
213	TILT TOWARD BEING THOSE 0.55 OF 123 WHERE FIRST COUSIN MARRIAGE IS NOT PERMITTED (198)	213	TILT TOWARD BEING THOSE 0.69 OF 35 WHERE FIRST COUSIN MARRIAGE IS PERMITTED (172)	55 24 68 11 XSQ= 5.29 PHI= -0.183 XP = 0.0215
234	TILT LESS TOWARD BEING THOSE 0.54 OF 102 WHERE THE COUSIN TERMINOLOGY IS OF CROW, OMAHA, OR IROQUOIS TYPE, RATHER THAN ESKIMO OR HAWAIIAN TYPE (152)	234	TILT MORE TOWARD BEING THOSE 0.77 OF 35 WHERE THE COUSIN TERMINOLOGY IS OF CROW, OMAHA, OR IROQUOIS TYPE, RATHER THAN ESKIMO OR HAWAIIAN TYPE (152)	55 27 47 8 XSQ= 4.92 PHI= -0.190 XP = 0.0265
240	TILT TOWARD BEING THOSE 0.60 OF 70 WHERE THE FAMILY, IF EXTENDED, IS SMALL OR STEM, RATHER THAN LARGE (135)	240	TILT TOWARD BEING THOSE 0.67 OF 24 WHERE THE FAMILY, IF EXTENDED, IS LARGE, RATHER THAN SMALL OR STEM (78)	28 16 42 8 XSQ= 4.09 PHI= -0.209 XP = 0.0431
242	DRIFT MORE TOWARD BEING THOSE 0.92 OF 125 WHERE MARRIAGE IS COMMONLY OR OCCASIONALLY POLYGYNOUS, RATHER THAN MONOGAMOUS (314)	242	DRIFT LESS TOWARD BEING THOSE 0.79 OF 38 WHERE MARRIAGE IS COMMONLY OR OCCASIONALLY POLYGYNOUS, RATHER THAN MONOGAMOUS (314)	115 30 10 8 XSQ= 3.81 PHI= 0.153 XP = 0.0509
254	IN ALL CASES ARE THOSE 1.00 OF 5 WHERE HOUSEHOLD AUTHORITY IS ON THE FATHER'S SIDE, RATHER THAN THE MOTHER'S (9) CA	254	TILT TOWARD BEING THOSE 0.75 OF 4 WHERE HOUSEHOLD AUTHORITY IS ON THE MOTHER'S SIDE, RATHER THAN THE FATHER'S (6) DA	5 1 0 3 XSQ= 2.76 PHI= 0.553 EP = 0.0476
262	TILT MORE TOWARD BEING THOSE 0.80 OF 125 WHERE WIVES ARE OBTAINED BY MEANS INVOLVING THE PRESENCE OF SOME CONSIDERATION (305)	262	TILT LESS TOWARD BEING THOSE 0.62 OF 37 WHERE WIVES ARE OBTAINED BY MEANS INVOLVING THE PRESENCE OF SOME CONSIDERATION (305)	100 23 25 14 XSQ= 4.04 PHI= 0.158 XP = 0.0444
272	TILT TOWARD BEING THOSE 0.64 OF 22 WHERE THE DIVORCE RATE IS LOW (28) CA	272	IN ALL CASES ARE THOSE 1.00 OF 4 WHERE THE DIVORCE RATE IS HIGH (29) CA	8 4 14 0 XSQ= 3.25 PHI= -0.354 EP = 0.0331
370	TILT TOWARD BEING THOSE 0.56 OF 78 WHERE THE SEGREGATION OF ADOLESCENT BOYS IS ABSENT (148)	370	TILT TOWARD BEING THOSE 0.71 OF 21 WHERE THE SEGREGATION OF ADOLESCENT BOYS IS COMPLETE OR PARTIAL (95)	34 15 44 6 XSQ= 4.08 PHI= -0.203 XP = 0.0435

377	DRIFT LESS TCWARD BEING THCSE 0.71 OF 107 WHERE MALE GENITAL MUTILATION IS ABSENT (242)	377	DRIFT MORE TOWARD BEING THCSE 0.90 CF 30 WHERE MALE GENITAL MUTILATICN IS ABSENT (242)	31 3 76 27 XSQ= 3.56 PHI= 0.161 XP = 0.0592
390	DRIFT LESS TCWARD BEING THCSE 0.80 OF 64 WHERE PREMARITAL SEX RELATIONS ARE WEAKLY PUNISHED ANC IN FACT NOT RARE OR PUNISHED CNLY IF PREGNANCY RESULTS, OR FREELY PERMITTEC (132) JTW,EA	390	IN ALL CASES ARE THCSE 1.00 CF 18 WHERE PREMARITAL SEX RELATIONS ARE WEAKLY PUNISHED AND IN FACT NOT RARE OR PUNISHED ONLY IF PREGNANCY RESULTS, OR FREELY PERMITTED (132) JTW,EA	13 0 51 18 XSQ= 2.96 PHI= 0.190 XP = 0.0856
392	LEAN TOWARD BEING THOSE 0.66 OF 64 WHERE PREMARITAL SEX RELATIONS ARE STRCNGLY PUNISHEC AND IN FACT RARE, OR WEAKLY PUNISHED ANC IN FACT NCT RARE, OR PUNISHED CNLY IF PREGNANCY RESULTS (112) JTW,EA	392	LEAN TOWARD BEING THOSE 0.72 OF 18 WHERE PREMARITAL SEX RELATICNS ARE FREELY PERMITTED (67) JTW,EA	42 5 22 13 XSQ= 6.75 PHI= 0.287 XP = 0.0094
403	DRIFT TOWARD BEING THCSE 0.75 OF 24 WHERE EXPLANATICNS OF ILLNESS OF AN ANAL NATURE ARE ABSENT (38) W-C	403	DRIFT TOWARD BEING THOSE 0.75 CF 4 WHERE EXPLANATICNS OF ILLNESS OF AN ANAL NATURE ARE PRESENT (23) W-C	6 3 18 1 XSQ= 1.97 PHI= -0.265 EP = 0.0841
437	DRIFT TCWARD BEING THCSE 0.61 OF 18 WHERE FEAR OF GHCSTS, SPIRITS, HUMANS CR ANIMALS IS HIGH (21) W-C,JFG	437	IN ALL CASES ARE THOSE 1.00 CF 4 WHERE FEAR OF GHOSTS, SPIRITS, HUMANS OR ANIMALS IS LOW (23) W-C,JFG	11 0 7 4 XSQ= 2.75 PHI= 0.354 EP = 0.0902

91 CULTURES WHERE SOCIETAL COMPLEXITY IS HIGH (18) F-W	91 CULTURES WHERE SOCIETAL COMPLEXITY IS LOW (22) F-W

BACKGROUND ON PAGE 85

BOTH SUBJECT AND PREDICATE

18 IN LEFT COLUMN

ASHANTI, BALINESE, CHAGGA, CREEK, CUNA, CZECHS, HANO, HEBREWS, KOREANS, LAPPS, LEPCHA, MAORI, MBUNDU, NAVAHO, RIFFIANS, ROMANS, VENDA, VIETNAMESE

22 IN RIGHT COLUMN

ANDAMANESE, ARANDA, AZANDE, CAYAPA, CHUKCHEE, COPR ESKIMO, CROW, IFUGAO, JIVARO, KAZAK, KURTATCHI, LAKHER, NAMA, SANPOIL, SIRIONO, SIWANS, THONGA, TUPINAMBA, WOLEAIANS, YAKUT, YARURO, YUROK

360 EXCLUDED BECAUSE UNASCERTAINED

	Left column (societal complexity high)			Right column (societal complexity low)		Statistics
4	DRIFT LESS TOWARD BEING THOSE LOCATED OUTSIDE OF THE CIRCUM-MEDITERRANEAN (355)	0.72 OF 18	4	DRIFT MORE TOWARD BEING THOSE LOCATED OUTSIDE OF THE CIRCUM-MEDITERRANEAN (355)	0.95 OF 22	5 1 13 21 XSQ= 2.57 PHI= 0.253 EP = 0.0734
44	TILT MORE TOWARD BEING THOSE WHERE SETTLEMENTS ARE FIXED (222)	0.88 OF 17	44	TILT LESS TOWARD BEING THOSE WHERE SETTLEMENTS ARE FIXED (222)	0.55 OF 22	15 12 2 10 XSQ= 3.65 PHI= 0.306 EP = 0.0365
46	TILT MORE TOWARD BEING THOSE OTHER THAN WHERE SETTLEMENTS ARE NON-FIXED AND MOVEMENT IS NOMADIC (260)	0.94 OF 17	46	TILT LESS TOWARD BEING THOSE OTHER THAN WHERE SETTLEMENTS ARE NON-FIXED AND MOVEMENT IS NOMADIC (260)	0.55 OF 22	1 10 16 12 XSQ= 5.59 PHI= -0.379 EP = 0.0106
51	TILT TOWARD BEING THOSE WHERE SUBSISTENCE IS PRIMARILY BY FOOD PRODUCTION -- I. E., AGRICULTURE OR HUSBANDRY -- RATHER THAN BY GATHERING (253)	0.83 OF 18	51	TILT TOWARD BEING THOSE WHERE SUBSISTENCE IS PRIMARILY BY FOOD GATHERING -- I. E., HUNTING, FISHING, OR COLLECTING -- RATHER THAN FOOD PRODUCTION (147)	0.55 OF 22	15 10 3 12 XSQ= 4.55 PHI= 0.337 EP = 0.0217
53	TILT TOWARD BEING THOSE WHERE FOOD PRODUCTION IS BY INTENSIVE AGRICULTURE, RATHER THAN BY SIMPLE AGRICULTURE OR INCIPIENT FOOD PRODUCTION (91)	0.63 OF 16	53	TILT TOWARD BEING THOSE WHERE FOOD PRODUCTION IS BY SIMPLE AGRICULTURE OR INCIPIENT FOOD PRODUCTION, RATHER THAN BY INTENSIVE AGRICULTURE (147)	0.86 OF 14	10 2 6 12 XSQ= 5.36 PHI= 0.423 EP = 0.0106

55	TILT TOWARD BEING THOSE WHERE FOOD PRODUCTION IS BY INTENSIVE AGRICULTURE, RATHER THAN BY SIMPLE AGRICULTURE (91)	0.77 OF 13	55	TILT TOWARD BEING THOSE WHERE FOOD PRODUCTION IS BY SIMPLE AGRICULTURE, RATHER THAN BY INTENSIVE AGRICULTURE (101)	0.78 OF 9	10 2 3 7 XSQ= 4.40 PHI= 0.447 EP = 0.0274
80	LEAN LESS TOWARD BEING THOSE WHERE NO CITY OR TOWN IS PRESENT (185)	0.60 OF 15	80	IN ALL CASES ARE THOSE WHERE NO CITY OR TOWN IS PRESENT (185)	1.00 OF 18	6 0 9 18 XSQ= 6.32 PHI= 0.438 EP = 0.0045
81	TEND TO BE THOSE WHERE A CITY OR TOWN IS PRESENT, OR THE AVERAGE COMMUNITY SIZE IS 200 OR GREATER (89)	0.80 OF 15	81	TEND TO BE THOSE WHERE NO CITY OR TOWN IS PRESENT, AND THE AVERAGE COMMUNITY SIZE IS SMALLER THAN 200 (135)	0.83 OF 18	12 3 3 15 XSQ= 10.81 PHI= 0.572 EP = 0.0004
83	LEAN TOWARD BEING THOSE WHERE, WITH NO CITY AND NO TOWN PRESENT, THE AVERAGE COMMUNITY SIZE IS BETWEEN 200 AND 999, RATHER THAN SMALLER THAN 200 (45)	0.67 OF 9	83	LEAN TOWARD BEING THOSE WHERE, WITH NO CITY AND NO TOWN PRESENT, THE AVERAGE COMMUNITY SIZE IS SMALLER THAN 200, RATHER THAN BETWEEN 200 AND 999 (135)	0.88 OF 17	6 2 3 15 XSQ= 5.95 PHI= 0.478 EP = 0.0077
85	TILT TOWARD BEING THOSE WHERE THE LEVEL OF POLITICAL INTEGRATION IS THE LARGE STATE, OR THE LITTLE STATE (70) GPM	0.60 OF 15	85	TILT TOWARD BEING THOSE WHERE THE LEVEL OF POLITICAL INTEGRATION IS THE MINIMAL STATE, THE AUTONOMOUS COMMUNITY, OR THE FAMILY (234) GPM	0.80 OF 20	9 4 6 16 XSQ= 4.29 PHI= 0.350 EP = 0.0322
86	LEAN TOWARD BEING THOSE WHERE THE LEVEL OF POLITICAL INTEGRATION IS THE LARGE STATE, THE LITTLE STATE, OR THE MINIMAL STATE (148) GPM	0.87 OF 15	86	LEAN TOWARD BEING THOSE WHERE THE LEVEL OF POLITICAL INTEGRATION IS THE AUTONOMOUS COMMUNITY, OR THE FAMILY (156) GPM	0.60 OF 20	13 8 2 12 XSQ= 5.95 PHI= 0.412 EP = 0.0069
96	DRIFT TOWARD BEING THOSE WHERE THE HIERARCHY OF NATIONAL JURISDICTION HAS FOUR, THREE, TWO OR ONE LEVEL (174) GES,EA	0.75 OF 16	96	DRIFT TOWARD BEING THOSE WHERE THE HIERARCHY OF NATIONAL JURISDICTION HAS NO LEVELS (156) GES,EA	0.59 OF 22	12 9 4 13 XSQ= 3.08 PHI= 0.285 EP = 0.0516
102	DRIFT MORE TOWARD BEING THOSE WHERE CLASS STRATIFICATION IS PRESENT (203)	0.83 OF 18	102	DRIFT LESS TOWARD BEING THOSE WHERE CLASS STRATIFICATION IS PRESENT (203)	0.55 OF 22	15 12 3 10 XSQ= 2.54 PHI= 0.252 EP = 0.0896
109	DRIFT LESS TOWARD BEING THOSE WHERE CASTES ARE ABSENT (317)	0.82 OF 17	109	IN ALL CASES ARE THOSE WHERE CASTES ARE ABSENT (317)	1.00 OF 21	3 0 14 21 XSQ= 1.96 PHI= 0.227 EP = 0.0806

116	TILT TOWARD BEING THOSE WHERE OCCUPATIONAL SPECIALIZATION IS FULL-TIME, WHETHER OR NOT FOR SURPLUS PRODUCTION (20) JMH	0.57 OF	7	116	TILT TOWARD BEING THOSE WHERE OCCUPATIONAL SPECIALIZATION IS PART-TIME ONLY (34) JMH	0.88 OF	16	4 2 3 14 XSQ= 2.98 PHI= 0.360 EP = 0.0450
118	IN ALL CASES ARE THOSE WHERE THE PERCENTAGE OF OCCUPATIONS THAT ARE SPECIALIZED IS HIGH OR MEDIUM (24) WME	1.00 OF	7	118	LEAN TOWARD BEING THOSE WHERE THE PERCENTAGE OF OCCUPATIONS THAT ARE SPECIALIZED IS LOW (25) WME	0.70 OF	10	7 3 0 7 XSQ= 5.69 PHI= 0.579 EP = 0.0098
127	TILT TOWARD BEING THOSE WHERE THE FEMALES' CONTRIBUTION TO SUBSISTENCE IS LOW (32) JKB	0.80 OF	5	127	TILT TOWARD BEING THOSE WHERE THE FEMALES' CONTRIBUTION TO SUBSISTENCE IS HIGH (33) JKB	0.79 OF	14	1 11 4 3 XSQ= 3.21 PHI= -0.411 EP = 0.0379
132	IN ALL CASES ARE THOSE WHERE ECONOMIC EXCHANGE INVOLVES THE USE OF MONEY (37) JMH	1.00 OF	7	132	LEAN TOWARD BEING THOSE WHERE ECONOMIC EXCHANGE DOES NOT INVOLVE THE USE OF MONEY (17) JMH	0.63 OF	16	7 6 0 10 XSQ= 5.41 PHI= 0.485 EP = 0.0075
139	DRIFT TOWARD BEING THOSE WHERE SUPERORDINATE PUNISHMENT IS PRESENT (15) BBW	0.71 OF	7	139	DRIFT TOWARD BEING THOSE WHERE SUPERORDINATE PUNISHMENT IS ABSENT (25) BBW	0.75 OF	12	5 3 2 9 XSQ= 2.24 PHI= 0.343 EP = 0.0739
141	IN ALL CASES ARE THOSE WHERE THE LEVEL OF SOCIAL SANCTION IS PUBLIC CORPOREAL SANCTION, RATHER THAN PUBLIC PROPERTY SANCTION OR PRIVATE SETTLEMENT (28) JMH	1.00 OF	7	141	TILT TOWARD BEING THOSE WHERE THE LEVEL OF SOCIAL SANCTION IS PUBLIC PROPERTY SANCTION OR PRIVATE SETTLEMENT, RATHER THAN PUBLIC CORPOREAL SANCTION (26) JMH	0.56 OF	16	7 7 0 9 XSQ= 4.32 PHI= 0.434 EP = 0.0189
147	IN ALL CASES ARE THOSE WHERE CODIFIED LAWS ARE PRESENT (20) LWS	1.00 OF	5	147	TILT TOWARD BEING THOSE WHERE CODIFIED LAWS ARE UNIMPORTANT OR ABSENT (13) LWS	0.75 OF	4	5 1 0 3 XSQ= 2.76 PHI= 0.553 EP = 0.0476
152	IN ALL CASES ARE THOSE WHERE THE DIFFERENTIATION OF THE JURIDICAL AGENCY FROM THE MEDICAL AGENCY IS HIGH (10) MJ	1.00 OF	2	152	IN ALL CASES ARE THOSE WHERE THE DIFFERENTIATION OF THE JURIDICAL AGENCY FROM THE MEDICAL AGENCY IS LOW (10) MJ	1.00 OF	4	2 0 0 4 XSQ= 2.34 PHI= 0.625 EP = 0.0667
196	TEND TO BE THOSE WHERE INDIVIDUAL RIGHTS IN REAL PROPERTY, AND RULES FOR INHERITANCE, ARE PRESENT (194)	0.92 OF	13	196	TEND TO BE THOSE WHERE INDIVIDUAL RIGHTS IN REAL PROPERTY, OR RULES FOR INHERITANCE, ARE ABSENT (87)	0.73 OF	15	12 4 1 11 XSQ= 9.72 PHI= 0.589 EP = 0.0006

319	DRIFT TOWARD BEING THOSE 0.78 OF 9 WHERE PROTECTION OF THE INFANT FROM ENVIRONMENTAL DISCOMFORTS IS HIGH (35) B-B-C	319	DRIFT TOWARD BEING THOSE 0.67 OF 12 WHERE PROTECTION OF THE INFANT FROM ENVIRONMENTAL DISCOMFORTS IS LOW (30) B-B-C	7 4 2 8 XSQ= 2.49 PHI= 0.344 EP = 0.0805
326	DRIFT TOWARD BEING THOSE 0.80 OF 10 WHERE THE INFERRED TRANSITION ANXIETY BETWEEN INFANCY AND CHILDHOOD IS HIGH (32) B-B-C	326	DRIFT TOWARD BEING THOSE 0.64 OF 11 WHERE THE INFERRED TRANSITION ANXIETY BETWEEN INFANCY AND CHILDHOOD IS LOW (35) B-B-C	8 4 2 7 XSQ= 2.49 PHI= 0.344 EP = 0.0805
390	TILT LESS TOWARD BEING THOSE 0.69 OF 13 WHERE PREMARITAL SEX RELATIONS ARE WEAKLY PUNISHED AND IN FACT NOT RARE OR PUNISHED ONLY IF PREGNANCY RESULTS, OR FREELY PERMITTED (132) JTW,EA	390	IN ALL CASES ARE THOSE 1.00 OF 15 WHERE PREMARITAL SEX RELATIONS ARE WEAKLY PUNISHED AND IN FACT NOT RARE OR PUNISHED ONLY IF PREGNANCY RESULTS, OR FREELY PERMITTED (132) JTW,EA	4 0 9 15 XSQ= 3.16 PHI= 0.336 EP = 0.0349
391	TILT TOWARD BEING THOSE 0.62 OF 13 WHERE PREMARITAL SEX RELATIONS ARE STRONGLY PUNISHED AND IN FACT RARE, OR WEAKLY PUNISHED AND IN FACT NOT RARE (89) JTW,EA	391	TILT TOWARD BEING THOSE 0.87 OF 15 WHERE PREMARITAL SEX RELATIONS ARE PUNISHED ONLY IF PREGNANCY RESULTS, OR FREELY PERMITTED (90) JTW,EA	8 2 5 13 XSQ= 5.11 PHI= 0.427 EP = 0.0163
392	TILT TOWARD BEING THOSE 0.85 OF 13 WHERE PREMARITAL SEX RELATIONS ARE STRONGLY PUNISHED AND IN FACT RARE, OR WEAKLY PUNISHED AND IN FACT NOT RARE, OR PUNISHED ONLY IF PREGNANCY RESULTS (112) JTW,EA	392	TILT TOWARD BEING THOSE 0.60 OF 15 WHERE PREMARITAL SEX RELATIONS ARE FREELY PERMITTED (67) JTW,EA	11 6 2 9 XSQ= 4.09 PHI= 0.382 EP = 0.0238
399	TILT TOWARD BEING THOSE 0.83 OF 6 WHERE INTENSITY OF CASTRATION ANXIETY IS LOW (22) WNS	399	TILT TOWARD BEING THOSE 0.78 OF 9 WHERE INTENSITY OF CASTRATION ANXIETY IS HIGH (23) WNS	1 7 5 2 XSQ= 3.23 PHI= -0.464 EP = 0.0406
403	TILT TOWARD BEING THOSE 0.60 OF 10 WHERE EXPLANATIONS OF ILLNESS OF AN ANAL NATURE ARE PRESENT (23) W-C	403	TILT TOWARD BEING THOSE 0.91 OF 11 WHERE EXPLANATIONS OF ILLNESS OF AN ANAL NATURE ARE ABSENT (38) W-C	6 1 4 10 XSQ= 4.03 PHI= 0.438 EP = 0.0237
431	IN ALL CASES ARE THOSE 1.00 OF 2 WHERE SUPERNATURAL SANCTIONS FOR MORALITY, HAVING AN EFFECT ON AN INDIVIDUAL'S AFTER LIFE, ARE PRESENT (10) GES	431	IN ALL CASES ARE THOSE 1.00 OF 7 WHERE SUPERNATURAL SANCTIONS FOR MORALITY, HAVING AN EFFECT ON AN INDIVIDUAL'S AFTERLIFE, ARE ABSENT OR UNREPORTED (25) GES	2 0 0 7 XSQ= 4.14 PHI= 0.679 EP = 0.0278
468	TILT TOWARD BEING THOSE 0.57 OF 7 WHERE CONTACT WITH OTHER CULTURES IS FREQUENT, RATHER THAN REGULAR OR IRREGULAR (17) JMH	468	TILT TOWARD BEING THOSE 0.94 OF 16 WHERE CONTACT WITH OTHER CULTURES IS REGULAR OR IRREGULAR, RATHER THAN FREQUENT (37) JMH	4 1 3 15 XSQ= 4.72 PHI= 0.453 EP = 0.0173

```
476  DRIFT TCWARD BEING THCSE         0.70 OF  1C        476  DRIFT TOWARD BEING THOSE        0.75 CF  12              3     9
     WHERE THE DEGREE OF INSCBRIETY IS                        WHERE THE DEGREE OF INSOBRIETY IS                             7     3
     MODERATE CR SLIGHT  (18) CH                              STRONG   (31) DH                                      XSQ=      2.82
                                                                                                                    PHI=    -0.358
                                                                                                                    EP =    0.0836

477  IN ALL CASES ARE THCSE           1.00 OF   5        477  DRIFT TOWARD BEING THCSE        0.63 OF   8              0     5
     WHERE ALCCHOLIC AGGRESSION IS                            WHERE ALCOHOLIC AGGRESSION IS                                 5     3
     MODERATE CR SLIGHT  (19) CH                              STRONG   (15) DH                                      XSQ=      2.78
                                                                                                                    PHI=    -0.462
                                                                                                                    EP =    0.0754
```

92 CULTURES WHOSE INDEX OF SOCIAL DEVELOPMENT IS HIGH (10) RN	92 CULTURES WHOSE INDEX OF SOCIAL DEVELOPMENT IS LOW (10) RN

BACKGROUND ON PAGE 85

SUBJECT ONLY

10 IN LEFT COLUMN

AZTEC CROW CUNA FON HANO INCA NUER NUPE SAMOANS TIKOPIA

10 IN RIGHT COLUMN

AINU LEPCHA LESU NAMA ONA SELUNG TIMBIRA TODA YAGUA YAHGAN

380 EXCLUDED BECAUSE UNASCERTAINED

5	IN ALL CASES ARE THOSE LOCATED OUTSIDE OF EAST EURASIA (330)	1.00 OF 10	5	DRIFT LESS TOWARD BEING THOSE LOCATED OUTSIDE OF EAST EURASIA (330)	0.60 OF 10	0 4 10 6 XSQ= 2.81 PHI= -0.375 EP = 0.0867
51	TILT TOWARD BEING THOSE WHERE SUBSISTENCE IS PRIMARILY BY FOOD PRODUCTION -- I. E., AGRICULTURE OR HUSBANDRY -- RATHER THAN BY GATHERING (253)	0.80 OF 10	51	TILT TOWARD BEING THOSE WHERE SUBSISTENCE IS PRIMARILY BY FOOD GATHERING -- I. E., HUNTING, FISHING, OR COLLECTING -- RATHER THAN FOOD PRODUCTION (147)	0.80 OF 10	8 2 2 8 XSQ= 5.00 PHI= 0.500 EP = 0.0230
54	IN ALL CASES ARE THOSE WHERE FOOD PRODUCTION IS BY INTENSIVE OR SIMPLE AGRICULTURE, RATHER THAN BY INCIPIENT FOOD PRODUCTION (192)	1.00 OF 7	54	TILT TOWARD BEING THOSE WHERE FOOD PRODUCTION IS BY INCIPIENT FOOD PRODUCTION, RATHER THAN BY INTENSIVE OR SIMPLE AGRICULTURE (46)	0.75 OF 4	7 1 0 3 XSQ= 3.93 PHI= 0.598 EP = 0.0242
56	IN ALL CASES ARE THOSE WHERE FOOD PRODUCTION IS BY SIMPLE AGRICULTURE, RATHER THAN BY INCIPIENT FOOD PRODUCTION (101)	1.00 OF 4	56	IN ALL CASES ARE THOSE WHERE FOOD PRODUCTION IS BY INCIPIENT FOOD PRODUCTION, RATHER THAN BY SIMPLE AGRICULTURE (46)	1.00 OF 3	4 0 0 3 XSQ= 3.51 PHI= 0.708 EP = 0.0286
81	TILT TOWARD BEING THOSE WHERE A CITY OR TOWN IS PRESENT, OR THE AVERAGE COMMUNITY SIZE IS 200 OR GREATER (89)	0.75 OF 8	81	TILT TOWARD BEING THOSE WHERE NO CITY OR TOWN IS PRESENT, AND THE AVERAGE COMMUNITY SIZE IS SMALLER THAN 200 (135)	0.88 OF 8	6 1 2 7 XSQ= 4.06 PHI= 0.504 EP = 0.0406

85	DRIFT LESS TOWARD BEING THOSE 0.57 OF 7 WHERE THE LEVEL OF POLITICAL INTEGRATION IS THE MINIMAL STATE, THE AUTONOMOUS COMMUNITY, OR THE FAMILY (234) GPM	85	IN ALL CASES ARE THOSE 1.00 OF 8 WHERE THE LEVEL OF POLITICAL INTEGRATION IS THE MINIMAL STATE, THE AUTONOMOUS COMMUNITY, OR THE FAMILY (234) GPM	3 0 4 8 XSQ= 2.03 PHI= 0.367 EP = 0.0769
86	TILT TOWARD BEING THOSE 0.86 OF 7 WHERE THE LEVEL OF POLITICAL INTEGRATION IS THE LARGE STATE, THE LITTLE STATE, OR THE MINIMAL STATE (148) GPM	86	TILT TOWARD BEING THOSE 0.88 OF 8 WHERE THE LEVEL OF POLITICAL INTEGRATION IS THE AUTONOMOUS COMMUNITY, OR THE FAMILY (156) GPM	6 1 1 7 XSQ= 5.37 PHI= 0.598 EP = 0.0101
95	TILT TOWARD BEING THOSE 0.50 OF 10 WHERE THE HIERARCHY OF NATIONAL JURISDICTION HAS FOUR, THREE, OR TWO LEVELS (76) GES,EA	95	IN ALL CASES ARE THOSE 1.00 OF 10 WHERE THE HIERARCHY OF NATIONAL JURISDICTION HAS ONE OR NO LEVELS (254) GES,EA	5 0 5 10 XSQ= 4.27 PHI= 0.462 EP = 0.0325
96	DRIFT TOWARD BEING THOSE 0.80 OF 10 WHERE THE HIERARCHY OF NATIONAL JURISDICTION HAS FOUR, THREE, TWO OR ONE LEVEL (174) GES,EA	96	DRIFT TOWARD BEING THOSE 0.70 OF 10 WHERE THE HIERARCHY OF NATIONAL JURISDICTION HAS NO LEVELS (156) GES,EA	8 3 2 7 XSQ= 3.23 PHI= 0.402 EP = 0.0698
100	IN ALL CASES ARE THOSE 1.00 OF 10 WHERE HIERARCHIES ARE MORE COMPLEX THAN THE 'SIMPLEST,' I. E., MORE COMPLEX THAN TWO LOCAL LEVELS WITH NO NATIONAL LEVELS (267) GES,EA	100	DRIFT LESS TOWARD BEING THOSE 0.60 OF 10 WHERE HIERARCHIES ARE MORE COMPLEX THAN THE 'SIMPLEST,' I. E., MORE COMPLEX THAN TWO LOCAL LEVELS WITH NO NATIONAL LEVELS (267) GES,EA	10 6 0 4 XSQ= 2.81 PHI= 0.375 EP = 0.0867
102	DRIFT TOWARD BEING THOSE 0.70 OF 10 WHERE CLASS STRATIFICATION IS PRESENT (203)	102	DRIFT TOWARD BEING THOSE 0.80 OF 10 WHERE CLASS STRATIFICATION IS ABSENT (180)	7 2 3 8 XSQ= 3.23 PHI= 0.402 EP = 0.0698
106	DRIFT TOWARD BEING THOSE 0.86 OF 7 WHERE CLASS STRATIFICATION, IF PRESENT, IS BASED ON SOMETHING OTHER THAN WEALTH (126)	106	IN ALL CASES ARE THOSE 1.00 OF 2 WHERE CLASS STRATIFICATION, IF PRESENT, IS BASED ON WEALTH (77)	1 2 6 0 XSQ= 2.01 PHI= -0.472 EP = 0.0833
196	TILT TOWARD BEING THOSE 0.75 OF 8 WHERE INDIVIDUAL RIGHTS IN REAL PROPERTY, AND RULES FOR INHERITANCE, ARE PRESENT (194)	196	TILT TOWARD BEING THOSE 0.86 OF 7 WHERE INDIVIDUAL RIGHTS IN REAL PROPERTY, OR RULES FOR INHERITANCE, ARE ABSENT (87)	6 1 2 6 XSQ= 3.36 PHI= 0.473 EP = 0.0406
349	TILT TOWARD BEING THOSE 0.67 OF 6 WHERE THE CHILD'S INFERRED ANXIETY OVER NON-PERFORMANCE OF ACHIEVEMENT BEHAVIOR IS HIGH (34) B-B-C	349	IN ALL CASES ARE THOSE 1.00 OF 7 WHERE THE CHILD'S INFERRED ANXIETY OVER NON-PERFORMANCE OF ACHIEVEMENT BEHAVIOR IS LOW (28) B-B-C	4 0 2 7 XSQ= 3.97 PHI= 0.553 EP = 0.0210

No.	Statement		N	No.	Statement		N	Statistics
350	DRIFT TOWARD BEING THOSE WHERE THE CHILD'S INFERRED ANXIETY OVER PERFORMANCE OF ACHIEVEMENT BEHAVIOR IS HIGH (34) B-B-C	0.50 OF	6	350	IN ALL CASES ARE THOSE WHERE THE CHILD'S INFERRED ANXIETY OVER PERFORMANCE OF ACHIEVEMENT BEHAVIOR IS LOW (26) B-B-C	1.00 OF	7	3 0 3 7 XSQ= 2.17 PHI= 0.408 EP = 0.0699
351	DRIFT TOWARD BEING THOSE WHERE THE CHILD'S INFERRED CONFLICT REGARDING ACHIEVEMENT BEHAVIOR IS HIGH (26) B-B-C	0.50 OF	6	351	IN ALL CASES ARE THOSE WHERE THE CHILD'S INFERRED CONFLICT REGARDING ACHIEVEMENT BEHAVIOR IS LOW (34) B-B-C	1.00 OF	7	3 0 3 7 XSQ= 2.17 PHI= 0.408 EP = 0.0699
395	IN ALL CASES ARE THOSE WHERE BELIEF IN THE UNCLEANNESS OF WOMEN IS UNIMPORTANT OR ABSENT (15) LWS	1.00 OF	4	395	IN ALL CASES ARE THOSE WHERE BELIEF IN THE UNCLEANNESS OF WOMEN IS PRESENT (18) LWS	1.00 OF	3	0 3 4 0 XSQ= 3.51 PHI= -0.708 EP = 0.0286
417	IN ALL CASES ARE THOSE WHERE WARFARE IS PREVALENT (34) LWS	1.00 OF	6	417	TILT TOWARD BEING THOSE WHERE WARFARE IS NOT PREVALENT (9) LWS	0.75 OF	4	6 1 0 3 XSQ= 3.35 PHI= 0.579 EP = 0.0333
421	DRIFT LESS TOWARD BEING THOSE WHERE KILLING, TORTURING, OR MUTILATING OF THE ENEMY IS NEGLIGIBLY EMPHASIZED (47) PES	0.56 OF	9	421	IN ALL CASES ARE THOSE WHERE KILLING, TORTURING, OR MUTILATING OF THE ENEMY IS NEGLIGIBLY EMPHASIZED (47) PES	1.00 OF	7	4 0 5 7 XSQ= 2.12 PHI= 0.364 EP = 0.0885
452	IN ALL CASES ARE THOSE WHERE TOTEMISM WITH FOOD TABOOS IS PRESENT (19) WNS	1.00 OF	3	452	TILT TOWARD BEING THOSE WHERE TOTEMISM WITH FOOD TABOOS IS ABSENT (24) WNS	0.83 OF	6	3 1 0 5 XSQ= 2.76 PHI= 0.553 EP = 0.0476
459	TILT TOWARD BEING THOSE WHERE GAMES, IF PRESENT, INCLUDE GAMES OF CHANCE (82) R-A-B,EA	0.83 OF	6	459	TILT TOWARD BEING THOSE WHERE GAMES, IF PRESENT, DO NOT INCLUDE GAMES OF CHANCE (89) R-A-B,EA	0.89 OF	9	5 1 1 8 XSQ= 5.10 PHI= 0.583 EP = 0.0110
460	TILT TOWARD BEING THOSE WHERE GAMES, IF PRESENT, ARE NOT LIMITED TO GAMES OF SKILL ONLY (104) R-A-B,EA	0.83 OF	6	460	TILT TOWARD BEING THOSE WHERE GAMES, IF PRESENT, ARE LIMITED TO GAMES OF SKILL ONLY (67) R-A-B,EA	0.89 OF	9	1 8 5 1 XSQ= 5.10 PHI= -0.583 EP = 0.0110
472	TILT TOWARD BEING THOSE WHERE THE COMPOSITE NARCISSISM INDEX IS HIGH (47) PES	0.78 OF	9	472	TILT TOWARD BEING THOSE WHERE THE COMPOSITE NARCISSISM INDEX IS LOW (43) PES	0.88 OF	8	7 1 2 7 XSQ= 4.86 PHI= 0.535 EP = 0.0152

92/

474	TILT TOWARD BEING THOSE WHERE BOASTFULNESS IS EXTREME	0.56 OF 9 (41) PES	474	IN ALL CASES ARE THOSE WHERE BOASTFULNESS IS MODERATE, NEGLIBIBLE, OR UNREPORTED (48) PES	1.00 OF 8

	5	0
	4	8
XSQ=	3.90	
PHI=	0.479	
EP =	0.0294	

93 CULTURES WHERE OVERALL SOCIAL STRUCTURAL COMPLEXITY IS HIGH (10) MJ

93 CULTURES WHERE OVERALL SOCIAL STRUCTURAL COMPLEXITY IS LOW (10) MJ

BACKGROUND ON PAGE 85

SUBJECT ONLY

10 IN LEFT COLUMN

BEMBA BURMESE JAVANESE KIKUYU LAMBA NUPE SAMOANS THAI TROBRIAND VIETNAMESE

10 IN RIGHT COLUMN

ANDAMANESE COMANCHE COPR ESKIMO JIVARO KUNG MUNDURUCU MURNGIN NAMA NAVAHO SIUAI

380 EXCLUDED BECAUSE UNASCERTAINED

	High complexity	Ratio	N		Low complexity	Ratio	N	Statistics
36	IN ALL CASES ARE THOSE WHERE THE NATURAL ENVIRONMENT IS OTHER THAN 'VERY HARSH,' OR SUB-TROPICAL BUSH, OR TEMPERATE GRASSLAND (292) FWM	1.00 OF	10	36	TILT TOWARD BEING THOSE WHERE THE NATURAL ENVIRONMENT IS 'VERY HARSH,' OR SUB-TROPICAL BUSH, OR TEMPERATE GRASSLAND (108) FWM	0.60 OF	10	0 6 10 4 XSQ= 5.95 PHI= -0.546 EP = 0.0108
44	TILT TOWARD BEING THOSE WHERE SETTLEMENTS ARE FIXED (222)	0.89 OF	9	44	TILT TOWARD BEING THOSE WHERE SETTLEMENTS ARE NON-FIXED (110)	0.78 OF	9	8 2 1 7 XSQ= 5.63 PHI= 0.559 EP = 0.0152
45	DRIFT TOWARD BEING THOSE WHERE SETTLEMENTS, IF FIXED, ARE COMPACT, RATHER THAN NON-COMPACT (149)	0.88 OF	8	45	IN ALL CASES ARE THOSE WHERE SETTLEMENTS, IF FIXED, ARE NON-COMPACT, RATHER THAN COMPACT (73)	1.00 OF	2	7 0 1 2 XSQ= 2.41 PHI= 0.491 EP = 0.0667
46	IN ALL CASES ARE THOSE OTHER THAN WHERE SETTLEMENTS ARE NON-FIXED AND MOVEMENT IS NOMADIC (260)	1.00 OF	9	46	TILT TOWARD BEING THOSE WHERE SETTLEMENTS ARE NON-FIXED AND MOVEMENT IS NOMADIC (72)	0.56 OF	9	0 5 9 4 XSQ= 4.43 PHI= -0.496 EP = 0.0294
51	IN ALL CASES ARE THOSE WHERE SUBSISTENCE IS PRIMARILY BY FOOD PRODUCTION -- I. E., AGRICULTURE OR HUSBANDRY -- RATHER THAN BY GATHERING (253)	1.00 OF	10	51	TEND TO BE THOSE WHERE SUBSISTENCE IS PRIMARILY BY FOOD GATHERING -- I. E., HUNTING, FISHING, OR COLLECTING -- RATHER THAN FOOD PRODUCTION (147)	0.80 OF	10	10 2 0 8 XSQ= 10.21 PHI= 0.714 EP = 0.0007

54	IN ALL CASES ARE THOSE WHERE FOOD PRODUCTION IS BY INTENSIVE OR SIMPLE AGRICULTURE, RATHER THAN BY INCIPIENT FOOD PRODUCTION (192)	1.00 OF 9	54	TILT TOWARD BEING THOSE WHERE FOOD PRODUCTION IS BY INCIPIENT FOOD PRODUCTION, RATHER THAN BY INTENSIVE OR SIMPLE AGRICULTURE (46)	0.60 OF 5	9 2 0 3 XSQ= 3.77 PHI= 0.519 EP = 0.0275
82	IN ALL CASES ARE THOSE WHERE A CITY OR TOWN IS PRESENT, OR THE AVERAGE COMMUNITY SIZE IS FIFTY OR GREATER (178)	1.00 OF 8	82	TILT TOWARD BEING THOSE WHERE NO CITY OR TOWN IS PRESENT, AND THE AVERAGE COMMUNITY SIZE IS SMALLER THAN FIFTY (46)	0.57 OF 7	8 3 0 4 XSQ= 3.65 PHI= 0.494 EP = 0.0256
84	TILT TOWARD BEING THOSE WHERE THE LEVEL OF POLITICAL INTEGRATION IS THE LARGE STATE (42) GPM	0.56 OF 9	84	IN ALL CASES ARE THOSE WHERE THE LEVEL OF POLITICAL INTEGRATION IS THE LITTLE STATE, THE MINIMAL STATE, THE AUTONOMOUS COMMUNITY, OR THE FAMILY (262) GPM	1.00 OF 8	5 0 4 8 XSQ= 3.90 PHI= 0.479 EP = 0.0294
86	LEAN TOWARD BEING THOSE WHERE THE LEVEL OF POLITICAL INTEGRATION IS THE LARGE STATE, THE LITTLE STATE, OR THE MINIMAL STATE (148) GPM	0.89 OF 9	86	LEAN TOWARD BEING THOSE WHERE THE LEVEL OF POLITICAL INTEGRATION IS THE AUTONOMOUS COMMUNITY, OR THE FAMILY (156) GPM	0.88 OF 8	8 1 1 7 XSQ= 7.09 PHI= 0.646 EP = 0.0034
95	LEAN TOWARD BEING THOSE WHERE THE HIERARCHY OF NATIONAL JURISDICTION HAS FOUR, THREE, OR TWO LEVELS (76) GES,EA	0.78 OF 9	95	IN ALL CASES ARE THOSE WHERE THE HIERARCHY OF NATIONAL JURISDICTION HAS ONE OR NO LEVELS (254) GES,EA	1.00 OF 9	7 0 2 9 XSQ= 8.42 PHI= 0.684 EP = 0.0023
96	LEAN TOWARD BEING THOSE WHERE THE HIERARCHY OF NATIONAL JURISDICTION HAS FOUR, THREE, TWO OR ONE LEVEL (174) GES,EA	0.89 OF 9	96	LEAN TOWARD BEING THOSE WHERE THE HIERARCHY OF NATIONAL JURISDICTION HAS NO LEVELS (156) GES,EA	0.89 OF 9	8 1 1 8 XSQ= 8.00 PHI= 0.667 EP = 0.0034
100	IN ALL CASES ARE THOSE WHERE HIERARCHIES ARE MORE COMPLEX THAN THE 'SIMPLEST,' I. E., MORE COMPLEX THAN TWO LOCAL LEVELS WITH NO NATIONAL LEVELS (267) GES,EA	1.00 OF 9	100	DRIFT LESS TOWARD BEING THOSE WHERE HIERARCHIES ARE MORE COMPLEX THAN THE 'SIMPLEST,' I. E., MORE COMPLEX THAN TWO LOCAL LEVELS WITH NO NATIONAL LEVELS (267) GES,EA	0.56 OF 9	9 5 0 4 XSQ= 2.89 PHI= 0.401 EP = 0.0824
102	LEAN TOWARD BEING THOSE WHERE CLASS STRATIFICATION IS PRESENT (203)	0.90 OF 10	102	LEAN TOWARD BEING THOSE WHERE CLASS STRATIFICATION IS ABSENT (180)	0.80 OF 10	9 2 1 8 XSQ= 7.27 PHI= 0.603 EP = 0.0055
106	DRIFT TOWARD BEING THOSE WHERE CLASS STRATIFICATION, IF PRESENT, IS BASED ON SOMETHING OTHER THAN WEALTH (126)	0.89 OF 9	106	IN ALL CASES ARE THOSE WHERE CLASS STRATIFICATION, IF PRESENT, IS BASED ON WEALTH (77)	1.00 OF 2	1 2 8 0 XSQ= 2.81 PHI= -0.505 EP = 0.0545

152	TILT TOWARD BEING THOSE 0.80 OF 10 WHERE THE DIFFERENTIATION OF THE JURIDICAL AGENCY FROM THE MEDICAL AGENCY IS HIGH (10) MJ	152	TILT TOWARD BEING THOSE 0.80 OF 10 WHERE THE DIFFERENTIATION OF THE JURIDICAL AGENCY FROM THE MEDICAL AGENCY IS LOW (10) MJ	8 2 2 8 XSQ= 5.00 PHI= 0.500 EP = 0.0230
163	TILT TOWARD BEING THOSE 0.75 OF 8 WHERE THE EMPHASIS ON INDIVIDUAL VOLITION AS THE CAUSE OF CRIME IS HIGH (7) MJ	163	TILT TOWARD BEING THOSE 0.89 OF 9 WHERE THE EMPHASIS ON INDIVIDUAL VOLITION AS THE CAUSE OF CRIME IS LOW (10) MJ	6 1 2 8 XSQ= 4.74 PHI= 0.528 EP = 0.0152
196	IN ALL CASES ARE THOSE 1.00 OF 8 WHERE INDIVIDUAL RIGHTS IN REAL PROPERTY, AND RULES FOR INHERITANCE, ARE PRESENT (194)	196	LEAN TOWARD BEING THOSE 0.88 OF 8 WHERE INDIVIDUAL RIGHTS IN REAL PROPERTY, OR RULES FOR INHERITANCE, ARE ABSENT (87)	8 1 0 7 XSQ= 9.14 PHI= 0.756 EP = 0.0014
330	IN ALL CASES ARE THOSE 1.00 OF 4 WHERE THE AGE OF THE INFANT AT TIME OF WEANING IS LOWER THAN 2.5 YEARS (36) B-B-C	330	IN ALL CASES ARE THOSE 1.00 OF 4 WHERE THE AGE OF THE INFANT AT TIME OF WEANING IS 2.5 YEARS OR HIGHER (34) B-B-C	0 4 4 0 XSQ= 4.50 PHI= -0.750 EP = 0.0286
390	TILT TOWARD BEING THOSE 0.71 OF 7 WHERE PREMARITAL SEX RELATIONS ARE STRONGLY PUNISHED AND IN FACT RARE (47) JTW,EA	390	IN ALL CASES ARE THOSE 1.00 OF 5 WHERE PREMARITAL SEX RELATIONS ARE WEAKLY PUNISHED AND IN FACT NOT RARE OR PUNISHED ONLY IF PREGNANCY RESULTS, OR FREELY PERMITTED (132) JTW,EA	5 0 2 5 XSQ= 3.54 PHI= 0.543 EP = 0.0278
426	DRIFT TOWARD BEING THOSE 0.75 OF 8 WHERE A HIGH GOD IS PRESENT (156) GES,EA	426	DRIFT TOWARD BEING THOSE 0.78 OF 9 WHERE A HIGH GOD IS ABSENT (104) GES,EA	6 2 2 7 XSQ= 2.85 PHI= 0.410 EP = 0.0567
435	IN ALL CASES ARE THOSE 1.00 OF 2 WHERE ABANDONMENT OF THE HOUSE OF THE DEAD IS NOT PRACTICED (19) LWS	435	IN ALL CASES ARE THOSE 1.00 OF 5 WHERE ABANDONMENT OF THE HOUSE OF THE DEAD IS PRACTICED (12) LWS	0 5 2 0 XSQ= 2.96 PHI= -0.650 EP = 0.0476
437	IN ALL CASES ARE THOSE 1.00 OF 2 WHERE FEAR OF GHOSTS, SPIRITS, HUMANS OR ANIMALS IS LOW (23) W-C,JFG	437	IN ALL CASES ARE THOSE 1.00 OF 4 WHERE FEAR OF GHOSTS, SPIRITS, HUMANS OR ANIMALS IS HIGH (21) W-C,JFG	0 4 2 0 XSQ= 2.34 PHI= -0.625 EP = 0.0667
451	IN ALL CASES ARE THOSE 1.00 OF 2 WHERE TOTEMISM IS PRESENT (15) LWS	451	IN ALL CASES ARE THOSE 1.00 OF 4 WHERE TOTEMISM IS UNIMPORTANT OR ABSENT (12) LWS	2 0 0 4 XSQ= 2.34 PHI= 0.625 EP = 0.0667

```
452  IN ALL CASES ARE THCSE           1.00 OF   2        452  IN ALL CASES ARE THCSE          1.00 OF   4              2     0
     WHERE TCTEMISM WITH FCCC TABCOS                          WHERE TOTEMISM WITH FOOD TABCOS                           0     4
     IS PRESENT  (19) WNS                                     IS ABSENT  (24) WNS                           XSQ=      2.34
                                                                                                            PHI=     0.625
                                                                                                            EP =    0.0667

473  DRIFT TCWARD BEING THCSE         0.75 OF   4        473  DRIFT TOWARD BEING THOSE        0.86 CF   7              3     1
     WHERE SENSITIVITY TC INSULT                              WHERE SENSITIVITY TO INSULT                               1     6
     IS EXTREME  (32) PES                                     IS MODERATE OR NEGLIGIBLE  (56) PES           XSQ=      1.86
                                                                                                            PHI=     0.411
                                                                                                            EP =    0.0879

480  IN ALL CASES ARE THCSE           1.00 OF   2        48C  IN ALL CASES ARE THOSE          1.00 OF   4              2     0
     WHERE CCMPLEXITY OF ARTISTIC CESIGN                      WHERE COMPLEXITY OF ARTISTIC DESIGN                       0     4
     IS HIGH  (14) HB                                         IS LOW  (15) HB                               XSQ=      2.34
                                                                                                            PHI=     0.625
                                                                                                            EP =    0.0667
```

94 CULTURES:
WHERE THE HIERARCHY
OF NATIONAL JURISDICTION HAS
FOUR OR THREE LEVELS (34) GES,EA

94 CULTURES
WHERE THE HIERARCHY
OF NATIONAL JURISDICTION HAS
TWO, ONE, OR NO LEVELS (296) GES,EA

BACKGROUND ON PAGE 86

BOTH SUBJECT AND PREDICATE

34 IN LEFT COLUMN

AMERICANS	BAMILEKE	BRAZILIANS	BULGARIANS	CAMBODIANS	CZECHS	DAGUR	DUTCH	EGYPTIANS	FON
GANDA	INCA	JAPANESE	JAVANESE	KABYLE	KAZAK	KHALKA	LOZI	MACASSARESE	MERINA
MIN CHINESE	NYORO	REGEIBAT	RUNDI	SERBS	SINHALESE	SONGHAI	SOTHO	SWAZI	THAI
TURKMEN	VIETNAMESE	WALLOONS	YORUBA						

296 IN RIGHT COLUMN

ABIPON	ABOR	AINU	AKHA	ALACALUF	ALBANIANS	ALORESE	AMBA	ANDAMANESE	APINAYE
ARANDA	ARAPESH	ARAUCANIANS	ASHANTI	ATAYAL	ATSUGEWI	AWEIKOMA	AZANDE	AZTEC	BABWA
BACAIRI	BAMBARA	BANDA	BARABRA	BARI	BASSERI	BAYA	BEJA	BEMBA	BHIL
BHUIYA	BIRIFOR	BLACK CARIB	BOERS	BORORO	BOTOCUDO	BOZO	BUNLAP	BURUSHO	CADUVEO
CAGABA	CALLINAGO	CAMAYURA	CARIB	CAYAPA	CHAGGA	CHAMACOCO	CHENCHU	CHERKESS	CHEROKEE
CHEYENNE	CHIBCHA	CHIR-APACHE	CHIRIGUANO	CHOCO	CHOROTI	CHORTI	CHUKCHEE	COCHITI	COORG
COPR ESKIMO	CREE	CREEK	CROW	CUNA	DARD	DELAWARE	DIEGUENO	DIERI	DILLING
DOGON	DOROBO	ELLICE	ENGA	EYAK	FANG	FOX	FUTAJALONKE	GARO	GILYAK
GISU	GOAJIRO	GOND	GROS VENTRE	GUAHIBO	GUATO	GURE	HAIDA	HANO	HANUNOO
HASINAI	HAVASUPAI	HAWAIIANS	HAZARA	HEBREWS	HERERO	HUICHOL	HUKUNDIKA	HURON	IBAN
IFUGAO	ILA	INGALIK	INGASSANA	IRAQW	IRISH	JEMEZ	JIVARO	JUKUN	KACHIN
KAPAUKU	KARIERA	KASKA	KATAB	KERAKI	KERALA	KHASI	KIKUYU	KISSI	KOHISTANI
KOL	KOREANS	KORYAK	KPE	KUBA	KUNG	KURTATCHI	KUTENAI	KWAKIUTL	LAKHER
LAMBA	LAMET	LANGO	LAPPS	LAU	LEPCHA	LESU	LHOTA NAGA	LOLO	LUO
MALAYS	MAM	MAMBILA	MAMVU	MANDAN	MANGAIANS	MANIHIKI	MANUS	MAORI	MARGI
MARICOPA	MARQUESANS	MARSHALLESE	MASAI	MATACO	MATAKAM	MAYA	MBUNDU	MBUTI	MENDE
MIAMI	MIAO	MINCHIA	MISKITO	MIWOK	MNONG GAR	MONGO	MONGUOR	MOSSI	MOTA
MOTILON	MUNDURUCU	MURINBATA	MURNGIN	MZAB	NABESNA	NAMA	NAMBICUARA	NANDI	NATCHEZ
NAVAHO	NDEMBU	NICOBARESE	NOMLAKI	NUER	NUNIVAK	NUPE	NURI	NYAKYUSA	OJIBWA
OKINAWANS	OMAHA	ONA	ONTONG-JAVA	ORAON	PAEZ	PAIWAN	PALAUANS	PAPAGO	PARAUJANO
PATHAN	PAWNEE	PONAPEANS	PUKAPUKA	PURARI	PURUM	RIFFIANS	RWALA	SAGADA	SAMOANS
SAMOYED	SANDAWE	SANPOIL	SANTAL	SARSI	SELUNG	SEMANG	SENIANG	SHERENTE	SHILLUK
SHLUH	SIRIONO	SIUAI	SIWANS	SOMALI	SUBANUN	SYRIANS	TAGBANUA	TALAMANCA	TALLENSI
TANALA	TAOS	TAPIRAPE	TARAHUMARA	TAREUMIUT	TEDA	TEHUELCHE	TENDA	TENETEHARA	TENINO
TERA	TERENA	TESO	THONGA	TIGRINYA	TIKOPIA	TIMBIRA	TIMUCUA	TIV	TIWI
TODA	TOKELAU	TOLOWA	TORAJA	TOTONAC	TRISTAN	TROBRIAND	TRUKESE	TRUMAI	TSHIMSHIAN
TUBATULABAL	TUCANO	TUCUNA	TUNEBO	TUPINAMBA	TURKANA	TWANA	ULAWANS	UTE	VEDDA
VENDA	WAICA	WANTOAT	WAPISHANA	WARRAU	WASHO	WICHITA	WIKMUNKAN	WITOTO	WOGEO
WOLEAIANS	WOLOF	YABARANA	YAGUA	YAHGAN	YAKO	YAKUT	YAO	YAPESE	YARURO
YOKUTS	YOMBE	YUKAGHIR	YUKI	YUROK	ZUNI				

70 EXCLUDED BECAUSE UNASCERTAINED

4	TEND LESS TO BE THCSE LCCATED CUTSIDE CF THE CIRCUM-MEDITERRANEAN (355)	0.68 OF 34	4	TEND MORE TO BE THOSE LOCATED OUTSIDE OF THE CIRCUM-MEDITERRANEAN (355)	0.93 CF 296	11 21 23 275 XSQ= 19.43 PHI= 0.243 XP = 0.0000
5	TILT LESS TOWARC BEING THCSE LOCATED CUTSIDE CF EAST EURASIA (330)	0.68 OF 34	5	TILT MORE TOWARD BEING THOSE LOCATED OUTSIDE OF EAST EURASIA (330)	0.84 OF 296	11 48 23 248 XSQ= 4.37 PHI= 0.115 XP = 0.0367
8	IN ALL CASES ARE THCSE LOCATED CUTSIDE CF NORTH AMERICA (330)	1.00 OF 34	8	LEAN LESS TOWARD BEING THOSE LOCATED OUTSIDE OF NORTH AMERICA (330)	0.80 CF 296	0 59 34 237 XSQ= 6.95 PHI= -0.145 XP = 0.0084
9	TILT MCRE TOWARC BEING THCSE LOCATED CUTSICE CF SCUTH AMERICA (335)	0.97 OF 34	9	TILT LESS TOWARD BEING THOSE LOCATED OUTSIDE OF SOUTH AMERICA (335)	0.81 OF 296	1 57 33 239 XSQ= 4.53 PHI= -0.117 XP = 0.0332
44	LEAN MCRE TOWARC BEING THCSE WHERE SETTLEMENTS ARE FIXEC (222)	0.88 OF 34	44	LEAN LESS TOWARD BEING THOSE WHERE SETTLEMENTS ARE FIXED (222)	0.64 CF 295	30 189 4 106 XSQ= 6.95 PHI= 0.145 XP = 0.0084
46	DRIFT MCRE TCWARC BEING THCSE CTHER THAN WHERE SETTLEMENTS ARE NON-FIXED AND MCVEMENT IS NCMADIC (260)	0.91 OF 34	46	DRIFT LESS TOWARD BEING THOSE OTHER THAN WHERE SETTLEMENTS ARE NON-FIXED AND MOVEMENT IS NOMADIC (260)	0.77 OF 295	3 69 31 226 XSQ= 2.98 PHI= -0.095 XP = 0.0843
51	TEND MORE TO BE THCSE WHERE SUBSISTENCE IS PRIMARILY BY FOOD PRCDUCTICN -- I. E., AGRICULTURE OR HUSBANDRY -- RATHER THAN BY GATHERING (253)	0.97 OF 34	51	TEND LESS TO BE THOSE WHERE SUBSISTENCE IS PRIMARILY BY FOOD PRODUCTION -- I. E., AGRICULTURE OR HUSBANDRY -- RATHER THAN BY GATHERING (253)	0.57 CF 296	33 170 1 126 XSQ= 18.59 PHI= 0.237 XP = 0.0000
53	TEND TC BE THCSE WHERE FCCD PRCDUCTICN IS BY INTENSIVE AGRICULTURE, RATHER THAN BY SIMPLE AGRICULTURE CR INCIPIENT FOCD PRCDUCTICN (91)	0.84 OF 31	53	TEND TO BE THOSE WHERE FOOD PRODUCTION IS BY SIMPLE AGRICULTURE OR INCIPIENT FOOD PRODUCTION, RATHER THAN BY INTENSIVE AGRICULTURE (147)	0.69 OF 197	26 62 5 135 XSQ= 28.86 PHI= 0.356 XP = 0.0000
55	TEND TC BE THCSE WHERE FCCD PRODUCTICN IS BY INTENSIVE AGRICULTURE, RATHER THAN BY SIMPLE AGRICULTURE (91)	0.87 OF 30	55	TEND TO BE THOSE WHERE FOOD PRODUCTION IS BY SIMPLE AGRICULTURE, RATHER THAN BY INTENSIVE AGRICULTURE (101)	0.61 CF 159	26 62 4 97 XSQ= 21.18 PHI= 0.335 XP = 0.0000

62	TEND MORE TO BE THOSE WHERE HUSBANDRY OF SOME KIND IS PRESENT (228)	0.97 OF 34	62	TEND LESS TO BE THOSE WHERE HUSBANDRY OF SOME KIND IS PRESENT (228)	0.64 OF 296	33 190 1 106 XSQ= 13.58 PHI= 0.203 XP = 0.0002
63	LEAN MORE TOWARD BEING THOSE WHERE HUSBANDRY, IF PRESENT, IS PRINCIPALLY IN THE FORM OF BOVINE, EQUINE, CAMEL-LIKE, OR DEER-LIKE ANIMALS, RATHER THAN PIGS, SHEEP, OR GOATS (152)	0.91 OF 33	63	LEAN LESS TOWARD BEING THOSE WHERE HUSBANDRY, IF PRESENT, IS PRINCIPALLY IN THE FORM OF BOVINE, EQUINE, CAMEL-LIKE, OR DEER-LIKE ANIMALS, RATHER THAN PIGS, SHEEP, OR GOATS (152)	0.63 OF 190	30 119 3 71 XSQ= 8.90 PHI= 0.200 XP = 0.0028
71	IN ALL CASES ARE THOSE WHERE METAL WORKING IS PRESENT (98)	1.00 OF 21	71	TEND TO BE THOSE WHERE METAL WORKING IS ABSENT (153)	0.66 OF 220	21 74 0 146 XSQ= 32.63 PHI= 0.368 XP = 0.
73	TILT TOWARD BEING THOSE WHERE WEAVING IS PRESENT (118)	0.73 OF 22	73	TILT TOWARD BEING THOSE WHERE WEAVING IS ABSENT (130)	0.55 OF 217	16 98 6 119 XSQ= 5.03 PHI= 0.145 XP = 0.0249
74	LEAN MORE TOWARD BEING THOSE WHERE POTTERY IS PRESENT (145)	0.95 OF 19	74	LEAN LESS TOWARD BEING THOSE WHERE POTTERY IS PRESENT (145)	0.59 OF 210	18 124 1 86 XSQ= 7.97 PHI= 0.187 XP = 0.0048
77	IN ALL CASES ARE THOSE WHERE THE WRITING SYSTEM IS ALPHABETIC-OR-PHONETIC, RATHER THAN BEING MNEMONIC OR ABSENT (15) JMH	1.00 OF 3	77	TILT TOWARD BEING THOSE WHERE THE WRITING SYSTEM IS MNEMONIC OR ABSENT, RATHER THAN BEING ALPHABETIC-OR-PHONETIC (39) JMH	0.78 OF 49	3 11 0 38 XSQ= 5.15 PHI= 0.315 XP = 0.0233
79	TEND TO BE THOSE WHERE A CITY IS PRESENT (23)	0.57 OF 28	79	TEND TO BE THOSE WHERE NO CITY IS PRESENT (201)	0.97 OF 193	16 6 12 187 XSQ= 73.73 PHI= 0.578 XP = 0.
80	TEND TO BE THOSE WHERE A CITY OR TOWN IS PRESENT (39)	0.75 OF 28	80	TEND TO BE THOSE WHERE NO CITY OR TOWN IS PRESENT (185)	0.92 OF 193	21 16 7 177 XSQ= 73.35 PHI= 0.576 XP = 0.
81	TEND TO BE THOSE WHERE A CITY OR TOWN IS PRESENT, OR THE AVERAGE COMMUNITY SIZE IS 200 OR GREATER (89)	0.86 OF 28	81	TEND TO BE THOSE WHERE NO CITY OR TOWN IS PRESENT, AND THE AVERAGE COMMUNITY SIZE IS SMALLER THAN 200 (135)	0.68 OF 193	24 62 4 131 XSQ= 27.33 PHI= 0.352 XP = 0.0000

84	TEND TO BE THOSE 0.81 OF 26 WHERE THE LEVEL OF POLITICAL INTEGRATION IS THE LARGE STATE (42) GPM	84	TEND TO BE THOSE 0.94 OF 232 WHERE THE LEVEL OF POLITICAL INTEGRATION IS THE LITTLE STATE, THE MINIMAL STATE, THE AUTONOMOUS COMMUNITY, OR THE FAMILY (262) GPM	21 14 5 218 XSQ= 105.08 PHI= 0.638 XP = 0.
85	IN ALL CASES ARE THOSE 1.00 OF 26 WHERE THE LEVEL OF POLITICAL INTEGRATION IS THE LARGE STATE, OR THE LITTLE STATE (70) GPM	85	TEND TO BE THOSE 0.87 OF 232 WHERE THE LEVEL OF POLITICAL INTEGRATION IS THE MINIMAL STATE, THE AUTONOMOUS COMMUNITY, OR THE FAMILY (234) GPM	26 31 0 201 XSQ= 96.99 PHI= 0.613 XP = 0.
88	DRIFT TOWARD BEING THOSE 0.58 OF 26 WHERE, IF A HEADMANSHIP IS PRESENT, SUCCESSION IS NON-HEREDITARY (106)	88	DRIFT TOWARD BEING THOSE 0.64 OF 205 WHERE, IF A HEADMANSHIP IS PRESENT, SUCCESSION IS HEREDITARY (165)	15 74 11 131 XSQ= 3.68 PHI= 0.126 XP = 0.0552
95	IN ALL CASES ARE THOSE 1.00 OF 34 WHERE THE HIERARCHY OF NATIONAL JURISDICTION HAS FOUR, THREE, OR TWO LEVELS (76) GES,EA	95	TEND TO BE THOSE 0.86 OF 296 WHERE THE HIERARCHY OF NATIONAL JURISDICTION HAS ONE OR NO LEVELS (254) GES,EA	34 42 0 254 XSQ= 121.89 PHI= 0.608 XP = 0.
102	TEND TO BE THOSE 0.94 OF 33 WHERE CLASS STRATIFICATION IS PRESENT (203)	102	TEND TO BE THOSE 0.52 OF 287 WHERE CLASS STRATIFICATION IS ABSENT (180)	31 137 2 150 XSQ= 23.52 PHI= 0.271 XP = 0.0000
106	IN ALL CASES ARE THOSE 1.00 OF 31 WHERE CLASS STRATIFICATION, IF PRESENT, IS BASED ON SOMETHING OTHER THAN WEALTH (126)	106	TEND LESS TO BE THOSE 0.51 OF 137 WHERE CLASS STRATIFICATION, IF PRESENT, IS BASED ON SOMETHING OTHER THAN WEALTH (126)	0 67 31 70 XSQ= 23.22 PHI= -0.372 XP = 0.0000
107	TEND TO BE THOSE 0.61 OF 31 WHERE CLASS STRATIFICATION, IF PRESENT, IS BASED ON OCCUPATIONAL STATUS (43)	107	TEND TO BE THOSE 0.88 OF 137 WHERE CLASS STRATIFICATION, IF PRESENT, IS BASED ON SOMETHING OTHER THAN OCCUPATIONAL STATUS (160)	19 17 12 120 XSQ= 33.03 PHI= 0.443 XP = 0.
110	TILT TOWARD BEING THOSE 0.62 OF 34 WHERE SLAVERY IS PRESENT (163)	110	TILT TOWARD BEING THOSE 0.61 OF 285 WHERE SLAVERY IS ABSENT (218)	21 112 13 173 XSQ= 5.42 PHI= 0.130 XP = 0.0199
116	IN ALL CASES ARE THOSE 1.00 OF 3 WHERE OCCUPATIONAL SPECIALIZATION IS FULL-TIME, WHETHER OR NOT FOR SURPLUS PRODUCTION (20) JMH	116	DRIFT TOWARD BEING THOSE 0.67 OF 49 WHERE OCCUPATIONAL SPECIALIZATION IS PART-TIME ONLY (34) JMH	3 16 0 33 XSQ= 3.01 PHI= 0.240 XP = 0.0829

130	TILT TOWARD BEING THOSE 0.88 OF 8 WHERE LEATHER WORKING IS MAINLY DONE BY MALES (39)	130	TILT TOWARD BEING THOSE 0.58 OF 72 WHERE LEATHER WORKING IS MAINLY DONE BY FEMALES (45)	7 30 1 42 XSQ= 4.38 PHI= 0.234 XP = 0.0364
163	IN ALL CASES ARE THOSE 1.00 OF 3 WHERE THE EMPHASIS ON INDIVIDUAL VOLITION AS THE CAUSE OF CRIME IS HIGH (7) MJ	163	TILT TOWARD BEING THOSE 0.75 OF 12 WHERE THE EMPHASIS ON INDIVIDUAL VOLITION AS THE CAUSE OF CRIME IS LOW (10) MJ	3 3 0 9 XSQ= 2.93 PHI= 0.442 EP = 0.0440
164	IN ALL CASES ARE THOSE 1.00 OF 3 WHERE THE EMPHASIS ON INDIVIDUAL VOLITION AS THE CAUSE OR SOURCE OF ILLNESS IS LOW (9) MJ	164	DRIFT TOWARD BEING THOSE 0.64 OF 14 WHERE THE EMPHASIS ON INDIVIDUAL VOLITION AS THE CAUSE OR SOURCE OF ILLNESS IS HIGH (9) MJ	0 9 3 5 XSQ= 1.92 PHI= -0.336 EP = 0.0824
182	DRIFT LESS TOWARD BEING THOSE 0.52 OF 33 OTHER THAN WHERE THE COMMUNITY IS STRUCTURED ON A NON-CLAN BASIS AND AGAMOUS (256)	182	DRIFT MORE TOWARD BEING THOSE 0.69 OF 284 OTHER THAN WHERE THE COMMUNITY IS STRUCTURED ON A NON-CLAN BASIS AND AGAMOUS (256)	16 87 17 197 XSQ= 3.52 PHI= 0.105 XP = 0.0606
183	IN ALL CASES ARE THOSE 1.00 OF 20 WHERE THE LARGEST NON-COGNATIC KIN GROUP IS SMALLER THAN A MOEITY, I. E., A PHRATRY OR SIB OR LINEAGE (218)	183	DRIFT LESS TOWARD BEING THOSE 0.83 OF 190 WHERE THE LARGEST NON-COGNATIC KIN GROUP IS SMALLER THAN A MOEITY, I. E., A PHRATRY OR SIB OR LINEAGE (218)	0 32 20 158 XSQ= 2.78 PHI= -0.115 XP = 0.0956
186	DRIFT TOWARD BEING THOSE 0.53 OF 34 WHERE THE KIN GROUP IS EXCLUSIVELY PATRILINEAL (150)	186	DRIFT TOWARD BEING THOSE 0.65 OF 296 WHERE THE KIN GROUP IS OTHER THAN EXCLUSIVELY PATRILINEAL (250)	18 104 16 192 XSQ= 3.42 PHI= 0.102 XP = 0.0644
187	IN ALL CASES ARE THOSE 1.00 OF 34 WHERE THE KIN GROUP IS OTHER THAN EXCLUSIVELY MATRILINEAL (344)	187	TILT LESS TOWARD BEING THOSE 0.84 OF 295 WHERE THE KIN GROUP IS OTHER THAN EXCLUSIVELY MATRILINEAL (344)	0 46 34 249 XSQ= 4.94 PHI= -0.122 XP = 0.0263
190	IN ALL CASES ARE THOSE 1.00 OF 19 WHERE THE KIN GROUP IS PATRILINEAL OR DOUBLE-DESCENT, RATHER THAN MATRILINEAL (186)	190	TILT LESS TOWARD BEING THOSE 0.73 OF 186 WHERE THE KIN GROUP IS PATRILINEAL OR DOUBLE-DESCENT, RATHER THAN MATRILINEAL (186)	19 135 0 51 XSQ= 5.55 PHI= 0.164 XP = 0.0185
196	TILT MORE TOWARD BEING THOSE 0.90 OF 30 WHERE INDIVIDUAL RIGHTS IN REAL PROPERTY, AND RULES FOR INHERITANCE, ARE PRESENT (194)	196	TILT LESS TOWARD BEING THOSE 0.65 OF 209 WHERE INDIVIDUAL RIGHTS IN REAL PROPERTY, AND RULES FOR INHERITANCE, ARE PRESENT (194)	27 135 3 74 XSQ= 6.63 PHI= 0.167 XP = 0.0100

197	TILT LESS TOWARD BEING THOSE WHERE RULES FOR THE INHERITANCE OF REAL PROPERTY, IF PRESENT, FAVOR EITHER THE MALE HEIR OR LINE, OR THE FEMALE HEIR OR LINE (165)	0.70 OF 27	197	TILT MORE TOWARD BEING THOSE WHERE RULES FOR THE INHERITANCE OF REAL PROPERTY, IF PRESENT, FAVOR EITHER THE MALE HEIR OR LINE, OR THE FEMALE HEIR OR LINE (165)	0.90 OF 135	19 121 8 14 XSQ= 5.56 PHI= -0.185 XP = 0.0183
213	TILT TOWARD BEING THOSE WHERE FIRST COUSIN MARRIAGE IS PERMITTED (172)	0.65 OF 31	213	TILT TOWARD BEING THOSE WHERE FIRST COUSIN MARRIAGE IS NOT PERMITTED (198)	0.57 OF 277	20 118 11 159 XSQ= 4.57 PHI= 0.122 XP = 0.0326
214	IN ALL CASES ARE THOSE WHERE FIRST COUSIN MARRIAGE, IF PERMITTED, IS OTHER THAN UNILATERAL (144)	1.00 OF 20	214	DRIFT LESS TOWARD BEING THOSE WHERE FIRST COUSIN MARRIAGE, IF PERMITTED, IS OTHER THAN UNILATERAL (144)	0.81 OF 118	0 22 20 96 XSQ= 3.15 PHI= -0.151 XP = 0.0758
240	TILT MORE TOWARD BEING THOSE WHERE THE FAMILY, IF EXTENDED, IS SMALL OR STEM, RATHER THAN LARGE (135)	0.89 OF 18	240	TILT LESS TOWARD BEING THOSE WHERE THE FAMILY, IF EXTENDED, IS SMALL OR STEM, RATHER THAN LARGE (135)	0.61 OF 160	2 62 16 98 XSQ= 4.23 PHI= -0.154 XP = 0.0396
241	DRIFT LESS TOWARD BEING THOSE WHERE THE FAMILY, IF EXTENDED, IS LARGE OR SMALL, RATHER THAN STEM (187)	0.72 OF 18	241	DRIFT MORE TOWARD BEING THOSE WHERE THE FAMILY, IF EXTENDED, IS LARGE OR SMALL, RATHER THAN STEM (187)	0.91 OF 160	13 145 5 15 XSQ= 3.80 PHI= -0.146 XP = 0.0511
242	TILT LESS TOWARD BEING THOSE WHERE MARRIAGE IS COMMONLY OR OCCASIONALLY POLYGYNOUS, RATHER THAN MONOGAMOUS (314)	0.65 OF 34	242	TILT MORE TOWARD BEING THOSE WHERE MARRIAGE IS COMMONLY OR OCCASIONALLY POLYGYNOUS, RATHER THAN MONOGAMOUS (314)	0.84 OF 293	22 246 12 47 XSQ= 6.39 PHI= -0.140 XP = 0.0115
319	IN ALL CASES ARE THOSE WHERE PROTECTION OF THE INFANT FROM ENVIRONMENTAL DISCOMFORTS IS LOW (30) B-B-C	1.00 OF 5	319	DRIFT TOWARD BEING THOSE WHERE PROTECTION OF THE INFANT FROM ENVIRONMENTAL DISCOMFORTS IS HIGH (35) B-B-C	0.56 OF 55	0 31 5 24 XSQ= 3.79 PHI= -0.251 XP = 0.0515
326	IN ALL CASES ARE THOSE WHERE THE INFERRED TRANSITION ANXIETY BETWEEN INFANCY AND CHILDHOOD IS HIGH (32) B-B-C	1.00 OF 4	326	DRIFT TOWARD BEING THOSE WHERE THE INFERRED TRANSITION ANXIETY BETWEEN INFANCY AND CHILDHOOD IS LOW (35) B-B-C	0.57 OF 58	4 25 0 33 XSQ= 2.85 PHI= 0.214 XP = 0.0915
337	IN ALL CASES ARE THOSE WHERE THE CHILD'S INFERRED ANXIETY OVER NON-PERFORMANCE OF RESPONSIBLE BEHAVIOR IS HIGH (38) B-B-C	1.00 OF 5	337	DRIFT LESS TOWARD BEING THOSE WHERE THE CHILD'S INFERRED ANXIETY OVER NON-PERFORMANCE OF RESPONSIBLE BEHAVIOR IS HIGH (38) B-B-C	0.51 OF 63	5 32 0 31 XSQ= 2.76 PHI= 0.201 XP = 0.0969

344	IN ALL CASES ARE THOSE 1.00 OF 5 WHERE THE TOTAL POSITIVE PRESSURE TOWARD DEVELOPING SELF-RELIANT BEHAVIOR IN THE CHILD IS HIGH (36) B-B-C	344	DRIFT TOWARD BEING THOSE 0.56 OF 66 WHERE THE TOTAL POSITIVE PRESSURE TOWARD DEVELOPING SELF-RELIANT BEHAVIOR IN THE CHILD IS LOW (40) B-B-C	5 29 0 37 XSQ= 3.82 PHI= 0.232 XP = 0.0506
345	IN ALL CASES ARE THOSE 1.00 OF 5 WHERE THE CHILD'S INFERRED ANXIETY OVER NON-PERFORMANCE OF SELF-RELIANT BEHAVIOR IS HIGH (37) B-B-C	345	TILT TOWARD BEING THOSE 0.58 OF 66 WHERE THE CHILD'S INFERRED ANXIETY OVER NON-PERFORMANCE OF SELF-RELIANT BEHAVIOR IS LOW (39) B-B-C	5 28 0 38 XSQ= 4.10 PHI= 0.240 XP = 0.0430
370	TILT MORE TOWARD BEING THOSE 0.83 OF 23 WHERE THE SEGREGATION OF ADOLESCENT BOYS IS ABSENT (148)	370	TILT LESS TOWARD BEING THOSE 0.58 OF 217 WHERE THE SEGREGATION OF ADOLESCENT BOYS IS ABSENT (148)	4 91 19 126 XSQ= 4.26 PHI= -0.133 XP = 0.0390
377	TILT LESS TOWARD BEING THOSE 0.56 OF 32 WHERE MALE GENITAL MUTILATION IS ABSENT (242)	377	TILT MORE TOWARD BEING THOSE 0.76 OF 290 WHERE MALE GENITAL MUTILATION IS ABSENT (242)	14 69 18 221 XSQ= 5.00 PHI= 0.125 XP = 0.0253
390	TILT TOWARD BEING THOSE 0.53 OF 19 WHERE PREMARITAL SEX RELATIONS ARE STRONGLY PUNISHED AND IN FACT RARE (47) JTW,EA	390	TILT TOWARD BEING THOSE 0.77 OF 150 WHERE PREMARITAL SEX RELATIONS ARE WEAKLY PUNISHED AND IN FACT NOT RARE OR PUNISHED ONLY IF PREGNANCY RESULTS, OR FREELY PERMITTED (132) JTW,EA	10 35 9 115 XSQ= 5.99 PHI= 0.188 XP = 0.0144
391	TEND TO BE THOSE 0.89 OF 19 WHERE PREMARITAL SEX RELATIONS ARE STRONGLY PUNISHED AND IN FACT RARE, OR WEAKLY PUNISHED AND IN FACT NOT RARE (89) JTW,EA	391	TEND TO BE THOSE 0.54 OF 150 WHERE PREMARITAL SEX RELATIONS ARE PUNISHED ONLY IF PREGNANCY RESULTS, OR FREELY PERMITTED (90) JTW,EA	17 69 2 81 XSQ= 11.07 PHI= 0.256 XP = 0.0009
424	IN ALL CASES ARE THOSE 1.00 OF 3 WHERE RELIGIOUS SPECIALISTS ARE FULL-TIME, RATHER THAN PART-TIME (21) JMH	424	DRIFT TOWARD BEING THOSE 0.65 OF 49 WHERE RELIGIOUS SPECIALISTS ARE PART-TIME, RATHER THAN FULL-TIME (33) JMH	3 17 0 32 XSQ= 2.71 PHI= 0.228 XP = 0.0998
426	LEAN MORE TOWARD BEING THOSE 0.85 OF 27 WHERE A HIGH GOD IS PRESENT (156) GES,EA	426	LEAN LESS TOWARD BEING THOSE 0.57 OF 230 WHERE A HIGH GOD IS PRESENT (156) GES,EA	23 131 4 99 XSQ= 6.89 PHI= 0.164 XP = 0.0087
428	IN ALL CASES ARE THOSE 1.00 OF 16 WHERE A HIGH GOD, IF PRESENT AND ACTIVE, SUPPORTS HUMAN MORALITY, RATHER THAN NOT SUPPORTING IT (61) GES,EA	428	LEAN LESS TOWARD BEING THOSE 0.62 OF 69 WHERE A HIGH GOD, IF PRESENT AND ACTIVE, SUPPORTS HUMAN MORALITY, RATHER THAN NOT SUPPORTING IT (61) GES,EA	16 43 0 26 XSQ= 7.00 PHI= 0.287 XP = 0.0081

```
458 TEND TO BE THOSE              0.93 OF  15    458 TEND TO BE THOSE              0.75 OF 154       14   38
    WHERE GAMES, IF PRESENT,                         WHERE GAMES, IF PRESENT,                          1  116
    INCLUDE GAMES OF STRATEGY  (52) R-A-B,EA         DO NOT INCLUDE                             XSQ=   27.11
                                                     GAMES OF STRATEGY  (119) R-A-B,EA          PHI=   0.401
                                                                                                XP =  0.0000

459 DRIFT TOWARD BEING THOSE      0.73 OF  15    459 DRIFT TOWARD BEING THOSE      0.55 OF 154       11   69
    WHERE GAMES, IF PRESENT,                         WHERE GAMES, IF PRESENT,                          4   85
    INCLUDE GAMES OF CHANCE  (82) R-A-B,EA           DO NOT INCLUDE                             XSQ=    3.39
                                                     GAMES OF CHANCE  (89) R-A-B,EA             PHI=   0.142
                                                                                                XP =  0.0655

460 TILT MORE TOWARD BEING THOSE  0.93 OF  15    460 TILT LESS TOWARD BEING THOSE  0.57 OF 154        1   66
    WHERE GAMES, IF PRESENT,                         WHERE GAMES, IF PRESENT,                         14   88
    ARE NOT LIMITED TO                               ARE NOT LIMITED TO                         XSQ=    6.05
    GAMES OF SKILL ONLY  (104) R-A-B,EA              GAMES OF SKILL ONLY  (104) R-A-B,EA        PHI=  -0.189
                                                                                                XP =  0.0139

468 IN ALL CASES ARE THOSE        1.00 OF   3    468 TILT TOWARD BEING THOSE       0.73 OF  49        3   13
    WHERE CONTACT WITH OTHER CULTURES                WHERE CONTACT WITH OTHER CULTURES                 0   36
    IS FREQUENT, RATHER THAN                         IS REGULAR OR IRREGULAR, RATHER THAN       XSQ=    4.13
    REGULAR OR IRREGULAR  (17) JMH                   FREQUENT  (37) JMH                         PHI=   0.282
                                                                                                XP =  0.0421

473 IN ALL CASES ARE THOSE        1.00 OF   7    473 DRIFT LESS TOWARD BEING THOSE 0.60 OF  77        0   31
    WHERE SENSITIVITY TO INSULT                      WHERE SENSITIVITY TO INSULT                       7   46
    IS MODERATE OR NEGLIGIBLE  (56) PES              IS MODERATE OR NEGLIGIBLE  (56) PES        XSQ=    2.90
                                                                                                PHI=  -0.186
                                                                                                XP =  0.0883
```

95 CULTURES
WHERE THE HIERARCHY
OF NATIONAL JURISDICTION HAS
FOUR, THREE, OR TWO LEVELS (76) GES,EA

95 CULTURES
WHERE THE HIERARCHY
OF NATIONAL JURISDICTION HAS
ONE OR NO LEVELS (254) GES,EA

BACKGROUND ON PAGE 86

BOTH SUBJECT AND PREDICATE

76 IN LEFT COLUMN

ALBANIANS	ALCRESE	AMERICANS	ASHANTI	AZANDE	AZTEC	BABWA	BAMILEKE	BEMBA	BOERS
BRAZILIANS	BULGARIANS	CAMBODIANS	CHEROKEE	CHIBCHA	COORG	CZECHS	DAGUR	DARC	DUTCH
EGYPTIANS	FCN	FUTAJALCNKE	GANCA	HASINAI	HAWAIIANS	HEBREWS	INCA	IRISH	JAPANESE
JAVANESE	KABYLE	KAZAK	KERALA	KHALKA	KOREANS	KUBA	LAMBA	LAU	LOZI
MACASSARESE	MALAYS	MASAI	MBUNDU	MERINA	MIN CHINESE	MONGO	MOSSI	NDEMBU	NUPE
NYAKYUSA	NYCRO	OKINAWANS	PALAUANS	PATHAN	PONAPEANS	REGEIBAT	RUNDI	SAMOANS	SERBS
SINHALESE	SOMALI	SONGHAI	SOTHO	SWAZI	SYRIANS	THAI	THONGA	TIGRINYA	TURKMEN
VENDA	VIETNAMESE	WALLCONS	WOLOF	YAKUT	YORUBA				

254 IN RIGHT COLUMN

ABIPON	ABCR	AINU	AKHA	ALACALUF	AMBA	ANDAMANESE	APINAYE	ARANDA	ARAPESH
ARAUCANIANS	ATAYAL	ATSUGEWI	AWEIKOMA	BACAIRI	BAMBARA	BANDA	BARABRA	BARI	BASSERI
BAYA	BEJA	BHIL	BHUIYA	BIRIFOR	BLACK CARIB	BORORO	BOTOCUDO	BOZO	BUNLAP
BURUSHO	CADUVEO	CAGABA	CALLINAGO	CAMAYURA	CARIB	CAYAPA	CHAGGA	CHAMACOCO	CHENCHU
CHERKESS	CHEYENNE	CHIR-APACHE	CHIRIGUANO	CHOCO	CHOROTI	CHORTI	CHUKCHEE	COCHITI	COPR ESKIMO
CREE	CREEK	CROW	CUNA	DELAWARE	DIEGUENO	DIERI	DILLING	DOGON	DOROBO
ELLICE	ENGA	EYAK	FANG	FOX	GARO	GILYAK	GISU	GOAJIRO	GOND
GROS VENTRE	GUAHIBO	GUATO	GURE	HAIDA	HANO	HANUNOO	HAVASUPAI	HAZARA	HERERO
HUICHOL	HUKUNDIKA	HURON	IBAN	IFUGAO	ILA	INGALIK	INGASSANA	IRAQW	JEMEZ
JIVARO	JUKUN	KACHIN	KAPAUKU	KARIERA	KASKA	KATAB	KERAKI	KHASI	KIKUYU
KISSI	KOHISTANI	KOL	KORYAK	KPE	KUNG	KURTATCHI	KUTENAI	KWAKIUTL	LAKHER
LAMET	LANGO	LAPPS	LEPCHA	LESU	LHOTA NAGA	LOLO	LUC	MAM	MAMBILA
MAMVU	MANDAN	MANGAIANS	MANIHIKI	MANUS	MAORI	MARGI	MARICOPA	MARQUESANS	MARSHALLESE
MATACO	MATAKAM	MAYA	MBUTI	MENDE	MIAMI	MIAO	MINCHIA	MISKITO	MIWOK
MNONG GAR	MONGUOR	MOTA	MOTILON	MUNDURUCU	MURINBATA	MURNGIN	MZAB	NABESNA	NAMA
NAMBICUARA	NANDI	NATCHEZ	NAVAHO	NICOBARESE	NOMLAKI	NUER	NUNIVAK	NURI	OJIBWA
OMAHA	ONA	ONTONG-JAVA	ORAON	PAEZ	PAIWAN	PAPAGO	PARAUJANO	PAWNEE	PUKAPUKA
PURARI	PURUM	RIFFIANS	RWALA	SAGADA	SAMOYED	SANDAWE	SANPOIL	SANTAL	SARSI
SELUNG	SEMANG	SENIANG	SHERENTE	SHILLUK	SHLUH	SIRIONO	SIUAI	SIWANS	SUBANUN
TAGBANUA	TALAMANCA	TALLENSI	TANALA	TAOS	TAPIRAPE	TARAHUMARA	TAREUMIUT	TEDA	TEHUELCHE
TENDA	TENETEHARA	TENINO	TERA	TERENA	TESO	TIKOPIA	TIMBIRA	TIMUCUA	TIV
TIWI	TODA	TOKELAU	TOLOWA	TORAJA	TOTONAC	TRISTAN	TROBRIAND	TRUKESE	TRUMAI
TSHIMSHIAN	TUBATULABAL	TUCANO	TUCUNA	TUNEBO	TUPINAMBA	TURKANA	TWANA	ULAWANS	UTE
VEDDA	WAICA	WANTOAT	WAPISHANA	WARRAU	WASHO	WICHITA	WIKMUNKAN	WITOTO	WOGEO
WOLEAIANS	YABARANA	YAGUA	YAHGAN	YAKO	YAO	YAPESE	YARURO	YOKUTS	YOMBE
YUKAGHIR	YUKI	YUROK	ZUNI						

70 EXCLUDED BECAUSE UNASCERTAINED

3	LEAN LESS TOWARC BEING THOSE LOCATED CUTSIDE CF AFRICA (320)	0.67 OF 76	3	LEAN MORE TOWARD BEING THOSE LOCATED OUTSIDE OF AFRICA (320)	0.83 OF 254	25 44 51 210 XSQ= 7.66 PHI= 0.152 XP = 0.0056
4	TEND LESS TO BE THCSE LOCATED CUTSIDE CF THE CIRCUM-MEDITERRANEAN (355)	0.75 OF 76	4	TEND MORE TO BE THOSE LOCATED OUTSIDE OF THE CIRCUM-MEDITERRANEAN (355)	0.95 OF 254	19 13 57 241 XSQ= 24.18 PHI= 0.271 XP = 0.0000
5	DRIFT LESS TCWARD BEING THOSE LOCATED OUTSIDE CF EAST EURASIA (330)	0.75 OF 76	5	DRIFT MORE TOWARD BEING THOSE LOCATED OUTSIDE OF EAST EURASIA (330)	0.84 OF 254	19 40 57 214 XSQ= 2.81 PHI= 0.092 XP = 0.0937
8	TEND MORE TO BE THCSE LOCATED CUTSIDE CF NORTH AMERICA (330)	0.96 OF 76	8	TEND LESS TO BE THOSE LOCATED OUTSIDE OF NORTH AMERICA (330)	0.78 OF 254	3 56 73 198 XSQ= 11.85 PHI= -0.189 XP = 0.0006
9	TEND MORE TO BE THCSE LOCATED CUTSIDE CF SOUTH AMERICA (335)	0.97 OF 76	9	TEND LESS TO BE THOSE LOCATED OUTSIDE OF SOUTH AMERICA (335)	0.78 OF 254	2 56 74 198 XSQ= 13.91 PHI= -0.205 XP = 0.0002
44	TEND MORE TO BE THCSE WHERE SETTLEMENTS ARE FIXEC (222)	0.84 OF 76	44	TEND LESS TO BE THOSE WHERE SETTLEMENTS ARE FIXED (222)	0.61 OF 253	64 155 12 98 XSQ= 12.81 PHI= 0.197 XP = 0.0003
46	LEAN MORE TOWARC BEING THCSE OTHER THAN WHERE SETTLEMENTS ARE NON-FIXED AND MCVEMENT IS NOMADIC (260)	0.92 OF 76	46	LEAN LESS TOWARD BEING THOSE OTHER THAN WHERE SETTLEMENTS ARE NON-FIXED AND MOVEMENT IS NOMADIC (260)	0.74 OF 253	6 66 70 187 XSQ= 10.28 PHI= -0.177 XP = 0.0013
51	TEND MORE TO BE THCSE WHERE SUBSISTENCE IS PRIMARILY BY FOOD PRODUCTION -- I. E., AGRICULTURE OR HUSBANDRY -- RATHER THAN BY GATHERING (253)	0.93 OF 76	51	TEND LESS TO BE THOSE WHERE SUBSISTENCE IS PRIMARILY BY FOOD PRODUCTION -- I. E., AGRICULTURE OR HUSBANDRY -- RATHER THAN BY GATHERING (253)	0.52 OF 254	71 132 5 122 XSQ= 40.73 PHI= 0.351 XP = 0.
53	TEND TO BE THOSE WHERE FOOD PRODUCTION IS BY INTENSIVE AGRICULTURE, RATHER THAN BY SIMPLE AGRICULTURE CR INCIPIENT FOCD PRODUCTION (91)	0.62 OF 69	53	TEND TO BE THOSE WHERE FOOD PRODUCTION IS BY SIMPLE AGRICULTURE OR INCIPIENT FOOD PRODUCTION, RATHER THAN BY INTENSIVE AGRICULTURE (147)	0.72 OF 159	43 45 26 114 XSQ= 22.08 PHI= 0.311 XP = 0.0000

55	TEND TO BE THOSE WHERE FOOD PRODUCTION IS BY INTENSIVE AGRICULTURE, RATHER THAN BY SIMPLE AGRICULTURE (91)	0.66 OF 65	55	TEND TO BE THOSE WHERE FOOD PRODUCTION IS BY SIMPLE AGRICULTURE, RATHER THAN BY INTENSIVE AGRICULTURE (101)	0.64 OF 124	43 45 22 79 XSQ= 14.11 PHI= 0.273 XP = 0.0002
62	TEND MORE TO BE THOSE WHERE HUSBANDRY OF SOME KIND IS PRESENT (228)	0.89 OF 76	62	TEND LESS TO BE THOSE WHERE HUSBANDRY OF SOME KIND IS PRESENT (228)	0.61 OF 254	68 155 8 99 XSQ= 20.33 PHI= 0.248 XP = 0.0000
63	TILT MORE TOWARD BEING THOSE WHERE HUSBANDRY, IF PRESENT, IS PRINCIPALLY IN THE FORM OF BOVINE, EQUINE, CAMEL-LIKE, OR DEER-LIKE ANIMALS, RATHER THAN PIGS, SHEEP, OR GOATS (152)	0.78 OF 68	63	TILT LESS TOWARD BEING THOSE WHERE HUSBANDRY, IF PRESENT, IS PRINCIPALLY IN THE FORM OF BOVINE, EQUINE, CAMEL-LIKE, OR DEER-LIKE ANIMALS, RATHER THAN PIGS, SHEEP, OR GOATS (152)	0.62 OF 155	53 96 15 59 XSQ= 4.76 PHI= 0.146 XP = 0.0291
71	TEND TO BE THOSE WHERE METAL WORKING IS PRESENT (98)	0.85 OF 52	71	TEND TO BE THOSE WHERE METAL WORKING IS ABSENT (153)	0.73 OF 189	44 51 8 138 XSQ= 54.33 PHI= 0.475 XP = 0.
73	LEAN TOWARD BEING THOSE WHERE WEAVING IS PRESENT (118)	0.67 OF 51	73	LEAN TOWARD BEING THOSE WHERE WEAVING IS ABSENT (130)	0.57 OF 188	34 80 17 108 XSQ= 8.41 PHI= 0.188 XP = 0.0037
74	LEAN MORE TOWARD BEING THOSE WHERE POTTERY IS PRESENT (145)	0.81 OF 48	74	LEAN LESS TOWARD BEING THOSE WHERE POTTERY IS PRESENT (145)	0.57 OF 181	39 103 9 78 XSQ= 8.54 PHI= 0.193 XP = 0.0035
77	DRIFT TOWARD BEING THOSE WHERE THE WRITING SYSTEM IS ALPHABETIC-OR-PHONETIC, RATHER THAN BEING MNEMONIC OR ABSENT (15) JMH	0.50 OF 12	77	DRIFT TOWARD BEING THOSE WHERE THE WRITING SYSTEM IS MNEMONIC OR ABSENT, RATHER THAN BEING ALPHABETIC-OR-PHONETIC (39) JMH	0.80 OF 40	6 8 6 32 XSQ= 2.84 PHI= 0.234 XP = 0.0922
79	TEND LESS TO BE THOSE WHERE NO CITY IS PRESENT (201)	0.63 OF 60	79	IN ALL CASES ARE THOSE WHERE NO CITY IS PRESENT (201)	1.00 OF 161	22 0 38 161 XSQ= 61.53 PHI= 0.528 XP = 0.
80	TEND TO BE THOSE WHERE A CITY OR TOWN IS PRESENT (39)	0.52 OF 60	80	TEND TO BE THOSE WHERE NO CITY OR TOWN IS PRESENT (185)	0.96 OF 161	31 6 29 155 XSQ= 68.67 PHI= 0.557 XP = 0.

81	TEND TO BE THOSE WHERE A CITY OR TOWN IS PRESENT, OR THE AVERAGE COMMUNITY SIZE IS 200 OR GREATER (89)	0.68 OF 60	81	TEND TO BE THOSE WHERE NO CITY OR TOWN IS PRESENT, AND THE AVERAGE COMMUNITY SIZE IS SMALLER THAN 200 (135)	0.72 OF 161	41 45 19 116 XSQ= 28.31 PHI= 0.358 XP = 0.0000
84	TEND TO BE THOSE WHERE THE LEVEL OF POLITICAL INTEGRATION IS THE LARGE STATE (42) GPM	0.55 OF 60	84	TEND TO BE THOSE WHERE THE LEVEL OF POLITICAL INTEGRATION IS THE LITTLE STATE, THE MINIMAL STATE, THE AUTONOMOUS COMMUNITY, OR THE FAMILY (262) GPM	0.99 OF 198	33 2 27 196 XSQ= 109.91 PHI= 0.653 XP = 0.
85	TEND TO BE THOSE WHERE THE LEVEL OF POLITICAL INTEGRATION IS THE LARGE STATE, OR THE LITTLE STATE (70) GPM	0.82 OF 60	85	TEND TO BE THOSE WHERE THE LEVEL OF POLITICAL INTEGRATION IS THE MINIMAL STATE, THE AUTONOMOUS COMMUNITY, OR THE FAMILY (234) GPM	0.96 OF 198	49 8 11 190 XSQ= 156.73 PHI= 0.779 XP = 0.
86	TEND TO BE THOSE WHERE THE LEVEL OF POLITICAL INTEGRATION IS THE LARGE STATE, THE LITTLE STATE, OR THE MINIMAL STATE (148) GPM	0.98 OF 60	86	TEND TO BE THOSE WHERE THE LEVEL OF POLITICAL INTEGRATION IS THE AUTONOMOUS COMMUNITY, OR THE FAMILY (156) GPM	0.68 OF 198	59 63 1 135 XSQ= 79.08 PHI= 0.554 XP = 0.
87	IN ALL CASES ARE THOSE WHERE THE LEVEL OF POLITICAL INTEGRATION IS THE LARGE STATE, THE LITTLE STATE, THE MINIMAL STATE, OR THE AUTONOMOUS COMMUNITY (281) GPM	1.00 OF 60	87	TILT LESS TOWARD BEING THOSE WHERE THE LEVEL OF POLITICAL INTEGRATION IS THE LARGE STATE, THE LITTLE STATE, THE MINIMAL STATE, OR THE AUTONOMOUS COMMUNITY (281) GPM	0.91 OF 198	60 180 0 18 XSQ= 4.55 PHI= 0.133 XP = 0.0330
98	DRIFT MORE TOWARD BEING THOSE WHERE THE HIERARCHY OF LOCAL JURISDICTION HAS FOUR OR THREE LEVELS (238) GES,EA	0.80 OF 76	98	DRIFT LESS TOWARD BEING THOSE WHERE THE HIERARCHY OF LOCAL JURISDICTION HAS FOUR OR THREE LEVELS (238) GES,EA	0.69 OF 254	61 176 15 78 XSQ= 2.96 PHI= 0.095 XP = 0.0854
102	TEND TO BE THOSE WHERE CLASS STRATIFICATION IS PRESENT (203)	0.88 OF 74	102	TEND TO BE THOSE WHERE CLASS STRATIFICATION IS ABSENT (180)	0.58 OF 246	65 103 9 143 XSQ= 46.38 PHI= 0.381 XP = 0.
106	TEND TO BE THOSE WHERE CLASS STRATIFICATION, IF PRESENT, IS BASED ON SOMETHING OTHER THAN WEALTH (126)	0.92 OF 65	106	TEND TO BE THOSE WHERE CLASS STRATIFICATION, IF PRESENT, IS BASED ON WEALTH (77)	0.60 OF 103	5 62 60 41 XSQ= 43.65 PHI= -0.510 XP = 0.
107	TEND LESS TO BE THOSE WHERE CLASS STRATIFICATION, IF PRESENT, IS BASED ON SOMETHING OTHER THAN OCCUPATIONAL STATUS (160)	0.54 OF 65	107	TEND MORE TO BE THOSE WHERE CLASS STRATIFICATION, IF PRESENT, IS BASED ON SOMETHING OTHER THAN OCCUPATIONAL STATUS (160)	0.94 OF 103	30 6 35 97 XSQ= 36.14 PHI= 0.464 XP = 0.

109	TEND LESS TC BE THCSE WHERE CASTES ARE ABSENT (317)	0.70 OF 69	109	TEND MORE TO BE THOSE WHERE CASTES ARE ABSENT (317)	0.91 CF 240	21 22 48 218 XSQ= 18.50 PHI= 0.245 XP = 0.0000
110	TEND TC BE THCSE WHERE SLAVERY IS PRESENT (163)	0.67 OF 75	110	TEND TO BE THOSE WHERE SLAVERY IS ABSENT (218)	0.66 OF 244	50 83 25 161 XSQ= 23.83 PHI= 0.273 XP = 0.0000
116	TEND TC BE THCSE WHERE CCCUPATIONAL SPECIALIZATION IS FULL-TIME, WHETHER OR NCT FOR SURPLUS PRCDUCTICN (20) JMH	0.83 OF 12	116	TEND TO BE THOSE WHERE OCCUPATIONAL SPECIALIZATICN IS PART-TIME ONLY (34) JMH	0.77 CF 40	10 9 2 31 XSQ= 12.23 PHI= 0.485 XP = 0.0005
129	LEAN TCWARD BEING THOSE WHERE WEAVING IS MAINLY DONE BY MALES (31)	0.54 OF 26	129	LEAN TOWARD BEING THOSE WHERE WEAVING IS MAINLY DONE BY FEMALES (73)	0.79 OF 76	14 16 12 60 XSQ= 8.52 PHI= 0.289 XP = 0.0035
130	LEAN TCWARD BEING THCSE WHERE LEATHER WCRKING IS MAINLY DCNE BY MALES (39)	0.81 OF 16	130	LEAN TOWARD BEING THOSE WHERE LEATHER WORKING IS MAINLY DONE BY FEMALES (45)	0.63 CF 64	13 24 3 40 XSQ= 8.17 PHI= 0.320 XP = 0.0042
136	DRIFT TCWARD BEING THCSE WHERE FULL-TIME ENTREPRENEURS ARE PRESENT (18) JV	0.88 OF 8	136	DRIFT TOWARD BEING THOSE WHERE FULL-TIME ENTREPRENEURS ARE ABSENT (14) JV	0.55 OF 22	7 10 1 12 XSQ= 2.68 PHI= 0.299 EP = 0.0924
137	TILT TCWARD BEING THCSE WHERE INVIDICUS DISPLAY OF WEALTH IS STRONGLY EMPHASIZEC (37) PES	0.63 OF 24	137	TILT TOWARD BEING THOSE WHERE INVIDIOUS DISPLAY OF WEALTH IS MODERATELY, LITTLE, CR NEGATIVELY EMPHASIZED (52) PES	0.69 CF 61	15 19 9 42 XSQ= 5.81 PHI= 0.261 XP = 0.0159
138	IN ALL CASES ARE THOSE WHERE SUPERORDINATE JUSTICE IS PRESENT (22) BBW	1.00 OF 8	138	LEAN TOWARD BEING THOSE WHERE SUPERORDINATE JUSTICE IS ABSENT (18) BBW	0.57 OF 30	8 13 0 17 XSQ= 6.07 PHI= 0.400 EP = 0.0047
147	IN ALL CASES ARE THCSE WHERE CCDIFIED LAWS ARE PRESENT (20) LWS	1.00 OF 7	147	TILT LESS TOWARD BEING THOSE WHERE CODIFIED LAWS ARE PRESENT (20) LWS	0.52 CF 25	7 13 0 12 XSQ= 3.52 PHI= 0.332 EP = 0.0288

149	TILT TOWARD BEING THOSE WHERE THE INCIDENCE OF THEFT IS HIGH (18) B-B-C	0.88 OF 8	149	TILT TOWARD BEING THOSE WHERE THE INCIDENCE OF THEFT IS LOW (19) B-B-C	0.65 OF 26	7 9 1 17 XSQ= 4.91 PHI= 0.380 EP = 0.0145
152	IN ALL CASES ARE THOSE WHERE THE DIFFERENTIATION OF THE JURIDICAL AGENCY FROM THE MEDICAL AGENCY IS HIGH (10) MJ	1.00 OF 7	152	LEAN TOWARD BEING THOSE WHERE THE DIFFERENTIATION OF THE JURIDICAL AGENCY FROM THE MEDICAL AGENCY IS LOW (10) MJ	0.82 OF 11	7 2 0 9 XSQ= 8.42 PHI= 0.684 EP = 0.0023
163	TILT TOWARD BEING THOSE WHERE THE EMPHASIS ON INDIVIDUAL VOLITION AS THE CAUSE OF CRIME IS HIGH (7) MJ	0.83 OF 6	163	TILT TOWARD BEING THOSE WHERE THE EMPHASIS ON INDIVIDUAL VOLITION AS THE CAUSE OF CRIME IS LOW (10) MJ	0.89 OF 9	5 1 1 8 XSQ= 5.10 PHI= 0.583 EP = 0.0110
175	DRIFT MORE TOWARD BEING THOSE WHERE THE COMMUNITY IS 'KIN-HETEROGENEOUS,' I. E. OTHER THAN A CLAN COMMUNITY OR A DEME (260)	0.78 OF 73	175	DRIFT LESS TOWARD BEING THOSE WHERE THE COMMUNITY IS 'KIN-HETEROGENEOUS,' I. E. OTHER THAN A CLAN COMMUNITY OR A DEME (260)	0.67 OF 244	16 81 57 163 XSQ= 2.86 PHI= -0.095 XP = 0.0910
181	TILT MORE TOWARD BEING THOSE WHERE THE COMMUNITY IS OTHER THAN A DEME (337)	0.97 OF 73	181	TILT LESS TOWARD BEING THOSE WHERE THE COMMUNITY IS OTHER THAN A DEME (337)	0.87 OF 244	2 31 71 213 XSQ= 4.96 PHI= -0.125 XP = 0.0259
182	TILT LESS TOWARD BEING THOSE OTHER THAN WHERE THE COMMUNITY IS STRUCTURED ON A NON-CLAN BASIS AND AGAMOUS (256)	0.56 OF 73	182	TILT MORE TOWARD BEING THOSE OTHER THAN WHERE THE COMMUNITY IS STRUCTURED ON A NON-CLAN BASIS AND AGAMOUS (256)	0.71 OF 244	32 71 41 173 XSQ= 4.91 PHI= 0.124 XP = 0.0267
183	IN ALL CASES ARE THOSE WHERE THE LARGEST NON-COGNATIC KIN GROUP IS SMALLER THAN A MOEITY, I. E., A PHRATRY OR SIB OR LINEAGE (218)	1.00 OF 54	183	TEND LESS TO BE THOSE WHERE THE LARGEST NON-COGNATIC KIN GROUP IS SMALLER THAN A MOEITY, I. E., A PHRATRY OR SIB OR LINEAGE (218)	0.79 OF 156	0 32 54 124 XSQ= 11.53 PHI= -0.234 XP = 0.0007
190	DRIFT MORE TOWARD BEING THOSE WHERE THE KIN GROUP IS PATRILINEAL OR DOUBLE-DESCENT, RATHER THAN MATRILINEAL (186)	0.85 OF 53	190	DRIFT LESS TOWARD BEING THOSE WHERE THE KIN GROUP IS PATRILINEAL OR DOUBLE-DESCENT, RATHER THAN MATRILINEAL (186)	0.72 OF 152	45 109 8 43 XSQ= 2.99 PHI= 0.121 XP = 0.0838
196	TEND MORE TO BE THOSE WHERE INDIVIDUAL RIGHTS IN REAL PROPERTY, AND RULES FOR INHERITANCE, ARE PRESENT (194)	0.89 OF 61	196	TEND LESS TO BE THOSE WHERE INDIVIDUAL RIGHTS IN REAL PROPERTY, AND RULES FOR INHERITANCE, ARE PRESENT (194)	0.61 OF 178	54 108 7 70 XSQ= 14.89 PHI= 0.250 XP = 0.0001

209	LEAN MORE TOWARD BEING THOSE WHERE MARITAL RESIDENCE IS PATRILOCAL, VIRILOCAL, OR AVUNCULOCAL, RATHER THAN MATRILOCAL OR UXORILOCAL (270)	0.92 OF 65	209	LEAN LESS TOWARD BEING THOSE WHERE MARITAL RESIDENCE IS PATRILOCAL, VIRILOCAL, OR AVUNCULOCAL, RATHER THAN MATRILOCAL OR UXORILOCAL (270)	0.76 OF 214	60 162 5 52 XSQ= 7.47 PHI= 0.164 XP = 0.0063
210	TILT MORE TOWARD BEING THOSE WHERE MARITAL RESIDENCE IS PATRILOCAL, RATHER THAN MATRILOCAL (169)	0.95 OF 42	210	TILT LESS TOWARD BEING THOSE WHERE MARITAL RESIDENCE IS PATRILOCAL, RATHER THAN MATRILOCAL (169)	0.80 OF 125	40 100 2 25 XSQ= 4.32 PHI= 0.161 XP = 0.0377
213	DRIFT TOWARD BEING THOSE WHERE FIRST COUSIN MARRIAGE IS PERMITTED (172)	0.56 OF 70	213	DRIFT TOWARD BEING THOSE WHERE FIRST COUSIN MARRIAGE IS NOT PERMITTED (198)	0.58 OF 238	39 99 31 139 XSQ= 3.81 PHI= 0.111 XP = 0.0510
214	IN ALL CASES ARE THOSE WHERE FIRST COUSIN MARRIAGE, IF PERMITTED, IS OTHER THAN UNILATERAL (144)	1.00 OF 39	214	LEAN LESS TOWARD BEING THOSE WHERE FIRST COUSIN MARRIAGE, IF PERMITTED, IS OTHER THAN UNILATERAL (144)	0.78 OF 99	0 22 39 77 XSQ= 8.72 PHI= -0.251 XP = 0.0031
254	IN ALL CASES ARE THOSE WHERE HOUSEHOLD AUTHORITY IS ON THE FATHER'S SIDE, RATHER THAN THE MOTHER'S (9) CA	1.00 OF 5	254	TILT TOWARD BEING THOSE WHERE HOUSEHOLD AUTHORITY IS ON THE MOTHER'S SIDE, RATHER THAN THE FATHER'S (6) DA	0.75 OF 8	5 2 0 6 XSQ= 4.27 PHI= 0.573 EP = 0.0210
278	TILT TOWARD BEING THOSE WHERE PROPERTY RIGHTS IN WOMEN ARE PRESENT (8) LWS	0.83 OF 6	278	TILT TOWARD BEING THOSE WHERE PROPERTY RIGHTS IN WOMEN ARE UNIMPORTANT OR ABSENT (14) LWS	0.80 OF 15	5 3 1 12 XSQ= 4.85 PHI= 0.481 EP = 0.0139
282	TILT TOWARD BEING THOSE WHERE THE STRENGTH OF DESIRE FOR CHILDREN IS HIGH (16) BCA	0.86 OF 7	282	TILT TOWARD BEING THOSE WHERE THE STRENGTH OF DESIRE FOR CHILDREN IS LOW OR ABSENT (20) BCA	0.68 OF 25	6 8 1 17 XSQ= 4.41 PHI= 0.371 EP = 0.0265
286	DRIFT TOWARD BEING THOSE WHERE THE NUMBER OF FOOD TABOOS DURING PREGNANCY IS LOW OR ABSENT (14) BCA	0.71 OF 7	286	DRIFT TOWARD BEING THOSE WHERE THE NUMBER OF FOOD TABOOS DURING PREGNANCY IS HIGH (20) BCA	0.68 OF 25	2 17 5 8 XSQ= 2.08 PHI= -0.255 EP = 0.0906
295	IN ALL CASES ARE THOSE WHERE THE SEVERITY OF PUNISHMENT FOR ABORTION IS HIGH (11) BCA	1.00 OF 6	295	TILT TOWARD BEING THOSE WHERE THE SEVERITY OF PUNISHMENT FOR ABORTION IS LOW OR ABSENT (12) BCA	0.71 OF 14	6 4 0 10 XSQ= 5.95 PHI= 0.546 EP = 0.0108

309	TILT TOWARD BEING THOSE 0.90 OF 10 WHERE ORAL SOCIALIZATION ANXIETY IS HIGH (26) W-C	309	TILT TOWARD BEING THOSE 0.59 OF 39 WHERE ORAL SOCIALIZATION ANXIETY IS LOW (27) W-C		9 16 1 23 XSQ= 5.81 PHI= 0.344 XP = 0.0160
314	LEAN TOWARD BEING THOSE 0.57 OF 14 WHERE THE INCIDENCE OF MOTHER-CHILD HOUSEHOLDS IS HIGH (19) W-D,S	314	LEAN TOWARD BEING THOSE 0.83 OF 60 WHERE THE INCIDENCE OF MOTHER-CHILD HOUSEHOLDS IS LOW (61) W-D,S		8 10 6 50 XSQ= 8.02 PHI= 0.329 XP = 0.0046
317	LEAN TOWARD BEING THOSE 0.79 OF 14 WHERE DISPLAY OF AFFECTION TOWARD THE INFANT IS LOW (29) B-B-C	317	LEAN TOWARD BEING THOSE 0.67 OF 49 WHERE DISPLAY OF AFFECTION TOWARD THE INFANT IS HIGH (39) B-B-C		3 33 11 16 XSQ= 7.59 PHI= -0.347 XP = 0.0059
318	LEAN TOWARD BEING THOSE 0.75 OF 16 WHERE THE OVERALL INDULGENCE OF THE INFANT IS LOW (31) B-B-C	318	LEAN TOWARD BEING THOSE 0.66 OF 50 WHERE THE OVERALL INDULGENCE OF THE INFANT IS HIGH (40) B-B-C		4 33 12 17 XSQ= 6.69 PHI= -0.318 XP = 0.0097
319	LEAN TOWARD BEING THOSE 0.86 OF 14 WHERE PROTECTION OF THE INFANT FROM ENVIRONMENTAL DISCOMFORTS IS LOW (30) B-B-C	319	LEAN TOWARD BEING THOSE 0.63 OF 46 WHERE PROTECTION OF THE INFANT FROM ENVIRONMENTAL DISCOMFORTS IS HIGH (35) B-B-C		2 29 12 17 XSQ= 8.36 PHI= -0.373 XP = 0.0038
320	DRIFT TOWARD BEING THOSE 0.56 OF 16 WHERE THE DEGREE OF REDUCTION OF THE INFANT'S DRIVES IS LOW (24) B-B-C	320	DRIFT TOWARD BEING THOSE 0.73 OF 48 WHERE THE DEGREE OF REDUCTION OF THE INFANT'S DRIVES IS HIGH (45) B-B-C		7 35 9 13 XSQ= 3.32 PHI= -0.228 XP = 0.0682
326	TILT TOWARD BEING THOSE 0.75 OF 16 WHERE THE INFERRED TRANSITION ANXIETY BETWEEN INFANCY AND CHILDHOOD IS HIGH (32) B-B-C	326	TILT TOWARD BEING THOSE 0.63 OF 46 WHERE THE INFERRED TRANSITION ANXIETY BETWEEN INFANCY AND CHILDHOOD IS LOW (35) B-B-C		12 17 4 29 XSQ= 5.46 PHI= 0.297 XP = 0.0195
334	LEAN TOWARD BEING THOSE 0.82 OF 17 WHERE THE INDULGENCE OF THE CHILD IS LOW (38) B-B-C	334	LEAN TOWARD BEING THOSE 0.61 OF 56 WHERE THE INDULGENCE OF THE CHILD IS HIGH (40) B-B-C		3 34 14 22 XSQ= 8.03 PHI= -0.332 XP = 0.0046
336	TILT TOWARD BEING THOSE 0.82 OF 17 WHERE THE TOTAL POSITIVE PRESSURE TOWARD DEVELOPING RESPONSIBLE BEHAVIOR IN THE CHILD IS HIGH (43) B-B-C	336	TILT TOWARD BEING THOSE 0.51 OF 53 WHERE THE TOTAL POSITIVE PRESSURE TOWARD DEVELOPING RESPONSIBLE BEHAVIOR IN THE CHILD IS LOW (32) B-B-C		14 26 3 27 XSQ= 4.55 PHI= 0.255 XP = 0.0330

No.		No.		
337	IN ALL CASES ARE THOSE 1.00 OF 16 WHERE THE CHILD'S INFERREC ANXIETY OVER NCN-PERFCRMANCE CF RESPCNSIBLE BEFAVIOR IS HIGH (38) B-B-C	337	TEND TO BE THOSE 0.60 OF 52 WHERE THE CHILD'S INFERRED ANXIETY OVER NON-PERFORMANCE OF RESPCNSIBLE BEHAVIOR IS LOW (35) B-B-C	16 21 0 31 XSQ= 15.21 PHI= 0.473 XP = 0.0001
338	IN ALL CASES ARE THCSE 1.00 OF 16 WHERE THE CHILD'S INFERREC ANXIETY OVER PERFORMANCE OF RESPCNSIBLE BEFAVIOR IS HIGH (44) B-B-C	338	TEND TO BE THOSE 0.52 CF 52 WHERE THE CHILD'S INFERRED ANXIETY OVER PERFORMANCE OF RESPONSIBLE BEHAVIOR IS LOW (29) B-B-C	16 25 0 27 XSQ= 11.70 PHI= 0.415 XP = 0.0006
339	TEND TO BE THCSE 0.88 OF 16 WHERE THE CHILD'S INFERREC CONFLICT REGARDING RESPCNSIBLE BEHAVIOR IS HIGH (31) B-B-C	339	TEND TO BE THOSE 0.69 OF 52 WHERE THE CHILD'S INFERRED CONFLICT REGARDING RESPCNSIBLE BEHAVICR IS LOW (42) B-B-C	14 16 2 36 XSQ= 13.75 PHI= 0.450 XP = 0.0002
346	DRIFT TCWARD BEING THCSE 0.71 OF 17 WHERE THE CHILD'S INFERREC ANXIETY OVER PERFORMANCE CF SELF-RELIANT BEFAVIOR IS HIGH (37) B-B-C	346	DRIFT TOWARD BEING THOSE 0.59 CF 54 WHERE THE CHILD'S INFERRED ANXIETY OVER PERFORMANCE OF SELF-RELIANT BEHAVIOR IS LOW (39) B-B-C	12 22 5 32 XSQ= 3.50 PHI= 0.222 XP = 0.0615
347	TILT TCWARD BEING THOSE 0.76 OF 17 WHERE THE CHILD'S INFERREC CONFLICT REGARDING SELF-RELIANT BEFAVIOR IS HIGH (37) B-B-C	347	TILT TOWARD BEING THOSE 0.61 OF 54 WHERE THE CHILD'S INFERRED CONFLICT REGARDING SELF-RELIANT BEHAVIOR IS LOW (39) B-B-C	13 21 4 33 XSQ= 5.89 PHI= 0.288 XP = 0.0152
350	TILT TCWARD BEING THCSE 0.85 OF 13 WHERE THE CHILD'S INFERREC ANXIETY OVER PERFCRMANCE CF ACHIEVEMENT BEFAVIOR IS HIGH (34) B-B-C	350	TILT TOWARD BEING THOSE 0.52 CF 42 WHERE THE CHILD'S INFERRED ANXIETY OVER PERFORMANCE OF ACHIEVEMENT BEHAVIOR IS LOW (26) B-B-C	11 20 2 22 XSQ= 4.12 PHI= 0.274 XP = 0.0423
351	TILT TCWARD BEING THOSE 0.69 OF 13 WHERE THE CHILD'S INFERREC CCNFLICT REGARDING ACHIEVEMENT BEHAVIOR IS HIGH (26) B-B-C	351	TILT TOWARD BEING THOSE 0.67 OF 42 WHERE THE CHILD'S INFERRED CCNFLICT REGARDING ACHIEVEMENT BEHAVIOR IS LOW (34) B-B-C	9 14 4 28 XSQ= 3.89 PHI= 0.266 XP = 0.0487
352	LEAN MCRE TOWARC BEING THCSE 0.94 OF 16 WHERE THE TOTAL POSITIVE PRESSURE TOWARD DEVELCPING OBEDIENT BEHAVICR IN THE CHILD IS HIGH (44) B-B-C	352	LEAN LESS TOWARD BEING THOSE 0.53 CF 51 WHERE THE TOTAL POSITIVE PRESSURE TOWARC DEVELOPING OBEDIENT BEHAVICR IN THE CHILD IS HIGH (44) B-B-C	15 27 1 24 XSQ= 7.01 PHI= 0.324 XP = 0.0081
353	LEAN TOWARD BEING THOSE 0.94 OF 16 WHERE THE CHILD'S INFERREC ANXIETY OVER NCN-PERFCRMANCE CF CBECIENT BEFAVIOR IS HIGH (42) B-B-C	353	LEAN TOWARD BEING THOSE 0.51 OF 53 WHERE THE CHILD-S INFERRED ANXIETY CVER NON-PERFORMANCE OF OBEDIENT BEHAVIOR IS LOW (32) B-B-C	15 26 1 27 XSQ= 8.41 PHI= 0.349 XP = 0.0037

```
354  LEAN TOWARD BEING THOSE          0.81 OF  16    354  LEAN TOWARD BEING THOSE          0.62 OF  52          13   20
     WHERE THE CHILD'S INFERREC ANXIETY OVER              WHERE THE CHILD'S INFERRED ANXIETY OVER                   3   32
     PERFORMANCE OF CBECIENT BEHAVIOR                     PERFORMANCE OF OBEDIENT BEHAVIOR                 XSQ=      7.34
     IS HIGH  (36) B-B-C                                  IS LOW  (37) B-B-C                               PHI=     0.328
                                                                                                           XP =    0.0068

355  TILT TOWARD BEING THCSE          0.81 OF  16    355  TILT TOWARD BEING THOSE          0.60 OF  52          13   21
     WHERE THE CHILD'S INFERREC CONFLICT                  WHERE THE CHILD'S INFERRED CONFLICT                       3   31
     REGARDING CBEDIENT BEHAVIOR                          REGARDING OBEDIENT BEHAVIOR                      XSQ=      6.62
     IS HIGH  (35) B-B-C                                  IS LOW  (38) B-B-C                               PHI=     0.312
                                                                                                           XP =    0.0101

358  IN ALL CASES ARE THCSE           1.00 OF  12    358  DRIFT LESS TOWARD BEING THCSE  0.71 OF  38            12   27
     WHERE ADOLESCENT PEER GROUPS ARE PRESENT             WHERE ADOLESCENT PEER GRCUPS ARE PRESENT                  0   11
     IN A SETTING OF WORK AND PUBLIC GATHERINGS           IN A SETTING OF WORK AND PUBLIC GATHERINGS       XSQ=      2.93
     AND LEISURE, CR CF                                   AND LEISURE, OR OF                               PHI=     0.242
     PUBLIC GATHERINGS AND LEISURE, OR                    PUBLIC GATHERINGS AND LEISURE, OR                XP =    0.0871
     OF LEISURE ONLY  (41) JKH                            OF LEISURE ONLY  (41) JKH

377  TEND LESS TO BE THCSE            0.57 OF  72    377  TEND MORE TO BE THOSE            0.79 OF 250          31   52
     WHERE MALE GENITAL MUTILATION                        WHERE MALE GENITAL MUTILATICN                            41  198
     IS ABSENT  (242)                                     IS ABSENT  (242)                                 XSQ=     13.33
                                                                                                           PHI=     0.203
                                                                                                           XP =    0.0003

391  TILT TCWARD BEING THOSE          0.66 OF  44    391  TILT TOWARD BEING THOSE          0.54 CF 125          29   57
     WHERE PREMARITAL SEX RELATIONS ARE                   WHERE PREMARITAL SEX RELATICNS ARE                       15   68
     STRCNGLY PUNISHED AND IN FACT RARE, OR               PUNISHED ONLY IF PREGNANCY RESULTS, OR           XSQ=      4.59
     WEAKLY PUNISHED AND                                  FREELY PERMITTED  (90) JTW,EA                    PHI=     0.165
     IN FACT NCT RARE  (89) JTW,EA                                                                         XP =    0.0322

393  DRIFT TOWARD BEING THOSE         0.77 OF  13    393  DRIFT TOWARD BEING THOSE         0.55 OF  64          10   29
     WHERE EXTRAMARITAL COITUS                            WHERE EXTRAMARITAL COITUS IS                              3   35
     IS PUNISHED, RATHER THAN                             PERMITTED, RATHER THAN                           XSQ=      3.15
     PERMITTED  (43) F-B                                  PUNISHED  (41) F-B                               PHI=     0.202
                                                                                                           XP =    0.0760

399  DRIFT TOWARD BEING THCSE         0.80 OF  10    399  DRIFT TOWARD BEING THOSE         0.58 CF  33           8   14
     WHERE INTENSITY OF CASTRATION ANXIETY                WHERE INTENSITY OF CASTRATICN ANXIETY                     2   19
     IS HIGH  (23) WNS                                    IS LOW  (22) WNS                                 XSQ=      2.96
                                                                                                           PHI=     0.263
                                                                                                           XP =    0.0852

420  DRIFT TOWARD BEING THOSE         0.65 OF  23    420  DRIFT TOWARD BEING THOSE         0.60 OF  60          15   24
     WHERE BELLICOSITY                                    WHERE BELLICOSITY                                         8   36
     IS EXTREME  (41) PES                                 IS MODERATE OR NEGLIGIBLE  (46) PES              XSQ=      3.29
                                                                                                           PHI=     0.199
                                                                                                           XP =    0.0696

424  TEND TO BE THOSE                 0.83 OF  12    424  TEND TO BE THOSE                 0.75 CF  40          10   10
     WHERE RELIGIOUS SPECIALISTS ARE                      WHERE RELIGIOUS SPECIALISTS ARE                           2   30
     FULL-TIME, RATHER THAN                               PART-TIME, RATHER THAN                           XSQ=     10.92
     PART-TIME  (21) JMH                                  FULL-TIME  (33) JMH                              PHI=     0.458
                                                                                                           XP =    0.0010
```

426	TEND MORE TO BE THCSE WHERE A HIGH GOD IS PRESENT (156) GES,EA	0.81 OF 63	426	TEND LESS TO BE THOSE WHERE A HIGH GOD IS PRESENT (156) GES,EA	0.53 OF 194	51 103 12 91 XSQ= 14.23 PHI= 0.235 XP = 0.0002
427	DRIFT TOWARD BEING THCSE WHERE A HIGH GOD, IF PRESENT, IS ACTIVE, RATHER THAN INACTIVE (87) GES,EA	0.67 OF 51	427	DRIFT TOWARD BEING THOSE WHERE A HIGH GOD, IF PRESENT, IS INACTIVE, RATHER THAN ACTIVE (69) GES,EA	0.50 CF 103	34 51 17 52 XSQ= 3.39 PHI= 0.148 XP = 0.0654
428	TILT MORE TOWARD BEING THCSE WHERE A HIGH GOD, IF PRESENT AND ACTIVE, SUPPORTS HUMAN MORALITY, RATHER THAN NOT SUPPORTING IT (61) GES,EA	0.85 OF 34	428	TILT LESS TOWARD BEING THOSE WHERE A HIGH GOD, IF PRESENT AND ACTIVE, SUPPORTS HUMAN MORALITY, RATHER THAN NOT SUPPORTING IT (61) GES,EA	0.59 CF 51	29 30 5 21 XSQ= 5.54 PHI= 0.255 XP = 0.0186
435	IN ALL CASES ARE THCSE WHERE ABANDONMENT OF THE HOUSE OF THE DEAD IS NOT PRACTICED (19) LWS	1.00 OF 6	435	DRIFT LESS TOWARD BEING THCSE WHERE ABANDONMENT OF THE HOUSE CF THE DEAD IS NOT PRACTICED (19) LWS	0.52 CF 25	0 12 6 13 XSQ= 2.89 PHI= -0.306 EP = 0.0585
441	DRIFT TOWARD BEING THCSE WHERE FEAR OF HUMAN BEINGS IS LOW (32) W-C	0.80 OF 10	441	DRIFT TOWARD BEING THOSE WHERE FEAR OF HUMAN BEINGS IS HIGH (29) W-C	0.57 OF 46	2 26 8 20 XSQ= 3.04 PHI= -0.233 XP = 0.0811
443	TILT TOWARD BEING THCSE WHERE OVERALL FEAR OF OTHERS IS LOW (30) W-C	0.80 OF 10	443	TILT TOWARD BEING THOSE WHERE OVERALL FEAR OF OTHERS IS HIGH (31) W-C	0.61 OF 46	2 28 8 18 XSQ= 4.00 PHI= -0.267 XP = 0.0456
450	TILT TOWARD BEING THOSE WHERE THE OBSERVATION OF FOOD TABOOS IS LOW, RATHER THAN HIGH OR MEDIUM (26) JRL	0.50 OF 22	450	TILT TOWARD BEING THOSE WHERE THE OBSERVATION OF FOOD TABOOS IS HIGH OR MEDIUM, RATHER THAN LOW (60) JRL	0.78 OF 60	11 47 11 13 XSQ= 4.95 PHI= -0.246 XP = 0.0261
458	TEND TO BE THOSE WHERE GAMES, IF PRESENT, INCLUDE GAMES OF STRATEGY (52) R-A-B,EA	0.83 OF 42	458	TEND TO BE THOSE WHERE GAMES, IF PRESENT, DO NOT INCLUDE GAMES OF STRATEGY (119) R-A-B,EA	0.87 CF 127	35 17 7 110 XSQ= 69.25 PHI= 0.640 XP = 0.
459	LEAN TOWARD BEING THOSE WHERE GAMES, IF PRESENT, INCLUDE GAMES OF CHANCE (82) R-A-B,EA	0.67 OF 42	459	LEAN TOWARD BEING THOSE WHERE GAMES, IF PRESENT, DO NOT INCLUDE GAMES OF CHANCE (89) R-A-B,EA	0.59 CF 127	28 52 14 75 XSQ= 7.38 PHI= 0.209 XP = 0.0066

```
460  TEND TO BE THOSE                0.93 OF  42      460  TEND TO BE THOSE                0.50 OF 127          3    64
     WHERE GAMES, IF PRESENT,                              WHERE GAMES, IF PRESENT,                            39    63
     ARE NOT LIMITED TO                                    ARE LIMITED TO                               XSQ=    22.90
     GAMES OF SKILL ONLY  (104) R-A-B,EA                   GAMES OF SKILL ONLY  (67) R-A-B,EA           PHI=   -0.368
                                                                                                        XP =   0.0000

468  LEAN TOWARD BEING THOSE         0.67 OF  12      468  LEAN TOWARD BEING THOSE         0.80 OF  40          8     8
     WHERE CONTACT WITH OTHER CULTURES                     WHERE CONTACT WITH OTHER CULTURES                    4    32
     IS FREQUENT, RATHER THAN                              IS REGULAR OR IRREGULAR, RATHER THAN         XSQ=     7.37
     REGULAR OR IRREGULAR  (17) JMH                        FREQUENT  (37) JMH                           PHI=    0.377
                                                                                                        XP =   0.0066

470  DRIFT TOWARD BEING THOSE        0.67 OF  12      470  DRIFT TOWARD BEING THOSE        0.70 OF  40          8    12
     WHERE INNOVATIONS ARE                                 WHERE INNOVATIONS ARE                                4    28
     GENERALLY ACCEPTED  (21) JMH                          ACCEPTED ONLY SELECTIVELY  (33) JMH          XSQ=     3.81
                                                                                                        PHI=    0.271
                                                                                                        XP =   0.0510

473  TILT TOWARD BEING THOSE         0.57 OF  23      473  TILT TOWARD BEING THOSE         0.70 OF  61         13    18
     WHERE SENSITIVITY TO INSULT                           WHERE SENSITIVITY TO INSULT                         10    43
     IS EXTREME  (32) PES                                  IS MODERATE OR NEGLIGIBLE  (56) PES          XSQ=     4.14
                                                                                                        PHI=    0.222
                                                                                                        XP =   0.0419

476  DRIFT TOWARD BEING THOSE        0.64 OF  11      476  DRIFT TOWARD BEING THOSE        0.71 OF  35          4    25
     WHERE THE DEGREE OF INSOBRIETY IS                     WHERE THE DEGREE OF INSOBRIETY IS                    7    10
     MODERATE OR SLIGHT  (18) CH                           STRONG  (31) DH                              XSQ=     3.04
                                                                                                        PHI=   -0.257
                                                                                                        XP =   0.0812
```

96 CULTURES
WHERE THE HIERARCHY
OF NATICNAL JURISDICTION HAS
FOUR, THREE, TWC OR
CNE LEVEL (174) GES,EA

96 CULTURES
WHERE THE HIERARCHY
OF NATIONAL JURISDICTION HAS
NO LEVELS (156) GES,EA

BACKGROUND ON PAGE 86

BOTH SUBJECT AND PREDICATE

174 IN LEFT COLUMN

AINU	ALBANIANS	ALCRESE	AMERICANS	ASHANTI	ATAYAL	AZANDE	AZTEC	BABWA	BAMBARA
BAMILEKE	BASSERI	BEJA	BEMBA	BHIL	BHUIYA	BOERS	BORORO	BOZO	BRAZILIANS
BULGARIANS	BURUSHO	CADUVEC	CAMBODIANS	CHAGGA	CHAMACOCO	CHERKESS	CHEROKEE	CHEYENNE	CHIBCHA
CHIRIGUANO	CHORTI	COORG	CREEK	CROW	CUNA	CZECHS	DAGUR	DARC	DILLING
DOGON	DUTCH	EGYPTIANS	ELLICE	EYAK	FON	FOX	FUTAJALONKE	GANDA	GARO
GISU	GOND	GROS VENTRE	HASINAI	HAWAIIANS	HAZARA	HEBREWS	HURON	ILA	INCA
IRAQW	IRISH	JAPANESE	JAVANESE	KABYLE	KACHIN	KAPAUKU	KAZAK	KERALA	KHALKA
KHASI	KISSI	KOHISTANI	KOL	KOREANS	KUBA	KUTENAI	KWAKIUTL	LAKHER	LAMBA
LAU	LOZI	LUO	MACASSARESE	MALAYS	MANDAN	MANGAIANS	MANIHIKI	MAORI	MARGI
MARICOPA	MARQUESANS	MARSHALLESE	MASAI	MAYA	MBUNDU	MENDE	MERINA	MIAMI	MIAO
MIN CHINESE	MINCHIA	MISKITO	MONGO	MONGUOR	MOSSI	NAMA	NANDI	NATCHEZ	NDEMBU
NUPE	NURI	NYAKYUSA	NYORO	OJIBWA	OKINAWANS	OMAHA	ORAON	PAEZ	PAIWAN
PALAUANS	PARAUJANO	PATHAN	PAWNEE	PONAPEANS	PUKAPUKA	REGEIBAT	RIFFIANS	RUNDI	RWALA
SAMOANS	SANDAWE	SANTAL	SARSI	SERBS	SHILLUK	SHLUH	SINHALESE	SOMALI	SONGHAI
SOTHO	SWAZI	SYRIANS	TANALA	TEDA	TENDA	TERA	TESO	THAI	THONGA
TIGRINYA	TIKOPIA	TIMUCUA	TIV	TODA	TOKELAU	TORAJA	TOTONAC	TROBRIAND	TSHIMSHIAN
TUBATULABAL	TUPINAMBA	TURKMEN	VENDA	VIETNAMESE	WALLOONS	WICHITA	WOLEAIANS	WOLOF	YAKUT
YAO	YAPESE	YOMBE	YORUBA						

156 IN RIGHT COLUMN

ABIPON	ABOR	AKHA	ALACALUF	AMBA	ANDAMANESE	APINAYE	ARANDA	ARAPESH	ARAUCANIANS
ATSUGEWI	AWEIKOMA	BACAIRI	BANDA	BARABRA	BARI	BAYA	BIRIFOR	BLACK CARIB	BOTOCUDO
BUNLAP	CAGABA	CALLINAGO	CAMAYURA	CARIB	CAYAPA	CHENCHU	CHIR-APACHE	CHOCO	CHOROTI
CHUKCHEE	COCHITI	COPR ESKIMO	CREE	DELAWARE	DIEGUENO	DIERI	DOROBO	ENGA	FANG
GILYAK	GOAJIRO	GUAHIBO	GUATO	GURE	HAIDA	HANO	HANUNOO	HAVASUPAI	HERERO
HUICHOL	HUKUNDIKA	IBAN	IFUGAO	INGALIK	INGASSANA	JEMEZ	JIVARO	JUKUN	KARIERA
KASKA	KATAB	KERAKI	KIKUYU	KORYAK	KPE	KUNG	KURTATCHI	LAMET	LANGO
LAPPS	LEPCHA	LESU	LHOTA NAGA	LOLO	MAM	MAMBILA	MAMVU	MANUS	MATACO
MATAKAM	MBUTI	MIWOK	MNONG GAR	MOTA	MOTILON	MUNDURUCU	MURINBATA	MURNGIN	MZAB
NABESNA	NAMBICUARA	NAVAHO	NICOBARESE	NOMLAKI	NUER	NUNIVAK	ONA	ONTONG-JAVA	PAPAGO
PURARI	PURUM	SAGADA	SAMOYED	SANPOIL	SELUNG	SEMANG	SENIANG	SHERENTE	SIRIONO
SIUAI	SIWANS	SUBANUN	TAGBANUA	TALAMANCA	TALLENSI	TAOS	TAPIRAPE	TARAHUMARA	TAREUMIUT
TEHUELCHE	TENETEHARA	TENINO	TERENA	TIMBIRA	TIWI	TOLOWA	TRISTAN	TRUKESE	TRUMAI
TUCANO	TUCUNA	TUNEBO	TURKANA	TWANA	ULAWANS	UTE	VEDDA	WAICA	WANTOAT
WAPISHANA	WARRAU	WASHO	WIKMUNKAN	WITOTO	WOGEO	YABARANA	YAGUA	YAHGAN	YAKO
YARURO	YOKUTS	YUKAGHIR	YUKI	YUROK	ZUNI				

70 EXCLUDED BECAUSE UNASCERTAINED

3	TILT LESS TOWARD BEING THOSE LOCATED OUTSIDE OF AFRICA (320)	0.74 OF 174	3	TILT MORE TOWARD BEING THOSE LOCATED OUTSIDE OF AFRICA (320)	0.85 OF 156	45 24 129 132 XSQ= 4.85 PHI= 0.121 XP = 0.0277
4	TEND LESS TO BE THOSE LOCATED OUTSIDE OF THE CIRCUM-MEDITERRANEAN (355)	0.84 OF 174	4	TEND MORE TO BE THOSE LOCATED OUTSIDE OF THE CIRCUM-MEDITERRANEAN (355)	0.97 OF 156	27 5 147 151 XSQ= 12.87 PHI= 0.197 XP = 0.0003
5	TILT LESS TOWARD BEING THOSE LOCATED OUTSIDE OF EAST EURASIA (330)	0.77 OF 174	5	TILT MORE TOWARD BEING THOSE LOCATED OUTSIDE OF EAST EURASIA (330)	0.88 OF 156	40 19 134 137 XSQ= 5.83 PHI= 0.133 XP = 0.0158
9	TEND MORE TO BE THOSE LOCATED OUTSIDE OF SOUTH AMERICA (335)	0.93 OF 174	9	TEND LESS TO BE THOSE LOCATED OUTSIDE OF SOUTH AMERICA (335)	0.71 OF 156	13 45 161 111 XSQ= 24.49 PHI= -0.272 XP = 0.0000
11	DRIFT MORE TOWARD BEING THOSE WHERE THE LATITUDE IS LESS THAN SIXTY DEGREES (385)	0.98 OF 174	11	DRIFT LESS TOWARD BEING THOSE WHERE THE LATITUDE IS LESS THAN SIXTY DEGREES (385)	0.94 OF 156	3 10 171 146 XSQ= 3.62 PHI= -0.105 XP = 0.0573
33	TILT MORE TOWARD BEING THOSE WHERE THE NATURAL ENVIRONMENT IS OTHER THAN 'VERY HARSH,' I.E., DESERT, DESERT GRASSES AND SHRUBS, TUNDRA, OR HIGH PLATEAU STEPPE (341) FWM	0.89 OF 174	33	TILT LESS TOWARD BEING THOSE WHERE THE NATURAL ENVIRONMENT IS OTHER THAN 'VERY HARSH,' I.E., DESERT, DESERT GRASSES AND SHRUBS, TUNDRA, OR HIGH PLATEAU STEPPE (341) FWM	0.79 OF 156	19 32 155 124 XSQ= 5.08 PHI= -0.124 XP = 0.0242
44	TEND MORE TO BE THOSE WHERE SETTLEMENTS ARE FIXED (222)	0.77 OF 174	44	TEND LESS TO BE THOSE WHERE SETTLEMENTS ARE FIXED (222)	0.55 OF 155	134 85 40 70 XSQ= 17.13 PHI= 0.228 XP = 0.0000
46	TEND MORE TO BE THOSE OTHER THAN WHERE SETTLEMENTS ARE NON-FIXED AND MOVEMENT IS NOMADIC (260)	0.87 OF 174	46	TEND LESS TO BE THOSE OTHER THAN WHERE SETTLEMENTS ARE NON-FIXED AND MOVEMENT IS NOMADIC (260)	0.68 OF 155	22 50 152 105 XSQ= 17.32 PHI= -0.229 XP = 0.0000
51	TEND TO BE THOSE WHERE SUBSISTENCE IS PRIMARILY BY FOOD PRODUCTION -- I. E., AGRICULTURE OR HUSBANDRY -- RATHER THAN BY GATHERING (253)	0.78 OF 174	51	TEND TO BE THOSE WHERE SUBSISTENCE IS PRIMARILY BY FOOD GATHERING -- I. E., HUNTING, FISHING, OR COLLECTING -- RATHER THAN FOOD PRODUCTION (147)	0.57 OF 156	136 67 38 89 XSQ= 41.61 PHI= 0.355 XP = 0.

53	TEND LESS TO BE THOSE WHERE FOOD PRODUCTION IS BY SIMPLE AGRICULTURE OR INCIPIENT FOOD PRODUCTION, RATHER THAN BY INTENSIVE AGRICULTURE (147)	0.51 OF 140	53	TEND MORE TO BE THOSE WHERE FOOD PRODUCTION IS BY SIMPLE AGRICULTURE OR INCIPIENT FOOD PRODUCTION, RATHER THAN BY INTENSIVE AGRICULTURE (147)	0.77 OF 88	68 20 72 68 XSQ= 14.16 PHI= 0.249 XP = 0.0002
54	TEND MORE TO BE THOSE WHERE FOOD PRODUCTION IS BY INTENSIVE OR SIMPLE AGRICULTURE, RATHER THAN BY INCIPIENT FOOD PRODUCTION (192)	0.90 OF 140	54	TEND LESS TO BE THOSE WHERE FOOD PRODUCTION IS BY INTENSIVE OR SIMPLE AGRICULTURE, RATHER THAN BY INCIPIENT FOOD PRODUCTION (192)	0.72 OF 88	126 63 14 25 XSQ= 11.65 PHI= 0.226 XP = 0.0006
55	LEAN TOWARD BEING THOSE WHERE FOOD PRODUCTION IS BY INTENSIVE AGRICULTURE, RATHER THAN BY SIMPLE AGRICULTURE (91)	0.54 OF 126	55	LEAN TOWARD BEING THOSE WHERE FOOD PRODUCTION IS BY SIMPLE AGRICULTURE, RATHER THAN BY INTENSIVE AGRICULTURE (101)	0.68 OF 63	68 20 58 43 XSQ= 7.47 PHI= 0.199 XP = 0.0063
56	TILT MORE TOWARD BEING THOSE WHERE FOOD PRODUCTION IS BY SIMPLE AGRICULTURE, RATHER THAN BY INCIPIENT FOOD PRODUCTION (101)	0.81 OF 72	56	TILT LESS TOWARD BEING THOSE WHERE FOOD PRODUCTION IS BY SIMPLE AGRICULTURE, RATHER THAN BY INCIPIENT FOOD PRODUCTION (101)	0.63 OF 68	58 43 14 25 XSQ= 4.39 PHI= 0.177 XP = 0.0361
62	TEND MORE TO BE THOSE WHERE HUSBANDRY OF SOME KIND IS PRESENT (228)	0.80 OF 174	62	TEND LESS TO BE THOSE WHERE HUSBANDRY OF SOME KIND IS PRESENT (228)	0.53 OF 156	140 83 34 73 XSQ= 26.66 PHI= 0.284 XP = 0.0000
63	TEND TO BE THOSE WHERE HUSBANDRY, IF PRESENT, IS PRINCIPALLY IN THE FORM OF BOVINE, EQUINE, CAMEL-LIKE, OR DEER-LIKE ANIMALS, RATHER THAN PIGS, SHEEP, OR GOATS (152)	0.77 OF 140	63	TEND TO BE THOSE WHERE HUSBANDRY, IF PRESENT, IS PRINCIPALLY IN THE FORM OF PIGS, SHEEP, OR GOATS, RATHER THAN BOVINE, EQUINE, CAMEL-LIKE, OR DEER-LIKE ANIMALS (74)	0.51 OF 83	108 41 32 42 XSQ= 16.86 PHI= 0.275 XP = 0.0000
71	TEND TO BE THOSE WHERE METAL WORKING IS PRESENT (98)	0.60 OF 124	71	TEND TO BE THOSE WHERE METAL WORKING IS ABSENT (153)	0.82 OF 117	74 21 50 96 XSQ= 42.17 PHI= 0.418 XP = 0.
73	LEAN TOWARD BEING THOSE WHERE WEAVING IS PRESENT (118)	0.58 OF 122	73	LEAN TOWARD BEING THOSE WHERE WEAVING IS ABSENT (130)	0.63 OF 117	71 43 51 74 XSQ= 10.17 PHI= 0.206 XP = 0.0014
74	TEND MORE TO BE THOSE WHERE POTTERY IS PRESENT (145)	0.73 OF 113	74	TEND LESS TO BE THOSE WHERE POTTERY IS PRESENT (145)	0.51 OF 116	83 59 30 57 XSQ= 11.46 PHI= 0.224 XP = 0.0007

79	TEND LESS TC BE THCSE WHERE NC CITY IS PRESENT (201)	0.80 OF 112	79	IN ALL CASES ARE THOSE WHERE NO CITY IS PRESENT (201)	1.00 OF 109	22 0 90 109 XSQ= 21.64 PHI= 0.313 XP = 0.0000
81	TEND TO BE THCSE WHERE A CITY CR TOWN IS PRESENT, OR THE AVERAGE CCMMUNITY SIZE IS 200 OR GREATER (89)	0.55 OF 112	81	TEND TO BE THOSE WHERE NO CITY OR TOWN IS PRESENT, AND THE AVERAGE COMMUNITY SIZE IS SMALLER THAN 200 (135)	0.78 OF 109	62 24 50 85 XSQ= 24.45 PHI= 0.333 XP = 0.0000
83	LEAN LESS TOWARC BEING THCSE WHERE, WITH NC CITY ANC NC TOWN PRESENT, THE AVERAGE COMMUNITY SIZE IS SMALLER THAN 200, RATHER THAN BETWEEN 200 AND 999 (135)	0.65 OF 77	83	LEAN MORE TOWARD BEING THOSE WHERE, WITH NO CITY AND NO TOWN PRESENT, THE AVERAGE COMMUNITY SIZE IS SMALLER THAN 200, RATHER THAN BETWEEN 200 AND 999 (135)	0.83 OF 102	27 17 50 85 XSQ= 7.05 PHI= 0.198 XP = 0.0079
84	TEND LESS TO BE THCSE WHERE THE LEVEL OF POLITICAL INTEGRATION IS THE LITTLE STATE, THE MINIMAL STATE, THE AUTONCMOUS COMMUNITY, CR THE FAMILY (262) GPM	0.74 OF 135	84	IN ALL CASES ARE THOSE WHERE THE LEVEL OF POLITICAL INTEGRATION IS THE LITTLE STATE, THE MINIMAL STATE, THE AUTONOMOUS COMMUNITY, CR THE FAMILY (262) GPM	1.00 OF 123	35 0 100 123 XSQ= 34.72 PHI= 0.367 XP = 0.
86	TEND TC BE THCSE WHERE THE LEVEL OF POLITICAL INTEGRATION IS THE LARGE STATE, THE LITTLE STATE, OR THE MINIMAL STATE (148) GPM	0.86 OF 135	86	TEND TO BE THOSE WHERE THE LEVEL OF POLITICAL INTEGRATION IS THE AUTONOMOUS COMMUNITY, CR THE FAMILY (156) GPM	0.95 OF 123	116 6 19 117 XSQ= 166.37 PHI= 0.803 XP = 0.
87	IN ALL CASES ARE THOSE WHERE THE LEVEL CF PCLITICAL INTEGRATION IS THE LARGE STATE, THE LITTLE STATE, THE MINIMAL STATE, OR THE AUTCNCMOUS COMMUNITY (281) GPM	1.00 OF 135	87	TEND LESS TO BE THOSE WHERE THE LEVEL OF POLITICAL INTEGRATICN IS THE LARGE STATE, THE LITTLE STATE, THE MINIMAL STATE, OR THE AUTONOMOUS COMMUNITY (281) GPM	0.85 OF 123	135 105 0 18 XSQ= 19.04 PHI= 0.272 XP = 0.0000
90	TILT LESS TOWARC BEING THCSE WHERE, IF A HEREDITARY HEACMANSHIP IS PRESENT, SUCCESSION IS PATRILINEAL, RATHER THAN MATRILINEAL (127)	0.71 OF 82	90	TILT MORE TOWARD BEING THOSE WHERE, IF A HEREDITARY HEADMANSHIP IS PRESENT, SUCCESSION IS PATRILINEAL, RATHER THAN MATRILINEAL (127)	0.87 OF 60	58 52 24 8 XSQ= 4.17 PHI= -0.171 XP = 0.0412
91	DRIFT TOWARD BEING THCSE WHERE SCCIETAL CCMPLEXITY IS HIGH (18) F-W	0.57 OF 21	91	DRIFT TOWARD BEING THOSE WHERE SOCIETAL COMPLEXITY IS LOW (22) F-W	0.76 OF 17	12 4 9 13 XSQ= 3.08 PHI= 0.285 EP = 0.0516
97	TILT LESS TOWARC BEING THCSE WHERE THE HIERARCHY OF LOCAL JURISDICTION HAS THREE OR TWO LEVELS (273) GES,EA	0.78 OF 174	97	TILT MORE TOWARD BEING THOSE WHERE THE HIERARCHY OF LOCAL JURISDICTION HAS THREE OR TWO LEVELS (273) GES,EA	0.88 OF 156	39 19 135 137 XSQ= 5.26 PHI= 0.126 XP = 0.0218

98	TEND MORE TO BE THOSE 0.83 OF 174 WHERE THE HIERARCHY OF LOCAL JURISDICTION HAS FOUR OR THREE LEVELS (238) GES,EA	98	TEND LESS TO BE THOSE 0.60 OF 156 WHERE THE HIERARCHY OF LOCAL JURISDICTION HAS FOUR OR THREE LEVELS (238) GES,EA	144 93 30 63 XSQ= 20.64 PHI= 0.250 XP = 0.0000
102	TEND TO BE THOSE 0.71 OF 165 WHERE CLASS STRATIFICATION IS PRESENT (203)	102	TEND TO BE THOSE 0.67 OF 155 WHERE CLASS STRATIFICATION IS ABSENT (180)	117 51 48 104 XSQ= 44.78 PHI= 0.374 XP = 0.
106	TEND TO BE THOSE 0.79 OF 117 WHERE CLASS STRATIFICATION, IF PRESENT, IS BASED ON SOMETHING OTHER THAN WEALTH (126)	106	TEND TO BE THOSE 0.84 OF 51 WHERE CLASS STRATIFICATION, IF PRESENT, IS BASED ON WEALTH (77)	24 43 93 8 XSQ= 57.67 PHI= -0.586 XP = 0.
107	TEND LESS TO BE THOSE 0.69 OF 117 WHERE CLASS STRATIFICATION, IF PRESENT, IS BASED ON SOMETHING OTHER THAN OCCUPATIONAL STATUS (160)	107	IN ALL CASES ARE THOSE 1.00 OF 51 WHERE CLASS STRATIFICATION, IF PRESENT, IS BASED ON SOMETHING OTHER THAN OCCUPATIONAL STATUS (160)	36 0 81 51 XSQ= 18.19 PHI= 0.329 XP = 0.0000
108	TEND LESS TO BE THOSE 0.56 OF 117 WHERE CLASS STRATIFICATION, IF PRESENT, IS BASED ON SOMETHING OTHER THAN A HEREDITARY ARISTOCRACY (129)	108	TEND MORE TO BE THOSE 0.84 OF 51 WHERE CLASS STRATIFICATION, IF PRESENT, IS BASED ON SOMETHING OTHER THAN A HEREDITARY ARISTOCRACY (129)	52 8 65 43 XSQ= 11.57 PHI= 0.262 XP = 0.0007
109	TEND LESS TO BE THOSE 0.76 OF 159 WHERE CASTES ARE ABSENT (317)	109	TEND MORE TO BE THOSE 0.97 OF 150 WHERE CASTES ARE ABSENT (317)	38 5 121 145 XSQ= 25.56 PHI= 0.288 XP = 0.0000
110	TEND TO BE THOSE 0.55 OF 167 WHERE SLAVERY IS PRESENT (163)	110	TEND TO BE THOSE 0.73 OF 152 WHERE SLAVERY IS ABSENT (218)	92 41 75 111 XSQ= 24.73 PHI= 0.278 XP = 0.0000
116	LEAN TOWARD BEING THOSE 0.55 OF 31 WHERE OCCUPATIONAL SPECIALIZATION IS FULL-TIME, WHETHER OR NOT FOR SURPLUS PRODUCTION (20) JMH	116	LEAN TOWARD BEING THOSE 0.90 OF 21 WHERE OCCUPATIONAL SPECIALIZATION IS PART-TIME ONLY (34) JMH	17 2 14 19 XSQ= 9.22 PHI= 0.421 XP = 0.0024
129	TILT LESS TOWARD BEING THOSE 0.62 OF 60 WHERE WEAVING IS MAINLY DONE BY FEMALES (73)	129	TILT MORE TOWARD BEING THOSE 0.83 OF 42 WHERE WEAVING IS MAINLY DONE BY FEMALES (73)	23 7 37 35 XSQ= 4.59 PHI= 0.212 XP = 0.0321

137	TILT TOWARD BEING THOSE 0.51 OF 47 WHERE INVIDIOUS DISPLAY OF WEALTH IS STRONGLY EMPHASIZED (37) PES	TILT TOWARD BEING THOSE 0.74 OF 38 WHERE INVIDIOUS DISPLAY OF WEALTH IS MODERATELY, LITTLE, OR NEGATIVELY EMPHASIZED (52) PES	24 10 23 28 XSQ= 4.38 PHI= 0.227 XP = 0.0364
138	TEND TO BE THOSE 0.89 OF 19 WHERE SUPERORDINATE JUSTICE IS PRESENT (22) BBW	TEND TO BE THOSE 0.79 OF 19 WHERE SUPERORDINATE JUSTICE IS ABSENT (18) BBW	17 4 2 15 XSQ= 15.33 PHI= 0.635 EP = 0.0000
139	DRIFT TOWARD BEING THOSE 0.53 OF 19 WHERE SUPERORDINATE PUNISHMENT IS PRESENT (15) BBW	DRIFT TOWARD BEING THOSE 0.79 OF 19 WHERE SUPERORDINATE PUNISHMENT IS ABSENT (25) BBW	10 4 9 15 XSQ= 2.83 PHI= 0.273 EP = 0.0911
142	DRIFT MORE TOWARD BEING THOSE 0.81 OF 31 WHERE THE LEVEL OF SOCIAL SANCTION IS PUBLIC CORPOREAL SANCTION OR PUBLIC PROPERTY SANCTION, RATHER THAN PRIVATE SETTLEMENT (38) JMH	DRIFT LESS TOWARD BEING THOSE 0.52 OF 21 WHERE THE LEVEL OF SOCIAL SANCTION IS PUBLIC CORPOREAL SANCTION OR PUBLIC PROPERTY SANCTION, RATHER THAN PRIVATE SETTLEMENT (38) JMH	25 11 6 10 XSQ= 3.46 PHI= 0.258 XP = 0.0628
147	LEAN TOWARD BEING THOSE 0.88 OF 16 WHERE CODIFIED LAWS ARE PRESENT (20) LWS	LEAN TOWARD BEING THOSE 0.63 OF 16 WHERE CODIFIED LAWS ARE UNIMPORTANT OR ABSENT (13) LWS	14 6 2 10 XSQ= 6.53 PHI= 0.452 EP = 0.0091
152	DRIFT TOWARD BEING THOSE 0.78 OF 9 WHERE THE DIFFERENTIATION OF THE JURIDICAL AGENCY FROM THE MEDICAL AGENCY IS HIGH (10) MJ	DRIFT TOWARD BEING THOSE 0.78 OF 9 WHERE THE DIFFERENTIATION OF THE JURIDICAL AGENCY FROM THE MEDICAL AGENCY IS LOW (10) MJ	7 2 2 7 XSQ= 3.56 PHI= 0.444 EP = 0.0567
163	TILT TOWARD BEING THOSE 0.71 OF 7 WHERE THE EMPHASIS ON INDIVIDUAL VOLITION AS THE CAUSE OF CRIME IS HIGH (7) MJ	TILT TOWARD BEING THOSE 0.88 OF 8 WHERE THE EMPHASIS ON INDIVIDUAL VOLITION AS THE CAUSE OF CRIME IS LOW (10) MJ	5 1 2 7 XSQ= 3.23 PHI= 0.464 EP = 0.0406
175	TILT MORE TOWARD BEING THOSE 0.75 OF 163 WHERE THE COMMUNITY IS 'KIN-HETEROGENEOUS,' I. E. OTHER THAN A CLAN COMMUNITY OR A DEME (260)	TILT LESS TOWARD BEING THOSE 0.64 OF 154 WHERE THE COMMUNITY IS 'KIN-HETEROGENEOUS,' I. E. OTHER THAN A CLAN COMMUNITY OR A DEME (260)	41 56 122 98 XSQ= 4.17 PHI= -0.115 XP = 0.0411
181	TILT MORE TOWARD BEING THOSE 0.93 OF 163 WHERE THE COMMUNITY IS OTHER THAN A DEME (337)	TILT LESS TOWARD BEING THOSE 0.86 OF 154 WHERE THE COMMUNITY IS OTHER THAN A DEME (337)	11 22 152 132 XSQ= 4.05 PHI= -0.113 XP = 0.0442

183	TEND MORE TO BE THOSE 0.95 OF 125 WHERE THE LARGEST NON-COGNATIC KIN GROUP IS SMALLER THAN A MOEITY, I. E., A PHRATRY OR SIB OR LINEAGE (218)	183	TEND LESS TO BE THOSE 0.69 OF 85 WHERE THE LARGEST NON-COGNATIC KIN GROUP IS SMALLER THAN A MOEITY, I. E., A PHRATRY OR SIB OR LINEAGE (218)	6 26 119 59 XSQ= 24.09 PHI= -0.339 XP = 0.0000
184	TILT MORE TOWARD BEING THOSE 0.74 OF 125 WHERE THE LARGEST NON-COGNATIC KIN GROUP IS SMALLER THAN A PHRATRY, I. E. A SIB OR LINEAGE (175)	184	TILT LESS TOWARD BEING THOSE 0.58 OF 85 WHERE THE LARGEST NON-COGNATIC KIN GROUP IS SMALLER THAN A PHRATRY, I. E. A SIB OR LINEAGE (175)	32 36 93 49 XSQ= 5.74 PHI= -0.165 XP = 0.0166
186	TILT LESS TOWARD BEING THOSE 0.57 OF 174 WHERE THE KIN GROUP IS OTHER THAN EXCLUSIVELY PATRILINEAL (250)	186	TILT MORE TOWARD BEING THOSE 0.69 OF 156 WHERE THE KIN GROUP IS OTHER THAN EXCLUSIVELY PATRILINEAL (250)	74 48 100 108 XSQ= 4.39 PHI= 0.115 XP = 0.0362
188	LEAN MORE TOWARD BEING THOSE 0.72 OF 174 WHERE THE KIN GROUP IS OTHER THAN EXCLUSIVELY COGNATIC (252)	188	LEAN LESS TOWARD BEING THOSE 0.54 OF 156 WHERE THE KIN GROUP IS OTHER THAN EXCLUSIVELY COGNATIC (252)	49 71 125 85 XSQ= 9.97 PHI= -0.174 XP = 0.0016
192	LEAN MORE TOWARD BEING THOSE 0.80 OF 174 OTHER THAN WHERE THE ONLY KIN GROUP PRESENT IS A KINDRED OR ELSE BILATERAL DESCENT IS INFERRED (289)	192	LEAN LESS TOWARD BEING THOSE 0.65 OF 156 OTHER THAN WHERE THE ONLY KIN GROUP PRESENT IS A KINDRED OR ELSE BILATERAL DESCENT IS INFERRED (289)	35 55 139 101 XSQ= 8.76 PHI= -0.163 XP = 0.0031
196	TEND MORE TO BE THOSE 0.82 OF 130 WHERE INDIVIDUAL RIGHTS IN REAL PROPERTY, AND RULES FOR INHERITANCE, ARE PRESENT (194)	196	TEND LESS TO BE THOSE 0.50 OF 109 WHERE INDIVIDUAL RIGHTS IN REAL PROPERTY, AND RULES FOR INHERITANCE, ARE PRESENT (194)	107 55 23 54 XSQ= 26.10 PHI= 0.330 XP = 0.0000
201	DRIFT MORE TOWARD BEING THOSE 0.89 OF 174 WHERE MARITAL RESIDENCE IS NON-OPTIONAL, RATHER THAN AMBILOCAL OR NEOLOCAL (334)	201	DRIFT LESS TOWARD BEING THOSE 0.81 OF 155 WHERE MARITAL RESIDENCE IS NON-OPTIONAL, RATHER THAN AMBILOCAL OR NEOLOCAL (334)	154 125 20 30 XSQ= 3.34 PHI= 0.101 XP = 0.0675
204	TILT MORE TOWARD BEING THOSE 0.87 OF 151 WHERE MARITAL RESIDENCE IS PATRILOCAL, VIRILOCAL, OR AVUNCULOCAL, RATHER THAN AMBILOCAL OR NEOLOCAL (270)	204	TILT LESS TOWARD BEING THOSE 0.75 OF 121 WHERE MARITAL RESIDENCE IS PATRILOCAL, VIRILOCAL, OR AVUNCULOCAL, RATHER THAN AMBILOCAL OR NEOLOCAL (270)	131 91 20 30 XSQ= 5.23 PHI= 0.139 XP = 0.0223
209	TILT MORE TOWARD BEING THOSE 0.85 OF 154 WHERE MARITAL RESIDENCE IS PATRILOCAL, VIRILOCAL, OR AVUNCULOCAL, RATHER THAN MATRILOCAL OR UXORILOCAL (270)	209	TILT LESS TOWARD BEING THOSE 0.73 OF 125 WHERE MARITAL RESIDENCE IS PATRILOCAL, VIRILOCAL, OR AVUNCULOCAL, RATHER THAN MATRILOCAL OR UXORILOCAL (270)	131 91 23 34 XSQ= 5.65 PHI= 0.142 XP = 0.0174

210	DRIFT MORE TOWARD BEING THOSE WHERE MARITAL RESIDENCE IS PATRILOCAL, RATHER THAN MATRILOCAL (169)	0.89 OF 98	210	DRIFT LESS TOWARD BEING THOSE WHERE MARITAL RESIDENCE IS PATRILOCAL, RATHER THAN MATRILOCAL (169)	0.77 OF 69	87 53 11 16 XSQ= 3.44 PHI= 0.144 XP = 0.0637
213	DRIFT TOWARD BEING THOSE WHERE FIRST COUSIN MARRIAGE IS PERMITTED (172)	0.50 OF 160	213	DRIFT TOWARD BEING THOSE WHERE FIRST COUSIN MARRIAGE IS NOT PERMITTED (198)	0.61 OF 148	80 58 80 90 XSQ= 3.21 PHI= 0.102 XP = 0.0732
214	TILT MORE TOWARD BEING THOSE WHERE FIRST COUSIN MARRIAGE, IF PERMITTED, IS OTHER THAN UNILATERAL (144)	0.90 OF 80	214	TILT LESS TOWARD BEING THOSE WHERE FIRST COUSIN MARRIAGE, IF PERMITTED, IS OTHER THAN UNILATERAL (144)	0.76 OF 58	8 14 72 44 XSQ= 4.02 PHI= -0.171 XP = 0.0451
236	LEAN TOWARD BEING THOSE WHERE THE FAMILY IS OF AN EXTENDED TYPE, RATHER THAN AN INDEPENDENT TYPE (213)	0.61 OF 173	236	LEAN TOWARD BEING THOSE WHERE THE FAMILY IS OF AN INDEPENDENT TYPE, RATHER THAN AN EXTENDED TYPE (185)	0.54 OF 156	106 72 67 84 XSQ= 6.95 PHI= 0.145 XP = 0.0084
257	TILT TOWARD BEING THOSE WHERE THE SEVERITY OF SISTER AVOIDANCE IS HIGH (10) WNS	0.64 OF 11	257	TILT TOWARD BEING THOSE WHERE THE SEVERITY OF SISTER AVOIDANCE IS LOW (17) WNS	0.80 OF 15	7 3 4 12 XSQ= 3.43 PHI= 0.363 EP = 0.0426
277	DRIFT TOWARD BEING THOSE WHERE THE STATUS OF WOMEN IS INFERIOR OR SUBJECTED (14) LWS	0.56 OF 18	277	DRIFT TOWARD BEING THOSE WHERE THE STATUS OF WOMEN IS NOT STRONGLY INFERIOR OR SUBJECTED (22) LWS	0.76 OF 17	10 4 8 13 XSQ= 2.52 PHI= 0.268 EP = 0.0858
278	TILT TOWARD BEING THOSE WHERE PROPERTY RIGHTS IN WOMEN ARE PRESENT (8) LWS	0.64 OF 11	278	TILT TOWARD BEING THOSE WHERE PROPERTY RIGHTS IN WOMEN ARE UNIMPORTANT OR ABSENT (14) LWS	0.90 OF 10	7 1 4 9 XSQ= 4.32 PHI= 0.453 EP = 0.0237
286	DRIFT TOWARD BEING THOSE WHERE THE NUMBER OF FOOD TABOOS DURING PREGNANCY IS LOW OR ABSENT (14) BCA	0.56 OF 18	286	DRIFT TOWARD BEING THOSE WHERE THE NUMBER OF FOOD TABOOS DURING PREGNANCY IS HIGH (20) BCA	0.79 OF 14	8 11 10 3 XSQ= 2.52 PHI= -0.281 EP = 0.0751
302	TILT TOWARD BEING THOSE WHERE THE AVERAGE EARLY SATISFACTION POTENTIAL IS LOW (17) W-C	0.60 OF 20	302	TILT TOWARD BEING THOSE WHERE THE AVERAGE EARLY SATISFACTION POTENTIAL IS HIGH (23) W-C	0.75 OF 16	8 12 12 4 XSQ= 3.11 PHI= -0.294 EP = 0.0485

No.				No.				
303	LEAN TOWARD BEING THOSE WHERE THE EARLY ORAL SATISFACTION POTENTIAL IS LOW (25) W-C	0.67 OF	24	303	LEAN TOWARD BEING THOSE WHERE THE EARLY ORAL SATISFACTION POTENTIAL IS HIGH (32) W-C	0.79 OF	28	8 22 16 6 XSQ= 9.06 PHI= -0.417 XP = 0.0026
309	TEND TO BE THOSE WHERE ORAL SOCIALIZATION ANXIETY IS HIGH (26) W-C	0.78 OF	23	309	TEND TO BE THOSE WHERE ORAL SOCIALIZATION ANXIETY IS LOW (27) W-C	0.73 OF	26	18 7 5 19 XSQ= 10.90 PHI= 0.472 XP = 0.0010
317	TILT TOWARD BEING THOSE WHERE DISPLAY OF AFFECTION TOWARD THE INFANT IS LOW (29) B-B-C	0.58 OF	31	317	TILT TOWARD BEING THOSE WHERE DISPLAY OF AFFECTION TOWARD THE INFANT IS HIGH (39) B-B-C	0.72 OF	32	13 23 18 9 XSQ= 4.61 PHI= -0.270 XP = 0.0319
318	TILT TOWARD BEING THOSE WHERE THE OVERALL INDULGENCE OF THE INFANT IS LOW (31) B-B-C	0.61 OF	33	318	TILT TOWARD BEING THOSE WHERE THE OVERALL INDULGENCE OF THE INFANT IS HIGH (40) B-B-C	0.73 OF	33	13 24 20 9 XSQ= 6.15 PHI= -0.305 XP = 0.0131
321	LEAN TOWARD BEING THOSE WHERE THE IMMEDIACY OF REDUCTION OF THE INFANT'S DRIVES IS LOW (25) B-B-C	0.59 OF	29	321	LEAN TOWARD BEING THOSE WHERE THE IMMEDIACY OF REDUCTION OF THE INFANT'S DRIVES IS HIGH (35) B-B-C	0.81 OF	26	12 21 17 5 XSQ= 7.30 PHI= -0.364 XP = 0.0069
322	DRIFT TOWARD BEING THOSE WHERE THE CONSISTENCY OF REDUCTION OF THE INFANT'S DRIVES IS LOW (32) B-B-C	0.68 OF	28	322	DRIFT TOWARD BEING THOSE WHERE THE CONSISTENCY OF REDUCTION OF THE INFANT'S DRIVES IS HIGH (27) B-B-C	0.62 OF	26	9 16 19 10 XSQ= 3.58 PHI= -0.257 XP = 0.0586
323	DRIFT TOWARD BEING THOSE WHERE THE CONSTANCY OF PRESENCE OF THE INFANT'S NURTURANT AGENT IS LOW (45) B-B-C	0.74 OF	34	323	DRIFT TOWARD BEING THOSE WHERE THE CONSTANCY OF PRESENCE OF THE INFANT'S NURTURANT AGENT IS HIGH (29) B-B-C	0.51 OF	35	9 18 25 17 XSQ= 3.52 PHI= -0.226 XP = 0.0605
324	TILT TOWARD BEING THOSE WHERE THE PAIN INFLICTED ON THE INFANT BY THE NURTURANT AGENT IS HIGH (34) B-B-C	0.69 OF	32	324	TILT TOWARD BEING THOSE WHERE THE PAIN INFLICTED ON THE INFANT BY THE NURTURANT AGENT IS LOW OR NEGLIGIBLE (32) B-B-C	0.62 OF	29	22 11 10 18 XSQ= 4.64 PHI= 0.276 XP = 0.0312
326	LEAN TOWARD BEING THOSE WHERE THE INFERRED TRANSITION ANXIETY BETWEEN INFANCY AND CHILDHOOD IS HIGH (32) B-B-C	0.64 OF	33	326	LEAN TOWARD BEING THOSE WHERE THE INFERRED TRANSITION ANXIETY BETWEEN INFANCY AND CHILDHOOD IS LOW (35) B-B-C	0.72 OF	29	21 8 12 21 XSQ= 6.67 PHI= 0.328 XP = 0.0098

328	DRIFT TOWARD BEING THOSE 0.65 OF 20 WHERE THE AGE OF THE INFANT AT THE ONSET OF SERIOUS SOCIALIZATION, OTHER THAN WEANING, IS TWO YEARS OR LOWER (20) B-B-C	328 DRIFT TOWARD BEING THOSE 0.67 OF 18 WHERE THE AGE OF THE INFANT AT THE ONSET OF SERIOUS SOCIALIZATION, OTHER THAN WEANING, IS HIGHER THAN TWO YEARS (21) B-B-C	7 12 13 6 XSQ= 2.64 PHI= -0.264 EP = 0.0624
334	TILT TOWARD BEING THOSE 0.62 OF 37 WHERE THE INDULGENCE OF THE CHILD IS LOW (38) B-B-C	334 TILT TOWARD BEING THOSE 0.64 OF 36 WHERE THE INDULGENCE OF THE CHILD IS HIGH (40) B-B-C	14 23 23 13 XSQ= 3.97 PHI= -0.233 XP = 0.0464
337	DRIFT TOWARD BEING THOSE 0.66 OF 35 WHERE THE CHILD'S INFERRED ANXIETY OVER NON-PERFORMANCE OF RESPONSIBLE BEHAVIOR IS HIGH (38) B-B-C	337 DRIFT TOWARD BEING THOSE 0.58 OF 33 WHERE THE CHILD'S INFERRED ANXIETY OVER NON-PERFORMANCE OF RESPONSIBLE BEHAVIOR IS LOW (35) B-B-C	23 14 12 19 XSQ= 2.83 PHI= 0.204 XP = 0.0923
345	DRIFT TOWARD BEING THOSE 0.58 OF 36 WHERE THE CHILD'S INFERRED ANXIETY OVER NON-PERFORMANCE OF SELF-RELIANT BEHAVIOR IS HIGH (37) B-B-C	345 DRIFT TOWARD BEING THOSE 0.66 OF 35 WHERE THE CHILD'S INFERRED ANXIETY OVER NON-PERFORMANCE OF SELF-RELIANT BEHAVIOR IS LOW (39) B-B-C	21 12 15 23 XSQ= 3.22 PHI= 0.213 XP = 0.0729
349	LEAN TOWARD BEING THOSE 0.75 OF 28 WHERE THE CHILD'S INFERRED ANXIETY OVER NON-PERFORMANCE OF ACHIEVEMENT BEHAVIOR IS HIGH (34) B-B-C	349 LEAN TOWARD BEING THOSE 0.66 OF 29 WHERE THE CHILD'S INFERRED ANXIETY OVER NON-PERFORMANCE OF ACHIEVEMENT BEHAVIOR IS LOW (28) B-B-C	21 10 7 19 XSQ= 7.86 PHI= 0.371 XP = 0.0050
350	TEND TO BE THOSE 0.81 OF 27 WHERE THE CHILD'S INFERRED ANXIETY OVER PERFORMANCE OF ACHIEVEMENT BEHAVIOR IS HIGH (34) B-B-C	350 TEND TO BE THOSE 0.68 OF 28 WHERE THE CHILD'S INFERRED ANXIETY OVER PERFORMANCE OF ACHIEVEMENT BEHAVIOR IS LOW (26) B-B-C	22 9 5 19 XSQ= 11.67 PHI= 0.461 XP = 0.0006
351	DRIFT TOWARD BEING THOSE 0.56 OF 27 WHERE THE CHILD'S INFERRED CONFLICT REGARDING ACHIEVEMENT BEHAVIOR IS HIGH (26) B-B-C	351 DRIFT TOWARD BEING THOSE 0.71 OF 28 WHERE THE CHILD'S INFERRED CONFLICT REGARDING ACHIEVEMENT BEHAVIOR IS LOW (34) B-B-C	15 8 12 20 XSQ= 3.08 PHI= 0.237 XP = 0.0793
352	TILT TOWARD BEING THOSE 0.78 OF 36 WHERE THE TOTAL POSITIVE PRESSURE TOWARD DEVELOPING OBEDIENT BEHAVIOR IN THE CHILD IS HIGH (44) B-B-C	352 TILT TOWARD BEING THOSE 0.55 OF 31 WHERE THE TOTAL POSITIVE PRESSURE TOWARD DEVELOPING OBEDIENT BEHAVIOR IN THE CHILD IS LOW (28) B-B-C	28 14 8 17 XSQ= 6.25 PHI= 0.305 XP = 0.0125
353	TILT TOWARD BEING THOSE 0.75 OF 36 WHERE THE CHILD'S INFERRED ANXIETY OVER NON-PERFORMANCE OF OBEDIENT BEHAVIOR IS HIGH (42) B-B-C	353 TILT TOWARD BEING THOSE 0.58 OF 33 WHERE THE CHILD-S INFERRED ANXIETY OVER NON-PERFORMANCE OF OBEDIENT BEHAVIOR IS LOW (32) B-B-C	27 14 9 19 XSQ= 6.29 PHI= 0.302 XP = 0.0122

354	TEND TO BE THOSE 0.69 OF 36 WHERE THE CHILD'S INFERRED ANXIETY OVER PERFORMANCE OF OBEDIENT BEHAVIOR IS HIGH (36) B-B-C	354	TEND TO BE THOSE 0.75 OF 32 WHERE THE CHILD'S INFERRED ANXIETY OVER PERFORMANCE OF OBEDIENT BEHAVIOR IS LOW (37) B-B-C	25 8 11 24 XSQ= 11.68 PHI= 0.414 XP = 0.0006
355	LEAN TOWARD BEING THOSE 0.69 OF 36 WHERE THE CHILD'S INFERRED CONFLICT REGARDING OBEDIENT BEHAVIOR IS HIGH (35) B-B-C	355	LEAN TOWARD BEING THOSE 0.72 OF 32 WHERE THE CHILD'S INFERRED CONFLICT REGARDING OBEDIENT BEHAVIOR IS LOW (38) B-B-C	25 9 11 23 XSQ= 9.98 PHI= 0.383 XP = 0.0016
356	DRIFT TOWARD BEING THOSE 0.72 OF 25 WHERE ADOLESCENT PEER GROUPS OR PAIRS ARE PRESENT IN A SETTING OF COURTSHIP (29) JKH	356	DRIFT TOWARD BEING THOSE 0.58 OF 24 WHERE NEITHER ADOLESCENT PEER GROUPS NOR PAIRS ARE PRESENT IN A SETTING OF COURTSHIP (22) JKH	18 10 7 14 XSQ= 3.45 PHI= 0.265 XP = 0.0634
358	LEAN MORE TOWARD BEING THOSE 0.96 OF 25 WHERE ADOLESCENT PEER GROUPS ARE PRESENT IN A SETTING OF WORK AND PUBLIC GATHERINGS AND LEISURE, OR OF PUBLIC GATHERINGS AND LEISURE, OR OF LEISURE ONLY (41) JKH	358	LEAN LESS TOWARD BEING THOSE 0.60 OF 25 WHERE ADOLESCENT PEER GROUPS ARE PRESENT IN A SETTING OF WORK AND PUBLIC GATHERINGS AND LEISURE, OR OF PUBLIC GATHERINGS AND LEISURE, OR OF LEISURE ONLY (41) JKH	24 15 1 10 XSQ= 7.46 PHI= 0.386 XP = 0.0063
360	DRIFT TOWARD BEING THOSE 0.56 OF 16 WHERE ADOLESCENT PEER GROUPS ARE PRESENT IN A SETTING OF WORK AND PUBLIC GATHERINGS AND LEISURE, OR AT LEAST OF PUBLIC GATHERINGS AND LEISURE (14) JKH	360	DRIFT TOWARD BEING THOSE 0.76 OF 21 WHERE ADOLESCENT PEER GROUPS ARE PRESENT ONLY IN A SETTING OF LEISURE, OR ELSE ARE ABSENT (23) JKH	9 5 7 16 XSQ= 2.80 PHI= 0.275 EP = 0.0857
377	TEND LESS TO BE THOSE 0.62 OF 168 WHERE MALE GENITAL MUTILATION IS ABSENT (242)	377	TEND MORE TO BE THOSE 0.88 OF 154 WHERE MALE GENITAL MUTILATION IS ABSENT (242)	64 19 104 135 XSQ= 26.53 PHI= 0.287 XP = 0.0000
393	TILT TOWARD BEING THOSE 0.64 OF 39 WHERE EXTRAMARITAL COITUS IS PUNISHED, RATHER THAN PERMITTED (43) F-B	393	TILT TOWARD BEING THOSE 0.63 OF 38 WHERE EXTRAMARITAL COITUS IS PERMITTED, RATHER THAN PUNISHED (41) F-B	25 14 14 24 XSQ= 4.68 PHI= 0.247 XP = 0.0305
399	DRIFT TOWARD BEING THOSE 0.65 OF 23 WHERE INTENSITY OF CASTRATION ANXIETY IS HIGH (23) WNS	399	DRIFT TOWARD BEING THOSE 0.65 OF 20 WHERE INTENSITY OF CASTRATION ANXIETY IS LOW (22) WNS	15 7 8 13 XSQ= 2.79 PHI= 0.255 XP = 0.0946
419	TILT MORE TOWARD BEING THOSE 0.76 OF 45 WHERE MILITARY GLORY IS STRONGLY OR MODERATELY EMPHASIZED (55) PES	419	TILT LESS TOWARD BEING THOSE 0.51 OF 37 WHERE MILITARY GLORY IS STRONGLY OR MODERATELY EMPHASIZED (55) PES	34 19 11 18 XSQ= 4.20 PHI= 0.226 XP = 0.0404

420	DRIFT TOWARD BEING THOSE WHERE BELLICOSITY IS EXTREME (41) PES	0.58 OF 45	420	DRIFT TOWARD BEING THOSE WHERE BELLICOSITY IS MODERATE OR NEGLIGIBLE (46) PES	0.66 OF 38	26 13 19 25 XSQ= 3.70 PHI= 0.211 XP = 0.0545
424	LEAN TOWARD BEING THOSE WHERE RELIGIOUS SPECIALISTS ARE FULL-TIME, RATHER THAN PART-TIME (21) JMH	0.55 OF 31	424	LEAN TOWARD BEING THOSE WHERE RELIGIOUS SPECIALISTS ARE PART-TIME, RATHER THAN FULL-TIME (33) JMH	0.86 OF 21	17 3 14 18 XSQ= 7.07 PHI= 0.369 XP = 0.0078
426	TEND TO BE THOSE WHERE A HIGH GOD IS PRESENT (156) GES,EA	0.73 OF 133	426	TEND TO BE THOSE WHERE A HIGH GOD IS ABSENT (104) GES,EA	0.54 OF 124	97 57 36 67 XSQ= 18.32 PHI= 0.267 XP = 0.0000
428	LEAN TOWARD BEING THOSE WHERE A HIGH GOD, IF PRESENT AND ACTIVE, SUPPORTS HUMAN MORALITY, RATHER THAN NOT SUPPORTING IT (61) GES,EA	0.80 OF 56	428	LEAN TOWARD BEING THOSE WHERE A HIGH GOD, IF PRESENT AND ACTIVE, DOES NOT SUPPORT HUMAN MORALITY, RATHER THAN SUPPORTING IT (26) GES,EA	0.52 OF 29	45 14 11 15 XSQ= 7.81 PHI= 0.303 XP = 0.0052
435	TILT TOWARD BEING THOSE WHERE ABANDONMENT OF THE HOUSE OF THE DEAD IS NOT PRACTICED (19) LWS	0.86 OF 14	435	TILT TOWARD BEING THOSE WHERE ABANDONMENT OF THE HOUSE OF THE DEAD IS PRACTICED (12) LWS	0.59 OF 17	2 10 12 7 XSQ= 4.68 PHI= -0.389 EP = 0.0245
441	DRIFT TOWARD BEING THOSE WHERE FEAR OF HUMAN BEINGS IS LOW (32) W-C	0.65 OF 26	441	DRIFT TOWARD BEING THOSE WHERE FEAR OF HUMAN BEINGS IS HIGH (29) W-C	0.63 OF 30	9 19 17 11 XSQ= 3.52 PHI= -0.251 XP = 0.0607
453	LEAN TOWARD BEING THOSE WHERE THE ROLE OF RELIGIOUS EXPERTS IS CONDUCIVE TO THE DEVELOPMENT OF THE INDIVIDUAL'S NEED TO ACHIEVE (13) DCM	0.53 OF 19	453	LEAN TOWARD BEING THOSE WHERE THE ROLE OF RELIGIOUS EXPERTS IS NOT CONDUCIVE TO THE DEVELOPMENT OF THE INDIVIDUAL'S NEED TO ACHIEVE (23) DCM	0.93 OF 14	10 1 9 13 XSQ= 5.60 PHI= 0.412 EP = 0.0089
458	TEND TO BE THOSE WHERE GAMES, IF PRESENT, INCLUDE GAMES OF STRATEGY (52) R-A-B,EA	0.54 OF 87	458	TEND TO BE THOSE WHERE GAMES, IF PRESENT, DO NOT INCLUDE GAMES OF STRATEGY (119) R-A-B,EA	0.94 OF 82	47 5 40 77 XSQ= 43.29 PHI= 0.506 XP = 0.
460	TEND TO BE THOSE WHERE GAMES, IF PRESENT, ARE NOT LIMITED TO GAMES OF SKILL ONLY (104) R-A-B,EA	0.74 OF 87	460	TEND TO BE THOSE WHERE GAMES, IF PRESENT, ARE LIMITED TO GAMES OF SKILL ONLY (67) R-A-B,EA	0.54 OF 82	23 44 64 38 XSQ= 11.96 PHI= -0.266 XP = 0.0005

468	TILT LESS TOWARD BEING THOSE 0.55 OF 31 WHERE CONTACT WITH OTHER CULTURES IS REGULAR OR IRREGULAR, RATHER THAN FREQUENT (37) JMH	468	TILT MORE TOWARD BEING THOSE 0.90 OF 21 WHERE CONTACT WITH OTHER CULTURES IS REGULAR OR IRREGULAR, RATHER THAN FREQUENT (37) JMH		14 2 17 19 XSQ= 5.88 PHI= 0.336 XP = 0.0153
472	DRIFT TOWARD BEING THOSE 0.62 OF 47 WHERE THE COMPOSITE NARCISSISM INDEX IS HIGH (47) PES	472	DRIFT TOWARD BEING THOSE 0.59 OF 39 WHERE THE COMPOSITE NARCISSISM INDEX IS LOW (43) PES		29 16 18 23 XSQ= 2.87 PHI= 0.183 XP = 0.0902
473	TILT LESS TOWARD BEING THOSE 0.52 OF 46 WHERE SENSITIVITY TO INSULT IS MODERATE OR NEGLIGIBLE (56) PES	473	TILT MORE TOWARD BEING THOSE 0.76 OF 38 WHERE SENSITIVITY TO INSULT IS MODERATE OR NEGLIGIBLE (56) PES		22 9 24 29 XSQ= 4.22 PHI= 0.224 XP = 0.0399
476	DRIFT TOWARD BEING THOSE 0.50 OF 26 WHERE THE DEGREE OF INSOBRIETY IS MODERATE OR SLIGHT (18) DH	476	DRIFT TOWARD BEING THOSE 0.80 OF 20 WHERE THE DEGREE OF INSOBRIETY IS STRONG (31) DH		13 16 13 4 XSQ= 3.17 PHI= -0.263 XP = 0.0748
477	TILT TOWARD BEING THOSE 0.73 OF 15 WHERE ALCOHOLIC AGGRESSION IS MODERATE OR SLIGHT (19) DH	477	TILT TOWARD BEING THOSE 0.65 OF 17 WHERE ALCOHOLIC AGGRESSION IS STRONG (15) DH		4 11 11 6 XSQ= 3.23 PHI= -0.318 EP = 0.0416

****

97 CULTURES WHERE THE HIERARCHY OF LOCAL JURISDICTION HAS FOUR LEVELS (58) GES,EA	97 CULTURES WHERE THE HIERARCHY OF LOCAL JURISDICTION HAS THREE OR TWO LEVELS (273) GES,EA

BACKGROUND ON PAGE 86 BOTH SUBJECT AND PREDICATE

58 IN LEFT COLUMN

ARAUCANIANS	ASHANTI	BABWA	BACAIRI	BAMBARA	BIRIFOR	BORORO	BOZO	BURUSHO	CHORTI
COORG	CREEK	CAGUR	DOGON	EGYPTIANS	ENGA	FOX	FUTAJALONKE	GURE	HANO
JUKUN	KABYLE	KACHIN	KATAB	KERALA	KHASI	KISSI	MAM	MAMBILA	MANGAIANS
MAORI	MARGI	MATAKAM	MENDE	MIAO	MINCHIA	MONGO	MOSSI	ONTONG-JAVA	ORAON
PALAUANS	PATHAN	PURARI	REGEIBAT	SAMOANS	SHLUH	SIWANS	TALLENSI	TANALA	TERA
TERENA	TIMBIRA	TIV	TSHIMSHIAN	TURKMEN	YAKO	YORUBA	ZUNI		

273 IN RIGHT COLUMN

ABIPON	ABOR	AINU	AKHA	ALACALUF	ALBANIANS	ALORESE	AMBA	AMERICANS	ANDAMANESE
APINAYE	ARANDA	ARAPESH	ATAYAL	ATSUGEWI	AWEIKOMA	AYMARA	AZANDE	AZTEC	BAMILEKE
BANDA	BARABRA	BARI	BASSERI	BAYA	BEJA	BEMBA	BHIL	BHUIYA	BLACK CARIB
BOERS	BOTOCUDO	BRAZILIANS	BULGARIANS	BUNLAP	CADUVEO	CAGABA	CALLINAGO	CAMAYURA	CAMBODIANS
CARIB	CAYAPA	CHAGGA	CHAMACOCO	CHENCHU	CHERKESS	CHEROKEE	CHEYENNE	CHIBCHA	CHIR-APACHE
CHIRIGUANO	CHOCO	CHOROTI	CHUKCHEE	COCHITI	COPR ESKIMO	CREE	CROW	CUNA	CZECHS
DARD	DELAWARE	DIEGUENO	DIERI	DILLING	DOROBO	DUTCH	ELLICE	EYAK	FANG
FON	GANDA	GARO	GILYAK	GISU	GOAJIRO	GOND	GROS VENTRE	GUAHIBO	GUATO
HAIDA	HANUNOO	HASINAI	HAVASUPAI	HAWAIIANS	HAZARA	HEBREWS	HERERO	HUICHOL	HUKUNDIKA
HURON	IBAN	IFUGAO	ILA	INCA	INGALIK	INGASSANA	IRAQW	IRISH	JAPANESE
JAVANESE	JEMEZ	JIVARO	KAPAUKU	KARIERA	KASKA	KAZAK	KERAKI	KHALKA	KIKUYU
KOHISTANI	KOL	KOREANS	KORYAK	KPE	KUBA	KUNG	KURTATCHI	KUTENAI	KWAKIUTL
LAKHER	LAMBA	LAMET	LANGO	LAPPS	LAU	LEPCHA	LESU	LHOTA NAGA	LOLO
LOZI	LUO	MACASSARESE	MALAYS	MAMVU	MANDAN	MANIHIKI	MANUS	MARICOPA	MARQUESANS
MARSHALLESE	MASAI	MATACO	MAYA	MBUNDU	MBUTI	MERINA	MIAMI	MIN CHINESE	MISKITO
MIWOK	MNONG GAR	MONGUOR	MOTA	MOTILON	MUNDURUCU	MURINBATA	MURNGIN	MZAB	NABESNA
NAMA	NAMBICUARA	NANDI	NATCHEZ	NAVAHO	NDEMBU	NICOBARESE	NOMLAKI	NUER	NUNIVAK
NUPE	NURI	NYAKYUSA	NYORO	OJIBWA	OKINAWANS	OMAHA	ONA	PAEZ	PAIWAN
PAPAGO	PARAUJANO	PAWNEE	PONAPEANS	PUKAPUKA	PURUM	RIFFIANS	RUNDI	RWALA	SAGADA
SAMOYED	SANDAWE	SANPOIL	SANTAL	SARSI	SELUNG	SEMANG	SENIANG	SERBS	SHERENTE
SHILLUK	SINHALESE	SIRIONO	SIUAI	SOMALI	SONGHAI	SOTHO	SUBANUN	SWAZI	SYRIANS
TAGBANUA	TALAMANCA	TAOS	TAPIRAPE	TARAHUMARA	TAREUMIUT	TEDA	TEHUELCHE	TENDA	TENETEHARA
TENINO	TESO	THAI	THONGA	TIGRINYA	TIKOPIA	TIMUCUA	TIWI	TODA	TOKELAU
TOLOWA	TORAJA	TOTONAC	TRISTAN	TROBRIAND	TRUKESE	TRUMAI	TUBATULABAL	TUCANO	TUCUNA
TUNEBO	TUPINAMBA	TURKANA	TWANA	ULAWANS	UTE	VEDDA	VENDA	VIETNAMESE	WAICA
WALLOONS	WANTOAT	WAPISHANA	WARRAU	WASHO	WICHITA	WIKMUNKAN	WITOTO	WOGEO	WOLEAIANS
WOLOF	YABARANA	YAGUA	YAHGAN	YAKUT	YAO	YAPESE	YARURO	YOKUTS	YOMBE
YUKAGHIR	YUKI	YUROK							

69 EXCLUDED BECAUSE UNASCERTAINED

3	LEAN LESS TOWARD BEING THOSE LOCATED OUTSIDE OF AFRICA (320)	0.64 OF 58	3	LEAN MORE TOWARD BEING THOSE LOCATED OUTSIDE OF AFRICA (320)	0.82 OF 273	21 48 37 225 XSQ= 8.96 PHI= 0.165 XP = 0.0028
8	DRIFT MORE TOWARD BEING THOSE LOCATED OUTSIDE OF NORTH AMERICA (330)	0.91 OF 58	8	DRIFT LESS TOWARD BEING THOSE LOCATED OUTSIDE OF NORTH AMERICA (330)	0.80 OF 273	5 54 53 219 XSQ= 3.34 PHI= -0.100 XP = 0.0676
12	DRIFT MORE TOWARD BEING THOSE WHERE THE LATITUDE IS LESS THAN FIFTY DEGREES (367)	0.98 OF 58	12	DRIFT LESS TOWARD BEING THOSE WHERE THE LATITUDE IS LESS THAN FIFTY DEGREES (367)	0.90 OF 273	1 28 57 245 XSQ= 3.35 PHI= -0.101 XP = 0.0670
13	TILT MORE TOWARD BEING THOSE WHERE THE LATITUDE IS LESS THAN FORTY DEGREES (329)	0.95 OF 58	13	TILT LESS TOWARD BEING THOSE WHERE THE LATITUDE IS LESS THAN FORTY DEGREES (329)	0.81 OF 273	3 52 55 221 XSQ= 5.68 PHI= -0.131 XP = 0.0171
36	DRIFT MORE TOWARD BEING THOSE WHERE THE NATURAL ENVIRONMENT IS OTHER THAN 'VERY HARSH,' OR SUB-TROPICAL BUSH, OR TEMPERATE GRASSLAND (292) FWM	0.84 OF 58	36	DRIFT LESS TOWARD BEING THOSE WHERE THE NATURAL ENVIRONMENT IS OTHER THAN 'VERY HARSH,' OR SUB-TROPICAL BUSH, OR TEMPERATE GRASSLAND (292) FWM	0.71 OF 273	9 78 49 195 XSQ= 3.56 PHI= -0.104 XP = 0.0592
44	TEND MORE TO BE THOSE WHERE SETTLEMENTS ARE FIXED (222)	0.88 OF 58	44	TEND LESS TO BE THOSE WHERE SETTLEMENTS ARE FIXED (222)	0.62 OF 272	51 169 7 103 XSQ= 13.18 PHI= 0.200 XP = 0.0003
46	LEAN MORE TOWARD BEING THOSE OTHER THAN WHERE SETTLEMENTS ARE NON-FIXED AND MOVEMENT IS NOMADIC (260)	0.93 OF 58	46	LEAN LESS TOWARD BEING THOSE OTHER THAN WHERE SETTLEMENTS ARE NON-FIXED AND MOVEMENT IS NOMADIC (260)	0.75 OF 272	4 68 54 204 XSQ= 8.15 PHI= -0.157 XP = 0.0043
51	LEAN MORE TOWARD BEING THOSE WHERE SUBSISTENCE IS PRIMARILY BY FOOD PRODUCTION -- I. E., AGRICULTURE OR HUSBANDRY -- RATHER THAN BY GATHERING (253)	0.81 OF 58	51	LEAN LESS TOWARD BEING THOSE WHERE SUBSISTENCE IS PRIMARILY BY FOOD PRODUCTION -- I. E., AGRICULTURE OR HUSBANDRY -- RATHER THAN BY GATHERING (253)	0.58 OF 273	47 157 11 116 XSQ= 10.22 PHI= 0.176 XP = 0.0014
62	TILT MORE TOWARD BEING THOSE WHERE HUSBANDRY OF SOME KIND IS PRESENT (228)	0.83 OF 58	62	TILT LESS TOWARD BEING THOSE WHERE HUSBANDRY OF SOME KIND IS PRESENT (228)	0.64 OF 273	48 176 10 97 XSQ= 6.50 PHI= 0.140 XP = 0.0108

71	DRIFT TCWARD BEING THCSE WHERE METAL WCRKING IS PRESENT (98)	0.56 OF 36	71	DRIFT TOWARD BEING THOSE WHERE METAL WORKING IS ABSENT (153)	0.63 OF 206	20 76 16 130 XSQ= 3.71 PHI= 0.124 XP = 0.0540
73	TILT TCWARD BEING THOSE WHERE WEAVING IS PRESENT (118)	0.67 OF 33	73	TILT TOWARD BEING THOSE WHERE WEAVING IS ABSENT (130)	0.55 OF 207	22 93 11 114 XSQ= 4.55 PHI= 0.138 XP = 0.0328
81	TEND TC BE THOSE WHERE A CITY CR TOWN IS PRESENT, OR THE AVERAGE COMMUNITY SIZE IS 200 OR GREATER (89)	0.68 OF 34	81	TEND TO BE THOSE WHERE NO CITY OR TOWN IS PRESENT, AND THE AVERAGE·COMMUNITY SIZE IS SMALLER THAN 200 (135)	0.66 OF 188	23 64 11 124 XSQ= 12.27 PHI= 0.235 XP = 0.0005
83	TEND TO BE THCSE WHERE, WITH NC CITY ANC NC TOWN PRESENT, THE AVERAGE COMMUNITY SIZE IS BETWEEN 200 AND 999, RATHER THAN SMALLER THAN 200 (45)	0.54 OF 24	83	TEND TO BE THOSE WHERE, WITH NO CITY AND NO TOWN PRESENT, THE AVERAGE COMMUNITY SIZE IS SMALLER THAN 200, RATHER THAN BETWEEN 200 AND 999 (135)	0.79 CF 156	13 32 11 124 XSQ= 10.83 PHI= 0.245 XP = 0.0010
86	LEAN TOWARD BEING THOSE WHERE THE LEVEL OF POLITICAL INTEGRATION IS THE LARGE STATE, THE LITTLE STATE, OR THE MINIMAL STATE (148) GPM	0.67 OF 43	86	LEAN TOWARD BEING THOSE WHERE THE LEVEL OF PCLITICAL INTEGRATICN IS THE AUTONOMOUS COMMUNITY, OR THE FAMILY (156) GPM	0.57 OF 215	29 93 14 122 XSQ= 7.47 PHI= 0.170 XP = 0.0063
96	TILT TCWARD BEING THOSE WHERE THE HIERARCHY OF NATICNAL JURISDICTICN HAS FCUR, THREE, TWC OR CNE LEVEL (174) GES,EA	0.67 OF 58	96	TILT TOWARD BEING THOSE WHERE THE HIERARCHY OF NATIONAL JURISDICTION HAS NO LEVELS (156) GES,EA	0.50 OF 272	39 135 19 137 XSQ= 5.26 PHI= 0.126 XP = 0.0218
106	TILT MCRE TOWARC BEING THCSE WHERE CLASS STRATIFICATION, IF PRESENT, IS BASED CN SCMETHING CTHER THAN WEALTH (126)	0.81 OF 31	106	TILT LESS TOWARD BEING THOSE WHERE CLASS STRATIFICATICN, IF PRESENT, IS BASED ON SOMETHING OTHER THAN WEALTH (126)	0.55 OF 138	6 62 25 76 XSQ= 5.86 PHI= -0.186 XP = 0.0155
109	LEAN LESS TOWARC BEING THCSE WHERE CASTES ARE ABSENT (317)	0.73 OF 52	109	LEAN MORE TOWARD BEING THOSE WHERE CASTES ARE ABSENT (317)	0.89 CF 258	14 29 38 229 XSQ= 7.65 PHI= 0.157 XP = 0.0057
110	TEND TC BE THCSE WHERE SLAVERY IS PRESENT (163)	0.64 OF 56	110	TEND TO BE THOSE WHERE SLAVERY IS ABSENT (218)	0.63 CF 264	36 97 20 167 XSQ= 13.32 PHI= 0.204 XP = 0.0003

128	DRIFT TOWARD BEING THOSE WHERE, IF SUBSISTENCE IS PRIMARILY BY AGRICULTURE, THE WORK IS MAINLY DONE BY MALES (40)	0.72 OF 18	128	DRIFT TOWARD BEING THOSE WHERE, IF SUBSISTENCE IS PRIMARILY BY AGRICULTURE, THE WORK IS MAINLY DONE BY FEMALES (37)	0.55 OF 58	13 26 5 32 XSQ= 3.10 PHI= 0.202 XP = 0.0782
129	TILT TOWARD BEING THOSE WHERE WEAVING IS MAINLY DONE BY MALES (31)	0.50 OF 20	129	TILT TOWARD BEING THOSE WHERE WEAVING IS MAINLY DONE BY FEMALES (73)	0.76 OF 82	10 20 10 62 XSQ= 3.92 PHI= 0.196 XP = 0.0477
130	DRIFT TOWARD BEING THOSE WHERE LEATHER WORKING IS MAINLY DONE BY MALES (39)	0.75 OF 12	130	DRIFT TOWARD BEING THOSE WHERE LEATHER WORKING IS MAINLY DONE BY FEMALES (45)	0.58 OF 69	9 29 3 40 XSQ= 3.24 PHI= 0.200 XP = 0.0720
131	IN ALL CASES ARE THOSE WHERE THE CONSTRUCTION OF PERMANENT HOUSES OR THE ERECTION OF TEMPORARY DWELLINGS IS MAINLY DONE BY MALES (136)	1.00 OF 26	131	DRIFT LESS TOWARD BEING THOSE WHERE THE CONSTRUCTION OF PERMANENT HOUSES OR THE ERECTION OF TEMPORARY DWELLINGS IS MAINLY DONE BY MALES (136)	0.84 OF 127	26 107 0 20 XSQ= 3.43 PHI= 0.150 XP = 0.0642
176	TEND TO BE THOSE WHERE THE COMMUNITY IS A CLAN-COMMUNITY OR A COMMUNITY STRUCTURED OR SEGMENTED ON A CLAN BASIS (169)	0.68 OF 56	176	TEND TO BE THOSE WHERE THE COMMUNITY IS OTHER THAN A CLAN-COMMUNITY OR A COMMUNITY STRUCTURED OR SEGMENTED ON A CLAN BASIS (213)	0.60 OF 262	38 104 18 158 XSQ= 13.69 PHI= 0.207 XP = 0.0002
178	TEND LESS TO BE THOSE WHERE THE COMMUNITY IS OTHER THAN SEGMENTED ON A CLAN BASIS AND NON-EXOGAMOUS (295)	0.55 OF 56	178	TEND MORE TO BE THOSE WHERE THE COMMUNITY IS OTHER THAN SEGMENTED ON A CLAN BASIS AND NON-EXOGAMOUS (295)	0.81 OF 262	25 49 31 213 XSQ= 15.97 PHI= 0.224 XP = 0.0001
182	LEAN MORE TOWARD BEING THOSE OTHER THAN WHERE THE COMMUNITY IS STRUCTURED ON A NON-CLAN BASIS AND AGAMOUS (256)	0.84 OF 56	182	LEAN LESS TOWARD BEING THOSE OTHER THAN WHERE THE COMMUNITY IS STRUCTURED ON A NON-CLAN BASIS AND AGAMOUS (256)	0.64 OF 262	9 94 47 168 XSQ= 7.39 PHI= -0.152 XP = 0.0066
186	LEAN TOWARD BEING THOSE WHERE THE KIN GROUP IS EXCLUSIVELY PATRILINEAL (150)	0.53 OF 58	186	LEAN TOWARD BEING THOSE WHERE THE KIN GROUP IS OTHER THAN EXCLUSIVELY PATRILINEAL (250)	0.66 OF 273	31 92 27 181 XSQ= 7.17 PHI= 0.147 XP = 0.0074
188	TEND MORE TO BE THOSE WHERE THE KIN GROUP IS OTHER THAN EXCLUSIVELY COGNATIC (252)	0.84 OF 58	188	TEND LESS TO BE THOSE WHERE THE KIN GROUP IS OTHER THAN EXCLUSIVELY COGNATIC (252)	0.59 OF 273	9 111 49 162 XSQ= 12.02 PHI= -0.191 XP = 0.0005

192	TEND MORE TO BE THOSE OTHER THAN WHERE THE ONLY KIN GROUP PRESENT IS A KINDRED OR ELSE BILATERAL DESCENT IS INFERRED (289)	0.98 OF 58	192	TEND LESS TO BE THOSE OTHER THAN WHERE THE ONLY KIN GROUP PRESENT IS A KINDRED OR ELSE BILATERAL DESCENT IS INFERRED (289)	0.67 OF 273	1 89 57 184 XSQ= 21.50 PHI= -0.255 XP = 0.0000
196	TEND MORE TO BE THOSE WHERE INDIVIDUAL RIGHTS IN REAL PROPERTY, AND RULES FOR INHERITANCE, ARE PRESENT (194)	0.91 OF 44	196	TEND LESS TO BE THOSE WHERE INDIVIDUAL RIGHTS IN REAL PROPERTY, AND RULES FOR INHERITANCE, ARE PRESENT (194)	0.63 OF 196	40 123 4 73 XSQ= 11.81 PHI= 0.222 XP = 0.0006
197	TILT MORE TOWARD BEING THOSE WHERE RULES FOR THE INHERITANCE OF REAL PROPERTY, IF PRESENT, FAVOR EITHER THE MALE HEIR OR LINE, OR THE FEMALE HEIR OR LINE (165)	0.97 OF 40	197	TILT LESS TOWARD BEING THOSE WHERE RULES FOR THE INHERITANCE OF REAL PROPERTY, IF PRESENT, FAVOR EITHER THE MALE HEIR OR LINE, OR THE FEMALE HEIR OR LINE (165)	0.83 OF 123	39 102 1 21 XSQ= 4.31 PHI= 0.163 XP = 0.0378
236	TEND TO BE THOSE WHERE THE FAMILY IS OF AN EXTENDED TYPE, RATHER THAN AN INDEPENDENT TYPE (213)	0.91 OF 58	236	TEND TO BE THOSE WHERE THE FAMILY IS OF AN INDEPENDENT TYPE, RATHER THAN AN EXTENDED TYPE (185)	0.54 OF 272	53 126 5 146 XSQ= 37.31 PHI= 0.336 XP = 0.
241	IN ALL CASES ARE THOSE WHERE THE FAMILY, IF EXTENDED, IS LARGE OR SMALL, RATHER THAN STEM (187)	1.00 OF 53	241	LEAN LESS TOWARD BEING THOSE WHERE THE FAMILY, IF EXTENDED, IS LARGE OR SMALL, RATHER THAN STEM (187)	0.84 OF 126	53 106 0 20 XSQ= 7.94 PHI= 0.211 XP = 0.0048
263	DRIFT MORE TOWARD BEING THOSE WHERE WIVES ARE OBTAINED BY RELATIVELY DIFFICULT MEANS, NAMELY BY BRIDE-PRICE, BRIDE-SERVICE, OR EXCHANGING A FEMALE RELATIVE (233)	0.71 OF 58	263	DRIFT LESS TOWARD BEING THOSE WHERE WIVES ARE OBTAINED BY RELATIVELY DIFFICULT MEANS, NAMELY BY BRIDE-PRICE, BRIDE-SERVICE, OR EXCHANGING A FEMALE RELATIVE (233)	0.57 OF 270	41 154 17 116 XSQ= 3.15 PHI= 0.098 XP = 0.0761
302	DRIFT TOWARD BEING THOSE WHERE THE AVERAGE EARLY SATISFACTION POTENTIAL IS LOW (17) W-C	0.83 OF 6	302	DRIFT TOWARD BEING THOSE WHERE THE AVERAGE EARLY SATISFACTION POTENTIAL IS HIGH (23) W-C	0.63 OF 30	1 19 5 11 XSQ= 2.72 PHI= -0.275 EP = 0.0689
305	DRIFT TOWARD BEING THOSE WHERE THE EARLY SEXUAL SATISFACTION POTENTIAL IS LOW (24) W-C	0.86 OF 7	305	DRIFT TOWARD BEING THOSE WHERE THE EARLY SEXUAL SATISFACTION POTENTIAL IS HIGH (27) W-C	0.60 OF 40	1 24 6 16 XSQ= 3.33 PHI= -0.266 XP = 0.0679
308	IN ALL CASES ARE THOSE WHERE AVERAGE SOCIALIZATION ANXIETY IS HIGH (22) W-C	1.00 OF 6	308	TILT TOWARD BEING THOSE WHERE AVERAGE SOCIALIZATION ANXIETY IS LOW (18) W-C	0.50 OF 30	6 15 0 15 XSQ= 3.29 PHI= 0.302 EP = 0.0304

320	DRIFT MORE TOWARD BEING THOSE WHERE THE DEGREE OF REDUCTION OF THE INFANT'S DRIVES IS HIGH (45) B-B-C	0.91 OF 11	320	DRIFT LESS TOWARD BEING THOSE WHERE THE DEGREE OF REDUCTION OF THE INFANT'S DRIVES IS HIGH (45) B-B-C	0.59 OF 54	10 32 1 22 XSQ= 2.74 PHI= 0.205 XP = 0.0979
377	LEAN LESS TOWARD BEING THOSE WHERE MALE GENITAL MUTILATION IS ABSENT (242)	0.57 OF 56	377	LEAN MORE TOWARD BEING THOSE WHERE MALE GENITAL MUTILATION IS ABSENT (242)	0.78 OF 267	24 59 32 208 XSQ= 9.39 PHI= 0.170 XP = 0.0022
382	DRIFT TOWARD BEING THOSE WHERE FEMALE INITIATION RITES ARE ABSENT (27) JKB	0.75 OF 8	382	DRIFT TOWARD BEING THOSE WHERE FEMALE INITIATION RITES ARE PRESENT (38) JKB	0.64 OF 53	2 34 6 19 XSQ= 2.93 PHI= -0.219 XP = 0.0867
399	TILT TOWARD BEING THOSE WHERE INTENSITY OF CASTRATION ANXIETY IS LOW (22) WNS	0.80 OF 10	399	TILT TOWARD BEING THOSE WHERE INTENSITY OF CASTRATION ANXIETY IS HIGH (23) WNS	0.62 OF 34	2 21 8 13 XSQ= 3.86 PHI= -0.296 XP = 0.0495
425	LEAN TOWARD BEING THOSE WHERE SUPERNATURALS ARE MAINLY BENEVOLENT, RATHER THAN AGGRESSIVE (16) L-T-W	0.86 OF 7	425	LEAN TOWARD BEING THOSE WHERE SUPERNATURALS ARE MAINLY AGGRESSIVE, RATHER THAN BENEVOLENT (20) L-T-W	0.73 OF 26	6 7 1 19 XSQ= 5.71 PHI= 0.416 EP = 0.0084
426	TILT MORE TOWARD BEING THOSE WHERE A HIGH GOD IS PRESENT (156) GES,EA	0.75 OF 44	426	TILT LESS TOWARD BEING THOSE WHERE A HIGH GOD IS PRESENT (156) GES,EA	0.57 OF 214	33 122 11 92 XSQ= 4.20 PHI= 0.128 XP = 0.0403
444	TILT TOWARD BEING THOSE WHERE THE USE OF DREAMS TO SEEK AND CONTROL SUPERNATURAL POWERS IS LOW (27) RGD	0.89 OF 9	444	TILT TOWARD BEING THOSE WHERE THE USE OF DREAMS TO SEEK AND CONTROL SUPERNATURAL POWERS IS HIGH (28) RGD	0.60 OF 42	1 25 8 17 XSQ= 5.15 PHI= -0.318 XP = 0.0233

98 CULTURES
WHERE THE HIERARCHY
OF LOCAL JURISDICTION HAS
FOUR CR THREE LEVELS (238) GES,EA

98 CULTURES
WHERE THE HIERARCHY
OF LOCAL JURISDICTION HAS
TWO LEVELS (93) GES,EA

BACKGROUND ON PAGE 86

BOTH SUBJECT AND PREDICATE

238 IN LEFT CCLUMN

ABOR	AINU	ALBANIANS	ALORESE	AMBA	APINAYE	ARAUCANIANS	ASHANTI	ATAYAL	AYMARA
AZANDE	AZTEC	BABWA	BACAIRI	BAMBARA	BAMILEKE	BANDA	BARABRA	BAYA	BEJA
BEMBA	BHIL	BIRIFOR	BOERS	BORORO	BOZO	BULGARIANS	BUNLAP	BURUSHO	CADUVEO
CAGABA	CALLINAGC	CAMAYURA	CAYAPA	CHENCHU	CHERKESS	CHEROKEE	CHEYENNE	CHIBCHA	CHIR-APACHE
CHIRIGUANC	CHCRTI	CHUKCHEE	COCHITI	COORG	CREE	CREEK	CUNA	DAGUR	DARD
DELAWARE	DILLING	DOGCN	DUTCH	EGYPTIANS	ELLICE	ENGA	EYAK	FANG	FON
FOX	FUTAJALONKE	GARC	GISU	GOND	GUAHIBO	GURE	HAIDA	HANO	HASINAI
HAVASUPAI	HAWAIIANS	HAZARA	HEBREWS	HERERO	HUICHOL	HURON	IBAN	IFUGAO	ILA
INGASSANA	IRAQW	JAPANESE	JEMEZ	JUKUN	KABYLE	KACHIN	KAPAUKU	KATAB	KAZAK
KERALA	KHALKA	KHASI	KIKUYU	KISSI	KOHISTANI	KOL	KOREANS	KORYAK	KPE
KUBA	KUNG	KURTATCHI	KWAKIUTL	LAKHER	LAMET	LANGO	LAU	LEPCHA	LESU
LHOTA NAGA	LOLC	LUO	MACASSARESE	MALAYS	MAM	MAMBILA	MANDAN	MANGAIANS	MANIHIKI
MANUS	MACRI	MARGI	MARICOPA	MARQUESANS	MARSHALLESE	MATAKAM	MAYA	MBUNCU	MENDE
MERINA	MIAMI	MIAC	MIN CHINESE	MINCHIA	MISKITO	MNONG GAR	MCNGO	MONGUOR	MOSSI
MOTA	MOTILON	MUNDURUCU	MZAB	NAMBICUARA	NATCHEZ	NAVAHO	NICOBARESE	NUER	NUNIVAK
NUPE	NURI	OJIBWA	OKINAWANS	OMAHA	ONTONG-JAVA	ORAON	PAIWAN	PALAUANS	PAPAGO
PATHAN	PAWNEE	PCNAPEANS	PUKAPUKA	PURARI	PURUM	REGEIBAT	RIFFIANS	RUNCI	RWALA
SAGADA	SAMCANS	SAMOYEC	SANPOIL	SANTAL	SERBS	SHERENTE	SHILLUK	SHLUH	SINHALESE
SIRIONC	SIUAI	SIWANS	SOMALI	SONGHAI	SOTHO	SWAZI	SYRIANS	TALLENSI	TANALA
TAPIRAPE	TAREUMIUT	TECA	TEHUELCHE	TENDA	TENETEHARA	TENINO	TERA	TERENA	TESO
THAI	THCNGA	TIGRINYA	TIKOPIA	TIMBIRA	TIMUCUA	TIV	TIWI	TODA	TOKELAU
TORAJA	TOTCNAC	TRUKESE	TRUMAI	TSHIMSHIAN	TUPINAMBA	TURKMEN	TWANA	ULAWANS	VECCA
VENDA	VIETNAMESE	WAPISHANA	WARRAU	WICHITA	WOGEO	WOLEAIANS	WOLOF	YAKO	YAKUT
YAO	YAPESE	YCKUTS	YOMBE	YORUBA	YUKAGHIR	YUROK	ZUNI		

93 IN RIGHT CCLUMN

ABIPON	AKHA	ALACALUF	AMERICANS	ANDAMANESE	ARANDA	ARAPESH	ATSUGEWI	AWEIKOMA	BARI
BASSERI	BHUIYA	BLACK CARIB	BOTOCUCO	BRAZILIANS	CAMBODIANS	CARIB	CHAGGA	CHAMACOCO	CHOCO
CHOROTI	COPR ESKIMO	CRCW	CZECHS	DIEGUENO	DIERI	DOROBO	GANDA	GILYAK	GOAJIRO
GROS VENTRE	GUATO	HANUNOC	HUKUNDIKA	INCA	INGALIK	IRISH	JAVANESE	JIVARO	KARIERA
KASKA	KERAKI	KUTENAI	LAMBA	LAPPS	LOZI	MAMVU	MASAI	MATACO	MBUTI
MIWOK	MURINBATA	MURNGIN	NABESNA	NAMA	NANDI	NDEMBU	NOMLAKI	NYAKYUSA	NYORO
ONA	PAEZ	PARAUJANO	SANCAWE	SARSI	SELUNG	SEMANG	SENIANG	SUBANUN	TAGBANUA
TALAMANCA	TACS	TARAHUMARA	TOLOWA	TRISTAN	TROBRIAND	TUBATULABAL	TUCANO	TUCUNA	TUNEBO
TURKANA	UTE	WAICA	WALLOONS	WANTOAT	WASHO	WIKMUNKAN	WITOTO	YABARANA	YAGUA
YAHGAN	YARURC	YUKI							

69 EXCLUDED BECAUSE UNASCERTAINEC

5	LEAN LESS TOWARD BEING THOSE LOCATED OUTSIDE OF EAST EURASIA (330)	0.79 OF 238	5	LEAN MORE TOWARD BEING THOSE LOCATED OUTSIDE OF EAST EURASIA (330)	0.91 OF 93	51 8 187 85 XSQ= 6.66 PHI= 0.142 XP = 0.0099
9	LEAN MORE TOWARD BEING THOSE LOCATED OUTSIDE OF SOUTH AMERICA (335)	0.87 OF 238	9	LEAN LESS TOWARD BEING THOSE LOCATED OUTSIDE OF SOUTH AMERICA (335)	0.71 OF 93	32 27 206 66 XSQ= 10.05 PHI= -0.174 XP = 0.0015
12	TILT MORE TOWARD BEING THOSE WHERE THE LATITUDE IS LESS THAN FIFTY DEGREES (367)	0.94 OF 238	12	TILT LESS TOWARD BEING THOSE WHERE THE LATITUDE IS LESS THAN FIFTY DEGREES (367)	0.85 OF 93	15 14 223 79 XSQ= 5.36 PHI= -0.127 XP = 0.0206
13	DRIFT MORE TOWARD BEING THOSE WHERE THE LATITUDE IS LESS THAN FORTY DEGREES (329)	0.86 OF 238	13	DRIFT LESS TOWARD BEING THOSE WHERE THE LATITUDE IS LESS THAN FORTY DEGREES (329)	0.77 OF 93	34 21 204 72 XSQ= 2.75 PHI= -0.091 XP = 0.0973
36	TILT MORE TOWARD BEING THOSE WHERE THE NATURAL ENVIRONMENT IS OTHER THAN 'VERY HARSH,' OR SUB-TROPICAL BUSH, OR TEMPERATE GRASSLAND (292) FWM	0.77 OF 238	36	TILT LESS TOWARD BEING THOSE WHERE THE NATURAL ENVIRONMENT IS OTHER THAN 'VERY HARSH,' OR SUB-TROPICAL BUSH, OR TEMPERATE GRASSLAND (292) FWM	0.66 OF 93	55 32. 183 61 XSQ= 3.84 PHI= -0.108 XP = 0.0500
44	TEND TO BE THOSE WHERE SETTLEMENTS ARE FIXED (222)	0.75 OF 237	44	TEND TO BE THOSE WHERE SETTLEMENTS ARE NON-FIXED (110)	0.55 OF 93	178 42 59 51 XSQ= 25.62 PHI= 0.279 XP = 0.0000
46	TEND MORE TO BE THOSE OTHER THAN WHERE SETTLEMENTS ARE NON-FIXED AND MOVEMENT IS NOMADIC (260)	0.87 OF 237	46	TEND LESS TO BE THOSE OTHER THAN WHERE SETTLEMENTS ARE NON-FIXED AND MOVEMENT IS NOMADIC (260)	0.55 OF 93	30 42 207 51 XSQ= 39.48 PHI= -0.346 XP = 0.
47	LEAN LESS TOWARD BEING THOSE WHERE, IF SETTLEMENTS ARE NON-FIXED, MOVEMENT IS NOMADIC, RATHER THAN NON-NOMADIC (72)	0.51 OF 59	47	LEAN MORE TOWARD BEING THOSE WHERE, IF SETTLEMENTS ARE NON-FIXED, MOVEMENT IS NOMADIC, RATHER THAN NON-NOMADIC (72)	0.82 OF 51	30 42 29 9 XSQ= 10.66 PHI= -0.311 XP = 0.0011
51	TEND TO BE THOSE WHERE SUBSISTENCE IS PRIMARILY BY FOOD PRODUCTION -- I. E., AGRICULTURE OR HUSBANDRY -- RATHER THAN BY GATHERING (253)	0.69 OF 238	51	TEND TO BE THOSE WHERE SUBSISTENCE IS PRIMARILY BY FOOD GATHERING -- I. E., HUNTING, FISHING, OR COLLECTING -- RATHER THAN FOOD PRODUCTION (147)	0.57 OF 93	164 40 74 53 XSQ= 17.89 PHI= 0.232 XP = 0.0000

62	TEND MORE TO BE THOSE WHERE HUSBANDRY OF SOME KIND IS PRESENT (228)	0.74 OF 238	62	TEND LESS TO BE THOSE WHERE HUSBANDRY OF SOME KIND IS PRESENT (228)	0.51 OF 93	177 47 61 46 XSQ= 16.29 PHI= 0.222 XP = 0.0001
71	LEAN LESS TOWARD BEING THOSE WHERE METAL WORKING IS ABSENT (153)	0.54 OF 167	71	LEAN MORE TOWARD BEING THOSE WHERE METAL WORKING IS ABSENT (153)	0.73 OF 75	76 20 91 55 XSQ= 6.91 PHI= 0.169 XP = 0.0086
73	TEND TO BE THOSE WHERE WEAVING IS PRESENT (118)	0.56 OF 165	73	TEND TO BE THOSE WHERE WEAVING IS ABSENT (130)	0.71 OF 75	93 22 72 53 XSQ= 14.03 PHI= 0.242 XP = 0.0002
81	LEAN LESS TOWARD BEING THOSE WHERE NO CITY OR TOWN IS PRESENT, AND THE AVERAGE COMMUNITY SIZE IS SMALLER THAN 200 (135)	0.55 OF 161	81	LEAN MORE TOWARD BEING THOSE WHERE NO CITY OR TOWN IS PRESENT, AND THE AVERAGE COMMUNITY SIZE IS SMALLER THAN 200 (135)	0.77 OF 61	73 14 88 47 XSQ= 8.39 PHI= 0.194 XP = 0.0038
82	TEND MORE TO BE THOSE WHERE A CITY OR TOWN IS PRESENT, OR THE AVERAGE COMMUNITY SIZE IS FIFTY OR GREATER (178)	0.88 OF 161	82	TEND LESS TO BE THOSE WHERE A CITY OR TOWN IS PRESENT, OR THE AVERAGE COMMUNITY SIZE IS FIFTY OR GREATER (178)	0.57 OF 61	141 35 20 26 XSQ= 22.76 PHI= 0.320 XP = 0.0000
83	LEAN LESS TOWARD BEING THOSE WHERE, WITH NO CITY AND NO TOWN PRESENT, THE AVERAGE COMMUNITY SIZE IS SMALLER THAN 200, RATHER THAN BETWEEN 200 AND 999 (135)	0.68 OF 129	83	LEAN MORE TOWARD BEING THOSE WHERE, WITH NO CITY AND NO TOWN PRESENT, THE AVERAGE COMMUNITY SIZE IS SMALLER THAN 200, RATHER THAN BETWEEN 200 AND 999 (135)	0.92 OF 51	41 4 88 47 XSQ= 9.93 PHI= 0.235 XP = 0.0016
86	TEND TO BE THOSE WHERE THE LEVEL OF POLITICAL INTEGRATION IS THE LARGE STATE, THE LITTLE STATE, OR THE MINIMAL STATE (148) GPM	0.54 OF 186	86	TEND TO BE THOSE WHERE THE LEVEL OF POLITICAL INTEGRATION IS THE AUTONOMOUS COMMUNITY, OR THE FAMILY (156) GPM	0.71 OF 72	101 21 85 51 XSQ= 12.17 PHI= 0.217 XP = 0.0005
96	TEND TO BE THOSE WHERE THE HIERARCHY OF NATIONAL JURISDICTION HAS FOUR, THREE, TWO OR ONE LEVEL (174) GES,EA	0.61 OF 237	96	TEND TO BE THOSE WHERE THE HIERARCHY OF NATIONAL JURISDICTION HAS NO LEVELS (156) GES,EA	0.68 OF 93	144 30 93 63 XSQ= 20.64 PHI= 0.250 XP = 0.0000
102	TEND TO BE THOSE WHERE CLASS STRATIFICATION IS PRESENT (203)	0.61 OF 231	102	TEND TO BE THOSE WHERE CLASS STRATIFICATION IS ABSENT (180)	0.69 OF 90	141 28 90 62 XSQ= 22.08 PHI= 0.262 XP = 0.0000

109	LEAN LESS TOWARD BEING THOSE 0.82 OF 218 WHERE CASTES ARE ABSENT (317)	109	LEAN MORE TOWARD BEING THOSE 0.96 OF 92 WHERE CASTES ARE ABSENT (317)		39 4 179 88 XSQ= 8.83 PHI= 0.169 XP = 0.0030
110	TEND TO BE THOSE 0.51 OF 228 WHERE SLAVERY IS PRESENT (163)	110	TEND TO BE THOSE 0.83 OF 92 WHERE SLAVERY IS ABSENT (218)		117 16 111 76 XSQ= 29.68 PHI= 0.305 XP = 0.0000
116	DRIFT LESS TOWARD BEING THOSE 0.56 OF 41 WHERE OCCUPATIONAL SPECIALIZATION IS PART-TIME ONLY (34) JMH	116	DRIFT MORE TOWARD BEING THOSE 0.91 OF 11 WHERE OCCUPATIONAL SPECIALIZATION IS PART-TIME ONLY (34) JMH		18 1 23 10 XSQ= 3.16 PHI= 0.246 XP = 0.0757
129	TILT LESS TOWARD BEING THOSE 0.66 OF 85 WHERE WEAVING IS MAINLY DONE BY FEMALES (73)	129	TILT MORE TOWARD BEING THOSE 0.94 OF 17 WHERE WEAVING IS MAINLY DONE BY FEMALES (73)		29 1 56 16 XSQ= 4.16 PHI= 0.202 XP = 0.0413
131	LEAN MORE TOWARD BEING THOSE 0.93 OF 110 WHERE THE CONSTRUCTION OF PERMANENT HOUSES OR THE ERECTION OF TEMPORARY DWELLINGS IS MAINLY DONE BY MALES (136)	131	LEAN LESS TOWARD BEING THOSE 0.72 OF 43 WHERE THE CONSTRUCTION OF PERMANENT HOUSES OR THE ERECTION OF TEMPORARY DWELLINGS IS MAINLY DONE BY MALES (136)		102 31 8 12 XSQ= 9.84 PHI= 0.254 XP = 0.0017
132	TILT TOWARD BEING THOSE 0.76 OF 41 WHERE ECONOMIC EXCHANGE INVOLVES THE USE OF MONEY (37) JMH	132	TILT TOWARD BEING THOSE 0.64 OF 11 WHERE ECONOMIC EXCHANGE DOES NOT INVOLVE THE USE OF MONEY (17) JMH		31 4 10 7 XSQ= 4.42 PHI= 0.291 XP = 0.0356
138	DRIFT TOWARD BEING THOSE 0.65 OF 26 WHERE SUPERORDINATE JUSTICE IS PRESENT (22) BBW	138	DRIFT TOWARD BEING THOSE 0.67 OF 12 WHERE SUPERORDINATE JUSTICE IS ABSENT (18) BBW		17 4 9 8 XSQ= 2.24 PHI= 0.243 EP = 0.0873
144	TILT TOWARD BEING THOSE 0.66 OF 35 WHERE THE RATIO OF RESTITUTIVE TO REPRESSIVE SANCTIONS IS HIGH OR MEDIUM (27) WME	144	TILT TOWARD BEING THOSE 0.75 OF 16 WHERE THE RATIO OF RESTITUTIVE TO REPRESSIVE SANCTIONS IS LOW (25) WME		23 4 12 12 XSQ= 5.76 PHI= 0.336 XP = 0.0164
175	LEAN MORE TOWARD BEING THOSE 0.74 OF 228 WHERE THE COMMUNITY IS 'KIN-HETEROGENEOUS,' I. E. OTHER THAN A CLAN COMMUNITY OR A DEME (260)	175	LEAN LESS TOWARD BEING THOSE 0.57 OF 90 WHERE THE COMMUNITY IS 'KIN-HETEROGENEOUS,' I. E. OTHER THAN A CLAN COMMUNITY OR A DEME (260)		59 39 169 51 XSQ= 8.42 PHI= -0.163 XP = 0.0037

176	TILT LESS TOWARD BEING THOSE 0.51 OF 228 WHERE THE COMMUNITY IS OTHER THAN A CLAN-COMMUNITY OR A COMMUNITY STRUCTURED OR SEGMENTED ON A CLAN BASIS (213)	176	TILT MORE TOWARD BEING THOSE 0.67 OF 90 WHERE THE COMMUNITY IS OTHER THAN A CLAN-COMMUNITY OR A COMMUNITY STRUCTURED OR SEGMENTED ON A CLAN BASIS (213)	112 30 116 60 XSQ= 5.89 PHI= 0.136 XP = 0.0153
177	TILT MORE TOWARD BEING THOSE 0.83 OF 228 WHERE THE COMMUNITY IS OTHER THAN A SINGLE CLAN-COMMUNITY AND EXOGAMOUS (305)	177	TILT LESS TOWARD BEING THOSE 0.72 OF 90 WHERE THE COMMUNITY IS OTHER THAN A SINGLE CLAN-COMMUNITY AND EXOGAMOUS (305)	39 25 189 65 XSQ= 3.93 PHI= -0.111 XP = 0.0474
178	TEND LESS TO BE THOSE 0.70 OF 228 WHERE THE COMMUNITY IS OTHER THAN SEGMENTED ON A CLAN BASIS AND NON-EXOGAMOUS (295)	178	TEND MORE TO BE THOSE 0.94 OF 90 WHERE THE COMMUNITY IS OTHER THAN SEGMENTED ON A CLAN BASIS AND NON-EXOGAMOUS (295)	69 5 159 85 XSQ= 20.70 PHI= 0.255 XP = 0.0000
179	DRIFT MORE TOWARD BEING THOSE 0.90 OF 228 WHERE THE COMMUNITY IS OTHER THAN STRUCTURED ON A NON-CLAN BASIS AND COMMONLY EXOGAMOUS (340)	179	DRIFT LESS TOWARD BEING THOSE 0.82 OF 90 WHERE THE COMMUNITY IS OTHER THAN STRUCTURED ON A NON-CLAN BASIS AND COMMONLY EXOGAMOUS (340)	23 16 205 74 XSQ= 2.87 PHI= -0.095 XP = 0.0904
180	LEAN MORE TOWARD BEING THOSE 0.71 OF 228 WHERE THE COMMUNITY IS COMMONLY NON-EXOGAMOUS, RATHER THAN EXOGAMOUS (258)	18C	LEAN LESS TOWARD BEING THOSE 0.54 OF 90 WHERE THE COMMUNITY IS COMMONLY NON-EXOGAMOUS, RATHER THAN EXOGAMOUS (258)	66 41 162 49 XSQ= 7.25 PHI= -0.151 XP = 0.0071
183	TILT MORE TOWARD BEING THOSE 0.88 OF 168 WHERE THE LARGEST NON-COGNATIC KIN GROUP IS SMALLER THAN A MOEITY, I. E., A PHRATRY OR SIB OR LINEAGE (218)	183	TILT LESS TOWARD BEING THOSE 0.72 OF 43 WHERE THE LARGEST NON-COGNATIC KIN GROUP IS SMALLER THAN A MOEITY, I. E., A PHRATRY OR SIB OR LINEAGE (218)	20 12 148 31 XSQ= 5.63 PHI= -0.163 XP = 0.0177
188	TEND TO BE THOSE 0.71 OF 238 WHERE THE KIN GROUP IS OTHER THAN EXCLUSIVELY COGNATIC (252)	188	TEND TO BE THOSE 0.54 OF 93 WHERE THE KIN GROUP IS EXCLUSIVELY COGNATIC (148)	70 50 168 43 XSQ= 16.12 PHI= -0.221 XP = 0.0001
192	TEND TO BE THOSE 0.82 OF 238 OTHER THAN WHERE THE ONLY KIN GROUP PRESENT IS A KINDRED OR ELSE BILATERAL DESCENT IS INFERRED (289)	192	TEND TO BE THOSE 0.51 OF 93 WHERE THE ONLY KIN GROUP PRESENT IS A KINDRED OR ELSE BILATERAL DESCENT IS INFERRED (111)	43 47 195 46 XSQ= 33.99 PHI= -0.320 XP = 0.
196	TEND TO BE THOSE 0.77 OF 173 WHERE INDIVIDUAL RIGHTS IN REAL PROPERTY, AND RULES FOR INHERITANCE, ARE PRESENT (194)	196	TEND TO BE THOSE 0.55 OF 67 WHERE INDIVIDUAL RIGHTS IN REAL PROPERTY, OR RULES FOR INHERITANCE, ARE ABSENT (87)	133 30 40 37 XSQ= 21.39 PHI= 0.299 XP = 0.0000

197	TILT MORE TOWARC BEING THCSE WHERE RULES FCR THE INHERITANCE OF REAL PRCPERTY, IF PRESENT, FAVCR EITHER THE MALE HEIR OR LINE, OR THE FEMALE HEIR CR LINE (165)	0.89 OF 133	197	TILT LESS TOWARD BEING THOSE WHERE RULES FOR THE INHERITANCE CF REAL PROPERTY, IF PRESENT, FAVOR EITHER THE MALE HEIR OR LINE, OR THE FEMALE HEIR OR LINE (165)	0.73 CF 30	119 22 14 8 XSQ= 4.17 PHI= 0.160 XP = 0.0412
201	TEND MORE TO BE THCSE WHERE MARITAL RESICENCE IS NCN-OPTIONAL, RATHER THAN, AMBILCCAL CR NECLOCAL (334)	0.90 OF 238	201	TEND LESS TO BE THOSE WHERE MARITAL RESIDENCE IS NON-OPTIONAL, RATHER THAN AMBILOCAL OR NEOLOCAL (334)	0.71 CF 92	215 65 23 27 XSQ= 18.50 PHI= 0.237 XP = 0.0000
204	TEND MORE TO BE THCSE WHERE MARITAL RESICENCE IS PATRILCCAL, VIRILOCAL, OR AVUNCULOCAL, RATHER THAN AMBILCCAL CR NECLOCAL (270)	0.88 OF 193	2C4	TEND LESS TO BE THOSE WHERE MARITAL RESIDENCE IS PATRILOCAL, VIRILOCAL, CR AVUNCULOCAL, RATHER THAN AMBILOCAL OR NEOLOCAL (270)	0.66 CF 80	170 53 23 27 XSQ= 16.59 PHI= 0.247 XP = 0.0000
207	TEND TO BE THCSE WHERE MARITAL RESICENCE IS MATRILCCAL OR UXCRILOCAL, RATHER THAN AMBILCCAL CR NECLOCAL (64)	0.66 OF 68	2C7	TEND TO BE THOSE WHERE MARITAL RESIDENCE IS AMBILOCAL OR NEOLOCAL, RATHER THAN MATRILOCAL OR UXORILOCAL (64)	0.69 CF 39	45 12 23 27 XSQ= 11.10 PHI= 0.322 XP = 0.0009
220	DRIFT LESS TOWARC BEING THCSE WHERE FIRST CCUSIN MARRIAGE IN SOME FCRM CR CTHER IS NCT PRESCRIBED CR PREFERREC (273)	0.71 OF 224	22C	DRIFT MORE TOWARD BEING THCSE WHERE FIRST COUSIN MARRIAGE IN SOME FORM OR OTHER IS NOT PRESCRIBED OR PREFERRED (273)	0.82 CF 85	65 15 159 70 XSQ= 3.58 PHI= 0.108 XP = 0.0585
236	TEND TO BE THOSE WHERE THE FAMILY IS OF AN EXTENDED TYPE, RATHER THAN AN INDEPENDENT TYPE (213)	0.70 OF 237	236	TEND TO BE THOSE WHERE THE FAMILY IS OF AN INDEPENDENT TYPE, RATHER THAN AN EXTENDED TYPE (185)	0.85 CF 93	165 14 72 79 XSQ= 77.94 PHI= 0.486 XP = 0.
241	DRIFT MORE TCWARC BEING THCSE WHERE THE FAMILY, IF EXTENCED, IS LARGE CR SMALL, RATHER THAN STEM (187)	0.90 OF 165	241	DRIFT LESS TOWARD BEING THCSE WHERE THE FAMILY, IF EXTENDED, IS LARGE OR SMALL, RATHER THAN STEM (187)	0.71 CF 14	149 10 16 4 XSQ= 2.93 PHI= 0.128 XP = 0.0872
366	DRIFT TCWARD BEING THCSE WHERE DISSCCIATICN CF THE SEXES AT ADCLESCENCE IS MEDIUM CR LCW (41) JKH	0.79 OF 43	366	DRIFT TOWARD BEING THOSE WHERE DISSOCIATION OF THE SEXES AT ADOLESCENCE IS HIGH (16) JKH	0.54 CF 13	9 7 34 6 XSQ= 3.81 PHI= -0.261 XP = 0.0510
377	LEAN LESS TOWARC BEING THCSE WHERE MALE GENITAL MUTILATION IS ABSENT (242)	0.70 OF 231	377	LEAN MORE TOWARD BEING THOSE WHERE MALE GENITAL MUTILATICN IS ABSENT (242)	0.86 CF 92	70 13 161 79 XSQ= 8.19 PHI= 0.159 XP = 0.0042

```
404  DRIFT LESS TOWARD BEING THOSE  0.60 OF  40    404  DRIFT MORE TOWARD BEING THOSE  0.88 OF  16          16     2
     WHERE EXPLANATIONS OF ILLNESS                       WHERE EXPLANATIONS OF ILLNESS                         24    14
     OF A SEXUAL NATURE                                  OF A SEXUAL NATURE                               XSQ=     2.80
     ARE ABSENT  (42) W-C                                ARE ABSENT  (42) W-C                             PHI=    0.224
                                                                                                          XP =   0.0941

427  DRIFT TOWARD BEING THOSE       0.60 OF 111    427  DRIFT TOWARD BEING THOSE       0.57 OF  44          67    19
     WHERE A HIGH GOD, IF PRESENT, IS                    WHERE A HIGH GOD, IF PRESENT, IS                      44    25
     ACTIVE, RATHER THAN                                 INACTIVE, RATHER THAN                            XSQ=     3.10
     INACTIVE  (87) GES,EA                               ACTIVE  (69) GES,EA                              PHI=    0.141
                                                                                                          XP =   0.0782

434  DRIFT TOWARD BEING THOSE       0.52 OF  48    434  DRIFT TOWARD BEING THOSE       0.76 OF  17          23    13
     WHERE ASCETICISM IN MOURNING BEHAVIOR               WHERE ASCETICISM IN MOURNING BEHAVIOR                 25     4
     IS LOW  (30) JFG                                    IS HIGH  (37) JFG                                XSQ=     3.07
                                                                                                          PHI=   -0.217
                                                                                                          XP =   0.0799

435  LEAN TOWARD BEING THOSE        0.80 OF  20    435  LEAN TOWARD BEING THOSE        0.73 OF  11           4     8
     WHERE ABANDONMENT OF THE HOUSE OF THE DEAD          WHERE ABANDONMENT OF THE HOUSE OF THE DEAD            16     3
     IS NOT PRACTICED  (19) LWS                          IS PRACTICED  (12) LWS                           XSQ=     6.24
                                                                                                          PHI=   -0.449
                                                                                                          EP =   0.0070

436  TILT LESS TOWARD BEING THOSE   0.61 OF  23    436  IN ALL CASES ARE THOSE         1.00 OF  11          14    11
     WHERE ACTIVE ANCESTRAL SPIRITS                      WHERE ACTIVE ANCESTRAL SPIRITS                         9     0
     ARE PRESENT  (27) GES                               ARE PRESENT  (27) GES                            XSQ=     4.02
                                                                                                          PHI=   -0.344
                                                                                                          EP =   0.0172
```

****

99 CULTURES
WHERE, WITH NATIONAL HIERARCHY ABSENT,
THE HIERARCHY OF LOCAL JURISDICTION HAS
FOUR OR THREE LEVELS (93) GES,EA

99 CULTURES
WHERE, WITH NATIONAL HIERARCHY ABSENT,
THE HIERARCHY OF LOCAL JURISDICTION HAS
TWO LEVELS (63) GES,EA

BACKGROUND ON PAGE 86

BOTH SUBJECT AND PREDICATE

93 IN LEFT COLUMN

ABOR	AMBA	APINAYE	ARAUCANIANS	BACAIRI	BANDA	BARABRA	BAYA	BIRIFOR	BUNLAP
CAGABA	CALLINAGO	CAMAYURA	CAYAPA	CHENCHU	CHIR-APACHE	CHUKCHEE	COCHITI	CREE	DELAWARE
ENGA	FANG	GUAHIBO	GURE	HAIDA	HANO	HAVASUPAI	HERERO	HUICHOL	IBAN
IFUGAO	INGASSANA	JEMEZ	JUKUN	KATAB	KIKUYU	KORYAK	KPE	KUNG	KURTATCHI
LAMET	LANGO	LEPCHA	LESU	LHOTA NAGA	LOLO	MAM	MAMBILA	MANUS	MATAKAM
MNONG GAR	MOTA	MOTILON	MUNDURUCU	MZAB	NAMBICUARA	NAVAHO	NICOBARESE	NUER	NUNIVAK
ONTONG-JAVA	PAPAGO	PURARI	PURUM	SAGADA	SAMOYED	SANPOIL	SHERENTE	SIRIONO	SIUAI
SIWANS	TALLENSI	TAPIRAPE	TAREUMIUT	TEHUELCHE	TENETEHARA	TENINO	TERENA	TIMBIRA	TIWI
TRUKESE	TRUMAI	TWANA	ULAWANS	VEDDA	WAPISHANA	WARRAU	WOGEO	YAKO	YOKUTS
YUKAGHIR	YUROK	ZUNI							

63 IN RIGHT COLUMN

ABIPON	AKHA	ALACALUF	ANDAMANESE	ARANDA	ARAPESH	ATSUGEWI	AWEIKOMA	BARI	BLACK CARIB
BOTOCUDO	CARIB	CHOCO	CHOROTI	COPR ESKIMO	DIEGUENO	DIERI	DOROBO	GILYAK	GOAJIRO
GUATO	HANUNOO	HUKUNDIKA	INGALIK	JIVARO	KARIERA	KASKA	KERAKI	LAPPS	MAMVU
MATACO	MBUTI	MIWOK	MURINBATA	MURNGIN	NABESNA	NOMLAKI	ONA	SELUNG	SEMANG
SENIANG	SUBANUN	TAGBANUA	TALAMANCA	TAOS	TARAHUMARA	TOLOWA	TRISTAN	TUCANO	TUCUNA
TUNEBO	TURKANA	UTE	WAICA	WANTOAT	WASHO	WIKMUNKAN	WITOTO	YABARANA	YAGUA
YAHGAN	YARURO	YUKI							

174 EXCLUDED BECAUSE IRRELEVANT (SEE LEFT COLUMN, PARAGRAPH 96)

70 EXCLUDED BECAUSE UNASCERTAINED

---

3 DRIFT LESS TOWARD BEING THOSE 0.80 OF 93
LOCATED OUTSIDE OF
AFRICA (320)

3 DRIFT MORE TOWARD BEING THOSE 0.92 OF 63
LOCATED OUTSIDE OF
AFRICA (320)

19 5
74 58
XSQ= 3.59
PHI= 0.152
XP = 0.0580

44 TEND TO BE THOSE 0.66 OF 92
WHERE SETTLEMENTS ARE FIXED (222)

44 TEND TO BE THOSE 0.62 OF 63
WHERE SETTLEMENTS ARE NON-FIXED (110)

61 24
31 39
XSQ= 10.90
PHI= 0.265
XP = 0.0010

46	TEND TO BE THOSE OTHER THAN WHERE SETTLEMENTS ARE NON-FIXED AND MOVEMENT IS NOMADIC (260)	0.82 OF 92	46	TEND TO BE THOSE WHERE SETTLEMENTS ARE NON-FIXED AND MOVEMENT IS NOMADIC (72)	0.52 OF 63	17 33 75 30 XSQ= 18.15 PHI= -0.342 XP = 0.0000
47	TILT LESS TOWARD BEING THOSE WHERE, IF SETTLEMENTS ARE NON-FIXED, MOVEMENT IS NOMADIC, RATHER THAN NON-NOMADIC (72)	0.55 OF 31	47	TILT MORE TOWARD BEING THOSE WHERE, IF SETTLEMENTS ARE NON-FIXED, MOVEMENT IS NOMADIC, RATHER THAN NON-NOMADIC (72)	0.85 OF 39	17 33 14 6 XSQ= 6.12 PHI= -0.296 XP = 0.0134
48	DRIFT TOWARD BEING THOSE WHERE THE FOOD SUPPLY IS NOT SECURE, AND FOOD SHORTAGES ARE FREQUENT OR ANNUAL (41) MGW	0.73 OF 26	48	DRIFT TOWARD BEING THOSE WHERE THE FOOD SUPPLY IS SECURE, AND FOOD SHORTAGES ARE RARE OR OCCASIONAL (38) MGW	0.58 OF 12	7 7 19 5 XSQ= 2.26 PHI= -0.244 EP = 0.0812
51	TILT TOWARD BEING THOSE WHERE SUBSISTENCE IS PRIMARILY BY FOOD PRODUCTION -- I. E., AGRICULTURE OR HUSBANDRY -- RATHER THAN BY GATHERING (253)	0.52 OF 93	51	TILT TOWARD BEING THOSE WHERE SUBSISTENCE IS PRIMARILY BY FOOD GATHERING -- I. E., HUNTING, FISHING, OR COLLECTING -- RATHER THAN FOOD PRODUCTION (147)	0.70 OF 63	48 19 45 44 XSQ= 6.21 PHI= 0.199 XP = 0.0127
53	DRIFT LESS TOWARD BEING THOSE WHERE FOOD PRODUCTION IS BY SIMPLE AGRICULTURE OR INCIPIENT FOOD PRODUCTION, RATHER THAN BY INTENSIVE AGRICULTURE (147)	0.72 OF 64	53	DRIFT MORE TOWARD BEING THOSE WHERE FOOD PRODUCTION IS BY SIMPLE AGRICULTURE OR INCIPIENT FOOD PRODUCTION, RATHER THAN BY INTENSIVE AGRICULTURE (147)	0.92 OF 24	18 2 46 22 XSQ= 2.85 PHI= 0.180 XP = 0.0915
55	DRIFT LESS TOWARD BEING THOSE WHERE FOOD PRODUCTION IS BY SIMPLE AGRICULTURE, RATHER THAN BY INTENSIVE AGRICULTURE (101)	0.61 OF 46	55	DRIFT MORE TOWARD BEING THOSE WHERE FOOD PRODUCTION IS BY SIMPLE AGRICULTURE, RATHER THAN BY INTENSIVE AGRICULTURE (101)	0.88 OF 17	18 2 28 15 XSQ= 3.12 PHI= 0.223 XP = 0.0773
62	TEND TO BE THOSE WHERE HUSBANDRY OF SOME KIND IS PRESENT (228)	0.66 OF 93	62	TEND TO BE THOSE WHERE HUSBANDRY OF ANY KIND IS ABSENT (172)	0.65 OF 63	61 22 32 41 XSQ= 12.99 PHI= 0.289 XP = 0.0003
71	TILT LESS TOWARD BEING THOSE WHERE METAL WORKING IS ABSENT (153)	0.74 OF 65	71	TILT MORE TOWARD BEING THOSE WHERE METAL WORKING IS ABSENT (153)	0.92 OF 52	17 4 48 48 XSQ= 5.49 PHI= 0.217 XP = 0.0191
73	TILT LESS TOWARD BEING THOSE WHERE WEAVING IS ABSENT (130)	0.53 OF 64	73	TILT MORE TOWARD BEING THOSE WHERE WEAVING IS ABSENT (130)	0.75 OF 53	30 13 34 40 XSQ= 5.30 PHI= 0.213 XP = 0.0213

82	TEND TO BE THOSE 0.79 OF 68 WHERE A CITY OR TOWN IS PRESENT, OR THE AVERAGE COMMUNITY SIZE IS FIFTY OR GREATER (178)	82	TEND TO BE THOSE 0.56 OF 41 WHERE NO CITY OR TOWN IS PRESENT, AND THE AVERAGE COMMUNITY SIZE IS SMALLER THAN FIFTY (46)	54 18 14 23 XSQ= 12.84 PHI= 0.343 XP = 0.0003
83	LEAN LESS TOWARD BEING THOSE 0.74 OF 62 WHERE, WITH NO CITY AND NO TOWN PRESENT, THE AVERAGE COMMUNITY SIZE IS SMALLER THAN 200, RATHER THAN BETWEEN 200 AND 999 (135)	83	LEAN MORE TOWARD BEING THOSE 0.97 OF 40 WHERE, WITH NO CITY AND NO TOWN PRESENT, THE AVERAGE COMMUNITY SIZE IS SMALLER THAN 200, RATHER THAN BETWEEN 200 AND 999 (135)	16 1 46 39 XSQ= 7.90 PHI= 0.278 XP = 0.0049
87	LEAN MORE TOWARD BEING THOSE 0.93 OF 73 WHERE THE LEVEL OF POLITICAL INTEGRATION IS THE LARGE STATE, THE LITTLE STATE, THE MINIMAL STATE, OR THE AUTONOMOUS COMMUNITY (281) GPM	87	LEAN LESS TOWARD BEING THOSE 0.74 OF 50 WHERE THE LEVEL OF POLITICAL INTEGRATION IS THE LARGE STATE, THE LITTLE STATE, THE MINIMAL STATE, OR THE AUTONOMOUS COMMUNITY (281) GPM	68 37 5 13 XSQ= 7.25 PHI= 0.243 XP = 0.0071
89	DRIFT TOWARD BEING THOSE 0.54 OF 26 WHERE, IF A NON-HEREDITARY HEADMANSHIP IS PRESENT, SUCCESSION IS BY MEANS OTHER THAN CONSENSUS (43)	89	DRIFT TOWARD BEING THOSE 0.80 OF 15 WHERE, IF A NON-HEREDITARY HEADMANSHIP IS PRESENT, SUCCESSION IS BY CONSENSUS (63)	12 12 14 3 XSQ= 3.20 PHI= -0.280 XP = 0.0735
102	LEAN LESS TOWARD BEING THOSE 0.58 OF 92 WHERE CLASS STRATIFICATION IS ABSENT (180)	102	LEAN MORE TOWARD BEING THOSE 0.81 OF 63 WHERE CLASS STRATIFICATION IS ABSENT (180)	39 12 53 51 XSQ= 8.20 PHI= 0.230 XP = 0.0042
110	TEND LESS TO BE THOSE 0.61 OF 90 WHERE SLAVERY IS ABSENT (218)	110	TEND MORE TO BE THOSE 0.90 OF 62 WHERE SLAVERY IS ABSENT (218)	35 6 55 56 XSQ= 14.45 PHI= 0.308 XP = 0.0001
131	DRIFT MORE TOWARD BEING THOSE 0.90 OF 42 WHERE THE CONSTRUCTION OF PERMANENT HOUSES OR THE ERECTION OF TEMPORARY DWELLINGS IS MAINLY DONE BY MALES (136)	131	DRIFT LESS TOWARD BEING THOSE 0.70 OF 30 WHERE THE CONSTRUCTION OF PERMANENT HOUSES OR THE ERECTION OF TEMPORARY DWELLINGS IS MAINLY DONE BY MALES (136)	38 21 4 9 XSQ= 3.67 PHI= 0.226 XP = 0.0553
132	DRIFT TOWARD BEING THOSE 0.67 OF 15 WHERE ECONOMIC EXCHANGE INVOLVES THE USE OF MONEY (37) JMH	132	DRIFT TOWARD BEING THOSE 0.83 OF 6 WHERE ECONOMIC EXCHANGE DOES NOT INVOLVE THE USE OF MONEY (17) JMH	10 1 5 5 XSQ= 2.52 PHI= 0.347 EP = 0.0635
144	DRIFT TOWARD BEING THOSE 0.67 OF 12 WHERE THE RATIO OF RESTITUTIVE TO REPRESSIVE SANCTIONS IS HIGH OR MEDIUM (27) WME	144	DRIFT TOWARD BEING THOSE 0.78 OF 9 WHERE THE RATIO OF RESTITUTIVE TO REPRESSIVE SANCTIONS IS LOW (25) WME	8 2 4 7 XSQ= 2.49 PHI= 0.344 EP = 0.0805

No.			No.			
175	LEAN TOWARD BEING THOSE WHERE THE COMMUNITY IS 'KIN-HETEROGENEOUS,' I. E. OTHER THAN A CLAN COMMUNITY OR A DEME (260)	0.73 OF 93	175	LEAN TOWARD BEING THOSE WHERE THE COMMUNITY IS 'KIN-HOMOGENEOUS,' I. E. A CLAN COMMUNITY OR A DEME (122)	0.51 OF 61	25 31 68 30 XSQ= 8.12 PHI= -0.230 XP = 0.0044
177	TILT MORE TOWARD BEING THOSE WHERE THE COMMUNITY IS OTHER THAN A SINGLE CLAN-COMMUNITY AND EXOGAMOUS (305)	0.85 OF 93	177	TILT LESS TOWARD BEING THOSE WHERE THE COMMUNITY IS OTHER THAN A SINGLE CLAN-COMMUNITY AND EXOGAMOUS (305)	0.67 OF 61	14 20 79 41 XSQ= 5.74 PHI= -0.193 XP = 0.0166
178	TEND LESS TO BE THOSE WHERE THE COMMUNITY IS OTHER THAN SEGMENTED ON A CLAN BASIS AND NON-EXOGAMOUS (295)	0.70 OF 93	178	TEND MORE TO BE THOSE WHERE THE COMMUNITY IS OTHER THAN SEGMENTED ON A CLAN BASIS AND NON-EXOGAMOUS (295)	0.95 OF 61	28 3 65 58 XSQ= 13.01 PHI= 0.291 XP = 0.0003
180	LEAN TOWARD BEING THOSE WHERE THE COMMUNITY IS COMMONLY NON-EXOGAMOUS, RATHER THAN EXOGAMOUS (258)	0.72 OF 93	180	LEAN TOWARD BEING THOSE WHERE THE COMMUNITY IS COMMONLY EXOGAMOUS, RATHER THAN NON-EXOGAMOUS (124)	0.51 OF 61	26 31 67 30 XSQ= 7.31 PHI= -0.218 XP = 0.0069
187	TILT LESS TOWARD BEING THOSE WHERE THE KIN GROUP IS OTHER THAN EXCLUSIVELY MATRILINEAL (344)	0.78 OF 93	187	TILT MORE TOWARD BEING THOSE WHERE THE KIN GROUP IS OTHER THAN EXCLUSIVELY MATRILINEAL (344)	0.92 OF 63	20 5 73 58 XSQ= 4.18 PHI= 0.164 XP = 0.0409
190	DRIFT LESS TOWARD BEING THOSE WHERE THE KIN GROUP IS PATRILINEAL OR DOUBLE-DESCENT, RATHER THAN MATRILINEAL (186)	0.62 OF 55	190	DRIFT MORE TOWARD BEING THOSE WHERE THE KIN GROUP IS PATRILINEAL OR DOUBLE-DESCENT, RATHER THAN MATRILINEAL (186)	0.83 OF 29	34 24 21 5 XSQ= 2.98 PHI= -0.188 XP = 0.0844
192	LEAN TOWARD BEING THOSE OTHER THAN WHERE THE ONLY KIN GROUP PRESENT IS A KINDRED OR ELSE BILATERAL DESCENT IS INFERRED (289)	0.75 OF 93	192	LEAN TOWARD BEING THOSE WHERE THE ONLY KIN GROUP PRESENT IS A KINDRED OR ELSE BILATERAL DESCENT IS INFERRED (111)	0.51 OF 63	23 32 70 31 XSQ= 10.06 PHI= -0.254 XP = 0.0015
196	LEAN TOWARD BEING THOSE WHERE INDIVIDUAL RIGHTS IN REAL PROPERTY, AND RULES FOR INHERITANCE, ARE PRESENT (194)	0.62 OF 65	196	LEAN TOWARD BEING THOSE WHERE INDIVIDUAL RIGHTS IN REAL PROPERTY, OR RULES FOR INHERITANCE, ARE ABSENT (87)	0.66 OF 44	40 15 25 29 XSQ= 6.85 PHI= 0.251 XP = 0.0089
201	TILT MORE TOWARD BEING THOSE WHERE MARITAL RESIDENCE IS NON-OPTIONAL, RATHER THAN AMBILOCAL OR NEOLOCAL (334)	0.87 OF 93	201	TILT LESS TOWARD BEING THOSE WHERE MARITAL RESIDENCE IS NON-OPTIONAL, RATHER THAN AMBILOCAL OR NEOLOCAL (334)	0.71 OF 62	81 44 12 18 XSQ= 5.21 PHI= 0.183 XP = 0.0225

No.	Statement	Ratio	N	No.	Statement	Ratio	N	Statistics
204	DRIFT MORE TOWARD BEING THOSE WHERE MARITAL RESIDENCE IS PATRILOCAL, VIRILOCAL, OR AVUNCULOCAL, RATHER THAN AMBILOCAL OR NEOLOCAL (270)	0.83 OF	69	204	DRIFT LESS TOWARD BEING THOSE WHERE MARITAL RESIDENCE IS PATRILOCAL, VIRILOCAL, OR AVUNCULOCAL, RATHER THAN AMBILOCAL OR NEOLOCAL (270)	0.65 OF	52	57 34 12 18 XSQ= 3.84 PHI= 0.178 XP = 0.0501
207	TILT TOWARD BEING THOSE WHERE MARITAL RESIDENCE IS MATRILOCAL OR UXORILOCAL, RATHER THAN AMBILOCAL OR NEOLOCAL (64)	0.67 OF	36	207	TILT TOWARD BEING THOSE WHERE MARITAL RESIDENCE IS AMBILOCAL OR NEOLOCAL, RATHER THAN MATRILOCAL OR UXORILOCAL (64)	0.64 OF	28	24 10 12 18 XSQ= 4.88 PHI= 0.276 XP = 0.0272
210	DRIFT LESS TOWARD BEING THOSE WHERE MARITAL RESIDENCE IS PATRILOCAL, RATHER THAN MATRILOCAL (169)	0.68 OF	44	210	DRIFT MORE TOWARD BEING THOSE WHERE MARITAL RESIDENCE IS PATRILOCAL, RATHER THAN MATRILOCAL (169)	0.92 OF	25	30 23 14 2 XSQ= 3.83 PHI= -0.236 XP = 0.0504
224	TILT TOWARD BEING THOSE WHERE COUSIN MARRIAGE IS PREFERENTIALLY OR PERMISSIVELY EITHER PATRI- OR MATRILATERAL, RATHER THAN SYMMETRICAL (66)	0.57 OF	35	224	TILT TOWARD BEING THOSE WHERE COUSIN MARRIAGE IS PREFERENTIALLY OR PERMISSIVELY SYMMETRICAL, RATHER THAN EITHER PATRI- OR MATRILATERAL (106)	0.78 OF	23	20 5 15 18 XSQ= 5.72 PHI= 0.314 XP = 0.0167
236	TEND TO BE THOSE WHERE THE FAMILY IS OF AN EXTENDED TYPE, RATHER THAN AN INDEPENDENT TYPE (213)	0.66 OF	93	236	TEND TO BE THOSE WHERE THE FAMILY IS OF AN INDEPENDENT TYPE, RATHER THAN AN EXTENDED TYPE (185)	0.83 OF	63	61 11 32 52 XSQ= 33.10 PHI= 0.461 XP = 0.
299	DRIFT LESS TOWARD BEING THOSE WHERE THE POST-PARTUM SEX TABOO LASTS ONE YEAR OR LESS (89)	0.61 OF	36	299	DRIFT MORE TOWARD BEING THOSE WHERE THE POST-PARTUM SEX TABOO LASTS ONE YEAR OR LESS (89)	0.85 OF	26	14 4 22 22 XSQ= 2.99 PHI= 0.220 XP = 0.0839
434	DRIFT TOWARD BEING THOSE WHERE ASCETICISM IN MOURNING BEHAVIOR IS LOW (30) JFG	0.55 OF	20	434	DRIFT TOWARD BEING THOSE WHERE ASCETICISM IN MOURNING BEHAVIOR IS HIGH (37) JFG	0.82 OF	11	9 9 11 2 XSQ= 2.58 PHI= -0.289 EP = 0.0656
475	DRIFT TOWARD BEING THOSE WHERE EXHIBITIONISTIC DANCING IS STRONGLY OR MODERATELY EMPHASIZED (48) PES	0.59 OF	27	475	DRIFT TOWARD BEING THOSE WHERE EXHIBITIONISTIC DANCING IS NEGLIGIBLY EMPHASIZED (38) PES	0.75 OF	12	16 3 11 9 XSQ= 2.65 PHI= 0.261 EP = 0.0824

****

100 CULTURES WHERE HIERARCHIES ARE MORE COMPLEX THAN THE 'SIMPLEST,' I. E., MORE COMPLEX THAN TWO LOCAL LEVELS WITH NO NATIONAL LEVELS (267) GES,EA	100 CULTURES WHERE HIERARCHIES ARE THE 'SIMPLEST' I. E., WHERE THERE ARE ONLY TWO LOCAL LEVELS WITH NO NATIONAL LEVELS (63) GES,EA

BACKGROUND ON PAGE 86 BOTH SUBJECT AND PREDICATE

....

267 IN LEFT COLUMN

ABOR	AINU	ALBANIANS	ALORESE	AMBA	AMERICANS	APINAYE	ARAUCANIANS	ASHANTI	ATAYAL
AZANDE	AZTEC	BABWA	BACAIRI	BAMBARA	BAMILEKE	BANDA	BARABRA	BASSERI	BAYA
BEJA	BEMBA	BHIL	BHUIYA	BIRIFOR	BOERS	BORORO	BOZO	BRAZILIANS	BULGARIANS
BUNLAP	BURUSHO	CADUVEO	CAGABA	CALLINAGO	CAMAYURA	CAMBODIANS	CAYAPA	CHAGGA	CHAMACOCO
CHENCHU	CHERKESS	CHEROKEE	CHEYENNE	CHIBCHA	CHIR-APACHE	CHIRIGUANO	CHORTI	CHUKCHEE	COCHITI
COORG	CREE	CREEK	CROW	CUNA	CZECHS	DAGUR	DARD	DELAWARE	DILLING
DOGON	DUTCH	EGYPTIANS	ELLICE	ENGA	EYAK	FANG	FON	FOX	FUTAJALONKE
GANDA	GARO	GISU	GOND	GROS VENTRE	GUAHIBO	GURE	HAIDA	HANO	HASINAI
HAVASUPAI	HAWAIIANS	HAZARA	HEBREWS	HERERO	HUICHOL	HURON	IBAN	IFUGAO	ILA
INCA	INGASSANA	IRAQW	IRISH	JAPANESE	JAVANESE	JEMEZ	JUKUN	KABYLE	KACHIN
KAPAUKU	KATAB	KAZAK	KERALA	KHALKA	KHASI	KIKUYU	KISSI	KOHISTANI	KOL
KOREANS	KORYAK	KPE	KUBA	KUNG	KURTATCHI	KUTENAI	KWAKIUTL	LAKHER	LAMBA
LAMET	LANGO	LAU	LEPCHA	LESU	LHOTA NAGA	LOLO	LOZI	LUO	MACASSARESE
MALAYS	MAM	MAMBILA	MANDAN	MANGAIANS	MANIHIKI	MANUS	MAORI	MARGI	MARICOPA
MARQUESANS	MARSHALLESE	MASAI	MATAKAM	MAYA	MBUNDU	MENDE	MERINA	MIAMI	MIAO
MIN CHINESE	MINCHIA	MISKITO	MNONG GAR	MONGO	MONGUOR	MOSSI	MOTA	MOTILON	MUNDURUCU
MZAB	NAMA	NAMBICUARA	NANDI	NATCHEZ	NAVAHO	NDEMBU	NICOBARESE	NUER	NUNIVAK
NUPE	NURI	NYAKYUSA	NYORO	OJIBWA	OKINAWANS	OMAHA	ONTONG-JAVA	ORAON	PAEZ
PAIWAN	PALAUANS	PAPAGO	PARAUJANO	PATHAN	PAWNEE	PONAPEANS	PUKAPUKA	PURARI	PURUM
REGEIBAT	RIFFIANS	RUNDI	RWALA	SAGADA	SAMOANS	SAMOYED	SANDAWE	SANPOIL	SANTAL
SARSI	SERBS	SHERENTE	SHILLUK	SHLUH	SINHALESE	SIRIONO	SIUAI	SIWANS	SOMALI
SONGHAI	SOTHO	SWAZI	SYRIANS	TALLENSI	TANALA	TAPIRAPE	TAREUMIUT	TEDA	TEHUELCHE
TENDA	TENETEHARA	TENINO	TERA	TERENA	TESO	THAI	THONGA	TIGRINYA	TIKOPIA
TIMBIRA	TIMUCUA	TIV	TIWI	TODA	TOKELAU	TORAJA	TOTONAC	TROBRIAND	TRUKESE
TRUMAI	TSHIMSHIAN	TUBATULABAL	TUPINAMBA	TURKMEN	TWANA	ULAWANS	VEDDA	VENDA	VIETNAMESE
WALLOONS	WAPISHANA	WARRAU	WICHITA	WOGEO	WOLEAIANS	WOLOF	YAKO	YAKUT	YAO
YAPESE	YOKUTS	YOMBE	YORUBA	YUKAGHIR	YUROK	ZUNI			

63 IN RIGHT COLUMN

ABIPON	AKHA	ALACALUF	ANDAMANESE	ARANDA	ARAPESH	ATSUGEWI	AWEIKOMA	BARI	BLACK CARIB
BOTOCUDO	CARIB	CHOCO	CHOROTI	COPR ESKIMO	DIEGUENO	DIERI	DOROBO	GILYAK	GOAJIRO
GUATO	HANUNOO	HUKUNDIKA	INGALIK	JIVARO	KARIERA	KASKA	KERAKI	LAPPS	MAMVU
MATACO	MBUTI	MIWOK	MURINBATA	MURNGIN	NABESNA	NOMLAKI	ONA	SELUNG	SEMANG
SENIANG	SUBANUN	TAGBANUA	TALAMANCA	TAOS	TARAHUMARA	TOLOWA	TRISTAN	TUCANO	TUCUNA
TUNEBO	TURKANA	UTE	WAICA	WANTOAT	WASHO	WIKMUNKAN	WITOTO	YABARANA	YAGUA
YAHGAN	YARURO	YUKI							

70 EXCLUDED BECAUSE UNASCERTAINED

3	LEAN LESS TOWARC BEING THCSE LOCATED CUTSIDE CF AFRICA (320)	0.76 OF 267	3	LEAN MORE TOWARD BEING THOSE LOCATED OUTSIDE OF AFRICA (320)	0.92 CF 63	64 5 203 58 XSQ= 6.98 PHI= 0.145 XP = 0.0082
4	DRIFT LESS TOWARC BEING THCSE LOCATED CUTSIDE CF THE CIRCUM-MEDITERRANEAN (355)	0.89 OF 267	4	DRIFT MORE TOWARD BEING THOSE LOCATED OUTSIDE OF THE CIRCUM-MEDITERRANEAN (355)	0.97 OF 63	30 2 237 61 XSQ= 2.92 PHI= 0.094 XP = 0.0876
5	TILT LESS TOWARC BEING THCSE LOCATED CUTSIDE OF EAST EURASIA (330)	0.80 OF 267	5	TILT MORE TOWARD BEING THOSE LOCATED OUTSIDE OF EAST EURASIA (330)	0.92 CF 63	54 5 213 58 XSQ= 4.44 PHI= 0.116 XP = 0.0351
9	TEND MORE TO BE THCSE LOCATED CUTSIDE CF SOUTH AMERICA (335)	0.87 OF 267	9	TEND LESS TO BE THOSE LOCATED OUTSIDE OF SOUTH AMERICA (335)	0.63 OF 63	35 23 232 40 XSQ= 17.68 PHI= -0.231 XP = 0.0000
44	TEND TC BE THCSE WHERE SETTLEMENTS ARE FIXEC (222)	0.73 OF 266	44	TEND TO BE THOSE WHERE SETTLEMENTS ARE NON-FIXED (110)	0.62 CF 63	195 24 71 39 XSQ= 26.82 PHI= 0.286 XP = 0.0000
46	TEND TC BE THCSE CTHER THAN WHERE SETTLEMENTS ARE NCN-FIXED AND MCVEMENT IS NCMADIC (260)	0.85 OF 266	46	TEND TO BE THOSE WHERE SETTLEMENTS ARE NON-FIXED AND MOVEMENT IS NOMADIC (72)	0.52 OF 63	39 33 227 30 XSQ= 40.21 PHI= -0.350 XP = 0.
47	LEAN LESS TOWARC BEING THCSE WHERE, IF SETTLEMENTS ARE NON-FIXEC, MOVEMENT IS NCMADIC, RATHER THAN NCN-NCMADIC (72)	0.55 OF 71	47	LEAN MORE TOWARD BEING THOSE WHERE, IF SETTLEMENTS ARE NON-FIXED, MOVEMENT IS NOMADIC, RATHER THAN NON-NOMADIC (72)	0.85 CF 39	39 33 32 6 XSQ= 8.54 PHI= -0.279 XP = 0.0035
51	TEND TC BE THCSE WHERE SUBSISTENCE IS PRIMARILY BY FCCD PRCDUCTION -- I. E., AGRICULTURE OR HUSBANDRY -- RATHER THAN BY GATHERING (253)	0.69 OF 267	51	TEND TO BE THOSE WHERE SUBSISTENCE IS PRIMARILY BY FOOD GATHERING -- I. E., HUNTING, FISHING, OR COLLECTING -- RATHER THAN FOOD PRODUCTION (147)	0.70 OF 63	184 19 83 44 XSQ= 30.72 PHI= 0.305 XP = 0.
53	LEAN LESS TOWARC BEING THCSE WHERE FCOD PRODUCTICN IS BY SIMPLE AGRICULTURE OR INCIPIENT FOCD PRODUCTICN, RATHER THAN BY INTENSIVE AGRICULTURE (147)	0.58 OF 204	53	LEAN MORE TOWARD BEING THOSE WHERE FOOD PRODUCTION IS BY SIMPLE AGRICULTURE OR INCIPIENT FOOD PRODUCTICN, RATHER THAN BY INTENSIVE AGRICULTURE (147)	0.92 CF 24	86 2 118 22 XSQ= 8.99 PHI= 0.199 XP = 0.0027

55	LEAN TOWARD BEING THOSE WHERE FOOD PRODUCTION IS BY INTENSIVE AGRICULTURE, RATHER THAN BY SIMPLE AGRICULTURE (91)	0.50 OF 172	55	LEAN TOWARD BEING THOSE WHERE FOOD PRODUCTION IS BY SIMPLE AGRICULTURE, RATHER THAN BY INTENSIVE AGRICULTURE (101)	0.88 OF 17	86 2 86 15 XSQ= 7.62 PHI= 0.201 XP = 0.0058
62	TEND TO BE THOSE WHERE HUSBANDRY OF SOME KIND IS PRESENT (228)	0.75 OF 267	62	TEND TO BE THOSE WHERE HUSBANDRY OF ANY KIND IS ABSENT (172)	0.65 OF 63	201 22 66 41 XSQ= 36.08 PHI= 0.331 XP = 0.
71	TEND LESS TO BE THOSE WHERE METAL WORKING IS ABSENT (153)	0.52 OF 189	71	TEND MORE TO BE THOSE WHERE METAL WORKING IS ABSENT (153)	0.92 OF 52	91 4 98 48 XSQ= 26.28 PHI= 0.330 XP = 0.0000
73	TEND TO BE THOSE WHERE WEAVING IS PRESENT (118)	0.54 OF 186	73	TEND TO BE THOSE WHERE WEAVING IS ABSENT (130)	0.75 OF 53	101 13 85 40 XSQ= 13.49 PHI= 0.238 XP = 0.0002
74	TILT TOWARD BEING THOSE WHERE POTTERY IS PRESENT (145)	0.67 OF 177	74	TILT TOWARD BEING THOSE WHERE POTTERY IS ABSENT (93)	0.54 OF 52	118 24 59 28 XSQ= 6.33 PHI= 0.166 XP = 0.0118
80	LEAN LESS TOWARD BEING THOSE WHERE NO CITY OR TOWN IS PRESENT (185)	0.79 OF 180	80	IN ALL CASES ARE THOSE WHERE NO CITY OR TOWN IS PRESENT (185)	1.00 OF 41	37 0 143 41 XSQ= 8.70 PHI= 0.198 XP = 0.0032
82	TEND TO BE THOSE WHERE A CITY OR TOWN IS PRESENT, OR THE AVERAGE COMMUNITY SIZE IS FIFTY OR GREATER (178)	0.87 OF 180	82	TEND TO BE THOSE WHERE NO CITY OR TOWN IS PRESENT, AND THE AVERAGE COMMUNITY SIZE IS SMALLER THAN FIFTY (46)	0.56 OF 41	157 18 23 23 XSQ= 35.44 PHI= 0.400 XP = 0.
83	TEND LESS TO BE THOSE WHERE, WITH NO CITY AND NO TOWN PRESENT, THE AVERAGE COMMUNITY SIZE IS SMALLER THAN 200, RATHER THAN BETWEEN 200 AND 999 (135)	0.69 OF 139	83	TEND MORE TO BE THOSE WHERE, WITH NO CITY AND NO TOWN PRESENT, THE AVERAGE COMMUNITY SIZE IS SMALLER THAN 200, RATHER THAN BETWEEN 200 AND 999 (135)	0.97 OF 40	43 1 96 39 XSQ= 12.06 PHI= 0.260 XP = 0.0005
85	TEND LESS TO BE THOSE WHERE THE LEVEL OF POLITICAL INTEGRATION IS THE MINIMAL STATE, THE AUTONOMOUS COMMUNITY, OR THE FAMILY (234) GPM	0.73 OF 208	85	IN ALL CASES ARE THOSE WHERE THE LEVEL OF POLITICAL INTEGRATION IS THE MINIMAL STATE, THE AUTONOMOUS COMMUNITY, OR THE FAMILY (234) GPM	1.00 OF 50	57 0 151 50 XSQ= 16.03 PHI= 0.249 XP = 0.0001

86 TEND TO BE THOSE 0.58 OF 208 WHERE THE LEVEL OF POLITICAL INTEGRATION IS THE LARGE STATE, THE LITTLE STATE, OR THE MINIMAL STATE (148) GPM	86 TEND TO BE THOSE 0.96 OF 50 WHERE THE LEVEL OF POLITICAL INTEGRATION IS THE AUTONOMOUS COMMUNITY, OR THE FAMILY (156) GPM	120 2 88 48 XSQ= 44.49 PHI= 0.415 XP = 0.
90 DRIFT LESS TOWARD BEING THOSE 0.74 OF 121 WHERE, IF A HEREDITARY HEADMANSHIP IS PRESENT, SUCCESSION IS PATRILINEAL, RATHER THAN MATRILINEAL (127)	90 DRIFT MORE TOWARD BEING THOSE 0.95 OF 21 WHERE, IF A HEREDITARY HEADMANSHIP IS PRESENT, SUCCESSION IS PATRILINEAL, RATHER THAN MATRILINEAL (127)	90 20 31 1 XSQ= 3.34 PHI= -0.153 XP = 0.0674
102 TEND TO BE THOSE 0.61 OF 257 WHERE CLASS STRATIFICATION IS PRESENT (203)	102 TEND TO BE THOSE 0.81 OF 63 WHERE CLASS STRATIFICATION IS ABSENT (180)	156 12 101 51 XSQ= 33.55 PHI= 0.324 XP = 0.
106 LEAN TOWARD BEING THOSE 0.63 OF 156 WHERE CLASS STRATIFICATION, IF PRESENT, IS BASED ON SOMETHING OTHER THAN WEALTH (126)	106 LEAN TOWARD BEING THOSE 0.83 OF 12 WHERE CLASS STRATIFICATION, IF PRESENT, IS BASED ON WEALTH (77)	57 10 99 2 XSQ= 8.32 PHI= -0.223 XP = 0.0039
109 LEAN LESS TOWARD BEING THOSE 0.83 OF 246 WHERE CASTES ARE ABSENT (317)	109 LEAN MORE TOWARD BEING THOSE 0.98 OF 63 WHERE CASTES ARE ABSENT (317)	42 1 204 62 XSQ= 8.79 PHI= 0.169 XP = 0.0030
110 TEND LESS TO BE THOSE 0.51 OF 257 WHERE SLAVERY IS ABSENT (218)	110 TEND MORE TO BE THOSE 0.90 OF 62 WHERE SLAVERY IS ABSENT (218)	127 6 130 56 XSQ= 30.83 PHI= 0.311 XP = 0.
131 LEAN MORE TOWARD BEING THOSE 0.91 OF 122 WHERE THE CONSTRUCTION OF PERMANENT HOUSES OR THE ERECTION OF TEMPORARY DWELLINGS IS MAINLY DONE BY MALES (136)	131 LEAN LESS TOWARD BEING THOSE 0.70 OF 30 WHERE THE CONSTRUCTION OF PERMANENT HOUSES OR THE ERECTION OF TEMPORARY DWELLINGS IS MAINLY DONE BY MALES (136)	111 21 11 9 XSQ= 7.53 PHI= 0.223 XP = 0.0061
132 TILT TOWARD BEING THOSE 0.74 OF 46 WHERE ECONOMIC EXCHANGE INVOLVES THE USE OF MONEY (37) JMH	132 TILT TOWARD BEING THOSE 0.83 OF 6 WHERE ECONOMIC EXCHANGE DOES NOT INVOLVE THE USE OF MONEY (17) JMH	34 1 12 5 XSQ= 5.52 PHI= 0.326 XP = 0.0188
136 DRIFT TOWARD BEING THOSE 0.63 OF 27 WHERE FULL-TIME ENTREPRENEURS ARE PRESENT (18) JV	136 IN ALL CASES ARE THOSE 1.00 OF 3 WHERE FULL-TIME ENTREPRENEURS ARE ABSENT (14) JV	17 0 10 3 XSQ= 2.17 PHI= 0.269 EP = 0.0704

137	DRIFT LESS TOWARD BEING THOSE 0.55 OF 74 WHERE INVIDIOUS DISPLAY OF WEALTH IS MODERATELY, LITTLE, OR NEGATIVELY EMPHASIZED (52) PES	137	DRIFT MORE TOWARD BEING THOSE 0.91 OF 11 WHERE INVIDIOUS DISPLAY OF WEALTH IS MODERATELY, LITTLE, OR NEGATIVELY EMPHASIZED (52) PES	33 1 41 10 XSQ= 3.66 PHI= 0.207 XP = 0.0558
138	LEAN TOWARD BEING THOSE 0.68 OF 31 WHERE SUPERORDINATE JUSTICE IS PRESENT (22) BBW	138	IN ALL CASES ARE THOSE 1.00 OF 7 WHERE SUPERORDINATE JUSTICE IS ABSENT (18) BBW	21 0 10 7 XSQ= 8.04 PHI= 0.460 EP = 0.0015
139	TILT LESS TOWARD BEING THOSE 0.55 OF 31 WHERE SUPERORDINATE PUNISHMENT IS ABSENT (25) BBW	139	IN ALL CASES ARE THOSE 1.00 OF 7 WHERE SUPERORDINATE PUNISHMENT IS ABSENT (25) BBW	14 0 17 7 XSQ= 3.25 PHI= 0.293 EP = 0.0334
144	DRIFT TOWARD BEING THOSE 0.60 OF 42 WHERE THE RATIO OF RESTITUTIVE TO REPRESSIVE SANCTIONS IS HIGH OR MEDIUM (27) WME	144	DRIFT TOWARD BEING THOSE 0.78 OF 9 WHERE THE RATIO OF RESTITUTIVE TO REPRESSIVE SANCTIONS IS LOW (25) WME	25 2 17 7 XSQ= 2.78 PHI= 0.233 XP = 0.0956
147	DRIFT TOWARD BEING THOSE 0.72 OF 25 WHERE CODIFIED LAWS ARE PRESENT (20) LWS	147	DRIFT TOWARD BEING THOSE 0.71 OF 7 WHERE CODIFIED LAWS ARE UNIMPORTANT OR ABSENT (13) LWS	18 2 7 5 XSQ= 2.74 PHI= 0.293 EP = 0.0735
152	DRIFT TOWARD BEING THOSE 0.64 OF 14 WHERE THE DIFFERENTIATION OF THE JURIDICAL AGENCY FROM THE MEDICAL AGENCY IS HIGH (10) MJ	152	IN ALL CASES ARE THOSE 1.00 OF 4 WHERE THE DIFFERENTIATION OF THE JURIDICAL AGENCY FROM THE MEDICAL AGENCY IS LOW (10) MJ	9 0 5 4 XSQ= 2.89 PHI= 0.401 EP = 0.0824
175	TEND TO BE THOSE 0.74 OF 256 WHERE THE COMMUNITY IS 'KIN-HETEROGENEOUS,' I. E. OTHER THAN A CLAN COMMUNITY OR A DEME (260)	175	TEND TO BE THOSE 0.51 OF 61 WHERE THE COMMUNITY IS 'KIN-HOMOGENEOUS,' I. E. A CLAN COMMUNITY OR A DEME (122)	66 31 190 30 XSQ= 13.39 PHI= -0.206 XP = 0.0003
177	TILT MORE TOWARD BEING THOSE 0.83 OF 256 WHERE THE COMMUNITY IS OTHER THAN A SINGLE CLAN-COMMUNITY AND EXOGAMOUS (305)	177	TILT LESS TOWARD BEING THOSE 0.67 OF 61 WHERE THE COMMUNITY IS OTHER THAN A SINGLE CLAN-COMMUNITY AND EXOGAMOUS (305)	44 20 212 41 XSQ= 6.50 PHI= -0.143 XP = 0.0108
178	TEND LESS TO BE THOSE 0.72 OF 256 WHERE THE COMMUNITY IS OTHER THAN SEGMENTED ON A CLAN BASIS AND NON-EXOGAMOUS (295)	178	TEND MORE TO BE THOSE 0.95 OF 61 WHERE THE COMMUNITY IS OTHER THAN SEGMENTED ON A CLAN BASIS AND NON-EXOGAMOUS (295)	71 3 185 58 XSQ= 13.08 PHI= 0.203 XP = 0.0003

No.		No.		
180	LEAN TOWARD BEING THOSE 0.70 OF 256 WHERE THE COMMUNITY IS COMMONLY NON-EXOGAMOUS, RATHER THAN EXOGAMOUS (258)	180	LEAN TOWARD BEING THOSE 0.51 OF 61 WHERE THE COMMUNITY IS COMMONLY EXOGAMOUS, RATHER THAN NON-EXOGAMOUS (124)	76 31 180 30 XSQ= 8.92 PHI= -0.168 XP = 0.0028
181	DRIFT MORE TOWARD BEING THOSE 0.91 OF 256 WHERE THE COMMUNITY IS OTHER THAN A DEME (337)	181	DRIFT LESS TOWARD BEING THOSE 0.82 OF 61 WHERE THE COMMUNITY IS OTHER THAN A DEME (337)	22 11 234 50 XSQ= 3.75 PHI= -0.109 XP = 0.0529
183	TEND MORE TO BE THOSE 0.89 OF 181 WHERE THE LARGEST NON-COGNATIC KIN GROUP IS SMALLER THAN A MOEITY, I. E., A PHRATRY OR SIB OR LINEAGE (218)	183	TEND LESS TO BE THOSE 0.59 OF 29 WHERE THE LARGEST NON-COGNATIC KIN GROUP IS SMALLER THAN A MOEITY, I. E., A PHRATRY OR SIB OR LINEAGE (218)	20 12 161 17 XSQ= 15.53 PHI= -0.272 XP = 0.0001
184	DRIFT MORE TOWARD BEING THOSE 0.70 OF 181 WHERE THE LARGEST NON-COGNATIC KIN GROUP IS SMALLER THAN A PHRATRY, I. E. A SIB OR LINEAGE (175)	184	DRIFT LESS TOWARD BEING THOSE 0.52 OF 29 WHERE THE LARGEST NON-COGNATIC KIN GROUP IS SMALLER THAN A PHRATRY, I. E. A SIB OR LINEAGE (175)	54 14 127 15 XSQ= 3.09 PHI= -0.121 XP = 0.0790
188	LEAN TOWARD BEING THOSE 0.68 OF 267 WHERE THE KIN GROUP IS OTHER THAN EXCLUSIVELY COGNATIC (252)	188	LEAN TOWARD BEING THOSE 0.54 OF 63 WHERE THE KIN GROUP IS EXCLUSIVELY COGNATIC (148)	86 34 181 29 XSQ= 9.51 PHI= -0.170 XP = 0.0020
192	TEND TO BE THOSE 0.78 OF 267 OTHER THAN WHERE THE ONLY KIN GROUP PRESENT IS A KINDRED OR ELSE BILATERAL DESCENT IS INFERRED (289)	192	TEND TO BE THOSE 0.51 OF 63 WHERE THE ONLY KIN GROUP PRESENT IS A KINDRED OR ELSE BILATERAL DESCENT IS INFERRED (111)	58 32 209 31 XSQ= 20.28 PHI= -0.248 XP = 0.0000
196	TEND TO BE THOSE 0.75 OF 195 WHERE INDIVIDUAL RIGHTS IN REAL PROPERTY, AND RULES FOR INHERITANCE, ARE PRESENT (194)	196	TEND TO BE THOSE 0.66 OF 44 WHERE INDIVIDUAL RIGHTS IN REAL PROPERTY, OR RULES FOR INHERITANCE, ARE ABSENT (87)	147 15 48 29 XSQ= 26.17 PHI= 0.331 XP = 0.0000
201	LEAN MORE TOWARD BEING THOSE 0.88 OF 267 WHERE MARITAL RESIDENCE IS NON-OPTIONAL, RATHER THAN AMBILOCAL OR NEOLOCAL (334)	201	LEAN LESS TOWARD BEING THOSE 0.71 OF 62 WHERE MARITAL RESIDENCE IS NON-OPTIONAL, RATHER THAN AMBILOCAL OR NEOLOCAL (334)	235 44 32 18 XSQ= 10.06 PHI= 0.175 XP = 0.0015
204	LEAN MORE TOWARD BEING THOSE 0.85 OF 220 WHERE MARITAL RESIDENCE IS PATRILOCAL, VIRILOCAL, OR AVUNCULOCAL, RATHER THAN AMBILOCAL OR NEOLOCAL (270)	204	LEAN LESS TOWARD BEING THOSE 0.65 OF 52 WHERE MARITAL RESIDENCE IS PATRILOCAL, VIRILOCAL, OR AVUNCULOCAL, RATHER THAN AMBILOCAL OR NEOLOCAL (270)	188 34 32 18 XSQ= 9.99 PHI= 0.192 XP = 0.0016

207	DRIFT TOWARD BEING THOSE 0.59 OF 79 WHERE MARITAL RESIDENCE IS MATRILOCAL OR UXORILOCAL, RATHER THAN AMBILOCAL OR NEOLOCAL (64)	207	DRIFT TOWARD BEING THOSE 0.64 OF 28 WHERE MARITAL RESIDENCE IS AMBILOCAL OR NEOLOCAL, RATHER THAN MATRILOCAL OR UXORILOCAL (64)	47 10 32 18 XSQ= 3.79 PHI= 0.188 XP = 0.0516
236	TEND TO BE THOSE 0.63 OF 266 WHERE THE FAMILY IS OF AN EXTENDED TYPE, RATHER THAN AN INDEPENDENT TYPE (213)	236	TEND TO BE THOSE 0.83 OF 63 WHERE THE FAMILY IS OF AN INDEPENDENT TYPE, RATHER THAN AN EXTENDED TYPE (185)	167 11 99 52 XSQ= 40.33 PHI= 0.350 XP = 0.
262	DRIFT MORE TOWARD BEING THOSE 0.79 OF 266 WHERE WIVES ARE OBTAINED BY MEANS INVOLVING THE PRESENCE OF SOME CONSIDERATION (305)	262	DRIFT LESS TOWARD BEING THOSE 0.67 OF 61 WHERE WIVES ARE OBTAINED BY MEANS INVOLVING THE PRESENCE OF SOME CONSIDERATION (305)	211 41 55 20 XSQ= 3.46 PHI= 0.103 XP = 0.0629
318	DRIFT LESS TOWARD BEING THOSE 0.51 OF 57 WHERE THE OVERALL INDULGENCE OF THE INFANT IS HIGH (40) B-B-C	318	DRIFT MORE TOWARD BEING THOSE 0.89 OF 9 WHERE THE OVERALL INDULGENCE OF THE INFANT IS HIGH (40) B-B-C	29 8 28 1 XSQ= 3.15 PHI= -0.218 XP = 0.0761
323	DRIFT TOWARD BEING THOSE 0.66 OF 59 WHERE THE CONSTANCY OF PRESENCE OF THE INFANT'S NURTURANT AGENT IS LOW (45) B-B-C	323	DRIFT TOWARD BEING THOSE 0.70 OF 10 WHERE THE CONSTANCY OF PRESENCE OF THE INFANT'S NURTURANT AGENT IS HIGH (29) B-B-C	20 7 39 3 XSQ= 3.29 PHI= -0.218 XP = 0.0699
349	DRIFT TOWARD BEING THOSE 0.60 OF 48 WHERE THE CHILD'S INFERRED ANXIETY OVER NON-PERFORMANCE OF ACHIEVEMENT BEHAVIOR IS HIGH (34) B-B-C	349	DRIFT TOWARD BEING THOSE 0.78 OF 9 WHERE THE CHILD'S INFERRED ANXIETY OVER NON-PERFORMANCE OF ACHIEVEMENT BEHAVIOR IS LOW (28) B-B-C	29 2 19 7 XSQ= 3.05 PHI= 0.231 XP = 0.0807
350	LEAN TOWARD BEING THOSE 0.65 OF 46 WHERE THE CHILD'S INFERRED ANXIETY OVER PERFORMANCE OF ACHIEVEMENT BEHAVIOR IS HIGH (34) B-B-C	350	LEAN TOWARD BEING THOSE 0.89 OF 9 WHERE THE CHILD'S INFERRED ANXIETY OVER PERFORMANCE OF ACHIEVEMENT BEHAVIOR IS LOW (26) B-B-C	30 1 16 8 XSQ= 6.89 PHI= 0.354 XP = 0.0086
358	DRIFT TOWARD BEING THOSE 0.84 OF 43 WHERE ADOLESCENT PEER GROUPS ARE PRESENT IN A SETTING OF WORK AND PUBLIC GATHERINGS AND LEISURE, OR OF PUBLIC GATHERINGS AND LEISURE, OR OF LEISURE ONLY (41) JKH	358	DRIFT TOWARD BEING THOSE 0.57 OF 7 WHERE ADOLESCENT PEER GROUPS ARE ABSENT IN A SETTING OF WORK, AND OF PUBLIC GATHERINGS, AND OF LEISURE (11) JKH	36 3 7 4 XSQ= 3.72 PHI= 0.273 XP = 0.0538
360	DRIFT LESS TOWARD BEING THOSE 0.55 OF 31 WHERE ADOLESCENT PEER GROUPS ARE PRESENT ONLY IN A SETTING OF LEISURE, OR ELSE ARE ABSENT (23) JKH	360	IN ALL CASES ARE THOSE 1.00 OF 6 WHERE ADOLESCENT PEER GROUPS ARE PRESENT ONLY IN A SETTING OF LEISURE, OR ELSE ARE ABSENT (23) JKH	14 0 17 6 XSQ= 2.65 PHI= 0.268 EP = 0.0645

377	LEAN LESS TOWARD BEING THOSE WHERE MALE GENITAL MUTILATION IS ABSENT (242)	0.70 OF 259	377	LEAN MORE TOWARD BEING THOSE WHERE MALE GENITAL MUTILATION IS ABSENT (242)	0.90 OF 63	77 6 182 57 XSQ= 9.78 PHI= 0.174 XP = 0.0018
417	TILT TOWARD BEING THOSE WHERE WARFARE IS PREVALENT (34) LWS	0.88 OF 33	417	TILT TOWARD BEING THOSE WHERE WARFARE IS NOT PREVALENT (9) LWS	0.56 OF 9	29 4 4 5 XSQ= 5.55 PHI= 0.364 XP = 0.0184
434	DRIFT TOWARD BEING THOSE WHERE ASCETICISM IN MOURNING BEHAVIOR IS LOW (30) JFG	0.51 OF 53	434	DRIFT TOWARD BEING THOSE WHERE ASCETICISM IN MOURNING BEHAVIOR IS HIGH (37) JFG	0.82 OF 11	26 9 27 2 XSQ= 2.73 PHI= -0.207 XP = 0.0982
435	TILT TOWARD BEING THOSE WHERE ABANDONMENT OF THE HOUSE OF THE DEAD IS NOT PRACTICED (19) LWS	0.74 OF 23	435	TILT TOWARD BEING THOSE WHERE ABANDONMENT OF THE HOUSE OF THE DEAD IS PRACTICED (12) LWS	0.75 OF 8	6 6 17 2 XSQ= 4.10 PHI= -0.364 EP = 0.0316
441	TILT TOWARD BEING THOSE WHERE FEAR OF HUMAN BEINGS IS LOW (32) W-C	0.58 OF 45	441	TILT TOWARD BEING THOSE WHERE FEAR OF HUMAN BEINGS IS HIGH (29) W-C	0.82 OF 11	19 9 26 2 XSQ= 4.07 PHI= -0.270 XP = 0.0436
444	DRIFT TOWARD BEING THOSE WHERE THE USE OF DREAMS TO SEEK AND CONTROL SUPERNATURAL POWERS IS LOW (27) RGD	0.55 OF 42	444	DRIFT TOWARD BEING THOSE WHERE THE USE OF DREAMS TO SEEK AND CONTROL SUPERNATURAL POWERS IS HIGH (28) RGD	0.88 OF 8	19 7 23 1 XSQ= 3.26 PHI= -0.256 XP = 0.0708
452	DRIFT TOWARD BEING THOSE WHERE TOTEMISM WITH FOOD TABOOS IS PRESENT (19) WNS	0.55 OF 33	452	DRIFT TOWARD BEING THOSE WHERE TOTEMISM WITH FOOD TABOOS IS ABSENT (24) WNS	0.88 OF 8	18 1 15 7 XSQ= 3.04 PHI= 0.272 XP = 0.0811
458	TEND LESS TO BE THOSE WHERE GAMES, IF PRESENT, DO NOT INCLUDE GAMES OF STRATEGY (119) R-A-B,EA	0.63 OF 136	458	TEND MORE TO BE THOSE WHERE GAMES, IF PRESENT, DO NOT INCLUDE GAMES OF STRATEGY (119) R-A-B,EA	0.97 OF 33	51 1 85 32 XSQ= 13.24 PHI= 0.280 XP = 0.0003
472	DRIFT TOWARD BEING THOSE WHERE THE COMPOSITE NARCISSISM INDEX IS HIGH (47) PES	0.57 OF 74	472	DRIFT TOWARD BEING THOSE WHERE THE COMPOSITE NARCISSISM INDEX IS LOW (43) PES	0.75 OF 12	42 3 32 9 XSQ= 3.00 PHI= 0.187 XP = 0.0833

475	TILT TOWARD BEING THOSE WHERE EXHIBITIONISTIC DANCING IS STRONGLY OR MODERATELY EMPHASIZED (48) PES	0.61 OF 70	475	TILT TOWARD BEING THOSE WHERE EXHIBITIONISTIC DANCING IS NEGLIGIBLY EMPHASIZED (38) PES	0.75 OF 12	43 3 27 9 XSQ= 4.14 PHI= 0.225 XP = 0.0419
476	TILT LESS TOWARD BEING THOSE WHERE THE DEGREE OF INSOBRIETY IS STRONG (31) DH	0.55 OF 38	476	IN ALL CASES ARE THOSE WHERE THE DEGREE OF INSOBRIETY IS STRONG (31) DH	1.00 OF 8	21 8 17 0 XSQ= 3.92 PHI= -0.292 XP = 0.0477

101 CULTURES WHERE THE NUMBER OF SPECIALTIES IN COMMUNAL ACTIVITIES IS HIGH (17) GES	101 CULTURES WHERE THE NUMBER OF SPECIALTIES IN COMMUNAL ACTIVITIES IS LOW (20) GES

BACKGROUND ON PAGE 88 — SUBJECT ONLY

17 IN LEFT COLUMN

ARANDA, AYMARA, AZANDE, AZTEC, BEMBA, CUNA, GANDA, LOZI, MARQUESANS, NAMA, NANDI, ROMANS, TANALA, TIMBIRA, TRUMAI, YOKUTS, ZUNI

20 IN RIGHT COLUMN

ARAPESH, COPR ESKIMO, DOBUANS, HEBREWS, IBAN, IFUGAO, KAREN, KASKA, MIAO, NUER, NYAKYUSA, SANPOIL, TALLENSI, TIV, TODA, WINNEBAGO, WOLEAIANS, YAGUA, YAHGAN, YUROK

363 EXCLUDED BECAUSE UNASCERTAINED

	Left column			Right column			Statistics
13	DRIFT MORE TOWARD BEING THOSE WHERE THE LATITUDE IS LESS THAN FORTY DEGREES (329)	0.94 OF 17	13	DRIFT LESS TOWARD BEING THOSE WHERE THE LATITUDE IS LESS THAN FORTY DEGREES (329)	0.70 OF 20		1 6 16 14 XSQ= 2.09 PHI= -0.238 EP = 0.0975
82	DRIFT TOWARD BEING THOSE WHERE A CITY OR TOWN IS PRESENT, OR THE AVERAGE COMMUNITY SIZE IS FIFTY OR GREATER (178)	0.87 OF 15	82	DRIFT TOWARD BEING THOSE WHERE NO CITY OR TOWN IS PRESENT, AND THE AVERAGE COMMUNITY SIZE IS SMALLER THAN FIFTY (46)	0.50 OF 12		13 6 2 6 XSQ= 2.72 PHI= 0.317 EP = 0.0870
86	TILT TOWARD BEING THOSE WHERE THE LEVEL OF POLITICAL INTEGRATION IS THE LARGE STATE, THE LITTLE STATE, OR THE MINIMAL STATE (148) GPM	0.67 OF 15	86	TILT TOWARD BEING THOSE WHERE THE LEVEL OF POLITICAL INTEGRATION IS THE AUTONOMOUS COMMUNITY, OR THE FAMILY (156) GPM	0.76 OF 17		10 4 5 13 XSQ= 4.40 PHI= 0.371 EP = 0.0307
102	TILT TOWARD BEING THOSE WHERE CLASS STRATIFICATION IS PRESENT (203)	0.71 OF 17	102	TILT TOWARD BEING THOSE WHERE CLASS STRATIFICATION IS ABSENT (180)	0.70 OF 20		12 6 5 14 XSQ= 4.54 PHI= 0.350 EP = 0.0217
106	TILT TOWARD BEING THOSE WHERE CLASS STRATIFICATION, IF PRESENT, IS BASED ON SOMETHING OTHER THAN WEALTH (126)	0.67 OF 12	106	IN ALL CASES ARE THOSE WHERE CLASS STRATIFICATION, IF PRESENT, IS BASED ON WEALTH (77)	1.00 OF 6		4 6 8 0 XSQ= 4.75 PHI= -0.514 EP = 0.0128

108	DRIFT TOWARD BEING THCSE WHERE CLASS STRATIFICATION, IF PRESENT, IS BASED CN A HEREDITARY ARISTCCRACY (74)	0.50 OF 12	108	IN ALL CASES ARE THOSE WHERE CLASS STRATIFICATION, IF PRESENT, IS BASED ON SOMETHING OTHER THAN A HEREDITARY ARISTOCRACY (129)	1.00 OF 6	6 0 6 6 XSQ= 2.53 PHI= 0.375 EP = 0.0537
132	TILT TOWARD BEING THOSE WHERE ECONCMIC EXCHANGE DOES NCT INVCLVE THE USE CF MCNEY (17) JMH	0.71 OF 7	132	TILT TOWARD BEING THOSE WHERE ECONOMIC EXCHANGE INVOLVES THE USE OF MONEY (37) JMH	0.83 OF 12	2 10 5 2 XSQ= 3.59 PHI= -0.435 EP = 0.0449
135	TILT TOWARD BEING THOSE WHERE INDIVIDUAL OWNERSHIP OF ECONOMICALLY SIGNIFICANT PROPERTY IS NEGLIGIBLE OR ABSENT (14) GES	0.59 OF 17	135	TILT TOWARD BEING THOSE WHERE INDIVIDUAL OWNERSHIP OF ECONOMICALLY SIGNIFICANT PROPERTY IS PRESENT (24) GES	0.80 OF 20	7 16 10 4 XSQ= 4.35 PHI= -0.343 EP = 0.0210
143	IN ALL CASES ARE THCSE WHERE THE RATIO CF RESTITUTIVE TC REPRESSIVE SANCTICNS IS MEDIUM CR LOW (32) WME	1.00 OF 7	143	LEAN TOWARD BEING THOSE WHERE THE RATIO OF RESTITUTIVE TO REPRESSIVE SANCTIONS IS HIGH (20) WME	0.70 OF 10	0 7 7 3 XSQ= 5.69 PHI= -0.579 EP = 0.0098
144	TILT TCWARD BEING THCSE WHERE THE RATIO OF RESTITUTIVE TO REPRESSIVE SANCTICNS IS LOW (25) WME	0.86 OF 7	144	TILT TOWARD BEING THOSE WHERE THE RATIO OF RESTITUTIVE TO REPRESSIVE SANCTICNS IS HIGH OR MEDIUM (27) WME	0.70 OF 10	1 7 6 3 XSQ= 3.14 PHI= -0.430 EP = 0.0498
180	DRIFT TCWARD BEING THOSE WHERE THE COMMUNITY IS COMMONLY NCN-EXCGAMOUS, RATHER THAN EXCGAMCUS (258)	0.76 OF 17	180	DRIFT TOWARD BEING THOSE WHERE THE COMMUNITY IS COMMONLY EXOGAMOUS, RATHER THAN NON-EXOGAMOUS (124)	0.53 OF 19	4 10 13 9 XSQ= 2.09 PHI= -0.241 EP = 0.0967
317	DRIFT TCWARD BEING THCSE WHERE DISPLAY OF AFFECTION TOWARD THE INFANT IS LCW (29) B-B-C	0.67 OF 9	317	DRIFT TOWARD BEING THOSE WHERE DISPLAY OF AFFECTICN TOWARD THE INFANT IS HIGH (39) B-B-C	0.86 CF 7	3 6 6 1 XSQ= 2.52 PHI= -0.397 EP = 0.0601
321	DRIFT TCWARD BEING THCSE WHERE THE IMMEDIACY OF REDUCTION OF THE INFANT'S DRIVES IS LCW (25) B-B-C	0.57 OF 7	321	IN ALL CASES ARE THOSE WHERE THE IMMEDIACY OF REDUCTION OF THE INFANT'S DRIVES IS HIGH (35) B-B-C	1.00 OF 7	3 7 4 0 XSQ= 3.15 PHI= -0.474 EP = 0.0699
327	IN ALL CASES ARE THOSE WHERE THE AGE OF THE INFANT AT TIME OF REDUCED CONTACT WITH MOTHER IS TWC YEARS CR LOWER (27) B-B-C	1.00 OF 4	327	DRIFT TOWARD BEING THOSE WHERE THE AGE OF THE INFANT AT TIME OF REDUCED CONTACT WITH MOTHER IS HIGHER THAN TWO YEARS (28) B-B-C	0.63 CF 8	0 5 4 3 XSQ= 2.10 PHI= -0.418 EP = 0.0808

342	IN ALL CASES ARE THOSE 1.00 OF 2 WHERE THE CHILD'S INFERREC ANXIETY OVER PERFORMANCE OF NURTURANT BEHAVIOR IS HIGH (18) B-B-C	342	DRIFT TOWARD BEING THOSE 0.80 OF 10 WHERE THE CHILD'S INFERRED ANXIETY OVER PERFORMANCE OF NURTURANT BEHAVIOR IS LOW (28) B-B-C	2 2 0 8 XSQ= 1.88 PHI= 0.395 EP = 0.0909
356	DRIFT TOWARD BEING THCSE 0.60 OF 5 WHERE NEITHER ACOLESCENT PEER GROUPS NCR PAIRS ARE PRESENT IN A SETTING CF COURTSHIP (22) JKH	356	IN ALL CASES ARE THOSE 1.00 CF 6 WHERE ADOLESCENT PEER GROUPS OR PAIRS ARE PRESENT IN A SETTING OF COURTSHIP (29) JKH	2 6 3 0 XSQ= 2.39 PHI= -0.466 EP = 0.0606
372	DRIFT TCWARD BEING THCSE 0.64 OF 11 WHERE MALE INITIATICN RITES ARE PRESENT (48) ASA	372	DRIFT TOWARD BEING THOSE 0.88 OF 8 WHERE MALE INITIATICN RITES ARE ABSENT (63) ASA	7 1 4 7 XSQ= 3.09 PHI= 0.403 EP = 0.0587
430	TILT TCWARD BEING THCSE 0.82 OF 17 WHERE SUPERNATURAL SANCTICNS FOR MORALITY, HAVING AN EFFECT ON AN INDIVIDUAL'S HEALTH, ARE ABSENT OR UNREPCRTED (22) GES	430	TILT TOWARD BEING THOSE 0.60 OF 20 WHERE SUPERNATURAL SANCTIONS FOR MORALITY, HAVING AN EFFECT ON AN INDIVIDUAL'S HEALTH, ARE PRESENT (16) GES	3 12 14 8 XSQ= 5.19 PHI= -0.375 EP = 0.0176

102 CULTURES WHERE CLASS STRATIFICATION IS PRESENT (203)

102 CULTURES WHERE CLASS STRATIFICATION IS ABSENT (180)

BACKGROUND ON PAGE 88 — BOTH SUBJECT AND PREDICATE

203 IN LEFT COLUMN

ABIPON	ABOR	ALORESE	AMERICANS	ARAUCANIANS	ASHANTI	ATSUGEWI	AYMARA	AZANDE	AZTEC
BALINESE	BAMBARA	BAMILEKE	BARABRA	BARI	BASQUES	BASSERI	BELU	BEMBA	BENGALI
BHIL	BOERS	BRAZILIANS	BULGARIANS	BURMESE	BURUSHO	BURYAT	CAGABA	CAMBA	CAMBODIANS
CHAGGA	CHAMACOCO	CHEREMIS	CHERKESS	CHIBCHA	CHUKCHEE	COORG	CUNA	CZECHS	DARD
DOGON	DUSUN	DUTCH	EGYPTIANS	ELLICE	EYAK	FANG	FON	FUTAJALONKE	GANDA
GARO	GILBERTESE	GISU	GOAJIRO	GOND	HAIDA	HASANIA	HASINAI	HAWAIIANS	HAZARA
HEBREWS	HEHE	HERERO	HO	HUICHOL	HURON	HUTSUL	ICELANDERS	IFUGAO	ILA
INCA	INGALIK	IRAQW	IRISH	JAPANESE	JAVANESE	JUKUN	KACHIN	KAPAUKU	KAREN
KAZAK	KERALA	KHALKA	KHASI	KIKUYU	KOHISTANI	KOREANS	KORYAK	KPE	KUBA
KURTATCHI	KWAKIUTL	LAKALAI	LAKHER	LAMET	LANGO	LAPPS	LAU	LEPCHA	LHOTA NAGA
LIFU	LOLO	LOZI	LUBA	LUO	MACASSARESE	MAGUZAWA	MALAYS	MAM	MANCHU
MANGAIANS	MANIHIKI	MANUS	MAORI	MARQUESANS	MARSHALLESE	MAYA	MBUGWE	MBUNDU	MENDE
MERINA	MIN CHINESE	MINANGKABAU	MINCHIA	MNONG GAR	MONGUOR	MOSSI	MOTA	MZAB	NAMA
NATCHEZ	NGONI	NOMLAKI	NUNIVAK	NUPE	NURI	NYANEKA	NYORO	OKINAWANS	ONTONG-JAVA
PAIWAN	PALAUANS	PATHAN	PAWNEE	PENDE	PONAPEANS	PORTUGUESE	PURUM	REGEIBAT	RIFFIANS
ROMANS	ROTINESE	RUNDI	RWALA	SAGADA	SAMOANS	SAMOYED	SENIANG	SERBS	SHILLUK
SINDHI	SIUAI	SIWANS	SOMALI	SONGHAI	SOTHO	SWAZI	SYRIANS	TAGBANUA	TALLENSI
TAMIL	TANALA	TANIMBARESE	TARAHUMARA	TAREUMIUT	TENINO	TERA	TERENA	THAI	THONGA
TIBETANS	TIGRINYA	TIKOPIA	TIMUCUA	TOLOWA	TORAJA	TROBRIAND	TSHIMSHIAN	TUPINAMBA	TURKMEN
TWANA	VENDA	VIETNAMESE	WALLOONS	WOLOF	WUTE	YAKUT	YAPESE	YOKUTS	YOMBE
YORUBA	YUKI	YUROK							

180 IN RIGHT COLUMN

AINU	AJIE	AKHA	ALACALUF	ALBANIANS	AMBA	ANDAMANESE	APINAYE	ARANDA	ARAPESH
ATAYAL	AWEIKOMA	BABWA	BACAIRI	BAJUN	BANDA	BATAK	BAYA	BEJA	BERGDAMA
BETE	BIRIFOR	BLACK CARIB	BORORO	BOTOCUDO	BOZO	BUDUMA	CADUVEO	CALLINAGO	CAMAYURA
CARAJA	CARIB	CAYAPA	CHENCHU	CHEROKEE	CHEYENNE	CHIR-APACHE	CHOCO	CHOROTI	CHORTI
COCHITI	COMANCHE	COPR ESKIMO	CREE	CREEK	CROW	DAGUR	DELAWARE	DIEGUENO	DIERI
DILLING	DOBUANS	DOROBO	ENGA	FOX	GILYAK	GROS VENTRE	GUAHIBO	GUATO	GURE
HANO	HANUNOO	HAVASUPAI	HUKUNDIKA	IBAN	INGASSANA	JEMEZ	JIVARO	KABYLE	KALMYK
KARIERA	KASKA	KATAB	KERAKI	KET	KHEVSUR	KIOW-APACHE	KISSI	KONSO	KUNG
KUTENAI	LAMBA	LESU	MAMBILA	MAMVU	MANDAN	MARGI	MARICOPA	MASAI	MATACO
MATAKAM	MBUTI	MENTAWEI	MIAMI	MIAO	MISKITO	MIWOK	MONGO	MOTILON	MUNDURUCU
MURINBATA	MURNGIN	NABESNA	NAMBICUARA	NANDI	NASKAPI	NAVAHO	NICOBARESE	NUER	NYAKYUSA
NYARO	OJIBWA	OMAHA	ONA	PALIKUR	PAPAGO	PARAUJANO	PENOBSCOT	POPOLUCA	PUKAPUKA
PURARI	RAROIANS	ROTUMANS	SANDAWE	SANPOIL	SANTAL	SARAMACCA	SARSI	SELUNG	SEMANG
SEMINOLE	SERI	SHERENTE	SHLUH	SIRIONO	SUBANUN	TALAMANCA	TAOS	TAPIRAPE	TEHUELCHE
TENDA	TENETEHARA	TESO	TETON	TIMBIRA	TIV	TIWI	TODA	TOKELAU	TRISTAN

TRUKESE TRUMAI TUBATULABAL TUCANO TUCUNA TUNEBO TURKANA ULAWANS UTE VEDDA
WAICA WANTOAT WAPISHANA WAROPEN WARRAU WASHO WICHITA WIKMUNKAN WINNEBAGO WITOTO
WOGEO WOLEAIANS YABARANA YAGUA YAHGAN YAKO YAO YARURO YUKAGHIR ZUNI

17 EXCLUDED BECAUSE UNASCERTAINEC

4	TEND LESS TO BE THCSE LOCATED CUTSIDE CF THE CIRCUM-MEDITERRANEAN (355)	0.83 OF 203	4	TEND MORE TO BE THOSE LOCATED OUTSIDE OF THE CIRCUM-MEDITERRANEAN (355)	0.95 OF 180	34 9 169 171 XSQ= 12.06 PHI= 0.177 XP = 0.0005
5	TEND LESS TO BE THCSE LOCATED CUTSIDE CF EAST EURASIA (330)	0.75 OF 203	5	TEND MORE TO BE THOSE LOCATED OUTSIDE OF EAST EURASIA (330)	0.92 OF 180	50 15 153 165 XSQ= 16.84 PHI= 0.210 XP = 0.0000
8	LEAN MCRE TOWARC BEING THCSE LOCATED CUTSIDE CF NORTH AMERICA (330)	0.89 OF 203	8	LEAN LESS TOWARD BEING THOSE LOCATED OUTSIDE OF NORTH AMERICA (330)	0.76 OF 180	23 44 180 136 XSQ= 10.48 PHI= -0.165 XP = 0.0012
9	TEND MORE TO BE THCSE LOCATED CUTSIDE CF SOUTH AMERICA (335)	0.93 OF 203	9	TEND LESS TO BE THOSE LOCATED OUTSIDE OF SOUTH AMERICA (335)	0.74 OF 180	14 47 189 133 XSQ= 24.89 PHI= -0.255 XP = 0.0000
15	DRIFT TCWARD BEING THCSE WHERE THE LATITUDE IS TWENTY DEGREES CR GREATER (183)	0.50 OF 203	15	DRIFT TOWARD BEING THOSE WHERE THE LATITUDE IS LESS THAN TWENTY DEGREES (217)	0.59 OF 180	102 73 101 107 XSQ= 3.23 PHI= 0.092 XP = 0.0723
44	TEND MORE TO BE THCSE WHERE SETTLEMENTS ARE FIXEC (222)	0.78 OF 171	44	TEND LESS TO BE THOSE WHERE SETTLEMENTS ARE FIXED (222)	0.54 OF 151	133 82 38 69 XSQ= 18.87 PHI= 0.242 XP = 0.0000
46	TEND MCRE TO BE THCSE OTHER THAN WHERE SETTLEMENTS ARE NON-FIXED AND MCVEMENT IS NOMADIC (260)	0.88 OF 171	46	TEND LESS TO BE THOSE OTHER THAN WHERE SETTLEMENTS ARE NON-FIXED AND MOVEMENT IS NOMADIC (260)	0.66 OF 151	20 51 151 100 XSQ= 21.48 PHI= -0.258 XP = 0.0000

47	TILT LESS TOWARD BEING THOSE WHERE, IF SETTLEMENTS ARE NON-FIXED, MOVEMENT IS NOMADIC, RATHER THAN NON-NOMADIC (72)	0.53 OF 38	47	TILT MORE TOWARD BEING THOSE WHERE, IF SETTLEMENTS ARE NON-FIXED, MOVEMENT IS NOMADIC, RATHER THAN NON-NOMADIC (72)	0.74 OF 69	20 51 18 18 XSQ= 4.06 PHI= -0.195 XP = 0.0438
51	TEND TO BE THOSE WHERE SUBSISTENCE IS PRIMARILY BY FOOD PRODUCTION -- I. E., AGRICULTURE OR HUSBANDRY -- RATHER THAN BY GATHERING (253)	0.79 OF 203	51	TEND TO BE THOSE WHERE SUBSISTENCE IS PRIMARILY BY FOOD GATHERING -- I. E., HUNTING, FISHING, OR COLLECTING -- RATHER THAN FOOD PRODUCTION (147)	0.58 OF 180	161 75 42 105 XSQ= 55.58 PHI= 0.381 XP = 0.
53	TEND LESS TO BE THOSE WHERE FOOD PRODUCTION IS BY SIMPLE AGRICULTURE OR INCIPIENT FOOD PRODUCTION, RATHER THAN BY INTENSIVE AGRICULTURE (147)	0.53 OF 140	53	TEND MORE TO BE THOSE WHERE FOOD PRODUCTION IS BY SIMPLE AGRICULTURE OR INCIPIENT FOOD PRODUCTION, RATHER THAN BY INTENSIVE AGRICULTURE (147)	0.77 OF 88	66 20 74 68 XSQ= 12.69 PHI= 0.236 XP = 0.0004
54	TEND MORE TO BE THOSE WHERE FOOD PRODUCTION IS BY INTENSIVE OR SIMPLE AGRICULTURE, RATHER THAN BY INCIPIENT FOOD PRODUCTION (192)	0.88 OF 140	54	TEND LESS TO BE THOSE WHERE FOOD PRODUCTION IS BY INTENSIVE OR SIMPLE AGRICULTURE, RATHER THAN BY INCIPIENT FOOD PRODUCTION (192)	0.67 OF 88	123 59 17 29 XSQ= 13.27 PHI= 0.241 XP = 0.0003
55	TILT TOWARD BEING THOSE WHERE FOOD PRODUCTION IS BY INTENSIVE AGRICULTURE, RATHER THAN BY SIMPLE AGRICULTURE (91)	0.54 OF 123	55	TILT TOWARD BEING THOSE WHERE FOOD PRODUCTION IS BY SIMPLE AGRICULTURE, RATHER THAN BY INTENSIVE AGRICULTURE (101)	0.66 OF 59	66 20 57 39 XSQ= 5.48 PHI= 0.174 XP = 0.0192
56	TILT MORE TOWARD BEING THOSE WHERE FOOD PRODUCTION IS BY SIMPLE AGRICULTURE, RATHER THAN BY INCIPIENT FOOD PRODUCTION (101)	0.77 OF 74	56	TILT LESS TOWARD BEING THOSE WHERE FOOD PRODUCTION IS BY SIMPLE AGRICULTURE, RATHER THAN BY INCIPIENT FOOD PRODUCTION (101)	0.57 OF 68	57 39 17 29 XSQ= 5.40 PHI= 0.195 XP = 0.0202
62	TEND TO BE THOSE WHERE HUSBANDRY OF SOME KIND IS PRESENT (228)	0.70 OF 203	62	TEND TO BE THOSE WHERE HUSBANDRY OF ANY KIND IS ABSENT (172)	0.57 OF 180	142 78 61 102 XSQ= 26.57 PHI= 0.263 XP = 0.0000
63	LEAN MORE TOWARD BEING THOSE WHERE HUSBANDRY, IF PRESENT, IS PRINCIPALLY IN THE FORM OF BOVINE, EQUINE, CAMEL-LIKE, OR DEER-LIKE ANIMALS, RATHER THAN PIGS, SHEEP, OR GOATS (152)	0.74 OF 141	63	LEAN LESS TOWARD BEING THOSE WHERE HUSBANDRY, IF PRESENT, IS PRINCIPALLY IN THE FORM OF BOVINE, EQUINE, CAMEL-LIKE, OR DEER-LIKE ANIMALS, RATHER THAN PIGS, SHEEP, OR GOATS (152)	0.55 OF 77	104 42 37 35 XSQ= 7.47 PHI= 0.185 XP = 0.0063
71	TEND TO BE THOSE WHERE METAL WORKING IS PRESENT (98)	0.57 OF 129	71	TEND TO BE THOSE WHERE METAL WORKING IS ABSENT (153)	0.82 OF 117	74 21 55 96 XSQ= 38.57 PHI= 0.396 XP = 0.

73	LEAN TCWARD BEING THOSE WHERE WEAVING IS PRESENT (118)	0.57 OF 129	73	LEAN TOWARD BEING THOSE WHERE WEAVING IS ABSENT (130)	0.64 CF 114	74 41 55 73 XSQ= 10.28 PHI= 0.206 XP = 0.0013
74	TILT MORE TOWARC BEING THCSE WHERE PCTTERY IS PRESENT (145)	0.67 OF 120	74	TILT LESS TOWARD BEING THOSE WHERE POTTERY IS PRESENT (145)	0.53 OF 114	81 60 39 54 XSQ= 4.79 PHI= 0.143 XP = 0.0286
79	TEND LESS TO BE THCSE WHERE NC CITY IS PRESENT (201)	0.82 OF 123	79	IN ALL CASES ARE THOSE WHERE NO CITY IS PRESENT (201)	1.00 CF 96	22 0 101 96 XSQ= 17.16 PHI= 0.280 XP = 0.0000
81	TEND TO BE THCSE WHERE A CITY CR TOWN IS PRESENT, OR THE AVERAGE COMMUNITY SIZE IS 200 CR GREATER (89)	0.52 OF 123	81	TEND TO BE THOSE WHERE NO CITY OR TOWN IS PRESENT, AND THE AVERAGE COMMUNITY SIZE IS SMALLER THAN 200 (135)	0.76 OF 96	64 23 59 73 XSQ= 16.59 PHI= 0.275 XP = 0.0000
84	TEND LESS TO BE THCSE WHERE THE LEVEL CF POLITICAL INTEGRATION IS THE LITTLE STATE, THE MINIMAL STATE, THE AUTCNCMOUS CCMMUNITY, CR THE FAMILY (262) GPM	0.74 OF 151	84	IN ALL CASES ARE THOSE WHERE THE LEVEL OF POLITICAL INTEGRATION IS THE LITTLE STATE, THE MINIMAL STATE, THE AUTONOMOUS COMMUNITY, CR THE FAMILY (262) GPM	1.00 CF 146	39 0 112 146 XSQ= 41.17 PHI= 0.372 XP = 0.
86	TEND TO BE THCSE WHERE THE LEVEL CF POLITICAL INTEGRATION IS THE LARGE STATE, THE LITTLE STATE, OR THE MINIMAL STATE (148) GPM	0.68 OF 151	86	TEND TO BE THOSE WHERE THE LEVEL OF POLITICAL INTEGRATION IS THE AUTONOMOUS COMMUNITY, OR THE FAMILY (156) GPM	0.73 OF 146	102 40 49 106 XSQ= 46.37 PHI= 0.395 XP = 0.
88	TILT MCRE TOWARC BEING THCSE WHERE, IF A HEACMANSHIP IS PRESENT, SUCCESSICN IS HERECITARY (165)	0.67 CF 147	88	TILT LESS TOWARD BEING THOSE WHERE, IF A HEADMANSHIP IS PRESENT, SUCCESSION IS HEREDITARY (165)	0.54 OF 116	48 53 99 63 XSQ= 4.12 PHI= -0.125 XP = 0.0423
91	DRIFT TCWARD BEING THOSE WHERE SCCIETAL CCMPLEXITY IS HIGH (18) F-W	0.56 OF 27	91	DRIFT TOWARD BEING THOSE WHERE SOCIETAL COMPLEXITY IS LOW (22) F-W	0.77 OF 13	15 3 12 10 XSQ= 2.54 PHI= 0.252 EP = 0.0896
96	TEND TC BE THCSE WHERE THE HIERARCHY OF NATICNAL JURISDICTICN HAS FOUR, THREE, TWC OR CNE LEVEL (174) GES,EA	0.70 OF 168	96	TEND TO BE THOSE WHERE THE HIERARCHY OF NATIONAL JURISDICTION HAS NO LEVELS (156) GES,EA	0.68 CF 152	117 48 51 104 XSQ= 44.78 PHI= 0.374 XP = 0.

98	TEND MORE TO BE THOSE 0.83 OF 169 WHERE THE HIERARCHY OF LOCAL JURISDICTION HAS FOUR OR THREE LEVELS (238) GES,EA	98	TEND LESS TO BE THOSE 0.59 OF 152 WHERE THE HIERARCHY OF LOCAL JURISDICTION HAS FOUR OR THREE LEVELS (238) GES,EA	141 90 28 62 XSQ= 22.08 PHI= 0.262 XP = 0.0000
99	LEAN MORE TOWARD BEING THOSE 0.76 OF 51 WHERE, WITH NATIONAL HIERARCHY ABSENT, THE HIERARCHY OF LOCAL JURISDICTION HAS FOUR OR THREE LEVELS (93) GES,EA	99	LEAN LESS TOWARD BEING THOSE 0.51 OF 104 WHERE, WITH NATIONAL HIERARCHY ABSENT, THE HIERARCHY OF LOCAL JURISDICTION HAS FOUR OR THREE LEVELS (93) GES,EA	39 53 12 51 XSQ= 8.20 PHI= 0.230 XP = 0.0042
100	TEND MORE TO BE THOSE 0.93 OF 168 WHERE HIERARCHIES ARE MORE COMPLEX THAN THE 'SIMPLEST,' I. E., MORE COMPLEX THAN TWO LOCAL LEVELS WITH NO NATIONAL LEVELS (267) GES,EA	100	TEND LESS TO BE THOSE 0.66 OF 152 WHERE HIERARCHIES ARE MORE COMPLEX THAN THE 'SIMPLEST,' I. E., MORE COMPLEX THAN TWO LOCAL LEVELS WITH NO NATIONAL LEVELS (267) GES,EA	156 101 12 51 XSQ= 33.55 PHI= 0.324 XP = 0.
109	TEND LESS TO BE THOSE 0.80 OF 182 WHERE CASTES ARE ABSENT (317)	109	TEND MORE TO BE THOSE 0.94 OF 176 WHERE CASTES ARE ABSENT (317)	36 10 146 166 XSQ= 14.65 PHI= 0.202 XP = 0.0001
110	TEND TO BE THOSE 0.61 OF 195 WHERE SLAVERY IS PRESENT (163)	110	TEND TO BE THOSE 0.77 OF 177 WHERE SLAVERY IS ABSENT (218)	119 40 76 137 XSQ= 54.42 PHI= 0.382 XP = 0.
116	TILT TOWARD BEING THOSE 0.50 OF 32 WHERE OCCUPATIONAL SPECIALIZATION IS FULL-TIME, WHETHER OR NOT FOR SURPLUS PRODUCTION (20) JMH	116	TILT TOWARD BEING THOSE 0.82 OF 22 WHERE OCCUPATIONAL SPECIALIZATION IS PART-TIME ONLY (34) JMH	16 4 16 18 XSQ= 4.38 PHI= 0.285 XP = 0.0364
118	DRIFT TOWARD BEING THOSE 0.60 OF 30 WHERE THE PERCENTAGE OF OCCUPATIONS THAT ARE SPECIALIZED IS HIGH OR MEDIUM (24) WME	118	DRIFT TOWARD BEING THOSE 0.68 OF 19 WHERE THE PERCENTAGE OF OCCUPATIONS THAT ARE SPECIALIZED IS LOW (25) WME	18 6 12 13 XSQ= 2.71 PHI= 0.235 XP = 0.0998
130	TILT TOWARD BEING THOSE 0.59 OF 46 WHERE LEATHER WORKING IS MAINLY DONE BY MALES (39)	130	TILT TOWARD BEING THOSE 0.72 OF 36 WHERE LEATHER WORKING IS MAINLY DONE BY FEMALES (45)	27 10 19 26 XSQ= 6.60 PHI= 0.284 XP = 0.0102
131	TEND MORE TO BE THOSE 0.95 OF 85 WHERE THE CONSTRUCTION OF PERMANENT HOUSES OR THE ERECTION OF TEMPORARY DWELLINGS IS MAINLY DONE BY MALES (136)	131	TEND LESS TO BE THOSE 0.75 OF 69 WHERE THE CONSTRUCTION OF PERMANENT HOUSES OR THE ERECTION OF TEMPORARY DWELLINGS IS MAINLY DONE BY MALES (136)	81 52 4 17 XSQ= 11.21 PHI= 0.270 XP = 0.0008

132	TILT TOWARD BEING THOSE WHERE ECONOMIC EXCHANGE INVOLVES THE USE OF MONEY (37) JMH	0.81 OF 32	132	TILT TOWARD BEING THOSE WHERE ECONOMIC EXCHANGE DOES NOT INVOLVE THE USE OF MONEY (17) JMH	0.50 OF 22	26 11 6 11 XSQ= 4.54 PHI= 0.290 XP = 0.0331
149	TILT TOWARD BEING THOSE WHERE THE INCIDENCE OF THEFT IS HIGH (18) B-B-C	0.67 OF 21	149	TILT TOWARD BEING THOSE WHERE THE INCIDENCE OF THEFT IS LOW (19) B-B-C	0.75 OF 16	14 4 7 12 XSQ= 4.75 PHI= 0.358 EP = 0.0201
152	DRIFT TOWARD BEING THOSE WHERE THE DIFFERENTIATION OF THE JURIDICAL AGENCY FROM THE MEDICAL AGENCY IS HIGH (10) MJ	0.73 OF 11	152	DRIFT TOWARD BEING THOSE WHERE THE DIFFERENTIATION OF THE JURIDICAL AGENCY FROM THE MEDICAL AGENCY IS LOW (10) MJ	0.78 OF 9	8 2 3 7 XSQ= 3.23 PHI= 0.402 EP = 0.0698
163	LEAN TOWARD BEING THOSE WHERE THE EMPHASIS ON INDIVIDUAL VOLITION AS THE CAUSE OF CRIME IS HIGH (7) MJ	0.70 OF 10	163	IN ALL CASES ARE THOSE WHERE THE EMPHASIS ON INDIVIDUAL VOLITION AS THE CAUSE OF CRIME IS LOW (10) MJ	1.00 OF 7	7 0 3 7 XSQ= 5.69 PHI= 0.579 EP = 0.0098
180	DRIFT MORE TOWARD BEING THOSE WHERE THE COMMUNITY IS COMMONLY NON-EXOGAMOUS, RATHER THAN EXOGAMOUS (258)	0.72 OF 197	180	DRIFT LESS TOWARD BEING THOSE WHERE THE COMMUNITY IS COMMONLY NON-EXOGAMOUS, RATHER THAN EXOGAMOUS (258)	0.62 OF 170	55 64 142 106 XSQ= 3.51 PHI= -0.098 XP = 0.0610
182	TILT LESS TOWARD BEING THOSE OTHER THAN WHERE THE COMMUNITY IS STRUCTURED ON A NON-CLAN BASIS AND AGAMOUS (256)	0.62 OF 197	182	TILT MORE TOWARD BEING THOSE OTHER THAN WHERE THE COMMUNITY IS STRUCTURED ON A NON-CLAN BASIS AND AGAMOUS (256)	0.72 OF 170	75 47 122 123 XSQ= 4.01 PHI= 0.105 XP = 0.0452
183	TEND MORE TO BE THOSE WHERE THE LARGEST NON-COGNATIC KIN GROUP IS SMALLER THAN A MOEITY, I. E., A PHRATRY OR SIB OR LINEAGE (218)	0.96 OF 137	183	TEND LESS TO BE THOSE WHERE THE LARGEST NON-COGNATIC KIN GROUP IS SMALLER THAN A MOEITY, I. E., A PHRATRY OR SIB OR LINEAGE (218)	0.75 OF 108	6 27 131 81 XSQ= 20.30 PHI= -0.288 XP = 0.0000
184	DRIFT MORE TOWARD BEING THOSE WHERE THE LARGEST NON-COGNATIC KIN GROUP IS SMALLER THAN A PHRATRY, I. E. A SIB OR LINEAGE (175)	0.74 OF 137	184	DRIFT LESS TOWARD BEING THOSE WHERE THE LARGEST NON-COGNATIC KIN GROUP IS SMALLER THAN A PHRATRY, I. E. A SIB OR LINEAGE (175)	0.63 OF 108	36 40 101 68 XSQ= 2.78 PHI= -0.107 XP = 0.0952
186	TILT LESS TOWARD BEING THOSE WHERE THE KIN GROUP IS OTHER THAN EXCLUSIVELY PATRILINEAL (250)	0.56 OF 203	186	TILT MORE TOWARD BEING THOSE WHERE THE KIN GROUP IS OTHER THAN EXCLUSIVELY PATRILINEAL (250)	0.69 OF 180	90 56 113 124 XSQ= 6.52 PHI= 0.131 XP = 0.0106

187	DRIFT MORE TOWARD BEING THOSE 0.89 OF 203 WHERE THE KIN GROUP IS OTHER THAN EXCLUSIVELY MATRILINEAL (344)	187	DRIFT LESS TOWARD BEING THOSE 0.82 OF 179 WHERE THE KIN GROUP IS OTHER THAN EXCLUSIVELY MATRILINEAL (344)	22 32 181 147 XSQ= 3.33 PHI= -0.093 XP = 0.0682
190	DRIFT MORE TOWARD BEING THOSE 0.80 OF 134 WHERE THE KIN GROUP IS PATRILINEAL OR DOUBLE-DESCENT, RATHER THAN MATRILINEAL (186)	190	DRIFT LESS TOWARD BEING THOSE 0.69 OF 106 WHERE THE KIN GROUP IS PATRILINEAL OR DOUBLE-DESCENT, RATHER THAN MATRILINEAL (186)	107 73 27 33 XSQ= 3.24 PHI= 0.116 XP = 0.0717
196	TEND MORE TO BE THOSE 0.80 OF 153 WHERE INDIVIDUAL RIGHTS IN REAL PROPERTY, AND RULES FOR INHERITANCE, ARE PRESENT (194)	196	TEND LESS TO BE THOSE 0.54 OF 120 WHERE INDIVIDUAL RIGHTS IN REAL PROPERTY, AND RULES FOR INHERITANCE, ARE PRESENT (194)	122 65 31 55 XSQ= 19.21 PHI= 0.265 XP = 0.0000
204	TILT MORE TOWARD BEING THOSE 0.86 OF 181 WHERE MARITAL RESIDENCE IS PATRILOCAL, VIRILOCAL, OR AVUNCULOCAL, RATHER THAN AMBILOCAL OR NEOLOCAL (270)	204	TILT LESS TOWARD BEING THOSE 0.75 OF 136 WHERE MARITAL RESIDENCE IS PATRILOCAL, VIRILOCAL, OR AVUNCULOCAL, RATHER THAN AMBILOCAL OR NEOLOCAL (270)	155 102 26 34 XSQ= 5.05 PHI= 0.126 XP = 0.0246
209	TEND MORE TO BE THOSE 0.88 OF 176 WHERE MARITAL RESIDENCE IS PATRILOCAL, VIRILOCAL, OR AVUNCULOCAL, RATHER THAN MATRILOCAL OR UXORILOCAL (270)	209	TEND LESS TO BE THOSE 0.70 OF 145 WHERE MARITAL RESIDENCE IS PATRILOCAL, VIRILOCAL, OR AVUNCULOCAL, RATHER THAN MATRILOCAL OR UXORILOCAL (270)	155 102 21 43 XSQ= 14.55 PHI= 0.213 XP = 0.0001
210	LEAN MORE TOWARD BEING THOSE 0.92 OF 110 WHERE MARITAL RESIDENCE IS PATRILOCAL, RATHER THAN MATRILOCAL (169)	210	LEAN LESS TOWARD BEING THOSE 0.73 OF 83 WHERE MARITAL RESIDENCE IS PATRILOCAL, RATHER THAN MATRILOCAL (169)	101 61 9 22 XSQ= 10.46 PHI= 0.233 XP = 0.0012
213	DRIFT TOWARD BEING THOSE 0.52 OF 188 WHERE FIRST COUSIN MARRIAGE IS PERMITTED (172)	213	DRIFT TOWARD BEING THOSE 0.59 OF 167 WHERE FIRST COUSIN MARRIAGE IS NOT PERMITTED (198)	98 69 90 98 XSQ= 3.73 PHI= 0.102 XP = 0.0536
234	DRIFT TOWARD BEING THOSE 0.57 OF 159 WHERE THE COUSIN TERMINOLOGY IS OF ESKIMO OR HAWAIIAN TYPE, RATHER THAN CROW, OMAHA, OR IROQUOIS TYPE (170)	234	DRIFT TOWARD BEING THOSE 0.53 OF 148 WHERE THE COUSIN TERMINOLOGY IS OF CROW, OMAHA, OR IROQUOIS TYPE, RATHER THAN ESKIMO OR HAWAIIAN TYPE (152)	68 79 91 69 XSQ= 3.05 PHI= -0.100 XP = 0.0809
236	DRIFT TOWARD BEING THOSE 0.59 OF 203 WHERE THE FAMILY IS OF AN EXTENDED TYPE, RATHER THAN AN INDEPENDENT TYPE (213)	236	DRIFT TOWARD BEING THOSE 0.51 OF 179 WHERE THE FAMILY IS OF AN INDEPENDENT TYPE, RATHER THAN AN EXTENDED TYPE (185)	119 87 84 92 XSQ= 3.45 PHI= 0.095 XP = 0.0633

255	TILT LESS TOWARD BEING THOSE WHERE GRANDPARENTAL AUTHORITY OVER PARENTS IS ABSENT (26) DA	0.60 OF 15	255	TILT MORE TOWARD BEING THOSE WHERE GRANDPARENTAL AUTHORITY OVER PARENTS IS ABSENT (26) DA	0.94 OF 17	6 1 9 16 XSQ= 3.61 PHI= 0.336 EP = 0.0330
262	LEAN MORE TOWARD BEING THOSE WHERE WIVES ARE OBTAINED BY MEANS INVOLVING THE PRESENCE OF SOME CONSIDERATION (305)	0.84 OF 202	262	LEAN LESS TOWARD BEING THOSE WHERE WIVES ARE OBTAINED BY MEANS INVOLVING THE PRESENCE OF SOME CONSIDERATION (305)	0.70 OF 177	169 124 33 53 XSQ= 9.20 PHI= 0.156 XP = 0.0024
278	TILT TOWARD BEING THOSE WHERE PROPERTY RIGHTS IN WOMEN ARE PRESENT (8) LWS	0.58 OF 12	278	TILT TOWARD BEING THOSE WHERE PROPERTY RIGHTS IN WOMEN ARE UNIMPORTANT OR ABSENT (14) LWS	0.90 OF 10	7 1 5 9 XSQ= 3.62 PHI= 0.405 EP = 0.0310
306	DRIFT TOWARD BEING THOSE WHERE THE EARLY DEPENDENCE SATISFACTION POTENTIAL IS LOW (24) W-C	0.59 OF 29	306	DRIFT TOWARD BEING THOSE WHERE THE EARLY DEPENDENCE SATISFACTION POTENTIAL IS HIGH (28) W-C	0.70 OF 23	12 16 17 7 XSQ= 3.04 PHI= -0.242 XP = 0.0810
307	DRIFT TOWARD BEING THOSE WHERE THE EARLY AGGRESSION SATISFACTION POTENTIAL IS HIGH (33) W-C	0.77 OF 26	307	DRIFT TOWARD BEING THOSE WHERE THE EARLY AGGRESSION SATISFACTION POTENTIAL IS LOW (19) W-C	0.50 OF 26	20 13 6 13 XSQ= 2.99 PHI= 0.240 XP = 0.0840
314	DRIFT LESS TOWARD BEING THOSE WHERE THE INCIDENCE OF MOTHER-CHILD HOUSEHOLDS IS LOW (61) W-C,S	0.66 OF 41	314	DRIFT MORE TOWARD BEING THOSE WHERE THE INCIDENCE OF MOTHER-CHILD HOUSEHOLDS IS LOW (61) W-D,S	0.87 OF 38	14 5 27 33 XSQ= 3.68 PHI= 0.216 XP = 0.0552
318	TILT TOWARD BEING THOSE WHERE THE OVERALL INDULGENCE OF THE INFANT IS LOW (31) B-B-C	0.57 OF 35	318	TILT TOWARD BEING THOSE WHERE THE OVERALL INDULGENCE OF THE INFANT IS HIGH (40) B-B-C	0.69 OF 36	15 25 20 11 XSQ= 4.08 PHI= -0.240 XP = 0.0435
319	TILT TOWARD BEING THOSE WHERE PROTECTION OF THE INFANT FROM ENVIRONMENTAL DISCOMFORTS IS LOW (30) B-B-C	0.63 OF 32	319	TILT TOWARD BEING THOSE WHERE PROTECTION OF THE INFANT FROM ENVIRONMENTAL DISCOMFORTS IS HIGH (35) B-B-C	0.70 OF 33	12 23 20 10 XSQ= 5.54 PHI= -0.292 XP = 0.0186
320	TILT LESS TOWARD BEING THOSE WHERE THE DEGREE OF REDUCTION OF THE INFANT'S DRIVES IS HIGH (45) B-B-C	0.51 OF 35	320	TILT MORE TOWARD BEING THOSE WHERE THE DEGREE OF REDUCTION OF THE INFANT'S DRIVES IS HIGH (45) B-B-C	0.79 OF 34	18 27 17 7 XSQ= 4.78 PHI= -0.263 XP = 0.0287

No.		No.		
335	DRIFT TOWARD BEING THOSE 0.62 OF 21 WHERE INITIAL INDULGENCE OF DEPENDENCY IS LOW (18) WNS	335	DRIFT TOWARD BEING THOSE 0.71 OF 17 WHERE INITIAL INDULGENCE OF DEPENDENCY IS HIGH (20) WNS	8 12 13 5 XSQ= 2.78 PHI= -0.271 EP = 0.0585
336	TILT TOWARD BEING THOSE 0.71 OF 35 WHERE THE TOTAL POSITIVE PRESSURE TOWARD DEVELOPING RESPONSIBLE BEHAVIOR IN THE CHILD IS HIGH (43) B-B-C	336	TILT TOWARD BEING THOSE 0.55 OF 40 WHERE THE TOTAL POSITIVE PRESSURE TOWARD DEVELOPING RESPONSIBLE BEHAVIOR IN THE CHILD IS LOW (32) B-B-C	25 18 10 22 XSQ= 4.30 PHI= 0.240 XP = 0.0380
337	TILT TOWARD BEING THOSE 0.69 OF 35 WHERE THE CHILD'S INFERRED ANXIETY OVER NON-PERFORMANCE OF RESPONSIBLE BEHAVIOR IS HIGH (38) B-B-C	337	TILT TOWARD BEING THOSE 0.63 OF 38 WHERE THE CHILD'S INFERRED ANXIETY OVER NON-PERFORMANCE OF RESPONSIBLE BEHAVIOR IS LOW (35) B-B-C	24 14 11 24 XSQ= 6.13 PHI= 0.290 XP = 0.0133
339	LEAN TOWARD BEING THOSE 0.60 OF 35 WHERE THE CHILD'S INFERRED CONFLICT REGARDING RESPONSIBLE BEHAVIOR IS HIGH (31) B-B-C	339	LEAN TOWARD BEING THOSE 0.74 OF 38 WHERE THE CHILD'S INFERRED CONFLICT REGARDING RESPONSIBLE BEHAVIOR IS LOW (42) B-B-C	21 10 14 28 XSQ= 7.14 PHI= 0.313 XP = 0.0075
342	DRIFT TOWARD BEING THOSE 0.58 OF 19 WHERE THE CHILD'S INFERRED ANXIETY OVER PERFORMANCE OF NURTURANT BEHAVIOR IS HIGH (18) B-B-C	342	DRIFT TOWARD BEING THOSE 0.74 OF 27 WHERE THE CHILD'S INFERRED ANXIETY OVER PERFORMANCE OF NURTURANT BEHAVIOR IS LOW (28) B-B-C	11 7 8 20 XSQ= 3.54 PHI= 0.277 XP = 0.0600
377	LEAN LESS TOWARD BEING THOSE 0.68 OF 165 WHERE MALE GENITAL MUTILATION IS ABSENT (242)	377	LEAN MORE TOWARD BEING THOSE 0.83 OF 151 WHERE MALE GENITAL MUTILATION IS ABSENT (242)	53 26 112 125 XSQ= 8.56 PHI= 0.165 XP = 0.0034
382	TILT TOWARD BEING THOSE 0.56 OF 36 WHERE FEMALE INITIATION RITES ARE ABSENT (27) JKB	382	TILT TOWARD BEING THOSE 0.75 OF 28 WHERE FEMALE INITIATION RITES ARE PRESENT (38) JKB	16 21 20 7 XSQ= 4.84 PHI= -0.275 XP = 0.0278
390	TILT LESS TOWARD BEING THOSE 0.68 OF 109 WHERE PREMARITAL SEX RELATIONS ARE WEAKLY PUNISHED AND IN FACT NOT RARE OR PUNISHED ONLY IF PREGNANCY RESULTS, OR FREELY PERMITTED (132) JTW,EA	390	TILT MORE TOWARD BEING THOSE 0.84 OF 67 WHERE PREMARITAL SEX RELATIONS ARE WEAKLY PUNISHED AND IN FACT NOT RARE OR PUNISHED ONLY IF PREGNANCY RESULTS, OR FREELY PERMITED (132) JTW,EA	35 11 74 56 XSQ= 4.51 PHI= 0.160 XP = 0.0337
392	TILT MORE TOWARD BEING THOSE 0.70 OF 109 WHERE PREMARITAL SEX RELATIONS ARE STRONGLY PUNISHED AND IN FACT RARE, OR WEAKLY PUNISHED AND IN FACT NOT RARE, OR PUNISHED ONLY IF PREGNANCY RESULTS (112) JTW,EA	392	TILT LESS TOWARD BEING THOSE 0.52 OF 67 WHERE PREMARITAL SEX RELATIONS ARE STRONGLY PUNISHED AND IN FACT RARE, OR WEAKLY PUNISHED AND IN FACT NOT RARE, OR PUNISHED ONLY IF PREGNANCY RESULTS (112) JTW,EA	76 35 33 32 XSQ= 4.72 PHI= 0.164 XP = 0.0298

405	DRIFT TOWARD BEING THOSE WHERE EXPLANATIONS OF ILLNESS OF A DEPENDENCE NATURE ARE PRESENT (34) W-C	0.70 OF 30	405	DRIFT TOWARD BEING THOSE WHERE EXPLANATIONS OF ILLNESS OF A DEPENDENCE NATURE ARE ABSENT (27) W-C	0.58 OF 31	21 13 9 18 XSQ= 3.80 PHI= 0.249 XP = 0.0514
417	TILT MORE TOWARD BEING THOSE WHERE WARFARE IS PREVALENT (34) LWS	0.95 OF 22	417	TILT LESS TOWARD BEING THOSE WHERE WARFARE IS PREVALENT (34) LWS	0.62 OF 21	21 13 1 8 XSQ= 5.42 PHI= 0.355 XP = 0.0199
424	TILT TOWARD BEING THOSE WHERE RELIGIOUS SPECIALISTS ARE FULL-TIME, RATHER THAN PART-TIME (21) JMH	0.53 OF 32	424	TILT TOWARD BEING THOSE WHERE RELIGIOUS SPECIALISTS ARE PART-TIME, RATHER THAN FULL-TIME (33) JMH	0.82 OF 22	17 4 15 18 XSQ= 5.31 PHI= 0.314 XP = 0.0212
426	LEAN MORE TOWARD BEING THOSE WHERE A HIGH GOD IS PRESENT (156) GES,EA	0.67 OF 144	426	LEAN LESS TOWARD BEING THOSE WHERE A HIGH GOD IS PRESENT (156) GES,EA	0.50 OF 113	97 57 47 56 XSQ= 6.86 PHI= 0.163 XP = 0.0088
427	TILT TOWARD BEING THOSE WHERE A HIGH GOD, IF PRESENT, IS ACTIVE, RATHER THAN INACTIVE (87) GES,EA	0.64 OF 97	427	TILT TOWARD BEING THOSE WHERE A HIGH GOD, IF PRESENT, IS INACTIVE, RATHER THAN ACTIVE (69) GES,EA	0.58 OF 57	62 24 35 33 XSQ= 6.07 PHI= 0.199 XP = 0.0137
435	DRIFT TOWARD BEING THOSE WHERE ABANDONMENT OF THE HOUSE OF THE DEAD IS NOT PRACTICED (19) LWS	0.80 OF 15	435	DRIFT TOWARD BEING THOSE WHERE ABANDONMENT OF THE HOUSE OF THE DEAD IS PRACTICED (12) LWS	0.56 OF 16	3 9 12 7 XSQ= 2.90 PHI= -0.306 EP = 0.0659
444	DRIFT TOWARD BEING THOSE WHERE THE USE OF DREAMS TO SEEK AND CONTROL SUPERNATURAL POWERS IS LOW (27) RGD	0.61 OF 33	444	DRIFT TOWARD BEING THOSE WHERE THE USE OF DREAMS TO SEEK AND CONTROL SUPERNATURAL POWERS IS HIGH (28) RGD	0.68 OF 22	13 15 20 7 XSQ= 3.30 PHI= -0.245 XP = 0.0692
450	TILT LESS TOWARD BEING THOSE WHERE THE OBSERVATION OF FOOD TABOOS IS HIGH OR MEDIUM, RATHER THAN LOW (60) JRL	0.59 OF 49	450	TILT MORE TOWARD BEING THOSE WHERE THE OBSERVATION OF FOOD TABOOS IS HIGH OR MEDIUM, RATHER THAN LOW (60) JRL	0.84 OF 37	29 31 20 6 XSQ= 4.94 PHI= -0.240 XP = 0.0263
458	TEND LESS TO BE THOSE WHERE GAMES, IF PRESENT, DO NOT INCLUDE GAMES OF STRATEGY (119) R-A-B,EA	0.55 OF 97	458	TEND MORE TO BE THOSE WHERE GAMES, IF PRESENT, DO NOT INCLUDE GAMES OF STRATEGY (119) R-A-B,EA	0.89 OF 71	44 8 53 63 XSQ= 20.73 PHI= 0.351 XP = 0.0000

460	DRIFT MORE TOWARD BEING THOSE 0.68 OF 97 WHERE GAMES, IF PRESENT, ARE NOT LIMITED TO GAMES OF SKILL ONLY (104) R-A-B,EA	460	DRIFT LESS TOWARD BEING THOSE 0.52 OF 71 WHERE GAMES, IF PRESENT, ARE NOT LIMITED TO GAMES OF SKILL ONLY (104) R-A-B,EA	31 34 66 37 XSQ= 3.74 PHI= -0.149 XP = 0.0532
468	TILT LESS TOWARD BEING THOSE 0.56 OF 32 WHERE CONTACT WITH OTHER CULTURES IS REGULAR OR IRREGULAR, RATHER THAN FREQUENT (37) JMH	468	TILT MORE TOWARD BEING THOSE 0.86 OF 22 WHERE CONTACT WITH OTHER CULTURES IS REGULAR OR IRREGULAR, RATHER THAN FREQUENT (37) JMH	14 3 18 19 XSQ= 4.17 PHI= 0.278 XP = 0.0411
473	TILT LESS TOWARD BEING THOSE 0.51 OF 49 WHERE SENSITIVITY TO INSULT IS MODERATE OR NEGLIGIBLE (56) PES	473	TILT MORE TOWARD BEING THOSE 0.79 OF 39 WHERE SENSITIVITY TO INSULT IS MODERATE OR NEGLIGIBLE (56) PES	24 8 25 31 XSQ= 6.42 PHI= 0.270 XP = 0.0113
475	DRIFT TOWARD BEING THOSE 0.65 OF 46 WHERE EXHIBITIONISTIC DANCING IS STRONGLY OR MODERATELY EMPHASIZED (48) PES	475	DRIFT TOWARD BEING THOSE 0.55 OF 40 WHERE EXHIBITIONISTIC DANCING IS NEGLIGIBLY EMPHASIZED (38) PES	30 18 16 22 XSQ= 2.77 PHI= 0.180 XP = 0.0958
480	TILT TOWARD BEING THOSE 0.71 OF 14 WHERE COMPLEXITY OF ARTISTIC DESIGN IS HIGH (14) HB	480	TILT TOWARD BEING THOSE 0.73 OF 15 WHERE COMPLEXITY OF ARTISTIC DESIGN IS LOW (15) HB	10 4 4 11 XSQ= 4.16 PHI= 0.379 EP = 0.0268

103 CULTURES
WHERE CLASS STRATIFICATION IS PRESENT
AND BASED ON CRITERIA OTHER THAN
WEALTH (126)

103 CULTURES
WHERE CLASS STRATIFICATION IS PRESENT
AND BASED ON WEALTH, OR ELSE IS
ABSENT (257)

BACKGROUND ON PAGE 88

SUBJECT ONLY

126 IN LEFT COLUMN

ABIPON	AMERICANS	ASHANTI	AZANDE	AZTEC	BALINESE	BAMBARA	BAMILEKE	BASQUES	BELU
BEMBA	BENGALI	BHIL	BOERS	BRAZILIANS	BULGARIANS	BURMESE	BURUSHO	BURYAT	CAMBA
CAMBODIANS	CHAGGA	CHAMACOCO	CHEREMIS	CHERKESS	CHIBCHA	COORG	CZECHS	CARO	DUTCH
EGYPTIANS	ELLICE	FON	FUTAJALONKE	GANDA	HAIDA	HASINAI	HAWAIIANS	HEHE	HO
ICELANDERS	INCA	IRISH	JAPANESE	JAVANESE	JUKUN	KACHIN	KAZAK	KERALA	KHALKA
KHASI	KOHISTANI	KOREANS	KUBA	KURTATCHI	KWAKIUTL	LAKHER	LIFU	LOLO	LOZI
LUBA	MACASSARESE	MAGUZAWA	MALAYS	MANGAIANS	MANIHIKI	MAORI	MARQUESANS	MARSHALLESE	MAYA
MBUNDU	MENDE	MERINA	MIN CHINESE	MINCHIA	MONGUOR	MOSSI	MZAB	NATCHEZ	NGONI
NUPE	NYANEKA	NYORO	OKINAWANS	PAIWAN	PALAUANS	PATHAN	PAWNEE	PENDE	PONAPEANS
PORTUGUESE	REGEIBAT	ROMANS	ROTINESE	RUNDI	SAMOANS	SERBS	SHILLUK	SINDHI	SONGHAI
SOTHO	SWAZI	SYRIANS	TAGBANUA	TAMIL	TANALA	TANIMBARESE	TERA	TERENA	THAI
THONGA	TIBETANS	TIGRINYA	TIKOPIA	TIMUCUA	TROBRIAND	TSHIMSHIAN	TURKMEN	VENDA	VIETNAMESE
WALLOONS	WOLOF	WUTE	YAPESE	YOMBE	YORUBA				

257 IN RIGHT COLUMN

ABOR	AINU	AJIE	AKHA	ALACALUF	ALBANIANS	ALORESE	AMBA	ANDAMANESE	APINAYE
ARANDA	ARAPESH	ARAUCANIANS	ATAYAL	ATSUGEWI	AWEIKOMA	AYMARA	BABWA	BACAIRI	BAJUN
BANDA	BARABRA	BARI	BASSERI	BATAK	BAYA	BEJA	BERGDAMA	BETE	BIRIFOR
BLACK CARIB	BORORO	BOTOCUDO	BOZO	BUDUMA	CADUVEO	CAGABA	CALLINAGO	CAMAYURA	CARAJA
CARIB	CAYAPA	CHENCHU	CHEROKEE	CHEYENNE	CHIR-APACHE	CHOCO	CHOROTI	CHORTI	CHUKCHEE
COCHITI	COMANCHE	COPR ESKIMO	CREE	CREEK	CROW	CUNA	DAGUR	DELAWARE	DIEGUENO
DIERI	DILLING	DOBUANS	DOGON	DOROBO	DUSUN	ENGA	EYAK	FANG	FOX
GARO	GILBERTESE	GILYAK	GISU	GOAJIRO	GOND	GROS VENTRE	GUAHIBO	GUATO	GURE
HANO	HANUNOO	HASANIA	HAVASUPAI	HAZARA	HEBREWS	HERERO	HUICHOL	HUKUNDIKA	HURON
HUTSUL	IBAN	IFUGAO	ILA	INGALIK	INGASSANA	IRAQW	JEMEZ	JIVARO	KABYLE
KALMYK	KAPAUKU	KAREN	KARIERA	KASKA	KATAB	KERAKI	KET	KHEVSUR	KIKUYU
KIOW-APACHE	KISSI	KONSO	KORYAK	KPE	KUNG	KUTENAI	LAKALAI	LAMBA	LAMET
LANGO	LAPPS	LAU	LEPCHA	LESU	LHOTA NAGA	LUO	MAM	MAMBILA	MAMVU
MANCHU	MANDAN	MANUS	MARGI	MARICOPA	MASAI	MATACO	MATAKAM	MBUGWE	MBUTI
MENTAWEI	MIAMI	MIAO	MINANGKABAU	MISKITO	MIWOK	MNONG GAR	MONGO	MOTA	MOTILON
MUNDURUCU	MURINBATA	MURNGIN	NABESNA	NAMA	NAMBICUARA	NANDI	NASKAPI	NAVAHO	NICOBARESE
NOMLAKI	NUER	NUNIVAK	NURI	NYAKYUSA	NYARO	OJIBWA	OMAHA	ONA	ONTONG-JAVA
PALIKUR	PAPAGO	PARAUJANO	PENOBSCOT	POPOLUCA	PUKAPUKA	PURARI	PURUM	RARCIANS	RIFFIANS
ROTUMANS	RWALA	SAGADA	SAMOYED	SANDAWE	SANPOIL	SANTAL	SARAMACCA	SARSI	SELUNG
SEMANG	SEMINOLE	SENIANG	SERI	SHERENTE	SHLUH	SIRIONO	SIUAI	SIWANS	SOMALI
SUBANUN	TALAMANCA	TALLENSI	TAOS	TAPIRAPE	TARAHUMARA	TAREUMIUT	TEHUELCHE	TENDA	TENETEHARA
TENINO	TESO	TETON	TIMBIRA	TIV	TIWI	TODA	TOKELAU	TOLOWA	TORAJA
TRISTAN	TRUKESE	TRUMAI	TUBATULABAL	TUCANO	TUCUNA	TUNEBO	TUPINAMBA	TURKANA	TWANA

ULAWANS WIKMUNKAN YAO UTE WINNEBAGO YARURO VEDDA WITOTO YOKUTS WAICA WOGEO YUKAGHIR WANTOAT WOLEAIANS YUKI WAPISHANA YABARANA YUROK WAROPEN YAGUA ZUNI WARRAU YAHGAN WASHO YAKO WICHITA YAKUT

17 EXCLUDED BECAUSE UNASCERTAINED

4	LEAN LESS TOWARD BEING THOSE LOCATED OUTSIDE OF THE CIRCUM-MEDITERRANEAN (355)	0.81 OF 126	4	LEAN MORE TOWARD BEING THOSE LOCATED OUTSIDE OF THE CIRCUM-MEDITERRANEAN (355)	0.93 OF 257	24 19 102 238 XSQ= 10.38 PHI= 0.165 XP = 0.0013
5	LEAN LESS TOWARD BEING THOSE LOCATED OUTSIDE OF EAST EURASIA (330)	0.74 OF 126	5	LEAN MORE TOWARD BEING THOSE LOCATED OUTSIDE OF EAST EURASIA (330)	0.88 OF 257	33 32 93 225 XSQ= 10.37 PHI= 0.165 XP = 0.0013
8	TEND MORE TO BE THOSE LOCATED OUTSIDE OF NORTH AMERICA (330)	0.94 OF 126	8	TEND LESS TO BE THOSE LOCATED OUTSIDE OF NORTH AMERICA (330)	0.77 OF 257	8 59 118 198 XSQ= 15.03 PHI= -0.198 XP = 0.0001
9	TEND MORE TO BE THOSE LOCATED OUTSIDE OF SOUTH AMERICA (335)	0.94 OF 126	9	TEND LESS TO BE THOSE LOCATED OUTSIDE OF SOUTH AMERICA (335)	0.79 OF 257	7 54 119 203 XSQ= 13.95 PHI= -0.191 XP = 0.0002
33	LEAN MORE TOWARD BEING THOSE WHERE THE NATURAL ENVIRONMENT IS OTHER THAN 'VERY HARSH,' I.E., DESERT, DESERT GRASSES AND SHRUBS, TUNDRA, OR HIGH PLATEAU STEPPE (341) FWM	0.93 OF 126	33	LEAN LESS TOWARD BEING THOSE WHERE THE NATURAL ENVIRONMENT IS OTHER THAN 'VERY HARSH,' I.E., DESERT, DESERT GRASSES AND SHRUBS, TUNDRA, OR HIGH PLATEAU STEPPE (341) FWM	0.81 OF 257	9 49 117 208 XSQ= 8.45 PHI= -0.149 XP = 0.0037
44	TEND MORE TO BE THOSE WHERE SETTLEMENTS ARE FIXED (222)	0.86 OF 102	44	TEND LESS TO BE THOSE WHERE SETTLEMENTS ARE FIXED (222)	0.58 OF 220	88 127 14 93 XSQ= 24.33 PHI= 0.275 XP = 0.0000
46	TEND MORE TO BE THOSE OTHER THAN WHERE SETTLEMENTS ARE NON-FIXED AND MOVEMENT IS NOMADIC (260)	0.94 OF 102	46	TEND LESS TO BE THOSE OTHER THAN WHERE SETTLEMENTS ARE NON-FIXED AND MOVEMENT IS NOMADIC (260)	0.70 OF 220	6 65 96 155 XSQ= 21.35 PHI= -0.257 XP = 0.0000

47	DRIFT TOWARD BEING THOSE 0.57 OF 14 WHERE, IF SETTLEMENTS ARE NON-FIXED, MOVEMENT IS NON-NOMADIC, RATHER THAN NOMADIC (38)	47	DRIFT TOWARD BEING THOSE 0.70 OF 93 WHERE, IF SETTLEMENTS ARE NON-FIXED, MOVEMENT IS NOMADIC, RATHER THAN NON-NOMADIC (72)	6 65 8 28 XSQ= 2.86 PHI= -0.164 XP = 0.0905
48	DRIFT TOWARD BEING THOSE 0.65 OF 23 WHERE THE FOOD SUPPLY IS SECURE, AND FOOD SHORTAGES ARE RARE OR OCCASIONAL (38) MGW	48	DRIFT TOWARD BEING THOSE 0.59 OF 56 WHERE THE FOOD SUPPLY IS NOT SECURE, AND FOOD SHORTAGES ARE FREQUENT OR ANNUAL (41) MGW	15 23 8 33 XSQ= 2.90 PHI= 0.192 XP = 0.0885
51	TEND TO BE THOSE 0.86 OF 126 WHERE SUBSISTENCE IS PRIMARILY BY FOOD PRODUCTION -- I. E., AGRICULTURE OR HUSBANDRY -- RATHER THAN BY GATHERING (253)	51	TEND TO BE THOSE 0.50 OF 257 WHERE SUBSISTENCE IS PRIMARILY BY FOOD GATHERING -- I. E., HUNTING, FISHING, OR COLLECTING -- RATHER THAN FOOD PRODUCTION (147)	108 128 18 129 XSQ= 44.59 PHI= 0.341 XP = 0.
53	TEND TO BE THOSE 0.53 OF 91 WHERE FOOD PRODUCTION IS BY INTENSIVE AGRICULTURE, RATHER THAN BY SIMPLE AGRICULTURE OR INCIPIENT FOOD PRODUCTION (91)	53	TEND TO BE THOSE 0.72 OF 137 WHERE FOOD PRODUCTION IS BY SIMPLE AGRICULTURE OR INCIPIENT FOOD PRODUCTION, RATHER THAN BY INTENSIVE AGRICULTURE (147)	48 38 43 99 XSQ= 13.51 PHI= 0.243 XP = 0.0002
55	LEAN TOWARD BEING THOSE 0.59 OF 82 WHERE FOOD PRODUCTION IS BY INTENSIVE AGRICULTURE, RATHER THAN BY SIMPLE AGRICULTURE (91)	55	LEAN TOWARD BEING THOSE 0.62 OF 100 WHERE FOOD PRODUCTION IS BY SIMPLE AGRICULTURE, RATHER THAN BY INTENSIVE AGRICULTURE (101)	48 38 34 62 XSQ= 6.82 PHI= 0.194 XP = 0.0090
56	DRIFT MORE TOWARD BEING THOSE 0.79 OF 43 WHERE FOOD PRODUCTION IS BY SIMPLE AGRICULTURE, RATHER THAN BY INCIPIENT FOOD PRODUCTION (101)	56	DRIFT LESS TOWARD BEING THOSE 0.63 OF 99 WHERE FOOD PRODUCTION IS BY SIMPLE AGRICULTURE, RATHER THAN BY INCIPIENT FOOD PRODUCTION (101)	34 62 9 37 XSQ= 2.99 PHI= 0.145 XP = 0.0839
62	TEND MORE TO BE THOSE 0.70 OF 126 WHERE HUSBANDRY OF SOME KIND IS PRESENT (228)	62	TEND LESS TO BE THOSE 0.51 OF 257 WHERE HUSBANDRY OF SOME KIND IS PRESENT (228)	88 132 38 125 XSQ= 11.07 PHI= 0.170 XP = 0.0009
63	DRIFT MORE TOWARD BEING THOSE 0.75 OF 87 WHERE HUSBANDRY, IF PRESENT, IS PRINCIPALLY IN THE FORM OF BOVINE, EQUINE, CAMEL-LIKE, OR DEER-LIKE ANIMALS, RATHER THAN PIGS, SHEEP, OR GOATS (152)	63	DRIFT LESS TOWARD BEING THOSE 0.62 OF 131 WHERE HUSBANDRY, IF PRESENT, IS PRINCIPALLY IN THE FORM OF BOVINE, EQUINE, CAMEL-LIKE, OR DEER-LIKE ANIMALS, RATHER THAN PIGS, SHEEP, OR GOATS (152)	65 81 22 50 XSQ= 3.36 PHI= 0.124 XP = 0.0668
71	TEND TO BE THOSE 0.68 OF 73 WHERE METAL WORKING IS PRESENT (98)	71	TEND TO BE THOSE 0.74 OF 173 WHERE METAL WORKING IS ABSENT (153)	50 45 23 128 XSQ= 37.31 PHI= 0.389 XP = 0.

73	TEND TO BE THOSE WHERE WEAVING IS PRESENT (118)	0.67 OF 73	73	TEND TO BE THOSE WHERE WEAVING IS ABSENT (130)	0.61 OF 170	49 66 24 104 XSQ= 15.29 PHI= 0.251 XP = 0.0001
74	LEAN MORE TOWARD BEING THOSE WHERE POTTERY IS PRESENT (145)	0.75 OF 64	74	LEAN LESS TOWARD BEING THOSE WHERE POTTERY IS PRESENT (145)	0.55 OF 170	48 93 16 77 XSQ= 7.17 PHI= 0.175 XP = 0.0074
79	TEND LESS TO BE THOSE WHERE NO CITY IS PRESENT (201)	0.69 OF 71	79	IN ALL CASES ARE THOSE WHERE NO CITY IS PRESENT (201)	1.00 OF 148	22 0 49 148 XSQ= 47.61 PHI= 0.466 XP = 0.
81	TEND TO BE THOSE WHERE A CITY OR TOWN IS PRESENT, OR THE AVERAGE COMMUNITY SIZE IS 200 OR GREATER (89)	0.70 OF 71	81	TEND TO BE THOSE WHERE NO CITY OR TOWN IS PRESENT, AND THE AVERAGE COMMUNITY SIZE IS SMALLER THAN 200 (135)	0.75 OF 148	50 37 21 111 XSQ= 39.47 PHI= 0.425 XP = 0.
83	LEAN LESS TOWARD BEING THOSE WHERE, WITH NO CITY AND NO TOWN PRESENT, THE AVERAGE COMMUNITY SIZE IS SMALLER THAN 200, RATHER THAN BETWEEN 200 AND 999 (135)	0.57 OF 37	83	LEAN MORE TOWARD BEING THOSE WHERE, WITH NO CITY AND NO TOWN PRESENT, THE AVERAGE COMMUNITY SIZE IS SMALLER THAN 200, RATHER THAN BETWEEN 200 AND 999 (135)	0.79 OF 140	16 29 21 111 XSQ= 6.69 PHI= 0.194 XP = 0.0097
85	TEND TO BE THOSE WHERE THE LEVEL OF POLITICAL INTEGRATION IS THE LARGE STATE, OR THE LITTLE STATE (70) GPM	0.62 OF 94	85	TEND TO BE THOSE WHERE THE LEVEL OF POLITICAL INTEGRATION IS THE MINIMAL STATE, THE AUTONOMOUS COMMUNITY, OR THE FAMILY (234) GPM	0.96 OF 203	58 9 36 194 XSQ= 117.36 PHI= 0.629 XP = 0.
86	TEND TO BE THOSE WHERE THE LEVEL OF POLITICAL INTEGRATION IS THE LARGE STATE, THE LITTLE STATE, OR THE MINIMAL STATE (148) GPM	0.91 OF 94	86	TEND TO BE THOSE WHERE THE LEVEL OF POLITICAL INTEGRATION IS THE AUTONOMOUS COMMUNITY, OR THE FAMILY (156) GPM	0.72 OF 203	86 56 8 147 XSQ= 102.60 PHI= 0.588 XP = 0.
87	IN ALL CASES ARE THOSE WHERE THE LEVEL OF POLITICAL INTEGRATION IS THE LARGE STATE, THE LITTLE STATE, THE MINIMAL STATE, OR THE AUTONOMOUS COMMUNITY (281) GPM	1.00 OF 94	87	LEAN LESS TOWARD BEING THOSE WHERE THE LEVEL OF POLITICAL INTEGRATION IS THE LARGE STATE, THE LITTLE STATE, THE MINIMAL STATE, OR THE AUTONOMOUS COMMUNITY (281) GPM	0.89 OF 203	94 180 0 23 XSQ= 10.01 PHI= 0.184 XP = 0.0016
91	DRIFT TOWARD BEING THOSE WHERE SOCIETAL COMPLEXITY IS HIGH (18) F-W	0.67 OF 15	91	DRIFT TOWARD BEING THOSE WHERE SOCIETAL COMPLEXITY IS LOW (22) F-W	0.68 OF 25	10 8 5 17 XSQ= 3.26 PHI= 0.285 EP = 0.0504

95	TEND TC BE THCSE WHERE THE HIERARCHY OF NATICNAL JURISDICTICN HAS FOUR, THREE, OR TWC LEVELS (76) GES,EA	0.59 OF 101	95	TEND TO BE THOSE WHERE THE HIERARCHY OF NATIONAL JURISDICTION HAS ONE OR NO LEVELS (254) GES,EA	0.94 OF 219	60 14 41 205 XSQ= 106.31 PHI= 0.576 XP = 0.
96	TEND TC BE THCSE WHERE THE HIERARCHY OF NATICNAL JURISDICTICN HAS FOUR, THREE, TWC OR CNE LEVEL (174) GES,EA	0.92 OF 101	96	TEND TO BE THOSE WHERE THE HIERARCHY OF NATIONAL JURISDICTION HAS NO LEVELS (156) GES,EA	0.67 OF 219	93 72 8 147 XSQ= 94.65 PHI= 0.544 XP = 0.
97	TILT LESS TOWARC BEING THCSE WHERE THE HIERARCHY OF LCCAL JURISDICTION HAS THREE OR TWO LEVELS (273) GES,EA	0.75 OF 101	97	TILT MORE TOWARD BEING THOSE WHERE THE HIERARCHY OF LOCAL JURISDICTION HAS THREE OR TWO LEVELS (273) GES,EA	0.85 OF 220	25 32 76 188 XSQ= 4.26 PHI= 0.115 XP = 0.0389
98	LEAN MORE TOWARC BEING THCSE WHERE THE HIERARCHY OF LCCAL JURISDICTICN HAS FOUR CR THREE LEVELS (238) GES,EA	0.84 OF 101	98	LEAN LESS TOWARD BEING THOSE WHERE THE HIERARCHY OF LOCAL JURISDICTION HAS FOUR OR THREE LEVELS (238) GES,EA	0.66 OF 220	85 146 16 74 XSQ= 10.00 PHI= 0.176 XP = 0.0016
100	TEND MORE TO BE THCSE WHERE HIERARCHIES ARE MORE COMPLEX THAN THE 'SIMPLEST,' I. E., MORE COMPLEX THAN TWC LCCAL LEVELS WITH NC NATICNAL LEVELS (267) GES,EA	0.98 OF 101	100	TEND LESS TO BE THOSE WHERE HIERARCHIES ARE MORE COMPLEX THAN THE 'SIMPLEST,' I. E., MORE COMPLEX THAN TWO LOCAL LEVELS WITH NO NATIONAL LEVELS (267) GES,EA	0.72 OF 219	99 158 2 61 XSQ= 27.65 PHI= 0.294 XP = 0.0000
109	TEND LESS TO BE THCSE WHERE CASTES ARE ABSENT (317)	0.75 OF 112	1C9	TEND MORE TO BE THOSE WHERE CASTES ARE ABSENT (317)	0.93 OF 246	28 18 84 228 XSQ= 19.94 PHI= 0.236 XP = 0.0000
110	TEND TO BE THCSE WHERE SLAVERY IS PRESENT (163)	0.67 OF 120	11C	TEND TO BE THOSE WHERE SLAVERY IS ABSENT (218)	0.69 OF 252	81 78 39 174 XSQ= 42.89 PHI= 0.340 XP = 0.
116	LEAN TOWARD BEING THCSE WHERE CCCUPATICNAL SPECIALIZATION IS FULL-TIME, WHETHER OR NCT FOR SURPLUS PRCDUCTICN (20) JMH	0.65 OF 20	116	LEAN TOWARD BEING THOSE WHERE OCCUPATIONAL SPECIALIZATION IS PART-TIME ONLY (34) JMH	0.79 OF 34	13 7 7 27 XSQ= 8.83 PHI= 0.404 XP = 0.0030
118	DRIFT TOWARD BEING THCSE WHERE THE PERCENTAGE CF OCCUPATIONS THAT ARE SPECIALIZED IS HIGH CR MEDIUM (24) WME	0.73 OF 15	118	DRIFT TOWARD BEING THOSE WHERE THE PERCENTAGE OF OCCUPATICNS THAT ARE SPECIALIZED IS LOW (25) WME	0.62 OF 34	11 13 4 21 XSQ= 3.82 PHI= 0.279 XP = 0.0506

120	DRIFT MORE TOWARD BEING THOSE 0.88 OF 17 WHERE THE CRAFT SPECIALIZATION SCORE IS HIGH OR MEDIUM (36) WME	120	DRIFT LESS TOWARD BEING THOSE 0.58 OF 36 WHERE THE CRAFT SPECIALIZATION SCORE IS HIGH OR MEDIUM (36) WME	15 21 2 15 XSQ= 3.47 PHI= 0.256 XP = 0.0627
129	TILT LESS TOWARD BEING THOSE 0.56 OF 39 WHERE WEAVING IS MAINLY DONE BY FEMALES (73)	129	TILT MORE TOWARD BEING THOSE 0.77 OF 62 WHERE WEAVING IS MAINLY DONE BY FEMALES (73)	17 14 22 48 XSQ= 4.03 PHI= 0.200 XP = 0.0447
130	LEAN TOWARD BEING THOSE 0.74 OF 19 WHERE LEATHER WORKING IS MAINLY DONE BY MALES (39)	130	LEAN TOWARD BEING THOSE 0.63 OF 63 WHERE LEATHER WORKING IS MAINLY DONE BY FEMALES (45)	14 23 5 40 XSQ= 6.72 PHI= 0.286 XP = 0.0096
131	LEAN MORE TOWARD BEING THOSE 0.98 OF 52 WHERE THE CONSTRUCTION OF PERMANENT HOUSES OR THE ERECTION OF TEMPORARY DWELLINGS IS MAINLY DONE BY MALES (136)	131	LEAN LESS TOWARD BEING THOSE 0.80 OF 102 WHERE THE CONSTRUCTION OF PERMANENT HOUSES OR THE ERECTION OF TEMPORARY DWELLINGS IS MAINLY DONE BY MALES (136)	51 82 1 20 XSQ= 7.71 PHI= 0.224 XP = 0.0055
132	DRIFT MORE TOWARD BEING THOSE 0.85 OF 20 WHERE ECONOMIC EXCHANGE INVOLVES THE USE OF MONEY (37) JMH	132	DRIFT LESS TOWARD BEING THOSE 0.59 OF 34 WHERE ECONOMIC EXCHANGE INVOLVES THE USE OF MONEY (37) JMH	17 20 3 14 XSQ= 2.88 PHI= 0.231 XP = 0.0898
138	TILT TOWARD BEING THOSE 0.79 OF 14 WHERE SUPERORDINATE JUSTICE IS PRESENT (22) BBW	138	TILT TOWARD BEING THOSE 0.58 OF 26 WHERE SUPERORDINATE JUSTICE IS ABSENT (18) BBW	11 11 3 15 XSQ= 3.48 PHI= 0.295 EP = 0.0456
141	DRIFT TOWARD BEING THOSE 0.70 OF 20 WHERE THE LEVEL OF SOCIAL SANCTION IS PUBLIC CORPOREAL SANCTION, RATHER THAN PUBLIC PROPERTY SANCTION OR PRIVATE SETTLEMENT (28) JMH	141	DRIFT TOWARD BEING THOSE 0.59 OF 34 WHERE THE LEVEL OF SOCIAL SANCTION IS PUBLIC PROPERTY SANCTION OR PRIVATE SETTLEMENT, RATHER THAN PUBLIC CORPOREAL SANCTION (26) JMH	14 14 6 20 XSQ= 3.12 PHI= 0.240 XP = 0.0776
149	LEAN TOWARD BEING THOSE 0.79 OF 14 WHERE THE INCIDENCE OF THEFT IS HIGH (18) B-B-C	149	LEAN TOWARD BEING THOSE 0.70 OF 23 WHERE THE INCIDENCE OF THEFT IS LOW (19) B-B-C	11 7 3 16 XSQ= 6.26 PHI= 0.411 EP = 0.0069
152	TILT TOWARD BEING THOSE 0.88 OF 8 WHERE THE DIFFERENTIATION OF THE JURIDICAL AGENCY FROM THE MEDICAL AGENCY IS HIGH (10) MJ	152	TILT TOWARD BEING THOSE 0.75 OF 12 WHERE THE DIFFERENTIATION OF THE JURIDICAL AGENCY FROM THE MEDICAL AGENCY IS LOW (10) MJ	7 3 1 9 XSQ= 5.21 PHI= 0.510 EP = 0.0198

```
163  LEAN TOWARD BEING THOSE          0.86 OF   7     163  LEAN TOWARD BEING THOSE          0.90 OF  10          6    1
     WHERE THE EMPHASIS ON INDIVIDUAL VOLITION             WHERE THE EMPHASIS ON INDIVIDUAL VOLITION             1    9
     AS THE CAUSE OF CRIME                                 AS THE CAUSE OF CRIME                            XSQ=    6.87
     IS HIGH  (7) MJ                                       IS LOW  (10) MJ                                  PHI=   0.636
                                                                                                            EP =  0.0037

175  TILT MORE TOWARD BEING THOSE   0.76 OF 122     175  TILT LESS TOWARD BEING THOSE   0.64 OF 245         29   88
     WHERE THE COMMUNITY IS                                WHERE THE COMMUNITY IS                               93  157
     'KIN-HETEROGENEOUS,' I. E.                            'KIN-HETEROGENEOUS,' I. E.                       XSQ=    4.99
     OTHER THAN                                            OTHER THAN                                       PHI=  -0.117
     A CLAN COMMUNITY OR A DEME  (260)                     A CLAN COMMUNITY OR A DEME  (260)                XP =  0.0255

177  TILT MORE TOWARD BEING THOSE   0.86 OF 122     177  TILT LESS TOWARD BEING THOSE   0.76 OF 245         17   58
     WHERE THE COMMUNITY IS OTHER THAN                     WHERE THE COMMUNITY IS OTHER THAN                   105  187
     A SINGLE CLAN-COMMUNITY AND                           A SINGLE CLAN-COMMUNITY AND                      XSQ=    4.17
     EXOGAMOUS  (305)                                      EXOGAMOUS  (305)                                 PHI=  -0.107
                                                                                                            XP =  0.0411

179  TILT MORE TOWARD BEING THOSE   0.94 OF 122     179  TILT LESS TOWARD BEING THOSE   0.87 OF 245          7   32
     WHERE THE COMMUNITY IS OTHER THAN                     WHERE THE COMMUNITY IS OTHER THAN                   115  213
     STRUCTURED ON A NON-CLAN BASIS AND                    STRUCTURED ON A NON-CLAN BASIS AND               XSQ=    3.86
     COMMONLY EXOGAMOUS  (340)                             COMMONLY EXOGAMOUS  (340)                        PHI=  -0.103
                                                                                                            XP =  0.0494

180  LEAN MORE TOWARD BEING THOSE   0.79 OF 122     180  LEAN LESS TOWARD BEING THOSE   0.62 OF 245         26   93
     WHERE THE COMMUNITY IS                                WHERE THE COMMUNITY IS                               96  152
     COMMONLY NON-EXOGAMOUS, RATHER THAN                   COMMONLY NON-EXOGAMOUS, RATHER THAN              XSQ=    9.56
     EXOGAMOUS  (258)                                      EXOGAMOUS  (258)                                 PHI=  -0.161
                                                                                                            XP =  0.0020

182  TILT LESS TOWARD BEING THOSE   0.58 OF 122     182  TILT MORE TOWARD BEING THOSE   0.71 OF 245         51   71
     OTHER THAN WHERE THE COMMUNITY IS                     OTHER THAN WHERE THE COMMUNITY IS                    71  174
     STRUCTURED ON A NON-CLAN BASIS AND                    STRUCTURED ON A NON-CLAN BASIS AND               XSQ=    5.47
     AGAMOUS  (256)                                        AGAMOUS  (256)                                   PHI=   0.122
                                                                                                            XP =  0.0193

183  TEND MORE TO BE THOSE          0.99 OF  83     183  TEND LESS TO BE THOSE          0.80 OF 162          1   32
     WHERE THE LARGEST NON-COGNATIC KIN GROUP              WHERE THE LARGEST NON-COGNATIC KIN GROUP             82  130
     IS SMALLER THAN A MOEITY, I. E.,                      IS SMALLER THAN A MOEITY, I. E.,                 XSQ=   14.65
     A PHRATRY OR SIB OR LINEAGE  (218)                    A PHRATRY OR SIB OR LINEAGE  (218)               PHI=  -0.245
                                                                                                            XP =  0.0001

184  LEAN MORE TOWARD BEING THOSE   0.82 OF  83     184  LEAN LESS TOWARD BEING THOSE   0.62 OF 162         15   61
     WHERE THE LARGEST NON-COGNATIC KIN GROUP              WHERE THE LARGEST NON-COGNATIC KIN GROUP             68  101
     IS SMALLER THAN A PHRATRY, I. E.                      IS SMALLER THAN A PHRATRY, I. E.                 XSQ=    8.94
     A SIB OR LINEAGE  (175)                               A SIB OR LINEAGE  (175)                          PHI=  -0.191
                                                                                                            XP =  0.0028

196  TEND MORE TO BE THOSE          0.89 OF  95     196  TEND LESS TO BE THOSE          0.57 OF 178         85  102
     WHERE INDIVIDUAL RIGHTS IN REAL PROPERTY,             WHERE INDIVIDUAL RIGHTS IN REAL PROPERTY,            10   76
     AND RULES FOR INHERITANCE,                            AND RULES FOR INHERITANCE,                       XSQ=   28.24
     ARE PRESENT  (194)                                    ARE PRESENT  (194)                               PHI=   0.322
                                                                                                            XP =  0.0000
```

207	DRIFT TOWARD BEING THOSE WHERE MARITAL RESIDENCE IS AMBILOCAL OR NEOLOCAL, RATHER THAN MATRILOCAL OR UXORILOCAL (64)	0.63 OF 30	207	DRIFT TOWARD BEING THOSE WHERE MARITAL RESIDENCE IS MATRILOCAL OR UXORILOCAL, RATHER THAN AMBILOCAL OR NEOLOCAL (64)	0.56 OF 94	11 53 19 41 XSQ= 2.79 PHI= -0.150 XP = 0.0946
209	LEAN MORE TOWARD BEING THOSE WHERE MARITAL RESIDENCE IS PATRILOCAL, VIRILOCAL, OR AVUNCULOCAL, RATHER THAN MATRILOCAL OR UXORILOCAL (270)	0.90 OF 107	209	LEAN LESS TOWARD BEING THOSE WHERE MARITAL RESIDENCE IS PATRILOCAL, VIRILOCAL, OR AVUNCULOCAL, RATHER THAN MATRILOCAL OR UXORILOCAL (270)	0.75 OF 214	96 161 11 53 XSQ= 8.49 PHI= 0.163 XP = 0.0036
210	TILT MORE TOWARD BEING THOSE WHERE MARITAL RESIDENCE IS PATRILOCAL, RATHER THAN MATRILOCAL (169)	0.92 OF 66	210	TILT LESS TOWARD BEING THOSE WHERE MARITAL RESIDENCE IS PATRILOCAL, RATHER THAN MATRILOCAL (169)	0.80 OF 127	61 101 5 26 XSQ= 4.44 PHI= 0.152 XP = 0.0350
213	TILT TOWARD BEING THOSE WHERE FIRST COUSIN MARRIAGE IS PERMITTED (172)	0.57 OF 114	213	TILT TOWARD BEING THOSE WHERE FIRST COUSIN MARRIAGE IS NOT PERMITTED (198)	0.58 OF 241	65 102 49 139 XSQ= 6.13 PHI= 0.131 XP = 0.0133
234	TILT TOWARD BEING THOSE WHERE THE COUSIN TERMINOLOGY IS OF ESKIMO OR HAWAIIAN TYPE, RATHER THAN CROW, OMAHA, OR IROQUOIS TYPE (170)	0.61 OF 98	234	TILT TOWARD BEING THOSE WHERE THE COUSIN TERMINOLOGY IS OF CROW, OMAHA, OR IROQUOIS TYPE, RATHER THAN ESKIMO OR HAWAIIAN TYPE (152)	0.52 OF 209	38 109 60 100 XSQ= 4.26 PHI= -0.118 XP = 0.0389
236	DRIFT MORE TOWARD BEING THOSE WHERE THE FAMILY IS OF AN EXTENDED TYPE, RATHER THAN AN INDEPENDENT TYPE (213)	0.60 OF 126	236	DRIFT LESS TOWARD BEING THOSE WHERE THE FAMILY IS OF AN EXTENDED TYPE, RATHER THAN AN INDEPENDENT TYPE (213)	0.51 OF 256	76 130 50 126 XSQ= 2.72 PHI= 0.084 XP = 0.0992
272	DRIFT TOWARD BEING THOSE WHERE THE DIVORCE RATE IS LOW (28) CA	0.67 OF 21	272	DRIFT TOWARD BEING THOSE WHERE THE DIVORCE RATE IS HIGH (29) CA	0.61 OF 36	7 22 14 14 XSQ= 3.06 PHI= -0.232 XP = 0.0803
304	DRIFT TOWARD BEING THOSE WHERE THE EARLY ANAL SATISFACTION POTENTIAL IS LOW (22) W-C	0.75 OF 16	304	DRIFT TOWARD BEING THOSE WHERE THE EARLY ANAL SATISFACTION POTENTIAL IS HIGH (19) W-C	0.60 OF 25	4 15 12 10 XSQ= 3.50 PHI= -0.292 XP = 0.0613
314	LEAN LESS TOWARD BEING THOSE WHERE THE INCIDENCE OF MOTHER-CHILD HOUSEHOLDS IS LOW (61) W-D,S	0.52 OF 23	314	LEAN MORE TOWARD BEING THOSE WHERE THE INCIDENCE OF MOTHER-CHILD HOUSEHOLDS IS LOW (61) W-D,S	0.86 OF 56	11 8 12 48 XSQ= 8.29 PHI= 0.324 XP = 0.0040

318	TILT TOWARD BEING THOSE 0.65 OF 20 WHERE THE OVERALL INDULGENCE OF THE INFANT IS LOW (31) B-B-C	318	TILT TOWARD BEING THOSE 0.65 OF 51 WHERE THE OVERALL INDULGENCE OF THE INFANT IS HIGH (40) B-B-C		7 33 13 18 XSQ= 4.02 PHI= -0.238 XP = 0.0450
324	DRIFT TOWARD BEING THOSE 0.70 OF 20 WHERE THE PAIN INFLICTED ON THE INFANT BY THE NURTURANT AGENT IS HIGH (34) B-B-C	324	DRIFT TOWARD BEING THOSE 0.57 OF 46 WHERE THE PAIN INFLICTED ON THE INFANT BY THE NURTURANT AGENT IS LOW OR NEGLIGIBLE (32) B-B-C		14 20 6 26 XSQ= 2.94 PHI= 0.211 XP = 0.0866
333	IN ALL CASES ARE THOSE 1.00 OF 6 WHERE THE AGE AT BEGINNING OF TRAINING IN HETEROSEXUAL PLAY INHIBITION IS EIGHT YEARS OR HIGHER (8) W-C	333	LEAN TOWARD BEING THOSE 0.80 OF 10 WHERE THE AGE AT BEGINNING OF TRAINING IN HETEROSEXUAL PLAY INHIBITION IS LOWER THAN EIGHT YEARS (8) W-C		6 2 0 8 XSQ= 6.67 PHI= 0.645 EP = 0.0070
338	DRIFT MORE TOWARD BEING THOSE 0.80 OF 20 WHERE THE CHILD'S INFERRED ANXIETY OVER PERFORMANCE OF RESPONSIBLE BEHAVIOR IS HIGH (44) B-B-C	338	DRIFT LESS TOWARD BEING THOSE 0.53 OF 53 WHERE THE CHILD'S INFERRED ANXIETY OVER PERFORMANCE OF RESPONSIBLE BEHAVIOR IS HIGH (44) B-B-C		16 28 4 25 XSQ= 3.41 PHI= 0.216 XP = 0.0647
339	TILT TOWARD BEING THOSE 0.65 OF 20 WHERE THE CHILD'S INFERRED CONFLICT REGARDING RESPONSIBLE BEHAVIOR IS HIGH (31) B-B-C	339	TILT TOWARD BEING THOSE 0.66 OF 53 WHERE THE CHILD'S INFERRED CONFLICT REGARDING RESPONSIBLE BEHAVIOR IS LOW (42) B-B-C		13 18 7 35 XSQ= 4.53 PHI= 0.249 XP = 0.0334
342	DRIFT TOWARD BEING THOSE 0.67 OF 12 WHERE THE CHILD'S INFERRED ANXIETY OVER PERFORMANCE OF NURTURANT BEHAVIOR IS HIGH (18) B-B-C	342	DRIFT TOWARD BEING THOSE 0.71 OF 34 WHERE THE CHILD'S INFERRED ANXIETY OVER PERFORMANCE OF NURTURANT BEHAVIOR IS LOW (28) B-B-C		8 10 4 24 XSQ= 3.72 PHI= 0.284 XP = 0.0537
350	TILT TOWARD BEING THOSE 0.81 OF 16 WHERE THE CHILD'S INFERRED ANXIETY OVER PERFORMANCE OF ACHIEVEMENT BEHAVIOR IS HIGH (34) B-B-C	350	TILT TOWARD BEING THOSE 0.52 OF 44 WHERE THE CHILD'S INFERRED ANXIETY OVER PERFORMANCE OF ACHIEVEMENT BEHAVIOR IS LOW (26) B-B-C		13 21 3 23 XSQ= 4.09 PHI= 0.261 XP = 0.0431
354	DRIFT TOWARD BEING THOSE 0.70 OF 20 WHERE THE CHILD'S INFERRED ANXIETY OVER PERFORMANCE OF OBEDIENT BEHAVIOR IS HIGH (36) B-B-C	354	DRIFT TOWARD BEING THOSE 0.58 OF 53 WHERE THE CHILD'S INFERRED ANXIETY OVER PERFORMANCE OF OBEDIENT BEHAVIOR IS LOW (37) B-B-C		14 22 6 31 XSQ= 3.64 PHI= 0.223 XP = 0.0563
358	DRIFT MORE TOWARD BEING THOSE 0.95 OF 19 WHERE ADOLESCENT PEER GROUPS ARE PRESENT IN A SETTING OF WORK AND PUBLIC GATHERINGS AND LEISURE, OR OF PUBLIC GATHERINGS AND LEISURE, OR OF LEISURE ONLY (41) JKH	358	DRIFT LESS TOWARD BEING THOSE 0.69 OF 32 WHERE ADOLESCENT PEER GROUPS ARE PRESENT IN A SETTING OF WORK AND PUBLIC GATHERINGS AND LEISURE, OR OF PUBLIC GATHERINGS AND LEISURE, OR OF LEISURE ONLY (41) JKH		18 22 1 10 XSQ= 3.35 PHI= 0.256 XP = 0.0673

```
360  DRIFT TOWARD BEING THOSE          0.58 OF  12     360  DRIFT TOWARD BEING THOSE          0.75 OF  24            7     6
     WHERE ADOLESCENT PEER GROUPS ARE PRESENT               WHERE ADOLESCENT PEER GROUPS ARE PRESENT                 5    18
     IN A SETTING OF WORK AND PUBLIC GATHERINGS             ONLY IN A SETTING OF LEISURE, OR ELSE             XSQ=     2.54
     AND LEISURE, OR AT LEAST OF                            ARE ABSENT  (23) JKH                              PHI=    0.266
     PUBLIC GATHERINGS AND LEISURE  (14) JKH                                                                  EP =   0.0714

365  LEAN TOWARD BEING THOSE           0.94 OF  16     365  LEAN TOWARD BEING THOSE           0.50 OF  28           15    14
     WHERE THE TIME SPENT IN                                WHERE THE TIME SPENT IN                                  1    14
     ADOLESCENT PEER GROUP ACTIVITY                         ADOLESCENT PEER GROUP ACTIVITY                    XSQ=     6.84
     IS HIGH OR HIGH-MEDIUM  (30) JKH                       IS LOW-MEDIUM OR LOW  (15) JKH                    PHI=    0.394
                                                                                                              XP =   0.0089

377  TEND LESS TO BE THOSE             0.62 OF  98     377  TEND MORE TO BE THOSE             0.81 OF 218           37    42
     WHERE MALE GENITAL MUTILATION                          WHERE MALE GENITAL MUTILATION                           61   176
     IS ABSENT  (242)                                       IS ABSENT  (242)                                  XSQ=    11.36
                                                                                                              PHI=    0.190
                                                                                                              XP =   0.0008

417  IN ALL CASES ARE THOSE            1.00 OF  12     417  DRIFT LESS TOWARD BEING THOSE     0.71 OF  31           12    22
     WHERE WARFARE IS                                       WHERE WARFARE IS                                         0     9
     PREVALENT  (34) LWS                                    PREVALENT  (34) LWS                               XSQ=     2.83
                                                                                                              PHI=    0.256
                                                                                                              XP =   0.0927

419  TILT MORE TOWARD BEING THOSE      0.81 OF  27     419  TILT LESS TOWARD BEING THOSE      0.56 OF  59           22    33
     WHERE MILITARY GLORY                                   WHERE MILITARY GLORY                                     5    26
     IS STRONGLY OR                                         IS STRONGLY OR                                    XSQ=     4.20
     MODERATELY EMPHASIZED  (55) PES                        MODERATELY EMPHASIZED  (55) PES                   PHI=    0.221
                                                                                                              XP =   0.0405

420  DRIFT TOWARD BEING THOSE          0.63 OF  27     420  DRIFT TOWARD BEING THOSE          0.60 OF  60           17    24
     WHERE BELLICOSITY                                      WHERE BELLICOSITY                                       10    36
     IS EXTREME  (41) PES                                   IS MODERATE OR NEGLIGIBLE  (46) PES               XSQ=     3.07
                                                                                                              PHI=    0.188
                                                                                                              XP =   0.0796

424  TEND TO BE THOSE                  0.70 OF  20     424  TEND TO BE THOSE                  0.79 OF  34           14     7
     WHERE RELIGIOUS SPECIALISTS ARE                        WHERE RELIGIOUS SPECIALISTS ARE                          6    27
     FULL-TIME, RATHER THAN                                 PART-TIME, RATHER THAN                            XSQ=    10.94
     PART-TIME  (21) JMH                                    FULL-TIME  (33) JMH                               PHI=    0.450
                                                                                                              XP =   0.0009

426  DRIFT MORE TOWARD BEING THOSE     0.69 OF  83     426  DRIFT LESS TOWARD BEING THOSE     0.56 OF 174           57    97
     WHERE A HIGH GOD IS                                    WHERE A HIGH GOD IS                                     26    77
     PRESENT  (156) GES,EA                                  PRESENT  (156) GES,EA                             XSQ=     3.39
                                                                                                              PHI=    0.115
                                                                                                              XP =   0.0656

444  TILT TOWARD BEING THOSE           0.75 OF  16     444  TILT TOWARD BEING THOSE           0.62 OF  39            4    24
     WHERE THE USE OF DREAMS                                WHERE THE USE OF DREAMS                                 12    15
     TO SEEK AND CONTROL SUPERNATURAL POWERS                TO SEEK AND CONTROL SUPERNATURAL POWERS           XSQ=     4.69
     IS LOW  (27) RGD                                       IS HIGH  (28) RGD                                 PHI=   -0.292
                                                                                                              XP =   0.0304
```

No.			No.			
450	LEAN TOWARD BEING THOSE WHERE THE OBSERVATION OF FOOD TABOOS IS LOW, RATHER THAN HIGH OR MEDIUM (26) JRL	0.52 OF 31	450	LEAN TOWARD BEING THOSE WHERE THE OBSERVATION OF FOOD TABOOS IS HIGH OR MEDIUM, RATHER THAN LOW (60) JRL	0.82 OF 55	15 45 16 10 XSQ= 8.98 PHI= -0.323 XP = 0.0027
452	DRIFT TOWARD BEING THOSE WHERE TOTEMISM WITH FOOD TABOOS IS PRESENT (19) WNS	0.67 OF 15	452	DRIFT TOWARD BEING THOSE WHERE TOTEMISM WITH FOOD TABOOS IS ABSENT (24) WNS	0.68 OF 28	10 9 5 19 XSQ= 3.42 PHI= 0.282 XP = 0.0642
458	TEND TO BE THOSE WHERE GAMES, IF PRESENT, INCLUDE GAMES OF STRATEGY (52) R-A-B,EA	0.61 OF 57	458	TEND TO BE THOSE WHERE GAMES, IF PRESENT, DO NOT INCLUDE GAMES OF STRATEGY (119) R-A-B,EA	0.85 OF 111	35 17 22 94 XSQ= 35.31 PHI= 0.458 XP = 0.
460	DRIFT MORE TOWARD BEING THOSE WHERE GAMES, IF PRESENT, ARE NOT LIMITED TO GAMES OF SKILL ONLY (104) R-A-B,EA	0.72 OF 57	460	DRIFT LESS TOWARD BEING THOSE WHERE GAMES, IF PRESENT, ARE NOT LIMITED TO GAMES OF SKILL ONLY (104) R-A-B,EA	0.56 OF 111	16 49 41 62 XSQ= 3.45 PHI= -0.143 XP = 0.0632
468	LEAN TOWARD BEING THOSE WHERE CONTACT WITH OTHER CULTURES IS FREQUENT, RATHER THAN REGULAR OR IRREGULAR (17) JMH	0.60 OF 20	468	LEAN TOWARD BEING THOSE WHERE CONTACT WITH OTHER CULTURES IS REGULAR OR IRREGULAR, RATHER THAN FREQUENT (37) JMH	0.85 OF 34	12 5 8 29 XSQ= 9.97 PHI= 0.430 XP = 0.0016
472	TILT TOWARD BEING THOSE WHERE THE COMPOSITE NARCISSISM INDEX IS HIGH (47) PES	0.72 OF 29	472	TILT TOWARD BEING THOSE WHERE THE COMPOSITE NARCISSISM INDEX IS LOW (43) PES	0.57 OF 61	21 26 8 35 XSQ= 5.85 PHI= 0.255 XP = 0.0156
473	LEAN TOWARD BEING THOSE WHERE SENSITIVITY TO INSULT IS EXTREME (32) PES	0.59 OF 29	473	LEAN TOWARD BEING THOSE WHERE SENSITIVITY TO INSULT IS MODERATE OR NEGLIGIBLE (56) PES	0.75 OF 59	17 15 12 44 XSQ= 7.88 PHI= 0.299 XP = 0.0050
475	TILT TOWARD BEING THOSE WHERE EXHIBITIONISTIC DANCING IS STRONGLY OR MODERATELY EMPHASIZED (48) PES	0.74 OF 27	475	TILT TOWARD BEING THOSE WHERE EXHIBITIONISTIC DANCING IS NEGLIGIBLY EMPHASIZED (38) PES	0.53 OF 59	20 28 7 31 XSQ= 4.30 PHI= 0.224 XP = 0.0382
480	DRIFT TOWARD BEING THOSE WHERE COMPLEXITY OF ARTISTIC DESIGN IS HIGH (14) HB	0.73 OF 11	480	DRIFT TOWARD BEING THOSE WHERE COMPLEXITY OF ARTISTIC DESIGN IS LOW (15) HB	0.67 OF 18	8 6 3 12 XSQ= 2.81 PHI= 0.311 EP = 0.0604

104 CULTURES
WHERE CLASS STRATIFICATICN
BASED CN WEALTH OR OCCUPATIONAL STATUS
IS PRESENT (120)

104 CULTURES
WHERE CLASS STRATIFICATION
BASED ON WEALTH OR OCCUPATICNAL STATUS
IS ABSENT (263)

BACKGROUND ON PAGE 88

SUBJECT ONLY

120 IN LEFT CCLUMN

ABOR	ALCRESE	AMERICANS	ARAUCANIANS	ATSUGEWI	AYMARA	AZTEC	BARABRA	BARI	BASQUES
BASSERI	BENGALI	BHIL	BRAZILIANS	BULGARIANS	BURMESE	BURUSHO	CAGABA	CAMBODIANS	CHUKCHEE
COORG	CUNA	CZECHS	DOGON	DUSUN	DUTCH	EGYPTIANS	EYAK	FANG	GARO
GILBERTESE	GISU	GOAJIRC	GOND	HASANIA	HAŻARA	HEBREWS	HERERO	HUICHOL	HURON
HUTSUL	IFUGAO	ILA	INCA	INGALIK	IRAQW	IRISH	JAPANESE	JAVANESE	KAPAUKU
KAREN	KERALA	KHASI	KIKUYU	KOREANS	KORYAK	KPE	LAKALAI	LAMET	LANGO
LAPPS	LAU	LEPCHA	LHOTA NAGA	LUO	MALAYS	MAM	MANCHU	MANUS	MAYA
MBUGWE	MIN CHINESE	MINANGKABAU	MINCHIA	MNONG GAR	MOSSI	MOTA	NAMA	NOMLAKI	NUNIVAK
NUPE	NURI	CNTCNG-JAVA	PATHAN	PORTUGUESE	PURUM	REGEIBAT	RIFFIANS	ROMANS	RUNDI
RWALA	SAGADA	SAMOYEC	SENIANG	SERBS	SHILLUK	SIUAI	SIWANS	SOMALI	SONGHAI
TALLENSI	TAMIL	TARAHUMARA	TAREUMIUT	TENINO	THAI	TIBETANS	TIGRINYA	TOLOWA	TORAJA
TUPINAMBA	TWANA	VIETNAMESE	WALLOONS	WOLOF	YAKUT	YOKUTS	YORUBA	YUKI	YUROK

263 IN RIGHT CCLUMN

ABIPON	AINU	AJIE	AKHA	ALACALUF	ALBANIANS	AMBA	ANDAMANESE	APINAYE	ARANDA
ARAPESH	ASHANTI	ATAYAL	AWEIKOMA	AZANDE	BABWA	BACAIRI	BAJUN	BALINESE	BAMBARA
BAMILEKE	BANDA	BATAK	BAYA	BEJA	BELU	BEMBA	BERGDAMA	BETE	BIRIFOR
BLACK CARIB	BCERS	BORCRO	BOTOCUDO	BOZO	BUDUMA	BURYAT	CADUVEO	CALLINAGO	CAMAYURA
CAMBA	CARAJA	CARIB	CAYAPA	CHAGGA	CHAMACOCO	CHENCHU	CHEREMIS	CHERKESS	CHEROKEE
CHEYENNE	CHIBCHA	CHIR-APACHE	CHOCO	CHOROTI	CHORTI	COCHITI	COMANCHE	COPR ESKIMO	CREE
CREEK	CRCW	DAGUR	DARC	DELAWARE	DIEGUENO	DIERI	DILLING	DOBUANS	DOROBO
ELLICE	ENGA	FCN	FOX	FUTAJALONKE	GANDA	GILYAK	GRCS VENTRE	GUAHIBO	GUATO
GURE	HAIDA	HANO	HANUNOO	HASINAI	HAVASUPAI	HAWAIIANS	HEHE	HO	HUKUNDIKA
IBAN	ICELANDERS	INGASSANA	JEMEZ	JIVARO	JUKUN	KABYLE	KACHIN	KALMYK	KARIERA
KASKA	KATAB	KAZAK	KERAKI	KET	KHALKA	KHEVSUR	KICW-APACHE	KISSI	KOHISTANI
KONSO	KUBA	KUNG	KURTATCHI	KUTENAI	KWAKIUTL	LAKHER	LAMBA	LESU	LIFU
LOLO	LOZI	LUBA	MACASSARESE	MAGUZAWA	MAMBILA	MAMVU	MANDAN	MANGAIANS	MANIHIKI
MAORI	MARGI	MARICOPA	MARQUESANS	MARSHALLESE	MASAI	MATACO	MATAKAM	MBUNDU	MBUTI
MENDE	MENTAWEI	MERINA	MIAMI	MIAO	MISKITO	MIWOK	MCNGO	MONGUOR	MOTILON
MUNDURUCU	MURINBATA	MURNGIN	MZAB	NABESNA	NAMBICUARA	NANDI	NASKAPI	NATCHEZ	NAVAHO
NGONI	NICCBARESE	NUER	NYAKYUSA	NYANEKA	NYARO	NYORO	OJIBWA	OKINAWANS	OMAHA
ONA	PAIWAN	PALAUANS	PALIKUR	PAPAGO	PARAUJANO	PAWNEE	PENDE	PENCBSCOT	PONAPEANS
POPCLUCA	PUKAPUKA	PURARI	RAROIANS	ROTINESE	ROTUMANS	SAMOANS	SANDAWE	SANPOIL	SANTAL
SARAMACCA	SARSI	SELUNG	SEMANG	SEMINOLE	SERI	SHERENTE	SHLUH	SINCHI	SIRIONO
SOTHO	SUBANUN	SWAZI	SYRIANS	TAGBANUA	TALAMANCA	TANALA	TANIMBARESE	TAOS	TAPIRAPE
TEHUELCHE	TENDA	TENETEHARA	TERA	TERENA	TESO	TETON	THCNGA	TIKOPIA	TIMBIRA
TIMUCUA	TIV	TIWI	TOCA	TOKELAU	TRISTAN	TROBRIAND	TRUKESE	TRUMAI	TSHIMSHIAN
TUBATULABAL	TUCANO	TUCUNA	TUNEBO	TURKANA	TURKMEN	ULAWANS	UTE	VEDCA	VENCA

WAICA WANTOAT WAPISHANA WAROPEN WARRAU WASHO WICHITA WIKMUNKAN WINNEBAGO WITOTO
WOGEO WOLEAIANS WUTE YABARANA YAGUA YAHGAN YAKO YAO YAPESE YARURO
YOMBE YUKAGHIR ZUNI

17 EXCLUDED BECAUSE UNASCERTAINED

3	DRIFT MORE TOWARD BEING THOSE LOCATED OUTSIDE OF AFRICA (320)	0.85 OF 120	3	DRIFT LESS TOWARD BEING THOSE LOCATED OUTSIDE OF AFRICA (320)	0.77 OF 263	18 61 102 202 XSQ= 2.90 PHI= -0.087 XP = 0.0887
4	TEND LESS TO BE THOSE LOCATED OUTSIDE OF THE CIRCUM-MEDITERRANEAN (355)	0.78 OF 120	4	TEND MORE TO BE THOSE LOCATED OUTSIDE OF THE CIRCUM-MEDITERRANEAN (355)	0.94 OF 263	26 17 94 246 XSQ= 17.61 PHI= 0.214 XP = 0.0000
5	TEND LESS TO BE THOSE LOCATED OUTSIDE OF EAST EURASIA (330)	0.71 OF 120	5	TEND MORE TO BE THOSE LOCATED OUTSIDE OF EAST EURASIA (330)	0.89 OF 263	35 30 85 233 XSQ= 17.21 PHI= 0.212 XP = 0.0000
9	LEAN MORE TOWARD BEING THOSE LOCATED OUTSIDE OF SOUTH AMERICA (335)	0.92 OF 120	9	LEAN LESS TOWARD BEING THOSE LOCATED OUTSIDE OF SOUTH AMERICA (335)	0.80 OF 263	9 52 111 211 XSQ= 8.37 PHI= -0.148 XP = 0.0038
15	DRIFT TOWARD BEING THOSE WHERE THE LATITUDE IS TWENTY DEGREES OR GREATER (183)	0.53 OF 120	15	DRIFT TOWARD BEING THOSE WHERE THE LATITUDE IS LESS THAN TWENTY DEGREES (217)	0.58 OF 263	64 111 56 152 XSQ= 3.68 PHI= 0.098 XP = 0.0552
44	TILT MORE TOWARD BEING THOSE WHERE SETTLEMENTS ARE FIXED (222)	0.75 OF 106	44	TILT LESS TOWARD BEING THOSE WHERE SETTLEMENTS ARE FIXED (222)	0.63 OF 216	80 135 26 81 XSQ= 4.82 PHI= 0.122 XP = 0.0281
46	TILT MORE TOWARD BEING THOSE OTHER THAN WHERE SETTLEMENTS ARE NON-FIXED AND MOVEMENT IS NOMADIC (260)	0.86 OF 106	46	TILT LESS TOWARD BEING THOSE OTHER THAN WHERE SETTLEMENTS ARE NON-FIXED AND MOVEMENT IS NOMADIC (260)	0.74 OF 216	15 56 91 160 XSQ= 5.07 PHI= -0.125 XP = 0.0243

51	TEND MORE TO BE THOSE WHERE SUBSISTENCE IS PRIMARILY BY FOOD PRODUCTION -- I. E., AGRICULTURE OR HUSBANDRY -- RATHER THAN BY GATHERING (253)	0.79 OF 120	51	TEND LESS TO BE THOSE WHERE SUBSISTENCE IS PRIMARILY BY FOOD PRODUCTION -- I. E., AGRICULTURE OR HUSBANDRY -- RATHER THAN BY GATHERING (253)	0.54 OF 263	95 141 25 122 XSQ= 21.69 PHI= 0.238 XP = 0.0000
53	TEND TO BE THOSE WHERE FOOD PRODUCTION IS BY INTENSIVE AGRICULTURE, RATHER THAN BY SIMPLE AGRICULTURE OR INCIPIENT FOOD PRODUCTION (91)	0.55 OF 85	53	TEND TO BE THOSE WHERE FOOD PRODUCTION IS BY SIMPLE AGRICULTURE OR INCIPIENT FOOD PRODUCTION, RATHER THAN BY INTENSIVE AGRICULTURE (147)	0.73 OF 143	47 39 38 104 XSQ= 16.65 PHI= 0.270 XP = 0.0000
55	LEAN TOWARD BEING THOSE WHERE FOOD PRODUCTION IS BY INTENSIVE AGRICULTURE, RATHER THAN BY SIMPLE AGRICULTURE (91)	0.62 OF 76	55	LEAN TOWARD BEING THOSE WHERE FOOD PRODUCTION IS BY SIMPLE AGRICULTURE, RATHER THAN BY INTENSIVE AGRICULTURE (101)	0.63 OF 106	47 39 29 67 XSQ= 10.16 PHI= 0.236 XP = 0.0014
62	TEND TO BE THOSE WHERE HUSBANDRY OF SOME KIND IS PRESENT (228)	0.74 OF 120	62	TEND TO BE THOSE WHERE HUSBANDRY OF ANY KIND IS ABSENT (172)	0.50 OF 263	89 131 31 132 XSQ= 19.01 PHI= 0.223 XP = 0.0000
63	TEND MORE TO BE THOSE WHERE HUSBANDRY, IF PRESENT, IS PRINCIPALLY IN THE FORM OF BOVINE, EQUINE, CAMEL-LIKE, OR DEER-LIKE ANIMALS, RATHER THAN PIGS, SHEEP, OR GOATS (152)	0.81 OF 89	63	TEND LESS TO BE THOSE WHERE HUSBANDRY, IF PRESENT, IS PRINCIPALLY IN THE FORM OF BOVINE, EQUINE, CAMEL-LIKE, OR DEER-LIKE ANIMALS, RATHER THAN PIGS, SHEEP, OR GOATS (152)	0.57 OF 129	72 74 17 55 XSQ= 12.14 PHI= 0.236 XP = 0.0005
71	TEND TO BE THOSE WHERE METAL WORKING IS PRESENT (98)	0.60 OF 80	71	TEND TO BE THOSE WHERE METAL WORKING IS ABSENT (153)	0.72 OF 166	48 47 32 119 XSQ= 21.55 PHI= 0.296 XP = 0.0000
73	TILT TOWARD BEING THOSE WHERE WEAVING IS PRESENT (118)	0.57 OF 80	73	TILT TOWARD BEING THOSE WHERE WEAVING IS ABSENT (130)	0.58 OF 163	46 69 34 94 XSQ= 4.36 PHI= 0.134 XP = 0.0367
74	TILT MORE TOWARD BEING THOSE WHERE POTTERY IS PRESENT (145)	0.71 OF 78	74	TILT LESS TOWARD BEING THOSE WHERE POTTERY IS PRESENT (145)	0.55 OF 156	55 86 23 70 XSQ= 4.52 PHI= 0.139 XP = 0.0336
77	TILT TOWARD BEING THOSE WHERE THE WRITING SYSTEM IS ALPHABETIC-OR-PHONETIC, RATHER THAN BEING MNEMONIC OR ABSENT (15) JMH	0.50 OF 20	77	TILT TOWARD BEING THOSE WHERE THE WRITING SYSTEM IS MNEMONIC OR ABSENT, RATHER THAN BEING ALPHABETIC-OR-PHONETIC (39) JMH	0.85 OF 34	10 5 10 29 XSQ= 6.16 PHI= 0.338 XP = 0.0131

81	LEAN TOWARD BEING THOSE 0.51 OF 86 WHERE A CITY OR TOWN IS PRESENT, OR THE AVERAGE COMMUNITY SIZE IS 200 OR GREATER (89)	81	LEAN TOWARD BEING THOSE 0.68 OF 133 WHERE NO CITY OR TOWN IS PRESENT, AND THE AVERAGE COMMUNITY SIZE IS SMALLER THAN 200 (135)	44 43 42 90 XSQ= 6.97 PHI= 0.178 XP = 0.0083
84	TEND LESS TO BE THOSE 0.70 OF 86 WHERE THE LEVEL OF POLITICAL INTEGRATION IS THE LITTLE STATE, THE MINIMAL STATE, THE AUTONOMOUS COMMUNITY, OR THE FAMILY (262) GPM	84	TEND MORE TO BE THOSE 0.94 OF 211 WHERE THE LEVEL OF POLITICAL INTEGRATION IS THE LITTLE STATE, THE MINIMAL STATE, THE AUTONOMOUS COMMUNITY, OR THE FAMILY (262) GPM	26 13 60 198 XSQ= 28.96 PHI= 0.312 XP = 0.0000
85	TEND LESS TO BE THOSE 0.64 OF 86 WHERE THE LEVEL OF POLITICAL INTEGRATION IS THE MINIMAL STATE, THE AUTONOMOUS COMMUNITY, OR THE FAMILY (234) GPM	85	TEND MORE TO BE THOSE 0.83 OF 211 WHERE THE LEVEL OF POLITICAL INTEGRATION IS THE MINIMAL STATE, THE AUTONOMOUS COMMUNITY, OR THE FAMILY (234) GPM	31 36 55 175 XSQ= 11.54 PHI= 0.197 XP = 0.0007
94	LEAN LESS TOWARD BEING THOSE 0.82 OF 103 WHERE THE HIERARCHY OF NATIONAL JURISDICTION HAS TWO, ONE, OR NO LEVELS (296) GES,EA	94	LEAN MORE TOWARD BEING THOSE 0.94 OF 217 WHERE THE HIERARCHY OF NATIONAL JURISDICTION HAS TWO, ONE, OR NO LEVELS (296) GES,EA	19 14 84 203 XSQ= 9.61 PHI= 0.173 XP = 0.0019
95	LEAN LESS TOWARD BEING THOSE 0.66 OF 103 WHERE THE HIERARCHY OF NATIONAL JURISDICTION HAS ONE OR NO LEVELS (254) GES,EA	95	LEAN MORE TOWARD BEING THOSE 0.82 OF 217 WHERE THE HIERARCHY OF NATIONAL JURISDICTION HAS ONE OR NO LEVELS (254) GES,EA	35 39 68 178 XSQ= 9.19 PHI= 0.169 XP = 0.0024
98	TILT MORE TOWARD BEING THOSE 0.81 OF 104 WHERE THE HIERARCHY OF LOCAL JURISDICTION HAS FOUR OR THREE LEVELS (238) GES,EA	98	TILT LESS TOWARD BEING THOSE 0.68 OF 217 WHERE THE HIERARCHY OF LOCAL JURISDICTION HAS FOUR OR THREE LEVELS (238) GES,EA	84 147 20 70 XSQ= 5.29 PHI= 0.128 XP = 0.0215
99	TILT MORE TOWARD BEING THOSE 0.77 OF 43 WHERE, WITH NATIONAL HIERARCHY ABSENT, THE HIERARCHY OF LOCAL JURISDICTION HAS FOUR OR THREE LEVELS (93) GES,EA	99	TILT LESS TOWARD BEING THOSE 0.53 OF 112 WHERE, WITH NATIONAL HIERARCHY ABSENT, THE HIERARCHY OF LOCAL JURISDICTION HAS FOUR OR THREE LEVELS (93) GES,EA	33 59 10 53 XSQ= 6.49 PHI= 0.205 XP = 0.0108
100	LEAN MORE TOWARD BEING THOSE 0.90 OF 103 WHERE HIERARCHIES ARE MORE COMPLEX THAN THE 'SIMPLEST,' I. E., MORE COMPLEX THAN TWO LOCAL LEVELS WITH NO NATIONAL LEVELS (267) GES,EA	100	LEAN LESS TOWARD BEING THOSE 0.76 OF 217 WHERE HIERARCHIES ARE MORE COMPLEX THAN THE 'SIMPLEST,' I. E., MORE COMPLEX THAN TWO LOCAL LEVELS WITH NO NATIONAL LEVELS (267) GES,EA	93 164 10 53 XSQ= 8.66 PHI= 0.164 XP = 0.0033
109	TEND LESS TO BE THOSE 0.77 OF 107 WHERE CASTES ARE ABSENT (317)	109	TEND MORE TO BE THOSE 0.92 OF 251 WHERE CASTES ARE ABSENT (317)	25 21 82 230 XSQ= 13.76 PHI= 0.196 XP = 0.0002

```
110  LEAN TOWARD BEING THOSE         0.53 OF 117    110  LEAN TOWARD BEING THOSE         0.62 OF 255       62   97
     WHERE SLAVERY IS PRESENT   (163)                    WHERE SLAVERY IS ABSENT   (218)                      55  158
                                                                                                       XSQ=     6.73
                                                                                                       PHI=    0.134
                                                                                                       XP =   0.0095

116  DRIFT TOWARD BEING THOSE        0.55 OF  20    116  DRIFT TOWARD BEING THOSE        0.74 OF  34       11    9
     WHERE OCCUPATIONAL SPECIALIZATION IS                WHERE OCCUPATIONAL SPECIALIZATION IS              9   25
     FULL-TIME, WHETHER OR NOT FOR                       PART-TIME ONLY  (34) JMH                   XSQ=     3.26
     SURPLUS PRODUCTION  (20) JMH                                                                   PHI=    0.246
                                                                                                       XP =   0.0711

128  LEAN TOWARD BEING THOSE         0.72 OF  32    128  LEAN TOWARD BEING THOSE         0.64 OF  42       23   15
     WHERE, IF SUBSISTENCE IS PRIMARILY BY               WHERE, IF SUBSISTENCE IS PRIMARILY BY              9   27
     AGRICULTURE, THE WORK IS                            AGRICULTURE, THE WORK IS                    XSQ=     8.11
     MAINLY DONE BY MALES  (40)                          MAINLY DONE BY FEMALES  (37)                PHI=    0.331
                                                                                                       XP =   0.0044

131  DRIFT MORE TOWARD BEING THOSE  0.94 OF  51    131  DRIFT LESS TOWARD BEING THOSE  0.83 OF 103       48   85
     WHERE THE CONSTRUCTION OF PERMANENT HOUSES          WHERE THE CONSTRUCTION OF PERMANENT HOUSES         3   18
     OR THE ERECTION OF TEMPORARY DWELLINGS              OR THE ERECTION OF TEMPORARY DWELLINGS      XSQ=     2.97
     IS MAINLY DONE BY MALES  (136)                      IS MAINLY DONE BY MALES  (136)              PHI=    0.139
                                                                                                       XP =   0.0848

132  DRIFT MORE TOWARD BEING THOSE  0.85 OF  20    132  DRIFT LESS TOWARD BEING THOSE  0.59 OF  34       17   20
     WHERE ECONOMIC EXCHANGE                             WHERE ECONOMIC EXCHANGE                            3   14
     INVOLVES THE USE OF MONEY  (37) JMH                 INVOLVES THE USE OF MONEY  (37) JMH         XSQ=     2.88
                                                                                                       PHI=    0.231
                                                                                                       XP =   0.0898

135  DRIFT MORE TOWARD BEING THOSE  0.85 OF  13    135  DRIFT LESS TOWARD BEING THOSE  0.52 OF  25       11   13
     WHERE INDIVIDUAL OWNERSHIP OF                       WHERE INDIVIDUAL OWNERSHIP OF                      2   12
     ECONOMICALLY SIGNIFICANT PROPERTY                   ECONOMICALLY SIGNIFICANT PROPERTY           XSQ=     2.63
     IS PRESENT  (24) GES                                IS PRESENT  (24) GES                        PHI=    0.263
                                                                                                       EP =   0.0773

163  TILT TOWARD BEING THOSE         0.75 OF   8    163  TILT TOWARD BEING THOSE         0.89 OF   9        6    1
     WHERE THE EMPHASIS ON INDIVIDUAL VOLITION           WHERE THE EMPHASIS ON INDIVIDUAL VOLITION          2    8
     AS THE CAUSE OF CRIME                               AS THE CAUSE OF CRIME                       XSQ=     4.74
     IS HIGH  (7) MJ                                     IS LOW  (10) MJ                             PHI=    0.528
                                                                                                       EP =   0.0152

164  TILT TOWARD BEING THOSE         0.86 OF   7    164  TILT TOWARD BEING THOSE         0.73 OF  11        1    8
     WHERE THE EMPHASIS ON INDIVIDUAL VOLITION           WHERE THE EMPHASIS ON INDIVIDUAL VOLITION          6    3
     AS THE CAUSE OR SOURCE OF ILLNESS                   AS THE CAUSE OR SOURCE OF ILLNESS           XSQ=     3.74
     IS LOW  (9) MJ                                      IS HIGH  (9) MJ                             PHI=   -0.456
                                                                                                       EP =   0.0498

182  DRIFT LESS TOWARD BEING THOSE  0.60 OF 118    182  DRIFT MORE TOWARD BEING THOSE  0.70 OF 249       47   75
     OTHER THAN WHERE THE COMMUNITY IS                   OTHER THAN WHERE THE COMMUNITY IS                 71  174
     STRUCTURED ON A NON-CLAN BASIS AND                  STRUCTURED ON A NON-CLAN BASIS AND          XSQ=     2.98
     AGAMOUS  (256)                                      AGAMOUS  (256)                              PHI=    0.090
                                                                                                       XP =   0.0844
```

183	TILT MORE TOWARD BEING THOSE 0.94 OF 79 WHERE THE LARGEST NON-COGNATIC KIN GROUP IS SMALLER THAN A MOEITY, I. E., A PHRATRY OR SIB OR LINEAGE (218)	183	TILT LESS TOWARD BEING THOSE 0.83 OF 166 WHERE THE LARGEST NON-COGNATIC KIN GROUP IS SMALLER THAN A MOEITY, I. E., A PHRATRY OR SIB OR LINEAGE (218)	5 28 74 138 XSQ= 4.24 PHI= -0.131 XP = 0.0396
186	DRIFT LESS TOWARD BEING THOSE 0.55 OF 120 WHERE THE KIN GROUP IS OTHER THAN EXCLUSIVELY PATRILINEAL (250)	186	DRIFT MORE TOWARD BEING THOSE 0.65 OF 263 WHERE THE KIN GROUP IS OTHER THAN EXCLUSIVELY PATRILINEAL (250)	54 92 66 171 XSQ= 3.09 PHI= 0.090 XP = 0.0785
187	DRIFT MORE TOWARD BEING THOSE 0.91 OF 120 WHERE THE KIN GROUP IS OTHER THAN EXCLUSIVELY MATRILINEAL (344)	187	DRIFT LESS TOWARD BEING THOSE 0.84 OF 262 WHERE THE KIN GROUP IS OTHER THAN EXCLUSIVELY MATRILINEAL (344)	11 43 109 219 XSQ= 2.99 PHI= -0.088 XP = 0.0839
190	TILT MORE TOWARD BEING THOSE 0.85 OF 78 WHERE THE KIN GROUP IS PATRILINEAL OR DOUBLE-DESCENT, RATHER THAN MATRILINEAL (186)	190	TILT LESS TOWARD BEING THOSE 0.70 OF 162 WHERE THE KIN GROUP IS PATRILINEAL OR DOUBLE-DESCENT, RATHER THAN MATRILINEAL (186)	66 114 12 48 XSQ= 4.96 PHI= 0.144 XP = 0.0259
196	DRIFT MORE TOWARD BEING THOSE 0.77 OF 94 WHERE INDIVIDUAL RIGHTS IN REAL PROPERTY, AND RULES FOR INHERITANCE, ARE PRESENT (194)	196	DRIFT LESS TOWARD BEING THOSE 0.64 OF 179 WHERE INDIVIDUAL RIGHTS IN REAL PROPERTY, AND RULES FOR INHERITANCE, ARE PRESENT (194)	72 115 22 64 XSQ= 3.80 PHI= 0.118 XP = 0.0512
198	TILT MORE TOWARD BEING THOSE 0.95 OF 59 WHERE RULES FOR THE INHERITANCE OF REAL PROPERTY, IF PRESENT, FAVOR THE MALE HEIR OR LINE, RATHER THAN THE FEMALE (144)	198	TILT LESS TOWARD BEING THOSE 0.82 OF 100 WHERE RULES FOR THE INHERITANCE OF REAL PROPERTY, IF PRESENT, FAVOR THE MALE HEIR OR LINE, RATHER THAN THE FEMALE (144)	56 82 3 18 XSQ= 4.33 PHI= 0.165 XP = 0.0374
209	DRIFT MORE TOWARD BEING THOSE 0.87 OF 105 WHERE MARITAL RESIDENCE IS PATRILOCAL, VIRILOCAL, OR AVUNCULOCAL, RATHER THAN MATRILOCAL OR UXORILOCAL (270)	209	DRIFT LESS TOWARD BEING THOSE 0.77 OF 216 WHERE MARITAL RESIDENCE IS PATRILOCAL, VIRILOCAL, OR AVUNCULOCAL, RATHER THAN MATRILOCAL OR UXORILOCAL (270)	91 166 14 50 XSQ= 3.67 PHI= 0.107 XP = 0.0554
210	TILT MORE TOWARD BEING THOSE 0.93 OF 67 WHERE MARITAL RESIDENCE IS PATRILOCAL, RATHER THAN MATRILOCAL (169)	210	TILT LESS TOWARD BEING THOSE 0.79 OF 126 WHERE MARITAL RESIDENCE IS PATRILOCAL, RATHER THAN MATRILOCAL (169)	62 100 5 26 XSQ= 4.69 PHI= 0.156 XP = 0.0303
234	TILT TOWARD BEING THOSE 0.62 OF 95 WHERE THE COUSIN TERMINOLOGY IS OF ESKIMO OR HAWAIIAN TYPE, RATHER THAN CROW, OMAHA, OR IROQUOIS TYPE (170)	234	TILT TOWARD BEING THOSE 0.52 OF 212 WHERE THE COUSIN TERMINOLOGY IS OF CROW, OMAHA, OR IROQUOIS TYPE, RATHER THAN ESKIMO OR HAWAIIAN TYPE (152)	36 111 59 101 XSQ= 4.94 PHI= -0.127 XP = 0.0263

240	DRIFT MCRE TCWARD BEING THOSE WHERE THE FAMILY, IF EXTENCEC, IS SMALL CR STEM, RATHER THAN LARGE (135)	0.72 OF 72	240	DRIFT LESS TOWARD BEING THCSE WHERE THE FAMILY, IF EXTENDED, IS SMALL OR STEM, RATHER THAN LARGE (135)	0.57 CF 134	20 57 52 77 XSQ= 3.75 PHI= -0.135 XP = 0.0528
241	LEAN LESS TOWARC BEING THCSE WHERE THE FAMILY, IF EXTENCEC, IS LARGE CR SMALL, RATHER THAN STEM (187)	0.79 OF 72	241	LEAN MORE TOWARD BEING THOSE WHERE THE FAMILY, IF EXTENDED, IS LARGE OR SMALL, RATHER THAN STEM (187)	0.93 OF 134	57 124 15 10 XSQ= 6.65 PHI= -0.180 XP = 0.0099
242	DRIFT LESS TCWARD BEING THOSE WHERE MARRIAGE IS COMMCNLY CR CCCASICNALLY PCLYGYNOUS, RATHER THAN MCNCGAMOUS (314)	0.74 OF 119	242	DRIFT MORE TOWARD BEING THCSE WHERE MARRIAGE IS COMMONLY OR OCCASIONALLY PCLYGYNOUS, RATHER THAN MONCGAMOUS (314)	0.82 CF 260	88 213 31 47 XSQ= 2.71 PHI= -0.085 XP = 0.1000
255	TILT TCWARC BEING THOSE WHERE GRANCPARENTAL AUTHORITY OVER PARENTS IS PRESENT (7) CA	0.50 OF 8	255	TILT TOWARD BEING THOSE WHERE GRANDPARENTAL AUTHCRITY OVER PARENTS IS ABSENT (26) DA	0.88 OF 24	4 3 4 21 XSQ= 2.99 PHI= 0.306 EP = 0.0469
277	DRIFT TCWARD BEING THCSE WHERE THE STATUS OF WCMEN IS INFERICR CR SUBJECTEC (14) LWS	0.64 OF 11	277	DRIFT TOWARD BEING THOSE WHERE THE STATUS OF WOMEN IS NOT STRONGLY INFERIOR OR SUBJECTED (22) LWS	0.72 OF 25	7 7 4 18 XSQ= 2.72 PHI= 0.275 EP = 0.0665
284	IN ALL CASES ARE THOSE WHERE CCNTRACEPTION IS NCT PRACTICED (7) CSF	1.00 OF 3	284	DRIFT TOWARD BEING THOSE WHERE CONTRACEPTION IS PRACTICED (10) CSF	0.71 OF 14	0 10 3 4 XSQ= 2.67 PHI= -0.397 FP = 0.0515
316	TILT TCWARD BEING THCSE WHERE EXCLUSIVE MOTHER-SON SLEEPING ARRANGEMENTS LAST LESS THAN ONE YEAR (25) W-K-A	0.92 OF 12	316	TILT TOWARD BEING THOSE WHERE EXCLUSIVE MOTHER-SON SLEEPING ARRANGEMENTS LAST CNE YEAR OR LONGER (19) W-K-A	0.56 OF 32	1 18 11 14 XSQ= 6.33 PHI= -0.379 XP = 0.0119
335	DRIFT TCWARD BEING THCSE WHERE INITIAL INDULGENCE CF CEPENCENCY IS LCW (18) WNS	0.83 OF 6	335	DRIFT TOWARD BEING THOSE WHERE INITIAL INDULGENCE CF DEPENDENCY IS HIGH (20) WNS	0.59 OF 32	1 19 5 13 XSQ= 2.18 PHI= -0.240 EP = 0.0828
354	DRIFT TCWARD BEING THCSE WHERE THE CHILD'S INFERREC ANXIETY OVER PERFORMANCE CF CBECIENT BEHAVIOR IS LCW (37) B-B-C	0.75 OF 16	354	DRIFT TOWARD BEING THCSE WHERE THE CHILD'S INFERRED ANXIETY OVER PERFORMANCE OF OBEDIENT BEHAVIOR IS HIGH (36) B-B-C	0.56 CF 57	4 32 12 25 XSQ= 3.68 PHI= -0.225 XP = 0.0550

No.		No.		
368	TILT TOWARD BEING THOSE 0.89 OF 9 WHERE DISSOCIATION OF THE SEXES AT ADOLESCENCE IS LOW (21) JKH	368	TILT TOWARD BEING THOSE 0.56 OF 27 WHERE DISSOCIATION OF THE SEXES AT ADOLESCENCE IS HIGH OR MEDIUM (16) JKH	1 15 8 12 XSQ= 3.75 PHI= -0.323 EP = 0.0260
369	LEAN TOWARD BEING THOSE 0.60 OF 15 WHERE BOTH DISSOCIATION OF THE SEXES AT ADOLESCENCE, AND CUSTOMS OF INITIATION AT ADOLESCENCE, ARE ABSENT (15) JKH	369	LEAN TOWARD BEING THOSE 0.85 OF 41 WHERE DISSOCIATION OF THE SEXES AT ADOLESCENCE, OR CUSTOMS OF INITIATION AT ADOLESCENCE, ARE PRESENT (42) JKH	6 35 9 6 XSQ= 9.33 PHI= -0.408 XP = 0.0023
373	TILT TOWARD BEING THOSE 0.92 OF 12 WHERE MALE INITIATION CEREMONIES AT PUBERTY ARE ABSENT (27) W-K-A	373	TILT TOWARD BEING THOSE 0.50 OF 32 WHERE MALE INITIATION CEREMONIES AT PUBERTY ARE PRESENT (17) W-K-A	1 16 11 16 XSQ= 4.75 PHI= -0.329 XP = 0.0292
382	TILT TOWARD BEING THOSE 0.63 OF 24 WHERE FEMALE INITIATION RITES ARE ABSENT (27) JKB	382	TILT TOWARD BEING THOSE 0.70 OF 40 WHERE FEMALE INITIATION RITES ARE PRESENT (38) JKB	9 28 15 12 XSQ= 5.23 PHI= -0.286 XP = 0.0222
391	TEND TO BE THOSE 0.68 OF 71 WHERE PREMARITAL SEX RELATIONS ARE STRONGLY PUNISHED AND IN FACT RARE, OR WEAKLY PUNISHED AND IN FACT NOT RARE (89) JTW,EA	391	TEND TO BE THOSE 0.62 OF 105 WHERE PREMARITAL SEX RELATIONS ARE PUNISHED ONLY IF PREGNANCY RESULTS, OR FREELY PERMITTED (90) JTW,EA	48 40 23 65 XSQ= 13.60 PHI= 0.278 XP = 0.0002
405	DRIFT TOWARD BEING THOSE 0.83 OF 12 WHERE EXPLANATIONS OF ILLNESS OF A DEPENDENCE NATURE ARE PRESENT (34) W-C	405	DRIFT TOWARD BEING THOSE 0.51 OF 49 WHERE EXPLANATIONS OF ILLNESS OF A DEPENDENCE NATURE ARE ABSENT (27) W-C	10 24 2 25 XSQ= 3.32 PHI= 0.233 XP = 0.0683
426	LEAN MORE TOWARD BEING THOSE 0.73 OF 91 WHERE A HIGH GOD IS PRESENT (156) GES,EA	426	LEAN LESS TOWARD BEING THOSE 0.53 OF 166 WHERE A HIGH GOD IS PRESENT (156) GES,EA	66 88 25 78 XSQ= 8.53 PHI= 0.182 XP = 0.0035
427	TILT TOWARD BEING THOSE 0.68 OF 66 WHERE A HIGH GOD, IF PRESENT, IS ACTIVE, RATHER THAN INACTIVE (87) GES,EA	427	TILT TOWARD BEING THOSE 0.53 OF 88 WHERE A HIGH GOD, IF PRESENT, IS INACTIVE, RATHER THAN ACTIVE (69) GES,EA	45 41 21 47 XSQ= 6.28 PHI= 0.202 XP = 0.0122
450	DRIFT LESS TOWARD BEING THOSE 0.58 OF 33 WHERE THE OBSERVATION OF FOOD TABOOS IS HIGH OR MEDIUM, RATHER THAN LOW (60) JRL	450	DRIFT MORE TOWARD BEING THOSE 0.77 OF 53 WHERE THE OBSERVATION OF FOOD TABOOS IS HIGH OR MEDIUM, RATHER THAN LOW (60) JRL	19 41 14 12 XSQ= 2.89 PHI= -0.183 XP = 0.0889

454	DRIFT TOWARD BEING THOSE 0.86 OF 7 WHERE THE OBJECTIVE OF THE INDIVIDUAL'S CONTACT WITH THE DIVINE IS CONDUCIVE TO THE DEVELOPMENT OF THE INDIVIDUAL'S NEED TO ACHIEVE (18) DCM	454	DRIFT TOWARD BEING THOSE 0.59 OF 29 WHERE THE OBJECTIVE OF THE INDIVIDUAL'S CONTACT WITH THE DIVINE IS NOT CONDUCIVE TO THE DEVELOPMENT OF THE INDIVIDUAL'S NEED TO ACHIEVE (18) DCM	6 12 1 17 XSQ= 2.84 PHI= 0.281 EP = 0.0877
458	TILT LESS TOWARD BEING THOSE 0.58 OF 60 WHERE GAMES, IF PRESENT, DO NOT INCLUDE GAMES OF STRATEGY (119) R-A-B,EA	458	TILT MORE TOWARD BEING THOSE 0.75 OF 108 WHERE GAMES, IF PRESENT, DO NOT INCLUDE GAMES OF STRATEGY (119) R-A-B,EA	25 27 35 81 XSQ= 4.26 PHI= 0.159 XP = 0.0389
468	DRIFT TOWARD BEING THOSE 0.50 OF 20 WHERE CONTACT WITH OTHER CULTURES IS FREQUENT, RATHER THAN REGULAR OR IRREGULAR (17) JMH	468	DRIFT TOWARD BEING THOSE 0.79 OF 34 WHERE CONTACT WITH OTHER CULTURES IS REGULAR OR IRREGULAR, RATHER THAN FREQUENT (37) JMH	10 7 10 27 XSQ= 3.78 PHI= 0.265 XP = 0.0519

****

105 CULTURES
WHERE CLASS STRATIFICATICN
BASED ON CCCUPATICNAL STATUS
IS PRESENT (43)

105 CULTURES
WHERE CLASS STRATIFICATION
BASED ON OCCUPATIONAL STATUS
IS ABSENT (340)

BACKGROUND ON PAGE 88

SUBJECT ONLY

43 IN LEFT CCLUMN

AMERICANS	AZTEC	BASQUES	BENGALI	BHIL	BRAZILIANS	BULGARIANS	BURMESE	BURUSHO	CAMBODIANS
COORG	CZECHS	DUTCH	EGYPTIANS	INCA	IRISH	JAPANESE	JAVANESE	KERALA	KHASI
KOREANS	MALAYS	MAYA	MIN CHINESE	MINCHIA	MOSSI	NUPE	PATHAN	PORTUGUESE	REGEIBAT
ROMANS	RUNDI	SERBS	SHILLUK	SONGHAI	TAMIL	THAI	TIBETANS	TIGRINYA	VIETNAMESE
WALLCONS	WOLCF	YORUBA							

340 IN RIGHT CCLUMN

ABIPCN	ABCR	AINU	AJIE	AKHA	ALACALUF	ALBANIANS	ALCRESE	AMBA	ANCAMANESE
APINAYE	ARANDA	ARAPESH	ARAUCANIANS	ASHANTI	ATAYAL	ATSUGEWI	AWEIKOMA	AYMARA	AZANDE
BABWA	BACAIRI	BAJUN	BALINESE	BAMBARA	BAMILEKE	BANDA	BARABRA	BARI	BASSERI
BATAK	BAYA	BEJA	BELU	BEMBA	BERGDAMA	BETE	BIRIFOR	BLACK CARIB	BOERS
BORORO	BOTOCUDO	BOZO	BUCUMA	BURYAT	CADUVEO	CAGABA	CALLINAGO	CAMAYURA	CAMBA
CARAJA	CARIB	CAYAPA	CHAGGA	CHAMACOCO	CHENCHU	CHEREMIS	CHERKESS	CHEROKEE	CHEYENNE
CHIBCHA	CHIR-APACHE	CHOCO	CHOROTI	CHORTI	CHUKCHEE	COCHITI	COMANCHE	COPR ESKIMO	CREE
CREEK	CROW	CUNA	DAGUR	DARD	DELAWARE	DIEGUENO	DIERI	DILLING	DOBUANS
DOGON	DORCBC	DUSUN	ELLICE	ENGA	EYAK	FANG	FON	FOX	FUTAJALONKE
GANDA	GARC	GILBERTESE	GILYAK	GISU	GOAJIRO	GOND	GRCS VENTRE	GUAHIBO	GUATO
GURE	HAIDA	HANC	HANUNOO	HASANIA	HASINAI	HAVASUPAI	HAWAIIANS	HAZARA	HEBREWS
HEHE	HERERC	HC	HUICHOL	HUKUNDIKA	HURON	HUTSUL	IBAN	ICELANDERS	IFUGAO
ILA	INGALIK	INGASSANA	IRAQW	JEMEZ	JIVARO	JUKUN	KABYLE	KACHIN	KALMYK
KAPAUKU	KAREN	KARIERA	KASKA	KATAB	KAZAK	KERAKI	KET	KHALKA	KHEVSUR
KIKUYU	KICW-APACHE	KISSI	KOHISTANI	KONSO	KORYAK	KPE	KUBA	KUNG	KURTATCHI
KUTENAI	KWAKIUTL	LAKALAI	LAKHER	LAMBA	LAMET	LANGO	LAPPS	LAU	LEPCHA
LESU	LHCTA NAGA	LIFU	LOLO	LOZI	LUBA	LUO	MACASSARESE	MAGUZAWA	MAM
MAMBILA	MAMVU	MANCHU	MANDAN	MANGAIANS	MANIHIKI	MANUS	MAORI	MARGI	MARICOPA
MARQUESANS	MARSHALLESE	MASAI	MATACO	MATAKAM	MBUGWE	MBUNDU	MBUTI	MENDE	MENTAWEI
MERINA	MIAMI	MIAC	MINANGKABAU	MISKITO	MIWOK	MNONG GAR	MONGO	MONGUOR	MOTA
MOTILON	MUNDURUCU	MURINBATA	MURNGIN	MZAB	NABESNA	NAMA	NAMBICUARA	NANDI	NASKAPI
NATCHEZ	NAVAHO	NGONI	NICOBARESE	NOMLAKI	NUER	NUNIVAK	NURI	NYAKYUSA	NYANEKA
NYARO	NYCRO	OJIBWA	OKINAWANS	OMAHA	ONA	ONTONG-JAVA	PAIWAN	PALAUANS	PALIKUR
PAPAGO	PARAUJANC	PAWNEE	PENDE	PENOBSCOT	PONAPEANS	POPOLUCA	PUKAPUKA	PURARI	PURUM
RARCIANS	RIFFIANS	ROTINESE	ROTUMANS	RWALA	SAGADA	SAMOANS	SAMOYED	SANCAWE	SANPOIL
SANTAL	SARAMACCA	SARSI	SELUNG	SEMANG	SEMINOLE	SENIANG	SERI	SHERENTE	SHLUH
SINDHI	SIRIONC	SIUAI	SIWANS	SOMALI	SOTHO	SUBANUN	SWAZI	SYRIANS	TAGBANUA
TALAMANCA	TALLENSI	TANALA	TANIMBARESE	TAOS	TAPIRAPE	TARAHUMARA	TAREUMIUT	TEHUELCHE	TENDA
TENETEHARA	TENINO	TERA	TERENA	TESO	TETON	THONGA	TIKOPIA	TIMBIRA	TIMUCUA
TIV	TIWI	TCCA	TOKELAU	TOLOWA	TORAJA	TRISTAN	TROBRIAND	TRUKESE	TRUMAI
TSHIMSHIAN	TUBATULABAL	TUCANO	TUCUNA	TUNEBO	TUPINAMBA	TURKANA	TURKMEN	TWANA	ULAWANS

UTE	VEDDA	VENDA	WAICA	WANTOAT	WAPISHANA	WAROPEN	WARRAU	WASHO	WICHITA
WIKMUNKAN	WINNEBAGO	WITOTO	WOGEO	WOLEAIANS	WUTE	YABARANA	YAGUA	YAHGAN	YAKO
YAKUT	YAO	YAPESE	YARURO	YOKUTS	YOMBE	YUKAGHIR	YUKI	YUROK	ZUNI

17 EXCLUDED BECAUSE UNASCERTAINED

4	TEND LESS TO BE THOSE LOCATED OUTSIDE OF THE CIRCUM-MEDITERRANEAN (355)	0.63 OF 43	4	TEND MORE TO BE THOSE LOCATED OUTSIDE OF THE CIRCUM-MEDITERRANEAN (355)	0.92 OF 340	16 27 27 313 XSQ= 29.94 PHI= 0.280 XP = 0.0000
5	TEND LESS TO BE THOSE LOCATED OUTSIDE OF EAST EURASIA (330)	0.58 OF 43	5	TEND MORE TO BE THOSE LOCATED OUTSIDE OF EAST EURASIA (330)	0.86 OF 340	18 47 25 293 XSQ= 19.35 PHI= 0.225 XP = 0.0000
6	LEAN MORE TOWARD BEING THOSE LOCATED OUTSIDE OF THE INSULAR PACIFIC (330)	0.98 OF 43	6	LEAN LESS TOWARD BEING THOSE LOCATED OUTSIDE OF THE INSULAR PACIFIC (330)	0.80 OF 340	1 67 42 273 XSQ= 6.75 PHI= -0.133 XP = 0.0094
8	TILT MORE TOWARD BEING THOSE LOCATED OUTSIDE OF NORTH AMERICA (330)	0.98 OF 43	8	TILT LESS TOWARD BEING THOSE LOCATED OUTSIDE OF NORTH AMERICA (330)	0.81 OF 340	1 66 42 274 XSQ= 6.58 PHI= -0.131 XP = 0.0103
9	DRIFT MORE TOWARD BEING THOSE LOCATED OUTSIDE OF SOUTH AMERICA (335)	0.95 OF 43	9	DRIFT LESS TOWARD BEING THOSE LOCATED OUTSIDE OF SOUTH AMERICA (335)	0.83 OF 340	2 59 41 281 XSQ= 3.70 PHI= -0.098 XP = 0.0544
16	LEAN MORE TOWARD BEING THOSE WHERE THE LATITUDE IS TEN DEGREES OR GREATER (277)	0.88 OF 43	16	LEAN LESS TOWARD BEING THOSE WHERE THE LATITUDE IS TEN DEGREES OR GREATER (277)	0.66 OF 340	38 226 5 114 XSQ= 7.56 PHI= 0.140 XP = 0.0060
44	TEND MORE TO BE THOSE WHERE SETTLEMENTS ARE FIXED (222)	0.95 OF 37	44	TEND LESS TO BE THOSE WHERE SETTLEMENTS ARE FIXED (222)	0.63 OF 285	35 180 2 105 XSQ= 13.20 PHI= 0.203 XP = 0.0003

46	LEAN MORE TOWARD BEING THOSE OTHER THAN WHERE SETTLEMENTS ARE NON-FIXED AND MOVEMENT IS NOMADIC (260)	0.97 OF 37	46	LEAN LESS TOWARD BEING THOSE OTHER THAN WHERE SETTLEMENTS ARE NON-FIXED AND MOVEMENT IS NOMADIC (260)	0.75 OF 285	1 70 36 215 XSQ= 7.88 PHI= -0.156 XP = 0.0050
51	TEND MORE TO BE THOSE WHERE SUBSISTENCE IS PRIMARILY BY FOOD PRODUCTION -- I. E., AGRICULTURE OR HUSBANDRY -- RATHER THAN BY GATHERING (253)	0.98 OF 43	51	TEND LESS TO BE THOSE WHERE SUBSISTENCE IS PRIMARILY BY FOOD PRODUCTION -- I. E., AGRICULTURE OR HUSBANDRY -- RATHER THAN BY GATHERING (253)	0.57 OF 340	42 194 1 146 XSQ= 24.94 PHI= 0.255 XP = 0.0000
53	TEND TO BE THOSE WHERE FOOD PRODUCTION IS BY INTENSIVE AGRICULTURE, RATHER THAN BY SIMPLE AGRICULTURE OR INCIPIENT FOOD PRODUCTION (91)	0.81 OF 36	53	TEND TO BE THOSE WHERE FOOD PRODUCTION IS BY SIMPLE AGRICULTURE OR INCIPIENT FOOD PRODUCTION, RATHER THAN BY INTENSIVE AGRICULTURE (147)	0.70 OF 192	29 57 7 135 XSQ= 31.26 PHI= 0.370 XP = 0.
55	TEND TO BE THOSE WHERE FOOD PRODUCTION IS BY INTENSIVE AGRICULTURE, RATHER THAN BY SIMPLE AGRICULTURE (91)	0.83 OF 35	55	TEND TO BE THOSE WHERE FOOD PRODUCTION IS BY SIMPLE AGRICULTURE, RATHER THAN BY INTENSIVE AGRICULTURE (101)	0.61 OF 147	29 57 6 90 XSQ= 20.31 PHI= 0.334 XP = 0.0000
62	LEAN MORE TOWARD BEING THOSE WHERE HUSBANDRY OF SOME KIND IS PRESENT (228)	0.81 OF 43	62	LEAN LESS TOWARD BEING THOSE WHERE HUSBANDRY OF SOME KIND IS PRESENT (228)	0.54 OF 340	35 185 8 155 XSQ= 10.29 PHI= 0.164 XP = 0.0013
63	TEND MORE TO BE THOSE WHERE HUSBANDRY, IF PRESENT, IS PRINCIPALLY IN THE FORM OF BOVINE, EQUINE, CAMEL-LIKE, OR DEER-LIKE ANIMALS, RATHER THAN PIGS, SHEEP, OR GOATS (152)	0.94 OF 35	63	TEND LESS TO BE THOSE WHERE HUSBANDRY, IF PRESENT, IS PRINCIPALLY IN THE FORM OF BOVINE, EQUINE, CAMEL-LIKE, OR DEER-LIKE ANIMALS, RATHER THAN PIGS, SHEEP, OR GOATS (152)	0.62 OF 183	33 113 2 70 XSQ= 12.63 PHI= 0.241 XP = 0.0004
71	IN ALL CASES ARE THOSE WHERE METAL WORKING IS PRESENT (98)	1.00 OF 24	71	TEND TO BE THOSE WHERE METAL WORKING IS ABSENT (153)	0.68 OF 222	24 71 0 151 XSQ= 39.45 PHI= 0.400 XP = 0.
73	TEND TO BE THOSE WHERE WEAVING IS PRESENT (118)	0.88 OF 24	73	TEND TO BE THOSE WHERE WEAVING IS ABSENT (130)	0.57 OF 219	21 94 3 125 XSQ= 15.50 PHI= 0.253 XP = 0.0001
74	IN ALL CASES ARE THOSE WHERE POTTERY IS PRESENT (145)	1.00 OF 22	74	TEND LESS TO BE THOSE WHERE POTTERY IS PRESENT (145)	0.56 OF 212	22 119 0 93 XSQ= 14.24 PHI= 0.247 XP = 0.0002

77	LEAN TOWARD BEING THOSE 0.75 OF 8 WHERE THE WRITING SYSTEM IS ALPHABETIC-OR-PHCNETIC, RATHER THAN BEING MNEMONIC CR ABSENT (15) JMH	77	LEAN TOWARD BEING THOSE 0.80 OF 46 WHERE THE WRITING SYSTEM IS MNEMONIC OR ABSENT, RATHER THAN BEING ALPHABETIC-OR-PHONETIC (39) JMH	6 9 2 37 XSQ= 7.86 PHI= 0.381 XP = 0.0051
79	TEND TC BE THCSE 0.59 OF 34 WHERE A CITY IS PRESENT (23)	79	TEND TO BE THOSE 0.99 OF 185 WHERE NO CITY IS PRESENT (201)	20 2 14 183 XSQ= 99.68 PHI= 0.675 XP = 0.
80	TEND TC BE THCSE 0.74 OF 34 WHERE A CITY CR TCWN IS PRESENT (39)	80	TEND TO BE THOSE 0.94 CF 185 WHERE NO CITY OR TOWN IS PRESENT (185)	25 12 9 173 XSQ= 87.23 PHI= 0.631 XP = 0.
81	TEND TC BE THCSE 0.88 OF 34 WHERE A CITY CR TOWN IS PRESENT, OR THE AVERAGE COMMUNITY SIZE IS 200 CR GREATER (89)	81	TEND TO BE THOSE 0.69 OF 185 WHERE NO CITY OR TOWN IS PRESENT, AND THE AVERAGE COMMUNITY SIZE IS SMALLER THAN 200 (135)	30 57 4 128 XSQ= 37.19 PHI= 0.412 XP = 0.
82	IN ALL CASES ARE THCSE 1.00 OF 34 WHERE A CITY CR TOWN IS PRESENT, OR THE AVERAGE COMMUNITY SIZE IS FIFTY OR GREATER (178)	82	LEAN LESS TOWARD BEING THOSE 0.76 OF 185 WHERE A CITY OR TOWN IS PRESENT, OR THE AVERAGE COMMUNITY SIZE IS FIFTY OR GREATER (178)	34 141 0 44 XSQ= 8.69 PHI= 0.199 XP = 0.0032
83	DRIFT TOWARD BEING THCSE 0.56 OF 9 WHERE, WITH NC CITY ANC NC TOWN PRESENT, THE AVERAGE COMMUNITY SIZE IS BETWEEN 200 AND 999, RATHER THAN SMALLER THAN 200 (45)	83	DRIFT TOWARD BEING THOSE 0.76 OF 168 WHERE, WITH NO CITY AND NC TOWN PRESENT, THE AVERAGE COMMUNITY SIZE IS SMALLER THAN 200, RATHER THAN BETWEEN 200 AND 999 (135)	5 40 4 128 XSQ= 3.02 PHI= 0.131 XP = 0.0822
84	TEND TC BE THCSE 0.86 OF 29 WHERE THE LEVEL OF PCLITICAL INTEGRATION IS THE LARGE STATE (42) GPM	84	TEND TO BE THOSE 0.95 CF 268 WHERE THE LEVEL OF POLITICAL INTEGRATION IS THE LITTLE STATE, THE MINIMAL STATE, THE AUTONOMOUS COMMUNITY, CR THE FAMILY (262) GPM	25 14 4 254 XSQ= 143.43 PHI= 0.695 XP = 0.
85	TEND TO BE THOSE 0.93 OF 29 WHERE THE LEVEL OF POLITICAL INTEGRATION IS THE LARGE STATE, CR THE LITTLE STATE (70) GPM	85	TEND TO BE THOSE 0.85 OF 268 WHERE THE LEVEL OF POLITICAL INTEGRATION IS THE MINIMAL STATE, THE AUTONOMOUS COMMUNITY, CR THE FAMILY (234) GPM	27 40 2 228 XSQ= 87.13 PHI= 0.542 XP = 0.
86	IN ALL CASES ARE THCSE 1.00 OF 29 WHERE THE LEVEL OF POLITICAL INTEGRATION IS THE LARGE STATE, THE LITTLE STATE, OR THE MINIMAL STATE (148) GPM	86	TEND TO BE THOSE 0.58 CF 268 WHERE THE LEVEL OF POLITICAL INTEGRATION IS THE AUTONOMOUS COMMUNITY, OR THE FAMILY (156) GPM	29 113 0 155 XSQ= 32.80 PHI= 0.332 XP = 0.

88	TEND TC BE THCSE WHERE, IF A HEACMANSHIP IS PRESENT, SUCCESSION IS NCN-HEREDITARY (106)	0.69 OF 29	88	TEND TO BE THOSE WHERE, IF A HEADMANSHIP IS PRESENT, SUCCESSION IS HEREDITARY (165)	0.65 CF 234	20 81 9 153 XSQ= 11.46 PHI= 0.209 XP = 0.0007
91	IN ALL CASES ARE THOSE WHERE SOCIETAL COMPLEXITY IS HIGH (18) F-W	1.00 OF 4	91	TILT TOWARD BEING THOSE WHERE SOCIETAL COMPLEXITY IS LOW (22) F-W	0.61 OF 36	4 14 0 22 XSQ= 3.24 PHI= 0.285 EP = 0.0335
94	TEND TO BE THOSE WHERE THE HIERARCHY OF NATIONAL JURISDICTION HAS FOUR CR THREE LEVELS (34) GES,EA	0.53 OF 36	94	TEND TO BE THOSE WHERE THE HIERARCHY OF NATIONAL JURISDICTION HAS TWO, ONE, OR NO LEVELS (296) GES,EA	0.95 CF 284	19 14 17 270 XSQ= 74.00 PHI= 0.481 XP = 0.
95	TEND TC BE THOSE WHERE THE HIERARCHY OF NATICNAL JURISDICTICN HAS FOUR, THREE, CR TWC LEVELS (76) GES,EA	0.83 OF 36	95	TEND TO BE THOSE WHERE THE HIERARCHY OF NATIONAL JURISDICTICN HAS ONE OR NO LEVELS (254) GES,EA	0.85 OF 284	30 44 6 240 XSQ= 78.94 PHI= 0.497 XP = 0.
96	IN ALL CASES ARE THCSE WHERE THE HIERARCHY OF NATICNAL JURISDICTICN HAS FOUR, THREE, TWC OR ONE LEVEL (174) GES,EA	1.00 OF 36	96	TEND TO BE THOSE WHERE THE HIERARCHY OF NATIONAL JURISDICTION HAS NO LEVELS (156) GES,EA	0.55 CF 284	36 129 0 155 XSQ= 35.95 PHI= 0.335 XP = 0.
109	TEND LESS TO BE THCSE WHERE CASTES ARE ABSENT (317)	0.54 OF 37	109	TEND MORE TO BE THOSE WHERE CASTES ARE ABSENT (317)	0.91 OF 321	17 29 20 292 XSQ= 37.14 PHI= 0.322 XP = 0.
110	DRIFT TCWARD BEING THCSE WHERE SLAVERY IS PRESENT (163)	0.57 OF 42	11C	DRIFT TOWARD BEING THOSE WHERE SLAVERY IS ABSENT (218)	0.59 OF 330	24 135 18 195 XSQ= 3.38 PHI= 0.095 XP = 0.0661
116	IN ALL CASES ARE THCSE WHERE OCCUPATIONAL SPECIALIZATION IS FULL-TIME, WHETHER OR NCT FOR SURPLUS PRCDUCTICN (20) JMH	1.00 OF 8	116	TEND TO BE THOSE WHERE OCCUPATIONAL SPECIALIZATICN IS PART-TIME ONLY (34) JMH	0.74 OF 46	8 12 0 34 XSQ= 12.95 PHI= 0.490 XP = 0.0003
118	IN ALL CASES ARE THOSE WHERE THE PERCENTAGE CF OCCUPATIONS THAT ARE SPECIALIZED IS HIGH OR MEDIUM (24) WME	1.00 OF 6	118	TILT TOWARD BEING THOSE WHERE THE PERCENTAGE CF CCCUPATICNS THAT ARE SPECIALIZED IS LOW (25) WME	0.58 CF 43	6 18 0 25 XSQ= 4.99 PHI= 0.319 XP = 0.0256

128	TILT TOWARD BEING THOSE WHERE, IF SUBSISTENCE IS PRIMARILY BY AGRICULTURE, THE WORK IS MAINLY DONE BY MALES (40)	0.85 OF 13	128	TILT TOWARD BEING THOSE WHERE, IF SUBSISTENCE IS PRIMARILY BY AGRICULTURE, THE WORK IS MAINLY DONE BY FEMALES (37)	0.56 OF 61	11 27 2 34 XSQ= 5.46 PHI= 0.272 XP = 0.0194
130	DRIFT TOWARD BEING THOSE WHERE LEATHER WORKING IS MAINLY DONE BY MALES (39)	0.86 OF 7	130	DRIFT TOWARD BEING THOSE WHERE LEATHER WORKING IS MAINLY DONE BY FEMALES (45)	0.59 OF 75	6 31 1 44 XSQ= 3.46 PHI= 0.205 XP = 0.0629
132	IN ALL CASES ARE THOSE WHERE ECONOMIC EXCHANGE INVOLVES THE USE OF MONEY (37) JMH	1.00 OF 8	132	DRIFT LESS TOWARD BEING THOSE WHERE ECONOMIC EXCHANGE INVOLVES THE USE OF MONEY (37) JMH	0.63 OF 46	8 29 0 17 XSQ= 2.77 PHI= 0.227 XP = 0.0959
152	IN ALL CASES ARE THOSE WHERE THE DIFFERENTIATION OF THE JURIDICAL AGENCY FROM THE MEDICAL AGENCY IS HIGH (10) MJ	1.00 OF 5	152	TILT TOWARD BEING THOSE WHERE THE DIFFERENTIATION OF THE JURIDICAL AGENCY FROM THE MEDICAL AGENCY IS LOW (10) MJ	0.67 OF 15	5 5 0 10 XSQ= 4.27 PHI= 0.462 EP = 0.0325
163	IN ALL CASES ARE THOSE WHERE THE EMPHASIS ON INDIVIDUAL VOLITION AS THE CAUSE OF CRIME IS HIGH (7) MJ	1.00 OF 5	163	LEAN TOWARD BEING THOSE WHERE THE EMPHASIS ON INDIVIDUAL VOLITION AS THE CAUSE OF CRIME IS LOW (10) MJ	0.83 OF 12	5 2 0 10 XSQ= 6.97 PHI= 0.640 EP = 0.0034
164	IN ALL CASES ARE THOSE WHERE THE EMPHASIS ON INDIVIDUAL VOLITION AS THE CAUSE OR SOURCE OF ILLNESS IS LOW (9) MJ	1.00 OF 5	164	TILT TOWARD BEING THOSE WHERE THE EMPHASIS ON INDIVIDUAL VOLITION AS THE CAUSE OR SOURCE OF ILLNESS IS HIGH (9) MJ	0.69 OF 13	0 9 5 4 XSQ= 4.43 PHI= -0.496 EP = 0.0294
175	DRIFT MORE TOWARD BEING THOSE WHERE THE COMMUNITY IS 'KIN-HETEROGENEOUS,' I. E. OTHER THAN A CLAN COMMUNITY OR A DEME (260)	0.81 OF 43	175	DRIFT LESS TOWARD BEING THOSE WHERE THE COMMUNITY IS 'KIN-HETEROGENEOUS,' I. E. OTHER THAN A CLAN COMMUNITY OR A DEME (260)	0.66 OF 324	8 109 35 215 XSQ= 3.29 PHI= -0.095 XP = 0.0697
176	DRIFT MORE TOWARD BEING THOSE WHERE THE COMMUNITY IS OTHER THAN A CLAN-COMMUNITY OR A COMMUNITY STRUCTURED OR SEGMENTED ON A CLAN BASIS (213)	0.70 OF 43	176	DRIFT LESS TOWARD BEING THOSE WHERE THE COMMUNITY IS OTHER THAN A CLAN-COMMUNITY OR A COMMUNITY STRUCTURED OR SEGMENTED ON A CLAN BASIS (213)	0.53 OF 324	13 151 30 173 XSQ= 3.48 PHI= -0.097 XP = 0.0621
177	TILT MORE TOWARD BEING THOSE WHERE THE COMMUNITY IS OTHER THAN A SINGLE CLAN-COMMUNITY AND EXOGAMOUS (305)	0.93 OF 43	177	TILT LESS TOWARD BEING THOSE WHERE THE COMMUNITY IS OTHER THAN A SINGLE CLAN-COMMUNITY AND EXOGAMOUS (305)	0.78 OF 324	3 72 40 252 XSQ= 4.53 PHI= -0.111 XP = 0.0333

180	TILT MORE TOWARD BEING THOSE 0.84 OF 43 WHERE THE COMMUNITY IS COMMONLY NON-EXOGAMOUS, RATHER THAN EXOGAMOUS (258)	180	TILT LESS TOWARD BEING THOSE 0.65 OF 324 WHERE THE COMMUNITY IS COMMONLY NON-EXOGAMOUS, RATHER THAN EXOGAMOUS (258)	7 112 36 212 XSQ= 4.99 PHI= -0.117 XP = 0.0255
182	LEAN TOWARD BEING THOSE 0.53 OF 43 WHERE THE COMMUNITY IS STRUCTURED ON A NON-CLAN BASIS AND AGAMOUS (126)	182	LEAN TOWARD BEING THOSE 0.69 OF 324 OTHER THAN WHERE THE COMMUNITY IS STRUCTURED ON A NON-CLAN BASIS AND AGAMOUS (256)	23 99 20 225 XSQ= 7.99 PHI= 0.148 XP = 0.0047
183	IN ALL CASES ARE THOSE 1.00 OF 25 WHERE THE LARGEST NON-COGNATIC KIN GROUP IS SMALLER THAN A MOEITY, I. E., A PHRATRY OR SIB OR LINEAGE (218)	183	DRIFT LESS TOWARD BEING THOSE 0.85 OF 220 WHERE THE LARGEST NON-COGNATIC KIN GROUP IS SMALLER THAN A MOEITY, I. E., A PHRATRY OR SIB OR LINEAGE (218)	0 33 25 187 XSQ= 3.14 PHI= -0.113 XP = 0.0763
184	DRIFT MORE TOWARD BEING THOSE 0.88 OF 25 WHERE THE LARGEST NON-COGNATIC KIN GROUP IS SMALLER THAN A PHRATRY, I. E. A SIB OR LINEAGE (175)	184	DRIFT LESS TOWARD BEING THOSE 0.67 OF 220 WHERE THE LARGEST NON-COGNATIC KIN GROUP IS SMALLER THAN A PHRATRY, I. E. A SIB OR LINEAGE (175)	3 73 22 147 XSQ= 3.77 PHI= -0.124 XP = 0.0522
187	DRIFT MORE TOWARD BEING THOSE 0.95 OF 43 WHERE THE KIN GROUP IS OTHER THAN EXCLUSIVELY MATRILINEAL (344)	187	DRIFT LESS TOWARD BEING THOSE 0.85 OF 339 WHERE THE KIN GROUP IS OTHER THAN EXCLUSIVELY MATRILINEAL (344)	2 52 41 287 XSQ= 2.76 PHI= -0.085 XP = 0.0964
190	DRIFT MORE TOWARD BEING THOSE 0.92 OF 25 WHERE THE KIN GROUP IS PATRILINEAL OR DOUBLE-DESCENT, RATHER THAN MATRILINEAL (186)	190	DRIFT LESS TOWARD BEING THOSE 0.73 OF 215 WHERE THE KIN GROUP IS PATRILINEAL OR DOUBLE-DESCENT, RATHER THAN MATRILINEAL (186)	23 157 2 58 XSQ= 3.35 PHI= 0.118 XP = 0.0673
192	DRIFT LESS TOWARD BEING THOSE 0.60 OF 43 OTHER THAN WHERE THE ONLY KIN GROUP PRESENT IS A KINDRED OR ELSE BILATERAL DESCENT IS INFERRED (289)	192	DRIFT MORE TOWARD BEING THOSE 0.75 OF 340 OTHER THAN WHERE THE ONLY KIN GROUP PRESENT IS A KINDRED OR ELSE BILATERAL DESCENT IS INFERRED (289)	17 86 26 254 XSQ= 3.25 PHI= 0.092 XP = 0.0716
196	TEND MORE TO BE THOSE 0.97 OF 36 WHERE INDIVIDUAL RIGHTS IN REAL PROPERTY, AND RULES FOR INHERITANCE, ARE PRESENT (194)	196	TEND LESS TO BE THOSE 0.64 OF 237 WHERE INDIVIDUAL RIGHTS IN REAL PROPERTY, AND RULES FOR INHERITANCE, ARE PRESENT (194)	35 152 1 85 XSQ= 14.36 PHI= 0.229 XP = 0.0002
197	DRIFT LESS TOWARD BEING THOSE 0.74 OF 35 WHERE RULES FOR THE INHERITANCE OF REAL PROPERTY, IF PRESENT, FAVOR EITHER THE MALE HEIR OR LINE, OR THE FEMALE HEIR OR LINE (165)	197	DRIFT MORE TOWARD BEING THOSE 0.88 OF 152 WHERE RULES FOR THE INHERITANCE OF REAL PROPERTY, IF PRESENT, FAVOR EITHER THE MALE HEIR OR LINE, OR THE FEMALE HEIR OR LINE (165)	26 133 9 19 XSQ= 2.93 PHI= -0.125 XP = 0.0868

213	TILT TOWARD BEING THOSE 0.67 OF 39 WHERE FIRST COUSIN MARRIAGE IS PERMITTED (172)	213	TILT TOWARD BEING THOSE 0.55 OF 316 WHERE FIRST COUSIN MARRIAGE IS NOT PERMITTED (198)	26 141 13 175 XSQ= 5.92 PHI= 0.129 XP = 0.0150
234	TEND TO BE THOSE 0.82 OF 34 WHERE THE COUSIN TERMINOLOGY IS OF ESKIMO OR HAWAIIAN TYPE, RATHER THAN CROW, OMAHA, OR IROQUOIS TYPE (170)	234	TEND TO BE THOSE 0.52 OF 273 WHERE THE COUSIN TERMINOLOGY IS OF CROW, OMAHA, OR IROQUOIS TYPE, RATHER THAN ESKIMO OR HAWAIIAN TYPE (152)	6 141 28 132 XSQ= 12.68 PHI= -0.203 XP = 0.0004
236	DRIFT MORE TOWARD BEING THOSE 0.67 OF 43 WHERE THE FAMILY IS OF AN EXTENDED TYPE, RATHER THAN AN INDEPENDENT TYPE (213)	236	DRIFT LESS TOWARD BEING THOSE 0.52 OF 339 WHERE THE FAMILY IS OF AN EXTENDED TYPE, RATHER THAN AN INDEPENDENT TYPE (213)	29 177 14 162 XSQ= 2.98 PHI= 0.088 XP = 0.0845
240	DRIFT MORE TOWARD BEING THOSE 0.79 OF 29 WHERE THE FAMILY, IF EXTENDED, IS SMALL OR STEM, RATHER THAN LARGE (135)	240	DRIFT LESS TOWARD BEING THOSE 0.60 OF 177 WHERE THE FAMILY, IF EXTENDED, IS SMALL OR STEM, RATHER THAN LARGE (135)	6 71 23 106 XSQ= 3.23 PHI= -0.125 XP = 0.0723
241	TEND LESS TO BE THOSE 0.66 OF 29 WHERE THE FAMILY, IF EXTENDED, IS LARGE OR SMALL, RATHER THAN STEM (187)	241	TEND MORE TO BE THOSE 0.92 OF 177 WHERE THE FAMILY, IF EXTENDED, IS LARGE OR SMALL, RATHER THAN STEM (187)	19 162 10 15 XSQ= 13.46 PHI= -0.256 XP = 0.0002
242	TEND LESS TO BE THOSE 0.55 OF 42 WHERE MARRIAGE IS COMMONLY OR OCCASIONALLY POLYGYNOUS, RATHER THAN MONOGAMOUS (314)	242	TEND MORE TO BE THOSE 0.82 OF 337 WHERE MARRIAGE IS COMMONLY OR OCCASIONALLY POLYGYNOUS, RATHER THAN MONOGAMOUS (314)	23 278 19 59 XSQ= 15.91 PHI= -0.205 XP = 0.0001
263	LEAN TOWARD BEING THOSE 0.63 OF 43 WHERE WIVES ARE OBTAINED BY RELATIVELY EASY MEANS, NAMELY BY TOKEN BRIDE-PRICE, GIFT EXCHANGE, ABSENCE OF ANY CONSIDERATION, OR RECEIPT OF DOWRY (162)	263	LEAN TOWARD BEING THOSE 0.62 OF 336 WHERE WIVES ARE OBTAINED BY RELATIVELY DIFFICULT MEANS, NAMELY BY BRIDE-PRICE, BRIDE-SERVICE, OR EXCHANGING A FEMALE RELATIVE (233)	16 207 27 129 XSQ= 8.39 PHI= -0.149 XP = 0.0038
272	TILT TOWARD BEING THOSE 0.88 OF 8 WHERE THE DIVORCE RATE IS LOW (28) CA	272	TILT TOWARD BEING THOSE 0.57 OF 49 WHERE THE DIVORCE RATE IS HIGH (29) CA	1 28 7 21 XSQ= 3.84 PHI= -0.260 XP = 0.0499
370	TILT MORE TOWARD BEING THOSE 0.81 OF 31 WHERE THE SEGREGATION OF ADOLESCENT BOYS IS ABSENT (148)	370	TILT LESS TOWARD BEING THOSE 0.59 OF 205 WHERE THE SEGREGATION OF ADOLESCENT BOYS IS ABSENT (148)	6 85 25 120 XSQ= 4.66 PHI= -0.141 XP = 0.0308

390	TEND TO BE THOSE WHERE PREMARITAL SEX RELATIONS ARE STRONGLY PUNISHED AND IN FACT RARE (47) JTW,EA	0.61 OF 23	390	TEND TO BE THOSE WHERE PREMARITAL SEX RELATIONS ARE WEAKLY PUNISHED AND IN FACT NOT RARE OR PUNISHED ONLY IF PREGNANCY RESULTS, OR FREELY PERMITTED (132) JTW,EA	0.79 OF 153	14 32 9 121 XSQ= 14.53 PHI= 0.287 XP = 0.0001
391	IN ALL CASES ARE THOSE WHERE PREMARITAL SEX RELATIONS ARE STRONGLY PUNISHED AND IN FACT RARE, OR WEAKLY PUNISHED AND IN FACT NOT RARE (89) JTW,EA	1.00 OF 23	391	TEND TO BE THOSE WHERE PREMARITAL SEX RELATIONS ARE PUNISHED ONLY IF PREGNANCY RESULTS, OR FREELY PERMITTED (90) JTW,EA	0.58 OF 153	23 65 0 88 XSQ= 24.21 PHI= 0.371 XP = 0.0000
424	IN ALL CASES ARE THOSE WHERE RELIGIOUS SPECIALISTS ARE FULL-TIME, RATHER THAN PART-TIME (21) JMH	1.00 OF 8	424	TEND TO BE THOSE WHERE RELIGIOUS SPECIALISTS ARE PART-TIME, RATHER THAN FULL-TIME (33) JMH	0.72 OF 46	8 13 0 33 XSQ= 11.89 PHI= 0.469 XP = 0.0006
426	LEAN MORE TOWARD BEING THOSE WHERE A HIGH GOD IS PRESENT (156) GES,EA	0.87 OF 30	426	LEAN LESS TOWARD BEING THOSE WHERE A HIGH GOD IS PRESENT (156) GES,EA	0.56 OF 227	26 128 4 99 XSQ= 8.89 PHI= 0.186 XP = 0.0029
427	TILT MORE TOWARD BEING THOSE WHERE A HIGH GOD, IF PRESENT, IS ACTIVE, RATHER THAN INACTIVE (87) GES,EA	0.77 OF 26	427	TILT LESS TOWARD BEING THOSE WHERE A HIGH GOD, IF PRESENT, IS ACTIVE, RATHER THAN INACTIVE (87) GES,EA	0.52 OF 128	20 66 6 62 XSQ= 4.66 PHI= 0.174 XP = 0.0310
428	TILT MORE TOWARD BEING THOSE WHERE A HIGH GOD, IF PRESENT AND ACTIVE, SUPPORTS HUMAN MORALITY, RATHER THAN NOT SUPPORTING IT (61) GES,EA	0.90 OF 20	428	TILT LESS TOWARD BEING THOSE WHERE A HIGH GOD, IF PRESENT AND ACTIVE, SUPPORTS HUMAN MORALITY, RATHER THAN NOT SUPPORTING IT (61) GES,EA	0.64 OF 66	18 42 2 24 XSQ= 3.89 PHI= 0.213 XP = 0.0487
436	IN ALL CASES ARE THOSE WHERE ACTIVE ANCESTRAL SPIRITS ARE ABSENT (11) GES	1.00 OF 2	436	DRIFT TOWARD BEING THOSE WHERE ACTIVE ANCESTRAL SPIRITS ARE PRESENT (27) GES	0.75 OF 36	0 27 2 9 XSQ= 2.18 PHI= -0.239 EP = 0.0782
444	DRIFT TOWARD BEING THOSE WHERE THE USE OF DREAMS TO SEEK AND CONTROL SUPERNATURAL POWERS IS LOW (27) RGD	0.86 OF 7	444	DRIFT TOWARD BEING THOSE WHERE THE USE OF DREAMS TO SEEK AND CONTROL SUPERNATURAL POWERS IS HIGH (28) RGD	0.56 OF 48	1 27 6 21 XSQ= 2.79 PHI= -0.225 XP = 0.0949
450	LEAN TOWARD BEING THOSE WHERE THE OBSERVATION OF FOOD TABOOS IS LOW, RATHER THAN HIGH OR MEDIUM (26) JRL	0.67 OF 15	450	LEAN TOWARD BEING THOSE WHERE THE OBSERVATION OF FOOD TABOOS IS HIGH OR MEDIUM, RATHER THAN LOW (60) JRL	0.77 OF 71	5 55 10 16 XSQ= 9.44 PHI= -0.331 XP = 0.0021

458	TEND TO BE THOSE 0.80 OF 20 WHERE GAMES, IF PRESENT, INCLUDE GAMES OF STRATEGY (52) R-A-B,EA	458	TEND TO BE THOSE 0.76 OF 148 WHERE GAMES, IF PRESENT, DO NOT INCLUDE GAMES OF STRATEGY (119) R-A-B,EA	16 36 4 112 XSQ= 23.02 PHI= 0.370 XP = 0.0000
459	DRIFT TOWARD BEING THOSE 0.70 OF 20 WHERE GAMES, IF PRESENT, INCLUDE GAMES OF CHANCE (82) R-A-B,EA	459	DRIFT TOWARD BEING THOSE 0.55 OF 148 WHERE GAMES, IF PRESENT, DO NOT INCLUDE GAMES OF CHANCE (89) R-A-B,EA	14 67 6 81 XSQ= 3.38 PHI= 0.142 XP = 0.0659
460	TILT MORE TOWARD BEING THOSE 0.85 OF 20 WHERE GAMES, IF PRESENT, ARE NOT LIMITED TO GAMES OF SKILL ONLY (104) R-A-B,EA	460	TILT LESS TOWARD BEING THOSE 0.58 OF 148 WHERE GAMES, IF PRESENT, ARE NOT LIMITED TO GAMES OF SKILL ONLY (104) R-A-B,EA	3 62 17 86 XSQ= 4.30 PHI= -0.160 XP = 0.0382
468	IN ALL CASES ARE THOSE 1.00 OF 8 WHERE CONTACT WITH OTHER CULTURES IS FREQUENT, RATHER THAN REGULAR OR IRREGULAR (17) JMH	468	TEND TO BE THOSE 0.80 OF 46 WHERE CONTACT WITH OTHER CULTURES IS REGULAR OR IRREGULAR, RATHER THAN FREQUENT (37) JMH	8 9 0 37 XSQ= 16.88 PHI= 0.559 XP = 0.0000
470	DRIFT TOWARD BEING THOSE 0.75 OF 8 WHERE INNOVATIONS ARE GENERALLY ACCEPTED (21) JMH	470	DRIFT TOWARD BEING THOSE 0.67 OF 46 WHERE INNOVATIONS ARE ACCEPTED ONLY SELECTIVELY (33) JMH	6 15 2 31 XSQ= 3.52 PHI= 0.255 XP = 0.0605

****

106 CULTURES
WHERE CLASS STRATIFICATION, IF PRESENT,
IS BASED CN WEALTH (77)

106 CULTURES
WHERE CLASS STRATIFICATION, IF PRESENT,
IS BASED ON SOMETHING OTHER THAN
WEALTH (126)

BACKGROUND ON PAGE 88

BOTH SUBJECT AND PREDICATE

....

77 IN LEFT CCLUMN

ABOR	ALCRESE	ARAUCANIANS	ATSUGEWI	AYMARA	BARABRA	BARI	BASSERI	CAGABA	CHUKCHEE
CUNA	DOGCN	DUSUN	EYAK	FANG	GARO	GILBERTESE	GISU	GOAJIRO	GOND
HASANIA	HAZARA	HEBREWS	HERERO	HUICHOL	HURON	HUTSUL	IFUGAO	ILA	INGALIK
IRAQW	KAPAUKU	KAREN	KIKUYU	KORYAK	KPE	LAKALAI	LAMET	LANGO	LAPPS
LAU	LEPCHA	LHCTA NAGA	LUO	MAM	MANCHU	MANUS	MBUGWE	MINANGKABAU	MNONG GAR
MOTA	NAMA	NOMLAKI	NUNIVAK	NURI	ONTONG-JAVA	PURUM	RIFFIANS	RWALA	SAGADA
SAMOYED	SENIANG	SIUAI	SIWANS	SOMALI	TALLENSI	TARAHUMARA	TAREUMIUT	TENINO	TOLOWA
TORAJA	TUPINAMBA	TWANA	YAKUT	YOKUTS	YUKI	YUROK			

126 IN RIGHT CCLUMN

ABIPON	AMERICANS	ASHANTI	AZANDE	AZTEC	BALINESE	BAMBARA	BAMILEKE	BASQUES	BELU
BEMBA	BENGALI	BHIL	BOERS	BRAZILIANS	BULGARIANS	BURMESE	BURUSHO	BURYAT	CAMBA
CAMBODIANS	CHAGGA	CHAMACCCO	CHEREMIS	CHERKESS	CHIBCHA	COORG	CZECHS	DARD	DUTCH
EGYPTIANS	ELLICE	FCN	FUTAJALONKE	GANDA	HAIDA	HASINAI	HAWAIIANS	HEHE	HO
ICELANDERS	INCA	IRISH	JAPANESE	JAVANESE	JUKUN	KACHIN	KAZAK	KERALA	KHALKA
KHASI	KOHISTANI	KOREANS	KUBA	KURTATCHI	KWAKIUTL	LAKHER	LIFU	LOLO	LOZI
LUBA	MACASSARESE	MAGUZAWA	MALAYS	MANGAIANS	MANIHIKI	MAORI	MARQUESANS	MARSHALLESE	MAYA
MBUNDU	MENDE	MERINA	MIN CHINESE	MINCHIA	MONGUOR	MOSSI	MZAB	NATCHEZ	NGONI
NUPE	NYANEKA	NYCRO	OKINAWANS	PAIWAN	PALAUANS	PATHAN	PAWNEE	PENDE	PONAPEANS
PORTUGUESE	REGEIBAT	ROMANS	ROTINESE	RUNDI	SAMOANS	SERBS	SHILLUK	SINDHI	SONGHAI
SOTHO	SWAZI	SYRIANS	TAGBANUA	TAMIL	TANALA	TANIMBARESE	TERA	TERENA	THAI
THONGA	TIBETANS	TIGRINYA	TIKOPIA	TIMUCUA	TROBRIAND	TSHIMSHIAN	TURKMEN	VENCA	VIETNAMESE
WALLOONS	WOLCF	WUTE	YAPESE	YOMBE	YORUBA				

180 EXCLUDED BECAUSE IRRELEVANT (SEE RIGHT COLUMN, PARAGRAPH 102)

17 EXCLUDED BECAUSE UNASCERTAINEC

----

8 LEAN LESS TOWARD BEING THOSE 0.81 OF 77
LOCATED OUTSIDE OF
NORTH AMERICA (330)

8 LEAN MORE TOWARD BEING THOSE 0.94 OF 126
LOCATED OUTSIDE OF
NORTH AMERICA (330)

15	8
62	118
XSQ=	6.95
PHI=	0.185
XP =	0.0084

11	LEAN LESS TOWARD BEING THOSE WHERE THE LATITUDE IS LESS THAN SIXTY DEGREES (385)	0.88 OF 77	11	LEAN MORE TOWARD BEING THOSE WHERE THE LATITUDE IS LESS THAN SIXTY DEGREES (385)	0.98 OF 126	9 2 68 124 XSQ= 7.65 PHI= 0.194 XP = 0.0057
33	LEAN LESS TOWARD BEING THOSE WHERE THE NATURAL ENVIRONMENT IS OTHER THAN 'VERY HARSH,' I.E., DESERT, DESERT GRASSES AND SHRUBS, TUNDRA, OR HIGH PLATEAU STEPPE (341) FWM	0.77 OF 77	33	LEAN MORE TOWARD BEING THOSE WHERE THE NATURAL ENVIRONMENT IS OTHER THAN 'VERY HARSH,' I.E., DESERT, DESERT GRASSES AND SHRUBS, TUNDRA, OR HIGH PLATEAU STEPPE (341) FWM	0.93 OF 126	18 9 59 117 XSQ= 9.56 PHI= 0.217 XP = 0.0020
44	LEAN LESS TOWARD BEING THOSE WHERE SETTLEMENTS ARE FIXED (222)	0.65 OF 69	44	LEAN MORE TOWARD BEING THOSE WHERE SETTLEMENTS ARE FIXED (222)	0.86 OF 102	45 88 24 14 XSQ= 9.38 PHI= -0.234 XP = 0.0022
46	LEAN LESS TOWARD BEING THOSE OTHER THAN WHERE SETTLEMENTS ARE NON-FIXED AND MOVEMENT IS NOMADIC (260)	0.80 OF 69	46	LEAN MORE TOWARD BEING THOSE OTHER THAN WHERE SETTLEMENTS ARE NON-FIXED AND MOVEMENT IS NOMADIC (260)	0.94 OF 102	14 6 55 96 XSQ= 6.94 PHI= 0.201 XP = 0.0084
51	LEAN LESS TOWARD BEING THOSE WHERE SUBSISTENCE IS PRIMARILY BY FOOD PRODUCTION -- I. E., AGRICULTURE OR HUSBANDRY -- RATHER THAN BY GATHERING (253)	0.69 OF 77	51	LEAN MORE TOWARD BEING THOSE WHERE SUBSISTENCE IS PRIMARILY BY FOOD PRODUCTION -- I. E., AGRICULTURE OR HUSBANDRY -- RATHER THAN BY GATHERING (253)	0.86 OF 126	53 108 24 18 XSQ= 7.31 PHI= -0.190 XP = 0.0069
71	LEAN TOWARD BEING THOSE WHERE METAL WORKING IS ABSENT (153)	0.57 OF 56	71	LEAN TOWARD BEING THOSE WHERE METAL WORKING IS PRESENT (98)	0.68 OF 73	24 50 32 23 XSQ= 7.50 PHI= -0.241 XP = 0.0062
73	TILT TOWARD BEING THOSE WHERE WEAVING IS ABSENT (130)	0.55 OF 56	73	TILT TOWARD BEING THOSE WHERE WEAVING IS PRESENT (118)	0.67 OF 73	25 49 31 24 XSQ= 5.66 PHI= -0.209 XP = 0.0173
74	DRIFT LESS TOWARD BEING THOSE WHERE POTTERY IS PRESENT (145)	0.59 OF 56	74	DRIFT MORE TOWARD BEING THOSE WHERE POTTERY IS PRESENT (145)	0.75 OF 64	33 48 23 16 XSQ= 2.82 PHI= -0.153 XP = 0.0930
79	IN ALL CASES ARE THOSE WHERE NO CITY IS PRESENT (201)	1.00 OF 52	79	TEND LESS TO BE THOSE WHERE NO CITY IS PRESENT (201)	0.69 OF 71	0 22 52 49 XSQ= 17.57 PHI= -0.378 XP = 0.0000

81	TEND TO BE THOSE 0.73 OF 52 WHERE NO CITY OR TOWN IS PRESENT, AND THE AVERAGE COMMUNITY SIZE IS SMALLER THAN 200 (135)	81	TEND TO BE THOSE 0.70 OF 71 WHERE A CITY OR TOWN IS PRESENT, OR THE AVERAGE COMMUNITY SIZE IS 200 OR GREATER (89)	14 50 38 21 XSQ= 21.05 PHI= -0.414 XP = 0.0000
83	TILT MORE TOWARD BEING THOSE 0.81 OF 47 WHERE, WITH NO CITY AND NO TOWN PRESENT, THE AVERAGE COMMUNITY SIZE IS SMALLER THAN 200, RATHER THAN BETWEEN 200 AND 999 (135)	83	TILT LESS TOWARD BEING THOSE 0.57 OF 37 WHERE, WITH NO CITY AND NO TOWN PRESENT, THE AVERAGE COMMUNITY SIZE IS SMALLER THAN 200, RATHER THAN BETWEEN 200 AND 999 (135)	9 16 38 21 XSQ= 4.65 PHI= -0.235 XP = 0.0310
85	TEND TO BE THOSE 0.93 OF 57 WHERE THE LEVEL OF POLITICAL INTEGRATION IS THE MINIMAL STATE, THE AUTONOMOUS COMMUNITY, OR THE FAMILY (234) GPM	85	TEND TO BE THOSE 0.62 OF 94 WHERE THE LEVEL OF POLITICAL INTEGRATION IS THE LARGE STATE, OR THE LITTLE STATE (70) GPM	4 58 53 36 XSQ= 41.62 PHI= -0.525 XP = 0.
86	TEND TO BE THOSE 0.72 OF 57 WHERE THE LEVEL OF POLITICAL INTEGRATION IS THE AUTONOMOUS COMMUNITY, OR THE FAMILY (156) GPM	86	TEND TO BE THOSE 0.91 OF 94 WHERE THE LEVEL OF POLITICAL INTEGRATION IS THE LARGE STATE, THE LITTLE STATE, OR THE MINIMAL STATE (148) GPM	16 86 41 8 XSQ= 62.25 PHI= -0.642 XP = 0.
94	IN ALL CASES ARE THOSE 1.00 OF 67 WHERE THE HIERARCHY OF NATIONAL JURISDICTION HAS TWO, ONE, OR NO LEVELS (296) GES,EA	94	TEND LESS TO BE THOSE 0.69 OF 101 WHERE THE HIERARCHY OF NATIONAL JURISDICTION HAS TWO, ONE, OR NO LEVELS (296) GES,EA	0 31 67 70 XSQ= 23.22 PHI= -0.372 XP = 0.0000
95	TEND TO BE THOSE 0.93 OF 67 WHERE THE HIERARCHY OF NATIONAL JURISDICTION HAS ONE OR NO LEVELS (254) GES,EA	95	TEND TO BE THOSE 0.59 OF 101 WHERE THE HIERARCHY OF NATIONAL JURISDICTION HAS FOUR, THREE, OR TWO LEVELS (76) GES,EA	5 60 62 41 XSQ= 43.65 PHI= -0.510 XP = 0.
96	TEND TO BE THOSE 0.64 OF 67 WHERE THE HIERARCHY OF NATIONAL JURISDICTION HAS NO LEVELS (156) GES,EA	96	TEND TO BE THOSE 0.92 OF 101 WHERE THE HIERARCHY OF NATIONAL JURISDICTION HAS FOUR, THREE, TWO OR ONE LEVEL (174) GES,EA	24 93 43 8 XSQ= 57.67 PHI= -0.586 XP = 0.
97	TILT MORE TOWARD BEING THOSE 0.91 OF 68 WHERE THE HIERARCHY OF LOCAL JURISDICTION HAS THREE OR TWO LEVELS (273) GES,EA	97	TILT LESS TOWARD BEING THOSE 0.75 OF 101 WHERE THE HIERARCHY OF LOCAL JURISDICTION HAS THREE OR TWO LEVELS (273) GES,EA	6 25 62 76 XSQ= 5.86 PHI= -0.186 XP = 0.0155
100	LEAN LESS TOWARD BEING THOSE 0.85 OF 67 WHERE HIERARCHIES ARE MORE COMPLEX THAN THE 'SIMPLEST,' I. E., MORE COMPLEX THAN TWO LOCAL LEVELS WITH NO NATIONAL LEVELS (267) GES,EA	100	LEAN MORE TOWARD BEING THOSE 0.98 OF 101 WHERE HIERARCHIES ARE MORE COMPLEX THAN THE 'SIMPLEST,' I. E., MORE COMPLEX THAN TWO LOCAL LEVELS WITH NO NATIONAL LEVELS (267) GES,EA	57 99 10 2 XSQ= 8.32 PHI= -0.223 XP = 0.0039

109	TILT MORE TOWARC BEING THCSE 0.89 OF 70 WHERE CASTES ARE ABSENT (317)	109	TILT LESS TOWARD BEING THOSE 0.75 OF 112 WHERE CASTES ARE ABSENT (317)	8 28 62 84 XSQ= 4.18 PHI= -0.152 XP = 0.0409
110	TILT LESS TOWARC BEING THCSE 0.51 OF 75 WHERE SLAVERY IS PRESENT (163)	110	TILT MORE TOWARD BEING THOSE 0.67 CF 120 WHERE SLAVERY IS PRESENT (163)	38 81 37 39 XSQ= 4.81 PHI= -0.157 XP = 0.0282
116	DRIFT TCWARD BEING THCSE 0.75 OF 12 WHERE OCCUPATIONAL SPECIALIZATION IS PART-TIME CNLY (34) JMH	116	DRIFT TOWARD BEING THOSE 0.65 OF 20 WHERE OCCUPATIONAL SPECIALIZATICN IS FULL-TIME, WHETHER OR NCT FOR SURPLUS PRODUCTION (20) JMH	3 13 9 7 XSQ= 3.33 PHI= -0.323 EP = 0.0659
142	DRIFT LESS TCWARC BEING THOSE 0.58 OF 12 WHERE THE LEVEL CF SOCIAL SANCTION IS PUBLIC CORPOREAL SANCTION CR PUBLIC PRCPERTY SANCTICN, RATHER THAN PRIVATE SETTLEMENT (38) JMH	142	DRIFT MORE TOWARD BEING THCSE 0.90 CF 20 WHERE THE LEVEL OF SOCIAL SANCTICN IS PUBLIC CORPOREAL SANCTION CR PUBLIC PROPERTY SANCTICN, RATHER THAN PRIVATE SETTLEMENT (38) JMH	7 18 5 2 XSQ= 2.74 PHI= -0.293 EP = 0.0735
143	DRIFT TCWARD BEING THCSE 0.60 OF 15 WHERE THE RATIO OF RESTITUTIVE TC REPRESSIVE SANCTICNS IS HIGH (20) WME	143	DRIFT TOWARD BEING THOSE 0.76 OF 17 WHERE THE RATIO OF RESTITUTIVE TO REPRESSIVE SANCTICNS IS MEDIUM OR LOW (32) WME	9 4 6 13 XSQ= 3.01 PHI= 0.307 EP = 0.0702
144	TILT TCWARD BEING THCSE 0.80 OF 15 WHERE THE RATIC CF RESTITUTIVE TC REPRESSIVE SANCTIONS IS HIGH CR MEDIUM (27) WME	144	TILT TOWARD BEING THOSE 0.65 CF 17 WHERE THE RATIO OF RESTITUTIVE TO REPRESSIVE SANCTIONS IS LOW (25) WME	12 6 3 11 XSQ= 4.78 PHI= 0.387 EP = 0.0155
175	DRIFT LESS TCWARD BEING THOSE 0.64 OF 75 WHERE THE COMMUNITY IS 'KIN-HETERCGENECUS,' I. E. OTHER THAN A CLAN COMMUNITY OR A CEME (260)	175	DRIFT MORE TOWARD BEING THCSE 0.76 OF 122 WHERE THE COMMUNITY IS 'KIN-HETEROGENEOUS,' I. E. OTHER THAN A CLAN COMMUNITY OR A DEME (260)	27 29 48 93 XSQ= 2.84 PHI= 0.120 XP = 0.0920
177	DRIFT LESS TCWARC BEING THOSE 0.75 OF 75 WHERE THE COMMUNITY IS OTHER THAN A SINGLE CLAN-CCMMUNITY ANC EXCGAMCUS (305)	177	DRIFT MORE TOWARD BEING THCSE 0.86 CF 122 WHERE THE COMMUNITY IS OTHER THAN A SINGLE CLAN-COMMUNITY AND EXOGAMOUS (305)	19 17 56 105 XSQ= 3.31 PHI= 0.130 XP = 0.0687
180	TILT LESS TOWARC BEING THCSE 0.61 OF 75 WHERE THE COMMUNITY IS COMMCNLY NCN-EXCGAMCUS, RATHER THAN EXCGAMCUS (258)	180	TILT MORE TOWARD BEING THOSE 0.79 OF 122 WHERE THE COMMUNITY IS COMMONLY NON-EXOGAMOUS, RATHER THAN EXOGAMOUS (258)	29 26 46 96 XSQ= 6.12 PHI= 0.176 XP = 0.0134

183	DRIFT LESS TOWARD BEING THOSE 0.91 OF 54 WHERE THE LARGEST NON-COGNATIC KIN GROUP IS SMALLER THAN A MOEITY, I. E., A PHRATRY OR SIB OR LINEAGE (218)	183	DRIFT MORE TOWARD BEING THOSE 0.99 OF 83 WHERE THE LARGEST NON-COGNATIC KIN GROUP IS SMALLER THAN A MOEITY, I. E., A PHRATRY OR SIB OR LINEAGE (218)	5 1 49 82 XSQ= 3.33 PHI= 0.156 XP = 0.0681
184	TILT LESS TOWARD BEING THOSE 0.61 OF 54 WHERE THE LARGEST NON-COGNATIC KIN GROUP IS SMALLER THAN A PHRATRY, I. E. A SIB OR LINEAGE (175)	184	TILT MORE TOWARD BEING THOSE 0.82 OF 83 WHERE THE LARGEST NON-COGNATIC KIN GROUP IS SMALLER THAN A PHRATRY, I. E. A SIB OR LINEAGE (175)	21 15 33 68 XSQ= 6.28 PHI= 0.214 XP = 0.0122
196	TEND LESS TO BE THOSE 0.64 OF 58 WHERE INDIVIDUAL RIGHTS IN REAL PROPERTY, AND RULES FOR INHERITANCE, ARE PRESENT (194)	196	TEND MORE TO BE THOSE 0.89 OF 95 WHERE INDIVIDUAL RIGHTS IN REAL PROPERTY, AND RULES FOR INHERITANCE, ARE PRESENT (194)	37 85 21 10 XSQ= 13.15 PHI= -0.293 XP = 0.0003
263	DRIFT MORE TOWARD BEING THOSE 0.69 OF 77 WHERE WIVES ARE OBTAINED BY RELATIVELY DIFFICULT MEANS, NAMELY BY BRIDE-PRICE, BRIDE-SERVICE, OR EXCHANGING A FEMALE RELATIVE (233)	263	DRIFT LESS TOWARD BEING THOSE 0.55 OF 125 WHERE WIVES ARE OBTAINED BY RELATIVELY DIFFICULT MEANS, NAMELY BY BRIDE-PRICE, BRIDE-SERVICE, OR EXCHANGING A FEMALE RELATIVE (233)	53 69 24 56 XSQ= 3.15 PHI= 0.125 XP = 0.0758
272	TILT TOWARD BEING THOSE 0.73 OF 15 WHERE THE DIVORCE RATE IS HIGH (29) CA	272	TILT TOWARD BEING THOSE 0.67 OF 21 WHERE THE DIVORCE RATE IS LOW (28) CA	11 7 4 14 XSQ= 4.11 PHI= 0.338 EP = 0.0409
314	DRIFT MORE TOWARD BEING THOSE 0.83 OF 18 WHERE THE INCIDENCE OF MOTHER-CHILD HOUSEHOLDS IS LOW (61) W-C,S	314	DRIFT LESS TOWARD BEING THOSE 0.52 OF 23 WHERE THE INCIDENCE OF MOTHER-CHILD HOUSEHOLDS IS LOW (61) W-D,S	3 11 15 12 XSQ= 3.08 PHI= -0.274 XP = 0.0791
316	DRIFT TOWARD BEING THOSE 0.88 OF 8 WHERE EXCLUSIVE MOTHER-SON SLEEPING ARRANGEMENTS LAST LESS THAN ONE YEAR (25) W-K-A	316	DRIFT TOWARD BEING THOSE 0.50 OF 18 WHERE EXCLUSIVE MOTHER-SON SLEEPING ARRANGEMENTS LAST ONE YEAR OR LONGER (19) W-K-A	1 9 7 9 XSQ= 1.90 PHI= -0.270 EP = 0.0989
333	TILT TOWARD BEING THOSE 0.75 OF 4 WHERE THE AGE AT BEGINNING OF TRAINING IN HETEROSEXUAL PLAY INHIBITION IS LOWER THAN EIGHT YEARS (8) W-C	333	IN ALL CASES ARE THOSE 1.00 OF 6 WHERE THE AGE AT BEGINNING OF TRAINING IN HETEROSEXUAL PLAY INHIBITION IS EIGHT YEARS OR HIGHER (8) W-C	1 6 3 0 XSQ= 3.35 PHI= -0.579 EP = 0.0333
345	TILT TOWARD BEING THOSE 0.73 OF 15 WHERE THE CHILD'S INFERRED ANXIETY OVER NON-PERFORMANCE OF SELF-RELIANT BEHAVIOR IS LOW (39) B-B-C	345	TILT TOWARD BEING THOSE 0.65 OF 20 WHERE THE CHILD'S INFERRED ANXIETY OVER NON-PERFORMANCE OF SELF-RELIANT BEHAVIOR IS HIGH (37) B-B-C	4 13 11 7 XSQ= 3.62 PHI= -0.322 EP = 0.0409

350	DRIFT TOWARD BEING THOSE WHERE THE CHILD'S INFERRED ANXIETY OVER PERFORMANCE OF ACHIEVEMENT BEHAVIOR IS LOW (26) B-B-C	0.56 OF 9	350	DRIFT TOWARD BEING THOSE WHERE THE CHILD'S INFERRED ANXIETY OVER PERFORMANCE OF ACHIEVEMENT BEHAVIOR IS HIGH (34) B-B-C	0.81 OF 16	4 13 5 3 XSQ= 2.09 PHI= -0.289 EP = 0.0870
354	TILT TOWARD BEING THOSE WHERE THE CHILD'S INFERRED ANXIETY OVER PERFORMANCE OF OBEDIENT BEHAVIOR IS LOW (37) B-B-C	0.73 OF 15	354	TILT TOWARD BEING THOSE WHERE THE CHILD'S INFERRED ANXIETY OVER PERFORMANCE OF OBEDIENT BEHAVIOR IS HIGH (36) B-B-C	0.70 OF 20	4 14 11 6 XSQ= 4.83 PHI= -0.371 EP = 0.0176
365	LEAN TOWARD BEING THOSE WHERE THE TIME SPENT IN ADOLESCENT PEER GROUP ACTIVITY IS LOW-MEDIUM OR LOW (15) JKH	0.63 OF 8	365	LEAN TOWARD BEING THOSE WHERE THE TIME SPENT IN ADOLESCENT PEER GROUP ACTIVITY IS HIGH OR HIGH-MEDIUM (30) JKH	0.94 OF 16	3 15 5 1 XSQ= 6.25 PHI= -0.510 EP = 0.0069
369	DRIFT TOWARD BEING THOSE WHERE BOTH DISSOCIATION OF THE SEXES AT ADOLESCENCE, AND CUSTOMS OF INITIATION AT ADOLESCENCE, ARE ABSENT (15) JKH	0.64 OF 11	369	DRIFT TOWARD BEING THOSE WHERE DISSOCIATION OF THE SEXES AT ADOLESCENCE, OR CUSTOMS OF INITIATION AT ADOLESCENCE, ARE PRESENT (42) JKH	0.77 OF 22	4 17 7 5 XSQ= 3.68 PHI= -0.334 EP = 0.0518
377	DRIFT MORE TOWARD BEING THOSE WHERE MALE GENITAL MUTILATION IS ABSENT (242)	0.76 OF 67	377	DRIFT LESS TOWARD BEING THOSE WHERE MALE GENITAL MUTILATION IS ABSENT (242)	0.62 OF 98	16 37 51 61 XSQ= 2.91 PHI= -0.133 XP = 0.0883
424	TILT TOWARD BEING THOSE WHERE RELIGIOUS SPECIALISTS ARE PART-TIME, RATHER THAN FULL-TIME (33) JMH	0.75 OF 12	424	TILT TOWARD BEING THOSE WHERE RELIGIOUS SPECIALISTS ARE FULL-TIME, RATHER THAN PART-TIME (21) JMH	0.70 OF 20	3 14 9 6 XSQ= 4.43 PHI= -0.372 EP = 0.0269
450	DRIFT TOWARD BEING THOSE WHERE THE OBSERVATION OF FOOD TABOOS IS HIGH OR MEDIUM, RATHER THAN LOW (60) JRL	0.78 OF 18	450	DRIFT TOWARD BEING THOSE WHERE THE OBSERVATION OF FOOD TABOOS IS LOW, RATHER THAN HIGH OR MEDIUM (26) JRL	0.52 OF 31	14 15 4 16 XSQ= 2.95 PHI= 0.245 XP = 0.0861
458	TEND TO BE THOSE WHERE GAMES, IF PRESENT, DO NOT INCLUDE GAMES OF STRATEGY (119) R-A-B,EA	0.77 OF 40	458	TEND TO BE THOSE WHERE GAMES, IF PRESENT, INCLUDE GAMES OF STRATEGY (52) R-A-B,EA	0.61 OF 57	9 35 31 22 XSQ= 12.83 PHI= -0.364 XP = 0.0003
468	TILT TOWARD BEING THOSE WHERE CONTACT WITH OTHER CULTURES IS REGULAR OR IRREGULAR, RATHER THAN FREQUENT (37) JMH	0.83 OF 12	468	TILT TOWARD BEING THOSE WHERE CONTACT WITH OTHER CULTURES IS FREQUENT, RATHER THAN REGULAR OR IRREGULAR (17) JMH	0.60 OF 20	2 12 10 8 XSQ= 4.10 PHI= -0.358 EP = 0.0276

```
472  DRIFT TOWARD BEING THOSE         0.57 OF  21      472  DRIFT TOWARD BEING THOSE         0.72 OF  29          9    21
     WHERE THE COMPOSITE NARCISSISM INCEX                  WHERE THE COMPOSITE NARCISSISM INDEX                12     8
     IS LOW  (43) PES                                      IS HIGH  (47) PES                           XSQ=     3.29
                                                                                                       PHI=   -0.256
                                                                                                       XP =   0.0698
```

107 CULTURES
WHERE CLASS STRATIFICATION, IF PRESENT,
IS BASED ON
OCCUPATIONAL STATUS (43)

107 CULTURES
WHERE CLASS STRATIFICATION, IF PRESENT,
IS BASED ON SOMETHING OTHER THAN
OCCUPATIONAL STATUS (160)

BACKGROUND ON PAGE 88

BOTH SUBJECT AND PREDICATE

43 IN LEFT COLUMN

AMERICANS	AZTEC	BASQUES	BENGALI	BHIL	BRAZILIANS	BULGARIANS	BURMESE	BURUSHO	CAMBODIANS
COORG	CZECHS	DUTCH	EGYPTIANS	INCA	IRISH	JAPANESE	JAVANESE	KERALA	KHASI
KOREANS	MALAYS	MAYA	MIN CHINESE	MINCHIA	MOSSI	NUPE	PATHAN	PORTUGUESE	REGEIBAT
ROMANS	RUNDI	SERBS	SHILLUK	SONGHAI	TAMIL	THAI	TIBETANS	TIGRINYA	VIETNAMESE
WALLOONS	WOLOF	YORUBA							

160 IN RIGHT COLUMN

ABIPON	ABOR	ALORESE	ARAUCANIANS	ASHANTI	ATSUGEWI	AYMARA	AZANDE	BALINESE	BAMBARA
BAMILEKE	BARABRA	BARI	BASSERI	BELU	BEMBA	BOERS	BURYAT	CAGABA	CAMBA
CHAGGA	CHAMACOCO	CHEREMIS	CHERKESS	CHIBCHA	CHUKCHEE	CUNA	DARD	COGON	DUSUN
ELLICE	EYAK	FANG	FON	FUTAJALONKE	GANDA	GARO	GILBERTESE	GISU	GOAJIRO
GOND	HAIDA	HASANIA	HASINAI	HAWAIIANS	HAZARA	HEBREWS	HEHE	HERERO	HO
HUICHOL	HURON	HUTSUL	ICELANDERS	IFUGAO	ILA	INGALIK	IRAQW	JUKUN	KACHIN
KAPAUKU	KAREN	KAZAK	KHALKA	KIKUYU	KOHISTANI	KORYAK	KPE	KUBA	KURTATCHI
KWAKIUTL	LAKALAI	LAKHER	LAMET	LANGO	LAPPS	LAU	LEPCHA	LHOTA NAGA	LIFU
LOLO	LOZI	LUBA	LUO	MACASSARESE	MAGUZAWA	MAM	MANCHU	MANGAIANS	MANIHIKI
MANUS	MAORI	MARQUESANS	MARSHALLESE	MBUGWE	MBUNDU	MENDE	MERINA	MINANGKABAU	MNONG GAR
MONGUOR	MOTA	MZAB	NAMA	NATCHEZ	NGONI	NOMLAKI	NUNIVAK	NURI	NYANEKA
NYORO	OKINAWANS	ONTONG-JAVA	PAIWAN	PALAUANS	PAWNEE	PENDE	PONAPEANS	PURUM	RIFFIANS
ROTINESE	RWALA	SAGADA	SAMOANS	SAMOYED	SENIANG	SINDHI	SIUAI	SIWANS	SOMALI
SOTHO	SWAZI	SYRIANS	TAGBANUA	TALLENSI	TANALA	TANIMBARESE	TARAHUMARA	TAREUMIUT	TENINO
TERA	TERENA	THONGA	TIKOPIA	TIMUCUA	TOLOWA	TORAJA	TROBRIAND	TSHIMSHIAN	TUPINAMBA
TURKMEN	TWANA	VENDA	WUTE	YAKUT	YAPESE	YOKUTS	YOMBE	YUKI	YUROK

180 EXCLUDED BECAUSE IRRELEVANT (SEE RIGHT COLUMN, PARAGRAPH 102)

17 EXCLUDED BECAUSE UNASCERTAINED

4 TEND LESS TO BE THOSE LOCATED OUTSIDE OF THE CIRCUM-MEDITERRANEAN (355) — 0.63 OF 43

4 TEND MORE TO BE THOSE LOCATED OUTSIDE OF THE CIRCUM-MEDITERRANEAN (355) — 0.89 OF 160

16	18
27	142

XSQ= 14.57
PHI= 0.268
XP = 0.0001

```
 5  LEAN LESS TOWARD BEING THOSE     0.58 OF  43     5  LEAN MORE TOWARD BEING THOSE     0.80 OF 160          18   32
    LOCATED OUTSIDE OF                                  LOCATED OUTSIDE OF                                    25  128
    EAST EURASIA  (330)                                 EAST EURASIA  (330)                            XSQ=     7.59
                                                                                                       PHI=    0.193
                                                                                                       XP =   0.0059

 6  LEAN MORE TOWARD BEING THOSE     0.98 OF  43     6  LEAN LESS TOWARD BEING THOSE     0.77 OF 160           1   37
    LOCATED OUTSIDE OF                                  LOCATED OUTSIDE OF                                    42  123
    THE INSULAR PACIFIC  (330)                          THE INSULAR PACIFIC  (330)                     XSQ=     8.32
                                                                                                       PHI=   -0.202
                                                                                                       XP =   0.0039

 8  DRIFT MORE TOWARD BEING THOSE    0.98 OF  43     8  DRIFT LESS TOWARD BEING THOSE    0.86 OF 160           1   22
    LOCATED OUTSIDE OF                                  LOCATED OUTSIDE OF                                    42  138
    NORTH AMERICA  (330)                                NORTH AMERICA  (330)                           XSQ=     3.34
                                                                                                       PHI=   -0.128
                                                                                                       XP =   0.0676

16  TILT MORE TOWARD BEING THOSE     0.88 OF  43    16  TILT LESS TOWARD BEING THOSE     0.69 OF 160          38  110
    WHERE THE LATITUDE IS                               WHERE THE LATITUDE IS                                  5   50
    TEN DEGREES OR GREATER  (277)                       TEN DEGREES OR GREATER  (277)                  XSQ=     5.65
                                                                                                       PHI=    0.167
                                                                                                       XP =   0.0175

44  TILT MORE TOWARD BEING THOSE     0.95 OF  37    44  TILT LESS TOWARD BEING THOSE     0.73 OF 134          35   98
    WHERE SETTLEMENTS ARE FIXED  (222)                  WHERE SETTLEMENTS ARE FIXED  (222)                     2   36
                                                                                                       XSQ=     6.53
                                                                                                       PHI=    0.195
                                                                                                       XP =   0.0106

51  LEAN MORE TOWARD BEING THOSE     0.98 OF  43    51  LEAN LESS TOWARD BEING THOSE     0.74 OF 160          42  119
    WHERE SUBSISTENCE IS PRIMARILY BY                   WHERE SUBSISTENCE IS PRIMARILY BY                      1   41
    FOOD PRODUCTION -- I. E., AGRICULTURE               FOOD PRODUCTION -- I. E., AGRICULTURE          XSQ=     9.84
    OR HUSBANDRY -- RATHER THAN BY                      OR HUSBANDRY -- RATHER THAN BY                 PHI=    0.220
    GATHERING  (253)                                    GATHERING  (253)                               XP =   0.0017

53  TEND TO BE THOSE                 0.81 OF  36    53  TEND TO BE THOSE                 0.64 OF 104          29   37
    WHERE FOOD PRODUCTION IS BY                         WHERE FOOD PRODUCTION IS BY                            7   67
    INTENSIVE AGRICULTURE, RATHER THAN BY               SIMPLE AGRICULTURE OR                          XSQ=    19.94
    SIMPLE AGRICULTURE OR                               INCIPIENT FOOD PRODUCTION, RATHER THAN BY      PHI=    0.377
    INCIPIENT FOOD PRODUCTION  (91)                     INTENSIVE AGRICULTURE  (147)                   XP =   0.0000

55  TEND TO BE THOSE                 0.83 OF  35    55  TEND TO BE THOSE                 0.58 OF  88          29   37
    WHERE FOOD PRODUCTION IS BY                         WHERE FOOD PRODUCTION IS BY                            6   51
    INTENSIVE AGRICULTURE, RATHER THAN BY               SIMPLE AGRICULTURE, RATHER THAN BY             XSQ=    15.17
    SIMPLE AGRICULTURE  (91)                            INTENSIVE AGRICULTURE  (101)                   PHI=    0.351
                                                                                                       XP =   0.0001

62  DRIFT MORE TOWARD BEING THOSE    0.81 OF  43    62  DRIFT LESS TOWARD BEING THOSE    0.67 OF 160          35  107
    WHERE HUSBANDRY OF SOME KIND                        WHERE HUSBANDRY OF SOME KIND                           8   53
    IS PRESENT  (228)                                   IS PRESENT  (228)                              XSQ=     2.74
                                                                                                       PHI=    0.116
                                                                                                       XP =   0.0976
```

63	LEAN MCRE TOWARC BEING THCSE WHERE HUSBANDRY, IF PRESENT, IS PRINCIPALLY IN THE FCRM OF BOVINE, EQUINE, CAMEL-LIKE, OR DEER-LIKE ANIMALS, RATHER THAN PIGS, SHEEP, CR GCATS (152)	0.94 OF 35	63	LEAN LESS TOWARD BEING THOSE WHERE HUSBANDRY, IF PRESENT, IS PRINCIPALLY IN THE FCRM OF BOVINE, EQUINE, CAMEL-LIKE, OR DEER-LIKE ANIMALS, RATHER THAN PIGS, SHEEP, OR GOATS (152)	0.67 OF 106	33 71 2 35 XSQ= 8.77 PHI= 0.249 XP = 0.0031
71	IN ALL CASES ARE THOSE WHERE METAL WCRKING IS PRESENT (98)	1.00 OF 24	71	TEND TO BE THOSE WHERE METAL WORKING IS ABSENT (153)	0.52 OF 105	24 50 0 55 XSQ= 19.83 PHI= 0.392 XP = 0.0000
73	LEAN MCRE TOWARC BEING THCSE WHERE WEAVING IS PRESENT (118)	0.88 OF 24	73	LEAN LESS TOWARD BEING THOSE WHERE WEAVING IS PRESENT (118)	0.50 OF 105	21 53 3 52 XSQ= 9.49 PHI= 0.271 XP = 0.0021
74	IN ALL CASES ARE THCSE WHERE PCTTERY IS PRESENT (145)	1.00 OF 22	74	TEND LESS TO BE THOSE WHERE POTTERY IS PRESENT (145)	0.60 OF 98	22 59 0 39 XSQ= 11.22 PHI= 0.306 XP = 0.0008
77	TILT TCWARD BEING THOSE WHERE THE WRITING SYSTEM IS ALPHABETIC-OR-PHCNETIC, RATHER THAN BEING MNEMCNIC CR ABSENT (15) JMH	0.75 OF 8	77	TILT TOWARD BEING THOSE WHERE THE WRITING SYSTEM IS MNEMONIC OR ABSENT, RATHER THAN BEING ALPHABETIC-OR-PHONETIC (39) JMH	0.75 CF 24	6 6 2 18 XSQ= 4.44 PHI= 0.373 EP = 0.0302
79	TEND TO BE THOSE WHERE A CITY IS PRESENT (23)	0.59 OF 34	79	TEND TO BE THOSE WHERE NO CITY IS PRESENT (201)	0.98 OF 89	20 2 14 87 XSQ= 49.83 PHI= 0.637 XP = 0.
80	TEND TC BE THCSE WHERE A CITY OR TOWN IS PRESENT (39)	0.74 OF 34	80	TEND TO BE THOSE WHERE NO CITY OR TOWN IS PRESENT (185)	0.88 CF 89	25 11 9 78 XSQ= 41.56 PHI= 0.581 XP = 0.
81	TEND TO BE THCSE WHERE A CITY CR TOWN IS PRESENT, OR THE AVERAGE COMMUNITY SIZE IS 200 OR GREATER (89)	0.88 OF 34	81	TEND TO BE THOSE WHERE NO CITY OR TOWN IS PRESENT, AND THE AVERAGE COMMUNITY SIZE IS SMALLER THAN 200 (135)	0.62 OF 89	30 34 4 55 XSQ= 22.71 PHI= 0.430 XP = 0.0000
84	TEND TC BE THCSE WHERE THE LEVEL OF POLITICAL INTEGRATION IS THE LARGE STATE (42) GPM	0.86 OF 29	84	TEND TO BE THOSE WHERE THE LEVEL OF POLITICAL INTEGRATION IS THE LITTLE STATE, THE MINIMAL STATE, THE AUTONOMOUS COMMUNITY, CR THE FAMILY (262) GPM	0.89 CF 122	25 14 4 108 XSQ= 64.46 PHI= 0.653 XP = 0.

```
 85  TEND TO BE THOSE                 0.93 OF  29      85  TEND TO BE THOSE                 0.71 OF 122            27   35
     WHERE THE LEVEL OF POLITICAL INTEGRATION              WHERE THE LEVEL OF POLITICAL INTEGRATION                2   87
     IS THE LARGE STATE, OR                                IS THE MINIMAL STATE,                             XSQ=   37.55
     THE LITTLE STATE  (70) GPM                            THE AUTONOMOUS COMMUNITY, OR                      PHI=   0.499
                                                           THE FAMILY  (234) GPM                             XP =   0.

 86  IN ALL CASES ARE THOSE           1.00 OF  29      86  TEND LESS TO BE THOSE            0.60 OF 122            29   73
     WHERE THE LEVEL OF POLITICAL INTEGRATION              WHERE THE LEVEL OF POLITICAL INTEGRATION                0   49
     IS THE LARGE STATE, THE LITTLE STATE,                 IS THE LARGE STATE, THE LITTLE STATE,             XSQ=   15.46
     OR THE MINIMAL STATE  (148) GPM                       OR THE MINIMAL STATE  (148) GPM                   PHI=   0.320
                                                                                                             XP =   0.0001

 88  TEND TO BE THOSE                 0.69 OF  29      88  TEND TO BE THOSE                 0.76 OF 118            20   28
     WHERE, IF A HEADMANSHIP IS PRESENT,                   WHERE, IF A HEADMANSHIP IS PRESENT,                     9   90
     SUCCESSION IS NON-HEREDITARY  (106)                   SUCCESSION IS HEREDITARY  (165)                   XSQ=   19.65
                                                                                                             PHI=   0.366
                                                                                                             XP =   0.0000

 94  TEND TO BE THOSE                 0.53 OF  36      94  TEND TO BE THOSE                 0.91 OF 132            19   12
     WHERE THE HIERARCHY                                   WHERE THE HIERARCHY                                    17  120
     OF NATIONAL JURISDICTION HAS                          OF NATIONAL JURISDICTION HAS                      XSQ=   33.03
     FOUR OR THREE LEVELS  (34) GES,EA                     TWO, ONE, OR NO LEVELS  (296) GES,EA              PHI=   0.443
                                                                                                             XP =   0.

 95  TEND TO BE THOSE                 0.83 OF  36      95  TEND TO BE THOSE                 0.73 OF 132            30   35
     WHERE THE HIERARCHY                                   WHERE THE HIERARCHY                                     6   97
     OF NATIONAL JURISDICTION HAS                          OF NATIONAL JURISDICTION HAS                      XSQ=   36.14
     FOUR, THREE, OR TWO LEVELS  (76) GES,EA               ONE OR NO LEVELS  (254) GES,EA                    PHI=   0.464
                                                                                                             XP =   0.

 96  IN ALL CASES ARE THOSE           1.00 OF  36      96  TEND LESS TO BE THOSE            0.61 OF 132            36   81
     WHERE THE HIERARCHY                                   WHERE THE HIERARCHY                                     0   51
     OF NATIONAL JURISDICTION HAS                          OF NATIONAL JURISDICTION HAS                      XSQ=   18.19
     FOUR, THREE, TWO OR                                   FOUR, THREE, TWO OR                               PHI=   0.329
     ONE LEVEL  (174) GES,EA                               ONE LEVEL  (174) GES,EA                           XP =   0.0000

109  TEND LESS TO BE THOSE            0.54 OF  37     109  TEND MORE TO BE THOSE            0.87 OF 145            17   19
     WHERE CASTES ARE ABSENT  (317)                        WHERE CASTES ARE ABSENT  (317)                         20  126
                                                                                                             XSQ=   18.02
                                                                                                             PHI=   0.315
                                                                                                             XP =   0.0000

116  IN ALL CASES ARE THOSE           1.00 OF   8     116  LEAN TOWARD BEING THOSE          0.67 OF  24             8    8
     WHERE OCCUPATIONAL SPECIALIZATION IS                  WHERE OCCUPATIONAL SPECIALIZATION IS                    0   16
     FULL-TIME, WHETHER OR NOT FOR                         PART-TIME ONLY  (34) JMH                          XSQ=    8.17
     SURPLUS PRODUCTION  (20) JMH                                                                            PHI=   0.505
                                                                                                             EP =   0.0024

118  IN ALL CASES ARE THOSE           1.00 OF   6     118  DRIFT TOWARD BEING THOSE         0.50 OF  24             6   12
     WHERE THE PERCENTAGE OF OCCUPATIONS                   WHERE THE PERCENTAGE OF OCCUPATIONS                     0   12
     THAT ARE SPECIALIZED                                  THAT ARE SPECIALIZED                              XSQ=    3.13
     IS HIGH OR MEDIUM  (24) WME                           IS LOW  (25) WME                                  PHI=   0.323
                                                                                                             EP =   0.0568
```

128	TILT TOWARD BEING THOSE 0.85 OF 13 WHERE, IF SUBSISTENCE IS PRIMARILY BY AGRICULTURE, THE WORK IS MAINLY DONE BY MALES (40)	128	TILT TOWARD BEING THOSE 0.55 OF 42 WHERE, IF SUBSISTENCE IS PRIMARILY BY AGRICULTURE, THE WORK IS MAINLY DONE BY FEMALES (37)	11 19 2 23 XSQ= 4.72 PHI= 0.293 XP = 0.0298
176	DRIFT MORE TOWARD BEING THOSE 0.70 OF 43 WHERE THE COMMUNITY IS OTHER THAN A CLAN-COMMUNITY OR A COMMUNITY STRUCTURED OR SEGMENTED ON A CLAN BASIS (213)	176	DRIFT LESS TOWARD BEING THOSE 0.53 OF 154 WHERE THE COMMUNITY IS OTHER THAN A CLAN-COMMUNITY OR A COMMUNITY STRUCTURED OR SEGMENTED ON A CLAN BASIS (213)	13 73 30 81 XSQ= 3.36 PHI= -0.131 XP = 0.0668
177	DRIFT MORE TOWARD BEING THOSE 0.93 OF 43 WHERE THE COMMUNITY IS OTHER THAN A SINGLE CLAN-COMMUNITY AND EXOGAMOUS (305)	177	DRIFT LESS TOWARD BEING THOSE 0.79 OF 154 WHERE THE COMMUNITY IS OTHER THAN A SINGLE CLAN-COMMUNITY AND EXOGAMOUS (305)	3 33 40 121 XSQ= 3.78 PHI= -0.139 XP = 0.0518
180	DRIFT MORE TOWARD BEING THOSE 0.84 OF 43 WHERE THE COMMUNITY IS COMMONLY NON-EXOGAMOUS, RATHER THAN EXOGAMOUS (258)	180	DRIFT LESS TOWARD BEING THOSE 0.69 OF 154 WHERE THE COMMUNITY IS COMMONLY NON-EXOGAMOUS, RATHER THAN EXOGAMOUS (258)	7 48 36 106 XSQ= 3.00 PHI= -0.123 XP = 0.0832
182	TILT TOWARD BEING THOSE 0.53 OF 43 WHERE THE COMMUNITY IS STRUCTURED ON A NON-CLAN BASIS AND AGAMOUS (126)	182	TILT TOWARD BEING THOSE 0.66 OF 154 OTHER THAN WHERE THE COMMUNITY IS STRUCTURED ON A NON-CLAN BASIS AND AGAMOUS (256)	23 52 20 102 XSQ= 4.74 PHI= 0.155 XP = 0.0295
192	TILT LESS TOWARD BEING THOSE 0.60 OF 43 OTHER THAN WHERE THE ONLY KIN GROUP PRESENT IS A KINDRED OR ELSE BILATERAL DESCENT IS INFERRED (289)	192	TILT MORE TOWARD BEING THOSE 0.81 OF 160 OTHER THAN WHERE THE ONLY KIN GROUP PRESENT IS A KINDRED OR ELSE BILATERAL DESCENT IS INFERRED (289)	17 31 26 129 XSQ= 6.55 PHI= 0.180 XP = 0.0105
196	LEAN MORE TOWARD BEING THOSE 0.97 OF 36 WHERE INDIVIDUAL RIGHTS IN REAL PROPERTY, AND RULES FOR INHERITANCE, ARE PRESENT (194)	196	LEAN LESS TOWARD BEING THOSE 0.74 OF 117 WHERE INDIVIDUAL RIGHTS IN REAL PROPERTY, AND RULES FOR INHERITANCE, ARE PRESENT (194)	35 87 1 30 XSQ= 7.55 PHI= 0.222 XP = 0.0060
197	DRIFT LESS TOWARD BEING THOSE 0.74 OF 35 WHERE RULES FOR THE INHERITANCE OF REAL PROPERTY, IF PRESENT, FAVOR EITHER THE MALE HEIR OR LINE, OR THE FEMALE HEIR OR LINE (165)	197	DRIFT MORE TOWARD BEING THOSE 0.89 OF 87 WHERE RULES FOR THE INHERITANCE OF REAL PROPERTY, IF PRESENT, FAVOR EITHER THE MALE HEIR OR LINE, OR THE FEMALE HEIR OR LINE (165)	26 77 9 10 XSQ= 2.83 PHI= -0.152 XP = 0.0923
213	DRIFT TOWARD BEING THOSE 0.67 OF 39 WHERE FIRST COUSIN MARRIAGE IS PERMITTED (172)	213	DRIFT TOWARD BEING THOSE 0.52 OF 149 WHERE FIRST COUSIN MARRIAGE IS NOT PERMITTED (198)	26 72 13 77 XSQ= 3.47 PHI= 0.136 XP = 0.0627

221	DRIFT MORE TOWARD BEING THOSE 0.97 OF 39 WHERE MATRILATERAL CROSS-COUSIN MARRIAGE IS NOT PRESCRIBED OR PREFERRED (335)	221	DRIFT LESS TOWARD BEING THOSE 0.86 OF 149 WHERE MATRILATERAL CROSS-COUSIN MARRIAGE IS NOT PRESCRIBED OR PREFERRED (335)	1 21 38 128 XSQ= 2.94 PHI= -0.125 XP = 0.0865
224	TILT TOWARD BEING THOSE 0.77 OF 26 WHERE COUSIN MARRIAGE IS PREFERENTIALLY OR PERMISSIVELY SYMMETRICAL, RATHER THAN EITHER PATRI- OR MATRILATERAL (106)	224	TILT TOWARD BEING THOSE 0.51 OF 72 WHERE COUSIN MARRIAGE IS PREFERENTIALLY OR PERMISSIVELY EITHER PATRI- OR MATRILATERAL, RATHER THAN SYMMETRICAL (66)	6 37 20 35 XSQ= 5.12 PHI= -0.229 XP = 0.0236
234	LEAN MORE TOWARD BEING THOSE 0.82 OF 34 WHERE THE COUSIN TERMINOLOGY IS OF ESKIMO OR HAWAIIAN TYPE, RATHER THAN CROW, OMAHA, OR IROQUOIS TYPE (170)	234	LEAN LESS TOWARD BEING THOSE 0.50 OF 125 WHERE THE COUSIN TERMINOLOGY IS OF ESKIMO OR HAWAIIAN TYPE, RATHER THAN CROW, OMAHA, OR IROQUOIS TYPE (170)	6 62 28 63 XSQ= 9.88 PHI= -0.249 XP = 0.0017
241	LEAN LESS TOWARD BEING THOSE 0.66 OF 29 WHERE THE FAMILY, IF EXTENDED, IS LARGE OR SMALL, RATHER THAN STEM (187)	241	LEAN MORE TOWARD BEING THOSE 0.91 OF 90 WHERE THE FAMILY, IF EXTENDED, IS LARGE OR SMALL, RATHER THAN STEM (187)	19 82 10 8 XSQ= 9.29 PHI= -0.279 XP = 0.0023
242	TEND LESS TO BE THOSE 0.55 OF 42 WHERE MARRIAGE IS COMMONLY OR OCCASIONALLY POLYGYNOUS, RATHER THAN MONOGAMOUS (314)	242	TEND MORE TO BE THOSE 0.86 OF 159 WHERE MARRIAGE IS COMMONLY OR OCCASIONALLY POLYGYNOUS, RATHER THAN MONOGAMOUS (314)	23 137 19 22 XSQ= 18.29 PHI= -0.302 XP = 0.0000
263	TEND TO BE THOSE 0.63 OF 43 WHERE WIVES ARE OBTAINED BY RELATIVELY EASY MEANS, NAMELY BY TOKEN BRIDE-PRICE, GIFT EXCHANGE, ABSENCE OF ANY CONSIDERATION, OR RECEIPT OF DOWRY (162)	263	TEND TO BE THOSE 0.67 OF 159 WHERE WIVES ARE OBTAINED BY RELATIVELY DIFFICULT MEANS, NAMELY BY BRIDE-PRICE, BRIDE-SERVICE, OR EXCHANGING A FEMALE RELATIVE (233)	16 106 27 53 XSQ= 11.08 PHI= -0.234 XP = 0.0009
272	TILT TOWARD BEING THOSE 0.88 OF 8 WHERE THE DIVORCE RATE IS LOW (28) CA	272	TILT TOWARD BEING THOSE 0.61 OF 28 WHERE THE DIVORCE RATE IS HIGH (29) CA	1 17 7 11 XSQ= 4.02 PHI= -0.334 EP = 0.0408
370	LEAN TOWARD BEING THOSE 0.81 OF 31 WHERE THE SEGREGATION OF ADOLESCENT BOYS IS ABSENT (148)	370	LEAN TOWARD BEING THOSE 0.51 OF 97 WHERE THE SEGREGATION OF ADOLESCENT BOYS IS COMPLETE OR PARTIAL (95)	6 49 25 48 XSQ= 8.08 PHI= -0.251 XP = 0.0045
390	LEAN TOWARD BEING THOSE 0.61 OF 23 WHERE PREMARITAL SEX RELATIONS ARE STRONGLY PUNISHED AND IN FACT RARE (47) JTW,EA	390	LEAN TOWARD BEING THOSE 0.76 OF 86 WHERE PREMARITAL SEX RELATIONS ARE WEAKLY PUNISHED AND IN FACT NOT RARE OR PUNISHED ONLY IF PREGNANCY RESULTS, OR FREELY PERMITTED (132) JTW,EA	14 21 9 65 XSQ= 9.45 PHI= 0.294 XP = 0.0021

391	IN ALL CASES ARE THOSE WHERE PREMARITAL SEX RELATIONS ARE STRONGLY PUNISHED AND IN FACT RARE, OR WEAKLY PUNISHED AND IN FACT NOT RARE (89) JTW,EA	1.00 OF 23	391	TEND TO BE THOSE WHERE PREMARITAL SEX RELATIONS ARE PUNISHED ONLY IF PREGNANCY RESULTS, OR FREELY PERMITTED (90) JTW,EA	0.58 OF 86	23 36 0 50 XSQ= 22.42 PHI= 0.454 XP = 0.0000
424	IN ALL CASES ARE THOSE WHERE RELIGIOUS SPECIALISTS ARE FULL-TIME, RATHER THAN PART-TIME (21) JMH	1.00 OF 8	424	LEAN TOWARD BEING THOSE WHERE RELIGIOUS SPECIALISTS ARE PART-TIME, RATHER THAN FULL-TIME (33) JMH	0.63 OF 24	8 9 0 15 XSQ= 7.07 PHI= 0.470 EP = 0.0029
426	TILT MORE TOWARD BEING THOSE WHERE A HIGH GOD IS PRESENT (156) GES,EA	0.87 OF 30	426	TILT LESS TOWARD BEING THOSE WHERE A HIGH GOD IS PRESENT (156) GES,EA	0.62 OF 114	26 71 4 43 XSQ= 5.36 PHI= 0.193 XP = 0.0206
428	TILT MORE TOWARD BEING THOSE WHERE A HIGH GOD, IF PRESENT AND ACTIVE, SUPPORTS HUMAN MORALITY, RATHER THAN NOT SUPPORTING IT (61) GES,EA	0.90 OF 20	428	TILT LESS TOWARD BEING THOSE WHERE A HIGH GOD, IF PRESENT AND ACTIVE, SUPPORTS HUMAN MORALITY, RATHER THAN NOT SUPPORTING IT (61) GES,EA	0.62 OF 42	18 26 2 16 XSQ= 3.92 PHI= 0.251 XP = 0.0478
450	TILT TOWARD BEING THOSE WHERE THE OBSERVATION OF FOOD TABOOS IS LOW, RATHER THAN HIGH OR MEDIUM (26) JRL	0.67 OF 15	450	TILT TOWARD BEING THOSE WHERE THE OBSERVATION OF FOOD TABOOS IS HIGH OR MEDIUM, RATHER THAN LOW (60) JRL	0.71 OF 34	5 24 10 10 XSQ= 4.54 PHI= -0.304 XP = 0.0332
458	LEAN TOWARD BEING THOSE WHERE GAMES, IF PRESENT, INCLUDE GAMES OF STRATEGY (52) R-A-B,EA	0.80 OF 20	458	LEAN TOWARD BEING THOSE WHERE GAMES, IF PRESENT, DO NOT INCLUDE GAMES OF STRATEGY (119) R-A-B,EA	0.64 OF 77	16 28 4 49 XSQ= 10.50 PHI= 0.329 XP = 0.0012
468	IN ALL CASES ARE THOSE WHERE CONTACT WITH OTHER CULTURES IS FREQUENT, RATHER THAN REGULAR OR IRREGULAR (17) JMH	1.00 OF 8	468	TEND TO BE THOSE WHERE CONTACT WITH OTHER CULTURES IS REGULAR OR IRREGULAR, RATHER THAN FREQUENT (37) JMH	0.75 OF 24	8 6 0 18 XSQ= 10.84 PHI= 0.582 EP = 0.0003

108 CULTURES
WHERE CLASS STRATIFICATION, IF PRESENT,
IS BASED ON
A HEREDITARY ARISTOCRACY (74)

108 CULTURES
WHERE CLASS STRATIFICATION, IF PRESENT,
IS BASED ON SOMETHING OTHER THAN
A HEREDITARY ARISTOCRACY (129)

BACKGROUND ON PAGE 88

BOTH SUBJECT AND PREDICATE

74 IN LEFT COLUMN

ABIPON, ASHANTI, AZANDE, BALINESE, BAMBARA, BAMILEKE, BELU, BEMBA, BURYAT, CHAGGA,
CHAMACOCO, CHERKESS, CHIBCHA, DARC, ELLICE, FON, FUTAJALONKE, GANDA, HAIDA, HASINAI,
HAWAIIANS, HEHE, HO, JUKUN, KACHIN, KAZAK, KHALKA, KUBA, KURTATCHI, KWAKIUTL,
LAKHER, LIFU, LOLO, LOZI, LUBA, MACASSARESE, MAGUZAWA, MANGAIANS, MANIHIKI, MAORI,
MARQUESANS, MARSHALLESE, MBUNDU, MENDE, MERINA, MONGUOR, MZAB, NGONI, NYANEKA, NYORO,
OKINAWANS, PAIWAN, PALAUANS, PAWNEE, PENDE, PONAPEANS, ROTINESE, SAMOANS, SOTHO, SWAZI,
TAGBANUA, TANALA, TANIMBARESE, TERA, TERENA, THONGA, TIKOPIA, TIMUCUA, TROBRIAND, TSHIMSHIAN,
TURKMEN, VENDA, WUTE, YOMBE

129 IN RIGHT COLUMN

ABOR, ALCRESE, AMERICANS, ARAUCANIANS, ATSUGEWI, AYMARA, AZTEC, BARABRA, BARI, BASQUES,
BASSERI, BENGALI, BHIL, BOERS, BRAZILIANS, BULGARIANS, BURMESE, BURUSHO, CAGABA, CAMBA,
CAMBODIANS, CHEREMIS, CHUKCHEE, COORG, CUNA, CZECHS, DOGON, DUSUN, DUTCH, EGYPTIANS,
EYAK, FANG, GARO, GILBERTESE, GISU, GOAJIRO, GOND, HASANIA, HAZARA, HEBREWS,
HERERO, HUICHOL, HURON, HUTSUL, ICELANDERS, IFUGAO, ILA, INCA, INGALIK, IRAQW,
IRISH, JAPANESE, JAVANESE, KAPAUKU, KAREN, KERALA, KHASI, KIKUYU, KOHISTANI, KOREANS,
KORYAK, KPE, LAKALAI, LAMET, LANGO, LAPPS, LAU, LEPCHA, LHOTA NAGA, LUO,
MALAYS, MAM, MANCHU, MANUS, MAYA, MBUGWE, MIN CHINESE, MINANGKABAU, MINCHIA, MNONG GAR,
MOSSI, MOTA, NAMA, NATCHEZ, NOMLAKI, NUNIVAK, NUPE, NURI, ONTONG-JAVA, PATHAN,
PORTUGUESE, PURUM, REGEIBAT, RIFFIANS, ROMANS, RUNDI, RWALA, SAGADA, SAMOYED, SENIANG,
SERBS, SHILLUK, SINDHI, SIUAI, SIWANS, SOMALI, SONGHAI, SYRIANS, TALLENSI, TAMIL,
TARAHUMARA, TAREUMIUT, TENINO, THAI, TIBETANS, TIGRINYA, TOLOWA, TORAJA, TUPINAMBA, TWANA,
VIETNAMESE, WALLOONS, WOLOF, YAKUT, YAPESE, YOKUTS, YORUBA, YUKI, YUROK

180 EXCLUDED BECAUSE IRRELEVANT (SEE RIGHT COLUMN, PARAGRAPH 102)

17 EXCLUDED BECAUSE UNASCERTAINED

---

3 TEND LESS TO BE THOSE LOCATED OUTSIDE OF AFRICA (320) — 0.65 OF 74

3 TEND MORE TO BE THOSE LOCATED OUTSIDE OF AFRICA (320) — 0.86 OF 129

26	18
48	111

XSQ= 11.21
PHI= 0.235
XP = 0.0008

4	LEAN MORE TOWARD BEING THOSE LOCATED OUTSIDE OF THE CIRCUM-MEDITERRANEAN (355)	0.95 OF 74	4	LEAN LESS TOWARD BEING THOSE LOCATED OUTSIDE OF THE CIRCUM-MEDITERRANEAN (355)	0.77 OF 129	4 30 70 99 XSQ= 9.50 PHI= -0.216 XP = 0.0021
6	TILT LESS TOWARD BEING THOSE LOCATED OUTSIDE OF THE INSULAR PACIFIC (330)	0.72 OF 74	6	TILT MORE TOWARD BEING THOSE LOCATED OUTSIDE OF THE INSULAR PACIFIC (330)	0.87 OF 129	21 17 53 112 XSQ= 6.18 PHI= 0.174 XP = 0.0129
13	TILT MORE TOWARD BEING THOSE WHERE THE LATITUDE IS LESS THAN FORTY DEGREES (329)	0.89 OF 74	13	TILT LESS TOWARD BEING THOSE WHERE THE LATITUDE IS LESS THAN FORTY DEGREES (329)	0.77 OF 129	8 30 66 99 XSQ= 4.00 PHI= -0.140 XP = 0.0454
14	TILT MORE TOWARD BEING THOSE WHERE THE LATITUDE IS LESS THAN THIRTY DEGREES (281)	0.81 OF 74	14	TILT LESS TOWARD BEING THOSE WHERE THE LATITUDE IS LESS THAN THIRTY DEGREES (281)	0.64 OF 129	14 47 60 82 XSQ= 6.06 PHI= -0.173 XP = 0.0139
16	TILT LESS TOWARD BEING THOSE WHERE THE LATITUDE IS TEN DEGREES OR GREATER (277)	0.64 OF 74	16	TILT MORE TOWARD BEING THOSE WHERE THE LATITUDE IS TEN DEGREES OR GREATER (277)	0.78 OF 129	47 101 27 28 XSQ= 4.48 PHI= -0.149 XP = 0.0343
33	TILT MORE TOWARD BEING THOSE WHERE THE NATURAL ENVIRONMENT IS OTHER THAN 'VERY HARSH,' I.E., DESERT, DESERT GRASSES AND SHRUBS, TUNDRA, OR HIGH PLATEAU STEPPE (341) FWM	0.95 OF 74	33	TILT LESS TOWARD BEING THOSE WHERE THE NATURAL ENVIRONMENT IS OTHER THAN 'VERY HARSH,' I.E., DESERT, DESERT GRASSES AND SHRUBS, TUNDRA, OR HIGH PLATEAU STEPPE (341) FWM	0.82 OF 129	4 23 70 106 XSQ= 5.26 PHI= -0.161 XP = 0.0218
53	TILT TOWARD BEING THOSE WHERE FOOD PRODUCTION IS BY SIMPLE AGRICULTURE OR INCIPIENT FOOD PRODUCTION, RATHER THAN BY INTENSIVE AGRICULTURE (147)	0.66 OF 50	53	TILT TOWARD BEING THOSE WHERE FOOD PRODUCTION IS BY INTENSIVE AGRICULTURE, RATHER THAN BY SIMPLE AGRICULTURE OR INCIPIENT FOOD PRODUCTION (91)	0.54 OF 90	17 49 33 41 XSQ= 4.60 PHI= -0.181 XP = 0.0319
55	TILT TOWARD BEING THOSE WHERE FOOD PRODUCTION IS BY SIMPLE AGRICULTURE, RATHER THAN BY INTENSIVE AGRICULTURE (101)	0.61 OF 44	55	TILT TOWARD BEING THOSE WHERE FOOD PRODUCTION IS BY INTENSIVE AGRICULTURE, RATHER THAN BY SIMPLE AGRICULTURE (91)	0.62 OF 79	17 49 27 30 XSQ= 5.31 PHI= -0.208 XP = 0.0212
63	TILT LESS TOWARD BEING THOSE WHERE HUSBANDRY, IF PRESENT, IS PRINCIPALLY IN THE FORM OF BOVINE, EQUINE, CAMEL-LIKE, OR DEER-LIKE ANIMALS, RATHER THAN PIGS, SHEEP, OR GOATS (152)	0.60 OF 48	63	TILT MORE TOWARD BEING THOSE WHERE HUSBANDRY, IF PRESENT, IS PRINCIPALLY IN THE FORM OF BOVINE, EQUINE, CAMEL-LIKE, OR DEER-LIKE ANIMALS, RATHER THAN PIGS, SHEEP, OR GOATS (152)	0.81 OF 93	29 75 19 18 XSQ= 5.69 PHI= -0.201 XP = 0.0171

77	DRIFT TOWARD BEING THOSE 0.83 OF 12 WHERE THE WRITING SYSTEM IS MNEMONIC OR ABSENT, RATHER THAN BEING ALPHABETIC-OR-PHONETIC (39) JMH	77	DRIFT TOWARD BEING THOSE 0.50 OF 20 WHERE THE WRITING SYSTEM IS ALPHABETIC-OR-PHONETIC, RATHER THAN BEING MNEMONIC OR ABSENT (15) JMH	2 10 10 10 XSQ= 2.28 PHI= -0.267 EP = 0.0753
79	TILT MORE TOWARD BEING THOSE 0.97 OF 35 WHERE NO CITY IS PRESENT (201)	79	TILT LESS TOWARD BEING THOSE 0.76 OF 88 WHERE NO CITY IS PRESENT (201)	1 21 34 67 XSQ= 6.16 PHI= -0.224 XP = 0.0131
86	TEND MORE TO BE THOSE 0.87 OF 61 WHERE THE LEVEL OF POLITICAL INTEGRATION IS THE LARGE STATE, THE LITTLE STATE, OR THE MINIMAL STATE (148) GPM	86	TEND LESS TO BE THOSE 0.54 OF 90 WHERE THE LEVEL OF POLITICAL INTEGRATION IS THE LARGE STATE, THE LITTLE STATE, OR THE MINIMAL STATE (148) GPM	53 49 8 41 XSQ= 16.01 PHI= 0.326 XP = 0.0001
88	TEND MORE TO BE THOSE 0.87 OF 60 WHERE, IF A HEADMANSHIP IS PRESENT, SUCCESSION IS HEREDITARY (165)	88	TEND LESS TO BE THOSE 0.54 OF 87 WHERE, IF A HEADMANSHIP IS PRESENT, SUCCESSION IS HEREDITARY (165)	8 40 52 47 XSQ= 15.75 PHI= -0.327 XP = 0.0001
96	TEND MORE TO BE THOSE 0.87 OF 60 WHERE THE HIERARCHY OF NATIONAL JURISDICTION HAS FOUR, THREE, TWO OR ONE LEVEL (174) GES,EA	96	TEND LESS TO BE THOSE 0.60 OF 108 WHERE THE HIERARCHY OF NATIONAL JURISDICTION HAS FOUR, THREE, TWO OR ONE LEVEL (174) GES,EA	52 65 8 43 XSQ= 11.57 PHI= 0.262 XP = 0.0007
109	TILT MORE TOWARD BEING THOSE 0.90 OF 68 WHERE CASTES ARE ABSENT (317)	109	TILT LESS TOWARD BEING THOSE 0.75 OF 114 WHERE CASTES ARE ABSENT (317)	7 29 61 85 XSQ= 5.24 PHI= -0.170 XP = 0.0221
110	LEAN MORE TOWARD BEING THOSE 0.76 OF 71 WHERE SLAVERY IS PRESENT (163)	110	LEAN LESS TOWARD BEING THOSE 0.52 OF 124 WHERE SLAVERY IS PRESENT (163)	54 65 17 59 XSQ= 9.64 PHI= 0.222 XP = 0.0019
128	LEAN TOWARD BEING THOSE 0.71 OF 21 WHERE, IF SUBSISTENCE IS PRIMARILY BY AGRICULTURE, THE WORK IS MAINLY DONE BY FEMALES (37)	128	LEAN TOWARD BEING THOSE 0.71 OF 34 WHERE, IF SUBSISTENCE IS PRIMARILY BY AGRICULTURE, THE WORK IS MAINLY DONE BY MALES (40)	6 24 15 10 XSQ= 7.63 PHI= -0.372 XP = 0.0058
176	DRIFT TOWARD BEING THOSE 0.53 OF 70 WHERE THE COMMUNITY IS A CLAN-COMMUNITY OR A COMMUNITY STRUCTURED OR SEGMENTED ON A CLAN BASIS (169)	176	DRIFT TOWARD BEING THOSE 0.61 OF 127 WHERE THE COMMUNITY IS OTHER THAN A CLAN-COMMUNITY OR A COMMUNITY STRUCTURED OR SEGMENTED ON A CLAN BASIS (213)	37 49 33 78 XSQ= 3.18 PHI= 0.127 XP = 0.0745

178	TILT LESS TOWARD BEING THOSE 0.67 OF 70 WHERE THE COMMUNITY IS OTHER THAN SEGMENTED ON A CLAN BASIS AND NON-EXOGAMOUS (295)	178	TILT MORE TOWARD BEING THOSE 0.81 OF 127 WHERE THE COMMUNITY IS OTHER THAN SEGMENTED ON A CLAN BASIS AND NON-EXOGAMOUS (295)	23 24 47 103 XSQ= 4.10 PHI= 0.144 XP = 0.0428
190	DRIFT LESS TOWARD BEING THOSE 0.71 OF 52 WHERE THE KIN GROUP IS PATRILINEAL OR DOUBLE-DESCENT, RATHER THAN MATRILINEAL (186)	190	DRIFT MORE TOWARD BEING THOSE 0.85 OF 82 WHERE THE KIN GROUP IS PATRILINEAL OR DOUBLE-DESCENT, RATHER THAN MATRILINEAL (186)	37 70 15 12 XSQ= 3.16 PHI= -0.154 XP = 0.0755
192	TEND MORE TO BE THOSE 0.91 OF 74 OTHER THAN WHERE THE ONLY KIN GROUP PRESENT IS A KINDRED OR ELSE BILATERAL DESCENT IS INFERRED (289)	192	TEND LESS TO BE THOSE 0.68 OF 129 OTHER THAN WHERE THE ONLY KIN GROUP PRESENT IS A KINDRED OR ELSE BILATERAL DESCENT IS INFERRED (289)	7 41 67 88 XSQ= 11.77 PHI= -0.241 XP = 0.0006
198	LEAN LESS TOWARD BEING THOSE 0.76 OF 41 WHERE RULES FOR THE INHERITANCE OF REAL PROPERTY, IF PRESENT, FAVOR THE MALE HEIR OR LINE, RATHER THAN THE FEMALE (144)	198	LEAN MORE TOWARD BEING THOSE 0.95 OF 62 WHERE RULES FOR THE INHERITANCE OF REAL PROPERTY, IF PRESENT, FAVOR THE MALE HEIR OR LINE, RATHER THAN THE FEMALE (144)	31 59 10 3 XSQ= 6.87 PHI= -0.258 XP = 0.0087
221	TILT LESS TOWARD BEING THOSE 0.81 OF 69 WHERE MATRILATERAL CROSS-COUSIN MARRIAGE IS NOT PRESCRIBED OR PREFERRED (335)	221	TILT MORE TOWARD BEING THOSE 0.92 OF 119 WHERE MATRILATERAL CROSS-COUSIN MARRIAGE IS NOT PRESCRIBED OR PREFERRED (335)	13 9 56 110 XSQ= 4.34 PHI= 0.152 XP = 0.0372
240	TILT LESS TOWARD BEING THOSE 0.51 OF 41 WHERE THE FAMILY, IF EXTENDED, IS SMALL OR STEM, RATHER THAN LARGE (135)	240	TILT MORE TOWARD BEING THOSE 0.74 OF 78 WHERE THE FAMILY, IF EXTENDED, IS SMALL OR STEM, RATHER THAN LARGE (135)	20 20 21 58 XSQ= 5.45 PHI= 0.214 XP = 0.0195
242	TEND MORE TO BE THOSE 0.93 OF 73 WHERE MARRIAGE IS COMMONLY OR OCCASIONALLY POLYGYNOUS, RATHER THAN MONOGAMOUS (314)	242	TEND LESS TO BE THOSE 0.72 OF 128 WHERE MARRIAGE IS COMMONLY OR OCCASIONALLY POLYGYNOUS, RATHER THAN MONOGAMOUS (314)	68 92 5 36 XSQ= 11.68 PHI= 0.241 XP = 0.0006
263	DRIFT MORE TOWARD BEING THOSE 0.70 OF 73 WHERE WIVES ARE OBTAINED BY RELATIVELY DIFFICULT MEANS, NAMELY BY BRIDE-PRICE, BRIDE-SERVICE, OR EXCHANGING A FEMALE RELATIVE (233)	263	DRIFT LESS TOWARD BEING THOSE 0.55 OF 129 WHERE WIVES ARE OBTAINED BY RELATIVELY DIFFICULT MEANS, NAMELY BY BRIDE-PRICE, BRIDE-SERVICE, OR EXCHANGING A FEMALE RELATIVE (233)	51 71 22 58 XSQ= 3.69 PHI= 0.135 XP = 0.0549
277	DRIFT TOWARD BEING THOSE 0.86 OF 7 WHERE THE STATUS OF WOMEN IS NOT STRONGLY INFERIOR OR SUBJECTED (22) LWS	277	DRIFT TOWARD BEING THOSE 0.64 OF 11 WHERE THE STATUS OF WOMEN IS INFERIOR OR SUBJECTED (14) LWS	1 7 6 4 XSQ= 2.46 PHI= -0.369 EP = 0.0656

No.	Statement	Proportion	No.	Statement	Proportion	Statistics
314	TILT TOWARD BEING THOSE WHERE THE INCIDENCE OF MOTHER-CHILD HOUSEHOLDS IS HIGH (19) W-D,S	0.55 OF 20	314	TILT TOWARD BEING THOSE WHERE THE INCIDENCE OF MOTHER-CHILD HOUSEHOLDS IS LOW (61) W-D,S	0.86 OF 21	11 3 9 18 XSQ= 5.85 PHI= 0.378 XP = 0.0156
316	TILT TOWARD BEING THOSE WHERE EXCLUSIVE MOTHER-SON SLEEPING ARRANGEMENTS LAST ONE YEAR OR LONGER (19) W-K-A	0.62 OF 13	316	TILT TOWARD BEING THOSE WHERE EXCLUSIVE MOTHER-SON SLEEPING ARRANGEMENTS LAST LESS THAN ONE YEAR (25) W-K-A	0.85 OF 13	8 2 5 11 XSQ= 4.06 PHI= 0.395 EP = 0.0414
333	IN ALL CASES ARE THOSE WHERE THE AGE AT BEGINNING OF TRAINING IN HETEROSEXUAL PLAY INHIBITION IS EIGHT YEARS OR HIGHER (8) W-C	1.00 OF 6	333	TILT TOWARD BEING THOSE WHERE THE AGE AT BEGINNING OF TRAINING IN HETEROSEXUAL PLAY INHIBITION IS LOWER THAN EIGHT YEARS (8) W-C	0.75 OF 4	6 1 0 3 XSQ= 3.35 PHI= 0.579 EP = 0.0333
345	DRIFT TOWARD BEING THOSE WHERE THE CHILD'S INFERRED ANXIETY OVER NON-PERFORMANCE OF SELF-RELIANT BEHAVIOR IS HIGH (37) B-B-C	0.63 OF 19	345	DRIFT TOWARD BEING THOSE WHERE THE CHILD'S INFERRED ANXIETY OVER NON-PERFORMANCE OF SELF-RELIANT BEHAVIOR IS LOW (39) B-B-C	0.69 OF 16	12 5 7 11 XSQ= 2.38 PHI= 0.261 EP = 0.0922
351	DRIFT TOWARD BEING THOSE WHERE THE CHILD'S INFERRED CONFLICT REGARDING ACHIEVEMENT BEHAVIOR IS HIGH (26) B-B-C	0.60 OF 15	351	DRIFT TOWARD BEING THOSE WHERE THE CHILD'S INFERRED CONFLICT REGARDING ACHIEVEMENT BEHAVIOR IS LOW (34) B-B-C	0.80 OF 10	9 2 6 8 XSQ= 2.44 PHI= 0.313 EP = 0.0992
354	LEAN TOWARD BEING THOSE WHERE THE CHILD'S INFERRED ANXIETY OVER PERFORMANCE OF OBEDIENT BEHAVIOR IS HIGH (36) B-B-C	0.74 OF 19	354	LEAN TOWARD BEING THOSE WHERE THE CHILD'S INFERRED ANXIETY OVER PERFORMANCE OF OBEDIENT BEHAVIOR IS LOW (37) B-B-C	0.75 OF 16	14 4 5 12 XSQ= 6.41 PHI= 0.428 EP = 0.0067
355	DRIFT TOWARD BEING THOSE WHERE THE CHILD'S INFERRED CONFLICT REGARDING OBEDIENT BEHAVIOR IS HIGH (35) B-B-C	0.63 OF 19	355	DRIFT TOWARD BEING THOSE WHERE THE CHILD'S INFERRED CONFLICT REGARDING OBEDIENT BEHAVIOR IS LOW (38) B-B-C	0.69 OF 16	12 5 7 11 XSQ= 2.38 PHI= 0.261 EP = 0.0922
369	TILT TOWARD BEING THOSE WHERE DISSOCIATION OF THE SEXES AT ADOLESCENCE, OR CUSTOMS OF INITIATION AT ADOLESCENCE, ARE PRESENT (42) JKH	0.82 OF 17	369	TILT TOWARD BEING THOSE WHERE BOTH DISSOCIATION OF THE SEXES AT ADOLESCENCE, AND CUSTOMS OF INITIATION AT ADOLESCENCE, ARE ABSENT (15) JKH	0.56 OF 16	14 7 3 9 XSQ= 3.77 PHI= 0.338 EP = 0.0324
370	TILT TOWARD BEING THOSE WHERE THE SEGREGATION OF ADOLESCENT BOYS IS COMPLETE OR PARTIAL (95)	0.59 OF 41	370	TILT TOWARD BEING THOSE WHERE THE SEGREGATION OF ADOLESCENT BOYS IS ABSENT (148)	0.64 OF 87	24 31 17 56 XSQ= 5.07 PHI= 0.199 XP = 0.0244

No.	Statement	Ratio	No.	Statement	Ratio	Statistics
373	DRIFT LESS TOWARD BEING THOSE WHERE MALE INITIATION CEREMONIES AT PUBERTY ARE ABSENT (27) W-K-A	0.54 OF 13	373	DRIFT MORE TOWARD BEING THOSE WHERE MALE INITIATION CEREMONIES AT PUBERTY ARE ABSENT (27) W-K-A	0.92 OF 13	6 1 7 12 XSQ= 3.13 PHI= 0.347 EP = 0.0730
391	LEAN TOWARD BEING THOSE WHERE PREMARITAL SEX RELATIONS ARE PUNISHED ONLY IF PREGNANCY RESULTS, OR FREELY PERMITTED (90) JTW,EA	0.69 OF 36	391	LEAN TOWARD BEING THOSE WHERE PREMARITAL SEX RELATIONS ARE STRONGLY PUNISHED AND IN FACT RARE, OR WEAKLY PUNISHED AND IN FACT NOT RARE (89) JTW,EA	0.66 OF 73	11 48 25 25 XSQ= 10.65 PHI= -0.313 XP = 0.0011
419	LEAN MORE TOWARD BEING THOSE WHERE MILITARY GLORY IS STRONGLY OR MODERATELY EMPHASIZED (55) PES	0.95 OF 19	419	LEAN LESS TOWARD BEING THOSE WHERE MILITARY GLORY IS STRONGLY OR MODERATELY EMPHASIZED (55) PES	0.54 OF 28	18 15 1 13 XSQ= 7.31 PHI= 0.394 XP = 0.0069
420	DRIFT TOWARD BEING THOSE WHERE BELLICOSITY IS EXTREME (41) PES	0.74 OF 19	420	DRIFT TOWARD BEING THOSE WHERE BELLICOSITY IS MODERATE OR NEGLIGIBLE (46) PES	0.57 OF 28	14 12 5 16 XSQ= 3.19 PHI= 0.261 XP = 0.0739
426	TILT LESS TOWARD BEING THOSE WHERE A HIGH GOD IS PRESENT (156) GES,EA	0.55 OF 49	426	TILT MORE TOWARD BEING THOSE WHERE A HIGH GOD IS PRESENT (156) GES,EA	0.74 OF 95	27 70 22 25 XSQ= 4.27 PHI= -0.172 XP = 0.0389
452	DRIFT TOWARD BEING THOSE WHERE TOTEMISM WITH FOOD TABOOS IS PRESENT (19) WNS	0.71 OF 14	452	DRIFT TOWARD BEING THOSE WHERE TOTEMISM WITH FOOD TABOOS IS ABSENT (24) WNS	0.67 OF 15	10 5 4 10 XSQ= 2.82 PHI= 0.312 EP = 0.0656
472	TILT TOWARD BEING THOSE WHERE THE COMPOSITE NARCISSISM INDEX IS HIGH (47) PES	0.81 OF 21	472	TILT TOWARD BEING THOSE WHERE THE COMPOSITE NARCISSISM INDEX IS LOW (43) PES	0.55 OF 29	17 13 4 16 XSQ= 5.20 PHI= 0.323 XP = 0.0225
476	DRIFT TOWARD BEING THOSE WHERE THE DEGREE OF INSOBRIETY IS MODERATE OR SLIGHT (18) CH	0.62 OF 13	476	DRIFT TOWARD BEING THOSE WHERE THE DEGREE OF INSOBRIETY IS STRONG (31) DH	0.75 OF 16	5 12 8 4 XSQ= 2.58 PHI= -0.299 EP = 0.0667

109 CULTURES
WHERE CASTES ARE PRESENT (51)

109 CULTURES
WHERE CASTES ARE ABSENT (317)

BACKGROUND ON PAGE 90

BCTH SUBJECT AND PREDICATE

51 IN LEFT COLUMN

AMBA	ARYANS	BAJUN	BALINESE	BAMBARA	BARI	BASSERI	BELU	BENGALI	BHIL
BOERS	BCZC	BRAZILIANS	BUCUMA	BURUSHO	COORG	DARD	DOGCN	EGYPTIANS	FANG
FUTAJALCNKE	JAPANESE	KERALA	KOHISTANI	KOL	KONSO	KOREANS	KUBA	MARGI	MASAI
MONGO	MOSSI	MZAB	NATCHEZ	NUER	NURI	ORAON	PATHAN	REGEIBAT	RIFFIANS
RUNDI	RWALA	SINHALESE	SOMALI	SONGHAI	TAMIL	TEDA	TENDA	TIGRINYA	WOLOF
YAPESE									

317 IN RIGHT CCLUMN

ABIPCN	ABCR	AINU	AJIE	AKHA	ALACALUF	ALORESE	AMERICANS	ANDAMANESE	APINAYE
ARANDA	ARAPESH	ARAUCANIANS	ASHANTI	ATAYAL	ATSUGEWI	AWEIKOMA	AYMARA	AZANDE	AZTEC
BABWA	BACAIRI	BAMILEKE	BANCA	BASQUES	BATAK	BAYA	BEMBA	BERGCAMA	BETE
BLACK CARIB	BORCRO	BOTOCUCO	BULGARIANS	CADUVEO	CAGABA	CALLINAGO	CAMAYURA	CAMBA	CAMBODIANS
CARAJA	CARIB	CAYAPA	CHAGGA	CHAMACOCO	CHENCHU	CHEREMIS	CHERKESS	CHERCKEE	CHEYENNE
CHIBCHA	CHINANTEC	CHIR-APACHE	CHIRIGUANO	CHOCO	CHOROTI	CHORTI	CHUKCHEE	COCHITI	COMANCHE
COPR ESKIMO	CREE	CREEK	CROW	CUNA	CZECHS	DAGUR	DELAWARE	DIEGUENO	DIERI
DILLING	DOBUANS	DCROBO	DUSUN	DUTCH	ELLICE	ENGA	EYAK	FON	FOX
GANDA	GARC	GILBERTESE	GILYAK	GISU	GOAJIRO	GROS VENTRE	GUAHIBC	GUATC	GURE
HAIDA	HANC	HANUNCC	HASINAI	HAVASUPAI	HAWAIIANS	HEBREWS	HEHE	HERERO	HUICHOL
HUKUNDIKA	HURCN	HUTSUL	IBAN	ICELANDERS	IFUGAO	ILA	INCA	INGALIK	INGASSANA
IRISH	JAVANESE	JEMEZ	JIVARO	JUKUN	KACHIN	KALMYK	KAPAUKU	KAREN	KARIERA
KASKA	KATAB	KAZAK	KERAKI	KET	KHEVSUR	KIKUYU	KICW-APACHE	KISSI	KORYAK
KPE	KUNG	KURTATCHI	KUTENAI	KWAKIUTL	LAKALAI	LAKHER	LAMBA	LAMET	LANGO
LAPPS	LAU	LESU	LHOTA NAGA	LIFU	LOZI	LUBA	LUC	MACASSARESE	MAGUZAWA
MAM	MAMBILA	MAMVU	MANCHU	MANDAN	MANGAIANS	MANIHIKI	MANUS	MAORI	MARICOPA
MARQUESANS	MARSHALLESE	MATACC	MATAKAM	MAYA	MBUGWE	MBUNDU	MBUTI	MENCE	MENTAWEI
MERINA	MIAMI	MIAC	MINANGKABAU	MISKITO	MIWOK	MNONG GAR	MOTA	MOTILON	MUNDURUCU
MURINBATA	MURNGIN	NABESNA	NAMA	NAMBICUARA	NANDI	NASKAPI	NAVAHO	NDEMBU	NGONI
NICOBARESE	NOMLAKI	NUNIVAK	NUPE	NYAKYUSA	NYANEKA	NYARO	NYORO	OJIBWA	OKINAWANS
OMAHA	CNA	CNTCNG-JAVA	PAEZ	PAIWAN	PALAUANS	PALIKUR	PAPAGO	PARAUJANO	PAWNEE
PENDE	PENCBSCOT	PCNAPEANS	POPOLUCA	PORTUGUESE	PUKAPUKA	PURARI	PURUM	RARCIANS	ROMANS
ROTINESE	ROTUMANS	SAGACA	SAMOANS	SAMOYED	SANDAWE	SANPOIL	SANTAL	SARAMACCA	SARSI
SELUNG	SEMANG	SEMINOLE	SENIANG	SERBS	SERI	SHERENTE	SHILLUK	SHLUH	SIRIONO
SIUAI	SOTHO	SUBANUN	SWAZI	TAGBANUA	TALAMANCA	TALLENSI	TANALA	TANIMBARESE	TAOS
TAPIRAPE	TARAHUMARA	TAREUMIUT	TEHUELCHE	TENETEHARA	TENINO	TERA	TERENA	TESC	TETON
THAI	THCNGA	TIKOPIA	TIMBIRA	TIMUCUA	TIV	TIWI	TODA	TOKELAU	TOLOWA
TORAJA	TOTCNAC	TRISTAN	TROBRIAND	TRUKESE	TRUMAI	TSHIMSHIAN	TUBATULABAL	TUCANO	TUCUNA
TUNEBO	TUPINAMBA	TURKANA	TWANA	ULAWANS	UTE	VEDDA	VENDA	VIETNAMESE	WAICA
WALLOONS	WANTOAT	WAPISHANA	WAROPEN	WARRAU	WASHO	WICHITA	WIKMUNKAN	WINNEBAGO	WITOTO

WOGEO YOKUTS WOLEAIANS YOMBE WUTE YORUBA YABARANA YUKAGHIR YAGUA YUKI YAHGAN YUROK YAKO ZUNI YAKUT YAO YARURO

32 EXCLUDED BECAUSE UNASCERTAINED

3	DRIFT LESS TOWARD BEING THOSE LOCATED OUTSIDE OF AFRICA (320)	0.69 OF 51	3	DRIFT MORE TOWARD BEING THOSE LOCATED OUTSIDE OF AFRICA (320)	0.80 OF 317	16 63 35 254 XSQ= 2.80 PHI= 0.087 XP = 0.0944
4	TEND LESS TO BE THOSE LOCATED OUTSIDE OF THE CIRCUM-MEDITERRANEAN (355)	0.73 OF 51	4	TEND MORE TO BE THOSE LOCATED OUTSIDE OF THE CIRCUM-MEDITERRANEAN (355)	0.93 OF 317	14 22 37 295 XSQ= 18.68 PHI= 0.225 XP = 0.0000
5	TEND LESS TO BE THOSE LOCATED OUTSIDE OF EAST EURASIA (330)	0.67 OF 51	5	TEND MORE TO BE THOSE LOCATED OUTSIDE OF EAST EURASIA (330)	0.89 OF 317	17 36 34 281 XSQ= 15.48 PHI= 0.205 XP = 0.0001
6	TILT MORE TOWARD BEING THOSE LOCATED OUTSIDE OF THE INSULAR PACIFIC (330)	0.94 OF 51	6	TILT LESS TOWARD BEING THOSE LOCATED OUTSIDE OF THE INSULAR PACIFIC (330)	0.79 OF 317	3 65 48 252 XSQ= 5.30 PHI= -0.120 XP = 0.0213
8	LEAN MORE TOWARD BEING THOSE LOCATED OUTSIDE OF NORTH AMERICA (330)	0.98 OF 51	8	LEAN LESS TOWARD BEING THOSE LOCATED OUTSIDE OF NORTH AMERICA (330)	0.79 OF 317	1 68 50 249 XSQ= 9.71 PHI= -0.162 XP = 0.0018
9	IN ALL CASES ARE THOSE LOCATED OUTSIDE OF SOUTH AMERICA (335)	1.00 OF 51	9	TEND LESS TO BE THOSE LOCATED OUTSIDE OF SOUTH AMERICA (335)	0.80 OF 317	0 63 51 254 XSQ= 10.87 PHI= -0.172 XP = 0.0010
13	IN ALL CASES ARE THOSE WHERE THE LATITUDE IS LESS THAN FORTY DEGREES (329)	1.00 OF 51	13	TEND LESS TO BE THOSE WHERE THE LATITUDE IS LESS THAN FORTY DEGREES (329)	0.79 OF 317	0 67 51 250 XSQ= 11.80 PHI= -0.179 XP = 0.0006
51	TEND MORE TO BE THOSE WHERE SUBSISTENCE IS PRIMARILY BY FOOD PRODUCTION -- I. E., AGRICULTURE OR HUSBANDRY -- RATHER THAN BY GATHERING (253)	0.90 OF 51	51	TEND LESS TO BE THOSE WHERE SUBSISTENCE IS PRIMARILY BY FOOD PRODUCTION -- I. E., AGRICULTURE OR HUSBANDRY -- RATHER THAN BY GATHERING (253)	0.55 OF 317	46 175 5 142 XSQ= 20.99 PHI= 0.239 XP = 0.0000

53	TEND TO BE THOSE 0.67 OF 36 WHERE FOOD PRODUCTION IS BY INTENSIVE AGRICULTURE, RATHER THAN BY SIMPLE AGRICULTURE OR INCIPIENT FOOD PRODUCTION (91)	53	TEND TO BE THOSE 0.71 OF 183 WHERE FOOD PRODUCTION IS BY SIMPLE AGRICULTURE OR INCIPIENT FOOD PRODUCTION, RATHER THAN BY INTENSIVE AGRICULTURE (147)	24 53 12 130 XSQ= 17.14 PHI= 0.280 XP = 0.0000
55	TEND TO BE THOSE 0.73 OF 33 WHERE FOOD PRODUCTION IS BY INTENSIVE AGRICULTURE, RATHER THAN BY SIMPLE AGRICULTURE (91)	55	TEND TO BE THOSE 0.62 OF 140 WHERE FOOD PRODUCTION IS BY SIMPLE AGRICULTURE, RATHER THAN BY INTENSIVE AGRICULTURE (101)	24 53 9 87 XSQ= 11.77 PHI= 0.261 XP = 0.0006
62	TEND MORE TO BE THOSE 0.80 OF 51 WHERE HUSBANDRY OF SOME KIND IS PRESENT (228)	62	TEND LESS TO BE THOSE 0.52 OF 317 WHERE HUSBANDRY OF SOME KIND IS PRESENT (228)	41 165 10 152 XSQ= 13.19 PHI= 0.189 XP = 0.0003
63	TILT MORE TOWARD BEING THOSE 0.83 OF 41 WHERE HUSBANDRY, IF PRESENT, IS PRINCIPALLY IN THE FORM OF BOVINE, EQUINE, CAMEL-LIKE, OR DEER-LIKE ANIMALS, RATHER THAN PIGS, SHEEP, OR GOATS (152)	63	TILT LESS TOWARD BEING THOSE 0.60 OF 164 WHERE HUSBANDRY, IF PRESENT, IS PRINCIPALLY IN THE FORM OF BOVINE, EQUINE, CAMEL-LIKE, OR DEER-LIKE ANIMALS, RATHER THAN PIGS, SHEEP, OR GOATS (152)	34 99 7 65 XSQ= 6.37 PHI= 0.176 XP = 0.0116
71	TEND TO BE THOSE 0.87 OF 31 WHERE METAL WORKING IS PRESENT (98)	71	TEND TO BE THOSE 0.70 OF 209 WHERE METAL WORKING IS ABSENT (153)	27 63 4 146 XSQ= 34.97 PHI= 0.382 XP = 0.
73	LEAN TOWARD BEING THOSE 0.72 OF 29 WHERE WEAVING IS PRESENT (118)	73	LEAN TOWARD BEING THOSE 0.58 OF 208 WHERE WEAVING IS ABSENT (130)	21 88 8 120 XSQ= 8.11 PHI= 0.185 XP = 0.0044
81	LEAN TOWARD BEING THOSE 0.63 OF 30 WHERE A CITY OR TOWN IS PRESENT, OR THE AVERAGE COMMUNITY SIZE IS 200 OR GREATER (89)	81	LEAN TOWARD BEING THOSE 0.64 OF 177 WHERE NO CITY OR TOWN IS PRESENT, AND THE AVERAGE COMMUNITY SIZE IS SMALLER THAN 200 (135)	19 64 11 113 XSQ= 6.80 PHI= 0.181 XP = 0.0091
85	TEND TO BE THOSE 0.56 OF 34 WHERE THE LEVEL OF POLITICAL INTEGRATION IS THE LARGE STATE, OR THE LITTLE STATE (70) GPM	85	TEND TO BE THOSE 0.82 OF 251 WHERE THE LEVEL OF POLITICAL INTEGRATION IS THE MINIMAL STATE, THE AUTONOMOUS COMMUNITY, OR THE FAMILY (234) GPM	19 44 15 207 XSQ= 23.40 PHI= 0.287 XP = 0.0000
86	TEND TO BE THOSE 0.85 OF 34 WHERE THE LEVEL OF POLITICAL INTEGRATION IS THE LARGE STATE, THE LITTLE STATE, OR THE MINIMAL STATE (148) GPM	86	TEND TO BE THOSE 0.59 OF 251 WHERE THE LEVEL OF POLITICAL INTEGRATION IS THE AUTONOMOUS COMMUNITY, OR THE FAMILY (156) GPM	29 104 5 147 XSQ= 21.42 PHI= 0.274 XP = 0.0000

No.	Statement	Proportion	No.	Statement	Proportion	Statistics
91	IN ALL CASES ARE THOSE WHERE SOCIETAL COMPLEXITY IS HIGH (18) F-W	1.00 OF 3	91	DRIFT TOWARD BEING THOSE WHERE SOCIETAL COMPLEXITY IS LOW (22) F-W	0.60 OF 35	3 14 0 21 XSQ= 1.96 PHI= 0.227 EP = 0.0806
96	TEND TC BE THCSE WHERE THE HIERARCHY OF NATICNAL JURISDICTION HAS FCUR, THREE, TWC OR ONE LEVEL (174) GES,EA	0.88 OF 43	96	TEND TO BE THOSE WHERE THE HIERARCHY OF NATIONAL JURISDICTICN HAS NO LEVELS (156) GES,EA	0.55 CF 266	38 121 5 145 XSQ= 25.56 PHI= 0.288 XP = 0.0000
97	LEAN LESS TOWARC BEING THCSE WHERE THE HIERARCHY OF LCCAL JURISDICTION HAS THREE OR TWO LEVELS (273) GES,EA	0.67 OF 43	97	LEAN MORE TOWARD BEING THOSE WHERE THE HIERARCHY OF LOCAL JURISDICTICN HAS THREE OR TWO LEVELS (273) GES,EA	0.86 OF 267	14 38 29 229 XSQ= 7.65 PHI= 0.157 XP = 0.0057
98	LEAN MORE TOWARC BEING THCSE WHERE THE HIERARCHY OF LOCAL JURISDICTION HAS FOUR CR THREE LEVELS (238) GES,EA	0.91 OF 43	98	LEAN LESS TOWARD BEING THOSE WHERE THE HIERARCHY OF LOCAL JURISDICTION HAS FOUR OR THREE LEVELS (238) GES,EA	0.67 CF 267	39 179 4 88 XSQ= 8.83 PHI= 0.169 XP = 0.0030
100	LEAN MORE TOWARC BEING THCSE WHERE HIERARCHIES ARE MORE COMPLEX THAN THE 'SIMPLEST,' I. E., MORE COMPLEX THAN TWO LCCAL LEVELS WITH NO NATICNAL LEVELS (267) GES,EA	0.98 OF 43	100	LEAN LESS TOWARD BEING THOSE WHERE HIERARCHIES ARE MORE COMPLEX THAN THE 'SIMPLEST,' I. E., MORE COMPLEX THAN TWO LOCAL LEVELS WITH NO NATIONAL LEVELS (267) GES,EA	0.77 CF 266	42 204 1 62 XSQ= 8.79 PHI= 0.169 XP = 0.0030
102	TEND TC BE THCSE WHERE CLASS STRATIFICATION IS PRESENT (203)	0.78 OF 46	102	TEND TO BE THOSE WHERE CLASS STRATIFICATICN IS ABSENT (180)	0.53 CF 312	36 146 10 166 XSQ= 14.65 PHI= 0.202 XP = 0.0001
106	TILT MORE TOWARC BEING THCSE WHERE CLASS STRATIFICATICN, IF PRESENT, IS BASED CN SOMETHING CTHER THAN WEALTH (126)	0.78 OF 36	106	TILT LESS TOWARD BEING THOSE WHERE CLASS STRATIFICATION, IF PRESENT, IS BASED ON SOMETHING CTHER THAN WEALTH (126)	0.58 CF 146	8 62 28 84 XSQ= 4.18 PHI= -0.152 XP = 0.0409
107	TEND LESS TC BE THCSE WHERE CLASS STRATIFICATION, IF PRESENT, IS BASED CN SCMETHING OTHER THAN OCCUPATICNAL STATUS (160)	0.53 OF 36	107	TEND MORE TC BE THOSE WHERE CLASS STRATIFICATION, IF PRESENT, IS BASED ON SOMETHING CTHER THAN OCCUPATIONAL STATUS (160)	0.86 CF 146	17 20 19 126 XSQ= 18.02 PHI= 0.315 XP = 0.0000
108	TILT MORE TOWARC BEING THCSE WHERE CLASS STRATIFICATICN, IF PRESENT, IS BASED CN SCMETHING CTHER THAN A HEREDITARY ARISTCCRACY (129)	0.81 OF 36	108	TILT LESS TOWARD BEING THOSE WHERE CLASS STRATIFICATION, IF PRESENT, IS BASED ON SOMETHING CTHER THAN A HEREDITARY ARISTOCRACY (129)	0.58 OF 146	7 61 29 85 XSQ= 5.24 PHI= -0.170 XP = 0.0221

110	LEAN TOWARD BEING THOSE WHERE SLAVERY IS PRESENT (163)	0.63 OF 46	110	LEAN TOWARD BEING THOSE WHERE SLAVERY IS ABSENT (218)	0.62 OF 311	29 117 17 194 XSQ= 9.69 PHI= 0.165 XP = 0.0019
116	DRIFT TOWARD BEING THOSE WHERE OCCUPATIONAL SPECIALIZATION IS FULL-TIME, WHETHER OR NOT FOR SURPLUS PRODUCTION (20) JMH	0.80 OF 5	116	DRIFT TOWARD BEING THOSE WHERE OCCUPATIONAL SPECIALIZATION IS PART-TIME ONLY (34) JMH	0.70 OF 46	4 14 1 32 XSQ= 2.92 PHI= 0.239 XP = 0.0873
118	IN ALL CASES ARE THOSE WHERE THE PERCENTAGE OF OCCUPATIONS THAT ARE SPECIALIZED IS HIGH OR MEDIUM (24) WME	1.00 OF 4	118	DRIFT TOWARD BEING THOSE WHERE THE PERCENTAGE OF OCCUPATIONS THAT ARE SPECIALIZED IS LOW (25) WME	0.59 OF 41	4 17 0 24 XSQ= 2.94 PHI= 0.256 XP = 0.0864
129	TEND TO BE THOSE WHERE WEAVING IS MAINLY DONE BY MALES (31)	0.67 OF 18	129	TEND TO BE THOSE WHERE WEAVING IS MAINLY DONE BY FEMALES (73)	0.80 OF 79	12 16 6 63 XSQ= 13.20 PHI= 0.369 XP = 0.0003
130	LEAN TOWARD BEING THOSE WHERE LEATHER WORKING IS MAINLY DONE BY MALES (39)	0.83 OF 12	130	LEAN TOWARD BEING THOSE WHERE LEATHER WORKING IS MAINLY DONE BY FEMALES (45)	0.62 OF 69	10 26 2 43 XSQ= 6.88 PHI= 0.291 XP = 0.0087
183	TILT MORE TOWARD BEING THOSE WHERE THE LARGEST NON-COGNATIC KIN GROUP IS SMALLER THAN A MOEITY, I. E., A PHRATRY OR SIB OR LINEAGE (218)	0.98 OF 44	183	TILT LESS TOWARD BEING THOSE WHERE THE LARGEST NON-COGNATIC KIN GROUP IS SMALLER THAN A MOEITY, I. E., A PHRATRY OR SIB OR LINEAGE (218)	0.83 OF 182	1 31 43 151 XSQ= 5.20 PHI= -0.152 XP = 0.0227
184	DRIFT MORE TOWARD BEING THOSE WHERE THE LARGEST NON-COGNATIC KIN GROUP IS SMALLER THAN A PHRATRY, I. E. A SIB OR LINEAGE (175)	0.82 OF 44	184	DRIFT LESS TOWARD BEING THOSE WHERE THE LARGEST NON-COGNATIC KIN GROUP IS SMALLER THAN A PHRATRY, I. E. A SIB OR LINEAGE (175)	0.66 OF 182	8 61 36 121 XSQ= 3.24 PHI= -0.120 XP = 0.0719
186	TEND TO BE THOSE WHERE THE KIN GROUP IS EXCLUSIVELY PATRILINEAL (150)	0.65 OF 51	186	TEND TO BE THOSE WHERE THE KIN GROUP IS OTHER THAN EXCLUSIVELY PATRILINEAL (250)	0.69 OF 317	33 97 18 220 XSQ= 20.90 PHI= 0.238 XP = 0.0000
188	TEND MORE TO BE THOSE WHERE THE KIN GROUP IS OTHER THAN EXCLUSIVELY COGNATIC (252)	0.86 OF 51	188	TEND LESS TO BE THOSE WHERE THE KIN GROUP IS OTHER THAN EXCLUSIVELY COGNATIC (252)	0.57 OF 317	7 135 44 182 XSQ= 14.25 PHI= -0.197 XP = 0.0002

190	LEAN MORE TOWARD BEING THOSE 0.91 OF 44 WHERE THE KIN GROUP IS PATRILINEAL OR DOUBLE-DESCENT, RATHER THAN MATRILINEAL (186)	190	LEAN LESS TOWARD BEING THOSE 0.68 OF 177 WHERE THE KIN GROUP IS PATRILINEAL OR DOUBLE-DESCENT, RATHER THAN MATRILINEAL (186)	40 121 4 56 XSQ= 7.95 PHI= 0.190 XP = 0.0048
192	LEAN MORE TOWARD BEING THOSE 0.90 OF 51 OTHER THAN WHERE THE ONLY KIN GROUP PRESENT IS A KINDRED OR ELSE BILATERAL DESCENT IS INFERRED (289)	192	LEAN LESS TOWARD BEING THOSE 0.68 OF 317 OTHER THAN WHERE THE ONLY KIN GROUP PRESENT IS A KINDRED OR ELSE BILATERAL DESCENT IS INFERRED (289)	5 101 46 216 XSQ= 9.37 PHI= -0.160 XP = 0.0022
196	LEAN MORE TOWARD BEING THOSE 0.90 OF 41 WHERE INDIVIDUAL RIGHTS IN REAL PROPERTY, AND RULES FOR INHERITANCE, ARE PRESENT (194)	196	LEAN LESS TOWARD BEING THOSE 0.63 OF 220 WHERE INDIVIDUAL RIGHTS IN REAL PROPERTY, AND RULES FOR INHERITANCE, ARE PRESENT (194)	37 138 4 82 XSQ= 10.63 PHI= 0.202 XP = 0.0011
198	DRIFT MORE TOWARD BEING THOSE 0.97 OF 34 WHERE RULES FOR THE INHERITANCE OF REAL PROPERTY, IF PRESENT, FAVOR THE MALE HEIR OR LINE, RATHER THAN THE FEMALE (144)	198	DRIFT LESS TOWARD BEING THOSE 0.83 OF 113 WHERE RULES FOR THE INHERITANCE OF REAL PROPERTY, IF PRESENT, FAVOR THE MALE HEIR OR LINE, RATHER THAN THE FEMALE (144)	33 94 1 19 XSQ= 3.18 PHI= 0.147 XP = 0.0745
201	TILT MORE TOWARD BEING THOSE 0.96 OF 51 WHERE MARITAL RESIDENCE IS NON-OPTIONAL, RATHER THAN AMBILOCAL OR NEOLOCAL (334)	201	TILT LESS TOWARD BEING THOSE 0.81 OF 315 WHERE MARITAL RESIDENCE IS NON-OPTIONAL, RATHER THAN AMBILOCAL OR NEOLOCAL (334)	49 256 2 59 XSQ= 5.91 PHI= 0.127 XP = 0.0151
204	LEAN MORE TOWARD BEING THOSE 0.96 OF 50 WHERE MARITAL RESIDENCE IS PATRILOCAL, VIRILOCAL, OR AVUNCULOCAL, RATHER THAN AMBILOCAL OR NEOLOCAL (270)	204	LEAN LESS TOWARD BEING THOSE 0.77 OF 254 WHERE MARITAL RESIDENCE IS PATRILOCAL, VIRILOCAL, OR AVUNCULOCAL, RATHER THAN AMBILOCAL OR NEOLOCAL (270)	48 195 2 59 XSQ= 8.47 PHI= 0.167 XP = 0.0036
209	LEAN MORE TOWARD BEING THOSE 0.98 OF 49 WHERE MARITAL RESIDENCE IS PATRILOCAL, VIRILOCAL, OR AVUNCULOCAL, RATHER THAN MATRILOCAL OR UXORILOCAL (270)	209	LEAN LESS TOWARD BEING THOSE 0.76 OF 256 WHERE MARITAL RESIDENCE IS PATRILOCAL, VIRILOCAL, OR AVUNCULOCAL, RATHER THAN MATRILOCAL OR UXORILOCAL (270)	48 195 1 61 XSQ= 10.75 PHI= 0.188 XP = 0.0010
210	TILT MORE TOWARD BEING THOSE 0.97 OF 40 WHERE MARITAL RESIDENCE IS PATRILOCAL, RATHER THAN MATRILOCAL (169)	210	TILT LESS TOWARD BEING THOSE 0.78 OF 134 WHERE MARITAL RESIDENCE IS PATRILOCAL, RATHER THAN MATRILOCAL (169)	39 105 1 29 XSQ= 6.63 PHI= 0.195 XP = 0.0101
225	TILT TOWARD BEING THOSE 0.64 OF 11 WHERE COUSIN MARRIAGE IS PREFERENTIALLY OR PERMISSIVELY PATRILATERAL, RATHER THAN MATRILATERAL (23)	225	TILT TOWARD BEING THOSE 0.76 OF 42 WHERE COUSIN MARRIAGE IS PREFERENTIALLY OR PERMISSIVELY MATRILATERAL, RATHER THAN PATRILATERAL (43)	7 10 4 32 XSQ= 4.65 PHI= 0.296 XP = 0.0311

236	DRIFT MORE TOWARD BEING THOSE 0.67 OF 51 WHERE THE FAMILY IS OF AN EXTENDED TYPE, RATHER THAN AN INDEPENDENT TYPE (213)	236	DRIFT LESS TOWARD BEING THOSE 0.51 OF 315 WHERE THE FAMILY IS OF AN EXTENDED TYPE, RATHER THAN AN INDEPENDENT TYPE (213)	34 160 17 155 XSQ= 3.83 PHI= 0.102 XP = 0.0505
263	TILT MORE TOWARD BEING THOSE 0.71 OF 51 WHERE WIVES ARE OBTAINED BY RELATIVELY DIFFICULT MEANS, NAMELY BY BRIDE-PRICE, BRIDE-SERVICE, OR EXCHANGING A FEMALE RELATIVE (233)	263	TILT LESS TOWARD BEING THOSE 0.55 OF 313 WHERE WIVES ARE OBTAINED BY RELATIVELY DIFFICULT MEANS, NAMELY BY BRIDE-PRICE, BRIDE-SERVICE, OR EXCHANGING A FEMALE RELATIVE (233)	36 171 15 142 XSQ= 3.92 PHI= 0.104 XP = 0.0476
377	TEND TO BE THOSE 0.57 OF 42 WHERE MALE GENITAL MUTILATION IS PRESENT (83)	377	TEND TO BE THOSE 0.81 OF 262 WHERE MALE GENITAL MUTILATION IS ABSENT (242)	24 49 18 213 XSQ= 27.24 PHI= 0.299 XP = 0.0000
382	TILT TOWARD BEING THOSE 0.78 OF 9 WHERE FEMALE INITIATION RITES ARE ABSENT (27) JKB	382	TILT TOWARD BEING THOSE 0.66 OF 53 WHERE FEMALE INITIATION RITES ARE PRESENT (38) JKB	2 35 7 18 XSQ= 4.45 PHI= -0.268 XP = 0.0349
426	TEND MORE TO BE THOSE 0.88 OF 33 WHERE A HIGH GOD IS PRESENT (156) GES,EA	426	TEND LESS TO BE THOSE 0.54 OF 211 WHERE A HIGH GOD IS PRESENT (156) GES,EA	29 113 4 98 XSQ= 12.44 PHI= 0.226 XP = 0.0004
427	TILT TOWARD BEING THOSE 0.72 OF 29 WHERE A HIGH GOD, IF PRESENT, IS ACTIVE, RATHER THAN INACTIVE (87) GES,EA	427	TILT TOWARD BEING THOSE 0.51 OF 113 WHERE A HIGH GOD, IF PRESENT, IS INACTIVE, RATHER THAN ACTIVE (69) GES,EA	21 55 8 58 XSQ= 4.32 PHI= 0.174 XP = 0.0377
428	TILT MORE TOWARD BEING THOSE 0.90 OF 21 WHERE A HIGH GOD, IF PRESENT AND ACTIVE, SUPPORTS HUMAN MORALITY, RATHER THAN NOT SUPPORTING IT (61) GES,EA	428	TILT LESS TOWARD BEING THOSE 0.60 OF 55 WHERE A HIGH GOD, IF PRESENT AND ACTIVE, SUPPORTS HUMAN MORALITY, RATHER THAN NOT SUPPORTING IT (61) GES,EA	19 33 2 22 XSQ= 5.20 PHI= 0.262 XP = 0.0226
450	DRIFT TOWARD BEING THOSE 0.50 OF 14 WHERE THE OBSERVATION OF FOOD TABOOS IS LOW, RATHER THAN HIGH OR MEDIUM (26) JRL	450	DRIFT TOWARD BEING THOSE 0.77 OF 66 WHERE THE OBSERVATION OF FOOD TABOOS IS HIGH OR MEDIUM, RATHER THAN LOW (60) JRL	7 51 7 15 XSQ= 3.05 PHI= -0.195 XP = 0.0808
458	TEND TO BE THOSE 0.71 OF 17 WHERE GAMES, IF PRESENT, INCLUDE GAMES OF STRATEGY (52) R-A-B,EA	458	TEND TO BE THOSE 0.75 OF 146 WHERE GAMES, IF PRESENT, DO NOT INCLUDE GAMES OF STRATEGY (119) R-A-B,EA	12 36 5 110 XSQ= 13.33 PHI= 0.286 XP = 0.0003

109/

```
473  LEAN TOWARD BEING THOSE          0.89 OF   9        473  LEAN TOWARD BEING THOSE         0.71 OF  75             8    22
     WHERE SENSITIVITY TO INSULT                                 WHERE SENSITIVITY TO INSULT                                   1    53
     IS EXTREME  (32) PES                                        IS MODERATE OR NEGLIGIBLE  (56) PES               XSQ=      9.96
                                                                                                                   PHI=     0.344
                                                                                                                   XP =    0.0016
```

****

110 CULTURES
WHERE SLAVERY IS PRESENT (163)

110 CULTURES
WHERE SLAVERY IS ABSENT (218)

BACKGROUND ON PAGE 90

BCTH SUBJECT AND PREDICATE

....

163 IN LEFT CCLUMN

ABIPON	ABOR	ALCRESE	ARAUCANIANS	ASHANTI	ATAYAL	AZANDE	AZTEC	BABWA	BAJUN
BALINESE	BAMBARA	BAMILEKE	BANDA	BARABRA	BATAK	BAYA	BELU	BEMBA	BERGDAMA
BIRIFOR	BOERS	BOZO	BRAZILIANS	BUDUMA	BURMESE	BURYAT	CALLINAGO	CAMBODIANS	CARAJA
CHAMACOCO	CHERKESS	CHIBCHA	CHUKCHEE	COMANCHE	COORG	CUNA	DILLING	DOGON	EGYPTIANS
EYAK	FON	FOX	FUTAJALONKE	GANDA	GARO	GILBERTESE	GISU	GOAJIRO	GURE
HAIDA	HASANIA	HASINAI	HAWAIIANS	HAZARA	HEBREWS	HEHE	HERERO	IBAN	ICELANDERS
IFUGAO	ILA	JUKUN	KABYLE	KACHIN	KAREN	KATAB	KAZAK	KHALKA	KISSI
KOREANS	KORYAK	KPE	KUBA	KUTENAI	KWAKIUTL	LAKHER	LAMBA	LANGO	LEPCHA
LHOTA NAGA	LIFU	LOLO	LOZI	LUBA	MACASSARESE	MAGUZAWA	MALAYS	MAMBILA	MAMVU
MANCHU	MAORI	MARGI	MAYA	MBUNDU	MENDE	MERINA	MIAMI	MIN CHINESE	MNONG GAR
MONGO	MONGUOR	MOSSI	MZAB	NAVAHO	NDEMBU	NGONI	NUPE	NURI	NYAKYUSA
NYANEKA	NYARO	NYORO	OMAHA	ORAON	PATHAN	PAWNEE	PENDE	REGEIBAT	ROMANS
ROTINESE	RUNDI	RWALA	SHILLUK	SINDHI	SIWANS	SOMALI	SONGHAI	TAGBANUA	TALLENSI
TANALA	TANIMBARESE	TECA	TEHUELCHE	TENINO	TERA	TERENA	TESO	THAI	TIBETANS
TIGRINYA	TIV	TOLOWA	TORAJA	TOTONAC	TRUMAI	TSHIMSHIAN	TUPINAMBA	TURKMEN	TWANA
VENDA	VIETNAMESE	WAROPEN	WITOTO	WOLOF	WUTE	YAKO	YAKUT	YAO	YOMBE
YORUBA	YUKAGHIR	YUROK							

218 IN RIGHT CCLUMN

AINU	AJIE	AKHA	ALACALUF	ALBANIANS	AMBA	AMERICANS	ANDAMANESE	APINAYE	ARANDA
ARAPESH	ATSUGEWI	AWEIKOMA	AYMARA	BACAIRI	BARI	BASQUES	BASSERI	BEJA	BENGALI
BETE	BHIL	BHUIYA	BLACK CARIB	BORORO	BOTOCUDO	BULGARIANS	CADUVEO	CAGABA	CAMAYURA
CAMBA	CARIB	CAYAPA	CHAGGA	CHENCHU	CHEREMIS	CHEROKEE	CHEYENNE	CHINANTEC	CHIR-APACHE
CHOCO	CHOROTI	CHORTI	COCHITI	COPR ESKIMO	CREE	CREEK	CROW	CZECHS	DAGUR
DELAWARE	DIEGUENO	DIERI	DOBUANS	DOROBO	DUSUN	DUTCH	ELLICE	ENGA	FANG
GILYAK	GOND	GROS VENTRE	GUAHIBO	GUATO	HANO	HANUNOO	HAVASUPAI	HUICHOL	HUKUNDIKA
HURON	HUTSUL	INCA	INGALIK	INGASSANA	IRISH	JAPANESE	JAVANESE	JEMEZ	JIVARO
KAPAUKU	KARIERA	KASKA	KERAKI	KERALA	KET	KHASI	KHEVSUR	KIKUYU	KIOW-APACHE
KOL	KONSO	KUNG	KURTATCHI	LAKALAI	LAMET	LAPPS	LAU	LESU	LUO
MAM	MANDAN	MANGAIANS	MANIHIKI	MANUS	MARICOPA	MARQUESANS	MARSHALLESE	MASAI	MATACO
MBUGWE	MBUTI	MENTAWEI	MIAO	MINANGKABAU	MINCHIA	MISKITO	MIWOK	MOTA	MOTILON
MUNDURUCU	MURINBATA	MURNGIN	NABESNA	NAMA	NAMBICUARA	NANDI	NASKAPI	NICOBARESE	NOMLAKI
NUER	NUNIVAK	OJIBWA	OKINAWANS	ONA	ONTONG-JAVA	PAEZ	PAIWAN	PALAUANS	PALIKUR
PAPAGO	PARAUJANO	PENOBSCOT	PONAPEANS	POPOLUCA	PORTUGUESE	PUKAPUKA	PURARI	RARCIANS	RIFFIANS
ROTUMANS	SAGADA	SAMOANS	SAMOYED	SANDAWE	SANPOIL	SANTAL	SARAMACCA	SARSI	SELUNG
SEMANG	SEMINOLE	SENIANG	SERBS	SERI	SHERENTE	SHLUH	SINHALESE	SIRIONO	SIUAI
SOTHO	SUBANUN	SWAZI	SYRIANS	TALAMANCA	TAMIL	TAOS	TAPIRAPE	TARAHUMARA	TAREUMIUT
TENDA	TENETEHARA	TETON	THONGA	TIKOPIA	TIMBIRA	TIWI	TODA	TOKELAU	TRISTAN

TROBRIAND TRUKESE TUBATULABAL TUCANO TUCUNA TURKANA ULAWANS UTE VECCA WAICA
WALLCONS WANTOAT WAPISHANA WARRAU WASHO WICHITA WIKMUNKAN WINNEBAGO WOGEO WOLEAIANS
YABARANA YAGUA YAHGAN YAPESE YARURO YOKUTS YUKI ZUNI

19 EXCLUDED BECAUSE UNASCERTAINED

3	TEND LESS TO BE THOSE LOCATED OUTSIDE OF AFRICA (320)	0.65 OF 163	3	TEND MORE TO BE THOSE LOCATED OUTSIDE OF AFRICA (320)	0.90 OF 218	57 22 106 196 XSQ= 33.62 PHI= 0.297 XP = 0.
5	TILT LESS TOWARD BEING THOSE LOCATED OUTSIDE OF EAST EURASIA (330)	0.79 OF 163	5	TILT MORE TOWARD BEING THOSE LOCATED OUTSIDE OF EAST EURASIA (330)	0.87 OF 218	35 29 128 189 XSQ= 3.89 PHI= 0.101 XP = 0.0486
6	LEAN MORE TOWARD BEING THOSE LOCATED OUTSIDE OF THE INSULAR PACIFIC (330)	0.90 OF 163	6	LEAN LESS TOWARD BEING THOSE LOCATED OUTSIDE OF THE INSULAR PACIFIC (330)	0.77 OF 218	17 51 146 167 XSQ= 9.83 PHI= -0.161 XP = 0.0017
8	LEAN MORE TOWARD BEING THOSE LOCATED OUTSIDE OF NORTH AMERICA (330)	0.89 OF 163	8	LEAN LESS TOWARD BEING THOSE LOCATED OUTSIDE OF NORTH AMERICA (330)	0.78 OF 218	18 49 145 169 XSQ= 7.64 PHI= -0.142 XP = 0.0057
9	LEAN MORE TOWARD BEING THOSE LOCATED OUTSIDE OF SOUTH AMERICA (335)	0.91 OF 163	9	LEAN LESS TOWARD BEING THOSE LOCATED OUTSIDE OF SOUTH AMERICA (335)	0.78 OF 218	14 47 149 171 XSQ= 10.72 PHI= -0.168 XP = 0.0011
42	DRIFT MORE TOWARD BEING THOSE WHERE THE NATURAL ENVIRONMENT IS OTHER THAN TROPICAL OR SUB-TROPICAL RAIN FOREST, OR MONSOON FOREST (244) FWM	0.66 OF 163	42	DRIFT LESS TOWARD BEING THOSE WHERE THE NATURAL ENVIRONMENT IS OTHER THAN TROPICAL OR SUB-TROPICAL RAIN FOREST, OR MONSOON FOREST (244) FWM	0.56 OF 218	55 96 108 122 XSQ= 3.71 PHI= -0.099 XP = 0.0540
44	TILT MORE TOWARD BEING THOSE WHERE SETTLEMENTS ARE FIXED (222)	0.75 OF 134	44	TILT LESS TOWARD BEING THOSE WHERE SETTLEMENTS ARE FIXED (222)	0.61 OF 187	100 114 34 73 XSQ= 5.96 PHI= 0.136 XP = 0.0146

46	LEAN MORE TOWARD BEING THOSE OTHER THAN WHERE SETTLEMENTS ARE NON-FIXED AND MOVEMENT IS NOMADIC (260)	0.87 OF 134	46	LEAN LESS TOWARD BEING THOSE OTHER THAN WHERE SETTLEMENTS ARE NON-FIXED AND MOVEMENT IS NOMADIC (260)	0.71 OF 187	18 54 116 133 XSQ= 9.83 PHI= -0.175 XP = 0.0017
47	DRIFT LESS TOWARD BEING THOSE WHERE, IF SETTLEMENTS ARE NON-FIXED, MOVEMENT IS NOMADIC, RATHER THAN NON-NOMADIC (72)	0.53 OF 34	47	DRIFT MORE TOWARD BEING THOSE WHERE, IF SETTLEMENTS ARE NON-FIXED, MOVEMENT IS NOMADIC, RATHER THAN NON-NOMADIC (72)	0.74 OF 73	18 54 16 19 XSQ= 3.75 PHI= -0.187 XP = 0.0527
51	TEND MORE TO BE THOSE WHERE SUBSISTENCE IS PRIMARILY BY FOOD PRODUCTION -- I. E., AGRICULTURE OR HUSBANDRY -- RATHER THAN BY GATHERING (253)	0.75 OF 163	51	TEND LESS TO BE THOSE WHERE SUBSISTENCE IS PRIMARILY BY FOOD PRODUCTION -- I. E., AGRICULTURE OR HUSBANDRY -- RATHER THAN BY GATHERING (253)	0.52 OF 218	123 113 40 105 XSQ= 21.09 PHI= 0.235 XP = 0.0000
54	DRIFT MORE TOWARD BEING THOSE WHERE FOOD PRODUCTION IS BY INTENSIVE OR SIMPLE AGRICULTURE, RATHER THAN BY INCIPIENT FOOD PRODUCTION (192)	0.86 OF 111	54	DRIFT LESS TOWARD BEING THOSE WHERE FOOD PRODUCTION IS BY INTENSIVE OR SIMPLE AGRICULTURE, RATHER THAN BY INCIPIENT FOOD PRODUCTION (192)	0.76 OF 116	95 88 16 28 XSQ= 2.84 PHI= 0.112 XP = 0.0921
62	LEAN MORE TOWARD BEING THOSE WHERE HUSBANDRY OF SOME KIND IS PRESENT (228)	0.67 OF 163	62	LEAN LESS TOWARD BEING THOSE WHERE HUSBANDRY OF SOME KIND IS PRESENT (228)	0.50 OF 218	110 110 53 108 XSQ= 10.39 PHI= 0.165 XP = 0.0013
63	DRIFT MORE TOWARD BEING THOSE WHERE HUSBANDRY, IF PRESENT, IS PRINCIPALLY IN THE FORM OF BOVINE, EQUINE, CAMEL-LIKE, OR DEER-LIKE ANIMALS, RATHER THAN PIGS, SHEEP, OR GOATS (152)	0.73 OF 109	63	DRIFT LESS TOWARD BEING THOSE WHERE HUSBANDRY, IF PRESENT, IS PRINCIPALLY IN THE FORM OF BOVINE, EQUINE, CAMEL-LIKE, OR DEER-LIKE ANIMALS, RATHER THAN PIGS, SHEEP, OR GOATS (152)	0.61 OF 110	80 67 29 43 XSQ= 3.32 PHI= 0.123 XP = 0.0683
71	TEND TO BE THOSE WHERE METAL WORKING IS PRESENT (98)	0.65 OF 93	71	TEND TO BE THOSE WHERE METAL WORKING IS ABSENT (153)	0.77 OF 149	60 34 33 115 XSQ= 40.17 PHI= 0.407 XP = 0.
73	TEND TO BE THOSE WHERE WEAVING IS PRESENT (118)	0.65 OF 89	73	TEND TO BE THOSE WHERE WEAVING IS ABSENT (130)	0.65 OF 150	58 53 31 97 XSQ= 18.81 PHI= 0.281 XP = 0.0000
74	LEAN MORE TOWARD BEING THOSE WHERE POTTERY IS PRESENT (145)	0.74 OF 82	74	LEAN LESS TOWARD BEING THOSE WHERE POTTERY IS PRESENT (145)	0.52 OF 147	61 77 21 70 XSQ= 9.75 PHI= 0.206 XP = 0.0018

77	DRIFT LESS TOWARD BEING THOSE 0.57 OF 23 WHERE THE WRITING SYSTEM IS MNEMONIC OR ABSENT, RATHER THAN BEING ALPHABETIC-OR-PHONETIC (39) JMH	77	DRIFT MORE TOWARD BEING THOSE 0.83 OF 29 WHERE THE WRITING SYSTEM IS MNEMONIC OR ABSENT, RATHER THAN BEING ALPHABETIC-OR-PHONETIC (39) JMH	10 5 13 24 XSQ= 3.12 PHI= 0.245 XP = 0.0774
80	TILT LESS TOWARD BEING THOSE 0.75 OF 91 WHERE NO CITY OR TOWN IS PRESENT (185)	80	TILT MORE TOWARD BEING THOSE 0.87 OF 127 WHERE NO CITY OR TOWN IS PRESENT (185)	23 16 68 111 XSQ= 4.97 PHI= 0.151 XP = 0.0258
81	TILT LESS TOWARD BEING THOSE 0.51 OF 91 WHERE NO CITY OR TOWN IS PRESENT, AND THE AVERAGE COMMUNITY SIZE IS SMALLER THAN 200 (135)	81	TILT MORE TOWARD BEING THOSE 0.68 OF 127 WHERE NO CITY OR TOWN IS PRESENT, AND THE AVERAGE COMMUNITY SIZE IS SMALLER THAN 200 (135)	45 41 46 86 XSQ= 5.84 PHI= 0.164 XP = 0.0157
82	LEAN MORE TOWARD BEING THOSE 0.90 OF 91 WHERE A CITY OR TOWN IS PRESENT, OR THE AVERAGE COMMUNITY SIZE IS FIFTY OR GREATER (178)	82	LEAN LESS TOWARD BEING THOSE 0.72 OF 127 WHERE A CITY OR TOWN IS PRESENT, OR THE AVERAGE COMMUNITY SIZE IS FIFTY OR GREATER (178)	82 91 9 36 XSQ= 9.93 PHI= 0.213 XP = 0.0016
86	TEND TO BE THOSE 0.65 OF 127 WHERE THE LEVEL OF POLITICAL INTEGRATION IS THE LARGE STATE, THE LITTLE STATE, OR THE MINIMAL STATE (148) GPM	86	TEND TO BE THOSE 0.66 OF 166 WHERE THE LEVEL OF POLITICAL INTEGRATION IS THE AUTONOMOUS COMMUNITY, OR THE FAMILY (156) GPM	83 57 44 109 XSQ= 26.51 PHI= 0.301 XP = 0.0000
96	TEND TO BE THOSE 0.69 OF 133 WHERE THE HIERARCHY OF NATIONAL JURISDICTION HAS FOUR, THREE, TWO OR ONE LEVEL (174) GES,EA	96	TEND TO BE THOSE 0.60 OF 186 WHERE THE HIERARCHY OF NATIONAL JURISDICTION HAS NO LEVELS (156) GES,EA	92 75 41 111 XSQ= 24.73 PHI= 0.278 XP = 0.0000
97	TEND LESS TO BE THOSE 0.73 OF 133 WHERE THE HIERARCHY OF LOCAL JURISDICTION HAS THREE OR TWO LEVELS (273) GES,EA	97	TEND MORE TO BE THOSE 0.89 OF 187 WHERE THE HIERARCHY OF LOCAL JURISDICTION HAS THREE OR TWO LEVELS (273) GES,EA	36 20 97 167 XSQ= 13.32 PHI= 0.204 XP = 0.0003
98	TEND MORE TO BE THOSE 0.88 OF 133 WHERE THE HIERARCHY OF LOCAL JURISDICTION HAS FOUR OR THREE LEVELS (238) GES,EA	98	TEND LESS TO BE THOSE 0.59 OF 187 WHERE THE HIERARCHY OF LOCAL JURISDICTION HAS FOUR OR THREE LEVELS (238) GES,EA	117 111 16 76 XSQ= 29.68 PHI= 0.305 XP = 0.0000
99	TEND TO BE THOSE 0.85 OF 41 WHERE, WITH NATIONAL HIERARCHY ABSENT, THE HIERARCHY OF LOCAL JURISDICTION HAS FOUR OR THREE LEVELS (93) GES,EA	99	TEND TO BE THOSE 0.50 OF 111 WHERE, WITH NATIONAL HIERARCHY ABSENT, THE HIERARCHY OF LOCAL JURISDICTION HAS TWO LEVELS (63) GES,EA	35 55 6 56 XSQ= 14.45 PHI= 0.308 XP = 0.0001

100	TEND MORE TO BE THOSE 0.95 OF 133 WHERE HIERARCHIES ARE MORE COMPLEX THAN THE 'SIMPLEST,' I. E., MORE COMPLEX THAN TWO LOCAL LEVELS WITH NO NATIONAL LEVELS (267) GES,EA	100	TEND LESS TO BE THOSE 0.70 OF 186 WHERE HIERARCHIES ARE MORE COMPLEX THAN THE 'SIMPLEST,' I. E., MORE COMPLEX THAN TWO LOCAL LEVELS WITH NO NATIONAL LEVELS (267) GES,EA	127 130 6 56 XSQ= 30.83 PHI= 0.311 XP = 0.
102	TEND TO BE THOSE 0.75 OF 159 WHERE CLASS STRATIFICATION IS PRESENT (203)	102	TEND TO BE THOSE 0.64 OF 213 WHERE CLASS STRATIFICATION IS ABSENT (180)	119 76 40 137 XSQ= 54.42 PHI= 0.382 XP = 0.
106	TILT MORE TOWARD BEING THOSE 0.68 OF 119 WHERE CLASS STRATIFICATION, IF PRESENT, IS BASED ON SOMETHING OTHER THAN WEALTH (126)	106	TILT LESS TOWARD BEING THOSE 0.51 OF 76 WHERE CLASS STRATIFICATION, IF PRESENT, IS BASED ON SOMETHING OTHER THAN WEALTH (126)	38 37 81 39 XSQ= 4.81 PHI= -0.157 XP = 0.0282
108	LEAN LESS TOWARD BEING THOSE 0.55 OF 119 WHERE CLASS STRATIFICATION, IF PRESENT, IS BASED ON SOMETHING OTHER THAN A HEREDITARY ARISTOCRACY (129)	108	LEAN MORE TOWARD BEING THOSE 0.78 OF 76 WHERE CLASS STRATIFICATION, IF PRESENT, IS BASED ON SOMETHING OTHER THAN A HEREDITARY ARISTOCRACY (129)	54 17 65 59 XSQ= 9.64 PHI= 0.222 XP = 0.0019
109	LEAN LESS TOWARD BEING THOSE 0.80 OF 146 WHERE CASTES ARE ABSENT (317)	109	LEAN MORE TOWARD BEING THOSE 0.92 OF 211 WHERE CASTES ARE ABSENT (317)	29 17 117 194 XSQ= 9.69 PHI= 0.165 XP = 0.0019
120	DRIFT MORE TOWARD BEING THOSE 0.83 OF 23 WHERE THE CRAFT SPECIALIZATION SCORE IS HIGH OR MEDIUM (36) WME	120	DRIFT LESS TOWARD BEING THOSE 0.57 OF 30 WHERE THE CRAFT SPECIALIZATION SCORE IS HIGH OR MEDIUM (36) WME	19 17 4 13 XSQ= 2.92 PHI= 0.235 XP = 0.0875
127	TILT TOWARD BEING THOSE 0.66 OF 29 WHERE THE FEMALES' CONTRIBUTION TO SUBSISTENCE IS LOW (32) JKB	127	TILT TOWARD BEING THOSE 0.64 OF 36 WHERE THE FEMALES' CONTRIBUTION TO SUBSISTENCE IS HIGH (33) JKB	10 23 19 13 XSQ= 4.44 PHI= -0.261 XP = 0.0351
129	TILT LESS TOWARD BEING THOSE 0.62 OF 52 WHERE WEAVING IS MAINLY DONE BY FEMALES (73)	129	TILT MORE TOWARD BEING THOSE 0.82 OF 45 WHERE WEAVING IS MAINLY DONE BY FEMALES (73)	20 8 32 37 XSQ= 4.07 PHI= 0.205 XP = 0.0437
133	DRIFT TOWARD BEING THOSE 0.69 OF 16 WHERE CONTRACTED DEBTS ARE SIGNIFICANTLY PRESENT (17) GES	133	DRIFT TOWARD BEING THOSE 0.67 OF 18 WHERE CONTRACTED DEBTS ARE MODERATELY PRESENT OR ABSENT (17) GES	11 6 5 12 XSQ= 2.95 PHI= 0.295 EP = 0.0844

152	TILT TOWARD BEING THOSE 0.88 OF 8 WHERE THE DIFFERENTIATION OF THE JURIDICAL AGENCY FROM THE MEDICAL AGENCY IS HIGH (10) MJ	152	TILT TOWARD BEING THOSE 0.75 OF 12 WHERE THE DIFFERENTIATION OF THE JURIDICAL AGENCY FROM THE MEDICAL AGENCY IS LOW (10) MJ	7 3 1 9 XSQ= 5.21 PHI= 0.510 EP = 0.0198
181	DRIFT MORE TOWARD BEING THOSE 0.92 OF 155 WHERE THE COMMUNITY IS OTHER THAN A DEME (337)	181	DRIFT LESS TOWARD BEING THOSE 0.86 OF 209 WHERE THE COMMUNITY IS OTHER THAN A DEME (337)	12 30 143 179 XSQ= 3.19 PHI= -0.094 XP = 0.0740
183	TEND MORE TO BE THOSE 0.95 OF 120 WHERE THE LARGEST NON-COGNATIC KIN GROUP IS SMALLER THAN A MOEITY, I. E., A PHRATRY OR SIB OR LINEAGE (218)	183	TEND LESS TO BE THOSE 0.77 OF 120 WHERE THE LARGEST NON-COGNATIC KIN GROUP IS SMALLER THAN A MOEITY, I. E., A PHRATRY OR SIB OR LINEAGE (218)	6 27 114 93 XSQ= 14.05 PHI= -0.242 XP = 0.0002
184	TILT MORE TOWARD BEING THOSE 0.77 OF 120 WHERE THE LARGEST NON-COGNATIC KIN GROUP IS SMALLER THAN A PHRATRY, I. E. A SIB OR LINEAGE (175)	184	TILT LESS TOWARD BEING THOSE 0.62 OF 120 WHERE THE LARGEST NON-COGNATIC KIN GROUP IS SMALLER THAN A PHRATRY, I. E. A SIB OR LINEAGE (175)	27 46 93 74 XSQ= 6.38 PHI= -0.163 XP = 0.0116
185	TILT LESS TOWARD BEING THOSE 0.70 OF 120 WHERE THE LARGEST NON-COGNATIC KIN GROUP IS THE MOEITY OR PHRATRY OR SIB (194)	185	TILT MORE TOWARD BEING THOSE 0.82 OF 120 WHERE THE LARGEST NON-COGNATIC KIN GROUP IS THE MOEITY OR PHRATRY OR SIB (194)	84 98 36 22 XSQ= 3.84 PHI= -0.127 XP = 0.0500
186	TEND LESS TO BE THOSE 0.51 OF 163 WHERE THE KIN GROUP IS OTHER THAN EXCLUSIVELY PATRILINEAL (250)	186	TEND MORE TO BE THOSE 0.72 OF 218 WHERE THE KIN GROUP IS OTHER THAN EXCLUSIVELY PATRILINEAL (250)	80 62 83 156 XSQ= 16.12 PHI= 0.206 XP = 0.0001
188	TEND MORE TO BE THOSE 0.74 OF 163 WHERE THE KIN GROUP IS OTHER THAN EXCLUSIVELY COGNATIC (252)	188	TEND LESS TO BE THOSE 0.55 OF 218 WHERE THE KIN GROUP IS OTHER THAN EXCLUSIVELY COGNATIC (252)	43 98 120 120 XSQ= 13.02 PHI= -0.185 XP = 0.0003
190	LEAN MORE TOWARD BEING THOSE 0.83 OF 117 WHERE THE KIN GROUP IS PATRILINEAL OR DOUBLE-DESCENT, RATHER THAN MATRILINEAL (186)	190	LEAN LESS TOWARD BEING THOSE 0.66 OF 118 WHERE THE KIN GROUP IS PATRILINEAL OR DOUBLE-DESCENT, RATHER THAN MATRILINEAL (186)	97 78 20 40 XSQ= 7.86 PHI= 0.183 XP = 0.0050
192	TEND MORE TO BE THOSE 0.83 OF 163 OTHER THAN WHERE THE ONLY KIN GROUP PRESENT IS A KINDRED OR ELSE BILATERAL DESCENT IS INFERRED (289)	192	TEND LESS TO BE THOSE 0.65 OF 218 OTHER THAN WHERE THE ONLY KIN GROUP PRESENT IS A KINDRED OR ELSE BILATERAL DESCENT IS INFERRED (289)	28 77 135 141 XSQ= 14.48 PHI= -0.195 XP = 0.0001

196	TEND MORE TO BE THOSE 0.81 OF 122 WHERE INDIVIDUAL RIGHTS IN REAL PROPERTY, AND RULES FOR INHERITANCE, ARE PRESENT (194)	196	TEND LESS TO BE THOSE 0.58 OF 150 WHERE INDIVIDUAL RIGHTS IN REAL PROPERTY, AND RULES FOR INHERITANCE, ARE PRESENT (194)	99 87 23 63 XSQ= 15.62 PHI= 0.240 XP = 0.0001
198	TILT MORE TOWARD BEING THOSE 0.93 OF 87 WHERE RULES FOR THE INHERITANCE OF REAL PROPERTY, IF PRESENT, FAVOR THE MALE HEIR OR LINE, RATHER THAN THE FEMALE (144)	198	TILT LESS TOWARD BEING THOSE 0.80 OF 70 WHERE RULES FOR THE INHERITANCE OF REAL PROPERTY, IF PRESENT, FAVOR THE MALE HEIR OR LINE, RATHER THAN THE FEMALE (144)	81 56 6 14 XSQ= 4.87 PHI= 0.176 XP = 0.0273
201	DRIFT MORE TOWARD BEING THOSE 0.88 OF 163 WHERE MARITAL RESIDENCE IS NON-OPTIONAL, RATHER THAN AMBILOCAL OR NEOLOCAL (334)	201	DRIFT LESS TOWARD BEING THOSE 0.81 OF 216 WHERE MARITAL RESIDENCE IS NON-OPTIONAL, RATHER THAN AMBILOCAL OR NEOLOCAL (334)	144 174 19 42 XSQ= 3.62 PHI= 0.098 XP = 0.0572
204	TILT MORE TOWARD BEING THOSE 0.87 OF 145 WHERE MARITAL RESIDENCE IS PATRILOCAL, VIRILOCAL, OR AVUNCULOCAL, RATHER THAN AMBILOCAL OR NEOLOCAL (270)	204	TILT LESS TOWARD BEING THOSE 0.75 OF 171 WHERE MARITAL RESIDENCE IS PATRILOCAL, VIRILOCAL, OR AVUNCULOCAL, RATHER THAN AMBILOCAL OR NEOLOCAL (270)	126 129 19 42 XSQ= 5.90 PHI= 0.137 XP = 0.0152
209	LEAN MORE TOWARD BEING THOSE 0.88 OF 144 WHERE MARITAL RESIDENCE IS PATRILOCAL, VIRILOCAL, OR AVUNCULOCAL, RATHER THAN MATRILOCAL OR UXORILOCAL (270)	209	LEAN LESS TOWARD BEING THOSE 0.74 OF 174 WHERE MARITAL RESIDENCE IS PATRILOCAL, VIRILOCAL, OR AVUNCULOCAL, RATHER THAN MATRILOCAL OR UXORILOCAL (270)	126 129 18 45 XSQ= 8.03 PHI= 0.159 XP = 0.0046
210	TILT MORE TOWARD BEING THOSE 0.91 OF 93 WHERE MARITAL RESIDENCE IS PATRILOCAL, RATHER THAN MATRILOCAL (169)	210	TILT LESS TOWARD BEING THOSE 0.77 OF 95 WHERE MARITAL RESIDENCE IS PATRILOCAL, RATHER THAN MATRILOCAL (169)	85 73 8 22 XSQ= 6.38 PHI= 0.184 XP = 0.0116
213	TILT TOWARD BEING THOSE 0.55 OF 154 WHERE FIRST COUSIN MARRIAGE IS PERMITTED (172)	213	TILT TOWARD BEING THOSE 0.59 OF 201 WHERE FIRST COUSIN MARRIAGE IS NOT PERMITTED (198)	85 83 69 118 XSQ= 6.21 PHI= 0.132 XP = 0.0127
220	TILT LESS TOWARD BEING THOSE 0.68 OF 154 WHERE FIRST COUSIN MARRIAGE IN SOME FORM OR OTHER IS NOT PRESCRIBED OR PREFERRED (273)	220	TILT MORE TOWARD BEING THOSE 0.78 OF 201 WHERE FIRST COUSIN MARRIAGE IN SOME FORM OR OTHER IS NOT PRESCRIBED OR PREFERRED (273)	50 45 104 156 XSQ= 4.02 PHI= 0.106 XP = 0.0450
221	TILT LESS TOWARD BEING THOSE 0.86 OF 154 WHERE MATRILATERAL CROSS-COUSIN MARRIAGE IS NOT PRESCRIBED OR PREFERRED (335)	221	TILT MORE TOWARD BEING THOSE 0.94 OF 201 WHERE MATRILATERAL CROSS-COUSIN MARRIAGE IS NOT PRESCRIBED OR PREFERRED (335)	21 12 133 189 XSQ= 5.20 PHI= 0.121 XP = 0.0226

<table>
<tr><td>224 LEAN LESS TOWARD BEING THOSE 0.51 OF 85
WHERE COUSIN MARRIAGE IS
PREFERENTIALLY OR PERMISSIVELY
SYMMETRICAL, RATHER THAN
EITHER PATRI- OR MATRILATERAL (106)</td><td>224 LEAN MORE TOWARD BEING THOSE 0.75 OF 83
WHERE COUSIN MARRIAGE IS
PREFERENTIALLY OR PERMISSIVELY
SYMMETRICAL, RATHER THAN
EITHER PATRI- OR MATRILATERAL (106)</td><td>42 21
43 62
XSQ= 9.41
PHI= 0.237
XP = 0.0022</td></tr>
<tr><td>236 DRIFT TOWARD BEING THOSE 0.59 OF 162
WHERE THE FAMILY IS
OF AN EXTENDED TYPE, RATHER THAN
AN INDEPENDENT TYPE (213)</td><td>236 DRIFT TOWARD BEING THOSE 0.51 OF 217
WHERE THE FAMILY IS
OF AN INDEPENDENT TYPE, RATHER THAN
AN EXTENDED TYPE (185)</td><td>96 107
66 110
XSQ= 3.30
PHI= 0.093
XP = 0.0692</td></tr>
<tr><td>242 TEND MORE TO BE THOSE 0.88 OF 161
WHERE MARRIAGE IS
COMMONLY OR OCCASIONALLY POLYGYNOUS,
RATHER THAN MONOGAMOUS (314)</td><td>242 TEND LESS TO BE THOSE 0.71 OF 215
WHERE MARRIAGE IS
COMMONLY OR OCCASIONALLY POLYGYNOUS,
RATHER THAN MONOGAMOUS (314)</td><td>142 153
19 62
XSQ= 14.82
PHI= 0.199
XP = 0.0001</td></tr>
<tr><td>262 TEND MORE TO BE THOSE 0.91 OF 163
WHERE WIVES ARE OBTAINED BY
MEANS INVOLVING THE PRESENCE
OF SOME CONSIDERATION (305)</td><td>262 TEND LESS TO BE THOSE 0.66 OF 215
WHERE WIVES ARE OBTAINED BY
MEANS INVOLVING THE PRESENCE
OF SOME CONSIDERATION (305)</td><td>148 142
15 73
XSQ= 30.43
PHI= 0.284
XP = 0.</td></tr>
<tr><td>263 TEND TO BE THOSE 0.71 OF 163
WHERE WIVES ARE OBTAINED BY
RELATIVELY DIFFICULT MEANS, NAMELY BY
BRIDE-PRICE, BRIDE-SERVICE, OR
EXCHANGING A FEMALE RELATIVE (233)</td><td>263 TEND TO BE THOSE 0.52 OF 215
WHERE WIVES ARE OBTAINED
BY RELATIVELY EASY MEANS, NAMELY BY
TOKEN BRIDE-PRICE, GIFT EXCHANGE,
ABSENCE OF ANY CONSIDERATION, OR
RECEIPT OF DOWRY (162)</td><td>116 104
47 111
XSQ= 18.87
PHI= 0.223
XP = 0.0000</td></tr>
<tr><td>286 DRIFT TOWARD BEING THOSE 0.60 OF 15
WHERE THE NUMBER OF FOOD TABOOS
DURING PREGNANCY
IS LOW OR ABSENT (14) BCA</td><td>286 DRIFT TOWARD BEING THOSE 0.74 OF 19
WHERE THE NUMBER OF FOOD TABOOS
DURING PREGNANCY
IS HIGH (20) BCA</td><td>6 14
9 5
XSQ= 2.66
PHI= -0.280
EP = 0.0800</td></tr>
<tr><td>295 TILT TOWARD BEING THOSE 0.86 OF 7
WHERE THE SEVERITY OF PUNISHMENT
FOR ABORTION
IS HIGH (11) BCA</td><td>295 TILT TOWARD BEING THOSE 0.69 OF 16
WHERE THE SEVERITY OF PUNISHMENT
FOR ABORTION
IS LOW OR ABSENT (12) BCA</td><td>6 5
1 11
XSQ= 3.81
PHI= 0.407
EP = 0.0272</td></tr>
<tr><td>300 TILT TOWARD BEING THOSE 0.57 OF 44
WHERE THE POST-PARTUM SEX TABOO LASTS
LONGER THAN SIX MONTHS (51)</td><td>300 TILT TOWARD BEING THOSE 0.68 OF 76
WHERE THE POST-PARTUM SEX TABOO LASTS
SIX MONTHS OR LESS (73)</td><td>25 24
19 52
XSQ= 6.34
PHI= 0.230
XP = 0.0118</td></tr>
<tr><td>314 TILT LESS TOWARD BEING THOSE 0.62 OF 34
WHERE THE INCIDENCE OF MOTHER-CHILD
HOUSEHOLDS IS LOW (61) W-D,S</td><td>314 TILT MORE TOWARD BEING THOSE 0.87 OF 45
WHERE THE INCIDENCE OF MOTHER-CHILD
HOUSEHOLDS IS LOW (61) W-D,S</td><td>13 6
21 39
XSQ= 5.28
PHI= 0.259
XP = 0.0215</td></tr>
</table>

318	TILT TOWARD BEING THOSE WHERE THE OVERALL INDULGENCE OF THE INFANT IS LOW (31) B-B-C	0.64 OF 25	318	TILT TOWARD BEING THOSE WHERE THE OVERALL INDULGENCE OF THE INFANT IS HIGH (40) B-B-C	0.67 OF 46	9 31 16 15 XSQ= 5.28 PHI= -0.273 XP = 0.0216
324	TILT TOWARD BEING THOSE WHERE THE PAIN INFLICTED ON THE INFANT BY THE NURTURANT AGENT IS HIGH (34) B-B-C	0.73 OF 22	324	TILT TOWARD BEING THOSE WHERE THE PAIN INFLICTED ON THE INFANT BY THE NURTURANT AGENT IS LOW OR NEGLIGIBLE (32) B-B-C	0.59 OF 44	16 18 6 26 XSQ= 4.74 PHI= 0.268 XP = 0.0295
344	DRIFT TOWARD BEING THOSE WHERE THE TOTAL POSITIVE PRESSURE TOWARD DEVELOPING SELF-RELIANT BEHAVIOR IN THE CHILD IS HIGH (36) B-B-C	0.63 OF 27	344	DRIFT TOWARD BEING THOSE WHERE THE TOTAL POSITIVE PRESSURE TOWARD DEVELOPING SELF-RELIANT BEHAVIOR IN THE CHILD IS LOW (40) B-B-C	0.61 OF 49	17 19 10 30 XSQ= 3.17 PHI= 0.204 XP = 0.0749
373	DRIFT TOWARD BEING THOSE WHERE MALE INITIATION CEREMONIES AT PUBERTY ARE ABSENT (27) W-K-A	0.79 OF 19	373	DRIFT TOWARD BEING THOSE WHERE MALE INITIATION CEREMONIES AT PUBERTY ARE PRESENT (17) W-K-A	0.52 OF 25	4 13 15 12 XSQ= 3.15 PHI= -0.268 XP = 0.0758
377	TEND LESS TO BE THOSE WHERE MALE GENITAL MUTILATION IS ABSENT (242)	0.62 OF 129	377	TEND MORE TO BE THOSE WHERE MALE GENITAL MUTILATION IS ABSENT (242)	0.84 OF 185	49 30 80 155 XSQ= 17.99 PHI= 0.239 XP = 0.0000
391	TILT TOWARD BEING THOSE WHERE PREMARITAL SEX RELATIONS ARE STRONGLY PUNISHED AND IN FACT RARE, OR WEAKLY PUNISHED AND IN FACT NOT RARE (89) JTW,EA	0.59 OF 73	391	TILT TOWARD BEING THOSE WHERE PREMARITAL SEX RELATIONS ARE PUNISHED ONLY IF PREGNANCY RESULTS, OR FREELY PERMITTED (90) JTW,EA	0.57 OF 103	43 44 30 59 XSQ= 3.85 PHI= 0.148 XP = 0.0496
393	LEAN TOWARD BEING THOSE WHERE EXTRAMARITAL COITUS IS PUNISHED, RATHER THAN PERMITTED (43) F-B	0.77 OF 30	393	LEAN TOWARD BEING THOSE WHERE EXTRAMARITAL COITUS IS PERMITTED, RATHER THAN PUNISHED (41) F-B	0.62 OF 53	23 20 7 33 XSQ= 10.12 PHI= 0.349 XP = 0.0015
417	TILT MORE TOWARD BEING THOSE WHERE WARFARE IS PREVALENT (34) LWS	0.95 OF 21	417	TILT LESS TOWARD BEING THOSE WHERE WARFARE IS PREVALENT (34) LWS	0.64 OF 22	20 14 1 8 XSQ= 4.71 PHI= 0.331 XP = 0.0299
419	DRIFT MORE TOWARD BEING THOSE WHERE MILITARY GLORY IS STRONGLY OR MODERATELY EMPHASIZED (55) PES	0.76 OF 38	419	DRIFT LESS TOWARD BEING THOSE WHERE MILITARY GLORY IS STRONGLY OR MODERATELY EMPHASIZED (55) PES	0.54 OF 48	29 26 9 22 XSQ= 3.60 PHI= 0.205 XP = 0.0576

426	TEND TC BE THCSE WHERE A HIGH GCC IS PRESENT (156) GES,EA	0.74 OF 105	426	TEND TO BE THOSE WHERE A HIGH GOD IS ABSENT (104) GES,EA	0.50 OF 146	78 73 27 73 XSQ= 14.03 PHI= 0.236 XP = 0.0002
436	DRIFT LESS TCWARD BEING THCSE WHERE ACTIVE ANCESTRAL SPIRITS ARE PRESENT (27) GES	0.56 OF 18	436	DRIFT MORE TOWARD BEING THCSE WHERE ACTIVE ANCESTRAL SPIRITS ARE PRESENT (27) GES	0.85 OF 20	10 17 8 3 XSQ= 2.69 PHI= -0.266 EP = 0.0741
450	TILT LESS TOWARD BEING THCSE WHERE THE CBSERVATICN CF FCOC TABOOS IS HIGH CR MEDIUM, RATHER THAN LCW (60) JRL	0.58 OF 36	450	TILT MORE TOWARD BEING THOSE WHERE THE OBSERVATION OF FCCD TABOOS IS HIGH OR MEDIUM, RATHER THAN LOW (6C) JRL	0.81 OF 48	21 39 15 9 XSQ= 4.23 PHI= -0.224 XP = 0.0397
454	DRIFT TCWARD BEING THCSE WHERE THE CBJECTIVE CF THE INCIVICUAL'S CONTACT WITH THE DIVINE IS CCNDUCIVE TO THE DEVELCPMENT OF THE INDIVIDUAL'S NEED TC ACHIEVE (18) CCM	0.75 OF 12	454	DRIFT TOWARD BEING THOSE WHERE THE OBJECTIVE OF THE INDIVIDUAL'S CONTACT WITH THE DIVINE IS NOT CONDUCIVE TO THE DEVELOPMENT OF THE INDIVIDUAL'S NEED TO ACHIEVE (18) DCM	0.63 CF 24	9 9 3 15 XSQ= 3.12 PHI= 0.295 EP = 0.0750
458	TEND TO BE THCSE WHERE GAMES, IF PRESENT, INCLUDE GAMES CF STRATEGY (52) R-A-B,EA	0.51 OF 61	458	TEND TO BE THOSE WHERE GAMES, IF PRESENT, DO NOT INCLUDE GAMES OF STRATEGY (119) R-A-B,EA	0.82 CF 105	31 19 30 86 XSQ= 18.11 PHI= 0.330 XP = 0.0000
460	TEND MCRE TO BE THCSE WHERE GAMES, IF PRESENT, ARE NCT LIMITED TC GAMES OF SKILL CNLY (104) R-A-B,EA	0.79 OF 61	460	TEND LESS TO BE THOSE WHERE GAMES, IF PRESENT, ARE NOT LIMITED TO GAMES OF SKILL ONLY (104) R-A-B,EA	0.50 CF 105	13 52 48 53 XSQ= 11.73 PHI= -0.266 XP = 0.0006
470	DRIFT TCWARD BEING THCSE WHERE INNCVATICNS ARE GENERALLY ACCEPTED (21) JMH	0.52 OF 23	470	DRIFT TOWARD BEING THOSE WHERE INNOVATICNS ARE ACCEPTED ONLY SELECTIVELY (33) JMH	0.76 CF 29	12 7 11 22 XSQ= 3.22 PHI= 0.249 XP = 0.0726
472	DRIFT TCWARD BEING THCSE WHERE THE CCMPOSITE NARCISSISM INCEX IS HIGH (47) PES	0.64 OF 39	472	DRIFT TOWARD BEING THOSE WHERE THE COMPOSITE NARCISSISM INDEX IS LOW (43) PES	0.57 OF 51	25 22 14 29 XSQ= 3.10 PHI= 0.186 XP = 0.0784
473	DRIFT LESS TCWARD BEING THOSE WHERE SENSITIVITY TO INSULT IS MCDERATE CR NEGLIGIBLE (56) PES	0.51 OF 37	473	DRIFT MORE TOWARD BEING THCSE WHERE SENSITIVITY TO INSULT IS MODERATE OR NEGLIGIBLE (56) PES	0.73 OF 51	18 14 19 37 XSQ= 3.30 PHI= 0.194 XP = 0.0694

474	TILT TOWARD BEING THOSE WHERE BOASTFULNESS IS EXTREME (41) PES	0.61 OF 38	474	TILT TOWARD BEING THOSE WHERE BOASTFULNESS IS MODERATE, NEGLIBIBLE, OR UNREPORTED (48) PES	0.65 OF 51	23 18 15 33 XSQ= 4.61 PHI= 0.228 XP = 0.0318
479	TILT TOWARD BEING THOSE WHERE THE NEED TO ACHIEVE, AS INFERRED FROM FOLKTALES, IS HIGH (18) JV	0.83 OF 12	479	TILT TOWARD BEING THOSE WHERE THE NEED TO ACHIEVE, AS INFERRED FROM FOLKTALES, IS LOW (18) JV	0.67 OF 24	10 8 2 16 XSQ= 6.12 PHI= 0.412 EP = 0.0116

111 CULTURES
WHERE WORK ORGANIZATIONS
HAVING A VOLUNTARY ASPECT
ARE REPORTED (34) SHU

111 CULTURES
WHERE WORK ORGANIZATIONS
HAVING A VOLUNTARY ASPECT
ARE NOT REPORTED (71) SHU

BACKGROUND ON PAGE 91

SUBJECT ONLY

34 IN LEFT COLUMN

ABIPON	ANDAMANESE	ARANDA	AZANDE	BEMBA	CARIB	COPR ESKIMO	DARD	DOGON	GILYAK
HAVASUPAI	IBAN	IFUGAO	ILA	JIVARO	JUKUN	KAREN	KURTATCHI	LAPPS	MANGAIANS
MARICOPA	MURNGIN	NAMA	NAMBICUARA	NAVAHO	ONA	SANPOIL	SEMANG	SIRIONO	TENETEHARA
TERENA	TIV	TRUMAI	TUBATULABAL						

71 IN RIGHT COLUMN

ASHANTI	ATAYAL	AWEIKOMA	AYMARA	BELU	BURMESE	BURUSHO	CAGABA	CAMAYURA	CAMBODIANS
CAYAPA	CHAGGA	CHUKCHEE	CROW	CUNA	FANG	FON	GOND	HAIDA	HANO
HAZARA	HUTSUL	KABYLE	KAZAK	KIKUYU	KWAKIUTL	LAU	MACASSARESE	MALAYS	MAM
MAORI	MARSHALLESE	MBUNDU	MIN CHINESE	MZAB	NUER	NUPE	NYORO	OJIBWA	PAPAGO
PENOBSCOT	POPOLUCA	PUKAPUKA	RIFFIANS	ROMANS	RWALA	SAMOANS	SAMOYED	SENIANG	SOMALI
SONGHAI	SOTHO	TALLENSI	TAOS	TARAHUMARA	THAI	THONGA	TIBETANS	TIKOPIA	TIMBIRA
TROBRIAND	TUPINAMBA	TURKANA	WAPISHANA	WINNEBAGO	WOGEO	WOLEAIANS	WOLOF	YAGUA	YOKUTS
ZUNI									

295 EXCLUDED BECAUSE UNASCERTAINED

44	TEND TO BE THOSE WHERE SETTLEMENTS ARE NON-FIXED (110) 0.61 OF 33	44	TEND TO BE THOSE WHERE SETTLEMENTS ARE FIXED (222) 0.77 OF 65		13 50 20 15 XSQ= 11.84 PHI= -0.348 XP = 0.0006
45	DRIFT TOWARD BEING THOSE WHERE SETTLEMENTS, IF FIXED, ARE NON-COMPACT, RATHER THAN COMPACT (73) 0.54 OF 13	45	DRIFT TOWARD BEING THOSE WHERE SETTLEMENTS, IF FIXED, ARE COMPACT, RATHER THAN NON-COMPACT (149) 0.78 OF 50		6 39 7 11 XSQ= 3.69 PHI= -0.242 XP = 0.0549
46	LEAN LESS TOWARD BEING THOSE OTHER THAN WHERE SETTLEMENTS ARE NON-FIXED AND MOVEMENT IS NOMADIC (260) 0.55 OF 33	46	LEAN MORE TOWARD BEING THOSE OTHER THAN WHERE SETTLEMENTS ARE NON-FIXED AND MOVEMENT IS NOMADIC (260) 0.83 OF 65		15 11 18 54 XSQ= 7.74 PHI= 0.281 XP = 0.0054

51	LEAN TOWARD BEING THOSE 0.56 OF 34 WHERE SUBSISTENCE IS PRIMARILY BY FOOD GATHERING -- I. E., HUNTING, FISHING, OR COLLECTING -- RATHER THAN FOOD PRODUCTION (147)	51	LEAN TOWARD BEING THOSE 0.73 OF 71 WHERE SUBSISTENCE IS PRIMARILY BY FOOD PRODUCTION -- I. E., AGRICULTURE OR HUSBANDRY -- RATHER THAN BY GATHERING (253)	15 52 19 19 XSQ= 7.23 PHI= -0.262 XP = 0.0072
53	DRIFT MORE TOWARD BEING THOSE 0.84 OF 19 WHERE FOOD PRODUCTION IS BY SIMPLE AGRICULTURE OR INCIPIENT FOOD PRODUCTION, RATHER THAN BY INTENSIVE AGRICULTURE (147)	53	DRIFT LESS TOWARD BEING THOSE 0.57 OF 54 WHERE FOOD PRODUCTION IS BY SIMPLE AGRICULTURE OR INCIPIENT FOOD PRODUCTION, RATHER THAN BY INTENSIVE AGRICULTURE (147)	3 23 16 31 XSQ= 3.31 PHI= -0.213 XP = 0.0688
62	TILT TOWARD BEING THOSE 0.53 OF 34 WHERE HUSBANDRY OF ANY KIND IS ABSENT (172)	62	TILT TOWARD BEING THOSE 0.75 OF 71 WHERE HUSBANDRY OF SOME KIND IS PRESENT (228)	16 53 18 18 XSQ= 6.59 PHI= -0.251 XP = 0.0103
80	IN ALL CASES ARE THOSE 1.00 OF 26 WHERE NO CITY OR TOWN IS PRESENT (185)	80	TILT LESS TOWARD BEING THOSE 0.80 OF 51 WHERE NO CITY OR TOWN IS PRESENT (185)	0 10 26 41 XSQ= 4.25 PHI= -0.235 XP = 0.0392
81	LEAN TOWARD BEING THOSE 0.81 OF 26 WHERE NO CITY OR TOWN IS PRESENT, AND THE AVERAGE COMMUNITY SIZE IS SMALLER THAN 200 (135)	81	LEAN TOWARD BEING THOSE 0.53 OF 51 WHERE A CITY OR TOWN IS PRESENT, OR THE AVERAGE COMMUNITY SIZE IS 200 OR GREATER (89)	5 27 21 24 XSQ= 6.73 PHI= -0.296 XP = 0.0095
86	LEAN TOWARD BEING THOSE 0.75 OF 32 WHERE THE LEVEL OF POLITICAL INTEGRATION IS THE AUTONOMOUS COMMUNITY, OR THE FAMILY (156) GPM	86	LEAN TOWARD BEING THOSE 0.57 OF 61 WHERE THE LEVEL OF POLITICAL INTEGRATION IS THE LARGE STATE, THE LITTLE STATE, OR THE MINIMAL STATE (148) GPM	8 35 24 26 XSQ= 7.60 PHI= -0.286 XP = 0.0058
94	IN ALL CASES ARE THOSE 1.00 OF 33 WHERE THE HIERARCHY OF NATIONAL JURISDICTION HAS TWO, ONE, OR NO LEVELS (296) GES,EA	94	TILT LESS TOWARD BEING THOSE 0.84 OF 62 WHERE THE HIERARCHY OF NATIONAL JURISDICTION HAS TWO, ONE, OR NO LEVELS (296) GES,EA	0 10 33 52 XSQ= 4.36 PHI= -0.214 XP = 0.0368
96	TILT TOWARD BEING THOSE 0.70 OF 33 WHERE THE HIERARCHY OF NATIONAL JURISDICTION HAS NO LEVELS (156) GES,EA	96	TILT TOWARD BEING THOSE 0.60 OF 62 WHERE THE HIERARCHY OF NATIONAL JURISDICTION HAS FOUR, THREE, TWO OR ONE LEVEL (174) GES,EA	10 37 23 25 XSQ= 6.31 PHI= -0.258 XP = 0.0120
98	TILT LESS TOWARD BEING THOSE 0.61 OF 33 WHERE THE HIERARCHY OF LOCAL JURISDICTION HAS FOUR OR THREE LEVELS 238) GES,EA	98	TILT MORE TOWARD BEING THOSE 0.83 OF 63 WHERE THE HIERARCHY OF LOCAL JURISDICTION HAS FOUR OR THREE LEVELS (238) GES,EA	20 52 13 11 XSQ= 4.45 PHI= -0.215 XP = 0.0349

100	LEAN LESS TOWARD BEING THOSE 0.67 OF 33 WHERE HIERARCHIES ARE MORE COMPLEX THAN THE 'SIMPLEST,' I. E., MORE COMPLEX THAN TWO LOCAL LEVELS WITH NO NATIONAL LEVELS (267) GES,EA	100	LEAN MORE TOWARD BEING THOSE 0.90 OF 62 WHERE HIERARCHIES ARE MORE COMPLEX THAN THE 'SIMPLEST,' I. E., MORE COMPLEX THAN TWO LOCAL LEVELS WITH NO NATIONAL LEVELS (267) GES,EA	22 56 11 6 XSQ= 6.67 PHI= -0.265 XP = 0.0098
102	TILT TOWARD BEING THOSE 0.59 OF 34 WHERE CLASS STRATIFICATION IS ABSENT (180)	102	TILT TOWARD BEING THOSE 0.69 OF 71 WHERE CLASS STRATIFICATION IS PRESENT (203)	14 49 20 22 XSQ= 6.31 PHI= -0.245 XP = 0.0120
128	TILT TOWARD BEING THOSE 0.88 OF 8 WHERE, IF SUBSISTENCE IS PRIMARILY BY AGRICULTURE, THE WORK IS MAINLY DONE BY FEMALES (37)	128	TILT TOWARD BEING THOSE 0.58 OF 19 WHERE, IF SUBSISTENCE IS PRIMARILY BY AGRICULTURE, THE WORK IS MAINLY DONE BY MALES (40)	1 11 7 8 XSQ= 3.04 PHI= -0.336 EP = 0.0433
132	TILT TOWARD BEING THOSE 0.60 OF 15 WHERE ECONOMIC EXCHANGE DOES NOT INVOLVE THE USE OF MONEY (17) JMH	132	TILT TOWARD BEING THOSE 0.74 OF 23 WHERE ECONOMIC EXCHANGE INVOLVES THE USE OF MONEY (37) JMH	6 17 9 6 XSQ= 3.07 PHI= -0.284 EP = 0.0486
138	DRIFT TOWARD BEING THOSE 0.70 OF 10 WHERE SUPERORDINATE JUSTICE IS ABSENT (18) BBW	138	DRIFT TOWARD BEING THOSE 0.71 OF 14 WHERE SUPERORDINATE JUSTICE IS PRESENT (22) BBW	3 10 7 4 XSQ= 2.54 PHI= -0.325 EP = 0.0953
163	IN ALL CASES ARE THOSE 1.00 OF 7 WHERE THE EMPHASIS ON INDIVIDUAL VOLITION AS THE CAUSE OF CRIME IS LOW (10) MJ	163	TILT TOWARD BEING THOSE 0.80 OF 5 WHERE THE EMPHASIS ON INDIVIDUAL VOLITION AS THE CAUSE OF CRIME IS HIGH (7) MJ	0 4 7 1 XSQ= 5.19 PHI= -0.657 EP = 0.0101
176	TEND TO BE THOSE 0.79 OF 34 WHERE THE COMMUNITY IS OTHER THAN A CLAN-COMMUNITY OR A COMMUNITY STRUCTURED OR SEGMENTED ON A CLAN BASIS (213)	176	TEND TO BE THOSE 0.57 OF 70 WHERE THE COMMUNITY IS A CLAN-COMMUNITY OR A COMMUNITY STRUCTURED OR SEGMENTED ON A CLAN BASIS (169)	7 40 27 30 XSQ= 10.91 PHI= -0.324 XP = 0.0010
177	DRIFT MORE TOWARD BEING THOSE 0.88 OF 34 WHERE THE COMMUNITY IS OTHER THAN A SINGLE CLAN-COMMUNITY AND EXOGAMOUS (305)	177	DRIFT LESS TOWARD BEING THOSE 0.71 OF 70 WHERE THE COMMUNITY IS OTHER THAN A SINGLE CLAN-COMMUNITY AND EXOGAMOUS (305)	4 20 30 50 XSQ= 2.76 PHI= -0.163 XP = 0.0969
178	TILT MORE TOWARD BEING THOSE 0.94 OF 34 WHERE THE COMMUNITY IS OTHER THAN SEGMENTED ON A CLAN BASIS AND NON-EXOGAMOUS (295)	178	TILT LESS TOWARD BEING THOSE 0.73 OF 70 WHERE THE COMMUNITY IS OTHER THAN SEGMENTED ON A CLAN BASIS AND NON-EXOGAMOUS (295)	2 19 32 51 XSQ= 5.17 PHI= -0.223 XP = 0.0230

182	TILT TOWARD BEING THOSE WHERE THE COMMUNITY IS STRUCTURED ON A NON-CLAN BASIS AND AGAMOUS (126)	0.50 OF 34	182	TILT TOWARD BEING THOSE OTHER THAN WHERE THE COMMUNITY IS STRUCTURED ON A NON-CLAN BASIS AND AGAMOUS (256)	0.74 OF 70	17 18 17 52 XSQ= 5.01 PHI= 0.219 XP = 0.0253
186	TILT MORE TOWARD BEING THOSE WHERE THE KIN GROUP IS OTHER THAN EXCLUSIVELY PATRILINEAL (250)	0.82 OF 34	186	TILT LESS TOWARD BEING THOSE WHERE THE KIN GROUP IS OTHER THAN EXCLUSIVELY PATRILINEAL (250)	0.58 OF 71	6 30 28 41 XSQ= 5.13 PHI= -0.221 XP = 0.0235
188	TILT TOWARD BEING THOSE WHERE THE KIN GROUP IS EXCLUSIVELY COGNATIC (148)	0.56 OF 34	188	TILT TOWARD BEING THOSE WHERE THE KIN GROUP IS OTHER THAN EXCLUSIVELY COGNATIC (252)	0.68 OF 71	19 23 15 48 XSQ= 4.35 PHI= 0.204 XP = 0.0370
196	TEND TO BE THOSE WHERE INDIVIDUAL RIGHTS IN REAL PROPERTY, OR RULES FOR INHERITANCE, ARE ABSENT (87)	0.68 OF 25	196	TEND TO BE THOSE WHERE INDIVIDUAL RIGHTS IN REAL PROPERTY, AND RULES FOR INHERITANCE, ARE PRESENT (194)	0.75 OF 53	8 40 17 13 XSQ= 11.79 PHI= -0.389 XP = 0.0006
214	TILT LESS TOWARD BEING THOSE WHERE FIRST COUSIN MARRIAGE, IF PERMITTED, IS OTHER THAN UNILATERAL (144)	0.60 OF 10	214	TILT MORE TOWARD BEING THOSE WHERE FIRST COUSIN MARRIAGE, IF PERMITTED, IS OTHER THAN UNILATERAL (144)	0.94 OF 33	4 2 6 31 XSQ= 4.81 PHI= 0.334 XP = 0.0283
240	DRIFT TOWARD BEING THOSE WHERE THE FAMILY, IF EXTENDED, IS LARGE, RATHER THAN SMALL OR STEM (78)	0.67 OF 15	240	DRIFT TOWARD BEING THOSE WHERE THE FAMILY, IF EXTENDED, IS SMALL OR STEM, RATHER THAN LARGE (135)	0.63 OF 43	10 16 5 27 XSQ= 2.80 PHI= 0.220 XP = 0.0942
243	TILT TOWARD BEING THOSE WHERE POLYGYNY, IF PRESENT, HAS A HIGH INCIDENCE (24) W-C,S	0.64 OF 14	243	TILT TOWARD BEING THOSE WHERE POLYGYNY, IF PRESENT, HAS A LOW INCIDENCE (36) W-D,S	0.73 OF 22	9 6 5 16 XSQ= 3.42 PHI= 0.308 EP = 0.0410
303	LEAN TOWARD BEING THOSE WHERE THE EARLY ORAL SATISFACTION POTENTIAL IS HIGH (32) W-C	0.91 OF 11	303	LEAN TOWARD BEING THOSE WHERE THE EARLY ORAL SATISFACTION POTENTIAL IS LOW (25) W-C	0.63 OF 19	10 7 1 12 XSQ= 6.24 PHI= 0.456 EP = 0.0067
326	TILT TOWARD BEING THOSE WHERE THE INFERRED TRANSITION ANXIETY BETWEEN INFANCY AND CHILDHOOD IS LOW (35) B-B-C	0.88 OF 8	326	TILT TOWARD BEING THOSE WHERE THE INFERRED TRANSITION ANXIETY BETWEEN INFANCY AND CHILDHOOD IS HIGH (32) B-B-C	0.59 OF 29	1 17 7 12 XSQ= 3.65 PHI= -0.314 EP = 0.0422

```
327  TILT TOWARD BEING THOSE          0.86 OF   7    327  TILT TOWARD BEING THOSE          0.65 OF  26           6     9
     WHERE THE AGE OF THE INFANT                         WHERE THE AGE OF THE INFANT                                1    17
     AT TIME OF REDUCED CONTACT WITH MOTHER              AT TIME OF REDUCED CONTACT WITH MOTHER              XSQ=     3.93
     IS HIGHER THAN TWO YEARS  (28) B-B-C                IS TWO YEARS OR LOWER  (27) B-B-C                   PHI=    0.345
                                                                                                             EP =   0.0300

335  DRIFT TOWARD BEING THOSE         0.89 OF   9    335  DRIFT TOWARD BEING THOSE         0.50 OF  14           8     7
     WHERE INITIAL INDULGENCE OF DEPENDENCY              WHERE INITIAL INDULGENCE OF DEPENDENCY                     1     7
     IS HIGH  (20) WNS                                   IS LOW  (18) WNS                                    XSQ=     2.14
                                                                                                             PHI=    0.305
                                                                                                             EP =   0.0858

397  DRIFT LESS TOWARD BEING THOSE  0.62 OF  13    397  DRIFT MORE TOWARD BEING THOSE  0.94 OF  16           5     1
     WHERE SEX DISABILITY                                WHERE SEX DISABILITY                                       8    15
     IS ABSENT  (42) JKH                                 IS ABSENT  (42) JKH                                 XSQ=     2.78
                                                                                                             PHI=    0.310
                                                                                                             EP =   0.0638

417  TILT LESS TOWARD BEING THOSE   0.56 OF   9    417  IN ALL CASES ARE THOSE           1.00 OF  13           5    13
     WHERE WARFARE IS                                    WHERE WARFARE IS                                           4     0
     PREVALENT  (34) LWS                                 PREVALENT  (34) LWS                                 XSQ=     4.39
                                                                                                             PHI=   -0.447
                                                                                                             EP =   0.0172

424  DRIFT MORE TOWARD BEING THOSE  0.87 OF  15    424  DRIFT LESS TOWARD BEING THOSE  0.57 OF  23           2    10
     WHERE RELIGIOUS SPECIALISTS ARE                     WHERE RELIGIOUS SPECIALISTS ARE                           13    13
     PART-TIME, RATHER THAN                              PART-TIME, RATHER THAN                              XSQ=     2.55
     FULL-TIME  (33) JMH                                 FULL-TIME  (33) JMH                                 PHI=   -0.259
                                                                                                             EP =   0.0770

425  IN ALL CASES ARE THOSE           1.00 OF   5    425  DRIFT TOWARD BEING THOSE         0.53 OF  19           0    10
     WHERE SUPERNATURALS ARE MAINLY                      WHERE SUPERNATURALS ARE MAINLY                             5     9
     AGGRESSIVE, RATHER THAN                             BENEVOLENT, RATHER THAN                             XSQ=     2.61
     BENEVOLENT  (20) L-T-W                              AGGRESSIVE  (16) L-T-W                              PHI=   -0.330
                                                                                                             EP =   0.0530

428  TILT TOWARD BEING THOSE          0.80 OF   5    428  TILT TOWARD BEING THOSE          0.80 OF  25           1    20
     WHERE A HIGH GOD, IF PRESENT AND ACTIVE,            WHERE A HIGH GOD, IF PRESENT AND ACTIVE,                   4     5
     DOES NOT SUPPORT HUMAN MORALITY,                    SUPPORTS HUMAN MORALITY, RATHER THAN                XSQ=     4.57
     RATHER THAN SUPPORTING IT  (26) GES,EA              NOT SUPPORTING IT  (61) GES,EA                      PHI=   -0.390
                                                                                                             EP =   0.0195

435  TILT TOWARD BEING THOSE          0.75 OF   8    435  TILT TOWARD BEING THOSE          0.89 OF   9           6     1
     WHERE ABANDONMENT OF THE HOUSE OF THE DEAD          WHERE ABANDONMENT OF THE HOUSE OF THE DEAD                 2     8
     IS PRACTICED  (12) LWS                              IS NOT PRACTICED  (19) LWS                          XSQ=     4.74
                                                                                                             PHI=    0.528
                                                                                                             EP =   0.0152

451  TILT TOWARD BEING THOSE          0.86 OF   7    451  TILT TOWARD BEING THOSE          0.86 OF   7           1     6
     WHERE TOTEMISM IS                                   WHERE TOTEMISM IS                                          6     1
     UNIMPORTANT OR ABSENT  (12) LWS                     PRESENT  (15) LWS                                   XSQ=     4.57
                                                                                                             PHI=   -0.571
                                                                                                             EP =   0.0291
```

111/

```
480  IN ALL CASES ARE THOSE          1.00 OF   4       480  DRIFT TOWARD BEING THOSE       0.58 OF  12             0     7
     WHERE CCMPLEXITY OF ARTISTIC CESIGN                    WHERE COMPLEXITY OF ARTISTIC DESIGN                   4     5
     IS LOW  (15) HB                                        IS HIGH  (14) HB                                XSQ=     2.12
                                                                                                            PHI=   -0.364
                                                                                                            EP =   0.0885
```

112 CULTURES
WHERE WORK ORGANIZATICNS
HAVING A CCNTRACTUAL ASPECT
ARE REPCRTED (50) SHU

112 CULTURES
WHERE WORK ORGANIZATIONS
HAVING A CONTRACTUAL ASPECT
ARE NOT REPORTED (55) SHU

BACKGROUND ON PAGE 91

SUBJECT ONLY

50 IN LEFT COLUMN

ATAYAL	AYMARA	BURMESE	BURUSHO	CAMAYURA	CAMBODIANS	CHAGGA	CHUKCHEE	CROW	CUNA
DOGON	FANG	FON	GILYAK	HAIDA	HANO	HAVASUPAI	HUTSUL	IBAN	IFUGAO
KABYLE	KAREN	KURTATCHI	KWAKIUTL	LAPPS	MACASSARESE	MALAYS	MAM	MAORI	MIN CHINESE
NUPE	NYCRO	PENOBSCOT	PUKAPUKA	ROMANS	RWALA	SAMOANS	SANPOIL	SOMALI	TALLENSI
TARAHUMARA	THAI	TIBETANS	TIMBIRA	TIV	TROBRIAND	TURKANA	WOLEAIANS	WOLOF	ZUNI

55 IN RIGHT COLUMN

ABIPON	ANDAMANESE	ARANDA	ASHANTI	AWEIKOMA	AZANDE	BELU	BEMBA	CAGABA	CARIB
CAYAPA	COPR ESKIMO	CARC	GOND	HAZARA	ILA	JIVARO	JUKUN	KAZAK	KIKUYU
LAU	MANGAIANS	MARICOPA	MARSHALLESE	MBUNDU	MURNGIN	MZAB	NAMA	NAMBICUARA	NAVAHO
NUER	OJIBWA	CNA	PAPAGO	POPOLUCA	RIFFIANS	SAMOYED	SEMANG	SENIANG	SIRIONO
SONGHAI	SOTHO	TAOS	TENETEHARA	TERENA	THONGA	TIKOPIA	TRUMAI	TUBATULABAL	TUPINAMBA
WAPISHANA	WINNEBAGO	WOGEO	YAGUA	YOKUTS					

295 EXCLUDED BECAUSE UNASCERTAINED

9	TILT MORE TOWARD BEING THOSE LOCATED OUTSIDE OF SOUTH AMERICA (335)	0.90 OF 50	9	TILT LESS TOWARD BEING THOSE LOCATED OUTSIDE OF SOUTH AMERICA (335)	0.73 OF 55		5 15 45 40 XSQ= 4.01 PHI= -0.195 XP = 0.0453
44	TILT MORE TOWARD BEING THOSE WHERE SETTLEMENTS ARE FIXED (222)	0.76 OF 46	44	TILT LESS TOWARD BEING THOSE WHERE SETTLEMENTS ARE FIXED (222)	0.54 OF 52		35 28 11 24 XSQ= 4.33 PHI= 0.210 XP = 0.0373
46	DRIFT MORE TOWARD BEING THOSE OTHER THAN WHERE SETTLEMENTS ARE NON-FIXED AND MOVEMENT IS NOMADIC (260)	0.83 OF 46	46	DRIFT LESS TOWARD BEING THOSE OTHER THAN WHERE SETTLEMENTS ARE NON-FIXED AND MOVEMENT IS NOMADIC (260)	0.65 OF 52		8 18 38 34 XSQ= 2.88 PHI= -0.172 XP = 0.0895
51	TILT MORE TOWARD BEING THOSE WHERE SUBSISTENCE IS PRIMARILY BY FOOD PRODUCTION -- I. E., AGRICULTURE OR HUSBANDRY -- RATHER THAN BY GATHERING (253)	0.76 OF 50	51	TILT LESS TOWARD BEING THOSE WHERE SUBSISTENCE IS PRIMARILY BY FOOD PRODUCTION -- I. E., AGRICULTURE OR HUSBANDRY -- RATHER THAN BY GATHERING (253)	0.53 OF 55		38 29 12 26 XSQ= 5.18 PHI= 0.222 XP = 0.0229

53	DRIFT LESS TOWARD BEING THOSE 0.53 OF 38 WHERE FOOD PRODUCTION IS BY SIMPLE AGRICULTURE OR INCIPIENT FOOD PRODUCTION, RATHER THAN BY INTENSIVE AGRICULTURE (147)	53	DRIFT MORE TOWARD BEING THOSE 0.77 OF 35 WHERE FOOD PRODUCTION IS BY SIMPLE AGRICULTURE OR INCIPIENT FOOD PRODUCTION, RATHER THAN BY INTENSIVE AGRICULTURE (147)	18 8 20 27 XSQ= 3.76 PHI= 0.227 XP = 0.0524
62	TILT MORE TOWARD BEING THOSE 0.78 OF 50 WHERE HUSBANDRY OF SOME KIND IS PRESENT (228)	62	TILT LESS TOWARD BEING THOSE 0.55 OF 55 WHERE HUSBANDRY OF SOME KIND IS PRESENT (228)	39 30 11 25 XSQ= 5.40 PHI= 0.227 XP = 0.0202
71	TILT TOWARD BEING THOSE 0.60 OF 30 WHERE METAL WORKING IS PRESENT (98)	71	TILT TOWARD BEING THOSE 0.72 OF 46 WHERE METAL WORKING IS ABSENT (153)	18 13 12 33 XSQ= 6.32 PHI= 0.288 XP = 0.0120
82	LEAN MORE TOWARD BEING THOSE 0.92 OF 38 WHERE A CITY OR TOWN IS PRESENT, OR THE AVERAGE COMMUNITY SIZE IS FIFTY OR GREATER (178)	82	LEAN LESS TOWARD BEING THOSE 0.64 OF 39 WHERE A CITY OR TOWN IS PRESENT, OR THE AVERAGE COMMUNITY SIZE IS FIFTY OR GREATER (178)	35 25 3 14 XSQ= 7.22 PHI= 0.306 XP = 0.0072
97	TILT LESS TOWARD BEING THOSE 0.75 OF 44 WHERE THE HIERARCHY OF LOCAL JURISDICTION HAS THREE OR TWO LEVELS (273) GES,EA	97	TILT MORE TOWARD BEING THOSE 0.92 OF 52 WHERE THE HIERARCHY OF LOCAL JURISDICTION HAS THREE OR TWO LEVELS (273) GES,EA	11 4 33 48 XSQ= 4.18 PHI= 0.209 XP = 0.0409
100	DRIFT MORE TOWARD BEING THOSE 0.91 OF 43 WHERE HIERARCHIES ARE MORE COMPLEX THAN THE 'SIMPLEST,' I. E., MORE COMPLEX THAN TWO LOCAL LEVELS WITH NO NATIONAL LEVELS (267) GES,EA	100	DRIFT LESS TOWARD BEING THOSE 0.75 OF 52 WHERE HIERARCHIES ARE MORE COMPLEX THAN THE 'SIMPLEST,' I. E., MORE COMPLEX THAN TWO LOCAL LEVELS WITH NO NATIONAL LEVELS (267) GES,EA	39 39 4 13 XSQ= 2.95 PHI= 0.176 XP = 0.0858
107	TILT LESS TOWARD BEING THOSE 0.71 OF 34 WHERE CLASS STRATIFICATION, IF PRESENT, IS BASED ON SOMETHING OTHER THAN OCCUPATIONAL STATUS (160)	107	TILT MORE TOWARD BEING THOSE 0.97 OF 29 WHERE CLASS STRATIFICATION, IF PRESENT, IS BASED ON SOMETHING OTHER THAN OCCUPATIONAL STATUS (160)	10 1 24 28 XSQ= 5.63 PHI= 0.299 XP = 0.0177
108	DRIFT TOWARD BEING THOSE 0.71 OF 34 WHERE CLASS STRATIFICATION, IF PRESENT, IS BASED ON SOMETHING OTHER THAN A HEREDITARY ARISTOCRACY (129)	108	DRIFT TOWARD BEING THOSE 0.55 OF 29 WHERE CLASS STRATIFICATION, IF PRESENT, IS BASED ON A HEREDITARY ARISTOCRACY (74)	10 16 24 13 XSQ= 3.29 PHI= -0.228 XP = 0.0698
110	TILT TOWARD BEING THOSE 0.55 OF 49 WHERE SLAVERY IS PRESENT (163)	110	TILT TOWARD BEING THOSE 0.70 OF 54 WHERE SLAVERY IS ABSENT (218)	27 16 22 38 XSQ= 5.85 PHI= 0.238 XP = 0.0156

No.			No.			
132	TILT TOWARD BEING THOSE WHERE ECONOMIC EXCHANGE INVOLVES THE USE OF MONEY (37) JMH	0.79 OF 19	132	TILT TOWARD BEING THOSE WHERE ECONOMIC EXCHANGE DOES NOT INVOLVE THE USE OF MONEY (17) JMH	0.58 OF 19	15 8 4 11 XSQ= 3.97 PHI= 0.323 EP = 0.0448
133	TILT TOWARD BEING THOSE WHERE CONTRACTED DEBTS ARE SIGNIFICANTLY PRESENT (17) GES	0.67 OF 9	133	TILT TOWARD BEING THOSE WHERE CONTRACTED DEBTS ARE MODERATELY PRESENT OR ABSENT (17) GES	0.89 OF 9	6 1 3 8 XSQ= 3.74 PHI= 0.456 EP = 0.0498
136	TILT TOWARD BEING THOSE WHERE FULL-TIME ENTREPRENEURS ARE ABSENT (14) JV	0.57 OF 7	136	IN ALL CASES ARE THOSE WHERE FULL-TIME ENTREPRENEURS ARE PRESENT (18) JV	1.00 OF 11	3 11 4 0 XSQ= 5.11 PHI= -0.533 EP = 0.0114
143	DRIFT TOWARD BEING THOSE WHERE THE RATIO OF RESTITUTIVE TO REPRESSIVE SANCTIONS IS HIGH (20) WME	0.58 OF 12	143	DRIFT TOWARD BEING THOSE WHERE THE RATIO OF RESTITUTIVE TO REPRESSIVE SANCTIONS IS MEDIUM OR LOW (32) WME	0.78 OF 18	7 4 5 14 XSQ= 2.64 PHI= 0.297 EP = 0.0626
144	DRIFT TOWARD BEING THOSE WHERE THE RATIO OF RESTITUTIVE TO REPRESSIVE SANCTIONS IS HIGH OR MEDIUM (27) WME	0.75 OF 12	144	DRIFT TOWARD BEING THOSE WHERE THE RATIO OF RESTITUTIVE TO REPRESSIVE SANCTIONS IS LOW (25) WME	0.67 OF 18	9 6 3 12 XSQ= 3.47 PHI= 0.340 EP = 0.0604
163	IN ALL CASES ARE THOSE WHERE THE EMPHASIS ON INDIVIDUAL VOLITION AS THE CAUSE OF CRIME IS HIGH (7) MJ	1.00 OF 4	163	IN ALL CASES ARE THOSE WHERE THE EMPHASIS ON INDIVIDUAL VOLITION AS THE CAUSE OF CRIME IS LOW (10) MJ	1.00 OF 8	4 0 0 8 XSQ= 7.92 PHI= 0.812 EP = 0.0020
178	TILT LESS TOWARD BEING THOSE WHERE THE COMMUNITY IS OTHER THAN SEGMENTED ON A CLAN BASIS AND NON-EXOGAMOUS (295)	0.70 OF 50	178	TILT MORE TOWARD BEING THOSE WHERE THE COMMUNITY IS OTHER THAN SEGMENTED ON A CLAN BASIS AND NON-EXOGAMOUS (295)	0.89 OF 54	15 6 35 48 XSQ= 4.64 PHI= 0.211 XP = 0.0313
196	LEAN TOWARD BEING THOSE WHERE INDIVIDUAL RIGHTS IN REAL PROPERTY, AND RULES FOR INHERITANCE, ARE PRESENT (194)	0.77 OF 40	196	LEAN TOWARD BEING THOSE WHERE INDIVIDUAL RIGHTS IN REAL PROPERTY, OR RULES FOR INHERITANCE, ARE ABSENT (87)	0.55 OF 38	31 17 9 21 XSQ= 7.51 PHI= 0.310 XP = 0.0061
220	TILT MORE TOWARD BEING THOSE WHERE FIRST COUSIN MARRIAGE IN SOME FORM OR OTHER IS NOT PRESCRIBED OR PREFERRED (273)	0.90 OF 48	220	TILT LESS TOWARD BEING THOSE WHERE FIRST COUSIN MARRIAGE IN SOME FORM OR OTHER IS NOT PRESCRIBED OR PREFERRED (273)	0.69 OF 54	5 17 43 37 XSQ= 5.48 PHI= -0.232 XP = 0.0193

234	DRIFT TCWARD BEING THCSE 0.67 OF 43 WHERE THE COUSIN TERMINCLCGY IS OF ESKIMO CR HAWAIIAN TYPE, RATHER THAN CROW, OMAHA, CR IRCQUCIS TYPE (170)	234	DRIFT TOWARD BEING THOSE 0.56 OF 45 WHERE THE COUSIN TERMINCLCGY IS OF CROW, OMAHA, OR IROQUOIS TYPE, RATHER THAN ESKIMO OR HAWAIIAN TYPE (152)	14 25 29 20 XSQ= 3.83 PHI= -0.209 XP = 0.0504
242	DRIFT LESS TOWARD BEING THOSE 0.69 OF 49 WHERE MARRIAGE IS COMMCNLY CR CCCASICNALLY PCLYGYNOUS, RATHER THAN MCNCGAMCUS (314)	242	DRIFT MORE TOWARD BEING THOSE 0.85 OF 55 WHERE MARRIAGE IS COMMONLY OR OCCASIONALLY PCLYGYNCUS, RATHER THAN MONOGAMCUS (314)	34 47 15 8 XSQ= 3.01 PHI= -0.170 XP = 0.0829
262	DRIFT MCRE TCWARD BEING THCSE 0.88 OF 50 WHERE WIVES ARE CBTAINEC BY MEANS INVCLVING THE PRESENCE CF SOME CCNSIDERATION (305)	262	DRIFT LESS TOWARD BEING THCSE 0.72 OF 54 WHERE WIVES ARE OBTAINED BY MEANS INVOLVING THE PRESENCE OF SOME CONSIDERATION (305)	44 39 6 15 XSQ= 3.09 PHI= 0.172 XP = 0.0787
302	DRIFT TCWARD BEING THCSE 0.64 OF 11 WHERE THE AVERAGE EARLY SATISFACTION POTENTIAL IS LOW (17) W-C	302	DRIFT TOWARD BEING THOSE 0.78 OF 9 WHERE THE AVERAGE EARLY SATISFACTICN POTENTIAL IS HIGH (23) W-C	4 7 7 2 XSQ= 1.96 PHI= -0.313 EP = 0.0923
309	DRIFT TCWARD BEING THCSE 0.77 OF 13 WHERE CRAL SCCIALIZATICN ANXIETY IS HIGH (26) W-C	3C9	DRIFT TOWARD BEING THOSE 0.64 OF 14 WHERE ORAL SOCIALIZATICN ANXIETY IS LOW (27) W-C	10 5 3 9 XSQ= 3.12 PHI= 0.340 EP = 0.0542
342	DRIFT TOWARD BEING THCSE 0.73 OF 11 WHERE THE CHILD'S INFERREC ANXIETY OVER PERFCRMANCE CF NURTURANT BEHAVIOR IS HIGH (18) B-B-C	342	DRIFT TOWARD BEING THOSE 0.69 OF 16 WHERE THE CHILD'S INFERRED ANXIETY OVER PERFORMANCE OF NURTURANT BEHAVIOR IS LOW (28) B-B-C	8 5 3 11 XSQ= 2.98 PHI= 0.332 EP = 0.0542
404	DRIFT LESS TCWARD BEING THCSE 0.53 OF 15 WHERE EXPLANATICNS CF ILLNESS OF A SEXUAL NATURE ARE ABSENT (42) W-C	404	DRIFT MORE TOWARD BEING THCSE 0.84 OF 19 WHERE EXPLANATIONS OF ILLNESS OF A SEXUAL NATURE ARE ABSENT (42) W-C	7 3 8 16 XSQ= 2.51 PHI= 0.271 EP = 0.0680
435	TILT TCWARD BEING THOSE 0.89 OF 9 WHERE ABANDONMENT CF THE HOUSE OF THE CEAD IS NCT PRACTICEC (19) LWS	435	TILT TOWARD BEING THOSE 0.75 OF 8 WHERE ABANDONMENT OF THE HOUSE OF THE DEAD IS PRACTICED (12) LWS	1 6 8 2 XSQ= 4.74 PHI= -0.528 EP = 0.0152
450	DRIFT LESS TCWARD BEING THCSE 0.56 OF 25 WHERE THE CBSERVATICN CF FCOD TABOOS IS HIGH CR MEDIUM, RATHER THAN LOW (60) JRL	45C	DRIFT MORE TOWARD BEING THCSE 0.83 OF 29 WHERE THE OBSERVATICN CF FCCD TABOCS IS HIGH OR MEDIUM, RATHER THAN LOW (60) JRL	14 24 11 5 XSQ= 3.42 PHI= -0.252 XP = 0.0645

112/

```
480  LEAN TOWARD BEING THOSE          0.88 OF   8      480  IN ALL CASES ARE THOSE          1.00 OF   8           7     0
     WHERE COMPLEXITY OF ARTISTIC DESIGN                   WHERE COMPLEXITY OF ARTISTIC DESIGN                    1     8
     IS HIGH  (14) HB                                      IS LOW  (15) HB                                  XSQ=    9.14
                                                                                                             PHI=   0.756
                                                                                                             EP =   0.0014
```

****

113 CULTURES WHERE WCRK ORGANIZATICNS HAVING A CUSTODIAL ASPECT ARE REPCRTED (46) SHU	113 CULTURES WHERE WORK ORGANIZATIONS HAVING A CUSTODIAL ASPECT ARE NOT REPORTED (59) SHU

BACKGROUND ON PAGE 91 — SUBJECT ONLY

46 IN LEFT CCLUMN

ASHANTI	ATAYAL	AYMARA	AZANCE	BEMBA	BURMESE	BURUSHO	CAGABA	CAMAYURA	CAMBODIANS
CHAGGA	CRCW	CUNA	GONC	HANO	KURTATCHI	LAU	MACASSARESE	MALAYS	MANGAIANS
MAORI	MARSHALLESE	MBUNDU	MIN CHINESE	NUPE	OJIBWA	PAPAGO	PENCBSCCT	PUKAPUKA	ROMANS
RWALA	SAMCANS	SOMALI	SOTHO	TAOS	THAI	THONGA	TIBETANS	TIV	TROBRIAND
WAPISHANA	WINNEBAGC	WCGEC	WOLEAIANS	WOLOF	YOKUTS				

59 IN RIGHT CCLUMN

ABIPCN	ANDAMANESE	ARANCA	AWEIKOMA	BELU	CARIB	CAYAPA	CHUKCHEE	COPR ESKIMO	DARC
DOGCN	FANG	FON	GILYAK	HAIDA	HAVASUPAI	HAZARA	HUTSUL	IBAN	IFUGAO
ILA	JIVARC	JUKUN	KABYLE	KAREN	KAZAK	KIKUYU	KWAKIUTL	LAPPS	MAM
MARICOPA	MURNGIN	MZAB	NAMA	NAMBICUARA	NAVAHO	NUER	NYCRO	CNA	POPOLUCA
RIFFIANS	SAMCYED	SANPCIL	SEMANG	SENIANG	SIRIONO	SONGHAI	TALLENSI	TARAHUMARA	TENETEHARA
TERENA	TIKCPIA	TIMBIRA	TRUMAI	TUBATULABAL	TUPINAMBA	TURKANA	YAGUA	ZUNI	

295 EXCLUDED BECAUSE UNASCERTAINEC

12	DRIFT MCRE TCWARD BEING THOSE 0.98 OF 46 WHERE THE LATITUDE IS LESS THAN FIFTY DEGREES (367)	12	DRIFT LESS TOWARD BEING THOSE 0.86 OF 59 WHERE THE LATITUDE IS LESS THAN FIFTY DEGREES (367)	1 8 / 45 51 / XSQ= 2.95 / PHI= -0.168 / XP = 0.0861
44	TILT MCRE TCWARC BEING THCSE 0.79 OF 42 WHERE SETTLEMENTS ARE FIXEC (222)	44	TILT LESS TOWARD BEING THOSE 0.54 CF 56 WHERE SETTLEMENTS ARE FIXED (222)	33 30 / 9 26 / XSQ= 5.49 / PHI= 0.237 / XP = 0.0191
46	LEAN MCRE TOWARC BEING THCSE 0.88 OF 42 CTHER THAN WHERE SETTLEMENTS ARE NON-FIXED AND MCVEMENT IS NCMADIC (260)	46	LEAN LESS TOWARD BEING THOSE 0.63 CF 56 OTHER THAN WHERE SETTLEMENTS ARE NON-FIXED AND MOVEMENT IS NOMADIC (260)	5 21 / 37 35 / XSQ= 6.81 / PHI= -0.264 / XP = 0.0091
51	LEAN MCRE TOWARC BEING THCSE 0.80 OF 46 WHERE SUBSISTENCE IS PRIMARILY BY FCCD PRODUCTION -- I. E., AGRICULTURE OR HUSBANDRY -- RATHER THAN BY GATHERING (253)	51	LEAN LESS TOWARD BEING THOSE 0.51 OF 59 WHERE SUBSISTENCE IS PRIMARILY BY FOOD PRODUCTION -- I. E., AGRICULTURE OR HUSBANDRY -- RATHER THAN BY GATHERING (253)	37 30 / 9 29 / XSQ= 8.56 / PHI= 0.286 / XP = 0.0034

No.	Statement	Proportion	No.	Statement	Proportion	Table / Statistics
56	TILT TOWARD BEING THOSE WHERE FOOD PRODUCTION IS BY SIMPLE AGRICULTURE, RATHER THAN BY INCIPIENT FOOD PRODUCTION (101)	0.81 OF 26	56	TILT TOWARD BEING THOSE WHERE FOOD PRODUCTION IS BY INCIPIENT FOOD PRODUCTION, RATHER THAN BY SIMPLE AGRICULTURE (46)	0.52 OF 21	21 10 5 11 XSQ= 4.31 PHI= 0.303 XP = 0.0380
79	DRIFT LESS TOWARD BEING THOSE WHERE NO CITY IS PRESENT (201)	0.88 OF 33	79	IN ALL CASES ARE THOSE WHERE NO CITY IS PRESENT (201)	1.00 OF 44	4 0 29 44 XSQ= 3.43 PHI= 0.211 XP = 0.0639
82	LEAN MORE TOWARD BEING THOSE WHERE A CITY OR TOWN IS PRESENT, OR THE AVERAGE COMMUNITY SIZE IS FIFTY OR GREATER (178)	0.94 OF 33	82	LEAN LESS TOWARD BEING THOSE WHERE A CITY OR TOWN IS PRESENT, OR THE AVERAGE COMMUNITY SIZE IS FIFTY OR GREATER (178)	0.66 OF 44	31 29 2 15 XSQ= 7.06 PHI= 0.303 XP = 0.0079
86	TEND TO BE THOSE WHERE THE LEVEL OF POLITICAL INTEGRATION IS THE LARGE STATE, THE LITTLE STATE, OR THE MINIMAL STATE (148) GPM	0.71 OF 41	86	TEND TO BE THOSE WHERE THE LEVEL OF POLITICAL INTEGRATION IS THE AUTONOMOUS COMMUNITY, OR THE FAMILY (156) GPM	0.73 OF 52	29 14 12 38 XSQ= 15.98 PHI= 0.415 XP = 0.0001
91	DRIFT TOWARD BEING THOSE WHERE SOCIETAL COMPLEXITY IS HIGH (18) F-W	0.58 OF 12	91	DRIFT TOWARD BEING THOSE WHERE SOCIETAL COMPLEXITY IS LOW (22) F-W	0.80 OF 15	7 3 5 12 XSQ= 2.72 PHI= 0.317 EP = 0.0568
96	TEND TO BE THOSE WHERE THE HIERARCHY OF NATIONAL JURISDICTION HAS FOUR, THREE, TWO OR ONE LEVEL (174) GES,EA	0.77 OF 40	96	TEND TO BE THOSE WHERE THE HIERARCHY OF NATIONAL JURISDICTION HAS NO LEVELS (156) GES,EA	0.71 OF 55	31 16 9 39 XSQ= 19.82 PHI= 0.457 XP = 0.0000
98	TILT MORE TOWARD BEING THOSE WHERE THE HIERARCHY OF LOCAL JURISDICTION HAS FOUR OR THREE LEVELS (238) GES,EA	0.88 OF 41	98	TILT LESS TOWARD BEING THOSE WHERE THE HIERARCHY OF LOCAL JURISDICTION HAS FOUR OR THREE LEVELS (238) GES,EA	0.65 OF 55	36 36 5 19 XSQ= 5.12 PHI= 0.231 XP = 0.0236
100	LEAN MORE TOWARD BEING THOSE WHERE HIERARCHIES ARE MORE COMPLEX THAN THE 'SIMPLEST,' I. E., MORE COMPLEX THAN TWO LOCAL LEVELS WITH NO NATIONAL LEVELS (267) GES,EA	0.97 OF 40	100	LEAN LESS TOWARD BEING THOSE WHERE HIERARCHIES ARE MORE COMPLEX THAN THE 'SIMPLEST,' I. E., MORE COMPLEX THAN TWO LOCAL LEVELS WITH NO NATIONAL LEVELS (267) GES,EA	0.71 OF 55	39 39 1 16 XSQ= 9.41 PHI= 0.315 XP = 0.0022
106	TILT TOWARD BEING THOSE WHERE CLASS STRATIFICATION, IF PRESENT, IS BASED ON SOMETHING OTHER THAN WEALTH (126)	0.75 OF 32	106	TILT TOWARD BEING THOSE WHERE CLASS STRATIFICATION, IF PRESENT, IS BASED ON WEALTH (77)	0.58 OF 31	8 18 24 13 XSQ= 5.80 PHI= -0.304 XP = 0.0160

107	LEAN LESS TOWARD BEING THOSE 0.69 OF 32 WHERE CLASS STRATIFICATION, IF PRESENT, IS BASED ON SOMETHING OTHER THAN OCCUPATIONAL STATUS (160)	107 LEAN MORE TOWARD BEING THOSE 0.97 OF 31 WHERE CLASS STRATIFICATION, IF PRESENT, IS BASED ON SOMETHING OTHER THAN OCCUPATIONAL STATUS (160)	10 1 22 30 XSQ= 6.75 PHI= 0.327 XP = 0.0094
116	TILT TOWARD BEING THOSE 0.53 OF 19 WHERE OCCUPATIONAL SPECIALIZATION IS FULL-TIME, WHETHER OR NOT FOR SURPLUS PRODUCTION (20) JMH	116 TILT TOWARD BEING THOSE 0.84 OF 19 WHERE OCCUPATIONAL SPECIALIZATION IS PART-TIME ONLY (34) JMH	10 3 9 16 XSQ= 4.21 PHI= 0.333 EP = 0.0382
129	TILT TOWARD BEING THOSE 0.67 OF 15 WHERE WEAVING IS MAINLY DONE BY MALES (31)	129 TILT TOWARD BEING THOSE 0.71 OF 21 WHERE WEAVING IS MAINLY DONE BY FEMALES (73)	10 6 5 15 XSQ= 3.72 PHI= 0.321 EP = 0.0409
132	LEAN TOWARD BEING THOSE 0.84 OF 19 WHERE ECONOMIC EXCHANGE INVOLVES THE USE OF MONEY (37) JMH	132 LEAN TOWARD BEING THOSE 0.63 OF 19 WHERE ECONOMIC EXCHANGE DOES NOT INVOLVE THE USE OF MONEY (17) JMH	16 7 3 12 XSQ= 7.05 PHI= 0.431 EP = 0.0069
137	TILT TOWARD BEING THOSE 0.54 OF 24 WHERE INVIDIOUS DISPLAY OF WEALTH IS STRONGLY EMPHASIZED (37) PES	137 TILT TOWARD BEING THOSE 0.80 OF 25 WHERE INVIDIOUS DISPLAY OF WEALTH IS MODERATELY, LITTLE, OR NEGATIVELY EMPHASIZED (52) PES	13 5 11 20 XSQ= 4.77 PHI= 0.312 XP = 0.0290
147	IN ALL CASES ARE THOSE 1.00 OF 5 WHERE CODIFIED LAWS ARE PRESENT (20) LWS	147 TILT TOWARD BEING THOSE 0.73 OF 11 WHERE CODIFIED LAWS ARE UNIMPORTANT OR ABSENT (13) LWS	5 3 0 8 XSQ= 4.65 PHI= 0.539 EP = 0.0256
152	TILT TOWARD BEING THOSE 0.83 OF 6 WHERE THE DIFFERENTIATION OF THE JURIDICAL AGENCY FROM THE MEDICAL AGENCY IS HIGH (10) MJ	152 TILT TOWARD BEING THOSE 0.86 OF 7 WHERE THE DIFFERENTIATION OF THE JURIDICAL AGENCY FROM THE MEDICAL AGENCY IS LOW (10) MJ	5 1 1 6 XSQ= 3.73 PHI= 0.536 EP = 0.0291
163	TILT TOWARD BEING THOSE 0.80 OF 5 WHERE THE EMPHASIS ON INDIVIDUAL VOLITION AS THE CAUSE OF CRIME IS HIGH (7) MJ	163 IN ALL CASES ARE THOSE 1.00 OF 7 WHERE THE EMPHASIS ON INDIVIDUAL VOLITION AS THE CAUSE OF CRIME IS LOW (10) MJ	4 0 1 7 XSQ= 5.19 PHI= 0.657 EP = 0.0101
196	TILT MORE TOWARD BEING THOSE 0.76 OF 33 WHERE INDIVIDUAL RIGHTS IN REAL PROPERTY, AND RULES FOR INHERITANCE, ARE PRESENT (194)	196 TILT LESS TOWARD BEING THOSE 0.51 OF 45 WHERE INDIVIDUAL RIGHTS IN REAL PROPERTY, AND RULES FOR INHERITANCE, ARE PRESENT (194)	25 23 8 22 XSQ= 3.90 PHI= 0.224 XP = 0.0483

326 TILT TOWARD BEING THOSE 0.64 OF 22 WHERE THE INFERRED TRANSITION ANXIETY BETWEEN INFANCY AND CHILDHOOD IS HIGH (32) B-B-C	326 TILT TOWARD BEING THOSE 0.73 OF 15 WHERE THE INFERRED TRANSITION ANXIETY BETWEEN INFANCY AND CHILDHOOD IS LOW (35) B-B-C	14 4 8 11 XSQ= 3.51 PHI= 0.308 EP = 0.0448
346 TILT TOWARD BEING THOSE 0.65 OF 23 WHERE THE CHILD'S INFERRED ANXIETY OVER PERFORMANCE OF SELF-RELIANT BEHAVIOR IS HIGH (37) B-B-C	346 TILT TOWARD BEING THOSE 0.70 OF 20 WHERE THE CHILD'S INFERRED ANXIETY OVER PERFORMANCE OF SELF-RELIANT BEHAVIOR IS LOW (39) B-B-C	15 6 8 14 XSQ= 3.99 PHI= 0.305 XP = 0.0457
347 TILT TOWARD BEING THOSE 0.65 OF 23 WHERE THE CHILD'S INFERRED CONFLICT REGARDING SELF-RELIANT BEHAVIOR IS HIGH (37) B-B-C	347 TILT TOWARD BEING THOSE 0.75 OF 20 WHERE THE CHILD'S INFERRED CONFLICT REGARDING SELF-RELIANT BEHAVIOR IS LOW (39) B-B-C	15 5 8 15 XSQ= 5.43 PHI= 0.355 XP = 0.0198
350 DRIFT TOWARD BEING THOSE 0.74 OF 19 WHERE THE CHILD'S INFERRED ANXIETY OVER PERFORMANCE OF ACHIEVEMENT BEHAVIOR IS HIGH (34) B-B-C	350 DRIFT TOWARD BEING THOSE 0.60 OF 15 WHERE THE CHILD'S INFERRED ANXIETY OVER PERFORMANCE OF ACHIEVEMENT BEHAVIOR IS LOW (26) B-B-C	14 6 5 9 XSQ= 2.66 PHI= 0.280 EP = 0.0800
354 DRIFT TOWARD BEING THOSE 0.61 OF 23 WHERE THE CHILD'S INFERRED ANXIETY OVER PERFORMANCE OF OBEDIENT BEHAVIOR IS HIGH (36) B-B-C	354 DRIFT TOWARD BEING THOSE 0.71 OF 17 WHERE THE CHILD'S INFERRED ANXIETY OVER PERFORMANCE OF OBEDIENT BEHAVIOR IS LOW (37) B-B-C	14 5 9 12 XSQ= 2.72 PHI= 0.261 EP = 0.0624
355 DRIFT TOWARD BEING THOSE 0.61 OF 23 WHERE THE CHILD'S INFERRED CONFLICT REGARDING OBEDIENT BEHAVIOR IS HIGH (35) B-B-C	355 DRIFT TOWARD BEING THOSE 0.71 OF 17 WHERE THE CHILD'S INFERRED CONFLICT REGARDING OBEDIENT BEHAVIOR IS LOW (38) B-B-C	14 5 9 12 XSQ= 2.72 PHI= 0.261 EP = 0.0624
424 DRIFT LESS TOWARD BEING THOSE 0.53 OF 19 WHERE RELIGIOUS SPECIALISTS ARE PART-TIME, RATHER THAN FULL-TIME (33) JMH	424 DRIFT MORE TOWARD BEING THOSE 0.84 OF 19 WHERE RELIGIOUS SPECIALISTS ARE PART-TIME, RATHER THAN FULL-TIME (33) JMH	9 3 10 16 XSQ= 3.04 PHI= 0.283 EP = 0.0789
452 LEAN TOWARD BEING THOSE 0.77 OF 13 WHERE TOTEMISM WITH FOOD TABOOS IS PRESENT (19) WNS	452 LEAN TOWARD BEING THOSE 0.83 OF 12 WHERE TOTEMISM WITH FOOD TABOOS IS ABSENT (24) WNS	10 2 3 10 XSQ= 6.82 PHI= 0.522 EP = 0.0048
453 TILT TOWARD BEING THOSE 0.57 OF 14 WHERE THE ROLE OF RELIGIOUS EXPERTS IS CONDUCIVE TO THE DEVELOPMENT OF THE INDIVIDUAL'S NEED TO ACHIEVE (13) DCM	453 IN ALL CASES ARE THOSE 1.00 OF 5 WHERE THE ROLE OF RELIGIOUS EXPERTS IS NOT CONDUCIVE TO THE DEVELOPMENT OF THE INDIVIDUAL'S NEED TO ACHIEVE (23) DCM	8 0 6 5 XSQ= 2.87 PHI= 0.389 EP = 0.0445

469	LEAN MORE TOWARD BEING THOSE WHERE CONTACT WITH OTHER CULTURES IS FREQUENT OR REGULAR, RATHER THAN IRREGULAR (43) JMH	0.95 OF 19	469	LEAN LESS TOWARD BEING THOSE WHERE CONTACT WITH OTHER CULTURES IS FREQUENT OR REGULAR, RATHER THAN IRREGULAR (43) JMH	0.53 OF 19		18	10
							1	9
						XSQ=		6.65
						PHI=		0.418
						EP =		0.0078
475	TILT TOWARD BEING THOSE WHERE EXHIBITIONISTIC DANCING IS STRONGLY OR MODERATELY EMPHASIZED (48) PES	0.83 OF 23	475	TILT TOWARD BEING THOSE WHERE EXHIBITIONISTIC DANCING IS NEGLIGIBLY EMPHASIZED (38) PES	0.56 OF 25		19	11
							4	14
						XSQ=		6.06
						PHI=		0.355
						XP =		0.0138
476	DRIFT TOWARD BEING THOSE WHERE THE DEGREE OF INSOBRIETY IS MODERATE OR SLIGHT (18) CH	0.58 OF 12	476	DRIFT TOWARD BEING THOSE WHERE THE DEGREE OF INSOBRIETY IS STRONG (31) DH	0.80 OF 15		5	12
							7	3
						XSQ=		2.72
						PHI=		-0.317
						EP =		0.0568

114 CULTURES
WHERE WORK ORGANIZATIONS
HAVING A FAMILIAL ASPECT
ARE REPORTED (87) SHU

114 CULTURES
WHERE WORK ORGANIZATIONS
HAVING A FAMILIAL ASPECT
ARE NOT REPORTED (18) SHU

BACKGROUND ON PAGE 91

SUBJECT ONLY

87 IN LEFT COLUMN

ASHANTI	ATAYAL	AWEIKOMA	AYMARA	BELU	BEMBA	BURMESE	BURUSHO	CAGABA	CAMAYURA
CAMBODIANS	CARIB	CAYAPA	CHAGGA	CHUKCHEE	COPR ESKIMO	CROW	CUNA	DOGON	FON
GILYAK	GOND	HAIDA	HANO	HAVASUPAI	HAZARA	HUTSUL	IBAN	IFUGAO	ILA
JIVARO	JUKUN	KABYLE	KAREN	KAZAK	KIKUYU	KURTATCHI	KWAKIUTL	LAPPS	LAU
MACASSARESE	MAM	MANGAIANS	MAORI	MARICOPA	MARSHALLESE	MBUNDU	MIN CHINESE	MURNGIN	MZAB
NAMA	NAMBICUARA	NAVAHO	NUER	NUPE	OJIBWA	ONA	PAPAGO	PENOBSCOT	POPOLUCA
PUKAPUKA	SAMOANS	SAMOYED	SENIANG	SIRIONO	SOMALI	SONGHAI	TALLENSI	TAOS	TARAHUMARA
TENETEHARA	TERENA	THAI	THONGA	TIBETANS	TIKOPIA	TIMBIRA	TIV	TROBRIAND	TUPINAMBA
TURKANA	WOGEO	WOLEAIANS	WOLOF	YAGUA	YOKUTS	ZUNI			

18 IN RIGHT COLUMN

ABIPON	ANDAMANESE	ARANDA	AZANDE	DARD	FANG	MALAYS	NYORO	RIFFIANS	ROMANS
RWALA	SANPOIL	SEMANG	SOTHO	TRUMAI	TUBATULABAL	WAPISHANA	WINNEBAGO		

295 EXCLUDED BECAUSE UNASCERTAINED

---

63 DRIFT LESS TOWARD BEING THOSE 0.53 OF 60 WHERE HUSBANDRY, IF PRESENT, IS PRINCIPALLY IN THE FORM OF BOVINE, EQUINE, CAMEL-LIKE, OR DEER-LIKE ANIMALS, RATHER THAN PIGS, SHEEP, OR GOATS (152)	63 DRIFT MORE TOWARD BEING THOSE 0.89 OF 9 WHERE HUSBANDRY, IF PRESENT, IS PRINCIPALLY IN THE FORM OF BOVINE, EQUINE, CAMEL-LIKE, OR DEER-LIKE ANIMALS, RATHER THAN PIGS, SHEEP, OR GOATS (152)	32 8 28 1 XSQ= 2.73 PHI= -0.199 XP = 0.0983
78 DRIFT LESS TOWARD BEING THOSE 0.52 OF 33 WHERE THE WRITING SYSTEM IS ALPHABETIC-OR-PHONETIC, OR MNEMONIC, RATHER THAN BEING ABSENT (36) JMH	78 IN ALL CASES ARE THOSE 1.00 OF 5 WHERE THE WRITING SYSTEM IS ALPHABETIC-OR-PHONETIC, OR MNEMONIC, RATHER THAN BEING ABSENT (36) JMH	17 5 16 0 XSQ= 2.43 PHI= -0.253 EP = 0.0612
88 DRIFT LESS TOWARD BEING THOSE 0.61 OF 66 WHERE, IF A HEADMANSHIP IS PRESENT, SUCCESSION IS HEREDITARY (165)	88 DRIFT MORE TOWARD BEING THOSE 0.92 OF 12 WHERE, IF A HEADMANSHIP IS PRESENT, SUCCESSION IS HEREDITARY (165)	26 1 40 11 XSQ= 3.06 PHI= 0.198 XP = 0.0800

131	DRIFT MORE TOWARD BEING THOSE 0.86 OF 44 WHERE THE CONSTRUCTION OF PERMANENT HOUSES OR THE ERECTION OF TEMPORARY DWELLINGS IS MAINLY DONE BY MALES (136)	131	DRIFT LESS TOWARD BEING THOSE 0.56 OF 9 WHERE THE CONSTRUCTION OF PERMANENT HOUSES OR THE ERECTION OF TEMPORARY DWELLINGS IS MAINLY DONE BY MALES (136)	38 5 6 4 XSQ= 2.84 PHI= 0.231 XP = 0.0920
137	DRIFT LESS TOWARD BEING THOSE 0.56 OF 41 WHERE INVIDIOUS DISPLAY OF WEALTH IS MODERATELY, LITTLE, OR NEGATIVELY EMPHASIZED (52) PES	137	IN ALL CASES ARE THOSE 1.00 OF 8 WHERE INVIDIOUS DISPLAY OF WEALTH IS MODERATELY, LITTLE, OR NEGATIVELY EMPHASIZED (52) PES	18 0 23 8 XSQ= 3.82 PHI= 0.279 XP = 0.0505
182	DRIFT TOWARD BEING THOSE 0.71 OF 86 OTHER THAN WHERE THE COMMUNITY IS STRUCTURED ON A NON-CLAN BASIS AND AGAMOUS (256)	182	DRIFT TOWARD BEING THOSE 0.56 OF 18 WHERE THE COMMUNITY IS STRUCTURED ON A NON-CLAN BASIS AND AGAMOUS (126)	25 10 61 8 XSQ= 3.57 PHI= -0.185 XP = 0.0590
196	DRIFT TOWARD BEING THOSE 0.68 OF 62 WHERE INDIVIDUAL RIGHTS IN REAL PROPERTY, AND RULES FOR INHERITANCE, ARE PRESENT (194)	196	DRIFT TOWARD BEING THOSE 0.63 OF 16 WHERE INDIVIDUAL RIGHTS IN REAL PROPERTY, OR RULES FOR INHERITANCE, ARE ABSENT (87)	42 6 20 10 XSQ= 3.72 PHI= 0.218 XP = 0.0538
243	DRIFT TOWARD BEING THOSE 0.64 OF 33 WHERE POLYGYNY, IF PRESENT, HAS A LOW INCIDENCE (36) W-D,S	243	IN ALL CASES ARE THOSE 1.00 OF 3 WHERE POLYGYNY, IF PRESENT, HAS A HIGH INCIDENCE (24) W-D,S	12 3 21 0 XSQ= 2.34 PHI= -0.255 EP = 0.0637
277	DRIFT TOWARD BEING THOSE 0.86 OF 14 WHERE THE STATUS OF WOMEN IS NOT STRONGLY INFERIOR OR SUBJECTED (22) LWS	277	DRIFT TOWARD BEING THOSE 0.60 OF 5 WHERE THE STATUS OF WOMEN IS INFERIOR OR SUBJECTED (14) LWS	2 3 12 2 XSQ= 1.96 PHI= -0.321 EP = 0.0844
356	TILT TOWARD BEING THOSE 0.64 OF 22 WHERE ADOLESCENT PEER GROUPS OR PAIRS ARE PRESENT IN A SETTING OF COURTSHIP (29) JKH	356	IN ALL CASES ARE THOSE 1.00 OF 4 WHERE NEITHER ADOLESCENT PEER GROUPS NOR PAIRS ARE PRESENT IN A SETTING OF COURTSHIP (22) JKH	14 0 8 4 XSQ= 3.25 PHI= 0.354 EP = 0.0331
366	TILT TOWARD BEING THOSE 0.80 OF 25 WHERE DISSOCIATION OF THE SEXES AT ADOLESCENCE IS MEDIUM OR LOW (41) JKH	366	TILT TOWARD BEING THOSE 0.80 OF 5 WHERE DISSOCIATION OF THE SEXES AT ADOLESCENCE IS HIGH (16) JKH	5 4 20 1 XSQ= 4.57 PHI= -0.390 EP = 0.0195
397	TILT TOWARD BEING THOSE 0.88 OF 24 WHERE SEX DISABILITY IS ABSENT (42) JKH	397	TILT TOWARD BEING THOSE 0.60 OF 5 WHERE SEX DISABILITY IS PRESENT (14) JKH	3 3 21 2 XSQ= 3.16 PHI= -0.330 EP = 0.0456

417	TILT TOWARD BEING THOSE WHERE WARFARE IS PREVALENT (34) LWS	0.94 OF	16	417	TILT TOWARD BEING THOSE WHERE WARFARE IS NOT PREVALENT (9) LWS	0.50 OF	6	15 3 1 3 XSQ= 3.06 PHI= 0.373 EP = 0.0458
433	TILT TOWARD BEING THOSE WHERE BELIEF IN REINCARNATION IS ABSENT (28) GES	0.94 OF	17	433	TILT TOWARD BEING THOSE WHERE BELIEF IN REINCARNATION IS PRESENT (10) GES	0.60 OF	5	1 3 16 2 XSQ= 4.40 PHI= -0.447 EP = 0.0239
436	TILT TOWARD BEING THOSE WHERE ACTIVE ANCESTRAL SPIRITS ARE PRESENT (27) GES	0.82 OF	17	436	TILT TOWARD BEING THOSE WHERE ACTIVE ANCESTRAL SPIRITS ARE ABSENT (11) GES	0.80 OF	5	14 1 3 4 XSQ= 4.35 PHI= 0.445 EP = 0.0207
438	TILT TOWARD BEING THOSE WHERE OTHER-WORLDLY FEARS OF GHOSTS OR SPIRITS ARE GREATER THAN THIS-WORLDLY FEARS OF HUMANS OR ANIMALS (27) W-C,JFG	0.73 OF	22	438	TILT TOWARD BEING THOSE WHERE THIS-WORLDLY FEARS OF HUMANS OR ANIMALS ARE GREATER THAN OTHER-WORLDLY FEARS OF GHOSTS OR SPIRITS (17) W-C,JFG	0.80 OF	5	16 1 6 4 XSQ= 2.86 PHI= 0.325 EP = 0.0473
439	DRIFT TOWARD BEING THOSE WHERE FEAR OF GHOSTS IS HIGH (30) W-C	0.59 OF	27	439	DRIFT TOWARD BEING THOSE WHERE FEAR OF GHOSTS IS LOW (31) W-C	0.86 OF	7	16 1 11 6 XSQ= 2.88 PHI= 0.291 EP = 0.0854
455	TILT TOWARD BEING THOSE WHERE THE MODE OF THE INDIVIDUAL'S CONTACT WITH THE DIVINE IS NOT CONDUCIVE TO THE DEVELOPMENT OF THE INDIVIDUAL'S NEED TO ACHIEVE (19) DCM	0.67 OF	15	455	IN ALL CASES ARE THOSE WHERE THE MODE OF THE INDIVIDUAL'S CONTACT WITH THE DIVINE IS CONDUCIVE TO THE DEVELOPMENT OF THE INDIVIDUAL'S NEED TO ACHIEVE (17) DCM	1.00 OF	4	5 4 10 0 XSQ= 3.27 PHI= -0.415 EP = 0.0325

115	CULTURES WHERE OCCUPATIONAL SPECIALIZATION IS FULL-TIME AND FOR SURPLUS PRODUCTION (7) JMH		115	CULTURES WHERE OCCUPATIONAL SPECIALIZATION IS FULL-TIME BUT NOT FOR SURPLUS PRODUCTION, OR PART-TIME ONLY (47) JMH		

BACKGROUND ON PAGE 93 — SUBJECT ONLY

7 IN LEFT COLUMN

AZTEC, BULGARIANS, BURMESE, CAMBODIANS, KHASI, KOREANS, NAVAHO

47 IN RIGHT COLUMN

ANDAMANESE, ARANDA, ARAUCANIANS, AZANDE, BEMBA, BURUSHO, CAYAPA, CHAGGA, CHUKCHEE, COPR ESKIMO, CREEK, CROW, CUNA, DARD, GILYAK, IBAN, JIVARO, KAREN, KASKA, KORYAK, KURTATCHI, LOLO, MANCAN, MARSHALLESE, MBUNDU, MIAO, NAMA, NUER, OJIBWA, PUKAPUKA, RWALA, SAMOANS, SAMOYED, SIRIONO, TALLENSI, TEHUELCHE, THONGA, TIKOPIA, TIMBIRA, TIV, TODA, TROBRIANDS, TUPINAMBA, VIETNAMESE, WOLEAIANS, YAKUT, YUROK

346 EXCLUDED BECAUSE UNASCERTAINED

73	IN ALL CASES ARE THOSE WHERE WEAVING IS PRESENT (118)	1.00 OF 5	73	TILT TOWARD BEING THOSE WHERE WEAVING IS ABSENT (130)	0.59 OF 44	5 18 0 26 XSQ= 4.15 PHI= 0.291 XP = 0.0417
77	LEAN TOWARD BEING THOSE WHERE THE WRITING SYSTEM IS ALPHABETIC-OR-PHONETIC, RATHER THAN BEING MNEMONIC OR ABSENT (15) JMH	0.86 OF 7	77	LEAN TOWARD BEING THOSE WHERE THE WRITING SYSTEM IS MNEMONIC OR ABSENT, RATHER THAN BEING ALPHABETIC-OR-PHONETIC (39) JMH	0.81 OF 47	6 9 1 38 XSQ= 10.34 PHI= 0.438 XP = 0.0013
79	TEND TO BE THOSE WHERE A CITY IS PRESENT (23)	0.67 OF 6	79	TEND TO BE THOSE WHERE NO CITY IS PRESENT (201)	0.97 OF 39	4 1 2 38 XSQ= 15.63 PHI= 0.589 XP = 0.0001
81	TILT TOWARD BEING THOSE WHERE A CITY OR TOWN IS PRESENT, OR THE AVERAGE COMMUNITY SIZE IS 200 OR GREATER (89)	0.83 OF 6	81	TILT TOWARD BEING THOSE WHERE NO CITY OR TOWN IS PRESENT, AND THE AVERAGE COMMUNITY SIZE IS SMALLER THAN 200 (135)	0.72 OF 39	5 11 1 28 XSQ= 4.70 PHI= 0.323 XP = 0.0301

84	TEND TO BE THOSE 0.71 OF 7 WHERE THE LEVEL OF POLITICAL INTEGRATION IS THE LARGE STATE (42) GPM	84	TEND TO BE THOSE 0.95 OF 43 WHERE THE LEVEL OF POLITICAL INTEGRATION IS THE LITTLE STATE, THE MINIMAL STATE, THE AUTONOMOUS COMMUNITY, OR THE FAMILY (262) GPM	5 2 2 41 XSQ= 17.09 PHI= 0.585 XP = 0.0000
91	IN ALL CASES ARE THOSE 1.00 OF 2 WHERE SOCIETAL COMPLEXITY IS HIGH (18) F-W	91	DRIFT TOWARD BEING THOSE 0.76 OF 21 WHERE SOCIETAL COMPLEXITY IS LOW (22) F-W	2 5 0 16 XSQ= 2.05 PHI= 0.299 EP = 0.0830
95	TILT TOWARD BEING THOSE 0.67 OF 6 WHERE THE HIERARCHY OF NATIONAL JURISDICTION HAS FOUR, THREE, OR TWO LEVELS (76) GES,EA	95	TILT TOWARD BEING THOSE 0.83 OF 46 WHERE THE HIERARCHY OF NATIONAL JURISDICTION HAS ONE OR NO LEVELS (254) GES,EA	4 8 2 38 XSQ= 4.75 PHI= 0.302 XP = 0.0293
107	IN ALL CASES ARE THOSE 1.00 OF 6 WHERE CLASS STRATIFICATION, IF PRESENT, IS BASED ON OCCUPATIONAL STATUS (43)	107	TEND TO BE THOSE 0.92 OF 26 WHERE CLASS STRATIFICATION, IF PRESENT, IS BASED ON SOMETHING OTHER THAN OCCUPATIONAL STATUS (160)	6 2 0 24 XSQ= 17.50 PHI= 0.740 EP = 0.0000
130	IN ALL CASES ARE THOSE 1.00 OF 2 WHERE LEATHER WORKING IS MAINLY DONE BY MALES (39)	130	TILT TOWARD BEING THOSE 0.88 OF 16 WHERE LEATHER WORKING IS MAINLY DONE BY FEMALES (45)	2 2 0 14 XSQ= 3.63 PHI= 0.449 EP = 0.0392
196	IN ALL CASES ARE THOSE 1.00 OF 6 WHERE INDIVIDUAL RIGHTS IN REAL PROPERTY, AND RULES FOR INHERITANCE, ARE PRESENT (194)	196	DRIFT LESS TOWARD BEING THOSE 0.53 OF 32 WHERE INDIVIDUAL RIGHTS IN REAL PROPERTY, AND RULES FOR INHERITANCE, ARE PRESENT (194)	6 17 0 15 XSQ= 2.89 PHI= 0.276 EP = 0.0634
391	IN ALL CASES ARE THOSE 1.00 OF 4 WHERE PREMARITAL SEX RELATIONS ARE STRONGLY PUNISHED AND IN FACT RARE, OR WEAKLY PUNISHED AND IN FACT NOT RARE (89) JTW,EA	391	TILT TOWARD BEING THOSE 0.70 OF 33 WHERE PREMARITAL SEX RELATIONS ARE PUNISHED ONLY IF PREGNANCY RESULTS, OR FREELY PERMITTED (90) JTW,EA	4 10 0 23 XSQ= 4.70 PHI= 0.357 EP = 0.0152
424	TILT TOWARD BEING THOSE 0.86 OF 7 WHERE RELIGIOUS SPECIALISTS ARE FULL-TIME, RATHER THAN PART-TIME (21) JMH	424	TILT TOWARD BEING THOSE 0.68 OF 47 WHERE RELIGIOUS SPECIALISTS ARE PART-TIME, RATHER THAN FULL-TIME (33) JMH	6 15 1 32 XSQ= 5.33 PHI= 0.314 XP = 0.0210
468	LEAN TOWARD BEING THOSE 0.86 OF 7 WHERE CONTACT WITH OTHER CULTURES IS FREQUENT, RATHER THAN REGULAR OR IRREGULAR (17) JMH	468	LEAN TOWARD BEING THOSE 0.77 OF 47 WHERE CONTACT WITH OTHER CULTURES IS REGULAR OR IRREGULAR, RATHER THAN FREQUENT (37) JMH	6 11 1 36 XSQ= 8.27 PHI= 0.391 XP = 0.0040

116 CULTURES WHERE OCCUPATIONAL SPECIALIZATION IS FULL-TIME, WHETHER OR NOT FOR SURPLUS PRODUCTION (20) JMH

116 CULTURES WHERE OCCUPATIONAL SPECIALIZATION IS PART-TIME ONLY (34) JMH

BACKGROUND ON PAGE 93

BOTH SUBJECT AND PREDICATE

20 IN LEFT COLUMN

AZANDE	AZTEC	BULGARIANS	BURMESE	BURUSHO	CAMBODIANS	DARD	KHASI	KOREANS	MARSHALLESE
MBUNDU	NAVAHO	PUKAPUKA	RWALA	SAMOANS	SAMOYED	TIV	TODA	VIETNAMESE	YAKUT

34 IN RIGHT COLUMN

ANDAMANESE	ARANDA	ARAUCANIANS	BEMBA	CAYAPA	CHAGGA	CHUKCHEE	COPR ESKIMO	CREEK	CROW
CUNA	GILYAK	IBAN	JIVARO	KAREN	KASKA	KORYAK	KURTATCHI	LOLO	MANDAN
MIAO	NAMA	NUER	OJIBWA	SIRIONO	TALLENSI	TEHUELCHE	THONGA	TIKOPIA	TIMBIRA
TROBRIAND	TUPINAMBA	WOLEAIANS	YUROK						

346 EXCLUDED BECAUSE UNASCERTAINED

5	DRIFT TOWARD BEING THOSE LOCATED IN EAST EURASIA (70)	0.50 OF 20	5	DRIFT TOWARD BEING THOSE LOCATED OUTSIDE OF EAST EURASIA (330)	0.79 OF 34	10 7 10 27	XSQ= 3.78 PHI= 0.265 XP = 0.0519
9	IN ALL CASES ARE THOSE LOCATED OUTSIDE OF SOUTH AMERICA (335)	1.00 OF 20	9	DRIFT LESS TOWARD BEING THOSE LOCATED OUTSIDE OF SOUTH AMERICA (335)	0.76 OF 34	0 8 20 26	XSQ= 3.82 PHI= -0.266 XP = 0.0507
51	TILT TOWARD BEING THOSE WHERE SUBSISTENCE IS PRIMARILY BY FOOD PRODUCTION -- I. E., AGRICULTURE OR HUSBANDRY -- RATHER THAN BY GATHERING (253)	0.85 OF 20	51	TILT TOWARD BEING THOSE WHERE SUBSISTENCE IS PRIMARILY BY FOOD GATHERING -- I. E., HUNTING, FISHING, OR COLLECTING -- RATHER THAN FOOD PRODUCTION (147)	0.50 OF 34	17 17 3 17	XSQ= 5.20 PHI= 0.310 XP = 0.0226
77	LEAN TOWARD BEING THOSE WHERE THE WRITING SYSTEM IS ALPHABETIC-OR-PHONETIC, RATHER THAN BEING MNEMONIC OR ABSENT (15) JMH	0.55 OF 20	77	LEAN TOWARD BEING THOSE WHERE THE WRITING SYSTEM IS MNEMONIC OR ABSENT, RATHER THAN BEING ALPHABETIC-OR-PHONETIC (39) JMH	0.88 OF 34	11 4 9 30	XSQ= 9.68 PHI= 0.423 XP = 0.0019

80	TILT LESS TOWARD BEING THOSE 0.72 OF 18 WHERE NO CITY OR TOWN IS PRESENT (185)	80 IN ALL CASES ARE THOSE 1.00 OF 27 WHERE NO CITY OR TOWN IS PRESENT (185)	5 0 13 27 XSQ= 5.86 PHI= 0.361 XP = 0.0155
81	TILT TOWARD BEING THOSE 0.56 OF 18 WHERE A CITY OR TOWN IS PRESENT, OR THE AVERAGE COMMUNITY SIZE IS 200 OR GREATER (89)	81 TILT TOWARD BEING THOSE 0.78 OF 27 WHERE NO CITY OR TOWN IS PRESENT, AND THE AVERAGE COMMUNITY SIZE IS SMALLER THAN 200 (135)	10 6 8 21 XSQ= 3.88 PHI= 0.294 XP = 0.0488
85	TEND TO BE THOSE 0.63 OF 19 WHERE THE LEVEL OF POLITICAL INTEGRATION IS THE LARGE STATE, OR THE LITTLE STATE (70) GPM	85 TEND TO BE THOSE 0.90 OF 31 WHERE THE LEVEL OF POLITICAL INTEGRATION IS THE MINIMAL STATE, THE AUTONOMOUS COMMUNITY, OR THE FAMILY (234) GPM	12 3 7 28 XSQ= 13.60 PHI= 0.522 XP = 0.0002
86	LEAN TOWARD BEING THOSE 0.79 OF 19 WHERE THE LEVEL OF POLITICAL INTEGRATION IS THE LARGE STATE, THE LITTLE STATE, OR THE MINIMAL STATE (148) GPM	86 LEAN TOWARD BEING THOSE 0.71 OF 31 WHERE THE LEVEL OF POLITICAL INTEGRATION IS THE AUTONOMOUS COMMUNITY, OR THE FAMILY (156) GPM	15 9 4 22 XSQ= 9.84 PHI= 0.444 XP = 0.0017
91	TILT TOWARD BEING THOSE 0.67 OF 6 WHERE SOCIETAL COMPLEXITY IS HIGH (18) F-W	91 TILT TOWARD BEING THOSE 0.82 OF 17 WHERE SOCIETAL COMPLEXITY IS LOW (22) F-W	4 3 2 14 XSQ= 2.98 PHI= 0.360 EP = 0.0450
94	DRIFT LESS TOWARD BEING THOSE 0.84 OF 19 WHERE THE HIERARCHY OF NATIONAL JURISDICTION HAS TWO, ONE, OR NO LEVELS (296) GES,EA	94 IN ALL CASES ARE THOSE 1.00 OF 33 WHERE THE HIERARCHY OF NATIONAL JURISDICTION HAS TWO, ONE, OR NO LEVELS (296) GES,EA	3 0 16 33 XSQ= 3.01 PHI= 0.240 XP = 0.0829
95	TEND TO BE THOSE 0.53 OF 19 WHERE THE HIERARCHY OF NATIONAL JURISDICTION HAS FOUR, THREE, OR TWO LEVELS (76) GES,EA	95 TEND TO BE THOSE 0.94 OF 33 WHERE THE HIERARCHY OF NATIONAL JURISDICTION HAS ONE OR NO LEVELS (254) GES,EA	10 2 9 31 XSQ= 12.23 PHI= 0.485 XP = 0.0005
96	LEAN TOWARD BEING THOSE 0.89 OF 19 WHERE THE HIERARCHY OF NATIONAL JURISDICTION HAS FOUR, THREE, TWO OR ONE LEVEL (174) GES,EA	96 LEAN TOWARD BEING THOSE 0.58 OF 33 WHERE THE HIERARCHY OF NATIONAL JURISDICTION HAS NO LEVELS (156) GES,EA	17 14 2 19 XSQ= 9.22 PHI= 0.421 XP = 0.0024
98	DRIFT MORE TOWARD BEING THOSE 0.95 OF 19 WHERE THE HIERARCHY OF LOCAL JURISDICTION HAS FOUR OR THREE LEVELS (238) GES,EA	98 DRIFT LESS TOWARD BEING THOSE 0.70 OF 33 WHERE THE HIERARCHY OF LOCAL JURISDICTION HAS FOUR OR THREE LEVELS (238) GES,EA	18 23 1 10 XSQ= 3.16 PHI= 0.246 XP = 0.0757

102	TILT TOWARD BEING THOSE WHERE CLASS STRATIFICATION IS PRESENT (203)	0.80 OF 20	102	TILT TOWARD BEING THOSE WHERE CLASS STRATIFICATION IS ABSENT (180)	0.53 OF 34	16 16 4 18 XSQ= 4.38 PHI= 0.285 XP = 0.0364
106	DRIFT TOWARD BEING THOSE WHERE CLASS STRATIFICATION, IF PRESENT, IS BASED ON SOMETHING OTHER THAN WEALTH (126)	0.81 OF 16	106	DRIFT TOWARD BEING THOSE WHERE CLASS STRATIFICATION, IF PRESENT, IS BASED ON WEALTH (77)	0.56 OF 16	3 9 13 7 XSQ= 3.33 PHI= -0.323 EP = 0.0659
107	LEAN TOWARD BEING THOSE WHERE CLASS STRATIFICATION, IF PRESENT, IS BASED ON OCCUPATIONAL STATUS (43)	0.50 OF 16	107	IN ALL CASES ARE THOSE WHERE CLASS STRATIFICATION, IF PRESENT, IS BASED ON SOMETHING OTHER THAN OCCUPATIONAL STATUS (160)	1.00 OF 16	8 0 8 16 XSQ= 8.17 PHI= 0.505 EP = 0.0024
109	DRIFT LESS TOWARD BEING THOSE WHERE CASTES ARE ABSENT (317)	0.78 OF 18	109	DRIFT MORE TOWARD BEING THOSE WHERE CASTES ARE ABSENT (317)	0.97 OF 33	4 1 14 32 XSQ= 2.92 PHI= 0.239 XP = 0.0873
132	LEAN MORE TOWARD BEING THOSE WHERE ECONOMIC EXCHANGE INVOLVES THE USE OF MONEY (37) JMH	0.95 OF 20	132	LEAN LESS TOWARD BEING THOSE WHERE ECONOMIC EXCHANGE INVOLVES THE USE OF MONEY (37) JMH	0.53 OF 34	19 18 1 16 XSQ= 8.47 PHI= 0.396 XP = 0.0036
133	IN ALL CASES ARE THOSE WHERE CONTRACTED DEBTS ARE SIGNIFICANTLY PRESENT (17) GES	1.00 OF 4	133	DRIFT TOWARD BEING THOSE WHERE CONTRACTED DEBTS ARE MODERATELY PRESENT OR ABSENT (17) GES	0.67 OF 12	4 4 0 8 XSQ= 3.00 PHI= 0.433 EP = 0.0769
142	TILT MORE TOWARD BEING THOSE WHERE THE LEVEL OF SOCIAL SANCTION IS PUBLIC CORPOREAL SANCTION OR PUBLIC PROPERTY SANCTION, RATHER THAN PRIVATE SETTLEMENT (38) JMH	0.90 OF 20	142	TILT LESS TOWARD BEING THOSE WHERE THE LEVEL OF SOCIAL SANCTION IS PUBLIC CORPOREAL SANCTION OR PUBLIC PROPERTY SANCTION, RATHER THAN PRIVATE SETTLEMENT (38) JMH	0.59 OF 34	18 20 2 14 XSQ= 4.47 PHI= 0.288 XP = 0.0345
152	IN ALL CASES ARE THOSE WHERE THE DIFFERENTIATION OF THE JURIDICAL AGENCY FROM THE MEDICAL AGENCY IS HIGH (10) MJ	1.00 OF 4	152	TILT TOWARD BEING THOSE WHERE THE DIFFERENTIATION OF THE JURIDICAL AGENCY FROM THE MEDICAL AGENCY IS LOW (10) MJ	0.83 OF 6	4 1 0 5 XSQ= 3.75 PHI= 0.612 EP = 0.0476
163	TILT TOWARD BEING THOSE WHERE THE EMPHASIS ON INDIVIDUAL VOLITION AS THE CAUSE OF CRIME IS HIGH (7) MJ	0.75 OF 4	163	IN ALL CASES ARE THOSE WHERE THE EMPHASIS ON INDIVIDUAL VOLITION AS THE CAUSE OF CRIME IS LOW (10) MJ	1.00 OF 5	3 0 1 5 XSQ= 2.76 PHI= 0.553 EP = 0.0476

```
183  IN ALL CASES ARE THOSE          1.00 OF  15    183  DRIFT LESS TOWARD BEING THOSE  0.78 OF  23           0     5
     WHERE THE LARGEST NON-COGNATIC KIN GROUP            WHERE THE LARGEST NON-COGNATIC KIN GROUP               15    18
     IS SMALLER THAN A MOEITY, I. E.,                    IS SMALLER THAN A MOEITY, I. E.,                XSQ=     2.09
     A PHRATRY OR SIB OR LINEAGE  (218)                  A PHRATRY OR SIB OR LINEAGE  (218)              PHI=   -0.235
                                                                                                         EP =   0.0730

214  IN ALL CASES ARE THOSE          1.00 OF   9    214  DRIFT LESS TOWARD BEING THOSE  0.60 OF  15           0     6
     WHERE FIRST COUSIN MARRIAGE,                        WHERE FIRST COUSIN MARRIAGE,                            9     9
     IF PERMITTED,                                       IF PERMITTED,                                   XSQ=     2.90
     IS OTHER THAN UNILATERAL  (144)                     IS OTHER THAN UNILATERAL  (144)                 PHI=   -0.348
                                                                                                         EP =   0.0519

286  TILT TOWARD BEING THOSE         0.60 OF   5    286  IN ALL CASES ARE THOSE         1.00 OF   7           2     7
     WHERE THE NUMBER OF FOOD TABOOS                     WHERE THE NUMBER OF FOOD TABOOS                         3     0
     DURING PREGNANCY                                    DURING PREGNANCY                                XSQ=     2.86
     IS LOW OR ABSENT  (14) BCA                          IS HIGH  (20) BCA                               PHI=   -0.488
                                                                                                         EP =   0.0455

309  IN ALL CASES ARE THOSE          1.00 OF   6    309  TILT TOWARD BEING THOSE        0.67 OF   9           6     3
     WHERE ORAL SOCIALIZATION ANXIETY                    WHERE ORAL SOCIALIZATION ANXIETY                        0     6
     IS HIGH  (26) W-C                                   IS LOW  (27) W-C                                XSQ=     4.18
                                                                                                         PHI=    0.528
                                                                                                         EP =   0.0278

317  IN ALL CASES ARE THOSE          1.00 OF   6    317  LEAN TOWARD BEING THOSE        0.76 OF  21           0    16
     WHERE DISPLAY OF AFFECTION TOWARD                   WHERE DISPLAY OF AFFECTION TOWARD                       6     5
     THE INFANT IS LOW  (29) B-B-C                       THE INFANT IS HIGH  (39) B-B-C                  XSQ=     8.29
                                                                                                         PHI=   -0.554
                                                                                                         EP =   0.0016

318  TILT TOWARD BEING THOSE         0.83 OF   6    318  TILT TOWARD BEING THOSE        0.71 OF  21           1    15
     WHERE THE OVERALL INDULGENCE                        WHERE THE OVERALL INDULGENCE                            5     6
     OF THE INFANT                                       OF THE INFANT                                   XSQ=     3.75
     IS LOW  (31) B-B-C                                  IS HIGH  (40) B-B-C                             PHI=   -0.373
                                                                                                         EP =   0.0265

334  TILT TOWARD BEING THOSE         0.86 OF   7    334  TILT TOWARD BEING THOSE        0.64 OF  22           1    14
     WHERE THE INDULGENCE OF THE CHILD                   WHERE THE INDULGENCE OF THE CHILD                       6     8
     IS LOW  (38) B-B-C                                  IS HIGH  (40) B-B-C                             XSQ=     3.39
                                                                                                         PHI=   -0.342
                                                                                                         EP =   0.0352

344  DRIFT TOWARD BEING THOSE        0.86 OF   7    344  DRIFT TOWARD BEING THOSE       0.57 OF  21           1    12
     WHERE THE TOTAL POSITIVE PRESSURE TOWARD            WHERE THE TOTAL POSITIVE PRESSURE TOWARD                6     9
     DEVELOPING SELF-RELIANT BEHAVIOR                    DEVELOPING SELF-RELIANT BEHAVIOR                XSQ=     2.35
     IN THE CHILD                                        IN THE CHILD                                    PHI=   -0.289
     IS LOW  (40) B-B-C                                  IS HIGH  (36) B-B-C                             EP =   0.0836

345  IN ALL CASES ARE THOSE          1.00 OF   7    345  TILT TOWARD BEING THOSE        0.57 OF  21           0    12
     WHERE THE CHILD'S INFERRED ANXIETY OVER             WHERE THE CHILD'S INFERRED ANXIETY OVER                 7     9
     NON-PERFORMANCE OF SELF-RELIANT BEHAVIOR            NON-PERFORMANCE OF SELF-RELIANT BEHAVIOR        XSQ=     4.86
     IS LOW  (39) B-B-C                                  IS HIGH  (37) B-B-C                             PHI=   -0.417
                                                                                                         EP =   0.0103
```

351	DRIFT TOWARD BEING THOSE 0.83 OF 6 WHERE THE CHILD'S INFERRED CONFLICT REGARDING ACHIEVEMENT BEHAVIOR IS HIGH (26) B-B-C	351	DRIFT TOWARD BEING THOSE 0.67 OF 15 WHERE THE CHILD'S INFERRED CONFLICT REGARDING ACHIEVEMENT BEHAVIOR IS LOW (34) B-B-C	5 5 1 10 XSQ= 2.52 PHI= 0.347 EP = 0.0635
353	IN ALL CASES ARE THOSE 1.00 OF 7 WHERE THE CHILD'S INFERRED ANXIETY OVER NON-PERFORMANCE OF OBEDIENT BEHAVIOR IS HIGH (42) B-B-C	353	LEAN TOWARD BEING THOSE 0.60 OF 20 WHERE THE CHILD-S INFERRED ANXIETY OVER NON-PERFORMANCE OF OBEDIENT BEHAVIOR IS LOW (32) B-B-C	7 8 0 12 XSQ= 5.33 PHI= 0.444 EP = 0.0081
355	TILT TOWARD BEING THOSE 0.86 OF 7 WHERE THE CHILD'S INFERRED CONFLICT REGARDING OBEDIENT BEHAVIOR IS HIGH (35) B-B-C	355	TILT TOWARD BEING THOSE 0.65 OF 20 WHERE THE CHILD'S INFERRED CONFLICT REGARDING OBEDIENT BEHAVIOR IS LOW (38) B-B-C	6 7 1 13 XSQ= 3.50 PHI= 0.360 EP = 0.0329
386	DRIFT TOWARD BEING THOSE 0.71 OF 7 WHERE SEXUAL EXPRESSION BY THE YOUNG IS PERMITTED (40) F-B	386	DRIFT TOWARD BEING THOSE 0.68 OF 19 WHERE SEXUAL EXPRESSION BY THE YOUNG IS RESTRICTED OR SEMI-RESTRICTED (46) F-B	2 13 5 6 XSQ= 1.90 PHI= -0.270 EP = 0.0946
406	DRIFT TOWARD BEING THOSE 0.75 OF 8 WHERE EXPLANATIONS OF ILLNESS OF AN AGGRESSION NATURE ARE PRESENT (28) W-C	406	DRIFT TOWARD BEING THOSE 0.78 OF 9 WHERE EXPLANATIONS OF ILLNESS OF AN AGGRESSION NATURE ARE ABSENT (33) W-C	6 2 2 7 XSQ= 2.85 PHI= 0.410 EP = 0.0567
424	TEND TO BE THOSE 0.85 OF 20 WHERE RELIGIOUS SPECIALISTS ARE FULL-TIME, RATHER THAN PART-TIME (21) JMH	424	TEND TO BE THOSE 0.88 OF 34 WHERE RELIGIOUS SPECIALISTS ARE PART-TIME, RATHER THAN FULL-TIME (33) JMH	17 4 3 30 XSQ= 25.42 PHI= 0.686 XP = 0.0000
436	TILT TOWARD BEING THOSE 0.80 OF 5 WHERE ACTIVE ANCESTRAL SPIRITS ARE ABSENT (11) GES	436	TILT TOWARD BEING THOSE 0.79 OF 14 WHERE ACTIVE ANCESTRAL SPIRITS ARE PRESENT (27) GES	1 11 4 3 XSQ= 3.21 PHI= -0.411 EP = 0.0379
458	TILT TOWARD BEING THOSE 0.56 OF 16 WHERE GAMES, IF PRESENT, INCLUDE GAMES OF STRATEGY (52) R-A-B,EA	458	TILT TOWARD BEING THOSE 0.82 OF 22 WHERE GAMES, IF PRESENT, DO NOT INCLUDE GAMES OF STRATEGY (119) R-A-B,EA	9 4 7 18 XSQ= 4.39 PHI= 0.340 EP = 0.0356
468	TEND TO BE THOSE 0.65 OF 20 WHERE CONTACT WITH OTHER CULTURES IS FREQUENT, RATHER THAN REGULAR OR IRREGULAR (17) JMH	468	TEND TO BE THOSE 0.88 OF 34 WHERE CONTACT WITH OTHER CULTURES IS REGULAR OR IRREGULAR, RATHER THAN FREQUENT (37) JMH	13 4 7 30 XSQ= 14.17 PHI= 0.512 XP = 0.0002

```
470  LEAN TOWARD BEING THOSE          0.65 OF  20     470  LEAN TOWARD BEING THOSE          0.76 OF  34            13     8
     WHERE INNOVATIONS ARE                                WHERE INNOVATIONS ARE                                      7    26
     GENERALLY ACCEPTED  (21) JMH                         ACCEPTED ONLY SELECTIVELY  (33) JMH              XSQ=      7.45
                                                                                                           PHI=     0.371
                                                                                                           XP =    0.0063

476  TILT TOWARD BEING THOSE          0.71 OF   7     476  TILT TOWARD BEING THOSE          0.91 OF  11             2    10
     WHERE THE DEGREE OF INSOBRIETY IS                    WHERE THE DEGREE OF INSOBRIETY IS                          5     1
     MODERATE OR SLIGHT  (18) CH                          STRONG  (31) DH                                  XSQ=      4.94
                                                                                                           PHI=    -0.524
                                                                                                           EP =    0.0128
```

117 CULTURES
WHERE THE PERCENTAGE OF OCCUPATIONS
THAT ARE SPECIALIZED
IS HIGH (19) WME

117 CULTURES
WHERE THE PERCENTAGE OF OCCUPATIONS
THAT ARE SPECIALIZED
IS MEDIUM OR LOW (30) WME

BACKGROUND ON PAGE 93

NEITHER SUBJECT NOR PREDICATE

19 IN LEFT COLUMN

ALBANIANS	ASHANTI	AZANDE	BHIL	CZECHS	GOAJIRO	INCA	KOREANS	LAPPS	LEPCHA
MAGUZAWA	MISKITO	NAMA	SIWANS	SOMALI	TIKOPIA	VIETNAMESE	WOLOF	YAO	

30 IN RIGHT COLUMN

ALORESE	ARANDA	CARIB	CHAGGA	COPR ESKIMO	GOND	HAVASUPAI	IBAN	IFUGAO	JIVARO
KACHIN	KAPAUKU	MATACO	MUNDURUCU	NAMBICUARA	NYAKYUSA	OJIBWA	PAPAGO	SENIANG	TALLENSI
TANALA	THONGA	TIMBIRA	TIV	TODA	TROBRIAND	YAHGAN	YAKUT	YOKUTS	YUROK

351 EXCLUDED BECAUSE UNASCERTAINED

****

118 CULTURES WHERE THE PERCENTAGE OF OCCUPATIONS THAT ARE SPECIALIZED IS HIGH OR MEDIUM (24) WME	118 CULTURES WHERE THE PERCENTAGE OF OCCUPATIONS THAT ARE SPECIALIZED IS LOW (25) WME

BACKGROUND ON PAGE 93 — BOTH SUBJECT AND PREDICATE

24 IN LEFT COLUMN

ALBANIANS	ASHANTI	AZANDE	BHIL	CHAGGA	CZECHS	GOAJIRO	INCA	KOREANS	LAPPS
LEPCHA	MAGUZAWA	MATACO	MISKITO	NAMA	PAPAGO	SIWANS	SOMALI	TALLENSI	TIKOPIA
TODA	VIETNAMESE	WOLOF	YAO						

25 IN RIGHT COLUMN

ALORESE	ARANDA	CARIB	COPR ESKIMO	GOND	HAVASUPAI	IBAN	IFUGAO	JIVARO	KACHIN
KAPAUKU	MUNDURUCU	NAMBICUARA	NYAKYUSA	OJIBWA	SENIANG	TANALA	THONGA	TIMBIRA	TIV
TROBRIAND	YAHGAN	YAKUT	YOKUTS	YUROK					

351 EXCLUDED BECAUSE UNASCERTAINED

4	TILT LESS TOWARD BEING THOSE LOCATED OUTSIDE OF THE CIRCUM-MEDITERRANEAN (355)	0.71 OF 24	IN ALL CASES ARE THOSE LOCATED OUTSIDE OF THE CIRCUM-MEDITERRANEAN (355)	1.00 OF 25	7 0 / 17 25 / XSQ= 6.29 / PHI= 0.358 / XP = 0.0121
6	DRIFT MORE TOWARD BEING THOSE LOCATED OUTSIDE OF THE INSULAR PACIFIC (330)	0.96 OF 24	DRIFT LESS TOWARD BEING THOSE LOCATED OUTSIDE OF THE INSULAR PACIFIC (330)	0.72 OF 25	1 7 / 23 18 / XSQ= 3.50 / PHI= -0.267 / XP = 0.0615
53	TILT TOWARD BEING THOSE WHERE FOOD PRODUCTION IS BY INTENSIVE AGRICULTURE, RATHER THAN BY SIMPLE AGRICULTURE OR INCIPIENT FOOD PRODUCTION (91)	0.56 OF 16	TILT TOWARD BEING THOSE WHERE FOOD PRODUCTION IS BY SIMPLE AGRICULTURE OR INCIPIENT FOOD PRODUCTION, RATHER THAN BY INTENSIVE AGRICULTURE (147)	0.83 OF 18	9 3 / 7 15 / XSQ= 4.21 / PHI= 0.352 / EP = 0.0299
55	TILT TOWARD BEING THOSE WHERE FOOD PRODUCTION IS BY INTENSIVE AGRICULTURE, RATHER THAN BY SIMPLE AGRICULTURE (91)	0.69 OF 13	TILT TOWARD BEING THOSE WHERE FOOD PRODUCTION IS BY SIMPLE AGRICULTURE, RATHER THAN BY INTENSIVE AGRICULTURE (101)	0.77 OF 13	9 3 / 4 10 / XSQ= 3.87 / PHI= 0.386 / EP = 0.0472

63	LEAN TOWARD BEING THOSE WHERE HUSBANDRY, IF PRESENT, IS PRINCIPALLY IN THE FORM OF BOVINE, EQUINE, CAMEL-LIKE, OR DEER-LIKE ANIMALS, RATHER THAN PIGS, SHEEP, OR GOATS (152)	0.89 OF 19	63	LEAN TOWARD BEING THOSE WHERE HUSBANDRY, IF PRESENT, IS PRINCIPALLY IN THE FORM OF PIGS, SHEEP, OR GOATS, RATHER THAN BOVINE, EQUINE, CAMEL-LIKE, OR DEER-LIKE ANIMALS (74)	0.67 OF 15	17 5 2 10 XSQ= 9.24 PHI= 0.521 EP = 0.0011
74	TILT TOWARD BEING THOSE WHERE POTTERY IS PRESENT (145)	0.80 OF 20	74	TILT TOWARD BEING THOSE WHERE POTTERY IS ABSENT (93)	0.55 OF 22	16 10 4 12 XSQ= 3.94 PHI= 0.306 XP = 0.0472
80	DRIFT LESS TOWARD BEING THOSE WHERE NO CITY OR TOWN IS PRESENT (185)	0.77 OF 22	80	IN ALL CASES ARE THOSE WHERE NO CITY OR TOWN IS PRESENT (185)	1.00 OF 21	5 0 17 21 XSQ= 3.42 PHI= 0.282 XP = 0.0646
81	TILT LESS TOWARD BEING THOSE WHERE NO CITY OR TOWN IS PRESENT, AND THE AVERAGE COMMUNITY SIZE IS SMALLER THAN 200 (135)	0.55 OF 22	81	TILT MORE TOWARD BEING THOSE WHERE NO CITY OR TOWN IS PRESENT, AND THE AVERAGE COMMUNITY SIZE IS SMALLER THAN 200 (135)	0.90 OF 21	10 2 12 19 XSQ= 5.22 PHI= 0.349 XP = 0.0223
84	TILT LESS TOWARD BEING THOSE WHERE THE LEVEL OF POLITICAL INTEGRATION IS THE LITTLE STATE, THE MINIMAL STATE, THE AUTONOMOUS COMMUNITY, OR THE FAMILY (262) GPM	0.68 OF 22	84	IN ALL CASES ARE THOSE WHERE THE LEVEL OF POLITICAL INTEGRATION IS THE LITTLE STATE, THE MINIMAL STATE, THE AUTONOMOUS COMMUNITY, OR THE FAMILY (262) GPM	1.00 OF 23	7 0 15 23 XSQ= 6.41 PHI= 0.378 XP = 0.0113
86	DRIFT TOWARD BEING THOSE WHERE THE LEVEL OF POLITICAL INTEGRATION IS THE LARGE STATE, THE LITTLE STATE, OR THE MINIMAL STATE (148) GPM	0.68 OF 22	86	DRIFT TOWARD BEING THOSE WHERE THE LEVEL OF POLITICAL INTEGRATION IS THE AUTONOMOUS COMMUNITY, OR THE FAMILY (156) GPM	0.61 OF 23	15 9 7 14 XSQ= 2.74 PHI= 0.247 XP = 0.0982
87	IN ALL CASES ARE THOSE WHERE THE LEVEL OF POLITICAL INTEGRATION IS THE LARGE STATE, THE LITTLE STATE, THE MINIMAL STATE, OR THE AUTONOMOUS COMMUNITY (281) GPM	1.00 OF 22	87	DRIFT LESS TOWARD BEING THOSE WHERE THE LEVEL OF POLITICAL INTEGRATION IS THE LARGE STATE, THE LITTLE STATE, THE MINIMAL STATE, OR THE AUTONOMOUS COMMUNITY (281) GPM	0.78 OF 23	22 18 0 5 XSQ= 3.40 PHI= 0.275 XP = 0.0650
91	LEAN TOWARD BEING THOSE WHERE SOCIETAL COMPLEXITY IS HIGH (18) F-W	0.70 OF 10	91	IN ALL CASES ARE THOSE WHERE SOCIETAL COMPLEXITY IS LOW (22) F-W	1.00 OF 7	7 0 3 7 XSQ= 5.69 PHI= 0.579 EP = 0.0098
102	DRIFT TOWARD BEING THOSE WHERE CLASS STRATIFICATION IS PRESENT (203)	0.75 OF 24	102	DRIFT TOWARD BEING THOSE WHERE CLASS STRATIFICATION IS ABSENT (180)	0.52 OF 25	18 12 6 13 XSQ= 2.71 PHI= 0.235 XP = 0.0998

107	DRIFT LESS TOWARD BEING THOSE 0.67 OF 18 WHERE CLASS STRATIFICATION, IF PRESENT, IS BASED ON SOMETHING OTHER THAN OCCUPATIONAL STATUS (160)	107	IN ALL CASES ARE THOSE 1.00 OF 12 WHERE CLASS STRATIFICATION, IF PRESENT, IS BASED ON SOMETHING OTHER THAN OCCUPATIONAL STATUS (160)	6 0 12 12 XSQ= 3.13 PHI= 0.323 EP = 0.0568
109	DRIFT LESS TOWARD BEING THOSE 0.81 OF 21 WHERE CASTES ARE ABSENT (317)	109	IN ALL CASES ARE THOSE 1.00 OF 24 WHERE CASTES ARE ABSENT (317)	4 0 17 24 XSQ= 2.94 PHI= 0.256 XP = 0.0864
120	IN ALL CASES ARE THOSE 1.00 OF 24 WHERE THE CRAFT SPECIALIZATION SCORE IS HIGH OR MEDIUM (36) WME	120	TEND TO BE THOSE 0.64 OF 25 WHERE THE CRAFT SPECIALIZATION SCORE IS LOW (17) WME	24 9 0 16 XSQ= 19.99 PHI= 0.639 XP = 0.0000
137	TILT TOWARD BEING THOSE 0.74 OF 19 WHERE INVIDIOUS DISPLAY OF WEALTH IS MODERATELY, LITTLE, OR NEGATIVELY EMPHASIZED (52) PES	137	TILT TOWARD BEING THOSE 0.63 OF 16 WHERE INVIDIOUS DISPLAY OF WEALTH IS STRONGLY EMPHASIZED (37) PES	5 10 14 6 XSQ= 3.28 PHI= -0.306 EP = 0.0442
138	IN ALL CASES ARE THOSE 1.00 OF 5 WHERE SUPERORDINATE JUSTICE IS PRESENT (22) BBW	138	TILT TOWARD BEING THOSE 0.70 OF 10 WHERE SUPERORDINATE JUSTICE IS ABSENT (18) BBW	5 3 0 7 XSQ= 4.05 PHI= 0.520 EP = 0.0256
139	DRIFT TOWARD BEING THOSE 0.60 OF 5 WHERE SUPERORDINATE PUNISHMENT IS PRESENT (15) BBW	139	DRIFT TOWARD BEING THOSE 0.90 OF 10 WHERE SUPERORDINATE PUNISHMENT IS ABSENT (25) BBW	3 1 2 9 XSQ= 2.09 PHI= 0.373 EP = 0.0769
183	IN ALL CASES ARE THOSE 1.00 OF 18 WHERE THE LARGEST NON-COGNATIC KIN GROUP IS SMALLER THAN A MOEITY, I. E., A PHRATRY OR SIB OR LINEAGE (218)	183	TILT LESS TOWARD BEING THOSE 0.75 OF 16 WHERE THE LARGEST NON-COGNATIC KIN GROUP IS SMALLER THAN A MOEITY, I. E., A PHRATRY OR SIB OR LINEAGE (218)	0 4 18 12 XSQ= 2.98 PHI= -0.296 EP = 0.0392
184	TEND TO BE THOSE 0.94 OF 18 WHERE THE LARGEST NON-COGNATIC KIN GROUP IS SMALLER THAN A PHRATRY, I. E. A SIB OR LINEAGE (175)	184	TEND TO BE THOSE 0.63 OF 16 WHERE THE LARGEST NON-COGNATIC KIN GROUP IS THE MOEITY OR PHRATRY (77)	1 10 17 6 XSQ= 10.08 PHI= -0.545 EP = 0.0006
196	TILT TOWARD BEING THOSE 0.81 OF 21 WHERE INDIVIDUAL RIGHTS IN REAL PROPERTY, AND RULES FOR INHERITANCE, ARE PRESENT (194)	196	TILT TOWARD BEING THOSE 0.59 OF 17 WHERE INDIVIDUAL RIGHTS IN REAL PROPERTY, OR RULES FOR INHERITANCE, ARE ABSENT (87)	17 7 4 10 XSQ= 4.79 PHI= 0.355 EP = 0.0184

201	IN ALL CASES ARE THCSE 1.00 OF 24 WHERE MARITAL RESICENCE IS NCN-OPTICNAL, RATHER THAN AMBILCCAL CR NECLOCAL (334)	201	DRIFT LESS TOWARD BEING THCSE 0.80 OF 25 WHERE MARITAL RESIDENCE IS NON-OPTIONAL, RATHER THAN AMBILOCAL OR NEOLOCAL (334)	24 20 0 5 XSQ= 3.39 PHI= 0.263 XP = 0.0658
204	IN ALL CASES ARE THOSE 1.00 OF 21 WHERE MARITAL RESICENCE IS PATRILCCAL, VIRILOCAL, OR AVUNCULOCAL, RATHER THAN AMBILCCAL CR NECLOCAL (270)	204	DRIFT LESS TOWARD BEING THCSE 0.78 OF 23 WHERE MARITAL RESIDENCE IS PATRILOCAL, VIRILCCAL, CR AVUNCULOCAL, RATHER THAN AMBILOCAL OR NEOLOCAL (270)	21 18 0 5 XSQ= 3.22 PHI= 0.270 XP = 0.0728
234	DRIFT TCWARD BEING THCSE 0.68 OF 19 WHERE THE COUSIN TERMINCLCGY IS OF ESKIMO CR HAWAIIAN TYPE, RATHER THAN CRCW, CMAHA, CR IRCQUCIS TYPE (170)	234	DRIFT TOWARD BEING THOSE 0.64 CF 22 WHERE THE COUSIN TERMINCLOGY IS OF CROW, OMAHA, OR IROQUOIS TYPE, RATHER THAN ESKIMO OR HAWAIIAN TYPE (152)	6 14 13 8 XSQ= 3.01 PHI= -0.271 XP = 0.0828
336	DRIFT TCWARD BEING THCSE 0.86 OF 7 WHERE THE TCTAL PCSITIVE PRESSURE TOWARD DEVELCPING RESPCNSIBLE BEHAVIOR IN THE CHILD IS HIGH (43) B-B-C	336	DRIFT TOWARD BEING THOSE 0.62 CF 13 WHERE THE TOTAL POSITIVE PRESSURE TOWARC DEVELOPING RESPONSIBLE BEHAVIOR IN THE CHILD IS LOW (32) B-B-C	6 5 1 8 XSQ= 2.42 PHI= 0.348 EP = 0.0703
344	IN ALL CASES ARE THCSE 1.00 OF 7 WHERE THE TOTAL POSITIVE PRESSURE TOWARD DEVELCPING SELF-RELIANT BEHAVIOR IN THE CHILD IS LCW (40) B-B-C	344	LEAN TOWARD BEING THCSE 0.69 CF 13 WHERE THE TOTAL POSITIVE PRESSURE TCWARC DEVELOPING SELF-RELIANT BEHAVICR IN THE CHILD IS HIGH (36) B-B-C	0 9 7 4 XSQ= 6.24 PHI= -0.558 EP = 0.0047
356	TILT TOWARD BEING THOSE 0.75 OF 4 WHERE NEITHER ADCLESCENT PEER GROUPS NCR PAIRS ARE PRESENT IN A SETTING CF COURTSHIP (22) JKH	356	TILT TOWARD BEING THOSE 0.90 OF 10 WHERE ADOLESCENT PEER GRCUPS OR PAIRS ARE PRESENT IN A SETTING OF COURTSHIP (29) JKH	1 9 3 1 XSQ= 3.16 PHI= -0.475 EP = 0.0410
382	DRIFT TCWARD BEING THCSE 0.73 OF 11 WHERE FEMALE INITIATICN RITES ARE ABSENT (27) JKB	382	DRIFT TOWARD BEING THOSE 0.67 CF 12 WHERE FEMALE INITIATION RITES ARE PRESENT (38) JKB	3 8 8 4 XSQ= 2.17 PHI= -0.307 EP = 0.0995
392	TILT TCWARD BEING THOSE 0.80 OF 20 WHERE PREMARITAL SEX RELATIONS ARE STRCNGLY PUNISHEC AND IN FACT RARE, OR WEAKLY PUNISHED ANC IN FACT NCT RARE, OR PUNISHED CNLY IF PREGNANCY RESULTS (112) JTW,EA	392	TILT TOWARD BEING THOSE 0.56 OF 16 WHERE PREMARITAL SEX RELATICNS ARE FREELY PERMITTED (67) JTW,EA	16 7 4 9 XSQ= 3.61 PHI= 0.317 EP = 0.0379
398	DRIFT TCWARD BEING THCSE 0.80 OF 5 WHERE THE INTENSITY OF SEX ANXIETY IS HIGH (16) WNS	398	DRIFT TOWARD BEING THOSE 0.83 OF 6 WHERE THE INTENSITY OF SEX ANXIETY IS LOW (16) WNS	4 1 1 5 XSQ= 2.23 PHI= 0.450 EP = 0.0801

402	DRIFT TCWARD BEING THCSE WHERE EXPLANATICNS CF ILLNESS OF AN ORAL NATURE ARE ABSENT (30) W-C	0.71 OF 7	402	DRIFT TOWARD BEING THOSE WHERE EXPLANATIONS OF ILLNESS OF AN ORAL NATURE ARE PRESENT (31) W-C	0.80 OF 10	2 8 5 2 XSQ= 2.62 PHI= -0.393 EP = 0.0584
424	TILT TOWARD BEING THOSE WHERE RELIGICUS SPECIALISTS ARE FULL-TIME, RATHER THAN PART-TIME (21) JMH	0.63 OF 8	424	TILT TOWARD BEING THOSE WHERE RELIGIOUS SPECIALISTS ARE PART-TIME, RATHER THAN FULL-TIME (33) JMH	0.91 OF 11	5 1 3 10 XSQ= 3.89 PHI= 0.453 EP = 0.0408
427	TILT TCWARD BEING THCSE WHERE A HIGH GOC, IF PRESENT, IS ACTIVE, RATHER THAN INACTIVE (87) GES,EA	0.86 OF 14	427	TILT TOWARD BEING THOSE WHERE A HIGH GOD, IF PRESENT, IS INACTIVE, RATHER THAN ACTIVE (69) GES,EA	0.67 CF 12	12 4 2 8 XSQ= 5.44 PHI= 0.457 EP = 0.0138
433	DRIFT TCWARD BEING THCSE WHERE BELIEF IN REINCARNATION IS PRESENT (10) GES	0.60 OF 5	433	DRIFT TOWARD BEING THOSE WHERE BELIEF IN REINCARNATICN IS ABSENT (28) GES	0.91 OF 11	3 1 2 10 XSQ= 2.42 PHI= 0.389 EP = 0.0632
444	DRIFT TCWARD BEING THCSE WHERE THE USE CF DREAMS TO SEEK AND CCNTROL SUPERNATURAL POWERS IS LOW (27) RGC	0.64 OF 11	444	DRIFT TOWARD BEING THOSE WHERE THE USE OF DREAMS TO SEEK AND CONTROL SUPERNATURAL PCWERS IS HIGH (28) RGD	0.75 CF 12	4 9 7 3 XSQ= 2.09 PHI= -0.302 EP = 0.0995

****

119 CULTURES
WHERE THE CRAFT SPECIALIZATION SCORE
IS HIGH (16) WME

119 CULTURES
WHERE THE CRAFT SPECIALIZATION SCORE
IS MEDIUM OR LOW (37) WME

BACKGROUND ON PAGE 93

NEITHER SUBJECT NOR PREDICATE

....

16 IN LEFT CCLUMN

ALBANIANS	ASHANTI	AZANDE	BHIL	COORG	CZECHS	GOAJIRO	INCA	KAZAK	KOREANS
LAPPS	MAGUZAWA	SOMALI	TIV	VIETNAMESE	WOLOF				

37 IN RIGHT CCLUMN

ALORESE	ARANDA	CARIB	CHAGGA	COPR ESKIMO	GOND	HAVASUPAI	IBAN	IFUGAO	JIVARO
KACHIN	KAPAUKU	LEPCHA	MATACO	MISKITO	MUNDURUCU	NAMA	NAMBICUARA	NUER	NYAKYUSA
OJIBWA	PAPAGC	RIFFIANS	SENIANG	SIWANS	TALLENSI	TANALA	THCNGA	TIKOPIA	TIMBIRA
TODA	TRCBRIANC	YAHGAN	YAKUT	YAO	YOKUTS	YUROK			

347 EXCLUDED BECAUSE UNASCERTAINEC

----

120 CULTURES WHERE THE CRAFT SPECIALIZATION SCORE IS HIGH OR MEDIUM (36) WME

120 CULTURES WHERE THE CRAFT SPECIALIZATION SCORE IS LOW (17) WME

BACKGROUND ON PAGE 93

BOTH SUBJECT AND PREDICATE

36 IN LEFT COLUMN

ALBANIANS	ARANDA	ASHANTI	AZANDE	BHIL	CHAGGA	COORG	CZECHS	GOAJIRO	IBAN
IFUGAO	INCA	JIVARO	KAZAK	KOREANS	LAPPS	LEPCHA	MAGUZAWA	MATACO	MISKITO
NAMA	OJIBWA	PAPAGO	RIFFIANS	SIWANS	SOMALI	TALLENSI	TANALA	TIKOPIA	TIV
TODA	TROBRIAND	VIETNAMESE	WOLOF	YAO	YUROK				

17 IN RIGHT COLUMN

ALORESE	CARIB	COPR ESKIMO	GOND	HAVASUPAI	KACHIN	KAPAUKU	MUNDURUCU	NAMBICUARA	NUER
NYAKYUSA	SENIANG	THONGA	TIMBIRA	YAHGAN	YAKUT	YOKUTS			

347 EXCLUDED BECAUSE UNASCERTAINED

4	DRIFT LESS TOWARD BEING THOSE LOCATED OUTSIDE OF THE CIRCUM-MEDITERRANEAN (355)	0.78 OF 36	4	IN ALL CASES ARE THOSE LOCATED OUTSIDE OF THE CIRCUM-MEDITERRANEAN (355)	1.00 OF 17	8 0 28 17 XSQ= 2.88 PHI= 0.233 XP = 0.0894
45	DRIFT TOWARD BEING THOSE WHERE SETTLEMENTS, IF FIXED, ARE NON-COMPACT, RATHER THAN COMPACT (73)	0.50 OF 24	45	DRIFT TOWARD BEING THOSE WHERE SETTLEMENTS, IF FIXED, ARE COMPACT, RATHER THAN NON-COMPACT (149)	0.89 OF 9	12 8 12 1 XSQ= 2.68 PHI= -0.285 EP = 0.0560
51	DRIFT TOWARD BEING THOSE WHERE SUBSISTENCE IS PRIMARILY BY FOOD PRODUCTION -- I. E., AGRICULTURE OR HUSBANDRY -- RATHER THAN BY GATHERING (253)	0.75 OF 36	51	DRIFT TOWARD BEING THOSE WHERE SUBSISTENCE IS PRIMARILY BY FOOD GATHERING -- I. E., HUNTING, FISHING, OR COLLECTING -- RATHER THAN FOOD PRODUCTION (147)	0.53 OF 17	27 8 9 9 XSQ= 2.87 PHI= 0.233 XP = 0.0902
53	TILT TOWARD BEING THOSE WHERE FOOD PRODUCTION IS BY INTENSIVE AGRICULTURE, RATHER THAN BY SIMPLE AGRICULTURE OR INCIPIENT FOOD PRODUCTION (91)	0.54 OF 24	53	TILT TOWARD BEING THOSE WHERE FOOD PRODUCTION IS BY SIMPLE AGRICULTURE OR INCIPIENT FOOD PRODUCTION, RATHER THAN BY INTENSIVE AGRICULTURE (147)	0.92 OF 12	13 1 11 11 XSQ= 5.27 PHI= 0.383 EP = 0.0111

55	DRIFT TOWARD BEING THCSE 0.62 OF 21 WHERE FCCD PRODUCTICN IS BY INTENSIVE AGRICULTURE, RATHER THAN BY SIMPLE AGRICULTURE (91)	55 DRIFT TOWARD BEING THOSE 0.86 CF 7 WHERE FOOD PRODUCTICN IS BY SIMPLE AGRICULTURE, RATHER THAN BY INTENSIVE AGRICULTURE (101)	13 1 8 6 XSQ= 3.05 PHI= 0.330 EP = 0.0768
71	DRIFT TCWARD BEING THCSE 0.58 OF 31 WHERE METAL WCRKING IS PRESENT (98)	71 DRIFT TOWARD BEING THOSE 0.73 CF 15 WHERE METAL WORKING IS ABSENT (153)	18 4 13 11 XSQ= 2.83 PHI= 0.248 XP = 0.0923
73	DRIFT TCWARD BEING THCSE 0.67 OF 30 WHERE WEAVING IS PRESENT (118)	73 DRIFT TOWARD BEING THOSE 0.67 OF 15 WHERE WEAVING IS ABSENT (130)	20 5 10 10 XSQ= 3.25 PHI= 0.269 XP = 0.0714
78	TILT TCWARD BEING THCSE 0.80 OF 15 WHERE THE WRITING SYSTEM IS ALPHABETIC-OR-PHCNETIC, CR MNEMONIC, RATHER THAN BEING ABSENT (36) JMH	78 TILT TOWARD BEING THOSE 0.80 CF 5 WHERE A WRITING SYSTEM IS ABSENT, RATHER THAN BEING PRESENT IN EITHER ALPHABETIC-OR-PHCNETIC FORM CR MNEMONIC FORM (18) JMH	12 1 3 4 XSQ= 3.59 PHI= 0.424 EP = 0.0307
81	DRIFT LESS TCWARD BEING THCSE 0.63 OF 32 WHERE NC CITY CR TCWN IS PRESENT, AND THE AVERAGE COMMUNITY SIZE IS SMALLER THAN 200 (135)	81 DRIFT MORE TOWARD BEING THCSE 0.93 OF 14 WHERE NO CITY OR TOWN IS PRESENT, AND THE AVERAGE COMMUNITY SIZE IS SMALLER THAN 200 (135)	12 1 20 13 XSQ= 3.06 PHI= 0.258 XP = 0.0804
84	DRIFT LESS TCWARD BEING THCSE 0.74 OF 34 WHERE THE LEVEL CF POLITICAL INTEGRATION IS THE LITTLE STATE, THE MINIMAL STATE, THE AUTCNCMOUS COMMUNITY, CR THE FAMILY (262) GPM	84 IN ALL CASES ARE THOSE 1.00 CF 14 WHERE THE LEVEL OF POLITICAL INTEGRATION IS THE LITTLE STATE, THE MINIMAL STATE, THE AUTONOMOUS COMMUNITY, CR THE FAMILY (262) GPM	9 0 25 14 XSQ= 2.99 PHI= 0.250 XP = 0.0838
110	DRIFT TCWARD BEING THCSE 0.53 OF 36 WHERE SLAVERY IS PRESENT (163)	11C DRIFT TOWARD BEING THOSE 0.76 OF 17 WHERE SLAVERY IS ABSENT (218)	19 4 17 13 XSQ= 2.92 PHI= 0.235 XP = 0.0875
118	TEND TO BE THOSE 0.73 OF 33 WHERE THE PERCENTAGE CF OCCUPATIONS THAT ARE SPECIALIZED IS HIGH CR MEDIUM (24) WME	118 IN ALL CASES ARE THOSE 1.00 CF 16 WHERE THE PERCENTAGE OF OCCUPATICNS THAT ARE SPECIALIZED IS LOW (25) WME	24 0 9 16 XSQ= 19.99 PHI= 0.639 XP = 0.0000
130	TILT TCWARD BEING THOSE 0.77 OF 13 WHERE LEATHER WCRKING IS MAINLY DCNE BY MALES (39)	130 IN ALL CASES ARE THOSE 1.00 OF 3 WHERE LEATHER WORKING IS MAINLY DONE BY FEMALES (45)	10 0 3 3 XSQ= 3.31 PHI= 0.455 EP = 0.0357

133 TILT TOWARD BEING THOSE 0.64 OF 11 WHERE CONTRACTED DEBTS ARE SIGNIFICANTLY PRESENT (17) GES	133 IN ALL CASES ARE THOSE 1.00 OF 6 WHERE CONTRACTED DEBTS ARE MODERATELY PRESENT OR ABSENT (17) GES	7 0 4 6 XSQ= 4.13 PHI= 0.493 EP = 0.0175
184 TILT TOWARD BEING THOSE 0.81 OF 26 WHERE THE LARGEST NON-COGNATIC KIN GROUP IS SMALLER THAN A PHRATRY, I. E. A SIB OR LINEAGE (175)	184 TILT TOWARD BEING THOSE 0.58 OF 12 WHERE THE LARGEST NON-COGNATIC KIN GROUP IS THE MOEITY OR PHRATRY (77)	5 7 21 5 XSQ= 4.14 PHI= -0.330 EP = 0.0258
196 TILT TOWARD BEING THOSE 0.77 OF 30 WHERE INDIVIDUAL RIGHTS IN REAL PROPERTY, AND RULES FOR INHERITANCE, ARE PRESENT (194)	196 TILT TOWARD BEING THOSE 0.67 OF 12 WHERE INDIVIDUAL RIGHTS IN REAL PROPERTY, OR RULES FOR INHERITANCE, ARE ABSENT (87)	23 4 7 8 XSQ= 5.25 PHI= 0.354 XP = 0.0219
340 DRIFT TOWARD BEING THOSE 0.89 OF 9 WHERE THE TOTAL POSITIVE PRESSURE TOWARD DEVELOPING NURTURANT BEHAVIOR IN THE CHILD IS HIGH (28) B-B-C	340 DRIFT TOWARD BEING THOSE 0.60 OF 5 WHERE THE TOTAL POSITIVE PRESSURE TOWARD DEVELOPING NURTURANT BEHAVIOR IN THE CHILD IS LOW (20) B-B-C	8 2 1 3 XSQ= 1.75 PHI= 0.354 EP = 0.0949
341 DRIFT TOWARD BEING THOSE 0.89 OF 9 WHERE THE CHILD'S INFERRED ANXIETY OVER NON-PERFORMANCE OF NURTURANT BEHAVIOR IS HIGH (30) B-B-C	341 DRIFT TOWARD BEING THOSE 0.60 OF 5 WHERE THE CHILD'S INFERRED ANXIETY OVER NON-PERFORMANCE OF NURTURANT BEHAVIOR IS LOW (16) B-B-C	8 2 1 3 XSQ= 1.75 PHI= 0.354 EP = 0.0949
356 DRIFT LESS TOWARD BEING THOSE 0.56 OF 9 WHERE ADOLESCENT PEER GROUPS OR PAIRS ARE PRESENT IN A SETTING OF COURTSHIP (29) JKH	356 IN ALL CASES ARE THOSE 1.00 OF 7 WHERE ADOLESCENT PEER GROUPS OR PAIRS ARE PRESENT IN A SETTING OF COURTSHIP (29) JKH	5 7 4 0 XSQ= 2.12 PHI= -0.364 EP = 0.0885
377 DRIFT LESS TOWARD BEING THOSE 0.65 OF 34 WHERE MALE GENITAL MUTILATION IS ABSENT (242)	377 DRIFT MORE TOWARD BEING THOSE 0.94 OF 17 WHERE MALE GENITAL MUTILATION IS ABSENT (242)	12 1 22 16 XSQ= 3.73 PHI= 0.270 XP = 0.0535
432 TILT TOWARD BEING THOSE 0.90 OF 10 WHERE AN ATTRACTIVE AFTERLIFE IS BELIEVED IN (27) LWS	432 IN ALL CASES ARE THOSE 1.00 OF 2 WHERE AN ATTRACTIVE AFTERLIFE IS NOT BELIEVED IN (11) LWS	9 0 1 2 XSQ= 3.20 PHI= 0.516 EP = 0.0455
444 TILT TOWARD BEING THOSE 0.58 OF 19 WHERE THE USE OF DREAMS TO SEEK AND CONTROL SUPERNATURAL POWERS IS LOW (27) RGD	444 IN ALL CASES ARE THOSE 1.00 OF 5 WHERE THE USE OF DREAMS TO SEEK AND CONTROL SUPERNATURAL POWERS IS HIGH (28) RGD	8 5 11 0 XSQ= 3.27 PHI= -0.369 EP = 0.0411

121 CULTURES
WHERE, WITH A STATE PRESENT,
THE CRAFT SPECIALIZATICN SCORE
IS HIGH CR MEDIUM (21) GPM/WME

121 CULTURES
WHERE, WITH A STATE PRESENT,
THE CRAFT SPECIALIZATICN SCORE
IS LOW (6) GPM/WME

BACKGROUND ON PAGE 93

NEITHER SUBJECT NOR PREDICATE

21 IN LEFT CCLUMN

ALBANIANS ASHANTI AZANDE CHAGGA COORG CZECHS INCA KAZAK KOREANS MAGUZAWA
MISKITO NAMA RIFFIANS SIWANS SOMALI TANALA TIV TRCBRIAND VIETNAMESE WOLOF
YAO

6 IN RIGHT CCLUMN

GOND KACHIN NYAKYUSA SENIANG THONGA YAKUT

29 EXCLUDED BECAUSE IRRELEVANT

ALORESE ARANDA BHIL CARIB COPR ESKIMO GOAJIRO HANO HAVASUPAI IBAN IFUGAO
JIVARO KAPAUKU LAPPS LEPCHA MATACO MUNDURUCU NAMBICUARA NUER OJIBWA PAPAGO
SEMANG TALLENSI TIKOPIA TIMBIRA TODA TRUKESE YAHGAN YOKUTS YURCK

344 EXCLUDED BECAUSE UNASCERTAINED

122 CULTURES
WHERE, WITHOUT A STATE PRESENT,
THE CRAFT SPECIALIZATION SCORE
IS HIGH OR MEDIUM (13) GPM/WME

122 CULTURES
WHERE, WITHOUT A STATE PRESENT,
THE CRAFT SPECIALIZATION SCORE
IS LOW (8) GPM/WME

BACKGROUND ON PAGE 93

NEITHER SUBJECT NOR PREDICATE

13 IN LEFT COLUMN

ARANDA GOAJIRO IBAN IFUGAO JIVARO LAPPS MATACO OJIBWA PAPAGO TALLENSI
TIKOPIA TODA YUROK

8 IN RIGHT COLUMN

ALORESE CARIB HAVASUPAI MUNDURUCU NAMBICUARA TIMBIRA YAHGAN YOKUTS

38 EXCLUDED BECAUSE IRRELEVANT

ALBANIANS ASHANTI AZANDE BHIL CHAGGA CHEYENNE COORG COPR ESKIMO CZECHS DARD
GANDA GOND HANO INCA KACHIN KAPAUKU KAZAK KOREANS LEPCHA MAGUZAWA
MAORI MISKITO NAMA NUER NYAKYUSA RIFFIANS RWALA SENIANG SIWANS SOMALI
TANALA THONGA TIV TROBRIAND VIETNAMESE WOLOF YAKUT YAC

341 EXCLUDED BECAUSE UNASCERTAINED

123 CULTURES
WHERE, WITH STRATIFICATION PRESENT,
THE CRAFT SPECIALIZATION SCORE
IS HIGH OR MEDIUM (25) EA/WME

123 CULTURES
WHERE, WITH STRATIFICATION PRESENT,
THE CRAFT SPECIALIZATION SCORE
IS LOW (8) EA/WME

BACKGROUND ON PAGE 93

NEITHER SUBJECT NOR PREDICATE

25 IN LEFT COLUMN

ASHANTI, AZANDE, BHIL, CHAGGA, COORG, CZECHS, GOAJIRO, IFUGAO, INCA, KAZAK,
KOREANS, LAPPS, LEPCHA, MACUZAWA, NAMA, RIFFIANS, SIWANS, SOMALI, TALLENSI, TANALA,
TIKOPIA, TROBRIAND, VIETNAMESE, WOLOF, YUROK

8 IN RIGHT COLUMN

ALORESE, GOND, KACHIN, KAPAUKU, SENIANG, THONGA, YAKUT, YOKUTS

24 EXCLUDED BECAUSE IRRELEVANT

ALBANIANS, ARANDA, CARIB, CHEYENNE, COPR ESKIMO, HANO, HAVASUPAI, IBAN, JIVARO, MATACO,
MISKITO, MUNDURUCU, NAMBICUARA, NUER, NYAKYUSA, OJIBWA, PAPAGO, SEMANG, TIMBIRA, TIV,
TODA, TRUKESE, YAHGAN, YAO

343 EXCLUDED BECAUSE UNASCERTAINED

124 CULTURES
WHERE, WITHOUT STRATIFICATION PRESENT,
THE CRAFT SPECIALIZATION SCORE
IS HIGH OR MEDIUM (11) EA/WME

124 CULTURES
WHERE, WITHOUT STRATIFICATION PRESENT,
THE CRAFT SPECIALIZATION SCORE
IS LOW (9) EA/WME

BACKGROUND ON PAGE 93

NEITHER SUBJECT NOR PREDICATE

11 IN LEFT COLUMN

ALBANIANS ARANDA IBAN JIVARO MATACO MISKITO OJIBWA PAPAGO TIV TOCA
YAO

9 IN RIGHT COLUMN

CARIB COPR ESKIMO HAVASUPAI MUNDURUCU NAMBICUARA NUER NYAKYUSA TIMB'RA YAHGAN

37 EXCLUDED BECAUSE IRRELEVANT

ALORESE	ASHANTI	AZANDE	BHIL	CHAGGA	COORG	CZECHS	DARD	GANDA	GOAJIRO
GOND	IFUGAO	INCA	KACHIN	KAPAUKU	KAZAK	KOREANS	LAPPS	LEPCHA	MACUZAWA
MAORI	NAMA	RIFFIANS	RWALA	SENIANG	SIWANS	SOMALI	TALLENSI	TANALA	THONGA
TIKOPIA	TROBRIAND	VIETNAMESE	WOLOF	YAKUT	YOKUTS	YUROK			

343 EXCLUDED BECAUSE UNASCERTAINED

125 CULTURES
WHERE THE RATIO OF MALE TO FEMALE
OCCUPATIONAL SPECIALIZATION
IS HIGH (15) WME

125 CULTURES
WHERE THE RATIO OF MALE TO FEMALE
OCCUPATIONAL SPECIALIZATION
IS MEDIUM OR LOW (32) WME

BACKGROUND ON PAGE 94

NEITHER SUBJECT NOR PREDICATE

15 IN LEFT COLUMN

AZANDE, CHAGGA, COPR ESKIMO, GOND, HAVASUPAI, IBAN, JIVARO, KAPAUKU, MAGUZAWA, NAMBICUARA,
TANALA, THONGA, TODA, TROBRIAND, YOKUTS

32 IN RIGHT COLUMN

ALBANIANS, ALORESE, ARANDA, ASHANTI, BHIL, CARIB, GOAJIRO, IFUGAO, INCA, KACHIN,
KOREANS, LAPPS, LEPCHA, MATACO, MISKITO, MUNDURUCU, NAMA, NYAKYUSA, OJIBWA, PAPAGO,
SENIANG, SIWANS, SOMALI, TALLENSI, TIKOPIA, TIMBIRA, TIV, WOLOF, YAHGAN, YAKUT,
YAO, YUROK

353 EXCLUDED BECAUSE UNASCERTAINED

****

126 CULTURES WHERE THE RATIC CF MALE TC FEMALE OCCUPATICNAL SPECIALIZATICN IS HIGH CR MEDIUM (22) WME	126 CULTURES WHERE THE RATIC OF MALE TO FEMALE OCCUPATIONAL SPECIALIZATICN IS LOW (25) WME

BACKGROUND ON PAGE 94 — NEITHER SUBJECT NOR PREDICATE

22 IN LEFT CCLUMN

AZANDE	CHAGGA	CCPR ESKIMC	GOAJIRO	GOND	HAVASUPAI	IBAN	JIVARO	KAPAUKU	LAPPS
MAGUZAWA	NAMBICUARA	NYAKYUSA	SENIANG	TALLENSI	TANALA	THONGA	TIKOPIA	TODA	TROBRIAND
WOLOF	YCKUTS								

25 IN RIGHT CCLUMN

ALBANIANS	ALCRESE	ARANDA	ASHANTI	BHIL	CARIB	IFUGAO	INCA	KACHIN	KOREANS
LEPCHA	MATACO	MISKITC	MUNDURUCU	NAMA	OJIBWA	PAPAGO	SIWANS	SOMALI	TIMBIRA
TIV	YAHGAN	YAKUT	YAO	YUROK					

353 EXCLUDED BECAUSE UNASCERTAINED

---

127 CULTURES
WHERE THE FEMALES' CONTRIBUTION
TO SUBSISTENCE
IS HIGH (33) JKB

127 CULTURES
WHERE THE FEMALES' CONTRIBUTION
TO SUBSISTENCE
IS LOW (32) JKB

BACKGROUND ON PAGE 95

BOTH SUBJECT AND PREDICATE

33 IN LEFT COLUMN

ALORESE	ANDAMANESE	ARANDA	AYMARA	AZANDE	BHIL	BULGARIANS	CAGABA	CARIB	CAYAPA
CHAMACOCO	CHIR-APACHE	CHOROTI	FON	GANDA	GOAJIRO	JIVARO	KAZAK	KURTATCHI	LEPCHA
LESU	MENDE	NAMA	NAMBICUARA	NASKAPI	NUER	OJIBWA	PUKAPUKA	THONGA	TIMBIRA
TUBATULABAL	TUPINAMBA	WOLEAIANS							

32 IN RIGHT COLUMN

AINU	AMERICANS	ARAUCANIANS	BALINESE	BEMBA	BURMESE	CHEYENNE	COPR ESKIMO	CUNA	DILLING
EGYPTIANS	JAPANESE	KHASI	LAMBA	LAPPS	MAGUZAWA	MOSSI	MUNDURUCU	NAVAHO	PAPAGO
RWALA	SAMOYED	SANPOIL	SOMALI	TALLENSI	TANALA	TEDA	TEHUELCHE	THAI	TODA
YAGUA	YUROK								

335 EXCLUDED BECAUSE UNASCERTAINED

---

4 DRIFT MORE TOWARD BEING THOSE 0.97 OF 33
LOCATED OUTSIDE OF
THE CIRCUM-MEDITERRANEAN (355)

4 DRIFT LESS TOWARD BEING THOSE 0.78 OF 32
LOCATED OUTSIDE OF
THE CIRCUM-MEDITERRANEAN (355)

1 7
32 25
XSQ= 3.74
PHI= -0.240
XP = 0.0531

14 TILT MORE TOWARD BEING THOSE 0.82 OF 33
WHERE THE LATITUDE IS
LESS THAN THIRTY DEGREES (281)

14 TILT LESS TOWARD BEING THOSE 0.56 OF 32
WHERE THE LATITUDE IS
LESS THAN THIRTY DEGREES (281)

6 14
27 18
XSQ= 3.86
PHI= -0.244
XP = 0.0495

16 TILT LESS TOWARD BEING THOSE 0.58 OF 33
WHERE THE LATITUDE IS
TEN DEGREES OR GREATER (277)

16 TILT MORE TOWARD BEING THOSE 0.84 OF 32
WHERE THE LATITUDE IS
TEN DEGREES OR GREATER (277)

19 27
14 5
XSQ= 4.42
PHI= -0.261
XP = 0.0355

53 TILT TOWARD BEING THOSE 0.81 OF 21
WHERE FOOD PRODUCTION IS BY
SIMPLE AGRICULTURE OR
INCIPIENT FOOD PRODUCTION, RATHER THAN BY
INTENSIVE AGRICULTURE (147)

53 TILT TOWARD BEING THOSE 0.56 OF 18
WHERE FOOD PRODUCTION IS BY
INTENSIVE AGRICULTURE, RATHER THAN BY
SIMPLE AGRICULTURE OR
INCIPIENT FOOD PRODUCTION (91)

4 10
17 8
XSQ= 4.14
PHI= -0.326
EP = 0.0237

55	TILT TOWARD BEING THOSE 0.73 OF 15 WHERE FOOD PRODUCTION IS BY SIMPLE AGRICULTURE, RATHER THAN BY INTENSIVE AGRICULTURE (101)	55	TILT TOWARD BEING THOSE 0.71 OF 14 WHERE FOOD PRODUCTION IS BY INTENSIVE AGRICULTURE, RATHER THAN BY SIMPLE AGRICULTURE (91)	4 10 11 4 XSQ= 4.16 PHI= -0.379 EP = 0.0268
63	DRIFT TOWARD BEING THOSE 0.50 OF 22 WHERE HUSBANDRY, IF PRESENT, IS PRINCIPALLY IN THE FORM OF PIGS, SHEEP, OR GOATS, RATHER THAN BOVINE, EQUINE, CAMEL-LIKE, OR DEER-LIKE ANIMALS (74)	63	DRIFT TOWARD BEING THOSE 0.81 OF 21 WHERE HUSBANDRY, IF PRESENT, IS PRINCIPALLY IN THE FORM OF BOVINE, EQUINE, CAMEL-LIKE, OR DEER-LIKE ANIMALS, RATHER THAN PIGS, SHEEP, OR GOATS (152)	11 17 11 4 XSQ= 3.27 PHI= -0.276 XP = 0.0705
71	DRIFT TOWARD BEING THOSE 0.70 OF 30 WHERE METAL WORKING IS ABSENT (153)	71	DRIFT TOWARD BEING THOSE 0.58 OF 26 WHERE METAL WORKING IS PRESENT (98)	9 15 21 11 XSQ= 3.30 PHI= -0.243 XP = 0.0691
86	TILT TOWARD BEING THOSE 0.69 OF 29 WHERE THE LEVEL OF POLITICAL INTEGRATION IS THE AUTONOMOUS COMMUNITY, OR THE FAMILY (156) GPM	86	TILT TOWARD BEING THOSE 0.61 OF 28 WHERE THE LEVEL OF POLITICAL INTEGRATION IS THE LARGE STATE, THE LITTLE STATE, OR THE MINIMAL STATE (148) GPM	9 17 20 11 XSQ= 3.93 PHI= -0.263 XP = 0.0474
91	TILT TOWARD BEING THOSE 0.92 OF 12 WHERE SOCIETAL COMPLEXITY IS LOW (22) F-W	91	TILT TOWARD BEING THOSE 0.57 OF 7 WHERE SOCIETAL COMPLEXITY IS HIGH (18) F-W	1 4 11 3 XSQ= 3.21 PHI= -0.411 EP = 0.0379
110	TILT TOWARD BEING THOSE 0.70 OF 33 WHERE SLAVERY IS ABSENT (218)	110	TILT TOWARD BEING THOSE 0.59 OF 32 WHERE SLAVERY IS PRESENT (163)	10 19 23 13 XSQ= 4.44 PHI= -0.261 XP = 0.0351
128	IN ALL CASES ARE THOSE 1.00 OF 9 WHERE, IF SUBSISTENCE IS PRIMARILY BY AGRICULTURE, THE WORK IS MAINLY DONE BY FEMALES (37)	128	LEAN TOWARD BEING THOSE 0.71 OF 7 WHERE, IF SUBSISTENCE IS PRIMARILY BY AGRICULTURE, THE WORK IS MAINLY DONE BY MALES (40)	0 5 9 2 XSQ= 6.32 PHI= -0.629 EP = 0.0048
139	DRIFT TOWARD BEING THOSE 0.78 OF 9 WHERE SUPERORDINATE PUNISHMENT IS ABSENT (25) BBW	139	DRIFT TOWARD BEING THOSE 0.75 OF 8 WHERE SUPERORDINATE PUNISHMENT IS PRESENT (15) BBW	2 6 7 2 XSQ= 2.85 PHI= -0.410 EP = 0.0567
213	DRIFT TOWARD BEING THOSE 0.68 OF 31 WHERE FIRST COUSIN MARRIAGE IS NOT PERMITTED (198)	213	DRIFT TOWARD BEING THOSE 0.59 OF 32 WHERE FIRST COUSIN MARRIAGE IS PERMITTED (172)	10 19 21 13 XSQ= 3.63 PHI= -0.240 XP = 0.0566

No.	Statement	Ratio	No.	Statement	Ratio	Statistics
236	DRIFT TOWARD BEING THOSE WHERE THE FAMILY IS OF AN INDEPENDENT TYPE, RATHER THAN AN EXTENDED TYPE (185)	0.55 OF 33	236	DRIFT TOWARD BEING THOSE WHERE THE FAMILY IS OF AN EXTENDED TYPE, RATHER THAN AN INDEPENDENT TYPE (213)	0.69 OF 32	15 22 18 10 XSQ= 2.71 PHI= -0.204 XP = 0.0998
243	DRIFT TOWARD BEING THOSE WHERE POLYGYNY, IF PRESENT, HAS A HIGH INCIDENCE (24) W-C,S	0.58 OF 19	243	DRIFT TOWARD BEING THOSE WHERE POLYGYNY, IF PRESENT, HAS A LOW INCIDENCE (36) W-D,S	0.73 OF 15	11 4 8 11 XSQ= 2.17 PHI= 0.253 EP = 0.0915
272	TILT TOWARD BEING THOSE WHERE THE DIVORCE RATE IS LOW (28) CA	0.70 OF 10	272	TILT TOWARD BEING THOSE WHERE THE DIVORCE RATE IS HIGH (29) CA	0.82 OF 11	3 9 7 2 XSQ= 3.82 PHI= -0.427 EP = 0.0300
300	DRIFT TOWARD BEING THOSE WHERE THE POST-PARTUM SEX TABOO LASTS LONGER THAN SIX MONTHS (51)	0.57 OF 21	300	DRIFT TOWARD BEING THOSE WHERE THE POST-PARTUM SEX TABOO LASTS SIX MONTHS OR LESS (73)	0.74 OF 19	12 5 9 14 XSQ= 2.72 PHI= 0.261 EP = 0.0624
316	LEAN TOWARD BEING THOSE WHERE EXCLUSIVE MOTHER-SON SLEEPING ARRANGEMENTS LAST ONE YEAR OR LONGER (19) W-K-A	0.69 OF 13	316	LEAN TOWARD BEING THOSE WHERE EXCLUSIVE MOTHER-SON SLEEPING ARRANGEMENTS LAST LESS THAN ONE YEAR (25) W-K-A	0.93 OF 14	9 1 4 13 XSQ= 8.64 PHI= 0.566 EP = 0.0013
354	DRIFT TOWARD BEING THOSE WHERE THE CHILD'S INFERRED ANXIETY OVER PERFORMANCE OF OBEDIENT BEHAVIOR IS HIGH (36) B-B-C	0.69 OF 16	354	DRIFT TOWARD BEING THOSE WHERE THE CHILD'S INFERRED ANXIETY OVER PERFORMANCE OF OBEDIENT BEHAVIOR IS LOW (37) B-B-C	0.73 OF 11	11 3 5 8 XSQ= 2.98 PHI= 0.332 EP = 0.0542
372	LEAN TOWARD BEING THOSE WHERE MALE INITIATION RITES ARE PRESENT (48) ASA	0.57 OF 21	372	LEAN TOWARD BEING THOSE WHERE MALE INITIATION RITES ARE ABSENT (63) ASA	0.93 OF 14	12 1 9 13 XSQ= 6.98 PHI= 0.447 EP = 0.0039
373	TEND TO BE THOSE WHERE MALE INITIATION CEREMONIES AT PUBERTY ARE PRESENT (17) W-K-A	0.77 OF 13	373	TEND TO BE THOSE WHERE MALE INITIATION CEREMONIES AT PUBERTY ARE ABSENT (27) W-K-A	0.93 OF 14	10 1 3 13 XSQ= 10.86 PHI= 0.634 EP = 0.0003
390	DRIFT MORE TOWARD BEING THOSE WHERE PREMARITAL SEX RELATIONS ARE WEAKLY PUNISHED AND IN FACT NOT RARE OR PUNISHED ONLY IF PREGNANCY RESULTS, OR FREELY PERMITTED (132) JTW,EA	0.91 OF 23	390	DRIFT LESS TOWARD BEING THOSE WHERE PREMARITAL SEX RELATIONS ARE WEAKLY PUNISHED AND IN FACT NOT RARE OR PUNISHED ONLY IF PREGNANCY RESULTS, OR FREELY PERMITTED (132) JTW,EA	0.65 OF 20	2 7 21 13 XSQ= 3.02 PHI= -0.265 XP = 0.0820

```
402  LEAN TCWARD BEING THCSE          0.91 OF  11      402  LEAN TOWARD BEING THOSE          0.73 CF  11         10     3
     WHERE EXPLANATICNS CF ILLNESS                         WHERE EXPLANATIONS OF ILLNESS                          1     8
     CF AN CRAL NATURE                                     OF AN ORAL NATURE                                XSQ=     6.77
     ARE PRESENT  (31) W-C                                 ARE ABSENT  (30) W-C                             PHI=    0.555
                                                                                                            EP =   0.0075

404  DRIFT TCWARD BEING THCSE         0.73 OF  11      404  DRIFT TOWARD BEING THOSE         0.73 OF  11          8     3
     WHERE EXPLANATICNS CF ILLNESS                         WHERE EXPLANATIONS OF ILLNESS                          3     8
     OF A SEXUAL NATURE                                    OF A SEXUAL NATURE                               XSQ=     2.91
     ARE PRESENT  (19) W-C                                 ARE ABSENT  (42) W-C                             PHI=    0.364
                                                                                                            EP =   0.0861

421  DRIFT TCWARD BEING THCSE         0.53 OF  19      421  DRIFT TOWARD BEING THOSE         0.78 CF  18         10     4
     WHERE KILLING, TCRTURING, CR MUTILATING               WHERE KILLING, TORTURING, CR MUTILATING                9    14
     OF THE ENEMY                                          OF THE ENEMY                                     XSQ=     2.46
     IS STRCNGLY CR MCDERATELY                             IS NEGLIGIBLY EMPHASIZED  (47) PES               PHI=    0.258
     EMPHASIZED  (37) PES                                                                                   EP =   0.0911

425  DRIFT TCWARD BEING THCSE         0.91 OF  11      425  DRIFT TOWARD BEING THOSE         0.60 CF   5          1     3
     WHERE SUPERNATURALS ARE MAINLY                        WHERE SUPERNATURALS ARE MAINLY                        10     2
     AGGRESSIVE, RATHER THAN                               BENEVOLENT, RATHER THAN                          XSQ=     2.42
     BENEVCLENT  (20) L-T-W                                AGGRESSIVE  (16) L-T-W                           PHI=   -0.389
                                                                                                            EP =   0.0632
```

****

128	CULTURES WHERE, IF SUBSISTENCE IS PRIMARILY BY AGRICULTURE, THE WORK IS MAINLY DONE BY MALES (40)	128	CULTURES WHERE, IF SUBSISTENCE IS PRIMARILY BY AGRICULTURE, THE WORK IS MAINLY DONE BY FEMALES (37)

BACKGROUND ON PAGE 95 — BOTH SUBJECT AND PREDICATE

....

40 IN LEFT COLUMN

AMERICANS	ARAUCANIANS	AZTEC	BAMBARA	BIRIFOR	BRAZILIANS	CHIRIGUANO	CHORTI	COORG	CUNA
DOGON	DUTCH	EGYPTIANS	HUICHOL	HUTSUL	INCA	JEMEZ	KACHIN	KATAB	LAU
LHOTA NAGA	MACASSARESE	MARQUESANS	MARSHALLESE	MAYA	MIAO	NICOBARESE	NUPE	NYAKYUSA	PONAPEANS
PURUM	RIFFIANS	SIWANS	SONGHAI	SYRIANS	TALLENSI	TAOS	TARAHUMARA	TOTONAC	YORUBA

37 IN RIGHT COLUMN

ALORESE	AMBA	AZANDE	BAMILEKE	BEMBA	BLACK CARIB	CAYAPA	DARD	ENGA	FANG
FON	GANDA	GISU	ILA	JAVANESE	JIVARO	KHASI	KIKUYU	KPE	KUBA
KURTATCHI	MAMVU	MANDAN	MANGAIANS	MBUNDU	MONGO	NANDI	NDEMBU	NURI	NYORO
PALAUANS	PUKAPUKA	SWAZI	THONGA	VENDA	YAO	YAPESE			

214 EXCLUDED BECAUSE IRRELEVANT

109 EXCLUDED BECAUSE UNASCERTAINED

3	TEND TO BE THOSE LOCATED OUTSIDE OF AFRICA (320)	0.80 OF 40	3	TEND TO BE THOSE LOCATED IN AFRICA (80)	0.59 OF 37	8 22 32 15 XSQ= 10.98 PHI= -0.378 XP = 0.0009
4	LEAN LESS TOWARD BEING THOSE LOCATED OUTSIDE OF THE CIRCUM-MEDITERRANEAN (355)	0.77 OF 40	4	IN ALL CASES ARE THOSE LOCATED OUTSIDE OF THE CIRCUM-MEDITERRANEAN (355)	1.00 OF 37	9 0 31 37 XSQ= 7.37 PHI= 0.309 XP = 0.0066
16	LEAN TOWARD BEING THOSE WHERE THE LATITUDE IS TEN DEGREES OR GREATER (277)	0.77 OF 40	16	LEAN TOWARD BEING THOSE WHERE THE LATITUDE IS LESS THAN TEN DEGREES (123)	0.59 OF 37	31 15 9 22 XSQ= 9.43 PHI= 0.350 XP = 0.0021
44	IN ALL CASES ARE THOSE WHERE SETTLEMENTS ARE FIXED (222)	1.00 OF 40	44	TILT LESS TOWARD BEING THOSE WHERE SETTLEMENTS ARE FIXED (222)	0.84 OF 37	40 31 0 6 XSQ= 4.96 PHI= 0.254 XP = 0.0260

53	LEAN TOWARD BEING THOSE 0.57 OF 40 WHERE FOOD PRODUCTION IS BY INTENSIVE AGRICULTURE, RATHER THAN BY SIMPLE AGRICULTURE OR INCIPIENT FOOD PRODUCTION (91)	53	LEAN TOWARD BEING THOSE 0.76 OF 37 WHERE FOOD PRODUCTION IS BY SIMPLE AGRICULTURE OR INCIPIENT FOOD PRODUCTION, RATHER THAN BY INTENSIVE AGRICULTURE (147)	23 9 17 28 XSQ= 7.40 PHI= 0.310 XP = 0.0065
55	LEAN TOWARD BEING THOSE 0.57 OF 40 WHERE FOOD PRODUCTION IS BY INTENSIVE AGRICULTURE, RATHER THAN BY SIMPLE AGRICULTURE (91)	55	LEAN TOWARD BEING THOSE 0.76 OF 37 WHERE FOOD PRODUCTION IS BY SIMPLE AGRICULTURE, RATHER THAN BY INTENSIVE AGRICULTURE (101)	23 9 17 28 XSQ= 7.40 PHI= 0.310 XP = 0.0065
73	TEND TO BE THOSE 0.81 OF 37 WHERE WEAVING IS PRESENT (118)	73	TEND TO BE THOSE 0.64 OF 36 WHERE WEAVING IS ABSENT (130)	30 13 7 23 XSQ= 13.44 PHI= 0.429 XP = 0.0002
77	TILT TOWARD BEING THOSE 0.50 OF 6 WHERE THE WRITING SYSTEM IS ALPHABETIC-OR-PHONETIC, RATHER THAN BEING MNEMONIC OR ABSENT (15) JMH	77	IN ALL CASES ARE THOSE 1.00 OF 11 WHERE THE WRITING SYSTEM IS MNEMONIC OR ABSENT, RATHER THAN BEING ALPHABETIC-OR-PHONETIC (39) JMH	3 0 3 11 XSQ= 3.68 PHI= 0.465 EP = 0.0294
80	TILT LESS TOWARD BEING THOSE 0.58 OF 33 WHERE NO CITY OR TOWN IS PRESENT (185)	80	TILT MORE TOWARD BEING THOSE 0.89 OF 27 WHERE NO CITY OR TOWN IS PRESENT (185)	14 3 19 24 XSQ= 5.71 PHI= 0.309 XP = 0.0169
88	TILT TOWARD BEING THOSE 0.52 OF 31 WHERE, IF A HEADMANSHIP IS PRESENT, SUCCESSION IS NON-HEREDITARY (106)	88	TILT TOWARD BEING THOSE 0.80 OF 30 WHERE, IF A HEADMANSHIP IS PRESENT, SUCCESSION IS HEREDITARY (165)	16 6 15 24 XSQ= 5.31 PHI= 0.295 XP = 0.0212
89	TILT TOWARD BEING THOSE 0.75 OF 16 WHERE, IF A NON-HEREDITARY HEADMANSHIP IS PRESENT, SUCCESSION IS BY CONSENSUS (63)	89	TILT TOWARD BEING THOSE 0.83 OF 6 WHERE, IF A NON-HEREDITARY HEADMANSHIP IS PRESENT, SUCCESSION IS BY MEANS OTHER THAN CONSENSUS (43)	12 1 4 5 XSQ= 3.97 PHI= 0.425 EP = 0.0461
97	DRIFT LESS TOWARD BEING THOSE 0.67 OF 39 WHERE THE HIERARCHY OF LOCAL JURISDICTION HAS THREE OR TWO LEVELS (273) GES,EA	97	DRIFT MORE TOWARD BEING THOSE 0.86 OF 37 WHERE THE HIERARCHY OF LOCAL JURISDICTION HAS THREE OR TWO LEVELS (273) GES,EA	13 5 26 32 XSQ= 3.10 PHI= 0.202 XP = 0.0782
107	TILT LESS TOWARD BEING THOSE 0.63 OF 30 WHERE CLASS STRATIFICATION, IF PRESENT, IS BASED ON SOMETHING OTHER THAN OCCUPATIONAL STATUS (160)	107	TILT MORE TOWARD BEING THOSE 0.92 OF 25 WHERE CLASS STRATIFICATION, IF PRESENT, IS BASED ON SOMETHING OTHER THAN OCCUPATIONAL STATUS (160)	11 2 19 23 XSQ= 4.72 PHI= 0.293 XP = 0.0298

```
108  LEAN TOWARD BEING THOSE           0.80 OF  30    108  LEAN TOWARD BEING THOSE           0.60 OF  25          6   15
     WHERE CLASS STRATIFICATICN, IF PRESENT,              WHERE CLASS STRATIFICATICN, IF PRESENT,             24   10
     IS BASED CN SCMETHING CTHER THAN                     IS BASED ON                                  XSQ=      7.63
     A HEREDITARY ARISTCCRACY  (129)                      A HEREDITARY ARISTOCRACY  (74)               PHI=    -0.372
                                                                                                       XP =    0.0058

127  IN ALL CASES ARE THCSE            1.00 OF   5    127  LEAN TOWARD BEING THOSE           0.82 OF  11          0    9
     WHERE THE FEMALES' CONTRIBUTION                      WHERE THE FEMALES' CONTRIBUTION                      5    2
     TO SUBSISTENCE                                       TO SUBSISTENCE                               XSQ=      6.32
     IS LCW  (32) JKB                                     IS HIGH  (33) JKB                            PHI=    -0.629
                                                                                                       EP =    0.0048

129  TILT TCWARD BEING THCSE           0.75 OF  24    129  TILT TOWARD BEING THOSE           0.62 OF  13          6    8
     WHERE WEAVING IS                                     WHERE WEAVING IS                                    18    5
     MAINLY DONE BY FEMALES  (73)                         MAINLY DONE BY MALES  (31)                   XSQ=      3.36
                                                                                                       PHI=    -0.301
                                                                                                       EP =    0.0395

181  TILT LESS TOWARC BEING THCSE  0.77 OF  39        181  TILT MORE TOWARD BEING THOSE  0.97 OF  36              9    1
     WHERE THE COMMUNITY IS OTHER THAN                    WHERE THE COMMUNITY IS OTHER THAN                   30   35
     A DEME  (337)                                        A DEME  (337)                                XSQ=      5.03
                                                                                                       PHI=     0.259
                                                                                                       XP =    0.0249

185  DRIFT LESS TCWARD BEING THCSE 0.63 OF  24        185  DRIFT MORE TOWARD BEING THCSE 0.88 OF  32             15   28
     WHERE THE LARGEST NCN-COGNATIC KIN GROUP             WHERE THE LARGEST NON-COGNATIC KIN GROUP             9    4
     IS THE MOEITY CR PHRATRY CR SIB  (194)               IS THE MOEITY OR PHRATRY CR SIB  (194)       XSQ=      3.51
                                                                                                       PHI=    -0.250
                                                                                                       XP =    0.0611

188  TILT LESS TCWARC BEING THCSE  0.60 OF  40        188  TILT MORE TOWARD BEING THOSE  0.86 CF  37             16    5
     WHERE THE KIN GRCUP IS                               WHERE THE KIN GROUP IS                              24   32
     OTHER THAN                                           OTHER THAN                                   XSQ=      5.53
     EXCLUSIVELY COGNATIC  (252)                          EXCLUSIVELY COGNATIC  (252)                  PHI=     0.268
                                                                                                       XP =    0.0187

192  TILT LESS TOWARC BEING THCSE  0.65 OF  40        192  TILT MORE TOWARD BEING THOSE  0.92 OF  37             14    3
     OTHER THAN WHERE THE CNLY KIN GROUP                  OTHER THAN WHERE THE ONLY KIN GRCUP                 26   34
     PRESENT IS A KINDRED CR ELSE                         PRESENT IS A KINDRED OR ELSE                 XSQ=      6.59
     BILATERAL DESCENT IS INFERREC  (289)                 BILATERAL DESCENT IS INFERRED  (289)         PHI=     0.293
                                                                                                       XP =    0.0102

201  TILT LESS TCWARC BEING THCSE  0.70 OF  40        201  TILT MORE TOWARD BEING THCSE  0.92 OF  37             28   34
     WHERE MARITAL RESICENCE IS                           WHERE MARITAL RESIDENCE IS                          12    3
     NON-CPTICNAL, RATHER THAN                            NON-OPTIONAL, RATHER THAN                    XSQ=      4.56
     AMBILCCAL CR NECLOCAL  (334)                         AMBILOCAL OR NEOLOCAL  (334)                 PHI=    -0.243
                                                                                                       XP =    0.0327

204  TILT LESS TOWARC BEING THCSE  0.68 OF  37        204  TILT MORE TOWARD BEING THOSE  0.91 OF  33             25   30
     WHERE MARITAL RESICENCE IS                           WHERE MARITAL RESIDENCE IS                          12    3
     PATRILCCAL, VIRILOCAL, OR AVUNCULOCAL,               PATRILOCAL, VIRILOCAL, CR AVUNCULOCAL,       XSQ=      4.34
     RATHER THAN                                          RATHER THAN                                  PHI=    -0.249
     AMBILCCAL CR NECLOCAL  (270)                         AMBILOCAL OR NEOLOCAL  (270)                 XP =    0.0372
```

213	TILT TOWARD BEING THOSE 0.64 OF 39 WHERE FIRST COUSIN MARRIAGE IS PERMITTED (172)	213	TILT TOWARD BEING THOSE 0.64 OF 36 WHERE FIRST COUSIN MARRIAGE IS NOT PERMITTED (198)	25 13 14 23 XSQ= 4.80 PHI= 0.253 XP = 0.0284
234	TILT TOWARD BEING THOSE 0.65 OF 34 WHERE THE COUSIN TERMINOLOGY IS OF ESKIMO OR HAWAIIAN TYPE, RATHER THAN CROW, OMAHA, OR IROQUOIS TYPE (170)	234	TILT TOWARD BEING THOSE 0.68 OF 31 WHERE THE COUSIN TERMINOLOGY IS OF CROW, OMAHA, OR IROQUOIS TYPE, RATHER THAN ESKIMO OR HAWAIIAN TYPE (152)	12 21 22 10 XSQ= 5.59 PHI= -0.293 XP = 0.0180
242	DRIFT LESS TOWARD BEING THOSE 0.71 OF 38 WHERE MARRIAGE IS COMMONLY OR OCCASIONALLY POLYGYNOUS, RATHER THAN MONOGAMOUS (314)	242	DRIFT MORE TOWARD BEING THOSE 0.89 OF 37 WHERE MARRIAGE IS COMMONLY OR OCCASIONALLY POLYGYNOUS, RATHER THAN MONOGAMOUS (314)	27 33 11 4 XSQ= 2.80 PHI= -0.193 XP = 0.0940
316	DRIFT TOWARD BEING THOSE 0.80 OF 5 WHERE EXCLUSIVE MOTHER-SON SLEEPING ARRANGEMENTS LAST LESS THAN ONE YEAR (25) W-K-A	316	DRIFT TOWARD BEING THOSE 0.86 OF 7 WHERE EXCLUSIVE MOTHER-SON SLEEPING ARRANGEMENTS LAST ONE YEAR OR LONGER (19) W-K-A	1 6 4 1 XSQ= 2.83 PHI= -0.486 EP = 0.0720
334	DRIFT TOWARD BEING THOSE 0.71 OF 7 WHERE THE INDULGENCE OF THE CHILD IS HIGH (40) B-B-C	334	DRIFT TOWARD BEING THOSE 0.77 OF 13 WHERE THE INDULGENCE OF THE CHILD IS LOW (38) B-B-C	5 3 2 10 XSQ= 2.65 PHI= 0.364 EP = 0.0623
339	DRIFT TOWARD BEING THOSE 0.86 OF 7 WHERE THE CHILD'S INFERRED CONFLICT REGARDING RESPONSIBLE BEHAVIOR IS LOW (42) B-B-C	339	DRIFT TOWARD BEING THOSE 0.69 OF 13 WHERE THE CHILD'S INFERRED CONFLICT REGARDING RESPONSIBLE BEHAVIOR IS HIGH (31) B-B-C	1 9 6 4 XSQ= 3.52 PHI= -0.419 EP = 0.0573
354	DRIFT TOWARD BEING THOSE 0.86 OF 7 WHERE THE CHILD'S INFERRED ANXIETY OVER PERFORMANCE OF OBEDIENT BEHAVIOR IS LOW (37) B-B-C	354	DRIFT TOWARD BEING THOSE 0.67 OF 12 WHERE THE CHILD'S INFERRED ANXIETY OVER PERFORMANCE OF OBEDIENT BEHAVIOR IS HIGH (36) B-B-C	1 8 6 4 XSQ= 2.99 PHI= -0.397 EP = 0.0573
370	LEAN TOWARD BEING THOSE 0.78 OF 32 WHERE THE SEGREGATION OF ADOLESCENT BOYS IS ABSENT (148)	370	LEAN TOWARD BEING THOSE 0.59 OF 32 WHERE THE SEGREGATION OF ADOLESCENT BOYS IS COMPLETE OR PARTIAL (95)	7 19 25 13 XSQ= 7.84 PHI= -0.350 XP = 0.0051
372	DRIFT TOWARD BEING THOSE 0.67 OF 12 WHERE MALE INITIATION RITES ARE ABSENT (63) ASA	372	DRIFT TOWARD BEING THOSE 0.73 OF 15 WHERE MALE INITIATION RITES ARE PRESENT (48) ASA	4 11 8 4 XSQ= 2.85 PHI= -0.325 EP = 0.0574

373	IN ALL CASES ARE THOSE WHERE MALE INITIATION CEREMONIES AT PUBERTY ARE ABSENT (27) W-K-A	1.00 OF	5	373	DRIFT TOWARD BEING THOSE WHERE MALE INITIATION CEREMONIES AT PUBERTY ARE PRESENT (17) W-K-A	0.57 OF	7	0 4 5 3 XSQ= 2.10 PHI= -0.418 EP = 0.0808
399	DRIFT TOWARD BEING THOSE WHERE INTENSITY OF CASTRATION ANXIETY IS LOW (22) WNS	0.75 OF	4	399	DRIFT TOWARD BEING THOSE WHERE INTENSITY OF CASTRATION ANXIETY IS HIGH (23) WNS	0.88 OF	8	1 7 3 1 XSQ= 2.30 PHI= -0.437 EP = 0.0667
427	LEAN TOWARD BEING THOSE WHERE A HIGH GOD, IF PRESENT, IS ACTIVE, RATHER THAN INACTIVE (87) GES,EA	0.78 OF	23	427	LEAN TOWARD BEING THOSE WHERE A HIGH GOD, IF PRESENT, IS INACTIVE, RATHER THAN ACTIVE (69) GES,EA	0.74 OF	23	18 6 5 17 XSQ= 10.54 PHI= 0.479 XP = 0.0012
443	IN ALL CASES ARE THOSE WHERE OVERALL FEAR OF OTHERS IS HIGH (31) W-C	1.00 OF	4	443	DRIFT TOWARD BEING THOSE WHERE OVERALL FEAR OF OTHERS IS LOW (30) W-C	0.75 OF	8	4 2 0 6 XSQ= 3.38 PHI= 0.530 EP = 0.0606
458	DRIFT TOWARD BEING THOSE WHERE GAMES, IF PRESENT, DO NOT INCLUDE GAMES OF STRATEGY (119) R-A-B,EA	0.64 OF	22	458	DRIFT TOWARD BEING THOSE WHERE GAMES, IF PRESENT, INCLUDE GAMES OF STRATEGY (52) R-A-B,EA	0.67 OF	18	8 12 14 6 XSQ= 2.53 PHI= -0.251 EP = 0.0679

129 CULTURES
WHERE WEAVING IS
MAINLY DCNE BY MALES (31)

129 CULTURES
WHERE WEAVING IS
MAINLY DONE BY FEMALES (73)

BACKGROUND ON PAGE 95

BOTH SUBJECT AND PREDICATE

31 IN LEFT CCLUMN

ASHANTI	AZANDE	BAMBARA	BAMILEKE	BIRIFOR	BURUSHO	CAGABA	DARD	EGYPTIANS	FON
JEMEZ	JIVARC	KCHISTANI	KUBA	MARICOPA	MENDE	MONGO	MCNGUOR	MOSSI	NAMBICUARA
NUPE	NURI	CNTCNG-JAVA	PAPAGO	SANTAL	SOMALI	SONGHAI	TIBETANS	TIV	WOLOF
YAKUT									

73 IN RIGHT CCLUMN

ABIPCN	ABCR	AINU	ALBANIANS	ARAUCANIANS	AZTEC	BASSERI	BULGARIANS	CALLINAGO	CAMAYURA
CARIB	CAYAPA	CHIRIGUANO	CHOROTI	CHORTI	CREEK	CUNA	DIEGUENC	GARC	GOAJIRO
GUATC	HAIDA	HUICHCL	HUTSUL	IBAN	INCA	JAVANESE	KAZAK	KHASI	KOREANS
KWAKIUTL	LAKHER	LEPCHA	LHOTA NAGA	MACASSARESE	MATACO	MAYA	MIAMI	MIAC	MISKITO
MNONG GAR	MUNDURUCU	NATCHEZ	NAVAHO	OKINAWANS	OMAHA	PAEZ	PALAUANS	PONAPEANS	PURUM
RIFFIANS	RWALA	SAGACA	SERBS	SIRIONO	SIWANS	TALAMANCA	TANALA	TAPIRAPE	TARAHUMARA
TEHUELCHE	TERENA	TCTCNAC	TRUKESE	TRUMAI	TSHIMSHIAN	TUCUNA	TUNEBO	TUPINAMBA	TWANA
WCLEAIANS	YABARANA	YAPESE							

3 EXCLUDED BECAUSE AMBIGUOUS

AYMARA	TENDA	YCRUBA

136 EXCLUDED BECAUSE IRRELEVANT

ALACALUF	ALCRESE	AMBA	AMERICANS	ANDAMANESE	APINAYE	ARANDA	ATSUGEWI	AWEIKOMA	BACAIRI
BARI	BEMBA	BHIL	BLACK CARIB	BORORO	BOTOCUDO	BRAZILIANS	CHENCHU	CHEYENNE	CHIR-APACHE
CHOCO	CHUKCHEE	CCMANCHE	COPR ESKIMO	CREE	CROW	CZECHS	DIERI	DUTCH	ELLICE
ENGA	EYAK	FANG	FOX	GANDA	GILBERTESE	GILYAK	GISU	GONC	GROS VENTRE
HASINAI	HAWAIIANS	HUKUNDIKA	HURON	ILA	INGALIK	JAPANESE	KAPAUKU	KARIERA	KASKA
KATAB	KERAKI	KHALKA	KIKUYU	KIOW-APACHE	KORYAK	KUNG	KURTATCHI	KUTENAI	LAMET
LAU	LESU	LOZI	LUO	MAMVU	MANDAN	MANGAIANS	MANIHIKI	MARQUESANS	MARSHALLESE
MASAI	MATAKAM	MBUNCU	MBUTI	MENTAWEI	MOTA	MURINBATA	MURNGIN	NABESNA	NAMA
NANDI	NDEMBU	NICOBARESE	NOMLAKI	NUER	NUNIVAK	NYORO	OJIBWA	ONA	PUKAPUKA
PURARI	RARCIANS	RUNCI	SAMOANS	SAMOYED	SANPOIL	SARSI	SEMANG	SENIANG	SHILLUK
SWAZI	SYRIANS	TALLENSI	TAOS	TAREUMIUT	TEDA	TENINO	THONGA	TIKOPIA	TIMBIRA
TIMUCUA	TIWI	TOCA	TOKELAU	TOLOWA	TRISTAN	TROBRIAND	TUBATULABAL	TUCANO	ULAWANS
UTE	VEDDA	VENCA	WAICA	WANTOAT	WASHO	WIKMUNKAN	WITCTO	WOGEC	YAGUA
YAHGAN	YAC	YARURO	YOKUTS	YUKI	YUROK				

157 EXCLUDED BECAUSE UNASCERTAINEC

3	TEND LESS TO BE THOSE LOCATED OUTSIDE OF AFRICA (320)	0.61 OF 31	3	IN ALL CASES ARE THOSE LOCATED OUTSIDE OF AFRICA (320)	1.00 OF 73	12 0 19 73 XSQ= 28.26 PHI= 0.521 XP = 0.0000
9	LEAN MORE TOWARD BEING THOSE LOCATED OUTSIDE OF SOUTH AMERICA (335)	0.90 OF 31	9	LEAN LESS TOWARD BEING THOSE LOCATED OUTSIDE OF SOUTH AMERICA (335)	0.62 OF 73	3 28 28 45 XSQ= 7.24 PHI= -0.264 XP = 0.0071
13	DRIFT MORE TOWARD BEING THOSE WHERE THE LATITUDE IS LESS THAN FORTY DEGREES (329)	0.97 OF 31	13	DRIFT LESS TOWARD BEING THOSE WHERE THE LATITUDE IS LESS THAN FORTY DEGREES (329)	0.82 OF 73	1 13 30 60 XSQ= 2.82 PHI= -0.165 XP = 0.0932
33	TILT LESS TOWARD BEING THOSE WHERE THE NATURAL ENVIRONMENT IS OTHER THAN 'VERY HARSH,' I.E., DESERT, DESERT GRASSES AND SHRUBS, TUNDRA, OR HIGH PLATEAU STEPPE (341) FWM	0.68 OF 31	33	TILT MORE TOWARD BEING THOSE WHERE THE NATURAL ENVIRONMENT IS OTHER THAN 'VERY HARSH,' I.E., DESERT, DESERT GRASSES AND SHRUBS, TUNDRA, OR HIGH PLATEAU STEPPE (341) FWM	0.88 OF 73	10 9 21 64 XSQ= 4.53 PHI= 0.209 XP = 0.0333
42	DRIFT TOWARD BEING THOSE WHERE THE NATURAL ENVIRONMENT IS OTHER THAN TROPICAL OR SUB-TROPICAL RAIN FOREST, OR MONSOON FOREST (244) FWM	0.71 OF 31	42	DRIFT TOWARD BEING THOSE WHERE THE NATURAL ENVIRONMENT IS TROPICAL OR SUB-TROPICAL RAIN FOREST, OR MONSOON FOREST (156) FWM	0.52 OF 73	9 38 22 35 XSQ= 3.77 PHI= -0.190 XP = 0.0521
51	TILT MORE TOWARD BEING THOSE WHERE SUBSISTENCE IS PRIMARILY BY FOOD PRODUCTION -- I. E., AGRICULTURE OR HUSBANDRY -- RATHER THAN BY GATHERING (253)	0.84 OF 31	51	TILT LESS TOWARD BEING THOSE WHERE SUBSISTENCE IS PRIMARILY BY FOOD PRODUCTION -- I. E., AGRICULTURE OR HUSBANDRY -- RATHER THAN BY GATHERING (253)	0.59 OF 73	26 43 5 30 XSQ= 5.01 PHI= 0.219 XP = 0.0252
71	LEAN TOWARD BEING THOSE WHERE METAL WORKING IS PRESENT (98)	0.77 OF 31	71	LEAN TOWARD BEING THOSE WHERE METAL WORKING IS ABSENT (153)	0.59 OF 69	24 28 7 41 XSQ= 10.20 PHI= 0.319 XP = 0.0014
85	LEAN TOWARD BEING THOSE WHERE THE LEVEL OF POLITICAL INTEGRATION IS THE LARGE STATE, OR THE LITTLE STATE (70) GPM	0.52 OF 27	85	LEAN TOWARD BEING THOSE WHERE THE LEVEL OF POLITICAL INTEGRATION IS THE MINIMAL STATE, THE AUTONOMOUS COMMUNITY, OR THE FAMILY (234) GPM	0.80 OF 56	14 11 13 45 XSQ= 7.51 PHI= 0.301 XP = 0.0061
90	IN ALL CASES ARE THOSE WHERE, IF A HEREDITARY HEADMANSHIP IS PRESENT, SUCCESSION IS PATRILINEAL, RATHER THAN MATRILINEAL (127)	1.00 OF 12	90	TILT LESS TOWARD BEING THOSE WHERE, IF A HEREDITARY HEADMANSHIP IS PRESENT, SUCCESSION IS PATRILINEAL, RATHER THAN MATRILINEAL (127)	0.66 OF 35	12 23 0 12 XSQ= 3.87 PHI= 0.287 XP = 0.0492

95	LEAN LESS TOWARC BEING THCSE WHERE THE HIERARCHY OF NATICNAL JURISDICTICN HAS CNE CR NC LEVELS (254) GES,EA	0.53 OF 30	95	LEAN MORE TOWARD BEING THOSE WHERE THE HIERARCHY OF NATIONAL JURISDICTICN HAS ONE OR NO LEVELS (254) GES,EA	0.83 OF 72	14 12 16 60 XSQ= 8.52 PHI= 0.289 XP = 0.0035
96	TILT MORE TOWARC BEING THCSE WHERE THE HIERARCHY OF NATIONAL JURISDICTICN HAS FOUR, THREE, TWC CR ONE LEVEL (174) GES,EA	0.77 OF 30	96	TILT LESS TOWARD BEING THOSE WHERE THE HIERARCHY OF NATIONAL JURISDICTICN HAS FOUR, THREE, TWC OR ONE LEVEL (174) GES,EA	0.51 OF 72	23 37 7 35 XSQ= 4.59 PHI= 0.212 XP = 0.0321
97	TILT LESS TOWARC BEING THCSE WHERE THE HIERARCHY CF LCCAL JURISDICTION HAS THREE CR TWO LEVELS (273) GES,EA	0.67 OF 30	97	TILT MORE TOWARD BEING THOSE WHERE THE HIERARCHY OF LOCAL JURISDICTION HAS THREE OR TWO LEVELS (273) GES,EA	0.86 OF 72	10 10 20 62 XSQ= 3.92 PHI= 0.196 XP = 0.0477
98	TILT MORE TCWARD BEING THCSE WHERE THE HIERARCHY CF LCCAL JURISDICTION HAS FOUR CR THREE LEVELS (238) GES,EA	0.97 OF 30	98	TILT LESS TOWARD BEING THOSE WHERE THE HIERARCHY OF LOCAL JURISDICTION HAS FOUR OR THREE LEVELS (238) GES,EA	0.78 CF 72	29 56 1 16 XSQ= 4.16 PHI= 0.202 XP = 0.0413
109	TEND LESS TO BE THCSE WHERE CASTES ARE ABSENT (317)	0.57 OF 28	109	TEND MORE TO BE THOSE WHERE CASTES ARE ABSENT (317)	0.91 OF 69	12 6 16 63 XSQ= 13.20 PHI= 0.369 XP = 0.0003
110	TILT TCWARD BEING THCSE WHERE SLAVERY IS PRESENT (163)	0.71 OF 28	110	TILT TOWARD BEING THOSE WHERE SLAVERY IS ABSENT (218)	0.54 CF 69	20 32 8 37 XSQ= 4.07 PHI= 0.205 XP = 0.0437
128	TILT TCWARD BEING THCSE WHERE, IF SUBSISTENCE IS PRIMARILY BY AGRICULTURE, THE WCRK IS MAINLY DCNE BY FEMALES (37)	0.57 OF 14	128	TILT TOWARD BEING THOSE WHERE, IF SUBSISTENCE IS PRIMARILY BY AGRICULTURE, THE WORK IS MAINLY DONE BY MALES (40)	0.78 OF 23	6 18 8 5 XSQ= 3.36 PHI= -0.301 EP = 0.0395
186	TEND TC BE THOSE WHERE THE KIN GRCUP IS EXCLUSIVELY PATRILINEAL (150)	0.65 OF 31	186	TEND TO BE THOSE WHERE THE KIN GROUP IS OTHER THAN EXCLUSIVELY PATRILINEAL (250)	0.74 CF 73	20 19 11 54 XSQ= 12.16 PHI= 0.342 XP = 0.0005
188	LEAN MORE TOWARC BEING THCSE WHERE THE KIN GRCUP IS OTHER THAN EXCLUSIVELY CCGNATIC (252)	0.84 OF 31	188	LEAN LESS TOWARD BEING THOSE WHERE THE KIN GROUP IS OTHER THAN EXCLUSIVELY COGNATIC (252)	0.55 CF 73	5 33 26 40 XSQ= 6.73 PHI= -0.254 XP = 0.0095

No.	Statement	Proportion	No.	Statement	Proportion	Statistics
190	TILT MORE TOWARD BEING THOSE WHERE THE KIN GROUP IS PATRILINEAL OR DOUBLE-DESCENT, RATHER THAN MATRILINEAL (186)	0.92 OF 26	190	TILT LESS TOWARD BEING THOSE WHERE THE KIN GROUP IS PATRILINEAL OR DOUBLE-DESCENT, RATHER THAN MATRILINEAL (186)	0.61 OF 38	24 23 2 15 XSQ= 6.45 PHI= 0.317 XP = 0.0111
192	TILT MORE TOWARD BEING THOSE OTHER THAN WHERE THE ONLY KIN GROUP PRESENT IS A KINDRED OR ELSE BILATERAL DESCENT IS INFERRED (289)	0.90 OF 31	192	TILT LESS TOWARD BEING THOSE OTHER THAN WHERE THE ONLY KIN GROUP PRESENT IS A KINDRED OR ELSE BILATERAL DESCENT IS INFERRED (289)	0.67 OF 73	3 24 28 49 XSQ= 4.95 PHI= -0.218 XP = 0.0262
201	DRIFT MORE TOWARD BEING THOSE WHERE MARITAL RESIDENCE IS NON-OPTIONAL, RATHER THAN AMBILOCAL OR NEOLOCAL (334)	0.97 OF 31	201	DRIFT LESS TOWARD BEING THOSE WHERE MARITAL RESIDENCE IS NON-OPTIONAL, RATHER THAN AMBILOCAL OR NEOLOCAL (334)	0.81 OF 73	30 59 1 14 XSQ= 3.29 PHI= 0.178 XP = 0.0698
204	TILT MORE TOWARD BEING THOSE WHERE MARITAL RESIDENCE IS PATRILOCAL, VIRILOCAL, OR AVUNCULOCAL, RATHER THAN AMBILOCAL OR NEOLOCAL (270)	0.97 OF 29	204	TILT LESS TOWARD BEING THOSE WHERE MARITAL RESIDENCE IS PATRILOCAL, VIRILOCAL, OR AVUNCULOCAL, RATHER THAN AMBILOCAL OR NEOLOCAL (270)	0.74 OF 54	28 40 1 14 XSQ= 5.01 PHI= 0.246 XP = 0.0252
209	TILT MORE TOWARD BEING THOSE WHERE MARITAL RESIDENCE IS PATRILOCAL, VIRILOCAL, OR AVUNCULOCAL, RATHER THAN MATRILOCAL OR UXORILOCAL (270)	0.93 OF 30	209	TILT LESS TOWARD BEING THOSE WHERE MARITAL RESIDENCE IS PATRILOCAL, VIRILOCAL, OR AVUNCULOCAL, RATHER THAN MATRILOCAL OR UXORILOCAL (270)	0.68 OF 59	28 40 2 19 XSQ= 5.85 PHI= 0.256 XP = 0.0156
210	IN ALL CASES ARE THOSE WHERE MARITAL RESIDENCE IS PATRILOCAL, RATHER THAN MATRILOCAL (169)	1.00 OF 21	210	LEAN LESS TOWARD BEING THOSE WHERE MARITAL RESIDENCE IS PATRILOCAL, RATHER THAN MATRILOCAL (169)	0.67 OF 30	21 20 0 10 XSQ= 6.72 PHI= 0.363 XP = 0.0095
242	TILT MORE TOWARD BEING THOSE WHERE MARRIAGE IS COMMONLY OR OCCASIONALLY POLYGYNOUS, RATHER THAN MONOGAMOUS (314)	0.97 OF 30	242	TILT LESS TOWARD BEING THOSE WHERE MARRIAGE IS COMMONLY OR OCCASIONALLY POLYGYNOUS, RATHER THAN MONOGAMOUS (314)	0.78 OF 72	29 56 1 16 XSQ= 4.16 PHI= 0.202 XP = 0.0413
263	TILT TOWARD BEING THOSE WHERE WIVES ARE OBTAINED BY RELATIVELY DIFFICULT MEANS, NAMELY BY BRIDE-PRICE, BRIDE-SERVICE, OR EXCHANGING A FEMALE RELATIVE (233)	0.74 OF 31	263	TILT TOWARD BEING THOSE WHERE WIVES ARE OBTAINED BY RELATIVELY EASY MEANS, NAMELY BY TOKEN BRIDE-PRICE, GIFT EXCHANGE, ABSENCE OF ANY CONSIDERATION, OR RECEIPT OF DOWRY (162)	0.53 OF 72	23 34 8 38 XSQ= 5.33 PHI= 0.228 XP = 0.0209
299	LEAN LESS TOWARD BEING THOSE WHERE THE POST-PARTUM SEX TABOO LASTS ONE YEAR OR LESS (89)	0.53 OF 19	299	LEAN MORE TOWARD BEING THOSE WHERE THE POST-PARTUM SEX TABOO LASTS ONE YEAR OR LESS (89)	0.94 OF 31	9 2 10 29 XSQ= 9.23 PHI= 0.430 XP = 0.0024

314	TILT TCWARD BEING THOSE WHERE THE INCIDENCE OF MOTHER-CHILD HOUSEHOLDS IS HIGH (19) W-D,S	0.50 OF 10	314	TILT TOWARD BEING THOSE WHERE THE INCIDENCE OF MOTHER-CHILD HOUSEHOLDS IS LOW (61) W-D,S	0.89 OF 19	5 2 5 17 XSQ= 3.63 PHI= 0.354 EP = 0.0302
377	TEND TC BE THCSE WHERE MALE GENITAL MUTILATION IS PRESENT (83)	0.57 OF 28	377	TEND TO BE THOSE WHERE MALE GENITAL MUTILATION IS ABSENT (242)	0.86 OF 72	16 10 12 62 XSQ= 17.42 PHI= 0.417 XP = 0.0000
400	IN ALL CASES ARE THCSE WHERE HOMCSEXUAL ACTIVITY IS PERMITTED (36) F-B	1.00 OF 6	400	DRIFT TOWARD BEING THOSE WHERE HOMOSEXUAL ACTIVITY IS PROHIBITED (22) F-B	0.50 OF 16	0 8 6 8 XSQ= 2.80 PHI= -0.357 EP = 0.0511
405	DRIFT TCWARD BEING THCSE WHERE EXPLANATICNS CF ILLNESS OF A DEPENDENCE NATURE ARE ABSENT (27) W-C	0.75 OF 8	405	DRIFT TOWARD BEING THOSE WHERE EXPLANATIONS OF ILLNESS OF A DEPENDENCE NATURE ARE PRESENT (34) W-C	0.73 OF 11	2 8 6 3 XSQ= 2.53 PHI= -0.365 EP = 0.0698
426	TILT MORE TOWARD BEING THCSE WHERE A HIGH GCD IS PRESENT (156) GES,EA	0.81 OF 27	426	TILT LESS TOWARD BEING THOSE WHERE A HIGH GOD IS PRESENT (156) GES,EA	0.56 OF 64	22 36 5 28 XSQ= 4.20 PHI= 0.215 XP = 0.0405
446	IN ALL CASES ARE THCSE WHERE WITCHCRAFT IS SIGNIFICANTLY PRESENT (14) GES	1.00 OF 2	446	DRIFT TOWARD BEING THOSE WHERE WITCHCRAFT IS MODERATELY PRESENT OR ABSENT (24) GES	0.88 OF 8	2 1 0 7 XSQ= 2.41 PHI= 0.491 EP = 0.0667
458	TEND TO BE THCSE WHERE GAMES, IF PRESENT, INCLUDE GAMES OF STRATEGY (52) R-A-B,EA	0.81 OF 16	458	TEND TO BE THOSE WHERE GAMES, IF PRESENT, DO NOT INCLUDE GAMES OF STRATEGY (119) R-A-B,EA	0.73 OF 49	13 13 3 36 XSQ= 12.85 PHI= 0.445 XP = 0.0003
460	IN ALL CASES ARE THOSE WHERE GAMES, IF PRESENT, ARE NCT LIMITED TC GAMES OF SKILL CNLY (104) R-A-B,EA	1.00 OF 16	460	LEAN LESS TOWARD BEING THOSE WHERE GAMES, IF PRESENT, ARE NOT LIMITED TO GAMES OF SKILL ONLY (104) R-A-B,EA	0.61 OF 49	0 19 16 30 XSQ= 6.99 PHI= -0.328 XP = 0.0082
476	DRIFT TCWARD BEING THCSE WHERE THE DEGREE OF INSCBRIETY IS MODERATE CR SLIGHT (18) CH	0.63 OF 8	476	DRIFT TOWARD BEING THOSE WHERE THE DEGREE OF INSOBRIETY IS STRONG (31) DH	0.83 OF 18	3 15 5 3 XSQ= 3.52 PHI= -0.368 EP = 0.0601

130 CULTURES
WHERE LEATHER WORKING IS
MAINLY DONE BY MALES (39)

130 CULTURES
WHERE LEATHER WORKING IS
MAINLY DONE BY FEMALES (45)

BACKGROUND ON PAGE 95

BOTH SUBJECT AND PREDICATE

39 IN LEFT COLUMN

ALBANIANS	ATSUGEWI	AYMARA	AZTEC	BAMBARA	BRAZILIANS	CHIRIGUANO	CHORTI	DIEGUENO	DOGON
EGYPTIANS	GANDA	GOAJIRO	HUTSUL	KHALKA	KIKUYU	KUNG	LOZI	MARICOPA	MOSSI
NAVAHO	NOMLAKI	NUPE	NURI	NYORO	PAPAGO	RIFFIANS	SIWANS	SOMALI	SWAZI
TALLENSI	TANALA	TECA	TERENA	TRISTAN	TUBATULABAL	WASHO	WOLOF	YUROK	

45 IN RIGHT COLUMN

ABIPON	ARAUCANIANS	CHAMACOCO	CHEYENNE	CHIR-APACHE	CHOROTI	CHUKCHEE	COMANCHE	COPR ESKIMO	CREE
CREEK	CROW	DELAWARE	EYAK	FOX	GILYAK	GROS VENTRE	HAIDA	HASINAI	HURON
ILA	INGALIK	KASKA	KIOW-APACHE	KORYAK	KUTENAI	MATACO	MIAMI	NABESNA	NAMA
NANDI	NUNIVAK	OJIBWA	OMAHA	ONA	RWALA	SAMOYED	SARSI	SONGHAI	TAREUMIUT
TEHUELCHE	TWANA	UTE	YAHGAN	YAKUT					

56 EXCLUDED BECAUSE IRRELEVANT

ALACALUF	AMERICANS	ANDAMANESE	ARANDA	AZANDE	BAJUN	BLACK CARIB	CARIB	CHENCHU	CZECHS
DUTCH	ELLICE	GARO	GILBERTESE	HAWAIIANS	INCA	JAVANESE	KAPAUKU	KERAKI	KURTATCHI
LAKHER	LAU	LESU	LHOTA NAGA	MANGAIANS	MANIHIKI	MARQUESANS	MARSHALLESE	MONGO	MURNGIN
NYAKYUSA	ONTONG-JAVA	PALIKUR	PONAPEANS	PUKAPUKA	RAROIANS	SAGADA	SAMOANS	SENIANG	SIRIONO
TALAMANCA	TAPIRAPE	THONGA	TIKOPIA	TIMBIRA	TOKELAU	TROBRIAND	TRUKESE	TUPINAMBA	ULAWANS
WITOTO	WOGEO	WOLEAIANS	YABARANA	YAO	YAPESE				

260 EXCLUDED BECAUSE UNASCERTAINED

---

3 TILT LESS TOWARD BEING THOSE LOCATED OUTSIDE OF AFRICA (320) 0.72 OF 39

3 TILT MORE TOWARD BEING THOSE LOCATED OUTSIDE OF AFRICA (320) 0.93 OF 45

11	3
28	42

XSQ= 5.51
PHI= 0.256
XP = 0.0189

TILT LESS TOWARD BEING THOSE LOCATED OUTSIDE OF THE CIRCUM-MEDITERRANEAN (355) 0.74 OF 39

4 TILT MORE TOWARD BEING THOSE LOCATED OUTSIDE OF THE CIRCUM-MEDITERRANEAN (355) 0.96 OF 45

10	2
29	43

XSQ= 6.03
PHI= 0.268
XP = 0.0140

8	LEAN TOWARD BEING THOSE LOCATED OUTSIDE OF NORTH AMERICA (330)	0.74 OF 39	8	LEAN TOWARD BEING THOSE LOCATED IN NORTH AMERICA (70)	0.60 OF 45	10 27 29 18 XSQ= 8.66 PHI= -0.321 XP = 0.0032
13	TEND TO BE THOSE WHERE THE LATITUDE IS LESS THAN FORTY DEGREES (329)	0.87 OF 39	13	TEND TO BE THOSE WHERE THE LATITUDE IS FORTY DEGREES OR GREATER (71)	0.62 OF 45	5 28 34 17 XSQ= 19.36 PHI= -0.480 XP = 0.0000
14	TEND TO BE THOSE WHERE THE LATITUDE IS LESS THAN THIRTY DEGREES (281)	0.62 OF 39	14	TEND TO BE THOSE WHERE THE LATITUDE IS THIRTY DEGREES OR GREATER (119)	0.82 OF 45	15 37 24 8 XSQ= 15.16 PHI= -0.425 XP = 0.0001
42	TILT LESS TOWARD BEING THOSE WHERE THE NATURAL ENVIRONMENT IS OTHER THAN TROPICAL OR SUB-TROPICAL RAIN FOREST, OR MONSOON FOREST (244) FWM	0.87 OF 39	42	IN ALL CASES ARE THOSE WHERE THE NATURAL ENVIRONMENT IS OTHER THAN TROPICAL OR SUB-TROPICAL RAIN FOREST, OR MONSOON FOREST (244) FWM	1.00 OF 45	5 0 34 45 XSQ= 4.06 PHI= 0.220 XP = 0.0440
44	TEND TO BE THOSE WHERE SETTLEMENTS ARE FIXED (222)	0.64 OF 39	44	TEND TO BE THOSE WHERE SETTLEMENTS ARE NON-FIXED (110)	0.81 OF 42	25 8 14 34 XSQ= 15.19 PHI= 0.433 XP = 0.0001
46	LEAN TOWARD BEING THOSE OTHER THAN WHERE SETTLEMENTS ARE NON-FIXED AND MOVEMENT IS NOMADIC (260)	0.74 OF 39	46	LEAN TOWARD BEING THOSE WHERE SETTLEMENTS ARE NON-FIXED AND MOVEMENT IS NOMADIC (72)	0.62 OF 42	10 26 29 16 XSQ= 9.35 PHI= -0.340 XP = 0.0022
51	TEND TO BE THOSE WHERE SUBSISTENCE IS PRIMARILY BY FOOD PRODUCTION -- I. E., AGRICULTURE OR HUSBANDRY -- RATHER THAN BY GATHERING (253)	0.67 OF 39	51	TEND TO BE THOSE WHERE SUBSISTENCE IS PRIMARILY BY FOOD GATHERING -- I. E., HUNTING, FISHING, OR COLLECTING -- RATHER THAN FOOD PRODUCTION (147)	0.89 OF 45	26 5 13 40 XSQ= 25.36 PHI= 0.549 XP = 0.0000
53	TILT TOWARD BEING THOSE WHERE FOOD PRODUCTION IS BY INTENSIVE AGRICULTURE, RATHER THAN BY SIMPLE AGRICULTURE OR INCIPIENT FOOD PRODUCTION (91)	0.64 OF 28	53	TILT TOWARD BEING THOSE WHERE FOOD PRODUCTION IS BY SIMPLE AGRICULTURE OR INCIPIENT FOOD PRODUCTION, RATHER THAN BY INTENSIVE AGRICULTURE (147)	0.79 OF 14	18 3 10 11 XSQ= 5.25 PHI= 0.354 XP = 0.0219
54	LEAN TOWARD BEING THOSE WHERE FOOD PRODUCTION IS BY INTENSIVE OR SIMPLE AGRICULTURE, RATHER THAN BY INCIPIENT FOOD PRODUCTION (192)	0.82 OF 28	54	LEAN TOWARD BEING THOSE WHERE FOOD PRODUCTION IS BY INCIPIENT FOOD PRODUCTION, RATHER THAN BY INTENSIVE OR SIMPLE AGRICULTURE (46)	0.71 OF 14	23 4 5 10 XSQ= 9.45 PHI= 0.474 XP = 0.0021

56	DRIFT TOWARD BEING THOSE 0.50 OF 10 WHERE FOOD PRODUCTION IS BY SIMPLE AGRICULTURE, RATHER THAN BY INCIPIENT FOOD PRODUCTION (101)	56	DRIFT TOWARD BEING THOSE 0.91 OF 11 WHERE FOOD PRODUCTION IS BY INCIPIENT FOOD PRODUCTION, RATHER THAN BY SIMPLE AGRICULTURE (46)	5 1 5 10 XSQ= 2.52 PHI= 0.347 EP = 0.0635
62	DRIFT TOWARD BEING THOSE 0.72 OF 39 WHERE HUSBANDRY OF SOME KIND IS PRESENT (228)	62	DRIFT TOWARD BEING THOSE 0.51 OF 45 WHERE HUSBANDRY OF ANY KIND IS ABSENT (172)	28 22 11 23 XSQ= 3.65 PHI= 0.208 XP = 0.0561
71	LEAN TOWARD BEING THOSE 0.64 OF 39 WHERE METAL WORKING IS PRESENT (98)	71	LEAN TOWARD BEING THOSE 0.73 OF 45 WHERE METAL WORKING IS ABSENT (153)	25 12 14 33 XSQ= 10.41 PHI= 0.352 XP = 0.0013
73	TILT TOWARD BEING THOSE 0.61 OF 38 WHERE WEAVING IS PRESENT (118)	73	TILT TOWARD BEING THOSE 0.68 OF 44 WHERE WEAVING IS ABSENT (130)	23 14 15 30 XSQ= 5.68 PHI= 0.263 XP = 0.0172
81	TILT TOWARD BEING THOSE 0.53 OF 32 WHERE A CITY OR TOWN IS PRESENT, OR THE AVERAGE COMMUNITY SIZE IS 200 OR GREATER (89)	81	TILT TOWARD BEING THOSE 0.81 OF 27 WHERE NO CITY OR TOWN IS PRESENT, AND THE AVERAGE COMMUNITY SIZE IS SMALLER THAN 200 (135)	17 5 15 22 XSQ= 6.09 PHI= 0.321 XP = 0.0136
84	LEAN LESS TOWARD BEING THOSE 0.77 OF 30 WHERE THE LEVEL OF POLITICAL INTEGRATION IS THE LITTLE STATE, THE MINIMAL STATE, THE AUTONOMOUS COMMUNITY, OR THE FAMILY (262) GPM	84	IN ALL CASES ARE THOSE 1.00 OF 37 WHERE THE LEVEL OF POLITICAL INTEGRATION IS THE LITTLE STATE, THE MINIMAL STATE, THE AUTONOMOUS COMMUNITY, OR THE FAMILY (262) GPM	7 0 23 37 XSQ= 7.31 PHI= 0.330 XP = 0.0069
85	DRIFT LESS TOWARD BEING THOSE 0.70 OF 30 WHERE THE LEVEL OF POLITICAL INTEGRATION IS THE MINIMAL STATE, THE AUTONOMOUS COMMUNITY, OR THE FAMILY (234) GPM	85	DRIFT MORE TOWARD BEING THOSE 0.89 OF 37 WHERE THE LEVEL OF POLITICAL INTEGRATION IS THE MINIMAL STATE, THE AUTONOMOUS COMMUNITY, OR THE FAMILY (234) GPM	9 4 21 33 XSQ= 2.77 PHI= 0.203 XP = 0.0960
90	TILT MORE TOWARD BEING THOSE 0.95 OF 19 WHERE, IF A HEREDITARY HEADMANSHIP IS PRESENT, SUCCESSION IS PATRILINEAL, RATHER THAN MATRILINEAL (127)	90	TILT LESS TOWARD BEING THOSE 0.60 OF 15 WHERE, IF A HEREDITARY HEADMANSHIP IS PRESENT, SUCCESSION IS PATRILINEAL, RATHER THAN MATRILINEAL (127)	18 9 1 6 XSQ= 4.24 PHI= 0.353 EP = 0.0282
94	TILT LESS TOWARD BEING THOSE 0.81 OF 37 WHERE THE HIERARCHY OF NATIONAL JURISDICTION HAS TWO, ONE, OR NO LEVELS (296) GES,EA	94	TILT MORE TOWARD BEING THOSE 0.98 OF 43 WHERE THE HIERARCHY OF NATIONAL JURISDICTION HAS TWO, ONE, OR NO LEVELS (296) GES,EA	7 1 30 42 XSQ= 4.38 PHI= 0.234 XP = 0.0364

95	LEAN LESS TOWARC BEING THCSE 0.65 OF 37 WHERE THE HIERARCHY OF NATICNAL JURISDICTICN HAS CNE OR NC LEVELS (254) GES,EA	95	LEAN MORE TOWARD BEING THOSE 0.93 OF 43 WHERE THE HIERARCHY OF NATIONAL JURISDICTICN HAS ONE OR NO LEVELS (254) GES,EA	13 3 24 40 XSQ= 8.17 PHI= 0.320 XP = 0.0042
97	DRIFT LESS TCWARC BEING THCSE 0.76 OF 38 WHERE THE HIERARCHY CF LOCAL JURISDICTION HAS THREE OR TWO LEVELS (273) GES,EA	97	DRIFT MORE TOWARD BEING THCSE 0.93 CF 43 WHERE THE HIERARCHY OF LOCAL JURISDICTION HAS THREE OR TWO LEVELS (273) GES,EA	9 3 29 40 XSQ= 3.24 PHI= 0.200 XP = 0.0720
102	TILT TOWARD BEING THOSE 0.73 OF 37 WHERE CLASS STRATIFICATION IS PRESENT (203)	102	TILT TOWARD BEING THOSE 0.58 OF 45 WHERE CLASS STRATIFICATICN IS ABSENT (180)	27 19 10 26 XSQ= 6.60 PHI= 0.284 XP = 0.0102
109	LEAN LESS TCWARC BEING THCSE 0.72 OF 36 WHERE CASTES ARE ABSENT (317)	109	LEAN MORE TOWARD BEING THOSE 0.96 CF 45 WHERE CASTES ARE ABSENT (317)	10 2 26 43 XSQ= 6.88 PHI= 0.291 XP = 0.0087
120	IN ALL CASES ARE THOSE 1.00 OF 10 WHERE THE CRAFT SPECIALIZATION SCORE IS HIGH CR MEDIUM (36) WME	120	TILT TOWARD BEING THOSE 0.50 CF 6 WHERE THE CRAFT SPECIALIZATICN SCORE IS LOW (17) WME	10 3 0 3 XSQ= 3.31 PHI= 0.455 EP = 0.0357
131	LEAN MCRE TOWARC BEING THCSE 0.92 OF 24 WHERE THE CONSTRUCTION OF PERMANENT HOUSES CR THE ERECTICN CF TEMPORARY CWELLINGS IS MAINLY DCNE BY MALES (136)	131	LEAN LESS TOWARD BEING THCSE 0.54 CF 26 WHERE THE CONSTRUCTION OF PERMANENT HOUSES OR THE ERECTION OF TEMPORARY DWELLINGS IS MAINLY DONE BY MALES (136)	22 14 2 12 XSQ= 7.08 PHI= 0.376 XP = 0.0078
175	DRIFT LESS TOWARC BEING THOSE 0.64 OF 39 WHERE THE COMMUNITY IS 'KIN-HETERCGENECUS,' I. E. CTHER THAN A CLAN CCMMUNITY OR A CEME (260)	175	DRIFT MORE TOWARD BEING THCSE 0.84 OF 44 WHERE THE COMMUNITY IS 'KIN-HETEROGENEOUS,' I. E. OTHER THAN A CLAN COMMUNITY OR A DEME (260)	14 7 25 37 XSQ= 3.38 PHI= 0.202 XP = 0.0661
182	TILT TCWARD BEING THCSE 0.74 OF 39 CTHER THAN WHERE THE COMMUNITY IS STRUCTURED ON A NON-CLAN BASIS ANC AGAMCUS (256)	182	TILT TOWARD BEING THOSE 0.50 CF 44 WHERE THE COMMUNITY IS STRUCTURED ON A NON-CLAN BASIS AND AGAMOUS (126)	10 22 29 22 XSQ= 4.20 PHI= -0.225 XP = 0.0404
183	IN ALL CASES ARE THOSE 1.00 OF 25 WHERE THE LARGEST NON-CCGNATIC KIN GROUP IS SMALLER THAN A MOEITY, I. E., A PHRATRY CR SIB CR LINEAGE (218)	183	TILT LESS TOWARD BEING THOSE 0.76 CF 21 WHERE THE LARGEST NCN-COGNATIC KIN GROUP IS SMALLER THAN A MOEITY, I. E., A PHRATRY OR SIB OR LINEAGE (218)	0 5 25 16 XSQ= 4.45 PHI= -0.311 XP = 0.0350

184	TILT MORE TOWARD BEING THOSE 0.88 OF 25 WHERE THE LARGEST NON-COGNATIC KIN GROUP IS SMALLER THAN A PHRATRY, I. E. A SIB OR LINEAGE (175)	184	TILT LESS TOWARD BEING THOSE 0.52 OF 21 WHERE THE LARGEST NON-COGNATIC KIN GROUP IS SMALLER THAN A PHRATRY, I. E. A SIB OR LINEAGE (175)	3 10 22 11 XSQ= 5.49 PHI= -0.346 XP = 0.0191
186	LEAN TOWARD BEING THOSE 0.51 OF 39 WHERE THE KIN GROUP IS EXCLUSIVELY PATRILINEAL (150)	186	LEAN TOWARD BEING THOSE 0.82 OF 45 WHERE THE KIN GROUP IS OTHER THAN EXCLUSIVELY PATRILINEAL (250)	20 8 19 37 XSQ= 9.10 PHI= 0.329 XP = 0.0026
190	TILT MORE TOWARD BEING THOSE 0.91 OF 23 WHERE THE KIN GROUP IS PATRILINEAL OR DOUBLE-DESCENT, RATHER THAN MATRILINEAL (186)	190	TILT LESS TOWARD BEING THOSE 0.62 OF 21 WHERE THE KIN GROUP IS PATRILINEAL OR DOUBLE-DESCENT, RATHER THAN MATRILINEAL (186)	21 13 2 8 XSQ= 3.86 PHI= 0.296 XP = 0.0495
196	TEND TO BE THOSE 0.86 OF 35 WHERE INDIVIDUAL RIGHTS IN REAL PROPERTY, AND RULES FOR INHERITANCE, ARE PRESENT (194)	196	TEND TO BE THOSE 0.72 OF 36 WHERE INDIVIDUAL RIGHTS IN REAL PROPERTY, OR RULES FOR INHERITANCE, ARE ABSENT (87)	30 10 5 26 XSQ= 21.92 PHI= 0.556 XP = 0.0000
198	IN ALL CASES ARE THOSE 1.00 OF 26 WHERE RULES FOR THE INHERITANCE OF REAL PROPERTY, IF PRESENT, FAVOR THE MALE HEIR OR LINE, RATHER THAN THE FEMALE (144)	198	DRIFT LESS TOWARD BEING THOSE 0.78 OF 9 WHERE RULES FOR THE INHERITANCE OF REAL PROPERTY, IF PRESENT, FAVOR THE MALE HEIR OR LINE, RATHER THAN THE FEMALE (144)	26 7 0 2 XSQ= 2.70 PHI= 0.278 EP = 0.0605
207	TILT TOWARD BEING THOSE 0.88 OF 8 WHERE MARITAL RESIDENCE IS AMBILOCAL OR NEOLOCAL, RATHER THAN MATRILOCAL OR UXORILOCAL (64)	207	TILT TOWARD BEING THOSE 0.62 OF 21 WHERE MARITAL RESIDENCE IS MATRILOCAL OR UXORILOCAL, RATHER THAN AMBILOCAL OR NEOLOCAL (64)	1 13 7 8 XSQ= 3.86 PHI= -0.365 EP = 0.0352
209	LEAN MORE TOWARD BEING THOSE 0.97 OF 32 WHERE MARITAL RESIDENCE IS PATRILOCAL, VIRILOCAL, OR AVUNCULOCAL, RATHER THAN MATRILOCAL OR UXORILOCAL (270)	209	LEAN LESS TOWARD BEING THOSE 0.65 OF 37 WHERE MARITAL RESIDENCE IS PATRILOCAL, VIRILOCAL, OR AVUNCULOCAL, RATHER THAN MATRILOCAL OR UXORILOCAL (270)	31 24 1 13 XSQ= 8.98 PHI= 0.361 XP = 0.0027
210	TILT MORE TOWARD BEING THOSE 0.96 OF 23 WHERE MARITAL RESIDENCE IS PATRILOCAL, RATHER THAN MATRILOCAL (169)	210	TILT LESS TOWARD BEING THOSE 0.69 OF 13 WHERE MARITAL RESIDENCE IS PATRILOCAL, RATHER THAN MATRILOCAL (169)	22 9 1 4 XSQ= 2.89 PHI= 0.283 EP = 0.0470
314	TILT LESS TOWARD BEING THOSE 0.60 OF 10 WHERE THE INCIDENCE OF MOTHER-CHILD HOUSEHOLDS IS LOW (61) W-D,S	314	IN ALL CASES ARE THOSE 1.00 OF 11 WHERE THE INCIDENCE OF MOTHER-CHILD HOUSEHOLDS IS LOW (61) W-D,S	4 0 6 11 XSQ= 3.15 PHI= 0.387 EP = 0.0351

No.			No.			
315	TILT TOWARD BEING THOSE WHERE MOTHER AND NURSING CHILD CUSTOMARILY SLEEP IN THE SAME BED (37) W-C,S	0.88 OF 8	315	TILT TOWARD BEING THOSE WHERE MOTHER AND NURSING CHILD CUSTOMARILY SLEEP IN DIFFERENT BEDS (14) W-D,S	0.75 OF 8	7 2 1 6 XSQ= 4.06 PHI= 0.504 EP = 0.0406
318	TILT TOWARD BEING THOSE WHERE THE OVERALL INDULGENCE OF THE INFANT IS LOW (31) B-B-C	0.88 OF 8	318	TILT TOWARD BEING THOSE WHERE THE OVERALL INDULGENCE OF THE INFANT IS HIGH (40) B-B-C	0.69 OF 13	1 9 7 4 XSQ= 4.32 PHI= -0.453 EP = 0.0237
336	DRIFT TOWARD BEING THOSE WHERE THE TOTAL POSITIVE PRESSURE TOWARD DEVELOPING RESPONSIBLE BEHAVIOR IN THE CHILD IS HIGH (43) B-B-C	0.88 OF 8	336	DRIFT TOWARD BEING THOSE WHERE THE TOTAL POSITIVE PRESSURE TOWARD DEVELOPING RESPONSIBLE BEHAVIOR IN THE CHILD IS LOW (32) B-B-C	0.54 OF 13	7 6 1 7 XSQ= 2.05 PHI= 0.312 EP = 0.0850
337	DRIFT TOWARD BEING THOSE WHERE THE CHILD'S INFERRED ANXIETY OVER NON-PERFORMANCE OF RESPONSIBLE BEHAVIOR IS HIGH (38) B-B-C	0.75 OF 8	337	DRIFT TOWARD BEING THOSE WHERE THE CHILD'S INFERRED ANXIETY OVER NON-PERFORMANCE OF RESPONSIBLE BEHAVIOR IS LOW (35) B-B-C	0.69 OF 13	6 4 2 9 XSQ= 2.31 PHI= 0.332 EP = 0.0805
344	DRIFT TOWARD BEING THOSE WHERE THE TOTAL POSITIVE PRESSURE TOWARD DEVELOPING SELF-RELIANT BEHAVIOR IN THE CHILD IS LOW (40) B-B-C	0.75 OF 8	344	DRIFT TOWARD BEING THOSE WHERE THE TOTAL POSITIVE PRESSURE TOWARD DEVELOPING SELF-RELIANT BEHAVIOR IN THE CHILD IS HIGH (36) B-B-C	0.69 OF 13	2 9 6 4 XSQ= 2.31 PHI= -0.332 EP = 0.0805
353	DRIFT TOWARD BEING THOSE WHERE THE CHILD'S INFERRED ANXIETY OVER NON-PERFORMANCE OF OBEDIENT BEHAVIOR IS HIGH (42) B-B-C	0.88 OF 8	353	DRIFT TOWARD BEING THOSE WHERE THE CHILD-S INFERRED ANXIETY OVER NON-PERFORMANCE OF OBEDIENT BEHAVIOR IS LOW (32) B-B-C	0.54 OF 13	7 6 1 7 XSQ= 2.05 PHI= 0.312 EP = 0.0850
377	LEAN LESS TOWARD BEING THOSE WHERE MALE GENITAL MUTILATION IS ABSENT (242)	0.66 OF 38	377	LEAN MORE TOWARD BEING THOSE WHERE MALE GENITAL MUTILATION IS ABSENT (242)	0.93 OF 43	13 3 25 40 XSQ= 7.80 PHI= 0.310 XP = 0.0052
440	IN ALL CASES ARE THOSE WHERE FEAR OF SPIRITS IS HIGH (32) W-C	1.00 OF 4	440	DRIFT TOWARD BEING THOSE WHERE FEAR OF SPIRITS IS LOW (29) W-C	0.75 OF 8	4 2 0 6 XSQ= 3.38 PHI= 0.530 EP = 0.0606
444	LEAN TOWARD BEING THOSE WHERE THE USE OF DREAMS TO SEEK AND CONTROL SUPERNATURAL POWERS IS LOW (27) RGC	0.80 OF 10	444	LEAN TOWARD BEING THOSE WHERE THE USE OF DREAMS TO SEEK AND CONTROL SUPERNATURAL POWERS IS HIGH (28) RGD	0.83 OF 12	2 10 8 2 XSQ= 6.45 PHI= -0.542 EP = 0.0083

```
458  LEAN LESS TOWARD BEING THOSE   0.56 OF  25        458  LEAN MORE TOWARD BEING THOSE   0.91 OF  34          11    3
     WHERE GAMES, IF PRESENT,                               WHERE GAMES, IF PRESENT,                                14   31
     DO NOT INCLUDE                                         DO NOT INCLUDE                                   XSQ=     8.00
     GAMES OF STRATEGY  (119) R-A-B,EA                      GAMES OF STRATEGY  (119) R-A-B,EA                PHI=    0.368
                                                                                                             XP =   0.0047
```

131 CULTURES
WHERE THE CONSTRUCTION OF PERMANENT HOUSES
OR THE ERECTION OF TEMPORARY DWELLINGS
IS MAINLY DONE BY MALES (136)

131 CULTURES
WHERE THE CONSTRUCTION OF PERMANENT HOUSES
OR THE ERECTION OF TEMPORARY DWELLINGS
IS MAINLY DONE BY FEMALES (21)

BACKGROUND ON PAGE 95

BOTH SUBJECT AND PREDICATE

136 IN LEFT COLUMN

ALACALUF	ALORESE	AMBA	AMERICANS	ARAUCANIANS	ATSUGEWI	AYMARA	AZANDE	AZTEC	BACAIRI
BAMBARA	BAMILEKE	BHIL	BLACK CARIB	BORORO	BRAZILIANS	BULGARIANS	BURUSHO	CAGABA	CALLINAGO
CAMAYURA	CARIB	CHENCHU	CHIRIGUANO	CHORTI	COORG	COPR ESKIMO	CREEK	CUNA	CZECHS
DARD	DELAWARE	DUTCH	ELLICE	EYAK	GANDA	GARO	GILYAK	GOAJIRO	HAIDA
HASINAI	HAWAIIANS	HUICHOL	HURON	HUTSUL	IBAN	INCA	INGALIK	JAPANESE	JAVANESE
JIVARO	KACHIN	KAPAUKU	KASKA	KATAB	KERAKI	KHALKA	KHASI	KOHISTANI	KOREANS
KURTATCHI	KWAKIUTL	LAKHER	LAMET	LAU	LEPCHA	LESU	LHOTA NAGA	LOLO	MACASSARESE
MANGAIANS	MACRI	MARICOPA	MARQUESANS	MARSHALLESE	MATAKAM	MBUNDU	MIAO	MNONG GAR	MONGO
MOSSI	MUNDURUCU	NAMBICUARA	NATCHEZ	NAVAHO	NICOBARESE	NOMLAKI	NUNIVAK	NYAKYUSA	OKINAWANS
PAEZ	PALAUANS	PALIKUR	PUKAPUKA	PURARI	RAROIANS	RIFFIANS	SAGADA	SAMOANS	SERBS
SIRIONO	SYRIANS	TANALA	TOTONAC	TARAHUMARA	TENINO	TERENA	THONGA	TIKOPIA	TIMBIRA
TIV	TODA	TUPINAMBA	TRISTAN	TROBRIAND	TRUKESE	TRUMAI	TSHIMSHIAN	TUBATULABAL	TUCANO
TUCUNA	TUPINAMBA	TWANA	ULAWANS	WITOTO	WOGEO	WOLEAIANS	WOLOF	YABARANA	YAGUA
YAKUT	YAO	YARURO	YORUBA	YUKI	YUROK				

21 IN RIGHT COLUMN

ANDAMANESE	ARANDA	AWEIKOMA	CHEYENNE	CHIR-APACHE	CROW	GROS VENTRE	KAZAK	KIOW-APACHE	KUNG
MATACO	MBUTI	MURNGIN	NABESNA	RWALA	SAMOYED	SARSI	SEMANG	SOMALI	TEHUELCHE
UTE									

29 EXCLUDED BECAUSE AMBIGUOUS

AINU	BASSERI	BEMBA	BIRIFOR	CHOROTI	CHUKCHEE	CREE	GOND	ILA	KIKUYU
KUTENAI	LOZI	MISKITO	NAMA	NANDI	NUPE	NYORO	OMAHA	ONTONG-JAVA	RUNDI
SANTAL	SHILLUK	SONGHAI	SWAZI	TALLENSI	TAREUMIUT	VENDA	WASHO	YAHGAN	

214 EXCLUDED BECAUSE UNASCERTAINED

---

8 DRIFT MORE TOWARD BEING THOSE LOCATED OUTSIDE OF NORTH AMERICA (330) — 0.81 OF 136

8 DRIFT LESS TOWARD BEING THOSE LOCATED OUTSIDE OF NORTH AMERICA (330) — 0.62 OF 21

26	8
110	13
XSQ=	2.82
PHI=	-0.134
XP =	0.0929

14 TILT TOWARD BEING THOSE WHERE THE LATITUDE IS LESS THAN THIRTY DEGREES (281) — 0.69 OF 136

14 TILT TOWARD BEING THOSE WHERE THE LATITUDE IS THIRTY DEGREES OR GREATER (119) — 0.57 OF 21

42	12
94	9
XSQ=	4.46
PHI=	-0.168
XP =	0.0348

15	TILT TOWARD BEING THOSE 0.54 OF 136 WHERE THE LATITUDE IS LESS THAN TWENTY DEGREES (217)	15	TILT TOWARD BEING THOSE 0.76 OF 21 WHERE THE LATITUDE IS TWENTY DEGREES OR GREATER (183)	63 16 73 5 XSQ= 5.35 PHI= -0.185 XP = 0.0207
33	LEAN MORE TOWARD BEING THOSE 0.90 OF 136 WHERE THE NATURAL ENVIRONMENT IS OTHER THAN 'VERY HARSH,' I.É., DESERT, DESERT GRASSES AND SHRUBS, TUNDRA, OR HIGH PLATEAU STEPPE (341) FWM	33	LEAN LESS TOWARD BEING THOSE 0.62 OF 21 WHERE THE NATURAL ENVIRONMENT IS OTHER THAN 'VERY HARSH,' I.E., DESERT, DESERT GRASSES AND SHRUBS, TUNDRA, OR HIGH PLATEAU STEPPE (341) FWM	14 8 122 13 XSQ= 9.48 PHI= -0.246 XP = 0.0021
36	TEND TO BE THOSE 0.83 OF 136 WHERE THE NATURAL ENVIRONMENT IS OTHER THAN 'VERY HARSH,' OR SUB-TROPICAL BUSH, OR TEMPERATE GRASSLAND (292) FWM	36	TEND TO BE THOSE 0.71 OF 21 WHERE THE NATURAL ENVIRONMENT IS 'VERY HARSH,' OR SUB-TROPICAL BUSH, OR TEMPERATE GRASSLAND (108) FWM	23 15 113 6 XSQ= 26.57 PHI= -0.411 XP = 0.0000
42	TILT LESS TOWARD BEING THOSE 0.54 OF 136 WHERE THE NATURAL ENVIRONMENT IS OTHER THAN TROPICAL OR SUB-TROPICAL RAIN FOREST, OR MONSOON FOREST (244) FWM	42	TILT MORE TOWARD BEING THOSE 0.81 OF 21 WHERE THE NATURAL ENVIRONMENT IS OTHER THAN TROPICAL OR SUB-TROPICAL RAIN FOREST, OR MONSOON FOREST (244) FWM	63 4 73 17 XSQ= 4.47 PHI= 0.169 XP = 0.0344
44	TEND TO BE THOSE 0.77 OF 134 WHERE SETTLEMENTS ARE FIXED (222)	44	IN ALL CASES ARE THOSE 1.00 OF 20 WHERE SETTLEMENTS ARE NON-FIXED (110)	103 0 31 20 XSQ= 43.02 PHI= 0.529 XP = 0.
46	TEND TO BE THOSE 0.89 OF 134 OTHER THAN WHERE SETTLEMENTS ARE NON-FIXED AND MOVEMENT IS NOMADIC (260)	46	IN ALL CASES ARE THOSE 1.00 OF 20 WHERE SETTLEMENTS ARE NON-FIXED AND MOVEMENT IS NOMADIC (72)	15 20 119 0 XSQ= 73.17 PHI= -0.689 XP = 0.
47	TEND TO BE THOSE 0.52 OF 31 WHERE, IF SETTLEMENTS ARE NON-FIXED, MOVEMENT IS NON-NOMADIC, RATHER THAN NOMADIC (38)	47	IN ALL CASES ARE THOSE 1.00 OF 20 WHERE, IF SETTLEMENTS ARE NON-FIXED, MOVEMENT IS NOMADIC, RATHER THAN NON-NOMADIC (72)	15 20 16 0 XSQ= 12.74 PHI= -0.500 XP = 0.0004
51	TEND TO BE THOSE 0.59 OF 136 WHERE SUBSISTENCE IS PRIMARILY BY FOOD PRODUCTION -- I. E., AGRICULTURE OR HUSBANDRY -- RATHER THAN BY GATHERING (253)	51	TEND TO BE THOSE 0.86 OF 21 WHERE SUBSISTENCE IS PRIMARILY BY FOOD GATHERING -- I. E., HUNTING, FISHING, OR COLLECTING -- RATHER THAN FOOD PRODUCTION (147)	80 3 56 18 XSQ= 12.75 PHI= 0.285 XP = 0.0004
63	DRIFT LESS TOWARD BEING THOSE 0.58 OF 86 WHERE HUSBANDRY, IF PRESENT, IS PRINCIPALLY IN THE FORM OF BOVINE, EQUINE, CAMEL-LIKE, OR DEER-LIKE ANIMALS, RATHER THAN PIGS, SHEEP, OR GOATS (152)	63	DRIFT MORE TOWARD BEING THOSE 0.92 OF 12 WHERE HUSBANDRY, IF PRESENT, IS PRINCIPALLY IN THE FORM OF BOVINE, EQUINE, CAMEL-LIKE, OR DEER-LIKE ANIMALS, RATHER THAN PIGS, SHEEP, OR GOATS (152)	50 11 36 1 XSQ= 3.71 PHI= -0.195 XP = 0.0540

```
71  DRIFT LESS TOWARD BEING THOSE  0.58 OF 130    71  DRIFT MORE TOWARD BEING THOSE  0.81 OF  21        54    4
    WHERE METAL WORKING IS                            WHERE METAL WORKING IS                            76   17
    ABSENT  (153)                                     ABSENT  (153)                               XSQ=     2.97
                                                                                                  PHI=    0.140
                                                                                                  XP =   0.0846

73  LEAN TOWARD BEING THOSE        0.58 OF 133    73  LEAN TOWARD BEING THOSE        0.76 OF  21        77    5
    WHERE WEAVING IS                                  WHERE WEAVING IS                                  56   16
    PRESENT  (118)                                    ABSENT  (130)                               XSQ=     7.15
                                                                                                  PHI=    0.215
                                                                                                  XP =   0.0075

74  TILT TOWARD BEING THOSE        0.64 OF 127    74  TILT TOWARD BEING THOSE        0.65 OF  20        81    7
    WHERE POTTERY IS                                  WHERE POTTERY IS                                  46   13
    PRESENT  (145)                                    ABSENT  (93)                                XSQ=     4.82
                                                                                                  PHI=    0.181
                                                                                                  XP =   0.0282

81  TILT LESS TOWARD BEING THOSE   0.63 OF  99    81  IN ALL CASES ARE THOSE         1.00 OF  14        37    0
    WHERE NO CITY OR TOWN IS PRESENT, AND             WHERE NO CITY OR TOWN IS PRESENT, AND             62   14
    THE AVERAGE COMMUNITY SIZE IS                     THE AVERAGE COMMUNITY SIZE IS               XSQ=     6.18
    SMALLER THAN 200  (135)                           SMALLER THAN 200  (135)                     PHI=    0.234
                                                                                                  XP =   0.0130

82  TEND TO BE THOSE               0.84 OF  99    82  TEND TO BE THOSE               0.71 OF  14        83    4
    WHERE A CITY OR TOWN IS PRESENT, OR               WHERE NO CITY OR TOWN IS PRESENT, AND             16   10
    THE AVERAGE COMMUNITY SIZE IS                     THE AVERAGE COMMUNITY SIZE IS               XSQ=    18.14
    FIFTY OR GREATER  (178)                           SMALLER THAN FIFTY  (46)                    PHI=    0.401
                                                                                                  XP =   0.0000

88  DRIFT TOWARD BEING THOSE       0.65 OF 104    88  DRIFT TOWARD BEING THOSE       0.64 OF  14        36    9
    WHERE, IF A HEADMANSHIP IS PRESENT,               WHERE, IF A HEADMANSHIP IS PRESENT,               68    5
    SUCCESSION IS HEREDITARY  (165)                   SUCCESSION IS NON-HEREDITARY  (106)         XSQ=     3.43
                                                                                                  PHI=   -0.171
                                                                                                  XP =   0.0639

97  DRIFT LESS TOWARD BEING THOSE  0.80 OF 133    97  IN ALL CASES ARE THOSE         1.00 OF  20        26    0
    WHERE THE HIERARCHY                               WHERE THE HIERARCHY                              107   20
    OF LOCAL JURISDICTION HAS                         OF LOCAL JURISDICTION HAS                   XSQ=     3.43
    THREE OR TWO LEVELS  (273) GES,EA                 THREE OR TWO LEVELS  (273) GES,EA           PHI=    0.150
                                                                                                  XP =   0.0642

98  LEAN TOWARD BEING THOSE        0.77 OF 133    98  LEAN TOWARD BEING THOSE        0.60 OF  20       102    8
    WHERE THE HIERARCHY                               WHERE THE HIERARCHY                               31   12
    OF LOCAL JURISDICTION HAS                         OF LOCAL JURISDICTION HAS                   XSQ=     9.84
    FOUR OR THREE LEVELS  (238) GES,EA                TWO LEVELS  (93) GES,EA                     PHI=    0.254
                                                                                                  XP =   0.0017

99  DRIFT TOWARD BEING THOSE       0.64 OF  59    99  DRIFT TOWARD BEING THOSE       0.69 OF  13        38    4
    WHERE, WITH NATIONAL HIERARCHY ABSENT,            WHERE, WITH NATIONAL HIERARCHY ABSENT,            21    9
    THE HIERARCHY OF LOCAL JURISDICTION HAS           THE HIERARCHY OF LOCAL JURISDICTION HAS     XSQ=     3.67
    FOUR OR THREE LEVELS  (93) GES,EA                 TWO LEVELS  (63) GES,EA                     PHI=    0.226
                                                                                                  XP =   0.0553
```

```
100  LEAN MORE TOWARD BEING THOSE   0.84 OF 132    100  LEAN LESS TOWARD BEING THOSE   0.55 OF  20        111   11
     WHERE HIERARCHIES ARE MORE COMPLEX THAN            WHERE HIERARCHIES ARE MORE COMPLEX THAN             21    9
     THE 'SIMPLEST,' I. E., MORE COMPLEX THAN           THE 'SIMPLEST,' I. E., MORE COMPLEX THAN      XSQ=     7.53
     TWO LOCAL LEVELS WITH                              TWO LOCAL LEVELS WITH                         PHI=    0.223
     NO NATIONAL LEVELS  (267) GES,EA                   NO NATIONAL LEVELS  (267) GES,EA              XP =   0.0061

102  TEND TO BE THOSE               0.61 OF 133    102  TEND TO BE THOSE               0.81 OF  21         81    4
     WHERE CLASS STRATIFICATION IS                      WHERE CLASS STRATIFICATION IS                       52   17
     PRESENT  (203)                                     ABSENT  (180)                                 XSQ=    11.21
                                                                                                      PHI=    0.270
                                                                                                      XP =   0.0008

130  LEAN TOWARD BEING THOSE        0.61 OF  36    130  LEAN TOWARD BEING THOSE        0.86 OF  14         22    2
     WHERE LEATHER WORKING IS                           WHERE LEATHER WORKING IS                            14   12
     MAINLY DONE BY MALES  (39)                         MAINLY DONE BY FEMALES  (45)                  XSQ=     7.08
                                                                                                      PHI=    0.376
                                                                                                      XP =   0.0078

132  DRIFT TOWARD BEING THOSE       0.76 OF  34    132  DRIFT TOWARD BEING THOSE       0.67 OF   6         26    2
     WHERE ECONOMIC EXCHANGE                            WHERE ECONOMIC EXCHANGE                              8    4
     INVOLVES THE USE OF MONEY  (37) JMH                DOES NOT INVOLVE                              XSQ=     2.70
                                                        THE USE OF MONEY  (17) JMH                    PHI=    0.260
                                                                                                      EP =   0.0548

142  DRIFT TOWARD BEING THOSE       0.76 OF  34    142  DRIFT TOWARD BEING THOSE       0.67 OF   6         26    2
     WHERE THE LEVEL OF SOCIAL SANCTION IS              WHERE THE LEVEL OF SOCIAL SANCTION IS                8    4
     PUBLIC CORPOREAL SANCTION OR                       PRIVATE SETTLEMENT, RATHER THAN               XSQ=     2.70
     PUBLIC PROPERTY SANCTION, RATHER THAN              PUBLIC CORPOREAL SANCTION OR                  PHI=    0.260
     PRIVATE SETTLEMENT  (38) JMH                       PUBLIC PROPERTY SETTLEMENT  (16) JMH          EP =   0.0548

178  TILT LESS TOWARD BEING THOSE   0.71 OF 133    178  IN ALL CASES ARE THOSE         1.00 OF  21         38    0
     WHERE THE COMMUNITY IS OTHER THAN                  WHERE THE COMMUNITY IS OTHER THAN                   95   21
     SEGMENTED ON A CLAN BASIS AND                      SEGMENTED ON A CLAN BASIS AND                 XSQ=     6.50
     NON-EXOGAMOUS  (295)                               NON-EXOGAMOUS  (295)                          PHI=    0.205
                                                                                                      XP =   0.0108

179  TILT MORE TOWARD BEING THOSE   0.88 OF 133    179  TILT LESS TOWARD BEING THOSE   0.67 OF  21         16    7
     WHERE THE COMMUNITY IS OTHER THAN                  WHERE THE COMMUNITY IS OTHER THAN                  117   14
     STRUCTURED ON A NON-CLAN BASIS AND                 STRUCTURED ON A NON-CLAN BASIS AND            XSQ=     4.91
     COMMONLY EXOGAMOUS  (340)                          COMMONLY EXOGAMOUS  (340)                     PHI=   -0.179
                                                                                                      XP =   0.0267

180  LEAN TOWARD BEING THOSE        0.71 OF 133    180  LEAN TOWARD BEING THOSE        0.62 OF  21         39   13
     WHERE THE COMMUNITY IS                             WHERE THE COMMUNITY IS                              94    8
     COMMONLY NON-EXOGAMOUS, RATHER THAN                COMMONLY EXOGAMOUS, RATHER THAN               XSQ=     7.21
     EXOGAMOUS  (258)                                   NON-EXOGAMOUS  (124)                          PHI=   -0.216
                                                                                                      XP =   0.0072

184  LEAN TOWARD BEING THOSE        0.69 OF  80    184  LEAN TOWARD BEING THOSE        0.89 OF   9         25    8
     WHERE THE LARGEST NON-COGNATIC KIN GROUP           WHERE THE LARGEST NON-COGNATIC KIN GROUP            55    1
     IS SMALLER THAN A PHRATRY, I. E.                   IS THE MOEITY OR PHRATRY  (77)                XSQ=     9.18
     A SIB OR LINEAGE  (175)                                                                          PHI=   -0.321
                                                                                                      XP =   0.0024
```

No.		Ratio	No.		Ratio	Stats
192	TILT TOWARD BEING THOSE OTHER THAN WHERE THE ONLY KIN GROUP PRESENT IS A KINDRED OR ELSE BILATERAL DESCENT IS INFERRED (289)	0.72 OF 136	192	TILT TOWARD BEING THOSE WHERE THE ONLY KIN GROUP PRESENT IS A KINDRED OR ELSE BILATERAL DESCENT IS INFERRED (111)	0.57 OF 21	38 12 98 9 XSQ= 5.86 PHI= -0.193 XP = 0.0154
196	TEND TO BE THOSE WHERE INDIVIDUAL RIGHTS IN REAL PROPERTY, AND RULES FOR INHERITANCE, ARE PRESENT (194)	0.72 OF 93	196	TEND TO BE THOSE WHERE INDIVIDUAL RIGHTS IN REAL PROPERTY, OR RULES FOR INHERITANCE, ARE ABSENT (87)	0.95 OF 20	67 1 26 19 XSQ= 28.14 PHI= 0.499 XP = 0.0000
257	DRIFT TOWARD BEING THOSE WHERE THE SEVERITY OF SISTER AVOIDANCE IS LOW (17) WNS	0.67 OF 12	257	IN ALL CASES ARE THOSE WHERE THE SEVERITY OF SISTER AVOIDANCE IS HIGH (10) WNS	1.00 OF 3	4 3 8 0 XSQ= 2.03 PHI= -0.367 EP = 0.0769
259	DRIFT TOWARD BEING THOSE WHERE THE SEVERITY OF MOTHER-IN-LAW AVOIDANCE IS LOW (20) WNS	0.52 OF 21	259	IN ALL CASES ARE THOSE WHERE THE SEVERITY OF MOTHER-IN-LAW AVOIDANCE IS HIGH (26) WNS	1.00 OF 6	10 6 11 0 XSQ= 3.36 PHI= -0.353 EP = 0.0536
386	DRIFT TOWARD BEING THOSE WHERE SEXUAL EXPRESSION BY THE YOUNG IS PERMITTED (40) F-B	0.58 OF 38	386	DRIFT TOWARD BEING THOSE WHERE SEXUAL EXPRESSION BY THE YOUNG IS RESTRICTED OR SEMI-RESTRICTED (46) F-B	0.88 OF 8	16 7 22 1 XSQ= 3.78 PHI= -0.287 XP = 0.0518
391	TILT TOWARD BEING THOSE WHERE PREMARITAL SEX RELATIONS ARE PUNISHED ONLY IF PREGNANCY RESULTS, OR FREELY PERMITTED (90) JTW,EA	0.58 OF 88	391	TILT TOWARD BEING THOSE WHERE PREMARITAL SEX RELATIONS ARE STRONGLY PUNISHED AND IN FACT RARE, OR WEAKLY PUNISHED AND IN FACT NOT RARE (89) JTW,EA	0.77 OF 13	37 10 51 3 XSQ= 4.22 PHI= -0.205 XP = 0.0398
397	DRIFT TOWARD BEING THOSE WHERE SEX DISABILITY IS ABSENT (42) JKH	0.83 OF 30	397	DRIFT TOWARD BEING THOSE WHERE SEX DISABILITY IS PRESENT (14) JKH	0.60 OF 5	5 3 25 2 XSQ= 2.44 PHI= -0.264 EP = 0.0665
417	DRIFT MORE TOWARD BEING THOSE WHERE WARFARE IS PREVALENT (34) LWS	0.93 OF 15	417	DRIFT LESS TOWARD BEING THOSE WHERE WARFARE IS PREVALENT (34) LWS	0.57 OF 7	14 4 1 3 XSQ= 2.12 PHI= 0.311 EP = 0.0766
420	DRIFT TOWARD BEING THOSE WHERE BELLICOSITY IS MODERATE OR NEGLIGIBLE (46) PES	0.59 OF 49	420	DRIFT TOWARD BEING THOSE WHERE BELLICOSITY IS EXTREME (41) PES	0.78 OF 9	20 7 29 2 XSQ= 2.82 PHI= -0.221 XP = 0.0930

```
435  TILT TOWARD BEING THOSE          0.82 OF  11     435  TILT TOWARD BEING THOSE          0.80 OF   5           2     4
     WHERE ABANDONMENT CF THE HOUSE OF THE DEAD           WHERE ABANDONMENT OF THE HOUSE OF THE DEAD             9     1
     IS NCT PRACTICED  (19) LWS                           IS PRACTICED  (12) LWS                         XSQ=    3.28
                                                                                                         PHI=  -0.453
                                                                                                         EP =  0.0357

455  DRIFT TCWARD BEING THCSE        0.64 OF  14     455  IN ALL CASES ARE THOSE           1.00 CF   4           5     4
     WHERE THE MODE CF THE INDIVICUAL'S                   WHERE THE MODE OF THE INDIVIDUAL'S                     9     0
     CONTACT WITH THE DIVINE                              CONTACT WITH THE DIVINE                        XSQ=    2.89
     IS NCT CCNDUCIVE TC THE CEVELOPMENT OF THE           IS CONDUCIVE TO THE DEVELOPMENT OF THE         PHI=  -0.401
     INDIVIDUAL'S NEED TC ACHIEVE  (19) CCM               INDIVIDUAL'S NEED TC ACHIEVE  (17) DCM         EP =  0.0824
```

132 CULTURES WHERE ECONOMIC EXCHANGE INVOLVES THE USE OF MONEY (37) JMH	132 CULTURES WHERE ECONOMIC EXCHANGE DOES NOT INVOLVE THE USE OF MONEY (17) JMH

BACKGROUND ON PAGE 96

BOTH SUBJECT AND PREDICATE

37 IN LEFT COLUMN

ARAUCANIANS	AZTEC	BULGARIANS	BURMESE	BURUSHO	CAMBODIANS	CAYAPA	CHAGGA	CREEK	CUNA
DARD	IBAN	KAREN	KASKA	KHASI	KOREANS	KORYAK	KURTATCHI	LOLO	MARSHALLESE
MBUNDU	MIAO	NAVAHO	OJIBWA	PUKAPUKA	RWALA	SAMOANS	SAMOYED	TALLENSI	THONGA
TIV	TODA	TROBRIAND	VIETNAMESE	WOLEAIANS	YAKUT	YUROK			

17 IN RIGHT COLUMN

ANDAMANESE	ARANDA	AZANDE	BEMBA	CHUKCHEE	COPR ESKIMO	CROW	GILYAK	JIVARO	MANDAN
NAMA	NUER	SIRIONO	TEHUELCHE	TIKOPIA	TIMBIRA	TUPINAMBA			

346 EXCLUDED BECAUSE UNASCERTAINED

44 LEAN TOWARD BEING THOSE WHERE SETTLEMENTS ARE FIXED (222) 0.74 OF 35	44 LEAN TOWARD BEING THOSE WHERE SETTLEMENTS ARE NON-FIXED (110) 0.71 OF 17	26 5 9 12 XSQ= 7.80 PHI= 0.387 XP = 0.0052
46 LEAN TOWARD BEING THOSE OTHER THAN WHERE SETTLEMENTS ARE NON-FIXED AND MOVEMENT IS NOMADIC (260) 0.86 OF 35	46 LEAN TOWARD BEING THOSE WHERE SETTLEMENTS ARE NON-FIXED AND MOVEMENT IS NOMADIC (72) 0.59 OF 17	5 10 30 7 XSQ= 8.99 PHI= -0.416 XP = 0.0027
51 LEAN TOWARD BEING THOSE WHERE SUBSISTENCE IS PRIMARILY BY FOOD PRODUCTION -- I. E., AGRICULTURE OR HUSBANDRY -- RATHER THAN BY GATHERING (253) 0.78 OF 37	51 LEAN TOWARD BEING THOSE WHERE SUBSISTENCE IS PRIMARILY BY FOOD GATHERING -- I. E., HUNTING, FISHING, OR COLLECTING -- RATHER THAN FOOD PRODUCTION (147) 0.71 OF 17	29 5 8 12 XSQ= 9.97 PHI= 0.430 XP = 0.0016
54 TILT TOWARD BEING THOSE WHERE FOOD PRODUCTION IS BY INTENSIVE OR SIMPLE AGRICULTURE, RATHER THAN BY INCIPIENT FOOD PRODUCTION (192) 0.86 OF 29	54 TILT TOWARD BEING THOSE WHERE FOOD PRODUCTION IS BY INCIPIENT FOOD PRODUCTION, RATHER THAN BY INTENSIVE OR SIMPLE AGRICULTURE (46) 0.50 OF 8	25 4 4 4 XSQ= 2.95 PHI= 0.282 EP = 0.0487

62	DRIFT MORE TOWARD BEING THOSE 0.81 OF 37 WHERE HUSBANDRY OF SOME KIND IS PRESENT (228)	62	DRIFT LESS TOWARD BEING THOSE 0.53 OF 17 WHERE HUSBANDRY OF SOME KIND IS PRESENT (228)	30 9 7 8 XSQ= 3.30 PHI= 0.247 XP = 0.0692
77	LEAN LESS TOWARD BEING THOSE 0.59 OF 37 WHERE THE WRITING SYSTEM IS MNEMONIC OR ABSENT, RATHER THAN BEING ALPHABETIC-OR-PHONETIC (39) JMH	77	IN ALL CASES ARE THOSE 1.00 OF 17 WHERE THE WRITING SYSTEM IS MNEMONIC OR ABSENT, RATHER THAN BEING ALPHABETIC-OR-PHONETIC (39) JMH	15 0 22 17 XSQ= 7.63 PHI= 0.376 XP = 0.0057
78	DRIFT TOWARD BEING THOSE 0.76 OF 37 WHERE THE WRITING SYSTEM IS ALPHABETIC-OR-PHONETIC, OR MNEMONIC, RATHER THAN BEING ABSENT (36) JMH	78	DRIFT TOWARD BEING THOSE 0.53 OF 17 WHERE A WRITING SYSTEM IS ABSENT, RATHER THAN BEING PRESENT IN EITHER ALPHABETIC-OR-PHONETIC FORM OR MNEMONIC FORM (18) JMH	28 8 9 9 XSQ= 3.10 PHI= 0.240 XP = 0.0782
91	LEAN TOWARD BEING THOSE 0.54 OF 13 WHERE SOCIETAL COMPLEXITY IS HIGH (18) F-W	91	IN ALL CASES ARE THOSE 1.00 OF 10 WHERE SOCIETAL COMPLEXITY IS LOW (22) F-W	7 0 6 10 XSQ= 5.41 PHI= 0.485 EP = 0.0075
98	TILT MORE TOWARD BEING THOSE 0.89 OF 35 WHERE THE HIERARCHY OF LOCAL JURISDICTION HAS FOUR OR THREE LEVELS (238) GES,EA	98	TILT LESS TOWARD BEING THOSE 0.59 OF 17 WHERE THE HIERARCHY OF LOCAL JURISDICTION HAS FOUR OR THREE LEVELS (238) GES,EA	31 10 4 7 XSQ= 4.42 PHI= 0.291 XP = 0.0356
99	DRIFT TOWARD BEING THOSE 0.91 OF 11 WHERE, WITH NATIONAL HIERARCHY ABSENT, THE HIERARCHY OF LOCAL JURISDICTION HAS FOUR OR THREE LEVELS (93) GES,EA	99	DRIFT TOWARD BEING THOSE 0.50 OF 10 WHERE, WITH NATIONAL HIERARCHY ABSENT, THE HIERARCHY OF LOCAL JURISDICTION HAS TWO LEVELS (63) GES,EA	10 5 1 5 XSQ= 2.52 PHI= 0.347 EP = 0.0635
100	TILT MORE TOWARD BEING THOSE 0.97 OF 35 WHERE HIERARCHIES ARE MORE COMPLEX THAN THE 'SIMPLEST,' I. E., MORE COMPLEX THAN TWO LOCAL LEVELS WITH NO NATIONAL LEVELS (267) GES,EA	100	TILT LESS TOWARD BEING THOSE 0.71 OF 17 WHERE HIERARCHIES ARE MORE COMPLEX THAN THE 'SIMPLEST,' I. E., MORE COMPLEX THAN TWO LOCAL LEVELS WITH NO NATIONAL LEVELS (267) GES,EA	34 12 1 5 XSQ= 5.52 PHI= 0.326 XP = 0.0188
102	TILT TOWARD BEING THOSE 0.70 OF 37 WHERE CLASS STRATIFICATION IS PRESENT (203)	102	TILT TOWARD BEING THOSE 0.65 OF 17 WHERE CLASS STRATIFICATION IS ABSENT (180)	26 6 11 11 XSQ= 4.54 PHI= 0.290 XP = 0.0331
116	LEAN TOWARD BEING THOSE 0.51 OF 37 WHERE OCCUPATIONAL SPECIALIZATION IS FULL-TIME, WHETHER OR NOT FOR SURPLUS PRODUCTION (20) JMH	116	LEAN TOWARD BEING THOSE 0.94 OF 17 WHERE OCCUPATIONAL SPECIALIZATION IS PART-TIME ONLY (34) JMH	19 1 18 16 XSQ= 8.47 PHI= 0.396 XP = 0.0036

131	DRIFT MORE TOWARD BEING THOSE 0.93 OF 28 WHERE THE CONSTRUCTION OF PERMANENT HOUSES OR THE ERECTION OF TEMPORARY DWELLINGS IS MAINLY DONE BY MALES (136)	131	DRIFT LESS TOWARD BEING THOSE 0.67 OF 12 WHERE THE CONSTRUCTION OF PERMANENT HOUSES OR THE ERECTION OF TEMPORARY DWELLINGS IS MAINLY DONE BY MALES (136)	26 8 2 4 XSQ= 2.70 PHI= 0.260 EP = 0.0548
137	DRIFT TOWARD BEING THOSE 0.52 OF 23 WHERE INVIDIOUS DISPLAY OF WEALTH IS STRONGLY EMPHASIZED (37) PES	137	DRIFT TOWARD BEING THOSE 0.83 OF 12 WHERE INVIDIOUS DISPLAY OF WEALTH IS MODERATELY, LITTLE, OR NEGATIVELY EMPHASIZED (52) PES	12 2 11 10 XSQ= 2.80 PHI= 0.283 EP = 0.0697
142	LEAN TOWARD BEING THOSE 0.84 OF 37 WHERE THE LEVEL OF SOCIAL SANCTION IS PUBLIC CORPOREAL SANCTION OR PUBLIC PROPERTY SANCTION, RATHER THAN PRIVATE SETTLEMENT (38) JMH	142	LEAN TOWARD BEING THOSE 0.59 OF 17 WHERE THE LEVEL OF SOCIAL SANCTION IS PRIVATE SETTLEMENT, RATHER THAN PUBLIC CORPOREAL SANCTION OR PUBLIC PROPERTY SETTLEMENT (16) JMH	31 7 6 10 XSQ= 8.20 PHI= 0.390 XP = 0.0042
143	DRIFT TOWARD BEING THOSE 0.58 OF 12 WHERE THE RATIO OF RESTITUTIVE TO REPRESSIVE SANCTIONS IS HIGH (20) WME	143	DRIFT TOWARD BEING THOSE 0.88 OF 8 WHERE THE RATIO OF RESTITUTIVE TO REPRESSIVE SANCTIONS IS MEDIUM OR LOW (32) WME	7 1 5 7 XSQ= 2.51 PHI= 0.354 EP = 0.0697
144	DRIFT TOWARD BEING THOSE 0.75 OF 12 WHERE THE RATIO OF RESTITUTIVE TO REPRESSIVE SANCTIONS IS HIGH OR MEDIUM (27) WME	144	DRIFT TOWARD BEING THOSE 0.75 OF 8 WHERE THE RATIO OF RESTITUTIVE TO REPRESSIVE SANCTIONS IS LOW (25) WME	9 2 3 6 XSQ= 3.04 PHI= 0.390 EP = 0.0648
147	IN ALL CASES ARE THOSE 1.00 OF 8 WHERE CODIFIED LAWS ARE PRESENT (20) LWS	147	IN ALL CASES ARE THOSE 1.00 OF 3 WHERE CODIFIED LAWS ARE UNIMPORTANT OR ABSENT (13) LWS	8 0 0 3 XSQ= 6.54 PHI= 0.771 EP = 0.0061
163	TILT TOWARD BEING THOSE 0.75 OF 4 WHERE THE EMPHASIS ON INDIVIDUAL VOLITION AS THE CAUSE OF CRIME IS HIGH (7) MJ	163	IN ALL CASES ARE THOSE 1.00 OF 5 WHERE THE EMPHASIS ON INDIVIDUAL VOLITION AS THE CAUSE OF CRIME IS LOW (10) MJ	3 0 1 5 XSQ= 2.76 PHI= 0.553 EP = 0.0476
196	LEAN TOWARD BEING THOSE 0.78 OF 23 WHERE INDIVIDUAL RIGHTS IN REAL PROPERTY, AND RULES FOR INHERITANCE, ARE PRESENT (194)	196	LEAN TOWARD BEING THOSE 0.67 OF 15 WHERE INDIVIDUAL RIGHTS IN REAL PROPERTY, OR RULES FOR INHERITANCE, ARE ABSENT (87)	18 5 5 10 XSQ= 5.91 PHI= 0.394 EP = 0.0082
309	TILT TOWARD BEING THOSE 0.89 OF 9 WHERE ORAL SOCIALIZATION ANXIETY IS HIGH (26) W-C	309	TILT TOWARD BEING THOSE 0.83 OF 6 WHERE ORAL SOCIALIZATION ANXIETY IS LOW (27) W-C	8 1 1 5 XSQ= 5.10 PHI= 0.583 EP = 0.0110

320	DRIFT TOWARD BEING THOSE WHERE THE DEGREE OF REDUCTION OF THE INFANT'S DRIVES IS LOW (24) B-B-C	0.50 OF 16	320	DRIFT TOWARD BEING THOSE WHERE THE DEGREE OF REDUCTION OF THE INFANT'S DRIVES IS HIGH (45) B-B-C	0.90 OF 10	8 9 8 1 XSQ= 2.76 PHI= -0.326 EP = 0.0873
322	DRIFT TOWARD BEING THOSE WHERE THE CONSISTENCY OF REDUCTION OF THE INFANT'S DRIVES IS LOW (32) B-B-C	0.75 OF 12	322	DRIFT TOWARD BEING THOSE WHERE THE CONSISTENCY OF REDUCTION OF THE INFANT'S DRIVES IS HIGH (27) B-B-C	0.75 OF 8	3 6 9 2 XSQ= 3.04 PHI= -0.390 EP = 0.0648
323	TILT TOWARD BEING THOSE WHERE THE CONSTANCY OF PRESENCE OF THE INFANT'S NURTURANT AGENT IS LOW (45) B-B-C	0.81 OF 16	323	TILT TOWARD BEING THOSE WHERE THE CONSTANCY OF PRESENCE OF THE INFANT'S NURTURANT AGENT IS HIGH (29) B-B-C	0.58 OF 12	3 7 13 5 XSQ= 3.11 PHI= -0.334 EP = 0.0497
326	DRIFT TOWARD BEING THOSE WHERE THE INFERRED TRANSITION ANXIETY BETWEEN INFANCY AND CHILDHOOD IS HIGH (32) B-B-C	0.56 OF 16	326	DRIFT TOWARD BEING THOSE WHERE THE INFERRED TRANSITION ANXIETY BETWEEN INFANCY AND CHILDHOOD IS LOW (35) B-B-C	0.86 OF 7	9 1 7 6 XSQ= 1.99 PHI= 0.294 EP = 0.0886
334	LEAN TOWARD BEING THOSE WHERE THE INDULGENCE OF THE CHILD IS LOW (38) B-B-C	0.71 OF 17	334	LEAN TOWARD BEING THOSE WHERE THE INDULGENCE OF THE CHILD IS HIGH (40) B-B-C	0.83 OF 12	5 10 12 2 XSQ= 6.17 PHI= -0.461 EP = 0.0078
346	TILT TOWARD BEING THOSE WHERE THE CHILD'S INFERRED ANXIETY OVER PERFORMANCE OF SELF-RELIANT BEHAVIOR IS HIGH (37) B-B-C	0.76 OF 17	346	TILT TOWARD BEING THOSE WHERE THE CHILD'S INFERRED ANXIETY OVER PERFORMANCE OF SELF-RELIANT BEHAVIOR IS LOW (39) B-B-C	0.73 OF 11	13 3 4 8 XSQ= 4.74 PHI= 0.412 EP = 0.0189
353	DRIFT TOWARD BEING THOSE WHERE THE CHILD'S INFERRED ANXIETY OVER NON-PERFORMANCE OF OBEDIENT BEHAVIOR IS HIGH (42) B-B-C	0.71 OF 17	353	DRIFT TOWARD BEING THOSE WHERE THE CHILD-S INFERRED ANXIETY OVER NON-PERFORMANCE OF OBEDIENT BEHAVIOR IS LOW (32) B-B-C	0.70 OF 10	12 3 5 7 XSQ= 2.72 PHI= 0.317 EP = 0.0568
403	TILT TOWARD BEING THOSE WHERE EXPLANATIONS OF ILLNESS OF AN ANAL NATURE ARE PRESENT (23) W-C	0.55 OF 11	403	IN ALL CASES ARE THOSE WHERE EXPLANATIONS OF ILLNESS OF AN ANAL NATURE ARE ABSENT (38) W-C	1.00 OF 6	6 0 5 6 XSQ= 2.95 PHI= 0.417 EP = 0.0427
424	TILT TOWARD BEING THOSE WHERE RELIGIOUS SPECIALISTS ARE FULL-TIME, RATHER THAN PART-TIME (21) JMH	0.51 OF 37	424	TILT TOWARD BEING THOSE WHERE RELIGIOUS SPECIALISTS ARE PART-TIME, RATHER THAN FULL-TIME (33) JMH	0.88 OF 17	19 2 18 15 XSQ= 6.11 PHI= 0.336 XP = 0.0135

435	TILT TOWARD BEING THOSE 0.88 OF 8 WHERE ABANDONMENT OF THE HOUSE OF THE DEAD IS NOT PRACTICED (19) LWS	435	TILT TOWARD BEING THOSE 0.83 OF 6 WHERE ABANDONMENT OF THE HOUSE OF THE DEAD IS PRACTICED (12) LWS	1 5 7 1 XSQ= 4.43 PHI= -0.562 EP = 0.0256
450	DRIFT LESS TOWARD BEING THOSE 0.65 OF 26 WHERE THE OBSERVATION OF FOOD TABOOS IS HIGH OR MEDIUM, RATHER THAN LOW (60) JRL	450	DRIFT MORE TOWARD BEING THOSE 0.94 OF 16 WHERE THE OBSERVATION OF FOOD TABOOS IS HIGH OR MEDIUM, RATHER THAN LOW (60) JRL	17 15 9 1 XSQ= 2.97 PHI= -0.266 XP = 0.0849
455	LEAN TOWARD BEING THOSE 0.75 OF 12 WHERE THE MODE OF THE INDIVIDUAL'S CONTACT WITH THE DIVINE IS NOT CONDUCIVE TO THE DEVELOPMENT OF THE INDIVIDUAL'S NEED TO ACHIEVE (19) DCM	455	IN ALL CASES ARE THOSE 1.00 OF 5 WHERE THE MODE OF THE INDIVIDUAL'S CONTACT WITH THE DIVINE IS CONDUCIVE TO THE DEVELOPMENT OF THE INDIVIDUAL'S NEED TO ACHIEVE (17) DCM	3 5 9 0 XSQ= 5.24 PHI= -0.555 EP = 0.0090
468	LEAN LESS TOWARD BEING THOSE 0.54 OF 37 WHERE CONTACT WITH OTHER CULTURES IS REGULAR OR IRREGULAR, RATHER THAN FREQUENT (37) JMH	468	IN ALL CASES ARE THOSE 1.00 OF 17 WHERE CONTACT WITH OTHER CULTURES IS REGULAR OR IRREGULAR, RATHER THAN FREQUENT (37) JMH	17 0 20 17 XSQ= 9.37 PHI= 0.417 XP = 0.0022
469	LEAN MORE TOWARD BEING THOSE 0.92 OF 37 WHERE CONTACT WITH OTHER CULTURES IS FREQUENT OR REGULAR, RATHER THAN IRREGULAR (43) JMH	469	LEAN LESS TOWARD BEING THOSE 0.53 OF 17 WHERE CONTACT WITH OTHER CULTURES IS FREQUENT OR REGULAR, RATHER THAN IRREGULAR (43) JMH	34 9 3 8 XSQ= 8.63 PHI= 0.400 XP = 0.0033
470	LEAN TOWARD BEING THOSE 0.54 OF 37 WHERE INNOVATIONS ARE GENERALLY ACCEPTED (21) JMH	470	LEAN TOWARD BEING THOSE 0.94 OF 17 WHERE INNOVATIONS ARE ACCEPTED ONLY SELECTIVELY (33) JMH	20 1 17 16 XSQ= 9.44 PHI= 0.418 XP = 0.0021

****

133 CULTURES WHERE CONTRACTED DEBTS ARE SIGNIFICANTLY PRESENT (17) GES	133 CULTURES WHERE CONTRACTED DEBTS ARE MODERATELY PRESENT OR ABSENT (17) GES

BACKGROUND ON PAGE 97 BOTH SUBJECT AND PREDICATE

....

17 IN LEFT COLUMN

ARAPESH	AZANDE	AZTEC	CUNA	DOBUANS	GANDA	HEBREWS	IBAN	IFUGAO	KASKA
LEPCHA	MARQUESANS	ROMANS	TIV	TODA	YUROK	ZUNI			

17 IN RIGHT COLUMN

ARANDA	COPR ESKIMO	LOZI	MIAO	NAMA	NANDI	NUER	NYAKYUSA	TALLENSI	TANALA
TIMBIRA	TRUMAI	WINNEBAGO	WOLEAIANS	YAGUA	YAHGAN	YOKUTS			

366 EXCLUDED BECAUSE UNASCERTAINED

46	DRIFT MORE TOWARD BEING THOSE OTHER THAN WHERE SETTLEMENTS ARE NON-FIXED AND MOVEMENT IS NOMADIC (260)	0.94 OF 16	46	DRIFT LESS TOWARD BEING THOSE OTHER THAN WHERE SETTLEMENTS ARE NON-FIXED AND MOVEMENT IS NOMADIC (260)	0.63 OF 16	1 6 15 10 XSQ= 2.93 PHI= -0.302 EP = 0.0829
51	TILT TOWARD BEING THOSE WHERE SUBSISTENCE IS PRIMARILY BY FOOD PRODUCTION -- I. E., AGRICULTURE OR HUSBANDRY -- RATHER THAN BY GATHERING (253)	0.88 OF 17	51	TILT TOWARD BEING THOSE WHERE SUBSISTENCE IS PRIMARILY BY FOOD GATHERING -- I. E., HUNTING, FISHING, OR COLLECTING -- RATHER THAN FOOD PRODUCTION (147)	0.59 OF 17	15 7 2 10 XSQ= 6.31 PHI= 0.431 EP = 0.0104
54	IN ALL CASES ARE THOSE WHERE FOOD PRODUCTION IS BY INTENSIVE OR SIMPLE AGRICULTURE, RATHER THAN BY INCIPIENT FOOD PRODUCTION (192)	1.00 OF 13	54	TILT LESS TOWARD BEING THOSE WHERE FOOD PRODUCTION IS BY INTENSIVE OR SIMPLE AGRICULTURE, RATHER THAN BY INCIPIENT FOOD PRODUCTION (192)	0.55 OF 11	13 6 0 5 XSQ= 4.96 PHI= 0.455 EP = 0.0109
56	IN ALL CASES ARE THOSE WHERE FOOD PRODUCTION IS BY SIMPLE AGRICULTURE, RATHER THAN BY INCIPIENT FOOD PRODUCTION (101)	1.00 OF 6	56	TILT TOWARD BEING THOSE WHERE FOOD PRODUCTION IS BY INCIPIENT FOOD PRODUCTION, RATHER THAN BY SIMPLE AGRICULTURE (46)	0.83 OF 6	6 1 0 5 XSQ= 5.49 PHI= 0.676 EP = 0.0152
63	DRIFT TOWARD BEING THOSE WHERE HUSBANDRY, IF PRESENT, IS PRINCIPALLY IN THE FORM OF PIGS, SHEEP, OR GOATS, RATHER THAN BOVINE, EQUINE, CAMEL-LIKE, OR DEER-LIKE ANIMALS (74)	0.58 OF 12	63	DRIFT TOWARD BEING THOSE WHERE HUSBANDRY, IF PRESENT, IS PRINCIPALLY IN THE FORM OF BOVINE, EQUINE, CAMEL-LIKE, OR DEER-LIKE ANIMALS, RATHER THAN PIGS, SHEEP, OR GOATS (152)	0.80 OF 10	5 8 7 2 XSQ= 1.92 PHI= -0.295 EP = 0.0991

78	IN ALL CASES ARE THOSE WHERE THE WRITING SYSTEM IS ALPHABETIC-OR-PHONETIC, OR MNEMONIC, RATHER THAN BEING ABSENT (36) JMH	1.00 OF	8	78	TILT TOWARD BEING THOSE WHERE A WRITING SYSTEM IS ABSENT, RATHER THAN BEING PRESENT IN EITHER ALPHABETIC-OR-PHONETIC FORM OR MNEMONIC FORM (18) JMH	0.63 OF	8	8 3 0 5 XSQ= 4.65 PHI= 0.539 EP = 0.0256
110	DRIFT TOWARD BEING THOSE WHERE SLAVERY IS PRESENT (163)	0.65 OF	17	110	DRIFT TOWARD BEING THOSE WHERE SLAVERY IS ABSENT (218)	0.71 OF	17	11 5 6 12 XSQ= 2.95 PHI= 0.295 EP = 0.0844
116	DRIFT TOWARD BEING THOSE WHERE OCCUPATIONAL SPECIALIZATION IS FULL-TIME, WHETHER OR NOT FOR SURPLUS PRODUCTION (20) JMH	0.50 OF	8	116	IN ALL CASES ARE THOSE WHERE OCCUPATIONAL SPECIALIZATION IS PART-TIME ONLY (34) JMH	1.00 OF	8	4 0 4 8 XSQ= 3.00 PHI= 0.433 EP = 0.0769
120	IN ALL CASES ARE THOSE WHERE THE CRAFT SPECIALIZATION SCORE IS HIGH OR MEDIUM (36) WME	1.00 OF	7	120	TILT TOWARD BEING THOSE WHERE THE CRAFT SPECIALIZATION SCORE IS LOW (17) WME	0.60 OF	10	7 4 0 6 XSQ= 4.13 PHI= 0.493 EP = 0.0175
137	LEAN TOWARD BEING THOSE WHERE INVIDIOUS DISPLAY OF WEALTH IS STRONGLY EMPHASIZED (37) PES	0.63 OF	16	137	LEAN TOWARD BEING THOSE WHERE INVIDIOUS DISPLAY OF WEALTH IS MODERATELY, LITTLE, OR NEGATIVELY EMPHASIZED (52) PES	0.92 OF	12	10 1 6 11 XSQ= 6.32 PHI= 0.475 EP = 0.0060
143	DRIFT TOWARD BEING THOSE WHERE THE RATIO OF RESTITUTIVE TO REPRESSIVE SANCTIONS IS HIGH (20) WME	0.75 OF	8	143	DRIFT TOWARD BEING THOSE WHERE THE RATIO OF RESTITUTIVE TO REPRESSIVE SANCTIONS IS MEDIUM OR LOW (32) WME	0.80 OF	10	6 2 2 8 XSQ= 3.45 PHI= 0.437 EP = 0.0536
147	IN ALL CASES ARE THOSE WHERE CODIFIED LAWS ARE PRESENT (20) LWS	1.00 OF	4	147	IN ALL CASES ARE THOSE WHERE CODIFIED LAWS ARE UNIMPORTANT OR ABSENT (13) LWS	1.00 OF	2	4 0 0 2 XSQ= 2.34 PHI= 0.625 EP = 0.0667
320	TILT TOWARD BEING THOSE WHERE THE DEGREE OF REDUCTION OF THE INFANT'S DRIVES IS LOW (24) B-B-C	0.56 OF	9	320	IN ALL CASES ARE THOSE WHERE THE DEGREE OF REDUCTION OF THE INFANT'S DRIVES IS HIGH (45) B-B-C	1.00 OF	8	4 8 5 0 XSQ= 3.90 PHI= -0.479 EP = 0.0294
339	TILT TOWARD BEING THOSE WHERE THE CHILD'S INFERRED CONFLICT REGARDING RESPONSIBLE BEHAVIOR IS HIGH (31) B-B-C	0.50 OF	10	339	IN ALL CASES ARE THOSE WHERE THE CHILD'S INFERRED CONFLICT REGARDING RESPONSIBLE BEHAVIOR IS LOW (42) B-B-C	1.00 OF	10	5 0 5 10 XSQ= 4.27 PHI= 0.462 EP = 0.0325

341	IN ALL CASES ARE THOSE 1.00 OF 4 WHERE THE CHILD'S INFERRED ANXIETY OVER NON-PERFORMANCE OF NURTURANT BEHAVIOR IS HIGH (30) B-B-C	341 DRIFT TOWARD BEING THOSE 0.63 OF 8 WHERE THE CHILD'S INFERRED ANXIETY OVER NON-PERFORMANCE OF NURTURANT BEHAVIOR IS LOW (16) B-B-C	4 3 0 5 XSQ= 2.10 PHI= 0.418 EP = 0.0808
393	TILT TOWARD BEING THOSE 0.63 OF 8 WHERE EXTRAMARITAL COITUS IS PUNISHED, RATHER THAN PERMITTED (43) F-B	393 IN ALL CASES ARE THOSE 1.00 OF 6 WHERE EXTRAMARITAL COITUS IS PERMITTED, RATHER THAN PUNISHED (41) F-B	5 0 3 6 XSQ= 3.43 PHI= 0.495 EP = 0.0310
421	LEAN TOWARD BEING THOSE 0.63 OF 16 WHERE KILLING, TORTURING, OR MUTILATING OF THE ENEMY IS STRONGLY OR MODERATELY EMPHASIZED (37) PES	421 LEAN TOWARD BEING THOSE 0.91 OF 11 WHERE KILLING, TORTURING, OR MUTILATING OF THE ENEMY IS NEGLIGIBLY EMPHASIZED (47) PES	10 1 6 10 XSQ= 5.65 PHI= 0.457 EP = 0.0076
424	DRIFT TOWARD BEING THOSE 0.50 OF 8 WHERE RELIGIOUS SPECIALISTS ARE FULL-TIME, RATHER THAN PART-TIME (21) JMH	424 IN ALL CASES ARE THOSE 1.00 OF 8 WHERE RELIGIOUS SPECIALISTS ARE PART-TIME, RATHER THAN FULL-TIME (33) JMH	4 0 4 8 XSQ= 3.00 PHI= 0.433 EP = 0.0769
429	TILT MORE TOWARD BEING THOSE 0.94 OF 16 WHERE SUPERNATURAL SANCTIONS FOR MORALITY ARE PRESENT (28) GES	429 TILT LESS TOWARD BEING THOSE 0.59 OF 17 WHERE SUPERNATURAL SANCTIONS FOR MORALITY ARE PRESENT (28) GES	15 10 1 7 XSQ= 3.74 PHI= 0.337 EP = 0.0391
435	IN ALL CASES ARE THOSE 1.00 OF 4 WHERE ABANDONMENT OF THE HOUSE OF THE DEAD IS NOT PRACTICED (19) LWS	435 IN ALL CASES ARE THOSE 1.00 OF 3 WHERE ABANDONMENT OF THE HOUSE OF THE DEAD IS PRACTICED (12) LWS	0 3 4 0 XSQ= 3.51 PHI= -0.708 EP = 0.0286
436	DRIFT LESS TOWARD BEING THOSE 0.53 OF 17 WHERE ACTIVE ANCESTRAL SPIRITS ARE PRESENT (27) GES	436 DRIFT MORE TOWARD BEING THOSE 0.88 OF 17 WHERE ACTIVE ANCESTRAL SPIRITS ARE PRESENT (27) GES	9 15 8 2 XSQ= 3.54 PHI= -0.323 EP = 0.0570

134 CULTURES
WHERE INCOME-PRODUCING PROPERTY IS
ONE HUNDRED PERCENT
INDIVIDUALLY OWNED (16) JV

134 CULTURES
WHERE INCOME-PRODUCING PROPERTY
IS LESS THAN ONE HUNDRED PERCENT
INDIVIDUALLY OWNED (18) JV

BACKGROUND ON PAGE 97

SUBJECT ONLY

16 IN LEFT COLUMN

AINU	ARAPESH	AZANDE	CHENCHU	CHIR-APACHE	COMANCHE	KASKA	LEPCHA	MANDAN	MARQUESANS
MBUNDU	SOTHO	TETON	VENDA	WINNEBAGO	YORUBA				

18 IN RIGHT COLUMN

ARANDA	ARAUCANIANS	ASHANTI	CHAGGA	CHUKCHEE	CROW	CUNA	KIKUYU	KORYAK	KURTATCHI
MASAI	NAVAHO	OJIBWA	PAPAGO	PUKAPUKA	TENETEHARA	THONGA	WOLEAIANS		

366 EXCLUDED BECAUSE UNASCERTAINED

33	DRIFT MORE TOWARD BEING THOSE 0.94 OF 16 WHERE THE NATURAL ENVIRONMENT IS OTHER THAN 'VERY HARSH,' I.E., DESERT, DESERT GRASSES AND SHRUBS, TUNDRA, OR HIGH PLATEAU STEPPE (341) FWM	33	DRIFT LESS TOWARD BEING THOSE 0.67 OF 18 WHERE THE NATURAL ENVIRONMENT IS OTHER THAN 'VERY HARSH,' I.E., DESERT, DESERT GRASSES AND SHRUBS, TUNDRA, OR HIGH PLATEAU STEPPE (341) FWM	1 6 15 12 XSQ= 2.32 PHI= -0.261 EP = 0.0900
213	DRIFT TOWARD BEING THOSE 0.56 OF 16 WHERE FIRST COUSIN MARRIAGE IS PERMITTED (172)	213	DRIFT TOWARD BEING THOSE 0.78 OF 18 WHERE FIRST COUSIN MARRIAGE IS NOT PERMITTED (198)	9 4 7 14 XSQ= 2.84 PHI= 0.289 EP = 0.0764
258	IN ALL CASES ARE THOSE 1.00 OF 4 WHERE THE SEVERITY OF SON'S WIFE AVOIDANCE IS LOW (16) WNS	258	DRIFT TOWARD BEING THOSE 0.71 OF 7 WHERE THE SEVERITY OF SON'S WIFE AVOIDANCE IS HIGH (15) WNS	0 5 4 2 XSQ= 2.75 PHI= -0.500 EP = 0.0606
342	DRIFT TOWARD BEING THOSE 0.91 OF 11 WHERE THE CHILD'S INFERRED ANXIETY OVER PERFORMANCE OF NURTURANT BEHAVIOR IS LOW (28) B-B-C	342	DRIFT TOWARD BEING THOSE 0.55 OF 11 WHERE THE CHILD'S INFERRED ANXIETY OVER PERFORMANCE OF NURTURANT BEHAVIOR IS HIGH (18) B-B-C	1 6 10 5 XSQ= 3.35 PHI= -0.390 EP = 0.0635
348	DRIFT TOWARD BEING THOSE 0.57 OF 14 WHERE THE TOTAL POSITIVE PRESSURE TOWARD DEVELOPING ACHIEVEMENT BEHAVIOR IN THE CHILD IS LOW (31) B-B-C	348	DRIFT TOWARD BEING THOSE 0.81 OF 16 WHERE THE TOTAL POSITIVE PRESSURE TOWARD DEVELOPING ACHIEVEMENT BEHAVIOR IN THE CHILD IS HIGH (32) B-B-C	6 13 8 3 XSQ= 3.23 PHI= -0.328 EP = 0.0567

349	DRIFT TOWARD BEING THOSE 0.50 OF 14 WHERE THE CHILD'S INFERRED ANXIETY OVER NON-PERFORMANCE OF ACHIEVEMENT BEHAVIOR IS LOW (28) B-B-C	349	DRIFT TOWARD BEING THOSE 0.87 OF 15 WHERE THE CHILD'S INFERRED ANXIETY OVER NON-PERFORMANCE OF ACHIEVEMENT BEHAVIOR IS HIGH (34) B-B-C	 XSQ= PHI= EP =	7 13 7 2 3.00 -0.321 0.0502
355	DRIFT TOWARD BEING THOSE 0.73 OF 15 WHERE THE CHILD'S INFERRED CONFLICT REGARDING OBEDIENT BEHAVIOR IS LOW (38) B-B-C	355	DRIFT TOWARD BEING THOSE 0.59 OF 17 WHERE THE CHILD'S INFERRED CONFLICT REGARDING OBEDIENT BEHAVIOR IS HIGH (35) B-B-C	 XSQ= PHI= EP =	4 10 11 7 2.17 -0.260 0.0870
382	TILT TOWARD BEING THOSE 0.75 OF 4 WHERE FEMALE INITIATION RITES ARE ABSENT (27) JKB	382	TILT TOWARD BEING THOSE 0.90 OF 10 WHERE FEMALE INITIATION RITES ARE PRESENT (38) JKB	 XSQ= PHI= EP =	1 9 3 1 3.16 -0.475 0.0410
424	DRIFT TOWARD BEING THOSE 0.75 OF 4 WHERE RELIGIOUS SPECIALISTS ARE FULL-TIME, RATHER THAN PART-TIME (21) JMH	424	DRIFT TOWARD BEING THOSE 0.85 OF 13 WHERE RELIGIOUS SPECIALISTS ARE PART-TIME, RATHER THAN FULL-TIME (33) JMH	 XSQ= PHI= EP =	3 2 1 11 2.76 0.403 0.0525
429	IN ALL CASES ARE THOSE 1.00 OF 6 WHERE SUPERNATURAL SANCTIONS FOR MORALITY ARE PRESENT (28) GES	429	DRIFT TOWARD BEING THOSE 0.67 OF 3 WHERE SUPERNATURAL SANCTIONS FOR MORALITY ARE ABSENT OR UNREPORTED (9) GES	 XSQ= PHI= EP =	6 1 0 2 2.01 0.472 0.0833

135 CULTURES
WHERE INDIVIDUAL OWNERSHIP OF
ECONOMICALLY SIGNIFICANT PROPERTY
IS PRESENT (24) GES

135 CULTURES
WHERE INDIVIDUAL OWNERSHIP OF
ECONOMICALLY SIGNIFICANT PROPERTY
IS NEGLIGIBLE OR ABSENT (14) GES

BACKGROUND ON PAGE 98

BOTH SUBJECT AND PREDICATE

24 IN LEFT COLUMN

ARAPESH	AYMARA	BEMBA	CUNA	DOBUANS	HEBREWS	IBAN	IFUGAO	KAREN	KASKA
LEPCHA	LOZI	MIAO	NAMA	NUER	NYAKYUSA	ROMANS	SAMOYED	TALLENSI	TANALA
TIV	TODA	WINNEBAGO	YURUK						

14 IN RIGHT COLUMN

ARANDA	AZANDE	AZTEC	COPR ESKIMO	GANDA	MARQUESANS	NANDI	TIMBIRA	TRUMAI	WOLEAIANS
YAGUA	YAHGAN	YOKUTS	ZUNI						

362 EXCLUDED BECAUSE UNASCERTAINED

---

5 DRIFT LESS TOWARD BEING THOSE 0.75 OF 24
LOCATED OUTSIDE OF
EAST EURASIA (330)

5 IN ALL CASES ARE THOSE 1.00 OF 14
LOCATED OUTSIDE OF
EAST EURASIA (330)

6 0
18 14
XSQ= 2.49
PHI= 0.256
EP = 0.0672

62 TILT TOWARD BEING THOSE 0.79 OF 24
WHERE HUSBANDRY OF SOME KIND
IS PRESENT (228)

62 TILT TOWARD BEING THOSE 0.57 OF 14
WHERE HUSBANDRY OF ANY KIND
IS ABSENT (172)

19 6
5 8
XSQ= 3.69
PHI= 0.312
EP = 0.0353

143 LEAN TOWARD BEING THOSE 0.73 OF 11
WHERE THE RATIO OF RESTITUTIVE
TO REPRESSIVE SANCTIONS
IS HIGH (20) WME

143 IN ALL CASES ARE THOSE 1.00 OF 7
WHERE THE RATIO OF RESTITUTIVE
TO REPRESSIVE SANCTIONS
IS MEDIUM OR LOW (32) WME

8 0
3 7
XSQ= 6.45
PHI= 0.599
EP = 0.0040

144 TILT TOWARD BEING THOSE 0.73 OF 11
WHERE THE RATIO OF RESTITUTIVE
TO REPRESSIVE SANCTIONS
IS HIGH OR MEDIUM (27) WME

144 TILT TOWARD BEING THOSE 0.86 OF 7
WHERE THE RATIO OF RESTITUTIVE
TO REPRESSIVE SANCTIONS
IS LOW (25) WME

8 1
3 6
XSQ= 3.74
PHI= 0.456
EP = 0.0498

196 DRIFT TOWARD BEING THOSE 0.81 OF 16
WHERE INDIVIDUAL RIGHTS IN REAL PROPERTY,
AND RULES FOR INHERITANCE,
ARE PRESENT (194)

196 DRIFT TOWARD BEING THOSE 0.54 OF 13
WHERE INDIVIDUAL RIGHTS IN REAL PROPERTY,
OR RULES FOR INHERITANCE,
ARE ABSENT (87)

13 6
3 7
XSQ= 2.51
PHI= 0.294
EP = 0.0641

No.		No.		
213	DRIFT LESS TOWARD BEING THOSE 0.57 OF 23 WHERE FIRST COUSIN MARRIAGE IS NOT PERMITTED (198)	213	DRIFT MORE TOWARD BEING THOSE 0.86 OF 14 WHERE FIRST COUSIN MARRIAGE IS NOT PERMITTED (198)	10 2 13 12 XSQ= 2.18 PHI= 0.243 EP = 0.0836
323	DRIFT TOWARD BEING THOSE 0.60 OF 10 WHERE THE CONSTANCY OF PRESENCE OF THE INFANT'S NURTURANT AGENT IS LOW (45) B-B-C	323	DRIFT TOWARD BEING THOSE 0.89 OF 9 WHERE THE CONSTANCY OF PRESENCE OF THE INFANT'S NURTURANT AGENT IS HIGH (29) B-B-C	4 8 6 1 XSQ= 2.99 PHI= -0.397 EP = 0.0573
340	IN ALL CASES ARE THOSE 1.00 OF 9 WHERE THE TOTAL POSITIVE PRESSURE TOWARD DEVELOPING NURTURANT BEHAVIOR IN THE CHILD IS HIGH (28) B-B-C	340	TILT TOWARD BEING THOSE 0.60 OF 5 WHERE THE TOTAL POSITIVE PRESSURE TOWARD DEVELOPING NURTURANT BEHAVIOR IN THE CHILD IS LOW (20) B-B-C	9 2 0 3 XSQ= 3.77 PHI= 0.519 EP = 0.0275
354	DRIFT TOWARD BEING THOSE 0.82 OF 11 WHERE THE CHILD'S INFERRED ANXIETY OVER PERFORMANCE OF OBEDIENT BEHAVIOR IS LOW (37) B-B-C	354	DRIFT TOWARD BEING THOSE 0.63 OF 8 WHERE THE CHILD'S INFERRED ANXIETY OVER PERFORMANCE OF OBEDIENT BEHAVIOR IS HIGH (36) B-B-C	2 5 9 3 XSQ= 2.24 PHI= -0.343 EP = 0.0739
355	DRIFT TOWARD BEING THOSE 0.82 OF 11 WHERE THE CHILD'S INFERRED CONFLICT REGARDING OBEDIENT BEHAVIOR IS LOW (38) B-B-C	355	DRIFT TOWARD BEING THOSE 0.63 OF 8 WHERE THE CHILD'S INFERRED CONFLICT REGARDING OBEDIENT BEHAVIOR IS HIGH (35) B-B-C	2 5 9 3 XSQ= 2.24 PHI= -0.343 EP = 0.0739
372	DRIFT TOWARD BEING THOSE 0.82 OF 11 WHERE MALE INITIATION RITES ARE ABSENT (63) ASA	372	DRIFT TOWARD BEING THOSE 0.67 OF 9 WHERE MALE INITIATION RITES ARE PRESENT (48) ASA	2 6 9 3 XSQ= 3.04 PHI= -0.390 EP = 0.0648
403	TILT TOWARD BEING THOSE 0.83 OF 6 WHERE EXPLANATIONS OF ILLNESS OF AN ANAL NATURE ARE PRESENT (23) W-C	403	IN ALL CASES ARE THOSE 1.00 OF 5 WHERE EXPLANATIONS OF ILLNESS OF AN ANAL NATURE ARE ABSENT (38) W-C	5 0 1 5 XSQ= 4.65 PHI= 0.650 EP = 0.0152
429	DRIFT MORE TOWARD BEING THOSE 0.87 OF 23 WHERE SUPERNATURAL SANCTIONS FOR MORALITY ARE PRESENT (28) GES	429	DRIFT LESS TOWARD BEING THOSE 0.57 OF 14 WHERE SUPERNATURAL SANCTIONS FOR MORALITY ARE PRESENT (28) GES	20 8 3 6 XSQ= 2.74 PHI= 0.272 EP = 0.0569
430	DRIFT TOWARD BEING THOSE 0.54 OF 24 WHERE SUPERNATURAL SANCTIONS FOR MORALITY, HAVING AN EFFECT ON AN INDIVIDUAL'S HEALTH, ARE PRESENT (16) GES	430	DRIFT TOWARD BEING THOSE 0.79 OF 14 WHERE SUPERNATURAL SANCTIONS FOR MORALITY, HAVING AN EFFECT ON AN INDIVIDUAL'S HEALTH, ARE ABSENT OR UNREPORTED (22) GES	13 3 11 11 XSQ= 2.66 PHI= 0.265 EP = 0.0877

443	DRIFT TOWARD BEING THOSE WHERE OVERALL FEAR OF OTHERS IS HIGH (31) W-C	0.83 OF 6	443	DRIFT TOWARD BEING THOSE WHERE OVERALL FEAR OF OTHERS IS LOW (30) W-C	0.80 OF 5		5 1
							1 4
						XSQ=	2.23
						PHI=	0.450
						EP =	0.0801

136 CULTURES
WHERE FULL-TIME ENTREPRENEURS
ARE PRESENT (18) JV

136 CULTURES
WHERE FULL-TIME ENTREPRENEURS
ARE ABSENT (14) JV

BACKGROUND ON PAGE 98

BOTH SUBJECT AND PREDICATE

18 IN LEFT COLUMN

ASHANTI	AZANDE	CHUKCHEE	CROW	CUNA	KIKUYU	KORYAK	MARQUESANS	MASAI	MBUNDU
NAVAHO	OJIBWA	PAPAGO	SOTHO	TENETEHARA	THONGA	WINNEBAGO	YORUBA		

14 IN RIGHT COLUMN

AINU	ARAPESH	ARAUCANIANS	CHAGGA	CHENCHU	KASKA	KURTATCHI	LEPCHA	PUKAPUKA	TETON
TUCUNA	VENDA	WICHITA	WOLEAIANS						

368 EXCLUDED BECAUSE UNASCERTAINED

33	DRIFT LESS TOWARD BEING THOSE 0.72 OF 18 WHERE THE NATURAL ENVIRONMENT IS OTHER THAN 'VERY HARSH,' I.E., DESERT, DESERT GRASSES AND SHRUBS, TUNDRA, OR HIGH PLATEAU STEPPE (341) FWM	33	IN ALL CASES ARE THOSE 1.00 OF 14 WHERE THE NATURAL ENVIRONMENT IS OTHER THAN 'VERY HARSH,' I.E., DESERT, DESERT GRASSES AND SHRUBS, TUNDRA, OR HIGH PLATEAU STEPPE (341) FWM	5 0 13 14 XSQ= 2.74 PHI= 0.293 EP = 0.0525
71	TILT TOWARD BEING THOSE 0.67 OF 15 WHERE METAL WORKING IS PRESENT (98)	71	TILT TOWARD BEING THOSE 0.90 OF 10 WHERE METAL WORKING IS ABSENT (153)	10 1 5 9 XSQ= 5.69 PHI= 0.477 EP = 0.0119
85	DRIFT LESS TOWARD BEING THOSE 0.65 OF 17 WHERE THE LEVEL OF POLITICAL INTEGRATION IS THE MINIMAL STATE, THE AUTONOMOUS COMMUNITY, OR THE FAMILY (234) GPM	85	IN ALL CASES ARE THOSE 1.00 OF 10 WHERE THE LEVEL OF POLITICAL INTEGRATION IS THE MINIMAL STATE, THE AUTONOMOUS COMMUNITY, OR THE FAMILY (234) GPM	6 0 11 10 XSQ= 2.73 PHI= 0.318 EP = 0.0570
95	DRIFT LESS TOWARD BEING THOSE 0.59 OF 17 WHERE THE HIERARCHY OF NATIONAL JURISDICTION HAS ONE OR NO LEVELS (254) GES,EA	95	DRIFT MORE TOWARD BEING THOSE 0.92 OF 13 WHERE THE HIERARCHY OF NATIONAL JURISDICTION HAS ONE OR NO LEVELS (254) GES,EA	7 1 10 12 XSQ= 2.68 PHI= 0.299 EP = 0.0924
100	IN ALL CASES ARE THOSE 1.00 OF 17 WHERE HIERARCHIES ARE MORE COMPLEX THAN THE 'SIMPLEST,' I. E., MORE COMPLEX THAN TWO LOCAL LEVELS WITH NO NATIONAL LEVELS (267) GES,EA	100	DRIFT LESS TOWARD BEING THOSE 0.77 OF 13 WHERE HIERARCHIES ARE MORE COMPLEX THAN THE 'SIMPLEST,' I. E., MORE COMPLEX THAN TWO LOCAL LEVELS WITH NO NATIONAL LEVELS (267) GES,EA	17 10 0 3 XSQ= 2.17 PHI= 0.269 EP = 0.0704

No.	Statement	Ratio	N	No.	Statement	Ratio	N	Statistics
143	IN ALL CASES ARE THOSE WHERE THE RATIO OF RESTITUTIVE TO REPRESSIVE SANCTIONS IS MEDIUM OR LOW (32) WME	1.00 OF	5	143	IN ALL CASES ARE THOSE WHERE THE RATIO OF RESTITUTIVE TO REPRESSIVE SANCTIONS IS HIGH (20) WME	1.00 OF	2	0 2 5 0 XSQ= 2.96 PHI= -0.650 EP = 0.0476
178	DRIFT MORE TOWARD BEING THOSE WHERE THE COMMUNITY IS OTHER THAN SEGMENTED ON A CLAN BASIS AND NON-EXOGAMOUS (295)	0.89 OF	18	178	DRIFT LESS TOWARD BEING THOSE WHERE THE COMMUNITY IS OTHER THAN SEGMENTED ON A CLAN BASIS AND NON-EXOGAMOUS (295)	0.57 OF	14	2 6 16 8 XSQ= 2.71 PHI= -0.291 EP = 0.0964
182	TILT TOWARD BEING THOSE WHERE THE COMMUNITY IS STRUCTURED ON A NON-CLAN BASIS AND AGAMOUS (126)	0.50 OF	18	182	TILT TOWARD BEING THOSE OTHER THAN WHERE THE COMMUNITY IS STRUCTURED ON A NON-CLAN BASIS AND AGAMOUS (256)	0.93 OF	14	9 1 9 13 XSQ= 4.89 PHI= 0.391 EP = 0.0189
201	IN ALL CASES ARE THOSE WHERE MARITAL RESIDENCE IS NON-OPTIONAL, RATHER THAN AMBILOCAL OR NEOLOCAL (334)	1.00 OF	18	201	DRIFT LESS TOWARD BEING THOSE WHERE MARITAL RESIDENCE IS NON-OPTIONAL, RATHER THAN AMBILOCAL OR NEOLOCAL (334)	0.79 OF	14	18 11 0 3 XSQ= 2.11 PHI= 0.257 EP = 0.0734
204	IN ALL CASES ARE THOSE WHERE MARITAL RESIDENCE IS PATRILOCAL, VIRILOCAL, OR AVUNCULOCAL, RATHER THAN AMBILOCAL OR NEOLOCAL (270)	1.00 OF	15	204	DRIFT LESS TOWARD BEING THOSE WHERE MARITAL RESIDENCE IS PATRILOCAL, VIRILOCAL, OR AVUNCULOCAL, RATHER THAN AMBILOCAL OR NEOLOCAL (270)	0.75 OF	12	15 9 0 3 XSQ= 2.07 PHI= 0.277 EP = 0.0752
242	IN ALL CASES ARE THOSE WHERE MARRIAGE IS COMMONLY OR OCCASIONALLY POLYGYNOUS, RATHER THAN MONOGAMOUS (314)	1.00 OF	17	242	TILT LESS TOWARD BEING THOSE WHERE MARRIAGE IS COMMONLY OR OCCASIONALLY POLYGYNOUS, RATHER THAN MONOGAMOUS (314)	0.71 OF	14	17 10 0 4 XSQ= 3.32 PHI= 0.327 EP = 0.0318
286	TILT TOWARD BEING THOSE WHERE THE NUMBER OF FOOD TABOOS DURING PREGNANCY IS LOW OR ABSENT (14) BCA	0.83 OF	6	286	TILT TOWARD BEING THOSE WHERE THE NUMBER OF FOOD TABOOS DURING PREGNANCY IS HIGH (20) BCA	0.86 OF	7	1 6 5 1 XSQ= 3.73 PHI= -0.536 EP = 0.0291
309	DRIFT TOWARD BEING THOSE WHERE ORAL SOCIALIZATION ANXIETY IS HIGH (26) W-C	0.86 OF	7	309	DRIFT TOWARD BEING THOSE WHERE ORAL SOCIALIZATION ANXIETY IS LOW (27) W-C	0.67 OF	9	6 3 1 6 XSQ= 2.52 PHI= 0.397 EP = 0.0601
351	DRIFT TOWARD BEING THOSE WHERE THE CHILD'S INFERRED CONFLICT REGARDING ACHIEVEMENT BEHAVIOR IS HIGH (26) B-B-C	0.63 OF	16	351	DRIFT TOWARD BEING THOSE WHERE THE CHILD'S INFERRED CONFLICT REGARDING ACHIEVEMENT BEHAVIOR IS LOW (34) B-B-C	0.80 OF	10	10 2 6 8 XSQ= 2.93 PHI= 0.335 EP = 0.0511

352	DRIFT MORE TOWARD BEING THOSE 0.88 OF 16 WHERE THE TOTAL POSITIVE PRESSURE TOWARD DEVELOPING OBEDIENT BEHAVIOR IN THE CHILD IS HIGH (44) B-B-C	352	DRIFT LESS TOWARD BEING THOSE 0.54 OF 13 WHERE THE TOTAL POSITIVE PRESSURE TOWARD DEVELOPING OBEDIENT BEHAVIOR IN THE CHILD IS HIGH (44) B-B-C	14 7 2 6 XSQ= 2.56 PHI= 0.297 EP = 0.0923
380	IN ALL CASES ARE THOSE 1.00 OF 6 WHERE SEGREGATION OF GIRLS AT MENARCHE IS PRESENT (35) F-B	380	DRIFT TOWARD BEING THOSE 0.67 OF 3 WHERE SEGREGATION OF GIRLS AT MENARCHE IS ABSENT (20) F-B	6 1 0 2 XSQ= 2.01 PHI= 0.472 EP = 0.0833
390	DRIFT LESS TOWARD BEING THOSE 0.67 OF 12 WHERE PREMARITAL SEX RELATIONS ARE WEAKLY PUNISHED AND IN FACT NOT RARE OR PUNISHED ONLY IF PREGNANCY RESULTS, OR FREELY PERMITTED (132) JTW,EA	390	IN ALL CASES ARE THOSE 1.00 OF 11 WHERE PREMARITAL SEX RELATIONS ARE WEAKLY PUNISHED AND IN FACT NOT RARE OR PUNISHED ONLY IF PREGNANCY RESULTS, OR FREELY PERMITTED (132) JTW,EA	4 0 8 11 XSQ= 2.42 PHI= 0.324 EP = 0.0932
472	TILT TOWARD BEING THOSE 0.73 OF 11 WHERE THE COMPOSITE NARCISSISM INDEX IS HIGH (47) PES	472	TILT TOWARD BEING THOSE 0.82 OF 11 WHERE THE COMPOSITE NARCISSISM INDEX IS LOW (43) PES	8 2 3 9 XSQ= 4.58 PHI= 0.456 EP = 0.0300
479	DRIFT TOWARD BEING THOSE 0.61 OF 18 WHERE THE NEED TO ACHIEVE, AS INFERRED FROM FOLKTALES, IS HIGH (18) JV	479	DRIFT TOWARD BEING THOSE 0.71 OF 14 WHERE THE NEED TO ACHIEVE, AS INFERRED FROM FOLKTALES, IS LOW (18) JV	11 4 7 10 XSQ= 2.17 PHI= 0.260 EP = 0.0870

137 CULTURES
WHERE INVIDIOUS DISPLAY OF WEALTH
IS STRONGLY EMPHASIZED (37) PES

137 CULTURES
WHERE INVIDIOUS DISPLAY OF WEALTH
IS MODERATELY, LITTLE, OR
NEGATIVELY EMPHASIZED (52) PES

BACKGROUND ON PAGE 99

BOTH SUBJECT AND PREDICATE

37 IN LEFT COLUMN

ALORESE	AMERICANS	ASHANTI	AYMARA	AZTEC	BEMBA	CHAGGA	CHEYENNE	COMANCHE	CROW
DOBUANS	FON	GANDA	HAIDA	HEBREWS	IBAN	IFUGAO	KASKA	KOREANS	KWAKIUTL
LAKHER	LAU	LESU	MANUS	MARQUESANS	NYAKYUSA	OJIBWA	SAMOANS	SIWANS	TAPIRAPE
THONGA	TIV	TROBRIAND	WOGEO	WOLOF	YAKUT	YUROK			

52 IN RIGHT COLUMN

ABIPON	AINU	ALBANIANS	ANDAMANESE	ARANDA	ARAPESH	ARAUCANIANS	AZANDE	BALINESE	BHIL
CHENCHU	CHIR-APACHE	CHUKCHEE	COPR ESKIMO	CREEK	CUNA	CZECHS	GOND	HANO	INCA
KAZAK	KURTATCHI	LANGO	LAPPS	LEPCHA	MAORI	MASAI	MURNGIN	NAMA	NAVAHO
NUER	PAPAGO	PUKAPUKA	RIFFIANS	RWALA	SANPOIL	SIRIONO	SOMALI	TALLENSI	TANALA
TIKOPIA	TIMBIRA	TODA	TRUMAI	VENDA	VIETNAMESE	WARRAU	WITOTO	WOLEAIANS	YAGUA
YAHGAN	ZUNI								

311 EXCLUDED BECAUSE UNASCERTAINED

---

9 DRIFT MORE TOWARD BEING THOSE 0.95 OF 37
LOCATED OUTSIDE OF
SOUTH AMERICA (335)

9 DRIFT LESS TOWARD BEING THOSE 0.79 OF 52
LOCATED OUTSIDE OF
SOUTH AMERICA (335)

2	11
35	41
XSQ=	3.13
PHI=	-0.187
XP =	0.0769

33 LEAN MORE TOWARD BEING THOSE 0.97 OF 37
WHERE THE NATURAL ENVIRONMENT IS
OTHER THAN 'VERY HARSH,' I.E., DESERT,
DESERT GRASSES AND SHRUBS, TUNDRA, OR
HIGH PLATEAU STEPPE (341) FWM

33 LEAN LESS TOWARD BEING THOSE 0.71 OF 52
WHERE THE NATURAL ENVIRONMENT IS
OTHER THAN 'VERY HARSH,' I.E., DESERT,
DESERT GRASSES AND SHRUBS, TUNDRA, OR
HIGH PLATEAU STEPPE (341) FWM

1	15
36	37
XSQ=	8.33
PHI=	-0.306
XP =	0.0039

36 TILT MORE TOWARD BEING THOSE 0.84 OF 37
WHERE THE NATURAL ENVIRONMENT IS
OTHER THAN
'VERY HARSH,' OR SUB-TROPICAL BUSH, OR
TEMPERATE GRASSLAND (292) FWM

36 TILT LESS TOWARD BEING THOSE 0.56 OF 52
WHERE THE NATURAL ENVIRONMENT IS
OTHER THAN
'VERY HARSH,' OR SUB-TROPICAL BUSH, OR
TEMPERATE GRASSLAND (292) FWM

6	23
31	29
XSQ=	6.50
PHI=	-0.270
XP =	0.0108

44 TILT MORE TOWARD BEING THOSE 0.80 OF 35
WHERE SETTLEMENTS ARE FIXED (222)

44 TILT LESS TOWARD BEING THOSE 0.57 OF 51
WHERE SETTLEMENTS ARE FIXED (222)

28	29
7	22
XSQ=	3.99
PHI=	0.215
XP =	0.0458

```
46  DRIFT MORE TOWARD BEING THOSE  0.86 OF  35      46  DRIFT LESS TOWARD BEING THOSE  0.67 OF  51          5    17
    OTHER THAN WHERE SETTLEMENTS ARE                    OTHER THAN WHERE SETTLEMENTS ARE                   30    34
    NON-FIXED AND MOVEMENT IS                           NON-FIXED AND MOVEMENT IS                    XSQ=     3.02
    NOMADIC  (260)                                      NOMADIC  (260)                               PHI=   -0.187
                                                                                                     XP =   0.0823

54  DRIFT MORE TOWARD BEING THOSE  0.89 OF  27      54  DRIFT LESS TOWARD BEING THOSE  0.67 OF  30         24    20
    WHERE FOOD PRODUCTION IS BY                         WHERE FOOD PRODUCTION IS BY                         3    10
    INTENSIVE OR SIMPLE                                 INTENSIVE OR SIMPLE                          XSQ=     2.82
    AGRICULTURE, RATHER THAN BY                         AGRICULTURE, RATHER THAN BY                  PHI=    0.223
    INCIPIENT FOOD PRODUCTION  (192)                    INCIPIENT FOOD PRODUCTION  (192)             XP =   0.0929

56  TILT TOWARD BEING THOSE        0.82 OF  17      56  TILT TOWARD BEING THOSE        0.56 OF  18         14     8
    WHERE FOOD PRODUCTION IS BY                         WHERE FOOD PRODUCTION IS BY                         3    10
    SIMPLE AGRICULTURE, RATHER THAN BY                  INCIPIENT FOOD PRODUCTION, RATHER THAN BY    XSQ=     3.88
    INCIPIENT FOOD PRODUCTION,  (101)                   SIMPLE AGRICULTURE  (46)                     PHI=    0.333
                                                                                                     EP =   0.0354

82  TILT MORE TOWARD BEING THOSE   0.93 OF  28      82  TILT LESS TOWARD BEING THOSE   0.67 OF  43         26    29
    WHERE A CITY OR TOWN IS PRESENT, OR                 WHERE A CITY OR TOWN IS PRESENT, OR                 2    14
    THE AVERAGE COMMUNITY SIZE IS                       THE AVERAGE COMMUNITY SIZE IS                XSQ=     4.90
    FIFTY OR GREATER  (178)                             FIFTY OR GREATER  (178)                      PHI=    0.263
                                                                                                     XP =   0.0268

86  TILT TOWARD BEING THOSE        0.65 OF  34      86  TILT TOWARD BEING THOSE        0.63 OF  43         22    16
    WHERE THE LEVEL OF POLITICAL INTEGRATION            WHERE THE LEVEL OF POLITICAL INTEGRATION           12    27
    IS THE LARGE STATE, THE LITTLE STATE,               IS THE AUTONOMOUS COMMUNITY, OR              XSQ=     4.70
    OR THE MINIMAL STATE  (148) GPM                     THE FAMILY  (156) GPM                        PHI=    0.247
                                                                                                     XP =   0.0302

96  TILT TOWARD BEING THOSE        0.71 OF  34      96  TILT TOWARD BEING THOSE        0.55 OF  51         24    23
    WHERE THE HIERARCHY                                 WHERE THE HIERARCHY                                10    28
    OF NATIONAL JURISDICTION HAS                        OF NATIONAL JURISDICTION HAS                 XSQ=     4.38
    FOUR, THREE, TWO OR                                 NO LEVELS  (156) GES,EA                      PHI=    0.227
    ONE LEVEL  (174) GES,EA                                                                          XP =   0.0364

100 DRIFT MORE TOWARD BEING THOSE  0.97 OF  34     100  DRIFT LESS TOWARD BEING THOSE  0.80 OF  51         33    41
    WHERE HIERARCHIES ARE MORE COMPLEX THAN             WHERE HIERARCHIES ARE MORE COMPLEX THAN             1    10
    THE 'SIMPLEST,' I. E., MORE COMPLEX THAN            THE 'SIMPLEST,' I. E., MORE COMPLEX THAN     XSQ=     3.66
    TWO LOCAL LEVELS WITH                               TWO LOCAL LEVELS WITH                        PHI=    0.207
    NO NATIONAL LEVELS  (267) GES,EA                    NO NATIONAL LEVELS  (267) GES,EA             XP =   0.0558

118 TILT TOWARD BEING THOSE        0.67 OF  15     118  TILT TOWARD BEING THOSE        0.70 OF  20          5    14
    WHERE THE PERCENTAGE OF OCCUPATIONS                 WHERE THE PERCENTAGE OF OCCUPATIONS                10     6
    THAT ARE SPECIALIZED                                THAT ARE SPECIALIZED                         XSQ=     3.28
    IS LOW  (25) WME                                    IS HIGH OR MEDIUM  (24) WME                  PHI=   -0.306
                                                                                                     EP =   0.0442

132 DRIFT MORE TOWARD BEING THOSE  0.86 OF  14     132  DRIFT LESS TOWARD BEING THOSE  0.52 OF  21         12    11
    WHERE ECONOMIC EXCHANGE                             WHERE ECONOMIC EXCHANGE                             2    10
    INVOLVES THE USE OF MONEY  (37) JMH                 INVOLVES THE USE OF MONEY  (37) JMH          XSQ=     2.80
                                                                                                     PHI=    0.283
                                                                                                     EP =   0.0697
```

No.			No.			
133	LEAN TOWARD BEING THOSE WHERE CONTRACTED DEBTS ARE SIGNIFICANTLY PRESENT (17) GES	0.91 OF 11	133	LEAN TOWARD BEING THOSE WHERE CONTRACTED DEBTS ARE MODERATELY PRESENT OR ABSENT (17) GES	0.65 OF 17	10 6 1 11 XSQ= 6.32 PHI= 0.475 EP = 0.0060
149	DRIFT TOWARD BEING THOSE WHERE THE INCIDENCE OF THEFT IS HIGH (18) B-B-C	0.67 OF 15	149	DRIFT TOWARD BEING THOSE WHERE THE INCIDENCE OF THEFT IS LOW (19) B-B-C	0.68 OF 19	10 6 5 13 XSQ= 2.85 PHI= 0.290 EP = 0.0824
258	DRIFT TOWARD BEING THOSE WHERE THE SEVERITY OF SON'S WIFE AVOIDANCE IS HIGH (15) WNS	0.67 OF 12	258	DRIFT TOWARD BEING THOSE WHERE THE SEVERITY OF SON'S WIFE AVOIDANCE IS LOW (16) WNS	0.75 OF 12	8 3 4 9 XSQ= 2.69 PHI= 0.334 EP = 0.0995
272	DRIFT TOWARD BEING THOSE WHERE THE DIVORCE RATE IS HIGH (29) CA	0.77 OF 13	272	DRIFT TOWARD BEING THOSE WHERE THE DIVORCE RATE IS LOW (28) CA	0.59 OF 17	10 7 3 10 XSQ= 2.52 PHI= 0.290 EP = 0.0711
285	DRIFT TOWARD BEING THOSE WHERE THE SEX TABOO DURING PREGNANCY IS PRESENT (14) BCA	0.69 OF 13	285	DRIFT TOWARD BEING THOSE WHERE THE SEX TABOO DURING PREGNANCY IS ABSENT OR INFERRED ABSENT (17) BCA	0.69 OF 16	9 5 4 11 XSQ= 2.76 PHI= 0.309 EP = 0.0656
309	TILT TOWARD BEING THOSE WHERE ORAL SOCIALIZATION ANXIETY IS HIGH (26) W-C	0.76 OF 17	309	TILT TOWARD BEING THOSE WHERE ORAL SOCIALIZATION ANXIETY IS LOW (27) W-C	0.65 OF 26	13 9 4 17 XSQ= 5.63 PHI= 0.362 XP = 0.0177
316	TILT TOWARD BEING THOSE WHERE EXCLUSIVE MOTHER-SON SLEEPING ARRANGEMENTS LAST ONE YEAR OR LONGER (19) W-K-A	0.69 OF 16	316	TILT TOWARD BEING THOSE WHERE EXCLUSIVE MOTHER-SON SLEEPING ARRANGEMENTS LAST LESS THAN ONE YEAR (25) W-K-A	0.76 OF 17	11 4 5 13 XSQ= 5.10 PHI= 0.393 EP = 0.0149
317	DRIFT TOWARD BEING THOSE WHERE DISPLAY OF AFFECTION TOWARD THE INFANT IS LOW (29) B-B-C	0.62 OF 21	317	DRIFT TOWARD BEING THOSE WHERE DISPLAY OF AFFECTION TOWARD THE INFANT IS HIGH (39) B-B-C	0.69 OF 29	8 20 13 9 XSQ= 3.54 PHI= -0.266 XP = 0.0599
320	LEAN TOWARD BEING THOSE WHERE THE DEGREE OF REDUCTION OF THE INFANT'S DRIVES IS LOW (24) B-B-C	0.57 OF 23	320	LEAN TOWARD BEING THOSE WHERE THE DEGREE OF REDUCTION OF THE INFANT'S DRIVES IS HIGH (45) B-B-C	0.83 OF 29	10 24 13 5 XSQ= 7.09 PHI= -0.369 XP = 0.0077

```
321 DRIFT TOWARD BEING THOSE          0.65 OF  20    321 DRIFT TOWARD BEING THOSE          0.68 OF  25          7    17
    WHERE THE IMMEDIACY OF REDUCTION                     WHERE THE IMMEDIACY OF REDUCTION                        13     8
    OF THE INFANT'S DRIVES                               OF THE INFANT'S DRIVES                            XSQ=     3.63
    IS LOW   (25) B-B-C                                  IS HIGH  (35) B-B-C                               PHI=   -0.284
                                                                                                           XP =   0.0569

322 TILT TOWARD BEING THOSE           0.79 OF  19    322 TILT TOWARD BEING THOSE           0.56 OF  25          4    14
    WHERE THE CONSISTENCY OF REDUCTION                   WHERE THE CONSISTENCY OF REDUCTION                      15    11
    OF THE INFANT'S DRIVES                               OF THE INFANT'S DRIVES                            XSQ=     4.10
    IS LOW   (32) B-B-C                                  IS HIGH  (27) B-B-C                               PHI=   -0.305
                                                                                                           XP =   0.0428

335 TILT TOWARD BEING THOSE           0.71 OF  14    335 TILT TOWARD BEING THOSE           0.73 OF  22          4    16
    WHERE INITIAL INDULGENCE OF DEPENDENCY               WHERE INITIAL INDULGENCE OF DEPENDENCY                  10     6
    IS LOW   (18) WNS                                    IS HIGH  (20) WNS                                 XSQ=     5.09
                                                                                                           PHI=   -0.376
                                                                                                           EP =   0.0159

341 DRIFT TOWARD BEING THOSE          0.82 OF  17    341 DRIFT TOWARD BEING THOSE          0.53 OF  17         14     8
    WHERE THE CHILD'S INFERRED ANXIETY OVER              WHERE THE CHILD'S INFERRED ANXIETY OVER                  3     9
    NON-PERFORMANCE OF NURTURANT BEHAVIOR                NON-PERFORMANCE OF NURTURANT BEHAVIOR             XSQ=     3.22
    IS HIGH  (30) B-B-C                                  IS LOW   (16) B-B-C                               PHI=    0.308
                                                                                                           EP =   0.0707

344 DRIFT TOWARD BEING THOSE          0.67 OF  24    344 DRIFT TOWARD BEING THOSE          0.60 OF  30         16    12
    WHERE THE TOTAL POSITIVE PRESSURE TOWARD             WHERE THE TOTAL POSITIVE PRESSURE TOWARD                 8    18
    DEVELOPING SELF-RELIANT BEHAVIOR                     DEVELOPING SELF-RELIANT BEHAVIOR                  XSQ=     2.80
    IN THE CHILD                                         IN THE CHILD                                      PHI=    0.228
    IS HIGH  (36) B-B-C                                  IS LOW   (40) B-B-C                               XP =   0.0940

348 DRIFT TOWARD BEING THOSE          0.74 OF  19    348 DRIFT TOWARD BEING THOSE          0.56 OF  27         14    12
    WHERE THE TOTAL POSITIVE PRESSURE TOWARD             WHERE THE TOTAL POSITIVE PRESSURE TOWARD                 5    15
    DEVELOPING ACHIEVEMENT BEHAVIOR                      DEVELOPING ACHIEVEMENT BEHAVIOR                   XSQ=     2.78
    IN THE CHILD                                         IN THE CHILD                                      PHI=    0.246
    IS HIGH  (32) B-B-C                                  IS LOW   (31) B-B-C                               XP =   0.0954

349 TILT TOWARD BEING THOSE           0.79 OF  19    349 TILT TOWARD BEING THOSE           0.58 OF  26         15    11
    WHERE THE CHILD'S INFERRED ANXIETY OVER              WHERE THE CHILD'S INFERRED ANXIETY OVER                  4    15
    NON-PERFORMANCE OF ACHIEVEMENT BEHAVIOR              NON-PERFORMANCE OF ACHIEVEMENT BEHAVIOR           XSQ=     4.63
    IS HIGH  (34) B-B-C                                  IS LOW   (28) B-B-C                               PHI=    0.321
                                                                                                           XP =   0.0314

355 DRIFT TOWARD BEING THOSE          0.67 OF  24    355 DRIFT TOWARD BEING THOSE          0.64 OF  28         16    10
    WHERE THE CHILD'S INFERRED CONFLICT                  WHERE THE CHILD'S INFERRED CONFLICT                      8    18
    REGARDING OBEDIENT BEHAVIOR                          REGARDING OBEDIENT BEHAVIOR                       XSQ=     3.79
    IS HIGH  (35) B-B-C                                  IS LOW   (38) B-B-C                               PHI=    0.270
                                                                                                           XP =   0.0515

358 IN ALL CASES ARE THOSE            1.00 OF  13    358 TILT LESS TOWARD BEING THOSE  0.65 OF  23         13    15
    WHERE ADOLESCENT PEER GROUPS ARE PRESENT             WHERE ADOLESCENT PEER GROUPS ARE PRESENT                 0     8
    IN A SETTING OF WORK AND PUBLIC GATHERINGS           IN A SETTING OF WORK AND PUBLIC GATHERINGS        XSQ=     3.98
    AND LEISURE, OR OF                                   AND LEISURE, OR OF                                PHI=    0.332
    PUBLIC GATHERINGS AND LEISURE, OR                    PUBLIC GATHERINGS AND LEISURE, OR                 EP =   0.0319
    OF LEISURE ONLY  (41) JKH                            OF LEISURE ONLY  (41) JKH
```

360	TILT TOWARD BEING THOSE 0.80 OF 5 WHERE ADOLESCENT PEER GROUPS ARE PRESENT IN A SETTING OF WORK AND PUBLIC GATHERINGS AND LEISURE, OR AT LEAST OF PUBLIC GATHERINGS AND LEISURE (14) JKH	360	TILT TOWARD BEING THOSE 0.83 OF 18 WHERE ADOLESCENT PEER GROUPS ARE PRESENT ONLY IN A SETTING OF LEISURE,' OR ELSE ARE ABSENT (23) JKH	4 3 1 15 XSQ= 4.72 PHI= 0.453 EP = 0.0173
393	DRIFT TOWARD BEING THOSE 0.75 OF 16 WHERE EXTRAMARITAL COITUS IS PUNISHED, RATHER THAN PERMITTED (43) F-B	393	DRIFT TOWARD BEING THOSE 0.57 OF 28 WHERE EXTRAMARITAL COITUS IS PERMITTED, RATHER THAN PUNISHED (41) F-B	12 12 4 16 XSQ= 3.05 PHI= 0.263 XP = 0.0810
402	TILT TOWARD BEING THOSE 0.78 OF 18 WHERE EXPLANATIONS OF ILLNESS OF AN ORAL NATURE ARE PRESENT (31) W-C	402	TILT TOWARD BEING THOSE 0.60 OF 30 WHERE EXPLANATIONS OF ILLNESS OF AN ORAL NATURE ARE ABSENT (30) W-C	14 12 4 18 XSQ= 5.03 PHI= 0.324 XP = 0.0248
417	IN ALL CASES ARE THOSE 1.00 OF 11 WHERE WARFARE IS PREVALENT (34) LWS	417	DRIFT LESS TOWARD BEING THOSE 0.70 OF 20 WHERE WARFARE IS PREVALENT (34) LWS	11 14 0 6 XSQ= 2.40 PHI= 0.278 EP = 0.0658
419	DRIFT MORE TOWARD BEING THOSE 0.76 OF 34 WHERE MILITARY GLORY IS STRONGLY OR MODERATELY EMPHASIZED (55) PES	419	DRIFT LESS TOWARD BEING THOSE 0.55 OF 51 WHERE MILITARY GLORY IS STRONGLY OR MODERATELY EMPHASIZED (55) PES	26 28 8 23 XSQ= 3.22 PHI= 0.195 XP = 0.0728
434	TILT TOWARD BEING THOSE 0.79 OF 19 WHERE ASCETICISM IN MOURNING BEHAVIOR IS HIGH (37) JFG	434	TILT TOWARD BEING THOSE 0.55 OF 31 WHERE ASCETICISM IN MOURNING BEHAVIOR IS LOW (30) JFG	15 14 4 17 XSQ= 4.22 PHI= 0.291 XP = 0.0399
435	DRIFT TOWARD BEING THOSE 0.89 OF 9 WHERE ABANDONMENT OF THE HOUSE OF THE DEAD IS NOT PRACTICED (19) LWS	435	DRIFT TOWARD BEING THOSE 0.50 OF 14 WHERE ABANDONMENT OF THE HOUSE OF THE DEAD IS PRACTICED (12) LWS	1 7 8 7 XSQ= 2.14 PHI= -0.305 EP = 0.0858
472	TEND TO BE THOSE 0.78 OF 37 WHERE THE COMPOSITE NARCISSISM INDEX IS HIGH (47) PES	472	TEND TO BE THOSE 0.67 OF 52 WHERE THE COMPOSITE NARCISSISM INDEX IS LOW (43) PES	29 17 8 35 XSQ= 16.29 PHI= 0.428 XP = 0.0001
473	TILT TOWARD BEING THOSE 0.50 OF 36 WHERE SENSITIVITY TO INSULT IS EXTREME (32) PES	473	TILT TOWARD BEING THOSE 0.75 OF 51 WHERE SENSITIVITY TO INSULT IS MODERATE OR NEGLIGIBLE (56) PES	18 13 18 38 XSQ= 4.51 PHI= 0.228 XP = 0.0337

474	TILT TOWARD BEING THOSE WHERE BOASTFULNESS IS EXTREME	0.61 OF 36 (41) PES	474	TILT TOWARD BEING THOSE WHERE BOASTFULNESS IS MODERATE, NEGLIBIBLE, OR UNREPORTED (48) PES	0.65 OF 52	22 18 14 34 XSQ= 5.00 PHI= 0.238 XP = 0.0253
475	LEAN TOWARD BEING THOSE WHERE EXHIBITIONISTIC DANCING IS STRONGLY OR MODERATELY EMPHASIZED (48) PES	0.75 OF 36	475	LEAN TOWARD BEING THOSE WHERE EXHIBITIONISTIC DANCING IS NEGLIGIBLY EMPHASIZED (38) PES	0.57 OF 49	27 21 9 28 XSQ= 7.46 PHI= 0.296 XP = 0.0063

138 CULTURES WHERE SUPERORDINATE JUSTICE IS PRESENT (22) BBW

138 CULTURES WHERE SUPERORDINATE JUSTICE IS ABSENT (18) BBW

BACKGROUND ON PAGE 100

BOTH SUBJECT AND PREDICATE

22 IN LEFT COLUMN

ASHANTI, AZANDE, BALINESE, CAYAPA, CHAGGA, CHEYENNE, CROW, GOND, JAPANESE, KAZAK, KWAKIUTL, LAMBA, LEPCHA, MASAI, ONTONG-JAVA, RIFFIANS, SAMOANS, SANPOIL, TANALA, TIKOPIA, TIV, VENDA

18 IN RIGHT COLUMN

ARANDA, CARIB, CHUKCHEE, COPR ESKIMO, DELAWARE, DIERI, DOBUANS, IFUGAO, JIVARO, KURTATCHI, LANGO, LESU, MAORI, MURNGIN, TROBRIAND, WITOTO, YUROK, ZUNI

360 EXCLUDED BECAUSE UNASCERTAINED

	Left column (present)			Right column (absent)		Statistics
3	DRIFT LESS TOWARD BEING THOSE LOCATED OUTSIDE OF AFRICA (320)	0.68 OF 22	3	DRIFT MORE TOWARD BEING THOSE LOCATED OUTSIDE OF AFRICA (320)	0.94 OF 18	7 1 / 15 17 / XSQ= 2.78 / PHI= 0.264 / EP = 0.0537
6	TILT TOWARD BEING THOSE LOCATED OUTSIDE OF THE INSULAR PACIFIC (330)	0.82 OF 22	6	TILT TOWARD BEING THOSE LOCATED IN THE INSULAR PACIFIC (70)	0.50 OF 18	4 9 / 18 9 / XSQ= 3.23 / PHI= -0.284 / EP = 0.0458
33	TILT MORE TOWARD BEING THOSE WHERE THE NATURAL ENVIRONMENT IS OTHER THAN 'VERY HARSH,' I.E., DESERT, DESERT GRASSES AND SHRUBS, TUNDRA, OR HIGH PLATEAU STEPPE (341) FWM	0.95 OF 22	33	TILT LESS TOWARD BEING THOSE WHERE THE NATURAL ENVIRONMENT IS OTHER THAN 'VERY HARSH,' I.E., DESERT, DESERT GRASSES AND SHRUBS, TUNDRA, OR HIGH PLATEAU STEPPE (341) FWM	0.67 OF 18	1 6 / 21 12 / XSQ= 3.86 / PHI= -0.311 / EP = 0.0328
48	DRIFT TOWARD BEING THOSE WHERE THE FOOD SUPPLY IS NOT SECURE, AND FOOD SHORTAGES ARE FREQUENT OR ANNUAL (41) MGW	0.60 OF 15	48	DRIFT TOWARD BEING THOSE WHERE THE FOOD SUPPLY IS SECURE, AND FOOD SHORTAGES ARE RARE OR OCCASIONAL (38) MGW	0.88 OF 8	6 7 / 9 1 / XSQ= 3.05 / PHI= -0.364 / EP = 0.0743
51	DRIFT TOWARD BEING THOSE WHERE SUBSISTENCE IS PRIMARILY BY FOOD PRODUCTION -- I. E., AGRICULTURE OR HUSBANDRY -- RATHER THAN BY GATHERING (253)	0.73 OF 22	51	DRIFT TOWARD BEING THOSE WHERE SUBSISTENCE IS PRIMARILY BY FOOD GATHERING -- I. E., HUNTING, FISHING, OR COLLECTING -- RATHER THAN FOOD PRODUCTION (147)	0.61 OF 18	16 7 / 6 11 / XSQ= 3.36 / PHI= 0.290 / EP = 0.0534

```
54  IN ALL CASES ARE THOSE          1.00 OF 13    54  LEAN TOWARD BEING THOSE          0.50 OF 12            13    6
    WHERE FOOD PRODUCTION IS BY                      WHERE FOOD PRODUCTION IS BY                              0    6
    INTENSIVE OR SIMPLE                              INCIPIENT FOOD PRODUCTION, RATHER THAN BY        XSQ=     6.03
    AGRICULTURE, RATHER THAN BY                      INTENSIVE OR SIMPLE AGRICULTURE  (46)            PHI=    0.491
    INCIPIENT FOOD PRODUCTION  (192)                                                                  EP =   0.0052

56  IN ALL CASES ARE THOSE          1.00 OF  7    56  TILT TOWARD BEING THOSE          0.60 OF 10             7    4
    WHERE FOOD PRODUCTION IS BY                      WHERE FOOD PRODUCTION IS BY                              0    6
    SIMPLE AGRICULTURE, RATHER THAN BY               INCIPIENT FOOD PRODUCTION, RATHER THAN BY        XSQ=     4.13
    INCIPIENT FOOD PRODUCTION  (101)                 SIMPLE AGRICULTURE  (46)                         PHI=    0.493
                                                                                                      EP =   0.0175

63  DRIFT TOWARD BEING THOSE        0.67 OF 15    63  DRIFT TOWARD BEING THOSE         0.75 OF  8            10    2
    WHERE HUSBANDRY, IF PRESENT,                     WHERE HUSBANDRY, IF PRESENT,                             5    6
    IS PRINCIPALLY IN THE FORM OF                    IS PRINCIPALLY IN THE FORM OF                    XSQ=     2.15
    BOVINE, EQUINE, CAMEL-LIKE, OR DEER-LIKE         PIGS, SHEEP, OR GOATS, RATHER THAN               PHI=    0.306
    ANIMALS, RATHER THAN                             BOVINE, EQUINE, CAMEL-LIKE, OR DEER-LIKE         EP =   0.0894
    PIGS, SHEEP, OR GOATS  (152)                     ANIMALS  (74)

71  TILT LESS TOWARD BEING THOSE    0.53 OF 19    71  TILT MORE TOWARD BEING THOSE     0.93 OF 14             9    1
    WHERE METAL WORKING IS                           WHERE METAL WORKING IS                                  10   13
    ABSENT  (153)                                    ABSENT  (153)                                    XSQ=     4.42
                                                                                                      PHI=    0.366
                                                                                                      EP =   0.0209

73  DRIFT TOWARD BEING THOSE        0.58 OF 19    73  DRIFT TOWARD BEING THOSE         0.77 OF 13            11    3
    WHERE WEAVING IS                                 WHERE WEAVING IS                                         8   10
    PRESENT  (118)                                   ABSENT  (130)                                    XSQ=     2.52
                                                                                                      PHI=    0.281
                                                                                                      EP =   0.0751

82  TILT TOWARD BEING THOSE         0.94 OF 16    82  TILT TOWARD BEING THOSE          0.50 OF 14            15    7
    WHERE A CITY OR TOWN IS PRESENT, OR              WHERE NO CITY OR TOWN IS PRESENT, AND                    1    7
    THE AVERAGE COMMUNITY SIZE IS                    THE AVERAGE COMMUNITY SIZE IS                    XSQ=     5.24
    FIFTY OR GREATER  (178)                          SMALLER THAN FIFTY  (46)                         PHI=    0.418
                                                                                                      EP =   0.0121

85  TILT LESS TOWARD BEING THOSE    0.71 OF 17    85  IN ALL CASES ARE THOSE           1.00 OF 17             5    0
    WHERE THE LEVEL OF POLITICAL INTEGRATION         WHERE THE LEVEL OF POLITICAL INTEGRATION                12   17
    IS THE MINIMAL STATE,                            IS THE MINIMAL STATE,                            XSQ=     3.75
    THE AUTONOMOUS COMMUNITY, OR                     THE AUTONOMOUS COMMUNITY, OR                     PHI=    0.332
    THE FAMILY  (234) GPM                            THE FAMILY  (234) GPM                            EP =   0.0445

86  TEND TO BE THOSE                0.82 OF 17    86  TEND TO BE THOSE                 0.88 OF 17            14    2
    WHERE THE LEVEL OF POLITICAL INTEGRATION         WHERE THE LEVEL OF POLITICAL INTEGRATION                 3   15
    IS THE LARGE STATE, THE LITTLE STATE,            IS THE AUTONOMOUS COMMUNITY, OR                  XSQ=    14.28
    OR THE MINIMAL STATE  (148) GPM                  THE FAMILY  (156) GPM                            PHI=    0.648
                                                                                                      EP =   0.0001

95  LEAN LESS TOWARD BEING THOSE    0.62 OF 21    95  IN ALL CASES ARE THOSE           1.00 OF 17             8    0
    WHERE THE HIERARCHY                              WHERE THE HIERARCHY                                     13   17
    OF NATIONAL JURISDICTION HAS                     OF NATIONAL JURISDICTION HAS                     XSQ=     6.07
    ONE OR NO LEVELS  (254) GES,EA                   ONE OR NO LEVELS  (254) GES,EA                   PHI=    0.400
                                                                                                      EP =   0.0047
```

```
 96  TEND TO BE THOSE                  0.81 OF  21     96  TEND TO BE THOSE                  0.88 OF  17       17    2
     WHERE THE HIERARCHY                                   WHERE THE HIERARCHY                                  4   15
     OF NATIONAL JURISDICTION HAS                          OF NATIONAL JURISDICTION HAS                 XSQ=    15.33
     FOUR, THREE, TWO OR                                   NO LEVELS  (156) GES,EA                      PHI=    0.635
     ONE LEVEL  (174) GES,EA                                                                            EP =   0.0000

 98  DRIFT MORE TOWARD BEING THOSE     0.81 OF  21     98  DRIFT LESS TOWARD BEING THOSE     0.53 OF  17       17    9
     WHERE THE HIERARCHY                                   WHERE THE HIERARCHY                                  4    8
     OF LOCAL JURISDICTION HAS                             OF LOCAL JURISDICTION HAS                    XSQ=     2.24
     FOUR OR THREE LEVELS  (238) GES,EA                    FOUR OR THREE LEVELS  (238) GES,EA           PHI=    0.243
                                                                                                        EP =   0.0873

100  IN ALL CASES ARE THOSE            1.00 OF  21    100  LEAN LESS TOWARD BEING THOSE      0.59 OF  17       21   10
     WHERE HIERARCHIES ARE MORE COMPLEX THAN               WHERE HIERARCHIES ARE MORE COMPLEX THAN              0    7
     THE 'SIMPLEST,' I. E., MORE COMPLEX THAN              THE 'SIMPLEST,' I. E., MORE COMPLEX THAN     XSQ=     8.04
     TWO LOCAL LEVELS WITH                                 TWO LOCAL LEVELS WITH                        PHI=    0.460
     NO NATIONAL LEVELS  (267) GES,EA                      NO NATIONAL LEVELS  (267) GES,EA             EP =   0.0015

118  TILT TOWARD BEING THOSE           0.63 OF   8    118  IN ALL CASES ARE THOSE            1.00 OF   7        5    0
     WHERE THE PERCENTAGE OF OCCUPATIONS                   WHERE THE PERCENTAGE OF OCCUPATIONS                  3    7
     THAT ARE SPECIALIZED                                  THAT ARE SPECIALIZED                         XSQ=     4.05
     IS HIGH OR MEDIUM  (24) WME                           IS LOW  (25) WME                             PHI=    0.520
                                                                                                        EP =   0.0256

139  TEND TO BE THOSE                  0.68 OF  22    139  IN ALL CASES ARE THOSE            1.00 OF  18       15    0
     WHERE SUPERORDINATE PUNISHMENT IS                     WHERE SUPERORDINATE PUNISHMENT IS                    7   18
     PRESENT  (15) BBW                                     ABSENT  (25) BBW                             XSQ=    16.84
                                                                                                        PHI=    0.649
                                                                                                        EP =   0.0000

142  IN ALL CASES ARE THOSE            1.00 OF   7    142  DRIFT TOWARD BEING THOSE          0.57 OF   7        7    3
     WHERE THE LEVEL OF SOCIAL SANCTION IS                 WHERE THE LEVEL OF SOCIAL SANCTION IS                0    4
     PUBLIC CORPOREAL SANCTION OR                          PRIVATE SETTLEMENT, RATHER THAN              XSQ=     3.15
     PUBLIC PROPERTY SANCTION, RATHER THAN                 PUBLIC CORPOREAL SANCTION OR                 PHI=    0.474
     PRIVATE SETTLEMENT  (38) JMH                          PUBLIC PROPERTY SETTLEMENT  (16) JMH         EP =   0.0699

152  IN ALL CASES ARE THOSE            1.00 OF   2    152  IN ALL CASES ARE THOSE            1.00 OF   4        2    0
     WHERE THE DIFFERENTIATION OF THE                      WHERE THE DIFFERENTIATION OF THE                     0    4
     JURIDICAL AGENCY FROM THE MEDICAL                     JURIDICAL AGENCY FROM THE MEDICAL            XSQ=     2.34
     AGENCY IS HIGH  (10) MJ                               AGENCY IS LOW  (10) MJ                       PHI=    0.625
                                                                                                        EP =   0.0667

183  IN ALL CASES ARE THOSE            1.00 OF  14    183  TILT LESS TOWARD BEING THOSE      0.64 OF  11        0    4
     WHERE THE LARGEST NON-COGNATIC KIN GROUP              WHERE THE LARGEST NON-COGNATIC KIN GROUP            14    7
     IS SMALLER THAN A MOEITY, I. E.,                      IS SMALLER THAN A MOEITY, I. E.,             XSQ=     3.66
     A PHRATRY OR SIB OR LINEAGE  (218)                    A PHRATRY OR SIB OR LINEAGE  (218)           PHI=   -0.382
                                                                                                        EP =   0.0261

186  DRIFT LESS TOWARD BEING THOSE     0.64 OF  22    186  DRIFT MORE TOWARD BEING THOSE     0.89 OF  18        8    2
     WHERE THE KIN GROUP IS                                WHERE THE KIN GROUP IS                              14   16
     OTHER THAN                                            OTHER THAN                                   XSQ=     2.15
     EXCLUSIVELY PATRILINEAL  (250)                        EXCLUSIVELY PATRILINEAL  (250)               PHI=    0.232
                                                                                                        EP =   0.0823
```

```
190  TILT TOWARD BEING THOSE          0.85 OF  13     190  TILT TOWARD BEING THOSE          0.64 OF  11          11     4
     WHERE THE KIN GROUP IS                               WHERE THE KIN GROUP IS                                  2     7
     PATRILINEAL OR DOUBLE-DESCENT,                       MATRILINEAL, RATHER THAN                          XSQ=     4.04
     RATHER THAN MATRILINEAL  (186)                       PATRILINEAL OR DOUBLE-DESCENT  (61)               PHI=    0.410
                                                                                                            EP =   0.0327

198  DRIFT TOWARD BEING THOSE         0.89 OF   9     198  DRIFT TOWARD BEING THOSE         0.67 OF   6           8     2
     WHERE RULES FOR THE INHERITANCE OF                   WHERE RULES FOR THE INHERITANCE OF                      1     4
     REAL PROPERTY, IF PRESENT,                           REAL PROPERTY, IF PRESENT,                        XSQ=     2.81
     FAVOR THE MALE HEIR OR LINE, RATHER THAN             FAVOR THE FEMALE HEIR OR LINE, RATHER THAN        PHI=    0.433
     THE FEMALE  (144)                                    THE MALE  (21)                                    EP =   0.0889

204  DRIFT MORE TOWARD BEING THOSE  0.90 OF  20     204  DRIFT LESS TOWARD BEING THOSE  0.60 OF  15          18     9
     WHERE MARITAL RESIDENCE IS                           WHERE MARITAL RESIDENCE IS                              2     6
     PATRILOCAL, VIRILOCAL, OR AVUNCULOCAL,               PATRILOCAL, VIRILOCAL, OR AVUNCULOCAL,            XSQ=     2.84
     RATHER THAN                                          RATHER THAN                                       PHI=    0.285
     AMBILOCAL OR NEOLOCAL  (270)                         AMBILOCAL OR NEOLOCAL  (270)                      EP =   0.0515

210  IN ALL CASES ARE THOSE           1.00 OF   9     210  DRIFT LESS TOWARD BEING THOSE  0.57 OF   7           9     4
     WHERE MARITAL RESIDENCE IS                           WHERE MARITAL RESIDENCE IS                              0     3
     PATRILOCAL, RATHER THAN                              PATRILOCAL, RATHER THAN                           XSQ=     2.35
     MATRILOCAL  (169)                                    MATRILOCAL  (169)                                 PHI=    0.383
                                                                                                            EP =   0.0625

236  DRIFT TOWARD BEING THOSE         0.73 OF  22     236  DRIFT TOWARD BEING THOSE         0.61 OF  18          16     7
     WHERE THE FAMILY IS                                  WHERE THE FAMILY IS                                     6    11
     OF AN EXTENDED TYPE, RATHER THAN                     OF AN INDEPENDENT TYPE, RATHER THAN               XSQ=     3.36
     AN INDEPENDENT TYPE  (213)                           AN EXTENDED TYPE  (185)                           PHI=    0.290
                                                                                                            EP =   0.0534

272  TILT TOWARD BEING THOSE          0.86 OF   7     272  IN ALL CASES ARE THOSE           1.00 OF   4           1     4
     WHERE THE DIVORCE RATE IS                            WHERE THE DIVORCE RATE IS                               6     0
     LOW  (28) CA                                         HIGH  (29) CA                                     XSQ=     4.48
                                                                                                            PHI=   -0.638
                                                                                                            EP =   0.0152

278  IN ALL CASES ARE THOSE           1.00 OF   2     278  IN ALL CASES ARE THOSE           1.00 OF   5           2     0
     WHERE PROPERTY RIGHTS IN WOMEN ARE                   WHERE PROPERTY RIGHTS IN WOMEN ARE                      0     5
     PRESENT  (8) LWS                                     UNIMPORTANT OR ABSENT  (14) LWS                   XSQ=     2.96
                                                                                                            PHI=    0.650
                                                                                                            EP =   0.0476

311  DRIFT TOWARD BEING THOSE         0.69 OF  16     311  DRIFT TOWARD BEING THOSE         0.75 OF   8          11     2
     WHERE SEXUAL SOCIALIZATION ANXIETY                   WHERE SEXUAL SOCIALIZATION ANXIETY                      5     6
     IS HIGH  (28) W-C                                    IS LOW  (23) W-C                                  XSQ=     2.54
                                                                                                            PHI=    0.325
                                                                                                            EP =   0.0825

317  DRIFT TOWARD BEING THOSE         0.54 OF  13     317  DRIFT TOWARD BEING THOSE         0.89 OF   9           6     8
     WHERE DISPLAY OF AFFECTION TOWARD                    WHERE DISPLAY OF AFFECTION TOWARD                       7     1
     THE INFANT IS LOW  (29) B-B-C                        THE INFANT IS HIGH  (39) B-B-C                    XSQ=     2.55
                                                                                                            PHI=   -0.341
                                                                                                            EP =   0.0743
```

318	TILT TCWARD BEING THCSE WHERE THE CVERALL INDULGENCE OF THE INFANT IS LOW (31) B-B-C	0.60 OF 15	318	TILT TOWARD BEING THOSE WHERE THE OVERALL INDULGENCE OF THE INFANT IS HIGH (40) B-B-C	0.89 OF 9	6 8 9 1 XSQ= 3.70 PHI= -0.393 EP = 0.0333
352	TILT TCWARD BEING THOSE WHERE THE TOTAL POSITIVE PRESSURE TOWARD DEVELCPING OBEDIENT BEHAVICR IN THE CHILD IS HIGH (44) B-B-C	0.75 OF 16	352	TILT TOWARD BEING THCSE WHERE THE TOTAL POSITIVE PRESSURE TOWARD DEVELOPING OBEDIENT BEHAVICR IN THE CHILD IS LOW (28) B-B-C	0.80 OF 10	12 2 4 8 XSQ= 5.44 PHI= 0.457 EP = 0.0138
353	TILT TCWARD BEING THOSE WHERE THE CHILD'S INFERREC ANXIETY OVER NCN-PERFCRMANCE CF CBECIENT BEHAVIOR IS HIGH (42) B-B-C	0.81 OF 16	353	TILT TOWARD BEING THOSE WHERE THE CHILD-S INFERRED ANXIETY CVER NON-PERFORMANCE OF OBEDIENT BEHAVICR IS LOW (32) B-B-C	0.70 OF 10	13 3 3 7 XSQ= 4.84 PHI= 0.431 EP = 0.0152
354	TILT TCWARD BEING THOSE WHERE THE CHILD'S INFERREC ANXIETY OVER PERFCRMANCE CF CBECIENT BEHAVIOR IS HIGH (36) B-B-C	0.81 OF 16	354	TILT TOWARD BEING THCSE WHERE THE CHILD'S INFERRED ANXIETY OVER PERFORMANCE OF OBEDIENT BEHAVICR IS LOW (37) B-B-C	0.70 CF 10	13 3 3 7 XSQ= 4.84 PHI= 0.431 EP = 0.0152
355	LEAN TOWARD BEING THCSE WHERE THE CHILD'S INFERREC CONFLICT REGARDING CBEDIENT BEHAVICR IS HIGH (35) B-B-C	0.81 OF 16	355	LEAN TOWARD BEING THCSE WHERE THE CHILD'S INFERRED CCNFLICT REGARDING OBEDIENT BEHAVICR IS LOW (38) B-B-C	0.80 OF 10	13 2 3 8 XSQ= 7.12 PHI= 0.523 EP = 0.0040
382	TILT TCWARD BEING THOSE WHERE FEMALE INITIATION RITES ARE ABSENT (27) JKB	0.70 OF 10	382	TILT TOWARD BEING THOSE WHERE FEMALE INITIATION RITES ARE PRESENT (38) JKB	0.86 OF 7	3 6 7 1 XSQ= 3.14 PHI= -0.430 EP = 0.0498
392	TILT TCWARD BEING THOSE WHERE PREMARITAL SEX RELATIONS ARE STRCNGLY PUNISHEC ANC IN FACT RARE, OR WEAKLY PUNISHED ANC IN FACT NCT RARE, OR PUNISHED CNLY IF PREGNANCY RESULTS (112) JTW,EA	0.71 OF 17	392	TILT TOWARD BEING THOSE WHERE PREMARITAL SEX RELATICNS ARE FREELY PERMITTED (67) JTW,EA	0.80 OF 10	12 2 5 8 XSQ= 4.59 PHI= 0.412 EP = 0.0183
396	DRIFT TCWARD BEING THCSE WHERE THE STRENGTH CF MENSTRUAL TABOOS IS HIGH (18) WNS	0.53 OF 15	396	DRIFT TOWARD BEING THOSE WHERE THE STRENGTH OF MENSTRUAL TABCCS IS LOW (35) WNS	0.89 CF 9	8 1 7 8 XSQ= 2.67 PHI= 0.333 EP = 0.0803
424	DRIFT TCWARD BEING THCSE WHERE RELIGICUS SPECIALISTS ARE FULL-TIME, RATHER THAN PART-TIME (21) JMH	0.57 OF 7	424	IN ALL CASES ARE THOSE WHERE RELIGIOUS SPECIALISTS ARE PART-TIME, RATHER THAN FULL-TIME (33) JMH	1.00 CF 7	4 0 3 7 XSQ= 3.15 PHI= 0.474 EP = 0.0699

430	IN ALL CASES ARE THOSE WHERE SUPERNATURAL SANCTIONS FOR MORALITY, HAVING AN EFFECT ON AN INDIVIDUAL'S HEALTH, ARE PRESENT (16) GES	1.00 OF 4	430	DRIFT TOWARD BEING THOSE WHERE SUPERNATURAL SANCTIONS FOR MORALITY, HAVING AN EFFECT ON AN INDIVIDUAL'S HEALTH, ARE ABSENT OR UNREPORTED (22) GES	0.67 OF 6	4 2 0 4 XSQ= 2.10 PHI= 0.458 EP = 0.0762
441	TILT TOWARD BEING THOSE WHERE FEAR OF HUMAN BEINGS IS LOW (32) W-C	0.56 OF 16	441	TILT TOWARD BEING THOSE WHERE FEAR OF HUMAN BEINGS IS HIGH (29) W-C	0.91 OF 11	7 10 9 1 XSQ= 4.36 PHI= -0.402 EP = 0.0183
458	LEAN TOWARD BEING THOSE WHERE GAMES, IF PRESENT, INCLUDE GAMES OF STRATEGY (52) R-A-B,EA	0.59 OF 17	458	LEAN TOWARD BEING THOSE WHERE GAMES, IF PRESENT, DO NOT INCLUDE GAMES OF STRATEGY (119) R-A-B,EA	0.92 OF 12	10 1 7 11 XSQ= 5.62 PHI= 0.440 EP = 0.0080
460	LEAN TOWARD BEING THOSE WHERE GAMES, IF PRESENT, ARE NOT LIMITED TO GAMES OF SKILL ONLY (104) R-A-B,EA	0.88 OF 17	460	LEAN TOWARD BEING THOSE WHERE GAMES, IF PRESENT, ARE LIMITED TO GAMES OF SKILL ONLY (67) R-A-B,EA	0.67 OF 12	2 8 15 4 XSQ= 7.11 PHI= -0.495 EP = 0.0045
476	TILT TOWARD BEING THOSE WHERE THE DEGREE OF INSOBRIETY IS MODERATE OR SLIGHT (18) DH	0.85 OF 13	476	TILT TOWARD BEING THOSE WHERE THE DEGREE OF INSOBRIETY IS STRONG (31) DH	0.75 OF 8	2 6 11 2 XSQ= 5.15 PHI= -0.495 EP = 0.0176
477	LEAN TOWARD BEING THOSE WHERE ALCOHOLIC AGGRESSION IS MODERATE OR SLIGHT (19) DH	0.88 OF 8	477	IN ALL CASES ARE THOSE WHERE ALCOHOLIC AGGRESSION IS STRONG (15) DH	1.00 OF 6	1 6 7 0 XSQ= 7.29 PHI= -0.722 EP = 0.0047

****

139 CULTURES WHERE SUPERORDINATE PUNISHMENT IS PRESENT (15) BBW	139 CULTURES WHERE SUPERORDINATE PUNISHMENT IS ABSENT (25) BBW

BACKGROUND ON PAGE 100

BOTH SUBJECT AND PREDICATE

....

15 IN LEFT COLUMN

ASHANTI	BALINESE	CAYAPA	CHEYENNE	CROW	JAPANESE	LAMBA	LEPCHA	ONTONG-JAVA	RIFFIANS
SAMOANS	SANPOIL	TANALA	TIKOPIA	VENDA					

25 IN RIGHT COLUMN

ARANDA	AZANDE	CARIB	CHAGGA	CHUKCHEE	COPR ESKIMO	DELAWARE	DIERI	DOBUANS	GOND
IFUGAO	JIVARO	KAZAK	KURTATCHI	KWAKIUTL	LANGO	LESU	MAORI	MASAI	MURNGIN
TIV	TROBRIAND	WITOTO	YUROK	ZUNI					

360 EXCLUDED BECAUSE UNASCERTAINED

	Left column (present)			Right column (absent)		
33	IN ALL CASES ARE THOSE WHERE THE NATURAL ENVIRONMENT IS OTHER THAN 'VERY HARSH,' I.E., DESERT, DESERT GRASSES AND SHRUBS, TUNDRA, OR HIGH PLATEAU STEPPE (341) FWM	1.00 OF 15	33	TILT LESS TOWARD BEING THOSE WHERE THE NATURAL ENVIRONMENT IS OTHER THAN 'VERY HARSH,' I.E., DESERT, DESERT GRASSES AND SHRUBS, TUNDRA, OR HIGH PLATEAU STEPPE (341) FWM	0.72 OF 25	0 7 15 18 XSQ= 3.34 PHI= -0.289 EP = 0.0328
53	DRIFT TOWARD BEING THOSE WHERE FOOD PRODUCTION IS BY INTENSIVE AGRICULTURE, RATHER THAN BY SIMPLE AGRICULTURE OR INCIPIENT FOOD PRODUCTION (91)	0.56 OF 9	53	DRIFT TOWARD BEING THOSE WHERE FOOD PRODUCTION IS BY SIMPLE AGRICULTURE OR INCIPIENT FOOD PRODUCTION, RATHER THAN BY INTENSIVE AGRICULTURE (147)	0.81 OF 16	5 3 4 13 XSQ= 2.09 PHI= 0.289 EP = 0.0870
54	IN ALL CASES ARE THOSE WHERE FOOD PRODUCTION IS BY INTENSIVE OR SIMPLE AGRICULTURE, RATHER THAN BY INCIPIENT FOOD PRODUCTION (192)	1.00 OF 9	54	DRIFT LESS TOWARD BEING THOSE WHERE FOOD PRODUCTION IS BY INTENSIVE OR SIMPLE AGRICULTURE, RATHER THAN BY INCIPIENT FOOD PRODUCTION (192)	0.63 OF 16	9 10 0 6 XSQ= 2.62 PHI= 0.324 EP = 0.0571
80	TILT LESS TOWARD BEING THOSE WHERE NO CITY OR TOWN IS PRESENT (185)	0.70 OF 10	80	IN ALL CASES ARE THOSE WHERE NO CITY OR TOWN IS PRESENT (185)	1.00 OF 20	3 0 7 20 XSQ= 3.75 PHI= 0.354 EP = 0.0296
82	IN ALL CASES ARE THOSE WHERE A CITY OR TOWN IS PRESENT, OR THE AVERAGE COMMUNITY SIZE IS FIFTY OR GREATER (178)	1.00 OF 10	82	TILT LESS TOWARD BEING THOSE WHERE A CITY OR TOWN IS PRESENT, OR THE AVERAGE COMMUNITY SIZE IS FIFTY OR GREATER (178)	0.60 OF 20	10 12 0 8 XSQ= 3.60 PHI= 0.346 EP = 0.0288

86	TILT TOWARD BEING THOSE 0.75 OF 12 WHERE THE LEVEL OF POLITICAL INTEGRATION IS THE LARGE STATE, THE LITTLE STATE, OR THE MINIMAL STATE (148) GPM	86	TILT TOWARD BEING THOSE 0.68 OF 22 WHERE THE LEVEL OF POLITICAL INTEGRATION IS THE AUTONOMOUS COMMUNITY, OR THE FAMILY (156) GPM	9 7 3 15 XSQ= 4.21 PHI= 0.352 EP = 0.0299
91	DRIFT TOWARD BEING THOSE 0.63 OF 8 WHERE SOCIETAL COMPLEXITY IS HIGH (18) F-W	91	DRIFT TOWARD BEING THOSE 0.82 OF 11 WHERE SOCIETAL COMPLEXITY IS LOW (22) F-W	5 2 3 9 XSQ= 2.24 PHI= 0.343 EP = 0.0739
96	DRIFT TOWARD BEING THOSE 0.71 OF 14 WHERE THE HIERARCHY OF NATIONAL JURISDICTION HAS FOUR, THREE, TWO OR ONE LEVEL (174) GES,EA	96	DRIFT TOWARD BEING THOSE 0.63 OF 24 WHERE THE HIERARCHY OF NATIONAL JURISDICTION HAS NO LEVELS (156) GES,EA	10 9 4 15 XSQ= 2.83 PHI= 0.273 EP = 0.0911
100	IN ALL CASES ARE THOSE 1.00 OF 14 WHERE HIERARCHIES ARE MORE COMPLEX THAN THE 'SIMPLEST,' I. E., MORE COMPLEX THAN TWO LOCAL LEVELS WITH NO NATIONAL LEVELS (267) GES,EA	100	TILT LESS TOWARD BEING THOSE 0.71 OF 24 WHERE HIERARCHIES ARE MORE COMPLEX THAN THE 'SIMPLEST,' I. E., MORE COMPLEX THAN TWO LOCAL LEVELS WITH NO NATIONAL LEVELS (267) GES,EA	14 17 0 7 XSQ= 3.25 PHI= 0.293 EP = 0.0334
118	DRIFT TOWARD BEING THOSE 0.75 OF 4 WHERE THE PERCENTAGE OF OCCUPATIONS THAT ARE SPECIALIZED IS HIGH OR MEDIUM (24) WME	118	DRIFT TOWARD BEING THOSE 0.82 OF 11 WHERE THE PERCENTAGE OF OCCUPATIONS THAT ARE SPECIALIZED IS LOW (25) WME	3 2 1 9 XSQ= 2.09 PHI= 0.373 EP = 0.0769
127	DRIFT TOWARD BEING THOSE 0.75 OF 8 WHERE THE FEMALES' CONTRIBUTION TO SUBSISTENCE IS LOW (32) JKB	127	DRIFT TOWARD BEING THOSE 0.78 OF 9 WHERE THE FEMALES' CONTRIBUTION TO SUBSISTENCE IS HIGH (33) JKB	2 7 6 2 XSQ= 2.85 PHI= -0.410 EP = 0.0567
138	IN ALL CASES ARE THOSE 1.00 OF 15 WHERE SUPERORDINATE JUSTICE IS PRESENT (22) BBW	138	TEND TO BE THOSE 0.72 OF 25 WHERE SUPERORDINATE JUSTICE IS ABSENT (18) BBW	15 7 0 18 XSQ= 16.84 PHI= 0.649 EP = 0.0000
152	IN ALL CASES ARE THOSE 1.00 OF 2 WHERE THE DIFFERENTIATION OF THE JURIDICAL AGENCY FROM THE MEDICAL AGENCY IS HIGH (10) MJ	152	IN ALL CASES ARE THOSE 1.00 OF 4 WHERE THE DIFFERENTIATION OF THE JURIDICAL AGENCY FROM THE MEDICAL AGENCY IS LOW (10) MJ	2 0 0 4 XSQ= 2.34 PHI= 0.625 EP = 0.0667
175	DRIFT MORE TOWARD BEING THOSE 0.87 OF 15 WHERE THE COMMUNITY IS 'KIN-HETEROGENEOUS,' I. E. OTHER THAN A CLAN COMMUNITY OR A DEME (260)	175	DRIFT LESS TOWARD BEING THOSE 0.60 OF 25 WHERE THE COMMUNITY IS 'KIN-HETEROGENEOUS,' I. E. OTHER THAN A CLAN COMMUNITY OR A DEME (260)	2 10 13 15 XSQ= 2.03 PHI= -0.225 EP = 0.0911

184	DRIFT TOWARD BEING THCSE 0.88 OF 8 WHERE THE LARGEST NCN-CCGNATIC KIN GROUP IS SMALLER THAN A PHRATRY, I. E. A SIB CR LINEAGE (175)	184	DRIFT TOWARD BEING THOSE 0.53 CF 17 WHERE THE LARGEST NON-COGNATIC KIN GROUP IS THE MOEITY CR PHRATRY (77)	1 9 7 8 XSQ= 2.21 PHI= -0.298 EP = 0.0875
236	TILT TCWARD BEING THOSE 0.80 OF 15 WHERE THE FAMILY IS OF AN EXTENDED TYPE, RATHER THAN AN INDEPENDENT TYPE (213)	236	TILT TOWARD BEING THOSE 0.56 CF 25 WHERE THE FAMILY IS OF AN INDEPENDENT TYPE, RATHER THAN AN EXTENDED TYPE (185)	12 11 3 14 XSQ= 3.61 PHI= 0.300 EP = 0.0464
263	LEAN TCWARD BEING THCSE 0.67 OF 15 WHERE WIVES ARE CBTAINEC BY RELATIVELY EASY MEANS, NAMELY BY TCKEN BRIDE-PRICE, GIFT EXCHANGE, ABSENCE CF ANY CCNSIDERATICN, OR RECEIPT CF DCWRY (162)	263	LEAN TOWARD BEING THOSE 0.80 CF 25 WHERE WIVES ARE OBTAINED BY RELATIVELY DIFFICULT MEANS, NAMELY BY BRIDE-PRICE, BRIDE-SERVICE, CR EXCHANGING A FEMALE RELATIVE (233)	5 20 10 5 XSQ= 6.83 PHI= -0.413 EP = 0.0062
300	DRIFT TCWARD BEING THCSE 0.88 OF 8 WHERE THE POST-PARTUM SEX TABCO LASTS SIX MCNTHS OR LESS (73)	300	DRIFT TOWARD BEING THCSE 0.60 CF 15 WHERE THE POST-PARTUM SEX TABOO LASTS LONGER THAN SIX MONTHS (51)	1 9 7 6 XSQ= 3.05 PHI= -0.364 EP = 0.0743
338	LEAN TCWARD BEING THCSE 0.60 OF 10 WHERE THE CHILD'S INFERREC ANXIETY OVER PERFCRMANCE CF RESPONSIBLE BEHAVIOR IS LCW (29) B-B-C	338	LEAN TOWARD BEING THOSE 0.93 CF 15 WHERE THE CHILD'S INFERRED ANXIETY OVER PERFORMANCE OF RESPONSIBLE BEHAVICR IS HIGH (44) B-B-C	4 14 6 1 XSQ= 6.03 PHI= -0.491 EP = 0.0068
370	DRIFT TCWARD BEING THCSE 0.75 OF 12 WHERE THE SEGREGATICN CF ADOLESCENT BOYS IS ABSENT (148)	370	DRIFT TOWARD BEING THOSE 0.60 OF 20 WHERE THE SEGREGATION OF ADOLESCENT BOYS IS COMPLETE OR PARTIAL (95)	3 12 9 8 XSQ= 2.42 PHI= -0.275 EP = 0.0759
402	TILT TOWARD BEING THCSE 0.73 OF 11 WHERE EXPLANATICNS OF ILLNESS CF AN CRAL NATURE ARE ABSENT (30) W-C	402	TILT TOWARD BEING THOSE 0.75 OF 16 WHERE EXPLANATIONS OF ILLNESS OF AN ORAL NATURE ARE PRESENT (31) W-C	3 12 8 4 XSQ= 4.24 PHI= -0.396 EP = 0.0220
424	TILT TCWARC BEING THOSE 0.75 OF 4 WHERE RELIGICUS SPECIALISTS ARE FULL-TIME, RATHER THAN PART-TIME (21) JMH	424	TILT TOWARD BEING THOSE 0.90 OF 10 WHERE RELIGIOUS SPECIALISTS ARE PART-TIME, RATHER THAN FULL-TIME (33) JMH	3 1 1 9 XSQ= 3.16 PHI= 0.475 EP = 0.0410
431	IN ALL CASES ARE THCSE 1.00 OF 2 WHERE SUPERNATURAL SANCTICNS FOR MORALITY, HAVING AN EFFECT ON AN INDIVIDUAL'S AFTER LIFE, ARE PRESENT (10) GES	431	IN ALL CASES ARE THOSE 1.00 OF 8 WHERE SUPERNATURAL SANCTIONS FOR MORALITY, HAVING AN EFFECT ON AN INDIVIDUAL'S AFTERLIFE, ARE ABSENT OR UNREPORTED (25) GES	2 0 0 8 XSQ= 4.73 PHI= 0.687 EP = 0.0222

```
441  LEAN TOWARD BEING THOSE         0.73 OF  11      441  LEAN TOWARD BEING THOSE        0.88 OF  16             3    14
     WHERE FEAR OF HUMAN BEINGS                           WHERE FEAR OF HUMAN BEINGS                             8     2
     IS LOW  (32) W-C                                     IS HIGH  (29) W-C                              XSQ=     7.72
                                                                                                         PHI=   -0.535
                                                                                                         EP =   0.0034
```

140 CULTURES
WHERE THE LEVEL OF SOCIAL SANCTION IS
PUBLIC CORPOREAL SANCTION, RATHER THAN
PRIVATE SETTLEMENT (28) JMH

140 CULTURES
WHERE THE LEVEL OF SOCIAL SANCTION IS
PRIVATE SETTLEMENT, RATHER THAN
PUBLIC CORPOREAL SANCTION (16) JMH

BACKGROUND ON PAGE 100

SUBJECT ONLY

28 IN LEFT COLUMN

ARAUCANIANS	AZANDE	AZTEC	BURMESE	BURUSHO	CAMBODIANS	CAYAPA	CHAGGA	COPR ESKIMO	CREEK
CROW	CUNA	CARC	IBAN	KASKA	KOREANS	KURTATCHI	MARSHALLESE	MBUNDU	NAMA
NAVAHO	NUER	OJIBWA	SAMOYED	TIKOPIA	TROBRIAND	VIETNAMESE	YAKUT		

16 IN RIGHT COLUMN

ANDAMANESE	ARANDA	BEMBA	CHUKCHEE	JIVARO	KORYAK	LOLO	MANDAN	MIAO	PUKAPUKA
RWALA	SIRIONO	TEHUELCHE	TIMBIRA	TUPINAMBA	YUROK				

10 EXCLUDED BECAUSE IRRELEVANT

BULGARIANS	GILYAK	KAREN	KHASI	SAMOANS	TALLENSI	THONGA	TIV	TODA	WOLEAIANS

346 EXCLUDED BECAUSE UNASCERTAINED

81	TILT TOWARD BEING THOSE 0.52 OF 23 WHERE A CITY OR TOWN IS PRESENT, OR THE AVERAGE COMMUNITY SIZE IS 200 OR GREATER (89)	81	TILT TOWARD BEING THOSE 0.92 OF 13 WHERE NO CITY OR TOWN IS PRESENT, AND THE AVERAGE COMMUNITY SIZE IS SMALLER THAN 200 (135)	12 1 11 12 XSQ= 5.33 PHI= 0.385 EP = 0.0111
83	TILT LESS TOWARD BEING THOSE 0.58 OF 19 WHERE, WITH NO CITY AND NO TOWN PRESENT, THE AVERAGE COMMUNITY SIZE IS SMALLER THAN 200, RATHER THAN BETWEEN 200 AND 999 (135)	83	TILT MORE TOWARD BEING THOSE 0.92 OF 13 WHERE, WITH NO CITY AND NO TOWN PRESENT, THE AVERAGE COMMUNITY SIZE IS SMALLER THAN 200, RATHER THAN BETWEEN 200 AND 999 (135)	8 1 11 12 XSQ= 2.98 PHI= 0.305 EP = 0.0497
86	LEAN TOWARD BEING THOSE 0.64 OF 25 WHERE THE LEVEL OF POLITICAL INTEGRATION IS THE LARGE STATE, THE LITTLE STATE, OR THE MINIMAL STATE (148) GPM	86	LEAN TOWARD BEING THOSE 0.80 OF 15 WHERE THE LEVEL OF POLITICAL INTEGRATION IS THE AUTONOMOUS COMMUNITY, OR THE FAMILY (156) GPM	16 3 9 12 XSQ= 5.62 PHI= 0.375 EP = 0.0098
91	TILT TOWARD BEING THOSE 0.50 OF 14 WHERE SOCIETAL COMPLEXITY IS HIGH (18) F-W	91	IN ALL CASES ARE THOSE 1.00 OF 7 WHERE SOCIETAL COMPLEXITY IS LOW (22) F-W	7 0 7 7 XSQ= 3.24 PHI= 0.393 EP = 0.0468

106	DRIFT TOWARD BEING THOSE WHERE CLASS STRATIFICATION, IF PRESENT, IS BASED ON SOMETHING OTHER THAN WEALTH (126)	0.74 OF 19	106	DRIFT TOWARD BEING THOSE WHERE CLASS STRATIFICATION, IF PRESENT, IS BASED ON WEALTH (77)	0.71 OF 7	5 5 14 2 XSQ= 2.70 PHI= -0.322 EP = 0.0687
116	DRIFT LESS TOWARD BEING THOSE WHERE OCCUPATIONAL SPECIALIZATION IS PART-TIME ONLY (34) JMH	0.54 OF 28	116	DRIFT MORE TOWARD BEING THOSE WHERE OCCUPATIONAL SPECIALIZATION IS PART-TIME ONLY (34) JMH	0.88 OF 16	13 2 15 14 XSQ= 3.82 PHI= 0.294 XP = 0.0508
132	TILT TOWARD BEING THOSE WHERE ECONOMIC EXCHANGE INVOLVES THE USE OF MONEY (37) JMH	0.79 OF 28	132	TILT TOWARD BEING THOSE WHERE ECONOMIC EXCHANGE DOES NOT INVOLVE THE USE OF MONEY (17) JMH	0.63 OF 16	22 6 6 10 XSQ= 5.75 PHI= 0.362 XP = 0.0165
138	DRIFT TOWARD BEING THOSE WHERE SUPERORDINATE JUSTICE IS PRESENT (22) BBW	0.63 OF 8	138	IN ALL CASES ARE THOSE WHERE SUPERORDINATE JUSTICE IS ABSENT (18) BBW	1.00 OF 4	5 0 3 4 XSQ= 2.10 PHI= 0.418 EP = 0.0808
186	TILT LESS TOWARD BEING THOSE WHERE THE KIN GROUP IS OTHER THAN EXCLUSIVELY PATRILINEAL (250)	0.61 OF 28	186	TILT MORE TOWARD BEING THOSE WHERE THE KIN GROUP IS OTHER THAN EXCLUSIVELY PATRILINEAL (250)	0.94 OF 16	11 1 17 15 XSQ= 4.06 PHI= 0.304 XP = 0.0439
196	DRIFT TOWARD BEING THOSE WHERE INDIVIDUAL RIGHTS IN REAL PROPERTY, AND RULES FOR INHERITANCE, ARE PRESENT (194)	0.79 OF 19	196	DRIFT TOWARD BEING THOSE WHERE INDIVIDUAL RIGHTS IN REAL PROPERTY, OR RULES FOR INHERITANCE, ARE ABSENT (87)	0.58 OF 12	15 5 4 7 XSQ= 2.99 PHI= 0.310 EP = 0.0564
279	IN ALL CASES ARE THOSE WHERE WIFE-LENDING AND WIFE EXCHANGE ARE UNIMPORTANT OR ABSENT (19) LWS	1.00 OF 4	279	IN ALL CASES ARE THOSE WHERE WIFE-LENDING OR WIFE-EXCHANGE IS PRESENT (10) LWS	1.00 OF 4	0 4 4 0 XSQ= 4.50 PHI= -0.750 EP = 0.0286
323	TILT TOWARD BEING THOSE WHERE THE CONSTANCY OF PRESENCE OF THE INFANT'S NURTURANT AGENT IS LOW (45) B-B-C	0.86 OF 14	323	TILT TOWARD BEING THOSE WHERE THE CONSTANCY OF PRESENCE OF THE INFANT'S NURTURANT AGENT IS HIGH (29) B-B-C	0.70 OF 10	2 7 12 3 XSQ= 5.53 PHI= -0.480 EP = 0.0104
334	TILT TOWARD BEING THOSE WHERE THE INDULGENCE OF THE CHILD IS LOW (38) B-B-C	0.64 OF 14	334	TILT TOWARD BEING THOSE WHERE THE INDULGENCE OF THE CHILD IS HIGH (40) B-B-C	0.80 OF 10	5 8 9 2 XSQ= 3.00 PHI= -0.353 EP = 0.0472

346	LEAN TOWARC BEING THOSE 0.71 OF 14 WHERE THE CHILD'S INFERREC ANXIETY OVER PERFCRMANCE CF SELF-RELIANT BEHAVIOR IS HIGH (37) B-B-C	346	LEAN TOWARD BEING THOSE 0.89 CF 9 WHERE THE CHILD'S INFERRED ANXIETY CVER PERFORMANCE OF SELF-RELIANT BEHAVICR IS LOW (39) B-B-C	10 1 4 8 XSQ= 5.75 PHI= 0.500 EP = 0.0094
347	LEAN TCWARC BEING THCSE 0.71 OF 14 WHERE THE CHILD'S INFERREC CONFLICT REGARDING SELF-RELIANT BEHAVIOR IS HIGH (37) B-B-C	347	LEAN TOWARD BEING THOSE 0.89 OF 9 WHERE THE CHILD'S INFERRED CCNFLICT REGARDING SELF-RELIANT BEHAVICR IS LOW (39) B-B-C	10 1 4 8 XSQ= 5.75 PHI= 0.500 EP = 0.0094
392	DRIFT TCWARD BEING THOSE 0.74 OF 19 WHERE PREMARITAL SEX RELATIONS ARE STRCNGLY PUNISHEC AND IN FACT RARE, OR WEAKLY PUNISHED ANC IN FACT NCT RARE, OR PUNISHED CNLY IF PREGNANCY RESULTS (112) JTW,EA	392	DRIFT TOWARD BEING THCSE 0.64 OF 11 WHERE PREMARITAL SEX RELATICNS ARE FREELY PERMITTED (67) JTW,EA	14 4 5 7 XSQ= 2.64 PHI= 0.297 EP = 0.0626
419	TILT TCWARD BEING THCSE 0.84 OF 19 WHERE MILITARY GLORY IS STRCNGLY CR MODERATELY EMPHASIZED (55) PES	419	TILT TOWARD BEING THOSE 0.60 CF 10 WHERE MILITARY GLORY IS NEGLIGIBLY EMPHASIZED (31) PES	16 4 3 6 XSQ= 4.10 PHI= 0.376 EP = 0.0317
424	TILT TOWARD BEING THOSE 0.54 OF 28 WHERE RELIGICUS SPECIALISTS ARE FULL-TIME, RATHER THAN PART-TIME (21) JMH	424	TILT TOWARD BEING THOSE 0.88 OF 16 WHERE RELIGIOUS SPECIALISTS ARE PART-TIME, RATHER THAN FULL-TIME (33) JMH	15 2 13 14 XSQ= 5.62 PHI= 0.357 XP = 0.0178
429	IN ALL CASES ARE THCSE 1.00 OF 9 WHERE SUPERNATURAL SANCTICNS FOR MORALITY ARE PRESENT (28) GES	429	LEAN TOWARD BEING THOSE 0.80 CF 5 WHERE SUPERNATURAL SANCTIONS FCR MCRALITY ARE ABSENT OR UNREPORTED (9) GES	9 1 0 4 XSQ= 6.54 PHI= 0.684 EP = 0.0050
458	TILT LESS TOWARC BEING THCSE 0.52 OF 21 WHERE GAMES, IF PRESENT, DC NCT INCLUDE GAMES OF STRATEGY (119) R-A-B,EA	458	IN ALL CASES ARE THOSE 1.00 OF 10 WHERE GAMES, IF PRESENT, DO NOT INCLUDE GAMES OF STRATEGY (119) R-A-B,EA	10 0 11 10 XSQ= 5.02 PHI= 0.402 EP = 0.0118
460	TILT TCWARD BEING THCSE 0.76 OF 21 WHERE GAMES, IF PRESENT, ARE NCT LIMITED TC GAMES CF SKILL CNLY (104) R-A-B,EA	460	TILT TOWARD BEING THOSE 0.70 CF 10 WHERE GAMES, IF PRESENT, ARE LIMITED TO GAMES OF SKILL ONLY (67) R-A-B,EA	5 7 16 3 XSQ= 4.30 PHI= -0.372 EP = 0.0214

141 CULTURES
WHERE THE LEVEL OF SOCIAL SANCTION IS
PUBLIC CORPOREAL SANCTION, RATHER THAN
PUBLIC PROPERTY SANCTION OR
PRIVATE SETTLEMENT (28) JMH

141 CULTURES
WHERE THE LEVEL OF SOCIAL SANCTION IS
PUBLIC PROPERTY SANCTION OR
PRIVATE SETTLEMENT, RATHER THAN
PUBLIC CORPOREAL SANCTION (26) JMH

BACKGROUND ON PAGE 100

PREDICATE ONLY

28 IN LEFT COLUMN

ARAUCANIANS	AZANDE	AZTEC	BURMESE	BURUSHO	CAMBODIANS	CAYAPA	CHAGGA	COPR ESKIMO	CREEK
CROW	CUNA	CARC	IBAN	KASKA	KOREANS	KURTATCHI	MARSHALLESE	MBUNDU	NAMA
NAVAHO	NUER	OJIBWA	SAMOYED	TIKOPIA	TROBRIAND	VIETNAMESE	YAKUT		

26 IN RIGHT COLUMN

ANDAMANESE	ARANDA	BEMBA	BULGARIANS	CHUKCHEE	GILYAK	JIVARO	KAREN	KHASI	KORYAK
LOLO	MANDAN	MIAO	PUKAPUKA	RWALA	SAMOANS	SIRIONO	TALLENSI	TEHUELCHE	THONGA
TIMBIRA	TIV	TODA	TUPINAMBA	WOLEAIANS	YUROK				

346 EXCLUDED BECAUSE UNASCERTAINED

142 CULTURES
WHERE THE LEVEL OF SOCIAL SANCTION IS
PUBLIC CORPOREAL SANCTION OR
PUBLIC PROPERTY SANCTION, RATHER THAN
PRIVATE SETTLEMENT (38) JMH

142 CULTURES
WHERE THE LEVEL OF SOCIAL SANCTION IS
PRIVATE SETTLEMENT, RATHER THAN
PUBLIC CORPOREAL SANCTION OR
PUBLIC PROPERTY SETTLEMENT (16) JMH

BACKGROUND ON PAGE 100

PREDICATE ONLY

38 IN LEFT COLUMN

ARAUCANIANS	AZANDE	AZTEC	BULGARIANS	BURMESE	BURUSHO	CAMBODIANS	CAYAPA	CHAGGA	COPR ESKIMO
CREEK	CROW	CUNA	DARD	GILYAK	IBAN	KAREN	KASKA	KHASI	KOREANS
KURTATCHI	MARSHALLESE	MBUNDU	NAMA	NAVAHO	NUER	OJIBWA	SAMOANS	SAMOYED	TALLENSI
THONGA	TIKOPIA	TIV	TODA	TROBRIAND	VIETNAMESE	WOLEAIANS	YAKUT		

16 IN RIGHT COLUMN

ANDAMANESE	ARANDA	BEMBA	CHUKCHEE	JIVARO	KORYAK	LOLO	MANDAN	MIAO	PUKAPUKA
RWALA	SIRIONO	TEHUELCHE	TIMBIRA	TUPINAMBA	YUROK				

346 EXCLUDED BECAUSE UNASCERTAINED

143 CULTURES
WHERE THE RATIC CF RESTITUTIVE
TC REPRESSIVE SANCTICNS
IS HIGH (20) WME

143 CULTURES
WHERE THE RATIO OF RESTITUTIVE
TO REPRESSIVE SANCTICNS
IS MEDIUM OR LOW (32) WME

BACKGROUND ON PAGE 101

PREDICATE ONLY

20 IN LEFT CCLUMN

ALBANIANS	ALCRESE	CHAGGA	CZECHS	IBAN	IFUGAO	KACHIN	KAZAK	LAPPS	LEPCHA
NUER	RIFFIANS	SEMANG	SOMALI	TALLENSI	TIV	TODA	YAKUT	YAO	YUROK

32 IN RIGHT CCLUMN

ARANDA	ASHANTI	AZANCE	BHIL	CARIB	COORG	COPR ESKIMO	GANDA	GONC	HAVASUPAI
INCA	JIVARC	KCREANS	MAGUZAWA	MATACO	MISKITO	MUNDURUCU	NAMA	NYAKYUSA	OJIBWA
PAPAGO	RWALA	SENIANG	SIWANS	TANALA	THONGA	TIKOPIA	TIMBIRA	TROBRIAND	WOLOF
YAHGAN	YCKUTS								

348 EXCLUDED BECAUSE UNASCERTAINEC

```
**********************************************************************************************************************

144  CULTURES                                      144  CULTURES
     WHERE THE RATIC CF RESTITUTIVE                     WHERE THE RATIO OF RESTITUTIVE
     TC REPRESSIVE SANCTICNS                            TO REPRESSIVE SANCTIONS
     IS HIGH OR MEDIUM  (27) WME                        IS LOW  (25) WME


BACKGROUND ON PAGE 101                                                         BOTH SUBJECT AND PREDICATE
......................................................................................................................

      27  IN LEFT CCLUMN

ALBANIANS  ALCRESE    BHIL       CHAGGA     CZECHS     GOND       IBAN       IFUGAO     KACHIN     KAZAK
LAPPS      LEPCHA     MISKITC    NUER       RIFFIANS   RWALA      SEMANG     SIWANS     SOMALI     TALLENSI
THONGA     TIMBIRA    TIV        TOCA       YAKUT      YAO        YUROK

      25  IN RIGHT CCLUMN

ARANDA     ASHANTI    AZANDE     CARIB      COORG      COPR ESKIMO GANDA     HAVASUPAI  INCA       JIVARO
KOREANS    MAGUZAWA   MATACO     MUNCURUCU  NAMA       NYAKYUSA   OJIBWA     PAPAGO     SENIANG    TANALA
TIKOPIA    TRCBRIANC  WOLCF      YAHGAN     YOKUTS

     348  EXCLUDED BECAUSE UNASCERTAINEC

----------------------------------------------------------------------------------------------------------------------
 48  TILT TCWARD BEING THCSE         0.80 OF  10    48  TILT TOWARD BEING THOSE         0.64 CF  14           2      9
     WHERE THE FOCD SUPPLY IS NCT SECURE,               WHERE THE FOOD SUPPLY IS SECURE,                        8      5
     AND FCCD SHORTAGES ARE                             AND FOOD SHORTAGES ARE                             XSQ=    3.00
     FREQUENT CR ANNUAL  (41) MGW                       RARE OR OCCASIONAL  (38) MGW                       PHI=  -0.353
                                                                                                           EP =  0.0472

 51  DRIFT MORE TCWARD BEING THCSE 0.78 OF  27      51  DRIFT LESS TOWARD BEING THOSE  0.52 OF  25         21     13
     WHERE SUBSISTENCE IS PRIMARILY BY                  WHERE SUBSISTENCE IS PRIMARILY BY                   6     12
     FCCD PRCDUCTICN -- I. E., AGRICULTURE              FOOD PRODUCTION -- I. E., AGRICULTURE              XSQ=    2.76
     OR HUSBANDRY -- RATHER THAN BY                     OR HUSBANDRY -- RATHER THAN BY                     PHI=   0.230
     GATHERING  (253)                                   GATHERING  (253)                                   XP =  0.0968

 62  LEAN MCRE TOWARC BEING THCSE    0.89 OF  27    62  LEAN LESS TOWARD BEING THOSE    0.52 CF  25        24     13
     WHERE HUSBANDRY CF SCME KIND                       WHERE HUSBANDRY OF SOME KIND                        3     12
     IS PRESENT  (228)                                  IS PRESENT  (228)                                  XSQ=    6.90
                                                                                                           PHI=   0.364
                                                                                                           XP =  0.0086

 98  TILT TCWARD BEING THOSE         0.85 OF  27    98  TILT TOWARD BEING THOSE         0.50 OF  24        23     12
     WHERE THE HIERARCHY                                WHERE THE HIERARCHY                                 4     12
     CF LCCAL JURISDICTION HAS                          OF LOCAL JURISDICTION HAS                          XSQ=    5.76
     FOUR CR THREE LEVELS  (238) GES,EA                 TWO LEVELS  (93) GES,EA                            PHI=   0.336
                                                                                                           XP =  0.0164
```

99	DRIFT TOWARD BEING THOSE 0.80 OF 10 WHERE, WITH NATIONAL HIERARCHY ABSENT, THE HIERARCHY OF LOCAL JURISDICTION HAS FOUR OR THREE LEVELS (93) GES,EA	99	DRIFT TOWARD BEING THOSE 0.64 OF 11 WHERE, WITH NATIONAL HIERARCHY ABSENT, THE HIERARCHY OF LOCAL JURISDICTION HAS TWO LEVELS (63) GES,EA	8 4 2 7 XSQ= 2.49 PHI= 0.344 EP = 0.0805
100	DRIFT MORE TOWARD BEING THOSE 0.93 OF 27 WHERE HIERARCHIES ARE MORE COMPLEX THAN THE 'SIMPLEST,' I. E., MORE COMPLEX THAN TWO LOCAL LEVELS WITH NO NATIONAL LEVELS (267) GES,EA	100	DRIFT LESS TOWARD BEING THOSE 0.71 OF 24 WHERE HIERARCHIES ARE MORE COMPLEX THAN THE 'SIMPLEST,' I. E., MORE COMPLEX THAN TWO LOCAL LEVELS WITH NO NATIONAL LEVELS (267) GES,EA	25 17 2 7 XSQ= 2.78 PHI= 0.233 XP = 0.0956
106	TILT TOWARD BEING THOSE 0.67 OF 18 WHERE CLASS STRATIFICATION, IF PRESENT, IS BASED ON WEALTH (77)	106	TILT TOWARD BEING THOSE 0.79 OF 14 WHERE CLASS STRATIFICATION, IF PRESENT, IS BASED ON SOMETHING OTHER THAN WEALTH (126)	12 3 6 11 XSQ= 4.78 PHI= 0.387 EP = 0.0155
132	DRIFT TOWARD BEING THOSE 0.82 OF 11 WHERE ECONOMIC EXCHANGE INVOLVES THE USE OF MONEY (37) JMH	132	DRIFT TOWARD BEING THOSE 0.67 OF 9 WHERE ECONOMIC EXCHANGE DOES NOT INVOLVE THE USE OF MONEY (17) JMH	9 3 2 6 XSQ= 3.04 PHI= 0.390 EP = 0.0648
135	TILT TOWARD BEING THOSE 0.89 OF 9 WHERE INDIVIDUAL OWNERSHIP OF ECONOMICALLY SIGNIFICANT PROPERTY IS PRESENT (24) GES	135	TILT TOWARD BEING THOSE 0.67 OF 9 WHERE INDIVIDUAL OWNERSHIP OF ECONOMICALLY SIGNIFICANT PROPERTY IS NEGLIGIBLE OR ABSENT (14) GES	8 3 1 6 XSQ= 3.74 PHI= 0.456 EP = 0.0498
141	DRIFT TOWARD BEING THOSE 0.64 OF 11 WHERE THE LEVEL OF SOCIAL SANCTION IS PUBLIC PROPERTY SANCTION OR PRIVATE SETTLEMENT, RATHER THAN PUBLIC CORPOREAL SANCTION (26) JMH	141	DRIFT TOWARD BEING THOSE 0.78 OF 9 WHERE THE LEVEL OF SOCIAL SANCTION IS PUBLIC CORPOREAL SANCTION, RATHER THAN PUBLIC PROPERTY SANCTION OR PRIVATE SETTLEMENT (28) JMH	4 7 7 2 XSQ= 1.96 PHI= -0.313 EP = 0.0923
185	IN ALL CASES ARE THOSE 1.00 OF 20 WHERE THE LARGEST NON-COGNATIC KIN GROUP IS THE MOEITY OR PHRATRY OR SIB (194)	185	DRIFT LESS TOWARD BEING THOSE 0.82 OF 17 WHERE THE LARGEST NON-COGNATIC KIN GROUP IS THE MOEITY OR PHRATRY OR SIB (194)	20 14 0 3 XSQ= 1.84 PHI= 0.223 EP = 0.0875
309	TILT TOWARD BEING THOSE 0.88 OF 8 WHERE ORAL SOCIALIZATION ANXIETY IS HIGH (26) W-C	309	TILT TOWARD BEING THOSE 0.67 OF 9 WHERE ORAL SOCIALIZATION ANXIETY IS LOW (27) W-C	7 3 1 6 XSQ= 3.14 PHI= 0.430 EP = 0.0498
323	DRIFT TOWARD BEING THOSE 0.78 OF 9 WHERE THE CONSTANCY OF PRESENCE OF THE INFANT'S NURTURANT AGENT IS LOW (45) B-B-C	323	DRIFT TOWARD BEING THOSE 0.64 OF 11 WHERE THE CONSTANCY OF PRESENCE OF THE INFANT'S NURTURANT AGENT IS HIGH (29) B-B-C	2 7 7 4 XSQ= 1.96 PHI= -0.313 EP = 0.0923

337	DRIFT TOWARD BEING THOSE WHERE THE CHILD'S INFERRED ANXIETY OVER NON-PERFORMANCE OF RESPONSIBLE BEHAVIOR IS HIGH (38) B-B-C	0.80 OF 10	337	DRIFT TOWARD BEING THOSE WHERE THE CHILD'S INFERRED ANXIETY OVER NON-PERFORMANCE OF RESPONSIBLE BEHAVIOR IS LOW (35) B-B-C	0.58 OF 12	8 5 2 7 XSQ= 1.92 PHI= 0.295 EP = 0.0991
382	TILT TOWARD BEING THOSE WHERE FEMALE INITIATION RITES ARE ABSENT (27) JKB	0.85 OF 13	382	TILT TOWARD BEING THOSE WHERE FEMALE INITIATION RITES ARE PRESENT (38) JKB	0.67 OF 12	2 8 11 4 XSQ= 4.87 PHI= -0.441 EP = 0.0154
402	DRIFT TOWARD BEING THOSE WHERE EXPLANATIONS OF ILLNESS OF AN ORAL NATURE ARE PRESENT (31) W-C	0.80 OF 10	402	DRIFT TOWARD BEING THOSE WHERE EXPLANATIONS OF ILLNESS OF AN ORAL NATURE ARE ABSENT (30) W-C	0.67 OF 9	8 3 2 6 XSQ= 2.53 PHI= 0.365 EP = 0.0698
427	TILT TOWARD BEING THOSE WHERE A HIGH GOD, IF PRESENT, IS ACTIVE, RATHER THAN INACTIVE (87) GES,EA	0.84 OF 19	427	TILT TOWARD BEING THOSE WHERE A HIGH GOD, IF PRESENT, IS INACTIVE, RATHER THAN ACTIVE (69) GES,EA	0.64 OF 11	16 4 3 7 XSQ= 5.19 PHI= 0.416 EP = 0.0147
435	IN ALL CASES ARE THOSE WHERE ABANDONMENT OF THE HOUSE OF THE DEAD IS NOT PRACTICED (19) LWS	1.00 OF 4	435	DRIFT TOWARD BEING THOSE WHERE ABANDONMENT OF THE HOUSE OF THE DEAD IS PRACTICED (12) LWS	0.67 OF 6	0 4 4 2 XSQ= 2.10 PHI= -0.458 EP = 0.0762
446	DRIFT TOWARD BEING THOSE WHERE WITCHCRAFT IS MODERATELY PRESENT OR ABSENT (24) GES	0.78 OF 9	446	DRIFT TOWARD BEING THOSE WHERE WITCHCRAFT IS SIGNIFICANTLY PRESENT (14) GES	0.78 OF 9	2 7 7 2 XSQ= 3.56 PHI= -0.444 EP = 0.0567
474	DRIFT TOWARD BEING THOSE WHERE BOASTFULNESS IS MODERATE, NEGLIBIBLE, OR UNREPORTED (48) PES	0.70 OF 23	474	DRIFT TOWARD BEING THOSE WHERE BOASTFULNESS IS EXTREME (41) PES	0.63 OF 16	7 10 16 6 XSQ= 2.75 PHI= -0.266 EP = 0.0586

****

145 CULTURES WHERE THE LEGAL ROLE DIFFERENTIATION IS HIGH (28) WME	145 CULTURES WHERE THE LEGAL ROLE DIFFERENTIATION IS MEDIUM OR LOW (21) WME

BACKGROUND ON PAGE 101 — NEITHER SUBJECT NOR PREDICATE

....

28 IN LEFT COLUMN

ALORESE	ASHANTI	AZANDE	CHAGGA	CZECHS	DARD	GANDA	GOND	INCA	KAZAK
LAPPS	LEPCHA	MAGUZAWA	NAMA	NYAKYUSA	OJIBWA	RIFFIANS	SEMANG	SIWANS	TANALA
THONGA	TIKOPIA	TROBRIAND	VIETNAMESE	WOLOF	YAKUT	YAO	YOKUTS		

21 IN RIGHT COLUMN

ARANDA	CARIB	COORG	COPR ESKIMO	HAVASUPAI	IBAN	IFUGAO	KACHIN	KAPAUKU	MATACO
MISKITO	NAMBICUARA	NUER	PAPAGO	SENIANG	TALLENSI	TIMBIRA	TIV	TODA	YAHGAN
YUROK									

351 EXCLUDED BECAUSE UNASCERTAINED

----

146 CULTURES
WHERE THE LEGAL RCLE CIFFERENTIATICN
IS HIGH CR MEDIUM (36) WME

146 CULTURES
WHERE THE LEGAL ROLE DIFFERENTIATICN
IS LOW (13) WME

BACKGROUND ON PAGE 101

NEITHER SUBJECT NOR PREDICATE

36 IN LEFT CCLUMN

ALORESE	ASHANTI	AZANDE	CHAGGA	COORG	CZECHS	DARD	GANDA	GOND	HAVASUPAI
INCA	KACHIN	KAPAUKU	KAZAK	LAPPS	LEPCHA	MAGUZAWA	MATACO	MISKITO	NAMA
NAMBICUARA	NYAKYUSA	OJIBWA	RIFFIANS	SENIANG	SIWANS	TANALA	THCNGA	TIKCPIA	TIMBIRA
TROBRIAND	VIETNAMESE	WCLCF	YAKUT	YAO	YOKUTS				

13 IN RIGHT CCLUMN

ARANDA	CARIB	CCPR ESKIMO IBAN	IFUGAO	NUER	PAPAGO	SEMANG	TALLENSI	TIV
TODA	YAHGAN	YURCK						

351 EXCLUDED BECAUSE UNASCERTAINED

****

147 CULTURES WHERE CODIFIED LAWS ARE PRESENT (20) LWS	147 CULTURES WHERE CODIFIED LAWS ARE UNIMPORTANT OR ABSENT (13) LWS

BACKGROUND ON PAGE 101

BOTH SUBJECT AND PREDICATE

20 IN LEFT COLUMN

AINU, INCA, ALBANIANS, KAZAK, ARAUCANIANS, LANGO, ASHANTI, LAPPS, AZTEC, OMAHA, CREEK, RWALA, DIERI, SAMOANS, HANO, SHILLUK, HEBREWS, TODA, IBAN, TROBRIAND

13 IN RIGHT COLUMN

ABIPON, VEDDA, ANDAMANESE, WITOTO, CHUKCHEE, YAHGAN, FANG, HAIDA, KUNG, KWAKIUTL, NAMA, SEMANG, SERI

367 EXCLUDED BECAUSE UNASCERTAINED

44	DRIFT TOWARD BEING THOSE WHERE SETTLEMENTS ARE FIXED (222)	0.70 OF 20	44	DRIFT TOWARD BEING THOSE WHERE SETTLEMENTS ARE NON-FIXED (110)	0.67 OF 12	14 4 6 8 XSQ= 2.74 PHI= 0.293 EP = 0.0683
46	TILT TOWARD BEING THOSE OTHER THAN WHERE SETTLEMENTS ARE NON-FIXED AND MOVEMENT IS NOMADIC (260)	0.80 OF 20	46	TILT TOWARD BEING THOSE WHERE SETTLEMENTS ARE NON-FIXED AND MOVEMENT IS NOMADIC (72)	0.67 OF 12	4 8 16 4 XSQ= 5.12 PHI= -0.400 EP = 0.0213
51	TEND TO BE THOSE WHERE SUBSISTENCE IS PRIMARILY BY FOOD PRODUCTION -- I. E., AGRICULTURE OR HUSBANDRY -- RATHER THAN BY GATHERING (253)	0.80 OF 20	51	TEND TO BE THOSE WHERE SUBSISTENCE IS PRIMARILY BY FOOD GATHERING -- I. E., HUNTING, FISHING, OR COLLECTING -- RATHER THAN FOOD PRODUCTION (147)	0.92 OF 13	16 1 4 12 XSQ= 13.72 PHI= 0.645 EP = 0.0001
54	TILT TOWARD BEING THOSE WHERE FOOD PRODUCTION IS BY INTENSIVE OR SIMPLE AGRICULTURE, RATHER THAN BY INCIPIENT FOOD PRODUCTION (192)	0.92 OF 13	54	TILT TOWARD BEING THOSE WHERE FOOD PRODUCTION IS BY INCIPIENT FOOD PRODUCTION, RATHER THAN BY INTENSIVE OR SIMPLE AGRICULTURE (46)	0.75 OF 4	12 1 1 3 XSQ= 4.42 PHI= 0.510 EP = 0.0223
56	DRIFT TOWARD BEING THOSE WHERE FOOD PRODUCTION IS BY SIMPLE AGRICULTURE, RATHER THAN BY INCIPIENT FOOD PRODUCTION (101)	0.86 OF 7	56	DRIFT TOWARD BEING THOSE WHERE FOOD PRODUCTION IS BY INCIPIENT FOOD PRODUCTION, RATHER THAN BY SIMPLE AGRICULTURE (46)	0.75 OF 4	6 1 1 3 XSQ= 1.86 PHI= 0.411 EP = 0.0879

62	LEAN TOWARD BEING THOSE WHERE HUSBANDRY OF SOME KIND IS PRESENT (228)	0.80 OF 20	62	LEAN TOWARD BEING THOSE WHERE HUSBANDRY OF ANY KIND IS ABSENT (172)	0.69 OF 13	16 4 4 9 XSQ= 6.07 PHI= 0.429 EP = 0.0096
73	DRIFT TOWARD BEING THOSE WHERE WEAVING IS PRESENT (118)	0.69 OF 16	73	DRIFT TOWARD BEING THOSE WHERE WEAVING IS ABSENT (130)	0.75 OF 12	11 3 5 9 XSQ= 3.65 PHI= 0.361 EP = 0.0542
81	DRIFT LESS TOWARD BEING THOSE WHERE NO CITY OR TOWN IS PRESENT, AND THE AVERAGE COMMUNITY SIZE IS SMALLER THAN 200 (135)	0.59 OF 17	81	IN ALL CASES ARE THOSE WHERE NO CITY OR TOWN IS PRESENT, AND THE AVERAGE COMMUNITY SIZE IS SMALLER THAN 200 (135)	1.00 OF 8	7 0 10 8 XSQ= 2.76 PHI= 0.332 EP = 0.0573
82	LEAN TOWARD BEING THOSE WHERE A CITY OR TOWN IS PRESENT, OR THE AVERAGE COMMUNITY SIZE IS FIFTY OR GREATER (178)	0.82 OF 17	82	LEAN TOWARD BEING THOSE WHERE NO CITY OR TOWN IS PRESENT, AND THE AVERAGE COMMUNITY SIZE IS SMALLER THAN FIFTY (46)	0.75 OF 8	14 2 3 6 XSQ= 5.48 PHI= 0.468 EP = 0.0099
85	LEAN LESS TOWARD BEING THOSE WHERE THE LEVEL OF POLITICAL INTEGRATION IS THE MINIMAL STATE, THE AUTONOMOUS COMMUNITY, OR THE FAMILY (234) GPM	0.56 OF 18	85	IN ALL CASES ARE THOSE WHERE THE LEVEL OF POLITICAL INTEGRATION IS THE MINIMAL STATE, THE AUTONOMOUS COMMUNITY, OR THE FAMILY (234) GPM	1.00 OF 12	8 0 10 12 XSQ= 5.18 PHI= 0.415 EP = 0.0100
86	LEAN TOWARD BEING THOSE WHERE THE LEVEL OF POLITICAL INTEGRATION IS THE LARGE STATE, THE LITTLE STATE, OR THE MINIMAL STATE (148) GPM	0.67 OF 18	86	LEAN TOWARD BEING THOSE WHERE THE LEVEL OF POLITICAL INTEGRATION IS THE AUTONOMOUS COMMUNITY, OR THE FAMILY (156) GPM	0.92 OF 12	12 1 6 11 XSQ= 7.74 PHI= 0.508 EP = 0.0024
87	IN ALL CASES ARE THOSE WHERE THE LEVEL OF POLITICAL INTEGRATION IS THE LARGE STATE, THE LITTLE STATE, THE MINIMAL STATE, OR THE AUTONOMOUS COMMUNITY (281) GPM	1.00 OF 18	87	DRIFT LESS TOWARD BEING THOSE WHERE THE LEVEL OF POLITICAL INTEGRATION IS THE LARGE STATE, THE LITTLE STATE, THE MINIMAL STATE, OR THE AUTONOMOUS COMMUNITY (281) GPM	0.75 OF 12	18 9 0 3 XSQ= 2.61 PHI= 0.295 EP = 0.0542
91	TILT TOWARD BEING THOSE WHERE SOCIETAL COMPLEXITY IS HIGH (18) F-W	0.83 OF 6	91	IN ALL CASES ARE THOSE WHERE SOCIETAL COMPLEXITY IS LOW (22) F-W	1.00 OF 3	5 0 1 3 XSQ= 2.76 PHI= 0.553 EP = 0.0476
95	TILT LESS TOWARD BEING THOSE WHERE THE HIERARCHY OF NATIONAL JURISDICTION HAS ONE OR NO LEVELS (254) GES,EA	0.65 OF 20	95	IN ALL CASES ARE THOSE WHERE THE HIERARCHY OF NATIONAL JURISDICTION HAS ONE OR NO LEVELS (254) GES,EA	1.00 OF 12	7 0 13 12 XSQ= 3.52 PHI= 0.332 EP = 0.0288

```
 96  LEAN TOWARD BEING THOSE          0.70 OF  20    96  LEAN TOWARD BEING THOSE           0.83 OF  12          14    2
     WHERE THE HIERARCHY                                WHERE THE HIERARCHY                                       6   10
     OF NATIONAL JURISDICTION HAS                       OF NATIONAL JURISDICTION HAS                     XSQ=     6.53
     FOUR, THREE, TWO OR                                NO LEVELS  (156) GES,EA                          PHI=    0.452
     ONE LEVEL  (174) GES,EA                                                                             EP =   0.0091

100  DRIFT MORE TOWARD BEING THOSE  0.90 OF  20   100  DRIFT LESS TOWARD BEING THOSE  0.58 OF  12          18    7
     WHERE HIERARCHIES ARE MORE COMPLEX THAN            WHERE HIERARCHIES ARE MORE COMPLEX THAN                   2    5
     THE 'SIMPLEST,' I. E., MORE COMPLEX THAN           THE 'SIMPLEST,' I. E., MORE COMPLEX THAN         XSQ=     2.74
     TWO LOCAL LEVELS WITH                              TWO LOCAL LEVELS WITH                            PHI=    0.293
     NO NATIONAL LEVELS  (267) GES,EA                   NO NATIONAL LEVELS  (267) GES,EA                 EP =   0.0735

132  IN ALL CASES ARE THOSE           1.00 OF   8   132  IN ALL CASES ARE THOSE            1.00 OF   3           8    0
     WHERE ECONOMIC EXCHANGE                            WHERE ECONOMIC EXCHANGE                                   0    3
     INVOLVES THE USE OF MONEY  (37) JMH                DOES NOT INVOLVE                                 XSQ=     6.54
                                                        THE USE OF MONEY  (17) JMH                       PHI=    0.771
                                                                                                         EP =   0.0061

133  IN ALL CASES ARE THOSE           1.00 OF   4   133  IN ALL CASES ARE THOSE            1.00 OF   2           4    0
     WHERE CONTRACTED DEBTS ARE                         WHERE CONTRACTED DEBTS ARE                                0    2
     SIGNIFICANTLY PRESENT  (17) GES                    MODERATELY PRESENT OR ABSENT  (17) GES           XSQ=     2.34
                                                                                                         PHI=    0.625
                                                                                                         EP =   0.0667

178  TILT LESS TOWARD BEING THOSE   0.63 OF  19   178  IN ALL CASES ARE THOSE            1.00 OF  13           7    0
     WHERE THE COMMUNITY IS OTHER THAN                  WHERE THE COMMUNITY IS OTHER THAN                        12   13
     SEGMENTED ON A CLAN BASIS AND                      SEGMENTED ON A CLAN BASIS AND                    XSQ=     4.16
     NON-EXOGAMOUS  (295)                               NON-EXOGAMOUS  (295)                             PHI=    0.361
                                                                                                         EP =   0.0252

180  DRIFT TOWARD BEING THOSE         0.68 OF  19   180  DRIFT TOWARD BEING THOSE          0.69 OF  13           6    9
     WHERE THE COMMUNITY IS                             WHERE THE COMMUNITY IS                                   13    4
     COMMONLY NON-EXOGAMOUS, RATHER THAN                COMMONLY EXOGAMOUS, RATHER THAN                  XSQ=     3.01
     EXOGAMOUS  (258)                                   NON-EXOGAMOUS  (124)                             PHI=   -0.307
                                                                                                         EP =   0.0702

188  DRIFT TOWARD BEING THOSE         0.75 OF  20   188  DRIFT TOWARD BEING THOSE          0.62 OF  13           5    8
     WHERE THE KIN GROUP IS                             WHERE THE KIN GROUP IS                                   15    5
     OTHER THAN                                         EXCLUSIVELY COGNATIC  (148)                      XSQ=     3.01
     EXCLUSIVELY COGNATIC  (252)                                                                         PHI=   -0.302
                                                                                                         EP =   0.0673

192  TILT TOWARD BEING THOSE          0.85 OF  20   192  TILT TOWARD BEING THOSE           0.54 OF  13           3    7
     OTHER THAN WHERE THE ONLY KIN GROUP                WHERE THE ONLY KIN GROUP PRESENT                         17    6
     PRESENT IS A KINDRED OR ELSE                       IS A KINDRED OR ELSE                             XSQ=     3.94
     BILATERAL DESCENT IS INFERRED  (289)               BILATERAL DESCENT IS INFERRED  (111)             PHI=   -0.346
                                                                                                         EP =   0.0259

196  TILT TOWARD BEING THOSE          0.73 OF  15   196  TILT TOWARD BEING THOSE           0.82 OF  11          11    2
     WHERE INDIVIDUAL RIGHTS IN REAL PROPERTY,          WHERE INDIVIDUAL RIGHTS IN REAL PROPERTY,                 4    9
     AND RULES FOR INHERITANCE,                         OR RULES FOR INHERITANCE,                        XSQ=     5.67
     ARE PRESENT  (194)                                 ARE ABSENT  (87)                                 PHI=    0.467
                                                                                                         EP =   0.0154
```

278	DRIFT TOWARD BEING THOSE WHERE PROPERTY RIGHTS IN WOMEN ARE PRESENT (8) LWS	0.58 OF 12	278	DRIFT TOWARD BEING THOSE WHERE PROPERTY RIGHTS IN WOMEN ARE UNIMPORTANT OR ABSENT (14) LWS	0.88 OF 8	 XSQ= PHI= EP =	7 1 5 7 2.51 0.354 0.0697
382	IN ALL CASES ARE THOSE WHERE FEMALE INITIATION RITES ARE ABSENT (27) JKB	1.00 OF 6	382	IN ALL CASES ARE THOSE WHERE FEMALE INITIATION RITES ARE PRESENT (38) JKB	1.00 OF 2	 XSQ= PHI= EP =	0 2 6 0 3.56 -0.667 0.0357
435	TILT TOWARD BEING THOSE WHERE ABANDONMENT OF THE HOUSE OF THE DEAD IS NOT PRACTICED (19) LWS	0.85 OF 13	435	TILT TOWARD BEING THOSE WHERE ABANDONMENT OF THE HOUSE OF THE DEAD IS PRACTICED (12) LWS	0.60 OF 10	 XSQ= PHI= EP =	2 6 11 4 3.19 -0.372 0.0393
451	TILT TOWARD BEING THOSE WHERE TOTEMISM IS PRESENT (15) LWS	0.83 OF 12	451	TILT TOWARD BEING THOSE WHERE TOTEMISM IS UNIMPORTANT OR ABSENT (12) LWS	0.67 OF 9	 XSQ= PHI= EP =	10 3 2 6 3.54 0.410 0.0318
476	DRIFT TOWARD BEING THOSE WHERE THE DEGREE OF INSOBRIETY IS MODERATE OR SLIGHT (18) CF	0.63 OF 8	476	IN ALL CASES ARE THOSE WHERE THE DEGREE OF INSOBRIETY IS STRONG (31) DH	1.00 OF 4	 XSQ= PHI= EP =	3 4 5 0 2.10 -0.418 0.0808

148 CULTURES
WHERE THE INCIDENCE OF PERSONAL CRIME
IS HIGH (12) B-B-C

148 CULTURES
WHERE THE INCIDENCE OF PERSONAL CRIME
IS LOW (21) B-B-C

BACKGROUND ON PAGE 102

BOTH SUBJECT AND PREDICATE

12 IN LEFT COLUMN

ASHANTI, AZANDE, CHAGGA, CHUKCHEE, COMANCHE, JIVARO, KURTATCHI, KWAKIUTL, MANUS, MAORI, NAVAHO, TIKOPIA

21 IN RIGHT COLUMN

ANDAMANESE, ARAPESH, AYMARA, CHENCHU, CHEYENNE, CUNA, FON, HANO, KASKA, LEPCHA, LESU, MBUNDU, PAPAGO, PUKAPUKA, SAMOANS, TANALA, THONGA, TROBRIAND, TRUKESE, YAGUA, YAKUT

367 EXCLUDED BECAUSE UNASCERTAINED

149	TILT TOWARD BEING THOSE WHERE THE INCIDENCE OF THEFT IS HIGH (18) B-B-C	0.83 OF 12	149	TILT TOWARD BEING THOSE WHERE THE INCIDENCE OF THEFT IS LOW (19) B-B-C	0.67 OF 21	10 7 / 2 14 / XSQ= 5.77 / PHI= 0.418 / EP = 0.0104
176	TILT TOWARD BEING THOSE WHERE THE COMMUNITY IS OTHER THAN A CLAN-COMMUNITY OR A COMMUNITY STRUCTURED OR SEGMENTED ON A CLAN BASIS (213)	0.75 OF 12	176	TILT TOWARD BEING THOSE WHERE THE COMMUNITY IS A CLAN-COMMUNITY OR A COMMUNITY STRUCTURED OR SEGMENTED ON A CLAN BASIS (169)	0.67 OF 21	3 14 / 9 7 / XSQ= 3.77 / PHI= -0.338 / EP = 0.0324
182	DRIFT LESS TOWARD BEING THOSE OTHER THAN WHERE THE COMMUNITY IS STRUCTURED ON A NON-CLAN BASIS AND AGAMOUS (256)	0.58 OF 12	182	DRIFT MORE TOWARD BEING THOSE OTHER THAN WHERE THE COMMUNITY IS STRUCTURED ON A NON-CLAN BASIS AND AGAMOUS (256)	0.90 OF 21	5 2 / 7 19 / XSQ= 2.99 / PHI= 0.301 / EP = 0.0709
242	IN ALL CASES ARE THOSE WHERE MARRIAGE IS COMMONLY OR OCCASIONALLY POLYGYNOUS, RATHER THAN MONOGAMOUS (314)	1.00 OF 12	242	TILT LESS TOWARD BEING THOSE WHERE MARRIAGE IS COMMONLY OR OCCASIONALLY POLYGYNOUS, RATHER THAN MONOGAMOUS (314)	0.62 OF 21	12 13 / 0 8 / XSQ= 4.14 / PHI= 0.354 / EP = 0.0159
258	DRIFT TOWARD BEING THOSE WHERE THE SEVERITY OF SON'S WIFE AVOIDANCE IS HIGH (15) WNS	0.71 OF 7	258	IN ALL CASES ARE THOSE WHERE THE SEVERITY OF SON'S WIFE AVOIDANCE IS LOW (16) WNS	1.00 OF 4	5 0 / 2 4 / XSQ= 2.75 / PHI= 0.500 / EP = 0.0606

No.			No.			
345	LEAN TOWARD BEING THOSE WHERE THE CHILD'S INFERRED ANXIETY OVER NON-PERFORMANCE OF SELF-RELIANT BEHAVIOR IS HIGH (37) B-B-C	0.75 OF 12	345	LEAN TOWARD BEING THOSE WHERE THE CHILD'S INFERRED ANXIETY OVER NON-PERFORMANCE OF SELF-RELIANT BEHAVIOR IS LOW (39) B-B-C	0.75 OF 20	9 5 3 15 XSQ= 5.72 PHI= 0.423 EP = 0.0100
348	LEAN TOWARD BEING THOSE WHERE THE TOTAL POSITIVE PRESSURE TOWARD DEVELOPING ACHIEVEMENT BEHAVIOR IN THE CHILD IS HIGH (32) B-B-C	0.90 OF 10	348	LEAN TOWARD BEING THOSE WHERE THE TOTAL POSITIVE PRESSURE TOWARD DEVELOPING ACHIEVEMENT BEHAVIOR IN THE CHILD IS LOW (31) B-B-C	0.71 OF 17	9 5 1 12 XSQ= 6.99 PHI= 0.509 EP = 0.0044
349	TILT TOWARD BEING THOSE WHERE THE CHILD'S INFERRED ANXIETY OVER NON-PERFORMANCE OF ACHIEVEMENT BEHAVIOR IS HIGH (34) B-B-C	0.90 OF 10	349	TILT TOWARD BEING THOSE WHERE THE CHILD'S INFERRED ANXIETY OVER NON-PERFORMANCE OF ACHIEVEMENT BEHAVIOR IS LOW (28) B-B-C	0.59 OF 17	9 7 1 10 XSQ= 4.36 PHI= 0.402 EP = 0.0183
392	DRIFT TOWARD BEING THOSE WHERE PREMARITAL SEX RELATIONS ARE STRONGLY PUNISHED AND IN FACT RARE, OR WEAKLY PUNISHED AND IN FACT NOT RARE, OR PUNISHED ONLY IF PREGNANCY RESULTS (112) JTW,EA	0.73 OF 11	392	DRIFT TOWARD BEING THOSE WHERE PREMARITAL SEX RELATIONS ARE FREELY PERMITTED (67) JTW,EA	0.71 OF 17	8 5 3 12 XSQ= 3.45 PHI= 0.351 EP = 0.0510
393	TILT TOWARD BEING THOSE WHERE EXTRAMARITAL COITUS IS PUNISHED, RATHER THAN PERMITTED (43) F-B	0.83 OF 6	393	TILT TOWARD BEING THOSE WHERE EXTRAMARITAL COITUS IS PERMITTED, RATHER THAN PUNISHED (41) F-B	0.79 OF 14	5 3 1 11 XSQ= 4.38 PHI= 0.468 EP = 0.0181
398	DRIFT TOWARD BEING THOSE WHERE THE INTENSITY OF SEX ANXIETY IS HIGH (16) WNS	0.88 OF 8	398	DRIFT TOWARD BEING THOSE WHERE THE INTENSITY OF SEX ANXIETY IS LOW (16) WNS	0.64 OF 11	7 4 1 7 XSQ= 3.09 PHI= 0.403 EP = 0.0587
399	DRIFT TOWARD BEING THOSE WHERE INTENSITY OF CASTRATION ANXIETY IS HIGH (23) WNS	0.78 OF 9	399	DRIFT TOWARD BEING THOSE WHERE INTENSITY OF CASTRATION ANXIETY IS LOW (22) WNS	0.64 OF 14	7 5 2 9 XSQ= 2.38 PHI= 0.322 EP = 0.0894
419	IN ALL CASES ARE THOSE WHERE MILITARY GLORY IS STRONGLY OR MODERATELY EMPHASIZED (55) PES	1.00 OF 12	419	TEND TO BE THOSE WHERE MILITARY GLORY IS NEGLIGIBLY EMPHASIZED (31) PES	0.61 OF 18	12 7 0 11 XSQ= 9.10 PHI= 0.551 EP = 0.0006
445	IN ALL CASES ARE THOSE WHERE SORCERY IS IMPORTANT (26) EBW,DH	1.00 OF 6	445	TILT TOWARD BEING THOSE WHERE SORCERY IS UNIMPORTANT (23) BBW,DH	0.67 OF 9	6 3 0 6 XSQ= 4.18 PHI= 0.528 EP = 0.0278

```
451  IN ALL CASES ARE THCSE          1.00 OF   3     451  IN ALL CASES ARE THOSE          1.00 OF   4           0    4
     WHERE TOTEMISM IS                                    WHERE TOTEMISM IS                                         3    0
     UNIMPORTANT OR ABSENT   (12) LWS                     PRESENT   (15) LWS                                 XSQ=      3.51
                                                                                                             PHI=    -0.708
                                                                                                             EP  =   0.0286

472  LEAN TOWARD BEING THOSE        0.83 OF  12     472  LEAN TOWARD BEING THOSE        0.68 OF  19          10    6
     WHERE THE COMPOSITE NARCISSISM INDEX                 WHERE THE COMPOSITE NARCISSISM INDEX                      2   13
     IS HIGH   (47) PES                                   IS LOW   (43) PES                                  XSQ=      5.95
                                                                                                             PHI=     0.438
                                                                                                             EP  =   0.0091

473  TILT TOWARD BEING THOSE        0.58 OF  12     473  TILT TOWARD BEING THOSE        0.89 OF  18           7    2
     WHERE SENSITIVITY TC INSULT                          WHERE SENSITIVITY TO INSULT                               5   16
     IS EXTREME   (32) PES                                IS MODERATE OR NEGLIGIBLE   (56) PES               XSQ=      5.56
                                                                                                             PHI=     0.431
                                                                                                             EP  =   0.0125

474  DRIFT TOWARD BEING THCSE       0.67 OF  12     474  DRIFT TOWARD BEING THOSE       0.74 OF  19           8    5
     WHERE BOASTFULNESS IS EXTREME  (41) PES              WHERE BOASTFULNESS IS MODERATE,                           4   14
                                                          NEGLIBIBLE, OR UNREPORTED   (48) PES              XSQ=      3.40
                                                                                                             PHI=     0.331
                                                                                                             EP  =   0.0596
```

149	CULTURES WHERE THE INCIDENCE OF THEFT IS HIGH (18) B-B-C	149	CULTURES WHERE THE INCIDENCE OF THEFT IS LOW (19) B-B-C

BACKGROUND ON PAGE 102 — BOTH SUBJECT AND PREDICATE

18 IN LEFT COLUMN

ASHANTI, AYMARA, AZANDE, CHAGGA, CHUKCHEE, COMANCHE, FON, KASKA, KURTATCHI, KWAKIUTL, LAU, MAORI, MBUNDU, NAVAHO, SAMOANS, THONGA, TIKOPIA, TRUKESE

19 IN RIGHT COLUMN

ANDAMANESE, ARAPESH, BALINESE, CHENCHU, CHEYENNE, CUNA, HANO, JIVARO, LEPCHA, LESU, MANUS, PAPAGO, PUKAPUKA, SIRIONO, TANALA, TROBRIAND, WOLEAIANS, YAGUA, YAKUT

363 EXCLUDED BECAUSE UNASCERTAINED

3	LEAN LESS TOWARD BEING THOSE LOCATED OUTSIDE OF AFRICA (320)	0.67 OF 18	3	IN ALL CASES ARE THOSE LOCATED OUTSIDE OF AFRICA (320)	1.00 OF 19	6 0 / 12 19 / XSQ= 5.30 / PHI= 0.379 / EP = 0.0080
71	DRIFT TOWARD BEING THOSE WHERE METAL WORKING IS PRESENT (98)	0.50 OF 16	71	DRIFT TOWARD BEING THOSE WHERE METAL WORKING IS ABSENT (153)	0.88 OF 16	8 2 / 8 14 / XSQ= 3.64 / PHI= 0.337 / EP = 0.0538
95	TILT LESS TOWARD BEING THOSE WHERE THE HIERARCHY OF NATIONAL JURISDICTION HAS ONE OR NO LEVELS (254) GES,EA	0.56 OF 16	95	TILT MORE TOWARD BEING THOSE WHERE THE HIERARCHY OF NATIONAL JURISDICTION HAS ONE OR NO LEVELS (254) GES,EA	0.94 OF 18	7 1 / 9 17 / XSQ= 4.91 / PHI= 0.380 / EP = 0.0145
102	TILT TOWARD BEING THOSE WHERE CLASS STRATIFICATION IS PRESENT (203)	0.78 OF 18	102	TILT TOWARD BEING THOSE WHERE CLASS STRATIFICATION IS ABSENT (180)	0.63 OF 19	14 7 / 4 12 / XSQ= 4.75 / PHI= 0.358 / EP = 0.0201
137	DRIFT TOWARD BEING THOSE WHERE INVIDIOUS DISPLAY OF WEALTH IS STRONGLY EMPHASIZED (37) PES	0.63 OF 16	137	DRIFT TOWARD BEING THOSE WHERE INVIDIOUS DISPLAY OF WEALTH IS MODERATELY, LITTLE, OR NEGATIVELY EMPHASIZED (52) PES	0.72 OF 18	10 5 / 6 13 / XSQ= 2.85 / PHI= 0.290 / EP = 0.0824

148	TILT TOWARD BEING THOSE WHERE THE INCIDENCE OF PERSONAL CRIME IS HIGH (12) B-B-C	0.59 OF	17	148	TILT TOWARD BEING THOSE WHERE THE INCIDENCE OF PERSONAL CRIME IS LOW (21) B-B-C	0.88 OF	16	10 2 7 14 XSQ= 5.77 PHI= 0.418 EP = 0.0104
305	DRIFT TOWARD BEING THOSE WHERE THE EARLY SEXUAL SATISFACTION POTENTIAL IS LOW (24) W-C	0.67 OF	12	305	DRIFT TOWARD BEING THOSE WHERE THE EARLY SEXUAL SATISFACTION POTENTIAL IS HIGH (27) W-C	0.73 OF	15	4 11 8 4 XSQ= 2.85 PHI= -0.325 EP = 0.0574
308	DRIFT TOWARD BEING THOSE WHERE AVERAGE SOCIALIZATION ANXIETY IS HIGH (22) W-C	0.75 OF	12	308	DRIFT TOWARD BEING THOSE WHERE AVERAGE SOCIALIZATION ANXIETY IS LOW (18) W-C	0.64 OF	14	9 5 3 9 XSQ= 2.59 PHI= 0.315 EP = 0.0618
309	DRIFT TOWARD BEING THOSE WHERE ORAL SOCIALIZATION ANXIETY IS HIGH (26) W-C	0.75 OF	12	309	DRIFT TOWARD BEING THOSE WHERE ORAL SOCIALIZATION ANXIETY IS LOW (27) W-C	0.63 OF	16	9 6 3 10 XSQ= 2.52 PHI= 0.300 EP = 0.0671
317	TILT TOWARD BEING THOSE WHERE DISPLAY OF AFFECTION TOWARD THE INFANT IS LOW (29) B-B-C	0.67 OF	18	317	TILT TOWARD BEING THOSE WHERE DISPLAY OF AFFECTION TOWARD THE INFANT IS HIGH (39) B-B-C	0.78 OF	18	6 14 12 4 XSQ= 5.51 PHI= -0.391 EP = 0.0176
318	DRIFT TOWARD BEING THOSE WHERE THE OVERALL INDULGENCE OF THE INFANT IS LOW (31) B-B-C	0.56 OF	18	318	DRIFT TOWARD BEING THOSE WHERE THE OVERALL INDULGENCE OF THE INFANT IS HIGH (40) B-B-C	0.74 OF	19	8 14 10 5 XSQ= 2.18 PHI= -0.243 EP = 0.0991
323	DRIFT TOWARD BEING THOSE WHERE THE CONSTANCY OF PRESENCE OF THE INFANT'S NURTURANT AGENT IS LOW (45) B-B-C	0.78 OF	18	323	DRIFT TOWARD BEING THOSE WHERE THE CONSTANCY OF PRESENCE OF THE INFANT'S NURTURANT AGENT IS HIGH (29) B-B-C	0.53 OF	19	4 10 14 9 XSQ= 2.46 PHI= -0.258 EP = 0.0911
334	LEAN TOWARD BEING THOSE WHERE THE INDULGENCE OF THE CHILD IS LOW (38) B-B-C	0.72 OF	18	334	LEAN TOWARD BEING THOSE WHERE THE INDULGENCE OF THE CHILD IS HIGH (40) B-B-C	0.74 OF	19	5 14 13 5 XSQ= 6.07 PHI= -0.405 EP = 0.0086
337	LEAN TOWARD BEING THOSE WHERE THE CHILD'S INFERRED ANXIETY OVER NON-PERFORMANCE OF RESPONSIBLE BEHAVIOR IS HIGH (38) B-B-C	0.72 OF	18	337	LEAN TOWARD BEING THOSE WHERE THE CHILD'S INFERRED ANXIETY OVER NON-PERFORMANCE OF RESPONSIBLE BEHAVIOR IS LOW (35) B-B-C	0.76 OF	17	13 4 5 13 XSQ= 6.46 PHI= 0.430 EP = 0.0067

338	TEND TO BE THOSE 0.94 OF 18 WHERE THE CHILD'S INFERRED ANXIETY OVER PERFORMANCE OF RESPONSIBLE BEHAVIOR IS HIGH (44) B-B-C	338	TEND TO BE THOSE 0.59 OF 17 WHERE THE CHILD'S INFERRED ANXIETY OVER PERFORMANCE OF RESPONSIBLE BEHAVIOR IS LOW (29) B-B-C	17 7 1 10 XSQ= 9.17 PHI= 0.512 EP = 0.0009
339	LEAN TOWARD BEING THOSE 0.78 OF 18 WHERE THE CHILD'S INFERRED CONFLICT REGARDING RESPONSIBLE BEHAVIOR IS HIGH (31) B-B-C	339	LEAN TOWARD BEING THOSE 0.76 OF 17 WHERE THE CHILD'S INFERRED CONFLICT REGARDING RESPONSIBLE BEHAVIOR IS LOW (42) B-B-C	14 4 4 13 XSQ= 8.24 PHI= 0.485 EP = 0.0022
345	TILT TOWARD BEING THOSE 0.67 OF 18 WHERE THE CHILD'S INFERRED ANXIETY OVER NON-PERFORMANCE OF SELF-RELIANT BEHAVIOR IS HIGH (37) B-B-C	345	TILT TOWARD BEING THOSE 0.72 OF 18 WHERE THE CHILD'S INFERRED ANXIETY OVER NON-PERFORMANCE OF SELF-RELIANT BEHAVIOR IS LOW (39) B-B-C	12 5 6 13 XSQ= 4.01 PHI= 0.334 EP = 0.0437
350	DRIFT TOWARD BEING THOSE 0.73 OF 15 WHERE THE CHILD'S INFERRED ANXIETY OVER PERFORMANCE OF ACHIEVEMENT BEHAVIOR IS HIGH (34) B-B-C	350	DRIFT TOWARD BEING THOSE 0.69 OF 13 WHERE THE CHILD'S INFERRED ANXIETY OVER PERFORMANCE OF ACHIEVEMENT BEHAVIOR IS LOW (26) B-B-C	11 4 4 9 XSQ= 3.51 PHI= 0.354 EP = 0.0557
351	DRIFT TOWARD BEING THOSE 0.53 OF 15 WHERE THE CHILD'S INFERRED CONFLICT REGARDING ACHIEVEMENT BEHAVIOR IS HIGH (26) B-B-C	351	DRIFT TOWARD BEING THOSE 0.85 OF 13 WHERE THE CHILD'S INFERRED CONFLICT REGARDING ACHIEVEMENT BEHAVIOR IS LOW (34) B-B-C	8 2 7 11 XSQ= 2.87 PHI= 0.320 EP = 0.0546
354	DRIFT TOWARD BEING THOSE 0.71 OF 17 WHERE THE CHILD'S INFERRED ANXIETY OVER PERFORMANCE OF OBEDIENT BEHAVIOR IS HIGH (36) B-B-C	354	DRIFT TOWARD BEING THOSE 0.65 OF 17 WHERE THE CHILD'S INFERRED ANXIETY OVER PERFORMANCE OF OBEDIENT BEHAVIOR IS LOW (37) B-B-C	12 6 5 11 XSQ= 2.95 PHI= 0.295 EP = 0.0844
355	TILT TOWARD BEING THOSE 0.65 OF 17 WHERE THE CHILD'S INFERRED CONFLICT REGARDING OBEDIENT BEHAVIOR IS HIGH (35) B-B-C	355	TILT TOWARD BEING THOSE 0.76 OF 17 WHERE THE CHILD'S INFERRED CONFLICT REGARDING OBEDIENT BEHAVIOR IS LOW (38) B-B-C	11 4 6 13 XSQ= 4.29 PHI= 0.355 EP = 0.0366
377	DRIFT LESS TOWARD BEING THOSE 0.59 OF 17 WHERE MALE GENITAL MUTILATION IS ABSENT (242)	377	DRIFT MORE TOWARD BEING THOSE 0.89 OF 18 WHERE MALE GENITAL MUTILATION IS ABSENT (242)	7 2 10 16 XSQ= 2.71 PHI= 0.278 EP = 0.0599
392	DRIFT TOWARD BEING THOSE 0.63 OF 16 WHERE PREMARITAL SEX RELATIONS ARE STRONGLY PUNISHED AND IN FACT RARE, OR WEAKLY PUNISHED AND IN FACT NOT RARE, OR PUNISHED ONLY IF PREGNANCY RESULTS (112) JTW,EA	392	DRIFT TOWARD BEING THOSE 0.73 OF 15 WHERE PREMARITAL SEX RELATIONS ARE FREELY PERMITTED (67) JTW,EA	10 4 6 11 XSQ= 2.70 PHI= 0.295 EP = 0.0732

393	LEAN TOWARD BEING THOSE 0.70 OF 10 WHERE EXTRAMARITAL COITUS IS PUNISHED, RATHER THAN PERMITTED (43) F-B	393	LEAN TOWARD BEING THOSE 0.91 OF 11 WHERE EXTRAMARITAL COITUS IS PERMITTED, RATHER THAN PUNISHED (41) F-B	7 1 3 10 XSQ= 5.86 PHI= 0.528 EP = 0.0075
398	TILT TOWARD BEING THOSE 0.88 OF 8 WHERE THE INTENSITY OF SEX ANXIETY IS HIGH (16) WNS	398	TILT TOWARD BEING THOSE 0.69 OF 13 WHERE THE INTENSITY OF SEX ANXIETY IS LOW (16) WNS	7 4 1 9 XSQ= 4.32 PHI= 0.453 EP = 0.0237
419	LEAN TOWARD BEING THOSE 0.87 OF 15 WHERE MILITARY GLORY IS STRONGLY OR MODERATELY EMPHASIZED (55) PES	419	LEAN TOWARD BEING THOSE 0.68 OF 19 WHERE MILITARY GLORY IS NEGLIGIBLY EMPHASIZED (31) PES	13 6 2 13 XSQ= 8.20 PHI= 0.491 EP = 0.0019
421	TILT TOWARD BEING THOSE 0.56 OF 16 WHERE KILLING, TORTURING, OR MUTILATING OF THE ENEMY IS STRONGLY OR MODERATELY EMPHASIZED (37) PES	421	TILT TOWARD BEING THOSE 0.88 OF 17 WHERE KILLING, TORTURING, OR MUTILATING OF THE ENEMY IS NEGLIGIBLY EMPHASIZED (47) PES	9 2 7 15 XSQ= 5.47 PHI= 0.407 EP = 0.0104
434	DRIFT TOWARD BEING THOSE 0.79 OF 14 WHERE ASCETICISM IN MOURNING BEHAVIOR IS HIGH (37) JFG	434	DRIFT TOWARD BEING THOSE 0.60 OF 15 WHERE ASCETICISM IN MOURNING BEHAVIOR IS LOW (30) JFG	11 6 3 9 XSQ= 2.99 PHI= 0.321 EP = 0.0604
440	DRIFT TOWARD BEING THOSE 0.75 OF 12 WHERE FEAR OF SPIRITS IS LOW (29) W-C	440	DRIFT TOWARD BEING THOSE 0.63 OF 16 WHERE FEAR OF SPIRITS IS HIGH (32) W-C	3 10 9 6 XSQ= 2.52 PHI= -0.300 EP = 0.0671
445	DRIFT TOWARD BEING THOSE 0.86 OF 7 WHERE SORCERY IS IMPORTANT (26) EBW,DH	445	DRIFT TOWARD BEING THOSE 0.67 OF 9 WHERE SORCERY IS UNIMPORTANT (23) BBW,DH	6 3 1 6 XSQ= 2.52 PHI= 0.397 EP = 0.0601
459	TILT TOWARD BEING THOSE 0.65 OF 17 WHERE GAMES, IF PRESENT, INCLUDE GAMES OF CHANCE (82) R-A-B,EA	459	TILT TOWARD BEING THOSE 0.77 OF 13 WHERE GAMES, IF PRESENT, DO NOT INCLUDE GAMES OF CHANCE (89) R-A-B,EA	11 3 6 10 XSQ= 3.59 PHI= 0.346 EP = 0.0329
460	DRIFT TOWARD BEING THOSE 0.76 OF 17 WHERE GAMES, IF PRESENT, ARE NOT LIMITED TO GAMES OF SKILL ONLY (104) R-A-B,EA	460	DRIFT TOWARD BEING THOSE 0.62 OF 13 WHERE GAMES, IF PRESENT, ARE LIMITED TO GAMES OF SKILL ONLY (67) R-A-B,EA	4 8 13 5 XSQ= 2.99 PHI= -0.316 EP = 0.0610

149/

472	TILT TOWARD BEING THOSE WHERE THE COMPOSITE NARCISSISM INDEX IS HIGH (47) PES	0.69 OF 16	472	TILT TOWARD BEING THOSE WHERE THE COMPOSITE NARCISSISM INDEX IS LOW (43) PES	0.68 OF 19

```
        11     6
         5    13
XSQ=      3.43
PHI=      0.313
EP =      0.0437
```

****

150	CULTURES WHERE THE DIFFERENTIATION OF THE JURIDICAL AGENCY FROM ALL OTHER AGENCIES IN THE SOCIETY IS HIGH (10) MJ	150	CULTURES WHERE THE DIFFERENTIATION OF THE JURIDICAL AGENCY FROM ALL OTHER AGENCIES IN THE SOCIETY IS LOW (10) MJ

BACKGROUND ON PAGE 102 SUBJECT ONLY

....

10 IN LEFT COLUMN

BEMBA BURMESE JAVANESE LAMBA NAMA NUPE SAMOANS SIUAI THAI VIETNAMESE

10 IN RIGHT COLUMN

ANDAMANESE COMANCHE COPR ESKIMO JIVARO KIKUYU KUNG MUNDURUCU MURNGIN NAVAHO TROBRIAND

380 EXCLUDED BECAUSE UNASCERTAINED

51	TILT TOWARD BEING THOSE WHERE SUBSISTENCE IS PRIMARILY BY FOOD PRODUCTION -- I. E., AGRICULTURE OR HUSBANDRY -- RATHER THAN BY GATHERING (253)	0.90 OF 10	51	TILT TOWARD BEING THOSE WHERE SUBSISTENCE IS PRIMARILY BY FOOD GATHERING -- I. E., HUNTING, FISHING, OR COLLECTING -- RATHER THAN FOOD PRODUCTION (147)	0.70 OF 10	9 3 1 7 XSQ= 5.21 PHI= 0.510 EP = 0.0198
71	TILT TOWARD BEING THOSE WHERE METAL WORKING IS PRESENT (98)	0.83 OF 6	71	TILT TOWARD BEING THOSE WHERE METAL WORKING IS ABSENT (153)	0.80 OF 10	5 2 1 8 XSQ= 3.81 PHI= 0.488 EP = 0.0350
80	DRIFT LESS TOWARD BEING THOSE WHERE NO CITY OR TOWN IS PRESENT (185)	0.57 OF 7	80	IN ALL CASES ARE THOSE WHERE NO CITY OR TOWN IS PRESENT (185)	1.00 OF 8	3 0 4 8 XSQ= 2.03 PHI= 0.367 EP = 0.0769
82	IN ALL CASES ARE THOSE WHERE A CITY OR TOWN IS PRESENT, OR THE AVERAGE COMMUNITY SIZE IS FIFTY OR GREATER (178)	1.00 OF 7	82	DRIFT TOWARD BEING THOSE WHERE NO CITY OR TOWN IS PRESENT, AND THE AVERAGE COMMUNITY SIZE IS SMALLER THAN FIFTY (46)	0.50 OF 8	7 4 0 4 XSQ= 2.56 PHI= 0.413 EP = 0.0769
85	TILT TOWARD BEING THOSE WHERE THE LEVEL OF POLITICAL INTEGRATION IS THE LARGE STATE, OR THE LITTLE STATE (70) GPM	0.56 OF 9	85	IN ALL CASES ARE THOSE WHERE THE LEVEL OF POLITICAL INTEGRATION IS THE MINIMAL STATE, THE AUTONOMOUS COMMUNITY, OR THE FAMILY (234) GPM	1.00 OF 8	5 0 4 8 XSQ= 3.90 PHI= 0.479 EP = 0.0294

86	LEAN TOWARD BEING THOSE 0.89 OF 9 WHERE THE LEVEL OF POLITICAL INTEGRATION IS THE LARGE STATE, THE LITTLE STATE, OR THE MINIMAL STATE (148) GPM	86	LEAN TOWARD BEING THOSE 0.88 OF 8 WHERE THE LEVEL OF POLITICAL INTEGRATION IS THE AUTONOMOUS COMMUNITY, OR THE FAMILY (156) GPM	8 1 1 7 XSQ= 7.09 PHI= 0.646 EP = 0.0034
95	LEAN TOWARD BEING THOSE 0.78 OF 9 WHERE THE HIERARCHY OF NATIONAL JURISDICTION HAS FOUR, THREE, OR TWO LEVELS (76) GES,EA	95	IN ALL CASES ARE THOSE 1.00 OF 9 WHERE THE HIERARCHY OF NATIONAL JURISDICTION HAS ONE OR NO LEVELS (254) GES,EA	7 0 2 9 XSQ= 8.42 PHI= 0.684 EP = 0.0023
96	LEAN TOWARD BEING THOSE 0.89 OF 9 WHERE THE HIERARCHY OF NATIONAL JURISDICTION HAS FOUR, THREE, TWO OR ONE LEVEL (174) GES,EA	96	LEAN TOWARD BEING THOSE 0.89 OF 9 WHERE THE HIERARCHY OF NATIONAL JURISDICTION HAS NO LEVELS (156) GES,EA	8 1 1 8 XSQ= 8.00 PHI= 0.667 EP = 0.0034
100	IN ALL CASES ARE THOSE 1.00 OF 9 WHERE HIERARCHIES ARE MORE COMPLEX THAN THE 'SIMPLEST,' I. E., MORE COMPLEX THAN TWO LOCAL LEVELS WITH NO NATIONAL LEVELS (267) GES,EA	100	DRIFT LESS TOWARD BEING THOSE 0.56 OF 9 WHERE HIERARCHIES ARE MORE COMPLEX THAN THE 'SIMPLEST,' I. E., MORE COMPLEX THAN TWO LOCAL LEVELS WITH NO NATIONAL LEVELS (267) GES,EA	9 5 0 4 XSQ= 2.89 PHI= 0.401 EP = 0.0824
102	LEAN TOWARD BEING THOSE 0.90 OF 10 WHERE CLASS STRATIFICATION IS PRESENT (203)	102	LEAN TOWARD BEING THOSE 0.80 OF 10 WHERE CLASS STRATIFICATION IS ABSENT (180)	9 2 1 8 XSQ= 7.27 PHI= 0.603 EP = 0.0055
118	IN ALL CASES ARE THOSE 1.00 OF 2 WHERE THE PERCENTAGE OF OCCUPATIONS THAT ARE SPECIALIZED IS HIGH OR MEDIUM (24) WME	118	IN ALL CASES ARE THOSE 1.00 OF 4 WHERE THE PERCENTAGE OF OCCUPATIONS THAT ARE SPECIALIZED IS LOW (25) WME	2 0 0 4 XSQ= 2.34 PHI= 0.625 EP = 0.0667
138	IN ALL CASES ARE THOSE 1.00 OF 2 WHERE SUPERORDINATE JUSTICE IS PRESENT (22) BBW	138	IN ALL CASES ARE THOSE 1.00 OF 4 WHERE SUPERORDINATE JUSTICE IS ABSENT (18) BBW	2 0 0 4 XSQ= 2.34 PHI= 0.625 EP = 0.0667
139	IN ALL CASES ARE THOSE 1.00 OF 2 WHERE SUPERORDINATE PUNISHMENT IS PRESENT (15) BBW	139	IN ALL CASES ARE THOSE 1.00 OF 4 WHERE SUPERORDINATE PUNISHMENT IS ABSENT (25) BBW	2 0 0 4 XSQ= 2.34 PHI= 0.625 EP = 0.0667
152	LEAN TOWARD BEING THOSE 0.90 OF 10 WHERE THE DIFFERENTIATION OF THE JURIDICAL AGENCY FROM THE MEDICAL AGENCY IS HIGH (10) MJ	152	LEAN TOWARD BEING THOSE 0.90 OF 10 WHERE THE DIFFERENTIATION OF THE JURIDICAL AGENCY FROM THE MEDICAL AGENCY IS LOW (10) MJ	9 1 1 9 XSQ= 9.80 PHI= 0.700 EP = 0.0011

163	LEAN TOWARD BEING THOSE 0.78 OF 9 WHERE THE EMPHASIS ON INDIVIDUAL VOLITION AS THE CAUSE OF CRIME IS HIGH (7) MJ	163	IN ALL CASES ARE THOSE 1.00 OF 8 WHERE THE EMPHASIS ON INDIVIDUAL VOLITION AS THE CAUSE OF CRIME IS LOW (10) MJ	 XSQ= PHI= EP =	7 0 2 8 7.61 0.669 0.0023
164	DRIFT TOWARD BEING THOSE 0.78 OF 9 WHERE THE EMPHASIS ON INDIVIDUAL VOLITION AS THE CAUSE OR SOURCE OF ILLNESS IS LOW (9) MJ	164	DRIFT TOWARD BEING THOSE 0.78 OF 9 WHERE THE EMPHASIS ON INDIVIDUAL VOLITION AS THE CAUSE OR SOURCE OF ILLNESS IS HIGH (9) MJ	 XSQ= PHI= EP =	2 7 7 2 3.56 -0.444 0.0567
184	IN ALL CASES ARE THOSE 1.00 OF 6 WHERE THE LARGEST NON-COGNATIC KIN GROUP IS SMALLER THAN A PHRATRY, I. E. A SIB OR LINEAGE (175)	184	TILT TOWARD BEING THOSE 0.80 OF 5 WHERE THE LARGEST NON-COGNATIC KIN GROUP IS THE MOEITY OR PHRATRY (77)	 XSQ= PHI= EP =	0 4 6 1 4.48 -0.638 0.0152
196	TILT TOWARD BEING THOSE 0.88 OF 8 WHERE INDIVIDUAL RIGHTS IN REAL PROPERTY, AND RULES FOR INHERITANCE, ARE PRESENT (194)	196	TILT TOWARD BEING THOSE 0.75 OF 8 WHERE INDIVIDUAL RIGHTS IN REAL PROPERTY, OR RULES FOR INHERITANCE, ARE ABSENT (87)	 XSQ= PHI= EP =	7 2 1 6 4.06 0.504 0.0406
214	IN ALL CASES ARE THOSE 1.00 OF 8 WHERE FIRST COUSIN MARRIAGE, IF PERMITTED, IS OTHER THAN UNILATERAL (144)	214	DRIFT TOWARD BEING THOSE 0.50 OF 4 WHERE FIRST COUSIN MARRIAGE, IF PERMITTED, IS UNILATERAL (28)	 XSQ= PHI= EP =	0 2 8 2 1.88 -0.395 0.0909
303	IN ALL CASES ARE THOSE 1.00 OF 2 WHERE THE EARLY ORAL SATISFACTION POTENTIAL IS LOW (25) W-C	303	DRIFT TOWARD BEING THOSE 0.86 OF 7 WHERE THE EARLY ORAL SATISFACTION POTENTIAL IS HIGH (32) W-C	 XSQ= PHI= EP =	0 6 2 1 2.01 -0.472 0.0833
444	TILT TOWARD BEING THOSE 0.80 OF 5 WHERE THE USE OF DREAMS TO SEEK AND CONTROL SUPERNATURAL POWERS IS LOW (27) RGD	444	IN ALL CASES ARE THOSE 1.00 OF 6 WHERE THE USE OF DREAMS TO SEEK AND CONTROL SUPERNATURAL POWERS IS HIGH (28) RGD	 XSQ= PHI= EP =	1 6 4 0 4.48 -0.638 0.0152
458	DRIFT TOWARD BEING THOSE 0.80 OF 5 WHERE GAMES, IF PRESENT, INCLUDE GAMES OF STRATEGY (52) R-A-B,EA	458	DRIFT TOWARD BEING THOSE 0.83 OF 6 WHERE GAMES, IF PRESENT, DO NOT INCLUDE GAMES OF STRATEGY (119) R-A-B,EA	 XSQ= PHI= EP =	4 1 1 5 2.23 0.450 0.0801

151 CULTURES
WHERE THE DIFFERENTIATION OF THE MEDICAL AGENCY FROM ALL OTHER AGENCIES IN THE SOCIETY IS HIGH (10) MJ

151 CULTURES
WHERE THE DIFFERENTIATION OF THE MEDICAL AGENCY FROM ALL OTHER AGENCIES IN THE SOCIETY IS LOW (10) MJ

BACKGROUND ON PAGE 102

SUBJECT ONLY

10 IN LEFT COLUMN

BEMBA BURMESE JAVANESE LAMBA NAVAHO NUPE SAMOANS SIUAI THAI VIETNAMESE

10 IN RIGHT COLUMN

ANDAMANESE COMANCHE COPR ESKIMO JIVARO KIKUYU KUNG MUNDURUCU MURNGIN NAMA TROBRIAND

380 EXCLUDED BECAUSE UNASCERTAINED

46	IN ALL CASES ARE THOSE OTHER THAN WHERE SETTLEMENTS ARE NON-FIXED AND MOVEMENT IS NOMADIC (260)	1.00 OF	9	46	TILT TOWARD BEING THOSE WHERE SETTLEMENTS ARE NON-FIXED AND MOVEMENT IS NOMADIC (72)	0.56 OF	9		0 5 9 4 XSQ= 4.43 PHI= -0.496 EP = 0.0294
51	TILT TOWARD BEING THOSE WHERE SUBSISTENCE IS PRIMARILY BY FOOD PRODUCTION -- I. E., AGRICULTURE OR HUSBANDRY -- RATHER THAN BY GATHERING (253)	0.90 OF	10	51	TILT TOWARD BEING THOSE WHERE SUBSISTENCE IS PRIMARILY BY FOOD GATHERING -- I. E., HUNTING, FISHING, OR COLLECTING -- RATHER THAN FOOD PRODUCTION (147)	0.70 OF	10		9 3 1 7 XSQ= 5.21 PHI= 0.510 EP = 0.0198
71	TILT TOWARD BEING THOSE WHERE METAL WORKING IS PRESENT (98)	0.83 OF	6	71	TILT TOWARD BEING THOSE WHERE METAL WORKING IS ABSENT (153)	0.80 OF	10		5 2 1 8 XSQ= 3.81 PHI= 0.488 EP = 0.0350
80	DRIFT LESS TOWARD BEING THOSE WHERE NO CITY OR TOWN IS PRESENT (185)	0.57 OF	7	80	IN ALL CASES ARE THOSE WHERE NO CITY OR TOWN IS PRESENT (185)	1.00 OF	8		3 0 4 8 XSQ= 2.03 PHI= 0.367 EP = 0.0769
81	TILT TOWARD BEING THOSE WHERE A CITY OR TOWN IS PRESENT, OR THE AVERAGE COMMUNITY SIZE IS 200 OR GREATER (89)	0.71 OF	7	81	TILT TOWARD BEING THOSE WHERE NO CITY OR TOWN IS PRESENT, AND THE AVERAGE COMMUNITY SIZE IS SMALLER THAN 200 (135)	0.88 OF	8		5 1 2 7 XSQ= 3.23 PHI= 0.464 EP = 0.0406

82	IN ALL CASES ARE THOSE WHERE A CITY OR TOWN IS PRESENT, OR THE AVERAGE COMMUNITY SIZE IS FIFTY OR GREATER (178)	1.00 OF 7	82	DRIFT TOWARD BEING THOSE WHERE NO CITY OR TOWN IS PRESENT, AND THE AVERAGE COMMUNITY SIZE IS SMALLER THAN FIFTY (46)	0.50 OF 8	7 4 0 4 XSQ= 2.56 PHI= 0.413 EP = 0.0769
85	TILT TOWARD BEING THOSE WHERE THE LEVEL OF POLITICAL INTEGRATION IS THE LARGE STATE, OR THE LITTLE STATE (70) GPM	0.56 OF 9	85	IN ALL CASES ARE THOSE WHERE THE LEVEL OF POLITICAL INTEGRATION IS THE MINIMAL STATE, THE AUTONOMOUS COMMUNITY, OR THE FAMILY (234) GPM	1.00 OF 8	5 0 4 8 XSQ= 3.90 PHI= 0.479 EP = 0.0294
86	DRIFT TOWARD BEING THOSE WHERE THE LEVEL OF POLITICAL INTEGRATION IS THE LARGE STATE, THE LITTLE STATE, OR THE MINIMAL STATE (148) GPM	0.78 OF 9	86	DRIFT TOWARD BEING THOSE WHERE THE LEVEL OF POLITICAL INTEGRATION IS THE AUTONOMOUS COMMUNITY, OR THE FAMILY (156) GPM	0.75 OF 8	7 2 2 6 XSQ= 2.85 PHI= 0.410 EP = 0.0567
91	IN ALL CASES ARE THOSE WHERE SOCIETAL COMPLEXITY IS HIGH (18) F-W	1.00 OF 2	91	IN ALL CASES ARE THOSE WHERE SOCIETAL COMPLEXITY IS LOW (22) F-W	1.00 OF 4	2 0 0 4 XSQ= 2.34 PHI= 0.625 EP = 0.0667
95	LEAN TOWARD BEING THOSE WHERE THE HIERARCHY OF NATIONAL JURISDICTION HAS FOUR, THREE, OR TWO LEVELS (76) GES,EA	0.78 OF 9	95	IN ALL CASES ARE THOSE WHERE THE HIERARCHY OF NATIONAL JURISDICTION HAS ONE OR NO LEVELS (254) GES,EA	1.00 OF 9	7 0 2 9 XSQ= 8.42 PHI= 0.684 EP = 0.0023
96	DRIFT TOWARD BEING THOSE WHERE THE HIERARCHY OF NATIONAL JURISDICTION HAS FOUR, THREE, TWO OR ONE LEVEL (174) GES,EA	0.78 OF 9	96	DRIFT TOWARD BEING THOSE WHERE THE HIERARCHY OF NATIONAL JURISDICTION HAS NO LEVELS (156) GES,EA	0.78 OF 9	7 2 2 7 XSQ= 3.56 PHI= 0.444 EP = 0.0567
100	IN ALL CASES ARE THOSE WHERE HIERARCHIES ARE MORE COMPLEX THAN THE 'SIMPLEST,' I. E., MORE COMPLEX THAN TWO LOCAL LEVELS WITH NO NATIONAL LEVELS (267) GES,EA	1.00 OF 9	100	DRIFT LESS TOWARD BEING THOSE WHERE HIERARCHIES ARE MORE COMPLEX THAN THE 'SIMPLEST,' I. E., MORE COMPLEX THAN TWO LOCAL LEVELS WITH NO NATIONAL LEVELS (267) GES,EA	0.56 OF 9	9 5 0 4 XSQ= 2.89 PHI= 0.401 EP = 0.0824
102	DRIFT TOWARD BEING THOSE WHERE CLASS STRATIFICATION IS PRESENT (203)	0.80 OF 10	102	DRIFT TOWARD BEING THOSE WHERE CLASS STRATIFICATION IS ABSENT (180)	0.70 OF 10	8 3 2 7 XSQ= 3.23 PHI= 0.402 EP = 0.0698
110	TILT TOWARD BEING THOSE WHERE SLAVERY IS PRESENT (163)	0.70 OF 10	110	TILT TOWARD BEING THOSE WHERE SLAVERY IS ABSENT (218)	0.90 OF 10	7 1 3 9 XSQ= 5.21 PHI= 0.510 EP = 0.0198

116	TILT TOWARD BEING THOSE 0.80 OF 5 WHERE OCCUPATIONAL SPECIALIZATION IS FULL-TIME, WHETHER OR NOT FOR SURPLUS PRODUCTION (20) JMH	116	IN ALL CASES ARE THOSE 1.00 OF 5 WHERE OCCUPATIONAL SPECIALIZATION IS PART-TIME ONLY (34) JMH	4 0 1 5 XSQ= 3.75 PHI= 0.612 EP = 0.0476
138	IN ALL CASES ARE THOSE 1.00 OF 2 WHERE SUPERORDINATE JUSTICE IS PRESENT (22) BBW	138	IN ALL CASES ARE THOSE 1.00 OF 4 WHERE SUPERORDINATE JUSTICE IS ABSENT (18) BBW	2 0 0 4 XSQ= 2.34 PHI= 0.625 EP = 0.0667
139	IN ALL CASES ARE THOSE 1.00 OF 2 WHERE SUPERORDINATE PUNISHMENT IS PRESENT (15) BBW	139	IN ALL CASES ARE THOSE 1.00 OF 4 WHERE SUPERORDINATE PUNISHMENT IS ABSENT (25) BBW	2 0 0 4 XSQ= 2.34 PHI= 0.625 EP = 0.0667
152	IN ALL CASES ARE THOSE 1.00 OF 10 WHERE THE DIFFERENTIATION OF THE JURIDICAL AGENCY FROM THE MEDICAL AGENCY IS HIGH (10) MJ	152	IN ALL CASES ARE THOSE 1.00 OF 10 WHERE THE DIFFERENTIATION OF THE JURIDICAL AGENCY FROM THE MEDICAL AGENCY IS LOW (10) MJ	10 0 0 10 XSQ= 16.20 PHI= 0.900 EP = 0.0000
163	LEAN TOWARD BEING THOSE 0.78 OF 9 WHERE THE EMPHASIS ON INDIVIDUAL VOLITION AS THE CAUSE OF CRIME IS HIGH (7) MJ	163	IN ALL CASES ARE THOSE 1.00 OF 8 WHERE THE EMPHASIS ON INDIVIDUAL VOLITION AS THE CAUSE OF CRIME IS LOW (10) MJ	7 0 2 8 XSQ= 7.61 PHI= 0.669 EP = 0.0023
175	DRIFT TOWARD BEING THOSE 0.90 OF 10 WHERE THE COMMUNITY IS 'KIN-HETEROGENEOUS,' I. E. OTHER THAN A CLAN COMMUNITY OR A DEME (260)	175	DRIFT TOWARD BEING THOSE 0.60 OF 10 WHERE THE COMMUNITY IS 'KIN-HOMOGENEOUS,' I. E. A CLAN COMMUNITY OR A DEME (122)	1 6 9 4 XSQ= 3.52 PHI= -0.419 EP = 0.0573
180	IN ALL CASES ARE THOSE 1.00 OF 10 WHERE THE COMMUNITY IS COMMONLY NON-EXOGAMOUS, RATHER THAN EXOGAMOUS (258)	180	DRIFT LESS TOWARD BEING THOSE 0.60 OF 10 WHERE THE COMMUNITY IS COMMONLY NON-EXOGAMOUS, RATHER THAN EXOGAMOUS (258)	0 4 10 6 XSQ= 2.81 PHI= -0.375 EP = 0.0867
196	IN ALL CASES ARE THOSE 1.00 OF 7 WHERE INDIVIDUAL RIGHTS IN REAL PROPERTY, AND RULES FOR INHERITANCE, ARE PRESENT (194)	196	LEAN TOWARD BEING THOSE 0.78 OF 9 WHERE INDIVIDUAL RIGHTS IN REAL PROPERTY, OR RULES FOR INHERITANCE, ARE ABSENT (87)	7 2 0 7 XSQ= 6.78 PHI= 0.651 EP = 0.0032
334	DRIFT TOWARD BEING THOSE 0.67 OF 3 WHERE THE INDULGENCE OF THE CHILD IS LOW (38) B-B-C	334	IN ALL CASES ARE THOSE 1.00 OF 6 WHERE THE INDULGENCE OF THE CHILD IS HIGH (40) B-B-C	1 6 2 0 XSQ= 2.01 PHI= -0.472 EP = 0.0833

```
355  IN ALL CASES ARE THOSE            1.00 OF   3     355  IN ALL CASES ARE THOSE             1.00 OF   5             3     0
     WHERE THE CHILD'S INFERRED CONFLICT                  WHERE THE CHILD'S INFERRED CONFLICT                        0     5
     REGARDING OBEDIENT BEHAVIOR                          REGARDING OBEDIENT BEHAVIOR                        XSQ=      4.30
     IS HIGH   (35) B-B-C                                 IS LOW   (38) B-B-C                                PHI=     0.733
                                                                                                             EP =    0.0179

391  DRIFT TOWARD BEING THOSE          0.86 OF   7     391  DRIFT TOWARD BEING THOSE           0.80 OF   5             6     1
     WHERE PREMARITAL SEX RELATIONS ARE                   WHERE PREMARITAL SEX RELATIONS ARE                         1     4
     STRONGLY PUNISHED AND IN FACT RARE, OR               PUNISHED ONLY IF PREGNANCY RESULTS, OR             XSQ=      2.83
     WEAKLY PUNISHED AND                                  FREELY PERMITTED   (90) JTW,EA                     PHI=     0.486
     IN FACT NOT RARE   (89) JTW,EA                                                                          EP =    0.0720

398  IN ALL CASES ARE THOSE            1.00 OF   2     398  IN ALL CASES ARE THOSE             1.00 OF   4             2     0
     WHERE THE INTENSITY OF SEX ANXIETY                   WHERE THE INTENSITY OF SEX ANXIETY                         0     4
     IS HIGH   (16) WNS                                   IS LOW   (16) WNS                                  XSQ=      2.34
                                                                                                             PHI=     0.625
                                                                                                             EP.=    0.0667

444  DRIFT TOWARD BEING THOSE          0.75 OF   4     444  DRIFT TOWARD BEING THOSE           0.86 OF   7             1     6
     WHERE THE USE OF DREAMS                              WHERE THE USE OF DREAMS                                    3     1
     TO SEEK AND CONTROL SUPERNATURAL POWERS              TO SEEK AND CONTROL SUPERNATURAL POWERS            XSQ=      1.86
     IS LOW   (27) RGD                                    IS HIGH   (28) RGD                                 PHI=    -0.411
                                                                                                             EP =    0.0879

470  TILT TOWARD BEING THOSE           0.80 OF   5     470  IN ALL CASES ARE THOSE             1.00 OF   5             4     0
     WHERE INNOVATIONS ARE                                WHERE INNOVATIONS ARE                                      1     5
     GENERALLY ACCEPTED   (21) JMH                        ACCEPTED ONLY SELECTIVELY   (33) JMH               XSQ=      3.75
                                                                                                             PHI=     0.612
                                                                                                             EP =    0.0476
```

152 CULTURES WHERE THE DIFFERENTIATION OF THE JURIDICAL AGENCY FROM THE MEDICAL AGENCY IS HIGH (10) MJ

152 CULTURES WHERE THE DIFFERENTIATION OF THE JURIDICAL AGENCY FROM THE MEDICAL AGENCY IS LOW (10) MJ

BACKGROUND ON PAGE 102

BOTH SUBJECT AND PREDICATE

10 IN LEFT COLUMN

BEMBA BURMESE JAVANESE LAMBA NAVAHO NUPE SAMOANS SIUAI THAI VIETNAMESE

10 IN RIGHT COLUMN

ANDAMANESE COMANCHE COPR ESKIMO JIVARO KIKUYU KUNG MUNDURUCU MURNGIN NAMA TROBRIAND

380 EXCLUDED BECAUSE UNASCERTAINED

	High (left column)				Low (right column)			
46	IN ALL CASES ARE THOSE OTHER THAN WHERE SETTLEMENTS ARE NON-FIXED AND MOVEMENT IS NOMADIC (260)	1.00 OF 9	46	TILT TOWARD BEING THOSE WHERE SETTLEMENTS ARE NON-FIXED AND MOVEMENT IS NOMADIC (72)	0.56 OF 9	0 5 9 4	XSQ= 4.43 PHI= -0.496 EP = 0.0294
51	TILT TOWARD BEING THOSE WHERE SUBSISTENCE IS PRIMARILY BY FOOD PRODUCTION -- I. E., AGRICULTURE OR HUSBANDRY -- RATHER THAN BY GATHERING (253)	0.90 OF 10	51	TILT TOWARD BEING THOSE WHERE SUBSISTENCE IS PRIMARILY BY FOOD GATHERING -- I. E., HUNTING, FISHING, OR COLLECTING -- RATHER THAN FOOD PRODUCTION (147)	0.70 OF 10	9 3 1 7	XSQ= 5.21 PHI= 0.510 EP = 0.0198
71	TILT TOWARD BEING THOSE WHERE METAL WORKING IS PRESENT (98)	0.83 OF 6	71	TILT TOWARD BEING THOSE WHERE METAL WORKING IS ABSENT (153)	0.80 OF 10	5 2 1 8	XSQ= 3.81 PHI= 0.488 EP = 0.0350
80	DRIFT LESS TOWARD BEING THOSE WHERE NO CITY OR TOWN IS PRESENT (185)	0.57 OF 7	80	IN ALL CASES ARE THOSE WHERE NO CITY OR TOWN IS PRESENT (185)	1.00 OF 8	3 0 4 8	XSQ= 2.03 PHI= 0.367 EP = 0.0769
81	TILT TOWARD BEING THOSE WHERE A CITY OR TOWN IS PRESENT, OR THE AVERAGE COMMUNITY SIZE IS 200 OR GREATER (89)	0.71 OF 7	81	TILT TOWARD BEING THOSE WHERE NO CITY OR TOWN IS PRESENT, AND THE AVERAGE COMMUNITY SIZE IS SMALLER THAN 200 (135)	0.88 OF 8	5 1 2 7	XSQ= 3.23 PHI= 0.464 EP = 0.0406

82	IN ALL CASES ARE THCSE WHERE A CITY CR TOWN IS PRESENT, OR THE AVERAGE COMMUNITY SIZE IS FIFTY OR GREATER (178)	1.00 OF 7	82	DRIFT TOWARD BEING THCSE WHERE NO CITY OR TOWN IS PRESENT, AND THE AVERAGE COMMUNITY SIZE IS SMALLER THAN FIFTY (46)	0.50 OF 8	7 4 0 4 XSQ= 2.56 PHI= 0.413 EP = 0.0769
85	TILT TOWARD BEING THCSE WHERE THE LEVEL CF POLITICAL INTEGRATICN IS THE LARGE STATE, CR THE LITTLE STATE (70) GPM	0.56 OF 9	85	IN ALL CASES ARE THOSE WHERE THE LEVEL OF POLITICAL INTEGRATION IS THE MINIMAL STATE, THE AUTONOMOUS COMMUNITY, CR THE FAMILY (234) GPM	1.00 CF 8	5 0 4 8 XSQ= 3.90 PHI= 0.479 EP = 0.0294
86	DRIFT TCWARD BEING THCSE WHERE THE LEVEL CF PCLITICAL INTEGRATICN IS THE LARGE STATE, THE LITTLE STATE, OR THE MINIMAL STATE (148) GPM	0.78 OF 9	86	DRIFT TOWARD BEING THOSE WHERE THE LEVEL OF PCLITICAL INTEGRATION IS THE AUTONOMOUS COMMUNITY, OR THE FAMILY (156) GPM	0.75 OF 8	7 2 2 6 XSQ= 2.85 PHI= 0.410 EP = 0.0567
91	IN ALL CASES ARE THCSE WHERE SOCIETAL CCMPLEXITY IS HIGH (18) F-W	1.00 OF 2	91	IN ALL CASES ARE THOSE WHERE SOCIETAL COMPLEXITY IS LOW (22) F-W	1.) CF 4	2 0 0 4 XSQ= 2.34 PHI= 0.625 EP = 0.0667
95	LEAN TCWARD BEING THCSE WHERE THE HIERARCHY OF NATICNAL JURISDICTICN HAS FOUR, THREE, OR TWC LEVELS (76) GES,EA	0.78 OF 9	95	IN ALL CASES ARE THOSE WHERE THE HIERARCHY OF NATIONAL JURISDICTION HAS ONE OR NO LEVELS (254) GES,EA	1.CO OF 9	7 0 2 9 XSQ= 8.42 PHI= 0.684 EP = 0.0023
96	DRIFT TCWARD BEING THCSE WHERE THE HIERARCHY OF NATICNAL JURISDICTION HAS FCUR, THREE, TWC OR ONE LEVEL (174) GES,EA	0.78 OF 9	96	DRIFT TOWARD BEING THOSE WHERE THE HIERARCHY OF NATIONAL JURISDICTICN HAS NO LEVELS (156) GES,EA	0.78 OF 9	7 2 2 7 XSQ= 3.56 PHI= 0.444 EP = 0.0567
100	IN ALL CASES ARE THCSE WHERE HIERARCHIES ARE MORE COMPLEX THAN THE 'SIMPLEST,' I. E., MORE COMPLEX THAN TWO LCCAL LEVELS WITH NC NATICNAL LEVELS (267) GES,EA	1.00 OF 9	100	DRIFT LESS TOWARD BEING THCSE WHERE HIERARCHIES ARE MORE COMPLEX THAN THE 'SIMPLEST,' I. E., MORE COMPLEX THAN TWO LOCAL LEVELS WITH NO NATIONAL LEVELS (267) GES,EA	0.56 CF 9	9 5 0 4 XSQ= 2.89 PHI= 0.401 EP = 0.0824
102	DRIFT TOWARD BEING THOSE WHERE CLASS STRATIFICATICN IS PRESENT (203)	0.80 OF 1C	102	DRIFT TOWARD BEING THOSE WHERE CLASS STRATIFICATION IS ABSENT (180)	0.70 CF 10	8 3 2 7 XSQ= 3.23 PHI= 0.402 EP = 0.0698
110	TILT TCWARD BEING THCSE WHERE SLAVERY IS PRESENT (163)	0.70 OF 1C	110	TILT TOWARD BEING THOSE WHERE SLAVERY IS ABSENT (218)	0.90 OF 10	7 1 3 9 XSQ= 5.21 PHI= 0.51C EP = 0.0198

116	TILT TOWARD BEING THOSE WHERE OCCUPATIONAL SPECIALIZATION IS FULL-TIME, WHETHER OR NOT FOR SURPLUS PRODUCTION (20) JMH	0.80 OF 5	116	IN ALL CASES ARE THOSE WHERE OCCUPATIONAL SPECIALIZATION IS PART-TIME ONLY (34) JMH	1.00 OF 5	 XSQ= PHI= EP =	4 0 1 5 3.75 0.612 0.0476
138	IN ALL CASES ARE THOSE WHERE SUPERORDINATE JUSTICE IS PRESENT (22) BBW	1.00 OF 2	138	IN ALL CASES ARE THOSE WHERE SUPERORDINATE JUSTICE IS ABSENT (18) BBW	1.00 OF 4	 XSQ= PHI= EP =	2 0 0 4 2.34 0.625 0.0667
139	IN ALL CASES ARE THOSE WHERE SUPERORDINATE PUNISHMENT IS PRESENT (15) BBW	1.00 OF 2	139	IN ALL CASES ARE THOSE WHERE SUPERORDINATE PUNISHMENT IS ABSENT (25) BBW	1.00 OF 4	 XSQ= PHI= EP =	2 0 0 4 2.34 0.625 0.0667
163	LEAN TOWARD BEING THOSE WHERE THE EMPHASIS ON INDIVIDUAL VOLITION AS THE CAUSE OF CRIME IS HIGH (7) MJ	0.78 OF 9	163	IN ALL CASES ARE THOSE WHERE THE EMPHASIS ON INDIVIDUAL VOLITION AS THE CAUSE OF CRIME IS LOW (10) MJ	1.00 OF 8	 XSQ= PHI= EP =	7 0 2 8 7.61 0.669 0.0023
175	DRIFT TOWARD BEING THOSE WHERE THE COMMUNITY IS 'KIN-HETEROGENEOUS,' I. E. OTHER THAN A CLAN COMMUNITY OR A DEME (260)	0.90 OF 10	175	DRIFT TOWARD BEING THOSE WHERE THE COMMUNITY IS 'KIN-HOMOGENEOUS,' I. E. A CLAN COMMUNITY OR A DEME (122)	0.60 OF 10	 XSQ= PHI= EP =	1 6 9 4 3.52 -0.419 0.0573
180	IN ALL CASES ARE THOSE WHERE THE COMMUNITY IS COMMONLY NON-EXOGAMOUS, RATHER THAN EXOGAMOUS (258)	1.00 OF 10	180	DRIFT LESS TOWARD BEING THOSE WHERE THE COMMUNITY IS COMMONLY NON-EXOGAMOUS, RATHER THAN EXOGAMOUS (258)	0.60 OF 10	 XSQ= PHI= EP =	0 4 10 6 2.81 -0.375 0.0867
196	IN ALL CASES ARE THOSE WHERE INDIVIDUAL RIGHTS IN REAL PROPERTY, AND RULES FOR INHERITANCE, ARE PRESENT (194)	1.00 OF 7	196	LEAN TOWARD BEING THOSE WHERE INDIVIDUAL RIGHTS IN REAL PROPERTY, OR RULES FOR INHERITANCE, ARE ABSENT (87)	0.78 OF 9	 XSQ= PHI= EP =	7 2 0 7 6.78 0.651 0.0032
334	DRIFT TOWARD BEING THOSE WHERE THE INDULGENCE OF THE CHILD IS LOW (38) B-B-C	0.67 OF 3	334	IN ALL CASES ARE THOSE WHERE THE INDULGENCE OF THE CHILD IS HIGH (40) B-B-C	1.00 OF 6	 XSQ= PHI= EP =	1 6 2 0 2.01 -0.472 0.0833
355	IN ALL CASES ARE THOSE WHERE THE CHILD'S INFERRED CONFLICT REGARDING OBEDIENT BEHAVIOR IS HIGH (35) B-B-C	1.00 OF 3	355	IN ALL CASES ARE THOSE WHERE THE CHILD'S INFERRED CONFLICT REGARDING OBEDIENT BEHAVIOR IS LOW (38) B-B-C	1.00 OF 5	 XSQ= PHI= EP =	3 0 0 5 4.30 0.733 0.0179

```
391  DRIFT TOWARD BEING THOSE         0.86 OF   7    391  DRIFT TOWARD BEING THOSE         0.80 OF   5            6     1
     WHERE PREMARITAL SEX RELATIONS ARE                   WHERE PREMARITAL SEX RELATIONS ARE                        1     4
     STRONGLY PUNISHED AND IN FACT RARE, OR               PUNISHED ONLY IF PREGNANCY RESULTS, OR            XSQ=     2.83
     WEAKLY PUNISHED AND                                  FREELY PERMITTED  (90) JTW,EA                     PHI=    0.486
     IN FACT NOT RARE  (89) JTW,EA                                                                          EP =   0.0720

398  IN ALL CASES ARE THOSE           1.00 OF   2    398  IN ALL CASES ARE THOSE           1.00 OF   4            2     0
     WHERE THE INTENSITY OF SEX ANXIETY                   WHERE THE INTENSITY OF SEX ANXIETY                        0     4
     IS HIGH  (16) WNS                                    IS LOW  (16) WNS                                  XSQ=     2.34
                                                                                                            PHI=    0.625
                                                                                                            EP =   0.0667

444  DRIFT TOWARD BEING THOSE         0.75 OF   4    444  DRIFT TOWARD BEING THOSE         0.86 OF   7            1     6
     WHERE THE USE OF DREAMS                              WHERE THE USE OF DREAMS                                   3     1
     TO SEEK AND CONTROL SUPERNATURAL POWERS              TO SEEK AND CONTROL SUPERNATURAL POWERS           XSQ=     1.86
     IS LOW  (27) RGD                                     IS HIGH  (28) RGD                                 PHI=   -0.411
                                                                                                            EP =   0.0879

470  TILT TOWARD BEING THOSE          0.80 OF   5    470  IN ALL CASES ARE THOSE           1.00 OF   5            4     0
     WHERE INNOVATIONS ARE                                WHERE INNOVATIONS ARE                                     1     5
     GENERALLY ACCEPTED  (21) JMH                         ACCEPTED ONLY SELECTIVELY  (33) JMH               XSQ=     3.75
                                                                                                            PHI=    0.612
                                                                                                            EP =   0.0476
```

153 CULTURES
WHERE THE DEGREE OF DIVISION OF LABOR
AMONG JURIDICAL SPECIALISTS AND SUB-UNITS
IS HIGH (10) MJ

153 CULTURES
WHERE THE DEGREE OF DIVISION OF LABOR
AMONG JURIDICAL SPECIALISTS AND SUB-UNITS
IS LOW (10) MJ

BACKGROUND ON PAGE 102

NEITHER SUBJECT NOR PREDICATE

10 IN LEFT COLUMN

BEMBA BURMESE JAVANESE KIKUYU LAMBA NUPE SAMOANS THAI TROBRIAND VIETNAMESE

10 IN RIGHT COLUMN

ANDAMANESE COMANCHE COPR ESKIMO JIVARO KUNG MUNDURUCU MURNGIN NAMA NAVAHO SIUAI

380 EXCLUDED BECAUSE UNASCERTAINED

****

154 CULTURES WHERE THE DEGREE OF DIVISION OF LABOR AMONG MEDICAL SPECIALISTS AND SUB-UNITS IS HIGH (10) MJ	154 CULTURES WHERE THE DEGREE OF DIVISION OF LABOR AMONG MEDICAL SPECIALISTS AND SUB-UNITS IS LOW (10) MJ

BACKGROUND ON PAGE 102

NEITHER SUBJECT NOR PREDICATE

10 IN LEFT COLUMN

BEMBA BURMESE JAVANESE KIKUYU LAMBA NAVAHO NUPE THAI TROBRIAND VIETNAMESE

10 IN RIGHT COLUMN

ANDAMANESE COMANCHE COPR ESKIMO JIVARO KUNG MUNDURUCU MURNGIN NAMA SAMOANS SIUAI

380 EXCLUDED BECAUSE UNASCERTAINED

---

155 CULTURES
WHERE THE EXTENT OF TRAINING
OF JURIDICAL SPECIALISTS
IS HIGH (9) MJ

155 CULTURES
WHERE THE EXTENT OF TRAINING
OF JURIDICAL SPECIALISTS
IS LOW (11) MJ

BACKGROUND ON PAGE 102

NEITHER SUBJECT NOR PREDICATE

9 IN LEFT COLUMN

BEMBA BURMESE JAVANESE KIKUYU LAMBA NUPE SAMOANS THAI VIETNAMESE

11 IN RIGHT COLUMN

ANDAMANESE COMANCHE COPR ESKIMO JIVARO KUNG MUNDURUCU MURNGIN NAMA NAVAHO SIUAI TROBRIAND

380 EXCLUDED BECAUSE UNASCERTAINED

156 CULTURES WHERE THE EXTENT OF TRAINING OF MEDICAL SPECIALISTS IS HIGH (9) MJ	156 CULTURES WHERE THE EXTENT OF TRAINING OF MEDICAL SPECIALISTS IS LOW (8) MJ

BACKGROUND ON PAGE 102

NEITHER SUBJECT NOR PREDICATE

9 IN LEFT COLUMN

BEMBA BURMESE JAVANESE KIKUYU LAMBA NAVAHO NUPE THAI VIETNAMESE

8 IN RIGHT COLUMN

COMANCHE COPR ESKIMO JIVARO KUNG MUNDURUCU MURNGIN NAMA TROBRIAND

383 EXCLUDED BECAUSE UNASCERTAINED

157 CULTURES
WHERE THE EXTENT OF HIERARCHICIZATION
OF THE JURIDICAL AGENCY
IS HIGH (9) MJ

157 CULTURES
WHERE THE EXTENT OF HIERARCHICIZATION
OF THE JURIDICAL AGENCY
IS LOW (11) MJ

BACKGROUND ON PAGE 102

NEITHER SUBJECT NOR PREDICATE

9 IN LEFT COLUMN

BEMBA BURMESE JAVANESE KIKUYU LAMBA NUPE SAMOANS THAI VIETNAMESE

11 IN RIGHT COLUMN

ANDAMANESE COMANCHE COPR ESKIMO JIVARO KUNG MUNDURUCU MURNGIN NAMA NAVAHO SIUAI
TROBRIAND

380 EXCLUDED BECAUSE UNASCERTAINED

158 CULTURES
WHERE THE EXTENT OF DEVELOPMENT
OF MEDICAL SUB-SYSTEMS
IS HIGH (11) MJ

158 CULTURES
WHERE THE EXTENT OF DEVELOPMENT
OF MEDICAL SUB-SYSTEMS
IS LOW (9) MJ

BACKGROUND ON PAGE 102

NEITHER SUBJECT NOR PREDICATE

11 IN LEFT COLUMN

BEMBA BURMESE JAVANESE KIKUYU LAMBA NAVAHO NUPE SAMOANS THAI TROBRIAND
VIETNAMESE

9 IN RIGHT COLUMN

ANDAMANESE COMANCHE COPR ESKIMO JIVARO KUNG MUNDURUCU MURNGIN NAMA SIUAI

380 EXCLUDED BECAUSE UNASCERTAINED

159 CULTURES WHERE THE DEGREE OF LOCALIZATION OF JURIDICAL ACTIVITY IS HIGH (10) MJ	159 CULTURES WHERE THE DEGREE OF LOCALIZATION OF JURIDICAL ACTIVITY IS LOW (10) MJ

BACKGROUND ON PAGE 102

NEITHER SUBJECT NOR PREDICATE

10 IN LEFT COLUMN

BEMBA BURMESE JAVANESE KIKUYU LAMBA NUPE SAMOANS SIUAI THAI VIETNAMESE

10 IN RIGHT COLUMN

ANDAMANESE COMANCHE COPR ESKIMO JIVARO KUNG MUNDURUCU MURNGIN NAMA NAVAHO TROBRIAND

380 EXCLUDED BECAUSE UNASCERTAINED

****

160 CULTURES WHERE THE DEGREE OF LOCALIZATION OF MEDICAL ACTIVITY IS HIGH (10) MJ	160 CULTURES WHERE THE DEGREE OF LOCALIZATION OF MEDICAL ACTIVITY IS LOW (10) MJ

BACKGROUND ON PAGE 102

NEITHER SUBJECT NOR PREDICATE

....

10 IN LEFT COLUMN

BEMBA	BURMESE	COMANCHE	JAVANESE	KIKUYU	LAMBA	NAMA	NUPE	THAI	VIETNAMESE

10 IN RIGHT COLUMN

ANDAMANESE	COPR ESKIMO	JIVARO	KUNG	MUNDURUCU	MURNGIN	NAVAHO	SAMOANS	SIUAI	TROBRIAND

380 EXCLUDED BECAUSE UNASCERTAINED

----

161 CULTURES WHERE THE DEGREE OF CONTROL OVER CLIENTS BY THE JURIDICAL AGENCY IS HIGH (10) MJ	161 CULTURES WHERE THE DEGREE OF CONTROL OVER CLIENTS BY THE JURIDICAL AGENCY IS LOW (10) MJ

BACKGROUND ON PAGE 102 — NEITHER SUBJECT NOR PREDICATE

10 IN LEFT COLUMN

BEMBA BURMESE JAVANESE KIKUYU LAMBA NUPE SAMOANS SIUAI THAI VIETNAMESE

10 IN RIGHT COLUMN

ANDAMANESE COMANCHE COPR ESKIMO JIVARO KUNG MUNDURUCU MURNGIN NAMA NAVAHO TROBRIAND

380 EXCLUDED BECAUSE UNASCERTAINED

162 CULTURES WHERE THE DEGREE OF CONTRCL OVER CLIENTS BY THE MEDICAL AGENCY IS HIGH (10) MJ	162 CULTURES WHERE THE DEGREE OF CONTROL OVER CLIENTS BY THE MEDICAL AGENCY IS LOW (10) MJ

BACKGROUND ON PAGE 102

NEITHER SUBJECT NOR PREDICATE

10 IN LEFT CCLUMN

BEMBA BURMESE JAVANESE KIKUYU LAMBA NAMA NUPE THAI TROBRIAND VIETNAMESE

10 IN RIGHT CCLUMN

ANDAMANESE COMANCHE COPR ESKIMO JIVARO KUNG MUNDURUCU MURNGIN NAVAHO SAMCANS SIUAI

380 EXCLUDED BECAUSE UNASCERTAINEC

163 CULTURES
WHERE THE EMPHASIS ON INDIVIDUAL VOLITION
AS THE CAUSE OF CRIME
IS HIGH (7) MJ

163 CULTURES
WHERE THE EMPHASIS ON INDIVIDUAL VOLITION
AS THE CAUSE OF CRIME
IS LOW (10) MJ

BACKGROUND ON PAGE 102

BOTH SUBJECT AND PREDICATE

7 IN LEFT COLUMN

BURMESE JAVANESE NUPE SAMOANS SIUAI THAI VIETNAMESE

10 IN RIGHT COLUMN

ANDAMANESE BEMBA COMANCHE COPR ESKIMO JIVARO KIKUYU KUNG MURNGIN NAMA NAVAHO

383 EXCLUDED BECAUSE UNASCERTAINED

	Left column				Right column			
36	IN ALL CASES ARE THOSE WHERE THE NATURAL ENVIRONMENT IS OTHER THAN 'VERY HARSH,' OR SUB-TROPICAL BUSH, OR TEMPERATE GRASSLAND (292) FWM	1.00 OF 7	36	TILT TOWARD BEING THOSE WHERE THE NATURAL ENVIRONMENT IS 'VERY HARSH,' OR SUB-TROPICAL BUSH, OR TEMPERATE GRASSLAND (108) FWM	0.60 OF 10	0 6 7 4	XSQ= 4.13 PHI= -0.493 EP = 0.0175
42	LEAN TOWARD BEING THOSE WHERE THE NATURAL ENVIRONMENT IS TROPICAL OR SUB-TROPICAL RAIN FOREST, OR MONSOON FOREST (156) FWM	0.86 OF 7	42	LEAN TOWARD BEING THOSE WHERE THE NATURAL ENVIRONMENT IS OTHER THAN TROPICAL OR SUB-TROPICAL RAIN FOREST, OR MONSOON FOREST (244) FWM	0.90 OF 10	6 1 1 9	XSQ= 6.87 PHI= 0.636 EP = 0.0037
44	IN ALL CASES ARE THOSE WHERE SETTLEMENTS ARE FIXED (222)	1.00 OF 6	44	LEAN TOWARD BEING THOSE WHERE SETTLEMENTS ARE NON-FIXED (110)	0.78 OF 9	6 2 0 7	XSQ= 5.90 PHI= 0.627 EP = 0.0070
51	IN ALL CASES ARE THOSE WHERE SUBSISTENCE IS PRIMARILY BY FOOD PRODUCTION -- I. E., AGRICULTURE OR HUSBANDRY -- RATHER THAN BY GATHERING (253)	1.00 OF 7	51	LEAN TOWARD BEING THOSE WHERE SUBSISTENCE IS PRIMARILY BY FOOD GATHERING -- I. E., HUNTING, FISHING, OR COLLECTING -- RATHER THAN FOOD PRODUCTION (147)	0.70 OF 10	7 3 0 7	XSQ= 5.69 PHI= 0.579 EP = 0.0098
80	TILT TOWARD BEING THOSE WHERE A CITY OR TOWN IS PRESENT (39)	0.60 OF 5	80	IN ALL CASES ARE THOSE WHERE NO CITY OR TOWN IS PRESENT (185)	1.00 OF 8	3 0 2 8	XSQ= 3.32 PHI= 0.505 EP = 0.0350

84	DRIFT TOWARD BEING THOSE 0.67 OF 6 WHERE THE LEVEL OF POLITICAL INTEGRATION IS THE LARGE STATE (42) GPM	84	DRIFT TOWARD BEING THOSE 0.88 OF 8 WHERE THE LEVEL OF POLITICAL INTEGRATION IS THE LITTLE STATE, THE MINIMAL STATE, THE AUTONOMOUS COMMUNITY, OR THE FAMILY (262) GPM	4 1 2 7 XSQ= 2.34 PHI= 0.409 EP = 0.0909
85	DRIFT TOWARD BEING THOSE 0.67 OF 6 WHERE THE LEVEL OF POLITICAL INTEGRATION IS THE LARGE STATE, OR THE LITTLE STATE (70) GPM	85	DRIFT TOWARD BEING THOSE 0.88 OF 8 WHERE THE LEVEL OF POLITICAL INTEGRATION IS THE MINIMAL STATE, THE AUTONOMOUS COMMUNITY, OR THE FAMILY (234) GPM	4 1 2 7 XSQ= 2.34 PHI= 0.409 EP = 0.0909
94	TILT TOWARD BEING THOSE 0.50 OF 6 WHERE THE HIERARCHY OF NATIONAL JURISDICTION HAS FOUR OR THREE LEVELS (34) GES,EA	94	IN ALL CASES ARE THOSE 1.00 OF 9 WHERE THE HIERARCHY OF NATIONAL JURISDICTION HAS TWO, ONE, OR NO LEVELS (296) GES,EA	3 0 3 9 XSQ= 2.93 PHI= 0.442 EP = 0.0440
95	TILT TOWARD BEING THOSE 0.83 OF 6 WHERE THE HIERARCHY OF NATIONAL JURISDICTION HAS FOUR, THREE, OR TWO LEVELS (76) GES,EA	95	TILT TOWARD BEING THOSE 0.89 OF 9 WHERE THE HIERARCHY OF NATIONAL JURISDICTION HAS ONE OR NO LEVELS (254) GES,EA	5 1 1 8 XSQ= 5.10 PHI= 0.583 EP = 0.0110
96	TILT TOWARD BEING THOSE 0.83 OF 6 WHERE THE HIERARCHY OF NATIONAL JURISDICTION HAS FOUR, THREE, TWO OR ONE LEVEL (174) GES,EA	96	TILT TOWARD BEING THOSE 0.78 OF 9 WHERE THE HIERARCHY OF NATIONAL JURISDICTION HAS NO LEVELS (156) GES,EA	5 2 1 7 XSQ= 3.23 PHI= 0.464 EP = 0.0406
102	IN ALL CASES ARE THOSE 1.00 OF 7 WHERE CLASS STRATIFICATION IS PRESENT (203)	102	LEAN TOWARD BEING THOSE 0.70 OF 10 WHERE CLASS STRATIFICATION IS ABSENT (180)	7 3 0 7 XSQ= 5.69 PHI= 0.579 EP = 0.0098
116	IN ALL CASES ARE THOSE 1.00 OF 3 WHERE OCCUPATIONAL SPECIALIZATION IS FULL-TIME, WHETHER OR NOT FOR SURPLUS PRODUCTION (20) JMH	116	TILT TOWARD BEING THOSE 0.83 OF 6 WHERE OCCUPATIONAL SPECIALIZATION IS PART-TIME ONLY (34) JMH	3 1 0 5 XSQ= 2.76 PHI= 0.553 EP = 0.0476
132	IN ALL CASES ARE THOSE 1.00 OF 3 WHERE ECONOMIC EXCHANGE INVOLVES THE USE OF MONEY (37) JMH	132	TILT TOWARD BEING THOSE 0.83 OF 6 WHERE ECONOMIC EXCHANGE DOES NOT INVOLVE THE USE OF MONEY (17) JMH	3 1 0 5 XSQ= 2.76 PHI= 0.553 EP = 0.0476
152	IN ALL CASES ARE THOSE 1.00 OF 7 WHERE THE DIFFERENTIATION OF THE JURIDICAL AGENCY FROM THE MEDICAL AGENCY IS HIGH (10) MJ	152	LEAN TOWARD BEING THOSE 0.80 OF 10 WHERE THE DIFFERENTIATION OF THE JURIDICAL AGENCY FROM THE MEDICAL AGENCY IS LOW (10) MJ	7 2 0 8 XSQ= 7.61 PHI= 0.669 EP = 0.0023

178	DRIFT LESS TOWARD BEING THOSE 0.57 OF 7 WHERE THE COMMUNITY IS OTHER THAN SEGMENTED ON A CLAN BASIS AND NON-EXOGAMOUS (295)	178	IN ALL CASES ARE THOSE 1.00 OF 10 WHERE THE COMMUNITY IS OTHER THAN SEGMENTED ON A CLAN BASIS AND NON-EXOGAMOUS (295)	3 0 4 10 XSQ= 2.67 PHI= 0.397 EP = 0.0515
196	IN ALL CASES ARE THOSE 1.00 OF 6 WHERE INDIVIDUAL RIGHTS IN REAL PROPERTY, AND RULES FOR INHERITANCE, ARE PRESENT (194)	196	LEAN TOWARD BEING THOSE 0.75 OF 8 WHERE INDIVIDUAL RIGHTS IN REAL PROPERTY, OR RULES FOR INHERITANCE, ARE ABSENT (87)	6 2 0 6 XSQ= 5.11 PHI= 0.604 EP = 0.0097
234	IN ALL CASES ARE THOSE 1.00 OF 7 WHERE THE COUSIN TERMINOLOGY IS OF ESKIMO OR HAWAIIAN TYPE, RATHER THAN CROW, OMAHA, OR IROQUOIS TYPE (170)	234	DRIFT TOWARD BEING THOSE 0.50 OF 8 WHERE THE COUSIN TERMINOLOGY IS OF CROW, OMAHA, OR IROQUOIS TYPE, RATHER THAN ESKIMO OR HAWAIIAN TYPE (152)	0 4 7 4 XSQ= 2.56 PHI= -0.413 EP = 0.0769
299	DRIFT TOWARD BEING THOSE 0.75 OF 4 WHERE THE POST-PARTUM SEX TABOO LASTS LONGER THAN ONE YEAR (35)	299	DRIFT TOWARD BEING THOSE 0.86 OF 7 WHERE THE POST-PARTUM SEX TABOO LASTS ONE YEAR OR LESS (89)	3 1 1 6 XSQ= 1.86 PHI= 0.411 EP = 0.0879
300	DRIFT TOWARD BEING THOSE 0.75 OF 4 WHERE THE POST-PARTUM SEX TABOO LASTS LONGER THAN SIX MONTHS (51)	300	DRIFT TOWARD BEING THOSE 0.86 OF 7 WHERE THE POST-PARTUM SEX TABOO LASTS SIX MONTHS OR LESS (73)	3 1 1 6 XSQ= 1.86 PHI= 0.411 EP = 0.0879
424	IN ALL CASES ARE THOSE 1.00 OF 3 WHERE RELIGIOUS SPECIALISTS ARE FULL-TIME, RATHER THAN PART-TIME (21) JMH	424	IN ALL CASES ARE THOSE 1.00 OF 6 WHERE RELIGIOUS SPECIALISTS ARE PART-TIME, RATHER THAN FULL-TIME (33) JMH	3 0 0 6 XSQ= 5.06 PHI= 0.750 EP = 0.0119
444	IN ALL CASES ARE THOSE 1.00 OF 3 WHERE THE USE OF DREAMS TO SEEK AND CONTROL SUPERNATURAL POWERS IS LOW (27) RGD	444	TILT TOWARD BEING THOSE 0.83 OF 6 WHERE THE USE OF DREAMS TO SEEK AND CONTROL SUPERNATURAL POWERS IS HIGH (28) RGD	0 5 3 1 XSQ= 2.76 PHI= -0.553 EP = 0.0476
450	DRIFT TOWARD BEING THOSE 0.67 OF 3 WHERE THE OBSERVATION OF FOOD TABOOS IS LOW, RATHER THAN HIGH OR MEDIUM (26) JRL	450	IN ALL CASES ARE THOSE 1.00 OF 8 WHERE THE OBSERVATION OF FOOD TABOOS IS HIGH OR MEDIUM, RATHER THAN LOW (60) JRL	1 8 2 0 XSQ= 2.81 PHI= -0.505 EP = 0.0545
468	DRIFT TOWARD BEING THOSE 0.67 OF 3 WHERE CONTACT WITH OTHER CULTURES IS FREQUENT, RATHER THAN REGULAR OR IRREGULAR (17) JMH	468	IN ALL CASES ARE THOSE 1.00 OF 6 WHERE CONTACT WITH OTHER CULTURES IS REGULAR OR IRREGULAR, RATHER THAN FREQUENT (37) JMH	2 0 1 6 XSQ= 2.01 PHI= 0.472 EP = 0.0833

164	CULTURES WHERE THE EMPHASIS ON INDIVIDUAL VOLITION AS THE CAUSE OR SOURCE OF ILLNESS IS HIGH (9) MJ	164	CULTURES WHERE THE EMPHASIS ON INDIVIDUAL VOLITION AS THE CAUSE OR SOURCE OF ILLNESS IS LOW (9) MJ

BACKGROUND ON PAGE 102 — BOTH SUBJECT AND PREDICATE

9 IN LEFT COLUMN

COPR ESKIMO KIKUYU, KUNG, LAMBA, MUNDURUCU, MURNGIN, NAVAHO, SAMOANS, TROBRIAND

9 IN RIGHT COLUMN

ANDAMANESE, BEMBA, BURMESE, JAVANESE, JIVARO, NAMA, NUPE, THAI, VIETNAMESE

382 EXCLUDED BECAUSE UNASCERTAINED

5	IN ALL CASES ARE THOSE LOCATED OUTSIDE OF EAST EURASIA (330)	1.00 OF 9	5	DRIFT LESS TOWARD BEING THOSE LOCATED OUTSIDE OF EAST EURASIA (330)	0.56 OF 9	 XSQ= PHI= EP =	0 9 	4 5 2.89 -0.401 0.0824
80	IN ALL CASES ARE THOSE WHERE NO CITY OR TOWN IS PRESENT (185)	1.00 OF 8	80	DRIFT LESS TOWARD BEING THOSE WHERE NO CITY OR TOWN IS PRESENT (185)	0.57 OF 7	 XSQ= PHI= EP =	0 8 	3 4 2.03 -0.367 0.0769
85	IN ALL CASES ARE THOSE WHERE THE LEVEL OF POLITICAL INTEGRATION IS THE MINIMAL STATE, THE AUTONOMOUS COMMUNITY, OR THE FAMILY (234) GPM	1.00 OF 8	85	TILT TOWARD BEING THOSE WHERE THE LEVEL OF POLITICAL INTEGRATION IS THE LARGE STATE, OR THE LITTLE STATE (70) GPM	0.63 OF 8	 XSQ= PHI= EP =	0 8 	5 3 4.65 -0.539 0.0256
88	TILT TOWARD BEING THOSE WHERE, IF A HEADMANSHIP IS PRESENT, SUCCESSION IS HEREDITARY (165)	0.86 OF 7	88	TILT TOWARD BEING THOSE WHERE, IF A HEADMANSHIP IS PRESENT, SUCCESSION IS NON-HEREDITARY (106)	0.78 OF 9	 XSQ= PHI= EP =	1 6 	7 2 4.06 -0.504 0.0406
94	IN ALL CASES ARE THOSE WHERE THE HIERARCHY OF NATIONAL JURISDICTION HAS TWO, ONE, OR NO LEVELS (296) GES,EA	1.00 OF 9	94	DRIFT LESS TOWARD BEING THOSE WHERE THE HIERARCHY OF NATIONAL JURISDICTION HAS TWO, ONE, OR NO LEVELS (296) GES,EA	0.63 OF 8	 XSQ= PHI= EP =	0 9 	3 5 1.92 -0.336 0.0824

```
184  DRIFT TOWARD BEING THOSE         0.67 OF   6     184  IN ALL CASES ARE THOSE         1.00 OF   4            4     0
     WHERE THE LARGEST NON-COGNATIC KIN GROUP              WHERE THE LARGEST NON-COGNATIC KIN GROUP             2     4
     IS THE MOEITY OR PHRATRY  (77)                        IS SMALLER THAN A PHRATRY, I. E.             XSQ=     2.10
                                                           A SIB OR LINEAGE  (175)                      PHI=    0.458
                                                                                                        EP =   0.0762

224  TILT TOWARD BEING THOSE          0.75 OF   4     224  IN ALL CASES ARE THOSE         1.00 OF   7            3     0
     WHERE COUSIN MARRIAGE IS                              WHERE COUSIN MARRIAGE IS                             1     7
     PREFERENTIALLY OR PERMISSIVELY                        PREFERENTIALLY OR PERMISSIVELY               XSQ=     3.93
     EITHER PATRI- OR MATRILATERAL,                        SYMMETRICAL, RATHER THAN                     PHI=    0.598
     RATHER THAN SYMMETRICAL  (66)                         EITHER PATRI- OR MATRILATERAL  (106)         EP =   0.0242
```

****

165 CULTURES WHERE THE JURIDICAL CLIENT'S COMMENTS ARE DISREGARDED OR USED AGAINST HIM, TO A HIGH EXTENT (7) MJ	165 CULTURES WHERE THE JURIDICAL CLIENT'S COMMENTS ARE DISREGARDED OR USED AGAINST HIM, TO A LOW EXTENT (9) MJ

BACKGROUND ON PAGE 102 SUBJECT ONLY

....

7 IN LEFT COLUMN

BEMBA BURMESE COMANCHE JAVANESE NUPE THAI VIETNAMESE

9 IN RIGHT COLUMN

JIVARO KIKUYU LAMBA MUNDURUCU NAMA NAVAHO SAMOANS SIUAI TROBRIAND

384 EXCLUDED BECAUSE UNASCERTAINED

	Left column				Right column				
5	DRIFT LESS TOWARD BEING THOSE LOCATED OUTSIDE OF EAST EURASIA (330)	0.57 OF	7	5	IN ALL CASES ARE THOSE LOCATED OUTSIDE OF EAST EURASIA (330)	1.00 OF	9	 XSQ= PHI= EP =	3 0 4 9 2.35 0.383 0.0625
53	DRIFT TOWARD BEING THOSE WHERE FOOD PRODUCTION IS BY INTENSIVE AGRICULTURE, RATHER THAN BY SIMPLE AGRICULTURE OR INCIPIENT FOOD PRODUCTION (91)	0.60 OF	5	53	DRIFT TOWARD BEING THOSE WHERE FOOD PRODUCTION IS BY SIMPLE AGRICULTURE OR INCIPIENT FOOD PRODUCTION, RATHER THAN BY INTENSIVE AGRICULTURE (147)	0.89 OF	9	 XSQ= PHI= EP =	3 1 2 8 1.75 0.354 0.0949
80	DRIFT TOWARD BEING THOSE WHERE A CITY OR TOWN IS PRESENT (39)	0.60 OF	5	80	IN ALL CASES ARE THOSE WHERE NO CITY OR TOWN IS PRESENT (185)	1.00 OF	6	 XSQ= PHI= EP =	3 0 2 6 2.39 0.466 0.0606
84	IN ALL CASES ARE THOSE WHERE THE LEVEL OF POLITICAL INTEGRATION IS THE LARGE STATE (42) GPM	1.00 OF	5	84	IN ALL CASES ARE THOSE WHERE THE LEVEL OF POLITICAL INTEGRATION IS THE LITTLE STATE, THE MINIMAL STATE, THE AUTONOMOUS COMMUNITY, OR THE FAMILY (262) GPM	1.00 OF	9	 XSQ= PHI= EP =	5 0 0 9 9.98 0.844 0.0005
85	IN ALL CASES ARE THOSE WHERE THE LEVEL OF POLITICAL INTEGRATION IS THE LARGE STATE, OR THE LITTLE STATE (70) GPM	1.00 OF	5	85	IN ALL CASES ARE THOSE WHERE THE LEVEL OF POLITICAL INTEGRATION IS THE MINIMAL STATE, THE AUTONOMOUS COMMUNITY, OR THE FAMILY (234) GPM	1.00 OF	9	 XSQ= PHI= EP =	5 0 0 9 9.98 0.844 0.0005

94	TILT TOWARD BEING THCSE WHERE THE HIERARCHY OF NATICNAL JURISDICTICN HAS FOUR CR THREE LEVELS (34) GES,EA	0.60 OF	5	94	IN ALL CASES ARE THOSE WHERE THE HIERARCHY OF NATIONAL JURISDICTICN HAS TWO, ONE, OR NO LEVELS (296) GES,EA	1.00 OF	9	 XSQ= PHI= EP =	3 0 2 9 3.77 0.519 0.0275
95	IN ALL CASES ARE THCSE WHERE THE HIERARCHY OF NATIONAL JURISDICTICN HAS FOUR, THREE, OR TWC LEVELS (76) GES,EA	1.00 OF	5	95	TILT TOWARD BEING THOSE WHERE THE HIERARCHY OF NATIONAL JURISDICTICN HAS ONE OR NO LEVELS (254) GES,EA	0.78 OF	9	 XSQ= PHI= EP =	5 2 0 7 4.98 0.596 0.0210
106	IN ALL CASES ARE THCSE WHERE CLASS STRATIFICATION, IF PRESENT, IS BASED CN SCMETHING CTHER THAN WEALTH (126)	1.00 OF	6	106	DRIFT TOWARD BEING THOSE WHERE CLASS STRATIFICATION, IF PRESENT, IS BASED ON WEALTH (77)	0.60 OF	5	 XSQ= PHI= EP =	0 3 6 2 2.39 -0.466 0.0606
107	TILT TOWARD BEING THOSE WHERE CLASS STRATIFICATION, IF PRESENT, IS BASED CN OCCUPATIONAL STATUS (43)	0.83 OF	6	107	IN ALL CASES ARE THOSE WHERE CLASS STRATIFICATICN, IF PRESENT, IS BASED ON SOMETHING OTHER THAN OCCUPATIONAL STATUS (160)	1.00 OF	5	 XSQ= PHI= EP =	5 0 1 5 4.65 0.650 0.0152
110	TILT TOWARD BEING THCSE WHERE SLAVERY IS PRESENT (163)	0.86 OF	7	110	TILT TOWARD BEING THOSE WHERE SLAVERY IS ABSENT (218)	0.78 OF	9	 XSQ= PHI= EP =	6 2 1 7 4.06 0.504 0.0406
164	IN ALL CASES ARE THOSE WHERE THE EMPHASIS ON INDIVIDUAL VOLITION AS THE CAUSE OR SOURCE OF ILLNESS IS LOW (9) MJ	1.00 OF	6	164	LEAN TOWARD BEING THOSE WHERE THE EMPHASIS CN INDIVIDUAL VCLITICN AS THE CAUSE OR SOURCE OF ILLNESS IS HIGH (9) MJ	0.75 OF	8	 XSQ= PHI= EP =	0 6 6 2 5.11 -0.604 0.0097
187	IN ALL CASES ARE THCSE WHERE THE KIN GRCUP IS OTHER THAN EXCLUSIVELY MATRILINEAL (344)	1.00 OF	7	187	DRIFT LESS TOWARD BEING THCSE WHERE THE KIN GROUP IS OTHER THAN EXCLUSIVELY MATRILINEAL (344)	0.56 OF	9	 XSQ= PHI= EP =	0 4 7 5 2.12 -0.364 0.0885
192	DRIFT LESS TOWARD BEING THCSE OTHER THAN WHERE THE CNLY KIN GROUP PRESENT IS A KINDRED CR ELSE BILATERAL DESCENT IS INFERREC (289)	0.57 OF	7	192	IN ALL CASES ARE THOSE OTHER THAN WHERE THE ONLY KIN GRCUP PRESENT IS A KINDRED OR ELSE BILATERAL DESCENT IS INFERRED (289)	1.00 OF	9	 XSQ= PHI= EP =	3 0 4 9 2.35 0.383 0.0625
390	IN ALL CASES ARE THCSE WHERE PREMARITAL SEX RELATIONS ARE STRCNGLY PUNISHED AND IN FACT RARE (47) JTW,EA	1.00 OF	4	390	TILT TOWARD BEING THOSE WHERE PREMARITAL SEX RELATIONS ARE WEAKLY PUNISHED AND IN FACT NOT RARE OR PUNISHED ONLY IF PREGNANCY RESULTS, CR FREELY PERMITIED (132) JTW,EA	0.86 OF	7	 XSQ= PHI= EP =	4 1 0 6 4.48 0.638 0.0152

```
166 CULTURES                                          166 CULTURES
    WHERE THE MEDICAL CLIENT'S COMMENTS                   WHERE THE MEDICAL CLIENT'S COMMENTS
    ARE REGARDED AS RELEVANT                              ARE REGARDED AS RELEVANT
    IN DIAGNOSIS AND CURE,                                IN DIAGNOSIS AND CURE,
    TO A HIGH EXTENT  (10) MJ                             TO A LOW EXTENT  (10) MJ

BACKGROUND ON PAGE 102                                                                    SUBJECT ONLY

     10  IN LEFT COLUMN

BEMBA       BURMESE     JAVANESE    KIKUYU      LAMBA       NAMA        NAVAHO      NUPE        THAI        VIETNAMESE

     10  IN RIGHT COLUMN

ANDAMANESE  COMANCHE    COPR ESKIMO JIVARO      KUNG        MUNDURUCU   MURNGIN     SAMOANS     SIUAI       TROBRIAND

     380  EXCLUDED BECAUSE UNASCERTAINED

------------------------------------------------------------------------------------------------------------------
 48 IN ALL CASES ARE THOSE          1.00 OF  3     48 IN ALL CASES ARE THOSE          1.00 OF  5        0     5
    WHERE THE FOOD SUPPLY IS NOT SECURE,              WHERE THE FOOD SUPPLY IS SECURE,                  3     0
    AND FOOD SHORTAGES ARE                            AND FOOD SHORTAGES ARE                     XSQ=     4.30
    FREQUENT OR ANNUAL  (41) MGW                      RARE OR OCCASIONAL  (38) MGW               PHI=   -0.733
                                                                                                 EP =   0.0179

 63 DRIFT TOWARD BEING THOSE        0.63 OF  8     63 IN ALL CASES ARE THOSE          1.00 OF  4        5     0
    WHERE HUSBANDRY, IF PRESENT,                      WHERE HUSBANDRY, IF PRESENT,                      3     4
    IS PRINCIPALLY IN THE FORM OF                     IS PRINCIPALLY IN THE FORM OF              XSQ=     2.10
    BOVINE, EQUINE, CAMEL-LIKE, OR DEER-LIKE          PIGS, SHEEP, OR GOATS, RATHER THAN         PHI=    0.418
    ANIMALS, RATHER THAN                              BOVINE, EQUINE, CAMEL-LIKE, OR DEER-LIKE   EP =   0.0808
    PIGS, SHEEP, OR GOATS  (152)                      ANIMALS  (74)

 71 IN ALL CASES ARE THOSE          1.00 OF  7     71 IN ALL CASES ARE THOSE          1.00 OF  9        7     0
    WHERE METAL WORKING IS                            WHERE METAL WORKING IS                            0     9
    PRESENT  (98)                                     ABSENT  (153)                              XSQ=    12.19
                                                                                                 PHI=    0.873
                                                                                                 EP =   0.0001

 74 IN ALL CASES ARE THOSE          1.00 OF  7     74 TILT TOWARD BEING THOSE         0.56 OF  9        7     4
    WHERE POTTERY IS                                  WHERE POTTERY IS                                  0     5
    PRESENT  (145)                                    ABSENT  (93)                               XSQ=     3.37
                                                                                                 PHI=    0.459
                                                                                                 EP =   0.0337

 81 LEAN TOWARD BEING THOSE         0.75 OF  8     81 IN ALL CASES ARE THOSE          1.00 OF  7        6     0
    WHERE A CITY OR TOWN IS PRESENT, OR               WHERE NO CITY OR TOWN IS PRESENT, AND             2     7
    THE AVERAGE COMMUNITY SIZE IS                     THE AVERAGE COMMUNITY SIZE IS              XSQ=     5.90
    200 OR GREATER  (89)                              SMALLER THAN 200  (135)                    PHI=    0.627
                                                                                                 EP =   0.0070
```

82	IN ALL CASES ARE THOSE WHERE A CITY OR TOWN IS PRESENT, OR THE AVERAGE COMMUNITY SIZE IS FIFTY OR GREATER (178)	1.00 OF	8	82	TILT TOWARD BEING THOSE WHERE NO CITY OR TOWN IS PRESENT, AND THE AVERAGE COMMUNITY SIZE IS SMALLER THAN FIFTY (46)	0.57 OF	7	8 3 0 4 XSQ= 3.65 PHI= 0.494 EP = 0.0256
83	TILT TOWARD BEING THOSE WHERE, WITH NO CITY AND NO TOWN PRESENT, THE AVERAGE COMMUNITY SIZE IS BETWEEN 200 AND 999, RATHER THAN SMALLER THAN 200 (45)	0.60 OF	5	83	IN ALL CASES ARE THOSE WHERE, WITH NO CITY AND NO TOWN PRESENT, THE AVERAGE COMMUNITY SIZE IS SMALLER THAN 200, RATHER THAN BETWEEN 200 AND 999 (135)	1.00 OF	7	3 0 2 7 XSQ= 2.86 PHI= 0.488 EP = 0.0455
85	TILT TOWARD BEING THOSE WHERE THE LEVEL OF POLITICAL INTEGRATION IS THE LARGE STATE, OR THE LITTLE STATE (70) GPM	0.56 OF	9	85	IN ALL CASES ARE THOSE WHERE THE LEVEL OF POLITICAL INTEGRATION IS THE MINIMAL STATE, THE AUTONOMOUS COMMUNITY, OR THE FAMILY (234) GPM	1.00 OF	8	5 0 4 8 XSQ= 3.90 PHI= 0.479 EP = 0.0294
86	DRIFT TOWARD BEING THOSE WHERE THE LEVEL OF POLITICAL INTEGRATION IS THE LARGE STATE, THE LITTLE STATE, OR THE MINIMAL STATE (148) GPM	0.78 OF	9	86	DRIFT TOWARD BEING THOSE WHERE THE LEVEL OF POLITICAL INTEGRATION IS THE AUTONOMOUS COMMUNITY, OR THE FAMILY (156) GPM	0.75 OF	8	7 2 2 6 XSQ= 2.85 PHI= 0.410 EP = 0.0567
95	TILT TOWARD BEING THOSE WHERE THE HIERARCHY OF NATIONAL JURISDICTION HAS FOUR, THREE, OR TWO LEVELS (76) GES,EA	0.67 OF	9	95	TILT TOWARD BEING THOSE WHERE THE HIERARCHY OF NATIONAL JURISDICTION HAS ONE OR NO LEVELS (254) GES,EA	0.89 OF	9	6 1 3 8 XSQ= 3.74 PHI= 0.456 EP = 0.0498
96	DRIFT TOWARD BEING THOSE WHERE THE HIERARCHY OF NATIONAL JURISDICTION HAS FOUR, THREE, TWO OR ONE LEVEL (174) GES,EA	0.78 OF	9	96	DRIFT TOWARD BEING THOSE WHERE THE HIERARCHY OF NATIONAL JURISDICTION HAS NO LEVELS (156) GES,EA	0.78 OF	9	7 2 2 7 XSQ= 3.56 PHI= 0.444 EP = 0.0567
100	IN ALL CASES ARE THOSE WHERE HIERARCHIES ARE MORE COMPLEX THAN THE 'SIMPLEST,' I. E., MORE COMPLEX THAN TWO LOCAL LEVELS WITH NO NATIONAL LEVELS (267) GES,EA	1.00 OF	9	100	DRIFT LESS TOWARD BEING THOSE WHERE HIERARCHIES ARE MORE COMPLEX THAN THE 'SIMPLEST,' I. E., MORE COMPLEX THAN TWO LOCAL LEVELS WITH NO NATIONAL LEVELS (267) GES,EA	0.56 OF	9	9 5 0 4 XSQ= 2.89 PHI= 0.401 EP = 0.0824
102	DRIFT TOWARD BEING THOSE WHERE CLASS STRATIFICATION IS PRESENT (203)	0.80 OF	10	102	DRIFT TOWARD BEING THOSE WHERE CLASS STRATIFICATION IS ABSENT (180)	0.70 OF	10	8 3 2 7 XSQ= 3.23 PHI= 0.402 EP = 0.0698
110	TILT TOWARD BEING THOSE WHERE SLAVERY IS PRESENT (163)	0.70 OF	10	110	TILT TOWARD BEING THOSE WHERE SLAVERY IS ABSENT (218)	0.90 OF	10	7 1 3 9 XSQ= 5.21 PHI= 0.510 EP = 0.0198

118	IN ALL CASES ARE THOSE 1.00 OF 2 WHERE THE PERCENTAGE OF OCCUPATIONS THAT ARE SPECIALIZED IS HIGH OR MEDIUM (24) WME	118	IN ALL CASES ARE THOSE 1.00 OF 4 WHERE THE PERCENTAGE OF OCCUPATIONS THAT ARE SPECIALIZED IS LOW (25) WME	2 0 0 4 XSQ= 2.34 PHI= 0.625 EP = 0.0667
152	TILT TOWARD BEING THOSE 0.80 OF 10 WHERE THE DIFFERENTIATION OF THE JURIDICAL AGENCY FROM THE MEDICAL AGENCY IS HIGH (10) MJ	152	TILT TOWARD BEING THOSE 0.80 OF 10 WHERE THE DIFFERENTIATION OF THE JURIDICAL AGENCY FROM THE MEDICAL AGENCY IS LOW (10) MJ	8 2 2 8 XSQ= 5.00 PHI= 0.500 EP = 0.0230
184	DRIFT TOWARD BEING THOSE 0.86 OF 7 WHERE THE LARGEST NON-COGNATIC KIN GROUP IS SMALLER THAN A PHRATRY, I. E. A SIB OR LINEAGE (175)	184	DRIFT TOWARD BEING THOSE 0.75 OF 4 WHERE THE LARGEST NON-COGNATIC KIN GROUP IS THE MOEITY OR PHRATRY (77)	1 3 6 1 XSQ= 1.86 PHI= -0.411 EP = 0.0879
196	TILT TOWARD BEING THOSE 0.88 OF 8 WHERE INDIVIDUAL RIGHTS IN REAL PROPERTY, AND RULES FOR INHERITANCE, ARE PRESENT (194)	196	TILT TOWARD BEING THOSE 0.75 OF 8 WHERE INDIVIDUAL RIGHTS IN REAL PROPERTY, OR RULES FOR INHERITANCE, ARE ABSENT (87)	7 2 1 6 XSQ= 4.06 PHI= 0.504 EP = 0.0406
318	IN ALL CASES ARE THOSE 1.00 OF 3 WHERE THE OVERALL INDULGENCE OF THE INFANT IS LOW (31) B-B-C	318	IN ALL CASES ARE THOSE 1.00 OF 5 WHERE THE OVERALL INDULGENCE OF THE INFANT IS HIGH (40) B-B-C	0 5 3 0 XSQ= 4.30 PHI= -0.733 EP = 0.0179
324	IN ALL CASES ARE THOSE 1.00 OF 2 WHERE THE PAIN INFLICTED ON THE INFANT BY THE NURTURANT AGENT IS HIGH (34) B-B-C	324	IN ALL CASES ARE THOSE 1.00 OF 4 WHERE THE PAIN INFLICTED ON THE INFANT BY THE NURTURANT AGENT IS LOW OR NEGLIGIBLE (32) B-B-C	2 0 0 4 XSQ= 2.34 PHI= 0.625 EP = 0.0667
334	DRIFT TOWARD BEING THOSE 0.67 OF 3 WHERE THE INDULGENCE OF THE CHILD IS LOW (38) B-B-C	334	IN ALL CASES ARE THOSE 1.00 OF 6 WHERE THE INDULGENCE OF THE CHILD IS HIGH (40) B-B-C	1 6 2 0 XSQ= 2.01 PHI= -0.472 EP = 0.0833
390	TILT TOWARD BEING THOSE 0.71 OF 7 WHERE PREMARITAL SEX RELATIONS ARE STRONGLY PUNISHED AND IN FACT RARE (47) JTW,EA	390	IN ALL CASES ARE THOSE 1.00 OF 5 WHERE PREMARITAL SEX RELATIONS ARE WEAKLY PUNISHED AND IN FACT NOT RARE OR PUNISHED ONLY IF PREGNANCY RESULTS, OR FREELY PERMITTED (132) JTW,EA	5 0 2 5 XSQ= 3.54 PHI= 0.543 EP = 0.0278
391	DRIFT TOWARD BEING THOSE 0.86 OF 7 WHERE PREMARITAL SEX RELATIONS ARE STRONGLY PUNISHED AND IN FACT RARE, OR WEAKLY PUNISHED AND IN FACT NOT RARE (89) JTW,EA	391	DRIFT TOWARD BEING THOSE 0.80 OF 5 WHERE PREMARITAL SEX RELATIONS ARE PUNISHED ONLY IF PREGNANCY RESULTS, OR FREELY PERMITTED (90) JTW,EA	6 1 1 4 XSQ= 2.83 PHI= 0.486 EP = 0.0720

392	IN ALL CASES ARE THOSE WHERE PREMARITAL SEX RELATIONS ARE STRONGLY PUNISHED AND IN FACT RARE, OR WEAKLY PUNISHED AND IN FACT NOT RARE, OR PUNISHED ONLY IF PREGNANCY RESULTS (112) JTW,EA	1.00 OF 7	392	TILT TOWARD BEING THOSE WHERE PREMARITAL SEX RELATIONS ARE FREELY PERMITTED (67) JTW,EA	0.80 OF 5	7 1 0 4 XSQ= 5.19 PHI= 0.657 EP = 0.0101
398	IN ALL CASES ARE THOSE WHERE THE INTENSITY OF SEX ANXIETY IS HIGH (16) WNS	1.00 OF 2	398	IN ALL CASES ARE THOSE WHERE THE INTENSITY OF SEX ANXIETY IS LOW (16) WNS	1.00 OF 4	2 0 0 4 XSQ= 2.34 PHI= 0.625 EP = 0.0667
444	DRIFT TOWARD BEING THOSE WHERE THE USE OF DREAMS TO SEEK AND CONTROL SUPERNATURAL POWERS IS LOW (27) RGD	0.75 OF 4	444	DRIFT TOWARD BEING THOSE WHERE THE USE OF DREAMS TO SEEK AND CONTROL SUPERNATURAL POWERS IS HIGH (28) RGD	0.86 OF 7	1 6 3 1 XSQ= 1.86 PHI= -0.411 EP = 0.0879
458	TILT TOWARD BEING THOSE WHERE GAMES, IF PRESENT, INCLUDE GAMES OF STRATEGY (52) R-A-B,EA	0.83 OF 6	458	IN ALL CASES ARE THOSE WHERE GAMES, IF PRESENT, DO NOT INCLUDE GAMES OF STRATEGY (119) R-A-B,EA	1.00 OF 5	5 0 1 5 XSQ= 4.65 PHI= 0.650 EP = 0.0152
460	IN ALL CASES ARE THOSE WHERE GAMES, IF PRESENT, ARE NOT LIMITED TO GAMES OF SKILL ONLY (104) R-A-B,EA	1.00 OF 6	460	DRIFT TOWARD BEING THOSE WHERE GAMES, IF PRESENT, ARE LIMITED TO GAMES OF SKILL ONLY (67) R-A-B,EA	0.60 OF 5	0 3 6 2 XSQ= 2.39 PHI= -0.466 EP = 0.0606
470	TILT TOWARD BEING THOSE WHERE INNOVATIONS ARE GENERALLY ACCEPTED (21) JMH	0.80 OF 5	470	IN ALL CASES ARE THOSE WHERE INNOVATIONS ARE ACCEPTED ONLY SELECTIVELY (33) JMH	1.00 OF 5	4 0 1 5 XSQ= 3.75 PHI= 0.612 EP = 0.0476

167 CULTURES
WHERE JURIDICAL SOLUTICN IS BASED
CN THE CLIENT'S ACTICNS
TO A HIGH EXTENT (9) MJ

167 CULTURES
WHERE JURIDICAL SOLUTICN IS BASED
ON THE CLIENT'S ACTIONS
TO A LOW EXTENT (7) MJ

BACKGROUND ON PAGE 102

NEITHER SUBJECT NOR PREDICATE

9 IN LEFT COLUMN

ANDAMANESE BURMESE COPR ESKIMO JAVANESE KUNG MURNGIN SAMOANS THAI VIETNAMESE

7 IN RIGHT CCLUMN

BEMBA COMANCHE JIVARO KIKUYU MUNDURUCU NAMA NAVAHO

384 EXCLUDED BECAUSE UNASCERTAINEC

168 CULTURES WHERE DIAGNOSIS AND CURE ARE BASED ON THE CLIENT'S MORAL AND SOCIAL ACTIONS TO A HIGH EXTENT (9) MJ	168 CULTURES WHERE DIAGNOSIS AND CURE ARE BASED ON THE CLIENT'S MORAL AND SOCIAL ACTIONS TO A LOW EXTENT (10) MJ

BACKGROUND ON PAGE 102 — NEITHER SUBJECT NOR PREDICATE

9 IN LEFT COLUMN

ANDAMANESE COPR ESKIMO JIVARO KIKUYU KUNG LAMBA MUNDURUCU NAMA NAVAHO

10 IN RIGHT COLUMN

BEMBA BURMESE COMANCHE JAVANESE MURNGIN NUPE SAMOANS THAI TROBRIAND VIETNAMESE

381 EXCLUDED BECAUSE UNASCERTAINED

169 CULTURES WHERE THE DEGREE OF MANIPULATION OF THE CLIENT IN JURIDICAL MATTERS IS HIGH (10) MJ	169 CULTURES WHERE THE DEGREE OF MANIPULATION OF THE CLIENT IN JURIDICAL MATTERS IS LOW (10) MJ

BACKGROUND ON PAGE 102 NEITHER SUBJECT NOR PREDICATE

10 IN LEFT COLUMN

BEMBA BURMESE JAVANESE KIKUYU NAMA NAVAHO NUPE SAMOANS THAI VIETNAMESE

10 IN RIGHT COLUMN

ANDAMANESE COMANCHE COPR ESKIMO JIVARO KUNG LAMBA MUNDURUCU MURNGIN SIUAI TROBRIAND

380 EXCLUDED BECAUSE UNASCERTAINED

170 CULTURES
WHERE THE DEGREE OF MANIPULATION
OF THE CLIENT IN MEDICAL MATTERS
IS HIGH (10) MJ

170 CULTURES
WHERE THE DEGREE OF MANIPULATION
OF THE CLIENT IN MEDICAL MATTERS
IS LOW (10) MJ

BACKGROUND ON PAGE 102

NEITHER SUBJECT NOR PREDICATE

10 IN LEFT COLUMN

ANDAMANESE BEMBA COMANCHE JIVARO KIKUYU KUNG LAMBA MURNGIN NAMA NAVAHO

10 IN RIGHT COLUMN

BURMESE COPR ESKIMO JAVANESE MUNDURUCU NUPE SAMOANS SIUAI THAI TROBRIAND VIETNAMESE

380 EXCLUDED BECAUSE UNASCERTAINED

171 CULTURES
WHERE THE JURIDICAL CLIENT IS HAMPERED
FROM RETURNING TO NORMAL SOCIAL ROLES
AS A CONSEQUENCE OF CRIME,
TO A HIGH EXTENT (10) MJ

171 CULTURES
WHERE THE JURIDICAL CLIENT IS HAMPERED
FROM RETURNING TO NORMAL SOCIAL ROLES
AS A CONSEQUENCE OF CRIME,
TO A LOW EXTENT (10) MJ

BACKGROUND ON PAGE 102

NEITHER SUBJECT NOR PREDICATE

10 IN LEFT COLUMN

BEMBA BURMESE JAVANESE KIKUYU LAMBA NAMA NUPE SAMOANS THAI VIETNAMESE

10 IN RIGHT COLUMN

ANDAMANESE COMANCHE COPR ESKIMO JIVARO KUNG MUNDURUCU MURNGIN NAVAHO SIUAI TROBRIAND

380 EXCLUDED BECAUSE UNASCERTAINED

****

172 CULTURES WHERE THE MEDICAL CLIENT IS HAMPERED FROM RETURNING TO NORMAL SOCIAL ROLES AS A CONSEQUENCE OF ILLNESS, TO A HIGH EXTENT (9) MJ	172 CULTURES WHERE THE MEDICAL CLIENT IS HAMPERED FROM RETURNING TO NORMAL SOCIAL ROLES AS A CONSEQUENCE OF ILLNESS, TO A LOW EXTENT (11) MJ

BACKGROUND ON PAGE 102 NEITHER SUBJECT NOR PREDICATE

....

9 IN LEFT COLUMN

BEMBA JIVARO KIKUYU LAMBA MURNGIN NAMA NAVAHO SAMOANS TROBRIAND

11 IN RIGHT COLUMN

ANDAMANESE BURMESE COMANCHE COPR ESKIMO JAVANESE KUNG MUNDURUCU NUPE SIUAI THAI
VIETNAMESE

380 EXCLUDED BECAUSE UNASCERTAINED

----

173 CULTURES
WHERE THE SOCIAL AND EMOTIONAL SUPPORT
GIVEN TO THE JURIDICAL CLIENT
DURING JUDGMENT AND PUNISHMENT
IS HIGH (10) MJ

173 CULTURES
WHERE THE SOCIAL AND EMOTIONAL SUPPORT
GIVEN TO THE JURIDICAL CLIENT
DURING JUDGMENT AND PUNISHMENT
IS LOW (10) MJ

BACKGROUND ON PAGE 102

NEITHER SUBJECT NOR PREDICATE

10 IN LEFT COLUMN

ANDAMANESE COMANCHE COPR ESKIMO JIVARO KUNG MUNDURUCU MURNGIN NAMA NAVAHO TROBRIAND

10 IN RIGHT COLUMN

BEMBA BURMESE JAVANESE KIKUYU LAMBA NUPE SAMOANS SIUAI THAI VIETNAMESE

380 EXCLUDED BECAUSE UNASCERTAINED

174 CULTURES
WHERE THE SOCIAL AND EMOTIONAL SUPPORT
GIVEN TO THE MEDICAL CLIENT
DURING DIAGNOSIS AND TREATMENT
IS HIGH (9) MJ

174 CULTURES
WHERE THE SOCIAL AND EMOTIONAL SUPPORT
GIVEN TO THE MEDICAL CLIENT
DURING DIAGNOSIS AND TREATMENT
IS LOW (11) MJ

BACKGROUND ON PAGE 102

NEITHER SUBJECT NOR PREDICATE

9 IN LEFT COLUMN

BURMESE JAVANESE MUNDURUCU NAVAHO NUPE SIUAI THAI TROBRIAND VIETNAMESE

11 IN RIGHT COLUMN

ANDAMANESE BEMBA COMANCHE COPR ESKIMO JIVARO KIKUYU KUNG LAMBA MURNGIN NAMA SAMOANS

380 EXCLUDED BECAUSE UNASCERTAINED

****

175 CULTURES WHERE THE COMMUNITY IS 'KIN-HOMOGENEOUS,' I. E. A CLAN COMMUNITY OR A DEME (122)	175 CULTURES WHERE THE COMMUNITY IS 'KIN-HETEROGENEOUS,' I. E. OTHER THAN A CLAN COMMUNITY OR A DEME (260)

BACKGROUND ON PAGE 105 — BOTH SUBJECT AND PREDICATE

....

122 IN LEFT COLUMN

AINU	AJIE	AMBA	ARANDA	AWEIKOMA	AYMARA	BABWA	BACAIRI	BALINESE	BANDA
BARI	BASSERI	BAYA	BEJA	BETE	BHUIYA	BIRIFOR	BURMESE	BURYAT	CARAJA
CARINYA	CHAGGA	CHINANTEC	CHOCO	COCHITI	COMANCHE	COPR ESKIMO	CUNA	DAGUR	DIEGUENO
DOBUANS	DOROBO	DUSUN	EGYPTIANS	ENGA	FANG	GISU	GOND	HAIDA	HAVASUPAI
HAZARA	HEHE	HO	HUICHOL	HUKUNDIKA	HUTSUL	INCA	INGASSANA	JEMEZ	JIVARO
KALMYK	KAPAUKU	KARIERA	KATAB	KAZAK	KERAKI	KHEVSUR	KIKUYU	KUMYK	LAU
LIFU	LOLO	LUO	MAMVU	MANCHU	MATAKAM	MBUNDU	MBUTI	MIN CHINESE	MINCHIA
MIWOK	MONGO	MURINBATA	MURNGIN	NAMA	NDEMBU	NOMLAKI	NUER	NYANEKA	OJIBWA
PAIWAN	PARAUJANO	PAWNEE	PENDE	PORTUGUESE	REGEIBAT	RIFFIANS	RWALA	SANDAWE	SEMINOLE
SENIANG	SINDHI	SIWANS	SOMALI	SWAZI	TAGBANUA	TALLENSI	TAOS	TAPIRAPE	TARAHUMARA
TENETEHARA	TERA	TERENA	THONGA	TIV	TODA	TOKELAU	TOLOWA	TRISTAN	TUCANO
TUCUNA	TUNEBO	VEDDA	WANTOAT	WARRAU	WIKMUNKAN	WITOTO	WOLOF	YAGUA	YAKUT
YARURO	YOMBE								

260 IN RIGHT COLUMN

18 EXCLUDED BECAUSE UNASCERTAINED

BOZO	BUDUMA	CADUVEO	CHIBCHA	GUATO	HEBREWS	IRAQW	KET	MANDAN	MANIHIKI
MIAMI	PAEZ	PALIKUR	POPOLUCA	ROTINESE	TALAMANCA	TOTONAC	TURKMEN		

3	DRIFT LESS TOWARD BEING THOSE 0.74 OF 122 LOCATED OUTSIDE OF AFRICA (320)	3	DRIFT MORE TOWARD BEING THOSE 0.82 OF 260 LOCATED OUTSIDE OF AFRICA (320)	32 47 90 213 XSQ= 2.89 PHI= 0.087 XP = 0.0894
12	DRIFT MORE TOWARD BEING THOSE 0.96 OF 122 WHERE THE LATITUDE IS LESS THAN FIFTY DEGREES (367)	12	DRIFT LESS TOWARD BEING THOSE 0.90 OF 260 WHERE THE LATITUDE IS LESS THAN FIFTY DEGREES (367)	5 27 117 233 XSQ= 3.50 PHI= -0.096 XP = 0.0615
51	TILT MORE TOWARD BEING THOSE 0.71 OF 122 WHERE SUBSISTENCE IS PRIMARILY BY FOOD PRODUCTION -- I. E., AGRICULTURE OR HUSBANDRY -- RATHER THAN BY GATHERING (253)	51	TILT LESS TOWARD BEING THOSE 0.60 OF 260 WHERE SUBSISTENCE IS PRIMARILY BY FOOD PRODUCTION -- I. E., AGRICULTURE OR HUSBANDRY -- RATHER THAN BY GATHERING (253)	87 156 35 104 XSQ= 4.11 PHI= 0.104 XP = 0.0425

73	DRIFT TOWARD BEING THOSE WHERE WEAVING IS ABSENT (130)	0.63 OF 75	73	DRIFT TOWARD BEING THOSE WHERE WEAVING IS PRESENT (118)	0.51 OF 165	28 84 47 81 XSQ= 3.29 PHI= -0.117 XP = 0.0696
79	TILT MORE TOWARD BEING THOSE WHERE NO CITY IS PRESENT (201)	0.97 OF 66	79	TILT LESS TOWARD BEING THOSE WHERE NO CITY IS PRESENT (201)	0.86 OF 154	2 21 64 133 XSQ= 4.48 PHI= -0.143 XP = 0.0344
80	TILT MORE TOWARD BEING THOSE WHERE NO CITY OR TOWN IS PRESENT (185)	0.92 OF 66	80	TILT LESS TOWARD BEING THOSE WHERE NO CITY OR TOWN IS PRESENT (185)	0.79 OF 154	5 32 61 122 XSQ= 4.85 PHI= -0.149 XP = 0.0276
90	TILT MORE TOWARD BEING THOSE WHERE, IF A HEREDITARY HEADMANSHIP IS PRESENT, SUCCESSION IS PATRILINEAL, RATHER THAN MATRILINEAL (127)	0.90 OF 48	90	TILT LESS TOWARD BEING THOSE WHERE, IF A HEREDITARY HEADMANSHIP IS PRESENT, SUCCESSION IS PATRILINEAL, RATHER THAN MATRILINEAL (127)	0.72 OF 113	43 81 5 32 XSQ= 5.13 PHI= 0.179 XP = 0.0235
96	TILT TOWARD BEING THOSE WHERE THE HIERARCHY OF NATIONAL JURISDICTION HAS NO LEVELS (156) GES,EA	0.58 OF 97	96	TILT TOWARD BEING THOSE WHERE THE HIERARCHY OF NATIONAL JURISDICTION HAS FOUR, THREE, TWO OR ONE LEVEL (174) GES,EA	0.55 OF 220	41 122 56 98 XSQ= 4.17 PHI= -0.115 XP = 0.0411
98	LEAN LESS TOWARD BEING THOSE WHERE THE HIERARCHY OF LOCAL JURISDICTION HAS FOUR OR THREE LEVELS (238) GES,EA	0.60 OF 98	98	LEAN MORE TOWARD BEING THOSE WHERE THE HIERARCHY OF LOCAL JURISDICTION HAS FOUR OR THREE LEVELS (238) GES,EA	0.77 OF 220	59 169 39 51 XSQ= 8.42 PHI= -0.163 XP = 0.0037
99	LEAN TOWARD BEING THOSE WHERE, WITH NATIONAL HIERARCHY ABSENT, THE HIERARCHY OF LOCAL JURISDICTION HAS TWO LEVELS (63) GES,EA	0.55 OF 56	99	LEAN TOWARD BEING THOSE WHERE, WITH NATIONAL HIERARCHY ABSENT, THE HIERARCHY OF LOCAL JURISDICTION HAS FOUR OR THREE LEVELS (93) GES,EA	0.69 OF 98	25 68 31 30 XSQ= 8.12 PHI= -0.230 XP = 0.0044
100	TEND LESS TO BE THOSE WHERE HIERARCHIES ARE MORE COMPLEX THAN THE 'SIMPLEST,' I. E., MORE COMPLEX THAN TWO LOCAL LEVELS WITH NO NATIONAL LEVELS (267) GES,EA	0.68 OF 97	100	TEND MORE TO BE THOSE WHERE HIERARCHIES ARE MORE COMPLEX THAN THE 'SIMPLEST,' I. E., MORE COMPLEX THAN TWO LOCAL LEVELS WITH NO NATIONAL LEVELS (267) GES,EA	0.86 OF 220	66 190 31 30 XSQ= 13.39 PHI= -0.206 XP = 0.0003
106	DRIFT LESS TOWARD BEING THOSE WHERE CLASS STRATIFICATION, IF PRESENT, IS BASED ON SOMETHING OTHER THAN WEALTH (126)	0.52 OF 56	106	DRIFT MORE TOWARD BEING THOSE WHERE CLASS STRATIFICATION, IF PRESENT, IS BASED ON SOMETHING OTHER THAN WEALTH (126)	0.66 OF 141	27 48 29 93 XSQ= 2.84 PHI= 0.120 XP = 0.0920

130	DRIFT TOWARD BEING THOSE WHERE LEATHER WORKING IS MAINLY DONE BY MALES (39)	0.67 OF 21	130	DRIFT TOWARD BEING THOSE WHERE LEATHER WORKING IS MAINLY DONE BY FEMALES (45)	0.60 OF 62	14 25 7 37 XSQ= 3.38 PHI= 0.202 XP = 0.0661
139	DRIFT MORE TOWARD BEING THOSE WHERE SUPERORDINATE PUNISHMENT IS ABSENT (25) BBW	0.83 OF 12	139	DRIFT LESS TOWARD BEING THOSE WHERE SUPERORDINATE PUNISHMENT IS ABSENT (25) BBW	0.54 OF 28	2 13 10 15 XSQ= 2.03 PHI= -0.225 EP = 0.0911
152	DRIFT TOWARD BEING THOSE WHERE THE DIFFERENTIATION OF THE JURIDICAL AGENCY FROM THE MEDICAL AGENCY IS LOW (10) MJ	0.86 OF 7	152	DRIFT TOWARD BEING THOSE WHERE THE DIFFERENTIATION OF THE JURIDICAL AGENCY FROM THE MEDICAL AGENCY IS HIGH (10) MJ	0.69 OF 13	1 9 6 4 XSQ= 3.52 PHI= -0.419 EP = 0.0573
186	TEND TO BE THOSE WHERE THE KIN GROUP IS EXCLUSIVELY PATRILINEAL (150)	0.53 OF 122	186	TEND TO BE THOSE WHERE THE KIN GROUP IS OTHER THAN EXCLUSIVELY PATRILINEAL (250)	0.70 OF 260	65 77 57 183 XSQ= 18.91 PHI= 0.222 XP = 0.0000
187	DRIFT MORE TOWARD BEING THOSE WHERE THE KIN GROUP IS OTHER THAN EXCLUSIVELY MATRILINEAL (344)	0.91 OF 121	187	DRIFT LESS TOWARD BEING THOSE WHERE THE KIN GROUP IS OTHER THAN EXCLUSIVELY MATRILINEAL (344)	0.84 OF 260	11 42 110 218 XSQ= 2.88 PHI= -0.087 XP = 0.0900
188	TILT MORE TOWARD BEING THOSE WHERE THE KIN GROUP IS OTHER THAN EXCLUSIVELY COGNATIC (252)	0.72 OF 122	188	TILT LESS TOWARD BEING THOSE WHERE THE KIN GROUP IS OTHER THAN EXCLUSIVELY COGNATIC (252)	0.59 OF 260	34 107 88 153 XSQ= 5.74 PHI= -0.123 XP = 0.0166
190	LEAN MORE TOWARD BEING THOSE WHERE THE KIN GROUP IS PATRILINEAL OR DOUBLE-DESCENT, RATHER THAN MATRILINEAL (186)	0.87 OF 86	190	LEAN LESS TOWARD BEING THOSE WHERE THE KIN GROUP IS PATRILINEAL OR DOUBLE-DESCENT, RATHER THAN MATRILINEAL (186)	0.68 OF 150	75 102 11 48 XSQ= 9.76 PHI= 0.203 XP = 0.0018
192	DRIFT MORE TOWARD BEING THOSE OTHER THAN WHERE THE ONLY KIN GROUP PRESENT IS A KINDRED OR ELSE BILATERAL DESCENT IS INFERRED (289)	0.80 OF 122	192	DRIFT LESS TOWARD BEING THOSE OTHER THAN WHERE THE ONLY KIN GROUP PRESENT IS A KINDRED OR ELSE BILATERAL DESCENT IS INFERRED (289)	0.70 OF 260	25 79 97 181 XSQ= 3.62 PHI= -0.097 XP = 0.0572
209	TILT MORE TOWARD BEING THOSE WHERE MARITAL RESIDENCE IS PATRILOCAL, VIRILOCAL, OR AVUNCULOCAL, RATHER THAN MATRILOCAL OR UXORILOCAL (270)	0.88 OF 105	209	TILT LESS TOWARD BEING THOSE WHERE MARITAL RESIDENCE IS PATRILOCAL, VIRILOCAL, OR AVUNCULOCAL, RATHER THAN MATRILOCAL OR UXORILOCAL (270)	0.77 OF 213	92 165 13 48 XSQ= 4.05 PHI= 0.113 XP = 0.0443

210	LEAN MORE TOWARD BEING THOSE WHERE MARITAL RESIDENCE IS PATRILOCAL, RATHER THAN MATRILOCAL (169)	0.95 OF 76	210	LEAN LESS TOWARD BEING THOSE WHERE MARITAL RESIDENCE IS PATRILOCAL, RATHER THAN MATRILOCAL (169)	0.78 OF 115	72 90 4 25 XSQ= 8.41 PHI= 0.210 XP = 0.0037
221	DRIFT MORE TOWARD BEING THOSE WHERE MATRILATERAL CROSS-COUSIN MARRIAGE IS NOT PRESCRIBED OR PREFERRED (335)	0.95 OF 116	221	DRIFT LESS TOWARD BEING THOSE WHERE MATRILATERAL CROSS-COUSIN MARRIAGE IS NOT PRESCRIBED OR PREFERRED (335)	0.88 OF 243	6 28 110 215 XSQ= 2.99 PHI= -0.091 XP = 0.0838
234	DRIFT TOWARD BEING THOSE WHERE THE COUSIN TERMINOLOGY IS OF CROW, OMAHA, OR IROQUOIS TYPE, RATHER THAN ESKIMO OR HAWAIIAN TYPE (152)	0.55 OF 94	234	DRIFT TOWARD BEING THOSE WHERE THE COUSIN TERMINOLOGY IS OF ESKIMO OR HAWAIIAN TYPE, RATHER THAN CROW, OMAHA, OR IROQUOIS TYPE (170)	0.56 OF 215	52 94 42 121 XSQ= 3.08 PHI= 0.100 XP = 0.0793
263	DRIFT MORE TOWARD BEING THOSE WHERE WIVES ARE OBTAINED BY RELATIVELY DIFFICULT MEANS, NAMELY BY BRIDE-PRICE, BRIDE-SERVICE, OR EXCHANGING A FEMALE RELATIVE (233)	0.67 OF 120	263	DRIFT LESS TOWARD BEING THOSE WHERE WIVES ARE OBTAINED BY RELATIVELY DIFFICULT MEANS, NAMELY BY BRIDE-PRICE, BRIDE-SERVICE, OR EXCHANGING A FEMALE RELATIVE (233)	0.56 OF 258	80 144 40 114 XSQ= 3.56 PHI= 0.097 XP = 0.0592
279	DRIFT TOWARD BEING THOSE WHERE WIFE-LENDING OR WIFE-EXCHANGE IS PRESENT (10) LWS	0.60 OF 10	279	DRIFT TOWARD BEING THOSE WHERE WIFE-LENDING AND WIFE EXCHANGE ARE UNIMPORTANT OR ABSENT (19) LWS	0.78 OF 18	6 4 4 14 XSQ= 2.52 PHI= 0.300 EP = 0.0974
318	DRIFT TOWARD BEING THOSE WHERE THE OVERALL INDULGENCE OF THE INFANT IS LOW (31) B-B-C	0.63 OF 19	318	DRIFT TOWARD BEING THOSE WHERE THE OVERALL INDULGENCE OF THE INFANT IS HIGH (40) B-B-C	0.63 OF 52	7 33 12 19 XSQ= 3.00 PHI= -0.206 XP = 0.0833
324	TILT TOWARD BEING THOSE WHERE THE PAIN INFLICTED ON THE INFANT BY THE NURTURANT AGENT IS HIGH (34) B-B-C	0.78 OF 18	324	TILT TOWARD BEING THOSE WHERE THE PAIN INFLICTED ON THE INFANT BY THE NURTURANT AGENT IS LOW OR NEGLIGIBLE (32) B-B-C	0.58 OF 48	14 20 4 28 XSQ= 5.47 PHI= 0.288 XP = 0.0194
377	TILT LESS TOWARD BEING THOSE WHERE MALE GENITAL MUTILATION IS ABSENT (242)	0.66 OF 98	377	TILT MORE TOWARD BEING THOSE WHERE MALE GENITAL MUTILATION IS ABSENT (242)	0.79 OF 214	33 44 65 170 XSQ= 5.53 PHI= 0.133 XP = 0.0187
393	DRIFT TOWARD BEING THOSE WHERE EXTRAMARITAL COITUS IS PUNISHED, RATHER THAN PERMITTED (43) F-B	0.68 OF 25	393	DRIFT TOWARD BEING THOSE WHERE EXTRAMARITAL COITUS IS PERMITTED, RATHER THAN PUNISHED (41) F-B	0.56 OF 59	17 26 8 33 XSQ= 3.12 PHI= 0.193 XP = 0.0771

175/

395	DRIFT TOWARD BEING THOSE WHERE BELIEF IN THE UNCLEANNESS OF WOMEN IS PRESENT (18) LWS	0.80 OF 10	395	DRIFT TOWARD BEING THOSE WHERE BELIEF IN THE UNCLEANNESS OF WOMEN IS UNIMPORTANT OR ABSENT (15) LWS	0.59 OF 22	8 9 2 13 XSQ= 2.80 PHI= 0.296 EP = 0.0605

****

176 CULTURES
WHERE THE COMMUNITY IS
A CLAN-COMMUNITY OR A COMMUNITY
STRUCTURED OR SEGMENTED
ON A CLAN BASIS (169)

176 CULTURES
WHERE THE COMMUNITY IS OTHER THAN
A CLAN-COMMUNITY OR A COMMUNITY
STRUCTURED OR SEGMENTED
ON A CLAN BASIS (213)

BACKGROUND ON PAGE 105

BOTH SUBJECT AND PREDICATE

....

169 IN LEFT COLUMN

AJIE	AMBA	APINAYE	ARANDA	ARAPESH	ARAUCANIANS	ARYANS	AZTEC	BABWA	BAMBARA
BAMILEKE	BANDA	BARI	BAYA	BEJA	BELU	BENGALI	BETE	BHUIYA	BIRIFOR
BORORO	BUNLAP	BURYAT	CALLINAGO	CHAGGA	CHEROKEE	COORG	DAGUR	DELAWARE	DIEGUENO
DILLING	DOBUANS	DOGON	DOROBO	ELLICE	ENGA	FANG	FON	FUTAJALONKE	GILBERTESE
GILYAK	GISU	GOND	GUAHIBO	GURE	HAIDA	HANO	HAWAIIANS	HAZARA	HEHE
HO	HURON	KABYLE	KACHIN	KALMYK	KAPAUKU	KARIERA	KASKA	KATAB	KAZAK
KERAKI	KHASI	KHEVSUR	KIKUYU	KISSI	KOHISTANI	KPE	KUBA	LAKALAI	LAMET
LAU	LESU	LHOTA NAGA	LIFU	LOLO	LUO	MACASSARESE	MAM	MAMBILA	MAMVU
MANCHU	MANUS	MACRI	MARGI	MARSHALLESE	MATAKAM	MBUNDU	MBUTI	MENDE	MENTAWEI
MIAO	MIN CHINESE	MINANGKABAU	MIWOK	MNONG GAR	MONGO	MONGUOR	MOSSI	MOTA	MURINBATA
MURNGIN	MZAB	NAMA	NDEMBU	NOMLAKI	NUER	NUPE	NYANEKA	NYARO	NYORO
OJIBWA	OMAHA	PALAUANS	PENDE	PUKAPUKA	PURARI	REGEIBAT	RIFFIANS	ROTUMANS	RUNDI
RWALA	SAMCANS	SANDAWE	SARAMACCA	SEMINOLE	SENIANG	SERBS	SHERENTE	SHILLUK	SHLUH
SIMBOESE	SIRIONO	SIUAI	SOMALI	SWAZI	TALLENSI	TANALA	TESO	THONGA	TIMBIRA
TIMUCUA	TIV	TODA	TOLOWA	TROBRIAND	TRUKESE	TUCANO	TUCUNA	ULAWANS	VEDDA
VENDA	WANTOAT	WAROPEN	WIKMUNKAN	WINNEBAGO	WITOTO	WOGEO	WOLEAIANS	WOLOF	WUTE
YAGUA	YAKO	YAKUT	YAO	YAPESE	YOKUTS	YOMBE	YORUBA	ZUNI	

213 IN RIGHT COLUMN

18 EXCLUDED BECAUSE UNASCERTAINED

3	TEND LESS TO BE THOSE LOCATED OUTSIDE OF AFRICA (320)	0.67 OF 169	3	TEND MORE TO BE THOSE LOCATED OUTSIDE OF AFRICA (320)	0.89 OF 213	56 23 113 190 XSQ= 27.32 PHI= 0.267 XP = 0.0000
4	TILT MORE TOWARD BEING THOSE LOCATED OUTSIDE OF THE CIRCUM-MEDITERRANEAN (355)	0.93 OF 169	4	TILT LESS TOWARD BEING THOSE LOCATED OUTSIDE OF THE CIRCUM-MEDITERRANEAN (355)	0.86 OF 213	12 30 157 183 XSQ= 4.01 PHI= -0.102 XP = 0.0452
6	TEND LESS TO BE THOSE LOCATED OUTSIDE OF THE INSULAR PACIFIC (330)	0.75 OF 169	6	TEND MORE TO BE THOSE LOCATED OUTSIDE OF THE INSULAR PACIFIC (330)	0.88 OF 213	43 25 126 188 XSQ= 11.18 PHI= 0.171 XP = 0.0008

8	LEAN MORE TOWARD BEING THOSE LOCATED OUTSIDE OF NORTH AMERICA (330)	0.89 OF 169	8	LEAN LESS TOWARD BEING THOSE LOCATED OUTSIDE OF NORTH AMERICA (330)	0.77 OF 213	18 48 151 165 XSQ= 8.50 PHI= -0.149 XP = 0.0036
9	TEND MORE TO BE THOSE LOCATED OUTSIDE OF SOUTH AMERICA (335)	0.92 OF 169	9	TEND LESS TO BE THOSE LOCATED OUTSIDE OF SOUTH AMERICA (335)	0.79 OF 213	14 45 155 168 XSQ= 10.94 PHI= -0.169 XP = 0.0009
15	TEND TO BE THOSE WHERE THE LATITUDE IS LESS THAN TWENTY DEGREES (217)	0.64 OF 169	15	TEND TO BE THOSE WHERE THE LATITUDE IS TWENTY DEGREES OR GREATER (183)	0.54 OF 213	60 116 109 97 XSQ= 12.88 PHI= -0.184 XP = 0.0003
33	LEAN MORE TOWARD BEING THOSE WHERE THE NATURAL ENVIRONMENT IS OTHER THAN 'VERY HARSH,' I.E., DESERT, DESERT GRASSES AND SHRUBS, TUNDRA, OR HIGH PLATEAU STEPPE (341) FWM	0.92 OF 169	33	LEAN LESS TOWARD BEING THOSE WHERE THE NATURAL ENVIRONMENT IS OTHER THAN 'VERY HARSH,' I.E., DESERT, DESERT GRASSES AND SHRUBS, TUNDRA, OR HIGH PLATEAU STEPPE (341) FWM	0.80 OF 213	14 43 155 170 XSQ= 9.60 PHI= -0.159 XP = 0.0019
36	LEAN MORE TOWARD BEING THOSE WHERE THE NATURAL ENVIRONMENT IS OTHER THAN 'VERY HARSH,' OR SUB-TROPICAL BUSH, OR TEMPERATE GRASSLAND (292) FWM	0.79 OF 169	36	LEAN LESS TOWARD BEING THOSE WHERE THE NATURAL ENVIRONMENT IS OTHER THAN 'VERY HARSH,' OR SUB-TROPICAL BUSH, OR TEMPERATE GRASSLAND (292) FWM	0.67 OF 213	35 71 134 142 XSQ= 6.87 PHI= -0.134 XP = 0.0087
44	DRIFT MORE TOWARD BEING THOSE WHERE SETTLEMENTS ARE FIXED (222)	0.73 OF 142	44	DRIFT LESS TOWARD BEING THOSE WHERE SETTLEMENTS ARE FIXED (222)	0.63 OF 177	103 111 39 66 XSQ= 3.01 PHI= 0.097 XP = 0.0826
45	DRIFT LESS TOWARD BEING THOSE WHERE SETTLEMENTS, IF FIXED, ARE COMPACT, RATHER THAN NON-COMPACT (149)	0.61 OF 103	45	DRIFT MORE TOWARD BEING THOSE WHERE SETTLEMENTS, IF FIXED, ARE COMPACT, RATHER THAN NON-COMPACT (149)	0.73 OF 111	63 81 40 30 XSQ= 2.87 PHI= -0.116 XP = 0.0903
46	DRIFT MORE TOWARD BEING THOSE OTHER THAN WHERE SETTLEMENTS ARE NON-FIXED AND MOVEMENT IS NOMADIC (260)	0.83 OF 142	46	DRIFT LESS TOWARD BEING THOSE OTHER THAN WHERE SETTLEMENTS ARE NON-FIXED AND MOVEMENT IS NOMADIC (260)	0.74 OF 177	24 46 118 131 XSQ= 3.29 PHI= -0.102 XP = 0.0698
51	LEAN MORE TOWARD BEING THOSE WHERE SUBSISTENCE IS PRIMARILY BY FOOD PRODUCTION -- I. E., AGRICULTURE OR HUSBANDRY -- RATHER THAN BY GATHERING (253)	0.72 OF 169	51	LEAN LESS TOWARD BEING THOSE WHERE SUBSISTENCE IS PRIMARILY BY FOOD PRODUCTION -- I. E., AGRICULTURE OR HUSBANDRY -- RATHER THAN BY GATHERING (253)	0.57 OF 213	122 121 47 92 XSQ= 8.98 PHI= 0.153 XP = 0.0027

53	DRIFT MORE TOWARD BEING THOSE 0.69 OF 109 WHERE FOOD PRODUCTION IS BY SIMPLE AGRICULTURE OR INCIPIENT FOOD PRODUCTION, RATHER THAN BY INTENSIVE AGRICULTURE (147)	53	DRIFT LESS TOWARD BEING THOSE 0.57 OF 118 WHERE FOOD PRODUCTION IS BY SIMPLE AGRICULTURE OR INCIPIENT FOOD PRODUCTION, RATHER THAN BY INTENSIVE AGRICULTURE (147)	34 51 75 67 XSQ= 3.00 PHI= -0.115 XP = 0.0830
55	TILT TOWARD BEING THOSE 0.63 OF 93 WHERE FOOD PRODUCTION IS BY SIMPLE AGRICULTURE, RATHER THAN BY INTENSIVE AGRICULTURE (101)	55	TILT TOWARD BEING THOSE 0.56 OF 91 WHERE FOOD PRODUCTION IS BY INTENSIVE AGRICULTURE, RATHER THAN BY SIMPLE AGRICULTURE (91)	34 51 59 40 XSQ= 6.26 PHI= -0.185 XP = 0.0123
56	TILT MORE TOWARD BEING THOSE 0.79 OF 75 WHERE FOOD PRODUCTION IS BY SIMPLE AGRICULTURE, RATHER THAN BY INCIPIENT FOOD PRODUCTION (101)	56	TILT LESS TOWARD BEING THOSE 0.60 OF 67 WHERE FOOD PRODUCTION IS BY SIMPLE AGRICULTURE, RATHER THAN BY INCIPIENT FOOD PRODUCTION (101)	59 40 16 27 XSQ= 5.16 PHI= 0.191 XP = 0.0231
62	TILT MORE TOWARD BEING THOSE 0.64 OF 169 WHERE HUSBANDRY OF SOME KIND IS PRESENT (228)	62	TILT LESS TOWARD BEING THOSE 0.53 OF 213 WHERE HUSBANDRY OF SOME KIND IS PRESENT (228)	108 113 61 100 XSQ= 4.12 PHI= 0.104 XP = 0.0424
63	TEND LESS TO BE THOSE 0.54 OF 106 WHERE HUSBANDRY, IF PRESENT, IS PRINCIPALLY IN THE FORM OF BOVINE, EQUINE, CAMEL-LIKE, OR DEER-LIKE ANIMALS, RATHER THAN PIGS, SHEEP, OR GOATS (152)	63	TEND MORE TO BE THOSE 0.79 OF 113 WHERE HUSBANDRY, IF PRESENT, IS PRINCIPALLY IN THE FORM OF BOVINE, EQUINE, CAMEL-LIKE, OR DEER-LIKE ANIMALS, RATHER THAN PIGS, SHEEP, OR GOATS (152)	57 89 49 24 XSQ= 14.26 PHI= -0.255 XP = 0.0002
73	TILT TOWARD BEING THOSE 0.62 OF 104 WHERE WEAVING IS ABSENT (130)	73	TILT TOWARD BEING THOSE 0.53 OF 136 WHERE WEAVING IS PRESENT (118)	40 72 64 64 XSQ= 4.40 PHI= -0.135 XP = 0.0359
79	TILT MORE TOWARD BEING THOSE 0.96 OF 95 WHERE NO CITY IS PRESENT (201)	79	TILT LESS TOWARD BEING THOSE 0.85 OF 125 WHERE NO CITY IS PRESENT (201)	4 19 91 106 XSQ= 5.84 PHI= -0.163 XP = 0.0157
80	TILT MORE TOWARD BEING THOSE 0.89 OF 95 WHERE NO CITY OR TOWN IS PRESENT (185)	80	TILT LESS TOWARD BEING THOSE 0.78 OF 125 WHERE NO CITY OR TOWN IS PRESENT (185)	10 27 85 98 XSQ= 3.97 PHI= -0.134 XP = 0.0462
88	LEAN MORE TOWARD BEING THOSE 0.71 OF 119 WHERE, IF A HEADMANSHIP IS PRESENT, SUCCESSION IS HEREDITARY (165)	88	LEAN LESS TOWARD BEING THOSE 0.53 OF 145 WHERE, IF A HEADMANSHIP IS PRESENT, SUCCESSION IS HEREDITARY (165)	35 68 84 77 XSQ= 7.68 PHI= -0.171 XP = 0.0056

No.		No.		
97	TEND LESS TO BE THOSE 0.73 OF 142 WHERE THE HIERARCHY OF LOCAL JURISDICTION HAS THREE OR TWO LEVELS (273) GES,EA	97	TEND MORE TO BE THOSE 0.90 OF 176 WHERE THE HIERARCHY OF LOCAL JURISDICTION HAS THREE OR TWO LEVELS (273) GES,EA	38 18 104 158 XSQ= 13.69 PHI= 0.207 XP = 0.0002
98	TILT MORE TOWARD BEING THOSE 0.79 OF 142 WHERE THE HIERARCHY OF LOCAL JURISDICTION HAS FOUR OR THREE LEVELS (238) GES,EA	98	TILT LESS TOWARD BEING THOSE 0.66 OF 176 WHERE THE HIERARCHY OF LOCAL JURISDICTION HAS FOUR OR THREE LEVELS (238) GES,EA	112 116 30 60 XSQ= 5.89 PHI= 0.136 XP = 0.0153
107	DRIFT MORE TOWARD BEING THOSE 0.85 OF 86 WHERE CLASS STRATIFICATION, IF PRESENT, IS BASED ON SOMETHING OTHER THAN OCCUPATIONAL STATUS (160)	107	DRIFT LESS TOWARD BEING THOSE 0.73 OF 111 WHERE CLASS STRATIFICATION, IF PRESENT, IS BASED ON SOMETHING OTHER THAN OCCUPATIONAL STATUS (160)	13 30 73 81 XSQ= 3.36 PHI= -0.131 XP = 0.0668
108	DRIFT LESS TOWARD BEING THOSE 0.57 OF 86 WHERE CLASS STRATIFICATION, IF PRESENT, IS BASED ON SOMETHING OTHER THAN A HEREDITARY ARISTOCRACY (129)	108	DRIFT MORE TOWARD BEING THOSE 0.70 OF 111 WHERE CLASS STRATIFICATION, IF PRESENT, IS BASED ON SOMETHING OTHER THAN A HEREDITARY ARISTOCRACY (129)	37 33 49 78 XSQ= 3.18 PHI= 0.127 XP = 0.0745
148	TILT TOWARD BEING THOSE 0.82 OF 17 WHERE THE INCIDENCE OF PERSONAL CRIME IS LOW (21) B-B-C	148	TILT TOWARD BEING THOSE 0.56 OF 16 WHERE THE INCIDENCE OF PERSONAL CRIME IS HIGH (12) B-B-C	3 9 14 7 XSQ= 3.77 PHI= -0.338 EP = 0.0324
186	TEND TO BE THOSE 0.56 OF 169 WHERE THE KIN GROUP IS EXCLUSIVELY PATRILINEAL (150)	186	TEND TO BE THOSE 0.78 OF 213 WHERE THE KIN GROUP IS OTHER THAN EXCLUSIVELY PATRILINEAL (250)	95 47 74 166 XSQ= 45.60 PHI= 0.345 XP = 0.
187	LEAN LESS TOWARD BEING THOSE 0.79 OF 169 WHERE THE KIN GROUP IS OTHER THAN EXCLUSIVELY MATRILINEAL (344)	187	LEAN MORE TOWARD BEING THOSE 0.92 OF 212 WHERE THE KIN GROUP IS OTHER THAN EXCLUSIVELY MATRILINEAL (344)	35 18 134 194 XSQ= 10.73 PHI= 0.168 XP = 0.0011
188	TEND TO BE THOSE 0.93 OF 169 WHERE THE KIN GROUP IS OTHER THAN EXCLUSIVELY COGNATIC (252)	188	TEND TO BE THOSE 0.61 OF 213 WHERE THE KIN GROUP IS EXCLUSIVELY COGNATIC (148)	11 130 158 83 XSQ= 117.97 PHI= -0.556 XP = 0.
192	IN ALL CASES ARE THOSE 1.00 OF 169 OTHER THAN WHERE THE ONLY KIN GROUP PRESENT IS A KINDRED OR ELSE BILATERAL DESCENT IS INFERRED (289)	192	TEND LESS TO BE THOSE 0.51 OF 213 OTHER THAN WHERE THE ONLY KIN GROUP PRESENT IS A KINDRED OR ELSE BILATERAL DESCENT IS INFERRED (289)	0 104 169 109 XSQ= 110.93 PHI= -0.539 XP = 0.

197	TEND MORE TO BE THOSE 0.98 OF 90 WHERE RULES FOR THE INHERITANCE OF REAL PROPERTY, IF PRESENT, FAVOR EITHER THE MALE HEIR OR LINE, OR THE FEMALE HEIR OR LINE (165)	197	TEND LESS TO BE THOSE 0.72 OF 98 WHERE RULES FOR THE INHERITANCE OF REAL PROPERTY, IF PRESENT, FAVOR EITHER THE MALE HEIR OR LINE, OR THE FEMALE HEIR OR LINE (165)	88 71 2 27 XSQ= 21.17 PHI= 0.336 XP = 0.0000
201	TEND MORE TO BE THOSE 0.94 OF 168 WHERE MARITAL RESIDENCE IS NON-OPTIONAL, RATHER THAN AMBILOCAL OR NEOLOCAL (334)	201	TEND LESS TO BE THOSE 0.75 OF 212 WHERE MARITAL RESIDENCE IS NON-OPTIONAL, RATHER THAN AMBILOCAL OR NEOLOCAL (334)	158 160 10 52 XSQ= 22.35 PHI= 0.242 XP = 0.0000
204	TEND MORE TO BE THOSE 0.93 OF 146 WHERE MARITAL RESIDENCE IS PATRILOCAL, VIRILOCAL, OR AVUNCULOCAL, RATHER THAN AMBILOCAL OR NEOLOCAL (270)	204	TEND LESS TO BE THOSE 0.70 OF 173 WHERE MARITAL RESIDENCE IS PATRILOCAL, VIRILOCAL, OR AVUNCULOCAL, RATHER THAN AMBILOCAL OR NEOLOCAL (270)	136 121 10 52 XSQ= 25.77 PHI= 0.284 XP = 0.0000
207	TILT TOWARD BEING THOSE 0.69 OF 32 WHERE MARITAL RESIDENCE IS MATRILOCAL OR UXORILOCAL, RATHER THAN AMBILOCAL OR NEOLOCAL (64)	207	TILT TOWARD BEING THOSE 0.57 OF 91 WHERE MARITAL RESIDENCE IS AMBILOCAL OR NEOLOCAL, RATHER THAN MATRILOCAL OR UXORILOCAL (64)	22 39 10 52 XSQ= 5.36 PHI= 0.209 XP = 0.0207
209	TILT MORE TOWARD BEING THOSE 0.86 OF 158 WHERE MARITAL RESIDENCE IS PATRILOCAL, VIRILOCAL, OR AVUNCULOCAL, RATHER THAN MATRILOCAL OR UXORILOCAL (270)	209	TILT LESS TOWARD BEING THOSE 0.76 OF 160 WHERE MARITAL RESIDENCE IS PATRILOCAL, VIRILOCAL, OR AVUNCULOCAL, RATHER THAN MATRILOCAL OR UXORILOCAL (270)	136 121 22 39 XSQ= 4.95 PHI= 0.125 XP = 0.0261
214	LEAN LESS TOWARD BEING THOSE 0.75 OF 80 WHERE FIRST COUSIN MARRIAGE, IF PERMITTED, IS OTHER THAN UNILATERAL (144)	214	LEAN MORE TOWARD BEING THOSE 0.92 OF 85 WHERE FIRST COUSIN MARRIAGE, IF PERMITTED, IS OTHER THAN UNILATERAL (144)	20 7 60 78 XSQ= 7.28 PHI= 0.210 XP = 0.0070
220	DRIFT LESS TOWARD BEING THOSE 0.69 OF 161 WHERE FIRST COUSIN MARRIAGE IN SOME FORM OR OTHER IS NOT PRESCRIBED OR PREFERRED (273)	220	DRIFT MORE TOWARD BEING THOSE 0.77 OF 198 WHERE FIRST COUSIN MARRIAGE IN SOME FORM OR OTHER IS NOT PRESCRIBED OR PREFERRED (273)	50 45 111 153 XSQ= 2.75 PHI= 0.088 XP = 0.0972
221	DRIFT LESS TOWARD BEING THOSE 0.87 OF 161 WHERE MATRILATERAL CROSS-COUSIN MARRIAGE IS NOT PRESCRIBED OR PREFERRED (335)	221	DRIFT MORE TOWARD BEING THOSE 0.93 OF 198 WHERE MATRILATERAL CROSS-COUSIN MARRIAGE IS NOT PRESCRIBED OR PREFERRED (335)	21 13 140 185 XSQ= 3.62 PHI= 0.100 XP = 0.0570
224	DRIFT LESS TOWARD BEING THOSE 0.54 OF 80 WHERE COUSIN MARRIAGE IS PREFERENTIALLY OR PERMISSIVELY SYMMETRICAL, RATHER THAN EITHER PATRI- OR MATRILATERAL (106)	224	DRIFT MORE TOWARD BEING THOSE 0.68 OF 85 WHERE COUSIN MARRIAGE IS PREFERENTIALLY OR PERMISSIVELY SYMMETRICAL, RATHER THAN EITHER PATRI- OR MATRILATERAL (106)	37 27 43 58 XSQ= 3.06 PHI= 0.136 XP = 0.0804

234	TEND TO BE THOSE WHERE THE COUSIN TERMINOLOGY IS OF CROW, OMAHA, OR IROQUOIS TYPE, RATHER THAN ESKIMO OR HAWAIIAN TYPE (152)	0.67 OF 134	234	TEND TO BE THOSE WHERE THE COUSIN TERMINOLOGY IS OF ESKIMO OR HAWAIIAN TYPE, RATHER THAN CROW, OMAHA, OR IROQUOIS TYPE (170)	0.68 OF 175	90 56 44 119 XSQ= 36.25 PHI= 0.343 XP = 0.
240	LEAN LESS TOWARD BEING THOSE WHERE THE FAMILY, IF EXTENDED, IS SMALL OR STEM, RATHER THAN LARGE (135)	0.51 OF 89	240	LEAN MORE TOWARD BEING THOSE WHERE THE FAMILY, IF EXTENDED, IS SMALL OR STEM, RATHER THAN LARGE (135)	0.73 OF 117	44 32 45 85 XSQ= 9.66 PHI= 0.217 XP = 0.0019
241	TEND MORE TO BE THOSE WHERE THE FAMILY, IF EXTENDED, IS LARGE OR SMALL, RATHER THAN STEM (187)	0.99 OF 89	241	TEND LESS TO BE THOSE WHERE THE FAMILY, IF EXTENDED, IS LARGE OR SMALL, RATHER THAN STEM (187)	0.79 OF 117	88 92 1 25 XSQ= 16.99 PHI= 0.287 XP = 0.0000
242	DRIFT MORE TOWARD BEING THOSE WHERE MARRIAGE IS COMMONLY OR OCCASIONALLY POLYGYNOUS, RATHER THAN MONOGAMOUS (314)	0.84 OF 167	242	DRIFT LESS TOWARD BEING THOSE WHERE MARRIAGE IS COMMONLY OR OCCASIONALLY POLYGYNOUS, RATHER THAN MONOGAMOUS (314)	0.75 OF 211	140 159 27 52 XSQ= 3.56 PHI= 0.097 XP = 0.0594
243	DRIFT TOWARD BEING THOSE WHERE POLYGYNY, IF PRESENT, HAS A HIGH INCIDENCE (24) W-C,S	0.53 OF 30	243	DRIFT TOWARD BEING THOSE WHERE POLYGYNY, IF PRESENT, HAS A LOW INCIDENCE (36) W-D,S	0.73 OF 30	16 8 14 22 XSQ= 3.40 PHI= 0.238 XP = 0.0651
262	LEAN MORE TOWARD BEING THOSE WHERE WIVES ARE OBTAINED BY MEANS INVOLVING THE PRESENCE OF SOME CONSIDERATION (305)	0.86 OF 166	262	LEAN LESS TOWARD BEING THOSE WHERE WIVES ARE OBTAINED BY MEANS INVOLVING THE PRESENCE OF SOME CONSIDERATION (305)	0.72 OF 212	143 152 23 60 XSQ= 10.51 PHI= 0.167 XP = 0.0012
263	TEND MORE TO BE THOSE WHERE WIVES ARE OBTAINED BY RELATIVELY DIFFICULT MEANS, NAMELY BY BRIDE-PRICE, BRIDE-SERVICE, OR EXCHANGING A FEMALE RELATIVE (233)	0.70 OF 166	263	TEND LESS TO BE THOSE WHERE WIVES ARE OBTAINED BY RELATIVELY DIFFICULT MEANS, NAMELY BY BRIDE-PRICE, BRIDE-SERVICE, OR EXCHANGING A FEMALE RELATIVE (233)	0.51 OF 212	116 108 50 104 XSQ= 13.05 PHI= 0.186 XP = 0.0003
280	TILT TOWARD BEING THOSE WHERE THE COMPOSITE FERTILITY LEVEL IS LOW (12) MN	0.71 OF 14	280	TILT TOWARD BEING THOSE WHERE THE COMPOSITE FERTILITY LEVEL IS HIGH (13) MN	0.82 OF 11	4 9 10 2 XSQ= 5.03 PHI= -0.448 EP = 0.0154
300	TILT TOWARD BEING THOSE WHERE THE POST-PARTUM SEX TABOO LASTS LONGER THAN SIX MONTHS (51)	0.52 OF 63	300	TILT TOWARD BEING THOSE WHERE THE POST-PARTUM SEX TABOO LASTS SIX MONTHS OR LESS (73)	0.70 OF 61	33 18 30 43 XSQ= 5.78 PHI= 0.216 XP = 0.0162

340	DRIFT TOWARD BEING THOSE 0.56 OF 25 WHERE THE TOTAL POSITIVE PRESSURE TOWARD DEVELOPING NURTURANT BEHAVIOR IN THE CHILD IS LOW (20) B-B-C	340	DRIFT TOWARD BEING THOSE 0.73 OF 22 WHERE THE TOTAL POSITIVE PRESSURE TOWARD DEVELOPING NURTURANT BEHAVIOR IN THE CHILD IS HIGH (28) B-B-C	11 16 14 6 XSQ= 2.86 PHI= -0.247 XP = 0.0907
370	TEND TO BE THOSE 0.52 OF 111 WHERE THE SEGREGATION OF ADOLESCENT BOYS IS COMPLETE OR PARTIAL (95)	370	TEND TO BE THOSE 0.72 OF 128 WHERE THE SEGREGATION OF ADOLESCENT BOYS IS ABSENT (148)	58 36 53 92 XSQ= 13.51 PHI= 0.238 XP = 0.0002
372	DRIFT TOWARD BEING THOSE 0.53 OF 55 WHERE MALE INITIATION RITES ARE PRESENT (48) ASA	372	DRIFT TOWARD BEING THOSE 0.66 OF 56 WHERE MALE INITIATION RITES ARE ABSENT (63) ASA	29 19 26 37 XSQ= 3.27 PHI= 0.172 XP = 0.0707
377	TEND LESS TO BE THOSE 0.63 OF 138 WHERE MALE GENITAL MUTILATION IS ABSENT (242)	377	TEND MORE TO BE THOSE 0.85 OF 174 WHERE MALE GENITAL MUTILATION IS ABSENT (242)	51 26 87 148 XSQ= 18.90 PHI= 0.246 XP = 0.0000
427	TILT TOWARD BEING THOSE 0.57 OF 69 WHERE A HIGH GOD, IF PRESENT, IS INACTIVE, RATHER THAN ACTIVE (69) GES,EA	427	TILT TOWARD BEING THOSE 0.63 OF 82 WHERE A HIGH GOD, IF PRESENT, IS ACTIVE, RATHER THAN INACTIVE (87) GES,EA	30 52 39 30 XSQ= 5.23 PHI= -0.186 XP = 0.0223
435	DRIFT TOWARD BEING THOSE 0.80 OF 15 WHERE ABANDONMENT OF THE HOUSE OF THE DEAD IS NOT PRACTICED (19) LWS	435	DRIFT TOWARD BEING THOSE 0.60 OF 15 WHERE ABANDONMENT OF THE HOUSE OF THE DEAD IS PRACTICED (12) LWS	3 9 12 6 XSQ= 3.47 PHI= -0.340 EP = 0.0604
441	DRIFT TOWARD BEING THOSE 0.63 OF 27 WHERE FEAR OF HUMAN BEINGS IS HIGH (29) W-C	441	DRIFT TOWARD BEING THOSE 0.65 OF 34 WHERE FEAR OF HUMAN BEINGS IS LOW (32) W-C	17 12 10 22 XSQ= 3.58 PHI= 0.242 XP = 0.0586
451	TILT TOWARD BEING THOSE 0.79 OF 14 WHERE TOTEMISM IS PRESENT (15) LWS	451	TILT TOWARD BEING THOSE 0.69 OF 13 WHERE TOTEMISM IS UNIMPORTANT OR ABSENT (12) LWS	11 4 3 9 XSQ= 4.45 PHI= 0.406 EP = 0.0213
476	TILT TOWARD BEING THOSE 0.58 OF 19 WHERE THE DEGREE OF INSOBRIETY IS MODERATE OR SLIGHT (18) DH	476	TILT TOWARD BEING THOSE 0.77 OF 30 WHERE THE DEGREE OF INSOBRIETY IS STRONG (31) DH	8 23 11 7 XSQ= 4.58 PHI= -0.306 XP = 0.0323

177 CULTURES WHERE THE COMMUNITY IS A SINGLE CLAN-COMMUNITY AND EXOGAMOUS (77)

177 CULTURES WHERE THE COMMUNITY IS OTHER THAN A SINGLE CLAN-COMMUNITY AND EXOGAMOUS (305)

BACKGROUND ON PAGE 105

BOTH SUBJECT AND PREDICATE

77 IN LEFT COLUMN

AJIE	AMBA	ARANDA	BABWA	BANDA	BARI	BAYA	BEJA	BETE	BHUIYA
BIRIFOR	BURYAT	CHAGGA	DAGUR	DIEGUENO	DOBUANS	DOROBO	ENGA	FANG	GISU
GOND	HAIDA	HAZARA	HEHE	HO	KALMYK	KAPAUKU	KARIERA	KATAB	KAZAK
KERAKI	KHEVSUR	KIKUYU	LAU	LIFU	LOLO	LUO	MAMVU	MANCHU	MATAKAM
MBUNDU	MBUTI	MIN CHINESE	MIWOK	MONGO	MURINBATA	MURNGIN	NAMA	NDEMBU	NOMLAKI
NUER	NYANEKA	OJIBWA	PENDE	REGEIBAT	RIFFIANS	RWALA	SANDAWE	SEMINOLE	SENIANG
SOMALI	SWAZI	TALLENSI	THONGA	TIV	TODA	TOLOWA	TUCANO	TUCUNA	VEDDA
WANTOAT	WIKMUNKAN	WITOTO	WOLOF	YAGUA	YAKUT	YOMBE			

305 IN RIGHT COLUMN

18 EXCLUDED BECAUSE UNASCERTAINED

	Left column			Right column			
3	TEND LESS TO BE THOSE LOCATED OUTSIDE OF AFRICA (320)	0.60 OF 77	3	TEND MORE TO BE THOSE LOCATED OUTSIDE OF AFRICA (320)	0.84 OF 305	31 48 46 257 XSQ= 21.07 PHI= 0.235 XP = 0.0000
8	DRIFT MORE TOWARD BEING THOSE LOCATED OUTSIDE OF NORTH AMERICA (330)	0.91 OF 77	8	DRIFT LESS TOWARD BEING THOSE LOCATED OUTSIDE OF NORTH AMERICA (330)	0.81 OF 305	7 59 70 246 XSQ= 3.83 PHI= -0.100 XP = 0.0502
9	LEAN MORE TOWARD BEING THOSE LOCATED OUTSIDE OF SOUTH AMERICA (335)	0.95 OF 77	9	LEAN LESS TOWARD BEING THOSE LOCATED OUTSIDE OF SOUTH AMERICA (335)	0.82 OF 305	4 55 73 250 XSQ= 6.81 PHI= -0.133 XP = 0.0091
14	DRIFT MORE TOWARD BEING THOSE WHERE THE LATITUDE IS LESS THAN THIRTY DEGREES (281)	0.79 OF 77	14	DRIFT LESS TOWARD BEING THOSE WHERE THE LATITUDE IS LESS THAN THIRTY DEGREES (281)	0.68 OF 305	16 98 61 207 XSQ= 3.26 PHI= -0.092 XP = 0.0709

16	DRIFT LESS TOWARD BEING THOSE 0.60 OF 77 WHERE THE LATITUDE IS TEN DEGREES OR GREATER (277)	16 DRIFT MORE TOWARD BEING THOSE 0.71 OF 305 WHERE THE LATITUDE IS TEN DEGREES OR GREATER (277)	46 218 31 87 XSQ= 3.44 PHI= -0.095 XP = 0.0638
51	TILT MORE TOWARD BEING THOSE 0.74 OF 77 WHERE SUBSISTENCE IS PRIMARILY BY FOOD PRODUCTION -- I. E., AGRICULTURE OR HUSBANDRY -- RATHER THAN BY GATHERING (253)	51 TILT LESS TOWARD BEING THOSE 0.61 OF 305 WHERE SUBSISTENCE IS PRIMARILY BY FOOD PRODUCTION -- I. E., AGRICULTURE OR HUSBANDRY -- RATHER THAN BY GATHERING (253)	57 186 20 119 XSQ= 3.97 PHI= 0.102 XP = 0.0463
55	TILT TOWARD BEING THOSE 0.70 OF 37 WHERE FOOD PRODUCTION IS BY SIMPLE AGRICULTURE, RATHER THAN BY INTENSIVE AGRICULTURE (101)	55 TILT TOWARD BEING THOSE 0.50 OF 147 WHERE FOOD PRODUCTION IS BY INTENSIVE AGRICULTURE, RATHER THAN BY SIMPLE AGRICULTURE (91)	11 74 26 73 XSQ= 4.26 PHI= -0.152 XP = 0.0391
56	TILT MORE TOWARD BEING THOSE 0.87 OF 30 WHERE FOOD PRODUCTION IS BY SIMPLE AGRICULTURE, RATHER THAN BY INCIPIENT FOOD PRODUCTION (101)	56 TILT LESS TOWARD BEING THOSE 0.65 OF 112 WHERE FOOD PRODUCTION IS BY SIMPLE AGRICULTURE, RATHER THAN BY INCIPIENT FOOD PRODUCTION (101)	26 73 4 39 XSQ= 4.21 PHI= 0.172 XP = 0.0402
73	LEAN TOWARD BEING THOSE 0.74 OF 50 WHERE WEAVING IS ABSENT (130)	73 LEAN TOWARD BEING THOSE 0.52 OF 190 WHERE WEAVING IS PRESENT (118)	13 99 37 91 XSQ= 9.81 PHI= -0.202 XP = 0.0017
79	DRIFT MORE TOWARD BEING THOSE 0.98 OF 44 WHERE NO CITY IS PRESENT (201)	79 DRIFT LESS TOWARD BEING THOSE 0.88 OF 176 WHERE NO CITY IS PRESENT (201)	1 22 43 154 XSQ= 2.92 PHI= -0.115 XP = 0.0877
80	TILT MORE TOWARD BEING THOSE 0.95 OF 44 WHERE NO CITY OR TOWN IS PRESENT (185)	80 TILT LESS TOWARD BEING THOSE 0.80 OF 176 WHERE NO CITY OR TOWN IS PRESENT (185)	2 35 42 141 XSQ= 4.88 PHI= -0.149 XP = 0.0272
81	TILT MORE TOWARD BEING THOSE 0.75 OF 44 WHERE NO CITY OR TOWN IS PRESENT, AND THE AVERAGE COMMUNITY SIZE IS SMALLER THAN 200 (135)	81 TILT LESS TOWARD BEING THOSE 0.57 OF 176 WHERE NO CITY OR TOWN IS PRESENT, AND THE AVERAGE COMMUNITY SIZE IS SMALLER THAN 200 (135)	11 75 33 101 XSQ= 3.88 PHI= -0.133 XP = 0.0490
84	DRIFT MORE TOWARD BEING THOSE 0.95 OF 56 WHERE THE LEVEL OF POLITICAL INTEGRATION IS THE LITTLE STATE, THE MINIMAL STATE, THE AUTONOMOUS COMMUNITY, OR THE FAMILY (262) GPM	84 DRIFT LESS TOWARD BEING THOSE 0.84 OF 231 WHERE THE LEVEL OF POLITICAL INTEGRATION IS THE LITTLE STATE, THE MINIMAL STATE, THE AUTONOMOUS COMMUNITY, OR THE FAMILY (262) GPM	3 37 53 194 XSQ= 3.43 PHI= -0.109 XP = 0.0641

98	TILT LESS TOWARD BEING THOSE WHERE THE HIERARCHY OF LOCAL JURISDICTION HAS FOUR OR THREE LEVELS (238) GES,EA	0.61 OF 64	98	TILT MORE TOWARD BEING THOSE WHERE THE HIERARCHY OF LOCAL JURISDICTION HAS FOUR OR THREE LEVELS (238) GES,EA	0.74 OF 254	39 189 25 65 XSQ= 3.93 PHI= -0.111 XP = 0.0474
99	TILT TOWARD BEING THOSE WHERE, WITH NATIONAL HIERARCHY ABSENT, THE HIERARCHY OF LOCAL JURISDICTION HAS TWO LEVELS (63) GES,EA	0.59 OF 34	99	TILT TOWARD BEING THOSE WHERE, WITH NATIONAL HIERARCHY ABSENT, THE HIERARCHY OF LOCAL JURISDICTION HAS FOUR OR THREE LEVELS (93) GES,EA	0.66 OF 120	14 79 20 41 XSQ= 5.74 PHI= -0.193 XP = 0.0166
100	TILT LESS TOWARD BEING THOSE WHERE HIERARCHIES ARE MORE COMPLEX THAN THE 'SIMPLEST,' I. E., MORE COMPLEX THAN TWO LOCAL LEVELS WITH NO NATIONAL LEVELS (267) GES,EA	0.69 OF 64	100	TILT MORE TOWARD BEING THOSE WHERE HIERARCHIES ARE MORE COMPLEX THAN THE 'SIMPLEST,' I. E., MORE COMPLEX THAN TWO LOCAL LEVELS WITH NO NATIONAL LEVELS (267) GES,EA	0.84 OF 253	44 212 20 41 XSQ= 6.50 PHI= -0.143 XP = 0.0108
106	DRIFT TOWARD BEING THOSE WHERE CLASS STRATIFICATION, IF PRESENT, IS BASED ON WEALTH (77)	0.53 OF 36	106	DRIFT TOWARD BEING THOSE WHERE CLASS STRATIFICATION, IF PRESENT, IS BASED ON SOMETHING OTHER THAN WEALTH (126)	0.65 OF 161	19 56 17 105 XSQ= 3.31 PHI= 0.130 XP = 0.0687
107	DRIFT MORE TOWARD BEING THOSE WHERE CLASS STRATIFICATION, IF PRESENT, IS BASED ON SOMETHING OTHER THAN OCCUPATIONAL STATUS (160)	0.92 OF 36	107	DRIFT LESS TOWARD BEING THOSE WHERE CLASS STRATIFICATION, IF PRESENT, IS BASED ON SOMETHING OTHER THAN OCCUPATIONAL STATUS (160)	0.75 OF 161	3 40 33 121 XSQ= 3.78 PHI= -0.139 XP = 0.0518
186	TEND TO BE THOSE WHERE THE KIN GROUP IS EXCLUSIVELY PATRILINEAL (150)	0.75 OF 77	186	TEND TO BE THOSE WHERE THE KIN GROUP IS OTHER THAN EXCLUSIVELY PATRILINEAL (250)	0.72 OF 305	58 84 19 221 XSQ= 58.08 PHI= 0.390 XP = 0.
188	IN ALL CASES ARE THOSE WHERE THE KIN GROUP IS OTHER THAN EXCLUSIVELY COGNATIC (252)	1.00 OF 77	188	TEND LESS TO BE THOSE WHERE THE KIN GROUP IS OTHER THAN EXCLUSIVELY COGNATIC (252)	0.54 OF 305	0 141 77 164 XSQ= 54.46 PHI= -0.378 XP = 0.
190	TEND MORE TO BE THOSE WHERE THE KIN GROUP IS PATRILINEAL OR DOUBLE-DESCENT, RATHER THAN MATRILINEAL (186)	0.89 OF 76	190	TEND LESS TO BE THOSE WHERE THE KIN GROUP IS PATRILINEAL OR DOUBLE-DESCENT, RATHER THAN MATRILINEAL (186)	0.68 OF 160	68 109 8 51 XSQ= 11.41 PHI= 0.220 XP = 0.0007
192	IN ALL CASES ARE THOSE OTHER THAN WHERE THE ONLY KIN GROUP PRESENT IS A KINDRED OR ELSE BILATERAL DESCENT IS INFERRED (289)	1.00 OF 77	192	TEND LESS TO BE THOSE OTHER THAN WHERE THE ONLY KIN GROUP PRESENT IS A KINDRED OR ELSE BILATERAL DESCENT IS INFERRED (289)	0.66 OF 305	0 104 77 201 XSQ= 34.38 PHI= -0.300 XP = 0.

197	IN ALL CASES ARE THOSE WHERE RULES FOR THE INHERITANCE OF REAL PROPERTY, IF PRESENT, FAVOR EITHER THE MALE HEIR OR LINE, OR THE FEMALE HEIR OR LINE (165)	1.00 OF 38	197	LEAN LESS TOWARD BEING THOSE WHERE RULES FOR THE INHERITANCE OF REAL PROPERTY, IF PRESENT, FAVOR EITHER THE MALE HEIR OR LINE, OR THE FEMALE HEIR OR LINE (165)	0.81 OF 150	38 121 0 29 XSQ= 7.27 PHI= 0.197 XP = 0.0070
201	TEND MORE TO BE THOSE WHERE MARITAL RESIDENCE IS NON-OPTIONAL, RATHER THAN AMBILOCAL OR NEOLOCAL (334)	0.99 OF 77	201	TEND LESS TO BE THOSE WHERE MARITAL RESIDENCE IS NON-OPTIONAL, RATHER THAN AMBILOCAL OR NEOLOCAL (334)	0.80 OF 303	76 242 1 61 XSQ= 14.60 PHI= 0.196 XP = 0.0001
204	TEND MORE TO BE THOSE WHERE MARITAL RESIDENCE IS PATRILOCAL, VIRILOCAL, OR AVUNCULOCAL, RATHER THAN AMBILOCAL OR NEOLOCAL (270)	0.99 OF 75	204	TEND LESS TO BE THOSE WHERE MARITAL RESIDENCE IS PATRILOCAL, VIRILOCAL, OR AVUNCULOCAL, RATHER THAN AMBILOCAL OR NEOLOCAL (270)	0.75 OF 244	74 183 1 61 XSQ= 19.04 PHI= 0.244 XP = 0.0000
209	TEND MORE TO BE THOSE WHERE MARITAL RESIDENCE IS PATRILOCAL, VIRILOCAL, OR AVUNCULOCAL, RATHER THAN MATRILOCAL OR UXORILOCAL (270)	0.97 OF 76	209	TEND LESS TO BE THOSE WHERE MARITAL RESIDENCE IS PATRILOCAL, VIRILOCAL, OR AVUNCULOCAL, RATHER THAN MATRILOCAL OR UXORILOCAL (270)	0.76 OF 242	74 183 2 59 XSQ= 16.27 PHI= 0.226 XP = 0.0001
210	LEAN MORE TOWARD BEING THOSE WHERE MARITAL RESIDENCE IS PATRILOCAL, RATHER THAN MATRILOCAL (169)	0.97 OF 67	210	LEAN LESS TOWARD BEING THOSE WHERE MARITAL RESIDENCE IS PATRILOCAL, RATHER THAN MATRILOCAL (169)	0.78 OF 124	65 97 2 27 XSQ= 10.51 PHI= 0.235 XP = 0.0012
234	TEND TO BE THOSE WHERE THE COUSIN TERMINOLOGY IS OF CROW, OMAHA, OR IROQUOIS TYPE, RATHER THAN ESKIMO OR HAWAIIAN TYPE (152)	0.84 OF 56	234	TEND TO BE THOSE WHERE THE COUSIN TERMINOLOGY IS OF ESKIMO OR HAWAIIAN TYPE, RATHER THAN CROW, OMAHA, OR IROQUOIS TYPE (170)	0.61 OF 253	47 99 9 154 XSQ= 35.14 PHI= 0.337 XP = 0.
236	DRIFT TOWARD BEING THOSE WHERE THE FAMILY IS OF AN INDEPENDENT TYPE, RATHER THAN AN EXTENDED TYPE (185)	0.55 OF 76	236	DRIFT TOWARD BEING THOSE WHERE THE FAMILY IS OF AN EXTENDED TYPE, RATHER THAN AN INDEPENDENT TYPE (213)	0.56 OF 305	34 172 42 133 XSQ= 2.88 PHI= -0.087 XP = 0.0899
242	TILT MORE TOWARD BEING THOSE WHERE MARRIAGE IS COMMONLY OR OCCASIONALLY POLYGYNOUS, RATHER THAN MONOGAMOUS (314)	0.89 OF 75	242	TILT LESS TOWARD BEING THOSE WHERE MARRIAGE IS COMMONLY OR OCCASIONALLY POLYGYNOUS, RATHER THAN MONOGAMOUS (314)	0.77 OF 303	67 232 8 71 XSQ= 5.18 PHI= 0.117 XP = 0.0229
255	DRIFT TOWARD BEING THOSE WHERE GRANDPARENTAL AUTHORITY OVER PARENTS IS PRESENT (7) CA	0.50 OF 6	255	DRIFT TOWARD BEING THOSE WHERE GRANDPARENTAL AUTHORITY OVER PARENTS IS ABSENT (26) DA	0.85 OF 27	3 4 3 23 XSQ= 1.84 PHI= 0.236 EP = 0.0929

257	TILT TOWARD BEING THOSE WHERE THE SEVERITY OF SISTER AVOIDANCE IS HIGH (10) WNS	0.80 OF 5	257	TILT TOWARD BEING THOSE WHERE THE SEVERITY OF SISTER AVOIDANCE IS LOW (17) WNS	0.73 OF 22	4 6 1 16 XSQ= 2.86 PHI= 0.325 EP = 0.0473
259	DRIFT TOWARD BEING THOSE WHERE THE SEVERITY OF MOTHER-IN-LAW AVOIDANCE IS HIGH (26) WNS	0.89 OF 9	259	DRIFT TOWARD BEING THOSE WHERE THE SEVERITY OF MOTHER-IN-LAW AVOIDANCE IS LOW (20) WNS	0.51 OF 37	8 18 1 19 XSQ= 3.27 PHI= 0.267 XP = 0.0704
262	TEND MORE TO BE THOSE WHERE WIVES ARE OBTAINED BY MEANS INVOLVING THE PRESENCE OF SOME CONSIDERATION (305)	0.95 OF 76	262	TEND LESS TO BE THOSE WHERE WIVES ARE OBTAINED BY MEANS INVOLVING THE PRESENCE OF SOME CONSIDERATION (305)	0.74 OF 302	72 223 4 79 XSQ= 14.28 PHI= 0.194 XP = 0.0002
263	TEND MORE TO BE THOSE WHERE WIVES ARE OBTAINED BY RELATIVELY DIFFICULT MEANS, NAMELY BY BRIDE-PRICE, BRIDE-SERVICE, OR EXCHANGING A FEMALE RELATIVE (233)	0.82 OF 76	263	TEND LESS TO BE THOSE WHERE WIVES ARE OBTAINED BY RELATIVELY DIFFICULT MEANS, NAMELY BY BRIDE-PRICE, BRIDE-SERVICE, OR EXCHANGING A FEMALE RELATIVE (233)	0.54 OF 302	62 162 14 140 XSQ= 18.49 PHI= 0.221 XP = 0.0000
324	TILT TOWARD BEING THOSE WHERE THE PAIN INFLICTED ON THE INFANT BY THE NURTURANT AGENT IS HIGH (34) B-B-C	0.83 OF 12	324	TILT TOWARD BEING THOSE WHERE THE PAIN INFLICTED ON THE INFANT BY THE NURTURANT AGENT IS LOW OR NEGLIGIBLE (32) B-B-C	0.56 OF 54	10 24 2 30 XSQ= 4.49 PHI= 0.261 XP = 0.0341
336	DRIFT MORE TOWARD BEING THOSE WHERE THE TOTAL POSITIVE PRESSURE TOWARD DEVELOPING RESPONSIBLE BEHAVIOR IN THE CHILD IS HIGH (43) B-B-C	0.80 OF 15	336	DRIFT LESS TOWARD BEING THOSE WHERE THE TOTAL POSITIVE PRESSURE TOWARD DEVELOPING RESPONSIBLE BEHAVIOR IN THE CHILD IS HIGH (43) B-B-C	0.51 OF 59	12 30 3 29 XSQ= 3.04 PHI= 0.203 XP = 0.0813
337	TILT TOWARD BEING THOSE WHERE THE CHILD'S INFERRED ANXIETY OVER NON-PERFORMANCE OF RESPONSIBLE BEHAVIOR IS HIGH (38) B-B-C	0.80 OF 15	337	TILT TOWARD BEING THOSE WHERE THE CHILD'S INFERRED ANXIETY OVER NON-PERFORMANCE OF RESPONSIBLE BEHAVIOR IS LOW (35) B-B-C	0.56 OF 57	12 25 3 32 XSQ= 4.85 PHI= 0.259 XP = 0.0277
346	TILT TOWARD BEING THOSE WHERE THE CHILD'S INFERRED ANXIETY OVER PERFORMANCE OF SELF-RELIANT BEHAVIOR IS HIGH (37) B-B-C	0.80 OF 15	346	TILT TOWARD BEING THOSE WHERE THE CHILD'S INFERRED ANXIETY OVER PERFORMANCE OF SELF-RELIANT BEHAVIOR IS LOW (39) B-B-C	0.60 OF 60	12 24 3 36 XSQ= 6.17 PHI= 0.287 XP = 0.0130
347	DRIFT TOWARD BEING THOSE WHERE THE CHILD'S INFERRED CONFLICT REGARDING SELF-RELIANT BEHAVIOR IS HIGH (37) B-B-C	0.73 OF 15	347	DRIFT TOWARD BEING THOSE WHERE THE CHILD'S INFERRED CONFLICT REGARDING SELF-RELIANT BEHAVIOR IS LOW (39) B-B-C	0.58 OF 60	11 25 4 35 XSQ= 3.64 PHI= 0.220 XP = 0.0565

370	LEAN TOWARD BEING THOSE 0.58 OF 50 WHERE THE SEGREGATION CF ACOLESCENT BOYS IS COMPLETE CR PARTIAL (95)	370	LEAN TOWARD BEING THOSE 0.66 OF 189 WHERE THE SEGREGATICN OF ADCLESCENT BOYS IS ABSENT (148)	29 65 21 124 XSQ= 8.27 PHI= 0.186 XP = 0.0040
377	TEND LESS TO BE THCSE 0.57 OF 63 WHERE MALE GENITAL MUTILATION IS ABSENT (242)	377	TEND MORE TO BE THOSE 0.80 CF 249 WHERE MALE GENITAL MUTILATICN IS ABSENT (242)	27 50 36 199 XSQ= 12.83 PHI= 0.203 XP = 0.0003
431	IN ALL CASES ARE THOSE 1.00 OF 8 WHERE SUPERNATURAL SANCTICNS FOR MORALITY, HAVING AN EFFECT ON AN INDIVIDUAL'S AFTERLIFE, ARE ABSENT OR UNREPORTEC (25) GES	431	DRIFT LESS TOWARD BEING THCSE 0.63 OF 27 WHERE SUPERNATURAL SANCTIONS FOR MORALITY, HAVING AN EFFECT ON AN INDIVIDUAL'S AFTERLIFE, ARE ABSENT OR UNREPORTED (25) GES	0 10 8 17 XSQ= 2.53 PHI= -0.269 EP = 0.0734
476	DRIFT TCWARD BEING THCSE 0.64 OF 11 WHERE THE DEGREE OF INSCBRIETY IS MODERATE CR SLIGHT (18) CH	476	DRIFT TOWARD BEING THOSE 0.71 OF 38 WHERE THE DEGREE OF INSOBRIETY IS STRONG (31) DH	4 27 7 11 XSQ= 3.05 PHI= -0.250 XP = 0.0807

178 CULTURES
WHERE THE COMMUNITY IS
SEGMENTED ON A CLAN BASIS AND
NON-EXOGAMOUS (87)

178 CULTURES
WHERE THE COMMUNITY IS OTHER THAN
SEGMENTED ON A CLAN BASIS AND
NON-EXOGAMOUS (295)

BACKGROUND ON PAGE 105

BOTH SUBJECT AND PREDICATE

87 IN LEFT COLUMN

APINAYE	ARAPESH	ARAUCANIANS	ARYANS	AZTEC	BAMBARA	BAMILEKE	BELU	BORORO	BUNLAP
CALLINAGO	CHEROKEE	DELAWARE	DILLING	ELLICE	FON	FUTAJALONKE	GILBERTESE	GILYAK	GUAHIBO
GURE	HANC	HAWAIIANS	HURON	KABYLE	KACHIN	KASKA	KHASI	KCHISTANI	KPE
KUBA	LAKALAI	LAMET	LESU	LHOTA NAGA	MACASSARESE	MAM	MAMBILA	MANUS	MAORI
MARGI	MARSHALLESE	MENDE	MENTAWEI	MIAO	MINANGKABAU	MNONG GAR	MONGUOR	MOSSI	MOTA
MZAB	NUPE	NYARO	NYORO	OMAHA	PALAUANS	PUKAPUKA	PURARI	ROTUMANS	RUNDI
SAMOANS	SARAMACCA	SERBS	SHERENTE	SHILLUK	SHLUH	SIMBOESE	SIRIONO	SIUAI	TANALA
TESO	TIMBIRA	TIMUCUA	TROBRIAND	TRUKESE	ULAWANS	VENDA	WAROPEN	WINNEBAGO	WOLEAIANS
WUTE	YAKO	YAO	YAPESE	YOKUTS	YORUBA	ZUNI			

295 IN RIGHT COLUMN

18 EXCLUDED BECAUSE UNASCERTAINED

4	TILT MORE TOWARD BEING THOSE LOCATED OUTSIDE OF THE CIRCUM-MEDITERRANEAN (355)	0.95 OF 87	4	TILT LESS TOWARD BEING THOSE LOCATED OUTSIDE OF THE CIRCUM-MEDITERRANEAN (355)	0.87 OF 295	4 38 83 257 XSQ= 3.90 PHI= -0.101 XP = 0.0482
6	TEND LESS TO BE THOSE LOCATED OUTSIDE OF THE INSULAR PACIFIC (330)	0.68 OF 87	6	TEND MORE TO BE THOSE LOCATED OUTSIDE OF THE INSULAR PACIFIC (330)	0.86 OF 295	28 40 59 255 XSQ= 14.68 PHI= 0.196 XP = 0.0001
11	IN ALL CASES ARE THOSE WHERE THE LATITUDE IS LESS THAN SIXTY DEGREES (385)	1.00 OF 87	11	DRIFT LESS TOWARD BEING THOSE WHERE THE LATITUDE IS LESS THAN SIXTY DEGREES (385)	0.95 OF 295	0 14 87 281 XSQ= 3.05 PHI= -0.089 XP = 0.0809
15	LEAN TOWARD BEING THOSE WHERE THE LATITUDE IS LESS THAN TWENTY DEGREES (217)	0.68 OF 87	15	LEAN TOWARD BEING THOSE WHERE THE LATITUDE IS TWENTY DEGREES OR GREATER (183)	0.50 OF 295	28 148 59 147 XSQ= 8.04 PHI= -0.145 XP = 0.0046

33	LEAN MORE TOWARD BEING THOSE 0.95 OF 87 WHERE THE NATURAL ENVIRONMENT IS OTHER THAN 'VERY HARSH,' I.E., DESERT, DESERT GRASSES AND SHRUBS, TUNDRA, OR HIGH PLATEAU STEPPE (341) FWM	33	LEAN LESS TOWARD BEING THOSE 0.82 OF 295 WHERE THE NATURAL ENVIRONMENT IS OTHER THAN 'VERY HARSH,' I.E., DESERT, DESERT GRASSES AND SHRUBS, TUNDRA, OR HIGH PLATEAU STEPPE (341) FWM	4 53 83 242 XSQ= 8.43 PHI= -0.149 XP = 0.0037
36	LEAN MORE TOWARD BEING THOSE 0.85 OF 87 WHERE THE NATURAL ENVIRONMENT IS OTHER THAN 'VERY HARSH,' OR SUB-TROPICAL BUSH, OR TEMPERATE GRASSLAND (292) FWM	36	LEAN LESS TOWARD BEING THOSE 0.68 OF 295 WHERE THE NATURAL ENVIRONMENT IS OTHER THAN 'VERY HARSH,' OR SUB-TROPICAL BUSH, OR TEMPERATE GRASSLAND (292) FWM	13 93 74 202 XSQ= 8.41 PHI= -0.148 XP = 0.0037
42	DRIFT LESS TOWARD BEING THOSE 0.52 OF 87 WHERE THE NATURAL ENVIRONMENT IS OTHER THAN TROPICAL OR SUB-TROPICAL RAIN FOREST, OR MONSOON FOREST (244) FWM	42	DRIFT MORE TOWARD BEING THOSE 0.64 OF 295 WHERE THE NATURAL ENVIRONMENT IS OTHER THAN TROPICAL OR SUB-TROPICAL RAIN FOREST, OR MONSOON FOREST (244) FWM	42 107 45 188 XSQ= 3.58 PHI= 0.097 XP = 0.0585
44	TEND MORE TO BE THOSE 0.84 OF 74 WHERE SETTLEMENTS ARE FIXED (222)	44	TEND LESS TO BE THOSE 0.62 OF 245 WHERE SETTLEMENTS ARE FIXED (222)	62 152 12 93 XSQ= 11.20 PHI= 0.187 XP = 0.0008
46	LEAN MORE TOWARD BEING THOSE 0.92 OF 74 OTHER THAN WHERE SETTLEMENTS ARE NON-FIXED AND MOVEMENT IS NOMADIC (260)	46	LEAN LESS TOWARD BEING THOSE 0.74 OF 245 OTHER THAN WHERE SETTLEMENTS ARE NON-FIXED AND MOVEMENT IS NOMADIC (260)	6 64 68 181 XSQ= 9.74 PHI= -0.175 XP = 0.0018
48	DRIFT TOWARD BEING THOSE 0.65 OF 23 WHERE THE FOOD SUPPLY IS SECURE, AND FOOD SHORTAGES ARE RARE OR OCCASIONAL (38) MGW	48	DRIFT TOWARD BEING THOSE 0.59 OF 56 WHERE THE FOOD SUPPLY IS NOT SECURE, AND FOOD SHORTAGES ARE FREQUENT OR ANNUAL (41) MGW	15 23 8 33 XSQ= 2.90 PHI= 0.192 XP = 0.0885
62	DRIFT MORE TOWARD BEING THOSE 0.67 OF 87 WHERE HUSBANDRY OF SOME KIND IS PRESENT (228)	62	DRIFT LESS TOWARD BEING THOSE 0.55 OF 295 WHERE HUSBANDRY OF SOME KIND IS PRESENT (228)	58 163 29 132 XSQ= 3.14 PHI= 0.091 XP = 0.0766
63	TEND TO BE THOSE 0.52 OF 58 WHERE HUSBANDRY, IF PRESENT, IS PRINCIPALLY IN THE FORM OF PIGS, SHEEP, OR GOATS, RATHER THAN BOVINE, EQUINE, CAMEL-LIKE, OR DEER-LIKE ANIMALS (74)	63	TEND TO BE THOSE 0.73 OF 161 WHERE HUSBANDRY, IF PRESENT, IS PRINCIPALLY IN THE FORM OF BOVINE, EQUINE, CAMEL-LIKE, OR DEER-LIKE ANIMALS, RATHER THAN PIGS, SHEEP, OR GOATS (152)	28 118 30 43 XSQ= 10.91 PHI= -0.223 XP = 0.0010
82	TILT MORE TOWARD BEING THOSE 0.94 OF 47 WHERE A CITY OR TOWN IS PRESENT, OR THE AVERAGE COMMUNITY SIZE IS FIFTY OR GREATER (178)	82	TILT LESS TOWARD BEING THOSE 0.75 OF 173 WHERE A CITY OR TOWN IS PRESENT, OR THE AVERAGE COMMUNITY SIZE IS FIFTY OR GREATER (178)	44 130 3 43 XSQ= 6.55 PHI= 0.173 XP = 0.0105

90	LEAN LESS TOWARC BEING THCSE WHERE, IF A HEREDITARY HEACMANSHIP IS PRESENT, SUCCESSICN IS PATRILINEAL, RATHER THAN MATRILINEAL (127)	0.60 OF 45	90	LEAN MORE TOWARD BEING THOSE WHERE, IF A HEREDITARY HEADMANSHIP IS PRESENT, SUCCESSION IS PATRILINEAL, RATHER THAN MATRILINEAL (127)	0.84 OF 116	27 97 18 19 XSQ= 8.93 PHI= -0.236 XP = 0.0028
97	TEND LESS TO BE THCSE WHERE THE HIERARCHY OF LOCAL JURISDICTION HAS THREE OR TWO LEVELS (273) GES,EA	0.66 OF 74	97	TEND MORE TO BE THOSE WHERE THE HIERARCHY OF LOCAL JURISDICTION HAS THREE OR TWO LEVELS (273) GES,EA	0.87 CF 244	25 31 49 213 XSQ= 15.97 PHI= 0.224 XP = 0.0001
98	TEND MORE TO BE THCSE WHERE THE HIERARCHY OF LCCAL JURISDICTICN HAS FOUR CR THREE LEVELS (238) GES,EA	0.93 OF 74	98	TEND LESS TO BE THOSE WHERE THE HIERARCHY OF LOCAL JURISDICTION HAS FOUR OR THREE LEVELS (238) GES,EA	0.65 CF 244	69 159 5 85 XSQ= 20.70 PHI= 0.255 XP = 0.0000
99	TEND MORE TO BE THCSE WHERE, WITH NATICNAL HIERARCHY ABSENT, THE HIERARCHY OF LCCAL JURISDICTION HAS FOUR CR THREE LEVELS (93) GES,EA	0.90 OF 31	99	TEND LESS TO BE THOSE WHERE, WITH NATIONAL HIERARCHY ABSENT, THE HIERARCHY OF LOCAL JURISDICTION HAS FOUR OR THREE LEVELS (93) GES,EA	0.53 CF 123	28 65 3 58 XSQ= 13.01 PHI= 0.291 XP = 0.0003
100	TEND MORE TO BE THCSE WHERE HIERARCHIES ARE MORE COMPLEX THAN THE 'SIMPLEST,' I. E., MORE COMPLEX THAN TWC LCCAL LEVELS WITH NO NATIONAL LEVELS (267) GES,EA	0.96 OF 74	100	TEND LESS TO BE THOSE WHERE HIERARCHIES ARE MORE COMPLEX THAN THE 'SIMPLEST,' I. E., MORE COMPLEX THAN TWO LOCAL LEVELS WITH NO NATIONAL LEVELS (267) GES,EA	0.76 CF 243	71 185 3 58 XSQ= 13.08 PHI= 0.203 XP = 0.0003
108	TILT LESS TOWARC BEING THCSE WHERE CLASS STRATIFICATION, IF PRESENT, IS BASED CN SOMETHING OTHER THAN A HEREDITARY ARISTCCRACY (129)	0.51 OF 47	108	TILT MORE TOWARD BEING THOSE WHERE CLASS STRATIFICATION, IF PRESENT, IS BASED ON SOMETHING OTHER THAN A HEREDITARY ARISTOCRACY (129)	0.69 CF 150	23 47 24 103 XSQ= 4.10 PHI= 0.144 XP = 0.0428
131	IN ALL CASES ARE THOSE WHERE THE CONSTRUCTION CF PERMANENT HOUSES OR THE ERECTICN CF TEMPORARY CWELLINGS IS MAINLY DONE BY MALES (136)	1.00 OF 38	131	TILT LESS TOWARD BEING THOSE WHERE THE CONSTRUCTION OF PERMANENT HOUSES OR THE ERECTION OF TEMPORARY DWELLINGS IS MAINLY DONE BY MALES (136)	0.82 OF 116	38 95 0 21 XSQ= 6.50 PHI= 0.205 XP = 0.0108
136	DRIFT TCWARD BEING THCSE WHERE FULL-TIME ENTREPRENEURS ARE ABSENT (14) JV	0.75 OF 8	136	DRIFT TOWARD BEING THOSE WHERE FULL-TIME ENTREPRENEURS ARE PRESENT (18) JV	0.67 OF 24	2 16 6 8 XSQ= 2.71 PHI= -0.291 EP = 0.0964
147	IN ALL CASES ARE THOSE WHERE CODIFIED LAWS ARE PRESENT (20) LWS	1.00 OF 7	147	TILT TOWARD BEING THOSE WHERE CODIFIED LAWS ARE UNIMPORTANT OR ABSENT (13) LWS	0.52 OF 25	7 12 0 13 XSQ= 4.16 PHI= 0.361 EP = 0.0252

No.		No.		
163	IN ALL CASES ARE THOSE 1.00 OF 3 WHERE THE EMPHASIS ON INDIVIDUAL VOLITION AS THE CAUSE OF CRIME IS HIGH (7) MJ	163	DRIFT TOWARD BEING THOSE 0.71 OF 14 WHERE THE EMPHASIS ON INDIVIDUAL VOLITION AS THE CAUSE OF CRIME IS LOW (10) MJ	3 4 0 10 XSQ= 2.67 PHI= 0.397 EP = 0.0515
187	TEND LESS TO BE THOSE 0.69 OF 87 WHERE THE KIN GROUP IS OTHER THAN EXCLUSIVELY MATRILINEAL (344)	187	TEND MORE TO BE THOSE 0.91 OF 294 WHERE THE KIN GROUP IS OTHER THAN EXCLUSIVELY MATRILINEAL (344)	27 26 60 268 XSQ= 25.78 PHI= 0.260 XP = 0.0000
188	TEND MORE TO BE THOSE 0.87 OF 87 WHERE THE KIN GROUP IS OTHER THAN EXCLUSIVELY COGNATIC (252)	188	TEND LESS TO BE THOSE 0.56 OF 295 WHERE THE KIN GROUP IS OTHER THAN EXCLUSIVELY COGNATIC (252)	11 130 76 165 XSQ= 27.16 PHI= -0.267 XP = 0.0000
190	TEND LESS TO BE THOSE 0.58 OF 74 WHERE THE KIN GROUP IS PATRILINEAL OR DOUBLE-DESCENT, RATHER THAN MATRILINEAL (186)	190	TEND MORE TO BE THOSE 0.83 OF 162 WHERE THE KIN GROUP IS PATRILINEAL OR DOUBLE-DESCENT, RATHER THAN MATRILINEAL (186)	43 134 31 28 XSQ= 15.12 PHI= -0.253 XP = 0.0001
192	IN ALL CASES ARE THOSE 1.00 OF 87 OTHER THAN WHERE THE ONLY KIN GROUP PRESENT IS A KINDRED OR ELSE BILATERAL DESCENT IS INFERRED (289)	192	TEND LESS TO BE THOSE 0.65 OF 295 OTHER THAN WHERE THE ONLY KIN GROUP PRESENT IS A KINDRED OR ELSE BILATERAL DESCENT IS INFERRED (289)	0 104 87 191 XSQ= 40.38 PHI= -0.325 XP = 0.
196	TILT MORE TOWARD BEING THOSE 0.81 OF 59 WHERE INDIVIDUAL RIGHTS IN REAL PROPERTY, AND RULES FOR INHERITANCE, ARE PRESENT (194)	196	TILT LESS TOWARD BEING THOSE 0.65 OF 214 WHERE INDIVIDUAL RIGHTS IN REAL PROPERTY, AND RULES FOR INHERITANCE, ARE PRESENT (194)	48 140 11 74 XSQ= 4.76 PHI= 0.132 XP = 0.0291
197	TILT MORE TOWARD BEING THOSE 0.96 OF 48 WHERE RULES FOR THE INHERITANCE OF REAL PROPERTY, IF PRESENT, FAVOR EITHER THE MALE HEIR OR LINE, OR THE FEMALE HEIR OR LINE (165)	197	TILT LESS TOWARD BEING THOSE 0.81 OF 140 WHERE RULES FOR THE INHERITANCE OF REAL PROPERTY, IF PRESENT, FAVOR EITHER THE MALE HEIR OR LINE, OR THE FEMALE HEIR OR LINE (165)	46 113 2 27 XSQ= 5.16 PHI= 0.166 XP = 0.0231
198	TILT LESS TOWARD BEING THOSE 0.78 OF 46 WHERE RULES FOR THE INHERITANCE OF REAL PROPERTY, IF PRESENT, FAVOR THE MALE HEIR OR LINE, RATHER THAN THE FEMALE (144)	198	TILT MORE TOWARD BEING THOSE 0.92 OF 113 WHERE RULES FOR THE INHERITANCE OF REAL PROPERTY, IF PRESENT, FAVOR THE MALE HEIR OR LINE, RATHER THAN THE FEMALE (144)	36 104 10 9 XSQ= 4.66 PHI= -0.171 XP = 0.0309
207	TILT TOWARD BEING THOSE 0.69 OF 29 WHERE MARITAL RESIDENCE IS MATRILOCAL OR UXORILOCAL, RATHER THAN AMBILOCAL OR NEOLOCAL (64)	207	TILT TOWARD BEING THOSE 0.56 OF 94 WHERE MARITAL RESIDENCE IS AMBILOCAL OR NEOLOCAL, RATHER THAN MATRILOCAL OR UXORILOCAL (64)	20 41 9 53 XSQ= 4.73 PHI= 0.196 XP = 0.0297

210	TEND LESS TO BE THOSE WHERE MARITAL RESIDENCE IS PATRILOCAL, RATHER THAN MATRILOCAL (169)	0.69 OF 64	210	TEND MORE TO BE THOSE WHERE MARITAL RESIDENCE IS PATRILOCAL, RATHER THAN MATRILOCAL (169)	0.93 OF 127	44 118 20 9 XSQ= 17.46 PHI= -0.302 XP = 0.0000
214	TEND LESS TO BE THOSE WHERE FIRST COUSIN MARRIAGE, IF PERMITTED, IS OTHER THAN UNILATERAL (144)	0.64 OF 39	214	TEND MORE TO BE THOSE WHERE FIRST COUSIN MARRIAGE, IF PERMITTED, IS OTHER THAN UNILATERAL (144)	0.90 OF 126	14 13 25 113 XSQ= 12.43 PHI= 0.274 XP = 0.0004
221	TILT LESS TOWARD BEING THOSE WHERE MATRILATERAL CROSS-COUSIN MARRIAGE IS NOT PRESCRIBED OR PREFERRED (335)	0.83 OF 81	221	TILT MORE TOWARD BEING THOSE WHERE MATRILATERAL CROSS-COUSIN MARRIAGE IS NOT PRESCRIBED OR PREFERRED (335)	0.93 OF 278	14 20 67 258 XSQ= 6.32 PHI= 0.133 XP = 0.0120
240	LEAN TOWARD BEING THOSE WHERE THE FAMILY, IF EXTENDED, IS LARGE, RATHER THAN SMALL OR STEM (78)	0.55 OF 51	240	LEAN TOWARD BEING THOSE WHERE THE FAMILY, IF EXTENDED, IS SMALL OR STEM, RATHER THAN LARGE (135)	0.69 OF 155	28 48 23 107 XSQ= 8.44 PHI= 0.202 XP = 0.0037
241	IN ALL CASES ARE THOSE WHERE THE FAMILY, IF EXTENDED, IS LARGE OR SMALL, RATHER THAN STEM (187)	1.00 OF 51	241	LEAN LESS TOWARD BEING THOSE WHERE THE FAMILY, IF EXTENDED, IS LARGE OR SMALL, RATHER THAN STEM (187)	0.83 OF 155	51 129 0 26 XSQ= 8.33 PHI= 0.201 XP = 0.0039
280	TILT TOWARD BEING THOSE WHERE THE COMPOSITE FERTILITY LEVEL IS LOW (12) MN	0.86 OF 7	280	TILT TOWARD BEING THOSE WHERE THE COMPOSITE FERTILITY LEVEL IS HIGH (13) MN	0.67 OF 18	1 12 6 6 XSQ= 3.64 PHI= -0.382 EP = 0.0302
300	TILT TOWARD BEING THOSE WHERE THE POST-PARTUM SEX TABOO LASTS LONGER THAN SIX MONTHS (51)	0.62 OF 29	300	TILT TOWARD BEING THOSE WHERE THE POST-PARTUM SEX TABOO LASTS SIX MONTHS OR LESS (73)	0.65 OF 95	18 33 11 62 XSQ= 5.77 PHI= 0.216 XP = 0.0163
336	LEAN TOWARD BEING THOSE WHERE THE TOTAL POSITIVE PRESSURE TOWARD DEVELOPING RESPONSIBLE BEHAVIOR IN THE CHILD IS LOW (32) B-B-C	0.71 OF 21	336	LEAN TOWARD BEING THOSE WHERE THE TOTAL POSITIVE PRESSURE TOWARD DEVELOPING RESPONSIBLE BEHAVIOR IN THE CHILD IS HIGH (43) B-B-C	0.68 OF 53	6 36 15 17 XSQ= 7.95 PHI= -0.328 XP = 0.0048
337	TILT TOWARD BEING THOSE WHERE THE CHILD'S INFERRED ANXIETY OVER NON-PERFORMANCE OF RESPONSIBLE BEHAVIOR IS LOW (35) B-B-C	0.70 OF 20	337	TILT TOWARD BEING THOSE WHERE THE CHILD'S INFERRED ANXIETY OVER NON-PERFORMANCE OF RESPONSIBLE BEHAVIOR IS HIGH (38) B-B-C	0.60 OF 52	6 31 14 21 XSQ= 3.96 PHI= -0.234 XP = 0.0467

339	DRIFT TOWARD BEING THOSE WHERE THE CHILD'S INFERRED CONFLICT REGARDING RESPONSIBLE BEHAVIOR IS LOW (42) B-B-C	0.75 OF 20	339	DRIFT TOWARD BEING THOSE WHERE THE CHILD'S INFERRED CONFLICT REGARDING RESPONSIBLE BEHAVIOR IS HIGH (31) B-B-C	0.50 OF 52	5 26 15 26 XSQ= 2.73 PHI= -0.195 XP = 0.0983
352	DRIFT TOWARD BEING THOSE WHERE THE TOTAL POSITIVE PRESSURE TOWARD DEVELOPING OBEDIENT BEHAVIOR IN THE CHILD IS LOW (28) B-B-C	0.58 OF 19	352	DRIFT TOWARD BEING THOSE WHERE THE TOTAL POSITIVE PRESSURE TOWARD DEVELOPING OBEDIENT BEHAVIOR IN THE CHILD IS HIGH (44) B-B-C	0.67 OF 52	8 35 11 17 XSQ= 2.72 PHI= -0.196 XP = 0.0991
393	DRIFT TOWARD BEING THOSE WHERE EXTRAMARITAL COITUS IS PERMITTED, RATHER THAN PUNISHED (41) F-B	0.70 OF 20	393	DRIFT TOWARD BEING THOSE WHERE EXTRAMARITAL COITUS IS PUNISHED, RATHER THAN PERMITTED (43) F-B	0.58 OF 64	6 37 14 27 XSQ= 3.67 PHI= -0.209 XP = 0.0554
397	IN ALL CASES ARE THOSE WHERE SEX DISABILITY IS ABSENT (42) JKH	1.00 OF 15	397	TILT LESS TOWARD BEING THOSE WHERE SEX DISABILITY IS ABSENT (42) JKH	0.66 OF 41	0 14 15 27 XSQ= 5.13 PHI= -0.303 XP = 0.0235
399	DRIFT TOWARD BEING THOSE WHERE INTENSITY OF CASTRATION ANXIETY IS LOW (22) WNS	0.71 OF 14	399	DRIFT TOWARD BEING THOSE WHERE INTENSITY OF CASTRATION ANXIETY IS HIGH (23) WNS	0.61 OF 31	4 19 10 12 XSQ= 2.93 PHI= -0.255 XP = 0.0872
435	IN ALL CASES ARE THOSE WHERE ABANDONMENT OF THE HOUSE OF THE DEAD IS NOT PRACTICED (19) LWS	1.00 OF 8	435	LEAN TOWARD BEING THOSE WHERE ABANDONMENT OF THE HOUSE OF THE DEAD IS PRACTICED (12) LWS	0.55 OF 22	0 12 8 10 XSQ= 5.18 PHI= -0.415 EP = 0.0100
451	TILT TOWARD BEING THOSE WHERE TOTEMISM IS PRESENT (15) LWS	0.88 OF 8	451	TILT TOWARD BEING THOSE WHERE TOTEMISM IS UNIMPORTANT OR ABSENT (12) LWS	0.58 OF 19	7 8 1 11 XSQ= 3.04 PHI= 0.336 EP = 0.0433
480	DRIFT TOWARD BEING THOSE WHERE COMPLEXITY OF ARTISTIC DESIGN IS HIGH (14) HB	0.78 OF 9	480	DRIFT TOWARD BEING THOSE WHERE COMPLEXITY OF ARTISTIC DESIGN IS LOW (15) HB	0.65 OF 20	7 7 2 13 XSQ= 3.00 PHI= 0.321 EP = 0.0502

179 CULTURES
WHERE THE COMMUNITY IS
STRUCTURED ON A NON-CLAN BASIS AND
COMMONLY EXOGAMOUS (42)

179 CULTURES
WHERE THE COMMUNITY IS OTHER THAN
STRUCTURED ON A NON-CLAN BASIS AND
COMMONLY EXOGAMOUS (340)

BACKGROUND ON PAGE 105

BOTH SUBJECT AND PREDICATE

42 IN LEFT COLUMN

ALBANIANS	ALCRESE	ATSUGEWI	BERGDAMA	BHIL	BOTOCUDO	CHENCHU	CHEYENNE	CHORCTI	CHORTI
CROW	DIERI	GANDA	GROS VENTRE	HERERO	KOL	KONSO	KOREANS	KUNG	KURTATCHI
KWAKIUTL	LAPPS	LEPCHA	LOZI	MANGAIANS	MATACO	NYAKYUSA	ONA	ORAON	SAMOYED
SANTAL	SEMANG	TEDA	TENINO	TETON	TURKANA	TWANA	WAPISHANA	YABARANA	YAHGAN
YUKAGHIR	YUROK								

340 IN RIGHT COLUMN

18 EXCLUDED BECAUSE UNASCERTAINED

15	LEAN TOWARD BEING THOSE WHERE THE LATITUDE IS TWENTY DEGREES OR GREATER (183) — 0.69 OF 42	15	LEAN TOWARD BEING THOSE WHERE THE LATITUDE IS LESS THAN TWENTY DEGREES (217) — 0.57 OF 340	29 147 13 193 XSQ= 9.01 PHI= 0.154 XP = 0.0027
36	DRIFT LESS TOWARD BEING THOSE WHERE THE NATURAL ENVIRONMENT IS OTHER THAN 'VERY HARSH,' OR SUB-TROPICAL BUSH, OR TEMPERATE GRASSLAND (292) FWM — 0.60 OF 42	36	DRIFT MORE TOWARD BEING THOSE WHERE THE NATURAL ENVIRONMENT IS OTHER THAN 'VERY HARSH,' OR SUB-TROPICAL BUSH, OR TEMPERATE GRASSLAND (292) FWM — 0.74 OF 340	17 89 25 251 XSQ= 3.13 PHI= 0.091 XP = 0.0767
44	LEAN TOWARD BEING THOSE WHERE SETTLEMENTS ARE NON-FIXED (110) — 0.56 OF 39	44	LEAN TOWARD BEING THOSE WHERE SETTLEMENTS ARE FIXED (222) — 0.70 OF 280	17 197 22 83 XSQ= 9.93 PHI= -0.176 XP = 0.0016
46	TEND LESS TO BE THOSE OTHER THAN WHERE SETTLEMENTS ARE NON-FIXED AND MOVEMENT IS NOMADIC (260) — 0.54 OF 39	46	TEND MORE TO BE THOSE OTHER THAN WHERE SETTLEMENTS ARE NON-FIXED AND MOVEMENT IS NOMADIC (260) — 0.81 OF 280	18 52 21 228 XSQ= 13.64 PHI= 0.207 XP = 0.0002
51	TEND TO BE THOSE WHERE SUBSISTENCE IS PRIMARILY BY FOOD GATHERING -- I. E., HUNTING, FISHING, OR COLLECTING -- RATHER THAN FOOD PRODUCTION (147) — 0.62 OF 42	51	TEND TO BE THOSE WHERE SUBSISTENCE IS PRIMARILY BY FOOD PRODUCTION -- I. E., AGRICULTURE OR HUSBANDRY -- RATHER THAN BY GATHERING (253) — 0.67 OF 340	16 227 26 113 XSQ= 12.06 PHI= -0.178 XP = 0.0005

56	DRIFT TOWARD BEING THOSE 0.60 OF 10 WHERE FOOD PRODUCTION IS BY INCIPIENT FOOD PRODUCTION, RATHER THAN BY SIMPLE AGRICULTURE (46)	56	DRIFT TOWARD BEING THOSE 0.72 OF 132 WHERE FOOD PRODUCTION IS BY SIMPLE AGRICULTURE, RATHER THAN BY INCIPIENT FOOD PRODUCTION (101)	4 95 6 37 XSQ= 3.11 PHI= -0.148 XP = 0.0777
81	TILT MORE TOWARD BEING THOSE 0.85 OF 26 WHERE NO CITY OR TOWN IS PRESENT, AND THE AVERAGE COMMUNITY SIZE IS SMALLER THAN 200 (135)	81	TILT LESS TOWARD BEING THOSE 0.58 OF 194 WHERE NO CITY OR TOWN IS PRESENT, AND THE AVERAGE COMMUNITY SIZE IS SMALLER THAN 200 (135)	4 82 22 112 XSQ= 5.88 PHI= -0.163 XP = 0.0153
82	LEAN LESS TOWARD BEING THOSE 0.58 OF 26 WHERE A CITY OR TOWN IS PRESENT, OR THE AVERAGE COMMUNITY SIZE IS FIFTY OR GREATER (178)	82	LEAN MORE TOWARD BEING THOSE 0.82 OF 194 WHERE A CITY OR TOWN IS PRESENT, OR THE AVERAGE COMMUNITY SIZE IS FIFTY OR GREATER (178)	15 159 11 35 XSQ= 6.76 PHI= -0.175 XP = 0.0093
83	DRIFT MORE TOWARD BEING THOSE 0.92 OF 24 WHERE, WITH NO CITY AND NO TOWN PRESENT, THE AVERAGE COMMUNITY SIZE IS SMALLER THAN 200, RATHER THAN BETWEEN 200 AND 999 (135)	83	DRIFT LESS TOWARD BEING THOSE 0.73 OF 154 WHERE, WITH NO CITY AND NO TOWN PRESENT, THE AVERAGE COMMUNITY SIZE IS SMALLER THAN 200, RATHER THAN BETWEEN 200 AND 999 (135)	2 42 22 112 XSQ= 3.05 PHI= -0.131 XP = 0.0808
85	DRIFT MORE TOWARD BEING THOSE 0.91 OF 32 WHERE THE LEVEL OF POLITICAL INTEGRATION IS THE MINIMAL STATE, THE AUTONOMOUS COMMUNITY, OR THE FAMILY (234) GPM	85	DRIFT LESS TOWARD BEING THOSE 0.75 OF 255 WHERE THE LEVEL OF POLITICAL INTEGRATION IS THE MINIMAL STATE, THE AUTONOMOUS COMMUNITY, OR THE FAMILY (234) GPM	3 63 29 192 XSQ= 2.96 PHI= -0.102 XP = 0.0855
98	DRIFT LESS TOWARD BEING THOSE 0.59 OF 39 WHERE THE HIERARCHY OF LOCAL JURISDICTION HAS FOUR OR THREE LEVELS (238) GES,EA	98	DRIFT MORE TOWARD BEING THOSE 0.73 OF 279 WHERE THE HIERARCHY OF LOCAL JURISDICTION HAS FOUR OR THREE LEVELS (238) GES,EA	23 205 16 74 XSQ= 2.87 PHI= -0.095 XP = 0.0904
131	TILT LESS TOWARD BEING THOSE 0.70 OF 23 WHERE THE CONSTRUCTION OF PERMANENT HOUSES OR THE ERECTION OF TEMPORARY DWELLINGS IS MAINLY DONE BY MALES (136)	131	TILT MORE TOWARD BEING THOSE 0.89 OF 131 WHERE THE CONSTRUCTION OF PERMANENT HOUSES OR THE ERECTION OF TEMPORARY DWELLINGS IS MAINLY DONE BY MALES (136)	16 117 7 14 XSQ= 4.91 PHI= -0.179 XP = 0.0267
188	LEAN TOWARD BEING THOSE 0.57 OF 42 WHERE THE KIN GROUP IS EXCLUSIVELY COGNATIC (148)	188	LEAN TOWARD BEING THOSE 0.66 OF 340 WHERE THE KIN GROUP IS OTHER THAN EXCLUSIVELY COGNATIC (252)	24 117 18 223 XSQ= 7.35 PHI= 0.139 XP = 0.0067
192	LEAN LESS TOWARD BEING THOSE 0.55 OF 42 OTHER THAN WHERE THE ONLY KIN GROUP PRESENT IS A KINDRED OR ELSE BILATERAL DESCENT IS INFERRED (289)	192	LEAN MORE TOWARD BEING THOSE 0.75 OF 340 OTHER THAN WHERE THE ONLY KIN GROUP PRESENT IS A KINDRED OR ELSE BILATERAL DESCENT IS INFERRED (289)	19 85 23 255 XSQ= 6.74 PHI= 0.133 XP = 0.0094

```
196  TILT LESS TOWARD BEING THOSE   0.52 OF  33      196  TILT MORE TOWARD BEING THOSE   0.71 OF 240         17   171
     WHERE INDIVIDUAL RIGHTS IN REAL PROPERTY,             WHERE INDIVIDUAL RIGHTS IN REAL PROPERTY,          16    69
     AND RULES FOR INHERITANCE,                            AND RULES FOR INHERITANCE,                    XSQ=     4.39
     ARE PRESENT  (194)                                    ARE PRESENT  (194)                            PHI=   -0.127
                                                                                                         XP =   0.0362

213  LEAN MORE TOWARD BEING THOSE   0.79 OF  42      213  LEAN LESS TOWARD BEING THOSE   0.51 OF 317          9   156
     WHERE FIRST COUSIN MARRIAGE IS                        WHERE FIRST COUSIN MARRIAGE IS                     33   161
     NOT PERMITTED  (198)                                  NOT PERMITTED  (198)                          XSQ=    10.43
                                                                                                         PHI=   -0.170
                                                                                                         XP =   0.0012

220  DRIFT MORE TOWARD BEING THOSE  0.86 OF  42      220  DRIFT LESS TOWARD BEING THOSE  0.72 OF 317          6    89
     WHERE FIRST COUSIN MARRIAGE                           WHERE FIRST COUSIN MARRIAGE                        36   228
     IN SOME FORM OR OTHER                                 IN SOME FORM OR OTHER                         XSQ=     2.95
     IS NOT PRESCRIBED OR PREFERRED  (273)                 IS NOT PRESCRIBED OR PREFERRED  (273)         PHI=   -0.091
                                                                                                         XP =   0.0859

240  TILT MORE TOWARD BEING THOSE   0.88 OF  24      240  TILT LESS TOWARD BEING THOSE   0.60 OF 182          3    73
     WHERE THE FAMILY, IF EXTENDED, IS                     WHERE THE FAMILY, IF EXTENDED, IS                  21   109
     SMALL OR STEM, RATHER THAN                            SMALL OR STEM, RATHER THAN                    XSQ=     5.81
     LARGE  (135)                                          LARGE  (135)                                  PHI=   -0.168
                                                                                                         XP =   0.0160

242  DRIFT MORE TOWARD BEING THOSE  0.90 OF  42      242  DRIFT LESS TOWARD BEING THOSE  0.78 OF 336         38   261
     WHERE MARRIAGE IS                                     WHERE MARRIAGE IS                                   4    75
     COMMONLY OR OCCASIONALLY POLYGYNOUS,                  COMMONLY OR OCCASIONALLY POLYGYNOUS,          XSQ=     2.97
     RATHER THAN MONOGAMOUS  (314)                         RATHER THAN MONOGAMOUS  (314)                 PHI=    0.089
                                                                                                         XP =   0.0851

310  TILT TOWARD BEING THOSE        0.88 OF   8      310  TILT TOWARD BEING THOSE        0.64 OF  33          1    21
     WHERE ANAL SOCIALIZATION ANXIETY                      WHERE ANAL SOCIALIZATION ANXIETY                    7    12
     IS LOW  (19) W-C                                      IS HIGH  (22) W-C                             XSQ=     4.87
                                                                                                         PHI=   -0.345
                                                                                                         XP =   0.0273

377  TILT MORE TOWARD BEING THOSE   0.90 OF  39      377  TILT LESS TOWARD BEING THOSE   0.73 OF 273          4    73
     WHERE MALE GENITAL MUTILATION                         WHERE MALE GENITAL MUTILATION                      35   200
     IS ABSENT  (242)                                      IS ABSENT  (242)                              XSQ=     4.14
                                                                                                         PHI=   -0.115
                                                                                                         XP =   0.0419

391  DRIFT TOWARD BEING THOSE       0.70 OF  23      391  DRIFT TOWARD BEING THOSE       0.53 OF 152         16    72
     WHERE PREMARITAL SEX RELATIONS ARE                    WHERE PREMARITAL SEX RELATIONS ARE                  7    80
     STRONGLY PUNISHED AND IN FACT RARE, OR                PUNISHED ONLY IF PREGNANCY RESULTS, OR        XSQ=     3.10
     WEAKLY PUNISHED AND                                   FREELY PERMITTED  (90) JTW,EA                 PHI=    0.133
     IN FACT NOT RARE  (89) JTW,EA                                                                       XP =   0.0783

451  DRIFT TOWARD BEING THOSE       0.83 OF   6      451  DRIFT TOWARD BEING THOSE       0.67 OF  21          1    14
     WHERE TOTEMISM IS                                     WHERE TOTEMISM IS                                   5     7
     UNIMPORTANT OR ABSENT  (12) LWS                       PRESENT  (15) LWS                             XSQ=     2.92
                                                                                                         PHI=   -0.329
                                                                                                         EP =   0.0602
```

180 CULTURES
WHERE THE COMMUNITY IS
COMMONLY EXOGAMOUS, RATHER THAN
NON-EXOGAMOUS (124)

180 CULTURES
WHERE THE COMMUNITY IS
COMMONLY NON-EXOGAMOUS, RATHER THAN
EXOGAMOUS (258)

BACKGROUND ON PAGE 105

BOTH SUBJECT AND PREDICATE

124 IN LEFT COLUMN

AJIE	ALBANIANS	ALORESE	AMBA	ARANDA	ATSUGEWI	BABWA	BANDA	BARI	BAYA
BEJA	BENGALI	BERGDAMA	BETE	BHIL	BHUIYA	BIRIFOR	BOTOCUDO	BURYAT	CHAGGA
CHENCHU	CHEYENNE	CHOROTI	CHORTI	COORG	CROW	DAGUR	DIEGUENO	DIERI	DOBUANS
DOGON	DOROBO	ENGA	FANG	GANDA	GISU	GOND	GROS VENTRE	HAIDA	HAZARA
HEHE	HERERO	HO	KALMYK	KAPAUKU	KARIERA	KATAB	KAZAK	KERAKI	KHEVSUR
KIKUYU	KISSI	KOL	KONSO	KOREANS	KUNG	KURTATCHI	KWAKIUTL	LAPPS	LAU
LEPCHA	LIFU	LOLO	LOZI	LUO	MAMVU	MANCHU	MANGAIANS	MATACO	MATAKAM
MBUNDU	MBUTI	MIN CHINESE	MIWOK	MONGO	MURINBATA	MURNGIN	NAMA	NDEMBU	NOMLAKI
NUER	NYAKYUSA	NYANEKA	OJIBWA	ONA	ORAON	PENDE	REGEIBAT	RIFFIANS	RWALA
SAMOYED	SANDAWE	SANTAL	SEMANG	SEMINOLE	SENIANG	SOMALI	SWAZI	TALLENSI	TEDA
TENINO	TETON	THONGA	TIV	TODA	TOLOWA	TUCANO	TUCUNA	TURKANA	TWANA
VEDDA	WANTOAT	WAPISHANA	WIKMUNKAN	WITOTO	WOGEO	WOLOF	YABARANA	YAGUA	YAHGAN
YAKUT	YOMBE	YUKAGHIR	YUROK						

258 IN RIGHT COLUMN

ABIPON	ABOR	AINU	AKHA	ALACALUF	AMERICANS	ANDAMANESE	APINAYE	ARAPESH	ARAUCANIANS
ARYANS	ASHANTI	ATAYAL	AWEIKOMA	AYMARA	AZANDE	AZTEC	BACAIRI	BAJUN	BALINESE
BAMBARA	BAMILEKE	BARABRA	BASQUES	BASSERI	BATAK	BELU	BEMBA	BLACK CARIB	BOERS
BORORO	BRAZILIANS	BULGARIANS	BUNLAP	BURMESE	BURUSHO	CAGABA	CALLINAGO	CAMAYURA	CAMBA
CAMBODIANS	CARAJA	CARIB	CARINYA	CAYAPA	CHAMACOCO	CHEREMIS	CHERKESS	CHEROKEE	CHINANTEC
CHIR-APACHE	CHIRIGUANO	CHOCO	CHUKCHEE	COCHITI	COMANCHE	COPR ESKIMO	CREE	CREEK	CUNA
CZECHS	DARD	DELAWARE	DILLING	DUSUN	DUTCH	EGYPTIANS	ELLICE	EYAK	FON
FOX	FUTAJALONKE	GARO	GILBERTESE	GILYAK	GOAJIRO	GUAHIBO	GURE	HANO	HANUNOO
HASANIA	HASINAI	HAVASUPAI	HAWAIIANS	HUICHOL	HUKUNDIKA	HURON	HUTSUL	IBAN	ICELANDERS
IFUGAO	ILA	INCA	INGALIK	INGASSANA	IRISH	JAPANESE	JAVANESE	JEMEZ	JIVARO
JUKUN	KABYLE	KACHIN	KAREN	KASKA	KERALA	KHALKA	KHASI	KIOW-APACHE	KOHISTANI
KORYAK	KPE	KUBA	KUMYK	KUTENAI	LAKALAI	LAKHER	LAMBA	LAMET	LANGO
LESU	LHOTA NAGA	LUBA	MACASSARESE	MAGUZAWA	MALAYS	MAM	MAMBILA	MANUS	MAORI
MARGI	MARICOPA	MARQUESANS	MARSHALLESE	MASAI	MAYA	MNONG GAR	MAZATECO	MBUGWE	MENDE
MERINA	MIAO	MINANGKABAU	MINCHIA	MISKITO	MONGUOR	MOSSI	MOTA	MENTAWEI	
MUNDURUCU	MZAB	NABESNA	NAMBICUARA	NANDI	NASKAPI	NATCHEZ	NAVAHO	NGONI	NICOBARESE
NUNIVAK	NUPE	NURI	NYARO	NYORO	OKINAWANS	OMAHA	ONTONG-JAVA	PAIWAN	PALAUANS
PAPAGO	PARAUJANO	PATHAN	PAWNEE	PENOBSCOT	PONAPEANS	PORTUGUESE	PUKAPUKA	PURARI	PURUM
RAROIANS	ROMANS	ROTUMANS	RUNDI	SAGADA	SAMOANS	SANPOIL	SARAMACCA	SARSI	SELUNG
SERBS	SERI	SHERENTE	SHILLUK	SHLUH	SIMBOESE	SINDHI	SINHALESE	SIRIONO	SIUAI
SIWANS	SONGHAI	SOTHO	SUBANUN	SYRIANS	TAGBANUA	TAMIL	TANALA	TANIMBARESE	TAOS
TAPIRAPE	TARAHUMARA	TAREUMIUT	TEHUELCHE	TENDA	TENETEHARA	TERA	TERENA	TESO	THAI
TIBETANS	TIGRINYA	TIKOPIA	TIMBIRA	TIMUCUA	TIWI	TOKELAU	TORAJA	TRISTAN	TROBRIAND

TRUKESE	TRUMAI	TSHIMSHIAN	TUBATULABAL	TUNEBO	TUPINAMBA	TZELTAL	ULAWANS	UTE	VENCA
VIETNAMESE	WAICA	WALLCONS	WAROPEN	WARRAU	WASHO	WICHITA	WINNEBAGO	WOLEAIANS	WUTE
YAKO	YAC	YAPESE	YARURO	YOKUTS	YORUBA	YUKI	ZUNI		

18 EXCLUDED BECAUSE UNASCERTAINEC

No.			No.			
3	TEND LESS TO BE THCSE LOCATED OUTSIDE OF AFRICA (320)	0.68 OF 124	3	TEND MORE TO BE THOSE LOCATED OUTSIDE OF AFRICA (320)	0.85 CF 258	40 39 84 219 XSQ= 13.98 PHI= 0.191 XP = 0.0002
9	TILT MORE TOWARC BEING THCSE LOCATED CUTSIDE CF SOUTH AMERICA (335)	0.90 OF 124	9	TILT LESS TOWARD BEING THOSE LOCATED OUTSIDE OF SOUTH AMERICA (335)	0.82 OF 258	12 47 112 211 XSQ= 4.05 PHI= -0.103 XP = 0.0443
44	TEND LESS TO BE THCSE WHERE SETTLEMENTS ARE FIXEC (222)	0.54 OF 107	44	TEND MORE TO BE THOSE WHERE SETTLEMENTS ARE FIXED (222)	0.74 CF 212	58 156 49 56 XSQ= 11.23 PHI= -0.188 XP = 0.0008
46	TEND LESS TO BE THCSE OTHER THAN WHERE SETTLEMENTS ARE NCN-FIXED AND MCVEMENT IS NOMADIC (260)	0.66 OF 107	46	TEND MORE TO BE THOSE OTHER THAN WHERE SETTLEMENTS ARE NON-FIXED AND MOVEMENT IS NOMADIC (260)	0.84 OF 212	36 34 71 178 XSQ= 11.86 PHI= 0.193 XP = 0.0006
73	TEND TC BE THOSE WHERE WEAVING IS ABSENT (130)	0.71 OF 83	73	TEND TO BE THOSE WHERE WEAVING IS PRESENT (118)	0.56 CF 157	24 88 59 69 XSQ= 14.99 PHI= -0.250 XP = 0.0001
74	DRIFT LESS TCWARC BEING THCSE WHERE PCTTERY IS PRESENT (145)	0.51 OF 78	74	DRIFT MORE TOWARD BEING THCSE WHERE POTTERY IS PRESENT (145)	0.64 OF 152	40 98 38 54 XSQ= 3.21 PHI= -0.118 XP = 0.0733
79	TILT MORE TOWARC BEING THCSE WHERE NC CITY IS PRESENT (201)	0.97 OF 74	79	TILT LESS TOWARD BEING THOSE WHERE NO CITY IS PRESENT (201)	0.86 CF 146	2 21 72 125 XSQ= 5.96 PHI= -0.165 XP = 0.0146

80	LEAN MORE TOWARD BEING THOSE 0.95 OF 74 WHERE NO CITY OR TOWN IS PRESENT (185)	80	LEAN LESS TOWARD BEING THOSE 0.77 OF 146 WHERE NO CITY OR TOWN IS PRESENT (185)	4 33 70 113 XSQ= 9.19 PHI= -0.204 XP = 0.0024
81	TEND MORE TO BE THOSE 0.80 OF 74 WHERE NO CITY OR TOWN IS PRESENT, AND THE AVERAGE COMMUNITY SIZE IS SMALLER THAN 200 (135)	81	TEND LESS TO BE THOSE 0.51 OF 146 WHERE NO CITY OR TOWN IS PRESENT, AND THE AVERAGE COMMUNITY SIZE IS SMALLER THAN 200 (135)	15 71 59 75 XSQ= 15.42 PHI= -0.265 XP = 0.0001
82	LEAN LESS TOWARD BEING THOSE 0.68 OF 74 WHERE A CITY OR TOWN IS PRESENT, OR THE AVERAGE COMMUNITY SIZE IS FIFTY OR GREATER (178)	82	LEAN MORE TOWARD BEING THOSE 0.85 OF 146 WHERE A CITY OR TOWN IS PRESENT, OR THE AVERAGE COMMUNITY SIZE IS FIFTY OR GREATER (178)	50 124 24 22 XSQ= 7.93 PHI= -0.190 XP = 0.0049
83	TILT MORE TOWARD BEING THOSE 0.84 OF 70 WHERE, WITH NO CITY AND NO TOWN PRESENT, THE AVERAGE COMMUNITY SIZE IS SMALLER THAN 200, RATHER THAN BETWEEN 200 AND 999 (135)	83	TILT LESS TOWARD BEING THOSE 0.69 OF 108 WHERE, WITH NO CITY AND NO TOWN PRESENT, THE AVERAGE COMMUNITY SIZE IS SMALLER THAN 200, RATHER THAN BETWEEN 200 AND 999 (135)	11 33 59 75 XSQ= 4.26 PHI= -0.155 XP = 0.0390
84	DRIFT MORE TOWARD BEING THOSE 0.92 OF 92 WHERE THE LEVEL OF POLITICAL INTEGRATION IS THE LITTLE STATE, THE MINIMAL STATE, THE AUTONOMOUS COMMUNITY, OR THE FAMILY (262) GPM	84	DRIFT LESS TOWARD BEING THOSE 0.83 OF 195 WHERE THE LEVEL OF POLITICAL INTEGRATION IS THE LITTLE STATE, THE MINIMAL STATE, THE AUTONOMOUS COMMUNITY, OR THE FAMILY (262) GPM	7 33 85 162 XSQ= 3.78 PHI= -0.115 XP = 0.0519
85	DRIFT MORE TOWARD BEING THOSE 0.84 OF 92 WHERE THE LEVEL OF POLITICAL INTEGRATION IS THE MINIMAL STATE, THE AUTONOMOUS COMMUNITY, OR THE FAMILY (234) GPM	85	DRIFT LESS TOWARD BEING THOSE 0.74 OF 195 WHERE THE LEVEL OF POLITICAL INTEGRATION IS THE MINIMAL STATE, THE AUTONOMOUS COMMUNITY, OR THE FAMILY (234) GPM	15 51 77 144 XSQ= 2.89 PHI= -0.100 XP = 0.0891
90	TILT MORE TOWARD BEING THOSE 0.89 OF 54 WHERE, IF A HEREDITARY HEADMANSHIP IS PRESENT, SUCCESSION IS PATRILINEAL, RATHER THAN MATRILINEAL (127)	90	TILT LESS TOWARD BEING THOSE 0.71 OF 107 WHERE, IF A HEREDITARY HEADMANSHIP IS PRESENT, SUCCESSION IS PATRILINEAL, RATHER THAN MATRILINEAL (127)	48 76 6 31 XSQ= 5.50 PHI= 0.185 XP = 0.0190
98	LEAN LESS TOWARD BEING THOSE 0.62 OF 107 WHERE THE HIERARCHY OF LOCAL JURISDICTION HAS FOUR OR THREE LEVELS (238) GES,EA	98	LEAN MORE TOWARD BEING THOSE 0.77 OF 211 WHERE THE HIERARCHY OF LOCAL JURISDICTION HAS FOUR OR THREE LEVELS (238) GES,EA	66 162 41 49 XSQ= 7.25 PHI= -0.151 XP = 0.0071
99	LEAN TOWARD BEING THOSE 0.54 OF 57 WHERE, WITH NATIONAL HIERARCHY ABSENT, THE HIERARCHY OF LOCAL JURISDICTION HAS TWO LEVELS (63) GES,EA	99	LEAN TOWARD BEING THOSE 0.69 OF 97 WHERE, WITH NATIONAL HIERARCHY ABSENT, THE HIERARCHY OF LOCAL JURISDICTION HAS FOUR OR THREE LEVELS (93) GES,EA	26 67 31 30 XSQ= 7.31 PHI= -0.218 XP = 0.0069

100	LEAN LESS TOWARD BEING THOSE 0.71 OF 107 WHERE HIERARCHIES ARE MORE COMPLEX THAN THE 'SIMPLEST,' I. E., MORE COMPLEX THAN TWO LOCAL LEVELS WITH NO NATIONAL LEVELS (267) GES,EA	100	LEAN MORE TOWARD BEING THOSE 0.86 OF 210 WHERE HIERARCHIES ARE MORE COMPLEX THAN THE 'SIMPLEST,' I. E., MORE COMPLEX THAN TWO LOCAL LEVELS WITH NO NATIONAL LEVELS (267) GES,EA	76 180 31 30 XSQ= 8.92 PHI= -0.168 XP = 0.0028
102	DRIFT TOWARD BEING THOSE 0.54 OF 119 WHERE CLASS STRATIFICATION IS ABSENT (180)	102	DRIFT TOWARD BEING THOSE 0.57 OF 248 WHERE CLASS STRATIFICATION IS PRESENT (203)	55 142 64 106 XSQ= 3.51 PHI= -0.098 XP = 0.0610
106	TILT TOWARD BEING THOSE 0.53 OF 55 WHERE CLASS STRATIFICATION, IF PRESENT, IS BASED ON WEALTH (77)	106	TILT TOWARD BEING THOSE 0.68 OF 142 WHERE CLASS STRATIFICATION, IF PRESENT, IS BASED ON SOMETHING OTHER THAN WEALTH (126)	29 46 26 96 XSQ= 6.12 PHI= 0.176 XP = 0.0134
107	DRIFT MORE TOWARD BEING THOSE 0.87 OF 55 WHERE CLASS STRATIFICATION, IF PRESENT, IS BASED ON SOMETHING OTHER THAN OCCUPATIONAL STATUS (160)	107	DRIFT LESS TOWARD BEING THOSE 0.75 OF 142 WHERE CLASS STRATIFICATION, IF PRESENT, IS BASED ON SOMETHING OTHER THAN OCCUPATIONAL STATUS (160)	7 36 48 106 XSQ= 3.00 PHI= -0.123 XP = 0.0832
131	LEAN LESS TOWARD BEING THOSE 0.75 OF 52 WHERE THE CONSTRUCTION OF PERMANENT HOUSES OR THE ERECTION OF TEMPORARY DWELLINGS IS MAINLY DONE BY MALES (136)	131	LEAN MORE TOWARD BEING THOSE 0.92 OF 102 WHERE THE CONSTRUCTION OF PERMANENT HOUSES OR THE ERECTION OF TEMPORARY DWELLINGS IS MAINLY DONE BY MALES (136)	39 94 13 8 XSQ= 7.21 PHI= -0.216 XP = 0.0072
143	DRIFT TOWARD BEING THOSE 0.50 OF 30 WHERE THE RATIO OF RESTITUTIVE TO REPRESSIVE SANCTIONS IS HIGH (20) WME	143	DRIFT TOWARD BEING THOSE 0.77 OF 22 WHERE THE RATIO OF RESTITUTIVE TO REPRESSIVE SANCTIONS IS MEDIUM OR LOW (32) WME	15 5 15 17 XSQ= 2.92 PHI= 0.237 XP = 0.0875
147	DRIFT TOWARD BEING THOSE 0.60 OF 15 WHERE CODIFIED LAWS ARE UNIMPORTANT OR ABSENT (13) LWS	147	DRIFT TOWARD BEING THOSE 0.76 OF 17 WHERE CODIFIED LAWS ARE PRESENT (20) LWS	6 13 9 4 XSQ= 3.01 PHI= -0.307 EP = 0.0702
152	IN ALL CASES ARE THOSE 1.00 OF 4 WHERE THE DIFFERENTIATION OF THE JURIDICAL AGENCY FROM THE MEDICAL AGENCY IS LOW (10) MJ	152	DRIFT TOWARD BEING THOSE 0.63 OF 16 WHERE THE DIFFERENTIATION OF THE JURIDICAL AGENCY FROM THE MEDICAL AGENCY IS HIGH (10) MJ	0 10 4 6 XSQ= 2.81 PHI= -0.375 EP = 0.0867
186	TEND TO BE THOSE 0.58 OF 124 WHERE THE KIN GROUP IS EXCLUSIVELY PATRILINEAL (150)	186	TEND TO BE THOSE 0.73 OF 258 WHERE THE KIN GROUP IS OTHER THAN EXCLUSIVELY PATRILINEAL (250)	72 70 52 188 XSQ= 33.00 PHI= 0.294 XP = 0.

187	TILT MORE TOWARD BEING THOSE WHERE THE KIN GROUP IS OTHER THAN EXCLUSIVELY MATRILINEAL (344)	0.92 OF 124	187	TILT LESS TOWARD BEING THOSE WHERE THE KIN GROUP IS OTHER THAN EXCLUSIVELY MATRILINEAL (344)	0.83 OF 257	10 43 114 214 XSQ= 4.55 PHI= -0.109 XP = 0.0330
188	TEND MORE TO BE THOSE WHERE THE KIN GROUP IS OTHER THAN EXCLUSIVELY COGNATIC (252)	0.81 OF 124	188	TEND LESS TO BE THOSE WHERE THE KIN GROUP IS OTHER THAN EXCLUSIVELY COGNATIC (252)	0.55 OF 258	24 117 100 141 XSQ= 23.20 PHI= -0.246 XP = 0.0000
190	TEND MORE TO BE THOSE WHERE THE KIN GROUP IS PATRILINEAL OR DOUBLE-DESCENT, RATHER THAN MATRILINEAL (186)	0.89 OF 99	190	TEND LESS TO BE THOSE WHERE THE KIN GROUP IS PATRILINEAL OR DOUBLE-DESCENT, RATHER THAN MATRILINEAL (186)	0.65 OF 137	88 89 11 48 XSQ= 16.29 PHI= 0.263 XP = 0.0001
192	TEND MORE TO BE THOSE OTHER THAN WHERE THE ONLY KIN GROUP PRESENT IS A KINDRED OR ELSE BILATERAL DESCENT IS INFERRED (289)	0.85 OF 124	192	TEND LESS TO BE THOSE OTHER THAN WHERE THE ONLY KIN GROUP PRESENT IS A KINDRED OR ELSE BILATERAL DESCENT IS INFERRED (289)	0.67 OF 258	19 85 105 173 XSQ= 12.25 PHI= -0.179 XP = 0.0005
197	TEND MORE TO BE THOSE WHERE RULES FOR THE INHERITANCE OF REAL PROPERTY, IF PRESENT, FAVOR EITHER THE MALE HEIR OR LINE, OR THE FEMALE HEIR OR LINE (165)	0.98 OF 59	197	TEND LESS TO BE THOSE WHERE RULES FOR THE INHERITANCE OF REAL PROPERTY, IF PRESENT, FAVOR EITHER THE MALE HEIR OR LINE, OR THE FEMALE HEIR OR LINE (165)	0.78 OF 129	58 101 1 28 XSQ= 10.94 PHI= 0.241 XP = 0.0009
201	TEND MORE TO BE THOSE WHERE MARITAL RESIDENCE IS NON-OPTIONAL, RATHER THAN AMBILOCAL OR NEOLOCAL (334)	0.95 OF 123	201	TEND LESS TO BE THOSE WHERE MARITAL RESIDENCE IS NON-OPTIONAL, RATHER THAN AMBILOCAL OR NEOLOCAL (334)	0.78 OF 257	117 201 6 56 XSQ= 16.21 PHI= 0.207 XP = 0.0001
204	TEND MORE TO BE THOSE WHERE MARITAL RESIDENCE IS PATRILOCAL, VIRILOCAL, OR AVUNCULOCAL, RATHER THAN AMBILOCAL OR NEOLOCAL (270)	0.95 OF 116	204	TEND LESS TO BE THOSE WHERE MARITAL RESIDENCE IS PATRILOCAL, VIRILOCAL, OR AVUNCULOCAL, RATHER THAN AMBILOCAL OR NEOLOCAL (270)	0.72 OF 203	110 147 6 56 XSQ= 22.27 PHI= 0.264 XP = 0.0000
209	TEND MORE TO BE THOSE WHERE MARITAL RESIDENCE IS PATRILOCAL, VIRILOCAL, OR AVUNCULOCAL, RATHER THAN MATRILOCAL OR UXORILOCAL (270)	0.94 OF 117	209	TEND LESS TO BE THOSE WHERE MARITAL RESIDENCE IS PATRILOCAL, VIRILOCAL, OR AVUNCULOCAL, RATHER THAN MATRILOCAL OR UXORILOCAL (270)	0.73 OF 201	110 147 7 54 XSQ= 19.48 PHI= 0.247 XP = 0.0000
210	TEND MORE TO BE THOSE WHERE MARITAL RESIDENCE IS PATRILOCAL, RATHER THAN MATRILOCAL (169)	0.98 OF 83	210	TEND LESS TO BE THOSE WHERE MARITAL RESIDENCE IS PATRILOCAL, RATHER THAN MATRILOCAL (169)	0.75 OF 108	81 81 2 27 XSQ= 16.89 PHI= 0.297 XP = 0.0000

234	TEND TO BE THOSE 0.64 OF 97 WHERE THE COUSIN TERMINOLOGY IS OF CROW, OMAHA, OR IROQUOIS TYPE, RATHER THAN ESKIMO OR HAWAIIAN TYPE (152)	234	TEND TO BE THOSE 0.60 OF 212 WHERE THE COUSIN TERMINOLOGY IS OF ESKIMO OR HAWAIIAN TYPE, RATHER THAN CROW, OMAHA, OR IROQUOIS TYPE (170)	62 84 35 128 XSQ= 14.80 PHI= 0.219 XP = 0.0001
242	LEAN MORE TOWARD BEING THOSE 0.89 OF 122 WHERE MARRIAGE IS COMMONLY OR OCCASIONALLY POLYGYNOUS, RATHER THAN MONOGAMOUS (314)	242	LEAN LESS TOWARD BEING THOSE 0.74 OF 256 WHERE MARRIAGE IS COMMONLY OR OCCASIONALLY POLYGYNOUS, RATHER THAN MONOGAMOUS (314)	109 190 13 66 XSQ= 10.54 PHI= 0.167 XP = 0.0012
255	TILT LESS TOWARD BEING THOSE 0.55 OF 11 WHERE GRANDPARENTAL AUTHORITY OVER PARENTS IS ABSENT (26) CA	255	TILT MORE TOWARD BEING THOSE 0.91 OF 22 WHERE GRANDPARENTAL AUTHORITY OVER PARENTS IS ABSENT (26) DA	5 2 6 20 XSQ= 3.83 PHI= 0.341 EP = 0.0274
259	TILT TOWARD BEING THOSE 0.78 OF 18 WHERE THE SEVERITY OF MOTHER-IN-LAW AVOIDANCE IS HIGH (26) WNS	259	TILT TOWARD BEING THOSE 0.57 OF 28 WHERE THE SEVERITY OF MOTHER-IN-LAW AVOIDANCE IS LOW (20) WNS	14 12 4 16 XSQ= 4.11 PHI= 0.299 XP = 0.0427
262	TEND MORE TO BE THOSE 0.91 OF 123 WHERE WIVES ARE OBTAINED BY MEANS INVOLVING THE PRESENCE OF SOME CONSIDERATION (305)	262	TEND LESS TO BE THOSE 0.72 OF 255 WHERE WIVES ARE OBTAINED BY MEANS INVOLVING THE PRESENCE OF SOME CONSIDERATION (305)	112 183 11 72 XSQ= 16.91 PHI= 0.212 XP = 0.0000
263	TEND MORE TO BE THOSE 0.76 OF 123 WHERE WIVES ARE OBTAINED BY RELATIVELY DIFFICULT MEANS, NAMELY BY BRIDE-PRICE, BRIDE-SERVICE, OR EXCHANGING A FEMALE RELATIVE (233)	263	TEND LESS TO BE THOSE 0.51 OF 255 WHERE WIVES ARE OBTAINED BY RELATIVELY DIFFICULT MEANS, NAMELY BY BRIDE-PRICE, BRIDE-SERVICE, OR EXCHANGING A FEMALE RELATIVE (233)	94 130 29 125 XSQ= 21.21 PHI= 0.237 XP = 0.0000
310	DRIFT TOWARD BEING THOSE 0.67 OF 15 WHERE ANAL SOCIALIZATION ANXIETY IS LOW (19) W-C	310	DRIFT TOWARD BEING THOSE 0.65 OF 26 WHERE ANAL SOCIALIZATION ANXIETY IS HIGH (22) W-C	5 17 10 9 XSQ= 2.75 PHI= -0.259 XP = 0.0975
337	DRIFT TOWARD BEING THOSE 0.66 OF 29 WHERE THE CHILD'S INFERRED ANXIETY OVER NON-PERFORMANCE OF RESPONSIBLE BEHAVIOR IS HIGH (38) B-B-C	337	DRIFT TOWARD BEING THOSE 0.58 OF 43 WHERE THE CHILD'S INFERRED ANXIETY OVER NON-PERFORMANCE OF RESPONSIBLE BEHAVIOR IS LOW (35) B-B-C	19 18 10 25 XSQ= 2.99 PHI= 0.204 XP = 0.0837
346	DRIFT TOWARD BEING THOSE 0.62 OF 29 WHERE THE CHILD'S INFERRED ANXIETY OVER PERFORMANCE OF SELF-RELIANT BEHAVIOR IS HIGH (37) B-B-C	346	DRIFT TOWARD BEING THOSE 0.61 OF 46 WHERE THE CHILD'S INFERRED ANXIETY OVER PERFORMANCE OF SELF-RELIANT BEHAVIOR IS LOW (39) B-B-C	18 18 11 28 XSQ= 2.89 PHI= 0.196 XP = 0.0893

```
347  DRIFT TOWARD BEING THOSE         0.62 OF  29      347  DRIFT TOWARD BEING THOSE         0.61 OF  46          18   18
     WHERE THE CHILD'S INFERRED CONFLICT                   WHERE THE CHILD'S INFERRED CONFLICT                   11   28
     REGARDING SELF-RELIANT BEHAVIOR                       REGARDING SELF-RELIANT BEHAVIOR                  XSQ=      2.89
     IS HIGH  (37) B-B-C                                   IS LOW  (39) B-B-C                               PHI=     0.196
                                                                                                            XP =    0.0893

370  DRIFT LESS TOWARD BEING THOSE  0.51 OF  78      370  DRIFT MORE TOWARD BEING THOSE  0.65 OF 161              38   56
     WHERE THE SEGREGATION OF ADOLESCENT BOYS              WHERE THE SEGREGATION OF ADOLESCENT BOYS              40  105
     IS ABSENT  (148)                                      IS ABSENT. (148)                                 XSQ=      3.71
                                                                                                            PHI=     0.125
                                                                                                            XP =    0.0540

377  DRIFT LESS TOWARD BEING THOSE  0.69 OF 106      377  DRIFT MORE TOWARD BEING THOSE  0.79 OF 206              33   44
     WHERE MALE GENITAL MUTILATION                         WHERE MALE GENITAL MUTILATION                         73  162
     IS ABSENT  (242)                                      IS ABSENT  (242)                                 XSQ=      3.09
                                                                                                            PHI=     0.100
                                                                                                            XP =    0.0788

392  DRIFT MORE TOWARD BEING THOSE  0.73 OF  63      392  DRIFT LESS TOWARD BEING THOSE  0.57 OF 112              46   64
     WHERE PREMARITAL SEX RELATIONS ARE                    WHERE PREMARITAL SEX RELATIONS ARE                    17   48
     STRONGLY PUNISHED AND IN FACT RARE, OR                STRONGLY PUNISHED AND IN FACT RARE, OR           XSQ=      3.70
     WEAKLY PUNISHED AND IN FACT NOT RARE, OR              WEAKLY PUNISHED AND IN FACT NOT RARE, OR         PHI=     0.145
     PUNISHED ONLY IF                                      PUNISHED ONLY IF                                 XP =    0.0545
     PREGNANCY RESULTS  (112) JTW,EA                       PREGNANCY RESULTS  (112) JTW,EA

417  DRIFT LESS TOWARD BEING THOSE  0.63 OF  19      417  DRIFT MORE TOWARD BEING THOSE  0.91 OF  23              12   21
     WHERE WARFARE IS                                      WHERE WARFARE IS                                       7    2
     PREVALENT  (34) LWS                                   PREVALENT  (34) LWS                              XSQ=      3.37
                                                                                                            PHI=    -0.283
                                                                                                            XP =    0.0665

434  DRIFT TOWARD BEING THOSE         0.71 OF  24      434  DRIFT TOWARD BEING THOSE         0.53 OF  43          17   20
     WHERE ASCETICISM IN MOURNING BEHAVIOR                 WHERE ASCETICISM IN MOURNING BEHAVIOR                  7   23
     IS HIGH  (37) JFG                                     IS LOW  (30) JFG                                 XSQ=      2.77
                                                                                                            PHI=     0.203
                                                                                                            XP =    0.0962

446  TILT TOWARD BEING THOSE          0.60 OF  15      446  TILT TOWARD BEING THOSE          0.77 OF  22           9    5
     WHERE WITCHCRAFT                                      WHERE WITCHCRAFT                                       6   17
     IS SIGNIFICANTLY PRESENT  (14) GES                    IS MODERATELY PRESENT OR                         XSQ=      3.80
                                                           ABSENT  (24) GES                                 PHI=     0.321
                                                                                                            EP =    0.0379

479  DRIFT TOWARD BEING THOSE         0.75 OF  12      479  DRIFT TOWARD BEING THOSE         0.61 OF  23           3   14
     WHERE THE NEED TO ACHIEVE,                            WHERE THE NEED TO ACHIEVE,                             9    9
     AS INFERRED FROM FOLKTALES,                           AS INFERRED FROM FOLKTALES,                      XSQ=      2.75
     IS LOW  (18) JV                                       IS HIGH  (18) JV                                 PHI=    -0.280
                                                                                                            EP =    0.0750
```

181 CULTURES
WHERE THE COMMUNITY IS
A DEME (45)

181 CULTURES
WHERE THE COMMUNITY IS OTHER THAN
A DEME (337)

BACKGROUND ON PAGE 105

BOTH SUBJECT AND PREDICATE

45 IN LEFT COLUMN

AINU	AWEIKOMA	AYMARA	BACAIRI	BALINESE	BASSERI	BURMESE	CARAJA	CARINYA	CHINANTEC
CHOCO	COCHITI	COMANCHE	COPR ESKIMO	CUNA	DUSUN	EGYPTIANS	HAVASUPAI	HUICHOL	HUKUNDIKA
HUTSUL	INCA	INGASSANA	JEMEZ	JIVARO	KUMYK	MINCHIA	PAIWAN	PARAUJANO	PAWNEE
PORTUGUESE	SINDHI	SIWANS	TAGBANUA	TAOS	TAPIRAPE	TARAHUMARA	TENETEHARA	TERA	TERENA
TOKELAU	TRISTAN	TUNEBO	WARRAU	YARURO					

337 IN RIGHT COLUMN

18 EXCLUDED BECAUSE UNASCERTAINED

	Left column (45)			Right column (337)		Statistics
3	LEAN MORE TOWARD BEING THOSE LOCATED OUTSIDE OF AFRICA (320)	0.98 OF 45	3	LEAN LESS TOWARD BEING THOSE LOCATED OUTSIDE OF AFRICA (320)	0.77 OF 337	1 78 / 44 259 / XSQ= 9.36 / PHI= -0.157 / XP = 0.0022
9	TEND LESS TO BE THOSE LOCATED OUTSIDE OF SOUTH AMERICA (335)	0.64 OF 45	9	TEND MORE TO BE THOSE LOCATED OUTSIDE OF SOUTH AMERICA (335)	0.87 OF 337	16 43 / 29 294 / XSQ= 14.10 / PHI= 0.192 / XP = 0.0002
33	DRIFT LESS TOWARD BEING THOSE WHERE THE NATURAL ENVIRONMENT IS OTHER THAN 'VERY HARSH,' I.E., DESERT, DESERT GRASSES AND SHRUBS, TUNDRA, OR HIGH PLATEAU STEPPE (341) FWM	0.76 OF 45	33	DRIFT MORE TOWARD BEING THOSE WHERE THE NATURAL ENVIRONMENT IS OTHER THAN 'VERY HARSH,' I.E., DESERT, DESERT GRASSES AND SHRUBS, TUNDRA, OR HIGH PLATEAU STEPPE (341) FWM	0.86 OF 337	11 46 / 34 291 / XSQ= 2.84 / PHI= 0.086 / XP = 0.0918
81	DRIFT TOWARD BEING THOSE WHERE A CITY OR TOWN IS PRESENT, OR THE AVERAGE COMMUNITY SIZE IS 200 OR GREATER (89)	0.59 OF 22	81	DRIFT TOWARD BEING THOSE WHERE NO CITY OR TOWN IS PRESENT, AND THE AVERAGE COMMUNITY SIZE IS SMALLER THAN 200 (135)	0.63 OF 198	13 73 / 9 125 / XSQ= 3.23 / PHI= 0.121 / XP = 0.0725
83	TILT TOWARD BEING THOSE WHERE, WITH NO CITY AND NO TOWN PRESENT, THE AVERAGE COMMUNITY SIZE IS BETWEEN 200 AND 999, RATHER THAN SMALLER THAN 200 (45)	0.50 OF 18	83	TILT TOWARD BEING THOSE WHERE, WITH NO CITY AND NO TOWN PRESENT, THE AVERAGE COMMUNITY SIZE IS SMALLER THAN 200, RATHER THAN BETWEEN 200 AND 999 (135)	0.78 OF 160	9 35 / 9 125 / XSQ= 5.45 / PHI= 0.175 / XP = 0.0196

88	TILT TOWARD BEING THOSE 0.60 OF 30 WHERE, IF A HEADMANSHIP IS PRESENT, SUCCESSION IS NON-HEREDITARY (106)	88	TILT TOWARD BEING THOSE 0.64 OF 234 WHERE, IF A HEADMANSHIP IS PRESENT, SUCCESSION IS HEREDITARY (165)	18 85 12 149 XSQ= 5.31 PHI= 0.142 XP = 0.0212
96	TILT TOWARD BEING THOSE 0.67 OF 33 WHERE THE HIERARCHY OF NATIONAL JURISDICTION HAS NO LEVELS (156) GES,EA	96	TILT TOWARD BEING THOSE 0.54 OF 284 WHERE THE HIERARCHY OF NATIONAL JURISDICTION HAS FOUR, THREE, TWO OR ONE LEVEL (174) GES,EA	11 152 22 132 XSQ= 4.05 PHI= -0.113 XP = 0.0442
100	DRIFT LESS TOWARD BEING THOSE 0.67 OF 33 WHERE HIERARCHIES ARE MORE COMPLEX THAN THE 'SIMPLEST,' I. E., MORE COMPLEX THAN TWO LOCAL LEVELS WITH NO NATIONAL LEVELS (267) GES,EA	100	DRIFT MORE TOWARD BEING THOSE 0.82 OF 284 WHERE HIERARCHIES ARE MORE COMPLEX THAN THE 'SIMPLEST,' I. E., MORE COMPLEX THAN TWO LOCAL LEVELS WITH NO NATIONAL LEVELS (267) GES,EA	22 234 11 50 XSQ= 3.75 PHI= -0.109 XP = 0.0529
110	DRIFT MORE TOWARD BEING THOSE 0.71 OF 42 WHERE SLAVERY IS ABSENT (218)	110	DRIFT LESS TOWARD BEING THOSE 0.56 OF 322 WHERE SLAVERY IS ABSENT (218)	12 143 30 179 XSQ= 3.19 PHI= -0.094 XP = 0.0740
128	TILT TOWARD BEING THOSE 0.90 OF 10 WHERE, IF SUBSISTENCE IS PRIMARILY BY AGRICULTURE, THE WORK IS MAINLY DONE BY MALES (40)	128	TILT TOWARD BEING THOSE 0.54 OF 65 WHERE, IF SUBSISTENCE IS PRIMARILY BY AGRICULTURE, THE WORK IS MAINLY DONE BY FEMALES (37)	9 30 1 35 XSQ= 5.03 PHI= 0.259 XP = 0.0249
185	LEAN TOWARD BEING THOSE 0.64 OF 11 WHERE THE LARGEST NON-COGNATIC KIN GROUP IS SMALLER THAN A SIB, I. E., THE LINEAGE (58)	185	LEAN TOWARD BEING THOSE 0.79 OF 230 WHERE THE LARGEST NON-COGNATIC KIN GROUP IS THE MOEITY OR PHRATRY OR SIB (194)	4 181 7 49 XSQ= 8.31 PHI= -0.186 XP = 0.0039
186	LEAN MORE TOWARD BEING THOSE 0.84 OF 45 WHERE THE KIN GROUP IS OTHER THAN EXCLUSIVELY PATRILINEAL (250)	186	LEAN LESS TOWARD BEING THOSE 0.60 OF 337 WHERE THE KIN GROUP IS OTHER THAN EXCLUSIVELY PATRILINEAL (250)	7 135 38 202 XSQ= 9.18 PHI= -0.155 XP = 0.0024
188	TEND TO BE THOSE 0.76 OF 45 WHERE THE KIN GROUP IS EXCLUSIVELY COGNATIC (148)	188	TEND TO BE THOSE 0.68 OF 337 WHERE THE KIN GROUP IS OTHER THAN EXCLUSIVELY COGNATIC (252)	34 107 11 230 XSQ= 30.86 PHI= 0.284 XP = 0.
192	TEND TO BE THOSE 0.56 OF 45 WHERE THE ONLY KIN GROUP PRESENT IS A KINDRED OR ELSE BILATERAL DESCENT IS INFERRED (111)	192	TEND TO BE THOSE 0.77 OF 337 OTHER THAN WHERE THE ONLY KIN GROUP PRESENT IS A KINDRED OR ELSE BILATERAL DESCENT IS INFERRED (289)	25 79 20 258 XSQ= 19.07 PHI= 0.223 XP = 0.0000

```
197  LEAN LESS TOWARD BEING THOSE   0.59 OF  17     197  LEAN MORE TOWARD BEING THOSE   0.87 OF 171        10  149
     WHERE RULES FOR THE INHERITANCE OF                  WHERE RULES FOR THE INHERITANCE OF                  7   22
     REAL PROPERTY, IF PRESENT,                          REAL PROPERTY, IF PRESENT,                   XSQ=     7.45
     FAVOR EITHER THE MALE HEIR OR LINE,                 FAVOR EITHER THE MALE HEIR OR LINE,          PHI=   -0.199
     OR THE FEMALE HEIR OR LINE  (165)                   OR THE FEMALE HEIR OR LINE  (165)            XP =   0.0063

201  TEND LESS TO BE THOSE          0.64 OF  45     201  TEND MORE TO BE THOSE          0.86 OF 335        29  289
     WHERE MARITAL RESIDENCE IS                          WHERE MARITAL RESIDENCE IS                         16   46
     NON-OPTIONAL, RATHER THAN                           NON-OPTIONAL, RATHER THAN                    XSQ=    12.29
     AMBILOCAL OR NEOLOCAL  (334)                        AMBILOCAL OR NEOLOCAL  (334)                 PHI=   -0.180
                                                                                                      XP =   0.0005

204  TEND LESS TO BE THOSE          0.53 OF  34     204  TEND MORE TO BE THOSE          0.84 OF 285        18  239
     WHERE MARITAL RESIDENCE IS                          WHERE MARITAL RESIDENCE IS                         16   46
     PATRILOCAL, VIRILOCAL, OR AVUNCULOCAL,              PATRILOCAL, VIRILOCAL, OR AVUNCULOCAL,       XSQ=    16.62
     RATHER THAN                                         RATHER THAN                                  PHI=   -0.228
     AMBILOCAL OR NEOLOCAL  (270)                        AMBILOCAL OR NEOLOCAL  (270)                 XP =   0.0000

209  TILT LESS TOWARD BEING THOSE   0.62 OF  29     209  TILT MORE TOWARD BEING THOSE   0.83 OF 289        18  239
     WHERE MARITAL RESIDENCE IS                          WHERE MARITAL RESIDENCE IS                         11   50
     PATRILOCAL, VIRILOCAL, OR AVUNCULOCAL,              PATRILOCAL, VIRILOCAL, OR AVUNCULOCAL,       XSQ=     5.97
     RATHER THAN                                         RATHER THAN                                  PHI=   -0.137
     MATRILOCAL OR UXORILOCAL  (270)                     MATRILOCAL OR UXORILOCAL  (270)              XP =   0.0146

220  TILT MORE TOWARD BEING THOSE   0.90 OF  41     220  TILT LESS TOWARD BEING THOSE   0.71 OF 318         4   91
     WHERE FIRST COUSIN MARRIAGE                         WHERE FIRST COUSIN MARRIAGE                        37  227
     IN SOME FORM OR OTHER                               IN SOME FORM OR OTHER                        XSQ=     5.70
     IS NOT PRESCRIBED OR PREFERRED  (273)               IS NOT PRESCRIBED OR PREFERRED  (273)        PHI=   -0.126
                                                                                                      XP =   0.0169

221  IN ALL CASES ARE THOSE         1.00 OF  41     221  DRIFT LESS TOWARD BEING THOSE  0.89 OF 318         0   34
     WHERE MATRILATERAL CROSS-COUSIN MARRIAGE            WHERE MATRILATERAL CROSS-COUSIN MARRIAGE           41  284
     IS NOT PRESCRIBED OR PREFERRED  (335)               IS NOT PRESCRIBED OR PREFERRED  (335)        XSQ=     3.68
                                                                                                      PHI=   -0.101
                                                                                                      XP =   0.0552

225  IN ALL CASES ARE THOSE         1.00 OF   3     225  DRIFT TOWARD BEING THOSE       0.67 OF  61         3   20
     WHERE COUSIN MARRIAGE IS                            WHERE COUSIN MARRIAGE IS                            0   41
     PREFERENTIALLY OR PERMISSIVELY                      PREFERENTIALLY OR PERMISSIVELY               XSQ=     3.07
     PATRILATERAL, RATHER THAN                           MATRILATERAL, RATHER THAN                    PHI=    0.219
     MATRILATERAL  (23)                                  PATRILATERAL  (43)                           XP =   0.0797

234  TEND TO BE THOSE               0.87 OF  38     234  TEND TO BE THOSE               0.52 OF 271         5  141
     WHERE THE COUSIN TERMINOLOGY IS                     WHERE THE COUSIN TERMINOLOGY IS                    33  130
     OF ESKIMO OR HAWAIIAN TYPE,                         OF CROW, OMAHA, OR IROQUOIS TYPE,            XSQ=    18.67
     RATHER THAN                                         RATHER THAN                                  PHI=   -0.246
     CROW, OMAHA, OR IROQUOIS TYPE  (170)                ESKIMO OR HAWAIIAN TYPE  (152)               XP =   0.0000

242  TILT LESS TOWARD BEING THOSE   0.67 OF  45     242  TILT MORE TOWARD BEING THOSE   0.81 OF 333        30  269
     WHERE MARRIAGE IS                                   WHERE MARRIAGE IS                                  15   64
     COMMONLY OR OCCASIONALLY POLYGYNOUS,                COMMONLY OR OCCASIONALLY POLYGYNOUS,         XSQ=     3.96
     RATHER THAN MONOGAMOUS  (314)                       RATHER THAN MONOGAMOUS  (314)                PHI=   -0.102
                                                                                                      XP =   0.0466
```

```
262  TEND LESS TO BE THOSE              0.55 OF  44      262  TEND MORE TO BE THOSE              0.81 OF 334           24  271
     WHERE WIVES ARE OBTAINED BY                             WHERE WIVES ARE OBTAINED BY                                20   63
     MEANS INVOLVING THE PRESENCE                            MEANS INVOLVING THE PRESENCE                       XSQ=    14.53
     OF SOME CONSIDERATION  (305)                            OF SOME CONSIDERATION  (305)                       PHI=   -0.196
                                                                                                                XP =   0.0001

263  TILT TOWARD BEING THOSE            0.59 OF  44      263  TILT TOWARD BEING THOSE            0.62 OF 334           18  206
     WHERE WIVES ARE OBTAINED                                WHERE WIVES ARE OBTAINED BY                                26  128
     BY RELATIVELY EASY MEANS, NAMELY BY                     RELATIVELY DIFFICULT MEANS, NAMELY BY              XSQ=     6.11
     TOKEN BRIDE-PRICE, GIFT EXCHANGE,                       BRIDE-PRICE, BRIDE-SERVICE, OR                     PHI=   -0.127
     ABSENCE OF ANY CONSIDERATION, OR                        EXCHANGING A FEMALE RELATIVE  (233)                XP =   0.0134
     RECEIPT OF DOWRY  (162)

308  IN ALL CASES ARE THOSE             1.00 OF   3      308  DRIFT TOWARD BEING THOSE           0.59 OF  37            0   22
     WHERE AVERAGE SOCIALIZATION ANXIETY                     WHERE AVERAGE SOCIALIZATION ANXIETY                         3   15
     IS LOW  (18) W-C                                        IS HIGH  (22) W-C                                  XSQ=     1.93
                                                                                                                PHI=   -0.219
                                                                                                                EP =   0.0826

370  TILT MORE TOWARD BEING THOSE    0.82 OF  28      370  TILT LESS TOWARD BEING THOSE    0.58 OF 211            5   89
     WHERE THE SEGREGATION OF ADOLESCENT BOYS                WHERE THE SEGREGATION OF ADOLESCENT BOYS                  23  122
     IS ABSENT  (148)                                        IS ABSENT  (148)                                   XSQ=     5.15
                                                                                                                PHI=   -0.147
                                                                                                                XP =   0.0232

428  IN ALL CASES ARE THOSE             1.00 OF   9      428  DRIFT LESS TOWARD BEING THOSE  0.67 OF  73            9   49
     WHERE A HIGH GOD, IF PRESENT AND ACTIVE,                WHERE A HIGH GOD, IF PRESENT AND ACTIVE,                   0   24
     SUPPORTS HUMAN MORALITY, RATHER THAN                    SUPPORTS HUMAN MORALITY, RATHER THAN               XSQ=     2.75
     NOT SUPPORTING IT  (61) GES,EA                          NOT SUPPORTING IT  (61) GES,EA                     PHI=    0.183
                                                                                                                XP =   0.0975
```

182 CULTURES
WHERE THE COMMUNITY IS
STRUCTURED ON A NON-CLAN BASIS AND
AGAMOUS (126)

182 CULTURES
OTHER THAN WHERE THE COMMUNITY IS
STRUCTURED ON A NON-CLAN BASIS AND
AGAMOUS (256)

BACKGROUND ON PAGE 105

BOTH SUBJECT AND PREDICATE

126 IN LEFT COLUMN

ABIPON	ABOR	AKHA	ALACALUF	AMERICANS	ANDAMANESE	ASHANTI	ATAYAL	AZANDE	BAJUN
BARABRA	BASQUES	BATAK	BEMBA	BLACK CARIB	BOERS	BRAZILIANS	BULGARIANS	BURUSHO	CAGABA
CAMAYURA	CAMBA	CAMBODIANS	CARIB	CAYAPA	CHAMACOCO	CHEREMIS	CHERKESS	CHIR-APACHE	CHIRIGUANO
CHUKCHEE	CREE	CREEK	CZECHS	DARD	DUTCH	EYAK	FOX	GARO	GOAJIRO
HANUNCO	HASANIA	HASINAI	IBAN	ICELANDERS	IFUGAO	ILA	INGALIK	IRISH	JAPANESE
JAVANESE	JUKUN	KAREN	KERALA	KHALKA	KIOW-APACHE	KORYAK	KUTENAI	LAKHER	LAMBA
LANGO	LUBA	MAGUZAWA	MALAYS	MARICOPA	MARQUESANS	MASAI	MAYA	MAZATECO	MBUGWE
MERINA	MISKITO	MOTILON	MUNDURUCU	NABESNA	NAMBICUARA	NANDI	NASKAPI	NATCHEZ	NAVAHO
NGONI	NICOBARESE	NUNIVAK	NURI	OKINAWANS	ONTONG-JAVA	PAPAGO	PATHAN	PENOBSCOT	PONAPEANS
PURUM	RARCIANS	ROMANS	SAGADA	SANPOIL	SARSI	SELUNG	SERI	SINHALESE	SONGHAI
SOTHO	SUBANUN	SYRIANS	TAMIL	TANIMBARESE	TAREUMIUT	TEHUELCHE	TENDA	THAI	TIBETANS
TIGRINYA	TIKOPIA	TIWI	TORAJA	TRUMAI	TSHIMSHIAN	TUBATULABAL	TUPINAMBA	TZELTAL	UTE
VIETNAMESE	WAICA	WALLCONS	WASHO	WICHITA	YUKI				

256 IN RIGHT COLUMN

18 EXCLUDED BECAUSE UNASCERTAINED

	Left			Right		Stats
3	LEAN MORE TOWARD BEING THOSE LOCATED OUTSIDE OF AFRICA (320)	0.88 OF 126	3	LEAN LESS TOWARD BEING THOSE LOCATED OUTSIDE OF AFRICA (320)	0.75 OF 256	15 64 111 192 XSQ= 8.05 PHI= -0.145 XP = 0.0046
6	DRIFT MORE TOWARD BEING THOSE LOCATED OUTSIDE OF THE INSULAR PACIFIC (330)	0.87 OF 126	6	DRIFT LESS TOWARD BEING THOSE LOCATED OUTSIDE OF THE INSULAR PACIFIC (330)	0.80 OF 256	16 52 110 204 XSQ= 2.85 PHI= -0.086 XP = 0.0916
8	DRIFT LESS TOWARD BEING THOSE LOCATED OUTSIDE OF NORTH AMERICA (330)	0.78 OF 126	8	DRIFT MORE TOWARD BEING THOSE LOCATED OUTSIDE OF NORTH AMERICA (330)	0.85 OF 256	28 38 98 218 XSQ= 2.72 PHI= 0.084 XP = 0.0990

No.		No.		
11	TILT LESS TOWARD BEING THOSE 0.93 OF 126 WHERE THE LATITUDE IS LESS THAN SIXTY DEGREES (385)	11	TILT MORE TOWARD BEING THOSE 0.98 OF 256 WHERE THE LATITUDE IS LESS THAN SIXTY DEGREES (385)	9 5 117 251 XSQ= 5.06 PHI= 0.115 XP = 0.0245
12	LEAN LESS TOWARD BEING THOSE 0.85 OF 126 WHERE THE LATITUDE IS LESS THAN FIFTY DEGREES (367)	12	LEAN MORE TOWARD BEING THOSE 0.95 OF 256 WHERE THE LATITUDE IS LESS THAN FIFTY DEGREES (367)	19 13 107 243 XSQ= 9.74 PHI= 0.160 XP = 0.0018
13	TILT LESS TOWARD BEING THOSE 0.76 OF 126 WHERE THE LATITUDE IS LESS THAN FORTY DEGREES (329)	13	TILT MORE TOWARD BEING THOSE 0.85 OF 256 WHERE THE LATITUDE IS LESS THAN FORTY DEGREES (329)	30 38 96 218 XSQ= 4.05 PHI= 0.103 XP = 0.0443
14	LEAN LESS TOWARD BEING THOSE 0.61 OF 126 WHERE THE LATITUDE IS LESS THAN THIRTY DEGREES (281)	14	LEAN MORE TOWARD BEING THOSE 0.75 OF 256 WHERE THE LATITUDE IS LESS THAN THIRTY DEGREES (281)	49 65 77 191 XSQ= 6.72 PHI= 0.133 XP = 0.0095
16	LEAN MORE TOWARD BEING THOSE 0.79 OF 126 WHERE THE LATITUDE IS TEN DEGREES OR GREATER (277)	16	LEAN LESS TOWARD BEING THOSE 0.64 OF 256 WHERE THE LATITUDE IS TEN DEGREES OR GREATER (277)	99 165 27 91 XSQ= 7.24 PHI= 0.138 XP = 0.0071
63	TILT MORE TOWARD BEING THOSE 0.79 OF 68 WHERE HUSBANDRY, IF PRESENT, IS PRINCIPALLY IN THE FORM OF BOVINE, EQUINE, CAMEL-LIKE, OR DEER-LIKE ANIMALS, RATHER THAN PIGS, SHEEP, OR GOATS (152)	63	TILT LESS TOWARD BEING THOSE 0.61 OF 151 WHERE HUSBANDRY, IF PRESENT, IS PRINCIPALLY IN THE FORM OF BOVINE, EQUINE, CAMEL-LIKE, OR DEER-LIKE ANIMALS, RATHER THAN PIGS, SHEEP, OR GOATS (152)	54 92 14 59 XSQ= 6.40 PHI= 0.171 XP = 0.0114
73	TILT TOWARD BEING THOSE 0.58 OF 79 WHERE WEAVING IS PRESENT (118)	73	TILT TOWARD BEING THOSE 0.59 OF 161 WHERE WEAVING IS ABSENT (130)	46 66 33 95 XSQ= 5.65 PHI= 0.153 XP = 0.0174
79	TEND LESS TO BE THOSE 0.78 OF 77 WHERE NO CITY IS PRESENT (201)	79	TEND MORE TO BE THOSE 0.96 OF 143 WHERE NO CITY IS PRESENT (201)	17 6 60 137 XSQ= 15.24 PHI= 0.263 XP = 0.0001
80	LEAN LESS TOWARD BEING THOSE 0.71 OF 77 WHERE NO CITY OR TOWN IS PRESENT (185)	80	LEAN MORE TOWARD BEING THOSE 0.90 OF 143 WHERE NO CITY OR TOWN IS PRESENT (185)	22 15 55 128 XSQ= 10.44 PHI= 0.218 XP = 0.0012

84	DRIFT LESS TOWARD BEING THOSE 0.80 OF 101 WHERE THE LEVEL OF POLITICAL INTEGRATION IS THE LITTLE STATE, THE MINIMAL STATE, THE AUTONOMOUS COMMUNITY, OR THE FAMILY (262) GPM	84	DRIFT MORE TOWARD BEING THOSE 0.89 OF 186 WHERE THE LEVEL OF POLITICAL INTEGRATION IS THE LITTLE STATE, THE MINIMAL STATE, THE AUTONOMOUS COMMUNITY, OR THE FAMILY (262) GPM	20 20 81 166 XSQ= 3.75 PHI= 0.114 XP = 0.0529
85	TILT LESS TOWARD BEING THOSE 0.69 OF 101 WHERE THE LEVEL OF POLITICAL INTEGRATION IS THE MINIMAL STATE, THE AUTONOMOUS COMMUNITY, OR THE FAMILY (234) GPM	85	TILT MORE TOWARD BEING THOSE 0.81 OF 186 WHERE THE LEVEL OF POLITICAL INTEGRATION IS THE MINIMAL STATE, THE AUTONOMOUS COMMUNITY, OR THE FAMILY (234) GPM	31 35 70 151 XSQ= 4.56 PHI= 0.126 XP = 0.0326
94	DRIFT LESS TOWARD BEING THOSE 0.84 OF 103 WHERE THE HIERARCHY OF NATIONAL JURISDICTION HAS TWO, ONE, OR NO LEVELS (296) GES,EA	94	DRIFT MORE TOWARD BEING THOSE 0.92 OF 214 WHERE THE HIERARCHY OF NATIONAL JURISDICTION HAS TWO, ONE, OR NO LEVELS (296) GES,EA	16 17 87 197 XSQ= 3.52 PHI= 0.105 XP = 0.0606
95	TILT LESS TOWARD BEING THOSE 0.69 OF 103 WHERE THE HIERARCHY OF NATIONAL JURISDICTION HAS ONE OR NO LEVELS (254) GES,EA	95	TILT MORE TOWARD BEING THOSE 0.81 OF 214 WHERE THE HIERARCHY OF NATIONAL JURISDICTION HAS ONE OR NO LEVELS (254) GES,EA	32 41 71 173 XSQ= 4.91 PHI= 0.124 XP = 0.0267
97	LEAN MORE TOWARD BEING THOSE 0.91 OF 103 WHERE THE HIERARCHY OF LOCAL JURISDICTION HAS THREE OR TWO LEVELS (273) GES,EA	97	LEAN LESS TOWARD BEING THOSE 0.78 OF 215 WHERE THE HIERARCHY OF LOCAL JURISDICTION HAS THREE OR TWO LEVELS (273) GES,EA	9 47 94 168 XSQ= 7.39 PHI= -0.152 XP = 0.0066
102	TILT TOWARD BEING THOSE 0.61 OF 122 WHERE CLASS STRATIFICATION IS PRESENT (203)	102	TILT TOWARD BEING THOSE 0.50 OF 245 WHERE CLASS STRATIFICATION IS ABSENT (180)	75 122 47 123 XSQ= 4.01 PHI= 0.105 XP = 0.0452
107	TILT LESS TOWARD BEING THOSE 0.69 OF 75 WHERE CLASS STRATIFICATION, IF PRESENT, IS BASED ON SOMETHING OTHER THAN OCCUPATIONAL STATUS (160)	107	TILT MORE TOWARD BEING THOSE 0.84 OF 122 WHERE CLASS STRATIFICATION, IF PRESENT, IS BASED ON SOMETHING OTHER THAN OCCUPATIONAL STATUS (160)	23 20 52 102 XSQ= 4.74 PHI= 0.155 XP = 0.0295
130	TILT TOWARD BEING THOSE 0.69 OF 32 WHERE LEATHER WORKING IS MAINLY DONE BY FEMALES (45)	130	TILT TOWARD BEING THOSE 0.57 OF 51 WHERE LEATHER WORKING IS MAINLY DONE BY MALES (39)	10 29 22 22 XSQ= 4.20 PHI= -0.225 XP = 0.0404
136	TILT TOWARD BEING THOSE 0.90 OF 10 WHERE FULL-TIME ENTREPRENEURS ARE PRESENT (18) JV	136	TILT TOWARD BEING THOSE 0.59 OF 22 WHERE FULL-TIME ENTREPRENEURS ARE ABSENT (14) JV	9 9 1 13 XSQ= 4.89 PHI= 0.391 EP = 0.0189

No.		No.		
148	DRIFT TOWARD BEING THOSE 0.71 OF 7 WHERE THE INCIDENCE OF PERSONAL CRIME IS HIGH (12) B-B-C	148	DRIFT TOWARD BEING THOSE 0.73 OF 26 WHERE THE INCIDENCE OF PERSONAL CRIME IS LOW (21) B-B-C	5 7 2 19 XSQ= 2.99 PHI= 0.301 EP = 0.0709
186	TEND MORE TO BE THOSE 0.77 OF 126 WHERE THE KIN GROUP IS OTHER THAN EXCLUSIVELY PATRILINEAL (250)	186	TEND LESS TO BE THOSE 0.56 OF 256 WHERE THE KIN GROUP IS OTHER THAN EXCLUSIVELY PATRILINEAL (250)	29 113 97 143 XSQ= 15.24 PHI= -0.200 XP = 0.0001
188	TEND TO BE THOSE 0.57 OF 126 WHERE THE KIN GROUP IS EXCLUSIVELY COGNATIC (148)	188	TEND TO BE THOSE 0.73 OF 256 WHERE THE KIN GROUP IS OTHER THAN EXCLUSIVELY COGNATIC (252)	72 69 54 187 XSQ= 31.77 PHI= 0.288 XP = 0.
192	TEND LESS TO BE THOSE 0.52 OF 126 OTHER THAN WHERE THE ONLY KIN GROUP PRESENT IS A KINDRED OR ELSE BILATERAL DESCENT IS INFERRED (289)	192	TEND MORE TO BE THOSE 0.83 OF 256 OTHER THAN WHERE THE ONLY KIN GROUP PRESENT IS A KINDRED OR ELSE BILATERAL DESCENT IS INFERRED (289)	60 44 66 212 XSQ= 37.95 PHI= 0.315 XP = 0.
197	TEND LESS TO BE THOSE 0.70 OF 64 WHERE RULES FOR THE INHERITANCE OF REAL PROPERTY, IF PRESENT, FAVOR EITHER THE MALE HEIR OR LINE, OR THE FEMALE HEIR OR LINE (165)	197	TEND MORE TO BE THOSE 0.92 OF 124 WHERE RULES FOR THE INHERITANCE OF REAL PROPERTY, IF PRESENT, FAVOR EITHER THE MALE HEIR OR LINE, OR THE FEMALE HEIR OR LINE (165)	45 114 19 10 XSQ= 13.52 PHI= -0.268 XP = 0.0002
201	LEAN LESS TOWARD BEING THOSE 0.75 OF 126 WHERE MARITAL RESIDENCE IS NON-OPTIONAL, RATHER THAN AMBILOCAL OR NEOLOCAL (334)	201	LEAN MORE TOWARD BEING THOSE 0.88 OF 254 WHERE MARITAL RESIDENCE IS NON-OPTIONAL, RATHER THAN AMBILOCAL OR NEOLOCAL (334)	95 223 31 31 XSQ= 8.60 PHI= -0.150 XP = 0.0034
204	LEAN LESS TOWARD BEING THOSE 0.70 OF 103 WHERE MARITAL RESIDENCE IS PATRILOCAL, VIRILOCAL, OR AVUNCULOCAL, RATHER THAN AMBILOCAL OR NEOLOCAL (270)	204	LEAN MORE TOWARD BEING THOSE 0.86 OF 216 WHERE MARITAL RESIDENCE IS PATRILOCAL, VIRILOCAL, OR AVUNCULOCAL, RATHER THAN AMBILOCAL OR NEOLOCAL (270)	72 185 31 31 XSQ= 10.06 PHI= -0.178 XP = 0.0015
234	TILT TOWARD BEING THOSE 0.61 OF 101 WHERE THE COUSIN TERMINOLOGY IS OF ESKIMO OR HAWAIIAN TYPE, RATHER THAN CROW, OMAHA, OR IROQUOIS TYPE (170)	234	TILT TOWARD BEING THOSE 0.51 OF 208 WHERE THE COUSIN TERMINOLOGY IS OF CROW, OMAHA, OR IROQUOIS TYPE, RATHER THAN ESKIMO OR HAWAIIAN TYPE (152)	39 107 62 101 XSQ= 3.99 PHI= -0.114 XP = 0.0458
240	DRIFT MORE TOWARD BEING THOSE 0.72 OF 65 WHERE THE FAMILY, IF EXTENDED, IS SMALL OR STEM, RATHER THAN LARGE (135)	240	DRIFT LESS TOWARD BEING THOSE 0.59 OF 141 WHERE THE FAMILY, IF EXTENDED, IS SMALL OR STEM, RATHER THAN LARGE (135)	18 58 47 83 XSQ= 2.90 PHI= -0.119 XP = 0.0886

241	TEND LESS TO BE THOSE 0.74 OF 65 WHERE THE FAMILY, IF EXTENDED, IS LARGE OR SMALL, RATHER THAN STEM (187)	241	TEND MORE TO BE THOSE 0.94 OF 141 WHERE THE FAMILY, IF EXTENDED, IS LARGE OR SMALL, RATHER THAN STEM (187)	48 132 17 9 XSQ= 14.03 PHI= -0.261 XP = 0.0002
242	DRIFT LESS TOWARD BEING THOSE 0.73 OF 124 WHERE MARRIAGE IS COMMONLY OR OCCASIONALLY POLYGYNOUS, RATHER THAN MONOGAMOUS (314)	242	DRIFT MORE TOWARD BEING THOSE 0.82 OF 254 WHERE MARRIAGE IS COMMONLY OR OCCASIONALLY POLYGYNOUS, RATHER THAN MONOGAMOUS (314)	91 208 33 46 XSQ= 3.15 PHI= -0.091 XP = 0.0760
243	DRIFT MORE TOWARD BEING THOSE 0.81 OF 16 WHERE POLYGYNY, IF PRESENT, HAS A LOW INCIDENCE (36) W-D,S	243	DRIFT LESS TOWARD BEING THOSE 0.52 OF 44 WHERE POLYGYNY, IF PRESENT, HAS A LOW INCIDENCE (36) W-D,S	3 21 13 23 XSQ= 2.99 PHI= -0.223 XP = 0.0840
263	LEAN TOWARD BEING THOSE 0.52 OF 126 WHERE WIVES ARE OBTAINED BY RELATIVELY EASY MEANS, NAMELY BY TOKEN BRIDE-PRICE, GIFT EXCHANGE, ABSENCE OF ANY CONSIDERATION, OR RECEIPT OF DOWRY (162)	263	LEAN TOWARD BEING THOSE 0.65 OF 252 WHERE WIVES ARE OBTAINED BY RELATIVELY DIFFICULT MEANS, NAMELY BY BRIDE-PRICE, BRIDE-SERVICE, OR EXCHANGING A FEMALE RELATIVE (233)	61 163 65 89 XSQ= 8.55 PHI= -0.150 XP = 0.0035
280	IN ALL CASES ARE THOSE 1.00 OF 6 WHERE THE COMPOSITE FERTILITY LEVEL IS HIGH (13) MN	280	TILT TOWARD BEING THOSE 0.63 OF 19 WHERE THE COMPOSITE FERTILITY LEVEL IS LOW (12) MN	6 7 0 12 XSQ= 4.98 PHI= 0.446 EP = 0.0149
324	DRIFT TOWARD BEING THOSE 0.73 OF 15 WHERE THE PAIN INFLICTED ON THE INFANT BY THE NURTURANT AGENT IS LOW OR NEGLIGIBLE (32) B-B-C	324	DRIFT TOWARD BEING THOSE 0.59 OF 51 WHERE THE PAIN INFLICTED ON THE INFANT BY THE NURTURANT AGENT IS HIGH (34) B-B-C	4 30 11 21 XSQ= 3.60 PHI= -0.233 XP = 0.0579
377	TILT MORE TOWARD BEING THOSE 0.84 OF 100 WHERE MALE GENITAL MUTILATION IS ABSENT (242)	377	TILT LESS TOWARD BEING THOSE 0.71 OF 212 WHERE MALE GENITAL MUTILATION IS ABSENT (242)	16 61 84 151 XSQ= 5.30 PHI= -0.130 XP = 0.0214
382	DRIFT TOWARD BEING THOSE 0.75 OF 24 WHERE FEMALE INITIATION RITES ARE PRESENT (38) JKB	382	DRIFT TOWARD BEING THOSE 0.51 OF 41 WHERE FEMALE INITIATION RITES ARE ABSENT (27) JKB	18 20 6 21 XSQ= 3.27 PHI= 0.224 XP = 0.0704

****

183 CULTURES WHERE THE LARGEST NON-COGNATIC KIN GROUP IS THE MOEITY (34)	183 CULTURES WHERE THE LARGEST NON-COGNATIC KIN GROUP IS SMALLER THAN A MOEITY, I. E., A PHRATRY OR SIB OR LINEAGE (218)

BACKGROUND ON PAGE 107 BOTH SUBJECT AND PREDICATE

....

34 IN LEFT COLUMN

ABOR	APINAYE	ARANDA	ARAPESH	BIRIFOR	BORORO	BUNLAP	CREEK	DIERI	EYAK
GARO	HAIDA	KARIERA	KASKA	KERAKI	KONSO	LESU	MANDAN	MIWOK	MOTA
MUNDURUCU	MURINBATA	MURNGIN	OMAHA	PURARI	SHERENTE	TALAMANCA	TIMBIRA	TIWI	TUCUNA
WIKMUNKAN	WINNEBAGO	WOGEO	YOKUTS						

218 IN RIGHT COLUMN

AINU	AJIE	AKHA	ALBANIANS	ALORESE	AMBA	ARAUCANIANS	ARYANS	ASHANTI	ATAYAL
AYMARA	AZANDE	BABWA	BAJUN	BAMBARA	BAMILEKE	BANDA	BARABRA	BARI	BASSERI
BATAK	BAYA	BEJA	BELU	BEMBA	BENGALI	BETE	BHIL	BHUIYA	BOZO
BUDUMA	BURUSHO	BURYAT	CALLINAGO	CHAGGA	CHENCHU	CHERKESS	CHEROKEE	COCHITI	COORG
CROW	DAGUR	DARD	DELAWARE	DIEGUENO	DILLING	DOBUANS	DOGON	DOROBO	EGYPTIANS
ENGA	FANG	FON	FOX	FUTAJALONKE	GANDA	GILYAK	GISU	GOAJIRO	GOND
GUAHIBO	GURE	HANO	HASANIA	HAZARA	HEBREWS	HEHE	HERERO	HO	HURON
ILA	IRAQW	JEMEZ	KABYLE	KACHIN	KALMYK	KAPAUKU	KAREN	KATAB	KAZAK
KERALA	KET	KHALKA	KHASI	KHEVSUR	KIKUYU	KISSI	KOHISTANI	KOREANS	KPE
KUBA	KURTATCHI	LAKALAI	LAKHER	LAMBA	LAMET	LANGO	LAU	LEPCHA	LHOTA NAGA
LIFU	LOLO	LUBA	LUO	MAGUZAWA	MAM	MAMVU	MANCHU	MANUS	MARGI
MARICOPA	MARSHALLESE	MASAI	MATAKAM	MAYA	MBUGWE	MBUNDU	MBUTI	MENDE	MERINA
MIAMI	MIAO	MIN CHINESE	MINANGKABAU	MINCHIA	MNONG GAR	MONGO	MONGUOR	MOSSI	MZAB
NABESNA	NAMA	NANDI	NAVAHO	NDEMBU	NOMLAKI	NUER	NUPE	NURI	NYAKYUSA
NYANEKA	NYARO	NYORO	OJIBWA	OKINAWANS	ORAON	PALAUANS	PALIKUR	PATHAN	PAWNEE
PENDE	PONAPEANS	PUKAPUKA	PURUM	REGEIBAT	RIFFIANS	ROTINESE	ROTUMANS	RUNDI	RWALA
SAMOYED	SANDAWE	SANTAL	SARAMACCA	SEMINOLE	SENIANG	SERBS	SHILLUK	SHLUH	SINDHI
SIRIONO	SIUAI	SIWANS	SOMALI	SONGHAI	SOTHO	SWAZI	SYRIANS	TALLENSI	TAMIL
TANALA	TANIMBARESE	TEDA	TENDA	TERA	TESO	THONGA	TIBETANS	TIGRINYA	TIKOPIA
TIMUCUA	TIV	TODA	TOLOWA	TROBRIAND	TRUKESE	TSHIMSHIAN	TUCANO	TURKANA	TURKMEN
TZELTAL	VEDDA	VENDA	VIETNAMESE	WANTOAT	WAROPEN	WITOTO	WOLEAIANS	WOLOF	WUTE
YAGUA	YAKO	YAKUT	YAO	YAPESE	YOMBE	YORUBA	ZUNI		

148 EXCLUDED BECAUSE IRRELEVANT

3	TEND MORE TO BE THOSE LOCATED OUTSIDE OF AFRICA (320)	0.97 OF 34	3	TEND LESS TO BE THOSE LOCATED OUTSIDE OF AFRICA (320)	0.67 OF 218

	1	72
	33	146
XSQ=		11.52
PHI=		-0.214
XP =		0.0007

5	TILT MORE TOWARD BEING THOSE LOCATED OUTSIDE OF EAST EURASIA (330)	0.94 OF 34	5	TILT LESS TOWARD BEING THOSE LOCATED OUTSIDE OF EAST EURASIA (330)	0.75 OF 218	2 54 32 164 XSQ= 5.03 PHI= -0.141 XP = 0.0249
6	TEND LESS TO BE THOSE LOCATED OUTSIDE OF THE INSULAR PACIFIC (330)	0.59 OF 34	6	TEND MORE TO BE THOSE LOCATED OUTSIDE OF THE INSULAR PACIFIC (330)	0.86 OF 218	14 30 20 188 XSQ= 13.50 PHI= 0.231 XP = 0.0002
8	TILT LESS TOWARD BEING THOSE LOCATED OUTSIDE OF NORTH AMERICA (330)	0.74 OF 34	8	TILT MORE TOWARD BEING THOSE LOCATED OUTSIDE OF NORTH AMERICA (330)	0.90 OF 218	9 21 25 197 XSQ= 6.43 PHI= 0.160 XP = 0.0112
9	TILT LESS TOWARD BEING THOSE LOCATED OUTSIDE OF SOUTH AMERICA (335)	0.79 OF 34	9	TILT MORE TOWARD BEING THOSE LOCATED OUTSIDE OF SOUTH AMERICA (335)	0.94 OF 218	7 14 27 204 XSQ= 5.98 PHI= 0.154 XP = 0.0144
44	TILT LESS TOWARD BEING THOSE WHERE SETTLEMENTS ARE FIXED (222)	0.53 OF 32	44	TILT MORE TOWARD BEING THOSE WHERE SETTLEMENTS ARE FIXED (222)	0.74 OF 179	17 132 15 47 XSQ= 4.61 PHI= -0.148 XP = 0.0317
46	TILT LESS TOWARD BEING THOSE OTHER THAN WHERE SETTLEMENTS ARE NON-FIXED AND MOVEMENT IS NOMADIC (260)	0.69 OF 32	46	TILT MORE TOWARD BEING THOSE OTHER THAN WHERE SETTLEMENTS ARE NON-FIXED AND MOVEMENT IS NOMADIC (260)	0.85 OF 179	10 27 22 152 XSQ= 3.85 PHI= 0.135 XP = 0.0497
51	TEND TO BE THOSE WHERE SUBSISTENCE IS PRIMARILY BY FOOD GATHERING -- I. E., HUNTING, FISHING, OR COLLECTING -- RATHER THAN FOOD PRODUCTION (147)	0.71 OF 34	51	TEND TO BE THOSE WHERE SUBSISTENCE IS PRIMARILY BY FOOD PRODUCTION -- I. E., AGRICULTURE OR HUSBANDRY -- RATHER THAN BY GATHERING (253)	0.80 OF 218	10 174 24 44 XSQ= 35.41 PHI= -0.375 XP = 0.
53	LEAN MORE TOWARD BEING THOSE WHERE FOOD PRODUCTION IS BY SIMPLE AGRICULTURE OR INCIPIENT FOOD PRODUCTION, RATHER THAN BY INTENSIVE AGRICULTURE (147)	0.94 OF 17	53	LEAN LESS TOWARD BEING THOSE WHERE FOOD PRODUCTION IS BY SIMPLE AGRICULTURE OR INCIPIENT FOOD PRODUCTION, RATHER THAN BY INTENSIVE AGRICULTURE (147)	0.58 OF 150	1 63 16 87 XSQ= 6.97 PHI= -0.204 XP = 0.0083
54	TEND LESS TO BE THOSE WHERE FOOD PRODUCTION IS BY INTENSIVE OR SIMPLE AGRICULTURE, RATHER THAN BY INCIPIENT FOOD PRODUCTION (192)	0.53 OF 17	54	TEND MORE TO BE THOSE WHERE FOOD PRODUCTION IS BY INTENSIVE OR SIMPLE AGRICULTURE, RATHER THAN BY INCIPIENT FOOD PRODUCTION (192)	0.87 OF 150	9 131 8 19 XSQ= 10.91 PHI= -0.256 XP = 0.0010

```
55  DRIFT MORE TOWARD BEING THOSE  0.89 OF   9     55  DRIFT LESS TOWARD BEING THOSE  0.52 OF 131          1   63
    WHERE FOOD PRODUCTION IS BY                         WHERE FOOD PRODUCTION IS BY                            8   68
    SIMPLE AGRICULTURE, RATHER THAN BY                  SIMPLE AGRICULTURE, RATHER THAN BY             XSQ=     3.27
    INTENSIVE AGRICULTURE  (101)                        INTENSIVE AGRICULTURE  (101)                   PHI=   -0.153
                                                                                                       XP =   0.0705

56  TILT TOWARD BEING THOSE        0.50 OF  16     56  TILT TOWARD BEING THOSE        0.78 OF  87          8   68
    WHERE FOOD PRODUCTION IS BY                         WHERE FOOD PRODUCTION IS BY                            8   19
    INCIPIENT FOOD PRODUCTION, RATHER THAN BY           SIMPLE AGRICULTURE, RATHER THAN BY             XSQ=     4.18
    SIMPLE AGRICULTURE  (46)                            INCIPIENT FOOD PRODUCTION  (101)               PHI=   -0.201
                                                                                                       XP =   0.0409

62  LEAN TOWARD BEING THOSE        0.59 OF  34     62  LEAN TOWARD BEING THOSE        0.68 OF 218         14  149
    WHERE HUSBANDRY OF ANY KIND                         WHERE HUSBANDRY OF SOME KIND                          20   69
    IS ABSENT  (172)                                    IS PRESENT  (228)                              XSQ=     8.35
                                                                                                       PHI=   -0.182
                                                                                                       XP =   0.0038

63  TILT TOWARD BEING THOSE        0.64 OF  14     63  TILT TOWARD BEING THOSE        0.70 OF 147          5  103
    WHERE HUSBANDRY, IF PRESENT,                        WHERE HUSBANDRY, IF PRESENT,                           9   44
    IS PRINCIPALLY IN THE FORM OF                       IS PRINCIPALLY IN THE FORM OF                  XSQ=     5.36
    PIGS, SHEEP, OR GOATS, RATHER THAN                  BOVINE, EQUINE, CAMEL-LIKE, OR DEER-LIKE       PHI=   -0.183
    BOVINE, EQUINE, CAMEL-LIKE, OR DEER-LIKE            ANIMALS, RATHER THAN                           XP =   0.0206
    ANIMALS  (74)                                       PIGS, SHEEP, OR GOATS  (152)

71  TEND TO BE THOSE               0.89 OF  28     71  TEND TO BE THOSE               0.58 OF 130          3   76
    WHERE METAL WORKING IS                              WHERE METAL WORKING IS                                25   54
    ABSENT  (153)                                       PRESENT  (98)                                  XSQ=    19.14
                                                                                                       PHI=   -0.348
                                                                                                       XP =   0.0000

73  DRIFT TOWARD BEING THOSE       0.68 OF  28     73  DRIFT TOWARD BEING THOSE       0.52 OF 123          9   64
    WHERE WEAVING IS                                    WHERE WEAVING IS                                      19   59
    ABSENT  (130)                                       PRESENT  (118)                                 XSQ=     2.86
                                                                                                       PHI=   -0.138
                                                                                                       XP =   0.0908

74  LEAN TOWARD BEING THOSE        0.61 OF  28     74  LEAN TOWARD BEING THOSE        0.69 OF 118         11   81
    WHERE POTTERY IS                                    WHERE POTTERY IS                                      17   37
    ABSENT  (93)                                        PRESENT  (145)                                 XSQ=     7.16
                                                                                                       PHI=   -0.221
                                                                                                       XP =   0.0075

80  IN ALL CASES ARE THOSE         1.00 OF  22     80  DRIFT LESS TOWARD BEING THOSE  0.83 OF 126          0   21
    WHERE NO CITY OR TOWN IS PRESENT  (185)             WHERE NO CITY OR TOWN IS PRESENT  (185)               22  105
                                                                                                       XSQ=     3.01
                                                                                                       PHI=   -0.143
                                                                                                       XP =   0.0826

81  LEAN MORE TOWARD BEING THOSE   0.91 OF  22     81  LEAN LESS TOWARD BEING THOSE   0.54 OF 126          2   58
    WHERE NO CITY OR TOWN IS PRESENT, AND               WHERE NO CITY OR TOWN IS PRESENT, AND                 20   68
    THE AVERAGE COMMUNITY SIZE IS                       THE AVERAGE COMMUNITY SIZE IS                  XSQ=     9.13
    SMALLER THAN 200  (135)                             SMALLER THAN 200  (135)                        PHI=   -0.248
                                                                                                       XP =   0.0025
```

```
82  TILT LESS TOWARD BEING THOSE   0.64 OF  22     82  TILT MORE TOWARD BEING THOSE   0.87 OF 126          14  109
    WHERE A CITY OR TOWN IS PRESENT, OR                 WHERE A CITY OR TOWN IS PRESENT, OR                        8   17
    THE AVERAGE COMMUNITY SIZE IS                       THE AVERAGE COMMUNITY SIZE IS                     XSQ=      5.45
    FIFTY OR GREATER  (178)                             FIFTY OR GREATER  (178)                           PHI=    -0.192
                                                                                                          XP =    0.0196

83  TILT MORE TOWARD BEING THOSE   0.91 OF  22     83  TILT LESS TOWARD BEING THOSE   0.67 OF 102            2   34
    WHERE, WITH NO CITY AND NO TOWN PRESENT,            WHERE, WITH NO CITY AND NO TOWN PRESENT,                  20   68
    THE AVERAGE COMMUNITY SIZE IS                       THE AVERAGE COMMUNITY SIZE IS                     XSQ=      4.05
    SMALLER THAN 200, RATHER THAN                       SMALLER THAN 200, RATHER THAN                     PHI=    -0.181
    BETWEEN 200 AND 999  (135)                          BETWEEN 200 AND 999  (135)                        XP =    0.0441

84  IN ALL CASES ARE THOSE         1.00 OF  29     84  DRIFT LESS TOWARD BEING THOSE  0.85 OF 162            0   24
    WHERE THE LEVEL OF POLITICAL INTEGRATION            WHERE THE LEVEL OF POLITICAL INTEGRATION                  29  138
    IS THE LITTLE STATE, THE MINIMAL STATE,             IS THE LITTLE STATE, THE MINIMAL STATE,           XSQ=      3.66
    THE AUTONOMOUS COMMUNITY, OR                        THE AUTONOMOUS COMMUNITY, OR                      PHI=    -0.138
    THE FAMILY  (262) GPM                               THE FAMILY  (262) GPM                             XP =    0.0558

85  TILT MORE TOWARD BEING THOSE   0.97 OF  29     85  TILT LESS TOWARD BEING THOSE   0.73 OF 162            1   44
    WHERE THE LEVEL OF POLITICAL INTEGRATION            WHERE THE LEVEL OF POLITICAL INTEGRATION                  28  118
    IS THE MINIMAL STATE,                               IS THE MINIMAL STATE,                             XSQ=      6.42
    THE AUTONOMOUS COMMUNITY, OR                        THE AUTONOMOUS COMMUNITY, OR                      PHI=    -0.183
    THE FAMILY  (234) GPM                               THE FAMILY  (234) GPM                             XP =    0.0113

86  LEAN TOWARD BEING THOSE        0.72 OF  29     86  LEAN TOWARD BEING THOSE        0.58 OF 162            8   94
    WHERE THE LEVEL OF POLITICAL INTEGRATION            WHERE THE LEVEL OF POLITICAL INTEGRATION                  21   68
    IS THE AUTONOMOUS COMMUNITY, OR                     IS THE LARGE STATE, THE LITTLE STATE,             XSQ=      7.98
    THE FAMILY  (156) GPM                               OR THE MINIMAL STATE  (148) GPM                   PHI=    -0.204
                                                                                                          XP =    0.0047

89  IN ALL CASES ARE THOSE         1.00 OF   4     89  DRIFT TOWARD BEING THOSE       0.57 OF  56            0   32
    WHERE, IF A NON-HEREDITARY HEADMANSHIP              WHERE, IF A NON-HEREDITARY HEADMANSHIP                     4   24
    IS PRESENT, SUCCESSION IS BY MEANS                  IS PRESENT, SUCCESSION IS                         XSQ=      2.87
    OTHER THAN CONSENSUS  (43)                          BY CONSENSUS  (63)                                PHI=    -0.219
                                                                                                          XP =    0.0902

94  IN ALL CASES ARE THOSE         1.00 OF  32     94  DRIFT LESS TOWARD BEING THOSE  0.89 OF 178            0   20
    WHERE THE HIERARCHY                                 WHERE THE HIERARCHY                                       32  158
    OF NATIONAL JURISDICTION HAS                        OF NATIONAL JURISDICTION HAS                      XSQ=      2.78
    TWO, ONE, OR NO LEVELS  (296) GES,EA                TWO, ONE, OR NO LEVELS  (296) GES,EA              PHI=    -0.115
                                                                                                          XP =    0.0956

95  IN ALL CASES ARE THOSE         1.00 OF  32     95  TEND LESS TO BE THOSE          0.70 OF 178            0   54
    WHERE THE HIERARCHY                                 WHERE THE HIERARCHY                                       32  124
    OF NATIONAL JURISDICTION HAS                        OF NATIONAL JURISDICTION HAS                      XSQ=     11.53
    ONE OR NO LEVELS  (254) GES,EA                      ONE OR NO LEVELS  (254) GES,EA                    PHI=    -0.234
                                                                                                          XP =    0.0007

96  TEND TO BE THOSE               0.81 OF  32     96  TEND TO BE THOSE               0.67 OF 178            6  119
    WHERE THE HIERARCHY                                 WHERE THE HIERARCHY                                       26   59
    OF NATIONAL JURISDICTION HAS                        OF NATIONAL JURISDICTION HAS                      XSQ=     24.09
    NO LEVELS  (156) GES,EA                             FOUR, THREE, TWO OR                               PHI=    -0.339
                                                        ONE LEVEL  (174) GES,EA                           XP =    0.0000
```

98	TILT LESS TOWARD BEING THCSE WHERE THE HIERARCHY OF LCCAL JURISDICTICN HAS FCUR CR THREE LEVELS (238) GES,EA	0.63 OF 32	98	TILT MORE TOWARD BEING THOSE WHERE THE HIERARCHY OF LOCAL JURISDICTION HAS FOUR OR THREE LEVELS (238) GES,EA	0.83 OF 179	20 148 12 31 XSQ= 5.63 PHI= -0.163 XP = 0.0177
100	TEND LESS TO BE THCSE WHERE HIERARCHIES ARE MORE COMPLEX THAN THE 'SIMPLEST,' I. E., MORE CCMPLEX THAN TWO LCCAL LEVELS WITH NC NATICNAL LEVELS (267) GES,EA	0.63 OF 32	100	TEND MORE TO BE THOSE WHERE HIERARCHIES ARE MORE COMPLEX THAN THE 'SIMPLEST,' I. E., MORE COMPLEX THAN TWO LOCAL LEVELS WITH NO NATIONAL LEVELS (267) GES,EA	0.90 CF 178	20 161 12 17 XSQ= 15.53 PHI= -0.272 XP = 0.0001
102	TEND TO BE THCSE WHERE CLASS STRATIFICATICN IS ABSENT (180)	0.82 OF 33	102	TEND TO BE THOSE WHERE CLASS STRATIFICATION IS PRESENT (203)	0.62 CF 212	6 131 27 81 XSQ= 20.30 PHI= -0.288 XP = 0.0000
106	DRIFT TOWARD BEING THCSE WHERE CLASS STRATIFICATION, IF PRESENT, IS BASED CN WEALTH (77)	0.83 OF 6	106	DRIFT TOWARD BEING THOSE WHERE CLASS STRATIFICATION, IF PRESENT, IS BASED ON SOMETHING OTHER THAN WEALTH (126)	0.63 CF 131	5 49 1 82 XSQ= 3.33 PHI= 0.156 XP = 0.0681
109	TILT MORE TOWARC BEING THCSE WHERE CASTES ARE ABSENT (317)	0.97 OF 32	109	TILT LESS TOWARD BEING THOSE WHERE CASTES ARE ABSENT (317)	0.78 OF 194	1 43 31 151 XSQ= 5.20 PHI= -0.152 XP = 0.0227
110	TEND TC BE THCSE WHERE SLAVERY IS ABSENT (218)	0.82 OF 33	110	TEND TO BE THOSE WHERE SLAVERY IS PRESENT (163)	0.55 CF 207	6 114 27 93 XSQ= 14.05 PHI= -0.242 XP = 0.0002
116	IN ALL CASES ARE THCSE WHERE OCCUPATIONAL SPECIALIZATION IS PART-TIME CNLY (34) JMH	1.00 OF 5	116	DRIFT LESS TOWARD BEING THCSE WHERE OCCUPATIONAL SPECIALIZATICN IS PART-TIME ONLY (34) JMH	0.55 CF 33	0 15 5 18 XSQ= 2.09 PHI= -0.235 EP = 0.0730
118	IN ALL CASES ARE THCSE WHERE THE PERCENTAGE CF OCCUPATIONS THAT ARE SPECIALIZEC IS LOW (25) WME	1.00 OF 4	118	TILT TOWARD BEING THOSE WHERE THE PERCENTAGE OF OCCUPATICNS THAT ARE SPECIALIZED IS HIGH OR MEDIUM (24) WME	0.60 CF 30	0 18 4 12 XSQ= 2.98 PHI= -0.296 EP = 0.0392
120	DRIFT TOWARD BEING THCSE WHERE THE CRAFT SPECIALIZATION SCORE IS LOW (17) WME	0.75 OF 4	120	DRIFT TOWARD BEING THOSE WHERE THE CRAFT SPECIALIZATICN SCORE IS HIGH OR MEDIUM (36) WME	0.74 CF 34	1 25 3 9 XSQ= 1.98 PHI= -0.228 EP = 0.0842

130	IN ALL CASES ARE THOSE WHERE LEATHER WORKING IS MAINLY DONE BY FEMALES (45)	1.00 OF 5	130	TILT TOWARD BEING THOSE WHERE LEATHER WORKING IS MAINLY DONE BY MALES (39)	0.61 OF 41	0 25 5 16 XSQ= 4.45 PHI= -0.311 XP = 0.0350
138	IN ALL CASES ARE THOSE WHERE SUPERORDINATE JUSTICE IS ABSENT (18) BBW	1.00 OF 4	138	TILT TOWARD BEING THOSE WHERE SUPERORDINATE JUSTICE IS PRESENT (22) BBW	0.67 OF 21	0 14 4 7 XSQ= 3.66 PHI= -0.382 EP = 0.0261
142	DRIFT TOWARD BEING THOSE WHERE THE LEVEL OF SOCIAL SANCTION IS PRIVATE SETTLEMENT, RATHER THAN PUBLIC CORPOREAL SANCTION OR PUBLIC PROPERTY SETTLEMENT (16) JMH	0.60 OF 5	142	DRIFT TOWARD BEING THOSE WHERE THE LEVEL OF SOCIAL SANCTION IS PUBLIC CORPOREAL SANCTION OR PUBLIC PROPERTY SANCTION, RATHER THAN PRIVATE SETTLEMENT (38) JMH	0.82 OF 33	2 27 3 6 XSQ= 2.21 PHI= -0.241 EP = 0.0755
186	TILT TOWARD BEING THOSE WHERE THE KIN GROUP IS OTHER THAN EXCLUSIVELY PATRILINEAL (250)	0.59 OF 34	186	TILT TOWARD BEING THOSE WHERE THE KIN GROUP IS EXCLUSIVELY PATRILINEAL (150)	0.62 OF 218	14 136 20 82 XSQ= 4.65 PHI= -0.136 XP = 0.0311
187	LEAN LESS TOWARD BEING THOSE WHERE THE KIN GROUP IS OTHER THAN EXCLUSIVELY MATRILINEAL (344)	0.59 OF 34	187	LEAN MORE TOWARD BEING THOSE WHERE THE KIN GROUP IS OTHER THAN EXCLUSIVELY MATRILINEAL (344)	0.81 OF 217	14 41 20 176 XSQ= 7.28 PHI= 0.170 XP = 0.0070
190	TILT LESS TOWARD BEING THOSE WHERE THE KIN GROUP IS PATRILINEAL OR DOUBLE-DESCENT, RATHER THAN MATRILINEAL (186)	0.59 OF 34	190	TILT MORE TOWARD BEING THOSE WHERE THE KIN GROUP IS PATRILINEAL OR DOUBLE-DESCENT, RATHER THAN MATRILINEAL (186)	0.78 OF 213	20 166 14 47 XSQ= 4.78 PHI= -0.139 XP = 0.0289
196	TILT LESS TOWARD BEING THOSE WHERE INDIVIDUAL RIGHTS IN REAL PROPERTY, AND RULES FOR INHERITANCE, ARE PRESENT (194)	0.57 OF 21	196	TILT MORE TOWARD BEING THOSE WHERE INDIVIDUAL RIGHTS IN REAL PROPERTY, AND RULES FOR INHERITANCE, ARE PRESENT (194)	0.80 OF 161	12 128 9 33 XSQ= 4.05 PHI= -0.149 XP = 0.0442
209	LEAN LESS TOWARD BEING THOSE WHERE MARITAL RESIDENCE IS PATRILOCAL, VIRILOCAL, OR AVUNCULOCAL, RATHER THAN MATRILOCAL OR UXORILOCAL (270)	0.70 OF 33	209	LEAN MORE TOWARD BEING THOSE WHERE MARITAL RESIDENCE IS PATRILOCAL, VIRILOCAL, OR AVUNCULOCAL, RATHER THAN MATRILOCAL OR UXORILOCAL (270)	0.89 OF 205	23 182 10 23 XSQ= 7.14 PHI= -0.173 XP = 0.0075
210	LEAN LESS TOWARD BEING THOSE WHERE MARITAL RESIDENCE IS PATRILOCAL, RATHER THAN MATRILOCAL (169)	0.64 OF 25	210	LEAN MORE TOWARD BEING THOSE WHERE MARITAL RESIDENCE IS PATRILOCAL, RATHER THAN MATRILOCAL (169)	0.87 OF 174	16 152 9 22 XSQ= 7.38 PHI= -0.193 XP = 0.0066

```
214  TILT LESS TOWARD BEING THOSE    0.58 OF  19    214  TILT MORE TOWARD BEING THOSE    0.82 OF 109       8   20
     WHERE FIRST COUSIN MARRIAGE,                        WHERE FIRST COUSIN MARRIAGE,                     11   89
     IF PERMITTED,                                       IF PERMITTED,                              XSQ=    4.04
     IS OTHER THAN UNILATERAL  (144)                     IS OTHER THAN UNILATERAL  (144)            PHI=   0.178
                                                                                                    XP =  0.0443

234  TILT MORE TOWARD BEING THOSE    0.90 OF  30    234  TILT LESS TOWARD BEING THOSE    0.65 OF 159      27  104
     WHERE THE COUSIN TERMINOLOGY IS                     WHERE THE COUSIN TERMINOLOGY IS                   3   55
     OF CROW, OMAHA, OR IROQUOIS TYPE,                   OF CROW, OMAHA, OR IROQUOIS TYPE,          XSQ=    6.07
     RATHER THAN                                         RATHER THAN                                PHI=   0.179
     ESKIMO OR HAWAIIAN TYPE  (152)                      ESKIMO OR HAWAIIAN TYPE  (152)             XP =  0.0138

285  IN ALL CASES ARE THOSE          1.00 OF   3    285  DRIFT TOWARD BEING THOSE        0.60 OF  20       3    8
     WHERE THE SEX TABOO DURING PREGNANCY                WHERE THE SEX TABOO DURING PREGNANCY              0   12
     IS PRESENT  (14) BCA                                IS ABSENT OR INFERRED ABSENT  (17) BCA     XSQ=    1.74
                                                                                                    PHI=   0.275
                                                                                                    EP =  0.0932

318  IN ALL CASES ARE THOSE          1.00 OF   8    318  LEAN TOWARD BEING THOSE         0.57 OF  40       8   17
     WHERE THE OVERALL INDULGENCE                        WHERE THE OVERALL INDULGENCE                      0   23
     OF THE INFANT                                       OF THE INFANT                              XSQ=    6.68
     IS HIGH  (40) B-B-C                                 IS LOW  (31) B-B-C                         PHI=   0.373
                                                                                                    XP =  0.0098

322  TILT TOWARD BEING THOSE         0.88 OF   8    322  TILT TOWARD BEING THOSE         0.65 OF  34       7   12
     WHERE THE CONSISTENCY OF REDUCTION                  WHERE THE CONSISTENCY OF REDUCTION                1   22
     OF THE INFANT'S DRIVES                              OF THE INFANT'S DRIVES                     XSQ=    5.17
     IS HIGH  (27) B-B-C                                 IS LOW  (32) B-B-C                         PHI=   0.351
                                                                                                    XP =  0.0229

331  IN ALL CASES ARE THOSE          1.00 OF   3    331  DRIFT TOWARD BEING THOSE        0.65 OF  20       3    7
     WHERE THE AGE AT BEGINNING                          WHERE THE AGE AT BEGINNING                        0   13
     OF INDEPENDENCE TRAINING                            OF INDEPENDENCE TRAINING                   XSQ=    2.23
     IS 3.8 YEARS OR HIGHER  (16) W-C                    IS LOWER THAN 3.8 YEARS  (21) W-C          PHI=   0.311
                                                                                                    EP =  0.0678

336  TILT TOWARD BEING THOSE         0.73 OF  11    336  TILT TOWARD BEING THOSE         0.67 OF  42       3   28
     WHERE THE TOTAL POSITIVE PRESSURE TOWARD            WHERE THE TOTAL POSITIVE PRESSURE TOWARD          8   14
     DEVELOPING RESPONSIBLE BEHAVIOR                     DEVELOPING RESPONSIBLE BEHAVIOR            XSQ=    4.07
     IN THE CHILD                                        IN THE CHILD                               PHI=  -0.277
     IS LOW  (32) B-B-C                                  IS HIGH  (43) B-B-C                        XP =  0.0437

337  TILT TOWARD BEING THOSE         0.73 OF  11    337  TILT TOWARD BEING THOSE         0.70 OF  40       3   28
     WHERE THE CHILD'S INFERRED ANXIETY OVER             WHERE THE CHILD'S INFERRED ANXIETY OVER           8   12
     NON-PERFORMANCE OF RESPONSIBLE BEHAVIOR             NON-PERFORMANCE OF RESPONSIBLE BEHAVIOR    XSQ=    4.94
     IS LOW  (35) B-B-C                                  IS HIGH  (38) B-B-C                        PHI=  -0.311
                                                                                                    XP =  0.0263

340  DRIFT TOWARD BEING THOSE        0.88 OF   8    340  DRIFT TOWARD BEING THOSE        0.52 OF  25       7   12
     WHERE THE TOTAL POSITIVE PRESSURE TOWARD            WHERE THE TOTAL POSITIVE PRESSURE TOWARD          1   13
     DEVELOPING NURTURANT BEHAVIOR                       DEVELOPING NURTURANT BEHAVIOR              XSQ=    2.42
     IN THE CHILD                                        IN THE CHILD                               PHI=   0.271
     IS HIGH  (28) B-B-C                                 IS LOW  (20) B-B-C                         EP =  0.0982
```

370	LEAN TOWARD BEING THOSE WHERE THE SEGREGATION OF ADOLESCENT BOYS IS COMPLETE OR PARTIAL (95)	0.79 OF 24	370	LEAN TOWARD BEING THOSE WHERE THE SEGREGATION OF ADOLESCENT BOYS IS ABSENT (148)	0.53 OF 136	19 64 5 72 XSQ= 7.19 PHI= 0.212 XP = 0.0073
377	DRIFT MORE TOWARD BEING THOSE WHERE MALE GENITAL MUTILATION IS ABSENT (242)	0.81 OF 32	377	DRIFT LESS TOWARD BEING THOSE WHERE MALE GENITAL MUTILATION IS ABSENT (242)	0.62 OF 176	6 67 26 109 XSQ= 3.63 PHI= -0.132 XP = 0.0568
393	DRIFT TOWARD BEING THOSE WHERE EXTRAMARITAL COITUS IS PERMITTED, RATHER THAN PUNISHED (41) F-B	0.80 OF 10	393	DRIFT TOWARD BEING THOSE WHERE EXTRAMARITAL COITUS IS PUNISHED, RATHER THAN PERMITTED (43) F-B	0.58 OF 45	2 26 8 19 XSQ= 3.28 PHI= -0.244 XP = 0.0700
426	TEND TO BE THOSE WHERE A HIGH GOD IS ABSENT (104) GES,EA	0.78 OF 27	426	TEND TO BE THOSE WHERE A HIGH GOD IS PRESENT (156) GES,EA	0.69 OF 144	6 99 21 45 XSQ= 18.85 PHI= -0.332 XP = 0.0000
440	IN ALL CASES ARE THOSE WHERE FEAR OF SPIRITS IS LOW (29) W-C	1.00 OF 5	440	TILT TOWARD BEING THOSE WHERE FEAR OF SPIRITS IS HIGH (32) W-C	0.53 OF 32	0 17 5 15 XSQ= 3.01 PHI= -0.285 EP = 0.0498
441	IN ALL CASES ARE THOSE WHERE FEAR OF HUMAN BEINGS IS HIGH (29) W-C	1.00 OF 5	441	TILT TOWARD BEING THOSE WHERE FEAR OF HUMAN BEINGS IS LOW (32) W-C	0.59 OF 32	5 13 0 19 XSQ= 3.96 PHI= 0.327 EP = 0.0197
444	IN ALL CASES ARE THOSE WHERE THE USE OF DREAMS TO SEEK AND CONTROL SUPERNATURAL POWERS IS HIGH (28) RGD	1.00 OF 3	444	DRIFT TOWARD BEING THOSE WHERE THE USE OF DREAMS TO SEEK AND CONTROL SUPERNATURAL POWERS IS LOW (27) RGD	0.59 OF 32	3 13 0 19 XSQ= 1.87 PHI= 0.231 EP = 0.0856
458	IN ALL CASES ARE THOSE WHERE GAMES, IF PRESENT, DO NOT INCLUDE GAMES OF STRATEGY (119) R-A-B,EA	1.00 OF 21	458	TEND TO BE THOSE WHERE GAMES, IF PRESENT, INCLUDE GAMES OF STRATEGY (52) R-A-B,EA	0.51 OF 82	0 42 21 40 XSQ= 16.10 PHI= -0.395 XP = 0.0001
460	LEAN TOWARD BEING THOSE WHERE GAMES, IF PRESENT, ARE LIMITED TO GAMES OF SKILL ONLY (67) R-A-B,EA	0.67 OF 21	460	LEAN TOWARD BEING THOSE WHERE GAMES, IF PRESENT, ARE NOT LIMITED TO GAMES OF SKILL ONLY (104) R-A-B,EA	0.72 OF 82	14 23 7 59 XSQ= 9.22 PHI= 0.299 XP = 0.0024

183/

```
476  IN ALL CASES ARE THCSE           1.00 OF    4        476  TILT TOWARD BEING THOSE         0.63 CF  27              4   10
     WHERE THE DEGREE CF INSOBRIETY IS                         WHERE THE DEGREE OF INSCBRIETY IS                        0   17
     STRONG  (31) DH                                           MODERATE OR SLIGHT  (18) DH                        XSQ=     3.32
                                                                                                                  PHI=    0.327
                                                                                                                  EP =   0.0318
```

184 CULTURES
WHERE THE LARGEST NON-COGNATIC KIN GROUP
IS THE MOEITY OR PHRATRY (77)

184 CULTURES
WHERE THE LARGEST NON-COGNATIC KIN GROUP
IS SMALLER THAN A PHRATRY, I. E.
A SIB OR LINEAGE (175)

BACKGROUND ON PAGE 107

BOTH SUBJECT AND PREDICATE

77 IN LEFT COLUMN

ABOR	AJIE	APINAYE	ARANDA	ARAPESH	BASSERI	BEJA	BIRIFOR	BORCRO	BUNLAP
CHENCHU	CREEK	CROW	DAGUR	DIERI	DILLING	EGYPTIANS	ENGA	EYAK	FON
GARO	GOND	HAIDA	HASANIA	HAZARA	HEBREWS	HERERO	KALMYK	KAPAUKU	KARIERA
KASKA	KAZAK	KERAKI	KOHISTANI	KONSO	LAKALAI	LAU	LESU	LHOTA NAGA	LOLO
MANDAN	MERINA	MINANGKABAU	MIWOK	MOTA	MUNDURUCU	MURINBATA	MURNGIN	NABESNA	NAVAHO
OMAHA	PALAUANS	PATHAN	PURARI	REGEIBAT	RWALA	SAMOYED	SEMINOLE	SENIANG	SHERENTE
SOMALI	TALAMANCA	TIMBIRA	TIMUCUA	TIV	TIWI	TROBRIAND	TSHIMSHIAN	TUCUNA	TURKMEN
WIKMUNKAN	WINNEBAGO	WOGEO	WUTE	YAKUT	YOKUTS	ZUNI			

175 IN RIGHT COLUMN

AINU	AKHA	ALBANIANS	ALORESE	AMBA	ARAUCANIANS	ARYANS	ASHANTI	ATAYAL	AYMARA
AZANDE	BABWA	BAJUN	BAMBARA	BAMILEKE	BANDA	BARABRA	BARI	BATAK	BAYA
BELU	BEMBA	BENGALI	BETE	BHIL	BHUIYA	BOZO	BUDUMA	BURUSHO	BURYAT
CALLINAGO	CHAGGA	CHERKESS	CHEROKEE	COCHITI	COORG	DARD	DELAWARE	DIEGUENO	DOBUANS
DOGON	DORCBO	FANG	FOX	FUTAJALONKE	GANDA	GILYAK	GISU	GOAJIRO	GUAHIBO
GURE	HANO	HEHE	HO	HURON	ILA	IRAQW	JEMEZ	KABYLE	KACHIN
KAREN	KATAB	KERALA	KET	KHALKA	KHASI	KHEVSUR	KIKUYU	KISSI	KOREANS
KPE	KUBA	KURTATCHI	LAKHER	LAMBA	LAMET	LANGO	LEPCHA	LIFU	LUBA
LUO	MAGUZAWA	MAM	MAMVU	MANCHU	MANUS	MARGI	MARICOPA	MARSHALLESE	MASAI
MATAKAM	MAYA	MBUGWE	MBUNDU	MBUTI	MENDE	MIAMI	MIAO	MIN CHINESE	MINCHIA
MNONG GAR	MONGO	MONGUOR	MOSSI	MZAB	NAMA	NANDI	NDEMBU	NOMLAKI	NUER
NUPE	NURI	NYAKYUSA	NYANEKA	NYARO	NYORO	OJIBWA	OKINAWANS	ORAON	PALIKUR
PAWNEE	PENDE	PONAPEANS	PUKAPUKA	PURUM	RIFFIANS	ROTINESE	ROTUMANS	RUNDI	SANDAWE
SANTAL	SARAMACCA	SERBS	SHILLUK	SHLUH	SINDHI	SIRIONO	SIUAI	SIWANS	SONGHAI
SOTHO	SWAZI	SYRIANS	TALLENSI	TAMIL	TANALA	TANIMBARESE	TEDA	TENDA	TERA
TESO	THONGA	TIBETANS	TIGRINYA	TIKOPIA	TODA	TOLOWA	TRUKESE	TUCANO	TURKANA
TZELTAL	VEDDA	VENDA	VIETNAMESE	WANTOAT	WAROPEN	WITOTO	WOLEAIANS	WOLOF	YAGUA
YAKO	YAO	YAPESE	YOMBE	YORUBA					

148 EXCLUDED BECAUSE IRRELEVANT

3 TEND MORE TO BE THOSE LOCATED OUTSIDE OF AFRICA (320) — 0.92 OF 77

3 TEND LESS TO BE THOSE LOCATED OUTSIDE OF AFRICA (320) — 0.62 OF 175

6	67
71	108
XSQ=	22.70
PHI=	-0.300
XP =	0.0000

6	LEAN LESS TOWARD BEING THOSE LOCATED OUTSIDE OF THE INSULAR PACIFIC (330)	0.70 OF 77	6	LEAN MORE TOWARD BEING THOSE LOCATED OUTSIDE OF THE INSULAR PACIFIC (330)	0.88 OF 175	23 21 54 154 XSQ= 10.64 PHI= 0.205 XP = 0.0011
8	LEAN LESS TOWARD BEING THOSE LOCATED OUTSIDE OF NORTH AMERICA (330)	0.79 OF 77	8	LEAN MORE TOWARD BEING THOSE LOCATED OUTSIDE OF NORTH AMERICA (330)	0.92 OF 175	16 14 61 161 XSQ= 7.15 PHI= 0.168 XP = 0.0075
15	TILT TOWARD BEING THOSE WHERE THE LATITUDE IS TWENTY DEGREES OR GREATER (183)	0.53 OF 77	15	TILT TOWARD BEING THOSE WHERE THE LATITUDE IS LESS THAN TWENTY DEGREES (217)	0.62 OF 175	41 66 36 109 XSQ= 4.66 PHI= 0.136 XP = 0.0308
33	DRIFT LESS TOWARD BEING THOSE WHERE THE NATURAL ENVIRONMENT IS OTHER THAN 'VERY HARSH,' I.E., DESERT, DESERT GRASSES AND SHRUBS, TUNDRA, OR HIGH PLATEAU STEPPE (341) FWM	0.81 OF 77	33	DRIFT MORE TOWARD BEING THOSE WHERE THE NATURAL ENVIRONMENT IS OTHER THAN 'VERY HARSH,' I.E., DESERT, DESERT GRASSES AND SHRUBS, TUNDRA, OR HIGH PLATEAU STEPPE (341) FWM	0.90 OF 175	15 18 62 157 XSQ= 3.21 PHI= 0.113 XP = 0.0734
36	DRIFT LESS TOWARD BEING THOSE WHERE THE NATURAL ENVIRONMENT IS OTHER THAN 'VERY HARSH,' OR SUB-TROPICAL BUSH, OR TEMPERATE GRASSLAND (292) FWM	0.69 OF 77	36	DRIFT MORE TOWARD BEING THOSE WHERE THE NATURAL ENVIRONMENT IS OTHER THAN 'VERY HARSH,' OR SUB-TROPICAL BUSH, OR TEMPERATE GRASSLAND (292) FWM	0.80 OF 175	24 35 53 140 XSQ= 3.12 PHI= 0.111 XP = 0.0772
44	TEND LESS TO BE THOSE WHERE SETTLEMENTS ARE FIXED (222)	0.53 OF 68	44	TEND MORE TO BE THOSE WHERE SETTLEMENTS ARE FIXED (222)	0.79 OF 143	36 113 32 30 XSQ= 13.88 PHI= -0.256 XP = 0.0002
45	DRIFT MORE TOWARD BEING THOSE WHERE SETTLEMENTS, IF FIXED, ARE COMPACT, RATHER THAN NON-COMPACT (149)	0.81 OF 36	45	DRIFT LESS TOWARD BEING THOSE WHERE SETTLEMENTS, IF FIXED, ARE COMPACT, RATHER THAN NON-COMPACT (149)	0.61 OF 113	29 69 7 44 XSQ= 3.78 PHI= 0.159 XP = 0.0518
46	TEND LESS TO BE THOSE OTHER THAN WHERE SETTLEMENTS ARE NON-FIXED AND MOVEMENT IS NOMADIC (260)	0.69 OF 68	46	TEND MORE TO BE THOSE OTHER THAN WHERE SETTLEMENTS ARE NON-FIXED AND MOVEMENT IS NOMADIC (260)	0.89 OF 143	21 16 47 127 XSQ= 11.04 PHI= 0.229 XP = 0.0009
51	TEND LESS TO BE THOSE WHERE SUBSISTENCE IS PRIMARILY BY FOOD PRODUCTION -- I. E., AGRICULTURE OR HUSBANDRY -- RATHER THAN BY GATHERING (253)	0.57 OF 77	51	TEND MORE TO BE THOSE WHERE SUBSISTENCE IS PRIMARILY BY FOOD PRODUCTION -- I. E., AGRICULTURE OR HUSBANDRY -- RATHER THAN BY GATHERING (253)	0.80 OF 175	44 140 33 35 XSQ= 13.04 PHI= -0.228 XP = 0.0003

54	LEAN LESS TOWARD BEING THOSE WHERE FOOD PRODUCTION IS BY INTENSIVE OR SIMPLE AGRICULTURE, RATHER THAN BY INCIPIENT FOOD PRODUCTION (192)	0.70 OF 43	54	LEAN MORE TOWARD BEING THOSE WHERE FOOD PRODUCTION IS BY INTENSIVE OR SIMPLE AGRICULTURE, RATHER THAN BY INCIPIENT FOOD PRODUCTION (192)	0.89 OF 124	30 110 13 14 XSQ= 7.11 PHI= -0.206 XP = 0.0077
56	TILT LESS TOWARD BEING THOSE WHERE FOOD PRODUCTION IS BY SIMPLE AGRICULTURE, RATHER THAN BY INCIPIENT FOOD PRODUCTION (101)	0.58 OF 31	56	TILT MORE TOWARD BEING THOSE WHERE FOOD PRODUCTION IS BY SIMPLE AGRICULTURE, RATHER THAN BY INCIPIENT FOOD PRODUCTION (101)	0.81 OF 72	18 58 13 14 XSQ= 4.56 PHI= -0.211 XP = 0.0326
63	TILT LESS TOWARD BEING THOSE WHERE HUSBANDRY, IF PRESENT, IS PRINCIPALLY IN THE FORM OF BOVINE, EQUINE, CAMEL-LIKE, OR DEER-LIKE ANIMALS, RATHER THAN PIGS, SHEEP, OR GOATS (152)	0.54 OF 46	63	TILT MORE TOWARD BEING THOSE WHERE HUSBANDRY, IF PRESENT, IS PRINCIPALLY IN THE FORM OF BOVINE, EQUINE, CAMEL-LIKE, OR DEER-LIKE ANIMALS, RATHER THAN PIGS, SHEEP, OR GOATS (152)	0.72 OF 115	25 83 21 32 XSQ= 3.96 PHI= -0.157 XP = 0.0467
71	TEND TO BE THOSE WHERE METAL WORKING IS ABSENT (153)	0.72 OF 53	71	TEND TO BE THOSE WHERE METAL WORKING IS PRESENT (98)	0.61 OF 105	15 64 38 41 XSQ= 13.74 PHI= -0.295 XP = 0.0002
74	TEND TO BE THOSE WHERE POTTERY IS ABSENT (93)	0.57 OF 51	74	TEND TO BE THOSE WHERE POTTERY IS PRESENT (145)	0.74 OF 95	22 70 29 25 XSQ= 12.01 PHI= -0.287 XP = 0.0005
81	TILT MORE TOWARD BEING THOSE WHERE NO CITY OR TOWN IS PRESENT, AND THE AVERAGE COMMUNITY SIZE IS SMALLER THAN 200 (135)	0.75 OF 44	81	TILT LESS TOWARD BEING THOSE WHERE NO CITY OR TOWN IS PRESENT, AND THE AVERAGE COMMUNITY SIZE IS SMALLER THAN 200 (135)	0.53 OF 104	11 49 33 55 XSQ= 5.39 PHI= -0.191 XP = 0.0203
82	DRIFT LESS TOWARD BEING THOSE WHERE A CITY OR TOWN IS PRESENT, OR THE AVERAGE COMMUNITY SIZE IS FIFTY OR GREATER (178)	0.73 OF 44	82	DRIFT MORE TOWARD BEING THOSE WHERE A CITY OR TOWN IS PRESENT, OR THE AVERAGE COMMUNITY SIZE IS FIFTY OR GREATER (178)	0.88 OF 104	32 91 12 13 XSQ= 3.81 PHI= -0.160 XP = 0.0509
83	DRIFT MORE TOWARD BEING THOSE WHERE, WITH NO CITY AND NO TOWN PRESENT, THE AVERAGE COMMUNITY SIZE IS SMALLER THAN 200, RATHER THAN BETWEEN 200 AND 999 (135)	0.82 OF 40	83	DRIFT LESS TOWARD BEING THOSE WHERE, WITH NO CITY AND NO TOWN PRESENT, THE AVERAGE COMMUNITY SIZE IS SMALLER THAN 200, RATHER THAN BETWEEN 200 AND 999 (135)	0.65 OF 84	7 29 33 55 XSQ= 3.03 PHI= -0.156 XP = 0.0817
96	TILT TOWARD BEING THOSE WHERE THE HIERARCHY OF NATIONAL JURISDICTION HAS NO LEVELS (156) GES,EA	0.53 OF 68	96	TILT TOWARD BEING THOSE WHERE THE HIERARCHY OF NATIONAL JURISDICTION HAS FOUR, THREE, TWO OR ONE LEVEL (174) GES,EA	0.65 OF 142	32 93 36 49 XSQ= 5.74 PHI= -0.165 XP = 0.0166

100	DRIFT LESS TOWARD BEING THOSE 0.79 OF 68 WHERE HIERARCHIES ARE MORE COMPLEX THAN THE 'SIMPLEST,' I. E., MORE COMPLEX THAN TWO LOCAL LEVELS WITH NO NATIONAL LEVELS (267) GES,EA	100	DRIFT MORE TOWARD BEING THOSE 0.89 OF 142 WHERE HIERARCHIES ARE MORE COMPLEX THAN THE 'SIMPLEST,' I. E., MORE COMPLEX THAN TWO LOCAL LEVELS WITH NO NATIONAL LEVELS (267) GES,EA	54 127 14 15 XSQ= 3.09 PHI= -0.121 XP = 0.0790
102	DRIFT TOWARD BEING THOSE 0.53 OF 76 WHERE CLASS STRATIFICATION IS ABSENT (180)	102	DRIFT TOWARD BEING THOSE 0.60 OF 169 WHERE CLASS STRATIFICATION IS PRESENT (203)	36 101 40 68 XSQ= 2.78 PHI= -0.107 XP = 0.0952
106	TILT TOWARD BEING THOSE 0.58 OF 36 WHERE CLASS STRATIFICATION, IF PRESENT, IS BASED ON WEALTH (77)	106	TILT TOWARD BEING THOSE 0.67 OF 101 WHERE CLASS STRATIFICATION, IF PRESENT, IS BASED ON SOMETHING OTHER THAN WEALTH (126)	21 33 15 68 XSQ= 6.28 PHI= 0.214 XP = 0.0122
109	DRIFT MORE TOWARD BEING THOSE 0.88 OF 69 WHERE CASTES ARE ABSENT (317)	109	DRIFT LESS TOWARD BEING THOSE 0.77 OF 157 WHERE CASTES ARE ABSENT (317)	8 36 61 121 XSQ= 3.24 PHI= -0.120 XP = 0.0719
110	TILT TOWARD BEING THOSE 0.63 OF 73 WHERE SLAVERY IS ABSENT (218)	110	TILT TOWARD BEING THOSE 0.56 OF 167 WHERE SLAVERY IS PRESENT (163)	27 93 46 74 XSQ= 6.38 PHI= -0.163 XP = 0.0116
118	TEND TO BE THOSE 0.91 OF 11 WHERE THE PERCENTAGE OF OCCUPATIONS THAT ARE SPECIALIZED IS LOW (25) WME	118	TEND TO BE THOSE 0.74 OF 23 WHERE THE PERCENTAGE OF OCCUPATIONS THAT ARE SPECIALIZED IS HIGH OR MEDIUM (24) WME	1 17 10 6 XSQ= 10.08 PHI= -0.545 EP = 0.0006
120	TILT TOWARD BEING THOSE 0.58 OF 12 WHERE THE CRAFT SPECIALIZATION SCORE IS LOW (17) WME	120	TILT TOWARD BEING THOSE 0.81 OF 26 WHERE THE CRAFT SPECIALIZATION SCORE IS HIGH OR MEDIUM (36) WME	5 21 7 5 XSQ= 4.14 PHI= -0.330 EP = 0.0258
130	TILT TOWARD BEING THOSE 0.77 OF 13 WHERE LEATHER WORKING IS MAINLY DONE BY FEMALES (45)	130	TILT TOWARD BEING THOSE 0.67 OF 33 WHERE LEATHER WORKING IS MAINLY DONE BY MALES (39)	3 22 10 11 XSQ= 5.49 PHI= -0.346 XP = 0.0191
131	LEAN LESS TOWARD BEING THOSE 0.76 OF 33 WHERE THE CONSTRUCTION OF PERMANENT HOUSES OR THE ERECTION OF TEMPORARY DWELLINGS IS MAINLY DONE BY MALES (136)	131	LEAN MORE TOWARD BEING THOSE 0.98 OF 56 WHERE THE CONSTRUCTION OF PERMANENT HOUSES OR THE ERECTION OF TEMPORARY DWELLINGS IS MAINLY DONE BY MALES (136)	25 55 8 1 XSQ= 9.18 PHI= -0.321 XP = 0.0024

139	DRIFT MORE TOWARD BEING THOSE 0.90 OF 10 WHERE SUPERORDINATE PUNISHMENT IS ABSENT (25) BBW	139	DRIFT LESS TOWARD BEING THOSE 0.53 OF 15 WHERE SUPERORDINATE PUNISHMENT IS ABSENT (25) BBW	1 7 9 8 XSQ= 2.21 PHI= -0.298 EP = 0.0875
164	IN ALL CASES ARE THOSE 1.00 OF 4 WHERE THE EMPHASIS ON INDIVIDUAL VOLITION AS THE CAUSE OR SOURCE OF ILLNESS IS HIGH (9) MJ	164	DRIFT TOWARD BEING THOSE 0.67 OF 6 WHERE THE EMPHASIS ON INDIVIDUAL VOLITION AS THE CAUSE OR SOURCE OF ILLNESS IS LOW (9) MJ	4 2 0 4 XSQ= 2.10 PHI= 0.458 EP = 0.0762
187	DRIFT LESS TOWARD BEING THOSE 0.70 OF 77 WHERE THE KIN GROUP IS OTHER THAN EXCLUSIVELY MATRILINEAL (344)	187	DRIFT MORE TOWARD BEING THOSE 0.82 OF 174 WHERE THE KIN GROUP IS OTHER THAN EXCLUSIVELY MATRILINEAL (344)	23 32 54 142 XSQ= 3.47 PHI= 0.118 XP = 0.0626
190	DRIFT LESS TOWARD BEING THOSE 0.67 OF 76 WHERE THE KIN GROUP IS PATRILINEAL OR DOUBLE-DESCENT, RATHER THAN MATRILINEAL (186)	190	DRIFT MORE TOWARD BEING THOSE 0.79 OF 171 WHERE THE KIN GROUP IS PATRILINEAL OR DOUBLE-DESCENT, RATHER THAN MATRILINEAL (186)	51 135 25 36 XSQ= 3.36 PHI= -0.117 XP = 0.0669
196	LEAN LESS TOWARD BEING THOSE 0.62 OF 53 WHERE INDIVIDUAL RIGHTS IN REAL PROPERTY, AND RULES FOR INHERITANCE, ARE PRESENT (194)	196	LEAN MORE TOWARD BEING THOSE 0.83 OF 129 WHERE INDIVIDUAL RIGHTS IN REAL PROPERTY, AND RULES FOR INHERITANCE, ARE PRESENT (194)	33 107 20 22 XSQ= 7.92 PHI= -0.209 XP = 0.0049
198	TILT LESS TOWARD BEING THOSE 0.72 OF 32 WHERE RULES FOR THE INHERITANCE OF REAL PROPERTY, IF PRESENT, FAVOR THE MALE HEIR OR LINE, RATHER THAN THE FEMALE (144)	198	TILT MORE TOWARD BEING THOSE 0.89 OF 104 WHERE RULES FOR THE INHERITANCE OF REAL PROPERTY, IF PRESENT, FAVOR THE MALE HEIR OR LINE, RATHER THAN THE FEMALE (144)	23 93 9 11 XSQ= 4.69 PHI= -0.186 XP = 0.0303
209	DRIFT LESS TOWARD BEING THOSE 0.79 OF 73 WHERE MARITAL RESIDENCE IS PATRILOCAL, VIRILOCAL, OR AVUNCULOCAL, RATHER THAN MATRILOCAL OR UXORILOCAL (270)	209	DRIFT MORE TOWARD BEING THOSE 0.89 OF 165 WHERE MARITAL RESIDENCE IS PATRILOCAL, VIRILOCAL, OR AVUNCULOCAL, RATHER THAN MATRILOCAL OR UXORILOCAL (270)	58 147 15 18 XSQ= 3.17 PHI= -0.115 XP = 0.0749
225	TILT TOWARD BEING THOSE 0.52 OF 27 WHERE COUSIN MARRIAGE IS PREFERENTIALLY OR PERMISSIVELY PATRILATERAL, RATHER THAN MATRILATERAL (23)	225	TILT TOWARD BEING THOSE 0.79 OF 38 WHERE COUSIN MARRIAGE IS PREFERENTIALLY OR PERMISSIVELY MATRILATERAL, RATHER THAN PATRILATERAL (43)	14 8 13 30 XSQ= 5.38 PHI= 0.288 XP = 0.0203
234	LEAN MORE TOWARD BEING THOSE 0.84 OF 57 WHERE THE COUSIN TERMINOLOGY IS OF CROW, OMAHA, OR IROQUOIS TYPE, RATHER THAN ESKIMO OR HAWAIIAN TYPE (152)	234	LEAN LESS TOWARD BEING THOSE 0.63 OF 132 WHERE THE COUSIN TERMINOLOGY IS OF CROW, OMAHA, OR IROQUOIS TYPE, RATHER THAN ESKIMO OR HAWAIIAN TYPE (152)	48 83 9 49 XSQ= 7.54 PHI= 0.200 XP = 0.0060

304	DRIFT TOWARD BEING THOSE 0.67 OF 9 WHERE THE EARLY ANAL SATISFACTION POTENTIAL IS HIGH (19) W-C	304	DRIFT TOWARD BEING THOSE 0.72 OF 18 WHERE THE EARLY ANAL SATISFACTION POTENTIAL IS LOW (22) W-C	6 5 3 13 XSQ= 2.32 PHI= 0.293 EP = 0.0969
318	TILT TOWARD BEING THOSE 0.81 OF 16 WHERE THE OVERALL INDULGENCE OF THE INFANT IS HIGH (40) B-B-C	318	TILT TOWARD BEING THOSE 0.63 OF 32 WHERE THE OVERALL INDULGENCE OF THE INFANT IS LOW (31) B-B-C	13 12 3 20 XSQ= 6.52 PHI= 0.369 XP = 0.0107
329	IN ALL CASES ARE THOSE 1.00 OF 4 WHERE THE AGE AT TOILET TRAINING IS TWO YEARS OR HIGHER (10) W-C	329	DRIFT TOWARD BEING THOSE 0.75 OF 8 WHERE THE AGE AT TOILET TRAINING IS LOWER THAN TWO YEARS (11) W-C	4 2 0 6 XSQ= 3.38 PHI= 0.530 EP = 0.0606
335	TILT TOWARD BEING THOSE 0.88 OF 8 WHERE INITIAL INDULGENCE OF DEPENDENCY IS HIGH (20) WNS	335	TILT TOWARD BEING THOSE 0.61 OF 18 WHERE INITIAL INDULGENCE OF DEPENDENCY IS LOW (18) WNS	7 7 1 11 XSQ= 3.49 PHI= 0.366 EP = 0.0357
336	DRIFT TOWARD BEING THOSE 0.60 OF 20 WHERE THE TOTAL POSITIVE PRESSURE TOWARD DEVELOPING RESPONSIBLE BEHAVIOR IN THE CHILD IS LOW (32) B-B-C	336	DRIFT TOWARD BEING THOSE 0.70 OF 33 WHERE THE TOTAL POSITIVE PRESSURE TOWARD DEVELOPING RESPONSIBLE BEHAVIOR IN THE CHILD IS HIGH (43) B-B-C	8 23 12 10 XSQ= 3.38 PHI= -0.253 XP = 0.0659
337	LEAN TOWARD BEING THOSE 0.65 OF 20 WHERE THE CHILD'S INFERRED ANXIETY OVER NON-PERFORMANCE OF RESPONSIBLE BEHAVIOR IS LOW (35) B-B-C	337	LEAN TOWARD BEING THOSE 0.77 OF 31 WHERE THE CHILD'S INFERRED ANXIETY OVER NON-PERFORMANCE OF RESPONSIBLE BEHAVIOR IS HIGH (38) B-B-C	7 24 13 7 XSQ= 7.48 PHI= -0.383 XP = 0.0062
340	TILT TOWARD BEING THOSE 0.90 OF 10 WHERE THE TOTAL POSITIVE PRESSURE TOWARD DEVELOPING NURTURANT BEHAVIOR IN THE CHILD IS HIGH (28) B-B-C	340	TILT TOWARD BEING THOSE 0.57 OF 23 WHERE THE TOTAL POSITIVE PRESSURE TOWARD DEVELOPING NURTURANT BEHAVIOR IN THE CHILD IS LOW (20) B-B-C	9 10 1 13 XSQ= 4.42 PHI= 0.366 EP = 0.0209
360	IN ALL CASES ARE THOSE 1.00 OF 5 WHERE ADOLESCENT PEER GROUPS ARE PRESENT ONLY IN A SETTING OF LEISURE, OR ELSE ARE ABSENT (23) JKH	360	DRIFT TOWARD BEING THOSE 0.53 OF 15 WHERE ADOLESCENT PEER GROUPS ARE PRESENT IN A SETTING OF WORK AND PUBLIC GATHERINGS AND LEISURE, OR AT LEAST OF PUBLIC GATHERINGS AND LEISURE (14) JKH	0 8 5 7 XSQ= 2.50 PHI= -0.354 EP = 0.0547
369	IN ALL CASES ARE THOSE 1.00 OF 11 WHERE DISSOCIATION OF THE SEXES AT ADOLESCENCE, OR CUSTOMS OF INITIATION AT ADOLESCENCE, ARE PRESENT (42) JKH	369	TILT LESS TOWARD BEING THOSE 0.58 OF 24 WHERE DISSOCIATION OF THE SEXES AT ADOLESCENCE, OR CUSTOMS OF INITIATION AT ADOLESCENCE, ARE PRESENT (42) JKH	11 14 0 10 XSQ= 4.54 PHI= 0.360 EP = 0.0146

370	TILT TOWARD BEING THOSE WHERE THE SEGREGATION OF ADOLESCENT BOYS IS COMPLETE OR PARTIAL (95)	0.65 OF 49	370	TILT TOWARD BEING THOSE WHERE THE SEGREGATION OF ADOLESCENT BOYS IS ABSENT (148)	0.54 OF 111	32 51 17 60 XSQ= 4.36 PHI= 0.165 XP = 0.0368
405	TILT TOWARD BEING THOSE WHERE EXPLANATIONS OF ILLNESS OF A DEPENDENCE NATURE ARE ABSENT (27) W-C	0.71 OF 14	405	TILT TOWARD BEING THOSE WHERE EXPLANATIONS OF ILLNESS OF A DEPENDENCE NATURE ARE PRESENT (34) W-C	0.74 OF 23	4 17 10 6 XSQ= 5.56 PHI= -0.388 EP = 0.0152
426	TEND TO BE THOSE WHERE A HIGH GOD IS ABSENT (104) GES,EA	0.59 OF 58	426	TEND TO BE THOSE WHERE A HIGH GOD IS PRESENT (156) GES,EA	0.72 OF 113	24 81 34 32 XSQ= 13.60 PHI= -0.282 XP = 0.0002
427	DRIFT TOWARD BEING THOSE WHERE A HIGH GOD, IF PRESENT, IS ACTIVE, RATHER THAN INACTIVE (87) GES,EA	0.71 OF 24	427	DRIFT TOWARD BEING THOSE WHERE A HIGH GOD, IF PRESENT, IS INACTIVE, RATHER THAN ACTIVE (69) GES,EA	0.52 OF 81	17 39 7 42 XSQ= 2.97 PHI= 0.168 XP = 0.0848
444	TILT TOWARD BEING THOSE WHERE THE USE OF DREAMS TO SEEK AND CONTROL SUPERNATURAL POWERS IS HIGH (28) RGD	0.80 OF 10	444	TILT TOWARD BEING THOSE WHERE THE USE OF DREAMS TO SEEK AND CONTROL SUPERNATURAL POWERS IS LOW (27) RGD	0.68 OF 25	8 8 2 17 XSQ= 4.84 PHI= 0.372 EP = 0.0218
458	LEAN TOWARD BEING THOSE WHERE GAMES, IF PRESENT, DO NOT INCLUDE GAMES OF STRATEGY (119) R-A-B,EA	0.79 OF 38	458	LEAN TOWARD BEING THOSE WHERE GAMES, IF PRESENT, INCLUDE GAMES OF STRATEGY (52) R-A-B,EA	0.52 OF 65	8 34 30 31 XSQ= 8.45 PHI= -0.286 XP = 0.0037
460	TILT TOWARD BEING THOSE WHERE GAMES, IF PRESENT, ARE LIMITED TO GAMES OF SKILL ONLY (67) R-A-B,EA	0.50 OF 38	460	TILT TOWARD BEING THOSE WHERE GAMES, IF PRESENT, ARE NOT LIMITED TO GAMES OF SKILL ONLY (104) R-A-B,EA	0.72 OF 65	19 18 19 47 XSQ= 4.26 PHI= 0.203 XP = 0.0390

****

185 CULTURES WHERE THE LARGEST NON-COGNATIC KIN GROUP IS THE MOIETY OR PHRATRY OR SIB (194)	185 CULTURES WHERE THE LARGEST NON-COGNATIC KIN GROUP IS SMALLER THAN A SIB, I. E., THE LINEAGE (58)

BACKGROUND ON PAGE 107 BOTH SUBJECT AND PREDICATE

194 IN LEFT COLUMN

ABOR	AJIE	ALBANIANS	ALORESE	AMBA	APINAYE	ARANDA	ARAPESH	ARYANS	ASHANTI
AZANDE	BAMBARA	BARABRA	BARI	BASSERI	BATAK	BEJA	BEMBA	BENGALI	BHIL
BHUIYA	BIRIFOR	BORORO	BUNLAP	BURUSHO	BURYAT	CHAGGA	CHENCHU	CHERKESS	CHEROKEE
COCHITI	COORG	CREEK	CROW	DAGUR	DARD	DELAWARE	DIERI	DILLING	DOBUANS
DOROBO	EGYPTIANS	ENGA	EYAK	FANG	FON	FOX	GANDA	GARO	GILYAK
GISU	GOAJIRO	GOND	GURE	HAIDA	HASANIA	HAZARA	HEBREWS	HEHE	HERERO
HO	HURON	ILA	IRAQW	KABYLE	KACHIN	KALMYK	KAPAUKU	KARIERA	KASKA
KAZAK	KERAKI	KERALA	KET	KHALKA	KHASI	KHEVSUR	KIKUYU	KISSI	KOHISTANI
KONSO	KOREANS	KPE	KUBA	KURTATCHI	LAKALAI	LAKHER	LAMBA	LAMET	LANGO
LAU	LEPCHA	LESU	LHOTA NAGA	LOLO	LUO	MAGUZAWA	MANCHU	MANDAN	MARICOPA
MARSHALLESE	MASAI	MATAKAM	MBUGWE	MERINA	MIAMI	MIAO	MIN CHINESE	MINANGKABAU	MIWOK
MNONG GAR	MONGUOR	MOSSI	MOTA	MUNDURUCU	MURINBATA	MURNGIN	MZAB	NABESNA	NAMA
NANDI	NAVAHO	NDEMBU	NUER	NURI	NYANEKA	NYORO	OKINAWANS	OMAHA	ORAON
PALAUANS	PALIKUR	PATHAN	PENDE	PONAPEANS	PUKAPUKA	PURARI	PURUM	REGEIBAT	RIFFIANS
ROTINESE	RUNDI	RWALA	SAMOYED	SANTAL	SARAMACCA	SEMINOLE	SENIANG	SHERENTE	SHILLUK
SIUAI	SIWANS	SOMALI	SOTHO	SWAZI	TALAMANCA	TALLENSI	TANALA	TEDA	TENDA
TESO	THONGA	TIBETANS	TIKOPIA	TIMBIRA	TIMUCUA	TIV	TIWI	TODA	TROBRIAND
TRUKESE	TSHIMSHIAN	TUCANO	TUCUNA	TURKANA	TURKMEN	TZELTAL	VEDDA	VENDA	VIETNAMESE
WANTOAT	WAROPEN	WIKMUNKAN	WINNEBAGO	WOGEO	WOLEAIANS	WUTE	YAKUT	YAO	YAPESE
YOKUTS	YOMBE	YORUBA	ZUNI						

58 IN RIGHT COLUMN

AINU	AKHA	ARAUCANIANS	ATAYAL	AYMARA	BABWA	BAJUN	BAMILEKE	BANDA	BAYA
BELU	BETE	BOZO	BUDUMA	CALLINAGO	DIEGUENO	DOGON	FUTAJALONKE	GUAHIBO	HANO
JEMEZ	KAREN	KATAB	LIFU	LUBA	MAM	MAMVU	MANUS	MARGI	MAYA
MBUNDU	MBUTI	MENDE	MINCHIA	MONGO	NOMLAKI	NUPE	NYAKYUSA	NYARO	OJIBWA
PAWNEE	ROTUMANS	SANDAWE	SERBS	SHLUH	SINDHI	SIRIONO	SONGHAI	SYRIANS	TAMIL
TANIMBARESE	TERA	TIGRINYA	TOLOWA	WITOTO	WOLOF	YAGUA	YAKO		

148 EXCLUDED BECAUSE IRRELEVANT

---

5 TILT LESS TOWARD BEING THOSE LOCATED OUTSIDE OF EAST EURASIA (330)	0.74 OF 194	5 TILT MORE TOWARD BEING THOSE LOCATED OUTSIDE OF EAST EURASIA (330)	0.90 OF 58	50 6 144 52 XSQ= 5.29 PHI= 0.145 XP = 0.0215

9	TILT MORE TOWARD BEING THOSE 0.94 OF 194 LOCATED OUTSIDE OF SOUTH AMERICA (335)	9	TILT LESS TOWARD BEING THOSE 0.84 OF 58 LOCATED OUTSIDE OF SOUTH AMERICA (335)	12 9 182 49 XSQ= 3.94 PHI= -0.125 XP = 0.0471
15	TILT LESS TOWARD BEING THOSE 0.54 OF 194 WHERE THE LATITUDE IS LESS THAN TWENTY DEGREES (217)	15	TILT MORE TOWARD BEING THOSE 0.71 OF 58 WHERE THE LATITUDE IS LESS THAN TWENTY DEGREES (217)	90 17 104 41 XSQ= 4.66 PHI= 0.136 XP = 0.0309
44	DRIFT LESS TOWARD BEING THOSE 0.67 OF 165 WHERE SETTLEMENTS ARE FIXED (222)	44	DRIFT MORE TOWARD BEING THOSE 0.83 OF 46 WHERE SETTLEMENTS ARE FIXED (222)	111 38 54 8 XSQ= 3.37 PHI= -0.126 XP = 0.0663
73	DRIFT TOWARD BEING THOSE 0.55 OF 125 WHERE WEAVING IS ABSENT (130)	73	DRIFT TOWARD BEING THOSE 0.65 OF 26 WHERE WEAVING IS PRESENT (118)	56 17 69 9 XSQ= 2.87 PHI= -0.138 XP = 0.0900
86	DRIFT TOWARD BEING THOSE 0.57 OF 149 WHERE THE LEVEL OF POLITICAL INTEGRATION IS THE LARGE STATE, THE LITTLE STATE, OR THE MINIMAL STATE (148) GPM	86	DRIFT TOWARD BEING THOSE 0.60 OF 42 WHERE THE LEVEL OF POLITICAL INTEGRATION IS THE AUTONOMOUS COMMUNITY, OR THE FAMILY (156) GPM	85 17 64 25 XSQ= 2.98 PHI= 0.125 XP = 0.0843
90	LEAN LESS TOWARD BEING THOSE 0.64 OF 92 WHERE, IF A HEREDITARY HEADMANSHIP IS PRESENT, SUCCESSION IS PATRILINEAL, RATHER THAN MATRILINEAL (127)	90	LEAN MORE TOWARD BEING THOSE 0.93 OF 27 WHERE, IF A HEREDITARY HEADMANSHIP IS PRESENT, SUCCESSION IS PATRILINEAL, RATHER THAN MATRILINEAL (127)	59 25 33 2 XSQ= 6.83 PHI= -0.240 XP = 0.0090
110	TILT TOWARD BEING THOSE 0.54 OF 182 WHERE SLAVERY IS ABSENT (218)	110	TILT TOWARD BEING THOSE 0.62 OF 58 WHERE SLAVERY IS PRESENT (163)	84 36 98 22 XSQ= 3.84 PHI= -0.127 XP = 0.0500
128	DRIFT TOWARD BEING THOSE 0.65 OF 43 WHERE, IF SUBSISTENCE IS PRIMARILY BY AGRICULTURE, THE WORK IS MAINLY DONE BY FEMALES (37)	128	DRIFT TOWARD BEING THOSE 0.69 OF 13 WHERE, IF SUBSISTENCE IS PRIMARILY BY AGRICULTURE, THE WORK IS MAINLY DONE BY MALES (40)	15 9 28 4 XSQ= 3.51 PHI= -0.250 XP = 0.0611
144	DRIFT TOWARD BEING THOSE 0.59 OF 34 WHERE THE RATIO OF RESTITUTIVE TO REPRESSIVE SANCTIONS IS HIGH OR MEDIUM (27) WME	144	IN ALL CASES ARE THOSE 1.00 OF 3 WHERE THE RATIO OF RESTITUTIVE TO REPRESSIVE SANCTIONS IS LOW (25) WME	20 0 14 3 XSQ= 1.84 PHI= 0.223 EP = 0.0875

181	LEAN MORE TOWARD BEING THOSE 0.98 OF 185 WHERE THE COMMUNITY IS OTHER THAN A DEME (337)	181	LEAN LESS TOWARD BEING THOSE 0.88 OF 56 WHERE THE COMMUNITY IS OTHER THAN A DEME (337)	4 7 181 49 XSQ= 8.31 PHI= -0.186 XP = 0.0039
198	DRIFT LESS TOWARD BEING THOSE 0.82 OF 104 WHERE RULES FOR THE INHERITANCE OF REAL PROPERTY, IF PRESENT, FAVOR THE MALE HEIR OR LINE, RATHER THAN THE FEMALE (144)	198	DRIFT MORE TOWARD BEING THOSE 0.97 OF 32 WHERE RULES FOR THE INHERITANCE OF REAL PROPERTY, IF PRESENT, FAVOR THE MALE HEIR OR LINE, RATHER THAN THE FEMALE (144)	85 31 19 1 XSQ= 3.35 PHI= -0.157 XP = 0.0673
234	TILT MORE TOWARD BEING THOSE 0.73 OF 149 WHERE THE COUSIN TERMINOLOGY IS OF CROW, OMAHA, OR IROQUOIS TYPE, RATHER THAN ESKIMO OR HAWAIIAN TYPE (152)	234	TILT LESS TOWARD BEING THOSE 0.55 OF 40 WHERE THE COUSIN TERMINOLOGY IS OF CROW, OMAHA, OR IROQUOIS TYPE, RATHER THAN ESKIMO OR HAWAIIAN TYPE (152)	109 22 40 18 XSQ= 4.07 PHI= 0.147 XP = 0.0437
272	DRIFT TOWARD BEING THOSE 0.58 OF 26 WHERE THE DIVORCE RATE IS HIGH (29) CA	272	DRIFT TOWARD BEING THOSE 0.86 OF 7 WHERE THE DIVORCE RATE IS LOW (28) CA	15 1 11 6 XSQ= 2.60 PHI= 0.281 EP = 0.0854
309	DRIFT TOWARD BEING THOSE 0.65 OF 26 WHERE ORAL SOCIALIZATION ANXIETY IS HIGH (26) W-C	309	DRIFT TOWARD BEING THOSE 0.83 OF 6 WHERE ORAL SOCIALIZATION ANXIETY IS LOW (27) W-C	17 1 9 5 XSQ= 2.93 PHI= 0.303 EP = 0.0636
333	DRIFT TOWARD BEING THOSE 0.75 OF 8 WHERE THE AGE AT BEGINNING OF TRAINING IN HETEROSEXUAL PLAY INHIBITION IS EIGHT YEARS OR HIGHER (8) W-C	333	IN ALL CASES ARE THOSE 1.00 OF 3 WHERE THE AGE AT BEGINNING OF TRAINING IN HETEROSEXUAL PLAY INHIBITION IS LOWER THAN EIGHT YEARS (8) W-C	6 0 2 3 XSQ= 2.39 PHI= 0.466 EP = 0.0606
355	TILT TOWARD BEING THOSE 0.64 OF 42 WHERE THE CHILD'S INFERRED CONFLICT REGARDING OBEDIENT BEHAVIOR IS HIGH (35) B-B-C	355	TILT TOWARD BEING THOSE 0.80 OF 10 WHERE THE CHILD'S INFERRED CONFLICT REGARDING OBEDIENT BEHAVIOR IS LOW (38) B-B-C	27 2 15 8 XSQ= 4.75 PHI= 0.302 XP = 0.0293
426	DRIFT LESS TOWARD BEING THOSE 0.58 OF 139 WHERE A HIGH GOD IS PRESENT (156) GES,EA	426	DRIFT MORE TOWARD BEING THOSE 0.78 OF 32 WHERE A HIGH GOD IS PRESENT (156) GES,EA	80 25 59 7 XSQ= 3.82 PHI= -0.149 XP = 0.0507
440	DRIFT TOWARD BEING THOSE 0.61 OF 31 WHERE FEAR OF SPIRITS IS LOW (29) W-C	440	DRIFT TOWARD BEING THOSE 0.83 OF 6 WHERE FEAR OF SPIRITS IS HIGH (32) W-C	12 5 19 1 XSQ= 2.43 PHI= -0.256 EP = 0.0752

```
478  DRIFT TCWARD BEING THCSE        0.70 OF  10        478  IN ALL CASES ARE THOSE          1.00 OF   3             3    3
     WHERE THE ABANDCNMENT CR KILLING OF                     WHERE THE ABANDONMENT OR KILLING OF                       7    0
     OLD PECPLE IS                                           OLD PEOPLE IS                                     XSQ=     2.17
     UNIMPCRTANT CR ABSENT   (12) LWS                        PRESENT  (12) LWS                                 PHI=   -0.408
                                                                                                               EP =   0.0699
```

```
186  CULTURES                                        186  CULTURES
     WHERE THE KIN GROUP IS                               WHERE THE KIN GROUP IS
     EXCLUSIVELY PATRILINEAL  (150)                       OTHER THAN
                                                          EXCLUSIVELY PATRILINEAL  (250)

BACKGROUND ON PAGE 108                                                BOTH SUBJECT AND PREDICATE

     150  IN LEFT COLUMN

ABOR          AJIE        AKHA       AMBA        ARAPESH    ARAUCANIANS AYMARA     AZANDE      BABWA     BAJUN
BAMBARA       BAMILEKE    BANDA      BARABRA     BARI       BASSERI     BATAK      BAYA        BEJA      BETE
BHIL          BHUIYA      BOZO       BUDUMA      BURUSHO    BURYAT      CHAGGA     CHENCHU     CHERKESS  COORG
DAGUR         DARD        DIEGUENO   DILLING     DOGON      DOROBO      EGYPTIANS  ENGA        FANG      FON
FUTAJALONKE   GANDA       GILYAK     GISU        GOND       HASANIA     HAZARA     HEBREWS     HEHE      HO
KABYLE        KACHIN      KALMYK     KAPAUKU     KATAB      KAZAK       KERAKI     KET         KHEVSUR   KIKUYU
KISSI         KOHISTANI   KONSO      KOREANS     LAKHER     LAMET       LANGO      LAU         LEPCHA    LHOTA NAGA
LIFU          LOLO        LUBA       LUO         MAGUZAWA   MAM         MAMVU      MANCHU      MARGI     MARICOPA
MASAI         MATAKAM     MAYA       MBUTI       MENDE      MERINA      MIAMI      MIN CHINESE MINCHIA   MIWOK
MONGO         MONGUOR     MOSSI      MUNDURUCU   MURINBATA  MZAB        NAMA       NOMLAKI     NUER      NUPE
NURI          NYORO       OMAHA      ORAON       PALIKUR    PURARI      PURUM      REGEIBAT    RIFFIANS  ROTINESE
RUNDI         SAMOYED     SANDAWE    SANTAL      SENIANG    SERBS       SHERENTE   SHILLUK     SHLUH     SINDHI
SIWANS        SOMALI      SONGHAI    SOTHO       SWAZI      SYRIANS     TALLENSI   TAMIL       TANALA    TANIMBARESE
TEDA          TERA        TESO       THONGA      TIBETANS   TOLOWA      TUCANO     TUCUNA      TURKANA   TURKMEN
TZELTAL       VIETNAMESE  WARGPEN    WIKMUNKAN   WINNEBAGO  WITOTO      WUTE       YAGUA       YAKUT     YOKUTS

     250  IN RIGHT COLUMN

--------------------------------------------------------------------------------------------------------
  3  TEND LESS TO BE THOSE          0.67 OF 150      3  TEND MORE TO BE THOSE          0.88 OF 250       49   31
     LOCATED OUTSIDE OF                                 LOCATED OUTSIDE OF                              101  219
     AFRICA  (320)                                      AFRICA  (320)                               XSQ=   22.82
                                                                                                    PHI=   0.239
                                                                                                    XP =  0.0000

  4  DRIFT LESS TOWARD BEING THOSE  0.85 OF 150      4  DRIFT MORE TOWARD BEING THOSE  0.91 OF 250       23   22
     LOCATED OUTSIDE OF                                 LOCATED OUTSIDE OF                              127  228
     THE CIRCUM-MEDITERRANEAN  (355)                    THE CIRCUM-MEDITERRANEAN  (355)             XSQ=    3.38
                                                                                                    PHI=   0.092
                                                                                                    XP =  0.0660

  5  TEND LESS TO BE THOSE          0.72 OF 150      5  TEND MORE TO BE THOSE          0.89 OF 250       42   28
     LOCATED OUTSIDE OF                                 LOCATED OUTSIDE OF                              108  222
     EAST EURASIA  (330)                                EAST EURASIA  (330)                         XSQ=   17.18
                                                                                                    PHI=   0.207
                                                                                                    XP =  0.0000
```

6	LEAN MORE TOWARD BEING THOSE LOCATED OUTSIDE OF THE INSULAR PACIFIC (330)	0.90 OF 150	6	LEAN LESS TOWARD BEING THOSE LOCATED OUTSIDE OF THE INSULAR PACIFIC (330)	0.78 OF 250	15 55 135 195 XSQ= 8.54 PHI= -0.146 XP = 0.0035
8	TEND MORE TO BE THOSE LOCATED OUTSIDE OF NORTH AMERICA (330)	0.94 OF 150	8	TEND LESS TO BE THOSE LOCATED OUTSIDE OF NORTH AMERICA (330)	0.76 OF 250	9 61 141 189 XSQ= 20.73 PHI= -0.228 XP = 0.0000
9	TEND MORE TO BE THOSE LOCATED OUTSIDE OF SOUTH AMERICA (335)	0.92 OF 150	9	TEND LESS TO BE THOSE LOCATED OUTSIDE OF SOUTH AMERICA (335)	0.79 OF 250	12 53 138 197 XSQ= 11.05 PHI= -0.166 XP = 0.0009
12	LEAN MORE TOWARD BEING THOSE WHERE THE LATITUDE IS LESS THAN FIFTY DEGREES (367)	0.97 OF 150	12	LEAN LESS TOWARD BEING THOSE WHERE THE LATITUDE IS LESS THAN FIFTY DEGREES (367)	0.89 OF 250	5 28 145 222 XSQ= 6.66 PHI= -0.129 XP = 0.0099
13	LEAN MORE TOWARD BEING THOSE WHERE THE LATITUDE IS LESS THAN FORTY DEGREES (329)	0.89 OF 150	13	LEAN LESS TOWARD BEING THOSE WHERE THE LATITUDE IS LESS THAN FORTY DEGREES (329)	0.78 OF 250	16 55 134 195 XSQ= 7.49 PHI= -0.137 XP = 0.0062
42	DRIFT MORE TOWARD BEING THOSE WHERE THE NATURAL ENVIRONMENT IS OTHER THAN TROPICAL OR SUB-TROPICAL RAIN FOREST, OR MONSOON FOREST (244) FWM	0.67 OF 150	42	DRIFT LESS TOWARD BEING THOSE WHERE THE NATURAL ENVIRONMENT IS OTHER THAN TROPICAL OR SUB-TROPICAL RAIN FOREST, OR MONSOON FOREST (244) FWM	0.58 OF 250	50 106 100 144 XSQ= 2.87 PHI= -0.085 XP = 0.0903
44	TILT MORE TOWARD BEING THOSE WHERE SETTLEMENTS ARE FIXED (222)	0.74 OF 123	44	TILT LESS TOWARD BEING THOSE WHERE SETTLEMENTS ARE FIXED (222)	0.63 OF 209	91 131 32 78 XSQ= 3.97 PHI= 0.109 XP = 0.0463
46	TILT MORE TOWARD BEING THOSE OTHER THAN WHERE SETTLEMENTS ARE NON-FIXED AND MOVEMENT IS NOMADIC (260)	0.85 OF 123	46	TILT LESS TOWARD BEING THOSE OTHER THAN WHERE SETTLEMENTS ARE NON-FIXED AND MOVEMENT IS NOMADIC (260)	0.75 OF 209	19 53 104 156 XSQ= 3.91 PHI= -0.109 XP = 0.0479
51	TEND MORE TO BE THOSE WHERE SUBSISTENCE IS PRIMARILY BY FOOD PRODUCTION -- I. E., AGRICULTURE OR HUSBANDRY -- RATHER THAN BY GATHERING (253)	0.77 OF 150	51	TEND LESS TO BE THOSE WHERE SUBSISTENCE IS PRIMARILY BY FOOD PRODUCTION -- I. E., AGRICULTURE OR HUSBANDRY -- RATHER THAN BY GATHERING (253)	0.55 OF 250	115 138 35 112 XSQ= 17.67 PHI= 0.210 XP = 0.0000

53	TILT LESS TOWARD BEING THOSE 0.52 OF 103 WHERE FOOD PRODUCTION IS BY SIMPLE AGRICULTURE OR INCIPIENT FOOD PRODUCTION, RATHER THAN BY INTENSIVE AGRICULTURE (147)	53	TILT MORE TOWARD BEING THOSE 0.69 OF 135 WHERE FOOD PRODUCTION IS BY SIMPLE AGRICULTURE OR INCIPIENT FOOD PRODUCTION, RATHER THAN BY INTENSIVE AGRICULTURE (147)	49 42 54 93 XSQ= 6.03 PHI= 0.159 XP = 0.0141
55	TILT TOWARD BEING THOSE 0.56 OF 88 WHERE FOOD PRODUCTION IS BY INTENSIVE AGRICULTURE, RATHER THAN BY SIMPLE AGRICULTURE (91)	55	TILT TOWARD BEING THOSE 0.60 OF 104 WHERE FOOD PRODUCTION IS BY SIMPLE AGRICULTURE, RATHER THAN BY INTENSIVE AGRICULTURE (101)	49 42 39 62 XSQ= 3.88 PHI= 0.142 XP = 0.0488
62	TEND MORE TO BE THOSE 0.68 OF 150 WHERE HUSBANDRY OF SOME KIND IS PRESENT (228)	62	TEND LESS TO BE THOSE 0.50 OF 250 WHERE HUSBANDRY OF SOME KIND IS PRESENT (228)	102 126 48 124 XSQ= 11.14 PHI= 0.167 XP = 0.0008
63	LEAN MORE TOWARD BEING THOSE 0.77 OF 100 WHERE HUSBANDRY, IF PRESENT, IS PRINCIPALLY IN THE FORM OF BOVINE, EQUINE, CAMEL-LIKE, OR DEER-LIKE ANIMALS, RATHER THAN PIGS, SHEEP, OR GOATS (152)	63	LEAN LESS TOWARD BEING THOSE 0.60 OF 126 WHERE HUSBANDRY, IF PRESENT, IS PRINCIPALLY IN THE FORM OF BOVINE, EQUINE, CAMEL-LIKE, OR DEER-LIKE ANIMALS, RATHER THAN PIGS, SHEEP, OR GOATS (152)	77 75 23 51 XSQ= 6.96 PHI= 0.175 XP = 0.0083
71	TEND TO BE THOSE 0.63 OF 87 WHERE METAL WORKING IS PRESENT (98)	71	TEND TO BE THOSE 0.74 OF 164 WHERE METAL WORKING IS ABSENT (153)	55 43 32 121 XSQ= 31.16 PHI= 0.352 XP = 0.
82	TILT MORE TOWARD BEING THOSE 0.89 OF 82 WHERE A CITY OR TOWN IS PRESENT, OR THE AVERAGE COMMUNITY SIZE IS FIFTY OR GREATER (178)	82	TILT LESS TOWARD BEING THOSE 0.74 OF 142 WHERE A CITY OR TOWN IS PRESENT, OR THE AVERAGE COMMUNITY SIZE IS FIFTY OR GREATER (178)	73 105 9 37 XSQ= 6.35 PHI= 0.168 XP = 0.0117
86	LEAN TOWARD BEING THOSE 0.61 OF 110 WHERE THE LEVEL OF POLITICAL INTEGRATION IS THE LARGE STATE, THE LITTLE STATE, OR THE MINIMAL STATE (148) GPM	86	LEAN TOWARD BEING THOSE 0.58 OF 194 WHERE THE LEVEL OF POLITICAL INTEGRATION IS THE AUTONOMOUS COMMUNITY, OR THE FAMILY (156) GPM	67 81 43 113 XSQ= 9.56 PHI= 0.177 XP = 0.0020
90	IN ALL CASES ARE THOSE 1.00 OF 62 WHERE, IF A HEREDITARY HEADMANSHIP IS PRESENT, SUCCESSION IS PATRILINEAL, RATHER THAN MATRILINEAL (127)	90	TEND LESS TO BE THOSE 0.63 OF 103 WHERE, IF A HEREDITARY HEADMANSHIP IS PRESENT, SUCCESSION IS PATRILINEAL, RATHER THAN MATRILINEAL (127)	62 65 0 38 XSQ= 27.67 PHI= 0.410 XP = 0.0000
96	TILT TOWARD BEING THOSE 0.61 OF 122 WHERE THE HIERARCHY OF NATIONAL JURISDICTION HAS FOUR, THREE, TWO OR ONE LEVEL (174) GES,EA	96	TILT TOWARD BEING THOSE 0.52 OF 208 WHERE THE HIERARCHY OF NATIONAL JURISDICTION HAS NO LEVELS (156) GES,EA	74 100 48 108 XSQ= 4.39 PHI= 0.115 XP = 0.0362

No.			No.			
97	LEAN LESS TOWARC BEING THCSE WHERE THE HIERARCHY OF LCCAL JURISDICTICN HAS THREE CR TWO LEVELS (273) GES,EA	0.75 OF 123	97	LEAN MORE TOWARD BEING THCSE WHERE THE HIERARCHY OF LOCAL JURISDICTICN HAS THREE OR TWO LEVELS (273) GES,EA	0.87 CF 208	31 27 92 181 XSQ= 7.17 PHI= 0.147 XP = 0.0074
102	TILT TCWARD BEING THOSE WHERE CLASS STRATIFICATICN IS PRESENT (203)	0.62 OF 146	102	TILT TOWARD BEING THOSE WHERE CLASS STRATIFICATICN IS ABSENT (180)	0.52 CF 237	90 113 56 124 XSQ= 6.52 PHI= 0.131 XP = 0.0106
109	TEND LESS TO BE THCSE WHERE CASTES ARE ABSENT (317)	0.75 OF 130	109	TEND MORE TO BE THOSE WHERE CASTES ARE ABSENT (317)	0.92 CF 238	33 18 97 220 XSQ= 20.90 PHI= 0.238 XP = 0.0000
110	TEND TC BE THCSE WHERE SLAVERY IS PRESENT (163)	0.56 OF 142	110	TEND TO BE THOSE WHERE SLAVERY IS ABSENT (218)	0.65 CF 239	80 83 62 156 XSQ= 16.12 PHI= 0.206 XP = 0.0001
129	TEND TC BE THCSE WHERE WEAVING IS MAINLY DONE BY MALES (31)	0.51 OF 39	129	TEND TO BE THOSE WHERE WEAVING IS MAINLY DONE BY FEMALES (73)	0.83 CF 65	20 11 19 54 XSQ= 12.16 PHI= 0.342 XP = 0.0005
130	LEAN TCWARD BEING THCSE WHERE LEATHER WCRKING IS MAINLY DCNE BY MALES (39)	0.71 OF 28	130	LEAN TOWARD BEING THOSE WHERE LEATHER WORKING IS MAINLY DONE BY FEMALES (45)	0.66 CF 56	20 19 8 37 XSQ= 9.10 PHI= 0.329 XP = 0.0026
138	DRIFT TCWARD BEING THCSE WHERE SUPERORDINATE JUSTICE IS PRESENT (22) BBW	0.80 OF 10	138	DRIFT TOWARD BEING THOSE WHERE SUPERORDINATE JUSTICE IS ABSENT (18) BBW	0.53 CF 30	8 14 2 16 XSQ= 2.15 PHI= 0.232 EP = 0.0823
141	DRIFT TCWARD BEING THCSE WHERE THE LEVEL CF SOCIAL SANCTION IS PUBLIC CORPOREAL SANCTICN, RATHER THAN PUBLIC PRCPERTY SANCTICN CR PRIVATE SETTLEMENT (28) JMH	0.73 OF 15	141	DRIFT TOWARD BEING THOSE WHERE THE LEVEL OF SOCIAL SANCTICN IS PUBLIC PROPERTY SANCTICN OR PRIVATE SETTLEMENT, RATHER THAN PUBLIC CORPOREAL SANCTION (26) JMH	0.56 CF 39	11 17 4 22 XSQ= 2.74 PHI= 0.225 XP = 0.0979
175	TEND LESS TC BE THCSE WHERE THE COMMUNITY IS 'KIN-HETERCGENECUS,' I. E. OTHER THAN A CLAN CCMMUNITY OR A DEME (260)	0.54 OF 142	175	TEND MORE TO BE THOSE WHERE THE COMMUNITY IS 'KIN-HETEROGENEOUS,' I. E. OTHER THAN A CLAN COMMUNITY OR A DEME (260)	0.76 CF 240	65 57 77 183 XSQ= 18.91 PHI= 0.222 XP = 0.0000

176	TEND TO BE THOSE WHERE THE COMMUNITY IS A CLAN-COMMUNITY OR A COMMUNITY STRUCTURED OR SEGMENTED ON A CLAN BASIS (169)	0.67 OF 142	176	TEND TO BE THOSE WHERE THE COMMUNITY IS OTHER THAN A CLAN-COMMUNITY OR A COMMUNITY STRUCTURED OR SEGMENTED ON A CLAN BASIS (213)	0.69 OF 240	95 74 47 166 XSQ= 45.60 PHI= 0.345 XP = 0.
177	TEND LESS TO BE THOSE WHERE THE COMMUNITY IS OTHER THAN A SINGLE CLAN-COMMUNITY AND EXOGAMOUS (305)	0.59 OF 142	177	TEND MORE TO BE THOSE WHERE THE COMMUNITY IS OTHER THAN A SINGLE CLAN-COMMUNITY AND EXOGAMOUS (305)	0.92 OF 240	58 19 84 221 XSQ= 58.08 PHI= 0.390 XP = 0.
180	TEND TO BE THOSE WHERE THE COMMUNITY IS COMMONLY EXOGAMOUS, RATHER THAN NON-EXOGAMOUS (124)	0.51 OF 142	180	TEND TO BE THOSE WHERE THE COMMUNITY IS COMMONLY NON-EXOGAMOUS, RATHER THAN EXOGAMOUS (258)	0.78 OF 240	72 52 70 188 XSQ= 33.00 PHI= 0.294 XP = 0.
181	LEAN MORE TOWARD BEING THOSE WHERE THE COMMUNITY IS OTHER THAN A DEME (337)	0.95 OF 142	181	LEAN LESS TOWARD BEING THOSE WHERE THE COMMUNITY IS OTHER THAN A DEME (337)	0.84 OF 240	7. 38 135 202 XSQ= 9.18 PHI= -0.155 XP = 0.0024
182	TEND MORE TO BE THOSE OTHER THAN WHERE THE COMMUNITY IS STRUCTURED ON A NON-CLAN BASIS AND AGAMOUS (256)	0.80 OF 142	182	TEND LESS TO BE THOSE OTHER THAN WHERE THE COMMUNITY IS STRUCTURED ON A NON-CLAN BASIS AND AGAMOUS (256)	0.60 OF 240	29 97 113 143 XSQ= 15.24 PHI= -0.200 XP = 0.0001
183	TILT MORE TOWARD BEING THOSE WHERE THE LARGEST NON-COGNATIC KIN GROUP IS SMALLER THAN A MOEITY, I. E., A PHRATRY OR SIB OR LINEAGE (218)	0.91 OF 150	183	TILT LESS TOWARD BEING THOSE WHERE THE LARGEST NON-COGNATIC KIN GROUP IS SMALLER THAN A MOEITY, I. E., A PHRATRY OR SIB OR LINEAGE (218)	0.80 OF 102	14 20 136 82 XSQ= 4.65 PHI= -0.136 XP = 0.0311
190	IN ALL CASES ARE THOSE WHERE THE KIN GROUP IS PATRILINEAL OR DOUBLE-DESCENT, RATHER THAN MATRILINEAL (186)	1.00 OF 147	190	TEND TO BE THOSE WHERE THE KIN GROUP IS MATRILINEAL, RATHER THAN PATRILINEAL OR DOUBLE-DESCENT (61)	0.61 OF 100	147 39 0 61 XSQ= 115.82 PHI= 0.685 XP = 0.
192	IN ALL CASES ARE THOSE OTHER THAN WHERE THE ONLY KIN GROUP PRESENT IS A KINDRED OR ELSE BILATERAL DESCENT IS INFERRED (289)	1.00 OF 150	192	TEND LESS TO BE THOSE OTHER THAN WHERE THE ONLY KIN GROUP PRESENT IS A KINDRED OR ELSE BILATERAL DESCENT IS INFERRED (289)	0.56 OF 250	0 111 150 139 XSQ= 89.98 PHI= -0.474 XP = 0.
196	TEND MORE TO BE THOSE WHERE INDIVIDUAL RIGHTS IN REAL PROPERTY, AND RULES FOR INHERITANCE, ARE PRESENT (194)	0.81 OF 117	196	TEND LESS TO BE THOSE WHERE INDIVIDUAL RIGHTS IN REAL PROPERTY, AND RULES FOR INHERITANCE, ARE PRESENT (194)	0.60 OF 164	95 99 22 65 XSQ= 12.90 PHI= 0.214 XP = 0.0003

```
197  TEND MORE TO BE THOSE             0.96 OF  95    197  TEND LESS TO BE THOSE             0.75 OF  99        91    74
     WHERE RULES FOR THE INHERITANCE OF                    WHERE RULES FOR THE INHERITANCE OF                    4    25
     REAL PROPERTY, IF PRESENT,                            REAL PROPERTY, IF PRESENT,                     XSQ=   15.27
     FAVOR EITHER THE MALE HEIR OR LINE,                   FAVOR EITHER THE MALE HEIR OR LINE,            PHI=   0.281
     OR THE FEMALE HEIR OR LINE  (165)                     OR THE FEMALE HEIR OR LINE  (165)              XP =  0.0001

198  IN ALL CASES ARE THOSE            1.00 OF  91    198  TEND LESS TO BE THOSE             0.72 OF  74        91    53
     WHERE RULES FOR THE INHERITANCE OF                    WHERE RULES FOR THE INHERITANCE OF                    0    21
     REAL PROPERTY, IF PRESENT,                            REAL PROPERTY, IF PRESENT,                     XSQ=   27.09
     FAVOR THE MALE HEIR OR LINE, RATHER THAN              FAVOR THE MALE HEIR OR LINE, RATHER THAN       PHI=   0.405
     THE FEMALE  (144)                                     THE FEMALE  (144)                              XP =  0.0000

201  TEND MORE TO BE THOSE             0.98 OF 150    201  TEND LESS TO BE THOSE             0.75 OF 248       147   187
     WHERE MARITAL RESIDENCE IS                            WHERE MARITAL RESIDENCE IS                            3    61
     NON-OPTIONAL, RATHER THAN                             NON-OPTIONAL, RATHER THAN                      XSQ=   33.71
     AMBILOCAL OR NEOLOCAL  (334)                          AMBILOCAL OR NEOLOCAL  (334)                   PHI=   0.291
                                                                                                          XP =  0.

204  TEND MORE TO BE THOSE             0.98 OF 149    204  TEND LESS TO BE THOSE             0.67 OF 185       146   124
     WHERE MARITAL RESIDENCE IS                            WHERE MARITAL RESIDENCE IS                            3    61
     PATRILOCAL, VIRILOCAL, OR AVUNCULOCAL,                PATRILOCAL, VIRILOCAL, OR AVUNCULOCAL,         XSQ=   49.09
     RATHER THAN                                           RATHER THAN                                    PHI=   0.383
     AMBILOCAL OR NEOLOCAL  (270)                          AMBILOCAL OR NEOLOCAL  (270)                   XP =  0.

209  TEND MORE TO BE THOSE             0.99 OF 147    209  TEND LESS TO BE THOSE             0.66 OF 187       146   124
     WHERE MARITAL RESIDENCE IS                            WHERE MARITAL RESIDENCE IS                            1    63
     PATRILOCAL, VIRILOCAL, OR AVUNCULOCAL,                PATRILOCAL, VIRILOCAL, OR AVUNCULOCAL,         XSQ=   55.78
     RATHER THAN                                           RATHER THAN                                    PHI=   0.409
     MATRILOCAL OR UXORILOCAL  (270)                       MATRILOCAL OR UXORILOCAL  (270)                XP =  0.

210  IN ALL CASES ARE THOSE            1.00 OF 137    210  TEND LESS TO BE THOSE             0.51 OF  63       137    32
     WHERE MARITAL RESIDENCE IS                            WHERE MARITAL RESIDENCE IS                            0    31
     PATRILOCAL, RATHER THAN                               PATRILOCAL, RATHER THAN                        XSQ=   76.07
     MATRILOCAL  (169)                                     MATRILOCAL  (169)                              PHI=   0.617
                                                                                                          XP =  0.

213  TILT TOWARD BEING THOSE            0.55 OF 141    213  TILT TOWARD BEING THOSE           0.59 OF 229        77    95
     WHERE FIRST COUSIN MARRIAGE IS                        WHERE FIRST COUSIN MARRIAGE IS                       64   134
     PERMITTED  (172)                                      NOT PERMITTED  (198)                           XSQ=    5.53
                                                                                                          PHI=   0.122
                                                                                                          XP =  0.0187

214  DRIFT LESS TOWARD BEING THOSE     0.78 OF  77    214  DRIFT MORE TOWARD BEING THOSE     0.88 OF  95        17    11
     WHERE FIRST COUSIN MARRIAGE,                          WHERE FIRST COUSIN MARRIAGE,                         60    84
     IF PERMITTED,                                         IF PERMITTED,                                  XSQ=    2.71
     IS OTHER THAN UNILATERAL  (144)                       IS OTHER THAN UNILATERAL  (144)                PHI=   0.126
                                                                                                          XP =  0.0996

221  LEAN LESS TOWARD BEING THOSE      0.84 OF 141    221  LEAN MORE TOWARD BEING THOSE      0.94 OF 229        22    13
     WHERE MATRILATERAL CROSS-COUSIN MARRIAGE              WHERE MATRILATERAL CROSS-COUSIN MARRIAGE            119   216
     IS NOT PRESCRIBED OR PREFERRED  (335)                 IS NOT PRESCRIBED OR PREFERRED  (335)          XSQ=    8.91
                                                                                                          PHI=   0.155
                                                                                                          XP =  0.0028
```

224	LEAN TOWARD BEING THOSE 0.51 OF 77 WHERE COUSIN MARRIAGE IS PREFERENTIALLY OR PERMISSIVELY EITHER PATRI- OR MATRILATERAL, RATHER THAN SYMMETRICAL (66)	224	LEAN TOWARD BEING THOSE 0.72 OF 95 WHERE COUSIN MARRIAGE IS PREFERENTIALLY OR PERMISSIVELY SYMMETRICAL, RATHER THAN EITHER PATRI- OR MATRILATERAL (106)	39 27 38 68 XSQ= 7.97 PHI= 0.215 XP = 0.0048
234	TEND TO BE THOSE 0.68 OF 98 WHERE THE COUSIN TERMINOLOGY IS OF CROW, OMAHA, OR IROQUOIS TYPE, RATHER THAN ESKIMO OR HAWAIIAN TYPE (152)	234	TEND TO BE THOSE 0.62 OF 224 WHERE THE COUSIN TERMINOLOGY IS OF ESKIMO OR HAWAIIAN TYPE, RATHER THAN CROW, OMAHA, OR IROQUOIS TYPE (170)	67 85 31 139 XSQ= 24.11 PHI= 0.274 XP = 0.0000
242	TEND MORE TO BE THOSE 0.89 OF 148 WHERE MARRIAGE IS COMMONLY OR OCCASIONALLY POLYGYNOUS, RATHER THAN MONOGAMOUS (314)	242	TEND LESS TO BE THOSE 0.74 OF 247 WHERE MARRIAGE IS COMMONLY OR OCCASIONALLY POLYGYNOUS, RATHER THAN MONOGAMOUS (314)	131 183 17 64 XSQ= 10.94 PHI= 0.166 XP = 0.0009
243	DRIFT TOWARD BEING THOSE 0.57 OF 23 WHERE POLYGYNY, IF PRESENT, HAS A HIGH INCIDENCE (24) W-C,S	243	DRIFT TOWARD BEING THOSE 0.70 OF 37 WHERE POLYGYNY, IF PRESENT, HAS A LOW INCIDENCE (36) W-D,S	13 11 10 26 XSQ= 3.20 PHI= 0.231 XP = 0.0737
262	TEND MORE TO BE THOSE 0.92 OF 148 WHERE WIVES ARE OBTAINED BY MEANS INVOLVING THE PRESENCE OF SOME CONSIDERATION (305)	262	TEND LESS TO BE THOSE 0.68 OF 247 WHERE WIVES ARE OBTAINED BY MEANS INVOLVING THE PRESENCE OF SOME CONSIDERATION (305)	136 169 12 78 XSQ= 27.66 PHI= 0.265 XP = 0.0000
263	TEND TO BE THOSE 0.80 OF 148 WHERE WIVES ARE OBTAINED BY RELATIVELY DIFFICULT MEANS, NAMELY BY BRIDE-PRICE, BRIDE-SERVICE, OR EXCHANGING A FEMALE RELATIVE (233)	263	TEND TO BE THOSE 0.53 OF 247 WHERE WIVES ARE OBTAINED BY RELATIVELY EASY MEANS, NAMELY BY TOKEN BRIDE-PRICE, GIFT EXCHANGE, ABSENCE OF ANY CONSIDERATION, OR RECEIPT OF DOWRY (162)	118 115 30 132 XSQ= 40.73 PHI= 0.321 XP = 0.
314	LEAN LESS TOWARD BEING THOSE 0.57 OF 28 WHERE THE INCIDENCE OF MOTHER-CHILD HOUSEHOLDS IS LOW (61) W-C,S	314	LEAN MORE TOWARD BEING THOSE 0.87 OF 52 WHERE THE INCIDENCE OF MOTHER-CHILD HOUSEHOLDS IS LOW (61) W-D,S	12 7 16 45 XSQ= 7.14 PHI= 0.299 XP = 0.0076
334	TILT TOWARD BEING THOSE 0.69 OF 26 WHERE THE INDULGENCE OF THE CHILD IS LOW (38) B-B-C	334	TILT TOWARD BEING THOSE 0.62 OF 52 WHERE THE INDULGENCE OF THE CHILD IS HIGH (40) B-B-C	8 32 18 20 XSQ= 5.39 PHI= -0.263 XP = 0.0202
336	TILT TOWARD BEING THOSE 0.79 OF 24 WHERE THE TOTAL POSITIVE PRESSURE TOWARD DEVELOPING RESPONSIBLE BEHAVIOR IN THE CHILD IS HIGH (43) B-B-C	336	TILT TOWARD BEING THOSE 0.53 OF 51 WHERE THE TOTAL POSITIVE PRESSURE TOWARD DEVELOPING RESPONSIBLE BEHAVIOR IN THE CHILD IS LOW (32) B-B-C	19 24 5 27 XSQ= 5.63 PHI= 0.274 XP = 0.0177

337	TILT TOWARD BEING THOSE 0.71 OF 24 WHERE THE CHILD'S INFERREC ANXIETY OVER NON-PERFORMANCE OF RESPONSIBLE BEHAVIOR IS HIGH (38) B-B-C	337	TILT TOWARD BEING THOSE 0.57 OF 49 WHERE THE CHILD'S INFERRED ANXIETY OVER NON-PERFORMANCE OF RESPCNSIBLE BEHAVIOR IS LOW (35) B-B-C	17 21 7 28 XSQ= 3.99 PHI= 0.234 XP = 0.0457
339	TILT TCWARD BEING THOSE 0.63 OF 24 WHERE THE CHILD'S INFERREC CONFLICT REGARDING RESPONSIBLE BEHAVIOR IS HIGH (31) B-B-C	339	TILT TOWARD BEING THOSE 0.67 OF 49 WHERE THE CHILD'S INFERRED CONFLICT REGARDING RESPCNSIBLE BEHAVIOR IS LOW (42) B-B-C	15 16 9 33 XSQ= 4.72 PHI= 0.254 XP = 0.0299
353	DRIFT TCWARD BEING THCSE 0.75 OF 24 WHERE THE CHILD'S INFERREC ANXIETY OVER NCN-PERFCRMANCE CF CBECIENT BEHAVIOR IS HIGH (42) B-B-C	353	DRIFT TOWARD BEING THOSE 0.52 OF 50 WHERE THE CHILD-S INFERRED ANXIETY OVER NON-PERFORMANCE OF OBEDIENT BEHAVIOR IS LOW (32) B-B-C	18 24 6 26 XSQ= 3.78 PHI= 0.226 XP = 0.0519
368	DRIFT TCWARD BEING THCSE 0.89 OF 9 WHERE DISSCCIATICN CF THE SEXES AT ADCLESCENCE IS LCW (21) JKH	368	DRIFT TOWARD BEING THOSE 0.54 CF 28 WHERE DISSOCIATION OF THE SEXES AT ADOLESCENCE IS HIGH OR MEDIUM (16) JKH	1 15 8 13 XSQ= 3.42 PHI= -0.304 EP = 0.0501
370	LEAN TCWARD BEING THOSE 0.51 OF 91 WHERE THE SEGREGATICN CF ACOLESCENT BOYS IS COMPLETE CR PARTIAL (95)	37C	LEAN TOWARD BEING THOSE 0.68 OF 152 WHERE THE SEGREGATION CF ADCLESCENT BOYS IS ABSENT (148)	46 49 45 103 XSQ= 7.27 PHI= 0.173 XP = 0.0070
377	TEND LESS TO BE THCSE 0.57 OF 121 WHERE MALE GENITAL MUTILATION IS ABSENT (242)	377	TEND MORE TO BE THOSE 0.85 CF 204 WHERE MALE GENITAL MUTILATION IS ABSENT (242)	52 31 69 173 XSQ= 29.38 PHI= 0.301 XP = 0.0000
382	TILT TOWARD BEING THOSE 0.61 OF 23 WHERE FEMALE INITIATICN RITES ARE ABSENT (27) JKB	382	TILT TOWARD BEING THOSE 0.69 OF 42 WHERE FEMALE INITIATION RITES ARE PRESENT (38) JKB	9 29 14 13 XSQ= 4.31 PHI= -0.258 XP = 0.0378
390	DRIFT LESS TCWARD BEING THOSE 0.66 OF 71 WHERE PREMARITAL SEX RELATIONS ARE WEAKLY PUNISHED ANC IN FACT NCT RARE OR PUNISHED CNLY IF PREGNANCY RESULTS, OR FREELY PERMITTEC (132) JTW,EA	390	DRIFT MORE TOWARD BEING THCSE 0.79 CF 108 WHERE PREMARITAL SEX RELATIONS ARE WEAKLY PUNISHED AND IN FACT NOT RARE OR PUNISHED ONLY IF PREGNANCY RESULTS, OR FREELY PERMITTED (132) JTW,EA	24 23 47 85 XSQ= 2.84 PHI= 0.126 XP = 0.0917
392	DRIFT MORE TCWARD BEING THOSE 0.72 OF 71 WHERE PREMARITAL SEX RELATIONS ARE STRCNGLY PUNISHEC AND IN FACT RARE, OR WEAKLY PUNISHED ANC IN FACT NOT RARE, OR PUNISHED CNLY IF PREGNANCY RESULTS (112) JTW,EA	392	DRIFT LESS TOWARD BEING THCSE 0.56 OF 108 WHERE PREMARITAL SEX RELATICNS ARE STRONGLY PUNISHED AND IN FACT RARE, CR WEAKLY PUNISHED AND IN FACT NOT RARE, OR PUNISHED ONLY IF PREGNANCY RESULTS (112) JTW,EA	51 61 20 47 XSQ= 3.68 PHI= 0.143 XP = 0.0551

400	TILT MORE TOWARD BEING THOSE WHERE HOMOSEXUAL ACTIVITY IS PERMITTED (36) F-B	0.87 OF 15	400	TILT LESS TOWARD BEING THOSE WHERE HOMOSEXUAL ACTIVITY IS PERMITTED (36) F-B	0.53 OF 43	2 20 13 23 XSQ= 3.89 PHI= -0.259 XP = 0.0487
426	LEAN MORE TOWARD BEING THOSE WHERE A HIGH GOD IS PRESENT (156) GES,EA	0.71 OF 99	426	LEAN LESS TOWARD BEING THOSE WHERE A HIGH GOD IS PRESENT (156) GES,EA	0.53 OF 161	70 86 29 75 XSQ= 6.93 PHI= 0.163 XP = 0.0085
427	DRIFT TOWARD BEING THOSE WHERE A HIGH GOD, IF PRESENT, IS ACTIVE, RATHER THAN INACTIVE (87) GES,EA	0.64 OF 70	427	DRIFT TOWARD BEING THOSE WHERE A HIGH GOD, IF PRESENT, IS INACTIVE, RATHER THAN ACTIVE (69) GES,EA	0.51 OF 86	45 42 25 44 XSQ= 3.13 PHI= 0.142 XP = 0.0767
458	TEND TO BE THOSE WHERE GAMES, IF PRESENT, INCLUDE GAMES OF STRATEGY (52) R-A-B,EA	0.52 OF 54	458	TEND TO BE THOSE WHERE GAMES, IF PRESENT, DO NOT INCLUDE GAMES OF STRATEGY (119) R-A-B,EA	0.79 OF 117	28 24 26 93 XSQ= 15.70 PHI= 0.303 XP = 0.0001
460	TILT MORE TOWARD BEING THOSE WHERE GAMES, IF PRESENT, ARE NOT LIMITED TO GAMES OF SKILL ONLY (104) R-A-B,EA	0.74 OF 54	460	TILT LESS TOWARD BEING THOSE WHERE GAMES, IF PRESENT, ARE NOT LIMITED TO GAMES OF SKILL ONLY (104) R-A-B,EA	0.55 OF 117	14 53 40 64 XSQ= 5.03 PHI= -0.172 XP = 0.0248
470	DRIFT TOWARD BEING THOSE WHERE INNOVATIONS ARE GENERALLY ACCEPTED (21) JMH	0.60 OF 15	470	DRIFT TOWARD BEING THOSE WHERE INNOVATIONS ARE ACCEPTED ONLY SELECTIVELY (33) JMH	0.69 OF 39	9 12 6 27 XSQ= 2.76 PHI= 0.226 XP = 0.0965
476	DRIFT TOWARD BEING THOSE WHERE THE DEGREE OF INSOBRIETY IS MODERATE OR SLIGHT (18) DH	0.60 OF 15	476	DRIFT TOWARD BEING THOSE WHERE THE DEGREE OF INSOBRIETY IS STRONG (31) DH	0.74 OF 34	6 25 9 9 XSQ= 3.70 PHI= -0.275 XP = 0.0546

187 CULTURES WHERE THE KIN GROUP IS EXCLUSIVELY MATRILINEAL (55)	187 CULTURES WHERE THE KIN GROUP IS OTHER THAN EXCLUSIVELY MATRILINEAL (344)

BACKGROUND ON PAGE 108

BOTH SUBJECT AND PREDICATE

55 IN LEFT COLUMN

APINAYE	BELU	BORORO	CALLINAGO	CHEROKEE	COCHITI	CREEK	CROW	DELAWARE	DIERI
DOBUANS	EYAK	GARO	GOAJIRO	GUAHIBO	GURE	HAIDA	HANO	HURON	JEMEZ
KAREN	KASKA	KERALA	KHASI	KUBA	LAMBA	LESU	MANDAN	MINANGKABAU	MNONG GAR
MOTA	NABESNA	NAVAHO	NDEMBU	NYANEKA	PAWNEE	PENDE	PONAPEANS	ROTUMANS	SARAMACCA
SEMINOLE	SIRIONO	SIUAI	TALAMANCA	TENDA	TIMBIRA	TIMUCUA	TIWI	TROBRIAND	TRUKESE
TSHIMSHIAN	VEDDA	YAO	YOMBE	ZUNI					

344 IN RIGHT COLUMN

1 EXCLUDED BECAUSE UNASCERTAINED

AINU

	Left column			Right column		Statistics
4	IN ALL CASES ARE THOSE LOCATED OUTSIDE OF THE CIRCUM-MEDITERRANEAN (355)	1.00 OF 55	4	LEAN LESS TOWARD BEING THOSE LOCATED OUTSIDE OF THE CIRCUM-MEDITERRANEAN (355)	0.87 OF 344	0 45 55 299 XSQ= 6.85 PHI= -0.131 XP = 0.0088
8	TEND LESS TO BE THOSE LOCATED OUTSIDE OF NORTH AMERICA (330)	0.65 OF 55	8	TEND MORE TO BE THOSE LOCATED OUTSIDE OF NORTH AMERICA (330)	0.85 OF 344	19 51 36 293 XSQ= 11.42 PHI= 0.169 XP = 0.0007
36	DRIFT MORE TOWARD BEING THOSE WHERE THE NATURAL ENVIRONMENT IS OTHER THAN 'VERY HARSH,' OR SUB-TROPICAL BUSH, OR TEMPERATE GRASSLAND (292) FWM	0.84 OF 55	36	DRIFT LESS TOWARD BEING THOSE WHERE THE NATURAL ENVIRONMENT IS OTHER THAN 'VERY HARSH,' OR SUB-TROPICAL BUSH, OR TEMPERATE GRASSLAND (292) FWM	0.71 OF 344	9 99 46 245 XSQ= 3.10 PHI= -0.088 XP = 0.0783
53	TILT MORE TOWARD BEING THOSE WHERE FOOD PRODUCTION IS BY SIMPLE AGRICULTURE OR INCIPIENT FOOD PRODUCTION, RATHER THAN BY INTENSIVE AGRICULTURE (147)	0.81 OF 32	53	TILT LESS TOWARD BEING THOSE WHERE FOOD PRODUCTION IS BY SIMPLE AGRICULTURE OR INCIPIENT FOOD PRODUCTION, RATHER THAN BY INTENSIVE AGRICULTURE (147)	0.59 OF 206	6 85 26 121 XSQ= 5.03 PHI= -0.145 XP = 0.0249

55	DRIFT TOWARD BEING THOSE 0.73 OF 22 WHERE FOOD PRODUCTION IS BY SIMPLE AGRICULTURE, RATHER THAN BY INTENSIVE AGRICULTURE (101)	55	DRIFT TOWARD BEING THOSE 0.50 OF 170 WHERE FOOD PRODUCTION IS BY INTENSIVE AGRICULTURE, RATHER THAN BY SIMPLE AGRICULTURE (91)	6 85 16 85 XSQ= 3.18 PHI= -0.129 XP = 0.0748
62	DRIFT TOWARD BEING THOSE 0.55 OF 55 WHERE HUSBANDRY OF ANY KIND IS ABSENT (172)	62	DRIFT TOWARD BEING THOSE 0.59 OF 344 WHERE HUSBANDRY OF SOME KIND IS PRESENT (228)	25 203 30 141 XSQ= 3.03 PHI= -0.087 XP = 0.0819
63	TILT TOWARD BEING THOSE 0.56 OF 25 WHERE HUSBANDRY, IF PRESENT, IS PRINCIPALLY IN THE FORM OF PIGS, SHEEP, OR GOATS, RATHER THAN BOVINE, EQUINE, CAMEL-LIKE, OR DEER-LIKE ANIMALS (74)	63	TILT TOWARD BEING THOSE 0.70 OF 201 WHERE HUSBANDRY, IF PRESENT, IS PRINCIPALLY IN THE FORM OF BOVINE, EQUINE, CAMEL-LIKE, OR DEER-LIKE ANIMALS, RATHER THAN PIGS, SHEEP, OR GOATS (152)	11 141 14 60 XSQ= 5.77 PHI= -0.160 XP = 0.0163
71	DRIFT MORE TOWARD BEING THOSE 0.76 OF 37 WHERE METAL WORKING IS ABSENT (153)	71	DRIFT LESS TOWARD BEING THOSE 0.58 OF 213 WHERE METAL WORKING IS ABSENT (153)	9 89 28 124 XSQ= 3.33 PHI= -0.115 XP = 0.0679
80	TILT MORE TOWARD BEING THOSE 0.97 OF 33 WHERE NO CITY OR TOWN IS PRESENT (185)	80	TILT LESS TOWARD BEING THOSE 0.80 OF 191 WHERE NO CITY OR TOWN IS PRESENT (185)	1 38 32 153 XSQ= 4.45 PHI= -0.141 XP = 0.0348
84	TILT MORE TOWARD BEING THOSE 0.98 OF 46 WHERE THE LEVEL OF POLITICAL INTEGRATION IS THE LITTLE STATE, THE MINIMAL STATE, THE AUTONOMOUS COMMUNITY, OR THE FAMILY (262) GPM	84	TILT LESS TOWARD BEING THOSE 0.84 OF 258 WHERE THE LEVEL OF POLITICAL INTEGRATION IS THE LITTLE STATE, THE MINIMAL STATE, THE AUTONOMOUS COMMUNITY, OR THE FAMILY (262) GPM	1 41 45 217 XSQ= 5.07 PHI= -0.129 XP = 0.0243
85	DRIFT MORE TOWARD BEING THOSE 0.89 OF 46 WHERE THE LEVEL OF POLITICAL INTEGRATION IS THE MINIMAL STATE, THE AUTONOMOUS COMMUNITY, OR THE FAMILY (234) GPM	85	DRIFT LESS TOWARD BEING THOSE 0.75 OF 258 WHERE THE LEVEL OF POLITICAL INTEGRATION IS THE MINIMAL STATE, THE AUTONOMOUS COMMUNITY, OR THE FAMILY (234) GPM	5 65 41 193 XSQ= 3.75 PHI= -0.111 XP = 0.0529
88	DRIFT MORE TOWARD BEING THOSE 0.74 OF 43 WHERE, IF A HEADMANSHIP IS PRESENT, SUCCESSION IS HEREDITARY (165)	88	DRIFT LESS TOWARD BEING THOSE 0.58 OF 227 WHERE, IF A HEADMANSHIP IS PRESENT, SUCCESSION IS HEREDITARY (165)	11 95 32 132 XSQ= 3.36 PHI= -0.112 XP = 0.0668
90	TEND TO BE THOSE 0.81 OF 32 WHERE, IF A HEREDITARY HEADMANSHIP IS PRESENT, SUCCESSION IS MATRILINEAL, RATHER THAN PATRILINEAL (38)	90	TEND TO BE THOSE 0.91 OF 132 WHERE, IF A HEREDITARY HEADMANSHIP IS PRESENT, SUCCESSION IS PATRILINEAL, RATHER THAN MATRILINEAL (127)	6 120 26 12 XSQ= 71.34 PHI= -0.660 XP = 0.

```
 94  IN ALL CASES ARE THOSE              1.00 OF  46     94  TILT LESS TOWARD BEING THOSE    0.88 OF 283          0   34
     WHERE THE HIERARCHY                                    WHERE THE HIERARCHY                                 46  249
     OF NATIONAL JURISDICTION HAS                           OF NATIONAL JURISDICTION HAS                  XSQ=     4.94
     TWO, ONE, OR NO LEVELS  (296) GES,EA                   TWO, ONE, OR NO LEVELS  (296) GES,EA          PHI=   -0.122
                                                                                                          XP =   0.0263

 99  TILT MORE TOWARD BEING THOSE    0.80 OF  25     99  TILT LESS TOWARD BEING THOSE    0.56 OF 131         20   73
     WHERE, WITH NATIONAL HIERARCHY ABSENT,                 WHERE, WITH NATIONAL HIERARCHY ABSENT,               5   58
     THE HIERARCHY OF LOCAL JURISDICTION HAS                THE HIERARCHY OF LOCAL JURISDICTION HAS       XSQ=     4.18
     FOUR OR THREE LEVELS  (93) GES,EA                      FOUR OR THREE LEVELS  (93) GES,EA             PHI=    0.164
                                                                                                          XP =   0.0409

102  DRIFT TOWARD BEING THOSE           0.59 OF  54    102  DRIFT TOWARD BEING THOSE          0.55 OF 328         22  181
     WHERE CLASS STRATIFICATION IS                          WHERE CLASS STRATIFICATION IS                       32  147
     ABSENT  (180)                                          PRESENT  (203)                                XSQ=     3.33
                                                                                                          PHI=   -0.093
                                                                                                          XP =   0.0682

175  DRIFT MORE TOWARD BEING THOSE   0.79 OF  53    175  DRIFT LESS TOWARD BEING THOSE   0.66 OF 328         11  110
     WHERE THE COMMUNITY IS                                 WHERE THE COMMUNITY IS                              42  218
     'KIN-HETEROGENEOUS,' I. E.                             'KIN-HETEROGENEOUS,' I. E.                    XSQ=     2.88
     OTHER THAN                                             OTHER THAN                                    PHI=   -0.087
     A CLAN COMMUNITY OR A DEME  (260)                      A CLAN COMMUNITY OR A DEME  (260)             XP =   0.0900

176  LEAN TOWARD BEING THOSE            0.66 OF  53    176  LEAN TOWARD BEING THOSE           0.59 OF 328         35  134
     WHERE THE COMMUNITY IS                                 WHERE THE COMMUNITY IS OTHER THAN                   18  194
     A CLAN-COMMUNITY OR A COMMUNITY                        A CLAN-COMMUNITY OR A COMMUNITY               XSQ=    10.73
     STRUCTURED OR SEGMENTED                                STRUCTURED OR SEGMENTED                       PHI=    0.168
     ON A CLAN BASIS  (169)                                 ON A CLAN BASIS  (213)                        XP =   0.0011

178  TEND TO BE THOSE                   0.51 OF  53    178  TEND TO BE THOSE                  0.82 OF 328         27   60
     WHERE THE COMMUNITY IS                                 WHERE THE COMMUNITY IS OTHER THAN                   26  268
     SEGMENTED ON A CLAN BASIS AND                          SEGMENTED ON A CLAN BASIS AND                 XSQ=    25.78
     NON-EXOGAMOUS  (87)                                    NON-EXOGAMOUS  (295)                          PHI=    0.260
                                                                                                          XP =   0.0000

180  TILT MORE TOWARD BEING THOSE    0.81 OF  53    180  TILT LESS TOWARD BEING THOSE    0.65 OF 328         10  114
     WHERE THE COMMUNITY IS                                 WHERE THE COMMUNITY IS                              43  214
     COMMONLY NON-EXOGAMOUS, RATHER THAN                    COMMONLY NON-EXOGAMOUS, RATHER THAN           XSQ=     4.55
     EXOGAMOUS  (258)                                       EXOGAMOUS  (258)                              PHI=   -0.109
                                                                                                          XP =   0.0330

183  LEAN LESS TOWARD BEING THOSE    0.75 OF  55    183  LEAN MORE TOWARD BEING THOSE    0.90 OF 196         14   20
     WHERE THE LARGEST NON-COGNATIC KIN GROUP               WHERE THE LARGEST NON-COGNATIC KIN GROUP            41  176
     IS SMALLER THAN A MOEITY, I. E.,                       IS SMALLER THAN A MOEITY, I. E.,              XSQ=     7.28
     A PHRATRY OR SIB OR LINEAGE  (218)                     A PHRATRY OR SIB OR LINEAGE  (218)            PHI=    0.170
                                                                                                          XP =   0.0070

184  DRIFT LESS TOWARD BEING THOSE   0.58 OF  55    184  DRIFT MORE TOWARD BEING THOSE   0.72 OF 196         23   54
     WHERE THE LARGEST NON-COGNATIC KIN GROUP               WHERE THE LARGEST NON-COGNATIC KIN GROUP            32  142
     IS SMALLER THAN A PHRATRY, I. E.                       IS SMALLER THAN A PHRATRY, I. E.              XSQ=     3.47
     A SIB OR LINEAGE  (175)                                A SIB OR LINEAGE  (175)                       PHI=    0.118
                                                                                                          XP =   0.0626
```

187/

190	IN ALL CASES ARE THOSE WHERE THE KIN GROUP IS MATRILINEAL, RATHER THAN PATRILINEAL OR DOUBLE-DESCENT (61)	1.00 OF 55	190	TEND TO BE THOSE WHERE THE KIN GROUP IS PATRILINEAL OR DOUBLE-DESCENT, RATHER THAN MATRILINEAL (186)	0.97 OF 192	0 186 55 6 XSQ= 210.57 PHI= -0.923 XP = 0.
192	IN ALL CASES ARE THOSE OTHER THAN WHERE THE ONLY KIN GROUP PRESENT IS A KINDRED OR ELSE BILATERAL DESCENT IS INFERRED (289)	1.00 OF 55	192	TEND LESS TO BE THOSE OTHER THAN WHERE THE ONLY KIN GROUP PRESENT IS A KINDRED OR ELSE BILATERAL DESCENT IS INFERRED (289)	0.68 OF 344	0 111 55 233 XSQ= 23.01 PHI= -0.240 XP = 0.0000
198	TEND TO BE THOSE WHERE RULES FOR THE INHERITANCE OF REAL PROPERTY, IF PRESENT, FAVOR THE FEMALE HEIR OR LINE, RATHER THAN THE MALE (21)	0.89 OF 19	198	TEND TO BE THOSE WHERE RULES FOR THE INHERITANCE OF REAL PROPERTY, IF PRESENT, FAVOR THE MALE HEIR OR LINE, RATHER THAN THE FEMALE (144)	0.97 OF 146	2 142 17 4 XSQ= 106.19 PHI= -0.802 XP = 0.
201	TILT MORE TOWARD BEING THOSE WHERE MARITAL RESIDENCE IS NON-OPTIONAL, RATHER THAN AMBILOCAL OR NEOLOCAL (334)	0.94 OF 54	201	TILT LESS TOWARD BEING THOSE WHERE MARITAL RESIDENCE IS NON-OPTIONAL, RATHER THAN AMBILOCAL OR NEOLOCAL (334)	0.82 OF 343	51 282 3 61 XSQ= 4.29 PHI= 0.104 XP = 0.0382
207	TEND TO BE THOSE WHERE MARITAL RESIDENCE IS MATRILOCAL OR UXORILOCAL, RATHER THAN AMBILOCAL OR NEOLOCAL (64)	0.91 OF 35	207	TEND TO BE THOSE WHERE MARITAL RESIDENCE IS AMBILOCAL OR NEOLOCAL, RATHER THAN MATRILOCAL OR UXORILOCAL (64)	0.66 OF 93	32 32 3 61 XSQ= 30.83 PHI= 0.491 XP = 0.
209	TEND TO BE THOSE WHERE MARITAL RESIDENCE IS MATRILOCAL OR UXORILOCAL, RATHER THAN PATRILOCAL, VIRILOCAL, OR AVUNCULOCAL (64)	0.63 OF 51	209	TEND TO BE THOSE WHERE MARITAL RESIDENCE IS PATRILOCAL, VIRILOCAL, OR AVUNCULOCAL, RATHER THAN MATRILOCAL OR UXORILOCAL (270)	0.89 OF 282	19 250 32 32 XSQ= 70.21 PHI= -0.459 XP = 0.
210	IN ALL CASES ARE THOSE WHERE MARITAL RESIDENCE IS MATRILOCAL, RATHER THAN PATRILOCAL (31)	1.00 OF 31	210	IN ALL CASES ARE THOSE WHERE MARITAL RESIDENCE IS PATRILOCAL, RATHER THAN MATRILOCAL (169)	1.00 OF 169	0 169 31 0 XSQ= 192.44 PHI= -0.981 XP = 0.
214	DRIFT LESS TOWARD BEING THOSE WHERE FIRST COUSIN MARRIAGE, IF PERMITTED, IS OTHER THAN UNILATERAL (144)	0.70 OF 30	214	DRIFT MORE TOWARD BEING THOSE WHERE FIRST COUSIN MARRIAGE, IF PERMITTED, IS OTHER THAN UNILATERAL (144)	0.87 OF 141	9 19 21 122 XSQ= 3.80 PHI= 0.149 XP = 0.0513
220	TILT LESS TOWARD BEING THOSE WHERE FIRST COUSIN MARRIAGE IN SOME FORM OR OTHER IS NOT PRESCRIBED OR PREFERRED (273)	0.62 OF 52	220	TILT MORE TOWARD BEING THOSE WHERE FIRST COUSIN MARRIAGE IN SOME FORM OR OTHER IS NOT PRESCRIBED OR PREFERRED (273)	0.76 OF 317	20 77 32 240 XSQ= 3.93 PHI= 0.103 XP = 0.0475

221	DRIFT LESS TCWARD BEING THCSE 0.83 OF 52 WHERE MATRILATERAL CRCSS-COUSIN MARRIAGE IS NCT PRESCRIBED CR PREFERREC (335)	221	DRIFT MORE TOWARD BEING THCSE 0.92 CF 317 WHERE MATRILATERAL CRCSS-CCUSIN MARRIAGE IS NOT PRESCRIBED OR PREFERRED (335)	9 26 43 291 XSQ= 3.32 PHI= 0.095 XP = 0.0685
234	TEND TC BE THCSE 0.77 OF 52 WHERE THE COUSIN TERMINCLCGY IS OF CRCW, CMAHA, CR IRCQUOIS TYPE, RATHER THAN ESKIMC CR HAWAIIAN TYPE (152)	234	TEND TO BE THCSE 0.59 CF 270 WHERE THE COUSIN TERMINCLOGY IS OF ESKIMO OR HAWAIIAN TYPE, RATHER THAN CROW, OMAHA, OR IROQUOIS TYPE (170)	40 112 12 158 XSQ= 20.58 PHI= 0.253 XP = 0.0000
240	TILT TOWARD BEING THOSE 0.58 OF 33 WHERE THE FAMILY, IF EXTENCEC, IS LARGE, RATHER THAN SMALL CR STEM (78)	24C	TILT TOWARD BEING THOSE 0.67 OF 179 WHERE THE FAMILY, IF EXTENDED, IS SMALL OR STEM, RATHER THAN LARGE (135)	19 59 14 120 XSQ= 6.24 PHI= 0.172 XP = 0.0125
254	DRIFT TCWARD BEING THCSE 0.80 OF 5 WHERE HCUSEHCLD AUTHORITY IS ON THE MOTHER'S SICE, RATHER THAN THE FATHER'S (6) CA	254	DRIFT TOWARD BEING THOSE 0.80 CF 10 WHERE HOUSEHOLD AUTHORITY IS ON THE FATHER'S SIDE, RATHER THAN THE MOTHER'S (9) DA	1 8 4 2 XSQ= 2.81 PHI= -0.433 EP = 0.0889
262	TILT LESS TOWARC BEING THCSE 0.63 OF 54 WHERE WIVES ARE CBTAINEC BY MEANS INVCLVING THE PRESENCE CF SCME CCNSIDERATION (305)	262	TILT MORE TOWARD BEING THCSE 0.80 CF 340 WHERE WIVES ARE OBTAINED BY MEANS INVOLVING THE PRESENCE OF SOME CONSIDERATICN (305)	34 271 20 69 XSQ= 6.54 PHI= -0.129 XP = 0.0105
263	LEAN TCWARD BEING THCSE 0.59 OF 54 WHERE WIVES ARE CBTAINEC BY RELATIVELY EASY MEANS, NAMELY BY TOKEN BRIDE-PRICE, GIFT EXCHANGE, ABSENCE CF ANY CCNSIDERATICN, OR RECEIPT OF DCWRY (162)	263	LEAN TOWARD BEING THOSE 0.62 CF 340 WHERE WIVES ARE OBTAINED BY RELATIVELY DIFFICULT MEANS, NAMELY BY BRIDE-PRICE, BRIDE-SERVICE, CR EXCHANGING A FEMALE RELATIVE (233)	22 211 32 129 XSQ= 7.90 PHI= -0.142 XP = 0.0049
336	TILT TCWARD BEING THOSE 0.75 OF 12 WHERE THE TCTAL POSITIVE PRESSURE TOWARD DEVELCPING RESPCNSIBLE BEHAVIOR IN THE CHILD IS LCW (32) B-B-C	336	TILT TOWARD BEING THOSE 0.63 CF 62 WHERE THE TOTAL PCSITIVE PRESSURE TCWARC DEVELOPING RESPONSIBLE BEHAVIOR IN THE CHILD IS HIGH (43) B-B-C	3 39 9 23 XSQ= 4.44 PHI= -0.245 XP = 0.0351
370	TILT TOWARC BEING THCSE 0.59 OF 34 WHERE THE SEGREGATION CF ACOLESCENT BOYS IS COMPLETE CR PARTIAL (95)	37C	TILT TOWARD BEING THOSE 0.64 OF 208 WHERE THE SEGREGATION OF ADCLESCENT BOYS IS ABSENT (148)	20 75 14 133 XSQ= 5.43 PHI= 0.150 XP = 0.0198
390	IN ALL CASES ARE THCSE 1.00 OF 19 WHERE PREMARITAL SEX RELATIONS ARE WEAKLY PUNISHED ANC IN FACT NCT RARE OR PUNISHED CNLY IF PREGNANCY RESULTS, OR FREELY PERMITTEC (132) JTW,EA	39C	TILT LESS TOWARD BEING THOSE 0.70 CF 159 WHERE PREMARITAL SEX RELATICNS ARE WEAKLY PUNISHED AND IN FACT NOT RARE OR PUNISHED ONLY IF PREGNANCY RESULTS, OR FREELY PERMITTED (132) JTW,EA	0 47 19 112 XSQ= 6.19 PHI= -0.186 XP = 0.0129

391	DRIFT TCWARD BEING THCSE WHERE PREMARITAL SEX RELATIONS ARE PUNISHED CNLY IF PREGNANCY RESULTS, OR FREELY PERMITTEC (90) JTW,EA	0.74 OF 19	391	DRIFT TOWARD BEING THOSE WHERE PREMARITAL SEX RELATICNS ARE STRONGLY PUNISHED AND IN FACT RARE, OR WEAKLY PUNISHED AND IN FACT NOT RARE (89) JTW,EA	0.53 OF 159	 XSQ= PHI= XP =	5 84 14 75 3.77 -0.146 0.0522
399	DRIFT TCWARD BEING THCSE WHERE INTENSITY CF CASTRATION ANXIETY IS LOW (22) WNS	0.86 OF 7	399	DRIFT TOWARD BEING THOSE WHERE INTENSITY OF CASTRATICN ANXIETY IS HIGH (23) WNS	0.57 CF 37	 XSQ= PHI= XP =	1 21 6 16 2.72 -0.249 0.0992
403	TILT TOWARD BEING THOSE WHERE EXPLANATICNS CF ILLNESS OF AN ANAL NATURE ARE PRESENT (23) W-C	0.75 OF 8	403	TILT TOWARD BEING THOSE WHERE EXPLANATICNS CF ILLNESS OF AN ANAL NATURE ARE ABSENT (38) W-C	0.69 OF 52	 XSQ= PHI= XP =	6 16 2 36 4.09 0.261 0.0431
426	TILT TCWARD BEING THCSE WHERE A HIGH GCC IS ABSENT (104) GES,EA	0.59 OF 37	426	TILT TOWARD BEING THOSE WHERE A HIGH GOD IS PRESENT (156) GES,EA	0.64 CF 222	 XSQ= PHI= XP =	15 141 22 81 6.06 -0.153 0.0138
427	LEAN TOWARD BEING THOSE WHERE A HIGH GCC, IF PRESENT, IS INACTIVE, RATHER THAN ACTIVE (69) GES,EA	0.80 OF 15	427	LEAN TOWARD BEING THOSE WHERE A HIGH GOD, IF PRESENT, IS ACTIVE, RATHER THAN INACTIVE (87) GES,EA	0.60 OF 141	 XSQ= PHI= XP =	3 84 12 57 7.08 -0.213 0.0078
428	IN ALL CASES ARE THCSE WHERE A HIGH GOC, IF PRESENT AND ACTIVE, DOES NOT SUPPCRT HUMAN MORALITY, RATHER THAN SUPPORTING IT (26) GES,EA	1.00 OF 3	428	TILT TOWARD BEING THOSE WHERE A HIGH GOD, IF PRESENT AND ACTIVE, SUPPORTS HUMAN MORALITY, RATHER THAN NOT SUPPORTING IT (61) GES,EA	0.73 CF 84	 XSQ= PHI= XP =	0 61 3 23 4.24 -0.221 0.0396
449	DRIFT TCWARD BEING THCSE WHERE THE CBSERVATICN CF FCOC TABOOS IS HIGH, RATHER THAN MEDIUM OR LOW (25) JRL	0.60 OF 10	449	DRIFT TOWARD BEING THOSE WHERE THE OBSERVATION CF FCOD TABOOS IS MEDIUM OR LOW, RATHER THAN HIGH (61) JRL	0.75 OF 76	 XSQ= PHI= XP =	6 19 4 57 3.69 0.207 0.0547
471	TILT TCWARD BEING THOSE WHERE SECRET SOCIETIES ARE PRESENT (9) LWS	0.83 OF 6	471	TILT TOWARD BEING THOSE WHERE SECRET SOCIETIES ARE UMIMPORTANT OR ABSENT (14) LWS	0.75 OF 16	 XSQ= PHI= EP =	5 4 1 12 3.97 0.425 0.0461

188 CULTURES WHERE THE KIN GROUP IS EXCLUSIVELY COGNATIC (148)

188 CULTURES WHERE THE KIN GROUP IS OTHER THAN EXCLUSIVELY COGNATIC (252)

BACKGROUND ON PAGE 108 | BOTH SUBJECT AND PREDICATE

148 IN LEFT COLUMN

ABIPON	ALACALUF	AMERICANS	ANDAMANESE	ATSUGEWI	AWEIKOMA	AZTEC	BACAIRI	BALINESE	BASQUES
BERGDAMA	BLACK CARIB	BOERS	BOTOCUDO	BRAZILIANS	BULGARIANS	BURMESE	CADUVEO	CAGABA	CAMAYURA
CAMBA	CAMBODIANS	CARAJA	CARIB	CARINYA	CAYAPA	CHAMACOCO	CHEREMIS	CHEYENNE	CHIBCHA
CHINANTEC	CHIR-APACHE	CHIRIGUANO	CHOCO	CHOROTI	CHORTI	CHUKCHEE	COMANCHE	COPR ESKIMO	CREE
CUNA	CZECHS	DUSUN	DUTCH	ELLICE	GILBERTESE	GROS VENTRE	GUATO	HANUNOO	HASINAI
HAVASUPAI	HAWAIIANS	HUICHOL	HUKUNDIKA	HUTSUL	IBAN	ICELANDERS	IFUGAO	INCA	INGALIK
INGASSANA	IRISH	JAPANESE	JAVANESE	JIVARO	JUKUN	KIOW-APACHE	KCL	KORYAK	KUMYK
KUNG	KUTENAI	KWAKIUTL	LAPPS	LOZI	MACASSARESE	MALAYS	MAMBILA	MANGAIANS	MANIHIKI
MAORI	MARQUESANS	MATACO	MAZATECO	MENTAWEI	MISKITO	MOTILON	NAMBICUARA	NASKAPI	NATCHEZ
NGONI	NICOBARESE	NUNIVAK	ONA	ONTONG-JAVA	PAEZ	PAIWAN	PAPAGO	PARAUJANO	PENOBSCOT
POPOLUCA	PORTUGUESE	RARCIANS	ROMANS	SAGADA	SAMOANS	SANPOIL	SARSI	SELUNG	SEMANG
SERI	SIMBOESE	SINHALESE	SUBANUN	TAGBANUA	TAOS	TAPIRAPE	TARAHUMARA	TAREUMIUT	TEHUELCHE
TENETEHARA	TENINO	TERENA	TETON	THAI	TOKELAU	TORAJA	TOTONAC	TRISTAN	TRUMAI
TUBATULABAL	TUNEBO	TUPINAMBA	TWANA	ULAWANS	UTE	WAICA	WALLCONS	WAPISHANA	WARRAU
WASHO	WICHITA	YABARANA	YAHGAN	YARURO	YUKAGHIR	YUKI	YUROK		

252 IN RIGHT COLUMN

3	TEND MORE TO BE THOSE LOCATED OUTSIDE OF AFRICA (320)	0.95 OF 148	3	TEND LESS TO BE THOSE LOCATED OUTSIDE OF AFRICA (320)	0.71 OF 252	7 73 141 179 XSQ= 32.74 PHI= -0.286 XP = 0.
5	LEAN MORE TOWARD BEING THOSE LOCATED OUTSIDE OF EAST EURASIA (330)	0.91 OF 148	5	LEAN LESS TOWARD BEING THOSE LOCATED OUTSIDE OF EAST EURASIA (330)	0.78 OF 252	14 56 134 196 XSQ= 9.65 PHI= -0.155 XP = 0.0019
8	TEND LESS TO BE THOSE LOCATED OUTSIDE OF NORTH AMERICA (330)	0.73 OF 148	8	TEND MORE TO BE THOSE LOCATED OUTSIDE OF NORTH AMERICA (330)	0.88 OF 252	40 30 108 222 XSQ= 13.74 PHI= 0.185 XP = 0.0002

9	TEND LESS TO BE THOSE LOCATED OUTSIDE OF SOUTH AMERICA (335)	0.70 OF 148	9	TEND MORE TO BE THOSE LOCATED OUTSIDE OF SOUTH AMERICA (335)	0.92 OF 252	44 21 104 231 XSQ= 29.81 PHI= 0.273 XP = 0.0000
12	LEAN LESS TOWARD BEING THOSE WHERE THE LATITUDE IS LESS THAN FIFTY DEGREES (367)	0.86 OF 148	12	LEAN MORE TOWARD BEING THOSE WHERE THE LATITUDE IS LESS THAN FIFTY DEGREES (367)	0.95 OF 252	21 12 127 240 XSQ= 9.74 PHI= 0.156 XP = 0.0018
13	TEND LESS TO BE THOSE WHERE THE LATITUDE IS LESS THAN FORTY DEGREES (329)	0.73 OF 148	13	TEND MORE TO BE THOSE WHERE THE LATITUDE IS LESS THAN FORTY DEGREES (329)	0.88 OF 252	40 31 108 221 XSQ= 12.86 PHI= 0.179 XP = 0.0003
14	LEAN LESS TOWARD BEING THOSE WHERE THE LATITUDE IS LESS THAN THIRTY DEGREES (281)	0.62 OF 148	14	LEAN MORE TOWARD BEING THOSE WHERE THE LATITUDE IS LESS THAN THIRTY DEGREES (281)	0.75 OF 252	56 63 92 189 XSQ= 6.75 PHI= 0.130 XP = 0.0094
16	DRIFT MORE TOWARD BEING THOSE WHERE THE LATITUDE IS TEN DEGREES OR GREATER (277)	0.75 OF 148	16	DRIFT LESS TOWARD BEING THOSE WHERE THE LATITUDE IS TEN DEGREES OR GREATER (277)	0.66 OF 252	111 166 37 86 XSQ= 3.23 PHI= 0.090 XP = 0.0722
36	TILT LESS TOWARD BEING THOSE WHERE THE NATURAL ENVIRONMENT IS OTHER THAN 'VERY HARSH,' OR SUB-TROPICAL BUSH, OR TEMPERATE GRASSLAND (292) FWM	0.67 OF 148	36	TILT MORE TOWARD BEING THOSE WHERE THE NATURAL ENVIRONMENT IS OTHER THAN 'VERY HARSH,' OR SUB-TROPICAL BUSH, OR TEMPERATE GRASSLAND (292) FWM	0.77 OF 252	49 59 99 193 XSQ= 3.97 PHI= 0.100 XP = 0.0464
44	DRIFT LESS TOWARD BEING THOSE WHERE SETTLEMENTS ARE FIXED (222)	0.60 OF 121	44	DRIFT MORE TOWARD BEING THOSE WHERE SETTLEMENTS ARE FIXED (222)	0.71 OF 211	73 149 48 62 XSQ= 3.22 PHI= -0.099 XP = 0.0726
46	TILT LESS TOWARD BEING THOSE OTHER THAN WHERE SETTLEMENTS ARE NON-FIXED AND MOVEMENT IS NOMADIC (260)	0.71 OF 121	46	TILT MORE TOWARD BEING THOSE OTHER THAN WHERE SETTLEMENTS ARE NON-FIXED AND MOVEMENT IS NOMADIC (260)	0.82 OF 211	35 37 86 174 XSQ= 5.22 PHI= 0.125 XP = 0.0223
51	TEND TO BE THOSE WHERE SUBSISTENCE IS PRIMARILY BY FOOD GATHERING -- I. E., HUNTING, FISHING, OR COLLECTING -- RATHER THAN FOOD PRODUCTION (147)	0.53 OF 148	51	TEND TO BE THOSE WHERE SUBSISTENCE IS PRIMARILY BY FOOD PRODUCTION -- I. E., AGRICULTURE OR HUSBANDRY -- RATHER THAN BY GATHERING (253)	0.73 OF 252	69 184 79 68 XSQ= 26.82 PHI= -0.259 XP = 0.0000

54	DRIFT LESS TOWARD BEING THOSE 0.73 OF 71 WHERE FOOD PRODUCTION IS BY INTENSIVE OR SIMPLE AGRICULTURE, RATHER THAN BY INCIPIENT FOOD PRODUCTION (192)	54	DRIFT MORE TOWARD BEING THOSE 0.84 OF 167 WHERE FOOD PRODUCTION IS BY INTENSIVE OR SIMPLE AGRICULTURE, RATHER THAN BY INCIPIENT FOOD PRODUCTION (192)	52 140 19 27 XSQ= 2.94 PHI= -0.111 XP = 0.0865
56	DRIFT LESS TOWARD BEING THOSE 0.57 OF 44 WHERE FOOD PRODUCTION IS BY SIMPLE AGRICULTURE, RATHER THAN BY INCIPIENT FOOD PRODUCTION (101)	56	DRIFT MORE TOWARD BEING THOSE 0.74 OF 103 WHERE FOOD PRODUCTION IS BY SIMPLE AGRICULTURE, RATHER THAN BY INCIPIENT FOOD PRODUCTION (101)	25 76 19 27 XSQ= 3.38 PHI= -0.152 XP = 0.0661
62	TEND TO BE THOSE 0.56 OF 148 WHERE HUSBANDRY OF ANY KIND IS ABSENT (172)	62	TEND TO BE THOSE 0.65 OF 252 WHERE HUSBANDRY OF SOME KIND IS PRESENT (228)	65 163 83 89 XSQ= 15.56 PHI= -0.197 XP = 0.0001
71	TEND TO BE THOSE 0.80 OF 93 WHERE METAL WORKING IS ABSENT (153)	71	TEND TO BE THOSE 0.50 OF 158 WHERE METAL WORKING IS PRESENT (98)	19 79 74 79 XSQ= 20.28 PHI= -0.284 XP = 0.0000
79	LEAN LESS TOWARD BEING THOSE 0.82 OF 76 WHERE NO CITY IS PRESENT (201)	79	LEAN MORE TOWARD BEING THOSE 0.94 OF 148 WHERE NO CITY IS PRESENT (201)	14 9 62 139 XSQ= 7.01 PHI= 0.177 XP = 0.0081
82	DRIFT LESS TOWARD BEING THOSE 0.72 OF 76 WHERE A CITY OR TOWN IS PRESENT, OR THE AVERAGE COMMUNITY SIZE IS FIFTY OR GREATER (178)	82	DRIFT MORE TOWARD BEING THOSE 0.83 OF 148 WHERE A CITY OR TOWN IS PRESENT, OR THE AVERAGE COMMUNITY SIZE IS FIFTY OR GREATER (178)	55 123 21 25 XSQ= 2.92 PHI= -0.114 XP = 0.0874
83	DRIFT MORE TOWARD BEING THOSE 0.84 OF 56 WHERE, WITH NO CITY AND NO TOWN PRESENT, THE AVERAGE COMMUNITY SIZE IS SMALLER THAN 200, RATHER THAN BETWEEN 200 AND 999 (135)	83	DRIFT LESS TOWARD BEING THOSE 0.71 OF 124 WHERE, WITH NO CITY AND NO TOWN PRESENT, THE AVERAGE COMMUNITY SIZE IS SMALLER THAN 200, RATHER THAN BETWEEN 200 AND 999 (135)	9 36 47 88 XSQ= 2.80 PHI= -0.125 XP = 0.0943
86	TILT TOWARD BEING THOSE 0.59 OF 113 WHERE THE LEVEL OF POLITICAL INTEGRATION IS THE AUTONOMOUS COMMUNITY, OR THE FAMILY (156) GPM	86	TILT TOWARD BEING THOSE 0.53 OF 191 WHERE THE LEVEL OF POLITICAL INTEGRATION IS THE LARGE STATE, THE LITTLE STATE, OR THE MINIMAL STATE (148) GPM	46 102 67 89 XSQ= 4.09 PHI= -0.116 XP = 0.0432
88	TILT TOWARD BEING THOSE 0.50 OF 92 WHERE, IF A HEADMANSHIP IS PRESENT, SUCCESSION IS NON-HEREDITARY (106)	88	TILT TOWARD BEING THOSE 0.66 OF 179 WHERE, IF A HEADMANSHIP IS PRESENT, SUCCESSION IS HEREDITARY (165)	46 60 46 119 XSQ= 6.26 PHI= 0.152 XP = 0.0124

90	LEAN MORE TOWARD BEING THOSE 0.93 OF 46 WHERE, IF A HEREDITARY HEADMANSHIP IS PRESENT, SUCCESSION IS PATRILINEAL, RATHER THAN MATRILINEAL (127)	90	LEAN LESS TOWARD BEING THOSE 0.71 OF 119 WHERE, IF A HEREDITARY HEADMANSHIP IS PRESENT, SUCCESSION IS PATRILINEAL, RATHER THAN MATRILINEAL (127)	 XSQ= PHI= XP =	43 84 3 35 8.56 0.228 0.0034
96	LEAN TOWARD BEING THOSE 0.59 OF 120 WHERE THE HIERARCHY OF NATIONAL JURISDICTION HAS NO LEVELS (156) GES,EA	96	LEAN TOWARD BEING THOSE 0.60 OF 210 WHERE THE HIERARCHY OF NATIONAL JURISDICTION HAS FOUR, THREE, TWO OR ONE LEVEL (174) GES,EA	 XSQ= PHI= XP =	49 125 71 85 9.97 -0.174 0.0016
97	TEND MORE TO BE THOSE 0.92 OF 120 WHERE THE HIERARCHY OF LOCAL JURISDICTION HAS THREE OR TWO LEVELS (273) GES,EA	97	TEND LESS TO BE THOSE 0.77 OF 211 WHERE THE HIERARCHY OF LOCAL JURISDICTION HAS THREE OR TWO LEVELS (273) GES,EA	 XSQ= PHI= XP =	9 49 111 162 12.02 -0.191 0.0005
98	TEND LESS TO BE THOSE 0.58 OF 120 WHERE THE HIERARCHY OF LOCAL JURISDICTION HAS FOUR OR THREE LEVELS (238) GES,EA	98	TEND MORE TO BE THOSE 0.80 OF 211 WHERE THE HIERARCHY OF LOCAL JURISDICTION HAS FOUR OR THREE LEVELS (238) GES,EA	 XSQ= PHI= XP =	70 168 50 43 16.12 -0.221 0.0001
100	LEAN LESS TOWARD BEING THOSE 0.72 OF 120 WHERE HIERARCHIES ARE MORE COMPLEX THAN THE 'SIMPLEST,' I. E., MORE COMPLEX THAN TWO LOCAL LEVELS WITH NO NATIONAL LEVELS (267) GES,EA	100	LEAN MORE TOWARD BEING THOSE 0.86 OF 210 WHERE HIERARCHIES ARE MORE COMPLEX THAN THE 'SIMPLEST,' I. E., MORE COMPLEX THAN TWO LOCAL LEVELS WITH NO NATIONAL LEVELS (267) GES,EA	 XSQ= PHI= XP =	86 181 34 29 9.51 -0.170 0.0020
109	TEND MORE TO BE THOSE 0.95 OF 142 WHERE CASTES ARE ABSENT (317)	109	TEND LESS TO BE THOSE 0.81 OF 226 WHERE CASTES ARE ABSENT (317)	 XSQ= PHI= XP =	7 44 135 182 14.25 -0.197 0.0002
110	TEND TO BE THOSE 0.70 OF 141 WHERE SLAVERY IS ABSENT (218)	110	TEND TO BE THOSE 0.50 OF 240 WHERE SLAVERY IS PRESENT (163)	 XSQ= PHI= XP =	43 120 98 120 13.02 -0.185 0.0003
128	TILT TOWARD BEING THOSE 0.76 OF 21 WHERE, IF SUBSISTENCE IS PRIMARILY BY AGRICULTURE, THE WORK IS MAINLY DONE BY MALES (40)	128	TILT TOWARD BEING THOSE 0.57 OF 56 WHERE, IF SUBSISTENCE IS PRIMARILY BY AGRICULTURE, THE WORK IS MAINLY DONE BY FEMALES (37)	 XSQ= PHI= XP =	16 24 5 32 5.53 0.268 0.0187
129	LEAN MORE TOWARD BEING THOSE 0.87 OF 38 WHERE WEAVING IS MAINLY DONE BY FEMALES (73)	129	LEAN LESS TOWARD BEING THOSE 0.61 OF 66 WHERE WEAVING IS MAINLY DONE BY FEMALES (73)	 XSQ= PHI= XP =	5 26 33 40 6.73 -0.254 0.0095

No.		No.		
147	DRIFT TOWARD BEING THOSE 0.62 OF 13 WHERE CODIFIED LAWS ARE UNIMPORTANT OR ABSENT (13) LWS	147	DRIFT TOWARD BEING THOSE 0.75 OF 20 WHERE CODIFIED LAWS ARE PRESENT (20) LWS	5 15 8 5 XSQ= 3.01 PHI= -0.302 EP = 0.0673
175	TILT MORE TOWARD BEING THOSE 0.76 OF 141 WHERE THE COMMUNITY IS 'KIN-HETEROGENEOUS,' I. E. OTHER THAN A CLAN COMMUNITY OR A DEME (260)	175	TILT LESS TOWARD BEING THOSE 0.63 OF 241 WHERE THE COMMUNITY IS 'KIN-HETEROGENEOUS,' I. E. OTHER THAN A CLAN COMMUNITY OR A DEME (260)	34 88 107 153 XSQ= 5.74 PHI= -0.123 XP = 0.0166
176	TEND TO BE THOSE 0.92 OF 141 WHERE THE COMMUNITY IS OTHER THAN A CLAN-COMMUNITY OR A COMMUNITY STRUCTURED OR SEGMENTED ON A CLAN BASIS (213)	176	TEND TO BE THOSE 0.66 OF 241 WHERE THE COMMUNITY IS A CLAN-COMMUNITY OR A COMMUNITY STRUCTURED OR SEGMENTED ON A CLAN BASIS (169)	11 158 130 83 XSQ= 117.97 PHI= -0.556 XP = 0.
177	IN ALL CASES ARE THOSE 1.00 OF 141 WHERE THE COMMUNITY IS OTHER THAN A SINGLE CLAN-COMMUNITY AND EXOGAMOUS (305)	177	TEND LESS TO BE THOSE 0.68 OF 241 WHERE THE COMMUNITY IS OTHER THAN A SINGLE CLAN-COMMUNITY AND EXOGAMOUS (305)	0 77 141 164 XSQ= 54.46 PHI= -0.378 XP = 0.
178	TEND MORE TO BE THOSE 0.92 OF 141 WHERE THE COMMUNITY IS OTHER THAN SEGMENTED ON A CLAN BASIS AND NON-EXOGAMOUS (295)	178	TEND LESS TO BE THOSE 0.68 OF 241 WHERE THE COMMUNITY IS OTHER THAN SEGMENTED ON A CLAN BASIS AND NON-EXOGAMOUS (295)	11 76 130 165 XSQ= 27.16 PHI= -0.267 XP = 0.0000
179	LEAN LESS TOWARD BEING THOSE 0.83 OF 141 WHERE THE COMMUNITY IS OTHER THAN STRUCTURED ON A NON-CLAN BASIS AND COMMONLY EXOGAMOUS (340)	179	LEAN MORE TOWARD BEING THOSE 0.93 OF 241 WHERE THE COMMUNITY IS OTHER THAN STRUCTURED ON A NON-CLAN BASIS AND COMMONLY EXOGAMOUS (340)	24 18 117 223 XSQ= 7.35 PHI= 0.139 XP = 0.0067
180	TEND MORE TO BE THOSE 0.83 OF 141 WHERE THE COMMUNITY IS COMMONLY NON-EXOGAMOUS, RATHER THAN EXOGAMOUS (258)	180	TEND LESS TO BE THOSE 0.59 OF 241 WHERE THE COMMUNITY IS COMMONLY NON-EXOGAMOUS, RATHER THAN EXOGAMOUS (258)	24 100 117 141 XSQ= 23.20 PHI= -0.246 XP = 0.0000
181	TEND LESS TO BE THOSE 0.76 OF 141 WHERE THE COMMUNITY IS OTHER THAN A DEME (337)	181	TEND MORE TO BE THOSE 0.95 OF 241 WHERE THE COMMUNITY IS OTHER THAN A DEME (337)	34 11 107 230 XSQ= 30.86 PHI= 0.284 XP = 0.
182	TEND TO BE THOSE 0.51 OF 141 WHERE THE COMMUNITY IS STRUCTURED ON A NON-CLAN BASIS AND AGAMOUS (126)	182	TEND TO BE THOSE 0.78 OF 241 OTHER THAN WHERE THE COMMUNITY IS STRUCTURED ON A NON-CLAN BASIS AND AGAMOUS (256)	72 54 69 187 XSQ= 31.77 PHI= 0.288 XP = 0.

192	TEND TO BE THOSE WHERE THE ONLY KIN GROUP PRESENT IS A KINDRED OR ELSE BILATERAL DESCENT IS INFERRED (111)	0.75 OF 148	192	IN ALL CASES ARE THOSE OTHER THAN WHERE THE ONLY KIN GROUP PRESENT IS A KINDRED OR ELSE BILATERAL DESCENT IS INFERRED (289)	1.00 OF 252	111 0 37 252 XSQ= 257.86 PHI= 0.803 XP = 0.
196	TEND LESS TO BE THOSE WHERE INDIVIDUAL RIGHTS IN REAL PROPERTY, AND RULES FOR INHERITANCE, ARE PRESENT (194)	0.55 OF 99	196	TEND MORE TO BE THOSE WHERE INDIVIDUAL RIGHTS IN REAL PROPERTY, AND RULES FOR INHERITANCE, ARE PRESENT (194)	0.77 OF 182	54 140 45 42 XSQ= 13.99 PHI= -0.223 XP = 0.0002
197	TEND LESS TO BE THOSE WHERE RULES FOR THE INHERITANCE OF REAL PROPERTY, IF PRESENT, FAVOR EITHER THE MALE HEIR OR LINE, OR THE FEMALE HEIR OR LINE (165)	0.54 OF 54	197	TEND MORE TO BE THOSE WHERE RULES FOR THE INHERITANCE OF REAL PROPERTY, IF PRESENT, FAVOR EITHER THE MALE HEIR OR LINE, OR THE FEMALE HEIR OR LINE (165)	0.97 OF 140	29 136 25 4 XSQ= 54.47 PHI= -0.530 XP = 0.
201	TEND LESS TO BE THOSE WHERE MARITAL RESIDENCE IS NON-OPTIONAL, RATHER THAN AMBILOCAL OR NEOLOCAL (334)	0.65 OF 147	201	TEND MORE TO BE THOSE WHERE MARITAL RESIDENCE IS NON-OPTIONAL, RATHER THAN AMBILOCAL OR NEOLOCAL (334)	0.95 OF 251	96 238 51 13 XSQ= 57.68 PHI= -0.381 XP = 0.
204	TEND LESS TO BE THOSE WHERE MARITAL RESIDENCE IS PATRILOCAL, VIRILOCAL, OR AVUNCULOCAL, RATHER THAN AMBILOCAL OR NEOLOCAL (270)	0.56 OF 116	204	TEND MORE TO BE THOSE WHERE MARITAL RESIDENCE IS PATRILOCAL, VIRILOCAL, OR AVUNCULOCAL, RATHER THAN AMBILOCAL OR NEOLOCAL (270)	0.94 OF 218	65 205 51 13 XSQ= 68.16 PHI= -0.452 XP = 0.
207	TEND TO BE THOSE WHERE MARITAL RESIDENCE IS AMBILOCAL OR NEOLOCAL, RATHER THAN MATRILOCAL OR UXORILOCAL (64)	0.62 OF 82	207	TEND TO BE THOSE WHERE MARITAL RESIDENCE IS MATRILOCAL OR UXORILOCAL, RATHER THAN AMBILOCAL OR NEOLOCAL (64)	0.72 OF 46	31 33 51 13 XSQ= 12.25 PHI= -0.309 XP = 0.0005
209	TEND LESS TO BE THOSE WHERE MARITAL RESIDENCE IS PATRILOCAL, VIRILOCAL, OR AVUNCULOCAL, RATHER THAN MATRILOCAL OR UXORILOCAL (270)	0.68 OF 96	209	TEND MORE TO BE THOSE WHERE MARITAL RESIDENCE IS PATRILOCAL, VIRILOCAL, OR AVUNCULOCAL, RATHER THAN MATRILOCAL OR UXORILOCAL (270)	0.86 OF 238	65 205 31 33 XSQ= 13.83 PHI= -0.203 XP = 0.0002
213	TEND TO BE THOSE WHERE FIRST COUSIN MARRIAGE IS NOT PERMITTED (198)	0.66 OF 131	213	TEND TO BE THOSE WHERE FIRST COUSIN MARRIAGE IS PERMITTED (172)	0.54 OF 239	44 128 87 111 XSQ= 12.77 PHI= -0.186 XP = 0.0004
214	IN ALL CASES ARE THOSE WHERE FIRST COUSIN MARRIAGE, IF PERMITTED, IS OTHER THAN UNILATERAL (144)	1.00 OF 44	214	LEAN LESS TOWARD BEING THOSE WHERE FIRST COUSIN MARRIAGE, IF PERMITTED, IS OTHER THAN UNILATERAL (144)	0.78 OF 128	0 28 44 100 XSQ= 9.95 PHI= -0.240 XP = 0.0016

```
220  TEND MORE TO BE THOSE           0.89 OF 131    220  TEND LESS TO BE THOSE           0.66 OF 239       15    82
     WHERE FIRST COUSIN MARRIAGE                         WHERE FIRST COUSIN MARRIAGE                        116   157
     IN SOME FORM OR OTHER                               IN SOME FORM OR OTHER                            XSQ=   21.69
     IS NOT PRESCRIBED OR PREFERRED  (273)               IS NOT PRESCRIBED OR PREFERRED  (273)            PHI=  -0.242
                                                                                                          XP =  0.0000

221  IN ALL CASES ARE THOSE          1.00 OF 131    221  TEND LESS TO BE THOSE           0.85 OF 239        0    35
     WHERE MATRILATERAL CROSS-COUSIN MARRIAGE            WHERE MATRILATERAL CROSS-COUSIN MARRIAGE           131   204
     IS NOT PRESCRIBED OR PREFERRED  (335)               IS NOT PRESCRIBED OR PREFERRED  (335)            XSQ=   19.51
                                                                                                          PHI=  -0.230
                                                                                                          XP =  0.0000

224  TEND TO BE THOSE                0.98 OF  44    224  TEND TO BE THOSE                0.51 OF 128        1    65
     WHERE COUSIN MARRIAGE IS                            WHERE COUSIN MARRIAGE IS                            43    63
     PREFERENTIALLY OR PERMISSIVELY                      PREFERENTIALLY OR PERMISSIVELY                   XSQ=   30.56
     SYMMETRICAL, RATHER THAN                            EITHER PATRI- OR MATRILATERAL,                   PHI=  -0.422
     EITHER PATRI- OR MATRILATERAL  (106)                RATHER THAN SYMMETRICAL  (66)                    XP =  0.

234  TEND TO BE THOSE                0.84 OF 133    234  TEND TO BE THOSE                0.69 OF 189       21   131
     WHERE THE COUSIN TERMINOLOGY IS                     WHERE THE COUSIN TERMINOLOGY IS                    112    58
     OF ESKIMO OR HAWAIIAN TYPE,                         OF CROW, OMAHA, OR IROQUOIS TYPE,                XSQ=   87.60
     RATHER THAN                                         RATHER THAN                                      PHI=  -0.522
     CROW, OMAHA, OR IROQUOIS TYPE  (170)                ESKIMO OR HAWAIIAN TYPE  (152)                   XP =  0.

241  TILT LESS TOWARD BEING THOSE    0.81 OF  77    241  TILT MORE TOWARD BEING THOSE    0.92 OF 136       62   125
     WHERE THE FAMILY, IF EXTENDED, IS                   WHERE THE FAMILY, IF EXTENDED, IS                   15    11
     LARGE OR SMALL, RATHER THAN                         LARGE OR SMALL, RATHER THAN                      XSQ=    4.94
     STEM  (187)                                         STEM  (187)                                      PHI=  -0.152
                                                                                                          XP =  0.0263

242  TILT LESS TOWARD BEING THOSE    0.73 OF 146    242  TILT MORE TOWARD BEING THOSE    0.83 OF 249      107   207
     WHERE MARRIAGE IS                                   WHERE MARRIAGE IS                                   39    42
     COMMONLY OR OCCASIONALLY POLYGYNOUS,                COMMONLY OR OCCASIONALLY POLYGYNOUS,             XSQ=    4.88
     RATHER THAN MONOGAMOUS  (314)                       RATHER THAN MONOGAMOUS  (314)                    PHI=  -0.111
                                                                                                          XP =  0.0271

243  TILT TOWARD BEING THOSE         0.88 OF  17    243  TILT TOWARD BEING THOSE         0.51 OF  43        2    22
     WHERE POLYGYNY, IF PRESENT,                         WHERE POLYGYNY, IF PRESENT,                         15    21
     HAS A LOW INCIDENCE  (36) W-D,S                     HAS A HIGH INCIDENCE  (24) W-D,S                 XSQ=    6.32
                                                                                                          PHI=  -0.325
                                                                                                          XP =  0.0119

262  TEND LESS TO BE THOSE           0.64 OF 146    262  TEND MORE TO BE THOSE           0.85 OF 249       93   212
     WHERE WIVES ARE OBTAINED BY                         WHERE WIVES ARE OBTAINED BY                         53    37
     MEANS INVOLVING THE PRESENCE                        MEANS INVOLVING THE PRESENCE                     XSQ=   22.85
     OF SOME CONSIDERATION  (305)                        OF SOME CONSIDERATION  (305)                     PHI=  -0.241
                                                                                                          XP =  0.0000

263  TEND TO BE THOSE                0.60 OF 146    263  TEND TO BE THOSE                0.70 OF 249       58   175
     WHERE WIVES ARE OBTAINED                            WHERE WIVES ARE OBTAINED BY                         88    74
     BY RELATIVELY EASY MEANS, NAMELY BY                 RELATIVELY DIFFICULT MEANS, NAMELY BY            XSQ=   34.27
     TOKEN BRIDE-PRICE, GIFT EXCHANGE,                   BRIDE-PRICE, BRIDE-SERVICE, OR                   PHI=  -0.295
     ABSENCE OF ANY CONSIDERATION, OR                    EXCHANGING A FEMALE RELATIVE  (233)              XP =  0.
     RECEIPT OF DOWRY  (162)
```

314	LEAN MORE TOWARD BEING THOSE 0.96 OF 26 WHERE THE INCIDENCE OF MOTHER-CHILD HOUSEHOLDS IS LOW (61) W-D,S	314	LEAN LESS TOWARD BEING THOSE 0.67 OF 54 WHERE THE INCIDENCE OF MOTHER-CHILD HOUSEHOLDS IS LOW (61) W-D,S	1 18 25 36 XSQ= 6.88 PHI= -0.293 XP = 0.0087
326	LEAN TOWARD BEING THOSE 0.85 OF 20 WHERE THE INFERRED TRANSITION ANXIETY BETWEEN INFANCY AND CHILDHOOD IS LOW (35) B-B-C	326	LEAN TOWARD BEING THOSE 0.62 OF 47 WHERE THE INFERRED TRANSITION ANXIETY BETWEEN INFANCY AND CHILDHOOD IS HIGH (32) B-B-C	3 29 17 18 XSQ= 10.46 PHI= -0.395 XP = 0.0012
327	TEND TO BE THOSE 0.94 OF 16 WHERE THE AGE OF THE INFANT AT TIME OF REDUCED CONTACT WITH MOTHER IS HIGHER THAN TWO YEARS (28) B-B-C	327	TEND TO BE THOSE 0.67 OF 39 WHERE THE AGE OF THE INFANT AT TIME OF REDUCED CONTACT WITH MOTHER IS TWO YEARS OR LOWER (27) B-B-C	15 13 1 26 XSQ= 14.24 PHI= 0.509 XP = 0.0002
334	TEND TO BE THOSE 0.83 OF 23 WHERE THE INDULGENCE OF THE CHILD IS HIGH (40) B-B-C	334	TEND TO BE THOSE 0.62 OF 55 WHERE THE INDULGENCE OF THE CHILD IS LOW (38) B-B-C	19 21 4 34 XSQ= 11.10 PHI= 0.377 XP = 0.0009
337	TILT TOWARD BEING THOSE 0.68 OF 22 WHERE THE CHILD'S INFERRED ANXIETY OVER NON-PERFORMANCE OF RESPONSIBLE BEHAVIOR IS LOW (35) B-B-C	337	TILT TOWARD BEING THOSE 0.61 OF 51 WHERE THE CHILD'S INFERRED ANXIETY OVER NON-PERFORMANCE OF RESPONSIBLE BEHAVIOR IS HIGH (38) B-B-C	7 31 15 20 XSQ= 4.07 PHI= -0.236 XP = 0.0436
338	TILT TOWARD BEING THOSE 0.59 OF 22 WHERE THE CHILD'S INFERRED ANXIETY OVER PERFORMANCE OF RESPONSIBLE BEHAVIOR IS LOW (29) B-B-C	338	TILT TOWARD BEING THOSE 0.69 OF 51 WHERE THE CHILD'S INFERRED ANXIETY OVER PERFORMANCE OF RESPONSIBLE BEHAVIOR IS HIGH (44) B-B-C	9 35 13 16 XSQ= 3.84 PHI= -0.229 XP = 0.0500
339	TILT TOWARD BEING THOSE 0.77 OF 22 WHERE THE CHILD'S INFERRED CONFLICT REGARDING RESPONSIBLE BEHAVIOR IS LOW (42) B-B-C	339	TILT TOWARD BEING THOSE 0.51 OF 51 WHERE THE CHILD'S INFERRED CONFLICT REGARDING RESPONSIBLE BEHAVIOR IS HIGH (31) B-B-C	5 26 17 25 XSQ= 3.93 PHI= -0.232 XP = 0.0474
346	LEAN TOWARD BEING THOSE 0.82 OF 22 WHERE THE CHILD'S INFERRED ANXIETY OVER PERFORMANCE OF SELF-RELIANT BEHAVIOR IS LOW (39) B-B-C	346	LEAN TOWARD BEING THOSE 0.61 OF 54 WHERE THE CHILD'S INFERRED ANXIETY OVER PERFORMANCE OF SELF-RELIANT BEHAVIOR IS HIGH (37) B-B-C	4 33 18 21 XSQ= 9.88 PHI= -0.360 XP = 0.0017
347	LEAN TOWARD BEING THOSE 0.82 OF 22 WHERE THE CHILD'S INFERRED CONFLICT REGARDING SELF-RELIANT BEHAVIOR IS LOW (39) B-B-C	347	LEAN TOWARD BEING THOSE 0.61 OF 54 WHERE THE CHILD'S INFERRED CONFLICT REGARDING SELF-RELIANT BEHAVIOR IS HIGH (37) B-B-C	4 33 18 21 XSQ= 9.88 PHI= -0.360 XP = 0.0017

353	TILT TOWARD BEING THOSE 0.68 OF 22 WHERE THE CHILD-S INFERRED ANXIETY OVER NON-PERFORMANCE OF OBEDIENT BEHAVIOR IS LOW (32) B-B-C	353	TILT TOWARD BEING THOSE 0.67 OF 52 WHERE THE CHILD'S INFERRED ANXIETY OVER NON-PERFORMANCE OF OBEDIENT BEHAVIOR IS HIGH (42) B-B-C	7 35 15 17 XSQ= 6.55 PHI= -0.298 XP = 0.0105
355	DRIFT TOWARD BEING THOSE 0.71 OF 21 WHERE THE CHILD'S INFERRED CONFLICT REGARDING OBEDIENT BEHAVIOR IS LOW (38) B-B-C	355	DRIFT TOWARD BEING THOSE 0.56 OF 52 WHERE THE CHILD'S INFERRED CONFLICT REGARDING OBEDIENT BEHAVIOR IS HIGH (35) B-B-C	6 29 15 23 XSQ= 3.41 PHI= -0.216 XP = 0.0648
370	TEND TO BE THOSE 0.86 OF 83 WHERE THE SEGREGATION OF ADOLESCENT BOYS IS ABSENT (148)	370	TEND TO BE THOSE 0.52 OF 160 WHERE THE SEGREGATION OF ADOLESCENT BOYS IS COMPLETE OR PARTIAL (95)	12 83 71 77 XSQ= 30.58 PHI= -0.355 XP = 0.
377	TEND MORE TO BE THOSE 0.91 OF 117 WHERE MALE GENITAL MUTILATION IS ABSENT (242)	377	TEND LESS TO BE THOSE 0.65 OF 208 WHERE MALE GENITAL MUTILATION IS ABSENT (242)	10 73 107 135 XSQ= 26.38 PHI= -0.285 XP = 0.0000
382	DRIFT TOWARD BEING THOSE 0.73 OF 26 WHERE FEMALE INITIATION RITES ARE PRESENT (38) JKB	382	DRIFT TOWARD BEING THOSE 0.51 OF 39 WHERE FEMALE INITIATION RITES ARE ABSENT (27) JKB	19 19 7 20 XSQ= 2.87 PHI= 0.210 XP = 0.0900
403	TEND TO BE THOSE 0.92 OF 24 WHERE EXPLANATIONS OF ILLNESS OF AN ANAL NATURE ARE ABSENT (38) W-C	4C3	TEND TO BE THOSE 0.57 OF 37 WHERE EXPLANATIONS OF ILLNESS OF AN ANAL NATURE ARE PRESENT (23) W-C	2 21 22 16 XSQ= 12.54 PHI= -0.453 XP = 0.0004
433	IN ALL CASES ARE THOSE 1.00 OF 11 WHERE BELIEF IN REINCARNATION IS ABSENT (28) GES	433	TILT LESS TOWARD BEING THOSE 0.63 OF 27 WHERE BELIEF IN REINCARNATION IS ABSENT (28) GES	0 10 11 17 XSQ= 3.78 PHI= -0.316 EP = 0.0200
436	TILT TOWARD BEING THOSE 0.55 OF 11 WHERE ACTIVE ANCESTRAL SPIRITS ARE ABSENT (11) GES	436	TILT TOWARD BEING THOSE 0.81 OF 27 WHERE ACTIVE ANCESTRAL SPIRITS ARE PRESENT (27) GES	5 22 6 5 XSQ= 3.34 PHI= -0.296 EP = 0.0471
451	LEAN TOWARD BEING THOSE 0.80 OF 10 WHERE TOTEMISM IS UNIMPORTANT OR ABSENT (12) LWS	451	LEAN TOWARD BEING THOSE 0.76 OF 17 WHERE TOTEMISM IS PRESENT (15) LWS	2 13 8 4 XSQ= 6.01 PHI= -0.472 EP = 0.0069

455	DRIFT TOWARD BEING THOSE 0.73 OF 11 WHERE THE MODE OF THE INDIVIDUAL'S CONTACT WITH THE DIVINE IS CONDUCIVE TO THE DEVELOPMENT OF THE INDIVIDUAL'S NEED TO ACHIEVE (17) DCM	455	DRIFT TOWARD BEING THOSE 0.64 OF 25 WHERE THE MODE OF THE INDIVIDUAL'S CONTACT WITH THE DIVINE IS NOT CONDUCIVE TO THE DEVELOPMENT OF THE INDIVIDUAL'S NEED TO ACHIEVE (19) DCM	8 9 3 16 XSQ= 2.79 PHI= 0.278 EP = 0.0704
458	TEND MORE TO BE THOSE 0.85 OF 68 WHERE GAMES, IF PRESENT, DO NOT INCLUDE GAMES OF STRATEGY (119) R-A-B,EA	458	TEND LESS TO BE THOSE 0.59 OF 103 WHERE GAMES, IF PRESENT, DO NOT INCLUDE GAMES OF STRATEGY (119) R-A-B,EA	10 42 58 61 XSQ= 11.95 PHI= -0.264 XP = 0.0005
471	TILT TOWARD BEING THOSE 0.89 OF 9 WHERE SECRET SOCIETIES ARE UNIMPORTANT OR ABSENT (14) LWS	471	TILT TOWARD BEING THOSE 0.57 OF 14 WHERE SECRET SOCIETIES ARE PRESENT (9) LWS	1 8 8 6 XSQ= 3.13 PHI= -0.369 EP = 0.0397
476	LEAN TOWARD BEING THOSE 0.94 OF 18 WHERE THE DEGREE OF INSOBRIETY IS STRONG (31) DH	476	LEAN TOWARD BEING THOSE 0.55 OF 31 WHERE THE DEGREE OF INSOBRIETY IS MODERATE OR SLIGHT (18) DH	17 14 1 17 XSQ= 9.88 PHI= 0.449 XP = 0.0017

189 CULTURES WHERE THE KIN GROUP IS DOUBLE-DESCENT (20)

189 CULTURES WHERE THE KIN GROUP IS OTHER THAN DOUBLE DESCENT (378)

BACKGROUND ON PAGE 108 — SUBJECT ONLY

20 IN LEFT COLUMN

ARANDA	ASHANTI	BIRIFOR	BUNLAP	HERERO	ILA	IRAQW	KARIERA	KPE	MANUS
MBUGWE	MBUNDU	MURNGIN	NYARO	TODA	VENDA	WOGEO	WOLOF	YAKO	YAPESE

378 IN RIGHT COLUMN

1 EXCLUDED BECAUSE AMBIGUOUS

PUKAPUKA

1 EXCLUDED BECAUSE UNASCERTAINED

3	LEAN TOWARD BEING THOSE LOCATED IN AFRICA (80)	0.50 OF 20	3	LEAN TOWARD BEING THOSE LOCATED OUTSIDE OF AFRICA (320)	0.81 OF 378	10 70 10 308 XSQ= 9.84 PHI= 0.157 XP = 0.0017
6	DRIFT LESS TOWARD BEING THOSE LOCATED OUTSIDE OF THE INSULAR PACIFIC (330)	0.65 OF 20	6	DRIFT MORE TOWARD BEING THOSE LOCATED OUTSIDE OF THE INSULAR PACIFIC (330)	0.84 OF 378	7 62 13 316 XSQ= 3.38 PHI= 0.092 XP = 0.0661
8	IN ALL CASES ARE THOSE LOCATED OUTSIDE OF NORTH AMERICA (330)	1.00 OF 20	8	DRIFT LESS TOWARD BEING THOSE LOCATED OUTSIDE OF NORTH AMERICA (330)	0.81 OF 378	0 70 20 308 XSQ= 3.31 PHI= -0.091 XP = 0.0690
9	IN ALL CASES ARE THOSE LOCATED OUTSIDE OF SOUTH AMERICA (335)	1.00 OF 20	9	DRIFT LESS TOWARD BEING THOSE LOCATED OUTSIDE OF SOUTH AMERICA (335)	0.83 OF 378	0 65 20 313 XSQ= 2.95 PHI= -0.086 XP = 0.0860

14	IN ALL CASES ARE THOSE 1.00 OF 20 WHERE THE LATITUDE IS LESS THAN THIRTY DEGREES (281)	14	LEAN LESS TOWARD BEING THOSE 0.69 OF 378 WHERE THE LATITUDE IS LESS THAN THIRTY DEGREES (281)	0 118 20 260 XSQ= 7.44 PHI= -0.137 XP = 0.0064
15	TILT MORE TOWARD BEING THOSE 0.80 OF 20 WHERE THE LATITUDE IS LESS THAN TWENTY DEGREES (217)	15	TILT LESS TOWARD BEING THOSE 0.53 OF 378 WHERE THE LATITUDE IS LESS THAN TWENTY DEGREES (217)	4 178 16 200 XSQ= 4.58 PHI= -0.107 XP = 0.0324
55	DRIFT MORE TOWARD BEING THOSE 0.83 OF 12 WHERE FOOD PRODUCTION IS BY SIMPLE AGRICULTURE, RATHER THAN BY INTENSIVE AGRICULTURE (101)	55	DRIFT LESS TOWARD BEING THOSE 0.50 OF 179 WHERE FOOD PRODUCTION IS BY SIMPLE AGRICULTURE, RATHER THAN BY INTENSIVE AGRICULTURE (101)	2 89 10 90 XSQ= 3.69 PHI= -0.139 XP = 0.0547
56	IN ALL CASES ARE THOSE 1.00 OF 10 WHERE FOOD PRODUCTION IS BY SIMPLE AGRICULTURE, RATHER THAN BY INCIPIENT FOOD PRODUCTION (101)	56	DRIFT LESS TOWARD BEING THOSE 0.66 OF 136 WHERE FOOD PRODUCTION IS BY SIMPLE AGRICULTURE, RATHER THAN BY INCIPIENT FOOD PRODUCTION (101)	10 90 0 46 XSQ= 3.50 PHI= 0.155 XP = 0.0615
86	DRIFT TOWARD BEING THOSE 0.76 OF 17 WHERE THE LEVEL OF POLITICAL INTEGRATION IS THE AUTONOMOUS COMMUNITY, OR THE FAMILY (156) GPM	86	DRIFT TOWARD BEING THOSE 0.50 OF 286 WHERE THE LEVEL OF POLITICAL INTEGRATION IS THE LARGE STATE, THE LITTLE STATE, OR THE MINIMAL STATE (148) GPM	4 144 13 142 XSQ= 3.61 PHI= -0.109 XP = 0.0575
88	DRIFT MORE TOWARD BEING THOSE 0.87 OF 15 WHERE, IF A HEADMANSHIP IS PRESENT, SUCCESSION IS HEREDITARY (165)	88	DRIFT LESS TOWARD BEING THOSE 0.59 OF 254 WHERE, IF A HEADMANSHIP IS PRESENT, SUCCESSION IS HEREDITARY (165)	2 104 13 150 XSQ= 3.44 PHI= -0.113 XP = 0.0636
176	LEAN TOWARD BEING THOSE 0.79 OF 19 WHERE THE COMMUNITY IS A CLAN-COMMUNITY OR A COMMUNITY STRUCTURED OR SEGMENTED ON A CLAN BASIS (169)	176	LEAN TOWARD BEING THOSE 0.58 OF 361 WHERE THE COMMUNITY IS OTHER THAN A CLAN-COMMUNITY OR A COMMUNITY STRUCTURED OR SEGMENTED ON A CLAN BASIS (213)	15 153 4 208 XSQ= 8.36 PHI= 0.148 XP = 0.0038
183	DRIFT LESS TOWARD BEING THOSE 0.70 OF 20 WHERE THE LARGEST NON-COGNATIC KIN GROUP IS SMALLER THAN A MOEITY, I. E., A PHRATRY OR SIB OR LINEAGE (218)	183	DRIFT MORE TOWARD BEING THOSE 0.88 OF 230 WHERE THE LARGEST NON-COGNATIC KIN GROUP IS SMALLER THAN A MOEITY, I. E., A PHRATRY OR SIB OR LINEAGE (218)	6 28 14 202 XSQ= 3.57 PHI= 0.120 XP = 0.0587
190	IN ALL CASES ARE THOSE 1.00 OF 20 WHERE THE KIN GROUP IS PATRILINEAL OR DOUBLE-DESCENT, RATHER THAN MATRILINEAL (186)	190	TILT LESS TOWARD BEING THOSE 0.73 OF 227 WHERE THE KIN GROUP IS PATRILINEAL OR DOUBLE-DESCENT, RATHER THAN MATRILINEAL (186)	20 166 0 61 XSQ= 5.77 PHI= 0.153 XP = 0.0163

```
192  IN ALL CASES ARE THOSE           1.00 OF  20      192  LEAN LESS TOWARD BEING THOSE   0.71 OF 378          0  111
     OTHER THAN WHERE THE ONLY KIN GROUP                   OTHER THAN WHERE THE ONLY KIN GROUP               20  267
     PRESENT IS A KINDRED OR ELSE                          PRESENT IS A KINDRED OR ELSE                    XSQ=    6.75
     BILATERAL DESCENT IS INFERRED  (289)                  BILATERAL DESCENT IS INFERRED  (289)            PHI=  -0.130
                                                                                                           XP =  0.0094

204  IN ALL CASES ARE THOSE           1.00 OF  20      204  TILT LESS TOWARD BEING THOSE   0.79 OF 312         20  248
     WHERE MARITAL RESIDENCE IS                            WHERE MARITAL RESIDENCE IS                         0   64
     PATRILOCAL, VIRILOCAL, OR AVUNCULOCAL,                PATRILOCAL, VIRILOCAL, OR AVUNCULOCAL,          XSQ=    3.85
     RATHER THAN                                           RATHER THAN                                     PHI=   0.108
     AMBILOCAL OR NEOLOCAL  (270)                          AMBILOCAL OR NEOLOCAL  (270)                    XP =  0.0498

209  IN ALL CASES ARE THOSE           1.00 OF  20      209  TILT LESS TOWARD BEING THOSE   0.79 OF 312         20  248
     WHERE MARITAL RESIDENCE IS                            WHERE MARITAL RESIDENCE IS                         0   64
     PATRILOCAL, VIRILOCAL, OR AVUNCULOCAL,                PATRILOCAL, VIRILOCAL, OR AVUNCULOCAL,          XSQ=    3.85
     RATHER THAN                                           RATHER THAN                                     PHI=   0.108
     MATRILOCAL OR UXORILOCAL  (270)                       MATRILOCAL OR UXORILOCAL  (270)                 XP =  0.0498

220  LEAN TOWARD BEING THOSE          0.58 OF  19      220  LEAN TOWARD BEING THOSE        0.75 OF 349         11   86
     WHERE FIRST COUSIN MARRIAGE                           WHERE FIRST COUSIN MARRIAGE                        8  263
     IN SOME FORM OR OTHER                                 IN SOME FORM OR OTHER                           XSQ=    8.62
     IS PRESCRIBED OR PREFERRED  (97)                      IS NOT PRESCRIBED OR PREFERRED  (273)           PHI=   0.153
                                                                                                           XP =  0.0033

234  TEND TO BE THOSE                 0.93 OF  15      234  TEND TO BE THOSE               0.55 OF 306         14  138
     WHERE THE COUSIN TERMINOLOGY IS                       WHERE THE COUSIN TERMINOLOGY IS                    1  168
     OF CROW, OMAHA, OR IROQUOIS TYPE,                     OF ESKIMO OR HAWAIIAN TYPE,                     XSQ=   11.48
     RATHER THAN                                           RATHER THAN                                     PHI=   0.189
     ESKIMO OR HAWAIIAN TYPE  (152)                        CROW, OMAHA, OR IROQUOIS TYPE  (170)            XP =  0.0007

262  DRIFT MORE TOWARD BEING THOSE    0.95 OF  20      262  DRIFT LESS TOWARD BEING THOSE  0.76 OF 373         19  285
     WHERE WIVES ARE OBTAINED BY                           WHERE WIVES ARE OBTAINED BY                        1   88
     MEANS INVOLVING THE PRESENCE                          MEANS INVOLVING THE PRESENCE                    XSQ=    2.76
     OF SOME CONSIDERATION  (305)                          OF SOME CONSIDERATION  (305)                    PHI=   0.084
                                                                                                           XP =  0.0967

263  DRIFT MORE TOWARD BEING THOSE    0.80 OF  20      263  DRIFT LESS TOWARD BEING THOSE  0.58 OF 373         16  217
     WHERE WIVES ARE OBTAINED BY                           WHERE WIVES ARE OBTAINED BY                        4  156
     RELATIVELY DIFFICULT MEANS, NAMELY BY                 RELATIVELY DIFFICULT MEANS, NAMELY BY           XSQ=    2.90
     BRIDE-PRICE, BRIDE-SERVICE, OR                        BRIDE-PRICE, BRIDE-SERVICE, OR                  PHI=   0.086
     EXCHANGING A FEMALE RELATIVE  (233)                   EXCHANGING A FEMALE RELATIVE  (233)             XP =  0.0888

299  TILT TOWARD BEING THOSE          0.58 OF  12      299  TILT TOWARD BEING THOSE        0.75 OF 110          7   28
     WHERE THE POST-PARTUM SEX TABOO LASTS                 WHERE THE POST-PARTUM SEX TABOO LASTS              5   82
     LONGER THAN ONE YEAR  (35)                            ONE YEAR OR LESS  (89)                          XSQ=    4.22
                                                                                                           PHI=   0.186
                                                                                                           XP =  0.0399

330  DRIFT TOWARD BEING THOSE         0.86 OF   7      330  DRIFT TOWARD BEING THOSE       0.56 OF  61          6   27
     WHERE THE AGE OF THE INFANT                           WHERE THE AGE OF THE INFANT                        1   34
     AT TIME OF WEANING                                    AT TIME OF WEANING                              XSQ=    2.82
     IS 2.5 YEARS OR HIGHER  (34) B-B-C                    IS LOWER THAN 2.5 YEARS  (36) B-B-C             PHI=   0.204
                                                                                                           XP =  0.0931
```

370	LEAN TOWARD BEING THOSE WHERE THE SEGREGATION OF ADOLESCENT BOYS IS COMPLETE OR PARTIAL (95)	0.80 OF 15	370	LEAN TOWARD BEING THOSE WHERE THE SEGREGATION OF ADOLESCENT BOYS IS ABSENT (148)	0.63 OF 226	12 83 3 143 XSQ= 9.29 PHI= 0.196 XP = 0.0023
372	DRIFT TOWARD BEING THOSE WHERE MALE INITIATION RITES ARE PRESENT (48) ASA	0.78 OF 9	372	DRIFT TOWARD BEING THOSE WHERE MALE INITIATION RITES ARE ABSENT (63) ASA	0.60 OF 101	7 40 2 61 XSQ= 3.48 PHI= 0.178 XP = 0.0619
433	IN ALL CASES ARE THOSE WHERE BELIEF IN REINCARNATION IS PRESENT (10) GES	1.00 OF 2	433	DRIFT TOWARD BEING THOSE WHERE BELIEF IN REINCARNATION IS ABSENT (28) GES	0.78 OF 36	2 8 0 28 XSQ= 2.58 PHI= 0.261 EP = 0.0640

****

190 CULTURES WHERE THE KIN GRCUP IS PATRILINEAL CR CCUBLE-CESCENT, RATHER THAN MATRILINEAL (186)	190 CULTURES WHERE THE KIN GROUP IS MATRILINEAL, RATHER THAN PATRILINEAL OR DOUBLE-DESCENT (61)

BACKGROUND ON PAGE 108 — BOTH SUBJECT AND PREDICATE

186 IN LEFT CCLUMN

ABOR	AJIE	AKHA	ALBANIANS	ALORESE	AMBA	ARANDA	ARAPESH	ARAUCANIANS	ARYANS
ASHANTI	ATAYAL	AYMARA	AZANDE	BABWA	BAJUN	BAMBARA	BAMILEKE	BANCA	BARABRA
BARI	BASSERI	BATAK	BAYA	BEJA	BENGALI	BETE	BHIL	BHUIYA	BIRIFOR
BOZO	BUDUMA	BUNLAP	BURUSHO	BURYAT	CHAGGA	CHENCHU	CHERKESS	COORG	DAGUR
DARD	DIEGUENO	DILLING	DOGON	DOROBO	EGYPTIANS	ENGA	FANG	FON	FOX
FUTAJALONKE	GANDA	GILYAK	GISU	GOND	HASANIA	HAZARA	HEBREWS	HEHE	HERERO
HO	ILA	IRAQW	KABYLE	KACHIN	KALMYK	KAPAUKU	KARIERA	KATAB	KAZAK
KERAKI	KET	KHALKA	KHEVSUR	KIKUYU	KISSI	KOHISTANI	KONSO	KOREANS	KPE
LAKHER	LAMET	LANGO	LAU	LEPCHA	LHOTA NAGA	LIFU	LOLO	LUBA	LUO
MAGUZAWA	MAM	MAMVU	MANCHU	MANUS	MARGI	MARICOPA	MASAI	MATAKAM	MAYA
MBUGWE	MBUNDU	MBUTI	MENDE	MIAMI	MIAO	MIN CHINESE	MINCHIA	MIWOK	MONGO
MONGUOR	MOSSI	MUNDURUCU	MURINBATA	MURNGIN	MZAB	NAMA	NANDI	NOMLAKI	NUER
NUPE	NURI	NYAKYUSA	NYARO	NYORO	OJIBWA	OKINAWANS	OMAHA	ORAON	PALIKUR
PATHAN	PURARI	PURUM	REGEIBAT	RIFFIANS	ROTINESE	RUNDI	RWALA	SAMOYED	SANDAWE
SANTAL	SENIANG	SERBS	SHERENTE	SHILLUK	SHLUH	SINDHI	SIWANS	SOMALI	SONGHAI
SOTHO	SWAZI	SYRIANS	TAMIL	TANIMBARESE	TEDA	TERA	TESO	THONGA	TIBETANS
TIGRINYA	TIKOPIA	TIV	TODA	TOLOWA	TUCANO	TUCUNA	TURKANA	TURKMEN	TZELTAL
VENDA	VIETNAMESE	WANTCAT	WAROPEN	WIKMUNKAN	WINNEBAGO	WITOTO	WOGEO	WOLOF	WUTE
YAGUA	YAKO	YAKUT	YAPESE	YOKUTS	YORUBA				

61 IN RIGHT CCLUMN

APINAYE	BELU	BEMBA	BORORO	CALLINAGO	CHEROKEE	COCHITI	CREEK	CROW	DELAWARE
DIERI	DOBUANS	EYAK	GARO	GOAJIRO	GUAHIBO	GURE	HAIDA	HANO	HURON
JEMEZ	KAREN	KASKA	KERALA	KHASI	KUBA	KURTATCHI	LAKALAI	LAMBA	LESU
MANDAN	MARSHALLESE	MINANGKABAU	MNONG GAR	MOTA	NABESNA	NAVAHO	NDEMBU	NYANEKA	PALAUANS
PAWNEE	PENDE	PONAPEANS	ROTUMANS	SARAMACCA	SEMINOLE	SIRIONO	SIUAI	TALAMANCA	TENDA
TIMBIRA	TIMUCUA	TIWI	TROBRIAND	TRUKESE	TSHIMSHIAN	VEDDA	WOLEAIANS	YAO	YOMBE
ZUNI									

4 EXCLUDED BECAUSE AMBIGUOUS

MERINA PUKAPUKA TALLENSI TANALA

148 EXCLUDED BECAUSE IRRELEVANT

1 EXCLUDED BECAUSE UNASCERTAINED

3 TILT LESS TOWARD BEING THOSE 0.67 OF 186 LOCATED OUTSIDE OF AFRICA (320)	3 TILT MORE TOWARD BEING THOSE 0.84 OF 61 LOCATED OUTSIDE OF AFRICA (320)	62 10 124 51 XSQ= 5.59 PHI= 0.150 XP = 0.0181
4 LEAN LESS TOWARD BEING THOSE 0.85 OF 186 LOCATED OUTSIDE OF THE CIRCUM-MEDITERRANEAN (355)	4 IN ALL CASES ARE THOSE 1.00 OF 61 LOCATED OUTSIDE OF THE CIRCUM-MEDITERRANEAN (355)	28 0 158 61 XSQ= 8.91 PHI= 0.190 XP = 0.0028
5 TILT LESS TOWARD BEING THOSE 0.75 OF 186 LOCATED OUTSIDE OF EAST EURASIA (330)	5 TILT MORE TOWARD BEING THOSE 0.90 OF 61 LOCATED OUTSIDE OF EAST EURASIA (330)	47 6 139 55 XSQ= 5.61 PHI= 0.151 XP = 0.0179
6 TILT MORE TOWARD BEING THOSE 0.86 OF 186 LOCATED OUTSIDE OF THE INSULAR PACIFIC (330)	6 TILT LESS TOWARD BEING THOSE 0.72 OF 61 LOCATED OUTSIDE OF THE INSULAR PACIFIC (330)	26 17 160 44 XSQ= 5.24 PHI= -0.146 XP = 0.0221
8 TEND MORE TO BE THOSE 0.94 OF 186 LOCATED OUTSIDE OF NORTH AMERICA (330)	8 TEND LESS TO BE THOSE 0.69 OF 61 LOCATED OUTSIDE OF NORTH AMERICA (330)	11 19 175 42 XSQ= 25.10 PHI= -0.319 XP = 0.0000
9 DRIFT MORE TOWARD BEING THOSE 0.94 OF 186 LOCATED OUTSIDE OF SOUTH AMERICA (335)	9 DRIFT LESS TOWARD BEING THOSE 0.85 OF 61 LOCATED OUTSIDE OF SOUTH AMERICA (335)	12 9 174 52 XSQ= 3.07 PHI= -0.112 XP = 0.0796
36 DRIFT LESS TOWARD BEING THOSE 0.73 OF 186 WHERE THE NATURAL ENVIRONMENT IS OTHER THAN 'VERY HARSH,' OR SUB-TROPICAL BUSH, OR TEMPERATE GRASSLAND (292) FWM	36 DRIFT MORE TOWARD BEING THOSE 0.85 OF 61 WHERE THE NATURAL ENVIRONMENT IS OTHER THAN 'VERY HARSH,' OR SUB-TROPICAL BUSH, OR TEMPERATE GRASSLAND (292) FWM	50 9 136 52 XSQ= 3.08 PHI= 0.112 XP = 0.0793
42 DRIFT MORE TOWARD BEING THOSE 0.66 OF 186 WHERE THE NATURAL ENVIRONMENT IS OTHER THAN TROPICAL OR SUB-TROPICAL RAIN FOREST, OR MONSOON FOREST (244) FWM	42 DRIFT LESS TOWARD BEING THOSE 0.52 OF 61 WHERE THE NATURAL ENVIRONMENT IS OTHER THAN TROPICAL OR SUB-TROPICAL RAIN FOREST, OR MONSOON FOREST (244) FWM	63 29 123 32 XSQ= 3.11 PHI= -0.112 XP = 0.0778
51 LEAN MORE TOWARD BEING THOSE 0.77 OF 186 WHERE SUBSISTENCE IS PRIMARILY BY FOOD PRODUCTION -- I. E., AGRICULTURE OR HUSBANDRY -- RATHER THAN BY GATHERING (253)	51 LEAN LESS TOWARD BEING THOSE 0.59 OF 61 WHERE SUBSISTENCE IS PRIMARILY BY FOOD PRODUCTION -- I. E., AGRICULTURE OR HUSBANDRY -- RATHER THAN BY GATHERING (253)	144 36 42 25 XSQ= 6.97 PHI= 0.168 XP = 0.0083

53	LEAN LESS TOWARD BEING THOSE 0.56 OF 125 WHERE FOOD PRODUCTION IS BY SIMPLE AGRICULTURE OR INCIPIENT FOOD PRODUCTION, RATHER THAN BY INTENSIVE AGRICULTURE (147)	53	LEAN MORE TOWARD BEING THOSE 0.84 OF 38 WHERE FOOD PRODUCTION IS BY SIMPLE AGRICULTURE OR INCIPIENT FOOD PRODUCTION, RATHER THAN BY INTENSIVE AGRICULTURE (147)	55 6 70 32 XSQ= 8.74 PHI= 0.231 XP = 0.0031
54	TILT MORE TOWARD BEING THOSE 0.87 OF 125 WHERE FOOD PRODUCTION IS BY INTENSIVE OR SIMPLE AGRICULTURE, RATHER THAN BY INCIPIENT FOOD PRODUCTION (192)	54	TILT LESS TOWARD BEING THOSE 0.71 OF 38 WHERE FOOD PRODUCTION IS BY INTENSIVE OR SIMPLE AGRICULTURE, RATHER THAN BY INCIPIENT FOOD PRODUCTION (192)	109 27 16 11 XSQ= 4.39 PHI= 0.164 XP = 0.0361
55	TILT TOWARD BEING THOSE 0.50 OF 109 WHERE FOOD PRODUCTION IS BY INTENSIVE AGRICULTURE, RATHER THAN BY SIMPLE AGRICULTURE (91)	55	TILT TOWARD BEING THOSE 0.78 OF 27 WHERE FOOD PRODUCTION IS BY SIMPLE AGRICULTURE, RATHER THAN BY INTENSIVE AGRICULTURE (101)	55 6 54 21 XSQ= 5.88 PHI= 0.208 XP = 0.0153
62	LEAN TOWARD BEING THOSE 0.69 OF 186 WHERE HUSBANDRY OF SOME KIND IS PRESENT (228)	62	LEAN TOWARD BEING THOSE 0.51 OF 61 WHERE HUSBANDRY OF ANY KIND IS ABSENT (172)	129 30 57 31 XSQ= 7.30 PHI= 0.172 XP = 0.0069
63	TEND TO BE THOSE 0.74 OF 127 WHERE HUSBANDRY, IF PRESENT, IS PRINCIPALLY IN THE FORM OF BOVINE, EQUINE, CAMEL-LIKE, OR DEER-LIKE ANIMALS, RATHER THAN PIGS, SHEEP, OR GOATS (152)	63	TEND TO BE THOSE 0.63 OF 30 WHERE HUSBANDRY, IF PRESENT, IS PRINCIPALLY IN THE FORM OF PIGS, SHEEP, OR GOATS, RATHER THAN BOVINE, EQUINE, CAMEL-LIKE, OR DEER-LIKE ANIMALS (74)	94 11 33 19 XSQ= 13.64 PHI= 0.295 XP = 0.0002
71	TEND TO BE THOSE 0.60 OF 112 WHERE METAL WORKING IS PRESENT (98)	71	TEND TO BE THOSE 0.76 OF 42 WHERE METAL WORKING IS ABSENT (153)	67 10 45 32 XSQ= 14.44 PHI= 0.306 XP = 0.0001
80	DRIFT LESS TOWARD BEING THOSE 0.82 OF 108 WHERE NO CITY OR TOWN IS PRESENT (185)	80	DRIFT MORE TOWARD BEING THOSE 0.97 OF 36 WHERE NO CITY OR TOWN IS PRESENT (185)	19 1 89 35 XSQ= 3.79 PHI= 0.162 XP = 0.0515
84	DRIFT LESS TOWARD BEING THOSE 0.85 OF 136 WHERE THE LEVEL OF POLITICAL INTEGRATION IS THE LITTLE STATE, THE MINIMAL STATE, THE AUTONOMOUS COMMUNITY, OR THE FAMILY (262) GPM	84	DRIFT MORE TOWARD BEING THOSE 0.96 OF 51 WHERE THE LEVEL OF POLITICAL INTEGRATION IS THE LITTLE STATE, THE MINIMAL STATE, THE AUTONOMOUS COMMUNITY, OR THE FAMILY (262) GPM	21 2 115 49 XSQ= 3.56 PHI= 0.138 XP = 0.0593
85	TILT LESS TOWARD BEING THOSE 0.72 OF 136 WHERE THE LEVEL OF POLITICAL INTEGRATION IS THE MINIMAL STATE, THE AUTONOMOUS COMMUNITY, OR THE FAMILY (234) GPM	85	TILT MORE TOWARD BEING THOSE 0.88 OF 51 WHERE THE LEVEL OF POLITICAL INTEGRATION IS THE MINIMAL STATE, THE AUTONOMOUS COMMUNITY, OR THE FAMILY (234) GPM	38 6 98 45 XSQ= 4.53 PHI= 0.156 XP = 0.0333

90	TEND TO BE THOSE 0.95 OF 80 WHERE, IF A HEREDITARY HEADMANSHIP IS PRESENT, SUCCESSION IS PATRILINEAL, RATHER THAN MATRILINEAL (127)	90	TEND TO BE THOSE 0.84 OF 37 WHERE, IF A HEREDITARY HEADMANSHIP IS PRESENT, SUCCESSION IS MATRILINEAL, RATHER THAN PATRILINEAL (38)	76 6 4 31 XSQ= 71.19 PHI= 0.780 XP = 0.
94	TILT LESS TOWARD BEING THOSE 0.88 OF 154 WHERE THE HIERARCHY OF NATIONAL JURISDICTION HAS TWO, ONE, OR NO LEVELS (296) GES,EA	94	IN ALL CASES ARE THOSE 1.00 OF 51 WHERE THE HIERARCHY OF NATIONAL JURISDICTION HAS TWO, ONE, OR NO LEVELS (296) GES,EA	19 0 135 51 XSQ= 5.55 PHI= 0.164 XP = 0.0185
95	DRIFT LESS TOWARD BEING THOSE 0.71 OF 154 WHERE THE HIERARCHY OF NATIONAL JURISDICTION HAS ONE OR NO LEVELS (254) GES,EA	95	DRIFT MORE TOWARD BEING THOSE 0.84 OF 51 WHERE THE HIERARCHY OF NATIONAL JURISDICTION HAS ONE OR NO LEVELS (254) GES,EA	45 8 109 43 XSQ= 2.99 PHI= 0.121 XP = 0.0838
99	DRIFT LESS TOWARD BEING THOSE 0.59 OF 58 WHERE, WITH NATIONAL HIERARCHY ABSENT, THE HIERARCHY OF LOCAL JURISDICTION HAS FOUR OR THREE LEVELS (93) GES,EA	99	DRIFT MORE TOWARD BEING THOSE 0.81 OF 26 WHERE, WITH NATIONAL HIERARCHY ABSENT, THE HIERARCHY OF LOCAL JURISDICTION HAS FOUR OR THREE LEVELS (93) GES,EA	34 21 24 5 XSQ= 2.98 PHI= -0.188 XP = 0.0844
102	DRIFT TOWARD BEING THOSE 0.59 OF 180 WHERE CLASS STRATIFICATION IS PRESENT (203)	102	DRIFT TOWARD BEING THOSE 0.55 OF 60 WHERE CLASS STRATIFICATION IS ABSENT (180)	107 27 73 33 XSQ= 3.24 PHI= 0.116 XP = 0.0717
108	DRIFT TOWARD BEING THOSE 0.65 OF 107 WHERE CLASS STRATIFICATION, IF PRESENT, IS BASED ON SOMETHING OTHER THAN A HEREDITARY ARISTOCRACY (129)	108	DRIFT TOWARD BEING THOSE 0.56 OF 27 WHERE CLASS STRATIFICATION, IF PRESENT, IS BASED ON A HEREDITARY ARISTOCRACY (74)	37 15 70 12 XSQ= 3.16 PHI= -0.154 XP = 0.0755
109	LEAN LESS TOWARD BEING THOSE 0.75 OF 161 WHERE CASTES ARE ABSENT (317)	109	LEAN MORE TOWARD BEING THOSE 0.93 OF 60 WHERE CASTES ARE ABSENT (317)	40 4 121 56 XSQ= 7.95 PHI= 0.190 XP = 0.0048
110	LEAN TOWARD BEING THOSE 0.55 OF 175 WHERE SLAVERY IS PRESENT (163)	110	LEAN TOWARD BEING THOSE 0.67 OF 60 WHERE SLAVERY IS ABSENT (218)	97 20 78 40 XSQ= 7.86 PHI= 0.183 XP = 0.0050
129	TILT TOWARD BEING THOSE 0.51 OF 47 WHERE WEAVING IS MAINLY DONE BY MALES (31)	129	TILT TOWARD BEING THOSE 0.88 OF 17 WHERE WEAVING IS MAINLY DONE BY FEMALES (73)	24 2 23 15 XSQ= 6.45 PHI= 0.317 XP = 0.0111

130	TILT TOWARD BEING THOSE WHERE LEATHER WORKING IS MAINLY DONE BY MALES (39)	0.62 OF 34	130	TILT TOWARD BEING THOSE WHERE LEATHER WORKING IS MAINLY DONE BY FEMALES (45)	0.80 OF 10	21 2 13 8 XSQ= 3.86 PHI= 0.296 XP = 0.0495
138	TILT TOWARD BEING THOSE WHERE SUPERORDINATE JUSTICE IS PRESENT (22) BBW	0.73 OF 15	138	TILT TOWARD BEING THOSE WHERE SUPERORDINATE JUSTICE IS ABSENT (18) BBW	0.78 OF 9	11 2 4 7 XSQ= 4.04 PHI= 0.410 EP = 0.0327
175	LEAN LESS TOWARD BEING THOSE WHERE THE COMMUNITY IS 'KIN-HETEROGENEOUS,' I. E. OTHER THAN A CLAN COMMUNITY OR A DEME (260)	0.58 OF 177	175	LEAN MORE TOWARD BEING THOSE WHERE THE COMMUNITY IS 'KIN-HETEROGENEOUS,' I. E. OTHER THAN A CLAN COMMUNITY OR A DEME (260)	0.81 OF 59	75 11 102 48 XSQ= 9.76 PHI= 0.203 XP = 0.0018
177	TEND LESS TO BE THOSE WHERE THE COMMUNITY IS OTHER THAN A SINGLE CLAN-COMMUNITY AND EXOGAMOUS (305)	0.62 OF 177	177	TEND MORE TO BE THOSE WHERE THE COMMUNITY IS OTHER THAN A SINGLE CLAN-COMMUNITY AND EXOGAMOUS (305)	0.86 OF 59	68 8 109 51 XSQ= 11.41 PHI= 0.220 XP = 0.0007
178	TEND TO BE THOSE WHERE THE COMMUNITY IS OTHER THAN SEGMENTED ON A CLAN BASIS AND NON-EXOGAMOUS (295)	0.76 OF 177	178	TEND TO BE THOSE WHERE THE COMMUNITY IS SEGMENTED ON A CLAN BASIS AND NON-EXOGAMOUS (87)	0.53 OF 59	43 31 134 28 XSQ= 15.12 PHI= -0.253 XP = 0.0001
180	TEND LESS TO BE THOSE WHERE THE COMMUNITY IS COMMONLY NON-EXOGAMOUS, RATHER THAN EXOGAMOUS (258)	0.50 OF 177	180	TEND MORE TO BE THOSE WHERE THE COMMUNITY IS COMMONLY NON-EXOGAMOUS, RATHER THAN EXOGAMOUS (258)	0.81 OF 59	88 11 89 48 XSQ= 16.29 PHI= 0.263 XP = 0.0001
183	TILT MORE TOWARD BEING THOSE WHERE THE LARGEST NON-COGNATIC KIN GROUP IS SMALLER THAN A MOEITY, I. E., A PHRATRY OR SIB OR LINEAGE (218)	0.89 OF 186	183	TILT LESS TOWARD BEING THOSE WHERE THE LARGEST NON-COGNATIC KIN GROUP IS SMALLER THAN A MOEITY, I. E., A PHRATRY OR SIB OR LINEAGE (218)	0.77 OF 61	20 14 166 47 XSQ= 4.78 PHI= -0.139 XP = 0.0289
184	DRIFT MORE TOWARD BEING THOSE WHERE THE LARGEST NON-COGNATIC KIN GROUP IS SMALLER THAN A PHRATRY, I. E. A SIB OR LINEAGE (175)	0.73 OF 186	184	DRIFT LESS TOWARD BEING THOSE WHERE THE LARGEST NON-COGNATIC KIN GROUP IS SMALLER THAN A PHRATRY, I. E. A SIB OR LINEAGE (175)	0.59 OF 61	51 25 135 36 XSQ= 3.36 PHI= -0.117 XP = 0.0669
198	TEND TO BE THOSE WHERE RULES FOR THE INHERITANCE OF REAL PROPERTY, IF PRESENT, FAVOR THE MALE HEIR OR LINE, RATHER THAN THE FEMALE (144)	0.99 OF 113	198	TEND TO BE THOSE WHERE RULES FOR THE INHERITANCE OF REAL PROPERTY, IF PRESENT, FAVOR THE FEMALE HEIR OR LINE, RATHER THAN THE MALE (21)	0.90 OF 21	112 2 1 19 XSQ= 105.00 PHI= 0.885 XP = 0.

201	LEAN MORE TOWARD BEING THOSE WHERE MARITAL RESIDENCE IS NON-OPTIONAL, RATHER THAN AMBILOCAL OR NEOLOCAL (334)	0.97 OF 186	201	LEAN LESS TOWARD BEING THOSE WHERE MARITAL RESIDENCE IS NON-OPTIONAL, RATHER THAN AMBILOCAL OR NEOLOCAL (334)	0.87 OF 60	181 52 5 8 XSQ= 8.25 PHI= 0.183 XP = 0.0041
204	TEND MORE TO BE THOSE WHERE MARITAL RESIDENCE IS PATRILOCAL, VIRILOCAL, OR AVUNCULOCAL, RATHER THAN AMBILOCAL OR NEOLOCAL (270)	0.97 OF 185	204	TEND LESS TO BE THOSE WHERE MARITAL RESIDENCE IS PATRILOCAL, VIRILOCAL, OR AVUNCULOCAL, RATHER THAN AMBILOCAL OR NEOLOCAL (270)	0.71 OF 28	180 20 5 8 XSQ= 24.06 PHI= 0.336 XP = 0.0000
207	LEAN TOWARD BEING THOSE WHERE MARITAL RESIDENCE IS AMBILOCAL OR NEOLOCAL, RATHER THAN MATRILOCAL OR UXORILOCAL (64)	0.83 OF 6	207	LEAN TOWARD BEING THOSE WHERE MARITAL RESIDENCE IS MATRILOCAL OR UXORILOCAL, RATHER THAN AMBILOCAL OR NEOLOCAL (64)	0.80 OF 40	1 32 5 8 XSQ= 7.43 PHI= -0.402 XP = 0.0064
209	TEND TO BE THOSE WHERE MARITAL RESIDENCE IS PATRILOCAL, VIRILOCAL, OR AVUNCULOCAL, RATHER THAN MATRILOCAL OR UXORILOCAL (270)	0.99 OF 181	209	TEND TO BE THOSE WHERE MARITAL RESIDENCE IS MATRILOCAL OR UXORILOCAL, RATHER THAN PATRILOCAL, VIRILOCAL, OR AVUNCULOCAL (64)	0.62 OF 52	180 20 1 32 XSQ= 118.62 PHI= 0.713 XP = 0.
210	IN ALL CASES ARE THOSE WHERE MARITAL RESIDENCE IS PATRILOCAL, RATHER THAN MATRILOCAL (169)	1.00 OF 165	210	IN ALL CASES ARE THOSE WHERE MARITAL RESIDENCE IS MATRILOCAL, RATHER THAN PATRILOCAL (31)	1.00 OF 31	165 0 0 31 XSQ= 188.56 PHI= 0.981 XP = 0.
240	LEAN TOWARD BEING THOSE WHERE THE FAMILY, IF EXTENDED, IS SMALL OR STEM, RATHER THAN LARGE (135)	0.69 OF 97	240	LEAN TOWARD BEING THOSE WHERE THE FAMILY, IF EXTENDED, IS LARGE, RATHER THAN SMALL OR STEM (78)	0.58 OF 36	30 21 67 15 XSQ= 7.22 PHI= -0.233 XP = 0.0072
242	LEAN MORE TOWARD BEING THOSE WHERE MARRIAGE IS COMMONLY OR OCCASIONALLY POLYGYNOUS, RATHER THAN MONOGAMOUS (314)	0.87 OF 183	242	LEAN LESS TOWARD BEING THOSE WHERE MARRIAGE IS COMMONLY OR OCCASIONALLY POLYGYNOUS, RATHER THAN MONOGAMOUS (314)	0.70 OF 61	160 43 23 18 XSQ= 8.22 PHI= 0.184 XP = 0.0041
262	TEND MORE TO BE THOSE WHERE WIVES ARE OBTAINED BY MEANS INVOLVING THE PRESENCE OF SOME CONSIDERATION (305)	0.92 OF 184	262	TEND LESS TO BE THOSE WHERE WIVES ARE OBTAINED BY MEANS INVOLVING THE PRESENCE OF SOME CONSIDERATION (305)	0.63 OF 60	170 38 14 22 XSQ= 28.11 PHI= 0.339 XP = 0.0000
263	TEND TO BE THOSE WHERE WIVES ARE OBTAINED BY RELATIVELY DIFFICULT MEANS, NAMELY BY BRIDE-PRICE, BRIDE-SERVICE, OR EXCHANGING A FEMALE RELATIVE (233)	0.80 OF 184	263	TEND TO BE THOSE WHERE WIVES ARE OBTAINED BY RELATIVELY EASY MEANS, NAMELY BY TOKEN BRIDE-PRICE, GIFT EXCHANGE, ABSENCE OF ANY CONSIDERATION, OR RECEIPT OF DOWRY (162)	0.57 OF 60	148 26 36 34 XSQ= 28.66 PHI= 0.343 XP = 0.0000

282	DRIFT TOWARD BEING THOSE 0.56 OF 16 WHERE THE STRENGTH OF DESIRE FOR CHILDREN IS HIGH (16) BCA	282	DRIFT TOWARD BEING THOSE 0.86 OF 7 WHERE THE STRENGTH OF DESIRE FOR CHILDREN IS LOW OR ABSENT (20) BCA	9 1 7 6 XSQ= 1.99 PHI= 0.294 EP = 0.0886
295	TILT TOWARD BEING THOSE 0.78 OF 9 WHERE THE SEVERITY OF PUNISHMENT FOR ABORTION IS HIGH (11) BCA	295	IN ALL CASES ARE THOSE 1.00 OF 5 WHERE THE SEVERITY OF PUNISHMENT FOR ABORTION IS LOW OR ABSENT (12) BCA	7 0 2 5 XSQ= 4.98 PHI= 0.596 EP = 0.0210
336	TILT TOWARD BEING THOSE 0.71 OF 35 WHERE THE TOTAL POSITIVE PRESSURE TOWARD DEVELOPING RESPONSIBLE BEHAVIOR IN THE CHILD IS HIGH (43) B-B-C	336	TILT TOWARD BEING THOSE 0.71 OF 14 WHERE THE TOTAL POSITIVE PRESSURE TOWARD DEVELOPING RESPONSIBLE BEHAVIOR IN THE CHILD IS LOW (32) B-B-C	25 4 10 10 XSQ= 5.93 PHI= 0.348 XP = 0.0149
360	TILT TOWARD BEING THOSE 0.67 OF 12 WHERE ADOLESCENT PEER GROUPS ARE PRESENT IN A SETTING OF WORK AND PUBLIC GATHERINGS AND LEISURE, OR AT LEAST OF PUBLIC GATHERINGS AND LEISURE (14) JKH	360	IN ALL CASES ARE THOSE 1.00 OF 6 WHERE ADOLESCENT PEER GROUPS ARE PRESENT ONLY IN A SETTING OF LEISURE, OR ELSE ARE ABSENT (23) JKH	8 0 4 6 XSQ= 4.75 PHI= 0.514 EP = 0.0128
377	TEND LESS TO BE THOSE 0.58 OF 153 WHERE MALE GENITAL MUTILATION IS ABSENT (242)	377	TEND MORE TO BE THOSE 0.86 OF 50 WHERE MALE GENITAL MUTILATION IS ABSENT (242)	64 7 89 43 XSQ= 11.64 PHI= 0.239 XP = 0.0006
390	LEAN LESS TOWARD BEING THOSE 0.67 OF 84 WHERE PREMARITAL SEX RELATIONS ARE WEAKLY PUNISHED AND IN FACT NOT RARE OR PUNISHED ONLY IF PREGNANCY RESULTS, OR FREELY PERMITTED (132) JTW,EA	390	IN ALL CASES ARE THOSE 1.00 OF 23 WHERE PREMARITAL SEX RELATIONS ARE WEAKLY PUNISHED AND IN FACT NOT RARE OR PUNISHED ONLY IF PREGNANCY RESULTS, OR FREELY PERMITTED (132) JTW,EA	28 0 56 23 XSQ= 8.73 PHI= 0.286 XP = 0.0031
391	LEAN TOWARD BEING THOSE 0.57 OF 84 WHERE PREMARITAL SEX RELATIONS ARE STRONGLY PUNISHED AND IN FACT RARE, OR WEAKLY PUNISHED AND IN FACT NOT RARE (89) JTW,EA	391	LEAN TOWARD BEING THOSE 0.78 OF 23 WHERE PREMARITAL SEX RELATIONS ARE PUNISHED ONLY IF PREGNANCY RESULTS, OR FREELY PERMITTED (90) JTW,EA	48 5 36 18 XSQ= 7.69 PHI= 0.268 XP = 0.0055
392	TILT TOWARD BEING THOSE 0.74 OF 84 WHERE PREMARITAL SEX RELATIONS ARE STRONGLY PUNISHED AND IN FACT RARE, OR WEAKLY PUNISHED AND IN FACT NOT RARE, OR PUNISHED ONLY IF PREGNANCY RESULTS (112) JTW,EA	392	TILT TOWARD BEING THOSE 0.52 OF 23 WHERE PREMARITAL SEX RELATIONS ARE FREELY PERMITTED (67) JTW,EA	62 11 22 12 XSQ= 4.49 PHI= 0.205 XP = 0.0341
393	DRIFT TOWARD BEING THOSE 0.62 OF 34 WHERE EXTRAMARITAL COITUS IS PUNISHED, RATHER THAN PERMITTED (43) F-B	393	DRIFT TOWARD BEING THOSE 0.67 OF 18 WHERE EXTRAMARITAL COITUS IS PERMITTED, RATHER THAN PUNISHED (41) F-B	21 6 13 12 XSQ= 2.76 PHI= 0.230 XP = 0.0968

```
426  TEND TO BE THOSE                0.70 OF 125     426  TEND TO BE THOSE                0.62 OF  42        87    16
     WHERE A HIGH GOD IS                                  WHERE A HIGH GOD IS                                38    26
     PRESENT  (156) GES,EA                                ABSENT  (104) GES,EA                         XSQ=   11.90
                                                                                                       PHI=   0.267
                                                                                                       XP =   0.0006

427  TILT TOWARD BEING THOSE         0.60 OF  87     427  TILT TOWARD BEING THOSE         0.75 OF  16        52     4
     WHERE A HIGH GOD, IF PRESENT, IS                     WHERE A HIGH GOD, IF PRESENT, IS                   35    12
     ACTIVE, RATHER THAN                                  INACTIVE, RATHER THAN                        XSQ=    5.26
     INACTIVE  (87) GES,EA                                ACTIVE  (69) GES,EA                          PHI=   0.226
                                                                                                       XP =   0.0218

428  TILT TOWARD BEING THOSE         0.71 OF  52     428  IN ALL CASES ARE THOSE          1.00 OF   4        37     0
     WHERE A HIGH GOD, IF PRESENT AND ACTIVE,             WHERE A HIGH GOD, IF PRESENT AND ACTIVE,           15     4
     SUPPORTS HUMAN MORALITY, RATHER THAN                 DOES NOT SUPPORT HUMAN MORALITY,             XSQ=    5.51
     NOT SUPPORTING IT  (61) GES,EA                       RATHER THAN SUPPORTING IT  (26) GES,EA       PHI=   0.314
                                                                                                       XP =   0.0189

440  DRIFT TOWARD BEING THOSE        0.67 OF  24     440  DRIFT TOWARD BEING THOSE        0.70 OF  10         8     7
     WHERE FEAR OF SPIRITS                                WHERE FEAR OF SPIRITS                              16     3
     IS LOW  (29) W-C                                     IS HIGH  (32) W-C                            XSQ=    2.51
                                                                                                       PHI=  -0.271
                                                                                                       EP =   0.0680

449  TILT TOWARD BEING THOSE         0.76 OF  41     449  TILT TOWARD BEING THOSE         0.62 OF  13        10     8
     WHERE THE OBSERVATION OF FOOD TABOOS                 WHERE THE OBSERVATION OF FOOD TABOOS               31     5
     IS MEDIUM OR LOW, RATHER THAN                        IS HIGH, RATHER THAN                         XSQ=    4.57
     HIGH  (61) JRL                                       MEDIUM OR LOW  (25) JRL                      PHI=  -0.291
                                                                                                       XP =   0.0325

458  LEAN TOWARD BEING THOSE         0.52 OF  69     458  LEAN TOWARD BEING THOSE         0.83 OF  30        36     5
     WHERE GAMES, IF PRESENT,                             WHERE GAMES, IF PRESENT,                           33    25
     INCLUDE GAMES OF STRATEGY  (52) R-A-B,EA             DO NOT INCLUDE                               XSQ=    9.45
                                                          GAMES OF STRATEGY  (119) R-A-B,EA            PHI=   0.309
                                                                                                       XP =   0.0021

468  TILT TOWARD BEING THOSE         0.50 OF  22     468  TILT TOWARD BEING THOSE         0.93 OF  14        11     1
     WHERE CONTACT WITH OTHER CULTURES                    WHERE CONTACT WITH OTHER CULTURES                  11    13
     IS FREQUENT, RATHER THAN                             IS REGULAR OR IRREGULAR, RATHER THAN         XSQ=    5.27
     REGULAR OR IRREGULAR  (17) JMH                       FREQUENT  (37) JMH                           PHI=   0.383
                                                                                                       EP =   0.0111
```

```
********************************************************************************************************
191  CULTURES                                          191  CULTURES
     WHERE THE KIN GROUP IS                                 WHERE THE KIN GROUP IS
     THE PATRILINEAL OR DOUBLE-DESCENT TYPE,                THE QUASI-LINEAGE,
     RATHER THAN THE                                        RATHER THAN THE
     QUASI-LINEAGE  (185)                                   PATRILINEAL OR DOUBLE-DESCENT TYPE  (14)

BACKGROUND ON PAGE 108                                                                      SUBJECT ONLY
........................................................................................................

     185  IN LEFT COLUMN

ABOR        AJIE        AKHA        ALBANIANS   ALORESE     AMBA        ARANDA      ARAPESH     ARAUCANIANS ARYANS
ASHANTI     ATAYAL      AYMARA      AZANDE      BABWA       BAJUN       BAMBARA     BAMILEKE    BANDA       BARABRA
BARI        BASSERI     BATAK       BAYA        BEJA        BENGALI     BETE        BHIL        BHUIYA      BIRIFOR
BOZO        BUDUMA      BUNLAP      BURUSHO     BURYAT      CHAGGA      CHENCHU     CHERKESS    COORG       DAGUR
DARD        DIEGUENO    DILLING     DOGON       DOROBO      EGYPTIANS   ENGA        FANG        FON         FOX
FUTAJALONKE GANDA       GILYAK      GISU        GOND        HASANIA     HAZARA      HEBREWS     HEHE        HERERO
HO          ILA         IRAQW       KABYLE      KACHIN      KALMYK      KAPAUKU     KARIERA     KATAB       KAZAK
KERAKI      KET         KHALKA      KHEVSUR     KIKUYU      KISSI       KOHISTANI   KONSO       KOREANS     KPE
LAKHER      LAMET       LANGO       LAU         LEPCHA      LHOTA NAGA  LIFU        LOLO        LUBA        LUO
MAGUZAWA    MAM         MAMVU       MANCHU      MANUS       MARGI       MARICOPA    MASAI       MATAKAM     MAYA
MBUGWE      MBUNDU      MBUTI       MENDE       MIAMI       MIAO        MIN CHINESE MINCHIA     MIWOK       MONGO
MONGUOR     MOSSI       MUNDURUCU   MURINBATA   MURNGIN     MZAB        NAMA        NANDI       NOMLAKI     NUER
NUPE        NURI        NYAKYUSA    NYARO       NYORO       OKINAWANS   OMAHA       ORAON       PALIKUR     PATHAN
PURARI      PURUM       REGEIBAT    RIFFIANS    ROTINESE    RUNDI       RWALA       SAMOYED     SANDAWE     SANTAL
SENIANG     SERBS       SHERENTE    SHILLUK     SHLUH       SINDHI      SIWANS      SOMALI      SONGHAI     SOTHO
SWAZI       SYRIANS     TAMIL       TANIMBARESE TEDA        TERA        TESO        THONGA      TIBETANS    TIGRINYA
TIKOPIA     TIV         TODA        TOLOWA      TUCANO      TUCUNA      TURKANA     TURKMEN     TZELTAL     VENDA
VIETNAMESE  WANTOAT     WAROPEN     WIKMUNKAN   WINNEBAGO   WITOTO      WOGEO       WOLOF       WUTE        YAGUA
YAKO        YAKUT       YAPESE      YOKUTS      YORUBA

      14  IN RIGHT COLUMN

BACAIRI     CAMAYURA    CREE        HAVASUPAI   JIVARO      MISKITO     MOTILON     NGONI       NUNIVAK     SINHALESE
TRUMAI      TUPINAMBA   WAPISHANA   YABARANA

       2  EXCLUDED BECAUSE AMBIGUOUS

OJIBWA      PUKAPUKA

     198  EXCLUDED BECAUSE IRRELEVANT

       1  EXCLUDED BECAUSE UNASCERTAINED

--------------------------------------------------------------------------------------------------------
  3  DRIFT LESS TOWARD BEING THOSE  0.66 OF 185       3  DRIFT MORE TOWARD BEING THOSE  0.93 OF  14        62     1
     LOCATED OUTSIDE OF                                  LOCATED OUTSIDE OF                                123    13
     AFRICA  (320)                                       AFRICA  (320)                                  XSQ=     3.05
                                                                                                        PHI=    0.124
                                                                                                        XP =   0.0806
```

8	DRIFT MORE TOWARD BEING THOSE LOCATED OUTSIDE OF NORTH AMERICA (330)	0.95 OF 185	8	DRIFT LESS TOWARD BEING THOSE LOCATED OUTSIDE OF NORTH AMERICA (330)	0.79 OF 14	10 3 175 11 XSQ= 3.16 PHI= -0.126 XP = 0.0753
9	TEND TO BE THOSE LOCATED OUTSIDE OF SOUTH AMERICA (335)	0.94 OF 185	9	TEND TO BE THOSE LOCATED IN SOUTH AMERICA (65)	0.64 OF 14	12 9 173 5 XSQ= 40.14 PHI= -0.449 XP = 0.
51	TEND TO BE THOSE WHERE SUBSISTENCE IS PRIMARILY BY FOOD PRODUCTION -- I. E., AGRICULTURE OR HUSBANDRY -- RATHER THAN BY GATHERING (253)	0.78 OF 185	51	TEND TO BE THOSE WHERE SUBSISTENCE IS PRIMARILY BY FOOD GATHERING -- I. E., HUNTING, FISHING, OR COLLECTING -- RATHER THAN FOOD PRODUCTION (147)	0.79 OF 14	144 3 41 11 XSQ= 18.63 PHI= 0.306 XP = 0.0000
54	TEND TO BE THOSE WHERE FOOD PRODUCTION IS BY INTENSIVE OR SIMPLE AGRICULTURE, RATHER THAN BY INCIPIENT FOOD PRODUCTION (192)	0.87 OF 125	54	TEND TO BE THOSE WHERE FOOD PRODUCTION IS BY INCIPIENT FOOD PRODUCTION, RATHER THAN BY INTENSIVE OR SIMPLE AGRICULTURE (46)	0.78 OF 9	109 2 16 7 XSQ= 20.57 PHI= 0.392 XP = 0.0000
56	TEND TO BE THOSE WHERE FOOD PRODUCTION IS BY SIMPLE AGRICULTURE, RATHER THAN BY INCIPIENT FOOD PRODUCTION (101)	0.77 OF 70	56	TEND TO BE THOSE WHERE FOOD PRODUCTION IS BY INCIPIENT FOOD PRODUCTION, RATHER THAN BY SIMPLE AGRICULTURE (46)	0.88 OF 8	54 1 16 7 XSQ= 11.49 PHI= 0.384 XP = 0.0007
62	TEND TO BE THOSE WHERE HUSBANDRY OF SOME KIND IS PRESENT (228)	0.70 OF 185	62	TEND TO BE THOSE WHERE HUSBANDRY OF ANY KIND IS ABSENT (172)	0.79 OF 14	129 3 56 11 XSQ= 11.52 PHI= 0.241 XP = 0.0007
71	LEAN TOWARD BEING THOSE WHERE METAL WORKING IS PRESENT (98)	0.60 OF 111	71	IN ALL CASES ARE THOSE WHERE METAL WORKING IS ABSENT (153)	1.00 OF 9	67 0 44 9 XSQ= 9.97 PHI= 0.288 XP = 0.0016
82	DRIFT MORE TOWARD BEING THOSE WHERE A CITY OR TOWN IS PRESENT, OR THE AVERAGE COMMUNITY SIZE IS FIFTY OR GREATER (178)	0.86 OF 107	82	DRIFT LESS TOWARD BEING THOSE WHERE A CITY OR TOWN IS PRESENT, OR THE AVERAGE COMMUNITY SIZE IS FIFTY OR GREATER (178)	0.60 OF 10	92 6 15 4 XSQ= 2.83 PHI= 0.156 XP = 0.0926
86	TILT TOWARD BEING THOSE WHERE THE LEVEL OF POLITICAL INTEGRATION IS THE LARGE STATE, THE LITTLE STATE, OR THE MINIMAL STATE (148) GPM	0.57 OF 135	86	TILT TOWARD BEING THOSE WHERE THE LEVEL OF POLITICAL INTEGRATION IS THE AUTONOMOUS COMMUNITY, OR THE FAMILY (156) GPM	0.77 OF 13	77 3 58 10 XSQ= 4.22 PHI= 0.169 XP = 0.0399

96	TILT TOWARD BEING THOSE WHERE THE HIERARCHY OF NATIONAL JURISDICTION HAS FOUR, THREE, TWO OR ONE LEVEL (174) GES,EA	0.62 OF 153	96	TILT TOWARD BEING THOSE WHERE THE HIERARCHY OF NATIONAL JURISDICTION HAS NO LEVELS (156) GES,EA	0.77 OF 13	95 3 58 10 XSQ= 6.01 PHI= 0.190 XP = 0.0142
102	TILT TOWARD BEING THOSE WHERE CLASS STRATIFICATION IS PRESENT (203)	0.60 OF 179	102	TILT TOWARD BEING THOSE WHERE CLASS STRATIFICATION IS ABSENT (180)	0.77 OF 13	107 3 72 10 XSQ= 5.26 PHI= 0.165 XP = 0.0219
110	TILT TOWARD BEING THOSE WHERE SLAVERY IS PRESENT (163)	0.56 OF 174	110	TILT TOWARD BEING THOSE WHERE SLAVERY IS ABSENT (218)	0.79 OF 14	97 3 77 11 XSQ= 4.83 PHI= 0.160 XP = 0.0280
142	DRIFT TOWARD BEING THOSE WHERE THE LEVEL OF SOCIAL SANCTION IS PUBLIC CORPOREAL SANCTION OR PUBLIC PROPERTY SANCTION, RATHER THAN PRIVATE SETTLEMENT (38) JMH	0.81 OF 21	142	IN ALL CASES ARE THOSE WHERE THE LEVEL OF SOCIAL SANCTION IS PRIVATE SETTLEMENT, RATHER THAN PUBLIC CORPOREAL SANCTION OR PUBLIC PROPERTY SETTLEMENT (16) JMH	1.00 OF 2	17 0 4 2 XSQ= 2.72 PHI= 0.344 EP = 0.0593
176	TEND TO BE THOSE WHERE THE COMMUNITY IS A CLAN-COMMUNITY OR A COMMUNITY STRUCTURED OR SEGMENTED ON A CLAN BASIS (169)	0.65 OF 176	176	IN ALL CASES ARE THOSE WHERE THE COMMUNITY IS OTHER THAN A CLAN-COMMUNITY OR A COMMUNITY STRUCTURED OR SEGMENTED ON A CLAN BASIS (213)	1.00 OF 14	115 0 61 14 XSQ= 20.52 PHI= 0.329 XP = 0.0000
177	LEAN LESS TOWARD BEING THOSE WHERE THE COMMUNITY IS OTHER THAN A SINGLE CLAN-COMMUNITY AND EXOGAMOUS (305)	0.62 OF 176	177	IN ALL CASES ARE THOSE WHERE THE COMMUNITY IS OTHER THAN A SINGLE CLAN-COMMUNITY AND EXOGAMOUS (305)	1.00 OF 14	67 0 109 14 XSQ= 6.65 PHI= 0.187 XP = 0.0099
178	DRIFT LESS TOWARD BEING THOSE WHERE THE COMMUNITY IS OTHER THAN SEGMENTED ON A CLAN BASIS AND NON-EXOGAMOUS (295)	0.76 OF 176	178	IN ALL CASES ARE THOSE WHERE THE COMMUNITY IS OTHER THAN SEGMENTED ON A CLAN BASIS AND NON-EXOGAMOUS (295)	1.00 OF 14	43 0 133 14 XSQ= 3.14 PHI= 0.128 XP = 0.0766
180	TILT LESS TOWARD BEING THOSE WHERE THE COMMUNITY IS COMMONLY NON-EXOGAMOUS, RATHER THAN EXOGAMOUS (258)	0.51 OF 176	180	TILT MORE TOWARD BEING THOSE WHERE THE COMMUNITY IS COMMONLY NON-EXOGAMOUS, RATHER THAN EXOGAMOUS (258)	0.86 OF 14	87 2 89 12 XSQ= 5.10 PHI= 0.164 XP = 0.0239
181	TILT MORE TOWARD BEING THOSE WHERE THE COMMUNITY IS OTHER THAN A DEME (337)	0.96 OF 176	181	TILT LESS TOWARD BEING THOSE WHERE THE COMMUNITY IS OTHER THAN A DEME (337)	0.79 OF 14	7 3 169 11 XSQ= 4.81 PHI= -0.159 XP = 0.0283

182	LEAN TOWARD BEING THOSE OTHER THAN WHERE THE COMMUNITY IS STRUCTURED ON A NON-CLAN BASIS AND AGAMOUS (256)	0.78 OF 176	182	LEAN TOWARD BEING THOSE WHERE THE COMMUNITY IS STRUCTURED ON A NON-CLAN BASIS AND AGAMOUS (126)	0.64 OF 14	39 9 137 5 XSQ= 10.06 PHI= -0.230 XP = 0.0015
207	TILT TOWARD BEING THOSE WHERE MARITAL RESIDENCE IS AMBILOCAL OR NEOLOCAL, RATHER THAN MATRILOCAL OR UXORILOCAL (64)	0.83 OF 6	207	IN ALL CASES ARE THOSE WHERE MARITAL RESIDENCE IS MATRILOCAL OR UXORILOCAL, RATHER THAN AMBILOCAL OR NEOLOCAL (64)	1.00 OF 4	1 4 5 0 XSQ= 3.75 PHI= -0.612 EP = 0.0476
209	TEND MORE TO BE THOSE WHERE MARITAL RESIDENCE IS PATRILOCAL, VIRILOCAL, OR AVUNCULOCAL, RATHER THAN MATRILOCAL OR UXORILOCAL (270)	0.99 OF 180	209	TEND LESS TO BE THOSE WHERE MARITAL RESIDENCE IS PATRILOCAL, VIRILOCAL, OR AVUNCULOCAL, RATHER THAN MATRILOCAL OR UXORILOCAL (270)	0.71 OF 14	179 10 1 4 XSQ= 30.21 PHI= 0.395 XP = 0.0000
213	LEAN LESS TOWARD BEING THOSE WHERE FIRST COUSIN MARRIAGE IS PERMITTED (172)	0.52 OF 175	213	LEAN MORE TOWARD BEING THOSE WHERE FIRST COUSIN MARRIAGE IS PERMITTED (172)	0.93 OF 14	91 13 84 1 XSQ= 7.17 PHI= -0.195 XP = 0.0074
220	TILT TOWARD BEING THOSE WHERE FIRST COUSIN MARRIAGE IN SOME FORM OR OTHER IS NOT PRESCRIBED OR PREFERRED (273)	0.67 OF 175	220	TILT TOWARD BEING THOSE WHERE FIRST COUSIN MARRIAGE IN SOME FORM OR OTHER IS PRESCRIBED OR PREFERRED (97)	0.64 OF 14	58 9 117 5 XSQ= 4.22 PHI= -0.149 XP = 0.0400
224	TEND TO BE THOSE WHERE COUSIN MARRIAGE IS PREFERENTIALLY OR PERMISSIVELY EITHER PATRI- OR MATRILATERAL, RATHER THAN SYMMETRICAL (66)	0.54 OF 91	224	IN ALL CASES ARE THOSE WHERE COUSIN MARRIAGE IS PREFERENTIALLY OR PERMISSIVELY SYMMETRICAL, RATHER THAN EITHER PATRI- OR MATRILATERAL (106)	1.00 OF 13	49 0 42 13 XSQ= 11.16 PHI= 0.328 XP = 0.0008
234	TILT LESS TOWARD BEING THOSE WHERE THE COUSIN TERMINOLOGY IS OF CROW, OMAHA, OR IROQUOIS TYPE, RATHER THAN ESKIMO OR HAWAIIAN TYPE (152)	0.67 OF 126	234	IN ALL CASES ARE THOSE WHERE THE COUSIN TERMINOLOGY IS OF CROW, OMAHA, OR IROQUOIS TYPE, RATHER THAN ESKIMO OR HAWAIIAN TYPE (152)	1.00 OF 13	85 13 41 0 XSQ= 4.54 PHI= -0.181 XP = 0.0332
240	DRIFT TOWARD BEING THOSE WHERE THE FAMILY, IF EXTENDED, IS SMALL OR STEM, RATHER THAN LARGE (135)	0.69 OF 96	240	DRIFT TOWARD BEING THOSE WHERE THE FAMILY, IF EXTENDED, IS LARGE, RATHER THAN SMALL OR STEM (78)	0.67 OF 9	30 6 66 3 XSQ= 3.14 PHI= -0.173 XP = 0.0762
263	LEAN TOWARD BEING THOSE WHERE WIVES ARE OBTAINED BY RELATIVELY DIFFICULT MEANS, NAMELY BY BRIDE-PRICE, BRIDE-SERVICE, OR EXCHANGING A FEMALE RELATIVE (233)	0.81 OF 183	263	LEAN TOWARD BEING THOSE WHERE WIVES ARE OBTAINED BY RELATIVELY EASY MEANS, NAMELY BY TOKEN BRIDE-PRICE, GIFT EXCHANGE, ABSENCE OF ANY CONSIDERATION, OR RECEIPT OF DOWRY (162)	0.57 OF 14	148 6 35 8 XSQ= 8.90 PHI= 0.213 XP = 0.0029

```
280  DRIFT TOWARD BEING THOSE          0.63 OF  16    280  IN ALL CASES ARE THOSE            1.00 OF   3          6     3
     WHERE THE COMPOSITE FERTILITY LEVEL                    WHERE THE COMPOSITE FERTILITY LEVEL                   10     0
     IS LOW   (12) MN                                       IS HIGH   (13) MN                                 XSQ=      1.85
                                                                                                             PHI=    -0.312
                                                                                                             EP =    0.0867

323  DRIFT TOWARD BEING THOSE          0.59 OF  32    323  IN ALL CASES ARE THOSE            1.00 OF   3         13     3
     WHERE THE CONSTANCY OF PRESENCE                        WHERE THE CONSTANCY OF PRESENCE                       19     0
     OF THE INFANT'S NURTURANT AGENT                        OF THE INFANT'S NURTURANT AGENT               XSQ=      1.87
     IS LOW   (45) B-B-C                                    IS HIGH   (29) B-B-C                          PHI=    -0.231
                                                                                                             EP =    0.0856

334  DRIFT TOWARD BEING THOSE          0.64 OF  36    334  IN ALL CASES ARE THOSE            1.00 OF   3         13     3
     WHERE THE INDULGENCE OF THE CHILD                      WHERE THE INDULGENCE OF THE CHILD                     23     0
     IS LOW   (38) B-B-C                                    IS HIGH   (40) B-B-C                          XSQ=      2.40
                                                                                                             PHI=    -0.248
                                                                                                             EP =    0.0613

337  TILT TOWARD BEING THOSE           0.68 OF  34    337  IN ALL CASES ARE THOSE            1.00 OF   3         23     0
     WHERE THE CHILD'S INFERRED ANXIETY OVER                WHERE THE CHILD'S INFERRED ANXIETY OVER               11     3
     NON-PERFORMANCE OF RESPONSIBLE BEHAVIOR                NON-PERFORMANCE OF RESPONSIBLE BEHAVIOR       XSQ=      2.87
     IS HIGH   (38) B-B-C                                   IS LOW   (35) B-B-C                           PHI=     0.279
                                                                                                             EP =    0.0468

339  DRIFT TOWARD BEING THOSE          0.59 OF  34    339  IN ALL CASES ARE THOSE            1.00 OF   3         20     0
     WHERE THE CHILD'S INFERRED CONFLICT                    WHERE THE CHILD'S INFERRED CONFLICT                   14     3
     REGARDING RESPONSIBLE BEHAVIOR                         REGARDING RESPONSIBLE BEHAVIOR                XSQ=      1.84
     IS HIGH   (31) B-B-C                                   IS LOW   (42) B-B-C                           PHI=     0.223
                                                                                                             EP =    0.0875

354  DRIFT TOWARD BEING THOSE          0.59 OF  34    354  IN ALL CASES ARE THOSE            1.00 OF   3         20     0
     WHERE THE CHILD'S INFERRED ANXIETY OVER                WHERE THE CHILD'S INFERRED ANXIETY OVER               14     3
     PERFORMANCE OF OBEDIENT BEHAVIOR                       PERFORMANCE OF OBEDIENT BEHAVIOR              XSQ=      1.84
     IS HIGH   (36) B-B-C                                   IS LOW   (37) B-B-C                           PHI=     0.223
                                                                                                             EP =    0.0875

355  DRIFT TOWARD BEING THOSE          0.62 OF  34    355  IN ALL CASES ARE THOSE            1.00 OF   3         21     0
     WHERE THE CHILD'S INFERRED CONFLICT                    WHERE THE CHILD'S INFERRED CONFLICT                   13     3
     REGARDING OBEDIENT BEHAVIOR                            REGARDING OBEDIENT BEHAVIOR                   XSQ=      2.14
     IS HIGH   (35) B-B-C                                   IS LOW   (38) B-B-C                           PHI=     0.240
                                                                                                             EP =    0.0721

358  TILT TOWARD BEING THOSE           0.91 OF  22    358  IN ALL CASES ARE THOSE            1.00 OF   2         20     0
     WHERE ADOLESCENT PEER GROUPS ARE PRESENT               WHERE ADOLESCENT PEER GROUPS ARE ABSENT                2     2
     IN A SETTING OF WORK AND PUBLIC GATHERINGS             IN A SETTING OF WORK, AND OF                  XSQ=      5.35
     AND LEISURE, OR OF                                     PUBLIC GATHERINGS, AND OF                     PHI=     0.472
     PUBLIC GATHERINGS AND LEISURE, OR                      LEISURE   (11) JKH                            EP =    0.0217
     OF LEISURE ONLY   (41) JKH

365  DRIFT TOWARD BEING THOSE          0.78 OF  18    365  IN ALL CASES ARE THOSE            1.00 OF   2         14     0
     WHERE THE TIME SPENT IN                                WHERE THE TIME SPENT IN                                4     2
     ADOLESCENT PEER GROUP ACTIVITY                         ADOLESCENT PEER GROUP ACTIVITY                XSQ=      2.14
     IS HIGH OR HIGH-MEDIUM   (30) JKH                      IS LOW-MEDIUM OR LOW   (15) JKH               PHI=     0.327
                                                                                                             EP =    0.0789
```

377	LEAN LESS TOWARC BEING THCSE WHERE MALE GENITAL MUTILATION IS ABSENT (242)	0.58 OF 152	377	IN ALL CASES ARE THCSE WHERE MALE GENITAL MUTILATICN IS ABSENT (242)	1.00 CF 13	64 0 88 13 XSQ= 7.26 PHI= 0.210 XP = 0.0071
392	LEAN TOWARD BEING THOSE WHERE PREMARITAL SEX RELATIONS ARE STRCNGLY PUNISHED AND IN FACT RARE, OR WEAKLY PUNISHED ANC IN FACT NCT RARE, OR PUNISHED CNLY IF PREGNANCY RESULTS (112) JTW,EA	0.75 OF 83	392	IN ALL CASES ARE THOSE WHERE PREMARITAL SEX RELATICNS ARE FREELY PERMITTED (67) JTW,EA	1.00 OF 5	62 0 21 5 XSQ= 9.31 PHI= 0.325 XP = 0.0023
458	TILT TOWARD BEING THOSE WHERE GAMES, IF PRESENT, INCLUDE GAMES OF STRATEGY (52) R-A-B,EA	0.52 OF 69	458	IN ALL CASES ARE THOSE WHERE GAMES, IF PRESENT, DO NOT INCLUDE GAMES OF STRATEGY (119) R-A-B,EA	1.00 OF 7	36 0 33 7 XSQ= 5.00 PHI= 0.257 XP = 0.0253
460	TILT TCWARD BEING THCSE WHERE GAMES, IF PRESENT, ARE NCT LIMITED TO GAMES OF SKILL CNLY (104) R-A-B,EA	0.68 OF 69	460	TILT TOWARD BEING THOSE WHERE GAMES, IF PRESENT, ARE LIMITED TO GAMES OF SKILL ONLY (67) R-A-B,EA	0.86 CF 7	22 6 47 1 XSQ= 5.77 PHI= -0.276 XP = 0.0163
469	DRIFT TCWARD BEING THCSE WHERE CCNTACT WITH OTHER CULTURES IS FREQUENT CR REGULAR, RATHER THAN IRREGULAR (43) JMH	0.76 OF 21	469	IN ALL CASES ARE THOSE WHERE CONTACT WITH OTHER CULTURES IS IRREGULAR, RATHER THAN FREQUENT OR REGULAR (11) JMH	1.00 OF 2	16 0 5 2 XSQ= 2.05 PHI= 0.299 EP = 0.0830

****

192 CULTURES
WHERE THE ONLY KIN GROUP PRESENT
IS A KINDRED OR ELSE
BILATERAL DESCENT IS INFERRED (111)

192 CULTURES
OTHER THAN WHERE THE ONLY KIN GROUP
PRESENT IS A KINDRED OR ELSE
BILATERAL DESCENT IS INFERRED (289)

BACKGROUND ON PAGE 108

BOTH SUBJECT AND PREDICATE

....

111 IN LEFT COLUMN

ABIPON ALACALUF AMERICANS ANDAMANESE ATSUGEWI AWEIKOMA BASQUES BERGDAMA BLACK CARIB BOERS
BOTOCUDO BRAZILIANS BULGARIANS BURMESE CADUVEO CAGABA CAMBA CAMBODIANS CARAJA CARIB
CARINYA CAYAPA CHAMACOCO CHEREMIS CHEYENNE CHIBCHA CHINANTEC CHIR-APACHE CHIRIGUANO CHOCO
CHOROTI CHORTI CHUKCHEE COPR ESKIMO CUNA CZECHS DUSUN DUTCH GROS VENTRE GUATO
HANUNOO HASINAI HUICHOL HUKUNDIKA HUTSUL IBAN ICELANDERS IFUGAO INCA INGALIK
IRISH JAPANESE JAVANESE KIOW-APACHE KOL KORYAK KUMYK KUNG KUTENAI LAPPS
MALAYS MANIHIKI MARQUESANS MATACO MAZATECO NAMBICUARA NASKAPI NATCHEZ NICOBARESE ONA
PAEZ PAPAGO PARAUJANO PENOBSCOT POPOLUCA PORTUGUESE ROMANS SAGADA SANPOIL SARSI
SELUNG SEMANG SERI SUBANUN TAGBANUA TAOS TAPIRAPE TARAHUMARA TAREUMIUT TEHUELCHE
TENETEHARA TENINO TETON THAI TORAJA TOTONAC TRISTAN TUBATULABAL TUNEBO TWANA
UTE WAICA WALLONS WARRAU WASHO WICHITA YAHGAN YARURO YUKAGHIR YUKI
YUROK

289 IN RIGHT COLUMN

3	TEND MORE TO BE THOSE LOCATED OUTSIDE OF AFRICA (320)	0.98 OF 111	3	TEND LESS TO BE THOSE LOCATED OUTSIDE OF AFRICA (320)	0.73 OF 289	2 78 109 211 XSQ= 30.24 PHI= -0.275 XP = 0.0000
5	DRIFT MORE TOWARD BEING THOSE LOCATED OUTSIDE OF EAST EURASIA (330)	0.88 OF 111	5	DRIFT LESS TOWARD BEING THOSE LOCATED OUTSIDE OF EAST EURASIA (330)	0.80 OF 289	13 57 98 232 XSQ= 3.03 PHI= -0.087 XP = 0.0816
6	TILT MORE TOWARD BEING THOSE LOCATED OUTSIDE OF THE INSULAR PACIFIC (330)	0.90 OF 111	6	TILT LESS TOWARD BEING THOSE LOCATED OUTSIDE OF THE INSULAR PACIFIC (330)	0.80 OF 289	11 59 100 230 XSQ= 5.42 PHI= -0.116 XP = 0.0199
8	TEND LESS TO BE THOSE LOCATED OUTSIDE OF NORTH AMERICA (330)	0.69 OF 111	8	TEND MORE TO BE THOSE LOCATED OUTSIDE OF NORTH AMERICA (330)	0.88 OF 289	34 36 77 253 XSQ= 17.11 PHI= 0.207 XP = 0.0000

9	TEND LESS TO BE THOSE LOCATED OUTSIDE OF SOUTH AMERICA (335)	0.69 OF 111	9	TEND MORE TO BE THOSE LOCATED OUTSIDE OF SOUTH AMERICA (335)	0.89 OF 289	34 31 77 258 XSQ= 21.91 PHI= 0.234 XP = 0.0000
15	TEND TO BE THOSE WHERE THE LATITUDE IS TWENTY DEGREES OR GREATER (183)	0.59 OF 111	15	TEND TO BE THOSE WHERE THE LATITUDE IS LESS THAN TWENTY DEGREES (217)	0.60 OF 289	66 117 45 172 XSQ= 10.88 PHI= 0.165 XP = 0.0010
33	DRIFT LESS TOWARD BEING THOSE WHERE THE NATURAL ENVIRONMENT IS OTHER THAN 'VERY HARSH,' I.E., DESERT, DESERT GRASSES AND SHRUBS, TUNDRA, OR HIGH PLATEAU STEPPE (341) FWM	0.79 OF 111	33	DRIFT MORE TOWARD BEING THOSE WHERE THE NATURAL ENVIRONMENT IS OTHER THAN 'VERY HARSH,' I.E., DESERT, DESERT GRASSES AND SHRUBS, TUNDRA, OR HIGH PLATEAU STEPPE (341) FWM	0.88 OF 289	23 36 88 253 XSQ= 3.72 PHI= 0.096 XP = 0.0537
36	LEAN LESS TOWARD BEING THOSE WHERE THE NATURAL ENVIRONMENT IS OTHER THAN 'VERY HARSH,' OR SUB-TROPICAL BUSH, OR TEMPERATE GRASSLAND (292) FWM	0.63 OF 111	36	LEAN MORE TOWARD BEING THOSE WHERE THE NATURAL ENVIRONMENT IS OTHER THAN 'VERY HARSH,' OR SUB-TROPICAL BUSH, OR TEMPERATE GRASSLAND (292) FWM	0.77 OF 289	41 67 70 222 XSQ= 7.01 PHI= 0.132 XP = 0.0081
44	LEAN LESS TOWARD BEING THOSE WHERE SETTLEMENTS ARE FIXED (222)	0.54 OF 92	44	LEAN MORE TOWARD BEING THOSE WHERE SETTLEMENTS ARE FIXED (222)	0.72 OF 240	50 172 42 68 XSQ= 8.24 PHI= -0.158 XP = 0.0041
46	TEND LESS TO BE THOSE OTHER THAN WHERE SETTLEMENTS ARE NON-FIXED AND MOVEMENT IS NOMADIC (260)	0.63 OF 92	46	TEND MORE TO BE THOSE OTHER THAN WHERE SETTLEMENTS ARE NON-FIXED AND MOVEMENT IS NOMADIC (260)	0.84 OF 240	34 38 58 202 XSQ= 16.25 PHI= 0.221 XP = 0.0001
47	TILT MORE TOWARD BEING THOSE WHERE, IF SETTLEMENTS ARE NON-FIXED, MOVEMENT IS NOMADIC, RATHER THAN NON-NOMADIC (72)	0.81 OF 42	47	TILT LESS TOWARD BEING THOSE WHERE, IF SETTLEMENTS ARE NON-FIXED, MOVEMENT IS NOMADIC, RATHER THAN NON-NOMADIC (72)	0.56 OF 68	34 38 8 30 XSQ= 6.15 PHI= 0.236 XP = 0.0131
51	TEND TO BE THOSE WHERE SUBSISTENCE IS PRIMARILY BY FOOD GATHERING -- I. E., HUNTING, FISHING, OR COLLECTING -- RATHER THAN FOOD PRODUCTION (147)	0.51 OF 111	51	TEND TO BE THOSE WHERE SUBSISTENCE IS PRIMARILY BY FOOD PRODUCTION -- I. E., AGRICULTURE OR HUSBANDRY -- RATHER THAN BY GATHERING (253)	0.69 OF 289	54 199 57 90 XSQ= 13.24 PHI= -0.182 XP = 0.0003
62	LEAN TOWARD BEING THOSE WHERE HUSBANDRY OF ANY KIND IS ABSENT (172)	0.54 OF 111	62	LEAN TOWARD BEING THOSE WHERE HUSBANDRY OF SOME KIND IS PRESENT (228)	0.61 OF 289	51 177 60 112 XSQ= 7.05 PHI= -0.133 XP = 0.0079

71	LEAN MORE TOWARD BEING THOSE WHERE METAL WORKING IS ABSENT (153)	0.76 OF 68	71	LEAN LESS TOWARD BEING THOSE WHERE METAL WORKING IS ABSENT (153)	0.55 OF 183	16 82 52 101 XSQ= 8.56 PHI= -0.185 XP = 0.0034
79	LEAN LESS TOWARD BEING THOSE WHERE NO CITY IS PRESENT (201)	0.80 OF 59	79	LEAN MORE TOWARD BEING THOSE WHERE NO CITY IS PRESENT (201)	0.93 OF 165	12 11 47 154 XSQ= 7.40 PHI= 0.182 XP = 0.0065
80	TILT LESS TOWARD BEING THOSE WHERE NO CITY OR TOWN IS PRESENT (185)	0.73 OF 59	80	TILT MORE TOWARD BEING THOSE WHERE NO CITY OR TOWN IS PRESENT (185)	0.86 OF 165	16 23 43 142 XSQ= 4.37 PHI= 0.140 XP = 0.0365
82	DRIFT LESS TOWARD BEING THOSE WHERE A CITY OR TOWN IS PRESENT, OR THE AVERAGE COMMUNITY SIZE IS FIFTY OR GREATER (178)	0.71 OF 59	82	DRIFT MORE TOWARD BEING THOSE WHERE A CITY OR TOWN IS PRESENT, OR THE AVERAGE COMMUNITY SIZE IS FIFTY OR GREATER (178)	0.82 OF 165	42 136 17 29 XSQ= 2.71 PHI= -0.110 XP = 0.0997
83	DRIFT MORE TOWARD BEING THOSE WHERE, WITH NO CITY AND NO TOWN PRESENT, THE AVERAGE COMMUNITY SIZE IS SMALLER THAN 200, RATHER THAN BETWEEN 200 AND 999 (135)	0.88 OF 41	83	DRIFT LESS TOWARD BEING THOSE WHERE, WITH NO CITY AND NO TOWN PRESENT, THE AVERAGE COMMUNITY SIZE IS SMALLER THAN 200, RATHER THAN BETWEEN 200 AND 999 (135)	0.71 OF 139	5 40 36 99 XSQ= 3.80 PHI= -0.145 XP = 0.0512
86	DRIFT TOWARD BEING THOSE WHERE THE LEVEL OF POLITICAL INTEGRATION IS THE AUTONOMOUS COMMUNITY, OR THE FAMILY (156) GPM	0.61 OF 82	86	DRIFT TOWARD BEING THOSE WHERE THE LEVEL OF POLITICAL INTEGRATION IS THE LARGE STATE, THE LITTLE STATE, OR THE MINIMAL STATE (148) GPM	0.52 OF 222	32 116 50 106 XSQ= 3.68 PHI= -0.110 XP = 0.0550
88	TEND TO BE THOSE WHERE, IF A HEADMANSHIP IS PRESENT, SUCCESSION IS NON-HEREDITARY (106)	0.63 OF 65	88	TEND TO BE THOSE WHERE, IF A HEADMANSHIP IS PRESENT, SUCCESSION IS HEREDITARY (165)	0.68 OF 206	41 65 24 141 XSQ= 19.31 PHI= 0.267 XP = 0.0000
96	LEAN TOWARD BEING THOSE WHERE THE HIERARCHY OF NATIONAL JURISDICTION HAS NO LEVELS (156) GES,EA	0.61 OF 90	96	LEAN TOWARD BEING THOSE WHERE THE HIERARCHY OF NATIONAL JURISDICTION HAS FOUR, THREE, TWO OR ONE LEVEL (174) GES,EA	0.58 OF 240	35 139 55 101 XSQ= 8.76 PHI= -0.163 XP = 0.0031
98	TEND TO BE THOSE WHERE THE HIERARCHY OF LOCAL JURISDICTION HAS TWO LEVELS (93) GES,EA	0.52 OF 90	98	TEND TO BE THOSE WHERE THE HIERARCHY OF LOCAL JURISDICTION HAS FOUR OR THREE LEVELS (238) GES,EA	0.81 OF 241	43 195 47 46 XSQ= 33.99 PHI= -0.320 XP = 0.

99	LEAN TOWARD BEING THOSE 0.58 OF 55 WHERE, WITH NATIONAL HIERARCHY ABSENT, THE HIERARCHY OF LOCAL JURISDICTION HAS TWO LEVELS (63) GES,EA	99	LEAN TOWARD BEING THOSE 0.69 OF 101 WHERE, WITH NATIONAL HIERARCHY ABSENT, THE HIERARCHY OF LOCAL JURISDICTION HAS FOUR OR THREE LEVELS (93) GES,EA	23 70 32 31 XSQ= 10.06 PHI= -0.254 XP = 0.0015
100	TEND LESS TO BE THOSE 0.64 OF 90 WHERE HIERARCHIES ARE MORE COMPLEX THAN THE 'SIMPLEST,' I. E., MORE COMPLEX THAN TWO LOCAL LEVELS WITH NO NATIONAL LEVELS (267) GES,EA	100	TEND MORE TO BE THOSE 0.87 OF 240 WHERE HIERARCHIES ARE MORE COMPLEX THAN THE 'SIMPLEST,' I. E., MORE COMPLEX THAN TWO LOCAL LEVELS WITH NO NATIONAL LEVELS (267) GES,EA	58 209 32 31 XSQ= 20.28 PHI= -0.248 XP = 0.0000
107	TILT LESS TOWARD BEING THOSE 0.65 OF 48 WHERE CLASS STRATIFICATION, IF PRESENT, IS BASED ON SOMETHING OTHER THAN OCCUPATIONAL STATUS (160)	107	TILT MORE TOWARD BEING THOSE 0.83 OF 155 WHERE CLASS STRATIFICATION, IF PRESENT, IS BASED ON SOMETHING OTHER THAN OCCUPATIONAL STATUS (160)	17 26 31 129 XSQ= 6.55 PHI= 0.180 XP = 0.0105
108	TEND MORE TO BE THOSE 0.85 OF 48 WHERE CLASS STRATIFICATION, IF PRESENT, IS BASED ON SOMETHING OTHER THAN A HEREDITARY ARISTOCRACY (129)	108	TEND LESS TO BE THOSE 0.57 OF 155 WHERE CLASS STRATIFICATION, IF PRESENT, IS BASED ON SOMETHING OTHER THAN A HEREDITARY ARISTOCRACY (129)	7 67 41 88 XSQ= 11.77 PHI= -0.241 XP = 0.0006
109	LEAN MORE TOWARD BEING THOSE 0.95 OF 106 WHERE CASTES ARE ABSENT (317)	109	LEAN LESS TOWARD BEING THOSE 0.82 OF 262 WHERE CASTES ARE ABSENT (317)	5 46 101 216 XSQ= 9.37 PHI= -0.160 XP = 0.0022
110	TEND MORE TO BE THOSE 0.73 OF 105 WHERE SLAVERY IS ABSENT (218)	110	TEND LESS TO BE THOSE 0.51 OF 276 WHERE SLAVERY IS ABSENT (218)	28 135 77 141 XSQ= 14.48 PHI= -0.195 XP = 0.0001
128	TILT TOWARD BEING THOSE 0.82 OF 17 WHERE, IF SUBSISTENCE IS PRIMARILY BY AGRICULTURE, THE WORK IS MAINLY DONE BY MALES (40)	128	TILT TOWARD BEING THOSE 0.57 OF 60 WHERE, IF SUBSISTENCE IS PRIMARILY BY AGRICULTURE, THE WORK IS MAINLY DONE BY FEMALES (37)	14 26 3 34 XSQ= 6.59 PHI= 0.293 XP = 0.0102
129	TILT MORE TOWARD BEING THOSE 0.89 OF 27 WHERE WEAVING IS MAINLY DONE BY FEMALES (73)	129	TILT LESS TOWARD BEING THOSE 0.64 OF 77 WHERE WEAVING IS MAINLY DONE BY FEMALES (73)	3 28 24 49 XSQ= 4.95 PHI= -0.218 XP = 0.0262
131	TILT LESS TOWARD BEING THOSE 0.76 OF 50 WHERE THE CONSTRUCTION OF PERMANENT HOUSES OR THE ERECTION OF TEMPORARY DWELLINGS IS MAINLY DONE BY MALES (136)	131	TILT MORE TOWARD BEING THOSE 0.92 OF 107 WHERE THE CONSTRUCTION OF PERMANENT HOUSES OR THE ERECTION OF TEMPORARY DWELLINGS IS MAINLY DONE BY MALES (136)	38 98 12 9 XSQ= 5.86 PHI= -0.193 XP = 0.0154

No.			No.			
147	TILT TOWARD BEING THOSE WHERE CODIFIED LAWS ARE UNIMPORTANT OR ABSENT (13) LWS	0.70 OF 10	147	TILT TOWARD BEING THOSE WHERE CODIFIED LAWS ARE PRESENT (20) LWS	0.74 OF 23	3 17 7 6 XSQ= 3.94 PHI= -0.346 EP = 0.0259
175	DRIFT MORE TOWARD BEING THOSE WHERE THE COMMUNITY IS 'KIN-HETEROGENEOUS,' I. E. OTHER THAN A CLAN COMMUNITY OR A DEME (260)	0.76 OF 104	175	DRIFT LESS TOWARD BEING THOSE WHERE THE COMMUNITY IS 'KIN-HETEROGENEOUS,' I. E. OTHER THAN A CLAN COMMUNITY OR A DEME (260)	0.65 OF 278	25 97 79 181 XSQ= 3.62 PHI= -0.097 XP = 0.0572
176	IN ALL CASES ARE THOSE WHERE THE COMMUNITY IS OTHER THAN A CLAN-COMMUNITY OR A COMMUNITY STRUCTURED OR SEGMENTED ON A CLAN BASIS (213)	1.00 OF 104	176	TEND TO BE THOSE WHERE THE COMMUNITY IS A CLAN-COMMUNITY OR A COMMUNITY STRUCTURED OR SEGMENTED ON A CLAN BASIS (169)	0.61 OF 278	0 169 104 109 XSQ= 110.93 PHI= -0.539 XP = 0.
177	IN ALL CASES ARE THOSE WHERE THE COMMUNITY IS OTHER THAN A SINGLE CLAN-COMMUNITY AND EXOGAMOUS (305)	1.00 OF 104	177	TEND LESS TO BE THOSE WHERE THE COMMUNITY IS OTHER THAN A SINGLE CLAN-COMMUNITY AND EXOGAMOUS (305)	0.72 OF 278	0 77 104 201 XSQ= 34.38 PHI= -0.300 XP = 0.
178	IN ALL CASES ARE THOSE WHERE THE COMMUNITY IS OTHER THAN SEGMENTED ON A CLAN BASIS AND NON-EXOGAMOUS (295)	1.00 OF 104	178	TEND LESS TO BE THOSE WHERE THE COMMUNITY IS OTHER THAN SEGMENTED ON A CLAN BASIS AND NON-EXOGAMOUS (295)	0.69 OF 278	0 87 104 191 XSQ= 40.38 PHI= -0.325 XP = 0.
179	LEAN LESS TOWARD BEING THOSE WHERE THE COMMUNITY IS OTHER THAN STRUCTURED ON A NON-CLAN BASIS AND COMMONLY EXOGAMOUS (340)	0.82 OF 104	179	LEAN MORE TOWARD BEING THOSE WHERE THE COMMUNITY IS OTHER THAN STRUCTURED ON A NON-CLAN BASIS AND COMMONLY EXOGAMOUS (340)	0.92 OF 278	19 23 85 255 XSQ= 6.74 PHI= 0.133 XP = 0.0094
180	TEND MORE TO BE THOSE WHERE THE COMMUNITY IS COMMONLY NON-EXOGAMOUS, RATHER THAN EXOGAMOUS (258)	0.82 OF 104	180	TEND LESS TO BE THOSE WHERE THE COMMUNITY IS COMMONLY NON-EXOGAMOUS, RATHER THAN EXOGAMOUS (258)	0.62 OF 278	19 105 85 173 XSQ= 12.25 PHI= -0.179 XP = 0.0005
181	TEND LESS TO BE THOSE WHERE THE COMMUNITY IS OTHER THAN A DEME (337)	0.76 OF 104	181	TEND MORE TO BE THOSE WHERE THE COMMUNITY IS OTHER THAN A DEME (337)	0.93 OF 278	25 20 79 258 XSQ= 19.07 PHI= 0.223 XP = 0.0000
182	TEND TO BE THOSE WHERE THE COMMUNITY IS STRUCTURED ON A NON-CLAN BASIS AND AGAMOUS (126)	0.58 OF 104	182	TEND TO BE THOSE OTHER THAN WHERE THE COMMUNITY IS STRUCTURED ON A NON-CLAN BASIS AND AGAMOUS (256)	0.76 OF 278	60 66 44 212 XSQ= 37.95 PHI= 0.315 XP = 0.

196	TEND LESS TO BE THOSE 0.51 OF 81 WHERE INDIVIDUAL RIGHTS IN REAL PROPERTY, AND RULES FOR INHERITANCE, ARE PRESENT (194)	196	TEND MORE TO BE THOSE 0.76 OF 200 WHERE INDIVIDUAL RIGHTS IN REAL PROPERTY, AND RULES FOR INHERITANCE, ARE PRESENT (194)	41 153 40 47 XSQ= 16.88 PHI= -0.245 XP = 0.0000
197	TEND LESS TO BE THOSE 0.51 OF 41 WHERE RULES FOR THE INHERITANCE OF REAL PROPERTY, IF PRESENT, FAVOR EITHER THE MALE HEIR OR LINE, OR THE FEMALE HEIR OR LINE (165)	197	TEND MORE TO BE THOSE 0.94 OF 153 WHERE RULES FOR THE INHERITANCE OF REAL PROPERTY, IF PRESENT, FAVOR EITHER THE MALE HEIR OR LINE, OR THE FEMALE HEIR OR LINE (165)	21 144 20 9 XSQ= 43.49 PHI= -0.473 XP = 0.
201	TEND LESS TO BE THOSE 0.63 OF 110 WHERE MARITAL RESIDENCE IS NON-OPTIONAL, RATHER THAN AMBILOCAL OR NEOLOCAL (334)	201	TEND MORE TO BE THOSE 0.92 OF 288 WHERE MARITAL RESIDENCE IS NON-OPTIONAL, RATHER THAN AMBILOCAL OR NEOLOCAL (334)	69 265 41 23 XSQ= 48.44 PHI= -0.349 XP = 0.
204	TEND LESS TO BE THOSE 0.52 OF 85 WHERE MARITAL RESIDENCE IS PATRILOCAL, VIRILOCAL, OR AVUNCULOCAL, RATHER THAN AMBILOCAL OR NEOLOCAL (270)	204	TEND MORE TO BE THOSE 0.91 OF 249 WHERE MARITAL RESIDENCE IS PATRILOCAL, VIRILOCAL, OR AVUNCULOCAL, RATHER THAN AMBILOCAL OR NEOLOCAL (270)	44 226 41 23 XSQ= 59.73 PHI= -0.423 XP = 0.
207	LEAN TOWARD BEING THOSE 0.62 OF 66 WHERE MARITAL RESIDENCE IS AMBILOCAL OR NEOLOCAL, RATHER THAN MATRILOCAL OR UXORILOCAL (64)	207	LEAN TOWARD BEING THOSE 0.63 OF 62 WHERE MARITAL RESIDENCE IS MATRILOCAL OR UXORILOCAL, RATHER THAN AMBILOCAL OR NEOLOCAL (64)	25 39 41 23 XSQ= 7.04 PHI= -0.234 XP = 0.0080
209	TEND LESS TO BE THOSE 0.64 OF 69 WHERE MARITAL RESIDENCE IS PATRILOCAL, VIRILOCAL, OR AVUNCULOCAL, RATHER THAN MATRILOCAL OR UXORILOCAL (270)	209	TEND MORE TO BE THOSE 0.85 OF 265 WHERE MARITAL RESIDENCE IS PATRILOCAL, VIRILOCAL, OR AVUNCULOCAL, RATHER THAN MATRILOCAL OR UXORILOCAL (270)	44 226 25 39 XSQ= 15.00 PHI= -0.212 XP = 0.0001
213	TEND TO BE THOSE 0.71 OF 95 WHERE FIRST COUSIN MARRIAGE IS NOT PERMITTED (198)	213	TEND TO BE THOSE 0.52 OF 275 WHERE FIRST COUSIN MARRIAGE IS PERMITTED (172)	28 144 67 131 XSQ= 13.97 PHI= -0.194 XP = 0.0002
214	IN ALL CASES ARE THOSE 1.00 OF 28 WHERE FIRST COUSIN MARRIAGE, IF PERMITTED, IS OTHER THAN UNILATERAL (144)	214	TILT LESS TOWARD BEING THOSE 0.81 OF 144 WHERE FIRST COUSIN MARRIAGE, IF PERMITTED, IS OTHER THAN UNILATERAL (144)	0 28 28 116 XSQ= 5.15 PHI= -0.173 XP = 0.0232
220	TEND MORE TO BE THOSE 0.95 OF 95 WHERE FIRST COUSIN MARRIAGE IN SOME FORM OR OTHER IS NOT PRESCRIBED OR PREFERRED (273)	220	TEND LESS TO BE THOSE 0.67 OF 275 WHERE FIRST COUSIN MARRIAGE IN SOME FORM OR OTHER IS NOT PRESCRIBED OR PREFERRED (273)	5 92 90 183 XSQ= 27.57 PHI= -0.273 XP = 0.0000

221	IN ALL CASES ARE THOSE WHERE MATRILATERAL CROSS-COUSIN MARRIAGE IS NOT PRESCRIBED OR PREFERRED (335)	1.00 OF 95	221	TEND LESS TO BE THOSE WHERE MATRILATERAL CROSS-COUSIN MARRIAGE IS NOT PRESCRIBED OR PREFERRED (335)	0.87 OF 275	0 35 95 240 XSQ= 11.91 PHI= -0.179 XP = 0.0006
224	IN ALL CASES ARE THOSE WHERE COUSIN MARRIAGE IS PREFERENTIALLY OR PERMISSIVELY SYMMETRICAL, RATHER THAN EITHER PATRI- OR MATRILATERAL (106)	1.00 OF 28	224	TEND LESS TO BE THOSE WHERE COUSIN MARRIAGE IS PREFERENTIALLY OR PERMISSIVELY SYMMETRICAL, RATHER THAN EITHER PATRI- OR MATRILATERAL (106)	0.54 OF 144	0 66 28 78 XSQ= 18.93 PHI= -0.332 XP = 0.0000
234	TEND TO BE THOSE WHERE THE COUSIN TERMINOLOGY IS OF ESKIMO OR HAWAIIAN TYPE, RATHER THAN CROW, OMAHA, OR IROQUOIS TYPE (170)	0.93 OF 98	234	TEND TO BE THOSE WHERE THE COUSIN TERMINOLOGY IS OF CROW, OMAHA, OR IROQUOIS TYPE, RATHER THAN ESKIMO OR HAWAIIAN TYPE (152)	0.65 OF 224	7 145 91 79 XSQ= 88.43 PHI= -0.524 XP = 0.
240	TILT MORE TOWARD BEING THOSE WHERE THE FAMILY, IF EXTENDED, IS SMALL OR STEM, RATHER THAN LARGE (135)	0.79 OF 52	240	TILT LESS TOWARD BEING THOSE WHERE THE FAMILY, IF EXTENDED, IS SMALL OR STEM, RATHER THAN LARGE (135)	0.58 OF 161	11 67 41 94 XSQ= 6.24 PHI= -0.171 XP = 0.0125
241	TEND LESS TO BE THOSE WHERE THE FAMILY, IF EXTENDED, IS LARGE OR SMALL, RATHER THAN STEM (187)	0.73 OF 52	241	TEND MORE TO BE THOSE WHERE THE FAMILY, IF EXTENDED, IS LARGE OR SMALL, RATHER THAN STEM (187)	0.93 OF 161	38 149 14 12 XSQ= 12.15 PHI= -0.239 XP = 0.0005
242	TEND LESS TO BE THOSE WHERE MARRIAGE IS COMMONLY OR OCCASIONALLY POLYGYNOUS, RATHER THAN MONOGAMOUS (314)	0.67 OF 109	242	TEND MORE TO BE THOSE WHERE MARRIAGE IS COMMONLY OR OCCASIONALLY POLYGYNOUS, RATHER THAN MONOGAMOUS (314)	0.84 OF 286	73 241 36 45 XSQ= 13.44 PHI= -0.184 XP = 0.0002
243	TILT MORE TOWARD BEING THOSE WHERE POLYGYNY, IF PRESENT, HAS A LOW INCIDENCE (36) W-D,S	0.91 OF 11	243	TILT LESS TOWARD BEING THOSE WHERE POLYGYNY, IF PRESENT, HAS A LOW INCIDENCE (36) W-D,S	0.53 OF 49	1 23 10 26 XSQ= 3.90 PHI= -0.255 XP = 0.0483
262	TEND LESS TO BE THOSE WHERE WIVES ARE OBTAINED BY MEANS INVOLVING THE PRESENCE OF SOME CONSIDERATION (305)	0.61 OF 109	262	TEND MORE TO BE THOSE WHERE WIVES ARE OBTAINED BY MEANS INVOLVING THE PRESENCE OF SOME CONSIDERATION (305)	0.84 OF 286	66 239 43 47 XSQ= 22.47 PHI= -0.239 XP = 0.0000
263	TEND TO BE THOSE WHERE WIVES ARE OBTAINED BY RELATIVELY EASY MEANS, NAMELY BY TOKEN BRIDE-PRICE, GIFT EXCHANGE, ABSENCE OF ANY CONSIDERATION, OR RECEIPT OF DOWRY (162)	0.61 OF 109	263	TEND TO BE THOSE WHERE WIVES ARE OBTAINED BY RELATIVELY DIFFICULT MEANS, NAMELY BY BRIDE-PRICE, BRIDE-SERVICE, OR EXCHANGING A FEMALE RELATIVE (233)	0.66 OF 286	43 190 66 96 XSQ= 22.65 PHI= -0.239 XP = 0.0000

278	IN ALL CASES ARE THOSE 1.00 OF WHERE PROPERTY RIGHTS IN WOMEN ARE UNIMPORTANT OR ABSENT (14) LWS	6	278	DRIFT TOWARD BEING THOSE 0.50 OF WHERE PROPERTY RIGHTS IN WOMEN ARE PRESENT (8) LWS	16	0 8 6 8 XSQ= 2.80 PHI= -0.357 EP = 0.0511
300	DRIFT MORE TOWARD BEING THOSE 0.75 OF WHERE THE POST-PARTUM SEX TABOO LASTS SIX MONTHS OR LESS (73)	32	300	DRIFT LESS TOWARD BEING THOSE 0.53 OF WHERE THE POST-PARTUM SEX TABOO LASTS SIX MONTHS OR LESS (73)	92	8 43 24 49 XSQ= 3.78 PHI= -0.175 XP = 0.0519
314	DRIFT MORE TOWARD BEING THOSE 0.94 OF WHERE THE INCIDENCE OF MOTHER-CHILD HOUSEHOLDS IS LOW (61) W-D,S	18	314	DRIFT LESS TOWARD BEING THOSE 0.71 OF WHERE THE INCIDENCE OF MOTHER-CHILD HOUSEHOLDS IS LOW (61) W-D,S	62	1 18 17 44 XSQ= 3.05 PHI= -0.195 XP = 0.0808
326	IN ALL CASES ARE THOSE 1.00 OF WHERE THE INFERRED TRANSITION ANXIETY BETWEEN INFANCY AND CHILDHOOD IS LOW (35) B-B-C	11	326	LEAN TOWARD BEING THOSE 0.57 OF WHERE THE INFERRED TRANSITION ANXIETY BETWEEN INFANCY AND CHILDHOOD IS HIGH (32) B-B-C	56	0 32 11 24 XSQ= 9.85 PHI= -0.383 XP = 0.0017
327	IN ALL CASES ARE THOSE 1.00 OF WHERE THE AGE OF THE INFANT AT TIME OF REDUCED CONTACT WITH MOTHER IS HIGHER THAN TWO YEARS (28) B-B-C	8	327	LEAN TOWARD BEING THOSE 0.57 OF WHERE THE AGE OF THE INFANT AT TIME OF REDUCED CONTACT WITH MOTHER IS TWO YEARS OR LOWER (27) B-B-C	47	8 20 0 27 XSQ= 6.88 PHI= 0.354 XP = 0.0087
334	TILT TOWARD BEING THOSE 0.79 OF WHERE THE INDULGENCE OF THE CHILD IS HIGH (40) B-B-C	14	334	TILT TOWARD BEING THOSE 0.55 OF WHERE THE INDULGENCE OF THE CHILD IS LOW (38) B-B-C	64	11 29 3 35 XSQ= 3.84 PHI= 0.222 XP = 0.0500
338	TILT TOWARD BEING THOSE 0.69 OF WHERE THE CHILD'S INFERRED ANXIETY OVER PERFORMANCE OF RESPONSIBLE BEHAVIOR IS LOW (29) B-B-C	13	338	TILT TOWARD BEING THOSE 0.67 OF WHERE THE CHILD'S INFERRED ANXIETY OVER PERFORMANCE OF RESPONSIBLE BEHAVIOR IS HIGH (44) B-B-C	60	4 40 9 20 XSQ= 4.35 PHI= -0.244 XP = 0.0370
345	DRIFT TOWARD BEING THOSE 0.77 OF WHERE THE CHILD'S INFERRED ANXIETY OVER NON-PERFORMANCE OF SELF-RELIANT BEHAVIOR IS LOW (39) B-B-C	13	345	DRIFT TOWARD BEING THOSE 0.54 OF WHERE THE CHILD'S INFERRED ANXIETY OVER NON-PERFORMANCE OF SELF-RELIANT BEHAVIOR IS HIGH (37) B-B-C	63	3 34 10 29 XSQ= 2.97 PHI= -0.198 XP = 0.0847
346	LEAN TOWARD BEING THOSE 0.92 OF WHERE THE CHILD'S INFERRED ANXIETY OVER PERFORMANCE OF SELF-RELIANT BEHAVIOR IS LOW (39) B-B-C	13	346	LEAN TOWARD BEING THOSE 0.57 OF WHERE THE CHILD'S INFERRED ANXIETY OVER PERFORMANCE OF SELF-RELIANT BEHAVIOR IS HIGH (37) B-B-C	63	1 36 12 27 XSQ= 8.66 PHI= -0.338 XP = 0.0032

347	TILT TCWARD BEING THCSE 0.85 OF 13 WHERE THE CHILD'S INFERREC CONFLICT REGARDING SELF-RELIANT BEHAVIOR IS LCW (39) B-B-C	347	TILT TOWARD BEING THOSE 0.56 OF 63 WHERE THE CHILD'S INFERRED CCNFLICT REGARDING SELF-RELIANT BEHAVIOR IS HIGH (37) B-B-C	2 35 11 28 XSQ= 5.45 PHI= -0.268 XP = 0.0196
353	TILT TCWARD BEING THCSE 0.77 OF 13 WHERE THE CHILD-S INFERREC ANXIETY OVER NCN-PERFORMANCE CF CBECIENT BEHAVIOR IS LCW (32) B-B-C	353	TILT TOWARD BEING THOSE 0.64 OF 61 WHERE THE CHILD'S INFERRED ANXIETY OVER NON-PERFORMANCE OF OBEDIENT BEHAVIOR IS HIGH (42) B-B-C	3 39 10 22 XSQ= 5.72 PHI= -0.278 XP = 0.0168
370	TEND TC BE THCSE 0.93 OF 67 WHERE THE SEGREGATION CF ACOLESCENT BOYS IS ABSENT (148)	370	TEND TO BE THOSE 0.51 CF 176 WHERE THE SEGREGATION OF ADCLESCENT BOYS IS COMPLETE OR PARTIAL (95)	5 90 62 86 XSQ= 37.06 PHI= -0.391 XP = 0.
377	TEND MCRE TO BE THCSE 0.95 OF 91 WHERE MALE GENITAL MUTILATION IS ABSENT (242)	377	TEND LESS TO BE THOSE 0.67 CF 234 WHERE MALE GENITAL MUTILATICN IS ABSENT (242)	5 78 86 156 XSQ= 25.26 PHI= -0.279 XP = 0.0000
391	DRIFT TCWARD BEING THOSE 0.61 OF 49 WHERE PREMARITAL SEX RELATIONS ARE STRCNGLY PUNISHED AND IN FACT RARE, OR WEAKLY PUNISHED ANC IN FACT NCT RARE (89) JTW,EA	391	DRIFT TOWARD BEING THOSE 0.55 OF 130 WHERE PREMARITAL SEX RELATICNS ARE PUNISHED ONLY IF PREGNANCY RESULTS, OR FREELY PERMITTED (90) JTW,EA	30 59 19 71 XSQ= 2.97 PHI= 0.129 XP = 0.0850
402	TILT TCWARC BEING THCSE 0.75 OF 16 WHERE EXPLANATICNS CF ILLNESS OF AN CRAL NATURE ARE ABSENT (30) W-C	402	TILT TOWARD BEING THOSE 0.60 OF 45 WHERE EXPLANATICNS OF ILLNESS OF AN ORAL NATURE ARE PRESENT (31) W-C	4 27 12 18 XSQ= 4.47 PHI= -0.271 XP = 0.0345
403	LEAN MCRE TCWARC BEINC THCSE 0.94 OF 16 WHERE EXPLANATICNS OF ILLNESS CF AN ANAL NATURE ARE ABSENT (38) W-C	403	LEAN LESS TOWARD BEING THOSE 0.51 CF 45 WHERE EXPLANATIONS OF ILLNESS OF AN ANAL NATURE ARE ABSENT (38) W-C	1 22 15 23 XSQ= 7.41 PHI= -0.349 XP = 0.0065
417	DRIFT LESS TCWARD BEING THCSE 0.58 OF 12 WHERE WARFARE IS PREVALENT (34) LWS	417	DRIFT MORE TOWARD BEING THCSE 0.87 CF 31 WHERE WARFARE IS PREVALENT (34) LWS	7 27 5 4 XSQ= 2.76 PHI= -0.253 XP = 0.0966
427	DRIFT MORE TCWARD BEING THCSE 0.68 OF 41 WHERE A HIGH GCC, IF PRESENT, IS ACTIVE, RATHER THAN INACTIVE (87) GES,EA	427	DRIFT LESS TOWARD BEING THCSE 0.51 OF 115 WHERE A HIGH GOD, IF PRESENT, IS ACTIVE, RATHER THAN INACTIVE (87) GES,EA	28 59 13 56 XSQ= 2.88 PHI= 0.136 XP = 0.0896

433	IN ALL CASES ARE THOSE WHERE BELIEF IN REINCARNATION IS ABSENT (28) GES	1.00 OF 8	433	DRIFT LESS TOWARD BEING THOSE WHERE BELIEF IN REINCARNATION IS ABSENT (28) GES	0.67 OF 30	0 10 8 20 XSQ= 2.10 PHI= -0.235 EP = 0.0821
451	TILT TOWARD BEING THOSE WHERE TOTEMISM IS UNIMPORTANT OR ABSENT (12) LWS	0.86 OF 7	451	TILT TOWARD BEING THOSE WHERE TOTEMISM IS PRESENT (15) LWS	0.70 OF 20	1 14 6 6 XSQ= 4.46 PHI= -0.406 EP = 0.0237
458	LEAN MORE TOWARD BEING THOSE WHERE GAMES, IF PRESENT, DO NOT INCLUDE GAMES OF STRATEGY (119) R-A-B,EA	0.86 OF 50	458	LEAN LESS TOWARD BEING THOSE WHERE GAMES, IF PRESENT, DO NOT INCLUDE GAMES OF STRATEGY (119) R-A-B,EA	0.63 OF 121	7 45 43 76 XSQ= 7.93 PHI= -0.215 XP = 0.0049
459	TILT TOWARD BEING THOSE WHERE GAMES, IF PRESENT, INCLUDE GAMES OF CHANCE (82) R-A-B,EA	0.62 OF 50	459	TILT TOWARD BEING THOSE WHERE GAMES, IF PRESENT, DO NOT INCLUDE GAMES OF CHANCE (89) R-A-B,EA	0.58 OF 121	31 51 19 70 XSQ= 4.82 PHI= 0.168 XP = 0.0281
471	IN ALL CASES ARE THOSE WHERE SECRET SOCIETIES ARE UNIMPORTANT OR ABSENT (14) LWS	1.00 OF 7	471	TILT TOWARD BEING THOSE WHERE SECRET SOCIETIES ARE PRESENT (9) LWS	0.56 OF 16	0 9 7 7 XSQ= 4.32 PHI= -0.434 EP = 0.0189
476	IN ALL CASES ARE THOSE WHERE THE DEGREE OF INSOBRIETY IS STRONG (31) DH	1.00 OF 14	476	LEAN TOWARD BEING THOSE WHERE THE DEGREE OF INSOBRIETY IS MODERATE OR SLIGHT (18) DH	0.51 OF 35	14 17 0 18 XSQ= 9.28 PHI= 0.435 XP = 0.0023

193 CULTURES WHERE THE KINDRED IS SPECIFICALLY REPORTED PRESENT (68)	193 CULTURES WHERE THE KINDRED IS NOT SPECIFICALLY REPORTED PRESENT, OR IS ABSENT (332)

BACKGROUND ON PAGE 108 — SUBJECT ONLY

68 IN LEFT COLUMN

ALBANIANS	ALCRESE	AMERICANS	ARYANS	BEMBA	BENGALI	BURMESE	CARAJA	CHEYENNE	CHOCO
CZECHS	DUSUN	DUTCH	FOX	GILBERTESE	HANUNOO	HAWAIIANS	HUICHOL	HUTSUL	IBAN
ICELANDERS	IFUGAO	INGASSANA	IRISH	JAPANESE	JAVANESE	KHALKA	KIOW-APACHE	KUMYK	KUNG
KURTATCHI	KWAKIUTL	LAKALAI	LAPPS	LOZI	MALAYS	MAMBILA	MAORI	MARQUESANS	MARSHALLESE
MIAO	NANDI	NYAKYUSA	OKINAWANS	PAIWAN	PATHAN	PUKAPUKA	RAROIANS	RWALA	SAGADA
SIMBOESE	SUBANUN	TAGBANUA	TARAHUMARA	TAREUMIUT	TENINO	TETON	THAI	TIGRINYA	TIKOPIA
TOKELAU	TRISTAN	TWANA	WALLOONS	WANTOAT	WICHITA	WOLEAIANS	YORUBA		

332 IN RIGHT COLUMN

	Left column (68)			Right column (332)		Statistics
3	DRIFT MORE TOWARD BEING THOSE LOCATED OUTSIDE OF AFRICA (320)	0.88 OF 68	3	DRIFT LESS TOWARD BEING THOSE LOCATED OUTSIDE OF AFRICA (320)	0.78 OF 332	8 72 60 260 XSQ= 2.88 PHI= -0.085 XP = 0.0897
4	TILT LESS TOWARD BEING THOSE LOCATED OUTSIDE OF THE CIRCUM-MEDITERRANEAN (355)	0.81 OF 68	4	TILT MORE TOWARD BEING THOSE LOCATED OUTSIDE OF THE CIRCUM-MEDITERRANEAN (355)	0.90 OF 332	13 32 55 300 XSQ= 4.17 PHI= 0.102 XP = 0.0410
6	TEND LESS TO BE THOSE LOCATED OUTSIDE OF THE INSULAR PACIFIC (330)	0.65 OF 68	6	TEND MORE TO BE THOSE LOCATED OUTSIDE OF THE INSULAR PACIFIC (330)	0.86 OF 332	24 46 44 286 XSQ= 16.51 PHI= 0.203 XP = 0.0000
9	LEAN MORE TOWARD BEING THOSE LOCATED OUTSIDE OF SOUTH AMERICA (335)	0.97 OF 68	9	LEAN LESS TOWARD BEING THOSE LOCATED OUTSIDE OF SOUTH AMERICA (335)	0.81 OF 332	2 63 66 269 XSQ= 9.52 PHI= -0.154 XP = 0.0020
44	DRIFT MORE TOWARD BEING THOSE WHERE SETTLEMENTS ARE FIXED (222)	0.78 OF 55	44	DRIFT LESS TOWARD BEING THOSE WHERE SETTLEMENTS ARE FIXED (222)	0.65 OF 277	43 179 12 98 XSQ= 3.22 PHI= 0.099 XP = 0.0727

62	DRIFT MORE TOWARD BEING THOSE 0.68 OF 68 WHERE HUSBANDRY OF SOME KIND IS PRESENT (228)	62	DRIFT LESS TOWARD BEING THOSE 0.55 OF 332 WHERE HUSBANDRY OF SOME KIND IS PRESENT (228)	46 182 22 150 XSQ= 3.28 PHI= 0.091 XP = 0.0700
79	LEAN LESS TOWARD BEING THOSE 0.74 OF 39 WHERE NO CITY IS PRESENT (201)	79	LEAN MORE TOWARD BEING THOSE 0.93 OF 185 WHERE NO CITY IS PRESENT (201)	10 13 29 172 XSQ= 10.18 PHI= 0.213 XP = 0.0014
80	TILT LESS TOWARD BEING THOSE 0.69 OF 39 WHERE NO CITY OR TOWN IS PRESENT (185)	80	TILT MORE TOWARD BEING THOSE 0.85 OF 185 WHERE NO CITY OR TOWN IS PRESENT (185)	12 27 27 158 XSQ= 4.79 PHI= 0.146 XP = 0.0286
86	DRIFT TOWARD BEING THOSE 0.61 OF 44 WHERE THE LEVEL OF POLITICAL INTEGRATION IS THE LARGE STATE, THE LITTLE STATE, OR THE MINIMAL STATE (148) GPM	86	DRIFT TOWARD BEING THOSE 0.53 OF 260 WHERE THE LEVEL OF POLITICAL INTEGRATION IS THE AUTONOMOUS COMMUNITY, OR THE FAMILY (156) GPM	27 121 17 139 XSQ= 2.74 PHI= 0.095 XP = 0.0976
94	DRIFT LESS TOWARD BEING THOSE 0.81 OF 54 WHERE THE HIERARCHY OF NATIONAL JURISDICTION HAS TWO, ONE, OR NO LEVELS (296) GES,EA	94	DRIFT MORE TOWARD BEING THOSE 0.91 OF 276 WHERE THE HIERARCHY OF NATIONAL JURISDICTION HAS TWO, ONE, OR NO LEVELS (296) GES,EA	10 24 44 252 XSQ= 3.71 PHI= 0.106 XP = 0.0540
95	TILT LESS TOWARD BEING THOSE 0.63 OF 54 WHERE THE HIERARCHY OF NATIONAL JURISDICTION HAS ONE OR NO LEVELS (254) GES,EA	95	TILT MORE TOWARD BEING THOSE 0.80 OF 276 WHERE THE HIERARCHY OF NATIONAL JURISDICTION HAS ONE OR NO LEVELS (254) GES,EA	20 56 34 220 XSQ= 6.23 PHI= 0.137 XP = 0.0125
96	DRIFT MORE TOWARD BEING THOSE 0.65 OF 54 WHERE THE HIERARCHY OF NATIONAL JURISDICTION HAS FOUR, THREE, TWO OR ONE LEVEL (174) GES,EA	96	DRIFT LESS TOWARD BEING THOSE 0.50 OF 276 WHERE THE HIERARCHY OF NATIONAL JURISDICTION HAS FOUR, THREE, TWO OR ONE LEVEL (174) GES,EA	35 139 19 137 XSQ= 3.23 PHI= 0.099 XP = 0.0724
102	DRIFT MORE TOWARD BEING THOSE 0.65 OF 65 WHERE CLASS STRATIFICATION IS PRESENT (203)	102	DRIFT LESS TOWARD BEING THOSE 0.51 OF 318 WHERE CLASS STRATIFICATION IS PRESENT (203)	42 161 23 157 XSQ= 3.70 PHI= 0.098 XP = 0.0546
107	DRIFT LESS TOWARD BEING THOSE 0.67 OF 42 WHERE CLASS STRATIFICATION, IF PRESENT, IS BASED ON SOMETHING OTHER THAN OCCUPATIONAL STATUS (160)	107	DRIFT MORE TOWARD BEING THOSE 0.82 OF 161 WHERE CLASS STRATIFICATION, IF PRESENT, IS BASED ON SOMETHING OTHER THAN OCCUPATIONAL STATUS (160)	14 29 28 132 XSQ= 3.81 PHI= 0.137 XP = 0.0509

129	IN ALL CASES ARE THOSE WHERE WEAVING IS MAINLY DONE BY FEMALES (73)	1.00 OF 13	129	TILT LESS TOWARD BEING THOSE WHERE WEAVING IS MAINLY DONE BY FEMALES (73)	0.66 OF 91	0 31 13 60 XSQ= 4.79 PHI= -0.215 XP = 0.0287
175	DRIFT MORE TOWARD BEING THOSE WHERE THE COMMUNITY IS 'KIN-HETEROGENEOUS,' I. E. OTHER THAN A CLAN COMMUNITY OR A DEME (260)	0.78 OF 68	175	DRIFT LESS TOWARD BEING THOSE WHERE THE COMMUNITY IS 'KIN-HETEROGENEOUS,' I. E. OTHER THAN A CLAN COMMUNITY OR A DEME (260)	0.66 OF 314	15 107 53 207 XSQ= 3.18 PHI= -0.091 XP = 0.0745
176	TEND MORE TO BE THOSE WHERE THE COMMUNITY IS OTHER THAN A CLAN-COMMUNITY OR A COMMUNITY STRUCTURED OR SEGMENTED ON A CLAN BASIS (213)	0.78 OF 68	176	TEND LESS TO BE THOSE WHERE THE COMMUNITY IS OTHER THAN A CLAN-COMMUNITY OR A COMMUNITY STRUCTURED OR SEGMENTED ON A CLAN BASIS (213)	0.51 OF 314	15 154 53 160 XSQ= 15.42 PHI= -0.201 XP = 0.0001
177	TEND MORE TO BE THOSE WHERE THE COMMUNITY IS OTHER THAN A SINGLE CLAN-COMMUNITY AND EXOGAMOUS (305)	0.97 OF 68	177	TEND LESS TO BE THOSE WHERE THE COMMUNITY IS OTHER THAN A SINGLE CLAN-COMMUNITY AND EXOGAMOUS (305)	0.76 OF 314	2 75 66 239 XSQ= 13.96 PHI= -0.191 XP = 0.0002
179	DRIFT LESS TOWARD BEING THOSE WHERE THE COMMUNITY IS OTHER THAN STRUCTURED ON A NON-CLAN BASIS AND COMMONLY EXOGAMOUS (340)	0.82 OF 68	179	DRIFT MORE TOWARD BEING THOSE WHERE THE COMMUNITY IS OTHER THAN STRUCTURED ON A NON-CLAN BASIS AND COMMONLY EXOGAMOUS (340)	0.90 OF 314	12 30 56 284 XSQ= 2.96 PHI= 0.088 XP = 0.0854
180	DRIFT MORE TOWARD BEING THOSE WHERE THE COMMUNITY IS COMMONLY NON-EXOGAMOUS, RATHER THAN EXOGAMOUS (258)	0.78 OF 68	180	DRIFT LESS TOWARD BEING THOSE WHERE THE COMMUNITY IS COMMONLY NON-EXOGAMOUS, RATHER THAN EXOGAMOUS (258)	0.65 OF 314	15 109 53 205 XSQ= 3.53 PHI= -0.096 XP = 0.0604
181	DRIFT LESS TOWARD BEING THOSE WHERE THE COMMUNITY IS OTHER THAN A DEME (337)	0.81 OF 68	181	DRIFT MORE TOWARD BEING THOSE WHERE THE COMMUNITY IS OTHER THAN A DEME (337)	0.90 OF 314	13 32 55 282 XSQ= 3.47 PHI= 0.095 XP = 0.0625
188	TEND TO BE THOSE WHERE THE KIN GROUP IS EXCLUSIVELY COGNATIC (148)	0.68 OF 68	188	TEND TO BE THOSE WHERE THE KIN GROUP IS OTHER THAN EXCLUSIVELY COGNATIC (252)	0.69 OF 332	46 102 22 230 XSQ= 31.45 PHI= 0.280 XP = 0.
192	TEND TO BE THOSE WHERE THE ONLY KIN GROUP PRESENT IS A KINDRED OR ELSE BILATERAL DESCENT IS INFERRED (111)	0.51 OF 68	192	TEND TO BE THOSE OTHER THAN WHERE THE ONLY KIN GROUP PRESENT IS A KINDRED OR ELSE BILATERAL DESCENT IS INFERRED (289)	0.77 OF 332	35 76 33 256 XSQ= 21.59 PHI= 0.232 XP = 0.0000

```
196  DRIFT MORE TOWARD BEING THCSE  0.80 OF  50    196  DRIFT LESS TOWARD BEING THOSE  0.67 OF 231         40  154
     WHERE INDIVIDUAL RIGHTS IN REAL PROPERTY,          WHERE INDIVIDUAL RIGHTS IN REAL PROPERTY,            10   77
     AND RULES FOR INHERITANCE,                         AND RULES FOR INHERITANCE,                       XSQ=    2.82
     ARE PRESENT  (194)                                 ARE PRESENT  (194)                               PHI=   0.100
                                                                                                         XP =  0.0929

197  TEND LESS TO BE THCSE          0.63 OF  40    197  TEND MORE TO BE THOSE          0.91 OF 154         25  140
     WHERE RULES FOR THE INHERITANCE OF                 WHERE RULES FOR THE INHERITANCE OF                   15   14
     REAL PROPERTY, IF PRESENT,                         REAL PROPERTY, IF PRESENT,                       XSQ=   17.98
     FAVOR EITHER THE MALE HEIR OR LINE,                FAVOR EITHER THE MALE HEIR OR LINE,              PHI=  -0.304
     OR THE FEMALE HEIR CR LINE  (165)                  OR THE FEMALE HEIR OR LINE  (165)                XP =  0.0000

201  TEND LESS TO BE THCSE          0.60 OF  68    201  TEND MORE TO BE THOSE          0.89 OF 330         41  293
     WHERE MARITAL RESIDENCE IS                         WHERE MARITAL RESIDENCE IS                           27   37
     NON-OPTIONAL, RATHER THAN                          NON-OPTIONAL, RATHER THAN                        XSQ=   31.84
     AMBILOCAL CR NEOLOCAL  (334)                       AMBILOCAL OR NEOLOCAL  (334)                     PHI=  -0.283
                                                                                                         XP =  0.

204  TEND LESS TO BE THCSE          0.53 OF  58    204  TEND MORE TO BE THOSE          0.87 OF 276         31  239
     WHERE MARITAL RESIDENCE IS                         WHERE MARITAL RESIDENCE IS                           27   37
     PATRILOCAL, VIRILOCAL, OR AVUNCULOCAL,             PATRILOCAL, VIRILOCAL, OR AVUNCULOCAL,           XSQ=   31.89
     RATHER THAN                                        RATHER THAN                                      PHI=  -0.309
     AMBILOCAL CR NEOLOCAL  (270)                       AMBILOCAL OR NEOLOCAL  (270)                     XP =  0.

207  LEAN TOWARD BEING THOSE        0.73 OF  37    207  LEAN TOWARD BEING THOSE        0.59 OF  91         10   54
     WHERE MARITAL RESIDENCE IS                         WHERE MARITAL RESIDENCE IS                           27   37
     AMBILOCAL CR NEOLOCAL, RATHER THAN                 MATRILOCAL OR UXORILOCAL, RATHER THAN            XSQ=    9.73
     MATRILOCAL OR UXORILOCAL  (64)                     AMBILOCAL OR NEOLOCAL  (64)                      PHI=  -0.276
                                                                                                         XP =  0.0018

213  LEAN MORE TOWARD BEING THCSE   0.69 OF  62    213  LEAN LESS TOWARD BEING THOSE   0.50 OF 308         19  153
     WHERE FIRST COUSIN MARRIAGE IS                     WHERE FIRST COUSIN MARRIAGE IS                       43  155
     NOT PERMITTED  (198)                               NOT PERMITTED  (198)                             XSQ=    6.77
                                                                                                         PHI=  -0.135
                                                                                                         XP =  0.0093

214  IN ALL CASES ARE THCSE         1.00 OF  19    214  DRIFT LESS TOWARD BEING THOSE  0.82 CF 153          0   28
     WHERE FIRST COUSIN MARRIAGE,                       WHERE FIRST COUSIN MARRIAGE,                         19  125
     IF PERMITTED,                                      IF PERMITTED,                                    XSQ=    2.92
     IS OTHER THAN UNILATERAL  (144)                    IS OTHER THAN UNILATERAL  (144)                  PHI=  -0.130
                                                                                                         XP =  0.0875

220  TILT MORE TOWARD BEING THCSE   0.87 OF  62    220  TILT LESS TOWARD BEING THOSE   0.71 OF 308          8   89
     WHERE FIRST COUSIN MARRIAGE                        WHERE FIRST COUSIN MARRIAGE                          54  219
     IN SOME FORM CR OTHER                              IN SOME FORM OR OTHER                            XSQ=    6.02
     IS NOT PRESCRIBED CR PREFERREC  (273)              IS NOT PRESCRIBED OR PREFERRED  (273)            PHI=  -0.128
                                                                                                         XP =  0.0141

221  TILT MORE TOWARD BEING THCSE   0.98 OF  62    221  TILT LESS TOWARD BEING THOSE   0.89 OF 308          1   34
     WHERE MATRILATERAL CROSS-COUSIN MARRIAGE           WHERE MATRILATERAL CROSS-COUSIN MARRIAGE             61  274
     IS NOT PRESCRIBED CR PREFERREC  (335)              IS NOT PRESCRIBED OR PREFERRED  (335)            XSQ=    4.31
                                                                                                         PHI=  -0.108
                                                                                                         XP =  0.0379
```

224	DRIFT MORE TOWARD BEING THOSE WHERE COUSIN MARRIAGE IS PREFERENTIALLY OR PERMISSIVELY SYMMETRICAL, RATHER THAN EITHER PATRI- OR MATRILATERAL (106)	0.84 OF 19	224	DRIFT LESS TOWARD BEING THOSE WHERE COUSIN MARRIAGE IS PREFERENTIALLY OR PERMISSIVELY SYMMETRICAL, RATHER THAN EITHER PATRI- OR MATRILATERAL (106)	0.59 OF 153	3 63 16 90 XSQ= 3.60 PHI= -0.145 XP = 0.0579
234	TEND TO BE THOSE WHERE THE COUSIN TERMINOLOGY IS OF ESKIMO OR HAWAIIAN TYPE, RATHER THAN CROW, OMAHA, OR IROQUOIS TYPE (170)	0.82 OF 65	234	TEND TO BE THOSE WHERE THE COUSIN TERMINOLOGY IS OF CROW, OMAHA, OR IROQUOIS TYPE, RATHER THAN ESKIMO OR HAWAIIAN TYPE (152)	0.54 OF 257	12 140 53 117 XSQ= 25.57 PHI= -0.282 XP = 0.0000
241	LEAN LESS TOWARD BEING THOSE WHERE THE FAMILY, IF EXTENDED, IS LARGE OR SMALL, RATHER THAN STEM (187)	0.74 OF 38	241	LEAN MORE TOWARD BEING THOSE WHERE THE FAMILY, IF EXTENDED, IS LARGE OR SMALL, RATHER THAN STEM (187)	0.91 OF 175	28 159 10 16 XSQ= 7.06 PHI= -0.182 XP = 0.0079
242	LEAN LESS TOWARD BEING THOSE WHERE MARRIAGE IS COMMONLY OR OCCASIONALLY POLYGYNOUS, RATHER THAN MONOGAMOUS (314)	0.66 OF 67	242	LEAN MORE TOWARD BEING THOSE WHERE MARRIAGE IS COMMONLY OR OCCASIONALLY POLYGYNOUS, RATHER THAN MONOGAMOUS (314)	0.82 OF 328	44 270 23 58 XSQ= 8.46 PHI= -0.146 XP = 0.0036
256	IN ALL CASES ARE THOSE WHERE GRANDPARENT AND GRANDCHILD ARE FRIENDLY EQUALS (25) CA	1.00 OF 9	256	DRIFT LESS TOWARD BEING THOSE WHERE GRANDPARENT AND GRANDCHILD ARE FRIENDLY EQUALS (25) CA	0.67 OF 24	9 16 0 8 XSQ= 2.35 PHI= 0.267 EP = 0.0731
259	DRIFT TOWARD BEING THOSE WHERE THE SEVERITY OF MOTHER-IN-LAW AVOIDANCE IS LOW (20) WNS	0.73 OF 11	259	DRIFT TOWARD BEING THOSE WHERE THE SEVERITY OF MOTHER-IN-LAW AVOIDANCE IS HIGH (26) WNS	0.66 OF 35	3 23 8 12 XSQ= 3.59 PHI= -0.279 XP = 0.0581
263	DRIFT TOWARD BEING THOSE WHERE WIVES ARE OBTAINED BY RELATIVELY EASY MEANS, NAMELY BY TOKEN BRIDE-PRICE, GIFT EXCHANGE, ABSENCE OF ANY CONSIDERATION, OR RECEIPT OF DOWRY (162)	0.51 OF 68	263	DRIFT TOWARD BEING THOSE WHERE WIVES ARE OBTAINED BY RELATIVELY DIFFICULT MEANS, NAMELY BY BRIDE-PRICE, BRIDE-SERVICE, OR EXCHANGING A FEMALE RELATIVE (233)	0.61 OF 327	33 200 35 127 XSQ= 3.21 PHI= -0.090 XP = 0.0732
295	DRIFT TOWARD BEING THOSE WHERE THE SEVERITY OF PUNISHMENT FOR ABORTION IS LOW OR ABSENT (12) BCA	0.86 OF 7	295	DRIFT TOWARD BEING THOSE WHERE THE SEVERITY OF PUNISHMENT FOR ABORTION IS HIGH (11) BCA	0.63 OF 16	1 10 6 6 XSQ= 2.81 PHI= -0.350 EP = 0.0686
299	DRIFT MORE TOWARD BEING THOSE WHERE THE POST-PARTUM SEX TABOO LASTS ONE YEAR OR LESS (89)	0.90 OF 21	299	DRIFT LESS TOWARD BEING THOSE WHERE THE POST-PARTUM SEX TABOO LASTS ONE YEAR OR LESS (89)	0.68 OF 103	2 33 19 70 XSQ= 3.32 PHI= -0.164 XP = 0.0683

No.		No.		
304	TILT TOWARD BEING THOSE 0.80 OF 10 WHERE THE EARLY ANAL SATISFACTION POTENTIAL IS HIGH (19) W-C	304	TILT TOWARD BEING THOSE 0.65 OF 31 WHERE THE EARLY ANAL SATISFACTION POTENTIAL IS LOW (22) W-C	8 11 2 20 XSQ= 4.37 PHI= 0.326 XP = 0.0366
307	TILT MORE TOWARD BEING THOSE 0.92 OF 13 WHERE THE EARLY AGGRESSION SATISFACTION POTENTIAL IS HIGH (33) W-C	307	TILT LESS TOWARD BEING THOSE 0.54 OF 39 WHERE THE EARLY AGGRESSION SATISFACTION POTENTIAL IS HIGH (33) W-C	12 21 1 18 XSQ= 4.67 PHI= 0.300 XP = 0.0307
325	TILT TOWARD BEING THOSE 0.86 OF 14 WHERE THE DEGREE OF DIFFUSION AMONG THE INFANT'S NURTURANT AGENTS IS HIGH (42) B-B-C	325	TILT TOWARD BEING THOSE 0.50 OF 60 WHERE THE DEGREE OF DIFFUSION AMONG THE INFANT'S NURTURANT AGENTS IS LOW (32) B-B-C	12 30 2 30 XSQ= 4.53 PHI= 0.248 XP = 0.0332
370	TILT MORE TOWARD BEING THOSE 0.76 OF 46 WHERE THE SEGREGATION OF ADOLESCENT BOYS IS ABSENT (148)	370	TILT LESS TOWARD BEING THOSE 0.57 OF 197 WHERE THE SEGREGATION OF ADOLESCENT BOYS IS ABSENT (148)	11 84 35 113 XSQ= 4.73 PHI= -0.140 XP = 0.0296
385	IN ALL CASES ARE THOSE 1.00 OF 16 WHERE SEXUAL EXPRESSION BY THE YOUNG IS SEMI-RESTRICTED OR PERMITTED (64) F-B	385	TILT LESS TOWARD BEING THOSE 0.69 OF 70 WHERE SEXUAL EXPRESSION BY THE YOUNG IS SEMI-RESTRICTED OR PERMITTED (64) F-B	0 22 16 48 XSQ= 5.21 PHI= -0.246 XP = 0.0225
400	LEAN TOWARD BEING THOSE 0.88 OF 8 WHERE HOMOSEXUAL ACTIVITY IS PROHIBITED (22) F-B	400	LEAN TOWARD BEING THOSE 0.70 OF 50 WHERE HOMOSEXUAL ACTIVITY IS PERMITTED (36) F-B	7 15 1 35 XSQ= 7.40 PHI= 0.357 XP = 0.0065
405	TILT TOWARD BEING THOSE 0.86 OF 14 WHERE EXPLANATIONS OF ILLNESS OF A DEPENDENCE NATURE ARE PRESENT (34) W-C	405	TILT TOWARD BEING THOSE 0.53 OF 47 WHERE EXPLANATIONS OF ILLNESS OF A DEPENDENCE NATURE ARE ABSENT (27) W-C	12 22 2 25 XSQ= 5.14 PHI= 0.290 XP = 0.0234
428	DRIFT MORE TOWARD BEING THOSE 0.89 OF 19 WHERE A HIGH GOD, IF PRESENT AND ACTIVE, SUPPORTS HUMAN MORALITY, RATHER THAN NOT SUPPORTING IT (61) GES,EA	428	DRIFT LESS TOWARD BEING THOSE 0.65 OF 68 WHERE A HIGH GOD, IF PRESENT AND ACTIVE, SUPPORTS HUMAN MORALITY, RATHER THAN NOT SUPPORTING IT (61) GES,EA	17 44 2 24 XSQ= 3.25 PHI= 0.193 XP = 0.0716
438	IN ALL CASES ARE THOSE 1.00 OF 7 WHERE OTHER-WORLDLY FEARS OF GHOSTS OR SPIRITS ARE GREATER THAN THIS-WORLDLY FEARS OF HUMANS OR ANIMALS (27) W-C,JFG	438	DRIFT LESS TOWARD BEING THOSE 0.54 OF 37 WHERE OTHER-WORLDLY FEARS OF GHOSTS OR SPIRITS ARE GREATER THAN THIS-WORLDLY FEARS OF HUMANS OR ANIMALS (27) W-C,JFG	7 20 0 17 XSQ= 3.48 PHI= 0.281 XP = 0.0620

193/

451	IN ALL CASES ARE THOSE WHERE TOTEMISM IS UNIMPCRTANT CR ABSENT (12) LWS	1.00 OF 4	451	TILT TOWARD BEING THOSE WHERE TOTEMISM IS PRESENT (15) LWS	0.65 OF 23	0 15 4 8 XSQ= 3.53 PHI= -0.361 EP = 0.0282

194 CULTURES
WHERE THE RAMAGE IS PRESENT (27)

194 CULTURES
WHERE THE RAMAGE IS ABSENT (373)

BACKGROUND ON PAGE 108

SUBJECT ONLY

27 IN LEFT COLUMN

ATAYAL	AZTEC	BALINESE	DUSUN	ELLICE	GILBERTESE	HAWAIIANS	IFUGAO	JAVANESE	JUKUN
KWAKIUTL	LOZI	MACASSARESE	MAMBILA	MANGAIANS	MAORI	MENTAWEI	ONTONG-JAVA	PAIWAN	PALAUANS
RAROIANS	SAGADA	SAMOANS	SIMBOESE	TIV	TOKELAU	ULAWANS			

373 IN RIGHT COLUMN

	Present (27)			Absent (373)		Statistics
5	IN ALL CASES ARE THOSE LOCATED OUTSIDE OF EAST EURASIA (330)	1.00 OF 27	5	TILT LESS TOWARD BEING THOSE LOCATED OUTSIDE OF EAST EURASIA (330)	0.81 OF 373	0 70 27 303 XSQ= 4.91 PHI= -0.111 XP = 0.0267
6	TEND TO BE THOSE LOCATED IN THE INSULAR PACIFIC (70)	0.78 OF 27	6	TEND TO BE THOSE LOCATED OUTSIDE OF THE INSULAR PACIFIC (330)	0.87 OF 373	21 49 6 324 XSQ= 68.46 PHI= 0.414 XP = 0.
9	IN ALL CASES ARE THOSE LOCATED OUTSIDE OF SOUTH AMERICA (335)	1.00 OF 27	9	TILT LESS TOWARD BEING THOSE LOCATED OUTSIDE OF SOUTH AMERICA (335)	0.83 OF 373	0 65 27 308 XSQ= 4.41 PHI= -0.105 XP = 0.0357
16	TILT TOWARD BEING THOSE WHERE THE LATITUDE IS LESS THAN TEN DEGREES (123)	0.52 OF 27	16	TILT TOWARD BEING THOSE WHERE THE LATITUDE IS TEN DEGREES OR GREATER (277)	0.71 OF 373	13 264 14 109 XSQ= 5.04 PHI= -0.112 XP = 0.0248
33	IN ALL CASES ARE THOSE WHERE THE NATURAL ENVIRONMENT IS OTHER THAN 'VERY HARSH,' I.E., DESERT, DESERT GRASSES AND SHRUBS, TUNDRA, OR HIGH PLATEAU STEPPE (341) FWM	1.00 OF 27	33	DRIFT LESS TOWARD BEING THOSE WHERE THE NATURAL ENVIRONMENT IS OTHER THAN 'VERY HARSH,' I.E., DESERT, DESERT GRASSES AND SHRUBS, TUNDRA, OR HIGH PLATEAU STEPPE (341) FWM	0.84 OF 373	0 59 27 314 XSQ= 3.83 PHI= -0.098 XP = 0.0503

42	LEAN TOWARD BEING THOSE 0.67 OF 27 WHERE THE NATURAL ENVIRONMENT IS TROPICAL OR SUB-TROPICAL RAIN FOREST, OR MONSOON FOREST (156) FWM	42	LEAN TOWARD BEING THOSE 0.63 OF 373 WHERE THE NATURAL ENVIRONMENT IS OTHER THAN TROPICAL OR SUB-TROPICAL RAIN FOREST, OR MONSOON FOREST (244) FWM	18 138 9 235 XSQ= 8.11 PHI= 0.142 XP = 0.0044
44	TILT MORE TOWARD BEING THOSE 0.90 OF 21 WHERE SETTLEMENTS ARE FIXED (222)	44	TILT LESS TOWARD BEING THOSE 0.65 OF 311 WHERE SETTLEMENTS ARE FIXED (222)	19 203 2 108 XSQ= 4.56 PHI= 0.117 XP = 0.0327
46	IN ALL CASES ARE THOSE 1.00 OF 21 OTHER THAN WHERE SETTLEMENTS ARE NON-FIXED AND MOVEMENT IS NOMADIC (260)	46	TILT LESS TOWARD BEING THOSE 0.77 OF 311 OTHER THAN WHERE SETTLEMENTS ARE NON-FIXED AND MOVEMENT IS NOMADIC (260)	0 72 21 239 XSQ= 4.92 PHI= -0.122 XP = 0.0266
48	IN ALL CASES ARE THOSE 1.00 OF 6 WHERE THE FOOD SUPPLY IS SECURE, AND FOOD SHORTAGES ARE RARE OR OCCASIONAL (38) MGW	48	TILT TOWARD BEING THOSE 0.56 OF 73 WHERE THE FOOD SUPPLY IS NOT SECURE, AND FOOD SHORTAGES ARE FREQUENT OR ANNUAL (41) MGW	6 32 0 41 XSQ= 4.94 PHI= 0.250 XP = 0.0263
63	LEAN TOWARD BEING THOSE 0.73 OF 15 WHERE HUSBANDRY, IF PRESENT, IS PRINCIPALLY IN THE FORM OF PIGS, SHEEP, OR GOATS, RATHER THAN BOVINE, EQUINE, CAMEL-LIKE, OR DEER-LIKE ANIMALS (74)	63	LEAN TOWARD BEING THOSE 0.70 OF 211 WHERE HUSBANDRY, IF PRESENT, IS PRINCIPALLY IN THE FORM OF BOVINE, EQUINE, CAMEL-LIKE, OR DEER-LIKE ANIMALS, RATHER THAN PIGS, SHEEP, OR GOATS (152)	4 148 11 63 XSQ= 10.13 PHI= -0.212 XP = 0.0015
74	TILT TOWARD BEING THOSE 0.67 OF 18 WHERE POTTERY IS ABSENT (93)	74	TILT TOWARD BEING THOSE 0.63 OF 220 WHERE POTTERY IS PRESENT (145)	6 139 12 81 XSQ= 5.04 PHI= -0.145 XP = 0.0248
86	DRIFT TOWARD BEING THOSE 0.68 OF 22 WHERE THE LEVEL OF POLITICAL INTEGRATION IS THE LARGE STATE, THE LITTLE STATE, OR THE MINIMAL STATE (148) GPM	86	DRIFT TOWARD BEING THOSE 0.53 OF 282 WHERE THE LEVEL OF POLITICAL INTEGRATION IS THE AUTONOMOUS COMMUNITY, OR THE FAMILY (156) GPM	15 133 7 149 XSQ= 2.82 PHI= 0.096 XP = 0.0933
88	DRIFT MORE TOWARD BEING THOSE 0.84 OF 19 WHERE, IF A HEADMANSHIP IS PRESENT, SUCCESSION IS HEREDITARY (165)	88	DRIFT LESS TOWARD BEING THOSE 0.59 OF 252 WHERE, IF A HEADMANSHIP IS PRESENT, SUCCESSION IS HEREDITARY (165)	3 103 16 149 XSQ= 3.67 PHI= -0.116 XP = 0.0553
97	TILT LESS TOWARD BEING THOSE 0.62 OF 21 WHERE THE HIERARCHY OF LOCAL JURISDICTION HAS THREE OR TWO LEVELS (273) GES,EA	97	TILT MORE TOWARD BEING THOSE 0.84 OF 310 WHERE THE HIERARCHY OF LOCAL JURISDICTION HAS THREE OR TWO LEVELS (273) GES,EA	8 50 13 260 XSQ= 5.13 PHI= 0.125 XP = 0.0235

```
 98 DRIFT MORE TOWARD BEING THOSE  0.90 OF  21     98 DRIFT LESS TOWARD BEING THOSE  0.71 OF 310        19  219
    WHERE THE HIERARCHY                               WHERE THE HIERARCHY                                   2   91
    OF LOCAL JURISDICTION HAS                         OF LOCAL JURISDICTION HAS                     XSQ=     2.91
    FOUR OR THREE LEVELS  (238) GES,EA                FOUR OR THREE LEVELS  (238) GES,EA            PHI=    0.094
                                                                                                    XP =   0.0880

100 IN ALL CASES ARE THOSE          1.00 OF  21    100 TILT LESS TOWARD BEING THOSE   0.80 OF 309        21  246
    WHERE HIERARCHIES ARE MORE COMPLEX THAN           WHERE HIERARCHIES ARE MORE COMPLEX THAN               0   63
    THE 'SIMPLEST,' I. E., MORE COMPLEX THAN          THE 'SIMPLEST,' I. E., MORE COMPLEX THAN      XSQ=     4.05
    TWO LOCAL LEVELS WITH                             TWO LOCAL LEVELS WITH                         PHI=    0.111
    NO NATIONAL LEVELS  (267) GES,EA                  NO NATIONAL LEVELS  (267) GES,EA              XP =   0.0441

102 DRIFT MORE TOWARD BEING THOSE  0.73 OF  26    102 DRIFT LESS TOWARD BEING THOSE  0.52 OF 357        19  184
    WHERE CLASS STRATIFICATION IS                     WHERE CLASS STRATIFICATION IS                         7  173
    PRESENT  (203)                                    PRESENT  (203)                                XSQ=     3.69
                                                                                                    PHI=    0.098
                                                                                                    XP =   0.0548

108 TILT TOWARD BEING THOSE         0.63 OF  19    108 TILT TOWARD BEING THOSE         0.66 OF 184        12   62
    WHERE CLASS STRATIFICATION, IF PRESENT,           WHERE CLASS STRATIFICATION, IF PRESENT,               7  122
    IS BASED ON                                       IS BASED ON SOMETHING OTHER THAN              XSQ=     5.24
    A HEREDITARY ARISTOCRACY  (74)                    A HEREDITARY ARISTOCRACY  (129)               PHI=    0.161
                                                                                                    XP =   0.0220

116 IN ALL CASES ARE THOSE          1.00 OF   3    116 DRIFT TOWARD BEING THOSE        0.67 OF  51         3   17
    WHERE OCCUPATIONAL SPECIALIZATION IS              WHERE OCCUPATIONAL SPECIALIZATION IS                  0   34
    FULL-TIME, WHETHER OR NOT FOR                     PART-TIME ONLY  (34) JMH                      XSQ=     2.92
    SURPLUS PRODUCTION  (20) JMH                                                                    PHI=    0.233
                                                                                                    XP =   0.0875

177 TILT MORE TOWARD BEING THOSE   0.96 OF  27    177 TILT LESS TOWARD BEING THOSE   0.79 OF 355         1   76
    WHERE THE COMMUNITY IS OTHER THAN                 WHERE THE COMMUNITY IS OTHER THAN                    26  279
    A SINGLE CLAN-COMMUNITY AND                       A SINGLE CLAN-COMMUNITY AND                   XSQ=     3.85
    EXOGAMOUS  (305)                                  EXOGAMOUS  (305)                              PHI=   -0.100
                                                                                                    XP =   0.0498

178 TILT LESS TOWARD BEING THOSE   0.56 OF  27    178 TILT MORE TOWARD BEING THOSE   0.79 OF 355        12   75
    WHERE THE COMMUNITY IS OTHER THAN                 WHERE THE COMMUNITY IS OTHER THAN                    15  280
    SEGMENTED ON A CLAN BASIS AND                     SEGMENTED ON A CLAN BASIS AND                 XSQ=     6.49
    NON-EXOGAMOUS  (295)                              NON-EXOGAMOUS  (295)                          PHI=    0.130
                                                                                                    XP =   0.0109

180 DRIFT MORE TOWARD BEING THOSE  0.85 OF  27    180 DRIFT LESS TOWARD BEING THOSE  0.66 OF 355         4  120
    WHERE THE COMMUNITY IS                            WHERE THE COMMUNITY IS                               23  235
    COMMONLY NON-EXOGAMOUS, RATHER THAN               COMMONLY NON-EXOGAMOUS, RATHER THAN           XSQ=     3.31
    EXOGAMOUS  (258)                                  EXOGAMOUS  (258)                              PHI=   -0.093
                                                                                                    XP =   0.0690

188 TEND TO BE THOSE                0.89 OF  27    188 TEND TO BE THOSE                0.67 OF 373        24  124
    WHERE THE KIN GROUP IS                            WHERE THE KIN GROUP IS                                3  249
    EXCLUSIVELY COGNATIC  (148)                       OTHER THAN                                    XSQ=    31.10
                                                      EXCLUSIVELY COGNATIC  (252)                   PHI=    0.279
                                                                                                    XP =   0.
```

196	DRIFT MORE TOWARD BEING THOSE 0.94 OF 16 WHERE INDIVIDUAL RIGHTS IN REAL PROPERTY, AND RULES FOR INHERITANCE, ARE PRESENT (194)	196	DRIFT LESS TOWARD BEING THOSE 0.68 OF 265 WHERE INDIVIDUAL RIGHTS IN REAL PROPERTY, AND RULES FOR INHERITANCE, ARE PRESENT (194)	15 179 1 86 XSQ= 3.70 PHI= 0.115 XP = 0.0545
197	LEAN LESS TOWARD BEING THOSE 0.53 OF 15 WHERE RULES FOR THE INHERITANCE OF REAL PROPERTY, IF PRESENT, FAVOR EITHER THE MALE HEIR OR LINE, OR THE FEMALE HEIR OR LINE (165)	197	LEAN MORE TOWARD BEING THOSE 0.88 OF 179 WHERE RULES FOR THE INHERITANCE OF REAL PROPERTY, IF PRESENT, FAVOR EITHER THE MALE HEIR OR LINE, OR THE FEMALE HEIR OR LINE (165)	8 157 7 22 XSQ= 10.30 PHI= -0.230 XP = 0.0013
201	TILT LESS TOWARD BEING THOSE 0.67 OF 27 WHERE MARITAL RESIDENCE IS NON-OPTIONAL, RATHER THAN AMBILOCAL OR NEOLOCAL (334)	201	TILT MORE TOWARD BEING THOSE 0.85 OF 371 WHERE MARITAL RESIDENCE IS NON-OPTIONAL, RATHER THAN AMBILOCAL OR NEOLOCAL (334)	18 316 9 55 XSQ= 5.09 PHI= -0.113 XP = 0.0240
204	TILT LESS TOWARD BEING THOSE 0.63 OF 24 WHERE MARITAL RESIDENCE IS PATRILOCAL, VIRILOCAL, OR AVUNCULOCAL, RATHER THAN AMBILOCAL OR NEOLOCAL (270)	204	TILT MORE TOWARD BEING THOSE 0.82 OF 310 WHERE MARITAL RESIDENCE IS PATRILOCAL, VIRILOCAL, OR AVUNCULOCAL, RATHER THAN AMBILOCAL OR NEOLOCAL (270)	15 255 9 55 XSQ= 4.41 PHI= -0.115 XP = 0.0357
213	LEAN MORE TOWARD BEING THOSE 0.85 OF 26 WHERE FIRST COUSIN MARRIAGE IS NOT PERMITTED (198)	213	LEAN LESS TOWARD BEING THOSE 0.51 OF 344 WHERE FIRST COUSIN MARRIAGE IS NOT PERMITTED (198)	4 168 22 176 XSQ= 9.57 PHI= -0.161 XP = 0.0020
220	TILT MORE TOWARD BEING THOSE 0.96 OF 26 WHERE FIRST COUSIN MARRIAGE IN SOME FORM OR OTHER IS NOT PRESCRIBED OR PREFERRED (273)	220	TILT LESS TOWARD BEING THOSE 0.72 OF 344 WHERE FIRST COUSIN MARRIAGE IN SOME FORM OR OTHER IS NOT PRESCRIBED OR PREFERRED (273)	1 96 25 248 XSQ= 6.04 PHI= -0.128 XP = 0.0140
234	TEND TO BE THOSE 0.96 OF 26 WHERE THE COUSIN TERMINOLOGY IS OF ESKIMO OR HAWAIIAN TYPE, RATHER THAN CROW, OMAHA, OR IROQUOIS TYPE (170)	234	TEND TO BE THOSE 0.51 OF 296 WHERE THE COUSIN TERMINOLOGY IS OF CROW, OMAHA, OR IROQUOIS TYPE, RATHER THAN ESKIMO OR HAWAIIAN TYPE (152)	1 151 25 145 XSQ= 19.49 PHI= -0.246 XP = 0.0000
342	IN ALL CASES ARE THOSE 1.00 OF 5 WHERE THE CHILD'S INFERRED ANXIETY OVER PERFORMANCE OF NURTURANT BEHAVIOR IS HIGH (18) B-B-C	342	TILT TOWARD BEING THOSE 0.68 OF 41 WHERE THE CHILD'S INFERRED ANXIETY OVER PERFORMANCE OF NURTURANT BEHAVIOR IS LOW (28) B-B-C	5 13 0 28 XSQ= 6.09 PHI= 0.364 XP = 0.0136
380	TILT TOWARD BEING THOSE 0.83 OF 6 WHERE SEGREGATION OF GIRLS AT MENARCHE IS ABSENT (20) F-B	380	TILT TOWARD BEING THOSE 0.69 OF 49 WHERE SEGREGATION OF GIRLS AT MENARCHE IS PRESENT (35) F-B	1 34 5 15 XSQ= 4.34 PHI= -0.281 XP = 0.0371

```
472  IN ALL CASES ARE THCSE            1.00 OF   7      472  TILT TOWARD BEING THOSE          0.52 CF  83            7   40
     WHERE THE COMPOSITE NARCISSISM INCEX                    WHERE THE COMPOSITE NARCISSISM INDEX                  0   43
     IS HIGH  (47) PES                                       IS LOW  (43) PES                               XSQ=     5.02
                                                                                                            PHI=    0.236
                                                                                                            XP =   0.0250

473  TILT TOWARD BEING THOSE           0.86 OF   7      473  TILT TOWARD BEING THOSE          0.68 OF  81            6   26
     WHERE SENSITIVITY TO INSULT                             WHERE SENSITIVITY TO INSULT                           1   55
     IS EXTREME  (32) PES                                    IS MODERATE OR NEGLIGIBLE  (56) PES            XSQ=     5.85
                                                                                                            PHI=    0.258
                                                                                                            XP =   0.0155
```

195 CULTURES
WHERE THE KINDRED, RATHER THAN
THE RAMAGE, IS
SPECIFICALLY REPORTED PRESENT (54)

195 CULTURES
WHERE THE RAMAGE, RATHER THAN
THE KINDRED, IS
SPECIFICALLY REPORTED PRESENT (13)

BACKGROUND ON PAGE 108 — SUBJECT ONLY

54 IN LEFT COLUMN

ALBANIANS	ALORESE	AMERICANS	ARYANS	BEMBA	BENGALI	BURMESE	CARAJA	CHEYENNE	CHOCO
CZECHS	DUTCH	FOX	HANUNOO	HUICHOL	HUTSUL	IBAN	ICELANDERS	INGASSANA	IRISH
JAPANESE	KHALKA	KIOW-APACHE	KUMYK	KUNG	KURTATCHI	LAKALAI	LAPPS	MALAYS	MARQUESANS
MARSHALLESE	MIAO	NANDI	NYAKYUSA	OKINAWANS	PATHAN	PUKAPUKA	RWALA	SUBANUN	TAGBANUA
TARAHUMARA	TAREUMIUT	TENINO	TETON	THAI	TIGRINYA	TIKOPIA	TRISTAN	TWANA	WALLOONS
WANTOAT	WICHITA	WOLEAIANS	YORUBA						

13 IN RIGHT COLUMN

ATAYAL	AZTEC	BALINESE	ELLICE	JUKUN	MACASSARESE	MANGAIANS	MENTAWEI	ONTONG-JAVA	PALAUANS
SAMOANS	TIV	ULAWANS							

14 EXCLUDED BECAUSE AMBIGUOUS

DUSUN	GILBERTESE	HAWAIIANS	IFUGAO	JAVANESE	KWAKIUTL	LOZI	MAMBILA	MAORI	PAIWAN
RAROIANS	SAGADA	SIMBOESE	TOKELAU						

319 EXCLUDED BECAUSE IRRELEVANT

6 LEAN TOWARD BEING THOSE LOCATED OUTSIDE OF THE INSULAR PACIFIC (330) — 0.76 OF 54

6 LEAN TOWARD BEING THOSE LOCATED IN THE INSULAR PACIFIC (70) — 0.77 OF 13

13 10
41 3
XSQ= 10.74
PHI= -0.400
XP = 0.0010

14 LEAN LESS TOWARD BEING THOSE WHERE THE LATITUDE IS LESS THAN THIRTY DEGREES (281) — 0.56 OF 54

14 IN ALL CASES ARE THOSE WHERE THE LATITUDE IS LESS THAN THIRTY DEGREES (281) — 1.00 OF 13

24 0
30 13
XSQ= 7.17
PHI= 0.327
XP = 0.0074

15 TILT TOWARD BEING THOSE WHERE THE LATITUDE IS TWENTY DEGREES OR GREATER (183) — 0.57 OF 54

15 TILT TOWARD BEING THOSE WHERE THE LATITUDE IS LESS THAN TWENTY DEGREES (217) — 0.85 OF 13

31 2
23 11
XSQ= 5.82
PHI= 0.295
XP = 0.0159

```
 16  TILT TOWARD BEING THOSE          0.74 OF  54      16  TILT TOWARD BEING THOSE          0.62 OF  13          40     5
     WHERE THE LATITUDE IS                                 WHERE THE LATITUDE IS                                 14     8
     TEN DEGREES OR GREATER  (277)                         LESS THAN TEN DEGREES  (123)                    XSQ=      4.52
                                                                                                           PHI=     0.260
                                                                                                           XP =    0.0335

 36  DRIFT LESS TOWARD BEING THOSE 0.72 OF  54      36  IN ALL CASES ARE THOSE           1.00 OF  13          15     0
     WHERE THE NATURAL ENVIRONMENT IS                      WHERE THE NATURAL ENVIRONMENT IS                      39    13
     OTHER THAN                                            OTHER THAN                                      XSQ=      3.19
     'VERY HARSH,' OR SUB-TROPICAL BUSH, OR                'VERY HARSH,' OR SUB-TROPICAL BUSH, OR          PHI=     0.218
     TEMPERATE GRASSLAND  (292) FWM                        TEMPERATE GRASSLAND  (292) FWM                  XP =    0.0740

 42  DRIFT TOWARD BEING THOSE         0.57 OF  54      42  DRIFT TOWARD BEING THOSE         0.77 OF  13          23    10
     WHERE THE NATURAL ENVIRONMENT IS                      WHERE THE NATURAL ENVIRONMENT IS                      31     3
     OTHER THAN                                            TROPICAL OR SUB-TROPICAL RAIN FOREST, OR        XSQ=      3.66
     TROPICAL OR SUB-TROPICAL RAIN FOREST, OR              MONSOON FOREST  (156) FWM                       PHI=    -0.234
     MONSOON FOREST  (244) FWM                                                                             XP =    0.0556

 63  LEAN TOWARD BEING THOSE          0.72 OF  39      63  LEAN TOWARD BEING THOSE          0.88 OF   8          28     1
     WHERE HUSBANDRY, IF PRESENT,                          WHERE HUSBANDRY, IF PRESENT,                          11     7
     IS PRINCIPALLY IN THE FORM OF                         IS PRINCIPALLY IN THE FORM OF                   XSQ=      7.53
     BOVINE, EQUINE, CAMEL-LIKE, OR DEER-LIKE              PIGS, SHEEP, OR GOATS, RATHER THAN              PHI=     0.400
     ANIMALS, RATHER THAN                                  BOVINE, EQUINE, CAMEL-LIKE, OR DEER-LIKE        XP =    0.0061
     PIGS, SHEEP, OR GOATS  (152)                          ANIMALS  (74)

 88  DRIFT LESS TOWARD BEING THOSE 0.52 OF  31      88  DRIFT MORE TOWARD BEING THOSE 0.89 OF   9             15     1
     WHERE, IF A HEADMANSHIP IS PRESENT,                   WHERE, IF A HEADMANSHIP IS PRESENT,                   16     8
     SUCCESSION IS HEREDITARY  (165)                       SUCCESSION IS HEREDITARY  (165)                 XSQ=      2.63
                                                                                                           PHI=     0.257
                                                                                                           EP =    0.0605

 97  LEAN TOWARD BEING THOSE          0.91 OF  44      97  LEAN TOWARD BEING THOSE          0.55 OF  11           4     6
     WHERE THE HIERARCHY                                   WHERE THE HIERARCHY                                   40     5
     OF LOCAL JURISDICTION HAS                             OF LOCAL JURISDICTION HAS                       XSQ=      9.36
     THREE OR TWO LEVELS  (273) GES,EA                     FOUR LEVELS  (58) GES,EA                        PHI=    -0.412
                                                                                                           XP =    0.0022

 98  DRIFT LESS TOWARD BEING THOSE 0.68 OF  44      98  IN ALL CASES ARE THOSE           1.00 OF  11          30    11
     WHERE THE HIERARCHY                                   WHERE THE HIERARCHY                                   14     0
     OF LOCAL JURISDICTION HAS                             OF LOCAL JURISDICTION HAS                       XSQ=      3.17
     FOUR OR THREE LEVELS  (238) GES,EA                    FOUR OR THREE LEVELS  (238) GES,EA              PHI=    -0.240
                                                                                                           XP =    0.0751

108  TILT TOWARD BEING THOSE          0.75 OF  32     108  TILT TOWARD BEING THOSE          0.78 OF   9           8     7
     WHERE CLASS STRATIFICATION, IF PRESENT,               WHERE CLASS STRATIFICATION, IF PRESENT,               24     2
     IS BASED ON SOMETHING OTHER THAN                      IS BASED ON                                     XSQ=      6.31
     A HEREDITARY ARISTOCRACY  (129)                       A HEREDITARY ARISTOCRACY  (74)                  PHI=    -0.392
                                                                                                           XP =    0.0120

129  IN ALL CASES ARE THOSE           1.00 OF  10     129  DRIFT LESS TOWARD BEING THOSE 0.60 OF   5              0     2
     WHERE WEAVING IS                                      WHERE WEAVING IS                                      10     3
     MAINLY DONE BY FEMALES  (73)                          MAINLY DONE BY FEMALES  (73)                    XSQ=      1.80
                                                                                                           PHI=    -0.347
                                                                                                           EP =    0.0952
```

```
176  LEAN TOWARD BEING THOSE         0.81 OF  54    176  LEAN TOWARD BEING THOSE         0.62 OF  13          10     8
     WHERE THE COMMUNITY IS OTHER THAN                    WHERE THE COMMUNITY IS                                  44     5
     A CLAN-COMMUNITY OR A COMMUNITY                      A CLAN-COMMUNITY OR A COMMUNITY                   XSQ=      7.80
     STRUCTURED OR SEGMENTED                              STRUCTURED OR SEGMENTED                           PHI=    -0.341
     ON A CLAN BASIS  (213)                               ON A CLAN BASIS  (169)                            XP =    0.0052

178  LEAN TOWARD BEING THOSE         0.87 OF  54    178  LEAN TOWARD BEING THOSE         0.54 OF  13           7     7
     WHERE THE COMMUNITY IS OTHER THAN                    WHERE THE COMMUNITY IS                                  47     6
     SEGMENTED ON A CLAN BASIS AND                        SEGMENTED ON A CLAN BASIS AND                     XSQ=      8.27
     NON-EXOGAMOUS  (295)                                 NON-EXOGAMOUS  (87)                               PHI=    -0.351
                                                                                                            XP =    0.0040

184  DRIFT TOWARD BEING THOSE        0.86 OF  22    184  DRIFT TOWARD BEING THOSE        0.67 OF   3           3     2
     WHERE THE LARGEST NON-COGNATIC KIN GROUP             WHERE THE LARGEST NON-COGNATIC KIN GROUP                19     1
     IS SMALLER THAN A PHRATRY, I. E.                     IS THE MOEITY OR PHRATRY  (77)                    XSQ=      1.92
     A SIB OR LINEAGE  (175)                                                                                PHI=    -0.277
                                                                                                            EP =    0.0913

198  DRIFT MORE TOWARD BEING THOSE 0.95 OF  22      198  DRIFT LESS TOWARD BEING THOSE 0.60 OF   5            21     3
     WHERE RULES FOR THE INHERITANCE OF                   WHERE RULES FOR THE INHERITANCE OF                       1     2
     REAL PROPERTY, IF PRESENT,                           REAL PROPERTY, IF PRESENT,                        XSQ=      2.22
     FAVOR THE MALE HEIR OR LINE, RATHER THAN             FAVOR THE MALE HEIR OR LINE, RATHER THAN          PHI=     0.287
     THE FEMALE  (144)                                    THE FEMALE  (144)                                 EP =    0.0786

299  DRIFT TOWARD BEING THOSE        0.89 OF  18    299  DRIFT TOWARD BEING THOSE        0.67 OF   3           2     2
     WHERE THE POST-PARTUM SEX TABOO LASTS                WHERE THE POST-PARTUM SEX TABOO LASTS                   16     1
     ONE YEAR OR LESS  (89)                               LONGER THAN ONE YEAR  (35)                        XSQ=      2.17
                                                                                                            PHI=    -0.322
                                                                                                            EP =    0.0797

304  DRIFT TOWARD BEING THOSE        0.75 OF   8    304  IN ALL CASES ARE THOSE          1.00 OF   3           6     0
     WHERE THE EARLY ANAL SATISFACTION                    WHERE THE EARLY ANAL SATISFACTION                        2     3
     POTENTIAL IS HIGH  (19) W-C                          POTENTIAL IS LOW  (22) W-C                        XSQ=      2.39
                                                                                                            PHI=     0.466
                                                                                                            EP =    0.0606

393  DRIFT TOWARD BEING THOSE        0.82 OF  11    393  IN ALL CASES ARE THOSE          1.00 OF   2           2     2
     WHERE EXTRAMARITAL COITUS IS                         WHERE EXTRAMARITAL COITUS                                9     0
     PERMITTED, RATHER THAN                               IS PUNISHED, RATHER THAN                          XSQ=      2.17
     PUNISHED  (41) F-B                                   PERMITTED  (43) F-B                               PHI=    -0.409
                                                                                                            EP =    0.0769

405  DRIFT TOWARD BEING THOSE        0.80 OF  10    405  DRIFT TOWARD BEING THOSE        0.75 OF   4           8     1
     WHERE EXPLANATIONS OF ILLNESS                        WHERE EXPLANATIONS OF ILLNESS                            2     3
     OF A DEPENDENCE NATURE                               OF A DEPENDENCE NATURE                            XSQ=      1.75
     ARE PRESENT  (34) W-C                                ARE ABSENT  (27) W-C                              PHI=     0.354
                                                                                                            EP =    0.0949
```

196 CULTURES
WHERE INDIVIDUAL RIGHTS IN REAL PROPERTY,
AND RULES FOR INHERITANCE,
ARE PRESENT (194)

196 CULTURES
WHERE INDIVIDUAL RIGHTS IN REAL PROPERTY,
OR RULES FOR INHERITANCE,
ARE ABSENT (87)

BACKGROUND ON PAGE 111

BOTH SUBJECT AND PREDICATE

194 IN LEFT COLUMN

ABOR	AKHA	ALBANIANS	AMBA	AMERICANS	ARAPESH	ARAUCANIANS	ARYANS	ASHANTI	ATAYAL
ATSUGEWI	AYMARA	AZANDE	AZTEC	BABWA	BAJUN	BAMBARA	BAMILEKE	BANCA	BARABRA
BARI	BASQUES	BATAK	BAYA	BEMBA	BHIL	BIRIFOR	BOZC	BRAZILIANS	BULGARIANS
BURMESE	CAGABA	CAMBODIANS	CHAGGA	CHENCHU	CHEREMIS	CHERKESS	CHIBCHA	CHINANTEC	CHIRIGUANO
CHOCO	CHCRTI	CCCRG	CREE	CZECHS	DAGUR	DARD	DELAWARE	DILLING	DOBUANS
DOGON	DCRCBC	DUSUN	DUTCH	EGYPTIANS	ELLICE	ENGA	FCN	FUTAJALONKE	GANDA
GILBERTESE	GISU	HAICA	HANO	HASANIA	HAVASUPAI	HAWAIIANS	HAZARA	HO	HUICHOL
HUTSUL	IBAN	ICELANCERS	IRAQW	IRISH	JAPANESE	JAVANESE	KABYLE	KACHIN	KATAB
KERAKI	KHALKA	KHASI	KHEVSUR	KIKUYU	KISSI	KOHISTANI	KOL	KONSO	KOREANS
KORYAK	KUTENAI	LAKHER	LANGO	LAPPS	LEPCHA	LHOTA NAGA	LIFU	LOLC	LOZI
LUBA	LUC	MAGUZAWA	MALAYS	MAM	MANCHU	MANDAN	MACRI	MARGI	MARICOPA
MARQUESANS	MASAI	MAYA	MBUGWE	MBUNDU	MENTAWEI	MERINA	MIAC	MIN CHINESE	MINCHIA
MONGO	MONGUCR	MOSSI	MOTA	NANDI	NUER	NUPE	NURI	NYAKYUSA	NYANEKA
NYARO	NYCRO	OJIBWA	OKINAWANS	OMAHA	ORAON	PAIWAN	PALAUANS	PAPAGC	PATHAN
PENOBSCOT	PONAPEANS	POPCLUCA	PURARI	PURUM	RAROIANS	REGEIBAT	RIFFIANS	ROMANS	RUNDI
SAGADA	SANTAL	SHILLUK	SHLUH	SINHALESE	SIUAI	SIWANS	SOMALI	SONGHAI	SWAZI
TAGBANUA	TALAMANCA	TALLENSI	TANALA	TANIMBARESE	TARAHUMARA	TEDA	TENDA	TERA	TESO
THAI	TIBETANS	TIGRINYA	TIKOPIA	TIMUCUA	TORAJA	TRISTAN	TRCBRIAND	TRUKESE	TSHIMSHIAN
TURKANA	ULAWANS	VECCA	VIETNAMESE	WANTOAT	WOGEO	WOLOF	WUTE	YAKC	YAPESE
YARURO	YCMBE	YORUBA	ZUNI						

87 IN RIGHT COLUMN

ABIPON	ALACALUF	ANCAMANESE	ARANCA	AWEIKOMA	BASSERI	BERGDAMA	BETE	BOTCCUDO	CAMAYURA
CHEYENNE	CHIR-APACHE	CHCROTI	CHUKCHEE	COMANCHE	COPR ESKIMO	CROW	DIEGUENO	FANG	GARO
GILYAK	GOND	GROS VENTRE	GUAHIBO	HANUNOO	HERERO	HUKUNDIKA	ILA	INCA	INGALIK
KALMYK	KAZAK	KET	KIOW-APACHE	KPE	KUBA	KUNG	MANUS	MATACO	MBUTI
MENDE	MINANGKABAU	MIWCK	MUNCURUCU	MURNGIN	NABESNA	NAMA	NASKAPI	NICCBARESE	NUNIVAK
ONA	PAEZ	PAWNEE	RWALA	SANPOIL	SARSI	SEMANG	SERI	SIRIONO	SOTHO
SUBANUN	TAREUMIUT	TEHUELCHE	TENETEHARA	TENINO	TERENA	TETON	THONGA	TIMBIRA	TIV
TIWI	TODA	TOLOWA	TRUMAI	TUBATULABAL	TUCANO	TUCUNA	TWANA	UTE	VENDA
WASHO	YAGUA	YAHGAN	YAKUT	YOKUTS	YUKAGHIR	YUKI			

119 EXCLUDED BECAUSE UNASCERTAINEC

---

4 LEAN LESS TOWARC BEING THOSE 0.83 OF 194
LOCATED OUTSIDE OF
THE CIRCUM-MEDITERRANEAN (355)

4 LEAN MORE TOWARD BEING THOSE 0.98 OF 87
LOCATED OUTSIDE OF
THE CIRCUM-MEDITERRANEAN (355)

33	2
161	85

XSQ= 10.61
PHI= 0.194
XP = 0.0011

```
 6 DRIFT LESS TOWARD BEING THOSE  0.82 OF 194    6 DRIFT MORE TOWARD BEING THOSE  0.92 OF  87       34     7
   LOCATED OUTSIDE OF                              LOCATED OUTSIDE OF                               160    80
   THE INSULAR PACIFIC  (330)                      THE INSULAR PACIFIC  (330)                    XSQ=    3.60
                                                                                                  PHI=   0.113
                                                                                                  XP =  0.0576

 8 TEND MORE TO BE THOSE          0.89 OF 194    8 TEND LESS TO BE THOSE          0.68 OF  87       21    28
   LOCATED OUTSIDE OF                              LOCATED OUTSIDE OF                               173    59
   NORTH AMERICA  (330)                            NORTH AMERICA  (330)                          XSQ=   17.58
                                                                                                  PHI=  -0.250
                                                                                                  XP =  0.0000

 9 TEND MORE TO BE THOSE          0.94 OF 194    9 TEND LESS TO BE THOSE          0.75 OF  87       11    22
   LOCATED OUTSIDE OF                              LOCATED OUTSIDE OF                               183    65
   SOUTH AMERICA  (335)                            SOUTH AMERICA  (335)                          XSQ=   20.45
                                                                                                  PHI=  -0.270
                                                                                                  XP =  0.0000

15 LEAN TOWARD BEING THOSE        0.57 OF 194   15 LEAN TOWARD BEING THOSE        0.64 OF  87       84    56
   WHERE THE LATITUDE IS                           WHERE THE LATITUDE IS                            110    31
   LESS THAN TWENTY DEGREES  (217)                 TWENTY DEGREES OR GREATER  (183)              XSQ=    9.84
                                                                                                  PHI=  -0.187
                                                                                                  XP =  0.0017

33 LEAN MORE TOWARD BEING THOSE   0.88 OF 194   33 LEAN LESS TOWARD BEING THOSE   0.72 OF  87       24    24
   WHERE THE NATURAL ENVIRONMENT IS                WHERE THE NATURAL ENVIRONMENT IS                 170    63
   OTHER THAN 'VERY HARSH,' I.E., DESERT,          OTHER THAN 'VERY HARSH,' I.E., DESERT,        XSQ=    8.77
   DESERT GRASSES AND SHRUBS, TUNDRA, OR           DESERT GRASSES AND SHRUBS, TUNDRA, OR         PHI=  -0.177
   HIGH PLATEAU STEPPE  (341) FWM                  HIGH PLATEAU STEPPE  (341) FWM                XP =  0.0031

36 TEND TO BE THOSE               0.78 OF 194   36 TEND TO BE THOSE               0.51 OF  87       42    44
   WHERE THE NATURAL ENVIRONMENT IS                WHERE THE NATURAL ENVIRONMENT IS                 152    43
   OTHER THAN                                      'VERY HARSH,' OR SUB-TROPICAL BUSH, OR •      XSQ=   22.32
   'VERY HARSH,' OR SUB-TROPICAL BUSH, OR          TEMPERATE GRASSLAND  (108) FWM                PHI=  -0.282
   TEMPERATE GRASSLAND  (292) FWM                                                                XP =  0.0000

42 DRIFT LESS TOWARD BEING THOSE  0.61 OF 194   42 DRIFT MORE TOWARD BEING THOSE  0.72 OF  87       75    24
   WHERE THE NATURAL ENVIRONMENT IS                WHERE THE NATURAL ENVIRONMENT IS                 119    63
   OTHER THAN                                      OTHER THAN                                    XSQ=    2.76
   TROPICAL OR SUB-TROPICAL RAIN FOREST, OR        TROPICAL OR SUB-TROPICAL RAIN FOREST, OR      PHI=   0.099
   MONSOON FOREST  (244) FWM                       MONSOON FOREST  (244) FWM                     XP =  0.0966

44 TEND TO BE THOSE               0.82 OF 164   44 TEND TO BE THOSE               0.73 OF  77      134    21
   WHERE SETTLEMENTS ARE FIXED  (222)              WHERE SETTLEMENTS ARE NON-FIXED  (110)            30    56
                                                                                                  XSQ=   65.30
                                                                                                  PHI=   0.521
                                                                                                  XP =  0.

46 TEND TO BE THOSE               0.92 OF 164   46 TEND TO BE THOSE               0.56 OF  77       13    43
   OTHER THAN WHERE SETTLEMENTS ARE                WHERE SETTLEMENTS ARE                            151    34
   NON-FIXED AND MOVEMENT IS                       NON-FIXED AND MOVEMENT IS                     XSQ=   64.79
   NOMADIC  (260)                                  NOMADIC  (72)                                 PHI=  -0.518
                                                                                                  XP =  0.
```

47	LEAN TOWARD BEING THOSE WHERE, IF SETTLEMENTS ARE NON-FIXED, MOVEMENT IS NON-NOMADIC, RATHER THAN NOMADIC (38)	0.57 OF 30	47	LEAN TOWARD BEING THOSE WHERE, IF SETTLEMENTS ARE NON-FIXED, MOVEMENT IS NOMADIC, RATHER THAN NON-NOMADIC (72)	0.77 OF 56	13 43 17 13 XSQ= 8.21 PHI= -0.309 XP = 0.0042
51	TEND TO BE THOSE WHERE SUBSISTENCE IS PRIMARILY BY FOOD PRODUCTION -- I. E., AGRICULTURE OR HUSBANDRY -- RATHER THAN BY GATHERING (253)	0.82 OF 194	51	TEND TO BE THOSE WHERE SUBSISTENCE IS PRIMARILY BY FOOD GATHERING -- I. E., HUNTING, FISHING, OR COLLECTING -- RATHER THAN FOOD PRODUCTION (147)	0.70 OF 87	159 26 35 61 XSQ= 70.12 PHI= 0.500 XP = 0.
53	LEAN LESS TOWARD BEING THOSE WHERE FOOD PRODUCTION IS BY SIMPLE AGRICULTURE OR INCIPIENT FOOD PRODUCTION, RATHER THAN BY INTENSIVE AGRICULTURE (147)	0.50 OF 143	53	LEAN MORE TOWARD BEING THOSE WHERE FOOD PRODUCTION IS BY SIMPLE AGRICULTURE OR INCIPIENT FOOD PRODUCTION, RATHER THAN BY INTENSIVE AGRICULTURE (147)	0.85 OF 27	71 4 72 23 XSQ= 9.81 PHI= 0.240 XP = 0.0017
54	LEAN MORE TOWARD BEING THOSE WHERE FOOD PRODUCTION IS BY INTENSIVE OR SIMPLE AGRICULTURE, RATHER THAN BY INCIPIENT FOOD PRODUCTION (192)	0.91 OF 143	54	LEAN LESS TOWARD BEING THOSE WHERE FOOD PRODUCTION IS BY INTENSIVE OR SIMPLE AGRICULTURE, RATHER THAN BY INCIPIENT FOOD PRODUCTION (192)	0.67 OF 27	130 18 13 9 XSQ= 9.79 PHI= 0.240 XP = 0.0018
55	TILT TOWARD BEING THOSE WHERE FOOD PRODUCTION IS BY INTENSIVE AGRICULTURE, RATHER THAN BY SIMPLE AGRICULTURE (91)	0.55 OF 130	55	TILT TOWARD BEING THOSE WHERE FOOD PRODUCTION IS BY SIMPLE AGRICULTURE, RATHER THAN BY INTENSIVE AGRICULTURE (101)	0.78 OF 18	71 4 59 14 XSQ= 5.40 PHI= 0.191 XP = 0.0201
56	DRIFT MORE TOWARD BEING THOSE WHERE FOOD PRODUCTION IS BY SIMPLE AGRICULTURE, RATHER THAN BY INCIPIENT FOOD PRODUCTION (101)	0.82 OF 72	56	DRIFT LESS TOWARD BEING THOSE WHERE FOOD PRODUCTION IS BY SIMPLE AGRICULTURE, RATHER THAN BY INCIPIENT FOOD PRODUCTION (101)	0.61 OF 23	59 14 13 9 XSQ= 3.25 PHI= 0.185 XP = 0.0716
62	TEND TO BE THOSE WHERE HUSBANDRY OF SOME KIND IS PRESENT (228)	0.73 OF 194	62	TEND TO BE THOSE WHERE HUSBANDRY OF ANY KIND IS ABSENT (172)	0.56 OF 87	142 38 52 49 XSQ= 21.47 PHI= 0.276 XP = 0.0000
71	TEND TO BE THOSE WHERE METAL WORKING IS PRESENT (98)	0.60 OF 115	71	TEND TO BE THOSE WHERE METAL WORKING IS ABSENT (153)	0.76 OF 70	69 17 46 53 XSQ= 20.90 PHI= 0.336 XP = 0.0000
73	LEAN TOWARD BEING THOSE WHERE WEAVING IS PRESENT (118)	0.58 OF 114	73	LEAN TOWARD BEING THOSE WHERE WEAVING IS ABSENT (130)	0.68 OF 68	66 22 48 46 XSQ= 10.13 PHI= 0.236 XP = 0.0015

74 DRIFT MORE TOWARD BEING THOSE 0.67 OF 107 WHERE POTTERY IS PRESENT (145)	74 DRIFT LESS TOWARD BEING THOSE 0.53 OF 68 WHERE POTTERY IS PRESENT (145)	72 36 35 32 XSQ= 3.04 PHI= 0.132 XP = 0.0812
79 LEAN LESS TOWARD BEING THOSE 0.83 OF 110 WHERE NO CITY IS PRESENT (201)	79 IN ALL CASES ARE THOSE 1.00 OF 57 WHERE NO CITY IS PRESENT (201)	19 0 91 57 XSQ= 9.46 PHI= 0.238 XP = 0.0021
81 TEND TO BE THOSE 0.55 OF 110 WHERE A CITY OR TOWN IS PRESENT, OR THE AVERAGE COMMUNITY SIZE IS 200 OR GREATER (89)	81 TEND TO BE THOSE 0.86 OF 57 WHERE NO CITY OR TOWN IS PRESENT, AND THE AVERAGE COMMUNITY SIZE IS SMALLER THAN 200 (135)	61 8 49 49 XSQ= 24.88 PHI= 0.386 XP = 0.0000
83 LEAN LESS TOWARD BEING THOSE 0.66 OF 74 WHERE, WITH NO CITY AND NO TOWN PRESENT, THE AVERAGE COMMUNITY SIZE IS SMALLER THAN 200, RATHER THAN BETWEEN 200 AND 999 (135)	83 LEAN MORE TOWARD BEING THOSE 0.88 OF 56 WHERE, WITH NO CITY AND NO TOWN PRESENT, THE AVERAGE COMMUNITY SIZE IS SMALLER THAN 200, RATHER THAN BETWEEN 200 AND 999 (135)	25 7 49 49 XSQ= 6.68 PHI= 0.227 XP = 0.0098
86 TEND TO BE THOSE 0.63 OF 139 WHERE THE LEVEL OF POLITICAL INTEGRATION IS THE LARGE STATE, THE LITTLE STATE, OR THE MINIMAL STATE (148) GPM	86 TEND TO BE THOSE 0.74 OF 76 WHERE THE LEVEL OF POLITICAL INTEGRATION IS THE AUTONOMOUS COMMUNITY, OR THE FAMILY (156) GPM	87 20 52 56 XSQ= 24.43 PHI= 0.337 XP = 0.0000
90 DRIFT LESS TOWARD BEING THOSE 0.77 OF 75 WHERE, IF A HEREDITARY HEADMANSHIP IS PRESENT, SUCCESSION IS PATRILINEAL, RATHER THAN MATRILINEAL (127)	90 DRIFT MORE TOWARD BEING THOSE 0.92 OF 39 WHERE, IF A HEREDITARY HEADMANSHIP IS PRESENT, SUCCESSION IS PATRILINEAL, RATHER THAN MATRILINEAL (127)	58 36 17 3 XSQ= 3.01 PHI= -0.162 XP = 0.0828
91 TEND TO BE THOSE 0.75 OF 16 WHERE SOCIETAL COMPLEXITY IS HIGH (18) F-W	91 TEND TO BE THOSE 0.92 OF 12 WHERE SOCIETAL COMPLEXITY IS LOW (22) F-W	12 1 4 11 XSQ= 9.72 PHI= 0.589 EP = 0.0006
96 TEND TO BE THOSE 0.66 OF 162 WHERE THE HIERARCHY OF NATIONAL JURISDICTION HAS FOUR, THREE, TWO OR ONE LEVEL (174) GES,EA	96 TEND TO BE THOSE 0.70 OF 77 WHERE THE HIERARCHY OF NATIONAL JURISDICTION HAS NO LEVELS (156) GES,EA	107 23 55 54 XSQ= 26.10 PHI= 0.330 XP = 0.0000
97 TEND LESS TO BE THOSE 0.75 OF 163 WHERE THE HIERARCHY OF LOCAL JURISDICTION HAS THREE OR TWO LEVELS (273) GES,EA	97 TEND MORE TO BE THOSE 0.95 OF 77 WHERE THE HIERARCHY OF LOCAL JURISDICTION HAS THREE OR TWO LEVELS (273) GES,EA	40 4 123 73 XSQ= 11.81 PHI= 0.222 XP = 0.0006

98	TEND MORE TO BE THOSE 0.82 OF 163 WHERE THE HIERARCHY OF LOCAL JURISDICTION HAS FOUR OR THREE LEVELS (238) GES,EA	98	TEND LESS TO BE THOSE 0.52 OF 77 WHERE THE HIERARCHY OF LOCAL JURISDICTION HAS FOUR OR THREE LEVELS (238) GES,EA	133 40 30 37 XSQ= 21.39 PHI= 0.299 XP = 0.0000
99	LEAN TOWARD BEING THOSE 0.73 OF 55 WHERE, WITH NATIONAL HIERARCHY ABSENT, THE HIERARCHY OF LOCAL JURISDICTION HAS FOUR OR THREE LEVELS (93) GES,EA	99	LEAN TOWARD BEING THOSE 0.54 OF 54 WHERE, WITH NATIONAL HIERARCHY ABSENT, THE HIERARCHY OF LOCAL JURISDICTION HAS TWO LEVELS (63) GES,EA	40 25 15 29 XSQ= 6.85 PHI= 0.251 XP = 0.0089
100	TEND MORE TO BE THOSE 0.91 OF 162 WHERE HIERARCHIES ARE MORE COMPLEX THAN THE 'SIMPLEST,' I. E., MORE COMPLEX THAN TWO LOCAL LEVELS WITH NO NATIONAL LEVELS (267) GES,EA	100	TEND LESS TO BE THOSE 0.62 OF 77 WHERE HIERARCHIES ARE MORE COMPLEX THAN THE 'SIMPLEST,' I. E., MORE COMPLEX THAN TWO LOCAL LEVELS WITH NO NATIONAL LEVELS (267) GES,EA	147 48 15 29 XSQ= 26.17 PHI= 0.331 XP = 0.0000
102	TEND TO BE THOSE 0.65 OF 187 WHERE CLASS STRATIFICATION IS PRESENT (203)	102	TEND TO BE THOSE 0.64 OF 86 WHERE CLASS STRATIFICATION IS ABSENT (180)	122 31 65 55 XSQ= 19.21 PHI= 0.265 XP = 0.0000
106	TEND TO BE THOSE 0.70 OF 122 WHERE CLASS STRATIFICATION, IF PRESENT, IS BASED ON SOMETHING OTHER THAN WEALTH (126)	106	TEND TO BE THOSE 0.68 OF 31 WHERE CLASS STRATIFICATION, IF PRESENT, IS BASED ON WEALTH (77)	37 21 85 10 XSQ= 13.15 PHI= -0.293 XP = 0.0003
107	LEAN LESS TOWARD BEING THOSE 0.71 OF 122 WHERE CLASS STRATIFICATION, IF PRESENT, IS BASED ON SOMETHING OTHER THAN OCCUPATIONAL STATUS (160)	107	LEAN MORE TOWARD BEING THOSE 0.97 OF 31 WHERE CLASS STRATIFICATION, IF PRESENT, IS BASED ON SOMETHING OTHER THAN OCCUPATIONAL STATUS (160)	35 1 87 30 XSQ= 7.55 PHI= 0.222 XP = 0.0060
109	LEAN LESS TOWARD BEING THOSE 0.79 OF 175 WHERE CASTES ARE ABSENT (317)	109	LEAN MORE TOWARD BEING THOSE 0.95 OF 86 WHERE CASTES ARE ABSENT (317)	37 4 138 82 XSQ= 10.63 PHI= 0.202 XP = 0.0011
110	TEND TO BE THOSE 0.53 OF 186 WHERE SLAVERY IS PRESENT (163)	110	TEND TO BE THOSE 0.73 OF 86 WHERE SLAVERY IS ABSENT (218)	99 23 87 63 XSQ= 15.62 PHI= 0.240 XP = 0.0001
118	TILT TOWARD BEING THOSE 0.71 OF 24 WHERE THE PERCENTAGE OF OCCUPATIONS THAT ARE SPECIALIZED IS HIGH OR MEDIUM (24) WME	118	TILT TOWARD BEING THOSE 0.71 OF 14 WHERE THE PERCENTAGE OF OCCUPATIONS THAT ARE SPECIALIZED IS LOW (25) WME	17 4 7 10 XSQ= 4.79 PHI= 0.355 EP = 0.0184

120	TILT TOWARD BEING THOSE 0.85 OF 27 WHERE THE CRAFT SPECIALIZATION SCORE IS HIGH OR MEDIUM (36) WME	120	TILT TOWARD BEING THOSE 0.53 OF 15 WHERE THE CRAFT SPECIALIZATION SCORE IS LOW (17) WME	23 7 4 8 XSQ= 5.25 PHI= 0.354 XP = 0.0219
130	TEND TO BE THOSE 0.75 OF 40 WHERE LEATHER WORKING IS MAINLY DONE BY MALES (39)	130	TEND TO BE THOSE 0.84 OF 31 WHERE LEATHER WORKING IS MAINLY DONE BY FEMALES (45)	30 5 10 26 XSQ= 21.92 PHI= 0.556 XP = 0.0000
131	TEND MORE TO BE THOSE 0.99 OF 68 WHERE THE CONSTRUCTION OF PERMANENT HOUSES OR THE ERECTION OF TEMPORARY DWELLINGS IS MAINLY DONE BY MALES (136)	131	TEND LESS TO BE THOSE 0.58 OF 45 WHERE THE CONSTRUCTION OF PERMANENT HOUSES OR THE ERECTION OF TEMPORARY DWELLINGS IS MAINLY DONE BY MALES (136)	67 26 1 19 XSQ= 28.14 PHI= 0.499 XP = 0.0000
132	LEAN TOWARD BEING THOSE 0.78 OF 23 WHERE ECONOMIC EXCHANGE INVOLVES THE USE OF MONEY (37) JMH	132	LEAN TOWARD BEING THOSE 0.67 OF 15 WHERE ECONOMIC EXCHANGE DOES NOT INVOLVE THE USE OF MONEY (17) JMH	18 5 5 10 XSQ= 5.91 PHI= 0.394 EP = 0.0082
135	DRIFT TOWARD BEING THOSE 0.68 OF 19 WHERE INDIVIDUAL OWNERSHIP OF ECONOMICALLY SIGNIFICANT PROPERTY IS PRESENT (24) GES	135	DRIFT TOWARD BEING THOSE 0.70 OF 10 WHERE INDIVIDUAL OWNERSHIP OF ECONOMICALLY SIGNIFICANT PROPERTY IS NEGLIGIBLE OR ABSENT (14) GES	13 3 6 7 XSQ= 2.51 PHI= 0.294 EP = 0.0641
141	TILT TOWARD BEING THOSE 0.65 OF 23 WHERE THE LEVEL OF SOCIAL SANCTION IS PUBLIC CORPOREAL SANCTION, RATHER THAN PUBLIC PROPERTY SANCTION OR PRIVATE SETTLEMENT (28) JMH	141	TILT TOWARD BEING THOSE 0.73 OF 15 WHERE THE LEVEL OF SOCIAL SANCTION IS PUBLIC PROPERTY SANCTION OR PRIVATE SETTLEMENT, RATHER THAN PUBLIC CORPOREAL SANCTION (26) JMH	15 4 8 11 XSQ= 3.97 PHI= 0.323 EP = 0.0448
147	TILT TOWARD BEING THOSE 0.85 OF 13 WHERE CODIFIED LAWS ARE PRESENT (20) LWS	147	TILT TOWARD BEING THOSE 0.69 OF 13 WHERE CODIFIED LAWS ARE UNIMPORTANT OR ABSENT (13) LWS	11 4 2 9 XSQ= 5.67 PHI= 0.467 EP = 0.0154
152	LEAN TOWARD BEING THOSE 0.78 OF 9 WHERE THE DIFFERENTIATION OF THE JURIDICAL AGENCY FROM THE MEDICAL AGENCY IS HIGH (10) MJ	152	IN ALL CASES ARE THOSE 1.00 OF 7 WHERE THE DIFFERENTIATION OF THE JURIDICAL AGENCY FROM THE MEDICAL AGENCY IS LOW (10) MJ	7 0 2 7 XSQ= 6.78 PHI= 0.651 EP = 0.0032
163	LEAN TOWARD BEING THOSE 0.75 OF 8 WHERE THE EMPHASIS ON INDIVIDUAL VOLITION AS THE CAUSE OF CRIME IS HIGH (7) MJ	163	IN ALL CASES ARE THOSE 1.00 OF 6 WHERE THE EMPHASIS ON INDIVIDUAL VOLITION AS THE CAUSE OF CRIME IS LOW (10) MJ	6 0 2 6 XSQ= 5.11 PHI= 0.604 EP = 0.0097

178	TILT LESS TOWARD BEING THOSE 0.74 OF 188 WHERE THE COMMUNITY IS OTHER THAN SEGMENTED ON A CLAN BASIS AND NON-EXOGAMOUS (295)	178	TILT MORE TOWARD BEING THOSE 0.87 OF 85 WHERE THE COMMUNITY IS OTHER THAN SEGMENTED ON A CLAN BASIS AND NON-EXOGAMOUS (295)	48 11 140 74 XSQ= 4.76 PHI= 0.132 XP = 0.0291
179	TILT MORE TOWARD BEING THOSE 0.91 OF 188 WHERE THE COMMUNITY IS OTHER THAN STRUCTURED ON A NON-CLAN BASIS AND COMMONLY EXOGAMOUS (340)	179	TILT LESS TOWARD BEING THOSE 0.81 OF 85 WHERE THE COMMUNITY IS OTHER THAN STRUCTURED ON A NON-CLAN BASIS AND COMMONLY EXOGAMOUS (340)	17 16 171 69 XSQ= 4.39 PHI= -0.127 XP = 0.0362
183	TILT MORE TOWARD BEING THOSE 0.91 OF 140 WHERE THE LARGEST NON-COGNATIC KIN GROUP IS SMALLER THAN A MOEITY, I. E., A PHRATRY OR SIB OR LINEAGE (218)	183	TILT LESS TOWARD BEING THOSE 0.79 OF 42 WHERE THE LARGEST NON-COGNATIC KIN GROUP IS SMALLER THAN A MOEITY, I. E., A PHRATRY OR SIB OR LINEAGE (218)	12 9 128 33 XSQ= 4.05 PHI= -0.149 XP = 0.0442
184	LEAN MORE TOWARD BEING THOSE 0.76 OF 140 WHERE THE LARGEST NON-COGNATIC KIN GROUP IS SMALLER THAN A PHRATRY, I. E. A SIB OR LINEAGE (175)	184	LEAN LESS TOWARD BEING THOSE 0.52 OF 42 WHERE THE LARGEST NON-COGNATIC KIN GROUP IS SMALLER THAN A PHRATRY, I. E. A SIB OR LINEAGE (175)	33 20 107 22 XSQ= 7.92 PHI= -0.209 XP = 0.0049
186	TEND LESS TO BE THOSE 0.51 OF 194 WHERE THE KIN GROUP IS OTHER THAN EXCLUSIVELY PATRILINEAL (250)	186	TEND MORE TO BE THOSE 0.75 OF 87 WHERE THE KIN GROUP IS OTHER THAN EXCLUSIVELY PATRILINEAL (250)	95 22 99 65 XSQ= 12.90 PHI= 0.214 XP = 0.0003
188	TEND TO BE THOSE 0.72 OF 194 WHERE THE KIN GROUP IS OTHER THAN EXCLUSIVELY COGNATIC (252)	188	TEND TO BE THOSE 0.52 OF 87 WHERE THE KIN GROUP IS EXCLUSIVELY COGNATIC (148)	54 45 140 42 XSQ= 13.99 PHI= -0.223 XP = 0.0002
192	TEND MORE TO BE THOSE 0.79 OF 194 OTHER THAN WHERE THE ONLY KIN GROUP PRESENT IS A KINDRED OR ELSE BILATERAL DESCENT IS INFERRED (289)	192	TEND LESS TO BE THOSE 0.54 OF 87 OTHER THAN WHERE THE ONLY KIN GROUP PRESENT IS A KINDRED OR ELSE BILATERAL DESCENT IS INFERRED (289)	41 40 153 47 XSQ= 16.88 PHI= -0.245 XP = 0.0000
209	LEAN MORE TOWARD BEING THOSE 0.90 OF 168 WHERE MARITAL RESIDENCE IS PATRILOCAL, VIRILOCAL, OR AVUNCULOCAL, RATHER THAN MATRILOCAL OR UXORILOCAL (270)	209	LEAN LESS TOWARD BEING THOSE 0.76 OF 71 WHERE MARITAL RESIDENCE IS PATRILOCAL, VIRILOCAL, OR AVUNCULOCAL, RATHER THAN MATRILOCAL OR UXORILOCAL (270)	151 54 17 17 XSQ= 6.73 PHI= 0.168 XP = 0.0095
242	TILT LESS TOWARD BEING THOSE 0.76 OF 192 WHERE MARRIAGE IS COMMONLY OR OCCASIONALLY POLYGYNOUS, RATHER THAN MONOGAMOUS (314)	242	TILT MORE TOWARD BEING THOSE 0.90 OF 86 WHERE MARRIAGE IS COMMONLY OR OCCASIONALLY POLYGYNOUS, RATHER THAN MONOGAMOUS (314)	145 77 47 9 XSQ= 6.41 PHI= -0.152 XP = 0.0114

259	DRIFT TOWARD BEING THOSE 0.60 OF 20 WHERE THE SEVERITY OF MOTHER-IN-LAW AVOIDANCE IS LOW (20) WNS	259	DRIFT TOWARD BEING THOSE 0.73 OF 15 WHERE THE SEVERITY OF MOTHER-IN-LAW AVOIDANCE IS HIGH (26) WNS	8 11 12 4 XSQ= 2.61 PHI= -0.273 EP = 0.0866
262	DRIFT MORE TOWARD BEING THOSE 0.84 OF 193 WHERE WIVES ARE OBTAINED BY MEANS INVOLVING THE PRESENCE OF SOME CONSIDERATION (305)	262	DRIFT LESS TOWARD BEING THOSE 0.74 OF 87 WHERE WIVES ARE OBTAINED BY MEANS INVOLVING THE PRESENCE OF SOME CONSIDERATION (305)	162 64 31 23 XSQ= 3.51 PHI= 0.112 XP = 0.0611
286	DRIFT TOWARD BEING THOSE 0.56 OF 16 WHERE THE NUMBER OF FOOD TABOOS DURING PREGNANCY IS LOW OR ABSENT (14) BCA	286	DRIFT TOWARD BEING THOSE 0.88 OF 8 WHERE THE NUMBER OF FOOD TABOOS DURING PREGNANCY IS HIGH (20) BCA	7 7 9 1 XSQ= 2.59 PHI= -0.329 EP = 0.0791
326	DRIFT TOWARD BEING THOSE 0.55 OF 31 WHERE THE INFERRED TRANSITION ANXIETY BETWEEN INFANCY AND CHILDHOOD IS HIGH (32) B-B-C	326	DRIFT TOWARD BEING THOSE 0.76 OF 17 WHERE THE INFERRED TRANSITION ANXIETY BETWEEN INFANCY AND CHILDHOOD IS LOW (35) B-B-C	17 4 14 13 XSQ= 3.19 PHI= 0.258 XP = 0.0739
333	DRIFT TOWARD BEING THOSE 0.67 OF 6 WHERE THE AGE AT BEGINNING OF TRAINING IN HETEROSEXUAL PLAY INHIBITION IS EIGHT YEARS OR HIGHER (8) W-C	333	IN ALL CASES ARE THOSE 1.00 OF 5 WHERE THE AGE AT BEGINNING OF TRAINING IN HETEROSEXUAL PLAY INHIBITION IS LOWER THAN EIGHT YEARS (8) W-C	4 0 2 5 XSQ= 2.75 PHI= 0.500 EP = 0.0606
360	TILT TOWARD BEING THOSE 0.56 OF 16 WHERE ADOLESCENT PEER GROUPS ARE PRESENT IN A SETTING OF WORK AND PUBLIC GATHERINGS AND LEISURE, OR AT LEAST OF PUBLIC GATHERINGS AND LEISURE (14) JKH	360	TILT TOWARD BEING THOSE 0.90 OF 10 WHERE ADOLESCENT PEER GROUPS ARE PRESENT ONLY IN A SETTING OF LEISURE, OR ELSE ARE ABSENT (23) JKH	9 1 7 9 XSQ= 3.78 PHI= 0.381 EP = 0.0367
373	DRIFT TOWARD BEING THOSE 0.72 OF 25 WHERE MALE INITIATION CEREMONIES AT PUBERTY ARE ABSENT (27) W-K-A	373	DRIFT TOWARD BEING THOSE 0.67 OF 9 WHERE MALE INITIATION CEREMONIES AT PUBERTY ARE PRESENT (17) W-K-A	7 6 18 3 XSQ= 2.71 PHI= -0.282 EP = 0.0565
377	TILT LESS TOWARD BEING THOSE 0.69 OF 160 WHERE MALE GENITAL MUTILATION IS ABSENT (242)	377	TILT MORE TOWARD BEING THOSE 0.83 OF 77 WHERE MALE GENITAL MUTILATION IS ABSENT (242)	49 13 111 64 XSQ= 4.40 PHI= 0.136 XP = 0.0360
382	TILT TOWARD BEING THOSE 0.63 OF 27 WHERE FEMALE INITIATION RITES ARE ABSENT (27) JKB	382	TILT TOWARD BEING THOSE 0.74 OF 19 WHERE FEMALE INITIATION RITES ARE PRESENT (38) JKB	10 14 17 5 XSQ= 4.62 PHI= -0.317 XP = 0.0315

```
424  DRIFT TOWARD BEING THOSE         0.52 OF  23    424  DRIFT TOWARD BEING THOSE         0.80 OF  15         12     3
     WHERE RELIGIOUS SPECIALISTS ARE                      WHERE RELIGIOUS SPECIALISTS ARE                         11    12
     FULL-TIME, RATHER THAN                               PART-TIME, RATHER THAN                           XSQ=     2.70
     PART-TIME  (21) JMH                                  FULL-TIME  (33) JMH                              PHI=    0.267
                                                                                                           EP =   0.0884

427  TILT TOWARD BEING THOSE          0.66 OF  80    427  TILT TOWARD BEING THOSE          0.59 OF  34         53    14
     WHERE A HIGH GOD, IF PRESENT, IS                     WHERE A HIGH GOD, IF PRESENT, IS                        27    20
     ACTIVE, RATHER THAN                                  INACTIVE, RATHER THAN                            XSQ=     5.20
     INACTIVE  (87) GES,EA                                ACTIVE  (69) GES,EA                              PHI=    0.214
                                                                                                           XP =   0.0226

429  TILT TOWARD BEING THOSE          0.89 OF  19    429  TILT TOWARD BEING THOSE          0.56 OF   9         17     4
     WHERE SUPERNATURAL SANCTIONS FOR MORALITY            WHERE SUPERNATURAL SANCTIONS FOR MORALITY                2     5
     ARE PRESENT  (28) GES                                ARE ABSENT OR UNREPORTED  (9) GES                XSQ=     4.42
                                                                                                           PHI=    0.397
                                                                                                           EP =   0.0196

431  TILT LESS TOWARD BEING THOSE     0.61 OF  18    431  IN ALL CASES ARE THOSE           1.00 OF  10          7     0
     WHERE SUPERNATURAL SANCTIONS FOR MORALITY,           WHERE SUPERNATURAL SANCTIONS FOR MORALITY,              11    10
     HAVING AN EFFECT ON                                  HAVING AN EFFECT ON                              XSQ=     3.32
     AN INDIVIDUAL'S AFTERLIFE,                           AN INDIVIDUAL'S AFTERLIFE,                       PHI=    0.344
     ARE ABSENT OR UNREPORTED  (25) GES                   ARE ABSENT OR UNREPORTED  (25) GES               EP =   0.0302

435  DRIFT TOWARD BEING THOSE         0.82 OF  11    435  DRIFT TOWARD BEING THOSE         0.58 OF  12          2     7
     WHERE ABANDONMENT OF THE HOUSE OF THE DEAD           WHERE ABANDONMENT OF THE HOUSE. OF THE DEAD              9     5
     IS NOT PRACTICED  (19) LWS                           IS PRACTICED  (12) LWS                           XSQ=     2.38
                                                                                                           PHI=   -0.322
                                                                                                           EP =   0.0894

452  TILT TOWARD BEING THOSE          0.59 OF  22    452  TILT TOWARD BEING THOSE          0.83 OF  12         13     2
     WHERE TOTEMISM WITH FOOD TABOOS                      WHERE TOTEMISM WITH FOOD TABOOS                          9    10
     IS PRESENT  (19) WNS                                 IS ABSENT  (24) WNS                              XSQ=     4.08
                                                                                                           PHI=    0.346
                                                                                                           EP =   0.0297

455  DRIFT TOWARD BEING THOSE         0.67 OF  15    455  DRIFT TOWARD BEING THOSE         0.75 OF  12          5     9
     WHERE THE MODE OF THE INDIVIDUAL'S                   WHERE THE MODE OF THE INDIVIDUAL'S                      10     3
     CONTACT WITH THE DIVINE                              CONTACT WITH THE DIVINE                          XSQ=     3.12
     IS NOT CONDUCIVE TO THE DEVELOPMENT OF THE           IS CONDUCIVE TO THE DEVELOPMENT OF THE           PHI=   -0.340
     INDIVIDUAL'S NEED TO ACHIEVE  (19) DCM               INDIVIDUAL'S NEED TO ACHIEVE  (17) DCM           EP =   0.0542

458  LEAN LESS TOWARD BEING THOSE     0.51 OF  70    458  LEAN MORE TOWARD BEING THOSE     0.80 OF  54         34    11
     WHERE GAMES, IF PRESENT,                             WHERE GAMES, IF PRESENT,                                36    43
     DO NOT INCLUDE                                       DO NOT INCLUDE                                   XSQ=     9.30
     GAMES OF STRATEGY  (119) R-A-B,EA                    GAMES OF STRATEGY  (119) R-A-B,EA                PHI=    0.274
                                                                                                           XP =   0.0023

473  LEAN TOWARD BEING THOSE          0.50 OF  42    473  LEAN TOWARD BEING THOSE          0.92 OF  25         21     2
     WHERE SENSITIVITY TO INSULT                          WHERE SENSITIVITY TO INSULT                             21    23
     IS EXTREME  (32) PES                                 IS MODERATE OR NEGLIGIBLE  (56) PES              XSQ=    10.47
                                                                                                           PHI=    0.395
                                                                                                           XP =   0.0012
```

196/

```
480  DRIFT TCWARD BEING THCSE        0.62 OF  13        480  DRIFT TOWARD BEING THOSE        0.88 OF   8            8     1
     WHERE COMPLEXITY OF ARTISTIC CESIGN                      WHERE COMPLEXITY OF ARTISTIC DESIGN                        5     7
     IS HIGH  (14) HB                                         IS LOW  (15) HB                                     XSQ=    3.07
                                                                                                                  PHI=   0.382
                                                                                                                  EP =  0.0669
```

197 CULTURES
WHERE RULES FOR THE INHERITANCE OF
REAL PROPERTY, IF PRESENT,
FAVOR EITHER THE MALE HEIR OR LINE,
OR THE FEMALE HEIR OR LINE (165)

197 CULTURES
WHERE RULES FOR THE INHERITANCE OF
REAL PROPERTY, IF PRESENT,
DO NOT FAVOR EITHER THE MALE HEIR OR LINE,
OR THE FEMALE HEIR OR LINE (29)

BACKGROUND ON PAGE 111

BOTH SUBJECT AND PREDICATE

165 IN LEFT COLUMN

ABOR	AKHA	ALBANIANS	AMBA	ARAPESH	ARAUCANIANS	ARYANS	ASHANTI	ATAYAL	ATSUGEWI
AYMARA	AZANDE	AZTEC	BABWA	BAMBARA	BAMILEKE	BANDA	BARABRA	BARI	BATAK
BAYA	BEMBA	BHIL	BIRIFOR	BOZO	BULGARIANS	CAGABA	CAMBODIANS	CHAGGA	CHENCHU
CHERKESS	CHIBCHA	CHINANTEC	CHIRIGUANO	CHOCO	COORG	CREE	CZECHS	DAGUR	DARD
DELAWARE	DILLING	DOBUANS	DOGON	DOROBO	EGYPTIANS	ELLICE	ENGA	FON	FUTAJALONKE
GANDA	GILBERTESE	GISU	HAIDA	HANO	HASANIA	HAVASUPAI	HAZARA	HO	HUICHOL
HUTSUL	ICELANDERS	IRAQW	IRISH	JAPANESE	KABYLE	KACHIN	KATAB	KERAKI	KHALKA
KHASI	KHEVSUR	KIKUYU	KISSI	KOHISTANI	KOL	KONSO	KOREANS	KORYAK	LAKHER
LANGO	LAPPS	LEPCHA	LHOTA NAGA	LIFU	LOLO	LOZI	LUBA	LUO	MAGUZAWA
MALAYS	MAM	MANCHU	MANDAN	MAORI	MARGI	MASAI	MAYA	MBUGWE	MBUNDU
MENTAWEI	MIAO	MIN CHINESE	MINCHIA	MONGO	MONGUOR	MOSSI	MOTA	NANDI	NUER
NUPE	NURI	NYAKYUSA	NYANEKA	NYARO	NYORO	OJIBWA	OKINAWANS	OMAHA	ORAON
PALAUANS	PAPAGO	PATHAN	PENOBSCOT	PONAPEANS	POPOLUCA	PURARI	PURUM	REGEIBAT	RIFFIANS
RUNDI	SANTAL	SHILLUK	SHLUH	SIUAI	SIWANS	SOMALI	SONGHAI	SWAZI	TALAMANCA
TALLENSI	TANALA	TANIMBARESE	TEDA	TENDA	TERA	TESO	TIBETANS	TIGRINYA	TIKOPIA
TIMUCUA	TROBRIAND	TRUKESE	TSHIMSHIAN	TURKANA	VEDDA	WANTOAT	WOGEO	WOLOF	WUTE
YAKO	YAPESE	YOMBE	YORUBA	ZUNI					

29 IN RIGHT COLUMN

AMERICANS	BAJUN	BASQUES	BRAZILIANS	BURMESE	CHEREMIS	CHORTI	DUSUN	DUTCH	HAWAIIANS
IBAN	JAVANESE	KUTENAI	MARICOPA	MARQUESANS	MERINA	PAIWAN	RAROIANS	ROMANS	SAGADA
SINHALESE	TAGBANUA	TARAHUMARA	THAI	TORAJA	TRISTAN	ULAWANS	VIETNAMESE	YARURO	

87 EXCLUDED BECAUSE IRRELEVANT (SEE RIGHT COLUMN, PARAGRAPH 196)

119 EXCLUDED BECAUSE UNASCERTAINED

3 LEAN LESS TOWARD BEING THOSE LOCATED OUTSIDE OF AFRICA (320)	0.69 OF 165	3 LEAN MORE TOWARD BEING THOSE LOCATED OUTSIDE OF AFRICA (320)	0.97 OF 29	51 1 114 28 XSQ= 8.13 PHI= 0.205 XP = 0.0043
6 LEAN MORE TOWARD BEING THOSE LOCATED OUTSIDE OF THE INSULAR PACIFIC (330)	0.86 OF 165	6 LEAN LESS TOWARD BEING THOSE LOCATED OUTSIDE OF THE INSULAR PACIFIC (330)	0.62 OF 29	23 11 142 18 XSQ= 8.23 PHI= -0.206 XP = 0.0041

```
 42  TILT TOWARD BEING THOSE          0.65 OF 165     42  TILT TOWARD BEING THOSE          0.59 OF  29          58    17
     WHERE THE NATURAL ENVIRONMENT IS                     WHERE THE NATURAL ENVIRONMENT IS                     107    12
     OTHER THAN                                           TROPICAL OR SUB-TROPICAL RAIN FOREST, OR        XSQ=     4.78
     TROPICAL OR SUB-TROPICAL RAIN FOREST, OR             MONSOON FOREST  (156) FWM                       PHI=   -0.157
     MONSOON FOREST  (244) FWM                                                                            XP =   0.0288

 45  TILT LESS TOWARD BEING THOSE     0.59 OF 112     45  TILT MORE TOWARD BEING THOSE     0.86 OF  22          66    19
     WHERE SETTLEMENTS, IF FIXED, ARE                     WHERE SETTLEMENTS, IF FIXED, ARE                      46     3
     COMPACT, RATHER THAN                                 COMPACT, RATHER THAN                            XSQ=     4.84
     NON-COMPACT  (149)                                   NON-COMPACT  (149)                              PHI=   -0.190
                                                                                                          XP =   0.0278

 79  TEND TO BE THOSE                 0.88 OF  95     79  TEND TO BE THOSE                 0.53 OF  15          11     8
     WHERE NO CITY IS PRESENT  (201)                      WHERE A CITY IS PRESENT  (23)                         84     7
                                                                                                          XSQ=    13.02
                                                                                                          PHI=   -0.344
                                                                                                          XP =   0.0003

 80  TILT TOWARD BEING THOSE          0.76 OF  95     80  TILT TOWARD BEING THOSE          0.60 OF  15          23     9
     WHERE NO CITY OR TOWN IS PRESENT  (185)              WHERE A CITY OR TOWN IS PRESENT  (39)                 72     6
                                                                                                          XSQ=     6.40
                                                                                                          PHI=   -0.241
                                                                                                          XP =   0.0114

 84  TILT MORE TOWARD BEING THOSE     0.79 OF 119     84  TILT LESS TOWARD BEING THOSE     0.55 OF  20          25     9
     WHERE THE LEVEL OF POLITICAL INTEGRATION             WHERE THE LEVEL OF POLITICAL INTEGRATION              94    11
     IS THE LITTLE STATE, THE MINIMAL STATE,              IS THE LITTLE STATE, THE MINIMAL STATE,         XSQ=     4.11
     THE AUTONOMOUS COMMUNITY, OR                         THE AUTONOMOUS COMMUNITY, OR                    PHI=   -0.172
     THE FAMILY  (262) GPM                                THE FAMILY  (262) GPM                           XP =   0.0425

 94  TILT MORE TOWARD BEING THOSE     0.86 OF 140     94  TILT LESS TOWARD BEING THOSE     0.64 OF  22          19     8
     WHERE THE HIERARCHY                                  WHERE THE HIERARCHY                                  121    14
     OF NATIONAL JURISDICTION HAS                         OF NATIONAL JURISDICTION HAS                    XSQ=     5.56
     TWO, ONE, OR NO LEVELS  (296) GES,EA                 TWO, ONE, OR NO LEVELS  (296) GES,EA            PHI=   -0.185
                                                                                                          XP =   0.0183

 97  TILT LESS TOWARD BEING THOSE     0.72 OF 141     97  TILT MORE TOWARD BEING THOSE     0.95 OF  22          39     1
     WHERE THE HIERARCHY                                  WHERE THE HIERARCHY                                  102    21
     OF LOCAL JURISDICTION HAS                            OF LOCAL JURISDICTION HAS                       XSQ=     4.31
     THREE OR TWO LEVELS  (273) GES,EA                    THREE OR TWO LEVELS  (273) GES,EA               PHI=    0.163
                                                                                                          XP =   0.0378

 98  TILT MORE TOWARD BEING THOSE     0.84 OF 141     98  TILT LESS TOWARD BEING THOSE     0.64 OF  22         119    14
     WHERE THE HIERARCHY                                  WHERE THE HIERARCHY                                   22     8
     OF LOCAL JURISDICTION HAS                            OF LOCAL JURISDICTION HAS                       XSQ=     4.17
     FOUR OR THREE LEVELS  (238) GES,EA                   FOUR OR THREE LEVELS  (238) GES,EA              PHI=    0.160
                                                                                                          XP =   0.0412

107  DRIFT MORE TOWARD BEING THOSE  0.75 OF 103      107  DRIFT LESS TOWARD BEING THOSE  0.53 OF  19           26     9
     WHERE CLASS STRATIFICATION, IF PRESENT,              WHERE CLASS STRATIFICATION, IF PRESENT,               77    10
     IS BASED ON SOMETHING OTHER THAN                     IS BASED ON SOMETHING OTHER THAN                XSQ=     2.83
     OCCUPATIONAL STATUS  (160)                           OCCUPATIONAL STATUS  (160)                      PHI=   -0.152
                                                                                                          XP =   0.0923
```

176	TEND TO BE THOSE 0.55 OF 159 WHERE THE COMMUNITY IS A CLAN-COMMUNITY OR A COMMUNITY STRUCTURED OR SEGMENTED ON A CLAN BASIS (169)	176	TEND TO BE THOSE 0.93 OF 29 WHERE THE COMMUNITY IS OTHER THAN A CLAN-COMMUNITY OR A COMMUNITY STRUCTURED OR SEGMENTED ON A CLAN BASIS (213)	88 2 71 27 XSQ= 21.17 PHI= 0.336 XP = 0.0000
177	LEAN LESS TOWARD BEING THOSE 0.76 OF 159 WHERE THE COMMUNITY IS OTHER THAN A SINGLE CLAN-COMMUNITY AND EXOGAMOUS (305)	177	IN ALL CASES ARE THOSE 1.00 OF 29 WHERE THE COMMUNITY IS OTHER THAN A SINGLE CLAN-COMMUNITY AND EXOGAMOUS (305)	38 0 121 29 XSQ= 7.27 PHI= 0.197 XP = 0.0070
178	TILT LESS TOWARD BEING THOSE 0.71 OF 159 WHERE THE COMMUNITY IS OTHER THAN SEGMENTED ON A CLAN BASIS AND NON-EXOGAMOUS (295)	178	TILT MORE TOWARD BEING THOSE 0.93 OF 29 WHERE THE COMMUNITY IS OTHER THAN SEGMENTED ON A CLAN BASIS AND NON-EXOGAMOUS (295)	46 2 113 27 XSQ= 5.16 PHI= 0.166 XP = 0.0231
180	TEND LESS TO BE THOSE 0.64 OF 159 WHERE THE COMMUNITY IS COMMONLY NON-EXOGAMOUS, RATHER THAN EXOGAMOUS (258)	180	TEND MORE TO BE THOSE 0.97 OF 29 WHERE THE COMMUNITY IS COMMONLY NON-EXOGAMOUS, RATHER THAN EXOGAMOUS (258)	58 1 101 28 XSQ= 10.94 PHI= 0.241 XP = 0.0009
181	LEAN MORE TOWARD BEING THOSE 0.94 OF 159 WHERE THE COMMUNITY IS OTHER THAN A DEME (337)	181	LEAN LESS TOWARD BEING THOSE 0.76 OF 29 WHERE THE COMMUNITY IS OTHER THAN A DEME (337)	10 7 149 22 XSQ= 7.45 PHI= -0.199 XP = 0.0063
182	TEND TO BE THOSE 0.72 OF 159 OTHER THAN WHERE THE COMMUNITY IS STRUCTURED ON A NON-CLAN BASIS AND AGAMOUS (256)	182	TEND TO BE THOSE 0.66 OF 29 WHERE THE COMMUNITY IS STRUCTURED ON A NON-CLAN BASIS AND AGAMOUS (126)	45 19 114 10 XSQ= 13.52 PHI= -0.268 XP = 0.0002
186	TEND TO BE THOSE 0.55 OF 165 WHERE THE KIN GROUP IS EXCLUSIVELY PATRILINEAL (150)	186	TEND TO BE THOSE 0.86 OF 29 WHERE THE KIN GROUP IS OTHER THAN EXCLUSIVELY PATRILINEAL (250)	91 4 74 25 XSQ= 15.27 PHI= 0.281 XP = 0.0001
188	TEND TO BE THOSE 0.82 OF 165 WHERE THE KIN GROUP IS OTHER THAN EXCLUSIVELY COGNATIC (252)	188	TEND TO BE THOSE 0.86 OF 29 WHERE THE KIN GROUP IS EXCLUSIVELY COGNATIC (148)	29 25 136 4 XSQ= 54.47 PHI= -0.530 XP = 0.
192	TEND TO BE THOSE 0.87 OF 165 OTHER THAN WHERE THE ONLY KIN GROUP PRESENT IS A KINDRED OR ELSE BILATERAL DESCENT IS INFERRED (289)	192	TEND TO BE THOSE 0.69 OF 29 WHERE THE ONLY KIN GROUP PRESENT IS A KINDRED OR ELSE BILATERAL DESCENT IS INFERRED (111)	21 20 144 9 XSQ= 43.49 PHI= -0.473 XP = 0.

No.		No.		
201	TEND TO BE THOSE 0.93 OF 165 WHERE MARITAL RESIDENCE IS NON-OPTIONAL, RATHER THAN AMBILOCAL OR NEOLOCAL (334)	201	TEND TO BE THOSE 0.52 OF 29 WHERE MARITAL RESIDENCE IS AMBILOCAL OR NEOLOCAL, RATHER THAN NON-OPTIONAL (64)	154 14 11 15 XSQ= 39.35 PHI= 0.450 XP = 0.
204	TEND TO BE THOSE 0.93 OF 154 WHERE MARITAL RESIDENCE IS PATRILOCAL, VIRILOCAL, OR AVUNCULOCAL, RATHER THAN AMBILOCAL OR NEOLOCAL (270)	204	TEND TO BE THOSE 0.65 OF 23 WHERE MARITAL RESIDENCE IS AMBILOCAL OR NEOLOCAL, RATHER THAN PATRILOCAL, VIRILOCAL, OR AVUNCULOCAL (64)	143 8 11 15 XSQ= 49.32 PHI= 0.528 XP = 0.
209	TEND MORE TO BE THOSE 0.93 OF 154 WHERE MARITAL RESIDENCE IS PATRILOCAL, VIRILOCAL, OR AVUNCULOCAL, RATHER THAN MATRILOCAL OR UXORILOCAL (270)	209	TEND LESS TO BE THOSE 0.57 OF 14 WHERE MARITAL RESIDENCE IS PATRILOCAL, VIRILOCAL, OR AVUNCULOCAL, RATHER THAN MATRILOCAL OR UXORILOCAL (270)	143 8 11 6 XSQ= 14.29 PHI= 0.292 XP = 0.0002
224	TILT LESS TOWARD BEING THOSE 0.52 OF 69 WHERE COUSIN MARRIAGE IS PREFERENTIALLY OR PERMISSIVELY SYMMETRICAL, RATHER THAN EITHER PATRI- OR MATRILATERAL (106)	224	TILT MORE TOWARD BEING THOSE 0.91 OF 11 WHERE COUSIN MARRIAGE IS PREFERENTIALLY OR PERMISSIVELY SYMMETRICAL, RATHER THAN EITHER PATRI- OR MATRILATERAL (106)	33 1 36 10 XSQ= 4.35 PHI= 0.233 XP = 0.0371
234	TEND TO BE THOSE 0.52 OF 122 WHERE THE COUSIN TERMINOLOGY IS OF CROW, OMAHA, OR IROQUOIS TYPE, RATHER THAN ESKIMO OR HAWAIIAN TYPE (152)	234	TEND TO BE THOSE 0.92 OF 26 WHERE THE COUSIN TERMINOLOGY IS OF ESKIMO OR HAWAIIAN TYPE, RATHER THAN CROW, OMAHA, OR IROQUOIS TYPE (170)	64 2 58 24 XSQ= 15.62 PHI= 0.325 XP = 0.0001
241	LEAN TOWARD BEING THOSE 0.86 OF 94 WHERE THE FAMILY, IF EXTENDED, IS LARGE OR SMALL, RATHER THAN STEM (187)	241	LEAN TOWARD BEING THOSE 0.50 OF 12 WHERE THE FAMILY, IF EXTENDED, IS STEM, RATHER THAN LARGE OR SMALL (26)	81 6 13 6 XSQ= 7.16 PHI= 0.260 XP = 0.0074
242	TEND TO BE THOSE 0.80 OF 164 WHERE MARRIAGE IS COMMONLY OR OCCASIONALLY POLYGYNOUS, RATHER THAN MONOGAMOUS (314)	242	TEND TO BE THOSE 0.54 OF 28 WHERE MARRIAGE IS MONOGAMOUS, RATHER THAN COMMONLY OR OCCASIONALLY POLYGYNOUS (81)	132 13 32 15 XSQ= 13.22 PHI= 0.262 XP = 0.0003
262	TILT MORE TOWARD BEING THOSE 0.87 OF 164 WHERE WIVES ARE OBTAINED BY MEANS INVOLVING THE PRESENCE OF SOME CONSIDERATION (305)	262	TILT LESS TOWARD BEING THOSE 0.69 OF 29 WHERE WIVES ARE OBTAINED BY MEANS INVOLVING THE PRESENCE OF SOME CONSIDERATION (305)	142 20 22 9 XSQ= 4.44 PHI= 0.152 XP = 0.0350
263	TEND TO BE THOSE 0.73 OF 164 WHERE WIVES ARE OBTAINED BY RELATIVELY DIFFICULT MEANS, NAMELY BY BRIDE-PRICE, BRIDE-SERVICE, OR EXCHANGING A FEMALE RELATIVE (233)	263	TEND TO BE THOSE 0.69 OF 29 WHERE WIVES ARE OBTAINED BY RELATIVELY EASY MEANS, NAMELY BY TOKEN BRIDE-PRICE, GIFT EXCHANGE, ABSENCE OF ANY CONSIDERATION, OR RECEIPT OF DOWRY (162)	119 9 45 20 XSQ= 17.21 PHI= 0.299 XP = 0.0000

301	DRIFT TOWARD BEING THOSE WHERE THE POST-PARTUM SEX TABOO LASTS LONGER THAN ONE MONTH (96) 0.83 OF 47	301	DRIFT TOWARD BEING THOSE WHERE THE POST-PARTUM SEX TABOO LASTS ONE MONTH OR LESS (28) 0.60 OF 5	39 2 8 3 XSQ= 2.76 PHI= 0.230 XP = 0.0967
370	TILT LESS TOWARD BEING THOSE WHERE THE SEGREGATION OF ADOLESCENT BOYS IS ABSENT (148) 0.54 OF 109	370	TILT MORE TOWARD BEING THOSE WHERE THE SEGREGATION OF ADOLESCENT BOYS IS ABSENT (148) 0.83 OF 18	50 3 59 15 XSQ= 4.28 PHI= 0.184 XP = 0.0385
426	DRIFT TOWARD BEING THOSE WHERE A HIGH GOD IS PRESENT (156) GES,EA 0.68 OF 108	426	DRIFT TOWARD BEING THOSE WHERE A HIGH GOD IS ABSENT (104) GES,EA 0.59 OF 17	73 7 35 10 XSQ= 3.38 PHI= 0.164 XP = 0.0662
442	DRIFT TOWARD BEING THOSE WHERE FEAR OF ANIMAL SPIRITS IS HIGH (28) W-C 0.62 OF 21	442	IN ALL CASES ARE THOSE WHERE FEAR OF ANIMAL SPIRITS IS LOW (33) W-C 1.00 OF 3	13 0 8 3 XSQ= 1.94 PHI= 0.284 EP = 0.0815

198 CULTURES
WHERE RULES FOR THE INHERITANCE OF
REAL PROPERTY, IF PRESENT,
FAVOR THE MALE HEIR OR LINE, RATHER THAN
THE FEMALE (144)

198 CULTURES
WHERE RULES FOR THE INHERITANCE OF
REAL PROPERTY, IF PRESENT,
FAVOR THE FEMALE HEIR OR LINE, RATHER THAN
THE MALE (21)

BACKGROUND ON PAGE 111

BOTH SUBJECT AND PREDICATE

144 IN LEFT COLUMN

ABOR	AKHA	ALBANIANS	AMBA	ARAPESH	ARAUCANIANS	ARYANS	ATAYAL	ATSUGEWI	AYMARA
AZANDE	AZTEC	BABWA	BAMBARA	BAMILEKE	BANDA	BARABRA	BARI	BATAK	BAYA
BHIL	BIRIFOR	BOZO	BULGARIANS	CAGABA	CAMBODIANS	CHAGGA	CHENCHU	CHERKESS	CHIBCHA
CHINANTEC	CHIRIGUANO	CHCCO	COORG	CREE	CZECHS	DAGUR	DARD	DILLING	DOGON
DOROBO	EGYPTIANS	ELLICE	ENGA	FON	FUTAJALONKE	GANDA	GILBERTESE	GISU	HASANIA
HAVASUPAI	HAZARA	HC	HUICHOL	HUTSUL	ICELANDERS	IRAQW	IRISH	JAPANESE	KABYLE
KACHIN	KATAB	KERAKI	KHALKA	KHEVSUR	KIKUYU	KISSI	KOHISTANI	KOL	KONSO
KOREANS	KORYAK	LAKHER	LANGO	LAPPS	LEPCHA	LHOTA NAGA	LIFU	LOLO	LOZI
LUBA	LUC	MAGUZAWA	MALAYS	MAM	MANCHU	MAORI	MARGI	MASAI	MAYA
MBUGWE	MBUNDU	MIAC	MIN CHINESE	MINCHIA	MONGO	MONGUOR	MOSSI	NANDI	NUER
NUPE	NURI	NYAKYUSA	NYARO	NYORO	OJIBWA	OKINAWANS	OMAHA	ORAON	PAPAGO
PATHAN	PENOBSCOT	POPOLUCA	PURARI	PURUM	REGEIBAT	RIFFIANS	RUNDI	SANTAL	SHILLUK
SHLUH	SIWANS	SOMALI	SONGHAI	SWAZI	TALLENSI	TANALA	TANIMBARESE	TEDA	TERA
TESO	TIBETANS	TIGRINYA	TIKOPIA	TRUKESE	TURKANA	VEDDA	WANTOAT	WOGEO	WOLOF
WUTE	YAKC	YAPESE	YORUBA						

21 IN RIGHT COLUMN

ASHANTI	BEMBA	DELAWARE	DOBUANS	HAIDA	HANO	KHASI	MANDAN	MENTAWEI	MOTA
NYANEKA	PALAUANS	PONAPEANS	SIUAI	TALAMANCA	TENDA	TIMUCUA	TROBRIAND	TSHIMSHIAN	YOMBE
ZUNI									

116 EXCLUDED BECAUSE IRRELEVANT

ABIPON	ALACALUF	AMERICANS	ANDAMANESE	ARANDA	AWEIKOMA	BAJUN	BASQUES	BASSERI	BERGDAMA
BETE	BOTOCUDO	BRAZILIANS	BURMESE	CAMAYURA	CHEREMIS	CHEYENNE	CHIR-APACHE	CHOROTI	CHORTI
CHUKCHEE	COMANCHE	COPR ESKIMO	CROW	DIEGUENO	DUSUN	DUTCH	FANG	GARO	GILYAK
GOND	GROS VENTRE	GUAHIBO	HANUNOO	HAWAIIANS	HERERO	HUKUNDIKA	IBAN	ILA	INCA
INGALIK	JAVANESE	KALMYK	KAZAK	KET	KIOW-APACHE	KPE	KUBA	KUNG	KUTENAI
MANUS	MARICOPA	MARQUESANS	MATACO	MBUTI	MENDE	MERINA	MINANGKABAU	MIWOK	MUNDURUCU
MURNGIN	NABESNA	NAMA	NASKAPI	NICOBARESE	NUNIVAK	ONA	PAEZ	PAIWAN	PAWNEE
RAROIANS	ROMANS	RWALA	SAGADA	SANPOIL	SARSI	SEMANG	SERI	SINHALESE	SIRIONO
SOTHO	SUBANUN	TAGBANUA	TARAHUMARA	TAREUMIUT	TEHUELCHE	TENETEHARA	TENINO	TERENA	TETON
THAI	THONGA	TIMBIRA	TIV	TIWI	TODA	TOLOWA	TORAJA	TRISTAN	TRUMAI
TUBATULABAL	TUCANO	TUCUNA	TWANA	ULAWANS	UTE	VENDA	VIETNAMESE	WASHO	YAGUA
YAHGAN	YAKUT	YARURO	YOKUTS	YUKAGHIR	YUKI				

119 EXCLUDED BECAUSE UNASCERTAINED

4	DRIFT LESS TOWARD BEING THOSE 0.82 OF 144 LOCATED OUTSIDE OF THE CIRCUM-MEDITERRANEAN (355)	4	IN ALL CASES ARE THOSE 1.00 OF 21 LOCATED OUTSIDE OF THE CIRCUM-MEDITERRANEAN (355)	26 0 118 21 XSQ= 3.24 PHI= 0.140 XP = 0.0717
5	DRIFT LESS TOWARD BEING THOSE 0.74 OF 144 LOCATED OUTSIDE OF EAST EURASIA (330)	5	DRIFT MORE TOWARD BEING THOSE 0.95 OF 21 LOCATED OUTSIDE OF EAST EURASIA (330)	37 1 107 20 XSQ= 3.43 PHI= 0.144 XP = 0.0642
6	TILT MORE TOWARD BEING THOSE 0.89 OF 144 LOCATED OUTSIDE OF THE INSULAR PACIFIC (330)	6	TILT LESS TOWARD BEING THOSE 0.67 OF 21 LOCATED OUTSIDE OF THE INSULAR PACIFIC (330)	16 7 128 14 XSQ= 5.81 PHI= -0.188 XP = 0.0160
8	LEAN MORE TOWARD BEING THOSE 0.92 OF 144 LOCATED OUTSIDE OF NORTH AMERICA (330)	8	LEAN LESS TOWARD BEING THOSE 0.67 OF 21 LOCATED OUTSIDE OF NORTH AMERICA (330)	11 7 133 14 XSQ= 9.95 PHI= -0.246 XP = 0.0016
47	DRIFT TOWARD BEING THOSE 0.50 OF 24 WHERE, IF SETTLEMENTS ARE NON-FIXED, MOVEMENT IS NOMADIC, RATHER THAN NON-NOMADIC (72)	47	IN ALL CASES ARE THOSE 1.00 OF 5 WHERE, IF SETTLEMENTS ARE NON-FIXED, MOVEMENT IS NON-NOMADIC, RATHER THAN NOMADIC (38)	12 0 12 5 XSQ= 2.45 PHI= 0.291 EP = 0.0588
53	TILT TOWARD BEING THOSE 0.53 OF 107 WHERE FOOD PRODUCTION IS BY INTENSIVE AGRICULTURE, RATHER THAN BY SIMPLE AGRICULTURE OR INCIPIENT FOOD PRODUCTION (91)	53	TILT TOWARD BEING THOSE 0.81 OF 16 WHERE FOOD PRODUCTION IS BY SIMPLE AGRICULTURE OR INCIPIENT FOOD PRODUCTION, RATHER THAN BY INTENSIVE AGRICULTURE (147)	57 3 50 13 XSQ= 5.33 PHI= 0.208 XP = 0.0210
55	TILT TOWARD BEING THOSE 0.58 OF 98 WHERE FOOD PRODUCTION IS BY INTENSIVE AGRICULTURE, RATHER THAN BY SIMPLE AGRICULTURE (91)	55	TILT TOWARD BEING THOSE 0.79 OF 14 WHERE FOOD PRODUCTION IS BY SIMPLE AGRICULTURE, RATHER THAN BY INTENSIVE AGRICULTURE (101)	57 3 41 11 XSQ= 5.25 PHI= 0.217 XP = 0.0219
63	TEND TO BE THOSE 0.79 OF 106 WHERE HUSBANDRY, IF PRESENT, IS PRINCIPALLY IN THE FORM OF BOVINE, EQUINE, CAMEL-LIKE, OR DEER-LIKE ANIMALS, RATHER THAN PIGS, SHEEP, OR GOATS (152)	63	TEND TO BE THOSE 0.71 OF 14 WHERE HUSBANDRY, IF PRESENT, IS PRINCIPALLY IN THE FORM OF PIGS, SHEEP, OR GOATS, RATHER THAN BOVINE, EQUINE, CAMEL-LIKE, OR DEER-LIKE ANIMALS (74)	84 4 22 10 XSQ= 13.75 PHI= 0.339 XP = 0.0002
71	LEAN TOWARD BEING THOSE 0.69 OF 84 WHERE METAL WORKING IS PRESENT (98)	71	LEAN TOWARD BEING THOSE 0.73 OF 15 WHERE METAL WORKING IS ABSENT (153)	58 4 26 11 XSQ= 8.04 PHI= 0.285 XP = 0.0046

90	TEND TO BE THOSE 0.91 OF 57 WHERE, IF A HEREDITARY HEADMANSHIP IS PRESENT, SUCCESSION IS PATRILINEAL, RATHER THAN MATRILINEAL (127)	90	IN ALL CASES ARE THOSE 1.00 OF 12 WHERE, IF A HEREDITARY HEADMANSHIP IS PRESENT, SUCCESSION IS MATRILINEAL, RATHER THAN PATRILINEAL (38)	52 0 5 12 XSQ= 39.66 PHI= 0.758 XP = 0.
108	LEAN TOWARD BEING THOSE 0.66 OF 90 WHERE CLASS STRATIFICATION, IF PRESENT, IS BASED ON SOMETHING OTHER THAN A HEREDITARY ARISTOCRACY (129)	108	LEAN TOWARD BEING THOSE 0.77 OF 13 WHERE CLASS STRATIFICATION, IF PRESENT, IS BASED ON A HEREDITARY ARISTOCRACY (74)	31 10 59 3 XSQ= 6.87 PHI= -0.258 XP = 0.0087
109	DRIFT LESS TOWARD BEING THOSE 0.74 OF 127 WHERE CASTES ARE ABSENT (317)	109	DRIFT MORE TOWARD BEING THOSE 0.95 OF 20 WHERE CASTES ARE ABSENT (317)	33 1 94 19 XSQ= 3.18 PHI= 0.147 XP = 0.0745
110	TILT TOWARD BEING THOSE 0.59 OF 137 WHERE SLAVERY IS PRESENT (163)	110	TILT TOWARD BEING THOSE 0.70 OF 20 WHERE SLAVERY IS ABSENT (218)	81 6 56 14 XSQ= 4.87 PHI= 0.176 XP = 0.0273
130	DRIFT TOWARD BEING THOSE 0.79 OF 33 WHERE LEATHER WORKING IS MAINLY DONE BY MALES (39)	130	IN ALL CASES ARE THOSE 1.00 OF 2 WHERE LEATHER WORKING IS MAINLY DONE BY FEMALES (45)	26 0 7 2 XSQ= 2.70 PHI= 0.278 EP = 0.0605
138	DRIFT TOWARD BEING THOSE 0.80 OF 10 WHERE SUPERORDINATE JUSTICE IS PRESENT (22) BBW	138	DRIFT TOWARD BEING THOSE 0.80 OF 5 WHERE SUPERORDINATE JUSTICE IS ABSENT (18) BBW	8 1 2 4 XSQ= 2.81 PHI= 0.433 EP = 0.0889
178	TILT TOWARD BEING THOSE 0.74 OF 140 WHERE THE COMMUNITY IS OTHER THAN SEGMENTED ON A CLAN BASIS AND NON-EXOGAMOUS (295)	178	TILT TOWARD BEING THOSE 0.53 OF 19 WHERE THE COMMUNITY IS SEGMENTED ON A CLAN BASIS AND NON-EXOGAMOUS (87)	36 10 104 9 XSQ= 4.66 PHI= -0.171 XP = 0.0309
184	TILT MORE TOWARD BEING THOSE 0.80 OF 116 WHERE THE LARGEST NON-COGNATIC KIN GROUP IS SMALLER THAN A PHRATRY, I. E. A SIB OR LINEAGE (175)	184	TILT LESS TOWARD BEING THOSE 0.55 OF 20 WHERE THE LARGEST NON-COGNATIC KIN GROUP IS SMALLER THAN A PHRATRY, I. E. A SIB OR LINEAGE (175)	23 9 93 11 XSQ= 4.69 PHI= -0.186 XP = 0.0303
185	DRIFT LESS TOWARD BEING THOSE 0.73 OF 116 WHERE THE LARGEST NON-COGNATIC KIN GROUP IS THE MOEITY OR PHRATRY OR SIB (194)	185	DRIFT MORE TOWARD BEING THOSE 0.95 OF 20 WHERE THE LARGEST NON-COGNATIC KIN GROUP IS THE MOEITY OR PHRATRY OR SIB (194)	85 19 31 1 XSQ= 3.35 PHI= -0.157 XP = 0.0673

```
186  TEND TO BE THOSE                0.63 OF 144    186  IN ALL CASES ARE THOSE          1.00 OF  21        91     0
     WHERE THE KIN GROUP IS                              WHERE THE KIN GROUP IS                               53    21
     EXCLUSIVELY PATRILINEAL  (150)                      OTHER THAN                                      XSQ=   27.09
                                                         EXCLUSIVELY PATRILINEAL  (250)                  PHI=    0.405
                                                                                                         XP =   0.0000

187  TEND TO BE THOSE                0.99 OF 144    187  TEND TO BE THOSE                0.81 OF  21         2    17
     WHERE THE KIN GROUP IS                              WHERE THE KIN GROUP IS                              142     4
     OTHER THAN                                          EXCLUSIVELY MATRILINEAL  (55)                   XSQ=  106.19
     EXCLUSIVELY MATRILINEAL  (344)                                                                      PHI=  -0.802
                                                                                                         XP =   0.

190  TEND TO BE THOSE                0.98 OF 114    190  TEND TO BE THOSE                0.95 OF  20       112     1
     WHERE THE KIN GROUP IS                              WHERE THE KIN GROUP IS                                2    19
     PATRILINEAL OR DOUBLE-DESCENT,                      MATRILINEAL, RATHER THAN                        XSQ=  105.00
     RATHER THAN MATRILINEAL  (186)                      PATRILINEAL OR DOUBLE-DESCENT  (61)             PHI=    0.885
                                                                                                         XP =   0.

207  TILT TOWARD BEING THOSE         0.75 OF  12    207  TILT TOWARD BEING THOSE         0.80 OF  10         3     8
     WHERE MARITAL RESIDENCE IS                          WHERE MARITAL RESIDENCE IS                            9     2
     AMBILOCAL OR NEOLOCAL, RATHER THAN                  MATRILOCAL OR UXORILOCAL, RATHER THAN           XSQ=    4.58
     MATRILOCAL OR UXORILOCAL  (64)                      AMBILOCAL OR NEOLOCAL  (64)                     PHI=  -0.456
                                                                                                         EP =   0.0300

209  TEND MORE TO BE THOSE           0.98 OF 135    209  TEND LESS TO BE THOSE           0.58 OF  19       132    11
     WHERE MARITAL RESIDENCE IS                          WHERE MARITAL RESIDENCE IS                            3     8
     PATRILOCAL, VIRILOCAL, OR AVUNCULOCAL,              PATRILOCAL, VIRILOCAL, OR AVUNCULOCAL,          XSQ=   34.16
     RATHER THAN                                         RATHER THAN                                     PHI=    0.471
     MATRILOCAL OR UXORILOCAL  (270)                     MATRILOCAL OR UXORILOCAL  (270)                 XP =   0.

210  TEND TO BE THOSE                0.98 OF 107    210  IN ALL CASES ARE THOSE          1.00 OF   8       105     0
     WHERE MARITAL RESIDENCE IS                          WHERE MARITAL RESIDENCE IS                            2     8
     PATRILOCAL, RATHER THAN                             MATRILOCAL, RATHER THAN                         XSQ=   78.34
     MATRILOCAL  (169)                                   PATRILOCAL  (31)                                PHI=    0.825
                                                                                                         XP =   0.

234  DRIFT TOWARD BEING THOSE        0.51 OF 105    234  DRIFT TOWARD BEING THOSE        0.76 OF  17        51    13
     WHERE THE COUSIN TERMINOLOGY IS                     WHERE THE COUSIN TERMINOLOGY IS                      54     4
     OF ESKIMO OR HAWAIIAN TYPE,                         OF CROW, OMAHA, OR IROQUOIS TYPE,               XSQ=    3.52
     RATHER THAN                                         RATHER THAN                                     PHI=  -0.170
     CROW, OMAHA, OR IROQUOIS TYPE  (170)                ESKIMO OR HAWAIIAN TYPE  (152)                  XP =   0.0608

240  TILT TOWARD BEING THOSE         0.73 OF  83    240  TILT TOWARD BEING THOSE         0.64 OF  11        22     7
     WHERE THE FAMILY, IF EXTENDED, IS                   WHERE THE FAMILY, IF EXTENDED, IS                    61     4
     SMALL OR STEM, RATHER THAN                          LARGE, RATHER THAN                              XSQ=    4.66
     LARGE  (135)                                        SMALL OR STEM  (78)                             PHI=  -0.223
                                                                                                         XP =   0.0309

272  TILT TOWARD BEING THOSE         0.65 OF  20    272  IN ALL CASES ARE THOSE          1.00 OF   4         7     4
     WHERE THE DIVORCE RATE IS                           WHERE THE DIVORCE RATE IS                            13     0
     LOW  (28) CA                                        HIGH  (29) CA                                   XSQ=    3.36
                                                                                                         PHI=  -0.374
                                                                                                         EP =   0.0311
```

306	DRIFT TOWARD BEING THOSE WHERE THE EARLY DEPENDENCE SATISFACTION POTENTIAL IS HIGH (28) W-C	0.77 OF	13	306	DRIFT TOWARD BEING THOSE WHERE THE EARLY DEPENDENCE SATISFACTION POTENTIAL IS LOW (24) W-C	0.75 OF	4	10 1 3 3 XSQ= 1.70 PHI= 0.316 EP = 0.0987
319	TILT TOWARD BEING THOSE WHERE PROTECTION OF THE INFANT FROM ENVIRONMENTAL DISCOMFORTS IS LOW (30) B-B-C	0.56 OF	25	319	IN ALL CASES ARE THOSE WHERE PROTECTION OF THE INFANT FROM ENVIRONMENTAL DISCOMFORTS IS HIGH (35) B-B-C	1.00 OF	5	11 5 14 0 XSQ= 3.24 PHI= -0.329 EP = 0.0447
324	TILT TOWARD BEING THOSE WHERE THE PAIN INFLICTED ON THE INFANT BY THE NURTURANT AGENT IS HIGH (34) B-B-C	0.62 OF	26	324	IN ALL CASES ARE THOSE WHERE THE PAIN INFLICTED ON THE INFANT BY THE NURTURANT AGENT IS LOW OR NEGLIGIBLE (32) B-B-C	1.00 OF	4	16 0 10 4 XSQ= 3.09 PHI= 0.321 EP = 0.0365
328	TILT TOWARD BEING THOSE WHERE THE AGE OF THE INFANT AT THE ONSET OF SERIOUS SOCIALIZATION, OTHER THAN WEANING, IS HIGHER THAN TWO YEARS (21) B-B-C	0.75 OF	16	328	IN ALL CASES ARE THOSE WHERE THE AGE OF THE INFANT AT THE ONSET OF SERIOUS SOCIALIZATION, OTHER THAN WEANING, IS TWO YEARS OR LOWER (20) B-B-C	1.00 OF	3	12 0 4 3 XSQ= 3.31 PHI= 0.417 EP = 0.0361
351	TILT TOWARD BEING THOSE WHERE THE CHILD'S INFERRED CONFLICT REGARDING ACHIEVEMENT BEHAVIOR IS LOW (34) B-B-C	0.60 OF	25	351	IN ALL CASES ARE THOSE WHERE THE CHILD'S INFERRED CONFLICT REGARDING ACHIEVEMENT BEHAVIOR IS HIGH (26) B-B-C	1.00 OF	4	10 4 15 0 XSQ= 2.86 PHI= -0.314 EP = 0.0421
377	DRIFT LESS TOWARD BEING THOSE WHERE MALE GENITAL MUTILATION IS ABSENT (242)	0.64 OF	121	377	DRIFT MORE TOWARD BEING THOSE WHERE MALE GENITAL MUTILATION IS ABSENT (242)	0.89 OF	18	44 2 77 16 XSQ= 3.44 PHI= 0.157 XP = 0.0635
391	TILT TOWARD BEING THOSE WHERE PREMARITAL SEX RELATIONS ARE STRONGLY PUNISHED AND IN FACT RARE, OR WEAKLY PUNISHED AND IN FACT NOT RARE (89) JTW,EA	0.57 OF	69	391	TILT TOWARD BEING THOSE WHERE PREMARITAL SEX RELATIONS ARE PUNISHED ONLY IF PREGNANCY RESULTS, OR FREELY PERMITTED (90) JTW,EA	0.83 OF	12	39 2 30 10 XSQ= 5.00 PHI= 0.248 XP = 0.0254
392	DRIFT TOWARD BEING THOSE WHERE PREMARITAL SEX RELATIONS ARE STRONGLY PUNISHED AND IN FACT RARE, OR WEAKLY PUNISHED AND IN FACT NOT RARE, OR PUNISHED ONLY IF PREGNANCY RESULTS (112) JTW,EA	0.72 OF	69	392	DRIFT TOWARD BEING THOSE WHERE PREMARITAL SEX RELATIONS ARE FREELY PERMITTED (67) JTW,EA	0.58 OF	12	50 5 19 7 XSQ= 3.15 PHI= 0.197 XP = 0.0760
405	TILT TOWARD BEING THOSE WHERE EXPLANATIONS OF ILLNESS OF A DEPENDENCE NATURE ARE PRESENT (34) W-C	0.63 OF	16	405	IN ALL CASES ARE THOSE WHERE EXPLANATIONS OF ILLNESS OF A DEPENDENCE NATURE ARE ABSENT (27) W-C	1.00 OF	5	10 0 6 5 XSQ= 3.72 PHI= 0.421 EP = 0.0351

```
426  TILT TOWARD BEING THOSE          0.72 OF  93      426  TILT TOWARD BEING THOSE          0.60 OF  15          67     6
     WHERE A HIGH GOD IS                                   WHERE A HIGH GOD IS                                   26     9
     PRESENT  (156) GES,EA                                 ABSENT  (104) GES,EA                             XSQ=     4.68
                                                                                                            PHI=    0.208
                                                                                                            XP =   0.0305

428  TILT TOWARD BEING THOSE          0.73 OF  44      428  IN ALL CASES ARE THOSE           1.00 OF   3          32     0
     WHERE A HIGH GOD, IF PRESENT AND ACTIVE,              WHERE A HIGH GOD, IF PRESENT AND ACTIVE,              12     3
     SUPPORTS HUMAN MORALITY, RATHER THAN                  DOES NOT SUPPORT HUMAN MORALITY,                 XSQ=     3.90
     NOT SUPPORTING IT  (61) GES,EA                        RATHER THAN SUPPORTING IT  (26) GES,EA           PHI=    0.288
                                                                                                            XP =   0.0483

439  TILT TOWARD BEING THOSE          0.69 OF  16      439  IN ALL CASES ARE THOSE           1.00 OF   5          11     0
     WHERE FEAR OF GHOSTS                                  WHERE FEAR OF GHOSTS                                   5     5
     IS HIGH  (30) W-C                                     IS LOW  (31) W-C                                 XSQ=     4.73
                                                                                                            PHI=    0.474
                                                                                                            EP =   0.0124

471  TILT TOWARD BEING THOSE          0.80 OF   5      471  IN ALL CASES ARE THOSE           1.00 OF   4           1     4
     WHERE SECRET SOCIETIES ARE                            WHERE SECRET SOCIETIES ARE                             4     0
     UNIMPORTANT OR ABSENT  (14) LWS                       PRESENT  (9) LWS                                 XSQ=     2.98
                                                                                                            PHI=   -0.575
                                                                                                            EP =   0.0476
```

199 CULTURES
WHERE RULES FOR THE INHERITANCE OF
MOVABLE PROPERTY, IF PRESENT,
FAVOR EITHER THE MALE HEIR OR LINE,
OR THE FEMALE HEIR OR LINE (211)

199 CULTURES
WHERE RULES FOR THE INHERITANCE OF
MOVABLE PROPERTY, IF PRESENT,
DO NOT FAVOR EITHER THE MALE HEIR OR LINE,
OR THE FEMALE HEIR OR LINE (46)

BACKGROUND ON PAGE 111

SUBJECT ONLY

211 IN LEFT COLUMN

ABOR	AINU	AKHA	ALBANIANS	AMBA	ARANDA	ARAPESH	ARAUCANIANS	ARYANS	ASHANTI
ATAYAL	ATSUGEWI	AYMARA	AZANDE	AZTEC	BABWA	BAMBARA	BAMILEKE	BANDA	BARABRA
BARI	BASSERI	BATAK	BAYA	BEJA	BEMBA	BERGDAMA	BETE	BHIL	BHUIYA
BIRIFOR	BOZO	BUDUMA	CAGABA	CAMBA	CHAGGA	CHENCHU	CHERKESS	CHIBCHA	CHINANTEC
CHUKCHEE	COORG	CREE	CREEK	CROW	CZECHS	DAGUR	DARD	DILLING	DOBUANS
DOGON	EGYPTIANS	ELLICE	ENGA	EYAK	FANG	FON	FUTAJALONKE	GANDA	GARO
GILYAK	GISU	GOAJIRO	HAIDA	HASANIA	HAZARA	HEBREWS	HEHE	HERERO	HO
HUKUNDIKA	HUTSUL	ICELANDERS	ILA	INCA	INGALIK	IRAQW	IRISH	JAPANESE	JEMEZ
KABYLE	KACHIN	KALMYK	KASKA	KATAB	KAZAK	KERAKI	KET	KHALKA	KHASI
KHEVSUR	KIKUYU	KISSI	KOHISTANI	KOL	KOREANS	KORYAK	KPE	KUBA	KUNG
KWAKIUTL	LAKHER	LAMBA	LANGO	LAU	LEPCHA	LESU	LHOTA NAGA	LIFU	LOLO
LOZI	LUBA	LUO	MAGUZAWA	MALAYS	MAM	MAMBILA	MANCHU	MANDAN	MARGI
MARSHALLESE	MASAI	MAYA	MBUGWE	MBUNDU	MENDE	MIAO	MIN CHINESE	MINANGKABAU	MINCHIA
MONGO	MONGUOR	MOSSI	MOTA	NAMA	NANDI	NAVAHO	NDEMBU	NGONI	NUER
NUNIVAK	NUPE	NURI	NYAKYUSA	NYANEKA	NYARO	NYORO	OJIBWA	OKINAWANS	OMAHA
ORAON	PAEZ	PALAUANS	PATHAN	PAWNEE	PENDE	PENOBSCOT	PONAPEANS	POPOLUCA	PURARI
PURUM	REGEIBAT	RIFFIANS	RUNDI	RWALA	SANDAWE	SANPOIL	SANTAL	SARAMACCA	SHILLUK
SHLUH	SIWANS	SOMALI	SONGHAI	SOTHO	SWAZI	TALLENSI	TANIMBARESE	TAREUMIUT	TEDA
TENDA	TENETEHARA	TERA	TESO	THONGA	TIBETANS	TIGRINYA	TIMBIRA	TIMUCUA	TIV
TODA	TOLOWA	TROBRIAND	TRUKESE	TSHIMSHIAN	TUCUNA	TURKANA	VEDDA	VENDA	WANTOAT
WOGEO	WOLOF	WUTE	YAKO	YAKUT	YAO	YAPESE	YARURO	YOMBE	YORUBA
YUKAGHIR									

46 IN RIGHT COLUMN

AMERICANS	BAJUN	BASQUES	BRAZILIANS	BULGARIANS	BURMESE	CAMBODIANS	CHEREMIS	CHORTI	COCHITI
COPR ESKIMO	DOROBO	DUSUN	DUTCH	GILBERTESE	HANUNOO	HAWAIIANS	HUICHOL	IBAN	JAVANESE
KUTENAI	LAPPS	MARQUESANS	MERINA	MNONG GAR	NICOBARESE	PAIWAN	RAROIANS	ROMANS	SAGADA
SARSI	SEMANG	SINHALESE	SIUAI	SUBANUN	TAGBANUA	TANALA	TARAHUMARA	THAI	TOKELAU
TORAJA	TRISTAN	ULAWANS	VIETNAMESE	YUROK	ZUNI				

32 EXCLUDED BECAUSE IRRELEVANT

AWEIKOMA	CAMAYURA	CHEYENNE	CHIR-APACHE	CHOROTI	COMANCHE	DIEGUENO	FOX	GOND	GROS VENTRE
HAVASUPAI	KIOW-APACHE	MANUS	MARICOPA	MATACO	MIWOK	MUNDURUCU	NABESNA	NOMLAKI	ONA
PAPAGO	SERI	SIRIONO	TENINO	TUBATULABAL	UTE	WASHO	WICHITA	YAGUA	YAHGAN
YOKUTS	YUKI								

111 EXCLUDED BECAUSE UNASCERTAINED

3	TEND LESS TO BE THOSE LOCATED OUTSIDE OF AFRICA (320)	0.66 OF 211	3	TEND MORE TO BE THOSE LOCATED OUTSIDE OF AFRICA (320)	0.96 OF 46	72 2 139 44 XSQ= 14.91 PHI= 0.241 XP = 0.0001
6	TEND MORE TO BE THOSE LOCATED OUTSIDE OF THE INSULAR PACIFIC (330)	0.89 OF 211	6	TEND LESS TO BE THOSE LOCATED OUTSIDE OF THE INSULAR PACIFIC (330)	0.65 OF 46	23 16 188 30 XSQ= 14.93 PHI= -0.241 XP = 0.0001
42	TEND TO BE THOSE WHERE THE NATURAL ENVIRONMENT IS OTHER THAN TROPICAL OR SUB-TROPICAL RAIN FOREST, OR MONSOON FOREST (244) FWM	0.70 OF 211	42	TEND TO BE THOSE WHERE THE NATURAL ENVIRONMENT IS TROPICAL OR SUB-TROPICAL RAIN FOREST, OR MONSOON FOREST (156) FWM	0.59 OF 46	64 27 147 19 XSQ= 12.07 PHI= -0.217 XP = 0.0005
74	TILT TOWARD BEING THOSE WHERE POTTERY IS PRESENT (145)	0.68 OF 122	74	TILT TOWARD BEING THOSE WHERE POTTERY IS ABSENT (93)	0.58 OF 24	83 10 39 14 XSQ= 4.94 PHI= 0.184 XP = 0.0262
79	TEND MORE TO BE THOSE WHERE NO CITY IS PRESENT (201)	0.93 OF 122	79	TEND LESS TO BE THOSE WHERE NO CITY IS PRESENT (201)	0.64 OF 28	9 10 113 18 XSQ= 14.07 PHI= -0.306 XP = 0.0002
80	TILT MORE TOWARD BEING THOSE WHERE NO CITY OR TOWN IS PRESENT (185)	0.82 OF 122	80	TILT LESS TOWARD BEING THOSE WHERE NO CITY OR TOWN IS PRESENT (185)	0.61 OF 28	22 11 100 17 XSQ= 4.82 PHI= -0.179 XP = 0.0281
84	DRIFT MORE TOWARD BEING THOSE WHERE THE LEVEL OF POLITICAL INTEGRATION IS THE LITTLE STATE, THE MINIMAL STATE, THE AUTONOMOUS COMMUNITY, OR THE FAMILY (262) GPM	0.82 OF 154	84	DRIFT LESS TOWARD BEING THOSE WHERE THE LEVEL OF POLITICAL INTEGRATION IS THE LITTLE STATE, THE MINIMAL STATE, THE AUTONOMOUS COMMUNITY, OR THE FAMILY (262) GPM	0.68 OF 34	27 11 127 23 XSQ= 2.93 PHI= -0.125 XP = 0.0870
88	TEND TO BE THOSE WHERE, IF A HEADMANSHIP IS PRESENT, SUCCESSION IS HEREDITARY (165)	0.65 OF 153	88	TEND TO BE THOSE WHERE, IF A HEADMANSHIP IS PRESENT, SUCCESSION IS NON-HEREDITARY (106)	0.76 OF 29	54 22 99 7 XSQ= 14.87 PHI= -0.286 XP = 0.0001
94	TILT MORE TOWARD BEING THOSE WHERE THE HIERARCHY OF NATIONAL JURISDICTION HAS TWO, ONE, OR NO LEVELS (296) GES,EA	0.89 OF 178	94	TILT LESS TOWARD BEING THOSE WHERE THE HIERARCHY OF NATIONAL JURISDICTION HAS TWO, ONE, OR NO LEVELS (296) GES,EA	0.74 OF 38	20 10 158 28 XSQ= 4.76 PHI= -0.148 XP = 0.0291

```
 97  DRIFT LESS TOWARD BEING THOSE  0.78 OF 179    97  DRIFT MORE TOWARD BEING THOSE  0.92 OF  38        40     3
     WHERE THE HIERARCHY                               WHERE THE HIERARCHY                              139    35
     OF LOCAL JURISDICTION HAS                         OF LOCAL JURISDICTION HAS                      XSQ=    3.26
     THREE OR TWO LEVELS  (273) GES,EA                 THREE OR TWO LEVELS  (273) GES,EA              PHI=   0.123
                                                                                                      XP =  0.0710

 98  TILT MORE TOWARD BEING THOSE   0.80 OF 179    98  TILT LESS TOWARD BEING THOSE   0.61 OF  38       144    23
     WHERE THE HIERARCHY                               WHERE THE HIERARCHY                               35    15
     OF LOCAL JURISDICTION HAS                         OF LOCAL JURISDICTION HAS                      XSQ=    5.94
     FOUR OR THREE LEVELS  (238) GES,EA                FOUR OR THREE LEVELS  (238) GES,EA             PHI=   0.165
                                                                                                      XP =  0.0148

100  TILT MORE TOWARD BEING THOSE   0.91 OF 178   100  TILT LESS TOWARD BEING THOSE   0.76 OF  38       162    29
     WHERE HIERARCHIES ARE MORE COMPLEX THAN           WHERE HIERARCHIES ARE MORE COMPLEX THAN           16     9
     THE 'SIMPLEST,' I. E., MORE COMPLEX THAN          THE 'SIMPLEST,' I. E., MORE COMPLEX THAN       XSQ=    5.25
     TWO LOCAL LEVELS WITH                             TWO LOCAL LEVELS WITH                          PHI=   0.156
     NO NATIONAL LEVELS  (267) GES,EA                  NO NATIONAL LEVELS  (267) GES,EA               XP =  0.0219

107  TILT MORE TOWARD BEING THOSE   0.80 OF 127   107  TILT LESS TOWARD BEING THOSE   0.61 OF  28        25    11
     WHERE CLASS STRATIFICATION, IF PRESENT,           WHERE CLASS STRATIFICATION, IF PRESENT,          102    17
     IS BASED ON SOMETHING OTHER THAN                  IS BASED ON SOMETHING OTHER THAN               XSQ=    3.90
     OCCUPATIONAL STATUS  (160)                        OCCUPATIONAL STATUS  (160)                     PHI=  -0.159
                                                                                                      XP =  0.0481

109  DRIFT LESS TOWARD BEING THOSE  0.80 OF 191   109  DRIFT MORE TOWARD BEING THOSE  0.93 OF  45        38     3
     WHERE CASTES ARE ABSENT  (317)                    WHERE CASTES ARE ABSENT  (317)                   153    42
                                                                                                      XSQ=    3.57
                                                                                                      PHI=   0.123
                                                                                                      XP =  0.0590

110  TILT TOWARD BEING THOSE        0.55 OF 203   110  TILT TOWARD BEING THOSE        0.63 OF  46       112    17
     WHERE SLAVERY IS PRESENT  (163)                   WHERE SLAVERY IS ABSENT  (218)                    91    29
                                                                                                      XSQ=    4.28
                                                                                                      PHI=   0.131
                                                                                                      XP =  0.0385

128  DRIFT TOWARD BEING THOSE       0.52 OF  54   128  DRIFT TOWARD BEING THOSE       0.89 OF   9        26     8
     WHERE, IF SUBSISTENCE IS PRIMARILY BY             WHERE, IF SUBSISTENCE IS PRIMARILY BY             28     1
     AGRICULTURE, THE WORK IS                          AGRICULTURE, THE WORK IS                       XSQ=    3.64
     MAINLY DONE BY FEMALES  (37)                      MAINLY DONE BY MALES  (40)                     PHI=  -0.241
                                                                                                      XP =  0.0562

129  TILT LESS TOWARD BEING THOSE   0.58 OF  60   129  IN ALL CASES ARE THOSE         1.00 OF   9        25     0
     WHERE WEAVING IS                                  WHERE WEAVING IS                                  35     9
     MAINLY DONE BY FEMALES  (73)                      MAINLY DONE BY FEMALES  (73)                   XSQ=    4.22
                                                                                                      PHI=   0.247
                                                                                                      XP =  0.0401

163  DRIFT TOWARD BEING THOSE       0.83 OF   6   163  DRIFT TOWARD BEING THOSE       0.83 OF   6         1     5
     WHERE THE EMPHASIS ON INDIVIDUAL VOLITION         WHERE THE EMPHASIS ON INDIV.DUAL VOLITION          5     1
     AS THE CAUSE OF CRIME                             AS THE CAUSE OF CRIME                          XSQ=    3.00
     IS LOW  (10) MJ                                   IS HIGH  (7) MJ                                PHI=  -0.500
                                                                                                      EP =  0.0801
```

176	TEND TO BE THOSE WHERE THE COMMUNITY IS A CLAN-COMMUNITY OR A COMMUNITY STRUCTURED OR SEGMENTED ON A CLAN BASIS (169)	0.55 OF 202	176	TEND TO BE THOSE WHERE THE COMMUNITY IS OTHER THAN A CLAN-COMMUNITY OR A COMMUNITY STRUCTURED OR SEGMENTED ON A CLAN BASIS (213)	0.83 OF 46	112 8 90 38 XSQ= 20.23 PHI= 0.286 XP = 0.0000
177	TEND LESS TO BE THOSE WHERE THE COMMUNITY IS OTHER THAN A SINGLE CLAN-COMMUNITY AND EXOGAMOUS (305)	0.72 OF 202	177	TEND MORE TO BE THOSE WHERE THE COMMUNITY IS OTHER THAN A SINGLE CLAN-COMMUNITY AND EXOGAMOUS (305)	0.98 OF 46	57 1 145 45 XSQ= 12.77 PHI= 0.227 XP = 0.0004
180	TEND LESS TO BE THOSE WHERE THE COMMUNITY IS COMMONLY NON-EXOGAMOUS, RATHER THAN EXOGAMOUS (258)	0.60 OF 202	180	TEND MORE TO BE THOSE WHERE THE COMMUNITY IS COMMONLY NON-EXOGAMOUS, RATHER THAN EXOGAMOUS (258)	0.89 OF 46	81 5 121 41 XSQ= 12.87 PHI= 0.228 XP = 0.0003
181	LEAN MORE TOWARD BEING THOSE WHERE THE COMMUNITY IS OTHER THAN A DEME (337)	0.93 OF 202	181	LEAN LESS TOWARD BEING THOSE WHERE THE COMMUNITY IS OTHER THAN A DEME (337)	0.78 OF 46	15 10 187 36 XSQ= 6.96 PHI= -0.168 XP = 0.0083
182	LEAN TOWARD BEING THOSE OTHER THAN WHERE THE COMMUNITY IS STRUCTURED ON A NON-CLAN BASIS AND AGAMOUS (256)	0.73 OF 202	182	LEAN TOWARD BEING THOSE WHERE THE COMMUNITY IS STRUCTURED ON A NON-CLAN BASIS AND AGAMOUS (126)	0.52 OF 46	55 24 147 22 XSQ= 9.62 PHI= -0.197 XP = 0.0019
186	TEND TO BE THOSE WHERE THE KIN GROUP IS EXCLUSIVELY PATRILINEAL (150)	0.52 OF 211	186	TEND TO BE THOSE WHERE THE KIN GROUP IS OTHER THAN EXCLUSIVELY PATRILINEAL (250)	0.89 OF 46	109 5 102 41 XSQ= 23.83 PHI= 0.305 XP = 0.0000
188	TEND TO BE THOSE WHERE THE KIN GROUP IS OTHER THAN EXCLUSIVELY COGNATIC (252)	0.83 OF 211	188	TEND TO BE THOSE WHERE THE KIN GROUP IS EXCLUSIVELY COGNATIC (148)	0.80 OF 46	35 37 176 9 XSQ= 73.21 PHI= -0.534 XP = 0.
190	DRIFT TOWARD BEING THOSE WHERE THE KIN GROUP IS PATRILINEAL OR DOUBLE-DESCENT, RATHER THAN MATRILINEAL (186)	0.80 OF 174	190	DRIFT TOWARD BEING THOSE WHERE THE KIN GROUP IS MATRILINEAL, RATHER THAN PATRILINEAL OR DOUBLE-DESCENT (61)	0.57 OF 7	139 3 35 4 XSQ= 3.49 PHI= 0.139 XP = 0.0618
192	TEND TO BE THOSE OTHER THAN WHERE THE ONLY KIN GROUP PRESENT IS A KINDRED OR ELSE BILATERAL DESCENT IS INFERRED (289)	0.87 OF 211	192	TEND TO BE THOSE WHERE THE ONLY KIN GROUP PRESENT IS A KINDRED OR ELSE BILATERAL DESCENT IS INFERRED (111)	0.65 OF 46	27 30 184 16 XSQ= 57.13 PHI= -0.471 XP = 0.

197	TEND TO BE THOSE WHERE RULES FOR THE INHERITANCE OF REAL PROPERTY, IF PRESENT, FAVOR EITHER THE MALE HEIR OR LINE, OR THE FEMALE HEIR OR LINE (165)	0.99 OF 146	197	TEND TO BE THOSE WHERE RULES FOR THE INHERITANCE OF REAL PROPERTY, IF PRESENT, DO NOT FAVOR EITHER THE MALE HEIR OR LINE, OR THE FEMALE HEIR OR LINE (29)	0.75 OF 36	145 9 1 27 XSQ= 116.88 PHI= 0.801 XP = 0.
201	TEND MORE TO BE THOSE WHERE MARITAL RESIDENCE IS NON-OPTIONAL, RATHER THAN AMBILOCAL OR NEOLOCAL (334)	0.93 OF 210	201	TEND LESS TO BE THOSE WHERE MARITAL RESIDENCE IS NON-OPTIONAL, RATHER THAN AMBILOCAL OR NEOLOCAL (334)	0.59 OF 46	195 27 15 19 XSQ= 35.33 PHI= 0.371 XP = 0.
204	TEND TO BE THOSE WHERE MARITAL RESIDENCE IS PATRILOCAL, VIRILOCAL, OR AVUNCULOCAL, RATHER THAN AMBILOCAL OR NEOLOCAL (270)	0.92 OF 191	204	TEND TO BE THOSE WHERE MARITAL RESIDENCE IS AMBILOCAL OR NEOLOCAL, RATHER THAN PATRILOCAL, VIRILOCAL, OR AVUNCULOCAL (64)	0.54 OF 35	176 16 15 19 XSQ= 46.33 PHI= 0.453 XP = 0.
209	TEND MORE TO BE THOSE WHERE MARITAL RESIDENCE IS PATRILOCAL, VIRILOCAL, OR AVUNCULOCAL, RATHER THAN MATRILOCAL OR UXORILOCAL (270)	0.90 OF 195	209	TEND LESS TO BE THOSE WHERE MARITAL RESIDENCE IS PATRILOCAL, VIRILOCAL, OR AVUNCULOCAL, RATHER THAN MATRILOCAL OR UXORILOCAL (270)	0.59 OF 27	176 16 19 11 XSQ= 16.94 PHI= 0.276 XP = 0.0000
210	TILT TOWARD BEING THOSE WHERE MARITAL RESIDENCE IS PATRILOCAL, RATHER THAN MATRILOCAL (169)	0.90 OF 140	210	TILT TOWARD BEING THOSE WHERE MARITAL RESIDENCE IS MATRILOCAL, RATHER THAN PATRILOCAL (31)	0.50 OF 6	126 3 14 3 XSQ= 5.48 PHI= 0.194 XP = 0.0192
224	DRIFT LESS TOWARD BEING THOSE WHERE COUSIN MARRIAGE IS PREFERENTIALLY OR PERMISSIVELY SYMMETRICAL, RATHER THAN EITHER PATRI- OR MATRILATERAL (106)	0.54 OF 100	224	DRIFT MORE TOWARD BEING THOSE WHERE COUSIN MARRIAGE IS PREFERENTIALLY OR PERMISSIVELY SYMMETRICAL, RATHER THAN EITHER PATRI- OR MATRILATERAL (106)	0.81 OF 16	46 3 54 13 XSQ= 3.16 PHI= 0.165 XP = 0.0757
234	TEND TO BE THOSE WHERE THE COUSIN TERMINOLOGY IS OF CROW, OMAHA, OR IROQUOIS TYPE, RATHER THAN ESKIMO OR HAWAIIAN TYPE (152)	0.58 OF 159	234	TEND TO BE THOSE WHERE THE COUSIN TERMINOLOGY IS OF ESKIMO OR HAWAIIAN TYPE, RATHER THAN CROW, OMAHA, OR IROQUOIS TYPE (170)	0.86 OF 42	93 6 66 36 XSQ= 24.24 PHI= 0.347 XP = 0.0000
242	TEND MORE TO BE THOSE WHERE MARRIAGE IS COMMONLY OR OCCASIONALLY POLYGYNOUS, RATHER THAN MONOGAMOUS (314)	0.84 OF 209	242	TEND LESS TO BE THOSE WHERE MARRIAGE IS COMMONLY OR OCCASIONALLY POLYGYNOUS, RATHER THAN MONOGAMOUS (314)	0.53 OF 45	176 24 33 21 XSQ= 19.28 PHI= 0.276 XP = 0.0000
262	LEAN MORE TOWARD BEING THOSE WHERE WIVES ARE OBTAINED BY MEANS INVOLVING THE PRESENCE OF SOME CONSIDERATION (305)	0.87 OF 210	262	LEAN LESS TOWARD BEING THOSE WHERE WIVES ARE OBTAINED BY MEANS INVOLVING THE PRESENCE OF SOME CONSIDERATION (305)	0.67 OF 46	183 31 27 15 XSQ= 9.34 PHI= 0.191 XP = 0.0022

199/

No.			No.			
263	TEND TO BE THOSE WHERE WIVES ARE OBTAINED BY RELATIVELY DIFFICULT MEANS, NAMELY BY BRIDE-PRICE, BRIDE-SERVICE, OR EXCHANGING A FEMALE RELATIVE (233)	0.72 OF 210	263	TEND TO BE THOSE WHERE WIVES ARE OBTAINED BY RELATIVELY EASY MEANS, NAMELY BY TOKEN BRIDE-PRICE, GIFT EXCHANGE, ABSENCE OF ANY CONSIDERATION, OR RECEIPT OF DOWRY (162)	0.61 OF 46	152 18 58 28 XSQ= 17.24 PHI= 0.260 XP = 0.0000
300	DRIFT LESS TOWARD BEING THOSE WHERE THE POST-PARTUM SEX TABOO LASTS SIX MONTHS OR LESS (73)	0.57 OF 74	300	DRIFT MORE TOWARD BEING THOSE WHERE THE POST-PARTUM SEX TABOO LASTS SIX MONTHS OR LESS (73)	0.91 OF 11	32 1 42 10 XSQ= 3.37 PHI= 0.199 XP = 0.0662
369	DRIFT TOWARD BEING THOSE WHERE DISSOCIATION OF THE SEXES AT ADOLESCENCE, OR CUSTOMS OF INITIATION AT ADOLESCENCE, ARE PRESENT (42) JKH	0.74 OF 34	369	IN ALL CASES ARE THOSE WHERE BOTH DISSOCIATION OF THE SEXES AT ADOLESCENCE, AND CUSTOMS OF INITIATION AT ADOLESCENCE, ARE ABSENT (15) JKH	1.00 OF 2	25 0 9 2 XSQ= 1.97 PHI= 0.234 EP = 0.0873
370	LEAN TOWARD BEING THOSE WHERE THE SEGREGATION OF ADOLESCENT BOYS IS COMPLETE OR PARTIAL (95)	0.50 OF 137	370	LEAN TOWARD BEING THOSE WHERE THE SEGREGATION OF ADOLESCENT BOYS IS ABSENT (148)	0.84 OF 31	69 5 68 26 XSQ= 10.67 PHI= 0.252 XP = 0.0011
377	DRIFT LESS TOWARD BEING THOSE WHERE MALE GENITAL MUTILATION IS ABSENT (242)	0.65 OF 176	377	DRIFT MORE TOWARD BEING THOSE WHERE MALE GENITAL MUTILATION IS ABSENT (242)	0.83 OF 36	61 6 115 30 XSQ= 3.68 PHI= 0.132 XP = 0.0550
402	DRIFT TOWARD BEING THOSE WHERE EXPLANATIONS OF ILLNESS OF AN ORAL NATURE ARE PRESENT (31) W-C	0.59 OF 27	402	DRIFT TOWARD BEING THOSE WHERE EXPLANATIONS OF ILLNESS OF AN ORAL NATURE ARE ABSENT (30) W-C	0.86 OF 7	16 1 11 6 XSQ= 2.88 PHI= 0.291 EP = 0.0854
403	DRIFT TOWARD BEING THOSE WHERE EXPLANATIONS OF ILLNESS OF AN ANAL NATURE ARE PRESENT (23) W-C	0.56 OF 27	403	DRIFT TOWARD BEING THOSE WHERE EXPLANATIONS OF ILLNESS OF AN ANAL NATURE ARE ABSENT (38) W-C	0.86 OF 7	15 1 12 6 XSQ= 2.32 PHI= 0.261 EP = 0.0900
404	DRIFT LESS TOWARD BEING THOSE WHERE EXPLANATIONS OF ILLNESS OF A SEXUAL NATURE ARE ABSENT (42) W-C	0.59 OF 27	404	IN ALL CASES ARE THOSE WHERE EXPLANATIONS OF ILLNESS OF A SEXUAL NATURE ARE ABSENT (42) W-C	1.00 OF 7	11 0 16 7 XSQ= 2.56 PHI= 0.274 EP = 0.0693
426	TILT TOWARD BEING THOSE WHERE A HIGH GOD IS PRESENT (156) GES,EA	0.64 OF 142	426	TILT TOWARD BEING THOSE WHERE A HIGH GOD IS ABSENT (104) GES,EA	0.59 OF 27	91 11 51 16 XSQ= 4.24 PHI= 0.158 XP = 0.0396

```
433  DRIFT LESS TOWARD BEING THOSE  0.62 OF  21      433  IN ALL CASES ARE THOSE          1.00 OF   7            8     0
     WHERE BELIEF IN REINCARNATION                        WHERE BELIEF IN REINCARNATION                        13     7
     IS ABSENT  (28) GES                                  IS ABSENT  (28) GES                           XSQ=      2.10
                                                                                                        PHI=     0.274
                                                                                                        EP =    0.0749

442  DRIFT TOWARD BEING THOSE       0.56 OF  27      442  DRIFT TOWARD BEING THOSE        0.86 OF   7           15     1
     WHERE FEAR OF ANIMAL SPIRITS                         WHERE FEAR OF ANIMAL SPIRITS                         12     6
     IS HIGH  (28) W-C                                    IS LOW  (33) W-C                              XSQ=      2.32
                                                                                                        PHI=     0.261
                                                                                                        EP =    0.0900

451  TILT TOWARD BEING THOSE        0.69 OF  16      451  IN ALL CASES ARE THOSE          1.00 OF   4           11     0
     WHERE TOTEMISM IS                                    WHERE TOTEMISM IS                                     5     4
     PRESENT  (15) LWS                                    UNIMPORTANT OR ABSENT  (12) LWS               XSQ=      3.65
                                                                                                        PHI=     0.427
                                                                                                        EP =    0.0260
```

200 CULTURES
WHERE RULES FOR THE INHERITANCE OF
MOVABLE PRCPERTY, IF PRESENT,
FAVOR THE MALE HEIR OR LINE, RATHER THAN
THE FEMALE (176)

200 CULTURES
WHERE RULES FOR THE INHERITANCE OF
MOVABLE PROPERTY, IF PRESENT,
FAVOR THE FEMALE HEIR CR LINE, RATHER THAN
THE MALE (35)

BACKGROUND ON PAGE 111

SUBJECT ONLY

176 IN LEFT COLUMN

ABOR	AINU	AKHA	ALBANIANS	AMBA	ARANDA	ARAPESH	ARAUCANIANS	ARYANS	ATAYAL
ATSUGEWI	AYMARA	AZANDE	AZTEC	BABWA	BAMBARA	BAMILEKE	BANDA	BARABRA	BARI
BASSERI	BATAK	BAYA	BEJA	BERGDAMA	BETE	BHIL	BHUIYA	BOZC	BUDUMA
CAGABA	CAMBA	CHAGGA	CHENCHU	CHERKESS	CHIBCHA	CHINANTEC	CHUKCHEE	COORG	CREE
CREEK	CZECHS	CAGUR	DARC	DILLING	DOGON	EGYPTIANS	ELLICE	ENGA	FANG
FON	FUTAJALCNKE	GANCA	GILYAK	GISU	HASANIA	HAZARA	HEBREWS	HEHE	HO
HUKUNDIKA	HUTSUL	ICELANCERS	INCA	INGALIK	IRAQW	IRISH	JAPANESE	JEMEZ	KABYLE
KACHIN	KALMYK	KASKA	KATAB	KAZAK	KERAKI	KET	KHALKA	KHEVSUR	KIKUYU
KISSI	KOHISTANI	KOL	KOREANS	KORYAK	KPE	KUNG	KWAKIUTL	LAKHER	LANGO
LAU	LEPCHA	LHCTA NAGA	LIFU	LOLO	LOZI	LUBA	LUC	MAGUZAWA	MALAYS
MAM	MAMBILA	MANCHU	MARGI	MARSHALLESE	MASAI	MAYA	MBUGWE	MENDE	MIAO
MIN CHINESE	MINCHIA	MONGO	MONGUOR	MOSSI	NAMA	NANDI	NGCNI	NUER	NUNIVAK
NUPE	NURI	NYAKYUSA	NYORO	OJIBWA	OKINAWANS	OMAHA	ORAON	PAEZ	PALAUANS
PATHAN	PENCBSCOT	POPCLUCA	PURARI	PURUM	REGEIBAT	RIFFIANS	RUNDI	RWALA	SANDAWE
SANPOIL	SANTAL	SHILLUK	SHLUH	SIWANS	SOMALI	SONGHAI	SCTHO	SWAZI	TALLENSI
TANIMBARESE	TAREUMIUT	TECA	TENETEHARA	TERA	TESO	THONGA	TIBETANS	TIGRINYA	TIV
TODA	TOLCWA	TRUKESE	TUCUNA	TURKANA	VEDDA	VENDA	WANTOAT	WOGEO	WOLOF
WUTE	YAKUT	YAPESE	YARURO	YORUBA	YUKAGHIR				

35 IN RIGHT CCLUMN

ASHANTI	BEMBA	BIRIFOR	CROW	DOBUANS	EYAK	GARO	GOAJIRO	HAICA	HERERO
ILA	KHASI	KUBA	LAMBA	LESU	MANDAN	MBUNDU	MINANGKABAU	MOTA	NAVAHO
NDEMBU	NYANEKA	NYARO	PAWNEE	PENDE	PONAPEANS	SARAMACCA	TENDA	TIMBIRA	TIMUCUA
TROBRIAND	TSHIMSHIAN	YAKO	YAO	YOMBE					

78 EXCLUDED BECAUSE IRRELEVANT

111 EXCLUDED BECAUSE UNASCERTAINED

4 TILT LESS TOWARC BEING THCSE 0.84 OF 176
LOCATED CUTSIDE OF
THE CIRCUM-MEDITERRANEAN (355)

4 IN ALL CASES ARE THOSE 1.00 OF 35
LOCATED OUTSIDE OF
THE CIRCUM-MEDITERRANEAN (355)

28	0
148	35

XSQ= 5.11
PHI= 0.156
XP = 0.0238

5	TILT LESS TOWARD BEING THOSE 0.74 OF 176 LOCATED OUTSIDE OF EAST EURASIA (330)	TILT MORE TOWARD BEING THOSE 0.94 OF 35 LOCATED OUTSIDE OF EAST EURASIA (330)	45 2 131 33 XSQ= 5.55 PHI= 0.162 XP = 0.0185
8	DRIFT MORE TOWARD BEING THOSE 0.90 OF 176 LOCATED OUTSIDE OF NORTH AMERICA (330)	DRIFT LESS TOWARD BEING THOSE 0.77 OF 35 LOCATED OUTSIDE OF NORTH AMERICA (330)	18 8 158 27 XSQ= 3.22 PHI= -0.124 XP = 0.0727
36	DRIFT LESS TOWARD BEING THOSE 0.69 OF 176 WHERE THE NATURAL ENVIRONMENT IS OTHER THAN 'VERY HARSH,' OR SUB-TROPICAL BUSH, OR TEMPERATE GRASSLAND (292) FWM	DRIFT MORE TOWARD BEING THOSE 0.86 OF 35 WHERE THE NATURAL ENVIRONMENT IS OTHER THAN 'VERY HARSH,' OR SUB-TROPICAL BUSH, OR TEMPERATE GRASSLAND (292) FWM	54 5 122 30 XSQ= 3.12 PHI= 0.122 XP = 0.0771
47	DRIFT TOWARD BEING THOSE 0.63 OF 40 WHERE, IF SETTLEMENTS ARE NON-FIXED, MOVEMENT IS NOMADIC, RATHER THAN NON-NOMADIC (72)	DRIFT TOWARD BEING THOSE 0.73 OF 11 WHERE, IF SETTLEMENTS ARE NON-FIXED, MOVEMENT IS NON-NOMADIC, RATHER THAN NOMADIC (38)	25 3 15 8 XSQ= 3.02 PHI= 0.243 XP = 0.0823
53	TEND TO BE THOSE 0.51 OF 119 WHERE FOOD PRODUCTION IS BY INTENSIVE AGRICULTURE, RATHER THAN BY SIMPLE AGRICULTURE OR INCIPIENT FOOD PRODUCTION (91)	TEND TO BE THOSE 0.96 OF 24 WHERE FOOD PRODUCTION IS BY SIMPLE AGRICULTURE OR INCIPIENT FOOD PRODUCTION, RATHER THAN BY INTENSIVE AGRICULTURE (147)	61 1 58 23 XSQ= 16.17 PHI= 0.336 XP = 0.0001
55	TEND TO BE THOSE 0.57 OF 107 WHERE FOOD PRODUCTION IS BY INTENSIVE AGRICULTURE, RATHER THAN BY SIMPLE AGRICULTURE (91)	TEND TO BE THOSE 0.95 OF 19 WHERE FOOD PRODUCTION IS BY SIMPLE AGRICULTURE, RATHER THAN BY INTENSIVE AGRICULTURE (101)	61 1 46 18 XSQ= 15.28 PHI= 0.348 XP = 0.0001
63	DRIFT MORE TOWARD BEING THOSE 0.74 OF 124 WHERE HUSBANDRY, IF PRESENT, IS PRINCIPALLY IN THE FORM OF BOVINE, EQUINE, CAMEL-LIKE, OR DEER-LIKE ANIMALS, RATHER THAN PIGS, SHEEP, OR GOATS (152)	DRIFT LESS TOWARD BEING THOSE 0.52 OF 23 WHERE HUSBANDRY, IF PRESENT, IS PRINCIPALLY IN THE FORM OF BOVINE, EQUINE, CAMEL-LIKE, OR DEER-LIKE ANIMALS, RATHER THAN PIGS, SHEEP, OR GOATS (152)	92 12 32 11 XSQ= 3.54 PHI= 0.155 XP = 0.0598
88	DRIFT LESS TOWARD BEING THOSE 0.61 OF 122 WHERE, IF A HEADMANSHIP IS PRESENT, SUCCESSION IS HEREDITARY (165)	DRIFT MORE TOWARD BEING THOSE 0.81 OF 31 WHERE, IF A HEADMANSHIP IS PRESENT, SUCCESSION IS HEREDITARY (165)	48 6 74 25 XSQ= 3.49 PHI= 0.151 XP = 0.0616
90	TEND TO BE THOSE 0.89 OF 74 WHERE, IF A HEREDITARY HEADMANSHIP IS PRESENT, SUCCESSION IS PATRILINEAL, RATHER THAN MATRILINEAL (127)	TEND TO BE THOSE 0.84 OF 25 WHERE, IF A HEREDITARY HEADMANSHIP IS PRESENT, SUCCESSION IS MATRILINEAL, RATHER THAN PATRILINEAL (38)	66 4 8 21 XSQ= 44.86 PHI= 0.673 XP = 0.

94	DRIFT LESS TOWARD BEING THOSE 0.87 OF 149 WHERE THE HIERARCHY OF NATIONAL JURISDICTION HAS TWO, ONE, OR NO LEVELS (296) GES,EA	94	IN ALL CASES ARE THOSE 1.00 OF 29 WHERE THE HIERARCHY OF NATIONAL JURISDICTION HAS TWO, ONE, OR NO LEVELS (296) GES,EA	20 0 129 29 XSQ= 3.14 PHI= 0.133 XP = 0.0763
108	TILT TOWARD BEING THOSE 0.65 OF 106 WHERE CLASS STRATIFICATION, IF PRESENT, IS BASED ON SOMETHING OTHER THAN A HEREDITARY ARISTOCRACY (129)	108	TILT TOWARD BEING THOSE 0.62 OF 21 WHERE CLASS STRATIFICATION, IF PRESENT, IS BASED ON A HEREDITARY ARISTOCRACY (74)	37 13 69 8 XSQ= 4.28 PHI= -0.184 XP = 0.0385
109	DRIFT LESS TOWARD BEING THOSE 0.77 OF 158 WHERE CASTES ARE ABSENT (317)	109	DRIFT MORE TOWARD BEING THOSE 0.94 OF 33 WHERE CASTES ARE ABSENT (317)	36 2 122 31 XSQ= 3.80 PHI= 0.141 XP = 0.0513
183	TILT MORE TOWARD BEING THOSE 0.93 OF 141 WHERE THE LARGEST NON-COGNATIC KIN GROUP IS SMALLER THAN A MOEITY, I. E., A PHRATRY OR SIB OR LINEAGE (218)	183	TILT LESS TOWARD BEING THOSE 0.77 OF 35 WHERE THE LARGEST NON-COGNATIC KIN GROUP IS SMALLER THAN A MOEITY, I. E., A PHRATRY OR SIB OR LINEAGE (218)	10 8 131 27 XSQ= 5.97 PHI= -0.184 XP = 0.0145
184	DRIFT MORE TOWARD BEING THOSE 0.75 OF 141 WHERE THE LARGEST NON-COGNATIC KIN GROUP IS SMALLER THAN A PHRATRY, I. E. A SIB OR LINEAGE (175)	184	DRIFT LESS TOWARD BEING THOSE 0.57 OF 35 WHERE THE LARGEST NON-COGNATIC KIN GROUP IS SMALLER THAN A PHRATRY, I. E. A SIB OR LINEAGE (175)	35 15 106 20 XSQ= 3.64 PHI= -0.144 XP = 0.0564
186	TEND TO BE THOSE 0.62 OF 176 WHERE THE KIN GROUP IS EXCLUSIVELY PATRILINEAL (150)	186	IN ALL CASES ARE THOSE 1.00 OF 35 WHERE THE KIN GROUP IS OTHER THAN EXCLUSIVELY PATRILINEAL (250)	109 0 67 35 XSQ= 42.39 PHI= 0.448 XP = 0.
187	TEND TO BE THOSE 0.97 OF 175 WHERE THE KIN GROUP IS OTHER THAN EXCLUSIVELY MATRILINEAL (344)	187	TEND TO BE THOSE 0.77 OF 35 WHERE THE KIN GROUP IS EXCLUSIVELY MATRILINEAL (55)	5 27 170 8 XSQ= 118.93 PHI= -0.753 XP = 0.
188	LEAN LESS TOWARD BEING THOSE 0.80 OF 176 WHERE THE KIN GROUP IS OTHER THAN EXCLUSIVELY COGNATIC (252)	188	IN ALL CASES ARE THOSE 1.00 OF 35 WHERE THE KIN GROUP IS OTHER THAN EXCLUSIVELY COGNATIC (252)	35 0 141 35 XSQ= 6.97 PHI= 0.182 XP = 0.0083
190	TEND TO BE THOSE 0.95 OF 139 WHERE THE KIN GROUP IS PATRILINEAL OR DOUBLE-DESCENT, RATHER THAN MATRILINEAL (186)	190	TEND TO BE THOSE 0.80 OF 35 WHERE THE KIN GROUP IS MATRILINEAL, RATHER THAN PATRILINEAL OR DOUBLE-DESCENT (61)	132 7 7 28 XSQ= 93.17 PHI= 0.732 XP = 0.

```
192  TILT LESS TOWARC BEING THCSE    0.85 OF 176     192  IN ALL CASES ARE THOSE           1.00 OF  35           27    0
     OTHER THAN WHERE THE CNLY KIN GROUP                  OTHER THAN WHERE THE ONLY KIN GRCUP                   149   35
     PRESENT IS A KINCREC CR ELSE                         PRESENT IS A KINDRED OR ELSE                     XSQ=     4.86
     BILATERAL DESCENT IS INFERREC  (289)                 BILATERAL DESCENT IS INFERRED  (289)             PHI=    0.152
                                                                                                           XP =   0.0275

198  TEND TO BE THCSE                0.99 OF 127     198  TEND TO BE THOSE                 0.78 OF  18          126    4
     WHERE RULES FOR THE INHERITANCE OF                   WHERE RULES FOR THE INHERITANCE CF                      1   14
     REAL PRCPERTY, IF PRESENT,                           REAL PROPERTY, IF PRESENT,                       XSQ=    92.63
     FAVCR THE MALE HEIR OR LINE, RATHER THAN             FAVOR THE FEMALE HEIR CR LINE, RATHER THAN       PHI=    0.799
     THE FEMALE  (144)                                    THE MALE  (21)                                   XP =   0.

207  DRIFT TOWARD BEING THCSE        0.57 OF  21     2C7  DRIFT TOWARD BEING THOSE         0.77 OF  13            9   10
     WHERE MARITAL RESICENCE IS                           WHERE MARITAL RESIDENCE IS                             12    3
     AMBILCCAL CR NECLOCAL, RATHER THAN                   MATRILOCAL OR UXORILOCAL, RATHER THAN            XSQ=     2.52
     MATRILOCAL OR UXCRILOCAL  (64)                       AMBILOCAL OR NEOLOCAL  (64)                      PHI=   -0.272
                                                                                                           EP =   0.0790

209  TEND MORE TO BE THCSE           0.95 OF 164     209  TEND LESS TO BE THOSE            0.68 OF  31          155   21
     WHERE MARITAL RESICENCE IS                           WHERE MARITAL RESIDENCE IS                              9   10
     PATRILOCAL, VIRILOCAL, CR AVUNCULOCAL,               PATRILOCAL, VIRILOCAL, OR AVUNCULOCAL,           XSQ=    18.31
     RATHER THAN                                          RATHER THAN                                      PHI=    0.306
     MATRILOCAL OR UXCRILOCAL  (270)                      MATRILOCAL OR UXORILOCAL  (270)                  XP =   0.0000

210  TEND TO BE THCSE                0.97 OF 126     21C  TEND TO BE THOSE                 0.71 OF  14          122    4
     WHERE MARITAL RESICENCE IS                           WHERE MARITAL RESIDENCE IS                              4   10
     PATRILCCAL, RATHER THAN                              MATRILOCAL, RATHER THAN                          XSQ=    57.86
     MATRILOCAL  (169)                                    PATRILOCAL  (31)                                 PHI=    0.643
                                                                                                           XP =   0.

213  TILT TCWARD BEING THOSE         0.54 OF 166     213  TILT TOWARD BEING THOSE          0.71 OF  34           76   24
     WHERE FIRST COUSIN MARRIACE IS                       WHERE FIRST COUSIN MARRIAGE IS                         90   10
     NCT PERMITTED  (198)                                 PERMITTED  (172)                                 XSQ=     5.99
                                                                                                           PHI=   -0.173
                                                                                                           XP =   0.0144

220  TILT MORE TOWARC BEING THCSE    0.76 OF 166     22C  TILT LESS TOWARD BEING THOSE     0.53 OF  34           40   16
     WHERE FIRST COUSIN MARRIACE                          WHERE FIRST COUSIN MARRIAGE                           126   18
     IN SOME FCRM CR CTHER                                IN SOME FORM OR OTHER                            XSQ=     6.29
     IS NOT PRESCRIBED CR PREFERREC  (273)                IS NOT PRESCRIBED OR PREFERRED  (273)            PHI=   -0.177
                                                                                                           XP =   0.0122

234  TEND LESS TO BE THCSE           0.51 OF 128     234  TEND MORE TO BE THOSE            0.90 OF  31           65   28
     WHERE THE COUSIN TERMINOLOGY IS                      WHERE THE COUSIN TERMINOLOGY IS                        63    3
     OF CRCW, CMAHA, OR IRCQUCIS TYPE,                    OF CROW, OMAHA, OR IROQUOIS TYPE,                XSQ=    14.48
     RATHER THAN                                          RATHER THAN                                      PHI=   -0.302
     ESKIMC CR HAWAIIAN TYPE  (152)                       ESKIMO OR HAWAIIAN TYPE  (152)                   XP =   0.0001

277  DRIFT TCWARD BEING THCSE        0.60 OF  20     277  IN ALL CASES ARE THOSE           1.00 OF   4           12    0
     WHERE THE STATUS OF WOMEN IS                         WHERE THE STATUS OF WOMEN IS                            8    4
     INFERICR CR SUBJECTEC  (14) LWS                      NOT STRONGLY INFERIOR OR                         XSQ=     2.70
                                                          SUBJECTED  (22) LWS                              PHI=    0.335
                                                                                                           EP =   0.0932
```

312	TILT TOWARD BEING THOSE 0.56 OF 16 WHERE DEPENDENCE SOCIALIZATION ANXIETY IS LOW (23) W-C	312	IN ALL CASES ARE THOSE 1.00 OF 5 WHERE DEPENDENCE SOCIALIZATION ANXIETY IS HIGH (24) W-C	7 5 9 0 XSQ= 2.89 PHI= -0.371 EP = 0.0451
319	DRIFT TOWARD BEING THOSE 0.63 OF 32 WHERE PROTECTION OF THE INFANT FROM ENVIRONMENTAL DISCOMFORTS IS LOW (30) B-B-C	319	DRIFT TOWARD BEING THOSE 0.83 OF 6 WHERE PROTECTION OF THE INFANT FROM ENVIRONMENTAL DISCOMFORTS IS HIGH (35) B-B-C	12 5 20 1 XSQ= 2.64 PHI= -0.264 EP = 0.0712
370	TEND TO BE THOSE 0.57 OF 115 WHERE THE SEGREGATION OF ADOLESCENT BOYS IS ABSENT (148)	370	TEND TO BE THOSE 0.86 OF 22 WHERE THE SEGREGATION OF ADOLESCENT BOYS IS COMPLETE OR PARTIAL (95)	50 19 65 3 XSQ= 11.92 PHI= -0.295 XP = 0.0006
403	TILT TOWARD BEING THOSE 0.57 OF 21 WHERE EXPLANATIONS OF ILLNESS OF AN ANAL NATURE ARE ABSENT (38) W-C	403	IN ALL CASES ARE THOSE 1.00 OF 6 WHERE EXPLANATIONS OF ILLNESS OF AN ANAL NATURE ARE PRESENT (23) W-C	9 6 12 0 XSQ= 4.07 PHI= -0.388 EP = 0.0200
405	TILT TOWARD BEING THOSE 0.71 OF 21 WHERE EXPLANATIONS OF ILLNESS OF A DEPENDENCE NATURE ARE PRESENT (34) W-C	405	TILT TOWARD BEING THOSE 0.83 OF 6 WHERE EXPLANATIONS OF ILLNESS OF A DEPENDENCE NATURE ARE ABSENT (27) W-C	15 1 6 5 XSQ= 3.75 PHI= 0.373 EP = 0.0265
426	DRIFT TOWARD BEING THOSE 0.68 OF 118 WHERE A HIGH GOD IS PRESENT (156) GES,EA	426	DRIFT TOWARD BEING THOSE 0.54 OF 24 WHERE A HIGH GOD IS ABSENT (104) GES,EA	80 11 38 13 XSQ= 3.28 PHI= 0.152 XP = 0.0701
427	TILT TOWARD BEING THOSE 0.64 OF 80 WHERE A HIGH GOD, IF PRESENT, IS ACTIVE, RATHER THAN INACTIVE (87) GES,EA	427	TILT TOWARD BEING THOSE 0.82 OF 11 WHERE A HIGH GOD, IF PRESENT, IS INACTIVE, RATHER THAN ACTIVE (69) GES,EA	51 2 29 9 XSQ= 6.49 PHI= 0.267 XP = 0.0109
429	DRIFT TOWARD BEING THOSE 0.88 OF 17 WHERE SUPERNATURAL SANCTIONS FOR MORALITY ARE PRESENT (28) GES	429	DRIFT TOWARD BEING THOSE 0.67 OF 3 WHERE SUPERNATURAL SANCTIONS FOR MORALITY ARE ABSENT OR UNREPORTED (9) GES	15 1 2 2 XSQ= 1.99 PHI= 0.315 EP = 0.0877
471	TILT TOWARD BEING THOSE 0.77 OF 13 WHERE SECRET SOCIETIES ARE UNIMPORTANT OR ABSENT (14) LWS	471	IN ALL CASES ARE THOSE 1.00 OF 4 WHERE SECRET SOCIETIES ARE PRESENT (9) LWS	3 4 10 0 XSQ= 4.63 PHI= -0.522 EP = 0.0147

****

201 CULTURES
WHERE MARITAL RESIDENCE IS
NON-OPTIONAL, RATHER THAN
AMBILOCAL OR NEOLOCAL (334)

201 CULTURES
WHERE MARITAL RESIDENCE IS
AMBILOCAL OR NEOLOCAL, RATHER THAN
NON-OPTIONAL (64)

BACKGROUND ON PAGE 113

BOTH SUBJECT AND PREDICATE

....

334 IN LEFT COLUMN

ABOR	AINU	AJIE	AKHA	ALBANIANS	ALORESE	AMBA	APINAYE	ARANDA	ARAPESH
ARAUCANIANS	ARYANS	ASHANTI	ATAYAL	ATSUGEWI	AYMARA	AZANDE	AZTEC	BABWA	BACAIRI
BALINESE	BAMBARA	BAMILEKE	BANDA	BARABRA	BARI	BASSERI	BATAK	BAYA	BEJA
BELU	BENGALI	BERGDAMA	BETE	BHIL	BHUIYA	BIRIFOR	BOERS	BORORO	BOZO
BUDUMA	BULGARIANS	BUNLAP	BURMESE	BURUSHO	BURYAT	CADUVEO	CAGABA	CALLINAGO	CAMAYURA
CARAJA	CAYAPA	CHAGGA	CHAMACOCO	CHERKESS	CHEROKEE	CHEYENNE	CHIBCHA	CHINANTEC	CHIR-APACHE
CHIRIGUANO	CHOROTI	CHUKCHEE	COCHITI	COORG	CREE	CREEK	CROW	CUNA	CZECHS
DAGUR	DARD	DELAWARE	DIEGUENO	DIERI	DILLING	DOGON	DOROBO	DUSUN	EGYPTIANS
ELLICE	ENGA	EYAK	FANG	FON	FUTAJALONKE	GANDA	GARO	GILBERTESE	GILYAK
GISU	GOAJIRO	GOND	GROS VENTRE	GUAHIBO	GURE	HAIDA	HANO	HANUNOO	HASANIA
HASINAI	HAVASUPAI	HAZARA	HEBREWS	HEHE	HERERO	HO	HURON	ICELANDERS	ILA
INCA	INGALIK	IRAQW	IRISH	JAPANESE	JAVANESE	JIVARO	KABYLE	KACHIN	KALMYK
KAPAUKU	KAREN	KARIERA	KASKA	KATAB	KAZAK	KERAKI	KERALA	KET	KHALKA
KHASI	KHEVSUR	KIKUYU	KIOW-APACHE	KISSI	KOHISTANI	KOL	KONSO	KOREANS	KORYAK
KPE	KUBA	KWAKIUTL	LAKHER	LAMET	LANGO	LAPPS	LAU	LEPCHA	LESU
LHOTA NAGA	LIFU	LOLO	LOZI	LUBA	LUO	MAGUZAWA	MALAYS	MAM	MAMBILA
MAMVU	MANCHU	MANDAN	MANGAIANS	MANIHIKI	MANUS	MARGI	MARICOPA	MARQUESANS	MASAI
MATACO	MATAKAM	MAYA	MAZATECO	MBUGWE	MBUNDU	MBUTI	MENDE	MENTAWEI	MERINA
MIAMI	MIAO	MIN CHINESE	MINCHIA	MISKITO	MIWOK	MNONG GAR	MONGO	MONGUOR	MOSSI
MOTA	MOTILON	MUNDURUCU	MURINBATA	MURNGIN	MZAB	NABESNA	NAMA	NAMBICUARA	NANDI
NASKAPI	NATCHEZ	NAVAHO	NDEMBU	NGONI	NICOBARESE	NOMLAKI	NUER	NUNIVAK	NUPE
NURI	NYANEKA	NYARO	NYORO	OJIBWA	OKINAWANS	ONA	ONTONG-JAVA	ORAON	PAIWAN
PALAUANS	PALIKUR	PAPAGO	PATHAN	PAWNEE	PENDE	PONAPEANS	POPOLUCA	PORTUGUESE	PUKAPUKA
PURARI	PURUM	REGEIBAT	RIFFIANS	ROTINESE	ROTUMANS	RUNDI	RWALA	SAMOYED	SANDAWE
SANPOIL	SANTAL	SARAMACCA	SARSI	SEMANG	SEMINOLE	SENIANG	SERBS	SERI	SHERENTE
SHILLUK	SHLUH	SINCHI	SINHALESE	SIRIONO	SIUAI	SIWANS	SOMALI	SONGHAI	SOTHO
SWAZI	SYRIANS	TAGBANUA	TALAMANCA	TALLENSI	TAMIL	TANALA	TANIMBARESE	TAPIRAPE	TEDA
TEHUELCHE	TENDA	TENETEHARA	TENINO	TERA	TESO	TETON	THAI	THONGA	TIBETANS
TIGRINYA	TIKOPIA	TIMBIRA	TIMUCUA	TIV	TIWI	TODA	TOKELAU	TOLOWA	TORAJA
TOTONAC	TROBRIAND	TRUKESE	TRUMAI	TSHIMSHIAN	TUBATULABAL	TUCANO	TUCUNA	TUNEBO	TUPINAMBA
TURKANA	TURKMEN	TWANA	TZELTAL	ULAWANS	VEDDA	VENDA	VIETNAMESE	WANTOAT	WAPISHANA
WAROPEN	WARRAU	WICHITA	WIKMUNKAN	WINNEBAGO	WITOTO	WOGEO	WOLOF	WUTE	YABARANA
YAGUA	YAHGAN	YAKO	YAKUT	YAO	YAPESE	YARURO	YOKUTS	YOMBE	YORUBA
YUKAGHIR	YUKI	YUROK	ZUNI						

64 IN RIGHT COLUMN

ABIPON	ALACALUF	AMERICANS	ANDAMANESE	AWEIKOMA	BAJUN	BASQUES	BEMBA	BLACK CARIB	BRAZILIANS
CAMBA	CAMBODIANS	CARIB	CARINYA	CHENCHU	CHEREMIS	CHOCO	CHORTI	COMANCHE	COPR ESKIMO

DOBUANS	DUTCH	FOX	GUATO	HAWAIIANS	HUICHOL	HUKUNDIKA	HUTSUL	IBAN	IFUGAO
INGASSANA	JEMEZ	JUKUN	KUMYK	KUNG	KURTATCHI	KUTENAI	LAKALAI	LAMBA	MACASSARESE
MAORI	MARSHALLESE	NYAKYUSA	OMAHA	PAEZ	PARAUJANO	PENOBSCOT	RARCIANS	ROMANS	SAGADA
SAMOANS	SELUNG	SIMBCESE	SUBANUN	TAOS	TARAHUMARA	TAREUMIUT	TERENA	TRISTAN	UTE
WAICA	WALLOONS	WASHO	WOLEAIANS						

1 EXCLUDED BECAUSE IRRELEVANT

MINANGKABAU

1 EXCLUDED BECAUSE UNASCERTAINED

BOTOCUDO

3	DRIFT LESS TOWARD BEING THOSE LOCATED OUTSIDE OF AFRICA (320)	0.78 OF 334	3	DRIFT MORE TOWARD BEING THOSE LOCATED OUTSIDE OF AFRICA (320)	0.89 OF 64	73 7 261 57 XSQ= 3.34 PHI= 0.092 XP = 0.0678
5	TILT LESS TOWARD BEING THOSE LOCATED OUTSIDE OF EAST EURASIA (330)	0.80 OF 334	5	TILT MORE TOWARD BEING THOSE LOCATED OUTSIDE OF EAST EURASIA (330)	0.94 OF 64	66 4 268 60 XSQ= 5.86 PHI= 0.121 XP = 0.0155
87	LEAN MORE TOWARD BEING THOSE WHERE THE LEVEL OF POLITICAL INTEGRATION IS THE LARGE STATE, THE LITTLE STATE, THE MINIMAL STATE, OR THE AUTONOMOUS COMMUNITY (281) GPM	0.94 OF 259	87	LEAN LESS TOWARD BEING THOSE WHERE THE LEVEL OF POLITICAL INTEGRATION IS THE LARGE STATE, THE LITTLE STATE, THE MINIMAL STATE, OR THE AUTONOMOUS COMMUNITY (281) GPM	0.81 OF 43	244 35 15 8 XSQ= 6.88 PHI= 0.151 XP = 0.0087
89	DRIFT LESS TOWARD BEING THOSE WHERE, IF A NON-HEREDITARY HEADMANSHIP IS PRESENT, SUCCESSION IS BY CONSENSUS (63)	0.55 OF 86	89	DRIFT MORE TOWARD BEING THOSE WHERE, IF A NON-HEREDITARY HEADMANSHIP IS PRESENT, SUCCESSION IS BY CONSENSUS (63)	0.79 OF 19	47 15 39 4 XSQ= 2.86 PHI= -0.165 XP = 0.0908
96	DRIFT TOWARD BEING THOSE WHERE THE HIERARCHY OF NATIONAL JURISDICTION HAS FOUR, THREE, TWO OR ONE LEVEL (174) GES,EA	0.55 OF 279	96	DRIFT TOWARD BEING THOSE WHERE THE HIERARCHY OF NATIONAL JURISDICTION HAS NO LEVELS (156) GES,EA	0.60 OF 50	154 20 125 30 XSQ= 3.34 PHI= 0.101 XP = 0.0675
98	TEND TO BE THOSE WHERE THE HIERARCHY OF LOCAL JURISDICTION HAS FOUR OR THREE LEVELS (238) GES,EA	0.77 OF 280	98	TEND TO BE THOSE WHERE THE HIERARCHY OF LOCAL JURISDICTION HAS TWO LEVELS (93) GES,EA	0.54 OF 50	215 23 65 27 XSQ= 18.50 PHI= 0.237 XP = 0.0000

99	TILT TOWARD BEING THOSE 0.65 OF 125 WHERE, WITH NATIONAL HIERARCHY ABSENT, THE HIERARCHY OF LOCAL JURISDICTION HAS FOUR OR THREE LEVELS (93) GES,EA	99	TILT TOWARD BEING THOSE 0.60 OF 30 WHERE, WITH NATIONAL HIERARCHY ABSENT, THE HIERARCHY OF LOCAL JURISDICTION HAS TWO LEVELS (63) GES,EA	81 12 44 18 XSQ= 5.21 PHI= 0.183 XP = 0.0225
100	LEAN MORE TOWARD BEING THOSE 0.84 OF 279 WHERE HIERARCHIES ARE MORE COMPLEX THAN THE 'SIMPLEST,' I. E., MORE COMPLEX THAN TWO LOCAL LEVELS WITH NO NATIONAL LEVELS (267) GES,EA	100	LEAN LESS TOWARD BEING THOSE 0.64 OF 50 WHERE HIERARCHIES ARE MORE COMPLEX THAN THE 'SIMPLEST,' I. E., MORE COMPLEX THAN TWO LOCAL LEVELS WITH NO NATIONAL LEVELS (267) GES,EA	235 32 44 18 XSQ= 10.06 PHI= 0.175 XP = 0.0015
109	TILT LESS TOWARD BEING THOSE 0.84 OF 305 WHERE CASTES ARE ABSENT (317)	109	TILT MORE TOWARD BEING THOSE 0.97 OF 61 WHERE CASTES ARE ABSENT (317)	49 2 256 59 XSQ= 5.91 PHI= 0.127 XP = 0.0151
110	DRIFT LESS TOWARD BEING THOSE 0.55 OF 318 WHERE SLAVERY IS ABSENT (218)	110	DRIFT MORE TOWARD BEING THOSE 0.69 OF 61 WHERE SLAVERY IS ABSENT (218)	144 19 174 42 XSQ= 3.62 PHI= 0.098 XP = 0.0572
118	DRIFT TOWARD BEING THOSE 0.55 OF 44 WHERE THE PERCENTAGE OF OCCUPATIONS THAT ARE SPECIALIZED IS HIGH OR MEDIUM (24) WME	118	IN ALL CASES ARE THOSE 1.00 OF 5 WHERE THE PERCENTAGE OF OCCUPATIONS THAT ARE SPECIALIZED IS LOW (25) WME	24 0 20 5 XSQ= 3.39 PHI= 0.263 XP = 0.0658
128	TILT TOWARD BEING THOSE 0.55 OF 62 WHERE, IF SUBSISTENCE IS PRIMARILY BY AGRICULTURE, THE WORK IS MAINLY DONE BY FEMALES (37)	128	TILT TOWARD BEING THOSE 0.80 OF 15 WHERE, IF SUBSISTENCE IS PRIMARILY BY AGRICULTURE, THE WORK IS MAINLY DONE BY MALES (40)	28 12 34 3 XSQ= 4.56 PHI= -0.243 XP = 0.0327
129	DRIFT LESS TOWARD BEING THOSE 0.66 OF 89 WHERE WEAVING IS MAINLY DONE BY FEMALES (73)	129	DRIFT MORE TOWARD BEING THOSE 0.93 OF 15 WHERE WEAVING IS MAINLY DONE BY FEMALES (73)	30 1 59 14 XSQ= 3.29 PHI= 0.178 XP = 0.0698
136	DRIFT TOWARD BEING THOSE 0.62 OF 29 WHERE FULL-TIME ENTREPRENEURS ARE PRESENT (18) JV	136	IN ALL CASES ARE THOSE 1.00 OF 3 WHERE FULL-TIME ENTREPRENEURS ARE ABSENT (14) JV	18 0 11 3 XSQ= 2.11 PHI= 0.257 EP = 0.0734
176	TEND LESS TO BE THOSE 0.50 OF 318 WHERE THE COMMUNITY IS OTHER THAN A CLAN-COMMUNITY OR A COMMUNITY STRUCTURED OR SEGMENTED ON A CLAN BASIS (213)	176	TEND MORE TO BE THOSE 0.84 OF 62 WHERE THE COMMUNITY IS OTHER THAN A CLAN-COMMUNITY OR A COMMUNITY STRUCTURED OR SEGMENTED ON A CLAN BASIS (213)	158 10 160 52 XSQ= 22.35 PHI= 0.242 XP = 0.0000

177	TEND LESS TO BE THOSE 0.76 OF 318 WHERE THE COMMUNITY IS OTHER THAN A SINGLE CLAN-COMMUNITY AND EXOGAMOUS (305)	177	TEND MORE TO BE THOSE 0.98 OF 62 WHERE THE COMMUNITY IS OTHER THAN A SINGLE CLAN-COMMUNITY AND EXOGAMOUS (305)	76 1 242 61 XSQ= 14.60 PHI= 0.196 XP = 0.0001
180	TEND LESS TO BE THOSE 0.63 OF 318 WHERE THE COMMUNITY IS COMMONLY NON-EXOGAMOUS, RATHER THAN EXOGAMOUS (258)	180	TEND MORE TO BE THOSE 0.90 OF 62 WHERE THE COMMUNITY IS COMMONLY NON-EXOGAMOUS, RATHER THAN EXOGAMOUS (258)	117 6 201 56 XSQ= 16.21 PHI= 0.207 XP = 0.0001
181	TEND MORE TO BE THOSE 0.91 OF 318 WHERE THE COMMUNITY IS OTHER THAN A DEME (337)	181	TEND LESS TO BE THOSE 0.74 OF 62 WHERE THE COMMUNITY IS OTHER THAN A DEME (337)	29 16 289 46 XSQ= 12.29 PHI= -0.180 XP = 0.0005
182	LEAN TOWARD BEING THOSE 0.70 OF 318 OTHER THAN WHERE THE COMMUNITY IS STRUCTURED ON A NON-CLAN BASIS AND AGAMOUS (256)	182	LEAN TOWARD BEING THOSE 0.50 OF 62 WHERE THE COMMUNITY IS STRUCTURED ON A NON-CLAN BASIS AND AGAMOUS (126)	95 31 223 31 XSQ= 8.60 PHI= -0.150 XP = 0.0034
186	TEND LESS TO BE THOSE 0.56 OF 334 WHERE THE KIN GROUP IS OTHER THAN EXCLUSIVELY PATRILINEAL (250)	186	TEND MORE TO BE THOSE 0.95 OF 64 WHERE THE KIN GROUP IS OTHER THAN EXCLUSIVELY PATRILINEAL (250)	147 3 187 61 XSQ= 33.71 PHI= 0.291 XP = 0.
187	TILT LESS TOWARD BEING THOSE 0.85 OF 333 WHERE THE KIN GROUP IS OTHER THAN EXCLUSIVELY MATRILINEAL (344)	187	TILT MORE TOWARD BEING THOSE 0.95 OF 64 WHERE THE KIN GROUP IS OTHER THAN EXCLUSIVELY MATRILINEAL (344)	51 3 282 61 XSQ= 4.29 PHI= 0.104 XP = 0.0382
188	TEND TO BE THOSE 0.71 OF 334 WHERE THE KIN GROUP IS OTHER THAN EXCLUSIVELY COGNATIC (252)	188	TEND TO BE THOSE 0.80 OF 64 WHERE THE KIN GROUP IS EXCLUSIVELY COGNATIC (148)	96 51 238 13 XSQ= 57.68 PHI= -0.381 XP = 0.
190	LEAN TOWARD BEING THOSE 0.78 OF 233 WHERE THE KIN GROUP IS PATRILINEAL OR DOUBLE-DESCENT, RATHER THAN MATRILINEAL (186)	190	LEAN TOWARD BEING THOSE 0.62 OF 13 WHERE THE KIN GROUP IS MATRILINEAL, RATHER THAN PATRILINEAL OR DOUBLE-DESCENT (61)	181 5 52 8 XSQ= 8.25 PHI= 0.183 XP = 0.0041
192	TEND TO BE THOSE 0.79 OF 334 OTHER THAN WHERE THE ONLY KIN GROUP PRESENT IS A KINDRED OR ELSE BILATERAL DESCENT IS INFERRED (289)	192	TEND TO BE THOSE 0.64 OF 64 WHERE THE ONLY KIN GROUP PRESENT IS A KINDRED OR ELSE BILATERAL DESCENT IS INFERRED (111)	69 41 265 23 XSQ= 48.44 PHI= -0.349 XP = 0.

197	TEND TO BE THOSE 0.92 OF 168 WHERE RULES FOR THE INHERITANCE OF REAL PROPERTY, IF PRESENT, FAVOR EITHER THE MALE HEIR OR LINE, OR THE FEMALE HEIR OR LINE (165)	197	TEND TO BE THOSE 0.58 OF 26 WHERE RULES FOR THE INHERITANCE OF REAL PROPERTY, IF PRESENT, DO NOT FAVOR EITHER THE MALE HEIR OR LINE, OR THE FEMALE HEIR OR LINE (29)	154 11 14 15 XSQ= 39.35 PHI= 0.450 XP = 0.
213	TILT LESS TOWARD BEING THOSE 0.51 OF 314 WHERE FIRST COUSIN MARRIAGE IS NOT PERMITTED (198)	213	TILT MORE TOWARD BEING THOSE 0.69 OF 54 WHERE FIRST COUSIN MARRIAGE IS NOT PERMITTED (198)	153 17 161 37 XSQ= 4.84 PHI= 0.115 XP = 0.0278
220	TILT LESS TOWARD BEING THOSE 0.71 OF 314 WHERE FIRST COUSIN MARRIAGE IN SOME FORM OR OTHER IS NOT PRESCRIBED OR PREFERRED (273)	220	TILT MORE TOWARD BEING THOSE 0.89 OF 54 WHERE FIRST COUSIN MARRIAGE IN SOME FORM OR OTHER IS NOT PRESCRIBED OR PREFERRED (273)	90 6 224 48 XSQ= 6.48 PHI= 0.133 XP = 0.0109
234	TEND TO BE THOSE 0.53 OF 262 WHERE THE COUSIN TERMINOLOGY IS OF CROW, OMAHA, OR IROQUOIS TYPE, RATHER THAN ESKIMO OR HAWAIIAN TYPE (152)	234	TEND TO BE THOSE 0.76 OF 58 WHERE THE COUSIN TERMINOLOGY IS OF ESKIMO OR HAWAIIAN TYPE, RATHER THAN CROW, OMAHA, OR IROQUOIS TYPE (170)	138 14 124 44 XSQ= 14.38 PHI= 0.212 XP = 0.0001
236	TEND TO BE THOSE 0.57 OF 332 WHERE THE FAMILY IS OF AN EXTENDED TYPE, RATHER THAN AN INDEPENDENT TYPE (213)	236	TEND TO BE THOSE 0.67 OF 64 WHERE THE FAMILY IS OF AN INDEPENDENT TYPE, RATHER THAN AN EXTENDED TYPE (185)	190 21 142 43 XSQ= 11.89 PHI= 0.173 XP = 0.0006
242	TEND MORE TO BE THOSE 0.83 OF 329 WHERE MARRIAGE IS COMMONLY OR OCCASIONALLY POLYGYNOUS, RATHER THAN MONOGAMOUS (314)	242	TEND LESS TO BE THOSE 0.61 OF 64 WHERE MARRIAGE IS COMMONLY OR OCCASIONALLY POLYGYNOUS, RATHER THAN MONOGAMOUS (314)	273 39 56 25 XSQ= 14.59 PHI= 0.193 XP = 0.0001
262	TEND MORE TO BE THOSE 0.82 OF 331 WHERE WIVES ARE OBTAINED BY MEANS INVOLVING THE PRESENCE OF SOME CONSIDERATION (305)	262	TEND LESS TO BE THOSE 0.56 OF 62 WHERE WIVES ARE OBTAINED BY MEANS INVOLVING THE PRESENCE OF SOME CONSIDERATION (305)	270 35 61 27 XSQ= 17.54 PHI= 0.211 XP = 0.0000
263	LEAN TOWARD BEING THOSE 0.63 OF 331 WHERE WIVES ARE OBTAINED BY RELATIVELY DIFFICULT MEANS, NAMELY BY BRIDE-PRICE, BRIDE-SERVICE, OR EXCHANGING A FEMALE RELATIVE (233)	263	LEAN TOWARD BEING THOSE 0.60 OF 62 WHERE WIVES ARE OBTAINED BY RELATIVELY EASY MEANS, NAMELY BY TOKEN BRIDE-PRICE, GIFT EXCHANGE, ABSENCE OF ANY CONSIDERATION, OR RECEIPT OF DOWRY (162)	208 25 123 37 XSQ= 10.06 PHI= 0.160 XP = 0.0015
301	TILT MORE TOWARD BEING THOSE 0.81 OF 106 WHERE THE POST-PARTUM SEX TABOO LASTS LONGER THAN ONE MONTH (96)	301	TILT LESS TOWARD BEING THOSE 0.56 OF 18 WHERE THE POST-PARTUM SEX TABOO LASTS LONGER THAN ONE MONTH (96)	86 10 20 8 XSQ= 4.39 PHI= 0.188 XP = 0.0362

344	DRIFT TOWARD BEING THOSE 0.58 OF 66 WHERE THE TOTAL POSITIVE PRESSURE TOWARD DEVELOPING SELF-RELIANT BEHAVIOR IN THE CHILD IS LOW (40) B-B-C	344	DRIFT TOWARD BEING THOSE 0.80 OF 10 WHERE THE TOTAL POSITIVE PRESSURE TOWARD DEVELOPING SELF-RELIANT BEHAVIOR IN THE CHILD IS HIGH (36) B-B-C	28 8 38 2 XSQ= 3.53 PHI= -0.215 XP = 0.0604
349	DRIFT LESS TOWARD BEING THOSE 0.51 OF 57 WHERE THE CHILD'S INFERRED ANXIETY OVER NON-PERFORMANCE OF ACHIEVEMENT BEHAVIOR IS HIGH (34) B-B-C	349	IN ALL CASES ARE THOSE 1.00 OF 5 WHERE THE CHILD'S INFERRED ANXIETY OVER NON-PERFORMANCE OF ACHIEVEMENT BEHAVIOR IS HIGH (34) B-B-C	29 5 28 0 XSQ= 2.71 PHI= -0.209 XP = 0.0994
368	DRIFT TOWARD BEING THOSE 0.67 OF 27 WHERE DISSOCIATION OF THE SEXES AT ADOLESCENCE IS LOW (21) JKH	368	DRIFT TOWARD BEING THOSE 0.70 OF 10 WHERE DISSOCIATION OF THE SEXES AT ADOLESCENCE IS HIGH OR MEDIUM (16) JKH	9 7 18 3 XSQ= 2.64 PHI= -0.267 EP = 0.0667
370	TILT LESS TOWARD BEING THOSE 0.58 OF 205 WHERE THE SEGREGATION OF ADOLESCENT BOYS IS ABSENT (148)	370	TILT MORE TOWARD BEING THOSE 0.79 OF 38 WHERE THE SEGREGATION OF ADOLESCENT BOYS IS ABSENT (148)	87 8 118 30 XSQ= 5.29 PHI= 0.148 XP = 0.0214
377	LEAN LESS TOWARD BEING THOSE 0.71 OF 273 WHERE MALE GENITAL MUTILATION IS ABSENT (242)	377	LEAN MORE TOWARD BEING THOSE 0.92 OF 51 WHERE MALE GENITAL MUTILATION IS ABSENT (242)	79 4 194 47 XSQ= 8.96 PHI= 0.166 XP = 0.0028
392	TILT TOWARD BEING THOSE 0.67 OF 150 WHERE PREMARITAL SEX RELATIONS ARE STRONGLY PUNISHED AND IN FACT RARE, OR WEAKLY PUNISHED AND IN FACT NOT RARE, OR PUNISHED ONLY IF PREGNANCY RESULTS (112) JTW,EA	392	TILT TOWARD BEING THOSE 0.59 OF 29 WHERE PREMARITAL SEX RELATIONS ARE FREELY PERMITTED (67) JTW,EA	100 12 50 17 XSQ= 5.60 PHI= 0.177 XP = 0.0180
433	DRIFT LESS TOWARD BEING THOSE 0.67 OF 30 WHERE BELIEF IN REINCARNATION IS ABSENT (28) GES	433	IN ALL CASES ARE THOSE 1.00 OF 8 WHERE BELIEF IN REINCARNATION IS ABSENT (28) GES	10 0 20 8 XSQ= 2.10 PHI= 0.235 EP = 0.0821
453	TILT TOWARD BEING THOSE 0.70 OF 33 WHERE THE ROLE OF RELIGIOUS EXPERTS IS NOT CONDUCIVE TO THE DEVELOPMENT OF THE INDIVIDUAL'S NEED TO ACHIEVE (23) DCM	453	IN ALL CASES ARE THOSE 1.00 OF 3 WHERE THE ROLE OF RELIGIOUS EXPERTS IS CONDUCIVE TO THE DEVELOPMENT OF THE INDIVIDUAL'S NEED TO ACHIEVE (13) DCM	10 3 23 0 XSQ= 3.16 PHI= -0.296 EP = 0.0401
477	DRIFT TOWARD BEING THOSE 0.64 OF 28 WHERE ALCOHOLIC AGGRESSION IS MODERATE OR SLIGHT (19) DH	477	DRIFT TOWARD BEING THOSE 0.83 OF 6 WHERE ALCOHOLIC AGGRESSION IS STRONG (15) DH	10 5 18 1 XSQ= 2.82 PHI= -0.288 EP = 0.0663

202 CULTURES WHERE MARITAL RESIDENCE IS AMBILOCAL (41)

202 CULTURES WHERE MARITAL RESIDENCE IS OTHER THAN AMBILOCAL (357)

BACKGROUND ON PAGE 113

SUBJECT ONLY

41 IN LEFT COLUMN

ALACALUF	ANDAMANESE	AWEIKOMA	BASQUES	BEMBA	CARIB	CHENCHU	CHORTI	COMANCHE	DOBUANS
DUTCH	FOX	HAWAIIANS	HUICHOL	HUKUNDIKA	IBAN	IFUGAO	INGASSANA	JUKUN	KUNG
KURTATCHI	KUTENAI	LAKALAI	LAMBA	MACASSARESE	MAORI	MARSHALLESE	OMAHA	PARAUJANO	PENOBSCOT
RARCIANS	SAGADA	SAMOANS	SIMBOESE	SUBANUN	TAREUMIUT	TERENA	UTE	WAICA	WASHO
WOLEAIANS									

357 IN RIGHT COLUMN

1 EXCLUDED BECAUSE IRRELEVANT

MINANGKABAU

1 EXCLUDED BECAUSE UNASCERTAINED

	Left column (41)			Right column (357)		
5	TILT MORE TOWARD BEING THOSE LOCATED OUTSIDE OF EAST EURASIA (330)	0.95 OF 41	5	TILT LESS TOWARD BEING THOSE LOCATED OUTSIDE OF EAST EURASIA (330)	0.81 OF 357	2 68 39 289 XSQ= 4.16 PHI= -0.102 XP = 0.0413
6	LEAN LESS TOWARD BEING THOSE LOCATED OUTSIDE OF THE INSULAR PACIFIC (330)	0.63 OF 41	6	LEAN MORE TOWARD BEING THOSE LOCATED OUTSIDE OF THE INSULAR PACIFIC (330)	0.85 OF 357	15 54 26 303 XSQ= 10.37 PHI= 0.161 XP = 0.0013
51	TILT TOWARD BEING THOSE WHERE SUBSISTENCE IS PRIMARILY BY FOOD GATHERING -- I. E., HUNTING, FISHING, OR COLLECTING -- RATHER THAN FOOD PRODUCTION (147)	0.54 OF 41	51	TILT TOWARD BEING THOSE WHERE SUBSISTENCE IS PRIMARILY BY FOOD PRODUCTION -- I. E., AGRICULTURE OR HUSBANDRY -- RATHER THAN BY GATHERING (253)	0.65 OF 357	19 233 22 124 XSQ= 4.89 PHI= -0.111 XP = 0.0271
71	TILT MORE TOWARD BEING THOSE WHERE METAL WORKING IS ABSENT (153)	0.80 OF 30	71	TILT LESS TOWARD BEING THOSE WHERE METAL WORKING IS ABSENT (153)	0.58 OF 220	6 92 24 128 XSQ= 4.40 PHI= -0.133 XP = 0.0360

81	TILT MORE TOWARD BEING THOSE WHERE NO CITY OR TOWN IS PRESENT, AND THE AVERAGE COMMUNITY SIZE IS SMALLER THAN 200 (135)	0.85 OF 20	81	TILT LESS TOWARD BEING THOSE WHERE NO CITY OR TOWN IS PRESENT, AND THE AVERAGE COMMUNITY SIZE IS SMALLER THAN 200 (135)	0.58 OF 203	3 86 17 117 XSQ= 4.60 PHI= -0.144 XP = 0.0320
82	DRIFT LESS TOWARD BEING THOSE WHERE A CITY OR TOWN IS PRESENT, OR THE AVERAGE COMMUNITY SIZE IS FIFTY OR GREATER (178)	0.60 OF 20	82	DRIFT MORE TOWARD BEING THOSE WHERE A CITY OR TOWN IS PRESENT, OR THE AVERAGE COMMUNITY SIZE IS FIFTY OR GREATER (178)	0.81 OF 203	12 165 8 38 XSQ= 3.82 PHI= -0.131 XP = 0.0506
83	DRIFT MORE TOWARD BEING THOSE WHERE, WITH NO CITY AND NO TOWN PRESENT, THE AVERAGE COMMUNITY SIZE IS SMALLER THAN 200, RATHER THAN BETWEEN 200 AND 999 (135)	0.94 OF 18	83	DRIFT LESS TOWARD BEING THOSE WHERE, WITH NO CITY AND NO TOWN PRESENT, THE AVERAGE COMMUNITY SIZE IS SMALLER THAN 200, RATHER THAN BETWEEN 200 AND 999 (135)	0.73 OF 161	1 44 17 117 XSQ= 3.00 PHI= -0.130 XP = 0.0831
87	LEAN LESS TOWARD BEING THOSE WHERE THE LEVEL OF POLITICAL INTEGRATION IS THE LARGE STATE, THE LITTLE STATE, THE MINIMAL STATE, OR THE AUTONOMOUS COMMUNITY (281) GPM	0.78 OF 32	87	LEAN MORE TOWARD BEING THOSE WHERE THE LEVEL OF POLITICAL INTEGRATION IS THE LARGE STATE, THE LITTLE STATE, THE MINIMAL STATE, OR THE AUTONOMOUS COMMUNITY (281) GPM	0.94 OF 270	25 254 7 16 XSQ= 8.20 PHI= -0.165 XP = 0.0042
109	IN ALL CASES ARE THOSE WHERE CASTES ARE ABSENT (317)	1.00 OF 40	109	TILT LESS TOWARD BEING THOSE WHERE CASTES ARE ABSENT (317)	0.84 OF 326	0 51 40 275 XSQ= 6.02 PHI= -0.128 XP = 0.0141
129	IN ALL CASES ARE THOSE WHERE WEAVING IS MAINLY DONE BY FEMALES (73)	1.00 OF 9	129	DRIFT LESS TOWARD BEING THOSE WHERE WEAVING IS MAINLY DONE BY FEMALES (73)	0.67 OF 95	0 31 9 64 XSQ= 2.77 PHI= -0.163 XP = 0.0961
136	IN ALL CASES ARE THOSE WHERE FULL-TIME ENTREPRENEURS ARE ABSENT (14) JV	1.00 OF 3	136	DRIFT TOWARD BEING THOSE WHERE FULL-TIME ENTREPRENEURS ARE PRESENT (18) JV	0.62 OF 29	0 18 3 11 XSQ= 2.11 PHI= -0.257 EP = 0.0734
175	DRIFT MORE TOWARD BEING THOSE WHERE THE COMMUNITY IS 'KIN-HETEROGENEOUS,' I. E. OTHER THAN A CLAN COMMUNITY OR A DEME (260)	0.80 OF 41	175	DRIFT LESS TOWARD BEING THOSE WHERE THE COMMUNITY IS 'KIN-HETEROGENEOUS,' I. E. OTHER THAN A CLAN COMMUNITY OR A DEME (260)	0.66 OF 339	8 114 33 225 XSQ= 2.73 PHI= -0.085 XP = 0.0986
176	TILT MORE TOWARD BEING THOSE WHERE THE COMMUNITY IS OTHER THAN A CLAN-COMMUNITY OR A COMMUNITY STRUCTURED OR SEGMENTED ON A CLAN BASIS (213)	0.76 OF 41	176	TILT LESS TOWARD BEING THOSE WHERE THE COMMUNITY IS OTHER THAN A CLAN-COMMUNITY OR A COMMUNITY STRUCTURED OR SEGMENTED ON A CLAN BASIS (213)	0.53 OF 339	10 158 31 181 XSQ= 6.45 PHI= -0.130 XP = 0.0111

177	LEAN MORE TOWARD BEING THOSE WHERE THE COMMUNITY IS OTHER THAN A SINGLE CLAN-COMMUNITY AND EXOGAMOUS (305)	0.98 OF 41	177	LEAN LESS TOWARD BEING THOSE WHERE THE COMMUNITY IS OTHER THAN A SINGLE CLAN-COMMUNITY AND EXOGAMOUS (305)	0.78 OF 339	1 76 40 263 XSQ= 7.84 PHI= -0.144 XP = 0.0051
180	LEAN MORE TOWARD BEING THOSE WHERE THE COMMUNITY IS COMMONLY NON-EXOGAMOUS, RATHER THAN EXOGAMOUS (258)	0.88 OF 41	180	LEAN LESS TOWARD BEING THOSE WHERE THE COMMUNITY IS COMMONLY NON-EXOGAMOUS, RATHER THAN EXOGAMOUS (258)	0.65 OF 339	5 118 36 221 XSQ= 7.54 PHI= -0.141 XP = 0.0060
182	TILT LESS TOWARD BEING THOSE OTHER THAN WHERE THE COMMUNITY IS STRUCTURED ON A NON-CLAN BASIS AND AGAMOUS (256)	0.51 OF 41	182	TILT MORE TOWARD BEING THOSE OTHER THAN WHERE THE COMMUNITY IS STRUCTURED ON A NON-CLAN BASIS AND AGAMOUS (256)	0.69 OF 339	20 106 21 233 XSQ= 4.30 PHI= 0.106 XP = 0.0381
186	TEND MORE TO BE THOSE WHERE THE KIN GROUP IS OTHER THAN EXCLUSIVELY PATRILINEAL (250)	0.95 OF 41	186	TEND LESS TO BE THOSE WHERE THE KIN GROUP IS OTHER THAN EXCLUSIVELY PATRILINEAL (250)	0.59 OF 357	2 148 39 209 XSQ= 19.42 PHI= -0.221 XP = 0.0000
188	TEND TO BE THOSE WHERE THE KIN GROUP IS EXCLUSIVELY COGNATIC (148)	0.76 OF 41	188	TEND TO BE THOSE WHERE THE KIN GROUP IS OTHER THAN EXCLUSIVELY COGNATIC (252)	0.68 OF 357	31 116 10 241 XSQ= 27.53 PHI= 0.263 XP = 0.0000
190	LEAN TOWARD BEING THOSE WHERE THE KIN GROUP IS MATRILINEAL, RATHER THAN PATRILINEAL OR DOUBLE-DESCENT (61)	0.70 OF 10	190	LEAN TOWARD BEING THOSE WHERE THE KIN GROUP IS PATRILINEAL OR DOUBLE-DESCENT, RATHER THAN MATRILINEAL (186)	0.78 OF 236	3 183 7 53 XSQ= 9.32 PHI= -0.195 XP = 0.0023
192	TEND TO BE THOSE WHERE THE ONLY KIN GROUP PRESENT IS A KINDRED OR ELSE BILATERAL DESCENT IS INFERRED (111)	0.51 OF 41	192	TEND TO BE THOSE OTHER THAN WHERE THE ONLY KIN GROUP PRESENT IS A KINDRED OR ELSE BILATERAL DESCENT IS INFERRED (289)	0.75 OF 357	21 89 20 268 XSQ= 11.43 PHI= 0.169 XP = 0.0007
197	TEND TO BE THOSE WHERE RULES FOR THE INHERITANCE OF REAL PROPERTY, IF PRESENT, DO NOT FAVOR EITHER THE MALE HEIR OR LINE, OR THE FEMALE HEIR OR LINE (29)	0.53 OF 15	197	TEND TO BE THOSE WHERE RULES FOR THE INHERITANCE OF REAL PROPERTY, IF PRESENT, FAVOR EITHER THE MALE HEIR OR LINE, OR THE FEMALE HEIR OR LINE (165)	0.88 OF 179	7 158 8 21 XSQ= 15.71 PHI= -0.285 XP = 0.0001
213	DRIFT MORE TOWARD BEING THOSE WHERE FIRST COUSIN MARRIAGE IS NOT PERMITTED (198)	0.68 OF 38	213	DRIFT LESS TOWARD BEING THOSE WHERE FIRST COUSIN MARRIAGE IS NOT PERMITTED (198)	0.52 OF 330	12 158 26 172 XSQ= 3.02 PHI= -0.091 XP = 0.0824

```
220  DRIFT MORE TOWARD BEING THOSE  0.87 OF  38     220  DRIFT LESS TOWARD BEING THOSE  0.72 OF 330          5   91
     WHERE FIRST COUSIN MARRIAGE                        WHERE FIRST COUSIN MARRIAGE                        33  239
     IN SOME FORM OR OTHER                              IN SOME FORM OR OTHER                       XSQ=     2.96
     IS NOT PRESCRIBED OR PREFERRED  (273)              IS NOT PRESCRIBED OR PREFERRED  (273)       PHI=   -0.090
                                                                                                    XP =   0.0851

234  TILT TOWARD BEING THOSE        0.72 OF  39     234  TILT TOWARD BEING THOSE        0.50 OF 281         11  141
     WHERE THE COUSIN TERMINOLOGY IS                    WHERE THE COUSIN TERMINOLOGY IS                    28  140
     OF ESKIMO OR HAWAIIAN TYPE,                        OF CROW, OMAHA, OR IROQUOIS TYPE,           XSQ=     5.78
     RATHER THAN                                        RATHER THAN                                 PHI=   -0.134
     CROW, OMAHA, OR IROQUOIS TYPE  (170)               ESKIMO OR HAWAIIAN TYPE  (152)              XP =   0.0162

262  LEAN LESS TOWARD BEING THOSE   0.59 OF  41     262  LEAN MORE TOWARD BEING THOSE   0.80 OF 352         24  281
     WHERE WIVES ARE OBTAINED BY                        WHERE WIVES ARE OBTAINED BY                        17   71
     MEANS INVOLVING THE PRESENCE                       MEANS INVOLVING THE PRESENCE                XSQ=     8.39
     OF SOME CONSIDERATION  (305)                       OF SOME CONSIDERATION  (305)                PHI=   -0.146
                                                                                                    XP =   0.0038

263  DRIFT TOWARD BEING THOSE       0.56 OF  41     263  DRIFT TOWARD BEING THOSE       0.61 OF 352         18  215
     WHERE WIVES ARE OBTAINED                           WHERE WIVES ARE OBTAINED BY                        23  137
     BY RELATIVELY EASY MEANS, NAMELY BY                RELATIVELY DIFFICULT MEANS, NAMELY BY       XSQ=     3.81
     TOKEN BRIDE-PRICE, GIFT EXCHANGE,                  BRIDE-PRICE, BRIDE-SERVICE, OR              PHI=   -0.098
     ABSENCE OF ANY CONSIDERATION, OR                   EXCHANGING A FEMALE RELATIVE  (233)         XP =   0.0511
     RECEIPT OF DOWRY  (162)

377  TILT MORE TOWARD BEING THOSE   0.91 OF  33     377  TILT LESS TOWARD BEING THOSE   0.73 OF 291          3   80
     WHERE MALE GENITAL MUTILATION                      WHERE MALE GENITAL MUTILATION                      30  211
     IS ABSENT  (242)                                   IS ABSENT  (242)                            XSQ=     4.35
                                                                                                    PHI=   -0.116
                                                                                                    XP =   0.0371

382  IN ALL CASES ARE THOSE         1.00 OF   6     382  DRIFT LESS TOWARD BEING THOSE  0.54 OF  59          6   32
     WHERE FEMALE INITIATION RITES                      WHERE FEMALE INITIATION RITES                       0   27
     ARE PRESENT  (38) JKB                              ARE PRESENT  (38) JKB                       XSQ=     3.00
                                                                                                    PHI=    0.215
                                                                                                    XP =   0.0832

390  IN ALL CASES ARE THOSE         1.00 OF  21     390  LEAN LESS TOWARD BEING THOSE   0.70 OF 158          0   47
     WHERE PREMARITAL SEX RELATIONS ARE                 WHERE PREMARITAL SEX RELATIONS ARE                 21  111
     WEAKLY PUNISHED AND IN FACT NOT RARE OR            WEAKLY PUNISHED AND IN FACT NOT RARE OR     XSQ=     7.00
     PUNISHED ONLY IF PREGNANCY RESULTS, OR             PUNISHED ONLY IF PREGNANCY RESULTS, OR      PHI=   -0.198
     FREELY PERMITTED  (132) JTW,EA                     FREELY PERMITTED  (132) JTW,EA              XP =   0.0081

391  TILT TOWARD BEING THOSE        0.76 OF  21     391  TILT TOWARD BEING THOSE        0.53 OF 158          5   84
     WHERE PREMARITAL SEX RELATIONS ARE                 WHERE PREMARITAL SEX RELATIONS ARE                 16   74
     PUNISHED ONLY IF PREGNANCY RESULTS, OR             STRONGLY PUNISHED AND IN FACT RARE, OR      XSQ=     5.27
     FREELY PERMITTED  (90) JTW,EA                      WEAKLY PUNISHED AND                         PHI=   -0.172
                                                        IN FACT NOT RARE  (89) JTW,EA               XP =   0.0217

392  LEAN TOWARD BEING THOSE        0.71 OF  21     392  LEAN TOWARD BEING THOSE        0.67 OF 158          6  106
     WHERE PREMARITAL SEX RELATIONS ARE                 WHERE PREMARITAL SEX RELATIONS ARE                 15   52
     FREELY PERMITTED  (67) JTW,EA                      STRONGLY PUNISHED AND IN FACT RARE, OR      XSQ=    10.16
                                                        WEAKLY PUNISHED AND IN FACT NOT RARE, OR    PHI=   -0.238
                                                        PUNISHED ONLY IF                            XP =   0.0014
                                                        PREGNANCY RESULTS  (112) JTW,EA
```

453	IN ALL CASES ARE THCSE WHERE THE RCLE CF RELIGIOUS EXPERTS IS CCNDUCIVE TC THE DEVELCPMENT OF THE INDIVIDUAL'S NEED TC ACHIEVE (13) CCM	1.00 OF	3	453	TILT TOWARD BEING THOSE WHERE THE ROLE CF RELIGIOUS EXPERTS IS NOT CONDUCIVE TC THE DEVELOPMENT CF THE INDIVIDUAL'S NEED TC ACHIEVE (23) DCM	0.70 OF	33
						3	10
						0	23
						XSQ=	3.16
						PHI=	0.296
						EP =	0.0401
477	IN ALL CASES ARE THOSE WHERE ALCCHCLIC AGGRESSICN IS STRCNG (15) DH	1.00 OF	4	477	TILT TOWARD BEING THOSE WHERE ALCOHOLIC AGGRESSICN IS MODERATE OR SLIGHT (19) DH	0.63 CF	30
						4	11
						0	19
						XSQ=	3.46
						PHI=	0.319
						EP =	0.0294

203 CULTURES WHERE MARITAL RESIDENCE IS NEOLOCAL (23)

203 CULTURES WHERE MARITAL RESIDENCE IS OTHER THAN NEOLOCAL (375)

BACKGROUND ON PAGE 113

SUBJECT ONLY

23 IN LEFT COLUMN

ABIPON, AMERICANS, BAJUN, BLACK CARIB, BRAZILIANS, CAMBA, CAMBODIANS, CARINYA, CHEREMIS, CHOCO, COPR ESKIMO, GUATO, HUTSUL, JEMEZ, KUMYK, NYAKYUSA, PAEZ, ROMANS, SELUNG, TAOS, TARAHUMARA, TRISTAN, WALLOONS

375 IN RIGHT COLUMN

1 EXCLUDED BECAUSE IRRELEVANT

MINANGKABAU

1 EXCLUDED BECAUSE UNASCERTAINED

	Left column (23)			Right column (375)		Statistics
4	TEND LESS TO BE THOSE LOCATED OUTSIDE OF THE CIRCUM-MEDITERRANEAN (355)	0.65 OF 23	4	TEND MORE TO BE THOSE LOCATED OUTSIDE OF THE CIRCUM-MEDITERRANEAN (355)	0.90 OF 375	8 37 15 338 XSQ= 11.05 PHI= 0.167 XP = 0.0009
6	IN ALL CASES ARE THOSE LOCATED OUTSIDE OF THE INSULAR PACIFIC (330)	1.00 OF 23	6	TILT LESS TOWARD BEING THOSE LOCATED OUTSIDE OF THE INSULAR PACIFIC (330)	0.82 OF 375	0 69 23 306 XSQ= 3.92 PHI= -0.099 XP = 0.0478
53	LEAN TOWARD BEING THOSE WHERE FOOD PRODUCTION IS BY INTENSIVE AGRICULTURE, RATHER THAN BY SIMPLE AGRICULTURE OR INCIPIENT FOOD PRODUCTION (91)	0.79 OF 14	53	LEAN TOWARD BEING THOSE WHERE FOOD PRODUCTION IS BY SIMPLE AGRICULTURE OR INCIPIENT FOOD PRODUCTION, RATHER THAN BY INTENSIVE AGRICULTURE (147)	0.64 OF 224	11 80 3 144 XSQ= 8.51 PHI= 0.189 XP = 0.0035
55	TILT TOWARD BEING THOSE WHERE FOOD PRODUCTION IS BY INTENSIVE AGRICULTURE, RATHER THAN BY SIMPLE AGRICULTURE (91)	0.85 OF 13	55	TILT TOWARD BEING THOSE WHERE FOOD PRODUCTION IS BY SIMPLE AGRICULTURE, RATHER THAN BY INTENSIVE AGRICULTURE (101)	0.55 OF 179	11 80 2 99 XSQ= 6.23 PHI= 0.180 XP = 0.0126

63	IN ALL CASES ARE THOSE 1.00 OF 12 WHERE HUSBANDRY, IF PRESENT, IS PRINCIPALLY IN THE FORM OF BOVINE, EQUINE, CAMEL-LIKE, OR DEER-LIKE ANIMALS, RATHER THAN PIGS, SHEEP, OR GOATS (152)	63	TILT LESS TOWARD BEING THOSE 0.65 OF 214 WHERE HUSBANDRY, IF PRESENT, IS PRINCIPALLY IN THE FORM OF BOVINE, EQUINE, CAMEL-LIKE, OR DEER-LIKE ANIMALS, RATHER THAN PIGS, SHEEP, OR GOATS (152)	12 140 0 74 XSQ= 4.70 PHI= 0.144 XP = 0.0302
81	DRIFT TOWARD BEING THOSE 0.69 OF 13 WHERE A CITY OR TOWN IS PRESENT, OR THE AVERAGE COMMUNITY SIZE IS 200 OR GREATER (83)	81	DRIFT TOWARD BEING THOSE 0.62 OF 210 WHERE NO CITY OR TOWN IS PRESENT, AND THE AVERAGE COMMUNITY SIZE IS SMALLER THAN 200 (135)	9 80 4 130 XSQ= 3.74 PHI= 0.129 XP = 0.0533
88	LEAN TOWARD BEING THOSE 0.77 OF 13 WHERE, IF A HEADMANSHIP IS PRESENT, SUCCESSION IS NON-HEREDITARY (106)	88	LEAN TOWARD BEING THOSE 0.63 OF 256 WHERE, IF A HEADMANSHIP IS PRESENT, SUCCESSION IS HEREDITARY (165)	10 95 3 161 XSQ= 6.65 PHI= 0.157 XP = 0.0099
98	TEND TO BE THOSE 0.94 OF 16 WHERE THE HIERARCHY OF LOCAL JURISDICTION HAS TWO LEVELS (93) GES,EA	98	TEND TO BE THOSE 0.75 OF 314 WHERE THE HIERARCHY OF LOCAL JURISDICTION HAS FOUR OR THREE LEVELS (238) GES,EA	1 237 15 77 XSQ= 32.93 PHI= -0.316 XP = 0.
99	LEAN TOWARD BEING THOSE 0.90 OF 10 WHERE, WITH NATIONAL HIERARCHY ABSENT, THE HIERARCHY OF LOCAL JURISDICTION HAS TWO LEVELS (63) GES,EA	99	LEAN TOWARD BEING THOSE 0.63 OF 145 WHERE, WITH NATIONAL HIERARCHY ABSENT, THE HIERARCHY OF LOCAL JURISDICTION HAS FOUR OR THREE LEVELS (93) GES,EA	1 92 9 53 XSQ= 9.02 PHI= -0.241 XP = 0.0027
100	TEND TO BE THOSE 0.56 OF 16 WHERE HIERARCHIES ARE THE 'SIMPLEST' I. E., WHERE THERE ARE ONLY TWO LOCAL LEVELS WITH NO NATIONAL LEVELS (63) GES,EA	100	TEND TO BE THOSE 0.83 OF 313 WHERE HIERARCHIES ARE MORE COMPLEX THAN THE 'SIMPLEST,' I. E., MORE COMPLEX THAN TWO LOCAL LEVELS WITH NO NATIONAL LEVELS (267) GES,EA	7 260 9 53 XSQ= 12.92 PHI= -0.198 XP = 0.0003
107	DRIFT TOWARD BEING THOSE 0.50 OF 10 WHERE CLASS STRATIFICATION, IF PRESENT, IS BASED ON OCCUPATIONAL STATUS (43)	107	DRIFT TOWARD BEING THOSE 0.80 OF 192 WHERE CLASS STRATIFICATION, IF PRESENT, IS BASED ON SOMETHING OTHER THAN OCCUPATIONAL STATUS (160)	5 38 5 154 XSQ= 3.53 PHI= 0.132 XP = 0.0602
128	DRIFT TOWARD BEING THOSE 0.88 OF 8 WHERE, IF SUBSISTENCE IS PRIMARILY BY AGRICULTURE, THE WORK IS MAINLY DONE BY MALES (40)	128	DRIFT TOWARD BEING THOSE 0.52 OF 69 WHERE, IF SUBSISTENCE IS PRIMARILY BY AGRICULTURE, THE WORK IS MAINLY DONE BY FEMALES (37)	7 33 1 36 XSQ= 3.07 PHI= 0.200 XP = 0.0797
176	IN ALL CASES ARE THOSE 1.00 OF 21 WHERE THE COMMUNITY IS OTHER THAN A CLAN-COMMUNITY OR A COMMUNITY STRUCTURED OR SEGMENTED ON A CLAN BASIS (213)	176	TEND LESS TO BE THOSE 0.53 OF 359 WHERE THE COMMUNITY IS OTHER THAN A CLAN-COMMUNITY OR A COMMUNITY STRUCTURED OR SEGMENTED ON A CLAN BASIS (213)	0 168 21 191 XSQ= 15.77 PHI= -0.204 XP = 0.0001

177	IN ALL CASES ARE THOSE 1.00 OF 21 WHERE THE COMMUNITY IS OTHER THAN A SINGLE CLAN-COMMUNITY AND EXOGAMOUS (305)	177	TILT LESS TOWARD BEING THOSE 0.79 OF 359 WHERE THE COMMUNITY IS OTHER THAN A SINGLE CLAN-COMMUNITY AND EXOGAMOUS (305)	0 77 21 282 XSQ= 4.40 PHI= -0.108 XP = 0.0360
178	IN ALL CASES ARE THOSE 1.00 OF 21 WHERE THE COMMUNITY IS OTHER THAN SEGMENTED ON A CLAN BASIS AND NON-EXOGAMOUS (295)	178	TILT LESS TOWARD BEING THOSE 0.76 OF 359 WHERE THE COMMUNITY IS OTHER THAN SEGMENTED ON A CLAN BASIS AND NON-EXOGAMOUS (295)	0 86 21 273 XSQ= 5.21 PHI= -0.117 XP = 0.0225
180	TILT MORE TOWARD BEING THOSE 0.95 OF 21 WHERE THE COMMUNITY IS COMMONLY NON-EXOGAMOUS, RATHER THAN EXOGAMOUS (258)	180	TILT LESS TOWARD BEING THOSE 0.66 OF 359 WHERE THE COMMUNITY IS COMMONLY NON-EXOGAMOUS, RATHER THAN EXOGAMOUS (258)	1 122 20 237 XSQ= 6.46 PHI= -0.130 XP = 0.0110
181	TEND LESS TO BE THOSE 0.57 OF 21 WHERE THE COMMUNITY IS OTHER THAN A DEME (337)	181	TEND MORE TO BE THOSE 0.90 OF 359 WHERE THE COMMUNITY IS OTHER THAN A DEME (337)	9 36 12 323 XSQ= 17.46 PHI= 0.214 XP = 0.0000
182	DRIFT TOWARD BEING THOSE 0.52 OF 21 WHERE THE COMMUNITY IS STRUCTURED ON A NON-CLAN BASIS AND AGAMOUS (126)	182	DRIFT TOWARD BEING THOSE 0.68 OF 359 OTHER THAN WHERE THE COMMUNITY IS STRUCTURED ON A NON-CLAN BASIS AND AGAMOUS (256)	11 115 10 244 XSQ= 2.84 PHI= 0.087 XP = 0.0917
185	IN ALL CASES ARE THOSE 1.00 OF 3 WHERE THE LARGEST NON-COGNATIC KIN GROUP IS SMALLER THAN A SIB, I. E., THE LINEAGE (58)	185	TILT TOWARD BEING THOSE 0.78 OF 248 WHERE THE LARGEST NON-COGNATIC KIN GROUP IS THE MOEITY OR PHRATRY OR SIB (194)	0 193 3 55 XSQ= 6.20 PHI= -0.157 XP = 0.0128
186	LEAN MORE TOWARD BEING THOSE 0.96 OF 23 WHERE THE KIN GROUP IS OTHER THAN EXCLUSIVELY PATRILINEAL (250)	186	LEAN LESS TOWARD BEING THOSE 0.60 OF 375 WHERE THE KIN GROUP IS OTHER THAN EXCLUSIVELY PATRILINEAL (250)	1 149 22 226 XSQ= 10.10 PHI= -0.159 XP = 0.0015
188	TEND TO BE THOSE 0.87 OF 23 WHERE THE KIN GROUP IS EXCLUSIVELY COGNATIC (148)	188	TEND TO BE THOSE 0.66 OF 375 WHERE THE KIN GROUP IS OTHER THAN EXCLUSIVELY COGNATIC (252)	20 127 3 248 XSQ= 23.99 PHI= 0.246 XP = 0.0000
192	TEND TO BE THOSE 0.87 OF 23 WHERE THE ONLY KIN GROUP PRESENT IS A KINDRED OR ELSE BILATERAL DESCENT IS INFERRED (111)	192	TEND TO BE THOSE 0.76 OF 375 OTHER THAN WHERE THE ONLY KIN GROUP PRESENT IS A KINDRED OR ELSE BILATERAL DESCENT IS INFERRED (289)	20 90 3 285 XSQ= 39.86 PHI= 0.316 XP = 0.

No.		No.		
197	TEND TO BE THOSE 0.64 OF 11 WHERE RULES FOR THE INHERITANCE OF REAL PROPERTY, IF PRESENT, DO NOT FAVOR EITHER THE MALE HEIR OR LINE, OR THE FEMALE HEIR OR LINE (29)	197	TEND TO BE THOSE 0.88 OF 183 WHERE RULES FOR THE INHERITANCE OF REAL PROPERTY, IF PRESENT, FAVOR EITHER THE MALE HEIR OR LINE, OR THE FEMALE HEIR OR LINE (165)	4 161 7 22 XSQ= 17.87 PHI= -0.304 XP = 0.0000
234	LEAN MORE TOWARD BEING THOSE 0.84 OF 19 WHERE THE COUSIN TERMINOLOGY IS OF ESKIMO OR HAWAIIAN TYPE, RATHER THAN CROW, OMAHA, OR IROQUOIS TYPE (170)	234	LEAN LESS TOWARD BEING THOSE 0.50 OF 301 WHERE THE COUSIN TERMINOLOGY IS OF ESKIMO OR HAWAIIAN TYPE, RATHER THAN CROW, OMAHA, OR IROQUOIS TYPE (170)	3 149 16 152 XSQ= 6.85 PHI= -0.146 XP = 0.0089
236	IN ALL CASES ARE THOSE 1.00 OF 23 WHERE THE FAMILY IS OF AN INDEPENDENT TYPE, RATHER THAN AN EXTENDED TYPE (185)	236	TEND TO BE THOSE 0.57 OF 373 WHERE THE FAMILY IS OF AN EXTENDED TYPE, RATHER THAN AN INDEPENDENT TYPE (213)	0 211 23 162 XSQ= 25.62 PHI= -0.254 XP = 0.0000
242	TEND TO BE THOSE 0.57 OF 23 WHERE MARRIAGE IS MONOGAMOUS, RATHER THAN COMMONLY OR OCCASIONALLY POLYGYNOUS (81)	242	TEND TO BE THOSE 0.82 OF 370 WHERE MARRIAGE IS COMMONLY OR OCCASIONALLY POLYGYNOUS, RATHER THAN MONOGAMOUS (314)	10 302 13 68 XSQ= 16.99 PHI= -0.208 XP = 0.0000
262	LEAN LESS TOWARD BEING THOSE 0.52 OF 21 WHERE WIVES ARE OBTAINED BY MEANS INVOLVING THE PRESENCE OF SOME CONSIDERATION (305)	262	LEAN MORE TOWARD BEING THOSE 0.79 OF 372 WHERE WIVES ARE OBTAINED BY MEANS INVOLVING THE PRESENCE OF SOME CONSIDERATION (305)	11 294 10 78 XSQ= 6.66 PHI= -0.130 XP = 0.0098
263	TILT TOWARD BEING THOSE 0.67 OF 21 WHERE WIVES ARE OBTAINED BY RELATIVELY EASY MEANS, NAMELY BY TOKEN BRIDE-PRICE, GIFT EXCHANGE, ABSENCE OF ANY CONSIDERATION, OR RECEIPT OF DOWRY (162)	263	TILT TOWARD BEING THOSE 0.61 OF 372 WHERE WIVES ARE OBTAINED BY RELATIVELY DIFFICULT MEANS, NAMELY BY BRIDE-PRICE, BRIDE-SERVICE, OR EXCHANGING A FEMALE RELATIVE (233)	7 226 14 146 XSQ= 5.11 PHI= -0.114 XP = 0.0238
370	TILT MORE TOWARD BEING THOSE 0.93 OF 14 WHERE THE SEGREGATION OF ADOLESCENT BOYS IS ABSENT (148)	370	TILT LESS TOWARD BEING THOSE 0.59 OF 229 WHERE THE SEGREGATION OF ADOLESCENT BOYS IS ABSENT (148)	1 94 13 135 XSQ= 5.03 PHI= -0.144 XP = 0.0250
377	DRIFT MORE TOWARD BEING THOSE 0.94 OF 18 WHERE MALE GENITAL MUTILATION IS ABSENT (242)	377	DRIFT LESS TOWARD BEING THOSE 0.73 OF 306 WHERE MALE GENITAL MUTILATION IS ABSENT (242)	1 82 17 224 XSQ= 2.99 PHI= -0.096 XP = 0.0839
430	IN ALL CASES ARE THOSE 1.00 OF 3 WHERE SUPERNATURAL SANCTIONS FOR MORALITY, HAVING AN EFFECT ON AN INDIVIDUAL'S HEALTH, ARE PRESENT (16) GES	430	DRIFT TOWARD BEING THOSE 0.63 OF 35 WHERE SUPERNATURAL SANCTIONS FOR MORALITY, HAVING AN EFFECT ON AN INDIVIDUAL'S HEALTH, ARE ABSENT OR UNREPORTED (22) GES	3 13 0 22 XSQ= 2.27 PHI= 0.244 EP = 0.0664

****

204 CULTURES
WHERE MARITAL RESIDENCE IS
PATRILOCAL, VIRILOCAL, OR AVUNCULOCAL,
RATHER THAN
AMBILOCAL OR NEOLOCAL (270)

204 CULTURES
WHERE MARITAL RESIDENCE IS
AMBILOCAL OR NEOLOCAL, RATHER THAN
PATRILOCAL, VIRILOCAL, OR
AVUNCULOCAL (64)

BACKGROUND ON PAGE 113 BOTH SUBJECT AND PREDICATE

....

270 IN LEFT COLUMN

ABOR	AINU	AJIE	AKHA	ALBANIANS	ALORESE	AMBA	ARANDA	ARAPESH	ARAUCANIANS
ARYANS	ASHANTI	ATAYAL	ATSUGEWI	AYMARA	AZANDE	AZTEC	BABWA	BACAIRI	BALINESE
BAMBARA	BAMILEKE	BANDA	BARABRA	BARI	BASSERI	BATAK	BAYA	BEJA	BENGALI
BERGDAMA	BETE	BHIL	BHUIYA	BIRIFOR	BOERS	BOZO	BUDUMA	BULGARIANS	BUNLAP
BURUSHO	BURYAT	CAMAYURA	CAYAPA	CHAGGA	CHERKESS	CHIBCHA	CHINANTEC	CHIRIGUANO	CHUKCHEE
COORG	CREE	CROW	CZECHS	DAGUR	DARD	DIEGUENO	DIERI	DILLING	DOGON
DOROBO	DUSUN	EGYPTIANS	ELLICE	ENGA	EYAK	FANG	FON	FUTAJALONKE	GANDA
GILBERTESE	GILYAK	GISU	GOAJIRO	GOND	GROS VENTRE	GURE	HAIDA	HASANIA	HAVASUPAI
HAZARA	HEBREWS	HEHE	HERERO	HO	ICELANDERS	ILA	INCA	IRAQW	IRISH
JAPANESE	JIVARO	KABYLE	KACHIN	KALMYK	KAPAUKU	KARIERA	KATAB	KAZAK	KERAKI
KERALA	KET	KHALKA	KHEVSUR	KIKUYU	KISSI	KOHISTANI	KOL	KONSO	KOREANS
KORYAK	KPE	KUBA	KWAKIUTL	LAKHER	LAMET	LANGO	LAPPS	LAU	LEPCHA
LHOTA NAGA	LIFU	LOLO	LOZI	LUBA	LUO	MAGUZAWA	MALAYS	MAM	MAMBILA
MAMVU	MANCHU	MANGAIANS	MANIHIKI	MANUS	MARGI	MARICOPA	MARQUESANS	MASAI	MATAKAM
MAYA	MAZATECO	MBUGWE	MBUNDU	MBUTI	MENDE	MENTAWEI	MERINA	MIAMI	MIAO
MIN CHINESE	MINCHIA	MIWOK	MONGO	MONGUOR	MOSSI	MOTA	MURINBATA	MURNGIN	MZAB
NAMA	NAMBICUARA	NANDI	NASKAPI	NATCHEZ	NDEMBU	NGONI	NOMLAKI	NUER	NUNIVAK
NUPE	NURI	NYANEKA	NYARO	NYORO	OJIBWA	OKINAWANS	ONA	ORAON	PAIWAN
PALAUANS	PALIKUR	PAPAGO	PATHAN	PENDE	POPOLUCA	PORTUGUESE	PUKAPUKA	PURARI	PURUM
REGEIBAT	RIFFIANS	ROTINESE	RUNDI	RWALA	SAMOYED	SANDAWE	SANPOIL	SANTAL	SARAMACCA
SARSI	SEMANG	SENIANG	SERBS	SERI	SHERENTE	SHILLUK	SHLUH	SINDHI	SINHALESE
SIUAI	SIWANS	SOMALI	SONGHAI	SOTHO	SWAZI	SYRIANS	TALLENSI	TAMIL	TANALA
TANIMBARESE	TEDA	TEHUELCHE	TENDA	TENINO	TERA	TESO	TETON	THONGA	TIBETANS
TIGRINYA	TIKOPIA	TIV	TIWI	TODA	TOLOWA	TOTONAC	TROBRIAND	TRUMAI	TSHIMSHIAN
TUBATULABAL	TUCANO	TUCUNA	TUNEBO	TURKANA	TURKMEN	TWANA	TZELTAL	ULAWANS	VENDA
VIETNAMESE	WANTOAT	WAPISHANA	WAROPEN	WIKMUNKAN	WINNEBAGO	WITOTO	WOGEO	WOLOF	WUTE
YAGUA	YAHGAN	YAKO	YAKUT	YAPESE	YOKUTS	YOMBE	YORUBA	YUKI	YUROK

64 IN RIGHT COLUMN

ABIPON	ALACALUF	AMERICANS	ANDAMANESE	AWEIKOMA	BAJUN	BASQUES	BEMBA	BLACK CARIB	BRAZILIANS
CAMBA	CAMBODIANS	CARIB	CARINYA	CHENCHU	CHEREMIS	CHOCO	CHORTI	COMANCHE	COPR ESKIMO
DOBUANS	DUTCH	FOX	GUATO	HAWAIIANS	HUICHOL	HUKUNDIKA	HUTSUL	IBAN	IFUGAO
INGASSANA	JEMEZ	JUKUN	KUMYK	KUNG	KURTATCHI	KUTENAI	LAKALAI	LAMBA	MACASSARESE
MAORI	MARSHALLESE	NYAKYUSA	OMAHA	PAEZ	PARAUJANO	PENOBSCOT	RAROIANS	ROMANS	SAGADA
SAMOANS	SELUNG	SIMBOESE	SUBANUN	TAOS	TARAHUMARA	TAREUMIUT	TERENA	TRISTAN	UTE
WAICA	WALLOONS	WASHO	WOLEAIANS						

65 EXCLUDED BECAUSE IRRELEVANT

1 EXCLUDED BECAUSE UNASCERTAINEC

3	TILT LESS TOWARC BEING THCSE LOCATED CUTSIDE CF AFRICA (320)	0.73 OF 270	3	TILT MORE TOWARD BEING THOSE LOCATED OUTSIDE OF AFRICA (320)	0.89 CF 64	72 7 198 57 XSQ= 6.24 PHI= 0.137 XP = 0.0125
5	LEAN LESS TOWARC BEING THCSE LOCATED CUTSIDE CF EAST EURASIA (330)	0.79 OF 270	5	LEAN MORE TOWARD BEING THOSE LOCATED OUTSIDE OF EAST EURASIA (330)	0.94 OF 64	57 4 213 60 XSQ= 6.69 PHI= 0.142 XP = 0.0097
9	TILT MORE TOWARC BEING THCSE LOCATED CUTSIDE OF SOUTH AMERICA (335)	0.90 OF 270	9	TILT LESS TOWARD BEING THOSE LOCATED OUTSIDE OF SOUTH AMERICA (335)	0.78 CF 64	27 14 243 50 XSQ= 5.72 PHI= -0.131 XP = 0.0168
51	TILT MCRE TOWARC BEING THCSE WHERE SUBSISTENCE IS PRIMARILY BY FOOD PRCDUCTICN -- I. E., AGRICULTURE OR HUSBANDRY -- RATHER THAN BY GATHERING (253)	0.70 OF 270	51	TILT LESS TOWARD BEING THOSE WHERE SUBSISTENCE IS PRIMARILY BY FOOD PRODUCTION -- I. E., AGRICULTURE OR HUSBANDRY -- RATHER THAN BY GATHERING (253)	0.56 OF 64	190 36 80 28 XSQ= 4.09 PHI= 0.111 XP = 0.0431
71	TILT LESS TCWARC BEING THCSE WHERE METAL WCRKING IS ABSENT (153)	0.52 OF 163	71	TILT MORE TOWARD BEING THOSE WHERE METAL WORKING IS ABSENT (153)	0.73 OF 44	79 12 84 32 XSQ= 5.49 PHI= 0.163 XP = 0.0192
86	DRIFT TCWARD BEING THCSE WHERE THE LEVEL CF POLITICAL INTEGRATICN IS THE LARGE STATE, THE LITTLE STATE, OR THE MINIMAL STATE (148) GPM	0.53 OF 202	86	DRIFT TOWARD BEING THOSE WHERE THE LEVEL OF POLITICAL INTEGRATION IS THE AUTONOMOUS COMMUNITY, CR THE FAMILY (156) GPM	0.63 CF 43	107 16 95 27 XSQ= 2.92 PHI= 0.109 XP = 0.0875
89	DRIFT LESS TCWARC BEING THCSE WHERE, IF A NCN-HEREDITARY HEACMANSHIP IS PRESENT, SUCCESSION IS BY CONSENSUS (63)	0.51 OF 70	89	DRIFT MORE TOWARD BEING THCSE WHERE, IF A NON-HEREDITARY HEADMANSHIP IS PRESENT, SUCCESSION IS BY CONSENSUS (63)	0.79 CF 19	36 15 34 4 XSQ= 3.57 PHI= -0.200 XP = 0.0589
96	TILT TCWARD BEING THCSE WHERE THE HIERARCHY OF NATICNAL JURISDICTICN HAS FCUR, THREE, TWC OR ONE LEVEL (174) GES,EA	0.59 OF 222	96	TILT TOWARD BEING THOSE WHERE THE HIERARCHY OF NATIONAL JURISDICTION HAS NO LEVELS (156) GES,EA	0.60 CF 50	131 20 91 30 XSQ= 5.23 PHI= 0.139 XP = 0.0223

98	TEND TO BE THOSE WHERE THE HIERARCHY OF LOCAL JURISDICTION HAS FOUR OR THREE LEVELS (238) GES,EA	0.76 OF 223	98	TEND TO BE THOSE WHERE THE HIERARCHY OF LOCAL JURISDICTION HAS TWO LEVELS (93) GES,EA	0.54 OF 50		170 23 53 27 XSQ= 16.59 PHI= 0.247 XP = 0.0000
99	DRIFT TOWARD BEING THOSE WHERE, WITH NATIONAL HIERARCHY ABSENT, THE HIERARCHY OF LOCAL JURISDICTION HAS FOUR OR THREE LEVELS (93) GES,EA	0.63 OF 91	99	DRIFT TOWARD BEING THOSE WHERE, WITH NATIONAL HIERARCHY ABSENT, THE HIERARCHY OF LOCAL JURISDICTION HAS TWO LEVELS (63) GES,EA	0.60 OF 30		57 12 34 18 XSQ= 3.84 PHI= 0.178 XP = 0.0501
100	LEAN MORE TOWARD BEING THOSE WHERE HIERARCHIES ARE MORE COMPLEX THAN THE 'SIMPLEST,' I. E., MORE COMPLEX THAN TWO LOCAL LEVELS WITH NO NATIONAL LEVELS (267) GES,EA	0.85 OF 222	100	LEAN LESS TOWARD BEING THOSE WHERE HIERARCHIES ARE MORE COMPLEX THAN THE 'SIMPLEST,' I. E., MORE COMPLEX THAN TWO LOCAL LEVELS WITH NO NATIONAL LEVELS (267) GES,EA	0.64 OF 50		188 32 34 18 XSQ= 9.99 PHI= 0.192 XP = 0.0016
102	TILT TOWARD BEING THOSE WHERE CLASS STRATIFICATION IS PRESENT (203)	0.60 OF 257	102	TILT TOWARD BEING THOSE WHERE CLASS STRATIFICATION IS ABSENT (180)	0.57 OF 60		155 26 102 34 XSQ= 5.05 PHI= 0.126 XP = 0.0246
109	LEAN LESS TOWARD BEING THOSE WHERE CASTES ARE ABSENT (317)	0.80 OF 243	109	LEAN MORE TOWARD BEING THOSE WHERE CASTES ARE ABSENT (317)	0.97 OF 61		48 2 195 59 XSQ= 8.47 PHI= 0.167 XP = 0.0036
110	TILT LESS TOWARD BEING THOSE WHERE SLAVERY IS ABSENT (218)	0.51 OF 255	110	TILT MORE TOWARD BEING THOSE WHERE SLAVERY IS ABSENT (218)	0.69 OF 61		126 19 129 42 XSQ= 5.90 PHI= 0.137 XP = 0.0152
118	DRIFT TOWARD BEING THOSE WHERE THE PERCENTAGE OF OCCUPATIONS THAT ARE SPECIALIZED IS HIGH OR MEDIUM (24) WME	0.54 OF 39	118	IN ALL CASES ARE THOSE WHERE THE PERCENTAGE OF OCCUPATIONS THAT ARE SPECIALIZED IS LOW (25) WME	1.00 OF 5		21 0 18 5 XSQ= 3.22 PHI= 0.270 XP = 0.0728
128	TILT TOWARD BEING THOSE WHERE, IF SUBSISTENCE IS PRIMARILY BY AGRICULTURE, THE WORK IS MAINLY DONE BY FEMALES (37)	0.55 OF 55	128	TILT TOWARD BEING THOSE WHERE, IF SUBSISTENCE IS PRIMARILY BY AGRICULTURE, THE WORK IS MAINLY DONE BY MALES (40)	0.80 OF 15		25 12 30 3 XSQ= 4.34 PHI= -0.249 XP = 0.0372
129	TILT LESS TOWARD BEING THOSE WHERE WEAVING IS MAINLY DONE BY FEMALES (73)	0.59 OF 68	129	TILT MORE TOWARD BEING THOSE WHERE WEAVING IS MAINLY DONE BY FEMALES (73)	0.93 OF 15		28 1 40 14 XSQ= 5.01 PHI= 0.246 XP = 0.0252

136	DRIFT TOWARD BEING THOSE WHERE FULL-TIME ENTREPRENEURS ARE PRESENT (18) JV	0.63 OF 24	136	IN ALL CASES ARE THOSE WHERE FULL-TIME ENTREPRENEURS ARE ABSENT (14) JV	1.00 OF 3	15 0 9 3 XSQ= 2.07 PHI= 0.277 EP = 0.0752
138	DRIFT TOWARD BEING THOSE WHERE SUPERORDINATE JUSTICE IS PRESENT (22) BBW	0.67 OF 27	138	DRIFT TOWARD BEING THOSE WHERE SUPERORDINATE JUSTICE IS ABSENT (18) BBW	0.75 OF 8	18 2 9 6 XSQ= 2.84 PHI= 0.285 EP = 0.0515
176	TEND TO BE THOSE WHERE THE COMMUNITY IS A CLAN-COMMUNITY OR A COMMUNITY STRUCTURED OR SEGMENTED ON A CLAN BASIS (169)	0.53 OF 257	176	TEND TO BE THOSE WHERE THE COMMUNITY IS OTHER THAN A CLAN-COMMUNITY OR A COMMUNITY STRUCTURED OR SEGMENTED ON A CLAN BASIS (213)	0.84 OF 62	136 10 121 52 XSQ= 25.77 PHI= 0.284 XP = 0.0000
177	TEND LESS TO BE THOSE WHERE THE COMMUNITY IS OTHER THAN A SINGLE CLAN-COMMUNITY AND EXOGAMOUS (305)	0.71 OF 257	177	TEND MORE TO BE THOSE WHERE THE COMMUNITY IS OTHER THAN A SINGLE CLAN-COMMUNITY AND EXOGAMOUS (305)	0.98 OF 62	74 1 183 61 XSQ= 19.04 PHI= 0.244 XP = 0.0000
180	TEND LESS TO BE THOSE WHERE THE COMMUNITY IS COMMONLY NON-EXOGAMOUS, RATHER THAN EXOGAMOUS (258)	0.57 OF 257	180	TEND MORE TO BE THOSE WHERE THE COMMUNITY IS COMMONLY NON-EXOGAMOUS, RATHER THAN EXOGAMOUS (258)	0.90 OF 62	110 6 147 56 XSQ= 22.27 PHI= 0.264 XP = 0.0000
181	TEND MORE TO BE THOSE WHERE THE COMMUNITY IS OTHER THAN A DEME (337)	0.93 OF 257	181	TEND LESS TO BE THOSE WHERE THE COMMUNITY IS OTHER THAN A DEME (337)	0.74 OF 62	18 16 239 46 XSQ= 16.62 PHI= -0.228 XP = 0.0000
182	LEAN TOWARD BEING THOSE OTHER THAN WHERE THE COMMUNITY IS STRUCTURED ON A NON-CLAN BASIS AND AGAMOUS (256)	0.72 OF 257	182	LEAN TOWARD BEING THOSE WHERE THE COMMUNITY IS STRUCTURED ON A NON-CLAN BASIS AND AGAMOUS (126)	0.50 OF 62	72 31 185 31 XSQ= 10.06 PHI= -0.178 XP = 0.0015
186	TEND TO BE THOSE WHERE THE KIN GROUP IS EXCLUSIVELY PATRILINEAL (150)	0.54 OF 270	186	TEND TO BE THOSE WHERE THE KIN GROUP IS OTHER THAN EXCLUSIVELY PATRILINEAL (250)	0.95 OF 64	146 3 124 61 XSQ= 49.09 PHI= 0.383 XP = 0.
188	TEND TO BE THOSE WHERE THE KIN GROUP IS OTHER THAN EXCLUSIVELY COGNATIC (252)	0.76 OF 270	188	TEND TO BE THOSE WHERE THE KIN GROUP IS EXCLUSIVELY COGNATIC (148)	0.80 OF 64	65 51 205 13 XSQ= 68.16 PHI= -0.452 XP = 0.

No.			No.			
190	TEND TO BE THOSE WHERE THE KIN GROUP IS PATRILINEAL OR DOUBLE-DESCENT, RATHER THAN MATRILINEAL (186)	0.90 OF 200	190	TEND TO BE THOSE WHERE THE KIN GROUP IS MATRILINEAL, RATHER THAN PATRILINEAL OR DOUBLE-DESCENT (61)	0.62 OF 13	180 5 20 8 XSQ= 24.06 PHI= 0.336 XP = 0.0000
192	TEND TO BE THOSE OTHER THAN WHERE THE ONLY KIN GROUP PRESENT IS A KINDRED OR ELSE BILATERAL DESCENT IS INFERRED (289)	0.84 OF 270	192	TEND TO BE THOSE WHERE THE ONLY KIN GROUP PRESENT IS A KINDRED OR ELSE BILATERAL DESCENT IS INFERRED (111)	0.64 OF 64	44 41 226 23 XSQ= 59.73 PHI= -0.423 XP = 0.
197	TEND TO BE THOSE WHERE RULES FOR THE INHERITANCE OF REAL PROPERTY, IF PRESENT, FAVOR EITHER THE MALE HEIR OR LINE, OR THE FEMALE HEIR OR LINE (165)	0.95 OF 151	197	TEND TO BE THOSE WHERE RULES FOR THE INHERITANCE OF REAL PROPERTY, IF PRESENT, DO NOT FAVOR EITHER THE MALE HEIR OR LINE, OR THE FEMALE HEIR OR LINE (29)	0.58 OF 26	143 11 8 15 XSQ= 49.32 PHI= 0.528 XP = 0.
213	TILT TOWARD BEING THOSE WHERE FIRST COUSIN MARRIAGE IS PERMITTED (172)	0.50 OF 256	213	TILT TOWARD BEING THOSE WHERE FIRST COUSIN MARRIAGE IS NOT PERMITTED (198)	0.69 OF 54	128 17 128 37 XSQ= 5.42 PHI= 0.132 XP = 0.0199
220	TILT LESS TOWARD BEING THOSE WHERE FIRST COUSIN MARRIAGE IN SOME FORM OR OTHER IS NOT PRESCRIBED OR PREFERRED (273)	0.72 OF 256	220	TILT MORE TOWARD BEING THOSE WHERE FIRST COUSIN MARRIAGE IN SOME FORM OR OTHER IS NOT PRESCRIBED OR PREFERRED (273)	0.89 OF 54	72 6 184 48 XSQ= 5.98 PHI= 0.139 XP = 0.0145
224	DRIFT LESS TOWARD BEING THOSE WHERE COUSIN MARRIAGE IS PREFERENTIALLY OR PERMISSIVELY SYMMETRICAL, RATHER THAN EITHER PATRI- OR MATRILATERAL (106)	0.57 OF 128	224	DRIFT MORE TOWARD BEING THOSE WHERE COUSIN MARRIAGE IS PREFERENTIALLY OR PERMISSIVELY SYMMETRICAL, RATHER THAN EITHER PATRI- OR MATRILATERAL (106)	0.82 OF 17	55 3 73 14 XSQ= 3.02 PHI= 0.144 XP = 0.0821
234	TEND TO BE THOSE WHERE THE COUSIN TERMINOLOGY IS OF CROW, OMAHA, OR IROQUOIS TYPE, RATHER THAN ESKIMO OR HAWAIIAN TYPE (152)	0.53 OF 201	234	TEND TO BE THOSE WHERE THE COUSIN TERMINOLOGY IS OF ESKIMO OR HAWAIIAN TYPE, RATHER THAN CROW, OMAHA, OR IROQUOIS TYPE (170)	0.76 OF 58	107 14 94 44 XSQ= 14.16 PHI= 0.234 XP = 0.0002
236	LEAN TOWARD BEING THOSE WHERE THE FAMILY IS OF AN EXTENDED TYPE, RATHER THAN AN INDEPENDENT TYPE (213)	0.53 OF 268	236	LEAN TOWARD BEING THOSE WHERE THE FAMILY IS OF AN INDEPENDENT TYPE, RATHER THAN AN EXTENDED TYPE (185)	0.67 OF 64	141 21 127 43 XSQ= 7.33 PHI= 0.149 XP = 0.0068
242	TEND MORE TO BE THOSE WHERE MARRIAGE IS COMMONLY OR OCCASIONALLY POLYGYNOUS, RATHER THAN MONOGAMOUS (314)	0.86 OF 265	242	TEND LESS TO BE THOSE WHERE MARRIAGE IS COMMONLY OR OCCASIONALLY POLYGYNOUS, RATHER THAN MONOGAMOUS (314)	0.61 OF 64	227 39 38 25 XSQ= 18.79 PHI= 0.239 XP = 0.0000

262 TEND MORE TO BE THOSE 0.87 OF 268 WHERE WIVES ARE OBTAINED BY MEANS INVOLVING THE PRESENCE OF SOME CONSIDERATION (305)	262 TEND LESS TO BE THOSE 0.56 CF 62 WHERE WIVES ARE OBTAINED BY MEANS INVOLVING THE PRESENCE OF SOME CONSIDERATICN (305)	234 35 34 27 XSQ= 29.81 PHI= 0.301 XP = 0.0000
263 TEND TO BE THOSE 0.69 OF 268 WHERE WIVES ARE OBTAINED BY RELATIVELY DIFFICULT MEANS, NAMELY BY BRIDE-PRICE, BRIDE-SERVICE, OR EXCHANGING A FEMALE RELATIVE (233)	263 TEND TO BE THOSE 0.60 OF 62 WHERE WIVES ARE OBTAINED BY RELATIVELY EASY MEANS, NAMELY BY TOKEN BRIDE-PRICE, GIFT EXCHANGE, ABSENCE OF ANY CONSIDERATICN, OR RECEIPT OF DOWRY (162)	184 25 84 37 XSQ= 16.21 PHI= 0.222 XP = 0.0001
301 TILT MORE TOWARD BEING THOSE 0.81 OF 85 WHERE THE POST-PARTUM SEX TABOO LASTS LONGER THAN ONE MONTH (96)	301 TILT LESS TOWARD BEING THOSE 0.56 CF 18 WHERE THE POST-PARTUM SEX TABOO LASTS LONGER THAN ONE MONTH (96)	69 10 16 8 XSQ= 4.12 PHI= 0.200 XP = 0.0425
324 DRIFT TOWARD BEING THOSE 0.64 OF 44 WHERE THE PAIN INFLICTED ON THE INFANT BY THE NURTURANT AGENT IS HIGH (34) B-B-C	324 DRIFT TOWARD BEING THOSE 0.75 OF 8 WHERE THE PAIN INFLICTED ON THE INFANT BY THE NURTURANT AGENT IS LOW OR NEGLIGIBLE (32) B-B-C	28 2 16 6 XSQ= 2.71 PHI= 0.228 XP = 0.0998
327 DRIFT TOWARD BEING THOSE 0.60 OF 35 WHERE THE AGE OF THE INFANT AT TIME OF REDUCED CONTACT WITH MOTHER IS TWO YEARS OR LOWER (27) B-B-C	327 DRIFT TOWARD BEING THOSE 0.78 OF 9 WHERE THE AGE OF THE INFANT AT TIME OF REDUCED CONTACT WITH MCTHER IS HIGHER THAN TWO YEARS (28) B-B-C	14 7 21 2 XSQ= 2.72 PHI= -0.249 XP = 0.0990
344 DRIFT TOWARD BEING THOSE 0.56 OF 5C WHERE THE TOTAL POSITIVE PRESSURE TOWARD DEVELOPING SELF-RELIANT BEHAVIOR IN THE CHILD IS LOW (40) B-B-C	344 DRIFT TOWARD BEING THOSE 0.80 OF 10 WHERE THE TOTAL POSITIVE PRESSURE TOWARC DEVELOPING SELF-RELIANT BEHAVIOR IN THE CHILD IS HIGH (36) B-B-C	22 8 28 2 XSQ= 3.00 PHI= -0.224 XP = 0.0833
368 DRIFT TOWARD BEING THOSE 0.71 OF 21 WHERE DISSOCIATION OF THE SEXES AT ADOLESCENCE IS LOW (21) JKH	368 DRIFT TOWARD BEING THOSE 0.70 CF 10 WHERE DISSOCIATION OF THE SEXES AT ADOLESCENCE IS HIGH OR MEDIUM (16) JKH	6 7 15 3 XSQ= 3.23 PHI= -0.323 EP = 0.0515
370 LEAN LESS TOWARD BEING THOSE 0.53 OF 164 WHERE THE SEGREGATION OF ADOLESCENT BOYS IS ABSENT (148)	370 LEAN MORE TOWARD BEING THOSE 0.79 OF 38 WHERE THE SEGREGATION OF ADOLESCENT BOYS IS ABSENT (148)	77 8 87 30 XSQ= 7.46 PHI= 0.192 XP = 0.0063
377 TEND LESS TO BE THOSE 0.65 OF 217 WHERE MALE GENITAL MUTILATION IS ABSENT (242)	377 TEND MORE TO BE THOSE 0.92 CF 51 WHERE MALE GENITAL MUTILATICN IS ABSENT (242)	75 4 142 47 XSQ= 12.93 PHI= 0.220 XP = 0.0003

391 DRIFT TCWARD BEING THCSE 0.56 OF 124 WHERE PREMARITAL SEX RELATIONS ARE STRCNGLY PUNISHEC AND IN FACT RARE, OR WEAKLY PUNISHED ANC IN FACT NCT RARE (89) JTW,EA	391 DRIFT TOWARD BEING THCSE 0.66 CF 29 WHERE PREMARITAL SEX RELATIONS ARE PUNISHED ONLY IF PREGNANCY RESULTS, OR FREELY PERMITTED (90) JTW,EA	69 10 55 19 XSQ= 3.41 PHI= 0.149 XP = 0.0648
392 LEAN TCWARD BEING THOSE 0.69 OF 124 WHERE PREMARITAL SEX RELATIONS ARE STRCNGLY PUNISHEC ANC IN FACT RARE, OR WEAKLY PUNISHED ANC IN FACT NCT RARE, OR PUNISHED CNLY IF PREGNANCY RESULTS (112) JTW,EA	392 LEAN TOWARD BEING THOSE 0.59 CF 29 WHERE PREMARITAL SEX RELATICNS ARE FREELY PERMITTED (67) JTW,EA	86 12 38 17 XSQ= 6.82 PHI= 0.211 XP = 0.0090
453 TILT TCWARD BEING THOSE 0.76 OF 25 WHERE THE ROLE CF RELIGIOUS EXPERTS IS NOT CCNDUCIVE TC THE CEVELOPMENT OF THE INDIVIDUAL'S NEED TC ACHIEVE (23) CCM	453 IN ALL CASES ARE THOSE 1.00 OF 3 WHERE THE ROLE OF RELIGICUS EXPERTS IS CONDUCIVE TO THE DEVELOPMENT OF THE INDIVIDUAL'S NEED TO ACHIEVE (13) DCM	6 3 19 0 XSQ= 4.04 PHI= -0.380 EP = 0.0256
456 DRIFT TCWARD BEING THCSE 0.60 OF 25 WHERE THE INTERNALIZATICN CF THE INDIVIDUAL'S CONTACT WITH THE DIVINE IS NOT CONDUCIVE TC THE DEVELOPMENT OF THE INDIVIDUAL'S NEED TC ACHIEVE (17) DCM	456 IN ALL CASES ARE THOSE 1.00 CF 3 WHERE THE INTERNALIZATICN CF THE INDIVIDUAL'S CCNTACT WITH THE DIVINE IS CONDUCIVE TO THE DEVELOPMENT OF THE INDIVIDUAL'S NEED TC ACHIEVE (19) CCM	10 3 15 0 XSQ= 1.84 PHI= -0.256 EP = 0.0873

****

205 CULTURES
WHERE MARITAL RESICENCE IS
PATRILCCAL (169)

205 CULTURES
WHERE MARITAL RESIDENCE IS
OTHER THAN PATRILOCAL (229)

BACKGROUND ON PAGE 113 | SUBJECT ONLY

....

169 IN LEFT COLUMN

AJIE	AKHA	ALBANIANS	AMBA	ARANDA	ARAPESH	ARAUCANIANS	ARYANS	AYMARA	BABWA
BAMBARA	BAMILEKE	BANCA	BARABRA	BARI	BASSERI	BATAK	BAYA	BEJA	BENGALI
BETE	BHIL	BHUIYA	BIRIFOR	BOZO	BUDUMA	BUNLAP	BURUSHO	BURYAT	CHAGGA
CHERKESS	CCCRG	CAGUR	DARC	DIEGUENO	DILLING	DOGON	DORCBC	EGYPTIANS	ENGA
FANG	FCN	FUTAJALCNKE	GILYAK	GISU	GOND	HASANIA	HAZARA	HEBREWS	HEHE
HO	IRAQW	KABYLE	KACHIN	KALMYK	KAPAUKU	KARIERA	KATAB	KAZAK	KERAKI
KHALKA	KHEVSUR	KIKUYU	KISSI	KOHISTANI	KOL	KONSO	KOREANS	KPE	LAKHER
LAMET	LANGO	LAU	LEPCHA	LHOTA NAGA	LIFU	LOLO	LUBA	LUC	MAGUZAWA
MAM	MAMVU	MANCHU	MANUS	MARGI	MARICOPA	MASAI	MATAKAM	MBUGWE	MBUNDU
MBUTI	MENDE	MIAMI	MIAO	MIN CHINESE	MINCHIA	MONGO	MONGUOR	MOSSI	MURINBATA
MURNGIN	MZAB	NAMA	NANDI	NOMLAKI	NUPE	NURI	NYARO	NYORO	OKINAWANS
ORAON	PATHAN	PUKAPUKA	PURARI	PURUM	REGEIBAT	RIFFIANS	ROTINESE	RUNDI	RWALA
SAMOYED	SANDAWE	SANTAL	SENIANG	SERBS	SHERENTE	SHILLUK	SHLUH	SINCHI	SIWANS
SOMALI	SCNGHAI	SOTHO	SWAZI	SYRIANS	TALLENSI	TAMIL	TANALA	TANIMBARESE	TEDA
TERA	TESC	THCNGA	TIBETANS	TIGRINYA	TIKOPIA	TODA	TOLOWA	TUCANO	TUCUNA
TURKANA	TURKMEN	TZELTAL	VENDA	VIETNAMESE	WANTOAT	WAROPEN	WIKMUNKAN	WINNEBAGO	WITOTO
WOGEO	WCLOF	WUTE	YAGUA	YAKO	YAKUT	YAPESE	YOKUTS	YORUBA	

229 IN RIGHT COLUMN

1 EXCLUDED BECAUSE IRRELEVANT

MINANGKABAU

1 EXCLUDED BECAUSE UNASCERTAINED

----

3 TEND LESS TO BE THCSE LOCATED CUTSIDE CF AFRICA (320) — 0.68 OF 169

3 TEND MORE TO BE THOSE LOCATED OUTSIDE OF AFRICA (320) — 0.89 OF 229

54 26
115 203
XSQ= 24.42
PHI= 0.248
XP = 0.0000

4 LEAN LESS TCWARD BEING THCSE LOCATED CUTSIDE OF THE CIRCUM-MEDITERRANEAN (355) — 0.83 OF 169

4 LEAN MORE TOWARD BEING THOSE LOCATED OUTSIDE OF THE CIRCUM-MEDITERRANEAN (355) — 0.93 CF 229

28 17
141 212
XSQ= 7.22
PHI= 0.135
XP = 0.0072

5	TEND LESS TO BE THCSE LOCATED OUTSIDE CF EAST EURASIA (330)	0.73 OF 169	5	TEND MORE TO BE THOSE LOCATED OUTSIDE OF EAST EURASIA (330)	0.90 CF 229	46 24 123 205 XSQ= 17.66 PHI= 0.211 XP = 0.0000
8	TEND MORE TO BE THCSE LOCATED CUTSIDE CF NORTH AMERICA (330)	0.96 OF 169	8	TEND LESS TO BE THOSE LOCATED OUTSIDE OF NORTH AMERICA (330)	0.72 CF 229	7 63 162 166 XSQ= 35.04 PHI= -0.297 XP = 0.
9	TEND MCRE TO BE THCSE LOCATED OUTSIDE CF SOUTH AMERICA (335)	0.95 OF 169	9	TEND LESS TO BE THOSE LOCATED OUTSIDE OF SOUTH AMERICA (335)	0.76 OF 229	9 55 160 174 XSQ= 23.81 PHI= -0.245 XP = 0.0000
12	LEAN MORE TOWARC BEING THCSE WHERE THE LATITUDE IS LESS THAN FIFTY DEGREES (367)	0.97 OF 169	12	LEAN LESS TOWARD BEING THOSE WHERE THE LATITUDE IS LESS THAN FIFTY DEGREES (367)	0.88 CF 229	5 28 164 201 XSQ= 9.80 PHI= -0.157 XP = 0.0017
13	TEND MCRE TO BE THCSE WHERE THE LATITUDE IS LESS THAN FORTY DEGREES (329)	0.91 OF 169	13	TEND LESS TO BE THOSE WHERE THE LATITUDE IS LESS THAN FORTY DEGREES (329)	0.76 CF 229	16 55 153 174 XSQ= 13.07 PHI= -0.181 XP = 0.0003
14	TILT MORE TOWARC BEING THCSE WHERE THE LATITUDE IS LESS THAN THIRTY DEGREES (281)	0.76 OF 169	14	TILT LESS TOWARD BEING THOSE WHERE THE LATITUDE IS LESS THAN THIRTY DEGREES (281)	0.66 CF 229	40 79 129 150 XSQ= 4.94 PHI= -0.111 XP = 0.0263
44	LEAN MCRE TOWARC BEING THCSE WHERE SETTLEMENTS ARE FIXEC (222)	0.76 OF 141	44	LEAN LESS TOWARD BEING THOSE WHERE SETTLEMENTS ARE FIXED (222)	0.61 CF 190	107 115 34 75 XSQ= 7.96 PHI= 0.155 XP = 0.0048
46	DRIFT MORE TOWARD BEING THOSE OTHER THAN WHERE SETTLEMENTS ARE NON-FIXED AND MCVEMENT IS NOMADIC (260)	0.84 OF 141	46	DRIFT LESS TOWARD BEING THCSE OTHER THAN WHERE SETTLEMENTS ARE NON-FIXED AND MOVEMENT IS NOMADIC (260)	0.75 CF 190	23 48 118 142 XSQ= 3.34 PHI= -0.100 XP = 0.0678
51	TEND MCRE TO BE THCSE WHERE SUBSISTENCE IS PRIMARILY BY FOOD PRODUCTION -- I. E., AGRICULTURE OR HUSBANDRY -- RATHER THAN BY GATHERING (253)	0.81 OF 169	51	TEND LESS TO BE THOSE WHERE SUBSISTENCE IS PRIMARILY BY FOOD PRODUCTION -- I. E., AGRICULTURE OR HUSBANDRY -- RATHER THAN BY GATHERING (253)	0.50 CF 229	137 115 32 114 XSQ= 38.52 PHI= 0.311 XP = 0.

53	LEAN LESS TOWARD BEING THOSE 0.52 OF 116 WHERE FOOD PRODUCTION IS BY SIMPLE AGRICULTURE OR INCIPIENT FOOD PRODUCTION, RATHER THAN BY INTENSIVE AGRICULTURE (147)	53	LEAN MORE TOWARD BEING THOSE 0.71 OF 122 WHERE FOOD PRODUCTION IS BY SIMPLE AGRICULTURE OR INCIPIENT FOOD PRODUCTION, RATHER THAN BY INTENSIVE AGRICULTURE (147)	56 35 60 87 XSQ= 8.85 PHI= 0.193 XP = 0.0029
54	LEAN MORE TOWARD BEING THOSE 0.90 OF 116 WHERE FOOD PRODUCTION IS BY INTENSIVE OR SIMPLE AGRICULTURE, RATHER THAN BY INCIPIENT FOOD PRODUCTION (192)	54	LEAN LESS TOWARD BEING THOSE 0.72 OF 122 WHERE FOOD PRODUCTION IS BY INTENSIVE OR SIMPLE AGRICULTURE, RATHER THAN BY INCIPIENT FOOD PRODUCTION (192)	104 88 12 34 XSQ= 10.61 PHI= 0.211 XP = 0.0011
55	DRIFT TOWARD BEING THOSE 0.54 OF 104 WHERE FOOD PRODUCTION IS BY INTENSIVE AGRICULTURE, RATHER THAN BY SIMPLE AGRICULTURE (91)	55	DRIFT TOWARD BEING THOSE 0.60 OF 88 WHERE FOOD PRODUCTION IS BY SIMPLE AGRICULTURE, RATHER THAN BY INTENSIVE AGRICULTURE (101)	56 35 48 53 XSQ= 3.24 PHI= 0.130 XP = 0.0717
56	TILT MORE TOWARD BEING THOSE 0.80 OF 60 WHERE FOOD PRODUCTION IS BY SIMPLE AGRICULTURE, RATHER THAN BY INCIPIENT FOOD PRODUCTION (101)	56	TILT LESS TOWARD BEING THOSE 0.61 OF 87 WHERE FOOD PRODUCTION IS BY SIMPLE AGRICULTURE, RATHER THAN BY INCIPIENT FOOD PRODUCTION (101)	48 53 12 34 XSQ= 5.16 PHI= 0.187 XP = 0.0231
62	TEND TO BE THOSE 0.71 OF 169 WHERE HUSBANDRY OF SOME KIND IS PRESENT (228)	62	TEND TO BE THOSE 0.53 OF 229 WHERE HUSBANDRY OF ANY KIND IS ABSENT (172)	120 108 49 121 XSQ= 21.63 PHI= 0.233 XP = 0.0000
63	TILT MORE TOWARD BEING THOSE 0.75 OF 118 WHERE HUSBANDRY, IF PRESENT, IS PRINCIPALLY IN THE FORM OF BOVINE, EQUINE, CAMEL-LIKE, OR DEER-LIKE ANIMALS, RATHER THAN PIGS, SHEEP, OR GOATS (152)	63	TILT LESS TOWARD BEING THOSE 0.59 OF 108 WHERE HUSBANDRY, IF PRESENT, IS PRINCIPALLY IN THE FORM OF BOVINE, EQUINE, CAMEL-LIKE, OR DEER-LIKE ANIMALS, RATHER THAN PIGS, SHEEP, OR GOATS (152)	88 64 30 44 XSQ= 5.33 PHI= 0.154 XP = 0.0209
71	TEND TO BE THOSE 0.62 OF 99 WHERE METAL WORKING IS PRESENT (98)	71	TEND TO BE THOSE 0.75 OF 151 WHERE METAL WORKING IS ABSENT (153)	61 37 38 114 XSQ= 33.02 PHI= 0.363 XP = 0.
82	DRIFT MORE TOWARD BEING THOSE 0.86 OF 97 WHERE A CITY OR TOWN IS PRESENT, OR THE AVERAGE COMMUNITY SIZE IS FIFTY OR GREATER (178)	82	DRIFT LESS TOWARD BEING THOSE 0.75 OF 126 WHERE A CITY OR TOWN IS PRESENT, OR THE AVERAGE COMMUNITY SIZE IS FIFTY OR GREATER (178)	83 94 14 32 XSQ= 3.38 PHI= 0.123 XP = 0.0659
86	TILT TOWARD BEING THOSE 0.58 OF 120 WHERE THE LEVEL OF POLITICAL INTEGRATION IS THE LARGE STATE, THE LITTLE STATE, OR THE MINIMAL STATE (148) GPM	86	TILT TOWARD BEING THOSE 0.57 OF 182 WHERE THE LEVEL OF POLITICAL INTEGRATION IS THE AUTONOMOUS COMMUNITY, OR THE FAMILY (156) GPM	70 78 50 104 XSQ= 6.33 PHI= 0.145 XP = 0.0119

90	TEND MORE TO BE THOSE WHERE, IF A HEREDITARY HEADMANSHIP IS PRESENT, SUCCESSION IS PATRILINEAL, RATHER THAN MATRILINEAL (127)	0.96 OF 74	90	TEND LESS TO BE THOSE WHERE, IF A HEREDITARY HEADMANSHIP IS PRESENT, SUCCESSION IS PATRILINEAL, RATHER THAN MATRILINEAL (127)	0.62 OF 90	71 56 3 34 XSQ= 24.54 PHI= 0.387 XP = 0.0000
96	LEAN TOWARD BEING THOSE WHERE THE HIERARCHY OF NATIONAL JURISDICTION HAS FOUR, THREE, TWO OR ONE LEVEL (174) GES,EA	0.62 OF 140	96	LEAN TOWARD BEING THOSE WHERE THE HIERARCHY OF NATIONAL JURISDICTION HAS NO LEVELS (156) GES,EA	0.54 OF 189	87 87 53 102 XSQ= 7.74 PHI= 0.153 XP = 0.0054
97	LEAN LESS TOWARD BEING THOSE WHERE THE HIERARCHY OF LOCAL JURISDICTION HAS THREE OR TWO LEVELS (273) GES,EA	0.74 OF 141	97	LEAN MORE TOWARD BEING THOSE WHERE THE HIERARCHY OF LOCAL JURISDICTION HAS THREE OR TWO LEVELS (273) GES,EA	0.88 OF 189	36 22 105 167 XSQ= 9.82 PHI= 0.173 XP = 0.0017
98	DRIFT MORE TOWARD BEING THOSE WHERE THE HIERARCHY OF LOCAL JURISDICTION HAS FOUR OR THREE LEVELS (238) GES,EA	0.78 OF 141	98	DRIFT LESS TOWARD BEING THOSE WHERE THE HIERARCHY OF LOCAL JURISDICTION HAS FOUR OR THREE LEVELS (238) GES,EA	0.68 OF 189	110 128 31 61 XSQ= 3.76 PHI= 0.107 XP = 0.0526
102	LEAN TOWARD BEING THOSE WHERE CLASS STRATIFICATION IS PRESENT (203)	0.62 OF 162	102	LEAN TOWARD BEING THOSE WHERE CLASS STRATIFICATION IS ABSENT (180)	0.54 OF 219	101 101 61 118 XSQ= 9.20 PHI= 0.155 XP = 0.0024
109	TEND LESS TO BE THOSE WHERE CASTES ARE ABSENT (317)	0.73 OF 144	109	TEND MORE TO BE THOSE WHERE CASTES ARE ABSENT (317)	0.95 OF 222	39 12 105 210 XSQ= 32.44 PHI= 0.298 XP = 0.
110	TEND TO BE THOSE WHERE SLAVERY IS PRESENT (163)	0.54 OF 158	110	TEND TO BE THOSE WHERE SLAVERY IS ABSENT (218)	0.65 OF 221	85 78 73 143 XSQ= 12.13 PHI= 0.179 XP = 0.0005
129	TEND TO BE THOSE WHERE WEAVING IS MAINLY DONE BY MALES (31)	0.51 OF 41	129	TEND TO BE THOSE WHERE WEAVING IS MAINLY DONE BY FEMALES (73)	0.84 OF 63	21 10 20 53 XSQ= 13.19 PHI= 0.356 XP = 0.0003
130	LEAN TOWARD BEING THOSE WHERE LEATHER WORKING IS MAINLY DONE BY MALES (39)	0.71 OF 31	130	LEAN TOWARD BEING THOSE WHERE LEATHER WORKING IS MAINLY DONE BY FEMALES (45)	0.68 OF 53	22 17 9 36 XSQ= 10.38 PHI= 0.352 XP = 0.0013

175	TEND LESS TO BE THOSE WHERE THE COMMUNITY IS 'KIN-HETEROGENEOUS,' I. E. OTHER THAN A CLAN COMMUNITY OR A DEME (260)	0.56 OF 162	175	TEND MORE TO BE THOSE WHERE THE COMMUNITY IS 'KIN-HETEROGENEOUS,' I. E. OTHER THAN A CLAN COMMUNITY OR A DEME (260)	0.77 OF 218	72 50 90 168 XSQ= 18.75 PHI= 0.222 XP = 0.0000
176	TEND TO BE THOSE WHERE THE COMMUNITY IS A CLAN-COMMUNITY OR A COMMUNITY STRUCTURED OR SEGMENTED ON A CLAN BASIS (169)	0.70 OF 162	176	TEND TO BE THOSE WHERE THE COMMUNITY IS OTHER THAN A CLAN-COMMUNITY OR A COMMUNITY STRUCTURED OR SEGMENTED ON A CLAN BASIS (213)	0.75 OF 218	114 54 48 164 XSQ= 76.51 PHI= 0.449 XP = 0.
177	TEND LESS TO BE THOSE WHERE THE COMMUNITY IS OTHER THAN A SINGLE CLAN-COMMUNITY AND EXOGAMOUS (305)	0.60 OF 162	177	TEND MORE TO BE THOSE WHERE THE COMMUNITY IS OTHER THAN A SINGLE CLAN-COMMUNITY AND EXOGAMOUS (305)	0.94 OF 218	65 12 97 206 XSQ= 66.81 PHI= 0.419 XP = 0.
178	DRIFT LESS TOWARD BEING THOSE WHERE THE COMMUNITY IS OTHER THAN SEGMENTED ON A CLAN BASIS AND NON-EXOGAMOUS (295)	0.73 OF 162	178	DRIFT MORE TOWARD BEING THOSE WHERE THE COMMUNITY IS OTHER THAN SEGMENTED ON A CLAN BASIS AND NON-EXOGAMOUS (295)	0.81 OF 218	44 42 118 176 XSQ= 2.87 PHI= 0.087 XP = 0.0901
179	TILT MORE TOWARD BEING THOSE WHERE THE COMMUNITY IS OTHER THAN STRUCTURED ON A NON-CLAN BASIS AND COMMONLY EXOGAMOUS (340)	0.93 OF 162	179	TILT LESS TOWARD BEING THOSE WHERE THE COMMUNITY IS OTHER THAN STRUCTURED ON A NON-CLAN BASIS AND COMMONLY EXOGAMOUS (340)	0.86 OF 218	11 30 151 188 XSQ= 4.00 PHI= -0.103 XP = 0.0456
180	TEND TO BE THOSE WHERE THE COMMUNITY IS COMMONLY EXOGAMOUS, RATHER THAN NON-EXOGAMOUS (124)	0.50 OF 162	180	TEND TO BE THOSE WHERE THE COMMUNITY IS COMMONLY NON-EXOGAMOUS, RATHER THAN EXOGAMOUS (258)	0.81 OF 218	81 42 81 176 XSQ= 38.71 PHI= 0.319 XP = 0.
181	TEND MORE TO BE THOSE WHERE THE COMMUNITY IS OTHER THAN A DEME (337)	0.96 OF 162	181	TEND LESS TO BE THOSE WHERE THE COMMUNITY IS OTHER THAN A DEME (337)	0.83 OF 218	7 38 155 180 XSQ= 14.07 PHI= -0.192 XP = 0.0002
182	TEND MORE TO BE THOSE OTHER THAN WHERE THE COMMUNITY IS STRUCTURED ON A NON-CLAN BASIS AND AGAMOUS (256)	0.81 OF 162	182	TEND LESS TO BE THOSE OTHER THAN WHERE THE COMMUNITY IS STRUCTURED ON A NON-CLAN BASIS AND AGAMOUS (256)	0.56 OF 218	30 96 132 122 XSQ= 26.17 PHI= -0.262 XP = 0.0000
183	TILT MORE TOWARD BEING THOSE WHERE THE LARGEST NON-COGNATIC KIN GROUP IS SMALLER THAN A MOIETY, I. E., A PHRATRY OR SIB OR LINEAGE (218)	0.90 OF 168	183	TILT LESS TOWARD BEING THOSE WHERE THE LARGEST NON-COGNATIC KIN GROUP IS SMALLER THAN A MOIETY, I. E., A PHRATRY OR SIB OR LINEAGE (218)	0.78 OF 83	16 18 152 65 XSQ= 6.02 PHI= -0.155 XP = 0.0142

No.			No.			
184	DRIFT MORE TOWARD BEING THOSE WHERE THE LARGEST NON-COGNATIC KIN GROUP IS SMALLER THAN A PHRATRY, I. E. A SIB OR LINEAGE (175)	0.74 OF 168	184	DRIFT LESS TOWARD BEING THOSE WHERE THE LARGEST NON-COGNATIC KIN GROUP IS SMALLER THAN A PHRATRY, I. E. A SIB OR LINEAGE (175)	0.61 OF 83	44 32 124 51 XSQ= 3.46 PHI= -0.117 XP = 0.0629
186	TEND TO BE THOSE WHERE THE KIN GROUP IS EXCLUSIVELY PATRILINEAL (150)	0.81 OF 169	186	TEND TO BE THOSE WHERE THE KIN GROUP IS OTHER THAN EXCLUSIVELY PATRILINEAL (250)	0.94 OF 229	137 13 32 216 XSQ= 232.13 PHI= 0.764 XP = 0.
187	IN ALL CASES ARE THOSE WHERE THE KIN GROUP IS OTHER THAN EXCLUSIVELY MATRILINEAL (344)	1.00 OF 169	187	TEND LESS TO BE THOSE WHERE THE KIN GROUP IS OTHER THAN EXCLUSIVELY MATRILINEAL (344)	0.76 OF 228	0 54 169 174 XSQ= 44.33 PHI= -0.334 XP = 0.
188	TEND TO BE THOSE WHERE THE KIN GROUP IS OTHER THAN EXCLUSIVELY COGNATIC (252)	0.99 OF 169	188	TEND TO BE THOSE WHERE THE KIN GROUP IS EXCLUSIVELY COGNATIC (148)	0.64 OF 229	1 146 168 83 XSQ= 163.85 PHI= -0.642 XP = 0.
190	IN ALL CASES ARE THOSE WHERE THE KIN GROUP IS PATRILINEAL OR DOUBLE-DESCENT, RATHER THAN MATRILINEAL (186)	1.00 OF 165	190	TEND TO BE THOSE WHERE THE KIN GROUP IS MATRILINEAL, RATHER THAN PATRILINEAL OR DOUBLE-DESCENT (61)	0.74 OF 81	165 21 0 60 XSQ= 157.66 PHI= 0.801 XP = 0.
192	TEND MORE TO BE THOSE OTHER THAN WHERE THE ONLY KIN GROUP PRESENT IS A KINDRED OR ELSE BILATERAL DESCENT IS INFERRED (289)	0.99 OF 169	192	TEND LESS TO BE THOSE OTHER THAN WHERE THE ONLY KIN GROUP PRESENT IS A KINDRED OR ELSE BILATERAL DESCENT IS INFERRED (289)	0.52 OF 229	1 109 168 120 XSQ= 105.10 PHI= -0.514 XP = 0.
196	TEND MORE TO BE THOSE WHERE INDIVIDUAL RIGHTS IN REAL PROPERTY, AND RULES FOR INHERITANCE, ARE PRESENT (194)	0.80 OF 133	196	TEND LESS TO BE THOSE WHERE INDIVIDUAL RIGHTS IN REAL PROPERTY, AND RULES FOR INHERITANCE, ARE PRESENT (194)	0.60 OF 146	107 87 26 59 XSQ= 13.33 PHI= 0.219 XP = 0.0003
197	TEND MORE TO BE THOSE WHERE RULES FOR THE INHERITANCE OF REAL PROPERTY, IF PRESENT, FAVOR EITHER THE MALE HEIR OR LINE, OR THE FEMALE HEIR OR LINE (165)	0.98 OF 107	197	TEND LESS TO BE THOSE WHERE RULES FOR THE INHERITANCE OF REAL PROPERTY, IF PRESENT, FAVOR EITHER THE MALE HEIR OR LINE, OR THE FEMALE HEIR OR LINE (165)	0.69 OF 87	105 60 2 27 XSQ= 29.85 PHI= 0.392 XP = 0.0000
198	IN ALL CASES ARE THOSE WHERE RULES FOR THE INHERITANCE OF REAL PROPERTY, IF PRESENT, FAVOR THE MALE HEIR OR LINE, RATHER THAN THE FEMALE (144)	1.00 OF 105	198	TEND LESS TO BE THOSE WHERE RULES FOR THE INHERITANCE OF REAL PROPERTY, IF PRESENT, FAVOR THE MALE HEIR OR LINE, RATHER THAN THE FEMALE (144)	0.65 OF 60	105 39 0 21 XSQ= 39.02 PHI= 0.486 XP = 0.

213	DRIFT TOWARD BEING THOSE WHERE FIRST COUSIN MARRIAGE IS PERMITTED (172)	0.52 OF 161	213	DRIFT TOWARD BEING THOSE WHERE FIRST COUSIN MARRIAGE IS NOT PERMITTED (198)	0.58 OF 207	84 86 77 121 XSQ= 3.70 PHI= 0.100 XP = 0.0544
220	TILT LESS TOWARD BEING THOSE WHERE FIRST COUSIN MARRIAGE IN SOME FORM OR OTHER IS NOT PRESCRIBED OR PREFERRED (273)	0.67 OF 161	220	TILT MORE TOWARD BEING THOSE WHERE FIRST COUSIN MARRIAGE IN SOME FORM OR OTHER IS NOT PRESCRIBED OR PREFERRED (273)	0.79 OF 207	53 43 108 164 XSQ= 6.31 PHI= 0.131 XP = 0.0120
221	TEND LESS TO BE THOSE WHERE MATRILATERAL CROSS-COUSIN MARRIAGE IS NOT PRESCRIBED OR PREFERRED (335)	0.84 OF 161	221	TEND MORE TO BE THOSE WHERE MATRILATERAL CROSS-COUSIN MARRIAGE IS NOT PRESCRIBED OR PREFERRED (335)	0.95 OF 207	25 10 136 197 XSQ= 10.83 PHI= 0.172 XP = 0.0010
224	LEAN TOWARD BEING THOSE WHERE COUSIN MARRIAGE IS PREFERENTIALLY OR PERMISSIVELY EITHER PATRI- OR MATRILATERAL, RATHER THAN SYMMETRICAL (66)	0.51 OF 84	224	LEAN TOWARD BEING THOSE WHERE COUSIN MARRIAGE IS PREFERENTIALLY OR PERMISSIVELY SYMMETRICAL, RATHER THAN EITHER PATRI- OR MATRILATERAL (106)	0.73 OF 86	43 23 41 63 XSQ= 9.69 PHI= 0.239 XP = 0.0019
234	TEND TO BE THOSE WHERE THE COUSIN TERMINOLOGY IS OF CROW, OMAHA, OR IROQUOIS TYPE, RATHER THAN ESKIMO OR HAWAIIAN TYPE (152)	0.66 OF 118	234	TEND TO BE THOSE WHERE THE COUSIN TERMINOLOGY IS OF ESKIMO OR HAWAIIAN TYPE, RATHER THAN CROW, OMAHA, OR IROQUOIS TYPE (170)	0.63 OF 202	78 74 40 128 XSQ= 24.77 PHI= 0.278 XP = 0.0000
242	TEND MORE TO BE THOSE WHERE MARRIAGE IS COMMONLY OR OCCASIONALLY POLYGYNOUS, RATHER THAN MONOGAMOUS (314)	0.89 OF 166	242	TEND LESS TO BE THOSE WHERE MARRIAGE IS COMMONLY OR OCCASIONALLY POLYGYNOUS, RATHER THAN MONOGAMOUS (314)	0.72 OF 227	148 164 18 63 XSQ= 15.74 PHI= 0.200 XP = 0.0001
243	DRIFT TOWARD BEING THOSE WHERE POLYGYNY, IF PRESENT, HAS A HIGH INCIDENCE (24) W-D,S	0.54 OF 26	243	DRIFT TOWARD BEING THOSE WHERE POLYGYNY, IF PRESENT, HAS A LOW INCIDENCE (36) W-D,S	0.71 OF 34	14 10 12 24 XSQ= 2.72 PHI= 0.213 XP = 0.0992
262	TEND MORE TO BE THOSE WHERE WIVES ARE OBTAINED BY MEANS INVOLVING THE PRESENCE OF SOME CONSIDERATION (305)	0.93 OF 167	262	TEND LESS TO BE THOSE WHERE WIVES ARE OBTAINED BY MEANS INVOLVING THE PRESENCE OF SOME CONSIDERATION (305)	0.66 OF 226	156 149 11 77 XSQ= 40.18 PHI= 0.320 XP = 0.
263	TEND TO BE THOSE WHERE WIVES ARE OBTAINED BY RELATIVELY DIFFICULT MEANS, NAMELY BY BRIDE-PRICE, BRIDE-SERVICE, OR EXCHANGING A FEMALE RELATIVE (233)	0.80 OF 167	263	TEND TO BE THOSE WHERE WIVES ARE OBTAINED BY RELATIVELY EASY MEANS, NAMELY BY TOKEN BRIDE-PRICE, GIFT EXCHANGE, ABSENCE OF ANY CONSIDERATION, OR RECEIPT OF DOWRY (162)	0.56 OF 226	133 100 34 126 XSQ= 48.38 PHI= 0.351 XP = 0.

No.		No.		
277	DRIFT TCWARD BEING THCSE 0.62 OF 13 WHERE THE STATUS OF WCMEN IS INFERICR CR SUBJECTED (14) LWS	277	DRIFT TOWARD BEING THOSE 0.74 OF 23 WHERE THE STATUS OF WOMEN IS NOT STRONGLY INFERIOR OR SUBJECTED (22) LWS	8 6 5 17 XSQ= 3.03 PHI= 0.290 EP = 0.0732
278	DRIFT TOWARD BEING THCSE 0.60 OF 10 WHERE PROPERTY RIGHTS IN WCMEN ARE PRESENT (8) LWS	278	DRIFT TOWARD BEING THOSE 0.83 OF 12 WHERE PROPERTY RIGHTS IN WOMEN ARE UNIMPORTANT OR ABSENT (14) LWS	6 2 4 10 XSQ= 2.75 PHI= 0.354 EP = 0.0743
312	DRIFT TOWARD BEING THCSE 0.71 OF 17 WHERE DEPENDENCE SCCIALIZATION ANXIETY IS LCW (23) W-C	312	DRIFT TOWARD BEING THOSE 0.63 OF 30 WHERE DEPENDENCE SOCIALIZATION ANXIETY IS HIGH (24) W-C	5 19 12 11 XSQ= 3.73 PHI= -0.282 XP = 0.0534
315	DRIFT MORE TCWARD BEING THOSE 0.90 OF 20 WHERE MOTHER ANC NURSING CHILC CUSTOMARILY SLEEP IN THE SAME BED (37) W-C,S	315	DRIFT LESS TOWARD BEING THCSE 0.61 OF 31 WHERE MOTHER AND NURSING CHILD CUSTOMARILY SLEEP IN THE SAME BED (37) W-D,S	18 19 2 12 XSQ= 3.69 PHI= 0.269 XP = 0.0546
319	DRIFT TCWARD BEING THCSE 0.62 OF 26 WHERE PRCTECTION OF THE INFANT FROM ENVIRCNMENTAL DISCOMFCRTS IS LCW (30) B-B-C	319	DRIFT TOWARD BEING THOSE 0.64 OF 39 WHERE PROTECTION OF THE INFANT FROM ENVIRONMENTAL DISCOMFCRTS IS HIGH (35) B-B-C	10 25 16 14 XSQ= 3.16 PHI= -0.220 XP = 0.0755
325	TILT TCWARD BEING THOSE 0.61 OF 28 WHERE THE DEGREE OF DIFFUSION AMONG THE INFANT'S NURTURANT AGENTS IS LCW (32) B-B-C	325	TILT TOWARD BEING THOSE 0.67 OF 46 WHERE THE DEGREE OF DIFFUSION AMONG THE INFANT'S NURTURANT AGENTS IS HIGH (42) B-B-C	11 31 17 15 XSQ= 4.52 PHI= -0.247 XP = 0.0336
327	LEAN TCWARD BEING THCSE 0.73 OF 22 WHERE THE AGE CF THE INFANT AT TIME OF REDUCED CCNTACT WITH MOTHER IS TWC YEARS CR LOWER (27) B-B-C	327	LEAN TOWARD BEING THOSE 0.67 OF 33 WHERE THE AGE OF THE INFANT AT TIME OF REDUCED CONTACT WITH MOTHER IS HIGHER THAN TWO YEARS (28) B-B-C	6 22 16 11 XSQ= 6.70 PHI= -0.349 XP = 0.0097
334	TILT TCWARD BEING THOSE 0.67 OF 30 WHERE THE INDULGENCE CF THE CHILD IS LCW (38) B-B-C	334	TILT TOWARD BEING THOSE 0.63 OF 48 WHERE THE INDULGENCE OF THE CHILD IS HIGH (40) B-B-C	10 30 20 18 XSQ= 5.17 PHI= -0.258 XP = 0.0229
370	TILT LESS TCWARC BEING THCSE 0.51 OF 105 WHERE THE SEGREGATICN CF ACOLESCENT BOYS IS ABSENT (148)	370	TILT MORE TOWARD BEING THOSE 0.68 OF 138 WHERE THE SEGREGATION OF ADCLESCENT BOYS IS ABSENT (148)	51 44 54 94 XSQ= 6.29 PHI= 0.161 XP = 0.0121

372	DRIFT TOWARD BEING THOSE 0.55 OF 44 WHERE MALE INITIATION RITES ARE PRESENT (48) ASA	372	DRIFT TOWARD BEING THOSE 0.64 OF 67 WHERE MALE INITIATION RITES ARE ABSENT (63) ASA		24 24 20 43 3.07 0.166 0.0798
				XSQ= PHI= XP =	
377	TEND LESS TO BE THOSE 0.55 OF 139 WHERE MALE GENITAL MUTILATION IS ABSENT (242)	377	TEND MORE TO BE THOSE 0.89 OF 185 WHERE MALE GENITAL MUTILATION IS ABSENT (242)	XSQ= PHI= XP =	62 21 77 164 44.33 0.370 0.
382	TILT TOWARD BEING THOSE 0.61 OF 23 WHERE FEMALE INITIATION RITES ARE ABSENT (27) JKB	382	TILT TOWARD BEING THOSE 0.69 OF 42 WHERE FEMALE INITIATION RITES ARE PRESENT (38) JKB	XSQ= PHI= XP =	9 29 14 13 4.31 -0.258 0.0378
390	TILT LESS TOWARD BEING THOSE 0.65 OF 77 WHERE PREMARITAL SEX RELATIONS ARE WEAKLY PUNISHED AND IN FACT NOT RARE OR PUNISHED ONLY IF PREGNANCY RESULTS, OR FREELY PERMITTED (132) JTW,EA	390	TILT MORE TOWARD BEING THOSE 0.80 OF 102 WHERE PREMARITAL SEX RELATIONS ARE WEAKLY PUNISHED AND IN FACT NOT RARE OR PUNISHED ONLY IF PREGNANCY RESULTS, OR FREELY PERMITTED (132) JTW,EA	XSQ= PHI= XP =	27 20 50 82 4.65 0.161 0.0311
392	LEAN MORE TOWARD BEING THOSE 0.74 OF 77 WHERE PREMARITAL SEX RELATIONS ARE STRONGLY PUNISHED AND IN FACT RARE, OR WEAKLY PUNISHED AND IN FACT NOT RARE, OR PUNISHED ONLY IF PREGNANCY RESULTS (112) JTW,EA	392	LEAN LESS TOWARD BEING THOSE 0.54 OF 102 WHERE PREMARITAL SEX RELATIONS ARE STRONGLY PUNISHED AND IN FACT RARE, OR WEAKLY PUNISHED AND IN FACT NOT RARE, OR PUNISHED ONLY IF PREGNANCY RESULTS (112) JTW,EA	XSQ= PHI= XP =	57 55 20 47 6.74 0.194 0.0094
426	LEAN MORE TOWARD BEING THOSE 0.70 OF 114 WHERE A HIGH GOD IS PRESENT (156) GES,EA	426	LEAN LESS TOWARD BEING THOSE 0.52 OF 146 WHERE A HIGH GOD IS PRESENT (156) GES,EA	XSQ= PHI= XP =	80 76 34 70 8.02 0.176 0.0046
449	DRIFT MORE TOWARD BEING THOSE 0.82 OF 38 WHERE THE OBSERVATION OF FOOD TABOOS IS MEDIUM OR LOW, RATHER THAN HIGH (61) JRL	449	DRIFT LESS TOWARD BEING THOSE 0.63 OF 48 WHERE THE OBSERVATION OF FOOD TABOOS IS MEDIUM OR LOW, RATHER THAN HIGH (61) JRL	XSQ= PHI= XP =	7 18 31 30 2.88 -0.183 0.0899
458	TEND TO BE THOSE 0.50 OF 62 WHERE GAMES, IF PRESENT, INCLUDE GAMES OF STRATEGY (52) R-A-B,EA	458	TEND TO BE THOSE 0.81 OF 109 WHERE GAMES, IF PRESENT, DO NOT INCLUDE GAMES OF STRATEGY (119) R-A-B,EA	XSQ= PHI= XP =	31 21 31 88 16.22 0.308 0.0001
468	DRIFT TOWARD BEING THOSE 0.50 OF 20 WHERE CONTACT WITH OTHER CULTURES IS FREQUENT, RATHER THAN REGULAR OR IRREGULAR (17) JMH	468	DRIFT TOWARD BEING THOSE 0.79 OF 34 WHERE CONTACT WITH OTHER CULTURES IS REGULAR OR IRREGULAR, RATHER THAN FREQUENT (37) JMH	XSQ= PHI= XP =	10 7 10 27 3.78 0.265 0.0519

205/

476	TILT TOWARD BEING THOSE WHERE THE DEGREE OF INSOBRIETY IS MODERATE OR SLIGHT (18) CH	0.58 OF 19	476	TILT TOWARD BEING THOSE WHERE THE DEGREE OF INSOBRIETY IS STRONG (31) DH	0.77 OF 30	8 23 11 7 XSQ= 4.58 PHI= -0.306 XP = 0.0323

206	CULTURES WHERE MARITAL RESIDENCE IS AVUNCULOCAL (18)	206	CULTURES WHERE MARITAL RESIDENCE IS OTHER THAN AVUNCULOCAL (380)	

BACKGROUND ON PAGE 113

SUBJECT ONLY

18 IN LEFT COLUMN

ASHANTI, EYAK, GOAJIRO, GURE, HAIDA, KERALA, KUBA, MOTA, NDEMBU, NYANEKA, PALAUANS, PENDE, SARAMACCA, SIUAI, TENDA, TROBRIAND, TSHIMSHIAN, YOMBE

380 IN RIGHT COLUMN

1 EXCLUDED BECAUSE IRRELEVANT

MINANGKABAU

1 EXCLUDED BECAUSE UNASCERTAINED

	Left column (18)		Right column (380)	Statistics
3	TILT LESS TOWARD BEING THOSE LOCATED OUTSIDE OF AFRICA (320) — 0.56 OF 18	3	TILT MORE TOWARD BEING THOSE LOCATED OUTSIDE OF AFRICA (320) — 0.81 OF 380	8 72 / 10 308 / XSQ= 5.46 / PHI= 0.117 / XP = 0.0195
15	TILT MORE TOWARD BEING THOSE WHERE THE LATITUDE IS LESS THAN TWENTY DEGREES (217) — 0.83 OF 18	15	TILT LESS TOWARD BEING THOSE WHERE THE LATITUDE IS LESS THAN TWENTY DEGREES (217) — 0.53 OF 380	3 180 / 15 200 / XSQ= 5.34 / PHI= -0.116 / XP = 0.0208
36	DRIFT MORE TOWARD BEING THOSE WHERE THE NATURAL ENVIRONMENT IS OTHER THAN 'VERY HARSH,' OR SUB-TROPICAL BUSH, OR TEMPERATE GRASSLAND (292) FWM — 0.94 OF 18	36	DRIFT LESS TOWARD BEING THOSE WHERE THE NATURAL ENVIRONMENT IS OTHER THAN 'VERY HARSH,' OR SUB-TROPICAL BUSH, OR TEMPERATE GRASSLAND (292) FWM — 0.72 OF 380	1 107 / 17 273 / XSQ= 3.37 / PHI= -0.092 / XP = 0.0664
53	DRIFT MORE TOWARD BEING THOSE WHERE FOOD PRODUCTION IS BY SIMPLE AGRICULTURE OR INCIPIENT FOOD PRODUCTION, RATHER THAN BY INTENSIVE AGRICULTURE (147) — 0.92 OF 12	53	DRIFT LESS TOWARD BEING THOSE WHERE FOOD PRODUCTION IS BY SIMPLE AGRICULTURE OR INCIPIENT FOOD PRODUCTION, RATHER THAN BY INTENSIVE AGRICULTURE (147) — 0.60 OF 226	1 90 / 11 136 / XSQ= 3.54 / PHI= -0.122 / XP = 0.0598

55	TILT MORE TOWARD BEING THOSE WHERE FOOD PRODUCTION IS BY SIMPLE AGRICULTURE, RATHER THAN BY INTENSIVE AGRICULTURE (101)	0.91 OF 11	55	TILT LESS TOWARD BEING THOSE WHERE FOOD PRODUCTION IS BY SIMPLE AGRICULTURE, RATHER THAN BY INTENSIVE AGRICULTURE (101)	0.50 OF 181	1 90 10 91 XSQ= 5.33 PHI= -0.167 XP = 0.0209
63	LEAN TOWARD BEING THOSE WHERE HUSBANDRY, IF PRESENT, IS PRINCIPALLY IN THE FORM OF PIGS, SHEEP, OR GOATS, RATHER THAN BOVINE, EQUINE, CAMEL-LIKE, OR DEER-LIKE ANIMALS (74)	0.75 OF 12	63	LEAN TOWARD BEING THOSE WHERE HUSBANDRY, IF PRESENT, IS PRINCIPALLY IN THE FORM OF BOVINE, EQUINE, CAMEL-LIKE, OR DEER-LIKE ANIMALS, RATHER THAN PIGS, SHEEP, OR GOATS (152)	0.70 OF 214	3 149 9 65 XSQ= 8.35 PHI= -0.192 XP = 0.0039
90	IN ALL CASES ARE THOSE WHERE, IF A HEREDITARY HEADMANSHIP IS PRESENT, SUCCESSION IS MATRILINEAL, RATHER THAN PATRILINEAL (38)	1.00 OF 13	90	TEND TO BE THOSE WHERE, IF A HEREDITARY HEADMANSHIP IS PRESENT, SUCCESSION IS PATRILINEAL, RATHER THAN MATRILINEAL (127)	0.84 OF 151	0 127 13 24 XSQ= 43.77 PHI= -0.517 XP = 0.
102	TILT MORE TOWARD BEING THOSE WHERE CLASS STRATIFICATION IS PRESENT (203)	0.82 OF 17	102	TILT LESS TOWARD BEING THOSE WHERE CLASS STRATIFICATION IS PRESENT (203)	0.52 OF 364	14 188 3 176 XSQ= 4.98 PHI= 0.114 XP = 0.0257
108	DRIFT TOWARD BEING THOSE WHERE CLASS STRATIFICATION, IF PRESENT, IS BASED ON A HEREDITARY ARISTOCRACY (74)	0.64 OF 14	108	DRIFT TOWARD BEING THOSE WHERE CLASS STRATIFICATION, IF PRESENT, IS BASED ON SOMETHING OTHER THAN A HEREDITARY ARISTOCRACY (129)	0.65 OF 188	9 65 5 123 XSQ= 3.76 PHI= 0.136 XP = 0.0526
176	DRIFT TOWARD BEING THOSE WHERE THE COMMUNITY IS A CLAN-COMMUNITY OR A COMMUNITY STRUCTURED OR SEGMENTED ON A CLAN BASIS (169)	0.67 OF 18	176	DRIFT TOWARD BEING THOSE WHERE THE COMMUNITY IS OTHER THAN A CLAN-COMMUNITY OR A COMMUNITY STRUCTURED OR SEGMENTED ON A CLAN BASIS (213)	0.57 OF 362	12 156 6 206 XSQ= 2.97 PHI= 0.088 XP = 0.0850
185	IN ALL CASES ARE THOSE WHERE THE LARGEST NON-COGNATIC KIN GROUP IS THE MOEITY OR PHRATRY OR SIB (194)	1.00 OF 18	185	TILT LESS TOWARD BEING THOSE WHERE THE LARGEST NON-COGNATIC KIN GROUP IS THE MOEITY OR PHRATRY OR SIB (194)	0.75 OF 233	18 175 0 58 XSQ= 4.51 PHI= 0.134 XP = 0.0337
186	IN ALL CASES ARE THOSE WHERE THE KIN GROUP IS OTHER THAN EXCLUSIVELY PATRILINEAL (250)	1.00 OF 18	186	LEAN LESS TOWARD BEING THOSE WHERE THE KIN GROUP IS OTHER THAN EXCLUSIVELY PATRILINEAL (250)	0.61 OF 380	0 150 18 230 XSQ= 9.78 PHI= -0.157 XP = 0.0018
187	TEND TO BE THOSE WHERE THE KIN GROUP IS EXCLUSIVELY MATRILINEAL (55)	0.89 OF 18	187	TEND TO BE THOSE WHERE THE KIN GROUP IS OTHER THAN EXCLUSIVELY MATRILINEAL (344)	0.90 OF 379	16 38 2 341 XSQ= 84.35 PHI= 0.461 XP = 0.

188	IN ALL CASES ARE THCSE WHERE THE KIN GRCUP IS CTHER THAN EXCLUSIVELY CCGNATIC (252)	1.00 OF 18	188	LEAN LESS TOWARD BEING THOSE WHERE THE KIN GROUP IS OTHER THAN EXCLUSIVELY COGNATIC (252)	0.61 OF 380	0 147 18 233 XSQ= 9.44 PHI= -0.154 XP = 0.0021
190	TEND TC BE THCSE WHERE THE KIN GRCUP IS MATRILINEAL, RATHER THAN PATRILINEAL CR DCUBLE-DESCENT (61)	0.94 OF 18	190	TEND TO BE THOSE WHERE THE KIN GROUP IS PATRILINEAL OR DOUBLE-DESCENT, RATHER THAN MATRILINEAL (186)	0.81 CF 228	1 185 17 43 XSQ= 47.67 PHI= -0.440 XP = 0.
192	IN ALL CASES ARE THCSE CTHER THAN WHERE THE CNLY KIN GROUP PRESENT IS A KINDRED CR ELSE BILATERAL DESCENT IS INFERRED (289)	1.00 OF 18	192	TILT LESS TOWARD BEING THOSE OTHER THAN WHERE THE ONLY KIN GRCUP PRESENT IS A KINDRED OR ELSE BILATERAL DESCENT IS INFERRED (289)	0.71 CF 380	0 110 18 270 XSQ= 5.83 PHI= -0.121 XP = 0.0158
198	IN ALL CASES ARE THCSE WHERE RULES FCR THE INHERITANCE OF REAL PRCPERTY, IF PRESENT, FAVCR THE FEMALE HEIR CR LINE, RATHER THAN THE MALE (21)	1.00 OF 10	198	TEND TO BE THOSE WHERE RULES FOR THE INHERITANCE CF REAL PROPERTY, IF PRESENT, FAVOR THE MALE HEIR OR LINE, RATHER THAN THE FEMALE (144)	0.93 CF 155	0 144 10 11 XSQ= 64.87 PHI= -0.627 XP = 0.
213	TILT TOWARD BEING THOSE WHERE FIRST CCUSIN MARRIAGE IS PERMITTED (172)	0.72 OF 18	213	TILT TOWARD BEING THOSE WHERE FIRST COUSIN MARRIAGE IS NOT PERMITTED (198)	0.55 CF 350	13 157 5 193 XSQ= 4.12 PHI= 0.106 XP = 0.0425
242	IN ALL CASES ARE THCSE WHERE MARRIAGE IS COMMCNLY CR OCCASICNALLY PCLYGYNOUS, RATHER THAN MCNCGAMCUS (314)	1.00 OF 18	242	DRIFT LESS TOWARD BEING THCSE WHERE MARRIAGE IS COMMONLY OR OCCASIONALLY PCLYGYNCUS, RATHER THAN MONOGAMOUS (314)	0.78 CF 375	18 294 0 81 XSQ= 3.67 PHI= 0.097 XP = 0.0555
370	TEND TC BE THCSE WHERE THE SEGREGATION CF ADOLESCENT BOYS IS CCMPLETE CR PARTIAL (95)	0.92 OF 13	370	TEND TO BE THOSE WHERE THE SEGREGATION CF ADOLESCENT BOYS IS ABSENT (148)	0.64 CF 230	12 83 1 147 XSQ= 14.06 PHI= 0.241 XP = 0.0002
372	IN ALL CASES ARE THCSE WHERE MALE INITIATICN RITES ARE ABSENT (63) ASA	1.00 OF 6	372	DRIFT LESS TOWARD BEING THCSE WHERE MALE INITIATICN RITES ARE ABSENT (63) ASA	0.54 CF 105	0 48 6 57 XSQ= 3.15 PHI= -0.168 XP = 0.0759
471	IN ALL CASES ARE THOSE WHERE SECRET SOCIETIES ARE PRESENT (9) LWS	1.00 OF 3	471	TILT TOWARD BEING THOSE WHERE SECRET SOCIETIES ARE UMIMPORTANT OR ABSENT (14) LWS	0.70 CF 20	3 6 0 14 XSQ= 2.83 PHI= 0.351 EP = 0.0474

206/

473	IN ALL CASES ARE THCSE WHERE SENSITIVITY TC INSULT IS EXTREME (32) PES	1.00 OF 3	473	DRIFT TOWARD BEING THOSE WHERE SENSITIVITY TO INSULT IS MODERATE OR NEGLIGIBLE (56) PES	0.66 OF 85		3 29
							0 56
						XSQ=	2.96
						PHI=	0.183
						XP =	0.0853

207 CULTURES
WHERE MARITAL RESIDENCE IS
MATRILOCAL OR UXORILOCAL, RATHER THAN
AMBILOCAL OR NEOLOCAL (64)

207 CULTURES
WHERE MARITAL RESIDENCE IS
AMBILOCAL OR NEOLOCAL, RATHER THAN
MATRILOCAL OR UXORILOCAL (64)

BACKGROUND ON PAGE 113

BOTH SUBJECT AND PREDICATE

64 IN LEFT COLUMN

APINAYE	BELU	BORORO	BURMESE	CADUVEO	CAGABA	CALLINAGO	CARAJA	CHAMACOCO	CHEROKEE
CHEYENNE	CHIR-APACHE	CHOROTI	COCHITI	CREEK	CUNA	DELAWARE	GARO	GUAHIBO	HANO
HANUNOO	HASINAI	HURON	INGALIK	JAVANESE	KAREN	KASKA	KHASI	KIOW-APACHE	LESU
MANDAN	MATACO	MISKITO	MNONG GAR	MOTILON	MUNDURUCU	NABESNA	NAVAHO	NICOBARESE	ONTONG-JAVA
PAWNEE	PONAPEANS	ROTUMANS	SEMINOLE	SIRIONO	TAGBANUA	TALAMANCA	TAPIRAPE	TENETEHARA	THAI
TIMBIRA	TIMUCUA	TOKELAU	TORAJA	TRUKESE	TUPINAMBA	VEDDA	WARRAU	WICHITA	YABARANA
YAO	YARURO	YUKAGHIR	ZUNI						

64 IN RIGHT COLUMN

ABIPON	ALACALUF	AMERICANS	ANDAMANESE	AWEIKOMA	BAJUN	BASQUES	BEMBA	BLACK CARIB	BRAZILIANS
CAMBA	CAMBODIANS	CARIB	CARINYA	CHENCHU	CHEREMIS	CHOCO	CHORTI	COMANCHE	COPR ESKIMO
DOBUANS	DUTCH	FOX	GUATO	HAWAIIANS	HUICHOL	HUKUNDIKA	HUTSUL	IBAN	IFUGAO
INGASSANA	JEMEZ	JUKUN	KUMYK	KUNG	KURTATCHI	KUTENAI	LAKALAI	LAMBA	MACASSARESE
MAORI	MARSHALLESE	NYAKYUSA	OMAHA	PAEZ	PARAUJANO	PENOBSCOT	RAROIANS	ROMANS	SAGADA
SAMOANS	SELUNG	SIMBOESE	SUBANUN	TAOS	TARAHUMARA	TAREUMIUT	TERENA	TRISTAN	UTE
WAICA	WALLOONS	WASHO	WOLEAIANS						

271 EXCLUDED BECAUSE IRRELEVANT

1 EXCLUDED BECAUSE UNASCERTAINED

3	DRIFT MORE TOWARD BEING THOSE LOCATED OUTSIDE OF AFRICA (320)	0.98 OF 64	3	DRIFT LESS TOWARD BEING THOSE LOCATED OUTSIDE OF AFRICA (320)	0.89 OF 64	1 7 63 57 XSQ= 3.33 PHI= -0.161 XP = 0.0679
4	IN ALL CASES ARE THOSE LOCATED OUTSIDE OF THE CIRCUM-MEDITERRANEAN (355)	1.00 OF 64	4	LEAN LESS TOWARD BEING THOSE LOCATED OUTSIDE OF THE CIRCUM-MEDITERRANEAN (355)	0.84 OF 64	0 10 64 54 XSQ= 8.79 PHI= -0.262 XP = 0.0030
53	TILT MORE TOWARD BEING THOSE WHERE FOOD PRODUCTION IS BY SIMPLE AGRICULTURE OR INCIPIENT FOOD PRODUCTION, RATHER THAN BY INTENSIVE AGRICULTURE (147)	0.83 OF 36	53	TILT LESS TOWARD BEING THOSE WHERE FOOD PRODUCTION IS BY SIMPLE AGRICULTURE OR INCIPIENT FOOD PRODUCTION, RATHER THAN BY INTENSIVE AGRICULTURE (147)	0.54 OF 35	6 16 30 19 XSQ= 5.71 PHI= -0.284 XP = 0.0169

54	TILT LESS TOWARD BEING THOSE 0.58 OF 36 WHERE FOOD PRODUCTION IS BY INTENSIVE OR SIMPLE AGRICULTURE, RATHER THAN BY INCIPIENT FOOD PRODUCTION (192)	54	TILT MORE TOWARD BEING THOSE 0.83 OF 35 WHERE FOOD PRODUCTION IS BY INTENSIVE OR SIMPLE AGRICULTURE, RATHER THAN BY INCIPIENT FOOD PRODUCTION (192)	21 29 15 6 XSQ= 4.01 PHI= -0.238 XP = 0.0451
74	DRIFT MORE TOWARD BEING THOSE 0.77 OF 43 WHERE POTTERY IS PRESENT (145)	74	DRIFT LESS TOWARD BEING THOSE 0.57 OF 42 WHERE POTTERY IS PRESENT (145)	33 24 10 18 XSQ= 2.86 PHI= 0.183 XP = 0.0907
87	DRIFT MORE TOWARD BEING THOSE 0.95 OF 57 WHERE THE LEVEL OF POLITICAL INTEGRATION IS THE LARGE STATE, THE LITTLE STATE, THE MINIMAL STATE, OR THE AUTONOMOUS COMMUNITY (281) GPM	87	DRIFT LESS TOWARD BEING THOSE 0.81 OF 43 WHERE THE LEVEL OF POLITICAL INTEGRATION IS THE LARGE STATE, THE LITTLE STATE, THE MINIMAL STATE, OR THE AUTONOMOUS COMMUNITY (281) GPM	54 35 3 8 XSQ= 3.20 PHI= 0.179 XP = 0.0737
98	TEND TO BE THOSE 0.79 OF 57 WHERE THE HIERARCHY OF LOCAL JURISDICTION HAS FOUR OR THREE LEVELS (238) GES,EA	98	TEND TO BE THOSE 0.54 OF 50 WHERE THE HIERARCHY OF LOCAL JURISDICTION HAS TWO LEVELS (93) GES,EA	45 23 12 27 XSQ= 11.10 PHI= 0.322 XP = 0.0009
99	TILT TOWARD BEING THOSE 0.71 OF 34 WHERE, WITH NATIONAL HIERARCHY ABSENT, THE HIERARCHY OF LOCAL JURISDICTION HAS FOUR OR THREE LEVELS (93) GES,EA	99	TILT TOWARD BEING THOSE 0.60 OF 30 WHERE, WITH NATIONAL HIERARCHY ABSENT, THE HIERARCHY OF LOCAL JURISDICTION HAS TWO LEVELS (63) GES,EA	24 12 10 18 XSQ= 4.88 PHI= 0.276 XP = 0.0272
100	DRIFT MORE TOWARD BEING THOSE 0.82 OF 57 WHERE HIERARCHIES ARE MORE COMPLEX THAN THE 'SIMPLEST,' I. E., MORE COMPLEX THAN TWO LOCAL LEVELS WITH NO NATIONAL LEVELS (267) GES,EA	100	DRIFT LESS TOWARD BEING THOSE 0.64 OF 50 WHERE HIERARCHIES ARE MORE COMPLEX THAN THE 'SIMPLEST,' I. E., MORE COMPLEX THAN TWO LOCAL LEVELS WITH NO NATIONAL LEVELS (267) GES,EA	47 32 10 18 XSQ= 3.79 PHI= 0.188 XP = 0.0516
130	TILT MORE TOWARD BEING THOSE 0.93 OF 14 WHERE LEATHER WORKING IS MAINLY DONE BY FEMALES (45)	130	TILT LESS TOWARD BEING THOSE 0.53 OF 15 WHERE LEATHER WORKING IS MAINLY DONE BY FEMALES (45)	1 7 13 8 XSQ= 3.86 PHI= -0.365 EP = 0.0352
176	TILT LESS TOWARD BEING THOSE 0.64 OF 61 WHERE THE COMMUNITY IS OTHER THAN A CLAN-COMMUNITY OR A COMMUNITY STRUCTURED OR SEGMENTED ON A CLAN BASIS (213)	176	TILT MORE TOWARD BEING THOSE 0.84 OF 62 WHERE THE COMMUNITY IS OTHER THAN A CLAN-COMMUNITY OR A COMMUNITY STRUCTURED OR SEGMENTED ON A CLAN BASIS (213)	22 10 39 52 XSQ= 5.36 PHI= 0.209 XP = 0.0207
178	TILT LESS TOWARD BEING THOSE 0.67 OF 61 WHERE THE COMMUNITY IS OTHER THAN SEGMENTED ON A CLAN BASIS AND NON-EXOGAMOUS (295)	178	TILT MORE TOWARD BEING THOSE 0.85 OF 62 WHERE THE COMMUNITY IS OTHER THAN SEGMENTED ON A CLAN BASIS AND NON-EXOGAMOUS (295)	20 9 41 53 XSQ= 4.73 PHI= 0.196 XP = 0.0297

187	TEND TO BE THOSE WHERE THE KIN GROUP IS EXCLUSIVELY MATRILINEAL (55)	0.50 OF 64	187	TEND TO BE THOSE WHERE THE KIN GROUP IS OTHER THAN EXCLUSIVELY MATRILINEAL (344)	0.95 OF 64	32 3 32 61 XSQ= 30.83 PHI= 0.491 XP = 0.
188	TEND TO BE THOSE WHERE THE KIN GROUP IS OTHER THAN EXCLUSIVELY COGNATIC (252)	0.52 OF 64	188	TEND TO BE THOSE WHERE THE KIN GROUP IS EXCLUSIVELY COGNATIC (148)	0.80 OF 64	31 51 33 13 XSQ= 12.25 PHI= -0.309 XP = 0.0005
190	LEAN MORE TOWARD BEING THOSE WHERE THE KIN GROUP IS MATRILINEAL, RATHER THAN PATRILINEAL OR DOUBLE-DESCENT (61)	0.97 OF 33	190	LEAN LESS TOWARD BEING THOSE WHERE THE KIN GROUP IS MATRILINEAL, RATHER THAN PATRILINEAL OR DOUBLE-DESCENT (61)	0.62 OF 13	1 5 32 8 XSQ= 7.43 PHI= -0.402 XP = 0.0064
192	LEAN TOWARD BEING THOSE OTHER THAN WHERE THE ONLY KIN GROUP PRESENT IS A KINDRED OR ELSE BILATERAL DESCENT IS INFERRED (289)	0.61 OF 64	192	LEAN TOWARD BEING THOSE WHERE THE ONLY KIN GROUP PRESENT IS A KINDRED OR ELSE BILATERAL DESCENT IS INFERRED (111)	0.64 OF 64	25 41 39 23 XSQ= 7.04 PHI= -0.234 XP = 0.0080
198	TILT TOWARD BEING THOSE WHERE RULES FOR THE INHERITANCE OF REAL PROPERTY, IF PRESENT, FAVOR THE FEMALE HEIR OR LINE, RATHER THAN THE MALE (21)	0.73 OF 11	198	TILT TOWARD BEING THOSE WHERE RULES FOR THE INHERITANCE OF REAL PROPERTY, IF PRESENT, FAVOR THE MALE HEIR OR LINE, RATHER THAN THE FEMALE (144)	0.82 OF 11	3 9 8 2 XSQ= 4.58 PHI= -0.456 EP = 0.0300
214	DRIFT LESS TOWARD BEING THOSE WHERE FIRST COUSIN MARRIAGE, IF PERMITTED, IS OTHER THAN UNILATERAL (144)	0.76 OF 25	214	IN ALL CASES ARE THOSE WHERE FIRST COUSIN MARRIAGE, IF PERMITTED, IS OTHER THAN UNILATERAL (144)	1.00 OF 17	6 0 19 17 XSQ= 3.00 PHI= 0.267 XP = 0.0832
220	TILT LESS TOWARD BEING THOSE WHERE FIRST COUSIN MARRIAGE IN SOME FORM OR OTHER IS NOT PRESCRIBED OR PREFERRED (273)	0.69 OF 58	220	TILT MORE TOWARD BEING THOSE WHERE FIRST COUSIN MARRIAGE IN SOME FORM OR OTHER IS NOT PRESCRIBED OR PREFERRED (273)	0.89 OF 54	18 6 40 48 XSQ= 5.46 PHI= 0.221 XP = 0.0194
234	LEAN TOWARD BEING THOSE WHERE THE COUSIN TERMINOLOGY IS OF CROW, OMAHA, OR IROQUOIS TYPE, RATHER THAN ESKIMO OR HAWAIIAN TYPE (152)	0.51 OF 61	234	LEAN TOWARD BEING THOSE WHERE THE COUSIN TERMINOLOGY IS OF ESKIMO OR HAWAIIAN TYPE, RATHER THAN CROW, OMAHA, OR IROQUOIS TYPE (170)	0.76 OF 58	31 14 30 44 XSQ= 7.90 PHI= 0.258 XP = 0.0049
236	TEND TO BE THOSE WHERE THE FAMILY IS OF AN EXTENDED TYPE, RATHER THAN AN INDEPENDENT TYPE (213)	0.77 OF 64	236	TEND TO BE THOSE WHERE THE FAMILY IS OF AN INDEPENDENT TYPE, RATHER THAN AN EXTENDED TYPE (185)	0.67 OF 64	49 21 15 43 XSQ= 22.98 PHI= 0.424 XP = 0.0000

207/

259	DRIFT TOWARD BEING THOSE 0.78 OF 9 WHERE THE SEVERITY OF MOTHER-IN-LAW AVOIDANCE IS HIGH (26) WNS	DRIFT TOWARD BEING THOSE 0.67 OF 12 WHERE THE SEVERITY OF MOTHER-IN-LAW AVOIDANCE IS LOW (20) WNS	7 4 2 8 XSQ= 2.49 PHI= 0.344 EP = 0.0805
307	DRIFT TOWARD BEING THOSE 0.71 OF 7 WHERE THE EARLY AGGRESSION SATISFACTION POTENTIAL IS LOW (19) W-C	DRIFT TOWARD BEING THOSE 0.77 OF 13 WHERE THE EARLY AGGRESSION SATISFACTION POTENTIAL IS HIGH (33) W-C	2 10 5 3 XSQ= 2.65 PHI= -0.364 EP = 0.0623
344	DRIFT TOWARD BEING THOSE 0.63 OF 16 WHERE THE TOTAL POSITIVE PRESSURE TOWARD DEVELOPING SELF-RELIANT BEHAVIOR IN THE CHILD IS LOW (40) B-B-C	DRIFT TOWARD BEING THOSE 0.80 OF 10 WHERE THE TOTAL POSITIVE PRESSURE TOWARD DEVELOPING SELF-RELIANT BEHAVIOR IN THE CHILD IS HIGH (36) B-B-C	6 8 10 2 XSQ= 2.93 PHI= -0.335 EP = 0.0511
393	DRIFT TOWARD BEING THOSE 0.61 OF 18 WHERE EXTRAMARITAL COITUS IS PERMITTED, RATHER THAN PUNISHED (41) F-B	DRIFT TOWARD BEING THOSE 0.71 OF 14 WHERE EXTRAMARITAL COITUS IS PUNISHED, RATHER THAN PERMITTED (43) F-B	7 10 11 4 XSQ= 2.17 PHI= -0.260 EP = 0.0870
473	DRIFT MORE TOWARD BEING THOSE 0.92 OF 13 WHERE SENSITIVITY TO INSULT IS MODERATE OR NEGLIGIBLE (56) PES	DRIFT LESS TOWARD BEING THOSE 0.60 OF 15 WHERE SENSITIVITY TO INSULT IS MODERATE OR NEGLIGIBLE (56) PES	1 6 12 9 XSQ= 2.35 PHI= -0.289 EP = 0.0836
477	IN ALL CASES ARE THOSE 1.00 OF 4 WHERE ALCOHOLIC AGGRESSION IS MODERATE OR SLIGHT (19) CH	TILT TOWARD BEING THOSE 0.83 OF 6 WHERE ALCOHOLIC AGGRESSION IS STRONG (15) DH	0 5 4 1 XSQ= 3.75 PHI= -0.612 EP = 0.0476

208 CULTURES WHERE MARITAL RESIDENCE IS MATRILOCAL (31)	208 CULTURES WHERE MARITAL RESIDENCE IS OTHER THAN MATRILOCAL (367)

BACKGROUND ON PAGE 113 — SUBJECT ONLY

31 IN LEFT COLUMN

APINAYE	BELU	BORORO	CALLINAGO	CHEROKEE	COCHITI	CREEK	DELAWARE	GARO	GUAHIBO
HANO	HURON	KAREN	KASKA	KHASI	LESU	MANDAN	MNONG GAR	NAVAHO	PAWNEE
PONAPEANS	ROTUMANS	SEMINOLE	SIRIONO	TALAMANCA	TIMBIRA	TIMUCUA	TRUKESE	VEDDA	YAO
ZUNI									

367 IN RIGHT COLUMN

1 EXCLUDED BECAUSE IRRELEVANT

MINANGKABAU

1 EXCLUDED BECAUSE UNASCERTAINED

	Left column (matrilocal)			Right column (other than matrilocal)		Statistics
3	TILT MORE TOWARD BEING THOSE LOCATED OUTSIDE OF AFRICA (320)	0.97 OF 31	3	TILT LESS TOWARD BEING THOSE LOCATED OUTSIDE OF AFRICA (320)	0.78 OF 367	1 79 30 288 XSQ= 4.88 PHI= -0.111 XP = 0.0272
4	IN ALL CASES ARE THOSE LOCATED OUTSIDE OF THE CIRCUM-MEDITERRANEAN (355)	1.00 OF 31	4	DRIFT LESS TOWARD BEING THOSE LOCATED OUTSIDE OF THE CIRCUM-MEDITERRANEAN (355)	0.88 OF 367	0 45 31 322 XSQ= 3.15 PHI= -0.089 XP = 0.0759
8	TEND LESS TO BE THOSE LOCATED OUTSIDE OF NORTH AMERICA (330)	0.58 OF 31	8	TEND MORE TO BE THOSE LOCATED OUTSIDE OF NORTH AMERICA (330)	0.84 OF 367	13 57 18 310 XSQ= 11.99 PHI= 0.174 XP = 0.0005
54	LEAN LESS TOWARD BEING THOSE WHERE FOOD PRODUCTION IS BY INTENSIVE OR SIMPLE AGRICULTURE, RATHER THAN BY INCIPIENT FOOD PRODUCTION (192)	0.55 OF 20	54	LEAN MORE TOWARD BEING THOSE WHERE FOOD PRODUCTION IS BY INTENSIVE OR SIMPLE AGRICULTURE, RATHER THAN BY INCIPIENT FOOD PRODUCTION (192)	0.83 OF 218	11 181 9 37 XSQ= 7.52 PHI= -0.178 XP = 0.0061

56	TILT TOWARD BEING THOSE 0.56 OF 16 WHERE FOOD PRODUCTION IS BY INCIPIENT FOOD PRODUCTION, RATHER THAN BY SIMPLE AGRICULTURE (46)	56	TILT TOWARD BEING THOSE 0.72 OF 131 WHERE FOOD PRODUCTION IS BY SIMPLE AGRICULTURE, RATHER THAN BY INCIPIENT FOOD PRODUCTION (101)	7 94 9 37 XSQ= 3.98 PHI= -0.165 XP = 0.0460
80	IN ALL CASES ARE THOSE 1.00 OF 21 WHERE NO CITY OR TOWN IS PRESENT (185)	80	DRIFT LESS TOWARD BEING THOSE 0.81 OF 202 WHERE NO CITY OR TOWN IS PRESENT (185)	0 39 21 163 XSQ= 3.67 PHI= -0.128 XP = 0.0555
84	IN ALL CASES ARE THOSE 1.00 OF 28 WHERE THE LEVEL OF POLITICAL INTEGRATION IS THE LITTLE STATE, THE MINIMAL STATE, THE AUTONOMOUS COMMUNITY, OR THE FAMILY (262) GPM	84	DRIFT LESS TOWARD BEING THOSE 0.85 OF 274 WHERE THE LEVEL OF POLITICAL INTEGRATION IS THE LITTLE STATE, THE MINIMAL STATE, THE AUTONOMOUS COMMUNITY, OR THE FAMILY (262) GPM	0 42 28 232 XSQ= 3.79 PHI= -0.112 XP = 0.0516
85	DRIFT MORE TOWARD BEING THOSE 0.93 OF 28 WHERE THE LEVEL OF POLITICAL INTEGRATION IS THE MINIMAL STATE, THE AUTONOMOUS COMMUNITY, OR THE FAMILY (234) GPM	85	DRIFT LESS TOWARD BEING THOSE 0.75 OF 274 WHERE THE LEVEL OF POLITICAL INTEGRATION IS THE MINIMAL STATE, THE AUTONOMOUS COMMUNITY, OR THE FAMILY (234) GPM	2 68 26 206 XSQ= 3.52 PHI= -0.108 XP = 0.0606
90	TEND TO BE THOSE 0.71 OF 17 WHERE, IF A HEREDITARY HEADMANSHIP IS PRESENT, SUCCESSION IS MATRILINEAL, RATHER THAN PATRILINEAL (38)	90	TEND TO BE THOSE 0.83 OF 147 WHERE, IF A HEREDITARY HEADMANSHIP IS PRESENT, SUCCESSION IS PATRILINEAL, RATHER THAN MATRILINEAL (127)	5 122 12 25 XSQ= 22.07 PHI= -0.367 XP = 0.0000
95	DRIFT MORE TOWARD BEING THOSE 0.93 OF 27 WHERE THE HIERARCHY OF NATIONAL JURISDICTION HAS ONE OR NO LEVELS (254) GES,EA	95	DRIFT LESS TOWARD BEING THOSE 0.75 OF 302 WHERE THE HIERARCHY OF NATIONAL JURISDICTION HAS ONE OR NO LEVELS (254) GES,EA	2 74 25 228 XSQ= 3.17 PHI= -0.098 XP = 0.0749
98	TILT MORE TOWARD BEING THOSE 0.93 OF 27 WHERE THE HIERARCHY OF LOCAL JURISDICTION HAS FOUR OR THREE LEVELS (238) GES,EA	98	TILT LESS TOWARD BEING THOSE 0.70 OF 303 WHERE THE HIERARCHY OF LOCAL JURISDICTION HAS FOUR OR THREE LEVELS (238) GES,EA	25 213 2 90 XSQ= 5.07 PHI= 0.124 XP = 0.0243
99	TILT MORE TOWARD BEING THOSE 0.88 OF 16 WHERE, WITH NATIONAL HIERARCHY ABSENT, THE HIERARCHY OF LOCAL JURISDICTION HAS FOUR OR THREE LEVELS (93) GES,EA	99	TILT LESS TOWARD BEING THOSE 0.57 OF 139 WHERE, WITH NATIONAL HIERARCHY ABSENT, THE HIERARCHY OF LOCAL JURISDICTION HAS FOUR OR THREE LEVELS (93) GES,EA	14 79 2 60 XSQ= 4.42 PHI= 0.169 XP = 0.0356
102	LEAN TOWARD BEING THOSE 0.71 OF 31 WHERE CLASS STRATIFICATION IS ABSENT (180)	102	LEAN TOWARD BEING THOSE 0.55 OF 350 WHERE CLASS STRATIFICATION IS PRESENT (203)	9 193 22 157 XSQ= 6.78 PHI= -0.133 XP = 0.0092

110	DRIFT MORE TOWARD BEING THOSE 0.73 OF 30 WHERE SLAVERY IS ABSENT (218)	110	DRIFT LESS TOWARD BEING THOSE 0.56 OF 349 WHERE SLAVERY IS ABSENT (218)	8 155 22 194 XSQ= 2.86 PHI= -0.087 XP = 0.0907
129	IN ALL CASES ARE THOSE 1.00 OF 10 WHERE WEAVING IS MAINLY DONE BY FEMALES (73)	129	DRIFT LESS TOWARD BEING THOSE 0.67 OF 94 WHERE WEAVING IS MAINLY DONE BY FEMALES (73)	0 31 10 63 XSQ= 3.25 PHI= -0.177 XP = 0.0712
138	IN ALL CASES ARE THOSE 1.00 OF 3 WHERE SUPERORDINATE JUSTICE IS ABSENT (18) BBW	138	DRIFT TOWARD BEING THOSE 0.59 OF 37 WHERE SUPERORDINATE JUSTICE IS PRESENT (22) BBW	0 22 3 15 XSQ= 1.93 PHI= -0.219 EP = 0.0826
175	TILT MORE TOWARD BEING THOSE 0.86 OF 29 WHERE THE COMMUNITY IS 'KIN-HETEROGENEOUS,' I. E. OTHER THAN A CLAN COMMUNITY OR A DEME (260)	175	TILT LESS TOWARD BEING THOSE 0.66 OF 351 WHERE THE COMMUNITY IS 'KIN-HETEROGENEOUS,' I. E. OTHER THAN A CLAN COMMUNITY OR A DEME (260)	4 118 25 233 XSQ= 3.96 PHI= -0.102 XP = 0.0465
176	TEND TO BE THOSE 0.76 OF 29 WHERE THE COMMUNITY IS A CLAN-COMMUNITY OR A COMMUNITY STRUCTURED OR SEGMENTED ON A CLAN BASIS (169)	176	TEND TO BE THOSE 0.58 OF 351 WHERE THE COMMUNITY IS OTHER THAN A CLAN-COMMUNITY OR A COMMUNITY STRUCTURED OR SEGMENTED ON A CLAN BASIS (213)	22 146 7 205 XSQ= 11.40 PHI= 0.173 XP = 0.0007
178	TEND TO BE THOSE 0.69 OF 29 WHERE THE COMMUNITY IS SEGMENTED ON A CLAN BASIS AND NON-EXOGAMOUS (87)	178	TEND TO BE THOSE 0.81 OF 351 WHERE THE COMMUNITY IS OTHER THAN SEGMENTED ON A CLAN BASIS AND NON-EXOGAMOUS (295)	20 66 9 285 XSQ= 35.68 PHI= 0.306 XP = 0.
180	LEAN MORE TOWARD BEING THOSE 0.93 OF 29 WHERE THE COMMUNITY IS COMMONLY NON-EXOGAMOUS, RATHER THAN EXOGAMOUS (258)	180	LEAN LESS TOWARD BEING THOSE 0.66 OF 351 WHERE THE COMMUNITY IS COMMONLY NON-EXOGAMOUS, RATHER THAN EXOGAMOUS (258)	2 121 27 230 XSQ= 8.09 PHI= -0.146 XP = 0.0045
182	DRIFT MORE TOWARD BEING THOSE 0.83 OF 29 OTHER THAN WHERE THE COMMUNITY IS STRUCTURED ON A NON-CLAN BASIS AND AGAMOUS (256)	182	DRIFT LESS TOWARD BEING THOSE 0.66 OF 351 OTHER THAN WHERE THE COMMUNITY IS STRUCTURED ON A NON-CLAN BASIS AND AGAMOUS (256)	5 121 24 230 XSQ= 2.85 PHI= -0.087 XP = 0.0912
183	TILT LESS TOWARD BEING THOSE 0.71 OF 31 WHERE THE LARGEST NON-COGNATIC KIN GROUP IS SMALLER THAN A MOEITY, I. E., A PHRATRY OR SIB OR LINEAGE (218)	183	TILT MORE TOWARD BEING THOSE 0.89 OF 220 WHERE THE LARGEST NON-COGNATIC KIN GROUP IS SMALLER THAN A MOEITY, I. E., A PHRATRY OR SIB OR LINEAGE (218)	9 25 22 195 XSQ= 5.81 PHI= 0.152 XP = 0.0159

187	IN ALL CASES ARE THOSE WHERE THE KIN GROUP IS EXCLUSIVELY MATRILINEAL (55)	1.00 OF 31	187	TEND TO BE THOSE WHERE THE KIN GROUP IS OTHER THAN EXCLUSIVELY MATRILINEAL (344)	0.94 OF 366	31 23 0 343 XSQ= 205.69 PHI= 0.720 XP = 0.
198	TEND TO BE THOSE WHERE RULES FOR THE INHERITANCE OF REAL PROPERTY, IF PRESENT, FAVOR THE FEMALE HEIR OR LINE, RATHER THAN THE MALE (21)	0.80 OF 10	198	TEND TO BE THOSE WHERE RULES FOR THE INHERITANCE OF REAL PROPERTY, IF PRESENT, FAVOR THE MALE HEIR OR LINE, RATHER THAN THE FEMALE (144)	0.92 OF 155	2 142 8 13 XSQ= 37.16 PHI= -0.475 XP = 0.
214	TILT LESS TOWARD BEING THOSE WHERE FIRST COUSIN MARRIAGE, IF PERMITTED, IS OTHER THAN UNILATERAL (144)	0.57 OF 14	214	TILT MORE TOWARD BEING THOSE WHERE FIRST COUSIN MARRIAGE, IF PERMITTED, IS OTHER THAN UNILATERAL (144)	0.86 OF 156	6 22 8 134 XSQ= 5.77 PHI= 0.184 XP = 0.0163
234	TEND TO BE THOSE WHERE THE COUSIN TERMINOLOGY IS OF CROW, OMAHA, OR IROQUOIS TYPE, RATHER THAN ESKIMO OR HAWAIIAN TYPE (152)	0.81 OF 31	234	TEND TO BE THOSE WHERE THE COUSIN TERMINOLOGY IS OF ESKIMO OR HAWAIIAN TYPE, RATHER THAN CROW, OMAHA, OR IROQUOIS TYPE (170)	0.56 OF 289	25 127 6 162 XSQ= 13.69 PHI= 0.207 XP = 0.0002
236	LEAN MORE TOWARD BEING THOSE WHERE THE FAMILY IS OF AN EXTENDED TYPE, RATHER THAN AN INDEPENDENT TYPE (213)	0.81 OF 31	236	LEAN LESS TOWARD BEING THOSE WHERE THE FAMILY IS OF AN EXTENDED TYPE, RATHER THAN AN INDEPENDENT TYPE (213)	0.51 OF 365	25 186 6 179 XSQ= 8.96 PHI= 0.150 XP = 0.0028
240	TILT TOWARD BEING THOSE WHERE THE FAMILY, IF EXTENDED, IS LARGE, RATHER THAN SMALL OR STEM (78)	0.56 OF 25	240	TILT TOWARD BEING THOSE WHERE THE FAMILY, IF EXTENDED, IS SMALL OR STEM, RATHER THAN LARGE (135)	0.67 OF 186	14 62 11 124 XSQ= 3.98 PHI= 0.137 XP = 0.0461
242	LEAN LESS TOWARD BEING THOSE WHERE MARRIAGE IS COMMONLY OR OCCASIONALLY POLYGYNOUS, RATHER THAN MONOGAMOUS (314)	0.58 OF 31	242	LEAN MORE TOWARD BEING THOSE WHERE MARRIAGE IS COMMONLY OR OCCASIONALLY POLYGYNOUS, RATHER THAN MONOGAMOUS (314)	0.81 OF 362	18 294 13 68 XSQ= 7.99 PHI= -0.143 XP = 0.0047
262	TEND TO BE THOSE WHERE WIVES ARE OBTAINED BY MEANS INVOLVING THE ABSENCE OF ANY CONSIDERATION (90)	0.57 OF 30	262	TEND TO BE THOSE WHERE WIVES ARE OBTAINED BY MEANS INVOLVING THE PRESENCE OF SOME CONSIDERATION (305)	0.80 OF 363	13 292 17 71 XSQ= 19.87 PHI= -0.225 XP = 0.0000
263	TEND TO BE THOSE WHERE WIVES ARE OBTAINED BY RELATIVELY EASY MEANS, NAMELY BY TOKEN BRIDE-PRICE, GIFT EXCHANGE, ABSENCE OF ANY CONSIDERATION, OR RECEIPT OF DOWRY (162)	0.73 OF 30	263	TEND TO BE THOSE WHERE WIVES ARE OBTAINED BY RELATIVELY DIFFICULT MEANS, NAMELY BY BRIDE-PRICE, BRIDE-SERVICE, OR EXCHANGING A FEMALE RELATIVE (233)	0.62 OF 363	8 225 22 138 XSQ= 12.89 PHI= -0.181 XP = 0.0003

296	IN ALL CASES ARE THOSE WHERE INFANTICIDE IS ABSENT OR INFERRED ABSENT (15) BCA	1.00 OF 3	296	DRIFT TOWARD BEING THOSE WHERE INFANTICIDE IS PRESENT (18) BCA	0.60 OF 30	0 18 3 12 XSQ= 1.91 PHI= -0.241 EP = 0.0834
377	TILT MORE TOWARD BEING THOSE WHERE MALE GENITAL MUTILATION IS ABSENT (242)	0.93 OF 27	377	TILT LESS TOWARD BEING THOSE WHERE MALE GENITAL MUTILATION IS ABSENT (242)	0.73 OF 297	2 81 25 216 XSQ= 4.14 PHI= -0.113 XP = 0.0420
390	IN ALL CASES ARE THOSE WHERE PREMARITAL SEX RELATIONS ARE WEAKLY PUNISHED AND IN FACT NOT RARE OR PUNISHED ONLY IF PREGNANCY RESULTS, OR FREELY PERMITTED (132) JTW,EA	1.00 OF 13	390	DRIFT LESS TOWARD BEING THOSE WHERE PREMARITAL SEX RELATIONS ARE WEAKLY PUNISHED AND IN FACT NOT RARE OR PUNISHED ONLY IF PREGNANCY RESULTS, OR FREELY PERMITTED (132) JTW,EA	0.72 OF 166	0 47 13 119 XSQ= 3.64 PHI= -0.143 XP = 0.0565
391	DRIFT TOWARD BEING THOSE WHERE PREMARITAL SEX RELATIONS ARE PUNISHED ONLY IF PREGNANCY RESULTS, OR FREELY PERMITTED (90) JTW,EA	0.77 OF 13	391	DRIFT TOWARD BEING THOSE WHERE PREMARITAL SEX RELATIONS ARE STRONGLY PUNISHED AND IN FACT RARE, OR WEAKLY PUNISHED AND IN FACT NOT RARE (89) JTW,EA	0.52 OF 166	3 86 10 80 XSQ= 2.91 PHI= -0.128 XP = 0.0878
399	IN ALL CASES ARE THOSE WHERE INTENSITY OF CASTRATION ANXIETY IS LOW (22) WNS	1.00 OF 5	399	DRIFT TOWARD BEING THOSE WHERE INTENSITY OF CASTRATION ANXIETY IS HIGH (23) WNS	0.57 OF 40	0 23 5 17 XSQ= 3.80 PHI= -0.291 XP = 0.0511
420	DRIFT TOWARD BEING THOSE WHERE BELLICOSITY IS MODERATE OR NEGLIGIBLE (46) PES	0.88 OF 8	420	DRIFT TOWARD BEING THOSE WHERE BELLICOSITY IS EXTREME (41) PES	0.51 OF 79	1 40 7 39 XSQ= 2.85 PHI= -0.181 XP = 0.0915
426	DRIFT TOWARD BEING THOSE WHERE A HIGH GOD IS ABSENT (104) GES,EA	0.59 OF 22	426	DRIFT TOWARD BEING THOSE WHERE A HIGH GOD IS PRESENT (156) GES,EA	0.62 OF 238	9 147 13 91 XSQ= 2.83 PHI= -0.104 XP = 0.0924
427	DRIFT TOWARD BEING THOSE WHERE A HIGH GOD, IF PRESENT, IS INACTIVE, RATHER THAN ACTIVE (69) GES,EA	0.78 OF 9	427	DRIFT TOWARD BEING THOSE WHERE A HIGH GOD, IF PRESENT, IS ACTIVE, RATHER THAN INACTIVE (87) GES,EA	0.58 OF 147	2 85 7 62 XSQ= 3.03 PHI= -0.139 XP = 0.0815
449	DRIFT TOWARD BEING THOSE WHERE THE OBSERVATION OF FOOD TABOOS IS HIGH, RATHER THAN MEDIUM OR LOW (25) JRL	0.63 OF 8	449	DRIFT TOWARD BEING THOSE WHERE THE OBSERVATION OF FOOD TABOOS IS MEDIUM OR LOW, RATHER THAN HIGH (61) JRL	0.74 OF 78	5 20 3 58 XSQ= 3.16 PHI= 0.192 XP = 0.0754

208/

```
473  IN ALL CASES ARE THCSE           1.00 OF    8       473  DRIFT LESS TOWARD BEING THCSE  0.60 OF  80            0    32
     WHERE SENSITIVITY TC INSULT                              WHERE SENSITIVITY TO INSULT                              8    48
     IS MODERATE OR NEGLIGIBLE  (56) PES                      IS MODERATE OR NEGLIGIBLE  (56) PES              XSQ=     3.45
                                                                                                                PHI=   -0.198
                                                                                                                XP =   0.0633
```

****

209 CULTURES
WHERE MARITAL RESICENCE IS
PATRILOCAL, VIRILOCAL, OR AVUNCULOCAL,
RATHER THAN
MATRILCCAL OR UXCRILOCAL (270)

209 CULTURES
WHERE MARITAL RESIDENCE IS
MATRILOCAL OR UXORILOCAL, RATHER THAN
PATRILOCAL, VIRILOCAL, OR
AVUNCULOCAL (64)

BACKGROUND ON PAGE 113

BOTH SUBJECT AND PREDICATE

....

270 IN LEFT CCLUMN

ABOR	AINU	AJIE	AKHA	ALBANIANS	ALORESE	AMBA	ARANDA	ARAPESH	ARAUCANIANS
ARYANS	ASHANTI	ATAYAL	ATSUGEWI	AYMARA	AZANDE	AZTEC	BABWA	BACAIRI	BALINESE
BAMBARA	BAMILEKE	BANCA	BARABRA	BARI	BASSERI	BATAK	BAYA	BEJA	BENGALI
BERGDAMA	BETE	BHIL	BHUIYA	BIRIFOR	BOERS	BOZO	BUDUMA	BULGARIANS	BUNLAP
BURUSHO	BURYAT	CAMAYURA	CAYAPA	CHAGGA	CHERKESS	CHIBCHA	CHINANTEC	CHIRIGUANO	CHUKCHEE
COORG	CREE	CRCW	CZECHS	DAGUR	DARD	DIEGUENO	DIERI	DILLING	DOGON
DOROBO	DUSUN	EGYPTIANS	ELLICE	ENGA	EYAK	FANG	FON	FUTAJALONKE	GANCA
GILBERTESE	GILYAK	GISU	GOAJIRO	GOND	GROS VENTRE	GURE	HAIDA	HASANIA	HAVASUPAI
HAZARA	HEBREWS	HEHE	HERERO	HO	ICELANDERS	ILA	INCA	IRAQW	IRISH
JAPANESE	JIVARO	KABYLE	KACHIN	KALMYK	KAPAUKU	KARIERA	KATAB	KAZAK	KERAKI
KERALA	KET	KHALKA	KHEVSUR	KIKUYU	KISSI	KOHISTANI	KOL	KONSO	KOREANS
KORYAK	KPE	KUBA	KWAKIUTL	LAKHER	LAMET	LANGO	LAPPS	LAU	LEPCHA
LHOTA NAGA	LIFU	LOLC	LOZI	LUBA	LUO	MAGUZAWA	MALAYS	MAM	MAMBILA
MAMVU	MANCHU	MANGAIANS	MANIHIKI	MANUS	MARGI	MARICOPA	MARQUESANS	MASAI	MATAKAM
MAYA	MAZATECO	MBUGWE	MBUNCU	MBUTI	MENDE	MENTAWEI	MERINA	MIAMI	MIAO
MIN CHINESE	MINCHIA	MIWCK	MONGO	MONGUOR	MOSSI	MOTA	MURINBATA	MURNGIN	MZAB
NAMA	NAMBICUARA	NANCI	NASKAPI	NATCHEZ	NDEMBU	NGONI	NOMLAKI	NUER	NUNIVAK
NUPE	NURI	NYANEKA	NYARO	NYORO	OJIBWA	OKINAWANS	ONA	ORACN	PAIWAN
PALAUANS	PALIKUR	PAPAGO	PATHAN	PENDE	POPOLUCA	PORTUGUESE	PUKAPUKA	PURARI	PURUM
REGEIBAT	RIFFIANS	ROTINESE	RUNCI	RWALA	SAMOYED	SANDAWE	SANPOIL	SANTAL	SARAMACCA
SARSI	SEMANG	SENIANG	SERBS	SERI	SHERENTE	SHILLUK	SHLUH	SINCHI	SINHALESE
SIUAI	SIWANS	SOMALI	SONGHAI	SOTHO	SWAZI	SYRIANS	TALLENSI	TAMIL	TANALA
TANIMBARESE	TEDA	TEHUELCHE	TENCA	TENINO	TERA	TESO	TETCN	THONGA	TIBETANS
TIGRINYA	TIKOPIA	TIV	TIWI	TODA	TOLOWA	TOTONAC	TROBRIAND	TRUMAI	TSHIMSHIAN
TUBATULABAL	TUCANC	TUCUNA	TUNEBO	TURKANA	TURKMEN	TWANA	TZELTAL	ULAWANS	VENDA
VIETNAMESE	WANTOAT	WAPISHANA	WAROPEN	WIKMUNKAN	WINNEBAGO	WITOTO	WOGEO	WOLOF	WUTE
YAGUA	YAHGAN	YAKC	YAKUT	YAPESE	YOKUTS	YOMBE	YORUBA	YUKI	YUROK

64 IN RIGHT CCLUMN

APINAYE	BELU	BORORO	BURMESE	CADUVEO	CAGABA	CALLINAGO	CARAJA	CHAMACOCO	CHEROKEE
CHEYENNE	CHIR-APACHE	CHOROTI	COCHITI	CREEK	CUNA	DELAWARE	GARO	GUAHIBO	HANO
HANUNOO	HASINAI	HURON	INGALIK	JAVANESE	KAREN	KASKA	KHASI	KIOW-APACHE	LESU
MANDAN	MATACO	MISKITO	MNONG GAR	MOTILON	MUNDURUCU	NABESNA	NAVAHO	NICOBARESE	ONTONG-JAVA
PAWNEE	PONAPEANS	ROTUMANS	SEMINOLE	SIRIONO	TAGBANUA	TALAMANCA	TAPIRAPE	TENETEHARA	THAI
TIMBIRA	TIMUCUA	TOKELAU	TORAJA	TRUKESE	TUPINAMBA	VEDDA	WARRAU	WICHITA	YABARANA
YAO	YARURO	YUKAGHIR	ZUNI						

65 EXCLUDED BECAUSE IRRELEVANT

1 EXCLUDED BECAUSE UNASCERTAINED

3	TEND LESS TO BE THOSE LOCATED OUTSIDE OF AFRICA (320)	0.73 OF 270	3	TEND MORE TO BE THOSE LOCATED OUTSIDE OF AFRICA (320)	0.98 OF 64	72 1 198 63 XSQ= 17.65 PHI= 0.230 XP = 0.0000
4	LEAN LESS TOWARD BEING THOSE LOCATED OUTSIDE OF THE CIRCUM-MEDITERRANEAN (355)	0.87 OF 270	4	IN ALL CASES ARE THOSE LOCATED OUTSIDE OF THE CIRCUM-MEDITERRANEAN (355)	1.00 OF 64	35 0 235 64 XSQ= 7.94 PHI= 0.154 XP = 0.0048
8	LEAN MORE TOWARD BEING THOSE LOCATED OUTSIDE OF NORTH AMERICA (330)	0.87 OF 270	8	LEAN LESS TOWARD BEING THOSE LOCATED OUTSIDE OF NORTH AMERICA (330)	0.69 OF 64	36 20 234 44 XSQ= 10.65 PHI= -0.179 XP = 0.0011
9	TEND MORE TO BE THOSE LOCATED OUTSIDE OF SOUTH AMERICA (335)	0.90 OF 270	9	TEND LESS TO BE THOSE LOCATED OUTSIDE OF SOUTH AMERICA (335)	0.64 OF 64	27 23 243 41 XSQ= 25.34 PHI= -0.275 XP = 0.0000
42	LEAN TOWARD BEING THOSE WHERE THE NATURAL ENVIRONMENT IS OTHER THAN TROPICAL OR SUB-TROPICAL RAIN FOREST, OR MONSOON FOREST (244) FWM	0.66 OF 270	42	LEAN TOWARD BEING THOSE WHERE THE NATURAL ENVIRONMENT IS TROPICAL OR SUB-TROPICAL RAIN FOREST, OR MONSOON FOREST (156) FWM	0.55 OF 64	93 35 177 29 XSQ= 8.13 PHI= -0.156 XP = 0.0043
51	TEND TO BE THOSE WHERE SUBSISTENCE IS PRIMARILY BY FOOD PRODUCTION -- I. E., AGRICULTURE OR HUSBANDRY -- RATHER THAN BY GATHERING (253)	0.70 OF 270	51	TEND TO BE THOSE WHERE SUBSISTENCE IS PRIMARILY BY FOOD GATHERING -- I. E., HUNTING, FISHING, OR COLLECTING -- RATHER THAN FOOD PRODUCTION (147)	0.59 OF 64	190 26 80 38 XSQ= 18.75 PHI= 0.237 XP = 0.0000
53	LEAN LESS TOWARD BEING THOSE WHERE FOOD PRODUCTION IS BY SIMPLE AGRICULTURE OR INCIPIENT FOOD PRODUCTION, RATHER THAN BY INTENSIVE AGRICULTURE (147)	0.59 OF 167	53	LEAN MORE TOWARD BEING THOSE WHERE FOOD PRODUCTION IS BY SIMPLE AGRICULTURE OR INCIPIENT FOOD PRODUCTION, RATHER THAN BY INTENSIVE AGRICULTURE (147)	0.83 OF 36	69 6 98 30 XSQ= 6.70 PHI= 0.182 XP = 0.0096
54	TEND MORE TO BE THOSE WHERE FOOD PRODUCTION IS BY INTENSIVE OR SIMPLE AGRICULTURE, RATHER THAN BY INCIPIENT FOOD PRODUCTION (192)	0.85 OF 167	54	TEND LESS TO BE THOSE WHERE FOOD PRODUCTION IS BY INTENSIVE OR SIMPLE AGRICULTURE, RATHER THAN BY INCIPIENT FOOD PRODUCTION (192)	0.58 OF 36	142 21 25 15 XSQ= 11.71 PHI= 0.240 XP = 0.0006

56	TILT TCWARC BEING THCSE WHERE FCCD PRODUCTICN IS BY SIMPLE AGRICULTURE, RATHER THAN BY INCIPIENT FOCD PRODUCTICN (101)	0.74 OF 98	56	TILT TOWARD BEING THOSE WHERE FOOD PRODUCTION IS BY INCIPIENT FOOD PRODUCTION, RATHER THAN BY SIMPLE AGRICULTURE (46)	0.50 CF 30	73 15 25 15 XSQ= 5.32 PHI= 0.204 XP = 0.0211
62	TILT TCWARD BEING THCSE WHERE HUSBANDRY CF SOME KIND IS PRESENT (228)	0.61 OF 270	62	TILT TOWARD BEING THOSE WHERE HUSBANDRY OF ANY KIND IS ABSENT (172)	0.55 OF 64	165 29 105 35 XSQ= 4.67 PHI= 0.118 XP = 0.0306
71	TEND LESS TO BE THCSE WHERE METAL WORKING IS ABSENT (153)	0.52 OF 163	71	TEND MORE TO BE THOSE WHERE METAL WORKING IS ABSENT (153)	0.84 CF 43	79 7 84 36 XSQ= 13.20 PHI= 0.253 XP = 0.0003
74	TILT LESS TOWARC BEING THCSE WHERE PCTTERY IS PRESENT (145)	0.58 OF 152	74	TILT MORE TOWARD BEING THOSE WHERE POTTERY IS PRESENT (145)	0.77 OF 43	88 33 64 10 XSQ= 4.29 PHI= -0.148 XP = 0.0384
80	DRIFT LESS TCWARC BEING THCSE WHERE NC CITY CR TCWN IS PRESENT (185)	0.81 OF 154	80	DRIFT MORE TOWARD BEING THCSE WHERE NO CITY OR TOWN IS PRESENT (185)	0.94 CF 36	30 2 124 34 XSQ= 3.11 PHI= 0.128 XP = 0.0780
84	TILT LESS TOWARC BEING THCSE WHERE THE LEVEL CF POLITICAL INTEGRATICN IS THE LITTLE STATE, THE MINIMAL STATE, THE AUTCNCMOUS CCMMUNITY, CR THE FAMILY (262) GPM	0.83 OF 202	84	TILT MORE TOWARD BEING THOSE WHERE THE LEVEL OF POLITICAL INTEGRATION IS THE LITTLE STATE, THE MINIMAL STATE, THE AUTONOMOUS COMMUNITY, CR THE FAMILY (262) GPM	0.95 CF 57	34 3 168 54 XSQ= 3.96 PHI= 0.124 XP = 0.0466
85	LEAN LESS TOWARC BEING THCSE WHERE THE LEVEL CF PCLITICAL INTEGRATION IS THE MINIMAL STATE, THE AUTCNCMOUS COMMUNITY, CR THE FAMILY (234) GPM	0.72 OF 202	85	LEAN MORE TOWARD BEING THCSE WHERE THE LEVEL OF PCLITICAL INTEGRATION IS THE MINIMAL STATE, THE AUTONOMOUS COMMUNITY, CR THE FAMILY (234) GPM	0.91 CF 57	57 5 145 52 XSQ= 8.20 PHI= 0.178 XP = 0.0042
90	LEAN MORE TOWARC BEING THCSE WHERE, IF A HEREDITARY HEADMANSHIP IS PRESENT, SUCCESSICN IS PATRILINEAL, RATHER THAN MATRILINEAL (127)	0.83 OF 118	90	LEAN LESS TOWARD BEING THOSE WHERE, IF A HEREDITARY HEADMANSHIP IS PRESENT, SUCCESSION IS PATRILINEAL, RATHER THAN MATRILINEAL (127)	0.54 CF 26	98 14 20 12 XSQ= 8.89 PHI= 0.248 XP = 0.0029
96	TILT TCWARC BEING THCSE WHERE THE HIERARCHY CF NATICNAL JURISDICTICN HAS FOUR, THREE, TWC OR CNE LEVEL (174) GES,EA	0.59 OF 222	96	TILT TOWARD BEING THOSE WHERE THE HIERARCHY OF NATIONAL JURISDICTICN HAS NO LEVELS (156) GES,EA	0.60 CF 57	131 23 91 34 XSQ= 5.65 PHI= 0.142 XP = 0.0174

102	TEND TO BE THOSE WHERE CLASS STRATIFICATION IS PRESENT (203)	0.60 OF 257	102	TEND TO BE THOSE WHERE CLASS STRATIFICATION IS ABSENT (180)	0.67 OF 64	155 21 102 43 XSQ= 14.55 PHI= 0.213 XP = 0.0001
109	LEAN LESS TOWARD BEING THOSE WHERE CASTES ARE ABSENT (317)	0.80 OF 243	109	LEAN MORE TOWARD BEING THOSE WHERE CASTES ARE ABSENT (317)	0.98 OF 62	48 1 195 61 XSQ= 10.75 PHI= 0.188 XP = 0.0010
110	LEAN LESS TOWARD BEING THOSE WHERE SLAVERY IS ABSENT (218)	0.51 OF 255	110	LEAN MORE TOWARD BEING THOSE WHERE SLAVERY IS ABSENT (218)	0.71 OF 63	126 18 129 45 XSQ= 8.03 PHI= 0.159 XP = 0.0046
129	TILT LESS TOWARD BEING THOSE WHERE WEAVING IS MAINLY DONE BY FEMALES (73)	0.59 OF 68	129	TILT MORE TOWARD BEING THOSE WHERE WEAVING IS MAINLY DONE BY FEMALES (73)	0.90 OF 21	28 2 40 19 XSQ= 5.85 PHI= 0.256 XP = 0.0156
130	LEAN TOWARD BEING THOSE WHERE LEATHER WORKING IS MAINLY DONE BY MALES (39)	0.56 OF 55	130	LEAN TOWARD BEING THOSE WHERE LEATHER WORKING IS MAINLY DONE BY FEMALES (45)	0.93 OF 14	31 1 24 13 XSQ= 8.98 PHI= 0.361 XP = 0.0027
175	TILT LESS TOWARD BEING THOSE WHERE THE COMMUNITY IS 'KIN-HETEROGENEOUS,' I. E. OTHER THAN A CLAN COMMUNITY OR A DEME (260)	0.64 OF 257	175	TILT MORE TOWARD BEING THOSE WHERE THE COMMUNITY IS 'KIN-HETEROGENEOUS,' I. E. OTHER THAN A CLAN COMMUNITY OR A DEME (260)	0.79 OF 61	92 13 165 48 XSQ= 4.05 PHI= 0.113 XP = 0.0443
176	TILT TOWARD BEING THOSE WHERE THE COMMUNITY IS A CLAN-COMMUNITY OR A COMMUNITY STRUCTURED OR SEGMENTED ON A CLAN BASIS (169)	0.53 OF 257	176	TILT TOWARD BEING THOSE WHERE THE COMMUNITY IS OTHER THAN A CLAN-COMMUNITY OR A COMMUNITY STRUCTURED OR SEGMENTED ON A CLAN BASIS (213)	0.64 OF 61	136 22 121 39 XSQ= 4.95 PHI= 0.125 XP = 0.0261
177	TEND LESS TO BE THOSE WHERE THE COMMUNITY IS OTHER THAN A SINGLE CLAN-COMMUNITY AND EXOGAMOUS (305)	0.71 OF 257	177	TEND MORE TO BE THOSE WHERE THE COMMUNITY IS OTHER THAN A SINGLE CLAN-COMMUNITY AND EXOGAMOUS (305)	0.97 OF 61	74 2 183 59 XSQ= 16.27 PHI= 0.226 XP = 0.0001
180	TEND LESS TO BE THOSE WHERE THE COMMUNITY IS COMMONLY NON-EXOGAMOUS, RATHER THAN EXOGAMOUS (258)	0.57 OF 257	180	TEND MORE TO BE THOSE WHERE THE COMMUNITY IS COMMONLY NON-EXOGAMOUS, RATHER THAN EXOGAMOUS (258)	0.89 OF 61	110 7 147 54 XSQ= 19.48 PHI= 0.247 XP = 0.0000

181	TILT MORE TOWARD BEING THOSE 0.93 OF 257 WHERE THE COMMUNITY IS OTHER THAN A DEME (337)	181	TILT LESS TOWARD BEING THOSE 0.82 OF 61 WHERE THE COMMUNITY IS OTHER THAN A DEME (337)	18 11 239 50 XSQ= 5.97 PHI= -0.137 XP = 0.0146
183	LEAN MORE TOWARD BEING THOSE 0.89 OF 205 WHERE THE LARGEST NON-COGNATIC KIN GROUP IS SMALLER THAN A MOEITY, I. E., A PHRATRY OR SIB OR LINEAGE (218)	183	LEAN LESS TOWARD BEING THOSE 0.70 OF 33 WHERE THE LARGEST NON-COGNATIC KIN GROUP IS SMALLER THAN A MOEITY, I. E., A PHRATRY OR SIB OR LINEAGE (218)	23 10 182 23 XSQ= 7.14 PHI= -0.173 XP = 0.0075
184	DRIFT MORE TOWARD BEING THOSE 0.72 OF 205 WHERE THE LARGEST NON-COGNATIC KIN GROUP IS SMALLER THAN A PHRATRY, I. E. A SIB OR LINEAGE (175)	184	DRIFT LESS TOWARD BEING THOSE 0.55 OF 33 WHERE THE LARGEST NON-COGNATIC KIN GROUP IS SMALLER THAN A PHRATRY, I. E. A SIB OR LINEAGE (175)	58 15 147 18 XSQ= 3.17 PHI= -0.115 XP = 0.0749
186	TEND TO BE THOSE 0.54 OF 270 WHERE THE KIN GROUP IS EXCLUSIVELY PATRILINEAL (150)	186	TEND TO BE THOSE 0.98 OF 64 WHERE THE KIN GROUP IS OTHER THAN EXCLUSIVELY PATRILINEAL (250)	146 1 124 63 XSQ= 55.78 PHI= 0.409 XP = 0.
187	TEND TO BE THOSE 0.93 OF 269 WHERE THE KIN GROUP IS OTHER THAN EXCLUSIVELY MATRILINEAL (344)	187	TEND TO BE THOSE 0.50 OF 64 WHERE THE KIN GROUP IS EXCLUSIVELY MATRILINEAL (55)	19 32 250 32 XSQ= 70.21 PHI= -0.459 XP = 0.
188	TEND MORE TO BE THOSE 0.76 OF 270 WHERE THE KIN GROUP IS OTHER THAN EXCLUSIVELY COGNATIC (252)	188	TEND LESS TO BE THOSE 0.52 OF 64 WHERE THE KIN GROUP IS OTHER THAN EXCLUSIVELY COGNATIC (252)	65 31 205 33 XSQ= 13.83 PHI= -0.203 XP = 0.0002
190	TEND TO BE THOSE 0.90 OF 200 WHERE THE KIN GROUP IS PATRILINEAL OR DOUBLE-DESCENT, RATHER THAN MATRILINEAL (186)	190	TEND TO BE THOSE 0.97 OF 33 WHERE THE KIN GROUP IS MATRILINEAL, RATHER THAN PATRILINEAL OR DOUBLE-DESCENT (61)	180 1 20 32 XSQ= 118.62 PHI= 0.713 XP = 0.
192	TEND MORE TO BE THOSE 0.84 OF 270 OTHER THAN WHERE THE ONLY KIN GROUP PRESENT IS A KINDRED OR ELSE BILATERAL DESCENT IS INFERRED (289)	192	TEND LESS TO BE THOSE 0.61 OF 64 OTHER THAN WHERE THE ONLY KIN GROUP PRESENT IS A KINDRED OR ELSE BILATERAL DESCENT IS INFERRED (289)	44 25 226 39 XSQ= 15.00 PHI= -0.212 XP = 0.0001
196	LEAN TOWARD BEING THOSE 0.74 OF 205 WHERE INDIVIDUAL RIGHTS IN REAL PROPERTY, AND RULES FOR INHERITANCE, ARE PRESENT (194)	196	LEAN TOWARD BEING THOSE 0.50 OF 34 WHERE INDIVIDUAL RIGHTS IN REAL PROPERTY, OR RULES FOR INHERITANCE, ARE ABSENT (87)	151 17 54 17 XSQ= 6.73 PHI= 0.168 XP = 0.0095

197	TEND MORE TO BE THOSE 0.95 OF 151 WHERE RULES FOR THE INHERITANCE OF REAL PROPERTY, IF PRESENT, FAVOR EITHER THE MALE HEIR OR LINE, OR THE FEMALE HEIR OR LINE (165)	197	TEND LESS TO BE THOSE 0.65 OF 17 WHERE RULES FOR THE INHERITANCE OF REAL PROPERTY, IF PRESENT, FAVOR EITHER THE MALE HEIR OR LINE, OR THE FEMALE HEIR OR LINE (165)	143 11 8 6 XSQ= 14.29 PHI= 0.292 XP = 0.0002
198	TEND TO BE THOSE 0.92 OF 143 WHERE RULES FOR THE INHERITANCE OF REAL PROPERTY, IF PRESENT, FAVOR THE MALE HEIR OR LINE, RATHER THAN THE FEMALE (144)	198	TEND TO BE THOSE 0.73 OF 11 WHERE RULES FOR THE INHERITANCE OF REAL PROPERTY, IF PRESENT, FAVOR THE FEMALE HEIR OR LINE, RATHER THAN THE MALE (21)	132 3 11 8 XSQ= 34.16 PHI= 0.471 XP = 0.
236	TEND LESS TO BE THOSE 0.53 OF 268 WHERE THE FAMILY IS OF AN EXTENDED TYPE, RATHER THAN AN INDEPENDENT TYPE (213)	236	TEND MORE TO BE THOSE 0.77 OF 64 WHERE THE FAMILY IS OF AN EXTENDED TYPE, RATHER THAN AN INDEPENDENT TYPE (213)	141 49 127 15 XSQ= 11.15 PHI= -0.183 XP = 0.0008
240	TEND TO BE THOSE 0.72 OF 141 WHERE THE FAMILY, IF EXTENDED, IS SMALL OR STEM, RATHER THAN LARGE (135)	240	TEND TO BE THOSE 0.55 OF 49 WHERE THE FAMILY, IF EXTENDED, IS LARGE, RATHER THAN SMALL OR STEM (78)	39 27 102 22 XSQ= 10.90 PHI= -0.240 XP = 0.0010
242	TILT MORE TOWARD BEING THOSE 0.86 OF 265 WHERE MARRIAGE IS COMMONLY OR OCCASIONALLY POLYGYNOUS, RATHER THAN MONOGAMOUS (314)	242	TILT LESS TOWARD BEING THOSE 0.72 OF 64 WHERE MARRIAGE IS COMMONLY OR OCCASIONALLY POLYGYNOUS, RATHER THAN MONOGAMOUS (314)	227 46 38 18 XSQ= 5.99 PHI= 0.135 XP = 0.0144
262	TEND MORE TO BE THOSE 0.87 OF 268 WHERE WIVES ARE OBTAINED BY MEANS INVOLVING THE PRESENCE OF SOME CONSIDERATION (305)	262	TEND LESS TO BE THOSE 0.57 OF 63 WHERE WIVES ARE OBTAINED BY MEANS INVOLVING THE PRESENCE OF SOME CONSIDERATION (305)	234 36 34 27 XSQ= 28.91 PHI= 0.296 XP = 0.0000
263	TEND TO BE THOSE 0.69 OF 268 WHERE WIVES ARE OBTAINED BY RELATIVELY DIFFICULT MEANS, NAMELY BY BRIDE-PRICE, BRIDE-SERVICE, OR EXCHANGING A FEMALE RELATIVE (233)	263	TEND TO BE THOSE 0.62 OF 63 WHERE WIVES ARE OBTAINED BY RELATIVELY EASY MEANS, NAMELY BY TOKEN BRIDE-PRICE, GIFT EXCHANGE, ABSENCE OF ANY CONSIDERATION, OR RECEIPT OF DOWRY (162)	184 24 84 39 XSQ= 19.11 PHI= 0.240 XP = 0.0000
324	TILT TOWARD BEING THOSE 0.64 OF 44 WHERE THE PAIN INFLICTED ON THE INFANT BY THE NURTURANT AGENT IS HIGH (34) B-B-C	324	TILT TOWARD BEING THOSE 0.71 OF 14 WHERE THE PAIN INFLICTED ON THE INFANT BY THE NURTURANT AGENT IS LOW OR NEGLIGIBLE (32) B-B-C	28 4 16 10 XSQ= 3.96 PHI= 0.261 XP = 0.0467
339	DRIFT LESS TOWARD BEING THOSE 0.51 OF 49 WHERE THE CHILD'S INFERRED CONFLICT REGARDING RESPONSIBLE BEHAVIOR IS LOW (42) B-B-C	339	DRIFT MORE TOWARD BEING THOSE 0.80 OF 15 WHERE THE CHILD'S INFERRED CONFLICT REGARDING RESPONSIBLE BEHAVIOR IS LOW (42) B-B-C	24 3 25 12 XSQ= 2.86 PHI= 0.211 XP = 0.0911

360	TILT TOWARD BEING THOSE 0.52 OF 21 WHERE ADOLESCENT PEER GROUPS ARE PRESENT IN A SETTING OF WORK AND PUBLIC GATHERINGS AND LEISURE, OR AT LEAST OF PUBLIC GATHERINGS AND LEISURE (14) JKH	360	IN ALL CASES ARE THOSE 1.00 OF 7 WHERE ADOLESCENT PEER GROUPS ARE PRESENT ONLY IN A SETTING OF LEISURE, OR ELSE ARE ABSENT (23) JKH	11 0 10 7 XSQ= 4.04 PHI= 0.380 EP = 0.0233
370	TILT LESS TOWARD BEING THOSE 0.53 OF 164 WHERE THE SEGREGATION OF ADOLESCENT BOYS IS ABSENT (148)	370	TILT MORE TOWARD BEING THOSE 0.76 OF 41 WHERE THE SEGREGATION OF ADOLESCENT BOYS IS ABSENT (148)	77 10 87 31 XSQ= 5.94 PHI= 0.170 XP = 0.0148
377	TEND LESS TO BE THOSE 0.65 OF 217 WHERE MALE GENITAL MUTILATION IS ABSENT (242)	377	TEND MORE TO BE THOSE 0.93 OF 56 WHERE MALE GENITAL MUTILATION IS ABSENT (242)	75 4 142 52 XSQ= 14.97 PHI= 0.234 XP = 0.0001
382	TILT TOWARD BEING THOSE 0.53 OF 43 WHERE FEMALE INITIATION RITES ARE ABSENT (27) JKB	382	TILT TOWARD BEING THOSE 0.86 OF 14 WHERE FEMALE INITIATION RITES ARE PRESENT (38) JKB	20 12 23 2 XSQ= 5.10 PHI= -0.299 XP = 0.0240
386	DRIFT TOWARD BEING THOSE 0.52 OF 50 WHERE SEXUAL EXPRESSION BY THE YOUNG IS PERMITTED (40) F-B	386	DRIFT TOWARD BEING THOSE 0.74 OF 19 WHERE SEXUAL EXPRESSION BY THE YOUNG IS RESTRICTED OR SEMI-RESTRICTED (46) F-B	24 14 26 5 XSQ= 2.71 PHI= -0.198 XP = 0.1000
426	TILT TOWARD BEING THOSE 0.66 OF 177 WHERE A HIGH GOD IS PRESENT (156) GES,EA	426	TILT TOWARD BEING THOSE 0.57 OF 42 WHERE A HIGH GOD IS ABSENT (104) GES,EA	116 18 61 24 XSQ= 6.43 PHI= 0.171 XP = 0.0112
458	TILT LESS TOWARD BEING THOSE 0.64 OF 116 WHERE GAMES, IF PRESENT, DO NOT INCLUDE GAMES OF STRATEGY (119) R-A-B,EA	458	TILT MORE TOWARD BEING THOSE 0.89 OF 27 WHERE GAMES, IF PRESENT, DO NOT INCLUDE GAMES OF STRATEGY (119) R-A-B,EA	42 3 74 24 XSQ= 5.29 PHI= 0.192 XP = 0.0215
473	TILT LESS TOWARD BEING THOSE 0.58 OF 60 WHERE SENSITIVITY TO INSULT IS MODERATE OR NEGLIGIBLE (56) PES	473	TILT MORE TOWARD BEING THOSE 0.92 OF 13 WHERE SENSITIVITY TO INSULT IS MODERATE OR NEGLIGIBLE (56) PES	25 1 35 12 XSQ= 4.00 PHI= 0.234 XP = 0.0455

210 CULTURES
WHERE MARITAL RESIDENCE IS
PATRILOCAL, RATHER THAN
MATRILOCAL (169)

210 CULTURES
WHERE MARITAL RESIDENCE IS
MATRILOCAL, RATHER THAN
PATRILOCAL (31)

BACKGROUND ON PAGE 113

BOTH SUBJECT AND PREDICATE

169 IN LEFT COLUMN

AJIE AKHA ALBANIANS AMBA ARANDA ARAPESH ARAUCANIANS ARYANS AYMARA BABWA
BAMBARA BAMILEKE BANDA BARABRA BARI BASSERI BATAK BAYA BEJA BENGALI
BETE BHIL BHUIYA BIRIFOR BOZO BUDUMA BUNLAP BURUSHO BURYAT CHAGGA
CHERKESS COORG DAGUR DARD DIEGUENO DILLING DOGON DOROBO EGYPTIANS ENGA
FANG FON FUTAJALONKE GILYAK GISU GOND HASANIA HAZARA HEBREWS HEHE
HO IRAQW KABYLE KACHIN KALMYK KAPAUKU KARIERA KATAB KAZAK KERAKI
KHALKA KHEVSUR KIKUYU KISSI KOHISTANI KOL KONSO KOREANS KPE LAKHER
LAMET LANGO LAU LEPCHA LHOTA NAGA LIFU LOLO LUBA LUO MAGUZAWA
MAM MAMVU MANCHU MANUS MARGI MARICOPA MASAI MATAKAM MBUGWE MBUNDU
MBUTI MENDE MIAMI MIAO MIN CHINESE MINCHIA MONGO MONGUOR MOSSI MURINBATA
MURNGIN MZAB NAMA NANDI NOMLAKI NUPE NURI NYARO NYORO OKINAWANS
ORAON PATHAN PUKAPUKA PURARI PURUM REGEIBAT RIFFIANS ROTINESE RUNDI RWALA
SAMOYED SANDAWE SANTAL SENIANG SERBS SHERENTE SHILLUK SHLUH SINDHI SIWANS
SOMALI SONGHAI SOTHO SWAZI SYRIANS TALLENSI TAMIL TANALA TANIMBARESE TEDA
TERA TESO THONGA TIBETANS TIGRINYA TIKOPIA TODA TOLOWA TUCANO TUCUNA
TURKANA TURKMEN TZELTAL VENDA VIETNAMESE WANTOAT WAROPEN WIKMUNKAN WINNEBAGO WITOTO
WOGEO WOLOF WUTE YAGUA YAKO YAKUT YAPESE YOKUTS YORUBA

31 IN RIGHT COLUMN

APINAYE BELU BORORO CALLINAGO CHEROKEE COCHITI CREEK DELAWARE GARO GUAHIBO
HANO HURON KAREN KASKA KHASI LESU MANDAN MNONG GAR NAVAHO PAWNEE
PONAPEANS ROTUMANS SEMINOLE SIRIONO TALAMANCA TIMBIRA TIMUCUA TRUKESE VEDDA YAO
ZUNI

199 EXCLUDED BECAUSE IRRELEVANT

1 EXCLUDED BECAUSE UNASCERTAINED

---

3 LEAN LESS TOWARD BEING THOSE LOCATED OUTSIDE OF AFRICA (320) 0.68 OF 169

3 LEAN MORE TOWARD BEING THOSE LOCATED OUTSIDE OF AFRICA (320) 0.97 OF 31

54	1
115	30

XSQ= 9.45
PHI= 0.217
XP = 0.0021

```
 4  TILT LESS TOWARD BEING THOSE    0.83 OF 169      4  IN ALL CASES ARE THOSE          1.00 OF  31        28     0
    LOCATED OUTSIDE OF                                  LOCATED OUTSIDE OF                                 141    31
    THE CIRCUM-MEDITERRANEAN  (355)                     THE CIRCUM-MEDITERRANEAN  (355)                 XSQ=    4.68
                                                                                                        PHI=   0.153
                                                                                                        XP =  0.0306

 8  TEND MORE TO BE THOSE           0.96 OF 169      8  TEND LESS TO BE THOSE           0.58 OF  31         7    13
    LOCATED OUTSIDE OF                                  LOCATED OUTSIDE OF                                 162    18
    NORTH AMERICA  (330)                                NORTH AMERICA  (330)                            XSQ=   37.48
                                                                                                        PHI=  -0.433
                                                                                                        XP =  0.

 9  LEAN MORE TOWARD BEING THOSE    0.95 OF 169      9  LEAN LESS TOWARD BEING THOSE    0.77 OF  31         9     7
    LOCATED OUTSIDE OF                                  LOCATED OUTSIDE OF                                 160    24
    SOUTH AMERICA  (335)                                SOUTH AMERICA  (335)                            XSQ=    8.38
                                                                                                        PHI=  -0.205
                                                                                                        XP =  0.0038

51  TEND TO BE THOSE                0.81 OF 169     51  TEND TO BE THOSE                0.52 OF  31       137    15
    WHERE SUBSISTENCE IS PRIMARILY BY                   WHERE SUBSISTENCE IS PRIMARILY BY                   32    16
    FOOD PRODUCTION -- I. E., AGRICULTURE               FOOD GATHERING -- I. E., HUNTING,               XSQ=   13.60
    OR HUSBANDRY -- RATHER THAN BY                      FISHING, OR COLLECTING -- RATHER THAN           PHI=   0.261
    GATHERING  (253)                                    FOOD PRODUCTION  (147)                          XP =  0.0002

53  TILT LESS TOWARD BEING THOSE    0.52 OF 116     53  TILT MORE TOWARD BEING THOSE    0.80 OF  20        56     4
    WHERE FOOD PRODUCTION IS BY                         WHERE FOOD PRODUCTION IS BY                         60    16
    SIMPLE AGRICULTURE OR                               SIMPLE AGRICULTURE OR                           XSQ=    4.44
    INCIPIENT FOOD PRODUCTION, RATHER THAN BY           INCIPIENT FOOD PRODUCTION, RATHER THAN BY       PHI=   0.181
    INTENSIVE AGRICULTURE  (147)                        INTENSIVE AGRICULTURE  (147)                    XP =  0.0350

54  TEND MORE TO BE THOSE           0.90 OF 116     54  TEND LESS TO BE THOSE           0.55 OF  20       104    11
    WHERE FOOD PRODUCTION IS BY                         WHERE FOOD PRODUCTION IS BY                         12     9
    INTENSIVE OR SIMPLE                                 INTENSIVE OR SIMPLE                             XSQ=   13.15
    AGRICULTURE, RATHER THAN BY                         AGRICULTURE, RATHER THAN BY                     PHI=   0.311
    INCIPIENT FOOD PRODUCTION  (192)                    INCIPIENT FOOD PRODUCTION  (192)                XP =  0.0003

56  TILT TOWARD BEING THOSE         0.80 OF  60     56  TILT TOWARD BEING THOSE         0.56 OF  16        48     7
    WHERE FOOD PRODUCTION IS BY                         WHERE FOOD PRODUCTION IS BY                         12     9
    SIMPLE AGRICULTURE, RATHER THAN BY                  INCIPIENT FOOD PRODUCTION, RATHER THAN BY       XSQ=    6.59
    INCIPIENT FOOD PRODUCTION  (101)                    SIMPLE AGRICULTURE  (46)                        PHI=   0.294
                                                                                                        XP =  0.0103

62  LEAN TOWARD BEING THOSE         0.71 OF 169     62  LEAN TOWARD BEING THOSE         0.58 OF  31       120    13
    WHERE HUSBANDRY OF SOME KIND                        WHERE HUSBANDRY OF ANY KIND                         49    18
    IS PRESENT  (228)                                   IS ABSENT  (172)                                XSQ=    8.67
                                                                                                        PHI=   0.208
                                                                                                        XP =  0.0032

63  DRIFT TOWARD BEING THOSE        0.75 OF 118     63  DRIFT TOWARD BEING THOSE        0.54 OF  13        88     6
    WHERE HUSBANDRY, IF PRESENT,                        WHERE HUSBANDRY, IF PRESENT,                        30     7
    IS PRINCIPALLY IN THE FORM OF                       IS PRINCIPALLY IN THE FORM OF                   XSQ=    3.37
    BOVINE, EQUINE, CAMEL-LIKE, OR DEER-LIKE            PIGS, SHEEP, OR GOATS, RATHER THAN              PHI=   0.160
    ANIMALS, RATHER THAN                                BOVINE, EQUINE, CAMEL-LIKE, OR DEER-LIKE        XP =  0.0664
    PIGS, SHEEP, OR GOATS  (152)                        ANIMALS  (74)
```

71	LEAN TOWARD BEING THOSE 0.62 OF 99 WHERE METAL WORKING IS PRESENT (98)	71	LEAN TOWARD BEING THOSE 0.77 OF 22 WHERE METAL WORKING IS ABSENT (153)	61 5 38 17 XSQ= 9.47 PHI= 0.280 XP = 0.0021
80	DRIFT LESS TOWARD BEING THOSE 0.84 OF 97 WHERE NO CITY OR TOWN IS PRESENT (185)	80	IN ALL CASES ARE THOSE 1.00 OF 21 WHERE NO CITY OR TOWN IS PRESENT (185)	16 0 81 21 XSQ= 2.72 PHI= 0.152 XP = 0.0989
84	DRIFT LESS TOWARD BEING THOSE 0.84 OF 120 WHERE THE LEVEL OF POLITICAL INTEGRATION IS THE LITTLE STATE, THE MINIMAL STATE, THE AUTONOMOUS COMMUNITY, OR THE FAMILY (262) GPM	84	IN ALL CASES ARE THOSE 1.00 OF 28 WHERE THE LEVEL OF POLITICAL INTEGRATION IS THE LITTLE STATE, THE MINIMAL STATE, THE AUTONOMOUS COMMUNITY, OR THE FAMILY (262) GPM	19 0 101 28 XSQ= 3.77 PHI= 0.160 XP = 0.0522
85	TILT LESS TOWARD BEING THOSE 0.71 OF 120 WHERE THE LEVEL OF POLITICAL INTEGRATION IS THE MINIMAL STATE, THE AUTONOMOUS COMMUNITY, OR THE FAMILY (234) GPM	85	TILT MORE TOWARD BEING THOSE 0.93 OF 28 WHERE THE LEVEL OF POLITICAL INTEGRATION IS THE MINIMAL STATE, THE AUTONOMOUS COMMUNITY, OR THE FAMILY (234) GPM	35 2 85 26 XSQ= 4.76 PHI= 0.179 XP = 0.0292
90	TEND TO BE THOSE 0.96 OF 74 WHERE, IF A HEREDITARY HEADMANSHIP IS PRESENT, SUCCESSION IS PATRILINEAL, RATHER THAN MATRILINEAL (127)	90	TEND TO BE THOSE 0.71 OF 17 WHERE, IF A HEREDITARY HEADMANSHIP IS PRESENT, SUCCESSION IS MATRILINEAL, RATHER THAN PATRILINEAL (38)	71 5 3 12 XSQ= 39.75 PHI= 0.661 XP = 0.
96	DRIFT TOWARD BEING THOSE 0.62 OF 140 WHERE THE HIERARCHY OF NATIONAL JURISDICTION HAS FOUR, THREE, TWO OR ONE LEVEL (174) GES,EA	96	DRIFT TOWARD BEING THOSE 0.59 OF 27 WHERE THE HIERARCHY OF NATIONAL JURISDICTION HAS NO LEVELS (156) GES,EA	87 11 53 16 XSQ= 3.44 PHI= 0.144 XP = 0.0637
99	DRIFT LESS TOWARD BEING THOSE 0.57 OF 53 WHERE, WITH NATIONAL HIERARCHY ABSENT, THE HIERARCHY OF LOCAL JURISDICTION HAS FOUR OR THREE LEVELS (93) GES,EA	99	DRIFT MORE TOWARD BEING THOSE 0.88 OF 16 WHERE, WITH NATIONAL HIERARCHY ABSENT, THE HIERARCHY OF LOCAL JURISDICTION HAS FOUR OR THREE LEVELS (93) GES,EA	30 14 23 2 XSQ= 3.83 PHI= -0.236 XP = 0.0504
102	LEAN TOWARD BEING THOSE 0.62 OF 162 WHERE CLASS STRATIFICATION IS PRESENT (203)	102	LEAN TOWARD BEING THOSE 0.71 OF 31 WHERE CLASS STRATIFICATION IS ABSENT (180)	101 9 61 22 XSQ= 10.46 PHI= 0.233 XP = 0.0012
109	TILT LESS TOWARD BEING THOSE 0.73 OF 144 WHERE CASTES ARE ABSENT (317)	109	TILT MORE TOWARD BEING THOSE 0.97 OF 30 WHERE CASTES ARE ABSENT (317)	39 1 105 29 XSQ= 6.63 PHI= 0.195 XP = 0.0101

110	TILT TOWARD BEING THOSE WHERE SLAVERY IS PRESENT (163)	0.54 OF 158	110	TILT TOWARD BEING THOSE WHERE SLAVERY IS ABSENT (218)	0.73 OF 30	85 8 73 22 XSQ= 6.38 PHI= 0.184 XP = 0.0116
129	LEAN TOWARD BEING THOSE WHERE WEAVING IS MAINLY DONE BY MALES (31)	0.51 OF 41	129	IN ALL CASES ARE THOSE WHERE WEAVING IS MAINLY DONE BY FEMALES (73)	1.00 OF 10	21 0 20 10 XSQ= 6.72 PHI= 0.363 XP = 0.0095
130	TILT TOWARD BEING THOSE WHERE LEATHER WORKING IS MAINLY DONE BY MALES (39)	0.71 OF 31	130	TILT TOWARD BEING THOSE WHERE LEATHER WORKING IS MAINLY DONE BY FEMALES (45)	0.80 OF 5	22 1 9 4 XSQ= 2.89 PHI= 0.283 EP = 0.0470
138	DRIFT TOWARD BEING THOSE WHERE SUPERORDINATE JUSTICE IS PRESENT (22) BBW	0.69 OF 13	138	IN ALL CASES ARE THOSE WHERE SUPERORDINATE JUSTICE IS ABSENT (18) BBW	1.00 OF 3	9 0 4 3 XSQ= 2.35 PHI= 0.383 EP = 0.0625
175	LEAN LESS TOWARD BEING THOSE WHERE THE COMMUNITY IS 'KIN-HETEROGENEOUS,' I. E. OTHER THAN A CLAN COMMUNITY OR A DEME (260)	0.56 OF 162	175	LEAN MORE TOWARD BEING THOSE WHERE THE COMMUNITY IS 'KIN-HETEROGENEOUS,' I. E. OTHER THAN A CLAN COMMUNITY OR A DEME (260)	0.86 OF 29	72 4 90 25 XSQ= 8.41 PHI= 0.210 XP = 0.0037
177	LEAN LESS TOWARD BEING THOSE WHERE THE COMMUNITY IS OTHER THAN A SINGLE CLAN-COMMUNITY AND EXOGAMOUS (305)	0.60 OF 162	177	LEAN MORE TOWARD BEING THOSE WHERE THE COMMUNITY IS OTHER THAN A SINGLE CLAN-COMMUNITY AND EXOGAMOUS (305)	0.93 OF 29	65 2 97 27 XSQ= 10.51 PHI= 0.235 XP = 0.0012
178	TEND TO BE THOSE WHERE THE COMMUNITY IS OTHER THAN SEGMENTED ON A CLAN BASIS AND NON-EXOGAMOUS (295)	0.73 OF 162	178	TEND TO BE THOSE WHERE THE COMMUNITY IS SEGMENTED ON A CLAN BASIS AND NON-EXOGAMOUS (87)	0.69 OF 29	44 20 118 9 XSQ= 17.46 PHI= -0.302 XP = 0.0000
180	TEND TO BE THOSE WHERE THE COMMUNITY IS COMMONLY EXOGAMOUS, RATHER THAN NON-EXOGAMOUS (124)	0.50 OF 162	180	TEND TO BE THOSE WHERE THE COMMUNITY IS COMMONLY NON-EXOGAMOUS, RATHER THAN EXOGAMOUS (258)	0.93 OF 29	81 2 81 27 XSQ= 16.89 PHI= 0.297 XP = 0.0000
183	LEAN MORE TOWARD BEING THOSE WHERE THE LARGEST NON-COGNATIC KIN GROUP IS SMALLER THAN A MOEITY, I. E., A PHRATRY OR SIB OR LINEAGE (218)	0.90 OF 168	183	LEAN LESS TOWARD BEING THOSE WHERE THE LARGEST NON-COGNATIC KIN GROUP IS SMALLER THAN A MOEITY, I. E., A PHRATRY OR SIB OR LINEAGE (218)	0.71 OF 31	16 9 152 22 XSQ= 7.38 PHI= -0.193 XP = 0.0066

186	TEND TO BE THOSE WHERE THE KIN GROUP IS EXCLUSIVELY PATRILINEAL (150)	0.81 OF 169	186	IN ALL CASES ARE THOSE WHERE THE KIN GROUP IS OTHER THAN EXCLUSIVELY PATRILINEAL (250)	1.00 OF 31	137 0 32 31 XSQ= 76.07 PHI= 0.617 XP = 0.
187	IN ALL CASES ARE THOSE WHERE THE KIN GROUP IS OTHER THAN EXCLUSIVELY MATRILINEAL (344)	1.00 OF 169	187	IN ALL CASES ARE THOSE WHERE THE KIN GROUP IS EXCLUSIVELY MATRILINEAL (55)	1.00 OF 31	0 31 169 0 XSQ= 192.44 PHI= -0.981 XP = 0.
190	IN ALL CASES ARE THOSE WHERE THE KIN GROUP IS PATRILINEAL OR DOUBLE-DESCENT, RATHER THAN MATRILINEAL (186)	1.00 OF 165	190	IN ALL CASES ARE THOSE WHERE THE KIN GROUP IS MATRILINEAL, RATHER THAN PATRILINEAL OR DOUBLE-DESCENT (61)	1.00 OF 31	165 0 0 31 XSQ= 188.56 PHI= 0.981 XP = 0.
198	IN ALL CASES ARE THOSE WHERE RULES FOR THE INHERITANCE OF REAL PROPERTY, IF PRESENT, FAVOR THE MALE HEIR OR LINE, RATHER THAN THE FEMALE (144)	1.00 OF 105	198	TEND TO BE THOSE WHERE RULES FOR THE INHERITANCE OF REAL PROPERTY, IF PRESENT, FAVOR THE FEMALE HEIR OR LINE, RATHER THAN THE MALE (21)	0.80 OF 10	105 2 0 8 XSQ= 78.34 PHI= 0.825 XP = 0.
236	TILT LESS TOWARD BEING THOSE WHERE THE FAMILY IS OF AN EXTENDED TYPE, RATHER THAN AN INDEPENDENT TYPE (213)	0.54 OF 168	236	TILT MORE TOWARD BEING THOSE WHERE THE FAMILY IS OF AN EXTENDED TYPE, RATHER THAN AN INDEPENDENT TYPE (213)	0.81 OF 31	91 25 77 6 XSQ= 6.50 PHI= -0.181 XP = 0.0108
240	TILT TOWARD BEING THOSE WHERE THE FAMILY, IF EXTENDED, IS SMALL OR STEM, RATHER THAN LARGE (135)	0.70 OF 91	240	TILT TOWARD BEING THOSE WHERE THE FAMILY, IF EXTENDED, IS LARGE, RATHER THAN SMALL OR STEM (78)	0.56 OF 25	27 14 64 11 XSQ= 4.85 PHI= -0.205 XP = 0.0276
242	TEND MORE TO BE THOSE WHERE MARRIAGE IS COMMONLY OR OCCASIONALLY POLYGYNOUS, RATHER THAN MONOGAMOUS (314)	0.89 OF 166	242	TEND LESS TO BE THOSE WHERE MARRIAGE IS COMMONLY OR OCCASIONALLY POLYGYNOUS, RATHER THAN MONOGAMOUS (314)	0.58 OF 31	148 18 18 13 XSQ= 16.77 PHI= 0.292 XP = 0.0000
254	DRIFT TOWARD BEING THOSE WHERE HOUSEHOLD AUTHORITY IS ON THE FATHER'S SIDE, RATHER THAN THE MOTHER'S (9) DA	0.86 OF 7	254	DRIFT TOWARD BEING THOSE WHERE HOUSEHOLD AUTHORITY IS ON THE MOTHER'S SIDE, RATHER THAN THE FATHER'S (6) DA	0.75 OF 4	6 1 1 3 XSQ= 1.86 PHI= 0.411 EP = 0.0879
262	TEND TO BE THOSE WHERE WIVES ARE OBTAINED BY MEANS INVOLVING THE PRESENCE OF SOME CONSIDERATION (305)	0.93 OF 167	262	TEND TO BE THOSE WHERE WIVES ARE OBTAINED BY MEANS INVOLVING THE ABSENCE OF ANY CONSIDERATION (90)	0.57 OF 30	156 13 11 17 XSQ= 48.28 PHI= 0.495 XP = 0.

263	TEND TC BE THCSE 0.80 OF 167 WHERE WIVES ARE CBTAINEC BY RELATIVELY DIFFICULT MEANS, NAMELY BY BRIDE-PRICE, BRIDE-SERVICE, OR EXCHANGING A FEMALE RELATIVE (233)	263	TEND TO BE THOSE 0.73 CF 30 WHERE WIVES ARE OBTAINED BY RELATIVELY EASY MEANS, NAMELY BY TOKEN BRIDE-PRICE, GIFT EXCHANGE, ABSENCE OF ANY CONSIDERATICN, OR RECEIPT OF DOWRY (162)	133 8 34 22 XSQ= 32.52 PHI= 0.406 XP = 0.
296	DRIFT TCWARD BEING THCSE 0.67 CF 12 WHERE INFANTICICE IS PRESENT (18) BCA	296	IN ALL CASES ARE THCSE 1.00 CF 3 WHERE INFANTICIDE IS ABSENT OR INFERRED ABSENT (15) BCA	8 0 4 3 XSQ= 2.03 PHI= 0.367 EP = 0.0769
377	TEND LESS TO BE THCSE 0.55 OF 139 WHERE MALE GENITAL MUTILATION IS ABSENT (242)	377	TEND MORE TO BE THOSE 0.93 CF 27 WHERE MALE GENITAL MUTILATICN IS ABSENT (242)	62 2 77 25 XSQ= 11.68 PHI= 0.265 XP = 0.0006
390	TILT LESS TOWARC BEING THCSE 0.65 OF 77 WHERE PREMARITAL SEX RELATIONS ARE WEAKLY PUNISHED ANC IN FACT NCT RARE OR PUNISHED CNLY IF PREGNANCY RESULTS, OR FREELY PERMITTEC (132) JTW,EA	390	IN ALL CASES ARE THOSE 1.00 CF 13 WHERE PREMARITAL SEX RELATICNS ARE WEAKLY PUNISHED AND IN FACT NOT RARE OR PUNISHED ONLY IF PREGNANCY RESULTS, OR FREELY PERMITTED (132) JTW,EA	27 0 50 13 XSQ= 4.95 PHI= 0.235 XP = 0.0261
391	TILT TCWARD BEING THCSE 0.57 OF 77 WHERE PREMARITAL SEX RELATIONS ARE STRCNGLY PUNISHEC ANC IN FACT RARE, OR WEAKLY PUNISHED ANC IN FACT NCT RARE (89) JTW,EA	391	TILT TOWARD BEING THOSE 0.77 CF 13 WHERE PREMARITAL SEX RELATICNS ARE PUNISHED ONLY IF PREGNANCY RESULTS, CR FREELY PERMITTED (90) JTW,EA	44 3 33 10 XSQ= 3.90 PHI= 0.208 XP = 0.0483
426	TILT TCWARD BEING THCSE 0.70 OF 114 WHERE A HIGH GCC IS PRESENT (156) GES,EA	426	TILT TOWARD BEING THOSE 0.59 CF 22 WHERE A HIGH GOD IS ABSENT (104) GES,EA	80 9 34 13 XSQ= 5.75 PHI= 0.206 XP = 0.0165
427	DRIFT TOWARD BEING THCSE 0.61 OF 8C WHERE A HIGH GCC, IF PRESENT, IS ACTIVE, RATHER THAN INACTIVE (87) GES,EA	427	DRIFT TOWARD BEING THOSE 0.78 CF 9 WHERE A HIGH GOD, IF PRESENT, IS INACTIVE, RATHER THAN ACTIVE (69) GES,EA	49 2 31 7 XSQ= 3.57 PHI= 0.200 XP = 0.0589
449	TILT TCWARD BEING THCSE 0.82 OF 38 WHERE THE CBSERVATICN CF FCOC TABOOS IS MEDIUM CR LCW, RATHER THAN HIGH (61) JRL	449	TILT TOWARD BEING THCSE 0.63 CF 8 WHERE THE OBSERVATICN OF FCOD TABOCS IS HIGH, RATHER THAN MEDIUM OR LOW (25) JRL	7 5 31 3 XSQ= 4.57 PHI= -0.315 XP = 0.0325
458	TILT TCWARD BEING THOSE 0.50 OF 62 WHERE GAMES, IF PRESENT, INCLUDE GAMES CF STRATEGY (52) R-A-B,EA	458	TILT TOWARD BEING THOSE 0.86 CF 14 WHERE GAMES, IF PRESENT, DO NOT INCLUDE GAMES OF STRATEGY (119) R-A-B,EA	31 2 31 12 XSQ= 4.57 PHI= 0.245 XP = 0.0326

210/

468 DRIFT TOWARD BEING THOSE WHERE CONTACT WITH OTHER CULTURES IS FREQUENT, RATHER THAN REGULAR OR IRREGULAR (17) JMH	0.50 OF 20	468 DRIFT TOWARD BEING THOSE WHERE CONTACT WITH OTHER CULTURES IS REGULAR OR IRREGULAR, RATHER THAN FREQUENT (37) JMH	0.88 OF 8	10 1 10 7 XSQ= 1.98 PHI= 0.266 EP = 0.0987

211 CULTURES
WHERE MARITAL RESICENCE IS
VIRILCCAL, RATHER THAN
UXCRILCCAL (83)

211 CULTURES
WHERE MARITAL RESIDENCE IS
UXORILOCAL, RATHER THAN
VIRILOCAL (33)

BACKGROUND ON PAGE 113

SUBJECT ONLY

83 IN LEFT CCLUMN

ABOR	AINU	ALCRESE	ATAYAL	ATSUGEWI	AZANDE	AZTEC	BACAIRI	BALINESE	BERGDAMA
BOERS	BULGARIANS	CAMAYURA	CAYAPA	CHIBCHA	CHINANTEC	CHIRIGUANO	CHUKCHEE	CREE	CROW
CZECHS	DIERI	DUSUN	ELLICE	GANDA	GILBERTESE	GROS VENTRE	HAVASUPAI	HERERO	ICELANDERS
ILA	INCA	IRISH	JAPANESE	JIVARO	KET	KORYAK	KWAKIUTL	LAPPS	LOZI
MALAYS	MAMBILA	MANGAIANS	MANIHIKI	MARQUESANS	MAYA	MAZATECO	MENTAWEI	MERINA	MIWOK
NAMBICUARA	NASKAPI	NATCHEZ	NGONI	NUER	NUNIVAK	OJIBWA	ONA	PAIWAN	PALIKUR
PAPAGO	POPOLUCA	PORTUGUESE	SANPOIL	SARSI	SEMANG	SERI	SINHALESE	TEHUELCHE	TENINO
TETON	TIV	TIWI	TOTONAC	TRUMAI	TUBATULABAL	TUNEBO	TWANA	ULAWANS	WAPISHANA
YAHGAN	YUKI	YURCK							

33 IN RIGHT CCLUMN

BURMESE	CADUVEC	CAGABA	CARAJA	CHAMACOCO	CHEYENNE	CHIR-APACHE	CHCRCTI	CUNA	HANUNOO
HASINAI	INGALIK	JAVANESE	KIOW-APACHE	MATACO	MISKITO	MOTILON	MUNDURUCU	NABESNA	NICOBARESE
ONTONG-JAVA	TAGBANUA	TAPIRAPE	TENETEHARA	THAI	TOKELAU	TORAJA	TUPINAMBA	WARRAU	WICHITA
YABARANA	YARURC	YUKAGHIR							

283 EXCLUDED BECAUSE IRRELEVANT

1 EXCLUDED BECAUSE UNASCERTAINEC

---

3 DRIFT LESS TCWARC BEING THCSE LOCATED CUTSIDE CF AFRICA (320) — 0.88 OF 83

3 IN ALL CASES ARE THOSE LOCATED OUTSIDE OF AFRICA (320) — 1.00 CF 33

10	0
73	33
XSQ=	2.96
PHI=	0.160
XP =	0.0856

9 LEAN MORE TOWARC BEING THCSE LOCATED CUTSIDE CF SOUTH AMERICA (335) — 0.81 OF 83

9 LEAN LESS TOWARD BEING THOSE LOCATED OUTSIDE OF SOUTH AMERICA (335) — 0.52 OF 33

16	16
67	17
XSQ=	8.67
PHI=	-0.273
XP =	0.0032

13 TILT LESS TCWARC BEING THCSE WHERE THE LATITUDE IS LESS THAN FORTY CEGREES (329) — 0.66 OF 83

13 TILT MORE TOWARD BEING THOSE WHERE THE LATITUDE IS LESS THAN FORTY DEGREES (329) — 0.91 CF 33

28	3
55	30
XSQ=	6.12
PHI=	0.230
XP =	0.0134

33	DRIFT LESS TOWARD BEING THOSE 0.78 OF 83 WHERE THE NATURAL ENVIRONMENT IS OTHER THAN 'VERY HARSH,' I.E., DESERT, DESERT GRASSES AND SHRUBS, TUNDRA, OR HIGH PLATEAU STEPPE (341) FWM	33 DRIFT MORE TOWARD BEING THOSE 0.94 OF 33 WHERE THE NATURAL ENVIRONMENT IS OTHER THAN 'VERY HARSH,' I.E., DESERT, DESERT GRASSES AND SHRUBS, TUNDRA, OR HIGH PLATEAU STEPPE (341) FWM	18 2 65 31 XSQ= 3.02 PHI= 0.161 XP = 0.0823
42	TILT TOWARD BEING THOSE 0.67 OF 83 WHERE THE NATURAL ENVIRONMENT IS OTHER THAN TROPICAL OR SUB-TROPICAL RAIN FOREST, OR MONSOON FOREST (244) FWM	42 TILT TOWARD BEING THOSE 0.61 OF 33 WHERE THE NATURAL ENVIRONMENT IS TROPICAL OR SUB-TROPICAL RAIN FOREST, OR MONSOON FOREST (156) FWM	27 20 56 13 XSQ= 6.60 PHI= -0.239 XP = 0.0102
74	TILT TOWARD BEING THOSE 0.52 OF 54 WHERE POTTERY IS ABSENT (93)	74 TILT TOWARD BEING THOSE 0.81 OF 21 WHERE POTTERY IS PRESENT (145)	26 17 28 4 XSQ= 5.38 PHI= -0.268 XP = 0.0204
130	DRIFT LESS TOWARD BEING THOSE 0.62 OF 21 WHERE LEATHER WORKING IS MAINLY DONE BY FEMALES (45)	130 IN ALL CASES ARE THOSE 1.00 OF 9 WHERE LEATHER WORKING IS MAINLY DONE BY FEMALES (45)	8 0 13 9 XSQ= 2.93 PHI= 0.313 EP = 0.0665
176	DRIFT LESS TOWARD BEING THOSE 0.87 OF 77 WHERE THE COMMUNITY IS OTHER THAN A CLAN-COMMUNITY OR A COMMUNITY STRUCTURED OR SEGMENTED ON A CLAN BASIS (213)	176 IN ALL CASES ARE THOSE 1.00 OF 32 WHERE THE COMMUNITY IS OTHER THAN A CLAN-COMMUNITY OR A COMMUNITY STRUCTURED OR SEGMENTED ON A CLAN BASIS (213)	10 0 67 32 XSQ= 3.15 PHI= 0.170 XP = 0.0759
188	DRIFT LESS TOWARD BEING THOSE 0.77 OF 83 WHERE THE KIN GROUP IS EXCLUSIVELY COGNATIC (148)	188 DRIFT MORE TOWARD BEING THOSE 0.94 OF 33 WHERE THE KIN GROUP IS EXCLUSIVELY COGNATIC (148)	64 31 19 2 XSQ= 3.45 PHI= -0.172 XP = 0.0633
192	TILT LESS TOWARD BEING THOSE 0.52 OF 83 WHERE THE ONLY KIN GROUP PRESENT IS A KINDRED OR ELSE BILATERAL DESCENT IS INFERRED (111)	192 TILT MORE TOWARD BEING THOSE 0.76 OF 33 WHERE THE ONLY KIN GROUP PRESENT IS A KINDRED OR ELSE BILATERAL DESCENT IS INFERRED (111)	43 25 40 8 XSQ= 4.64 PHI= -0.200 XP = 0.0312
197	LEAN TOWARD BEING THOSE 0.82 OF 34 WHERE RULES FOR THE INHERITANCE OF REAL PROPERTY, IF PRESENT, FAVOR EITHER THE MALE HEIR OR LINE, OR THE FEMALE HEIR OR LINE (165)	197 LEAN TOWARD BEING THOSE 0.86 OF 7 WHERE RULES FOR THE INHERITANCE OF REAL PROPERTY, IF PRESENT, DO NOT FAVOR EITHER THE MALE HEIR OR LINE, OR THE FEMALE HEIR OR LINE (29)	28 1 6 6 XSQ= 9.91 PHI= 0.492 XP = 0.0016
236	DRIFT LESS TOWARD BEING THOSE 0.52 OF 82 WHERE THE FAMILY IS OF AN EXTENDED TYPE, RATHER THAN AN INDEPENDENT TYPE (213)	236 DRIFT MORE TOWARD BEING THOSE 0.73 OF 33 WHERE THE FAMILY IS OF AN EXTENDED TYPE, RATHER THAN AN INDEPENDENT TYPE (213)	43 24 39 9 XSQ= 3.19 PHI= -0.167 XP = 0.0740

240	LEAN TOWARD BEING THOSE WHERE THE FAMILY, IF EXTENDED, IS SMALL OR STEM, RATHER THAN LARGE (135)	0.81 OF 43	240	LEAN TOWARD BEING THOSE WHERE THE FAMILY, IF EXTENDED, IS LARGE, RATHER THAN SMALL OR STEM (78)	0.54 OF 24	8 13 35 11 XSQ= 7.47 PHI= -0.334 XP = 0.0063
304	DRIFT TOWARD BEING THOSE WHERE THE EARLY ANAL SATISFACTION POTENTIAL IS HIGH (19) W-C	0.70 OF 10	304	IN ALL CASES ARE THOSE WHERE THE EARLY ANAL SATISFACTION POTENTIAL IS LOW (22) W-C	1.00 OF 3	7 0 3 3 XSQ= 2.17 PHI= 0.408 EP = 0.0699
324	DRIFT TOWARD BEING THOSE WHERE THE PAIN INFLICTED ON THE INFANT BY THE NURTURANT AGENT IS HIGH (34) B-B-C	0.75 OF 16	324	DRIFT TOWARD BEING THOSE WHERE THE PAIN INFLICTED ON THE INFANT BY THE NURTURANT AGENT IS LOW OR NEGLIGIBLE (32) B-B-C	0.71 OF 7	12 2 4 5 XSQ= 2.67 PHI= 0.341 EP = 0.0657
326	DRIFT LESS TOWARD BEING THOSE WHERE THE INFERRED TRANSITION ANXIETY BETWEEN INFANCY AND CHILDHOOD IS LOW (35) B-B-C	0.59 OF 17	326	IN ALL CASES ARE THOSE WHERE THE INFERRED TRANSITION ANXIETY BETWEEN INFANCY AND CHILDHOOD IS LOW (35) B-B-C	1.00 OF 7	7 0 10 7 XSQ= 2.32 PHI= 0.311 EP = 0.0648
339	DRIFT LESS TOWARD BEING THOSE WHERE THE CHILD'S INFERRED CONFLICT REGARDING RESPONSIBLE BEHAVIOR IS LOW (42) B-B-C	0.58 OF 19	339	IN ALL CASES ARE THOSE WHERE THE CHILD'S INFERRED CONFLICT REGARDING RESPONSIBLE BEHAVIOR IS LOW (42) B-B-C	1.00 OF 7	8 0 11 7 XSQ= 2.51 PHI= 0.311 EP = 0.0622
346	DRIFT LESS TOWARD BEING THOSE WHERE THE CHILD'S INFERRED ANXIETY OVER PERFORMANCE OF SELF-RELIANT BEHAVIOR IS LOW (39) B-B-C	0.58 OF 19	346	IN ALL CASES ARE THOSE WHERE THE CHILD'S INFERRED ANXIETY OVER PERFORMANCE OF SELF-RELIANT BEHAVIOR IS LOW (39) B-B-C	1.00 OF 7	8 0 11 7 XSQ= 2.51 PHI= 0.311 EP = 0.0622
372	DRIFT LESS TOWARD BEING THOSE WHERE MALE INITIATION RITES ARE ABSENT (63) ASA	0.53 OF 19	372	DRIFT MORE TOWARD BEING THOSE WHERE MALE INITIATION RITES ARE ABSENT (63) ASA	0.89 OF 9	9 1 10 8 XSQ= 2.10 PHI= 0.274 EP = 0.0980
382	TILT LESS TOWARD BEING THOSE WHERE FEMALE INITIATION RITES ARE PRESENT (38) JKB	0.53 OF 19	382	IN ALL CASES ARE THOSE WHERE FEMALE INITIATION RITES ARE PRESENT (38) JKB	1.00 OF 10	10 10 9 0 XSQ= 4.83 PHI= -0.408 EP = 0.0114
385	LEAN TOWARD BEING THOSE WHERE SEXUAL EXPRESSION BY THE YOUNG IS SEMI-RESTRICTED OR PERMITTED (64) F-B	0.94 OF 18	385	LEAN TOWARD BEING THOSE WHERE SEXUAL EXPRESSION BY THE YOUNG IS RESTRICTED (22) F-B	0.56 OF 9	1 5 17 4 XSQ= 6.03 PHI= -0.472 EP = 0.0079

212 CULTURES
WHERE MARITAL RESICENCE IS
AVUNCULCCAL, RATHER THAN
MATRILCCAL (18)

212 CULTURES
WHERE MARITAL RESIDENCE IS
MATRILOCAL, RATHER THAN
AVUNCULOCAL (31)

BACKGROUND ON PAGE 113

SUBJECT ONLY

18 IN LEFT CCLUMN

ASHANTI, EYAK, GCAJIRC, GURE, HAIDA, KERALA, KUBA, MOTA, NDEMBU, NYANEKA, PALAUANS, PENDE, SARAMACCA, SIUAI, TENDA, TROBRIAND, TSHIMSHIAN, YOMBE

31 IN RIGHT CCLUMN

APINAYE, BELU, BCRCRO, CALLINAGO, CHEROKEE, COCHITI, CREEK, DELAWARE, GARC, GUAHIBO, HANC, HURCN, KAREN, KASKA, KHASI, LESU, MANDAN, MNONG GAR, NAVAHO, PAWNEE, PONAPEANS, ROTUMANS, SEMINCLE, SIRIONO, TALAMANCA, TIMBIRA, TIMUCUA, TRUKESE, VEDDA, YAO, ZUNI

350 EXCLUDED BECAUSE IRRELEVANT

1 EXCLUDED BECAUSE UNASCERTAINEC

	Left column			Right column			Statistics
3	LEAN LESS TOWARC BEING THCSE LOCATED CUTSIDE CF AFRICA (320)	0.56 OF 18	3	LEAN MORE TOWARD BEING THOSE LOCATED OUTSIDE OF AFRICA (320)	0.97 CF 31		8 1 10 30 XSQ= 10.30 PHI= 0.459 XP = 0.0013
15	DRIFT MORE TCWARD BEING THCSE WHERE THE LATITUDE IS LESS THAN TWENTY DEGREES (217)	0.83 OF 18	15	DRIFT LESS TOWARD BEING THCSE WHERE THE LATITUDE IS LESS THAN TWENTY DEGREES (217)	0.52 CF 31		3 15 15 16 XSQ= 3.66 PHI= -0.273 XP = 0.0557
51	DRIFT TCWARD BEING THCSE WHERE SUBSISTENCE IS PRIMARILY BY FCOD PRCDUCTION -- I. E., AGRICULTURE OR HUSBANDRY -- RATHER THAN BY GATHERING (253)	0.78 OF 18	51	DRIFT TOWARD BEING THOSE WHERE SUBSISTENCE IS PRIMARILY BY FOOD GATHERING -- I. E., HUNTING, FISHING, OR COLLECTING -- RATHER THAN FOOD PRODUCTION (147)	0.52 OF 31		14 15 4 16 XSQ= 2.95 PHI= 0.245 XP = 0.0861
54	TILT MCRE TOWARC BEING THCSE WHERE FCCD PRCDUCTICN IS BY INTENSIVE CR SIMPLE AGRICULTURE, RATHER THAN BY INCIPIENT FCCD PRODUCTICN (192)	0.92 OF 12	54	TILT LESS TOWARD BEING THOSE WHERE FOOD PRODUCTION IS BY INTENSIVE OR SIMPLE AGRICULTURE, RATHER THAN BY INCIPIENT FOOD PRODUCTICN (192)	0.55 CF 20		11 11 1 9 XSQ= 3.14 PHI= 0.313 EP = 0.0496

56	TILT TOWARD BEING THOSE 0.91 OF 11 WHERE FOOD PRODUCTION IS BY SIMPLE AGRICULTURE, RATHER THAN BY INCIPIENT FOOD PRODUCTION (101)	56	TILT TOWARD BEING THOSE 0.56 OF 16 WHERE FOOD PRODUCTION IS BY INCIPIENT FOOD PRODUCTION, RATHER THAN BY SIMPLE AGRICULTURE (46)	10 [illegible] 1 [illegible] XSQ= 4[illegible] PHI= 0.4[illegible] EP = 0.0183
80	DRIFT LESS TOWARD BEING THOSE 0.78 OF 9 WHERE NO CITY OR TOWN IS PRESENT (185)	80	IN ALL CASES ARE THOSE 1.00 OF 21 WHERE NO CITY OR TOWN IS PRESENT (185)	2 0 7 21 XSQ= 2.07 PHI= 0.262 EP = 0.0828
90	IN ALL CASES ARE THOSE 1.00 OF 13 WHERE, IF A HEREDITARY HEADMANSHIP IS PRESENT, SUCCESSION IS MATRILINEAL, RATHER THAN PATRILINEAL (38)	90	DRIFT LESS TOWARD BEING THOSE 0.71 OF 17 WHERE, IF A HEREDITARY HEADMANSHIP IS PRESENT, SUCCESSION IS MATRILINEAL, RATHER THAN PATRILINEAL (38)	0 5 13 12 XSQ= 2.71 PHI= -0.301 EP = 0.0525
95	DRIFT LESS TOWARD BEING THOSE 0.67 OF 15 WHERE THE HIERARCHY OF NATIONAL JURISDICTION HAS ONE OR NO LEVELS (254) GES,EA	95	DRIFT MORE TOWARD BEING THOSE 0.93 OF 27 WHERE THE HIERARCHY OF NATIONAL JURISDICTION HAS ONE OR NO LEVELS (254) GES,EA	5 2 10 25 XSQ= 2.99 PHI= 0.267 XP = 0.0840
102	LEAN TOWARD BEING THOSE 0.82 OF 17 WHERE CLASS STRATIFICATION IS PRESENT (203)	102	LEAN TOWARD BEING THOSE 0.71 OF 31 WHERE CLASS STRATIFICATION IS ABSENT (180)	14 9 3 22 XSQ= 10.46 PHI= 0.467 XP = 0.0012
110	TILT TOWARD BEING THOSE 0.61 OF 18 WHERE SLAVERY IS PRESENT (163)	110	TILT TOWARD BEING THOSE 0.73 OF 30 WHERE SLAVERY IS ABSENT (218)	11 8 7 22 XSQ= 4.23 PHI= 0.297 XP = 0.0396
137	IN ALL CASES ARE THOSE 1.00 OF 3 WHERE INVIDIOUS DISPLAY OF WEALTH IS STRONGLY EMPHASIZED (37) PES	137	DRIFT TOWARD BEING THOSE 0.75 OF 8 WHERE INVIDIOUS DISPLAY OF WEALTH IS MODERATELY, LITTLE, OR NEGATIVELY EMPHASIZED (52) PES	3 2 0 6 XSQ= 2.39 PHI= 0.466 EP = 0.0606
178	DRIFT TOWARD BEING THOSE 0.61 OF 18 WHERE THE COMMUNITY IS OTHER THAN SEGMENTED ON A CLAN BASIS AND NON-EXOGAMOUS (295)	178	DRIFT TOWARD BEING THOSE 0.69 OF 29 WHERE THE COMMUNITY IS SEGMENTED ON A CLAN BASIS AND NON-EXOGAMOUS (87)	7 20 11 9 XSQ= 2.97 PHI= -0.251 XP = 0.0847
185	IN ALL CASES ARE THOSE 1.00 OF 18 WHERE THE LARGEST NON-COGNATIC KIN GROUP IS THE MOEITY OR PHRATRY OR SIB (194)	185	DRIFT LESS TOWARD BEING THOSE 0.74 OF 31 WHERE THE LARGEST NON-COGNATIC KIN GROUP IS THE MOEITY OR PHRATRY OR SIB (194)	18 23 0 8 XSQ= 3.82 PHI= 0.279 XP = 0.0505

No.	Statement	Proportion	No.	Statement	Proportion	Statistics
236	LEAN TOWARD BEING THOSE WHERE THE FAMILY IS OF AN INDEPENDENT TYPE, RATHER THAN AN EXTENDED TYPE (185)	0.61 OF 18	236	LEAN TOWARD BEING THOSE WHERE THE FAMILY IS OF AN EXTENDED TYPE, RATHER THAN AN INDEPENDENT TYPE (213)	0.81 OF 31	7 25 11 6 XSQ= 7.02 PHI= -0.378 XP = 0.0081
242	IN ALL CASES ARE THOSE WHERE MARRIAGE IS COMMONLY OR OCCASIONALLY POLYGYNOUS, RATHER THAN MONOGAMOUS (314)	1.00 OF 18	242	LEAN LESS TOWARD BEING THOSE WHERE MARRIAGE IS COMMONLY OR OCCASIONALLY POLYGYNOUS, RATHER THAN MONOGAMOUS (314)	0.58 OF 31	18 18 0 13 XSQ= 8.24 PHI= 0.410 XP = 0.0041
262	LEAN TOWARD BEING THOSE WHERE WIVES ARE OBTAINED BY MEANS INVOLVING THE PRESENCE OF SOME CONSIDERATION (305)	0.94 OF 18	262	LEAN TOWARD BEING THOSE WHERE WIVES ARE OBTAINED BY MEANS INVOLVING THE ABSENCE OF ANY CONSIDERATION (90)	0.57 OF 30	17 13 1 17 XSQ= 10.45 PHI= 0.467 XP = 0.0012
263	LEAN TOWARD BEING THOSE WHERE WIVES ARE OBTAINED BY RELATIVELY DIFFICULT MEANS, NAMELY BY BRIDE-PRICE, BRIDE-SERVICE, OR EXCHANGING A FEMALE RELATIVE (233)	0.72 OF 18	263	LEAN TOWARD BEING THOSE WHERE WIVES ARE OBTAINED BY RELATIVELY EASY MEANS, NAMELY BY TOKEN BRIDE-PRICE, GIFT EXCHANGE, ABSENCE OF ANY CONSIDERATION, OR RECEIPT OF DOWRY (162)	0.73 OF 30	13 8 5 22 XSQ= 7.73 PHI= 0.401 XP = 0.0054
370	LEAN TOWARD BEING THOSE WHERE THE SEGREGATION OF ADOLESCENT BOYS IS COMPLETE OR PARTIAL (95)	0.92 OF 13	370	LEAN TOWARD BEING THOSE WHERE THE SEGREGATION OF ADOLESCENT BOYS IS ABSENT (148)	0.65 OF 20	12 7 1 13 XSQ= 8.38 PHI= 0.504 EP = 0.0014
372	IN ALL CASES ARE THOSE WHERE MALE INITIATION RITES ARE ABSENT (63) ASA	1.00 OF 6	372	TILT TOWARD BEING THOSE WHERE MALE INITIATION RITES ARE PRESENT (48) ASA	0.57 OF 14	0 8 6 6 XSQ= 3.58 PHI= -0.423 EP = 0.0419
420	IN ALL CASES ARE THOSE WHERE BELLICOSITY IS EXTREME (41) PES	1.00 OF 3	420	TILT TOWARD BEING THOSE WHERE BELLICOSITY IS MODERATE OR NEGLIGIBLE (46) PES	0.88 OF 8	3 1 0 7 XSQ= 3.93 PHI= 0.598 EP = 0.0242
472	IN ALL CASES ARE THOSE WHERE THE COMPOSITE NARCISSISM INDEX IS HIGH (47) PES	1.00 OF 3	472	DRIFT TOWARD BEING THOSE WHERE THE COMPOSITE NARCISSISM INDEX IS LOW (43) PES	0.75 OF 8	3 2 0 6 XSQ= 2.39 PHI= 0.466 EP = 0.0606
473	IN ALL CASES ARE THOSE WHERE SENSITIVITY TO INSULT IS EXTREME (32) PES	1.00 OF 3	473	IN ALL CASES ARE THOSE WHERE SENSITIVITY TO INSULT IS MODERATE OR NEGLIGIBLE (56) PES	1.00 OF 8	3 0 0 8 XSQ= 6.54 PHI= 0.771 EP = 0.0061

212/

```
474  IN ALL CASES ARE THOSE          1.00 OF   3        474  DRIFT TOWARD BEING THOSE       0.75 OF   8            3     2
     WHERE BOASTFULNESS IS EXTREME  (41) PES                 WHERE BOASTFULNESS IS MODERATE,                        0     6
                                                             NEGLIBIBLE, OR UNREPORTED  (48) PES           XSQ=      2.39
                                                                                                           PHI=     0.466
                                                                                                           EP =    0.0606
```

****

213 CULTURES
WHERE FIRST COUSIN MARRIAGE IS
PERMITTED (172)

213 CULTURES
WHERE FIRST COUSIN MARRIAGE IS
NOT PERMITTED (198)

BACKGROUND ON PAGE 117

BOTH SUBJECT AND PREDICATE

....

172 IN LEFT COLUMN

ABOR	AINU	AJIE	ALACALUF	ALBANIANS	AMERICANS	APINAYE	ARAUCANIANS	ASHANTI	AWEIKOMA
BACAIRI	BAJUN	BALINESE	BAMBARA	BARABRA	BASSERI	BATAK	BEJA	BELU	BEMBA
BERGDAMA	BHUIYA	BIRIFOR	BLACK CARIB	BORORO	BOTOCUDO	BOZO	BUDUMA	BURMESE	BURYAT
CALLINAGO	CAMAYURA	CAMBODIANS	CARAJA	CARIB	CHENCHU	CHIRIGUANO	CHUKCHEE	COORG	CREE
DILLING	DUTCH	EGYPTIANS	EYAK	FON	FUTAJALONKE	GARO	GILYAK	GOAJIRO	GOND
GUAHIBO	HAIDA	HASANIA	HAZARA	HEBREWS	HEHE	HERERO	HO	HUICHOL	ILA
INCA	JAPANESE	JAVANESE	JIVARO	KABYLE	KACHIN	KARIERA	KASKA	KERAKI	KERALA
KHASI	KISSI	KONSO	LAKALAI	LAKHER	LAMBA	LAMET	LAU	LHOTA NAGA	LOLO
MACASSARESE	MAGUZAWA	MALAYS	MANCHU	MANDAN	MANIHIKI	MARQUESANS	MARSHALLESE	MAYA	MBUNDU
MBUTI	MENDE	MENTAWEI	MERINA	MIAO	MIN CHINESE	MINANGKABAU	MINCHIA	MISKITO	MNONG GAR
MONGUOR	MOTILON	MUNDURUCU	MURNGIN	NABESNA	NAMA	NAMBICUARA	NASKAPI	NDEMBU	NGONI
NUNIVAK	NUPE	NYANEKA	OJIBWA	PATHAN	PENDE	PONAPEANS	PORTUGUESE	PURUM	REGEIBAT
RIFFIANS	ROMANS	ROTINESE	RUNDI	RWALA	SAMOYED	SANDAWE	SARAMACCA	SHERENTE	SINDHI
SINHALESE	SIRIONO	SIUAI	SIWANS	SONGHAI	SOTHO	SUBANUN	SWAZI	SYRIANS	TAMIL
TANALA	TANIMBARESE	TEHUELCHE	TENDA	TERA	THAI	TIBETANS	TIWI	TODA	TOLOWA
TROBRIAND	TRUMAI	TSHIMSHIAN	TUCANO	TUCUNA	TUPINAMBA	TURKMEN	TZELTAL	VEDDA	VENDA
WANTOAT	WAPISHANA	WAROPEN	WIKMUNKAN	WINNEBAGO	WITOTO	WOLOF	YABARANA	YAKO	YAKUT
YAO	YARURO								

198 IN RIGHT COLUMN

ABIPON	AKHA	ALORESE	AMBA	ANDAMANESE	ARANDA	ARAPESH	ARYANS	ATAYAL	ATSUGEWI
AYMARA	AZANDE	AZTEC	BAMILEKE	BANDA	BARI	BAYA	BENGALI	BETE	BHIL
BRAZILIANS	BUNLAP	BURUSHO	CAGABA	CAMBA	CARINYA	CAYAPA	CHAGGA	CHEREMIS	CHEROKEE
CHEYENNE	CHINANTEC	CHIR-APACHE	CHOCO	CHOROTI	CHORTI	COCHITI	COMANCHE	COPR ESKIMO	CREEK
CROW	CUNA	CZECHS	DAGUR	DARD	DIEGUENO	DIERI	DOBUANS	DOGON	DOROBO
DUSUN	ELLICE	ENGA	FANG	FOX	GANDA	GILBERTESE	GISU	GROS VENTRE	GURE
HANO	HANUNOO	HASINAI	HAVASUPAI	HAWAIIANS	HUKUNDIKA	HURON	IBAN	IFUGAO	INGALIK
INGASSANA	IRISH	JEMEZ	JUKUN	KALMYK	KAPAUKU	KATAB	KAZAK	KHALKA	KHEVSUR
KIKUYU	KIOW-APACHE	KOL	KOREANS	KORYAK	KPE	KUBA	KUNG	KURTATCHI	KUTENAI
KWAKIUTL	LANGO	LAPPS	LEPCHA	LESU	LIFU	LOZI	LUBA	LUO	MAM
MAMBILA	MANGAIANS	MANUS	MAORI	MARGI	MARICOPA	MASAI	MATACO	MATAKAM	MAZATECO
MBUGWE	MIAMI	MIWOK	MONGO	MOSSI	MOTA	MURINBATA	NANDI	NATCHEZ	NAVAHO
NICOBARESE	NOMLAKI	NUER	NURI	NYAKYUSA	NYARO	NYORO	OKINAWANS	OMAHA	ONA
ONTONG-JAVA	ORAON	PAIWAN	PALAUANS	PAPAGO	PARAUJANO	PAWNEE	PENOBSCOT	POPOLUCA	PUKAPUKA
PURARI	ROTUMANS	SAGADA	SAMOANS	SANPOIL	SANTAL	SARSI	SEMANG	SEMINOLE	SENIANG
SERI	SHILLUK	SIMBOESE	SOMALI	TAGBANUA	TALAMANCA	TALLENSI	TAOS	TAPIRAPE	TARAHUMARA
TAREUMIUT	TEDA	TENETEHARA	TENINO	TERENA	TESO	TETON	THONGA	TIGRINYA	TIKOPIA
TIMBIRA	TIV	TOKELAU	TORAJA	TOTONAC	TRUKESE	TUBATULABAL	TUNEBO	TURKANA	TWANA

ULAWANS	UTE	VIETNAMESE	WASHO	WICHITA	WOGEO	WOLEAIANS	WUTE	YAGUA	YAHGAN
YAPESE	YOKUTS	YOMBE	YORUBA	YUKAGHIR	YUKI	YUROK	ZUNI		

30 EXCLUDED BECAUSE UNASCERTAINED

BABWA	BASQUES	BOERS	BULGARIANS	CADUVEO	CHAMACOCO	CHERKESS	CHIBCHA	DELAWARE	GUATO
HUTSUL	ICELANDERS	IRAQW	KAREN	KET	KOHISTANI	KUMYK	MAMVU	MZAB	PAEZ
PALIKUR	RARCIANS	SELUNG	SERBS	SHLUH	TIMUCUA	TRISTAN	WAICA	WALLCONS	WARRAU

4	TILT LESS TOWARD BEING THOSE LOCATED OUTSIDE OF THE CIRCUM-MEDITERRANEAN (355)	0.87 OF 172	4	TILT MORE TOWARD BEING THOSE LOCATED OUTSIDE OF THE CIRCUM-MEDITERRANEAN (355)	0.95 OF 198	22 10 150 188 XSQ= 6.03 PHI= 0.128 XP = 0.0140
5	TEND LESS TO BE THOSE LOCATED OUTSIDE OF EAST EURASIA (330)	0.74 OF 172	5	TEND MORE TO BE THOSE LOCATED OUTSIDE OF EAST EURASIA (330)	0.89 OF 198	44 22 128 176 XSQ= 12.18 PHI= 0.181 XP = 0.0005
8	TEND MORE TO BE THOSE LOCATED OUTSIDE OF NORTH AMERICA (330)	0.92 OF 172	8	TEND LESS TO BE THOSE LOCATED OUTSIDE OF NORTH AMERICA (330)	0.72 OF 198	13 55 159 143 XSQ= 23.76 PHI= -0.253 XP = 0.0000
9	TILT LESS TOWARD BEING THOSE LOCATED OUTSIDE OF SOUTH AMERICA (335)	0.80 OF 172	9	TILT MORE TOWARD BEING THOSE LOCATED OUTSIDE OF SOUTH AMERICA (335)	0.89 OF 198	35 22 137 176 XSQ= 5.34 PHI= 0.120 XP = 0.0209
14	TILT MORE TOWARD BEING THOSE WHERE THE LATITUDE IS LESS THAN THIRTY DEGREES (281)	0.77 OF 172	14	TILT LESS TOWARD BEING THOSE WHERE THE LATITUDE IS LESS THAN THIRTY DEGREES (281)	0.67 OF 198	39 66 133 132 XSQ= 4.63 PHI= -0.112 XP = 0.0313
36	TILT MORE TOWARD BEING THOSE WHERE THE NATURAL ENVIRONMENT IS OTHER THAN 'VERY HARSH,' OR SUB-TROPICAL BUSH, OR TEMPERATE GRASSLAND (292) FWM	0.78 OF 172	36	TILT LESS TOWARD BEING THOSE WHERE THE NATURAL ENVIRONMENT IS OTHER THAN 'VERY HARSH,' OR SUB-TROPICAL BUSH, OR TEMPERATE GRASSLAND (292) FWM	0.67 OF 198	38 65 134 133 XSQ= 4.76 PHI= -0.113 XP = 0.0291
63	LEAN MORE TOWARD BEING THOSE WHERE HUSBANDRY, IF PRESENT, IS PRINCIPALLY IN THE FORM OF BOVINE, EQUINE, CAMEL-LIKE, OR DEER-LIKE ANIMALS, RATHER THAN PIGS, SHEEP, OR GOATS (152)	0.78 OF 93	63	LEAN LESS TOWARD BEING THOSE WHERE HUSBANDRY, IF PRESENT, IS PRINCIPALLY IN THE FORM OF BOVINE, EQUINE, CAMEL-LIKE, OR DEER-LIKE ANIMALS, RATHER THAN PIGS, SHEEP, OR GOATS (152)	0.57 OF 120	73 68 20 52 XSQ= 10.20 PHI= 0.219 XP = 0.0014

73	DRIFT TOWARD BEING THOSE WHERE WEAVING IS PRESENT (118) — 0.54 OF 105	73	DRIFT TOWARD BEING THOSE WHERE WEAVING IS ABSENT (130) — 0.59 OF 130	57 53 48 77 XSQ= 3.74 PHI= 0.126 XP = 0.0532
80	DRIFT LESS TOWARD BEING THOSE WHERE NO CITY OR TOWN IS PRESENT (185) — 0.79 OF 102	80	DRIFT MORE TOWARD BEING THOSE WHERE NO CITY OR TOWN IS PRESENT (185) — 0.89 OF 110	21 12 81 98 XSQ= 3.07 PHI= 0.120 XP = 0.0796
83	TILT MORE TOWARD BEING THOSE WHERE, WITH NO CITY AND NO TOWN PRESENT, THE AVERAGE COMMUNITY SIZE IS SMALLER THAN 200, RATHER THAN BETWEEN 200 AND 999 (135) — 0.84 OF 79	83	TILT LESS TOWARD BEING THOSE WHERE, WITH NO CITY AND NO TOWN PRESENT, THE AVERAGE COMMUNITY SIZE IS SMALLER THAN 200, RATHER THAN BETWEEN 200 AND 999 (135) — 0.67 OF 95	13 31 66 64 XSQ= 5.15 PHI= -0.172 XP = 0.0233
84	TILT LESS TOWARD BEING THOSE WHERE THE LEVEL OF POLITICAL INTEGRATION IS THE LITTLE STATE, THE MINIMAL STATE, THE AUTONOMOUS COMMUNITY, OR THE FAMILY (262) GPM — 0.81 OF 136	84	TILT MORE TOWARD BEING THOSE WHERE THE LEVEL OF POLITICAL INTEGRATION IS THE LITTLE STATE, THE MINIMAL STATE, THE AUTONOMOUS COMMUNITY, OR THE FAMILY (262) GPM — 0.90 OF 145	26 14 110 131 XSQ= 4.40 PHI= 0.125 XP = 0.0359
90	TILT LESS TOWARD BEING THOSE WHERE, IF A HEREDITARY HEADMANSHIP IS PRESENT, SUCCESSION IS PATRILINEAL, RATHER THAN MATRILINEAL (127) — 0.70 OF 79	90	TILT MORE TOWARD BEING THOSE WHERE, IF A HEREDITARY HEADMANSHIP IS PRESENT, SUCCESSION IS PATRILINEAL, RATHER THAN MATRILINEAL (127) — 0.86 OF 79	55 68 24 11 XSQ= 5.29 PHI= -0.183 XP = 0.0215
96	DRIFT TOWARD BEING THOSE WHERE THE HIERARCHY OF NATIONAL JURISDICTION HAS FOUR, THREE, TWO OR ONE LEVEL (174) GES,EA — 0.58 OF 138	96	DRIFT TOWARD BEING THOSE WHERE THE HIERARCHY OF NATIONAL JURISDICTION HAS NO LEVELS (156) GES,EA — 0.53 OF 170	80 80 58 90 XSQ= 3.21 PHI= 0.102 XP = 0.0732
102	DRIFT TOWARD BEING THOSE WHERE CLASS STRATIFICATION IS PRESENT (203) — 0.59 OF 167	102	DRIFT TOWARD BEING THOSE WHERE CLASS STRATIFICATION IS ABSENT (180) — 0.52 OF 188	98 90 69 98 XSQ= 3.73 PHI= 0.102 XP = 0.0536
107	DRIFT LESS TOWARD BEING THOSE WHERE CLASS STRATIFICATION, IF PRESENT, IS BASED ON SOMETHING OTHER THAN OCCUPATIONAL STATUS (160) — 0.73 OF 98	107	DRIFT MORE TOWARD BEING THOSE WHERE CLASS STRATIFICATION, IF PRESENT, IS BASED ON SOMETHING OTHER THAN OCCUPATIONAL STATUS (160) — 0.86 OF 90	26 13 72 77 XSQ= 3.47 PHI= 0.136 XP = 0.0627
110	TILT TOWARD BEING THOSE WHERE SLAVERY IS PRESENT (163) — 0.51 OF 168	110	TILT TOWARD BEING THOSE WHERE SLAVERY IS ABSENT (218) — 0.63 OF 187	85 69 83 118 XSQ= 6.21 PHI= 0.132 XP = 0.0127

```
127  DRIFT TOWARD BEING THOSE        0.66 OF  29     127  DRIFT TOWARD BEING THOSE         0.62 OF  34          10    21
     WHERE THE FEMALES' CONTRIBUTION                      WHERE THE FEMALES' CONTRIBUTION                       19    13
     TO SUBSISTENCE                                       TO SUBSISTENCE                               XSQ=       3.63
     IS LOW  (32) JKB                                     IS HIGH  (33) JKB                            PHI=     -0.240
                                                                                                       XP =     0.0566

128  TILT TOWARD BEING THOSE         0.66 OF  38     128  TILT TOWARD BEING THOSE          0.62 OF  37          25    14
     WHERE, IF SUBSISTENCE IS PRIMARILY BY                WHERE, IF SUBSISTENCE IS PRIMARILY BY                 13    23
     AGRICULTURE, THE WORK IS                             AGRICULTURE, THE WORK IS                     XSQ=       4.80
     MAINLY DONE BY MALES  (40)                           MAINLY DONE BY FEMALES  (37)                 PHI=      0.253
                                                                                                       XP =     0.0284

135  DRIFT MORE TOWARD BEING THOSE   0.83 OF  12     135  DRIFT LESS TOWARD BEING THOSE    0.52 OF  25          10    13
     WHERE INDIVIDUAL OWNERSHIP OF                        WHERE INDIVIDUAL OWNERSHIP OF                          2    12
     ECONOMICALLY SIGNIFICANT PROPERTY                    ECONOMICALLY SIGNIFICANT PROPERTY            XSQ=       2.18
     IS PRESENT  (24) GES                                 IS PRESENT  (24) GES                         PHI=      0.243
                                                                                                       EP =     0.0836

179  LEAN MORE TOWARD BEING THOSE    0.95 OF 165     179  LEAN LESS TOWARD BEING THOSE     0.83 OF 194           9    33
     WHERE THE COMMUNITY IS OTHER THAN                    WHERE THE COMMUNITY IS OTHER THAN                    156   161
     STRUCTURED ON A NON-CLAN BASIS AND                   STRUCTURED ON A NON-CLAN BASIS AND           XSQ=      10.43
     COMMONLY EXOGAMOUS  (340)                            COMMONLY EXOGAMOUS  (340)                    PHI=     -0.170
                                                                                                       XP =     0.0012

186  TILT LESS TOWARD BEING THOSE    0.55 OF 172     186  TILT MORE TOWARD BEING THOSE     0.68 OF 198          77    64
     WHERE THE KIN GROUP IS                               WHERE THE KIN GROUP IS                                95   134
     OTHER THAN                                           OTHER THAN                                   XSQ=       5.53
     EXCLUSIVELY PATRILINEAL  (250)                       EXCLUSIVELY PATRILINEAL  (250)               PHI=      0.122
                                                                                                       XP =     0.0187

188  TEND MORE TO BE THOSE           0.74 OF 172     188  TEND LESS TO BE THOSE            0.56 OF 198          44    87
     WHERE THE KIN GROUP IS                               WHERE THE KIN GROUP IS                               128   111
     OTHER THAN                                           OTHER THAN                                   XSQ=      12.77
     EXCLUSIVELY COGNATIC  (252)                          EXCLUSIVELY COGNATIC  (252)                  PHI=     -0.186
                                                                                                       XP =     0.0004

192  TEND MORE TO BE THOSE           0.84 OF 172     192  TEND LESS TO BE THOSE            0.66 OF 198          28    67
     OTHER THAN WHERE THE ONLY KIN GROUP                  OTHER THAN WHERE THE ONLY KIN GROUP                  144   131
     PRESENT IS A KINDRED OR ELSE                         PRESENT IS A KINDRED OR ELSE                 XSQ=      13.97
     BILATERAL DESCENT IS INFERRED  (289)                 BILATERAL DESCENT IS INFERRED  (289)         PHI=     -0.194
                                                                                                       XP =     0.0002

201  TILT MORE TOWARD BEING THOSE    0.90 OF 170     201  TILT LESS TOWARD BEING THOSE     0.81 OF 198         153   161
     WHERE MARITAL RESIDENCE IS                           WHERE MARITAL RESIDENCE IS                            17    37
     NON-OPTIONAL, RATHER THAN                            NON-OPTIONAL, RATHER THAN                    XSQ=       4.84
     AMBILOCAL OR NEOLOCAL  (334)                         AMBILOCAL OR NEOLOCAL  (334)                 PHI=      0.115
                                                                                                       XP =     0.0278

204  TILT MORE TOWARD BEING THOSE    0.88 OF 145     204  TILT LESS TOWARD BEING THOSE     0.78 OF 165         128   128
     WHERE MARITAL RESIDENCE IS                           WHERE MARITAL RESIDENCE IS                            17    37
     PATRILOCAL, VIRILOCAL, OR AVUNCULOCAL,               PATRILOCAL, VIRILOCAL, OR AVUNCULOCAL,       XSQ=       5.42
     RATHER THAN                                          RATHER THAN                                  PHI=      0.132
     AMBILOCAL OR NEOLOCAL  (270)                         AMBILOCAL OR NEOLOCAL  (270)                 XP =     0.0199
```

220	TEND TO BE THCSE 0.56 OF 172 WHERE FIRST CCUSIN MARRIACE IN SCME FCRM CR CTHER IS PRESCRIBED CR PREFERREC (97)	220	IN ALL CASES ARE THOSE 1.00 CF 198 WHERE FIRST COUSIN MARRIAGE IN SOME FORM OR OTHER IS NOT PRESCRIBED OR PREFERRED (273)	97 0 75 198 XSQ= 148.44 PHI= 0.633 XP = 0.
221	TEND LESS TC BE THCSE 0.80 OF 172 WHERE MATRILATERAL CRCSS-COUSIN MARRIACE IS NCT PRESCRIBEC CR PREFERREC (335)	221	IN ALL CASES ARE THOSE 1.00 CF 198 WHERE MATRILATERAL CROSS-CCUSIN MARRIAGE IS NOT PRESCRIBED OR PREFERRED (335)	35 0 137 198 XSQ= 42.16 PHI= 0.338 XP = 0.
234	TEND TO BE THCSE 0.70 OF 128 WHERE THE COUSIN TERMINCLCGY IS OF CRCW, CMAHA, CR IRCQUCIS TYPE, RATHER THAN ESKIMC CR HAWAIIAN TYPE (152)	234	TEND TO BE THOSE 0.66 OF 174 WHERE THE COUSIN TERMINCLOGY IS OF ESKIMO OR HAWAIIAN TYPE, RATHER THAN CROW, OMAHA, OR IROQUOIS TYPE (170)	89 60 39 114 XSQ= 34.85 PHI= 0.340 XP = 0.
242	TILT MCRE TOWARC BEING THCSE 0.88 OF 168 WHERE MARRIAGE IS COMMCNLY CR OCCASICNALLY PCLYGYNOUS, RATHER THAN MCNCGAMOUS (314)	242	TILT LESS TOWARD BEING THCSE 0.77 CF 197 WHERE MARRIAGE IS COMMONLY OR OCCASIONALLY PCLYGYNCUS, RATHER THAN MONOGAMCUS (314)	147 151 21 46 XSQ= 6.42 PHI= 0.133 XP = 0.0113
308	TILT TOWARD BEING THOSE 0.69 OF 13 WHERE AVERAGE SCCIALIZATICN ANXIETY IS LOW (18) W-C	308	TILT TOWARD BEING THOSE 0.67 OF 27 WHERE AVERAGE SOCIALIZATION ANXIETY IS HIGH (22) W-C	4 18 9 9 XSQ= 3.23 PHI= -0.284 EP = 0.0458
311	DRIFT TCWARD BEING THCSE 0.63 OF 19 WHERE SEXUAL SOCIALIZATICN ANXIETY IS LOW (23) W-C	311	DRIFT TOWARD BEING THOSE 0.66 OF 32 WHERE SEXUAL SOCIALIZATION ANXIETY IS HIGH (28) W-C	7 21 12 11 XSQ= 2.91 PHI= -0.239 XP = 0.0880
325	TEND TO BE THOSE 0.70 OF 27 WHERE THE DEGREE OF DIFFUSION AMONG THE INFANT'S NURTURANT AGENTS IS LCW (32) B-B-C	325	TEND TO BE THOSE 0.72 OF 47 WHERE THE DEGREE OF DIFFUSICN AMCNG THE INFANT'S NURTURANT AGENTS IS HIGH (42) B-B-C	8 34 19 13 XSQ= 11.07 PHI= -0.387 XP = 0.0009
339	DRIFT TCWARD BEING THCSE 0.60 OF 25 WHERE THE CHILD'S INFERREC CONFLICT REGARDING RESPONSIBLE BEHAVIOR IS HIGH (31) B-B-C	339	DRIFT TOWARD BEING THOSE 0.67 CF 48 WHERE THE CHILD'S INFERRED CONFLICT REGARDING RESPCNSIBLE BEHAVIOR IS LOW (42) B-B-C	15 16 10 32 XSQ= 3.76 PHI= 0.227 XP = 0.0526
391	DRIFT TCWARD BEING THOSE 0.59 OF 75 WHERE PREMARITAL SEX RELATIONS ARE PUNISHED CNLY IF PREGNANCY RESULTS, OR FREELY PERMITTEC (90) JTW,EA	391	DRIFT TOWARD BEING THOSE 0.56 OF 95 WHERE PREMARITAL SEX RELATICNS ARE STRONGLY PUNISHED AND IN FACT RARE, OR WEAKLY PUNISHED AND IN FACT NOT RARE (89) JTW,EA	31 53 44 42 XSQ= 2.95 PHI= -0.132 XP = 0.0859

```
398  DRIFT TOWARD BEING THOSE          0.71 OF  14     398  DRIFT TOWARD BEING THOSE         0.67 OF  18            4   12
     WHERE THE INTENSITY OF SEX ANXIETY                     WHERE THE INTENSITY OF SEX ANXIETY                   10    6
     IS LOW  (16) WNS                                       IS HIGH  (16) WNS                             XSQ=     3.17
                                                                                                          PHI=   -0.315
                                                                                                          EP =   0.0732

405  TILT TOWARD BEING THOSE           0.80 OF  20     405  TILT TOWARD BEING THOSE          0.55 OF  40           16   18
     WHERE EXPLANATIONS OF ILLNESS                          WHERE EXPLANATIONS OF ILLNESS                         4   22
     OF A DEPENDENCE NATURE                                 OF A DEPENDENCE NATURE                        XSQ=     5.30
     ARE PRESENT  (34) W-C                                  ARE ABSENT  (27) W-C                          PHI=    0.297
                                                                                                          XP =   0.0213

446  DRIFT MORE TOWARD BEING THOSE     0.83 OF  12     446  DRIFT LESS TOWARD BEING THOSE    0.52 OF  25            2   12
     WHERE WITCHCRAFT                                       WHERE WITCHCRAFT                                     10   13
     IS MODERATELY PRESENT OR                               IS MODERATELY PRESENT OR                      XSQ=     2.18
     ABSENT  (24) GES                                       ABSENT  (24) GES                              PHI=   -0.243
                                                                                                          EP =   0.0836

447  DRIFT TOWARD BEING THOSE          0.62 OF  13     447  DRIFT TOWARD BEING THOSE         0.75 OF  20            5   15
     WHERE LOVE MAGIC IS                                    WHERE LOVE MAGIC IS                                   8    5
     ABSENT  (13) S-R                                       PRESENT  (20) S-R                             XSQ=     3.01
                                                                                                          PHI=   -0.302
                                                                                                          EP =   0.0673

459  DRIFT TOWARD BEING THOSE          0.62 OF  66     459  DRIFT TOWARD BEING THOSE         0.54 OF 101           25   55
     WHERE GAMES, IF PRESENT,                               WHERE GAMES, IF PRESENT,                             41   46
     DO NOT INCLUDE                                         INCLUDE GAMES OF CHANCE  (82) R-A-B,EA        XSQ=     3.76
     GAMES OF CHANCE  (89) R-A-B,EA                                                                       PHI=   -0.150
                                                                                                          XP =   0.0526
```

****

214 CULTURES WHERE FIRST COUSIN MARRIAGE, IF PERMITTED, IS UNILATERAL (28)	214 CULTURES WHERE FIRST COUSIN MARRIAGE, IF PERMITTED, IS OTHER THAN UNILATERAL (144)

BACKGROUND ON PAGE 117 BOTH SUBJECT AND PREDICATE

....

28 IN LEFT COLUMN

ABOR	ARAUCANIANS	BATAK	BELU	CALLINAGO	GILYAK	HO	ILA	KACHIN	KASKA
KISSI	KONSO	LAMET	LHOTA NAGA	MANDAN	MAYA	MENDE	MNONG GAR	MURNGIN	PENDE
PURUM	SANDAWE	SHERENTE	SIRIONO	TIWI	TROBRIAND	WAROPEN	WIKMUNKAN		

144 IN RIGHT COLUMN

AINU	AJIE	ALACALUF	ALBANIANS	AMERICANS	APINAYE	ASHANTI	AWEIKOMA	BACAIRI	BAJUN
BALINESE	BAMBARA	BARABRA	BASSERI	BEJA	BEMBA	BERGDAMA	BHUIYA	BIRIFOR	BLACK CARIB
BORORO	BOTOCUDO	BOZO	BUDUMA	BURMESE	BURYAT	CAMAYURA	CAMBODIANS	CARAJA	CARIB
CHENCHU	CHIRIGUANO	CHUKCHEE	COORG	CREE	DILLING	DUTCH	EGYPTIANS	EYAK	FON
FUTAJALONKE	GARO	GOAJIRO	GOND	GUAHIBO	HAIDA	HASANIA	HAZARA	HEBREWS	HEHE
HERERO	HUICHOL	INCA	JAPANESE	JAVANESE	JIVARO	KABYLE	KARIERA	KERAKI	KERALA
KHASI	LAKALAI	LAKHER	LAMBA	LAU	LOLO	MACASSARESE	MAGUZAWA	MALAYS	MANCHU
MANIHIKI	MARQUESANS	MARSHALLESE	MBUNDU	MBUTI	MENTAWEI	MERINA	MIAO	MIN CHINESE	MINANGKABAU
MINCHIA	MISKITO	MONGUOR	MOTILON	MUNDURUCU	NABESNA	NAMA	NAMBICUARA	NASKAPI	NDEMBU
NGONI	NUNIVAK	NUPE	NYANEKA	OJIBWA	PATHAN	PONAPEANS	PORTUGUESE	REGEIBAT	RIFFIANS
ROMANS	ROTINESE	RUNDI	RWALA	SAMOYED	SARAMACCA	SINDHI	SINHALESE	SIUAI	SIWANS
SONGHAI	SOTHO	SUBANUN	SWAZI	SYRIANS	TAMIL	TANALA	TANIMBARESE	TEHUELCHE	TENDA
TERA	THAI	TIBETANS	TODA	TOLOWA	TRUMAI	TSHIMSHIAN	TUCANO	TUCUNA	TUPINAMBA
TURKMEN	TZELTAL	VEDDA	VENDA	WANTOAT	WAPISHANA	WINNEBAGO	WITOTO	WOLOF	YABARANA
YAKO	YAKUT	YAO	YARURO						

198 EXCLUDED BECAUSE IRRELEVANT (SEE RIGHT COLUMN, PARAGRAPH 213)

30 EXCLUDED BECAUSE UNASCERTAINED

33	IN ALL CASES ARE THOSE 1.00 OF 28 WHERE THE NATURAL ENVIRONMENT IS OTHER THAN 'VERY HARSH,' I.E., DESERT, DESERT GRASSES AND SHRUBS, TUNDRA, OR HIGH PLATEAU STEPPE (341) FWM	33	TILT LESS TOWARD BEING THOSE 0.84 OF 144 WHERE THE NATURAL ENVIRONMENT IS OTHER THAN 'VERY HARSH,' I.E., DESERT, DESERT GRASSES AND SHRUBS, TUNDRA, OR HIGH PLATEAU STEPPE (341) FWM	0 23 28 121 XSQ= 3.88 PHI= -0.150 XP = 0.0490
36	DRIFT MORE TOWARD BEING THOSE 0.93 OF 28 WHERE THE NATURAL ENVIRONMENT IS OTHER THAN 'VERY HARSH,' OR SUB-TROPICAL BUSH, OR TEMPERATE GRASSLAND (292) FWM	36	DRIFT LESS TOWARD BEING THOSE 0.75 OF 144 WHERE THE NATURAL ENVIRONMENT IS OTHER THAN 'VERY HARSH,' OR SUB-TROPICAL BUSH, OR TEMPERATE GRASSLAND (292) FWM	2 36 26 108 XSQ= 3.37 PHI= -0.140 XP = 0.0665

53	DRIFT MORE TOWARD BEING THOSE 0.87 OF 15 WHERE FOOD PRODUCTION IS BY SIMPLE AGRICULTURE OR INCIPIENT FOOD PRODUCTION, RATHER THAN BY INTENSIVE AGRICULTURE (147)	53	DRIFT LESS TOWARD BEING THOSE 0.58 OF 89 WHERE FOOD PRODUCTION IS BY SIMPLE AGRICULTURE OR INCIPIENT FOOD PRODUCTION, RATHER THAN BY INTENSIVE AGRICULTURE (147)	2 37 13 52 XSQ= 3.25 PHI= -0.177 XP = 0.0716
55	TILT TOWARD BEING THOSE 0.85 OF 13 WHERE FOOD PRODUCTION IS BY SIMPLE AGRICULTURE, RATHER THAN BY INTENSIVE AGRICULTURE (101)	55	TILT TOWARD BEING THOSE 0.54 OF 69 WHERE FOOD PRODUCTION IS BY INTENSIVE AGRICULTURE, RATHER THAN BY SIMPLE AGRICULTURE (91)	2 37 11 32 XSQ= 4.97 PHI= -0.246 XP = 0.0258
84	DRIFT MORE TOWARD BEING THOSE 0.96 OF 23 WHERE THE LEVEL OF POLITICAL INTEGRATION IS THE LITTLE STATE, THE MINIMAL STATE, THE AUTONOMOUS COMMUNITY, OR THE FAMILY (262) GPM	84	DRIFT LESS TOWARD BEING THOSE 0.78 OF 113 WHERE THE LEVEL OF POLITICAL INTEGRATION IS THE LITTLE STATE, THE MINIMAL STATE, THE AUTONOMOUS COMMUNITY, OR THE FAMILY (262) GPM	1 25 22 88 XSQ= 2.84 PHI= -0.145 XP = 0.0919
85	DRIFT MORE TOWARD BEING THOSE 0.91 OF 23 WHERE THE LEVEL OF POLITICAL INTEGRATION IS THE MINIMAL STATE, THE AUTONOMOUS COMMUNITY, OR THE FAMILY (234) GPM	85	DRIFT LESS TOWARD BEING THOSE 0.69 OF 113 WHERE THE LEVEL OF POLITICAL INTEGRATION IS THE MINIMAL STATE, THE AUTONOMOUS COMMUNITY, OR THE FAMILY (234) GPM	2 35 21 78 XSQ= 3.73 PHI= -0.166 XP = 0.0534
95	IN ALL CASES ARE THOSE 1.00 OF 22 WHERE THE HIERARCHY OF NATIONAL JURISDICTION HAS ONE OR NO LEVELS (254) GES,EA	95	LEAN LESS TOWARD BEING THOSE 0.66 OF 116 WHERE THE HIERARCHY OF NATIONAL JURISDICTION HAS ONE OR NO LEVELS (254) GES,EA	0 39 22 77 XSQ= 8.72 PHI= -0.251 XP = 0.0031
96	TILT TOWARD BEING THOSE 0.64 OF 22 WHERE THE HIERARCHY OF NATIONAL JURISDICTION HAS NO LEVELS (156) GES,EA	96	TILT TOWARD BEING THOSE 0.62 OF 116 WHERE THE HIERARCHY OF NATIONAL JURISDICTION HAS FOUR, THREE, TWO OR ONE LEVEL (174) GES,EA	8 72 14 44 XSQ= 4.02 PHI= -0.171 XP = 0.0451
116	IN ALL CASES ARE THOSE 1.00 OF 6 WHERE OCCUPATIONAL SPECIALIZATION IS PART-TIME ONLY (34) JMH	116	DRIFT TOWARD BEING THOSE 0.50 OF 18 WHERE OCCUPATIONAL SPECIALIZATION IS FULL-TIME, WHETHER OR NOT FOR SURPLUS PRODUCTION (20) JMH	0 9 6 9 XSQ= 2.90 PHI= -0.348 EP = 0.0519
176	LEAN TOWARD BEING THOSE 0.74 OF 27 WHERE THE COMMUNITY IS A CLAN-COMMUNITY OR A COMMUNITY STRUCTURED OR SEGMENTED ON A CLAN BASIS (169)	176	LEAN TOWARD BEING THOSE 0.57 OF 138 WHERE THE COMMUNITY IS OTHER THAN A CLAN-COMMUNITY OR A COMMUNITY STRUCTURED OR SEGMENTED ON A CLAN BASIS (213)	20 60 7 78 XSQ= 7.28 PHI= 0.210 XP = 0.0070
178	TEND TO BE THOSE 0.52 OF 27 WHERE THE COMMUNITY IS SEGMENTED ON A CLAN BASIS AND NON-EXOGAMOUS (87)	178	TEND TO BE THOSE 0.82 OF 138 WHERE THE COMMUNITY IS OTHER THAN SEGMENTED ON A CLAN BASIS AND NON-EXOGAMOUS (295)	14 25 13 113 XSQ= 12.43 PHI= 0.274 XP = 0.0004

183 TILT LESS TOWARD BEING THOSE 0.71 OF 28 WHERE THE LARGEST NON-COGNATIC KIN GROUP IS SMALLER THAN A MOEITY, I. E., A PHRATRY OR SIB OR LINEAGE (218)	183 TILT MORE TOWARD BEING THOSE 0.89 OF 100 WHERE THE LARGEST NON-COGNATIC KIN GROUP IS SMALLER THAN A MOEITY, I. E., A PHRATRY OR SIB OR LINEAGE (218)	8 11 20 89 XSQ= 4.04 PHI= 0.178 XP = 0.0443
186 DRIFT TOWARD BEING THOSE 0.61 OF 28 WHERE THE KIN GROUP IS EXCLUSIVELY PATRILINEAL (150)	186 DRIFT TOWARD BEING THOSE 0.58 OF 144 WHERE THE KIN GROUP IS OTHER THAN EXCLUSIVELY PATRILINEAL (250)	17 60 11 84 XSQ= 2.71 PHI= 0.126 XP = 0.0996
187 DRIFT LESS TOWARD BEING THOSE 0.68 OF 28 WHERE THE KIN GROUP IS OTHER THAN EXCLUSIVELY MATRILINEAL (344)	187 DRIFT MORE TOWARD BEING THOSE 0.85 OF 143 WHERE THE KIN GROUP IS OTHER THAN EXCLUSIVELY MATRILINEAL (344)	9 21 19 122 XSQ= 3.80 PHI= 0.149 XP = 0.0513
188 IN ALL CASES ARE THOSE 1.00 OF 28 WHERE THE KIN GROUP IS OTHER THAN EXCLUSIVELY COGNATIC (252)	188 LEAN LESS TOWARD BEING THOSE 0.69 OF 144 WHERE THE KIN GROUP IS OTHER THAN EXCLUSIVELY COGNATIC (252)	0 44 28 100 XSQ= 9.95 PHI= -0.240 XP = 0.0016
192 IN ALL CASES ARE THOSE 1.00 OF 28 OTHER THAN WHERE THE ONLY KIN GROUP PRESENT IS A KINDRED OR ELSE BILATERAL DESCENT IS INFERRED (289)	192 TILT LESS TOWARD BEING THOSE 0.81 OF 144 OTHER THAN WHERE THE ONLY KIN GROUP PRESENT IS A KINDRED OR ELSE BILATERAL DESCENT IS INFERRED (289)	0 28 28 116 XSQ= 5.15 PHI= -0.173 XP = 0.0232
207 IN ALL CASES ARE THOSE 1.00 OF 6 WHERE MARITAL RESIDENCE IS MATRILOCAL OR UXORILOCAL, RATHER THAN AMBILOCAL OR NEOLOCAL (64)	207 DRIFT LESS TOWARD BEING THOSE 0.53 OF 36 WHERE MARITAL RESIDENCE IS MATRILOCAL OR UXORILOCAL, RATHER THAN AMBILOCAL OR NEOLOCAL (64)	6 19 0 17 XSQ= 3.00 PHI= 0.267 XP = 0.0832
221 TEND TO BE THOSE 0.61 OF 28 WHERE MATRILATERAL CROSS-COUSIN MARRIAGE IS PRESCRIBED OR PREFERRED (35)	221 TEND TO BE THOSE 0.88 OF 144 WHERE MATRILATERAL CROSS-COUSIN MARRIAGE IS NOT PRESCRIBED OR PREFERRED (335)	17 18 11 126 XSQ= 30.71 PHI= 0.423 XP = 0.
224 IN ALL CASES ARE THOSE 1.00 OF 28 WHERE COUSIN MARRIAGE IS PREFERENTIALLY OR PERMISSIVELY EITHER PATRI- OR MATRILATERAL, RATHER THAN SYMMETRICAL (66)	224 TEND TO BE THOSE 0.74 OF 144 WHERE COUSIN MARRIAGE IS PREFERENTIALLY OR PERMISSIVELY SYMMETRICAL, RATHER THAN EITHER PATRI- OR MATRILATERAL (106)	28 38 0 106 XSQ= 50.65 PHI= 0.543 XP = 0.
225 DRIFT MORE TOWARD BEING THOSE 0.79 OF 28 WHERE COUSIN MARRIAGE IS PREFERENTIALLY OR PERMISSIVELY MATRILATERAL, RATHER THAN PATRILATERAL (43)	225 DRIFT LESS TOWARD BEING THOSE 0.55 OF 38 WHERE COUSIN MARRIAGE IS PREFERENTIALLY OR PERMISSIVELY MATRILATERAL, RATHER THAN PATRILATERAL (43)	6 17 22 21 XSQ= 2.90 PHI= -0.210 XP = 0.0886

303	IN ALL CASES ARE THOSE 1.00 OF 3 WHERE THE EARLY ORAL SATISFACTION POTENTIAL IS HIGH (32) W-C	303	DRIFT TOWARD BEING THOSE 0.63 OF 16 WHERE THE EARLY ORAL SATISFACTION POTENTIAL IS LOW (25) W-C	3 6 0 10 XSQ= 1.85 PHI= 0.312 EP = 0.0867
306	IN ALL CASES ARE THOSE 1.00 OF 3 WHERE THE EARLY DEPENDENCE SATISFACTION POTENTIAL IS HIGH (28) W-C	306	DRIFT TOWARD BEING THOSE 0.64 OF 14 WHERE THE EARLY DEPENDENCE SATISFACTION POTENTIAL IS LOW (24) W-C	3 5 0 9 XSQ= 1.92 PHI= 0.336 EP = 0.0824
352	DRIFT TOWARD BEING THOSE 0.71 OF 7 WHERE THE TOTAL POSITIVE PRESSURE TOWARD DEVELOPING OBEDIENT BEHAVIOR IN THE CHILD IS LOW (28) B-B-C	352	DRIFT TOWARD BEING THOSE 0.71 OF 21 WHERE THE TOTAL POSITIVE PRESSURE TOWARD DEVELOPING OBEDIENT BEHAVIOR IN THE CHILD IS HIGH (44) B-B-C	2 15 5 6 XSQ= 2.45 PHI= -0.296 EP = 0.0764
370	TILT TOWARD BEING THOSE 0.68 OF 19 WHERE THE SEGREGATION OF ADOLESCENT BOYS IS COMPLETE OR PARTIAL (95)	370	TILT TOWARD BEING THOSE 0.62 OF 85 WHERE THE SEGREGATION OF ADOLESCENT BOYS IS ABSENT (148)	13 32 6 53 XSQ= 4.80 PHI= 0.215 XP = 0.0284
393	IN ALL CASES ARE THOSE 1.00 OF 6 WHERE EXTRAMARITAL COITUS IS PERMITTED, RATHER THAN PUNISHED (41) F-B	393	TILT TOWARD BEING THOSE 0.55 OF 29 WHERE EXTRAMARITAL COITUS IS PUNISHED, RATHER THAN PERMITTED (43) F-B	0 16 6 13 XSQ= 4.08 PHI= -0.341 EP = 0.0216
395	IN ALL CASES ARE THOSE 1.00 OF 2 WHERE BELIEF IN THE UNCLEANNESS OF WOMEN IS UNIMPORTANT OR ABSENT (15) LWS	395	DRIFT TOWARD BEING THOSE 0.83 OF 12 WHERE BELIEF IN THE UNCLEANNESS OF WOMEN IS PRESENT (18) LWS	0 10 2 2 XSQ= 2.46 PHI= -0.420 EP = 0.0659
399	IN ALL CASES ARE THOSE 1.00 OF 4 WHERE INTENSITY OF CASTRATION ANXIETY IS LOW (22) WNS	399	DRIFT TOWARD BEING THOSE 0.62 OF 13 WHERE INTENSITY OF CASTRATION ANXIETY IS HIGH (23) WNS	0 8 4 5 XSQ= 2.51 PHI= -0.384 EP = 0.0824
427	TILT TOWARD BEING THOSE 0.78 OF 9 WHERE A HIGH GOD, IF PRESENT, IS INACTIVE, RATHER THAN ACTIVE (69) GES,EA	427	TILT TOWARD BEING THOSE 0.65 OF 57 WHERE A HIGH GOD, IF PRESENT, IS ACTIVE, RATHER THAN INACTIVE (87) GES,EA	2 37 7 20 XSQ= 4.23 PHI= -0.253 XP = 0.0398
428	IN ALL CASES ARE THOSE 1.00 OF 2 WHERE A HIGH GOD, IF PRESENT AND ACTIVE, DOES NOT SUPPORT HUMAN MORALITY, RATHER THAN SUPPORTING IT (26) GES,EA	428	DRIFT TOWARD BEING THOSE 0.78 OF 37 WHERE A HIGH GOD, IF PRESENT AND ACTIVE, SUPPORTS HUMAN MORALITY, RATHER THAN NOT SUPPORTING IT (61) GES,EA	0 29 2 8 XSQ= 2.69 PHI= -0.263 EP = 0.0607

214/

```
468  IN ALL CASES ARE THCSE          1.00 OF   6        468  DRIFT LESS TOWARD BEING THCSE  0.56 CF  18             0    8
     WHERE CCNTACT WITH CTHER CULTURES                       WHERE CONTACT WITH OTHER CULTURES                      6   10
     IS REGULAR CR IRREGULAR, RATHER THAN                    IS REGULAR OR IRREGULAR, RATHER THAN            XSQ=     2.25
     FREQUENT  (37) JMH                                      FREQUENT  (37) JMH                              PHI=   -0.306
                                                                                                             EP =   0.0664
```

215 CULTURES
WHERE FIRST CCUSIN MARRIAGE,
IF PERMITTED,
IS DUCLATERAL (85)

215 CULTURES
WHERE FIRST COUSIN MARRIAGE,
IF PERMITTED,
IS OTHER THAN DUOLATERAL (87)

BACKGROUND ON PAGE 117

SUBJECT ONLY

85 IN LEFT CCLUMN

AJIE	ALBANIANS	APINAYE	ASHANTI	BACAIRI	BAMBARA	BEMBA	BHUIYA	BIRIFOR	BLACK CARIB
BORORO	BURYAT	CAMAYURA	CARIB	CHENCHU	COORG	CREE	DILLING	EYAK	GARO
GOND	GUAHIBO	HAIDA	HEHE	HERERO	KARIERA	KERAKI	KERALA	KHASI	LAKALAI
LAKHER	LAMBA	LAU	LOLO	MAGUZAWA	MANCHU	MARQUESANS	MARSHALLESE	MBUNDU	MBUTI
MIAO	MIN CHINESE	MINANGKABAU	MISKITO	MONGUOR	MOTILON	MUNDURUCU	NABESNA	NAMA	NAMBICUARA
NASKAPI	NDEMBU	NGONI	NUPE	NYANEKA	OJIBWA	PONAPEANS	RUNDI	SINHALESE	SIUAI
SWAZI	TAMIL	TANALA	TANIMBARESE	TERA	TODA	TOLOWA	TRUMAI	TSHIMSHIAN	TUCANO
TUCUNA	TUPINAMBA	TURKMEN	TZELTAL	VEDDA	VENDA	WANTOAT	WAPISHANA	WINNEBAGO	WITOTO
WOLOF	YABARANA	YAKO	YAO	YARURO					

87 IN RIGHT CCLUMN

ABOR	AINU	ALACALUF	AMERICANS	ARAUCANIANS	AWEIKOMA	BAJUN	BALINESE	BARABRA	BASSERI
BATAK	BEJA	BELU	BERGDAMA	BOTOCUDO	BOZO	BUDUMA	BURMESE	CALLINAGO	CAMBODIANS
CARAJA	CHIRIGUANO	CHUKCHEE	DUTCH	EGYPTIANS	FON	FUTAJALONKE	GILYAK	GOAJIRO	HASANIA
HAZARA	HEBREWS	HO	HUICHOL	ILA	INCA	JAPANESE	JAVANESE	JIVARO	KABYLE
KACHIN	KASKA	KISSI	KONSO	LAMET	LHOTA NAGA	MACASSARESE	MALAYS	MANDAN	MANIHIKI
MAYA	MENDE	MENTAWEI	MERINA	MINCHIA	MNONG GAR	MURNGIN	NUNIVAK	PATHAN	PENDE
PORTUGUESE	PURUM	REGEIBAT	RIFFIANS	ROMANS	ROTINESE	RWALA	SAMOYED	SANDAWE	SARAMACCA
SHERENTE	SINDHI	SIRIONO	SIWANS	SONGHAI	SOTHO	SUBANUN	SYRIANS	TEHUELCHE	TENDA
THAI	TIBETANS	TIWI	TROBRIAND	WAROPEN	WIKMUNKAN	YAKUT			

198 EXCLUDED BECAUSE IRRELEVANT (SEE RIGHT COLUMN, PARAGRAPH 213)

30 EXCLUDED BECAUSE UNASCERTAINED

---

4 LEAN MORE TOWARD BEING THOSE 0.95 OF 85
LOCATED OUTSIDE OF
THE CIRCUM-MEDITERRANEAN (355)

4 LEAN LESS TOWARD BEING THOSE 0.79 OF 87
LOCATED OUTSIDE OF
THE CIRCUM-MEDITERRANEAN (355)

4 18
81 69
XSQ= 8.47
PHI= -0.222
XP = 0.0036

15 TILT TOWARD BEING THOSE 0.66 OF 85
WHERE THE LATITUDE IS
LESS THAN TWENTY DEGREES (217)

15 TILT TOWARD BEING THOSE 0.51 OF 87
WHERE THE LATITUDE IS
TWENTY DEGREES OR GREATER (183)

29 44
56 43
XSQ= 4.12
PHI= -0.155
XP = 0.0425

33	LEAN MORE TOWARD BEING THOSE 0.95 OF 85 WHERE THE NATURAL ENVIRONMENT IS OTHER THAN 'VERY HARSH,' I.E., DESERT, DESERT GRASSES AND SHRUBS, TUNDRA, OR HIGH PLATEAU STEPPE (341) FWM	33	LEAN LESS TOWARD BEING THOSE 0.78 OF 87 WHERE THE NATURAL ENVIRONMENT IS OTHER THAN 'VERY HARSH,' I.E., DESERT, DESERT GRASSES AND SHRUBS, TUNDRA, OR HIGH PLATEAU STEPPE (341) FWM	4 19 81 68 XSQ= 9.47 PHI= -0.235 XP = 0.0021
36	DRIFT MORE TOWARD BEING THOSE 0.85 OF 85 WHERE THE NATURAL ENVIRONMENT IS OTHER THAN 'VERY HARSH,' OR SUB-TROPICAL BUSH, OR TEMPERATE GRASSLAND (292) FWM	36	DRIFT LESS TOWARD BEING THOSE 0.71 OF 87 WHERE THE NATURAL ENVIRONMENT IS OTHER THAN 'VERY HARSH,' OR SUB-TROPICAL BUSH, OR TEMPERATE GRASSLAND (292) FWM	13 25 72 62 XSQ= 3.77 PHI= -0.148 XP = 0.0523
47	DRIFT TOWARD BEING THOSE 0.55 OF 22 WHERE, IF SETTLEMENTS ARE NON-FIXED, MOVEMENT IS NON-NOMADIC, RATHER THAN NOMADIC (38)	47	DRIFT TOWARD BEING THOSE 0.75 OF 24 WHERE, IF SETTLEMENTS ARE NON-FIXED, MOVEMENT IS NOMADIC, RATHER THAN NON-NOMADIC (72)	10 18 12 6 XSQ= 3.06 PHI= -0.258 XP = 0.0804
53	TILT TOWARD BEING THOSE 0.74 OF 54 WHERE FOOD PRODUCTION IS BY SIMPLE AGRICULTURE OR INCIPIENT FOOD PRODUCTION, RATHER THAN BY INTENSIVE AGRICULTURE (147)	53	TILT TOWARD BEING THOSE 0.50 OF 50 WHERE FOOD PRODUCTION IS BY INTENSIVE AGRICULTURE, RATHER THAN BY SIMPLE AGRICULTURE OR INCIPIENT FOOD PRODUCTION (91)	14 25 40 25 XSQ= 5.43 PHI= -0.229 XP = 0.0198
55	DRIFT TOWARD BEING THOSE 0.64 OF 39 WHERE FOOD PRODUCTION IS BY SIMPLE AGRICULTURE, RATHER THAN BY INTENSIVE AGRICULTURE (101)	55	DRIFT TOWARD BEING THOSE 0.58 OF 43 WHERE FOOD PRODUCTION IS BY INTENSIVE AGRICULTURE, RATHER THAN BY SIMPLE AGRICULTURE (91)	14 25 25 18 XSQ= 3.21 PHI= -0.198 XP = 0.0730
63	DRIFT LESS TOWARD BEING THOSE 0.69 OF 42 WHERE HUSBANDRY, IF PRESENT, IS PRINCIPALLY IN THE FORM OF BOVINE, EQUINE, CAMEL-LIKE, OR DEER-LIKE ANIMALS, RATHER THAN PIGS, SHEEP, OR GOATS (152)	63	DRIFT MORE TOWARD BEING THOSE 0.86 OF 51 WHERE HUSBANDRY, IF PRESENT, IS PRINCIPALLY IN THE FORM OF BOVINE, EQUINE, CAMEL-LIKE, OR DEER-LIKE ANIMALS, RATHER THAN PIGS, SHEEP, OR GOATS (152)	29 44 13 7 XSQ= 3.09 PHI= -0.182 XP = 0.0786
71	DRIFT TOWARD BEING THOSE 0.64 OF 58 WHERE METAL WORKING IS ABSENT (153)	71	DRIFT TOWARD BEING THOSE 0.54 OF 50 WHERE METAL WORKING IS PRESENT (98)	21 27 37 23 XSQ= 2.76 PHI= -0.160 XP = 0.0966
73	DRIFT TOWARD BEING THOSE 0.55 OF 56 WHERE WEAVING IS ABSENT (130)	73	DRIFT TOWARD BEING THOSE 0.65 OF 49 WHERE WEAVING IS PRESENT (118)	25 32 31 17 XSQ= 3.70 PHI= -0.188 XP = 0.0543
80	DRIFT MORE TOWARD BEING THOSE 0.88 OF 50 WHERE NO CITY OR TOWN IS PRESENT (185)	80	DRIFT LESS TOWARD BEING THOSE 0.71 OF 52 WHERE NO CITY OR TOWN IS PRESENT (185)	6 15 44 37 XSQ= 3.45 PHI= -0.184 XP = 0.0631

81	TILT MORE TOWARD BEING THOSE 0.76 OF 50 WHERE NO CITY OR TOWN IS PRESENT, AND THE AVERAGE COMMUNITY SIZE IS SMALLER THAN 200 (135)	81	TILT LESS TOWARD BEING THOSE 0.54 OF 52 WHERE NO CITY OR TOWN IS PRESENT, AND THE AVERAGE COMMUNITY SIZE IS SMALLER THAN 200 (135)	12 24 38 28 XSQ= 4.55 PHI= -0.211 XP = 0.0329
82	DRIFT LESS TOWARD BEING THOSE 0.66 OF 50 WHERE A CITY OR TOWN IS PRESENT, OR THE AVERAGE COMMUNITY SIZE IS FIFTY OR GREATER (178)	82	DRIFT MORE TOWARD BEING THOSE 0.83 OF 52 WHERE A CITY OR TOWN IS PRESENT, OR THE AVERAGE COMMUNITY SIZE IS FIFTY OR GREATER (178)	33 43 17 9 XSQ= 2.91 PHI= -0.169 XP = 0.0879
84	TILT MORE TOWARD BEING THOSE 0.89 OF 66 WHERE THE LEVEL OF POLITICAL INTEGRATION IS THE LITTLE STATE, THE MINIMAL STATE, THE AUTONOMOUS COMMUNITY, OR THE FAMILY (262) GPM	84	TILT LESS TOWARD BEING THOSE 0.73 OF 70 WHERE THE LEVEL OF POLITICAL INTEGRATION IS THE LITTLE STATE, THE MINIMAL STATE, THE AUTONOMOUS COMMUNITY, OR THE FAMILY (262) GPM	7 19 59 51 XSQ= 4.99 PHI= -0.191 XP = 0.0256
85	TILT MORE TOWARD BEING THOSE 0.82 OF 66 WHERE THE LEVEL OF POLITICAL INTEGRATION IS THE MINIMAL STATE, THE AUTONOMOUS COMMUNITY, OR THE FAMILY (234) GPM	85	TILT LESS TOWARD BEING THOSE 0.64 OF 70 WHERE THE LEVEL OF POLITICAL INTEGRATION IS THE MINIMAL STATE, THE AUTONOMOUS COMMUNITY, OR THE FAMILY (234) GPM	12 25 54 45 XSQ= 4.42 PHI= -0.180 XP = 0.0354
87	TILT MORE TOWARD BEING THOSE 0.98 OF 66 WHERE THE LEVEL OF POLITICAL INTEGRATION IS THE LARGE STATE, THE LITTLE STATE, THE MINIMAL STATE, OR THE AUTONOMOUS COMMUNITY (281) GPM	87	TILT LESS TOWARD BEING THOSE 0.89 OF 70 WHERE THE LEVEL OF POLITICAL INTEGRATION IS THE LARGE STATE, THE LITTLE STATE, THE MINIMAL STATE, OR THE AUTONOMOUS COMMUNITY (281) GPM	65 62 1 8 XSQ= 3.92 PHI= 0.170 XP = 0.0478
94	TILT MORE TOWARD BEING THOSE 0.93 OF 71 WHERE THE HIERARCHY OF NATIONAL JURISDICTION HAS TWO, ONE, OR NO LEVELS (296) GES,EA	94	TILT LESS TOWARD BEING THOSE 0.78 OF 67 WHERE THE HIERARCHY OF NATIONAL JURISDICTION HAS TWO, ONE, OR NO LEVELS (296) GES,EA	5 15 66 52 XSQ= 5.37 PHI= -0.197 XP = 0.0205
108	LEAN TOWARD BEING THOSE 0.53 OF 43 WHERE CLASS STRATIFICATION, IF PRESENT, IS BASED ON A HEREDITARY ARISTOCRACY (74)	108	LEAN TOWARD BEING THOSE 0.75 OF 55 WHERE CLASS STRATIFICATION, IF PRESENT, IS BASED ON SOMETHING OTHER THAN A HEREDITARY ARISTOCRACY (129)	23 14 20 41 XSQ= 6.92 PHI= 0.266 XP = 0.0085
109	DRIFT MORE TOWARD BEING THOSE 0.91 OF 74 WHERE CASTES ARE ABSENT (317)	109	DRIFT LESS TOWARD BEING THOSE 0.78 OF 74 WHERE CASTES ARE ABSENT (317)	7 16 67 58 XSQ= 3.29 PHI= -0.149 XP = 0.0695
176	TILT TOWARD BEING THOSE 0.57 OF 84 WHERE THE COMMUNITY IS A CLAN-COMMUNITY OR A COMMUNITY STRUCTURED OR SEGMENTED ON A CLAN BASIS (169)	176	TILT TOWARD BEING THOSE 0.60 OF 81 WHERE THE COMMUNITY IS OTHER THAN A CLAN-COMMUNITY OR A COMMUNITY STRUCTURED OR SEGMENTED ON A CLAN BASIS (213)	48 32 36 49 XSQ= 4.45 PHI= 0.164 XP = 0.0348

177	LEAN LESS TOWARD BEING THOSE WHERE THE COMMUNITY IS OTHER THAN A SINGLE CLAN-COMMUNITY AND EXOGAMOUS (305)	0.67 OF	84	177	LEAN MORE TOWARD BEING THOSE WHERE THE COMMUNITY IS OTHER THAN A SINGLE CLAN-COMMUNITY AND EXOGAMOUS (305)	0.86 OF	81	28 11 56 70 XSQ= 7.85 PHI= 0.218 XP = 0.0051
180	LEAN LESS TOWARD BEING THOSE WHERE THE COMMUNITY IS COMMONLY NON-EXOGAMOUS, RATHER THAN EXOGAMOUS (258)	0.60 OF	84	180	LEAN MORE TOWARD BEING THOSE WHERE THE COMMUNITY IS COMMONLY NON-EXOGAMOUS, RATHER THAN EXOGAMOUS (258)	0.80 OF	81	34 16 50 65 XSQ= 7.43 PHI= 0.212 XP = 0.0064
181	LEAN MORE TOWARD BEING THOSE WHERE THE COMMUNITY IS OTHER THAN A DEME (337)	0.96 OF	84	181	LEAN LESS TOWARD BEING THOSE WHERE THE COMMUNITY IS OTHER THAN A DEME (337)	0.83 OF	81	3 14 81 67 XSQ= 6.97 PHI= -0.206 XP = 0.0083
192	LEAN MORE TOWARD BEING THOSE OTHER THAN WHERE THE ONLY KIN GROUP PRESENT IS A KINDRED OR ELSE BILATERAL DESCENT IS INFERRED (289)	0.93 OF	85	192	LEAN LESS TOWARD BEING THOSE OTHER THAN WHERE THE ONLY KIN GROUP PRESENT IS A KINDRED OR ELSE BILATERAL DESCENT IS INFERRED (289)	0.75 OF	87	6 22 79 65 XSQ= 9.19 PHI= -0.231 XP = 0.0024
220	TEND TO BE THOSE WHERE FIRST COUSIN MARRIAGE IN SOME FORM OR OTHER IS PRESCRIBED OR PREFERRED (97)	0.71 OF	85	220	TEND TO BE THOSE WHERE FIRST COUSIN MARRIAGE IN SOME FORM OR OTHER IS NOT PRESCRIBED OR PREFERRED (273)	0.57 OF	87	60 37 25 50 XSQ= 12.65 PHI= 0.271 XP = 0.0004
224	TILT MORE TOWARD BEING THOSE WHERE COUSIN MARRIAGE IS PREFERENTIALLY OR PERMISSIVELY SYMMETRICAL, RATHER THAN EITHER PATRI- OR MATRILATERAL (106)	0.71 OF	85	224	TILT LESS TOWARD BEING THOSE WHERE COUSIN MARRIAGE IS PREFERENTIALLY OR PERMISSIVELY SYMMETRICAL, RATHER THAN EITHER PATRI- OR MATRILATERAL (106)	0.53 OF	87	25 41 60 46 XSQ= 4.98 PHI= -0.170 XP = 0.0256
225	DRIFT MORE TOWARD BEING THOSE WHERE COUSIN MARRIAGE IS PREFERENTIALLY OR PERMISSIVELY MATRILATERAL, RATHER THAN PATRILATERAL (43)	0.80 OF	25	225	DRIFT LESS TOWARD BEING THOSE WHERE COUSIN MARRIAGE IS PREFERENTIALLY OR PERMISSIVELY MATRILATERAL, RATHER THAN PATRILATERAL (43)	0.56 OF	41	5 18 20 23 XSQ= 2.93 PHI= -0.211 XP = 0.0872
234	TEND TO BE THOSE WHERE THE COUSIN TERMINOLOGY IS OF CROW, OMAHA, OR IROQUOIS TYPE, RATHER THAN ESKIMO OR HAWAIIAN TYPE (152)	0.85 OF	75	234	TEND TO BE THOSE WHERE THE COUSIN TERMINOLOGY IS OF ESKIMO OR HAWAIIAN TYPE, RATHER THAN CROW, OMAHA, OR IROQUOIS TYPE (170)	0.53 OF	53	64 25 11 28 XSQ= 19.59 PHI= 0.391 XP = 0.0000
240	TILT LESS TOWARD BEING THOSE WHERE THE FAMILY, IF EXTENDED, IS SMALL OR STEM, RATHER THAN LARGE (135)	0.54 OF	50	240	TILT MORE TOWARD BEING THOSE WHERE THE FAMILY, IF EXTENDED, IS SMALL OR STEM, RATHER THAN LARGE (135)	0.78 OF	46	23 10 27 36 XSQ= 5.22 PHI= 0.233 XP = 0.0223

315	DRIFT TCWARD BEING THCSE WHERE MOTHER ANC NURSING CHILC CUSTCMARILY SLEEP IN THE SAME BED (37) W-C,S	0.91 OF 11	315	DRIFT TOWARD BEING THOSE WHERE MOTHER AND NURSING CHILD CUSTOMARILY SLEEP IN DIFFERENT BEDS (14) W-D,S	0.55 CF 11	10 5 1 6 XSQ= 3.35 PHI= 0.390 EP = 0.0635
350	TILT TCWARC BEING THCSE WHERE THE CHILD'S INFERREC ANXIETY OVER PERFORMANCE OF ACHIEVEMENT BEHAVIOR IS HIGH (34) B-B-C	0.88 OF 8	350	TILT TOWARD BEING THOSE WHERE THE CHILD'S INFERRED ANXIETY OVER PERFORMANCE OF ACHIEVEMENT BEHAVICR IS LOW (26) B-B-C	0.73 CF 11	7 3 1 8 XSQ= 4.54 PHI= 0.489 EP = 0.0198
351	TILT TCWARD BEING THCSE WHERE THE CHILD'S INFERREC CONFLICT REGARDING ACHIEVEMENT BEHAVIOR IS HIGH (26) B-B-C	0.75 OF 8	351	TILT TOWARD BEING THOSE WHERE THE CHILD'S INFERRED CONFLICT REGARDING ACHIEVEMENT BEHAVIOR IS LOW (34) B-B-C	0.82 OF 11	6 2 2 9 XSQ= 4.02 PHI= 0.460 EP = 0.0237
377	LEAN MORE TOWARC BEING THCSE WHERE MALE GENITAL MUTILATION IS ABSENT (242)	0.83 OF 70	377	LEAN LESS TCWARD BEING THOSE WHERE MALE GENITAL MUTILATICN IS ABSENT (242)	0.62 CF 68	12 26 58 42 XSQ= 6.67 PHI= -0.220 XP = 0.0098
395	IN ALL CASES ARE THCSE WHERE BELIEF IN THE UNCLEANNESS CF WOMEN IS PRESENT (18) LWS	1.00 OF 7	395	DRIFT TOWARD BEING THOSE WHERE BELIEF IN THE UNCLEANNESS OF WOMEN IS UNIMPORTANT OR ABSENT (15) LWS	0.57 CF 7	7 3 0 4 XSQ= 3.15 PHI= 0.474 EP = 0.0699
426	DRIFT TCWARD BEING THCSE WHERE A HIGH GCC IS ABSENT (104) GES,EA	0.50 OF 56	426	DRIFT TOWARD BEING THOSE WHERE A HIGH GOD IS PRESENT (156) GES,EA	0.69 CF 55	28 38 28 17 XSQ= 3.44 PHI= -0.176 XP = 0.0636
427	TILT TCWARD BEING THCSE WHERE A HIGH GCC, IF PRESENT, IS INACTIVE, RATHER THAN ACTIVE (69) GES,EA	0.57 OF 28	427	TILT TOWARD BEING THOSE WHERE A HIGH GCD, IF PRESENT, IS ACTIVE, RATHER THAN INACTIVE (87) GES,EA	0.71 OF 38	12 27 16 11 XSQ= 4.20 PHI= -0.252 XP = 0.0404
439	DRIFT TCWARD BEING THCSE WHERE FEAR OF GHCSTS IS HIGH (30) W-C	0.70 OF 10	439	DRIFT TOWARD BEING THOSE WHERE FEAR OF GHOSTS IS LOW (31) W-C	0.80 OF 10	7 2 3 8 XSQ= 3.23 PHI= 0.402 EP = 0.0698
442	DRIFT TCWARD BEING THCSE WHERE FEAR OF ANIMAL SPIRITS IS LCW (33) W-C	0.70 OF 10	442	DRIFT TOWARD BEING THOSE WHERE FEAR OF ANIMAL SPIRITS IS HIGH (28) W-C	0.80 CF 10	3 8 7 2 XSQ= 3.23 PHI= -0.402 EP = 0.0698

459	TILT TOWARD BEING THOSE WHERE GAMES, IF PRESENT, DO NOT INCLUDE GAMES OF CHANCE (89) R-A-B,EA	0.75 OF 36	459	TILT TOWARD BEING THOSE WHERE GAMES, IF PRESENT, INCLUDE GAMES OF CHANCE (82) R-A-B,EA	0.53 OF 30	9 16 27 14 XSQ= 4.44 PHI= -0.259 XP = 0.0350
477	DRIFT TOWARD BEING THOSE WHERE ALCOHOLIC AGGRESSION IS MODERATE OR SLIGHT (19) DH	0.80 OF 10	477	DRIFT TOWARD BEING THOSE WHERE ALCOHOLIC AGGRESSION IS STRONG (15) DH	0.75 OF 8	2 6 8 2 XSQ= 3.45 PHI= -0.437 EP = 0.0536
480	DRIFT TOWARD BEING THOSE WHERE COMPLEXITY OF ARTISTIC DESIGN IS LOW (15) HB	0.75 OF 4	480	DRIFT TOWARD BEING THOSE WHERE COMPLEXITY OF ARTISTIC DESIGN IS HIGH (14) HB	0.86 OF 7	1 6 3 1 XSQ= 1.86 PHI= -0.411 EP = 0.0879

216 CULTURES
WHERE FIRST CCUSIN MARRIAGE,
IF PERMITTED,
IS TRILATERAL (13)

216 CULTURES
WHERE FIRST COUSIN MARRIAGE,
IF PERMITTED,
IS OTHER THAN TRILATERAL (159)

BACKGROUND ON PAGE 117 SUBJECT ONLY

13 IN LEFT CCLUMN

AINU	FCN	GCAJIRC	JIVARO	MENTAWEI	MERINA	RIFFIANS	RCTINESE	SAMCYEC	SARAMACCA
TENDA	TIBETANS	YAKUT							

159 IN RIGHT CCLUMN

ABOR	AJIE	ALACALUF	ALBANIANS	AMERICANS	APINAYE	ARAUCANIANS	ASHANTI	AWEIKOMA	BACAIRI
BAJUN	BALINESE	BAMBARA	BARABRA	BASSERI	BATAK	BEJA	BELU	BEMBA	BERGDAMA
BHUIYA	BIRIFOR	BLACK CARIB	BORORO	BOTOCUDO	BOZO	BUDUMA	BURMESE	BURYAT	CALLINAGO
CAMAYURA	CAMBODIANS	CARAJA	CARIB	CHENCHU	CHIRIGUANO	CHUKCHEE	COCRG	CREE	DILLING
DUTCH	EGYPTIANS	EYAK	FUTAJALCNKE	GARO	GILYAK	GOND	GUAHIBC	HAIDA	HASANIA
HAZARA	HEBREWS	HEHE	HERERO	HO	HUICHOL	ILA	INCA	JAPANESE	JAVANESE
KABYLE	KACHIN	KARIERA	KASKA	KERAKI	KERALA	KHASI	KISSI	KONSO	LAKALAI
LAKHER	LAMBA	LAMET	LAU	LHOTA NAGA	LOLO	MACASSARESE	MAGUZAWA	MALAYS	MANCHU
MANDAN	MANIHIKI	MARQUESANS	MARSHALLESE	MAYA	MBUNDU	MBUTI	MENDE	MIAC	MIN CHINESE
MINANGKABAU	MINCHIA	MISKITC	MNONG GAR	MONGUOR	MOTILON	MUNDURUCU	MURNGIN	NABESNA	NAMA
NAMBICUARA	NASKAPI	NCEMBU	NGONI	NUNIVAK	NUPE	NYANEKA	OJIBWA	PATHAN	PENDE
PONAPEANS	PORTUGUESE	PURUM	REGEIBAT	ROMANS	RUNDI	RWALA	SANDAWE	SHERENTE	SINDHI
SINHALESE	SIRIONC	SIUAI	SIWANS	SONGHAI	SOTHO	SUBANUN	SWAZI	SYRIANS	TAMIL
TANALA	TANIMBARESE	TEHUELCHE	TERA	THAI	TIWI	TZELTAL	VEDDA	TROBRIAND	TRUMAI
TSHIMSHIAN	TUCANC	TUCUNA	TUPINAMBA	TURKMEN	TZELTAL	VEDDA	VENDA	WANTOAT	WAPISHANA
WARCPEN	WIKMUNKAN	WINNEBAGO	WITOTO	WOLOF	YABARANA	YAKO	YAO	YARURO	

198 EXCLUCED BECAUSE IRRELEVANT (SEE RIGHT COLUMN, PARAGRAPH 213)

30 EXCLUDED BECAUSE UNASCERTAINEC

---

11 DRIFT LESS TCWARC BEING THOSE 0.85 OF 13
WHERE THE LATITUDE IS
LESS THAN SIXTY DEGREES (385)

11 DRIFT MORE TOWARD BEING THCSE 0.97 CF 159
WHERE THE LATITUDE IS
LESS THAN SIXTY DEGREES (385)

2	4
11	155
XSQ=	2.71
PHI=	0.125
XP =	0.0999

220 TILT TCWARD BEING THOSE 0.77 OF 13
WHERE FIRST CCUSIN MARRIAGE
IN SCME FCRM CR CTHER
IS NCT PRESCRIBED CR PREFERREC (273)

22C TILT TOWARD BEING THOSE 0.59 OF 159
WHERE FIRST COUSIN MARRIAGE
IN SOME FORM OR OTHER
IS PRESCRIBED OR PREFERRED (97)

3	94
10	65
XSQ=	4.97
PHI=	-0.170
XP =	0.0258

224	TILT MORE TOWARD BEING THOSE WHERE COUSIN MARRIAGE IS PREFERENTIALLY OR PERMISSIVELY SYMMETRICAL, RATHER THAN EITHER PATRI- OR MATRILATERAL (106)	0.92 OF 13	224	TILT LESS TOWARD BEING THOSE WHERE COUSIN MARRIAGE IS PREFERENTIALLY OR PERMISSIVELY SYMMETRICAL, RATHER THAN EITHER PATRI- OR MATRILATERAL (106)	0.59 OF 159	1 65 12 94 XSQ= 4.28 PHI= -0.158 XP = 0.0385
243	IN ALL CASES ARE THOSE WHERE POLYGYNY, IF PRESENT, HAS A HIGH INCIDENCE (24) W-C,S	1.00 OF 3	243	DRIFT TOWARD BEING THOSE WHERE POLYGYNY, IF PRESENT, HAS A LOW INCIDENCE (36) W-D,S	0.65 OF 23	3 8 0 15 XSQ= 2.34 PHI= 0.300 EP = 0.0635
303	IN ALL CASES ARE THOSE WHERE THE EARLY ORAL SATISFACTION POTENTIAL IS LOW (25) W-C	1.00 OF 4	303	DRIFT TOWARD BEING THOSE WHERE THE EARLY ORAL SATISFACTION POTENTIAL IS HIGH (32) W-C	0.60 OF 15	0 9 4 6 XSQ= 2.47 PHI= -0.361 EP = 0.0867
307	IN ALL CASES ARE THOSE WHERE THE EARLY AGGRESSION SATISFACTION POTENTIAL IS LOW (19) W-C	1.00 OF 4	307	LEAN TOWARD BEING THOSE WHERE THE EARLY AGGRESSION SATISFACTION POTENTIAL IS HIGH (33) W-C	0.85 OF 13	0 11 4 2 XSQ= 6.24 PHI= -0.606 EP = 0.0063
313	IN ALL CASES ARE THOSE WHERE AGGRESSION SOCIALIZATION ANXIETY IS HIGH (26) W-C	1.00 OF 4	313	TILT TOWARD BEING THOSE WHERE AGGRESSION SOCIALIZATION ANXIETY IS LOW (28) W-C	0.69 OF 13	4 4 0 9 XSQ= 3.43 PHI= 0.449 EP = 0.0294
320	IN ALL CASES ARE THOSE WHERE THE DEGREE OF REDUCTION OF THE INFANT'S DRIVES IS LOW (24) B-B-C	1.00 OF 3	320	DRIFT TOWARD BEING THOSE WHERE THE DEGREE OF REDUCTION OF THE INFANT'S DRIVES IS HIGH (45) B-B-C	0.62 OF 21	0 13 3 8 XSQ= 1.94 PHI= -0.284 EP = 0.0815
321	IN ALL CASES ARE THOSE WHERE THE IMMEDIACY OF REDUCTION OF THE INFANT'S DRIVES IS LOW (25) B-B-C	1.00 OF 3	321	DRIFT TOWARD BEING THOSE WHERE THE IMMEDIACY OF REDUCTION OF THE INFANT'S DRIVES IS HIGH (35) B-B-C	0.69 OF 16	0 11 3 5 XSQ= 2.48 PHI= -0.362 EP = 0.0578
350	IN ALL CASES ARE THOSE WHERE THE CHILD'S INFERRED ANXIETY OVER PERFORMANCE OF ACHIEVEMENT BEHAVIOR IS LOW (26) B-B-C	1.00 OF 3	350	DRIFT TOWARD BEING THOSE WHERE THE CHILD'S INFERRED ANXIETY OVER PERFORMANCE OF ACHIEVEMENT BEHAVIOR IS HIGH (34) B-B-C	0.63 OF 16	0 10 3 6 XSQ= 1.85 PHI= -0.312 EP = 0.0867
373	IN ALL CASES ARE THOSE WHERE MALE INITIATION CEREMONIES AT PUBERTY ARE PRESENT (17) W-K-A	1.00 OF 2	373	DRIFT TOWARD BEING THOSE WHERE MALE INITIATION CEREMONIES AT PUBERTY ARE ABSENT (27) W-K-A	0.85 OF 13	2 2 0 11 XSQ= 2.76 PHI= 0.429 EP = 0.0571

```
399  IN ALL CASES ARE THOSE           1.00 OF   3     399  DRIFT TOWARD BEING THOSE        0.64 OF  14          3     5
     WHERE INTENSITY OF CASTRATION ANXIETY                 WHERE INTENSITY OF CASTRATION ANXIETY                 0     9
     IS HIGH  (23) WNS                                     IS LOW  (22) WNS                              XSQ=     1.92
                                                                                                         PHI=    0.336
                                                                                                         EP =   0.0824

402  IN ALL CASES ARE THOSE           1.00 OF   5     402  TILT TOWARD BEING THOSE         0.60 OF  15          5     6
     WHERE EXPLANATIONS OF ILLNESS                         WHERE EXPLANATIONS OF ILLNESS                         0     9
     OF AN ORAL NATURE                                     OF AN ORAL NATURE                             XSQ=     3.30
     ARE PRESENT  (31) W-C                                 ARE ABSENT  (30) W-C                          PHI=    0.406
                                                                                                         EP =   0.0379

428  TILT TOWARD BEING THOSE          0.75 OF   4     428  TILT TOWARD BEING THOSE         0.80 OF  35          1    28
     WHERE A HIGH GOD, IF PRESENT AND ACTIVE,              WHERE A HIGH GOD, IF PRESENT AND ACTIVE,              3     7
     DOES NOT SUPPORT HUMAN MORALITY,                      SUPPORTS HUMAN MORALITY, RATHER THAN          XSQ=     3.18
     RATHER THAN SUPPORTING IT  (26) GES,EA                NOT SUPPORTING IT  (61) GES,EA                PHI=   -0.285
                                                                                                         EP =   0.0449

442  IN ALL CASES ARE THOSE           1.00 OF   5     442  TILT TOWARD BEING THOSE         0.60 OF  15          5     6
     WHERE FEAR OF ANIMAL SPIRITS                          WHERE FEAR OF ANIMAL SPIRITS                          0     9
     IS HIGH  (28) W-C                                     IS LOW  (33) W-C                              XSQ=     3.30
                                                                                                         PHI=    0.406
                                                                                                         EP =   0.0379
```

```
********************************************************************************************************

217  CULTURES                                          217  CULTURES
     WHERE FIRST COUSIN MARRIAGE,                           WHERE FIRST COUSIN MARRIAGE,
     IF PERMITTED,                                          IF PERMITTED,
     IS QUADRILATERAL  (46)                                 IS OTHER THAN QUADRILATERAL  (126)


BACKGROUND ON PAGE 117                                                                     SUBJECT ONLY
........................................................................................................

     46  IN LEFT COLUMN

ALACALUF    AMERICANS   AWEIKOMA    BAJUN       BALINESE    BARABRA     BASSERI     BEJA        BERGDAMA    BOTOCUDO
BOZO        BUDUMA      BURMESE     CAMBODIANS  CARAJA      CHIRIGUANO  CHUKCHEE    DUTCH       EGYPTIANS   FUTAJALONKE
HASANIA     HAZARA      HEBREWS     HUICHOL     INCA        JAPANESE    JAVANESE    KABYLE      MACASSARESE MALAYS
MANIHIKI    MINCHIA     NUNIVAK     PATHAN      PORTUGUESE  REGEIBAT    ROMANS      RWALA       SINDHI      SIWANS
SONGHAI     SOTHO       SUBANUN     SYRIANS     TEHUELCHE   THAI

    126  IN RIGHT COLUMN

ABOR        AINU        AJIE        ALBANIANS   APINAYE     ARAUCANIANS ASHANTI     BACAIRI     BAMBARA     BATAK
BELU        BEMBA       BHUIYA      BIRIFOR     BLACK CARIB BORORO      BURYAT      CALLINAGO   CAMAYURA    CARIB
CHENCHU     COORG       CREE        DILLING     EYAK        FON         GARO        GILYAK      GOAJIRO     GOND
GUAHIBO     HAIDA       HEHE        HERERO      HO          ILA         JIVARO      KACHIN      KARIERA     KASKA
KERAKI      KERALA      KHASI       KISSI       KONSO       LAKALAI     LAKHER      LAMBA       LAMET       LAU
LHOTA NAGA  LOLO        MAGUZAWA    MANCHU      MANDAN      MARQUESANS  MARSHALLESE MAYA        MBUNDU      MBUTI
MENDE       MENTAWEI    MERINA      MIAO        MIN CHINESE MINANGKABAU MISKITO     MNONG GAR   MONGUOR     MOTILON
MUNDURUCU   MURNGIN     NABESNA     NAMA        NAMBICUARA  NASKAPI     NDEMBU      NGONI       NUPE        NYANEKA
OJIBWA      PENDE       PONAPEANS   PURUM       RIFFIANS    ROTINESE    RUNDI       SAMOYED     SANDAWE     SARAMACCA
SHERENTE    SINHALESE   SIRIONO     SIUAI       SWAZI       TAMIL       TANALA      TANIMBARESE TENDA       TERA
TIBETANS    TIWI        TODA        TOLOWA      TROBRIAND   TRUMAI      TSHIMSHIAN  TUCANO      TUCUNA      TUPINAMBA
TURKMEN     TZELTAL     VEDDA       VENDA       WANTOAT     WAPISHANA   WAROPEN     WIKMUNKAN   WINNEBAGO   WITOTO
WOLOF       YABARANA    YAKO        YAKUT       YAO         YARURO

    198  EXCLUDED BECAUSE IRRELEVANT (SEE RIGHT COLUMN, PARAGRAPH 213)

     30  EXCLUDED BECAUSE UNASCERTAINED

--------------------------------------------------------------------------------------------------------
  4  TEND LESS TO BE THOSE           0.65 OF  46       4  TEND MORE TO BE THOSE          0.95 OF 126          16    6
     LOCATED OUTSIDE OF                                   LOCATED OUTSIDE OF                                   30  120
     THE CIRCUM-MEDITERRANEAN  (355)                      THE CIRCUM-MEDITERRANEAN  (355)               XSQ=   24.60
                                                                                                        PHI=   0.378
                                                                                                        XP =  0.0000

 15  LEAN TOWARD BEING THOSE         0.63 OF  46      15  LEAN TOWARD BEING THOSE        0.65 OF 126          29   44
     WHERE THE LATITUDE IS                                WHERE THE LATITUDE IS                                17   82
     TWENTY DEGREES OR GREATER  (183)                     LESS THAN TWENTY DEGREES  (217)               XSQ=    9.79
                                                                                                        PHI=   0.239
                                                                                                        XP =  0.0018
```

33	TEND LESS TO BE THOSE 0.67 OF 46 WHERE THE NATURAL ENVIRONMENT IS OTHER THAN 'VERY HARSH,' I.E., DESERT, DESERT GRASSES AND SHRUBS, TUNDRA, OR HIGH PLATEAU STEPPE (341) FWM	33	TEND MORE TO BE THOSE 0.94 OF 126 WHERE THE NATURAL ENVIRONMENT IS OTHER THAN 'VERY HARSH,' I.E., DESERT, DESERT GRASSES AND SHRUBS, TUNDRA, OR HIGH PLATEAU STEPPE (341) FWM	15 8 31 118 XSQ= 17.86 PHI= 0.322 XP = 0.0000
36	TEND LESS TO BE THOSE 0.59 OF 46 WHERE THE NATURAL ENVIRONMENT IS OTHER THAN 'VERY HARSH,' OR SUB-TROPICAL BUSH, OR TEMPERATE GRASSLAND (292) FWM	36	TEND MORE TO BE THOSE 0.85 OF 126 WHERE THE NATURAL ENVIRONMENT IS OTHER THAN 'VERY HARSH,' OR SUB-TROPICAL BUSH, OR TEMPERATE GRASSLAND (292) FWM	19 19 27 107 XSQ= 11.98 PHI= 0.264 XP = 0.0005
42	DRIFT MORE TOWARD BEING THOSE 0.72 OF 46 WHERE THE NATURAL ENVIRONMENT IS OTHER THAN TROPICAL OR SUB-TROPICAL RAIN FOREST, OR MONSOON FOREST (244) FWM	42	DRIFT LESS TOWARD BEING THOSE 0.54 OF 126 WHERE THE NATURAL ENVIRONMENT IS OTHER THAN TROPICAL OR SUB-TROPICAL RAIN FOREST, OR MONSOON FOREST (244) FWM	13 58 33 68 XSQ= 3.69 PHI= -0.146 XP = 0.0548
53	TEND TO BE THOSE 0.78 OF 27 WHERE FOOD PRODUCTION IS BY INTENSIVE AGRICULTURE, RATHER THAN BY SIMPLE AGRICULTURE OR INCIPIENT FOOD PRODUCTION (91)	53	TEND TO BE THOSE 0.77 OF 77 WHERE FOOD PRODUCTION IS BY SIMPLE AGRICULTURE OR INCIPIENT FOOD PRODUCTION, RATHER THAN BY INTENSIVE AGRICULTURE (147)	21 18 6 59 XSQ= 22.97 PHI= 0.470 XP = 0.0000
55	TEND TO BE THOSE 0.84 OF 25 WHERE FOOD PRODUCTION IS BY INTENSIVE AGRICULTURE, RATHER THAN BY SIMPLE AGRICULTURE (91)	55	TEND TO BE THOSE 0.68 OF 57 WHERE FOOD PRODUCTION IS BY SIMPLE AGRICULTURE, RATHER THAN BY INTENSIVE AGRICULTURE (101)	21 18 4 39 XSQ= 17.10 PHI= 0.457 XP = 0.0000
63	TILT MORE TOWARD BEING THOSE 0.93 OF 30 WHERE HUSBANDRY, IF PRESENT, IS PRINCIPALLY IN THE FORM OF BOVINE, EQUINE, CAMEL-LIKE, OR DEER-LIKE ANIMALS, RATHER THAN PIGS, SHEEP, OR GOATS (152)	63	TILT LESS TOWARD BEING THOSE 0.71 OF 63 WHERE HUSBANDRY, IF PRESENT, IS PRINCIPALLY IN THE FORM OF BOVINE, EQUINE, CAMEL-LIKE, OR DEER-LIKE ANIMALS, RATHER THAN PIGS, SHEEP, OR GOATS (152)	28 45 2 18 XSQ= 4.55 PHI= 0.221 XP = 0.0329
81	TEND TO BE THOSE 0.64 OF 28 WHERE A CITY OR TOWN IS PRESENT, OR THE AVERAGE COMMUNITY SIZE IS 200 OR GREATER (89)	81	TEND TO BE THOSE 0.76 OF 74 WHERE NO CITY OR TOWN IS PRESENT, AND THE AVERAGE COMMUNITY SIZE IS SMALLER THAN 200 (135)	18 18 10 56 XSQ= 12.51 PHI= 0.350 XP = 0.0004
83	TILT LESS TOWARD BEING THOSE 0.63 OF 16 WHERE, WITH NO CITY AND NO TOWN PRESENT, THE AVERAGE COMMUNITY SIZE IS SMALLER THAN 200, RATHER THAN BETWEEN 200 AND 999 (135)	83	TILT MORE TOWARD BEING THOSE 0.89 OF 63 WHERE, WITH NO CITY AND NO TOWN PRESENT, THE AVERAGE COMMUNITY SIZE IS SMALLER THAN 200, RATHER THAN BETWEEN 200 AND 999 (135)	6 7 10 56 XSQ= 4.69 PHI= 0.244 XP = 0.0304
85	TEND TO BE THOSE 0.54 OF 35 WHERE THE LEVEL OF POLITICAL INTEGRATION IS THE LARGE STATE, OR THE LITTLE STATE (70) GPM	85	TEND TO BE THOSE 0.82 OF 101 WHERE THE LEVEL OF POLITICAL INTEGRATION IS THE MINIMAL STATE, THE AUTONOMOUS COMMUNITY, OR THE FAMILY (234) GPM	19 18 16 83 XSQ= 15.66 PHI= 0.339 XP = 0.0001

86	DRIFT TOWARD BEING THOSE 0.66 OF 35 WHERE THE LEVEL OF POLITICAL INTEGRATION IS THE LARGE STATE, THE LITTLE STATE, OR THE MINIMAL STATE (148) GPM	86	DRIFT TOWARD BEING THOSE 0.52 OF 101 WHERE THE LEVEL OF POLITICAL INTEGRATION IS THE AUTONOMOUS COMMUNITY, OR THE FAMILY (156) GPM	23 48 12 53 XSQ= 2.76 PHI= 0.142 XP = 0.0969
88	LEAN TOWARD BEING THOSE 0.59 OF 29 WHERE, IF A HEADMANSHIP IS PRESENT, SUCCESSION IS NON-HEREDITARY (106)	88	LEAN TOWARD BEING THOSE 0.72 OF 93 WHERE, IF A HEADMANSHIP IS PRESENT, SUCCESSION IS HEREDITARY (165)	17 26 12 67 XSQ= 7.81 PHI= 0.253 XP = 0.0052
90	IN ALL CASES ARE THOSE 1.00 OF 12 WHERE, IF A HEREDITARY HEADMANSHIP IS PRESENT, SUCCESSION IS PATRILINEAL, RATHER THAN MATRILINEAL (127)	90	TILT LESS TOWARD BEING THOSE 0.64 OF 67 WHERE, IF A HEREDITARY HEADMANSHIP IS PRESENT, SUCCESSION IS PATRILINEAL, RATHER THAN MATRILINEAL (127)	12 43 0 24 XSQ= 4.60 PHI= 0.241 XP = 0.0320
95	LEAN TOWARD BEING THOSE 0.50 OF 36 WHERE THE HIERARCHY OF NATIONAL JURISDICTION HAS FOUR, THREE, OR TWO LEVELS (76) GES,EA	95	LEAN TOWARD BEING THOSE 0.79 OF 102 WHERE THE HIERARCHY OF NATIONAL JURISDICTION HAS ONE OR NO LEVELS (254) GES,EA	18 21 18 81 XSQ= 9.95 PHI= 0.269 XP = 0.0016
102	TILT MORE TOWARD BEING THOSE 0.73 OF 45 WHERE CLASS STRATIFICATION IS PRESENT (203)	102	TILT LESS TOWARD BEING THOSE 0.53 OF 122 WHERE CLASS STRATIFICATION IS PRESENT (203)	33 65 12 57 XSQ= 4.66 PHI= 0.167 XP = 0.0309
107	LEAN LESS TOWARD BEING THOSE 0.52 OF 33 WHERE CLASS STRATIFICATION, IF PRESENT, IS BASED ON SOMETHING OTHER THAN OCCUPATIONAL STATUS (160)	107	LEAN MORE TOWARD BEING THOSE 0.85 OF 65 WHERE CLASS STRATIFICATION, IF PRESENT, IS BASED ON SOMETHING OTHER THAN OCCUPATIONAL STATUS (160)	16 10 17 55 XSQ= 10.66 PHI= 0.330 XP = 0.0011
108	LEAN MORE TOWARD BEING THOSE 0.85 OF 33 WHERE CLASS STRATIFICATION, IF PRESENT, IS BASED ON SOMETHING OTHER THAN A HEREDITARY ARISTOCRACY (129)	108	LEAN LESS TOWARD BEING THOSE 0.51 OF 65 WHERE CLASS STRATIFICATION, IF PRESENT, IS BASED ON SOMETHING OTHER THAN A HEREDITARY ARISTOCRACY (129)	5 32 28 33 XSQ= 9.42 PHI= -0.310 XP = 0.0022
109	LEAN LESS TOWARD BEING THOSE 0.66 OF 35 WHERE CASTES ARE ABSENT (317)	109	LEAN MORE TOWARD BEING THOSE 0.90 OF 113 WHERE CASTES ARE ABSENT (317)	12 11 23 102 XSQ= 10.47 PHI= 0.266 XP = 0.0012
127	IN ALL CASES ARE THOSE 1.00 OF 8 WHERE THE FEMALES' CONTRIBUTION TO SUBSISTENCE IS LOW (32) JKB	127	TILT LESS TOWARD BEING THOSE 0.52 OF 21 WHERE THE FEMALES' CONTRIBUTION TO SUBSISTENCE IS LOW (32) JKB	0 10 8 11 XSQ= 3.90 PHI= -0.367 EP = 0.0265

128	DRIFT MORE TOWARD BEING THOSE 0.91 OF 11 WHERE, IF SUBSISTENCE IS PRIMARILY BY AGRICULTURE, THE WORK IS MAINLY DONE BY MALES (40)	128	DRIFT LESS TOWARD BEING THOSE 0.56 OF 27 WHERE, IF SUBSISTENCE IS PRIMARILY BY AGRICULTURE, THE WORK IS MAINLY DONE BY MALES (40)	10 15 1 12 XSQ= 2.91 PHI= 0.277 EP = 0.0597
176	TEND TO BE THOSE 0.83 OF 42 WHERE THE COMMUNITY IS OTHER THAN A CLAN-COMMUNITY OR A COMMUNITY STRUCTURED OR SEGMENTED ON A CLAN BASIS (213)	176	TEND TO BE THOSE 0.59 OF 123 WHERE THE COMMUNITY IS A CLAN-COMMUNITY OR A COMMUNITY STRUCTURED OR SEGMENTED ON A CLAN BASIS (169)	7 73 35 50 XSQ= 21.16 PHI= -0.358 XP = 0.0000
177	TILT MORE TOWARD BEING THOSE 0.90 OF 42 WHERE THE COMMUNITY IS OTHER THAN A SINGLE CLAN-COMMUNITY AND EXOGAMOUS (305)	177	TILT LESS TOWARD BEING THOSE 0.72 OF 123 WHERE THE COMMUNITY IS OTHER THAN A SINGLE CLAN-COMMUNITY AND EXOGAMOUS (305)	4 35 38 88 XSQ= 5.21 PHI= -0.178 XP = 0.0224
178	LEAN MORE TOWARD BEING THOSE 0.93 OF 42 WHERE THE COMMUNITY IS OTHER THAN SEGMENTED ON A CLAN BASIS AND NON-EXOGAMOUS (295)	178	LEAN LESS TOWARD BEING THOSE 0.71 OF 123 WHERE THE COMMUNITY IS OTHER THAN SEGMENTED ON A CLAN BASIS AND NON-EXOGAMOUS (295)	3 36 39 87 XSQ= 7.31 PHI= -0.210 XP = 0.0069
180	TILT MORE TOWARD BEING THOSE 0.86 OF 42 WHERE THE COMMUNITY IS COMMONLY NON-EXOGAMOUS, RATHER THAN EXOGAMOUS (258)	180	TILT LESS TOWARD BEING THOSE 0.64 OF 123 WHERE THE COMMUNITY IS COMMONLY NON-EXOGAMOUS, RATHER THAN EXOGAMOUS (258)	6 44 36 79 XSQ= 5.86 PHI= -0.189 XP = 0.0154
181	TEND LESS TO BE THOSE 0.71 OF 42 WHERE THE COMMUNITY IS OTHER THAN A DEME (337)	181	TEND MORE TO BE THOSE 0.96 OF 123 WHERE THE COMMUNITY IS OTHER THAN A DEME (337)	12 5 30 118 XSQ= 17.78 PHI= 0.328 XP = 0.0000
182	TILT TOWARD BEING THOSE 0.50 OF 42 WHERE THE COMMUNITY IS STRUCTURED ON A NON-CLAN BASIS AND AGAMOUS (126)	182	TILT TOWARD BEING THOSE 0.69 OF 123 OTHER THAN WHERE THE COMMUNITY IS STRUCTURED ON A NON-CLAN BASIS AND AGAMOUS (256)	21 38 21 85 XSQ= 4.18 PHI= 0.159 XP = 0.0409
183	IN ALL CASES ARE THOSE 1.00 OF 21 WHERE THE LARGEST NON-COGNATIC KIN GROUP IS SMALLER THAN A MOEITY, I. E., A PHRATRY OR SIB OR LINEAGE (218)	183	DRIFT LESS TOWARD BEING THOSE 0.82 OF 107 WHERE THE LARGEST NON-COGNATIC KIN GROUP IS SMALLER THAN A MOEITY, I. E., A PHRATRY OR SIB OR LINEAGE (218)	0 19 21 88 XSQ= 3.09 PHI= -0.155 XP = 0.0789
185	DRIFT LESS TOWARD BEING THOSE 0.62 OF 21 WHERE THE LARGEST NON-COGNATIC KIN GROUP IS THE MOEITY OR PHRATRY OR SIB (194)	185	DRIFT MORE TOWARD BEING THOSE 0.81 OF 107 WHERE THE LARGEST NON-COGNATIC KIN GROUP IS THE MOEITY OR PHRATRY OR SIB (194)	13 87 8 20 XSQ= 2.82 PHI= -0.148 XP = 0.0934

187	IN ALL CASES ARE THOSE WHERE THE KIN GROUP IS OTHER THAN EXCLUSIVELY MATRILINEAL (344)	1.00 OF 46	187	TEND LESS TO BE THOSE WHERE THE KIN GROUP IS OTHER THAN EXCLUSIVELY MATRILINEAL (344)	0.76 OF 125	0 30 46 95 XSQ= 11.78 PHI= -0.262 XP = 0.0006
188	TEND TO BE THOSE WHERE THE KIN GROUP IS EXCLUSIVELY COGNATIC (148)	0.54 OF 46	188	TEND TO BE THOSE WHERE THE KIN GROUP IS OTHER THAN EXCLUSIVELY COGNATIC (252)	0.85 OF 126	25 19 21 107 XSQ= 25.27 PHI= 0.383 XP = 0.0000
190	IN ALL CASES ARE THOSE WHERE THE KIN GROUP IS PATRILINEAL OR DOUBLE-DESCENT, RATHER THAN MATRILINEAL (186)	1.00 OF 21	190	LEAN LESS TOWARD BEING THOSE WHERE THE KIN GROUP IS PATRILINEAL OR DOUBLE-DESCENT, RATHER THAN MATRILINEAL (186)	0.68 OF 104	21 71 0 33 XSQ= 7.49 PHI= 0.245 XP = 0.0062
192	TEND LESS TO BE THOSE OTHER THAN WHERE THE ONLY KIN GROUP PRESENT IS A KINDRED OR ELSE BILATERAL DESCENT IS INFERRED (289)	0.52 OF 46	192	TEND MORE TO BE THOSE OTHER THAN WHERE THE ONLY KIN GROUP PRESENT IS A KINDRED OR ELSE BILATERAL DESCENT IS INFERRED (289)	0.95 OF 126	22 6 24 120 XSQ= 42.75 PHI= 0.499 XP = 0.
197	TILT LESS TOWARD BEING THOSE WHERE RULES FOR THE INHERITANCE OF REAL PROPERTY, IF PRESENT, FAVOR EITHER THE MALE HEIR OR LINE, OR THE FEMALE HEIR OR LINE (165)	0.71 OF 24	197	TILT MORE TOWARD BEING THOSE WHERE RULES FOR THE INHERITANCE OF REAL PROPERTY, IF PRESENT, FAVOR EITHER THE MALE HEIR OR LINE, OR THE FEMALE HEIR OR LINE (165)	0.93 OF 56	17 52 7 4 XSQ= 5.14 PHI= -0.253 XP = 0.0234
198	IN ALL CASES ARE THOSE WHERE RULES FOR THE INHERITANCE OF REAL PROPERTY, IF PRESENT, FAVOR THE MALE HEIR OR LINE, RATHER THAN THE FEMALE (144)	1.00 OF 17	198	DRIFT LESS TOWARD BEING THOSE WHERE RULES FOR THE INHERITANCE OF REAL PROPERTY, IF PRESENT, FAVOR THE MALE HEIR OR LINE, RATHER THAN THE FEMALE (144)	0.77 OF 52	17 40 0 12 XSQ= 3.28 PHI= 0.218 XP = 0.0702
201	LEAN LESS TOWARD BEING THOSE WHERE MARITAL RESIDENCE IS NON-OPTIONAL, RATHER THAN AMBILOCAL OR NEOLOCAL (334)	0.78 OF 45	201	LEAN MORE TOWARD BEING THOSE WHERE MARITAL RESIDENCE IS NON-OPTIONAL, RATHER THAN AMBILOCAL OR NEOLOCAL (334)	0.94 OF 125	35 118 10 7 XSQ= 8.40 PHI= -0.222 XP = 0.0038
204	LEAN LESS TOWARD BEING THOSE WHERE MARITAL RESIDENCE IS PATRILOCAL, VIRILOCAL, OR AVUNCULOCAL, RATHER THAN AMBILOCAL OR NEOLOCAL (270)	0.76 OF 41	204	LEAN MORE TOWARD BEING THOSE WHERE MARITAL RESIDENCE IS PATRILOCAL, VIRILOCAL, OR AVUNCULOCAL, RATHER THAN AMBILOCAL OR NEOLOCAL (270)	0.93 OF 104	31 97 10 7 XSQ= 7.24 PHI= -0.223 XP = 0.0071
207	TILT TOWARD BEING THOSE WHERE MARITAL RESIDENCE IS AMBILOCAL OR NEOLOCAL, RATHER THAN MATRILOCAL OR UXORILOCAL (64)	0.71 OF 14	207	TILT TOWARD BEING THOSE WHERE MARITAL RESIDENCE IS MATRILOCAL OR UXORILOCAL, RATHER THAN AMBILOCAL OR NEOLOCAL (64)	0.75 OF 28	4 21 10 7 XSQ= 6.53 PHI= -0.394 XP = 0.0106

210	IN ALL CASES ARE THOSE WHERE MARITAL RESIDENCE IS PATRILOCAL, RATHER THAN MATRILOCAL (169)	1.00 OF 20	210	DRIFT LESS TOWARD BEING THOSE WHERE MARITAL RESIDENCE IS PATRILOCAL, RATHER THAN MATRILOCAL (169)	0.82 OF 78	20 64 0 14 XSQ= 2.85 PHI= 0.171 XP = 0.0913
220	TEND TO BE THOSE WHERE FIRST COUSIN MARRIAGE IN SOME FORM OR OTHER IS NOT PRESCRIBED OR PREFERRED (273)	0.70 OF 46	220	TEND TO BE THOSE WHERE FIRST COUSIN MARRIAGE IN SOME FORM OR OTHER IS PRESCRIBED OR PREFERRED (97)	0.66 OF 126	14 83 32 43 XSQ= 15.80 PHI= -0.303 XP = 0.0001
221	IN ALL CASES ARE THOSE WHERE MATRILATERAL CROSS-COUSIN MARRIAGE IS NOT PRESCRIBED OR PREFERRED (335)	1.00 OF 46	221	TEND LESS TO BE THOSE WHERE MATRILATERAL CROSS-COUSIN MARRIAGE IS NOT PRESCRIBED OR PREFERRED (335)	0.72 OF 126	0 35 46 91 XSQ= 14.37 PHI= -0.289 XP = 0.0001
224	DRIFT MORE TOWARD BEING THOSE WHERE COUSIN MARRIAGE IS PREFERENTIALLY OR PERMISSIVELY SYMMETRICAL, RATHER THAN EITHER PATRI- OR MATRILATERAL (106)	0.74 OF 46	224	DRIFT LESS TOWARD BEING THOSE WHERE COUSIN MARRIAGE IS PREFERENTIALLY OR PERMISSIVELY SYMMETRICAL, RATHER THAN EITHER PATRI- OR MATRILATERAL (106)	0.57 OF 126	12 54 34 72 XSQ= 3.33 PHI= -0.139 XP = 0.0680
225	IN ALL CASES ARE THOSE WHERE COUSIN MARRIAGE IS PREFERENTIALLY OR PERMISSIVELY PATRILATERAL, RATHER THAN MATRILATERAL (23)	1.00 OF 12	225	TEND TO BE THOSE WHERE COUSIN MARRIAGE IS PREFERENTIALLY OR PERMISSIVELY MATRILATERAL, RATHER THAN PATRILATERAL (43)	0.80 OF 54	12 11 0 43 XSQ= 24.03 PHI= 0.603 XP = 0.0000
234	TEND TO BE THOSE WHERE THE COUSIN TERMINOLOGY IS OF ESKIMO OR HAWAIIAN TYPE, RATHER THAN CROW, OMAHA, OR IROQUOIS TYPE (170)	0.81 OF 26	234	TEND TO BE THOSE WHERE THE COUSIN TERMINOLOGY IS OF CROW, OMAHA, OR IROQUOIS TYPE, RATHER THAN ESKIMO OR HAWAIIAN TYPE (152)	0.82 OF 102	5 84 21 18 XSQ= 36.04 PHI= -0.531 XP = 0.
240	LEAN MORE TOWARD BEING THOSE WHERE THE FAMILY, IF EXTENDED, IS SMALL OR STEM, RATHER THAN LARGE (135)	0.92 OF 25	240	LEAN LESS TOWARD BEING THOSE WHERE THE FAMILY, IF EXTENDED, IS SMALL OR STEM, RATHER THAN LARGE (135)	0.56 OF 71	2 31 23 40 XSQ= 8.90 PHI= -0.305 XP = 0.0028
317	IN ALL CASES ARE THOSE WHERE DISPLAY OF AFFECTION TOWARD THE INFANT IS HIGH (39) B-B-C	1.00 OF 3	317	DRIFT TOWARD BEING THOSE WHERE DISPLAY OF AFFECTION TOWARD THE INFANT IS LOW (29) B-B-C	0.62 OF 21	3 8 0 13 XSQ= 1.94 PHI= 0.284 EP = 0.0815
370	LEAN TOWARD BEING THOSE WHERE THE SEGREGATION OF ADOLESCENT BOYS IS ABSENT (148)	0.88 OF 24	370	LEAN TOWARD BEING THOSE WHERE THE SEGREGATION OF ADOLESCENT BOYS IS COMPLETE OR PARTIAL (95)	0.52 OF 80	3 42 21 38 XSQ= 10.46 PHI= -0.317 XP = 0.0012

```
377  LEAN LESS TOWARD BEING THOSE     0.51 OF  37    377  LEAN MORE TOWARD BEING THOSE     0.80 OF 101          18    20
     WHERE MALE GENITAL MUTILATION                        WHERE MALE GENITAL MUTILATION                          19    81
     IS ABSENT  (242)                                     IS ABSENT  (242)                               XSQ=      9.89
                                                                                                         PHI=     0.268
                                                                                                         XP =    0.0017

390  TEND TO BE THOSE                 0.58 OF  19    390  TEND TO BE THOSE                 0.86 OF  56          11     8
     WHERE PREMARITAL SEX RELATIONS ARE                   WHERE PREMARITAL SEX RELATIONS ARE                      8    48
     STRONGLY PUNISHED AND                                WEAKLY PUNISHED AND IN FACT NOT RARE OR        XSQ=     12.05
     IN FACT RARE  (47) JTW,EA                            PUNISHED ONLY IF PREGNANCY RESULTS, OR         PHI=     0.401
                                                          FREELY PERMITTED  (132) JTW,EA                 XP =    0.0005

391  TEND TO BE THOSE                 0.79 OF  19    391  TEND TO BE THOSE                 0.71 OF  56          15    16
     WHERE PREMARITAL SEX RELATIONS ARE                   WHERE PREMARITAL SEX RELATIONS ARE                      4    40
     STRONGLY PUNISHED AND IN FACT RARE, OR               PUNISHED ONLY IF PREGNANCY RESULTS, OR         XSQ=     12.84
     WEAKLY PUNISHED AND                                  FREELY PERMITTED  (90) JTW,EA                  PHI=     0.414
     IN FACT NOT RARE  (89) JTW,EA                                                                       XP =    0.0003

392  TILT TOWARD BEING THOSE          0.79 OF  19    392  TILT TOWARD BEING THOSE          0.54 OF  56          15    26
     WHERE PREMARITAL SEX RELATIONS ARE                   WHERE PREMARITAL SEX RELATIONS ARE                      4    30
     STRONGLY PUNISHED AND IN FACT RARE, OR               FREELY PERMITTED  (67) JTW,EA                  XSQ=      4.81
     WEAKLY PUNISHED AND IN FACT NOT RARE, OR                                                            PHI=     0.253
     PUNISHED ONLY IF                                                                                    XP =    0.0283
     PREGNANCY RESULTS  (112) JTW,EA

426  TILT MORE TOWARD BEING THOSE     0.77 OF  30    426  TILT LESS TOWARD BEING THOSE     0.53 OF  81          23    43
     WHERE A HIGH GOD IS                                  WHERE A HIGH GOD IS                                     7    38
     PRESENT  (156) GES,EA                                PRESENT  (156) GES,EA                          XSQ=      4.12
                                                                                                         PHI=     0.193
                                                                                                         XP =    0.0424

427  TEND TO BE THOSE                 0.91 OF  23    427  TEND TO BE THOSE                 0.58 OF  43          21    18
     WHERE A HIGH GOD, IF PRESENT, IS                     WHERE A HIGH GOD, IF PRESENT, IS                        2    25
     ACTIVE, RATHER THAN                                  INACTIVE, RATHER THAN                          XSQ=     13.18
     INACTIVE  (87) GES,EA                                ACTIVE  (69) GES,EA                            PHI=     0.447
                                                                                                         XP =    0.0003

428  LEAN TOWARD BEING THOSE          0.95 OF  21    428  LEAN TOWARD BEING THOSE          0.50 OF  18          20     9
     WHERE A HIGH GOD, IF PRESENT AND ACTIVE,             WHERE A HIGH GOD, IF PRESENT AND ACTIVE,                1     9
     SUPPORTS HUMAN MORALITY, RATHER THAN                 DOES NOT SUPPORT HUMAN MORALITY,               XSQ=      8.17
     NOT SUPPORTING IT  (61) GES,EA                       RATHER THAN SUPPORTING IT  (26) GES,EA         PHI=     0.458
                                                                                                         EP =    0.0022

450  DRIFT TOWARD BEING THOSE         0.71 OF   7    450  DRIFT TOWARD BEING THOSE         0.69 OF  32           2    22
     WHERE THE OBSERVATION OF FOOD TABOOS                 WHERE THE OBSERVATION OF FOOD TABOOS                    5    10
     IS LOW, RATHER THAN                                  IS HIGH OR MEDIUM, RATHER THAN                 XSQ=      2.40
     HIGH OR MEDIUM  (26) JRL                             LOW  (60) JRL                                  PHI=    -0.248
                                                                                                         EP =    0.0846

459  TILT TOWARD BEING THOSE          0.67 OF  15    459  TILT TOWARD BEING THOSE          0.71 OF  51          10    15
     WHERE GAMES, IF PRESENT,                             WHERE GAMES, IF PRESENT,                                5    36
     INCLUDE GAMES OF CHANCE  (82) R-A-B,EA               DO NOT INCLUDE                                 XSQ=      5.35
                                                          GAMES OF CHANCE  (89) R-A-B,EA                 PHI=     0.285
                                                                                                         XP =    0.0208
```

217/

477	IN ALL CASES ARE THOSE WHERE ALCCHOLIC AGGRESSION IS STRCNG (15) DH	1.00 OF 3	477	DRIFT TOWARD BEING THOSE WHERE ALCOHOLIC AGGRESSICN IS MODERATE OR SLIGHT (19) DH	0.67 OF 15		3 5
							0 10
						XSQ=	2.20
						PHI=	0.350
						EP =	0.0686

219 CULTURES WHERE FIRST COUSIN MARRIAGE, IF PERMITTED, IS DUOLATERAL, RATHER THAN TRI- OR QUADRILATERAL (85)	219 CULTURES WHERE FIRST COUSIN MARRIAGE, IF PERMITTED, IS TRI- OR QUADRILATERAL, RATHER THAN DUOLATERAL (59)

BACKGROUND ON PAGE 117

NEITHER SUBJECT NOR PREDICATE

85 IN LEFT COLUMN

AJIE	ALBANIANS	APINAYE	ASHANTI	BACAIRI	BAMBARA	BEMBA	BHUIYA	BIRIFOR	BLACK CARIB
BORORO	BURYAT	CAMAYURA	CARIB	CHENCHU	COORG	CREE	DILLING	EYAK	GARO
GOND	GUAHIBO	HAIDA	HEHE	HERERO	KARIERA	KERAKI	KERALA	KHASI	LAKALAI
LAKHER	LAMBA	LAU	LOLO	MAGUZAWA	MANCHU	MARQUESANS	MARSHALLESE	MBUNDU	MBUTI
MIAO	MIN CHINESE	MINANGKABAU	MISKITO	MONGUOR	MOTILON	MUNDURUCU	NABESNA	NAMA	NAMBICUARA
NASKAPI	NDEMBU	NGONI	NUPE	NYANEKA	OJIBWA	PONAPEANS	RUNDI	SINHALESE	SIUAI
SWAZI	TAMIL	TANALA	TANIMBARESE	TERA	TODA	TOLOWA	TRUMAI	TSHIMSHIAN	TUCANO
TUCUNA	TUPINAMBA	TURKMEN	TZELTAL	VEDDA	VENDA	WANTOAT	WAPISHANA	WINNEBAGO	WITOTO
WOLOF	YABARANA	YAKO	YAO	YARURO					

59 IN RIGHT COLUMN

AINU	ALACALUF	AMERICANS	AWEIKOMA	BAJUN	BALINESE	BARABRA	BASSERI	BEJA	BERGDAMA
BOTOCUDO	BOZO	BUDUMA	BURMESE	CAMBODIANS	CARAJA	CHIRIGUANO	CHUKCHEE	DUTCH	EGYPTIANS
FON	FUTAJALONKE	GCAJIRO	HASANIA	HAZARA	HEBREWS	HUICHOL	INCA	JAPANESE	JAVANESE
JIVARO	KABYLE	MACASSARESE	MALAYS	MANIHIKI	MENTAWEI	MERINA	MINCHIA	NUNIVAK	PATHAN
PORTUGUESE	REGEIBAT	RIFFIANS	ROMANS	ROTINESE	RWALA	SAMOYED	SARAMACCA	SINDHI	SIWANS
SONGHAI	SOTHO	SUBANUN	SYRIANS	TEHUELCHE	TENDA	THAI	TIBETANS	YAKUT	

226 EXCLUDED BECAUSE IRRELEVANT

30 EXCLUDED BECAUSE UNASCERTAINED

```
220  CULTURES                                          220  CULTURES
     WHERE FIRST COUSIN MARRIAGE                            WHERE FIRST COUSIN MARRIAGE
     IN SOME FORM OR OTHER                                  IN SOME FORM OR OTHER
     IS PRESCRIBED OR PREFERRED   (97)                      IS NOT PRESCRIBED OR PREFERRED   (273)

BACKGROUND ON PAGE 117                                                          BOTH SUBJECT AND PREDICATE

     97  IN LEFT COLUMN

AJIE        ALBANIANS    APINAYE      ARAUCANIANS  ASHANTI     BAJUN        BALINESE     BAMBARA     BARABRA      BASSERI
BATAK       BEJA         BELU         BEMBA        BIRIFOR     CALLINAGO    CAMAYURA     CARIB       CHENCHU      COORG
CREE        EGYPTIANS    FUTAJALONKE  GARO         GILYAK      GOND         GUAHIBO      HAIDA       HASANIA      HAZARA
HEHE        HERERO       ILA          KACHIN       KARIERA     KASKA        KERALA       KISSI       LAKALAI      LAKHER
LAMBA       LAMET        LAU          LHOTA NAGA   LOLO        MAGUZAWA     MARQUESANS   MBUNDU      MENDE        MERINA
MIAO        MINANGKABAU  MISKITO      MNONG GAR    MOTILON     MUNDURUCU    MURNGIN      NABESNA     NAMBICUARA   NASKAPI
NDEMBU      PATHAN       PENDE        PONAPEANS    PURUM       REGEIBAT     ROTINESE     RUNDI       RWALA        SAMOYED
SANDAWE     SINHALESE    SIRIONO      SIUAI        SOTHO       SYRIANS      TAMIL        TANALA      TANIMBARESE  TODA
TRUMAI      TSHIMSHIAN   TUCANO       TUPINAMBA    TURKMEN     TZELTAL      VEDDA        VENDA       WANTOAT      WAPISHANA
WAROPEN     WIKMUNKAN    WOLOF        YABARANA     YAKO        YAO          YARURO

    273  IN RIGHT COLUMN

     30  EXCLUDED BECAUSE UNASCERTAINED

--------------------------------------------------------------------------------------------------------------
  5  TILT LESS TOWARD BEING THOSE   0.74 OF  97     5  TILT MORE TOWARD BEING THOSE   0.85 OF 273        25   41
     LOCATED OUTSIDE OF                               LOCATED OUTSIDE OF                                72  232
     EAST EURASIA  (330)                              EAST EURASIA  (330)                         XSQ=    4.94
                                                                                                  PHI=   0.116
                                                                                                  XP =  0.0263

  8  TEND MORE TO BE THOSE          0.94 OF  97     8  TEND LESS TO BE THOSE          0.77 OF 273         6   62
     LOCATED OUTSIDE OF                               LOCATED OUTSIDE OF                                91  211
     NORTH AMERICA  (330)                             NORTH AMERICA  (330)                        XSQ=   11.95
                                                                                                  PHI=  -0.180
                                                                                                  XP =  0.0005

 13  TILT MORE TOWARD BEING THOSE   0.91 OF  97    13  TILT LESS TOWARD BEING THOSE   0.81 OF 273         9   52
     WHERE THE LATITUDE IS                            WHERE THE LATITUDE IS                             88  221
     LESS THAN FORTY DEGREES  (329)                   LESS THAN FORTY DEGREES  (329)              XSQ=    4.28
                                                                                                  PHI=  -0.108
                                                                                                  XP =  0.0386

 14  LEAN MORE TOWARD BEING THOSE   0.84 OF  97    14  LEAN LESS TOWARD BEING THOSE   0.67 OF 273        16   89
     WHERE THE LATITUDE IS                            WHERE THE LATITUDE IS                             81  184
     LESS THAN THIRTY DEGREES  (281)                  LESS THAN THIRTY DEGREES  (281)             XSQ=    8.36
                                                                                                  PHI=  -0.150
                                                                                                  XP =  0.0038
```

15	DRIFT MORE TOWARD BEING THOSE 0.64 OF 97 WHERE THE LATITUDE IS LESS THAN TWENTY DEGREES (217)	15	DRIFT LESS TOWARD BEING THOSE 0.52 OF 273 WHERE THE LATITUDE IS LESS THAN TWENTY DEGREES (217)	35 131 62 142 XSQ= 3.63 PHI= -0.099 XP = 0.0567
81	DRIFT MORE TOWARD BEING THOSE 0.72 OF 61 WHERE NO CITY OR TOWN IS PRESENT, AND THE AVERAGE COMMUNITY SIZE IS SMALLER THAN 200 (135)	81	DRIFT LESS TOWARD BEING THOSE 0.57 OF 151 WHERE NO CITY OR TOWN IS PRESENT, AND THE AVERAGE COMMUNITY SIZE IS SMALLER THAN 200 (135)	17 65 44 86 XSQ= 3.60 PHI= -0.130 XP = 0.0576
88	DRIFT MORE TOWARD BEING THOSE 0.71 OF 69 WHERE, IF A HEADMANSHIP IS PRESENT, SUCCESSION IS HEREDITARY (165)	88	DRIFT LESS TOWARD BEING THOSE 0.57 OF 190 WHERE, IF A HEADMANSHIP IS PRESENT, SUCCESSION IS HEREDITARY (165)	20 81 49 109 XSQ= 3.41 PHI= -0.115 XP = 0.0648
98	DRIFT MORE TOWARD BEING THOSE 0.81 OF 80 WHERE THE HIERARCHY OF LOCAL JURISDICTION HAS FOUR OR THREE LEVELS (238) GES,EA	98	DRIFT LESS TOWARD BEING THOSE 0.69 OF 229 WHERE THE HIERARCHY OF LOCAL JURISDICTION HAS FOUR OR THREE LEVELS (238) GES,EA	65 159 15 70 XSQ= 3.58 PHI= 0.108 XP = 0.0585
110	TILT TOWARD BEING THOSE 0.53 OF 95 WHERE SLAVERY IS PRESENT (163)	110	TILT TOWARD BEING THOSE 0.60 OF 260 WHERE SLAVERY IS ABSENT (218)	50 104 45 156 XSQ= 4.02 PHI= 0.106 XP = 0.0450
176	DRIFT TOWARD BEING THOSE 0.53 OF 95 WHERE THE COMMUNITY IS A CLAN-COMMUNITY OR A COMMUNITY STRUCTURED OR SEGMENTED ON A CLAN BASIS (169)	176	DRIFT TOWARD BEING THOSE 0.58 OF 264 WHERE THE COMMUNITY IS OTHER THAN A CLAN-COMMUNITY OR A COMMUNITY STRUCTURED OR SEGMENTED ON A CLAN BASIS (213)	50 111 45 153 XSQ= 2.75 PHI= 0.088 XP = 0.0972
179	DRIFT MORE TOWARD BEING THOSE 0.94 OF 95 WHERE THE COMMUNITY IS OTHER THAN STRUCTURED ON A NON-CLAN BASIS AND COMMONLY EXOGAMOUS (340)	179	DRIFT LESS TOWARD BEING THOSE 0.86 OF 264 WHERE THE COMMUNITY IS OTHER THAN STRUCTURED ON A NON-CLAN BASIS AND COMMONLY EXOGAMOUS (340)	6 36 89 228 XSQ= 2.95 PHI= -0.091 XP = 0.0859
181	TILT MORE TOWARD BEING THOSE 0.96 OF 95 WHERE THE COMMUNITY IS OTHER THAN A DEME (337)	181	TILT LESS TOWARD BEING THOSE 0.86 OF 264 WHERE THE COMMUNITY IS OTHER THAN A DEME (337)	4 37 91 227 XSQ= 5.70 PHI= -0.126 XP = 0.0169
187	TILT LESS TOWARD BEING THOSE 0.79 OF 97 WHERE THE KIN GROUP IS OTHER THAN EXCLUSIVELY MATRILINEAL (344)	187	TILT MORE TOWARD BEING THOSE 0.88 OF 272 WHERE THE KIN GROUP IS OTHER THAN EXCLUSIVELY MATRILINEAL (344)	20 32 77 240 XSQ= 3.93 PHI= 0.103 XP = 0.0475

188	TEND MORE TO BE THCSE WHERE THE KIN GRCUP IS OTHER THAN EXCLUSIVELY COGNATIC (252)	0.85 OF 97	188	TEND LESS TO BE THOSE WHERE THE KIN GROUP IS OTHER THAN EXCLUSIVELY COGNATIC (252)	0.58 OF 273	15 116 82 157 XSQ= 21.69 PHI= -0.242 XP = 0.0000
192	TEND MORE TO BE THCSE OTHER THAN WHERE THE CNLY KIN GROUP PRESENT IS A KINCREC OR ELSE BILATERAL DESCENT IS INFERREC (289)	0.95 OF 97	192	TEND LESS TO BE THOSE OTHER THAN WHERE THE ONLY KIN GRCUP PRESENT IS A KINDRED OR ELSE BILATERAL DESCENT IS INFERRED (289)	0.67 OF 273	5 90 92 183 XSQ= 27.57 PHI= -0.273 XP = 0.0000
201	TILT MORE TOWARC BEING THOSE WHERE MARITAL RESICENCE IS NON-CPTICNAL, RATHER THAN AMBILCCAL CR NECLOCAL (334)	0.94 OF 96	201	TILT LESS TOWARD BEING THOSE WHERE MARITAL RESIDENCE IS NON-OPTIONAL, RATHER THAN AMBILOCAL OR NEOLOCAL (334)	0.82 OF 272	90 224 6 48 XSQ= 6.48 PHI= 0.133 XP = 0.0109
204	TILT MORE TOWARC BEING THCSE WHERE MARITAL RESICENCE IS PATRILCCAL, VIRILOCAL, OR AVUNCULOCAL, RATHER THAN AMBILCCAL CR NECLOCAL (270)	0.92 OF 78	204	TILT LESS TOWARD BEING THOSE WHERE MARITAL RESIDENCE IS PATRILOCAL, VIRILOCAL, OR AVUNCULOCAL, RATHER THAN AMBILOCAL OR NEOLOCAL (270)	0.79 OF 232	72 184 6 48 XSQ= 5.98 PHI= 0.139 XP = 0.0145
207	TILT TCWARD BEING THOSE WHERE MARITAL RESICENCE IS MATRILOCAL OR UXCRILOCAL, RATHER THAN AMBILCCAL CR NECLOCAL (64)	0.75 OF 24	207	TILT TOWARD BEING THOSE WHERE MARITAL RESIDENCE IS AMBILOCAL OR NEOLOCAL, RATHER THAN MATRILOCAL OR UXORILOCAL (64)	0.55 OF 88	18 40 6 48 XSQ= 5.46 PHI= 0.221 XP = 0.0194
213	IN ALL CASES ARE THOSE WHERE FIRST COUSIN MARRIAGE IS PERMITTED (172)	1.00 OF 97	213	TEND TO BE THOSE WHERE FIRST COUSIN MARRIAGE IS NOT PERMITTED (198)	0.73 OF 273	97 75 0 198 XSQ= 148.44 PHI= 0.633 XP = 0.
221	TEND LESS TO BE THCSE WHERE MATRILATERAL CROSS-COUSIN MARRIAGE IS NCT PRESCRIBED CR PREFERREC (335)	0.64 OF 97	221	IN ALL CASES ARE THOSE WHERE MATRILATERAL CROSS-CCUSIN MARRIAGE IS NOT PRESCRIBED OR PREFERRED (335)	1.00 OF 273	35 0 62 273 XSQ= 104.62 PHI= 0.532 XP = 0.
224	TEND TC BE THCSE WHERE CCUSIN MARRIAGE IS PREFERENTIALLY CR PERMISSIVELY EITHER PATRI- CR MATRILATERAL, RATHER THAN SYMMETRICAL (66)	0.57 OF 97	224	TEND TO BE THOSE WHERE COUSIN MARRIAGE IS PREFERENTIALLY OR PERMISSIVELY SYMMETRICAL, RATHER THAN EITHER PATRI- OR MATRILATERAL (106)	0.85 CF 75	55 11 42 64 XSQ= 29.85 PHI= 0.417 XP = 0.0000
234	TEND TC BE THCSE WHERE THE COUSIN TERMINCLCGY IS OF CRCW, CMAHA, CR IRCQUCIS TYPE, RATHER THAN ESKIMC CR HAWAIIAN TYPE (152)	0.81 OF 78	234	TEND TO BE THOSE WHERE THE COUSIN TERMINCLOGY IS OF ESKIMO OR HAWAIIAN TYPE, RATHER THAN CROW, OMAHA, OR IROQUOIS TYPE (170)	0.62 OF 224	63 86 15 138 XSQ= 39.89 PHI= 0.363 XP = 0.

242	LEAN MORE TOWARD BEING THOSE 0.91 OF 94 WHERE MARRIAGE IS COMMONLY OR OCCASIONALLY POLYGYNOUS, RATHER THAN MONOGAMOUS (314)	LEAN LESS TOWARD BEING THOSE 0.78 OF 271 WHERE MARRIAGE IS COMMONLY OR OCCASIONALLY POLYGYNOUS, RATHER THAN MONOGAMOUS (314)	86 212 8 59 XSQ= 7.33 PHI= 0.142 XP = 0.0068
256	TILT TOWARD BEING THOSE 0.75 OF 4 WHERE GRANDPARENT AND GRANDCHILD ARE NOT FRIENDLY EQUALS (8) DA	TILT TOWARD BEING THOSE 0.83 OF 29 WHERE GRANDPARENT AND GRANDCHILD ARE FRIENDLY EQUALS (25) DA	1 24 3 5 XSQ= 3.63 PHI= -0.332 EP = 0.0359
262	TEND MORE TO BE THOSE 0.91 OF 97 WHERE WIVES ARE OBTAINED BY MEANS INVOLVING THE PRESENCE OF SOME CONSIDERATION (305)	TEND LESS TO BE THOSE 0.74 OF 270 WHERE WIVES ARE OBTAINED BY MEANS INVOLVING THE PRESENCE OF SOME CONSIDERATION (305)	88 199 9 71 XSQ= 11.15 PHI= 0.174 XP = 0.0008
263	LEAN MORE TOWARD BEING THOSE 0.72 OF 97 WHERE WIVES ARE OBTAINED BY RELATIVELY DIFFICULT MEANS, NAMELY BY BRIDE-PRICE, BRIDE-SERVICE, OR EXCHANGING A FEMALE RELATIVE (233)	LEAN LESS TOWARD BEING THOSE 0.56 OF 270 WHERE WIVES ARE OBTAINED BY RELATIVELY DIFFICULT MEANS, NAMELY BY BRIDE-PRICE, BRIDE-SERVICE, OR EXCHANGING A FEMALE RELATIVE (233)	70 151 27 119 XSQ= 7.19 PHI= 0.140 XP = 0.0073
278	TILT TOWARD BEING THOSE 0.80 OF 5 WHERE PROPERTY RIGHTS IN WOMEN ARE PRESENT (8) LWS	TILT TOWARD BEING THOSE 0.76 OF 17 WHERE PROPERTY RIGHTS IN WOMEN ARE UNIMPORTANT OR ABSENT (14) LWS	4 4 1 13 XSQ= 3.16 PHI= 0.379 EP = 0.0393
295	IN ALL CASES ARE THOSE 1.00 OF 3 WHERE THE SEVERITY OF PUNISHMENT FOR ABORTION IS HIGH (11) BCA	DRIFT TOWARD BEING THOSE 0.60 OF 20 WHERE THE SEVERITY OF PUNISHMENT FOR ABORTION IS LOW OR ABSENT (12) BCA	3 8 0 12 XSQ= 1.74 PHI= 0.275 EP = 0.0932
301	DRIFT LESS TOWARD BEING THOSE 0.66 OF 35 WHERE THE POST-PARTUM SEX TABOO LASTS LONGER THAN ONE MONTH (96)	DRIFT MORE TOWARD BEING THOSE 0.82 OF 87 WHERE THE POST-PARTUM SEX TABOO LASTS LONGER THAN ONE MONTH (96)	23 71 12 16 XSQ= 2.72 PHI= -0.149 XP = 0.0989
391	TILT TOWARD BEING THOSE 0.68 OF 41 WHERE PREMARITAL SEX RELATIONS ARE PUNISHED ONLY IF PREGNANCY RESULTS, OR FREELY PERMITTED (90) JTW,EA	TILT TOWARD BEING THOSE 0.55 OF 129 WHERE PREMARITAL SEX RELATIONS ARE STRONGLY PUNISHED AND IN FACT RARE, OR WEAKLY PUNISHED AND IN FACT NOT RARE (89) JTW,EA	13 71 28 58 XSQ= 5.87 PHI= -0.186 XP = 0.0154
405	TILT TOWARD BEING THOSE 0.92 OF 12 WHERE EXPLANATIONS OF ILLNESS OF A DEPENDENCE NATURE ARE PRESENT (34) W-C	TILT TOWARD BEING THOSE 0.52 OF 48 WHERE EXPLANATIONS OF ILLNESS OF A DEPENDENCE NATURE ARE ABSENT (27) W-C	11 23 1 25 XSQ= 5.81 PHI= 0.311 XP = 0.0160

447	LEAN TOWARD BEING THOSE WHERE LOVE MAGIC IS ABSENT (13) S-R	0.88 OF 8	447	LEAN TOWARD BEING THOSE WHERE LOVE MAGIC IS PRESENT (20) S-R	0.76 OF 25	1 19 7 6 XSQ= 7.75 PHI= -0.485 EP = 0.0026
453	IN ALL CASES ARE THOSE WHERE THE ROLE OF RELIGIOUS EXPERTS IS NOT CONDUCIVE TO THE DEVELOPMENT OF THE INDIVIDUAL'S NEED TO ACHIEVE (23) DCM	1.00 OF 7	453	TILT LESS TOWARD BEING THOSE WHERE THE ROLE OF RELIGIOUS EXPERTS IS NOT CONDUCIVE TO THE DEVELOPMENT OF THE INDIVIDUAL'S NEED TO ACHIEVE (23) DCM	0.55 OF 29	0 13 7 16 XSQ= 3.16 PHI= -0.296 EP = 0.0343
458	DRIFT LESS TOWARD BEING THOSE WHERE GAMES, IF PRESENT, DO NOT INCLUDE GAMES OF STRATEGY (119) R-A-B,EA	0.56 OF 34	458	DRIFT MORE TOWARD BEING THOSE WHERE GAMES, IF PRESENT, DO NOT INCLUDE GAMES OF STRATEGY (119) R-A-B,EA	0.73 OF 133	15 36 19 97 XSQ= 2.95 PHI= 0.133 XP = 0.0858
459	DRIFT TOWARD BEING THOSE WHERE GAMES, IF PRESENT, DO NOT INCLUDE GAMES OF CHANCE (89) R-A-B,EA	0.68 OF 34	459	DRIFT TOWARD BEING THOSE WHERE GAMES, IF PRESENT, INCLUDE GAMES OF CHANCE (82) R-A-B,EA	0.52 OF 133	11 69 23 64 XSQ= 3.39 PHI= -0.143 XP = 0.0655

221 CULTURES WHERE MATRILATERAL CROSS-COUSIN MARRIAGE IS PRESCRIBED OR PREFERRED (35)	221 CULTURES WHERE MATRILATERAL CROSS-COUSIN MARRIAGE IS NOT PRESCRIBED OR PREFERRED (335)

BACKGROUND ON PAGE 117

BOTH SUBJECT AND PREDICATE

35 IN LEFT COLUMN

ALBANIANS	ARAUCANIANS	BAMBARA	BATAK	BELU	CHENCHU	GARO	GILYAK	HEHE	KACHIN
KASKA	KERALA	KISSI	LAKHER	LAMBA	LAMET	LHOTA NAGA	LOLO	MAGUZAWA	MBUNDU
MENDE	MNONG GAR	MURNGIN	PURUM	SAMOYED	SANDAWE	SIRIONO	SIUAI	TANIMBARESE	TSHIMSHIAN
TURKMEN	TZELTAL	VENDA	WAROPEN	WIKMUNKAN					

335 IN RIGHT COLUMN

30 EXCLUDED BECAUSE UNASCERTAINED

	Left column (35)			Right column (335)			Statistics
5	LEAN LESS TOWARD BEING THOSE LOCATED OUTSIDE OF EAST EURASIA (330)	0.63 OF 35	5	LEAN MORE TOWARD BEING THOSE LOCATED OUTSIDE OF EAST EURASIA (330)	0.84 OF 335		13 53 22 282 XSQ= 8.43 PHI= 0.151 XP = 0.0037
8	DRIFT MORE TOWARD BEING THOSE LOCATED OUTSIDE OF NORTH AMERICA (330)	0.94 OF 35	8	DRIFT LESS TOWARD BEING THOSE LOCATED OUTSIDE OF NORTH AMERICA (330)	0.80 OF 335		2 66 33 269 XSQ= 3.25 PHI= -0.094 XP = 0.0713
33	DRIFT MORE TOWARD BEING THOSE WHERE THE NATURAL ENVIRONMENT IS OTHER THAN 'VERY HARSH,' I.E., DESERT, DESERT GRASSES AND SHRUBS, TUNDRA, OR HIGH PLATEAU STEPPE (341) FWM	0.97 OF 35	33	DRIFT LESS TOWARD BEING THOSE WHERE THE NATURAL ENVIRONMENT IS OTHER THAN 'VERY HARSH,' I.E., DESERT, DESERT GRASSES AND SHRUBS, TUNDRA, OR HIGH PLATEAU STEPPE (341) FWM	0.84 OF 335		1 55 34 280 XSQ= 3.54 PHI= -0.098 XP = 0.0598
36	DRIFT MORE TOWARD BEING THOSE WHERE THE NATURAL ENVIRONMENT IS OTHER THAN 'VERY HARSH,' OR SUB-TROPICAL BUSH, OR TEMPERATE GRASSLAND (292) FWM	0.86 OF 35	36	DRIFT LESS TOWARD BEING THOSE WHERE THE NATURAL ENVIRONMENT IS OTHER THAN 'VERY HARSH,' OR SUB-TROPICAL BUSH, OR TEMPERATE GRASSLAND (292) FWM	0.71 OF 335		5 98 30 237 XSQ= 2.83 PHI= -0.087 XP = 0.0926
63	DRIFT MORE TOWARD BEING THOSE WHERE HUSBANDRY, IF PRESENT, IS PRINCIPALLY IN THE FORM OF BOVINE, EQUINE, CAMEL-LIKE, OR DEER-LIKE ANIMALS, RATHER THAN PIGS, SHEEP, OR GOATS (152)	0.86 OF 21	63	DRIFT LESS TOWARD BEING THOSE WHERE HUSBANDRY, IF PRESENT, IS PRINCIPALLY IN THE FORM OF BOVINE, EQUINE, CAMEL-LIKE, OR DEER-LIKE ANIMALS, RATHER THAN PIGS, SHEEP, OR GOATS (152)	0.64 OF 192		18 123 3 69 XSQ= 3.06 PHI= 0.120 XP = 0.0804

88	TILT MORE TOWARD BEING THOSE 0.83 OF 24 WHERE, IF A HEADMANSHIP IS PRESENT, SUCCESSION IS HEREDITARY (165)	88	TILT LESS TOWARD BEING THOSE 0.59 OF 235 WHERE, IF A HEADMANSHIP IS PRESENT, SUCCESSION IS HEREDITARY (165)	4 97 20 138 XSQ= 4.56 PHI= -0.133 XP = 0.0328
107	DRIFT MORE TOWARD BEING THOSE 0.95 OF 22 WHERE CLASS STRATIFICATION, IF PRESENT, IS BASED ON SOMETHING OTHER THAN OCCUPATIONAL STATUS (160)	107	DRIFT LESS TOWARD BEING THOSE 0.77 OF 166 WHERE CLASS STRATIFICATION, IF PRESENT, IS BASED ON SOMETHING OTHER THAN OCCUPATIONAL STATUS (160)	1 38 21 128 XSQ= 2.94 PHI= -0.125 XP = 0.0865
108	TILT TOWARD BEING THOSE 0.59 OF 22 WHERE CLASS STRATIFICATION, IF PRESENT, IS BASED ON A HEREDITARY ARISTOCRACY (74)	108	TILT TOWARD BEING THOSE 0.66 OF 166 WHERE CLASS STRATIFICATION, IF PRESENT, IS BASED ON SOMETHING OTHER THAN A HEREDITARY ARISTOCRACY (129)	13 56 9 110 XSQ= 4.34 PHI= 0.152 XP = 0.0372
110	TILT TOWARD BEING THOSE 0.64 OF 33 WHERE SLAVERY IS PRESENT (163)	110	TILT TOWARD BEING THOSE 0.59 OF 322 WHERE SLAVERY IS ABSENT (218)	21 133 12 189 XSQ= 5.20 PHI= 0.121 XP = 0.0226
175	DRIFT MORE TOWARD BEING THOSE 0.82 OF 34 WHERE THE COMMUNITY IS 'KIN-HETEROGENEOUS,' I. E. OTHER THAN A CLAN COMMUNITY OR A DEME (260)	175	DRIFT LESS TOWARD BEING THOSE 0.66 OF 325 WHERE THE COMMUNITY IS 'KIN-HETEROGENEOUS,' I. E. OTHER THAN A CLAN COMMUNITY OR A DEME (260)	6 110 28 215 XSQ= 2.99 PHI= -0.091 XP = 0.0838
176	DRIFT TOWARD BEING THOSE 0.62 OF 34 WHERE THE COMMUNITY IS A CLAN-COMMUNITY OR A COMMUNITY STRUCTURED OR SEGMENTED ON A CLAN BASIS (169)	176	DRIFT TOWARD BEING THOSE 0.57 OF 325 WHERE THE COMMUNITY IS OTHER THAN A CLAN-COMMUNITY OR A COMMUNITY STRUCTURED OR SEGMENTED ON A CLAN BASIS (213)	21 140 13 185 XSQ= 3.62 PHI= 0.100 XP = 0.0570
178	TILT LESS TOWARD BEING THOSE 0.59 OF 34 WHERE THE COMMUNITY IS OTHER THAN SEGMENTED ON A CLAN BASIS AND NON-EXOGAMOUS (295)	178	TILT MORE TOWARD BEING THOSE 0.79 OF 325 WHERE THE COMMUNITY IS OTHER THAN SEGMENTED ON A CLAN BASIS AND NON-EXOGAMOUS (295)	14 67 20 258 XSQ= 6.32 PHI= 0.133 XP = 0.0120
181	IN ALL CASES ARE THOSE 1.00 OF 34 WHERE THE COMMUNITY IS OTHER THAN A DEME (337)	181	DRIFT LESS TOWARD BEING THOSE 0.87 OF 325 WHERE THE COMMUNITY IS OTHER THAN A DEME (337)	0 41 34 284 XSQ= 3.68 PHI= -0.101 XP = 0.0552
186	LEAN TOWARD BEING THOSE 0.63 OF 35 WHERE THE KIN GROUP IS EXCLUSIVELY PATRILINEAL (150)	186	LEAN TOWARD BEING THOSE 0.64 OF 335 WHERE THE KIN GROUP IS OTHER THAN EXCLUSIVELY PATRILINEAL (250)	22 119 13 216 XSQ= 8.91 PHI= 0.155 XP = 0.0028

```
187  DRIFT LESS TOWARD BEING THOSE  0.74 OF  35    187  DRIFT MORE TOWARD BEING THOSE  0.87 OF 334          9   43
     WHERE THE KIN GROUP IS                              WHERE THE KIN GROUP IS                                 26  291
     OTHER THAN                                          OTHER THAN                                      XSQ=     3.32
     EXCLUSIVELY MATRILINEAL  (344)                      EXCLUSIVELY MATRILINEAL  (344)                  PHI=    0.095
                                                                                                         XP =   0.0685

188  IN ALL CASES ARE THOSE         1.00 OF  35    188  TEND LESS TO BE THOSE          0.61 OF 335          0  131
     WHERE THE KIN GROUP IS                              WHERE THE KIN GROUP IS                                 35  204
     OTHER THAN                                          OTHER THAN                                      XSQ=    19.51
     EXCLUSIVELY COGNATIC  (252)                         EXCLUSIVELY COGNATIC  (252)                     PHI=   -0.230
                                                                                                         XP =   0.0000

192  IN ALL CASES ARE THOSE         1.00 OF  35    192  TEND LESS TO BE THOSE          0.72 OF 335          0   95
     OTHER THAN WHERE THE ONLY KIN GROUP                 OTHER THAN WHERE THE ONLY KIN GROUP                    35  240
     PRESENT IS A KINDRED OR ELSE                        PRESENT IS A KINDRED OR ELSE                    XSQ=    11.91
     BILATERAL DESCENT IS INFERRED  (289)                BILATERAL DESCENT IS INFERRED  (289)            PHI=   -0.179
                                                                                                         XP =   0.0006

213  IN ALL CASES ARE THOSE         1.00 OF  35    213  TEND TO BE THOSE               0.59 OF 335         35  137
     WHERE FIRST COUSIN MARRIAGE IS                      WHERE FIRST COUSIN MARRIAGE IS                          0  198
     PERMITTED  (172)                                    NOT PERMITTED  (198)                            XSQ=    42.16
                                                                                                         PHI=    0.338
                                                                                                         XP =   0.

214  TEND LESS TO BE THOSE          0.51 OF  35    214  TEND MORE TO BE THOSE          0.92 OF 137         17   11
     WHERE FIRST COUSIN MARRIAGE,                        WHERE FIRST COUSIN MARRIAGE,                           18  126
     IF PERMITTED,                                       IF PERMITTED,                                   XSQ=    30.71
     IS OTHER THAN UNILATERAL  (144)                     IS OTHER THAN UNILATERAL  (144)                 PHI=    0.423
                                                                                                         XP =   0.

220  IN ALL CASES ARE THOSE         1.00 OF  35    220  TEND TO BE THOSE               0.81 OF 335         35   62
     WHERE FIRST COUSIN MARRIAGE                         WHERE FIRST COUSIN MARRIAGE                             0  273
     IN SOME FORM OR OTHER                               IN SOME FORM OR OTHER                           XSQ=   104.62
     IS PRESCRIBED OR PREFERRED  (97)                    IS NOT PRESCRIBED OR PREFERRED  (273)           PHI=    0.532
                                                                                                         XP =   0.

224  IN ALL CASES ARE THOSE         1.00 OF  35    224  TEND TO BE THOSE               0.77 OF 137         35   31
     WHERE COUSIN MARRIAGE IS                            WHERE COUSIN MARRIAGE IS                                0  106
     PREFERENTIALLY OR PERMISSIVELY                      PREFERENTIALLY OR PERMISSIVELY                  XSQ=    67.34
     EITHER PATRI- OR MATRILATERAL,                      SYMMETRICAL, RATHER THAN                        PHI=    0.626
     RATHER THAN SYMMETRICAL  (66)                       EITHER PATRI- OR MATRILATERAL  (106)            XP =   0.

234  LEAN TOWARD BEING THOSE        0.75 OF  28    234  LEAN TOWARD BEING THOSE        0.53 OF 274         21  128
     WHERE THE COUSIN TERMINOLOGY IS                     WHERE THE COUSIN TERMINOLOGY IS                         7  146
     OF CROW, OMAHA, OR IROQUOIS TYPE,                   OF ESKIMO OR HAWAIIAN TYPE,                     XSQ=     7.04
     RATHER THAN                                         RATHER THAN                                     PHI=    0.153
     ESKIMO OR HAWAIIAN TYPE  (152)                      CROW, OMAHA, OR IROQUOIS TYPE  (170)            XP =   0.0080

242  DRIFT MORE TOWARD BEING THOSE  0.94 OF  35    242  DRIFT LESS TOWARD BEING THOSE  0.80 OF 330         33  265
     WHERE MARRIAGE IS                                   WHERE MARRIAGE IS                                       2   65
     COMMONLY OR OCCASIONALLY POLYGYNOUS,                COMMONLY OR OCCASIONALLY POLYGYNOUS,            XSQ=     3.25
     RATHER THAN MONOGAMOUS  (314)                       RATHER THAN MONOGAMOUS  (314)                   PHI=    0.094
                                                                                                         XP =   0.0715
```

262	DRIFT MORE TOWARD BEING THOSE WHERE WIVES ARE OBTAINED BY MEANS INVOLVING THE PRESENCE OF SOME CONSIDERATION (305)	0.91 OF 35	262	DRIFT LESS TOWARD BEING THOSE WHERE WIVES ARE OBTAINED BY MEANS INVOLVING THE PRESENCE OF SOME CONSIDERATION (305)	0.77 OF 332	32 255 3 77 XSQ= 3.16 PHI= 0.093 XP = 0.0755
263	LEAN MORE TOWARD BEING THOSE WHERE WIVES ARE OBTAINED BY RELATIVELY DIFFICULT MEANS, NAMELY BY BRIDE-PRICE, BRIDE-SERVICE, OR EXCHANGING A FEMALE RELATIVE (233)	0.86 OF 35	263	LEAN LESS TOWARD BEING THOSE WHERE WIVES ARE OBTAINED BY RELATIVELY DIFFICULT MEANS, NAMELY BY BRIDE-PRICE, BRIDE-SERVICE, OR EXCHANGING A FEMALE RELATIVE (233)	0.58 OF 332	30 191 5 141 XSQ= 9.36 PHI= 0.160 XP = 0.0022
308	IN ALL CASES ARE THOSE WHERE AVERAGE SOCIALIZATION ANXIETY IS LOW (18) W-C	1.00 OF 4	308	TILT TOWARD BEING THOSE WHERE AVERAGE SOCIALIZATION ANXIETY IS HIGH (22) W-C	0.61 OF 36	0 22 4 14 XSQ= 3.24 PHI= -0.285 EP = 0.0335
339	DRIFT TOWARD BEING THOSE WHERE THE CHILD'S INFERRED CONFLICT REGARDING RESPONSIBLE BEHAVIOR IS HIGH (31) B-B-C	0.83 OF 6	339	DRIFT TOWARD BEING THOSE WHERE THE CHILD'S INFERRED CONFLICT REGARDING RESPONSIBLE BEHAVIOR IS LOW (42) B-B-C	0.61 OF 67	5 26 1 41 XSQ= 2.83 PHI= 0.197 XP = 0.0924
391	DRIFT TOWARD BEING THOSE WHERE PREMARITAL SEX RELATIONS ARE PUNISHED ONLY IF PREGNANCY RESULTS, OR FREELY PERMITTED (90) JTW,EA	0.75 OF 16	391	DRIFT TOWARD BEING THOSE WHERE PREMARITAL SEX RELATIONS ARE STRONGLY PUNISHED AND IN FACT RARE, OR WEAKLY PUNISHED AND IN FACT NOT RARE (89) JTW,EA	0.52 OF 154	4 80 12 74 XSQ= 3.20 PHI= -0.137 XP = 0.0736
400	IN ALL CASES ARE THOSE WHERE HOMOSEXUAL ACTIVITY IS PROHIBITED (22) F-B	1.00 OF 3	400	DRIFT TOWARD BEING THOSE WHERE HOMOSEXUAL ACTIVITY IS PERMITTED (36) F-B	0.65 OF 55	3 19 0 36 XSQ= 2.77 PHI= 0.219 XP = 0.0960
405	IN ALL CASES ARE THOSE WHERE EXPLANATIONS OF ILLNESS OF A DEPENDENCE NATURE ARE PRESENT (34) W-C	1.00 OF 6	405	DRIFT LESS TOWARD BEING THOSE WHERE EXPLANATIONS OF ILLNESS OF A DEPENDENCE NATURE ARE PRESENT (34) W-C	0.52 OF 54	6 28 0 26 XSQ= 3.33 PHI= 0.235 XP = 0.0682
447	TILT TOWARD BEING THOSE WHERE LOVE MAGIC IS ABSENT (13) S-R	0.83 OF 6	447	TILT TOWARD BEING THOSE WHERE LOVE MAGIC IS PRESENT (20) S-R	0.70 OF 27	1 19 5 8 XSQ= 3.89 PHI= -0.344 EP = 0.0248
458	DRIFT TOWARD BEING THOSE WHERE GAMES, IF PRESENT, INCLUDE GAMES OF STRATEGY (52) R-A-B,EA	0.60 OF 10	458	DRIFT TOWARD BEING THOSE WHERE GAMES, IF PRESENT, DO NOT INCLUDE GAMES OF STRATEGY (119) R-A-B,EA	0.71 OF 157	6 45 4 112 XSQ= 3.00 PHI= 0.134 XP = 0.0832

222 CULTURES
WHERE, WITH THE KIN GROUP PATRILINEAL,
MATRILATERAL CROSS-COUSIN MARRIAGE
IS PRESCRIBED OR PREFERRED (23)

222 CULTURES
WHERE, WITH THE KIN GROUP PATRILINEAL,
MATRILATERAL CROSS-COUSIN MARRIAGE
IS NOT PRESCRIBED OR PREFERRED (137)

BACKGROUND ON PAGE 117 SUBJECT ONLY

23 IN LEFT COLUMN

ALBANIANS ARAUCANIANS BAMBARA BATAK CHENCHU GILYAK HEHE KACHIN KISSI LAKHER
LAMET LHOTA NAGA LOLO MAGUZAWA MENDE PURUM SAMOYED SANDAWE TANIMBARESE TURKMEN
TZELTAL WARCPEN WIKMUNKAN

137 IN RIGHT COLUMN

ABOR AJIE AKHA ALORESE AMBA ARAPESH ARYANS ATAYAL AYMARA AZANDE
BAJUN BAMILEKE BANDA BARABRA BARI BASSERI BAYA BEJA BENGALI BETE
BHIL BHUIYA BOZO BUCUMA BURUSHO BURYAT CHAGGA COORG DAGUR CARD
DIEGUENO DILLING DOGON DOROBO EGYPTIANS ENGA FANG FON FOX FUTAJALONKE
GANDA GISU GOND HASANIA HAZARA HEBREWS HO KABYLE KALMYK KAPAUKU
KATAB KAZAK KERAKI KHALKA KHEVSUR KIKUYU KONSO KOREANS LANGO LAU
LEPCHA LIFU LUBA LUO MAM MANCHU MARGI MARICOPA MASAI MATAKAM
MAYA MBUTI MERINA MIAMI MIAO MIN CHINESE MINCHIA MIWOK MONGO MONGUOR
MOSSI MUNDURUCU MURINBATA NAMA NANDI NOMLAKI NUER NUPE NURI NYAKYUSA
NYORO OJIBWA OKINAWANS OMAHA ORAON PATHAN PURARI REGEIBAT RIFFIANS ROTINESE
RUNDI RWALA SANTAL SENIANG SHERENTE SHILLUK SINDHI SIWANS SOMALI SONGHAI
SOTHO SWAZI SYRIANS TALLENSI TAMIL TANALA TEDA TERA TESO THONGA
TIBETANS TIGRINYA TIKOPIA TIV TOLOWA TUCANO TUCUNA TURKANA VIETNAMESE WANTOAT
WINNEBAGO WITOTO WUTE YAGUA YAKUT YOKUTS YORUBA

1 EXCLUDED BECAUSE AMBIGUOUS

PUKAPUKA

208 EXCLUDED BECAUSE IRRELEVANT

31 EXCLUDED BECAUSE UNASCERTAINED

---

107 IN ALL CASES ARE THOSE 1.00 OF 14
WHERE CLASS STRATIFICATION, IF PRESENT,
IS BASED ON SOMETHING OTHER THAN
OCCUPATIONAL STATUS (160)

107 DRIFT LESS TOWARD BEING THOSE 0.74 OF 81
WHERE CLASS STRATIFICATION, IF PRESENT,
IS BASED ON SOMETHING OTHER THAN
OCCUPATIONAL STATUS (160)

	0	21
	14	60
XSQ=		3.28
PHI=		-0.186
XP =		0.0703

```
108  TILT TOWARD BEING THOSE          0.64 OF  14     108  TILT TOWARD BEING THOSE          0.69 OF  81          9    25
     WHERE CLASS STRATIFICATION, IF PRESENT,               WHERE CLASS STRATIFICATION, IF PRESENT,              5    56
     IS BASED ON                                           IS BASED ON SOMETHING OTHER THAN                XSQ=     4.44
     A HEREDITARY ARISTOCRACY  (74)                        A HEREDITARY ARISTOCRACY  (129)                 PHI=    0.216
                                                                                                           XP =   0.0351

109  DRIFT MORE TOWARD BEING THOSE  0.95 OF  19      109  DRIFT LESS TOWARD BEING THOSE  0.71 OF 119           1    35
     WHERE CASTES ARE ABSENT  (317)                        WHERE CASTES ARE ABSENT  (317)                      18    84
                                                                                                           XSQ=     3.78
                                                                                                           PHI=   -0.166
                                                                                                           XP =   0.0518

128  IN ALL CASES ARE THOSE           1.00 OF   5     128  TILT TOWARD BEING THOSE          0.53 OF  32          5    15
     WHERE, IF SUBSISTENCE IS PRIMARILY BY                 WHERE, IF SUBSISTENCE IS PRIMARILY BY                0    17
     AGRICULTURE, THE WORK IS                              AGRICULTURE, THE WORK IS                        XSQ=     3.01
     MAINLY DONE BY MALES  (40)                            MAINLY DONE BY FEMALES  (37)                    PHI=    0.285
                                                                                                           EP =   0.0498

175  TILT MORE TOWARD BEING THOSE   0.82 OF  22      175  TILT LESS TOWARD BEING THOSE   0.52 OF 132           4    63
     WHERE THE COMMUNITY IS                                WHERE THE COMMUNITY IS                              18    69
     'KIN-HETEROGENEOUS,' I. E.                            'KIN-HETEROGENEOUS,' I. E.                      XSQ=     5.55
     OTHER THAN                                            OTHER THAN                                      PHI=   -0.190
     A CLAN COMMUNITY OR A DEME  (260)                     A CLAN COMMUNITY OR A DEME  (260)               XP =   0.0185

177  DRIFT MORE TOWARD BEING THOSE  0.82 OF  22      177  DRIFT LESS TOWARD BEING THOSE  0.58 OF 132           4    56
     WHERE THE COMMUNITY IS OTHER THAN                     WHERE THE COMMUNITY IS OTHER THAN                   18    76
     A SINGLE CLAN-COMMUNITY AND                           A SINGLE CLAN-COMMUNITY AND                     XSQ=     3.70
     EXOGAMOUS  (305)                                      EXOGAMOUS  (305)                                PHI=   -0.155
                                                                                                           XP =   0.0545

213  IN ALL CASES ARE THOSE           1.00 OF  23     213  TEND TO BE THOSE                 0.56 OF 137         23    60
     WHERE FIRST COUSIN MARRIAGE IS                        WHERE FIRST COUSIN MARRIAGE IS                       0    77
     PERMITTED  (172)                                      NOT PERMITTED  (198)                            XSQ=    22.72
                                                                                                           PHI=    0.377
                                                                                                           XP =   0.0000

214  TEND TO BE THOSE                 0.52 OF  23     214  TEND TO BE THOSE                 0.92 OF  60         12     5
     WHERE FIRST COUSIN MARRIAGE,                          WHERE FIRST COUSIN MARRIAGE,                        11    55
     IF PERMITTED,                                         IF PERMITTED,                                   XSQ=    17.02
     IS UNILATERAL  (28)                                   IS OTHER THAN UNILATERAL  (144)                 PHI=    0.453
                                                                                                           XP =   0.0000

220  IN ALL CASES ARE THOSE           1.00 OF  23     220  TEND TO BE THOSE                 0.81 OF 137         23    26
     WHERE FIRST COUSIN MARRIAGE                           WHERE FIRST COUSIN MARRIAGE                          0   111
     IN SOME FORM OR OTHER                                 IN SOME FORM OR OTHER                           XSQ=    57.10
     IS PRESCRIBED OR PREFERRED  (97)                      IS NOT PRESCRIBED OR PREFERRED  (273)           PHI=    0.597
                                                                                                           XP =   0.

224  IN ALL CASES ARE THOSE           1.00 OF  23     224  TEND TO BE THOSE                 0.68 OF  60         23    19
     WHERE COUSIN MARRIAGE IS                              WHERE COUSIN MARRIAGE IS                             0    41
     PREFERENTIALLY OR PERMISSIVELY                        PREFERENTIALLY OR PERMISSIVELY                  XSQ=    28.39
     EITHER PATRI- OR MATRILATERAL,                        SYMMETRICAL, RATHER THAN                        PHI=    0.585
     RATHER THAN SYMMETRICAL  (66)                         EITHER PATRI- OR MATRILATERAL  (106)            XP =   0.0000
```

225	IN ALL CASES ARE THOSE 1.00 OF 23 WHERE COUSIN MARRIAGE IS PREFERENTIALLY OR PERMISSIVELY MATRILATERAL, RATHER THAN PATRILATERAL (43)	225	TEND TO BE THOSE 0.63 OF 19 WHERE COUSIN MARRIAGE IS PREFERENTIALLY OR PERMISSIVELY PATRILATERAL, RATHER THAN MATRILATERAL (23)	 XSQ= PHI= XP =	0 12 23 7 17.36 -0.643 0.0000
263	DRIFT MORE TOWARD BEING THOSE 0.96 OF 23 WHERE WIVES ARE OBTAINED BY RELATIVELY DIFFICULT MEANS, NAMELY BY BRIDE-PRICE, BRIDE-SERVICE, OR EXCHANGING A FEMALE RELATIVE (233)	263	DRIFT LESS TOWARD BEING THOSE 0.77 OF 135 WHERE WIVES ARE OBTAINED BY RELATIVELY DIFFICULT MEANS, NAMELY BY BRIDE-PRICE, BRIDE-SERVICE, OR EXCHANGING A FEMALE RELATIVE (233)	 XSQ= PHI= XP =	22 104 1 31 3.14 0.141 0.0763
337	IN ALL CASES ARE THOSE 1.00 OF 2 WHERE THE CHILD'S INFERRED ANXIETY OVER NON-PERFORMANCE OF RESPONSIBLE BEHAVIOR IS LOW (35) B-B-C	337	DRIFT TOWARD BEING THOSE 0.75 OF 28 WHERE THE CHILD'S INFERRED ANXIETY OVER NON-PERFORMANCE OF RESPONSIBLE BEHAVIOR IS HIGH (38) B-B-C	 XSQ= PHI= EP =	0 21 2 7 2.07 -0.262 0.0828
369	IN ALL CASES ARE THOSE 1.00 OF 3 WHERE BOTH DISSOCIATION OF THE SEXES AT ADOLESCENCE, AND CUSTOMS OF INITIATION AT ADOLESCENCE, ARE ABSENT (15) JKH	369	TILT TOWARD BEING THOSE 0.74 OF 19 WHERE DISSOCIATION OF THE SEXES AT ADOLESCENCE, OR CUSTOMS OF INITIATION AT ADOLESCENCE, ARE PRESENT (42) JKH	 XSQ= PHI= EP =	0 14 3 5 3.31 -0.388 0.0364
391	DRIFT TOWARD BEING THOSE 0.73 OF 11 WHERE PREMARITAL SEX RELATIONS ARE PUNISHED ONLY IF PREGNANCY RESULTS, OR FREELY PERMITTED (90) JTW,EA	391	DRIFT TOWARD BEING THOSE 0.59 OF 64 WHERE PREMARITAL SEX RELATIONS ARE STRONGLY PUNISHED AND IN FACT RARE, OR WEAKLY PUNISHED AND IN FACT NOT RARE (89) JTW,EA	 XSQ= PHI= XP =	3 38 8 26 2.72 -0.190 0.0994
399	IN ALL CASES ARE THOSE 1.00 OF 3 WHERE INTENSITY OF CASTRATION ANXIETY IS LOW (22) WNS	399	TILT TOWARD BEING THOSE 0.73 OF 15 WHERE INTENSITY OF CASTRATION ANXIETY IS HIGH (23) WNS	 XSQ= PHI= EP =	0 11 3 4 2.99 -0.408 0.0429
447	IN ALL CASES ARE THOSE 1.00 OF 2 WHERE LOVE MAGIC IS ABSENT (13) S-R	447	DRIFT TOWARD BEING THOSE 0.80 OF 10 WHERE LOVE MAGIC IS PRESENT (20) S-R	 XSQ= PHI= EP =	0 8 2 2 1.88 -0.395 0.0909

223 CULTURES WHERE, WITH THE KIN GROUP MATRILINEAL, MATRILATERAL CROSS-COUSIN MARRIAGE IS PRESCRIBED OR PREFERRED (9)	223 CULTURES WHERE, WITH THE KIN GROUP MATRILINEAL, MATRILATERAL CROSS-COUSIN MARRIAGE IS NOT PRESCRIBED OR PREFERRED (50)

BACKGROUND ON PAGE 117 SUBJECT ONLY

9 IN LEFT COLUMN

BELU GARO KASKA KERALA LAMBA MNONG GAR SIRIONO SIUAI TSHIMSHIAN

50 IN RIGHT COLUMN

AINU	APINAYE	BEMBA	BORORO	CALLINAGO	CHEROKEE	COCHITI	CREEK	CROW	DIERI
DOBUANS	EYAK	GOAJIRO	GUAHIBO	GURE	HAIDA	HANO	HURON	JEMEZ	KHASI
KUBA	KURTATCHI	LAKALAI	LESU	MANDAN	MARSHALLESE	MINANGKABAU	MOTA	NABESNA	NAVAHO
NDEMBU	NYANEKA	PALAUANS	PAWNEE	PENDE	PONAPEANS	ROTUMANS	SARAMACCA	SEMINOLE	TALAMANCA
TENDA	TIMBIRA	TIWI	TROBRIAND	TRUKESE	VEDDA	WOLEAIANS	YAO	YOMBE	ZUNI

1 EXCLUDED BECAUSE AMBIGUOUS

PUKAPUKA

310 EXCLUDED BECAUSE IRRELEVANT

30 EXCLUDED BECAUSE UNASCERTAINED

5	DRIFT LESS TOWARD BEING THOSE LOCATED OUTSIDE OF EAST EURASIA (330)	0.67 OF 9	5	DRIFT MORE TOWARD BEING THOSE LOCATED OUTSIDE OF EAST EURASIA (330)	0.94 OF 50	3 3 6 47 XSQ= 3.60 PHI= 0.247 XP = 0.0576
213	IN ALL CASES ARE THOSE WHERE FIRST COUSIN MARRIAGE IS PERMITTED (172)	1.00 OF 9	213	TILT TOWARD BEING THOSE WHERE FIRST COUSIN MARRIAGE IS NOT PERMITTED (198)	0.50 OF 50	9 25 0 25 XSQ= 5.90 PHI= 0.316 XP = 0.0152
220	IN ALL CASES ARE THOSE WHERE FIRST COUSIN MARRIAGE IN SOME FORM OR OTHER IS PRESCRIBED OR PREFERRED (97)	1.00 OF 9	220	TEND TO BE THOSE WHERE FIRST COUSIN MARRIAGE IN SOME FORM OR OTHER IS NOT PRESCRIBED OR PREFERRED (273)	0.74 OF 50	9 13 0 37 XSQ= 14.84 PHI= 0.501 XP = 0.0001

223/

```
224  IN ALL CASES ARE THOSE            1.00 OF   9     224  TEND TO BE THOSE                  0.72 OF  25          9     7
     WHERE COUSIN MARRIAGE IS                               WHERE COUSIN MARRIAGE IS                                0    18
     PREFERENTIALLY OR PERMISSIVELY                         PREFERENTIALLY OR PERMISSIVELY                   XSQ=   11.03
     EITHER PATRI- OR MATRILATERAL,                         SYMMETRICAL, RATHER THAN                         PHI=   0.570
     RATHER THAN SYMMETRICAL  (66)                          EITHER PATRI- OR MATRILATERAL  (106)             EP =  0.0002

225  IN ALL CASES ARE THOSE            1.00 OF   9     225  TEND TO BE THOSE                  0.86 OF   7          0     6
     WHERE COUSIN MARRIAGE IS                               WHERE COUSIN MARRIAGE IS                                9     1
     PREFERENTIALLY OR PERMISSIVELY                         PREFERENTIALLY OR PERMISSIVELY                   XSQ=    8.96
     MATRILATERAL, RATHER THAN                              PATRILATERAL, RATHER THAN                        PHI=  -0.748
     PATRILATERAL  (43)                                     MATRILATERAL  (23)                               EP =  0.0009

325  IN ALL CASES ARE THOSE            1.00 OF   3     325  TILT TOWARD BEING THOSE           0.83 OF  12          0    10
     WHERE THE DEGREE OF DIFFUSION AMONG                    WHERE THE DEGREE OF DIFFUSION AMONG                     3     2
     THE INFANT'S NURTURANT AGENTS                          THE INFANT'S NURTURANT AGENTS                    XSQ=    4.22
     IS LOW  (32) B-B-C                                     IS HIGH  (42) B-B-C                              PHI=  -0.530
                                                                                                             EP =  0.0220

344  IN ALL CASES ARE THOSE            1.00 OF   3     344  DRIFT TOWARD BEING THOSE          0.67 OF  12          3     4
     WHERE THE TOTAL POSITIVE PRESSURE TOWARD               WHERE THE TOTAL POSITIVE PRESSURE TOWARD                0     8
     DEVELOPING SELF-RELIANT BEHAVIOR                       DEVELOPING SELF-RELIANT BEHAVIOR                 XSQ=    2.03
     IN THE CHILD                                           IN THE CHILD                                     PHI=   0.367
     IS HIGH  (36) B-B-C                                    IS LOW  (40) B-B-C                               EP =  0.0769

365  IN ALL CASES ARE THOSE            1.00 OF   2     365  IN ALL CASES ARE THOSE            1.00 OF   6          0     6
     WHERE THE TIME SPENT IN                                WHERE THE TIME SPENT IN                                 2     0
     ADOLESCENT PEER GROUP ACTIVITY                         ADOLESCENT PEER GROUP ACTIVITY                   XSQ=    3.56
     IS LOW-MEDIUM OR LOW  (15) JKH                         IS HIGH OR HIGH-MEDIUM  (30) JKH                 PHI=  -0.667
                                                                                                             EP =  0.0357

385  IN ALL CASES ARE THOSE            1.00 OF   2     385  TILT TOWARD BEING THOSE           0.88 OF  17          2     2
     WHERE SEXUAL EXPRESSION BY THE YOUNG                   WHERE SEXUAL EXPRESSION BY THE YOUNG                    0    15
     IS RESTRICTED  (22) F-B                                IS SEMI-RESTRICTED OR                            XSQ=    3.91
                                                            PERMITTED  (64) F-B                              PHI=   0.454
                                                                                                             EP =  0.0351

447  IN ALL CASES ARE THOSE            1.00 OF   2     447  IN ALL CASES ARE THOSE            1.00 OF   6          0     6
     WHERE LOVE MAGIC IS                                    WHERE LOVE MAGIC IS                                     2     0
     ABSENT  (13) S-R                                       PRESENT  (20) S-R                                XSQ=    3.56
                                                                                                             PHI=  -0.667
                                                                                                             EP =  0.0357
```

224 CULTURES
WHERE CCUSIN MARRIAGE IS
PREFERENTIALLY CR PERMISSIVELY
EITHER PATRI- OR MATRILATERAL,
RATHER THAN SYMMETRICAL (66)

224 CULTURES
WHERE COUSIN MARRIAGE IS
PREFERENTIALLY OR PERMISSIVELY
SYMMETRICAL, RATHER THAN
EITHER PATRI- OR MATRILATERAL (106)

BACKGROUND ON PAGE 117

BCTH SUBJECT AND PREDICATE

66 IN LEFT CCLUMN

ABOR	ALBANIANS	ARAUCANIANS	BAJUN	BALINESE	BAMBARA .	BARABRA	BASSERI	BATAK	BEJA
BELU	BIRIFOR	BURYAT	CALLINAGO	CHENCHU	EGYPTIANS	GARO	GILYAK	HAIDA	HASANIA
HAZARA	HEHE	HERERC	HO	ILA	KACHIN	KASKA	KERALA	KISSI	KONSO
LAKHER	LAMBA	LAMET	LHOTA NAGA	LOLO	MAGUZAWA	MANDAN	MAYA	MBUNDU	MENDE
MIN CHINESE	MNCNG GAR	MURNGIN	PATHAN	PENDE	PURUM	REGEIBAT	RWALA	SAMCYED	SANDAWE
SHERENTE	SIRIONO	SIUAI	SYRIANS	TANIMBARESE	TIWI	TOLOWA	TRCBRIAND	TSHIMSHIAN	TURKMEN
TZELTAL	VEDDA	VENCA	WAROPEN	WIKMUNKAN	YAKO				

106 IN RIGHT CCLUMN

AINU	AJIE	ALACALUF	AMERICANS	APINAYE	ASHANTI	AWEIKOMA	BACAIRI	BEMBA	BERGDAMA
BHUIYA	BLACK CARIB	BCRCRC	BOTOCUDO	BOZO	BUDUMA	BURMESE	CAMAYURA	CAMBODIANS	CARAJA
CARIB	CHIRIGUANC	CHUKCHEE	COORG	CREE	DILLING	DUTCH	EYAK	FON	FUTAJALONKE
GOAJIRO	GOND	GUAHIBC	HEBREWS	HUICHOL	INCA	JAPANESE	JAVANESE	JIVARO	KABYLE
KARIERA	KERAKI	KHASI	LAKALAI	LAU	MACASSARESE	MALAYS	MANCHU	MANIHIKI	MARQUESANS
MARSHALLESE	MBUTI	MENTAWEI	MERINA	MIAO	MINANGKABAU	MINCHIA	MISKITC	MONGUOR	MOTILON
MUNDURUCU	NABESNA	NAMA	NAMBICUARA	NASKAPI	NDEMBU	NGCNI	NUNIVAK	NUPE	NYANEKA
OJIBWA	PONAPEANS	PORTUGUESE	RIFFIANS	ROMANS	ROTINESE	RUNDI	SARAMACCA	SINCHI	SINHALESE
SIWANS	SONGHAI	SOTHO	SUBANUN	SWAZI	TAMIL	TANALA	TEHUELCHE	TENDA	TERA
THAI	TIBETANS	TOCA	TRUMAI	TUCANO	TUCUNA	TUPINAMBA	WANTOAT	WAPISHANA	WINNEBAGO
WITOTC	WCLCF	YABARANA	YAKUT	YAO	YARURO				

198 EXCLUDED BECAUSE IRRELEVANT

30 EXCLUDED BECAUSE UNASCERTAINEC

9	LEAN MORE TOWARC BEING THCSE 0.91 OF 66 LOCATED CUTSIDE OF SCUTH AMERICA (335)	9	LEAN LESS TOWARD BEING THOSE 0.73 OF 106 LOCATED OUTSIDE OF SOUTH AMERICA (335)	6 29 60 77 XSQ= 7.29 PHI= -0.206 XP = 0.0070
51	DRIFT MORE TOWARD BEING THCSE 0.74 OF 66 WHERE SUBSISTENCE IS PRIMARILY BY FOOD PRCDUCTICN -- I. E., AGRICULTURE CR HUSBANDRY -- RATHER THAN BY GATHERING (253)	51	DRIFT LESS TOWARD BEING THCSE 0.60 OF 106 WHERE SUBSISTENCE IS PRIMARILY BY FOOD PRODUCTION -- I. E., AGRICULTURE OR HUSBANDRY -- RATHER THAN BY GATHERING (253)	49 64 17 42 XSQ= 2.88 PHI= 0.129 XP = 0.0896

54	TILT MORE TOWARD BEING THOSE 0.91 OF 35 WHERE FOOD PRODUCTION IS BY INTENSIVE OR SIMPLE AGRICULTURE, RATHER THAN BY INCIPIENT FOOD PRODUCTION (192)	54	TILT LESS TOWARD BEING THOSE 0.72 OF 69 WHERE FOOD PRODUCTION IS BY INTENSIVE OR SIMPLE AGRICULTURE, RATHER THAN BY INCIPIENT FOOD PRODUCTION (192)	32 50 3 19 XSQ= 3.93 PHI= 0.195 XP = 0.0473
56	TILT MORE TOWARD BEING THOSE 0.86 OF 21 WHERE FOOD PRODUCTION IS BY SIMPLE AGRICULTURE, RATHER THAN BY INCIPIENT FOOD PRODUCTION (101)	56	TILT LESS TOWARD BEING THOSE 0.57 OF 44 WHERE FOOD PRODUCTION IS BY SIMPLE AGRICULTURE, RATHER THAN BY INCIPIENT FOOD PRODUCTION (101)	18 25 3 19 XSQ= 4.09 PHI= 0.251 XP = 0.0432
84	DRIFT MORE TOWARD BEING THOSE 0.90 OF 50 WHERE THE LEVEL OF POLITICAL INTEGRATION IS THE LITTLE STATE, THE MINIMAL STATE, THE AUTONOMOUS COMMUNITY, OR THE FAMILY (262) GPM	84	DRIFT LESS TOWARD BEING THOSE 0.76 OF 86 WHERE THE LEVEL OF POLITICAL INTEGRATION IS THE LITTLE STATE, THE MINIMAL STATE, THE AUTONOMOUS COMMUNITY, OR THE FAMILY (262) GPM	5 21 45 65 XSQ= 3.37 PHI= -0.157 XP = 0.0664
88	DRIFT MORE TOWARD BEING THOSE 0.76 OF 45 WHERE, IF A HEADMANSHIP IS PRESENT, SUCCESSION IS HEREDITARY (165)	88	DRIFT LESS TOWARD BEING THOSE 0.58 OF 77 WHERE, IF A HEADMANSHIP IS PRESENT, SUCCESSION IS HEREDITARY (165)	11 32 34 45 XSQ= 2.93 PHI= -0.155 XP = 0.0868
99	TILT TOWARD BEING THOSE 0.80 OF 25 WHERE, WITH NATIONAL HIERARCHY ABSENT, THE HIERARCHY OF LOCAL JURISDICTION HAS FOUR OR THREE LEVELS (93) GES,EA	99	TILT TOWARD BEING THOSE 0.55 OF 33 WHERE, WITH NATIONAL HIERARCHY ABSENT, THE HIERARCHY OF LOCAL JURISDICTION HAS TWO LEVELS (63) GES,EA	20 15 5 18 XSQ= 5.72 PHI= 0.314 XP = 0.0167
107	TILT MORE TOWARD BEING THOSE 0.86 OF 43 WHERE CLASS STRATIFICATION, IF PRESENT, IS BASED ON SOMETHING OTHER THAN OCCUPATIONAL STATUS (160)	107	TILT LESS TOWARD BEING THOSE 0.64 OF 55 WHERE CLASS STRATIFICATION, IF PRESENT, IS BASED ON SOMETHING OTHER THAN OCCUPATIONAL STATUS (160)	6 20 37 35 XSQ= 5.12 PHI= -0.229 XP = 0.0236
110	LEAN TOWARD BEING THOSE 0.67 OF 63 WHERE SLAVERY IS PRESENT (163)	110	LEAN TOWARD BEING THOSE 0.59 OF 105 WHERE SLAVERY IS ABSENT (218)	42 43 21 62 XSQ= 9.41 PHI= 0.237 XP = 0.0022
164	IN ALL CASES ARE THOSE 1.00 OF 3 WHERE THE EMPHASIS ON INDIVIDUAL VOLITION AS THE CAUSE OR SOURCE OF ILLNESS IS HIGH (9) MJ	164	TILT TOWARD BEING THOSE 0.88 OF 8 WHERE THE EMPHASIS ON INDIVIDUAL VOLITION AS THE CAUSE OR SOURCE OF ILLNESS IS LOW (9) MJ	3 1 0 7 XSQ= 3.93 PHI= 0.598 EP = 0.0242
176	DRIFT TOWARD BEING THOSE 0.58 OF 64 WHERE THE COMMUNITY IS A CLAN-COMMUNITY OR A COMMUNITY STRUCTURED OR SEGMENTED ON A CLAN BASIS (169)	176	DRIFT TOWARD BEING THOSE 0.57 OF 101 WHERE THE COMMUNITY IS OTHER THAN A CLAN-COMMUNITY OR A COMMUNITY STRUCTURED OR SEGMENTED ON A CLAN BASIS (213)	37 43 27 58 XSQ= 3.06 PHI= 0.136 XP = 0.0804

186	LEAN TOWARD BEING THOSE WHERE THE KIN GROUP IS EXCLUSIVELY PATRILINEAL (150)	0.59 OF 66	186	LEAN TOWARD BEING THOSE WHERE THE KIN GROUP IS OTHER THAN EXCLUSIVELY PATRILINEAL (250)	0.64 OF 106	39 38 27 68 XSQ= 7.97 PHI= 0.215 XP = 0.0048
188	TEND MORE TO BE THOSE WHERE THE KIN GROUP IS OTHER THAN EXCLUSIVELY COGNATIC (252)	0.98 OF 66	188	TEND LESS TO BE THOSE WHERE THE KIN GROUP IS OTHER THAN EXCLUSIVELY COGNATIC (252)	0.59 OF 106	1 43 65 63 XSQ= 30.56 PHI= -0.422 XP = 0.
192	IN ALL CASES ARE THOSE OTHER THAN WHERE THE ONLY KIN GROUP PRESENT IS A KINDRED OR ELSE BILATERAL DESCENT IS INFERRED (289)	1.00 OF 66	192	TEND LESS TO BE THOSE OTHER THAN WHERE THE ONLY KIN GROUP PRESENT IS A KINDRED OR ELSE BILATERAL DESCENT IS INFERRED (289)	0.74 OF 106	0 28 66 78 XSQ= 18.93 PHI= -0.332 XP = 0.0000
197	TILT MORE TOWARD BEING THOSE WHERE RULES FOR THE INHERITANCE OF REAL PROPERTY, IF PRESENT, FAVOR EITHER THE MALE HEIR OR LINE, OR THE FEMALE HEIR OR LINE (165)	0.97 OF 34	197	TILT LESS TOWARD BEING THOSE WHERE RULES FOR THE INHERITANCE OF REAL PROPERTY, IF PRESENT, FAVOR EITHER THE MALE HEIR OR LINE, OR THE FEMALE HEIR OR LINE (165)	0.78 OF 46	33 36 1 10 XSQ= 4.35 PHI= 0.233 XP = 0.0371
204	DRIFT MORE TOWARD BEING THOSE WHERE MARITAL RESIDENCE IS PATRILOCAL, VIRILOCAL, OR AVUNCULOCAL, RATHER THAN AMBILOCAL OR NEOLOCAL (270)	0.95 OF 58	204	DRIFT LESS TOWARD BEING THOSE WHERE MARITAL RESIDENCE IS PATRILOCAL, VIRILOCAL, OR AVUNCULOCAL, RATHER THAN AMBILOCAL OR NEOLOCAL (270)	0.84 OF 87	55 73 3 14 XSQ= 3.02 PHI= 0.144 XP = 0.0821
214	TEND LESS TO BE THOSE WHERE FIRST COUSIN MARRIAGE, IF PERMITTED, IS OTHER THAN UNILATERAL (144)	0.58 OF 66	214	IN ALL CASES ARE THOSE WHERE FIRST COUSIN MARRIAGE, IF PERMITTED, IS OTHER THAN UNILATERAL (144)	1.00 OF 106	28 0 38 106 XSQ= 50.65 PHI= 0.543 XP = 0.
220	TEND TO BE THOSE WHERE FIRST COUSIN MARRIAGE IN SOME FORM OR OTHER IS PRESCRIBED OR PREFERRED (97)	0.83 OF 66	220	TEND TO BE THOSE WHERE FIRST COUSIN MARRIAGE IN SOME FORM OR OTHER IS NOT PRESCRIBED OR PREFERRED (273)	0.60 OF 106	55 42 11 64 XSQ= 29.85 PHI= 0.417 XP = 0.0000
221	TEND TO BE THOSE WHERE MATRILATERAL CROSS-COUSIN MARRIAGE IS PRESCRIBED OR PREFERRED (35)	0.53 OF 66	221	IN ALL CASES ARE THOSE WHERE MATRILATERAL CROSS-COUSIN MARRIAGE IS NOT PRESCRIBED OR PREFERRED (335)	1.00 OF 106	35 0 31 106 XSQ= 67.34 PHI= 0.626 XP = 0.
262	TILT MORE TOWARD BEING THOSE WHERE WIVES ARE OBTAINED BY MEANS INVOLVING THE PRESENCE OF SOME CONSIDERATION (305)	0.91 OF 66	262	TILT LESS TOWARD BEING THOSE WHERE WIVES ARE OBTAINED BY MEANS INVOLVING THE PRESENCE OF SOME CONSIDERATION (305)	0.76 OF 105	60 80 6 25 XSQ= 4.97 PHI= 0.170 XP = 0.0259

263	TEND MORE TO BE THOSE WHERE WIVES ARE OBTAINED BY RELATIVELY DIFFICULT MEANS, NAMELY BY BRIDE-PRICE, BRIDE-SERVICE, OR EXCHANGING A FEMALE RELATIVE (233)	0.82 OF 66	263	TEND LESS TO BE THOSE WHERE WIVES ARE OBTAINED BY RELATIVELY DIFFICULT MEANS, NAMELY BY BRIDE-PRICE, BRIDE-SERVICE, OR EXCHANGING A FEMALE RELATIVE (233)	0.54 OF 105	54 57 12 48 XSQ= 12.31 PHI= 0.268 XP = 0.0005
296	DRIFT TOWARD BEING THOSE WHERE INFANTICIDE IS ABSENT OR INFERRED ABSENT (15) BCA	0.80 OF 5	296	DRIFT TOWARD BEING THOSE WHERE INFANTICIDE IS PRESENT (18) BCA	0.83 OF 6	1 5 4 1 XSQ= 2.23 PHI= -0.450 EP = 0.0801
302	LEAN TOWARD BEING THOSE WHERE THE AVERAGE EARLY SATISFACTION POTENTIAL IS HIGH (23) W-C	0.86 OF 7	302	IN ALL CASES ARE THOSE WHERE THE AVERAGE EARLY SATISFACTION POTENTIAL IS LOW (17) W-C	1.00 OF 6	6 0 1 6 XSQ= 6.41 PHI= 0.702 EP = 0.0047
307	IN ALL CASES ARE THOSE WHERE THE EARLY AGGRESSION SATISFACTION POTENTIAL IS HIGH (33) W-C	1.00 OF 9	307	LEAN TOWARD BEING THOSE WHERE THE EARLY AGGRESSION SATISFACTION POTENTIAL IS LOW (19) W-C	0.75 OF 8	9 2 0 6 XSQ= 7.41 PHI= 0.660 EP = 0.0023
313	DRIFT TOWARD BEING THOSE WHERE AGGRESSION SOCIALIZATION ANXIETY IS LOW (28) W-C	0.78 OF 9	313	DRIFT TOWARD BEING THOSE WHERE AGGRESSION SOCIALIZATION ANXIETY IS HIGH (26) W-C	0.75 OF 8	2 6 7 2 XSQ= 2.85 PHI= -0.410 EP = 0.0567
323	TILT MORE TOWARD BEING THOSE WHERE THE CONSTANCY OF PRESENCE OF THE INFANT'S NURTURANT AGENT IS LOW (45) B-B-C	0.92 OF 12	323	TILT LESS TOWARD BEING THOSE WHERE THE CONSTANCY OF PRESENCE OF THE INFANT'S NURTURANT AGENT IS LOW (45) B-B-C	0.53 OF 15	1 7 11 8 XSQ= 3.04 PHI= -0.336 EP = 0.0433
373	IN ALL CASES ARE THOSE WHERE MALE INITIATION CEREMONIES AT PUBERTY ARE ABSENT (27) W-K-A	1.00 OF 7	373	DRIFT TOWARD BEING THOSE WHERE MALE INITIATION CEREMONIES AT PUBERTY ARE PRESENT (17) W-K-A	0.50 OF 8	0 4 7 4 XSQ= 2.56 PHI= -0.413 EP = 0.0769
382	DRIFT TOWARD BEING THOSE WHERE FEMALE INITIATION RITES ARE ABSENT (27) JKB	0.75 OF 8	382	DRIFT TOWARD BEING THOSE WHERE FEMALE INITIATION RITES ARE PRESENT (38) JKB	0.67 OF 21	2 14 6 7 XSQ= 2.56 PHI= -0.297 EP = 0.0923
399	DRIFT TOWARD BEING THOSE WHERE INTENSITY OF CASTRATION ANXIETY IS LOW (22) WNS	0.78 OF 9	399	DRIFT TOWARD BEING THOSE WHERE INTENSITY OF CASTRATION ANXIETY IS HIGH (23) WNS	0.75 OF 8	2 6 7 2 XSQ= 2.85 PHI= -0.410 EP = 0.0567

```
400  TILT TOWARD BEING THOSE        0.75 OF   8     400  TILT TOWARD BEING THOSE        0.75 OF  16           6    4
     WHERE HOMOSEXUAL ACTIVITY                           WHERE HOMOSEXUAL ACTIVITY                             2   12
     IS PROHIBITED  (22) F-B                             IS PERMITTED  (36) F-B                      XSQ=     3.62
                                                                                                     PHI=    0.388
                                                                                                     EP  =  0.0324

460  DRIFT TOWARD BEING THOSE       0.70 OF  23     460  DRIFT TOWARD BEING THOSE       0.56 OF  43           7   24
     WHERE GAMES, IF PRESENT,                            WHERE GAMES, IF PRESENT,                             16   19
     ARE NOT LIMITED TO                                  ARE LIMITED TO                              XSQ=     2.92
     GAMES OF SKILL ONLY  (104) R-A-B,EA                 GAMES OF SKILL ONLY  (67) R-A-B,EA          PHI=   -0.210
                                                                                                     XP  =  0.0873
```

****

	Left column		Right column
225	CULTURES WHERE COUSIN MARRIAGE IS PREFERENTIALLY OR PERMISSIVELY PATRILATERAL, RATHER THAN MATRILATERAL (23)	225	CULTURES WHERE COUSIN MARRIAGE IS PREFERENTIALLY OR PERMISSIVELY MATRILATERAL, RATHER THAN PATRILATERAL (43)

BACKGROUND ON PAGE 117

BOTH SUBJECT AND PREDICATE

....

23 IN LEFT COLUMN

BAJUN, BALINESE, BARABRA, BASSERI, BEJA, BIRIFOR, CALLINAGO, EGYPTIANS, HAIDA, HASANIA, HAZARA, HERERO, ILA, PATHAN, PENDE, REGEIBAT, RWALA, SHERENTE, SYRIANS, TIWI, TROBRIAND, VEDDA, YAKO

43 IN RIGHT COLUMN

ABOR, ALBANIANS, ARAUCANIANS, BAMBARA, BATAK, BELU, BURYAT, CHENCHU, GARO, GILYAK, HEHE, HO, KACHIN, KASKA, KERALA, KISSI, KONSO, LAKHER, LAMBA, LAMET, LHOTA NAGA, LOLO, MAGUZAWA, MANDAN, MAYA, MBUNDU, MENDE, MIN CHINESE, MNONG GAR, MURNGIN, PURUM, SAMOYED, SANDAWE, SIRIONO, SIUAI, TANIMBARESE, TOLOWA, TSHIMSHIAN, TURKMEN, TZELTAL, VENDA, WARDPEN, WIKMUNKAN

304 EXCLUDED BECAUSE IRRELEVANT

30 EXCLUDED BECAUSE UNASCERTAINED

	Left column				Right column			Statistics
4	TILT LESS TOWARD BEING THOSE LOCATED OUTSIDE OF THE CIRCUM-MEDITERRANEAN (355)	0.70 OF 23		4	TILT MORE TOWARD BEING THOSE LOCATED OUTSIDE OF THE CIRCUM-MEDITERRANEAN (355)	0.93 OF 43		7 3 16 40 XSQ= 4.72 PHI= 0.267 XP = 0.0298
33	TEND LESS TO BE THOSE WHERE THE NATURAL ENVIRONMENT IS OTHER THAN 'VERY HARSH,' I.E., DESERT, DESERT GRASSES AND SHRUBS, TUNDRA, OR HIGH PLATEAU STEPPE (341) FWM	0.61 OF 23		33	TEND MORE TO BE THOSE WHERE THE NATURAL ENVIRONMENT IS OTHER THAN 'VERY HARSH,' I.E., DESERT, DESERT GRASSES AND SHRUBS, TUNDRA, OR HIGH PLATEAU STEPPE (341) FWM	0.98 OF 43		9 1 14 42 XSQ= 13.06 PHI= 0.445 XP = 0.0003
36	TILT LESS TOWARD BEING THOSE WHERE THE NATURAL ENVIRONMENT IS OTHER THAN 'VERY HARSH,' OR SUB-TROPICAL BUSH, OR TEMPERATE GRASSLAND (292) FWM	0.57 OF 23		36	TILT MORE TOWARD BEING THOSE WHERE THE NATURAL ENVIRONMENT IS OTHER THAN 'VERY HARSH,' OR SUB-TROPICAL BUSH, OR TEMPERATE GRASSLAND (292) FWM	0.86 OF 43		10 6 13 37 XSQ= 5.60 PHI= 0.291 XP = 0.0180
89	DRIFT TOWARD BEING THOSE WHERE, IF A NON-HEREDITARY HEADMANSHIP IS PRESENT, SUCCESSION IS BY CONSENSUS (63)	0.80 OF 5		89	DRIFT TOWARD BEING THOSE WHERE, IF A NON-HEREDITARY HEADMANSHIP IS PRESENT, SUCCESSION IS BY MEANS OTHER THAN CONSENSUS (43)	0.83 OF 6		4 1 1 5 XSQ= 2.23 PHI= 0.450 EP = 0.0801

109	TILT LESS TOWARD BEING THOSE 0.59 OF 17 WHERE CASTES ARE ABSENT (317)	109	TILT MORE TOWARD BEING THOSE 0.89 OF 36 WHERE CASTES ARE ABSENT (317)	7 4 10 32 XSQ= 4.65 PHI= 0.296 XP = 0.0311
181	DRIFT LESS TOWARD BEING THOSE 0.87 OF 23 WHERE THE COMMUNITY IS OTHER THAN A DEME (337)	181	IN ALL CASES ARE THOSE 1.00 OF 41 WHERE THE COMMUNITY IS OTHER THAN A DEME (337)	3 0 20 41 XSQ= 3.07 PHI= 0.219 XP = 0.0797
184	TILT TOWARD BEING THOSE 0.64 OF 22 WHERE THE LARGEST NON-COGNATIC KIN GROUP IS THE MOEITY OR PHRATRY (77)	184	TILT TOWARD BEING THOSE 0.70 OF 43 WHERE THE LARGEST NON-COGNATIC KIN GROUP IS SMALLER THAN A PHRATRY, I. E. A SIB OR LINEAGE (175)	14 13 8 30 XSQ= 5.38 PHI= 0.288 XP = 0.0203
214	DRIFT TOWARD BEING THOSE 0.74 OF 23 WHERE FIRST COUSIN MARRIAGE, IF PERMITTED, IS OTHER THAN UNILATERAL (144)	214	DRIFT TOWARD BEING THOSE 0.51 OF 43 WHERE FIRST COUSIN MARRIAGE, IF PERMITTED, IS UNILATERAL (28)	6 22 17 21 XSQ= 2.90 PHI= -0.210 XP = 0.0886
221	IN ALL CASES ARE THOSE 1.00 OF 23 WHERE MATRILATERAL CROSS-COUSIN MARRIAGE IS NOT PRESCRIBED OR PREFERRED (335)	221	TEND TO BE THOSE 0.81 OF 43 WHERE MATRILATERAL CROSS-COUSIN MARRIAGE IS PRESCRIBED OR PREFERRED (35)	0 35 23 8 XSQ= 36.66 PHI= -0.745 XP = 0.
377	TILT TOWARD BEING THOSE 0.53 OF 19 WHERE MALE GENITAL MUTILATION IS PRESENT (83)	377	TILT TOWARD BEING THOSE 0.82 OF 33 WHERE MALE GENITAL MUTILATION IS ABSENT (242)	10 6 9 27 XSQ= 5.20 PHI= 0.316 XP = 0.0226
386	IN ALL CASES ARE THOSE 1.00 OF 3 WHERE SEXUAL EXPRESSION BY THE YOUNG IS PERMITTED (40) F-B	386	TILT TOWARD BEING THOSE 0.86 OF 7 WHERE SEXUAL EXPRESSION BY THE YOUNG IS RESTRICTED OR SEMI-RESTRICTED (46) F-B	0 6 3 1 XSQ= 3.35 PHI= -0.579 EP = 0.0333
428	IN ALL CASES ARE THOSE 1.00 OF 9 WHERE A HIGH GOD, IF PRESENT AND ACTIVE, SUPPORTS HUMAN MORALITY, RATHER THAN NOT SUPPORTING IT (61) GES,EA	428	LEAN TOWARD BEING THOSE 0.63 OF 8 WHERE A HIGH GOD, IF PRESENT AND ACTIVE, DOES NOT SUPPORT HUMAN MORALITY, RATHER THAN SUPPORTING IT (26) GES,EA	9 3 0 5 XSQ= 5.24 PHI= 0.555 EP = 0.0090
473	DRIFT TOWARD BEING THOSE 0.75 OF 4 WHERE SENSITIVITY TO INSULT IS EXTREME (32) PES	473	DRIFT TOWARD BEING THOSE 0.88 OF 8 WHERE SENSITIVITY TO INSULT IS MODERATE OR NEGLIGIBLE (56) PES	3 1 1 7 XSQ= 2.30 PHI= 0.437 EP = 0.0667

****

226 CULTURES
WHERE THE COUSIN TERMINOLOGY IS
OF CROW, OMAHA, OR IROQUOIS TYPE (152)

226 CULTURES
WHERE THE COUSIN TERMINOLOGY IS OTHER THAN
OF CROW, OMAHA, OR IROQUOIS TYPE (212)

BACKGROUND ON PAGE 121 SUBJECT ONLY

....

152 IN LEFT COLUMN

AJIE	AKHA	AMBA	APINAYE	ARANDA	ARAPESH	ARAUCANIANS	BACAIRI	BAMBARA	BANDA
BARI	BEMBA	BIRIFOR	BLACK CARIB	BORORO	BUDUMA	BUNLAP	CALLINAGO	CAMAYURA	CARIB
CHAGGA	CHENCHU	CHEROKEE	COORG	CREE	CREEK	CROW	DAGUR	DIEGUENO	DIERI
DOBUANS	DOGON	DOROBO	ENGA	EYAK	FANG	FOX	FUTAJALONKE	GANDA	GARO
GILYAK	GOAJIRO	GOND	GUAHIBO	GUATO	HAIDA	HANO	HAVASUPAI	HEHE	HERERO
HO	HURON	ILA	IRAQW	KACHIN	KALMYK	KAPAUKU	KARIERA	KASKA	KAZAK
KERAKI	KERALA	KHALKA	KHASI	KIKUYU	KONSO	KURTATCHI	LAKALAI	LAKHER	LAMBA
LAMET	LANGO	LAU	LESU	LHOTA NAGA	MANCHU	MANDAN	MARICOPA	MARSHALLESE	MASAI
MATAKAM	MBUGWE	MBUNDU	MIAMI	MISKITO	MIWOK	MNONG GAR	MONGO	MOTA	MOTILON
MURINBATA	NABESNA	NAMA	NAMBICUARA	NANDI	NASKAPI	NAVAHO	NDEMBU	NGONI	NOMLAKI
NUNIVAK	NYAKYUSA	NYANEKA	NYORO	OJIBWA	OMAHA	PAWNEE	PENDE	PONAPEANS	ROTINESE
RUNDI	SEMINOLE	SENIANG	SHERENTE	SINHALESE	SIRIONO	SONGHAI	SOTHO	SWAZI	TAMIL
TANALA	TAREUMIUT	TEDA	TERA	TETON	THONGA	TIMBIRA	TIMUCUA	TODA	TOKELAU
TOLOWA	TROBRIAND	TRUKESE	TRUMAI	TSHIMSHIAN	TUCANO	TUCUNA	TUPINAMBA	TZELTAL	VEDDA
VENDA	WANTOAT	WAPISHANA	WAROPEN	WIKMUNKAN	WINNEBAGO	WOGEO	YABARANA	YAKO	YAO
YAPESE	ZUNI								

212 IN RIGHT COLUMN

36 EXCLUDED BECAUSE UNASCERTAINED

ABOR	ALACALUF	BAMILEKE	BASSERI	BAYA	BETE	BOZO	CHAMACOCO	CHEREMIS	CHIRIGUANO
JIVARO	KABYLE	KET	KHEVSUR	KPE	LUBA	MBUTI	MENTAWEI	MIN CHINESE	MONGUOR
MZAB	NURI	NYARO	PAEZ	PALIKUR	RIFFIANS	SAMOYED	SHLUH	TEHUELCHE	TENDA
WAICA	WITOTO	WUTE	YAGUA	YOMBE	YUKAGHIR				

----

3 TILT LESS TOWARD BEING THOSE LOCATED OUTSIDE OF AFRICA (320) 0.75 OF 152

3 TILT MORE TOWARD BEING THOSE LOCATED OUTSIDE OF AFRICA (320) 0.85 OF 212

38	31
114	181

XSQ= 5.55
PHI= 0.123
XP = 0.0185

4 LEAN MORE TOWARD BEING THOSE LOCATED OUTSIDE OF THE CIRCUM-MEDITERRANEAN (355) 0.95 OF 152

4 LEAN LESS TOWARD BEING THOSE LOCATED OUTSIDE OF THE CIRCUM-MEDITERRANEAN (355) 0.85 OF 212

7	32
145	180

XSQ= 9.11
PHI= -0.158
XP = 0.0025

No.			No.			
15	DRIFT MORE TOWARD BEING THOSE WHERE THE LATITUDE IS LESS THAN TWENTY DEGREES (217)	0.61 OF 152	15	DRIFT LESS TOWARD BEING THOSE WHERE THE LATITUDE IS LESS THAN TWENTY DEGREES (217)	0.50 OF 212	60 105 92 107 XSQ= 3.22 PHI= -0.094 XP = 0.0729
53	LEAN MORE TOWARD BEING THOSE WHERE FOOD PRODUCTION IS BY SIMPLE AGRICULTURE OR INCIPIENT FOOD PRODUCTION, RATHER THAN BY INTENSIVE AGRICULTURE (147)	0.74 OF 92	53	LEAN LESS TOWARD BEING THOSE WHERE FOOD PRODUCTION IS BY SIMPLE AGRICULTURE OR INCIPIENT FOOD PRODUCTION, RATHER THAN BY INTENSIVE AGRICULTURE (147)	0.53 OF 126	24 59 68 67 XSQ= 8.84 PHI= -0.201 XP = 0.0029
54	TILT LESS TOWARD BEING THOSE WHERE FOOD PRODUCTION IS BY INTENSIVE OR SIMPLE AGRICULTURE, RATHER THAN BY INCIPIENT FOOD PRODUCTION (192)	0.74 OF 92	54	TILT MORE TOWARD BEING THOSE WHERE FOOD PRODUCTION IS BY INTENSIVE OR SIMPLE AGRICULTURE, RATHER THAN BY INCIPIENT FOOD PRODUCTION (192)	0.87 OF 126	68 109 24 17 XSQ= 4.73 PHI= -0.147 XP = 0.0296
55	TILT TOWARD BEING THOSE WHERE FOOD PRODUCTION IS BY SIMPLE AGRICULTURE, RATHER THAN BY INTENSIVE AGRICULTURE (101)	0.65 OF 68	55	TILT TOWARD BEING THOSE WHERE FOOD PRODUCTION IS BY INTENSIVE AGRICULTURE, RATHER THAN BY SIMPLE AGRICULTURE (91)	0.54 OF 109	24 59 44 50 XSQ= 5.23 PHI= -0.172 XP = 0.0222
73	LEAN TOWARD BEING THOSE WHERE WEAVING IS ABSENT (130)	0.64 OF 101	73	LEAN TOWARD BEING THOSE WHERE WEAVING IS PRESENT (118)	0.54 OF 127	36 69 65 58 XSQ= 7.17 PHI= -0.177 XP = 0.0074
81	TEND TO BE THOSE WHERE NO CITY OR TOWN IS PRESENT, AND THE AVERAGE COMMUNITY SIZE IS SMALLER THAN 200 (135)	0.74 OF 92	81	TEND TO BE THOSE WHERE A CITY OR TOWN IS PRESENT, OR THE AVERAGE COMMUNITY SIZE IS 200 OR GREATER (89)	0.50 OF 114	24 57 68 57 XSQ= 11.22 PHI= -0.233 XP = 0.0008
84	LEAN MORE TOWARD BEING THOSE WHERE THE LEVEL OF POLITICAL INTEGRATION IS THE LITTLE STATE, THE MINIMAL STATE, THE AUTONOMOUS COMMUNITY, OR THE FAMILY (262) GPM	0.92 OF 120	84	LEAN LESS TOWARD BEING THOSE WHERE THE LEVEL OF POLITICAL INTEGRATION IS THE LITTLE STATE, THE MINIMAL STATE, THE AUTONOMOUS COMMUNITY, OR THE FAMILY (262) GPM	0.79 OF 155	10 32 110 123 XSQ= 7.00 PHI= -0.160 XP = 0.0082
85	LEAN MORE TOWARD BEING THOSE WHERE THE LEVEL OF POLITICAL INTEGRATION IS THE MINIMAL STATE, THE AUTONOMOUS COMMUNITY, OR THE FAMILY (234) GPM	0.83 OF 120	85	LEAN LESS TOWARD BEING THOSE WHERE THE LEVEL OF POLITICAL INTEGRATION IS THE MINIMAL STATE, THE AUTONOMOUS COMMUNITY, OR THE FAMILY (234) GPM	0.69 OF 155	20 48 100 107 XSQ= 6.68 PHI= -0.156 XP = 0.0097
88	TEND MORE TO BE THOSE WHERE, IF A HEADMANSHIP IS PRESENT, SUCCESSION IS HEREDITARY (165)	0.74 OF 111	88	TEND LESS TO BE THOSE WHERE, IF A HEADMANSHIP IS PRESENT, SUCCESSION IS HEREDITARY (165)	0.51 OF 137	29 67 82 70 XSQ= 12.47 PHI= -0.224 XP = 0.0004

90	LEAN LESS TOWARD BEING THOSE 0.67 OF 82 WHERE, IF A HEREDITARY HEADMANSHIP IS PRESENT, SUCCESSION IS PATRILINEAL, RATHER THAN MATRILINEAL (127)	90	LEAN MORE TOWARD BEING THOSE 0.87 OF 70 WHERE, IF A HEREDITARY HEADMANSHIP IS PRESENT, SUCCESSION IS PATRILINEAL, RATHER THAN MATRILINEAL (127)	55 61 27 9 XSQ= 7.34 PHI= -0.220 XP = 0.0067
102	TILT TOWARD BEING THOSE 0.54 OF 147 WHERE CLASS STRATIFICATION IS ABSENT (180)	102	TILT TOWARD BEING THOSE 0.59 OF 202 WHERE CLASS STRATIFICATION IS PRESENT (203)	68 120 79 82 XSQ= 5.40 PHI= -0.124 XP = 0.0201
107	LEAN MORE TOWARD BEING THOSE 0.91 OF 68 WHERE CLASS STRATIFICATION, IF PRESENT, IS BASED ON SOMETHING OTHER THAN OCCUPATIONAL STATUS (160)	107	LEAN LESS TOWARD BEING THOSE 0.70 OF 120 WHERE CLASS STRATIFICATION, IF PRESENT, IS BASED ON SOMETHING OTHER THAN OCCUPATIONAL STATUS (160)	6 36 62 84 XSQ= 10.03 PHI= -0.231 XP = 0.0015
108	TILT LESS TOWARD BEING THOSE 0.54 OF 68 WHERE CLASS STRATIFICATION, IF PRESENT, IS BASED ON SOMETHING OTHER THAN A HEREDITARY ARISTOCRACY (129)	108	TILT MORE TOWARD BEING THOSE 0.70 OF 120 WHERE CLASS STRATIFICATION, IF PRESENT, IS BASED ON SOMETHING OTHER THAN A HEREDITARY ARISTOCRACY (129)	31 36 37 84 XSQ= 3.94 PHI= 0.145 XP = 0.0470
118	TILT TOWARD BEING THOSE 0.70 OF 20 WHERE THE PERCENTAGE OF OCCUPATIONS THAT ARE SPECIALIZED IS LOW (25) WME	118	TILT TOWARD BEING THOSE 0.64 OF 28 WHERE THE PERCENTAGE OF OCCUPATIONS THAT ARE SPECIALIZED IS HIGH OR MEDIUM (24) WME	6 18 14 10 XSQ= 4.20 PHI= -0.296 XP = 0.0404
128	TILT TOWARD BEING THOSE 0.64 OF 33 WHERE, IF SUBSISTENCE IS PRIMARILY BY AGRICULTURE, THE WORK IS MAINLY DONE BY FEMALES (37)	128	TILT TOWARD BEING THOSE 0.68 OF 38 WHERE, IF SUBSISTENCE IS PRIMARILY BY AGRICULTURE, THE WORK IS MAINLY DONE BY MALES (40)	12 26 21 12 XSQ= 6.06 PHI= -0.292 XP = 0.0138
129	DRIFT MORE TOWARD BEING THOSE 0.83 OF 35 WHERE WEAVING IS MAINLY DONE BY FEMALES (73)	129	DRIFT LESS TOWARD BEING THOSE 0.64 OF 59 WHERE WEAVING IS MAINLY DONE BY FEMALES (73)	6 21 29 38 XSQ= 2.81 PHI= -0.173 XP = 0.0938
163	IN ALL CASES ARE THOSE 1.00 OF 4 WHERE THE EMPHASIS ON INDIVIDUAL VOLITION AS THE CAUSE OF CRIME IS LOW (10) MJ	163	DRIFT TOWARD BEING THOSE 0.58 OF 12 WHERE THE EMPHASIS ON INDIVIDUAL VOLITION AS THE CAUSE OF CRIME IS HIGH (7) MJ	0 7 4 5 XSQ= 2.12 PHI= -0.364 EP = 0.0885
176	TEND TO BE THOSE 0.62 OF 146 WHERE THE COMMUNITY IS A CLAN-COMMUNITY OR A COMMUNITY STRUCTURED OR SEGMENTED ON A CLAN BASIS (169)	176	TEND TO BE THOSE 0.70 OF 204 WHERE THE COMMUNITY IS OTHER THAN A CLAN-COMMUNITY OR A COMMUNITY STRUCTURED OR SEGMENTED ON A CLAN BASIS (213)	90 61 56 143 XSQ= 33.67 PHI= 0.310 XP = 0.

177	TEND LESS TO BE THOSE 0.68 OF 146 WHERE THE COMMUNITY IS OTHER THAN A SINGLE CLAN-COMMUNITY AND EXOGAMOUS (305)	177	TEND MORE TO BE THOSE 0.90 OF 204 WHERE THE COMMUNITY IS OTHER THAN A SINGLE CLAN-COMMUNITY AND EXOGAMOUS (305)	47 21 99 183 XSQ= 24.69 PHI= 0.266 XP = 0.0000
178	DRIFT LESS TOWARD BEING THOSE 0.73 OF 146 WHERE THE COMMUNITY IS OTHER THAN SEGMENTED ON A CLAN BASIS AND NON-EXOGAMOUS (295)	178	DRIFT MORE TOWARD BEING THOSE 0.81 OF 204 WHERE THE COMMUNITY IS OTHER THAN SEGMENTED ON A CLAN BASIS AND NON-EXOGAMOUS (295)	40 38 106 166 XSQ= 3.29 PHI= 0.097 XP = 0.0697
180	TEND LESS TO BE THOSE 0.58 OF 146 WHERE THE COMMUNITY IS COMMONLY NON-EXOGAMOUS, RATHER THAN EXOGAMOUS (258)	180	TEND MORE TO BE THOSE 0.75 OF 204 WHERE THE COMMUNITY IS COMMONLY NON-EXOGAMOUS, RATHER THAN EXOGAMOUS (258)	62 51 84 153 XSQ= 11.09 PHI= 0.178 XP = 0.0009
181	TEND MORE TO BE THOSE 0.97 OF 146 WHERE THE COMMUNITY IS OTHER THAN A DEME (337)	181	TEND LESS TO BE THOSE 0.81 OF 204 WHERE THE COMMUNITY IS OTHER THAN A DEME (337)	5 38 141 166 XSQ= 16.87 PHI= -0.220 XP = 0.0000
182	TILT MORE TOWARD BEING THOSE 0.73 OF 146 OTHER THAN WHERE THE COMMUNITY IS STRUCTURED ON A NON-CLAN BASIS AND AGAMOUS (256)	182	TILT LESS TOWARD BEING THOSE 0.62 OF 204 OTHER THAN WHERE THE COMMUNITY IS STRUCTURED ON A NON-CLAN BASIS AND AGAMOUS (256)	39 77 107 127 XSQ= 4.19 PHI= -0.109 XP = 0.0407
183	LEAN LESS TOWARD BEING THOSE 0.79 OF 131 WHERE THE LARGEST NON-COGNATIC KIN GROUP IS SMALLER THAN A MOEITY, I. E., A PHRATRY OR SIB OR LINEAGE (218)	183	LEAN MORE TOWARD BEING THOSE 0.94 OF 95 WHERE THE LARGEST NON-COGNATIC KIN GROUP IS SMALLER THAN A MOEITY, I. E., A PHRATRY OR SIB OR LINEAGE (218)	27 6 104 89 XSQ= 7.91 PHI= 0.187 XP = 0.0049
185	DRIFT MORE TOWARD BEING THOSE 0.83 OF 131 WHERE THE LARGEST NON-COGNATIC KIN GROUP IS THE MOEITY OR PHRATRY OR SIB (194)	185	DRIFT LESS TOWARD BEING THOSE 0.73 OF 95 WHERE THE LARGEST NON-COGNATIC KIN GROUP IS THE MOEITY OR PHRATRY OR SIB (194)	109 69 22 26 XSQ= 3.08 PHI= 0.117 XP = 0.0795
186	LEAN LESS TOWARD BEING THOSE 0.56 OF 152 WHERE THE KIN GROUP IS OTHER THAN EXCLUSIVELY PATRILINEAL (250)	186	LEAN MORE TOWARD BEING THOSE 0.71 OF 212 WHERE THE KIN GROUP IS OTHER THAN EXCLUSIVELY PATRILINEAL (250)	67 61 85 151 XSQ= 8.44 PHI= 0.152 XP = 0.0037
187	TEND LESS TO BE THOSE 0.74 OF 152 WHERE THE KIN GROUP IS OTHER THAN EXCLUSIVELY MATRILINEAL (344)	187	TEND MORE TO BE THOSE 0.94 OF 211 WHERE THE KIN GROUP IS OTHER THAN EXCLUSIVELY MATRILINEAL (344)	40 13 112 198 XSQ= 27.19 PHI= 0.274 XP = 0.0000

188	TEND TO BE THOSE WHERE THE KIN GROUP IS OTHER THAN EXCLUSIVELY COGNATIC (252)	0.86 OF 152	188	TEND TO BE THOSE WHERE THE KIN GROUP IS EXCLUSIVELY COGNATIC (148)	0.55 OF 212	21 117 131 95 XSQ= 62.63 PHI= -0.415 XP = 0.
190	LEAN LESS TOWARD BEING THOSE WHERE THE KIN GROUP IS PATRILINEAL OR DOUBLE-DESCENT, RATHER THAN MATRILINEAL (186)	0.66 OF 130	190	LEAN MORE TOWARD BEING THOSE WHERE THE KIN GROUP IS PATRILINEAL OR DOUBLE-DESCENT, RATHER THAN MATRILINEAL (186)	0.84 OF 91	86 76 44 15 XSQ= 7.38 PHI= -0.183 XP = 0.0066
192	TEND MORE TO BE THOSE OTHER THAN WHERE THE ONLY KIN GROUP PRESENT IS A KINDRED OR ELSE BILATERAL DESCENT IS INFERRED (289)	0.95 OF 152	192	TEND LESS TO BE THOSE OTHER THAN WHERE THE ONLY KIN GROUP PRESENT IS A KINDRED OR ELSE BILATERAL DESCENT IS INFERRED (289)	0.55 OF 212	7 96 145 116 XSQ= 70.21 PHI= -0.439 XP = 0.
197	TEND MORE TO BE THOSE WHERE RULES FOR THE INHERITANCE OF REAL PROPERTY, IF PRESENT, FAVOR EITHER THE MALE HEIR OR LINE, OR THE FEMALE HEIR OR LINE (165)	0.97 OF 66	197	TEND LESS TO BE THOSE WHERE RULES FOR THE INHERITANCE OF REAL PROPERTY, IF PRESENT, FAVOR EITHER THE MALE HEIR OR LINE, OR THE FEMALE HEIR OR LINE (165)	0.76 OF 109	64 83 2 26 XSQ= 11.76 PHI= 0.259 XP = 0.0006
198	TILT LESS TOWARD BEING THOSE WHERE RULES FOR THE INHERITANCE OF REAL PROPERTY, IF PRESENT, FAVOR THE MALE HEIR OR LINE, RATHER THAN THE FEMALE (144)	0.80 OF 64	198	TILT MORE TOWARD BEING THOSE WHERE RULES FOR THE INHERITANCE OF REAL PROPERTY, IF PRESENT, FAVOR THE MALE HEIR OR LINE, RATHER THAN THE FEMALE (144)	0.94 OF 83	51 78 13 5 XSQ= 5.60 PHI= -0.195 XP = 0.0180
201	LEAN MORE TOWARD BEING THOSE WHERE MARITAL RESIDENCE IS NON-OPTIONAL, RATHER THAN AMBILOCAL OR NEOLOCAL (334)	0.91 OF 152	201	LEAN LESS TOWARD BEING THOSE WHERE MARITAL RESIDENCE IS NON-OPTIONAL, RATHER THAN AMBILOCAL OR NEOLOCAL (334)	0.78 OF 210	138 164 14 46 XSQ= 9.38 PHI= 0.161 XP = 0.0022
204	LEAN MORE TOWARD BEING THOSE WHERE MARITAL RESIDENCE IS PATRILOCAL, VIRILOCAL, OR AVUNCULOCAL, RATHER THAN AMBILOCAL OR NEOLOCAL (270)	0.88 OF 121	204	LEAN LESS TOWARD BEING THOSE WHERE MARITAL RESIDENCE IS PATRILOCAL, VIRILOCAL, OR AVUNCULOCAL, RATHER THAN AMBILOCAL OR NEOLOCAL (270)	0.74 OF 179	107 133 14 46 XSQ= 8.15 PHI= 0.165 XP = 0.0043
207	LEAN TOWARD BEING THOSE WHERE MARITAL RESIDENCE IS MATRILOCAL OR UXORILOCAL, RATHER THAN AMBILOCAL OR NEOLOCAL (64)	0.69 OF 45	207	LEAN TOWARD BEING THOSE WHERE MARITAL RESIDENCE IS AMBILOCAL OR NEOLOCAL, RATHER THAN MATRILOCAL OR UXORILOCAL (64)	0.60 OF 77	31 31 14 46 XSQ= 8.20 PHI= 0.259 XP = 0.0042
210	LEAN LESS TOWARD BEING THOSE WHERE MARITAL RESIDENCE IS PATRILOCAL, RATHER THAN MATRILOCAL (169)	0.76 OF 103	210	LEAN MORE TOWARD BEING THOSE WHERE MARITAL RESIDENCE IS PATRILOCAL, RATHER THAN MATRILOCAL (169)	0.92 OF 76	78 70 25 6 XSQ= 7.09 PHI= -0.199 XP = 0.0078

213	TEND TO BE THOSE 0.60 OF 149 WHERE FIRST CCUSIN MARRIAGE IS PERMITTED (172)	213	TEND TO BE THOSE 0.65 OF 192 WHERE FIRST COUSIN MARRIAGE IS NOT PERMITTED (198)	89 67 60 125 XSQ= 19.86 PHI= 0.241 XP = 0.0000
220	TEND LESS TO BE THCSE 0.58 OF 149 WHERE FIRST CCUSIN MARRIAGE IN SOME FORM CR CTHER IS NCT PRESCRIBED CR PREFERREC (273)	220	TEND MORE TO BE THOSE 0.83 OF 192 WHERE FIRST COUSIN MARRIAGE IN SOME FORM OR OTHER IS NOT PRESCRIBED OR PREFERRED (273)	63 32 86 160 XSQ= 26.13 PHI= 0.277 XP = 0.0000
221	TILT LESS TOWARC BEING THCSE 0.86 OF 149 WHERE MATRILATERAL CRCSS-COUSIN MARRIAGE IS NCT PRESCRIBEC CR PREFERREC (335)	221	TILT MORE TOWARD BEING THOSE 0.93 OF 192 WHERE MATRILATERAL CROSS-CCUSIN MARRIAGE IS NOT PRESCRIBED OR PREFERRED (335)	21 13 128 179 XSQ= 4.23 PHI= 0.111 XP = 0.0397
236	DRIFT TCWARD BEING THCSE 0.51 OF 151 WHERE THE FAMILY IS OF AN INDEPENDENT TYPE, RATHER THAN AN EXTENDED TYPE (185)	236	DRIFT TOWARD BEING THOSE 0.59 OF 211 WHERE THE FAMILY IS OF AN EXTENDED TYPE, RATHER THAN AN INDEPENDENT TYPE (213)	74 125 77 86 XSQ= 3.32 PHI= -0.096 XP = 0.0683
240	TILT LESS TOWARC BEING THCSE 0.53 OF 74 WHERE THE FAMILY, IF EXTENCEC, IS SMALL OR STEM, RATHER THAN LARGE (135)	240	TILT MORE TOWARD BEING THOSE 0.68 OF 125 WHERE THE FAMILY, IF EXTENDED, IS SMALL OR STEM, RATHER THAN LARGE (135)	35 40 39 85 XSQ= 4.00 PHI= 0.142 XP = 0.0454
242	TILT MCRE TOWARC BEING THOSE 0.85 OF 150 WHERE MARRIAGE IS COMMCNLY CR OCCASICNALLY PCLYGYNOUS, RATHER THAN MCNCGAMCUS (314)	242	TILT LESS TOWARD BEING THOSE 0.76 OF 209 WHERE MARRIAGE IS COMMONLY OR OCCASIONALLY PCLYGYNCUS, RATHER THAN MONOGAMOUS (314)	128 158 22 51 XSQ= 4.53 PHI= 0.112 XP = 0.0334
243	DRIFT TOWARD BEING THOSE 0.52 OF 27 WHERE PCLYGYNY, IF PRESENT, HAS A HIGH INCICENCE (24) W-C,S	243	DRIFT TOWARD BEING THOSE 0.73 OF 30 WHERE POLYGYNY, IF PRESENT, HAS A LOW INCIDENCE (36) W-D,S	14 8 13 22 XSQ= 2.81 PHI= 0.222 XP = 0.0934
256	DRIFT LESS TCWARD BEING THOSE 0.55 OF 11 WHERE GRANDPARENT AND GRANCCHILD ARE FRIENDLY EQUALS (25) CA	256	DRIFT MORE TOWARD BEING THCSE 0.86 OF 22 WHERE GRANDPARENT AND GRANDCHILD ARE FRIENDLY EQUALS (25) DA	6 19 5 3 XSQ= 2.50 PHI= -0.275 EP = 0.0825
259	TILT TOWARD BEING THOSE 0.76 OF 21 WHERE THE SEVERITY OF MOTHER-IN-LAW AVOIDANCE IS HIGH (26) WNS	259	TILT TOWARD BEING THOSE 0.60 OF 25 WHERE THE SEVERITY OF MOTHER-IN-LAW AVOIDANCE IS LOW (20) WNS	16 10 5 15 XSQ= 4.70 PHI= 0.320 XP = 0.0302

302	DRIFT TCWARD BEING THCSE 0.75 OF 16 WHERE THE AVERAGE EARLY SATISFACTION PCTENTIAL IS HIGH (23) W-C	302	DRIFT TOWARD BEING THOSE 0.57 CF 23 WHERE THE AVERAGE EARLY SATISFACTION POTENTIAL IS LCW (17) W-C	12 10 4 13 XSQ= 2.64 PHI= 0.260 EP = 0.0994
327	DRIFT TCWARD BEING THCSE 0.63 OF 27 WHERE THE AGE CF THE INFANT AT TIME CF REDUCED CONTACT WITH MOTHER IS TWC YEARS CR LOWER (27) B-B-C	327	DRIFT TOWARD BEING THOSE 0.65 CF 26 WHERE THE AGE OF THE INFANT AT TIME OF REDUCED CONTACT WITH MOTHER IS HIGHER THAN TWO YEARS (28) B-B-C	10 17 17 9 XSQ= 3.20 PHI= -0.246 XP = 0.0736
346	TILT TOWARD BEING THCSE 0.63 OF 38 WHERE THE CHILD'S INFERREC ANXIETY OVER PERFORMANCE CF SELF-RELIANT BEHAVIOR IS HIGH (37) B-B-C	346	TILT TOWARD BEING THOSE 0.64 OF 36 WHERE THE CHILD'S INFERRED ANXIETY OVER PERFORMANCE OF SELF-RELIANT BEHAVIOR IS LOW (39) B-B-C	24 13 14 23 XSQ= 4.38 PHI= 0.243 XP = 0.0363
347	LEAN TCWARD BEING THOSE 0.68 OF 38 WHERE THE CHILD'S INFERREC CONFLICT REGARDING SELF-RELIANT BEHAVIOR IS HIGH (37) B-B-C	347	LEAN TOWARD BEI.G THOSE 0.69 CF 36 WHERE THE CHILD'S INFERRED CONFLICT REGARDING SELF-RELIANT BEHAVIOR IS LOW (39) B-B-C	26 11 12 25 XSQ= 9.14 PHI= 0.351 XP = 0.0025
370	TEND TC BE THCSE 0.59 OF 94 WHERE THE SEGREGATICN CF ADOLESCENT BOYS IS COMPLETE CR PARTIAL (95)	37C	TEND TO BE THOSE 0.73 OF 132 WHERE THE SEGREGATION OF ADCLESCENT BOYS IS ABSENT (148)	55 36 39 96 XSQ= 20.99 PHI= 0.305 XP = 0.0000
380	TILT TOWARD BEING THOSE 0.79 OF 28 WHERE SEGREGATICN CF GIRLS AT MENARCHE IS PRESENT (35) F-B	380	TILT TOWARD BEING THOSE 0.54 CF 26 WHERE SEGREGATION OF GIRLS AT MENARCHE IS ABSENT (20) F-B	22 12 6 14 XSQ= 4.76 PHI= 0.297 XP = 0.0290
391	TEND TC BE THCSE 0.69 OF 62 WHERE PREMARITAL SEX RELATIONS ARE PUNISHED CNLY IF PREGNANCY RESULTS, OR FREELY PERMITTEC (90) JTW,EA	391	TEND TO BE THOSE 0.60 OF 103 WHERE PREMARITAL SEX RELATICNS ARE STRONGLY PUNISHED AND IN FACT RARE, OR WEAKLY PUNISHED AND IN FACT NOT RARE (89) JTW,EA	19 62 43 41 XSQ= 12.37 PHI= -0.274 XP = 0.0004
426	LEAN TOWARD BEING THOSE 0.52 OF 102 WHERE A HIGH GOC IS ABSENT (104) GES,EA	426	LEAN TOWARD BEING THOSE 0.66 OF 140 WHERE A HIGH GOD IS PRESENT (156) GES,EA	49 92 53 48 XSQ= 6.87 PHI= -0.169 XP = 0.0088
427	LEAN TOWARD BEING THCSE 0.61 OF 49 WHERE A HIGH GOC, IF PRESENT, IS INACTIVE, RATHER THAN ACTIVE (69) GES,EA	427	LEAN TOWARD BEING THOSE 0.64 OF 92 WHERE A HIGH GOD, IF PRESENT, IS ACTIVE, RATHER THAN INACTIVE (87) GES,EA	19 59 30 33 XSQ= 7.32 PHI= -0.228 XP = 0.0068

428	TILT TOWARD BEING THOSE 0.53 OF 19 WHERE A HIGH GOD, IF PRESENT AND ACTIVE, DOES NOT SUPPORT HUMAN MORALITY, RATHER THAN SUPPORTING IT (26) GES,EA	428	TILT TOWARD BEING THOSE 0.76 OF 59 WHERE A HIGH GOD, IF PRESENT AND ACTIVE, SUPPORTS HUMAN MORALITY, RATHER THAN NOT SUPPORTING IT (61) GES,EA	9 45 10 14 XSQ= 4.36 PHI= -0.236 XP = 0.0368
430	DRIFT TOWARD BEING THOSE 0.73 OF 15 WHERE SUPERNATURAL SANCTIONS FOR MORALITY, HAVING AN EFFECT ON AN INDIVIDUAL'S HEALTH, ARE ABSENT OR UNREPORTED (22) GES	430	DRIFT TOWARD BEING THOSE 0.57 OF 21 WHERE SUPERNATURAL SANCTIONS FOR MORALITY, HAVING AN EFFECT ON AN INDIVIDUAL'S HEALTH, ARE PRESENT (16) GES	4 12 11 9 XSQ= 2.17 PHI= -0.246 EP = 0.0958
450	LEAN MORE TOWARD BEING THOSE 0.89 OF 36 WHERE THE OBSERVATION OF FOOD TABOOS IS HIGH OR MEDIUM, RATHER THAN LOW (60) JRL	450	LEAN LESS TOWARD BEING THOSE 0.55 OF 47 WHERE THE OBSERVATION OF FOOD TABOOS IS HIGH OR MEDIUM, RATHER THAN LOW (60) JRL	32 26 4 21 XSQ= 9.38 PHI= 0.336 XP = 0.0022
459	TILT TOWARD BEING THOSE 0.63 OF 70 WHERE GAMES, IF PRESENT, DO NOT INCLUDE GAMES OF CHANCE (89) R-A-B,EA	459	TILT TOWARD BEING THOSE 0.55 OF 94 WHERE GAMES, IF PRESENT, INCLUDE GAMES OF CHANCE (82) R-A-B,EA	26 52 44 42 XSQ= 4.61 PHI= -0.168 XP = 0.0318
471	TILT TOWARD BEING THOSE 0.70 OF 10 WHERE SECRET SOCIETIES ARE PRESENT (9) LWS	471	TILT TOWARD BEING THOSE 0.83 OF 12 WHERE SECRET SOCIETIES ARE UMIMPORTANT OR ABSENT (14) LWS	7 2 3 10 XSQ= 4.40 PHI= 0.447 EP = 0.0274
473	TILT MORE TOWARD BEING THOSE 0.79 OF 34 WHERE SENSITIVITY TO INSULT IS MODERATE OR NEGLIGIBLE (56) PES	473	TILT LESS TOWARD BEING THOSE 0.54 OF 50 WHERE SENSITIVITY TO INSULT IS MODERATE OR NEGLIGIBLE (56) PES	7 23 27 27 XSQ= 4.64 PHI= -0.235 XP = 0.0312

227 CULTURES WHERE THE COUSIN TERMINOLOGY IS OF CROW OR OMAHA TYPE (59)	227 CULTURES WHERE THE COUSIN TERMINOLOGY IS OTHER THAN OF CROW OR OMAHA TYPE (305)

BACKGROUND ON PAGE 121

SUBJECT ONLY

59 IN LEFT COLUMN

AMBA	APINAYE	ARAPESH	ARAUCANIANS	BANDA	BARI	BIRIFOR	BORORO	CHAGGA	CHEROKEE
CREEK	CROW	DOROBO	FANG	FOX	GOAJIRO	HAIDA	HANO	IRAQW	KALMYK
KASKA	KAZAK	KHALKA	KIKUYU	KONSO	LAKHER	LAMET	LANGO	LHOTA NAGA	MANDAN
MASAI	MATAKAM	MBUGWE	MIAMI	MIWOK	MNONG GAR	MONGO	MOTA	NANDI	NOMLAKI
NYORO	OMAHA	PAWNEE	PENDE	PONAPEANS	SEMINOLE	SENIANG	SHERENTE	SIRIONO	THONGA
TIMBIRA	TIMUCUA	TOKELAU	TROBRIAND	TRUKESE	TZELTAL	WINNEBAGO	YAPESE	ZUNI	

305 IN RIGHT COLUMN

36 EXCLUDED BECAUSE UNASCERTAINED

3	DRIFT LESS TOWARD BEING THOSE LOCATED OUTSIDE OF AFRICA (320) 0.71 OF 59	3	DRIFT MORE TOWARD BEING THOSE LOCATED OUTSIDE OF AFRICA (320) 0.83 OF 305	17 52 42 253 XSQ= 3.72 PHI= 0.101 XP = 0.0537
8	DRIFT LESS TOWARD BEING THOSE LOCATED OUTSIDE OF NORTH AMERICA (330) 0.71 OF 59	8	DRIFT MORE TOWARD BEING THOSE LOCATED OUTSIDE OF NORTH AMERICA (330) 0.83 OF 305	17 53 42 252 XSQ= 3.46 PHI= 0.097 XP = 0.0629
16	TILT LESS TOWARD BEING THOSE WHERE THE LATITUDE IS TEN DEGREES OR GREATER (277) 0.58 OF 59	16	TILT MORE TOWARD BEING THOSE WHERE THE LATITUDE IS TEN DEGREES OR GREATER (277) 0.73 OF 305	34 222 25 83 XSQ= 4.74 PHI= -0.114 XP = 0.0294
80	IN ALL CASES ARE THOSE WHERE NO CITY OR TOWN IS PRESENT (185) 1.00 OF 32	80	LEAN LESS TOWARD BEING THOSE WHERE NO CITY OR TOWN IS PRESENT (185) 0.79 OF 174	0 36 32 138 XSQ= 6.65 PHI= -0.180 XP = 0.0099

84	TILT MORE TOWARD BEING THOSE 0.96 OF 51 WHERE THE LEVEL OF POLITICAL INTEGRATION IS THE LITTLE STATE, THE MINIMAL STATE, THE AUTONOMOUS COMMUNITY, OR THE FAMILY (262) GPM	84	TILT LESS TOWARD BEING THOSE 0.82 OF 224 WHERE THE LEVEL OF POLITICAL INTEGRATION IS THE LITTLE STATE, THE MINIMAL STATE, THE AUTONOMOUS COMMUNITY, OR THE FAMILY (262) GPM	2 40 49 184 XSQ= 5.20 PHI= -0.138 XP = 0.0225
85	DRIFT MORE TOWARD BEING THOSE 0.86 OF 51 WHERE THE LEVEL OF POLITICAL INTEGRATION IS THE MINIMAL STATE, THE AUTONOMOUS COMMUNITY, OR THE FAMILY (234) GPM	85	DRIFT LESS TOWARD BEING THOSE 0.73 OF 224 WHERE THE LEVEL OF POLITICAL INTEGRATION IS THE MINIMAL STATE, THE AUTONOMOUS COMMUNITY, OR THE FAMILY (234) GPM	7 61 44 163 XSQ= 3.38 PHI= -0.111 XP = 0.0661
88	TEND MORE TO BE THOSE 0.86 OF 44 WHERE, IF A HEADMANSHIP IS PRESENT, SUCCESSION IS HEREDITARY (165)	88	TEND LESS TO BE THOSE 0.56 OF 204 WHERE, IF A HEADMANSHIP IS PRESENT, SUCCESSION IS HEREDITARY (165)	6 90 38 114 XSQ= 12.92 PHI= -0.228 XP = 0.0003
89	DRIFT TOWARD BEING THOSE 0.83 OF 6 WHERE, IF A NON-HEREDITARY HEADMANSHIP IS PRESENT, SUCCESSION IS BY MEANS OTHER THAN CONSENSUS (43)	89	DRIFT TOWARD BEING THOSE 0.62 OF 90 WHERE, IF A NON-HEREDITARY HEADMANSHIP IS PRESENT, SUCCESSION IS BY CONSENSUS (63)	1 56 5 34 XSQ= 3.14 PHI= -0.181 XP = 0.0766
107	IN ALL CASES ARE THOSE 1.00 OF 27 WHERE CLASS STRATIFICATION, IF PRESENT, IS BASED ON SOMETHING OTHER THAN OCCUPATIONAL STATUS (160)	107	LEAN LESS TOWARD BEING THOSE 0.74 OF 161 WHERE CLASS STRATIFICATION, IF PRESENT, IS BASED ON SOMETHING OTHER THAN OCCUPATIONAL STATUS (160)	0 42 27 119 XSQ= 7.63 PHI= -0.201 XP = 0.0057
116	IN ALL CASES ARE THOSE 1.00 OF 10 WHERE OCCUPATIONAL SPECIALIZATION IS PART-TIME ONLY (34) JMH	116	TILT LESS TOWARD BEING THOSE 0.54 OF 41 WHERE OCCUPATIONAL SPECIALIZATION IS PART-TIME ONLY (34) JMH	0 19 10 22 XSQ= 5.54 PHI= -0.329 XP = 0.0186
176	TEND TO BE THOSE 0.73 OF 56 WHERE THE COMMUNITY IS A CLAN-COMMUNITY OR A COMMUNITY STRUCTURED OR SEGMENTED ON A CLAN BASIS (169)	176	TEND TO BE THOSE 0.63 OF 294 WHERE THE COMMUNITY IS OTHER THAN A CLAN-COMMUNITY OR A COMMUNITY STRUCTURED OR SEGMENTED ON A CLAN BASIS (213)	41 110 15 184 XSQ= 23.14 PHI= 0.257 XP = 0.0000
177	LEAN LESS TOWARD BEING THOSE 0.66 OF 56 WHERE THE COMMUNITY IS OTHER THAN A SINGLE CLAN-COMMUNITY AND EXOGAMOUS (305)	177	LEAN MORE TOWARD BEING THOSE 0.83 OF 294 WHERE THE COMMUNITY IS OTHER THAN A SINGLE CLAN-COMMUNITY AND EXOGAMOUS (305)	19 49 37 245 XSQ= 7.89 PHI= 0.150 XP = 0.0050
178	LEAN LESS TOWARD BEING THOSE 0.61 OF 56 WHERE THE COMMUNITY IS OTHER THAN SEGMENTED ON A CLAN BASIS AND NON-EXOGAMOUS (295)	178	LEAN MORE TOWARD BEING THOSE 0.81 OF 294 WHERE THE COMMUNITY IS OTHER THAN SEGMENTED ON A CLAN BASIS AND NON-EXOGAMOUS (295)	22 56 34 238 XSQ= 9.99 PHI= 0.169 XP = 0.0016

No.		No.		
179	DRIFT MORE TOWARD BEING THOSE 0.96 OF 56 WHERE THE COMMUNITY IS OTHER THAN STRUCTURED ON A NON-CLAN BASIS AND COMMONLY EXOGAMOUS (340)	179	DRIFT LESS TOWARD BEING THOSE 0.87 OF 294 WHERE THE COMMUNITY IS OTHER THAN STRUCTURED ON A NON-CLAN BASIS AND COMMONLY EXOGAMOUS (340)	2 38 54 256 XSQ= 3.19 PHI= -0.096 XP = 0.0739
181	DRIFT MORE TOWARD BEING THOSE 0.96 OF 56 WHERE THE COMMUNITY IS OTHER THAN A DEME (337)	181	DRIFT LESS TOWARD BEING THOSE 0.86 OF 294 WHERE THE COMMUNITY IS OTHER THAN A DEME (337)	2 41 54 253 XSQ= 3.78 PHI= -0.104 XP = 0.0517
182	TILT MORE TOWARD BEING THOSE 0.80 OF 56 OTHER THAN WHERE THE COMMUNITY IS STRUCTURED ON A NON-CLAN BASIS AND AGAMOUS (256)	182	TILT LESS TOWARD BEING THOSE 0.64 OF 294 OTHER THAN WHERE THE COMMUNITY IS STRUCTURED ON A NON-CLAN BASIS AND AGAMOUS (256)	11 105 45 189 XSQ= 4.78 PHI= -0.117 XP = 0.0288
183	LEAN LESS TOWARD BEING THOSE 0.74 OF 58 WHERE THE LARGEST NON-COGNATIC KIN GROUP IS SMALLER THAN A MOEITY, I. E., A PHRATRY OR SIB OR LINEAGE (218)	183	LEAN MORE TOWARD BEING THOSE 0.89 OF 168 WHERE THE LARGEST NON-COGNATIC KIN GROUP IS SMALLER THAN A MOEITY, I. E., A PHRATRY OR SIB OR LINEAGE (218)	15 18 43 150 XSQ= 6.77 PHI= 0.173 XP = 0.0093
185	DRIFT MORE TOWARD BEING THOSE 0.88 OF 58 WHERE THE LARGEST NON-COGNATIC KIN GROUP IS THE MOEITY OR PHRATRY OR SIB (194)	185	DRIFT LESS TOWARD BEING THOSE 0.76 OF 168 WHERE THE LARGEST NON-COGNATIC KIN GROUP IS THE MOEITY OR PHRATRY OR SIB (194)	51 127 7 41 XSQ= 3.22 PHI= 0.119 XP = 0.0728
186	TILT LESS TOWARD BEING THOSE 0.51 OF 59 WHERE THE KIN GROUP IS OTHER THAN EXCLUSIVELY PATRILINEAL (250)	186	TILT MORE TOWARD BEING THOSE 0.68 OF 305 WHERE THE KIN GROUP IS OTHER THAN EXCLUSIVELY PATRILINEAL (250)	29 99 30 206 XSQ= 5.33 PHI= 0.121 XP = 0.0209
187	TEND LESS TO BE THOSE 0.63 OF 59 WHERE THE KIN GROUP IS OTHER THAN EXCLUSIVELY MATRILINEAL (344)	187	TEND MORE TO BE THOSE 0.90 OF 304 WHERE THE KIN GROUP IS OTHER THAN EXCLUSIVELY MATRILINEAL (344)	22 31 37 273 XSQ= 26.95 PHI= 0.272 XP = 0.0000
188	TEND MORE TO BE THOSE 0.98 OF 59 WHERE THE KIN GROUP IS OTHER THAN EXCLUSIVELY COGNATIC (252)	188	TEND LESS TO BE THOSE 0.55 OF 305 WHERE THE KIN GROUP IS OTHER THAN EXCLUSIVELY COGNATIC (252)	1 137 58 168 XSQ= 37.42 PHI= -0.321 XP = 0.
190	TILT LESS TOWARD BEING THOSE 0.62 OF 58 WHERE THE KIN GROUP IS PATRILINEAL OR DOUBLE-DESCENT, RATHER THAN MATRILINEAL (186)	190	TILT MORE TOWARD BEING THOSE 0.77 OF 163 WHERE THE KIN GROUP IS PATRILINEAL OR DOUBLE-DESCENT, RATHER THAN MATRILINEAL (186)	36 126 22 37 XSQ= 4.32 PHI= -0.140 XP = 0.0376

```
192  IN ALL CASES ARE THOSE            1.00 OF  59    192  TEND LESS TO BE THOSE            0.66 OF 305            0   103
     OTHER THAN WHERE THE ONLY KIN GROUP                    OTHER THAN WHERE THE ONLY KIN GROUP                  59   202
     PRESENT IS A KINDRED OR ELSE                           PRESENT IS A KINDRED OR ELSE                  XSQ=     26.15
     BILATERAL DESCENT IS INFERRED  (289)                   BILATERAL DESCENT IS INFERRED  (289)          PHI=    -0.268
                                                                                                           XP =    0.0000

197  IN ALL CASES ARE THOSE            1.00 OF  31    197  TILT LESS TOWARD BEING THOSE    0.81 OF 144           31   116
     WHERE RULES FOR THE INHERITANCE OF                     WHERE RULES FOR THE INHERITANCE OF                    0    28
     REAL PROPERTY, IF PRESENT,                             REAL PROPERTY, IF PRESENT,                    XSQ=      5.80
     FAVOR EITHER THE MALE HEIR OR LINE,                    FAVOR EITHER THE MALE HEIR OR LINE,           PHI=     0.182
     OR THE FEMALE HEIR OR LINE  (165)                      OR THE FEMALE HEIR OR LINE  (165)             XP =    0.0160

198  TILT LESS TOWARD BEING THOSE   0.74 OF  31       198  TILT MORE TOWARD BEING THOSE    0.91 OF 116           23   106
     WHERE RULES FOR THE INHERITANCE OF                     WHERE RULES FOR THE INHERITANCE OF                    8    10
     REAL PROPERTY, IF PRESENT,                             REAL PROPERTY, IF PRESENT,                    XSQ=      5.22
     FAVOR THE MALE HEIR OR LINE, RATHER THAN               FAVOR THE MALE HEIR OR LINE, RATHER THAN      PHI=    -0.188
     THE FEMALE  (144)                                      THE FEMALE  (144)                             XP =    0.0223

201  LEAN MORE TOWARD BEING THOSE   0.97 OF  59       201  LEAN LESS TOWARD BEING THOSE    0.81 OF 303           57   245
     WHERE MARITAL RESIDENCE IS                             WHERE MARITAL RESIDENCE IS                            2    58
     NON-OPTIONAL, RATHER THAN                              NON-OPTIONAL, RATHER THAN                     XSQ=      7.76
     AMBILOCAL OR NEOLOCAL  (334)                           AMBILOCAL OR NEOLOCAL  (334)                  PHI=     0.146
                                                                                                           XP =    0.0053

204  TILT MORE TOWARD BEING THOSE   0.95 OF  42       204  TILT LESS TOWARD BEING THOSE    0.78 OF 258           40   200
     WHERE MARITAL RESIDENCE IS                             WHERE MARITAL RESIDENCE IS                            2    58
     PATRILOCAL, VIRILOCAL, OR AVUNCULOCAL,                 PATRILOCAL, VIRILOCAL, OR AVUNCULOCAL,        XSQ=      6.02
     RATHER THAN                                            RATHER THAN                                   PHI=     0.142
     AMBILOCAL OR NEOLOCAL  (270)                           AMBILOCAL OR NEOLOCAL  (270)                  XP =    0.0141

207  TEND TO BE THOSE                  0.89 OF  19    207  TEND TO BE THOSE                0.56 OF 103           17    45
     WHERE MARITAL RESIDENCE IS                             WHERE MARITAL RESIDENCE IS                            2    58
     MATRILOCAL OR UXORILOCAL, RATHER THAN                  AMBILOCAL OR NEOLOCAL, RATHER THAN            XSQ=     11.68
     AMBILOCAL OR NEOLOCAL  (64)                            MATRILOCAL OR UXORILOCAL  (64)                PHI=     0.309
                                                                                                           XP =    0.0006

209  DRIFT LESS TOWARD BEING THOSE  0.70 OF  57       209  DRIFT MORE TOWARD BEING THOSE   0.82 OF 245           40   200
     WHERE MARITAL RESIDENCE IS                             WHERE MARITAL RESIDENCE IS                           17    45
     PATRILOCAL, VIRILOCAL, OR AVUNCULOCAL,                 PATRILOCAL, VIRILOCAL, OR AVUNCULOCAL,        XSQ=      3.05
     RATHER THAN                                            RATHER THAN                                   PHI=    -0.101
     MATRILOCAL OR UXORILOCAL  (270)                        MATRILOCAL OR UXORILOCAL  (270)               XP =    0.0807

210  LEAN LESS TOWARD BEING THOSE   0.67 OF  49       210  LEAN MORE TOWARD BEING THOSE    0.88 OF 130           33   115
     WHERE MARITAL RESIDENCE IS                             WHERE MARITAL RESIDENCE IS                           16    15
     PATRILOCAL, RATHER THAN                                PATRILOCAL, RATHER THAN                       XSQ=      9.65
     MATRILOCAL  (169)                                      MATRILOCAL  (169)                             PHI=    -0.232
                                                                                                           XP =    0.0019

214  TEND TO BE THOSE                  0.55 OF  20    214  TEND TO BE THOSE                0.88 OF 136           11    16
     WHERE FIRST COUSIN MARRIAGE,                           WHERE FIRST COUSIN MARRIAGE,                          9   120
     IF PERMITTED,                                          IF PERMITTED,                                 XSQ=     19.85
     IS UNILATERAL  (28)                                    IS OTHER THAN UNILATERAL  (144)               PHI=     0.357
                                                                                                           XP =    0.0000
```

224	LEAN TOWARD BEING THOSE 0.75 OF 20 WHERE COUSIN MARRIAGE IS PREFERENTIALLY OR PERMISSIVELY EITHER PATRI- OR MATRILATERAL, RATHER THAN SYMMETRICAL (66)	224	LEAN TOWARD BEING THOSE 0.65 OF 136 WHERE COUSIN MARRIAGE IS PREFERENTIALLY OR PERMISSIVELY SYMMETRICAL, RATHER THAN EITHER PATRI- OR MATRILATERAL (106)	15 47 5 89 XSQ= 10.28 PHI= 0.257 XP = 0.0013
260	DRIFT TOWARD BEING THOSE 0.60 OF 10 WHERE THE AGE OF MALES AT MARRIAGE IS TWENTY OR OVER (17) JKH	260	DRIFT TOWARD BEING THOSE 0.74 OF 43 WHERE THE AGE OF MALES AT MARRIAGE IS LESS THAN TWENTY (38) JKH	4 32 6 11 XSQ= 2.97 PHI= -0.237 XP = 0.0847
304	DRIFT TOWARD BEING THOSE 0.86 OF 7 WHERE THE EARLY ANAL SATISFACTION POTENTIAL IS LOW (22) W-C	304	DRIFT TOWARD BEING THOSE 0.53 OF 32 WHERE THE EARLY ANAL SATISFACTION POTENTIAL IS HIGH (19) W-C	1 17 6 15 XSQ= 2.10 PHI= -0.232 EP = 0.0985
330	DRIFT TOWARD BEING THOSE 0.72 OF 18 WHERE THE AGE OF THE INFANT AT TIME OF WEANING IS LOWER THAN 2.5 YEARS (36) B-B-C	330	DRIFT TOWARD BEING THOSE 0.56 OF 50 WHERE THE AGE OF THE INFANT AT TIME OF WEANING IS 2.5 YEARS OR HIGHER (34) B-B-C	5 28 13 22 XSQ= 3.17 PHI= -0.216 XP = 0.0752
370	TILT TOWARD BEING THOSE 0.58 OF 36 WHERE THE SEGREGATION OF ADOLESCENT BOYS IS COMPLETE OR PARTIAL (95)	370	TILT TOWARD BEING THOSE 0.63 OF 190 WHERE THE SEGREGATION OF ADOLESCENT BOYS IS ABSENT (148)	21 70 15 120 XSQ= 4.95 PHI= 0.148 XP = 0.0261
391	DRIFT TOWARD BEING THOSE 0.69 OF 26 WHERE PREMARITAL SEX RELATIONS ARE PUNISHED ONLY IF PREGNANCY RESULTS, OR FREELY PERMITTED (90) JTW,EA	391	DRIFT TOWARD BEING THOSE 0.53 OF 139 WHERE PREMARITAL SEX RELATIONS ARE STRONGLY PUNISHED AND IN FACT RARE, OR WEAKLY PUNISHED AND IN FACT NOT RARE (89) JTW,EA	8 73 18 66 XSQ= 3.32 PHI= -0.142 XP = 0.0684
392	DRIFT TOWARD BEING THOSE 0.54 OF 26 WHERE PREMARITAL SEX RELATIONS ARE FREELY PERMITTED (67) JTW,EA	392	DRIFT TOWARD BEING THOSE 0.65 OF 139 WHERE PREMARITAL SEX RELATIONS ARE STRONGLY PUNISHED AND IN FACT RARE, OR WEAKLY PUNISHED AND IN FACT NOT RARE, OR PUNISHED ONLY IF PREGNANCY RESULTS (112) JTW,EA	12 91 14 48 XSQ= 2.71 PHI= -0.128 XP = 0.0998
417	IN ALL CASES ARE THOSE 1.00 OF 11 WHERE WARFARE IS PREVALENT (34) LWS	417	DRIFT LESS TOWARD BEING THOSE 0.72 OF 29 WHERE WARFARE IS PREVALENT (34) LWS	11 21 0 8 XSQ= 2.26 PHI= 0.238 EP = 0.0803
428	DRIFT TOWARD BEING THOSE 0.63 OF 8 WHERE A HIGH GOD, IF PRESENT AND ACTIVE, DOES NOT SUPPORT HUMAN MORALITY, RATHER THAN SUPPORTING IT (26) GES,EA	428	DRIFT TOWARD BEING THOSE 0.73 OF 70 WHERE A HIGH GOD, IF PRESENT AND ACTIVE, SUPPORTS HUMAN MORALITY, RATHER THAN NOT SUPPORTING IT (61) GES,EA	3 51 5 19 XSQ= 2.72 PHI= -0.187 XP = 0.0993

450	DRIFT MORE TOWARD BEING THOSE WHERE THE OBSERVATION OF FOOD TABOOS IS HIGH OR MEDIUM, RATHER THAN LOW (60) JRL	0.93 OF	14	450	DRIFT LESS TOWARD BEING THOSE WHERE THE OBSERVATION OF FOOD TABOOS IS HIGH OR MEDIUM, RATHER THAN LOW (60) JRL	0.65 OF	69	13 45 1 24 XSQ= 3.01 PHI= 0.191 XP = 0.0826
451	DRIFT TOWARD BEING THOSE WHERE TOTEMISM IS PRESENT (15) LWS	0.88 OF	8	451	DRIFT TOWARD BEING THOSE WHERE TOTEMISM IS UNIMPORTANT OR ABSENT (12) LWS	0.53 OF	17	7 8 1 9 XSQ= 2.21 PHI= 0.298 EP = 0.0875
471	LEAN TOWARD BEING THOSE WHERE SECRET SOCIETIES ARE PRESENT (9) LWS	0.86 OF	7	471	LEAN TOWARD BEING THOSE WHERE SECRET SOCIETIES ARE UMIMPORTANT OR ABSENT (14) LWS	0.80 OF	15	6 3 1 12 XSQ= 6.02 PHI= 0.523 EP = 0.0066

228 CULTURES WHERE THE COUSIN TERMINOLOGY IS OF CROW TYPE (28)

228 CULTURES WHERE THE COUSIN TERMINOLOGY IS OTHER THAN OF CROW TYPE (336)

BACKGROUND ON PAGE 121 — SUBJECT ONLY

28 IN LEFT COLUMN

APINAYE	BIRIFOR	BORORO	CHEROKEE	CREEK	CROW	GOAJIRO	HAIDA	HANO	IRAQW
KASKA	MANDAN	MBUGWE	MNONG GAR	MONGO	MOTA	PAWNEE	PENDE	PONAPEANS	SEMINOLE
SENIANG	SIRIONO	TIMBIRA	TIMUCUA	TROBRIAND	TRUKESE	YAPESE	ZUNI		

336 IN RIGHT COLUMN

36 EXCLUDED BECAUSE UNASCERTAINED

	Left column			Right column		Statistics
5	DRIFT MORE TOWARD BEING THOSE LOCATED OUTSIDE OF EAST EURASIA (330)	0.96 OF 28	5	DRIFT LESS TOWARD BEING THOSE LOCATED OUTSIDE OF EAST EURASIA (330)	0.82 OF 336	1 61 27 275 XSQ= 2.93 PHI= -0.090 XP = 0.0872
8	TILT LESS TOWARD BEING THOSE LOCATED OUTSIDE OF NORTH AMERICA (330)	0.61 OF 28	8	TILT MORE TOWARD BEING THOSE LOCATED OUTSIDE OF NORTH AMERICA (330)	0.82 OF 336	11 59 17 277 XSQ= 6.52 PHI= 0.134 XP = 0.0107
71	DRIFT MORE TOWARD BEING THOSE WHERE METAL WORKING IS ABSENT (153)	0.81 OF 21	71	DRIFT LESS TOWARD BEING THOSE WHERE METAL WORKING IS ABSENT (153)	0.59 OF 209	4 85 17 124 XSQ= 2.90 PHI= -0.112 XP = 0.0883
84	IN ALL CASES ARE THOSE WHERE THE LEVEL OF POLITICAL INTEGRATION IS THE LITTLE STATE, THE MINIMAL STATE, THE AUTONOMOUS COMMUNITY, OR THE FAMILY. (262) GPM	1.00 OF 24	84	DRIFT LESS TOWARD BEING THOSE WHERE THE LEVEL OF POLITICAL INTEGRATION IS THE LITTLE STATE, THE MINIMAL STATE, THE AUTONOMOUS COMMUNITY, OR THE FAMILY (262) GPM	0.83 OF 251	0 42 24 209 XSQ= 3.53 PHI= -0.113 XP = 0.0601
85	DRIFT MORE TOWARD BEING THOSE WHERE THE LEVEL OF POLITICAL INTEGRATION IS THE MINIMAL STATE, THE AUTONOMOUS COMMUNITY, OR THE FAMILY (234) GPM	0.92 OF 24	85	DRIFT LESS TOWARD BEING THOSE WHERE THE LEVEL OF POLITICAL INTEGRATION IS THE MINIMAL STATE, THE AUTONOMOUS COMMUNITY, OR THE FAMILY (234) GPM	0.74 OF 251	2 66 22 185 XSQ= 2.89 PHI= -0.103 XP = 0.0890

88	DRIFT MORE TOWARD BEING THOSE 0.84 OF 19 WHERE, IF A HEADMANSHIP IS PRESENT, SUCCESSION IS HEREDITARY (165)	88	DRIFT LESS TOWARD BEING THOSE 0.59 OF 229 WHERE, IF A HEADMANSHIP IS PRESENT, SUCCESSION IS HEREDITARY (165)	3 93 16 136 XSQ= 3.57 PHI= -0.120 XP = 0.0588
90	TEND TO BE THOSE 0.75 OF 16 WHERE, IF A HEREDITARY HEADMANSHIP IS PRESENT, SUCCESSION IS MATRILINEAL, RATHER THAN PATRILINEAL (38)	90	TEND TO BE THOSE 0.82 OF 136 WHERE, IF A HEREDITARY HEADMANSHIP IS PRESENT, SUCCESSION IS PATRILINEAL, RATHER THAN MATRILINEAL (127)	4 112 12 24 XSQ= 22.98 PHI= -0.389 XP = 0.0000
107	IN ALL CASES ARE THOSE 1.00 OF 13 WHERE CLASS STRATIFICATION, IF PRESENT, IS BASED ON SOMETHING OTHER THAN OCCUPATIONAL STATUS (160)	107	DRIFT LESS TOWARD BEING THOSE 0.76 OF 175 WHERE CLASS STRATIFICATION, IF PRESENT, IS BASED ON SOMETHING OTHER THAN OCCUPATIONAL STATUS (160)	0 42 13 133 XSQ= 2.75 PHI= -0.121 XP = 0.0971
116	IN ALL CASES ARE THOSE 1.00 OF 7 WHERE OCCUPATIONAL SPECIALIZATION IS PART-TIME ONLY (34) JMH	116	DRIFT LESS TOWARD BEING THOSE 0.57 OF 44 WHERE OCCUPATIONAL SPECIALIZATION IS PART-TIME ONLY (34) JMH	0 19 7 25 XSQ= 3.15 PHI= -0.248 XP = 0.0761
176	TEND TO BE THOSE 0.77 OF 26 WHERE THE COMMUNITY IS A CLAN-COMMUNITY OR A COMMUNITY STRUCTURED OR SEGMENTED ON A CLAN BASIS (169)	176	TEND TO BE THOSE 0.60 OF 324 WHERE THE COMMUNITY IS OTHER THAN A CLAN-COMMUNITY OR A COMMUNITY STRUCTURED OR SEGMENTED ON A CLAN BASIS (213)	20 131 6 193 XSQ= 11.62 PHI= 0.182 XP = 0.0007
178	TEND TO BE THOSE 0.54 OF 26 WHERE THE COMMUNITY IS SEGMENTED ON A CLAN BASIS AND NON-EXOGAMOUS (87)	178	TEND TO BE THOSE 0.80 OF 324 WHERE THE COMMUNITY IS OTHER THAN SEGMENTED ON A CLAN BASIS AND NON-EXOGAMOUS (295)	14 64 12 260 XSQ= 14.24 PHI= 0.202 XP = 0.0002
182	DRIFT MORE TOWARD BEING THOSE 0.85 OF 26 OTHER THAN WHERE THE COMMUNITY IS STRUCTURED ON A NON-CLAN BASIS AND AGAMOUS (256)	182	DRIFT LESS TOWARD BEING THOSE 0.65 OF 324 OTHER THAN WHERE THE COMMUNITY IS STRUCTURED ON A NON-CLAN BASIS AND AGAMOUS (256)	4 112 22 212 XSQ= 3.18 PHI= -0.095 XP = 0.0746
184	TILT TOWARD BEING THOSE 0.54 OF 28 WHERE THE LARGEST NON-COGNATIC KIN GROUP IS THE MOIETY OR PHRATRY (77)	184	TILT TOWARD BEING THOSE 0.71 OF 198 WHERE THE LARGEST NON-COGNATIC KIN GROUP IS SMALLER THAN A PHRATRY, I. E. A SIB OR LINEAGE (175)	15 58 13 140 XSQ= 5.55 PHI= 0.157 XP = 0.0185
186	LEAN MORE TOWARD BEING THOSE 0.93 OF 28 WHERE THE KIN GROUP IS OTHER THAN EXCLUSIVELY PATRILINEAL (250)	186	LEAN LESS TOWARD BEING THOSE 0.63 OF 336 WHERE THE KIN GROUP IS OTHER THAN EXCLUSIVELY PATRILINEAL (250)	2 126 26 210 XSQ= 9.16 PHI= -0.159 XP = 0.0025

187	TEND TO BE THCSE WHERE THE KIN GRCUP IS EXCLUSIVELY MATRILINEAL (55)	0.79 OF 28	187	TEND TO BE THOSE WHERE THE KIN GROUP IS OTHER THAN EXCLUSIVELY MATRILINEAL (344)	0.91 CF 335	22 31 6 304 XSQ= 94.10 PHI= 0.509 XP = 0.
188	IN ALL CASES ARE THCSE WHERE THE KIN GRCUP IS CTHER THAN EXCLUSIVELY CCGNATIC (252)	1.00 OF 28	188	TEND LESS TO BE THOSE WHERE THE KIN GROUP IS OTHER THAN EXCLUSIVELY COGNATIC (252)	0.59 CF 336	0 138 28 198 XSQ= 16.82 PHI= -0.215 XP = 0.0000
190	TEND TC BE THCSE WHERE THE KIN GRCUP IS MATRILINEAL, RATHER THAN PATRILINEAL CR CCUBLE-DESCENT (61)	0.79 OF 28	19C	TEND TO BE THOSE WHERE THE KIN GROUP IS PATRILINEAL OR DOUBLE-DESCENT, RATHER THAN MATRILINEAL (186)	0.81 CF 193	6 156 22 37 XSQ= 41.10 PHI= -0.431 XP = 0.
192	IN ALL CASES ARE THCSE OTHER THAN WHERE THE CNLY KIN GROUP PRESENT IS A KINDRED CR ELSE BILATERAL DESCENT IS INFERREC (289)	1.00 OF 28	192	LEAN LESS TOWARD BEING THOSE OTHER THAN WHERE THE ONLY KIN GRCUP PRESENT IS A KINDRED OR ELSE BILATERAL DESCENT IS INFERRED (289)	0.69 OF 336	0 103 28 233 XSQ= 10.51 PHI= -0.170 XP = 0.0012
198	TEND TC BE THCSE WHERE RULES FCR THE INHERITANCE OF REAL PRCPERTY, IF PRESENT, FAVOR THE FEMALE HEIR CR LINE, RATHER THAN THE MALE (21)	0.57 OF 14	198	TEND TO BE THOSE WHERE RULES FOR THE INHERITANCE CF REAL PROPERTY, IF PRESENT, FAVOR THE MALE HEIR OR LINE, RATHER THAN THE FEMALE (144)	0.92 CF 133	6 123 8 10 XSQ= 24.59 PHI= -0.409 XP = 0.0000
201	IN ALL CASES ARE THCSE WHERE MARITAL RESICENCE IS NON-OPTICNAL, RATHER THAN AMBILCCAL CR NECLOCAL (334)	1.00 OF 28	201	TILT LESS TOWARD BEING THOSE WHERE MARITAL RESIDENCE IS NON-OPTIONAL, RATHER THAN AMBILOCAL OR NEOLOCAL (334)	0.82 OF 334	28 274 0 60 XSQ= 4.80 PHI= 0.115 XP = 0.0285
207	IN ALL CASES ARE THCSE WHERE MARITAL RESICENCE IS MATRILCCAL OR UXCRILOCAL, RATHER THAN AMBILCCAL CR NECLOCAL (64)	1.00 OF 16	2C7	TEND TO BE THOSE WHERE MARITAL RESIDENCE IS AMBILOCAL OR NEOLOCAL, RATHER THAN MATRILOCAL OR UXORILCCAL (64)	0.57 CF 106	16 46 0 60 XSQ= 15.63 PHI= 0.358 XP = 0.0001
209	TEND TC BE THCSE WHERE MARITAL RESICENCE IS MATRILCCAL OR UXCRILOCAL, RATHER THAN PATRILCCAL, VIRILOCAL, CR AVUNCULCCAL (64)	0.57 OF 28	2C9	TEND TO BE THOSE WHERE MARITAL RESIDENCE IS PATRILOCAL, VIRILOCAL, CR AVUNCULOCAL, RATHER THAN MATRILOCAL OR UXORILCCAL (270)	0.83 CF 274	12 228 16 46 XSQ= 22.94 PHI= -0.276 XP = 0.0000
210	TEND TC BE THCSE WHERE MARITAL RESICENCE IS MATRILCCAL, RATHER THAN PATRILCCAL (31)	0.73 OF 22	21C	TEND TO BE THOSE WHERE MARITAL RESIDENCE IS PATRILOCAL, RATHER THAN MATRILOCAL (169)	0.90 CF 157	6 142 16 15 XSQ= 49.46 PHI= -0.526 XP = 0.

214	LEAN TOWARD BEING THOSE WHERE FIRST COUSIN MARRIAGE, IF PERMITTED, IS UNILATERAL (28)	0.50 OF 12	214	LEAN TOWARD BEING THOSE WHERE FIRST COUSIN MARRIAGE, IF PERMITTED, IS OTHER THAN UNILATERAL (144)	0.85 OF 144	6 21 6 123 XSQ= 7.39 PHI= 0.218 XP = 0.0066
224	DRIFT TOWARD BEING THOSE WHERE COUSIN MARRIAGE IS PREFERENTIALLY OR PERMISSIVELY EITHER PATRI- OR MATRILATERAL, RATHER THAN SYMMETRICAL (66)	0.67 OF 12	224	DRIFT TOWARD BEING THOSE WHERE COUSIN MARRIAGE IS PREFERENTIALLY OR PERMISSIVELY SYMMETRICAL, RATHER THAN EITHER PATRI- OR MATRILATERAL (106)	0.63 OF 144	8 54 4 90 XSQ= 2.81 PHI= 0.134 XP = 0.0936
296	IN ALL CASES ARE THOSE WHERE INFANTICIDE IS ABSENT OR INFERRED ABSENT (15) BCA	1.00 OF 3	296	DRIFT TOWARD BEING THOSE WHERE INFANTICIDE IS PRESENT (18) BCA	0.59 OF 29	0 17 3 12 XSQ= 1.77 PHI= -0.235 EP = 0.0917
330	DRIFT TOWARD BEING THOSE WHERE THE AGE OF THE INFANT AT TIME OF WEANING IS LOWER THAN 2.5 YEARS (36) B-B-C	0.88 OF 8	330	DRIFT TOWARD BEING THOSE WHERE THE AGE OF THE INFANT AT TIME OF WEANING IS 2.5 YEARS OR HIGHER (34) B-B-C	0.53 OF 60	1 32 7 28 XSQ= 3.22 PHI= -0.218 XP = 0.0728
336	DRIFT TOWARD BEING THOSE WHERE THE TOTAL POSITIVE PRESSURE TOWARD DEVELOPING RESPONSIBLE BEHAVIOR IN THE CHILD IS LOW (32) B-B-C	0.78 OF 9	336	DRIFT TOWARD BEING THOSE WHERE THE TOTAL POSITIVE PRESSURE TOWARD DEVELOPING RESPONSIBLE BEHAVIOR IN THE CHILD IS HIGH (43) B-B-C	0.63 OF 64	2 40 7 24 XSQ= 3.72 PHI= -0.226 XP = 0.0538
377	DRIFT MORE TOWARD BEING THOSE WHERE MALE GENITAL MUTILATION IS ABSENT (242)	0.92 OF 25	377	DRIFT LESS TOWARD BEING THOSE WHERE MALE GENITAL MUTILATION IS ABSENT (242)	0.75 OF 274	2 69 23 205 XSQ= 2.85 PHI= -0.098 XP = 0.0916
390	IN ALL CASES ARE THOSE WHERE PREMARITAL SEX RELATIONS ARE WEAKLY PUNISHED AND IN FACT NOT RARE OR PUNISHED ONLY IF PREGNANCY RESULTS, OR FREELY PERMITTED (132) JTW,EA	1.00 OF 12	390	DRIFT LESS TOWARD BEING THOSE WHERE PREMARITAL SEX RELATIONS ARE WEAKLY PUNISHED AND IN FACT NOT RARE OR PUNISHED ONLY IF PREGNANCY RESULTS, OR FREELY PERMITTED (132) JTW,EA	0.72 OF 153	0 43 12 110 XSQ= 3.22 PHI= -0.140 XP = 0.0728
391	TILT TOWARD BEING THOSE WHERE PREMARITAL SEX RELATIONS ARE PUNISHED ONLY IF PREGNANCY RESULTS, OR FREELY PERMITTED (90) JTW,EA	0.83 OF 12	391	TILT TOWARD BEING THOSE WHERE PREMARITAL SEX RELATIONS ARE STRONGLY PUNISHED AND IN FACT RARE, OR WEAKLY PUNISHED AND IN FACT NOT RARE (89) JTW,EA	0.52 OF 153	2 79 10 74 XSQ= 4.13 PHI= -0.158 XP = 0.0420
392	DRIFT TOWARD BEING THOSE WHERE PREMARITAL SEX RELATIONS ARE FREELY PERMITTED (67) JTW,EA	0.67 OF 12	392	DRIFT TOWARD BEING THOSE WHERE PREMARITAL SEX RELATIONS ARE STRONGLY PUNISHED AND IN FACT RARE, OR WEAKLY PUNISHED AND IN FACT NOT RARE, OR PUNISHED ONLY IF PREGNANCY RESULTS (112) JTW,EA	0.65 OF 153	4 99 8 54 XSQ= 3.43 PHI= -0.144 XP = 0.0641

398	IN ALL CASES ARE THOSE WHERE THE INTENSITY OF SEX ANXIETY IS LOW (16) WNS	1.00 OF 3	398	DRIFT TOWARD BEING THOSE WHERE THE INTENSITY OF SEX ANXIETY IS HIGH (16) WNS	0.58 OF 26	0 15 3 11 XSQ= 1.65 PHI= -0.238 EP = 0.0996
426	TILT TOWARD BEING THOSE WHERE A HIGH GOD IS ABSENT (104) GES,EA	0.67 OF 18	426	TILT TOWARD BEING THOSE WHERE A HIGH GOD IS PRESENT (156) GES,EA	0.60 OF 224	6 135 12 89 XSQ= 3.92 PHI= -0.127 XP = 0.0476
458	DRIFT MORE TOWARD BEING THOSE WHERE GAMES, IF PRESENT, DO NOT INCLUDE GAMES OF STRATEGY (119) R-A-B,EA	0.93 OF 15	458	DRIFT LESS TOWARD BEING THOSE WHERE GAMES, IF PRESENT, DO NOT INCLUDE GAMES OF STRATEGY (119) R-A-B,EA	0.67 OF 149	1 49 14 100 XSQ= 3.27 PHI= -0.141 XP = 0.0706
471	IN ALL CASES ARE THOSE WHERE SECRET SOCIETIES ARE PRESENT (9) LWS	1.00 OF 4	471	TILT TOWARD BEING THOSE WHERE SECRET SOCIETIES ARE UMIMPORTANT OR ABSENT (14) LWS	0.72 OF 18	4 5 0 13 XSQ= 4.39 PHI= 0.447 EP = 0.0172

229 CULTURES WHERE THE COUSIN TERMINOLOGY IS OF OMAHA TYPE (31)

229 CULTURES WHERE THE COUSIN TERMINOLOGY IS OTHER THAN OF OMAHA TYPE (333)

BACKGROUND ON PAGE 121 — SUBJECT ONLY

31 IN LEFT COLUMN

AMBA	ARAPESH	ARAUCANIANS	BANCA	BARI	CHAGGA	DOROBO	FANG	FOX	KALMYK
KAZAK	KHALKA	KIKUYU	KONSO	LAKHER	LAMET	LANGO	LHCTA NAGA	MASAI	MATAKAM
MIAMI	MIWCK	NANCI	NOMLAKI	NYORO	OMAHA	SHERENTE	THCNGA	TOKELAU	TZELTAL
WINNEBAGO									

333 IN RIGHT COLUMN

36 EXCLUDED BECAUSE UNASCERTAINED

	Left column			Right column		
3	LEAN LESS TOWARD BEING THOSE LOCATED OUTSIDE OF AFRICA (320)	0.58 OF 31	3	LEAN MORE TOWARD BEING THOSE LOCATED OUTSIDE OF AFRICA (320)	0.83 OF 333	13 56 18 277 XSQ= 10.07 PHI= 0.166 XP = 0.0015
16	TILT LESS TOWARD BEING THOSE WHERE THE LATITUDE IS TEN DEGREES OR GREATER (277)	0.52 OF 31	16	TILT MORE TOWARD BEING THOSE WHERE THE LATITUDE IS TEN DEGREES OR GREATER (277)	0.72 OF 333	16 240 15 93 XSQ= 4.75 PHI= -0.114 XP = 0.0293
71	TILT TOWARD BEING THOSE WHERE METAL WORKING IS PRESENT (98)	0.68 OF 19	71	TILT TOWARD BEING THOSE WHERE METAL WORKING IS ABSENT (153)	0.64 OF 211	13 76 6 135 XSQ= 6.41 PHI= 0.167 XP = 0.0114
88	LEAN MORE TOWARD BEING THOSE WHERE, IF A HEADMANSHIP IS PRESENT, SUCCESSION IS HEREDITARY (165)	0.88 OF 25	88	LEAN LESS TOWARD BEING THOSE WHERE, IF A HEADMANSHIP IS PRESENT, SUCCESSION IS HEREDITARY (165)	0.58 OF 223	3 93 22 130 XSQ= 7.15 PHI= -0.170 XP = 0.0075
90	IN ALL CASES ARE THOSE WHERE, IF A HEREDITARY HEADMANSHIP IS PRESENT, SUCCESSION IS PATRILINEAL, RATHER THAN MATRILINEAL (127)	1.00 OF 22	90	TILT LESS TOWARD BEING THOSE WHERE, IF A HEREDITARY HEADMANSHIP IS PRESENT, SUCCESSION IS PATRILINEAL, RATHER THAN MATRILINEAL (127)	0.72 OF 130	22 94 0 36 XSQ= 6.52 PHI= 0.207 XP = 0.0106

107	IN ALL CASES ARE THOSE 1.00 OF 14 WHERE CLASS STRATIFICATION, IF PRESENT, IS BASED ON SOMETHING OTHER THAN OCCUPATIONAL STATUS (160)	107	DRIFT LESS TOWARD BEING THOSE 0.76 OF 174 WHERE CLASS STRATIFICATION, IF PRESENT, IS BASED ON SOMETHING OTHER THAN OCCUPATIONAL STATUS (160)	0 42 14 132 XSQ= 3.07 PHI= -0.128 XP = 0.0797
176	LEAN TOWARD BEING THOSE 0.70 OF 30 WHERE THE COMMUNITY IS A CLAN-COMMUNITY OR A COMMUNITY STRUCTURED OR SEGMENTED ON A CLAN BASIS (169)	176	LEAN TOWARD BEING THOSE 0.59 OF 320 WHERE THE COMMUNITY IS OTHER THAN A CLAN-COMMUNITY OR A COMMUNITY STRUCTURED OR SEGMENTED ON A CLAN BASIS (213)	21 130 9 190 XSQ= 8.49 PHI= 0.156 XP = 0.0036
177	LEAN LESS TOWARD BEING THOSE 0.57 OF 30 WHERE THE COMMUNITY IS OTHER THAN A SINGLE CLAN-COMMUNITY AND EXOGAMOUS (305)	177	LEAN MORE TOWARD BEING THOSE 0.83 OF 320 WHERE THE COMMUNITY IS OTHER THAN A SINGLE CLAN-COMMUNITY AND EXOGAMOUS (305)	13 55 17 265 XSQ= 10.37 PHI= 0.172 XP = 0.0013
186	TEND TO BE THOSE 0.87 OF 31 WHERE THE KIN GROUP IS EXCLUSIVELY PATRILINEAL (150)	186	TEND TO BE THOSE 0.70 OF 333 WHERE THE KIN GROUP IS OTHER THAN EXCLUSIVELY PATRILINEAL (250)	27 101 4 232 XSQ= 37.63 PHI= 0.322 XP = 0.
187	IN ALL CASES ARE THOSE 1.00 OF 31 WHERE THE KIN GROUP IS OTHER THAN EXCLUSIVELY MATRILINEAL (344)	187	TILT LESS TOWARD BEING THOSE 0.84 OF 332 WHERE THE KIN GROUP IS OTHER THAN EXCLUSIVELY MATRILINEAL (344)	0 53 31 279 XSQ= 4.59 PHI= -0.112 XP = 0.0322
188	TEND MORE TO BE THOSE 0.97 OF 31 WHERE THE KIN GROUP IS OTHER THAN EXCLUSIVELY COGNATIC (252)	188	TEND LESS TO BE THOSE 0.59 OF 333 WHERE THE KIN GROUP IS OTHER THAN EXCLUSIVELY COGNATIC (252)	1 137 30 196 XSQ= 15.75 PHI= -0.208 XP = 0.0001
190	IN ALL CASES ARE THOSE 1.00 OF 30 WHERE THE KIN GROUP IS PATRILINEAL OR DOUBLE-DESCENT, RATHER THAN MATRILINEAL (186)	190	TEND LESS TO BE THOSE 0.69 OF 191 WHERE THE KIN GROUP IS PATRILINEAL OR DOUBLE-DESCENT, RATHER THAN MATRILINEAL (186)	30 132 0 59 XSQ= 11.11 PHI= 0.224 XP = 0.0009
192	IN ALL CASES ARE THOSE 1.00 OF 31 OTHER THAN WHERE THE ONLY KIN GROUP PRESENT IS A KINDRED OR ELSE BILATERAL DESCENT IS INFERRED (289)	192	TEND LESS TO BE THOSE 0.69 OF 333 OTHER THAN WHERE THE ONLY KIN GROUP PRESENT IS A KINDRED OR ELSE BILATERAL DESCENT IS INFERRED (289)	0 103 31 230 XSQ= 11.89 PHI= -0.181 XP = 0.0006
204	DRIFT MORE TOWARD BEING THOSE 0.93 OF 30 WHERE MARITAL RESIDENCE IS PATRILOCAL, VIRILOCAL, OR AVUNCULOCAL, RATHER THAN AMBILOCAL OR NEOLOCAL (270)	204	DRIFT LESS TOWARD BEING THOSE 0.79 OF 270 WHERE MARITAL RESIDENCE IS PATRILOCAL, VIRILOCAL, OR AVUNCULOCAL, RATHER THAN AMBILOCAL OR NEOLOCAL (270)	28 212 2 58 XSQ= 2.84 PHI= 0.097 XP = 0.0922

209	TILT MORE TOWARD BEING THOSE 0.97 OF 29 WHERE MARITAL RESIDENCE IS PATRILOCAL, VIRILOCAL, OR AVUNCULOCAL, RATHER THAN MATRILOCAL OR UXORILOCAL (270)	209	TILT LESS TOWARD BEING THOSE 0.78 OF 273 WHERE MARITAL RESIDENCE IS PATRILOCAL, VIRILOCAL, OR AVUNCULOCAL, RATHER THAN MATRILOCAL OR UXORILOCAL (270)	28 212 1 61 XSQ= 4.64 PHI= 0.124 XP = 0.0313
210	IN ALL CASES ARE THOSE 1.00 OF 27 WHERE MARITAL RESIDENCE IS PATRILOCAL, RATHER THAN MATRILOCAL (169)	210	TILT LESS TOWARD BEING THOSE 0.80 OF 152 WHERE MARITAL RESIDENCE IS PATRILOCAL, RATHER THAN MATRILOCAL (169)	27 121 0 31 XSQ= 5.31 PHI= 0.172 XP = 0.0212
213	TILT MORE TOWARD BEING THOSE 0.74 OF 31 WHERE FIRST COUSIN MARRIAGE IS NOT PERMITTED (198)	213	TILT LESS TOWARD BEING THOSE 0.52 OF 310 WHERE FIRST COUSIN MARRIAGE IS NOT PERMITTED (198)	8 148 23 162 XSQ= 4.62 PHI= -0.116 XP = 0.0317
214	LEAN TOWARD BEING THOSE 0.63 OF 8 WHERE FIRST COUSIN MARRIAGE, IF PERMITTED, IS UNILATERAL (28)	214	LEAN TOWARD BEING THOSE 0.85 OF 148 WHERE FIRST COUSIN MARRIAGE, IF PERMITTED, IS OTHER THAN UNILATERAL (144)	5 22 3 126 XSQ= 8.93 PHI= 0.239 XP = 0.0028
224	TILT TOWARD BEING THOSE 0.88 OF 8 WHERE COUSIN MARRIAGE IS PREFERENTIALLY OR PERMISSIVELY EITHER PATRI- OR MATRILATERAL, RATHER THAN SYMMETRICAL (66)	224	TILT TOWARD BEING THOSE 0.63 OF 148 WHERE COUSIN MARRIAGE IS PREFERENTIALLY OR PERMISSIVELY SYMMETRICAL, RATHER THAN EITHER PATRI- OR MATRILATERAL (106)	7 55 1 93 XSQ= 6.07 PHI= 0.197 XP = 0.0138
242	DRIFT MORE TOWARD BEING THOSE 0.94 OF 31 WHERE MARRIAGE IS COMMONLY OR OCCASIONALLY POLYGYNOUS, RATHER THAN MONOGAMOUS (314)	242	DRIFT LESS TOWARD BEING THOSE 0.78 OF 328 WHERE MARRIAGE IS COMMONLY OR OCCASIONALLY POLYGYNOUS, RATHER THAN MONOGAMOUS (314)	29 257 2 71 XSQ= 3.15 PHI= 0.094 XP = 0.0758
260	DRIFT TOWARD BEING THOSE 0.80 OF 5 WHERE THE AGE OF MALES AT MARRIAGE IS TWENTY OR OVER (17) JKH	260	DRIFT TOWARD BEING THOSE 0.73 OF 48 WHERE THE AGE OF MALES AT MARRIAGE IS LESS THAN TWENTY (38) JKH	1 35 4 13 XSQ= 3.64 PHI= -0.262 XP = 0.0563
263	DRIFT MORE TOWARD BEING THOSE 0.73 OF 30 WHERE WIVES ARE OBTAINED BY RELATIVELY DIFFICULT MEANS, NAMELY BY BRIDE-PRICE, BRIDE-SERVICE, OR EXCHANGING A FEMALE RELATIVE (233)	263	DRIFT LESS TOWARD BEING THOSE 0.55 OF 329 WHERE WIVES ARE OBTAINED BY RELATIVELY DIFFICULT MEANS, NAMELY BY BRIDE-PRICE, BRIDE-SERVICE, OR EXCHANGING A FEMALE RELATIVE (233)	22 181 8 148 XSQ= 3.05 PHI= 0.092 XP = 0.0809
282	DRIFT TOWARD BEING THOSE 0.83 OF 6 WHERE THE STRENGTH OF DESIRE FOR CHILDREN IS HIGH (16) BCA	282	DRIFT TOWARD BEING THOSE 0.64 OF 28 WHERE THE STRENGTH OF DESIRE FOR CHILDREN IS LOW OR ABSENT (20) BCA	5 10 1 18 XSQ= 2.82 PHI= 0.288 EP = 0.0663

229/

```
370  DRIFT TOWARD BEING THOSE         0.63 OF  19      370  DRIFT TOWARD BEING THOSE         0.62 OF 207         12   79
     WHERE THE SEGREGATION CF ADOLESCENT BOYS               WHERE THE SEGREGATION OF ADOLESCENT BOYS               7  128
     IS COMPLETE OR PARTIAL  (95)                           IS ABSENT  (148)                               XSQ=     3.54
                                                                                                           PHI=    0.125
                                                                                                           XP =   0.0599

420  DRIFT TOWARD BEING THOSE         0.86 OF   7      420  DRIFT TOWARD BEING THOSE         0.58 OF  76          6   32
     WHERE BELLICOSITY                                      WHERE BELLICOSITY                                      1   44
     IS EXTREME  (41) PES                                   IS MODERATE OR NEGLIGIBLE  (46) PES            XSQ=     3.31
                                                                                                           PHI=    0.200
                                                                                                           XP =   0.0688
```

****

230 CULTURES WHERE THE COUSIN TERMINOLOGY IS OF IROQUOIS TYPE (93)	230 CULTURES WHERE THE COUSIN TERMINOLOGY IS OTHER THAN OF IROQUOIS TYPE (271)

BACKGROUND ON PAGE 121 — SUBJECT ONLY

93 IN LEFT COLUMN

AJIE	AKHA	ARANDA	BACAIRI	BAMBARA	BEMBA	BLACK CARIB	BUDUMA	BUNLAP	CALLINAGO
CAMAYURA	CARIB	CHENCHU	COORG	CREE	DAGUR	DIEGUENO	DIERI	DOBUANS	DOGON
ENGA	EYAK	FUTAJALONKE	GANDA	GARO	GILYAK	GOND	GUAHIBO	GUATC	HAVASUPAI
HEHE	HERERO	HO	HURON	ILA	KACHIN	KAPAUKU	KARIERA	KERAKI	KERALA
KHASI	KURTATCHI	LAKALAI	LAMBA	LAU	LESU	MANCHU	MARICOPA	MARSHALLESE	MBUNDU
MISKITO	MOTILON	MURINBATA	NABESNA	NAMA	NAMBICUARA	NASKAPI	NAVAHO	NDEMBU	NGONI
NUNIVAK	NYAKYUSA	NYANEKA	OJIBWA	ROTINESE	RUNDI	SINHALESE	SONGHAI	SOTHO	SWAZI
TAMIL	TANALA	TAREUMIUT	TECA	TERA	TETON	TODA	TOLOWA	TRUMAI	TSHIMSHIAN
TUCANO	TUCUNA	TUPINAMBA	VEDDA	VENDA	WANTOAT	WAPISHANA	WAROPEN	WIKMUNKAN	WOGEO
YABARANA	YAKO	YAO							

271 IN RIGHT COLUMN

36 EXCLUDED BECAUSE UNASCERTAINED

	Left column		Right column	Statistics
4	TILT MORE TOWARD BEING THOSE 0.96 OF 93 LOCATED OUTSIDE OF THE CIRCUM-MEDITERRANEAN (355)	4	TILT LESS TOWARD BEING THOSE 0.87 OF 271 LOCATED OUTSIDE OF THE CIRCUM-MEDITERRANEAN (355)	4 35 89 236 XSQ= 4.51 PHI= -0.111 XP = 0.0337
14	TILT MORE TOWARD BEING THOSE 0.81 OF 93 WHERE THE LATITUDE IS LESS THAN THIRTY DEGREES (281)	14	TILT LESS TOWARD BEING THOSE 0.68 OF 271 WHERE THE LATITUDE IS LESS THAN THIRTY DEGREES (281)	18 87 75 184 XSQ= 4.88 PHI= -0.116 XP = 0.0272
51	TILT LESS TOWARD BEING THOSE 0.54 OF 93 WHERE SUBSISTENCE IS PRIMARILY BY FOOD PRODUCTION -- I. E., AGRICULTURE OR HUSBANDRY -- RATHER THAN BY GATHERING (253)	51	TILT MORE TOWARD BEING THOSE 0.67 OF 271 WHERE SUBSISTENCE IS PRIMARILY BY FOOD PRODUCTION -- I. E., AGRICULTURE OR HUSBANDRY -- RATHER THAN BY GATHERING (253)	50 181 43 90 XSQ= 4.52 PHI= -0.111 XP = 0.0335
53	DRIFT MORE TOWARD BEING THOSE 0.74 OF 54 WHERE FOOD PRODUCTION IS BY SIMPLE AGRICULTURE OR INCIPIENT FOOD PRODUCTION, RATHER THAN BY INTENSIVE AGRICULTURE (147)	53	DRIFT LESS TOWARD BEING THOSE 0.58 OF 164 WHERE FOOD PRODUCTION IS BY SIMPLE AGRICULTURE OR INCIPIENT FOOD PRODUCTION, RATHER THAN BY INTENSIVE AGRICULTURE (147)	14 69 40 95 XSQ= 3.83 PHI= -0.133 XP = 0.0502

54	DRIFT LESS TOWARD BEING THOSE WHERE FOOD PRODUCTION IS BY INTENSIVE OR SIMPLE AGRICULTURE, RATHER THAN BY INCIPIENT FOOD PRODUCTION (192)	0.72 OF 54	54	DRIFT MORE TOWARD BEING THOSE WHERE FOOD PRODUCTION IS BY INTENSIVE OR SIMPLE AGRICULTURE, RATHER THAN BY INCIPIENT FOOD PRODUCTION (192)	0.84 OF 164	39 138 15 26 XSQ= 3.04 PHI= -0.118 XP = 0.0811
62	LEAN TOWARD BEING THOSE WHERE HUSBANDRY OF ANY KIND IS ABSENT (172)	0.55 OF 93	62	LEAN TOWARD BEING THOSE WHERE HUSBANDRY OF SOME KIND IS PRESENT (228)	0.62 OF 271	42 169 51 102 XSQ= 7.72 PHI= -0.146 XP = 0.0055
73	TILT TOWARD BEING THOSE WHERE WEAVING IS ABSENT (130)	0.67 OF 61	73	TILT TOWARD BEING THOSE WHERE WEAVING IS PRESENT (118)	0.51 OF 167	20 85 41 82 XSQ= 5.19 PHI= -0.151 XP = 0.0227
79	DRIFT MORE TOWARD BEING THOSE WHERE NO CITY IS PRESENT (201)	0.97 OF 60	79	DRIFT LESS TOWARD BEING THOSE WHERE NO CITY IS PRESENT (201)	0.86 OF 146	2 20 58 126 XSQ= 3.76 PHI= -0.135 XP = 0.0523
81	TILT MORE TOWARD BEING THOSE WHERE NO CITY OR TOWN IS PRESENT, AND THE AVERAGE COMMUNITY SIZE IS SMALLER THAN 200 (135)	0.73 OF 60	81	TILT LESS TOWARD BEING THOSE WHERE NO CITY OR TOWN IS PRESENT, AND THE AVERAGE COMMUNITY SIZE IS SMALLER THAN 200 (135)	0.55 OF 146	16 65 44 81 XSQ= 4.96 PHI= -0.155 XP = 0.0260
82	LEAN LESS TOWARD BEING THOSE WHERE A CITY OR TOWN IS PRESENT, OR THE AVERAGE COMMUNITY SIZE IS FIFTY OR GREATER (178)	0.67 OF 60	82	LEAN MORE TOWARD BEING THOSE WHERE A CITY OR TOWN IS PRESENT, OR THE AVERAGE COMMUNITY SIZE IS FIFTY OR GREATER (178)	0.86 OF 146	40 125 20 21 XSQ= 8.43 PHI= -0.202 XP = 0.0037
90	DRIFT LESS TOWARD BEING THOSE WHERE, IF A HEREDITARY HEADMANSHIP IS PRESENT, SUCCESSION IS PATRILINEAL, RATHER THAN MATRILINEAL (127)	0.66 OF 44	90	DRIFT MORE TOWARD BEING THOSE WHERE, IF A HEREDITARY HEADMANSHIP IS PRESENT, SUCCESSION IS PATRILINEAL, RATHER THAN MATRILINEAL (127)	0.81 OF 108	29 87 15 21 XSQ= 2.94 PHI= -0.139 XP = 0.0862
176	TILT TOWARD BEING THOSE WHERE THE COMMUNITY IS A CLAN-COMMUNITY OR A COMMUNITY STRUCTURED OR SEGMENTED ON A CLAN BASIS (169)	0.54 OF 90	176	TILT TOWARD BEING THOSE WHERE THE COMMUNITY IS OTHER THAN A CLAN-COMMUNITY OR A COMMUNITY STRUCTURED OR SEGMENTED ON A CLAN BASIS (213)	0.61 OF 260	49 102 41 158 XSQ= 5.70 PHI= 0.128 XP = 0.0169
177	LEAN LESS TOWARD BEING THOSE WHERE THE COMMUNITY IS OTHER THAN A SINGLE CLAN-COMMUNITY AND EXOGAMOUS (305)	0.69 OF 90	177	LEAN MORE TOWARD BEING THOSE WHERE THE COMMUNITY IS OTHER THAN A SINGLE CLAN-COMMUNITY AND EXOGAMOUS (305)	0.85 OF 260	28 40 62 220 XSQ= 9.58 PHI= 0.165 XP = 0.0020

180	LEAN LESS TOWARD BEING THOSE WHERE THE COMMUNITY IS COMMONLY NON-EXOGAMOUS, RATHER THAN EXOGAMOUS (258)	0.54 OF 90	180	LEAN MORE TOWARD BEING THOSE WHERE THE COMMUNITY IS COMMONLY NON-EXOGAMOUS, RATHER THAN EXOGAMOUS (258)	0.72 OF 260	41 72 49 188 XSQ= 8.96 PHI= 0.160 XP = 0.0028
181	LEAN MORE TOWARD BEING THOSE WHERE THE COMMUNITY IS OTHER THAN A DEME (337)	0.97 OF 90	181	LEAN LESS TOWARD BEING THOSE WHERE THE COMMUNITY IS OTHER THAN A DEME (337)	0.85 OF 260	3 40 87 220 XSQ= 7.93 PHI= -0.150 XP = 0.0049
188	TEND MORE TO BE THOSE WHERE THE KIN GROUP IS OTHER THAN EXCLUSIVELY COGNATIC (252)	0.78 OF 93	188	TEND LESS TO BE THOSE WHERE THE KIN GROUP IS OTHER THAN EXCLUSIVELY COGNATIC (252)	0.56 OF 271	20 118 73 153 XSQ= 13.36 PHI= -0.192 XP = 0.0003
192	TEND MORE TO BE THOSE OTHER THAN WHERE THE ONLY KIN GROUP PRESENT IS A KINDRED OR ELSE BILATERAL DESCENT IS INFERRED (289)	0.92 OF 93	192	TEND LESS TO BE THOSE OTHER THAN WHERE THE ONLY KIN GROUP PRESENT IS A KINDRED OR ELSE BILATERAL DESCENT IS INFERRED (289)	0.65 OF 271	7 96 86 175 XSQ= 25.20 PHI= -0.263 XP = 0.0000
213	TEND TO BE THOSE WHERE FIRST COUSIN MARRIAGE IS PERMITTED (172)	0.75 OF 92	213	TEND TO BE THOSE WHERE FIRST COUSIN MARRIAGE IS NOT PERMITTED (198)	0.65 OF 249	69 87 23 162 XSQ= 41.84 PHI= 0.350 XP = 0.
214	DRIFT MORE TOWARD BEING THOSE WHERE FIRST COUSIN MARRIAGE, IF PERMITTED, IS OTHER THAN UNILATERAL (144)	0.90 OF 69	214	DRIFT LESS TOWARD BEING THOSE WHERE FIRST COUSIN MARRIAGE, IF PERMITTED, IS OTHER THAN UNILATERAL (144)	0.77 OF 87	7 20 62 67 XSQ= 3.58 PHI= -0.152 XP = 0.0584
220	TEND TO BE THOSE WHERE FIRST COUSIN MARRIAGE IN SOME FORM OR OTHER IS PRESCRIBED OR PREFERRED (97)	0.54 OF 92	220	TEND TO BE THOSE WHERE FIRST COUSIN MARRIAGE IN SOME FORM OR OTHER IS NOT PRESCRIBED OR PREFERRED (273)	0.82 OF 249	50 45 42 204 XSQ= 42.20 PHI= 0.352 XP = 0.
224	TILT MORE TOWARD BEING THOSE WHERE COUSIN MARRIAGE IS PREFERENTIALLY OR PERMISSIVELY SYMMETRICAL, RATHER THAN EITHER PATRI- OR MATRILATERAL (106)	0.71 OF 69	224	TILT LESS TOWARD BEING THOSE WHERE COUSIN MARRIAGE IS PREFERENTIALLY OR PERMISSIVELY SYMMETRICAL, RATHER THAN EITHER PATRI- OR MATRILATERAL (106)	0.52 OF 87	20 42 49 45 XSQ= 5.20 PHI= -0.183 XP = 0.0226
236	DRIFT TOWARD BEING THOSE WHERE THE FAMILY IS OF AN INDEPENDENT TYPE, RATHER THAN AN EXTENDED TYPE (185)	0.53 OF 92	236	DRIFT TOWARD BEING THOSE WHERE THE FAMILY IS OF AN EXTENDED TYPE, RATHER THAN AN INDEPENDENT TYPE (213)	0.58 OF 270	43 156 49 114 XSQ= 2.95 PHI= -0.090 XP = 0.0861

242	TILT MORE TOWARD BEING THOSE 0.88 OF 91 WHERE MARRIAGE IS COMMONLY OR OCCASIONALLY POLYGYNOUS, RATHER THAN MONOGAMOUS (314)	TILT LESS TOWARD BEING THOSE 0.77 OF 268 WHERE MARRIAGE IS COMMONLY OR OCCASIONALLY POLYGYNOUS, RATHER THAN MONOGAMOUS (314)	80 206 11 62 XSQ= 4.46 PHI= 0.111 XP = 0.0347
259	DRIFT TOWARD BEING THOSE 0.83 OF 12 WHERE THE SEVERITY OF MOTHER-IN-LAW AVOIDANCE IS HIGH (26) WNS	DRIFT TOWARD BEING THOSE 0.53 OF 34 WHERE THE SEVERITY OF MOTHER-IN-LAW AVOIDANCE IS LOW (20) WNS	10 16 2 18 XSQ= 3.39 PHI= 0.271 XP = 0.0657
306	DRIFT TOWARD BEING THOSE 0.82 OF 11 WHERE THE EARLY DEPENDENCE SATISFACTION POTENTIAL IS HIGH (28) W-C	DRIFT TOWARD BEING THOSE 0.54 OF 39 WHERE THE EARLY DEPENDENCE SATISFACTION POTENTIAL IS LOW (24) W-C	9 18 2 21 XSQ= 3.07 PHI= 0.248 XP = 0.0795
325	DRIFT TOWARD BEING THOSE 0.63 OF 19 WHERE THE DEGREE OF DIFFUSION AMONG THE INFANT'S NURTURANT AGENTS IS LOW (32) B-B-C	DRIFT TOWARD BEING THOSE 0.66 OF 53 WHERE THE DEGREE OF DIFFUSION AMONG THE INFANT'S NURTURANT AGENTS IS HIGH (42) B-B-C	7 35 12 18 XSQ= 3.78 PHI= -0.229 XP = 0.0520
335	DRIFT TOWARD BEING THOSE 0.86 OF 7 WHERE INITIAL INDULGENCE OF DEPENDENCY IS HIGH (20) WNS	DRIFT TOWARD BEING THOSE 0.55 OF 29 WHERE INITIAL INDULGENCE OF DEPENDENCY IS LOW (18) WNS	6 13 1 16 XSQ= 2.32 PHI= 0.254 EP = 0.0918
347	DRIFT TOWARD BEING THOSE 0.70 OF 20 WHERE THE CHILD'S INFERRED CONFLICT REGARDING SELF-RELIANT BEHAVIOR IS HIGH (37) B-B-C	DRIFT TOWARD BEING THOSE 0.57 OF 54 WHERE THE CHILD'S INFERRED CONFLICT REGARDING SELF-RELIANT BEHAVIOR IS LOW (39) B-B-C	14 23 6 31 XSQ= 3.36 PHI= 0.213 XP = 0.0669
352	DRIFT MORE TOWARD BEING THOSE 0.80 OF 20 WHERE THE TOTAL POSITIVE PRESSURE TOWARD DEVELOPING OBEDIENT BEHAVIOR IN THE CHILD IS HIGH (44) B-B-C	DRIFT LESS TOWARD BEING THOSE 0.54 OF 50 WHERE THE TOTAL POSITIVE PRESSURE TOWARD DEVELOPING OBEDIENT BEHAVIOR IN THE CHILD IS HIGH (44) B-B-C	16 27 4 23 XSQ= 3.05 PHI= 0.209 XP = 0.0806
370	LEAN TOWARD BEING THOSE 0.59 OF 58 WHERE THE SEGREGATION OF ADOLESCENT BOYS IS COMPLETE OR PARTIAL (95)	LEAN TOWARD BEING THOSE 0.66 OF 168 WHERE THE SEGREGATION OF ADOLESCENT BOYS IS ABSENT (148)	34 57 24 111 XSQ= 9.93 PHI= 0.210 XP = 0.0016
382	TILT TOWARD BEING THOSE 0.82 OF 17 WHERE FEMALE INITIATION RITES ARE PRESENT (38) JKB	TILT TOWARD BEING THOSE 0.53 OF 43 WHERE FEMALE INITIATION RITES ARE ABSENT (27) JKB	14 20 3 23 XSQ= 5.00 PHI= 0.289 XP = 0.0254

391	TILT TOWARD BEING THOSE 0.69 OF 36 WHERE PREMARITAL SEX RELATIONS ARE PUNISHED ONLY IF PREGNANCY RESULTS, OR FREELY PERMITTED (90) JTW,EA	391	TILT TOWARD BEING THOSE 0.54 OF 129 WHERE PREMARITAL SEX RELATIONS ARE STRONGLY PUNISHED AND IN FACT RARE, OR WEAKLY PUNISHED AND IN FACT NOT RARE (89) JTW,EA	 XSQ= PHI= XP =	11 70 25 59 5.42 -0.181 0.0199
406	DRIFT TOWARD BEING THOSE 0.83 OF 12 WHERE EXPLANATIONS OF ILLNESS OF AN AGGRESSION NATURE ARE ABSENT (33) W-C	406	DRIFT TOWARD BEING THOSE 0.52 OF 44 WHERE EXPLANATIONS OF ILLNESS OF AN AGGRESSION NATURE ARE PRESENT (28) W-C	 XSQ= PHI= XP =	2 23 10 21 3.50 -0.250 0.0612
426	TILT TOWARD BEING THOSE 0.54 OF 63 WHERE A HIGH GOD IS ABSENT (104) GES,EA	426	TILT TOWARD BEING THOSE 0.63 OF 179 WHERE A HIGH GOD IS PRESENT (156) GES,EA	 XSQ= PHI= XP =	29 112 34 67 4.58 -0.138 0.0323
427	DRIFT TOWARD BEING THOSE 0.62 OF 29 WHERE A HIGH GOD, IF PRESENT, IS INACTIVE, RATHER THAN ACTIVE (69) GES,EA	427	DRIFT TOWARD BEING THOSE 0.60 OF 112 WHERE A HIGH GOD, IF PRESENT, IS ACTIVE, RATHER THAN INACTIVE (87) GES,EA	 XSQ= PHI= XP =	11 67 18 45 3.62 -0.160 0.0569
435	TILT TOWARD BEING THOSE 0.83 OF 6 WHERE ABANDONMENT OF THE HOUSE OF THE DEAD IS PRACTICED (12) LWS	435	TILT TOWARD BEING THOSE 0.74 OF 23 WHERE ABANDONMENT OF THE HOUSE OF THE DEAD IS NOT PRACTICED (19) LWS	 XSQ= PHI= EP =	5 6 1 17 4.42 0.390 0.0185
446	TILT TOWARD BEING THOSE 0.67 OF 9 WHERE WITCHCRAFT IS SIGNIFICANTLY PRESENT (14) GES	446	TILT TOWARD BEING THOSE 0.74 OF 27 WHERE WITCHCRAFT IS MODERATELY PRESENT OR ABSENT (24) GES	 XSQ= PHI= EP =	6 7 3 20 3.25 0.301 0.0459
450	DRIFT MORE TOWARD BEING THOSE 0.86 OF 22 WHERE THE OBSERVATION OF FOOD TABOOS IS HIGH OR MEDIUM, RATHER THAN LOW (60) JRL	450	DRIFT LESS TOWARD BEING THOSE 0.64 OF 61 WHERE THE OBSERVATION OF FOOD TABOOS IS HIGH OR MEDIUM, RATHER THAN LOW (60) JRL	 XSQ= PHI= XP =	19 39 3 22 2.87 0.186 0.0901
459	LEAN TOWARD BEING THOSE 0.72 OF 40 WHERE GAMES, IF PRESENT, DO NOT INCLUDE GAMES OF CHANCE (89) R-A-B,EA	459	LEAN TOWARD BEING THOSE 0.54 OF 124 WHERE GAMES, IF PRESENT, INCLUDE GAMES OF CHANCE (82) R-A-B,EA	 XSQ= PHI= XP =	11 67 29 57 7.51 -0.214 0.0061
460	DRIFT TOWARD BEING THOSE 0.52 OF 40 WHERE GAMES, IF PRESENT, ARE LIMITED TO GAMES OF SKILL ONLY (67) R-A-B,EA	460	DRIFT TOWARD BEING THOSE 0.65 OF 124 WHERE GAMES, IF PRESENT, ARE NOT LIMITED TO GAMES OF SKILL ONLY (104) R-A-B,EA	 XSQ= PHI= XP =	21 43 19 81 3.32 0.142 0.0683

```
474  DRIFT TOWARD BEING THCSE        0.76 OF  17     474  DRIFT TOWARD BEING THOSE        0.51 OF  68          4   35
     WHERE BCASTFULNESS IS MODERATE,                      WHERE BOASTFULNESS IS EXTREME   (41) PES            13   33
     NEGLIBIBLE, CR UNREPORTED  (48) PES                                                               XSQ=      3.22
                                                                                                       PHI=    -0.195
                                                                                                       XP  =   0.0725

480  IN ALL CASES ARE THOSE          1.00 OF   4     48C  DRIFT TOWARD BEING THOSE        0.58 OF  24          0   14
     WHERE COMPLEXITY OF ARTISTIC CESIGN                  WHERE COMPLEXITY OF ARTISTIC DESIGN                  4   10
     IS LOW  (15) HB                                      IS HIGH  (14) HB                                 XSQ=      2.63
                                                                                                       PHI=    -0.306
                                                                                                       EP  =   0.0978
```

****

231 CULTURES
WHERE THE COUSIN TERMINOLOGY IS
OF ESKIMO OR HAWAIIAN TYPE (170)

231 CULTURES
WHERE THE COUSIN TERMINOLOGY IS OTHER THAN
OF ESKIMO OR HAWAIIAN TYPE (194)

BACKGROUND ON PAGE 121

SUBJECT ONLY

....

170 IN LEFT COLUMN

ABIPON	ALBANIANS	ALORESE	AMERICANS	ANDAMANESE	ARYANS	ATAYAL	ATSUGEWI	AWEIKOMA	AYMARA
AZTEC	BABWA	BALINESE	BASQUES	BELU	BENGALI	BHUIYA	BOERS	BOTOCUDO	BRAZILIANS
BURMESE	BURUSHO	CADUVEO	CACABA	CAMBA	CAMBODIANS	CARAJA	CARINYA	CAYAPA	CHERKESS
CHEYENNE	CHIBCHA	CHINANTEC	CHIR-APACHE	CHOCO	CHOROTI	CHORTI	CHUKCHEE	COCHITI	COMANCHE
COPR ESKIMO	CUNA	CZECHS	DARO	DELAWARE	DUSUN	DUTCH	ELLICE	GILBERTESE	GISU
GROS VENTRE	GURE	HANUNOO	HASINAI	HAWAIIANS	HEBREWS	HUICHOL	HUKUNDIKA	HUTSUL	IBAN
IFUGAO	INCA	INGALIK	INGASSANA	IRISH	JAPANESE	JAVANESE	JEMEZ	JUKUN	KAREN
KATAB	KIOW-APACHE	KISSI	KOL	KOREANS	KORYAK	KUBA	KUMYK	KUNG	KUTENAI
KWAKIUTL	LAPPS	LEPCHA	LIFU	LOZI	MACASSARESE	MAGUZAWA	MALAYS	MAM	MAMBILA
MAMVU	MANGAIANS	MANIHIKI	MAORI	MARGI	MARQUESANS	MATACO	MAYA	MAZATECO	MENDE
MERINA	MIAO	MINANGKABAU	MOSSI	NICOBARESE	NUPE	OKINAWANS	ONA	ONTONG-JAVA	ORAON
PAIWAN	PALAUANS	PAPAGO	PARAUJANO	PATHAN	PENOBSCOT	POPOLUCA	PORTUGUESE	PUKAPUKA	PURARI
RAROIANS	ROTUMANS	SAGADA	SAMOANS	SANPOIL	SARAMACCA	SARSI	SELUNG	SEMANG	SERBS
SERI	SIMBOESE	SIUAI	SUBANUN	TAGBANUA	TALAMANCA	TALLENSI	TANIMBARESE	TAOS	TAPIRAPE
TARAHUMARA	TENETEHARA	TENINO	TERENA	TESO	THAI	TIBETANS	TIKOPIA	TIV	TORAJA
TOTONAC	TRISTAN	TUBATULABAL	TUNEBO	TWANA	ULAWANS	UTE	VIETNAMESE	WALLOONS	WARRAU
WASHO	WICHITA	WOLEAIANS	WOLOF	YAHGAN	YARURO	YOKUTS	YORUBA	YUKI	YUROK

194 IN RIGHT COLUMN

36 EXCLUDED BECAUSE UNASCERTAINED

----

3 LEAN MORE TOWARD BEING THOSE 0.88 OF 170
LOCATED OUTSIDE OF
AFRICA (320)

3 LEAN LESS TOWARD BEING THOSE 0.75 OF 194
LOCATED OUTSIDE OF
AFRICA (320)

20 49
150 145
XSQ= 9.88
PHI= -0.165
XP = 0.0017

42 DRIFT LESS TOWARD BEING THOSE 0.56 OF 170
WHERE THE NATURAL ENVIRONMENT IS
OTHER THAN
TROPICAL OR SUB-TROPICAL RAIN FOREST, OR
MONSOON FOREST (244) FWM

42 DRIFT MORE TOWARD BEING THOSE 0.65 OF 194
WHERE THE NATURAL ENVIRONMENT IS
OTHER THAN
TROPICAL OR SUB-TROPICAL RAIN FOREST, OR
MONSOON FOREST (244) FWM

75 68
95 126
XSQ= 2.75
PHI= 0.087
XP = 0.0970

54 TILT MORE TOWARD BEING THOSE 0.89 OF 99
WHERE FOOD PRODUCTION IS BY
INTENSIVE OR SIMPLE
AGRICULTURE, RATHER THAN BY
INCIPIENT FOOD PRODUCTION (192)

54 TILT LESS TOWARD BEING THOSE 0.75 OF 119
WHERE FOOD PRODUCTION IS BY
INTENSIVE OR SIMPLE
AGRICULTURE, RATHER THAN BY
INCIPIENT FOOD PRODUCTION (192)

88 89
11 30
XSQ= 6.14
PHI= 0.168
XP = 0.0132

56	TILT MORE TOWARC BEING THCSE 0.80 OF 55 WHERE FCCD PRCDUCTICN IS BY SIMPLE AGRICULTURE, RATHER THAN BY INCIPIENT FCCD PRCDUCTION (101)	56	TILT LESS TOWARD BEING THOSE 0.63 OF 80 WHERE FOOD PRODUCTICN IS BY SIMPLE AGRICULTURE, RATHER THAN BY INCIPIENT FOOD PRODUCTICN (101)	44 50 11 30 XSQ= 3.93 PHI= 0.171 XP = 0.0475
81	LEAN TCWARD BEING THOSE 0.52 OF 89 WHERE A CITY CR TOWN IS PRESENT, OR THE AVERAGE COMMUNITY SIZE IS 200 CR GREATER (89)	81	LEAN TOWARD BEING THOSE 0.70 OF 117 WHERE NO CITY OR TOWN IS PRESENT, AND THE AVERAGE COMMUNITY SIZE IS SMALLER THAN 200 (135)	46 35 43 82 XSQ= 9.15 PHI= 0.211 XP = 0.0025
83	DRIFT LESS TCWARD BEING THCSE 0.67 OF 64 WHERE, WITH NC CITY ANC NC TOWN PRESENT, THE AVERAGE COMMUNITY SIZE IS SMALLER THAN 200, RATHER THAN BETWEEN 200 AND 999 (135)	83	DRIFT MORE TOWARD BEING THCSE 0.81 OF 101 WHERE, WITH NO CITY AND NC TOWN PRESENT, THE AVERAGE COMMUNITY SIZE IS SMALLER THAN 200, RATHER THAN BETWEEN 200 AND 999 (135)	21 19 43 82 XSQ= 3.45 PHI= 0.145 XP = 0.0631
84	TILT LESS TOWARC BEING THCSE 0.79 OF 126 WHERE THE LEVEL CF POLITICAL INTEGRATION IS THE LITTLE STATE, THE MINIMAL STATE, THE AUTONCMOUS CCMMUNITY, CR THE FAMILY (262) GPM	84	TILT MORE TOWARD BEING THOSE 0.89 OF 149 WHERE THE LEVEL OF POLITICAL INTEGRATION IS THE LITTLE STATE, THE MINIMAL STATE, THE AUTONOMOUS COMMUNITY, CR THE FAMILY (262) GPM	26 16 100 133 XSQ= 4.43 PHI= 0.127 XP = 0.0353
88	TEND TC BE THCSE 0.51 OF 112 WHERE, IF A HEACMANSHIP IS PRESENT, SUCCESSICN IS NCN-HERECITARY (106)	88	TEND TO BE THOSE 0.71 CF 136 WHERE, IF A HEADMANSHIP IS PRESENT, SUCCESSION IS HEREDITARY (165)	57 39 55 97 XSQ= 11.86 PHI= 0.219 XP = 0.0006
90	DRIFT MORE TCWARD BEING THCSE 0.85 OF 55 WHERE, IF A HERECITARY HEACMANSHIP IS PRESENT, SUCCESSICN IS PATRILINEAL, RATHER THAN MATRILINEAL (127)	90	DRIFT LESS TOWARD BEING THOSE 0.71 OF 97 WHERE, IF A HEREDITARY HEADMANSHIP IS PRESENT, SUCCESSION IS PATRILINEAL, RATHER THAN MATRILINEAL (127)	47 69 8 28 XSQ= 3.23 PHI= 0.146 XP = 0.0723
107	TILT LESS TOWARC BEING THCSE 0.69 OF 91 WHERE CLASS STRATIFICATION, IF PRESENT, IS BASED CN SCMETHING CTHER THAN OCCUPATICNAL STATUS (160)	1C7	TILT MORE TOWARD BEING THOSE 0.86 CF 97 WHERE CLASS STRATIFICATICN, IF PRESENT, IS BASED ON SOMETHING CTHER THAN OCCUPATIONAL STATUS (160)	28 14 63 83 XSQ= 6.31 PHI= 0.183 XP = 0.0120
128	TILT TCWARD BEING THOSE 0.69 OF 32 WHERE, IF SUBSISTENCE IS PRIMARILY BY AGRICULTURE, THE WCRK IS MAINLY DCNE BY MALES (40)	128	TILT TOWARD BEING THOSE 0.59 CF 39 WHERE, IF SUBSISTENCE IS PRIMARILY BY AGRICULTURE, THE WORK IS MAINLY DONE BY FEMALES (37)	22 16 10 23 XSQ= 4.37 PHI= 0.248 XP = 0.0365
163	TILT TOWARD BEING THCSE 0.64 OF 11 WHERE THE EMPHASIS ON INCIVICUAL VOLITION AS THE CAUSE CF CRIME IS HIGH (7) MJ	163	IN ALL CASES ARE THCSE 1.00 OF 5 WHERE THE EMPHASIS CN INDIVIDUAL VCLITICN AS THE CAUSE OF CRIME IS LOW (10) MJ	7 0 4 5 XSQ= 3.37 PHI= 0.459 EP = 0.0337

175	TILT MORE TOWARD BEING THOSE 0.74 OF 163 WHERE THE COMMUNITY IS 'KIN-HETEROGENEOUS,' I. E. OTHER THAN A CLAN COMMUNITY OR A DEME (260)	175	TILT LESS TOWARD BEING THOSE 0.63 OF 187 WHERE THE COMMUNITY IS 'KIN-HETEROGENEOUS,' I. E. OTHER THAN A CLAN COMMUNITY OR A DEME (260)	42 69 121 118 XSQ= 4.48 PHI= -0.113 XP = 0.0342
176	TEND TO BE THOSE 0.73 OF 163 WHERE THE COMMUNITY IS OTHER THAN A CLAN-COMMUNITY OR A COMMUNITY STRUCTURED OR SEGMENTED ON A CLAN BASIS (213)	176	TEND TO BE THOSE 0.57 OF 187 WHERE THE COMMUNITY IS A CLAN-COMMUNITY OR A COMMUNITY STRUCTURED OR SEGMENTED ON A CLAN BASIS (169)	44 107 119 80 XSQ= 31.21 PHI= -0.299 XP = 0.
177	TEND MORE TO BE THOSE 0.94 OF 163 WHERE THE COMMUNITY IS OTHER THAN A SINGLE CLAN-COMMUNITY AND EXOGAMOUS (305)	177	TEND LESS TO BE THOSE 0.68 OF 187 WHERE THE COMMUNITY IS OTHER THAN A SINGLE CLAN-COMMUNITY AND EXOGAMOUS (305)	9 59 154 128 XSQ= 36.05 PHI= -0.321 XP = 0.
180	TEND MORE TO BE THOSE 0.79 OF 163 WHERE THE COMMUNITY IS COMMONLY NON-EXOGAMOUS, RATHER THAN EXOGAMOUS (258)	180	TEND LESS TO BE THOSE 0.58 OF 187 WHERE THE COMMUNITY IS COMMONLY NON-EXOGAMOUS, RATHER THAN EXOGAMOUS (258)	35 78 128 109 XSQ= 15.40 PHI= -0.210 XP = 0.0001
181	TEND LESS TO BE THOSE 0.80 OF 163 WHERE THE COMMUNITY IS OTHER THAN A DEME (337)	181	TEND MORE TO BE THOSE 0.95 OF 187 WHERE THE COMMUNITY IS OTHER THAN A DEME (337)	33 10 130 177 XSQ= 16.58 PHI= 0.218 XP = 0.0000
182	DRIFT LESS TOWARD BEING THOSE 0.62 OF 163 OTHER THAN WHERE THE COMMUNITY IS STRUCTURED ON A NON-CLAN BASIS AND AGAMOUS (256)	182	DRIFT MORE TOWARD BEING THOSE 0.71 OF 187 OTHER THAN WHERE THE COMMUNITY IS STRUCTURED ON A NON-CLAN BASIS AND AGAMOUS (256)	62 54 101 133 XSQ= 2.90 PHI= 0.091 XP = 0.0887
183	TILT MORE TOWARD BEING THOSE 0.95 OF 58 WHERE THE LARGEST NON-COGNATIC KIN GROUP IS SMALLER THAN A MOEITY, I. E., A PHRATRY OR SIB OR LINEAGE (218)	183	TILT LESS TOWARD BEING THOSE 0.82 OF 168 WHERE THE LARGEST NON-COGNATIC KIN GROUP IS SMALLER THAN A MOEITY, I. E., A PHRATRY OR SIB OR LINEAGE (218)	3 30 55 138 XSQ= 4.59 PHI= -0.143 XP = 0.0321
184	LEAN MORE TOWARD BEING THOSE 0.84 OF 58 WHERE THE LARGEST NON-COGNATIC KIN GROUP IS SMALLER THAN A PHRATRY, I. E. A SIB OR LINEAGE (175)	184	LEAN LESS TOWARD BEING THOSE 0.62 OF 168 WHERE THE LARGEST NON-COGNATIC KIN GROUP IS SMALLER THAN A PHRATRY, I. E. A SIB OR LINEAGE (175)	9 64 49 104 XSQ= 9.04 PHI= -0.200 XP = 0.0026
185	DRIFT LESS TOWARD BEING THOSE 0.69 OF 58 WHERE THE LARGEST NON-COGNATIC KIN GROUP IS THE MOEITY OR PHRATRY OR SIB (194)	185	DRIFT MORE TOWARD BEING THOSE 0.82 OF 168 WHERE THE LARGEST NON-COGNATIC KIN GROUP IS THE MOEITY OR PHRATRY OR SIB (194)	40 138 18 30 XSQ= 3.72 PHI= -0.128 XP = 0.0537

186	TEND TO BE THOSE WHERE THE KIN GROUP IS OTHER THAN EXCLUSIVELY PATRILINEAL (250)	0.82 OF 170	186	TEND TO BE THOSE WHERE THE KIN GROUP IS EXCLUSIVELY PATRILINEAL (150)	0.50 OF 194	31 97 139 97 XSQ= 38.72 PHI= -0.326 XP = 0.
187	TEND MORE TO BE THOSE WHERE THE KIN GROUP IS OTHER THAN EXCLUSIVELY MATRILINEAL (344)	0.93 OF 170	187	TEND LESS TO BE THOSE WHERE THE KIN GROUP IS OTHER THAN EXCLUSIVELY MATRILINEAL (344)	0.79 OF 193	12 41 158 152 XSQ= 13.47 PHI= -0.193 XP = 0.0002
188	TEND TO BE THOSE WHERE THE KIN GROUP IS EXCLUSIVELY COGNATIC (148)	0.66 OF 170	188	TEND TO BE THOSE WHERE THE KIN GROUP IS OTHER THAN EXCLUSIVELY COGNATIC (252)	0.87 OF 194	112 26 58 168 XSQ= 103.79 PHI= 0.534 XP = 0.
192	TEND TO BE THOSE WHERE THE ONLY KIN GROUP PRESENT IS A KINDRED OR ELSE BILATERAL DESCENT IS INFERRED (111)	0.54 OF 170	192	TEND TO BE THOSE OTHER THAN WHERE THE ONLY KIN GROUP PRESENT IS A KINDRED OR ELSE BILATERAL DESCENT IS INFERRED (289)	0.94 OF 194	91 12 79 182 XSQ= 97.77 PHI= 0.518 XP = 0.
197	TEND LESS TO BE THOSE WHERE RULES FOR THE INHERITANCE OF REAL PROPERTY, IF PRESENT, FAVOR EITHER THE MALE HEIR OR LINE, OR THE FEMALE HEIR OR LINE (165)	0.71 OF 82	197	TEND MORE TO BE THOSE WHERE RULES FOR THE INHERITANCE OF REAL PROPERTY, IF PRESENT, FAVOR EITHER THE MALE HEIR OR LINE, OR THE FEMALE HEIR OR LINE (165)	0.96 OF 93	58 89 24 4 XSQ= 18.40 PHI= -0.324 XP = 0.0000
201	TEND LESS TO BE THOSE WHERE MARITAL RESIDENCE IS NON-OPTIONAL, RATHER THAN AMBILOCAL OR NEOLOCAL (334)	0.74 OF 168	201	TEND MORE TO BE THOSE WHERE MARITAL RESIDENCE IS NON-OPTIONAL, RATHER THAN AMBILOCAL OR NEOLOCAL (334)	0.92 OF 194	124 178 44 16 XSQ= 19.69 PHI= -0.233 XP = 0.0000
204	TEND LESS TO BE THOSE WHERE MARITAL RESIDENCE IS PATRILOCAL, VIRILOCAL, OR AVUNCULOCAL, RATHER THAN AMBILOCAL OR NEOLOCAL (270)	0.68 OF 138	204	TEND MORE TO BE THOSE WHERE MARITAL RESIDENCE IS PATRILOCAL, VIRILOCAL, OR AVUNCULOCAL, RATHER THAN AMBILOCAL OR NEOLOCAL (270)	0.90 OF 162	94 146 44 16 XSQ= 21.20 PHI= -0.266 XP = 0.0000
207	LEAN TOWARD BEING THOSE WHERE MARITAL RESIDENCE IS AMBILOCAL OR NEOLOCAL, RATHER THAN MATRILOCAL OR UXORILOCAL (64)	0.59 OF 74	207	LEAN TOWARD BEING THOSE WHERE MARITAL RESIDENCE IS MATRILOCAL OR UXORILOCAL, RATHER THAN AMBILOCAL OR NEOLOCAL (64)	0.67 OF 48	30 32 44 16 XSQ= 6.94 PHI= -0.239 XP = 0.0084
213	TEND TO BE THOSE WHERE FIRST COUSIN MARRIAGE IS NOT PERMITTED (198)	0.75 OF 153	213	TEND TO BE THOSE WHERE FIRST COUSIN MARRIAGE IS PERMITTED (172)	0.62 OF 188	39 117 114 71 XSQ= 44.42 PHI= -0.361 XP = 0.

220	TEND MORE TO BE THOSE 0.90 OF 153 WHERE FIRST COUSIN MARRIAGE IN SOME FORM OR OTHER IS NOT PRESCRIBED OR PREFERRED (273)	220	TEND LESS TO BE THOSE 0.57 OF 188 WHERE FIRST COUSIN MARRIAGE IN SOME FORM OR OTHER IS NOT PRESCRIBED OR PREFERRED (273)	15 80 138 108 XSQ= 43.40 PHI= -0.357 XP = 0.
221	LEAN MORE TOWARD BEING THOSE 0.95 OF 153 WHERE MATRILATERAL CROSS-COUSIN MARRIAGE IS NOT PRESCRIBED OR PREFERRED (335)	221	LEAN LESS TOWARD BEING THOSE 0.86 OF 188 WHERE MATRILATERAL CROSS-COUSIN MARRIAGE IS NOT PRESCRIBED OR PREFERRED (335)	7 27 146 161 XSQ= 7.94 PHI= -0.153 XP = 0.0048
224	DRIFT MORE TOWARD BEING THOSE 0.74 OF 39 WHERE COUSIN MARRIAGE IS PREFERENTIALLY OR PERMISSIVELY SYMMETRICAL, RATHER THAN EITHER PATRI- OR MATRILATERAL (106)	224	DRIFT LESS TOWARD BEING THOSE 0.56 OF 117 WHERE COUSIN MARRIAGE IS PREFERENTIALLY OR PERMISSIVELY SYMMETRICAL, RATHER THAN EITHER PATRI- OR MATRILATERAL (106)	10 52 29 65 XSQ= 3.57 PHI= -0.151 XP = 0.0589
241	TILT LESS TOWARD BEING THOSE 0.82 OF 100 WHERE THE FAMILY, IF EXTENDED, IS LARGE OR SMALL, RATHER THAN STEM (187)	241	TILT MORE TOWARD BEING THOSE 0.93 OF 99 WHERE THE FAMILY, IF EXTENDED, IS LARGE OR SMALL, RATHER THAN STEM (187)	82 92 18 7 XSQ= 4.46 PHI= -0.150 XP = 0.0347
242	LEAN LESS TOWARD BEING THOSE 0.72 OF 167 WHERE MARRIAGE IS COMMONLY OR OCCASIONALLY POLYGYNOUS, RATHER THAN MONOGAMOUS (314)	242	LEAN MORE TOWARD BEING THOSE 0.86 OF 192 WHERE MARRIAGE IS COMMONLY OR OCCASIONALLY POLYGYNOUS, RATHER THAN MONOGAMOUS (314)	121 165 46 27 XSQ= 9.21 PHI= -0.160 XP = 0.0024
243	TILT TOWARD BEING THOSE 0.85 OF 20 WHERE POLYGYNY, IF PRESENT, HAS A LOW INCIDENCE (36) W-D,S	243	TILT TOWARD BEING THOSE 0.51 OF 37 WHERE POLYGYNY, IF PRESENT, HAS A HIGH INCIDENCE (24) W-D,S	3 19 17 18 XSQ= 5.79 PHI= -0.319 XP = 0.0162
256	TILT MORE TOWARD BEING THOSE 0.94 OF 18 WHERE GRANDPARENT AND GRANDCHILD ARE FRIENDLY EQUALS (25) DA	256	TILT LESS TOWARD BEING THOSE 0.53 OF 15 WHERE GRANDPARENT AND GRANDCHILD ARE FRIENDLY EQUALS (25) DA	17 8 1 7 XSQ= 5.46 PHI= 0.407 EP = 0.0120
259	TILT TOWARD BEING THOSE 0.65 OF 20 WHERE THE SEVERITY OF MOTHER-IN-LAW AVOIDANCE IS LOW (20) WNS	259	TILT TOWARD BEING THOSE 0.73 OF 26 WHERE THE SEVERITY OF MOTHER-IN-LAW AVOIDANCE IS HIGH (26) WNS	7 19 13 7 XSQ= 5.21 PHI= -0.337 XP = 0.0225
262	LEAN LESS TOWARD BEING THOSE 0.69 OF 169 WHERE WIVES ARE OBTAINED BY MEANS INVOLVING THE PRESENCE OF SOME CONSIDERATION (305)	262	LEAN MORE TOWARD BEING THOSE 0.82 OF 190 WHERE WIVES ARE OBTAINED BY MEANS INVOLVING THE PRESENCE OF SOME CONSIDERATION (305)	117 156 52 34 XSQ= 7.45 PHI= -0.144 XP = 0.0064

No.		No.		
263	LEAN TOWARD BEING THOSE 0.53 OF 169 WHERE WIVES ARE OBTAINED BY RELATIVELY EASY MEANS, NAMELY BY TOKEN BRIDE-PRICE, GIFT EXCHANGE, ABSENCE OF ANY CONSIDERATION, OR RECEIPT OF DOWRY (162)	263	LEAN TOWARD BEING THOSE 0.65 OF 190 WHERE WIVES ARE OBTAINED BY RELATIVELY DIFFICULT MEANS, NAMELY BY BRIDE-PRICE, BRIDE-SERVICE, OR EXCHANGING A FEMALE RELATIVE (233)	80 123 89 67 XSQ= 10.32 PHI= -0.170 XP = 0.0013
279	TILT TOWARD BEING THOSE 0.91 OF 11 WHERE WIFE-LENDING AND WIFE EXCHANGE ARE UNIMPORTANT OR ABSENT (19) LWS	279	TILT TOWARD BEING THOSE 0.53 OF 15 WHERE WIFE-LENDING OR WIFE-EXCHANGE IS PRESENT (10) LWS	1 8 10 7 XSQ= 3.71 PHI= -0.378 EP = 0.0362
316	DRIFT TOWARD BEING THOSE 0.74 OF 19 WHERE EXCLUSIVE MOTHER-SON SLEEPING ARRANGEMENTS LAST LESS THAN ONE YEAR (25) W-K-A	316	DRIFT TOWARD BEING THOSE 0.57 OF 23 WHERE EXCLUSIVE MOTHER-SON SLEEPING ARRANGEMENTS LAST ONE YEAR OR LONGER (19) W-K-A	5 13 14 10 XSQ= 2.74 PHI= -0.255 XP = 0.0978
325	TILT TOWARD BEING THOSE 0.77 OF 26 WHERE THE DEGREE OF DIFFUSION AMONG THE INFANT'S NURTURANT AGENTS IS HIGH (42) B-B-C	325	TILT TOWARD BEING THOSE 0.52 OF 46 WHERE THE DEGREE OF DIFFUSION AMONG THE INFANT'S NURTURANT AGENTS IS LOW (32) B-B-C	20 22 6 24 XSQ= 4.65 PHI= 0.254 XP = 0.0310
327	LEAN TOWARD BEING THOSE 0.76 OF 21 WHERE THE AGE OF THE INFANT AT TIME OF REDUCED CONTACT WITH MOTHER IS HIGHER THAN TWO YEARS (28) B-B-C	327	LEAN TOWARD BEING THOSE 0.66 OF 32 WHERE THE AGE OF THE INFANT AT TIME OF REDUCED CONTACT WITH MOTHER IS TWO YEARS OR LOWER (27) B-B-C	16 11 5 21 XSQ= 7.28 PHI= 0.371 XP = 0.0070
334	DRIFT TOWARD BEING THOSE 0.64 OF 28 WHERE THE INDULGENCE OF THE CHILD IS HIGH (40) B-B-C	334	DRIFT TOWARD BEING THOSE 0.58 OF 48 WHERE THE INDULGENCE OF THE CHILD IS LOW (38) B-B-C	18 20 10 28 XSQ= 2.77 PHI= 0.191 XP = 0.0960
346	DRIFT TOWARD BEING THOSE 0.67 OF 27 WHERE THE CHILD'S INFERRED ANXIETY OVER PERFORMANCE OF SELF-RELIANT BEHAVIOR IS LOW (39) B-B-C	346	DRIFT TOWARD BEING THOSE 0.60 OF 47 WHERE THE CHILD'S INFERRED ANXIETY OVER PERFORMANCE OF SELF-RELIANT BEHAVIOR IS HIGH (37) B-B-C	9 28 18 19 XSQ= 3.73 PHI= -0.225 XP = 0.0534
347	LEAN TOWARD BEING THOSE 0.74 OF 27 WHERE THE CHILD'S INFERRED CONFLICT REGARDING SELF-RELIANT BEHAVIOR IS LOW (39) B-B-C	347	LEAN TOWARD BEING THOSE 0.64 OF 47 WHERE THE CHILD'S INFERRED CONFLICT REGARDING SELF-RELIANT BEHAVIOR IS HIGH (37) B-B-C	7 30 20 17 XSQ= 8.40 PHI= -0.337 XP = 0.0038
370	TEND TO BE THOSE 0.78 OF 105 WHERE THE SEGREGATION OF ADOLESCENT BOYS IS ABSENT (148)	370	TEND TO BE THOSE 0.56 OF 121 WHERE THE SEGREGATION OF ADOLESCENT BOYS IS COMPLETE OR PARTIAL (95)	23 68 82 53 XSQ= 26.08 PHI= -0.340 XP = 0.0000

377	DRIFT MORE TOWARD BEING THOSE WHERE MALE GENITAL MUTILATION IS ABSENT (242)	0.81 OF 135	377	DRIFT LESS TOWARD BEING THOSE WHERE MALE GENITAL MUTILATION IS ABSENT (242)	0.72 OF 164	25 46 110 118 XSQ= 3.21 PHI= -0.104 XP = 0.0733
380	TILT TOWARD BEING THOSE WHERE SEGREGATION OF GIRLS AT MENARCHE IS ABSENT (20) F-B	0.59 OF 22	380	TILT TOWARD BEING THOSE WHERE SEGREGATION OF GIRLS AT MENARCHE IS PRESENT (35) F-B	0.78 OF 32	9 25 13 7 XSQ= 6.23 PHI= -0.340 XP = 0.0126
391	TILT TOWARD BEING THOSE WHERE PREMARITAL SEX RELATIONS ARE STRONGLY PUNISHED AND IN FACT RARE, OR WEAKLY PUNISHED AND IN FACT NOT RARE (89) JTW,EA	0.58 OF 84	391	TILT TOWARD BEING THOSE WHERE PREMARITAL SEX RELATIONS ARE PUNISHED ONLY IF PREGNANCY RESULTS, OR FREELY PERMITTED (90) JTW,EA	0.60 OF 81	49 32 35 49 XSQ= 5.12 PHI= 0.176 XP = 0.0237
403	TILT TOWARD BEING THOSE WHERE EXPLANATIONS OF ILLNESS OF AN ANAL NATURE ARE ABSENT (38) W-C	0.80 OF 25	403	TILT TOWARD BEING THOSE WHERE EXPLANATIONS OF ILLNESS OF AN ANAL NATURE ARE PRESENT (23) W-C	0.55 OF 31	5 17 20 14 XSQ= 5.66 PHI= -0.318 XP = 0.0174
406	DRIFT TOWARD BEING THOSE WHERE EXPLANATIONS OF ILLNESS OF AN AGGRESSION NATURE ARE PRESENT (28) W-C	0.60 OF 25	406	DRIFT TOWARD BEING THOSE WHERE EXPLANATIONS OF ILLNESS OF AN AGGRESSION NATURE ARE ABSENT (33) W-C	0.68 OF 31	15 10 10 21 XSQ= 3.26 PHI= 0.241 XP = 0.0710
419	TILT TOWARD BEING THOSE WHERE MILITARY GLORY IS NEGLIGIBLY EMPHASIZED (31) PES	0.50 OF 36	419	TILT TOWARD BEING THOSE WHERE MILITARY GLORY IS STRONGLY OR MODERATELY EMPHASIZED (55) PES	0.74 OF 46	18 34 18 12 XSQ= 4.00 PHI= -0.221 XP = 0.0455
420	DRIFT TOWARD BEING THOSE WHERE BELLICOSITY IS MODERATE OR NEGLIGIBLE (46) PES	0.67 OF 39	420	DRIFT TOWARD BEING THOSE WHERE BELLICOSITY IS EXTREME (41) PES	0.57 OF 44	13 25 26 19 XSQ= 3.70 PHI= -0.211 XP = 0.0545
450	TILT LESS TOWARD BEING THOSE WHERE THE OBSERVATION OF FOOD TABOOS IS HIGH OR MEDIUM, RATHER THAN LOW (60) JRL	0.56 OF 39	450	TILT MORE TOWARD BEING THOSE WHERE THE OBSERVATION OF FOOD TABOOS IS HIGH OR MEDIUM, RATHER THAN LOW (60) JRL	0.82 OF 44	22 36 17 8 XSQ= 5.19 PHI= -0.250 XP = 0.0227
451	LEAN TOWARD BEING THOSE WHERE TOTEMISM IS UNIMPORTANT OR ABSENT (12) LWS	0.78 OF 9	451	LEAN TOWARD BEING THOSE WHERE TOTEMISM IS PRESENT (15) LWS	0.81 OF 16	2 13 7 3 XSQ= 6.08 PHI= -0.493 EP = 0.0090

```
452  DRIFT TOWARD BEING THCSE           0.71 OF  17      452  DRIFT TOWARD BEING THOSE           0.61 OF  23          5    14
     WHERE TOTEMISM WITH FCOD TABOOS                          WHERE TOTEMISM WITH FOOD TABCOS                        12     9
     IS ABSENT  (24) WNS                                      IS PRESENT  (19) WNS                            XSQ=      2.72
                                                                                                              PHI=    -0.261
                                                                                                              EP =    0.0624

459  LEAN TOWARD BEING THOSE            0.59 OF  79      459  LEAN TOWARD BEING THOSE            0.64 CF  85         47    31
     WHERE GAMES, IF PRESENT,                                 WHERE GAMES, IF PRESENT,                               32    54
     INCLUDE GAMES OF CHANCE  (82) R-A-B,EA                   DO NOT INCLUDE                                  XSQ=      7.80
                                                              GAMES OF CHANCE  (89) R-A-B,EA                  PHI=     0.218
                                                                                                              XP =    0.0052

471  DRIFT TOWARD BEING THCSE           0.88 OF   8      471  DRIFT TOWARD BEING THOSE           0.57 CF  14          1     8
     WHERE SECRET SOCIETIES ARE                               WHERE SECRET SOCIETIES ARE                              7     6
     UMIMPCRTANT CR ABSENT  (14) LWS                          PRESENT  (9) LWS                                XSQ=      2.55
                                                                                                              PHI=    -0.341
                                                                                                              EP =    0.0743

476  DRIFT TOWARD BEING THCSE           0.81 OF  16      476  DRIFT TOWARD BEING THOSE           0.50 CF  30         13    15
     WHERE THE DEGREE OF INSCBRIETY IS                        WHERE THE DEGREE OF INSCBRIETY IS                       3    15
     STRCNG  (31) DH                                          MODERATE OR SLIGHT  (18) DH                     XSQ=      3.07
                                                                                                              PHI=     0.258
                                                                                                              XP =    0.0799
```

232 CULTURES
WHERE THE COUSIN TERMINOLOGY IS
OF ESKIMO TYPE (47)

232 CULTURES
WHERE THE COUSIN TERMINOLOGY IS OTHER THAN
OF ESKIMO TYPE (317)

BACKGROUND ON PAGE 121 — SUBJECT ONLY

47 IN LEFT COLUMN

ABIPON	ALBANIANS	AMERICANS	ATSUGEWI	BASQUES	BOERS	BRAZILIANS	CAMBA	CAMBODIANS	CARINYA
CAYAPA	CHERKESS	CHIBCHA	CHOROTI	CHUKCHEE	COPR ESKIMO	CZECHS	DUSUN	DUTCH	HANUNOO
HEBREWS	HUTSUL	IBAN	IRISH	JAPANESE	JAVANESE	JEMEZ	KAREN	KOREANS	KORYAK
KUMYK	KUNG	LAPPS	MACASSARESE	NICOBARESE	OKINAWANS	ONA	PENOBSCOT	PORTUGUESE	SAGADA
SELUNG	TAGBANUA	TAOS	TIBETANS	TRISTAN	WALLOONS	YAHGAN			

317 IN RIGHT COLUMN

36 EXCLUDED BECAUSE UNASCERTAINED

Left column		Right column		Statistics
3 LEAN MORE TOWARD BEING THOSE LOCATED OUTSIDE OF AFRICA (320)	0.98 OF 47	3 LEAN LESS TOWARD BEING THOSE LOCATED OUTSIDE OF AFRICA (320)	0.79 OF 317	1 68 46 249 XSQ= 8.73 PHI= -0.155 XP = 0.0031
4 TEND LESS TO BE THOSE LOCATED OUTSIDE OF THE CIRCUM-MEDITERRANEAN (355)	0.66 OF 47	4 TEND MORE TO BE THOSE LOCATED OUTSIDE OF THE CIRCUM-MEDITERRANEAN (355)	0.93 OF 317	16 23 31 294 XSQ= 27.97 PHI= 0.277 XP = 0.0000
14 TEND TO BE THOSE WHERE THE LATITUDE IS THIRTY DEGREES OR GREATER (119)	0.55 OF 47	14 TEND TO BE THOSE WHERE THE LATITUDE IS LESS THAN THIRTY DEGREES (281)	0.75 OF 317	26 79 21 238 XSQ= 16.98 PHI= 0.216 XP = 0.0000
15 LEAN TOWARD BEING THOSE WHERE THE LATITUDE IS TWENTY DEGREES OR GREATER (183)	0.66 OF 47	15 LEAN TOWARD BEING THOSE WHERE THE LATITUDE IS LESS THAN TWENTY DEGREES (217)	0.58 OF 317	31 134 16 183 XSQ= 8.34 PHI= 0.151 XP = 0.0039
33 DRIFT LESS TOWARD BEING THOSE WHERE THE NATURAL ENVIRONMENT IS OTHER THAN 'VERY HARSH,' I.E., DESERT, DESERT GRASSES AND SHRUBS, TUNDRA, OR HIGH PLATEAU STEPPE (341) FWM	0.77 OF 47	33 DRIFT MORE TOWARD BEING THOSE WHERE THE NATURAL ENVIRONMENT IS OTHER THAN 'VERY HARSH,' I.E., DESERT, DESERT GRASSES AND SHRUBS, TUNDRA, OR HIGH PLATEAU STEPPE (341) FWM	0.88 OF 317	11 39 36 278 XSQ= 3.37 PHI= 0.096 XP = 0.0663

No.			No.			
53	TEND TO BE THOSE WHERE FOOD PRODUCTION IS BY INTENSIVE AGRICULTURE, RATHER THAN BY SIMPLE AGRICULTURE OR INCIPIENT FOOD PRODUCTION (91)	0.74 OF 27	53	TEND TO BE THOSE WHERE FOOD PRODUCTION IS BY SIMPLE AGRICULTURE OR INCIPIENT FOOD PRODUCTION, RATHER THAN BY INTENSIVE AGRICULTURE (147)	0.67 OF 191	20 63 7 128 XSQ= 15.24 PHI= 0.264 XP = 0.0001
55	TEND TO BE THOSE WHERE FOOD PRODUCTION IS BY INTENSIVE AGRICULTURE, RATHER THAN BY SIMPLE AGRICULTURE (91)	0.80 OF 25	55	TEND TO BE THOSE WHERE FOOD PRODUCTION IS BY SIMPLE AGRICULTURE, RATHER THAN BY INTENSIVE AGRICULTURE (101)	0.59 OF 152	20 63 5 89 XSQ= 11.31 PHI= 0.253 XP = 0.0008
63	TILT MORE TOWARD BEING THOSE WHERE HUSBANDRY, IF PRESENT, IS PRINCIPALLY IN THE FORM OF BOVINE, EQUINE, CAMEL-LIKE, OR DEER-LIKE ANIMALS, RATHER THAN PIGS, SHEEP, OR GOATS (152)	0.87 OF 30	63	TILT LESS TOWARD BEING THOSE WHERE HUSBANDRY, IF PRESENT, IS PRINCIPALLY IN THE FORM OF BOVINE, EQUINE, CAMEL-LIKE, OR DEER-LIKE ANIMALS, RATHER THAN PIGS, SHEEP, OR GOATS (152)	0.64 OF 179	26 115 4 64 XSQ= 4.91 PHI= 0.153 XP = 0.0267
71	LEAN TOWARD BEING THOSE WHERE METAL WORKING IS PRESENT (98)	0.64 OF 28	71	LEAN TOWARD BEING THOSE WHERE METAL WORKING IS ABSENT (153)	0.65 OF 202	18 71 10 131 XSQ= 7.62 PHI= 0.182 XP = 0.0058
73	DRIFT TOWARD BEING THOSE WHERE WEAVING IS PRESENT (118)	0.64 OF 28	73	DRIFT TOWARD BEING THOSE WHERE WEAVING IS ABSENT (130)	0.56 OF 200	18 87 10 113 XSQ= 3.48 PHI= 0.123 XP = 0.0623
81	TILT TOWARD BEING THOSE WHERE A CITY OR TOWN IS PRESENT, OR THE AVERAGE COMMUNITY SIZE IS 200 OR GREATER (89)	0.60 OF 30	81	TILT TOWARD BEING THOSE WHERE NO CITY OR TOWN IS PRESENT, AND THE AVERAGE COMMUNITY SIZE IS SMALLER THAN 200 (135)	0.64 OF 176	18 63 12 113 XSQ= 5.32 PHI= 0.161 XP = 0.0211
84	TILT LESS TOWARD BEING THOSE WHERE THE LEVEL OF POLITICAL INTEGRATION IS THE LITTLE STATE, THE MINIMAL STATE, THE AUTONOMOUS COMMUNITY, OR THE FAMILY (262) GPM	0.71 OF 34	84	TILT MORE TOWARD BEING THOSE WHERE THE LEVEL OF POLITICAL INTEGRATION IS THE LITTLE STATE, THE MINIMAL STATE, THE AUTONOMOUS COMMUNITY, OR THE FAMILY (262) GPM	0.87 OF 241	10 32 24 209 XSQ= 4.81 PHI= 0.132 XP = 0.0283
85	DRIFT LESS TOWARD BEING THOSE WHERE THE LEVEL OF POLITICAL INTEGRATION IS THE MINIMAL STATE, THE AUTONOMOUS COMMUNITY, OR THE FAMILY (234) GPM	0.62 OF 34	85	DRIFT MORE TOWARD BEING THOSE WHERE THE LEVEL OF POLITICAL INTEGRATION IS THE MINIMAL STATE, THE AUTONOMOUS COMMUNITY, OR THE FAMILY (234) GPM	0.77 OF 241	13 55 21 186 XSQ= 3.02 PHI= 0.105 XP = 0.0822
88	TILT TOWARD BEING THOSE WHERE, IF A HEADMANSHIP IS PRESENT, SUCCESSION IS NON-HEREDITARY (106)	0.64 OF 25	88	TILT TOWARD BEING THOSE WHERE, IF A HEADMANSHIP IS PRESENT, SUCCESSION IS HEREDITARY (165)	0.64 OF 223	16 80 9 143 XSQ= 6.36 PHI= 0.160 XP = 0.0117

94	LEAN LESS TOWARD BEING THOSE 0.76 OF 37 WHERE THE HIERARCHY OF NATIONAL JURISDICTION HAS TWO, ONE, OR NO LEVELS (296) GES,EA	94	LEAN MORE TOWARD BEING THOSE 0.92 OF 266 WHERE THE HIERARCHY OF NATIONAL JURISDICTION HAS TWO, ONE, OR NO LEVELS (296) GES,EA	9 22 28 244 XSQ= 7.45 PHI= 0.157 XP = 0.0063
95	LEAN LESS TOWARD BEING THOSE 0.57 OF 37 WHERE THE HIERARCHY OF NATIONAL JURISDICTION HAS ONE OR NO LEVELS (254) GES,EA	95	LEAN MORE TOWARD BEING THOSE 0.79 OF 266 WHERE THE HIERARCHY OF NATIONAL JURISDICTION HAS ONE OR NO LEVELS (254) GES,EA	16 57 21 209 XSQ= 7.30 PHI= 0.155 XP = 0.0069
97	IN ALL CASES ARE THOSE 1.00 OF 37 WHERE THE HIERARCHY OF LOCAL JURISDICTION HAS THREE OR TWO LEVELS (273) GES,EA	97	LEAN LESS TOWARD BEING THOSE 0.79 OF 267 WHERE THE HIERARCHY OF LOCAL JURISDICTION HAS THREE OR TWO LEVELS (273) GES,EA	0 55 37 212 XSQ= 7.97 PHI= -0.162 XP = 0.0048
98	LEAN TOWARD BEING THOSE 0.51 OF 37 WHERE THE HIERARCHY OF LOCAL JURISDICTION HAS TWO LEVELS (93) GES,EA	98	LEAN TOWARD BEING THOSE 0.76 OF 267 WHERE THE HIERARCHY OF LOCAL JURISDICTION HAS FOUR OR THREE LEVELS (238) GES,EA	18 202 19 65 XSQ= 10.54 PHI= -0.186 XP = 0.0012
99	DRIFT TOWARD BEING THOSE 0.60 OF 20 WHERE, WITH NATIONAL HIERARCHY ABSENT, THE HIERARCHY OF LOCAL JURISDICTION HAS TWO LEVELS (63) GES,EA	99	DRIFT TOWARD BEING THOSE 0.63 OF 123 WHERE, WITH NATIONAL HIERARCHY ABSENT, THE HIERARCHY OF LOCAL JURISDICTION HAS FOUR OR THREE LEVELS (93) GES,EA	8 78 12 45 XSQ= 3.02 PHI= -0.145 XP = 0.0823
100	TILT LESS TOWARD BEING THOSE 0.68 OF 37 WHERE HIERARCHIES ARE MORE COMPLEX THAN THE 'SIMPLEST,' I. E., MORE COMPLEX THAN TWO LOCAL LEVELS WITH NO NATIONAL LEVELS (267) GES,EA	100	TILT MORE TOWARD BEING THOSE 0.83 OF 266 WHERE HIERARCHIES ARE MORE COMPLEX THAN THE 'SIMPLEST,' I. E., MORE COMPLEX THAN TWO LOCAL LEVELS WITH NO NATIONAL LEVELS (267) GES,EA	25 221 12 45 XSQ= 4.15 PHI= -0.117 XP = 0.0415
102	DRIFT MORE TOWARD BEING THOSE 0.67 OF 45 WHERE CLASS STRATIFICATION IS PRESENT (203)	102	DRIFT LESS TOWARD BEING THOSE 0.52 OF 304 WHERE CLASS STRATIFICATION IS PRESENT (203)	30 158 15 146 XSQ= 2.84 PHI= 0.090 XP = 0.0920
107	LEAN LESS TOWARD BEING THOSE 0.57 OF 30 WHERE CLASS STRATIFICATION, IF PRESENT, IS BASED ON SOMETHING OTHER THAN OCCUPATIONAL STATUS (160)	107	LEAN MORE TOWARD BEING THOSE 0.82 OF 158 WHERE CLASS STRATIFICATION, IF PRESENT, IS BASED ON SOMETHING OTHER THAN OCCUPATIONAL STATUS (160)	13 29 17 129 XSQ= 7.68 PHI= 0.202 XP = 0.0056
108	DRIFT MORE TOWARD BEING THOSE 0.80 OF 30 WHERE CLASS STRATIFICATION, IF PRESENT, IS BASED ON SOMETHING OTHER THAN A HEREDITARY ARISTOCRACY (129)	108	DRIFT LESS TOWARD BEING THOSE 0.61 OF 158 WHERE CLASS STRATIFICATION, IF PRESENT, IS BASED ON SOMETHING OTHER THAN A HEREDITARY ARISTOCRACY (129)	6 61 24 97 XSQ= 3.04 PHI= -0.127 XP = 0.0813

No.			No.			
176	TEND MORE TO BE THOSE WHERE THE COMMUNITY IS OTHER THAN A CLAN-COMMUNITY OR A COMMUNITY STRUCTURED OR SEGMENTED ON A CLAN BASIS (213)	0.98 OF 45	176	TEND LESS TO BE THOSE WHERE THE COMMUNITY IS OTHER THAN A CLAN-COMMUNITY OR A COMMUNITY STRUCTURED OR SEGMENTED ON A CLAN BASIS (213)	0.51 OF 305	1 150 44 155 XSQ= 33.36 PHI= -0.309 XP = 0.
177	IN ALL CASES ARE THOSE WHERE THE COMMUNITY IS OTHER THAN A SINGLE CLAN-COMMUNITY AND EXOGAMOUS (305)	1.00 OF 45	177	TEND LESS TO BE THOSE WHERE THE COMMUNITY IS OTHER THAN A SINGLE CLAN-COMMUNITY AND EXOGAMOUS (305)	0.78 OF 305	0 68 45 237 XSQ= 11.07 PHI= -0.178 XP = 0.0009
178	LEAN MORE TOWARD BEING THOSE WHERE THE COMMUNITY IS OTHER THAN SEGMENTED ON A CLAN BASIS AND NON-EXOGAMOUS (295)	0.98 OF 45	178	LEAN LESS TOWARD BEING THOSE WHERE THE COMMUNITY IS OTHER THAN SEGMENTED ON A CLAN BASIS AND NON-EXOGAMOUS (295)	0.75 OF 305	1 77 44 228 XSQ= 10.71 PHI= -0.175 XP = 0.0011
180	TILT MORE TOWARD BEING THOSE WHERE THE COMMUNITY IS COMMONLY NON-EXOGAMOUS, RATHER THAN EXOGAMOUS (258)	0.82 OF 45	180	TILT LESS TOWARD BEING THOSE WHERE THE COMMUNITY IS COMMONLY NON-EXOGAMOUS, RATHER THAN EXOGAMOUS (258)	0.66 OF 305	8 105 37 200 XSQ= 4.24 PHI= -0.110 XP = 0.0395
181	DRIFT LESS TOWARD BEING THOSE WHERE THE COMMUNITY IS OTHER THAN A DEME (337)	0.78 OF 45	181	DRIFT MORE TOWARD BEING THOSE WHERE THE COMMUNITY IS OTHER THAN A DEME (337)	0.89 OF 305	10 33 35 272 XSQ= 3.73 PHI= 0.103 XP = 0.0534
182	TEND TO BE THOSE WHERE THE COMMUNITY IS STRUCTURED ON A NON-CLAN BASIS AND AGAMOUS (126)	0.58 OF 45	182	TEND TO BE THOSE OTHER THAN WHERE THE COMMUNITY IS STRUCTURED ON A NON-CLAN BASIS AND AGAMOUS (256)	0.70 OF 305	26 90 19 215 XSQ= 12.90 PHI= 0.192 XP = 0.0003
186	TEND MORE TO BE THOSE WHERE THE KIN GROUP IS OTHER THAN EXCLUSIVELY PATRILINEAL (250)	0.91 OF 47	186	TEND LESS TO BE THOSE WHERE THE KIN GROUP IS OTHER THAN EXCLUSIVELY PATRILINEAL (250)	0.61 OF 317	4 124 43 193 XSQ= 15.50 PHI= -0.206 XP = 0.0001
187	DRIFT MORE TOWARD BEING THOSE WHERE THE KIN GROUP IS OTHER THAN EXCLUSIVELY MATRILINEAL (344)	0.96 OF 47	187	DRIFT LESS TOWARD BEING THOSE WHERE THE KIN GROUP IS OTHER THAN EXCLUSIVELY MATRILINEAL (344)	0.84 OF 316	2 51 45 265 XSQ= 3.73 PHI= -0.101 XP = 0.0534
188	TEND TO BE THOSE WHERE THE KIN GROUP IS EXCLUSIVELY COGNATIC (148)	0.83 OF 47	188	TEND TO BE THOSE WHERE THE KIN GROUP IS OTHER THAN EXCLUSIVELY COGNATIC (252)	0.69 OF 317	39 99 8 218 XSQ= 44.39 PHI= 0.349 XP = 0.

192	TEND TO BE THOSE WHERE THE ONLY KIN GROUP PRESENT IS A KINDRED OR ELSE BILATERAL DESCENT IS INFERRED (111)	0.81 OF 47	192	TEND TO BE THOSE OTHER THAN WHERE THE ONLY KIN GROUP PRESENT IS A KINDRED OR ELSE BILATERAL DESCENT IS INFERRED (289)	0.79 OF 317	38 65 9 252 XSQ= 70.52 PHI= 0.440 XP = 0.
197	LEAN LESS TOWARD BEING THOSE WHERE RULES FOR THE INHERITANCE OF REAL PROPERTY, IF PRESENT, FAVOR EITHER THE MALE HEIR OR LINE, OR THE FEMALE HEIR OR LINE (165)	0.60 OF 25	197	LEAN MORE TOWARD BEING THOSE WHERE RULES FOR THE INHERITANCE OF REAL PROPERTY, IF PRESENT, FAVOR EITHER THE MALE HEIR OR LINE, OR THE FEMALE HEIR OR LINE (165)	0.88 OF 150	15 132 10 18 XSQ= 10.50 PHI= -0.245 XP = 0.0012
201	TEND LESS TO BE THOSE WHERE MARITAL RESIDENCE IS NON-OPTIONAL, RATHER THAN AMBILOCAL OR NEOLOCAL (334)	0.55 OF 47	201	TEND MORE TO BE THOSE WHERE MARITAL RESIDENCE IS NON-OPTIONAL, RATHER THAN AMBILOCAL OR NEOLOCAL (334)	0.88 OF 315	26 276 21 39 XSQ= 28.57 PHI= -0.281 XP = 0.0000
204	TEND TO BE THOSE WHERE MARITAL RESIDENCE IS AMBILOCAL OR NEOLOCAL, RATHER THAN PATRILOCAL, VIRILOCAL, OR AVUNCULOCAL (64)	0.51 OF 41	204	TEND TO BE THOSE WHERE MARITAL RESIDENCE IS PATRILOCAL, VIRILOCAL, OR AVUNCULOCAL, RATHER THAN AMBILOCAL OR NEOLOCAL (270)	0.85 OF 259	20 220 21 39 XSQ= 26.71 PHI= -0.298 XP = 0.0000
207	LEAN TOWARD BEING THOSE WHERE MARITAL RESIDENCE IS AMBILOCAL OR NEOLOCAL, RATHER THAN MATRILOCAL OR UXORILOCAL (64)	0.78 OF 27	207	LEAN TOWARD BEING THOSE WHERE MARITAL RESIDENCE IS MATRILOCAL OR UXORILOCAL, RATHER THAN AMBILOCAL OR NEOLOCAL (64)	0.59 OF 95	6 56 21 39 XSQ= 9.92 PHI= -0.285 XP = 0.0016
213	DRIFT MORE TOWARD BEING THOSE WHERE FIRST COUSIN MARRIAGE IS NOT PERMITTED (198)	0.70 OF 37	213	DRIFT LESS TOWARD BEING THOSE WHERE FIRST COUSIN MARRIAGE IS NOT PERMITTED (198)	0.52 OF 304	11 145 26 159 XSQ= 3.60 PHI= -0.103 XP = 0.0579
220	TEND MORE TO BE THOSE WHERE FIRST COUSIN MARRIAGE IN SOME FORM OR OTHER IS NOT PRESCRIBED OR PREFERRED (273)	0.97 OF 37	220	TEND LESS TO BE THOSE WHERE FIRST COUSIN MARRIAGE IN SOME FORM OR OTHER IS NOT PRESCRIBED OR PREFERRED (273)	0.69 OF 304	1 94 36 210 XSQ= 11.70 PHI= -0.185 XP = 0.0006
224	DRIFT MORE TOWARD BEING THOSE WHERE COUSIN MARRIAGE IS PREFERENTIALLY OR PERMISSIVELY SYMMETRICAL, RATHER THAN EITHER PATRI- OR MATRILATERAL (106)	0.91 OF 11	224	DRIFT LESS TOWARD BEING THOSE WHERE COUSIN MARRIAGE IS PREFERENTIALLY OR PERMISSIVELY SYMMETRICAL, RATHER THAN EITHER PATRI- OR MATRILATERAL (106)	0.58 OF 145	1 61 10 84 XSQ= 3.37 PHI= -0.147 XP = 0.0665
236	DRIFT TOWARD BEING THOSE WHERE THE FAMILY IS OF AN INDEPENDENT TYPE, RATHER THAN AN EXTENDED TYPE (185)	0.57 OF 47	236	DRIFT TOWARD BEING THOSE WHERE THE FAMILY IS OF AN EXTENDED TYPE, RATHER THAN AN INDEPENDENT TYPE (213)	0.57 OF 315	20 179 27 136 XSQ= 2.81 PHI= -0.088 XP = 0.0935

No.		No.		
241	TEND TO BE THOSE 0.55 OF 20 WHERE THE FAMILY, IF EXTENDED, IS STEM, RATHER THAN LARGE OR SMALL (26)	241	TEND TO BE THOSE 0.92 OF 179 WHERE THE FAMILY, IF EXTENDED, IS LARGE OR SMALL, RATHER THAN STEM (187)	9 165 11 14 XSQ= 32.29 PHI= -0.403 XP = 0.
242	TEND TO BE THOSE 0.52 OF 46 WHERE MARRIAGE IS MONOGAMOUS, RATHER THAN COMMONLY OR OCCASIONALLY POLYGYNOUS (81)	242	TEND TO BE THOSE 0.84 OF 313 WHERE MARRIAGE IS COMMONLY OR OCCASIONALLY POLYGYNOUS, RATHER THAN MONOGAMOUS (314)	22 264 24 49 XSQ= 30.80 PHI= -0.293 XP = 0.
255	IN ALL CASES ARE THOSE 1.00 OF 2 WHERE GRANDPARENTAL AUTHORITY OVER PARENTS IS PRESENT (7) CA	255	TILT TOWARD BEING THOSE 0.84 OF 31 WHERE GRANDPARENTAL AUTHORITY OVER PARENTS IS ABSENT (26) DA	2 5 0 26 XSQ= 3.69 PHI= 0.334 EP = 0.0398
262	DRIFT LESS TOWARD BEING THOSE 0.65 OF 46 WHERE WIVES ARE OBTAINED BY MEANS INVOLVING THE PRESENCE OF SOME CONSIDERATION (305)	262	DRIFT MORE TOWARD BEING THOSE 0.78 OF 313 WHERE WIVES ARE OBTAINED BY MEANS INVOLVING THE PRESENCE OF SOME CONSIDERATION (305)	30 243 16 70 XSQ= 2.75 PHI= -0.087 XP = 0.0974
263	TILT TOWARD BEING THOSE 0.59 OF 46 WHERE WIVES ARE OBTAINED BY RELATIVELY EASY MEANS, NAMELY BY TOKEN BRIDE-PRICE, GIFT EXCHANGE, ABSENCE OF ANY CONSIDERATION, OR RECEIPT OF DOWRY (162)	263	TILT TOWARD BEING THOSE 0.59 OF 313 WHERE WIVES ARE OBTAINED BY RELATIVELY DIFFICULT MEANS, NAMELY BY BRIDE-PRICE, BRIDE-SERVICE, OR EXCHANGING A FEMALE RELATIVE (233)	19 184 27 129 XSQ= 4.30 PHI= -0.109 XP = 0.0381
300	DRIFT MORE TOWARD BEING THOSE 0.92 OF 12 WHERE THE POST-PARTUM SEX TABOO LASTS SIX MONTHS OR LESS (73)	300	DRIFT LESS TOWARD BEING THOSE 0.58 OF 101 WHERE THE POST-PARTUM SEX TABOO LASTS SIX MONTHS OR LESS (73)	1 42 11 59 XSQ= 3.72 PHI= -0.181 XP = 0.0538
353	IN ALL CASES ARE THOSE 1.00 OF 4 WHERE THE CHILD-S INFERRED ANXIETY OVER NON-PERFORMANCE OF OBEDIENT BEHAVIOR IS LOW (32) B-B-C	353	DRIFT TOWARD BEING THOSE 0.60 OF 68 WHERE THE CHILD'S INFERRED ANXIETY OVER NON-PERFORMANCE OF OBEDIENT BEHAVIOR IS HIGH (42) B-B-C	0 41 4 27 XSQ= 3.41 PHI= -0.218 XP = 0.0647
370	TEND MORE TO BE THOSE 0.90 OF 31 WHERE THE SEGREGATION OF ADOLESCENT BOYS IS ABSENT (148)	370	TEND LESS TO BE THOSE 0.55 OF 195 WHERE THE SEGREGATION OF ADOLESCENT BOYS IS ABSENT (148)	3 88 28 107 XSQ= 12.54 PHI= -0.236 XP = 0.0004
377	DRIFT MORE TOWARD BEING THOSE 0.89 OF 38 WHERE MALE GENITAL MUTILATION IS ABSENT (242)	377	DRIFT LESS TOWARD BEING THOSE 0.74 OF 261 WHERE MALE GENITAL MUTILATION IS ABSENT (242)	4 67 34 194 XSQ= 3.41 PHI= -0.107 XP = 0.0649

380	IN ALL CASES ARE THOSE WHERE SEGREGATION OF GIRLS AT MENARCHE IS ABSENT (20) F-B	1.00 OF	3	380	DRIFT TOWARD BEING THOSE WHERE SEGREGATION OF GIRLS AT MENARCHE IS PRESENT (35) F-B	0.67 OF	51	 XSQ= PHI= XP =	0 34 3 17 2.92 -0.233 0.0875
382	DRIFT TOWARD BEING THOSE WHERE FEMALE INITIATION RITES ARE ABSENT (27) JKB	0.83 OF	6	382	DRIFT TOWARD BEING THOSE WHERE FEMALE INITIATION RITES ARE PRESENT (38) JKB	0.61 OF	54	 XSQ= PHI= XP =	1 33 5 21 2.72 -0.213 0.0989
391	TILT TOWARD BEING THOSE WHERE PREMARITAL SEX RELATIONS ARE STRONGLY PUNISHED AND IN FACT RARE, OR WEAKLY PUNISHED AND IN FACT NOT RARE (89) JTW,EA	0.69 OF	26	391	TILT TOWARD BEING THOSE WHERE PREMARITAL SEX RELATIONS ARE PUNISHED ONLY IF PREGNANCY RESULTS, OR FREELY PERMITTED (90) JTW,EA	0.55 OF	139	 XSQ= PHI= XP =	18 63 8 76 4.10 0.158 0.0429
402	IN ALL CASES ARE THOSE WHERE EXPLANATIONS OF ILLNESS OF AN ORAL NATURE ARE ABSENT (30) W-C	1.00 OF	5	402	DRIFT TOWARD BEING THOSE WHERE EXPLANATIONS OF ILLNESS OF AN ORAL NATURE ARE PRESENT (31) W-C	0.55 OF	51	 XSQ= PHI= XP =	0 28 5 23 3.51 -0.250 0.0609
427	TEND TO BE THOSE WHERE A HIGH GOD, IF PRESENT, IS ACTIVE, RATHER THAN INACTIVE (87) GES,EA	0.95 OF	20	427	TEND TO BE THOSE WHERE A HIGH GOD, IF PRESENT, IS INACTIVE, RATHER THAN ACTIVE (69) GES,EA	0.51 OF	121	 XSQ= PHI= XP =	19 59 1 62 13.03 0.304 0.0003
450	TILT TOWARD BEING THOSE WHERE THE OBSERVATION OF FOOD TABOOS IS LOW, RATHER THAN HIGH OR MEDIUM (26) JRL	0.67 OF	9	450	TILT TOWARD BEING THOSE WHERE THE OBSERVATION OF FOOD TABOOS IS HIGH OR MEDIUM, RATHER THAN LOW (60) JRL	0.74 OF	74	 XSQ= PHI= XP =	3 55 6 19 4.61 -0.236 0.0319
451	IN ALL CASES ARE THOSE WHERE TOTEMISM IS UNIMPORTANT OR ABSENT (12) LWS	1.00 OF	4	451	TILT TOWARD BEING THOSE WHERE TOTEMISM IS PRESENT (15) LWS	0.71 OF	21	 XSQ= PHI= EP =	0 15 4 6 4.48 -0.423 0.0166

233 CULTURES
WHERE THE COUSIN TERMINOLOGY IS
OF HAWAIIAN TYPE (123)

233 CULTURES
WHERE THE COUSIN TERMINOLOGY IS OTHER THAN
OF HAWAIIAN TYPE (241)

BACKGROUND ON PAGE 121 SUBJECT ONLY

123 IN LEFT COLUMN

ALORESE	ANDAMANESE	ARYANS	ATAYAL	AWEIKOMA	AYMARA	AZTEC	BABWA	BALINESE	BELU
BENGALI	BHUIYA	BOTOCUDO	BURMESE	BURUSHO	CADUVEO	CAGABA	CARAJA	CHEYENNE	CHINANTEC
CHIR-APACHE	CHOCO	CHORTI	COCHITI	COMANCHE	CUNA	DARD	DELAWARE	ELLICE	GILBERTESE
GISU	GROS VENTRE	GURE	HASINAI	HAWAIIANS	HUICHOL	HUKUNDIKA	IFUGAO	INCA	INGALIK
INGASSANA	JUKUN	KATAB	KIOW-APACHE	KISSI	KOL	KUBA	KUTENAI	KWAKIUTL	LEPCHA
LIFU	LOZI	MAGUZAWA	MALAYS	MAM	MAMBILA	MAMVU	MANGAIANS	MANIHIKI	MAORI
MARGI	MARQUESANS	MATACO	MAYA	MAZATECO	MENDE	MERINA	MIAO	MINANGKABAU	MOSSI
NUPE	ONTONG-JAVA	ORAON	PAIWAN	PALAUANS	PAPAGO	PARAUJANO	PATHAN	POPOLUCA	PUKAPUKA
PURARI	RARCIANS	ROTUMANS	SAMOANS	SANPOIL	SARAMACCA	SARSI	SEMANG	SERBS	SERI
SIMBOESE	SIUAI	SUBANUN	TALAMANCA	TALLENSI	TANIMBARESE	TAPIRAPE	TARAHUMARA	TENETEHARA	TENINO
TERENA	TESO	THAI	TIKOPIA	TIV	TORAJA	TOTONAC	TUBATULABAL	TUNEBO	TWANA
ULAWANS	UTE	VIETNAMESE	WARRAU	WASHO	WICHITA	WOLEAIANS	WOLOF	YARURO	YOKUTS
YORUBA	YUKI	YUROK							

241 IN RIGHT COLUMN

36 EXCLUDED BECAUSE UNASCERTAINED

4	TEND MORE TO BE THOSE LOCATED OUTSIDE OF THE CIRCUM-MEDITERRANEAN (355)	0.98 OF 123	4	TEND LESS TO BE THOSE LOCATED OUTSIDE OF THE CIRCUM-MEDITERRANEAN (355)	0.85 OF 241	3 36 120 205 XSQ= 12.02 PHI= -0.182 XP = 0.0005
6	DRIFT LESS TOWARD BEING THOSE LOCATED OUTSIDE OF THE INSULAR PACIFIC (330)	0.76 OF 123	6	DRIFT MORE TOWARD BEING THOSE LOCATED OUTSIDE OF THE INSULAR PACIFIC (330)	0.84 OF 241	30 39 93 202 XSQ= 3.06 PHI= 0.092 XP = 0.0804
8	TILT LESS TOWARD BEING THOSE LOCATED OUTSIDE OF NORTH AMERICA (330)	0.74 OF 123	8	TILT MORE TOWARD BEING THOSE LOCATED OUTSIDE OF NORTH AMERICA (330)	0.84 OF 241	32 38 91 203 XSQ= 4.87 PHI= 0.116 XP = 0.0274

12 TILT MORE TOWARD BEING THOSE 0.97 OF 123 WHERE THE LATITUDE IS LESS THAN FIFTY DEGREES (367)	12 TILT LESS TOWARD BEING THOSE 0.90 OF 241 WHERE THE LATITUDE IS LESS THAN FIFTY DEGREES (367)	4 25 119 216 XSQ= 4.70 PHI= -0.114 XP = 0.0301
13 TILT MORE TOWARD BEING THOSE 0.89 OF 123 WHERE THE LATITUDE IS LESS THAN FORTY DEGREES (329)	13 TILT LESS TOWARD BEING THOSE 0.79 OF 241 WHERE THE LATITUDE IS LESS THAN FORTY DEGREES (329)	13 51 110 190 XSQ= 5.60 PHI= -0.124 XP = 0.0180
42 TILT LESS TOWARD BEING THOSE 0.51 OF 123 WHERE THE NATURAL ENVIRONMENT IS OTHER THAN TROPICAL OR SUB-TROPICAL RAIN FOREST, OR MONSOON FOREST (244) FWM	42 TILT MORE TOWARD BEING THOSE 0.66 OF 241 WHERE THE NATURAL ENVIRONMENT IS OTHER THAN TROPICAL OR SUB-TROPICAL RAIN FOREST, OR MONSOON FOREST (244) FWM	60 83 63 158 XSQ= 6.43 PHI= 0.133 XP = 0.0112
56 TILT MORE TOWARD BEING THOSE 0.81 OF 48 WHERE FOOD PRODUCTION IS BY SIMPLE AGRICULTURE, RATHER THAN BY INCIPIENT FOOD PRODUCTION (101)	56 TILT LESS TOWARD BEING THOSE 0.63 OF 87 WHERE FOOD PRODUCTION IS BY SIMPLE AGRICULTURE, RATHER THAN BY INCIPIENT FOOD PRODUCTION (101)	39 55 9 32 XSQ= 3.94 PHI= 0.171 XP = 0.0471
63 LEAN LESS TOWARD BEING THOSE 0.54 OF 70 WHERE HUSBANDRY, IF PRESENT, IS PRINCIPALLY IN THE FORM OF BOVINE, EQUINE, CAMEL-LIKE, OR DEER-LIKE ANIMALS, RATHER THAN PIGS, SHEEP, OR GOATS (152)	63 LEAN MORE TOWARD BEING THOSE 0.74 OF 139 WHERE HUSBANDRY, IF PRESENT, IS PRINCIPALLY IN THE FORM OF BOVINE, EQUINE, CAMEL-LIKE, OR DEER-LIKE ANIMALS, RATHER THAN PIGS, SHEEP, OR GOATS (152)	38 103 32 36 XSQ= 7.45 PHI= -0.189 XP = 0.0063
71 TILT MORE TOWARD BEING THOSE 0.74 OF 73 WHERE METAL WORKING IS ABSENT (153)	71 TILT LESS TOWARD BEING THOSE 0.55 OF 157 WHERE METAL WORKING IS ABSENT (153)	19 70 54 87 XSQ= 6.47 PHI= -0.168 XP = 0.0109
83 DRIFT LESS TOWARD BEING THOSE 0.65 OF 48 WHERE, WITH NO CITY AND NO TOWN PRESENT, THE AVERAGE COMMUNITY SIZE IS SMALLER THAN 200, RATHER THAN BETWEEN 200 AND 999 (135)	83 DRIFT MORE TOWARD BEING THOSE 0.80 OF 117 WHERE, WITH NO CITY AND NO TOWN PRESENT, THE AVERAGE COMMUNITY SIZE IS SMALLER THAN 200, RATHER THAN BETWEEN 200 AND 999 (135)	17 23 31 94 XSQ= 3.78 PHI= 0.151 XP = 0.0517
88 DRIFT LESS TOWARD BEING THOSE 0.53 OF 87 WHERE, IF A HEADMANSHIP IS PRESENT, SUCCESSION IS HEREDITARY (165)	88 DRIFT MORE TOWARD BEING THOSE 0.66 OF 161 WHERE, IF A HEADMANSHIP IS PRESENT, SUCCESSION IS HEREDITARY (165)	41 55 46 106 XSQ= 3.47 PHI= 0.118 XP = 0.0624
97 DRIFT LESS TOWARD BEING THOSE 0.75 OF 102 WHERE THE HIERARCHY OF LOCAL JURISDICTION HAS THREE OR TWO LEVELS (273) GES,EA	97 DRIFT MORE TOWARD BEING THOSE 0.85 OF 202 WHERE THE HIERARCHY OF LOCAL JURISDICTION HAS THREE OR TWO LEVELS (273) GES,EA	25 30 77 172 XSQ= 3.64 PHI= 0.109 XP = 0.0564

163	TILT TOWARD BEING THOSE 0.75 OF 8 WHERE THE EMPHASIS ON INDIVIDUAL VOLITION AS THE CAUSE OF CRIME IS HIGH (7) MJ	163	TILT TOWARD BEING THOSE 0.88 OF 8 WHERE THE EMPHASIS ON INDIVIDUAL VOLITION AS THE CAUSE OF CRIME IS LOW (10) MJ	6 1 2 7 XSQ= 4.06 PHI= 0.504 EP = 0.0406
164	TILT TOWARD BEING THOSE 0.83 OF 6 WHERE THE EMPHASIS ON INDIVIDUAL VOLITION AS THE CAUSE OR SOURCE OF ILLNESS IS LOW (9) MJ	164	TILT TOWARD BEING THOSE 0.73 OF 11 WHERE THE EMPHASIS ON INDIVIDUAL VOLITION AS THE CAUSE OR SOURCE OF ILLNESS IS HIGH (9) MJ	1 8 5 3 XSQ= 2.91 PHI= -0.413 EP = 0.0498
176	DRIFT MORE TOWARD BEING THOSE 0.64 OF 118 WHERE THE COMMUNITY IS OTHER THAN A CLAN-COMMUNITY OR A COMMUNITY STRUCTURED OR SEGMENTED ON A CLAN BASIS (213)	176	DRIFT LESS TOWARD BEING THOSE 0.53 OF 232 WHERE THE COMMUNITY IS OTHER THAN A CLAN-COMMUNITY OR A COMMUNITY STRUCTURED OR SEGMENTED ON A CLAN BASIS (213)	43 108 75 124 XSQ= 2.86 PHI= -0.090 XP = 0.0908
177	TEND MORE TO BE THOSE 0.92 OF 118 WHERE THE COMMUNITY IS OTHER THAN A SINGLE CLAN-COMMUNITY AND EXOGAMOUS (305)	177	TEND LESS TO BE THOSE 0.75 OF 232 WHERE THE COMMUNITY IS OTHER THAN A SINGLE CLAN-COMMUNITY AND EXOGAMOUS (305)	9 59 109 173 XSQ= 14.72 PHI= -0.205 XP = 0.0001
180	TILT MORE TOWARD BEING THOSE 0.77 OF 118 WHERE THE COMMUNITY IS COMMONLY NON-EXOGAMOUS, RATHER THAN EXOGAMOUS (258)	180	TILT LESS TOWARD BEING THOSE 0.63 OF 232 WHERE THE COMMUNITY IS COMMONLY NON-EXOGAMOUS, RATHER THAN EXOGAMOUS (258)	27 86 91 146 XSQ= 6.57 PHI= -0.137 XP = 0.0104
181	LEAN LESS TOWARD BEING THOSE 0.81 OF 118 WHERE THE COMMUNITY IS OTHER THAN A DEME (337)	181	LEAN MORE TOWARD BEING THOSE 0.91 OF 232 WHERE THE COMMUNITY IS OTHER THAN A DEME (337)	23 20 95 212 XSQ= 7.60 PHI= 0.147 XP = 0.0058
183	DRIFT MORE TOWARD BEING THOSE 0.94 OF 50 WHERE THE LARGEST NON-COGNATIC KIN GROUP IS SMALLER THAN A MOEITY, I. E., A PHRATRY OR SIB OR LINEAGE (218)	183	DRIFT LESS TOWARD BEING THOSE 0.83 OF 176 WHERE THE LARGEST NON-COGNATIC KIN GROUP IS SMALLER THAN A MOEITY, I. E., A PHRATRY OR SIB OR LINEAGE (218)	3 30 47 146 XSQ= 2.98 PHI= -0.115 XP = 0.0845
184	LEAN MORE TOWARD BEING THOSE 0.84 OF 50 WHERE THE LARGEST NON-COGNATIC KIN GROUP IS SMALLER THAN A PHRATRY, I. E. A SIB OR LINEAGE (175)	184	LEAN LESS TOWARD BEING THOSE 0.63 OF 176 WHERE THE LARGEST NON-COGNATIC KIN GROUP IS SMALLER THAN A PHRATRY, I. E. A SIB OR LINEAGE (175)	8 65 42 111 XSQ= 6.87 PHI= -0.174 XP = 0.0087
185	DRIFT LESS TOWARD BEING THOSE 0.68 OF 50 WHERE THE LARGEST NON-COGNATIC KIN GROUP IS THE MOEITY OR PHRATRY OR SIB (194)	185	DRIFT MORE TOWARD BEING THOSE 0.82 OF 176 WHERE THE LARGEST NON-COGNATIC KIN GROUP IS THE MOEITY OR PHRATRY OR SIB (194)	34 144 16 32 XSQ= 3.66 PHI= -0.127 XP = 0.0558

186	TEND MORE TO BE THOSE WHERE THE KIN GROUP IS OTHER THAN EXCLUSIVELY PATRILINEAL (250)	0.78 OF 123	186	TEND LESS TO BE THOSE WHERE THE KIN GROUP IS OTHER THAN EXCLUSIVELY PATRILINEAL (250)	0.58 OF 241	27 101 96 140 XSQ= 13.37 PHI= -0.192 XP = 0.0003
187	TILT MORE TOWARD BEING THOSE WHERE THE KIN GROUP IS OTHER THAN EXCLUSIVELY MATRILINEAL (344)	0.92 OF 123	187	TILT LESS TOWARD BEING THOSE WHERE THE KIN GROUP IS OTHER THAN EXCLUSIVELY MATRILINEAL (344)	0.82 OF 240	10 43 113 197 XSQ= 5.49 PHI= -0.123 XP = 0.0192
188	TEND TO BE THOSE WHERE THE KIN GROUP IS EXCLUSIVELY COGNATIC (148)	0.59 OF 123	188	TEND TO BE THOSE WHERE THE KIN GROUP IS OTHER THAN EXCLUSIVELY COGNATIC (252)	0.73 OF 241	73 65 50 176 XSQ= 34.91 PHI= 0.310 XP = 0.
192	TEND LESS TO BE THOSE OTHER THAN WHERE THE ONLY KIN GROUP PRESENT IS A KINDRED OR ELSE BILATERAL DESCENT IS INFERRED (289)	0.57 OF 123	192	TEND MORE TO BE THOSE OTHER THAN WHERE THE ONLY KIN GROUP PRESENT IS A KINDRED OR ELSE BILATERAL DESCENT IS INFERRED (289)	0.79 OF 241	53 50 70 191 XSQ= 18.95 PHI= 0.228 XP = 0.0000
197	DRIFT LESS TOWARD BEING THOSE WHERE RULES FOR THE INHERITANCE OF REAL PROPERTY, IF PRESENT, FAVOR EITHER THE MALE HEIR OR LINE, OR THE FEMALE HEIR OR LINE (165)	0.75 OF 57	197	DRIFT MORE TOWARD BEING THOSE WHERE RULES FOR THE INHERITANCE OF REAL PROPERTY, IF PRESENT, FAVOR EITHER THE MALE HEIR OR LINE, OR THE FEMALE HEIR OR LINE (165)	0.88 OF 118	43 104 14 14 XSQ= 3.71 PHI= -0.146 XP = 0.0540
213	TEND TO BE THOSE WHERE FIRST COUSIN MARRIAGE IS NOT PERMITTED (198)	0.76 OF 116	213	TEND TO BE THOSE WHERE FIRST COUSIN MARRIAGE IS PERMITTED (172)	0.57 OF 225	28 128 88 97 XSQ= 31.77 PHI= -0.305 XP = 0.
220	TEND MORE TO BE THOSE WHERE FIRST COUSIN MARRIAGE IN SOME FORM OR OTHER IS NOT PRESCRIBED OR PREFERRED (273)	0.88 OF 116	220	TEND LESS TO BE THOSE WHERE FIRST COUSIN MARRIAGE IN SOME FORM OR OTHER IS NOT PRESCRIBED OR PREFERRED (273)	0.64 OF 225	14 81 102 144 XSQ= 20.64 PHI= -0.246 XP = 0.0000
221	DRIFT MORE TOWARD BEING THOSE WHERE MATRILATERAL CROSS-COUSIN MARRIAGE IS NOT PRESCRIBED OR PREFERRED (335)	0.95 OF 116	221	DRIFT LESS TOWARD BEING THOSE WHERE MATRILATERAL CROSS-COUSIN MARRIAGE IS NOT PRESCRIBED OR PREFERRED (335)	0.88 OF 225	6 28 110 197 XSQ= 3.74 PHI= -0.105 XP = 0.0533
236	LEAN TOWARD BEING THOSE WHERE THE FAMILY IS OF AN EXTENDED TYPE, RATHER THAN AN INDEPENDENT TYPE (213)	0.66 OF 122	236	LEAN TOWARD BEING THOSE WHERE THE FAMILY IS OF AN INDEPENDENT TYPE, RATHER THAN AN EXTENDED TYPE (185)	0.50 OF 240	80 119 42 121 XSQ= 7.72 PHI= 0.146 XP = 0.0055

240	DRIFT LESS TOWARD BEING THOSE 0.54 OF 80 WHERE THE FAMILY, IF EXTENDED, IS SMALL OR STEM, RATHER THAN LARGE (135)	240	DRIFT MORE TOWARD BEING THOSE 0.68 OF 119 WHERE THE FAMILY, IF EXTENDED, IS SMALL OR STEM, RATHER THAN LARGE (135)	37 38 43 81 XSQ= 3.59 PHI= 0.134 XP = 0.0582
243	TILT MORE TOWARD BEING THOSE 0.83 OF 18 WHERE POLYGYNY, IF PRESENT, HAS A LOW INCIDENCE (36) W-D,S	243	TILT LESS TOWARD BEING THOSE 0.51 OF 39 WHERE POLYGYNY, IF PRESENT, HAS A LOW INCIDENCE (36) W-D,S	3 19 15 20 XSQ= 4.07 PHI= -0.267 XP = 0.0436
255	DRIFT MORE TOWARD BEING THOSE 0.94 OF 16 WHERE GRANDPARENTAL AUTHORITY OVER PARENTS IS ABSENT (26) DA	255	DRIFT LESS TOWARD BEING THOSE 0.65 OF 17 WHERE GRANDPARENTAL AUTHORITY OVER PARENTS IS ABSENT (26) DA	1 6 15 11 XSQ= 2.60 PHI= -0.281 EP = 0.0854
256	IN ALL CASES ARE THOSE 1.00 OF 16 WHERE GRANDPARENT AND GRANDCHILD ARE FRIENDLY EQUALS (25) DA	256	LEAN LESS TOWARD BEING THOSE 0.53 OF 17 WHERE GRANDPARENT AND GRANDCHILD ARE FRIENDLY EQUALS (25) DA	16 9 0 8 XSQ= 7.54 PHI= 0.478 EP = 0.0027
259	DRIFT TOWARD BEING THOSE 0.63 OF 19 WHERE THE SEVERITY OF MOTHER-IN-LAW AVOIDANCE IS LOW (20) WNS	259	DRIFT TOWARD BEING THOSE 0.70 OF 27 WHERE THE SEVERITY OF MOTHER-IN-LAW AVOIDANCE IS HIGH (26) WNS	7 19 12 8 XSQ= 3.83 PHI= -0.288 XP = 0.0504
263	DRIFT TOWARD BEING THOSE 0.50 OF 123 WHERE WIVES ARE OBTAINED BY RELATIVELY EASY MEANS, NAMELY BY TOKEN BRIDE-PRICE, GIFT EXCHANGE, ABSENCE OF ANY CONSIDERATION, OR RECEIPT OF DOWRY (162)	263	DRIFT TOWARD BEING THOSE 0.60 OF 236 WHERE WIVES ARE OBTAINED BY RELATIVELY DIFFICULT MEANS, NAMELY BY BRIDE-PRICE, BRIDE-SERVICE, OR EXCHANGING A FEMALE RELATIVE (233)	61 142 62 94 XSQ= 3.26 PHI= -0.095 XP = 0.0709
279	IN ALL CASES ARE THOSE 1.00 OF 6 WHERE WIFE-LENDING AND WIFE EXCHANGE ARE UNIMPORTANT OR ABSENT (19) LWS	279	DRIFT LESS TOWARD BEING THOSE 0.55 OF 20 WHERE WIFE-LENDING AND WIFE EXCHANGE ARE UNIMPORTANT OR ABSENT (19) LWS	0 9 6 11 XSQ= 2.38 PHI= -0.303 EP = 0.0634
282	DRIFT TOWARD BEING THOSE 0.77 OF 13 WHERE THE STRENGTH OF DESIRE FOR CHILDREN IS LOW OR ABSENT (20) BCA	282	DRIFT TOWARD BEING THOSE 0.57 OF 21 WHERE THE STRENGTH OF DESIRE FOR CHILDREN IS HIGH (16) BCA	3 12 10 9 XSQ= 2.52 PHI= -0.272 EP = 0.0790
300	TILT TOWARD BEING THOSE 0.56 OF 32 WHERE THE POST-PARTUM SEX TABOO LASTS LONGER THAN SIX MONTHS (51)	300	TILT TOWARD BEING THOSE 0.69 OF 81 WHERE THE POST-PARTUM SEX TABOO LASTS SIX MONTHS OR LESS (73)	18 25 14 56 XSQ= 5.24 PHI= 0.215 XP = 0.0221

325	TILT TOWARD BEING THOSE 0.78 OF 23 WHERE THE DEGREE OF DIFFUSION AMONG THE INFANT'S NURTURANT AGENTS IS HIGH (42) B-B-C	325	TILT TOWARD BEING THOSE 0.51 OF 49 WHERE THE DEGREE OF DIFFUSION AMONG THE INFANT'S NURTURANT AGENTS IS LOW (32) B-B-C	18 24 5 25 XSQ= 4.38 PHI= 0.247 XP = 0.0363
327	TILT TOWARD BEING THOSE 0.74 OF 19 WHERE THE AGE OF THE INFANT AT TIME OF REDUCED CONTACT WITH MOTHER IS HIGHER THAN TWO YEARS (28) B-B-C	327	TILT TOWARD BEING THOSE 0.62 OF 34 WHERE THE AGE OF THE INFANT AT TIME OF REDUCED CONTACT WITH MOTHER IS TWO YEARS OR LOWER (27) B-B-C	14 13 5 21 XSQ= 4.79 PHI= 0.301 XP = 0.0286
339	DRIFT TOWARD BEING THOSE 0.74 OF 23 WHERE THE CHILD'S INFERRED CONFLICT REGARDING RESPONSIBLE BEHAVIOR IS LOW (42) B-B-C	339	DRIFT TOWARD BEING THOSE 0.52 OF 48 WHERE THE CHILD'S INFERRED CONFLICT REGARDING RESPONSIBLE BEHAVIOR IS HIGH (31) B-B-C	6 25 17 23 XSQ= 3.28 PHI= -0.215 XP = 0.0701
347	TILT TOWARD BEING THOSE 0.74 OF 23 WHERE THE CHILD'S INFERRED CONFLICT REGARDING SELF-RELIANT BEHAVIOR IS LOW (39) B-B-C	347	TILT TOWARD BEING THOSE 0.61 OF 51 WHERE THE CHILD'S INFERRED CONFLICT REGARDING SELF-RELIANT BEHAVIOR IS HIGH (37) B-B-C	6 31 17 20 XSQ= 6.31 PHI= -0.292 XP = 0.0120
370	LEAN MORE TOWARD BEING THOSE 0.73 OF 74 WHERE THE SEGREGATION OF ADOLESCENT BOYS IS ABSENT (148)	370	LEAN LESS TOWARD BEING THOSE 0.53 OF 152 WHERE THE SEGREGATION OF ADOLESCENT BOYS IS ABSENT (148)	20 71 54 81 XSQ= 7.22 PHI= -0.179 XP = 0.0072
459	TILT TOWARD BEING THOSE 0.62 OF 55 WHERE GAMES, IF PRESENT, INCLUDE GAMES OF CHANCE (82) R-A-B,EA	459	TILT TOWARD BEING THOSE 0.60 OF 109 WHERE GAMES, IF PRESENT, DO NOT INCLUDE GAMES OF CHANCE (89) R-A-B,EA	34 44 21 65 XSQ= 5.91 PHI= 0.190 XP = 0.0150
460	DRIFT MORE TOWARD BEING THOSE 0.71 OF 55 WHERE GAMES, IF PRESENT, ARE NOT LIMITED TO GAMES OF SKILL ONLY (104) R-A-B,EA	460	DRIFT LESS TOWARD BEING THOSE 0.56 OF 109 WHERE GAMES, IF PRESENT, ARE NOT LIMITED TO GAMES OF SKILL ONLY (104) R-A-B,EA	16 48 39 61 XSQ= 2.83 PHI= -0.131 XP = 0.0924
468	DRIFT TOWARD BEING THOSE 0.53 OF 15 WHERE CONTACT WITH OTHER CULTURES IS FREQUENT, RATHER THAN REGULAR OR IRREGULAR (17) JMH	468	DRIFT TOWARD BEING THOSE 0.78 OF 36 WHERE CONTACT WITH OTHER CULTURES IS REGULAR OR IRREGULAR, RATHER THAN FREQUENT (37) JMH	8 8 7 28 XSQ= 3.42 PHI= 0.259 XP = 0.0642
470	DRIFT TOWARD BEING THOSE 0.60 OF 15 WHERE INNOVATIONS ARE GENERALLY ACCEPTED (21) JMH	470	DRIFT TOWARD BEING THOSE 0.69 OF 36 WHERE INNOVATIONS ARE ACCEPTED ONLY SELECTIVELY (33) JMH	9 11 6 25 XSQ= 2.71 PHI= 0.231 XP = 0.0994

234 CULTURES
WHERE THE COUSIN TERMINOLOGY IS
OF CROW, OMAHA, OR IROQUOIS TYPE,
RATHER THAN
ESKIMO OR HAWAIIAN TYPE (152)

234 CULTURES
WHERE THE COUSIN TERMINOLOGY IS
OF ESKIMO OR HAWAIIAN TYPE,
RATHER THAN
CROW, OMAHA, OR IROQUOIS TYPE (170)

BACKGROUND ON PAGE 121

BOTH SUBJECT AND PREDICATE

152 IN LEFT COLUMN

AJIE	AKHA	AMBA	APINAYE	ARANDA	ARAPESH	ARAUCANIANS	BACAIRI	BAMBARA	BANDA
BARI	BEMBA	BIRIFOR	BLACK CARIB	BORORO	BUDUMA	BUNLAP	CALLINAGO	CAMAYURA	CARIB
CHAGGA	CHENCHU	CHEROKEE	COORG	CREE	CREEK	CROW	DAGUR	DIEGUENO	DIERI
DOBUANS	DOGON	DOROBO	ENGA	EYAK	FANG	FOX	FUTAJALONKE	GANDA	GARO
GILYAK	GOAJIRO	GOND	GUAHIBO	GUATO	HAIDA	HANO	HAVASUPAI	HEHE	HERERO
HO	HURON	ILA	IRAQW	KACHIN	KALMYK	KAPAUKU	KARIERA	KASKA	KAZAK
KERAKI	KERALA	KHALKA	KHASI	KIKUYU	KONSO	KURTATCHI	LAKALAI	LAKHER	LAMBA
LAMET	LANGO	LAU	LESU	LHOTA NAGA	MANCHU	MANDAN	MARICOPA	MARSHALLESE	MASAI
MATAKAM	MBUGWE	MBUNDU	MIAMI	MISKITO	MIWOK	MNONG GAR	MONGO	MOTA	MOTILON
MURINBATA	NABESNA	NAMA	NAMBICUARA	NANDI	NASKAPI	NAVAHO	NDEMBU	NGONI	NOMLAKI
NUNIVAK	NYAKYUSA	NYANEKA	NYORO	OJIBWA	OMAHA	PAWNEE	PENDE	PONAPEANS	ROTINESE
RUNDI	SEMINOLE	SENIANG	SHERENTE	SINHALESE	SIRIONO	SONGHAI	SOTHO	SWAZI	TAMIL
TANALA	TAREUMIUT	TECA	TERA	TETON	THONGA	TIMBIRA	TIMUCUA	TODA	TOKELAU
TOLOWA	TROBRIAND	TRUKESE	TRUMAI	TSHIMSHIAN	TUCANO	TUCUNA	TUPINAMBA	TZELTAL	VEDDA
VENDA	WANTOAT	WAPISHANA	WAROPEN	WIKMUNKAN	WINNEBAGO	WOGEO	YABARANA	YAKO	YAO
YAPESE	ZUNI								

170 IN RIGHT COLUMN

ABIPON	ALBANIANS	ALORESE	AMERICANS	ANDAMANESE	ARYANS	ATAYAL	ATSUGEWI	AWEIKOMA	AYMARA
AZTEC	BABWA	BALINESE	BASQUES	BELU	BENGALI	BHUIYA	BOERS	BOTOCUDO	BRAZILIANS
BURMESE	BURUSHO	CADUVEC	CAGABA	CAMBA	CAMBODIANS	CARAJA	CARINYA	CAYAPA	CHERKESS
CHEYENNE	CHIBCHA	CHINANTEC	CHIR-APACHE	CHOCO	CHOROTI	CHORTI	CHUKCHEE	COCHITI	COMANCHE
COPR ESKIMO	CUNA	CZECHS	DARD	DELAWARE	DUSUN	DUTCH	ELLICE	GILBERTESE	GISU
GROS VENTRE	GURE	HANUNOO	HASINAI	HAWAIIANS	HEBREWS	HUICHOL	HUKUNDIKA	HUTSUL	IBAN
IFUGAO	INCA	INGALIK	INGASSANA	IRISH	JAPANESE	JAVANESE	JEMEZ	JUKUN	KAREN
KATAB	KIOW-APACHE	KISSI	KOL	KOREANS	KORYAK	KUBA	KUMYK	KUNG	KUTENAI
KWAKIUTL	LAPPS	LEPCHA	LIFU	LOZI	MACASSARESE	MAGUZAWA	MALAYS	MAM	MAMBILA
MAMVU	MANGAIANS	MANIHIKI	MAORI	MARGI	MARQUESANS	MATACO	MAYA	MAZATECO	MENDE
MERINA	MIAO	MINANGKABAU	MOSSI	NICOBARESE	NUPE	OKINAWANS	ONA	ONTONG-JAVA	ORAON
PAIWAN	PALAUANS	PAPAGO	PARAUJANO	PATHAN	PENOBSCOT	POPOLUCA	PORTUGUESE	PUKAPUKA	PURARI
RAROIANS	ROTUMANS	SAGADA	SAMOANS	SANPOIL	SARAMACCA	SARSI	SELUNG	SEMANG	SERBS
SERI	SIMBOESE	SIUAI	SUBANUN	TAGBANUA	TALAMANCA	TALLENSI	TANIMBARESE	TAOS	TAPIRAPE
TARAHUMARA	TENETEHARA	TENINO	TERENA	TESO	THAI	TIBETANS	TIKOPIA	TIV	TORAJA
TOTONAC	TRISTAN	TUBATULABAL	TUNEBO	TWANA	ULAWANS	UTE	VIETNAMESE	WALLOONS	WARRAU
WASHO	WICHITA	WOLEAIANS	WOLOF	YAHGAN	YARURO	YOKUTS	YORUBA	YUKI	YUROK

42 EXCLUDED BECAUSE IRRELEVANT

36 EXCLUDED BECAUSE UNASCERTAINEC

3	LEAN LESS TOWARC BEING THCSE LOCATED CUTSIDE CF AFRICA (320)	0.75 OF 152	3	LEAN MORE TOWARD BEING THOSE LOCATED OUTSIDE OF AFRICA (320)	0.88 CF 170	38 20 114 150 XSQ= 8.64 PHI= 0.164 XP = 0.0033
4	DRIFT MORE TCWARD BEING THCSE LOCATED CUTSIDE CF THE CIRCUM-MEDITERRANEAN (355)	0.95 OF 152	4	DRIFT LESS TOWARD BEING THCSE LOCATED OUTSIDE OF THE CIRCUM-MEDITERRANEAN (355)	0.89 CF 170	7 19 145 151 XSQ= 3.83 PHI= -0.109 XP = 0.0505
53	TILT MORE TOWARC BEING THCSE WHERE FCCD PRCDUCTICN IS BY SIMPLE AGRICULTURE OR INCIPIENT FCCD PRCDUCTICN, RATHER THAN BY INTENSIVE AGRICULTURE (147)	0.74 OF 92	53	TILT LESS TOWARD BEING THOSE WHERE FOOD PRODUCTICN IS BY SIMPLE AGRICULTURE OR INCIPIENT FOOD PRODUCTICN, RATHER THAN BY INTENSIVE AGRICULTURE (147)	0.56 CF 99	24 44 68 55 XSQ= 6.23 PHI= -0.181 XP = 0.0126
54	TILT LESS TOWARC BEING THCSE WHERE FCCD PRCDUCTICN IS BY INTENSIVE CR SIMPLE AGRICULTURE, RATHER THAN BY INCIPIENT FCCD PRCDUCTICN (192)	0.74 OF 92	54	TILT MORE TOWARD BEING THOSE WHERE FOOD PRODUCTICN IS BY INTENSIVE OR SIMPLE AGRICULTURE, RATHER THAN BY INCIPIENT FOOD PRODUCTICN (192)	0.89 CF 99	68 88 24 11 XSQ= 6.18 PHI= -0.180 XP = 0.0129
55	DRIFT TOWARD BEING THCSE WHERE FCCD PRCDUCTICN IS BY SIMPLE AGRICULTURE, RATHER THAN BY INTENSIVE AGRICULTURE (101)	0.65 OF 68	55	DRIFT TOWARD BEING THOSE WHERE FOOD PRODUCTICN IS BY INTENSIVE AGRICULTURE, RATHER THAN BY SIMPLE AGRICULTURE (91)	0.50 CF 88	24 44 44 44 XSQ= 2.80 PHI= -0.134 XP = 0.0941
56	DRIFT LESS TCWARC BEING THCSE WHERE FCCD PRCDUCTICN IS BY SIMPLE AGRICULTURE, RATHER THAN BY INCIPIENT FCCD PRCDUCTICN (101)	0.65 OF 68	56	DRIFT MORE TOWARD BEING THCSE WHERE FOOD PRODUCTICN IS BY SIMPLE AGRICULTURE, RATHER THAN BY INCIPIENT FOOD PRODUCTICN (101)	0.80 CF 55	44 44 24 11 XSQ= 2.78 PHI= -0.150 XP = 0.0953
73	DRIFT TOWARD BEING THCSE WHERE WEAVING IS ABSENT (130)	0.64 OF 101	73	DRIFT TOWARD BEING THOSE WHERE WEAVING IS PRESENT (118)	0.50 CF 104	36 52 65 52 XSQ= 3.74 PHI= -0.135 XP = 0.0530
81	TEND TC BE THCSE WHERE NC CITY OR TCWN IS PRESENT, ANC THE AVERAGE COMMUNITY SIZE IS SMALLER THAN 200 (135)	0.74 OF 92	81	TEND TO BE THOSE WHERE A CITY OR TOWN IS PRESENT, OR THE AVERAGE COMMUNITY SIZE IS 20C OR GREATER (89)	0.52 CF 89	24 46 68 43 XSQ= 11.44 PHI= -0.251 XP = 0.0007

```
 83  DRIFT MORE TOWARD BEING THOSE  0.81 OF  84    83  DRIFT LESS TOWARD BEING THOSE  0.67 OF  64       16   21
     WHERE, WITH NO CITY AND NO TOWN PRESENT,          WHERE, WITH NO CITY AND NO TOWN PRESENT,          68   43
     THE AVERAGE COMMUNITY SIZE IS                     THE AVERAGE COMMUNITY SIZE IS               XSQ=     2.97
     SMALLER THAN 200, RATHER THAN                     SMALLER THAN 200, RATHER THAN               PHI=   -0.142
     BETWEEN 200 AND 999  (135)                        BETWEEN 200 AND 999  (135)                  XP =   0.0847

 84  TILT MORE TOWARD BEING THOSE   0.92 OF 120    84  TILT LESS TOWARD BEING THOSE   0.79 OF 126       10   26
     WHERE THE LEVEL OF POLITICAL INTEGRATION          WHERE THE LEVEL OF POLITICAL INTEGRATION         110  100
     IS THE LITTLE STATE, THE MINIMAL STATE,           IS THE LITTLE STATE, THE MINIMAL STATE,     XSQ=     6.49
     THE AUTONOMOUS COMMUNITY, OR                      THE AUTONOMOUS COMMUNITY, OR                PHI=   -0.162
     THE FAMILY  (262) GPM                             THE FAMILY  (262) GPM                       XP =   0.0108

 85  TILT MORE TOWARD BEING THOSE   0.83 OF 120    85  TILT LESS TOWARD BEING THOSE   0.71 OF 126       20   36
     WHERE THE LEVEL OF POLITICAL INTEGRATION          WHERE THE LEVEL OF POLITICAL INTEGRATION         100   90
     IS THE MINIMAL STATE,                             IS THE MINIMAL STATE,                       XSQ=     4.30
     THE AUTONOMOUS COMMUNITY, OR                      THE AUTONOMOUS COMMUNITY, OR                PHI=   -0.132
     THE FAMILY  (234) GPM                             THE FAMILY  (234) GPM                       XP =   0.0381

 88  TEND TO BE THOSE               0.74 OF 111    88  TEND TO BE THOSE               0.51 OF 112       29   57
     WHERE, IF A HEADMANSHIP IS PRESENT,               WHERE, IF A HEADMANSHIP IS PRESENT,               82   55
     SUCCESSION IS HEREDITARY  (165)                   SUCCESSION IS NON-HEREDITARY  (106)         XSQ=    13.41
                                                                                                   PHI=   -0.245
                                                                                                   XP =   0.0003

 90  TILT LESS TOWARD BEING THOSE   0.67 OF  82    90  TILT MORE TOWARD BEING THOSE   0.85 OF  55       55   47
     WHERE, IF A HEREDITARY HEADMANSHIP                WHERE, IF A HEREDITARY HEADMANSHIP                27    8
     IS PRESENT, SUCCESSION IS                         IS PRESENT, SUCCESSION IS                   XSQ=     4.92
     PATRILINEAL, RATHER THAN                          PATRILINEAL, RATHER THAN                    PHI=   -0.190
     MATRILINEAL  (127)                                MATRILINEAL  (127)                          XP =   0.0265

102  DRIFT TOWARD BEING THOSE       0.54 OF 147   102  DRIFT TOWARD BEING THOSE       0.57 OF 160       68   91
     WHERE CLASS STRATIFICATION IS                     WHERE CLASS STRATIFICATION IS                     79   69
     ABSENT  (180)                                     PRESENT  (203)                              XSQ=     3.05
                                                                                                   PHI=   -0.100
                                                                                                   XP =   0.0809

107  LEAN MORE TOWARD BEING THOSE   0.91 OF  68   107  LEAN LESS TOWARD BEING THOSE   0.69 OF  91        6   28
     WHERE CLASS STRATIFICATION, IF PRESENT,           WHERE CLASS STRATIFICATION, IF PRESENT,           62   63
     IS BASED ON SOMETHING OTHER THAN                  IS BASED ON SOMETHING OTHER THAN            XSQ=     9.88
     OCCUPATIONAL STATUS  (160)                        OCCUPATIONAL STATUS  (160)                  PHI=   -0.249
                                                                                                   XP =   0.0017

118  DRIFT TOWARD BEING THOSE       0.70 OF  20   118  DRIFT TOWARD BEING THOSE       0.62 OF  21        6   13
     WHERE THE PERCENTAGE OF OCCUPATIONS               WHERE THE PERCENTAGE OF OCCUPATIONS               14    8
     THAT ARE SPECIALIZED                              THAT ARE SPECIALIZED                        XSQ=     3.01
     IS LOW  (25) WME                                  IS HIGH OR MEDIUM  (24) WME                 PHI=   -0.271
                                                                                                   XP =   0.0828

128  TILT TOWARD BEING THOSE        0.64 OF  33   128  TILT TOWARD BEING THOSE        0.69 OF  32       12   22
     WHERE, IF SUBSISTENCE IS PRIMARILY BY             WHERE, IF SUBSISTENCE IS PRIMARILY BY             21   10
     AGRICULTURE, THE WORK IS                          AGRICULTURE, THE WORK IS                    XSQ=     5.59
     MAINLY DONE BY FEMALES  (37)                      MAINLY DONE BY MALES  (40)                  PHI=   -0.293
                                                                                                   XP =   0.0180
```

163	IN ALL CASES ARE THOSE 1.00 OF 4 WHERE THE EMPHASIS ON INDIVIDUAL VOLITION AS THE CAUSE OF CRIME IS LOW (10) MJ	163	DRIFT TOWARD BEING THOSE 0.64 OF 11 WHERE THE EMPHASIS ON INDIVIDUAL VOLITION AS THE CAUSE OF CRIME IS HIGH (7) MJ	0 7 4 4 XSQ= 2.56 PHI= -0.413 EP = 0.0769
175	DRIFT LESS TOWARD BEING THOSE 0.64 OF 146 WHERE THE COMMUNITY IS 'KIN-HETEROGENEOUS,' I. E. OTHER THAN A CLAN COMMUNITY OR A DEME (260)	175	DRIFT MORE TOWARD BEING THOSE 0.74 OF 163 WHERE THE COMMUNITY IS 'KIN-HETEROGENEOUS,' I. E. OTHER THAN A CLAN COMMUNITY OR A DEME (260)	52 42 94 121 XSQ= 3.08 PHI= 0.100 XP = 0.0793
176	TEND TO BE THOSE 0.62 OF 146 WHERE THE COMMUNITY IS A CLAN-COMMUNITY OR A COMMUNITY STRUCTURED OR SEGMENTED ON A CLAN BASIS (169)	176	TEND TO BE THOSE 0.73 OF 163 WHERE THE COMMUNITY IS OTHER THAN A CLAN-COMMUNITY OR A COMMUNITY STRUCTURED OR SEGMENTED ON A CLAN BASIS (213)	90 44 56 119 XSQ= 36.25 PHI= 0.343 XP = 0.
177	TEND LESS TO BE THOSE 0.68 OF 146 WHERE THE COMMUNITY IS OTHER THAN A SINGLE CLAN-COMMUNITY AND EXOGAMOUS (305)	177	TEND MORE TO BE THOSE 0.94 OF 163 WHERE THE COMMUNITY IS OTHER THAN A SINGLE CLAN-COMMUNITY AND EXOGAMOUS (305)	47 9 99 154 XSQ= 35.14 PHI= 0.337 XP = 0.
180	TEND LESS TO BE THOSE 0.58 OF 146 WHERE THE COMMUNITY IS COMMONLY NON-EXOGAMOUS, RATHER THAN EXOGAMOUS (258)	180	TEND MORE TO BE THOSE 0.79 OF 163 WHERE THE COMMUNITY IS COMMONLY NON-EXOGAMOUS, RATHER THAN EXOGAMOUS (258)	62 35 84 128 XSQ= 14.80 PHI= 0.219 XP = 0.0001
181	TEND MORE TO BE THOSE 0.97 OF 146 WHERE THE COMMUNITY IS OTHER THAN A DEME (337)	181	TEND LESS TO BE THOSE 0.80 OF 163 WHERE THE COMMUNITY IS OTHER THAN A DEME (337)	5 33 141 130 XSQ= 18.67 PHI= -0.246 XP = 0.0000
182	TILT MORE TOWARD BEING THOSE 0.73 OF 146 OTHER THAN WHERE THE COMMUNITY IS STRUCTURED ON A NON-CLAN BASIS AND AGAMOUS (256)	182	TILT LESS TOWARD BEING THOSE 0.62 OF 163 OTHER THAN WHERE THE COMMUNITY IS STRUCTURED ON A NON-CLAN BASIS AND AGAMOUS (256)	39 62 107 101 XSQ= 3.99 PHI= -0.114 XP = 0.0458
183	TILT LESS TOWARD BEING THOSE 0.79 OF 131 WHERE THE LARGEST NON-COGNATIC KIN GROUP IS SMALLER THAN A MOEITY, I. E., A PHRATRY OR SIB OR LINEAGE (218)	183	TILT MORE TOWARD BEING THOSE 0.95 OF 58 WHERE THE LARGEST NON-COGNATIC KIN GROUP IS SMALLER THAN A MOEITY, I. E., A PHRATRY OR SIB OR LINEAGE (218)	27 3 104 55 XSQ= 6.07 PHI= 0.179 XP = 0.0138
184	LEAN LESS TOWARD BEING THOSE 0.63 OF 131 WHERE THE LARGEST NON-COGNATIC KIN GROUP IS SMALLER THAN A PHRATRY, I. E. A SIB OR LINEAGE (175)	184	LEAN MORE TOWARD BEING THOSE 0.84 OF 58 WHERE THE LARGEST NON-COGNATIC KIN GROUP IS SMALLER THAN A PHRATRY, I. E. A SIB OR LINEAGE (175)	48 9 83 49 XSQ= 7.54 PHI= 0.200 XP = 0.0060

No.	Left		No.	Right		Statistics
185	TILT MORE TOWARD BEING THOSE WHERE THE LARGEST NON-COGNATIC KIN GROUP IS THE MOEITY OR PHRATRY OR SIB (194)	0.83 OF 131	185	TILT LESS TOWARD BEING THOSE WHERE THE LARGEST NON-COGNATIC KIN GROUP IS THE MOEITY OR PHRATRY OR SIB (194)	0.69 OF 58	109 40 22 18 XSQ= 4.07 PHI= 0.147 XP = 0.0437
186	TEND LESS TO BE THOSE WHERE THE KIN GROUP IS OTHER THAN EXCLUSIVELY PATRILINEAL (250)	0.56 OF 152	186	TEND MORE TO BE THOSE WHERE THE KIN GROUP IS OTHER THAN EXCLUSIVELY PATRILINEAL (250)	0.82 OF 170	67 31 85 139 XSQ= 24.11 PHI= 0.274 XP = 0.0000
187	TEND LESS TO BE THOSE WHERE THE KIN GROUP IS OTHER THAN EXCLUSIVELY MATRILINEAL (344)	0.74 OF 152	187	TEND MORE TO BE THOSE WHERE THE KIN GROUP IS OTHER THAN EXCLUSIVELY MATRILINEAL (344)	0.93 OF 170	40 12 112 158 XSQ= 20.58 PHI= 0.253 XP = 0.0000
188	TEND TO BE THOSE WHERE THE KIN GROUP IS OTHER THAN EXCLUSIVELY COGNATIC (252)	0.86 OF 152	188	TEND TO BE THOSE WHERE THE KIN GROUP IS EXCLUSIVELY COGNATIC (148)	0.66 OF 170	21 112 131 58 XSQ= 87.60 PHI= -0.522 XP = 0.
192	TEND TO BE THOSE OTHER THAN WHERE THE ONLY KIN GROUP PRESENT IS A KINDRED OR ELSE BILATERAL DESCENT IS INFERRED (289)	0.95 OF 152	192	TEND TO BE THOSE WHERE THE ONLY KIN GROUP PRESENT IS A KINDRED OR ELSE BILATERAL DESCENT IS INFERRED (111)	0.54 OF 170	7 91 145 79 XSQ= 88.43 PHI= -0.524 XP = 0.
197	TEND MORE TO BE THOSE WHERE RULES FOR THE INHERITANCE OF REAL PROPERTY, IF PRESENT, FAVOR EITHER THE MALE HEIR OR LINE, OR THE FEMALE HEIR OR LINE (165)	0.97 OF 66	197	TEND LESS TO BE THOSE WHERE RULES FOR THE INHERITANCE OF REAL PROPERTY, IF PRESENT, FAVOR EITHER THE MALE HEIR OR LINE, OR THE FEMALE HEIR OR LINE (165)	0.71 OF 82	64 58 2 24 XSQ= 15.62 PHI= 0.325 XP = 0.0001
198	DRIFT LESS TOWARD BEING THOSE WHERE RULES FOR THE INHERITANCE OF REAL PROPERTY, IF PRESENT, FAVOR THE MALE HEIR OR LINE, RATHER THAN THE FEMALE (144)	0.80 OF 64	198	DRIFT MORE TOWARD BEING THOSE WHERE RULES FOR THE INHERITANCE OF REAL PROPERTY, IF PRESENT, FAVOR THE MALE HEIR OR LINE, RATHER THAN THE FEMALE (144)	0.93 OF 58	51 54 13 4 XSQ= 3.52 PHI= -0.170 XP = 0.0608
201	TEND MORE TO BE THOSE WHERE MARITAL RESIDENCE IS NON-OPTIONAL, RATHER THAN AMBILOCAL OR NEOLOCAL (334)	0.91 OF 152	201	TEND LESS TO BE THOSE WHERE MARITAL RESIDENCE IS NON-OPTIONAL, RATHER THAN AMBILOCAL OR NEOLOCAL (334)	0.74 OF 168	138 124 14 44 XSQ= 14.38 PHI= 0.212 XP = 0.0001
204	TEND MORE TO BE THOSE WHERE MARITAL RESIDENCE IS PATRILOCAL, VIRILOCAL, OR AVUNCULOCAL, RATHER THAN AMBILOCAL OR NEOLOCAL (270)	0.88 OF 121	204	TEND LESS TO BE THOSE WHERE MARITAL RESIDENCE IS PATRILOCAL, VIRILOCAL, OR AVUNCULOCAL, RATHER THAN AMBILOCAL OR NEOLOCAL (270)	0.68 OF 138	107 94 14 44 XSQ= 14.16 PHI= 0.234 XP = 0.0002

207	LEAN TOWARD BEING THOSE 0.69 OF 45 WHERE MARITAL RESIDENCE IS MATRILOCAL OR UXORILOCAL, RATHER THAN AMBILOCAL OR NEOLOCAL (64)	207	LEAN TOWARD BEING THOSE 0.59 OF 74 WHERE MARITAL RESIDENCE IS AMBILOCAL OR NEOLOCAL, RATHER THAN MATRILOCAL OR UXORILOCAL (64)	31 30 14 44 XSQ= 7.90 PHI= 0.258 XP = 0.0049
213	TEND TO BE THOSE 0.60 OF 149 WHERE FIRST COUSIN MARRIAGE IS PERMITTED (172)	213	TEND TO BE THOSE 0.75 OF 153 WHERE FIRST COUSIN MARRIAGE IS NOT PERMITTED (198)	89 39 60 114 XSQ= 34.85 PHI= 0.340 XP = 0.
220	TEND LESS TO BE THOSE 0.58 OF 149 WHERE FIRST COUSIN MARRIAGE IN SOME FORM OR OTHER IS NOT PRESCRIBED OR PREFERRED (273)	220	TEND MORE TO BE THOSE 0.90 OF 153 WHERE FIRST COUSIN MARRIAGE IN SOME FORM OR OTHER IS NOT PRESCRIBED OR PREFERRED (273)	63 15 86 138 XSQ= 39.89 PHI= 0.363 XP = 0.
221	LEAN LESS TOWARD BEING THOSE 0.86 OF 149 WHERE MATRILATERAL CROSS-COUSIN MARRIAGE IS NOT PRESCRIBED OR PREFERRED (335)	221	LEAN MORE TOWARD BEING THOSE 0.95 OF 153 WHERE MATRILATERAL CROSS-COUSIN MARRIAGE IS NOT PRESCRIBED OR PREFERRED (335)	21 7 128 146 XSQ= 7.04 PHI= 0.153 XP = 0.0080
236	DRIFT TOWARD BEING THOSE 0.51 OF 151 WHERE THE FAMILY IS OF AN INDEPENDENT TYPE, RATHER THAN AN EXTENDED TYPE (185)	236	DRIFT TOWARD BEING THOSE 0.59 OF 169 WHERE THE FAMILY IS OF AN EXTENDED TYPE, RATHER THAN AN INDEPENDENT TYPE (213)	74 100 77 69 XSQ= 2.92 PHI= -0.096 XP = 0.0873
241	DRIFT MORE TOWARD BEING THOSE 0.92 OF 74 WHERE THE FAMILY, IF EXTENDED, IS LARGE OR SMALL, RATHER THAN STEM (187)	241	DRIFT LESS TOWARD BEING THOSE 0.82 OF 100 WHERE THE FAMILY, IF EXTENDED, IS LARGE OR SMALL, RATHER THAN STEM (187)	68 82 6 18 XSQ= 2.72 PHI= 0.125 XP = 0.0993
242	LEAN MORE TOWARD BEING THOSE 0.85 OF 150 WHERE MARRIAGE IS COMMONLY OR OCCASIONALLY POLYGYNOUS, RATHER THAN MONOGAMOUS (314)	242	LEAN LESS TOWARD BEING THOSE 0.72 OF 167 WHERE MARRIAGE IS COMMONLY OR OCCASIONALLY POLYGYNOUS, RATHER THAN MONOGAMOUS (314)	128 121 22 46 XSQ= 7.03 PHI= 0.149 XP = 0.0080
243	TILT TOWARD BEING THOSE 0.52 OF 27 WHERE POLYGYNY, IF PRESENT, HAS A HIGH INCIDENCE (24) W-D,S	243	TILT TOWARD BEING THOSE 0.85 OF 20 WHERE POLYGYNY, IF PRESENT, HAS A LOW INCIDENCE (36) W-D,S	14 3 13 17 XSQ= 5.26 PHI= 0.334 XP = 0.0219
256	TILT LESS TOWARD BEING THOSE 0.55 OF 11 WHERE GRANDPARENT AND GRANDCHILD ARE FRIENDLY EQUALS (25) CA	256	TILT MORE TOWARD BEING THOSE 0.94 OF 18 WHERE GRANDPARENT AND GRANDCHILD ARE FRIENDLY EQUALS (25) CA	6 17 5 1 XSQ= 4.42 PHI= -0.390 EP = 0.0185

259	TILT TOWARD BEING THOSE 0.76 OF 21 WHERE THE SEVERITY OF MOTHER-IN-LAW AVOIDANCE IS HIGH (26) WNS	259	TILT TOWARD BEING THOSE 0.65 OF 20 WHERE THE SEVERITY OF MOTHER-IN-LAW AVOIDANCE IS LOW (20) WNS	16 7 5 13 XSQ= 5.48 PHI= 0.366 XP = 0.0192
262	DRIFT MORE TOWARD BEING THOSE 0.79 OF 148 WHERE WIVES ARE OBTAINED BY MEANS INVOLVING THE PRESENCE OF SOME CONSIDERATION (305)	262	DRIFT LESS TOWARD BEING THOSE 0.69 OF 169 WHERE WIVES ARE OBTAINED BY MEANS INVOLVING THE PRESENCE OF SOME CONSIDERATION (305)	117 117 31 52 XSQ= 3.45 PHI= 0.104 XP = 0.0633
263	TILT TOWARD BEING THOSE 0.61 OF 148 WHERE WIVES ARE OBTAINED BY RELATIVELY DIFFICULT MEANS, NAMELY BY BRIDE-PRICE, BRIDE-SERVICE, OR EXCHANGING A FEMALE RELATIVE (233)	263	TILT TOWARD BEING THOSE 0.53 OF 169 WHERE WIVES ARE OBTAINED BY RELATIVELY EASY MEANS, NAMELY BY TOKEN BRIDE-PRICE, GIFT EXCHANGE, ABSENCE OF ANY CONSIDERATION, OR RECEIPT OF DOWRY (162)	90 80 58 89 XSQ= 5.23 PHI= 0.128 XP = 0.0222
279	DRIFT TOWARD BEING THOSE 0.55 OF 11 WHERE WIFE-LENDING OR WIFE-EXCHANGE IS PRESENT (10) LWS	279	DRIFT TOWARD BEING THOSE 0.91 OF 11 WHERE WIFE-LENDING AND WIFE EXCHANGE ARE UNIMPORTANT OR ABSENT (19) LWS	6 1 5 10 XSQ= 3.35 PHI= 0.390 EP = 0.0635
325	DRIFT LESS TOWARD BEING THOSE 0.51 OF 37 WHERE THE DEGREE OF DIFFUSION AMONG THE INFANT'S NURTURANT AGENTS IS HIGH (42) B-B-C	325	DRIFT MORE TOWARD BEING THOSE 0.77 OF 26 WHERE THE DEGREE OF DIFFUSION AMONG THE INFANT'S NURTURANT AGENTS IS HIGH (42) B-B-C	19 20 18 6 XSQ= 3.22 PHI= -0.226 XP = 0.0728
327	TILT TOWARD BEING THOSE 0.63 OF 27 WHERE THE AGE OF THE INFANT AT TIME OF REDUCED CONTACT WITH MOTHER IS TWO YEARS OR LOWER (27) B-B-C	327	TILT TOWARD BEING THOSE 0.76 OF 21 WHERE THE AGE OF THE INFANT AT TIME OF REDUCED CONTACT WITH MOTHER IS HIGHER THAN TWO YEARS (28) B-B-C	10 16 17 5 XSQ= 5.80 PHI= -0.348 XP = 0.0160
346	TILT TOWARD BEING THOSE 0.63 OF 38 WHERE THE CHILD'S INFERRED ANXIETY OVER PERFORMANCE OF SELF-RELIANT BEHAVIOR IS HIGH (37) B-B-C	346	TILT TOWARD BEING THOSE 0.67 OF 27 WHERE THE CHILD'S INFERRED ANXIETY OVER PERFORMANCE OF SELF-RELIANT BEHAVIOR IS LOW (39) B-B-C	24 9 14 18 XSQ= 4.49 PHI= 0.263 XP = 0.0341
347	LEAN TOWARD BEING THOSE 0.68 OF 38 WHERE THE CHILD'S INFERRED CONFLICT REGARDING SELF-RELIANT BEHAVIOR IS HIGH (37) B-B-C	347	LEAN TOWARD BEING THOSE 0.74 OF 27 WHERE THE CHILD'S INFERRED CONFLICT REGARDING SELF-RELIANT BEHAVIOR IS LOW (39) B-B-C	26 7 12 20 XSQ= 9.77 PHI= 0.388 XP = 0.0018
370	TEND TO BE THOSE 0.59 OF 94 WHERE THE SEGREGATION OF ADOLESCENT BOYS IS COMPLETE OR PARTIAL (95)	370	TEND TO BE THOSE 0.78 OF 105 WHERE THE SEGREGATION OF ADOLESCENT BOYS IS ABSENT (148)	55 23 39 82 XSQ= 26.37 PHI= 0.364 XP = 0.0000

380	TILT TOWARD BEING THOSE 0.79 OF 28 WHERE SEGREGATION OF GIRLS AT MENARCHE IS PRESENT (35) F-B	380	TILT TOWARD BEING THOSE 0.59 OF 22 WHERE SEGREGATION OF GIRLS AT MENARCHE IS ABSENT (20) F-B	22 9 6 13 XSQ= 5.90 PHI= 0.344 XP = 0.0151
391	LEAN TOWARD BEING THOSE 0.69 OF 62 WHERE PREMARITAL SEX RELATIONS ARE PUNISHED ONLY IF PREGNANCY RESULTS, OR FREELY PERMITTED (90) JTW,EA	391	LEAN TOWARD BEING THOSE 0.58 OF 84 WHERE PREMARITAL SEX RELATIONS ARE STRONGLY PUNISHED AND IN FACT RARE, OR WEAKLY PUNISHED AND IN FACT NOT RARE (89) JTW,EA	19 49 43 35 XSQ= 9.91 PHI= -0.260 XP = 0.0016
403	TILT TOWARD BEING THOSE 0.52 OF 23 WHERE EXPLANATIONS OF ILLNESS OF AN ANAL NATURE ARE PRESENT (23) W-C	403	TILT TOWARD BEING THOSE 0.80 OF 25 WHERE EXPLANATIONS OF ILLNESS OF AN ANAL NATURE ARE ABSENT (38) W-C	12 5 11 20 XSQ= 4.11 PHI= 0.292 XP = 0.0427
406	DRIFT TOWARD BEING THOSE 0.70 OF 23 WHERE EXPLANATIONS OF ILLNESS OF AN AGGRESSION NATURE ARE ABSENT (33) W-C	406	DRIFT TOWARD BEING THOSE 0.60 OF 25 WHERE EXPLANATIONS OF ILLNESS OF AN AGGRESSION NATURE ARE PRESENT (28) W-C	7 15 16 10 XSQ= 3.11 PHI= -0.255 XP = 0.0778
426	TILT TOWARD BEING THOSE 0.52 OF 102 WHERE A HIGH GOD IS ABSENT (104) GES,EA	426	TILT TOWARD BEING THOSE 0.63 OF 107 WHERE A HIGH GOD IS PRESENT (156) GES,EA	49 67 53 40 XSQ= 3.92 PHI= -0.137 XP = 0.0476
427	TILT TOWARD BEING THOSE 0.61 OF 49 WHERE A HIGH GOD, IF PRESENT, IS INACTIVE, RATHER THAN ACTIVE (69) GES,EA	427	TILT TOWARD BEING THOSE 0.61 OF 67 WHERE A HIGH GOD, IF PRESENT, IS ACTIVE, RATHER THAN INACTIVE (87) GES,EA	19 41 30 26 XSQ= 4.83 PHI= -0.204 XP = 0.0279
428	DRIFT TOWARD BEING THOSE 0.53 OF 19 WHERE A HIGH GOD, IF PRESENT AND ACTIVE, DOES NOT SUPPORT HUMAN MORALITY, RATHER THAN SUPPORTING IT (26) GES,EA	428	DRIFT TOWARD BEING THOSE 0.76 OF 41 WHERE A HIGH GOD, IF PRESENT AND ACTIVE, SUPPORTS HUMAN MORALITY, RATHER THAN NOT SUPPORTING IT (61) GES,EA	9 31 10 10 XSQ= 3.48 PHI= -0.241 XP = 0.0623
450	LEAN MORE TOWARD BEING THOSE 0.89 OF 36 WHERE THE OBSERVATION OF FOOD TABOOS IS HIGH OR MEDIUM, RATHER THAN LOW (60) JRL	450	LEAN LESS TOWARD BEING THOSE 0.56 OF 39 WHERE THE OBSERVATION OF FOOD TABOOS IS HIGH OR MEDIUM, RATHER THAN LOW (60) JRL	32 22 4 17 XSQ= 8.25 PHI= 0.332 XP = 0.0041
451	TILT TOWARD BEING THOSE 0.77 OF 13 WHERE TOTEMISM IS PRESENT (15) LWS	451	TILT TOWARD BEING THOSE 0.78 OF 9 WHERE TOTEMISM IS UNIMPORTANT OR ABSENT (12) LWS	10 2 3 7 XSQ= 4.40 PHI= 0.447 EP = 0.0274

452	DRIFT TOWARD BEING THOSE WHERE TOTEMISM WITH FOOD TABOOS IS PRESENT (19) WNS	0.63 OF 16	452	DRIFT TOWARD BEING THOSE WHERE TOTEMISM WITH FOOD TABOOS IS ABSENT (24) WNS	0.71 OF 17	10 5 6 12 XSQ= 2.43 PHI= 0.271 EP = 0.0844
459	TILT TOWARD BEING THOSE WHERE GAMES, IF PRESENT, DO NOT INCLUDE GAMES OF CHANCE (89) R-A-B,EA	0.63 OF 70	459	TILT TOWARD BEING THOSE WHERE GAMES, IF PRESENT, INCLUDE GAMES OF CHANCE (82) R-A-B,EA	0.59 OF 79	26 47 44 32 XSQ= 6.55 PHI= -0.210 XP = 0.0105
471	TILT TOWARD BEING THOSE WHERE SECRET SOCIETIES ARE PRESENT (9) LWS	0.70 OF 10	471	TILT TOWARD BEING THOSE WHERE SECRET SOCIETIES ARE UMIMPORTANT OR ABSENT (14) LWS	0.88 OF 8	7 1 3 7 XSQ= 3.85 PHI= 0.462 EP = 0.0248
473	DRIFT MORE TOWARD BEING THOSE WHERE SENSITIVITY TO INSULT IS MODERATE OR NEGLIGIBLE (56) PES	0.79 OF 34	473	DRIFT LESS TOWARD BEING THOSE WHERE SENSITIVITY TO INSULT IS MODERATE OR NEGLIGIBLE (56) PES	0.56 OF 39	7 17 27 22 XSQ= 3.37 PHI= -0.215 XP = 0.0662

235 CULTURES
WHERE THE COUSIN TERMINOLOGY IS
OF DESCRIPTIVE TYPE (30)

235 CULTURES
WHERE THE COUSIN TERMINOLOGY IS OTHER THAN
OF DESCRIPTIVE TYPE (334)

BACKGROUND ON PAGE 121 — SUBJECT ONLY

30 IN LEFT COLUMN

ASHANTI	AZANDE	BAJUN	BARABRA	BEJA	BERGDAMA	BHIL	BULGARIANS	DILLING	EGYPTIANS
FON	HASANIA	HAZARA	ICELANDERS	KOHISTANI	LOLO	LUO	MINCHIA	NUER	REGEIBAT
ROMANS	RWALA	SANTAL	SHILLUK	SINDHI	SIWANS	SOMALI	SYRIANS	TIGRINYA	TURKANA

334 IN RIGHT COLUMN

36 EXCLUDED BECAUSE UNASCERTAINED

	Left column (30)			Right column (334)		
3	DRIFT LESS TOWARD BEING THOSE LOCATED OUTSIDE OF AFRICA (320)	0.67 OF 30	3	DRIFT MORE TOWARD BEING THOSE LOCATED OUTSIDE OF AFRICA (320)	0.82 OF 334	10 59 20 275 XSQ= 3.44 PHI= 0.097 XP = 0.0637
4	TEND LESS TO BE THOSE LOCATED OUTSIDE OF THE CIRCUM-MEDITERRANEAN (355)	0.57 OF 30	4	TEND MORE TO BE THOSE LOCATED OUTSIDE OF THE CIRCUM-MEDITERRANEAN (355)	0.92 OF 334	13 26 17 308 XSQ= 32.74 PHI= 0.300 XP = 0.
6	IN ALL CASES ARE THOSE LOCATED OUTSIDE OF THE INSULAR PACIFIC (330)	1.00 OF 30	6	TILT LESS TOWARD BEING THOSE LOCATED OUTSIDE OF THE INSULAR PACIFIC (330)	0.79 OF 334	0 69 30 265 XSQ= 6.36 PHI= -0.132 XP = 0.0117
8	IN ALL CASES ARE THOSE LOCATED OUTSIDE OF NORTH AMERICA (330)	1.00 OF 30	8	TILT LESS TOWARD BEING THOSE LOCATED OUTSIDE OF NORTH AMERICA (330)	0.79 OF 334	0 70 30 264 XSQ= 6.49 PHI= -0.134 XP = 0.0108
9	IN ALL CASES ARE THOSE LOCATED OUTSIDE OF SOUTH AMERICA (335)	1.00 OF 30	9	TILT LESS TOWARD BEING THOSE LOCATED OUTSIDE OF SOUTH AMERICA (335)	0.84 OF 334	0 55 30 279 XSQ= 4.61 PHI= -0.112 XP = 0.0319

33	LEAN LESS TOWARD BEING THOSE 0.67 OF 30 WHERE THE NATURAL ENVIRONMENT IS OTHER THAN 'VERY HARSH,' I.E., DESERT, DESERT GRASSES AND SHRUBS, TUNDRA, OR HIGH PLATEAU STEPPE (341) FWM	33	LEAN MORE TOWARD BEING THOSE 0.88 OF 334 WHERE THE NATURAL ENVIRONMENT IS OTHER THAN 'VERY HARSH,' I.E., DESERT, DESERT GRASSES AND SHRUBS, TUNDRA, OR HIGH PLATEAU STEPPE (341) FWM	10 40 20 294 XSQ= 8.87 PHI= 0.156 XP = 0.0029
42	LEAN MORE TOWARD BEING THOSE 0.87 OF 30 WHERE THE NATURAL ENVIRONMENT IS OTHER THAN TROPICAL OR SUB-TROPICAL RAIN FOREST, OR MONSOON FOREST (244) FWM	42	LEAN LESS TOWARD BEING THOSE 0.58 OF 334 WHERE THE NATURAL ENVIRONMENT IS OTHER THAN TROPICAL OR SUB-TROPICAL RAIN FOREST, OR MONSOON FOREST (244) FWM	4 139 26 195 XSQ= 8.08 PHI= -0.149 XP = 0.0045
51	TILT MORE TOWARD BEING THOSE 0.83 OF 30 WHERE SUBSISTENCE IS PRIMARILY BY FOOD PRODUCTION -- I. E., AGRICULTURE OR HUSBANDRY -- RATHER THAN BY GATHERING (253)	51	TILT LESS TOWARD BEING THOSE 0.62 OF 334 WHERE SUBSISTENCE IS PRIMARILY BY FOOD PRODUCTION -- I. E., AGRICULTURE OR HUSBANDRY -- RATHER THAN BY GATHERING (253)	25 206 5 128 XSQ= 4.67 PHI= 0.113 XP = 0.0306
53	LEAN TOWARD BEING THOSE 0.67 OF 21 WHERE FOOD PRODUCTION IS BY INTENSIVE AGRICULTURE, RATHER THAN BY SIMPLE AGRICULTURE OR INCIPIENT FOOD PRODUCTION (91)	53	LEAN TOWARD BEING THOSE 0.65 OF 197 WHERE FOOD PRODUCTION IS BY SIMPLE AGRICULTURE OR INCIPIENT FOOD PRODUCTION, RATHER THAN BY INTENSIVE AGRICULTURE (147)	14 69 7 128 XSQ= 6.77 PHI= 0.176 XP = 0.0093
55	TILT TOWARD BEING THOSE 0.78 OF 18 WHERE FOOD PRODUCTION IS BY INTENSIVE AGRICULTURE, RATHER THAN BY SIMPLE AGRICULTURE (91)	55	TILT TOWARD BEING THOSE 0.57 OF 159 WHERE FOOD PRODUCTION IS BY SIMPLE AGRICULTURE, RATHER THAN BY INTENSIVE AGRICULTURE (101)	14 69 4 90 XSQ= 6.36 PHI= 0.190 XP = 0.0117
62	TILT MORE TOWARD BEING THOSE 0.80 OF 30 WHERE HUSBANDRY OF SOME KIND IS PRESENT (228)	62	TILT LESS TOWARD BEING THOSE 0.56 OF 334 WHERE HUSBANDRY OF SOME KIND IS PRESENT (228)	24 187 6 147 XSQ= 5.57 PHI= 0.124 XP = 0.0183
63	TILT MORE TOWARD BEING THOSE 0.92 OF 24 WHERE HUSBANDRY, IF PRESENT, IS PRINCIPALLY IN THE FORM OF BOVINE, EQUINE, CAMEL-LIKE, OR DEER-LIKE ANIMALS, RATHER THAN PIGS, SHEEP, OR GOATS (152)	63	TILT LESS TOWARD BEING THOSE 0.64 OF 185 WHERE HUSBANDRY, IF PRESENT, IS PRINCIPALLY IN THE FORM OF BOVINE, EQUINE, CAMEL-LIKE, OR DEER-LIKE ANIMALS, RATHER THAN PIGS, SHEEP, OR GOATS (152)	22 119 2 66 XSQ= 6.04 PHI= 0.170 XP = 0.0140
71	TEND TO BE THOSE 0.81 OF 16 WHERE METAL WORKING IS PRESENT (98)	71	TEND TO BE THOSE 0.64 OF 214 WHERE METAL WORKING IS ABSENT (153)	13 76 3 138 XSQ= 11.27 PHI= 0.221 XP = 0.0008
73	TILT TOWARD BEING THOSE 0.75 OF 16 WHERE WEAVING IS PRESENT (118)	73	TILT TOWARD BEING THOSE 0.56 OF 212 WHERE WEAVING IS ABSENT (130)	12 93 4 119 XSQ= 4.62 PHI= 0.142 XP = 0.0316

80	TILT LESS TOWARD BEING THOSE 0.61 OF 18 WHERE NO CITY OR TOWN IS PRESENT (185)	80	TILT MORE TOWARD BEING THOSE 0.85 OF 188 WHERE NO CITY OR TOWN IS PRESENT (185)	7 29 11 159 XSQ= 4.75 PHI= 0.152 XP = 0.0293
85	LEAN TOWARD BEING THOSE 0.53 OF 19 WHERE THE LEVEL OF POLITICAL INTEGRATION IS THE LARGE STATE, OR THE LITTLE STATE (70) GPM	85	LEAN TOWARD BEING THOSE 0.77 OF 256 WHERE THE LEVEL OF POLITICAL INTEGRATION IS THE MINIMAL STATE, THE AUTONOMOUS COMMUNITY, OR THE FAMILY (234) GPM	10 58 9 198 XSQ= 7.00 PHI= 0.160 XP = 0.0081
86	TILT TOWARD BEING THOSE 0.79 OF 19 WHERE THE LEVEL OF POLITICAL INTEGRATION IS THE LARGE STATE, THE LITTLE STATE, OR THE MINIMAL STATE (148) GPM	86	TILT TOWARD BEING THOSE 0.53 OF 256 WHERE THE LEVEL OF POLITICAL INTEGRATION IS THE AUTONOMOUS COMMUNITY, OR THE FAMILY (156) GPM	15 121 4 135 XSQ= 5.89 PHI= 0.146 XP = 0.0152
96	TILT MORE TOWARD BEING THOSE 0.79 OF 24 WHERE THE HIERARCHY OF NATIONAL JURISDICTION HAS FOUR, THREE, TWO OR ONE LEVEL (174) GES,EA	96	TILT LESS TOWARD BEING THOSE 0.51 OF 279 WHERE THE HIERARCHY OF NATIONAL JURISDICTION HAS FOUR, THREE, TWO OR ONE LEVEL (174) GES,EA	19 141 5 138 XSQ= 6.16 PHI= 0.143 XP = 0.0130
98	TILT MORE TOWARD BEING THOSE 0.96 OF 24 WHERE THE HIERARCHY OF LOCAL JURISDICTION HAS FOUR OR THREE LEVELS (238) GES,EA	98	TILT LESS TOWARD BEING THOSE 0.70 OF 280 WHERE THE HIERARCHY OF LOCAL JURISDICTION HAS FOUR OR THREE LEVELS (238) GES,EA	23 197 1 83 XSQ= 5.96 PHI= 0.140 XP = 0.0147
102	TILT MORE TOWARD BEING THOSE 0.77 OF 30 WHERE CLASS STRATIFICATION IS PRESENT (203)	102	TILT LESS TOWARD BEING THOSE 0.52 OF 319 WHERE CLASS STRATIFICATION IS PRESENT (203)	23 165 7 154 XSQ= 5.90 PHI= 0.130 XP = 0.0152
108	DRIFT MORE TOWARD BEING THOSE 0.83 OF 23 WHERE CLASS STRATIFICATION, IF PRESENT, IS BASED ON SOMETHING OTHER THAN A HEREDITARY ARISTOCRACY (129)	108	DRIFT LESS TOWARD BEING THOSE 0.62 OF 165 WHERE CLASS STRATIFICATION, IF PRESENT, IS BASED ON SOMETHING OTHER THAN A HEREDITARY ARISTOCRACY (129)	4 63 19 102 XSQ= 2.95 PHI= -0.125 XP = 0.0858
109	TEND LESS TO BE THOSE 0.57 OF 21 WHERE CASTES ARE ABSENT (317)	109	TEND MORE TO BE THOSE 0.89 OF 314 WHERE CASTES ARE ABSENT (317)	9 36 12 278 XSQ= 14.09 PHI= 0.205 XP = 0.0002
110	LEAN TOWARD BEING THOSE 0.69 OF 29 WHERE SLAVERY IS PRESENT (163)	110	LEAN TOWARD BEING THOSE 0.61 OF 317 WHERE SLAVERY IS ABSENT (218)	20 125 9 192 XSQ= 8.34 PHI= 0.155 XP = 0.0039

No.			No.			
118	IN ALL CASES ARE THOSE WHERE THE PERCENTAGE OF OCCUPATIONS THAT ARE SPECIALIZED IS HIGH OR MEDIUM (24) WME	1.00 OF 5	118	DRIFT TOWARD BEING THOSE WHERE THE PERCENTAGE OF OCCUPATIONS THAT ARE SPECIALIZED IS LOW (25) WME	0.56 OF 43	5 19 0 24 XSQ= 3.57 PHI= 0.273 XP = 0.0588
129	LEAN TOWARD BEING THOSE WHERE WEAVING IS MAINLY DONE BY MALES (31)	0.70 OF 10	129	LEAN TOWARD BEING THOSE WHERE WEAVING IS MAINLY DONE BY FEMALES (73)	0.76 OF 84	7 20 3 64 XSQ= 7.19 PHI= 0.277 XP = 0.0073
183	IN ALL CASES ARE THOSE WHERE THE LARGEST NON-COGNATIC KIN GROUP IS SMALLER THAN A MOEITY, I. E., A PHRATRY OR SIB OR LINEAGE (218)	1.00 OF 26	183	DRIFT LESS TOWARD BEING THOSE WHERE THE LARGEST NON-COGNATIC KIN GROUP IS SMALLER THAN A MOEITY, I. E., A PHRATRY OR SIB OR LINEAGE (218)	0.83 OF 200	0 33 26 167 XSQ= 3.79 PHI= -0.129 XP = 0.0516
186	TEND TO BE THOSE WHERE THE KIN GROUP IS EXCLUSIVELY PATRILINEAL (150)	0.77 OF 30	186	TEND TO BE THOSE WHERE THE KIN GROUP IS OTHER THAN EXCLUSIVELY PATRILINEAL (250)	0.69 OF 334	23 105 7 229 XSQ= 22.76 PHI= 0.250 XP = 0.0000
187	IN ALL CASES ARE THOSE WHERE THE KIN GROUP IS OTHER THAN EXCLUSIVELY MATRILINEAL (344)	1.00 OF 30	187	TILT LESS TOWARD BEING THOSE WHERE THE KIN GROUP IS OTHER THAN EXCLUSIVELY MATRILINEAL (344)	0.84 OF 333	0 53 30 280 XSQ= 4.39 PHI= -0.110 XP = 0.0362
188	LEAN MORE TOWARD BEING THOSE WHERE THE KIN GROUP IS OTHER THAN EXCLUSIVELY COGNATIC (252)	0.87 OF 30	188	LEAN LESS TOWARD BEING THOSE WHERE THE KIN GROUP IS OTHER THAN EXCLUSIVELY COGNATIC (252)	0.60 OF 334	4 134 26 200 XSQ= 7.29 PHI= -0.142 XP = 0.0069
190	IN ALL CASES ARE THOSE WHERE THE KIN GROUP IS PATRILINEAL OR DOUBLE-DESCENT, RATHER THAN MATRILINEAL (186)	1.00 OF 26	190	LEAN LESS TOWARD BEING THOSE WHERE THE KIN GROUP IS PATRILINEAL OR DOUBLE-DESCENT, RATHER THAN MATRILINEAL (186)	0.70 OF 195	26 136 0 59 XSQ= 9.24 PHI= 0.204 XP = 0.0024
192	DRIFT MORE TOWARD BEING THOSE OTHER THAN WHERE THE ONLY KIN GROUP PRESENT IS A KINDRED OR ELSE BILATERAL DESCENT IS INFERRED (289)	0.87 OF 30	192	DRIFT LESS TOWARD BEING THOSE OTHER THAN WHERE THE ONLY KIN GROUP PRESENT IS A KINDRED OR ELSE BILATERAL DESCENT IS INFERRED (289)	0.70 OF 334	4 99 26 235 XSQ= 2.85 PHI= -0.088 XP = 0.0914
196	TILT MORE TOWARD BEING THOSE WHERE INDIVIDUAL RIGHTS IN REAL PROPERTY, AND RULES FOR INHERITANCE, ARE PRESENT (194)	0.93 OF 27	196	TILT LESS TOWARD BEING THOSE WHERE INDIVIDUAL RIGHTS IN REAL PROPERTY, AND RULES FOR INHERITANCE, ARE PRESENT (194)	0.67 OF 225	25 150 2 75 XSQ= 6.46 PHI= 0.160 XP = 0.0110

204	DRIFT MORE TOWARD BEING THOSE WHERE MARITAL RESIDENCE IS PATRILOCAL, VIRILOCAL, OR AVUNCULOCAL, RATHER THAN AMBILOCAL OR NEOLOCAL (270)	0.93 OF 30	204	DRIFT LESS TOWARD BEING THOSE WHERE MARITAL RESIDENCE IS PATRILOCAL, VIRILOCAL, OR AVUNCULOCAL, RATHER THAN AMBILOCAL OR NEOLOCAL (270)	0.79 OF 270	28 212 2 58 XSQ= 2.84 PHI= 0.097 XP = 0.0922
209	IN ALL CASES ARE THOSE WHERE MARITAL RESIDENCE IS PATRILOCAL, VIRILOCAL, OR AVUNCULOCAL, RATHER THAN MATRILOCAL OR UXORILOCAL (270)	1.00 OF 28	209	LEAN LESS TOWARD BEING THOSE WHERE MARITAL RESIDENCE IS PATRILOCAL, VIRILOCAL, OR AVUNCULOCAL, RATHER THAN MATRILOCAL OR UXORILOCAL (270)	0.77 OF 274	28 212 0 62 XSQ= 6.65 PHI= 0.148 XP = 0.0099
210	IN ALL CASES ARE THOSE WHERE MARITAL RESIDENCE IS PATRILOCAL, RATHER THAN MATRILOCAL (169)	1.00 OF 22	210	TILT LESS TOWARD BEING THOSE WHERE MARITAL RESIDENCE IS PATRILOCAL, RATHER THAN MATRILOCAL (169)	0.80 OF 157	22 126 0 31 XSQ= 3.97 PHI= 0.149 XP = 0.0464
213	TILT TOWARD BEING THOSE WHERE FIRST COUSIN MARRIAGE IS PERMITTED (172)	0.67 OF 27	213	TILT TOWARD BEING THOSE WHERE FIRST COUSIN MARRIAGE IS NOT PERMITTED (198)	0.56 OF 314	18 138 9 176 XSQ= 4.30 PHI= 0.112 XP = 0.0382
214	IN ALL CASES ARE THOSE WHERE FIRST COUSIN MARRIAGE, IF PERMITTED, IS OTHER THAN UNILATERAL (144)	1.00 OF 18	214	DRIFT LESS TOWARD BEING THOSE WHERE FIRST COUSIN MARRIAGE, IF PERMITTED, IS OTHER THAN UNILATERAL (144)	0.80 OF 138	0 27 18 111 XSQ= 3.00 PHI= -0.139 XP = 0.0832
225	TEND TO BE THOSE WHERE COUSIN MARRIAGE IS PREFERENTIALLY OR PERMISSIVELY PATRILATERAL, RATHER THAN MATRILATERAL (23)	0.90 OF 10	225	TEND TO BE THOSE WHERE COUSIN MARRIAGE IS PREFERENTIALLY OR PERMISSIVELY MATRILATERAL, RATHER THAN PATRILATERAL (43)	0.75 OF 52	9 13 1 39 XSQ= 12.77 PHI= 0.454 XP = 0.0004
240	IN ALL CASES ARE THOSE WHERE THE FAMILY, IF EXTENDED, IS SMALL OR STEM, RATHER THAN LARGE (135)	1.00 OF 16	240	LEAN LESS TOWARD BEING THOSE WHERE THE FAMILY, IF EXTENDED, IS SMALL OR STEM, RATHER THAN LARGE (135)	0.59 OF 183	0 75 16 108 XSQ= 8.85 PHI= -0.211 XP = 0.0029
262	TILT MORE TOWARD BEING THOSE WHERE WIVES ARE OBTAINED BY MEANS INVOLVING THE PRESENCE OF SOME CONSIDERATION (305)	0.97 OF 30	262	TILT LESS TOWARD BEING THOSE WHERE WIVES ARE OBTAINED BY MEANS INVOLVING THE PRESENCE OF SOME CONSIDERATION (305)	0.74 OF 329	29 244 1 85 XSQ= 6.46 PHI= 0.134 XP = 0.0111
263	LEAN MORE TOWARD BEING THOSE WHERE WIVES ARE OBTAINED BY RELATIVELY DIFFICULT MEANS, NAMELY BY BRIDE-PRICE, BRIDE-SERVICE, OR EXCHANGING A FEMALE RELATIVE (233)	0.83 OF 30	263	LEAN LESS TOWARD BEING THOSE WHERE WIVES ARE OBTAINED BY RELATIVELY DIFFICULT MEANS, NAMELY BY BRIDE-PRICE, BRIDE-SERVICE, OR EXCHANGING A FEMALE RELATIVE (233)	0.54 OF 329	25 178 5 151 XSQ= 8.41 PHI= 0.153 XP = 0.0037

282	IN ALL CASES ARE THOSE WHERE THE STRENGTH OF DESIRE FOR CHILDREN IS HIGH (16) BCA	1.00 OF 3	282	DRIFT TOWARD BEING THOSE WHERE THE STRENGTH OF DESIRE FOR CHILDREN IS LOW OR ABSENT (20) BCA	0.61 OF 31	3 12 0 19 XSQ= 2.05 PHI= 0.246 EP = 0.0760
286	IN ALL CASES ARE THOSE WHERE THE NUMBER OF FOOD TABOOS DURING PREGNANCY IS LOW OR ABSENT (14) BCA	1.00 OF 3	286	DRIFT TOWARD BEING THOSE WHERE THE NUMBER OF FOOD TABOOS DURING PREGNANCY IS HIGH (20) BCA	0.63 OF 30	0 19 3 11 XSQ= 2.26 PHI= -0.262 EP = 0.0667
295	IN ALL CASES ARE THOSE WHERE THE SEVERITY OF PUNISHMENT FOR ABORTION IS HIGH (11) BCA	1.00 OF 3	295	DRIFT TOWARD BEING THOSE WHERE THE SEVERITY OF PUNISHMENT FOR ABORTION IS LOW OR ABSENT (12) BCA	0.63 OF 19	3 7 0 12 XSQ= 2.01 PHI= 0.302 EP = 0.0779
305	IN ALL CASES ARE THOSE WHERE THE EARLY SEXUAL SATISFACTION POTENTIAL IS LOW (24) W-C	1.00 OF 4	305	DRIFT TOWARD BEING THOSE WHERE THE EARLY SEXUAL SATISFACTION POTENTIAL IS HIGH (27) W-C	0.58 OF 45	0 26 4 19 XSQ= 2.88 PHI= -0.242 XP = 0.0898
314	TILT TOWARD BEING THOSE WHERE THE INCIDENCE OF MOTHER-CHILD HOUSEHOLDS IS HIGH (19) W-D,S	0.67 OF 6	314	TILT TOWARD BEING THOSE WHERE THE INCIDENCE OF MOTHER-CHILD HOUSEHOLDS IS LOW (61) W-D,S	0.79 OF 70	4 15 2 55 XSQ= 3.86 PHI= 0.225 XP = 0.0494
337	IN ALL CASES ARE THOSE WHERE THE CHILD'S INFERRED ANXIETY OVER NON-PERFORMANCE OF RESPONSIBLE BEHAVIOR IS HIGH (38) B-B-C	1.00 OF 5	337	DRIFT TOWARD BEING THOSE WHERE THE CHILD'S INFERRED ANXIETY OVER NON-PERFORMANCE OF RESPONSIBLE BEHAVIOR IS LOW (35) B-B-C	0.50 OF 66	5 33 0 33 XSQ= 2.88 PHI= 0.201 XP = 0.0898
377	TEND TO BE THOSE WHERE MALE GENITAL MUTILATION IS PRESENT (83)	0.58 OF 24	377	TEND TO BE THOSE WHERE MALE GENITAL MUTILATION IS ABSENT (242)	0.79 OF 275	14 57 10 218 XSQ= 15.23 PHI= 0.226 XP = 0.0001
382	LEAN TOWARD BEING THOSE WHERE FEMALE INITIATION RITES ARE ABSENT (27) JKB	0.89 OF 9	382	LEAN TOWARD BEING THOSE WHERE FEMALE INITIATION RITES ARE PRESENT (38) JKB	0.65 OF 51	1 33 8 18 XSQ= 6.90 PHI= -0.339 XP = 0.0086
390	LEAN TOWARD BEING THOSE WHERE PREMARITAL SEX RELATIONS ARE STRONGLY PUNISHED AND IN FACT RARE (47) JTW,EA	0.62 OF 13	390	LEAN TOWARD BEING THOSE WHERE PREMARITAL SEX RELATIONS ARE WEAKLY PUNISHED AND IN FACT NOT RARE OR PUNISHED ONLY IF PREGNANCY RESULTS, OR FREELY PERMITTED (132) JTW,EA	0.77 OF 152	8 35 5 117 XSQ= 7.33 PHI= 0.211 XP = 0.0068

391	TILT TOWARD BEING THOSE 0.85 OF 13 WHERE PREMARITAL SEX RELATIONS ARE STRONGLY PUNISHED AND IN FACT RARE, OR WEAKLY PUNISHED AND IN FACT NOT RARE (89) JTW,EA	391	TILT TOWARD BEING THOSE 0.54 OF 152 WHERE PREMARITAL SEX RELATIONS ARE PUNISHED ONLY IF PREGNANCY RESULTS, OR FREELY PERMITTED (90) JTW,EA	11 70 2 82 XSQ= 5.67 PHI= 0.185 XP = 0.0173
419	IN ALL CASES ARE THOSE 1.00 OF 7 WHERE MILITARY GLORY IS STRONGLY OR MODERATELY EMPHASIZED (55) PES	419	DRIFT LESS TOWARD BEING THOSE 0.60 OF 75 WHERE MILITARY GLORY IS STRONGLY OR MODERATELY EMPHASIZED (55) PES	7 45 0 30 XSQ= 2.86 PHI= 0.187 XP = 0.0908
420	TILT TOWARD BEING THOSE 0.88 OF 8 WHERE BELLICOSITY IS EXTREME (41) PES	420	TILT TOWARD BEING THOSE 0.59 OF 75 WHERE BELLICOSITY IS MODERATE OR NEGLIGIBLE (46) PES	7 31 1 44 XSQ= 4.49 PHI= 0.232 XP = 0.0342
426	LEAN MORE TOWARD BEING THOSE 0.87 OF 23 WHERE A HIGH GOD IS PRESENT (156) GES,EA	426	LEAN LESS TOWARD BEING THOSE 0.55 OF 219 WHERE A HIGH GOD IS PRESENT (156) GES,EA	20 121 3 98 XSQ= 7.35 PHI= 0.174 XP = 0.0067
427	TILT MORE TOWARD BEING THOSE 0.80 OF 20 WHERE A HIGH GOD, IF PRESENT, IS ACTIVE, RATHER THAN INACTIVE (87) GES,EA	427	TILT LESS TOWARD BEING THOSE 0.51 OF 121 WHERE A HIGH GOD, IF PRESENT, IS ACTIVE, RATHER THAN INACTIVE (87) GES,EA	16 62 4 59 XSQ= 4.64 PHI= 0.181 XP = 0.0313
430	IN ALL CASES ARE THOSE 1.00 OF 3 WHERE SUPERNATURAL SANCTIONS FOR MORALITY, HAVING AN EFFECT ON AN INDIVIDUAL'S HEALTH, ARE PRESENT (16) GES	430	DRIFT TOWARD BEING THOSE 0.61 OF 33 WHERE SUPERNATURAL SANCTIONS FOR MORALITY, HAVING AN EFFECT ON AN INDIVIDUAL'S HEALTH, ARE ABSENT OR UNREPORTED (22) GES	3 13 0 20 XSQ= 2.00 PHI= 0.236 EP = 0.0784
458	LEAN TOWARD BEING THOSE 0.80 OF 10 WHERE GAMES, IF PRESENT, INCLUDE GAMES OF STRATEGY (52) R-A-B,EA	458	LEAN TOWARD BEING THOSE 0.73 OF 154 WHERE GAMES, IF PRESENT, DO NOT INCLUDE GAMES OF STRATEGY (119) R-A-B,EA	8 42 2 112 XSQ= 9.96 PHI= 0.246 XP = 0.0016
473	TILT TOWARD BEING THOSE 0.75 OF 8 WHERE SENSITIVITY TO INSULT IS EXTREME (32) PES	473	TILT TOWARD BEING THOSE 0.68 OF 76 WHERE SENSITIVITY TO INSULT IS MODERATE OR NEGLIGIBLE (56) PES	6 24 2 52 XSQ= 4.20 PHI= 0.224 XP = 0.0404

236 CULTURES
WHERE THE FAMILY IS
OF AN EXTENDED TYPE, RATHER THAN
AN INDEPENDENT TYPE (213)

236 CULTURES
WHERE THE FAMILY IS
OF AN INDEPENDENT TYPE, RATHER THAN
AN EXTENDED TYPE (185)

BACKGROUND ON PAGE 122

BOTH SUBJECT AND PREDICATE

213 IN LEFT COLUMN

AINU	ALBANIANS	APINAYE	ARAUCANIANS	ARYANS	ASHANTI	ATAYAL	ATSUGEWI	AYMARA	BABWA
BACAIRI	BALINESE	BAMBARA	BASQUES	BATAK	BELU	BENGALI	BETE	BHIL	BIRIFOR
BOERS	BORORO	BOTOCUDO	BOZO	BULGARIANS	BURUSHO	BURYAT	CADUVEO	CALLINAGO	CAMAYURA
CARAJA	CAYAPA	CHEROKEE	CHEYENNE	CHINANTEC	CHIR-APACHE	CHIRIGUANO	CHORTI	CHUKCHEE	COCHITI
COMANCHE	COORG	CREEK	CUNA	CZECHS	DAGUR	DARD	DELAWARE	DOGON	DUTCH
EGYPTIANS	ELLICE	FANG	FOX	GARO	GOND	GUAHIBO	GURE	HAIDA	HANO
HANUNOO	HASINAI	HAVASUPAI	HAWAIIANS	HAZARA	HEBREWS	HEHE	HERERO	HUICHOL	HUKUNDIKA
HURON	IBAN	ICELANDERS	ILA	INGASSANA	IRISH	JAPANESE	JAVANESE	JIVARO	JUKUN
KABYLE	KACHIN	KALMYK	KAPAUKU	KASKA	KATAB	KAZAK	KERALA	KHALKA	KHASI
KIOW-APACHE	KISSI	KOL	KONSO	KOREANS	KORYAK	KUBA	KUNG	KWAKIUTL	LAKALAI
LANGO	LAU	LEPCHA	LIFU	LUO	MAGUZAWA	MALAYS	MAM	MAMBILA	MANCHU
MANDAN	MANGAIANS	MANIHIKI	MAORI	MARGI	MARSHALLESE	MATACO	MATAKAM	MBUGWE	MENDE
MIAO	MIN CHINESE	MINANGKABAU	MINCHIA	MISKITO	MONGO	MONGUOR	MOSSI	MOTILON	MUNDURUCU
NATCHEZ	NAVAHO	NUER	NUNIVAK	NUPE	NURI	NYANEKA	OJIBWA	OKINAWANS	ONTONG-JAVA
ORAON	PAIWAN	PAPAGO	PAWNEE	PORTUGUESE	PURUM	RAROIANS	REGEIBAT	RIFFIANS	SAMOANS
SAMOYED	SANPOIL	SANTAL	SERBS	SERI	SHLUH	SINDHI	SIRIONO	SIWANS	SOMALI
SWAZI	SYRIANS	TALAMANCA	TALLENSI	TAMIL	TANALA	TANIMBARESE	TAPIRAPE	TAREUMIUT	TEDA
TEHUELCHE	TENETEHARA	TENINO	TERA	TERENA	THAI	THONGA	TIBETANS	TIMBIRA	TIMUCUA
TIV	TIWI	TOKELAU	TORAJA	TRUKESE	TRUMAI	TSHIMSHIAN	TUPINAMBA	TURKANA	TURKMEN
TWANA	TZELTAL	UTE	VEDDA	VENDA	VIETNAMESE	WAROPEN	WARRAU	WICHITA	WINNEBAGO
WOLEAIANS	WOLOF	WUTE	YAKO	YAKUT	YAO	YAPESE	YARURO	YOKUTS	YORUBA
YUKAGHIR	YUROK	ZUNI							

185 IN RIGHT COLUMN

ABIPON	ABOR	AKHA	ALACALUF	ALORESE	AMBA	AMERICANS	ANDAMANESE	ARANDA	ARAPESH
AWEIKOMA	AZANDE	AZTEC	BAJUN	BAMILEKE	BANDA	BARABRA	BARI	BASSERI	BAYA
BEJA	BEMBA	BERGDAMA	BHUIYA	BLACK CARIB	BRAZILIANS	BUDUMA	BUNLAP	BURMESE	CAGABA
CAMBA	CAMBODIANS	CARIB	CARINYA	CHAGGA	CHAMACOCO	CHENCHU	CHEREMIS	CHERKESS	CHIBCHA
CHOCO	CHOROTI	COPR ESKIMO	CREE	CROW	DIEGUENO	DIERI	DILLING	DOBUANS	DOROBO
DUSUN	ENGA	EYAK	FON	FUTAJALONKE	GANDA	GILBERTESE	GILYAK	GISU	GOAJIRO
GROS VENTRE	GUATO	HASANIA	HO	HUTSUL	IFUGAO	INCA	INGALIK	IRAQW	JEMEZ
KAREN	KARIERA	KERAKI	KET	KHEVSUR	KIKUYU	KOHISTANI	KPE	KUMYK	KURTATCHI
KUTENAI	LAKHER	LAMBA	LAMET	LAPPS	LESU	LHOTA NAGA	LOLO	LOZI	LUBA
MACASSARESE	MAMVU	MANUS	MARICOPA	MARQUESANS	MASAI	MAYA	MAZATECO	MBUNDU	MBUTI
MENTAWEI	MERINA	MIAMI	MIWOK	MNONG GAR	MOTA	MURINBATA	MURNGIN	MZAB	NABESNA
NAMA	NAMBICUARA	NANDI	NASKAPI	NDEMBU	NGONI	NICOBARESE	NOMLAKI	NYAKYUSA	NYARO
NYORO	OMAHA	ONA	PAEZ	PALAUANS	PALIKUR	PARAUJANO	PATHAN	PENDE	PENOBSCOT
PONAPEANS	POPOLUCA	PUKAPUKA	PURARI	ROMANS	ROTINESE	ROTUMANS	RUNDI	RWALA	SAGADA

SANDAWE	SARAMACCA	SARSI	SELUNG	SEMANG	SEMINOLE	SENIANG	SHERENTE	SHILLUK	SIMBOESE
SINHALESE	SIUAI	SONGHAI	SOTHO	SUBANUN	TAGBANUA	TAOS	TARAHUMARA	TENDA	TESO
TETON	TIGRINYA	TIKOPIA	TODA	TOLOWA	TRISTAN	TROBRIAND	TUBATULABAL	TUCANO	TUCUNA
TUNEBO	ULAWANS	WAICA	WALLOONS	WANTOAT	WAPISHANA	WASHO	WIKMUNKAN	WITOTO	WOGEO
YABARANA	YAGUA	YAHGAN	YOMBE	YUKI					

2 EXCLUDED BECAUSE UNASCERTAINED

5	DRIFT LESS TOWARD BEING THOSE LOCATED OUTSIDE OF EAST EURASIA (330)	0.79 OF 213	5	DRIFT MORE TOWARD BEING THOSE LOCATED OUTSIDE OF EAST EURASIA (330)	0.86 OF 185	45 25 168 160 XSQ= 3.45 PHI= 0.093 XP = 0.0632
6	DRIFT MORE TOWARD BEING THOSE LOCATED OUTSIDE OF THE INSULAR PACIFIC (330)	0.86 OF 213	6	DRIFT LESS TOWARD BEING THOSE LOCATED OUTSIDE OF THE INSULAR PACIFIC (330)	0.79 OF 185	30 39 183 146 XSQ= 2.91 PHI= -0.086 XP = 0.0880
15	LEAN TOWARD BEING THOSE WHERE THE LATITUDE IS TWENTY DEGREES OR GREATER (183)	0.53 OF 213	15	LEAN TOWARD BEING THOSE WHERE THE LATITUDE IS LESS THAN TWENTY DEGREES (217)	0.63 OF 185	113 68 100 117 XSQ= 9.96 PHI= 0.158 XP = 0.0016
56	DRIFT LESS TOWARD BEING THOSE WHERE FOOD PRODUCTION IS BY SIMPLE AGRICULTURE, RATHER THAN BY INCIPIENT FOOD PRODUCTION (101)	0.62 OF 79	56	DRIFT MORE TOWARD BEING THOSE WHERE FOOD PRODUCTION IS BY SIMPLE AGRICULTURE, RATHER THAN BY INCIPIENT FOOD PRODUCTION (101)	0.76 OF 67	49 51 30 16 XSQ= 2.72 PHI= -0.136 XP = 0.0993
73	LEAN TOWARD BEING THOSE WHERE WEAVING IS PRESENT (118)	0.56 OF 131	73	LEAN TOWARD BEING THOSE WHERE WEAVING IS ABSENT (130)	0.63 OF 116	74 43 57 73 XSQ= 8.54 PHI= 0.186 XP = 0.0035
81	DRIFT LESS TOWARD BEING THOSE WHERE NO CITY OR TOWN IS PRESENT, AND THE AVERAGE COMMUNITY SIZE IS SMALLER THAN 200 (135)	0.54 OF 116	81	DRIFT MORE TOWARD BEING THOSE WHERE NO CITY OR TOWN IS PRESENT, AND THE AVERAGE COMMUNITY SIZE IS SMALLER THAN 200 (135)	0.67 OF 107	53 35 63 72 XSQ= 3.40 PHI= 0.123 XP = 0.0652
82	LEAN MORE TOWARD BEING THOSE WHERE A CITY OR TOWN IS PRESENT, OR THE AVERAGE COMMUNITY SIZE IS FIFTY OR GREATER (178)	0.88 OF 116	82	LEAN LESS TOWARD BEING THOSE WHERE A CITY OR TOWN IS PRESENT, OR THE AVERAGE COMMUNITY SIZE IS FIFTY OR GREATER (178)	0.70 OF 107	102 75 14 32 XSQ= 9.75 PHI= 0.209 XP = 0.0018

No.		No.		
83	DRIFT LESS TOWARD BEING THOSE 0.68 OF 92 WHERE, WITH NO CITY AND NO TOWN PRESENT, THE AVERAGE COMMUNITY SIZE IS SMALLER THAN 200, RATHER THAN BETWEEN 200 AND 999 (135)	83	DRIFT MORE TOWARD BEING THOSE 0.82 OF 88 WHERE, WITH NO CITY AND NO TOWN PRESENT, THE AVERAGE COMMUNITY SIZE IS SMALLER THAN 200, RATHER THAN BETWEEN 200 AND 999 (135)	29 16 63 72 XSQ= 3.59 PHI= 0.141 XP = 0.0582
86	DRIFT TOWARD BEING THOSE 0.54 OF 170 WHERE THE LEVEL OF POLITICAL INTEGRATION IS THE LARGE STATE, THE LITTLE STATE, OR THE MINIMAL STATE (148) GPM	86	DRIFT TOWARD BEING THOSE 0.58 OF 132 WHERE THE LEVEL OF POLITICAL INTEGRATION IS THE AUTONOMOUS COMMUNITY, OR THE FAMILY (156) GPM	91 55 79 77 XSQ= 3.73 PHI= 0.111 XP = 0.0536
96	LEAN TOWARD BEING THOSE 0.60 OF 178 WHERE THE HIERARCHY OF NATIONAL JURISDICTION HAS FOUR, THREE, TWO OR ONE LEVEL (174) GES,EA	96	LEAN TOWARD BEING THOSE 0.56 OF 151 WHERE THE HIERARCHY OF NATIONAL JURISDICTION HAS NO LEVELS (156) GES,EA	106 67 72 84 XSQ= 6.95 PHI= 0.145 XP = 0.0084
98	TEND TO BE THOSE 0.92 OF 179 WHERE THE HIERARCHY OF LOCAL JURISDICTION HAS FOUR OR THREE LEVELS (238) GES,EA	98	TEND TO BE THOSE 0.52 OF 151 WHERE THE HIERARCHY OF LOCAL JURISDICTION HAS TWO LEVELS (93) GES,EA	165 72 14 79 XSQ= 77.94 PHI= 0.486 XP = 0.
99	TEND TO BE THOSE 0.85 OF 72 WHERE, WITH NATIONAL HIERARCHY ABSENT, THE HIERARCHY OF LOCAL JURISDICTION HAS FOUR OR THREE LEVELS (93) GES,EA	99	TEND TO BE THOSE 0.62 OF 84 WHERE, WITH NATIONAL HIERARCHY ABSENT, THE HIERARCHY OF LOCAL JURISDICTION HAS TWO LEVELS (63) GES,EA	61 32 11 52 XSQ= 33.10 PHI= 0.461 XP = 0.
100	TEND MORE TO BE THOSE 0.94 OF 178 WHERE HIERARCHIES ARE MORE COMPLEX THAN THE 'SIMPLEST,' I. E., MORE COMPLEX THAN TWO LOCAL LEVELS WITH NO NATIONAL LEVELS (267) GES,EA	100	TEND LESS TO BE THOSE 0.66 OF 151 WHERE HIERARCHIES ARE MORE COMPLEX THAN THE 'SIMPLEST,' I. E., MORE COMPLEX THAN TWO LOCAL LEVELS WITH NO NATIONAL LEVELS (267) GES,EA	167 99 11 52 XSQ= 40.33 PHI= 0.350 XP = 0.
102	DRIFT TOWARD BEING THOSE 0.58 OF 206 WHERE CLASS STRATIFICATION IS PRESENT (203)	102	DRIFT TOWARD BEING THOSE 0.52 OF 176 WHERE CLASS STRATIFICATION IS ABSENT (180)	119 84 87 92 XSQ= 3.45 PHI= 0.095 XP = 0.0633
109	DRIFT LESS TOWARD BEING THOSE 0.82 OF 194 WHERE CASTES ARE ABSENT (317)	109	DRIFT MORE TOWARD BEING THOSE 0.90 OF 172 WHERE CASTES ARE ABSENT (317)	34 17 160 155 XSQ= 3.83 PHI= 0.102 XP = 0.0505
110	DRIFT LESS TOWARD BEING THOSE 0.53 OF 203 WHERE SLAVERY IS ABSENT (218)	110	DRIFT MORE TOWARD BEING THOSE 0.63 OF 176 WHERE SLAVERY IS ABSENT (218)	96 66 107 110 XSQ= 3.30 PHI= 0.093 XP = 0.0692

127	DRIFT TOWARD BEING THOSE 0.59 OF 37 WHERE THE FEMALES' CONTRIBUTION TO SUBSISTENCE IS LOW (32) JKB	127	DRIFT TOWARD BEING THOSE 0.64 OF 28 WHERE THE FEMALES' CONTRIBUTION TO SUBSISTENCE IS HIGH (33) JKB	15 18 22 10 XSQ= 2.71 PHI= -0.204 XP = 0.0998
138	DRIFT TOWARD BEING THOSE 0.70 OF 23 WHERE SUPERORDINATE JUSTICE IS PRESENT (22) BBW	138	DRIFT TOWARD BEING THOSE 0.65 OF 17 WHERE SUPERORDINATE JUSTICE IS ABSENT (18) BBW	16 6 7 11 XSQ= 3.36 PHI= 0.290 EP = 0.0534
139	TILT TOWARD BEING THOSE 0.52 OF 23 WHERE SUPERORDINATE PUNISHMENT IS PRESENT (15) BBW	139	TILT TOWARD BEING THOSE 0.82 OF 17 WHERE SUPERORDINATE PUNISHMENT IS ABSENT (25) BBW	12 3 11 14 XSQ= 3.61 PHI= 0.300 EP = 0.0464
177	DRIFT MORE TOWARD BEING THOSE 0.83 OF 206 WHERE THE COMMUNITY IS OTHER THAN A SINGLE CLAN-COMMUNITY AND EXOGAMOUS (305)	177	DRIFT LESS TOWARD BEING THOSE 0.76 OF 175 WHERE THE COMMUNITY IS OTHER THAN A SINGLE CLAN-COMMUNITY AND EXOGAMOUS (305)	34 42 172 133 XSQ= 2.88 PHI= -0.087 XP = 0.0899
201	TEND MORE TO BE THOSE 0.90 OF 211 WHERE MARITAL RESIDENCE IS NON-OPTIONAL, RATHER THAN AMBILOCAL OR NEOLOCAL (334)	201	TEND LESS TO BE THOSE 0.77 OF 185 WHERE MARITAL RESIDENCE IS NON-OPTIONAL, RATHER THAN AMBILOCAL OR NEOLOCAL (334)	190 142 21 43 XSQ= 11.89 PHI= 0.173 XP = 0.0006
204	LEAN MORE TOWARD BEING THOSE 0.87 OF 162 WHERE MARITAL RESIDENCE IS PATRILOCAL, VIRILOCAL, OR AVUNCULOCAL, RATHER THAN AMBILOCAL OR NEOLOCAL (270)	204	LEAN LESS TOWARD BEING THOSE 0.75 OF 170 WHERE MARITAL RESIDENCE IS PATRILOCAL, VIRILOCAL, OR AVUNCULOCAL, RATHER THAN AMBILOCAL OR NEOLOCAL (270)	141 127 21 43 XSQ= 7.33 PHI= 0.149 XP = 0.0068
207	TEND TO BE THOSE 0.70 OF 70 WHERE MARITAL RESIDENCE IS MATRILOCAL OR UXORILOCAL, RATHER THAN AMBILOCAL OR NEOLOCAL (64)	207	TEND TO BE THOSE 0.74 OF 58 WHERE MARITAL RESIDENCE IS AMBILOCAL OR NEOLOCAL, RATHER THAN MATRILOCAL OR UXORILOCAL (64)	49 15 21 43 XSQ= 22.98 PHI= 0.424 XP = 0.0000
209	TEND LESS TO BE THOSE 0.74 OF 190 WHERE MARITAL RESIDENCE IS PATRILOCAL, VIRILOCAL, OR AVUNCULOCAL, RATHER THAN MATRILOCAL OR UXORILOCAL (270)	209	TEND MORE TO BE THOSE 0.89 OF 142 WHERE MARITAL RESIDENCE IS PATRILOCAL, VIRILOCAL, OR AVUNCULOCAL, RATHER THAN MATRILOCAL OR UXORILOCAL (270)	141 127 49 15 XSQ= 11.15 PHI= -0.183 XP = 0.0008
210	TILT LESS TOWARD BEING THOSE 0.78 OF 116 WHERE MARITAL RESIDENCE IS PATRILOCAL, RATHER THAN MATRILOCAL (169)	210	TILT MORE TOWARD BEING THOSE 0.93 OF 83 WHERE MARITAL RESIDENCE IS PATRILOCAL, RATHER THAN MATRILOCAL (169)	91 77 25 6 XSQ= 6.50 PHI= -0.181 XP = 0.0108

234	DRIFT TOWARD BEING THOSE 0.57 OF 174 WHERE THE COUSIN TERMINOLOGY IS OF ESKIMO OR HAWAIIAN TYPE, RATHER THAN CROW, OMAHA, OR IROQUOIS TYPE (170)	234	DRIFT TOWARD BEING THOSE 0.53 OF 146 WHERE THE COUSIN TERMINOLOGY IS OF CROW, OMAHA, OR IROQUOIS TYPE, RATHER THAN ESKIMO OR HAWAIIAN TYPE (152)	74 77 100 69 XSQ= 2.92 PHI= -0.096 XP = 0.0873
285	TILT TOWARD BEING THOSE 0.72 OF 18 WHERE THE SEX TABOO DURING PREGNANCY IS ABSENT OR INFERRED ABSENT (17) BCA	285	TILT TOWARD BEING THOSE 0.69 OF 13 WHERE THE SEX TABOO DURING PREGNANCY IS PRESENT (14) BCA	5 9 13 4 XSQ= 3.70 PHI= -0.345 EP = 0.0325
307	TILT TOWARD BEING THOSE 0.54 OF 24 WHERE THE EARLY AGGRESSION SATISFACTION POTENTIAL IS LOW (19) W-C	307	TILT TOWARD BEING THOSE 0.79 OF 28 WHERE THE EARLY AGGRESSION SATISFACTION POTENTIAL IS HIGH (33) W-C	11 22 13 6 XSQ= 4.64 PHI= -0.299 XP = 0.0311
313	TILT TOWARD BEING THOSE 0.67 OF 24 WHERE AGGRESSION SOCIALIZATION ANXIETY IS HIGH (26) W-C	313	TILT TOWARD BEING THOSE 0.67 OF 30 WHERE AGGRESSION SOCIALIZATION ANXIETY IS LOW (28) W-C	16 10 8 20 XSQ= 4.67 PHI= 0.294 XP = 0.0306
319	DRIFT TOWARD BEING THOSE 0.64 OF 39 WHERE PROTECTION OF THE INFANT FROM ENVIRONMENTAL DISCOMFORTS IS HIGH (35) B-B-C	319	DRIFT TOWARD BEING THOSE 0.62 OF 26 WHERE PROTECTION OF THE INFANT FROM ENVIRONMENTAL DISCOMFORTS IS LOW (30) B-B-C	25 10 14 16 XSQ= 3.16 PHI= 0.220 XP = 0.0755
327	TILT TOWARD BEING THOSE 0.66 OF 32 WHERE THE AGE OF THE INFANT AT TIME OF REDUCED CONTACT WITH MOTHER IS HIGHER THAN TWO YEARS (28) B-B-C	327	TILT TOWARD BEING THOSE 0.70 OF 23 WHERE THE AGE OF THE INFANT AT TIME OF REDUCED CONTACT WITH MOTHER IS TWO YEARS OR LOWER (27) B-B-C	21 7 11 16 XSQ= 5.30 PHI= 0.310 XP = 0.0214
370	TILT MORE TOWARD BEING THOSE 0.66 OF 140 WHERE THE SEGREGATION OF ADOLESCENT BOYS IS ABSENT (148)	370	TILT LESS TOWARD BEING THOSE 0.53 OF 102 WHERE THE SEGREGATION OF ADOLESCENT BOYS IS ABSENT (148)	47 48 93 54 XSQ= 3.95 PHI= -0.128 XP = 0.0468
426	DRIFT MORE TOWARD BEING THOSE 0.65 OF 138 WHERE A HIGH GOD IS PRESENT (156) GES,EA	426	DRIFT LESS TOWARD BEING THOSE 0.54 OF 122 WHERE A HIGH GOD IS PRESENT (156) GES,EA	90 66 48 56 XSQ= 2.89 PHI= 0.105 XP = 0.0892
442	LEAN TOWARD BEING THOSE 0.67 OF 27 WHERE FEAR OF ANIMAL SPIRITS IS HIGH (28) W-C	442	LEAN TOWARD BEING THOSE 0.71 OF 34 WHERE FEAR OF ANIMAL SPIRITS IS LOW (33) W-C	18 10 9 24 XSQ= 6.98 PHI= 0.338 XP = 0.0083

458	DRIFT LESS TOWARD BEING THOSE 0.63 OF 93 WHERE GAMES, IF PRESENT, DO NOT INCLUDE GAMES OF STRATEGY (119) R-A-B,EA	458	DRIFT MORE TOWARD BEING THCSE 0.77 OF 78 WHERE GAMES, IF PRESENT, DO NOT INCLUDE GAMES OF STRATEGY (119) R-A-B,EA	34 18 59 60 XSQ= 3.03 PHI= 0.133 XP = 0.0815
460	DRIFT MORE TOWARD BEING THOSE 0.68 OF 93 WHERE GAMES, IF PRESENT, ARE NOT LIMITED TO GAMES OF SKILL ONLY (104) R-A-B,EA	460	DRIFT LESS TOWARD BEING THCSE 0.53 OF 78 WHERE GAMES, IF PRESENT, ARE NOT LIMITED TO GAMES OF SKILL ONLY (104) R-A-B,EA	30 37 63 41 XSQ= 3.49 PHI= -0.143 XP = 0.0618

237 CULTURES
WHERE THE FAMILY IS
OF THE LARGE EXTENDED TYPE (78)

237 CULTURES
WHERE THE FAMILY IS OTHER THAN
OF THE LARGE EXTENDED TYPE (320)

BACKGROUND ON PAGE 122

SUBJECT ONLY

78 IN LEFT COLUMN

APINAYE	ARYANS	AYMARA	BAMBARA	BELU	BENGALI	BIRIFOR	BOTOCUDO	BOZO	BURYAT
CALLINAGO	CAMAYURA	CHEYENNE	COMANCHE	CREEK	CUNA	DARD	DELAWARE	DOGON	FOX
GOND	GURE	HAIDA	HASINAI	HAVASUPAI	HAWAIIANS	HURON	JIVARO	JUKUN	KALMYK
KASKA	KERALA	KHASI	KIOW-APACHE	KISSI	KORYAK	LIFU	MAGUZAWA	MAMBILA	MANCHU
MAORI	MARSHALLESE	MATAKAM	MINANGKABAU	MISKITO	MONGO	MOSSI	MUNDURUCU	NUPE	ONTONG-JAVA
RAROIANS	RIFFIANS	SAMOANS	SIRIONO	SWAZI	TALAMANCA	TAPIRAPE	TENETEHARA	TERA	TERENA
THONGA	TIMUCUA	TIV	TOKELAU	TORAJA	TRUKESE	TRUMAI	TSHIMSHIAN	TUPINAMBA	TWANA
VENDA	WARCPEN	WARRAU	WOLEAIANS	YAO	YOKUTS	YORUBA	ZUNI		

320 IN RIGHT COLUMN

2 EXCLUDED BECAUSE UNASCERTAINED

4	DRIFT MORE TOWARD BEING THOSE 0.95 OF 78 LOCATED OUTSIDE OF THE CIRCUM-MEDITERRANEAN (355)	4 DRIFT LESS TOWARD BEING THOSE 0.87 OF 320 LOCATED OUTSIDE OF THE CIRCUM-MEDITERRANEAN (355)	4 41 74 279 XSQ= 2.97 PHI= -0.086 XP = 0.0850
46	DRIFT MORE TOWARD BEING THOSE 0.88 OF 65 OTHER THAN WHERE SETTLEMENTS ARE NON-FIXED AND MOVEMENT IS NOMADIC (260)	46 DRIFT LESS TOWARD BEING THOSE 0.76 OF 266 OTHER THAN WHERE SETTLEMENTS ARE NON-FIXED AND MOVEMENT IS NOMADIC (260)	8 64 57 202 XSQ= 3.58 PHI= -0.104 XP = 0.0586
47	TILT TOWARD BEING THOSE 0.58 OF 19 WHERE, IF SETTLEMENTS ARE NON-FIXED, MOVEMENT IS NON-NOMADIC, RATHER THAN NOMADIC (38)	47 TILT TOWARD BEING THOSE 0.70 OF 91 WHERE, IF SETTLEMENTS ARE NON-FIXED, MOVEMENT IS NOMADIC, RATHER THAN NON-NOMADIC (72)	8 64 11 27 XSQ= 4.36 PHI= -0.199 XP = 0.0368
51	DRIFT LESS TOWARD BEING THOSE 0.54 OF 78 WHERE SUBSISTENCE IS PRIMARILY BY FOOD PRODUCTION -- I. E., AGRICULTURE OR HUSBANDRY -- RATHER THAN BY GATHERING (253)	51 DRIFT MORE TOWARD BEING THOSE 0.65 OF 320 WHERE SUBSISTENCE IS PRIMARILY BY FOOD PRODUCTION -- I. E., AGRICULTURE OR HUSBANDRY -- RATHER THAN BY GATHERING (253)	42 209 36 111 XSQ= 3.06 PHI= -0.088 XP = 0.0800

```
53  TILT MORE TOWARD BEING THOSE     0.77 OF  48      53  TILT LESS TOWARD BEING THOSE    0.58 OF 189          11   80
    WHERE FOOD PRODUCTION IS BY                           WHERE FOOD PRODUCTION IS BY                          37  109
    SIMPLE AGRICULTURE OR                                 SIMPLE AGRICULTURE OR                          XSQ=      5.30
    INCIPIENT FOOD PRODUCTION, RATHER THAN BY             INCIPIENT FOOD PRODUCTION, RATHER THAN BY      PHI=    -0.150
    INTENSIVE AGRICULTURE  (147)                          INTENSIVE AGRICULTURE  (147)                   XP =    0.0213

54  TILT LESS TOWARD BEING THOSE     0.69 OF  48      54  TILT MORE TOWARD BEING THOSE    0.84 OF 189          33  158
    WHERE FOOD PRODUCTION IS BY                           WHERE FOOD PRODUCTION IS BY                          15   31
    INTENSIVE OR SIMPLE                                   INTENSIVE OR SIMPLE                            XSQ=      4.49
    AGRICULTURE, RATHER THAN BY                           AGRICULTURE, RATHER THAN BY                    PHI=    -0.138
    INCIPIENT FOOD PRODUCTION  (192)                      INCIPIENT FOOD PRODUCTION  (192)               XP =    0.0341

63  TILT TOWARD BEING THOSE          0.51 OF  39      63  TILT TOWARD BEING THOSE         0.71 OF 186          19  132
    WHERE HUSBANDRY, IF PRESENT,                          WHERE HUSBANDRY, IF PRESENT,                         20   54
    IS PRINCIPALLY IN THE FORM OF                         IS PRINCIPALLY IN THE FORM OF                  XSQ=      6.26
    PIGS, SHEEP, OR GOATS, RATHER THAN                    BOVINE, EQUINE, CAMEL-LIKE, OR DEER-LIKE       PHI=    -0.167
    BOVINE, EQUINE, CAMEL-LIKE, OR DEER-LIKE              ANIMALS, RATHER THAN                           XP =    0.0124
    ANIMALS  (74)                                         PIGS, SHEEP, OR GOATS  (152)

82  TILT MORE TOWARD BEING THOSE     0.95 OF  39      82  TILT LESS TOWARD BEING THOSE    0.76 OF 184          37  140
    WHERE A CITY OR TOWN IS PRESENT, OR                   WHERE A CITY OR TOWN IS PRESENT, OR                   2   44
    THE AVERAGE COMMUNITY SIZE IS                         THE AVERAGE COMMUNITY SIZE IS                  XSQ=      5.84
    FIFTY OR GREATER  (178)                               FIFTY OR GREATER  (178)                        PHI=     0.162
                                                                                                         XP =    0.0157

88  TILT MORE TOWARD BEING THOSE     0.75 OF  59      88  TILT LESS TOWARD BEING THOSE    0.57 OF 211          15   91
    WHERE, IF A HEADMANSHIP IS PRESENT,                   WHERE, IF A HEADMANSHIP IS PRESENT,                  44  120
    SUCCESSION IS HEREDITARY  (165)                       SUCCESSION IS HEREDITARY  (165)                XSQ=      5.34
                                                                                                         PHI=    -0.141
                                                                                                         XP =    0.0208

90  TILT LESS TOWARD BEING THOSE     0.64 OF  44      90  TILT MORE TOWARD BEING THOSE    0.82 OF 120          28   98
    WHERE, IF A HEREDITARY HEADMANSHIP                    WHERE, IF A HEREDITARY HEADMANSHIP                   16   22
    IS PRESENT, SUCCESSION IS                             IS PRESENT, SUCCESSION IS                      XSQ=      4.91
    PATRILINEAL, RATHER THAN                              PATRILINEAL, RATHER THAN                       PHI=    -0.173
    MATRILINEAL  (127)                                    MATRILINEAL  (127)                             XP =    0.0267

94  DRIFT MORE TOWARD BEING THOSE    0.97 OF  64      94  DRIFT LESS TOWARD BEING THOSE   0.88 OF 265           2   32
    WHERE THE HIERARCHY                                   WHERE THE HIERARCHY                                  62  233
    OF NATIONAL JURISDICTION HAS                          OF NATIONAL JURISDICTION HAS                   XSQ=      3.54
    TWO, ONE, OR NO LEVELS  (296) GES,EA                  TWO, ONE, OR NO LEVELS  (296) GES,EA           PHI=    -0.104
                                                                                                         XP =    0.0598

97  TEND LESS TO BE THOSE            0.63 OF  65      97  TEND MORE TO BE THOSE           0.87 OF 265          24   34
    WHERE THE HIERARCHY                                   WHERE THE HIERARCHY                                  41  231
    OF LOCAL JURISDICTION HAS                             OF LOCAL JURISDICTION HAS                      XSQ=     19.28
    THREE OR TWO LEVELS  (273) GES,EA                     THREE OR TWO LEVELS  (273) GES,EA              PHI=     0.242
                                                                                                         XP =    0.0000

98  TEND MORE TO BE THOSE            0.94 OF  65      98  TEND LESS TO BE THOSE           0.66 OF 265          61  176
    WHERE THE HIERARCHY                                   WHERE THE HIERARCHY                                   4   89
    OF LOCAL JURISDICTION HAS                             OF LOCAL JURISDICTION HAS                      XSQ=     18.07
    FOUR OR THREE LEVELS  (238) GES,EA                    FOUR OR THREE LEVELS  (238) GES,EA             PHI=     0.234
                                                                                                         XP =    0.0000
```

99	LEAN MORE TOWARD BEING THOSE WHERE, WITH NATIONAL HIERARCHY ABSENT, THE HIERARCHY OF LOCAL JURISDICTION HAS FOUR OR THREE LEVELS (93) GES,EA	0.86 OF 28	99	LEAN LESS TOWARD BEING THOSE WHERE, WITH NATIONAL HIERARCHY ABSENT, THE HIERARCHY OF LOCAL JURISDICTION HAS FOUR OR THREE LEVELS (93) GES,EA	0.54 OF 128	24 69 4 59 XSQ= 8.38 PHI= 0.232 XP = 0.0038
100	LEAN MORE TOWARD BEING THOSE WHERE HIERARCHIES ARE MORE COMPLEX THAN THE 'SIMPLEST,' I. E., MORE COMPLEX THAN TWO LOCAL LEVELS WITH NO NATIONAL LEVELS (267) GES,EA	0.94 OF 64	100	LEAN LESS TOWARD BEING THOSE WHERE HIERARCHIES ARE MORE COMPLEX THAN THE 'SIMPLEST,' I. E., MORE COMPLEX THAN TWO LOCAL LEVELS WITH NO NATIONAL LEVELS (267) GES,EA	0.78 OF 265	60 206 4 59 XSQ= 7.54 PHI= 0.151 XP = 0.0060
108	DRIFT TOWARD BEING THOSE WHERE CLASS STRATIFICATION, IF PRESENT, IS BASED ON A HEREDITARY ARISTOCRACY (74)	0.50 OF 40	108	DRIFT TOWARD BEING THOSE WHERE CLASS STRATIFICATION, IF PRESENT, IS BASED ON SOMETHING OTHER THAN A HEREDITARY ARISTOCRACY (129)	0.67 OF 163	20 54 20 109 XSQ= 3.25 PHI= 0.127 XP = 0.0713
176	LEAN TOWARD BEING THOSE WHERE THE COMMUNITY IS A CLAN-COMMUNITY OR A COMMUNITY STRUCTURED OR SEGMENTED ON A CLAN BASIS (169)	0.58 OF 76	176	LEAN TOWARD BEING THOSE WHERE THE COMMUNITY IS OTHER THAN A CLAN-COMMUNITY OR A COMMUNITY STRUCTURED OR SEGMENTED ON A CLAN BASIS (213)	0.59 OF 305	44 124 32 181 XSQ= 6.65 PHI= 0.132 XP = 0.0099
178	LEAN LESS TOWARD BEING THOSE WHERE THE COMMUNITY IS OTHER THAN SEGMENTED ON A CLAN BASIS AND NON-EXOGAMOUS (295)	0.63 OF 76	178	LEAN MORE TOWARD BEING THOSE WHERE THE COMMUNITY IS OTHER THAN SEGMENTED ON A CLAN BASIS AND NON-EXOGAMOUS (295)	0.81 OF 305	28 59 48 246 XSQ= 9.60 PHI= 0.159 XP = 0.0019
179	TILT MORE TOWARD BEING THOSE WHERE THE COMMUNITY IS OTHER THAN STRUCTURED ON A NON-CLAN BASIS AND COMMONLY EXOGAMOUS (340)	0.96 OF 76	179	TILT LESS TOWARD BEING THOSE WHERE THE COMMUNITY IS OTHER THAN STRUCTURED ON A NON-CLAN BASIS AND COMMONLY EXOGAMOUS (340)	0.87 OF 305	3 39 73 266 XSQ= 3.99 PHI= -0.102 XP = 0.0458
182	DRIFT MORE TOWARD BEING THOSE OTHER THAN WHERE THE COMMUNITY IS STRUCTURED ON A NON-CLAN BASIS AND AGAMOUS (256)	0.76 OF 76	182	DRIFT LESS TOWARD BEING THOSE OTHER THAN WHERE THE COMMUNITY IS STRUCTURED ON A NON-CLAN BASIS AND AGAMOUS (256)	0.65 OF 305	18 108 58 197 XSQ= 3.27 PHI= -0.093 XP = 0.0706
187	LEAN LESS TOWARD BEING THOSE WHERE THE KIN GROUP IS OTHER THAN EXCLUSIVELY MATRILINEAL (344)	0.76 OF 78	187	LEAN MORE TOWARD BEING THOSE WHERE THE KIN GROUP IS OTHER THAN EXCLUSIVELY MATRILINEAL (344)	0.89 OF 319	19 36 59 283 XSQ= 7.91 PHI= 0.141 XP = 0.0049
190	LEAN LESS TOWARD BEING THOSE WHERE THE KIN GROUP IS PATRILINEAL OR DOUBLE-DESCENT, RATHER THAN MATRILINEAL (186)	0.59 OF 51	190	LEAN MORE TOWARD BEING THOSE WHERE THE KIN GROUP IS PATRILINEAL OR DOUBLE-DESCENT, RATHER THAN MATRILINEAL (186)	0.79 OF 195	30 155 21 40 XSQ= 8.18 PHI= -0.182 XP = 0.0042

192	LEAN MORE TOWARD BEING THOSE 0.86 OF 78 OTHER THAN WHERE THE ONLY KIN GROUP PRESENT IS A KINDRED OR ELSE BILATERAL DESCENT IS INFERRED (289)	192	LEAN LESS TOWARD BEING THOSE 0.69 OF 320 OTHER THAN WHERE THE ONLY KIN GROUP PRESENT IS A KINDRED OR ELSE BILATERAL DESCENT IS INFERRED (289)	11 99 67 221 XSQ= 8.07 PHI= -0.142 XP = 0.0045
198	DRIFT LESS TOWARD BEING THOSE 0.76 OF 29 WHERE RULES FOR THE INHERITANCE OF REAL PROPERTY, IF PRESENT, FAVOR THE MALE HEIR OR LINE, RATHER THAN THE FEMALE (144)	198	DRIFT MORE TOWARD BEING THOSE 0.90 OF 136 WHERE RULES FOR THE INHERITANCE OF REAL PROPERTY, IF PRESENT, FAVOR THE MALE HEIR OR LINE, RATHER THAN THE FEMALE (144)	22 122 7 14 XSQ= 2.97 PHI= -0.134 XP = 0.0847
207	LEAN TOWARD BEING THOSE 0.73 OF 37 WHERE MARITAL RESIDENCE IS MATRILOCAL OR UXORILOCAL, RATHER THAN AMBILOCAL OR NEOLOCAL (64)	207	LEAN TOWARD BEING THOSE 0.59 OF 91 WHERE MARITAL RESIDENCE IS AMBILOCAL OR NEOLOCAL, RATHER THAN MATRILOCAL OR UXORILOCAL (64)	27 37 10 54 XSQ= 9.73 PHI= 0.276 XP = 0.0018
209	TEND LESS TO BE THOSE 0.59 OF 66 WHERE MARITAL RESIDENCE IS PATRILOCAL, VIRILOCAL, OR AVUNCULOCAL, RATHER THAN MATRILOCAL OR UXORILOCAL (270)	209	TEND MORE TO BE THOSE 0.86 OF 266 WHERE MARITAL RESIDENCE IS PATRILOCAL, VIRILOCAL, OR AVUNCULOCAL, RATHER THAN MATRILOCAL OR UXORILOCAL (270)	39 229 27 37 XSQ= 23.07 PHI= -0.264 XP = 0.0000
210	TEND LESS TO BE THOSE 0.66 OF 41 WHERE MARITAL RESIDENCE IS PATRILOCAL, RATHER THAN MATRILOCAL (169)	210	TEND MORE TO BE THOSE 0.89 OF 158 WHERE MARITAL RESIDENCE IS PATRILOCAL, RATHER THAN MATRILOCAL (169)	27 141 14 17 XSQ= 11.82 PHI= -0.244 XP = 0.0006
285	TILT TOWARD BEING THOSE 0.88 OF 8 WHERE THE SEX TABOO DURING PREGNANCY IS ABSENT OR INFERRED ABSENT (17) BCA	285	TILT TOWARD BEING THOSE 0.57 OF 23 WHERE THE SEX TABOO DURING PREGNANCY IS PRESENT (14) BCA	1 13 7 10 XSQ= 3.04 PHI= -0.313 EP = 0.0454
327	TILT TOWARD BEING THOSE 0.76 OF 17 WHERE THE AGE OF THE INFANT AT TIME OF REDUCED CONTACT WITH MOTHER IS HIGHER THAN TWO YEARS (28) B-B-C	327	TILT TOWARD BEING THOSE 0.61 OF 38 WHERE THE AGE OF THE INFANT AT TIME OF REDUCED CONTACT WITH MOTHER IS TWO YEARS OR LOWER (27) B-B-C	13 15 4 23 XSQ= 5.04 PHI= 0.303 XP = 0.0248
385	DRIFT LESS TOWARD BEING THOSE 0.56 OF 18 WHERE SEXUAL EXPRESSION BY THE YOUNG IS SEMI-RESTRICTED OR PERMITTED (64) F-B	385	DRIFT MORE TOWARD BEING THOSE 0.79 OF 68 WHERE SEXUAL EXPRESSION BY THE YOUNG IS SEMI-RESTRICTED OR PERMITTED (64) F-B	8 14 10 54 XSQ= 3.09 PHI= 0.190 XP = 0.0786
391	LEAN TOWARD BEING THOSE 0.75 OF 32 WHERE PREMARITAL SEX RELATIONS ARE PUNISHED ONLY IF PREGNANCY RESULTS, OR FREELY PERMITTED (90) JTW,EA	391	LEAN TOWARD BEING THOSE 0.55 OF 147 WHERE PREMARITAL SEX RELATIONS ARE STRONGLY PUNISHED AND IN FACT RARE, OR WEAKLY PUNISHED AND IN FACT NOT RARE (89) JTW,EA	8 81 24 66 XSQ= 8.36 PHI= -0.216 XP = 0.0038

237/

392 TILT TOWARD BEING THOSE WHERE PREMARITAL SEX RELATIONS ARE FREELY PERMITTED (67) JTW,EA	0.56 OF 32	392 TILT TOWARD BEING THOSE WHERE PREMARITAL SEX RELATIONS ARE STRONGLY PUNISHED AND IN FACT RARE, OR WEAKLY PUNISHED AND IN FACT NOT RARE, OR PUNISHED ONLY IF PREGNANCY RESULTS (112) JTW,EA	0.67 OF 147	14 98 18 49 XSQ= 4.96 PHI= -0.166 XP = 0.0260

238 CULTURES
WHERE THE FAMILY IS
OF THE SMALL EXTENDED TYPE (109)

238 CULTURES
WHERE THE FAMILY IS OTHER THAN
OF THE SMALL EXTENDED TYPE (289)

BACKGROUND ON PAGE 122

SUBJECT ONLY

109 IN LEFT COLUMN

AINU	ALBANIANS	ARAUCANIANS	ASHANTI	ATSUGEWI	BABWA	BACAIRI	BALINESE	BATAK	BETE
BHIL	BOERS	BORORO	BULGARIANS	BURUSHO	CADUVEO	CARAJA	CAYAPA	CHEROKEE	CHIR-APACHE
CHIRIGUANO	CHORTI	COCHITI	COORG	DAGUR	DUTCH	EGYPTIANS	ELLICE	FANG	GUAHIBO
HANO	HANUNOO	HAZARA	HEBREWS	HEHE	HERERO	HUICHOL	HUKUNDIKA	ICELANDERS	ILA
INGASSANA	KABYLE	KACHIN	KAPAUKU	KATAB	KAZAK	KOL	KUBA	KUNG	KWAKIUTL
LAKALAI	LAU	LEPCHA	LUO	MALAYS	MAM	MANDAN	MANGAIANS	MANIHIKI	MARGI
MATACO	MBUGWE	MENDE	MIAO	MIN CHINESE	MINCHIA	MONGUOR	MOTILON	NATCHEZ	NAVAHO
NUER	NUNIVAK	NURI	NYANEKA	ORAON	PAPAGO	PAWNEE	REGEIBAT	SAMOYED	SANTAL
SERBS	SERI	SHLUH	SINDHI	SIWANS	SOMALI	SYRIANS	TALLENSI	TANALA	TANIMBARESE
TAREUMIUT	TEDA	TEHUELCHE	TIMBIRA	TIWI	TURKANA	TURKMEN	TZELTAL	UTE	VEDDA
VIETNAMESE	WICHITA	WINNEBAGO	WOLOF	WUTE	YAKO	YAKUT	YAPESE	YUROK	

289 IN RIGHT COLUMN

2 EXCLUDED BECAUSE UNASCERTAINED

6	DRIFT MORE TOWARD BEING THOSE 0.89 OF 109 LOCATED OUTSIDE OF THE INSULAR PACIFIC (330)	6	DRIFT LESS TOWARD BEING THOSE 0.80 OF 289 LOCATED OUTSIDE OF THE INSULAR PACIFIC (330)	12 57 97 232 XSQ= 3.61 PHI= -0.095 XP = 0.0575
15	LEAN TOWARD BEING THOSE 0.57 OF 109 WHERE THE LATITUDE IS TWENTY DEGREES OR GREATER (183)	15	LEAN TOWARD BEING THOSE 0.59 OF 289 WHERE THE LATITUDE IS LESS THAN TWENTY DEGREES (217)	62 119 47 170 XSQ= 7.25 PHI= 0.135 XP = 0.0071
33	TILT LESS TOWARD BEING THOSE 0.79 OF 109 WHERE THE NATURAL ENVIRONMENT IS OTHER THAN 'VERY HARSH,' I.E., DESERT, DESERT GRASSES AND SHRUBS, TUNDRA, OR HIGH PLATEAU STEPPE (341) FWM	33	TILT MORE TOWARD BEING THOSE 0.88 OF 289 WHERE THE NATURAL ENVIRONMENT IS OTHER THAN 'VERY HARSH,' I.E., DESERT, DESERT GRASSES AND SHRUBS, TUNDRA, OR HIGH PLATEAU STEPPE (341) FWM	23 36 86 253 XSQ= 4.02 PHI= 0.101 XP = 0.0449
53	LEAN TOWARD BEING THOSE 0.52 OF 71 WHERE FOOD PRODUCTION IS BY INTENSIVE AGRICULTURE, RATHER THAN BY SIMPLE AGRICULTURE OR INCIPIENT FOOD PRODUCTION (91)	53	LEAN TOWARD BEING THOSE 0.67 OF 166 WHERE FOOD PRODUCTION IS BY SIMPLE AGRICULTURE OR INCIPIENT FOOD PRODUCTION, RATHER THAN BY INTENSIVE AGRICULTURE (147)	37 54 34 112 XSQ= 7.26 PHI= 0.175 XP = 0.0071

55	LEAN TOWARD BEING THOSE 0.64 OF 58 WHERE FOOD PRODUCTION IS BY INTENSIVE AGRICULTURE, RATHER THAN BY SIMPLE AGRICULTURE (91)	55	LEAN TOWARD BEING THOSE 0.59 OF 133 WHERE FOOD PRODUCTION IS BY SIMPLE AGRICULTURE, RATHER THAN BY INTENSIVE AGRICULTURE (101)	37 54 21 79 XSQ= 7.80 PHI= 0.202 XP = 0.0052
62	DRIFT MORE TOWARD BEING THOSE 0.65 OF 109 WHERE HUSBANDRY OF SOME KIND IS PRESENT (228)	62	DRIFT LESS TOWARD BEING THOSE 0.54 OF 289 WHERE HUSBANDRY OF SOME KIND IS PRESENT (228)	71 156 38 133 XSQ= 3.58 PHI= 0.095 XP = 0.0585
63	TILT MORE TOWARD BEING THOSE 0.79 OF 71 WHERE HUSBANDRY, IF PRESENT, IS PRINCIPALLY IN THE FORM OF BOVINE, EQUINE, CAMEL-LIKE, OR DEER-LIKE ANIMALS, RATHER THAN PIGS, SHEEP, OR GOATS (152)	63	TILT LESS TOWARD BEING THOSE 0.62 OF 154 WHERE HUSBANDRY, IF PRESENT, IS PRINCIPALLY IN THE FORM OF BOVINE, EQUINE, CAMEL-LIKE, OR DEER-LIKE ANIMALS, RATHER THAN PIGS, SHEEP, OR GOATS (152)	56 95 15 59 XSQ= 5.75 PHI= 0.160 XP = 0.0165
83	DRIFT LESS TOWARD BEING THOSE 0.65 OF 48 WHERE, WITH NO CITY AND NO TOWN PRESENT, THE AVERAGE COMMUNITY SIZE IS SMALLER THAN 200, RATHER THAN BETWEEN 200 AND 999 (135)	83	DRIFT MORE TOWARD BEING THOSE 0.79 OF 132 WHERE, WITH NO CITY AND NO TOWN PRESENT, THE AVERAGE COMMUNITY SIZE IS SMALLER THAN 200, RATHER THAN BETWEEN 200 AND 999 (135)	17 28 31 104 XSQ= 3.07 PHI= 0.131 XP = 0.0798
96	TILT TOWARD BEING THOSE 0.62 OF 94 WHERE THE HIERARCHY OF NATIONAL JURISDICTION HAS FOUR, THREE, TWO OR ONE LEVEL (174) GES,EA	96	TILT TOWARD BEING THOSE 0.51 OF 235 WHERE THE HIERARCHY OF NATIONAL JURISDICTION HAS NO LEVELS (156) GES,EA	58 115 36 120 XSQ= 3.89 PHI= 0.109 XP = 0.0485
97	TEND LESS TO BE THOSE 0.69 OF 94 WHERE THE HIERARCHY OF LOCAL JURISDICTION HAS THREE OR TWO LEVELS (273) GES,EA	97	TEND MORE TO BE THOSE 0.88 OF 236 WHERE THE HIERARCHY OF LOCAL JURISDICTION HAS THREE OR TWO LEVELS (273) GES,EA	29 29 65 207 XSQ= 14.73 PHI= 0.211 XP = 0.0001
98	TEND MORE TO BE THOSE 0.94 OF 94 WHERE THE HIERARCHY OF LOCAL JURISDICTION HAS FOUR OR THREE LEVELS (238) GES,EA	98	TEND LESS TO BE THOSE 0.63 OF 236 WHERE THE HIERARCHY OF LOCAL JURISDICTION HAS FOUR OR THREE LEVELS (238) GES,EA	88 149 6 87 XSQ= 29.37 PHI= 0.298 XP = 0.0000
99	LEAN MORE TOWARD BEING THOSE 0.83 OF 36 WHERE, WITH NATIONAL HIERARCHY ABSENT, THE HIERARCHY OF LOCAL JURISDICTION HAS FOUR OR THREE LEVELS (93) GES,EA	99	LEAN LESS TOWARD BEING THOSE 0.52 OF 120 WHERE, WITH NATIONAL HIERARCHY ABSENT, THE HIERARCHY OF LOCAL JURISDICTION HAS FOUR OR THREE LEVELS (93) GES,EA	30 63 6 57 XSQ= 9.69 PHI= 0.249 XP = 0.0019
100	TEND MORE TO BE THOSE 0.94 OF 94 WHERE HIERARCHIES ARE MORE COMPLEX THAN THE 'SIMPLEST,' I. E., MORE COMPLEX THAN TWO LOCAL LEVELS WITH NO NATIONAL LEVELS (267) GES,EA	100	TEND LESS TO BE THOSE 0.76 OF 235 WHERE HIERARCHIES ARE MORE COMPLEX THAN THE 'SIMPLEST,' I. E., MORE COMPLEX THAN TWO LOCAL LEVELS WITH NO NATIONAL LEVELS (267) GES,EA	88 178 6 57 XSQ= 12.72 PHI= 0.197 XP = 0.0004

109	DRIFT LESS TOWARD BEING THOSE 0.80 OF 96 WHERE CASTES ARE ABSENT (317)	109	DRIFT MORE TOWARD BEING THOSE 0.88 OF 270 WHERE CASTES ARE ABSENT (317)	19 32 77 238 XSQ= 3.09 PHI= 0.092 XP = 0.0788
135	DRIFT MORE TOWARD BEING THOSE 0.90 OF 10 WHERE INDIVIDUAL OWNERSHIP OF ECONOMICALLY SIGNIFICANT PROPERTY IS PRESENT (24) GES	135	DRIFT LESS TOWARD BEING THOSE 0.54 OF 28 WHERE INDIVIDUAL OWNERSHIP OF ECONOMICALLY SIGNIFICANT PROPERTY IS PRESENT (24) GES	9 15 1 13 XSQ= 2.78 PHI= 0.271 EP = 0.0594
138	DRIFT TOWARD BEING THOSE 0.88 OF 8 WHERE SUPERORDINATE JUSTICE IS PRESENT (22) BBW	138	DRIFT TOWARD BEING THOSE 0.53 OF 32 WHERE SUPERORDINATE JUSTICE IS ABSENT (18) BBW	7 15 1 17 XSQ= 2.78 PHI= 0.264 EP = 0.0537
179	DRIFT LESS TOWARD BEING THOSE 0.84 OF 104 WHERE THE COMMUNITY IS OTHER THAN STRUCTURED ON A NON-CLAN BASIS AND COMMONLY EXOGAMOUS (340)	179	DRIFT MORE TOWARD BEING THOSE 0.91 OF 277 WHERE THE COMMUNITY IS OTHER THAN STRUCTURED ON A NON-CLAN BASIS AND COMMONLY EXOGAMOUS (340)	17 25 87 252 XSQ= 3.42 PHI= 0.095 XP = 0.0645
183	DRIFT MORE TOWARD BEING THOSE 0.93 OF 74 WHERE THE LARGEST NON-COGNATIC KIN GROUP IS SMALLER THAN A MOEITY, I. E., A PHRATRY OR SIB OR LINEAGE (218)	183	DRIFT LESS TOWARD BEING THOSE 0.84 OF 177 WHERE THE LARGEST NON-COGNATIC KIN GROUP IS SMALLER THAN A MOEITY, I. E., A PHRATRY OR SIB OR LINEAGE (218)	5 29 69 148 XSQ= 3.35 PHI= -0.116 XP = 0.0672
186	TILT LESS TOWARD BEING THOSE 0.54 OF 109 WHERE THE KIN GROUP IS OTHER THAN EXCLUSIVELY PATRILINEAL (250)	186	TILT MORE TOWARD BEING THOSE 0.66 OF 289 WHERE THE KIN GROUP IS OTHER THAN EXCLUSIVELY PATRILINEAL (250)	50 99 59 190 XSQ= 4.08 PHI= 0.101 XP = 0.0435
197	TILT MORE TOWARD BEING THOSE 0.95 OF 55 WHERE RULES FOR THE INHERITANCE OF REAL PROPERTY, IF PRESENT, FAVOR EITHER THE MALE HEIR OR LINE, OR THE FEMALE HEIR OR LINE (165)	197	TILT LESS TOWARD BEING THOSE 0.81 OF 139 WHERE RULES FOR THE INHERITANCE OF REAL PROPERTY, IF PRESENT, FAVOR EITHER THE MALE HEIR OR LINE, OR THE FEMALE HEIR OR LINE (165)	52 113 3 26 XSQ= 4.45 PHI= 0.151 XP = 0.0349
201	TILT MORE TOWARD BEING THOSE 0.92 OF 109 WHERE MARITAL RESIDENCE IS NON-OPTIONAL, RATHER THAN AMBILOCAL OR NEOLOCAL (334)	201	TILT LESS TOWARD BEING THOSE 0.81 OF 287 WHERE MARITAL RESIDENCE IS NON-OPTIONAL, RATHER THAN AMBILOCAL OR NEOLOCAL (334)	100 232 9 55 XSQ= 6.15 PHI= 0.125 XP = 0.0131
204	TILT MORE TOWARD BEING THOSE 0.90 OF 92 WHERE MARITAL RESIDENCE IS PATRILOCAL, VIRILOCAL, OR AVUNCULOCAL, RATHER THAN AMBILOCAL OR NEOLOCAL (270)	204	TILT LESS TOWARD BEING THOSE 0.77 OF 240 WHERE MARITAL RESIDENCE IS PATRILOCAL, VIRILOCAL, OR AVUNCULOCAL, RATHER THAN AMBILOCAL OR NEOLOCAL (270)	83 185 9 55 XSQ= 6.55 PHI= 0.140 XP = 0.0105

255	TILT TOWARD BEING THOSE 0.50 OF 8 WHERE GRANDPARENTAL AUTHORITY OVER PARENTS IS PRESENT (7) CA	255	TILT TOWARD BEING THOSE 0.88 OF 25 WHERE GRANDPARENTAL AUTHORITY OVER PARENTS IS ABSENT (26) DA	4 3 4 22 XSQ= 3.21 PHI= 0.312 EP = 0.0418
284	IN ALL CASES ARE THOSE 1.00 OF 3 WHERE CONTRACEPTION IS NOT PRACTICED (7) CSF	284	DRIFT TOWARD BEING THOSE 0.71 OF 14 WHERE CONTRACEPTION IS PRACTICED (10) CSF	0 10 3 4 XSQ= 2.67 PHI= -0.397 EP = 0.0515
306	DRIFT TOWARD BEING THOSE 0.73 OF 11 WHERE THE EARLY DEPENDENCE SATISFACTION POTENTIAL IS LOW (24) W-C	306	DRIFT TOWARD BEING THOSE 0.61 OF 41 WHERE THE EARLY DEPENDENCE SATISFACTION POTENTIAL IS HIGH (28) W-C	3 25 8 16 XSQ= 2.72 PHI= -0.229 XP = 0.0989
307	TEND TO BE THOSE 0.91 OF 11 WHERE THE EARLY AGGRESSION SATISFACTION POTENTIAL IS LOW (19) W-C	307	TEND TO BE THOSE 0.78 OF 41 WHERE THE EARLY AGGRESSION SATISFACTION POTENTIAL IS HIGH (33) W-C	1 32 10 9 XSQ= 14.94 PHI= -0.536 XP = 0.0001
313	TILT TOWARD BEING THOSE 0.82 OF 11 WHERE AGGRESSION SOCIALIZATION ANXIETY IS HIGH (26) W-C	313	TILT TOWARD BEING THOSE 0.60 OF 43 WHERE AGGRESSION SOCIALIZATION ANXIETY IS LOW (28) W-C	9 17 2 26 XSQ= 4.69 PHI= 0.295 XP = 0.0303
319	LEAN TOWARD BEING THOSE 0.84 OF 19 WHERE PROTECTION OF THE INFANT FROM ENVIRONMENTAL DISCOMFORTS IS HIGH (35) B-B-C	319	LEAN TOWARD BEING THOSE 0.59 OF 46 WHERE PROTECTION OF THE INFANT FROM ENVIRONMENTAL DISCOMFORTS IS LOW (30) B-B-C	16 19 3 27 XSQ= 8.31 PHI= 0.358 XP = 0.0039
344	TILT TOWARD BEING THOSE 0.75 OF 20 WHERE THE TOTAL POSITIVE PRESSURE TOWARD DEVELOPING SELF-RELIANT BEHAVIOR IN THE CHILD IS LOW (40) B-B-C	344	TILT TOWARD BEING THOSE 0.55 OF 56 WHERE THE TOTAL POSITIVE PRESSURE TOWARD DEVELOPING SELF-RELIANT BEHAVIOR IN THE CHILD IS HIGH (36) B-B-C	5 31 15 25 XSQ= 4.30 PHI= -0.238 XP = 0.0382
360	TILT TOWARD BEING THOSE 0.62 OF 13 WHERE ADOLESCENT PEER GROUPS ARE PRESENT IN A SETTING OF WORK AND PUBLIC GATHERINGS AND LEISURE, OR AT LEAST OF PUBLIC GATHERINGS AND LEISURE (14) JKH	360	TILT TOWARD BEING THOSE 0.75 OF 24 WHERE ADOLESCENT PEER GROUPS ARE PRESENT ONLY IN A SETTING OF LEISURE, OR ELSE ARE ABSENT (23) JKH	8 6 5 18 XSQ= 3.36 PHI= 0.301 EP = 0.0395
382	LEAN TOWARD BEING THOSE 0.68 OF 22 WHERE FEMALE INITIATION RITES ARE ABSENT (27) JKB	382	LEAN TOWARD BEING THOSE 0.72 OF 43 WHERE FEMALE INITIATION RITES ARE PRESENT (38) JKB	7 31 15 12 XSQ= 8.13 PHI= -0.354 XP = 0.0043

390	DRIFT LESS TOWARD BEING THOSE 0.63 OF 49 WHERE PREMARITAL SEX RELATIONS ARE WEAKLY PUNISHED AND IN FACT NOT RARE OR PUNISHED ONLY IF PREGNANCY RESULTS, OR FREELY PERMITTED (132) JTW,EA	390	DRIFT MORE TOWARD BEING THOSE 0.78 OF 130 WHERE PREMARITAL SEX RELATIONS ARE WEAKLY PUNISHED AND IN FACT NOT RARE OR PUNISHED ONLY IF PREGNANCY RESULTS, OR FREELY PERMITTED (132) JTW,EA	18 29 31 101 XSQ= 3.12 PHI= 0.132 XP = 0.0775
403	TILT TOWARD BEING THOSE 0.73 OF 11 WHERE EXPLANATIONS OF ILLNESS OF AN ANAL NATURE ARE PRESENT (23) W-C	403	TILT TOWARD BEING THOSE 0.70 OF 50 WHERE EXPLANATIONS OF ILLNESS OF AN ANAL NATURE ARE ABSENT (38) W-C	8 15 3 35 XSQ= 5.31 PHI= 0.295 XP = 0.0212
427	TILT TOWARD BEING THOSE 0.70 OF 47 WHERE A HIGH GOD, IF PRESENT, IS ACTIVE, RATHER THAN INACTIVE (87) GES,EA	427	TILT TOWARD BEING THOSE 0.50 OF 109 WHERE A HIGH GOD, IF PRESENT, IS INACTIVE, RATHER THAN ACTIVE (69) GES,EA	33 54 14 55 XSQ= 4.88 PHI= 0.177 XP = 0.0271
430	DRIFT TOWARD BEING THOSE 0.70 OF 10 WHERE SUPERNATURAL SANCTIONS FOR MORALITY, HAVING AN EFFECT ON AN INDIVIDUAL'S HEALTH, ARE PRESENT (16) GES	430	DRIFT TOWARD BEING THOSE 0.68 OF 28 WHERE SUPERNATURAL SANCTIONS FOR MORALITY, HAVING AN EFFECT ON AN INDIVIDUAL'S HEALTH, ARE ABSENT OR UNREPORTED (22) GES	7 9 3 19 XSQ= 2.92 PHI= 0.277 EP = 0.0623
442	TILT TOWARD BEING THOSE 0.82 OF 11 WHERE FEAR OF ANIMAL SPIRITS IS HIGH (28) W-C	442	TILT TOWARD BEING THOSE 0.62 OF 50 WHERE FEAR OF ANIMAL SPIRITS IS LOW (33) W-C	9 19 2 31 XSQ= 5.32 PHI= 0.295 XP = 0.0211

239 CULTURES WHERE THE FAMILY IS OF THE STEM EXTENDED TYPE (26)

239 CULTURES WHERE THE FAMILY IS OTHER THAN OF THE STEM EXTENDED TYPE (372)

BACKGROUND ON PAGE 122

SUBJECT ONLY

26 IN LEFT COLUMN

ATAYAL	BASQUES	CHINANTEC	CHUKCHEE	CZECHS	GARO	IBAN	IRISH	JAPANESE	JAVANESE
KHALKA	KONSO	KOREANS	LANGO	OJIBWA	OKINAWANS	PAIWAN	PORTUGUESE	PURUM	SANPOIL
TAMIL	TENINO	THAI	TIBETANS	YARURO	YUKAGHIR				

372 IN RIGHT COLUMN

2 EXCLUDED BECAUSE UNASCERTAINED

	Left column (26)			Right column (372)		
3	DRIFT MORE TOWARD BEING THOSE LOCATED OUTSIDE OF AFRICA (320)	0.96 OF 26	3	DRIFT LESS TOWARD BEING THOSE LOCATED OUTSIDE OF AFRICA (320)	0.79 OF 372	1 79 25 293 XSQ= 3.56 PHI= -0.095 XP = 0.0593
5	LEAN LESS TOWARD BEING THOSE LOCATED OUTSIDE OF EAST EURASIA (330)	0.58 OF 26	5	LEAN MORE TOWARD BEING THOSE LOCATED OUTSIDE OF EAST EURASIA (330)	0.84 OF 372	11 59 15 313 XSQ= 9.97 PHI= 0.158 XP = 0.0016
14	TILT TOWARD BEING THOSE WHERE THE LATITUDE IS THIRTY DEGREES OR GREATER (119)	0.50 OF 26	14	TILT TOWARD BEING THOSE WHERE THE LATITUDE IS LESS THAN THIRTY DEGREES (281)	0.72 OF 372	13 106 13 266 XSQ= 4.39 PHI= 0.105 XP = 0.0363
15	TILT TOWARD BEING THOSE WHERE THE LATITUDE IS TWENTY DEGREES OR GREATER (183)	0.69 OF 26	15	TILT TOWARD BEING THOSE WHERE THE LATITUDE IS LESS THAN TWENTY DEGREES (217)	0.56 OF 372	18 163 8 209 XSQ= 5.35 PHI= 0.116 XP = 0.0208
45	DRIFT MORE TOWARD BEING THOSE WHERE SETTLEMENTS, IF FIXED, ARE COMPACT, RATHER THAN NON-COMPACT (149)	0.93 OF 14	45	DRIFT LESS TOWARD BEING THOSE WHERE SETTLEMENTS, IF FIXED, ARE COMPACT, RATHER THAN NON-COMPACT (149)	0.65 OF 207	13 135 1 72 XSQ= 3.37 PHI= 0.123 XP = 0.0666

79	TEND LESS TO BE THOSE WHERE NO CITY IS PRESENT (201)	0.61 OF 18	79	TEND MORE TO BE THOSE WHERE NO CITY IS PRESENT (201)	0.92 OF 205		7 16 11 189 XSQ= 14.09 PHI= 0.251 XP = 0.0002
80	TILT LESS TOWARD BEING THOSE WHERE NO CITY OR TOWN IS PRESENT (185)	0.61 OF 18	80	TILT MORE TOWARD BEING THOSE WHERE NO CITY OR TOWN IS PRESENT (185)	0.85 OF 205		7 31 11 174 XSQ= 5.04 PHI= 0.150 XP = 0.0248
84	LEAN LESS TOWARD BEING THOSE WHERE THE LEVEL OF POLITICAL INTEGRATION IS THE LITTLE STATE, THE MINIMAL STATE, THE AUTONOMOUS COMMUNITY, OR THE FAMILY (262) GPM	0.59 OF 17	84	LEAN MORE TOWARD BEING THOSE WHERE THE LEVEL OF POLITICAL INTEGRATION IS THE LITTLE STATE, THE MINIMAL STATE, THE AUTONOMOUS COMMUNITY, OR THE FAMILY (262) GPM	0.88 OF 285		7 34 10 251 XSQ= 9.34 PHI= 0.176 XP = 0.0022
85	TILT LESS TOWARD BEING THOSE WHERE THE LEVEL OF POLITICAL INTEGRATION IS THE MINIMAL STATE, THE AUTONOMOUS COMMUNITY, OR THE FAMILY (234) GPM	0.53 OF 17	85	TILT MORE TOWARD BEING THOSE WHERE THE LEVEL OF POLITICAL INTEGRATION IS THE MINIMAL STATE, THE AUTONOMOUS COMMUNITY, OR THE FAMILY (234) GPM	0.79 OF 285		8 61 9 224 XSQ= 4.62 PHI= 0.124 XP = 0.0315
94	DRIFT LESS TOWARD BEING THOSE WHERE THE HIERARCHY OF NATIONAL JURISDICTION HAS TWO, ONE, OR NO LEVELS (296) GES,EA	0.75 OF 20	94	DRIFT MORE TOWARD BEING THOSE WHERE THE HIERARCHY OF NATIONAL JURISDICTION HAS TWO, ONE, OR NO LEVELS (296) GES,EA	0.91 OF 309		5 29 15 280 XSQ= 3.40 PHI= 0.102 XP = 0.0651
97	IN ALL CASES ARE THOSE WHERE THE HIERARCHY OF LOCAL JURISDICTION HAS THREE OR TWO LEVELS (273) GES,EA	1.00 OF 20	97	DRIFT LESS TOWARD BEING THOSE WHERE THE HIERARCHY OF LOCAL JURISDICTION HAS THREE OR TWO LEVELS (273) GES,EA	0.81 OF 310		0 58 20 252 XSQ= 3.34 PHI= -0.101 XP = 0.0676
102	DRIFT MORE TOWARD BEING THOSE WHERE CLASS STRATIFICATION IS PRESENT (203)	0.72 OF 25	102	DRIFT LESS TOWARD BEING THOSE WHERE CLASS STRATIFICATION IS PRESENT (203)	0.52 OF 357		18 185 7 172 XSQ= 3.05 PHI= 0.089 XP = 0.0806
107	TEND TO BE THOSE WHERE CLASS STRATIFICATION, IF PRESENT, IS BASED ON OCCUPATIONAL STATUS (43)	0.56 OF 18	107	TEND TO BE THOSE WHERE CLASS STRATIFICATION, IF PRESENT, IS BASED ON SOMETHING OTHER THAN OCCUPATIONAL STATUS (160)	0.82 OF 185		10 33 8 152 XSQ= 11.81 PHI= 0.241 XP = 0.0006
176	TEND MORE TO BE THOSE WHERE THE COMMUNITY IS OTHER THAN A CLAN-COMMUNITY OR A COMMUNITY STRUCTURED OR SEGMENTED ON A CLAN BASIS (213)	0.96 OF 26	176	TEND LESS TO BE THOSE WHERE THE COMMUNITY IS OTHER THAN A CLAN-COMMUNITY OR A COMMUNITY STRUCTURED OR SEGMENTED ON A CLAN BASIS (213)	0.53 OF 355		1 167 25 188 XSQ= 16.63 PHI= -0.209 XP = 0.0000

177	DRIFT MORE TOWARD BEING THOSE 0.96 OF 26 WHERE THE COMMUNITY IS OTHER THAN A SINGLE CLAN-COMMUNITY AND EXOGAMOUS (305)	177	DRIFT LESS TOWARD BEING THOSE 0.79 OF 355 WHERE THE COMMUNITY IS OTHER THAN A SINGLE CLAN-COMMUNITY AND EXOGAMOUS (305)	1 75 25 280 XSQ= 3.51 PHI= -0.096 XP = 0.0609
178	IN ALL CASES ARE THOSE 1.00 OF 26 WHERE THE COMMUNITY IS OTHER THAN SEGMENTED ON A CLAN BASIS AND NON-EXOGAMOUS (295)	178	LEAN LESS TOWARD BEING THOSE 0.75 OF 355 WHERE THE COMMUNITY IS OTHER THAN SEGMENTED ON A CLAN BASIS AND NON-EXOGAMOUS (295)	0 87 26 268 XSQ= 6.93 PHI= -0.135 XP = 0.0085
182	TEND TO BE THOSE 0.65 OF 26 WHERE THE COMMUNITY IS STRUCTURED ON A NON-CLAN BASIS AND AGAMOUS (126)	182	TEND TO BE THOSE 0.69 OF 355 OTHER THAN WHERE THE COMMUNITY IS STRUCTURED ON A NON-CLAN BASIS AND AGAMOUS (256)	17 109 9 246 XSQ= 11.64 PHI= 0.175 XP = 0.0006
188	TILT TOWARD BEING THOSE 0.58 OF 26 WHERE THE KIN GROUP IS EXCLUSIVELY COGNATIC (148)	188	TILT TOWARD BEING THOSE 0.65 OF 372 WHERE THE KIN GROUP IS OTHER THAN EXCLUSIVELY COGNATIC (252)	15 132 11 240 XSQ= 4.24 PHI= 0.103 XP = 0.0396
192	LEAN TOWARD BEING THOSE 0.54 OF 26 WHERE THE ONLY KIN GROUP PRESENT IS A KINDRED OR ELSE BILATERAL DESCENT IS INFERRED (111)	192	LEAN TOWARD BEING THOSE 0.74 OF 372 OTHER THAN WHERE THE ONLY KIN GROUP PRESENT IS A KINDRED OR ELSE BILATERAL DESCENT IS INFERRED (289)	14 96 12 276 XSQ= 8.20 PHI= 0.144 XP = 0.0042
197	DRIFT LESS TOWARD BEING THOSE 0.68 OF 19 WHERE RULES FOR THE INHERITANCE OF REAL PROPERTY, IF PRESENT, FAVOR EITHER THE MALE HEIR OR LINE, OR THE FEMALE HEIR OR LINE (165)	197	DRIFT MORE TOWARD BEING THOSE 0.87 OF 175 WHERE RULES FOR THE INHERITANCE OF REAL PROPERTY, IF PRESENT, FAVOR EITHER THE MALE HEIR OR LINE, OR THE FEMALE HEIR OR LINE (165)	13 152 6 23 XSQ= 3.25 PHI= -0.129 XP = 0.0716
234	TILT MORE TOWARD BEING THOSE 0.75 OF 24 WHERE THE COUSIN TERMINOLOGY IS OF ESKIMO OR HAWAIIAN TYPE, RATHER THAN CROW, OMAHA, OR IROQUOIS TYPE (170)	234	TILT LESS TOWARD BEING THOSE 0.51 OF 296 WHERE THE COUSIN TERMINOLOGY IS OF ESKIMO OR HAWAIIAN TYPE, RATHER THAN CROW, OMAHA, OR IROQUOIS TYPE (170)	6 145 18 151 XSQ= 4.21 PHI= -0.115 XP = 0.0402
242	LEAN LESS TOWARD BEING THOSE 0.56 OF 25 WHERE MARRIAGE IS COMMONLY OR OCCASIONALLY POLYGYNOUS, RATHER THAN MONOGAMOUS (314)	242	LEAN MORE TOWARD BEING THOSE 0.81 OF 370 WHERE MARRIAGE IS COMMONLY OR OCCASIONALLY POLYGYNOUS, RATHER THAN MONOGAMOUS (314)	14 300 11 70 XSQ= 7.56 PHI= -0.138 XP = 0.0060
263	LEAN TOWARD BEING THOSE 0.69 OF 26 WHERE WIVES ARE OBTAINED BY RELATIVELY EASY MEANS, NAMELY BY TOKEN BRIDE-PRICE, GIFT EXCHANGE, ABSENCE OF ANY CONSIDERATION, OR RECEIPT OF DOWRY (162)	263	LEAN TOWARD BEING THOSE 0.61 OF 367 WHERE WIVES ARE OBTAINED BY RELATIVELY DIFFICULT MEANS, NAMELY BY BRIDE-PRICE, BRIDE-SERVICE, OR EXCHANGING A FEMALE RELATIVE (233)	8 224 18 143 XSQ= 7.99 PHI= -0.143 XP = 0.0047

300	IN ALL CASES ARE THCSE WHERE THE POST-PARTUM SEX TABOO LASTS SIX MCNTHS OR LESS (73)	1.00 OF 6	300	DRIFT LESS TOWARD BEING THCSE WHERE THE POST-PARTUM SEX TABOO LASTS SIX MONTHS OR LESS (73)	0.57 OF 118	0 51 6 67 XSQ= 2.80 PHI= -0.150 XP = 0.0942
377	DRIFT MORE TOWARD BEING THOSE WHERE MALE GENITAL MUTILATION IS ABSENT (242)	0.95 OF 20	377	DRIFT LESS TOWARD BEING THCSE WHERE MALE GENITAL MUTILATION IS ABSENT (242)	0.73 OF 304	1 81 19 223 XSQ= 3.58 PHI= -0.105 XP = 0.0586
391	DRIFT TOWARD BEING THCSE WHERE PREMARITAL SEX RELATIONS ARE STRONGLY PUNISHEC AND IN FACT RARE, OR WEAKLY PUNISHED AND IN FACT NCT RARE (89) JTW,EA	0.77 OF 13	391	DRIFT TOWARD BEING THOSE WHERE PREMARITAL SEX RELATICNS ARE PUNISHED ONLY IF PREGNANCY RESULTS, OR FREELY PERMITTED (90) JTW,EA	0.52 OF 166	10 79 3 87 XSQ= 3.06 PHI= 0.131 XP = 0.0803
459	TILT TOWARD BEING THOSE WHERE GAMES, IF PRESENT, INCLUDE GAMES OF CHANCE (82) R-A-B,EA	0.82 OF 11	459	TILT TOWARD BEING THOSE WHERE GAMES, IF PRESENT, DO NOT INCLUDE GAMES OF CHANCE (89) R-A-B,EA	0.54 CF 160	9 73 2 87 XSQ= 4.05 PHI= 0.154 XP = 0.0442
477	IN ALL CASES ARE THCSE WHERE ALCCHOLIC AGGRESSION IS STRONG (15) DH	1.00 OF 3	477	DRIFT TOWARD BEING THOSE WHERE ALCOHOLIC AGGRESSION IS MODERATE OR SLIGHT (19) DH	0.61 CF 31	3 12 0 19 XSQ= 2.05 PHI= 0.246 EP = 0.0760

240 CULTURES WHERE THE FAMILY, IF EXTENDED, IS LARGE, RATHER THAN SMALL OR STEM (78)

240 CULTURES WHERE THE FAMILY, IF EXTENDED, IS SMALL OR STEM, RATHER THAN LARGE (135)

BACKGROUND ON PAGE 122

PREDICATE ONLY

78 IN LEFT COLUMN

APINAYE	ARYANS	AYMARA	BAMBARA	BELU	BENGALI	BIRIFOR	BOTOCUDO	BOZO	BURYAT
CALLINAGO	CAMAYURA	CHEYENNE	COMANCHE	CREEK	CUNA	DARD	DELAWARE	DOGON	FOX
GOND	GURE	HAIDA	HASINAI	HAVASUPAI	HAWAIIANS	HURON	JIVARO	JUKUN	KALMYK
KASKA	KERALA	KHASI	KIOW-APACHE	KISSI	KORYAK	LIFU	MAGUZAWA	MAMBILA	MANCHU
MAORI	MARSHALLESE	MATAKAM	MINANGKABAU	MISKITO	MONGO	MOSSI	MUNDURUCU	NUPE	ONTONG-JAVA
RAROIANS	RIFFIANS	SAMOANS	SIRIONO	SWAZI	TALAMANCA	TAPIRAPE	TENETEHARA	TERA	TERENA
THONGA	TIMUCUA	TIV	TOKELAU	TORAJA	TRUKESE	TRUMAI	TSHIMSHIAN	TUPINAMBA	TWANA
VENDA	WAROPEN	WARRAU	WOLEAIANS	YAO	YOKUTS	YORUBA	ZUNI		

135 IN RIGHT COLUMN

AINU	ALBANIANS	ARAUCANIANS	ASHANTI	ATAYAL	ATSUGEWI	BABWA	BACAIRI	BALINESE	BASQUES
BATAK	BETE	BHIL	BOERS	BORORO	BULGARIANS	BURUSHO	CADUVEO	CARAJA	CAYAPA
CHEROKEE	CHINANTEC	CHIR-APACHE	CHIRIGUANO	CHORTI	CHUKCHEE	COCHITI	COORG	CZECHS	DAGUR
DUTCH	EGYPTIANS	ELLICE	FANG	GARO	GUAHIRO	HANO	HANUNOO	HAZARA	HEBREWS
HEHE	HERERO	HUICHOL	HUKUNDIKA	IBAN	ICELANDERS	ILA	INGASSANA	IRISH	JAPANESE
JAVANESE	KABYLE	KACHIN	KAPAUKU	KATAB	KAZAK	KHALKA	KOL	KONSO	KOREANS
KUBA	KUNG	KWAKIUTL	LAKALAI	LANGO	LAU	LEPCHA	LUO	MALAYS	MAM
MANDAN	MANGAIANS	MANIHIKI	MARGI	MATACO	MBUGWE	MENDE	MIAO	MIN CHINESE	MINCHIA
MONGUOR	MOTILON	NATCHEZ	NAVAHO	NUER	NUNIVAK	NURI	NYANEKA	OJIBWA	OKINAWANS
ORAON	PAIWAN	PAPAGO	PAWNEE	PORTUGUESE	PURUM	REGEIBAT	SAMOYED	SANPOIL	SANTAL
SERBS	SERI	SHLUH	SINDHI	SIWANS	SOMALI	SYRIANS	TALLENSI	TAMIL	TANALA
TANIMBARESE	TAREUMIUT	TEDA	TEHUELCHE	TENINO	THAI	TIBETANS	TIMBIRA	TIWI	TURKANA
TURKMEN	TZELTAL	UTE	VEDDA	VIETNAMESE	WICHITA	WINNEBAGO	WOLOF	WUTE	YAKO
YAKUT	YAPESE	YARURO	YUKAGHIR	YUROK					

185 EXCLUDED BECAUSE IRRELEVANT (SEE RIGHT COLUMN, PARAGRAPH 236)

2 EXCLUDED BECAUSE UNASCERTAINED

241 CULTURES
WHERE THE FAMILY, IF EXTENCEC, IS
LARGE CR SMALL, RATHER THAN
STEM (187)

241 CULTURES
WHERE THE FAMILY, IF EXTENDED, IS
STEM, RATHER THAN
LARGE OR SMALL (26)

BACKGROUND ON PAGE 122

PREDICATE ONLY

187 IN LEFT CCLUMN

AINU	ALBANIANS	APINAYE	ARAUCANIANS	ARYANS	ASHANTI	ATSUGEWI	AYMARA	BABWA	BACAIRI
BALINESE	BAMBARA	BATAK	BELU	BENGALI	BETE	BHIL	BIRIFOR	BOERS	BORORO
BOTOCUDO	BOZC	BULGARIANS	BURUSHO	BURYAT	CADUVEO	CALLINAGO	CAMAYURA	CARAJA	CAYAPA
CHEROKEE	CHEYENNE	CHIR-APACHE	CHIRIGUANO	CHORTI	COCHITI	COMANCHE	COCRG	CREEK	CUNA
DAGUR	DARD	DELAWARE	DOGON	DUTCH	EGYPTIANS	ELLICE	FANG	FOX	GOND
GUAHIBO	GURE	HAICA	HANO	HANUNOO	HASINAI	HAVASUPAI	HAWAIIANS	HAZARA	HEBREWS
HEHE	HERERO	HUICHOL	HUKUNDIKA	HURON	ICELANDERS	ILA	INGASSANA	JIVARO	JUKUN
KABYLE	KACHIN	KALMYK	KAPAUKU	KASKA	KATAB	KAZAK	KERALA	KHASI	KIOW-APACHE
KISSI	KOL	KORYAK	KUBA	KUNG	KWAKIUTL	LAKALAI	LAU	LEPCHA	LIFU
LUO	MAGUZAWA	MALAYS	MAM	MAMBILA	MANCHU	MANDAN	MANGAIANS	MANIHIKI	MAORI
MARGI	MARSHALLESE	MATACO	MATAKAM	MBUGWE	MENDE	MIAO	MIN CHINESE	MINANGKABAU	MINCHIA
MISKITO	MONGO	MONGUOR	MOSSI	MOTILON	MUNDURUCU	NATCHEZ	NAVAHO	NUER	NUNIVAK
NUPE	NURI	NYANEKA	ONTONG-JAVA	ORAON	PAPAGO	PAWNEE	RAROIANS	REGEIBAT	RIFFIANS
SAMOANS	SAMCYED	SANTAL	SERBS	SERI	SHLUH	SINDHI	SIRIONC	SIWANS	SOMALI
SWAZI	SYRIANS	TALAMANCA	TALLENSI	TANALA	TANIMBARESE	TAPIRAPE	TAREUMIUT	TEDA	TEHUELCHE
TENETEHARA	TERA	TERENA	THONGA	TIMBIRA	TIMUCUA	TIV	TIWI	TOKELAU	TORAJA
TRUKESE	TRUMAI	TSHIMSHIAN	TUPINAMBA	TURKANA	TURKMEN	TWANA	TZELTAL	UTE	VEDDA
VENDA	VIETNAMESE	WAROPEN	WARRAU	WICHITA	WINNEBAGO	WOLEAIANS	WOLOF	WUTE	YAKO
YAKUT	YAC	YAPESE	YOKUTS	YORUBA	YUROK	ZUNI			

26 IN RIGHT CCLUMN

ATAYAL	BASQUES	CHINANTEC	CHUKCHEE	CZECHS	GARO	IBAN	IRISH	JAPANESE	JAVANESE
KHALKA	KONSO	KCREANS	LANGO	OJIBWA	OKINAWANS	PAIWAN	PORTUGUESE	PURUM	SANPOIL
TAMIL	TENINC	THAI	TIBETANS	YARURO	YUKAGHIR				

185 EXCLUDED BECAUSE IRRELEVANT (SEE RIGHT COLUMN, PARAGRAPH 236)

2 EXCLUDED BECAUSE UNASCERTAINED

242 CULTURES
WHERE MARRIAGE IS
COMMONLY OR OCCASIONALLY POLYGYNOUS,
RATHER THAN MONOGAMOUS (314)

242 CULTURES
WHERE MARRIAGE IS MONOGAMOUS,
RATHER THAN COMMONLY OR OCCASIONALLY
POLYGYNOUS (81)

BACKGROUND ON PAGE 124

BOTH SUBJECT AND PREDICATE

314 IN LEFT COLUMN

ABIPON	ABOR	AINU	AKHA	ALACALUF	ALBANIANS	ALORESE	AMBA	ARANDA	ARAPESH
ARAUCANIANS	ARYANS	ASHANTI	ATSUGEWI	AWEIKOMA	AZANDE	AZTEC	BABWA	BACAIRI	BALINESE
BAMBARA	BAMILEKE	BANDA	BARABRA	BARI	BASSERI	BATAK	BAYA	BEJA	BELU
BEMBA	BENGALI	BERGDAMA	BETE	BHIL	BIRIFOR	BLACK CARIB	BORORO	BOTOCUDO	BOZO
BUDUMA	BUNLAP	BURUSHO	BURYAT	CADUVEO	CAGABA	CALLINAGO	CAMAYURA	CAMBODIANS	CARAJA
CARIB	CARINYA	CHAGGA	CHERKESS	CHEROKEE	CHEYENNE	CHIBCHA	CHIR-APACHE	CHIRIGUANO	CHOROTI
CHUKCHEE	COMANCHE	CREE	CREEK	CROW	CUNA	DARD	DELAWARE	DIEGUENO	DIERI
DILLING	DOGON	EGYPTIANS	ELLICE	ENGA	EYAK	FANG	FON	FOX	FUTAJALONKE
GANDA	GARO	GILBERTESE	GILYAK	GISU	GOAJIRO	GOND	GROS VENTRE	GUAHIBO	GUATO
GURE	HAIDA	HANUNOO	HASANIA	HASINAI	HAVASUPAI	HAWAIIANS	HAZARA	HEBREWS	HEHE
HERERO	HO	HUICHOL	HUKUNDIKA	ILA	INGALIK	IRAQW	JAVANESE	JIVARO	JUKUN
KABYLE	KACHIN	KALMYK	KAPAUKU	KARIERA	KATAB	KAZAK	KERAKI	KERALA	KHEVSUR
KIKUYU	KIOW-APACHE	KISSI	KOHISTANI	KOL	KONSO	KORYAK	KPE	KUBA	KUMYK
KUNG	KURTATCHI	KUTENAI	KWAKIUTL	LAKALAI	LAKHER	LAMBA	LAMET	LANGO	LAU
LEPCHA	LESU	LHOTA NAGA	LIFU	LOLO	LOZI	LUBA	LUO	MACASSARESE	MAGUZAWA
MALAYS	MAMBILA	MAMVU	MANDAN	MANGAIANS	MANIHIKI	MANUS	MAORI	MARGI	MARICOPA
MASAI	MATACO	MATAKAM	MAZATECO	MBUNDU	MBUTI	MENDE	MERINA	MIAMI	MIAO
MIN CHINESE	MINANGKABAU	MINCHIA	MISKITO	MIWOK	MNONG GAR	MONGO	MONGUOR	MOSSI	MOTA
MOTILON	MUNDURUCU	MURINBATA	MURNGIN	NAMA	NAMBICUARA	NANDI	NASKAPI	NATCHEZ	NAVAHO
NDEMBU	NGONI	NICOBARESE	NOMLAKI	NUER	NUNIVAK	NUPE	NURI	NYAKYUSA	NYANEKA
NYARO	NYORO	OJIBWA	OMAHA	ONA	ONTONG-JAVA	ORAON	PAEZ	PAIWAN	PALAUANS
PAPAGO	PARAUJANO	PATHAN	PAWNEE	PENDE	PENOBSCOT	PONAPEANS	POPOLUCA	PURARI	PURUM
RAROIANS	REGEIBAT	RIFFIANS	ROTINESE	RUNDI	RWALA	SAMOANS	SAMOYED	SANDAWE	SANPOIL
SANTAL	SARAMACCA	SARSI	SELUNG	SEMANG	SENIANG	SHERENTE	SHILLUK	SIMBOESE	SINDHI
SIRIONO	SIUAI	SIWANS	SOMALI	SONGHAI	SOTHO	SUBANUN	SWAZI	SYRIANS	TAGBANUA
TALAMANCA	TALLENSI	TAMIL	TANALA	TANIMBARESE	TARAHUMARA	TAREUMIUT	TEDA	TEHUELCHE	TENDA
TENETEHARA	TENINO	TERA	TERENA	TESO	TETON	THAI	THONGA	TIKOPIA	TIMUCUA
TIV	TIWI	TOKELAU	TOLOWA	TROBRIAND	TRUMAI	TSHIMSHIAN	TUCANO	TUCUNA	TUNEBO
TUPINAMBA	TURKANA	TURKMEN	TWANA	TZELTAL	ULAWANS	UTE	VENDA	VIETNAMESE	WAICA
WANTOAT	WAPISHANA	WAROPEN	WARRAU	WASHO	WICHITA	WIKMUNKAN	WINNEBAGO	WITOTO	WOGEO
WOLOF	WUTE	YABARANA	YAHGAN	YAKO	YAKUT	YAO	YARURO	YOKUTS	YOMBE
YORUBA	YUKAGHIR	YUKI	YUROK						

81 IN RIGHT COLUMN

AMERICANS	ANDAMANESE	APINAYE	ATAYAL	AYMARA	BAJUN	BASQUES	BHUIYA	BOERS	BRAZILIANS
BULGARIANS	BURMESE	CAMBA	CAYAPA	CHAMACOCO	CHENCHU	CHEREMIS	CHINANTEC	CHOCO	CHORTI
COCHITI	COORG	COPR ESKIMO	CZECHS	DAGUR	DOBUANS	DOROBO	DUSUN	DUTCH	HANO
HURON	HUTSUL	IBAN	ICELANDERS	IFUGAO	INCA	INGASSANA	IRISH	JAPANESE	JEMEZ

```
KAREN       KASKA      KET        KHALKA     KHASI        KOREANS    LAPPS      MAM         MANCHU     MARSHALLESE
MAYA        MBUGWE     MENTAWEI   MZAB       NABESNA      OKINAWANS  PALIKUR    PORTUGUESE  PUKAPUKA   ROMANS
ROTUMANS    SAGADA     SEMINOLE   SERBS      SERI         SHLUH      SINHALESE  TAOS        TAPIRAPE   TIGRINYA
TIMBIRA     TORAJA     TRISTAN    TRUKESE    TUBATULABAL  VEDDA      WALLOONS   WOLEAIANS   YAGUA      YAPESE
ZUNI

      3  EXCLUDED BECAUSE IRRELEVANT

MARQUESANS  TIBETANS   TOCA

      2  EXCLUDED BECAUSE UNASCERTAINEC

-----------------------------------------------------------------------------------------------------------------
 3  TEND LESS TO BE THCSE            0.76 OF 314      3  TEND MORE TO BE THOSE            0.95 OF  81         76     4
    LOCATED OUTSIDE CF                                   LOCATED OUTSIDE OF                                 238    77
    AFRICA  (320)                                        AFRICA  (320)                                 XSQ=    13.63
                                                                                                       PHI=    0.186
                                                                                                       XP =   0.0002

 4  TEND MORE TO BE THCSE            0.92 OF 314      4  TEND LESS TO BE THOSE            0.75 OF  81         25    20
    LOCATED CUTSIDE CF                                   LOCATED OUTSIDE OF                                 289    61
    THE CIRCUM-MEDITERRANEAN  (355)                      THE CIRCUM-MEDITERRANEAN  (355)               XSQ=    16.23
                                                                                                       PHI=   -0.203
                                                                                                       XP =   0.0001

12  DRIFT MORE TCWARD BEING THCSE    0.93 OF 314     12  DRIFT LESS TOWARD BEING THCSE    0.86 OF  81         22    11
    WHERE THE LATITUDE IS                                WHERE THE LATITUDE IS                              292    70
    LESS THAN FIFTY DEGREES  (367)                       LESS THAN FIFTY DEGREES  (367)                XSQ=     2.83
                                                                                                       PHI=   -0.085
                                                                                                       XP =   0.0927

13  TILT MORE TOWARD BEING THCSE     0.84 OF 314     13  TILT LESS TOWARD BEING THOSE     0.73 OF  81         49    22
    WHERE THE LATITUDE IS                                WHERE THE LATITUDE IS                              265    59
    LESS THAN FORTY DEGREES  (329)                       LESS THAN FORTY DEGREES  (329)                XSQ=     5.07
                                                                                                       PHI=   -0.113
                                                                                                       XP =   0.0243

14  TILT MORE TOWARD BEING THCSE     0.73 OF 314     14  TILT LESS TOWARD BEING THOSE     0.59 OF  81         85    33
    WHERE THE LATITUDE IS                                WHERE THE LATITUDE IS                              229    48
    LESS THAN THIRTY DEGREES  (281)                      LESS THAN THIRTY DEGREES  (281)               XSQ=     5.11
                                                                                                       PHI=   -0.114
                                                                                                       XP =   0.0238

44  TILT LESS TOWARD BEING THCSE     0.64 OF 267     44  TILT MORE TOWARD BEING THOSE     0.81 OF  62        170    50
    WHERE SETTLEMENTS ARE FIXEC  (222)                   WHERE SETTLEMENTS ARE FIXED  (222)                  97    12
                                                                                                       XSQ=     5.80
                                                                                                       PHI=   -0.133
                                                                                                       XP =   0.0160
```

45	DRIFT LESS TOWARD BEING THOSE 0.64 OF 170 WHERE SETTLEMENTS, IF FIXED, ARE COMPACT, RATHER THAN NON-COMPACT (149)	45	DRIFT MORE TOWARD BEING THOSE 0.78 OF 50 WHERE SETTLEMENTS, IF FIXED, ARE COMPACT, RATHER THAN NON-COMPACT (149)	109 39 61 11 XSQ= 2.78 PHI= -0.112 XP = 0.0954
51	TILT LESS TOWARD BEING THOSE 0.60 OF 314 WHERE SUBSISTENCE IS PRIMARILY BY FOOD PRODUCTION -- I. E., AGRICULTURE OR HUSBANDRY -- RATHER THAN BY GATHERING (253)	51	TILT MORE TOWARD BEING THOSE 0.74 OF 81 WHERE SUBSISTENCE IS PRIMARILY BY FOOD PRODUCTION -- I. E., AGRICULTURE OR HUSBANDRY -- RATHER THAN BY GATHERING (253)	188 60 126 21 XSQ= 4.97 PHI= -0.112 XP = 0.0258
53	LEAN TOWARD BEING THOSE 0.67 OF 186 WHERE FOOD PRODUCTION IS BY SIMPLE AGRICULTURE OR INCIPIENT FOOD PRODUCTION, RATHER THAN BY INTENSIVE AGRICULTURE (147)	53	LEAN TOWARD BEING THOSE 0.58 OF 50 WHERE FOOD PRODUCTION IS BY INTENSIVE AGRICULTURE, RATHER THAN BY SIMPLE AGRICULTURE OR INCIPIENT FOOD PRODUCTION (91)	62 29 124 21 XSQ= 9.11 PHI= -0.196 XP = 0.0025
55	LEAN TOWARD BEING THOSE 0.58 OF 147 WHERE FOOD PRODUCTION IS BY SIMPLE AGRICULTURE, RATHER THAN BY INTENSIVE AGRICULTURE (101)	55	LEAN TOWARD BEING THOSE 0.67 OF 43 WHERE FOOD PRODUCTION IS BY INTENSIVE AGRICULTURE, RATHER THAN BY SIMPLE AGRICULTURE (91)	62 29 85 14 XSQ= 7.53 PHI= -0.199 XP = 0.0061
81	TILT TOWARD BEING THOSE 0.64 OF 170 WHERE NO CITY OR TOWN IS PRESENT, AND THE AVERAGE COMMUNITY SIZE IS SMALLER THAN 200 (135)	81	TILT TOWARD BEING THOSE 0.53 OF 51 WHERE A CITY OR TOWN IS PRESENT, OR THE AVERAGE COMMUNITY SIZE IS 200 OR GREATER (89)	61 27 109 24 XSQ= 4.08 PHI= -0.136 XP = 0.0434
84	TILT MORE TOWARD BEING THOSE 0.89 OF 243 WHERE THE LEVEL OF POLITICAL INTEGRATION IS THE LITTLE STATE, THE MINIMAL STATE, THE AUTONOMOUS COMMUNITY, OR THE FAMILY (262) GPM	84	TILT LESS TOWARD BEING THOSE 0.77 OF 56 WHERE THE LEVEL OF POLITICAL INTEGRATION IS THE LITTLE STATE, THE MINIMAL STATE, THE AUTONOMOUS COMMUNITY, OR THE FAMILY (262) GPM	27 13 216 43 XSQ= 4.76 PHI= -0.126 XP = 0.0292
88	LEAN TOWARD BEING THOSE 0.66 OF 221 WHERE, IF A HEADMANSHIP IS PRESENT, SUCCESSION IS HEREDITARY (165)	88	LEAN TOWARD BEING THOSE 0.61 OF 46 WHERE, IF A HEADMANSHIP IS PRESENT, SUCCESSION IS NON-HEREDITARY (106)	76 28 145 18 XSQ= 10.14 PHI= -0.195 XP = 0.0014
89	TILT LESS TOWARD BEING THOSE 0.51 OF 76 WHERE, IF A NON-HEREDITARY HEADMANSHIP IS PRESENT, SUCCESSION IS BY CONSENSUS (63)	89	TILT MORE TOWARD BEING THOSE 0.79 OF 28 WHERE, IF A NON-HEREDITARY HEADMANSHIP IS PRESENT, SUCCESSION IS BY CONSENSUS (63)	39 22 37 6 XSQ= 5.19 PHI= -0.223 XP = 0.0227
90	DRIFT MORE TOWARD BEING THOSE 0.79 OF 145 WHERE, IF A HEREDITARY HEADMANSHIP IS PRESENT, SUCCESSION IS PATRILINEAL, RATHER THAN MATRILINEAL (127)	90	DRIFT LESS TOWARD BEING THOSE 0.56 OF 18 WHERE, IF A HEREDITARY HEADMANSHIP IS PRESENT, SUCCESSION IS PATRILINEAL, RATHER THAN MATRILINEAL (127)	115 10 30 8 XSQ= 3.81 PHI= 0.153 XP = 0.0509

94	TILT MORE TOWARD BEING THOSE 0.92 OF 268 WHERE THE HIERARCHY OF NATIONAL JURISDICTION HAS TWO, ONE, OR NO LEVELS (296) GES,EA	94	TILT LESS TOWARD BEING THOSE 0.80 OF 59 WHERE THE HIERARCHY OF NATIONAL JURISDICTION HAS TWO, ONE, OR NO LEVELS (296) GES,EA	22 12 246 47 XSQ= 6.39 PHI= -0.140 XP = 0.0115
107	TEND MORE TO BE THOSE 0.86 OF 160 WHERE CLASS STRATIFICATION, IF PRESENT, IS BASED ON SOMETHING OTHER THAN OCCUPATIONAL STATUS (160)	107	TEND LESS TO BE THOSE 0.54 OF 41 WHERE CLASS STRATIFICATION, IF PRESENT, IS BASED ON SOMETHING OTHER THAN OCCUPATIONAL STATUS (160)	23 19 137 22 XSQ= 18.29 PHI= -0.302 XP = 0.0000
108	TEND LESS TO BE THOSE 0.57 OF 160 WHERE CLASS STRATIFICATION, IF PRESENT, IS BASED ON SOMETHING OTHER THAN A HEREDITARY ARISTOCRACY (129)	108	TEND MORE TO BE THOSE 0.88 OF 41 WHERE CLASS STRATIFICATION, IF PRESENT, IS BASED ON SOMETHING OTHER THAN A HEREDITARY ARISTOCRACY (129)	68 5 92 36 XSQ= 11.68 PHI= 0.241 XP = 0.0006
110	TEND LESS TO BE THOSE 0.52 OF 295 WHERE SLAVERY IS ABSENT (218)	110	TEND MORE TO BE THOSE 0.77 OF 81 WHERE SLAVERY IS ABSENT (218)	142 19 153 62 XSQ= 14.82 PHI= 0.199 XP = 0.0001
128	DRIFT TOWARD BEING THOSE 0.55 OF 60 WHERE, IF SUBSISTENCE IS PRIMARILY BY AGRICULTURE, THE WORK IS MAINLY DONE BY FEMALES (37)	128	DRIFT TOWARD BEING THOSE 0.73 OF 15 WHERE, IF SUBSISTENCE IS PRIMARILY BY AGRICULTURE, THE WORK IS MAINLY DONE BY MALES (40)	27 11 33 4 XSQ= 2.80 PHI= -0.193 XP = 0.0940
129	TILT LESS TOWARD BEING THOSE 0.66 OF 85 WHERE WEAVING IS MAINLY DONE BY FEMALES (73)	129	TILT MORE TOWARD BEING THOSE 0.94 OF 17 WHERE WEAVING IS MAINLY DONE BY FEMALES (73)	29 1 56 16 XSQ= 4.16 PHI= 0.202 XP = 0.0413
136	TILT TOWARD BEING THOSE 0.63 OF 27 WHERE FULL-TIME ENTREPRENEURS ARE PRESENT (18) JV	136	IN ALL CASES ARE THOSE 1.00 OF 4 WHERE FULL-TIME ENTREPRENEURS ARE ABSENT (14) JV	17 0 10 4 XSQ= 3.32 PHI= 0.327 EP = 0.0318
148	TILT LESS TOWARD BEING THOSE 0.52 OF 25 WHERE THE INCIDENCE OF PERSONAL CRIME IS LOW (21) B-B-C	148	IN ALL CASES ARE THOSE 1.00 OF 8 WHERE THE INCIDENCE OF PERSONAL CRIME IS LOW (21) B-B-C	12 0 13 8 XSQ= 4.14 PHI= 0.354 EP = 0.0159
176	DRIFT LESS TOWARD BEING THOSE 0.53 OF 299 WHERE THE COMMUNITY IS OTHER THAN A CLAN-COMMUNITY OR A COMMUNITY STRUCTURED OR SEGMENTED ON A CLAN BASIS (213)	176	DRIFT MORE TOWARD BEING THOSE 0.66 OF 79 WHERE THE COMMUNITY IS OTHER THAN A CLAN-COMMUNITY OR A COMMUNITY STRUCTURED OR SEGMENTED ON A CLAN BASIS (213)	140 27 159 52 XSQ= 3.56 PHI= 0.097 XP = 0.0594

177	TILT LESS TOWARD BEING THOSE 0.78 OF 299 WHERE THE COMMUNITY IS OTHER THAN A SINGLE CLAN-COMMUNITY AND EXOGAMOUS (305)	177	TILT MORE TOWARD BEING THOSE 0.90 OF 79 WHERE THE COMMUNITY IS OTHER THAN A SINGLE CLAN-COMMUNITY AND EXOGAMOUS (305)	67 8 232 71 XSQ= 5.18 PHI= 0.117 XP = 0.0229
179	DRIFT LESS TOWARD BEING THOSE 0.87 OF 299 WHERE THE COMMUNITY IS OTHER THAN STRUCTURED ON A NON-CLAN BASIS AND COMMONLY EXOGAMOUS (340)	179	DRIFT MORE TOWARD BEING THOSE 0.95 OF 79 WHERE THE COMMUNITY IS OTHER THAN STRUCTURED ON A NON-CLAN BASIS AND COMMONLY EXOGAMOUS (340)	38 4 261 75 XSQ= 2.97 PHI= 0.089 XP = 0.0851
180	LEAN LESS TOWARD BEING THOSE 0.64 OF 299 WHERE THE COMMUNITY IS COMMONLY NON-EXOGAMOUS, RATHER THAN EXOGAMOUS (258)	180	LEAN MORE TOWARD BEING THOSE 0.84 OF 79 WHERE THE COMMUNITY IS COMMONLY NON-EXOGAMOUS, RATHER THAN EXOGAMOUS (258)	109 13 190 66 XSQ= 10.54 PHI= 0.167 XP = 0.0012
181	TILT MORE TOWARD BEING THOSE 0.90 OF 299 WHERE THE COMMUNITY IS OTHER THAN A DEME (337)	181	TILT LESS TOWARD BEING THOSE 0.81 OF 79 WHERE THE COMMUNITY IS OTHER THAN A DEME (337)	30 15 269 64 XSQ= 3.96 PHI= -0.102 XP = 0.0466
182	DRIFT MORE TOWARD BEING THOSE 0.70 OF 299 OTHER THAN WHERE THE COMMUNITY IS STRUCTURED ON A NON-CLAN BASIS AND AGAMOUS (256)	182	DRIFT LESS TOWARD BEING THOSE 0.58 OF 79 OTHER THAN WHERE THE COMMUNITY IS STRUCTURED ON A NON-CLAN BASIS AND AGAMOUS (256)	91 33 208 46 XSQ= 3.15 PHI= -0.091 XP = 0.0760
186	TEND LESS TO BE THOSE 0.58 OF 314 WHERE THE KIN GROUP IS OTHER THAN EXCLUSIVELY PATRILINEAL (250)	186	TEND MORE TO BE THOSE 0.79 OF 81 WHERE THE KIN GROUP IS OTHER THAN EXCLUSIVELY PATRILINEAL (250)	131 17 183 64 XSQ= 10.94 PHI= 0.166 XP = 0.0009
188	TILT MORE TOWARD BEING THOSE 0.66 OF 314 WHERE THE KIN GROUP IS OTHER THAN EXCLUSIVELY COGNATIC (252)	188	TILT LESS TOWARD BEING THOSE 0.52 OF 81 WHERE THE KIN GROUP IS OTHER THAN EXCLUSIVELY COGNATIC (252)	107 39 207 42 XSQ= 4.88 PHI= -0.111 XP = 0.0271
190	LEAN MORE TOWARD BEING THOSE 0.79 OF 203 WHERE THE KIN GROUP IS PATRILINEAL OR DOUBLE-DESCENT, RATHER THAN MATRILINEAL (186)	190	LEAN LESS TOWARD BEING THOSE 0.56 OF 41 WHERE THE KIN GROUP IS PATRILINEAL OR DOUBLE-DESCENT, RATHER THAN MATRILINEAL (186)	160 23 43 18 XSQ= 8.22 PHI= 0.184 XP = 0.0041
192	TEND MORE TO BE THOSE 0.77 OF 314 OTHER THAN WHERE THE ONLY KIN GROUP PRESENT IS A KINDRED OR ELSE BILATERAL DESCENT IS INFERRED (289)	192	TEND LESS TO BE THOSE 0.56 OF 81 OTHER THAN WHERE THE ONLY KIN GROUP PRESENT IS A KINDRED OR ELSE BILATERAL DESCENT IS INFERRED (289)	73 36 241 45 XSQ= 13.44 PHI= -0.184 XP = 0.0002

196	TILT LESS TOWARD BEING THOSE 0.65 OF 222 WHERE INDIVIDUAL RIGHTS IN REAL PROPERTY, AND RULES FOR INHERITANCE, ARE PRESENT (194)	196	TILT MORE TOWARD BEING THOSE 0.84 OF 56 WHERE INDIVIDUAL RIGHTS IN REAL PROPERTY, AND RULES FOR INHERITANCE, ARE PRESENT (194)	145 47 77 9 XSQ= 6.41 PHI= -0.152 XP = 0.0114
197	TEND MORE TO BE THOSE 0.91 OF 145 WHERE RULES FOR THE INHERITANCE OF REAL PROPERTY, IF PRESENT, FAVOR EITHER THE MALE HEIR OR LINE, OR THE FEMALE HEIR OR LINE (165)	197	TEND LESS TO BE THOSE 0.68 OF 47 WHERE RULES FOR THE INHERITANCE OF REAL PROPERTY, IF PRESENT, FAVOR EITHER THE MALE HEIR OR LINE, OR THE FEMALE HEIR OR LINE (165)	132 32 13 15 XSQ= 13.22 PHI= 0.262 XP = 0.0003
201	TEND MORE TO BE THOSE 0.88 OF 312 WHERE MARITAL RESIDENCE IS NON-OPTIONAL, RATHER THAN AMBILOCAL OR NEOLOCAL (334)	201	TEND LESS TO BE THOSE 0.69 OF 81 WHERE MARITAL RESIDENCE IS NON-OPTIONAL, RATHER THAN AMBILOCAL OR NEOLOCAL (334)	273 56 39 25 XSQ= 14.59 PHI= 0.193 XP = 0.0001
204	TEND MORE TO BE THOSE 0.85 OF 266 WHERE MARITAL RESIDENCE IS PATRILOCAL, VIRILOCAL, OR AVUNCULOCAL, RATHER THAN AMBILOCAL OR NEOLOCAL (270)	204	TEND LESS TO BE THOSE 0.60 OF 63 WHERE MARITAL RESIDENCE IS PATRILOCAL, VIRILOCAL, OR AVUNCULOCAL, RATHER THAN AMBILOCAL OR NEOLOCAL (270)	227 38 39 25 XSQ= 18.79 PHI= 0.239 XP = 0.0000
209	TILT MORE TOWARD BEING THOSE 0.83 OF 273 WHERE MARITAL RESIDENCE IS PATRILOCAL, VIRILOCAL, OR AVUNCULOCAL, RATHER THAN MATRILOCAL OR UXORILOCAL (270)	209	TILT LESS TOWARD BEING THOSE 0.68 OF 56 WHERE MARITAL RESIDENCE IS PATRILOCAL, VIRILOCAL, OR AVUNCULOCAL, RATHER THAN MATRILOCAL OR UXORILOCAL (270)	227 38 46 18 XSQ= 5.99 PHI= 0.135 XP = 0.0144
210	TEND MORE TO BE THOSE 0.89 OF 166 WHERE MARITAL RESIDENCE IS PATRILOCAL, RATHER THAN MATRILOCAL (169)	210	TEND LESS TO BE THOSE 0.58 OF 31 WHERE MARITAL RESIDENCE IS PATRILOCAL, RATHER THAN MATRILOCAL (169)	148 18 18 13 XSQ= 16.77 PHI= 0.292 XP = 0.0000
213	TILT LESS TOWARD BEING THOSE 0.51 OF 298 WHERE FIRST COUSIN MARRIAGE IS NOT PERMITTED (198)	213	TILT MORE TOWARD BEING THOSE 0.69 OF 67 WHERE FIRST COUSIN MARRIAGE IS NOT PERMITTED (198)	147 21 151 46 XSQ= 6.42 PHI= 0.133 XP = 0.0113
220	LEAN LESS TOWARD BEING THOSE 0.71 OF 298 WHERE FIRST COUSIN MARRIAGE IN SOME FORM OR OTHER IS NOT PRESCRIBED OR PREFERRED (273)	220	LEAN MORE TOWARD BEING THOSE 0.88 OF 67 WHERE FIRST COUSIN MARRIAGE IN SOME FORM OR OTHER IS NOT PRESCRIBED OR PREFERRED (273)	86 8 212 59 XSQ= 7.33 PHI= 0.142 XP = 0.0068
221	DRIFT LESS TOWARD BEING THOSE 0.89 OF 298 WHERE MATRILATERAL CROSS-COUSIN MARRIAGE IS NOT PRESCRIBED OR PREFERRED (335)	221	DRIFT MORE TOWARD BEING THOSE 0.97 OF 67 WHERE MATRILATERAL CROSS-COUSIN MARRIAGE IS NOT PRESCRIBED OR PREFERRED (335)	33 2 265 65 XSQ= 3.25 PHI= 0.094 XP = 0.0715

234	LEAN TOWARD BEING THOSE 0.51 OF 249 WHERE THE COUSIN TERMINOLOGY IS OF CROW, OMAHA, OR IROQUOIS TYPE, RATHER THAN ESKIMO OR HAWAIIAN TYPE (152)	234 LEAN TOWARD BEING THOSE 0.68 OF 68 WHERE THE COUSIN TERMINOLOGY IS OF ESKIMO OR HAWAIIAN TYPE, RATHER THAN CROW, OMAHA, OR IROQUOIS TYPE (170)	128 22 121 46 XSQ= 7.03 PHI= 0.149 XP = 0.0080
241	LEAN MORE TOWARD BEING THOSE 0.92 OF 170 WHERE THE FAMILY, IF EXTENDED, IS LARGE OR SMALL, RATHER THAN STEM (187)	241 LEAN LESS TOWARD BEING THOSE 0.74 OF 42 WHERE THE FAMILY, IF EXTENDED, IS LARGE OR SMALL, RATHER THAN STEM (187)	156 31 14 11 XSQ= 8.78 PHI= 0.204 XP = 0.0030
254	TILT TOWARD BEING THOSE 0.75 OF 12 WHERE HOUSEHOLD AUTHORITY IS ON THE FATHER'S SIDE, RATHER THAN THE MOTHER'S (9) CA	254 IN ALL CASES ARE THOSE 1.00 OF 3 WHERE HOUSEHOLD AUTHORITY IS ON THE MOTHER'S SIDE, RATHER THAN THE FATHER'S (6) DA	9 0 3 3 XSQ= 2.93 PHI= 0.442 EP = 0.0440
259	DRIFT TOWARD BEING THOSE 0.64 OF 39 WHERE THE SEVERITY OF MOTHER-IN-LAW AVOIDANCE IS HIGH (26) WNS	259 DRIFT TOWARD BEING THOSE 0.83 OF 6 WHERE THE SEVERITY OF MOTHER-IN-LAW AVOIDANCE IS LOW (20) WNS	25 1 14 5 XSQ= 3.05 PHI= 0.260 XP = 0.0808
262	TEND MORE TO BE THOSE 0.82 OF 309 WHERE WIVES ARE OBTAINED BY MEANS INVOLVING THE PRESENCE OF SOME CONSIDERATION (305)	262 TEND LESS TO BE THOSE 0.59 OF 81 WHERE WIVES ARE OBTAINED BY MEANS INVOLVING THE PRESENCE OF SOME CONSIDERATION (305)	253 48 56 33 XSQ= 17.38 PHI= 0.211 XP = 0.0000
263	TEND TO BE THOSE 0.66 OF 309 WHERE WIVES ARE OBTAINED BY RELATIVELY DIFFICULT MEANS, NAMELY BY BRIDE-PRICE, BRIDE-SERVICE, OR EXCHANGING A FEMALE RELATIVE (233)	263 TEND TO BE THOSE 0.67 OF 81 WHERE WIVES ARE OBTAINED BY RELATIVELY EASY MEANS, NAMELY BY TOKEN BRIDE-PRICE, GIFT EXCHANGE, ABSENCE OF ANY CONSIDERATION, OR RECEIPT OF DOWRY (162)	205 27 104 54 XSQ= 27.66 PHI= 0.266 XP = 0.0000
277	DRIFT LESS TOWARD BEING THOSE 0.55 OF 29 WHERE THE STATUS OF WOMEN IS NOT STRONGLY INFERIOR OR SUBJECTED (22) LWS	277 IN ALL CASES ARE THOSE 1.00 OF 6 WHERE THE STATUS OF WOMEN IS NOT STRONGLY INFERIOR OR SUBJECTED (22) LWS	13 0 16 6 XSQ= 2.57 PHI= 0.271 EP = 0.0645
295	TILT TOWARD BEING THOSE 0.61 OF 18 WHERE THE SEVERITY OF PUNISHMENT FOR ABORTION IS HIGH (11) BCA	295 IN ALL CASES ARE THOSE 1.00 OF 5 WHERE THE SEVERITY OF PUNISHMENT FOR ABORTION IS LOW OR ABSENT (12) BCA	11 0 7 5 XSQ= 3.66 PHI= 0.399 EP = 0.0373
299	TILT LESS TOWARD BEING THOSE 0.67 OF 102 WHERE THE POST-PARTUM SEX TABOO LASTS ONE YEAR OR LESS (89)	299 TILT MORE TOWARD BEING THOSE 0.95 OF 20 WHERE THE POST-PARTUM SEX TABOO LASTS ONE YEAR OR LESS (89)	34 1 68 19 XSQ= 5.25 PHI= 0.207 XP = 0.0220

314	TILT LESS TOWARC BEING THCSE 0.69 OF 62 WHERE THE INCIDENCE CF MCTHER-CHILC HCUSEHCLDS IS LCW (61) W-C,S	314	IN ALL CASES ARE THOSE 1.00 OF 17 WHERE THE INCIDENCE OF MOTHER-CHILD HOUSEHOLDS IS LOW (61) W-D,S	19 0 43 17 XSQ= 5.28 PHI= 0.259 XP = 0.0215
316	TILT TCWARD BEING THOSE 0.53 OF 34 WHERE EXCLUSIVE MOTHER-SCN SLEEPING ARRANGEMENTS LAST CNE YEAR OR LCNGER (19) W-K-A	316	TILT TOWARD BEING THOSE 0.90 OF 10 WHERE EXCLUSIVE MOTHER-SCN SLEEPING ARRANGEMENTS LAST LESS THAN ONE YEAR (25) W-K-A	18 1 16 9 XSQ= 4.19 PHI= 0.309 XP = 0.0407
324	DRIFT TCWARD BEING THCSE 0.56 OF 55 WHERE THE PAIN INFLICTEC ON THE INFANT BY THE NURTURANT AGENT IS HIGH (34) B-B-C	324	DRIFT TOWARD BEING THOSE 0.80 CF 10 WHERE THE PAIN INFLICTED ON THE INFANT BY THE NURTURANT AGENT IS LOW OR NEGLIGIBLE (32) B-B-C	31 2 24 8 XSQ= 3.14 PHI= 0.220 XP = 0.0764
326	TILT TCWARD BEING THOSE 0.58 OF 57 WHERE THE INFERRED TRANSITION ANXIETY BETWEEN INFANCY ANC CHILCHCOC IS LCW (35) B-B-C	326	TILT TOWARD BEING THOSE 0.89 OF 9 WHERE THE INFERRED TRANSITICN ANXIETY BETWEEN INFANCY AND CHILDHCCD IS HIGH (32) B-B-C	24 8 33 1 XSQ= 5.07 PHI= -0.277 XP = 0.0244
327	DRIFT TCWARD BEING THCSE 0.58 OF 45 WHERE THE AGE OF THE INFANT AT TIME CF REDUCED CONTACT WITH MOTHER IS HIGHER THAN TWO YEARS (28) B-B-C	327	DRIFT TOWARD BEING THOSE 0.80 CF 10 WHERE THE AGE OF THE INFANT AT TIME OF REDUCED CONTACT WITH MCTHER IS TWO YEARS OR LOWER (27) B-B-C	26 2 19 8 XSQ= 3.28 PHI= 0.244 XP = 0.0700
330	DRIFT TCWARD BEING THOSE 0.55 OF 58 WHERE THE AGE CF THE INFANT AT TIME CF WEANING IS 2.5 YEARS CR HIGHER (34) B-B-C	330	DRIFT TOWARD BEING THOSE 0.82 OF 11 WHERE THE AGE OF THE INFANT AT TIME OF WEANING IS LOWER THAN 2.5 YEARS (36) B-B-C	32 2 26 9 XSQ= 3.69 PHI= 0.231 XP = 0.0547
369	DRIFT TCWARD BEING THCSE 0.79 OF 48 WHERE DISSCCIATICN CF THE SEXES AT ADCLESCENCE, CR CUSTOMS CF INITIATION AT ACOLESCENCE, ARE PRESENT (42) JKH	369	DRIFT TOWARD BEING THOSE 0.56 CF 9 WHERE BOTH DISSOCIATION CF THE SEXES AT ADOLESCENCE, AND CUSTOMS OF INITIATION AT ADOLESCENCE, ARE ABSENT (15) JKH	38 4 10 5 XSQ= 3.09 PHI= 0.233 XP = 0.0787
370	LEAN LESS TCWARC BEING THCSE 0.56 OF 189 WHERE THE SEGREGATION CF ACOLESCENT BOYS IS ABSENT (148)	370	LEAN MORE TOWARD BEING THOSE 0.78 CF 51 WHERE THE SEGREGATION OF ADCLESCENT BOYS IS ABSENT (148)	84 11 105 40 XSQ= 7.86 PHI= 0.181 XP = 0.0051
377	LEAN LESS TOWARC BEING THCSE 0.71 OF 261 WHERE MALE GENITAL MUTILATION IS ABSENT (242)	377	LEAN MORE TCWARD BEING THCSE 0.90 CF 61 WHERE MALE GENITAL MUTILATICN IS ABSENT (242)	75 6 186 55 XSQ= 8.40 PHI= 0.162 XP = 0.0037

398	TILT TOWARD BEING THOSE 0.59 OF 27 WHERE THE INTENSITY OF SEX ANXIETY IS HIGH (16) WNS	398	IN ALL CASES ARE THOSE 1.00 OF 4 WHERE THE INTENSITY OF SEX ANXIETY IS LOW (16) WNS	16 0 11 4 XSQ= 2.81 PHI= 0.301 EP = 0.0434
404	DRIFT LESS TOWARD BEING THOSE 0.62 OF 47 WHERE EXPLANATIONS OF ILLNESS OF A SEXUAL NATURE ARE ABSENT (42) W-C	404	DRIFT MORE TOWARD BEING THOSE 0.92 OF 13 WHERE EXPLANATIONS OF ILLNESS OF A SEXUAL NATURE ARE ABSENT (42) W-C	18 1 29 12 XSQ= 3.11 PHI= 0.228 XP = 0.0779
419	LEAN TOWARD BEING THOSE 0.73 OF 66 WHERE MILITARY GLORY IS STRONGLY OR MODERATELY EMPHASIZED (55) PES	419	LEAN TOWARD BEING THOSE 0.63 OF 19 WHERE MILITARY GLORY IS NEGLIGIBLY EMPHASIZED (31) PES	48 7 18 12 XSQ= 6.82 PHI= 0.283 XP = 0.0090
420	TILT TOWARD BEING THOSE 0.55 OF 65 WHERE BELLICOSITY IS EXTREME (41) PES	420	TILT TOWARD BEING THOSE 0.80 OF 20 WHERE BELLICOSITY IS MODERATE OR NEGLIGIBLE (46) PES	36 4 29 16 XSQ= 6.33 PHI= 0.273 XP = 0.0119
428	TILT LESS TOWARD BEING THOSE 0.63 OF 68 WHERE A HIGH GOD, IF PRESENT AND ACTIVE, SUPPORTS HUMAN MORALITY, RATHER THAN NOT SUPPORTING IT (61) GES,EA	428	TILT MORE TOWARD BEING THOSE 0.95 OF 19 WHERE A HIGH GOD, IF PRESENT AND ACTIVE, SUPPORTS HUMAN MORALITY, RATHER THAN NOT SUPPORTING IT (61) GES,EA	43 18 25 1 XSQ= 5.61 PHI= -0.254 XP = 0.0179
447	DRIFT TOWARD BEING THOSE 0.70 OF 27 WHERE LOVE MAGIC IS PRESENT (20) S-R	447	DRIFT TOWARD BEING THOSE 0.80 OF 5 WHERE LOVE MAGIC IS ABSENT (13) S-R	19 1 8 4 XSQ= 2.67 PHI= 0.289 EP = 0.0531
472	TILT TOWARD BEING THOSE 0.60 OF 68 WHERE THE COMPOSITE NARCISSISM INDEX IS HIGH (47) PES	472	TILT TOWARD BEING THOSE 0.75 OF 20 WHERE THE COMPOSITE NARCISSISM INDEX IS LOW (43) PES	41 5 27 15 XSQ= 6.37 PHI= 0.269 XP = 0.0116
473	TILT LESS TOWARD BEING THOSE 0.56 OF 66 WHERE SENSITIVITY TO INSULT IS MODERATE OR NEGLIGIBLE (56) PES	473	TILT MORE TOWARD BEING THOSE 0.90 OF 20 WHERE SENSITIVITY TO INSULT IS MODERATE OR NEGLIGIBLE (56) PES	29 2 37 18 XSQ= 6.27 PHI= 0.270 XP = 0.0123

243 CULTURES
WHERE POLYGYNY, IF PRESENT,
HAS A HIGH INCIDENCE (24) W-D,S

243 CULTURES
WHERE POLYGYNY, IF PRESENT,
HAS A LOW INCIDENCE (36) W-D,S

BACKGROUND ON PAGE 124 — BOTH SUBJECT AND PREDICATE

24 IN LEFT COLUMN

ARANDA	ARAPESH	ARAUCANIANS	AZANDE	BEMBA	BHIL	FON	GANDA	JIVARO	KAPAUKU
KURTATCHI	MENDE	MURNGIN	NAMBICUARA	NUER	NYAKYUSA	RIFFIANS	SIRIONO	TALLENSI	TANALA
THONGA	TIV	VENDA	WOGEO						

36 IN RIGHT COLUMN

ALORESE	ASHANTI	BALINESE	CAGABA	CAMAYURA	CARIB	CHIR-APACHE	COMANCHE	COPR ESKIMO	EGYPTIANS
GILYAK	KAZAK	KORYAK	KUTENAI	LAMBA	LAU	LEPCHA	MANUS	MAORI	MUNDURUCU
NAMA	NAVAHO	OJIBWA	PAPAGO	SAMOANS	SENIANG	SIUAI	TARAHUMARA	THAI	TIKOPIA
TODA	TROBRIAND	TRUKESE	TURKANA	YAGUA	YUROK				

340 EXCLUDED BECAUSE UNASCERTAINED

	Left column			Right column		Statistics
3	LEAN LESS TOWARD BEING THOSE LOCATED OUTSIDE OF AFRICA (320)	0.54 OF 24	3	LEAN MORE TOWARD BEING THOSE LOCATED OUTSIDE OF AFRICA (320)	0.89 OF 36	11 4 13 32 XSQ= 7.50 PHI= 0.354 XP = 0.0062
8	IN ALL CASES ARE THOSE LOCATED OUTSIDE OF NORTH AMERICA (330)	1.00 OF 24	8	TILT LESS TOWARD BEING THOSE LOCATED OUTSIDE OF NORTH AMERICA (330)	0.75 OF 36	0 9 24 27 XSQ= 5.23 PHI= -0.295 XP = 0.0221
13	IN ALL CASES ARE THOSE WHERE THE LATITUDE IS LESS THAN FORTY DEGREES (329)	1.00 OF 24	13	DRIFT LESS TOWARD BEING THOSE WHERE THE LATITUDE IS LESS THAN FORTY DEGREES (329)	0.81 OF 36	0 7 24 29 XSQ= 3.56 PHI= -0.244 XP = 0.0590
14	DRIFT MORE TOWARD BEING THOSE WHERE THE LATITUDE IS LESS THAN THIRTY DEGREES (281)	0.92 OF 24	14	DRIFT LESS TOWARD BEING THOSE WHERE THE LATITUDE IS LESS THAN THIRTY DEGREES (281)	0.67 OF 36	2 12 22 24 XSQ= 3.73 PHI= -0.249 XP = 0.0534

51	TILT TOWARD BEING THOSE WHERE SUBSISTENCE IS PRIMARILY BY FOOD PRODUCTION -- I. E., AGRICULTURE OR HUSBANDRY -- RATHER THAN BY GATHERING (253)	0.79 OF 24	51	TILT TOWARD BEING THOSE WHERE SUBSISTENCE IS PRIMARILY BY FOOD GATHERING -- I. E., HUNTING, FISHING, OR COLLECTING -- RATHER THAN FOOD PRODUCTION (147)	0.56 OF 36	19 16 5 20 XSQ= 5.79 PHI= 0.311 XP = 0.0162
54	TILT MORE TOWARD BEING THOSE WHERE FOOD PRODUCTION IS BY INTENSIVE OR SIMPLE AGRICULTURE, RATHER THAN BY INCIPIENT FOOD PRODUCTION (192)	0.95 OF 19	54	TILT LESS TOWARD BEING THOSE WHERE FOOD PRODUCTION IS BY INTENSIVE OR SIMPLE AGRICULTURE, RATHER THAN BY INCIPIENT FOOD PRODUCTION (192)	0.62 OF 21	18 13 1 8 XSQ= 4.43 PHI= 0.333 EP = 0.0214
56	TILT MORE TOWARD BEING THOSE WHERE FOOD PRODUCTION IS BY SIMPLE AGRICULTURE, RATHER THAN BY INCIPIENT FOOD PRODUCTION (101)	0.92 OF 12	56	TILT LESS TOWARD BEING THOSE WHERE FOOD PRODUCTION IS BY SIMPLE AGRICULTURE, RATHER THAN BY INCIPIENT FOOD PRODUCTION (101)	0.53 OF 17	11 9 1 8 XSQ= 3.29 PHI= 0.337 EP = 0.0432
71	DRIFT TOWARD BEING THOSE WHERE METAL WORKING IS PRESENT (98)	0.57 OF 23	71	DRIFT TOWARD BEING THOSE WHERE METAL WORKING IS ABSENT (153)	0.73 OF 30	13 8 10 22 XSQ= 3.68 PHI= 0.264 XP = 0.0550
127	DRIFT TOWARD BEING THOSE WHERE THE FEMALES' CONTRIBUTION TO SUBSISTENCE IS HIGH (33) JKB	0.73 OF 15	127	DRIFT TOWARD BEING THOSE WHERE THE FEMALES' CONTRIBUTION TO SUBSISTENCE IS LOW (32) JKB	0.58 OF 19	11 8 4 11 XSQ= 2.17 PHI= 0.253 EP = 0.0915
176	DRIFT TOWARD BEING THOSE WHERE THE COMMUNITY IS A CLAN-COMMUNITY OR A COMMUNITY STRUCTURED OR SEGMENTED ON A CLAN BASIS (169)	0.67 OF 24	176	DRIFT TOWARD BEING THOSE WHERE THE COMMUNITY IS OTHER THAN A CLAN-COMMUNITY OR A COMMUNITY STRUCTURED OR SEGMENTED ON A CLAN BASIS (213)	0.61 OF 36	16 14 8 22 XSQ= 3.40 PHI= 0.238 XP = 0.0651
182	DRIFT MORE TOWARD BEING THOSE OTHER THAN WHERE THE COMMUNITY IS STRUCTURED ON A NON-CLAN BASIS AND AGAMOUS (256)	0.88 OF 24	182	DRIFT LESS TOWARD BEING THOSE OTHER THAN WHERE THE COMMUNITY IS STRUCTURED ON A NON-CLAN BASIS AND AGAMOUS (256)	0.64 OF 36	3 13 21 23 XSQ= 2.99 PHI= -0.223 XP = 0.0840
186	DRIFT TOWARD BEING THOSE WHERE THE KIN GROUP IS EXCLUSIVELY PATRILINEAL (150)	0.54 OF 24	186	DRIFT TOWARD BEING THOSE WHERE THE KIN GROUP IS OTHER THAN EXCLUSIVELY PATRILINEAL (250)	0.72 OF 36	13 10 11 26 XSQ= 3.20 PHI= 0.231 XP = 0.0737
188	TILT MORE TOWARD BEING THOSE WHERE THE KIN GROUP IS OTHER THAN EXCLUSIVELY COGNATIC (252)	0.92 OF 24	188	TILT LESS TOWARD BEING THOSE WHERE THE KIN GROUP IS OTHER THAN EXCLUSIVELY COGNATIC (252)	0.58 OF 36	2 15 22 21 XSQ= 6.32 PHI= -0.325 XP = 0.0119

192	TILT MORE TOWARD BEING THOSE OTHER THAN WHERE THE ONLY KIN GROUP PRESENT IS A KINDRED OR ELSE BILATERAL DESCENT IS INFERRED (289)	0.96 OF 24	192	TILT LESS TOWARD BEING THOSE OTHER THAN WHERE THE ONLY KIN GROUP PRESENT IS A KINDRED OR ELSE BILATERAL DESCENT IS INFERRED (289)	0.72 OF 36	 XSQ= PHI= XP =	1 10 23 26 3.90 -0.255 0.0483
234	TILT TOWARD BEING THOSE WHERE THE COUSIN TERMINOLOGY IS OF CROW, OMAHA, OR IROQUOIS TYPE, RATHER THAN ESKIMO OR HAWAIIAN TYPE (152)	0.82 OF 17	234	TILT TOWARD BEING THOSE WHERE THE COUSIN TERMINOLOGY IS OF ESKIMO OR HAWAIIAN TYPE, RATHER THAN CROW, OMAHA, OR IROQUOIS TYPE (170)	0.57 OF 30	 XSQ= PHI= XP =	14 13 3 17 5.26 0.334 0.0219
254	IN ALL CASES ARE THOSE WHERE HOUSEHOLD AUTHORITY IS ON THE FATHER'S SIDE, RATHER THAN THE MOTHER'S (9) CA	1.00 OF 5	254	TILT TOWARD BEING THOSE WHERE HOUSEHOLD AUTHORITY IS ON THE MOTHER'S SIDE, RATHER THAN THE FATHER'S (6) DA	0.75 OF 4	 XSQ= PHI= EP =	5 1 0 3 2.76 0.553 0.0476
260	DRIFT LESS TOWARD BEING THOSE WHERE THE AGE OF MALES AT MARRIAGE IS LESS THAN TWENTY (38) JKH	0.53 OF 15	260	DRIFT MORE TOWARD BEING THOSE WHERE THE AGE OF MALES AT MARRIAGE IS LESS THAN TWENTY (38) JKH	0.88 OF 16	 XSQ= PHI= EP =	8 14 7 2 2.88 -0.305 0.0538
263	DRIFT MORE TOWARD BEING THOSE WHERE WIVES ARE OBTAINED BY RELATIVELY DIFFICULT MEANS, NAMELY BY BRIDE-PRICE, BRIDE-SERVICE, OR EXCHANGING A FEMALE RELATIVE (233)	0.79 OF 24	263	DRIFT LESS TOWARD BEING THOSE WHERE WIVES ARE OBTAINED BY RELATIVELY DIFFICULT MEANS, NAMELY BY BRIDE-PRICE, BRIDE-SERVICE, OR EXCHANGING A FEMALE RELATIVE (233)	0.53 OF 36	 XSQ= PHI= XP =	19 19 5 17 3.26 0.233 0.0711
279	IN ALL CASES ARE THOSE WHERE WIFE-LENDING OR WIFE-EXCHANGE IS PRESENT (10) LWS	1.00 OF 3	279	TILT TOWARD BEING THOSE WHERE WIFE-LENDING AND WIFE EXCHANGE ARE UNIMPORTANT OR ABSENT (19) LWS	0.83 OF 6	 XSQ= PHI= EP =	3 1 0 5 2.76 0.553 0.0476
306	TILT TOWARD BEING THOSE WHERE THE EARLY DEPENDENCE SATISFACTION POTENTIAL IS HIGH (28) W-C	0.90 OF 10	306	TILT TOWARD BEING THOSE WHERE THE EARLY DEPENDENCE SATISFACTION POTENTIAL IS LOW (24) W-C	0.59 OF 17	 XSQ= PHI= EP =	9 7 1 10 4.36 0.402 0.0183
314	TEND TO BE THOSE WHERE THE INCIDENCE OF MOTHER-CHILD HOUSEHOLDS IS HIGH (19) W-D,S	0.65 OF 23	314	TEND TO BE THOSE WHERE THE INCIDENCE OF MOTHER-CHILD HOUSEHOLDS IS LOW (61) W-D,S	0.91 OF 32	 XSQ= PHI= XP =	15 3 8 29 16.50 0.548 0.0000
316	TILT TOWARD BEING THOSE WHERE EXCLUSIVE MOTHER-SON SLEEPING ARRANGEMENTS LAST ONE YEAR OR LONGER (19) W-K-A	0.75 OF 12	316	TILT TOWARD BEING THOSE WHERE EXCLUSIVE MOTHER-SON SLEEPING ARRANGEMENTS LAST LESS THAN ONE YEAR (25) W-K-A	0.68 OF 19	 XSQ= PHI= EP =	9 6 3 13 3.95 0.357 0.0290

No.	Left-hand item	Ratio	No.	Right-hand item	Ratio	Statistics
319	TILT TOWARD BEING THOSE WHERE PROTECTION OF THE INFANT FROM ENVIRONMENTAL DISCOMFORTS IS LOW (30) B-B-C	0.67 OF 15	319	TILT TOWARD BEING THOSE WHERE PROTECTION OF THE INFANT FROM ENVIRONMENTAL DISCOMFORTS IS HIGH (35) B-B-C	0.72 OF 18	5 13 10 5 XSQ= 3.55 PHI= -0.328 EP = 0.0383
324	LEAN TOWARD BEING THOSE WHERE THE PAIN INFLICTED ON THE INFANT BY THE NURTURANT AGENT IS HIGH (34) B-B-C	0.86 OF 14	324	LEAN TOWARD BEING THOSE WHERE THE PAIN INFLICTED ON THE INFANT BY THE NURTURANT AGENT IS LOW OR NEGLIGIBLE (32) B-B-C	0.75 OF 20	12 5 2 15 XSQ= 9.84 PHI= 0.538 EP = 0.0013
331	DRIFT TOWARD BEING THOSE WHERE THE AGE AT BEGINNING OF INDEPENDENCE TRAINING IS 3.8 YEARS OR HIGHER (16) W-C	0.63 OF 8	331	DRIFT TOWARD BEING THOSE WHERE THE AGE AT BEGINNING OF INDEPENDENCE TRAINING IS LOWER THAN 3.8 YEARS (21) W-C	0.86 OF 14	5 2 3 12 XSQ= 3.46 PHI= 0.397 EP = 0.0524
335	TILT TOWARD BEING THOSE WHERE INITIAL INDULGENCE OF DEPENDENCY IS HIGH (20) WNS	0.90 OF 10	335	TILT TOWARD BEING THOSE WHERE INITIAL INDULGENCE OF DEPENDENCY IS LOW (18) WNS	0.56 OF 16	9 7 1 9 XSQ= 3.78 PHI= 0.381 EP = 0.0367
370	DRIFT TOWARD BEING THOSE WHERE THE SEGREGATION OF ADOLESCENT BOYS IS COMPLETE OR PARTIAL (95)	0.65 OF 23	370	DRIFT TOWARD BEING THOSE WHERE THE SEGREGATION OF ADOLESCENT BOYS IS ABSENT (148)	0.63 OF 27	15 10 8 17 XSQ= 2.90 PHI= 0.241 XP = 0.0887
377	DRIFT LESS TOWARD BEING THOSE WHERE MALE GENITAL MUTILATION IS ABSENT (242)	0.63 OF 24	377	DRIFT MORE TOWARD BEING THOSE WHERE MALE GENITAL MUTILATION IS ABSENT (242)	0.85 OF 34	9 5 15 29 XSQ= 2.84 PHI= 0.221 XP = 0.0917
386	TILT TOWARD BEING THOSE WHERE SEXUAL EXPRESSION BY THE YOUNG IS RESTRICTED OR SEMI-RESTRICTED (46) F-B	0.90 OF 10	386	TILT TOWARD BEING THOSE WHERE SEXUAL EXPRESSION BY THE YOUNG IS PERMITTED (40) F-B	0.58 OF 24	9 10 1 14 XSQ= 4.87 PHI= 0.379 EP = 0.0204
441	TILT TOWARD BEING THOSE WHERE FEAR OF HUMAN BEINGS IS HIGH (29) W-C	0.69 OF 13	441	TILT TOWARD BEING THOSE WHERE FEAR OF HUMAN BEINGS IS LOW (32) W-C	0.72 OF 18	9 5 4 13 XSQ= 3.70 PHI= 0.345 EP = 0.0325
443	DRIFT TOWARD BEING THOSE WHERE OVERALL FEAR OF OTHERS IS HIGH (31) W-C	0.62 OF 13	443	DRIFT TOWARD BEING THOSE WHERE OVERALL FEAR OF OTHERS IS LOW (30) W-C	0.72 OF 18	8 5 5 13 XSQ= 2.28 PHI= 0.271 EP = 0.0785

452	LEAN TOWARD BEING THOSE WHERE TOTEMISM WITH FOOD TABOOS IS PRESENT (19) WNS	0.73 OF 11	452	LEAN TOWARD BEING THOSE WHERE TOTEMISM WITH FOOD TABOOS IS ABSENT (24) WNS	0.80 OF 20	8 4 3 16 XSQ= 6.24 PHI= 0.449 EP = 0.0070
458	DRIFT TOWARD BEING THOSE WHERE GAMES, IF PRESENT, INCLUDE GAMES OF STRATEGY (52) R-A-B,EA	0.56 OF 16	458	DRIFT TOWARD BEING THOSE WHERE GAMES, IF PRESENT, DO NOT INCLUDE GAMES OF STRATEGY (119) R-A-B,EA	0.74 OF 27	9 7 7 20 XSQ= 2.76 PHI= 0.253 XP = 0.0965

244 CULTURES
WHERE MARRIAGE, IF COMMONLY POLYGYNOUS, IS PREFERENTIALLY SORORAL, RATHER THAN NOT PREFERENTIALLY SORORAL (44)

244 CULTURES
WHERE MARRIAGE, IF COMMONLY POLYGYNOUS, IS NOT PREFERENTIALLY SORORAL, RATHER THAN PREFERENTIALLY SORORAL (108)

BACKGROUND ON PAGE 124

SUBJECT ONLY

44 IN LEFT COLUMN

ARANDA	ATSUGEWI	BANCA	BEMBA	BERGDAMA	BOTOCUDO	CHEYENNE	CHIR-APACHE	COMANCHE	CROW
DIEGUENO	DIERI	FOX	GONC	GROS VENTRE	GUATO	HUKUNDIKA	KARIERA	KIOW-APACHE	KURTATCHI
LAKALAI	LAU	LUC	MANCAN	MANGAIANS	MIAMI	MIWOK	MOTA	MURNGIN	NATCHEZ
NAVAHO	PAPAGO	PAWNEE	POPOLUCA	SARSI	SENIANG	SIRIONO	SWAZI	TETON	THONGA
VENDA	WARRAU	WICHITA	WIKMUNKAN						

108 IN RIGHT COLUMN

ALBANIANS	AMBA	ARAPESH	ARAUCANIANS	ARYANS	ASHANTI	AWEIKOMA	AZANDE	BABWA	BAMBARA
BAMILEKE	BARI	BAYA	BELU	BETE	BIRIFOR	BOZO	BUDUMA	CHAGGA	CHERKESS
CHIBCHA	CHUKCHEE	CARC	DILLING	EYAK	FANG	FON	FUTAJALONKE	GANCA	GISU
GOAJIRO	HASANIA	HEBREWS	HEHE	HERERO	HO	ILA	JIVARO	KAPAUKU	KATAB
KAZAK	KERAKI	KIKUYU	KISSI	KONSO	KPE	LANGO	LHOTA NAGA	LIFU	LOZI
LUBA	MAGUZAWA	MAMVU	MAORI	MARGI	MASAI	MBUNDU	MENDE	MONGO	MOSSI
MOTILON	MURINBATA	NDEMBU	NGONI	NUER	NUPE	NURI	NYAKYUSA	NYANEKA	NYORO
ONA	PAEZ	PENDE	PURARI	ROTINESE	RUNDI	RWALA	SANPOIL	SARAMACCA	SHILLUK
SOMALI	SOTHO	TALLENSI	TANALA	TEDA	TENINO	TERA	TESO	TIKOPIA	TIV
TIWI	TOLOWA	TSHIMSHIAN	TUNEBO	TUPINAMBA	TURKANA	VIETNAMESE	WANTOAT	WAPISHANA	WOGEO
WOLOF	WUTE	YAKO	YAKUT	YOKUTS	YOMBE	YORUBA	YUROK		

246 EXCLUDED BECAUSE IRRELEVANT

2 EXCLUDED BECAUSE UNASCERTAINED

---

3 TEND TO BE THOSE LOCATED OUTSIDE OF AFRICA (320) — 0.84 OF 44

3 TEND TO BE THOSE LOCATED IN AFRICA (80) — 0.50 OF 108

```
    7   54
   37   54
XSQ=  13.74
PHI=  -0.301
XP =  0.0002
```

4 IN ALL CASES ARE THOSE LOCATED OUTSIDE OF THE CIRCUM-MEDITERRANEAN (355) — 1.00 OF 44

4 TILT LESS TOWARD BEING THOSE LOCATED OUTSIDE OF THE CIRCUM-MEDITERRANEAN (355) — 0.89 OF 108

```
    0   12
   44   96
XSQ=   3.89
PHI=  -0.160
XP =  0.0486
```

6	DRIFT LESS TCWARC BEING THOSE LOCATED CUTSIDE OF THE INSULAR PACIFIC (330)	0.75 OF 44	6	DRIFT MORE TOWARD BEING THCSE LOCATED OUTSIDE OF THE INSULAR PACIFIC (330)	0.88 OF 108	11 13 33 95 XSQ= 3.04 PHI= 0.141 XP = 0.0814
8	TEND LESS TC BE THCSE LCCATED CUTSIDE CF NCRTH AMERICA (330)	0.52 OF 44	8	TEND MORE TO BE THOSE LOCATED OUTSIDE OF NORTH AMERICA (330)	0.94 CF 108	21 7 23 101 XSQ= 32.70 PHI= 0.464 XP = 0.
15	TEND TO BE THCSE WHERE THE LATITUDE IS TWENTY DEGREES CR GREATER (183)	0.66 OF 44	15	TEND TO BE THOSE WHERE THE LATITUDE IS LESS THAN TWENTY DEGREES (217)	0.74 CF 108	29 28 15 80 XSQ= 19.65 PHI= 0.360 XP = 0.0000
36	TEND TC BE THCSE WHERE THE NATURAL ENVIRONMENT IS 'VERY HARSH,' CR SUB-TROPICAL BUSH, OR TEMPERATE GRASSLANC (108) FWM	0.50 OF 44	36	TEND TO BE THOSE WHERE THE NATURAL ENVIRONMENT IS OTHER THAN 'VERY HARSH,' OR SUB-TROPICAL BUSH, OR TEMPERATE GRASSLAND (292) FWM	0.79 CF 108	22 23 22 85 XSQ= 11.02 PHI= 0.269 XP = 0.0009
44	TEND TC BE THCSE WHERE SETTLEMENTS ARE NCN-FIXEC (110)	0.66 OF 38	44	TEND TO BE THOSE WHERE SETTLEMENTS ARE FIXED (222)	0.70 CF 91	13 64 25 27 XSQ= 13.07 PHI= -0.318 XP = 0.0003
46	LEAN LESS TOWARC BEING THOSE CTHER THAN WHERE SETTLEMENTS ARE NCN-FIXED AND MCVEMENT IS NOMADIC (260)	0.55 OF 38	46	LEAN MORE TOWARD BEING THOSE OTHER THAN WHERE SETTLEMENTS ARE NON-FIXED AND MOVEMENT IS NOMADIC (260)	0.81 CF 91	17 17 21 74 XSQ= 8.08 PHI= 0.250 XP = 0.0045
51	TEND TC BE THCSE WHERE SUBSISTENCE IS PRIMARILY BY FCCD GATHERING -- I. E., HUNTING, FISHING, CR CCLLECTING -- RATHER THAN FCCD PRODUCTICN (147)	0.64 OF 44	51	TEND TO BE THOSE WHERE SUBSISTENCE IS PRIMARILY BY FOOD PRODUCTION -- I. E., AGRICULTURE OR HUSBANDRY -- RATHER THAN BY GATHERING (253)	0.77 OF 108	16 83 28 25 XSQ= 20.82 PHI= -0.370 XP = 0.0000
62	DRIFT TCWARD BEING THCSE WHERE HUSBANDRY CF ANY KINC IS ABSENT (172)	0.52 OF 44	62	DRIFT TOWARD BEING THOSE WHERE HUSBANDRY OF SOME KIND IS PRESENT (228)	0.64 OF 108	21 69 23 39 XSQ= 2.75 PHI= -0.134 XP = 0.0976
71	TEND TC BE THCSE WHERE METAL WCRKING IS ABSENT (153)	0.86 OF 35	71	TEND TO BE THOSE WHERE METAL WORKING IS PRESENT (98)	0.63 OF 67	5 42 30 25 XSQ= 19.77 PHI= -0.440 XP = 0.0000

73	TILT MORE TOWARD BEING THOSE 0.80 OF 35 WHERE WEAVING IS ABSENT (130)	73	TILT LESS TOWARD BEING THOSE 0.54 OF 67 WHERE WEAVING IS ABSENT (130)	7 31 28 36 XSQ= 5.71 PHI= -0.237 XP = 0.0169
81	TILT MORE TOWARD BEING THOSE 0.80 OF 20 WHERE NO CITY OR TOWN IS PRESENT, AND THE AVERAGE COMMUNITY SIZE IS SMALLER THAN 200 (135)	81	TILT LESS TOWARD BEING THOSE 0.52 OF 62 WHERE NO CITY OR TOWN IS PRESENT, AND THE AVERAGE COMMUNITY SIZE IS SMALLER THAN 200 (135)	4 30 16 32 XSQ= 3.92 PHI= -0.219 XP = 0.0477
84	TILT MORE TOWARD BEING THOSE 0.97 OF 38 WHERE THE LEVEL OF POLITICAL INTEGRATION IS THE LITTLE STATE, THE MINIMAL STATE, THE AUTONOMOUS COMMUNITY, OR THE FAMILY (262) GPM	84	TILT LESS TOWARD BEING THOSE 0.79 OF 81 WHERE THE LEVEL OF POLITICAL INTEGRATION IS THE LITTLE STATE, THE MINIMAL STATE, THE AUTONOMOUS COMMUNITY, OR THE FAMILY (262) GPM	1 17 37 64 XSQ= 5.43 PHI= -0.214 XP = 0.0197
85	TEND MORE TO BE THOSE 0.95 OF 38 WHERE THE LEVEL OF POLITICAL INTEGRATION IS THE MINIMAL STATE, THE AUTONOMOUS COMMUNITY, OR THE FAMILY (234) GPM	85	TEND LESS TO BE THOSE 0.63 OF 81 WHERE THE LEVEL OF POLITICAL INTEGRATION IS THE MINIMAL STATE, THE AUTONOMOUS COMMUNITY, OR THE FAMILY (234) GPM	2 30 36 51 XSQ= 11.72 PHI= -0.314 XP = 0.0006
95	DRIFT MORE TOWARD BEING THOSE 0.87 OF 38 WHERE THE HIERARCHY OF NATIONAL JURISDICTION HAS ONE OR NO LEVELS (254) GES,EA	95	DRIFT LESS TOWARD BEING THOSE 0.69 OF 91 WHERE THE HIERARCHY OF NATIONAL JURISDICTION HAS ONE OR NO LEVELS (254) GES,EA	5 28 33 63 XSQ= 3.49 PHI= -0.165 XP = 0.0617
97	TILT MORE TOWARD BEING THOSE 0.95 OF 38 WHERE THE HIERARCHY OF LOCAL JURISDICTION HAS THREE OR TWO LEVELS (273) GES,EA	97	TILT LESS TOWARD BEING THOSE 0.76 OF 91 WHERE THE HIERARCHY OF LOCAL JURISDICTION HAS THREE OR TWO LEVELS (273) GES,EA	2 22 36 69 XSQ= 5.14 PHI= -0.200 XP = 0.0233
98	DRIFT LESS TOWARD BEING THOSE 0.61 OF 38 WHERE THE HIERARCHY OF LOCAL JURISDICTION HAS FOUR OR THREE LEVELS (238) GES,EA	98	DRIFT MORE TOWARD BEING THOSE 0.77 OF 91 WHERE THE HIERARCHY OF LOCAL JURISDICTION HAS FOUR OR THREE LEVELS (238) GES,EA	23 70 15 21 XSQ= 2.81 PHI= -0.148 XP = 0.0935
100	TILT LESS TOWARD BEING THOSE 0.68 OF 38 WHERE HIERARCHIES ARE MORE COMPLEX THAN THE 'SIMPLEST,' I. E., MORE COMPLEX THAN TWO LOCAL LEVELS WITH NO NATIONAL LEVELS (267) GES,EA	100	TILT MORE TOWARD BEING THOSE 0.86 OF 91 WHERE HIERARCHIES ARE MORE COMPLEX THAN THE 'SIMPLEST,' I. E., MORE COMPLEX THAN TWO LOCAL LEVELS WITH NO NATIONAL LEVELS (267) GES,EA	26 78 12 13 XSQ= 4.08 PHI= -0.178 XP = 0.0433
102	LEAN TOWARD BEING THOSE 0.66 OF 44 WHERE CLASS STRATIFICATION IS ABSENT (180)	102	LEAN TOWARD BEING THOSE 0.64 OF 104 WHERE CLASS STRATIFICATION IS PRESENT (203)	15 67 29 37 XSQ= 10.32 PHI= -0.264 XP = 0.0013

109	LEAN MORE TOWARD BEING THOSE WHERE CASTES ARE ABSENT (317)	0.98 OF 43	109	LEAN LESS TOWARD BEING THOSE WHERE CASTES ARE ABSENT (317)	0.79 OF 104	1 22 42 82 XSQ= 6.81 PHI= -0.215 XP = 0.0091
110	TEND TO BE THOSE WHERE SLAVERY IS ABSENT (218)	0.79 OF 43	110	TEND TO BE THOSE WHERE SLAVERY IS PRESENT (163)	0.71 OF 104	9 74 34 30 XSQ= 29.21 PHI= -0.446 XP = 0.0000
129	TILT TOWARD BEING THOSE WHERE WEAVING IS MAINLY DONE BY FEMALES (73)	0.86 OF 7	129	TILT TOWARD BEING THOSE WHERE WEAVING IS MAINLY DONE BY MALES (31)	0.61 OF 28	1 17 6 11 XSQ= 3.15 PHI= -0.300 EP = 0.0408
130	DRIFT TOWARD BEING THOSE WHERE LEATHER WORKING IS MAINLY DONE BY FEMALES (45)	0.64 OF 14	130	DRIFT TOWARD BEING THOSE WHERE LEATHER WORKING IS MAINLY DONE BY MALES (39)	0.70 OF 23	5 16 9 7 XSQ= 2.80 PHI= -0.275 EP = 0.0857
131	LEAN TOWARD BEING THOSE WHERE THE CONSTRUCTION OF PERMANENT HOUSES OR THE ERECTION OF TEMPORARY DWELLINGS IS MAINLY DONE BY FEMALES (21)	0.50 OF 16	131	LEAN TOWARD BEING THOSE WHERE THE CONSTRUCTION OF PERMANENT HOUSES OR THE ERECTION OF TEMPORARY DWELLINGS IS MAINLY DONE BY MALES (136)	0.89 OF 36	8 32 8 4 XSQ= 7.37 PHI= -0.377 XP = 0.0066
176	DRIFT TOWARD BEING THOSE WHERE THE COMMUNITY IS OTHER THAN A CLAN-COMMUNITY OR A COMMUNITY STRUCTURED OR SEGMENTED ON A CLAN BASIS (213)	0.57 OF 40	176	DRIFT TOWARD BEING THOSE WHERE THE COMMUNITY IS A CLAN-COMMUNITY OR A COMMUNITY STRUCTURED OR SEGMENTED ON A CLAN BASIS (169)	0.62 OF 102	17 63 23 39 XSQ= 3.59 PHI= -0.159 XP = 0.0582
178	DRIFT MORE TOWARD BEING THOSE WHERE THE COMMUNITY IS OTHER THAN SEGMENTED ON A CLAN BASIS AND NON-EXOGAMOUS (295)	0.90 OF 40	178	DRIFT LESS TOWARD BEING THOSE WHERE THE COMMUNITY IS OTHER THAN SEGMENTED ON A CLAN BASIS AND NON-EXOGAMOUS (295)	0.74 OF 102	4 27 36 75 XSQ= 3.65 PHI= -0.160 XP = 0.0560
179	DRIFT LESS TOWARD BEING THOSE WHERE THE COMMUNITY IS OTHER THAN STRUCTURED ON A NON-CLAN BASIS AND COMMONLY EXOGAMOUS (340)	0.75 OF 40	179	DRIFT MORE TOWARD BEING THOSE WHERE THE COMMUNITY IS OTHER THAN STRUCTURED ON A NON-CLAN BASIS AND COMMONLY EXOGAMOUS (340)	0.88 OF 102	10 12 30 90 XSQ= 2.90 PHI= 0.143 XP = 0.0886
184	TILT TOWARD BEING THOSE WHERE THE LARGEST NON-COGNATIC KIN GROUP IS THE MOEITY OR PHRATRY (77)	0.54 OF 26	184	TILT TOWARD BEING THOSE WHERE THE LARGEST NON-COGNATIC KIN GROUP IS SMALLER THAN A PHRATRY, I. E. A SIB OR LINEAGE (175)	0.74 OF 92	14 24 12 68 XSQ= 5.94 PHI= 0.224 XP = 0.0148

No.			No.			
186	TEND TO BE THOSE WHERE THE KIN GROUP IS OTHER THAN EXCLUSIVELY PATRILINEAL (250)	0.75 OF 44	186	TEND TO BE THOSE WHERE THE KIN GROUP IS EXCLUSIVELY PATRILINEAL (150)	0.60 OF 108	11 65 33 43 XSQ= 14.11 PHI= -0.305 XP = 0.0002
188	LEAN LESS TOWARD BEING THOSE WHERE THE KIN GROUP IS OTHER THAN EXCLUSIVELY COGNATIC (252)	0.59 OF 44	188	LEAN MORE TOWARD BEING THOSE WHERE THE KIN GROUP IS OTHER THAN EXCLUSIVELY COGNATIC (252)	0.85 OF 108	18 16 26 92 XSQ= 10.80 PHI= 0.267 XP = 0.0010
190	LEAN LESS TOWARD BEING THOSE WHERE THE KIN GROUP IS PATRILINEAL OR DOUBLE-DESCENT, RATHER THAN MATRILINEAL (186)	0.62 OF 26	190	LEAN MORE TOWARD BEING THOSE WHERE THE KIN GROUP IS PATRILINEAL OR DOUBLE-DESCENT, RATHER THAN MATRILINEAL (186)	0.89 OF 90	16 80 10 10 XSQ= 8.75 PHI= -0.275 XP = 0.0031
192	TEND LESS TO BE THOSE OTHER THAN WHERE THE ONLY KIN GROUP PRESENT IS A KINDRED OR ELSE BILATERAL DESCENT IS INFERRED (289)	0.64 OF 44	192	TEND MORE TO BE THOSE OTHER THAN WHERE THE ONLY KIN GROUP PRESENT IS A KINDRED OR ELSE BILATERAL DESCENT IS INFERRED (289)	0.92 OF 108	16 9 28 99 XSQ= 15.89 PHI= 0.323 XP = 0.0001
196	TEND TO BE THOSE WHERE INDIVIDUAL RIGHTS IN REAL PROPERTY, OR RULES FOR INHERITANCE, ARE ABSENT (87)	0.69 OF 29	196	TEND TO BE THOSE WHERE INDIVIDUAL RIGHTS IN REAL PROPERTY, AND RULES FOR INHERITANCE, ARE PRESENT (194)	0.77 OF 88	9 68 20 20 XSQ= 18.72 PHI= -0.400 XP = 0.0000
198	TILT LESS TOWARD BEING THOSE WHERE RULES FOR THE INHERITANCE OF REAL PROPERTY, IF PRESENT, FAVOR THE MALE HEIR OR LINE, RATHER THAN THE FEMALE (144)	0.67 OF 9	198	TILT MORE TOWARD BEING THOSE WHERE RULES FOR THE INHERITANCE OF REAL PROPERTY, IF PRESENT, FAVOR THE MALE HEIR OR LINE, RATHER THAN THE FEMALE (144)	0.94 OF 67	6 63 3 4 XSQ= 4.21 PHI= -0.235 XP = 0.0402
201	TILT LESS TOWARD BEING THOSE WHERE MARITAL RESIDENCE IS NON-OPTIONAL, RATHER THAN AMBILOCAL OR NEOLOCAL (334)	0.84 OF 43	201	TILT MORE TOWARD BEING THOSE WHERE MARITAL RESIDENCE IS NON-OPTIONAL, RATHER THAN AMBILOCAL OR NEOLOCAL (334)	0.96 OF 108	36 104 7 4 XSQ= 5.46 PHI= -0.190 XP = 0.0195
204	LEAN LESS TOWARD BEING THOSE WHERE MARITAL RESIDENCE IS PATRILOCAL, VIRILOCAL, OR AVUNCULOCAL, RATHER THAN AMBILOCAL OR NEOLOCAL (270)	0.79 OF 34	204	LEAN MORE TOWARD BEING THOSE WHERE MARITAL RESIDENCE IS PATRILOCAL, VIRILOCAL, OR AVUNCULOCAL, RATHER THAN AMBILOCAL OR NEOLOCAL (270)	0.96 OF 105	27 101 7 4 XSQ= 7.75 PHI= -0.236 XP = 0.0054
209	TEND LESS TO BE THOSE WHERE MARITAL RESIDENCE IS PATRILOCAL, VIRILOCAL, OR AVUNCULOCAL, RATHER THAN MATRILOCAL OR UXORILOCAL (270)	0.75 OF 36	209	TEND MORE TO BE THOSE WHERE MARITAL RESIDENCE IS PATRILOCAL, VIRILOCAL, OR AVUNCULOCAL, RATHER THAN MATRILOCAL OR UXORILOCAL (270)	0.97 OF 104	27 101 9 3 XSQ= 13.99 PHI= -0.316 XP = 0.0002

210	LEAN LESS TOWARD BEING THOSE WHERE MARITAL RESIDENCE IS PATRILOCAL, RATHER THAN MATRILOCAL (169)	0.78 OF	18	210	LEAN MORE TOWARD BEING THOSE WHERE MARITAL RESIDENCE IS PATRILOCAL, RATHER THAN MATRILOCAL (169)	0.99 OF	75	14 74 4 1 XSQ= 8.68 PHI= -0.306 XP = 0.0032
213	DRIFT MORE TOWARD BEING THOSE WHERE FIRST COUSIN MARRIAGE IS NOT PERMITTED (198)	0.69 OF	42	213	DRIFT LESS TOWARD BEING THOSE WHERE FIRST COUSIN MARRIAGE IS NOT PERMITTED (198)	0.50 OF	103	13 51 29 52 XSQ= 3.45 PHI= -0.154 XP = 0.0632
260	TILT TOWARD BEING THOSE WHERE THE AGE OF MALES AT MARRIAGE IS LESS THAN TWENTY (38) JKH	0.91 OF	11	260	TILT TOWARD BEING THOSE WHERE THE AGE OF MALES AT MARRIAGE IS TWENTY OR OVER (17) JKH	0.53 OF	15	10 7 1 8 XSQ= 3.71 PHI= 0.378 EP = 0.0362
262	TEND LESS TO BE THOSE WHERE WIVES ARE OBTAINED BY MEANS INVOLVING THE PRESENCE OF SOME CONSIDERATION (305)	0.70 OF	43	262	TEND MORE TO BE THOSE WHERE WIVES ARE OBTAINED BY MEANS INVOLVING THE PRESENCE OF SOME CONSIDERATION (305)	0.94 OF	107	30 101 13 6 XSQ= 14.66 PHI= -0.313 XP = 0.0001
263	LEAN LESS TOWARD BEING THOSE WHERE WIVES ARE OBTAINED BY RELATIVELY DIFFICULT MEANS, NAMELY BY BRIDE-PRICE, BRIDE-SERVICE, OR EXCHANGING A FEMALE RELATIVE (233)	0.53 OF	43	263	LEAN MORE TOWARD BEING THOSE WHERE WIVES ARE OBTAINED BY RELATIVELY DIFFICULT MEANS, NAMELY BY BRIDE-PRICE, BRIDE-SERVICE, OR EXCHANGING A FEMALE RELATIVE (233)	0.80 OF	107	23 86 20 21 XSQ= 9.85 PHI= -0.256 XP = 0.0017
296	LEAN TOWARD BEING THOSE WHERE INFANTICIDE IS ABSENT OR INFERRED ABSENT (15) BCA	0.71 OF	7	296	LEAN TOWARD BEING THOSE WHERE INFANTICIDE IS PRESENT (18) BCA	0.92 OF	12	2 11 5 1 XSQ= 5.49 PHI= -0.537 EP = 0.0095
300	TILT TOWARD BEING THOSE WHERE THE POST-PARTUM SEX TABOO LASTS SIX MONTHS OR LESS (73)	0.74 OF	19	300	TILT TOWARD BEING THOSE WHERE THE POST-PARTUM SEX TABOO LASTS LONGER THAN SIX MONTHS (51)	0.62 OF	39	5 24 14 15 XSQ= 5.01 PHI= -0.294 XP = 0.0252
302	TILT TOWARD BEING THOSE WHERE THE AVERAGE EARLY SATISFACTION POTENTIAL IS HIGH (23) W-C	0.89 OF	9	302	TILT TOWARD BEING THOSE WHERE THE AVERAGE EARLY SATISFACTION POTENTIAL IS LOW (17) W-C	0.62 OF	13	8 5 1 8 XSQ= 3.70 PHI= 0.410 EP = 0.0306
303	TILT TOWARD BEING THOSE WHERE THE EARLY ORAL SATISFACTION POTENTIAL IS HIGH (32) W-C	0.92 OF	12	303	TILT TOWARD BEING THOSE WHERE THE EARLY ORAL SATISFACTION POTENTIAL IS LOW (25) W-C	0.56 OF	16	11 7 1 9 XSQ= 4.93 PHI= 0.420 EP = 0.0159

308	DRIFT TOWARD BEING THOSE WHERE AVERAGE SOCIALIZATION ANXIETY IS LOW (18) W-C	0.67 OF 9	308	DRIFT TOWARD BEING THOSE WHERE AVERAGE SOCIALIZATION ANXIETY IS HIGH (22) W-C	0.77 OF 13	3 10 6 3 XSQ= 2.57 PHI= -0.342 EP = 0.0789
309	DRIFT TOWARD BEING THOSE WHERE ORAL SOCIALIZATION ANXIETY IS LOW (27) W-C	0.82 OF 11	309	DRIFT TOWARD BEING THOSE WHERE ORAL SOCIALIZATION ANXIETY IS HIGH (26) W-C	0.60 OF 15	2 9 9 6 XSQ= 2.99 PHI= -0.339 EP = 0.0506
314	DRIFT TOWARD BEING THOSE WHERE THE INCIDENCE OF MOTHER-CHILD HOUSEHOLDS IS LOW (61) W-D,S	0.67 OF 12	314	DRIFT TOWARD BEING THOSE WHERE THE INCIDENCE OF MOTHER-CHILD HOUSEHOLDS IS HIGH (19) W-D,S	0.70 OF 20	4 14 8 6 XSQ= 2.74 PHI= -0.293 EP = 0.0683
327	DRIFT TOWARD BEING THOSE WHERE THE AGE OF THE INFANT AT TIME OF REDUCED CONTACT WITH MOTHER IS HIGHER THAN TWO YEARS (28) B-B-C	0.73 OF 11	327	DRIFT TOWARD BEING THOSE WHERE THE AGE OF THE INFANT AT TIME OF REDUCED CONTACT WITH MOTHER IS TWO YEARS OR LOWER (27) B-B-C	0.67 OF 18	8 6 3 12 XSQ= 2.81 PHI= 0.311 EP = 0.0604
351	LEAN TOWARD BEING THOSE WHERE THE CHILD'S INFERRED CONFLICT REGARDING ACHIEVEMENT BEHAVIOR IS HIGH (26) B-B-C	0.79 OF 14	351	LEAN TOWARD BEING THOSE WHERE THE CHILD'S INFERRED CONFLICT REGARDING ACHIEVEMENT BEHAVIOR IS LOW (34) B-B-C	0.70 OF 23	11 7 3 16 XSQ= 6.26 PHI= 0.411 EP = 0.0069
354	DRIFT TOWARD BEING THOSE WHERE THE CHILD'S INFERRED ANXIETY OVER PERFORMANCE OF OBEDIENT BEHAVIOR IS HIGH (36) B-B-C	0.71 OF 17	354	DRIFT TOWARD BEING THOSE WHERE THE CHILD'S INFERRED ANXIETY OVER PERFORMANCE OF OBEDIENT BEHAVIOR IS LOW (37) B-B-C	0.63 OF 24	12 9 5 15 XSQ= 3.14 PHI= 0.277 XP = 0.0765
377	DRIFT MORE TOWARD BEING THOSE WHERE MALE GENITAL MUTILATION IS ABSENT (242)	0.79 OF 38	377	DRIFT LESS TOWARD BEING THOSE WHERE MALE GENITAL MUTILATION IS ABSENT (242)	0.59 OF 88	8 36 30 52 XSQ= 3.77 PHI= -0.173 XP = 0.0521
382	IN ALL CASES ARE THOSE WHERE FEMALE INITIATION RITES ARE PRESENT (38) JKB	1.00 OF 8	382	TILT TOWARD BEING THOSE WHERE FEMALE INITIATION RITES ARE ABSENT (27) JKB	0.50 OF 20	8 10 0 10 XSQ= 4.23 PHI= 0.389 EP = 0.0251
424	IN ALL CASES ARE THOSE WHERE RELIGIOUS SPECIALISTS ARE PART-TIME, RATHER THAN FULL-TIME (33) JMH	1.00 OF 8	424	TILT TOWARD BEING THOSE WHERE RELIGIOUS SPECIALISTS ARE FULL-TIME, RATHER THAN PART-TIME (21) JMH	0.50 OF 16	0 8 8 8 XSQ= 3.96 PHI= -0.406 EP = 0.0222

426	TILT TOWARD BEING THOSE WHERE A HIGH GOD IS ABSENT (104) GES,EA	0.56 OF 27	426	TILT TOWARD BEING THOSE WHERE A HIGH GOD IS PRESENT (156) GES,EA	0.74 OF 74	12 55 / 15 19 / XSQ= 6.63 / PHI= -0.256 / XP = 0.0100
435	DRIFT TOWARD BEING THOSE WHERE ABANDONMENT OF THE HOUSE OF THE DEAD IS PRACTICED (12) LWS	0.80 OF 5	435	DRIFT TOWARD BEING THOSE WHERE ABANDONMENT OF THE HOUSE OF THE DEAD IS NOT PRACTICED (19) LWS	0.80 OF 10	4 2 / 1 8 / XSQ= 2.81 / PHI= 0.433 / EP = 0.0889
450	IN ALL CASES ARE THOSE WHERE THE OBSERVATION OF FOOD TABOOS IS HIGH OR MEDIUM, RATHER THAN LOW (60) JRL	1.00 OF 13	450	DRIFT LESS TOWARD BEING THOSE WHERE THE OBSERVATION OF FOOD TABOOS IS HIGH OR MEDIUM, RATHER THAN LOW (60) JRL	0.72 OF 29	13 21 / 0 8 / XSQ= 2.82 / PHI= 0.259 / XP = 0.0930
454	TILT TOWARD BEING THOSE WHERE THE OBJECTIVE OF THE INDIVIDUAL'S CONTACT WITH THE DIVINE IS NOT CONDUCIVE TO THE DEVELOPMENT OF THE INDIVIDUAL'S NEED TO ACHIEVE (18) DCM	0.77 OF 13	454	TILT TOWARD BEING THOSE WHERE THE OBJECTIVE OF THE INDIVIDUAL'S CONTACT WITH THE DIVINE IS CONDUCIVE TO THE DEVELOPMENT OF THE INDIVIDUAL'S NEED TO ACHIEVE (18) DCM	0.73 OF 11	3 8 / 10 3 / XSQ= 4.09 / PHI= -0.413 / EP = 0.0377
458	LEAN TOWARD BEING THOSE WHERE GAMES, IF PRESENT, DO NOT INCLUDE GAMES OF STRATEGY (119) R-A-B,EA	0.88 OF 24	458	LEAN TOWARD BEING THOSE WHERE GAMES, IF PRESENT, INCLUDE GAMES OF STRATEGY (52) R-A-B,EA	0.52 OF 44	3 23 / 21 21 / XSQ= 8.79 / PHI= -0.359 / XP = 0.0030
473	TILT TOWARD BEING THOSE WHERE SENSITIVITY TO INSULT IS MODERATE OR NEGLIGIBLE (56) PES	0.88 OF 16	473	TILT TOWARD BEING THOSE WHERE SENSITIVITY TO INSULT IS EXTREME (32) PES	0.50 OF 28	2 14 / 14 14 / XSQ= 4.67 / PHI= -0.326 / XP = 0.0306
480	IN ALL CASES ARE THOSE WHERE COMPLEXITY OF ARTISTIC DESIGN IS LOW (15) HB	1.00 OF 7	480	TILT TOWARD BEING THOSE WHERE COMPLEXITY OF ARTISTIC DESIGN IS HIGH (14) HB	0.67 OF 6	0 4 / 7 2 / XSQ= 3.97 / PHI= -0.553 / EP = 0.0210

245 CULTURES
WHERE MARRIAGE, IF COMMONLY POLYGYNOUS, IS THE TYPE WHERE CO-WIVES DWELL TOGETHER, RATHER THAN SEPARATELY (71)

245 CULTURES
WHERE MARRIAGE, IF COMMONLY POLYGYNOUS, IS THE TYPE WHERE CO-WIVES DWELL SEPARATELY, RATHER THAN TOGETHER (81)

BACKGROUND ON PAGE 124

SUBJECT ONLY

71 IN LEFT COLUMN

ALBANIANS ARANDA ARAPESH ARYANS ATSUGEWI AWEIKOMA BELU BOTOCUDO BOZO BUDUMA
CHERKESS CHEYENNE CHIBCHA CHIR-APACHE COMANCHE CROW DARD DIERI EYAK FOX
GOND GROS VENTRE GUATO HASANIA HEBREWS HEHE HO HUKUNDIKA JIVARO KAPAUKU
KARIERA KAZAK KERAKI KIOW-APACHE LAKALAI LAU LHOTA NAGA MANDAN MANGAIANS MAORI
MIAMI MIWOK MOTA MOTILON MURINBATA MURNGIN NATCHEZ ONA PAEZ PAPAGO
PAWNEE POPOLUCA PURARI ROTINESE SANPOIL SARSI SENIANG SIRIONO TENINO TETON
TIWI TOLOWA TSHIMSHIAN TUNEBO VIETNAMESE WAPISHANA WARRAU WICHITA WIKMUNKAN WOGEO
YUROK

81 IN RIGHT COLUMN

AMBA ARAUCANIANS ASHANTI AZANDE BABWA BAMBARA BAMILEKE BANDA BARI BAYA
BEMBA BERGDAMA BETE BIRIFOR CHAGGA CHUKCHEE DIEGUENO DILLING FANG FON
FUTAJALONKE GANDA GISU GOAJIRO HERERO ILA KATAB KIKUYU KISSI KONSO
KPE KURTATCHI LANGO LIFU LOZI LUBA LUO MAGUZAWA MAMVU MARGI
MASAI MBUNDU MENDE MONGO MOSSI NAVAHO NDEMBU NGONI NUER NUPE
NURI NYAKYUSA NYANEKA NYORO PENDE RUNDI RWALA SARAMACCA SHILLUK SOMALI
SOTHO SWAZI TALLENSI TANALA TEDA TERA TESO THONGA TIKOPIA TIV
TUPINAMBA TURKANA VENDA WANTOAT WOLOF WUTE YAKO YAKUT YOKUTS YOMBE
YORUBA

246 EXCLUDED BECAUSE IRRELEVANT

2 EXCLUDED BECAUSE UNASCERTAINED

3	TEND TO BE THOSE LOCATED OUTSIDE OF AFRICA (320)	0.97 OF 71	3	TEND TO BE THOSE LOCATED IN AFRICA (80)	0.73 OF 81	2 59 69 22 XSQ= 74.33 PHI= -0.699 XP = 0.
6	TEND LESS TO BE THOSE LOCATED OUTSIDE OF THE INSULAR PACIFIC (330)	0.72 OF 71	6	TEND MORE TO BE THOSE LOCATED OUTSIDE OF THE INSULAR PACIFIC (330)	0.95 OF 81	20 4 51 77 XSQ= 13.66 PHI= 0.300 XP = 0.0002

8	TEND LESS TO BE THCSE LOCATED CUTSIDE OF NORTH AMERICA (330)	0.65 OF 71	8	TEND MORE TO BE THOSE LOCATED OUTSIDE OF NORTH AMERICA (330)	0.96 OF 81	25 3 46 78 XSQ= 22.94 PHI= 0.388 XP = 0.0000
9	TILT LESS TOWARC BEING THCSE LCCATED OUTSIDE CF SOUTH AMERICA (335)	0.83 OF 71	9	TILT MORE TOWARD BEING THOSE LOCATED OUTSIDE OF SOUTH AMERICA (335)	0.95 OF 81	12 4 59 77 XSQ= 4.55 PHI= 0.173 XP = 0.0329
15	TEND TO BE THOSE WHERE THE LATITUDE IS TWENTY DEGREES CR GREATER (183)	0.56 OF 71	15	TEND TO BE THOSE WHERE THE LATITUDE IS LESS THAN TWENTY DEGREES (217)	0.79 OF 81	40 17 31 64 XSQ= 18.69 PHI= 0.351 XP = 0.0000
16	TEND TO BE THOSE WHERE THE LATITUDE IS TEN DEGREES CR GREATER (277)	0.79 OF 71	16	TEND TO BE THOSE WHERE THE LATITUDE IS LESS THAN TEN DEGREES (123)	0.53 OF 81	56 38 15 43 XSQ= 15.05 PHI= 0.315 XP = 0.0001
36	DRIFT LESS TOWARD BEING THCSE WHERE THE NATURAL ENVIRONMENT IS OTHER THAN 'VERY HARSH,' OR SUB-TROPICAL BUSH, OR TEMPERATE GRASSLAND (292) FWM	0.62 OF 71	36	DRIFT MORE TOWARD BEING THOSE WHERE THE NATURAL ENVIRONMENT IS OTHER THAN 'VERY HARSH,' OR SUB-TROPICAL BUSH, OR TEMPERATE GRASSLAND (292) FWM	0.78 OF 81	27 18 44 63 XSQ= 3.81 PHI= 0.158 XP = 0.0510
44	TEND TO BE THOSE WHERE SETTLEMENTS ARE NON-FIXED (110)	0.58 OF 59	44	TEND TO BE THOSE WHERE SETTLEMENTS ARE FIXED (222)	0.74 OF 70	25 52 34 18 XSQ= 12.26 PHI= -0.308 XP = 0.0005
45	TILT TOWARD BEING THOSE WHERE SETTLEMENTS, IF FIXEC, ARE COMPACT, RATHER THAN NON-COMPACT (149)	0.76 OF 25	45	TILT TOWARD BEING THOSE WHERE SETTLEMENTS, IF FIXED, ARE NON-COMPACT, RATHER THAN COMPACT (73)	0.52 OF 52	19 25 6 27 XSQ= 4.30 PHI= 0.236 XP = 0.0382
46	TILT LESS TOWARD BEING THOSE OTHER THAN WHERE SETTLEMENTS ARE NON-FIXED AND MOVEMENT IS NOMADIC (260)	0.63 OF 59	46	TILT MORE TOWARD BEING THOSE OTHER THAN WHERE SETTLEMENTS ARE NON-FIXED AND MOVEMENT IS NOMADIC (260)	0.83 OF 70	22 12 37 58 XSQ= 5.70 PHI= 0.210 XP = 0.0170
51	TEND TO BE THOSE WHERE SUBSISTENCE IS PRIMARILY BY FOOD GATHERING -- I. E., HUNTING, FISHING, OR COLLECTING -- RATHER THAN FOOD PRODUCTION (147)	0.58 OF 71	51	TEND TO BE THOSE WHERE SUBSISTENCE IS PRIMARILY BY FOOD PRODUCTION -- I. E., AGRICULTURE OR HUSBANDRY -- RATHER THAN BY GATHERING (253)	0.85 OF 81	30 69 41 12 XSQ= 28.85 PHI= -0.436 XP = 0.0000

62	TEND TO BE THOSE WHERE HUSBANDRY OF ANY KIND IS ABSENT (172)	0.63 OF 71	62	TEND TO BE THOSE WHERE HUSBANDRY OF SOME KIND IS PRESENT (228)	0.79 OF 81	26 64 45 17 XSQ= 26.43 PHI= -0.417 XP = 0.0000
71	TEND TO BE THOSE WHERE METAL WORKING IS ABSENT (153)	0.90 OF 49	71	TEND TO BE THOSE WHERE METAL WORKING IS PRESENT (98)	0.79 OF 53	5 42 44 11 XSQ= 46.11 PHI= -0.672 XP = 0.
74	TEND TO BE THOSE WHERE POTTERY IS ABSENT (93)	0.65 OF 48	74	TEND TO BE THOSE WHERE POTTERY IS PRESENT (145)	0.86 OF 50	17 43 31 7 XSQ= 24.31 PHI= -0.498 XP = 0.0000
81	TILT TOWARD BEING THOSE WHERE NO CITY OR TOWN IS PRESENT, AND THE AVERAGE COMMUNITY SIZE IS SMALLER THAN 200 (135)	0.77 OF 31	81	TILT TOWARD BEING THOSE WHERE A CITY OR TOWN IS PRESENT, OR THE AVERAGE COMMUNITY SIZE IS 200 OR GREATER (89)	0.53 OF 51	7 27 24 24 XSQ= 6.12 PHI= -0.273 XP = 0.0133
83	TILT MORE TOWARD BEING THOSE WHERE, WITH NO CITY AND NO TOWN PRESENT, THE AVERAGE COMMUNITY SIZE IS SMALLER THAN 200, RATHER THAN BETWEEN 200 AND 999 (135)	0.83 OF 29	83	TILT LESS TOWARD BEING THOSE WHERE, WITH NO CITY AND NO TOWN PRESENT, THE AVERAGE COMMUNITY SIZE IS SMALLER THAN 200, RATHER THAN BETWEEN 200 AND 999 (135)	0.55 OF 44	5 20 24 24 XSQ= 4.99 PHI= -0.261 XP = 0.0255
85	LEAN MORE TOWARD BEING THOSE WHERE THE LEVEL OF POLITICAL INTEGRATION IS THE MINIMAL STATE, THE AUTONOMOUS COMMUNITY, OR THE FAMILY (234) GPM	0.86 OF 57	85	LEAN LESS TOWARD BEING THOSE WHERE THE LEVEL OF POLITICAL INTEGRATION IS THE MINIMAL STATE, THE AUTONOMOUS COMMUNITY, OR THE FAMILY (234) GPM	0.61 OF 62	8 24 49 38 XSQ= 7.98 PHI= -0.259 XP = 0.0047
87	DRIFT LESS TOWARD BEING THOSE WHERE THE LEVEL OF POLITICAL INTEGRATION IS THE LARGE STATE, THE LITTLE STATE, THE MINIMAL STATE, OR THE AUTONOMOUS COMMUNITY (281) GPM	0.89 OF 57	87	DRIFT MORE TOWARD BEING THOSE WHERE THE LEVEL OF POLITICAL INTEGRATION IS THE LARGE STATE, THE LITTLE STATE, THE MINIMAL STATE, OR THE AUTONOMOUS COMMUNITY (281) GPM	0.98 OF 62	51 61 6 1 XSQ= 2.80 PHI= -0.153 XP = 0.0940
96	TILT TOWARD BEING THOSE WHERE THE HIERARCHY OF NATIONAL JURISDICTION HAS NO LEVELS (156) GES,EA	0.56 OF 59	96	TILT TOWARD BEING THOSE WHERE THE HIERARCHY OF NATIONAL JURISDICTION HAS FOUR, THREE, TWO OR ONE LEVEL (174) GES,EA	0.66 OF 70	26 46 33 24 XSQ= 5.24 PHI= -0.201 XP = 0.0221
97	TILT MORE TOWARD BEING THOSE WHERE THE HIERARCHY OF LOCAL JURISDICTION HAS THREE OR TWO LEVELS (273) GES,EA	0.90 OF 59	97	TILT LESS TOWARD BEING THOSE WHERE THE HIERARCHY OF LOCAL JURISDICTION HAS THREE OR TWO LEVELS (273) GES,EA	0.74 OF 70	6 18 53 52 XSQ= 4.13 PHI= -0.179 XP = 0.0420

98	TILT LESS TOWARD BEING THOSE 0.61 OF 59 WHERE THE HIERARCHY OF LOCAL JURISDICTION HAS FOUR OR THREE LEVELS (238) GES,EA	98	TILT MORE TOWARD BEING THOSE 0.81 OF 70 WHERE THE HIERARCHY OF LOCAL JURISDICTION HAS FOUR OR THREE LEVELS (238) GES,EA	36 57 23 13 XSQ= 5.65 PHI= -0.209 XP = 0.0174
99	TILT TOWARD BEING THOSE 0.58 OF 33 WHERE, WITH NATIONAL HIERARCHY ABSENT, THE HIERARCHY OF LOCAL JURISDICTION HAS TWO LEVELS (63) GES,EA	99	TILT TOWARD BEING THOSE 0.75 OF 24 WHERE, WITH NATIONAL HIERARCHY ABSENT, THE HIERARCHY OF LOCAL JURISDICTION HAS FOUR OR THREE LEVELS (93) GES,EA	14 18 19 6 XSQ= 4.74 PHI= -0.288 XP = 0.0295
100	LEAN LESS TOWARD BEING THOSE 0.68 OF 59 WHERE HIERARCHIES ARE MORE COMPLEX THAN THE 'SIMPLEST,' I. E., MORE COMPLEX THAN TWO LOCAL LEVELS WITH NO NATIONAL LEVELS (267) GES,EA	100	LEAN MORE TOWARD BEING THOSE 0.91 OF 70 WHERE HIERARCHIES ARE MORE COMPLEX THAN THE 'SIMPLEST,' I. E., MORE COMPLEX THAN TWO LOCAL LEVELS WITH NO NATIONAL LEVELS (267) GES,EA	40 64 19 6 XSQ= 9.98 PHI= -0.278 XP = 0.0016
102	LEAN TOWARD BEING THOSE 0.59 OF 69 WHERE CLASS STRATIFICATION IS ABSENT (180)	102	LEAN TOWARD BEING THOSE 0.68 OF 79 WHERE CLASS STRATIFICATION IS PRESENT (203)	28 54 41 25 XSQ= 10.40 PHI= -0.265 XP = 0.0013
109	DRIFT MORE TOWARD BEING THOSE 0.91 OF 67 WHERE CASTES ARE ABSENT (317)	109	DRIFT LESS TOWARD BEING THOSE 0.79 OF 80 WHERE CASTES ARE ABSENT (317)	6 17 61 63 XSQ= 3.30 PHI= -0.150 XP = 0.0694
110	TEND TO BE THOSE 0.67 OF 66 WHERE SLAVERY IS ABSENT (218)	110	TEND TO BE THOSE 0.75 OF 81 WHERE SLAVERY IS PRESENT (163)	22 61 44 20 XSQ= 24.39 PHI= -0.407 XP = 0.0000
129	TILT TOWARD BEING THOSE 0.77 OF 13 WHERE WEAVING IS MAINLY DONE BY FEMALES (73)	129	TILT TOWARD BEING THOSE 0.68 OF 22 WHERE WEAVING IS MAINLY DONE BY MALES (31)	3 15 10 7 XSQ= 4.97 PHI= -0.377 EP = 0.0153
130	LEAN TOWARD BEING THOSE 0.73 OF 15 WHERE LEATHER WORKING IS MAINLY DONE BY FEMALES (45)	130	LEAN TOWARD BEING THOSE 0.77 OF 22 WHERE LEATHER WORKING IS MAINLY DONE BY MALES (39)	4 17 11 5 XSQ= 7.36 PHI= -0.446 EP = 0.0059
131	TILT LESS TOWARD BEING THOSE 0.64 OF 28 WHERE THE CONSTRUCTION OF PERMANENT HOUSES OR THE ERECTION OF TEMPORARY DWELLINGS IS MAINLY DONE BY MALES (136)	131	TILT MORE TOWARD BEING THOSE 0.92 OF 24 WHERE THE CONSTRUCTION OF PERMANENT HOUSES OR THE ERECTION OF TEMPORARY DWELLINGS IS MAINLY DONE BY MALES (136)	18 22 10 2 XSQ= 4.02 PHI= -0.278 XP = 0.0448

149	DRIFT TOWARD BEING THCSE WHERE THE INCIDENCE OF THEFT IS LCW (19) B-B-C	0.63 OF 8	149	DRIFT TOWARD BEING THOSE WHERE THE INCIDENCE OF THEFT IS HIGH (18) B-B-C	0.83 OF 12	3 10 5 2 XSQ= 2.65 PHI= -0.364 EP = 0.0623
176	LEAN TOWARD BEING THCSE WHERE THE COMMUNITY IS CTHER THAN A CLAN-CCMMUNITY OR A COMMUNITY STRUCTURED OR SEGMENTEC CN A CLAN BASIS (213)	0.59 OF 61	176	LEAN TOWARD BEING THOSE WHERE THE COMMUNITY IS A CLAN-COMMUNITY OR A COMMUNITY STRUCTURED OR SEGMENTED ON A CLAN BASIS (169)	0.68 CF 81	25 55 36 26 XSQ= 9.18 PHI= -0.254 XP = 0.0024
177	DRIFT MORE TCWARC BEING THCSE WHERE THE COMMUNITY IS CTHER THAN A SINGLE CLAN-CCMMUNITY ANC EXCGAMCUS (305)	0.75 OF 61	177	DRIFT LESS TOWARD BEING THCSE WHERE THE COMMUNITY IS OTHER THAN A SINGLE CLAN-COMMUNITY AND EXOGAMOUS (305)	0.60 OF 81	15 32 46 49 XSQ= 2.85 PHI= -0.142 XP = 0.0911
181	TILT LESS TOWARC BEING THCSE WHERE THE COMMUNITY IS CTHER THAN A DEME (337)	0.89 OF 61	181	TILT MORE TOWARD BEING THCSE WHERE THE COMMUNITY IS CTHER THAN A DEME (337)	0.99 OF 81	7 1 54 80 XSQ= 5.07 PHI= 0.189 XP = 0.0243
184	TEND TO BE THCSE WHERE THE LARGEST NON-CCGNATIC KIN GROUP IS THE MCEITY OR PHRATRY (77)	0.62 OF 42	184	TEND TO BE THOSE WHERE THE LARGEST NON-COGNATIC KIN GROUP IS SMALLER THAN A PHRATRY, I. E. A SIB OR LINEAGE (175)	0.84 OF 76	26 12 16 64 XSQ= 24.28 PHI= 0.454 XP = 0.0000
186	TEND TC BE THCSE WHERE THE KIN GRCUP IS CTHER THAN EXCLUSIVELY PATRILINEAL (250)	0.66 OF 71	186	TEND TO BE THOSE WHERE THE KIN GROUP IS EXCLUSIVELY PATRILINEAL (150)	0.64 OF 81	24 52 47 29 XSQ= 12.79 PHI= -0.290 XP = 0.0003
188	TEND LESS TO BE THCSE WHERE THE KIN GRCUP IS CTHER THAN EXCLUSIVELY CCGNATIC (252)	0.59 OF 71	188	TEND MORE TO BE THOSE WHERE THE KIN GROUP IS OTHER THAN EXCLUSIVELY COGNATIC (252)	0.94 OF 81	29 5 42 76 XSQ= 24.23 PHI= 0.399 XP = 0.0000
190	DRIFT LESS TCWARC BEING THCSE WHERE THE KIN GRCUP IS PATRILINEAL OR DCUBLE-DESCENT, RATHER THAN MATRILINEAL (186)	0.74 OF 42	190	DRIFT MORE TOWARD BEING THCSE WHERE THE KIN GROUP IS PATRILINEAL OR DOUBLE-DESCENT, RATHER THAN MATRILINEAL (186)	0.88 OF 74	31 65 11 9 XSQ= 2.78 PHI= -0.155 XP = 0.0956
192	TEND LESS TO BE THCSE OTHER THAN WHERE THE CNLY KIN GROUP PRESENT IS A KINDREC CR ELSE BILATERAL DESCENT IS INFERREC (289)	0.68 OF 71	192	TEND MORE TO BE THOSE OTHER THAN WHERE THE ONLY KIN GROUP PRESENT IS A KINDRED OR ELSE BILATERAL DESCENT IS INFERRED (289)	0.98 OF 81	23 2 48 79 XSQ= 22.53 PHI= 0.385 XP = 0.0000

196	LEAN TOWARD BEING THOSE 0.53 OF 45 WHERE INDIVIDUAL RIGHTS IN REAL PROPERTY, OR RULES FOR INHERITANCE, ARE ABSENT (87)	196	LEAN TOWARD BEING THOSE 0.78 OF 72 WHERE INDIVIDUAL RIGHTS IN REAL PROPERTY, AND RULES FOR INHERITANCE, ARE PRESENT (194)	21 56 24 16 XSQ= 10.57 PHI= -0.301 XP = 0.0011
204	DRIFT LESS TOWARD BEING THOSE 0.87 OF 60 WHERE MARITAL RESIDENCE IS PATRILOCAL, VIRILOCAL, OR AVUNCULOCAL, RATHER THAN AMBILOCAL OR NEOLOCAL (270)	204	DRIFT MORE TOWARD BEING THOSE 0.96 OF 79 WHERE MARITAL RESIDENCE IS PATRILOCAL, VIRILOCAL, OR AVUNCULOCAL, RATHER THAN AMBILOCAL OR NEOLOCAL (270)	52 76 8 3 XSQ= 3.05 PHI= -0.148 XP = 0.0809
209	TILT LESS TOWARD BEING THOSE 0.84 OF 62 WHERE MARITAL RESIDENCE IS PATRILOCAL, VIRILOCAL, OR AVUNCULOCAL, RATHER THAN MATRILOCAL OR UXORILOCAL (270)	209	TILT MORE TOWARD BEING THOSE 0.97 OF 78 WHERE MARITAL RESIDENCE IS PATRILOCAL, VIRILOCAL, OR AVUNCULOCAL, RATHER THAN MATRILOCAL OR UXORILOCAL (270)	52 76 10 2 XSQ= 6.47 PHI= -0.215 XP = 0.0110
210	DRIFT LESS TOWARD BEING THOSE 0.88 OF 33 WHERE MARITAL RESIDENCE IS PATRILOCAL, RATHER THAN MATRILOCAL (169)	210	DRIFT MORE TOWARD BEING THOSE 0.98 OF 60 WHERE MARITAL RESIDENCE IS PATRILOCAL, RATHER THAN MATRILOCAL (169)	29 59 4 1 XSQ= 2.75 PHI= -0.172 XP = 0.0973
243	DRIFT TOWARD BEING THOSE 0.53 OF 15 WHERE POLYGYNY, IF PRESENT, HAS A LOW INCIDENCE (36) W-D,S	243	DRIFT TOWARD BEING THOSE 0.78 OF 18 WHERE POLYGYNY, IF PRESENT, HAS A HIGH INCIDENCE (24) W-D,S	7 14 8 4 XSQ= 2.21 PHI= -0.259 EP = 0.0827
260	TILT TOWARD BEING THOSE 0.92 OF 12 WHERE THE AGE OF MALES AT MARRIAGE IS LESS THAN TWENTY (38) JKH	260	TILT TOWARD BEING THOSE 0.57 OF 14 WHERE THE AGE OF MALES AT MARRIAGE IS TWENTY OR OVER (17) JKH	11 6 1 8 XSQ= 4.82 PHI= 0.430 EP = 0.0145
262	TEND LESS TO BE THOSE 0.77 OF 69 WHERE WIVES ARE OBTAINED BY MEANS INVOLVING THE PRESENCE OF SOME CONSIDERATION (305)	262	TEND MORE TO BE THOSE 0.96 OF 81 WHERE WIVES ARE OBTAINED BY MEANS INVOLVING THE PRESENCE OF SOME CONSIDERATION (305)	53 78 16 3 XSQ= 11.09 PHI= -0.272 XP = 0.0009
263	LEAN LESS TOWARD BEING THOSE 0.59 OF 69 WHERE WIVES ARE OBTAINED BY RELATIVELY DIFFICULT MEANS, NAMELY BY BRIDE-PRICE, BRIDE-SERVICE, OR EXCHANGING A FEMALE RELATIVE (233)	263	LEAN MORE TOWARD BEING THOSE 0.84 OF 81 WHERE WIVES ARE OBTAINED BY RELATIVELY DIFFICULT MEANS, NAMELY BY BRIDE-PRICE, BRIDE-SERVICE, OR EXCHANGING A FEMALE RELATIVE (233)	41 68 28 13 XSQ= 10.09 PHI= -0.259 XP = 0.0015
301	TILT LESS TOWARD BEING THOSE 0.57 OF 21 WHERE THE POST-PARTUM SEX TABOO LASTS LONGER THAN ONE MONTH (96)	301	TILT MORE TOWARD BEING THOSE 0.89 OF 37 WHERE THE POST-PARTUM SEX TABOO LASTS LONGER THAN ONE MONTH (96)	12 33 9 4 XSQ= 6.18 PHI= -0.326 XP = 0.0130

302	DRIFT TOWARD BEING THOSE WHERE THE AVERAGE EARLY SATISFACTION POTENTIAL IS HIGH (23) W-C	0.80 OF 10	302	DRIFT TOWARD BEING THOSE WHERE THE AVERAGE EARLY SATISFACTION POTENTIAL IS LOW (17) W-C	0.58 OF 12	8 5 / 2 7 / XSQ= 1.92 / PHI= 0.295 / EP = 0.0991
309	TILT TOWARD BEING THOSE WHERE ORAL SOCIALIZATION ANXIETY IS LOW (27) W-C	0.85 OF 13	309	TILT TOWARD BEING THOSE WHERE ORAL SOCIALIZATION ANXIETY IS HIGH (26) W-C	0.69 OF 13	2 9 / 11 4 / XSQ= 5.67 / PHI= -0.467 / EP = 0.0154
314	LEAN TOWARD BEING THOSE WHERE THE INCIDENCE OF MOTHER-CHILD HOUSEHOLDS IS LOW (61) W-C,S	0.77 OF 13	314	LEAN TOWARD BEING THOSE WHERE THE INCIDENCE OF MOTHER-CHILD HOUSEHOLDS IS HIGH (19) W-D,S	0.79 OF 19	3 15 / 10 4 / XSQ= 7.65 / PHI= -0.489 / EP = 0.0033
317	TILT TOWARD BEING THOSE WHERE DISPLAY OF AFFECTION TOWARD THE INFANT IS HIGH (39) B-B-C	0.81 OF 16	317	TILT TOWARD BEING THOSE WHERE DISPLAY OF AFFECTION TOWARD THE INFANT IS LOW (29) B-B-C	0.55 OF 22	13 10 / 3 12 / XSQ= 3.58 / PHI= 0.307 / EP = 0.0435
318	LEAN TOWARD BEING THOSE WHERE THE OVERALL INDULGENCE OF THE INFANT IS HIGH (40) B-B-C	0.87 OF 15	318	LEAN TOWARD BEING THOSE WHERE THE OVERALL INDULGENCE OF THE INFANT IS LOW (31) B-B-C	0.63 OF 24	13 9 / 2 15 / XSQ= 7.19 / PHI= 0.429 / EP = 0.0033
319	TILT TOWARD BEING THOSE WHERE PROTECTION OF THE INFANT FROM ENVIRONMENTAL DISCOMFORTS IS HIGH (35) B-B-C	0.73 OF 15	319	TILT TOWARD BEING THOSE WHERE PROTECTION OF THE INFANT FROM ENVIRONMENTAL DISCOMFORTS IS LOW (30) B-B-C	0.63 OF 24	11 9 / 4 15 / XSQ= 3.42 / PHI= 0.296 / EP = 0.0484
320	DRIFT MORE TOWARD BEING THOSE WHERE THE DEGREE OF REDUCTION OF THE INFANT'S DRIVES IS HIGH (45) B-B-C	0.93 OF 14	320	DRIFT LESS TOWARD BEING THOSE WHERE THE DEGREE OF REDUCTION OF THE INFANT'S DRIVES IS HIGH (45) B-B-C	0.61 OF 23	13 14 / 1 9 / XSQ= 3.04 / PHI= 0.287 / EP = 0.0559
324	DRIFT TOWARD BEING THOSE WHERE THE PAIN INFLICTED ON THE INFANT BY THE NURTURANT AGENT IS LOW OR NEGLIGIBLE (32) B-B-C	0.57 OF 14	324	DRIFT TOWARD BEING THOSE WHERE THE PAIN INFLICTED ON THE INFANT BY THE NURTURANT AGENT IS HIGH (34) B-B-C	0.74 OF 23	6 17 / 8 6 / XSQ= 2.37 / PHI= -0.253 / EP = 0.0851
327	DRIFT TOWARD BEING THOSE WHERE THE AGE OF THE INFANT AT TIME OF REDUCED CONTACT WITH MOTHER IS HIGHER THAN TWO YEARS (28) B-B-C	0.73 OF 11	327	DRIFT TOWARD BEING THOSE WHERE THE AGE OF THE INFANT AT TIME OF REDUCED CONTACT WITH MOTHER IS TWO YEARS OR LOWER (27) B-B-C	0.67 OF 18	8 6 / 3 12 / XSQ= 2.81 / PHI= 0.311 / EP = 0.0604

333	IN ALL CASES ARE THOSE WHERE THE AGE AT BEGINNING OF TRAINING IN HETEROSEXUAL PLAY INHIBITION IS LOWER THAN EIGHT YEARS (8) W-C	1.00 OF 5	333	IN ALL CASES ARE THOSE. WHERE THE AGE AT BEGINNING OF TRAINING IN HETEROSEXUAL PLAY INHIBITION IS EIGHT YEARS OR HIGHER (8) W-C	1.00 OF 3	0 3 5 0 XSQ= 4.30 PHI= -0.733 EP = 0.0179
334	LEAN TOWARD BEING THOSE WHERE THE INDULGENCE OF THE CHILD IS HIGH (40) B-B-C	0.76 OF 17	334	LEAN TOWARD BEING THOSE WHERE THE INDULGENCE OF THE CHILD IS LOW (38) B-B-C	0.69 OF 26	13 8 4 18 XSQ= 6.86 PHI= 0.399 XP = 0.0088
336	LEAN TOWARD BEING THOSE WHERE THE TOTAL POSITIVE PRESSURE TOWARD DEVELOPING RESPONSIBLE BEHAVIOR IN THE CHILD IS LOW (32) B-B-C	0.53 OF 17	336	LEAN TOWARD BEING THOSE WHERE THE TOTAL POSITIVE PRESSURE TOWARD DEVELOPING RESPONSIBLE BEHAVIOR IN THE CHILD IS HIGH (43) B-B-C	0.88 OF 26	8 23 9 3 XSQ= 6.82 PHI= -0.398 XP = 0.0090
337	LEAN TOWARD BEING THOSE WHERE THE CHILD'S INFERRED ANXIETY OVER NON-PERFORMANCE OF RESPONSIBLE BEHAVIOR IS LOW (35) B-B-C	0.69 OF 16	337	LEAN TOWARD BEING THOSE WHERE THE CHILD'S INFERRED ANXIETY OVER NON-PERFORMANCE OF RESPONSIBLE BEHAVIOR IS HIGH (38) B-B-C	0.81 OF 26	5 21 11 5 XSQ= 8.31 PHI= -0.445 XP = 0.0040
338	DRIFT TOWARD BEING THOSE WHERE THE CHILD'S INFERRED ANXIETY OVER PERFORMANCE OF RESPONSIBLE BEHAVIOR IS LOW (29) B-B-C	0.56 OF 16	338	DRIFT TOWARD BEING THOSE WHERE THE CHILD'S INFERRED ANXIETY OVER PERFORMANCE OF RESPONSIBLE BEHAVIOR IS HIGH (44) B-B-C	0.77 OF 26	7 20 9 6 XSQ= 3.41 PHI= -0.285 XP = 0.0647
339	LEAN TOWARD BEING THOSE WHERE THE CHILD'S INFERRED CONFLICT REGARDING RESPONSIBLE BEHAVIOR IS LOW (42) B-B-C	0.88 OF 16	339	LEAN TOWARD BEING THOSE WHERE THE CHILD'S INFERRED CONFLICT REGARDING RESPONSIBLE BEHAVIOR IS HIGH (31) B-B-C	0.62 OF 26	2 16 14 10 XSQ= 7.83 PHI= -0.432 XP = 0.0051
346	TILT TOWARD BEING THOSE WHERE THE CHILD'S INFERRED ANXIETY OVER PERFORMANCE OF SELF-RELIANT BEHAVIOR IS LOW (39) B-B-C	0.76 OF 17	346	TILT TOWARD BEING THOSE WHERE THE CHILD'S INFERRED ANXIETY OVER PERFORMANCE OF SELF-RELIANT BEHAVIOR IS HIGH (37) B-B-C	0.65 OF 26	4 17 13 9 XSQ= 5.63 PHI= -0.362 XP = 0.0177
347	TILT TOWARD BEING THOSE WHERE THE CHILD'S INFERRED CONFLICT REGARDING SELF-RELIANT BEHAVIOR IS LOW (39) B-B-C	0.71 OF 17	347	TILT TOWARD BEING THOSE WHERE THE CHILD'S INFERRED CONFLICT REGARDING SELF-RELIANT BEHAVIOR IS HIGH (37) B-B-C	0.69 OF 26	5 18 12 8 XSQ= 5.05 PHI= -0.343 XP = 0.0247
353	TILT TOWARD BEING THOSE WHERE THE CHILD-S INFERRED ANXIETY OVER NON-PERFORMANCE OF OBEDIENT BEHAVIOR IS LOW (32) B-B-C	0.69 OF 16	353	TILT TOWARD BEING THOSE WHERE THE CHILD'S INFERRED ANXIETY OVER NON-PERFORMANCE OF OBEDIENT BEHAVIOR IS HIGH (42) B-B-C	0.68 OF 25	5 17 11 8 XSQ= 3.92 PHI= -0.309 XP = 0.0476

365	TILT TOWARD BEING THOSE WHERE THE TIME SPENT IN ADOLESCENT PEER GROUP ACTIVITY IS LOW-MEDIUM OR LOW (15) JKH	0.67 OF 9	365	TILT TOWARD BEING THOSE WHERE THE TIME SPENT IN ADOLESCENT PEER GROUP ACTIVITY IS HIGH OR HIGH-MEDIUM (30) JKH	0.91 CF 11	3 10 6 1 XSQ= 4.90 PHI= -0.495 EP = 0.0166
377	LEAN MORE TOWARD BEING THOSE WHERE MALE GENITAL MUTILATION IS ABSENT (242)	0.81 OF 58	377	LEAN LESS TOWARD BEING THOSE WHERE MALE GENITAL MUTILATION IS ABSENT (242)	0.51 OF 68	11 33 47 35 XSQ= 10.77 PHI= -0.292 XP = 0.0010
393	DRIFT TOWARD BEING THOSE WHERE EXTRAMARITAL COITUS IS PERMITTED, RATHER THAN PUNISHED (41) F-B	0.63 OF 19	393	DRIFT TOWARD BEING THOSE WHERE EXTRAMARITAL COITUS IS PUNISHED, RATHER THAN PERMITTED (43) F-B	0.71 CF 17	7 12 12 5 XSQ= 2.86 PHI= -0.282 EP = 0.0543
419	LEAN LESS TOWARD BEING THOSE WHERE MILITARY GLORY IS STRONGLY OR MODERATELY EMPHASIZED (55) PES	0.52 OF 21	419	LEAN MORE TOWARD BEING THOSE WHERE MILITARY GLORY IS STRONGLY OR MODERATELY EMPHASIZED (55) PES	0.96 CF 24	11 23 10 1 XSQ= 9.22 PHI= -0.453 XP = 0.0024
426	LEAN TOWARD BEING THOSE WHERE A HIGH GOD IS ABSENT (104) GES,EA	0.51 OF 43	426	LEAN TOWARD BEING THOSE WHERE A HIGH GOD IS PRESENT (156) GES,EA	0.79 CF 58	21 46 22 12 XSQ= 8.95 PHI= -0.298 XP = 0.0028
428	TILT TOWARD BEING THOSE WHERE A HIGH GOD, IF PRESENT AND ACTIVE, SUPPORTS HUMAN MORALITY, RATHER THAN NOT SUPPORTING IT (61) GES,EA	0.77 OF 13	428	TILT TOWARD BEING THOSE WHERE A HIGH GOD, IF PRESENT AND ACTIVE, DOES NOT SUPPORT HUMAN MORALITY, RATHER THAN SUPPORTING IT (26) GES,EA	0.63 CF 19	10 7 3 12 XSQ= 3.50 PHI= 0.331 EP = 0.0359
455	TILT TOWARD BEING THOSE WHERE THE MODE OF THE INDIVIDUAL'S CONTACT WITH THE DIVINE IS CONDUCIVE TO THE DEVELOPMENT OF THE INDIVIDUAL'S NEED TO ACHIEVE (17) DCM	0.90 OF 10	455	TILT TOWARD BEING THOSE WHERE THE MODE OF THE INDIVIDUAL'S CONTACT WITH THE DIVINE IS NOT CONDUCIVE TO THE DEVELOPMENT OF THE INDIVIDUAL'S NEED TO ACHIEVE (19) DCM	0.57 CF 14	9 6 1 8 XSQ= 3.70 PHI= 0.393 EP = 0.0333
458	TEND TO BE THOSE WHERE GAMES, IF PRESENT, DO NOT INCLUDE GAMES OF STRATEGY (119) R-A-B,EA	0.88 OF 34	458	TEND TO BE THOSE WHERE GAMES, IF PRESENT, INCLUDE GAMES OF STRATEGY (52) R-A-B,EA	0.65 CF 34	4 22 30 12 XSQ= 18.00 PHI= -0.514 XP = 0.0000
460	TILT LESS TOWARD BEING THOSE WHERE GAMES, IF PRESENT, ARE NOT LIMITED TO GAMES OF SKILL ONLY (104) R-A-B,EA	0.53 OF 34	460	TILT MORE TOWARD BEING THOSE WHERE GAMES, IF PRESENT, ARE NOT LIMITED TO GAMES OF SKILL ONLY (104) R-A-B,EA	0.82 CF 34	16 6 18 28 XSQ= 5.44 PHI= 0.283 XP = 0.0197

```
*****************************************************************************************************

246  CULTURES                                      246  CULTURES
     WHERE THE FAMILY IS                                OTHER THAN WHERE THE FAMILY IS
     INDEPENDENT AND                                    INDEPENDENT AND
     MARRIAGE IS COMMONLY POLYGYNOUS AND                MARRIAGE IS COMMONLY POLYGYNOUS AND
     PREFERENTIALLY SORORAL, AND                        PREFERENTIALLY SORORAL AND
     CO-WIVES DWELL TOGETHER  (15)                      CO-WIVES DWELL TOGETHER  (383)

BACKGROUND ON PAGE 124                                                                  SUBJECT ONLY
.....................................................................................................

     15  IN LEFT COLUMN

ARANDA      CROW        DIERI       GROS VENTRE GUATO       KARIERA     MIAMI       MIWOK       MOTA        MURNGIN
POPOLUCA    SARSI       SENIANG     TETON       WIKMUNKAN

    383  IN RIGHT COLUMN

      2  EXCLUDED BECAUSE UNASCERTAINED

-----------------------------------------------------------------------------------------------------
  3  IN ALL CASES ARE THOSE          1.00 OF  15      3  DRIFT LESS TOWARD BEING THOSE  0.79 OF 383          0   80
     LOCATED OUTSIDE OF                                  LOCATED OUTSIDE OF                                 15  303
     AFRICA  (320)                                       AFRICA  (320)                               XSQ=     2.73
                                                                                                     PHI=   -0.083
                                                                                                     XP =   0.0986

  6  LEAN LESS TOWARD BEING THOSE    0.53 OF  15      6  LEAN MORE TOWARD BEING THOSE   0.84 OF 383          7   62
     LOCATED OUTSIDE OF                                  LOCATED OUTSIDE OF                                  8  321
     THE INSULAR PACIFIC  (330)                          THE INSULAR PACIFIC  (330)                  XSQ=     7.35
                                                                                                     PHI=    0.136
                                                                                                     XP =   0.0067

  8  LEAN LESS TOWARD BEING THOSE    0.53 OF  15      8  LEAN MORE TOWARD BEING THOSE   0.84 OF 383          7   62
     LOCATED OUTSIDE OF                                  LOCATED OUTSIDE OF                                  8  321
     NORTH AMERICA  (330)                                NORTH AMERICA  (330)                        XSQ=     7.35
                                                                                                     PHI=    0.136
                                                                                                     XP =   0.0067

 16  IN ALL CASES ARE THOSE          1.00 OF  15     16  TILT LESS TOWARD BEING THOSE   0.68 OF 383         15  260
     WHERE THE LATITUDE IS                               WHERE THE LATITUDE IS                               0  123
     TEN DEGREES OR GREATER  (277)                       TEN DEGREES OR GREATER  (277)               XSQ=     5.55
                                                                                                     PHI=    0.118
                                                                                                     XP =   0.0185

 44  TEND TO BE THOSE                0.85 OF  13     44  TEND TO BE THOSE               0.69 OF 318          2  219
     WHERE SETTLEMENTS ARE NON-FIXED  (110)              WHERE SETTLEMENTS ARE FIXED  (222)                 11   99
                                                                                                     XSQ=    13.78
                                                                                                     PHI=   -0.204
                                                                                                     XP =   0.0002
```

46	TEND TO BE THOSE WHERE SETTLEMENTS ARE NON-FIXED AND MOVEMENT IS NOMADIC (72)	0.69 OF 13	46	TEND TO BE THOSE OTHER THAN WHERE SETTLEMENTS ARE NON-FIXED AND MOVEMENT IS NOMADIC (260)	0.80 OF 318	9 63 4 255 XSQ= 15.14 PHI= 0.214 XP = 0.0001
51	LEAN TOWARD BEING THOSE WHERE SUBSISTENCE IS PRIMARILY BY FOOD GATHERING -- I. E., HUNTING, FISHING, OR COLLECTING -- RATHER THAN FOOD PRODUCTION (147)	0.80 OF 15	51	LEAN TOWARD BEING THOSE WHERE SUBSISTENCE IS PRIMARILY BY FOOD PRODUCTION -- I. E., AGRICULTURE OR HUSBANDRY -- RATHER THAN BY GATHERING (253)	0.65 OF 383	3 248 12 135 XSQ= 10.56 PHI= -0.163 XP = 0.0012
71	IN ALL CASES ARE THOSE WHERE METAL WORKING IS ABSENT (153)	1.00 OF 12	71	TILT LESS TOWARD BEING THOSE WHERE METAL WORKING IS ABSENT (153)	0.59 OF 238	0 98 12 140 XSQ= 6.49 PHI= -0.161 XP = 0.0108
73	DRIFT MORE TOWARD BEING THOSE WHERE WEAVING IS ABSENT (130)	0.83 OF 12	73	DRIFT LESS TOWARD BEING THOSE WHERE WEAVING IS ABSENT (130)	0.51 OF 235	2 115 10 120 XSQ= 3.56 PHI= -0.120 XP = 0.0591
74	TILT TOWARD BEING THOSE WHERE POTTERY IS ABSENT (93)	0.75 OF 12	74	TILT TOWARD BEING THOSE WHERE POTTERY IS PRESENT (145)	0.63 OF 225	3 141 9 84 XSQ= 5.29 PHI= -0.149 XP = 0.0214
82	TEND TO BE THOSE WHERE NO CITY OR TOWN IS PRESENT, AND THE AVERAGE COMMUNITY SIZE IS SMALLER THAN FIFTY (46)	0.83 OF 6	82	TEND TO BE THOSE WHERE A CITY OR TOWN IS PRESENT, OR THE AVERAGE COMMUNITY SIZE IS FIFTY OR GREATER (178)	0.81 OF 217	1 176 5 41 XSQ= 11.13 PHI= -0.223 XP = 0.0008
89	DRIFT TOWARD BEING THOSE WHERE, IF A NON-HEREDITARY HEADMANSHIP IS PRESENT, SUCCESSION IS BY MEANS OTHER THAN CONSENSUS (43)	0.83 OF 6	89	DRIFT TOWARD BEING THOSE WHERE, IF A NON-HEREDITARY HEADMANSHIP IS PRESENT, SUCCESSION IS BY CONSENSUS (63)	0.62 OF 100	1 62 5 38 XSQ= 3.13 PHI= -0.172 XP = 0.0770
95	IN ALL CASES ARE THOSE WHERE THE HIERARCHY OF NATIONAL JURISDICTION HAS ONE OR NO LEVELS (254) GES,EA	1.00 OF 13	95	DRIFT LESS TOWARD BEING THOSE WHERE THE HIERARCHY OF NATIONAL JURISDICTION HAS ONE OR NO LEVELS (254) GES,EA	0.76 OF 316	0 76 13 240 XSQ= 2.82 PHI= -0.093 XP = 0.0928
98	TEND TO BE THOSE WHERE THE HIERARCHY OF LOCAL JURISDICTION HAS TWO LEVELS (93) GES,EA	0.85 OF 13	98	TEND TO BE THOSE WHERE THE HIERARCHY OF LOCAL JURISDICTION HAS FOUR OR THREE LEVELS (238) GES,EA	0.74 OF 317	2 235 11 82 XSQ= 18.49 PHI= -0.237 XP = 0.0000

99	LEAN TOWARD BEING THOSE WHERE, WITH NATIONAL HIERARCHY ABSENT, THE HIERARCHY OF LOCAL JURISDICTION HAS TWO LEVELS (63) GES,EA	0.89 OF 9	99	LEAN TOWARD BEING THOSE WHERE, WITH NATIONAL HIERARCHY ABSENT, THE HIERARCHY OF LOCAL JURISDICTION HAS FOUR OR THREE LEVELS (93) GES,EA	0.63 OF 147	 XSQ= PHI= XP =	1 92 8 55 7.32 -0.217 0.0068
100	TEND TO BE THOSE WHERE HIERARCHIES ARE THE 'SIMPLEST' I. E., WHERE THERE ARE ONLY TWO LOCAL LEVELS WITH NO NATIONAL LEVELS (63) GES,EA	0.62 OF 13	100	TEND TO BE THOSE WHERE HIERARCHIES ARE MORE COMPLEX THAN THE 'SIMPLEST,' I. E., MORE COMPLEX THAN TWO LOCAL LEVELS WITH NO NATIONAL LEVELS (267) GES,EA	0.83 OF 316	 XSQ= PHI= XP =	5 261 8 55 12.99 -0.199 0.0003
102	LEAN TOWARD BEING THOSE WHERE CLASS STRATIFICATION IS ABSENT (180)	0.87 OF 15	102	LEAN TOWARD BEING THOSE WHERE CLASS STRATIFICATION IS PRESENT (203)	0.55 OF 367	 XSQ= PHI= XP =	2 201 13 166 8.34 -0.148 0.0039
110	LEAN MORE TOWARD BEING THOSE WHERE SLAVERY IS ABSENT (218)	0.93 OF 15	110	LEAN LESS TOWARD BEING THOSE WHERE SLAVERY IS ABSENT (218)	0.56 OF 364	 XSQ= PHI= XP =	1 161 14 203 6.84 -0.134 0.0089
131	IN ALL CASES ARE THOSE WHERE THE CONSTRUCTION OF PERMANENT HOUSES OR THE ERECTION OF TEMPORARY DWELLINGS IS MAINLY DONE BY FEMALES (21)	1.00 OF 5	131	TEND TO BE THOSE WHERE THE CONSTRUCTION OF PERMANENT HOUSES OR THE ERECTION OF TEMPORARY DWELLINGS IS MAINLY DONE BY MALES (136)	0.89 OF 151	 XSQ= PHI= XP =	0 135 5 16 25.98 -0.408 0.0000
177	TILT TOWARD BEING THOSE WHERE THE COMMUNITY IS A SINGLE CLAN-COMMUNITY AND EXOGAMOUS (77)	0.50 OF 12	177	TILT TOWARD BEING THOSE WHERE THE COMMUNITY IS OTHER THAN A SINGLE CLAN-COMMUNITY AND EXOGAMOUS (305)	0.81 OF 369	 XSQ= PHI= XP =	6 70 6 299 5.20 0.117 0.0226
179	TILT LESS TOWARD BEING THOSE WHERE THE COMMUNITY IS OTHER THAN STRUCTURED ON A NON-CLAN BASIS AND COMMONLY EXOGAMOUS (340)	0.67 OF 12	179	TILT MORE TOWARD BEING THOSE WHERE THE COMMUNITY IS OTHER THAN STRUCTURED ON A NON-CLAN BASIS AND COMMONLY EXOGAMOUS (340)	0.90 OF 369	 XSQ= PHI= XP =	4 38 8 331 4.16 0.104 0.0414
180	TEND TO BE THOSE WHERE THE COMMUNITY IS COMMONLY EXOGAMOUS, RATHER THAN NON-EXOGAMOUS (124)	0.83 OF 12	180	TEND TO BE THOSE WHERE THE COMMUNITY IS COMMONLY NON-EXOGAMOUS, RATHER THAN EXOGAMOUS (258)	0.69 OF 369	 XSQ= PHI= XP =	10 113 2 256 12.46 0.181 0.0004
183	TEND TO BE THOSE WHERE THE LARGEST NON-COGNATIC KIN GROUP IS THE MOEITY (34)	0.70 OF 10	183	TEND TO BE THOSE WHERE THE LARGEST NON-COGNATIC KIN GROUP IS SMALLER THAN A MOEITY, I. E., A PHRATRY OR SIB OR LINEAGE (218)	0.89 OF 241	 XSQ= PHI= XP =	7 27 3 214 23.55 0.306 0.0000

184	TEND TO BE THOSE WHERE THE LARGEST NON-COGNATIC KIN GROUP IS THE MOEITY OR PHRATRY (77)	0.90 OF 10	184	TEND TO BE THOSE WHERE THE LARGEST NON-COGNATIC KIN GROUP IS SMALLER THAN A PHRATRY, I. E. A SIB OR LINEAGE (175)	0.72 OF 241	9 67 1 174 XSQ= 14.77 PHI= 0.243 XP = 0.0001
196	LEAN TOWARD BEING THOSE WHERE INDIVIDUAL RIGHTS IN REAL PROPERTY, OR RULES FOR INHERITANCE, ARE ABSENT (87)	0.78 OF 9	196	LEAN TOWARD BEING THOSE WHERE INDIVIDUAL RIGHTS IN REAL PROPERTY, AND RULES FOR INHERITANCE, ARE PRESENT (194)	0.71 OF 272	2 192 7 80 XSQ= 7.41 PHI= -0.162 XP = 0.0065
234	TILT TOWARD BEING THOSE WHERE THE COUSIN TERMINOLOGY IS OF CROW, OMAHA, OR IROQUOIS TYPE, RATHER THAN ESKIMO OR HAWAIIAN TYPE (152)	0.79 OF 14	234	TILT TOWARD BEING THOSE WHERE THE COUSIN TERMINOLOGY IS OF ESKIMO OR HAWAIIAN TYPE, RATHER THAN CROW, OMAHA, OR IROQUOIS TYPE (170)	0.54 OF 306	11 140 3 166 XSQ= 4.54 PHI= 0.119 XP = 0.0330
279	IN ALL CASES ARE THOSE WHERE WIFE-LENDING OR WIFE-EXCHANGE IS PRESENT (10) LWS	1.00 OF 3	279	TILT TOWARD BEING THOSE WHERE WIFE-LENDING AND WIFE EXCHANGE ARE UNIMPORTANT OR ABSENT (19) LWS	0.73 OF 26	3 7 0 19 XSQ= 3.53 PHI= 0.349 EP = 0.0328
300	IN ALL CASES ARE THOSE WHERE THE POST-PARTUM SEX TABOO LASTS SIX MONTHS OR LESS (73)	1.00 OF 6	300	DRIFT LESS TOWARD BEING THOSE WHERE THE POST-PARTUM SEX TABOO LASTS SIX MONTHS OR LESS (73)	0.57 OF 118	0 51 6 67 XSQ= 2.80 PHI= -0.150 XP = 0.0942
351	IN ALL CASES ARE THOSE WHERE THE CHILD'S INFERRED CONFLICT REGARDING ACHIEVEMENT BEHAVIOR IS HIGH (26) B-B-C	1.00 OF 4	351	DRIFT TOWARD BEING THOSE WHERE THE CHILD'S INFERRED CONFLICT REGARDING ACHIEVEMENT BEHAVIOR IS LOW (34) B-B-C	0.61 OF 56	4 22 0 34 XSQ= 3.40 PHI= 0.238 XP = 0.0650
370	TILT TOWARD BEING THOSE WHERE THE SEGREGATION OF ADOLESCENT BOYS IS COMPLETE OR PARTIAL (95)	0.86 OF 7	370	TILT TOWARD BEING THOSE WHERE THE SEGREGATION OF ADOLESCENT BOYS IS ABSENT (148)	0.62 OF 235	6 89 1 146 XSQ= 4.67 PHI= 0.139 XP = 0.0306
380	IN ALL CASES ARE THOSE WHERE SEGREGATION OF GIRLS AT MENARCHE IS ABSENT (20) F-B	1.00 OF 3	380	DRIFT TOWARD BEING THOSE WHERE SEGREGATION OF GIRLS AT MENARCHE IS PRESENT (35) F-B	0.67 OF 52	0 35 3 17 XSQ= 3.03 PHI= -0.235 XP = 0.0820
455	IN ALL CASES ARE THOSE WHERE THE MODE OF THE INDIVIDUAL'S CONTACT WITH THE DIVINE IS CONDUCIVE TO THE DEVELOPMENT OF THE INDIVIDUAL'S NEED TO ACHIEVE (17) DCM	1.00 OF 3	455	DRIFT TOWARD BEING THOSE WHERE THE MODE OF THE INDIVIDUAL'S CONTACT WITH THE DIVINE IS NOT CONDUCIVE TO THE DEVELOPMENT OF THE INDIVIDUAL'S NEED TO ACHIEVE (19) DCM	0.58 OF 33	3 14 0 19 XSQ= 1.71 PHI= 0.218 EP = 0.0952

247 CULTURES
WHERE THE FAMILY IS
INDEPENDENT AND
MARRIAGE IS COMMCNLY PCLYGYNOUS AND
NOT PREFERENTIALLY SORORAL AND
CO-WIVES DWELL SEPARATELY (34)

247 CULTURES
OTHER THAN WHERE THE FAMILY IS
INDEPENDENT AND
MARRIAGE IS COMMONLY POLYGYNOUS AND
NOT PREFERENTIALLY SORORAL AND
CO-WIVES DWELL SEPARATELY (364)

BACKGROUND ON PAGE 124

SUBJECT ONLY

34 IN LEFT CCLUMN

AMBA	AZANDE	BAMILEKE	BARI	BAYA	CHAGGA	DILLING	FCN	FUTAJALONKE	GANDA
GISU	GOAJIRO	KIKUYU	KPE	LOZI	LUBA	MAMVU	MASAI	MBUNDU	NDEMBU
NGONI	NYAKYUSA	NYORO	PENDE	RUNDI	RWALA	SARAMACCA	SHILLUK	SOTHO	TESO
TIKOPIA	TODA	WANTCAT	YOMBE						

364 IN RIGHT CCLUMN

2 EXCLUDED BECAUSE UNASCERTAINED

	Left column			Right column		Statistics
3	TEND TO BE THOSE LOCATED IN AFRICA (80)	0.82 OF 34	3	TEND TO BE THOSE LOCATED OUTSIDE OF AFRICA (320)	0.86 OF 364	28 52 6 312 XSQ= 85.52 PHI= 0.464 XP = 0.
5	TILT MORE TOWARD BEING THOSE LOCATED OUTSIDE OF EAST EURASIA (330)	0.97 OF 34	5	TILT LESS TOWARD BEING THOSE LOCATED OUTSIDE OF EAST EURASIA (330)	0.81 OF 364	1 69 33 295 XSQ= 4.45 PHI= -0.106 XP = 0.0348
8	IN ALL CASES ARE THOSE LOCATED OUTSIDE OF NORTH AMERICA (330)	1.00 OF 34	8	TILT LESS TOWARD BEING THOSE LOCATED OUTSIDE OF NORTH AMERICA (330)	0.81 OF 364	0 69 34 295 XSQ= 6.53 PHI= -0.128 XP = 0.0106
13	IN ALL CASES ARE THOSE WHERE THE LATITUDE IS LESS THAN FORTY DEGREES (329)	1.00 OF 34	13	LEAN LESS TOWARD BEING THOSE WHERE THE LATITUDE IS LESS THAN FORTY DEGREES (329)	0.80 OF 364	0 71 34 293 XSQ= 6.80 PHI= -0.131 XP = 0.0091
16	TEND TO BE THOSE WHERE THE LATITUDE IS LESS THAN TEN DEGREES (123)	0.65 OF 34	16	TEND TO BE THOSE WHERE THE LATITUDE IS TEN DEGREES OR GREATER (277)	0.72 OF 364	12 263 22 101 XSQ= 18.20 PHI= -0.214 XP = 0.0000

```
45  TILT TOWARD BEING THOSE         0.58 OF  24    45  TILT TOWARD BEING THOSE         0.70 OF 197          10  138
    WHERE SETTLEMENTS, IF FIXED, ARE                   WHERE SETTLEMENTS, IF FIXED, ARE                     14   59
    NON-COMPACT, RATHER THAN                           COMPACT, RATHER THAN                            XSQ=     6.56
    COMPACT  (73)                                      NON-COMPACT  (149)                              PHI=   -0.172
                                                                                                       XP =   0.0104

51  LEAN MORE TOWARD BEING THOSE    0.88 OF  34    51  LEAN LESS TOWARD BEING THOSE    0.61 OF 364          30  221
    WHERE SUBSISTENCE IS PRIMARILY BY                  WHERE SUBSISTENCE IS PRIMARILY BY                     4  143
    FOOD PRODUCTION -- I. E., AGRICULTURE              FOOD PRODUCTION -- I. E., AGRICULTURE           XSQ=     8.96
    OR HUSBANDRY -- RATHER THAN BY                     OR HUSBANDRY -- RATHER THAN BY                  PHI=    0.150
    GATHERING  (253)                                   GATHERING  (253)                                XP =   0.0028

62  LEAN MORE TOWARD BEING THOSE    0.82 OF  34    62  LEAN LESS TOWARD BEING THOSE    0.55 OF 364          28  199
    WHERE HUSBANDRY OF SOME KIND                       WHERE HUSBANDRY OF SOME KIND                          6  165
    IS PRESENT  (228)                                  IS PRESENT  (228)                               XSQ=     8.63
                                                                                                       PHI=    0.147
                                                                                                       XP =   0.0033

71  TEND TO BE THOSE                0.77 OF  22    71  TEND TO BE THOSE                0.64 OF 228          17   81
    WHERE METAL WORKING IS                             WHERE METAL WORKING IS                                5  147
    PRESENT  (98)                                      ABSENT  (153)                                   XSQ=    12.97
                                                                                                       PHI=    0.228
                                                                                                       XP =   0.0003

73  DRIFT MORE TOWARD BEING THOSE   0.73 OF  22    73  DRIFT LESS TOWARD BEING THOSE   0.51 OF 225           6  111
    WHERE WEAVING IS                                   WHERE WEAVING IS                                     16  114
    ABSENT  (130)                                      ABSENT  (130)                                   XSQ=     3.08
                                                                                                       PHI=   -0.112
                                                                                                       XP =   0.0794

74  DRIFT MORE TOWARD BEING THOSE   0.81 OF  21    74  DRIFT LESS TOWARD BEING THOSE   0.59 OF 216          17  127
    WHERE POTTERY IS                                   WHERE POTTERY IS                                      4   89
    PRESENT  (145)                                     PRESENT  (145)                                  XSQ=     3.07
                                                                                                       PHI=    0.114
                                                                                                       XP =   0.0799

83  DRIFT LESS TOWARD BEING THOSE   0.55 OF  20    83  DRIFT MORE TOWARD BEING THOSE   0.77 OF 160           9   36
    WHERE, WITH NO CITY AND NO TOWN PRESENT,           WHERE, WITH NO CITY AND NO TOWN PRESENT,             11  124
    THE AVERAGE COMMUNITY SIZE IS                      THE AVERAGE COMMUNITY SIZE IS                   XSQ=     3.67
    SMALLER THAN 200, RATHER THAN                      SMALLER THAN 200, RATHER THAN                   PHI=    0.143
    BETWEEN 200 AND 999  (135)                         BETWEEN 200 AND 999  (135)                      XP =   0.0552

85  LEAN TOWARD BEING THOSE         0.52 OF  23    85  LEAN TOWARD BEING THOSE         0.80 OF 279          12   57
    WHERE THE LEVEL OF POLITICAL INTEGRATION           WHERE THE LEVEL OF POLITICAL INTEGRATION             11  222
    IS THE LARGE STATE, OR                             IS THE MINIMAL STATE,                           XSQ=    10.41
    THE LITTLE STATE  (70) GPM                         THE AUTONOMOUS COMMUNITY, OR                    PHI=    0.186
                                                       THE FAMILY  (234) GPM                           XP =   0.0013

86  DRIFT TOWARD BEING THOSE        0.70 OF  23    86  DRIFT TOWARD BEING THOSE        0.53 OF 279          16  130
    WHERE THE LEVEL OF POLITICAL INTEGRATION           WHERE THE LEVEL OF POLITICAL INTEGRATION              7  149
    IS THE LARGE STATE, THE LITTLE STATE,              IS THE AUTONOMOUS COMMUNITY, OR                 XSQ=     3.62
    OR THE MINIMAL STATE  (148) GPM                    THE FAMILY  (156) GPM                           PHI=    0.109
                                                                                                       XP =   0.0572
```

88	TILT MORE TOWARD BEING THOSE 0.81 OF 26 WHERE, IF A HEADMANSHIP IS PRESENT, SUCCESSION IS HEREDITARY (165)	88	TILT LESS TOWARD BEING THOSE 0.59 OF 244 WHERE, IF A HEADMANSHIP IS PRESENT, SUCCESSION IS HEREDITARY (165)	5 101 21 143 XSQ= 3.95 PHI= -0.121 XP = 0.0467
94	TILT LESS TOWARD BEING THOSE 0.77 OF 30 WHERE THE HIERARCHY OF NATIONAL JURISDICTION HAS TWO, ONE, OR NO LEVELS (296) GES,EA	94	TILT MORE TOWARD BEING THOSE 0.91 OF 299 WHERE THE HIERARCHY OF NATIONAL JURISDICTION HAS TWO, ONE, OR NO LEVELS (296) GES,EA	7 27 23 272 XSQ= 4.57 PHI= 0.118 XP = 0.0324
95	TILT LESS TOWARD BEING THOSE 0.57 OF 30 WHERE THE HIERARCHY OF NATIONAL JURISDICTION HAS ONE OR NO LEVELS (254) GES,EA	95	TILT MORE TOWARD BEING THOSE 0.79 OF 299 WHERE THE HIERARCHY OF NATIONAL JURISDICTION HAS ONE OR NO LEVELS (254) GES,EA	13 63 17 236 XSQ= 6.41 PHI= 0.140 XP = 0.0114
96	TILT MORE TOWARD BEING THOSE 0.73 OF 30 WHERE THE HIERARCHY OF NATIONAL JURISDICTION HAS FOUR, THREE, TWO OR ONE LEVEL (174) GES,EA	96	TILT LESS TOWARD BEING THOSE 0.51 OF 299 WHERE THE HIERARCHY OF NATIONAL JURISDICTION HAS FOUR, THREE, TWO OR ONE LEVEL (174) GES,EA	22 151 8 148 XSQ= 4.82 PHI= 0.121 XP = 0.0281
97	DRIFT MORE TOWARD BEING THOSE 0.97 OF 30 WHERE THE HIERARCHY OF LOCAL JURISDICTION HAS THREE OR TWO LEVELS (273) GES,EA	97	DRIFT LESS TOWARD BEING THOSE 0.81 OF 300 WHERE THE HIERARCHY OF LOCAL JURISDICTION HAS THREE OR TWO LEVELS (273) GES,EA	1 57 29 243 XSQ= 3.60 PHI= -0.104 XP = 0.0577
102	DRIFT MORE TOWARD BEING THOSE 0.70 OF 33 WHERE CLASS STRATIFICATION IS PRESENT (203)	102	DRIFT LESS TOWARD BEING THOSE 0.52 OF 349 WHERE CLASS STRATIFICATION IS PRESENT (203)	23 180 10 169 XSQ= 3.28 PHI= 0.093 XP = 0.0701
108	LEAN TOWARD BEING THOSE 0.65 OF 23 WHERE CLASS STRATIFICATION, IF PRESENT, IS BASED ON A HEREDITARY ARISTOCRACY (74)	108	LEAN TOWARD BEING THOSE 0.67 OF 180 WHERE CLASS STRATIFICATION, IF PRESENT, IS BASED ON SOMETHING OTHER THAN A HEREDITARY ARISTOCRACY (129)	15 59 8 121 XSQ= 7.92 PHI= 0.197 XP = 0.0049
110	LEAN TOWARD BEING THOSE 0.71 OF 34 WHERE SLAVERY IS PRESENT (163)	110	LEAN TOWARD BEING THOSE 0.60 OF 345 WHERE SLAVERY IS ABSENT (218)	24 138 10 207 XSQ= 10.62 PHI= 0.167 XP = 0.0011
128	LEAN TOWARD BEING THOSE 0.92 OF 13 WHERE, IF SUBSISTENCE IS PRIMARILY BY AGRICULTURE, THE WORK IS MAINLY DONE BY FEMALES (37)	128	LEAN TOWARD BEING THOSE 0.60 OF 63 WHERE, IF SUBSISTENCE IS PRIMARILY BY AGRICULTURE, THE WORK IS MAINLY DONE BY MALES (40)	1 38 12 25 XSQ= 9.93 PHI= -0.362 XP = 0.0016

149	IN ALL CASES ARE THOSE WHERE THE INCIDENCE OF THEFT IS HIGH (18) B-B-C	1.00 OF 5	149	TILT TOWARD BEING THOSE WHERE THE INCIDENCE OF THEFT IS LOW (19) B-B-C	0.59 OF 32	5 13 0 19 XSQ= 3.96 PHI= 0.327 EP = 0.0197
176	LEAN TOWARD BEING THOSE WHERE THE COMMUNITY IS A CLAN-COMMUNITY OR A COMMUNITY STRUCTURED OR SEGMENTED ON A CLAN BASIS (169)	0.71 OF 34	176	LEAN TOWARD BEING THOSE WHERE THE COMMUNITY IS OTHER THAN A CLAN-COMMUNITY OR A COMMUNITY STRUCTURED OR SEGMENTED ON A CLAN BASIS (213)	0.59 OF 347	24 144 10 203 XSQ= 9.48 PHI= 0.158 XP = 0.0021
177	LEAN LESS TOWARD BEING THOSE WHERE THE COMMUNITY IS OTHER THAN A SINGLE CLAN-COMMUNITY AND EXOGAMOUS (305)	0.59 OF 34	177	LEAN MORE TOWARD BEING THOSE WHERE THE COMMUNITY IS OTHER THAN A SINGLE CLAN-COMMUNITY AND EXOGAMOUS (305)	0.82 OF 347	14 62 20 285 XSQ= 9.13 PHI= 0.155 XP = 0.0025
180	TILT TOWARD BEING THOSE WHERE THE COMMUNITY IS COMMONLY EXOGAMOUS, RATHER THAN NON-EXOGAMOUS (124)	0.50 OF 34	180	TILT TOWARD BEING THOSE WHERE THE COMMUNITY IS COMMONLY NON-EXOGAMOUS, RATHER THAN EXOGAMOUS (258)	0.69 OF 347	17 106 17 241 XSQ= 4.51 PHI= 0.109 XP = 0.0338
181	IN ALL CASES ARE THOSE WHERE THE COMMUNITY IS OTHER THAN A DEME (337)	1.00 OF 34	181	DRIFT LESS TOWARD BEING THOSE WHERE THE COMMUNITY IS OTHER THAN A DEME (337)	0.87 OF 347	0 45 34 302 XSQ= 3.83 PHI= -0.100 XP = 0.0503
183	IN ALL CASES ARE THOSE WHERE THE LARGEST NON-COGNATIC KIN GROUP IS SMALLER THAN A MOEITY, I. E., A PHRATRY OR SIB OR LINEAGE (218)	1.00 OF 32	183	TILT LESS TOWARD BEING THOSE WHERE THE LARGEST NON-COGNATIC KIN GROUP IS SMALLER THAN A MOEITY, I. E., A PHRATRY OR SIB OR LINEAGE (218)	0.84 OF 219	0 34 32 185 XSQ= 4.50 PHI= -0.134 XP = 0.0340
184	TILT MORE TOWARD BEING THOSE WHERE THE LARGEST NON-COGNATIC KIN GROUP IS SMALLER THAN A PHRATRY, I. E. A SIB OR LINEAGE (175)	0.91 OF 32	184	TILT LESS TOWARD BEING THOSE WHERE THE LARGEST NON-COGNATIC KIN GROUP IS SMALLER THAN A PHRATRY, I. E. A SIB OR LINEAGE (175)	0.67 OF 219	3 73 29 146 XSQ= 6.50 PHI= -0.161 XP = 0.0108
186	TILT TOWARD BEING THOSE WHERE THE KIN GROUP IS EXCLUSIVELY PATRILINEAL (150)	0.59 OF 34	186	TILT TOWARD BEING THOSE WHERE THE KIN GROUP IS OTHER THAN EXCLUSIVELY PATRILINEAL (250)	0.65 OF 364	20 129 14 235 XSQ= 6.30 PHI= 0.126 XP = 0.0121
188	TEND MORE TO BE THOSE WHERE THE KIN GROUP IS OTHER THAN EXCLUSIVELY COGNATIC (252)	0.94 OF 34	188	TEND LESS TO BE THOSE WHERE THE KIN GROUP IS OTHER THAN EXCLUSIVELY COGNATIC (252)	0.60 OF 364	2 145 32 219 XSQ= 13.97 PHI= -0.187 XP = 0.0002

192	IN ALL CASES ARE THOSE 1.00 OF 34 OTHER THAN WHERE THE ONLY KIN GROUP PRESENT IS A KINDRED OR ELSE BILATERAL DESCENT IS INFERRED (289)	192	TEND LESS TO BE THOSE 0.70 OF 364 OTHER THAN WHERE THE ONLY KIN GROUP PRESENT IS A KINDRED OR ELSE BILATERAL DESCENT IS INFERRED (289)	0 110 34 254 XSQ= 12.73 PHI= -0.179 XP = 0.0004
196	DRIFT MORE TOWARD BEING THOSE 0.86 OF 28 WHERE INDIVIDUAL RIGHTS IN REAL PROPERTY, AND RULES FOR INHERITANCE, ARE PRESENT (194)	196	DRIFT LESS TOWARD BEING THOSE 0.67 OF 253 WHERE INDIVIDUAL RIGHTS IN REAL PROPERTY, AND RULES FOR INHERITANCE, ARE PRESENT (194)	24 170 4 83 XSQ= 3.23 PHI= 0.107 XP = 0.0725
197	IN ALL CASES ARE THOSE 1.00 OF 24 WHERE RULES FOR THE INHERITANCE OF REAL PROPERTY, IF PRESENT, FAVOR EITHER THE MALE HEIR OR LINE, OR THE FEMALE HEIR OR LINE (165)	197	DRIFT LESS TOWARD BEING THOSE 0.83 OF 170 WHERE RULES FOR THE INHERITANCE OF REAL PROPERTY, IF PRESENT, FAVOR EITHER THE MALE HEIR OR LINE, OR THE FEMALE HEIR OR LINE (165)	24 141 0 29 XSQ= 3.57 PHI= 0.136 XP = 0.0590
201	DRIFT MORE TOWARD BEING THOSE 0.97 OF 34 WHERE MARITAL RESIDENCE IS NON-OPTIONAL, RATHER THAN AMBILOCAL OR NEOLOCAL (334)	201	DRIFT LESS TOWARD BEING THOSE 0.83 OF 362 WHERE MARITAL RESIDENCE IS NON-OPTIONAL, RATHER THAN AMBILOCAL OR NEOLOCAL (334)	33 299 1 63 XSQ= 3.79 PHI= 0.098 XP = 0.0516
204	TILT MORE TOWARD BEING THOSE 0.97 OF 34 WHERE MARITAL RESIDENCE IS PATRILOCAL, VIRILOCAL, OR AVUNCULOCAL, RATHER THAN AMBILOCAL OR NEOLOCAL (270)	204	TILT LESS TOWARD BEING THOSE 0.79 OF 298 WHERE MARITAL RESIDENCE IS PATRILOCAL, VIRILOCAL, OR AVUNCULOCAL, RATHER THAN AMBILOCAL OR NEOLOCAL (270)	33 235 1 63 XSQ= 5.38 PHI= 0.127 XP = 0.0204
209	IN ALL CASES ARE THOSE 1.00 OF 33 WHERE MARITAL RESIDENCE IS PATRILOCAL, VIRILOCAL, OR AVUNCULOCAL, RATHER THAN MATRILOCAL OR UXORILOCAL (270)	209	LEAN LESS TOWARD BEING THOSE 0.79 OF 299 WHERE MARITAL RESIDENCE IS PATRILOCAL, VIRILOCAL, OR AVUNCULOCAL, RATHER THAN MATRILOCAL OR UXORILOCAL (270)	33 235 0 64 XSQ= 7.43 PHI= 0.150 XP = 0.0064
210	IN ALL CASES ARE THOSE 1.00 OF 24 WHERE MARITAL RESIDENCE IS PATRILOCAL, RATHER THAN MATRILOCAL (169)	210	DRIFT LESS TOWARD BEING THOSE 0.82 OF 175 WHERE MARITAL RESIDENCE IS PATRILOCAL, RATHER THAN MATRILOCAL (169)	24 144 0 31 XSQ= 3.78 PHI= 0.138 XP = 0.0519
234	LEAN TOWARD BEING THOSE 0.75 OF 24 WHERE THE COUSIN TERMINOLOGY IS OF CROW, OMAHA, OR IROQUOIS TYPE, RATHER THAN ESKIMO OR HAWAIIAN TYPE (152)	234	LEAN TOWARD BEING THOSE 0.55 OF 296 WHERE THE COUSIN TERMINOLOGY IS OF ESKIMO OR HAWAIIAN TYPE, RATHER THAN CROW, OMAHA, OR IROQUOIS TYPE (170)	18 133 6 163 XSQ= 6.89 PHI= 0.147 XP = 0.0087
258	DRIFT TOWARD BEING THOSE 0.83 OF 6 WHERE THE SEVERITY OF SON'S WIFE AVOIDANCE IS HIGH (15) WNS	258	DRIFT TOWARD BEING THOSE 0.60 OF 25 WHERE THE SEVERITY OF SON'S WIFE AVOIDANCE IS LOW (16) WNS	5 10 1 15 XSQ= 2.11 PHI= 0.261 EP = 0.0829

262	IN ALL CASES ARE THOSE WHERE WIVES ARE OBTAINED BY MEANS INVOLVING THE PRESENCE OF SOME CONSIDERATION (305)	1.00 OF 34	262	LEAN LESS TOWARD BEING THOSE WHERE WIVES ARE OBTAINED BY MEANS INVOLVING THE PRESENCE OF SOME CONSIDERATION (305)	0.75 OF 359	34 270 0 89 XSQ= 9.53 PHI= 0.156 XP = 0.0020
263	TILT MORE TOWARD BEING THOSE WHERE WIVES ARE OBTAINED BY RELATIVELY DIFFICULT MEANS, NAMELY BY BRIDE-PRICE, BRIDE-SERVICE, OR EXCHANGING A FEMALE RELATIVE (233)	0.79 OF 34	263	TILT LESS TOWARD BEING THOSE WHERE WIVES ARE OBTAINED BY RELATIVELY DIFFICULT MEANS, NAMELY BY BRIDE-PRICE, BRIDE-SERVICE, OR EXCHANGING A FEMALE RELATIVE (233)	0.57 OF 359	27 205 7 154 XSQ= 5.50 PHI= 0.118 XP = 0.0190
279	IN ALL CASES ARE THOSE WHERE WIFE-LENDING OR WIFE-EXCHANGE IS PRESENT (10) LWS	1.00 OF 3	279	TILT TOWARD BEING THOSE WHERE WIFE-LENDING AND WIFE EXCHANGE ARE UNIMPORTANT OR ABSENT (19) LWS	0.73 OF 26	3 7 0 19 XSQ= 3.53 PHI= 0.349 EP = 0.0328
296	IN ALL CASES ARE THOSE WHERE INFANTICIDE IS PRESENT (18) BCA	1.00 OF 5	296	TILT TOWARD BEING THOSE WHERE INFANTICIDE IS ABSENT OR INFERRED ABSENT (15) BCA	0.54 OF 28	5 13 0 15 XSQ= 2.99 PHI= 0.301 EP = 0.0488
314	TILT TOWARD BEING THOSE WHERE THE INCIDENCE OF MOTHER-CHILD HOUSEHOLDS IS HIGH (19) W-D,S	0.80 OF 5	314	TILT TOWARD BEING THOSE WHERE THE INCIDENCE OF MOTHER-CHILD HOUSEHOLDS IS LOW (61) W-D,S	0.80 OF 75	4 15 1 60 XSQ= 6.30 PHI= 0.281 XP = 0.0121
316	IN ALL CASES ARE THOSE WHERE EXCLUSIVE MOTHER-SON SLEEPING ARRANGEMENTS LAST ONE YEAR OR LONGER (19) W-K-A	1.00 OF 5	316	TILT TOWARD BEING THOSE WHERE EXCLUSIVE MOTHER-SON SLEEPING ARRANGEMENTS LAST LESS THAN ONE YEAR (25) W-K-A	0.64 OF 39	5 14 0 25 XSQ= 5.04 PHI= 0.338 XP = 0.0248
318	DRIFT TOWARD BEING THOSE WHERE THE OVERALL INDULGENCE OF THE INFANT IS LOW (31) B-B-C	0.78 OF 9	318	DRIFT TOWARD BEING THOSE WHERE THE OVERALL INDULGENCE OF THE INFANT IS HIGH (40) B-B-C	0.61 OF 62	2 38 7 24 XSQ= 3.42 PHI= -0.219 XP = 0.0645
319	DRIFT TOWARD BEING THOSE WHERE PROTECTION OF THE INFANT FROM ENVIRONMENTAL DISCOMFORTS IS LOW (30) B-B-C	0.78 OF 9	319	DRIFT TOWARD BEING THOSE WHERE PROTECTION OF THE INFANT FROM ENVIRONMENTAL DISCOMFORTS IS HIGH (35) B-B-C	0.59 OF 56	2 33 7 23 XSQ= 2.86 PHI= -0.210 XP = 0.0910
327	IN ALL CASES ARE THOSE WHERE THE AGE OF THE INFANT AT TIME OF REDUCED CONTACT WITH MOTHER IS TWO YEARS OR LOWER (27) B-B-C	1.00 OF 8	327	LEAN TOWARD BEING THOSE WHERE THE AGE OF THE INFANT AT TIME OF REDUCED CONTACT WITH MOTHER IS HIGHER THAN TWO YEARS (28) B-B-C	0.60 OF 47	0 28 8 19 XSQ= 7.47 PHI= -0.369 XP = 0.0063

No.		No.		
336	DRIFT MORE TOWARD BEING THOSE 0.90 OF 10 WHERE THE TOTAL POSITIVE PRESSURE TOWARD DEVELOPING RESPONSIBLE BEHAVIOR IN THE CHILD IS HIGH (43) B-B-C	336	DRIFT LESS TOWARD BEING THOSE 0.52 OF 65 WHERE THE TOTAL POSITIVE PRESSURE TOWARD DEVELOPING RESPONSIBLE BEHAVIOR IN THE CHILD IS HIGH (43) B-B-C	9 34 1 31 XSQ= 3.61 PHI= 0.219 XP = 0.0574
337	TILT TOWARD BEING THOSE 0.90 OF 10 WHERE THE CHILD'S INFERRED ANXIETY OVER NON-PERFORMANCE OF RESPONSIBLE BEHAVIOR IS HIGH (38) B-B-C	337	TILT TOWARD BEING THOSE 0.54 OF 63 WHERE THE CHILD'S INFERRED ANXIETY OVER NON-PERFORMANCE OF RESPONSIBLE BEHAVIOR IS LOW (35) B-B-C	9 29 1 34 XSQ= 5.04 PHI= 0.263 XP = 0.0248
347	DRIFT TOWARD BEING THOSE 0.80 OF 10 WHERE THE CHILD'S INFERRED CONFLICT REGARDING SELF-RELIANT BEHAVIOR IS HIGH (37) B-B-C	347	DRIFT TOWARD BEING THOSE 0.56 OF 66 WHERE THE CHILD'S INFERRED CONFLICT REGARDING SELF-RELIANT BEHAVIOR IS LOW (39) B-B-C	8 29 2 37 XSQ= 3.19 PHI= 0.205 XP = 0.0740
353	DRIFT MORE TOWARD BEING THOSE 0.89 OF 9 WHERE THE CHILD'S INFERRED ANXIETY OVER NON-PERFORMANCE OF OBEDIENT BEHAVIOR IS HIGH (42) B-B-C	353	DRIFT LESS TOWARD BEING THOSE 0.52 OF 65 WHERE THE CHILD'S INFERRED ANXIETY OVER NON-PERFORMANCE OF OBEDIENT BEHAVIOR IS HIGH (42) B-B-C	8 34 1 31 XSQ= 2.95 PHI= 0.200 XP = 0.0859
370	LEAN TOWARD BEING THOSE 0.71 OF 21 WHERE THE SEGREGATION OF ADOLESCENT BOYS IS COMPLETE OR PARTIAL (95)	370	LEAN TOWARD BEING THOSE 0.64 OF 221 WHERE THE SEGREGATION OF ADOLESCENT BOYS IS ABSENT (148)	15 80 6 141 XSQ= 8.56 PHI= 0.188 XP = 0.0034
377	LEAN TOWARD BEING THOSE 0.52 OF 29 WHERE MALE GENITAL MUTILATION IS PRESENT (83)	377	LEAN TOWARD BEING THOSE 0.77 OF 295 WHERE MALE GENITAL MUTILATION IS ABSENT (242)	15 67 14 228 XSQ= 10.27 PHI= 0.178 XP = 0.0014
424	DRIFT TOWARD BEING THOSE 0.83 OF 6 WHERE RELIGIOUS SPECIALISTS ARE FULL-TIME, RATHER THAN PART-TIME (21) JMH	424	DRIFT TOWARD BEING THOSE 0.67 OF 48 WHERE RELIGIOUS SPECIALISTS ARE PART-TIME, RATHER THAN FULL-TIME (33) JMH	5 16 1 32 XSQ= 3.70 PHI= 0.262 XP = 0.0543
427	TILT TOWARD BEING THOSE 0.74 OF 19 WHERE A HIGH GOD, IF PRESENT, IS INACTIVE, RATHER THAN ACTIVE (69) GES,EA	427	TILT TOWARD BEING THOSE 0.60 OF 137 WHERE A HIGH GOD, IF PRESENT, IS ACTIVE, RATHER THAN INACTIVE (87) GES,EA	5 82 14 55 XSQ= 6.31 PHI= -0.201 XP = 0.0120
446	DRIFT TOWARD BEING THOSE 0.80 OF 5 WHERE WITCHCRAFT IS SIGNIFICANTLY PRESENT (14) GES	446	DRIFT TOWARD BEING THOSE 0.70 OF 33 WHERE WITCHCRAFT IS MODERATELY PRESENT OR ABSENT (24) GES	4 10 1 23 XSQ= 2.72 PHI= 0.268 EP = 0.0519

```
458  LEAN TOWARD BEING THOSE          0.67 OF  15     458  LEAN TOWARD BEING THOSE          0.73 OF 156         10   42
     WHERE GAMES, IF PRESENT,                             WHERE GAMES, IF PRESENT,                                   5  114
     INCLUDE GAMES OF STRATEGY  (52) R-A-B,EA             DO NOT INCLUDE                                     XSQ=    8.42
                                                          GAMES OF STRATEGY  (119) R-A-B,EA                  PHI=   0.222
                                                                                                             XP =  0.0037

459  TILT TOWARD BEING THOSE          0.80 OF  15     459  TILT TOWARD BEING THOSE          0.51 OF 156          3   79
     WHERE GAMES, IF PRESENT,                             WHERE GAMES, IF PRESENT,                                  12   77
     DO NOT INCLUDE                                       INCLUDE GAMES OF CHANCE  (82) R-A-B,EA             XSQ=    3.99
     GAMES OF CHANCE  (89) R-A-B,EA                                                                          PHI=  -0.153
                                                                                                             XP =  0.0457
```

****

248 CULTURES WHERE, WITH THE EXTENDED FAMILY PRESENT, MARRIAGE IS COMMONLY OR OCCASIONALLY POLYGYNOUS, RATHER THAN MONOGAMOUS (170)	248 CULTURES WHERE, WITH THE EXTENDED FAMILY PRESENT, MARRIAGE IS MONOGAMOUS, RATHER THAN COMMONLY OR OCCASIONALLY POLYGYNOUS (42)

BACKGROUND ON PAGE 124 SUBJECT ONLY

....

170 IN LEFT COLUMN

AINU	ALBANIANS	ARAUCANIANS	ARYANS	ASHANTI	ATSUGEWI	BABWA	BACAIRI	BALINESE	BAMBARA
BATAK	BELU	BENGALI	BETE	BHIL	BIRIFOR	BORORO	BOTOCUDO	BOZO	BURUSHO
BURYAT	CADUVEO	CALLIÑAGO	CAMAYURA	CARAJA	CHEROKEE	CHEYENNE	CHIR-APACHE	CHIRIGUANO	CHUKCHEE
COMANCHE	CREEK	CUNA	DARC	DELAWARE	DOGON	EGYPTIANS	ELLICE	FANG	FOX
GARO	GOND	GUAHIBO	GURE	HAIDA	HANUNOO	HASINAI	HAVASUPAI	HAWAIIANS	HAZARA
HEBREWS	HEHE	HERERO	HUICHOL	HUKUNDIKA	ILA	JAVANESE	JIVARO	JUKUN	KABYLE
KACHIN	KALMYK	KAPAUKU	KATAB	KAZAK	KERALA	KIOW-APACHE	KISSI	KOL	KONSO
KORYAK	KUBA	KUNG	KWAKIUTL	LAKALAI	LANGO	LAU	LEPCHA	LIFU	LUO
MAGUZAWA	MALAYS	MAMBILA	MANDAN	MANGAIANS	MANIHIKI	MAORI	MARGI	MATACO	MATAKAM
MENDE	MIAO	MIN CHINESE	MINANGKABAU	MINCHIA	MISKITO	MONGO	MONGUOR	MOSSI	MOTILON
MUNDURUCU	NATCHEZ	NAVAHO	NUER	NUNIVAK	NUPE	NURI	NYANEKA	OJIBWA	ONTONG-JAVA
ORAON	PAIWAN	PAPAGO	PAWNEE	PURUM	RAROIANS	REGEIBAT	RIFFIANS	SAMOANS	SAMOYED
SANPOIL	SANTAL	SINDHI	SIRIONO	SIWANS	SOMALI	SWAZI	SYRIANS	TALAMANCA	TALLENSI
TAMIL	TANALA	TANIMBARESE	TAREUMIUT	TEDA	TEHUELCHE	TENETEHARA	TENINO	TERA	TERENA
THAI	THONGA	TIMUCUA	TIV	TIWI	TOKELAU	TRUMAI	TSHIMSHIAN	TUPINAMBA	TURKANA
TURKMEN	TWANA	TZELTAL	UTE	VENDA	VIETNAMESE	WAROPEN	WARRAU	WICHITA	WINNEBAGO
WOLOF	WUTE	YAKO	YAKUT	YAO	YARURO	YOKUTS	YORUBA	YUKAGHIR	YUROK

42 IN RIGHT COLUMN

APINAYE	ATAYAL	AYMARA	BASQUES	BOERS	BULGARIANS	CAYAPA	CHINANTEC	CHORTI	COCHITI
COORG	CZECHS	CAGUR	DUTCH	HANO	HURON	IBAN	ICELANDERS	INGASSANA	IRISH
JAPANESE	KASKA	KHALKA	KHASI	KOREANS	MAM	MANCHU	MARSHALLESE	MBUGWE	OKINAWANS
PORTUGUESE	SERBS	SERI	SHLUH	TAPIRAPE	TIMBIRA	TORAJA	TRUKESE	VEDDA	WOLEAIANS
YAPESE	ZUNI								

186 EXCLUDED BECAUSE IRRELEVANT

2 EXCLUDED BECAUSE UNASCERTAINED

----

3 TILT LESS TOWARD BEING THOSE LOCATED OUTSIDE OF AFRICA (320)	0.78 OF 170	3 TILT MORE TOWARD BEING THOSE LOCATED OUTSIDE OF AFRICA (320)	0.95 OF 42

38	2
132	40
XSQ=	5.71
PHI=	0.164
XP =	0.0169

4 TILT MORE TOWARD BEING THOSE 0.91 OF 170 LOCATED OUTSIDE OF THE CIRCUM-MEDITERRANEAN (355)	4 TILT LESS TOWARD BEING THOSE 0.76 OF 42 LOCATED OUTSIDE OF THE CIRCUM-MEDITERRANEAN (355)	15 10 155 32 XSQ= 5.90 PHI= -0.167 XP = 0.0151
13 DRIFT MORE TOWARD BEING THOSE 0.84 OF 170 WHERE THE LATITUDE IS LESS THAN FORTY DEGREES (329)	13 DRIFT LESS TOWARD BEING THOSE 0.69 OF 42 WHERE THE LATITUDE IS LESS THAN FORTY DEGREES (329)	28 13 142 29 XSQ= 3.65 PHI= -0.131 XP = 0.0562
44 LEAN LESS TOWARD BEING THOSE 0.63 OF 144 WHERE SETTLEMENTS ARE FIXED (222)	44 LEAN MORE TOWARD BEING THOSE 0.91 OF 35 WHERE SETTLEMENTS ARE FIXED (222)	91 32 53 3 XSQ= 9.17 PHI= -0.226 XP = 0.0025
51 TILT LESS TOWARD BEING THOSE 0.60 OF 170 WHERE SUBSISTENCE IS PRIMARILY BY FOOD PRODUCTION -- I. E., AGRICULTURE OR HUSBANDRY -- RATHER THAN BY GATHERING (253)	51 TILT MORE TOWARD BEING THOSE 0.79 OF 42 WHERE SUBSISTENCE IS PRIMARILY BY FOOD PRODUCTION -- I. E., AGRICULTURE OR HUSBANDRY -- RATHER THAN BY GATHERING (253)	102 33 68 9 XSQ= 4.25 PHI= -0.142 XP = 0.0392
77 DRIFT TOWARD BEING THOSE 0.79 OF 24 WHERE THE WRITING SYSTEM IS MNEMONIC OR ABSENT, RATHER THAN BEING ALPHABETIC-OR-PHONETIC (39) JMH	77 DRIFT TOWARD BEING THOSE 0.56 OF 9 WHERE THE WRITING SYSTEM IS ALPHABETIC-OR-PHONETIC, RATHER THAN BEING MNEMONIC OR ABSENT (15) JMH	5 5 19 4 XSQ= 2.27 PHI= -0.262 EP = 0.0895
79 LEAN MORE TOWARD BEING THOSE 0.91 OF 91 WHERE NO CITY IS PRESENT (201)	79 LEAN LESS TOWARD BEING THOSE 0.68 OF 25 WHERE NO CITY IS PRESENT (201)	8 8 83 17 XSQ= 7.04 PHI= -0.246 XP = 0.0080
80 DRIFT MORE TOWARD BEING THOSE 0.86 OF 91 WHERE NO CITY OR TOWN IS PRESENT (185)	80 DRIFT LESS TOWARD BEING THOSE 0.68 OF 25 WHERE NO CITY OR TOWN IS PRESENT (185)	13 8 78 17 XSQ= 3.04 PHI= -0.162 XP = 0.0811
84 DRIFT MORE TOWARD BEING THOSE 0.89 OF 138 WHERE THE LEVEL OF POLITICAL INTEGRATION IS THE LITTLE STATE, THE MINIMAL STATE, THE AUTONOMOUS COMMUNITY, OR THE FAMILY (262) GPM	84 DRIFT LESS TOWARD BEING THOSE 0.74 OF 31 WHERE THE LEVEL OF POLITICAL INTEGRATION IS THE LITTLE STATE, THE MINIMAL STATE, THE AUTONOMOUS COMMUNITY, OR THE FAMILY (262) GPM	15 8 123 23 XSQ= 3.62 PHI= -0.146 XP = 0.0572
88 DRIFT TOWARD BEING THOSE 0.65 OF 126 WHERE, IF A HEADMANSHIP IS PRESENT, SUCCESSION IS HEREDITARY (165)	88 DRIFT TOWARD BEING THOSE 0.56 OF 27 WHERE, IF A HEADMANSHIP IS PRESENT, SUCCESSION IS NON-HEREDITARY (106)	44 15 82 12 XSQ= 3.17 PHI= -0.144 XP = 0.0749

90	LEAN TOWARD BEING THOSE 0.80 OF 82 WHERE, IF A HEREDITARY HEADMANSHIP IS PRESENT, SUCCESSION IS PATRILINEAL, RATHER THAN MATRILINEAL (127)	90	LEAN TOWARD BEING THOSE 0.67 OF 12 WHERE, IF A HEREDITARY HEADMANSHIP IS PRESENT, SUCCESSION IS MATRILINEAL, RATHER THAN PATRILINEAL (38)	66 4 16 8 XSQ= 9.89 PHI= 0.324 XP = 0.0017
94	DRIFT MORE TOWARD BEING THOSE 0.92 OF 144 WHERE THE HIERARCHY OF NATIONAL JURISDICTION HAS TWO, ONE, OR NO LEVELS (296) GES,EA	94	DRIFT LESS TOWARD BEING THOSE 0.79 OF 34 WHERE THE HIERARCHY OF NATIONAL JURISDICTION HAS TWO, ONE, OR NO LEVELS (296) GES,EA	11 7 133 27 XSQ= 3.75 PHI= -0.145 XP = 0.0528
107	LEAN MORE TOWARD BEING THOSE 0.82 OF 95 WHERE CLASS STRATIFICATION, IF PRESENT, IS BASED ON SOMETHING OTHER THAN OCCUPATIONAL STATUS (160)	107	LEAN LESS TOWARD BEING THOSE 0.52 OF 23 WHERE CLASS STRATIFICATION, IF PRESENT, IS BASED ON SOMETHING OTHER THAN OCCUPATIONAL STATUS (160)	17 11 78 12 XSQ= 7.59 PHI= -0.254 XP = 0.0059
108	TILT LESS TOWARD BEING THOSE 0.60 OF 95 WHERE CLASS STRATIFICATION, IF PRESENT, IS BASED ON SOMETHING OTHER THAN A HEREDITARY ARISTOCRACY (129)	108	TILT MORE TOWARD BEING THOSE 0.87 OF 23 WHERE CLASS STRATIFICATION, IF PRESENT, IS BASED ON SOMETHING OTHER THAN A HEREDITARY ARISTOCRACY (129)	38 3 57 20 XSQ= 4.81 PHI= 0.202 XP = 0.0284
110	TEND TO BE THOSE 0.54 OF 160 WHERE SLAVERY IS PRESENT (163)	110	TEND TO BE THOSE 0.79 OF 42 WHERE SLAVERY IS ABSENT (218)	86 9 74 33 XSQ= 12.68 PHI= 0.251 XP = 0.0004
127	DRIFT TOWARD BEING THOSE 0.67 OF 30 WHERE THE FEMALES' CONTRIBUTION TO SUBSISTENCE IS LOW (32) JKB	127	DRIFT TOWARD BEING THOSE 0.71 OF 7 WHERE THE FEMALES' CONTRIBUTION TO SUBSISTENCE IS HIGH (33) JKB	10 5 20 2 XSQ= 2.02 PHI= -0.234 EP = 0.0953
129	TILT LESS TOWARD BEING THOSE 0.61 OF 54 WHERE WEAVING IS MAINLY DONE BY FEMALES (73)	129	IN ALL CASES ARE THOSE 1.00 OF 12 WHERE WEAVING IS MAINLY DONE BY FEMALES (73)	21 0 33 12 XSQ= 5.17 PHI= 0.280 XP = 0.0230
180	TILT LESS TOWARD BEING THOSE 0.66 OF 163 WHERE THE COMMUNITY IS COMMONLY NON-EXOGAMOUS, RATHER THAN EXOGAMOUS (258)	180	TILT MORE TOWARD BEING THOSE 0.86 OF 42 WHERE THE COMMUNITY IS COMMONLY NON-EXOGAMOUS, RATHER THAN EXOGAMOUS (258)	56 6 107 36 XSQ= 5.46 PHI= 0.163 XP = 0.0195
186	TILT LESS TOWARD BEING THOSE 0.59 OF 170 WHERE THE KIN GROUP IS OTHER THAN EXCLUSIVELY PATRILINEAL (250)	186	TILT MORE TOWARD BEING THOSE 0.81 OF 42 WHERE THE KIN GROUP IS OTHER THAN EXCLUSIVELY PATRILINEAL (250)	70 8 100 34 XSQ= 6.17 PHI= 0.171 XP = 0.0130

190	TILT MORE TOWARD BEING THOSE WHERE THE KIN GROUP IS PATRILINEAL OR DOUBLE-DESCENT, RATHER THAN MATRILINEAL (186)	0.78 OF 107	190	TILT LESS TOWARD BEING THOSE WHERE THE KIN GROUP IS PATRILINEAL OR DOUBLE-DESCENT, RATHER THAN MATRILINEAL (186)	0.52 OF 25	83 13 24 12 XSQ= 5.45 PHI= 0.203 XP = 0.0195
192	TILT MORE TOWARD BEING THOSE OTHER THAN WHERE THE ONLY KIN GROUP PRESENT IS A KINDRED OR ELSE BILATERAL DESCENT IS INFERRED (289)	0.79 OF 170	192	TILT LESS TOWARD BEING THOSE OTHER THAN WHERE THE ONLY KIN GROUP PRESENT IS A KINDRED OR ELSE BILATERAL DESCENT IS INFERRED (289)	0.62 OF 42	36 16 134 26 XSQ= 4.33 PHI= -0.143 XP = 0.0374
196	LEAN LESS TOWARD BEING THOSE WHERE INDIVIDUAL RIGHTS IN REAL PROPERTY, AND RULES FOR INHERITANCE, ARE PRESENT (194)	0.64 OF 120	196	LEAN MORE TOWARD BEING THOSE WHERE INDIVIDUAL RIGHTS IN REAL PROPERTY, AND RULES FOR INHERITANCE, ARE PRESENT (194)	0.93 OF 30	77 28 43 2 XSQ= 8.38 PHI= -0.236 XP = 0.0038
210	LEAN MORE TOWARD BEING THOSE WHERE MARITAL RESIDENCE IS PATRILOCAL, RATHER THAN MATRILOCAL (169)	0.84 OF 93	210	LEAN LESS TOWARD BEING THOSE WHERE MARITAL RESIDENCE IS PATRILOCAL, RATHER THAN MATRILOCAL (169)	0.55 OF 22	78 12 15 10 XSQ= 7.35 PHI= 0.253 XP = 0.0067
213	TILT TOWARD BEING THOSE WHERE FIRST COUSIN MARRIAGE IS PERMITTED (172)	0.52 OF 164	213	TILT TOWARD BEING THOSE WHERE FIRST COUSIN MARRIAGE IS NOT PERMITTED (198)	0.72 OF 36	85 10 79 26 XSQ= 5.92 PHI= 0.172 XP = 0.0150
220	TILT LESS TOWARD BEING THOSE WHERE FIRST COUSIN MARRIAGE IN SOME FORM OR OTHER IS NOT PRESCRIBED OR PREFERRED (273)	0.70 OF 164	220	TILT MORE TOWARD BEING THOSE WHERE FIRST COUSIN MARRIAGE IN SOME FORM OR OTHER IS NOT PRESCRIBED OR PREFERRED (273)	0.89 OF 36	50 4 114 32 XSQ= 4.68 PHI= 0.153 XP = 0.0305
241	LEAN MORE TOWARD BEING THOSE WHERE THE FAMILY, IF EXTENDED, IS LARGE OR SMALL, RATHER THAN STEM (187)	0.92 OF 170	241	LEAN LESS TOWARD BEING THOSE WHERE THE FAMILY, IF EXTENDED, IS LARGE OR SMALL, RATHER THAN STEM (187)	0.74 OF 42	156 31 14 11 XSQ= 8.78 PHI= 0.204 XP = 0.0030
254	DRIFT TOWARD BEING THOSE WHERE HOUSEHOLD AUTHORITY IS ON THE FATHER'S SIDE, RATHER THAN THE MOTHER'S (9) CA	0.75 OF 8	254	IN ALL CASES ARE THOSE WHERE HOUSEHOLD AUTHORITY IS ON THE MOTHER'S SIDE, RATHER THAN THE FATHER'S (6) DA	1.00 OF 3	6 0 2 3 XSQ= 2.39 PHI= 0.466 EP = 0.0606
262	LEAN MORE TOWARD BEING THOSE WHERE WIVES ARE OBTAINED BY MEANS INVOLVING THE PRESENCE OF SOME CONSIDERATION (305)	0.79 OF 168	262	LEAN LESS TOWARD BEING THOSE WHERE WIVES ARE OBTAINED BY MEANS INVOLVING THE PRESENCE OF SOME CONSIDERATION (305)	0.55 OF 42	133 23 35 19 XSQ= 9.24 PHI= 0.210 XP = 0.0024

No.	Statement		No.	Statement		Statistics
263	TEND TO BE THOSE WHERE WIVES ARE OBTAINED BY RELATIVELY DIFFICULT MEANS, NAMELY BY BRIDE-PRICE, BRIDE-SERVICE, OR EXCHANGING A FEMALE RELATIVE (233)	0.62 OF 168	263	TEND TO BE THOSE WHERE WIVES ARE OBTAINED BY RELATIVELY EASY MEANS, NAMELY BY TOKEN BRIDE-PRICE, GIFT EXCHANGE, ABSENCE OF ANY CONSIDERATION, OR RECEIPT OF DOWRY (162)	0.69 OF 42	104 13 64 29 XSQ= 11.82 PHI= 0.237 XP = 0.0006
299	TILT LESS TOWARD BEING THOSE WHERE THE POST-PARTUM SEX TABOO LASTS ONE YEAR OR LESS (89)	0.64 OF 55	299	IN ALL CASES ARE THOSE WHERE THE POST-PARTUM SEX TABOO LASTS ONE YEAR OR LESS (89)	1.00 OF 11	20 0 35 11 XSQ= 4.15 PHI= 0.251 XP = 0.0417
326	TILT TOWARD BEING THOSE WHERE THE INFERRED TRANSITION ANXIETY BETWEEN INFANCY AND CHILDHOOD IS LOW (35) B-B-C	0.58 OF 33	326	IN ALL CASES ARE THOSE WHERE THE INFERRED TRANSITION ANXIETY BETWEEN INFANCY AND CHILDHOOD IS HIGH (32) B-B-C	1.00 OF 6	14 6 19 0 XSQ= 4.63 PHI= -0.345 EP = 0.0202
327	LEAN TOWARD BEING THOSE WHERE THE AGE OF THE INFANT AT TIME OF REDUCED CONTACT WITH MOTHER IS HIGHER THAN TWO YEARS (28) B-B-C	0.78 OF 27	327	IN ALL CASES ARE THOSE WHERE THE AGE OF THE INFANT AT TIME OF REDUCED CONTACT WITH MOTHER IS TWO YEARS OR LOWER (27) B-B-C	1.00 OF 5	21 0 6 5 XSQ= 8.13 PHI= 0.504 EP = 0.0023
330	TILT TOWARD BEING THOSE WHERE THE AGE OF THE INFANT AT TIME OF WEANING IS 2.5 YEARS OR HIGHER (34) B-B-C	0.63 OF 32	330	TILT TOWARD BEING THOSE WHERE THE AGE OF THE INFANT AT TIME OF WEANING IS LOWER THAN 2.5 YEARS (36) B-B-C	0.86 OF 7	20 1 12 6 XSQ= 3.61 PHI= 0.304 EP = 0.0350
347	DRIFT TOWARD BEING THOSE WHERE THE CHILD'S INFERRED CONFLICT REGARDING SELF-RELIANT BEHAVIOR IS LOW (39) B-B-C	0.57 OF 37	347	DRIFT TOWARD BEING THOSE WHERE THE CHILD'S INFERRED CONFLICT REGARDING SELF-RELIANT BEHAVIOR IS HIGH (37) B-B-C	0.86 OF 7	16 6 21 1 XSQ= 2.72 PHI= -0.249 XP = 0.0992
348	DRIFT TOWARD BEING THOSE WHERE THE TOTAL POSITIVE PRESSURE TOWARD DEVELOPING ACHIEVEMENT BEHAVIOR IN THE CHILD IS HIGH (32) B-B-C	0.55 OF 33	348	DRIFT TOWARD BEING THOSE WHERE THE TOTAL POSITIVE PRESSURE TOWARD DEVELOPING ACHIEVEMENT BEHAVIOR IN THE CHILD IS LOW (31) B-B-C	0.86 OF 7	18 1 15 6 XSQ= 2.31 PHI= 0.240 EP = 0.0948
349	DRIFT TOWARD BEING THOSE WHERE THE CHILD'S INFERRED ANXIETY OVER NON-PERFORMANCE OF ACHIEVEMENT BEHAVIOR IS HIGH (34) B-B-C	0.61 OF 33	349	DRIFT TOWARD BEING THOSE WHERE THE CHILD'S INFERRED ANXIETY OVER NON-PERFORMANCE OF ACHIEVEMENT BEHAVIOR IS LOW (28) B-B-C	0.83 OF 6	20 1 13 5 XSQ= 2.37 PHI= 0.247 EP = 0.0775
377	TILT LESS TOWARD BEING THOSE WHERE MALE GENITAL MUTILATION IS ABSENT (242)	0.72 OF 138	377	TILT MORE TOWARD BEING THOSE WHERE MALE GENITAL MUTILATION IS ABSENT (242)	0.91 OF 34	39 3 99 31 XSQ= 4.58 PHI= 0.163 XP = 0.0323

```
382  DRIFT TOWARD BEING THOSE        0.57 OF  30     382  DRIFT TOWARD BEING THOSE        0.86 OF   7           17     1
     WHERE FEMALE INITIATION RITES                        WHERE FEMALE INITIATION RITES                          13     6
     ARE PRESENT  (38) JKB                                ARE ABSENT  (27) JKB                             XSQ=      2.56
                                                                                                           PHI=     0.263
                                                                                                           EP =    0.0897

420  DRIFT LESS TOWARD BEING THOSE  0.52 OF  42     420  DRIFT MORE TOWARD BEING THOSE  0.90 OF  10           20     1
     WHERE BELLICOSITY                                    WHERE BELLICOSITY                                      22     9
     IS MODERATE OR NEGLIGIBLE  (46) PES                  IS MODERATE OR NEGLIGIBLE  (46) PES              XSQ=      3.31
                                                                                                           PHI=     0.252
                                                                                                           XP =    0.0687

424  TILT TOWARD BEING THOSE         0.75 OF  24     424  TILT TOWARD BEING THOSE         0.67 OF   9            6     6
     WHERE RELIGIOUS SPECIALISTS ARE                      WHERE RELIGIOUS SPECIALISTS ARE                        18     3
     PART-TIME, RATHER THAN                               FULL-TIME, RATHER THAN                           XSQ=      3.28
     FULL-TIME  (33) JMH                                  PART-TIME  (21) JMH                              PHI=    -0.315
                                                                                                           EP =    0.0441

426  DRIFT TOWARD BEING THOSE        0.70 OF 109     426  DRIFT TOWARD BEING THOSE        0.52 OF  29           76    14
     WHERE A HIGH GOD IS                                  WHERE A HIGH GOD IS                                    33    15
     PRESENT  (156) GES,EA                                ABSENT  (104) GES,EA                             XSQ=      3.75
                                                                                                           PHI=     0.165
                                                                                                           XP =    0.0529

428  TILT LESS TOWARD BEING THOSE   0.60 OF  45     428  IN ALL CASES ARE THOSE          1.00 OF  10           27    10
     WHERE A HIGH GOD, IF PRESENT AND ACTIVE,             WHERE A HIGH GOD, IF PRESENT AND ACTIVE,               18     0
     SUPPORTS HUMAN MORALITY, RATHER THAN                 SUPPORTS HUMAN MORALITY, RATHER THAN             XSQ=      4.27
     NOT SUPPORTING IT  (61) GES,EA                       NOT SUPPORTING IT  (61) GES,EA                   PHI=    -0.279
                                                                                                           XP =    0.0388

472  DRIFT TOWARD BEING THOSE        0.58 OF  43     472  DRIFT TOWARD BEING THOSE        0.80 OF  10           25     2
     WHERE THE COMPOSITE NARCISSISM INDEX                 WHERE THE COMPOSITE NARCISSISM INDEX                   18     8
     IS HIGH  (47) PES                                    IS LOW  (43) PES                                 XSQ=      3.32
                                                                                                           PHI=     0.250
                                                                                                           XP =    0.0685
```

249 CULTURES
WHERE, WITH THE INDEPENDENT
FAMILY PRESENT,
MARRIAGE IS COMMONLY OR OCCASIONALLY
POLYGYNOUS, RATHER THAN
MONOGAMOUS (144)

249 CULTURES
WHERE, WITH THE INDEPENDENT
FAMILY PRESENT,
MARRIAGE IS MONOGAMOUS, RATHER THAN
COMMONLY OR OCCASIONALLY
POLYGYNOUS (39)

BACKGROUND ON PAGE 124

SUBJECT ONLY

144 IN LEFT COLUMN

ABIPON	ABOR	AKHA	ALACALUF	ALORESE	AMBA	ARANDA	ARAPESH	AWEIKOMA	AZANDE
AZTEC	BAMILEKE	BANDA	BARABRA	BARI	BASSERI	BAYA	BEJA	BEMBA	BERGDAMA
BLACK CARIB	BUDUMA	BUNLAP	CAGABA	CAMBODIANS	CARIB	CARINYA	CHAGGA	CHERKESS	CHIBCHA
CHOROTI	CREE	CROW	DIEGUENO	DIERI	DILLING	ENGA	EYAK	FON	FUTAJALONKE
GANDA	GILBERTESE	GILYAK	GISU	GOAJIRO	GROS VENTRE	GUATO	HASANIA	HO	INGALIK
IRAQW	KARIERA	KERAKI	KHEVSUR	KIKUYU	KOHISTANI	KPE	KUMYK	KURTATCHI	KUTENAI
LAKHER	LAMBA	LAMET	LESU	LHOTA NAGA	LOLO	LOZI	LUBA	MACASSARESE	MAMVU
MANUS	MARICOPA	MASAI	MAZATECO	MBUNDU	MBUTI	MERINA	MIAMI	MIWOK	MNONG GAR
MOTA	MURINBATA	MURNGIN	NAMA	NAMBICUARA	NANDI	NASKAPI	NDEMBU	NGONI	NICOBARESE
NOMLAKI	NYAKYUSA	NYARO	NYORO	OMAHA	ONA	PAEZ	PALAUANS	PARAUJANO	PATHAN
PENDE	PENOBSCOT	PONAPEANS	POPOLUCA	PURARI	ROTINESE	RUNDI	RWALA	SANDAWE	SARAMACCA
SARSI	SELUNG	SEMANG	SENIANG	SHERENTE	SHILLUK	SIMBOESE	SIUAI	SONGHAI	SOTHO
SUBANUN	TAGBANUA	TARAHUMARA	TENDA	TESO	TETON	TIKOPIA	TOLOWA	TROBRIAND	TUCANO
TUCUNA	TUNEBO	ULAWANS	WAICA	WANTOAT	WAPISHANA	WASHO	WIKMUNKAN	WITOTO	WOGEO
YABARANA	YAHGAN	YOMBE	YUKI						

39 IN RIGHT COLUMN

AMERICANS	ANDAMANESE	BAJUN	BHUIYA	BRAZILIANS	BURMESE	CAMBA	CHAMACOCO	CHENCHU	CHEREMIS
CHOCO	COPR ESKIMO	DOBUANS	DOROBO	DUSUN	HUTSUL	IFUGAO	INCA	JEMEZ	KAREN
KET	LAPPS	MAYA	MENTAWEI	MZAB	NABESNA	PALIKUR	PUKAPUKA	ROMANS	ROTUMANS
SAGADA	SEMINOLE	SINHALESE	TAOS	TIGRINYA	TRISTAN	TUBATULABAL	WALLOONS	YAGUA	

215 EXCLUDED BECAUSE IRRELEVANT

2 EXCLUDED BECAUSE UNASCERTAINED

3 LEAN LESS TOWARD BEING THOSE 0.74 OF 144
LOCATED OUTSIDE OF
AFRICA (320)

3 LEAN MORE TOWARD BEING THOSE 0.95 OF 39
LOCATED OUTSIDE OF
AFRICA (320)

38	2
106	37
XSQ=	6.92
PHI=	0.195
XP =	0.0085

4 LEAN MORE TOWARD BEING THOSE 0.93 OF 144
LOCATED OUTSIDE OF
THE CIRCUM-MEDITERRANEAN (355)

4 LEAN LESS TOWARD BEING THOSE 0.74 OF 39
LOCATED OUTSIDE OF
THE CIRCUM-MEDITERRANEAN (355)

10	10
134	29
XSQ=	9.18
PHI=	-0.224
XP =	0.0024

```
11  TILT MORE TOWARD BEING THOSE    0.99 OF 144     11  TILT LESS TOWARD BEING THOSE    0.90 OF  39          2     4
    WHERE THE LATITUDE IS                               WHERE THE LATITUDE IS                             142    35
    LESS THAN SIXTY DEGREES  (385)                      LESS THAN SIXTY DEGREES  (385)              XSQ=     5.07
                                                                                                    PHI=   -0.166
                                                                                                    XP =   0.0243

14  DRIFT MORE TOWARD BEING THOSE   0.79 OF 144     14  DRIFT LESS TOWARD BEING THOSE   0.64 OF  39         30    14
    WHERE THE LATITUDE IS                               WHERE THE LATITUDE IS                             114    25
    LESS THAN THIRTY DEGREES  (281)                     LESS THAN THIRTY DEGREES  (281)             XSQ=     3.03
                                                                                                    PHI=   -0.129
                                                                                                    XP =   0.0816

16  TILT LESS TOWARD BEING THOSE    0.60 OF 144     16  TILT MORE TOWARD BEING THOSE    0.79 OF  39         86    31
    WHERE THE LATITUDE IS                               WHERE THE LATITUDE IS                              58     8
    TEN DEGREES OR GREATER  (277)                       TEN DEGREES OR GREATER  (277)               XSQ=     4.38
                                                                                                    PHI=   -0.155
                                                                                                    XP =   0.0364

48  DRIFT TOWARD BEING THOSE        0.59 OF  27     48  DRIFT TOWARD BEING THOSE        0.83 OF   6         11     5
    WHERE THE FOOD SUPPLY IS NOT SECURE,                WHERE THE FOOD SUPPLY IS SECURE,                   16     1
    AND FOOD SHORTAGES ARE                              AND FOOD SHORTAGES ARE                      XSQ=     2.06
    FREQUENT OR ANNUAL  (41) MGW                        RARE OR OCCASIONAL  (38) MGW                PHI=   -0.250
                                                                                                    EP =   0.0854

53  LEAN TOWARD BEING THOSE         0.72 OF  83     53  LEAN TOWARD BEING THOSE         0.68 OF  19         23    13
    WHERE FOOD PRODUCTION IS BY                         WHERE FOOD PRODUCTION IS BY                        60     6
    SIMPLE AGRICULTURE OR                               INTENSIVE AGRICULTURE, RATHER THAN BY       XSQ=     9.51
    INCIPIENT FOOD PRODUCTION, RATHER THAN BY           SIMPLE AGRICULTURE OR                       PHI=   -0.305
    INTENSIVE AGRICULTURE  (147)                        INCIPIENT FOOD PRODUCTION  (91)             XP =   0.0020

55  LEAN TOWARD BEING THOSE         0.67 OF  69     55  LEAN TOWARD BEING THOSE         0.76 OF  17         23    13
    WHERE FOOD PRODUCTION IS BY                         WHERE FOOD PRODUCTION IS BY                        46     4
    SIMPLE AGRICULTURE, RATHER THAN BY                  INTENSIVE AGRICULTURE, RATHER THAN BY       XSQ=     8.73
    INTENSIVE AGRICULTURE  (101)                        SIMPLE AGRICULTURE  (91)                    PHI=   -0.319
                                                                                                    XP =   0.0031

81  DRIFT TOWARD BEING THOSE        0.72 OF  79     81  DRIFT TOWARD BEING THOSE        0.50 OF  26         22    13
    WHERE NO CITY OR TOWN IS PRESENT, AND               WHERE A CITY OR TOWN IS PRESENT, OR                57    13
    THE AVERAGE COMMUNITY SIZE IS                       THE AVERAGE COMMUNITY SIZE IS               XSQ=     3.38
    SMALLER THAN 200  (135)                             200 OR GREATER  (89)                        PHI=   -0.179
                                                                                                    XP =   0.0660

88  TILT TOWARD BEING THOSE         0.66 OF  95     88  TILT TOWARD BEING THOSE         0.68 OF  19         32    13
    WHERE, IF A HEADMANSHIP IS PRESENT,                 WHERE, IF A HEADMANSHIP IS PRESENT,                63     6
    SUCCESSION IS HEREDITARY  (165)                     SUCCESSION IS NON-HEREDITARY  (106)         XSQ=     6.61
                                                                                                    PHI=   -0.241
                                                                                                    XP =   0.0101

89  DRIFT TOWARD BEING THOSE        0.56 OF  32     89  DRIFT TOWARD BEING THOSE        0.77 OF  13         14    10
    WHERE, IF A NON-HEREDITARY HEADMANSHIP              WHERE, IF A NON-HEREDITARY HEADMANSHIP             18     3
    IS PRESENT, SUCCESSION IS BY MEANS                  IS PRESENT, SUCCESSION IS                   XSQ=     2.86
    OTHER THAN CONSENSUS  (43)                          BY CONSENSUS  (63)                          PHI=   -0.252
                                                                                                    XP =   0.0906
```

107	LEAN MORE TOWARD BEING THOSE 0.91 OF 65 WHERE CLASS STRATIFICATION, IF PRESENT, IS BASED ON SOMETHING OTHER THAN OCCUPATIONAL STATUS (160)	107	LEAN LESS TOWARD BEING THOSE 0.56 OF 18 WHERE CLASS STRATIFICATION, IF PRESENT, IS BASED ON SOMETHING OTHER THAN OCCUPATIONAL STATUS (160)	6 8 59 10 XSQ= 10.08 PHI= -0.349 XP = 0.0015
108	TILT LESS TOWARD BEING THOSE 0.54 OF 65 WHERE CLASS STRATIFICATION, IF PRESENT, IS BASED ON SOMETHING OTHER THAN A HEREDITARY ARISTOCRACY (129)	108	TILT MORE TOWARD BEING THOSE 0.89 OF 18 WHERE CLASS STRATIFICATION, IF PRESENT, IS BASED ON SOMETHING OTHER THAN A HEREDITARY ARISTOCRACY (129)	30 2 35 16 XSQ= 5.90 PHI= 0.267 XP = 0.0151
128	TILT TOWARD BEING THOSE 0.70 OF 27 WHERE, IF SUBSISTENCE IS PRIMARILY BY AGRICULTURE, THE WORK IS MAINLY DONE BY FEMALES (37)	128	TILT TOWARD BEING THOSE 0.88 OF 8 WHERE, IF SUBSISTENCE IS PRIMARILY BY AGRICULTURE, THE WORK IS MAINLY DONE BY MALES (40)	8 7 19 1 XSQ= 6.24 PHI= -0.422 EP = 0.0111
149	DRIFT TOWARD BEING THOSE 0.60 OF 10 WHERE THE INCIDENCE OF THEFT IS HIGH (18) B-B-C	149	IN ALL CASES ARE THOSE 1.00 OF 4 WHERE THE INCIDENCE OF THEFT IS LOW (19) B-B-C	6 0 4 4 XSQ= 2.11 PHI= 0.388 EP = 0.0849
176	LEAN TOWARD BEING THOSE 0.51 OF 136 WHERE THE COMMUNITY IS A CLAN-COMMUNITY OR A COMMUNITY STRUCTURED OR SEGMENTED ON A CLAN BASIS (169)	176	LEAN TOWARD BEING THOSE 0.76 OF 37 WHERE THE COMMUNITY IS OTHER THAN A CLAN-COMMUNITY OR A COMMUNITY STRUCTURED OR SEGMENTED ON A CLAN BASIS (213)	69 9 67 28 XSQ= 7.16 PHI= 0.203 XP = 0.0074
180	TILT LESS TOWARD BEING THOSE 0.61 OF 136 WHERE THE COMMUNITY IS COMMONLY NON-EXOGAMOUS, RATHER THAN EXOGAMOUS (258)	180	TILT MORE TOWARD BEING THOSE 0.81 OF 37 WHERE THE COMMUNITY IS COMMONLY NON-EXOGAMOUS, RATHER THAN EXOGAMOUS (258)	53 7 83 30 XSQ= 4.32 PHI= 0.158 XP = 0.0378
181	LEAN MORE TOWARD BEING THOSE 0.94 OF 136 WHERE THE COMMUNITY IS OTHER THAN A DEME (337)	181	LEAN LESS TOWARD BEING THOSE 0.76 OF 37 WHERE THE COMMUNITY IS OTHER THAN A DEME (337)	8 9 128 28 XSQ= 9.18 PHI= -0.230 XP = 0.0024
183	DRIFT LESS TOWARD BEING THOSE 0.80 OF 97 WHERE THE LARGEST NON-COGNATIC KIN GROUP IS SMALLER THAN A MOEITY, I. E., A PHRATRY OR SIB OR LINEAGE (218)	183	IN ALL CASES ARE THOSE 1.00 OF 17 WHERE THE LARGEST NON-COGNATIC KIN GROUP IS SMALLER THAN A MOEITY, I. E., A PHRATRY OR SIB OR LINEAGE (218)	19 0 78 17 XSQ= 2.71 PHI= 0.154 XP = 0.0997
186	TILT LESS TOWARD BEING THOSE 0.58 OF 144 WHERE THE KIN GROUP IS OTHER THAN EXCLUSIVELY PATRILINEAL (250)	186	TILT MORE TOWARD BEING THOSE 0.77 OF 39 WHERE THE KIN GROUP IS OTHER THAN EXCLUSIVELY PATRILINEAL (250)	61 9 83 30 XSQ= 4.05 PHI= 0.149 XP = 0.0442

188	TILT TOWARD BEING THOSE WHERE THE KIN GROUP IS OTHER THAN EXCLUSIVELY COGNATIC (252)	0.67 OF 144	188	TILT TOWARD BEING THOSE WHERE THE KIN GROUP IS EXCLUSIVELY COGNATIC (148)	0.56 OF 39	47 22 97 17 XSQ= 6.41 PHI= -0.187 XP = 0.0114
192	LEAN TOWARD BEING THOSE OTHER THAN WHERE THE ONLY KIN GROUP PRESENT IS A KINDRED OR ELSE BILATERAL DESCENT IS INFERRED (289)	0.74 OF 144	192	LEAN TOWARD BEING THOSE WHERE THE ONLY KIN GROUP PRESENT IS A KINDRED OR ELSE BILATERAL DESCENT IS INFERRED (111)	0.51 OF 39	37 20 107 19 XSQ= 8.21 PHI= -0.212 XP = 0.0042
197	TEND TO BE THOSE WHERE RULES FOR THE INHERITANCE OF REAL PROPERTY, IF PRESENT, FAVOR EITHER THE MALE HEIR OR LINE, OR THE FEMALE HEIR OR LINE (165)	0.91 OF 68	197	TEND TO BE THOSE WHERE RULES FOR THE INHERITANCE OF REAL PROPERTY, IF PRESENT, DO NOT FAVOR EITHER THE MALE HEIR OR LINE, OR THE FEMALE HEIR OR LINE (29)	0.53 OF 19	62 9 6 10 XSQ= 16.18 PHI= 0.431 XP = 0.0001
201	TEND MORE TO BE THOSE WHERE MARITAL RESIDENCE IS NON-OPTIONAL, RATHER THAN AMBILOCAL OR NEOLOCAL (334)	0.83 OF 144	201	TEND LESS TO BE THOSE WHERE MARITAL RESIDENCE IS NON-OPTIONAL, RATHER THAN AMBILOCAL OR NEOLOCAL (334)	0.54 OF 39	119 21 25 18 XSQ= 12.60 PHI= 0.262 XP = 0.0004
204	TEND TO BE THOSE WHERE MARITAL RESIDENCE IS PATRILOCAL, VIRILOCAL, OR AVUNCULOCAL, RATHER THAN AMBILOCAL OR NEOLOCAL (270)	0.81 OF 135	204	TEND TO BE THOSE WHERE MARITAL RESIDENCE IS AMBILOCAL OR NEOLOCAL, RATHER THAN PATRILOCAL, VIRILOCAL, OR AVUNCULOCAL (64)	0.55 OF 33	110 15 25 18 XSQ= 16.23 PHI= 0.311 XP = 0.0001
209	TILT MORE TOWARD BEING THOSE WHERE MARITAL RESIDENCE IS PATRILOCAL, VIRILOCAL, OR AVUNCULOCAL, RATHER THAN MATRILOCAL OR UXORILOCAL (270)	0.92 OF 119	209	TILT LESS TOWARD BEING THOSE WHERE MARITAL RESIDENCE IS PATRILOCAL, VIRILOCAL, OR AVUNCULOCAL, RATHER THAN MATRILOCAL OR UXORILOCAL (270)	0.71 OF 21	110 15 9 6 XSQ= 6.19 PHI= 0.210 XP = 0.0129
210	TILT MORE TOWARD BEING THOSE WHERE MARITAL RESIDENCE IS PATRILOCAL, RATHER THAN MATRILOCAL (169)	0.96 OF 73	210	TILT LESS TOWARD BEING THOSE WHERE MARITAL RESIDENCE IS PATRILOCAL, RATHER THAN MATRILOCAL (169)	0.67 OF 9	70 6 3 3 XSQ= 6.24 PHI= 0.276 XP = 0.0125
234	TEND TO BE THOSE WHERE THE COUSIN TERMINOLOGY IS OF CROW, OMAHA, OR IROQUOIS TYPE, RATHER THAN ESKIMO OR HAWAIIAN TYPE (152)	0.61 OF 115	234	TEND TO BE THOSE WHERE THE COUSIN TERMINOLOGY IS OF ESKIMO OR HAWAIIAN TYPE, RATHER THAN CROW, OMAHA, OR IROQUOIS TYPE (170)	0.79 OF 29	70 6 45 23 XSQ= 13.43 PHI= 0.305 XP = 0.0002
262	LEAN MORE TOWARD BEING THOSE WHERE WIVES ARE OBTAINED BY MEANS INVOLVING THE PRESENCE OF SOME CONSIDERATION (305)	0.85 OF 141	262	LEAN LESS TOWARD BEING THOSE WHERE WIVES ARE OBTAINED BY MEANS INVOLVING THE PRESENCE OF SOME CONSIDERATION (305)	0.64 OF 39	120 25 21 14 XSQ= 7.32 PHI= 0.202 XP = 0.0068

263	TEND TO BE THOSE 0.72 OF 141 WHERE WIVES ARE OBTAINED BY RELATIVELY DIFFICULT MEANS, NAMELY BY BRIDE-PRICE, BRIDE-SERVICE, OR EXCHANGING A FEMALE RELATIVE (233)	263	TEND TO BE THOSE 0.64 OF 39 WHERE WIVES ARE OBTAINED BY RELATIVELY EASY MEANS, NAMELY BY TOKEN BRIDE-PRICE, GIFT EXCHANGE, ABSENCE OF ANY CONSIDERATION, OR RECEIPT OF DOWRY (162)	101 14 40 25 XSQ= 15.40 PHI= 0.292 XP = 0.0001
311	DRIFT TOWARD BEING THOSE 0.62 OF 21 WHERE SEXUAL SOCIALIZATION ANXIETY IS HIGH (28) W-C	311	DRIFT TOWARD BEING THOSE 0.83 OF 6 WHERE SEXUAL SOCIALIZATION ANXIETY IS LOW (23) W-C	13 1 8 5 XSQ= 2.23 PHI= 0.287 EP = 0.0768
316	TILT TOWARD BEING THOSE 0.73 OF 11 WHERE EXCLUSIVE MOTHER-SON SLEEPING ARRANGEMENTS LAST ONE YEAR OR LONGER (19) W-K-A	316	IN ALL CASES ARE THOSE 1.00 OF 4 WHERE EXCLUSIVE MOTHER-SON SLEEPING ARRANGEMENTS LAST LESS THAN ONE YEAR (25) W-K-A	8 0 3 4 XSQ= 3.65 PHI= 0.494 EP = 0.0256
370	TILT TOWARD BEING THOSE 0.54 OF 79 WHERE THE SEGREGATION OF ADOLESCENT BOYS IS COMPLETE OR PARTIAL (95)	370	TILT TOWARD BEING THOSE 0.76 OF 21 WHERE THE SEGREGATION OF ADOLESCENT BOYS IS ABSENT (148)	43 5 36 16 XSQ= 5.07 PHI= 0.225 XP = 0.0244
377	DRIFT LESS TOWARD BEING THOSE 0.71 OF 123 WHERE MALE GENITAL MUTILATION IS ABSENT (242)	377	DRIFT MORE TOWARD BEING THOSE 0.89 OF 27 WHERE MALE GENITAL MUTILATION IS ABSENT (242)	36 3 87 24 XSQ= 2.91 PHI= 0.139 XP = 0.0881
391	DRIFT TOWARD BEING THOSE 0.58 OF 64 WHERE PREMARITAL SEX RELATIONS ARE STRONGLY PUNISHED AND IN FACT RARE, OR WEAKLY PUNISHED AND IN FACT NOT RARE (89) JTW,EA	391	DRIFT TOWARD BEING THOSE 0.68 OF 19 WHERE PREMARITAL SEX RELATIONS ARE PUNISHED ONLY IF PREGNANCY RESULTS, OR FREELY PERMITTED (90) JTW,EA	37 6 27 13 XSQ= 3.06 PHI= 0.192 XP = 0.0804
392	DRIFT TOWARD BEING THOSE 0.69 OF 64 WHERE PREMARITAL SEX RELATIONS ARE STRONGLY PUNISHED AND IN FACT RARE, OR WEAKLY PUNISHED AND IN FACT NOT RARE, OR PUNISHED ONLY IF PREGNANCY RESULTS (112) JTW,EA	392	DRIFT TOWARD BEING THOSE 0.58 OF 19 WHERE PREMARITAL SEX RELATIONS ARE FREELY PERMITTED (67) JTW,EA	44 8 20 11 XSQ= 3.38 PHI= 0.202 XP = 0.0660
398	DRIFT TOWARD BEING THOSE 0.71 OF 14 WHERE THE INTENSITY OF SEX ANXIETY IS HIGH (16) WNS	398	IN ALL CASES ARE THOSE 1.00 OF 3 WHERE THE INTENSITY OF SEX ANXIETY IS LOW (16) WNS	10 0 4 3 XSQ= 2.67 PHI= 0.397 EP = 0.0515

403	TILT TOWARD BEING THOSE WHERE EXPLANATIONS OF ILLNESS OF AN ANAL NATURE ARE PRESENT (23) W-C	0.52 OF 23	403	TILT TOWARD BEING THOSE WHERE EXPLANATIONS OF ILLNESS OF AN ANAL NATURE ARE ABSENT (38) W-C	0.90 OF 10	12 1 11 9 XSQ= 3.58 PHI= 0.329 EP = 0.0495
404	DRIFT LESS TOWARD BEING THOSE WHERE EXPLANATIONS OF ILLNESS OF A SEXUAL NATURE ARE ABSENT (42) W-C	0.52 OF 23	404	DRIFT MORE TOWARD BEING THOSE WHERE EXPLANATIONS OF ILLNESS OF A SEXUAL NATURE ARE ABSENT (42) W-C	0.90 OF 10	11 1 12 9 XSQ= 2.83 PHI= 0.293 EP = 0.0545
419	TILT TOWARD BEING THOSE WHERE MILITARY GLORY IS STRONGLY OR MODERATELY EMPHASIZED (55) PES	0.76 OF 25	419	TILT TOWARD BEING THOSE WHERE MILITARY GLORY IS NEGLIGIBLY EMPHASIZED (31) PES	0.67 OF 9	19 3 6 6 XSQ= 3.57 PHI= 0.324 EP = 0.0403
420	DRIFT TOWARD BEING THOSE WHERE BELLICOSITY IS EXTREME (41) PES	0.70 OF 23	420	DRIFT TOWARD BEING THOSE WHERE BELLICOSITY IS MODERATE OR NEGLIGIBLE (46) PES	0.70 OF 10	16 3 7 7 XSQ= 2.99 PHI= 0.301 EP = 0.0569

250 CULTURES WHERE, WITH THE PATRILINEAL KIN GROUP PRESENT, MARRIAGE IS COMMONLY OR OCCASIONALLY POLYGYNOUS, RATHER THAN MONOGAMOUS (146)	250 CULTURES WHERE, WITH THE PATRILINEAL KIN GROUP PRESENT, MARRIAGE IS MONOGAMOUS, RATHER THAN COMMONLY OR OCCASIONALLY POLYGYNOUS (21)

BACKGROUND ON PAGE 124 SUBJECT ONLY

146 IN LEFT COLUMN

ABOR	AKHA	ALBANIANS	ALORESE	AMBA	ARAPESH	ARAUCANIANS	ARYANS	AZANDE	BABWA
BAMBARA	BAMILEKE	BANCA	BARABRA	BARI	BASSERI	BATAK	BAYA	BEJA	BENGALI
BETE	BHIL	BOZO	BUDUMA	BURUSHO	BURYAT	CHAGGA	CHERKESS	DARD	DIEGUENO
DILLING	DOGON	EGYPTIANS	ENGA	FANG	FON	FOX	FUTAJALONKE	GANDA	GILYAK
GISU	GOND	HASANIA	HAZARA	HEBREWS	HEHE	HO	KABYLE	KACHIN	KALMYK
KAPAUKU	KATAB	KAZAK	KERAKI	KHEVSUR	KIKUYU	KISSI	KOHISTANI	KONSO	LAKHER
LAMET	LANGO	LAU	LEPCHA	LHOTA NAGA	LIFU	LOLO	LUBA	LUO	MAGUZAWA
MAMVU	MARGI	MARICOPA	MASAI	MATAKAM	MBUTI	MENDE	MERINA	MIAMI	MIAO
MIN CHINESE	MINCHIA	MIWOK	MONGO	MONGUOR	MOSSI	MUNDURUCU	MURINBATA	NAMA	NANDI
NOMLAKI	NUER	NUPE	NURI	NYAKYUSA	NYORO	OJIBWA	OMAHA	CRAON	PATHAN
PURARI	PURUM	REGEIBAT	RIFFIANS	ROTINESE	RUNDI	RWALA	SAMOYED	SANDAWE	SANTAL
SENIANG	SHERENTE	SHILLUK	SINDHI	SIWANS	SOMALI	SONGHAI	SOTHO	SWAZI	SYRIANS
TALLENSI	TAMIL	TANALA	TANIMBARESE	TEDA	TERA	TESO	THONGA	TIKOPIA	TIV
TOLOWA	TUCANO	TUCUNA	TURKANA	TURKMEN	TZELTAL	VIETNAMESE	WANTOAT	WAROPEN	WIKMUNKAN
WINNEBAGO	WITOTO	WUTE	YAKUT	YOKUTS	YORUBA				

21 IN RIGHT COLUMN

ATAYAL	AYMARA	BAJUN	BHUIYA	CHENCHU	COORG	DAGUR	DOROBO	KET	KHALKA
KOREANS	MAM	MANCHU	MAYA	MZAB	OKINAWANS	PALIKUR	SERBS	SHLUH	TIGRINYA
YAGUA									

1 EXCLUDED BECAUSE AMBIGUOUS

PUKAPUKA

230 EXCLUDED BECAUSE IRRELEVANT

2 EXCLUDED BECAUSE UNASCERTAINED

3 TILT LESS TOWARD BEING THOSE LOCATED OUTSIDE OF AFRICA (320) 0.65 OF 146	3 TILT MORE TOWARD BEING THOSE LOCATED OUTSIDE OF AFRICA (320) 0.90 OF 21	51 2 95 19 XSQ= 4.36 PHI= 0.162 XP = 0.0368

9	LEAN MORE TOWARD BEING THOSE 0.95 OF 146 LOCATED OUTSIDE OF SOUTH AMERICA (335)	9	LEAN LESS TOWARD BEING THOSE 0.76 OF 21 LOCATED OUTSIDE OF SOUTH AMERICA (335)	7 5 139 16 XSQ= 7.31 PHI= -0.209 XP = 0.0069
80	DRIFT MORE TOWARD BEING THOSE 0.85 OF 80 WHERE NO CITY OR TOWN IS PRESENT (185)	80	DRIFT LESS TOWARD BEING THOSE 0.60 OF 15 WHERE NO CITY OR TOWN IS PRESENT (185)	12 6 68 9 XSQ= 3.64 PHI= -0.196 XP = 0.0564
88	LEAN TOWARD BEING THOSE 0.65 OF 95 WHERE, IF A HEADMANSHIP IS PRESENT, SUCCESSION IS HEREDITARY (165)	88	LEAN TOWARD BEING THOSE 0.76 OF 17 WHERE, IF A HEADMANSHIP IS PRESENT, SUCCESSION IS NON-HEREDITARY (106)	33 13 62 4 XSQ= 8.72 PHI= -0.279 XP = 0.0031
89	DRIFT TOWARD BEING THOSE 0.58 OF 33 WHERE, IF A NON-HEREDITARY HEADMANSHIP IS PRESENT, SUCCESSION IS BY MEANS OTHER THAN CONSENSUS (43)	89	DRIFT TOWARD BEING THOSE 0.77 OF 13 WHERE, IF A NON-HEREDITARY HEADMANSHIP IS PRESENT, SUCCESSION IS BY CONSENSUS (63)	14 10 19 3 XSQ= 3.17 PHI= -0.263 XP = 0.0749
107	DRIFT MORE TOWARD BEING THOSE 0.82 OF 87 WHERE CLASS STRATIFICATION, IF PRESENT, IS BASED ON SOMETHING OTHER THAN OCCUPATIONAL STATUS (160)	107	DRIFT LESS TOWARD BEING THOSE 0.55 OF 11 WHERE CLASS STRATIFICATION, IF PRESENT, IS BASED ON SOMETHING OTHER THAN OCCUPATIONAL STATUS (160)	16 5 71 6 XSQ= 2.79 PHI= -0.169 XP = 0.0947
185	DRIFT MORE TOWARD BEING THOSE 0.77 OF 146 WHERE THE LARGEST NON-COGNATIC KIN GROUP IS THE MOEITY OR PHRATRY OR SIB (194)	185	DRIFT LESS TOWARD BEING THOSE 0.57 OF 21 WHERE THE LARGEST NON-COGNATIC KIN GROUP IS THE MOEITY OR PHRATRY OR SIB (194)	112 12 34 9 XSQ= 2.73 PHI= 0.128 XP = 0.0988
241	TILT MORE TOWARD BEING THOSE 0.94 OF 78 WHERE THE FAMILY, IF EXTENDED, IS LARGE OR SMALL, RATHER THAN STEM (187)	241	TILT LESS TOWARD BEING THOSE 0.64 OF 11 WHERE THE FAMILY, IF EXTENDED, IS LARGE OR SMALL, RATHER THAN STEM (187)	73 7 5 4 XSQ= 6.51 PHI= 0.270 XP = 0.0108
263	DRIFT MORE TOWARD BEING THOSE 0.83 OF 144 WHERE WIVES ARE OBTAINED BY RELATIVELY DIFFICULT MEANS, NAMELY BY BRIDE-PRICE, BRIDE-SERVICE, OR EXCHANGING A FEMALE RELATIVE (233)	263	DRIFT LESS TOWARD BEING THOSE 0.62 OF 21 WHERE WIVES ARE OBTAINED BY RELATIVELY DIFFICULT MEANS, NAMELY BY BRIDE-PRICE, BRIDE-SERVICE, OR EXCHANGING A FEMALE RELATIVE (233)	119 13 25 8 XSQ= 3.71 PHI= 0.150 XP = 0.0540
324	TILT TOWARD BEING THOSE 0.71 OF 24 WHERE THE PAIN INFLICTED ON THE INFANT BY THE NURTURANT AGENT IS HIGH (34) B-B-C	324	IN ALL CASES ARE THOSE 1.00 OF 3 WHERE THE PAIN INFLICTED ON THE INFANT BY THE NURTURANT AGENT IS LOW OR NEGLIGIBLE (32) B-B-C	17 0 7 3 XSQ= 3.10 PHI= 0.339 EP = 0.0410

370	DRIFT TOWARD BEING THOSE 0.51 OF 92 WHERE THE SEGREGATION OF ADOLESCENT BOYS IS COMPLETE OR PARTIAL (95)	370	DRIFT TOWARD BEING THOSE 0.83 OF 12 WHERE THE SEGREGATION OF ADOLESCENT BOYS IS ABSENT (148)	47 2 45 10 XSQ= 3.76 PHI= 0.190 XP = 0.0525
419	LEAN TOWARD BEING THOSE 0.78 OF 32 WHERE MILITARY GLORY IS STRONGLY OR MODERATELY EMPHASIZED (55) PES	419	IN ALL CASES ARE THOSE 1.00 OF 4 WHERE MILITARY GLORY IS NEGLIGIBLY EMPHASIZED (31) PES	25 0 7 4 XSQ= 6.88 PHI= 0.437 EP = 0.0056
420	TILT TOWARD BEING THOSE 0.63 OF 32 WHERE BELLICOSITY IS EXTREME (41) PES	420	IN ALL CASES ARE THOSE 1.00 OF 4 WHERE BELLICOSITY IS MODERATE OR NEGLIGIBLE (46) PES	20 0 12 4 XSQ= 3.38 PHI= 0.306 EP = 0.0309

251 CULTURES WHERE, WITH THE MATRILINEAL KIN GROUP PRESENT, MARRIAGE IS COMMONLY OR OCCASIONALLY POLYGYNOUS, RATHER THAN MONOGAMOUS (43)	251 CULTURES WHERE, WITH THE MATRILINEAL KIN GROUP PRESENT, MARRIAGE IS MONOGAMOUS, RATHER THAN COMMONLY OR OCCASIONALLY POLYGYNOUS (18)

BACKGROUND ON PAGE 124

SUBJECT ONLY

43 IN LEFT COLUMN

BELU	BEMBA	BORORO	CALLINAGO	CHEROKEE	CREEK	CROW	DELAWARE	DIERI	EYAK
GARO	GOAJIRO	GUAHIBO	GURE	HAIDA	KERALA	KUBA	KURTATCHI	LAKALAI	LAMBA
LESU	MANDAN	MINANGKABAU	MNONG GAR	MOTA	NAVAHO	NDEMBU	NYANEKA	PALAUANS	PAWNEE
PENDE	PONAPEANS	SARAMACCA	SIRIONO	SIUAI	TALAMANCA	TENDA	TIMUCUA	TIWI	TROBRIAND
TSHIMSHIAN	YAO	YOMBE							

18 IN RIGHT COLUMN

APINAYE	COCHITI	DOBUANS	HANO	HURON	JEMEZ	KAREN	KASKA	KHASI	MARSHALLESE
NABESNA	ROTUMANS	SEMINOLE	TIMBIRA	TRUKESE	VEDDA	WOLEAIANS	ZUNI		

1 EXCLUDED BECAUSE AMBIGUOUS

PUKAPUKA

337 EXCLUDED BECAUSE IRRELEVANT

1 EXCLUDED BECAUSE UNASCERTAINED

	Left column			Right column				
3	DRIFT LESS TOWARD BEING THOSE LOCATED OUTSIDE OF AFRICA (320)	0.77 OF 43	3	IN ALL CASES ARE THOSE LOCATED OUTSIDE OF AFRICA (320)	1.00 OF 18	10 0 33 18 XSQ= 3.45 PHI= 0.238 XP = 0.0631
53	TILT MORE TOWARD BEING THOSE WHERE FOOD PRODUCTION IS BY SIMPLE AGRICULTURE OR INCIPIENT FOOD PRODUCTION, RATHER THAN BY INTENSIVE AGRICULTURE (147)	0.93 OF 28	53	TILT LESS TOWARD BEING THOSE WHERE FOOD PRODUCTION IS BY SIMPLE AGRICULTURE OR INCIPIENT FOOD PRODUCTION, RATHER THAN BY INTENSIVE AGRICULTURE (147)	0.60 OF 10	2 4 26 6 XSQ= 3.77 PHI= -0.315 EP = 0.0314
55	TILT TOWARD BEING THOSE WHERE FOOD PRODUCTION IS BY SIMPLE AGRICULTURE, RATHER THAN BY INTENSIVE AGRICULTURE (101)	0.90 OF 20	55	TILT TOWARD BEING THOSE WHERE FOOD PRODUCTION IS BY INTENSIVE AGRICULTURE, RATHER THAN BY SIMPLE AGRICULTURE (91)	0.57 OF 7	2 4 18 3 XSQ= 4.22 PHI= -0.395 EP = 0.0239

```
 86  DRIFT TOWARD BEING THOSE         0.54 OF  37    86  DRIFT TOWARD BEING THOSE         0.79 OF  14        20     3
     WHERE THE LEVEL OF POLITICAL INTEGRATION            WHERE THE LEVEL OF POLITICAL INTEGRATION            17    11
     IS THE LARGE STATE, THE LITTLE STATE,               IS THE AUTONOMOUS COMMUNITY, OR                XSQ=     3.15
     OR THE MINIMAL STATE  (148) GPM                     THE FAMILY  (156) GPM                          PHI=    0.248
                                                                                                        XP =   0.0760

102  TILT TOWARD BEING THOSE          0.55 OF  42   102  TILT TOWARD BEING THOSE          0.78 OF  18        23     4
     WHERE CLASS STRATIFICATION IS                       WHERE CLASS STRATIFICATION IS                       19    14
     PRESENT  (203)                                      ABSENT  (180)                                  XSQ=     4.16
                                                                                                        PHI=    0.263
                                                                                                        XP =   0.0415

110  LEAN LESS TOWARD BEING THOSE     0.55 OF  42   110  LEAN MORE TOWARD BEING THOSE     0.94 OF  18        19     1
     WHERE SLAVERY IS ABSENT  (218)                      WHERE SLAVERY IS ABSENT  (218)                      23    17
                                                                                                        XSQ=     7.23
                                                                                                        PHI=    0.347
                                                                                                        XP =   0.0072

198  IN ALL CASES ARE THOSE           1.00 OF  15   198  DRIFT LESS TOWARD BEING THOSE    0.67 OF   6         0     2
     WHERE RULES FOR THE INHERITANCE OF                  WHERE RULES FOR THE INHERITANCE OF                  15     4
     REAL PROPERTY, IF PRESENT,                          REAL PROPERTY, IF PRESENT,                     XSQ=     2.33
     FAVOR THE FEMALE HEIR OR LINE, RATHER THAN          FAVOR THE FEMALE HEIR OR LINE, RATHER THAN     PHI=   -0.333
     THE MALE  (21)                                      THE MALE  (21)                                 EP =   0.0714

204  LEAN TOWARD BEING THOSE          0.83 OF  24   204  IN ALL CASES ARE THOSE           1.00 OF   4        20     0
     WHERE MARITAL RESIDENCE IS                          WHERE MARITAL RESIDENCE IS                           4     4
     PATRILOCAL, VIRILOCAL, OR AVUNCULOCAL,              AMBILOCAL OR NEOLOCAL, RATHER THAN             XSQ=     7.94
     RATHER THAN                                         PATRILOCAL, VIRILOCAL, OR                      PHI=    0.533
     AMBILOCAL OR NEOLOCAL  (270)                        AVUNCULOCAL  (64)                              EP =   0.0034

209  LEAN TOWARD BEING THOSE          0.53 OF  38   209  IN ALL CASES ARE THOSE           1.00 OF  14        20     0
     WHERE MARITAL RESIDENCE IS                          WHERE MARITAL RESIDENCE IS                          18    14
     PATRILOCAL, VIRILOCAL, OR AVUNCULOCAL,              MATRILOCAL OR UXORILOCAL, RATHER THAN          XSQ=     9.85
     RATHER THAN                                         PATRILOCAL, VIRILOCAL, OR                      PHI=    0.435
     MATRILOCAL OR UXORILOCAL  (270)                     AVUNCULOCAL  (64)                              XP =   0.0017

213  DRIFT TOWARD BEING THOSE         0.66 OF  41   213  DRIFT TOWARD BEING THOSE         0.65 OF  17        27     6
     WHERE FIRST COUSIN MARRIAGE IS                      WHERE FIRST COUSIN MARRIAGE IS                      14    11
     PERMITTED  (172)                                    NOT PERMITTED  (198)                           XSQ=     3.41
                                                                                                        PHI=    0.243
                                                                                                        XP =   0.0646

262  TILT TOWARD BEING THOSE          0.74 OF  42   262  TILT TOWARD BEING THOSE          0.61 OF  18        31     7
     WHERE WIVES ARE OBTAINED BY                         WHERE WIVES ARE OBTAINED                            11    11
     MEANS INVOLVING THE PRESENCE                        BY MEANS INVOLVING THE ABSENCE                 XSQ=     5.20
     OF SOME CONSIDERATION  (305)                        OF ANY CONSIDERATION  (90)                     PHI=    0.294
                                                                                                        XP =   0.0226

263  TILT TOWARD BEING THOSE          0.55 OF  42   263  TILT TOWARD BEING THOSE          0.83 OF  18        23     3
     WHERE WIVES ARE OBTAINED BY                         WHERE WIVES ARE OBTAINED                            19    15
     RELATIVELY DIFFICULT MEANS, NAMELY BY               BY RELATIVELY EASY MEANS, NAMELY BY            XSQ=     5.98
     BRIDE-PRICE, BRIDE-SERVICE, OR                      TOKEN BRIDE-PRICE, GIFT EXCHANGE,              PHI=    0.316
     EXCHANGING A FEMALE RELATIVE  (233)                 ABSENCE OF ANY CONSIDERATION, OR               XP =   0.0145
                                                         RECEIPT OF DOWRY  (162)
```

302	IN ALL CASES ARE THOSE WHERE THE AVERAGE EARLY SATISFACTION POTENTIAL IS HIGH (23) W-C	1.00 OF	5	302	IN ALL CASES ARE THOSE WHERE THE AVERAGE EARLY SATISFACTION POTENTIAL IS LOW (17) W-C	1.00 OF	2	 XSQ= PHI= EP =	5 0 0 2 2.96 0.650 0.0476
306	IN ALL CASES ARE THOSE WHERE THE EARLY DEPENDENCE SATISFACTION POTENTIAL IS HIGH (28) W-C	1.00 OF	5	306	IN ALL CASES ARE THOSE WHERE THE EARLY DEPENDENCE SATISFACTION POTENTIAL IS LOW (24) W-C	1.00 OF	3	 XSQ= PHI= EP =	5 0 0 3 4.30 0.733 0.0179
313	IN ALL CASES ARE THOSE WHERE AGGRESSION SOCIALIZATION ANXIETY IS LOW (28) W-C	1.00 OF	6	313	TILT TOWARD BEING THOSE WHERE AGGRESSION SOCIALIZATION ANXIETY IS HIGH (26) W-C	0.75 OF	4	 XSQ= PHI= EP =	0 3 6 1 3.35 -0.579 0.0333
322	DRIFT TOWARD BEING THOSE WHERE THE CONSISTENCY OF REDUCTION OF THE INFANT'S DRIVES IS LOW (32) B-B-C	0.83 OF	6	322	DRIFT TOWARD BEING THOSE WHERE THE CONSISTENCY OF REDUCTION OF THE INFANT'S DRIVES IS HIGH (27) B-B-C	0.83 OF	6	 XSQ= PHI= EP =	1 5 5 1 3.00 -0.500 0.0801
326	DRIFT TOWARD BEING THOSE WHERE THE INFERRED TRANSITION ANXIETY BETWEEN INFANCY AND CHILDHOOD IS LOW (35) B-B-C	0.57 OF	7	326	IN ALL CASES ARE THOSE WHERE THE INFERRED TRANSITION ANXIETY BETWEEN INFANCY AND CHILDHOOD IS HIGH (32) B-B-C	1.00 OF	5	 XSQ= PHI= EP =	3 5 4 0 2.10 -0.418 0.0808
327	DRIFT TOWARD BEING THOSE WHERE THE AGE OF THE INFANT AT TIME OF REDUCED CONTACT WITH MOTHER IS HIGHER THAN TWO YEARS (28) B-B-C	0.67 OF	6	327	IN ALL CASES ARE THOSE WHERE THE AGE OF THE INFANT AT TIME OF REDUCED CONTACT WITH MOTHER IS TWO YEARS OR LOWER (27) B-B-C	1.00 OF	4	 XSQ= PHI= EP =	4 0 2 4 2.10 0.458 0.0762
335	IN ALL CASES ARE THOSE WHERE INITIAL INDULGENCE OF DEPENDENCY IS HIGH (20) WNS	1.00 OF	4	335	IN ALL CASES ARE THOSE WHERE INITIAL INDULGENCE OF DEPENDENCY IS LOW (18) WNS	1.00 OF	2	 XSQ= PHI= EP =	4 0 0 2 2.34 0.625 0.0667
370	TILT TOWARD BEING THOSE WHERE THE SEGREGATION OF ADOLESCENT BOYS IS COMPLETE OR PARTIAL (95)	0.68 OF	28	370	TILT TOWARD BEING THOSE WHERE THE SEGREGATION OF ADOLESCENT BOYS IS ABSENT (148)	0.73 OF	11	 XSQ= PHI= EP =	19 3 9 8 3.77 0.311 0.0329
382	IN ALL CASES ARE THOSE WHERE FEMALE INITIATION RITES ARE PRESENT (38) JKB	1.00 OF	6	382	DRIFT TOWARD BEING THOSE WHERE FEMALE INITIATION RITES ARE ABSENT (27) JKB	0.67 OF	3	 XSQ= PHI= EP =	6 1 0 2 2.01 0.472 0.0833

```
402  IN ALL CASES ARE THOSE          1.00 OF   6     402  TILT TOWARD BEING THOSE         0.75 OF   4           6      1
     WHERE EXPLANATIONS OF ILLNESS                        WHERE EXPLANATIONS OF ILLNESS                           0      3
     OF AN ORAL NATURE                                    OF AN ORAL NATURE                               XSQ=      3.35
     ARE PRESENT  (31) W-C                                ARE ABSENT  (30) W-C                            PHI=     0.579
                                                                                                          EP =    0.0333

424  IN ALL CASES ARE THOSE          1.00 OF   8     424  DRIFT TOWARD BEING THOSE        0.50 OF   6           0      3
     WHERE RELIGIOUS SPECIALISTS ARE                      WHERE RELIGIOUS SPECIALISTS ARE                         8      3
     PART-TIME, RATHER THAN                               FULL-TIME, RATHER THAN                          XSQ=      2.55
     FULL-TIME  (33) JMH                                  PART-TIME  (21) JMH                             PHI=    -0.427
                                                                                                          EP =    0.0549

425  IN ALL CASES ARE THOSE          1.00 OF   4     425  IN ALL CASES ARE THOSE          1.00 OF   2           0      2
     WHERE SUPERNATURALS ARE MAINLY                       WHERE SUPERNATURALS ARE MAINLY                          4      0
     AGGRESSIVE, RATHER THAN                              BENEVOLENT, RATHER THAN                         XSQ=      2.34
     BENEVOLENT  (20) L-T-W                               AGGRESSIVE  (16) L-T-W                          PHI=    -0.625
                                                                                                          EP =    0.0667

472  TILT TOWARD BEING THOSE         0.67 OF   9     472  IN ALL CASES ARE THOSE          1.00 OF   6           6      0
     WHERE THE COMPOSITE NARCISSISM INDEX                 WHERE THE COMPOSITE NARCISSISM INDEX                    3      6
     IS HIGH  (47) PES                                    IS LOW  (43) PES                                XSQ=      4.18
                                                                                                          PHI=     0.528
                                                                                                          EP =    0.0278

474  TILT TOWARD BEING THOSE         0.67 OF   9     474  IN ALL CASES ARE THOSE          1.00 OF   6           6      0
     WHERE BOASTFULNESS IS EXTREME   (41) PES             WHERE BOASTFULNESS IS MODERATE,                         3      6
                                                          NEGLIBIBLE, OR UNREPORTED  (48) PES             XSQ=      4.18
                                                                                                          PHI=     0.528
                                                                                                          EP =    0.0278
```

252 CULTURES WHERE, WITH THE EXCLUSIVELY COGNATIC KIN GROUP PRESENT, MARRIAGE IS COMMONLY OR OCCASIONALLY POLYGYNOUS, RATHER THAN MONOGAMOUS (107)	252 CULTURES WHERE, WITH THE EXCLUSIVELY COGNATIC KIN GROUP PRESENT, MARRIAGE IS MONOGAMOUS, RATHER THAN COMMONLY OR OCCASIONALLY POLYGYNOUS (39)

BACKGROUND ON PAGE 124

SUBJECT ONLY

107 IN LEFT COLUMN

ABIPON	ALACALUF	ATSUGEWI	AWEIKOMA	AZTEC	BACAIRI	BALINESE	BERGDAMA	BLACK CARIB	BOTOCUDO
CADUVEO	CAGABA	CAMAYURA	CAMBODIANS	CARAJA	CARIB	CARINYA	CHEYENNE	CHIBCHA	CHIR-APACHE
CHIRIGUANO	CHOROTI	CHUKCHEE	COMANCHE	CREE	CUNA	ELLICE	GILBERTESE	GROS VENTRE	GUATO
HANUNOO	HASINAI	HAVASUPAI	HAWAIIANS	HUICHOL	HUKUNDIKA	INGALIK	JAVANESE	JIVARO	JUKUN
KIOW-APACHE	KOL	KORYAK	KUMYK	KUNG	KUTENAI	KWAKIUTL	LOZI	MACASSARESE	MALAYS
MAMBILA	MANGAIANS	MANIHIKI	MAORI	MATACO	MAZATECO	MISKITO	MOTILON	NAMBICUARA	NASKAPI
NATCHEZ	NGONI	NICOBARESE	NUNIVAK	ONA	ONTONG-JAVA	PAEZ	PAIWAN	PAPAGO	PARAUJANO
PENOBSCOT	POPOLUCA	RAROIANS	SAMOANS	SANPOIL	SARSI	SELUNG	SEMANG	SIMBOESE	SUBANUN
TAGBANUA	TARAHUMARA	TAREUMIUT	TEHUELCHE	TENETEHARA	TENINO	TERENA	TETON	THAI	TOKELAU
TRUMAI	TUNEBO	TUPINAMBA	TWANA	ULAWANS	UTE	WAICA	WAPISHANA	WARRAU	WASHO
WICHITA	YABARANA	YAHGAN	YARURO	YUKAGHIR	YUKI	YUROK			

39 IN RIGHT COLUMN

AMERICANS	ANDAMANESE	BASQUES	BOERS	BRAZILIANS	BULGARIANS	BURMESE	CAMBA	CAYAPA	CHAMACOCO
CHEREMIS	CHINANTEC	CHOCO	CHORTI	COPR ESKIMO	CZECHS	DUSUN	DUTCH	HUTSUL	IBAN
ICELANDERS	IFUGAC	INCA	INGASSANA	IRISH	JAPANESE	LAPPS	MENTAWEI	PORTUGUESE	ROMANS
SAGADA	SERI	SINHALESE	TAOS	TAPIRAPE	TORAJA	TRISTAN	TUBATULABAL	WALLOONS	

1 EXCLUDED BECAUSE AMBIGUOUS

PUKAPUKA

252 EXCLUDED BECAUSE IRRELEVANT

1 EXCLUDED BECAUSE UNASCERTAINED

4	TEND MORE TO BE THOSE LOCATED OUTSIDE OF THE CIRCUM-MEDITERRANEAN (355)	0.99 OF 107	4	TEND LESS TO BE THOSE LOCATED OUTSIDE OF THE CIRCUM-MEDITERRANEAN (355)	0.59 OF 39	1 16 106 23 XSQ= 40.84 PHI= -0.529 XP = 0.
8	TILT LESS TOWARD BEING THOSE LOCATED OUTSIDE OF NORTH AMERICA (330)	0.68 OF 107	8	TILT MORE TOWARD BEING THOSE LOCATED OUTSIDE OF NORTH AMERICA (330)	0.87 OF 39	34 5 73 34 XSQ= 4.32 PHI= 0.172 XP = 0.0376

No.			No.			
9	DRIFT LESS TOWARD BEING THOSE LOCATED OUTSIDE OF SOUTH AMERICA (335)	0.65 OF 107	9	DRIFT MORE TOWARD BEING THOSE LOCATED OUTSIDE OF SOUTH AMERICA (335)	0.82 OF 39	37 7 70 32 XSQ= 3.01 PHI= 0.143 XP = 0.0829
44	LEAN LESS TOWARD BEING THOSE WHERE SETTLEMENTS ARE FIXED (222)	0.52 OF 90	44	LEAN MORE TOWARD BEING THOSE WHERE SETTLEMENTS ARE FIXED (222)	0.83 OF 29	47 24 43 5 XSQ= 7.28 PHI= -0.247 XP = 0.0070
48	DRIFT TOWARD BEING THOSE WHERE THE FOOD SUPPLY IS NOT SECURE, AND FOOD SHORTAGES ARE FREQUENT OR ANNUAL (41) MGW	0.58 OF 24	48	IN ALL CASES ARE THOSE WHERE THE FOOD SUPPLY IS SECURE, AND FOOD SHORTAGES ARE RARE OR OCCASIONAL (38) MGW	1.00 OF 3	10 3 14 0 XSQ= 1.67 PHI= -0.249 EP = 0.0978
51	TEND TO BE THOSE WHERE SUBSISTENCE IS PRIMARILY BY FOOD GATHERING -- I. E., HUNTING, FISHING, OR COLLECTING -- RATHER THAN FOOD PRODUCTION (147)	0.66 OF 107	51	TEND TO BE THOSE WHERE SUBSISTENCE IS PRIMARILY BY FOOD PRODUCTION -- I. E., AGRICULTURE OR HUSBANDRY -- RATHER THAN BY GATHERING (253)	0.79 OF 39	36 31 71 8 XSQ= 22.38 PHI= -0.392 XP = 0.0000
53	LEAN TOWARD BEING THOSE WHERE FOOD PRODUCTION IS BY SIMPLE AGRICULTURE OR INCIPIENT FOOD PRODUCTION, RATHER THAN BY INTENSIVE AGRICULTURE (147)	0.76 OF 45	53	LEAN TOWARD BEING THOSE WHERE FOOD PRODUCTION IS BY INTENSIVE AGRICULTURE, RATHER THAN BY SIMPLE AGRICULTURE OR INCIPIENT FOOD PRODUCTION (91)	0.67 OF 24	11 16 34 8 XSQ= 10.01 PHI= -0.381 XP = 0.0016
55	TILT TOWARD BEING THOSE WHERE FOOD PRODUCTION IS BY SIMPLE AGRICULTURE, RATHER THAN BY INTENSIVE AGRICULTURE (101)	0.62 OF 29	55	TILT TOWARD BEING THOSE WHERE FOOD PRODUCTION IS BY INTENSIVE AGRICULTURE, RATHER THAN BY SIMPLE AGRICULTURE (91)	0.76 OF 21	11 16 18 5 XSQ= 5.72 PHI= -0.338 XP = 0.0168
62	TILT TOWARD BEING THOSE WHERE HUSBANDRY OF ANY KIND IS ABSENT (172)	0.63 OF 107	62	TILT TOWARD BEING THOSE WHERE HUSBANDRY OF SOME KIND IS PRESENT (228)	0.59 OF 39	40 23 67 16 XSQ= 4.59 PHI= -0.177 XP = 0.0322
71	TEND TO BE THOSE WHERE METAL WORKING IS ABSENT (153)	0.87 OF 71	71	TEND TO BE THOSE WHERE METAL WORKING IS PRESENT (98)	0.50 OF 20	9 10 62 10 XSQ= 11.00 PHI= -0.348 XP = 0.0009
73	DRIFT TOWARD BEING THOSE WHERE WEAVING IS ABSENT (130)	0.59 OF 74	73	DRIFT TOWARD BEING THOSE WHERE WEAVING IS PRESENT (118)	0.67 OF 21	30 14 44 7 XSQ= 3.50 PHI= -0.192 XP = 0.0613

74	DRIFT LESS TOWARD BEING THOSE WHERE POTTERY IS PRESENT (145)	0.52 OF 71	74	DRIFT MORE TOWARD BEING THOSE WHERE POTTERY IS PRESENT (145)	0.79 OF 19	37 15 34 4 XSQ= 3.39 PHI= -0.194 XP = 0.0655
80	TEND TO BE THOSE WHERE NO CITY OR TOWN IS PRESENT (185)	0.90 OF 51	80	TEND TO BE THOSE WHERE A CITY OR TOWN IS PRESENT (39)	0.52 OF 23	5 12 46 11 XSQ= 13.78 PHI= -0.431 XP = 0.0002
81	LEAN TOWARD BEING THOSE WHERE NO CITY OR TOWN IS PRESENT, AND THE AVERAGE COMMUNITY SIZE IS SMALLER THAN 200 (135)	0.75 OF 51	81	LEAN TOWARD BEING THOSE WHERE A CITY OR TOWN IS PRESENT, OR THE AVERAGE COMMUNITY SIZE IS 200 OR GREATER (89)	0.65 OF 23	13 15 38 8 XSQ= 9.01 PHI= -0.349 XP = 0.0027
84	TEND MORE TO BE THOSE WHERE THE LEVEL OF POLITICAL INTEGRATION IS THE LITTLE STATE, THE MINIMAL STATE, THE AUTONOMOUS COMMUNITY, OR THE FAMILY (262) GPM	0.92 OF 85	84	TEND LESS TO BE THOSE WHERE THE LEVEL OF POLITICAL INTEGRATION IS THE LITTLE STATE, THE MINIMAL STATE, THE AUTONOMOUS COMMUNITY, OR THE FAMILY (262) GPM	0.62 OF 26	7 10 78 16 XSQ= 11.79 PHI= -0.326 XP = 0.0006
85	LEAN MORE TOWARD BEING THOSE WHERE THE LEVEL OF POLITICAL INTEGRATION IS THE MINIMAL STATE, THE AUTONOMOUS COMMUNITY, OR THE FAMILY (234) GPM	0.86 OF 85	85	LEAN LESS TOWARD BEING THOSE WHERE THE LEVEL OF POLITICAL INTEGRATION IS THE MINIMAL STATE, THE AUTONOMOUS COMMUNITY, OR THE FAMILY (234) GPM	0.54 OF 26	12 12 73 14 XSQ= 10.24 PHI= -0.304 XP = 0.0014
88	TILT TOWARD BEING THOSE WHERE, IF A HEADMANSHIP IS PRESENT, SUCCESSION IS HEREDITARY (165)	0.55 OF 77	88	TILT TOWARD BEING THOSE WHERE, IF A HEADMANSHIP IS PRESENT, SUCCESSION IS NON-HEREDITARY (106)	0.79 OF 14	35 11 42 3 XSQ= 3.96 PHI= -0.209 XP = 0.0467
96	DRIFT TOWARD BEING THOSE WHERE THE HIERARCHY OF NATIONAL JURISDICTION HAS NO LEVELS (156) GES,EA	0.65 OF 91	96	DRIFT TOWARD BEING THOSE WHERE THE HIERARCHY OF NATIONAL JURISDICTION HAS FOUR, THREE, TWO OR ONE LEVEL (174) GES,EA	0.56 OF 27	32 15 59 12 XSQ= 2.81 PHI= -0.154 XP = 0.0936
102	TILT TOWARD BEING THOSE WHERE CLASS STRATIFICATION IS ABSENT (180)	0.59 OF 100	102	TILT TOWARD BEING THOSE WHERE CLASS STRATIFICATION IS PRESENT (203)	0.65 OF 37	41 24 59 13 XSQ= 5.25 PHI= -0.196 XP = 0.0220
107	TEND TO BE THOSE WHERE CLASS STRATIFICATION, IF PRESENT, IS BASED ON SOMETHING OTHER THAN OCCUPATIONAL STATUS (160)	0.88 OF 41	107	TEND TO BE THOSE WHERE CLASS STRATIFICATION, IF PRESENT, IS BASED ON OCCUPATIONAL STATUS (43)	0.54 OF 24	5 13 36 11 XSQ= 11.30 PHI= -0.417 XP = 0.0008

108	LEAN LESS TOWARD BEING THOSE 0.56 OF 41 WHERE CLASS STRATIFICATION, IF PRESENT, IS BASED ON SOMETHING OTHER THAN A HEREDITARY ARISTOCRACY (129)	108	LEAN MORE TOWARD BEING THOSE 0.96 OF 24 WHERE CLASS STRATIFICATION, IF PRESENT, IS BASED ON SOMETHING OTHER THAN A HEREDITARY ARISTOCRACY (129)	18 1 23 23 XSQ= 9.71 PHI= 0.387 XP = 0.0018
130	DRIFT TOWARD BEING THOSE 0.71 OF 31 WHERE LEATHER WORKING IS MAINLY DONE BY FEMALES (45)	130	DRIFT TOWARD BEING THOSE 0.71 OF 7 WHERE LEATHER WORKING IS MAINLY DONE BY MALES (39)	9 5 22 2 XSQ= 2.78 PHI= -0.270 EP = 0.0772
179	TILT LESS TOWARD BEING THOSE 0.78 OF 101 WHERE THE COMMUNITY IS OTHER THAN STRUCTURED ON A NON-CLAN BASIS AND COMMONLY EXOGAMOUS (340)	179	TILT MORE TOWARD BEING THOSE 0.95 OF 39 WHERE THE COMMUNITY IS OTHER THAN STRUCTURED ON A NON-CLAN BASIS AND COMMONLY EXOGAMOUS (340)	22 2 79 37 XSQ= 4.38 PHI= 0.177 XP = 0.0363
180	TILT LESS TOWARD BEING THOSE 0.78 OF 101 WHERE THE COMMUNITY IS COMMONLY NON-EXOGAMOUS, RATHER THAN EXOGAMOUS (258)	180	TILT MORE TOWARD BEING THOSE 0.95 OF 39 WHERE THE COMMUNITY IS COMMONLY NON-EXOGAMOUS, RATHER THAN EXOGAMOUS (258)	22 2 79 37 XSQ= 4.38 PHI= 0.177 XP = 0.0363
192	LEAN LESS TOWARD BEING THOSE 0.68 OF 107 WHERE THE ONLY KIN GROUP PRESENT IS A KINDRED OR ELSE BILATERAL DESCENT IS INFERRED (111)	192	LEAN MORE TOWARD BEING THOSE 0.92 OF 39 WHERE THE ONLY KIN GROUP PRESENT IS A KINDRED OR ELSE BILATERAL DESCENT IS INFERRED (111)	73 36 34 3 XSQ= 7.54 PHI= -0.227 XP = 0.0060
196	TEND TO BE THOSE 0.58 OF 69 WHERE INDIVIDUAL RIGHTS IN REAL PROPERTY, OR RULES FOR INHERITANCE, ARE ABSENT (87)	196	TEND TO BE THOSE 0.83 OF 29 WHERE INDIVIDUAL RIGHTS IN REAL PROPERTY, AND RULES FOR INHERITANCE, ARE PRESENT (194)	29 24 40 5 XSQ= 12.05 PHI= -0.351 XP = 0.0005
201	DRIFT MORE TOWARD BEING THOSE 0.70 OF 106 WHERE MARITAL RESIDENCE IS NON-OPTIONAL, RATHER THAN AMBILOCAL OR NEOLOCAL (334)	201	DRIFT LESS TOWARD BEING THOSE 0.51 OF 39 WHERE MARITAL RESIDENCE IS NON-OPTIONAL, RATHER THAN AMBILOCAL OR NEOLOCAL (334)	74 20 32 19 XSQ= 3.52 PHI= 0.156 XP = 0.0607
207	TILT LESS TOWARD BEING THOSE 0.54 OF 59 WHERE MARITAL RESIDENCE IS AMBILOCAL OR NEOLOCAL, RATHER THAN MATRILOCAL OR UXORILOCAL (64)	207	TILT MORE TOWARD BEING THOSE 0.83 OF 23 WHERE MARITAL RESIDENCE IS AMBILOCAL OR NEOLOCAL, RATHER THAN MATRILOCAL OR UXORILOCAL (64)	27 4 32 19 XSQ= 4.52 PHI= 0.235 XP = 0.0334
234	TILT LESS TOWARD BEING THOSE 0.80 OF 98 WHERE THE COUSIN TERMINOLOGY IS OF ESKIMO OR HAWAIIAN TYPE, RATHER THAN CROW, OMAHA, OR IROQUOIS TYPE (170)	234	TILT MORE TOWARD BEING THOSE 0.97 OF 33 WHERE THE COUSIN TERMINOLOGY IS OF ESKIMO OR HAWAIIAN TYPE, RATHER THAN CROW, OMAHA, OR IROQUOIS TYPE (170)	20 1 78 32 XSQ= 4.32 PHI= 0.182 XP = 0.0376

240	TILT LESS TOWARD BEING THCSE WHERE THE FAMILY, IF EXTENDED, IS SMALL OR STEM, RATHER THAN LARGE (135)	0.58 OF 60	240	TILT MORE TOWARD BEING THCSE WHERE THE FAMILY, IF EXTENDED, IS SMALL OR STEM, RATHER THAN LARGE (135)	0.88 OF 17	25 2 35 15 XSQ= 3.97 PHI= 0.227 XP = 0.0463
241	TILT MORE TOWARD BEING THCSE WHERE THE FAMILY, IF EXTENDED, IS LARGE CR SMALL, RATHER THAN STEM (187)	0.87 OF 60	241	TILT LESS TOWARD BEING THOSE WHERE THE FAMILY, IF EXTENDED, IS LARGE OR SMALL, RATHER THAN STEM (187)	0.59 CF 17	52 10 8 7 XSQ= 4.89 PHI= 0.252 XP = 0.0270
263	TILT LESS TOWARD BEING THCSE WHERE WIVES ARE OBTAINED BY RELATIVELY EASY MEANS; NAMELY BY TOKEN BRIDE-PRICE, GIFT EXCHANGE, ABSENCE CF ANY CCNSIDERATICN, OR RECEIPT CF DCWRY (162)	0.54 OF 105	263	TILT MORE TOWARD BEING THOSE WHERE WIVES ARE OBTAINED BY RELATIVELY EASY MEANS, NAMELY BY TOKEN BRIDE-PRICE, GIFT EXCHANGE, ABSENCE OF ANY CONSIDERATICN, CR RECEIPT OF DOWRY (162)	0.74 OF 39	48 10 57 29 XSQ= 3.97 PHI= 0.166 XP = 0.0464
272	TILT TOWARD BEING THOSE WHERE THE DIVORCE RATE IS HIGH (29) CA	0.69 OF 16	272	TILT TOWARD BEING THOSE WHERE THE DIVORCE RATE IS LOW (28) CA	0.86 OF 7	11 1 5 6 XSQ= 3.81 PHI= 0.407 EP = 0.0272
305	DRIFT TOWARD BEING THCSE WHERE THE EARLY SEXUAL SATISFACTION POTENTIAL IS LOW (24) W-C	0.79 OF 14	305	IN ALL CASES ARE THOSE WHERE THE EARLY SEXUAL SATISFACTION POTENTIAL IS HIGH (27) W-C	1.00 OF 2	3 2 11 0 XSQ= 2.04 PHI= -0.357 EP = 0.0833
311	DRIFT TOWARD BEING THCSE WHERE SEXUAL SOCIALIZATION ANXIETY IS HIGH (28) W-C	0.79 OF 14	311	IN ALL CASES ARE THOSE WHERE SEXUAL SOCIALIZATION ANXIETY IS LOW (23) W-C	1.00 OF 2	11 0 3 2 XSQ= 2.04 PHI= 0.357 EP = 0.0833
369	DRIFT TOWARD BEING THCSE WHERE DISSOCIATICN OF THE SEXES AT ADOLESCENCE, OR CUSTOMS OF INITIATION AT ADOLESCENCE, ARE PRESENT (42) JKH	0.88 OF 17	369	DRIFT TOWARD BEING THOSE WHERE BOTH DISSOCIATION OF THE SEXES AT ADOLESCENCE, AND CUSTOMS OF INITIATION AT ADOLESCENCE, ARE ABSENT (15) JKH	0.60 OF 5	15 2 2 3 XSQ= 2.74 PHI= 0.353 EP = 0.0549
373	DRIFT TOWARD BEING THOSE WHERE MALE INITIATION CEREMONIES AT PUBERTY ARE PRESENT (17) W-K-A	0.58 OF 12	373	IN ALL CASES ARE THOSE WHERE MALE INITIATION CEREMONIES AT PUBERTY ARE ABSENT (27) W-K-A	1.00 OF 4	7 0 5 4 XSQ= 2.12 PHI= 0.364 EP = 0.0885
382	LEAN TOWARD BEING THCSE WHERE FEMALE INITIATION RITES ARE PRESENT (38) JKB	0.94 OF 16	382	LEAN TOWARD BEING THOSE WHERE FEMALE INITIATION RITES ARE ABSENT (27) JKB	0.60 OF 10	15 4 1 6 XSQ= 6.51 PHI= 0.500 EP = 0.0053

430	TILT TOWARD BEING THOSE 0.83 OF 6 WHERE SUPERNATURAL SANCTIONS FOR MORALITY, HAVING AN EFFECT ON AN INDIVIDUAL'S HEALTH, ARE ABSENT OR UNREPORTED (22) GES	430	IN ALL CASES ARE THOSE 1.00 OF 4 WHERE SUPERNATURAL SANCTIONS FOR MORALITY, HAVING AN EFFECT ON AN INDIVIDUAL'S HEALTH, ARE PRESENT (16) GES	1 4 5 0 XSQ= 3.75 PHI= -0.612 EP = 0.0476
439	DRIFT TOWARD BEING THOSE 0.65 OF 17 WHERE FEAR OF GHOSTS IS LOW (31) W-C	439	DRIFT TOWARD BEING THOSE 0.83 OF 6 WHERE FEAR OF GHOSTS IS HIGH (30) W-C	6 5 11 1 XSQ= 2.40 PHI= -0.323 EP = 0.0686
458	TILT MORE TOWARD BEING THOSE 0.91 OF 54 WHERE GAMES, IF PRESENT, DO NOT INCLUDE GAMES OF STRATEGY (119) R-A-B,EA	458	TILT LESS TOWARD BEING THOSE 0.62 OF 13 WHERE GAMES, IF PRESENT, DO NOT INCLUDE GAMES OF STRATEGY (119) R-A-B,EA	5 5 49 8 XSQ= 4.92 PHI= -0.271 XP = 0.0265
473	TILT TOWARD BEING THOSE 0.59 OF 17 WHERE SENSITIVITY TO INSULT IS EXTREME (32) PES	473	TILT TOWARD BEING THOSE 0.89 OF 9 WHERE SENSITIVITY TO INSULT IS MODERATE OR NEGLIGIBLE (56) PES	10 1 7 8 XSQ= 3.71 PHI= 0.378 EP = 0.0362

253 CULTURES WHERE THE FAMILY IS INDEPENDENT AND MARRIAGE IS MONOGAMOUS (39)	253 CULTURES OTHER THAN WHERE THE FAMILY IS INDEPENDENT AND MARRIAGE IS MONOGAMOUS (359)

BACKGROUND ON PAGE 124

SUBJECT ONLY

39 IN LEFT COLUMN

AMERICANS	ANDAMANESE	BAJUN	BHUIYA	BRAZILIANS	BURMESE	CAMBA	CHAMACOCO	CHENCHU	CHEREMIS
CHOCO	COPR ESKIMO	DOBUANS	DOROBO	DUSUN	HUTSUL	IFUGAO	INCA	JEMEZ	KAREN
KET	LAPPS	MAYA	MENTAWEI	MZAB	NABESNA	PALIKUR	PUKAPUKA	ROMANS	ROTUMANS
SAGADA	SEMINOLE	SINHALESE	TAOS	TIGRINYA	TRISTAN	TUBATULABAL	WALLOONS	YAGUA	

359 IN RIGHT COLUMN

2 EXCLUDED BECAUSE UNASCERTAINED

	Left column		Right column		Statistics
3	TILT MORE TOWARD BEING THOSE LOCATED OUTSIDE OF AFRICA (320)	0.95 OF 39	TILT LESS TOWARD BEING THOSE LOCATED OUTSIDE OF AFRICA (320)	0.78 OF 359	2 78 37 281 XSQ= 5.05 PHI= -0.113 XP = 0.0247
4	LEAN LESS TOWARD BEING THOSE LOCATED OUTSIDE OF THE CIRCUM-MEDITERRANEAN (355)	0.74 OF 39	LEAN MORE TOWARD BEING THOSE LOCATED OUTSIDE OF THE CIRCUM-MEDITERRANEAN (355)	0.90 OF 359	10 35 29 324 XSQ= 7.35 PHI= 0.136 XP = 0.0067
11	DRIFT LESS TOWARD BEING THOSE WHERE THE LATITUDE IS LESS THAN SIXTY DEGREES (385)	0.90 OF 39	DRIFT MORE TOWARD BEING THOSE WHERE THE LATITUDE IS LESS THAN SIXTY DEGREES (385)	0.97 OF 359	4 11 35 348 XSQ= 3.23 PHI= 0.090 XP = 0.0723
53	TILT TOWARD BEING THOSE WHERE FOOD PRODUCTION IS BY INTENSIVE AGRICULTURE, RATHER THAN BY SIMPLE AGRICULTURE OR INCIPIENT FOOD PRODUCTION (91)	0.68 OF 19	TILT TOWARD BEING THOSE WHERE FOOD PRODUCTION IS BY SIMPLE AGRICULTURE OR INCIPIENT FOOD PRODUCTION, RATHER THAN BY INTENSIVE AGRICULTURE (147)	0.64 OF 218	13 78 6 140 XSQ= 6.55 PHI= 0.166 XP = 0.0105 •
55	TILT TOWARD BEING THOSE WHERE FOOD PRODUCTION IS BY INTENSIVE AGRICULTURE, RATHER THAN BY SIMPLE AGRICULTURE (91)	0.76 OF 17	TILT TOWARD BEING THOSE WHERE FOOD PRODUCTION IS BY SIMPLE AGRICULTURE, RATHER THAN BY INTENSIVE AGRICULTURE (101)	0.55 OF 174	13 78 4 96 XSQ= 5.01 PHI= 0.162 XP = 0.0252

80	LEAN LESS TOWARD BEING THOSE 0.62 OF 26 WHERE NO CITY OR TOWN IS PRESENT (185)	80	LEAN MORE TOWARD BEING THOSE 0.86 OF 197 WHERE NO CITY OR TOWN IS PRESENT (185)	10 28 16 169 XSQ= 7.92 PHI= 0.188 XP = 0.0049
87	TILT LESS TOWARD BEING THOSE 0.80 OF 25 WHERE THE LEVEL OF POLITICAL INTEGRATION IS THE LARGE STATE, THE LITTLE STATE, THE MINIMAL STATE, OR THE AUTONOMOUS COMMUNITY (281) GPM	87	TILT MORE TOWARD BEING THOSE 0.94 OF 277 WHERE THE LEVEL OF POLITICAL INTEGRATION IS THE LARGE STATE, THE LITTLE STATE, THE MINIMAL STATE, OR THE AUTONOMOUS COMMUNITY (281) GPM	20 259 5 18 XSQ= 4.18 PHI= -0.118 XP = 0.0410
88	TILT TOWARD BEING THOSE 0.68 OF 19 WHERE, IF A HEADMANSHIP IS PRESENT, SUCCESSION IS NON-HEREDITARY (106)	88	TILT TOWARD BEING THOSE 0.63 OF 251 WHERE, IF A HEADMANSHIP IS PRESENT, SUCCESSION IS HEREDITARY (165)	13 93 6 158 XSQ= 6.03 PHI= 0.149 XP = 0.0140
97	IN ALL CASES ARE THOSE 1.00 OF 25 WHERE THE HIERARCHY OF LOCAL JURISDICTION HAS THREE OR TWO LEVELS (273) GES,EA	97	TILT LESS TOWARD BEING THOSE 0.81 OF 305 WHERE THE HIERARCHY OF LOCAL JURISDICTION HAS THREE OR TWO LEVELS (273) GES,EA	0 58 25 247 XSQ= 4.53 PHI= -0.117 XP = 0.0333
98	TEND TO BE THOSE 0.64 OF 25 WHERE THE HIERARCHY OF LOCAL JURISDICTION HAS TWO LEVELS (93) GES,EA	98	TEND TO BE THOSE 0.75 OF 305 WHERE THE HIERARCHY OF LOCAL JURISDICTION HAS FOUR OR THREE LEVELS (238) GES,EA	9 228 16 77 XSQ= 15.28 PHI= -0.215 XP = 0.0001
100	TILT LESS TOWARD BEING THOSE 0.64 OF 25 WHERE HIERARCHIES ARE MORE COMPLEX THAN THE 'SIMPLEST,' I. E., MORE COMPLEX THAN TWO LOCAL LEVELS WITH NO NATIONAL LEVELS (267) GES,EA	100	TILT MORE TOWARD BEING THOSE 0.82 OF 304 WHERE HIERARCHIES ARE MORE COMPLEX THAN THE 'SIMPLEST,' I. E., MORE COMPLEX THAN TWO LOCAL LEVELS WITH NO NATIONAL LEVELS (267) GES,EA	16 250 9 54 XSQ= 3.85 PHI= -0.108 XP = 0.0496
107	TILT LESS TOWARD BEING THOSE 0.56 OF 18 WHERE CLASS STRATIFICATION, IF PRESENT, IS BASED ON SOMETHING OTHER THAN OCCUPATIONAL STATUS (160)	107	TILT MORE TOWARD BEING THOSE 0.81 OF 185 WHERE CLASS STRATIFICATION, IF PRESENT, IS BASED ON SOMETHING OTHER THAN OCCUPATIONAL STATUS (160)	8 35 10 150 XSQ= 4.96 PHI= 0.156 XP = 0.0259
108	TILT MORE TOWARD BEING THOSE 0.89 OF 18 WHERE CLASS STRATIFICATION, IF PRESENT, IS BASED ON SOMETHING OTHER THAN A HEREDITARY ARISTOCRACY (129)	108	TILT LESS TOWARD BEING THOSE 0.61 OF 185 WHERE CLASS STRATIFICATION, IF PRESENT, IS BASED ON SOMETHING OTHER THAN A HEREDITARY ARISTOCRACY (129)	2 72 16 113 XSQ= 4.34 PHI= -0.146 XP = 0.0372
110	TILT MORE TOWARD BEING THOSE 0.74 OF 39 WHERE SLAVERY IS ABSENT (218)	110	TILT LESS TOWARD BEING THOSE 0.55 OF 340 WHERE SLAVERY IS ABSENT (218)	10 152 29 188 XSQ= 4.45 PHI= -0.108 XP = 0.0350

128	DRIFT TOWARD BEING THOSE WHERE, IF SUBSISTENCE IS PRIMARILY BY AGRICULTURE, THE WORK IS MAINLY DONE BY MALES (40)	0.88 OF 8	128	DRIFT TOWARD BEING THOSE WHERE, IF SUBSISTENCE IS PRIMARILY BY AGRICULTURE, THE WORK IS MAINLY DONE BY FEMALES (37)	0.53 OF 68	7 32 1 36 XSQ= 3.21 PHI= 0.205 XP = 0.0733
138	IN ALL CASES ARE THOSE WHERE SUPERORDINATE JUSTICE IS ABSENT (18) BBW	1.00 OF 3	138	DRIFT TOWARD BEING THOSE WHERE SUPERORDINATE JUSTICE IS PRESENT (22) BBW	0.59 OF 37	0 22 3 15 XSQ= 1.93 PHI= -0.219 EP = 0.0826
176	TILT MORE TOWARD BEING THOSE WHERE THE COMMUNITY IS OTHER THAN A CLAN-COMMUNITY OR A COMMUNITY STRUCTURED OR SEGMENTED ON A CLAN BASIS (213)	0.76 OF 37	176	TILT LESS TOWARD BEING THOSE WHERE THE COMMUNITY IS OTHER THAN A CLAN-COMMUNITY OR A COMMUNITY STRUCTURED OR SEGMENTED ON A CLAN BASIS (213)	0.54 OF 344	9 159 28 185 XSQ= 5.64 PHI= -0.122 XP = 0.0176
181	TILT LESS TOWARD BEING THOSE WHERE THE COMMUNITY IS OTHER THAN A DEME (337)	0.76 OF 37	181	TILT MORE TOWARD BEING THOSE WHERE THE COMMUNITY IS OTHER THAN A DEME (337)	0.90 OF 344	9 36 28 308 XSQ= 4.90 PHI= 0.113 XP = 0.0268
186	DRIFT MORE TOWARD BEING THOSE WHERE THE KIN GROUP IS OTHER THAN EXCLUSIVELY PATRILINEAL (250)	0.77 OF 39	186	DRIFT LESS TOWARD BEING THOSE WHERE THE KIN GROUP IS OTHER THAN EXCLUSIVELY PATRILINEAL (250)	0.61 OF 359	9 140 30 219 XSQ= 3.16 PHI= -0.089 XP = 0.0756
188	TILT TOWARD BEING THOSE WHERE THE KIN GROUP IS EXCLUSIVELY COGNATIC (148)	0.56 OF 39	188	TILT TOWARD BEING THOSE WHERE THE KIN GROUP IS OTHER THAN EXCLUSIVELY COGNATIC (252)	0.65 OF 359	22 125 17 234 XSQ= 6.14 PHI= 0.124 XP = 0.0132
192	LEAN TOWARD BEING THOSE WHERE THE ONLY KIN GROUP PRESENT IS A KINDRED OR ELSE BILATERAL DESCENT IS INFERRED (111)	0.51 OF 39	192	LEAN TOWARD BEING THOSE OTHER THAN WHERE THE ONLY KIN GROUP PRESENT IS A KINDRED OR ELSE BILATERAL DESCENT IS INFERRED (289)	0.75 OF 359	20 90 19 269 XSQ= 10.81 PHI= 0.165 XP = 0.0010
197	TEND TO BE THOSE WHERE RULES FOR THE INHERITANCE OF REAL PROPERTY, IF PRESENT, DO NOT FAVOR EITHER THE MALE HEIR OR LINE, OR THE FEMALE HEIR OR LINE (29)	0.53 OF 19	197	TEND TO BE THOSE WHERE RULES FOR THE INHERITANCE OF REAL PROPERTY, IF PRESENT, FAVOR EITHER THE MALE HEIR OR LINE, OR THE FEMALE HEIR OR LINE (165)	0.89 OF 175	9 156 10 19 XSQ= 20.35 PHI= -0.324 XP = 0.0000
201	TEND LESS TO BE THOSE WHERE MARITAL RESIDENCE IS NON-OPTIONAL, RATHER THAN AMBILOCAL OR NEOLOCAL (334)	0.54 OF 39	201	TEND MORE TO BE THOSE WHERE MARITAL RESIDENCE IS NON-OPTIONAL, RATHER THAN AMBILOCAL OR NEOLOCAL (334)	0.87 OF 357	21 311 18 46 XSQ= 26.32 PHI= -0.258 XP = 0.0000

204	TEND TO BE THOSE WHERE MARITAL RESIDENCE IS AMBILOCAL OR NEOLOCAL, RATHER THAN PATRILOCAL, VIRILOCAL, OR AVUNCULOCAL (64)	0.55 OF 33	204	TEND TO BE THOSE WHERE MARITAL RESIDENCE IS PATRILOCAL, VIRILOCAL, OR AVUNCULOCAL, RATHER THAN AMBILOCAL OR NEOLOCAL (270)	0.85 OF 299	15 253 18 46 XSQ= 26.83 PHI= -0.284 XP = 0.0000
207	TILT TOWARD BEING THOSE WHERE MARITAL RESIDENCE IS AMBILOCAL OR NEOLOCAL, RATHER THAN MATRILOCAL OR UXORILOCAL (64)	0.75 OF 24	207	TILT TOWARD BEING THOSE WHERE MARITAL RESIDENCE IS MATRILOCAL OR UXORILOCAL, RATHER THAN AMBILOCAL OR NEOLOCAL (64)	0.56 OF 104	6 58 18 46 XSQ= 6.21 PHI= -0.220 XP = 0.0127
234	LEAN MORE TOWARD BEING THOSE WHERE THE COUSIN TERMINOLOGY IS OF ESKIMO OR HAWAIIAN TYPE, RATHER THAN CROW, OMAHA, OR IROQUOIS TYPE (170)	0.79 OF 29	234	LEAN LESS TOWARD BEING THOSE WHERE THE COUSIN TERMINOLOGY IS OF ESKIMO OR HAWAIIAN TYPE, RATHER THAN CROW, OMAHA, OR IROQUOIS TYPE (170)	0.50 OF 291	6 145 23 146 XSQ= 7.85 PHI= -0.157 XP = 0.0051
262	DRIFT LESS TOWARD BEING THOSE WHERE WIVES ARE OBTAINED BY MEANS INVOLVING THE PRESENCE OF SOME CONSIDERATION (305)	0.64 OF 39	262	DRIFT MORE TOWARD BEING THOSE WHERE WIVES ARE OBTAINED BY MEANS INVOLVING THE PRESENCE OF SOME CONSIDERATION (305)	0.79 OF 354	25 279 14 75 XSQ= 3.54 PHI= -0.095 XP = 0.0599
263	LEAN TOWARD BEING THOSE WHERE WIVES ARE OBTAINED BY RELATIVELY EASY MEANS, NAMELY BY TOKEN BRIDE-PRICE, GIFT EXCHANGE, ABSENCE OF ANY CONSIDERATION, OR RECEIPT OF DOWRY (162)	0.64 OF 39	263	LEAN TOWARD BEING THOSE WHERE WIVES ARE OBTAINED BY RELATIVELY DIFFICULT MEANS, NAMELY BY BRIDE-PRICE, BRIDE-SERVICE, OR EXCHANGING A FEMALE RELATIVE (233)	0.62 OF 354	14 218 25 136 XSQ= 8.55 PHI= -0.147 XP = 0.0035
392	DRIFT TOWARD BEING THOSE WHERE PREMARITAL SEX RELATIONS ARE FREELY PERMITTED (67) JTW,EA	0.58 OF 19	392	DRIFT TOWARD BEING THOSE WHERE PREMARITAL SEX RELATIONS ARE STRONGLY PUNISHED AND IN FACT RARE, OR WEAKLY PUNISHED AND IN FACT NOT RARE, OR PUNISHED ONLY IF PREGNANCY RESULTS (112) JTW,EA	0.65 OF 160	8 104 11 56 XSQ= 2.89 PHI= -0.127 XP = 0.0893
419	DRIFT TOWARD BEING THOSE WHERE MILITARY GLORY IS NEGLIGIBLY EMPHASIZED (31) PES	0.67 OF 9	419	DRIFT TOWARD BEING THOSE WHERE MILITARY GLORY IS STRONGLY OR MODERATELY EMPHASIZED (55) PES	0.68 OF 77	3 52 6 25 XSQ= 2.74 PHI= -0.178 XP = 0.0979
480	IN ALL CASES ARE THOSE WHERE COMPLEXITY OF ARTISTIC DESIGN IS LOW (15) HB	1.00 OF 4	480	DRIFT TOWARD BEING THOSE WHERE COMPLEXITY OF ARTISTIC DESIGN IS HIGH (14) HB	0.56 OF 25	0 14 4 11 XSQ= 2.38 PHI= -0.286 EP = 0.0996

254 CULTURES WHERE HOUSEHOLD AUTHORITY IS ON THE FATHER'S SIDE, RATHER THAN THE MOTHER'S (9) CA

254 CULTURES WHERE HOUSEHOLD AUTHORITY IS ON THE MOTHER'S SIDE, RATHER THAN THE FATHER'S (6) DA

BACKGROUND ON PAGE 127

BOTH SUBJECT AND PREDICATE

9 IN LEFT COLUMN

CHEROKEE COMANCHE FON HEHE KURTATCHI MURNGIN SWAZI THONGA VENDA

6 IN RIGHT COLUMN

HAIDA HANO MANUS MARSHALLESE NAVAHO TRUKESE

385 EXCLUDED BECAUSE UNASCERTAINED

	Left column			Right column		
3	TILT TOWARD BEING THOSE LOCATED IN AFRICA (80)	0.56 OF 9	3	IN ALL CASES ARE THOSE LOCATED OUTSIDE OF AFRICA (320)	1.00 OF 6	5 0 4 6 XSQ= 2.81 PHI= 0.433 EP = 0.0440
73	DRIFT TOWARD BEING THOSE WHERE WEAVING IS ABSENT (130)	0.86 OF 7	73	DRIFT TOWARD BEING THOSE WHERE WEAVING IS PRESENT (118)	0.75 OF 4	1 3 6 1 XSQ= 1.86 PHI= -0.411 EP = 0.0879
86	DRIFT TOWARD BEING THOSE WHERE THE LEVEL OF POLITICAL INTEGRATION IS THE LARGE STATE, THE LITTLE STATE, OR THE MINIMAL STATE (148) GPM	0.67 OF 6	86	IN ALL CASES ARE THOSE WHERE THE LEVEL OF POLITICAL INTEGRATION IS THE AUTONOMOUS COMMUNITY, OR THE FAMILY (156) GPM	1.00 OF 4	4 0 2 4 XSQ= 2.10 PHI= 0.458 EP = 0.0762
90	TILT TOWARD BEING THOSE WHERE, IF A HEREDITARY HEADMANSHIP IS PRESENT, SUCCESSION IS PATRILINEAL, RATHER THAN MATRILINEAL (127)	0.83 OF 6	90	IN ALL CASES ARE THOSE WHERE, IF A HEREDITARY HEADMANSHIP IS PRESENT, SUCCESSION IS MATRILINEAL, RATHER THAN PATRILINEAL (38)	1.00 OF 3	5 0 1 3 XSQ= 2.76 PHI= 0.553 EP = 0.0476
95	TILT TOWARD BEING THOSE WHERE THE HIERARCHY OF NATIONAL JURISDICTION HAS FOUR, THREE, OR TWO LEVELS (76) GES,EA	0.71 OF 7	95	IN ALL CASES ARE THOSE WHERE THE HIERARCHY OF NATIONAL JURISDICTION HAS ONE OR NO LEVELS (254) GES,EA	1.00 OF 6	5 0 2 6 XSQ= 4.27 PHI= 0.573 EP = 0.0210

```
187  DRIFT TOWARD BEING THOSE        0.89 OF   9     187  DRIFT TOWARD BEING THOSE        0.67 OF   6           1     4
     WHERE THE KIN GROUP IS                               WHERE THE KIN GROUP IS                                 8     2
     OTHER THAN                                           EXCLUSIVELY MATRILINEAL  (55)                  XSQ=     2.81
     EXCLUSIVELY MATRILINEAL  (344)                                                                      PHI=   -0.433
                                                                                                         EP =   0.0889

210  DRIFT TOWARD BEING THOSE        0.86 OF   7     210  DRIFT TOWARD BEING THOSE        0.75 OF   4           6     1
     WHERE MARITAL RESIDENCE IS                           WHERE MARITAL RESIDENCE IS                             1     3
     PATRILOCAL, RATHER THAN                              MATRILOCAL, RATHER THAN                        XSQ=     1.86
     MATRILOCAL  (169)                                    PATRILOCAL  (31)                               PHI=    0.411
                                                                                                         EP =   0.0879

242  IN ALL CASES ARE THOSE          1.00 OF   9     242  TILT TOWARD BEING THOSE         0.50 OF   6           9     3
     WHERE MARRIAGE IS                                    WHERE MARRIAGE IS MONOGAMOUS,                          0     3
     COMMONLY OR OCCASIONALLY POLYGYNOUS,                 RATHER THAN COMMONLY OR OCCASIONALLY           XSQ=     2.93
     RATHER THAN MONOGAMOUS  (314)                        POLYGYNOUS  (81)                               PHI=    0.442
                                                                                                         EP =   0.0440

243  TILT TOWARD BEING THOSE         0.83 OF   6     243  IN ALL CASES ARE THOSE          1.00 OF   3           5     0
     WHERE POLYGYNY, IF PRESENT,                          WHERE POLYGYNY, IF PRESENT,                            1     3
     HAS A HIGH INCIDENCE  (24) W-D,S                     HAS A LOW INCIDENCE  (36) W-D,S                XSQ=     2.76
                                                                                                         PHI=    0.553
                                                                                                         EP =   0.0476

263  TILT TOWARD BEING THOSE         0.78 OF   9     263  TILT TOWARD BEING THOSE         0.83 OF   6           7     1
     WHERE WIVES ARE OBTAINED BY                          WHERE WIVES ARE OBTAINED                               2     5
     RELATIVELY DIFFICULT MEANS, NAMELY BY                BY RELATIVELY EASY MEANS, NAMELY BY            XSQ=     3.23
     BRIDE-PRICE, BRIDE-SERVICE, OR                       TOKEN BRIDE-PRICE, GIFT EXCHANGE,              PHI=    0.464
     EXCHANGING A FEMALE RELATIVE  (233)                  ABSENCE OF ANY CONSIDERATION, OR               EP =   0.0406
                                                          RECEIPT OF DOWRY  (162)

314  DRIFT TOWARD BEING THOSE        0.67 OF   6     314  IN ALL CASES ARE THOSE          1.00 OF   4           4     0
     WHERE THE INCIDENCE OF MOTHER-CHILD                  WHERE THE INCIDENCE OF MOTHER-CHILD                    2     4
     HOUSEHOLDS IS HIGH  (19) W-D,S                       HOUSEHOLDS IS LOW  (61) W-D,S                  XSQ=     2.10
                                                                                                         PHI=    0.458
                                                                                                         EP =   0.0762

377  DRIFT TOWARD BEING THOSE        0.57 OF   7     377  IN ALL CASES ARE THOSE          1.00 OF   6           4     0
     WHERE MALE GENITAL MUTILATION                        WHERE MALE GENITAL MUTILATION                          3     6
     IS PRESENT  (83)                                     IS ABSENT  (242)                               XSQ=     2.63
                                                                                                         PHI=    0.450
                                                                                                         EP =   0.0699

440  IN ALL CASES ARE THOSE          1.00 OF   6     440  IN ALL CASES ARE THOSE          1.00 OF   4           0     4
     WHERE FEAR OF SPIRITS                                WHERE FEAR OF SPIRITS                                  6     0
     IS LOW  (29) W-C                                     IS HIGH  (32) W-C                              XSQ=     6.27
                                                                                                         PHI=   -0.792
                                                                                                         EP =   0.0048
```

```
*****************************************************************************************************

255  CULTURES                                      255  CULTURES
     WHERE GRANDPARENTAL AUTHORITY                      WHERE GRANDPARENTAL AUTHORITY
     OVER PARENTS IS PRESENT  (7) CA                    OVER PARENTS IS ABSENT  (26) DA


BACKGROUND ON PAGE 127                                                   BOTH SUBJECT AND PREDICATE
.....................................................................................................

       7  IN LEFT COLUMN

ASHANTI     ATSUGEWI    KOREANS     NAMA        SEMINOLE    TALLENSI    TANALA

      26  IN RIGHT COLUMN

ARAPESH     AZANDE      BHUIYA      BURMESE     CHEYENNE    CHIR-APACHE DILLING     FOX         JUKUN       KASKA
KATAB       KIOW-APACHE LAKHER      LESU        LOZI        NYAKYUSA    OJIBWA      ONTONG-JAVA PAPAGO      SANPOIL
SARAMACCA   SHILLUK     TARAHUMARA  TIKOPIA     TIMBIRA     WOLEAIANS

     367  EXCLUDED BECAUSE UNASCERTAINED

-----------------------------------------------------------------------------------------------------
 71  TILT TOWARD BEING THOSE          0.83 OF   6     71  TILT TOWARD BEING THOSE          0.74 OF  19          5    5
     WHERE METAL WORKING IS                               WHERE METAL WORKING IS                                1   14
     PRESENT  (98)                                        ABSENT  (153)                                  XSQ=     4.03
                                                                                                         PHI=    0.401
                                                                                                         EP =   0.0225

 80  DRIFT LESS TOWARD BEING THOSE    0.67 OF   6     80  IN ALL CASES ARE THOSE           1.00 OF  13          2    0
     WHERE NO CITY OR TOWN IS PRESENT  (185)              WHERE NO CITY OR TOWN IS PRESENT  (185)               4   13
                                                                                                         XSQ=     1.95
                                                                                                         PHI=    0.320
                                                                                                         EP =   0.0877

102  TILT TOWARD BEING THOSE          0.86 OF   7    102  TILT TOWARD BEING THOSE          0.64 OF  25          6    9
     WHERE CLASS STRATIFICATION IS                        WHERE CLASS STRATIFICATION IS                         1   16
     PRESENT  (203)                                       ABSENT  (180)                                  XSQ=     3.61
                                                                                                         PHI=    0.336
                                                                                                         EP =   0.0330

177  DRIFT LESS TOWARD BEING THOSE    0.57 OF   7    177  DRIFT MORE TOWARD BEING THOSE    0.88 OF  26          3    3
     WHERE THE COMMUNITY IS OTHER THAN                    WHERE THE COMMUNITY IS OTHER THAN                     4   23
     A SINGLE CLAN-COMMUNITY AND                          A SINGLE CLAN-COMMUNITY AND                    XSQ=     1.84
     EXOGAMOUS  (305)                                     EXOGAMOUS  (305)                               PHI=    0.236
                                                                                                         EP =   0.0929

180  TILT TOWARD BEING THOSE          0.71 OF   7    180  TILT TOWARD BEING THOSE          0.77 OF  26          5    6
     WHERE THE COMMUNITY IS                               WHERE THE COMMUNITY IS                                2   20
     COMMONLY EXOGAMOUS, RATHER THAN                      COMMONLY NON-EXOGAMOUS, RATHER THAN            XSQ=     3.83
     NON-EXOGAMOUS  (124)                                 EXOGAMOUS  (258)                               PHI=    0.341
                                                                                                         EP =   0.0274
```

255/

256	LEAN TOWARD BEING THOSE WHERE GRANDPARENT AND GRANCCHILD ARE NCT FRIENDLY ECUALS (8) CA	0.71 OF 7	256	LEAN TOWARD BEING THOSE WHERE GRANDPARENT AND GRANDCHILD ARE FRIENDLY EQUALS (25) DA	0.88 OF 26	 XSQ= PHI= EP =	2 23 5 3 7.76 -0.485 0.0041
318	IN ALL CASES ARE THOSE WHERE THE CVERALL INCULGENCE OF THE INFANT IS LCW (31) B-B-C	1.00 OF 3	318	TILT TOWARD BEING THOSE WHERE THE OVERALL INDULGENCE OF THE INFANT IS HIGH (40) B-B-C	0.83 OF 12	 XSQ= PHI= EP =	0 10 3 2 4.22 -0.530 0.0220
400	IN ALL CASES ARE THCSE WHERE HCMCSEXUAL ACTIVITY IS PERMITTED (36) F-B	1.00 OF 3	400	DRIFT TOWARD BEING THOSE WHERE HOMOSEXUAL ACTIVITY IS PROHIBITED (22) F-B	0.75 OF 8	 XSQ= PHI= EP =	0 6 3 2 2.39 -0.466 0.0606
444	IN ALL CASES ARE THOSE WHERE THE USE CF DREAMS TC SEEK AND CCNTROL SUPERNATURAL POWERS IS LCW (27) RGC	1.00 OF 4	444	DRIFT TOWARD BEING THOSE WHERE THE USE OF DREAMS TO SEEK AND CONTROL SUPERNATURAL POWERS IS HIGH (28) RGD	0.71 OF 7	 XSQ= PHI= EP =	0 5 4 2 2.75 -0.500 0.0606
449	DRIFT TCWARD BEING THOSE WHERE THE CBSERVATION CF FCOC TABOOS IS MEDIUM CR LOW, RATHER THAN HIGH (61) JRL	0.75 OF 4	449	DRIFT TOWARD BEING THOSE WHERE THE OBSERVATION OF FCOD TABOOS IS HIGH, RATHER THAN MEDIUM OR LOW (25) JRL	0.88 OF 8	 XSQ= PHI= EP =	1 7 3 1 2.30 -0.437 0.0667

```
**********************************************************************************************************

256  CULTURES                                        256  CULTURES
     WHERE GRANDPARENT AND GRANDCHILD                     WHERE GRANDPARENT AND GRANDCHILD
     ARE FRIENDLY EQUALS  (25) CA                         ARE NOT FRIENDLY EQUALS  (8) DA


BACKGROUND ON PAGE 127                                                          BOTH SUBJECT AND PREDICATE
..........................................................................................................

      25  IN LEFT COLUMN

ARAPESH     AZANDE       BHUIYA      BURMESE     CHEYENNE    CHIR-APACHE DILLING     FOX         JUKUN       KASKA
KATAB       KICW-APACHE  KCREANS     LESU        LOZI        NYAKYUSA    OJIBWA      ONTCNG-JAVA PAPAGO      SANPOIL
SARAMACCA   TALLENSI     TARAHUMARA  TIKOPIA     WOLEAIANS

       8  IN RIGHT CCLUMN

ASHANTI     ATSUGEWI     LAKHER      NAMA        SEMINOLE    SHILLUK     TANALA      TIMBIRA

     367  EXCLUDED BECAUSE UNASCERTAINED


----------------------------------------------------------------------------------------------------------
 71  DRIFT TCWARD BEING THOSE       0.72 OF  18        71  DRIFT TOWARD BEING THOSE       0.71 OF   7           5     5
     WHERE METAL WORKING IS                                 WHERE METAL WORKING IS                              13     2
     ABSENT  (153)                                          PRESENT  (98)                               XSQ=     2.39
                                                                                                        PHI=   -0.309
                                                                                                        EP =   0.0752

220  TILT MORE TOWARD BEING THOSE   0.96 OF  25       22C  TILT LESS TOWARD BEING THOSE   0.63 OF   8           1     3
     WHERE FIRST COUSIN MARRIAGE                            WHERE FIRST COUSIN MARRIAGE                         24     5
     IN SOME FORM OR OTHER                                  IN SOME FORM OR OTHER                       XSQ=     3.63
     IS NCT PRESCRIBED CR PREFERRED  (273)                  IS NOT PRESCRIBED OR PREFERRED  (273)       PHI=   -0.332
                                                                                                        EP =   0.0359

234  TILT TCWARD BEING THOSE        0.74 OF  23       234  TILT TOWARD BEING THOSE        0.83 OF   6           6     5
     WHERE THE COUSIN TERMINOLOGY IS                        WHERE THE COUSIN TERMINOLOGY IS                     17     1
     OF ESKIMO CR HAWAIIAN TYPE,                            OF CROW, OMAHA, OR IROQUOIS TYPE,           XSQ=     4.42
     RATHER THAN                                            RATHER THAN                                 PHI=   -0.390
     CROW, OMAHA, CR IRCQUOIS TYPE  (170)                   ESKIMO OR HAWAIIAN TYPE  (152)              EP =   0.0185

255  LEAN TOWARD BEING THOSE        0.92 OF  25       255  LEAN TOWARD BEING THOSE        0.63 OF   8           2     5
     WHERE GRANDPARENTAL AUTHORITY                          WHERE GRANDPARENTAL AUTHORITY                       23     3
     OVER PARENTS IS ABSENT  (26) CA                        OVER PARENTS IS PRESENT  (7) DA             XSQ=     7.76
                                                                                                        PHI=   -0.485
                                                                                                        EP =   0.0041

368  TILT TCWARD BEING THOSE        0.88 OF   8       368  IN ALL CASES ARE THOSE         1.00 OF   3           7     0
     WHERE DISSOCIATION OF THE SEXES                        WHERE DISSOCIATION OF THE SEXES                      1     3
     AT ADOLESCENCE                                         AT ADOLESCENCE                              XSQ=     3.93
     IS HIGH CR MEDIUM  (16) JKH                            IS LOW  (21) JKH                            PHI=    0.598
                                                                                                        EP =   0.0242
```

370	DRIFT TOWARD BEING THOSE 0.65 OF 17 WHERE THE SEGREGATION OF ADOLESCENT BOYS IS ABSENT (148)	370	DRIFT TOWARD BEING THOSE 0.86 OF 7 WHERE THE SEGREGATION OF ADOLESCENT BOYS IS COMPLETE OR PARTIAL (95)	6 6 11 1 XSQ= 3.23 PHI= -0.367 EP = 0.0686
398	IN ALL CASES ARE THOSE 1.00 OF 6 WHERE THE INTENSITY OF SEX ANXIETY IS HIGH (16) WNS	398	DRIFT TOWARD BEING THOSE 0.67 OF 3 WHERE THE INTENSITY OF SEX ANXIETY IS LOW (16) WNS	6 1 0 2 XSQ= 2.01 PHI= 0.472 EP = 0.0833

257 CULTURES
WHERE THE SEVERITY OF SISTER
AVOIDANCE IS HIGH (10) WNS

257 CULTURES
WHERE THE SEVERITY OF SISTER
AVOIDANCE IS LOW (17) WNS

BACKGROUND ON PAGE 127 — BOTH SUBJECT AND PREDICATE

10 IN LEFT COLUMN

CHEYENNE, CHIR-APACHE, LAU, MURNGIN, NAMA, OJIBWA, ONTONG-JAVA, PUKAPUKA, SAMOANS, TROBRIAND

17 IN RIGHT COLUMN

ALORESE, ARAPESH, ASHANTI, CHAGGA, CHENCHU, COMANCHE, HANO, IFUGAO, KURTATCHI, MANUS, MARSHALLESE, NAVAHO, PAPAGO, SIRIONO, SUBANUN, TARAHUMARA, TRUKESE

373 EXCLUDED BECAUSE UNASCERTAINED

	Left column			Right column		Statistics
45	IN ALL CASES ARE THOSE WHERE SETTLEMENTS, IF FIXED, ARE COMPACT, RATHER THAN NON-COMPACT (149)	1.00 OF 4	45	DRIFT TOWARD BEING THOSE WHERE SETTLEMENTS, IF FIXED, ARE NON-COMPACT, RATHER THAN COMPACT (73)	0.58 OF 12	4 5 0 7 XSQ= 2.12 PHI= 0.364 EP = 0.0885
46	TILT TOWARD BEING THOSE WHERE SETTLEMENTS ARE NON-FIXED AND MOVEMENT IS NOMADIC (72)	0.50 OF 10	46	TILT TOWARD BEING THOSE OTHER THAN WHERE SETTLEMENTS ARE NON-FIXED AND MOVEMENT IS NOMADIC (260)	0.94 OF 16	5 1 5 15 XSQ= 4.40 PHI= 0.411 EP = 0.0184
73	DRIFT TOWARD BEING THOSE WHERE WEAVING IS ABSENT (130)	0.90 OF 10	73	DRIFT TOWARD BEING THOSE WHERE WEAVING IS PRESENT (118)	0.55 OF 11	1 6 9 5 XSQ= 2.89 PHI= -0.371 EP = 0.0635
86	DRIFT TOWARD BEING THOSE WHERE THE LEVEL OF POLITICAL INTEGRATION IS THE LARGE STATE, THE LITTLE STATE, OR THE MINIMAL STATE (148) GPM	0.50 OF 10	86	DRIFT TOWARD BEING THOSE WHERE THE LEVEL OF POLITICAL INTEGRATION IS THE AUTONOMOUS COMMUNITY, OR THE FAMILY (156) GPM	0.86 OF 14	5 2 5 12 XSQ= 2.08 PHI= 0.294 EP = 0.0850
96	TILT TOWARD BEING THOSE WHERE THE HIERARCHY OF NATIONAL JURISDICTION HAS FOUR, THREE, TWO OR ONE LEVEL (174) GES,EA	0.70 OF 10	96	TILT TOWARD BEING THOSE WHERE THE HIERARCHY OF NATIONAL JURISDICTION HAS NO LEVELS (156) GES,EA	0.75 OF 16	7 4 3 12 XSQ= 3.43 PHI= 0.363 EP = 0.0426

131	DRIFT LESS TOWARD BEING THOSE 0.57 OF 7 WHERE THE CONSTRUCTION OF PERMANENT HOUSES OR THE ERECTION OF TEMPORARY DWELLINGS IS MAINLY DONE BY MALES (136)	131	IN ALL CASES ARE THOSE 1.00 OF 8 WHERE THE CONSTRUCTION OF PERMANENT HOUSES OR THE ERECTION OF TEMPORARY DWELLINGS IS MAINLY DONE BY MALES (136)	4 8 3 0 XSQ= 2.03 PHI= -0.367 EP = 0.0769
177	TILT LESS TOWARD BEING THOSE 0.60 OF 10 WHERE THE COMMUNITY IS OTHER THAN A SINGLE CLAN-COMMUNITY AND EXOGAMOUS (305)	177	TILT MORE TOWARD BEING THOSE 0.94 OF 17 WHERE THE COMMUNITY IS OTHER THAN A SINGLE CLAN-COMMUNITY AND EXOGAMOUS (305)	4 1 6 16 XSQ= 2.86 PHI= 0.325 EP = 0.0473
259	TILT TOWARD BEING THOSE 0.75 OF 8 WHERE THE SEVERITY OF MOTHER-IN-LAW AVOIDANCE IS HIGH (26) WNS	259	TILT TOWARD BEING THOSE 0.79 OF 14 WHERE THE SEVERITY OF MOTHER-IN-LAW AVOIDANCE IS LOW (20) WNS	6 3 2 11 XSQ= 4.03 PHI= 0.428 EP = 0.0260
263	DRIFT MORE TOWARD BEING THOSE 0.90 OF 10 WHERE WIVES ARE OBTAINED BY RELATIVELY EASY MEANS, NAMELY BY TOKEN BRIDE-PRICE, GIFT EXCHANGE, ABSENCE OF ANY CONSIDERATION, OR RECEIPT OF DOWRY (162)	263	DRIFT LESS TOWARD BEING THOSE 0.53 OF 17 WHERE WIVES ARE OBTAINED BY RELATIVELY EASY MEANS, NAMELY BY TOKEN BRIDE-PRICE, GIFT EXCHANGE, ABSENCE OF ANY CONSIDERATION, OR RECEIPT OF DOWRY (162)	1 8 9 9 XSQ= 2.40 PHI= -0.298 EP = 0.0912
315	DRIFT TOWARD BEING THOSE 0.67 OF 3 WHERE MOTHER AND NURSING CHILD CUSTOMARILY SLEEP IN DIFFERENT BEDS (14) W-D,S	315	DRIFT TOWARD BEING THOSE 0.92 OF 12 WHERE MOTHER AND NURSING CHILD CUSTOMARILY SLEEP IN THE SAME BED (37) W-D,S	1 11 2 1 XSQ= 2.11 PHI= -0.375 EP = 0.0813
355	DRIFT TOWARD BEING THOSE 0.78 OF 9 WHERE THE CHILD'S INFERRED CONFLICT REGARDING OBEDIENT BEHAVIOR IS HIGH (35) B-B-C	355	DRIFT TOWARD BEING THOSE 0.62 OF 13 WHERE THE CHILD'S INFERRED CONFLICT REGARDING OBEDIENT BEHAVIOR IS LOW (38) B-B-C	7 5 2 8 XSQ= 1.92 PHI= 0.295 EP = 0.0991

****

258	CULTURES WHERE THE SEVERITY OF SON'S WIFE AVOIDANCE IS HIGH (15) WNS	258	CULTURES WHERE THE SEVERITY OF SON'S WIFE AVOIDANCE IS LOW (16) WNS

BACKGROUND ON PAGE 127

BOTH SUBJECT AND PREDICATE

....

15 IN LEFT COLUMN

ARAUCANIANS ASHANTI CALLINAGO CHAGGA GANDA GISU IFUGAO LAU MANUS NAVAHO
NYAKYUSA OJIBWA OMAHA SEMANG TIKOPIA

16 IN RIGHT COLUMN

ALORESE CHENCHU CHIR-APACHE COMANCHE FON HANO KURTATCHI LANGO MARQUESANS MARSHALLESE
PAPAGO SANPOIL SIRIONO SUBANUN TALLENSI TARAHUMARA

369 EXCLUDED BECAUSE UNASCERTAINED

137	DRIFT TOWARD BEING THOSE 0.73 OF 11 WHERE INVIDIOUS DISPLAY OF WEALTH IS STRONGLY EMPHASIZED (37) PES	137	DRIFT TOWARD BEING THOSE 0.69 OF 13 WHERE INVIDIOUS DISPLAY OF WEALTH IS MODERATELY, LITTLE, OR NEGATIVELY EMPHASIZED (52) PES	8 4 3 9 XSQ= 2.69 PHI= 0.334 EP = 0.0995
148	IN ALL CASES ARE THOSE 1.00 OF 5 WHERE THE INCIDENCE OF PERSONAL CRIME IS HIGH (12) B-B-C	148	DRIFT TOWARD BEING THOSE 0.67 OF 6 WHERE THE INCIDENCE OF PERSONAL CRIME IS LOW (21) B-B-C	5 2 0 4 XSQ= 2.75 PHI= 0.500 EP = 0.0606
259	LEAN TOWARD BEING THOSE 0.77 OF 13 WHERE THE SEVERITY OF MOTHER-IN-LAW AVOIDANCE IS HIGH (26) WNS	259	LEAN TOWARD BEING THOSE 0.81 OF 16 WHERE THE SEVERITY OF MOTHER-IN-LAW AVOIDANCE IS LOW (20) WNS	10 3 3 13 XSQ= 7.60 PHI= 0.512 EP = 0.0029
282	TILT TOWARD BEING THOSE 0.83 OF 6 WHERE THE STRENGTH OF DESIRE FOR CHILDREN IS HIGH (16) BCA	282	TILT TOWARD BEING THOSE 0.88 OF 8 WHERE THE STRENGTH OF DESIRE FOR CHILDREN IS LOW OR ABSENT (20) BCA	5 1 1 7 XSQ= 4.43 PHI= 0.562 EP = 0.0256
348	IN ALL CASES ARE THOSE 1.00 OF 10 WHERE THE TOTAL POSITIVE PRESSURE TOWARD DEVELOPING ACHIEVEMENT BEHAVIOR IN THE CHILD IS HIGH (32) B-B-C	348	DRIFT LESS TOWARD BEING THOSE 0.57 OF 7 WHERE THE TOTAL POSITIVE PRESSURE TOWARD DEVELOPING ACHIEVEMENT BEHAVIOR IN THE CHILD IS HIGH (32) B-B-C	10 4 0 3 XSQ= 2.67 PHI= 0.397 EP = 0.0515

355	TILT TOWARD BEING THOSE WHERE THE CHILD'S INFERRED CONFLICT REGARDING OBEDIENT BEHAVIOR IS HIGH (35) B-B-C	0.67 OF 12	355	TILT TOWARD BEING THOSE WHERE THE CHILD'S INFERRED CONFLICT REGARDING OBEDIENT BEHAVIOR IS LOW (38) B-B-C	0.80 OF 10	8 2 4 8 XSQ= 3.09 PHI= 0.375 EP = 0.0427
393	IN ALL CASES ARE THOSE WHERE EXTRAMARITAL COITUS IS PUNISHED, RATHER THAN PERMITTED (43) F-B	1.00 OF 6	393	TILT TOWARD BEING THOSE WHERE EXTRAMARITAL COITUS IS PERMITTED, RATHER THAN PUNISHED (41) F-B	0.64 OF 11	6 4 0 7 XSQ= 4.13 PHI= 0.493 EP = 0.0175
419	TILT TOWARD BEING THOSE WHERE MILITARY GLORY IS STRONGLY OR MODERATELY EMPHASIZED (55) PES	0.91 OF 11	419	TILT TOWARD BEING THOSE WHERE MILITARY GLORY IS NEGLIGIBLY EMPHASIZED (31) PES	0.58 OF 12	10 5 1 7 XSQ= 4.16 PHI= 0.425 EP = 0.0272
472	TILT TOWARD BEING THOSE WHERE THE COMPOSITE NARCISSISM INDEX IS HIGH (47) PES	0.82 OF 11	472	TILT TOWARD BEING THOSE WHERE THE COMPOSITE NARCISSISM INDEX IS LOW (43) PES	0.69 OF 13	9 4 2 9 XSQ= 4.37 PHI= 0.427 EP = 0.0188
473	DRIFT TOWARD BEING THOSE WHERE SENSITIVITY TO INSULT IS EXTREME (32) PES	0.55 OF 11	473	DRIFT TOWARD BEING THOSE WHERE SENSITIVITY TO INSULT IS MODERATE OR NEGLIGIBLE (56) PES	0.85 OF 13	6 2 5 11 XSQ= 2.54 PHI= 0.325 EP = 0.0825
475	DRIFT MORE TOWARD BEING THOSE WHERE EXHIBITIONISTIC DANCING IS STRONGLY OR MODERATELY EMPHASIZED (48) PES	0.91 OF 11	475	DRIFT LESS TOWARD BEING THOSE WHERE EXHIBITIONISTIC DANCING IS STRONGLY OR MODERATELY EMPHASIZED (48) PES	0.54 OF 13	10 7 1 6 XSQ= 2.37 PHI= 0.314 EP = 0.0778

```
**********************************************************************************************************************

259  CULTURES                                              259  CULTURES
     WHERE THE SEVERITY OF MOTHER-IN-LAW                        WHERE THE SEVERITY OF MOTHER-IN-LAW
     AVOIDANCE IS HIGH  (26) WNS                                AVOIDANCE IS LOW  (20) WNS


BACKGROUND ON PAGE 127                                                                     BOTH SUBJECT AND PREDICATE
......................................................................................................................

     26  IN LEFT COLUMN

ARAUCANIANS BEMBA        CALLINAGO   CHEYENNE    CHIR-APACHE CROW        GANDA       GISU        GROS VENTRE KURTATCHI
LAMBA       LANGO        LAU         LESU        MANUS       MURNGIN     NAMA        NAVAHO      NUER        OJIBWA
OMAHA       SEMANG       THONGA      TIMBIRA     TIV         WARRAU

     20  IN RIGHT COLUMN

ALORESE     ASHANTI      CHENCHU     COMANCHE    FON         HANO        IBAN        IFUGAO      LEPCHA      MARQUESANS
MARSHALLESE PAPAGO       SAMOANS     SANPOIL     SIRIONO     SUBANUN     TALLENSI    TARAHUMARA  TIKOPIA     TROBRIAND

     354  EXCLUDED BECAUSE UNASCERTAINED

----------------------------------------------------------------------------------------------------------------------
 44  DRIFT TOWARD BEING THOSE        0.50 OF  26        44  DRIFT TOWARD BEING THOSE        0.79 OF  19          13   15
     WHERE SETTLEMENTS ARE NON-FIXED  (110)                 WHERE SETTLEMENTS ARE FIXED  (222)                    13    4
                                                                                                            XSQ=     2.78
                                                                                                            PHI=   -0.248
                                                                                                            XP =   0.0955

131  DRIFT LESS TOWARD BEING THOSE  0.63 OF  16       131  IN ALL CASES ARE THOSE           1.00 OF  11          10   11
     WHERE THE CONSTRUCTION OF PERMANENT HOUSES             WHERE THE CONSTRUCTION OF PERMANENT HOUSES            6    0
     OR THE ERECTION OF TEMPORARY DWELLINGS                 OR THE ERECTION OF TEMPORARY DWELLINGS          XSQ=     3.36
     IS MAINLY DONE BY MALES  (136)                         IS MAINLY DONE BY MALES  (136)                  PHI=   -0.353
                                                                                                            EP =   0.0536

177  DRIFT LESS TOWARD BEING THOSE  0.69 OF  26       177  DRIFT MORE TOWARD BEING THOSE  0.95 OF  20            8    1
     WHERE THE COMMUNITY IS OTHER THAN                      WHERE THE COMMUNITY IS OTHER THAN                    18   19
     A SINGLE CLAN-COMMUNITY AND                            A SINGLE CLAN-COMMUNITY AND                     XSQ=     3.27
     EXOGAMOUS  (305)                                       EXOGAMOUS  (305)                                PHI=    0.267
                                                                                                            XP =   0.0704

180  TILT TOWARD BEING THOSE         0.54 OF  26       180  TILT TOWARD BEING THOSE         0.80 OF  20          14    4
     WHERE THE COMMUNITY IS                                 WHERE THE COMMUNITY IS                               12   16
     COMMONLY EXOGAMOUS, RATHER THAN                        COMMONLY NON-EXOGAMOUS, RATHER THAN             XSQ=     4.11
     NON-EXOGAMOUS  (124)                                   EXOGAMOUS  (258)                                PHI=    0.299
                                                                                                            XP =   0.0427

196  DRIFT TOWARD BEING THOSE        0.58 OF  19       196  DRIFT TOWARD BEING THOSE        0.75 OF  16           8   12
     WHERE INDIVIDUAL RIGHTS IN REAL PROPERTY,              WHERE INDIVIDUAL RIGHTS IN REAL PROPERTY,            11    4
     OR RULES FOR INHERITANCE,                              AND RULES FOR INHERITANCE,                      XSQ=     2.61
     ARE ABSENT  (87)                                       ARE PRESENT  (194)                              PHI=   -0.273
                                                                                                            EP =   0.0866
```

207	DRIFT TOWARD BEING THOSE 0.64 OF 11 WHERE MARITAL RESIDENCE IS MATRILOCAL OR UXORILOCAL, RATHER THAN AMBILOCAL OR NEOLOCAL (64)	207	DRIFT TOWARD BEING THOSE 0.80 OF 10 WHERE MARITAL RESIDENCE IS AMBILOCAL OR NEOLOCAL, RATHER THAN MATRILOCAL OR UXORILOCAL (64)	7 2 4 8 XSQ= 2.49 PHI= 0.344 EP = 0.0805
234	TILT TOWARD BEING THOSE 0.70 OF 23 WHERE THE COUSIN TERMINOLOGY IS OF CROW, OMAHA, OR IROQUOIS TYPE, RATHER THAN ESKIMO OR HAWAIIAN TYPE (152)	234	TILT TOWARD BEING THOSE 0.72 OF 18 WHERE THE COUSIN TERMINOLOGY IS OF ESKIMO OR HAWAIIAN TYPE, RATHER THAN CROW, OMAHA, OR IROQUOIS TYPE (170)	16 5 7 13 XSQ= 5.48 PHI= 0.366 XP = 0.0192
242	DRIFT MORE TOWARD BEING THOSE 0.96 OF 26 WHERE MARRIAGE IS COMMONLY OR OCCASIONALLY POLYGYNOUS, RATHER THAN MONOGAMOUS (314)	242	DRIFT LESS TOWARD BEING THOSE 0.74 OF 19 WHERE MARRIAGE IS COMMONLY OR OCCASIONALLY POLYGYNOUS, RATHER THAN MONOGAMOUS (314)	25 14 1 5 XSQ= 3.05 PHI= 0.260 XP = 0.0808
257	TILT TOWARD BEING THOSE 0.67 OF 9 WHERE THE SEVERITY OF SISTER AVOIDANCE IS HIGH (10) WNS	257	TILT TOWARD BEING THOSE 0.85 OF 13 WHERE THE SEVERITY OF SISTER AVOIDANCE IS LOW (17) WNS	6 2 3 11 XSQ= 4.03 PHI= 0.428 EP = 0.0260
258	LEAN TOWARD BEING THOSE 0.77 OF 13 WHERE THE SEVERITY OF SON'S WIFE AVOIDANCE IS HIGH (15) WNS	258	LEAN TOWARD BEING THOSE 0.81 OF 16 WHERE THE SEVERITY OF SON'S WIFE AVOIDANCE IS LOW (16) WNS	10 3 3 13 XSQ= 7.60 PHI= 0.512 EP = 0.0029
301	TILT TOWARD BEING THOSE 0.84 OF 19 WHERE THE POST-PARTUM SEX TABOO LASTS LONGER THAN ONE MONTH (96)	301	TILT TOWARD BEING THOSE 0.58 OF 12 WHERE THE POST-PARTUM SEX TABOO LASTS ONE MONTH OR LESS (28)	16 5 3 7 XSQ= 4.30 PHI= 0.372 EP = 0.0214
341	DRIFT TOWARD BEING THOSE 0.55 OF 11 WHERE THE CHILD'S INFERRED ANXIETY OVER NON-PERFORMANCE OF NURTURANT BEHAVIOR IS LOW (16) B-B-C	341	DRIFT TOWARD BEING THOSE 0.89 OF 9 WHERE THE CHILD'S INFERRED ANXIETY OVER NON-PERFORMANCE OF NURTURANT BEHAVIOR IS HIGH (30) B-B-C	5 8 6 1 XSQ= 2.42 PHI= -0.348 EP = 0.0703
347	TILT TOWARD BEING THOSE 0.61 OF 18 WHERE THE CHILD'S INFERRED CONFLICT REGARDING SELF-RELIANT BEHAVIOR IS HIGH (37) B-B-C	347	TILT TOWARD BEING THOSE 0.87 OF 15 WHERE THE CHILD'S INFERRED CONFLICT REGARDING SELF-RELIANT BEHAVIOR IS LOW (39) B-B-C	11 2 7 13 XSQ= 5.95 PHI= 0.425 EP = 0.0110
348	DRIFT TOWARD BEING THOSE 0.81 OF 16 WHERE THE TOTAL POSITIVE PRESSURE TOWARD DEVELOPING ACHIEVEMENT BEHAVIOR IN THE CHILD IS HIGH (32) B-B-C	348	DRIFT TOWARD BEING THOSE 0.56 OF 9 WHERE THE TOTAL POSITIVE PRESSURE TOWARD DEVELOPING ACHIEVEMENT BEHAVIOR IN THE CHILD IS LOW (31) B-B-C	13 4 3 5 XSQ= 2.09 PHI= 0.289 EP = 0.0870

355	DRIFT TOWARD BEING THOSE 0.65 OF 17 WHERE THE CHILD'S INFERRED CONFLICT REGARDING OBEDIENT BEHAVIOR IS HIGH (35) B-B-C	355	DRIFT TOWARD BEING THOSE 0.71 OF 14 WHERE THE CHILD'S INFERRED CONFLICT REGARDING OBEDIENT BEHAVIOR IS LOW (38) B-B-C	11 4 6 10 XSQ= 2.70 PHI= 0.295 EP = 0.0732
370	TILT TOWARD BEING THOSE 0.61 OF 23 WHERE THE SEGREGATION OF ADOLESCENT BOYS IS COMPLETE OR PARTIAL (95)	370	TILT TOWARD BEING THOSE 0.78 OF 18 WHERE THE SEGREGATION OF ADOLESCENT BOYS IS ABSENT (148)	14 4 9 14 XSQ= 4.66 PHI= 0.337 XP = 0.0310
386	DRIFT TOWARD BEING THOSE 0.79 OF 14 WHERE SEXUAL EXPRESSION BY THE YOUNG IS RESTRICTED OR SEMI-RESTRICTED (46) F-B	386	DRIFT TOWARD BEING THOSE 0.64 OF 14 WHERE SEXUAL EXPRESSION BY THE YOUNG IS PERMITTED (40) F-B	11 5 3 9 XSQ= 3.65 PHI= 0.361 EP = 0.0542
392	TILT TOWARD BEING THOSE 0.88 OF 16 WHERE PREMARITAL SEX RELATIONS ARE STRONGLY PUNISHED AND IN FACT RARE, OR WEAKLY PUNISHED AND IN FACT NOT RARE, OR PUNISHED ONLY IF PREGNANCY RESULTS (112) JTW,EA	392	TILT TOWARD BEING THOSE 0.53 OF 17 WHERE PREMARITAL SEX RELATIONS ARE FREELY PERMITTED (67) JTW,EA	14 8 2 9 XSQ= 4.38 PHI= 0.364 EP = 0.0255
397	DRIFT TOWARD BEING THOSE 0.50 OF 14 WHERE SEX DISABILITY IS PRESENT (14) JKH	397	DRIFT TOWARD BEING THOSE 0.90 OF 10 WHERE SEX DISABILITY IS ABSENT (42) JKH	7 1 7 9 XSQ= 2.59 PHI= 0.329 EP = 0.0791
403	DRIFT TOWARD BEING THOSE 0.73 OF 11 WHERE EXPLANATIONS OF ILLNESS OF AN ANAL NATURE ARE PRESENT (23) W-C	403	DRIFT TOWARD BEING THOSE 0.69 OF 16 WHERE EXPLANATIONS OF ILLNESS OF AN ANAL NATURE ARE ABSENT (38) W-C	8 5 3 11 XSQ= 2.98 PHI= 0.332 EP = 0.0542
404	DRIFT TOWARD BEING THOSE 0.64 OF 11 WHERE EXPLANATIONS OF ILLNESS OF A SEXUAL NATURE ARE PRESENT (19) W-C	404	DRIFT TOWARD BEING THOSE 0.75 OF 16 WHERE EXPLANATIONS OF ILLNESS OF A SEXUAL NATURE ARE ABSENT (42) W-C	7 4 4 12 XSQ= 2.59 PHI= 0.310 EP = 0.0608
419	TILT TOWARD BEING THOSE 0.85 OF 20 WHERE MILITARY GLORY IS STRONGLY OR MODERATELY EMPHASIZED (55) PES	419	TILT TOWARD BEING THOSE 0.53 OF 15 WHERE MILITARY GLORY IS NEGLIGIBLY EMPHASIZED (31) PES	17 7 3 8 XSQ= 4.20 PHI= 0.346 EP = 0.0271
425	TILT TOWARD BEING THOSE 0.88 OF 8 WHERE SUPERNATURALS ARE MAINLY AGGRESSIVE, RATHER THAN BENEVOLENT (20) L-T-W	425	TILT TOWARD BEING THOSE 0.67 OF 12 WHERE SUPERNATURALS ARE MAINLY BENEVOLENT, RATHER THAN AGGRESSIVE (16) L-T-W	1 8 7 4 XSQ= 3.71 PHI= -0.431 EP = 0.0281

```
435  TILT TOWARD BEING THOSE            0.80 OF   5     435  IN ALL CASES ARE THOSE             1.00 OF   6            4     0
     WHERE ABANDONMENT OF THE HOUSE OF THE DEAD               WHERE ABANDONMENT OF THE HOUSE OF THE DEAD              1     6
     IS PRACTICED  (12) LWS                                   IS NOT PRACTICED  (19) LWS                        XSQ=     4.48
                                                                                                                 PHI=    0.638
                                                                                                                 EP =   0.0152

454  IN ALL CASES ARE THOSE             1.00 OF   8     454  TILT TOWARD BEING THOSE            0.60 OF   5            0     3
     WHERE THE OBJECTIVE OF THE INDIVIDUAL'S                  WHERE THE OBJECTIVE OF THE INDIVIDUAL'S                 8     2
     CONTACT WITH THE DIVINE                                  CONTACT WITH THE DIVINE                           XSQ=     3.32
     IS NOT CONDUCIVE TO THE DEVELOPMENT OF THE               IS CONDUCIVE TO THE DEVELOPMENT OF THE            PHI=   -0.505
     INDIVIDUAL'S NEED TO ACHIEVE  (18) DCM                   INDIVIDUAL'S NEED TO ACHIEVE  (18) DCM            EP =   0.0350

477  IN ALL CASES ARE THOSE             1.00 OF   4     477  TILT TOWARD BEING THOSE            0.80 OF   5            4     1
     WHERE ALCOHOLIC AGGRESSION IS                            WHERE ALCOHOLIC AGGRESSION IS                           0     4
     STRONG  (15) DH                                          MODERATE OR SLIGHT  (19) DH                       XSQ=     2.98
                                                                                                                 PHI=    0.575
                                                                                                                 EP =   0.0476
```

```
******************************************************************************************************************

260  CULTURES                                          260  CULTURES
     WHERE THE AGE OF MALES AT MARRIAGE                     WHERE THE AGE OF MALES AT MARRIAGE
     IS LESS THAN TWENTY  (38) JKH                          IS TWENTY OR OVER  (17) JKH


BACKGROUND ON PAGE 128                                                              BOTH SUBJECT AND PREDICATE
..................................................................................................................

      38  IN LEFT COLUMN

ALORESE     ANDAMANESE  AYMARA      BALINESE    CAGABA      CAMAYURA    CARIB       CHEYENNE    CHIR-APACHE CHUKCHEE
COPR ESKIMO CREEK       DIERI       EGYPTIANS   FON         IFUGAO      JIVARO      JUKUN       KAZAK       KURTATCHI
KWAKIUTL    LAMBA       LAU         LEPCHA      MIAO        MURNGIN     ORAON       PAPAGO      RIFFIANS    SAMOANS
SANPOIL     SERBS       SIRIONO     TANALA      VENDA       WARRAU      YAKO        YAPESE

      17  IN RIGHT COLUMN

ABIPON      ARAUCANIANS AZANDE      IRISH       JAPANESE    LAKHER      LESU        MACRI       MASAI       NUER
NYAKYUSA    ONTONG-JAVA TALLENSI    THONGA      TIMBIRA     TIV         TROBRIAND

     345  EXCLUDED BECAUSE UNASCERTAINED

------------------------------------------------------------------------------------------------------------------
  3  TILT MORE TOWARD BEING THOSE    0.87 OF  38          3  TILT LESS TOWARD BEING THOSE    0.59 OF  17          5     7
     LOCATED OUTSIDE OF                                      LOCATED OUTSIDE OF                                  33    10
     AFRICA  (320)                                           AFRICA  (320)                                    XSQ=   3.89
                                                                                                              PHI=  -0.266
                                                                                                              XP =  0.0486

243  DRIFT TOWARD BEING THOSE        0.64 OF  22        243  DRIFT TOWARD BEING THOSE        0.78 OF   9          8     7
     WHERE POLYGYNY, IF PRESENT,                             WHERE POLYGYNY, IF PRESENT,                         14     2
     HAS A LOW INCIDENCE  (36) W-D,S                         HAS A HIGH INCIDENCE  (24) W-D,S                 XSQ=   2.88
                                                                                                              PHI=  -0.305
                                                                                                              EP =  0.0538

301  TILT LESS TOWARD BEING THOSE    0.67 OF  21        301  IN ALL CASES ARE THOSE          1.00 OF  12         14    12
     WHERE THE POST-PARTUM SEX TABOO LASTS                   WHERE THE POST-PARTUM SEX TABOO LASTS                7     0
     LONGER THAN ONE MONTH  (96)                             LONGER THAN ONE MONTH  (96)                      XSQ=   3.28
                                                                                                              PHI=  -0.315
                                                                                                              EP =  0.0319

307  DRIFT LESS TOWARD BEING THOSE   0.53 OF  19        307  DRIFT MORE TOWARD BEING THOSE   0.89 OF   9         10     8
     WHERE THE EARLY AGGRESSION SATISFACTION                 WHERE THE EARLY AGGRESSION SATISFACTION              9     1
     POTENTIAL IS HIGH  (33) W-C                             POTENTIAL IS HIGH  (33) W-C                      XSQ=   2.10
                                                                                                              PHI=  -0.274
                                                                                                              EP =  0.0980
```

310	DRIFT TOWARD BEING THOSE WHERE ANAL SOCIALIZATION ANXIETY IS LOW (19) W-C	0.62 OF 13	310	DRIFT TOWARD BEING THOSE WHERE ANAL SOCIALIZATION ANXIETY IS HIGH (22) W-C	0.86 OF 7	5 6 8 1 XSQ= 2.42 PHI= -0.348 EP = 0.0703
314	TILT TOWARD BEING THOSE WHERE THE INCIDENCE OF MOTHER-CHILD HOUSEHOLDS IS LOW (61) W-C,S	0.84 OF 25	314	TILT TOWARD BEING THOSE WHERE THE INCIDENCE OF MOTHER-CHILD HOUSEHOLDS IS HIGH (19) W-D,S	0.55 OF 11	4 6 21 5 XSQ= 3.90 PHI= -0.329 EP = 0.0390
339	TILT TOWARD BEING THOSE WHERE THE CHILD'S INFERRED CONFLICT REGARDING RESPONSIBLE BEHAVIOR IS HIGH (31) B-B-C	0.63 OF 19	339	TILT TOWARD BEING THOSE WHERE THE CHILD'S INFERRED CONFLICT REGARDING RESPONSIBLE BEHAVIOR IS LOW (42) B-B-C	0.77 OF 13	12 3 7 10 XSQ= 3.50 PHI= 0.331 EP = 0.0359
345	DRIFT TOWARD BEING THOSE WHERE THE CHILD'S INFERRED ANXIETY OVER NON-PERFORMANCE OF SELF-RELIANT BEHAVIOR IS HIGH (37) B-B-C	0.57 OF 21	345	DRIFT TOWARD BEING THOSE WHERE THE CHILD'S INFERRED ANXIETY OVER NON-PERFORMANCE OF SELF-RELIANT BEHAVIOR IS LOW (39) B-B-C	0.77 OF 13	12 3 9 10 XSQ= 2.52 PHI= 0.272 EP = 0.0790
396	DRIFT LESS TOWARD BEING THOSE WHERE THE STRENGTH OF MENSTRUAL TABOOS IS LOW (35) WNS	0.57 OF 21	396	DRIFT MORE TOWARD BEING THOSE WHERE THE STRENGTH OF MENSTRUAL TABOOS IS LOW (35) WNS	0.92 OF 13	9 1 12 12 XSQ= 3.24 PHI= 0.309 EP = 0.0514
438	DRIFT TOWARD BEING THOSE WHERE OTHER-WORLDLY FEARS OF GHOSTS OR SPIRITS ARE GREATER THAN THIS-WORLDLY FEARS OF HUMANS OR ANIMALS (27) W-C,JFG	0.79 OF 19	438	DRIFT TOWARD BEING THOSE WHERE THIS-WORLDLY FEARS OF HUMANS OR ANIMALS ARE GREATER THAN OTHER-WORLDLY FEARS OF GHOSTS OR SPIRITS (17) W-C,JFG	0.63 OF 8	15 3 4 5 XSQ= 2.69 PHI= 0.315 EP = 0.0721
439	DRIFT TOWARD BEING THOSE WHERE FEAR OF GHOSTS IS HIGH (30) W-C	0.62 OF 21	439	DRIFT TOWARD BEING THOSE WHERE FEAR OF GHOSTS IS LOW (31) W-C	0.80 OF 10	13 2 8 8 XSQ= 3.23 PHI= 0.323 EP = 0.0538
472	TILT TOWARD BEING THOSE WHERE THE COMPOSITE NARCISSISM INDEX IS LOW (43) PES	0.50 OF 26	472	TILT TOWARD BEING THOSE WHERE THE COMPOSITE NARCISSISM INDEX IS HIGH (47) PES	0.86 OF 14	13 12 13 2 XSQ= 3.55 PHI= -0.298 EP = 0.0403
474	TILT TOWARD BEING THOSE WHERE BOASTFULNESS IS MODERATE, NEGLIBIBLE, OR UNREPORTED (48) PES	0.65 OF 26	474	TILT TOWARD BEING THOSE WHERE BOASTFULNESS IS EXTREME (41) PES	0.77 OF 13	9 10 17 3 XSQ= 4.63 PHI= -0.345 EP = 0.0187

```
261  CULTURES                                        261  CULTURES
     WHERE FEMALE MARRIAGE OCCURS                         WHERE FEMALE MARRIAGE OCCURS
     AT OR BEFORE PUBERTY  (19) JTW,EA                    AFTER PUBERTY  (183) JTW,EA


BACKGROUND ON PAGE 128                                                                      SUBJECT ONLY
........................................................................................................

     19  IN LEFT COLUMN

APINAYE     ARANDA      ARAPESH     BEMBA       BOTOCUDO    CREEK       GROS VENTRE KERAKI      KUNG        LUBA
MISKITO     MURNGIN     NABESNA     NAMBICUARA  NYAKYUSA    SAMOYED     TAPIRAPE    TERENA      TIWI

     183  IN RIGHT COLUMN

ABIPON      ABOR        AINU        AKHA        ALBANIANS   ALORESE     AMBA        AMERICANS   ANDAMANESE  ARAUCANIANS
ASHANTI     ATSUGEWI    AWEIKOMA    AYMARA      AZANDE      AZTEC       BARI        BASSERI     BATAK       BAYA
BHIL        BHUIYA      BORORO      BRAZILIANS  BURUSHO     CALLINAGO   CAMBODIANS  CARIB       CHAGGA      CHENCHU
CHEYENNE    CHIBCHA     CHIR-APACHE CHOROTI     CHUKCHEE    COORG       COPR ESKIMO CUNA        DELAWARE    DOBUANS
DUTCH       EGYPTIANS   ELLICE      ENGA        FANG        FON         FUTAJALONKE GANDA       GARO        GILBERTESE
GILYAK      GISU        GOAJIRO     GOND        HAIDA       HANO        HAWAIIANS   HAZARA      HEBREWS     HUTSUL
IBAN        IFUGAO      ILA         INCA        INGALIK     IRISH       JAPANESE    JAVANESE    JIVARO      KACHIN
KAPAUKU     KASKA       KAZAK       KHEVSUR     KIKUYU      KIOW-APACHE KOREANS     KORYAK      KURTATCHI   KUTENAI
KWAKIUTL    LAKHER      LAMET       LAPPS       LAU         LEPCHA      LOLO        LUO         MACASSARESE MAGUZAWA
MAM         MAMVU       MANGAIANS   MANIHIKI    MANUS       MAORI       MARQUESANS  MARSHALLESE MASAI       MATACO
MENTAWEI    MERINA      MINCHIA     MONGO       MONGUOR     MUNDURUCU   MZAB        NAMA        NATCHEZ     NAVAHO
NICOBARESE  NOMLAKI     NUPE        OJIBWA      OKINAWANS   OMAHA       ONA         PALAUANS    PARAUJANO   PONAPEANS
PUKAPUKA    PURUM       RAROIANS    RIFFIANS    RUNDI       RWALA       SAGADA      SAMOANS     SANPOIL     SANTAL
SARSI       SEMANG      SERBS       SHILLUK     SHLUH       SINHALESE   SIRIONO     SIUAI       SOMALI      SONGHAI
TALAMANCA   TALLENSI    TANALA      TAOS        TARAHUMARA  TAREUMIUT   TEDA        TEHUELCHE   TENDA       TENINO
THAI        THONGA      TIKOPIA     TIMBIRA     TIV         TODA        TOKELAU     TOLOWA      TRISTAN     TROBRIAND
TRUKESE     TRUMAI      TUBATULABAL TUCUNA      TUPINAMBA   TWANA       ULAWANS     UTE         VEDDA       VENDA
VIETNAMESE  WITOTO      WOGEO       WOLEAIANS   WOLOF       YABARANA    YAGUA       YAHGAN      YAKUT       YAO
YAPESE      YORUBA      YUKI

     198  EXCLUDED BECAUSE UNASCERTAINED

--------------------------------------------------------------------------------------------------------
 44  LEAN TOWARD BEING THOSE         0.67 OF  18       44  LEAN TOWARD BEING THOSE         0.70 OF 175          6  123
     WHERE SETTLEMENTS ARE NON-FIXED  (110)                WHERE SETTLEMENTS ARE FIXED  (222)                  12   52
                                                                                                        XSQ=     8.46
                                                                                                        PHI=   -0.209
                                                                                                        XP =   0.0036

 46  LEAN TOWARD BEING THOSE         0.56 OF  18       46  LEAN TOWARD BEING THOSE         0.79 OF 175         10   36
     WHERE SETTLEMENTS ARE                                 OTHER THAN WHERE SETTLEMENTS ARE                     8  139
     NON-FIXED AND MOVEMENT IS                             NON-FIXED AND MOVEMENT IS                    XSQ=     9.16
     NOMADIC  (72)                                         NOMADIC  (260)                               PHI=    0.218
                                                                                                        XP =   0.0025
```

51	LEAN TOWARD BEING THOSE WHERE SUBSISTENCE IS PRIMARILY BY FOOD GATHERING -- I. E., HUNTING, FISHING, OR COLLECTING -- RATHER THAN FOOD PRODUCTION (147)	0.79 OF 19	51	LEAN TOWARD BEING THOSE WHERE SUBSISTENCE IS PRIMARILY BY FOOD PRODUCTION -- I. E., AGRICULTURE OR HUSBANDRY -- RATHER THAN BY GATHERING (253)	0.63 OF 183	4 115 15 68 XSQ= 10.75 PHI= -0.231 XP = 0.0010
54	LEAN TOWARD BEING THOSE WHERE FOOD PRODUCTION IS BY INCIPIENT FOOD PRODUCTION, RATHER THAN BY INTENSIVE OR SIMPLE AGRICULTURE (46)	0.60 OF 10	54	LEAN TOWARD BEING THOSE WHERE FOOD PRODUCTION IS BY INTENSIVE OR SIMPLE AGRICULTURE, RATHER THAN BY INCIPIENT FOOD PRODUCTION (192)	0.86 OF 119	4 102 6 17 XSQ= 10.22 PHI= -0.282 XP = 0.0014
56	TILT TOWARD BEING THOSE WHERE FOOD PRODUCTION IS BY INCIPIENT FOOD PRODUCTION, RATHER THAN BY SIMPLE AGRICULTURE (46)	0.67 OF 9	56	TILT TOWARD BEING THOSE WHERE FOOD PRODUCTION IS BY SIMPLE AGRICULTURE, RATHER THAN BY INCIPIENT FOOD PRODUCTION (101)	0.75 OF 69	3 52 6 17 XSQ= 4.89 PHI= -0.250 XP = 0.0270
62	TILT TOWARD BEING THOSE WHERE HUSBANDRY OF ANY KIND IS ABSENT (172)	0.58 OF 19	62	TILT TOWARD BEING THOSE WHERE HUSBANDRY OF SOME KIND IS PRESENT (228)	0.70 OF 183	8 128 11 55 XSQ= 4.87 PHI= -0.155 XP = 0.0274
71	DRIFT MORE TOWARD BEING THOSE WHERE METAL WORKING IS ABSENT (153)	0.82 OF 17	71	DRIFT LESS TOWARD BEING THOSE WHERE METAL WORKING IS ABSENT (153)	0.56 OF 152	3 67 14 85 XSQ= 3.38 PHI= -0.141 XP = 0.0660
74	DRIFT TOWARD BEING THOSE WHERE POTTERY IS ABSENT (93)	0.63 OF 16	74	DRIFT TOWARD BEING THOSE WHERE POTTERY IS PRESENT (145)	0.62 OF 149	6 93 10 56 XSQ= 2.77 PHI= -0.130 XP = 0.0960
81	TILT MORE TOWARD BEING THOSE WHERE NO CITY OR TOWN IS PRESENT, AND THE AVERAGE COMMUNITY SIZE IS SMALLER THAN 200 (135)	0.93 OF 15	81	TILT LESS TOWARD BEING THOSE WHERE NO CITY OR TOWN IS PRESENT, AND THE AVERAGE COMMUNITY SIZE IS SMALLER THAN 200 (135)	0.62 OF 134	1 51 14 83 XSQ= 4.55 PHI= -0.175 XP = 0.0329
82	DRIFT LESS TOWARD BEING THOSE WHERE A CITY OR TOWN IS PRESENT, OR THE AVERAGE COMMUNITY SIZE IS FIFTY OR GREATER (178)	0.60 OF 15	82	DRIFT MORE TOWARD BEING THOSE WHERE A CITY OR TOWN IS PRESENT, OR THE AVERAGE COMMUNITY SIZE IS FIFTY OR GREATER (178)	0.84 OF 134	9 112 6 22 XSQ= 3.49 PHI= -0.153 XP = 0.0617
96	TILT TOWARD BEING THOSE WHERE THE HIERARCHY OF NATIONAL JURISDICTION HAS NO LEVELS (156) GES,EA	0.72 OF 18	96	TILT TOWARD BEING THOSE WHERE THE HIERARCHY OF NATIONAL JURISDICTION HAS FOUR, THREE, TWO OR ONE LEVEL (174) GES,EA	0.57 OF 173	5 98 13 75 XSQ= 4.37 PHI= -0.151 XP = 0.0366

102	LEAN TOWARD BEING THOSE 0.79 OF 19 WHERE CLASS STRATIFICATION IS ABSENT (180)	102	LEAN TOWARD BEING THOSE 0.61 OF 180 WHERE CLASS STRATIFICATION IS PRESENT (203)	4 110 15 70 XSQ= 9.69 PHI= -0.221 XP = 0.0018
131	LEAN TOWARD BEING THOSE 0.50 OF 12 WHERE THE CONSTRUCTION OF PERMANENT HOUSES OR THE ERECTION OF TEMPORARY DWELLINGS IS MAINLY DONE BY FEMALES (21)	131	LEAN TOWARD BEING THOSE 0.88 OF 105 WHERE THE CONSTRUCTION OF PERMANENT HOUSES OR THE ERECTION OF TEMPORARY DWELLINGS IS MAINLY DONE BY MALES (136)	6 92 6 13 XSQ= 8.61 PHI= -0.271 XP = 0.0033
183	TEND TO BE THOSE 0.58 OF 12 WHERE THE LARGEST NON-COGNATIC KIN GROUP IS THE MOEITY (34)	183	TEND TO BE THOSE 0.90 OF 114 WHERE THE LARGEST NON-COGNATIC KIN GROUP IS SMALLER THAN A MOEITY, I. E., A PHRATRY OR SIB OR LINEAGE (218)	7 11 5 103 XSQ= 17.23 PHI= 0.370 XP = 0.0000
184	LEAN TOWARD BEING THOSE 0.75 OF 12 WHERE THE LARGEST NON-COGNATIC KIN GROUP IS THE MOEITY OR PHRATRY (77)	184	LEAN TOWARD BEING THOSE 0.73 OF 114 WHERE THE LARGEST NON-COGNATIC KIN GROUP IS SMALLER THAN A PHRATRY, I. E. A SIB OR LINEAGE (175)	9 31 3 83 XSQ= 9.35 PHI= 0.272 XP = 0.0022
196	DRIFT TOWARD BEING THOSE 0.62 OF 13 WHERE INDIVIDUAL RIGHTS IN REAL PROPERTY, OR RULES FOR INHERITANCE, ARE ABSENT (87)	196	DRIFT TOWARD BEING THOSE 0.68 OF 145 WHERE INDIVIDUAL RIGHTS IN REAL PROPERTY, AND RULES FOR INHERITANCE, ARE PRESENT (194)	5 98 8 47 XSQ= 3.27 PHI= -0.144 XP = 0.0706
243	IN ALL CASES ARE THOSE 1.00 OF 6 WHERE POLYGYNY, IF PRESENT, HAS A HIGH INCIDENCE (24) W-D,S	243	TILT TOWARD BEING THOSE 0.63 OF 43 WHERE POLYGYNY, IF PRESENT, HAS A LOW INCIDENCE (36) W-D,S	6 16 0 27 XSQ= 6.04 PHI= 0.351 XP = 0.0139
299	IN ALL CASES ARE THOSE 1.00 OF 12 WHERE THE POST-PARTUM SEX TABOO LASTS ONE YEAR OR LESS (89)	299	DRIFT LESS TOWARD BEING THOSE 0.72 OF 86 WHERE THE POST-PARTUM SEX TABOO LASTS ONE YEAR OR LESS (89)	0 24 12 62 XSQ= 3.05 PHI= -0.177 XP = 0.0805
370	DRIFT TOWARD BEING THOSE 0.67 OF 12 WHERE THE SEGREGATION OF ADOLESCENT BOYS IS COMPLETE OR PARTIAL (95)	370	DRIFT TOWARD BEING THOSE 0.65 OF 139 WHERE THE SEGREGATION OF ADOLESCENT BOYS IS ABSENT (148)	8 48 4 91 XSQ= 3.61 PHI= 0.155 XP = 0.0575
372	DRIFT TOWARD BEING THOSE 0.86 OF 7 WHERE MALE INITIATION RITES ARE PRESENT (48) ASA	372	DRIFT TOWARD BEING THOSE 0.60 OF 67 WHERE MALE INITIATION RITES ARE ABSENT (63) ASA	6 27 1 40 XSQ= 3.61 PHI= 0.221 XP = 0.0574

262 CULTURES:
WHERE WIVES ARE OBTAINED BY
MEANS INVOLVING THE PRESENCE
OF SOME CONSIDERATION (305)

262 CULTURES
WHERE WIVES ARE OBTAINED
BY MEANS INVOLVING THE ABSENCE
OF ANY CONSIDERATION (90)

BACKGROUND ON PAGE 128

BOTH SUBJECT AND PREDICATE

305 IN LEFT COLUMN

ABIPON	ABOR	AJIE	ALBANIANS	ALORESE	AMBA	APINAYE	ARANDA	ARAUCANIANS	ARYANS
ASHANTI	ATAYAL	ATSUGEWI	AZANDE	AZTEC	BABWA	BAJUN	BALINESE	BAMBARA	BAMILEKE
BANDA	BARABRA	BARI	BASQUES	BASSERI	BATAK	BAYA	BEJA	BELU	BEMBA
BENGALI	BERGDAMA	BETE	BHIL	BHUIYA	BIRIFOR	BOERS	BOZO	BUDUMA	BUNLAP
BURMESE	BURUSHO	BURYAT	CAGABA	CALLINAGO	CAMAYURA	CAMBODIANS	CARIB	CHAGGA	CHAMACOCO
CHENCHU	CHEREMIS	CHERKESS	CHEYENNE	CHIBCHA	CHIRIGUANO	CHOROTI	CHORTI	CHUKCHEE	COPR ESKIMO
CREE	CREEK	CROW	CUNA	CZECHS	DAGUR	DARD	DIERI	DILLING	DOBUANS
DOGON	DOROBO	DUSUN	EGYPTIANS	ELLICE	ENGA	EYAK	FANG	FON	FOX
FUTAJALONKE	GANDA	GILBERTESE	GILYAK	GISU	GOAJIRO	GOND	GROS VENTRE	GUAHIBO	GURE
HAIDA	HANUNOO	HASANIA	HAVASUPAI	HAZARA	HEBREWS	HEHE	HERERO	HO	HUTSUL
ICELANDERS	IFUGAO	ILA	INGASSANA	IRAQW	IRISH	JAVANESE	JIVARO	JUKUN	KABYLE
KACHIN	KALMYK	KAPAUKU	KARIERA	KASKA	KATAB	KAZAK	KERAKI	KET	KHALKA
KHEVSUR	KIKUYU	KIOW-APACHE	KISSI	KOHISTANI	KOL	KORYAK	KPE	KUBA	KUMYK
KUNG	KURTATCHI	KWAKIUTL	LAKALAI	LAKHER	LAMBA	LAMET	LANGO	LAU	LEPCHA
LESU	LHOTA NAGA	LIFU	LOLO	LOZI	LUBA	LUO	MACASSARESE	MAGUZAWA	MALAYS
MAM	MAMBILA	MAMVU	MANCHU	MANUS	MAORI	MARGI	MARQUESANS	MASAI	MATACO
MATAKAM	MAYA	MBUGWE	MBUNDU	MBUTI	MENDE	MENTAWEI	MERINA	MIAMI	MIAO
MIN CHINESE	MINCHIA	MISKITO	MNONG GAR	MONGO	MONGUOR	MOSSI	MOTA	MUNDURUCU	MURNGIN
MZAB	NABESNA	NAMA	NANCI	NASKAPI	NAVAHO	NDEMBU	NGONI	NOMLAKI	NUER
NUPE	NURI	NYAKYUSA	NYANEKA	NYARO	NYORO	OKINAWANS	OMAHA	ONA	ORAON
PAIWAN	PALAUANS	PARAUJANO	PATHAN	PENDE	PENOBSCOT	PUKAPUKA	PURARI	PURUM	REGEIBAT
RIFFIANS	ROMANS	ROTINESE	RUNDI	RWALA	SAGADA	SAMOANS	SAMOYED	SANDAWE	SANPOIL
SANTAL	SARAMACCA	SARSI	SENIANG	SERBS	SERI	SHILLUK	SHLUH	SIMBOESE	SINDHI
SINHALESE	SIUAI	SIWANS	SOMALI	SONGHAI	SOTHO	SUBANUN	SWAZI	SYRIANS	TAGBANUA
TALAMANCA	TALLENSI	TAMIL	TANALA	TANIMBARESE	TARAHUMARA	TAREUMIUT	TEDA	TEHUELCHE	TENDA
TENETEHARA	TENINO	TERA	TESO	TETON	THAI	THONGA	TIBETANS	TIGRINYA	TIKOPIA
TIMBIRA	TIV	TIWI	TOCA	TOLOWA	TORAJA	TROBRIAND	TRUMAI	TSHIMSHIAN	TUBATULABAL
TUCANO	TUCUNA	TUNEBO	TUPINAMBA	TURKANA	TURKMEN	TWANA	TZELTAL	ULAWANS	VEDDA
VENDA	VIETNAMESE	WALLCONS	WANTOAT	WAPISHANA	WAROPEN	WARRAU	WICHITA	WIKMUNKAN	WITOTO
WOGEO	WOLOF	WUTE	YABARANA	YAGUA	YAHGAN	YAKO	YAKUT	YARURO	YOMBE
YORUBA	YUKAGHIR	YUKI	YUROK	ZUNI					

90 IN RIGHT COLUMN

AINU	AKHA	ALACALUF	AMERICANS	ANDAMANESE	ARAPESH	AWEIKOMA	AYMARA	BACAIRI	BLACK CARIB
BORORO	BOTOCUDO	BRAZILIANS	BULGARIANS	CADUVEO	CAMBA	CARAJA	CAYAPA	CHEROKEE	CHINANTEC
CHIR-APACHE	CHOCO	COCHITI	COMANCHE	COORG	DELAWARE	DIEGUENO	DUTCH	GARO	HANO
HASINAI	HAWAIIANS	HUICHOL	HUKUNDIKA	HURON	IBAN	INCA	INGALIK	JAPANESE	JEMEZ
KAREN	KERALA	KHASI	KONSO	KOREANS	KUTENAI	LAPPS	MANDAN	MANGAIANS	MANIHIKI

MARICOPA	MARSHALLESE	MAZATECO	MINANGKABAU	MIWOK	MOTILON	NAMBICUARA	NATCHEZ	NICOBARESE	NUNIVAK
OJIBWA	ONTONG-JAVA	PAEZ	PALIKUR	PAPAGO	PAWNEE	PONAPEANS	POPOLUCA	PORTUGUESE	RAROIANS
ROTUMANS	SELUNG	SEMANG	SEMINOLE	SHERENTE	SIRIONO	TAOS	TAPIRAPE	TERENA	TOKELAU
TOTONAC	TRISTAN	TRUKESE	UTE	WAICA	WASHO	WOLEAIANS	YAC	YAPESE	YOKUTS

5 EXCLUDED BECAUSE UNASCERTAINED

3	TEND LESS TO BE THOSE LOCATED OUTSIDE OF AFRICA (320)	0.74 OF 305	3	TEND MORE TO BE THOSE LOCATED OUTSIDE OF AFRICA (320)	0.99 OF 90	79 1 226 89 XSQ= 24.93 PHI= 0.251 XP = 0.0000
8	TEND MORE TO BE THOSE LOCATED OUTSIDE OF NORTH AMERICA (330)	0.88 OF 305	8	TEND LESS TO BE THOSE LOCATED OUTSIDE OF NORTH AMERICA (330)	0.66 OF 90	37 31 268 59 XSQ= 22.74 PHI= -0.240 XP = 0.0000
9	TILT MORE TOWARD BEING THOSE LOCATED OUTSIDE OF SOUTH AMERICA (335)	0.87 OF 305	9	TILT LESS TOWARD BEING THOSE LOCATED OUTSIDE OF SOUTH AMERICA (335)	0.76 OF 90	41 22 264 68 XSQ= 5.48 PHI= -0.118 XP = 0.0192
14	TILT MORE TOWARD BEING THOSE WHERE THE LATITUDE IS LESS THAN THIRTY DEGREES (281)	0.73 OF 305	14	TILT LESS TOWARD BEING THOSE WHERE THE LATITUDE IS LESS THAN THIRTY DEGREES (281)	0.61 OF 90	83 35 222 55 XSQ= 3.98 PHI= -0.100 XP = 0.0460
16	DRIFT LESS TOWARD BEING THOSE WHERE THE LATITUDE IS TEN DEGREES OR GREATER (277)	0.67 OF 305	16	DRIFT MORE TOWARD BEING THOSE WHERE THE LATITUDE IS TEN DEGREES OR GREATER (277)	0.78 OF 90	203 70 102 20 XSQ= 3.59 PHI= -0.095 XP = 0.0581
42	DRIFT MORE TOWARD BEING THOSE WHERE THE NATURAL ENVIRONMENT IS OTHER THAN TROPICAL OR SUB-TROPICAL RAIN FOREST, OR MONSOON FOREST (244) FWM	0.63 OF 305	42	DRIFT LESS TOWARD BEING THOSE WHERE THE NATURAL ENVIRONMENT IS OTHER THAN TROPICAL OR SUB-TROPICAL RAIN FOREST, OR MONSOON FOREST (244) FWM	0.52 OF 90	112 43 193 47 XSQ= 3.11 PHI= -0.089 XP = 0.0776
46	DRIFT MORE TOWARD BEING THOSE OTHER THAN WHERE SETTLEMENTS ARE NON-FIXED AND MOVEMENT IS NOMADIC (260)	0.81 OF 253	46	DRIFT LESS TOWARD BEING THOSE OTHER THAN WHERE SETTLEMENTS ARE NON-FIXED AND MOVEMENT IS NOMADIC (260)	0.71 OF 76	48 22 205 54 XSQ= 2.90 PHI= -0.094 XP = 0.0885

51	LEAN TOWARD BEING THOSE WHERE SUBSISTENCE IS PRIMARILY BY FOOD PRODUCTION -- I. E., AGRICULTURE OR HUSBANDRY -- RATHER THAN BY GATHERING (253)	0.68 OF 305	51	LEAN TOWARD BEING THOSE WHERE SUBSISTENCE IS PRIMARILY BY FOOD GATHERING -- I. E., HUNTING, FISHING, OR COLLECTING -- RATHER THAN FOOD PRODUCTION (147)	0.50 OF 90	207 45 98 45 XSQ= 8.85 PHI= 0.150 XP = 0.0029
62	TEND TO BE THOSE WHERE HUSBANDRY OF SOME KIND IS PRESENT (228)	0.63 OF 305	62	TEND TO BE THOSE WHERE HUSBANDRY OF ANY KIND IS ABSENT (172)	0.59 OF 90	191 37 114 53 XSQ= 12.31 PHI= 0.177 XP = 0.0005
71	TEND LESS TO BE THOSE WHERE METAL WORKING IS ABSENT (153)	0.54 OF 183	71	TEND MORE TO BE THOSE WHERE METAL WORKING IS ABSENT (153)	0.78 OF 65	84 14 99 51 XSQ= 10.91 PHI= 0.210 XP = 0.0010
85	DRIFT LESS TOWARD BEING THOSE WHERE THE LEVEL OF POLITICAL INTEGRATION IS THE MINIMAL STATE, THE AUTONOMOUS COMMUNITY, OR THE FAMILY (234) GPM	0.74 OF 228	85	DRIFT MORE TOWARD BEING THOSE WHERE THE LEVEL OF POLITICAL INTEGRATION IS THE MINIMAL STATE, THE AUTONOMOUS COMMUNITY, OR THE FAMILY (234) GPM	0.85 OF 73	59 11 169 62 XSQ= 3.04 PHI= 0.100 XP = 0.0813
89	TILT LESS TOWARD BEING THOSE WHERE, IF A NON-HEREDITARY HEADMANSHIP IS PRESENT, SUCCESSION IS BY CONSENSUS (63)	0.52 OF 82	89	TILT MORE TOWARD BEING THOSE WHERE, IF A NON-HEREDITARY HEADMANSHIP IS PRESENT, SUCCESSION IS BY CONSENSUS (63)	0.83 OF 24	43 20 39 4 XSQ= 6.12 PHI= -0.240 XP = 0.0133
90	TILT MORE TOWARD BEING THOSE WHERE, IF A HEREDITARY HEADMANSHIP IS PRESENT, SUCCESSION IS PATRILINEAL, RATHER THAN MATRILINEAL (127)	0.81 OF 123	90	TILT LESS TOWARD BEING THOSE WHERE, IF A HEREDITARY HEADMANSHIP IS PRESENT, SUCCESSION IS PATRILINEAL, RATHER THAN MATRILINEAL (127)	0.64 OF 39	100 25 23 14 XSQ= 4.04 PHI= 0.158 XP = 0.0444
100	DRIFT MORE TOWARD BEING THOSE WHERE HIERARCHIES ARE MORE COMPLEX THAN THE 'SIMPLEST,' I. E., MORE COMPLEX THAN TWO LOCAL LEVELS WITH NO NATIONAL LEVELS (267) GES,EA	0.84 OF 252	100	DRIFT LESS TOWARD BEING THOSE WHERE HIERARCHIES ARE MORE COMPLEX THAN THE 'SIMPLEST,' I. E., MORE COMPLEX THAN TWO LOCAL LEVELS WITH NO NATIONAL LEVELS (267) GES,EA	0.73 OF 75	211 55 41 20 XSQ= 3.46 PHI= 0.103 XP = 0.0629
102	LEAN TOWARD BEING THOSE WHERE CLASS STRATIFICATION IS PRESENT (203)	0.58 OF 293	102	LEAN TOWARD BEING THOSE WHERE CLASS STRATIFICATION IS ABSENT (180)	0.62 OF 86	169 33 124 53 XSQ= 9.20 PHI= 0.156 XP = 0.0024
110	TEND TO BE THOSE WHERE SLAVERY IS PRESENT (163)	0.51 OF 290	110	TEND TO BE THOSE WHERE SLAVERY IS ABSENT (218)	0.83 OF 88	148 15 142 73 XSQ= 30.43 PHI= 0.284 XP = 0.

176	LEAN LESS TOWARD BEING THOSE WHERE THE COMMUNITY IS OTHER THAN A CLAN-COMMUNITY OR A COMMUNITY STRUCTURED OR SEGMENTED ON A CLAN BASIS (213)	0.52 OF 295	176	LEAN MORE TOWARD BEING THOSE WHERE THE COMMUNITY IS OTHER THAN A CLAN-COMMUNITY OR A COMMUNITY STRUCTURED OR SEGMENTED ON A CLAN BASIS (213)	0.72 OF 83	143 23 152 60 XSQ= 10.51 PHI= 0.167 XP = 0.0012
177	TEND LESS TO BE THOSE WHERE THE COMMUNITY IS OTHER THAN A SINGLE CLAN-COMMUNITY AND EXOGAMOUS (305)	0.76 OF 295	177	TEND MORE TO BE THOSE WHERE THE COMMUNITY IS OTHER THAN A SINGLE CLAN-COMMUNITY AND EXOGAMOUS (305)	0.95 OF 83	72 4 223 79 XSQ= 14.28 PHI= 0.194 XP = 0.0002
180	TEND LESS TO BE THOSE WHERE THE COMMUNITY IS COMMONLY NON-EXOGAMOUS, RATHER THAN EXOGAMOUS (258)	0.62 OF 295	180	TEND MORE TO BE THOSE WHERE THE COMMUNITY IS COMMONLY NON-EXOGAMOUS, RATHER THAN EXOGAMOUS (258)	0.87 OF 83	112 11 183 72 XSQ= 16.91 PHI= 0.212 XP = 0.0000
181	TEND MORE TO BE THOSE WHERE THE COMMUNITY IS OTHER THAN A DEME (337)	0.92 OF 295	181	TEND LESS TO BE THOSE WHERE THE COMMUNITY IS OTHER THAN A DEME (337)	0.76 OF 83	24 20 271 63 XSQ= 14.53 PHI= -0.196 XP = 0.0001
186	TEND LESS TO BE THOSE WHERE THE KIN GROUP IS OTHER THAN EXCLUSIVELY PATRILINEAL (250)	0.55 OF 305	186	TEND MORE TO BE THOSE WHERE THE KIN GROUP IS OTHER THAN EXCLUSIVELY PATRILINEAL (250)	0.87 OF 90	136 12 169 78 XSQ= 27.66 PHI= 0.265 XP = 0.0000
187	TILT MORE TOWARD BEING THOSE WHERE THE KIN GROUP IS OTHER THAN EXCLUSIVELY MATRILINEAL (344)	0.89 OF 305	187	TILT LESS TOWARD BEING THOSE WHERE THE KIN GROUP IS OTHER THAN EXCLUSIVELY MATRILINEAL (344)	0.78 OF 89	34 20 271 69 XSQ= 6.54 PHI= -0.129 XP = 0.0105
188	TEND TO BE THOSE WHERE THE KIN GROUP IS OTHER THAN EXCLUSIVELY COGNATIC (252)	0.70 OF 305	188	TEND TO BE THOSE WHERE THE KIN GROUP IS EXCLUSIVELY COGNATIC (148)	0.59 OF 90	93 53 212 37 XSQ= 22.85 PHI= -0.241 XP = 0.0000
190	TEND TO BE THOSE WHERE THE KIN GROUP IS PATRILINEAL OR DOUBLE-DESCENT, RATHER THAN MATRILINEAL (186)	0.82 OF 208	190	TEND TO BE THOSE WHERE THE KIN GROUP IS MATRILINEAL, RATHER THAN PATRILINEAL OR DOUBLE-DESCENT (61)	0.61 OF 36	170 14 38 22 XSQ= 28.11 PHI= 0.339 XP = 0.0000
192	TEND MORE TO BE THOSE OTHER THAN WHERE THE ONLY KIN GROUP PRESENT IS A KINDRED OR ELSE BILATERAL DESCENT IS INFERRED (289)	0.78 OF 305	192	TEND LESS TO BE THOSE OTHER THAN WHERE THE ONLY KIN GROUP PRESENT IS A KINDRED OR ELSE BILATERAL DESCENT IS INFERRED (289)	0.52 OF 90	66 43 239 47 XSQ= 22.47 PHI= -0.239 XP = 0.0000

196	DRIFT MORE TOWARD BEING THOSE 0.72 OF 226 WHERE INDIVIDUAL RIGHTS IN REAL PROPERTY, AND RULES FOR INHERITANCE, ARE PRESENT (194)	196	DRIFT LESS TOWARD BEING THOSE 0.57 OF 54 WHERE INDIVIDUAL RIGHTS IN REAL PROPERTY, AND RULES FOR INHERITANCE, ARE PRESENT (194)	162 31 64 23 XSQ= 3.51 PHI= 0.112 XP = 0.0611
197	TILT MORE TOWARD BEING THOSE 0.88 OF 162 WHERE RULES FOR THE INHERITANCE OF REAL PROPERTY, IF PRESENT, FAVOR EITHER THE MALE HEIR OR LINE, OR THE FEMALE HEIR OR LINE (165)	197	TILT LESS TOWARD BEING THOSE 0.71 OF 31 WHERE RULES FOR THE INHERITANCE OF REAL PROPERTY, IF PRESENT, FAVOR EITHER THE MALE HEIR OR LINE, OR THE FEMALE HEIR OR LINE (165)	142 22 20 9 XSQ= 4.44 PHI= 0.152 XP = 0.0350
201	TEND MORE TO BE THOSE 0.89 OF 305 WHERE MARITAL RESIDENCE IS NON-OPTIONAL, RATHER THAN AMBILOCAL OR NEOLOCAL (334)	201	TEND LESS TO BE THOSE 0.69 OF 88 WHERE MARITAL RESIDENCE IS NON-OPTIONAL, RATHER THAN AMBILOCAL OR NEOLOCAL (334)	270 61 35 27 XSQ= 17.54 PHI= 0.211 XP = 0.0000
204	TEND MORE TO BE THOSE 0.87 OF 269 WHERE MARITAL RESIDENCE IS PATRILOCAL, VIRILOCAL, OR AVUNCULOCAL, RATHER THAN AMBILOCAL OR NEOLOCAL (270)	204	TEND LESS TO BE THOSE 0.56 OF 61 WHERE MARITAL RESIDENCE IS PATRILOCAL, VIRILOCAL, OR AVUNCULOCAL, RATHER THAN AMBILOCAL OR NEOLOCAL (270)	234 34 35 27 XSQ= 29.81 PHI= 0.301 XP = 0.0000
209	TEND MORE TO BE THOSE 0.87 OF 270 WHERE MARITAL RESIDENCE IS PATRILOCAL, VIRILOCAL, OR AVUNCULOCAL, RATHER THAN MATRILOCAL OR UXORILOCAL (270)	209	TEND LESS TO BE THOSE 0.56 OF 61 WHERE MARITAL RESIDENCE IS PATRILOCAL, VIRILOCAL, OR AVUNCULOCAL, RATHER THAN MATRILOCAL OR UXORILOCAL (270)	234 34 36 27 XSQ= 28.91 PHI= 0.296 XP = 0.0000
210	TEND TO BE THOSE 0.92 OF 169 WHERE MARITAL RESIDENCE IS PATRILOCAL, RATHER THAN MATRILOCAL (169)	210	TEND TO BE THOSE 0.61 OF 28 WHERE MARITAL RESIDENCE IS MATRILOCAL, RATHER THAN PATRILOCAL (31)	156 11 13 17 XSQ= 48.28 PHI= 0.495 XP = 0.
220	TEND LESS TO BE THOSE 0.69 OF 287 WHERE FIRST COUSIN MARRIAGE IN SOME FORM OR OTHER IS NOT PRESCRIBED OR PREFERRED (273)	220	TEND MORE TO BE THOSE 0.89 OF 80 WHERE FIRST COUSIN MARRIAGE IN SOME FORM OR OTHER IS NOT PRESCRIBED OR PREFERRED (273)	88 9 199 71 XSQ= 11.15 PHI= 0.174 XP = 0.0008
221	DRIFT LESS TOWARD BEING THOSE 0.89 OF 287 WHERE MATRILATERAL CROSS-COUSIN MARRIAGE IS NOT PRESCRIBED OR PREFERRED (335)	221	DRIFT MORE TOWARD BEING THOSE 0.96 OF 80 WHERE MATRILATERAL CROSS-COUSIN MARRIAGE IS NOT PRESCRIBED OR PREFERRED (335)	32 3 255 77 XSQ= 3.16 PHI= 0.093 XP = 0.0755
224	TILT LESS TOWARD BEING THOSE 0.57 OF 140 WHERE COUSIN MARRIAGE IS PREFERENTIALLY OR PERMISSIVELY SYMMETRICAL, RATHER THAN EITHER PATRI- OR MATRILATERAL (106)	224	TILT MORE TOWARD BEING THOSE 0.81 OF 31 WHERE COUSIN MARRIAGE IS PREFERENTIALLY OR PERMISSIVELY SYMMETRICAL, RATHER THAN EITHER PATRI- OR MATRILATERAL (106)	60 6 80 25 XSQ= 4.97 PHI= 0.170 XP = 0.0259

234	DRIFT TOWARD BEING THOSE 0.50 OF 234 WHERE THE COUSIN TERMINOLOGY IS OF CROW, OMAHA, OR IROQUOIS TYPE, RATHER THAN ESKIMO OR HAWAIIAN TYPE (152)	234	DRIFT TOWARD BEING THOSE 0.63 OF 83 WHERE THE COUSIN TERMINOLOGY IS OF ESKIMO OR HAWAIIAN TYPE, RATHER THAN CROW, OMAHA, OR IROQUOIS TYPE (170)	117 31 117 52 XSQ= 3.45 PHI= 0.104 XP = 0.0633
242	TEND MORE TO BE THOSE 0.84 OF 301 WHERE MARRIAGE IS COMMONLY OR OCCASIONALLY POLYGYNOUS, RATHER THAN MONOGAMOUS (314)	242	TEND LESS TO BE THOSE 0.63 OF 89 WHERE MARRIAGE IS COMMONLY OR OCCASIONALLY POLYGYNOUS, RATHER THAN MONOGAMOUS (314)	253 56 48 33 XSQ= 17.38 PHI= 0.211 XP = 0.0000
333	DRIFT TOWARD BEING THOSE 0.67 OF 12 WHERE THE AGE AT BEGINNING OF TRAINING IN HETEROSEXUAL PLAY INHIBITION IS EIGHT YEARS OR HIGHER (8) W-C	333	IN ALL CASES ARE THOSE 1.00 OF 4 WHERE THE AGE AT BEGINNING OF TRAINING IN HETEROSEXUAL PLAY INHIBITION IS LOWER THAN EIGHT YEARS (8) W-C	8 0 4 4 XSQ= 3.00 PHI= 0.433 EP = 0.0769
356	LEAN TOWARD BEING THOSE 0.67 OF 43 WHERE ADOLESCENT PEER GROUPS OR PAIRS ARE PRESENT IN A SETTING OF COURTSHIP (29) JKH	356	IN ALL CASES ARE THOSE 1.00 OF 8 WHERE NEITHER ADOLESCENT PEER GROUPS NOR PAIRS ARE PRESENT IN A SETTING OF COURTSHIP (22) JKH	29 0 14 8 XSQ= 9.91 PHI= 0.441 XP = 0.0016
370	LEAN LESS TOWARD BEING THOSE 0.56 OF 190 WHERE THE SEGREGATION OF ADOLESCENT BOYS IS ABSENT (148)	370	LEAN MORE TOWARD BEING THOSE 0.79 OF 53 WHERE THE SEGREGATION OF ADOLESCENT BOYS IS ABSENT (148)	84 11 106 42 XSQ= 8.62 PHI= 0.188 XP = 0.0033
377	TEND LESS TO BE THOSE 0.69 OF 249 WHERE MALE GENITAL MUTILATION IS ABSENT (242)	377	TEND MORE TO BE THOSE 0.93 OF 73 WHERE MALE GENITAL MUTILATION IS ABSENT (242)	77 5 172 68 XSQ= 15.99 PHI= 0.223 XP = 0.0001
391	DRIFT TOWARD BEING THOSE 0.54 OF 140 WHERE PREMARITAL SEX RELATIONS ARE STRONGLY PUNISHED AND IN FACT RARE, OR WEAKLY PUNISHED AND IN FACT NOT RARE (89) JTW,EA	391	DRIFT TOWARD BEING THOSE 0.64 OF 39 WHERE PREMARITAL SEX RELATIONS ARE PUNISHED ONLY IF PREGNANCY RESULTS, OR FREELY PERMITTED (90) JTW,EA	75 14 65 25 XSQ= 3.14 PHI= 0.132 XP = 0.0765
417	DRIFT TOWARD BEING THOSE 0.86 OF 35 WHERE WARFARE IS PREVALENT (34) LWS	417	DRIFT TOWARD BEING THOSE 0.50 OF 8 WHERE WARFARE IS NOT PREVALENT (9) LWS	30 4 5 4 XSQ= 3.09 PHI= 0.268 XP = 0.0786
419	DRIFT TOWARD BEING THOSE 0.70 OF 69 WHERE MILITARY GLORY IS STRONGLY OR MODERATELY EMPHASIZED (55) PES	419	DRIFT TOWARD BEING THOSE 0.59 OF 17 WHERE MILITARY GLORY IS NEGLIGIBLY EMPHASIZED (31) PES	48 7 21 10 XSQ= 3.62 PHI= 0.205 XP = 0.0572

```
420  DRIFT TOWARD BEING THOSE        0.53 OF  70    420  DRIFT TOWARD BEING THOSE        0.76 OF  17          37     4
     WHERE BELLICOSITY                                   WHERE BELLICOSITY                                    33    13
     IS EXTREME  (41) PES                                IS MODERATE OR NEGLIGIBLE  (46) PES             XSQ=     3.62
                                                                                                         PHI=    0.204
                                                                                                         XP =   0.0572

426  LEAN TOWARD BEING THOSE         0.66 OF 204    426  LEAN TOWARD BEING THOSE         0.59 OF  54         134    22
     WHERE A HIGH GOD IS                                 WHERE A HIGH GOD IS                                  70    32
     PRESENT  (156) GES,EA                               ABSENT  (104) GES,EA                            XSQ=    10.10
                                                                                                         PHI=    0.198
                                                                                                         XP =   0.0015

454  TILT TOWARD BEING THOSE         0.63 OF  27    454  TILT TOWARD BEING THOSE         0.88 OF   8          17     1
     WHERE THE OBJECTIVE OF THE INDIVIDUAL'S             WHERE THE OBJECTIVE OF THE INDIVIDUAL'S              10     7
     CONTACT WITH THE DIVINE                             CONTACT WITH THE DIVINE                         XSQ=     4.43
     IS CONDUCIVE TO THE DEVELOPMENT OF THE              IS NOT CONDUCIVE TO THE DEVELOPMENT OF THE      PHI=    0.356
     INDIVIDUAL'S NEED TO ACHIEVE  (18) DCM              INDIVIDUAL'S NEED TO ACHIEVE  (18) DCM          EP =   0.0178

458  TILT LESS TOWARD BEING THOSE    0.65 OF 127    458  TILT MORE TOWARD BEING THOSE    0.84 OF  44          45     7
     WHERE GAMES, IF PRESENT,                            WHERE GAMES, IF PRESENT,                             82    37
     DO NOT INCLUDE                                      DO NOT INCLUDE                                  XSQ=     5.00
     GAMES OF STRATEGY  (119) R-A-B,EA                   GAMES OF STRATEGY  (119) R-A-B,EA               PHI=    0.171
                                                                                                         XP =   0.0254

473  TILT LESS TOWARD BEING THOSE    0.58 OF  71    473  TILT MORE TOWARD BEING THOSE    0.88 OF  17          30     2
     WHERE SENSITIVITY TO INSULT                         WHERE SENSITIVITY TO INSULT                          41    15
     IS MODERATE OR NEGLIGIBLE  (56) PES                 IS MODERATE OR NEGLIGIBLE  (56) PES             XSQ=     4.27
                                                                                                         PHI=    0.220
                                                                                                         XP =   0.0388
```

263 CULTURES
WHERE WIVES ARE OBTAINED BY RELATIVELY DIFFICULT MEANS, NAMELY BY BRIDE-PRICE, BRIDE-SERVICE, OR EXCHANGING A FEMALE RELATIVE (233)

263 CULTURES
WHERE WIVES ARE OBTAINED BY RELATIVELY EASY MEANS, NAMELY BY TOKEN BRIDE-PRICE, GIFT EXCHANGE, ABSENCE OF ANY CONSIDERATION, OR RECEIPT OF DOWRY (162)

BACKGROUND ON PAGE 128

BOTH SUBJECT AND PREDICATE

233 IN LEFT COLUMN

ABIPON	ABOR	AJIE	ALBANIANS	ALORESE	AMBA	ARANDA	ARAUCANIANS	ARYANS	ASHANTI
ATAYAL	AZANDE	BAPWA	BAJUN	BAMBARA	BAMILEKE	BANDA	BARABRA	BARI	BASSERI
BATAK	BAYA	BEJA	BELU	BEMBA	BENGALI	BERGDAMA	BETE	BHIL	BHUIYA
BIRIFOR	BOZO	BUDUMA	BUNLAP	BURYAT	CAGABA	CALLINAGO	CAMAYURA	CAMBODIANS	CARIB
CHAGGA	CHAMACOCO	CHENCHU	CHERKESS	CHIBCHA	CHIRIGUANO	CHOROTI	CHORTI	CHUKCHEE	COPR ESKIMO
CREE	CUNA	DAGUR	DARD	DIERI	DILLING	DOGON	DOROBO	DUSUN	EGYPTIANS
ENGA	EYAK	FANG	FON	FOX	FUTAJALONKE	GANDA	GILBERTESE	GILYAK	GISU
GOAJIRO	GOND	GROS VENTRE	GUAHIBO	HAIDA	HANUNOO	HASANIA	HAZARA	HEBREWS	HEHE
HERERO	HO	IFUGAO	ILA	INGASSANA	IRAQW	JIVARO	JUKUN	KABYLE	KACHIN
KALMYK	KAPAUKU	KOHISTANI	KARIERA	KASKA	KAZAK	KERAKI	KET	KHALKA	KHEVSUR	KIKUYU
KISSI	KOHISTANI	KOL	KORYAK	KPE	KUBA	KUMYK	KUNG	KURTATCHI	LAKALAI
LAKHER	LAMBA	LAMET	LANGO	LEPCHA	LESU	LHOTA NAGA	LIFU	LOLO	LUBA
LUO	MACASSARESE	MAGUZAWA	MALAYS	MAMBILA	MAMVU	MANCHU	MARGI	MASAI	MATACO
MATAKAM	MAYA	MBUGWE	MBUNDU	MBUTI	MENDE	MENTAWEI	MIAO	MIN CHINESE	MINCHIA
MONGO	MONGUOR	MOSSI	MOTA	MUNDURUCU	MURNGIN	MZAB	NANDI	NASKAPI	NUER
NUPE	NURI	NYAKYUSA	NYANEKA	NYARO	NYORO	ONA	ORAON	PAIWAN	PALAUANS
PARAUJANO	PATHAN	PENOBSCOT	PURARI	PURUM	REGEIBAT	RIFFIANS	ROTINESE	RWALA	SAMOYED
SANDAWE	SANTAL	SARAMACCA	SARSI	SENIANG	SERI	SHILLUK	SHLUH	SIMBOESE	SIUAI
SIWANS	SOMALI	SONGHAI	SOTHO	SUBANUN	SWAZI	SYRIANS	TAGBANUA	TALAMANCA	TALLENSI
TANIMBARESE	TARAHUMARA	TAREUMIUT	TECA	TENDA	TENETEHARA	TERA	TESO	TETON	THONGA
TIMBIRA	TIV	TIWI	TOLOWA	TORAJA	TSHIMSHIAN	TUBATULABAL	TUCANO	TUCUNA	TUPINAMBA
TURKANA	TURKMEN	TZELTAL	ULAWANS	VENDA	WANTOAT	WAPISHANA	WARRAU	WICHITA	WIKMUNKAN
WITOTO	WOLOF	WUTE	YABARANA	YAGUA	YAHGAN	YAKO	YARURO	YOMBE	YORUBA
YUKAGHIR	YUROK	ZUNI							

162 IN RIGHT COLUMN

AINU	AKHA	ALACALUF	AMERICANS	ANDAMANESE	APINAYE	ARAPESH	ATSUGEWI	AWEIKOMA	AYMARA
AZTEC	BACAIRI	BALINESE	BASQUES	BLACK CARIB	BOERS	BORORO	BOTOCUDO	BRAZILIANS	BULGARIANS
BURMESE	BURUSHO	CADUVEO	CAMBA	CARAJA	CAYAPA	CHEREMIS	CHEROKEE	CHEYENNE	CHINANTEC
CHIR-APACHE	CHOCO	COCHITI	COMANCHE	COORG	CREEK	CROW	CZECHS	DELAWARE	DIEGUENO
DOBUANS	DUTCH	ELLICE	GARO	GURE	HANO	HASINAI	HAVASUPAI	HAWAIIANS	HUICHOL
HUKUNDIKA	HURON	HUTSUL	IBAN	ICELANDERS	INCA	INGALIK	IRISH	JAPANESE	JAVANESE
JEMEZ	KAREN	KATAB	KERALA	KHASI	KIOW-APACHE	KONSO	KOREANS	KUTENAI	KWAKIUTL
LAPPS	LAU	LOZI	MAM	MANDAN	MANGAIANS	MANIHIKI	MANUS	MAORI	MARICOPA
MARQUESANS	MARSHALLESE	MAZATECO	MERINA	MIAMI	MINANGKABAU	MISKITO	MIWOK	MNONG GAR	MOTILON
NABESNA	NAMA	NAMBICUARA	NATCHEZ	NAVAHO	NDEMBU	NGONI	NICOBARESE	NOMLAKI	NUNIVAK
OJIBWA	OKINAWANS	OMAHA	ONTONG-JAVA	PAEZ	PALIKUR	PAPAGO	PAWNEE	PENDE	PONAPEANS
POPOLUCA	PORTUGUESE	PUKAPUKA	RAROIANS	ROMANS	ROTUMANS	RUNDI	SAGADA	SAMOANS	SANPOIL

SELUNG	SEMANG	SEMINOLE	SERBS	SHERENTE	SINDHI	SINHALESE	SIRIONO	TAMIL	TANALA
TAOS	TAPIRAPE	TEHUELCHE	TENINO	TERENA	THAI	TIBETANS	TIGRINYA	TIKCPIA	TOCA
TOKELAU	TCTCNAC	TRISTAN	TROBRIAND	TRUKESE	TRUMAI	TUNEBO	TWANA	UTE	VEDDA
VIETNAMESE	WAICA	WALLCONS	WAROPEN	WASHO	WOGEO	WOLEAIANS	YAKUT	YAO	YAPESE
YOKUTS	YUKI								

5 EXCLUCED BECAUSE UNASCERTAINEC

3	TEND LESS TC BE THCSE LOCATED CUTSIDE CF AFRICA (320)	0.70 OF 233	3	TEND MORE TO BE THOSE LOCATED OUTSIDE OF AFRICA (320)	0.94 CF 162	71 9 162 153 XSQ= 35.21 PHI= 0.299 XP = 0.
8	TEND MCRE TC BE THCSE LCCATED CUTSIDE CF NCRTH AMERICA (330)	0.91 OF 233	8	TEND LESS TO BE THOSE LOCATED OUTSIDE OF NORTH AMERICA (330)	0.70 CF 162	20 48 213 114 XSQ= 28.24 PHI= -0.267 XP = 0.0000
13	TILT MCRE TOWARC BEING THCSE WHERE THE LATITUCE IS LESS THAN FCRTY DEGREES (329)	0.86 OF 233	13	TILT LESS TOWARD BEING THOSE WHERE THE LATITUDE IS LESS THAN FCRTY DEGREES (329)	0.77 CF 162	33 37 200 125 XSQ= 4.36 PHI= -0.105 XP = 0.0369
14	TEND MCRE TO BE THCSE WHERE THE LATITUCE IS LESS THAN THIRTY DEGREES (281)	0.77 OF 233	14	TEND LESS TO BE THOSE WHERE THE LATITUDE IS LESS THAN THIRTY DEGREES (281)	0.60 CF 162	53 65 180 97 XSQ= 12.96 PHI= -0.181 XP = 0.0003
16	TEND LESS TO BE THCSE WHERE THE LATITUCE IS TEN DEGREES CR GREATER (277)	0.62 OF 233	16	TEND MORE TO BE THOSE WHERE THE LATITUDE IS TEN DEGREES OR GREATER (277)	0.79 CF 162	145 128 88 34 XSQ= 11.83 PHI= -0.173 XP = 0.0006
45	TILT LESS TOWARC BEING THCSE WHERE SETTLEMENTS, IF FIXEC, ARE CCMPACT, RATHER THAN NON-CCMPACT (149)	0.61 OF 135	45	TILT MORE TOWARD BEING THCSE WHERE SETTLEMENTS, IF FIXED, ARE COMPACT, RATHER THAN NON-COMPACT (149)	0.76 CF 87	83 66 52 21 XSQ= 4.33 PHI= -0.140 XP = 0.0375
48	TILT TCWARD BEING THCSE WHERE THE FCCC SUPPLY IS NCT SECURE, AND FCCD SHORTAGES ARE FREQUENT CR ANNUAL (41) MGW	0.65 OF 46	48	TILT TOWARD BEING THOSE WHERE THE FOOD SUPPLY IS SECURE, AND FOOD SHORTAGES ARE RARE OR OCCASIONAL (38) MGW	0.66 CF 32	16 21 30 11 XSQ= 6.02 PHI= -0.278 XP = 0.0142

51	TEND MORE TO BE THOSE 0.71 OF 233 WHERE SUBSISTENCE IS PRIMARILY BY FOOD PRODUCTION -- I. E., AGRICULTURE OR HUSBANDRY -- RATHER THAN BY GATHERING (253)	51	TEND LESS TO BE THOSE 0.54 OF 162 WHERE SUBSISTENCE IS PRIMARILY BY FOOD PRODUCTION -- I. E., AGRICULTURE OR HUSBANDRY -- RATHER THAN BY GATHERING (253)	165 87 68 75 XSQ= 11.39 PHI= 0.170 XP = 0.0007
54	TILT MORE TOWARD BEING THOSE 0.86 OF 149 WHERE FOOD PRODUCTION IS BY INTENSIVE OR SIMPLE AGRICULTURE, RATHER THAN BY INCIPIENT FOOD PRODUCTION (192)	54	TILT LESS TOWARD BEING THOSE 0.74 OF 87 WHERE FOOD PRODUCTION IS BY INTENSIVE OR SIMPLE AGRICULTURE, RATHER THAN BY INCIPIENT FOOD PRODUCTION (192)	128 64 21 23 XSQ= 4.73 PHI= 0.142 XP = 0.0296
56	TILT MORE TOWARD BEING THOSE 0.77 OF 93 WHERE FOOD PRODUCTION IS BY SIMPLE AGRICULTURE, RATHER THAN BY INCIPIENT FOOD PRODUCTION (101)	56	TILT LESS TOWARD BEING THOSE 0.56 OF 52 WHERE FOOD PRODUCTION IS BY SIMPLE AGRICULTURE, RATHER THAN BY INCIPIENT FOOD PRODUCTION (101)	72 29 21 23 XSQ= 6.41 PHI= 0.210 XP = 0.0114
62	LEAN TOWARD BEING THOSE 0.64 OF 233 WHERE HUSBANDRY OF SOME KIND IS PRESENT (228)	62	LEAN TOWARD BEING THOSE 0.52 OF 162 WHERE HUSBANDRY OF ANY KIND IS ABSENT (172)	150 78 83 84 XSQ= 9.66 PHI= 0.156 XP = 0.0019
71	LEAN LESS TOWARD BEING THOSE 0.52 OF 135 WHERE METAL WORKING IS ABSENT (153)	71	LEAN MORE TOWARD BEING THOSE 0.71 OF 113 WHERE METAL WORKING IS ABSENT (153)	65 33 70 80 XSQ= 8.46 PHI= 0.185 XP = 0.0036
79	TEND MORE TO BE THOSE 0.96 OF 127 WHERE NO CITY IS PRESENT (201)	79	TEND LESS TO BE THOSE 0.81 OF 96 WHERE NO CITY IS PRESENT (201)	5 18 122 78 XSQ= 11.42 PHI= -0.226 XP = 0.0007
80	TILT MORE TOWARD BEING THOSE 0.87 OF 127 WHERE NO CITY OR TOWN IS PRESENT (185)	8C	TILT LESS TOWARD BEING THOSE 0.76 OF 96 WHERE NO CITY OR TOWN IS PRESENT (185)	16 23 111 73 XSQ= 4.13 PHI= -0.136 XP = 0.0420
84	DRIFT MORE TOWARD BEING THOSE 0.89 OF 177 WHERE THE LEVEL OF POLITICAL INTEGRATION IS THE LITTLE STATE, THE MINIMAL STATE, THE AUTONOMOUS COMMUNITY, OR THE FAMILY (262) GPM	84	DRIFT LESS TOWARD BEING THOSE 0.81 OF 124 WHERE THE LEVEL OF POLITICAL INTEGRATION IS THE LITTLE STATE, THE MINIMAL STATE, THE AUTONOMOUS COMMUNITY, OR THE FAMILY (262) GPM	19 23 158 101 XSQ= 3.09 PHI= -0.101 XP = 0.0790
89	DRIFT LESS TOWARD BEING THOSE 0.52 OF 60 WHERE, IF A NON-HEREDITARY HEADMANSHIP IS PRESENT, SUCCESSION IS BY CONSENSUS (63)	89	DRIFT MORE TOWARD BEING THOSE 0.70 OF 46 WHERE, IF A NON-HEREDITARY HEADMANSHIP IS PRESENT, SUCCESSION IS BY CONSENSUS (63)	31 32 29 14 XSQ= 2.76 PHI= -0.161 XP = 0.0968

97 DRIFT LESS TOWARD BEING THOSE 0.79 OF 195 WHERE THE HIERARCHY OF LOCAL JURISDICTION HAS THREE OR TWO LEVELS (273) GES,EA	97 DRIFT MORE TOWARD BEING THOSE 0.87 OF 133 WHERE THE HIERARCHY OF LOCAL JURISDICTION HAS THREE OR TWO LEVELS (273) GES,EA	41 17 154 116 XSQ= 3.15 PHI= 0.098 XP = 0.0761
106 DRIFT LESS TOWARD BEING THOSE 0.57 OF 122 WHERE CLASS STRATIFICATION, IF PRESENT, IS BASED ON SOMETHING OTHER THAN WEALTH (126)	106 DRIFT MORE TOWARD BEING THOSE 0.70 OF 80 WHERE CLASS STRATIFICATION, IF PRESENT, IS BASED ON SOMETHING OTHER THAN WEALTH (126)	53 24 69 56 XSQ= 3.15 PHI= 0.125 XP = 0.0758
107 TEND MORE TO BE THOSE 0.87 OF 122 WHERE CLASS STRATIFICATION, IF PRESENT, IS BASED ON SOMETHING OTHER THAN OCCUPATIONAL STATUS (160)	107 TEND LESS TO BE THOSE 0.66 OF 80 WHERE CLASS STRATIFICATION, IF PRESENT, IS BASED ON SOMETHING OTHER THAN OCCUPATIONAL STATUS (160)	16 27 106 53 XSQ= 11.08 PHI= -0.234 XP = 0.0009
108 DRIFT LESS TOWARD BEING THOSE 0.58 OF 122 WHERE CLASS STRATIFICATION, IF PRESENT, IS BASED ON SOMETHING OTHER THAN A HEREDITARY ARISTOCRACY (129)	108 DRIFT MORE TOWARD BEING THOSE 0.72 OF 80 WHERE CLASS STRATIFICATION, IF PRESENT, IS BASED ON SOMETHING OTHER THAN A HEREDITARY ARISTOCRACY (129)	51 22 71 58 XSQ= 3.69 PHI= 0.135 XP = 0.0549
109 TILT LESS TOWARD BEING THOSE 0.83 OF 207 WHERE CASTES ARE ABSENT (317)	109 TILT MORE TOWARD BEING THOSE 0.90 OF 157 WHERE CASTES ARE ABSENT (317)	36 15 171 142 XSQ= 3.92 PHI= 0.104 XP = 0.0476
110 TEND TO BE THOSE 0.53 OF 220 WHERE SLAVERY IS PRESENT (163)	110 TEND TO BE THOSE 0.70 OF 158 WHERE SLAVERY IS ABSENT (218)	116 47 104 111 XSQ= 18.87 PHI= 0.223 XP = 0.0000
129 TILT LESS TOWARD BEING THOSE 0.60 OF 57 WHERE WEAVING IS MAINLY DONE BY FEMALES (73)	129 TILT MORE TOWARD BEING THOSE 0.83 OF 46 WHERE WEAVING IS MAINLY DONE BY FEMALES (73)	23 8 34 38 XSQ= 5.33 PHI= 0.228 XP = 0.0209
139 LEAN TOWARD BEING THOSE 0.80 OF 25 WHERE SUPERORDINATE PUNISHMENT IS ABSENT (25) BBW	139 LEAN TOWARD BEING THOSE 0.67 OF 15 WHERE SUPERORDINATE PUNISHMENT IS PRESENT (15) BBW	5 10 20 5 XSQ= 6.83 PHI= -0.413 EP = 0.0062
175 DRIFT LESS TOWARD BEING THOSE 0.64 OF 224 WHERE THE COMMUNITY IS 'KIN-HETEROGENEOUS,' I. E. OTHER THAN A CLAN COMMUNITY OR A DEME (260)	175 DRIFT MORE TOWARD BEING THOSE 0.74 OF 154 WHERE THE COMMUNITY IS 'KIN-HETEROGENEOUS,' I. E. OTHER THAN A CLAN COMMUNITY OR A DEME (260)	80 40 144 114 XSQ= 3.56 PHI= 0.097 XP = 0.0592

176	TEND TO BE THOSE 0.52 OF 224 WHERE THE COMMUNITY IS A CLAN-COMMUNITY OR A COMMUNITY STRUCTURED OR SEGMENTED ON A CLAN BASIS (169)	176 TEND TO BE THOSE 0.68 OF 154 WHERE THE COMMUNITY IS OTHER THAN A CLAN-COMMUNITY OR A COMMUNITY STRUCTURED OR SEGMENTED ON A CLAN BASIS (213)	116 50 108 104 XSQ= 13.05 PHI= 0.186 XP = 0.0003
177	TEND LESS TO BE THOSE 0.72 OF 224 WHERE THE COMMUNITY IS OTHER THAN A SINGLE CLAN-COMMUNITY AND EXOGAMOUS (305)	177 TEND MORE TO BE THOSE 0.91 OF 154 WHERE THE COMMUNITY IS OTHER THAN A SINGLE CLAN-COMMUNITY AND EXOGAMOUS (305)	62 14 162 140 XSQ= 18.49 PHI= 0.221 XP = 0.0000
180	TEND LESS TO BE THOSE 0.58 OF 224 WHERE THE COMMUNITY IS COMMONLY NON-EXOGAMOUS, RATHER THAN EXOGAMOUS (258)	180 TEND MORE TO BE THOSE 0.81 OF 154 WHERE THE COMMUNITY IS COMMONLY NON-EXOGAMOUS, RATHER THAN EXOGAMOUS (258)	94 29 130 125 XSQ= 21.21 PHI= 0.237 XP = 0.0000
181	TILT MORE TOWARD BEING THOSE 0.92 OF 224 WHERE THE COMMUNITY IS OTHER THAN A DEME (337)	181 TILT LESS TOWARD BEING THOSE 0.83 OF 154 WHERE THE COMMUNITY IS OTHER THAN A DEME (337)	18 26 206 128 XSQ= 6.11 PHI= -0.127 XP = 0.0134
182	LEAN MORE TOWARD BEING THOSE 0.73 OF 224 OTHER THAN WHERE THE COMMUNITY IS STRUCTURED ON A NON-CLAN BASIS AND AGAMOUS (256)	182 LEAN LESS TOWARD BEING THOSE 0.58 OF 154 OTHER THAN WHERE THE COMMUNITY IS STRUCTURED ON A NON-CLAN BASIS AND AGAMOUS (256)	61 65 163 89 XSQ= 8.55 PHI= -0.150 XP = 0.0035
186	TEND TO BE THOSE 0.51 OF 233 WHERE THE KIN GROUP IS EXCLUSIVELY PATRILINEAL (150)	186 TEND TO BE THOSE 0.81 OF 162 WHERE THE KIN GROUP IS OTHER THAN EXCLUSIVELY PATRILINEAL (250)	118 30 115 132 XSQ= 40.73 PHI= 0.321 XP = 0.
187	LEAN MORE TOWARD BEING THOSE 0.91 OF 233 WHERE THE KIN GROUP IS OTHER THAN EXCLUSIVELY MATRILINEAL (344)	187 LEAN LESS TOWARD BEING THOSE 0.80 OF 161 WHERE THE KIN GROUP IS OTHER THAN EXCLUSIVELY MATRILINEAL (344)	22 32 211 129 XSQ= 7.90 PHI= -0.142 XP = 0.0049
188	TEND TO BE THOSE 0.75 OF 233 WHERE THE KIN GROUP IS OTHER THAN EXCLUSIVELY COGNATIC (252)	188 TEND TO BE THOSE 0.54 OF 162 WHERE THE KIN GROUP IS EXCLUSIVELY COGNATIC (148)	58 88 175 74 XSQ= 34.27 PHI= -0.295 XP = 0.
190	TEND MORE TO BE THOSE 0.85 OF 174 WHERE THE KIN GROUP IS PATRILINEAL OR DOUBLE-DESCENT, RATHER THAN MATRILINEAL (186)	190 TEND LESS TO BE THOSE 0.51 OF 70 WHERE THE KIN GROUP IS PATRILINEAL OR DOUBLE-DESCENT, RATHER THAN MATRILINEAL (186)	148 36 26 34 XSQ= 28.66 PHI= 0.343 XP = 0.0000

192	TEND MORE TO BE THOSE 0.82 OF 233 OTHER THAN WHERE THE ONLY KIN GROUP PRESENT IS A KINDRED OR ELSE BILATERAL DESCENT IS INFERRED (289)	192	TEND LESS TO BE THOSE 0.59 OF 162 OTHER THAN WHERE THE ONLY KIN GROUP PRESENT IS A KINDRED OR ELSE BILATERAL DESCENT IS INFERRED (289)	43 66 190 96 XSQ= 22.65 PHI= -0.239 XP = 0.0000
197	TEND MORE TO BE THOSE 0.93 OF 128 WHERE RULES FOR THE INHERITANCE OF REAL PROPERTY, IF PRESENT, FAVOR EITHER THE MALE HEIR OR LINE, OR THE FEMALE HEIR OR LINE (165)	197	TEND LESS TO BE THOSE 0.69 OF 65 WHERE RULES FOR THE INHERITANCE OF REAL PROPERTY, IF PRESENT, FAVOR EITHER THE MALE HEIR OR LINE, OR THE FEMALE HEIR OR LINE (165)	119 45 9 20 XSQ= 17.21 PHI= 0.299 XP = 0.0000
201	LEAN MORE TOWARD BEING THOSE 0.89 OF 233 WHERE MARITAL RESIDENCE IS NON-OPTIONAL, RATHER THAN AMBILOCAL OR NEOLOCAL (334)	201	LEAN LESS TOWARD BEING THOSE 0.77 OF 160 WHERE MARITAL RESIDENCE IS NON-OPTIONAL, RATHER THAN AMBILOCAL OR NEOLOCAL (334)	208 123 25 37 XSQ= 10.06 PHI= 0.160 XP = 0.0015
204	TEND MORE TO BE THOSE 0.88 OF 209 WHERE MARITAL RESIDENCE IS PATRILOCAL, VIRILOCAL, OR AVUNCULOCAL, RATHER THAN AMBILOCAL OR NEOLOCAL (270)	204	TEND LESS TO BE THOSE 0.69 OF 121 WHERE MARITAL RESIDENCE IS PATRILOCAL, VIRILOCAL, OR AVUNCULOCAL, RATHER THAN AMBILOCAL OR NEOLOCAL (270)	184 84 25 37 XSQ= 16.21 PHI= 0.222 XP = 0.0001
209	TEND MORE TO BE THOSE 0.88 OF 208 WHERE MARITAL RESIDENCE IS PATRILOCAL, VIRILOCAL, OR AVUNCULOCAL, RATHER THAN MATRILOCAL OR UXORILOCAL (270)	209	TEND LESS TO BE THOSE 0.68 OF 123 WHERE MARITAL RESIDENCE IS PATRILOCAL, VIRILOCAL, OR AVUNCULOCAL, RATHER THAN MATRILOCAL OR UXORILOCAL (270)	184 84 24 39 XSQ= 19.11 PHI= 0.240 XP = 0.0000
210	TEND MORE TO BE THOSE 0.94 OF 141 WHERE MARITAL RESIDENCE IS PATRILOCAL, RATHER THAN MATRILOCAL (169)	210	TEND LESS TO BE THOSE 0.61 OF 56 WHERE MARITAL RESIDENCE IS PATRILOCAL, RATHER THAN MATRILOCAL (169)	133 34 8 22 XSQ= 32.52 PHI= 0.406 XP = 0.
220	LEAN LESS TOWARD BEING THOSE 0.68 OF 221 WHERE FIRST COUSIN MARRIAGE IN SOME FORM OR OTHER IS NOT PRESCRIBED OR PREFERRED (273)	220	LEAN MORE TOWARD BEING THOSE 0.82 OF 146 WHERE FIRST COUSIN MARRIAGE IN SOME FORM OR OTHER IS NOT PRESCRIBED OR PREFERRED (273)	70 27 151 119 XSQ= 7.19 PHI= 0.140 XP = 0.0073
221	LEAN LESS TOWARD BEING THOSE 0.86 OF 221 WHERE MATRILATERAL CROSS-COUSIN MARRIAGE IS NOT PRESCRIBED OR PREFERRED (335)	221	LEAN MORE TOWARD BEING THOSE 0.97 OF 146 WHERE MATRILATERAL CROSS-COUSIN MARRIAGE IS NOT PRESCRIBED OR PREFERRED (335)	30 5 191 141 XSQ= 9.36 PHI= 0.160 XP = 0.0022
224	TEND LESS TO BE THOSE 0.51 OF 111 WHERE COUSIN MARRIAGE IS PREFERENTIALLY OR PERMISSIVELY SYMMETRICAL, RATHER THAN EITHER PATRI- OR MATRILATERAL (106)	224	TEND MORE TO BE THOSE 0.80 OF 60 WHERE COUSIN MARRIAGE IS PREFERENTIALLY OR PERMISSIVELY SYMMETRICAL, RATHER THAN EITHER PATRI- OR MATRILATERAL (106)	54 12 57 48 XSQ= 12.31 PHI= 0.268 XP = 0.0005

234	TILT TOWARD BEING THOSE 0.53 OF 170 WHERE THE COUSIN TERMINOLOGY IS OF CROW, OMAHA, OR IROQUOIS TYPE, RATHER THAN ESKIMO OR HAWAIIAN TYPE (152)	234	TILT TOWARD BEING THOSE 0.61 OF 147 WHERE THE COUSIN TERMINOLOGY IS OF ESKIMO OR HAWAIIAN TYPE, RATHER THAN CROW, OMAHA, OR IROQUOIS TYPE (170)	90 58 80 89 XSQ= 5.23 PHI= 0.128 XP = 0.0222
241	TILT MORE TOWARD BEING THOSE 0.93 OF 117 WHERE THE FAMILY, IF EXTENDED, IS LARGE OR SMALL, RATHER THAN STEM (187)	241	TILT LESS TOWARD BEING THOSE 0.81 OF 94 WHERE THE FAMILY, IF EXTENDED, IS LARGE OR SMALL, RATHER THAN STEM (187)	109 76 8 18 XSQ= 6.22 PHI= 0.172 XP = 0.0127
242	TEND MORE TO BE THOSE 0.88 OF 232 WHERE MARRIAGE IS COMMONLY OR OCCASIONALLY POLYGYNOUS, RATHER THAN MONOGAMOUS (314)	242	TEND LESS TO BE THOSE 0.66 OF 158 WHERE MARRIAGE IS COMMONLY OR OCCASIONALLY POLYGYNOUS, RATHER THAN MONOGAMOUS (314)	205 104 27 54 XSQ= 27.66 PHI= 0.266 XP = 0.0000
243	DRIFT TOWARD BEING THOSE 0.50 OF 38 WHERE POLYGYNY, IF PRESENT, HAS A HIGH INCIDENCE (24) W-D,S	243	DRIFT TOWARD BEING THOSE 0.77 OF 22 WHERE POLYGYNY, IF PRESENT, HAS A LOW INCIDENCE (36) W-D,S	19 5 19 17 XSQ= 3.26 PHI= 0.233 XP = 0.0711
254	TILT TOWARD BEING THOSE 0.88 OF 8 WHERE HOUSEHOLD AUTHORITY IS ON THE FATHER'S SIDE, RATHER THAN THE MOTHER'S (9) DA	254	TILT TOWARD BEING THOSE 0.71 OF 7 WHERE HOUSEHOLD AUTHORITY IS ON THE MOTHER'S SIDE, RATHER THAN THE FATHER'S (6) DA	7 2 1 5 XSQ= 3.23 PHI= 0.464 EP = 0.0406
257	DRIFT TOWARD BEING THOSE 0.89 OF 9 WHERE THE SEVERITY OF SISTER AVOIDANCE IS LOW (17) WNS	257	DRIFT TOWARD BEING THOSE 0.50 OF 18 WHERE THE SEVERITY OF SISTER AVOIDANCE IS HIGH (10) WNS	1 9 8 9 XSQ= 2.40 PHI= -0.298 EP = 0.0912
279	TILT TOWARD BEING THOSE 0.50 OF 18 WHERE WIFE-LENDING OR WIFE-EXCHANGE IS PRESENT (10) LWS	279	TILT TOWARD BEING THOSE 0.91 OF 11 WHERE WIFE-LENDING AND WIFE EXCHANGE ARE UNIMPORTANT OR ABSENT (19) LWS	9 1 9 10 XSQ= 3.41 PHI= 0.343 EP = 0.0436
280	TILT TOWARD BEING THOSE 0.67 OF 15 WHERE THE COMPOSITE FERTILITY LEVEL IS LOW (12) MN	280	TILT TOWARD BEING THOSE 0.80 OF 10 WHERE THE COMPOSITE FERTILITY LEVEL IS HIGH (13) MN	5 8 10 2 XSQ= 3.53 PHI= -0.376 EP = 0.0414
301	DRIFT MORE TOWARD BEING THOSE 0.83 OF 77 WHERE THE POST-PARTUM SEX TABOO LASTS LONGER THAN ONE MONTH (96)	301	DRIFT LESS TOWARD BEING THOSE 0.68 OF 47 WHERE THE POST-PARTUM SEX TABOO LASTS LONGER THAN ONE MONTH (96)	64 32 13 15 XSQ= 2.96 PHI= 0.155 XP = 0.0853

314	LEAN LESS TOWARD BEING THOSE 0.65 OF 48 WHERE THE INCIDENCE OF MOTHER-CHILD HOUSEHOLDS IS LOW (61) W-D,S	314	LEAN MORE TOWARD BEING THOSE 0.94 OF 32 WHERE THE INCIDENCE OF MOTHER-CHILD HOUSEHOLDS IS LOW (61) W-D,S	17 2 31 30 XSQ= 7.48 PHI= 0.306 XP = 0.0062
370	TEND TO BE THOSE 0.50 OF 145 WHERE THE SEGREGATION OF ADOLESCENT BOYS IS COMPLETE OR PARTIAL (95)	370	TEND TO BE THOSE 0.78 OF 98 WHERE THE SEGREGATION OF ADOLESCENT BOYS IS ABSENT (148)	73 22 72 76 XSQ= 17.96 PHI= 0.272 XP = 0.0000
377	TEND LESS TO BE THOSE 0.65 OF 193 WHERE MALE GENITAL MUTILATION IS ABSENT (242)	377	TEND MORE TO BE THOSE 0.88 OF 129 WHERE MALE GENITAL MUTILATION IS ABSENT (242)	67 15 126 114 XSQ= 20.51 PHI= 0.252 XP = 0.0000
386	DRIFT TOWARD BEING THOSE 0.63 OF 46 WHERE SEXUAL EXPRESSION BY THE YOUNG IS RESTRICTED OR SEMI-RESTRICTED (46) F-B	386	DRIFT TOWARD BEING THOSE 0.57 OF 40 WHERE SEXUAL EXPRESSION BY THE YOUNG IS PERMITTED (40) F-B	29 17 17 23 XSQ= 2.85 PHI= 0.182 XP = 0.0913
419	DRIFT MORE TOWARD BEING THOSE 0.74 OF 46 WHERE MILITARY GLORY IS STRONGLY OR MODERATELY EMPHASIZED (55) PES	419	DRIFT LESS TOWARD BEING THOSE 0.52 OF 40 WHERE MILITARY GLORY IS STRONGLY OR MODERATELY EMPHASIZED (55) PES	34 21 12 19 XSQ= 3.38 PHI= 0.198 XP = 0.0661
420	TILT TOWARD BEING THOSE 0.59 OF 46 WHERE BELLICOSITY IS EXTREME (41) PES	420	TILT TOWARD BEING THOSE 0.66 OF 41 WHERE BELLICOSITY IS MODERATE OR NEGLIGIBLE (46) PES	27 14 19 27 XSQ= 4.30 PHI= 0.222 XP = 0.0380
424	DRIFT TOWARD BEING THOSE 0.74 OF 27 WHERE RELIGIOUS SPECIALISTS ARE PART-TIME, RATHER THAN FULL-TIME (33) JMH	424	DRIFT TOWARD BEING THOSE 0.52 OF 27 WHERE RELIGIOUS SPECIALISTS ARE FULL-TIME, RATHER THAN PART-TIME (21) JMH	7 14 20 13 XSQ= 2.81 PHI= -0.228 XP = 0.0940
426	LEAN TOWARD BEING THOSE 0.68 OF 152 WHERE A HIGH GOD IS PRESENT (156) GES,EA	426	LEAN TOWARD BEING THOSE 0.51 OF 106 WHERE A HIGH GOD IS ABSENT (104) GES,EA	104 52 48 54 XSQ= 9.00 PHI= 0.187 XP = 0.0027
430	TILT TOWARD BEING THOSE 0.55 OF 22 WHERE SUPERNATURAL SANCTIONS FOR MORALITY, HAVING AN EFFECT ON AN INDIVIDUAL'S HEALTH, ARE PRESENT (16) GES	430	TILT TOWARD BEING THOSE 0.80 OF 15 WHERE SUPERNATURAL SANCTIONS FOR MORALITY, HAVING AN EFFECT ON AN INDIVIDUAL'S HEALTH, ARE ABSENT OR UNREPORTED (22) GES	12 3 10 12 XSQ= 3.10 PHI= 0.289 EP = 0.0471

437	TILT TOWARD BEING THOSE WHERE FEAR OF GHOSTS, SPIRITS, HUMANS OR ANIMALS IS LOW (23) W-C,JFG	0.68 OF 25	437	TILT TOWARD BEING THOSE WHERE FEAR OF GHOSTS, SPIRITS, HUMANS OR ANIMALS IS HIGH (21) W-C,JFG	0.68 OF 19	8 13 17 6 XSQ= 4.37 PHI= -0.315 XP = 0.0365
442	TILT TOWARD BEING THOSE WHERE FEAR OF ANIMAL SPIRITS IS LOW (33) W-C	0.71 OF 31	442	TILT TOWARD BEING THOSE WHERE FEAR OF ANIMAL SPIRITS IS HIGH (28) W-C	0.63 OF 30	9 19 22 11 XSQ= 5.91 PHI= -0.311 XP = 0.0151
443	TILT TOWARD BEING THOSE WHERE OVERALL FEAR OF OTHERS IS LOW (30) W-C	0.65 OF 31	443	TILT TOWARD BEING THOSE WHERE OVERALL FEAR OF OTHERS IS HIGH (31) W-C	0.67 OF 30	11 20 20 10 XSQ= 4.75 PHI= -0.279 XP = 0.0293
454	LEAN TOWARD BEING THOSE WHERE THE OBJECTIVE OF THE INDIVIDUAL'S CONTACT WITH THE DIVINE IS CONDUCIVE TO THE DEVELOPMENT OF THE INDIVIDUAL'S NEED TO ACHIEVE (18) DCM	0.73 OF 22	454	LEAN TOWARD BEING THOSE WHERE THE OBJECTIVE OF THE INDIVIDUAL'S CONTACT WITH THE DIVINE IS NOT CONDUCIVE TO THE DEVELOPMENT OF THE INDIVIDUAL'S NEED TO ACHIEVE (18) DCM	0.85 OF 13	16 2 6 11 XSQ= 8.58 PHI= 0.495 EP = 0.0016
458	TILT LESS TOWARD BEING THOSE WHERE GAMES, IF PRESENT, DO NOT INCLUDE GAMES OF STRATEGY (119) R-A-B,EA	0.61 OF 84	458	TILT MORE TOWARD BEING THOSE WHERE GAMES, IF PRESENT, DO NOT INCLUDE GAMES OF STRATEGY (119) R-A-B,EA	0.78 OF 87	33 19 51 68 XSQ= 5.35 PHI= 0.177 XP = 0.0207
459	DRIFT TOWARD BEING THOSE WHERE GAMES, IF PRESENT, DO NOT INCLUDE GAMES OF CHANCE (89) R-A-B,EA	0.60 OF 84	459	DRIFT TOWARD BEING THOSE WHERE GAMES, IF PRESENT, INCLUDE GAMES OF CHANCE (82) R-A-B,EA	0.55 OF 87	34 48 50 39 XSQ= 3.13 PHI= -0.135 XP = 0.0767
473	DRIFT LESS TOWARD BEING THOSE WHERE SENSITIVITY TO INSULT IS MODERATE OR NEGLIGIBLE (56) PES	0.54 OF 48	473	DRIFT MORE TOWARD BEING THOSE WHERE SENSITIVITY TO INSULT IS MODERATE OR NEGLIGIBLE (56) PES	0.75 OF 40	22 10 26 30 XSQ= 3.24 PHI= 0.192 XP = 0.0718

264 CULTURES
WHERE WIVES ARE OBTAINED BY
BRIDE-PRICE (163)

264 CULTURES
WHERE WIVES ARE OBTAINED BY
MEANS OTHER THAN
BRIDE-PRICE (232)

BACKGROUND ON PAGE 128

SUBJECT ONLY

163 IN LEFT COLUMN

ABIPON	ABOR	ALBANIANS	ALORESE	ARAUCANIANS	ARYANS	ASHANTI	ATAYAL	AZANDE	BABWA
BAJUN	BAMBARA	BAMILEKE	BARABRA	BARI	BASSERI	BATAK	BAYA	BEJA	BELU
BENGALI	BETE	BHIL	BHUIYA	BIRIFOR	BOZO	BUDUMA	BURYAT	CAMBODIANS	CHAGGA
CHENCHU	CHERKESS	CHIBCHA	DAGUR	DARD	DILLING	DOROBO	DUSUN	EGYPTIANS	ENGA
FANG	FON	FUTAJALONKE	GANDA	GILBERTESE	GILYAK	GISU	GOAJIRO	GOND	GROS VENTRE
HASANIA	HAZARA	HEBREWS	HEHE	HERERO	HO	IFUGAO	ILA	IRAQW	JUKUN
KABYLE	KACHIN	KALMYK	KAPAUKU	KAZAK	KET	KHALKA	KHEVSUR	KIKUYU	KISSI
KOHISTANI	KOL	KPE	KUBA	KUMYK	KURTATCHI	LAKALAI	LAKHER	LAMET	LANGO
LEPCHA	LESU	LHOTA NAGA	LIFU	LOLO	LUBA	LUO	MACASSARESE	MAGUZAWA	MALAYS
MAMVU	MANCHU	MARGI	MASAI	MATAKAM	MBUGWE	MBUNDU	MENDE	MIAO	MIN CHINESE
MINCHIA	MONGO	MONGUOR	MOSSI	MOTA	MZAB	NANDI	NUER	NUPE	NURI
NYAKYUSA	NYANEKA	NYARO	NYORO	ORAON	PAIWAN	PALAUANS	PARAUJANO	PATHAN	PURARI
REGEIBAT	RIFFIANS	ROTINESE	RWALA	SAMOYED	SANDAWE	SANTAL	SARAMACCA	SARSI	SENIANG
SERI	SHILLUK	SHLUH	SIMBOESE	SIUAI	SIWANS	SOMALI	SONGHAI	SOTHO	SUBANUN
SWAZI	SYRIANS	TALLENSI	TANIMBARESE	TEDA	TESO	TETON	THONGA	TIWI	TOLOWA
TORAJA	TSHIMSHIAN	TUBATULABAL	TURKANA	TURKMEN	ULAWANS	VENDA	WOLOF	WUTE	YAKO
YOMBE	YORUBA	YUROK							

232 IN RIGHT COLUMN

5 EXCLUDED BECAUSE UNASCERTAINED

3	TEND LESS TO BE THOSE LOCATED OUTSIDE OF AFRICA (320)	0.64 OF 163	3	TEND MORE TO BE THOSE LOCATED OUTSIDE OF AFRICA (320)	0.91 OF 232	59 21 104 211 XSQ= 42.01 PHI= 0.326 XP = 0.
4	DRIFT LESS TOWARD BEING THOSE LOCATED OUTSIDE OF THE CIRCUM-MEDITERRANEAN (355)	0.85 OF 163	4	DRIFT MORE TOWARD BEING THOSE LOCATED OUTSIDE OF THE CIRCUM-MEDITERRANEAN (355)	0.91 OF 232	25 20 138 212 XSQ= 3.64 PHI= 0.096 XP = 0.0564
5	TILT LESS TOWARD BEING THOSE LOCATED OUTSIDE OF EAST EURASIA (330)	0.77 OF 163	5	TILT MORE TOWARD BEING THOSE LOCATED OUTSIDE OF EAST EURASIA (330)	0.86 OF 232	38 32 125 200 XSQ= 5.32 PHI= 0.116 XP = 0.0211

8	TEND MORE TO BE THOSE LOCATED OUTSIDE OF NORTH AMERICA (330)	0.95 OF 163	8	TEND LESS TO BE THOSE LOCATED OUTSIDE OF NORTH AMERICA (330)	0.74 OF 232	8 60 155 172 XSQ= 28.04 PHI= -0.266 XP = 0.0000
9	TEND MORE TO BE THOSE LOCATED OUTSIDE OF SOUTH AMERICA (335)	0.96 OF 163	9	TEND LESS TO BE THOSE LOCATED OUTSIDE OF SOUTH AMERICA (335)	0.75 OF 232	6 57 157 175 XSQ= 29.62 PHI= -0.274 XP = 0.0000
12	TILT MORE TOWARD BEING THOSE WHERE THE LATITUDE IS LESS THAN FIFTY DEGREES (367)	0.96 OF 163	12	TILT LESS TOWARD BEING THOSE WHERE THE LATITUDE IS LESS THAN FIFTY DEGREES (367)	0.89 OF 232	7 26 156 206 XSQ= 5.11 PHI= -0.114 XP = 0.0238
13	TILT MORE TOWARD BEING THOSE WHERE THE LATITUDE IS LESS THAN FORTY DEGREES (329)	0.88 OF 163	13	TILT LESS TOWARD BEING THOSE WHERE THE LATITUDE IS LESS THAN FORTY DEGREES (329)	0.78 OF 232	19 51 144 181 XSQ= 6.31 PHI= -0.126 XP = 0.0120
14	TILT MORE TOWARD BEING THOSE WHERE THE LATITUDE IS LESS THAN THIRTY DEGREES (281)	0.77 OF 163	14	TILT LESS TOWARD BEING THOSE WHERE THE LATITUDE IS LESS THAN THIRTY DEGREES (281)	0.65 OF 232	37 81 126 151 XSQ= 6.25 PHI= -0.126 XP = 0.0124
16	LEAN LESS TOWARD BEING THOSE WHERE THE LATITUDE IS TEN DEGREES OR GREATER (277)	0.61 OF 163	16	LEAN MORE TOWARD BEING THOSE WHERE THE LATITUDE IS TEN DEGREES OR GREATER (277)	0.75 OF 232	100 173 63 59 XSQ= 7.23 PHI= -0.135 XP = 0.0072
44	TILT MORE TOWARD BEING THOSE WHERE SETTLEMENTS ARE FIXED (222)	0.76 OF 131	44	TILT LESS TOWARD BEING THOSE WHERE SETTLEMENTS ARE FIXED (222)	0.62 OF 198	99 123 32 75 XSQ= 5.90 PHI= 0.134 XP = 0.0151
45	TILT LESS TOWARD BEING THOSE WHERE SETTLEMENTS, IF FIXED, ARE COMPACT, RATHER THAN NON-COMPACT (149)	0.59 OF 99	45	TILT MORE TOWARD BEING THOSE WHERE SETTLEMENTS, IF FIXED, ARE COMPACT, RATHER THAN NON-COMPACT (149)	0.74 OF 123	58 91 41 32 XSQ= 5.22 PHI= -0.153 XP = 0.0224
46	DRIFT MORE TOWARD BEING THOSE OTHER THAN WHERE SETTLEMENTS ARE NON-FIXED AND MOVEMENT IS NOMADIC (260)	0.84 OF 131	46	DRIFT LESS TOWARD BEING THOSE OTHER THAN WHERE SETTLEMENTS ARE NON-FIXED AND MOVEMENT IS NOMADIC (260)	0.75 OF 198	21 49 110 149 XSQ= 3.08 PHI= -0.097 XP = 0.0795

48	DRIFT TOWARD BEING THOSE 0.67 OF 30 WHERE THE FOOD SUPPLY IS NOT SECURE, AND FOOD SHORTAGES ARE FREQUENT OR ANNUAL (41) MGW	48	DRIFT TOWARD BEING THOSE 0.56 OF 48 WHERE THE FOOD SUPPLY IS SECURE, AND FOOD SHORTAGES ARE RARE OR OCCASIONAL (38) MGW	10 27 20 21 XSQ= 3.02 PHI= -0.197 XP = 0.0821
51	TEND MORE TO BE THOSE 0.83 OF 163 WHERE SUBSISTENCE IS PRIMARILY BY FOOD PRODUCTION -- I. E., AGRICULTURE OR HUSBANDRY -- RATHER THAN BY GATHERING (253)	51	TEND LESS TO BE THOSE 0.50 OF 232 WHERE SUBSISTENCE IS PRIMARILY BY FOOD PRODUCTION -- I. E., AGRICULTURE OR HUSBANDRY -- RATHER THAN BY GATHERING (253)	135 117 28 115 XSQ= 42.10 PHI= 0.326 XP = 0.
53	TILT LESS TOWARD BEING THOSE 0.54 OF 110 WHERE FOOD PRODUCTION IS BY SIMPLE AGRICULTURE OR INCIPIENT FOOD PRODUCTION, RATHER THAN BY INTENSIVE AGRICULTURE (147)	53	TILT MORE TOWARD BEING THOSE 0.68 OF 126 WHERE FOOD PRODUCTION IS BY SIMPLE AGRICULTURE OR INCIPIENT FOOD PRODUCTION, RATHER THAN BY INTENSIVE AGRICULTURE (147)	51 40 59 86 XSQ= 4.70 PHI= 0.141 XP = 0.0302
54	TEND MORE TO BE THOSE 0.92 OF 110 WHERE FOOD PRODUCTION IS BY INTENSIVE OR SIMPLE AGRICULTURE, RATHER THAN BY INCIPIENT FOOD PRODUCTION (192)	54	TEND LESS TO BE THOSE 0.72 OF 126 WHERE FOOD PRODUCTION IS BY INTENSIVE OR SIMPLE AGRICULTURE, RATHER THAN BY INCIPIENT FOOD PRODUCTION (192)	101 91 9 35 XSQ= 13.60 PHI= 0.240 XP = 0.0002
56	LEAN MORE TOWARD BEING THOSE 0.85 OF 59 WHERE FOOD PRODUCTION IS BY SIMPLE AGRICULTURE, RATHER THAN BY INCIPIENT FOOD PRODUCTION (101)	56	LEAN LESS TOWARD BEING THOSE 0.59 OF 86 WHERE FOOD PRODUCTION IS BY SIMPLE AGRICULTURE, RATHER THAN BY INCIPIENT FOOD PRODUCTION (101)	50 51 9 35 XSQ= 9.55 PHI= 0.257 XP = 0.0020
62	TEND TO BE THOSE 0.74 OF 163 WHERE HUSBANDRY OF SOME KIND IS PRESENT (228)	62	TEND TO BE THOSE 0.53 OF 232 WHERE HUSBANDRY OF ANY KIND IS ABSENT (172)	120 108 43 124 XSQ= 27.64 PHI= 0.265 XP = 0.0000
71	TEND TO BE THOSE 0.66 OF 86 WHERE METAL WORKING IS PRESENT (98)	71	TEND TO BE THOSE 0.75 OF 162 WHERE METAL WORKING IS ABSENT (153)	57 41 29 121 XSQ= 37.76 PHI= 0.390 XP = 0.
82	TILT MORE TOWARD BEING THOSE 0.88 OF 85 WHERE A CITY OR TOWN IS PRESENT, OR THE AVERAGE COMMUNITY SIZE IS FIFTY OR GREATER (178)	82	TILT LESS TOWARD BEING THOSE 0.75 OF 138 WHERE A CITY OR TOWN IS PRESENT, OR THE AVERAGE COMMUNITY SIZE IS FIFTY OR GREATER (178)	75 103 10 35 XSQ= 5.22 PHI= 0.153 XP = 0.0223
83	TILT LESS TOWARD BEING THOSE 0.65 OF 69 WHERE, WITH NO CITY AND NO TOWN PRESENT, THE AVERAGE COMMUNITY SIZE IS SMALLER THAN 200, RATHER THAN BETWEEN 200 AND 999 (135)	83	TILT MORE TOWARD BEING THOSE 0.81 OF 110 WHERE, WITH NO CITY AND NO TOWN PRESENT, THE AVERAGE COMMUNITY SIZE IS SMALLER THAN 200, RATHER THAN BETWEEN 200 AND 999 (135)	24 21 45 89 XSQ= 4.75 PHI= 0.163 XP = 0.0294

86	LEAN TOWARD BEING THOSE 0.58 OF 120 WHERE THE LEVEL OF POLITICAL INTEGRATION IS THE LARGE STATE, THE LITTLE STATE, OR THE MINIMAL STATE (148) GPM	86	LEAN TOWARD BEING THOSE 0.58 OF 181 WHERE THE LEVEL OF POLITICAL INTEGRATION IS THE AUTONOMOUS COMMUNITY, OR THE FAMILY (156) GPM	70 76 50 105 XSQ= 7.08 PHI= 0.153 XP = 0.0078
96	TEND TO BE THOSE 0.67 OF 131 WHERE THE HIERARCHY OF NATIONAL JURISDICTION HAS FOUR, THREE, TWO OR ONE LEVEL (174) GES,EA	96	TEND TO BE THOSE 0.57 OF 196 WHERE THE HIERARCHY OF NATIONAL JURISDICTION HAS NO LEVELS (156) GES,EA	88 85 43 111 XSQ= 16.92 PHI= 0.227 XP = 0.0000
97	LEAN LESS TOWARD BEING THOSE 0.75 OF 131 WHERE THE HIERARCHY OF LOCAL JURISDICTION HAS THREE OR TWO LEVELS (273) GES,EA	97	LEAN MORE TOWARD BEING THOSE 0.87 OF 197 WHERE THE HIERARCHY OF LOCAL JURISDICTION HAS THREE OR TWO LEVELS (273) GES,EA	33 25 98 172 XSQ= 7.61 PHI= 0.152 XP = 0.0058
98	LEAN MORE TOWARD BEING THOSE 0.82 OF 131 WHERE THE HIERARCHY OF LOCAL JURISDICTION HAS FOUR OR THREE LEVELS (238) GES,EA	98	LEAN LESS TOWARD BEING THOSE 0.66 OF 197 WHERE THE HIERARCHY OF LOCAL JURISDICTION HAS FOUR OR THREE LEVELS (238) GES,EA	107 130 24 67 XSQ= 8.89 PHI= 0.165 XP = 0.0029
99	TILT MORE TOWARD BEING THOSE 0.77 OF 43 WHERE, WITH NATIONAL HIERARCHY ABSENT, THE HIERARCHY OF LOCAL JURISDICTION HAS FOUR OR THREE LEVELS (93) GES,EA	99	TILT LESS TOWARD BEING THOSE 0.54 OF 111 WHERE, WITH NATIONAL HIERARCHY ABSENT, THE HIERARCHY OF LOCAL JURISDICTION HAS FOUR OR THREE LEVELS (93) GES,EA	33 60 10 51 XSQ= 5.76 PHI= 0.193 XP = 0.0164
100	TEND MORE TO BE THOSE 0.92 OF 131 WHERE HIERARCHIES ARE MORE COMPLEX THAN THE 'SIMPLEST,' I. E., MORE COMPLEX THAN TWO LOCAL LEVELS WITH NO NATIONAL LEVELS (267) GES,EA	100	TEND LESS TO BE THOSE 0.74 OF 196 WHERE HIERARCHIES ARE MORE COMPLEX THAN THE 'SIMPLEST,' I. E., MORE COMPLEX THAN TWO LOCAL LEVELS WITH NO NATIONAL LEVELS (267) GES,EA	121 145 10 51 XSQ= 16.30 PHI= 0.223 XP = 0.0001
102	TEND TO BE THOSE 0.68 OF 156 WHERE CLASS STRATIFICATION IS PRESENT (203)	102	TEND TO BE THOSE 0.57 OF 223 WHERE CLASS STRATIFICATION IS ABSENT (180)	106 96 50 127 XSQ= 21.87 PHI= 0.240 XP = 0.0000
107	TILT MORE TOWARD BEING THOSE 0.86 OF 106 WHERE CLASS STRATIFICATION, IF PRESENT, IS BASED ON SOMETHING OTHER THAN OCCUPATIONAL STATUS (160)	107	TILT LESS TOWARD BEING THOSE 0.71 OF 96 WHERE CLASS STRATIFICATION, IF PRESENT, IS BASED ON SOMETHING OTHER THAN OCCUPATIONAL STATUS (160)	15 28 91 68 XSQ= 5.91 PHI= -0.171 XP = 0.0150
108	TILT LESS TOWARD BEING THOSE 0.57 OF 106 WHERE CLASS STRATIFICATION, IF PRESENT, IS BASED ON SOMETHING OTHER THAN A HEREDITARY ARISTOCRACY (129)	108	TILT MORE TOWARD BEING THOSE 0.72 OF 96 WHERE CLASS STRATIFICATION, IF PRESENT, IS BASED ON SOMETHING OTHER THAN A HEREDITARY ARISTOCRACY (129)	46 27 60 69 XSQ= 4.45 PHI= 0.148 XP = 0.0349

```
109  TEND LESS TO BE THOSE            0.76 OF 139     109  TEND MORE TO BE THOSE            0.92 OF 225        33   18
     WHERE CASTES ARE ABSENT   (317)                       WHERE CASTES ARE ABSENT   (317)                   106  207
                                                                                                        XSQ=    16.39
                                                                                                        PHI=    0.212
                                                                                                        XP =   0.0001

110  TEND TO BE THOSE                 0.62 OF 154     110  TEND TO BE THOSE                 0.70 OF 224        95   68
     WHERE SLAVERY IS PRESENT   (163)                      WHERE SLAVERY IS ABSENT   (218)                    59  156
                                                                                                        XSQ=    35.26
                                                                                                        PHI=    0.305
                                                                                                        XP =   0.

128  DRIFT TOWARD BEING THOSE         0.60 OF  40     128  DRIFT TOWARD BEING THOSE         0.65 OF  37        16   24
     WHERE, IF SUBSISTENCE IS PRIMARILY BY                 WHERE, IF SUBSISTENCE IS PRIMARILY BY              24   13
     AGRICULTURE, THE WORK IS                              AGRICULTURE, THE WORK IS                     XSQ=     3.82
     MAINLY DONE BY FEMALES   (37)                         MAINLY DONE BY MALES   (40)                  PHI=   -0.223
                                                                                                        XP =   0.0507

129  TEND TO BE THOSE                 0.54 OF  37     129  TEND TO BE THOSE                 0.83 OF  66        20   11
     WHERE WEAVING IS                                      WHERE WEAVING IS                                   17   55
     MAINLY DONE BY MALES   (31)                           MAINLY DONE BY FEMALES   (73)                XSQ=    14.03
                                                                                                        PHI=    0.369
                                                                                                        XP =   0.0002

130  TILT TOWARD BEING THOSE          0.67 OF  30     130  TILT TOWARD BEING THOSE          0.65 OF  54        20   19
     WHERE LEATHER WORKING IS                              WHERE LEATHER WORKING IS                           10   35
     MAINLY DONE BY MALES   (39)                           MAINLY DONE BY FEMALES   (45)                XSQ=     6.47
                                                                                                        PHI=    0.278
                                                                                                        XP =   0.0110

144  TILT TOWARD BEING THOSE          0.71 OF  24     144  TILT TOWARD BEING THOSE          0.64 OF  28        17   10
     WHERE THE RATIO OF RESTITUTIVE                        WHERE THE RATIO OF RESTITUTIVE                      7   18
     TO REPRESSIVE SANCTIONS                               TO REPRESSIVE SANCTIONS                      XSQ=     5.06
     IS HIGH OR MEDIUM   (27) WME                          IS LOW   (25) WME                            PHI=    0.312
                                                                                                        XP =   0.0245

176  TEND TO BE THOSE                 0.59 OF 155     176  TEND TO BE THOSE                 0.66 OF 223        91   75
     WHERE THE COMMUNITY IS                                WHERE THE COMMUNITY IS OTHER THAN                  64  148
     A CLAN-COMMUNITY OR A COMMUNITY                       A CLAN-COMMUNITY OR A COMMUNITY              XSQ=    22.34
     STRUCTURED OR SEGMENTED                               STRUCTURED OR SEGMENTED                      PHI=    0.243
     ON A CLAN BASIS   (169)                               ON A CLAN BASIS   (213)                      XP =   0.0000

177  TEND LESS TO BE THOSE            0.70 OF 155     177  TEND MORE TO BE THOSE            0.87 OF 223        46   30
     WHERE THE COMMUNITY IS OTHER THAN                     WHERE THE COMMUNITY IS OTHER THAN                 109  193
     A SINGLE CLAN-COMMUNITY AND                           A SINGLE CLAN-COMMUNITY AND                  XSQ=    13.99
     EXOGAMOUS   (305)                                     EXOGAMOUS   (305)                            PHI=    0.192
                                                                                                        XP =   0.0002

178  DRIFT LESS TOWARD BEING THOSE    0.72 OF 155     178  DRIFT MORE TOWARD BEING THOSE    0.81 OF 223        43   42
     WHERE THE COMMUNITY IS OTHER THAN                     WHERE THE COMMUNITY IS OTHER THAN                 112  181
     SEGMENTED ON A CLAN BASIS AND                         SEGMENTED ON A CLAN BASIS AND                XSQ=     3.67
     NON-EXOGAMOUS   (295)                                 NON-EXOGAMOUS   (295)                        PHI=    0.099
                                                                                                        XP =   0.0555
```

180	TEND LESS TO BE THOSE WHERE THE COMMUNITY IS COMMONLY NON-EXOGAMOUS, RATHER THAN EXOGAMOUS (258)	0.57 OF 155	180	TEND MORE TO BE THOSE WHERE THE COMMUNITY IS COMMONLY NON-EXOGAMOUS, RATHER THAN EXOGAMOUS (258)	0.74 OF 223	66 57 89 166 XSQ= 11.30 PHI= 0.173 XP = 0.0008
181	LEAN MORE TOWARD BEING THOSE WHERE THE COMMUNITY IS OTHER THAN A DEME (337)	0.95 OF 155	181	LEAN LESS TOWARD BEING THOSE WHERE THE COMMUNITY IS OTHER THAN A DEME (337)	0.84 OF 223	8 36 147 187 XSQ= 9.68 PHI= -0.160 XP = 0.0019
182	LEAN MORE TOWARD BEING THOSE OTHER THAN WHERE THE COMMUNITY IS STRUCTURED ON A NON-CLAN BASIS AND AGAMOUS (256)	0.75 OF 155	182	LEAN LESS TOWARD BEING THOSE OTHER THAN WHERE THE COMMUNITY IS STRUCTURED ON A NON-CLAN BASIS AND AGAMOUS (256)	0.61 OF 223	38 88 117 135 XSQ= 8.53 PHI= -0.150 XP = 0.0035
183	TEND MORE TO BE THOSE WHERE THE LARGEST NON-COGNATIC KIN GROUP IS SMALLER THAN A MOEITY, I. E., A PHRATRY OR SIB OR LINEAGE (218)	0.96 OF 140	183	TEND LESS TO BE THOSE WHERE THE LARGEST NON-COGNATIC KIN GROUP IS SMALLER THAN A MOEITY, I. E., A PHRATRY OR SIB OR LINEAGE (218)	0.76 OF 109	6 26 134 83 XSQ= 19.24 PHI= -0.278 XP = 0.0000
186	TEND TO BE THOSE WHERE THE KIN GROUP IS EXCLUSIVELY PATRILINEAL (150)	0.63 OF 163	186	TEND TO BE THOSE WHERE THE KIN GROUP IS OTHER THAN EXCLUSIVELY PATRILINEAL (250)	0.80 OF 232	102 46 61 186 XSQ= 72.86 PHI= 0.429 XP = 0.
187	LEAN MORE TOWARD BEING THOSE WHERE THE KIN GROUP IS OTHER THAN EXCLUSIVELY MATRILINEAL (344)	0.93 OF 163	187	LEAN LESS TOWARD BEING THOSE WHERE THE KIN GROUP IS OTHER THAN EXCLUSIVELY MATRILINEAL (344)	0.81 OF 231	11 43 152 188 XSQ= 10.40 PHI= -0.162 XP = 0.0013
188	TEND TO BE THOSE WHERE THE KIN GROUP IS OTHER THAN EXCLUSIVELY COGNATIC (252)	0.86 OF 163	188	TEND TO BE THOSE WHERE THE KIN GROUP IS EXCLUSIVELY COGNATIC (148)	0.53 OF 232	23 123 140 109 XSQ= 60.54 PHI= -0.391 XP = 0.
190	TEND MORE TO BE THOSE WHERE THE KIN GROUP IS PATRILINEAL OR DOUBLE-DESCENT, RATHER THAN MATRILINEAL (186)	0.90 OF 139	190	TEND LESS TO BE THOSE WHERE THE KIN GROUP IS PATRILINEAL OR DOUBLE-DESCENT, RATHER THAN MATRILINEAL (186)	0.56 OF 105	125 59 14 46 XSQ= 34.92 PHI= 0.378 XP = 0.
192	TEND MORE TO BE THOSE OTHER THAN WHERE THE ONLY KIN GROUP PRESENT IS A KINDRED OR ELSE BILATERAL DESCENT IS INFERRED (289)	0.90 OF 163	192	TEND LESS TO BE THOSE OTHER THAN WHERE THE ONLY KIN GROUP PRESENT IS A KINDRED OR ELSE BILATERAL DESCENT IS INFERRED (289)	0.60 OF 232	17 92 146 140 XSQ= 39.48 PHI= -0.316 XP = 0.

196	TEND MCRE TO BE THCSE 0.80 OF 131 WHERE INDIVIDUAL RIGHTS IN REAL PROPERTY, AND RULES FOR INHERITANCE, ARE PRESENT (194)	196	TEND LESS TO BE THOSE 0.59 CF 149 WHERE INDIVIDUAL RIGHTS IN REAL PRCPERTY, AND RULES FOR INHERITANCE, ARE PRESENT (194)	105 88 26 61 XSQ= 13.51 PHI= 0.220 XP = 0.0002
197	TEND MORE TC BE THCSE 0.95 OF 105 WHERE RULES FCR THE INHERITANCE OF REAL PRCPERTY, IF PRESENT, FAVOR EITHER THE MALE HEIR OR LINE, OR THE FEMALE HEIR CR LINE (165)	197	TEND LESS TO BE THOSE 0.73 CF 88 WHERE RULES FOR THE INHERITANCE CF REAL PROPERTY, IF PRESENT, FAVOR EITHER THE MALE HEIR CR LINE, OR THE FEMALE HEIR OR LINE (165)	100 64 5 24 XSQ= 17.28 PHI= 0.299 XP = 0.0000
198	TILT MCRE TOWARC BEING THCSE 0.93 OF 100 WHERE RULES FCR THE INHERITANCE OF REAL PRCPERTY, IF PRESENT, FAVOR THE MALE HEIR CR LINE, RATHER THAN THE FEMALE (144)	198	TILT LESS TOWARD BEING THOSE 0.80 OF 64 WHERE RULES FOR THE INHERITANCE CF REAL PROPERTY, IF PRESENT, FAVOR THE MALE HEIR OR LINE, RATHER THAN THE FEMALE (144)	93 51 7 13 XSQ= 5.28 PHI= 0.179 XP = 0.0216
201	LEAN MCRE TCWARC BEING THCSE 0.91 OF 163 WHERE MARITAL RESICENCE IS NCN-CPTICNAL, RATHER THAN AMBILCCAL CR NECLOCAL (334)	2C1	LEAN LESS TOWARD BEING THOSE 0.79 CF 230 WHERE MARITAL RESIDENCE IS NON-OPTIONAL, RATHER THAN AMBILOCAL OR NEOLOCAL (334)	149 182 14 48 XSQ= 9.92 PHI= 0.159 XP = 0.0016
204	TEND MCRE TO BE THCSE 0.91 OF 160 WHERE MARITAL RESICENCE IS PATRILCCAL, VIRILOCAL, OR AVUNCULOCAL, RATHER THAN AMBILCCAL CR NECLOCAL (270)	204	TEND LESS TO BE THOSE 0.72 CF 170 WHERE MARITAL RESIDENCE IS PATRILOCAL, VIRILOCAL, CR AVUNCULCCAL, RATHER THAN AMBILOCAL OR NECLOCAL (270)	146 122 14 48 XSQ= 19.25 PHI= 0.242 XP = 0.0000
207	LEAN TCWARC BEING THOSE 0.82 OF 17 WHERE MARITAL RESICENCE IS AMBILCCAL CR NECLOCAL, RATHER THAN MATRILCCAL OR UXCRILOCAL (64)	2C7	LEAN TOWARD BEING THOSE 0.56 CF 108 WHERE MARITAL RESIDENCE IS MATRILOCAL OR UXORILCCAL, RATHER THAN AMBILOCAL OR NECLOCAL (64)	3 60 14 48 XSQ= 7.00 PHI= -0.237 XP = 0.0082
209	TEND MCRE TO BE THCSE 0.98 OF 149 WHERE MARITAL RESICENCE IS PATRILCCAL, VIRILOCAL, CR AVUNCULOCAL, RATHER THAN MATRILCCAL OR UXCRILOCAL (270)	209	TEND LESS TO BE THOSE 0.67 CF 182 WHERE MARITAL RESIDENCE IS PATRILOCAL, VIRILOCAL, CR AVUNCULCCAL, RATHER THAN MATRILOCAL OR UXORILOCAL (270)	146 122 3 60 XSQ= 48.95 PHI= 0.385 XP = 0.
210	TEND MCRE TC BE THCSE 0.98 OF 116 WHERE MARITAL RESICENCE IS PATRILCCAL, RATHER THAN MATRILOCAL (169)	21C	TEND LESS TO BE THOSE 0.65 CF 81 WHERE MARITAL RESIDENCE IS PATRILOCAL, RATHER THAN MATRILOCAL (169)	114 53 2 28 XSQ= 37.35 PHI= 0.435 XP = 0.
221	LEAN LESS TOWARC BEING THCSE 0.84 OF 153 WHERE MATRILATERAL CRCSS-CCUSIN MARRIAGE IS NCT PRESCRIBED CR PREFERREC (335)	221	LEAN MORE TOWARD BEING THOSE 0.95 CF 214 WHERE MATRILATERAL CROSS-CCUSIN MARRIAGE IS NOT PRESCRIBED OR PREFERRED (335)	24 11 129 203 XSQ= 10.31 PHI= 0.168 XP = 0.0013

No.	First item	No.	Second item	Table and statistics
224	TEND TO BE THOSE 0.60 OF 75 WHERE COUSIN MARRIAGE IS PREFERENTIALLY OR PERMISSIVELY EITHER PATRI- OR MATRILATERAL, RATHER THAN SYMMETRICAL (66)	224	TEND TO BE THOSE 0.78 OF 96 WHERE COUSIN MARRIAGE IS PREFERENTIALLY OR PERMISSIVELY SYMMETRICAL, RATHER THAN EITHER PATRI- OR MATRILATERAL (106)	45 21 30 75 XSQ= 24.24 PHI= 0.377 XP = 0.0000
241	TILT MORE TOWARD BEING THOSE 0.95 OF 84 WHERE THE FAMILY, IF EXTENDED, IS LARGE OR SMALL, RATHER THAN STEM (187)	241	TILT LESS TOWARD BEING THOSE 0.83 OF 127 WHERE THE FAMILY, IF EXTENDED, IS LARGE OR SMALL, RATHER THAN STEM (187)	80 105 4 22 XSQ= 6.27 PHI= 0.172 XP = 0.0123
242	TEND MORE TO BE THOSE 0.90 OF 163 WHERE MARRIAGE IS COMMONLY OR OCCASIONALLY POLYGYNOUS, RATHER THAN MONOGAMOUS (314)	242	TEND LESS TO BE THOSE 0.72 OF 227 WHERE MARRIAGE IS COMMONLY OR OCCASIONALLY POLYGYNOUS, RATHER THAN MONOGAMOUS (314)	146 163 17 64 XSQ= 17.13 PHI= 0.210 XP = 0.0000
243	TILT TOWARD BEING THOSE 0.58 OF 24 WHERE POLYGYNY, IF PRESENT, HAS A HIGH INCIDENCE (24) W-C,S	243	TILT TOWARD BEING THOSE 0.72 OF 36 WHERE POLYGYNY, IF PRESENT, HAS A LOW INCIDENCE (36) W-D,S	14 10 10 26 XSQ= 4.40 PHI= 0.271 XP = 0.0359
254	IN ALL CASES ARE THOSE 1.00 OF 6 WHERE HOUSEHOLD AUTHORITY IS ON THE FATHER'S SIDE, RATHER THAN THE MOTHER'S (9) CA	254	TILT TOWARD BEING THOSE 0.67 OF 9 WHERE HOUSEHOLD AUTHORITY IS ON THE MOTHER'S SIDE, RATHER THAN THE FATHER'S (6) DA	6 3 0 6 XSQ= 4.18 PHI= 0.528 EP = 0.0278
257	IN ALL CASES ARE THOSE 1.00 OF 7 WHERE THE SEVERITY OF SISTER AVOIDANCE IS LOW (17) WNS	257	TILT TOWARD BEING THOSE 0.50 OF 20 WHERE THE SEVERITY OF SISTER AVOIDANCE IS HIGH (10) WNS	0 10 7 10 XSQ= 3.62 PHI= -0.366 EP = 0.0261
278	TILT TOWARD BEING THOSE 0.67 OF 9 WHERE PROPERTY RIGHTS IN WOMEN ARE PRESENT (8) LWS	278	TILT TOWARD BEING THOSE 0.85 OF 13 WHERE PROPERTY RIGHTS IN WOMEN ARE UNIMPORTANT OR ABSENT (14) LWS	6 2 3 11 XSQ= 4.03 PHI= 0.428 EP = 0.0260
280	TILT TOWARD BEING THOSE 0.67 OF 15 WHERE THE COMPOSITE FERTILITY LEVEL IS LOW (12) MN	280	TILT TOWARD BEING THOSE 0.80 OF 10 WHERE THE COMPOSITE FERTILITY LEVEL IS HIGH (13) MN	5 8 10 2 XSQ= 3.53 PHI= -0.376 EP = 0.0414
282	DRIFT TOWARD BEING THOSE 0.64 OF 14 WHERE THE STRENGTH OF DESIRE FOR CHILDREN IS HIGH (16) BCA	282	DRIFT TOWARD BEING THOSE 0.68 OF 22 WHERE THE STRENGTH OF DESIRE FOR CHILDREN IS LOW OR ABSENT (20) BCA	9 7 5 15 XSQ= 2.46 PHI= 0.261 EP = 0.0874

301	DRIFT MORE TOWARD BEING THOSE 0.88 OF 48 WHERE THE POST-PARTUM SEX TABOO LASTS LONGER THAN ONE MONTH (96)	301	DRIFT LESS TOWARD BEING THOSE 0.71 OF 76 WHERE THE POST-PARTUM SEX TABOO LASTS LONGER THAN ONE MONTH (96)	42 54 6 22 XSQ= 3.66 PHI= 0.172 XP = 0.0557
314	TEND TO BE THOSE 0.50 OF 28 WHERE THE INCIDENCE OF MOTHER-CHILD HOUSEHOLDS IS HIGH (19) W-D,S	314	TEND TO BE THOSE 0.90 OF 52 WHERE THE INCIDENCE OF MOTHER-CHILD HOUSEHOLDS IS LOW (61) W-D,S	14 5 14 47 XSQ= 14.24 PHI= 0.422 XP = 0.0002
319	TILT TOWARD BEING THOSE 0.70 OF 23 WHERE PROTECTION OF THE INFANT FROM ENVIRONMENTAL DISCOMFORTS IS LOW (30) B-B-C	319	TILT TOWARD BEING THOSE 0.66 OF 41 WHERE PROTECTION OF THE INFANT FROM ENVIRONMENTAL DISCOMFORTS IS HIGH (35) B-B-C	7 27 16 14 XSQ= 6.07 PHI= -0.308 XP = 0.0138
336	LEAN TOWARD BEING THOSE 0.84 OF 25 WHERE THE TOTAL POSITIVE PRESSURE TOWARD DEVELOPING RESPONSIBLE BEHAVIOR IN THE CHILD IS HIGH (43) B-B-C	336	LEAN TOWARD BEING THOSE 0.55 OF 49 WHERE THE TOTAL POSITIVE PRESSURE TOWARD DEVELOPING RESPONSIBLE BEHAVIOR IN THE CHILD IS LOW (32) B-B-C	21 22 4 27 XSQ= 8.85 PHI= 0.346 XP = 0.0029
337	TEND TO BE THOSE 0.84 OF 25 WHERE THE CHILD'S INFERRED ANXIETY OVER NON-PERFORMANCE OF RESPONSIBLE BEHAVIOR IS HIGH (38) B-B-C	337	TEND TO BE THOSE 0.64 OF 47 WHERE THE CHILD'S INFERRED ANXIETY OVER NON-PERFORMANCE OF RESPONSIBLE BEHAVIOR IS LOW (35) B-B-C	21 17 4 30 XSQ= 13.12 PHI= 0.427 XP = 0.0003
338	DRIFT MORE TOWARD BEING THOSE 0.76 OF 25 WHERE THE CHILD'S INFERRED ANXIETY OVER PERFORMANCE OF RESPONSIBLE BEHAVIOR IS HIGH (44) B-B-C	338	DRIFT LESS TOWARD BEING THOSE 0.51 OF 47 WHERE THE CHILD'S INFERRED ANXIETY OVER PERFORMANCE OF RESPONSIBLE BEHAVIOR IS HIGH (44) B-B-C	19 24 6 23 XSQ= 3.25 PHI= 0.212 XP = 0.0716
339	LEAN TOWARD BEING THOSE 0.68 OF 25 WHERE THE CHILD'S INFERRED CONFLICT REGARDING RESPONSIBLE BEHAVIOR IS HIGH (31) B-B-C	339	LEAN TOWARD BEING THOSE 0.70 OF 47 WHERE THE CHILD'S INFERRED CONFLICT REGARDING RESPONSIBLE BEHAVIOR IS LOW (42) B-B-C	17 14 8 33 XSQ= 8.22 PHI= 0.338 XP = 0.0041
370	TEND TO BE THOSE 0.55 OF 97 WHERE THE SEGREGATION OF ADOLESCENT BOYS IS COMPLETE OR PARTIAL (95)	370	TEND TO BE THOSE 0.71 OF 146 WHERE THE SEGREGATION OF ADOLESCENT BOYS IS ABSENT (148)	53 42 44 104 XSQ= 15.31 PHI= 0.251 XP = 0.0001
377	TEND LESS TO BE THOSE 0.56 OF 130 WHERE MALE GENITAL MUTILATION IS ABSENT (242)	377	TEND MORE TO BE THOSE 0.87 OF 192 WHERE MALE GENITAL MUTILATION IS ABSENT (242)	57 25 73 167 XSQ= 37.20 PHI= 0.340 XP = 0.

391	TILT TOWARD BEING THOSE WHERE PREMARITAL SEX RELATIONS ARE STRONGLY PUNISHED AND IN FACT RARE, OR WEAKLY PUNISHED AND IN FACT NOT RARE (89) JTW,EA	0.60 OF 72	391	TILT TOWARD BEING THOSE WHERE PREMARITAL SEX RELATIONS ARE PUNISHED ONLY IF PREGNANCY RESULTS, OR FREELY PERMITTED (90) JTW,EA	0.57 OF 107	43 46 29 61 XSQ= 4.17 PHI= 0.153 XP = 0.0411
417	IN ALL CASES ARE THOSE WHERE WARFARE IS PREVALENT (34) LWS	1.00 OF 13	417	DRIFT LESS TOWARD BEING THOSE WHERE WARFARE IS PREVALENT (34) LWS	0.70 OF 30	13 21 0 9 XSQ= 3.29 PHI= 0.276 XP = 0.0699
419	DRIFT MORE TOWARD BEING THOSE WHERE MILITARY GLORY IS STRONGLY OR MODERATELY EMPHASIZED (55) PES	0.77 OF 31	419	DRIFT LESS TOWARD BEING THOSE WHERE MILITARY GLORY IS STRONGLY OR MODERATELY EMPHASIZED (55) PES	0.56 OF 55	24 31 7 24 XSQ= 2.95 PHI= 0.185 XP = 0.0857
420	LEAN TOWARD BEING THOSE WHERE BELLICOSITY IS EXTREME (41) PES	0.70 OF 30	420	LEAN TOWARD BEING THOSE WHERE BELLICOSITY IS MODERATE OR NEGLIGIBLE (46) PES	0.65 OF 57	21 20 9 37 XSQ= 8.26 PHI= 0.308 XP = 0.0040
426	TEND MORE TO BE THOSE WHERE A HIGH GOD IS PRESENT (156) GES,EA	0.75 OF 104	426	TEND LESS TO BE THOSE WHERE A HIGH GOD IS PRESENT (156) GES,EA	0.51 OF 154	78 78 26 76 XSQ= 14.40 PHI= 0.236 XP = 0.0001
430	TILT TOWARD BEING THOSE WHERE SUPERNATURAL SANCTIONS FOR MORALITY, HAVING AN EFFECT ON AN INDIVIDUAL'S HEALTH, ARE PRESENT (16) GES	0.67 OF 12	430	TILT TOWARD BEING THOSE WHERE SUPERNATURAL SANCTIONS FOR MORALITY, HAVING AN EFFECT ON AN INDIVIDUAL'S HEALTH, ARE ABSENT OR UNREPORTED (22) GES	0.72 OF 25	8 7 4 18 XSQ= 3.55 PHI= 0.310 EP = 0.0360
443	TILT TOWARD BEING THOSE WHERE OVERALL FEAR OF OTHERS IS LOW (30) W-C	0.70 OF 20	443	TILT TOWARD BEING THOSE WHERE OVERALL FEAR OF OTHERS IS HIGH (31) W-C	0.61 OF 41	6 25 14 16 XSQ= 4.00 PHI= -0.256 XP = 0.0456
458	TEND TO BE THOSE WHERE GAMES, IF PRESENT, INCLUDE GAMES OF STRATEGY (52) R-A-B,EA	0.56 OF 52	458	TEND TO BE THOSE WHERE GAMES, IF PRESENT, DO NOT INCLUDE GAMES OF STRATEGY (119) R-A-B,EA	0.81 OF 119	29 23 23 96 XSQ= 21.02 PHI= 0.351 XP = 0.0000
472	DRIFT TOWARD BEING THOSE WHERE THE COMPOSITE NARCISSISM INDEX IS HIGH (47) PES	0.66 OF 32	472	DRIFT TOWARD BEING THOSE WHERE THE COMPOSITE NARCISSISM INDEX IS LOW (43) PES	0.55 OF 58	21 26 11 32 XSQ= 2.79 PHI= 0.176 XP = 0.0949

264/

473	TILT TOWARD BEING THOSE WHERE SENSITIVITY TO INSULT IS EXTREME (32) PES	0.53 OF 32	473	TILT TOWARD BEING THOSE WHERE SENSITIVITY TO INSULT IS MODERATE OR NEGLIGIBLE (56) PES	0.73 OF 56	17 15 15 41 XSQ= 5.02 PHI= 0.239 XP = 0.0251

265 CULTURES WHERE WIVES ARE OBTAINED BY BRIDE-SERVICE (54)	265 CULTURES WHERE WIVES ARE OBTAINED BY MEANS OTHER THAN BRIDE-SERVICE (341)

BACKGROUND ON PAGE 128

SUBJECT ONLY

54 IN LEFT COLUMN

BEMBA	BERGDAMA	CAGABA	CALLINAGO	CAMAYURA	CARIB	CHAMACOCO	CHIRIGUANO	CHOROTI	CHORTI
CHUKCHEE	COPPER ESKIMO	CREE	CUNA	DOGON	EYAK	FOX	GUAHIBO	HAICA	HANUNOO
INGASSANA	JIVARO	KASKA	KORYAK	KUNG	LAMBA	MATACO	MAYA	MENTAWEI	MUNDURUCU
MURNGIN	ONA	PENOBSCOT	PURUM	TAGBANUA	TALAMANCA	TARAHUMARA	TAREUMIUT	TENDA	TENETEHARA
TERA	TIMBIRA	TUPINAMBA	TZELTAL	WAPISHANA	WARRAU	WICHITA	WITOTO	YABARANA	YAGUA
YAHGAN	YARURO	YUKAGHIR	ZUNI						

341 IN RIGHT COLUMN

5 EXCLUDED BECAUSE UNASCERTAINED

	Left column			Right column			Statistics
4	TILT MORE TOWARD BEING THOSE LOCATED OUTSIDE OF THE CIRCUM-MEDITERRANEAN (355)	0.98 OF 54	4	TILT LESS TOWARD BEING THOSE LOCATED OUTSIDE OF THE CIRCUM-MEDITERRANEAN (355)	0.87 OF 341		1 44 53 297 XSQ= 4.60 PHI= -0.108 XP = 0.0320
5	DRIFT MORE TOWARD BEING THOSE LOCATED OUTSIDE OF EAST EURASIA (330)	0.93 OF 54	5	DRIFT LESS TOWARD BEING THOSE LOCATED OUTSIDE OF EAST EURASIA (330)	0.81 OF 341		4 66 50 275 XSQ= 3.78 PHI= -0.098 XP = 0.0518
6	DRIFT MORE TOWARD BEING THOSE LOCATED OUTSIDE OF THE INSULAR PACIFIC (330)	0.93 OF 54	6	DRIFT LESS TOWARD BEING THOSE LOCATED OUTSIDE OF THE INSULAR PACIFIC (330)	0.81 OF 341		4 65 50 276 XSQ= 3.62 PHI= -0.096 XP = 0.0571
9	TEND TO BE THOSE LOCATED IN SOUTH AMERICA (65)	0.50 OF 54	9	TEND TO BE THOSE LOCATED OUTSIDE OF SOUTH AMERICA (335)	0.89 OF 341		27 36 27 305 XSQ= 51.20 PHI= 0.360 XP = 0.

No.		Ratio	No.		Ratio	
11	LEAN LESS TOWARD BEING THOSE WHERE THE LATITUDE IS LESS THAN SIXTY DEGREES (385)	0.89 OF 54	11	LEAN MORE TOWARD BEING THOSE WHERE THE LATITUDE IS LESS THAN SIXTY DEGREES (385)	0.97 OF 341	6 9 48 332 XSQ= 6.99 PHI= 0.133 XP = 0.0082
12	LEAN LESS TOWARD BEING THOSE WHERE THE LATITUDE IS LESS THAN FIFTY DEGREES (367)	0.80 OF 54	12	LEAN MORE TOWARD BEING THOSE WHERE THE LATITUDE IS LESS THAN FIFTY DEGREES (367)	0.94 OF 341	11 22 43 319 XSQ= 10.05 PHI= 0.159 XP = 0.0015
51	TEND TO BE THOSE WHERE SUBSISTENCE IS PRIMARILY BY FOOD GATHERING -- I. E., HUNTING, FISHING, OR COLLECTING -- RATHER THAN FOOD PRODUCTION (147)	0.59 OF 54	51	TEND TO BE THOSE WHERE SUBSISTENCE IS PRIMARILY BY FOOD PRODUCTION -- I. E., AGRICULTURE OR HUSBANDRY -- RATHER THAN BY GATHERING (253)	0.67 OF 341	22 230 32 111 XSQ= 13.26 PHI= -0.183 XP = 0.0003
53	LEAN MORE TOWARD BEING THOSE WHERE FOOD PRODUCTION IS BY SIMPLE AGRICULTURE OR INCIPIENT FOOD PRODUCTION, RATHER THAN BY INTENSIVE AGRICULTURE (147)	0.87 OF 31	53	LEAN LESS TOWARD BEING THOSE WHERE FOOD PRODUCTION IS BY SIMPLE AGRICULTURE OR INCIPIENT FOOD PRODUCTION, RATHER THAN BY INTENSIVE AGRICULTURE (147)	0.58 OF 205	4 87 27 118 XSQ= 8.71 PHI= -0.192 XP = 0.0032
54	TILT LESS TOWARD BEING THOSE WHERE FOOD PRODUCTION IS BY INTENSIVE OR SIMPLE AGRICULTURE, RATHER THAN BY INCIPIENT FOOD PRODUCTION (192)	0.65 OF 31	54	TILT MORE TOWARD BEING THOSE WHERE FOOD PRODUCTION IS BY INTENSIVE OR SIMPLE AGRICULTURE, RATHER THAN BY INCIPIENT FOOD PRODUCTION (192)	0.84 OF 205	20 172 11 33 XSQ= 5.46 PHI= -0.152 XP = 0.0195
55	TILT TOWARD BEING THOSE WHERE FOOD PRODUCTION IS BY SIMPLE AGRICULTURE, RATHER THAN BY INTENSIVE AGRICULTURE (101)	0.80 OF 20	55	TILT TOWARD BEING THOSE WHERE FOOD PRODUCTION IS BY INTENSIVE AGRICULTURE, RATHER THAN BY SIMPLE AGRICULTURE (91)	0.51 OF 172	4 87 16 85 XSQ= 5.55 PHI= -0.170 XP = 0.0185
62	TILT TOWARD BEING THOSE WHERE HUSBANDRY OF ANY KIND IS ABSENT (172)	0.57 OF 54	62	TILT TOWARD BEING THOSE WHERE HUSBANDRY OF SOME KIND IS PRESENT (228)	0.60 OF 341	23 205 31 136 XSQ= 5.17 PHI= -0.114 XP = 0.0230
63	DRIFT TOWARD BEING THOSE WHERE HUSBANDRY, IF PRESENT, IS PRINCIPALLY IN THE FORM OF PIGS, SHEEP, OR GOATS, RATHER THAN BOVINE, EQUINE, CAMEL-LIKE, OR DEER-LIKE ANIMALS (74)	0.52 OF 23	63	DRIFT TOWARD BEING THOSE WHERE HUSBANDRY, IF PRESENT, IS PRINCIPALLY IN THE FORM OF BOVINE, EQUINE, CAMEL-LIKE, OR DEER-LIKE ANIMALS, RATHER THAN PIGS, SHEEP, OR GOATS (152)	0.69 OF 203	11 141 12 62 XSQ= 3.46 PHI= -0.124 XP = 0.0628
71	LEAN MORE TOWARD BEING THOSE WHERE METAL WORKING IS ABSENT (153)	0.82 OF 39	71	LEAN LESS TOWARD BEING THOSE WHERE METAL WORKING IS ABSENT (153)	0.56 OF 209	7 91 32 118 XSQ= 7.97 PHI= -0.179 XP = 0.0048

79	IN ALL CASES ARE THOSE 1.00 OF 31 WHERE NO CITY IS PRESENT (201)	79	DRIFT LESS TOWARD BEING THOSE 0.88 OF 192 WHERE NO CITY IS PRESENT (201)	0 23 31 169 XSQ= 2.95 PHI= -0.115 XP = 0.0860
80	TILT MORE TOWARD BEING THOSE 0.97 OF 31 WHERE NO CITY OR TOWN IS PRESENT (185)	80	TILT LESS TOWARD BEING THOSE 0.80 OF 192 WHERE NO CITY OR TOWN IS PRESENT (185)	1 38 30 154 XSQ= 3.99 PHI= -0.134 XP = 0.0457
81	TEND MORE TO BE THOSE 0.90 OF 31 WHERE NO CITY OR TOWN IS PRESENT, AND THE AVERAGE COMMUNITY SIZE IS SMALLER THAN 200 (135)	81	TEND LESS TO BE THOSE 0.55 OF 192 WHERE NO CITY OR TOWN IS PRESENT, AND THE AVERAGE COMMUNITY SIZE IS SMALLER THAN 200 (135)	3 86 28 106 XSQ= 12.30 PHI= -0.235 XP = 0.0005
82	TILT LESS TOWARD BEING THOSE 0.61 OF 31 WHERE A CITY OR TOWN IS PRESENT, OR THE AVERAGE COMMUNITY SIZE IS FIFTY OR GREATER (178)	82	TILT MORE TOWARD BEING THOSE 0.83 OF 192 WHERE A CITY OR TOWN IS PRESENT, OR THE AVERAGE COMMUNITY SIZE IS FIFTY OR GREATER (178)	19 159 12 33 XSQ= 6.40 PHI= -0.169 XP = 0.0114
83	LEAN MORE TOWARD BEING THOSE 0.97 OF 29 WHERE, WITH NO CITY AND NO TOWN PRESENT, THE AVERAGE COMMUNITY SIZE IS SMALLER THAN 200, RATHER THAN BETWEEN 200 AND 999 (135)	83	LEAN LESS TOWARD BEING THOSE 0.71 OF 150 WHERE, WITH NO CITY AND NO TOWN PRESENT, THE AVERAGE COMMUNITY SIZE IS SMALLER THAN 200, RATHER THAN BETWEEN 200 AND 999 (135)	1 44 28 106 XSQ= 7.33 PHI= -0.202 XP = 0.0068
86	TEND TO BE THOSE 0.76 OF 46 WHERE THE LEVEL OF POLITICAL INTEGRATION IS THE AUTONOMOUS COMMUNITY, OR THE FAMILY (156) GPM	86	TEND TO BE THOSE 0.53 OF 255 WHERE THE LEVEL OF POLITICAL INTEGRATION IS THE LARGE STATE, THE LITTLE STATE, OR THE MINIMAL STATE (148) GPM	11 135 35 120 XSQ= 12.01 PHI= -0.200 XP = 0.0005
94	IN ALL CASES ARE THOSE 1.00 OF 50 WHERE THE HIERARCHY OF NATIONAL JURISDICTION HAS TWO, ONE, OR NO LEVELS (296) GES,EA	94	TILT LESS TOWARD BEING THOSE 0.88 OF 277 WHERE THE HIERARCHY OF NATIONAL JURISDICTION HAS TWO, ONE, OR NO LEVELS (296) GES,EA	0 34 50 243 XSQ= 5.60 PHI= -0.131 XP = 0.0180
96	TEND TO BE THOSE 0.72 OF 50 WHERE THE HIERARCHY OF NATIONAL JURISDICTION HAS NO LEVELS (156) GES,EA	96	TEND TO BE THOSE 0.57 OF 277 WHERE THE HIERARCHY OF NATIONAL JURISDICTION HAS FOUR, THREE, TWO OR ONE LEVEL (174) GES,EA	14 159 36 118 XSQ= 13.54 PHI= -0.203 XP = 0.0002
100	LEAN LESS TOWARD BEING THOSE 0.66 OF 50 WHERE HIERARCHIES ARE MORE COMPLEX THAN THE 'SIMPLEST,' I. E., MORE COMPLEX THAN TWO LOCAL LEVELS WITH NO NATIONAL LEVELS (267) GES,EA	100	LEAN MORE TOWARD BEING THOSE 0.84 OF 277 WHERE HIERARCHIES ARE MORE COMPLEX THAN THE 'SIMPLEST,' I. E., MORE COMPLEX THAN TWO LOCAL LEVELS WITH NO NATIONAL LEVELS (267) GES,EA	33 233 17 44 XSQ= 8.00 PHI= -0.156 XP = 0.0047

102	TEND TO BE THOSE WHERE CLASS STRATIFICATION IS ABSENT (180)	0.69 OF 52	102	TEND TO BE THOSE WHERE CLASS STRATIFICATION IS PRESENT (203)	0.57 OF 327	16 186 36 141 XSQ= 11.26 PHI= -0.172 XP = 0.0008
106	DRIFT TOWARD BEING THOSE WHERE CLASS STRATIFICATION, IF PRESENT, IS BASED ON WEALTH (77)	0.63 OF 16	106	DRIFT TOWARD BEING THOSE WHERE CLASS STRATIFICATION, IF PRESENT, IS BASED ON SOMETHING OTHER THAN WEALTH (126)	0.64 OF 186	10 67 6 119 XSQ= 3.33 PHI= 0.128 XP = 0.0681
109	TILT MORE TOWARD BEING THOSE WHERE CASTES ARE ABSENT (317)	0.96 OF 53	109	TILT LESS TOWARD BEING THOSE WHERE CASTES ARE ABSENT (317)	0.84 OF 311	2 49 51 262 XSQ= 4.45 PHI= -0.111 XP = 0.0350
116	IN ALL CASES ARE THOSE WHERE OCCUPATIONAL SPECIALIZATION IS PART-TIME ONLY (34) JMH	1.00 OF 9	116	TILT LESS TOWARD BEING THOSE WHERE OCCUPATIONAL SPECIALIZATION IS PART-TIME ONLY (34) JMH	0.56 OF 45	0 20 9 25 XSQ= 4.59 PHI= -0.292 XP = 0.0322
120	DRIFT TOWARD BEING THOSE WHERE THE CRAFT SPECIALIZATION SCORE IS LOW (17) WME	0.71 OF 7	120	DRIFT TOWARD BEING THOSE WHERE THE CRAFT SPECIALIZATION SCORE IS HIGH OR MEDIUM (36) WME	0.74 OF 46	2 34 5 12 XSQ= 3.84 PHI= -0.269 XP = 0.0500
129	DRIFT MORE TOWARD BEING THOSE WHERE WEAVING IS MAINLY DONE BY FEMALES (73)	0.89 OF 18	129	DRIFT LESS TOWARD BEING THOSE WHERE WEAVING IS MAINLY DONE BY FEMALES (73)	0.66 OF 85	2 29 16 56 XSQ= 2.72 PHI= -0.163 XP = 0.0989
130	TILT TOWARD BEING THOSE WHERE LEATHER WORKING IS MAINLY DONE BY FEMALES (45)	0.78 OF 18	130	TILT TOWARD BEING THOSE WHERE LEATHER WORKING IS MAINLY DONE BY MALES (39)	0.53 OF 66	4 35 14 31 XSQ= 4.23 PHI= -0.224 XP = 0.0397
132	TILT TOWARD BEING THOSE WHERE ECONOMIC EXCHANGE DOES NOT INVOLVE THE USE OF MONEY (17) JMH	0.67 OF 9	132	TILT TOWARD BEING THOSE WHERE ECONOMIC EXCHANGE INVOLVES THE USE OF MONEY (37) JMH	0.76 OF 45	3 34 6 11 XSQ= 4.40 PHI= -0.285 XP = 0.0360
138	TILT TOWARD BEING THOSE WHERE SUPERORDINATE JUSTICE IS ABSENT (18) BBW	0.88 OF 8	138	TILT TOWARD BEING THOSE WHERE SUPERORDINATE JUSTICE IS PRESENT (22) BBW	0.66 OF 32	1 21 7 11 XSQ= 5.31 PHI= -0.364 EP = 0.0138

142	TILT TOWARD BEING THOSE 0.67 OF 9 WHERE THE LEVEL OF SOCIAL SANCTION IS PRIVATE SETTLEMENT, RATHER THAN PUBLIC CORPOREAL SANCTION OR PUBLIC PROPERTY SETTLEMENT (16) JMH	142	TILT TOWARD BEING THOSE 0.78 OF 45 WHERE THE LEVEL OF SOCIAL SANCTION IS PUBLIC CORPOREAL SANCTION OR PUBLIC PROPERTY SANCTION, RATHER THAN PRIVATE SETTLEMENT (38) JMH	3 35 6 10 XSQ= 5.13 PHI= -0.308 XP = 0.0235
143	IN ALL CASES ARE THOSE 1.00 OF 7 WHERE THE RATIO OF RESTITUTIVE TO REPRESSIVE SANCTIONS IS MEDIUM OR LOW (32) WME	143	DRIFT LESS TOWARD BEING THOSE 0.56 OF 45 WHERE THE RATIO OF RESTITUTIVE TO REPRESSIVE SANCTIONS IS MEDIUM OR LOW (32) WME	0 20 7 25 XSQ= 3.35 PHI= -0.254 XP = 0.0671
144	DRIFT TOWARD BEING THOSE 0.86 OF 7 WHERE THE RATIO OF RESTITUTIVE TO REPRESSIVE SANCTIONS IS LOW (25) WME	144	DRIFT TOWARD BEING THOSE 0.58 OF 45 WHERE THE RATIO OF RESTITUTIVE TO REPRESSIVE SANCTIONS IS HIGH OR MEDIUM (27) WME	1 26 6 19 XSQ= 3.01 PHI= -0.241 XP = 0.0826
147	IN ALL CASES ARE THOSE 1.00 OF 5 WHERE CODIFIED LAWS ARE UNIMPORTANT OR ABSENT (13) LWS	147	LEAN TOWARD BEING THOSE 0.71 OF 28 WHERE CODIFIED LAWS ARE PRESENT (20) LWS	0 20 5 8 XSQ= 6.32 PHI= -0.438 EP = 0.0054
163	IN ALL CASES ARE THOSE 1.00 OF 5 WHERE THE EMPHASIS ON INDIVIDUAL VOLITION AS THE CAUSE OF CRIME IS LOW (10) MJ	163	TILT TOWARD BEING THOSE 0.58 OF 12 WHERE THE EMPHASIS ON INDIVIDUAL VOLITION AS THE CAUSE OF CRIME IS HIGH (7) MJ	0 7 5 5 XSQ= 2.84 PHI= -0.409 EP = 0.0441
176	TEND MORE TO BE THOSE 0.79 OF 53 WHERE THE COMMUNITY IS OTHER THAN A CLAN-COMMUNITY OR A COMMUNITY STRUCTURED OR SEGMENTED ON A CLAN BASIS (213)	176	TEND LESS TO BE THOSE 0.52 OF 325 WHERE THE COMMUNITY IS OTHER THAN A CLAN-COMMUNITY OR A COMMUNITY STRUCTURED OR SEGMENTED ON A CLAN BASIS (213)	11 155 42 170 XSQ= 12.35 PHI= -0.181 XP = 0.0004
177	TILT MORE TOWARD BEING THOSE 0.92 OF 53 WHERE THE COMMUNITY IS OTHER THAN A SINGLE CLAN-COMMUNITY AND EXOGAMOUS (305)	177	TILT LESS TOWARD BEING THOSE 0.78 OF 325 WHERE THE COMMUNITY IS OTHER THAN A SINGLE CLAN-COMMUNITY AND EXOGAMOUS (305)	4 72 49 253 XSQ= 5.18 PHI= -0.117 XP = 0.0229
178	DRIFT MORE TOWARD BEING THOSE 0.89 OF 53 WHERE THE COMMUNITY IS OTHER THAN SEGMENTED ON A CLAN BASIS AND NON-EXOGAMOUS (295)	178	DRIFT LESS TOWARD BEING THOSE 0.76 OF 325 WHERE THE COMMUNITY IS OTHER THAN SEGMENTED ON A CLAN BASIS AND NON-EXOGAMOUS (295)	6 79 47 246 XSQ= 3.70 PHI= -0.099 XP = 0.0546
179	DRIFT LESS TOWARD BEING THOSE 0.81 OF 53 WHERE THE COMMUNITY IS OTHER THAN STRUCTURED ON A NON-CLAN BASIS AND COMMONLY EXOGAMOUS (340)	179	DRIFT MORE TOWARD BEING THOSE 0.90 OF 325 WHERE THE COMMUNITY IS OTHER THAN STRUCTURED ON A NON-CLAN BASIS AND COMMONLY EXOGAMOUS (340)	10 32 43 293 XSQ= 2.90 PHI= 0.088 XP = 0.0887

183	LEAN LESS TOWARD BEING THOSE 0.67 OF 21 WHERE THE LARGEST NON-COGNATIC KIN GROUP IS SMALLER THAN A MOEITY, I. E., A PHRATRY OR SIB OR LINEAGE (218)	183	LEAN MORE TOWARD BEING THOSE 0.89 OF 228 WHERE THE LARGEST NON-COGNATIC KIN GROUP IS SMALLER THAN A MOEITY, I. E., A PHRATRY OR SIB OR LINEAGE (218)	 XSQ= PHI= XP =	7 25 14 203 6.71 0.164 0.0096
186	TEND MORE TO BE THOSE 0.85 OF 54 WHERE THE KIN GROUP IS OTHER THAN EXCLUSIVELY PATRILINEAL (250)	186	TEND LESS TO BE THOSE 0.59 OF 341 WHERE THE KIN GROUP IS OTHER THAN EXCLUSIVELY PATRILINEAL (250)	 XSQ= PHI= XP =	8 140 46 201 12.60 -0.179 0.0004
188	TEND TO BE THOSE 0.61 OF 54 WHERE THE KIN GROUP IS EXCLUSIVELY COGNATIC (148)	188	TEND TO BE THOSE 0.67 OF 341 WHERE THE KIN GROUP IS OTHER THAN EXCLUSIVELY COGNATIC (252)	 XSQ= PHI= XP =	33 113 21 228 14.48 0.191 0.0001
190	LEAN TOWARD BEING THOSE 0.52 OF 21 WHERE THE KIN GROUP IS MATRILINEAL, RATHER THAN PATRILINEAL OR DOUBLE-DESCENT (61)	19C	LEAN TOWARD BEING THOSE 0.78 OF 223 WHERE THE KIN GROUP IS PATRILINEAL OR DOUBLE-DESCENT, RATHER THAN MATRILINEAL (186)	 XSQ= PHI= XP =	10 174 11 49 8.00 -0.181 0.0047
192	LEAN LESS TOWARD BEING THOSE 0.54 OF 54 OTHER THAN WHERE THE ONLY KIN GROUP PRESENT IS A KINDRED OR ELSE BILATERAL DESCENT IS INFERRED (289)	192	LEAN MORE TOWARD BEING THOSE 0.75 OF 341 OTHER THAN WHERE THE ONLY KIN GROUP PRESENT IS A KINDRED OR ELSE BILATERAL DESCENT IS INFERRED (289)	 XSQ= PHI= XP =	25 84 29 257 9.89 0.158 0.0017
196	TILT LESS TOWARD BEING THOSE 0.51 OF 37 WHERE INDIVIDUAL RIGHTS IN REAL PROPERTY, AND RULES FOR INHERITANCE, ARE PRESENT (194)	196	TILT MORE TOWARD BEING THOSE 0.72 OF 243 WHERE INDIVIDUAL RIGHTS IN REAL PROPERTY, AND RULES FOR INHERITANCE, ARE PRESENT (194)	 XSQ= PHI= XP =	19 174 18 69 5.24 -0.137 0.0221
198	LEAN LESS TOWARD BEING THOSE 0.60 OF 15 WHERE RULES FOR THE INHERITANCE OF REAL PROPERTY, IF PRESENT, FAVOR THE MALE HEIR OR LINE, RATHER THAN THE FEMALE (144)	198	LEAN MORE TOWARD BEING THOSE 0.91 OF 149 WHERE RULES FOR THE INHERITANCE OF REAL PROPERTY, IF PRESENT, FAVOR THE MALE HEIR OR LINE, RATHER THAN THE FEMALE (144)	 XSQ= PHI= XP =	9 135 6 14 9.23 -0.237 0.0024
204	TILT LESS TOWARD BEING THOSE 0.67 OF 33 WHERE MARITAL RESIDENCE IS PATRILOCAL, VIRILOCAL, OR AVUNCULOCAL, RATHER THAN AMBILOCAL OR NEOLOCAL (270)	2C4	TILT MORE TOWARD BEING THOSE 0.83 OF 297 WHERE MARITAL RESIDENCE IS PATRILOCAL, VIRILOCAL, OR AVUNCULOCAL, RATHER THAN AMBILOCAL OR NEOLOCAL (270)	 XSQ= PHI= XP =	22 246 11 51 4.08 -0.111 0.0434
207	DRIFT TOWARD BEING THOSE 0.66 OF 32 WHERE MARITAL RESIDENCE IS MATRILOCAL OR UXORILOCAL, RATHER THAN AMBILOCAL OR NEOLOCAL (64)	2C7	DRIFT TOWARD BEING THOSE 0.55 OF 93 WHERE MARITAL RESIDENCE IS AMBILOCAL OR NEOLOCAL, RATHER THAN MATRILOCAL OR UXORILOCAL (64)	 XSQ= PHI= XP =	21 42 11 51 3.21 0.160 0.0731

```
209  TEND LESS TC BE THCSE             0.51 OF  43     209  TEND MORE TO BE THOSE             0.85 CF 288          22  246
     WHERE MARITAL RESICENCE IS                              WHERE MARITAL RESIDENCE IS                                 21   42
     PATRILCCAL, VIRILOCAL, CR AVUNCULOCAL,                  PATRILOCAL, VIRILOCAL, CR AVUNCULCCAL,              XSQ=   26.31
     RATHER THAN                                             RATHER THAN                                         PHI=  -0.282
     MATRILCCAL CR UXCRILCCAL  (270)                         MATRILOCAL OR UXORILCCAL  (270)                     XP =   0.0000

210  LEAN LESS TCWARC BEING THCSE      0.54 OF  13     21C  LEAN MORE TOWARD BEING THCSE      0.87 CF 184           7  160
     WHERE MARITAL RESICENCF IS                              WHERE MARITAL RESIDENCE IS                                  6   24
     PATRILCCAL, RATHER THAN                                 PATRILOCAL, RATHER THAN                             XSQ=    7.91
     MATRILCCAL  (169)                                       MATRILOCAL  (169)                                   PHI=  -0.200
                                                                                                                 XP =   0.0049

240  DRIFT TCWARD BEING THCSE          0.52 OF  31     24C  DRIFT TOWARD BEING THOSE          0.66 CF 180          16   61
     WHERE THE FAMILY, IF EXTENCEC, IS                       WHERE THE FAMILY, IF EXTENDED, IS                          15  119
     LARGE, RATHER THAN                                      SMALL OR STEM, RATHER THAN                          XSQ=    2.86
     SMALL CR STEM  (78)                                     LARGE  (135)                                        PHI=   0.116
                                                                                                                 XP =   0.0908

323  DRIFT TCWARD BEING THCSE          0.63 OF  16     323  DRIFT TOWARD BEING THCSE          0.68 CF  57          10   18
     WHERE THE CCNSTANCY CF PRESENCE                         WHERE THE CONSTANCY CF PRESENCE                             6   39
     CF THE INFANT'S NURTURANT AGENT                         OF THE INFANT'S NURTURANT AGENT                     XSQ=    3.83
     IS HIGH  (29) B-B-C                                     IS LOW  (45) B-B-C                                  PHI=   0.229
                                                                                                                 XP =   0.0504

337  TILT TCWARC BEING THCSE           0.80 OF  15     337  TILT TOWARD BEING THOSE           0.61 CF  57           3   35
     WHERE THE CHILD'S INFERREC ANXIETY OVER                 WHERE THE CHILD'S INFERRED ANXIETY CVER                    12   22
     NCN-PERFCRMANCE CF RESPCNSIBLE BEHAVIOR                 NON-PERFORMANCE OF RESPCNSIBLE BEHAVIOR             XSQ=    6.59
     IS LCW  (35) B-B-C                                      IS HIGH  (38) B-B-C                                 PHI=  -0.303
                                                                                                                 XP =   0.0102

342  IN ALL CASES ARE THCSE            1.00 OF   6     342  DRIFT LESS TOWARD BEING THCSE  0.54 CF  39              0   18
     WHERE THE CHILC'S INFERREC ANXIETY OVER                 WHERE THE CHILD'S INFERRED ANXIETY CVER                     6   21
     PERFCRMANCE CF NURTURANT BEHAVIOR                       PERFORMANCE OF NURTURANT BEHAVICR                   XSQ=    2.89
     IS LCW  (28) B-B-C                                      IS LOW  (28) B-B-C                                  PHI=  -0.254
                                                                                                                 XP =   0.0890

349  TILT TCWARD BEING THCSE           0.77 OF  13     349  TILT TOWARD BEING THOSE           0.63 CF  48           3   30
     WHERE THE CHILD'S INFERREC ANXIETY OVER                 WHERE THE CHILD'S INFERRED ANXIETY CVER                    10   18
     NCN-PERFCRMANCE CF ACHIEVEMENT BEHAVIOR                 NON-PERFORMANCE OF ACHIEVEMENT BEHAVIOR             XSQ=    4.91
     IS LCW  (28) B-B-C                                      IS HIGH  (34) B-B-C                                 PHI=  -0.284
                                                                                                                 XP =   0.0267

350  TILT TCWARD BEING THOSE           0.77 OF  13     35C  TILT TOWARD BEING THOSE           0.65 OF  46           3   30
     WHERE THE CHILD'S INFERREC ANXIETY OVER                 WHERE THE CHILD'S INFERRED ANXIETY CVER                    10   16
     PERFCRMANCE CF ACHIEVEMENT BEHAVIOR                     PERFORMANCE OF ACHIEVEMENT BEHAVICR                 XSQ=    5.69
     IS LCW  (26) B-B-C                                      IS HIGH  (34) B-B-C                                 PHI=  -0.311
                                                                                                                 XP =   0.0170

351  DRIFT TCWARD BEING THCSE          0.85 OF  13     351  DRIFT TOWARD BEING THOSE          0.50 CF  46           2   23
     WHERE THE CHILC'S INFERREC CCNFLICT                     WHERE THE CHILD'S INFERRED CCNFLICT                        11   23
     REGARDING ACHIEVEMENT BEHAVICR                          REGARDING ACHIEVEMENT BEHAVICR                      XSQ=    3.66
     IS LCW  (34) B-B-C                                      IS HIGH  (26) B-B-C                                 PHI=  -0.249
                                                                                                                 XP =   0.0558
```

No.		No.		
354	TILT TOWARD BEING THOSE 0.79 OF 14 WHERE THE CHILD'S INFERRED ANXIETY OVER PERFORMANCE OF OBEDIENT BEHAVIOR IS LOW (37) B-B-C	354	TILT TOWARD BEING THOSE 0.57 OF 58 WHERE THE CHILD'S INFERRED ANXIETY OVER PERFORMANCE OF OBEDIENT BEHAVIOR IS HIGH (36) B-B-C	3 33 11 25 XSQ= 4.34 PHI= -0.246 XP = 0.0371
355	TILT TOWARD BEING THOSE 0.79 OF 14 WHERE THE CHILD'S INFERRED CONFLICT REGARDING OBEDIENT BEHAVIOR IS LOW (38) B-B-C	355	TILT TOWARD BEING THOSE 0.55 OF 58 WHERE THE CHILD'S INFERRED CONFLICT REGARDING OBEDIENT BEHAVIOR IS HIGH (35) B-B-C	3 32 11 26 XSQ= 3.88 PHI= -0.232 XP = 0.0489
358	LEAN TOWARD BEING THOSE 0.60 OF 10 WHERE ADOLESCENT PEER GROUPS ARE ABSENT IN A SETTING OF WORK, AND OF PUBLIC GATHERINGS, AND OF LEISURE (11) JKH	358	LEAN TOWARD BEING THOSE 0.88 OF 42 WHERE ADOLESCENT PEER GROUPS ARE PRESENT IN A SETTING OF WORK AND PUBLIC GATHERINGS AND LEISURE, OR OF PUBLIC GATHERINGS AND LEISURE, OR OF LEISURE ONLY (41) JKH	4 37 6 5 XSQ= 8.50 PHI= -0.404 XP = 0.0035
365	DRIFT TOWARD BEING THOSE 0.71 OF 7 WHERE THE TIME SPENT IN ADOLESCENT PEER GROUP ACTIVITY IS LOW-MEDIUM OR LOW (15) JKH	365	DRIFT TOWARD BEING THOSE 0.74 OF 38 WHERE THE TIME SPENT IN ADOLESCENT PEER GROUP ACTIVITY IS HIGH OR HIGH-MEDIUM (30) JKH	2 28 5 10 XSQ= 3.57 PHI= -0.282 XP = 0.0587
377	TILT MORE TOWARD BEING THOSE 0.90 OF 50 WHERE MALE GENITAL MUTILATION IS ABSENT (242)	377	TILT LESS TOWARD BEING THOSE 0.72 OF 272 WHERE MALE GENITAL MUTILATION IS ABSENT (242)	5 77 45 195 XSQ= 6.53 PHI= -0.142 XP = 0.0106
382	DRIFT MORE TOWARD BEING THOSE 0.85 OF 13 WHERE FEMALE INITIATION RITES ARE PRESENT (38) JKB	382	DRIFT LESS TOWARD BEING THOSE 0.52 OF 52 WHERE FEMALE INITIATION RITES ARE PRESENT (38) JKB	11 27 2 25 XSQ= 3.33 PHI= 0.226 XP = 0.0680
385	TILT TOWARD BEING THOSE 0.50 OF 16 WHERE SEXUAL EXPRESSION BY THE YOUNG IS RESTRICTED (22) F-B	385	TILT TOWARD BEING THOSE 0.80 OF 70 WHERE SEXUAL EXPRESSION BY THE YOUNG IS SEMI-RESTRICTED OR PERMITTED (64) F-B	8 14 8 56 XSQ= 4.68 PHI= 0.233 XP = 0.0305
392	TILT TOWARD BEING THOSE 0.59 OF 22 WHERE PREMARITAL SEX RELATIONS ARE FREELY PERMITTED (67) JTW,EA	392	TILT TOWARD BEING THOSE 0.66 OF 157 WHERE PREMARITAL SEX RELATIONS ARE STRONGLY PUNISHED AND IN FACT RARE, OR WEAKLY PUNISHED AND IN FACT NOT RARE, OR PUNISHED ONLY IF PREGNANCY RESULTS (112) JTW,EA	9 103 13 54 XSQ= 4.03 PHI= -0.150 XP = 0.0448

452	DRIFT TCWARD BEING THCSE 0.89 OF 9 WHERE TCTEMISM WITH FCCC TABCOS IS ABSENT (24) WNS	452	DRIFT TOWARD BEING THOSE 0.53 CF 34 WHERE TOTEMISM WITH FCOD TABCOS IS PRESENT (19) WNS	1 18 8 16 XSQ= 3.50 PHI= -0.285 XP = 0.0615
454	IN ALL CASES ARE THCSE 1.00 OF 6 WHERE THE CBJECTIVE CF THE INCIVICUAL'S CONTACT WITH THE DIVINE IS CCNDUCIVE TC THE DEVELCPMENT OF THE INDIVIDUAL'S NEEC TC ACHIEVE (18) CCM	454	TILT TOWARD BEING THOSE 0.59 CF 29 WHERE THE OBJECTIVE OF THE INDIVICUAL'S CONTACT WITH THE DIVINE IS NOT CONDUCIVE TO THE DEVELCPMENT CF THE INDIVIDUAL'S NEED TO ACHIEVE (18) DCM	6 12 0 17 XSQ= 4.69 PHI= 0.366 EP = 0.0191
458	DRIFT MCRE TCWARC BEING THCSE 0.88 OF 25 WHERE GAMES, IF PRESENT, DC NCT INCLUDE GAMES CF STRATEGY (119) R-A-B,EA	458	DRIFT LESS TOWARD BEING THCSE 0.66 CF 146 WHERE GAMES, IF PRESENT, DO NOT INCLUDE GAMES OF STRATEGY (119) R-A-B,EA	3 49 22 97 XSQ= 3.73 PHI= -0.148 XP = 0.0536
478	IN ALL CASES ARE THCSE 1.00 OF 4 WHERE THE ABANDCNMENT CR KILLING OF CLD PECPLE IS PRESENT (12) LWS	478	DRIFT TOWARD BEING THOSE 0.60 CF 20 WHERE THE ABANDONMENT CR KILLING CF OLD PEOPLE IS UNIMPORTANT OR ABSENT (12) LWS	4 8 0 12 XSQ= 2.70 PHI= 0.335 EP = 0.0932

266 CULTURES
WHERE WIVES ARE OBTAINED BY
BRIDE-PRICE, RATHER THAN
BRIDE-SERVICE (163)

266 CULTURES
WHERE WIVES ARE OBTAINED BY
BRIDE-SERVICE, RATHER THAN
BRIDE-PRICE (54)

BACKGROUND ON PAGE 128

SUBJECT ONLY

163 IN LEFT COLUMN

ABIPON	ABOR	ALBANIANS	ALORESE	ARAUCANIANS	ARYANS	ASHANTI	ATAYAL	AZANDE	BABWA
BAJUN	BAMBARA	BAMILEKE	BARABRA	BARI	BASSERI	BATAK	BAYA	BEJA	BELU
BENGALI	BETE	BHIL	BHUIYA	BIRIFOR	BOZO	BUDUMA	BURYAT	CAMBODIANS	CHAGGA
CHENCHU	CHERKESS	CHIBCHA	DAGUR	DARD	DILLING	DOROBO	DUSUN	EGYPTIANS	ENGA
FANG	FON	FUTAJALONKE	GANDA	GILBERTESE	GILYAK	GISU	GOAJIRO	GOND	GROS VENTRE
HASANIA	HAZARA	HEBREWS	HEHE	HERERO	HO	IFUGAO	ILA	IRAQW	JUKUN
KABYLE	KACHIN	KALMYK	KAPAUKU	KAZAK	KET	KHALKA	KHEVSUR	KIKUYU	KISSI
KOHISTANI	KOL	KPE	KUBA	KUMYK	KURTATCHI	LAKALAI	LAKHER	LAMET	LANGO
LEPCHA	LESU	LHOTA NAGA	LIFU	LOLO	LUBA	LUO	MACASSARESE	MAGUZAWA	MALAYS
MAMVU	MANCHU	MARGI	MASAI	MATAKAM	MBUGWE	MBUNDU	MENDE	MIAO	MIN CHINESE
MINCHIA	MONGO	MONDUOR	MOSSI	MOTA	MZAB	NANDI	NUER	NUPE	NURI
NYAKYUSA	NYANEKA	NYARO	NYORO	ORAON	PAIWAN	PALAUANS	PARAUJANO	PATHAN	PURARI
REGEIBAT	RIFFIANS	ROTINESE	RWALA	SAMOYED	SANDAWE	SANTAL	SARAMACCA	SARSI	SENIANG
SERI	SHILLUK	SHLUH	SIMBOESE	SIUAI	SIWANS	SOMALI	SONGHAI	SOTHO	SUBANUN
SWAZI	SYRIANS	TALLENSI	TANIMBARESE	TEDA	TESO	TETON	THONGA	TIWI	TOLOWA
TORAJA	TSHIMSHIAN	TUBATULABAL	TURKANA	TURKMEN	ULAWANS	VENDA	WOLOF	WUTE	YAKO
YOMBE	YORUBA	YUROK							

54 IN RIGHT COLUMN

BEMBA	BERGDAMA	CAGABA	CALLINAGO	CAMAYURA	CARIB	CHAMACOCO	CHIRIGUANO	CHOROTI	CHORTI
CHUKCHEE	COPPER ESKIMO	CREE	CUNA	DOGON	EYAK	FOX	GUAHIBO	HAICA	HANUNOO
INGASSANA	JIVARO	KASKA	KORYAK	KUNG	LAMBA	MATACO	MAYA	MENTAWEI	MUNDURUCU
MURNGIN	ONA	PENOBSCOT	PURUM	TAGBANUA	TALAMANCA	TARAHUMARA	TAREUMIUT	TENDA	TENETEHARA
TERA	TIMBIRA	TUPINAMBA	TZELTAL	WAPISHANA	WARRAU	WICHITA	WITOTO	YABARANA	YAGUA
YAHGAN	YARURO	YUKAGHIR	ZUNI						

178 EXCLUDED BECAUSE IRRELEVANT

5 EXCLUDED BECAUSE UNASCERTAINED

---

3 LEAN LESS TOWARD BEING THOSE 0.64 OF 163
LOCATED OUTSIDE OF
AFRICA (320)

3 LEAN MORE TOWARD BEING THOSE 0.87 OF 54
LOCATED OUTSIDE OF
AFRICA (320)

59	7
104	47

XSQ= 9.28
PHI= 0.207
XP = 0.0023

4	TILT LESS TCWARC BEINC THCSE LCCATED CUTSIDE CF THE CIRCUM-MEDITERRANEAN (355)	0.85 OF 163	4	TILT MORE TOWARD BEING THOSE LOCATED OUTSIDE CF THE CIRCUM-MEDITERRANEAN (355)	0.98 CF 54	25 1 138 53 XSQ= 5.77 PHI= 0.163 XP = 0.0163
5	TILT LESS TCWARC BEINC THCSE LCCATED CUTSIDE CF EAST EURASIA (330)	0.77 OF 163	5	TILT MORE TOWARD BEING THCSE LOCATED OUTSIDE OF EAST EURASIA (330)	0.93 CF 54	38 4 125 50 XSQ= 5.59 PHI= 0.161 XP = 0.0180
8	LEAN MORE TCWARC BEINC THCSE LCCATED CUTSIDE CF NCRTH AMERICA (330)	0.95 OF 163	8	LEAN LESS TCWARD BEING THOSE LOCATED OUTSIDE OF NORTH AMERICA (330)	0.80 CF 54	8 11 155 43 XSQ= 10.28 PHI= -0.218 XP = 0.0013
9	TEND TC BE THCSE LCCATED CUTSIDE CF SCUTH AMERICA (335)	0.96 OF 163	9	TEND TO BE THOSE LOCATED IN SOUTH AMERICA (65)	0.50 CF 54	6 27 157 27 XSQ= 63.94 PHI= -0.543 XP = 0.
11	TILT MCRE TOWARC BEING THCSE WHERE THE LATITUDE IS LESS THAN SIXTY CEGREES (385)	0.98 OF 163	11	TILT LESS TOWARD BEING THOSE WHERE THE LATITUDE IS LESS THAN SIXTY DEGREES (385)	0.89 CF 54	3 6 160 48 XSQ= 6.59 PHI= -0.174 XP = 0.0102
12	TEND MCRE TO BE THCSE WHERE THE LATITUCE IS LESS THAN FIFTY CEGREES (367)	0.96 OF 163	12	TEND LESS TO BE THCSE WHERE THE LATITUDE IS LESS THAN FIFTY DEGREES (367)	0.80 CF 54	7 11 156 43 XSQ= 11.75 PHI= -0.233 XP = 0.0006
13	TILT MORE TOWARC BEING THCSE WHERE THE LATITUCE IS LESS THAN FORTY CEGREES (329)	0.88 OF 163	13	TILT LESS TOWARD BEING THOSE WHERE THE LATITUDE IS LESS THAN FORTY DEGREES (329)	0.76 CF 54	19 13 144 41 XSQ= 4.04 PHI= -0.136 XP = 0.0445
44	TILT MCRE TCWARC BEING THCSE WHERE SETTLEMENTS ARE FIXEC (222)	0.76 OF 131	44	TILT LESS TOWARD BEING THCSE WHERE SETTLEMENTS ARE FIXED (222)	0.59 CF 49	99 29 32 20 XSQ= 3.9C PHI= 0.147 XP = 0.0483
51	TEND TC BE THCSE WHERE SUBSISTENCE IS PRIMARILY BY FCCD PRCDUCTICN -- I. E., AGRICULTURE CR HUSBANDRY -- RATHER THAN BY GATHERING (253)	0.83 OF 163	51	TEND TO BE THOSE WHERE SUBSISTENCE IS PRIMARILY BY FOOD GATHERING -- I. E., HUNTING, FISHING, OR COLLECTING -- RATHER THAN FOOD PRODUCTION (147)	0.59 CF 54	135 22 28 32 XSQ= 33.83 PHI= 0.395 XP = 0.

53	LEAN LESS TOWARD BEING THOSE 0.54 OF 110 WHERE FOOD PRODUCTION IS BY SIMPLE AGRICULTURE OR INCIPIENT FOOD PRODUCTION, RATHER THAN BY INTENSIVE AGRICULTURE (147)	53	LEAN MORE TOWARD BEING THOSE 0.87 OF 31 WHERE FOOD PRODUCTION IS BY SIMPLE AGRICULTURE OR INCIPIENT FOOD PRODUCTION, RATHER THAN BY INTENSIVE AGRICULTURE (147)	51 4 59 27 XSQ= 10.02 PHI= 0.267 XP = 0.0016
54	TEND MORE TO BE THOSE 0.92 OF 110 WHERE FOOD PRODUCTION IS BY INTENSIVE OR SIMPLE AGRICULTURE, RATHER THAN BY INCIPIENT FOOD PRODUCTION (192)	54	TEND LESS TO BE THOSE 0.65 OF 31 WHERE FOOD PRODUCTION IS BY INTENSIVE OR SIMPLE AGRICULTURE, RATHER THAN BY INCIPIENT FOOD PRODUCTION (192)	101 20 9 11 XSQ= 12.65 PHI= 0.300 XP = 0.0004
55	TILT TOWARD BEING THOSE 0.50 OF 101 WHERE FOOD PRODUCTION IS BY INTENSIVE AGRICULTURE, RATHER THAN BY SIMPLE AGRICULTURE (91)	55	TILT TOWARD BEING THOSE 0.80 OF 20 WHERE FOOD PRODUCTION IS BY SIMPLE AGRICULTURE, RATHER THAN BY INTENSIVE AGRICULTURE (101)	51 4 50 16 XSQ= 5.09 PHI= 0.205 XP = 0.0240
56	TILT MORE TOWARD BEING THOSE 0.85 OF 59 WHERE FOOD PRODUCTION IS BY SIMPLE AGRICULTURE, RATHER THAN BY INCIPIENT FOOD PRODUCTION (101)	56	TILT LESS TOWARD BEING THOSE 0.59 OF 27 WHERE FOOD PRODUCTION IS BY SIMPLE AGRICULTURE, RATHER THAN BY INCIPIENT FOOD PRODUCTION (101)	50 16 9 11 XSQ= 5.39 PHI= 0.250 XP = 0.0203
62	TEND TO BE THOSE 0.74 OF 163 WHERE HUSBANDRY OF SOME KIND IS PRESENT (228)	62	TEND TO BE THOSE 0.57 OF 54 WHERE HUSBANDRY OF ANY KIND IS ABSENT (172)	120 23 43 31 XSQ= 16.02 PHI= 0.272 XP = 0.0001
63	TILT TOWARD BEING THOSE 0.72 OF 118 WHERE HUSBANDRY, IF PRESENT, IS PRINCIPALLY IN THE FORM OF BOVINE, EQUINE, CAMEL-LIKE, OR DEER-LIKE ANIMALS, RATHER THAN PIGS, SHEEP, OR GOATS (152)	63	TILT TOWARD BEING THOSE 0.52 OF 23 WHERE HUSBANDRY, IF PRESENT, IS PRINCIPALLY IN THE FORM OF PIGS, SHEEP, OR GOATS, RATHER THAN BOVINE, EQUINE, CAMEL-LIKE, OR DEER-LIKE ANIMALS (74)	85 11 33 12 XSQ= 4.14 PHI= 0.171 XP = 0.0420
71	TEND TO BE THOSE 0.66 OF 86 WHERE METAL WORKING IS PRESENT (98)	71	TEND TO BE THOSE 0.82 OF 39 WHERE METAL WORKING IS ABSENT (153)	57 7 29 32 XSQ= 23.19 PHI= 0.431 XP = 0.0000
80	DRIFT LESS TOWARD BEING THOSE 0.82 OF 85 WHERE NO CITY OR TOWN IS PRESENT (185)	80	DRIFT MORE TOWARD BEING THOSE 0.97 OF 31 WHERE NO CITY OR TOWN IS PRESENT (185)	15 1 70 30 XSQ= 2.85 PHI= 0.157 XP = 0.0912
81	TEND LESS TO BE THOSE 0.53 OF 85 WHERE NO CITY OR TOWN IS PRESENT, AND THE AVERAGE COMMUNITY SIZE IS SMALLER THAN 200 (135)	81	TEND MORE TO BE THOSE 0.90 OF 31 WHERE NO CITY OR TOWN IS PRESENT, AND THE AVERAGE COMMUNITY SIZE IS SMALLER THAN 200 (135)	40 3 45 28 XSQ= 12.05 PHI= 0.322 XP = 0.0005

82	LEAN MORE TOWARD BEING THOSE 0.88 OF 85 WHERE A CITY OR TOWN IS PRESENT, OR THE AVERAGE COMMUNITY SIZE IS FIFTY OR GREATER (178)	82	LEAN LESS TOWARD BEING THOSE 0.61 OF 31 WHERE A CITY OR TOWN IS PRESENT, OR THE AVERAGE COMMUNITY SIZE IS FIFTY OR GREATER (178)	75 19 10 12 XSQ= 9.05 PHI= 0.279 XP = 0.0026
83	LEAN LESS TOWARD BEING THOSE 0.65 OF 69 WHERE, WITH NO CITY AND NO TOWN PRESENT, THE AVERAGE COMMUNITY SIZE IS SMALLER THAN 200, RATHER THAN BETWEEN 200 AND 999 (135)	83	LEAN MORE TOWARD BEING THOSE 0.97 OF 29 WHERE, WITH NO CITY AND NO TOWN PRESENT, THE AVERAGE COMMUNITY SIZE IS SMALLER THAN 200, RATHER THAN BETWEEN 200 AND 999 (135)	24 1 45 28 XSQ= 8.97 PHI= 0.302 XP = 0.0028
86	TEND TO BE THOSE 0.58 OF 120 WHERE THE LEVEL OF POLITICAL INTEGRATION IS THE LARGE STATE, THE LITTLE STATE, OR THE MINIMAL STATE (148) GPM	86	TEND TO BE THOSE 0.76 OF 46 WHERE THE LEVEL OF POLITICAL INTEGRATION IS THE AUTONOMOUS COMMUNITY, OR THE FAMILY (156) GPM	70 11 50 35 XSQ= 14.42 PHI= 0.295 XP = 0.0001
94	TILT LESS TOWARD BEING THOSE 0.86 OF 131 WHERE THE HIERARCHY OF NATIONAL JURISDICTION HAS TWO, ONE, OR NO LEVELS (296) GES,EA	94	IN ALL CASES ARE THOSE 1.00 OF 50 WHERE THE HIERARCHY OF NATIONAL JURISDICTION HAS TWO, ONE, OR NO LEVELS (296) GES,EA	18 0 113 50 XSQ= 6.17 PHI= 0.185 XP = 0.0130
96	TEND TO BE THOSE 0.67 OF 131 WHERE THE HIERARCHY OF NATIONAL JURISDICTION HAS FOUR, THREE, TWO OR ONE LEVEL (174) GES,EA	96	TEND TO BE THOSE 0.72 OF 50 WHERE THE HIERARCHY OF NATIONAL JURISDICTION HAS NO LEVELS (156) GES,EA	88 14 43 36 XSQ= 21.02 PHI= 0.341 XP = 0.0000
97	DRIFT LESS TOWARD BEING THOSE 0.75 OF 131 WHERE THE HIERARCHY OF LOCAL JURISDICTION HAS THREE OR TWO LEVELS (273) GES,EA	97	DRIFT MORE TOWARD BEING THOSE 0.88 OF 50 WHERE THE HIERARCHY OF LOCAL JURISDICTION HAS THREE OR TWO LEVELS (273) GES,EA	33 6 98 44 XSQ= 2.99 PHI= 0.128 XP = 0.0840
98	LEAN MORE TOWARD BEING THOSE 0.82 OF 131 WHERE THE HIERARCHY OF LOCAL JURISDICTION HAS FOUR OR THREE LEVELS (238) GES,EA	98	LEAN LESS TOWARD BEING THOSE 0.62 OF 50 WHERE THE HIERARCHY OF LOCAL JURISDICTION HAS FOUR OR THREE LEVELS (238) GES,EA	107 31 24 19 XSQ= 6.69 PHI= 0.192 XP = 0.0097
99	TILT MORE TOWARD BEING THOSE 0.77 OF 43 WHERE, WITH NATIONAL HIERARCHY ABSENT, THE HIERARCHY OF LOCAL JURISDICTION HAS FOUR OR THREE LEVELS (93) GES,EA	99	TILT LESS TOWARD BEING THOSE 0.53 OF 36 WHERE, WITH NATIONAL HIERARCHY ABSENT, THE HIERARCHY OF LOCAL JURISDICTION HAS FOUR OR THREE LEVELS (93) GES,EA	33 19 10 17 XSQ= 3.99 PHI= 0.225 XP = 0.0457
100	TEND MORE TO BE THOSE 0.92 OF 131 WHERE HIERARCHIES ARE MORE COMPLEX THAN THE 'SIMPLEST,' I. E., MORE COMPLEX THAN TWO LOCAL LEVELS WITH NO NATIONAL LEVELS (267) GES,EA	100	TEND LESS TO BE THOSE 0.66 OF 50 WHERE HIERARCHIES ARE MORE COMPLEX THAN THE 'SIMPLEST,' I. E., MORE COMPLEX THAN TWO LOCAL LEVELS WITH NO NATIONAL LEVELS (267) GES,EA	121 33 10 17 XSQ= 17.80 PHI= 0.314 XP = 0.0000

```
102  TEND TO BE THOSE                 0.68 OF 156    102  TEND TO BE THOSE                 0.69 OF  52       106    16
     WHERE CLASS STRATIFICATION IS                        WHERE CLASS STRATIFICATION IS                        50    36
     PRESENT  (203)                                       ABSENT  (180)                                  XSQ=    20.72
                                                                                                         PHI=    0.316
                                                                                                         XP =   0.0000

109  LEAN LESS TOWARD BEING THOSE     0.76 OF 139    109  LEAN MORE TOWARD BEING THOSE     0.96 OF  53        33     2
     WHERE CASTES ARE ABSENT  (317)                       WHERE CASTES ARE ABSENT  (317)                      106    51
                                                                                                         XSQ=     8.97
                                                                                                         PHI=    0.216
                                                                                                         XP =   0.0027

110  LEAN TOWARD BEING THOSE          0.62 OF 154    110  LEAN TOWARD BEING THOSE          0.65 OF  51        95    18
     WHERE SLAVERY IS PRESENT  (163)                      WHERE SLAVERY IS ABSENT  (218)                       59    33
                                                                                                         XSQ=     9.75
                                                                                                         PHI=    0.218
                                                                                                         XP =   0.0018

116  DRIFT LESS TOWARD BEING THOSE    0.63 OF  16    116  IN ALL CASES ARE THOSE           1.00 OF   9         6     0
     WHERE OCCUPATIONAL SPECIALIZATION IS                 WHERE OCCUPATIONAL SPECIALIZATION IS                 10     9
     PART-TIME ONLY  (34) JMH                             PART-TIME ONLY  (34) JMH                       XSQ=     2.62
                                                                                                         PHI=    0.324
                                                                                                         EP =   0.0571

118  DRIFT TOWARD BEING THOSE         0.57 OF  21    118  DRIFT TOWARD BEING THOSE         0.86 OF   7        12     1
     WHERE THE PERCENTAGE OF OCCUPATIONS                  WHERE THE PERCENTAGE OF OCCUPATIONS                   9     6
     THAT ARE SPECIALIZED                                 THAT ARE SPECIALIZED                           XSQ=     2.35
     IS HIGH OR MEDIUM  (24) WME                          IS LOW  (25) WME                               PHI=    0.289
                                                                                                         EP =   0.0836

120  DRIFT TOWARD BEING THOSE         0.67 OF  24    120  DRIFT TOWARD BEING THOSE         0.71 OF   7        16     2
     WHERE THE CRAFT SPECIALIZATION SCORE                 WHERE THE CRAFT SPECIALIZATION SCORE                  8     5
     IS HIGH OR MEDIUM  (36) WME                          IS LOW  (17) WME                               XSQ=     1.85
                                                                                                         PHI=    0.245
                                                                                                         EP =   0.0994

128  DRIFT TOWARD BEING THOSE         0.60 OF  40    128  DRIFT TOWARD BEING THOSE         0.78 OF   9        16     7
     WHERE, IF SUBSISTENCE IS PRIMARILY BY                WHERE, IF SUBSISTENCE IS PRIMARILY BY                24     2
     AGRICULTURE, THE WORK IS                             AGRICULTURE, THE WORK IS                       XSQ=     2.83
     MAINLY DONE BY FEMALES  (37)                         MAINLY DONE BY MALES  (40)                     PHI=   -0.240
                                                                                                         XP =   0.0925

129  LEAN TOWARD BEING THOSE          0.54 OF  37    129  LEAN TOWARD BEING THOSE          0.89 OF  18        20     2
     WHERE WEAVING IS                                     WHERE WEAVING IS                                     17    16
     MAINLY DONE BY MALES  (31)                           MAINLY DONE BY FEMALES  (73)                   XSQ=     7.60
                                                                                                         PHI=    0.372
                                                                                                         XP =   0.0058

130  LEAN TOWARD BEING THOSE          0.67 OF  30    130  LEAN TOWARD BEING THOSE          0.78 OF  18        20     4
     WHERE LEATHER WORKING IS                             WHERE LEATHER WORKING IS                             10    14
     MAINLY DONE BY MALES  (39)                           MAINLY DONE BY FEMALES  (45)                   XSQ=     7.20
                                                                                                         PHI=    0.387
                                                                                                         XP =   0.0073
```

132	TILT TOWARD BEING THOSE WHERE ECONOMIC EXCHANGE INVOLVES THE USE OF MONEY (37) JMH	0.81 OF 16	132	TILT TOWARD BEING THOSE WHERE ECONOMIC EXCHANGE DOES NOT INVOLVE THE USE OF MONEY (17) JMH	0.67 OF 9	13 3 3 6 XSQ= 3.85 PHI= 0.392 EP = 0.0308
138	TILT TOWARD BEING THOSE WHERE SUPERORDINATE JUSTICE IS PRESENT (22) BBW	0.64 OF 14	138	TILT TOWARD BEING THOSE WHERE SUPERORDINATE JUSTICE IS ABSENT (18) BBW	0.88 OF 8	9 1 5 7 XSQ= 3.62 PHI= 0.405 EP = 0.0310
142	DRIFT TOWARD BEING THOSE. WHERE THE LEVEL OF SOCIAL SANCTION IS PUBLIC CORPOREAL SANCTION OR PUBLIC PROPERTY SANCTION, RATHER THAN PRIVATE SETTLEMENT (38) JMH	0.75 OF 16	142	DRIFT TOWARD BEING THOSE WHERE THE LEVEL OF SOCIAL SANCTION IS PRIVATE SETTLEMENT, RATHER THAN PUBLIC CORPOREAL SANCTION OR PUBLIC PROPERTY SETTLEMENT (16) JMH	0.67 OF 9	12 3 4 6 XSQ= 2.61 PHI= 0.323 EP = 0.0872
143	TILT TOWARD BEING THOSE WHERE THE RATIO OF RESTITUTIVE TO REPRESSIVE SANCTIONS IS HIGH (20) WME	0.50 OF 24	143	IN ALL CASES ARE THOSE WHERE THE RATIO OF RESTITUTIVE TO REPRESSIVE SANCTIONS IS MEDIUM OR LOW (32) WME	1.00 OF 7	12 0 12 7 XSQ= 3.80 PHI= 0.350 EP = 0.0261
144	TILT TOWARD BEING THOSE WHERE THE RATIO OF RESTITUTIVE TO REPRESSIVE SANCTIONS IS HIGH OR MEDIUM (27) WME	0.71 OF 24	144	TILT TOWARD BEING THOSE WHERE THE RATIO OF RESTITUTIVE TO REPRESSIVE SANCTIONS IS LOW (25) WME	0.86 OF 7	17 1 7 6 XSQ= 4.98 PHI= 0.401 EP = 0.0245
147	TILT TOWARD BEING THOSE WHERE CODIFIED LAWS ARE PRESENT (20) LWS	0.73 OF 11	147	IN ALL CASES ARE THOSE WHERE CODIFIED LAWS ARE UNIMPORTANT OR ABSENT (13) LWS	1.00 OF 5	8 0 3 5 XSQ= 4.65 PHI= 0.539 EP = 0.0256
176	TEND TO BE THOSE WHERE THE COMMUNITY IS A CLAN-COMMUNITY OR A COMMUNITY STRUCTURED OR SEGMENTED ON A CLAN BASIS (169)	0.59 OF 155	176	TEND TO BE THOSE WHERE THE COMMUNITY IS OTHER THAN A CLAN-COMMUNITY OR A COMMUNITY STRUCTURED OR SEGMENTED ON A CLAN BASIS (213)	0.79 OF 53	91 11 64 42 XSQ= 21.27 PHI= 0.320 XP = 0.0000
177	LEAN LESS TOWARD BEING THOSE WHERE THE COMMUNITY IS OTHER THAN A SINGLE CLAN-COMMUNITY AND EXOGAMOUS (305)	0.70 OF 155	177	LEAN MORE TOWARD BEING THOSE WHERE THE COMMUNITY IS OTHER THAN A SINGLE CLAN-COMMUNITY AND EXOGAMOUS (305)	0.92 OF 53	46 4 109 49 XSQ= 9.42 PHI= 0.213 XP = 0.0022
178	TILT LESS TOWARD BEING THOSE WHERE THE COMMUNITY IS OTHER THAN SEGMENTED ON A CLAN BASIS AND NON-EXOGAMOUS (295)	0.72 OF 155	178	TILT MORE TOWARD BEING THOSE WHERE THE COMMUNITY IS OTHER THAN SEGMENTED ON A CLAN BASIS AND NON-EXOGAMOUS (295)	0.89 OF 53	43 6 112 47 XSQ= 5.04 PHI= 0.156 XP = 0.0248

No.		Ratio	No.		Ratio	
180	DRIFT LESS TCWARC BEING THCSE WHERE THE COMMUNITY IS COMMCNLY NCN-EXCGAMCUS, RATHER THAN EXCGAMCUS (258)	0.57 OF 155	180	DRIFT MORE TOWARD BEING THCSE WHERE THE COMMLNITY IS COMMONLY NON-EXOGAMOUS, RATHER THAN EXOGAMOUS (258)	0.72 CF 53	66 15 89 38 XSQ= 2.81 PHI= 0.116 XP = 0.0935
181	LEAN MCRE TOWARC BEING THCSE WHERE THE COMMUNITY IS CTHER THAN A DEME (337)	0.95 OF 155	181	LEAN LESS TOWARD BEING THOSE WHERE THE COMMUNITY IS CTHER THAN A DEME (337)	0.81 CF 53	8 10 147 43 XSQ= 7.73 PHI= -0.193 XP = 0.C054
182	TILT MCRE TOWARC BEING THCSE CTHER THAN WHERE THE COMMUNITY IS STRUCTURED ON A NON-CLAN BASIS ANC AGAMCUS (256)	0.75 OF 155	182	TILT LESS TOWARD BEING THOSE OTHER THAN WHERE THE COMMUNITY IS STRUCTURED ON A NON-CLAN BASIS AND AGAMOUS (256)	0.58 CF 53	38 22 117 31 XSQ= 4.76 PHI= -0.151 XP = 0.0291
183	TEND MCRE TC BE THCSE WHERE THE LARGEST NCN-CCGNATIC KIN GROUP IS SMALLER THAN A MCEITY, I. E., A PHRATRY CR SIB CR LINEACE (218)	0.96 OF 14C	183	TEND LESS TO BE THOSE WHERE THE LARGEST NCN-CCGNATIC KIN GROUP IS SMALLER THAN A MOEITY, I. E., A PHRATRY OR SIB OR LINEAGE (218)	0.67 CF 21	6 7 134 14 XSQ= 17.03 PHI= -0.325 XP = 0.000C
186	TEND TC BE THCSE WHERE THE KIN GRCUP IS EXCLUSIVELY PATRILINEAL (150)	0.63 OF 163	186	TEND TO BE THOSE WHERE THE KIN GROUP IS OTHER THAN EXCLLSIVELY PATRILINEAL (250)	0.85 CF 54	102 8 61 46 XSQ= 35.13 PHI= 0.402 XP = 0.
187	TILT MCRE TOWARC BEING THCSE WHERE THE KIN GRCUP IS CTHER THAN EXCLUSIVELY MATRILINEAL (344)	0.93 OF 163	187	TILT LESS TOWARD BEING THOSE WHERE THE KIN GROUP IS OTHER THAN EXCLUSIVELY MATRILINEAL (344)	0.81 CF 54	11 10 152 44 XSQ= 5.15 PHI= -0.154 XP = 0.0232
188	TEND TC BE THCSE WHERE THE KIN GRCUP IS OTHER THAN EXCLUSIVELY CCGNATIC (252)	0.86 OF 163	188	TEND TO BE THOSE WHERE THE KIN GROUP IS EXCLUSIVELY COGNATIC (148)	0.61 CF 54	23 33 140 21 XSQ= 44.38 PHI= -0.452 XP = 0.
190	TEND TC BE THCSE WHERE THE KIN GRCUP IS PATRILINEAL CR CCUBLE-CESCENT, RATHER THAN MATRILINEAL (186)	0.90 OF 139	19C	TEND TO BE THOSE WHERE THE KIN GROUP IS MATRILINEAL, RATHER THAN PATRILINEAL OR DOUBLE-DESCENT (61)	0.52 CF 21	125 10 14 11 XSQ= 21.67 PHI= 0.368 XP = 0.C000
192	TEND MCRE TC BE THCSE CTHER THAN WHERE THE CNLY KIN GROUP PRESENT IS A KINCREC CR ELSE BILATERAL CESCENT IS INFERREC (289)	0.90 OF 163	192	TEND LESS TO BE THOSE OTHER THAN WHERE THE ONLY KIN GRCUP PRESENT IS A KINDRED OR ELSE BILATERAL DESCENT IS INFERRED (289)	0.54 CF 54	17 25 146 29 XSQ= 31.17 PHI= -0.379 XP = 0.

```
196  TEND MORE TO BE THOSE              0.80 OF 131    196  TEND LESS TO BE THOSE              0.51 OF  37         105    19
     WHERE INDIVIDUAL RIGHTS IN REAL PROPERTY,              WHERE INDIVIDUAL RIGHTS IN REAL PROPERTY,               26    18
     AND RULES FOR INHERITANCE,                             AND RULES FOR INHERITANCE,                          XSQ=   10.94
     ARE PRESENT  (194)                                     ARE PRESENT  (194)                                  PHI=   0.255
                                                                                                                XP =  0.0009

197  TILT MORE TOWARD BEING THOSE       0.95 OF 105    197  TILT LESS TOWARD BEING THOSE       0.79 OF  19         100    15
     WHERE RULES FOR THE INHERITANCE OF                     WHERE RULES FOR THE INHERITANCE OF                       5     4
     REAL PROPERTY, IF PRESENT,                             REAL PROPERTY, IF PRESENT,                          XSQ=    4.15
     FAVOR EITHER THE MALE HEIR OR LINE,                    FAVOR EITHER THE MALE HEIR OR LINE,                 PHI=   0.183
     OR THE FEMALE HEIR OR LINE  (165)                      OR THE FEMALE HEIR OR LINE  (165)                   XP =  0.0415

198  TEND MORE TO BE THOSE              0.93 OF 100    198  TEND LESS TO BE THOSE              0.60 OF  15          93     9
     WHERE RULES FOR THE INHERITANCE OF                     WHERE RULES FOR THE INHERITANCE OF                       7     6
     REAL PROPERTY, IF PRESENT,                             REAL PROPERTY, IF PRESENT,                          XSQ=   11.07
     FAVOR THE MALE HEIR OR LINE, RATHER THAN               FAVOR THE MALE HEIR OR LINE, RATHER THAN            PHI=   0.310
     THE FEMALE  (144)                                      THE FEMALE  (144)                                   XP =  0.0009

201  TILT MORE TOWARD BEING THOSE       0.91 OF 163    201  TILT LESS TOWARD BEING THOSE       0.80 OF  54         149    43
     WHERE MARITAL RESIDENCE IS                             WHERE MARITAL RESIDENCE IS                              14    11
     NON-OPTIONAL, RATHER THAN                              NON-OPTIONAL, RATHER THAN                           XSQ=    4.43
     AMBILOCAL OR NEOLOCAL  (334)                           AMBILOCAL OR NEOLOCAL  (334)                        PHI=   0.143
                                                                                                                XP =  0.0354

204  TEND MORE TO BE THOSE              0.91 OF 160    204  TEND LESS TO BE THOSE              0.67 OF  33         146    22
     WHERE MARITAL RESIDENCE IS                             WHERE MARITAL RESIDENCE IS                              14    11
     PATRILOCAL, VIRILOCAL, OR AVUNCULOCAL,                 PATRILOCAL, VIRILOCAL, OR AVUNCULOCAL,              XSQ=   12.56
     RATHER THAN                                            RATHER THAN                                         PHI=   0.255
     AMBILOCAL OR NEOLOCAL  (270)                           AMBILOCAL OR NEOLOCAL  (270)                        XP =  0.0004

207  LEAN TOWARD BEING THOSE            0.82 OF  17    207  LEAN TOWARD BEING THOSE            0.66 OF  32           3    21
     WHERE MARITAL RESIDENCE IS                             WHERE MARITAL RESIDENCE IS                              14    11
     AMBILOCAL OR NEOLOCAL, RATHER THAN                     MATRILOCAL OR UXORILOCAL, RATHER THAN               XSQ=    8.40
     MATRILOCAL OR UXORILOCAL  (64)                         AMBILOCAL OR NEOLOCAL  (64)                         PHI=  -0.414
                                                                                                                XP =  0.0038

209  TEND MORE TO BE THOSE              0.98 OF 149    209  TEND LESS TO BE THOSE              0.51 OF  43         146    22
     WHERE MARITAL RESIDENCE IS                             WHERE MARITAL RESIDENCE IS                               3    21
     PATRILOCAL, VIRILOCAL, OR AVUNCULOCAL,                 PATRILOCAL, VIRILOCAL, OR AVUNCULOCAL,              XSQ=   62.68
     RATHER THAN                                            RATHER THAN                                         PHI=   0.571
     MATRILOCAL OR UXORILOCAL  (270)                        MATRILOCAL OR UXORILOCAL  (270)                     XP =  0.

210  TEND MORE TO BE THOSE              0.98 OF 116    210  TEND LESS TO BE THOSE              0.54 OF  13         114     7
     WHERE MARITAL RESIDENCE IS                             WHERE MARITAL RESIDENCE IS                               2     6
     PATRILOCAL, RATHER THAN                                PATRILOCAL, RATHER THAN                             XSQ=   32.40
     MATRILOCAL  (169)                                      MATRILOCAL  (169)                                   PHI=   0.501
                                                                                                                XP =  0.

224  TILT TOWARD BEING THOSE            0.60 OF  75    224  TILT TOWARD BEING THOSE            0.70 OF  27          45     8
     WHERE COUSIN MARRIAGE IS                               WHERE COUSIN MARRIAGE IS                                30    19
     PREFERENTIALLY OR PERMISSIVELY                         PREFERENTIALLY OR PERMISSIVELY                      XSQ=    6.17
     EITHER PATRI- OR MATRILATERAL,                         SYMMETRICAL, RATHER THAN                            PHI=   0.246
     RATHER THAN SYMMETRICAL  (66)                          EITHER PATRI- OR MATRILATERAL  (106)                XP =  0.0130
```

240	DRIFT TOWARD BEING THOSE WHERE THE FAMILY, IF EXTENDED, IS SMALL OR STEM, RATHER THAN LARGE (135)	0.69 OF 84	240	DRIFT TOWARD BEING THOSE WHERE THE FAMILY, IF EXTENDED, IS LARGE, RATHER THAN SMALL OR STEM (78)	0.52 OF 31	26 16 58 15 XSQ= 3.33 PHI= -0.170 XP = 0.0682
243	DRIFT TOWARD BEING THOSE WHERE POLYGYNY, IF PRESENT, HAS A HIGH INCIDENCE (24) W-C,S	0.58 OF 24	243	DRIFT TOWARD BEING THOSE WHERE POLYGYNY, IF PRESENT, HAS A LOW INCIDENCE (36) W-D,S	0.75 OF 12	14 3 10 9 XSQ= 2.35 PHI= 0.256 EP = 0.0830
309	DRIFT TOWARD BEING THOSE WHERE ORAL SOCIALIZATION ANXIETY IS HIGH (26) W-C	0.59 OF 17	309	DRIFT TOWARD BEING THOSE WHERE ORAL SOCIALIZATION ANXIETY IS LOW (27) W-C	0.86 OF 7	10 1 7 6 XSQ= 2.37 PHI= 0.314 EP = 0.0778
314	TILT TOWARD BEING THOSE WHERE THE INCIDENCE OF MOTHER-CHILD HOUSEHOLDS IS HIGH (19) W-D,S	0.50 OF 28	314	TILT TOWARD BEING THOSE WHERE THE INCIDENCE OF MOTHER-CHILD HOUSEHOLDS IS LOW (61) W-D,S	0.89 OF 18	14 2 14 16 XSQ= 5.69 PHI= 0.352 XP = 0.0171
319	TILT TOWARD BEING THOSE WHERE PROTECTION OF THE INFANT FROM ENVIRONMENTAL DISCOMFORTS IS LOW (30) B-B-C	0.70 OF 23	319	TILT TOWARD BEING THOSE WHERE PROTECTION OF THE INFANT FROM ENVIRONMENTAL DISCOMFORTS IS HIGH (35) B-B-C	0.69 OF 13	7 9 16 4 XSQ= 3.61 PHI= -0.317 EP = 0.0379
323	DRIFT TOWARD BEING THOSE WHERE THE CONSTANCY OF PRESENCE OF THE INFANT'S NURTURANT AGENT IS LOW (45) B-B-C	0.71 OF 24	323	DRIFT TOWARD BEING THOSE WHERE THE CONSTANCY OF PRESENCE OF THE INFANT'S NURTURANT AGENT IS HIGH (29) B-B-C	0.63 OF 16	7 10 17 6 XSQ= 3.11 PHI= -0.279 EP = 0.0531
336	LEAN TOWARD BEING THOSE WHERE THE TOTAL POSITIVE PRESSURE TOWARD DEVELOPING RESPONSIBLE BEHAVIOR IN THE CHILD IS HIGH (43) B-B-C	0.84 OF 25	336	LEAN TOWARD BEING THOSE WHERE THE TOTAL POSITIVE PRESSURE TOWARD DEVELOPING RESPONSIBLE BEHAVIOR IN THE CHILD IS LOW (32) B-B-C	0.63 OF 16	21 6 4 10 XSQ= 7.43 PHI= 0.426 XP = 0.0064
337	TEND TO BE THOSE WHERE THE CHILD'S INFERRED ANXIETY OVER NON-PERFORMANCE OF RESPONSIBLE BEHAVIOR IS HIGH (38) B-B-C	0.84 OF 25	337	TEND TO BE THOSE WHERE THE CHILD'S INFERRED ANXIETY OVER NON-PERFORMANCE OF RESPONSIBLE BEHAVIOR IS LOW (35) B-B-C	0.80 OF 15	21 3 4 12 XSQ= 13.44 PHI= 0.580 EP = 0.0001
338	TILT TOWARD BEING THOSE WHERE THE CHILD'S INFERRED ANXIETY OVER PERFORMANCE OF RESPONSIBLE BEHAVIOR IS HIGH (44) B-B-C	0.76 OF 25	338	TILT TOWARD BEING THOSE WHERE THE CHILD'S INFERRED ANXIETY OVER PERFORMANCE OF RESPONSIBLE BEHAVIOR IS LOW (29) B-B-C	0.60 OF 15	19 6 6 9 XSQ= 3.76 PHI= 0.307 EP = 0.0418

339	TILT TOWARD BEING THOSE 0.68 OF 25 WHERE THE CHILD'S INFERRED CONFLICT REGARDING RESPONSIBLE BEHAVIOR IS HIGH (31) B-B-C	339	TILT TOWARD BEING THOSE 0.73 OF 15 WHERE THE CHILD'S INFERRED CONFLICT REGARDING RESPONSIBLE BEHAVIOR IS LOW (42) B-B-C	17 4 8 11 XSQ= 4.87 PHI= 0.349 EP = 0.0211
349	DRIFT TOWARD BEING THOSE 0.57 OF 21 WHERE THE CHILD'S INFERRED ANXIETY OVER NON-PERFORMANCE OF ACHIEVEMENT BEHAVIOR IS HIGH (34) B-B-C	349	DRIFT TOWARD BEING THOSE 0.77 OF 13 WHERE THE CHILD'S INFERRED ANXIETY OVER NON-PERFORMANCE OF ACHIEVEMENT BEHAVIOR IS LOW (28) B-B-C	12 3 9 10 XSQ= 2.52 PHI= 0.272 EP = 0.0790
350	TILT TOWARD BEING THOSE 0.67 OF 21 WHERE THE CHILD'S INFERRED ANXIETY OVER PERFORMANCE OF ACHIEVEMENT BEHAVIOR IS HIGH (34) B-B-C	350	TILT TOWARD BEING THOSE 0.77 OF 13 WHERE THE CHILD'S INFERRED ANXIETY OVER PERFORMANCE OF ACHIEVEMENT BEHAVIOR IS LOW (26) B-B-C	14 3 7 10 XSQ= 4.48 PHI= 0.363 EP = 0.0324
351	DRIFT LESS TOWARD BEING THOSE 0.52 OF 21 WHERE THE CHILD'S INFERRED CONFLICT REGARDING ACHIEVEMENT BEHAVIOR IS LOW (34) B-B-C	351	DRIFT MORE TOWARD BEING THOSE 0.85 OF 13 WHERE THE CHILD'S INFERRED CONFLICT REGARDING ACHIEVEMENT BEHAVIOR IS LOW (34) B-B-C	10 2 11 11 XSQ= 2.38 PHI= 0.264 EP = 0.0750
358	TILT TOWARD BEING THOSE 0.86 OF 21 WHERE ADOLESCENT PEER GROUPS ARE PRESENT IN A SETTING OF WORK AND PUBLIC GATHERINGS AND LEISURE, OR OF PUBLIC GATHERINGS AND LEISURE, OR OF LEISURE ONLY (41) JKH	358	TILT TOWARD BEING THOSE 0.60 OF 10 WHERE ADOLESCENT PEER GROUPS ARE ABSENT IN A SETTING OF WORK, AND OF PUBLIC GATHERINGS, AND OF LEISURE (11) JKH	18 4 3 6 XSQ= 4.83 PHI= 0.395 EP = 0.0297
360	DRIFT TOWARD BEING THOSE 0.54 OF 13 WHERE ADOLESCENT PEER GROUPS ARE PRESENT IN A SETTING OF WORK AND PUBLIC GATHERINGS AND LEISURE, OR AT LEAST OF PUBLIC GATHERINGS AND LEISURE (14) JKH	360	DRIFT TOWARD BEING THOSE 0.89 OF 9 WHERE ADOLESCENT PEER GROUPS ARE PRESENT ONLY IN A SETTING OF LEISURE, OR ELSE ARE ABSENT (23) JKH	7 1 6 8 XSQ= 2.55 PHI= 0.341 EP = 0.0743
365	DRIFT TOWARD BEING THOSE 0.78 OF 18 WHERE THE TIME SPENT IN ADOLESCENT PEER GROUP ACTIVITY IS HIGH OR HIGH-MEDIUM (30) JKH	365	DRIFT TOWARD BEING THOSE 0.71 OF 7 WHERE THE TIME SPENT IN ADOLESCENT PEER GROUP ACTIVITY IS LOW-MEDIUM OR LOW (15) JKH	14 2 4 5 XSQ= 3.38 PHI= 0.367 EP = 0.0581
370	DRIFT TOWARD BEING THOSE 0.55 OF 97 WHERE THE SEGREGATION OF ADOLESCENT BOYS IS COMPLETE OR PARTIAL (95)	370	DRIFT TOWARD BEING THOSE 0.65 OF 37 WHERE THE SEGREGATION OF ADOLESCENT BOYS IS ABSENT (148)	53 13 44 24 XSQ= 3.33 PHI= 0.158 XP = 0.0679
377	TEND LESS TO BE THOSE 0.56 OF 130 WHERE MALE GENITAL MUTILATION IS ABSENT (242)	377	TEND MORE TO BE THOSE 0.90 OF 50 WHERE MALE GENITAL MUTILATION IS ABSENT (242)	57 5 73 45 XSQ= 16.85 PHI= 0.306 XP = 0.0000

382	TILT TOWARD BEING THOSE WHERE FEMALE INITIATION RITES ARE ABSENT (27) JKB	0.56 OF 25	382	TILT TOWARD BEING THOSE WHERE FEMALE INITIATION RITES ARE PRESENT (38) JKB	0.85 OF 13	11 11 14 2 XSQ= 4.24 PHI= -0.334 EP = 0.0201
391	TILT TOWARD BEING THOSE WHERE PREMARITAL SEX RELATIONS ARE STRONGLY PUNISHED AND IN FACT RARE, OR WEAKLY PUNISHED AND IN FACT NOT RARE (89) JTW,EA	0.60 OF 72	391	TILT TOWARD BEING THOSE WHERE PREMARITAL SEX RELATIONS ARE PUNISHED ONLY IF PREGNANCY RESULTS, OR FREELY PERMITTED (90) JTW,EA	0.68 OF 22	43 7 29 15 XSQ= 4.21 PHI= 0.212 XP = 0.0402
392	LEAN TOWARD BEING THOSE WHERE PREMARITAL SEX RELATIONS ARE STRONGLY PUNISHED AND IN FACT RARE, OR WEAKLY PUNISHED AND IN FACT NOT RARE, OR PUNISHED ONLY IF PREGNANCY RESULTS (112) JTW,EA	0.74 OF 72	392	LEAN TOWARD BEING THOSE WHERE PREMARITAL SEX RELATIONS ARE FREELY PERMITTED (67) JTW,EA	0.59 OF 22	53 9 19 13 XSQ= 6.64 PHI= 0.266 XP = 0.0100
426	DRIFT MORE TOWARD BEING THOSE WHERE A HIGH GOD IS PRESENT (156) GES,EA	0.75 OF 104	426	DRIFT LESS TOWARD BEING THOSE WHERE A HIGH GOD IS PRESENT (156) GES,EA	0.58 OF 38	78 22 26 16 XSQ= 3.13 PHI= 0.148 XP = 0.0768
451	DRIFT TOWARD BEING THOSE WHERE TOTEMISM IS PRESENT (15) LWS	0.83 OF 6	451	DRIFT TOWARD BEING THOSE WHERE TOTEMISM IS UNIMPORTANT OR ABSENT (12) LWS	0.80 OF 5	5 1 1 4 XSQ= 2.23 PHI= 0.450 EP = 0.0801
452	TILT TOWARD BEING THOSE WHERE TOTEMISM WITH FOOD TABOOS IS PRESENT (19) WNS	0.59 OF 17	452	TILT TOWARD BEING THOSE WHERE TOTEMISM WITH FOOD TABOOS IS ABSENT (24) WNS	0.89 OF 9	10 1 7 8 XSQ= 3.71 PHI= 0.378 EP = 0.0362
458	TEND TO BE THOSE WHERE GAMES, IF PRESENT, INCLUDE GAMES OF STRATEGY (52) R-A-B,EA	0.56 OF 52	458	TEND TO BE THOSE WHERE GAMES, IF PRESENT, DO NOT INCLUDE GAMES OF STRATEGY (119) R-A-B,EA	0.88 OF 25	29 3 23 22 XSQ= 11.58 PHI= 0.388 XP = 0.0007

267 CULTURES WHERE WIVES ARE OBTAINED BY TOKEN BRIDE-PRICE (31)	267 CULTURES WHERE WIVES ARE OBTAINED BY MEANS OTHER THAN TOKEN BRIDE-PRICE (364)

BACKGROUND ON PAGE 128 — SUBJECT ONLY

31 IN LEFT COLUMN

APINAYE, AZTEC, BALINESE, BURUSHO, CHEYENNE, CREEK, CROW, GURE, HAVASUPAI, JAVANESE, KATAB, LOZI, MAM, MERINA, MISKITO, NABESNA, NAVAHO, NDEMBU, NGONI, OKINAWANS, PENDE, RUNDI, SANPOIL, TAMIL, TANALA, THAI, TODA, TRUMAI, TUNEBO, VEDDA, VIETNAMESE

364 IN RIGHT COLUMN

5 EXCLUDED BECAUSE UNASCERTAINED

	Left column (31)		Right column (364)		Statistics
4	IN ALL CASES ARE THOSE LOCATED OUTSIDE OF THE CIRCUM-MEDITERRANEAN (355)	1.00 OF 31	DRIFT LESS TOWARD BEING THOSE LOCATED OUTSIDE OF THE CIRCUM-MEDITERRANEAN (355)	0.88 OF 364	0 45 / 31 319 / XSQ= 3.19 / PHI= -0.090 / XP = 0.0742
45	DRIFT MORE TOWARD BEING THOSE WHERE SETTLEMENTS, IF FIXED, ARE COMPACT, RATHER THAN NON-COMPACT (149)	0.88 OF 17	DRIFT LESS TOWARD BEING THOSE WHERE SETTLEMENTS, IF FIXED, ARE COMPACT, RATHER THAN NON-COMPACT (149)	0.65 OF 205	15 134 / 2 71 / XSQ= 2.76 / PHI= 0.111 / XP = 0.0969
56	DRIFT TOWARD BEING THOSE WHERE FOOD PRODUCTION IS BY INCIPIENT FOOD PRODUCTION, RATHER THAN BY SIMPLE AGRICULTURE (46)	0.60 OF 10	DRIFT TOWARD BEING THOSE WHERE FOOD PRODUCTION IS BY SIMPLE AGRICULTURE, RATHER THAN BY INCIPIENT FOOD PRODUCTION (101)	0.72 OF 135	4 97 / 6 38 / XSQ= 3.09 / PHI= -0.146 / XP = 0.0788
79	DRIFT LESS TOWARD BEING THOSE WHERE NO CITY IS PRESENT (201)	0.77 OF 22	DRIFT MORE TOWARD BEING THOSE WHERE NO CITY IS PRESENT (201)	0.91 OF 201	5 18 / 17 183 / XSQ= 2.71 / PHI= 0.110 / XP = 0.0995
84	TILT LESS TOWARD BEING THOSE WHERE THE LEVEL OF POLITICAL INTEGRATION IS THE LITTLE STATE, THE MINIMAL STATE, THE AUTONOMOUS COMMUNITY, OR THE FAMILY (262) GPM	0.67 OF 21	TILT MORE TOWARD BEING THOSE WHERE THE LEVEL OF POLITICAL INTEGRATION IS THE LITTLE STATE, THE MINIMAL STATE, THE AUTONOMOUS COMMUNITY, OR THE FAMILY (262) GPM	0.88 OF 280	7 35 / 14 245 / XSQ= 5.43 / PHI= 0.134 / XP = 0.0198

```
 85  TILT LESS TOWARD BEING THOSE    0.52 OF  21     85  TILT MORE TOWARD BEING THOSE    0.79 OF 280        10   60
     WHERE THE LEVEL OF POLITICAL INTEGRATION            WHERE THE LEVEL OF POLITICAL INTEGRATION           11  220
     IS THE MINIMAL STATE,                               IS THE MINIMAL STATE,                         XSQ=     6.11
     THE AUTONOMOUS COMMUNITY, OR                        THE AUTONOMOUS COMMUNITY, OR                  PHI=    0.142
     THE FAMILY  (234) GPM                               THE FAMILY  (234) GPM                         XP =   0.0134

 94  DRIFT LESS TOWARD BEING THOSE  0.78 OF  27      94  DRIFT MORE TOWARD BEING THOSE  0.91 OF 300          6   28
     WHERE THE HIERARCHY                                 WHERE THE HIERARCHY                                21  272
     OF NATIONAL JURISDICTION HAS                        OF NATIONAL JURISDICTION HAS                  XSQ=     3.14
     TWO, ONE, OR NO LEVELS  (296) GES,EA                TWO, ONE, OR NO LEVELS  (296) GES,EA          PHI=    0.098
                                                                                                       XP =   0.0763

106  TILT MORE TOWARD BEING THOSE    0.93 OF  15    106  TILT LESS TOWARD BEING THOSE    0.59 OF 187         1   76
     WHERE CLASS STRATIFICATION, IF PRESENT,             WHERE CLASS STRATIFICATION, IF PRESENT,            14  111
     IS BASED ON SOMETHING OTHER THAN                    IS BASED ON SOMETHING OTHER THAN              XSQ=     5.43
     WEALTH  (126)                                       WEALTH  (126)                                 PHI=   -0.164
                                                                                                       XP =   0.0198

107  TILT LESS TOWARD BEING THOSE    0.53 OF  15    107  TILT MORE TOWARD BEING THOSE    0.81 OF 187         7   36
     WHERE CLASS STRATIFICATION, IF PRESENT,             WHERE CLASS STRATIFICATION, IF PRESENT,             8  151
     IS BASED ON SOMETHING OTHER THAN                    IS BASED ON SOMETHING OTHER THAN              XSQ=     4.70
     OCCUPATIONAL STATUS  (160)                          OCCUPATIONAL STATUS  (160)                    PHI=    0.153
                                                                                                       XP =   0.0302

127  IN ALL CASES ARE THOSE          1.00 OF   7    127  TILT TOWARD BEING THOSE         0.57 OF  58         0   33
     WHERE THE FEMALES' CONTRIBUTION                     WHERE THE FEMALES' CONTRIBUTION                     7   25
     TO SUBSISTENCE                                      TO SUBSISTENCE                                XSQ=     5.97
     IS LOW  (32) JKB                                    IS HIGH  (33) JKB                             PHI=   -0.303
                                                                                                       XP =   0.0145

138  IN ALL CASES ARE THOSE          1.00 OF   5    138  DRIFT TOWARD BEING THOSE        0.51 OF  35         5   17
     WHERE SUPERORDINATE JUSTICE IS                      WHERE SUPERORDINATE JUSTICE IS                      0   18
     PRESENT  (22) BBW                                   ABSENT  (18)  BBW                             XSQ=     2.83
                                                                                                       PHI=    0.266
                                                                                                       EP =   0.0530

139  IN ALL CASES ARE THOSE          1.00 OF   5    139  LEAN TOWARD BEING THOSE         0.71 OF  35         5   10
     WHERE SUPERORDINATE PUNISHMENT IS                   WHERE SUPERORDINATE PUNISHMENT IS                   0   25
     PRESENT  (15) BBW                                   ABSENT  (25) BBW                              XSQ=     6.72
                                                                                                       PHI=    0.410
                                                                                                       EP =   0.0046

152  IN ALL CASES ARE THOSE          1.00 OF   4    152  DRIFT TOWARD BEING THOSE        0.63 OF  16         4    6
     WHERE THE DIFFERENTIATION OF THE                    WHERE THE DIFFERENTIATION OF THE                    0   10
     JURIDICAL AGENCY FROM THE MEDICAL                   JURIDICAL AGENCY FROM THE MEDICAL             XSQ=     2.81
     AGENCY IS HIGH  (10) MJ                             AGENCY IS LOW  (10) MJ                        PHI=    0.375
                                                                                                       EP =   0.0867

187  TILT LESS TOWARD BEING THOSE    0.71 OF  31    187  TILT MORE TOWARD BEING THOSE    0.88 OF 363         9   45
     WHERE THE KIN GROUP IS                              WHERE THE KIN GROUP IS                             22  318
     OTHER THAN                                          OTHER THAN                                    XSQ=     5.35
     EXCLUSIVELY MATRILINEAL  (344)                      EXCLUSIVELY MATRILINEAL  (344)                PHI=    0.117
                                                                                                       XP =   0.0207
```

```
190  TILT TOWARD BEING THOSE          0.53 OF  17      190  TILT TOWARD BEING THOSE          0.78 OF 227          8  176
     WHERE THE KIN GROUP IS                                WHERE THE KIN GROUP IS                                 9   51
     MATRILINEAL, RATHER THAN                              PATRILINEAL OR DOUBLE-DESCENT,                 XSQ=     6.36
     PATRILINEAL OR DOUBLE-DESCENT  (61)                   RATHER THAN MATRILINEAL  (186)                 PHI=   -0.161
                                                                                                          XP =   0.0117

201  IN ALL CASES ARE THOSE           1.00 OF  31      201  TILT LESS TOWARD BEING THOSE     0.83 OF 362         31  300
     WHERE MARITAL RESIDENCE IS                            WHERE MARITAL RESIDENCE IS                             0   62
     NON-OPTIONAL, RATHER THAN                             NON-OPTIONAL, RATHER THAN                      XSQ=     5.08
     AMBILOCAL OR NEOLOCAL  (334)                          AMBILOCAL OR NEOLOCAL  (334)                   PHI=    0.114
                                                                                                          XP =   0.0242

204  IN ALL CASES ARE THOSE           1.00 OF  22      204  TILT LESS TOWARD BEING THOSE     0.80 OF 308         22  246
     WHERE MARITAL RESIDENCE IS                            WHERE MARITAL RESIDENCE IS                             0   62
     PATRILOCAL, VIRILOCAL, OR AVUNCULOCAL,                PATRILOCAL, VIRILOCAL, OR AVUNCULOCAL,         XSQ=     4.21
     RATHER THAN                                           RATHER THAN                                    PHI=    0.113
     AMBILOCAL OR NEOLOCAL  (270)                          AMBILOCAL OR NEOLOCAL  (270)                   XP =   0.0401

207  IN ALL CASES ARE THOSE           1.00 OF   9      207  LEAN TOWARD BEING THOSE          0.53 OF 116          9   54
     WHERE MARITAL RESIDENCE IS                            WHERE MARITAL RESIDENCE IS                             0   62
     MATRILOCAL OR UXORILOCAL, RATHER THAN                 AMBILOCAL OR NEOLOCAL, RATHER THAN             XSQ=     7.53
     AMBILOCAL OR NEOLOCAL  (64)                           MATRILOCAL OR UXORILOCAL  (64)                 PHI=    0.245
                                                                                                          XP =   0.0061

220  DRIFT LESS TOWARD BEING THOSE    0.58 OF  31      220  DRIFT MORE TOWARD BEING THOSE    0.75 OF 336         13   84
     WHERE FIRST COUSIN MARRIAGE                           WHERE FIRST COUSIN MARRIAGE                           18  252
     IN SOME FORM OR OTHER                                 IN SOME FORM OR OTHER                          XSQ=     3.36
     IS NOT PRESCRIBED OR PREFERRED  (273)                 IS NOT PRESCRIBED OR PREFERRED  (273)          PHI=    0.096
                                                                                                          XP =   0.0668

225  IN ALL CASES ARE THOSE           1.00 OF   3      225  DRIFT TOWARD BEING THOSE         0.68 OF  63          3   20
     WHERE COUSIN MARRIAGE IS                              WHERE COUSIN MARRIAGE IS                               0   43
     PREFERENTIALLY OR PERMISSIVELY                        PREFERENTIALLY OR PERMISSIVELY                 XSQ=     3.25
     PATRILATERAL, RATHER THAN                             MATRILATERAL, RATHER THAN                      PHI=    0.222
     MATRILATERAL  (23)                                    PATRILATERAL  (43)                             XP =   0.0712

301  TILT TOWARD BEING THOSE          0.54 OF  13      301  TILT TOWARD BEING THOSE          0.81 OF 111          6   90
     WHERE THE POST-PARTUM SEX TABOO LASTS                 WHERE THE POST-PARTUM SEX TABOO LASTS                  7   21
     ONE MONTH OR LESS  (28)                               LONGER THAN ONE MONTH  (96)                    XSQ=     6.25
                                                                                                          PHI=   -0.224
                                                                                                          XP =   0.0125

391  DRIFT TOWARD BEING THOSE         0.75 OF  16      391  DRIFT TOWARD BEING THOSE         0.53 OF 163         12   77
     WHERE PREMARITAL SEX RELATIONS ARE                    WHERE PREMARITAL SEX RELATIONS ARE                     4   86
     STRONGLY PUNISHED AND IN FACT RARE, OR                PUNISHED ONLY IF PREGNANCY RESULTS, OR         XSQ=     3.45
     WEAKLY PUNISHED AND                                   FREELY PERMITTED  (90) JTW,EA                  PHI=    0.139
     IN FACT NOT RARE  (89) JTW,EA                                                                        XP =   0.0633
```

```
************************************************************************************************************

268  CULTURES                                            268  CULTURES
     WHERE WIVES ARE OBTAINED BY                              WHERE WIVES ARE OBTAINED BY
     BRIDE-PRICE, RATHER THAN                                 TOKEN BRIDE-PRICE, RATHER THAN
     TOKEN BRIDE PRICE  (163)                                 BRIDE-PRICE  (31)


BACKGROUND ON PAGE 128                                                                        SUBJECT ONLY
............................................................................................................

     163  IN LEFT COLUMN

ABIPON      ABOR        ALBANIANS   ALORESE     ARAUCANIANS ARYANS      ASHANTI     ATAYAL      AZANDE      BABWA
BAJUN       BAMBARA     BAMILEKE    BARABRA     BARI        BASSERI     BATAK       BAYA        BEJA        BELU
BENGALI     BETE        BHIL        BHUIYA      BIRIFOR     BOZO        BUDUMA      BURYAT      CAMBODIANS  CHAGGA
CHENCHU     CHERKESS    CHIBCHA     DAGUR       DARD        DILLING     DOROBO      DUSUN       EGYPTIANS   ENGA
FANG        FON         FUTAJALONKE GANDA       GILBERTESE  GILYAK      GISU        GOAJIRO     GOND        GROS VENTRE
HASANIA     HAZARA      HEBREWS     HEHE        HERERO      HO          IFUGAO      ILA         IRAQW       JUKUN
KABYLE      KACHIN      KALMYK      KAPAUKU     KAZAK       KET         KHALKA      KHEVSUR     KIKUYU      KISSI
KOHISTANI   KOL         KPE         KUBA        KUMYK       KURTATCHI   LAKALAI     LAKHER      LAMET       LANGO
LEPCHA      LESU        LHOTA NAGA  LIFU        LOLO        LUBA        LUO         MACASSARESE MAGUZAWA    MALAYS
MAMVU       MANCHU      MARGI       MASAI       MATAKAM     MBUGWE      MBUNDU      MENDE       MIAO        MIN CHINESE
MINCHIA     MONGO       MONGUOR     MOSSI       MOTA        MZAB        NANDI       NUER        NUPE        NURI
NYAKYUSA    NYANEKA     NYARO       NYORO       ORAON       PAIWAN      PALAUANS    PARAUJANO   PATHAN      PURARI
REGEIBAT    RIFFIANS    ROTINESE    RWALA       SAMOYED     SANDAWE     SANTAL      SARAMACCA   SARSI       SENIANG
SERI        SHILLUK     SHLUH       SIMBOESE    SIUAI       SIWANS      SOMALI      SONGHAI     SOTHO       SUBANUN
SWAZI       SYRIANS     TALLENSI    TANIMBARESE TEDA        TESO        TETON       THONGA      TIWI        TOLOWA
TORAJA      TSHIMSHIAN  TUBATULABAL TURKANA     TURKMEN     ULAWANS     VENDA       WOLOF       WUTE        YAKO
YOMBE       YORUBA      YUROK

      31  IN RIGHT COLUMN

APINAYE     AZTEC       BALINESE    BURUSHO     CHEYENNE    CREEK       CROW        GURE        HAVASUPAI   JAVANESE
KATAB       LOZI        MAM         MERINA      MISKITO     NABESNA     NAVAHO      NDEMBU      NGONI       OKINAWANS
PENDE       RUNDI       SANPOIL     TAMIL       TANALA      THAI        TODA        TRUMAI      TUNEBO      VEDDA
VIETNAMESE

     201  EXCLUDED BECAUSE IRRELEVANT

       5  EXCLUDED BECAUSE UNASCERTAINED

------------------------------------------------------------------------------------------------------------
   4  TILT LESS TOWARD BEING THOSE    0.85 OF 163          4  IN ALL CASES ARE THOSE          1.00 OF  31          25      0
      LOCATED OUTSIDE OF                                      LOCATED OUTSIDE OF                                  138     31
      THE CIRCUM-MEDITERRANEAN  (355)                         THE CIRCUM-MEDITERRANEAN  (355)                  XSQ=     4.18
                                                                                                               PHI=    0.147
                                                                                                               XP =   0.0410
```

8	TEND MORE TO BE THOSE LOCATED OUTSIDE OF NORTH AMERICA (330)	0.95 OF 163	8	TEND LESS TO BE THOSE LOCATED OUTSIDE OF NORTH AMERICA (330)	0.74 OF 31	8 8 155 23 XSQ= 12.40 PHI= -0.253 XP = 0.0004
9	TILT MORE TOWARD BEING THOSE LOCATED OUTSIDE OF SOUTH AMERICA (335)	0.96 OF 163	9	TILT LESS TOWARD BEING THOSE LOCATED OUTSIDE OF SOUTH AMERICA (335)	0.84 OF 31	6 5 157 26 XSQ= 5.40 PHI= -0.167 XP = 0.0202
45	TILT LESS TOWARD BEING THOSE WHERE SETTLEMENTS, IF FIXED, ARE COMPACT, RATHER THAN NON-COMPACT (149)	0.59 OF 99	45	TILT MORE TOWARD BEING THOSE WHERE SETTLEMENTS, IF FIXED, ARE COMPACT, RATHER THAN NON-COMPACT (149)	0.88 OF 17	58 15 41 2 XSQ= 4.27 PHI= -0.192 XP = 0.0388
51	TILT MORE TOWARD BEING THOSE WHERE SUBSISTENCE IS PRIMARILY BY FOOD PRODUCTION -- I. E., AGRICULTURE OR HUSBANDRY -- RATHER THAN BY GATHERING (253)	0.83 OF 163	51	TILT LESS TOWARD BEING THOSE WHERE SUBSISTENCE IS PRIMARILY BY FOOD PRODUCTION -- I. E., AGRICULTURE OR HUSBANDRY -- RATHER THAN BY GATHERING (253)	0.61 OF 31	135 19 28 12 XSQ= 6.12 PHI= 0.178 XP = 0.0134
54	TILT MORE TOWARD BEING THOSE WHERE FOOD PRODUCTION IS BY INTENSIVE OR SIMPLE AGRICULTURE, RATHER THAN BY INCIPIENT FOOD PRODUCTION (192)	0.92 OF 110	54	TILT LESS TOWARD BEING THOSE WHERE FOOD PRODUCTION IS BY INTENSIVE OR SIMPLE AGRICULTURE, RATHER THAN BY INCIPIENT FOOD PRODUCTION (192)	0.70 OF 20	101 14 9 6 XSQ= 5.90 PHI= 0.213 XP = 0.0151
56	LEAN TOWARD BEING THOSE WHERE FOOD PRODUCTION IS BY SIMPLE AGRICULTURE, RATHER THAN BY INCIPIENT FOOD PRODUCTION (101)	0.85 OF 59	56	LEAN TOWARD BEING THOSE WHERE FOOD PRODUCTION IS BY INCIPIENT FOOD PRODUCTION, RATHER THAN BY SIMPLE AGRICULTURE (46)	0.60 OF 10	50 4 9 6 XSQ= 7.60 PHI= 0.332 XP = 0.0058
79	TILT MORE TOWARD BEING THOSE WHERE NO CITY IS PRESENT (201)	0.94 OF 85	79	TILT LESS TOWARD BEING THOSE WHERE NO CITY IS PRESENT (201)	0.77 OF 22	5 5 80 17 XSQ= 4.03 PHI= -0.194 XP = 0.0446
84	DRIFT MORE TOWARD BEING THOSE WHERE THE LEVEL OF POLITICAL INTEGRATION IS THE LITTLE STATE, THE MINIMAL STATE, THE AUTONOMOUS COMMUNITY, OR THE FAMILY (262) GPM	0.85 OF 120	84	DRIFT LESS TOWARD BEING THOSE WHERE THE LEVEL OF POLITICAL INTEGRATION IS THE LITTLE STATE, THE MINIMAL STATE, THE AUTONOMOUS COMMUNITY, OR THE FAMILY (262) GPM	0.67 OF 21	18 7 102 14 XSQ= 2.96 PHI= -0.145 XP = 0.0855
102	DRIFT TOWARD BEING THOSE WHERE CLASS STRATIFICATION IS PRESENT (203)	0.68 OF 156	102	DRIFT TOWARD BEING THOSE WHERE CLASS STRATIFICATION IS ABSENT (180)	0.50 OF 30	106 15 50 15 XSQ= 2.82 PHI= 0.123 XP = 0.0931

106	TILT LESS TOWARD BEING THOSE 0.59 OF 106 WHERE CLASS STRATIFICATION, IF PRESENT, IS BASED ON SOMETHING OTHER THAN WEALTH (126)	106	TILT MORE TOWARD BEING THOSE 0.93 OF 15 WHERE CLASS STRATIFICATION, IF PRESENT, IS BASED ON SOMETHING OTHER THAN WEALTH (126)	43 1 63 14 XSQ= 5.14 PHI= 0.206 XP = 0.0233
107	LEAN MORE TOWARD BEING THOSE 0.86 OF 106 WHERE CLASS STRATIFICATION, IF PRESENT, IS BASED ON SOMETHING OTHER THAN OCCUPATIONAL STATUS (160)	107	LEAN LESS TOWARD BEING THOSE 0.53 OF 15 WHERE CLASS STRATIFICATION, IF PRESENT, IS BASED ON SOMETHING OTHER THAN OCCUPATIONAL STATUS (160)	15 7 91 8 XSQ= 7.28 PHI= -0.245 XP = 0.0070
127	TILT TOWARD BEING THOSE 0.56 OF 25 WHERE THE FEMALES' CONTRIBUTION TO SUBSISTENCE IS HIGH (33) JKB	127	IN ALL CASES ARE THOSE 1.00 OF 7 WHERE THE FEMALES' CONTRIBUTION TO SUBSISTENCE IS LOW (32) JKB	14 0 11 7 XSQ= 4.88 PHI= 0.390 EP = 0.0105
129	TILT TOWARD BEING THOSE 0.54 OF 37 WHERE WEAVING IS MAINLY DONE BY MALES (31)	129	TILT TOWARD BEING THOSE 0.90 OF 10 WHERE WEAVING IS MAINLY DONE BY FEMALES (73)	20 1 17 9 XSQ= 4.53 PHI= 0.310 XP = 0.0334
139	TILT TOWARD BEING THOSE 0.71 OF 14 WHERE SUPERORDINATE PUNISHMENT IS ABSENT (25) BBW	139	IN ALL CASES ARE THOSE 1.00 OF 5 WHERE SUPERORDINATE PUNISHMENT IS PRESENT (15) BBW	4 5 10 0 XSQ= 4.95 PHI= -0.510 EP = 0.0108
176	TILT TOWARD BEING THOSE 0.59 OF 155 WHERE THE COMMUNITY IS A CLAN-COMMUNITY OR A COMMUNITY STRUCTURED OR SEGMENTED ON A CLAN BASIS (169)	176	TILT TOWARD BEING THOSE 0.65 OF 31 WHERE THE COMMUNITY IS OTHER THAN A CLAN-COMMUNITY OR A COMMUNITY STRUCTURED OR SEGMENTED ON A CLAN BASIS (213)	91 11 64 20 XSQ= 4.73 PHI= 0.159 XP = 0.0297
182	TILT MORE TOWARD BEING THOSE 0.75 OF 155 OTHER THAN WHERE THE COMMUNITY IS STRUCTURED ON A NON-CLAN BASIS AND AGAMOUS (256)	182	TILT LESS TOWARD BEING THOSE 0.55 OF 31 OTHER THAN WHERE THE COMMUNITY IS STRUCTURED ON A NON-CLAN BASIS AND AGAMOUS (256)	38 14 117 17 XSQ= 4.49 PHI= -0.155 XP = 0.0341
186	TEND TO BE THOSE 0.63 OF 163 WHERE THE KIN GROUP IS EXCLUSIVELY PATRILINEAL (150)	186	TEND TO BE THOSE 0.74 OF 31 WHERE THE KIN GROUP IS OTHER THAN EXCLUSIVELY PATRILINEAL (250)	102 8 61 23 XSQ= 12.89 PHI= 0.258 XP = 0.0003
187	TEND MORE TO BE THOSE 0.93 OF 163 WHERE THE KIN GROUP IS OTHER THAN EXCLUSIVELY MATRILINEAL (344)	187	TEND LESS TO BE THOSE 0.71 OF 31 WHERE THE KIN GROUP IS OTHER THAN EXCLUSIVELY MATRILINEAL (344)	11 9 152 22 XSQ= 11.68 PHI= -0.245 XP = 0.0006

188	LEAN MORE TOWARD BEING THOSE WHERE THE KIN GROUP IS OTHER THAN EXCLUSIVELY COGNATIC (252)	0.86 OF 163	188	LEAN LESS TOWARD BEING THOSE WHERE THE KIN GROUP IS OTHER THAN EXCLUSIVELY COGNATIC (252)	0.61 OF 31	23 12 140 19 XSQ= 9.06 PHI= -0.216 XP = 0.0026
190	TEND TO BE THOSE WHERE THE KIN GROUP IS PATRILINEAL OR DOUBLE-DESCENT, RATHER THAN MATRILINEAL (186)	0.90 OF 139	190	TEND TO BE THOSE WHERE THE KIN GROUP IS MATRILINEAL, RATHER THAN PATRILINEAL OR DOUBLE-DESCENT (61)	0.53 OF 17	125 8 14 9 XSQ= 18.87 PHI= 0.348 XP = 0.0000
197	LEAN MORE TOWARD BEING THOSE WHERE RULES FOR THE INHERITANCE OF REAL PROPERTY, IF PRESENT, FAVOR EITHER THE MALE HEIR OR LINE, OR THE FEMALE HEIR OR LINE (165)	0.95 OF 105	197	LEAN LESS TOWARD BEING THOSE WHERE RULES FOR THE INHERITANCE OF REAL PROPERTY, IF PRESENT, FAVOR EITHER THE MALE HEIR OR LINE, OR THE FEMALE HEIR OR LINE (165)	0.69 OF 13	100 9 5 4 XSQ= 7.72 PHI= 0.256 XP = 0.0055
207	TEND TO BE THOSE WHERE MARITAL RESIDENCE IS AMBILOCAL OR NEOLOCAL, RATHER THAN MATRILOCAL OR UXORILOCAL (64)	0.82 OF 17	207	IN ALL CASES ARE THOSE WHERE MARITAL RESIDENCE IS MATRILOCAL OR UXORILOCAL, RATHER THAN AMBILOCAL OR NEOLOCAL (64)	1.00 OF 9	3 9 14 0 XSQ= 12.92 PHI= -0.705 EP = 0.0001
209	TEND MORE TO BE THOSE WHERE MARITAL RESIDENCE IS PATRILOCAL, VIRILOCAL, OR AVUNCULOCAL, RATHER THAN MATRILOCAL OR UXORILOCAL (270)	0.98 OF 149	209	TEND LESS TO BE THOSE WHERE MARITAL RESIDENCE IS PATRILOCAL, VIRILOCAL, OR AVUNCULOCAL, RATHER THAN MATRILOCAL OR UXORILOCAL (270)	0.71 OF 31	146 22 3 9 XSQ= 25.92 PHI= 0.379 XP = 0.0000
210	TEND MORE TO BE THOSE WHERE MARITAL RESIDENCE IS PATRILOCAL, RATHER THAN MATRILOCAL (169)	0.98 OF 116	210	TEND LESS TO BE THOSE WHERE MARITAL RESIDENCE IS PATRILOCAL, RATHER THAN MATRILOCAL (169)	0.69 OF 13	114 9 2 4 XSQ= 16.17 PHI= 0.354 XP = 0.0001
221	TILT LESS TOWARD BEING THOSE WHERE MATRILATERAL CROSS-COUSIN MARRIAGE IS NOT PRESCRIBED OR PREFERRED (335)	0.84 OF 153	221	IN ALL CASES ARE THOSE WHERE MATRILATERAL CROSS-COUSIN MARRIAGE IS NOT PRESCRIBED OR PREFERRED (335)	1.00 OF 31	24 0 129 31 XSQ= 4.29 PHI= 0.153 XP = 0.0382
224	LEAN TOWARD BEING THOSE WHERE COUSIN MARRIAGE IS PREFERENTIALLY OR PERMISSIVELY EITHER PATRI- OR MATRILATERAL, RATHER THAN SYMMETRICAL (66)	0.60 OF 75	224	LEAN TOWARD BEING THOSE WHERE COUSIN MARRIAGE IS PREFERENTIALLY OR PERMISSIVELY SYMMETRICAL, RATHER THAN EITHER PATRI- OR MATRILATERAL (106)	0.81 OF 16	45 3 30 13 XSQ= 7.42 PHI= 0.286 XP = 0.0064
241	TILT MORE TOWARD BEING THOSE WHERE THE FAMILY, IF EXTENDED, IS LARGE OR SMALL, RATHER THAN STEM (187)	0.95 OF 84	241	TILT LESS TOWARD BEING THOSE WHERE THE FAMILY, IF EXTENDED, IS LARGE OR SMALL, RATHER THAN STEM (187)	0.75 OF 20	80 15 4 5 XSQ= 6.01 PHI= 0.240 XP = 0.0143

301	LEAN TOWARD BEING THOSE WHERE THE POST-PARTUM SEX TABOO LASTS LONGER THAN ONE MONTH (96)	0.88 OF 48	301	LEAN TOWARD BEING THOSE WHERE THE POST-PARTUM SEX TABOO LASTS ONE MONTH OR LESS (28)	0.54 OF 13	42 6 6 7 XSQ= 8.11 PHI= 0.365 XP = 0.0044
307	DRIFT TOWARD BEING THOSE WHERE THE EARLY AGGRESSION SATISFACTION POTENTIAL IS HIGH (33) W-C	0.76 OF 17	307	DRIFT TOWARD BEING THOSE WHERE THE EARLY AGGRESSION SATISFACTION POTENTIAL IS LOW (19) W-C	0.75 OF 4	13 1 4 3 XSQ= 1.89 PHI= 0.300 EP = 0.0877
319	DRIFT TOWARD BEING THOSE WHERE PROTECTION OF THE INFANT FROM ENVIRONMENTAL DISCOMFORTS IS LOW (30) B-B-C	0.70 OF 23	319	DRIFT TOWARD BEING THOSE WHERE PROTECTION OF THE INFANT FROM ENVIRONMENTAL DISCOMFORTS IS HIGH (35) B-B-C	0.80 OF 5	7 4 16 1 XSQ= 2.41 PHI= -0.293 EP = 0.0618
337	TILT TOWARD BEING THOSE WHERE THE CHILD'S INFERRED ANXIETY OVER NON-PERFORMANCE OF RESPONSIBLE BEHAVIOR IS HIGH (38) B-B-C	0.84 OF 25	337	TILT TOWARD BEING THOSE WHERE THE CHILD'S INFERRED ANXIETY OVER NON-PERFORMANCE OF RESPONSIBLE BEHAVIOR IS LOW (35) B-B-C	0.80 OF 5	21 1 4 4 XSQ= 5.76 PHI= 0.438 EP = 0.0112
338	TILT TOWARD BEING THOSE WHERE THE CHILD'S INFERRED ANXIETY OVER PERFORMANCE OF RESPONSIBLE BEHAVIOR IS HIGH (44) B-B-C	0.76 OF 25	338	TILT TOWARD BEING THOSE WHERE THE CHILD'S INFERRED ANXIETY OVER PERFORMANCE OF RESPONSIBLE BEHAVIOR IS LOW (29) B-B-C	0.80 OF 5	19 1 6 4 XSQ= 3.63 PHI= 0.348 EP = 0.0312
370	TILT TOWARD BEING THOSE WHERE THE SEGREGATION OF ADOLESCENT BOYS IS COMPLETE OR PARTIAL (95)	0.55 OF 97	370	TILT TOWARD BEING THOSE WHERE THE SEGREGATION OF ADOLESCENT BOYS IS ABSENT (148)	0.78 OF 18	53 4 44 14 XSQ= 5.15 PHI= 0.212 XP = 0.0232
377	TILT LESS TOWARD BEING THOSE WHERE MALE GENITAL MUTILATION IS ABSENT (242)	0.56 OF 130	377	TILT MORE TOWARD BEING THOSE WHERE MALE GENITAL MUTILATION IS ABSENT (242)	0.80 OF 25	57 5 73 20 XSQ= 4.02 PHI= 0.161 XP = 0.0449
417	IN ALL CASES ARE THOSE WHERE WARFARE IS PREVALENT (34) LWS	1.00 OF 13	417	DRIFT LESS TOWARD BEING THOSE WHERE WARFARE IS PREVALENT (34) LWS	0.67 OF 6	13 4 0 2 XSQ= 1.95 PHI= 0.320 EP = 0.0877
440	TILT TOWARD BEING THOSE WHERE FEAR OF SPIRITS IS LOW (29) W-C	0.65 OF 20	440	IN ALL CASES ARE THOSE WHERE FEAR OF SPIRITS IS HIGH (32) W-C	1.00 OF 4	7 4 13 0 XSQ= 3.36 PHI= -0.374 EP = 0.0311

269 CULTURES WHERE WIVES ARE OBTAINED BY EXCHANGING A FEMALE RELATIVE (16)	269 CULTURES WHERE WIVES ARE OBTAINED BY MEANS OTHER THAN EXCHANGING A FEMALE RELATIVE (379)

BACKGROUND ON PAGE 128 SUBJECT ONLY

16 IN LEFT COLUMN

AJIE	AMBA	ARANDA	BANDA	BUNLAP	DIERI	KARIERA	KERAKI	MAMBILA	MBUTI
NASKAPI	TIV	TUCANO	TUCUNA	WANTOAT	WIKMUNKAN				

379 IN RIGHT COLUMN

5 EXCLUDED BECAUSE UNASCERTAINED

6	LEAN TOWARD BEING THOSE LOCATED IN THE INSULAR PACIFIC (70)	0.50 OF 16	6	LEAN TOWARD BEING THOSE LOCATED OUTSIDE OF THE INSULAR PACIFIC (330)	0.84 OF 379		8 61 8 318 XSQ= 10.00 PHI= 0.159 XP = 0.0016
16	TILT TOWARD BEING THOSE WHERE THE LATITUDE IS LESS THAN TEN DEGREES (123)	0.56 OF 16	16	TILT TOWARD BEING THOSE WHERE THE LATITUDE IS TEN DEGREES OR GREATER (277)	0.70 OF 379		7 266 9 113 XSQ= 3.86 PHI= -0.099 XP = 0.0493
63	IN ALL CASES ARE THOSE WHERE HUSBANDRY, IF PRESENT, IS PRINCIPALLY IN THE FORM OF PIGS, SHEEP, OR GOATS, RATHER THAN BOVINE, EQUINE, CAMEL-LIKE, OR DEER-LIKE ANIMALS (74)	1.00 OF 7	63	TEND TO BE THOSE WHERE HUSBANDRY, IF PRESENT, IS PRINCIPALLY IN THE FORM OF BOVINE, EQUINE, CAMEL-LIKE, OR DEER-LIKE ANIMALS, RATHER THAN PIGS, SHEEP, OR GOATS (152)	0.69 OF 219		0 152 7 67 XSQ= 11.85 PHI= -0.229 XP = 0.0006
73	DRIFT MORE TOWARD BEING THOSE WHERE WEAVING IS ABSENT (130)	0.82 OF 11	73	DRIFT LESS TOWARD BEING THOSE WHERE WEAVING IS ABSENT (130)	0.51 OF 234		2 115 9 119 XSQ= 2.89 PHI= -0.109 XP = 0.0890
82	TILT TOWARD BEING THOSE WHERE NO CITY OR TOWN IS PRESENT, AND THE AVERAGE COMMUNITY SIZE IS SMALLER THAN FIFTY (46)	0.55 OF 11	82	TILT TOWARD BEING THOSE WHERE A CITY OR TOWN IS PRESENT, OR THE AVERAGE COMMUNITY SIZE IS FIFTY OR GREATER (178)	0.82 OF 212		5 173 6 39 XSQ= 6.39 PHI= -0.169 XP = 0.0115

86	DRIFT MORE TOWARD BEING THOSE WHERE THE LEVEL OF POLITICAL INTEGRATION IS THE AUTONOMOUS COMMUNITY, OR THE FAMILY (156) GPM	0.82 OF 11	86	DRIFT LESS TOWARD BEING THOSE WHERE THE LEVEL OF POLITICAL INTEGRATION IS THE AUTONOMOUS COMMUNITY, OR THE FAMILY (156) GPM	0.50 OF 290	2 144 9 146 XSQ= 3.04 PHI= -0.100 XP = 0.0814
95	IN ALL CASES ARE THOSE WHERE THE HIERARCHY OF NATIONAL JURISDICTION HAS ONE OR NO LEVELS (254) GES,EA	1.00 OF 14	95	DRIFT LESS TOWARD BEING THOSE WHERE THE HIERARCHY OF NATIONAL JURISDICTION HAS ONE OR NO LEVELS (254) GES,EA	0.76 OF 313	0 76 14 237 XSQ= 3.17 PHI= -0.098 XP = 0.0749
96	LEAN TOWARD BEING THOSE WHERE THE HIERARCHY OF NATIONAL JURISDICTION HAS NO LEVELS (156) GES,EA	0.93 OF 14	96	LEAN TOWARD BEING THOSE WHERE THE HIERARCHY OF NATIONAL JURISDICTION HAS FOUR, THREE, TWO OR ONE LEVEL (174) GES,EA	0.55 OF 313	1 172 13 141 XSQ= 10.45 PHI= -0.179 XP = 0.0012
98	LEAN TOWARD BEING THOSE WHERE THE HIERARCHY OF LOCAL JURISDICTION HAS TWO LEVELS (93) GES,EA	0.64 OF 14	98	LEAN TOWARD BEING THOSE WHERE THE HIERARCHY OF LOCAL JURISDICTION HAS FOUR OR THREE LEVELS (238) GES,EA	0.74 OF 314	5 232 9 82 XSQ= 7.93 PHI= -0.155 XP = 0.0049
99	TILT TOWARD BEING THOSE WHERE, WITH NATIONAL HIERARCHY ABSENT, THE HIERARCHY OF LOCAL JURISDICTION HAS TWO LEVELS (63) GES,EA	0.69 OF 13	99	TILT TOWARD BEING THOSE WHERE, WITH NATIONAL HIERARCHY ABSENT, THE HIERARCHY OF LOCAL JURISDICTION HAS FOUR OR THREE LEVELS (93) GES,EA	0.63 OF 141	4 89 9 52 XSQ= 3.94 PHI= -0.160 XP = 0.0471
100	TEND TO BE THOSE WHERE HIERARCHIES ARE THE 'SIMPLEST' I. E., WHERE THERE ARE ONLY TWO LOCAL LEVELS WITH NO NATIONAL LEVELS (63) GES,EA	0.64 OF 14	100	TEND TO BE THOSE WHERE HIERARCHIES ARE MORE COMPLEX THAN THE 'SIMPLEST,' I. E., MORE COMPLEX THAN TWO LOCAL LEVELS WITH NO NATIONAL LEVELS (267) GES,EA	0.83 OF 313	5 261 9 52 XSQ= 17.05 PHI= -0.228 XP = 0.0000
102	IN ALL CASES ARE THOSE WHERE CLASS STRATIFICATION IS ABSENT (180)	1.00 OF 15	102	TEND TO BE THOSE WHERE CLASS STRATIFICATION IS PRESENT (203)	0.55 OF 364	0 202 15 162 XSQ= 15.66 PHI= -0.203 XP = 0.0001
175	TEND TO BE THOSE WHERE THE COMMUNITY IS 'KIN-HOMOGENEOUS,' I. E. A CLAN COMMUNITY OR A DEME (122)	0.75 OF 16	175	TEND TO BE THOSE WHERE THE COMMUNITY IS 'KIN-HETEROGENEOUS,' I. E. OTHER THAN A CLAN COMMUNITY OR A DEME (260)	0.70 OF 362	12 108 4 254 XSQ= 12.42 PHI= 0.181 XP = 0.0004
176	TEND TO BE THOSE WHERE THE COMMUNITY IS A CLAN-COMMUNITY OR A COMMUNITY STRUCTURED OR SEGMENTED ON A CLAN BASIS (169)	0.88 OF 16	176	TEND TO BE THOSE WHERE THE COMMUNITY IS OTHER THAN A CLAN-COMMUNITY OR A COMMUNITY STRUCTURED OR SEGMENTED ON A CLAN BASIS (213)	0.58 OF 362	14 152 2 210 XSQ= 11.10 PHI= 0.171 XP = 0.0009

177	TEND TO BE THOSE 0.75 OF 16 WHERE THE COMMUNITY IS A SINGLE CLAN-COMMUNITY AND EXOGAMOUS (77)	177	TEND TO BE THOSE 0.82 OF 362 WHERE THE COMMUNITY IS OTHER THAN A SINGLE CLAN-COMMUNITY AND EXOGAMOUS (305)	12 64 4 298 XSQ= 27.87 PHI= 0.272 XP = 0.0000
180	TEND TO BE THOSE 0.81 OF 16 WHERE THE COMMUNITY IS COMMONLY EXOGAMOUS, RATHER THAN NON-EXOGAMOUS (124)	18C	TEND TO BE THOSE 0.70 OF 362 WHERE THE COMMUNITY IS COMMONLY NON-EXOGAMOUS, RATHER THAN EXOGAMOUS (258)	13 110 3 252 XSQ= 15.82 PHI= 0.205 XP = 0.0001
182	TILT MORE TOWARD BEING THOSE 0.94 OF 16 OTHER THAN WHERE THE COMMUNITY IS STRUCTURED ON A NON-CLAN BASIS AND AGAMOUS (256)	182	TILT LESS TOWARD BEING THOSE 0.65 OF 362 OTHER THAN WHERE THE COMMUNITY IS STRUCTURED ON A NON-CLAN BASIS AND AGAMOUS (256)	1 125 15 237 XSQ= 4.32 PHI= -0.107 XP = 0.0378
183	TEND TO BE THOSE 0.50 OF 14 WHERE THE LARGEST NON-COGNATIC KIN GROUP IS THE MOEITY (34)	183	TEND TO BE THOSE 0.89 OF 235 WHERE THE LARGEST NON-COGNATIC KIN GROUP IS SMALLER THAN A MOEITY, I. E., A PHRATRY OR SIB OR LINEAGE (218)	7 25 7 210 XSQ= 14.93 PHI= 0.245 XP = 0.0001
184	LEAN TOWARD BEING THOSE 0.64 OF 14 WHERE THE LARGEST NON-COGNATIC KIN GROUP IS THE MOEITY OR PHRATRY (77)	184	LEAN TOWARD BEING THOSE 0.72 OF 235 WHERE THE LARGEST NON-COGNATIC KIN GROUP IS SMALLER THAN A PHRATRY, I. E. A SIB OR LINEAGE (175)	9 65 5 170 XSQ= 6.82 PHI= 0.166 XP = 0.0090
188	DRIFT MORE TOWARD BEING THOSE 0.88 OF 16 WHERE THE KIN GROUP IS OTHER THAN EXCLUSIVELY COGNATIC (252)	188	DRIFT LESS TOWARD BEING THOSE 0.62 OF 379 WHERE THE KIN GROUP IS OTHER THAN EXCLUSIVELY COGNATIC (252)	2 144 14 235 XSQ= 3.26 PHI= -0.091 XP = 0.0711
192	DRIFT MORE TOWARD BEING THOSE 0.94 OF 16 OTHER THAN WHERE THE ONLY KIN GROUP PRESENT IS A KINDRED OR ELSE BILATERAL DESCENT IS INFERRED (289)	192	DRIFT LESS TOWARD BEING THOSE 0.72 OF 379 OTHER THAN WHERE THE ONLY KIN GROUP PRESENT IS A KINDRED OR ELSE BILATERAL DESCENT IS INFERRED (289)	1 108 15 271 XSQ= 2.77 PHI= -0.084 XP = 0.0960
196	DRIFT TOWARD BEING THOSE 0.60 OF 10 WHERE INDIVIDUAL RIGHTS IN REAL PROPERTY, OR RULES FOR INHERITANCE, ARE ABSENT (87)	196	DRIFT TOWARD BEING THOSE 0.70 OF 270 WHERE INDIVIDUAL RIGHTS IN REAL PROPERTY, AND RULES FOR INHERITANCE, ARE PRESENT (194)	4 189 6 81 XSQ= 2.77 PHI= -0.100 XP = 0.0959
209	IN ALL CASES ARE THOSE 1.00 OF 16 WHERE MARITAL RESIDENCE IS PATRILOCAL, VIRILOCAL, OR AVUNCULOCAL, RATHER THAN MATRILOCAL OR UXORILOCAL (270)	209	DRIFT LESS TOWARD BEING THOSE 0.80 OF 315 WHERE MARITAL RESIDENCE IS PATRILOCAL, VIRILOCAL, OR AVUNCULOCAL, RATHER THAN MATRILOCAL OR UXORILOCAL (270)	16 252 0 63 XSQ= 2.76 PHI= 0.091 XP = 0.0966

```
234  LEAN TOWARD BEING THOSE        0.87 OF  15     234  LEAN TOWARD BEING THOSE        0.55 OF 302          13  135
     WHERE THE COUSIN TERMINOLOGY IS                     WHERE THE COUSIN TERMINOLOGY IS                       2  167
     OF CROW, OMAHA, OR IROQUOIS TYPE,                   OF ESKIMO OR HAWAIIAN TYPE,                   XSQ=     8.49
     RATHER THAN                                         RATHER THAN                                   PHI=    0.164
     ESKIMO OR HAWAIIAN TYPE  (152)                      CROW, OMAHA, OR IROQUOIS TYPE  (170)          XP =   0.0036

236  LEAN TOWARD BEING THOSE        0.87 OF  15     236  LEAN TOWARD BEING THOSE        0.55 OF 378           2  209
     WHERE THE FAMILY IS                                 WHERE THE FAMILY IS                                  13  169
     OF AN INDEPENDENT TYPE, RATHER THAN                 OF AN EXTENDED TYPE, RATHER THAN              XSQ=     8.60
     AN EXTENDED TYPE  (185)                             AN INDEPENDENT TYPE  (213)                    PHI=   -0.148
                                                                                                       XP =   0.0034

242  IN ALL CASES ARE THOSE         1.00 OF  15     242  DRIFT LESS TOWARD BEING THOSE  0.78 OF 375          15  294
     WHERE MARRIAGE IS                                   WHERE MARRIAGE IS                                     0   81
     COMMONLY OR OCCASIONALLY POLYGYNOUS,                COMMONLY OR OCCASIONALLY POLYGYNOUS,          XSQ=     2.88
     RATHER THAN MONOGAMOUS  (314)                       RATHER THAN MONOGAMOUS  (314)                 PHI=    0.086
                                                                                                       XP =   0.0896

372  IN ALL CASES ARE THOSE         1.00 OF   4     372  DRIFT TOWARD BEING THOSE       0.58 OF 106           4   44
     WHERE MALE INITIATION RITES ARE                     WHERE MALE INITIATION RITES ARE                       0   62
     PRESENT  (48) ASA                                   ABSENT  (63) ASA                              XSQ=     3.25
                                                                                                       PHI=    0.172
                                                                                                       XP =   0.0715

380  IN ALL CASES ARE THOSE         1.00 OF   3     380  DRIFT TOWARD BEING THOSE       0.67 OF  52           0   35
     WHERE SEGREGATION OF GIRLS AT MENARCHE              WHERE SEGREGATION OF GIRLS AT MENARCHE                3   17
     IS ABSENT  (20) F-B                                 IS PRESENT  (35) F-B                          XSQ=     3.03
                                                                                                       PHI=   -0.235
                                                                                                       XP =   0.0820

459  IN ALL CASES ARE THOSE         1.00 OF   7     459  TILT TOWARD BEING THOSE        0.50 OF 164           0   82
     WHERE GAMES, IF PRESENT,                            WHERE GAMES, IF PRESENT,                              7   82
     DO NOT INCLUDE                                      INCLUDE GAMES OF CHANCE  (82) R-A-B,EA        XSQ=     4.87
     GAMES OF CHANCE  (89) R-A-B,EA                                                                    PHI=   -0.169
                                                                                                       XP =   0.0273

460  TILT TOWARD BEING THOSE        0.86 OF   7     460  TILT TOWARD BEING THOSE        0.63 OF 164           6   61
     WHERE GAMES, IF PRESENT,                            WHERE GAMES, IF PRESENT,                              1  103
     ARE LIMITED TO                                      ARE NOT LIMITED TO                            XSQ=     4.75
     GAMES OF SKILL ONLY  (67) R-A-B,EA                  GAMES OF SKILL ONLY  (104) R-A-B,EA           PHI=    0.167
                                                                                                       XP =   0.0293
```

270 CULTURES WHERE WIVES ARE OBTAINED BY GIFT EXCHANGE (26)	270 CULTURES WHERE WIVES ARE OBTAINED BY MEANS OTHER THAN GIFT EXCHANGE (369)

BACKGROUND ON PAGE 128 — SUBJECT ONLY

26 IN LEFT COLUMN

ATSUGEWI	DOBUANS	ELLICE	KIOW-APACHE	KWAKIUTL	LAU	MANUS	MAORI	MARQUESANS	MIAMI
MNONG GAR	NAMA	NOMLAKI	OMAHA	PUKAPUKA	SAGADA	SAMOANS	TEHUELCHE	TENINO	TIKOPIA
TROBRIAND	TWANA	WARDPEN	WOGEO	YAKUT	YUKI				

369 IN RIGHT COLUMN

5 EXCLUDED BECAUSE UNASCERTAINED

	Left column			Right column		
3	DRIFT MORE TOWARD BEING THOSE LOCATED OUTSIDE OF AFRICA (320)	0.96 OF 26	3	DRIFT LESS TOWARD BEING THOSE LOCATED OUTSIDE OF AFRICA (320)	0.79 OF 369	1 79 25 290 XSQ= 3.62 PHI= -0.096 XP = 0.0573
6	TEND TO BE THOSE LOCATED IN THE INSULAR PACIFIC (70)	0.50 OF 26	6	TEND TO BE THOSE LOCATED OUTSIDE OF THE INSULAR PACIFIC (330)	0.85 OF 369	13 56 13 313 XSQ= 18.09 PHI= 0.214 XP = 0.0000
8	TILT LESS TOWARD BEING THOSE LOCATED OUTSIDE OF NORTH AMERICA (330)	0.65 OF 26	8	TILT MORE TOWARD BEING THOSE LOCATED OUTSIDE OF NORTH AMERICA (330)	0.84 OF 369	9 59 17 310 XSQ= 4.68 PHI= 0.109 XP = 0.0306
13	TILT LESS TOWARD BEING THOSE WHERE THE LATITUDE IS LESS THAN FORTY DEGREES (329)	0.65 OF 26	13	TILT MORE TOWARD BEING THOSE WHERE THE LATITUDE IS LESS THAN FORTY DEGREES (329)	0.83 OF 369	9 61 17 308 XSQ= 4.28 PHI= 0.104 XP = 0.0386
14	DRIFT LESS TOWARD BEING THOSE WHERE THE LATITUDE IS LESS THAN THIRTY DEGREES (281)	0.54 OF 26	14	DRIFT MORE TOWARD BEING THOSE WHERE THE LATITUDE IS LESS THAN THIRTY DEGREES (281)	0.71 OF 369	12 106 14 263 XSQ= 2.74 PHI= 0.083 XP = 0.0980

48	DRIFT TOWARD BEING THOSE WHERE THE FOOD SUPPLY IS SECURE, AND FOOD SHORTAGES ARE RARE OR OCCASIONAL (38) MGW	0.80 OF 10	48	DRIFT TOWARD BEING THOSE WHERE THE FOOD SUPPLY IS NOT SECURE, AND FOOD SHORTAGES ARE FREQUENT OR ANNUAL (41) MGW	0.57 OF 68	8 29 2 39 XSQ= 3.50 PHI= 0.212 XP = 0.0615
51	LEAN TOWARD BEING THOSE WHERE SUBSISTENCE IS PRIMARILY BY FOOD GATHERING -- I. E., HUNTING, FISHING, OR COLLECTING -- RATHER THAN FOOD PRODUCTION (147)	0.65 OF 26	51	LEAN TOWARD BEING THOSE WHERE SUBSISTENCE IS PRIMARILY BY FOOD PRODUCTION -- I. E., AGRICULTURE OR HUSBANDRY -- RATHER THAN BY GATHERING (253)	0.66 OF 369	9 243 17 126 XSQ= 8.95 PHI= -0.151 XP = 0.0028
53	DRIFT MORE TOWARD BEING THOSE WHERE FOOD PRODUCTION IS BY SIMPLE AGRICULTURE OR INCIPIENT FOOD PRODUCTION, RATHER THAN BY INTENSIVE AGRICULTURE (147)	0.92 OF 12	53	DRIFT LESS TOWARD BEING THOSE WHERE FOOD PRODUCTION IS BY SIMPLE AGRICULTURE OR INCIPIENT FOOD PRODUCTION, RATHER THAN BY INTENSIVE AGRICULTURE (147)	0.60 OF 224	1 90 11 134 XSQ= 3.62 PHI= -0.124 XP = 0.0570
55	DRIFT MORE TOWARD BEING THOSE WHERE FOOD PRODUCTION IS BY SIMPLE AGRICULTURE, RATHER THAN BY INTENSIVE AGRICULTURE (101)	0.88 OF 8	55	DRIFT LESS TOWARD BEING THOSE WHERE FOOD PRODUCTION IS BY SIMPLE AGRICULTURE, RATHER THAN BY INTENSIVE AGRICULTURE (101)	0.51 OF 184	1 90 7 94 XSQ= 2.75 PHI= -0.120 XP = 0.0974
63	DRIFT TOWARD BEING THOSE WHERE HUSBANDRY, IF PRESENT, IS PRINCIPALLY IN THE FORM OF PIGS, SHEEP, OR GOATS, RATHER THAN BOVINE, EQUINE, CAMEL-LIKE, OR DEER-LIKE ANIMALS (74)	0.57 OF 14	63	DRIFT TOWARD BEING THOSE WHERE HUSBANDRY, IF PRESENT, IS PRINCIPALLY IN THE FORM OF BOVINE, EQUINE, CAMEL-LIKE, OR DEER-LIKE ANIMALS, RATHER THAN PIGS, SHEEP, OR GOATS (152)	0.69 OF 212	6 146 8 66 XSQ= 2.94 PHI= -0.114 XP = 0.0864
74	TILT TOWARD BEING THOSE WHERE POTTERY IS ABSENT (93)	0.61 OF 23	74	TILT TOWARD BEING THOSE WHERE POTTERY IS PRESENT (145)	0.63 OF 212	9 134 14 78 XSQ= 4.09 PHI= -0.132 XP = 0.0432
80	IN ALL CASES ARE THOSE WHERE NO CITY OR TOWN IS PRESENT (185)	1.00 OF 20	80	DRIFT LESS TOWARD BEING THOSE WHERE NO CITY OR TOWN IS PRESENT (185)	0.81 OF 203	0 39 20 164 XSQ= 3.42 PHI= -0.124 XP = 0.0644
81	DRIFT MORE TOWARD BEING THOSE WHERE NO CITY OR TOWN IS PRESENT, AND THE AVERAGE COMMUNITY SIZE IS SMALLER THAN 200 (135)	0.80 OF 20	81	DRIFT LESS TOWARD BEING THOSE WHERE NO CITY OR TOWN IS PRESENT, AND THE AVERAGE COMMUNITY SIZE IS SMALLER THAN 200 (135)	0.58 OF 203	4 85 16 118 XSQ= 2.78 PHI= -0.112 XP = 0.0956
82	IN ALL CASES ARE THOSE WHERE A CITY OR TOWN IS PRESENT, OR THE AVERAGE COMMUNITY SIZE IS FIFTY OR GREATER (178)	1.00 OF 20	82	TILT LESS TOWARD BEING THOSE WHERE A CITY OR TOWN IS PRESENT, OR THE AVERAGE COMMUNITY SIZE IS FIFTY OR GREATER (178)	0.78 OF 203	20 158 0 45 XSQ= 4.26 PHI= 0.138 XP = 0.0389

85	DRIFT MORE TOWARD BEING THOSE WHERE THE LEVEL OF POLITICAL INTEGRATION IS THE MINIMAL STATE, THE AUTONOMOUS COMMUNITY, OR THE FAMILY (234) CPM	0.95 OF 21	85	DRIFT LESS TOWARD BEING THOSE WHERE THE LEVEL OF POLITICAL INTEGRATION IS THE MINIMAL STATE, THE AUTONOMOUS COMMUNITY, OR THE FAMILY (234) GPM	0.75 OF 280	1 69 20 211 XSQ= 3.28 PHI= -0.104 XP = 0.0700
106	DRIFT TOWARD BEING THOSE WHERE CLASS STRATIFICATION, IF PRESENT, IS BASED ON WEALTH (77)	0.61 OF 18	106	DRIFT TOWARD BEING THOSE WHERE CLASS STRATIFICATION, IF PRESENT, IS BASED ON SOMETHING OTHER THAN WEALTH (126)	0.64 OF 184	11 66 7 118 XSQ= 3.42 PHI= 0.130 XP = 0.0643
107	IN ALL CASES ARE THOSE WHERE CLASS STRATIFICATION, IF PRESENT, IS BASED ON SOMETHING OTHER THAN OCCUPATIONAL STATUS (160)	1.00 OF 18	107	TILT LESS TOWARD BEING THOSE WHERE CLASS STRATIFICATION, IF PRESENT, IS BASED ON SOMETHING OTHER THAN OCCUPATIONAL STATUS (160)	0.77 OF 184	0 43 18 141 XSQ= 4.04 PHI= -0.141 XP = 0.0444
109	IN ALL CASES ARE THOSE WHERE CASTES ARE ABSENT (317)	1.00 OF 26	109	DRIFT LESS TOWARD BEING THOSE WHERE CASTES ARE ABSENT (317)	0.85 OF 338	0 51 26 287 XSQ= 3.40 PHI= -0.097 XP = 0.0654
137	DRIFT TOWARD BEING THOSE WHERE INVIDIOUS DISPLAY OF WEALTH IS STRONGLY EMPHASIZED (37) PES	0.69 OF 13	137	DRIFT TOWARD BEING THOSE WHERE INVIDIOUS DISPLAY OF WEALTH IS MODERATELY, LITTLE, OR NEGATIVELY EMPHASIZED (52) PES	0.63 OF 76	9 28 4 48 XSQ= 3.55 PHI= 0.200 XP = 0.0594
257	TILT TOWARD BEING THOSE WHERE THE SEVERITY OF SISTER AVOIDANCE IS HIGH (10) WNS	0.83 OF 6	257	TILT TOWARD BEING THOSE WHERE THE SEVERITY OF SISTER AVOIDANCE IS LOW (17) WNS	0.76 OF 21	5 5 1 16 XSQ= 4.77 PHI= 0.420 EP = 0.0152
279	IN ALL CASES ARE THOSE WHERE WIFE-LENDING AND WIFE EXCHANGE ARE UNIMPORTANT OR ABSENT (19) LWS	1.00 OF 6	279	DRIFT LESS TOWARD BEING THOSE WHERE WIFE-LENDING AND WIFE EXCHANGE ARE UNIMPORTANT OR ABSENT (19) LWS	0.57 OF 23	0 10 6 13 XSQ= 2.29 PHI= -0.281 EP = 0.0676
309	TILT TOWARD BEING THOSE WHERE ORAL SOCIALIZATION ANXIETY IS HIGH (26) W-C	0.77 OF 13	309	TILT TOWARD BEING THOSE WHERE ORAL SOCIALIZATION ANXIETY IS LOW (27) W-C	0.60 OF 40	10 16 3 24 XSQ= 3.98 PHI= 0.274 XP = 0.0461
347	TILT TOWARD BEING THOSE WHERE THE CHILD'S INFERRED CONFLICT REGARDING SELF-RELIANT BEHAVIOR IS LOW (39) B-B-C	0.83 OF 12	347	TILT TOWARD BEING THOSE WHERE THE CHILD'S INFERRED CONFLICT REGARDING SELF-RELIANT BEHAVIOR IS HIGH (37) B-B-C	0.54 OF 63	2 34 10 29 XSQ= 4.22 PHI= -0.237 XP = 0.0399

No.	Statement	Ratio	No.	Statement	Ratio	Statistics
349	DRIFT TOWARD BEING THOSE WHERE THE CHILD'S INFERRED ANXIETY OVER NON-PERFORMANCE OF ACHIEVEMENT BEHAVIOR IS HIGH (34) B-B-C	0.88 OF 8	349	DRIFT TOWARD BEING THOSE WHERE THE CHILD'S INFERRED ANXIETY OVER NON-PERFORMANCE OF ACHIEVEMENT BEHAVIOR IS LOW (28) B-B-C	0.51 OF 53	7 26 1 27 XSQ= 2.73 PHI= 0.212 XP = 0.0983
372	DRIFT TOWARD BEING THOSE WHERE MALE INITIATION RITES ARE PRESENT (48) ASA	0.69 OF 13	372	DRIFT TOWARD BEING THOSE WHERE MALE INITIATION RITES ARE ABSENT (63) ASA	0.60 OF 97	9 39 4 58 XSQ= 2.84 PHI= 0.161 XP = 0.0922
386	TILT TOWARD BEING THOSE WHERE SEXUAL EXPRESSION BY THE YOUNG IS PERMITTED (40) F-B	0.79 OF 14	386	TILT TOWARD BEING THOSE WHERE SEXUAL EXPRESSION BY THE YOUNG IS RESTRICTED OR SEMI-RESTRICTED (46) F-B	0.60 OF 72	3 43 11 29 XSQ= 5.46 PHI= -0.252 XP = 0.0195
458	TILT MORE TOWARD BEING THOSE WHERE GAMES, IF PRESENT, DO NOT INCLUDE GAMES OF STRATEGY (119) R-A-B,EA	0.91 OF 22	458	TILT LESS TOWARD BEING THOSE WHERE GAMES, IF PRESENT, DO NOT INCLUDE GAMES OF STRATEGY (119) R-A-B,EA	0.66 OF 149	2 50 20 99 XSQ= 4.33 PHI= -0.159 XP = 0.0375
480	TILT TOWARD BEING THOSE WHERE COMPLEXITY OF ARTISTIC DESIGN IS HIGH (14) HB	0.86 OF 7	480	TILT TOWARD BEING THOSE WHERE COMPLEXITY OF ARTISTIC DESIGN IS LOW (15) HB	0.64 OF 22	6 8 1 14 XSQ= 3.39 PHI= 0.342 XP = 0.0352

****

271	CULTURES WHERE WIVES ARE CBTAINEC BY RECEIPT CF DCWRY (15)	271	CULTURES WHERE WIVES ARE OBTAINED BY MEANS OTHER THAN RECEIPT OF DOWRY (380)

BACKGROUND ON PAGE 128 — SUBJECT ONLY

....

15 IN LEFT CCLUMN

BASQUES, BCERS, BURMESE, CHEREMIS, CZECHS, HUTSUL, ICELANDERS, IRISH, ROMANS, SERBS, SINDHI, SINHALESE, TIBETANS, TIGRINYA, WALLOONS

380 IN RIGHT CCLUMN

5 EXCLUCED BECAUSE UNASCERTAINEC

	Left column			Right column		
3	IN ALL CASES ARE THCSE LCCATED CUTSIDE CF AFRICA (320)	1.00 OF 15	3	DRIFT LESS TOWARD BEING THCSE LOCATED OUTSIDE OF AFRICA (320)	0.79 CF 380	0 80 15 300 XSQ= 2.76 PHI= -0.084 XP = 0.0964
4	TEND TC BE THCSE LCCATED IN THE CIRCUM-MECITERRANEAN (45)	0.73 OF 15	4	TEND TO BE THOSE LOCATED OUTSIDE OF THE CIRCUM-MEDITERRANEAN (355)	0.91 CF 380	11 34 4 346 XSQ= 53.05 PHI= 0.366 XP = 0.
13	TEND TC BE THCSE WHERE THE LATITUCE IS FCRTY DEGREES CR GREATER (71)	0.60 OF 15	13	TEND TO BE THOSE WHERE THE LATITUDE IS LESS THAN FORTY DEGREES (329)	0.84 CF 380	9 61 6 319 XSQ= 16.22 PHI= 0.203 XP = 0.0001
14	LEAN TCWARD BEING THCSE WHERE THE LATITUCE IS THIRTY DEGREES CR GREATER (119)	0.67 OF 15	14	LEAN TOWARD BEING THOSE WHERE THE LATITUDE IS LESS THAN THIRTY DEGREES (281)	0.72 CF 380	10 108 5 272 XSQ= 8.33 PHI= 0.145 XP = 0.0039
15	TILT TCWARC BEING THCSE WHERE THE LATITUCE IS TWENTY DEGREES CR GREATER (183)	0.80 OF 15	15	TILT TOWARD BEING THOSE WHERE THE LATITUDE IS LESS THAN TWENTY DEGREES (217)	0.56 CF 380	12 169 3 211 XSQ= 5.98 PHI= 0.123 XP = 0.0145

42	DRIFT MORE TOWARD BEING THOSE 0.87 OF 15 WHERE THE NATURAL ENVIRONMENT IS OTHER THAN TROPICAL OR SUB-TROPICAL RAIN FOREST, OR MONSOON FOREST (244) FWM	42	DRIFT LESS TOWARD BEING THOSE 0.60 OF 380 WHERE THE NATURAL ENVIRONMENT IS OTHER THAN TROPICAL OR SUB-TROPICAL RAIN FOREST, OR MONSOON FOREST (244) FWM	2 153 13 227 XSQ= 3.33 PHI= -0.092 XP = 0.0679
44	IN ALL CASES ARE THOSE 1.00 OF 9 WHERE SETTLEMENTS ARE FIXED (222)	44	DRIFT LESS TOWARD BEING THOSE 0.67 OF 320 WHERE SETTLEMENTS ARE FIXED (222)	9 213 0 107 XSQ= 3.07 PHI= 0.097 XP = 0.0799
51	TILT MORE TOWARD BEING THOSE 0.93 OF 15 WHERE SUBSISTENCE IS PRIMARILY BY FOOD PRODUCTION -- I. E., AGRICULTURE OR HUSBANDRY -- RATHER THAN BY GATHERING (253)	51	TILT LESS TOWARD BEING THOSE 0.63 OF 380 WHERE SUBSISTENCE IS PRIMARILY BY FOOD PRODUCTION -- I. E., AGRICULTURE OR HUSBANDRY -- RATHER THAN BY GATHERING (253)	14 238 1 142 XSQ= 4.63 PHI= 0.108 XP = 0.0313
53	LEAN TOWARD BEING THOSE 0.89 OF 9 WHERE FOOD PRODUCTION IS BY INTENSIVE AGRICULTURE, RATHER THAN BY SIMPLE AGRICULTURE OR INCIPIENT FOOD PRODUCTION (91)	53	LEAN TOWARD BEING THOSE 0.63 OF 227 WHERE FOOD PRODUCTION IS BY SIMPLE AGRICULTURE OR INCIPIENT FOOD PRODUCTION, RATHER THAN BY INTENSIVE AGRICULTURE (147)	8 83 1 144 XSQ= 7.92 PHI= 0.183 XP = 0.0049
55	IN ALL CASES ARE THOSE 1.00 OF 8 WHERE FOOD PRODUCTION IS BY INTENSIVE AGRICULTURE, RATHER THAN BY SIMPLE AGRICULTURE (91)	55	LEAN TOWARD BEING THOSE 0.55 OF 184 WHERE FOOD PRODUCTION IS BY SIMPLE AGRICULTURE, RATHER THAN BY INTENSIVE AGRICULTURE (101)	8 83 0 101 XSQ= 7.19 PHI= 0.194 XP = 0.0073
63	IN ALL CASES ARE THOSE 1.00 OF 9 WHERE HUSBANDRY, IF PRESENT, IS PRINCIPALLY IN THE FORM OF BOVINE, EQUINE, CAMEL-LIKE, OR DEER-LIKE ANIMALS, RATHER THAN PIGS, SHEEP, OR GOATS (152)	63	DRIFT LESS TOWARD BEING THOSE 0.66 OF 217 WHERE HUSBANDRY, IF PRESENT, IS PRINCIPALLY IN THE FORM OF BOVINE, EQUINE, CAMEL-LIKE, OR DEER-LIKE ANIMALS, RATHER THAN PIGS, SHEEP, OR GOATS (152)	9 143 0 74 XSQ= 3.15 PHI= 0.118 XP = 0.0761
71	IN ALL CASES ARE THOSE 1.00 OF 4 WHERE METAL WORKING IS PRESENT (98)	71	TILT TOWARD BEING THOSE 0.61 OF 244 WHERE METAL WORKING IS ABSENT (153)	4 94 0 150 XSQ= 3.92 PHI= 0.126 XP = 0.0478
79	TEND TO BE THOSE 0.75 OF 8 WHERE A CITY IS PRESENT (23)	79	TEND TO BE THOSE 0.92 OF 215 WHERE NO CITY IS PRESENT (201)	6 17 2 198 XSQ= 30.63 PHI= 0.371 XP = 0.
80	IN ALL CASES ARE THOSE 1.00 OF 8 WHERE A CITY OR TOWN IS PRESENT (39)	80	TEND TO BE THOSE 0.86 OF 215 WHERE NO CITY OR TOWN IS PRESENT (185)	8 31 0 184 XSQ= 33.44 PHI= 0.387 XP = 0.

84	TEND TO BE THOSE WHERE THE LEVEL OF POLITICAL INTEGRATION IS THE LARGE STATE (42) GPM	0.78 OF 9	84	TEND TO BE THOSE WHERE THE LEVEL OF POLITICAL INTEGRATION IS THE LITTLE STATE, THE MINIMAL STATE, THE AUTONOMOUS COMMUNITY, OR THE FAMILY (262) GPM	0.88 OF 292	7 35 2 257 XSQ= 26.24 PHI= 0.295 XP = 0.0000
85	IN ALL CASES ARE THOSE WHERE THE LEVEL OF POLITICAL INTEGRATION IS THE LARGE STATE, OR THE LITTLE STATE (70) GPM	1.00 OF 9	85	TEND TO BE THOSE WHERE THE LEVEL OF POLITICAL INTEGRATION IS THE MINIMAL STATE, THE AUTONOMOUS COMMUNITY, OR THE FAMILY (234) GPM	0.79 OF 292	9 61 0 231 XSQ= 26.34 PHI= 0.296 XP = 0.0000
88	IN ALL CASES ARE THOSE WHERE, IF A HEADMANSHIP IS PRESENT, SUCCESSION IS NON-HEREDITARY (106)	1.00 OF 5	88	TILT TOWARD BEING THOSE WHERE, IF A HEADMANSHIP IS PRESENT, SUCCESSION IS HEREDITARY (165)	0.62 OF 263	5 101 0 162 XSQ= 5.42 PHI= 0.142 XP = 0.0199
94	TEND TO BE THOSE WHERE THE HIERARCHY OF NATIONAL JURISDICTION HAS FOUR OR THREE LEVELS (34) GES,EA	0.57 OF 7	94	TEND TO BE THOSE WHERE THE HIERARCHY OF NATIONAL JURISDICTION HAS TWO, ONE, OR NO LEVELS (296) GES,EA	0.91 OF 320	4 30 3 290 XSQ= 12.04 PHI= 0.192 XP = 0.0005
95	IN ALL CASES ARE THOSE WHERE THE HIERARCHY OF NATIONAL JURISDICTION HAS FOUR, THREE, OR TWO LEVELS (76) GES,EA	1.00 OF 7	95	TEND TO BE THOSE WHERE THE HIERARCHY OF NATIONAL JURISDICTION HAS ONE OR NO LEVELS (254) GES,EA	0.78 OF 320	7 69 0 251 XSQ= 19.43 PHI= 0.244 XP = 0.0000
102	IN ALL CASES ARE THOSE WHERE CLASS STRATIFICATION IS PRESENT (203)	1.00 OF 14	102	TEND LESS TO BE THOSE WHERE CLASS STRATIFICATION IS PRESENT (203)	0.52 OF 365	14 188 0 177 XSQ= 10.86 PHI= 0.169 XP = 0.0010
106	TILT MORE TOWARD BEING THOSE WHERE CLASS STRATIFICATION, IF PRESENT, IS BASED ON SOMETHING OTHER THAN WEALTH (126)	0.93 OF 14	106	TILT LESS TOWARD BEING THOSE WHERE CLASS STRATIFICATION, IF PRESENT, IS BASED ON SOMETHING OTHER THAN WEALTH (126)	0.60 OF 188	1 76 13 112 XSQ= 4.79 PHI= -0.154 XP = 0.0286
107	TEND TO BE THOSE WHERE CLASS STRATIFICATION, IF PRESENT, IS BASED ON OCCUPATIONAL STATUS (43)	0.64 OF 14	107	TEND TO BE THOSE WHERE CLASS STRATIFICATION, IF PRESENT, IS BASED ON SOMETHING OTHER THAN OCCUPATIONAL STATUS (160)	0.82 OF 188	9 34 5 154 XSQ= 13.96 PHI= 0.263 XP = 0.0002
108	IN ALL CASES ARE THOSE WHERE CLASS STRATIFICATION, IF PRESENT, IS BASED ON SOMETHING OTHER THAN A HEREDITARY ARISTOCRACY (129)	1.00 OF 14	108	LEAN LESS TOWARD BEING THOSE WHERE CLASS STRATIFICATION, IF PRESENT, IS BASED ON SOMETHING OTHER THAN A HEREDITARY ARISTOCRACY (129)	0.61 OF 188	0 73 14 115 XSQ= 6.91 PHI= -0.185 XP = 0.0086

176	LEAN MORE TOWARD BEING THOSE 0.93 OF 15 WHERE THE COMMUNITY IS OTHER THAN A CLAN-COMMUNITY OR A COMMUNITY STRUCTURED OR SEGMENTED ON A CLAN BASIS (213)	176	LEAN LESS TOWARD BEING THOSE 0.55 OF 363 WHERE THE COMMUNITY IS OTHER THAN A CLAN-COMMUNITY OR A COMMUNITY STRUCTURED OR SEGMENTED ON A CLAN BASIS (213)	1 165 14 198 XSQ= 7.29 PHI= -0.139 XP = 0.0069
177	IN ALL CASES ARE THOSE 1.00 OF 15 WHERE THE COMMUNITY IS OTHER THAN A SINGLE CLAN-COMMUNITY AND EXOGAMOUS (305)	177	DRIFT LESS TOWARD BEING THOSE 0.79 OF 363 WHERE THE COMMUNITY IS OTHER THAN A SINGLE CLAN-COMMUNITY AND EXOGAMOUS (305)	0 76 15 287 XSQ= 2.74 PHI= -0.085 XP = 0.0981
180	IN ALL CASES ARE THOSE 1.00 OF 15 WHERE THE COMMUNITY IS COMMONLY NON-EXOGAMOUS, RATHER THAN EXOGAMOUS (258)	180	TILT LESS TOWARD BEING THOSE 0.66 OF 363 WHERE THE COMMUNITY IS COMMONLY NON-EXOGAMOUS, RATHER THAN EXOGAMOUS (258)	0 123 15 240 XSQ= 6.07 PHI= -0.127 XP = 0.0138
182	LEAN TOWARD BEING THOSE 0.73 OF 15 WHERE THE COMMUNITY IS STRUCTURED ON A NON-CLAN BASIS AND AGAMOUS (126)	182	LEAN TOWARD BEING THOSE 0.68 OF 363 OTHER THAN WHERE THE COMMUNITY IS STRUCTURED ON A NON-CLAN BASIS AND AGAMOUS (256)	11 115 4 248 XSQ= 9.45 PHI= 0.158 XP = 0.0021
185	DRIFT TOWARD BEING THOSE 0.75 OF 4 WHERE THE LARGEST NON-COGNATIC KIN GROUP IS SMALLER THAN A SIB, I. E., THE LINEAGE (58)	185	DRIFT TOWARD BEING THOSE 0.78 OF 245 WHERE THE LARGEST NON-COGNATIC KIN GROUP IS THE MOEITY OR PHRATRY OR SIB (194)	1 190 3 55 XSQ= 3.50 PHI= -0.119 XP = 0.0615
188	LEAN TOWARD BEING THOSE 0.73 OF 15 WHERE THE KIN GROUP IS EXCLUSIVELY COGNATIC (148)	188	LEAN TOWARD BEING THOSE 0.64 OF 380 WHERE THE KIN GROUP IS OTHER THAN EXCLUSIVELY COGNATIC (252)	11 135 4 245 XSQ= 7.30 PHI= 0.136 XP = 0.0069
192	LEAN TOWARD BEING THOSE 0.67 OF 15 WHERE THE ONLY KIN GROUP PRESENT IS A KINDRED OR ELSE BILATERAL DESCENT IS INFERRED (111)	192	LEAN TOWARD BEING THOSE 0.74 OF 380 OTHER THAN WHERE THE ONLY KIN GROUP PRESENT IS A KINDRED OR ELSE BILATERAL DESCENT IS INFERRED (289)	10 99 5 281 XSQ= 9.97 PHI= 0.159 XP = 0.0016
196	IN ALL CASES ARE THOSE 1.00 OF 11 WHERE INDIVIDUAL RIGHTS IN REAL PROPERTY, AND RULES FOR INHERITANCE, ARE PRESENT (194)	196	DRIFT LESS TOWARD BEING THOSE 0.68 OF 269 WHERE INDIVIDUAL RIGHTS IN REAL PROPERTY, AND RULES FOR INHERITANCE, ARE PRESENT (194)	11 182 0 87 XSQ= 3.76 PHI= 0.116 XP = 0.0524
197	TILT LESS TOWARD BEING THOSE 0.55 OF 11 WHERE RULES FOR THE INHERITANCE OF REAL PROPERTY, IF PRESENT, FAVOR EITHER THE MALE HEIR OR LINE, OR THE FEMALE HEIR OR LINE (165)	197	TILT MORE TOWARD BEING THOSE 0.87 OF 182 WHERE RULES FOR THE INHERITANCE OF REAL PROPERTY, IF PRESENT, FAVOR EITHER THE MALE HEIR OR LINE, OR THE FEMALE HEIR OR LINE (165)	6 158 5 24 XSQ= 6.12 PHI= -0.178 XP = 0.0134

```
234  TILT MORE TOWARD BEING THOSE   0.90 OF  10   234  TILT LESS TOWARD BEING THOSE   0.52 OF 307          1  147
     WHERE THE COUSIN TERMINOLOGY IS                    WHERE THE COUSIN TERMINOLOGY IS                          9  160
     OF ESKIMO OR HAWAIIAN TYPE,                        OF ESKIMO OR HAWAIIAN TYPE,                      XSQ=     4.17
     RATHER THAN                                        RATHER THAN                                      PHI=   -0.115
     CROW, OMAHA, OR IROQUOIS TYPE  (170)               CROW, OMAHA, OR IROQUOIS TYPE  (170)             XP =   0.0413

240  IN ALL CASES ARE THOSE         1.00 OF   8   240  DRIFT LESS TOWARD BEING THOSE  0.62 OF 203          0   77
     WHERE THE FAMILY, IF EXTENDED, IS                  WHERE THE FAMILY, IF EXTENDED, IS                        8  126
     SMALL OR STEM, RATHER THAN                         SMALL OR STEM, RATHER THAN                       XSQ=     3.28
     LARGE  (135)                                       LARGE  (135)                                     PHI=   -0.125
                                                                                                         XP =   0.0701

241  LEAN TOWARD BEING THOSE        0.50 OF   8   241  LEAN TOWARD BEING THOSE        0.89 OF 203          4  181
     WHERE THE FAMILY, IF EXTENDED, IS                  WHERE THE FAMILY, IF EXTENDED, IS                        4   22
     STEM, RATHER THAN                                  LARGE OR SMALL, RATHER THAN                      XSQ=     7.60
     LARGE OR SMALL  (26)                               STEM  (187)                                      PHI=   -0.190
                                                                                                         XP =   0.0058

242  TEND TO BE THOSE               0.93 OF  14   242  TEND TO BE THOSE               0.82 OF 376          1  308
     WHERE MARRIAGE IS MONOGAMOUS,                      WHERE MARRIAGE IS                                       13   68
     RATHER THAN COMMONLY OR OCCASIONALLY               COMMONLY OR OCCASIONALLY POLYGYNOUS,             XSQ=    41.43
     POLYGYNOUS  (81)                                   RATHER THAN MONOGAMOUS  (314)                    PHI=   -0.326
                                                                                                         XP =   0.

370  IN ALL CASES ARE THOSE         1.00 OF   8   370  DRIFT LESS TOWARD BEING THOSE  0.60 OF 235          0   95
     WHERE THE SEGREGATION OF ADOLESCENT BOYS           WHERE THE SEGREGATION OF ADOLESCENT BOYS                 8  140
     IS ABSENT  (148)                                   IS ABSENT  (148)                                 XSQ=     3.75
                                                                                                         PHI=   -0.124
                                                                                                         XP =   0.0529

427  IN ALL CASES ARE THOSE         1.00 OF   7   427  TILT LESS TOWARD BEING THOSE   0.54 OF 149          7   80
     WHERE A HIGH GOD, IF PRESENT, IS                   WHERE A HIGH GOD, IF PRESENT, IS                         0   69
     ACTIVE, RATHER THAN                                ACTIVE, RATHER THAN                              XSQ=     4.09
     INACTIVE  (87) GES,EA                              INACTIVE  (87) GES,EA                            PHI=    0.162
                                                                                                         XP =   0.0432

450  IN ALL CASES ARE THOSE         1.00 OF   3   450  TILT TOWARD BEING THOSE        0.72 OF  83          0   60
     WHERE THE OBSERVATION OF FOOD TABOOS               WHERE THE OBSERVATION OF FOOD TABOOS                     3   23
     IS LOW, RATHER THAN                                IS HIGH OR MEDIUM, RATHER THAN                   XSQ=     4.16
     HIGH OR MEDIUM  (26) JRL                           LOW  (60) JRL                                    PHI=   -0.220
                                                                                                         XP =   0.0415
```

****

272 CULTURES WHERE THE DIVORCE RATE IS HIGH (29) CA	272 CULTURES WHERE THE DIVORCE RATE IS LOW (28) CA

BACKGROUND ON PAGE 130 BOTH SUBJECT AND PREDICATE

....

29 IN LEFT COLUMN

ABIPON	ALORESE	BEMBA	CHUKCHEE	COMANCHE	CUNA	FANG	IFUGAO	ILA	KHASI
LAU	LOZI	MAGUZAWA	MANDAN	MARQUESANS	MUNDURUCU	NAMBICUARA	OJIBWA	OMAHA	PAPAGO
SAMOANS	SEMANG	SIWANS	SOMALI	TARAHUMARA	TODA	YAO	YUROK	ZUNI	

28 IN RIGHT COLUMN

ANDAMANESE	ATAYAL	AWEIKOMA	AZANDE	AZTEC	BHIL	BURMESE	CALLINAGO	CAYAPA	GOND
IBAN	INCA	KAZAK	KIKUYU	KORYAK	LEPCHA	LOLO	MACASSARESE	MBUNDU	NYAKYUSA
PAWNEE	SIRIONO	THAI	TIKOPIA	TUBATULABAL	VEDDA	VIETNAMESE	YORUBA		

343 EXCLUDED BECAUSE UNASCERTAINED

	Left column		Right column	Statistics
5	DRIFT MORE TOWARD BEING THOSE 0.86 OF 29 LOCATED OUTSIDE OF EAST EURASIA (330)	5	DRIFT LESS TOWARD BEING THOSE 0.61 OF 28 LOCATED OUTSIDE OF EAST EURASIA (330)	4 11 25 17 XSQ= 3.55 PHI= -0.250 XP = 0.0595
44	DRIFT TOWARD BEING THOSE 0.52 OF 27 WHERE SETTLEMENTS ARE NON-FIXED (110)	44	DRIFT TOWARD BEING THOSE 0.74 OF 27 WHERE SETTLEMENTS ARE FIXED (222)	13 20 14 7 XSQ= 2.81 PHI= -0.228 XP = 0.0940
47	DRIFT TOWARD BEING THOSE 0.57 OF 14 WHERE, IF SETTLEMENTS ARE NON-FIXED, MOVEMENT IS NON-NOMADIC, RATHER THAN NOMADIC (38)	47	DRIFT TOWARD BEING THOSE 0.86 OF 7 WHERE, IF SETTLEMENTS ARE NON-FIXED, MOVEMENT IS NOMADIC, RATHER THAN NON-NOMADIC (72)	6 6 8 1 XSQ= 1.97 PHI= -0.306 EP = 0.0873
80	IN ALL CASES ARE THOSE 1.00 OF 23 WHERE NO CITY OR TOWN IS PRESENT (185)	80	DRIFT LESS TOWARD BEING THOSE 0.80 OF 25 WHERE NO CITY OR TOWN IS PRESENT (185)	0 5 23 20 XSQ= 3.22 PHI= -0.259 XP = 0.0730

85	DRIFT MORE TOWARD BEING THOSE 0.86 OF 28 WHERE THE LEVEL OF POLITICAL INTEGRATION IS THE MINIMAL STATE, THE AUTONOMOUS COMMUNITY, OR THE FAMILY (234) GPM	85	DRIFT LESS TOWARD BEING THOSE 0.62 OF 26 WHERE THE LEVEL OF POLITICAL INTEGRATION IS THE MINIMAL STATE, THE AUTONOMOUS COMMUNITY, OR THE FAMILY (234) GPM	4 10 24 16 XSQ= 2.94 PHI= -0.233 XP = 0.0864
90	TILT LESS TOWARD BEING THOSE 0.67 OF 12 WHERE, IF A HEREDITARY HEADMANSHIP IS PRESENT, SUCCESSION IS PATRILINEAL, RATHER THAN MATRILINEAL (127)	90	IN ALL CASES ARE THOSE 1.00 OF 14 WHERE, IF A HEREDITARY HEADMANSHIP IS PRESENT, SUCCESSION IS PATRILINEAL, RATHER THAN MATRILINEAL (127)	8 14 4 0 XSQ= 3.25 PHI= -0.354 EP = 0.0331
106	TILT TOWARD BEING THOSE 0.61 OF 18 WHERE CLASS STRATIFICATION, IF PRESENT, IS BASED ON WEALTH (77)	106	TILT TOWARD BEING THOSE 0.78 OF 18 WHERE CLASS STRATIFICATION, IF PRESENT, IS BASED ON SOMETHING OTHER THAN WEALTH (126)	11 4 7 14 XSQ= 4.11 PHI= 0.338 EP = 0.0409
107	TILT MORE TOWARD BEING THOSE 0.94 OF 18 WHERE CLASS STRATIFICATION, IF PRESENT, IS BASED ON SOMETHING OTHER THAN OCCUPATIONAL STATUS (160)	107	TILT LESS TOWARD BEING THOSE 0.61 OF 18 WHERE CLASS STRATIFICATION, IF PRESENT, IS BASED ON SOMETHING OTHER THAN OCCUPATIONAL STATUS (160)	1 7 17 11 XSQ= 4.02 PHI= -0.334 EP = 0.0408
127	TILT TOWARD BEING THOSE 0.75 OF 12 WHERE THE FEMALES' CONTRIBUTION TO SUBSISTENCE IS LOW (32) JKB	127	TILT TOWARD BEING THOSE 0.78 OF 9 WHERE THE FEMALES' CONTRIBUTION TO SUBSISTENCE IS HIGH (33) JKB	3 7 9 2 XSQ= 3.82 PHI= -0.427 EP = 0.0300
137	DRIFT TOWARD BEING THOSE 0.59 OF 17 WHERE INVIDIOUS DISPLAY OF WEALTH IS STRONGLY EMPHASIZED (37) PES	137	DRIFT TOWARD BEING THOSE 0.77 OF 13 WHERE INVIDIOUS DISPLAY OF WEALTH IS MODERATELY, LITTLE, OR NEGATIVELY EMPHASIZED (52) PES	10 3 7 10 XSQ= 2.52 PHI= 0.290 EP = 0.0711
138	TILT TOWARD BEING THOSE 0.80 OF 5 WHERE SUPERORDINATE JUSTICE IS ABSENT (18) BBW	138	IN ALL CASES ARE THOSE 1.00 OF 6 WHERE SUPERORDINATE JUSTICE IS PRESENT (22) BBW	1 6 4 0 XSQ= 4.48 PHI= -0.638 EP = 0.0152
141	DRIFT TOWARD BEING THOSE 0.78 OF 9 WHERE THE LEVEL OF SOCIAL SANCTION IS PUBLIC PROPERTY SANCTION OR PRIVATE SETTLEMENT, RATHER THAN PUBLIC CORPOREAL SANCTION (26) JMH	141	DRIFT TOWARD BEING THOSE 0.67 OF 12 WHERE THE LEVEL OF SOCIAL SANCTION IS PUBLIC CORPOREAL SANCTION, RATHER THAN PUBLIC PROPERTY SANCTION OR PRIVATE SETTLEMENT (28) JMH	2 8 7 4 XSQ= 2.49 PHI= -0.344 EP = 0.0805
185	DRIFT MORE TOWARD BEING THOSE 0.94 OF 16 WHERE THE LARGEST NON-COGNATIC KIN GROUP IS THE MOEITY OR PHRATRY OR SIB (194)	185	DRIFT LESS TOWARD BEING THOSE 0.65 OF 17 WHERE THE LARGEST NON-COGNATIC KIN GROUP IS THE MOEITY OR PHRATRY OR SIB (194)	15 11 1 6 XSQ= 2.60 PHI= 0.281 EP = 0.0854

198	TILT LESS TOWARD BEING THOSE 0.64 OF 11 WHERE RULES FOR THE INHERITANCE OF REAL PROPERTY, IF PRESENT, FAVOR THE MALE HEIR OR LINE, RATHER THAN THE FEMALE (144)	198	IN ALL CASES ARE THOSE 1.00 OF 13 WHERE RULES FOR THE INHERITANCE OF REAL PROPERTY, IF PRESENT, FAVOR THE MALE HEIR OR LINE, RATHER THAN THE FEMALE (144)	 XSQ= PHI= EP =	7 13 4 0 3.36 -0.374 0.0311
319	DRIFT TOWARD BEING THOSE 0.75 OF 12 WHERE PROTECTION OF THE INFANT FROM ENVIRONMENTAL DISCOMFORTS IS HIGH (35) B-B-C	319	DRIFT TOWARD BEING THOSE 0.75 OF 8 WHERE PROTECTION OF THE INFANT FROM ENVIRONMENTAL DISCOMFORTS IS LOW (30) B-B-C	 XSQ= PHI= EP =	9 2 3 6 3.04 0.390 0.0648
323	DRIFT TOWARD BEING THOSE 0.77 OF 13 WHERE THE CONSTANCY OF PRESENCE OF THE INFANT'S NURTURANT AGENT IS LOW (45) B-B-C	323	DRIFT TOWARD BEING THOSE 0.67 OF 9 WHERE THE CONSTANCY OF PRESENCE OF THE INFANT'S NURTURANT AGENT IS HIGH (29) B-B-C	 XSQ= PHI= EP =	3 6 10 3 2.57 -0.342 0.0789
329	IN ALL CASES ARE THOSE 1.00 OF 4 WHERE THE AGE AT TOILET TRAINING IS LOWER THAN TWO YEARS (11) W-C	329	IN ALL CASES ARE THOSE 1.00 OF 2 WHERE THE AGE AT TOILET TRAINING IS TWO YEARS OR HIGHER (10) W-C	 XSQ= PHI= EP =	0 2 4 0 2.34 -0.625 0.0667
330	DRIFT TOWARD BEING THOSE 0.64 OF 11 WHERE THE AGE OF THE INFANT AT TIME OF WEANING IS LOWER THAN 2.5 YEARS (36) B-B-C	330	DRIFT TOWARD BEING THOSE 0.78 OF 9 WHERE THE AGE OF THE INFANT AT TIME OF WEANING IS 2.5 YEARS OR HIGHER (34) B-B-C	 XSQ= PHI= EP =	4 7 7 2 1.96 -0.313 0.0923
349	DRIFT TOWARD BEING THOSE 0.80 OF 10 WHERE THE CHILD'S INFERRED ANXIETY OVER NON-PERFORMANCE OF ACHIEVEMENT BEHAVIOR IS HIGH (34) B-B-C	349	DRIFT TOWARD BEING THOSE 0.75 OF 8 WHERE THE CHILD'S INFERRED ANXIETY OVER NON-PERFORMANCE OF ACHIEVEMENT BEHAVIOR IS LOW (28) B-B-C	 XSQ= PHI= EP =	8 2 2 6 3.45 0.437 0.0536
430	TILT TOWARD BEING THOSE 0.88 OF 8 WHERE SUPERNATURAL SANCTIONS FOR MORALITY, HAVING AN EFFECT ON AN INDIVIDUAL'S HEALTH, ARE ABSENT OR UNREPORTED (22) GES	430	TILT TOWARD BEING THOSE 0.80 OF 5 WHERE SUPERNATURAL SANCTIONS FOR MORALITY, HAVING AN EFFECT ON AN INDIVIDUAL'S HEALTH, ARE PRESENT (16) GES	 XSQ= PHI= EP =	1 4 7 1 3.41 -0.512 0.0319
442	DRIFT TOWARD BEING THOSE 0.78 OF 9 WHERE FEAR OF ANIMAL SPIRITS IS LOW (33) W-C	442	DRIFT TOWARD BEING THOSE 0.80 OF 5 WHERE FEAR OF ANIMAL SPIRITS IS HIGH (28) W-C	 XSQ= PHI= EP =	2 4 7 1 2.34 -0.409 0.0909
444	TILT TOWARD BEING THOSE 0.79 OF 14 WHERE THE USE OF DREAMS TO SEEK AND CONTROL SUPERNATURAL POWERS IS HIGH (28) RGD	444	TILT TOWARD BEING THOSE 0.75 OF 12 WHERE THE USE OF DREAMS TO SEEK AND CONTROL SUPERNATURAL POWERS IS LOW (27) RGD	 XSQ= PHI= EP =	11 3 3 9 5.46 0.458 0.0162

```
454  DRIFT TOWARD BEING THOSE          0.57 OF   7      454  IN ALL CASES ARE THOSE           1.00 OF   6             3     6
     WHERE THE OBJECTIVE OF THE INDIVIDUAL'S                WHERE THE OBJECTIVE OF THE INDIVIDUAL'S                  4     0
     CONTACT WITH THE DIVINE                                CONTACT WITH THE DIVINE                          XSQ=      2.63
     IS NOT CONDUCIVE TO THE DEVELOPMENT OF THE             IS CONDUCIVE TO THE DEVELOPMENT OF THE           PHI=    -0.450
     INDIVIDUAL'S NEED TO ACHIEVE  (18) DOM                 INDIVIDUAL'S NEED TO ACHIEVE  (18) DOM           EP =    0.0699

476  DRIFT TOWARD BEING THOSE          0.80 OF  10      476  DRIFT TOWARD BEING THOSE         0.71 OF   7             8     2
     WHERE THE DEGREE OF INSOBRIETY IS                      WHERE THE DEGREE OF INSOBRIETY IS                        2     5
     STRONG  (31) DH                                        MODERATE OR SLIGHT  (18) DH                      XSQ=      2.62
                                                                                                             PHI=     0.393
                                                                                                             EP =    0.0584
```

```
*******************************************************************************************************
273  CULTURES                                        273  CULTURES
     WHERE, WITH THE KIN GROUP NON-COGNATIC,              WHERE, WITH THE KIN GROUP NON-COGNATIC,
     THE DIVORCE RATE IS                                  THE DIVORCE RATE IS
     HIGH  (16) EA/CA                                     LOW  (17) EA/CA


BACKGROUND ON PAGE 130                                                                   SUBJECT ONLY
.......................................................................................................

     16  IN LEFT COLUMN

ALORESE      BEMBA       FANG        ILA         KHASI       LAU         MAGUZAWA    MANDAN      MUNDURUCU   OJIBWA
OMAHA        SIWANS      SOMALI      TODA        YAO         ZUNI

     17  IN RIGHT COLUMN

ATAYAL       AZANDE      BHIL        CALLINAGO   GOND        KAZAK       KIKUYU      LEPCHA      LOLO        MBUNDU
NYAKYUSA     PAWNEE      SIRIONO     TIKOPIA     VEDDA       VIETNAMESE  YORUBA

     24  EXCLUDED BECAUSE IRRELEVANT

ABIPON       ANDAMANESE  AWEIKOMA    AZTEC       BURMESE     CAYAPA      CHUKCHEE    COMANCHE    CUNA        IBAN
IFUGAO       INCA        KORYAK      LOZI        MACASSARESE MARQUESANS  NAMBICUARA  PAPAGO      SAMOANS     SEMANG
TARAHUMARA   THAI        TUBATULABAL YUROK

    343  EXCLUDED BECAUSE UNASCERTAINED


-------------------------------------------------------------------------------------------------------
 44  DRIFT TOWARD BEING THOSE        0.53 OF  15       44  DRIFT TOWARD BEING THOSE        0.82 OF  17          7   14
     WHERE SETTLEMENTS ARE NON-FIXED  (110)                WHERE SETTLEMENTS ARE FIXED  (222)                   8    3
                                                                                                      XSQ=    3.06
                                                                                                      PHI=  -0.309
                                                                                                      EP =  0.0617

 47  DRIFT TOWARD BEING THOSE        0.75 OF   8       47  IN ALL CASES ARE THOSE          1.00 OF   3          2    3
     WHERE, IF SETTLEMENTS ARE NON-FIXED,                  WHERE, IF SETTLEMENTS ARE NON-FIXED,                 6    0
     MOVEMENT IS NON-NOMADIC, RATHER THAN                  MOVEMENT IS NOMADIC, RATHER THAN           XSQ=    2.39
     NOMADIC  (38)                                         NON-NOMADIC  (72)                          PHI=  -0.466
                                                                                                      EP =  0.0606

 90  TILT TOWARD BEING THOSE         0.57 OF   7       90  IN ALL CASES ARE THOSE          1.00 OF  10          3   10
     WHERE, IF A HEREDITARY HEADMANSHIP                    WHERE, IF A HEREDITARY HEADMANSHIP                   4    0
     IS PRESENT, SUCCESSION IS                             IS PRESENT, SUCCESSION IS                  XSQ=    4.63
     MATRILINEAL, RATHER THAN                              PATRILINEAL, RATHER THAN                   PHI=  -0.522
     PATRILINEAL  (38)                                     MATRILINEAL  (127)                         EP =  0.0147

106  DRIFT TOWARD BEING THOSE        0.67 OF   9      106  DRIFT TOWARD BEING THOSE        0.75 OF  12          6    3
     WHERE CLASS STRATIFICATION, IF PRESENT,               WHERE CLASS STRATIFICATION, IF PRESENT,              3    9
     IS BASED ON WEALTH  (77)                              IS BASED ON SOMETHING OTHER THAN           XSQ=    2.14
                                                           WEALTH  (126)                              PHI=   0.319
                                                                                                      EP =  0.0872
```

```
127  DRIFT TOWARD BEING THOSE         0.75 OF   8    127  IN ALL CASES ARE THOSE              1.00 OF   4         2     4
     WHERE THE FEMALES' CONTRIBUTION                     WHERE THE FEMALES' CONTRIBUTION                          6     0
     TO SUBSISTENCE                                      TO SUBSISTENCE                                     XSQ=     3.38
     IS LOW   (32) JKB                                   IS HIGH   (33) JKB                                 PHI=   -0.530
                                                                                                            EP =   0.0606

137  TILT TOWARD BEING THOSE          0.63 OF   8    137  TILT TOWARD BEING THOSE             0.89 OF   9         5     1
     WHERE INVIDIOUS DISPLAY OF WEALTH                   WHERE INVIDIOUS DISPLAY OF WEALTH                        3     8
     IS STRONGLY EMPHASIZED   (37) PES                   IS MODERATELY, LITTLE, OR                          XSQ=     2.91
                                                         NEGATIVELY EMPHASIZED   (52) PES                   PHI=    0.413
                                                                                                            EP =   0.0498

185  DRIFT MORE TOWARD BEING THOSE  0.94 OF  16     185  DRIFT LESS TOWARD BEING THOSE  0.65 OF  17             15    11
     WHERE THE LARGEST NON-COGNATIC KIN GROUP            WHERE THE LARGEST NON-COGNATIC KIN GROUP                  1     6
     IS THE MOEITY OR PHRATRY OR SIB   (194)             IS THE MOEITY OR PHRATRY OR SIB   (194)             XSQ=     2.60
                                                                                                            PHI=    0.281
                                                                                                            EP =   0.0854

198  TILT LESS TOWARD BEING THOSE   0.56 OF   9     198  IN ALL CASES ARE THOSE              1.00 OF  11          5    11
     WHERE RULES FOR THE INHERITANCE OF                  WHERE RULES FOR THE INHERITANCE OF                        4     0
     REAL PROPERTY, IF PRESENT,                          REAL PROPERTY, IF PRESENT,                         XSQ=     3.65
     FAVOR THE MALE HEIR OR LINE, RATHER THAN            FAVOR THE MALE HEIR OR LINE, RATHER THAN           PHI=   -0.427
     THE FEMALE   (144)                                  THE FEMALE   (144)                                 EP =   0.0260

213  DRIFT TOWARD BEING THOSE         0.69 OF  16    213  DRIFT TOWARD BEING THOSE            0.65 OF  17         11     6
     WHERE FIRST COUSIN MARRIAGE IS                      WHERE FIRST COUSIN MARRIAGE IS                            5    11
     PERMITTED   (172)                                   NOT PERMITTED   (198)                              XSQ=     2.48
                                                                                                            PHI=    0.274
                                                                                                            EP =   0.0844

224  TILT TOWARD BEING THOSE          0.73 OF  11    224  TILT TOWARD BEING THOSE             0.83 OF   6          3     5
     WHERE COUSIN MARRIAGE IS                            WHERE COUSIN MARRIAGE IS                                  8     1
     PREFERENTIALLY OR PERMISSIVELY                      PREFERENTIALLY OR PERMISSIVELY                     XSQ=     2.91
     SYMMETRICAL, RATHER THAN                            EITHER PATRI- OR MATRILATERAL,                     PHI=   -0.413
     EITHER PATRI- OR MATRILATERAL   (106)               RATHER THAN SYMMETRICAL   (66)                     EP =   0.0498

442  IN ALL CASES ARE THOSE           1.00 OF   3    442  IN ALL CASES ARE THOSE              1.00 OF   4          0     4
     WHERE FEAR OF ANIMAL SPIRITS                        WHERE FEAR OF ANIMAL SPIRITS                              3     0
     IS LOW   (33) W-C                                   IS HIGH   (28) W-C                                 XSQ=     3.51
                                                                                                            PHI=   -0.708
                                                                                                            EP =   0.0286

454  IN ALL CASES ARE THOSE           1.00 OF   2    454  IN ALL CASES ARE THOSE              1.00 OF   5          0     5
     WHERE THE OBJECTIVE OF THE INDIVIDUAL'S             WHERE THE OBJECTIVE OF THE INDIVIDUAL'S                   2     0
     CONTACT WITH THE DIVINE                             CONTACT WITH THE DIVINE                            XSQ=     2.96
     IS NOT CONDUCIVE TO THE DEVELOPMENT OF THE          IS CONDUCIVE TO THE DEVELOPMENT OF THE             PHI=   -0.650
     INDIVIDUAL'S NEED TO ACHIEVE   (18) DCM             INDIVIDUAL'S NEED TO ACHIEVE   (18) DCM            EP =   0.0476
```

274 CULTURES
WHERE, WITH THE KIN GROUP PATRILINEAL,
THE DIVORCE RATE IS
HIGH (9) EA/CA

274 CULTURES
WHERE, WITH THE KIN GROUP PATRILINEAL,
THE DIVORCE RATE IS
LOW (12) EA/CA

BACKGROUND ON PAGE 130

SUBJECT ONLY

9 IN LEFT COLUMN

ALORESE FANG LAU MAGUZAWA MUNDURUCU OJIBWA OMAHA SIWANS SOMALI

12 IN RIGHT COLUMN

ATAYAL AZANDE BHIL GOND KAZAK KIKUYU LEPCHA LOLO NYAKYUSA TIKOPIA VIETNAMESE YORUBA

36 EXCLUDED BECAUSE IRRELEVANT

ABIPON ANDAMANESE AWEIKOMA AZTEC BEMBA BURMESE CALLINAGO CAYAPA CHUKCHEE COMANCHE CUNA IBAN IFUGAO ILA INCA KHASI KORYAK LOZI MACASSARESE MANDAN MARQUESANS MBUNDU NAMBICUARA PAPAGO PAWNEE SAMOANS SEMANG SIRIONO TARAHUMARA THAI TODA TUBATULABAL VEDDA YAO YUROK ZUNI

343 EXCLUDED BECAUSE UNASCERTAINED

	Left column				Right column				Statistics
4	DRIFT LESS TOWARD BEING THOSE LOCATED OUTSIDE OF THE CIRCUM-MEDITERRANEAN (355)	0.67 OF	9	4	IN ALL CASES ARE THOSE LOCATED OUTSIDE OF THE CIRCUM-MEDITERRANEAN (355)	1.00 OF	12		3 0 / 6 12 / XSQ= 2.34 / PHI= 0.334 / EP = 0.0632
5	IN ALL CASES ARE THOSE LOCATED OUTSIDE OF EAST EURASIA (330)	1.00 OF	9	5	TILT TOWARD BEING THOSE LOCATED IN EAST EURASIA (70)	0.50 OF	12		0 6 / 9 6 / XSQ= 4.09 / PHI= -0.441 / EP = 0.0186
137	TILT TOWARD BEING THOSE WHERE INVIDIOUS DISPLAY OF WEALTH IS STRONGLY EMPHASIZED (37) PES	0.80 OF	5	137	TILT TOWARD BEING THOSE WHERE INVIDIOUS DISPLAY OF WEALTH IS MODERATELY, LITTLE, OR NEGATIVELY EMPHASIZED (52) PES	0.88 OF	8		4 1 / 1 7 / XSQ= 3.41 / PHI= 0.512 / EP = 0.0319
354	IN ALL CASES ARE THOSE WHERE THE CHILD'S INFERRED ANXIETY OVER PERFORMANCE OF OBEDIENT BEHAVIOR IS HIGH (36) B-B-C	1.00 OF	4	354	DRIFT TOWARD BEING THOSE WHERE THE CHILD'S INFERRED ANXIETY OVER PERFORMANCE OF OBEDIENT BEHAVIOR IS LOW (37) B-B-C	0.67 OF	6		4 2 / 0 4 / XSQ= 2.10 / PHI= 0.458 / EP = 0.0762

```
355  IN ALL CASES ARE THCSE          1.00 OF   4       355  DRIFT TOWARD BEING THOSE        0.67 CF   6            4    2
     WHERE THE CHILD'S INFERREC CONFLICT                     WHERE THE CHILD'S INFERRED CCNFLICT                     0    4
     REGARDING CBEDIENT BEHAVICR                             REGARDING OBEDIENT BEHAVIOR                      XSQ=     2.10
     IS HIGH  (35) B-B-C                                     IS LOW  (38) B-B-C                               PHI=    0.458
                                                                                                              EP =   0.0762
```

```
******************************************************************************************************

275  CULTURES                                        275  CULTURES
     WHERE, WITH THE KIN GROUP                            WHERE, WITH THE KIN GROUP
     EXCLUSIVELY COGNATIC,                                EXCLUSIVELY COGNATIC,
     THE DIVORCE RATE IS                                  THE DIVORCE RATE IS
     HIGH  (13) EA/CA                                     LOW  (11) EA/CA

BACKGROUND ON PAGE 130                                                                SUBJECT ONLY
......................................................................................................

      13   IN LEFT COLUMN

ABIPON       CHUKCHEE     COMANCHE     CUNA         IFUGAO       LOZI         MARQUESANS   NAMBICUARA   PAPAGO       SAMOANS
SEMANG       TARAHUMARA   YUROK

      11   IN RIGHT COLUMN

ANDAMANESE   AWEIKOMA     AZTEC        BURMESE      CAYAPA       IBAN         INCA         KORYAK       MACASSARESE  THAI
TUBATULABAL

      33   EXCLUDED BECAUSE IRRELEVANT

ALORESE      ATAYAL       AZANDE       BEMBA        BHIL         CALLINAGO    FANG         GOND         ILA          KAZAK
KHASI        KIKUYU       LAU          LEPCHA       LOLO         MAGUZAWA     MANDAN       MBUNDU       MUNDURUCU    NYAKYUSA
OJIBWA       OMAHA        PAWNEE       SIRIONO      SIWANS       SOMALI       TIKOPIA      TODA         VEDDA        VIETNAMESE
YAO          YORUBA       ZUNI

     343   EXCLUDED BECAUSE UNASCERTAINED

------------------------------------------------------------------------------------------------------
 81  IN ALL CASES ARE THOSE         1.00 OF   9        81  DRIFT LESS TOWARD BEING THOSE  0.56 OF   9            0    4
     WHERE NO CITY OR TOWN IS PRESENT, AND                  WHERE NO CITY OR TOWN IS PRESENT, AND                    9    5
     THE AVERAGE COMMUNITY SIZE IS                          THE AVERAGE COMMUNITY SIZE IS                    XSQ=    2.89
     SMALLER THAN 200  (135)                                SMALLER THAN 200  (135)                          PHI=  -0.401
                                                                                                             EP =  0.0824

 85  DRIFT MORE TOWARD BEING THOSE  0.92 OF  12        85  DRIFT LESS TOWARD BEING THOSE  0.55 OF  11            1    5
     WHERE THE LEVEL OF POLITICAL INTEGRATION               WHERE THE LEVEL OF POLITICAL INTEGRATION                11    6
     IS THE MINIMAL STATE,                                  IS THE MINIMAL STATE,                            XSQ=    2.40
     THE AUTONOMOUS COMMUNITY, OR                           THE AUTONOMOUS COMMUNITY, OR                     PHI=  -0.323
     THE FAMILY  (234) GPM                                  THE FAMILY  (234) GPM                            EP =  0.0686

107  IN ALL CASES ARE THOSE         1.00 OF   9       107  TILT TOWARD BEING THOSE        0.67 OF   6            0    4
     WHERE CLASS STRATIFICATION, IF PRESENT,                WHERE CLASS STRATIFICATION, IF PRESENT,                  9    2
     IS BASED ON SOMETHING OTHER THAN                       IS BASED ON                                      XSQ=    5.13
     OCCUPATIONAL STATUS  (160)                             OCCUPATIONAL STATUS  (43)                        PHI=  -0.585
                                                                                                             EP =  0.0110

242  TILT TOWARD BEING THOSE        0.92 OF  12       242  TILT TOWARD BEING THOSE        0.55 OF  11           11    5
     WHERE MARRIAGE IS                                      WHERE MARRIAGE IS MONOGAMOUS,                            1    6
     COMMONLY OR OCCASIONALLY POLYGYNOUS,                   RATHER THAN COMMONLY OR OCCASIONALLY             XSQ=    3.81
     RATHER THAN MONOGAMOUS  (314)                          POLYGYNOUS  (81)                                 PHI=   0.407
                                                                                                             EP =  0.0272
```

275/

```
323  DRIFT TOWARD BEING THOSE          0.86 OF    7        323  IN ALL CASES ARE THOSE           1.00 OF    2              1      2
     WHERE THE CONSTANCY OF PRESENCE                             WHERE THE CONSTANCY OF PRESENCE                             6      0
     OF THE INFANT'S NURTURANT AGENT                             OF THE INFANT'S NURTURANT AGENT                     XSQ=      2.01
     IS LOW   (45) B-B-C                                         IS HIGH   (29) B-B-C                                PHI=    -0.472
                                                                                                                     EP  =   0.0833
```

```
*******************************************************************************************************

276  CULTURES                                             276  CULTURES
     WHERE, WITH THE KINDREC THE ONLY KIN GROUP                WHERE, WITH THE KINDRED THE CNLY KIN GRCUP
     PRESENT, CR WITH BILATERAL DESCENT                        PRESENT, OR WITH BILATERAL DESCENT
     INFERRED, THE DIVCRCE RATE IS                             INFERRED, THE DIVORCE RATE IS
     HIGH  (9) EA/CA                                           LOW  (9) EA/CA

BACKGROUND ON PAGE 130                                                                        SUBJECT ONLY
.......................................................................................................

      9  IN LEFT CCLUMN

ABIPCN      CHUKCHEE    CUNA        MARQUESANS  NAMBICUARA  PAPAGO      SEMANG      TARAHUMARA  YURCK

      9  IN RIGHT CCLUMN

ANDAMANESE  AWEIKOMA    BURMESE     CAYAPA      IBAN        INCA        KORYAK      THAI        TUBATULABAL

     39  EXCLUDED BECAUSE IRRELEVANT

ALORESE     ATAYAL      AZANCE      AZTEC       BEMBA       BHIL        CALLINAGO   CCMANCHE    FANG        GONC
IFUGAC      ILA         KAZAK       KHASI       KIKUYU      LAU         LEPCHA      LCLC        LOZI        MACASSARESE
MAGLZAWA    MANDAN      MBUNCU      MUNCURUCU   NYAKYUSA    OJIBWA      OMAHA       PAWNEE      SAMCANS     SIRIONO
SIWANS      SCMALI      TIKCPIA     TOCA        VEDDA       VIETNAMESE  YAC         YCRUBA      ZUNI

    343  EXCLUCED BECAUSE UNASCERTAINEC

-------------------------------------------------------------------------------------------------------
107  IN ALL CASES ARE THCSE         1.00 OF   6      1C7  TILT TOWARD BEING THOSE        0.75 CF   4          0     3
     WHERE CLASS STRATIFICATICN, IF PRESENT,              WHERE CLASS STRATIFICATICN, IF PRESENT,              6     1
     IS BASED CN SCMETHING CTHER THAN                     IS BASED ON                                    XSQ=     3.35
     CCCUPATICNAL STATUS  (160)                           OCCUPATIONAL STATUS  (43)                      PHI=   -0.579
                                                                                                         EP =   0.0333

242  IN ALL CASES ARE THCSE         1.00 OF   8      242  LEAN TOWARD BEING THCSE        0.67 CF   9          8     3
     WHERE MARRIAGE IS                                    WHERE MARRIAGE IS MCNCGAMOUS,                        0     6
     COMMCNLY CR CCCASICNALLY PCLYGYNOUS,                 RATHER THAN COMMCNLY CR CCCASICNALLY           XSQ=     5.58
     RATHER THAN MCNCGAMCUS  (314)                        POLYGYNCUS  (81)                               PHI=    0.573
                                                                                                         EP =   0.0090
```

277 CULTURES WHERE THE STATUS OF WOMEN IS INFERIOR OR SUBJECTED (14) LWS	277 CULTURES WHERE THE STATUS OF WOMEN IS NOT STRONGLY INFERIOR OR SUBJECTED (22) LWS

BACKGROUND ON PAGE 132 — BOTH SUBJECT AND PREDICATE

14 IN LEFT COLUMN

AINU, ALBANIANS, ARANDA, ARAUCANIANS, AZTEC, CHUKCHEE, CREEK, FANG, HEBREWS, KUTENAI, MAORI, RWALA, TODA, YAKUT

22 IN RIGHT COLUMN

ANDAMANESE, ASHANTI, HAIDA, HANO, IBAN, JIVARO, KAZAK, KUNG, KWAKIUTL, LANGO, LAPPS, NAMA, NAVAHO, OMAHA, SAMOANS, SEMANG, SERI, SHILLUK, TROBRIAND, VEDDA, WITOTO, YAHGAN

364 EXCLUDED BECAUSE UNASCERTAINED

	Left column		Right column		Statistics
14	DRIFT TOWARD BEING THOSE WHERE THE LATITUDE IS THIRTY DEGREES OR GREATER (119)	0.71 OF 14	DRIFT TOWARD BEING THOSE WHERE THE LATITUDE IS LESS THAN THIRTY DEGREES (281)	0.64 OF 22	10 8 / 4 14 / XSQ= 2.92 / PHI= 0.285 / EP = 0.0858
42	DRIFT MORE TOWARD BEING THOSE WHERE THE NATURAL ENVIRONMENT IS OTHER THAN TROPICAL OR SUB-TROPICAL RAIN FOREST, OR MONSOON FOREST (244) FWM	0.93 OF 14	DRIFT LESS TOWARD BEING THOSE WHERE THE NATURAL ENVIRONMENT IS OTHER THAN TROPICAL OR SUB-TROPICAL RAIN FOREST, OR MONSOON FOREST (244) FWM	0.64 OF 22	1 8 / 13 14 / XSQ= 2.49 / PHI= -0.263 / EP = 0.0620
55	TILT TOWARD BEING THOSE WHERE FOOD PRODUCTION IS BY INTENSIVE AGRICULTURE, RATHER THAN BY SIMPLE AGRICULTURE (91)	0.80 OF 5	TILT TOWARD BEING THOSE WHERE FOOD PRODUCTION IS BY SIMPLE AGRICULTURE, RATHER THAN BY INTENSIVE AGRICULTURE (101)	0.88 OF 8	4 1 / 1 7 / XSQ= 3.41 / PHI= 0.512 / EP = 0.0319
96	DRIFT TOWARD BEING THOSE WHERE THE HIERARCHY OF NATIONAL JURISDICTION HAS FOUR, THREE, TWO OR ONE LEVEL (174) GES,EA	0.71 OF 14	DRIFT TOWARD BEING THOSE WHERE THE HIERARCHY OF NATIONAL JURISDICTION HAS NO LEVELS (156) GES,EA	0.62 OF 21	10 8 / 4 13 / XSQ= 2.52 / PHI= 0.268 / EP = 0.0858
108	DRIFT TOWARD BEING THOSE WHERE CLASS STRATIFICATION, IF PRESENT, IS BASED ON SOMETHING OTHER THAN A HEREDITARY ARISTOCRACY (129)	0.88 OF 8	DRIFT TOWARD BEING THOSE WHERE CLASS STRATIFICATION, IF PRESENT, IS BASED ON A HEREDITARY ARISTOCRACY (74)	0.60 OF 10	1 6 / 7 4 / XSQ= 2.46 / PHI= -0.369 / EP = 0.0656

242	IN ALL CASES ARE THOSE 1.00 OF 13 WHERE MARRIAGE IS COMMONLY OR OCCASIONALLY POLYGYNOUS, RATHER THAN MONOGAMOUS (314)	242	DRIFT LESS TOWARD BEING THOSE 0.73 OF 22 WHERE MARRIAGE IS COMMONLY OR OCCASIONALLY POLYGYNOUS, RATHER THAN MONOGAMOUS (314)	 XSQ= PHI= EP =	13 16 0 6 2.57 0.271 0.0645
279	DRIFT TOWARD BEING THOSE 0.56 OF 9 WHERE WIFE-LENDING OR WIFE-EXCHANGE IS PRESENT (10) LWS	279	DRIFT TOWARD BEING THOSE 0.88 OF 16 WHERE WIFE-LENDING AND WIFE EXCHANGE ARE UNIMPORTANT OR ABSENT (19) LWS	 XSQ= PHI= EP =	5 2 4 14 3.38 0.367 0.0581
304	IN ALL CASES ARE THOSE 1.00 OF 5 WHERE THE EARLY ANAL SATISFACTION POTENTIAL IS HIGH (19) W-C	304	DRIFT TOWARD BEING THOSE 0.67 OF 6 WHERE THE EARLY ANAL SATISFACTION POTENTIAL IS LOW (22) W-C	 XSQ= PHI= EP =	5 2 0 4 2.75 0.500 0.0606
319	TILT TOWARD BEING THOSE 0.60 OF 5 WHERE PROTECTION OF THE INFANT FROM ENVIRONMENTAL DISCOMFORTS IS LOW (30) B-B-C	319	IN ALL CASES ARE THOSE 1.00 OF 8 WHERE PROTECTION OF THE INFANT FROM ENVIRONMENTAL DISCOMFORTS IS HIGH (35) B-B-C	 XSQ= PHI= EP =	2 8 3 0 3.32 -0.505 0.0350
320	TILT TOWARD BEING THOSE 0.50 OF 6 WHERE THE DEGREE OF REDUCTION OF THE INFANT'S DRIVES IS LOW (24) B-B-C	320	IN ALL CASES ARE THOSE 1.00 OF 9 WHERE THE DEGREE OF REDUCTION OF THE INFANT'S DRIVES IS HIGH (45) B-B-C	 XSQ= PHI= EP =	3 9 3 0 2.93 -0.442 0.0440
324	IN ALL CASES ARE THOSE 1.00 OF 5 WHERE THE PAIN INFLICTED ON THE INFANT BY THE NURTURANT AGENT IS HIGH (34) B-B-C	324	TILT TOWARD BEING THOSE 0.67 OF 9 WHERE THE PAIN INFLICTED ON THE INFANT BY THE NURTURANT AGENT IS LOW OR NEGLIGIBLE (32) B-B-C	 XSQ= PHI= EP =	5 3 0 6 3.43 0.495 0.0310
325	TILT TOWARD BEING THOSE 0.67 OF 6 WHERE THE DEGREE OF DIFFUSION AMONG THE INFANT'S NURTURANT AGENTS IS LOW (32) B-B-C	325	TILT TOWARD BEING THOSE 0.90 OF 10 WHERE THE DEGREE OF DIFFUSION AMONG THE INFANT'S NURTURANT AGENTS IS HIGH (42) B-B-C	 XSQ= PHI= EP =	2 9 4 1 3.28 -0.453 0.0357
370	TILT TOWARD BEING THOSE 0.90 OF 10 WHERE THE SEGREGATION OF ADOLESCENT BOYS IS ABSENT (148)	370	TILT TOWARD BEING THOSE 0.50 OF 18 WHERE THE SEGREGATION OF ADOLESCENT BOYS IS COMPLETE OR PARTIAL (95)	 XSQ= PHI= EP =	1 9 9 9 2.91 -0.322 0.0484
435	DRIFT TOWARD BEING THOSE 0.90 OF 10 WHERE ABANDONMENT OF THE HOUSE OF THE DEAD IS NOT PRACTICED (19) LWS	435	DRIFT TOWARD BEING THOSE 0.50 OF 16 WHERE ABANDONMENT OF THE HOUSE OF THE DEAD IS PRACTICED (12) LWS	 XSQ= PHI= EP =	1 8 9 8 2.76 -0.326 0.0873

451 DRIFT TCWARD BEING THCSE WHERE TCTEMISM IS PRESENT (15) LWS — 0.86 OF 7

451 DRIFT TOWARD BEING THOSE WHERE TOTEMISM IS UNIMPORTANT OR ABSENT (12) LWS — 0.59 OF 17

	6	7
	1	10
XSQ=		2.37
PHI=		0.314
EP =		0.0778

****

278 CULTURES WHERE PROPERTY RIGHTS IN WOMEN ARE PRESENT (8) LWS	278 CULTURES WHERE PROPERTY RIGHTS IN WOMEN ARE UNIMPORTANT OR ABSENT (14) LWS

BACKGROUND ON PAGE 132 — BOTH SUBJECT AND PREDICATE

8 IN LEFT COLUMN

ALBANIANS ARAUCANIANS ASHANTI AZTEC HEBREWS KAZAK NAMA RWALA

14 IN RIGHT COLUMN

AINU ANDAMANESE CHUKCHEE DIERI IBAN KUNG LANGO MAORI SEMANG SERI
SHILLUK VEDDA WITOTO YAKUT

378 EXCLUDED BECAUSE UNASCERTAINED

	Left column			Right column		
4	TILT LESS TOWARD BEING THOSE LOCATED OUTSIDE OF THE CIRCUM-MEDITERRANEAN (355)	0.63 OF 8	4	IN ALL CASES ARE THOSE LOCATED OUTSIDE OF THE CIRCUM-MEDITERRANEAN (355)	1.00 OF 14	3 0 5 14 XSQ= 3.31 PHI= 0.388 EP = 0.0364
51	LEAN TOWARD BEING THOSE WHERE SUBSISTENCE IS PRIMARILY BY FOOD PRODUCTION -- I. E., AGRICULTURE OR HUSBANDRY -- RATHER THAN BY GATHERING (253)	0.88 OF 8	51	LEAN TOWARD BEING THOSE WHERE SUBSISTENCE IS PRIMARILY BY FOOD GATHERING -- I. E., HUNTING, FISHING, OR COLLECTING -- RATHER THAN FOOD PRODUCTION (147)	0.79 OF 14	7 3 1 11 XSQ= 6.50 PHI= 0.543 EP = 0.0062
53	TILT TOWARD BEING THOSE WHERE FOOD PRODUCTION IS BY INTENSIVE AGRICULTURE, RATHER THAN BY SIMPLE AGRICULTURE OR INCIPIENT FOOD PRODUCTION (91)	0.67 OF 6	53	IN ALL CASES ARE THOSE WHERE FOOD PRODUCTION IS BY SIMPLE AGRICULTURE OR INCIPIENT FOOD PRODUCTION, RATHER THAN BY INTENSIVE AGRICULTURE (147)	1.00 OF 7	4 0 2 7 XSQ= 3.97 PHI= 0.553 EP = 0.0210
62	TILT TOWARD BEING THOSE WHERE HUSBANDRY OF SOME KIND IS PRESENT (228)	0.88 OF 8	62	TILT TOWARD BEING THOSE WHERE HUSBANDRY OF ANY KIND IS ABSENT (172)	0.64 OF 14	7 5 1 9 XSQ= 3.62 PHI= 0.405 EP = 0.0310
71	IN ALL CASES ARE THOSE WHERE METAL WORKING IS PRESENT (98)	1.00 OF 7	71	TILT TOWARD BEING THOSE WHERE METAL WORKING IS ABSENT (153)	0.67 OF 12	7 4 0 8 XSQ= 5.56 PHI= 0.541 EP = 0.0128

73	DRIFT TOWARD BEING THOSE WHERE WEAVING IS PRESENT (118)	0.86 OF 7	73	DRIFT TOWARD BEING THOSE WHERE WEAVING IS ABSENT (130)	0.67 OF 12	6 4 1 8 XSQ= 2.99 PHI= 0.397 EP = 0.0573
82	IN ALL CASES ARE THOSE WHERE A CITY OR TOWN IS PRESENT, OR THE AVERAGE COMMUNITY SIZE IS FIFTY OR GREATER (178)	1.00 OF 7	82	TILT TOWARD BEING THOSE WHERE NO CITY OR TOWN IS PRESENT, AND THE AVERAGE COMMUNITY SIZE IS SMALLER THAN FIFTY (46)	0.67 OF 9	7 3 0 6 XSQ= 4.89 PHI= 0.553 EP = 0.0114
84	TILT TOWARD BEING THOSE WHERE THE LEVEL OF POLITICAL INTEGRATION IS THE LARGE STATE (42) GPM	0.50 OF 8	84	TILT TOWARD BEING THOSE WHERE THE LEVEL OF POLITICAL INTEGRATION IS THE LITTLE STATE, THE MINIMAL STATE, THE AUTONOMOUS COMMUNITY, OR THE FAMILY (262) GPM	0.92 OF 13	4 1 4 12 XSQ= 2.83 PHI= 0.367 EP = 0.0475
85	DRIFT TOWARD BEING THOSE WHERE THE LEVEL OF POLITICAL INTEGRATION IS THE LARGE STATE, OR THE LITTLE STATE (70) GPM	0.63 OF 8	85	DRIFT TOWARD BEING THOSE WHERE THE LEVEL OF POLITICAL INTEGRATION IS THE MINIMAL STATE, THE AUTONOMOUS COMMUNITY, OR THE FAMILY (234) GPM	0.85 OF 13	5 2 3 11 XSQ= 3.05 PHI= 0.381 EP = 0.0555
86	LEAN TOWARD BEING THOSE WHERE THE LEVEL OF POLITICAL INTEGRATION IS THE LARGE STATE, THE LITTLE STATE, OR THE MINIMAL STATE (148) GPM	0.88 OF 8	86	LEAN TOWARD BEING THOSE WHERE THE LEVEL OF POLITICAL INTEGRATION IS THE AUTONOMOUS COMMUNITY, OR THE FAMILY (156) GPM	0.77 OF 13	7 3 1 10 XSQ= 5.86 PHI= 0.528 EP = 0.0075
95	TILT TOWARD BEING THOSE WHERE THE HIERARCHY OF NATIONAL JURISDICTION HAS FOUR, THREE, OR TWO LEVELS (76) GES,EA	0.63 OF 8	95	TILT TOWARD BEING THOSE WHERE THE HIERARCHY OF NATIONAL JURISDICTION HAS ONE OR NO LEVELS (254) GES,EA	0.92 OF 13	5 1 3 12 XSQ= 4.85 PHI= 0.481 EP = 0.0139
96	TILT TOWARD BEING THOSE WHERE THE HIERARCHY OF NATIONAL JURISDICTION HAS FOUR, THREE, TWO OR ONE LEVEL (174) GES,EA	0.88 OF 8	96	TILT TOWARD BEING THOSE WHERE THE HIERARCHY OF NATIONAL JURISDICTION HAS NO LEVELS (156) GES,EA	0.69 OF 13	7 4 1 9 XSQ= 4.32 PHI= 0.453 EP = 0.0237
102	TILT TOWARD BEING THOSE WHERE CLASS STRATIFICATION IS PRESENT (203)	0.88 OF 8	102	TILT TOWARD BEING THOSE WHERE CLASS STRATIFICATION IS ABSENT (180)	0.64 OF 14	7 5 1 9 XSQ= 3.62 PHI= 0.405 EP = 0.0310
138	IN ALL CASES ARE THOSE WHERE SUPERORDINATE JUSTICE IS PRESENT (22) BBW	1.00 OF 2	138	IN ALL CASES ARE THOSE WHERE SUPERORDINATE JUSTICE IS ABSENT (18) BBW	1.00 OF 5	2 0 0 5 XSQ= 2.96 PHI= 0.650 EP = 0.0476

```
147  DRIFT TCWARD BEING THCSE           0.88 OF   8      147  DRIFT TOWARD REING THOSE           0.58 CF  12          7     5
     WHERE CCDIFIED LAWS ARE                                  WHERE CODIFIED LAWS ARE                                1     7
     PRESENT  (20) LWS                                        UNIMPORTANT OR ABSENT  (13) LWS                XSQ=    2.51
                                                                                                             PHI=   0.354
                                                                                                             EP =  0.0697

192  IN ALL CASES ARE THCSE             1.00 OF   8      192  DRIFT LESS TOWARD BEING THCSE  0.57 CF  14          0     6
     CTHER THAN WHERE THE CNLY KIN GROUP                      OTHER THAN WHERE THE CNLY KIN GRCUP                    8     8
     PRESENT IS A KINCREC CR ELSE                             PRESENT IS A KINDRED OR ELSE                   XSQ=    2.80
     BILATERAL DESCENT IS INFERREC  (289)                     BILATERAL DESCENT IS INFERRED  (289)           PHI=  -0.357
                                                                                                             EP =  0.0511

220  TILT TCWARD BEING THCSE            0.50 OF   8      220  TILT TOWARD BEING THOSE            0.93 CF  14          4     1
     WHERE FIRST CCUSIN MARRIACE                              WHERE FIRST CCUSIN MARRIAGE                            4    13
     IN SCME FCRM CR CTHER                                    IN SOME FORM OR OTHER                          XSQ=    3.16
     IS PRESCRIBED CR PREFERREC  (97)                         IS NOT PRESCRIBED CR PREFERRED  (273)          PHI=   0.379
                                                                                                             EP =  0.0393

311  IN ALL CASES ARE THCSE             1.00 OF   2      311  IN ALL CASES ARE THCSE             1.00 CF   5          2     0
     WHERE SEXUAL SCCIALIZATICN ANXIETY                       WHERE SEXUAL SOCIALIZATICN ANXIETY                     0     5
     IS HIGH  (28) W-C                                        IS LOW  (23) W-C                               XSQ=    2.96
                                                                                                             PHI=   0.650
                                                                                                             EP =  0.0476

390  TILT TCWARD BEING THCSE            0.50 OF   8      39C  IN ALL CASES ARE THOSE             1.00 CF  10          4     0
     WHERE PREMARITAL SEX RELATIONS ARE                       WHERE PREMARITAL SEX RELATICNS ARE                     4    10
     STRCNGLY PUNISHED ANC                                    WEAKLY PUNISHED AND IN FACT NCT RARE CR        XSQ=    3.86
     IN FACT RARE  (47) JTW,EA                                PUNISHED ONLY IF PREGNANCY RESULTS, CR         PHI=   0.463
                                                              FREELY PERMITTED  (132) JTW,EA                 EP =  0.0229

392  IN ALL CASES ARE THCSE             1.00 OF   8      392  TILT TOWARD BEING THOSE            0.50 CF  10          8     5
     WHERE PREMARITAL SEX RELATIONS ARE                       WHERE PREMARITAL SEX RELATICNS ARE                     0     5
     STRCNGLY PUNISHEC AND IN FACT RARE, OR                   FREELY PERMITTED  (67) JTW,EA                  XSQ=    3.33
     WEAKLY PUNISHED ANC IN FACT NCT RARE, OR                                                                PHI=   0.430
     PUNISHED CNLY IF                                                                                        EP =  0.0359
     PREGNANCY RESULTS  (112) JTW,EA

4C2  IN ALL CASES ARE THCSE             1.00 OF   2      4C2  IN ALL CASES ARE THOSE             1.00 CF   5          0     5
     WHERE EXPLANATICNS CF ILLNESS                            WHERE EXPLANATICNS OF ILLNESS                          2     0
     CF AN CRAL NATURE                                        OF AN ORAL NATURE                              XSQ=    2.96
     ARE ABSENT  (30) W-C                                     ARE PRESENT  (31) W-C                          PHI=  -0.650
                                                                                                             EP =  0.0476

428  DRIFT TCWARD BEING THCSE           0.67 OF   6      428  IN ALL CASES ARE THCSE             1.00 CF   5          4     0
     WHERE A HIGH GCC, IF PRESENT ANC ACTIVE,                 WHERE A HIGH GOD, IF PRESENT AND ACTIVE,               2     5
     SUPPCRTS HUMAN MCRALITY, RATHER THAN                     DOES NOT SUPPORT HUMAN MCRALITY,               XSQ=    2.75
     NCT SUPPCRTING IT  (61) GES,EA                           RATHER THAN SUPPCRTING IT  (26) GES,EA         PHI=   0.500
                                                                                                             EP =  0.0606

432  IN ALL CASES ARE THCSE             1.00 OF   7      432  DRIFT LESS TOWARD BEING THCSE  0.54 CF  13          7     7
     WHERE AN ATTRACTIVE AFTERLIFE IS                         WHERE AN ATTRACTIVE AFTERLIFE IS                       0     6
     BELIEVED IN  (27) LWS                                    BELIEVED IN  (27) LWS                          XSQ=    2.68
                                                                                                             PHI=   0.366
                                                                                                             EP =  0.0515
```

```
440  IN ALL CASES ARE THCSE           1.00 OF   2      440  IN ALL CASES ARE THCSE           1.00 CF   5           0     5
     WHERE FEAR OF SPIRITS                                  WHERE FEAR CF SPIRITS                                     2     0
     IS LCW  (29) W-C                                       IS HIGH  (32) W-C                               XSQ=      2.96
                                                                                                             PHI=    -0.650
                                                                                                             EP =    0.0476

458  TILT TCWARD BEING THCSE          0.71 OF   7      458  TILT TOWARD BEING THCSE          0.90 CF  10           5     1
     WHERE GAMES, IF PRESENT,                               WHERE GAMES, IF PRESENT,                                  2     9
     INCLUDE GAMES CF STRATEGY  (52) R-A-B,EA               DO NOT INCLUDE                                  XSQ=      4.38
                                                            GAMES OF STRATEGY  (119) R-A-B,EA               PHI=     0.508
                                                                                                             EP =    0.0345

460  TILT TCWARD BEING THCSE          0.86 OF   7      460  TILT TOWARD BEING THOSE          0.80 OF  10           1     8
     WHERE GAMES, IF PRESENT,                               WHERE GAMES, IF PRESENT,                                  6     2
     ARE NCT LIMITED TC                                     ARE LIMITED TO                                  XSQ=      4.74
     GAMES CF SKILL CNLY  (104) R-A-B,EA                    GAMES OF SKILL ONLY  (67) R-A-B,EA              PHI=    -0.528
                                                                                                             EP =    0.0152
```

****

279 CULTURES WHERE WIFE-LENDING OR WIFE-EXCHANGE IS PRESENT (10) LWS	279 CULTURES WHERE WIFE-LENDING AND WIFE EXCHANGE ARE UNIMPORTANT OR ABSENT (19) LWS

BACKGROUND ON PAGE 132 BOTH SUBJECT AND PREDICATE

....

10 IN LEFT COLUMN

ARANDA CHUKCHEE DIERI FANG FON HAIDA JIVARO MOTA RWALA TODA

19 IN RIGHT COLUMN

ASHANTI AZTEC HEBREWS IBAN KAZAK KUNG KWAKIUTL LANGO MAORI OMAHA
SAMOANS SEMANG SERI TROBRIAND VEDDA WITOTO YAHGAN YAKUT YUKAGHIR

371 EXCLUDED BECAUSE UNASCERTAINED

	Left column			Right column		
141	IN ALL CASES ARE THOSE 1.00 OF 5 WHERE THE LEVEL OF SOCIAL SANCTION IS PUBLIC PROPERTY SANCTION OR PRIVATE SETTLEMENT, RATHER THAN PUBLIC CORPOREAL SANCTION (26) JMH	141	TILT TOWARD BEING THOSE 0.80 OF 5 WHERE THE LEVEL OF SOCIAL SANCTION IS PUBLIC CORPOREAL SANCTION, RATHER THAN PUBLIC PROPERTY SANCTION OR PRIVATE SETTLEMENT (28) JMH	0 4 5 1 XSQ= 3.75 PHI= -0.612 EP = 0.0476
142	TILT TOWARD BEING THOSE 0.80 OF 5 WHERE THE LEVEL OF SOCIAL SANCTION IS PRIVATE SETTLEMENT, RATHER THAN PUBLIC CORPOREAL SANCTION OR PUBLIC PROPERTY SETTLEMENT (16) JMH	142	IN ALL CASES ARE THOSE 1.00 OF 5 WHERE THE LEVEL OF SOCIAL SANCTION IS PUBLIC CORPOREAL SANCTION OR PUBLIC PROPERTY SANCTION, RATHER THAN PRIVATE SETTLEMENT (38) JMH	1 5 4 0 XSQ= 3.75 PHI= -0.612 EP = 0.0476
175	DRIFT TOWARD BEING THOSE 0.60 OF 10 WHERE THE COMMUNITY IS 'KIN-HOMOGENEOUS,' I. E. A CLAN COMMUNITY OR A DEME (122)	175	DRIFT TOWARD BEING THOSE 0.78 OF 18 WHERE THE COMMUNITY IS 'KIN-HETEROGENEOUS,' I. E. OTHER THAN A CLAN COMMUNITY OR A DEME (260)	6 4 4 14 XSQ= 2.52 PHI= 0.300 EP = 0.0974
234	DRIFT TOWARD BEING THOSE 0.86 OF 7 WHERE THE COUSIN TERMINOLOGY IS OF CROW, OMAHA, OR IROQUOIS TYPE, RATHER THAN ESKIMO OR HAWAIIAN TYPE (152)	234	DRIFT TOWARD BEING THOSE 0.67 OF 15 WHERE THE COUSIN TERMINOLOGY IS OF ESKIMO OR HAWAIIAN TYPE, RATHER THAN CROW, OMAHA, OR IROQUOIS TYPE (170)	6 5 1 10 XSQ= 3.35 PHI= 0.390 EP = 0.0635
243	TILT TOWARD BEING THOSE 0.75 OF 4 WHERE POLYGYNY, IF PRESENT, HAS A HIGH INCIDENCE (24) W-D,S	243	IN ALL CASES ARE THOSE 1.00 OF 5 WHERE POLYGYNY, IF PRESENT, HAS A LOW INCIDENCE (36) W-D,S	3 0 1 5 XSQ= 2.76 PHI= 0.553 EP = 0.0476

263	TILT TOWARD BEING THOSE WHERE WIVES ARE OBTAINED BY RELATIVELY DIFFICULT MEANS, NAMELY BY BRIDE-PRICE, BRIDE-SERVICE, OR EXCHANGING A FEMALE RELATIVE (233)	0.90 OF 10	263	TILT TOWARD BEING THOSE WHERE WIVES ARE OBTAINED BY RELATIVELY EASY MEANS, NAMELY BY TOKEN BRIDE-PRICE, GIFT EXCHANGE, ABSENCE OF ANY CONSIDERATION, OR RECEIPT OF DOWRY (162)	0.53 OF 19	9 9 1 10 XSQ= 3.41 PHI= 0.343 EP = 0.0436
277	DRIFT TOWARD BEING THOSE WHERE THE STATUS OF WOMEN IS INFERIOR OR SUBJECTED (14) LWS	0.71 OF 7	277	DRIFT TOWARD BEING THOSE WHERE THE STATUS OF WOMEN IS NOT STRONGLY INFERIOR OR SUBJECTED (22) LWS	0.78 OF 18	5 4 2 14 XSQ= 3.38 PHI= 0.367 EP = 0.0581
323	DRIFT TOWARD BEING THOSE WHERE THE CONSTANCY OF PRESENCE OF THE INFANT'S NURTURANT AGENT IS HIGH (29) B-B-C	0.75 OF 4	323	DRIFT TOWARD BEING THOSE WHERE THE CONSTANCY OF PRESENCE OF THE INFANT'S NURTURANT AGENT IS LOW (45) B-B-C	0.88 OF 8	3 1 1 7 XSQ= 2.30 PHI= 0.437 EP = 0.0667
325	IN ALL CASES ARE THOSE WHERE THE DEGREE OF DIFFUSION AMONG THE INFANT'S NURTURANT AGENTS IS LOW (32) B-B-C	1.00 OF 4	325	TILT TOWARD BEING THOSE WHERE THE DEGREE OF DIFFUSION AMONG THE INFANT'S NURTURANT AGENTS IS HIGH (42) B-B-C	0.88 OF 8	0 7 4 1 XSQ= 5.19 PHI= -0.657 EP = 0.0101
377	DRIFT TOWARD BEING THOSE WHERE MALE GENITAL MUTILATION IS PRESENT (83)	0.50 OF 10	377	DRIFT TOWARD BEING THOSE WHERE MALE GENITAL MUTILATION IS ABSENT (242)	0.83 OF 18	5 3 5 15 XSQ= 2.06 PHI= 0.271 EP = 0.0913
391	DRIFT TOWARD BEING THOSE WHERE PREMARITAL SEX RELATIONS ARE PUNISHED ONLY IF PREGNANCY RESULTS, OR FREELY PERMITTED (90) JTW,EA	0.71 OF 7	391	DRIFT TOWARD BEING THOSE WHERE PREMARITAL SEX RELATIONS ARE STRONGLY PUNISHED AND IN FACT RARE, OR WEAKLY PUNISHED AND IN FACT NOT RARE (89) JTW,EA	0.73 OF 15	2 11 5 4 XSQ= 2.32 PHI= -0.325 EP = 0.0743
433	IN ALL CASES ARE THOSE WHERE BELIEF IN REINCARNATION IS PRESENT (10) GES	1.00 OF 2	433	IN ALL CASES ARE THOSE WHERE BELIEF IN REINCARNATION IS ABSENT (28) GES	1.00 OF 4	2 0 0 4 XSQ= 2.34 PHI= 0.625 EP = 0.0667

280 CULTURES
WHERE THE COMPOSITE FERTILITY LEVEL
IS HIGH (13) MN

280 CULTURES
WHERE THE COMPOSITE FERTILITY LEVEL
IS LOW (12) MN

BACKGROUND ON PAGE 133

BOTH SUBJECT AND PREDICATE

13 IN LEFT COLUMN

ALORESE, ASHANTI, HAVASUPAI, KOREANS, MASAI, NAVAHO, NGONI, OJIBWA, SINHALESE, TALLENSI, THONGA, TIKOPIA, YAO

12 IN RIGHT COLUMN

DUSUN, GANDA, KAPAUKU, LESU, MBUNDU, MENDE, MONGO, NUPE, PURARI, TODA, YAKO, YAPESE

375 EXCLUDED BECAUSE UNASCERTAINED

15	TILT LESS TOWARD BEING THOSE WHERE THE LATITUDE IS LESS THAN TWENTY DEGREES (217)	0.62 OF 13	15	IN ALL CASES ARE THOSE WHERE THE LATITUDE IS LESS THAN TWENTY DEGREES (217)	1.00 OF 12	5 0 8 12 XSQ= 3.62 PHI= 0.380 EP = 0.0391
16	TILT TOWARD BEING THOSE WHERE THE LATITUDE IS TEN DEGREES OR GREATER (277)	0.69 OF 13	16	TILT TOWARD BEING THOSE WHERE THE LATITUDE IS LESS THAN TEN DEGREES (123)	0.83 OF 12	9 2 4 10 XSQ= 5.03 PHI= 0.448 EP = 0.0154
42	TILT TOWARD BEING THOSE WHERE THE NATURAL ENVIRONMENT IS OTHER THAN TROPICAL OR SUB-TROPICAL RAIN FOREST, OR MONSOON FOREST (244) FWM	0.69 OF 13	42	TILT TOWARD BEING THOSE WHERE THE NATURAL ENVIRONMENT IS TROPICAL OR SUB-TROPICAL RAIN FOREST, OR MONSOON FOREST (156) FWM	0.75 OF 12	4 9 9 3 XSQ= 3.28 PHI= -0.362 EP = 0.0472
176	TILT TOWARD BEING THOSE WHERE THE COMMUNITY IS OTHER THAN A CLAN-COMMUNITY OR A COMMUNITY STRUCTURED OR SEGMENTED ON A CLAN BASIS (213)	0.69 OF 13	176	TILT TOWARD BEING THOSE WHERE THE COMMUNITY IS A CLAN-COMMUNITY OR A COMMUNITY STRUCTURED OR SEGMENTED ON A CLAN BASIS (169)	0.83 OF 12	4 10 9 2 XSQ= 5.03 PHI= -0.448 EP = 0.0154
178	TILT TOWARD BEING THOSE WHERE THE COMMUNITY IS OTHER THAN SEGMENTED ON A CLAN BASIS AND NON-EXOGAMOUS (295)	0.92 OF 13	178	TILT TOWARD BEING THOSE WHERE THE COMMUNITY IS SEGMENTED ON A CLAN BASIS AND NON-EXOGAMOUS (87)	0.50 OF 12	1 6 12 6 XSQ= 3.64 PHI= -0.382 EP = 0.0302

182	TILT LESS TOWARD BEING THOSE OTHER THAN WHERE THE COMMUNITY IS STRUCTURED ON A NON-CLAN BASIS AND AGAMOUS (256)	0.54 OF 13	182	IN ALL CASES ARE THOSE OTHER THAN WHERE THE COMMUNITY IS STRUCTURED ON A NON-CLAN BASIS AND AGAMOUS (256)	1.00 OF 12	6 0 7 12 XSQ= 4.98 PHI= 0.446 EP = 0.0149
263	TILT TOWARD BEING THOSE WHERE WIVES ARE OBTAINED BY RELATIVELY EASY MEANS, NAMELY BY TOKEN BRIDE-PRICE, GIFT EXCHANGE, ABSENCE OF ANY CONSIDERATION, OR RECEIPT OF DOWRY (162)	0.62 OF 13	263	TILT TOWARD BEING THOSE WHERE WIVES ARE OBTAINED BY RELATIVELY DIFFICULT MEANS, NAMELY BY BRIDE-PRICE, BRIDE-SERVICE, OR EXCHANGING A FEMALE RELATIVE (233)	0.83 OF 12	5 10 8 2 XSQ= 3.53 PHI= -0.376 EP = 0.0414
320	DRIFT TOWARD BEING THOSE WHERE THE DEGREE OF REDUCTION OF THE INFANT'S DRIVES IS HIGH (45) B-B-C	0.75 OF 8	320	IN ALL CASES ARE THOSE WHERE THE DEGREE OF REDUCTION OF THE INFANT'S DRIVES IS LOW (24) B-B-C	1.00 OF 3	6 0 2 3 XSQ= 2.39 PHI= 0.466 EP = 0.0606
331	IN ALL CASES ARE THOSE WHERE THE AGE AT BEGINNING OF INDEPENDENCE TRAINING IS LOWER THAN 3.8 YEARS (21) W-C	1.00 OF 4	331	IN ALL CASES ARE THOSE WHERE THE AGE AT BEGINNING OF INDEPENDENCE TRAINING IS 3.8 YEARS OR HIGHER (16) W-C	1.00 OF 2	0 2 4 0 XSQ= 2.34 PHI= -0.625 EP = 0.0667
370	TILT TOWARD BEING THOSE WHERE THE SEGREGATION OF ADOLESCENT BOYS IS ABSENT (148)	0.70 OF 10	370	TILT TOWARD BEING THOSE WHERE THE SEGREGATION OF ADOLESCENT BOYS IS COMPLETE OR PARTIAL (95)	0.90 OF 10	3 9 7 1 XSQ= 5.21 PHI= -0.510 EP = 0.0198
449	TILT TOWARD BEING THOSE WHERE THE OBSERVATION OF FOOD TABOOS IS HIGH, RATHER THAN MEDIUM OR LOW (25) JRL	0.83 OF 6	449	IN ALL CASES ARE THOSE WHERE THE OBSERVATION OF FOOD TABOOS IS MEDIUM OR LOW, RATHER THAN HIGH (61) JRL	1.00 OF 6	5 0 1 6 XSQ= 5.49 PHI= 0.676 EP = 0.0152
474	TILT TOWARD BEING THOSE WHERE BOASTFULNESS IS EXTREME (41) PES	0.78 OF 9	474	IN ALL CASES ARE THOSE WHERE BOASTFULNESS IS MODERATE, NEGLIBIBLE, OR UNREPORTED (48) PES	1.00 OF 3	7 0 2 3 XSQ= 2.86 PHI= 0.488 EP = 0.0455

281 CULTURES
WHERE THE INCIDENCE CF STERILITY
IS HIGH (10) MN

281 CULTURES
WHERE THE INCIDENCE CF STERILITY
IS LOW (5) MN

BACKGROUND ON PAGE 133

NEITHER SUBJECT NOR PRECICATE

10 IN LEFT CCLUMN

ASHANTI DUSUN GANCA KAPAUKU LESU MONGO NAVAHO NUPE TODA YAPESE

5 IN RIGHT CCLUMN

HAVASUPAI OJIBWA TALLENSI TIKOPIA YAKO

385 EXCLUCED BECAUSE UNASCERTAINEC

282 CULTURES
WHERE THE STRENGTH OF DESIRE FOR CHILDREN
IS HIGH (16) BCA

282 CULTURES
WHERE THE STRENGTH OF DESIRE FOR CHILDREN
IS LOW OR ABSENT (20) BCA

BACKGROUND ON PAGE 133

BOTH SUBJECT AND PREDICATE

16 IN LEFT COLUMN

AINU	ARAPESH	ASHANTI	AZANDE	BALINESE	CHAGGA	DUSUN	FON	IFUGAO	JIVARO
MAORI	MASAI	NAVAHO	OMAHA	THONGA	VENDA				

20 IN RIGHT COLUMN

ALORESE	CHIR-APACHE	COMANCHE	DOBUANS	HANO	KURTATCHI	KUTENAI	KWAKIUTL	LAKHER	LEPCHA
LESU	MARSHALLESE	PAPAGO	PUKAPUKA	TANALA	TIKOPIA	TIV	TROBRIAND	WOGEO	YAGUA

364 EXCLUDED BECAUSE UNASCERTAINED

3	TILT LESS TOWARD BEING THOSE LOCATED OUTSIDE OF AFRICA (320)	0.56 OF 16	3	TILT MORE TOWARD BEING THOSE LOCATED OUTSIDE OF AFRICA (320)	0.95 OF 20	7 1 / 9 19 / XSQ= 5.64 / PHI= 0.396 / EP = 0.0121
36	DRIFT TOWARD BEING THOSE WHERE THE NATURAL ENVIRONMENT IS 'VERY HARSH,' OR SUB-TROPICAL BUSH, OR TEMPERATE GRASSLAND (108) FWM	0.50 OF 16	36	DRIFT TOWARD BEING THOSE WHERE THE NATURAL ENVIRONMENT IS OTHER THAN 'VERY HARSH,' OR SUB-TROPICAL BUSH, OR TEMPERATE GRASSLAND (292) FWM	0.80 OF 20	8 4 / 8 16 / XSQ= 2.38 / PHI= 0.257 / EP = 0.0815
71	DRIFT TOWARD BEING THOSE WHERE METAL WORKING IS PRESENT (98)	0.55 OF 11	71	DRIFT TOWARD BEING THOSE WHERE METAL WORKING IS ABSENT (153)	0.81 OF 16	6 3 / 5 13 / XSQ= 2.32 / PHI= 0.293 / EP = 0.0969
73	DRIFT TOWARD BEING THOSE WHERE WEAVING IS PRESENT (118)	0.73 OF 11	73	DRIFT TOWARD BEING THOSE WHERE WEAVING IS ABSENT (130)	0.67 OF 18	8 6 / 3 12 / XSQ= 2.81 / PHI= 0.311 / EP = 0.0604
85	TILT LESS TOWARD BEING THOSE WHERE THE LEVEL OF POLITICAL INTEGRATION IS THE MINIMAL STATE, THE AUTONOMOUS COMMUNITY, OR THE FAMILY (234) GPM	0.62 OF 13	85	IN ALL CASES ARE THOSE WHERE THE LEVEL OF POLITICAL INTEGRATION IS THE MINIMAL STATE, THE AUTONOMOUS COMMUNITY, OR THE FAMILY (234) GPM	1.00 OF 15	5 0 / 8 15 / XSQ= 4.65 / PHI= 0.407 / EP = 0.0131

86	DRIFT TOWARD BEING THOSE 0.69 OF 13 WHERE THE LEVEL OF POLITICAL INTEGRATION IS THE LARGE STATE, THE LITTLE STATE, OR THE MINIMAL STATE (148) GPM	86	DRIFT TOWARD BEING THOSE 0.73 OF 15 WHERE THE LEVEL OF POLITICAL INTEGRATION IS THE AUTONOMOUS COMMUNITY, OR THE FAMILY (156) GPM	9 4 4 11 XSQ= 3.51 PHI= 0.354 EP = 0.0557
95	TILT LESS TOWARD BEING THOSE 0.57 OF 14 WHERE THE HIERARCHY OF NATIONAL JURISDICTION HAS ONE OR NO LEVELS (254) GES,EA	95	TILT MORE TOWARD BEING THOSE 0.94 OF 18 WHERE THE HIERARCHY OF NATIONAL JURISDICTION HAS ONE OR NO LEVELS (254) GES,EA	6 1 8 17 XSQ= 4.41 PHI= 0.371 EP = 0.0265
190	DRIFT MORE TOWARD BEING THOSE 0.90 OF 10 WHERE THE KIN GROUP IS PATRILINEAL OR DOUBLE-DESCENT, RATHER THAN MATRILINEAL (186)	190	DRIFT LESS TOWARD BEING THOSE 0.54 OF 13 WHERE THE KIN GROUP IS PATRILINEAL OR DOUBLE-DESCENT, RATHER THAN MATRILINEAL (186)	9 7 1 6 XSQ= 1.99 PHI= 0.294 EP = 0.0886
258	TILT TOWARD BEING THOSE 0.83 OF 6 WHERE THE SEVERITY OF SON'S WIFE AVOIDANCE IS HIGH (15) WNS	258	TILT TOWARD BEING THOSE 0.88 OF 8 WHERE THE SEVERITY OF SON'S WIFE AVOIDANCE IS LOW (16) WNS	5 1 1 7 XSQ= 4.43 PHI= 0.562 EP = 0.0256
295	DRIFT TOWARD BEING THOSE 0.70 OF 10 WHERE THE SEVERITY OF PUNISHMENT FOR ABORTION IS HIGH (11) BCA	295	DRIFT TOWARD BEING THOSE 0.75 OF 12 WHERE THE SEVERITY OF PUNISHMENT FOR ABORTION IS LOW OR ABSENT (12) BCA	7 3 3 9 XSQ= 2.82 PHI= 0.358 EP = 0.0836
318	TILT TOWARD BEING THOSE 0.73 OF 15 WHERE THE OVERALL INDULGENCE OF THE INFANT IS LOW (31) B-B-C	318	TILT TOWARD BEING THOSE 0.73 OF 15 WHERE THE OVERALL INDULGENCE OF THE INFANT IS HIGH (40) B-B-C	4 11 11 4 XSQ= 4.80 PHI= -0.400 EP = 0.0268
321	TILT TOWARD BEING THOSE 0.83 OF 12 WHERE THE IMMEDIACY OF REDUCTION OF THE INFANT'S DRIVES IS LOW (25) B-B-C	321	TILT TOWARD BEING THOSE 0.64 OF 14 WHERE THE IMMEDIACY OF REDUCTION OF THE INFANT'S DRIVES IS HIGH (35) B-B-C	2 9 10 5 XSQ= 4.21 PHI= -0.402 EP = 0.0214
324	LEAN TOWARD BEING THOSE 0.85 OF 13 WHERE THE PAIN INFLICTED ON THE INFANT BY THE NURTURANT AGENT IS HIGH (34) B-B-C	324	LEAN TOWARD BEING THOSE 0.73 OF 15 WHERE THE PAIN INFLICTED ON THE INFANT BY THE NURTURANT AGENT IS LOW OR NEGLIGIBLE (32) B-B-C	11 4 2 11 XSQ= 7.22 PHI= 0.508 EP = 0.0032
336	DRIFT TOWARD BEING THOSE 0.73 OF 15 WHERE THE TOTAL POSITIVE PRESSURE TOWARD DEVELOPING RESPONSIBLE BEHAVIOR IN THE CHILD IS HIGH (43) B-B-C	336	DRIFT TOWARD BEING THOSE 0.63 OF 16 WHERE THE TOTAL POSITIVE PRESSURE TOWARD DEVELOPING RESPONSIBLE BEHAVIOR IN THE CHILD IS LOW (32) B-B-C	11 6 4 10 XSQ= 2.70 PHI= 0.295 EP = 0.0732

339	DRIFT TOWARD BEING THOSE 0.67 OF 15 WHERE THE CHILD'S INFERRED CONFLICT REGARDING RESPONSIBLE BEHAVIOR IS HIGH (31) B-B-C	339	DRIFT TOWARD BEING THOSE 0.69 OF 16 WHERE THE CHILD'S INFERRED CONFLICT REGARDING RESPONSIBLE BEHAVIOR IS LOW (42) B-B-C	10 5 5 11 XSQ= 2.60 PHI= 0.290 EP = 0.0756
343	DRIFT TOWARD BEING THOSE 0.80 OF 10 WHERE THE CHILD'S INFERRED CONFLICT REGARDING NURTURANT BEHAVIOR IS HIGH (29) B-B-C	343	DRIFT TOWARD BEING THOSE 0.58 OF 12 WHERE THE CHILD'S INFERRED CONFLICT REGARDING NURTURANT BEHAVIOR IS LOW (18) B-B-C	8 5 2 7 XSQ= 1.92 PHI= 0.295 EP = 0.0991
345	DRIFT TOWARD BEING THOSE 0.67 OF 15 WHERE THE CHILD'S INFERRED ANXIETY OVER NON-PERFORMANCE OF SELF-RELIANT BEHAVIOR IS HIGH (37) B-B-C	345	DRIFT TOWARD BEING THOSE 0.69 OF 16 WHERE THE CHILD'S INFERRED ANXIETY OVER NON-PERFORMANCE OF SELF-RELIANT BEHAVIOR IS LOW (39) B-B-C	10 5 5 11 XSQ= 2.60 PHI= 0.290 EP = 0.0756
385	DRIFT LESS TOWARD BEING THOSE 0.62 OF 13 WHERE SEXUAL EXPRESSION BY THE YOUNG IS SEMI-RESTRICTED OR PERMITTED (64) F-B	385	DRIFT MORE TOWARD BEING THOSE 0.94 OF 16 WHERE SEXUAL EXPRESSION BY THE YOUNG IS SEMI-RESTRICTED OR PERMITTED (64) F-B	5 1 8 15 XSQ= 2.78 PHI= 0.310 EP = 0.0638
393	TILT TOWARD BEING THOSE 0.85 OF 13 WHERE EXTRAMARITAL COITUS IS PUNISHED, RATHER THAN PERMITTED (43) F-B	393	TILT TOWARD BEING THOSE 0.57 OF 14 WHERE EXTRAMARITAL COITUS IS PERMITTED, RATHER THAN PUNISHED (41) F-B	11 6 2 8 XSQ= 3.41 PHI= 0.355 EP = 0.0461
438	DRIFT TOWARD BEING THOSE 0.85 OF 13 WHERE OTHER-WORLDLY FEARS OF GHOSTS OR SPIRITS ARE GREATER THAN THIS-WORLDLY FEARS OF HUMANS OR ANIMALS (27) W-C,JFG	438	DRIFT TOWARD BEING THOSE 0.56 OF 16 WHERE THIS-WORLDLY FEARS OF HUMANS OR ANIMALS ARE GREATER THAN OTHER-WORLDLY FEARS OF GHOSTS OR SPIRITS (17) W-C,JFG	11 7 2 9 XSQ= 3.50 PHI= 0.347 EP = 0.0524
456	IN ALL CASES ARE THOSE 1.00 OF 9 WHERE THE INTERNALIZATION OF THE INDIVIDUAL'S CONTACT WITH THE DIVINE IS NOT CONDUCIVE TO THE DEVELOPMENT OF THE INDIVIDUAL'S NEED TO ACHIEVE (17) DCM	456	TILT TOWARD BEING THOSE 0.67 OF 6 WHERE THE INTERNALIZATION OF THE INDIVIDUAL'S CONTACT WITH THE DIVINE IS CONDUCIVE TO THE DEVELOPMENT OF THE INDIVIDUAL'S NEED TO ACHIEVE (19) DCM	0 4 9 2 XSQ= 5.13 PHI= -0.585 EP = 0.0110
458	TILT TOWARD BEING THOSE 0.64 OF 11 WHERE GAMES, IF PRESENT, INCLUDE GAMES OF STRATEGY (52) R-A-B,EA	458	TILT TOWARD BEING THOSE 0.81 OF 16 WHERE GAMES, IF PRESENT, DO NOT INCLUDE GAMES OF STRATEGY (119) R-A-B,EA	7 3 4 13 XSQ= 3.87 PHI= 0.379 EP = 0.0402
459	DRIFT TOWARD BEING THOSE 0.64 OF 11 WHERE GAMES, IF PRESENT, INCLUDE GAMES OF CHANCE (82) R-A-B,EA	459	DRIFT TOWARD BEING THOSE 0.75 OF 16 WHERE GAMES, IF PRESENT, DO NOT INCLUDE GAMES OF CHANCE (89) R-A-B,EA	7 4 4 12 XSQ= 2.59 PHI= 0.310 EP = 0.0608

282/

```
473  DRIFT TCWARD BEING THCSE        0.57 OF  14      473  DRIFT TOWARD BEING THCSE      0.78 CF  18            8    4
     WHERE SENSITIVITY TC INSULT                           WHERE SENSITIVITY TO INSULT                             6   14
     IS EXTREME  (32) PES                                  IS MODERATE OR NEGLIGIBLE  (56) PES          XSQ=     2.74
                                                                                                        PHI=    0.293
                                                                                                        EP =   0.0683
```

283 CULTURES
WHERE THE SEVERITY CF PENALTIES
FCR BARRENNESS
IS HIGH (14) BCA

283 CULTURES
WHERE THE SEVERITY CF PENALTIES
FOR BARRENNESS
IS LOW OR ABSENT (17) BCA

BACKGROUND ON PAGE 133 SUBJECT ONLY

14 IN LEFT CCLUMN

ALORESE	ASHANTI	AZANCE	BALINESE	CHAGGA	CHIR-APACHE FON	IFUGAC	JIVARO	MASAI
PAPAGC	SIRICNC	TANALA	THONGA					

17 IN RIGHT CCLUMN

AINU	DCBUANS	DUSUN	HANO	KURTATCHI	KUTENAI	KWAKIUTL	LAKHER	LEPCHA	LESU
MAORI	MARSHALLESE	PUKAPUKA	TIKOPIA	TROBRIAND	VENDA	YAGLA			

369 EXCLUDED BECAUSE UNASCERTAINEC

3	TILT LESS TOWARC BEING THCSE LCCATED CUTSIDE CF AFRICA (320)	0.57 OF 14	3	TILT MORE TOWARD BEING THOSE LOCATED OUTSIDE OF AFRICA (320)	0.94 CF 17	6 1 8 16 XSQ= 4.08 PHI= 0.363 EP = 0.0281
71	TILT TCWARD BEING THOSE WHERE METAL WCRKING IS PRESENT (98)	0.60 OF 10	71	TILT TOWARD BEING THOSE WHERE METAL WORKING IS ABSENT (153)	0.92 OF 13	6 1 4 12 XSQ= 5.04 PHI= 0.468 EP = 0.0186
85	TILT LESS TCWARC BEING THCSE WHERE THE LEVEL CF POLITICAL INTEGRATICN IS THE MINIMAL STATE, THE AUTCNCMOUS CCMMUNITY, CR THE FAMILY (234) GPM	0.62 OF 13	85	IN ALL CASES ARE THCSE WHERE THE LEVEL OF PCLITICAL INTEGRATION IS THE MINIMAL STATE, THE AUTONOMOUS COMMUNITY, CR THE FAMILY (234) GPM	1.00 CF 11	5 0 8 11 XSQ= 3.27 PHI= 0.369 EP = 0.0411
95	TILT LESS TCWARC BEING THCSE WHERE THE HIERARCHY CF NATICNAL JURISDICTICN HAS CNE CR NC LEVELS (254) GES,EA	0.54 OF 13	95	TILT MORE TOWARD BEING THCSE WHERE THE HIERARCHY OF NATIONAL JURISDICTICN HAS ONE OR NO LEVELS (254) GES,EA	0.93 CF 15	6 1 7 14 XSQ= 3.88 PHI= 0.372 EP = 0.0286
129	DRIFT TCWARD BEING THCSE WHERE WEAVING IS MAINLY DCNE BY MALES (31)	0.71 OF 7	129	IN ALL CASES ARE THOSE WHERE WEAVING IS MAINLY DONE BY FEMALES (73)	1.00 CF 4	5 0 2 4 XSQ= 2.75 PHI= 0.500 EP = 0.0606

136	TILT TOWARD BEING THOSE WHERE FULL-TIME ENTREPRENEURS ARE PRESENT (18) JV	0.83 OF 6	136	IN ALL CASES ARE THOSE WHERE FULL-TIME ENTREPRENEURS ARE ABSENT (14) JV	1.00 OF 5	5 0 1 5 XSQ= 4.65 PHI= 0.650 EP = 0.0152
242	DRIFT MORE TOWARD BEING THOSE WHERE MARRIAGE IS COMMONLY OR OCCASIONALLY POLYGYNOUS, RATHER THAN MONOGAMOUS (314)	0.93 OF 14	242	DRIFT LESS TOWARD BEING THOSE WHERE MARRIAGE IS COMMONLY OR OCCASIONALLY POLYGYNOUS, RATHER THAN MONOGAMOUS (314)	0.65 OF 17	13 11 1 6 XSQ= 2.06 PHI= 0.258 EP = 0.0940
282	TILT TOWARD BEING THOSE WHERE THE STRENGTH OF DESIRE FOR CHILDREN IS HIGH (16) BCA	0.69 OF 13	282	TILT TOWARD BEING THOSE WHERE THE STRENGTH OF DESIRE FOR CHILDREN IS LOW OR ABSENT (20) BCA	0.76 OF 17	9 4 4 13 XSQ= 4.54 PHI= 0.389 EP = 0.0247
295	LEAN TOWARD BEING THOSE WHERE THE SEVERITY OF PUNISHMENT FOR ABORTION IS HIGH (11) BCA	0.80 OF 10	295	LEAN TOWARD BEING THOSE WHERE THE SEVERITY OF PUNISHMENT FOR ABORTION IS LOW OR ABSENT (12) BCA	0.91 OF 11	8 1 2 10 XSQ= 8.05 PHI= 0.619 EP = 0.0019
318	TILT TOWARD BEING THOSE WHERE THE OVERALL INDULGENCE OF THE INFANT IS LOW (31) B-B-C	0.79 OF 14	318	TILT TOWARD BEING THOSE WHERE THE OVERALL INDULGENCE OF THE INFANT IS HIGH (40) B-B-C	0.67 OF 12	3 8 11 4 XSQ= 3.72 PHI= -0.378 EP = 0.0447
377	DRIFT LESS TOWARD BEING THOSE WHERE MALE GENITAL MUTILATION IS ABSENT (242)	0.54 OF 13	377	DRIFT MORE TOWARD BEING THOSE WHERE MALE GENITAL MUTILATION IS ABSENT (242)	0.87 OF 15	6 2 7 13 XSQ= 2.24 PHI= 0.283 EP = 0.0957
385	TEND TO BE THOSE WHERE SEXUAL EXPRESSION BY THE YOUNG IS RESTRICTED (22) F-B	0.58 OF 12	385	IN ALL CASES ARE THOSE WHERE SEXUAL EXPRESSION BY THE YOUNG IS SEMI-RESTRICTED OR PERMITTED (64) F-B	1.00 OF 16	7 0 5 16 XSQ= 9.53 PHI= 0.583 EP = 0.0007
386	LEAN TOWARD BEING THOSE WHERE SEXUAL EXPRESSION BY THE YOUNG IS RESTRICTED OR SEMI-RESTRICTED (46) F-B	0.83 OF 12	386	LEAN TOWARD BEING THOSE WHERE SEXUAL EXPRESSION BY THE YOUNG IS PERMITTED (40) F-B	0.69 OF 16	10 5 2 11 XSQ= 5.53 PHI= 0.444 EP = 0.0093
455	DRIFT TOWARD BEING THOSE WHERE THE MODE OF THE INDIVIDUAL'S CONTACT WITH THE DIVINE IS CONDUCIVE TO THE DEVELOPMENT OF THE INDIVIDUAL'S NEED TO ACHIEVE (17) DCM	0.57 OF 7	455	IN ALL CASES ARE THOSE WHERE THE MODE OF THE INDIVIDUAL'S CONTACT WITH THE DIVINE IS NOT CONDUCIVE TO THE DEVELOPMENT OF THE INDIVIDUAL'S NEED TO ACHIEVE (19) DCM	1.00 OF 5	4 0 3 5 XSQ= 2.10 PHI= 0.418 EP = 0.0808

```
458  TILT TOWARD BEING THOSE           0.70 OF  10      458  TILT TOWARD BEING THOSE           0.86 OF  14           7    2
     WHERE GAMES, IF PRESENT,                               WHERE GAMES, IF PRESENT,                                 3   12
     INCLUDE GAMES OF STRATEGY  (52) R-A-B,EA               DO NOT INCLUDE                                    XSQ=     5.53
                                                            GAMES OF STRATEGY  (119) R-A-B,EA                 PHI=    0.480
                                                                                                              EP =   0.0104

459  DRIFT TOWARD BEING THOSE          0.60 OF  10      459  DRIFT TOWARD BEING THOSE          0.79 OF  14           6    3
     WHERE GAMES, IF PRESENT,                               WHERE GAMES, IF PRESENT,                                 4   11
     INCLUDE GAMES OF CHANCE  (82) R-A-B,EA                 DO NOT INCLUDE                                    XSQ=     2.24
                                                            GAMES OF CHANCE  (89) R-A-B,EA                    PHI=    0.306
                                                                                                              EP =   0.0918

460  LEAN TOWARD BEING THOSE           0.90 OF  10      460  LEAN TOWARD BEING THOSE           0.71 OF  14           1   10
     WHERE GAMES, IF PRESENT,                               WHERE GAMES, IF PRESENT,                                 9    4
     ARE NOT LIMITED TO                                     ARE LIMITED TO                                    XSQ=     6.56
     GAMES OF SKILL ONLY  (104) R-A-B,EA                    GAMES OF SKILL ONLY  (67) R-A-B,EA                PHI=   -0.523
                                                                                                              EP =   0.0045
```

284 CULTURES WHERE CONTRACEPTION IS PRACTICED (10) CSF

284 CULTURES WHERE CONTRACEPTION IS NOT PRACTICED (7) CSF

BACKGROUND ON PAGE 134 — BOTH SUBJECT AND PREDICATE

10 IN LEFT COLUMN

APINAYE AZANDE CARIB KURTATCHI LESU MAORI MASAI SANPOIL THONGA TUBATULABAL

7 IN RIGHT COLUMN

AINU ARANDA IFUGAO KWAKIUTL LEPCHA TARAHUMARA TROBRIAND

383 EXCLUDED BECAUSE UNASCERTAINED

53	IN ALL CASES ARE THOSE WHERE FOOD PRODUCTION IS BY SIMPLE AGRICULTURE OR INCIPIENT FOOD PRODUCTION, RATHER THAN BY INTENSIVE AGRICULTURE (147)	1.00 OF 7	53	TILT TOWARD BEING THOSE WHERE FOOD PRODUCTION IS BY INTENSIVE AGRICULTURE, RATHER THAN BY SIMPLE AGRICULTURE OR INCIPIENT FOOD PRODUCTION (91)	0.75 OF 4		0 3 7 1 XSQ= 3.93 PHI= -0.598 EP = 0.0242
306	DRIFT TOWARD BEING THOSE WHERE THE EARLY DEPENDENCE SATISFACTION POTENTIAL IS HIGH (28) W-C	0.83 OF 6	306	DRIFT TOWARD BEING THOSE WHERE THE EARLY DEPENDENCE SATISFACTION POTENTIAL IS LOW (24) W-C	0.80 OF 5		5 1 1 4 XSQ= 2.23 PHI= 0.450 EP = 0.0801
347	DRIFT TOWARD BEING THOSE WHERE THE CHILD'S INFERRED CONFLICT REGARDING SELF-RELIANT BEHAVIOR IS HIGH (37) B-B-C	0.67 OF 6	347	IN ALL CASES ARE THOSE WHERE THE CHILD'S INFERRED CONFLICT REGARDING SELF-RELIANT BEHAVIOR IS LOW (39) B-B-C	1.00 OF 6		4 0 2 6 XSQ= 3.38 PHI= 0.530 EP = 0.0606
366	DRIFT TOWARD BEING THOSE WHERE DISSOCIATION OF THE SEXES AT ADOLESCENCE IS HIGH (16) JKH	0.63 OF 8	366	IN ALL CASES ARE THOSE WHERE DISSOCIATION OF THE SEXES AT ADOLESCENCE IS MEDIUM OR LOW (41) JKH	1.00 OF 4		5 0 3 4 XSQ= 2.10 PHI= 0.418 EP = 0.0808
369	IN ALL CASES ARE THOSE WHERE DISSOCIATION OF THE SEXES AT ADOLESCENCE, OR CUSTOMS OF INITIATION AT ADOLESCENCE, ARE PRESENT (42) JKH	1.00 OF 8	369	DRIFT TOWARD BEING THOSE WHERE BOTH DISSOCIATION OF THE SEXES AT ADOLESCENCE, AND CUSTOMS OF INITIATION AT ADOLESCENCE, ARE ABSENT (15) JKH	0.50 OF 4		8 2 0 2 XSQ= 1.88 PHI= 0.395 EP = 0.0909

```
453  IN ALL CASES ARE THCSE          1.00 OF   4       453  IN ALL CASES ARE THOSE          1.00 CF   3             4     0
     WHERE THE ROLE CF RELIGIOUS EXPERTS                    WHERE THE ROLE OF RELIGICUS EXPERTS                     0     3
     IS CCNDUCIVE TC THE CEVELCPMENT OF THE                 IS NOT CONDUCIVE TO THE DEVELOPMENT CF THE     XSQ=    3.51
     INDIVIDUAL'S NEED TC ACHIEVE  (13) CCM                 INDIVIDUAL'S NEED TC ACHIEVE  (23) DCM         PHI=   0.708
                                                                                                           EP =  0.0286
```

****

285	CULTURES WHERE THE SEX TABCC DURING PREGNANCY IS PRESENT (14) BCA	285	CULTURES WHERE THE SEX TABOO DURING PREGNANCY IS ABSENT OR INFERRED ABSENT (17) BCA

BACKGROUND ON PAGE 134

BCTH SUBJECT ANC PRECICATE

....

14 IN LEFT CCLUMN

AINU, ALCRESE, ARAPESH, ASHANTI, CHAGGA, CHIR-APACHE, COMANCHE, FCN, IFUGAO, LESU, MASAI, TANALA, TRCBRIAND, WOCEO

17 IN RIGHT CCLUMN

AZANDE, HANC, JIVARC, KURTATCHI, KWAKIUTL, LAKHER, LEPCHA, MACRI, MARSHALLESE, NAVAHO, PAPAGC, PUKAPUKA, SANPCIL, SIRIONO, THONGA, TIV, VENDA

369 EXCLUDED BECAUSE UNASCERTAINEC

16	DRIFT TCWARD BEING THCSE WHERE THE LATITUDE IS LESS THAN TEN DEGREES (123)	0.64 OF 14	16	DRIFT TOWARD BEING THOSE WHERE THE LATITUDE IS TEN DEGREES OR GREATER (277)	0.71 CF 17	5 12 9 5 XSQ= 2.49 PHI= -0.284 EP = 0.0759
42	TILT TCWARD BEING THOSE WHERE THE NATURAL ENVIRCNMENT IS TRCPICAL CR SUB-TRCPICAL RAIN FOREST, OR MCNSCCN FCREST (156) FWM	0.64 OF 14	42	TILT TOWARD BEING THOSE WHERE THE NATURAL ENVIRCNMENT IS OTHER THAN TROPICAL OR SUB-TROPICAL RAIN FOREST, OR MONSOON FOREST (244) FWM	0.76 CF 17	9 4 5 13 XSQ= 3.70 PHI= 0.345 EP = 0.0325
88	DRIFT TCWARD BEING THCSE WHERE, IF A HEACMANSHIP IS PRESENT, SUCCESSICN IS NCN-HEREDITARY (106)	0.50 OF 10	88	DRIFT TOWARD BEING THOSE WHERE, IF A HEADMANSHIP IS PRESENT, SUCCESSION IS HEREDITARY (165)	0.86 CF 14	5 2 5 12 XSQ= 2.08 PHI= 0.294 EP = 0.0850
137	DRIFT TCWARD BEING THCSE WHERE INVIDICUS DISPLAY CF WEALTH IS STRCNGLY EMPHASIZEC (37) PES	0.64 OF 14	137	DRIFT TOWARD BEING THOSE WHERE INVIDIOUS DISPLAY CF WEALTH IS MODERATELY, LITTLE, CR NEGATIVELY EMPHASIZED (52) PES	0.73 OF 15	9 4 5 11 XSQ= 2.76 PHI= 0.309 EP = 0.0656
183	DRIFT LESS TCWARC BEING THCSE WHERE THE LARGEST NCN-CCGNATIC KIN GROUP IS SMALLER THAN A MCEITY, I. E., A PHRATRY CR SIB OR LINEACE (218)	0.73 OF 11	183	IN ALL CASES ARE THCSE WHERE THE LARGEST NON-COGNATIC KIN GROUP IS SMALLER THAN A MOEITY, I. E., A PHRATRY OR SIB OR LINEAGE (218)	1.00 CF 12	3 0 8 12 XSQ= 1.74 PHI= 0.275 EP = 0.0932

236	TILT TOWARD BEING THOSE WHERE THE FAMILY IS OF AN INDEPENDENT TYPE, RATHER THAN AN EXTENDED TYPE (185)	0.64 OF 14	236	TILT TOWARD BEING THOSE WHERE THE FAMILY IS OF AN EXTENDED TYPE, RATHER THAN AN INDEPENDENT TYPE (213)	0.76 OF 17	5 13 9 4 XSQ= 3.70 PHI= -0.345 EP = 0.0325
331	DRIFT TOWARD BEING THOSE WHERE THE AGE AT BEGINNING OF INDEPENDENCE TRAINING IS 3.8 YEARS OR HIGHER (16) W-C	0.67 OF 12	331	DRIFT TOWARD BEING THOSE WHERE THE AGE AT BEGINNING OF INDEPENDENCE TRAINING IS LOWER THAN 3.8 YEARS (21) W-C	0.73 OF 11	8 3 4 8 XSQ= 2.17 PHI= 0.307 EP = 0.0995
351	TILT TOWARD BEING THOSE WHERE THE CHILD'S INFERRED CONFLICT REGARDING ACHIEVEMENT BEHAVIOR IS LOW (34) B-B-C	0.82 OF 11	351	TILT TOWARD BEING THOSE WHERE THE CHILD'S INFERRED CONFLICT REGARDING ACHIEVEMENT BEHAVIOR IS HIGH (26) B-B-C	0.67 OF 12	2 8 9 4 XSQ= 3.69 PHI= -0.401 EP = 0.0361
403	DRIFT TOWARD BEING THOSE WHERE EXPLANATIONS OF ILLNESS OF AN ANAL NATURE ARE PRESENT (23) W-C	0.71 OF 14	403	DRIFT TOWARD BEING THOSE WHERE EXPLANATIONS OF ILLNESS OF AN ANAL NATURE ARE ABSENT (38) W-C	0.65 OF 17	10 6 4 11 XSQ= 2.70 PHI= 0.295 EP = 0.0732
406	TILT TOWARD BEING THOSE WHERE EXPLANATIONS OF ILLNESS OF AN AGGRESSION NATURE ARE ABSENT (33) W-C	0.79 OF 14	406	TILT TOWARD BEING THOSE WHERE EXPLANATIONS OF ILLNESS OF AN AGGRESSION NATURE ARE PRESENT (28) W-C	0.71 OF 17	3 12 11 5 XSQ= 5.59 PHI= -0.425 EP = 0.0113
426	LEAN TOWARD BEING THOSE WHERE A HIGH GOD IS ABSENT (104) GES,EA	0.75 OF 12	426	LEAN TOWARD BEING THOSE WHERE A HIGH GOD IS PRESENT (156) GES,EA	0.80 OF 15	3 12 9 3 XSQ= 6.09 PHI= -0.475 EP = 0.0071
442	DRIFT TOWARD BEING THOSE WHERE FEAR OF ANIMAL SPIRITS IS LOW (33) W-C	0.57 OF 14	442	DRIFT TOWARD BEING THOSE WHERE FEAR OF ANIMAL SPIRITS IS HIGH (28) W-C	0.76 OF 17	6 13 8 4 XSQ= 2.38 PHI= -0.277 EP = 0.0751

286 CULTURES
WHERE THE NUMBER OF FOOD TABOOS
DURING PREGNANCY
IS HIGH (20) BCA

286 CULTURES
WHERE THE NUMBER OF FOOD TABOOS
DURING PREGNANCY
IS LOW OR ABSENT (14) BCA

BACKGROUND ON PAGE 134

BOTH SUBJECT AND PREDICATE

20 IN LEFT COLUMN

ANDAMANESE, ARAPESH, CHAGGA, CHIR-APACHE, DUSUN, IFUGAO, JIVARO, KURTATCHI, KUTENAI, KWAKIUTL, LEPCHA, LESU, PUKAPUKA, SANPOIL, SIRIONO, THONGA, TIV, TROBRIAND, VENDA, WOGEO

14 IN RIGHT COLUMN

AINU, ALORESE, ASHANTI, AZANDE, COMANCHE, FON, HANO, LAKHER, MAORI, MARSHALLESE, MASAI, NAVAHO, PAPAGO, TANALA

366 EXCLUDED BECAUSE UNASCERTAINED

45	TILT TOWARD BEING THOSE WHERE SETTLEMENTS, IF FIXED, ARE NON-COMPACT, RATHER THAN COMPACT (73)	0.57 OF 14	45	TILT TOWARD BEING THOSE WHERE SETTLEMENTS, IF FIXED, ARE COMPACT, RATHER THAN NON-COMPACT (149)	0.90 OF 10	6 9 / 8 1 / XSQ= 3.70 / PHI= -0.393 / EP = 0.0333
71	TILT TOWARD BEING THOSE WHERE METAL WORKING IS ABSENT (153)	0.87 OF 15	71	TILT TOWARD BEING THOSE WHERE METAL WORKING IS PRESENT (98)	0.58 OF 12	2 7 / 13 5 / XSQ= 4.22 / PHI= -0.395 / EP = 0.0369
73	DRIFT TOWARD BEING THOSE WHERE WEAVING IS ABSENT (130)	0.69 OF 16	73	DRIFT TOWARD BEING THOSE WHERE WEAVING IS PRESENT (118)	0.69 OF 13	5 9 / 11 4 / XSQ= 2.76 / PHI= -0.309 / EP = 0.0656
77	IN ALL CASES ARE THOSE WHERE THE WRITING SYSTEM IS MNEMONIC OR ABSENT, RATHER THAN BEING ALPHABETIC-OR-PHONETIC (39) JMH	1.00 OF 9	77	TILT TOWARD BEING THOSE WHERE THE WRITING SYSTEM IS ALPHABETIC-OR-PHONETIC, RATHER THAN BEING MNEMONIC OR ABSENT (15) JMH	0.67 OF 3	0 2 / 9 1 / XSQ= 3.20 / PHI= -0.516 / EP = 0.0455
96	DRIFT TOWARD BEING THOSE WHERE THE HIERARCHY OF NATIONAL JURISDICTION HAS NO LEVELS (156) GES,EA	0.58 OF 19	96	DRIFT TOWARD BEING THOSE WHERE THE HIERARCHY OF NATIONAL JURISDICTION HAS FOUR, THREE, TWO OR ONE LEVEL (174) GES,EA	0.77 OF 13	8 10 / 11 3 / XSQ= 2.52 / PHI= -0.281 / EP = 0.0751

110	DRIFT TOWARD BEING THOSE WHERE SLAVERY IS ABSENT (218)	0.70 OF 20	110	DRIFT TOWARD BEING THOSE WHERE SLAVERY IS PRESENT (163)	0.64 OF 14	6 9 14 5	XSQ= 2.66 PHI= -0.280 EP = 0.0800
116	TILT TOWARD BEING THOSE WHERE OCCUPATIONAL SPECIALIZATION IS PART-TIME ONLY (34) JMH	0.78 OF 9	116	IN ALL CASES ARE THOSE WHERE OCCUPATIONAL SPECIALIZATION IS FULL-TIME, WHETHER OR NOT FOR SURPLUS PRODUCTION (20) JMH	1.00 OF 3	2 3 7 0	XSQ= 2.86 PHI= -0.488 EP = 0.0455
136	TILT TOWARD BEING THOSE WHERE FULL-TIME ENTREPRENEURS ARE ABSENT (14) JV	0.86 OF 7	136	TILT TOWARD BEING THOSE WHERE FULL-TIME ENTREPRENEURS ARE PRESENT (18) JV	0.83 OF 6	1 5 6 1	XSQ= 3.73 PHI= -0.536 EP = 0.0291
196	DRIFT TOWARD BEING THOSE WHERE INDIVIDUAL RIGHTS IN REAL PROPERTY, OR RULES FOR INHERITANCE, ARE ABSENT (87)	0.50 OF 14	196	DRIFT TOWARD BEING THOSE WHERE INDIVIDUAL RIGHTS IN REAL PROPERTY, AND RULES FOR INHERITANCE, ARE PRESENT (194)	0.90 OF 10	7 9 7 1	XSQ= 2.59 PHI= -0.329 EP = 0.0791
299	DRIFT TOWARD BEING THOSE WHERE THE POST-PARTUM SEX TABOO LASTS LONGER THAN ONE YEAR (35)	0.50 OF 14	299	DRIFT TOWARD BEING THOSE WHERE THE POST-PARTUM SEX TABOO LASTS ONE YEAR OR LESS (89)	0.89 OF 9	7 1 7 8	XSQ= 2.14 PHI= 0.305 EP = 0.0858
316	DRIFT TOWARD BEING THOSE WHERE EXCLUSIVE MOTHER-SON SLEEPING ARRANGEMENTS LAST ONE YEAR OR LONGER (19) W-K-A	0.80 OF 10	316	DRIFT TOWARD BEING THOSE WHERE EXCLUSIVE MOTHER-SON SLEEPING ARRANGEMENTS LAST LESS THAN ONE YEAR (25) W-K-A	0.70 OF 10	8 3 2 7	XSQ= 3.23 PHI= 0.402 EP = 0.0698
317	TILT TOWARD BEING THOSE WHERE DISPLAY OF AFFECTION TOWARD THE INFANT IS HIGH (39) B-B-C	0.71 OF 14	317	TILT TOWARD BEING THOSE WHERE DISPLAY OF AFFECTION TOWARD THE INFANT IS LOW (29) B-B-C	0.75 OF 12	10 3 4 9	XSQ= 3.87 PHI= 0.386 EP = 0.0472
330	DRIFT TOWARD BEING THOSE WHERE THE AGE OF THE INFANT AT TIME OF WEANING IS 2.5 YEARS OR HIGHER (34) B-B-C	0.69 OF 16	330	DRIFT TOWARD BEING THOSE WHERE THE AGE OF THE INFANT AT TIME OF WEANING IS LOWER THAN 2.5 YEARS (36) B-B-C	0.75 OF 12	11 3 5 9	XSQ= 3.65 PHI= 0.361 EP = 0.0542
343	TILT TOWARD BEING THOSE WHERE THE CHILD'S INFERRED CONFLICT REGARDING NURTURANT BEHAVIOR IS LOW (18) B-B-C	0.62 OF 13	343	IN ALL CASES ARE THOSE WHERE THE CHILD'S INFERRED CONFLICT REGARDING NURTURANT BEHAVIOR IS HIGH (29) B-B-C	1.00 OF 6	5 6 8 0	XSQ= 4.10 PHI= -0.465 EP = 0.0181

441	TILT TCWARD BEING THOSE WHERE FEAR CF HUMAN BEINGS IS HIGH (29) W-C	0.65 OF 20	441	TILT TOWARD BEING THOSE WHERE FEAR OF HUMAN BEINGS IS LOW (32) W-C	0.79 OF 14	13 3 7 11 XSQ= 4.65 PHI= 0.370 EP = 0.0173
479	TILT TCWARD BEING THCSE WHERE THE NEED TC ACHIEVE, AS INFERRED FROM FCLKTALES, IS LCW (18) JV	0.88 OF 8	479	TILT TOWARD BEING THOSE WHERE THE NEED TO ACHIEVE, AS INFERRED FROM FCLKTALES, IS HIGH (18) JV	0.71 CF 7	1 5 7 2 XSQ= 3.23 PHI= -0.464 EP = 0.0406

287	CULTURES WHERE THE ISOLATION OF WOMEN IN CHILDBIRTH IS PRACTICED (16) CSF	287	CULTURES WHERE THE ISOLATION OF WOMEN IN CHILDBIRTH IS NOT PRACTICED (20) CSF	

BACKGROUND ON PAGE 134 — SUBJECT ONLY

16 IN LEFT COLUMN

APINAYE	ARANDA	ASHANTI	CREEK	CROW	GOND	JIVARO	KWAKIUTL	MAORI	MARICOPA
MBUNDU	OMAHA	PUKAPUKA	SAMOYED	TARAHUMARA	WITOTO				

20 IN RIGHT COLUMN

CARIB	CHUKCHEE	COPPER ESKIMO	DOBUANS	HANO	IFUGAO	KURTATCHI	LAKHER	LANGO	LEPCHA
LESU	MASAI	NAMA	RIFFIANS	SENIANG	TIKOPIA	TIV	TODA	TROBRIAND	VENDA

364 EXCLUDED BECAUSE UNASCERTAINED

51	DRIFT TOWARD BEING THOSE 0.63 OF 16 WHERE SUBSISTENCE IS PRIMARILY BY FOOD GATHERING -- I. E., HUNTING, FISHING, OR COLLECTING -- RATHER THAN FOOD PRODUCTION (147)	51	DRIFT TOWARD BEING THOSE 0.70 OF 20 WHERE SUBSISTENCE IS PRIMARILY BY FOOD PRODUCTION -- I. E., AGRICULTURE OR HUSBANDRY -- RATHER THAN BY GATHERING (253)	6 14 10 6 XSQ= 2.60 PHI= -0.269 EP = 0.0910
313	DRIFT TOWARD BEING THOSE 0.83 OF 6 WHERE AGGRESSION SOCIALIZATION ANXIETY IS HIGH (26) W-C	313	DRIFT TOWARD BEING THOSE 0.69 OF 13 WHERE AGGRESSION SOCIALIZATION ANXIETY IS LOW (28) W-C	5 4 1 9 XSQ= 2.69 PHI= 0.376 EP = 0.0573
336	TILT TOWARD BEING THOSE 0.89 OF 9 WHERE THE TOTAL POSITIVE PRESSURE TOWARD DEVELOPING RESPONSIBLE BEHAVIOR IN THE CHILD IS LOW (32) B-B-C	336	TILT TOWARD BEING THOSE 0.64 OF 11 WHERE THE TOTAL POSITIVE PRESSURE TOWARD DEVELOPING RESPONSIBLE BEHAVIOR IN THE CHILD IS HIGH (43) B-B-C	1 7 8 4 XSQ= 3.71 PHI= -0.431 EP = 0.0281
345	DRIFT TOWARD BEING THOSE 0.78 OF 9 WHERE THE CHILD'S INFERRED ANXIETY OVER NON-PERFORMANCE OF SELF-RELIANT BEHAVIOR IS HIGH (37) B-B-C	345	DRIFT TOWARD BEING THOSE 0.73 OF 11 WHERE THE CHILD'S INFERRED ANXIETY OVER NON-PERFORMANCE OF SELF-RELIANT BEHAVIOR IS LOW (39) B-B-C	7 3 2 8 XSQ= 3.23 PHI= 0.402 EP = 0.0698
391	TILT LESS TOWARD BEING THOSE 0.56 OF 9 WHERE PREMARITAL SEX RELATIONS ARE PUNISHED ONLY IF PREGNANCY RESULTS, OR FREELY PERMITTED (90) JTW,EA	391	TILT MORE TOWARD BEING THOSE 0.94 OF 16 WHERE PREMARITAL SEX RELATIONS ARE PUNISHED ONLY IF PREGNANCY RESULTS, OR FREELY PERMITTED (90) JTW,EA	4 1 5 15 XSQ= 3.14 PHI= 0.354 EP = 0.0403

287/

```
427  DRIFT TOWARD BEING THOSE        0.73 OF  11      427  DRIFT TOWARD BEING THOSE        0.75 OF   8               3    6
     WHERE A HIGH GOD, IF PRESENT, IS                          WHERE A HIGH GOD, IF PRESENT, IS                          8    2
     INACTIVE, RATHER THAN                                     ACTIVE, RATHER THAN                                XSQ=     2.53
     ACTIVE  (69) GES,EA                                       INACTIVE  (87) GES,EA                              PHI=   -0.365
                                                                                                                  EP =   0.0698
```

****

288	CULTURES WHERE THE DELIVERY OF A CHILD MAY BE ATTENDED BY THE HUSBAND (17) CSF	288	CULTURES WHERE THE DELIVERY OF A CHILD MAY NOT BE ATTENDED BY THE HUSBAND (11) CSF

BACKGROUND ON PAGE 134 SUBJECT ONLY

....

17 IN LEFT COLUMN

AINU ANDAMANESE CHUKCHEE COPR ESKIMO HANO IFUGAO KWAKIUTL LAKHER LEPCHA MAORI
MARICOPA MASAI TODA TUBATULABAL TUPINAMBA YAKUT YUKAGHIR

11 IN RIGHT COLUMN

APINAYE ARANDA ASHANTI CREEK CROW GOND JIVARO PUKAPUKA SAMOYED TARAHUMARA
WITOTO

372 EXCLUDED BECAUSE UNASCERTAINED

143	TILT TOWARD BEING THOSE WHERE THE RATIO OF RESTITUTIVE TO REPRESSIVE SANCTIONS IS HIGH (20) WME	0.80 OF 5	143	IN ALL CASES ARE THOSE WHERE THE RATIO OF RESTITUTIVE TO REPRESSIVE SANCTIONS IS MEDIUM OR LOW (32) WME	1.00 OF 4	4 0 1 4 XSQ= 2.98 PHI= 0.575 EP = 0.0476
184	TILT TOWARD BEING THOSE WHERE THE LARGEST NON-COGNATIC KIN GROUP IS SMALLER THAN A PHRATRY, I. E. A SIB OR LINEAGE (175)	0.88 OF 8	184	TILT TOWARD BEING THOSE WHERE THE LARGEST NON-COGNATIC KIN GROUP IS THE MOEITY OR PHRATRY (77)	0.67 OF 9	1 6 7 3 XSQ= 3.14 PHI= -0.430 EP = 0.0498
316	IN ALL CASES ARE THOSE WHERE EXCLUSIVE MOTHER-SON SLEEPING ARRANGEMENTS LAST LESS THAN ONE YEAR (25) W-K-A	1.00 OF 6	316	IN ALL CASES ARE THOSE WHERE EXCLUSIVE MOTHER-SON SLEEPING ARRANGEMENTS LAST ONE YEAR OR LONGER (19) W-K-A	1.00 OF 2	0 2 6 0 XSQ= 3.56 PHI= -0.667 EP = 0.0357
337	DRIFT TOWARD BEING THOSE WHERE THE CHILD'S INFERRED ANXIETY OVER NON-PERFORMANCE OF RESPONSIBLE BEHAVIOR IS HIGH (38) B-B-C	0.80 OF 10	337	DRIFT TOWARD BEING THOSE WHERE THE CHILD'S INFERRED ANXIETY OVER NON-PERFORMANCE OF RESPONSIBLE BEHAVIOR IS LOW (35) B-B-C	0.80 OF 5	8 1 2 4 XSQ= 2.81 PHI= 0.433 EP = 0.0889
339	DRIFT TOWARD BEING THOSE WHERE THE CHILD'S INFERRED CONFLICT REGARDING RESPONSIBLE BEHAVIOR IS HIGH (31) B-B-C	0.80 OF 10	339	DRIFT TOWARD BEING THOSE WHERE THE CHILD'S INFERRED CONFLICT REGARDING RESPONSIBLE BEHAVIOR IS LOW (42) B-B-C	0.80 OF 5	8 1 2 4 XSQ= 2.81 PHI= 0.433 EP = 0.0889

```
421  DRIFT TCWARD BEING THCSE        0.75 OF  12      421  DRIFT TOWARD BEING THOSE        0.75 OF   8              3     6
     WHERE KILLING, TCRTURINC, CR MUTILATINC               WHERE KILLING, TORTURING, CR MUTILATING                  9     2
     OF THE ENEMY                                          OF THE ENEMY                                     XSQ=     3.04
     IS NEGLIGIBLY EMPHASIZEC  (47) PES                    IS STRONGLY OR MODERATELY                        PHI=   -0.390
                                                           EMPHASIZED  (37) PES                             EP =   0.0648
```

```
289 CULTURES                                       289 CULTURES
    WHERE THE DELIVERY OF A CHILD                      WHERE THE DELIVERY OF A CHILD
    MAY BE ATTENDED BY                                 MAY NOT BE ATTENDED
    A MALE DOCTOR  (12) CSF                            BY A MALE DOCTOR  (9) CSF


BACKGROUND ON PAGE 134                                                                    SUBJECT ONLY
.............................................................................................

     12  IN LEFT COLUMN

COPR ESKIMO CREEK   CROW      HANO      MARICOPA   MASAI     OMAHA     PUKAPUKA   SANPOIL    THONGA
VENDA       YAKUT

     9  IN RIGHT COLUMN

APINAYE     ARANDA   ASHANTI   GOND      JIVARO     KWAKIUTL  MAORI     SAMOYED    WITOTO

    379  EXCLUDED BECAUSE UNASCERTAINED

---------------------------------------------------------------------------------------------
  8 DRIFT TOWARD BEING THOSE     0.58 OF  12     8 DRIFT TOWARD BEING THOSE       0.89 OF   9            7     1
    LOCATED IN NORTH AMERICA  (70)                 LOCATED OUTSIDE OF                                    5     8
                                                   NORTH AMERICA  (330)                           XSQ=      3.07
                                                                                                   PHI=     0.382
                                                                                                   EP =    0.0669

  9 IN ALL CASES ARE THOSE       1.00 OF  12     9 DRIFT LESS TOWARD BEING THOSE  0.67 OF   9            0     3
    LOCATED OUTSIDE OF                             LOCATED OUTSIDE OF                                   12     6
    SOUTH AMERICA  (335)                           SOUTH AMERICA  (335)                           XSQ=      2.34
                                                                                                   PHI=    -0.334
                                                                                                   EP =    0.0632

 48 TILT TOWARD BEING THOSE      0.75 OF   8    48 IN ALL CASES ARE THOSE         1.00 OF   5            2     5
    WHERE THE FOOD SUPPLY IS NOT SECURE,           WHERE THE FOOD SUPPLY IS SECURE,                      6     0
    AND FOOD SHORTAGES ARE                         AND FOOD SHORTAGES ARE                         XSQ=      4.27
    FREQUENT OR ANNUAL  (41) MGW                   RARE OR OCCASIONAL  (38) MGW                   PHI=    -0.573
                                                                                                   EP =    0.0210

 63 DRIFT TOWARD BEING THOSE     0.88 OF   8    63 DRIFT TOWARD BEING THOSE       0.75 OF   4            7     1
    WHERE HUSBANDRY, IF PRESENT,                   WHERE HUSBANDRY, IF PRESENT,                          1     3
    IS PRINCIPALLY IN THE FORM OF                  IS PRINCIPALLY IN THE FORM OF                  XSQ=      2.30
    BOVINE, EQUINE, CAMEL-LIKE, OR DEER-LIKE       PIGS, SHEEP, OR GOATS, RATHER THAN             PHI=     0.437
    ANIMALS, RATHER THAN                           BOVINE, EQUINE, CAMEL-LIKE, OR DEER-LIKE       EP =    0.0667
    PIGS, SHEEP, OR GOATS  (152)                   ANIMALS  (74)

148 IN ALL CASES ARE THOSE       1.00 OF   4   148 IN ALL CASES ARE THOSE         1.00 OF   4            0     4
    WHERE THE INCIDENCE OF PERSONAL CRIME          WHERE THE INCIDENCE OF PERSONAL CRIME                 4     0
    IS LOW  (21) B-B-C                             IS HIGH  (12) B-B-C                            XSQ=      4.50
                                                                                                   PHI=    -0.750
                                                                                                   EP =    0.0286
```

```
213  TILT TOWARD BEING THOSE         0.83 OF  12     213  TILT TOWARD BEING THOSE         0.67 OF   9            2    6
     WHERE FIRST COUSIN MARRIAGE IS                      WHERE FIRST COUSIN MARRIAGE IS                        10    3
     NOT PERMITTED  (198)                                PERMITTED  (172)                               XSQ=     3.54
                                                                                                        PHI=   -0.410
                                                                                                        EP =   0.0318

321  DRIFT TOWARD BEING THOSE        0.86 OF   7     321  DRIFT TOWARD BEING THOSE        0.75 OF   4            1    3
     WHERE THE IMMEDIACY OF REDUCTION                    WHERE THE IMMEDIACY OF REDUCTION                       6    1
     OF THE INFANT'S DRIVES                              OF THE INFANT'S DRIVES                         XSQ=     1.86
     IS LOW  (25) B-B-C                                  IS HIGH  (35) B-B-C                            PHI=   -0.411
                                                                                                        EP =   0.0879

346  TILT TOWARD BEING THOSE         0.75 OF   8     346  IN ALL CASES ARE THOSE          1.00 OF   5            6    0
     WHERE THE CHILD'S INFERRED ANXIETY OVER             WHERE THE CHILD'S INFERRED ANXIETY OVER                2    5
     PERFORMANCE OF SELF-RELIANT BEHAVIOR                PERFORMANCE OF SELF-RELIANT BEHAVIOR           XSQ=     4.27
     IS HIGH  (37) B-B-C                                 IS LOW  (39) B-B-C                             PHI=    0.573
                                                                                                        EP =   0.0210

347  TILT TOWARD BEING THOSE         0.75 OF   8     347  IN ALL CASES ARE THOSE          1.00 OF   5            6    0
     WHERE THE CHILD'S INFERRED CONFLICT                 WHERE THE CHILD'S INFERRED CONFLICT                    2    5
     REGARDING SELF-RELIANT BEHAVIOR                     REGARDING SELF-RELIANT BEHAVIOR                XSQ=     4.27
     IS HIGH  (37) B-B-C                                 IS LOW  (39) B-B-C                             PHI=    0.573
                                                                                                        EP =   0.0210

459  TILT TOWARD BEING THOSE         0.82 OF  11     459  TILT TOWARD BEING THOSE         0.83 OF   6            9    1
     WHERE GAMES, IF PRESENT,                            WHERE GAMES, IF PRESENT,                               2    5
     INCLUDE GAMES OF CHANCE  (82) R-A-B,EA              DO NOT INCLUDE                                 XSQ=     4.38
                                                         GAMES OF CHANCE  (89) R-A-B,EA                 PHI=    0.508
                                                                                                        EP =   0.0345

460  TILT TOWARD BEING THOSE         0.91 OF  11     460  TILT TOWARD BEING THOSE         0.67 OF   6            1    4
     WHERE GAMES, IF PRESENT,                            WHERE GAMES, IF PRESENT,                              10    2
     ARE NOT LIMITED TO                                  ARE LIMITED TO                                 XSQ=     3.74
     GAMES OF SKILL ONLY  (104) R-A-B,EA                 GAMES OF SKILL ONLY  (67) R-A-B,EA             PHI=   -0.469
                                                                                                        EP =   0.0276
```

290 CULTURES
WHERE WCMEN AFTER CELIVERY
ARE ISCLATED
IN A SPECIAL SHELTER (12) CSF

290 CULTURES
WHERE WOMEN AFTER DELIVERY
ARE NOT ISOLATED
IN A SPECIAL SHELTER (21) CSF

BACKGROUND ON PAGE 134

SUBJECT ONLY

12 IN LEFT CCLUMN

ASHANTI AZANDE CREEK GONC HANO LANGO MAORI MARICOPA RIFFIANS THONGA
TODA VENDA

21 IN RIGHT CCLUMN

APINAYE CHUKCHEE CCPR ESKIMO CROW DOBUANS IFUGAO JIVARO KURTATCHI KWAKIUTL LAKHER
LEPCHA LESU NAMA SANPOIL TANALA TARAHUMARA TIV TRCBRIAND TUBATULABAL YAKUT
YURCK

367 EXCLUDED BECAUSE UNASCERTAINEC

3	DRIFT LESS TCWARC BEING THCSE LCCATED CUTSIDE CF AFRICA (320)	0.58 OF	12	3	DRIFT MORE TOWARD BEING THCSE LOCATED OUTSIDE OF AFRICA (320)	0.90 CF	21		5 2 7 19 XSQ= 2.99 PHI= 0.301 EP = 0.0709
13	IN ALL CASES ARE THCSE WHERE THE LATITUCE IS LESS THAN FORTY CEGREES (329)	1.00 OF	12	13	TILT LESS TOWARD BEING THOSE WHERE THE LATITUDE IS LESS THAN FORTY DEGREES (329)	0.67 CF	21		0 7 12 14 XSQ= 3.28 PHI= -0.315 EP = 0.0319
45	TILT TCWARC BEING THCSE WHERE SETTLEMENTS, IF FIXEC, ARE CCMPACT, RATHER THAN NCN-CCMPACT (149)	0.91 OF	11	45	TILT TOWARD BEING THOSE WHERE SETTLEMENTS, IF FIXED, ARE NON-COMPACT, RATHER THAN COMPACT (73)	0.54 CF	13		10 6 1 7 XSQ= 3.55 PHI= 0.384 EP = 0.0335
46	IN ALL CASES ARE THCSE OTHER THAN WHERE SETTLEMENTS ARE NCN-FIXED AND MCVEMENT IS NCMADIC (260)	1.00 OF	12	46	TILT LESS TOWARD BEING THOSE OTHER THAN WHERE SETTLEMENTS ARE NON-FIXED AND MOVEMENT IS NOMADIC (260)	0.65 CF	20		0 7 12 13 XSQ= 3.52 PHI= -0.332 EP = 0.0288
81	DRIFT LESS TCWARC BEINC THCSE WHERE NC CITY CR TCWN IS PRESENT, ANC THE AVERAGE CCMMUNITY SIZE IS SMALLER THAN 200 (135)	0.55 OF	11	81	DRIFT MORE TOWARD BEING THCSE WHERE NO CITY OR TOWN IS PRESENT, ANC THE AVERAGE COMMUNITY SIZE IS SMALLER THAN 2CO (135)	0.87 OF	15		5 2 6 13 XSQ= 1.90 PHI= 0.270 EP = 0.0946

```
 85  TILT LESS TOWARD BEING THOSE     0.60 OF  10      85  TILT MORE TOWARD BEING THOSE    0.94 OF  17          4     1
     WHERE THE LEVEL OF POLITICAL INTEGRATION              WHERE THE LEVEL OF POLITICAL INTEGRATION             6    16
     IS THE MINIMAL STATE,                                 IS THE MINIMAL STATE,                         XSQ=     2.86
     THE AUTONOMOUS COMMUNITY, OR                          THE AUTONOMOUS COMMUNITY, OR                  PHI=    0.325
     THE FAMILY (234) GPM                                  THE FAMILY (234) GPM                          EP =   0.0473

 91  LEAN TOWARD BEING THOSE          0.75 OF   8      91  LEAN TOWARD BEING THOSE         0.92 OF  12          6     1
     WHERE SOCIETAL COMPLEXITY                             WHERE SOCIETAL COMPLEXITY                            2    11
     IS HIGH  (18) F-W                                     IS LOW  (22) F-W                              XSQ=     6.68
                                                                                                         PHI=    0.578
                                                                                                         EP =   0.0044

 96  DRIFT TOWARD BEING THOSE         0.83 OF  12      96  DRIFT TOWARD BEING THOSE        0.55 OF  20         10     9
     WHERE THE HIERARCHY                                   WHERE THE HIERARCHY                                  2    11
     OF NATIONAL JURISDICTION HAS                          OF NATIONAL JURISDICTION HAS                  XSQ=     3.12
     FOUR, THREE, TWO OR                                   NO LEVELS  (156) GES,EA                       PHI=    0.312
     ONE LEVEL  (174) GES,EA                                                                             EP =   0.0619

 98  IN ALL CASES ARE THOSE           1.00 OF  12      98  TILT LESS TOWARD BEING THOSE    0.65 OF  20         12    13
     WHERE THE HIERARCHY                                   WHERE THE HIERARCHY                                  0     7
     OF LOCAL JURISDICTION HAS                             OF LOCAL JURISDICTION HAS                     XSQ=     3.52
     FOUR OR THREE LEVELS  (238) GES,EA                    FOUR OR THREE LEVELS  (238) GES,EA            PHI=    0.332
                                                                                                         EP =   0.0288

137  DRIFT TOWARD BEING THOSE         0.82 OF  11     137  DRIFT TOWARD BEING THOSE        0.59 OF  17          2    10
     WHERE INVIDIOUS DISPLAY OF WEALTH                     WHERE INVIDIOUS DISPLAY OF WEALTH                    9     7
     IS MODERATELY, LITTLE, OR                             IS STRONGLY EMPHASIZED  (37) PES              XSQ=     3.00
     NEGATIVELY EMPHASIZED  (52) PES                                                                     PHI=   -0.327
                                                                                                         EP =   0.0540

147  IN ALL CASES ARE THOSE           1.00 OF   5     147  TILT TOWARD BEING THOSE         0.75 OF   4          5     1
     WHERE CODIFIED LAWS ARE                               WHERE CODIFIED LAWS ARE                              0     3
     PRESENT  (20) LWS                                     UNIMPORTANT OR ABSENT  (13) LWS               XSQ=     2.76
                                                                                                         PHI=    0.553
                                                                                                         EP =   0.0476

188  DRIFT MORE TOWARD BEING THOSE    0.92 OF  12     188  DRIFT LESS TOWARD BEING THOSE   0.57 OF  21          1     9
     WHERE THE KIN GROUP IS                                WHERE THE KIN GROUP IS                              11    12
     OTHER THAN                                            OTHER THAN                                    XSQ=     2.83
     EXCLUSIVELY COGNATIC  (252)                           EXCLUSIVELY COGNATIC  (252)                   PHI=   -0.293
                                                                                                         EP =   0.0545

192  IN ALL CASES ARE THOSE           1.00 OF  12     192  TILT LESS TOWARD BEING THOSE    0.67 OF  21          0     7
     OTHER THAN WHERE THE ONLY KIN GROUP                   OTHER THAN WHERE THE ONLY KIN GROUP                 12    14
     PRESENT IS A KINDRED OR ELSE                          PRESENT IS A KINDRED OR ELSE                  XSQ=     3.28
     BILATERAL DESCENT IS INFERRED  (289)                  BILATERAL DESCENT IS INFERRED  (289)          PHI=   -0.315
                                                                                                         EP =   0.0319

234  TILT TOWARD BEING THOSE          0.89 OF   9     234  TILT TOWARD BEING THOSE         0.53 OF  19          8     9
     WHERE THE COUSIN TERMINOLOGY IS                       WHERE THE COUSIN TERMINOLOGY IS                      1    10
     OF CROW, OMAHA, OR IROQUOIS TYPE,                     OF ESKIMO OR HAWAIIAN TYPE,                   XSQ=     2.84
     RATHER THAN                                           RATHER THAN                                   PHI=    0.319
     ESKIMO OR HAWAIIAN TYPE  (152)                        CROW, OMAHA, OR IROQUOIS TYPE  (170)          EP =   0.0491
```

282	TILT TOWARD BEING THOSE WHERE THE STRENGTH OF DESIRE FOR CHILDREN IS HIGH (16) BCA	0.83 OF 6	282	TILT TOWARD BEING THOSE WHERE THE STRENGTH OF DESIRE FOR CHILDREN IS LOW OR ABSENT (20) BCA	0.82 OF 11	5 2 1 9 XSQ= 4.38 PHI= 0.508 EP = 0.0345
305	IN ALL CASES ARE THOSE WHERE THE EARLY SEXUAL SATISFACTION POTENTIAL IS LOW (24) W-C	1.00 OF 6	305	LEAN TOWARD BEING THOSE WHERE THE EARLY SEXUAL SATISFACTION POTENTIAL IS HIGH (27) W-C	0.75 OF 12	0 9 6 3 XSQ= 6.25 PHI= -0.589 EP = 0.0090
393	TILT TOWARD BEING THOSE WHERE EXTRAMARITAL COITUS IS PUNISHED, RATHER THAN PERMITTED (43) F-B	0.90 OF 10	393	TILT TOWARD BEING THOSE WHERE EXTRAMARITAL COITUS IS PERMITTED, RATHER THAN PUNISHED (41) F-B	0.60 OF 15	9 6 1 9 XSQ= 4.34 PHI= 0.417 EP = 0.0177
400	IN ALL CASES ARE THOSE WHERE HOMOSEXUAL ACTIVITY IS PERMITTED (36) F-B	1.00 OF 6	400	DRIFT TOWARD BEING THOSE WHERE HOMOSEXUAL ACTIVITY IS PROHIBITED (22) F-B	0.50 OF 14	0 7 6 7 XSQ= 2.68 PHI= -0.366 EP = 0.0515
433	IN ALL CASES ARE THOSE WHERE BELIEF IN REINCARNATION IS PRESENT (10) GES	1.00 OF 2	433	DRIFT TOWARD BEING THOSE WHERE BELIEF IN REINCARNATION IS ABSENT (28) GES	0.88 OF 8	2 1 0 7 XSQ= 2.41 PHI= 0.491 EP = 0.0667

291 CULTURES
WHERE WOMEN AFTER DELIVERY
ARE CONFINED TO THE DWELLING (20) CSF

291 CULTURES
WHERE WOMEN AFTER DELIVERY
ARE NOT CONFINED
TO THE DWELLING (12) CSF

BACKGROUND ON PAGE 134

SUBJECT ONLY

20 IN LEFT COLUMN

APINAYE	CHUKCHEE	COPR ESKIMO	DOBUANS	IFUGAO	JIVARO	KURTATCHI	KWAKIUTL	LAKHER	LEPCHA
LESU	NAMA	SANPOIL	TANALA	TARAHUMARA	TIV	TROBRIAND	TUBATULABAL	YAKUT	YUROK

12 IN RIGHT COLUMN

AZANDE	CREEK	CROW	GOND	HANO	LANGO	MAORI	MARICOPA	RIFFIANS	THONGA
TODA	VENDA								

368 EXCLUDED BECAUSE UNASCERTAINED

36	DRIFT TOWARD BEING THOSE 0.70 OF 20 WHERE THE NATURAL ENVIRONMENT IS OTHER THAN 'VERY HARSH,' OR SUB-TROPICAL BUSH, OR TEMPERATE GRASSLAND (292) FWM	36	DRIFT TOWARD BEING THOSE 0.67 OF 12 WHERE THE NATURAL ENVIRONMENT IS 'VERY HARSH,' OR SUB-TROPICAL BUSH, OR TEMPERATE GRASSLAND (108) FWM	6 8 14 4 XSQ= 2.74 PHI= -0.293 EP = 0.0683
42	TILT LESS TOWARD BEING THOSE 0.60 OF 20 WHERE THE NATURAL ENVIRONMENT IS OTHER THAN TROPICAL OR SUB-TROPICAL RAIN FOREST, OR MONSOON FOREST (244) FWM	42	IN ALL CASES ARE THOSE 1.00 OF 12 WHERE THE NATURAL ENVIRONMENT IS OTHER THAN TROPICAL OR SUB-TROPICAL RAIN FOREST, OR MONSOON FOREST (244) FWM	8 0 12 12 XSQ= 4.44 PHI= 0.373 EP = 0.0135
45	DRIFT TOWARD BEING THOSE 0.54 OF 13 WHERE SETTLEMENTS, IF FIXED, ARE NON-COMPACT, RATHER THAN COMPACT (73)	45	DRIFT TOWARD BEING THOSE 0.90 OF 10 WHERE SETTLEMENTS, IF FIXED, ARE COMPACT, RATHER THAN NON-COMPACT (149)	6 9 7 1 XSQ= 3.05 PHI= -0.364 EP = 0.0743
86	DRIFT TOWARD BEING THOSE 0.63 OF 16 WHERE THE LEVEL OF POLITICAL INTEGRATION IS THE AUTONOMOUS COMMUNITY, OR THE FAMILY (156) GPM	86	DRIFT TOWARD BEING THOSE 0.80 OF 10 WHERE THE LEVEL OF POLITICAL INTEGRATION IS THE LARGE STATE, THE LITTLE STATE, OR THE MINIMAL STATE (148) GPM	6 8 10 2 XSQ= 2.93 PHI= -0.335 EP = 0.0511
91	TILT TOWARD BEING THOSE 0.91 OF 11 WHERE SOCIETAL COMPLEXITY IS LOW (22) F-W	91	TILT TOWARD BEING THOSE 0.63 OF 8 WHERE SOCIETAL COMPLEXITY IS HIGH (18) F-W	1 5 10 3 XSQ= 3.89 PHI= -0.453 EP = 0.0408

96	TILT TOWARD BEING THOSE WHERE THE HIERARCHY OF NATIONAL JURISDICTION HAS NO LEVELS (156) GES,EA	0.58 OF 19	96	TILT TOWARD BEING THOSE WHERE THE HIERARCHY OF NATIONAL JURISDICTION HAS FOUR, THREE, TWO OR ONE LEVEL (174) GES,EA	0.83 OF 12	8 10 11 2 XSQ= 3.58 PHI= -0.340 EP = 0.0317
188	TILT LESS TOWARD BEING THOSE WHERE THE KIN GROUP IS OTHER THAN EXCLUSIVELY COGNATIC (252)	0.55 OF 20	188	TILT MORE TOWARD BEING THOSE WHERE THE KIN GROUP IS OTHER THAN EXCLUSIVELY COGNATIC (252)	0.92 OF 12	9 1 11 11 XSQ= 3.14 PHI= 0.313 EP = 0.0496
192	TILT LESS TOWARD BEING THOSE OTHER THAN WHERE THE ONLY KIN GROUP PRESENT IS A KINDRED OR ELSE BILATERAL DESCENT IS INFERRED (289)	0.65 OF 20	192	IN ALL CASES ARE THOSE OTHER THAN WHERE THE ONLY KIN GROUP PRESENT IS A KINDRED OR ELSE BILATERAL DESCENT IS INFERRED (289)	1.00 OF 12	7 0 13 12 XSQ= 3.52 PHI= 0.332 EP = 0.0288
234	TILT TOWARD BEING THOSE WHERE THE COUSIN TERMINOLOGY IS OF ESKIMO OR HAWAIIAN TYPE, RATHER THAN CROW, OMAHA, OR IROQUOIS TYPE (170)	0.56 OF 18	234	TILT TOWARD BEING THOSE WHERE THE COUSIN TERMINOLOGY IS OF CROW, OMAHA, OR IROQUOIS TYPE, RATHER THAN ESKIMO OR HAWAIIAN TYPE (152)	0.90 OF 10	8 9 10 1 XSQ= 3.85 PHI= -0.371 EP = 0.0407
282	TILT TOWARD BEING THOSE WHERE THE STRENGTH OF DESIRE FOR CHILDREN IS LOW OR ABSENT (20) BCA	0.82 OF 11	282	TILT TOWARD BEING THOSE WHERE THE STRENGTH OF DESIRE FOR CHILDREN IS HIGH (16) BCA	0.80 OF 5	2 4 9 1 XSQ= 3.28 PHI= -0.453 EP = 0.0357
305	LEAN TOWARD BEING THOSE WHERE THE EARLY SEXUAL SATISFACTION POTENTIAL IS HIGH (27) W-C	0.75 OF 12	305	IN ALL CASES ARE THOSE WHERE THE EARLY SEXUAL SATISFACTION POTENTIAL IS LOW (24) W-C	1.00 OF 5	9 0 3 5 XSQ= 5.24 PHI= 0.555 EP = 0.0090
393	TILT TOWARD BEING THOSE WHERE EXTRAMARITAL COITUS IS PERMITTED, RATHER THAN PUNISHED (41) F-B	0.64 OF 14	393	TILT TOWARD BEING THOSE WHERE EXTRAMARITAL COITUS IS PUNISHED, RATHER THAN PERMITTED (43) F-B	0.90 OF 10	5 9 9 1 XSQ= 5.02 PHI= -0.457 EP = 0.0129
400	TILT TOWARD BEING THOSE WHERE HOMOSEXUAL ACTIVITY IS PROHIBITED (22) F-B	0.54 OF 13	400	IN ALL CASES ARE THOSE WHERE HOMOSEXUAL ACTIVITY IS PERMITTED (36) F-B	1.00 OF 7	7 0 6 7 XSQ= 3.67 PHI= 0.429 EP = 0.0233
433	DRIFT TOWARD BEING THOSE WHERE BELIEF IN REINCARNATION IS ABSENT (28) GES	0.88 OF 8	433	IN ALL CASES ARE THOSE WHERE BELIEF IN REINCARNATION IS PRESENT (10) GES	1.00 OF 2	1 2 7 0 XSQ= 2.41 PHI= -0.491 EP = 0.0667

292 CULTURES
WHERE PRACTICES TO BEAUTIFY
THE NEWBORN CHILD
ARE PRESENT (16) BCA

292 CULTURES
WHERE PRACTICES TO BEAUTIFY
THE NEWBORN CHILD
ARE ABSENT OR INFERRED ABSENT (16) BCA

BACKGROUND ON PAGE 135

SUBJECT ONLY

16 IN LEFT COLUMN

AINU	CHAGGA	CHIR-APACHE	HANO	JIVARO	KURTATCHI	KUTENAI	KWAKIUTL	LAKHER	NAVAHO
SANPOIL	SIRIONO	THONGA	TIV	TROBRIAND	VENDA				

16 IN RIGHT COLUMN

ALORESE	ARAPESH	ASHANTI	AZANDE	COMANCHE	FON	IFUGAO	LEPCHA	LESU	MAORI
MARSHALLESE	MASAI	PUKAPUKA	TANALA	WOGEO	YAGUA				

368 EXCLUDED BECAUSE UNASCERTAINED

6	DRIFT TOWARD BEING THOSE LOCATED OUTSIDE OF THE INSULAR PACIFIC (330)	0.88 OF 16		6	DRIFT TOWARD BEING THOSE LOCATED IN THE INSULAR PACIFIC (70)	0.50 OF 16		2 8 / 14 8 / XSQ= 3.64 / PHI= -0.337 / EP = 0.0538
8	DRIFT LESS TOWARD BEING THOSE LOCATED OUTSIDE OF NORTH AMERICA (330)	0.63 OF 16		8	DRIFT MORE TOWARD BEING THOSE LOCATED OUTSIDE OF NORTH AMERICA (330)	0.94 OF 16		6 1 / 10 15 / XSQ= 2.93 / PHI= 0.302 / EP = 0.0829
15	DRIFT TOWARD BEING THOSE WHERE THE LATITUDE IS TWENTY DEGREES OR GREATER (183)	0.63 OF 16		15	DRIFT TOWARD BEING THOSE WHERE THE LATITUDE IS LESS THAN TWENTY DEGREES (217)	0.75 OF 16		10 4 / 6 12 / XSQ= 3.17 / PHI= 0.315 / EP = 0.0732
16	DRIFT TOWARD BEING THOSE WHERE THE LATITUDE IS TEN DEGREES OR GREATER (277)	0.69 OF 16		16	DRIFT TOWARD BEING THOSE WHERE THE LATITUDE IS LESS THAN TEN DEGREES (123)	0.63 OF 16		11 6 / 5 10 / XSQ= 2.01 / PHI= 0.250 / EP = 0.0938
42	TILT TOWARD BEING THOSE WHERE THE NATURAL ENVIRONMENT IS OTHER THAN TROPICAL OR SUB-TROPICAL RAIN FOREST, OR MONSOON FOREST (244) FWM	0.81 OF 16		42	TILT TOWARD BEING THOSE WHERE THE NATURAL ENVIRONMENT IS TROPICAL OR SUB-TROPICAL RAIN FOREST, OR MONSOON FOREST (156) FWM	0.69 OF 16		3 11 / 13 5 / XSQ= 6.22 / PHI= -0.441 / EP = 0.0113

74	LEAN TOWARD BEING THOSE WHERE POTTERY IS PRESENT (145) 0.92 OF 13	74	LEAN TOWARD BEING THOSE WHERE POTTERY IS ABSENT (93) 0.71 OF 14	12 4 1 10 XSQ= 8.86 PHI= 0.573 EP = 0.0013
116	DRIFT TOWARD BEING THOSE WHERE OCCUPATIONAL SPECIALIZATION IS PART-TIME ONLY (34) JMH 0.75 OF 8	116	IN ALL CASES ARE THOSE WHERE OCCUPATIONAL SPECIALIZATION IS FULL-TIME, WHETHER OR NOT FOR SURPLUS PRODUCTION (20) JMH 1.00 OF 3	2 3 6 0 XSQ= 2.39 PHI= -0.466 EP = 0.0606
224	DRIFT TOWARD BEING THOSE WHERE COUSIN MARRIAGE IS PREFERENTIALLY OR PERMISSIVELY EITHER PATRI- OR MATRILATERAL, RATHER THAN SYMMETRICAL (66) 0.67 OF 6	224	IN ALL CASES ARE THOSE WHERE COUSIN MARRIAGE IS PREFERENTIALLY OR PERMISSIVELY SYMMETRICAL, RATHER THAN EITHER PATRI- OR MATRILATERAL (106) 1.00 OF 4	4 0 2 4 XSQ= 2.10 PHI= 0.458 EP = 0.0762
236	DRIFT TOWARD BEING THOSE WHERE THE FAMILY IS OF AN EXTENDED TYPE, RATHER THAN AN INDEPENDENT TYPE (213) 0.69 OF 16	236	DRIFT TOWARD BEING THOSE WHERE THE FAMILY IS OF AN INDEPENDENT TYPE, RATHER THAN AN EXTENDED TYPE (185) 0.63 OF 16	11 6 5 10 XSQ= 2.01 PHI= 0.250 EP = 0.0938
285	DRIFT TOWARD BEING THOSE WHERE THE SEX TABOO DURING PREGNANCY IS ABSENT OR INFERRED ABSENT (17) BCA 0.73 OF 15	285	DRIFT TOWARD BEING THOSE WHERE THE SEX TABOO DURING PREGNANCY IS PRESENT (14) BCA 0.67 OF 15	4 10 11 5 XSQ= 3.35 PHI= -0.334 EP = 0.0656
286	DRIFT TOWARD BEING THOSE WHERE THE NUMBER OF FOOD TABOOS DURING PREGNANCY IS HIGH (20) BCA 0.75 OF 16	286	DRIFT TOWARD BEING THOSE WHERE THE NUMBER OF FOOD TABOOS DURING PREGNANCY IS LOW OR ABSENT (14) BCA 0.60 OF 15	12 6 4 9 XSQ= 2.59 PHI= 0.289 EP = 0.0732
330	DRIFT TOWARD BEING THOSE WHERE THE AGE OF THE INFANT AT TIME OF WEANING IS 2.5 YEARS OR HIGHER (34) B-B-C 0.69 OF 13	330	DRIFT TOWARD BEING THOSE WHERE THE AGE OF THE INFANT AT TIME OF WEANING IS LOWER THAN 2.5 YEARS (36) B-B-C 0.71 OF 14	9 4 4 10 XSQ= 2.98 PHI= 0.332 EP = 0.0570
338	DRIFT MORE TOWARD BEING THOSE WHERE THE CHILD'S INFERRED ANXIETY OVER PERFORMANCE OF RESPONSIBLE BEHAVIOR IS HIGH (44) B-B-C 0.92 OF 12	338	DRIFT LESS TOWARD BEING THOSE WHERE THE CHILD'S INFERRED ANXIETY OVER PERFORMANCE OF RESPONSIBLE BEHAVIOR IS HIGH (44) B-B-C 0.60 OF 15	11 9 1 6 XSQ= 2.03 PHI= 0.274 EP = 0.0914
340	DRIFT TOWARD BEING THOSE WHERE THE TOTAL POSITIVE PRESSURE TOWARD DEVELOPING NURTURANT BEHAVIOR IN THE CHILD IS LOW (20) B-B-C 0.88 OF 8	340	DRIFT TOWARD BEING THOSE WHERE THE TOTAL POSITIVE PRESSURE TOWARD DEVELOPING NURTURANT BEHAVIOR IN THE CHILD IS HIGH (28) B-B-C 0.64 OF 11	1 7 7 4 XSQ= 3.09 PHI= -0.403 EP = 0.0587

343	DRIFT TOWARD BEING THOSE 0.75 OF 8 WHERE THE CHILD'S INFERRED CONFLICT REGARDING NURTURANT BEHAVIOR IS LOW (18) B-B-C	343	DRIFT TOWARD BEING THOSE 0.73 OF 11 WHERE THE CHILD'S INFERRED CONFLICT REGARDING NURTURANT BEHAVIOR IS HIGH (29) B-B-C	2 8 6 3 XSQ= 2.53 PHI= -0.365 EP = 0.0698
350	DRIFT TOWARD BEING THOSE 0.80 OF 10 WHERE THE CHILD'S INFERRED ANXIETY OVER PERFORMANCE OF ACHIEVEMENT BEHAVIOR IS HIGH (34) B-B-C	350	DRIFT TOWARD BEING THOSE 0.62 OF 13 WHERE THE CHILD'S INFERRED ANXIETY OVER PERFORMANCE OF ACHIEVEMENT BEHAVIOR IS LOW (26) B-B-C	8 5 2 8 XSQ= 2.46 PHI= 0.327 EP = 0.0903
351	TILT TOWARD BEING THOSE 0.70 OF 10 WHERE THE CHILD'S INFERRED CONFLICT REGARDING ACHIEVEMENT BEHAVIOR IS HIGH (26) B-B-C	351	TILT TOWARD BEING THOSE 0.85 OF 13 WHERE THE CHILD'S INFERRED CONFLICT REGARDING ACHIEVEMENT BEHAVIOR IS LOW (34) B-B-C	7 2 3 11 XSQ= 4.97 PHI= 0.465 EP = 0.0131
397	DRIFT LESS TOWARD BEING THOSE 0.64 OF 11 WHERE SEX DISABILITY IS ABSENT (42) JKH	397	IN ALL CASES ARE THOSE 1.00 OF 9 WHERE SEX DISABILITY IS ABSENT (42) JKH	4 0 7 9 XSQ= 2.13 PHI= 0.327 EP = 0.0941
424	IN ALL CASES ARE THOSE 1.00 OF 8 WHERE RELIGIOUS SPECIALISTS ARE PART-TIME, RATHER THAN FULL-TIME (33) JMH	424	IN ALL CASES ARE THOSE 1.00 OF 3 WHERE RELIGIOUS SPECIALISTS ARE FULL-TIME, RATHER THAN PART-TIME (21) JMH	0 3 8 0 XSQ= 6.54 PHI= -0.771 EP = 0.0061
440	DRIFT TOWARD BEING THOSE 0.69 OF 16 WHERE FEAR OF SPIRITS IS HIGH (32) W-C	440	DRIFT TOWARD BEING THOSE 0.69 OF 16 WHERE FEAR OF SPIRITS IS LOW (29) W-C	11 5 5 11 XSQ= 3.13 PHI= 0.312 EP = 0.0756
442	DRIFT TOWARD BEING THOSE 0.75 OF 16 WHERE FEAR OF ANIMAL SPIRITS IS HIGH (28) W-C	442	DRIFT TOWARD BEING THOSE 0.63 OF 16 WHERE FEAR OF ANIMAL SPIRITS IS LOW (33) W-C	12 6 4 10 XSQ= 3.17 PHI= 0.315 EP = 0.0732
443	DRIFT TOWARD BEING THOSE 0.75 OF 16 WHERE OVERALL FEAR OF OTHERS IS HIGH (31) W-C	443	DRIFT TOWARD BEING THOSE 0.63 OF 16 WHERE OVERALL FEAR OF OTHERS IS LOW (30) W-C	12 6 4 10 XSQ= 3.17 PHI= 0.315 EP = 0.0732
454	TILT TOWARD BEING THOSE 0.86 OF 7 WHERE THE OBJECTIVE OF THE INDIVIDUAL'S CONTACT WITH THE DIVINE IS NOT CONDUCIVE TO THE DEVELOPMENT OF THE INDIVIDUAL'S NEED TO ACHIEVE (18) DCM	454	TILT TOWARD BEING THOSE 0.86 OF 7 WHERE THE OBJECTIVE OF THE INDIVIDUAL'S CONTACT WITH THE DIVINE IS CONDUCIVE TO THE DEVELOPMENT OF THE INDIVIDUAL'S NEED TO ACHIEVE (18) DCM	1 6 6 1 XSQ= 4.57 PHI= -0.571 EP = 0.0291

```
459  DRIFT TOWARD BEING THOSE          0.57 OF  14        459  DRIFT TOWARD BEING THOSE          0.83 OF  12            8     2
     WHERE GAMES, IF PRESENT,                                  WHERE GAMES, IF PRESENT,                                  6    10
     INCLUDE GAMES OF CHANCE   (82) R-A-B,EA                   DO NOT INCLUDE                                     XSQ=     2.93
                                                               GAMES OF CHANCE   (89) R-A-B,EA                    PHI=    0.335
                                                                                                                  EP =   0.0511

475  DRIFT TOWARD BEING THOSE          0.73 OF  15        475  DRIFT TOWARD BEING THOSE          0.64 OF  14           11     5
     WHERE EXHIBITIONISTIC DANCING                             WHERE EXHIBITIONISTIC DANCING                             4     9
     IS STRONGLY OR MODERATELY                                 IS NEGLIGIBLY EMPHASIZED   (38) PES                XSQ=     2.76
     EMPHASIZED   (48) PES                                                                                        PHI=    0.309
                                                                                                                  EP =   0.0656
```

293 CULTURES
WHERE THE IMPORTANCE OF PRACTICES
TO BRING GOOD LUCK
TO THE NEWBORN CHILD
IS HIGH (20) BCA

293 CULTURES
WHERE THE IMPORTANCE OF PRACTICES
TO BRING GOOD LUCK
TO THE NEWBORN CHILD
IS LOW OR ABSENT (14) BCA

BACKGROUND ON PAGE 135 SUBJECT ONLY

20 IN LEFT COLUMN

AINU	ARAPESH	AZANDE	BALINESE	CHAGGA	CHIR-APACHE	FON	HANO	JIVARO	KWAKIUTL
LAKHER	LESU	MACRI	MARSHALLESE	NAVAHO	SIRIONO	THONGA	TIV	VENDA	WOGEO

14 IN RIGHT COLUMN

ALORESE	ASHANTI	COMANCHE	IFUGAO	KURTATCHI	KUTENAI	LEPCHA	MASAI	OMAHA	PUKAPUKA
SANPOIL	TANALA	TROBRIANDS	YAGUA						

366 EXCLUDED BECAUSE UNASCERTAINED

81	LEAN TOWARD BEING THOSE WHERE A CITY OR TOWN IS PRESENT, OR THE AVERAGE COMMUNITY SIZE IS 200 OR GREATER (89)	0.64 OF 11	81	LEAN TOWARD BEING THOSE WHERE NO CITY OR TOWN IS PRESENT, AND THE AVERAGE COMMUNITY SIZE IS SMALLER THAN 200 (135)	0.92 OF 12	7 1 / 4 11 / XSQ= 5.49 / PHI= 0.489 / EP = 0.0094
83	LEAN TOWARD BEING THOSE WHERE, WITH NO CITY AND NO TOWN PRESENT, THE AVERAGE COMMUNITY SIZE IS BETWEEN 200 AND 999, RATHER THAN SMALLER THAN 200 (45)	0.60 OF 10	83	IN ALL CASES ARE THOSE WHERE, WITH NO CITY AND NO TOWN PRESENT, THE AVERAGE COMMUNITY SIZE IS SMALLER THAN 200, RATHER THAN BETWEEN 200 AND 999 (135)	1.00 OF 11	6 0 / 4 11 / XSQ= 6.53 / PHI= 0.558 / EP = 0.0039
108	IN ALL CASES ARE THOSE WHERE CLASS STRATIFICATION, IF PRESENT, IS BASED ON A HEREDITARY ARISTOCRACY (74)	1.00 OF 10	108	DRIFT LESS TOWARD BEING THOSE WHERE CLASS STRATIFICATION, IF PRESENT, IS BASED ON A HEREDITARY ARISTOCRACY (74)	0.57 OF 7	10 4 / 0 3 / XSQ= 2.67 / PHI= 0.397 / EP = 0.0515
201	DRIFT MORE TOWARD BEING THOSE WHERE MARITAL RESIDENCE IS NON-OPTIONAL, RATHER THAN AMBILOCAL OR NEOLOCAL (334)	0.90 OF 20	201	DRIFT LESS TOWARD BEING THOSE WHERE MARITAL RESIDENCE IS NON-OPTIONAL, RATHER THAN AMBILOCAL OR NEOLOCAL (334)	0.64 OF 14	18 9 / 2 5 / XSQ= 1.94 / PHI= 0.239 / EP = 0.0969
207	TILT TOWARD BEING THOSE WHERE MARITAL RESIDENCE IS MATRILOCAL OR UXORILOCAL, RATHER THAN AMBILOCAL OR NEOLOCAL (64)	0.71 OF 7	207	IN ALL CASES ARE THOSE WHERE MARITAL RESIDENCE IS AMBILOCAL OR NEOLOCAL, RATHER THAN MATRILOCAL OR UXORILOCAL (64)	1.00 OF 5	5 0 / 2 5 / XSQ= 3.54 / PHI= 0.543 / EP = 0.0278

243	DRIFT TOWARD BEING THOSE WHERE POLYGYNY, IF PRESENT, HAS A HIGH INCIDENCE (24) W-C,S	0.69 OF 13	243	DRIFT TOWARD BEING THOSE WHERE POLYGYNY, IF PRESENT, HAS A LOW INCIDENCE (36) W-D,S	0.78 OF 9	9 2 4 7 XSQ= 3.01 PHI= 0.370 EP = 0.0805
324	DRIFT TOWARD BEING THOSE WHERE THE PAIN INFLICTED ON THE INFANT BY THE NURTURANT AGENT IS HIGH (34) B-B-C	0.75 OF 16	324	DRIFT TOWARD BEING THOSE WHERE THE PAIN INFLICTED ON THE INFANT BY THE NURTURANT AGENT IS LOW OR NEGLIGIBLE (32) B-B-C	0.64 OF 11	12 4 4 7 XSQ= 2.59 PHI= 0.310 EP = 0.0608
330	DRIFT TOWARD BEING THOSE WHERE THE AGE OF THE INFANT AT TIME OF WEANING IS 2.5 YEARS OR HIGHER (34) B-B-C	0.67 OF 18	330	DRIFT TOWARD BEING THOSE WHERE THE AGE OF THE INFANT AT TIME OF WEANING IS LOWER THAN 2.5 YEARS (36) B-B-C	0.73 OF 11	12 3 6 8 XSQ= 2.81 PHI= 0.311 EP = 0.0604
340	DRIFT TOWARD BEING THOSE WHERE THE TOTAL POSITIVE PRESSURE TOWARD DEVELOPING NURTURANT BEHAVIOR IN THE CHILD IS LOW (20) B-B-C	0.69 OF 13	340	DRIFT TOWARD BEING THOSE WHERE THE TOTAL POSITIVE PRESSURE TOWARD DEVELOPING NURTURANT BEHAVIOR IN THE CHILD IS HIGH (28) B-B-C	0.75 OF 8	4 6 9 2 XSQ= 2.31 PHI= -0.332 EP = 0.0805
369	TILT TOWARD BEING THOSE WHERE DISSOCIATION OF THE SEXES AT ADOLESCENCE, OR CUSTOMS OF INITIATION AT ADOLESCENCE, ARE PRESENT (42) JKH	0.92 OF 13	369	TILT TOWARD BEING THOSE WHERE BOTH DISSOCIATION OF THE SEXES AT ADOLESCENCE, AND CUSTOMS OF INITIATION AT ADOLESCENCE, ARE ABSENT (15) JKH	0.50 OF 8	12 4 1 4 XSQ= 2.83 PHI= 0.367 EP = 0.0475
372	DRIFT TOWARD BEING THOSE WHERE MALE INITIATION RITES ARE PRESENT (48) ASA	0.60 OF 15	372	DRIFT TOWARD BEING THOSE WHERE MALE INITIATION RITES ARE ABSENT (63) ASA	0.77 OF 13	9 3 6 10 XSQ= 2.52 PHI= 0.300 EP = 0.0671
373	TILT TOWARD BEING THOSE WHERE MALE INITIATION CEREMONIES AT PUBERTY ARE PRESENT (17) W-K-A	0.67 OF 15	373	IN ALL CASES ARE THOSE WHERE MALE INITIATION CEREMONIES AT PUBERTY ARE ABSENT (27) W-K-A	1.00 OF 6	10 0 5 6 XSQ= 5.20 PHI= 0.497 EP = 0.0124
442	TILT TOWARD BEING THOSE WHERE FEAR OF ANIMAL SPIRITS IS HIGH (28) W-C	0.75 OF 20	442	TILT TOWARD BEING THOSE WHERE FEAR OF ANIMAL SPIRITS IS LOW (33) W-C	0.71 OF 14	15 4 5 10 XSQ= 5.44 PHI= 0.400 EP = 0.0135
443	DRIFT TOWARD BEING THOSE WHERE OVERALL FEAR OF OTHERS IS HIGH (31) W-C	0.70 OF 20	443	DRIFT TOWARD BEING THOSE WHERE OVERALL FEAR OF OTHERS IS LOW (30) W-C	0.64 OF 14	14 5 6 9 XSQ= 2.66 PHI= 0.280 EP = 0.0800

294 CULTURES WHERE PRACTICES TO PROTECT THE NEWBORN CHILD FROM HARMFUL INFLUENCES ARE PRESENT (16) BCA	294 CULTURES WHERE PRACTICES TO PROTECT THE NEWBORN CHILD FROM HARMFUL INFLUENCES ARE ABSENT OR INFERRED ABSENT (18) BCA

BACKGROUND ON PAGE 135 SUBJECT ONLY

16 IN LEFT COLUMN

ALORESE ARAPESH AZANDE BALINESE CHAGGA CHIR-APACHE DUSUN JIVARO KURTATCHI KWAKIUTL
LAKHER MARSHALLESE NAVAHO TIV TROBRIAND VENDA

18 IN RIGHT COLUMN

AINU ASHANTI COMANCHE FON HANO IFUGAO KUTENAI LEPCHA LESU MAORI
MASAI PUKAPUKA SANPOIL SIRIONO TANALA THONGA WOGEO YAGUA

366 EXCLUDED BECAUSE UNASCERTAINED

16	DRIFT TOWARD BEING THOSE WHERE THE LATITUDE IS LESS THAN TEN DEGREES (123)	0.69 OF 16	16	DRIFT TOWARD BEING THOSE WHERE THE LATITUDE IS TEN DEGREES OR GREATER (277)	0.67 OF 18	5 12 11 6 XSQ= 2.95 PHI= -0.295 EP = 0.0844
78	TILT TOWARD BEING THOSE WHERE THE WRITING SYSTEM IS ALPHABETIC-OR-PHONETIC, OR MNEMONIC, RATHER THAN BEING ABSENT (36) JMH	0.88 OF 8	78	IN ALL CASES ARE THOSE WHERE A WRITING SYSTEM IS ABSENT, RATHER THAN BEING PRESENT IN EITHER ALPHABETIC-OR-PHONETIC FORM OR MNEMONIC FORM (18) JMH	1.00 OF 3	7 0 1 3 XSQ= 3.93 PHI= 0.598 EP = 0.0242
141	DRIFT TOWARD BEING THOSE WHERE THE LEVEL OF SOCIAL SANCTION IS PUBLIC CORPOREAL SANCTION, RATHER THAN PUBLIC PROPERTY SANCTION OR PRIVATE SETTLEMENT (28) JMH	0.75 OF 8	141	IN ALL CASES ARE THOSE WHERE THE LEVEL OF SOCIAL SANCTION IS PUBLIC PROPERTY SANCTION OR PRIVATE SETTLEMENT, RATHER THAN PUBLIC CORPOREAL SANCTION (26) JMH	1.00 OF 3	6 0 2 3 XSQ= 2.39 PHI= 0.466 EP = 0.0606
148	DRIFT TOWARD BEING THOSE WHERE THE INCIDENCE OF PERSONAL CRIME IS HIGH (12) B-B-C	0.75 OF 8	148	DRIFT TOWARD BEING THOSE WHERE THE INCIDENCE OF PERSONAL CRIME IS LOW (21) B-B-C	0.73 OF 11	6 3 2 8 XSQ= 2.53 PHI= 0.365 EP = 0.0698
185	IN ALL CASES ARE THOSE WHERE THE LARGEST NON-COGNATIC KIN GROUP IS THE MOEITY OR PHRATRY OR SIB (194)	1.00 OF 11	185	DRIFT LESS TOWARD BEING THOSE WHERE THE LARGEST NON-COGNATIC KIN GROUP IS THE MOEITY OR PHRATRY OR SIB (194)	0.69 OF 13	11 9 0 4 XSQ= 2.15 PHI= 0.299 EP = 0.0983

311	DRIFT TOWARD BEING THOSE 0.71 OF 14 WHERE SEXUAL SOCIALIZATION ANXIETY IS HIGH (28) W-C	311	DRIFT TOWARD BEING THOSE 0.61 OF 18 WHERE SEXUAL SOCIALIZATION ANXIETY IS LOW (23) W-C	10 7 4 11 XSQ= 2.17 PHI= 0.260 EP = 0.0870
347	DRIFT TOWARD BEING THOSE 0.62 OF 13 WHERE THE CHILD'S INFERRED CONFLICT REGARDING SELF-RELIANT BEHAVIOR IS HIGH (37) B-B-C	347	DRIFT TOWARD BEING THOSE 0.75 OF 16 WHERE THE CHILD'S INFERRED CONFLICT REGARDING SELF-RELIANT BEHAVIOR IS LOW (39) B-B-C	8 4 5 12 XSQ= 2.58 PHI= 0.299 EP = 0.0667
351	DRIFT TOWARD BEING THOSE 0.60 OF 10 WHERE THE CHILD'S INFERRED CONFLICT REGARDING ACHIEVEMENT BEHAVIOR IS HIGH (26) B-B-C	351	DRIFT TOWARD BEING THOSE 0.79 OF 14 WHERE THE CHILD'S INFERRED CONFLICT REGARDING ACHIEVEMENT BEHAVIOR IS LOW (34) B-B-C	6 3 4 11 XSQ= 2.24 PHI= 0.306 EP = 0.0918
354	DRIFT TOWARD BEING THOSE 0.77 OF 13 WHERE THE CHILD'S INFERRED ANXIETY OVER PERFORMANCE OF OBEDIENT BEHAVIOR IS HIGH (36) B-B-C	354	DRIFT TOWARD BEING THOSE 0.60 OF 15 WHERE THE CHILD'S INFERRED ANXIETY OVER PERFORMANCE OF OBEDIENT BEHAVIOR IS LOW (37) B-B-C	10 6 3 9 XSQ= 2.52 PHI= 0.300 EP = 0.0671
366	IN ALL CASES ARE THOSE 1.00 OF 11 WHERE DISSOCIATION OF THE SEXES AT ADOLESCENCE IS MEDIUM OR LOW (41) JKH	366	TILT LESS TOWARD BEING THOSE 0.60 OF 10 WHERE DISSOCIATION OF THE SEXES AT ADOLESCENCE IS MEDIUM OR LOW (41) JKH	0 4 11 6 XSQ= 3.15 PHI= -0.387 EP = 0.0351
392	DRIFT TOWARD BEING THOSE 0.77 OF 13 WHERE PREMARITAL SEX RELATIONS ARE STRONGLY PUNISHED AND IN FACT RARE, OR WEAKLY PUNISHED AND IN FACT NOT RARE, OR PUNISHED ONLY IF PREGNANCY RESULTS (112) JTW,EA	392	DRIFT TOWARD BEING THOSE 0.63 OF 16 WHERE PREMARITAL SEX RELATIONS ARE FREELY PERMITTED (67) JTW,EA	10 6 3 10 XSQ= 3.05 PHI= 0.325 EP = 0.0608
449	IN ALL CASES ARE THOSE 1.00 OF 6 WHERE THE OBSERVATION OF FOOD TABOOS IS HIGH, RATHER THAN MEDIUM OR LOW (25) JRL	449	LEAN TOWARD BEING THOSE 0.78 OF 9 WHERE THE OBSERVATION OF FOOD TABOOS IS MEDIUM OR LOW, RATHER THAN HIGH (61) JRL	6 2 0 7 XSQ= 5.90 PHI= 0.627 EP = 0.0070
475	TILT TOWARD BEING THOSE 0.79 OF 14 WHERE EXHIBITIONISTIC DANCING IS STRONGLY OR MODERATELY EMPHASIZED (48) PES	475	TILT TOWARD BEING THOSE 0.63 OF 16 WHERE EXHIBITIONISTIC DANCING IS NEGLIGIBLY EMPHASIZED (38) PES	11 6 3 10 XSQ= 3.59 PHI= 0.346 EP = 0.0329

295 CULTURES WHERE THE SEVERITY CF PUNISHMENT FCR ABCRTICN IS HIGH (11) BCA	295 CULTURES WHERE THE SEVERITY CF PUNISHMENT FOR ABORTION IS LOW OR ABSENT (12) BCA

BACKGROUND ON PAGE 135 BCTH SUBJECT ANC PREDICATE

11 IN LEFT CCLUMN

ALORESE ASHANTI AZANCE BALINESE CHIR-APACHE FON JIVARO MASAI SANPOIL VENCA
WOGEC

12 IN RIGHT CCLUMN

AINU CHAGGA DOBUANS DUSUN HANO KURTATCHI KWAKIUTL LESU MARSHALLESE PAPAGO
PUKAPUKA TIKCPIA

377 EXCLUDED BECAUSE UNASCERTAINEC

3	DRIFT LESS TCWARC BEING THCSE LCCATED CUTSIDE CF AFRICA (320)	0.55 OF 11	3	DRIFT MORE TOWARD BEING THCSE LOCATED OUTSIDE OF AFRICA (320)	0.92 CF 12	5 1 / 6 11 / XSQ= 2.40 / PHI= 0.323 / EP = 0.0686
71	DRIFT LESS TCWARC BEING THCSE WHERE METAL WCRKING IS ABSENT (153)	0.56 OF 9	71	IN ALL CASES ARE THOSE WHERE METAL WORKING IS ABSENT (153)	1.00 CF 7	4 0 / 5 7 / XSQ= 2.12 / PHI= 0.364 / EP = 0.0885
85	DRIFT TCWARD BEING THCSE WHERE THE LEVEL CF PCLITICAL INTEGRATICN IS THE LARGE STATE, CR THE LITTLE STATE (70) GPM	0.50 OF 8	85	IN ALL CASES ARE THCSE WHERE THE LEVEL OF PCLITICAL INTEGRATICN IS THE MINIMAL STATE, THE AUTONOMOUS COMMUNITY, CR THE FAMILY (234) GPM	1.00 CF 8	4 0 / 4 8 / XSQ= 3.00 / PHI= 0.433 / EP = 0.0769
95	TILT TCWARD BEING THCSE WHERE THE HIERARCHY OF NATICNAL JURISDICTICN HAS FCUR, THREE, CR TWC LEVELS (76) GES,EA	0.60 OF 10	95	IN ALL CASES ARE THOSE WHERE THE HIERARCHY OF NATIONAL JURISDICTICN HAS ONE OR NO LEVELS (254) GES,EA	1.00 CF 10	6 0 / 4 10 / XSQ= 5.95 / PHI= 0.546 / EP = 0.0108
110	TILT TCWARC BEING THCSE WHERE SLAVERY IS PRESENT (163)	0.55 OF 11	11C	TILT TOWARD BEING THOSE WHERE SLAVERY IS ABSENT (218)	0.92 CF 12	6 1 / 5 11 / XSQ= 3.81 / PHI= 0.407 / EP = 0.0272

190	IN ALL CASES ARE THCSE 1.00 OF 7 WHERE THE KIN GRCUP IS PATRILINEAL CR CCUELE-CESCENT, RATHER THAN MATRILINEAL (186)	19C	TILT TOWARD BEING THOSE 0.71 CF 7 WHERE THE KIN GRCUP IS MATRILINEAL, RATHER THAN PATRILINEAL OR DOUBLE-DESCENT (61)	7 2 0 5 XSQ= 4.98 PHI= 0.596 EP = 0.0210
220	DRIFT LESS TCWARC BEING THCSE 0.73 OF 11 WHERE FIRST CCUSIN MARRIAGE IN SOME FCRM CR CTHER IS NCT PRESCRIBEC CR PREFERREC (273)	22C	IN ALL CASES ARE THCSE 1.00 CF 12 WHERE FIRST COUSIN MARRIAGE IN SOME FORM OR OTHER IS NOT PRESCRIBED CR PREFERRED (273)	3 0 8 12 XSQ= 1.74 PHI= 0.275 EP = 0.0932
242	IN ALL CASES ARE THCSE 1.00 OF 11 WHERE MARRIAGE IS COMMCNLY CR CCCASICNALLY PCLYGYNOUS, RATHER THAN MCNCGAMCUS (314)	242	TILT LESS TOWARD BEING THCSE 0.58 CF 12 WHERE MARRIAGE IS COMMONLY OR OCCASICNALLY PCLYGYNCUS, RATHER THAN MONOGAMOUS (314)	11 7 0 5 XSQ= 3.66 PHI= 0.399 EP = 0.0373
282	DRIFT TCWARD BEING THCSE 0.70 OF 1C WHERE THE STRENGTH CF CESIRE FOR CHILCREN IS HIGH (16) BCA	282	DRIFT TOWARD BEING THCSE 0.75 CF 12 WHERE THE STRENGTH CF DESIRE FCR CHILDREN IS LOW OR ABSENT (20) BCA	7 3 3 9 XSQ= 2.82 PHI= 0.358 EP = 0.0836
344	DRIFT TCWARD BEING THCSE 0.70 OF 10 WHERE THE TOTAL POSITIVE PRESSURE TOWARC DEVELCPING SELF-RELIANT BEHAVIOR IN THE CHILD IS HIGH (36) B-B-C	344	DRIFT TOWARD BEING THOSE 0.78 OF 9 WHERE THE TOTAL POSITIVE PRESSURE TOWARC DEVELOPING SELF-RELIANT BEHAVIOR IN THE CHILD IS LOW (40) B-B-C	7 2 3 7 XSQ= 2.63 PHI= 0.372 EP = 0.0698
386	DRIFT TCWARD BEING THCSE 0.78 OF 9 WHERE SEXUAL EXPRESSICN BY THE YOUNG IS RESTRICTED CR SEMI-RESTRICTED (46) F-B	386	DRIFT TOWARD BEING THCSE 0.67 CF 12 WHERE SEXUAL EXPRESSION BY THE YCUNG IS PERMITTED (40) F-B	7 4 2 8 XSQ= 2.49 PHI= 0.344 EP = 0.0805
393	TILT TCWARD BEING THCSE 0.88 OF 8 WHERE EXTRAMARITAL CCITUS IS PUNISHED, RATHER THAN PERMITTED (43) F-B	393	TILT TOWARD BEING THOSE 0.67 OF 9 WHERE EXTRAMARITAL CCITUS IS PERMITTED, RATHER THAN PUNISHED (41) F-B	7 3 1 6 XSQ= 3.14 PHI= 0.430 EP = 0.0498
421	TILT TCWARD BEING THCSE 0.73 OF 11 WHERE KILLING, TCRTURING, CR MUTILATING CF THE ENEMY IS STRCNGLY CR MCDERATELY EMPHASIZED (37) PES	421	TILT TOWARD BEING THCSE 0.80 CF 10 WHERE KILLING, TORTURING, CR MUTILATING OF THE ENEMY IS NEGLIGIBLY EMPHASIZED (47) PES	8 2 3 8 XSQ= 3.92 PHI= 0.432 EP = 0.0300
458	TILT TCWARD BEING THOSE 0.63 OF 8 WHERE GAMES, IF PRESENT, INCLUDE GAMES CF STRATEGY (52) R-A-B,EA	458	TILT TOWARD BEING THOSE 0.89 OF 9 WHERE GAMES, IF PRESENT, DO NOT INCLUDE GAMES OF STRATEGY (119) R-A-B,EA	5 1 3 8 XSQ= 2.91 PHI= 0.413 EP = 0.0498

```
295/

460  TILT TOWARD BEING THOSE          0.88 OF   8        460  TILT TOWARD BEING THOSE          0.67 OF   9            1     6
     WHERE GAMES, IF PRESENT,                                 WHERE GAMES, IF PRESENT,                                7     3
     ARE NOT LIMITED TO                                       ARE LIMITED TO                                   XSQ=     3.14
     GAMES OF SKILL ONLY  (104) R-A-B,EA                      GAMES OF SKILL ONLY  (67) R-A-B,EA               PHI=   -0.430
                                                                                                               EP =   0.0498
```

296 CULTURES WHERE INFANTICIDE IS PRESENT (18) BCA

296 CULTURES WHERE INFANTICIDE IS ABSENT OR INFERRED ABSENT (15) BCA

BACKGROUND ON PAGE 135 — BOTH SUBJECT AND PREDICATE

18 IN LEFT COLUMN

AINU, ARAPESH, AZANDE, CHAGGA, CHIR-APACHE, DOBUANS, DUSUN, FON, JIVARO, KWAKIUTL, MAORI, MARSHALLESE, MASAI, SANPOIL, TANALA, TIKOPIA, VENDA, WOGEO

15 IN RIGHT COLUMN

ANDAMANESE, ASHANTI, BALINESE, HANO, IFUGAO, KURTATCHI, LAKHER, LEPCHA, NAVAHO, OMAHA, PAPAGO, PUKAPUKA, SIRIONO, THONGA, TROBRIAND

367 EXCLUDED BECAUSE UNASCERTAINED

74	DRIFT TOWARD BEING THOSE WHERE POTTERY IS ABSENT (93)	0.54 OF 13	74	DRIFT TOWARD BEING THOSE WHERE POTTERY IS PRESENT (145)	0.83 OF 12		6 10 / 7 2 / XSQ= 2.30 / PHI= -0.304 / EP = 0.0968
210	IN ALL CASES ARE THOSE WHERE MARITAL RESIDENCE IS PATRILOCAL, RATHER THAN MATRILOCAL (169)	1.00 OF 8	210	DRIFT LESS TOWARD BEING THOSE WHERE MARITAL RESIDENCE IS PATRILOCAL, RATHER THAN MATRILOCAL (169)	0.57 OF 7		8 4 / 0 3 / XSQ= 2.03 / PHI= 0.367 / EP = 0.0769
224	DRIFT TOWARD BEING THOSE WHERE COUSIN MARRIAGE IS PREFERENTIALLY OR PERMISSIVELY SYMMETRICAL, RATHER THAN EITHER PATRI- OR MATRILATERAL (106)	0.83 OF 6	224	DRIFT TOWARD BEING THOSE WHERE COUSIN MARRIAGE IS PREFERENTIALLY OR PERMISSIVELY EITHER PATRI- OR MATRILATERAL, RATHER THAN SYMMETRICAL (66)	0.80 OF 5		1 4 / 5 1 / XSQ= 2.23 / PHI= -0.450 / EP = 0.0801
302	TILT TOWARD BEING THOSE WHERE THE AVERAGE EARLY SATISFACTION POTENTIAL IS LOW (17) W-C	0.64 OF 14	302	TILT TOWARD BEING THOSE WHERE THE AVERAGE EARLY SATISFACTION POTENTIAL IS HIGH (23) W-C	0.83 OF 12		5 10 / 9 2 / XSQ= 4.21 / PHI= -0.402 / EP = 0.0214
303	TILT TOWARD BEING THOSE WHERE THE EARLY ORAL SATISFACTION POTENTIAL IS LOW (25) W-C	0.67 OF 18	303	TILT TOWARD BEING THOSE WHERE THE EARLY ORAL SATISFACTION POTENTIAL IS HIGH (32) W-C	0.73 OF 15		6 11 / 12 4 / XSQ= 3.76 / PHI= -0.338 / EP = 0.0366

313	DRIFT TOWARD BEING THOSE WHERE AGGRESSION SOCIALIZATION ANXIETY IS HIGH (26) W-C	0.67 OF	18	313	DRIFT TOWARD BEING THOSE WHERE AGGRESSION SOCIALIZATION ANXIETY IS LOW (28) W-C	0.67 OF	15	12 5 6 10 XSQ= 2.43 PHI= 0.271 EP = 0.0844
325	TILT TOWARD BEING THOSE WHERE THE DEGREE OF DIFFUSION AMONG THE INFANT'S NURTURANT AGENTS IS LOW (32) B-B-C	0.57 OF	14	325	TILT TOWARD BEING THOSE WHERE THE DEGREE OF DIFFUSION AMONG THE INFANT'S NURTURANT AGENTS IS HIGH (42) B-B-C	0.93 OF	14	6 13 8 1 XSQ= 5.89 PHI= -0.459 EP = 0.0128
331	DRIFT TOWARD BEING THOSE WHERE THE AGE AT BEGINNING OF INDEPENDENCE TRAINING IS 3.8 YEARS OR HIGHER (16) W-C	0.69 OF	13	331	DRIFT TOWARD BEING THOSE WHERE THE AGE AT BEGINNING OF INDEPENDENCE TRAINING IS LOWER THAN 3.8 YEARS (21) W-C	0.73 OF	11	9 3 4 8 XSQ= 2.69 PHI= 0.334 EP = 0.0995
373	DRIFT TOWARD BEING THOSE WHERE MALE INITIATION CEREMONIES AT PUBERTY ARE PRESENT (17) W-K-A	0.75 OF	8	373	DRIFT TOWARD BEING THOSE WHERE MALE INITIATION CEREMONIES AT PUBERTY ARE ABSENT (27) W-K-A	0.80 OF	10	6 2 2 8 XSQ= 3.45 PHI= 0.437 EP = 0.0536
377	DRIFT LESS TOWARD BEING THOSE WHERE MALE GENITAL MUTILATION IS ABSENT (242)	0.63 OF	16	377	DRIFT MORE TOWARD BEING THOSE WHERE MALE GENITAL MUTILATION IS ABSENT (242)	0.93 OF	14	6 1 10 13 XSQ= 2.34 PHI= 0.279 EP = 0.0860
399	DRIFT TOWARD BEING THOSE WHERE INTENSITY OF CASTRATION ANXIETY IS HIGH (23) WNS	0.67 OF	12	399	DRIFT TOWARD BEING THOSE WHERE INTENSITY OF CASTRATION ANXIETY IS LOW (22) WNS	0.75 OF	12	8 3 4 9 XSQ= 2.69 PHI= 0.334 EP = 0.0995
437	TILT TOWARD BEING THOSE WHERE FEAR OF GHOSTS, SPIRITS, HUMANS OR ANIMALS IS HIGH (21) W-C,JFG	0.92 OF	12	437	TILT TOWARD BEING THOSE WHERE FEAR OF GHOSTS, SPIRITS, HUMANS OR ANIMALS IS LOW (23) W-C,JFG	0.53 OF	15	11 7 1 8 XSQ= 4.22 PHI= 0.395 EP = 0.0192
443	DRIFT TOWARD BEING THOSE WHERE OVERALL FEAR OF OTHERS IS HIGH (31) W-C	0.72 OF	18	443	DRIFT TOWARD BEING THOSE WHERE OVERALL FEAR OF OTHERS IS LOW (30) W-C	0.60 OF	15	13 6 5 9 XSQ= 2.28 PHI= 0.263 EP = 0.0853
447	DRIFT TOWARD BEING THOSE WHERE LOVE MAGIC IS PRESENT (20) S-R	0.90 OF	10	447	DRIFT TOWARD BEING THOSE WHERE LOVE MAGIC IS ABSENT (13) S-R	0.55 OF	11	9 5 1 6 XSQ= 2.89 PHI= 0.371 EP = 0.0635

297 CULTURES
WHERE TWINS ARE UNWELCOME
AND ONE OR BOTH KILLED (13) CSF

297 CULTURES
WHERE TWINS ARE NOT UNWELCOME
AND NOT KILLED (9) CSF

BACKGROUND ON PAGE 136 — SUBJECT ONLY

13 IN LEFT COLUMN

AINU, ARANDA, CARIB, CHOROTI, COPR ESKIMO, DOBUANS, MURNGIN, THONGA, TIKOPIA, TODA, VENDA, WITOTO, YUROK

9 IN RIGHT COLUMN

ASHANTI, AZANDE, JIVARO, KWAKIUTL, LANGO, MASAI, MBUNDU, OMAHA, RIFFIANS

378 EXCLUDED BECAUSE UNASCERTAINED

3	DRIFT TOWARD BEING THOSE LOCATED OUTSIDE OF AFRICA (320)	0.85 OF 13	3	DRIFT TOWARD BEING THOSE LOCATED IN AFRICA (80)	0.56 OF 9	2 5 11 4 XSQ= 2.32 PHI= -0.325 EP = 0.0743
16	DRIFT TOWARD BEING THOSE WHERE THE LATITUDE IS TEN DEGREES OR GREATER (277)	0.85 OF 13	16	DRIFT TOWARD BEING THOSE WHERE THE LATITUDE IS LESS THAN TEN DEGREES (123)	0.56 OF 9	11 4 2 5 XSQ= 2.32 PHI= 0.325 EP = 0.0743
51	DRIFT TOWARD BEING THOSE WHERE SUBSISTENCE IS PRIMARILY BY FOOD GATHERING -- I. E., HUNTING, FISHING, OR COLLECTING -- RATHER THAN FOOD PRODUCTION (147)	0.69 OF 13	51	DRIFT TOWARD BEING THOSE WHERE SUBSISTENCE IS PRIMARILY BY FOOD PRODUCTION -- I. E., AGRICULTURE OR HUSBANDRY -- RATHER THAN BY GATHERING (253)	0.78 OF 9	4 7 9 2 XSQ= 3.01 PHI= -0.370 EP = 0.0805
62	TILT TOWARD BEING THOSE WHERE HUSBANDRY OF ANY KIND IS ABSENT (172)	0.77 OF 13	62	TILT TOWARD BEING THOSE WHERE HUSBANDRY OF SOME KIND IS PRESENT (228)	0.78 OF 9	3 7 10 2 XSQ= 4.40 PHI= -0.447 EP = 0.0274
71	LEAN TOWARD BEING THOSE WHERE METAL WORKING IS ABSENT (153)	0.92 OF 12	71	LEAN TOWARD BEING THOSE WHERE METAL WORKING IS PRESENT (98)	0.71 OF 7	1 5 11 2 XSQ= 5.49 PHI= -0.537 EP = 0.0095

73	DRIFT TCWARD BEING THCSE WHERE WEAVING IS ABSENT (130)	0.75 OF 12	73	DRIFT TOWARD BEING THOSE WHERE WEAVING IS PRESENT (118)	0.75 OF 8	3 6 9 2 XSQ= 3.04 PHI= -0.390 EP = 0.0648
82	TILT TCWARD BEING THCSE WHERE NC CITY CR TCWN IS PRESENT, AND THE AVERAGE CCMMUNITY SIZE IS SMALLER THAN FIFTY (46)	0.70 OF 10	82	TILT TOWARD BEING THOSE WHERE A CITY OR TOWN IS PRESENT, CR THE AVERAGE COMMUNITY SIZE IS FIFTY OR GREATER (178)	0.86 CF 7	3 6 7 1 XSQ= 3.14 PHI= -0.430 EP = 0.0498
86	TILT TCWARD BEING THOSE WHERE THE LEVEL CF PCLITICAL INTEGRATION IS THE AUTCNOMCUS CCMMUNITY, CR THE FAMILY (156) GPM	0.90 OF 10	86	TILT TOWARD BEING THCSE WHERE THE LEVEL CF PCLITICAL INTEGRATION IS THE LARGE STATE, THE LITTLE STATE, OR THE MINIMAL STATE (148) GPM	0.71 OF 7	1 5 9 2 XSQ= 4.38 PHI= -0.508 EP = 0.0345
1C0	DRIFT TCWARD BEING THCSE WHERE HIERARCHIES ARE THE 'SIMPLEST' I. E., WHERE THERE ARE CNLY TWC LCCAL LEVELS WITH NC NATICNAL LEVELS (63) GES,EA	0.50 OF 12	1CC	DRIFT TOWARD BEING THOSE WHERE HIERARCHIES ARE MCRE CCMPLEX THAN THE 'SIMPLEST,' I. E., MCRE CCMPLEX THAN TWO LOCAL LEVELS WITH NO NATIONAL LEVELS (267) GES,EA	0.89 CF 9	6 8 6 1 XSQ= 1.97 PHI= -0.306 EP = 0.0873
110	DRIFT TCWARD BEING THCSE WHERE SLAVERY IS ABSENT (218)	0.77 OF 13	11C	DRIFT TOWARD BEING THOSE WHERE SLAVERY IS PRESENT (163)	0.67 OF 9	3 6 10 3 XSQ= 2.57 PHI= -0.342 EP = 0.0789
186	DRIFT TCWARD BEING THCSE WHERE THE KIN GRCUP IS CTHER THAN EXCLUSIVELY PATRILINEAL (250)	0.85 OF 13	186	DRIFT TOWARD BEING THOSE WHERE THE KIN GROUP IS EXCLUSIVELY PATRILINEAL (150)	0.56 CF 9	2 5 11 4 XSQ= 2.32 PHI= -0.325 EP = 0.0743
196	LEAN TCWARD BEING THCSE WHERE INDIVIDUAL RIGHTS IN REAL PROPERTY, CR RULES FCR INHERITANCE, ARE ABSENT (87)	0.78 OF 9	196	IN ALL CASES ARE THCSE WHERE INDIVIDUAL RIGHTS IN REAL PRCPERTY, AND RULES FOR INHERITANCE, ARE PRESENT (194)	1.00 CF 7	2 7 7 0 XSQ= 6.78 PHI= -0.651 EP = 0.0032
277	TILT TCWARD BEING THCSE WHERE THE STATUS CF WOMEN IS INFERICR CR SUBJECTED (14) LWS	0.75 OF 4	277	IN ALL CASES ARE THCSE WHERE THE STATUS OF WOMEN IS NOT STRONGLY INFERICR CR SUBJECTED (22) LWS	1.00 CF 5	3 0 1 5 XSQ= 2.76 PHI= 0.553 EP = 0.0476
353	DRIFT TCWARD BEING THCSE WHERE THE CHILD-S INFERREC ANXIETY OVER NCN-PERFCRMANCE CF CBEDIENT BEHAVIOR IS LCW (32) B-B-C	0.50 OF 6	353	IN ALL CASES ARE THCSE WHERE THE CHILD'S INFERRED ANXIETY OVER NON-PERFORMANCE OF OBEDIENT BEHAVICR IS HIGH (42) B-B-C	1.00 OF 7	3 7 3 0 XSQ= 2.17 PHI= -0.408 EP = 0.0699

```
404  IN ALL CASES ARE THCSE           1.00 OF    8      4C4  TILT TOWARD BEING THOSE          0.57 CF    7            0      4
     WHERE EXPLANATICNS CF ILLNESS                           WHERE EXPLANATICNS CF ILLNESS                             8      3
     CF A SEXUAL NATURE                                      OF A SEXUAL NATURE                              XSQ=      3.65
     ARE ABSENT  (42) W-C                                    ARE PRESENT  (19) W-C                           PHI=    -0.494
                                                                                                             EP =    0.0256

417  TILT TCWARC BEING THCSE          0.75 OF    4      417  IN ALL CASES ARE THOSE           1.00 CF    5            1      5
     WHERE WARFARE IS                                        WHERE WARFARE IS                                          3      0
     NCT PREVALENT  (9) LWS                                  PREVALENT  (34) LWS                             XSQ=      2.76
                                                                                                             PHI=    -0.553
                                                                                                             EP =    0.0476

426  DRIFT TCWARD BEING THCSE         0.67 OF   12      426  DRIFT TOWARD BEING THOSE         0.86 CF    7            4      6
     WHERE A HIGH GCC IS                                     WHERE A HIGH GCD IS                                       8      1
     ABSENT  (104) GES,EA                                    PRESENT  (156) GES,EA                           XSQ=      2.99
                                                                                                             PHI=    -0.397
                                                                                                             EP =    0.0573

460  TILT TCWARC BEING THCSE          0.55 OF   11      460  IN ALL CASES ARE THOSE           1.00 CF    6            6      0
     WHERE GAMES, IF PRESENT,                                WHERE GAMES, IF PRESENT,                                  5      6
     ARE LIMITED TC                                          ARE NOT LIMITED TO                              XSQ=      2.95
     GAMES CF SKILL CNLY  (67) R-A-B,EA                      GAMES OF SKILL CNLY  (104) R-A-B,EA             PHI=     0.417
                                                                                                             EP =    0.0427

472  DRIFT TCWARD BEING THCSE         0.64 OF   11      472  DRIFT TOWARD BEING THOSE         0.86 CF    7            4      6
     WHERE THE CCMPCSITE NARCISSISM INCEX                    WHERE THE COMPOSITE NARCISSISM INDEX                      7      1
     IS LCW  (43) PES                                        IS HIGH  (47) PES                               XSQ=      2.46
                                                                                                             PHI=    -0.369
                                                                                                             EP =    0.0656

473  TILT TCWARC BEING THCSE          0.82 OF   11      473  TILT TOWARD BEING THOSE          0.86 CF    7            2      6
     WHERE SENSITIVITY TC INSULT                             WHERE SENSITIVITY TO INSULT                               9      1
     IS MCDERATE CR NEGLIGIBLE  (56) PES                     IS EXTREME  (32) PES                            XSQ=      5.40
                                                                                                             PHI=    -0.548
                                                                                                             EP =    0.0128

474  DRIFT TCWARD BEING THCSE         0.64 OF   11      474  DRIFT TOWARD BEING THOSE         0.86 CF    7            4      6
     WHERE BCASTFULNESS IS MCDERATE,                         WHERE BOASTFULNESS IS EXTREME  (41) PES                   7      1
     NEGLIBIBLE, CR UNREPCRTEC  (48) PES                                                                     XSQ=      2.46
                                                                                                             PHI=    -0.369
                                                                                                             EP =    0.0656
```

****

298 CULTURES WHERE THE PCST-PARTUM SEX TABCC LASTS LONGER THAN CNE YEAR, RATHER THAN CNE MCNTH CR LESS (35)	298 CULTURES WHERE THE POST-PARTUM SEX TABCC LASTS ONE MONTH OR LESS, RATHER THAN LONGER THAN ONE YEAR (28)

BACKGROUND ON PAGE 136 | SUBJECT ONLY

....

35 IN LEFT CCLUMN

ABIPCN	AZANDE	BAMILEKE	BIRIFOR	BUNLAP	BURUSHO	CHAMACOCO	CHIR-APACHE	FANG	GANDA
HAIDA	ILA	JIVARC	KATAB	KPE	KURTATCHI	LAU	LESU	MENDE	NUER
NUPE	SAMCANS	SHILLUK	SIUAI	TALLENSI	TENDA	TIV	TRCBRIAND	UTE	WICHITA
WITCTC	WCGEC	WOLCF	YAKO	YAO					

28 IN RIGHT CCLUMN

ALACALUF	AMERICANS	ARANDA	ASHANTI	ATSUGEWI	CARIB	CHENCHU	CHUKCHEE	COCHITI	CROW
DARD	GCND	KAPAUKU	LAMBA	MARQUESANS	MARSHALLESE	MISKITO	MCNGC	MURNGIN	OKINAWANS
PUKAPUKA	SANPOIL	SIRICNC	TANALA	TARAHUMARA	TAREUMIUT	TODA	VEDDA		

62 EXCLUCED BECAUSE IRRELEVANT

AINU	ALCRESE	ARAPESH	ARAUCANIANS	BAMBARA	BEMBA	BLACK CARIB	CALLINAGC	CHAGGA	COORG
CREEK	DIEGUENC	CCRCBC	EGYPTIANS	FON	GOAJIRO	GROS VENTRE	JAPANESE	JAVANESE	KASKA
KERAKI	KIKUYU	KUBA	KUNG	KWAKIUTL	LAPPS	LEPCHA	LUC	MACASSARESE	MASAI
MATACC	PIWCK	MOSSI	NAMA	NAMBICUARA	NANDI	NAVAHO	PCNAPEANS	PURUM	RIFFIANS
RUNDI	RWALA	SAGACA	SAMOYEC	SARSI	SOMALI	TAPIRAPE	TEHUELCHE	TENETEHARA	THONGA
TIMBIRA	TCLCWA	TUBATULABAL	TUCUNA	TWANA	WARRAU	WOLEAIANS	YABARANA	YAGUA	YAHGAN
YAPESE	YUKI								

275 EXCLUDED BECAUSE UNASCERTAINEC

---

3 LEAN LESS TOWARC BEING THCSE LOCATED CUTSICE CF AFRICA (320)	0.51 OF 35	3 LEAN MORE TOWARD BEING THOSE LOCATED OUTSIDE OF AFRICA (320)	0.89 CF 28	17 3 18 25 XSQ= 8.62 PHI= 0.370 XP = 0.0033
5 TILT MCRE TCWARC BEING THCSE LCCATED CUTSIDE CF EAST EURASIA (330)	0.97 OF 35	5 TILT LESS TOWARD BEING THCSE LOCATED OUTSIDE OF EAST EURASIA (330)	0.71 CF 28	1 8 34 20 XSQ= 6.43 PHI= -0.320 XP = 0.0112
15 TILT TCWARD BEING THCSE WHERE THE LATITUCE IS LESS THAN TWENTY DEGREES (217)	0.80 OF 35	15 TILT TOWARD BEING THOSE WHERE THE LATITUDE IS TWENTY DEGREES OR GREATER (183)	0.50 CF 28	7 14 28 14 XSQ= 5.02 PHI= -0.282 XP = 0.0250

44	DRIFT MORE TOWARD BEING THOSE WHERE SETTLEMENTS ARE FIXED (222)	0.77 OF 35	44	DRIFT LESS TOWARD BEING THOSE WHERE SETTLEMENTS ARE FIXED (222)	0.54 OF 28	27 15 8 13 XSQ= 2.90 PHI= 0.215 XP = 0.0885
51	TILT MORE TOWARD BEING THOSE WHERE SUBSISTENCE IS PRIMARILY BY FOOD PRODUCTION -- I. E., AGRICULTURE OR HUSBANDRY -- RATHER THAN BY GATHERING (253)	0.80 OF 35	51	TILT LESS TOWARD BEING THOSE WHERE SUBSISTENCE IS PRIMARILY BY FOOD PRODUCTION -- I. E., AGRICULTURE OR HUSBANDRY -- RATHER THAN BY GATHERING (253)	0.54 OF 28	28 15 7 13 XSQ= 3.87 PHI= 0.248 XP = 0.0492
62	TILT MORE TOWARD BEING THOSE WHERE HUSBANDRY OF SOME KIND IS PRESENT (228)	0.86 OF 35	62	TILT LESS TOWARD BEING THOSE WHERE HUSBANDRY OF SOME KIND IS PRESENT (228)	0.61 OF 28	30 17 5 11 XSQ= 3.90 PHI= 0.249 XP = 0.0484
74	TILT TOWARD BEING THOSE WHERE POTTERY IS PRESENT (145)	0.77 OF 31	74	TILT TOWARD BEING THOSE WHERE POTTERY IS ABSENT (93)	0.52 OF 27	24 13 7 14 XSQ= 4.16 PHI= 0.268 XP = 0.0414
82	TILT MORE TOWARD BEING THOSE WHERE A CITY OR TOWN IS PRESENT, OR THE AVERAGE COMMUNITY SIZE IS FIFTY OR GREATER (178)	0.96 OF 24	82	TILT LESS TOWARD BEING THOSE WHERE A CITY OR TOWN IS PRESENT, OR THE AVERAGE COMMUNITY SIZE IS FIFTY OR GREATER (178)	0.61 OF 23	23 14 1 9 XSQ= 6.61 PHI= 0.375 XP = 0.0101
83	DRIFT LESS TOWARD BEING THOSE WHERE, WITH NO CITY AND NO TOWN PRESENT, THE AVERAGE COMMUNITY SIZE IS SMALLER THAN 200, RATHER THAN BETWEEN 200 AND 999 (135)	0.59 OF 22	83	DRIFT MORE TOWARD BEING THOSE WHERE, WITH NO CITY AND NO TOWN PRESENT, THE AVERAGE COMMUNITY SIZE IS SMALLER THAN 200, RATHER THAN BETWEEN 200 AND 999 (135)	0.90 OF 20	9 2 13 18 XSQ= 3.70 PHI= 0.297 XP = 0.0543
89	DRIFT TOWARD BEING THOSE WHERE, IF A NON-HEREDITARY HEADMANSHIP IS PRESENT, SUCCESSION IS BY MEANS OTHER THAN CONSENSUS (43)	0.70 OF 10	89	DRIFT TOWARD BEING THOSE WHERE, IF A NON-HEREDITARY HEADMANSHIP IS PRESENT, SUCCESSION IS BY CONSENSUS (63)	0.75 OF 12	3 9 7 3 XSQ= 2.82 PHI= -0.358 EP = 0.0836
110	LEAN TOWARD BEING THOSE WHERE SLAVERY IS PRESENT (163)	0.58 OF 33	110	LEAN TOWARD BEING THOSE WHERE SLAVERY IS ABSENT (218)	0.81 OF 27	19 5 14 22 XSQ= 7.88 PHI= 0.362 XP = 0.0050
127	TILT TOWARD BEING THOSE WHERE THE FEMALES' CONTRIBUTION TO SUBSISTENCE IS HIGH (33) JKB	0.90 OF 10	127	TILT TOWARD BEING THOSE WHERE THE FEMALES' CONTRIBUTION TO SUBSISTENCE IS LOW (32) JKB	0.63 OF 8	9 3 1 5 XSQ= 3.40 PHI= 0.435 EP = 0.0430

129	DRIFT TOWARD BEING THOSE WHERE WEAVING IS MAINLY DONE BY MALES (31)	0.82 OF	11	129	DRIFT TOWARD BEING THOSE WHERE WEAVING IS MAINLY DONE BY FEMALES (73)	0.67 OF	9	9 3 2 6 XSQ= 3.04 PHI= 0.390 EP = 0.0648
176	DRIFT TOWARD BEING THOSE WHERE THE COMMUNITY IS A CLAN-COMMUNITY OR A COMMUNITY STRUCTURED OR SEGMENTED ON A CLAN BASIS (169)	0.66 OF	35	176	DRIFT TOWARD BEING THOSE WHERE THE COMMUNITY IS OTHER THAN A CLAN-COMMUNITY OR A COMMUNITY STRUCTURED OR SEGMENTED ON A CLAN BASIS (213)	0.61 OF	28	23 11 12 17 XSQ= 3.37 PHI= 0.231 XP = 0.0662
197	IN ALL CASES ARE THOSE WHERE RULES FOR THE INHERITANCE OF REAL PROPERTY, IF PRESENT, FAVOR EITHER THE MALE HEIR OR LINE, OR THE FEMALE HEIR OR LINE (165)	1.00 OF	16	197	DRIFT LESS TOWARD BEING THOSE WHERE RULES FOR THE INHERITANCE OF REAL PROPERTY, IF PRESENT, FAVOR EITHER THE MALE HEIR OR LINE, OR THE FEMALE HEIR OR LINE (165)	0.73 OF	11	16 8 0 3 XSQ= 2.54 PHI= 0.306 EP = 0.0564
241	IN ALL CASES ARE THOSE WHERE THE FAMILY, IF EXTENDED, IS LARGE OR SMALL, RATHER THAN STEM (187)	1.00 OF	20	241	DRIFT LESS TOWARD BEING THOSE WHERE THE FAMILY, IF EXTENDED, IS LARGE OR SMALL, RATHER THAN STEM (187)	0.81 OF	16	20 13 0 3 XSQ= 2.00 PHI= 0.236 EP = 0.0784
242	TILT MORE TOWARD BEING THOSE WHERE MARRIAGE IS COMMONLY OR OCCASIONALLY POLYGYNOUS, RATHER THAN MONOGAMOUS (314)	0.97 OF	35	242	TILT LESS TOWARD BEING THOSE WHERE MARRIAGE IS COMMONLY OR OCCASIONALLY POLYGYNOUS, RATHER THAN MONOGAMOUS (314)	0.73 OF	26	34 19 1 7 XSQ= 5.62 PHI= 0.303 XP = 0.0178
260	TILT TOWARD BEING THOSE WHERE THE AGE OF MALES AT MARRIAGE IS TWENTY OR OVER (17) JKH	0.54 OF	13	260	IN ALL CASES ARE THOSE WHERE THE AGE OF MALES AT MARRIAGE IS LESS THAN TWENTY (38) JKH	1.00 OF	7	6 7 7 0 XSQ= 3.67 PHI= -0.429 EP = 0.0233
263	TILT TOWARD BEING THOSE WHERE WIVES ARE OBTAINED BY RELATIVELY DIFFICULT MEANS, NAMELY BY BRIDE-PRICE, BRIDE-SERVICE, OR EXCHANGING A FEMALE RELATIVE (233)	0.74 OF	35	263	TILT TOWARD BEING THOSE WHERE WIVES ARE OBTAINED BY RELATIVELY EASY MEANS, NAMELY BY TOKEN BRIDE-PRICE, GIFT EXCHANGE, ABSENCE OF ANY CONSIDERATION, OR RECEIPT OF DOWRY (162)	0.54 OF	28	26 13 9 15 XSQ= 4.01 PHI= 0.252 XP = 0.0453
316	DRIFT TOWARD BEING THOSE WHERE EXCLUSIVE MOTHER-SON SLEEPING ARRANGEMENTS LAST ONE YEAR OR LONGER (19) W-K-A	0.90 OF	10	316	DRIFT TOWARD BEING THOSE WHERE EXCLUSIVE MOTHER-SON SLEEPING ARRANGEMENTS LAST LESS THAN ONE YEAR (25) W-K-A	0.60 OF	5	9 2 1 3 XSQ= 2.09 PHI= 0.373 EP = 0.0769
326	TILT TOWARD BEING THOSE WHERE THE INFERRED TRANSITION ANXIETY BETWEEN INFANCY AND CHILDHOOD IS LOW (35) B-B-C	0.85 OF	13	326	TILT TOWARD BEING THOSE WHERE THE INFERRED TRANSITION ANXIETY BETWEEN INFANCY AND CHILDHOOD IS HIGH (32) B-B-C	0.67 OF	9	2 6 11 3 XSQ= 4.03 PHI= -0.428 EP = 0.0260

342	TILT TOWARD BEING THOSE 0.71 OF 7 WHERE THE CHILD'S INFERRED ANXIETY OVER PERFORMANCE OF NURTURANT BEHAVIOR IS LOW (28) B-B-C	342	IN ALL CASES ARE THOSE 1.00 OF 5 WHERE THE CHILD'S INFERRED ANXIETY OVER PERFORMANCE OF NURTURANT BEHAVIOR IS HIGH (18) B-B-C	2 5 5 0 XSQ= 3.54 PHI= -0.543 EP = 0.0278
369	IN ALL CASES ARE THOSE 1.00 OF 14 WHERE DISSOCIATION OF THE SEXES AT ADOLESCENCE, OR CUSTOMS OF INITIATION AT ADOLESCENCE, ARE PRESENT (42) JKH	369	TILT LESS TOWARD BEING THOSE 0.57 OF 7 WHERE DISSOCIATION OF THE SEXES AT ADOLESCENCE, OR CUSTOMS OF INITIATION AT ADOLESCENCE, ARE PRESENT (42) JKH	14 4 0 3 XSQ= 3.94 PHI= 0.433 EP = 0.0263
370	DRIFT TOWARD BEING THOSE 0.59 OF 27 WHERE THE SEGREGATION OF ADOLESCENT BOYS IS COMPLETE OR PARTIAL (95)	370	DRIFT TOWARD BEING THOSE 0.70 OF 23 WHERE THE SEGREGATION OF ADOLESCENT BOYS IS ABSENT (148)	16 7 11 16 XSQ= 3.07 PHI= 0.248 XP = 0.0795
373	TILT TOWARD BEING THOSE 0.70 OF 10 WHERE MALE INITIATION CEREMONIES AT PUBERTY ARE PRESENT (17) W-K-A	373	IN ALL CASES ARE THOSE 1.00 OF 5 WHERE MALE INITIATION CEREMONIES AT PUBERTY ARE ABSENT (27) W-K-A	7 0 3 5 XSQ= 4.05 PHI= 0.520 EP = 0.0256
377	DRIFT LESS TOWARD BEING THOSE 0.57 OF 35 WHERE MALE GENITAL MUTILATION IS ABSENT (242)	377	DRIFT MORE TOWARD BEING THOSE 0.82 OF 28 WHERE MALE GENITAL MUTILATION IS ABSENT (242)	15 5 20 23 XSQ= 3.41 PHI= 0.233 XP = 0.0649
392	TILT TOWARD BEING THOSE 0.75 OF 24 WHERE PREMARITAL SEX RELATIONS ARE STRONGLY PUNISHED AND IN FACT RARE, OR WEAKLY PUNISHED AND IN FACT NOT RARE, OR PUNISHED ONLY IF PREGNANCY RESULTS (112) JTW,EA	392	TILT TOWARD BEING THOSE 0.65 OF 20 WHERE PREMARITAL SEX RELATIONS ARE FREELY PERMITTED (67) JTW,EA	18 7 6 13 XSQ= 5.58 PHI= 0.356 XP = 0.0182
405	LEAN TOWARD BEING THOSE 0.73 OF 11 WHERE EXPLANATIONS OF ILLNESS OF A DEPENDENCE NATURE ARE ABSENT (27) W-C	405	LEAN TOWARD BEING THOSE 0.90 OF 10 WHERE EXPLANATIONS OF ILLNESS OF A DEPENDENCE NATURE ARE PRESENT (34) W-C	3 9 8 1 XSQ= 6.05 PHI= -0.537 EP = 0.0075
417	IN ALL CASES ARE THOSE 1.00 OF 8 WHERE WARFARE IS PREVALENT (34) LWS	417	DRIFT TOWARD BEING THOSE 0.50 OF 6 WHERE WARFARE IS NOT PREVALENT (9) LWS	8 3 0 3 XSQ= 2.55 PHI= 0.427 EP = 0.0549
419	DRIFT TOWARD BEING THOSE 0.75 OF 16 WHERE MILITARY GLORY IS STRONGLY OR MODERATELY EMPHASIZED (55) PES	419	DRIFT TOWARD BEING THOSE 0.62 OF 13 WHERE MILITARY GLORY IS NEGLIGIBLY EMPHASIZED (31) PES	12 5 4 8 XSQ= 2.58 PHI= 0.299 EP = 0.0667

438	TILT TOWARD BEING THOSE WHERE THIS-WORLDLY FEARS OF HUMANS OR ANIMALS ARE GREATER THAN OTHER-WORLDLY FEARS OF GHOSTS OR SPIRITS (17) W-C,JFG	0.75 OF 8	438	TILT TOWARD BEING THOSE WHERE OTHER-WORLDLY FEARS OF GHOSTS OR SPIRITS ARE GREATER THAN THIS-WORLDLY FEARS OF HUMANS OR ANIMALS (27) W-C,JFG	0.89 OF 9	2 8 6 1	XSQ= 4.74 PHI= -0.528 EP = 0.0152
441	LEAN TOWARD BEING THOSE WHERE FEAR OF HUMAN BEINGS IS HIGH (29) W-C	0.91 OF 11	441	LEAN TOWARD BEING THOSE WHERE FEAR OF HUMAN BEINGS IS LOW (32) W-C	0.80 OF 10	10 2 1 8	XSQ= 8.05 PHI= 0.619 EP = 0.0019
447	TILT TOWARD BEING THOSE WHERE LOVE MAGIC IS PRESENT (20) S-R	0.86 OF 7	447	TILT TOWARD BEING THOSE WHERE LOVE MAGIC IS ABSENT (13) S-R	0.86 OF 7	6 1 1 6	XSQ= 4.57 PHI= 0.571 EP = 0.0291
449	LEAN TOWARD BEING THOSE WHERE THE OBSERVATION OF FOOD TABOOS IS HIGH, RATHER THAN MEDIUM OR LOW (25) JRL	0.67 OF 15	449	LEAN TOWARD BEING THOSE WHERE THE OBSERVATION OF FOOD TABOOS IS MEDIUM OR LOW, RATHER THAN HIGH (61) JRL	0.93 OF 15	10 1 5 14	XSQ= 9.19 PHI= 0.553 EP = 0.0017
472	TILT TOWARD BEING THOSE WHERE THE COMPOSITE NARCISSISM INDEX IS HIGH (47) PES	0.76 OF 17	472	TILT TOWARD BEING THOSE WHERE THE COMPOSITE NARCISSISM INDEX IS LOW (43) PES	0.71 OF 14	13 4 4 10	XSQ= 5.31 PHI= 0.414 EP = 0.0122
473	DRIFT LESS TOWARD BEING THOSE WHERE SENSITIVITY TO INSULT IS MODERATE OR NEGLIGIBLE (56) PES	0.53 OF 17	473	DRIFT MORE TOWARD BEING THOSE WHERE SENSITIVITY TO INSULT IS MODERATE OR NEGLIGIBLE (56) PES	0.86 OF 14	8 2 9 12	XSQ= 2.42 PHI= 0.280 EP = 0.0680

```
****************************************************************************************************

299  CULTURES                                      299  CULTURES
     WHERE THE POST-PARTUM SEX TABOO LASTS               WHERE THE POST-PARTUM SEX TABOO LASTS
     LONGER THAN ONE YEAR  (35)                          ONE YEAR OR LESS  (89)


BACKGROUND ON PAGE 136                                                              PREDICATE ONLY
....................................................................................................

     35  IN LEFT COLUMN

ABIPON      AZANDE      BAMILEKE    BIRIFOR     BUNLAP      BURUSHO     CHAMACOCO   CHIR-APACHE FANG        GANDA
HAIDA       ILA         JIVARO      KATAB       KPE         KURTATCHI   LAU         LESU        MENDE       NUER
NUPE        SAMOANS     SHILLUK     SIUAI       TALLENSI    TENDA       TIV         TROBRIAND   UTE         WICHITA
WITOTO      WOGEO       WOLOF       YAKO        YAO

     89  IN RIGHT COLUMN

AINU        ALACALUF    ALORESE     AMERICANS   ARANDA      ARAPESH     ARAUCANIANS ASHANTI     ATSUGEWI    BAMBARA
BEMBA       BLACK CARIB CALLINAGO   CARIB       CHAGGA      CHENCHU     CHUKCHEE    COCHITI     COORG       CREEK
CROW        DARD        DIEGUENO    DOROBO      EGYPTIANS   FON         GOAJIRO     GOND        GROS VENTRE JAPANESE
JAVANESE    KAPAUKU     KASKA       KERAKI      KIKUYU      KUBA        KUNG        KWAKIUTL    LAMBA       LAPPS
LUO         MACASSARESE MARQUESANS  MARSHALLESE MASAI       MATACO      MISKITO     MIWOK       MONGO       MOSSI
MURNGIN     NAMA        NAMBICUARA  NANDI       NAVAHO      OKINAWANS   PONAPEANS   PUKAPUKA    PURUM       RIFFIANS
RUNDI       RWALA       SACACA      SAMOYED     SANPOIL     SARSI       SIRIONO     SOMALI      TANALA      TAPIRAPE
TARAHUMARA  TAREUMIUT   TEHUELCHE   TENETEHARA  THONGA      TIMBIRA     TODA        TOLOWA      TUBATULABAL TUCUNA
TWANA       VEDDA       WARRAU      WOLEAIANS   YABARANA    YAGUA       YAHGAN      YAPESE      YUKI

      1  EXCLUDED BECAUSE IRRELEVANT

LEPCHA

    275  EXCLUDED BECAUSE UNASCERTAINED

----------------------------------------------------------------------------------------------------
```

```
************************************************************************************************************************

3C0  CULTURES                                           3CC  CULTURES
     WHERE THE POST-PARTUM SEX TABCC LASTS                   WHERE THE POST-PARTUM SEX TABCC LASTS
     LONGER THAN SIX MONTHS  (51)                            SIX MONTHS OR LESS  (73)


BACKGROUND ON PAGE 136                                                                                    PREDICATE ONLY
........................................................................................................................

      51   IN LEFT COLUMN

ABIPON       ALCRESE      ARAPESH      ARAUCANIANS AZANDE      BAMILEKE    BIRIFOR     BUNLAP      BURUSHO     CHAMACOCO
CHIR-APACHE  DIEGUENC     FANG         FON         GANDA       HAIDA       ILA         JIVARC      KATAB       KERAKI
KPE          KURTATCHI    KWAKIUTL     LAU         LESU        MASAI       MATACO      MENDE       MOSSI       NUER
NUPE         SAMCANS      SHILLUK      SIUAI       TALLENSI    TAPIRAPE    TEHUELCHE   TENDA       TIV         TROBRIAND
TUCUNA       UTE          WICHITA      WITOTO      WOGEO       WOLEAIANS   WOLOF       YAGUA       YAKO        YAO
YAPESE

      73   IN RIGHT COLUMN

AINU         ALACALUF     AMERICANS    ARANDA      ASHANTI     ATSUGEWI    BAMBARA     BEMBA       BLACK CARIB CALLINAGO
CARIB        CHAGGA       CHENCHU      CHUKCHEE    COCHITI     COORG       CREEK       CROW        DARC        COROBO
EGYPTIANS    GCAJIRO      GOND         GROS VENTRE JAPANESE    JAVANESE    KAPAUKU     KASKA       KIKUYU      KUBA
KUNG         LAMBA        LAPPS        LUO         MACASSARESE MARQUESANS  MARSHALLESE MISKITO     MIWOK       MONGO
MURNGIN      NAMA         NAMBICUARA   NANDI       NAVAHO      OKINAWANS   PONAPEANS   PUKAPUKA    PURUM       RIFFIANS
RUNDI        RWALA        SAGADA       SAMOYED     SANPOIL     SARSI       SIRIONO     SOMALI      TANALA      TARAHUMARA
TAREUMIUT    TENETEHARA   THONGA       TIMBIRA     TODA        TOLOWA      TUBATULABAL TWANA       VEDDA       WARRAU
YABARANA     YAHGAN       YUKI

      1   EXCLUDED BECAUSE IRRELEVANT

LEPCHA

      275   EXCLUDED BECAUSE UNASCERTAINED

------------------------------------------------------------------------------------------------------------------------
```

301 CULTURES
WHERE THE POST-PARTUM SEX TABOO LASTS
LONGER THAN ONE MONTH (96)

301 CULTURES
WHERE THE POST-PARTUM SEX TABOO LASTS
ONE MONTH OR LESS (28)

BACKGROUND ON PAGE 136

BOTH SUBJECT AND PREDICATE

96 IN LEFT COLUMN

ABIPON	AINU	ALORESE	ARAPESH	ARAUCANIANS	AZANDE	BAMBARA	BAMILEKE	BEMBA	BIRIFOR
BLACK CARIB	BUNLAP	BURUSHO	CALLINAGO	CHAGGA	CHAMACOCO	CHIR-APACHE	COORG	CREEK	DIEGUENO
DOROBO	EGYPTIANS	FANG	FON	GANDA	GOAJIRO	GROS VENTRE	HAIDA	ILA	JAPANESE
JAVANESE	JIVARO	KASKA	KATAB	KERAKI	KIKUYU	KPE	KUBA	KUNG	KURTATCHI
KWAKIUTL	LAPPS	LAU	LESU	LUO	MACASSARESE	MASAI	MATACO	MENDE	MIWOK
MOSSI	NAMA	NAMBICUARA	NANDI	NAVAHO	NUER	NUPE	PONAPEANS	PURUM	RIFFIANS
RUNDI	RWALA	SAGADA	SAMOANS	SAMOYED	SARSI	SHILLUK	SIUAI	SOMALI	TALLENSI
TAPIRAPE	TEHUELCHE	TENDA	TENETEHARA	THONGA	TIMBIRA	TIV	TOLOWA	TROBRIAND	TUBATULABAL
TUCUNA	TWANA	UTE	WARRAU	WICHITA	WITOTO	WOGEO	WOLEAIANS	WOLOF	YABARANA
YAGUA	YAHGAN	YAKO	YAO	YAPESE	YUKI				

28 IN RIGHT COLUMN

ALACALUF	AMERICANS	ARANDA	ASHANTI	ATSUGEWI	CARIB	CHENCHU	CHUKCHEE	COCHITI	CROW
DARD	GOND	KAPAUKU	LAMBA	MARQUESANS	MARSHALLESE	MISKITO	MONGO	MURNGIN	OKINAWANS
PUKAPUKA	SANPOIL	SIRIONO	TANALA	TARAHUMARA	TAREUMIUT	TODA	VEDDA		

1 EXCLUDED BECAUSE IRRELEVANT

LEPCHA

275 EXCLUDED BECAUSE UNASCERTAINED

3	TILT LESS TOWARD BEING THOSE LOCATED OUTSIDE OF AFRICA (320)	0.67 OF 96	3	TILT MORE TOWARD BEING THOSE LOCATED OUTSIDE OF AFRICA (320)	0.89 OF 28	32 3 64 25 XSQ= 4.41 PHI= 0.189 XP = 0.0356
5	LEAN MORE TOWARD BEING THOSE LOCATED OUTSIDE OF EAST EURASIA (330)	0.94 OF 96	5	LEAN LESS TOWARD BEING THOSE LOCATED OUTSIDE OF EAST EURASIA (330)	0.71 OF 28	6 8 90 20 XSQ= 8.67 PHI= -0.264 XP = 0.0032
110	TILT LESS TOWARD BEING THOSE WHERE SLAVERY IS ABSENT (218)	0.58 OF 93	110	TILT MORE TOWARD BEING THOSE WHERE SLAVERY IS ABSENT (218)	0.81 OF 27	39 5 54 22 XSQ= 3.98 PHI= 0.182 XP = 0.0459

197	DRIFT MORE TOWARD BEING THOSE 0.95 OF 41 WHERE RULES FOR THE INHERITANCE OF REAL PROPERTY, IF PRESENT, FAVOR EITHER THE MALE HEIR OR LINE, OR THE FEMALE HEIR OR LINE (165)	197	DRIFT LESS TOWARD BEING THOSE 0.73 OF 11 WHERE RULES FOR THE INHERITANCE OF REAL PROPERTY, IF PRESENT, FAVOR EITHER THE MALE HEIR OR LINE, OR THE FEMALE HEIR OR LINE (165)	39 8 2 3 XSQ= 2.76 PHI= 0.230 XP = 0.0967
201	TILT MORE TOWARD BEING THOSE 0.90 OF 96 WHERE MARITAL RESIDENCE IS NON-OPTIONAL, RATHER THAN AMBILOCAL OR NEOLOCAL (334)	201	TILT LESS TOWARD BEING THOSE 0.71 OF 28 WHERE MARITAL RESIDENCE IS NON-OPTIONAL, RATHER THAN AMBILOCAL OR NEOLOCAL (334)	86 20 10 8 XSQ= 4.39 PHI= 0.188 XP = 0.0362
204	TILT MORE TOWARD BEING THOSE 0.87 OF 79 WHERE MARITAL RESIDENCE IS PATRILOCAL, VIRILOCAL, OR AVUNCULOCAL, RATHER THAN AMBILOCAL OR NEOLOCAL (270)	204	TILT LESS TOWARD BEING THOSE 0.67 OF 24 WHERE MARITAL RESIDENCE IS PATRILOCAL, VIRILOCAL, OR AVUNCULOCAL, RATHER THAN AMBILOCAL OR NEOLOCAL (270)	69 16 10 8 XSQ= 4.12 PHI= 0.200 XP = 0.0425
220	DRIFT MORE TOWARD BEING THOSE 0.76 OF 94 WHERE FIRST COUSIN MARRIAGE IN SOME FORM OR OTHER IS NOT PRESCRIBED OR PREFERRED (273)	220	DRIFT LESS TOWARD BEING THOSE 0.57 OF 28 WHERE FIRST COUSIN MARRIAGE IN SOME FORM OR OTHER IS NOT PRESCRIBED OR PREFERRED (273)	23 12 71 16 XSQ= 2.72 PHI= -0.149 XP = 0.0989
259	TILT TOWARD BEING THOSE 0.76 OF 21 WHERE THE SEVERITY OF MOTHER-IN-LAW AVOIDANCE IS HIGH (26) WNS	259	TILT TOWARD BEING THOSE 0.70 OF 10 WHERE THE SEVERITY OF MOTHER-IN-LAW AVOIDANCE IS LOW (20) WNS	16 3 5 7 XSQ= 4.30 PHI= 0.372 EP = 0.0214
260	TILT LESS TOWARD BEING THOSE 0.54 OF 26 WHERE THE AGE OF MALES AT MARRIAGE IS LESS THAN TWENTY (38) JKH	260	IN ALL CASES ARE THOSE 1.00 OF 7 WHERE THE AGE OF MALES AT MARRIAGE IS LESS THAN TWENTY (38) JKH	14 7 12 0 XSQ= 3.28 PHI= -0.315 EP = 0.0319
263	DRIFT TOWARD BEING THOSE 0.67 OF 96 WHERE WIVES ARE OBTAINED BY RELATIVELY DIFFICULT MEANS, NAMELY BY BRIDE-PRICE, BRIDE-SERVICE, OR EXCHANGING A FEMALE RELATIVE (233)	263	DRIFT TOWARD BEING THOSE 0.54 OF 28 WHERE WIVES ARE OBTAINED BY RELATIVELY EASY MEANS, NAMELY BY TOKEN BRIDE-PRICE, GIFT EXCHANGE, ABSENCE OF ANY CONSIDERATION, OR RECEIPT OF DOWRY (162)	64 13 32 15 XSQ= 2.96 PHI= 0.155 XP = 0.0853
311	DRIFT TOWARD BEING THOSE 0.68 OF 22 WHERE SEXUAL SOCIALIZATION ANXIETY IS HIGH (28) W-C	311	DRIFT TOWARD BEING THOSE 0.70 OF 10 WHERE SEXUAL SOCIALIZATION ANXIETY IS LOW (23) W-C	15 3 7 7 XSQ= 2.67 PHI= 0.289 EP = 0.0623
342	TILT TOWARD BEING THOSE 0.61 OF 18 WHERE THE CHILD'S INFERRED ANXIETY OVER PERFORMANCE OF NURTURANT BEHAVIOR IS LOW (28) B-B-C	342	IN ALL CASES ARE THOSE 1.00 OF 5 WHERE THE CHILD'S INFERRED ANXIETY OVER PERFORMANCE OF NURTURANT BEHAVIOR IS HIGH (18) B-B-C	7 5 11 0 XSQ= 3.66 PHI= -0.399 EP = 0.0373

No.	Statement	Ratio	N	No.	Statement	Ratio	N	Statistics
369	DRIFT MORE TOWARD BEING THOSE WHERE DISSOCIATION OF THE SEXES AT ADOLESCENCE, OR CUSTOMS OF INITIATION AT ADOLESCENCE, ARE PRESENT (42) JKH	0.89 OF	27	369	DRIFT LESS TOWARD BEING THOSE WHERE DISSOCIATION OF THE SEXES AT ADOLESCENCE, OR CUSTOMS OF INITIATION AT ADOLESCENCE, ARE PRESENT (42) JKH	0.57 OF	7	24 4 3 3 XSQ= 1.98 PHI= 0.241 EP = 0.0857
373	DRIFT TOWARD BEING THOSE WHERE MALE INITIATION CEREMONIES AT PUBERTY ARE PRESENT (17) W-K-A	0.52 OF	23	373	IN ALL CASES ARE THOSE WHERE MALE INITIATION CEREMONIES AT PUBERTY ARE ABSENT (27) W-K-A	1.00 OF	5	12 0 11 5 XSQ= 2.68 PHI= 0.310 EP = 0.0525
391	DRIFT TOWARD BEING THOSE WHERE PREMARITAL SEX RELATIONS ARE STRONGLY PUNISHED AND IN FACT RARE, OR WEAKLY PUNISHED AND IN FACT NOT RARE (89) JTW,EA	0.57 OF	65	391	DRIFT TOWARD BEING THOSE WHERE PREMARITAL SEX RELATIONS ARE PUNISHED ONLY IF PREGNANCY RESULTS, OR FREELY PERMITTED (90) JTW,EA	0.70 OF	20	37 6 28 14 XSQ= 3.42 PHI= 0.201 XP = 0.0643
392	LEAN TOWARD BEING THOSE WHERE PREMARITAL SEX RELATIONS ARE STRONGLY PUNISHED AND IN FACT RARE, OR WEAKLY PUNISHED AND IN FACT NOT RARE, OR PUNISHED ONLY IF PREGNANCY RESULTS (112) JTW,EA	0.74 OF	65	392	LEAN TOWARD BEING THOSE WHERE PREMARITAL SEX RELATIONS ARE FREELY PERMITTED (67) JTW,EA	0.65 OF	20	48 7 17 13 XSQ= 8.48 PHI= 0.316 XP = 0.0036
393	DRIFT TOWARD BEING THOSE WHERE EXTRAMARITAL COITUS IS PUNISHED, RATHER THAN PERMITTED (43) F-B	0.62 OF	29	393	DRIFT TOWARD BEING THOSE WHERE EXTRAMARITAL COITUS IS PERMITTED, RATHER THAN PUNISHED (41) F-B	0.71 OF	14	18 4 11 10 XSQ= 3.01 PHI= 0.264 XP = 0.0830
405	TILT TOWARD BEING THOSE WHERE EXPLANATIONS OF ILLNESS OF A DEPENDENCE NATURE ARE ABSENT (27) W-C	0.56 OF	25	405	TILT TOWARD BEING THOSE WHERE EXPLANATIONS OF ILLNESS OF A DEPENDENCE NATURE ARE PRESENT (34) W-C	0.90 OF	10	11 9 14 1 XSQ= 4.44 PHI= -0.356 EP = 0.0220
419	DRIFT TOWARD BEING THOSE WHERE MILITARY GLORY IS STRONGLY OR MODERATELY EMPHASIZED (55) PES	0.72 OF	40	419	DRIFT TOWARD BEING THOSE WHERE MILITARY GLORY IS NEGLIGIBLY EMPHASIZED (31) PES	0.62 OF	13	29 5 11 8 XSQ= 3.57 PHI= 0.260 XP = 0.0587
425	DRIFT TOWARD BEING THOSE WHERE SUPERNATURALS ARE MAINLY AGGRESSIVE, RATHER THAN BENEVOLENT (20) L-T-W	0.80 OF	15	425	DRIFT TOWARD BEING THOSE WHERE SUPERNATURALS ARE MAINLY BENEVOLENT, RATHER THAN AGGRESSIVE (16) L-T-W	0.75 OF	4	3 3 12 1 XSQ= 2.24 PHI= -0.344 EP = 0.0709
441	TILT TOWARD BEING THOSE WHERE FEAR OF HUMAN BEINGS IS HIGH (29) W-C	0.64 OF	25	441	TILT TOWARD BEING THOSE WHERE FEAR OF HUMAN BEINGS IS LOW (32) W-C	0.80 OF	10	16 2 9 8 XSQ= 3.91 PHI= 0.334 EP = 0.0275

```
447  TEND TC BE THCSE              0.93 OF  15     447  TEND TO BE THOSE              0.86 CF   7           14     1
     WHERE LCVE MAGIC IS                                WHERE LOVE MAGIC IS                                  1     6
     PRESENT  (20) S-R                                  ABSENT  (13) S-R                             XSQ=    10.34
                                                                                                     PHI=    0.686
                                                                                                     EP =   0.0006

449  LEAN TOWARC BEING THOSE       0.50 OF  38     449  LEAN TOWARD BEING THOSE       0.93 OF  15          19     1
     WHERE THE CBSERVATICN CF FCOC TABOOS               WHERE THE OBSERVATICN OF FCCD TABOOS                19    14
     IS HIGH, RATHER THAN                               IS MEDIUM OR LOW, RATHER THAN                XSQ=     6.85
     MEDIUM CR LCW  (25) JRL                            HIGH  (61) JRL                               PHI=    0.360
                                                                                                     XP =   0.0089
```

```
302  CULTURES                                           302  CULTURES
     WHERE THE AVERAGE EARLY SATISFACTION                    WHERE THE AVERAGE EARLY SATISFACTICN
     PCTENTIAL IS HIGH  (23) W-C                             POTENTIAL IS LOW  (17) W-C

BACKGROUND ON PAGE 137                                                          BOTH SUBJECT AND PREDICATE

       23  IN LEFT COLUMN

ALORESE     ARAPESH     AZANDE      BALINESE    CHENCHU     COMANCHE    KURTATCHI   LAKHER      LEPCHA      LESU
MANUS       MACRI       NAVAHO      PAPAGO      PUKAPUKA    SIRIONO     TENINO      TETON       THONGA      TROBRIAND
VENDA       WOGEO       YAGUA

       17  IN RIGHT COLUMN

AINU        ASHANTI     CHAGGA      CHIR-APACHE DOBUANS     FON         HANO        KUTENAI     KWAKIUTL    MARQUESANS
ONTONG-JAVA RWALA       SAMOANS     SANPOIL     TANALA      TIKOPIA     YAKUT

      360  EXCLUDED BECAUSE UNASCERTAINED

-----------------------------------------------------------------------------------------------------------------
 12  IN ALL CASES ARE THOSE           1.00 OF  23      12  DRIFT LESS TOWARD BEING THOSE  0.82 OF  17           0    3
     WHERE THE LATITUDE IS                                 WHERE THE LATITUDE IS                              23   14
     LESS THAN FIFTY DEGREES  (367)                        LESS THAN FIFTY DEGREES  (367)               XSQ=     2.21
                                                                                                        PHI=   -0.235
                                                                                                        EP =   0.0688

 46  DRIFT MORE TOWARD BEING THOSE  0.95 OF  20        46  DRIFT LESS TOWARD BEING THOSE  0.69 OF  16           1    5
     OTHER THAN WHERE SETTLEMENTS ARE                      OTHER THAN WHERE SETTLEMENTS ARE                   19   11
     NON-FIXED AND MOVEMENT IS                             NON-FIXED AND MOVEMENT IS                    XSQ=     2.72
     NOMADIC  (260)                                        NOMADIC  (260)                               PHI=   -0.275
                                                                                                        EP =   0.0689

 47  DRIFT TOWARD BEING THOSE        0.80 OF   5       47  DRIFT TOWARD BEING THOSE       0.83 OF   6           1    5
     WHERE, IF SETTLEMENTS ARE NON-FIXED,                  WHERE, IF SETTLEMENTS ARE NON-FIXED,                4    1
     MOVEMENT IS NON-NOMADIC, RATHER THAN                  MOVEMENT IS NOMADIC, RATHER THAN             XSQ=     2.23
     NOMADIC  (38)                                         NON-NOMADIC  (72)                            PHI=   -0.450
                                                                                                        EP =   0.0801

 96  TILT TOWARD BEING THOSE         0.60 OF  20       96  TILT TOWARD BEING THOSE        0.75 OF  16           8   12
     WHERE THE HIERARCHY                                   WHERE THE HIERARCHY                                12    4
     OF NATIONAL JURISDICTION HAS                          OF NATIONAL JURISDICTION HAS                 XSQ=     3.11
     NO LEVELS  (156) GES,EA                               FOUR, THREE, TWO OR                          PHI=   -0.294
                                                           ONE LEVEL  (174) GES,EA                      EP =   0.0485

 97  DRIFT MORE TOWARD BEING THOSE  0.95 OF  20        97  DRIFT LESS TOWARD BEING THOSE  0.69 OF  16           1    5
     WHERE THE HIERARCHY                                   WHERE THE HIERARCHY                                19   11
     OF LOCAL JURISDICTION HAS                             OF LOCAL JURISDICTION HAS                    XSQ=     2.72
     THREE OR TWO LEVELS  (273) GES,EA                     THREE OR TWO LEVELS  (273) GES,EA            PHI=   -0.275
                                                                                                        EP =   0.0689
```

224	IN ALL CASES ARE THOSE WHERE COUSIN MARRIAGE IS PREFERENTIALLY OR PERMISSIVELY EITHER PATRI- OR MATRILATERAL, RATHER THAN SYMMETRICAL (66)	1.00 OF 6	224	LEAN TOWARD BEING THOSE WHERE COUSIN MARRIAGE IS PREFERENTIALLY OR PERMISSIVELY SYMMETRICAL, RATHER THAN EITHER PATRI- OR MATRILATERAL (106)	0.86 OF 7	6 1 0 6 XSQ= 6.41 PHI= 0.702 EP = 0.0047
296	TILT TOWARD BEING THOSE WHERE INFANTICIDE IS ABSENT OR INFERRED ABSENT (15) BCA	0.67 OF 15	296	TILT TOWARD BEING THOSE WHERE INFANTICIDE IS PRESENT (18) BCA	0.82 OF 11	5 9 10 2 XSQ= 4.21 PHI= -0.402 EP = 0.0214
303	LEAN TOWARD BEING THOSE WHERE THE EARLY ORAL SATISFACTION POTENTIAL IS HIGH (32) W-C	0.78 OF 23	303	LEAN TOWARD BEING THOSE WHERE THE EARLY ORAL SATISFACTION POTENTIAL IS LOW (25) W-C	0.76 OF 17	18 4 5 13 XSQ= 9.72 PHI= 0.493 EP = 0.0011
306	LEAN TOWARD BEING THOSE WHERE THE EARLY DEPENDENCE SATISFACTION POTENTIAL IS HIGH (28) W-C	0.74 OF 23	306	LEAN TOWARD BEING THOSE WHERE THE EARLY DEPENDENCE SATISFACTION POTENTIAL IS LOW (24) W-C	0.71 OF 17	17 5 6 12 XSQ= 6.13 PHI= 0.391 EP = 0.0095
307	TILT TOWARD BEING THOSE WHERE THE EARLY AGGRESSION SATISFACTION POTENTIAL IS HIGH (33) W-C	0.78 OF 23	307	TILT TOWARD BEING THOSE WHERE THE EARLY AGGRESSION SATISFACTION POTENTIAL IS LOW (19) W-C	0.59 OF 17	18 7 5 10 XSQ= 4.26 PHI= 0.326 EP = 0.0235
308	TILT TOWARD BEING THOSE WHERE AVERAGE SOCIALIZATION ANXIETY IS LOW (18) W-C	0.61 OF 23	308	TILT TOWARD BEING THOSE WHERE AVERAGE SOCIALIZATION ANXIETY IS HIGH (22) W-C	0.76 OF 17	9 13 14 4 XSQ= 4.10 PHI= -0.320 EP = 0.0267
313	TILT TOWARD BEING THOSE WHERE AGGRESSION SOCIALIZATION ANXIETY IS LOW (28) W-C	0.61 OF 23	313	TILT TOWARD BEING THOSE WHERE AGGRESSION SOCIALIZATION ANXIETY IS HIGH (26) W-C	0.76 OF 17	9 13 14 4 XSQ= 4.10 PHI= -0.320 EP = 0.0267
323	DRIFT LESS TOWARD BEING THOSE WHERE THE CONSTANCY OF PRESENCE OF THE INFANT'S NURTURANT AGENT IS LOW (45) B-B-C	0.52 OF 21	323	DRIFT MORE TOWARD BEING THOSE WHERE THE CONSTANCY OF PRESENCE OF THE INFANT'S NURTURANT AGENT IS LOW (45) B-B-C	0.85 OF 13	10 2 11 11 XSQ= 2.38 PHI= 0.264 EP = 0.0750
329	DRIFT TOWARD BEING THOSE WHERE THE AGE AT TOILET TRAINING IS TWO YEARS OR HIGHER (10) W-C	0.64 OF 14	329	DRIFT TOWARD BEING THOSE WHERE THE AGE AT TOILET TRAINING IS LOWER THAN TWO YEARS (11) W-C	0.86 OF 7	9 1 5 6 XSQ= 2.89 PHI= 0.371 EP = 0.0635

```
330  DRIFT TOWARD BEING THOSE          0.65 OF  20     330  DRIFT TOWARD BEING THOSE          0.73 OF  11         13    3
     WHERE THE AGE OF THE INFANT                            WHERE THE AGE OF THE INFANT                              7    8
     AT TIME OF WEANING                                     AT TIME OF WEANING                                 XSQ=    2.68
     IS 2.5 YEARS OR HIGHER  (34) B-B-C                     IS LOWER THAN 2.5 YEARS  (36) B-B-C                PHI=   0.294
                                                                                                               EP =  0.0659

335  LEAN TOWARD BEING THOSE           0.70 OF  20     335  LEAN TOWARD BEING THOSE           0.82 OF  11         14    2
     WHERE INITIAL INDULGENCE OF DEPENDENCY                 WHERE INITIAL INDULGENCE OF DEPENDENCY               6    9
     IS HIGH  (20) WNS                                      IS LOW  (18) WNS                                   XSQ=    5.70
                                                                                                               PHI=   0.429
                                                                                                               EP =  0.0091

337  TILT TOWARD BEING THOSE           0.65 OF  20     337  TILT TOWARD BEING THOSE           0.77 OF  13          7   10
     WHERE THE CHILD'S INFERRED ANXIETY OVER                WHERE THE CHILD'S INFERRED ANXIETY OVER             13    3
     NON-PERFORMANCE OF RESPONSIBLE BEHAVIOR                NON-PERFORMANCE OF RESPONSIBLE BEHAVIOR            XSQ=    3.99
     IS LOW  (35) B-B-C                                     IS HIGH  (38) B-B-C                                PHI=  -0.348
                                                                                                               EP =  0.0324

353  TILT TOWARD BEING THOSE           0.57 OF  21     353  TILT TOWARD BEING THOSE           0.83 OF  12          9   10
     WHERE THE CHILD-S INFERRED ANXIETY OVER                WHERE THE CHILD'S INFERRED ANXIETY OVER             12    2
     NON-PERFORMANCE OF OBEDIENT BEHAVIOR                   NON-PERFORMANCE OF OBEDIENT BEHAVIOR               XSQ=    3.60
     IS LOW  (32) B-B-C                                     IS HIGH  (42) B-B-C                                PHI=  -0.330
                                                                                                               EP =  0.0328

373  DRIFT TOWARD BEING THOSE          0.77 OF  13     373  DRIFT TOWARD BEING THOSE          0.67 OF   9          3    6
     WHERE MALE INITIATION CEREMONIES                       WHERE MALE INITIATION CEREMONIES                    10    3
     AT PUBERTY ARE ABSENT  (27) W-K-A                      AT PUBERTY ARE PRESENT  (17) W-K-A                 XSQ=    2.57
                                                                                                               PHI=  -0.342
                                                                                                               EP =  0.0789

377  DRIFT MORE TOWARD BEING THOSE     0.85 OF  20     377  DRIFT LESS TOWARD BEING THOSE     0.53 OF  15          3    7
     WHERE MALE GENITAL MUTILATION                          WHERE MALE GENITAL MUTILATION                       17    8
     IS ABSENT  (242)                                       IS ABSENT  (242)                                   XSQ=    2.80
                                                                                                               PHI=  -0.283
                                                                                                               EP =  0.0619

419  DRIFT TOWARD BEING THOSE          0.52 OF  21     419  DRIFT TOWARD BEING THOSE          0.85 OF  13         10   11
     WHERE MILITARY GLORY                                   WHERE MILITARY GLORY                                11    2
     IS NEGLIGIBLY EMPHASIZED  (31) PES                     IS STRONGLY OR                                     XSQ=    3.22
                                                            MODERATELY EMPHASIZED  (55) PES                    PHI=  -0.308
                                                                                                               EP =  0.0672

437  LEAN TOWARD BEING THOSE           0.71 OF  17     437  LEAN TOWARD BEING THOSE           0.83 OF  12          5   10
     WHERE FEAR OF GHOSTS, SPIRITS,                         WHERE FEAR OF GHOSTS, SPIRITS,                      12    2
     HUMANS OR ANIMALS                                      HUMANS OR ANIMALS                                  XSQ=    6.17
     IS LOW  (23) W-C,JFG                                   IS HIGH  (21) W-C,JFG                              PHI=  -0.461
                                                                                                               EP =  0.0078

452  DRIFT TOWARD BEING THOSE          0.58 OF  12     452  DRIFT TOWARD BEING THOSE          0.89 OF   9          5    8
     WHERE TOTEMISM WITH FOOD TABOOS                        WHERE TOTEMISM WITH FOOD TABOOS                      7    1
     IS ABSENT  (24) WNS                                    IS PRESENT  (19) WNS                               XSQ=    3.07
                                                                                                               PHI=  -0.382
                                                                                                               EP =  0.0669
```

303 CULTURES WHERE THE EARLY ORAL SATISFACTION POTENTIAL IS HIGH (32) W-C	303 CULTURES WHERE THE EARLY ORAL SATISFACTION POTENTIAL IS LOW (25) W-C

BACKGROUND ON PAGE 137 — BOTH SUBJECT AND PREDICATE

32 IN LEFT COLUMN

ANDAMANESE	ARAPESH	AZANDE	CHENCHU	COMANCHE	COPR ESKIMO	IFUGAO	KURTATCHI	KUTENAI	LAKHER
LAPPS	LEPCHA	MANUS	MURNGIN	NAVAHO	ONTONG-JAVA	PAPAGO	PUKAPUKA	SANPOIL	SENIANG
SIRIONO	TANALA	TENINO	TETON	THONGA	TROBRIAND	VENDA	WAPISHANA	WARRAU	WITOTO
WOGEO	YUKAGHIR								

25 IN RIGHT COLUMN

AINU	ALORESE	ASHANTI	BALINESE	CHAGGA	CHIR-APACHE	DOBUANS	DUSUN	FON	HANO
JIVARO	KWAKIUTL	LAMBA	LESU	MAORI	MARQUESANS	MARSHALLESE	MASAI	OMAHA	RWALA
SAMOANS	TAOS	TIKOPIA	YAGUA	YAKUT					

343 EXCLUDED BECAUSE UNASCERTAINED

81	DRIFT MORE TOWARD BEING THOSE WHERE NO CITY OR TOWN IS PRESENT, AND THE AVERAGE COMMUNITY SIZE IS SMALLER THAN 200 (135)	0.86 OF 22	81	DRIFT LESS TOWARD BEING THOSE WHERE NO CITY OR TOWN IS PRESENT, AND THE AVERAGE COMMUNITY SIZE IS SMALLER THAN 200 (135)	0.53 OF 15	3 7 / 19 8 / XSQ= 3.40 / PHI= -0.303 / EP = 0.0563
86	TILT TOWARD BEING THOSE WHERE THE LEVEL OF POLITICAL INTEGRATION IS THE AUTONOMOUS COMMUNITY, OR THE FAMILY (156) GPM	0.76 OF 25	86	TILT TOWARD BEING THOSE WHERE THE LEVEL OF POLITICAL INTEGRATION IS THE LARGE STATE, THE LITTLE STATE, OR THE MINIMAL STATE (148) GPM	0.60 OF 20	6 12 / 19 8 / XSQ= 4.59 / PHI= -0.320 / XP = 0.0321
96	LEAN TOWARD BEING THOSE WHERE THE HIERARCHY OF NATIONAL JURISDICTION HAS NO LEVELS (156) GES,EA	0.73 OF 30	96	LEAN TOWARD BEING THOSE WHERE THE HIERARCHY OF NATIONAL JURISDICTION HAS FOUR, THREE, TWO OR ONE LEVEL (174) GES,EA	0.73 OF 22	8 16 / 22 6 / XSQ= 9.06 / PHI= -0.417 / XP = 0.0026
214	DRIFT LESS TOWARD BEING THOSE WHERE FIRST COUSIN MARRIAGE, IF PERMITTED, IS OTHER THAN UNILATERAL (144)	0.67 OF 9	214	IN ALL CASES ARE THOSE WHERE FIRST COUSIN MARRIAGE, IF PERMITTED, IS OTHER THAN UNILATERAL (144)	1.00 OF 10	3 0 / 6 10 / XSQ= 1.85 / PHI= 0.312 / EP = 0.0867

```
296  TILT TOWARD BEING THOSE          0.65 OF  17     296  TILT TOWARD BEING THOSE          0.75 OF  16         6   12
     WHERE INFANTICIDE                                     WHERE INFANTICIDE                                     11    4
     IS ABSENT OR INFERRED ABSENT  (15) BCA                IS PRESENT  (18) BCA                           XSQ=      3.76
                                                                                                          PHI=    -0.338
                                                                                                          EP  =   0.0366

302  LEAN TOWARD BEING THOSE          0.82 OF  22     302  LEAN TOWARD BEING THOSE          0.72 OF  18        18    5
     WHERE THE AVERAGE EARLY SATISFACTION                  WHERE THE AVERAGE EARLY SATISFACTION                   4   13
     POTENTIAL IS HIGH  (23) W-C                           POTENTIAL IS LOW  (17) W-C                     XSQ=      9.72
                                                                                                          PHI=     0.493
                                                                                                          EP  =   0.0011

306  LEAN TOWARD BEING THOSE          0.73 OF  30     306  LEAN TOWARD BEING THOSE          0.71 OF  21        22    6
     WHERE THE EARLY DEPENDENCE SATISFACTION               WHERE THE EARLY DEPENDENCE SATISFACTION                8   15
     POTENTIAL IS HIGH  (28) W-C                           POTENTIAL IS LOW  (24) W-C                     XSQ=      8.27
                                                                                                          PHI=     0.403
                                                                                                          XP  =   0.0040

309  TILT TOWARD BEING THOSE          0.67 OF  30     309  TILT TOWARD BEING THOSE          0.70 OF  23        10   16
     WHERE ORAL SOCIALIZATION ANXIETY                      WHERE ORAL SOCIALIZATION ANXIETY                      20    7
     IS LOW  (27) W-C                                      IS HIGH  (26) W-C                              XSQ=      5.47
                                                                                                          PHI=    -0.321
                                                                                                          XP  =   0.0194

321  TILT TOWARD BEING THOSE          0.72 OF  18     321  TILT TOWARD BEING THOSE          0.67 OF  18        13    6
     WHERE THE IMMEDIACY OF REDUCTION                      WHERE THE IMMEDIACY OF REDUCTION                       5   12
     OF THE INFANT'S DRIVES                                OF THE INFANT'S DRIVES                         XSQ=      4.01
     IS HIGH  (35) B-B-C                                   IS LOW  (25) B-B-C                             PHI=     0.334
                                                                                                          EP  =   0.0437

323  TILT TOWARD BEING THOSE          0.52 OF  21     323  TILT TOWARD BEING THOSE          0.85 OF  20        11    3
     WHERE THE CONSTANCY OF PRESENCE                       WHERE THE CONSTANCY OF PRESENCE                       10   17
     OF THE INFANT'S NURTURANT AGENT                       OF THE INFANT'S NURTURANT AGENT                XSQ=      4.81
     IS HIGH  (29) B-B-C                                   IS LOW  (45) B-B-C                             PHI=     0.343
                                                                                                          XP  =   0.0283

330  TILT TOWARD BEING THOSE          0.70 OF  20     330  TILT TOWARD BEING THOSE          0.67 OF  18        14    6
     WHERE THE AGE OF THE INFANT                           WHERE THE AGE OF THE INFANT                            6   12
     AT TIME OF WEANING                                    AT TIME OF WEANING                             XSQ=      3.74
     IS 2.5 YEARS OR HIGHER  (34) B-B-C                    IS LOWER THAN 2.5 YEARS  (36) B-B-C            PHI=     0.314
                                                                                                          EP  =   0.0496

335  TILT TOWARD BEING THOSE          0.68 OF  25     335  TILT TOWARD BEING THOSE          0.77 OF  13        17    3
     WHERE INITIAL INDULGENCE OF DEPENDENCY                WHERE INITIAL INDULGENCE OF DEPENDENCY                 8   10
     IS HIGH  (20) WNS                                     IS LOW  (18) WNS                               XSQ=      5.24
                                                                                                          PHI=     0.371
                                                                                                          EP  =   0.0156

373  DRIFT TOWARD BEING THOSE         0.83 OF  12     373  DRIFT TOWARD BEING THOSE         0.57 OF  14         2    8
     WHERE MALE INITIATION CEREMONIES                      WHERE MALE INITIATION CEREMONIES                      10    6
     AT PUBERTY ARE ABSENT  (27) W-K-A                     AT PUBERTY ARE PRESENT  (17) W-K-A             XSQ=      2.93
                                                                                                          PHI=    -0.335
                                                                                                          EP  =   0.0511
```

430	TILT TOWARD BEING THOSE WHERE SUPERNATURAL SANCTIONS FOR MORALITY, HAVING AN EFFECT ON AN INDIVIDUAL'S HEALTH, ARE PRESENT (16) GES	0.83 OF 6	430	IN ALL CASES ARE THOSE WHERE SUPERNATURAL SANCTIONS FOR MORALITY, HAVING AN EFFECT ON AN INDIVIDUAL'S HEALTH, ARE ABSENT OR UNREPORTED (22) GES	1.00 OF 3	5 0 1 3 XSQ= 2.76 PHI= 0.553 EP = 0.0476
473	LEAN TOWARD BEING THOSE WHERE SENSITIVITY TO INSULT IS MODERATE OR NEGLIGIBLE (56) PES	0.84 OF 25	473	LEAN TOWARD BEING THOSE WHERE SENSITIVITY TO INSULT IS EXTREME (32) PES	0.58 OF 19	4 11 21 8 XSQ= 6.67 PHI= -0.389 XP = 0.0098
480	TILT TOWARD BEING THOSE WHERE COMPLEXITY OF ARTISTIC DESIGN IS LOW (15) HB	0.82 OF 11	480	TILT TOWARD BEING THOSE WHERE COMPLEXITY OF ARTISTIC DESIGN IS HIGH (14) HB	0.63 OF 16	2 10 9 6 XSQ= 3.55 PHI= -0.362 EP = 0.0473

```
304  CULTURES                                          304  CULTURES
     WHERE THE EARLY ANAL SATISFACTION                      WHERE THE EARLY ANAL SATISFACTION
     POTENTIAL IS HIGH  (19) W-C                            POTENTIAL IS LOW  (22) W-C


BACKGROUND ON PAGE 137                                                           BOTH SUBJECT AND PREDICATE
.........................................................................................................

      19  IN LEFT COLUMN

AINU        ALORESE     CHENCHU     COMANCHE    KUTENAI     KWAKIUTL    LESU        MAORI       MARQUESANS  NAVAHO
PAPAGO      RWALA       SIRIONO     TENINO      TETON       TIKOPIA     WOGEO       YAGUA       YAKUT

      22  IN RIGHT COLUMN

ARAPESH     ASHANTI     AZANDE      BALINESE    CHAGGA      CHIR-APACHE DOBUANS     FON         HANO        KURTATCHI
LAKHER      LEPCHA      MANUS       ONTONG-JAVA PUKAPUKA    SAMOANS     SANPOIL     TANALA      THONGA      TROBRIAND
VENDA       YUKAGHIR

     359  EXCLUDED BECAUSE UNASCERTAINED

---------------------------------------------------------------------------------------------------------
  3  IN ALL CASES ARE THOSE          1.00 OF  19        3  TILT LESS TOWARD BEING THOSE   0.73 OF  22          0     6
     LOCATED OUTSIDE OF                                    LOCATED OUTSIDE OF                                  19    16
     AFRICA  (320)                                         AFRICA  (320)                                 XSQ=     4.08
                                                                                                         PHI=   -0.316
                                                                                                         XP =   0.0433

 14  TILT TOWARD BEING THOSE         0.58 OF  19       14  TILT TOWARD BEING THOSE        0.82 OF  22         11     4
     WHERE THE LATITUDE IS                                 WHERE THE LATITUDE IS                                8    18
     THIRTY DEGREES OR GREATER  (119)                      LESS THAN THIRTY DEGREES  (281)               XSQ=     5.32
                                                                                                         PHI=    0.360
                                                                                                         XP =   0.0210

 51  LEAN TOWARD BEING THOSE         0.79 OF  19       51  LEAN TOWARD BEING THOSE        0.77 OF  22          4    17
     WHERE SUBSISTENCE IS PRIMARILY BY                     WHERE SUBSISTENCE IS PRIMARILY BY                   15     5
     FOOD GATHERING -- I. E., HUNTING,                     FOOD PRODUCTION -- I. E., AGRICULTURE         XSQ=    10.75
     FISHING, OR COLLECTING -- RATHER THAN                 OR HUSBANDRY -- RATHER THAN BY                PHI=   -0.512
     FOOD PRODUCTION  (147)                                GATHERING  (253)                              XP =   0.0010

 54  LEAN TOWARD BEING THOSE         0.63 OF   8       54  IN ALL CASES ARE THOSE         1.00 OF  15          3    15
     WHERE FOOD PRODUCTION IS BY                           WHERE FOOD PRODUCTION IS BY                          5     0
     INCIPIENT FOOD PRODUCTION, RATHER THAN BY             INTENSIVE OR SIMPLE                           XSQ=     8.59
     INTENSIVE OR SIMPLE AGRICULTURE  (46)                 AGRICULTURE, RATHER THAN BY                   PHI=   -0.611
                                                           INCIPIENT FOOD PRODUCTION  (192)              EP =   0.0017

 56  LEAN TOWARD BEING THOSE         0.63 OF   8       56  IN ALL CASES ARE THOSE         1.00 OF  10          3    10
     WHERE FOOD PRODUCTION IS BY                           WHERE FOOD PRODUCTION IS BY                          5     0
     INCIPIENT FOOD PRODUCTION, RATHER THAN BY             SIMPLE AGRICULTURE, RATHER THAN BY            XSQ=     5.82
     SIMPLE AGRICULTURE  (46)                              INCIPIENT FOOD PRODUCTION  (101)              PHI=   -0.569
                                                                                                         EP =   0.0065
```

77	TILT TOWARD BEING THOSE 0.60 OF 5 WHERE THE WRITING SYSTEM IS ALPHABETIC-OR-PHONETIC, RATHER THAN BEING MNEMONIC OR ABSENT (15) JMH	77	IN ALL CASES ARE THOSE 1.00 OF 7 WHERE THE WRITING SYSTEM IS MNEMONIC OR ABSENT, RATHER THAN BEING ALPHABETIC-OR-PHONETIC (39) JMH	3 0 2 7 XSQ= 2.86 PHI= 0.488 EP = 0.0455
184	DRIFT TOWARD BEING THOSE 0.55 OF 11 WHERE THE LARGEST NON-COGNATIC KIN GROUP IS THE MOEITY OR PHRATRY (77)	184	DRIFT TOWARD BEING THOSE 0.81 OF 16 WHERE THE LARGEST NON-COGNATIC KIN GROUP IS SMALLER THAN A PHRATRY, I. E. A SIB OR LINEAGE (175)	6 3 5 13 XSQ= 2.32 PHI= 0.293 EP = 0.0969
277	DRIFT TOWARD BEING THOSE 0.71 OF 7 WHERE THE STATUS OF WOMEN IS INFERIOR OR SUBJECTED (14) LWS	277	IN ALL CASES ARE THOSE 1.00 OF 4 WHERE THE STATUS OF WOMEN IS NOT STRONGLY INFERIOR OR SUBJECTED (22) LWS	5 0 2 4 XSQ= 2.75 PHI= 0.500 EP = 0.0606
310	LEAN TOWARD BEING THOSE 0.74 OF 19 WHERE ANAL SOCIALIZATION ANXIETY IS LOW (19) W-C	310	LEAN TOWARD BEING THOSE 0.77 OF 22 WHERE ANAL SOCIALIZATION ANXIETY IS HIGH (22) W-C	5 17 14 5 XSQ= 8.70 PHI= -0.461 XP = 0.0032
314	IN ALL CASES ARE THOSE 1.00 OF 13 WHERE THE INCIDENCE OF MOTHER-CHILD HOUSEHOLDS IS LOW (61) W-C,S	314	LEAN LESS TOWARD BEING THOSE 0.56 OF 18 WHERE THE INCIDENCE OF MOTHER-CHILD HOUSEHOLDS IS LOW (61) W-D,S	0 8 13 10 XSQ= 5.64 PHI= -0.427 EP = 0.0096
337	DRIFT TOWARD BEING THOSE 0.67 OF 15 WHERE THE CHILD'S INFERRED ANXIETY OVER NON-PERFORMANCE OF RESPONSIBLE BEHAVIOR IS LOW (35) B-B-C	337	DRIFT TOWARD BEING THOSE 0.67 OF 18 WHERE THE CHILD'S INFERRED ANXIETY OVER NON-PERFORMANCE OF RESPONSIBLE BEHAVIOR IS HIGH (38) B-B-C	5 12 10 6 XSQ= 2.43 PHI= -0.271 EP = 0.0844
346	DRIFT TOWARD BEING THOSE 0.75 OF 16 WHERE THE CHILD'S INFERRED ANXIETY OVER PERFORMANCE OF SELF-RELIANT BEHAVIOR IS LOW (39) B-B-C	346	DRIFT TOWARD BEING THOSE 0.56 OF 18 WHERE THE CHILD'S INFERRED ANXIETY OVER PERFORMANCE OF SELF-RELIANT BEHAVIOR IS HIGH (37) B-B-C	4 10 12 8 XSQ= 2.13 PHI= -0.250 EP = 0.0921
353	TILT TOWARD BEING THOSE 0.63 OF 16 WHERE THE CHILD-S INFERRED ANXIETY OVER NON-PERFORMANCE OF OBEDIENT BEHAVIOR IS LOW (32) B-B-C	353	TILT TOWARD BEING THOSE 0.76 OF 17 WHERE THE CHILD'S INFERRED ANXIETY OVER NON-PERFORMANCE OF OBEDIENT BEHAVIOR IS HIGH (42) B-B-C	6 13 10 4 XSQ= 3.65 PHI= -0.333 EP = 0.0366
370	TILT TOWARD BEING THOSE 0.87 OF 15 WHERE THE SEGREGATION OF ADOLESCENT BOYS IS ABSENT (148)	370	TILT TOWARD BEING THOSE 0.56 OF 18 WHERE THE SEGREGATION OF ADOLESCENT BOYS IS COMPLETE OR PARTIAL (95)	2 10 13 8 XSQ= 4.61 PHI= -0.374 EP = 0.0272

```
458  TILT TOWARD BEING THOSE          0.93 OF  15      458  TILT TOWARD BEING THOSE          0.50 OF  16             1     8
     WHERE GAMES, IF PRESENT,                               WHERE GAMES, IF PRESENT,                                   14     8
     DO NOT INCLUDE                                         INCLUDE GAMES OF STRATEGY  (52) R-A-B,EA          XSQ=     5.11
     GAMES OF STRATEGY  (119) R-A-B,EA                                                                       PHI=   -0.406
                                                                                                             EP =   0.0155

469  TILT TOWARD BEING THOSE          0.60 OF   5      469  IN ALL CASES ARE THOSE           1.00 OF   7             2     7
     WHERE CONTACT WITH OTHER CULTURES                      WHERE CONTACT WITH OTHER CULTURES                          3     0
     IS IRREGULAR, RATHER THAN                              IS FREQUENT OR REGULAR, RATHER THAN               XSQ=     2.86
     FREQUENT OR REGULAR  (11) JMH                          IRREGULAR  (43) JMH                               PHI=   -0.488
                                                                                                             EP =   0.0455

476  DRIFT TOWARD BEING THOSE         0.75 OF   4      476  DRIFT TOWARD BEING THOSE         0.80 OF  10             3     2
     WHERE THE DEGREE OF INSOBRIETY IS                      WHERE THE DEGREE OF INSOBRIETY IS                          1     8
     STRONG  (31) DH                                        MODERATE OR SLIGHT  (18) DH                       XSQ=     1.75
                                                                                                             PHI=    0.354
                                                                                                             EP =   0.0949
```

****

305 CULTURES WHERE THE EARLY SEXUAL SATISFACTION POTENTIAL IS HIGH (27) W-C	305 CULTURES WHERE THE EARLY SEXUAL SATISFACTION POTENTIAL IS LOW (24) W-C

BACKGROUND ON PAGE 137   BOTH SUBJECT AND PREDICATE

....

27 IN LEFT COLUMN

AINU	ALORESE	ANDAMANESE	ARAPESH	BALINESE	CHAGGA	CHENCHU	COMANCHE	IFUGAO	KURTATCHI
LAKHER	LAMBA	LEPCHA	LESU	MARQUESANS	MARSHALLESE	MASAI	MURNGIN	PUKAPUKA	SANPOIL
SIRIONO	TIKOPIA	TIV	TROBRIAND	WOGEO	YAGUA	YAKUT			

24 IN RIGHT COLUMN

ABIPON	ASHANTI	AZANDE	CHIR-APACHE	DOBUANS	FON	HANO	KUTENAI	KWAKIUTL	MANUS
MAORI	NAVAHO	ONTONG-JAVA	PAPAGO	RWALA	SAMOANS	SENIANG	TANALA	TENINO	TETON
THONGA	VENDA	WAPISHANA	WITOTO						

349 EXCLUDED BECAUSE UNASCERTAINED

8	TILT MORE TOWARD BEING THOSE LOCATED OUTSIDE OF NORTH AMERICA (330)	0.93 OF 27	8	TILT LESS TOWARD BEING THOSE LOCATED OUTSIDE OF NORTH AMERICA (330)	0.67 OF 24	2 8 25 16 XSQ= 3.90 PHI= -0.276 XP = 0.0483
15	TILT TOWARD BEING THOSE WHERE THE LATITUDE IS LESS THAN TWENTY DEGREES (217)	0.78 OF 27	15	TILT TOWARD BEING THOSE WHERE THE LATITUDE IS TWENTY DEGREES OR GREATER (183)	0.58 OF 24	6 14 21 10 XSQ= 5.52 PHI= -0.329 XP = 0.0188
45	TILT TOWARD BEING THOSE WHERE SETTLEMENTS, IF FIXED, ARE NON-COMPACT, RATHER THAN COMPACT (73)	0.50 OF 18	45	TILT TOWARD BEING THOSE WHERE SETTLEMENTS, IF FIXED, ARE COMPACT, RATHER THAN NON-COMPACT (149)	0.93 OF 14	9 13 9 1 XSQ= 4.89 PHI= -0.391 EP = 0.0189
73	DRIFT TOWARD BEING THOSE WHERE WEAVING IS ABSENT (130)	0.73 OF 22	73	DRIFT TOWARD BEING THOSE WHERE WEAVING IS PRESENT (118)	0.58 OF 19	6 11 16 8 XSQ= 2.78 PHI= -0.260 XP = 0.0956

82	DRIFT LESS TOWARD BEING THOSE 0.70 OF 20 WHERE A CITY OR TOWN IS PRESENT, OR THE AVERAGE COMMUNITY SIZE IS FIFTY OR GREATER (178)	82	IN ALL CASES ARE THOSE 1.00 OF 12 WHERE A CITY OR TOWN IS PRESENT, OR THE AVERAGE COMMUNITY SIZE IS FIFTY OR GREATER (178)		14 12 6 0 XSQ= 2.68 PHI= -0.289 EP = 0.0613
97	DRIFT MORE TOWARD BEING THOSE 0.96 OF 25 WHERE THE HIERARCHY OF LOCAL JURISDICTION HAS THREE OR TWO LEVELS (273) GES,EA	97	DRIFT LESS TOWARD BEING THOSE 0.73 OF 22 WHERE THE HIERARCHY OF LOCAL JURISDICTION HAS THREE OR TWO LEVELS (273) GES,EA		1 6 24 16 XSQ= 3.33 PHI= -0.266 XP = 0.0679
143	LEAN TOWARD BEING THOSE 0.75 OF 8 WHERE THE RATIO OF RESTITUTIVE TO REPRESSIVE SANCTIONS IS HIGH (20) WME	143	IN ALL CASES ARE THOSE 1.00 OF 7 WHERE THE RATIO OF RESTITUTIVE TO REPRESSIVE SANCTIONS IS MEDIUM OR LOW (32) WME		6 0 2 7 XSQ= 5.90 PHI= 0.627 EP = 0.0070
149	DRIFT TOWARD BEING THOSE 0.73 OF 15 WHERE THE INCIDENCE OF THEFT IS LOW (19) B-B-C	149	DRIFT TOWARD BEING THOSE 0.67 OF 12 WHERE THE INCIDENCE OF THEFT IS HIGH (18) B-B-C		4 8 11 4 XSQ= 2.85 PHI= -0.325 EP = 0.0574
308	TEND TO BE THOSE 0.75 OF 20 WHERE AVERAGE SOCIALIZATION ANXIETY IS LOW (18) W-C	308	TEND TO BE THOSE 0.85 OF 20 WHERE AVERAGE SOCIALIZATION ANXIETY IS HIGH (22) W-C		5 17 15 3 XSQ= 12.22 PHI= -0.553 EP = 0.0003
311	TEND TO BE THOSE 0.74 OF 27 WHERE SEXUAL SOCIALIZATION ANXIETY IS LOW (23) W-C	311	TEND TO BE THOSE 0.87 OF 23 WHERE SEXUAL SOCIALIZATION ANXIETY IS HIGH (28) W-C		7 20 20 3 XSQ= 16.25 PHI= -0.570 XP = 0.0001
313	TEND TO BE THOSE 0.78 OF 27 WHERE AGGRESSION SOCIALIZATION ANXIETY IS LOW (28) W-C	313	TEND TO BE THOSE 0.76 OF 21 WHERE AGGRESSION SOCIALIZATION ANXIETY IS HIGH (26) W-C		6 16 21 5 XSQ= 11.77 PHI= -0.495 XP = 0.0006
348	DRIFT TOWARD BEING THOSE 0.64 OF 14 WHERE THE TOTAL POSITIVE PRESSURE TOWARD DEVELOPING ACHIEVEMENT BEHAVIOR IN THE CHILD IS LOW (31) B-B-C	348	DRIFT TOWARD BEING THOSE 0.73 OF 15 WHERE THE TOTAL POSITIVE PRESSURE TOWARD DEVELOPING ACHIEVEMENT BEHAVIOR IN THE CHILD IS HIGH (32) B-B-C		5 11 9 4 XSQ= 2.76 PHI= -0.309 EP = 0.0656
349	LEAN TOWARD BEING THOSE 0.64 OF 14 WHERE THE CHILD'S INFERRED ANXIETY OVER NON-PERFORMANCE OF ACHIEVEMENT BEHAVIOR IS LOW (28) B-B-C	349	LEAN TOWARD BEING THOSE 0.87 OF 15 WHERE THE CHILD'S INFERRED ANXIETY OVER NON-PERFORMANCE OF ACHIEVEMENT BEHAVIOR IS HIGH (34) B-B-C		5 13 9 2 XSQ= 5.97 PHI= -0.454 EP = 0.0078

No.		No.		
350	LEAN TOWARD BEING THOSE 0.77 OF 13 WHERE THE CHILD'S INFERREC ANXIETY OVER PERFCRMANCE OF ACHIEVEMENT BEHAVIOR IS LCW (26) B-B-C	350	LEAN TOWARD BEING THOSE 0.87 OF 15 WHERE THE CHILD'S INFERRED ANXIETY OVER PERFORMANCE OF ACHIEVEMENT BEHAVIOR IS HIGH (34) B-B-C	3 13 10 2 XSQ= 9.05 PHI= -0.568 EP = 0.0016
351	LEAN TCWARD BEING THOSE 0.85 OF 13 WHERE THE CHILD'S INFERREC CONFLICT REGARDING ACHIEVEMENT BEHAVIOR IS LCW (34) B-B-C	351	LEAN TOWARD BEING THOSE 0.73 OF 15 WHERE THE CHILD'S INFERRED CONFLICT REGARDING ACHIEVEMENT BEHAVIOR IS HIGH (26) B-B-C	2 11 11 4 XSQ= 7.22 PHI= -0.508 EP = 0.0032
352	TILT TCWARD BEING THOSE 0.61 OF 23 WHERE THE TOTAL POSITIVE PRESSURE TOWARD DEVELCPING OBEDIENT BEHAVIOR IN THE CHILD IS LCW (28) B-B-C	352	TILT TOWARD BEING THOSE 0.80 OF 15 WHERE THE TOTAL POSITIVE PRESSURE TOWARC DEVELOPING OBEDIENT BEHAVICR IN THE CHILD IS HIGH (44) B-B-C	9 12 14 3 XSQ= 4.59 PHI= -0.348 EP = 0.0202
390	IN ALL CASES ARE THOSE 1.00 OF 21 WHERE PREMARITAL SEX RELATIONS ARE WEAKLY PUNISHED ANC IN FACT NOT RARE OR PUNISHED CNLY IF PREGNANCY RESULTS, OR FREELY PERMITTEC (132) JTW,EA	390	TEND LESS TO BE THOSE 0.58 OF 19 WHERE PREMARITAL SEX RELATIONS ARE WEAKLY PUNISHED AND IN FACT NOT RARE OR PUNISHED ONLY IF PREGNANCY RESULTS, OR FREELY PERMITTED (132) JTW,EA	0 8 21 11 XSQ= 8.58 PHI= -0.463 EP = 0.0010
391	LEAN TCWARD BEING THOSE 0.86 OF 21 WHERE PREMARITAL SEX RELATIONS ARE PUNISHED CNLY IF PREGNANCY RESULTS, OR FREELY PERMITTEC (90) JTW,EA	391	LEAN TOWARD BEING THOSE 0.58 OF 19 WHERE PREMARITAL SEX RELATICNS ARE STRONGLY PUNISHED AND IN FACT RARE, OR WEAKLY PUNISHED AND IN FACT NOT RARE (89) JTW,EA	3 11 18 8 XSQ= 6.53 PHI= -0.404 EP = 0.0072
392	TILT TCWARD BEING THOSE 0.62 OF 21 WHERE PREMARITAL SEX RELATIONS ARE FREELY PERMITTEC (67) JTW,EA	392	TILT TOWARD BEING THOSE 0.74 OF 19 WHERE PREMARITAL SEX RELATIONS ARE STRONGLY PUNISHED AND IN FACT RARE, OR WEAKLY PUNISHED AND IN FACT NOT RARE, OR PUNISHED ONLY IF PREGNANCY RESULTS (112) JTW,EA	8 14 13 5 XSQ= 3.77 PHI= -0.307 EP = 0.0309
393	DRIFT TCWARD BEING THOSE 0.59 OF 17 WHERE EXTRAMARITAL COITUS IS PERMITTED, RATHER THAN PUNISHED (41) F-B	393	DRIFT TOWARD BEING THOSE 0.76 OF 17 WHERE EXTRAMARITAL COITUS IS PUNISHED, RATHER THAN PERMITTED (43) F-B	7 13 10 4 XSQ= 3.04 PHI= -0.299 EP = 0.0799
398	DRIFT TCWARD BEING THCSE 0.61 OF 18 WHERE THE INTENSITY OF SEX ANXIETY IS LCW (16) WNS	398	DRIFT TOWARD BEING THOSE 0.75 OF 12 WHERE THE INTENSITY OF SEX ANXIETY IS HIGH (16) WNS	7 9 11 3 XSQ= 2.46 PHI= -0.286 EP = 0.0717
400	TILT TCWARD BEING THCSE 0.79 OF 14 WHERE HCMCSEXUAL ACTIVITY IS PRCHIBITED (22) F-B	400	TILT TOWARD BEING THOSE 0.69 OF 13 WHERE HOMOSEXUAL ACTIVITY IS PERMITTED (36) F-B	11 4 3 9 XSQ= 4.45 PHI= 0.406 EP = 0.0213

417	DRIFT TOWARD BEING THOSE WHERE WARFARE IS NOT PREVALENT (9) LWS	0.50 OF 4	417	IN ALL CASES ARE THOSE WHERE WARFARE IS PREVALENT (34) LWS	1.00 OF 11	2 11 2 0 XSQ= 2.76 PHI= -0.429 EP = 0.0571
419	TILT TOWARD BEING THOSE WHERE MILITARY GLORY IS NEGLIGIBLY EMPHASIZED (31) PES	0.50 OF 24	419	TILT TOWARD BEING THOSE WHERE MILITARY GLORY IS STRONGLY OR MODERATELY EMPHASIZED (55) PES	0.88 OF 17	12 15 12 2 XSQ= 4.88 PHI= -0.345 XP = 0.0272
445	DRIFT TOWARD BEING THOSE WHERE SORCERY IS UNIMPORTANT (23) BBW,DH	0.58 OF 12	445	DRIFT TOWARD BEING THOSE WHERE SORCERY IS IMPORTANT (26) BBW,DH	0.89 OF 9	5 8 7 1 XSQ= 3.07 PHI= -0.382 EP = 0.0669
447	TILT TOWARD BEING THOSE WHERE LOVE MAGIC IS ABSENT (13) S-R	0.55 OF 22	447	TILT TOWARD BEING THOSE WHERE LOVE MAGIC IS PRESENT (20) S-R	0.90 OF 10	10 9 12 1 XSQ= 3.96 PHI= -0.352 EP = 0.0237
455	TILT TOWARD BEING THOSE WHERE THE MODE OF THE INDIVIDUAL'S CONTACT WITH THE DIVINE IS NOT CONDUCIVE TO THE DEVELOPMENT OF THE INDIVIDUAL'S NEED TO ACHIEVE (19) DCM	0.89 OF 9	455	TILT TOWARD BEING THOSE WHERE THE MODE OF THE INDIVIDUAL'S CONTACT WITH THE DIVINE IS CONDUCIVE TO THE DEVELOPMENT OF THE INDIVIDUAL'S NEED TO ACHIEVE (17) DCM	0.63 OF 8	1 5 8 3 XSQ= 2.91 PHI= -0.413 EP = 0.0498
459	TILT TOWARD BEING THOSE WHERE GAMES, IF PRESENT, DO NOT INCLUDE GAMES OF CHANCE (89) R-A-B,EA	0.85 OF 20	459	TILT TOWARD BEING THOSE WHERE GAMES, IF PRESENT, INCLUDE GAMES OF CHANCE (82) R-A-B,EA	0.55 OF 20	3 11 17 9 XSQ= 5.38 PHI= -0.367 EP = 0.0187

306 CULTURES
WHERE THE EARLY DEPENDENCE SATISFACTION
POTENTIAL IS HIGH (28) W-C

306 CULTURES
WHERE THE EARLY DEPENDENCE SATISFACTION
POTENTIAL IS LOW (24) W-C

BACKGROUND ON PAGE 137

BOTH SUBJECT AND PREDICATE

28 IN LEFT COLUMN

ANDAMANESE	ARAPESH	AZANDE	CHAGGA	CHENCHU	COMANCHE	COPR ESKIMO	DUSUN	FON	KURTATCHI
LAPPS	LESU	MACRI	MURNGIN	NAVAHO	ONTONG-JAVA	PAPAGO	PUKAPUKA	SANPOIL	SIRIONO
TANALA	TENINO	TETON	TROBRIAND	VENDA	WAPISHANA	WOGEO	YAGUA		

24 IN RIGHT COLUMN

ABIPON	AINU	ALORESE	ASHANTI	BALINESE	CHIR-APACHE	DOBUANS	HANO	IFUGAO	KUTENAI
KWAKIUTL	LAKHER	LEPCHA	MANUS	MARQUESANS	MARSHALLESE	RWALA	SAMOANS	SENIANG	TAOS
THONGA	TIKOPIA	WITOTO	YAKUT						

348 EXCLUDED BECAUSE UNASCERTAINED

62	DRIFT TOWARD BEING THOSE WHERE HUSBANDRY OF ANY KIND IS ABSENT (172)	0.54 OF 28	62	DRIFT TOWARD BEING THOSE WHERE HUSBANDRY OF SOME KIND IS PRESENT (228)	0.75 OF 24	13 18 15 6 XSQ= 3.28 PHI= -0.251 XP = 0.0703
82	TILT LESS TOWARD BEING THOSE WHERE A CITY OR TOWN IS PRESENT, OR THE AVERAGE COMMUNITY SIZE IS FIFTY OR GREATER (178)	0.65 OF 20	82	IN ALL CASES ARE THOSE WHERE A CITY OR TOWN IS PRESENT, OR THE AVERAGE COMMUNITY SIZE IS FIFTY OR GREATER (178)	1.00 OF 13	13 13 7 0 XSQ= 3.87 PHI= -0.342 EP = 0.0266
102	DRIFT TOWARD BEING THOSE WHERE CLASS STRATIFICATION IS ABSENT (180)	0.57 OF 28	102	DRIFT TOWARD BEING THOSE WHERE CLASS STRATIFICATION IS PRESENT (203)	0.71 OF 24	12 17 16 7 XSQ= 3.04 PHI= -0.242 XP = 0.0810
198	DRIFT TOWARD BEING THOSE WHERE RULES FOR THE INHERITANCE OF REAL PROPERTY, IF PRESENT, FAVOR THE MALE HEIR OR LINE, RATHER THAN THE FEMALE (144)	0.91 OF 11	198	DRIFT TOWARD BEING THOSE WHERE RULES FOR THE INHERITANCE OF REAL PROPERTY, IF PRESENT, FAVOR THE FEMALE HEIR OR LINE, RATHER THAN THE MALE (21)	0.50 OF 6	10 3 1 3 XSQ= 1.70 PHI= 0.316 EP = 0.0987

No.	Statement	Proportion	N	No.	Statement	Proportion	N	Statistics
214	DRIFT LESS TOWARD BEING THOSE WHERE FIRST COUSIN MARRIAGE, IF PERMITTED, IS OTHER THAN UNILATERAL (144)	0.63 OF	8	214	IN ALL CASES ARE THOSE WHERE FIRST COUSIN MARRIAGE, IF PERMITTED, IS OTHER THAN UNILATERAL (144)	1.00 OF	9	3 0 5 9 XSQ= 1.92 PHI= 0.336 EP = 0.0824
243	TILT TOWARD BEING THOSE WHERE POLYGYNY, IF PRESENT, HAS A HIGH INCIDENCE (24) W-C,S	0.56 OF	16	243	TILT TOWARD BEING THOSE WHERE POLYGYNY, IF PRESENT, HAS A LOW INCIDENCE (36) W-D,S	0.91 OF	11	9 1 7 10 XSQ= 4.36 PHI= 0.402 EP = 0.0183
284	DRIFT TOWARD BEING THOSE WHERE CONTRACEPTION IS PRACTICED (10) CSF	0.83 OF	6	284	DRIFT TOWARD BEING THOSE WHERE CONTRACEPTION IS NOT PRACTICED (7) CSF	0.80 OF	5	5 1 1 4 XSQ= 2.23 PHI= 0.450 EP = 0.0801
302	LEAN TOWARD BEING THOSE WHERE THE AVERAGE EARLY SATISFACTION POTENTIAL IS HIGH (23) W-C	0.77 OF	22	302	LEAN TOWARD BEING THOSE WHERE THE AVERAGE EARLY SATISFACTION POTENTIAL IS LOW (17) W-C	0.67 OF	18	17 6 5 12 XSQ= 6.13 PHI= 0.391 EP = 0.0095
303	LEAN TOWARD BEING THOSE WHERE THE EARLY ORAL SATISFACTION POTENTIAL IS HIGH (32) W-C	0.79 OF	28	303	LEAN TOWARD BEING THOSE WHERE THE EARLY ORAL SATISFACTION POTENTIAL IS LOW (25) W-C	0.65 OF	23	22 8 6 15 XSQ= 8.27 PHI= 0.403 XP = 0.0040
317	DRIFT TOWARD BEING THOSE WHERE DISPLAY OF AFFECTION TOWARD THE INFANT IS HIGH (39) B-B-C	0.70 OF	20	317	DRIFT TOWARD BEING THOSE WHERE DISPLAY OF AFFECTION TOWARD THE INFANT IS LOW (29) B-B-C	0.64 OF	14	14 5 6 9 XSQ= 2.66 PHI= 0.280 EP = 0.0800
320	DRIFT TOWARD BEING THOSE WHERE THE DEGREE OF REDUCTION OF THE INFANT'S DRIVES IS HIGH (45) B-B-C	0.75 OF	20	320	DRIFT TOWARD BEING THOSE WHERE THE DEGREE OF REDUCTION OF THE INFANT'S DRIVES IS LOW (24) B-B-C	0.56 OF	16	15 7 5 9 XSQ= 2.46 PHI= 0.261 EP = 0.0874
323	TILT TOWARD BEING THOSE WHERE THE CONSTANCY OF PRESENCE OF THE INFANT'S NURTURANT AGENT IS HIGH (29) B-B-C	0.50 OF	22	323	TILT TOWARD BEING THOSE WHERE THE CONSTANCY OF PRESENCE OF THE INFANT'S NURTURANT AGENT IS LOW (45) B-B-C	0.87 OF	15	11 2 11 13 XSQ= 3.78 PHI= 0.319 EP = 0.0353
335	IN ALL CASES ARE THOSE WHERE INITIAL INDULGENCE OF DEPENDENCY IS HIGH (20) WNS	1.00 OF	20	335	IN ALL CASES ARE THOSE WHERE INITIAL INDULGENCE OF DEPENDENCY IS LOW (18) WNS	1.00 OF	18	20 0 0 18 XSQ= 34.09 PHI= 0.947 EP = 0.0000

337	DRIFT TOWARD BEING THOSE 0.60 OF 20 WHERE THE CHILD'S INFERRED ANXIETY OVER NON-PERFORMANCE OF RESPONSIBLE BEHAVIOR IS LOW (35) B-B-C	337	DRIFT TOWARD BEING THOSE 0.73 OF 15 WHERE THE CHILD'S INFERRED ANXIETY OVER NON-PERFORMANCE OF RESPONSIBLE BEHAVIOR IS HIGH (38) B-B-C	8 11 12 4 XSQ= 2.61 PHI= -0.273 EP = 0.0866
356	TILT TOWARD BEING THOSE 0.79 OF 14 WHERE NEITHER ADOLESCENT PEER GROUPS NOR PAIRS ARE PRESENT IN A SETTING OF COURTSHIP (22) JKH	356	TILT TOWARD BEING THOSE 0.70 OF 10 WHERE ADOLESCENT PEER GROUPS OR PAIRS ARE PRESENT IN A SETTING OF COURTSHIP (29) JKH	3 7 11 3 XSQ= 3.84 PHI= -0.400 EP = 0.0351
360	DRIFT TOWARD BEING THOSE 0.90 OF 10 WHERE ADOLESCENT PEER GROUPS ARE PRESENT ONLY IN A SETTING OF LEISURE, OR ELSE ARE ABSENT (23) JKH	360	DRIFT TOWARD BEING THOSE 0.60 OF 5 WHERE ADOLESCENT PEER GROUPS ARE PRESENT IN A SETTING OF WORK AND PUBLIC GATHERINGS AND LEISURE, OR AT LEAST OF PUBLIC GATHERINGS AND LEISURE (14) JKH	1 3 9 2 XSQ= 2.09 PHI= -0.373 EP = 0.0769
368	TILT TOWARD BEING THOSE 0.73 OF 11 WHERE DISSOCIATION OF THE SEXES AT ADOLESCENCE IS HIGH OR MEDIUM (16) JKH	368	TILT TOWARD BEING THOSE 0.83 OF 6 WHERE DISSOCIATION OF THE SEXES AT ADOLESCENCE IS LOW (21) JKH	8 1 3 5 XSQ= 2.91 PHI= 0.413 EP = 0.0498
393	LEAN TOWARD BEING THOSE 0.71 OF 17 WHERE EXTRAMARITAL COITUS IS PERMITTED, RATHER THAN PUNISHED (41) F-B	393	LEAN TOWARD BEING THOSE 0.78 OF 18 WHERE EXTRAMARITAL COITUS IS PUNISHED, RATHER THAN PERMITTED (43) F-B	5 14 12 4 XSQ= 6.41 PHI= -0.428 EP = 0.0067
421	DRIFT TOWARD BEING THOSE 0.74 OF 23 WHERE KILLING, TORTURING, OR MUTILATING OF THE ENEMY IS NEGLIGIBLY EMPHASIZED (47) PES	421	DRIFT TOWARD BEING THOSE 0.59 OF 17 WHERE KILLING, TORTURING, OR MUTILATING OF THE ENEMY IS STRONGLY OR MODERATELY EMPHASIZED (37) PES	6 10 17 7 XSQ= 3.11 PHI= -0.279 EP = 0.0531
424	TILT TOWARD BEING THOSE 0.78 OF 9 WHERE RELIGIOUS SPECIALISTS ARE PART-TIME, RATHER THAN FULL-TIME (33) JMH	424	TILT TOWARD BEING THOSE 0.83 OF 6 WHERE RELIGIOUS SPECIALISTS ARE FULL-TIME, RATHER THAN PART-TIME (21) JMH	2 5 7 1 XSQ= 3.23 PHI= -0.464 EP = 0.0406
473	DRIFT MORE TOWARD BEING THOSE 0.83 OF 23 WHERE SENSITIVITY TO INSULT IS MODERATE OR NEGLIGIBLE (56) PES	473	DRIFT LESS TOWARD BEING THOSE 0.53 OF 19 WHERE SENSITIVITY TO INSULT IS MODERATE OR NEGLIGIBLE (56) PES	4 9 19 10 XSQ= 3.08 PHI= -0.271 XP = 0.0790

307 CULTURES
WHERE THE EARLY AGGRESSION SATISFACTION
POTENTIAL IS HIGH (33) W-C

307 CULTURES
WHERE THE EARLY AGGRESSION SATISFACTION
POTENTIAL IS LOW (19) W-C

BACKGROUND ON PAGE 137

BOTH SUBJECT AND PREDICATE

33 IN LEFT COLUMN

ALORESE	AZANDE	BALINESE	CHAGGA	CHENCHU	COMANCHE	COPR ESKIMO	DUSUN	IFUGAO	KURTATCHI
KUTENAI	LAKHER	LAMBA	MANUS	MAORI	MARQUESANS	MARSHALLESE	MASAI	MURNGIN	ONTONG-JAVA
PUKAPUKA	RWALA	SAMOANS	SIRIONO	TENINO	TETON	THONGA	TIKOPIA	TIV	TROBRIAND
VENDA	WOGEO	YAGUA							

19 IN RIGHT COLUMN

AINU	ANDAMANESE	ARAPESH	ASHANTI	CHIR-APACHE	DOBUANS	FON	HANO	JIVARO	KWAKIUTL
LEPCHA	LESU	NAVAHO	OMAHA	PAPAGO	SANPOIL	TANALA	YAKUT	ZUNI	

348 EXCLUDED BECAUSE UNASCERTAINED

6	TILT LESS TOWARD BEING THOSE LOCATED OUTSIDE OF THE INSULAR PACIFIC (330)	0.52 OF 33	6	TILT MORE TOWARD BEING THOSE LOCATED OUTSIDE OF THE INSULAR PACIFIC (330)	0.84 OF 19	16 3 / 17 16 / XSQ= 4.24 / PHI= 0.285 / XP = 0.0395
8	DRIFT MORE TOWARD BEING THOSE LOCATED OUTSIDE OF NORTH AMERICA (330)	0.85 OF 33	8	DRIFT LESS TOWARD BEING THOSE LOCATED OUTSIDE OF NORTH AMERICA (330)	0.58 OF 19	5 8 / 28 11 / XSQ= 3.35 / PHI= -0.254 / XP = 0.0674
14	TILT TOWARD BEING THOSE WHERE THE LATITUDE IS LESS THAN THIRTY DEGREES (281)	0.79 OF 33	14	TILT TOWARD BEING THOSE WHERE THE LATITUDE IS THIRTY DEGREES OR GREATER (119)	0.53 OF 19	7 10 / 26 9 / XSQ= 4.08 / PHI= -0.280 / XP = 0.0435
15	TILT TOWARD BEING THOSE WHERE THE LATITUDE IS LESS THAN TWENTY DEGREES (217)	0.70 OF 33	15	TILT TOWARD BEING THOSE WHERE THE LATITUDE IS TWENTY DEGREES OR GREATER (183)	0.63 OF 19	10 12 / 23 7 / XSQ= 4.07 / PHI= -0.280 / XP = 0.0436

33	DRIFT MORE TOWARD BEING THOSE 0.91 OF 33 WHERE THE NATURAL ENVIRONMENT IS OTHER THAN 'VERY HARSH,' I.E., DESERT, DESERT GRASSES AND SHRUBS, TUNDRA, OR HIGH PLATEAU STEPPE (341) FWM	33	DRIFT LESS TOWARD BEING THOSE 0.68 OF 19 WHERE THE NATURAL ENVIRONMENT IS OTHER THAN 'VERY HARSH,' I.E., DESERT, DESERT GRASSES AND SHRUBS, TUNDRA, OR HIGH PLATEAU STEPPE (341) FWM	3 6 30 13 XSQ= 2.83 PHI= -0.233 XP = 0.0923
56	TILT TOWARD BEING THOSE 0.93 OF 14 WHERE FOOD PRODUCTION IS BY SIMPLE AGRICULTURE, RATHER THAN BY INCIPIENT FOOD PRODUCTION (101)	56	TILT TOWARD BEING THOSE 0.50 OF 8 WHERE FOOD PRODUCTION IS BY INCIPIENT FOOD PRODUCTION, RATHER THAN BY SIMPLE AGRICULTURE (46)	13 4 1 4 XSQ= 3.16 PHI= 0.379 EP = 0.0393
73	TILT TOWARD BEING THOSE 0.73 OF 26 WHERE WEAVING IS ABSENT (130)	73	TILT TOWARD BEING THOSE 0.73 OF 15 WHERE WEAVING IS PRESENT (118)	7 11 19 4 XSQ= 6.54 PHI= -0.399 XP = 0.0105
88	LEAN TOWARD BEING THOSE 0.80 OF 25 WHERE, IF A HEADMANSHIP IS PRESENT, SUCCESSION IS HEREDITARY (165)	88	LEAN TOWARD BEING THOSE 0.67 OF 15 WHERE, IF A HEADMANSHIP IS PRESENT, SUCCESSION IS NON-HEREDITARY (106)	5 10 20 5 XSQ= 6.83 PHI= -0.413 EP = 0.0062
102	DRIFT TOWARD BEING THOSE 0.61 OF 33 WHERE CLASS STRATIFICATION IS PRESENT (203)	102	DRIFT TOWARD BEING THOSE 0.68 OF 19 WHERE CLASS STRATIFICATION IS ABSENT (180)	20 6 13 13 XSQ= 2.99 PHI= 0.240 XP = 0.0840
207	DRIFT TOWARD BEING THOSE 0.83 OF 12 WHERE MARITAL RESIDENCE IS AMBILOCAL OR NEOLOCAL, RATHER THAN MATRILOCAL OR UXORILOCAL (64)	207	DRIFT TOWARD BEING THOSE 0.63 OF 8 WHERE MARITAL RESIDENCE IS MATRILOCAL OR UXORILOCAL, RATHER THAN AMBILOCAL OR NEOLOCAL (64)	2 5 10 3 XSQ= 2.65 PHI= -0.364 EP = 0.0623
224	LEAN TOWARD BEING THOSE 0.82 OF 11 WHERE COUSIN MARRIAGE IS PREFERENTIALLY OR PERMISSIVELY EITHER PATRI- OR MATRILATERAL, RATHER THAN SYMMETRICAL (66)	224	IN ALL CASES ARE THOSE 1.00 OF 6 WHERE COUSIN MARRIAGE IS PREFERENTIALLY OR PERMISSIVELY SYMMETRICAL, RATHER THAN EITHER PATRI- OR MATRILATERAL (106)	9 0 2 6 XSQ= 7.41 PHI= 0.660 EP = 0.0023
236	TILT TOWARD BEING THOSE 0.67 OF 33 WHERE THE FAMILY IS OF AN INDEPENDENT TYPE, RATHER THAN AN EXTENDED TYPE (185)	236	TILT TOWARD BEING THOSE 0.68 OF 19 WHERE THE FAMILY IS OF AN EXTENDED TYPE, RATHER THAN AN INDEPENDENT TYPE (213)	11 13 22 6 XSQ= 4.64 PHI= -0.299 XP = 0.0311
240	LEAN TOWARD BEING THOSE 0.82 OF 11 WHERE THE FAMILY, IF EXTENDED, IS LARGE, RATHER THAN SMALL OR STEM (78)	240	LEAN TOWARD BEING THOSE 0.85 OF 13 WHERE THE FAMILY, IF EXTENDED, IS SMALL OR STEM, RATHER THAN LARGE (135)	9 2 2 11 XSQ= 8.09 PHI= 0.580 EP = 0.0031

260	DRIFT LESS TOWARD BEING THOSE WHERE THE AGE OF MALES AT MARRIAGE IS LESS THAN TWENTY (38) JKH	0.56 OF 18	260	DRIFT MORE TOWARD BEING THOSE WHERE THE AGE OF MALES AT MARRIAGE IS LESS THAN TWENTY (38) JKH	0.90 OF 10	10 9 8 1 XSQ= 2.10 PHI= -0.274 EP = 0.0980
302	TILT TOWARD BEING THOSE WHERE THE AVERAGE EARLY SATISFACTION POTENTIAL IS HIGH (23) W-C	0.72 OF 25	302	TILT TOWARD BEING THOSE WHERE THE AVERAGE EARLY SATISFACTION POTENTIAL IS LOW (17) W-C	0.67 OF 15	18 5 7 10 XSQ= 4.26 PHI= 0.326 EP = 0.0235
313	TEND TO BE THOSE WHERE AGGRESSION SOCIALIZATION ANXIETY IS LOW (28) W-C	0.73 OF 33	313	TEND TO BE THOSE WHERE AGGRESSION SOCIALIZATION ANXIETY IS HIGH (26) W-C	0.84 OF 19	9 16 24 3 XSQ= 13.46 PHI= -0.509 XP = 0.0002
319	DRIFT TOWARD BEING THOSE WHERE PROTECTION OF THE INFANT FROM ENVIRONMENTAL DISCOMFORTS IS LOW (30) B-B-C	0.60 OF 20	319	DRIFT TOWARD BEING THOSE WHERE PROTECTION OF THE INFANT FROM ENVIRONMENTAL DISCOMFORTS IS HIGH (35) B-B-C	0.73 OF 15	8 11 12 4 XSQ= 2.61 PHI= -0.273 EP = 0.0866
352	TILT TOWARD BEING THOSE WHERE THE TOTAL POSITIVE PRESSURE TOWARD DEVELOPING OBEDIENT BEHAVIOR IN THE CHILD IS LOW (28) B-B-C	0.59 OF 27	352	TILT TOWARD BEING THOSE WHERE THE TOTAL POSITIVE PRESSURE TOWARD DEVELOPING OBEDIENT BEHAVIOR IN THE CHILD IS HIGH (44) B-B-C	0.79 OF 14	11 11 16 3 XSQ= 3.89 PHI= -0.308 XP = 0.0485
353	LEAN TOWARD BEING THOSE WHERE THE CHILD-S INFERRED ANXIETY OVER NON-PERFORMANCE OF OBEDIENT BEHAVIOR IS LOW (32) B-B-C	0.56 OF 27	353	LEAN TOWARD BEING THOSE WHERE THE CHILD'S INFERRED ANXIETY OVER NON-PERFORMANCE OF OBEDIENT BEHAVIOR IS HIGH (42) B-B-C	0.93 OF 14	12 13 15 1 XSQ= 7.16 PHI= -0.418 XP = 0.0075
356	TILT TOWARD BEING THOSE WHERE ADOLESCENT PEER GROUPS OR PAIRS ARE PRESENT IN A SETTING OF COURTSHIP (29) JKH	0.69 OF 16	356	TILT TOWARD BEING THOSE WHERE NEITHER ADOLESCENT PEER GROUPS NOR PAIRS ARE PRESENT IN A SETTING OF COURTSHIP (22) JKH	0.89 OF 9	11 1 5 8 XSQ= 5.53 PHI= 0.470 EP = 0.0112
403	DRIFT TOWARD BEING THOSE WHERE EXPLANATIONS OF ILLNESS OF AN ANAL NATURE ARE ABSENT (38) W-C	0.70 OF 33	403	DRIFT TOWARD BEING THOSE WHERE EXPLANATIONS OF ILLNESS OF AN ANAL NATURE ARE PRESENT (23) W-C	0.58 OF 19	10 11 23 8 XSQ= 2.75 PHI= -0.230 XP = 0.0971
405	DRIFT TOWARD BEING THOSE WHERE EXPLANATIONS OF ILLNESS OF A DEPENDENCE NATURE ARE PRESENT (34) W-C	0.67 OF 33	405	DRIFT TOWARD BEING THOSE WHERE EXPLANATIONS OF ILLNESS OF A DEPENDENCE NATURE ARE ABSENT (27) W-C	0.63 OF 19	22 7 11 12 XSQ= 3.22 PHI= 0.249 XP = 0.0726

437	TILT TOWARD BEING THOSE WHERE FEAR OF GHOSTS, SPIRITS, HUMANS OR ANIMALS IS LOW (23) W-C,JFG	0.65 OF 20	437	TILT TOWARD BEING THOSE WHERE FEAR OF GHOSTS, SPIRITS, HUMANS OR ANIMALS IS HIGH (21) W-C,JFG	0.76 OF 17	7 13 13 4 XSQ= 4.80 PHI= -0.360 EP = 0.0202
442	TILT TOWARD BEING THOSE WHERE FEAR OF ANIMAL SPIRITS IS LOW (33) W-C	0.67 OF 33	442	TILT TOWARD BEING THOSE WHERE FEAR OF ANIMAL SPIRITS IS HIGH (28) W-C	0.68 OF 19	11 13 22 6 XSQ= 4.64 PHI= -0.299 XP = 0.0311
453	TILT TOWARD BEING THOSE WHERE THE ROLE OF RELIGIOUS EXPERTS IS CONDUCIVE TO THE DEVELOPMENT OF THE INDIVIDUAL'S NEED TO ACHIEVE (13) DCM	0.50 OF 10	453	IN ALL CASES ARE THOSE WHERE THE ROLE OF RELIGIOUS EXPERTS IS NOT CONDUCIVE TO THE DEVELOPMENT OF THE INDIVIDUAL'S NEED TO ACHIEVE (23) DCM	1.00 OF 7	5 0 5 7 XSQ= 2.84 PHI= 0.409 EP = 0.0441
472	DRIFT TOWARD BEING THOSE WHERE THE COMPOSITE NARCISSISM INDEX IS HIGH (47) PES	0.65 OF 26	472	DRIFT TOWARD BEING THOSE WHERE THE COMPOSITE NARCISSISM INDEX IS LOW (43) PES	0.67 OF 18	17 6 9 12 XSQ= 3.19 PHI= 0.269 XP = 0.0741
474	TILT TOWARD BEING THOSE WHERE BOASTFULNESS IS EXTREME (41) PES	0.58 OF 26	474	TILT TOWARD BEING THOSE WHERE BOASTFULNESS IS MODERATE, NEGLIBIBLE, OR UNREPORTED (48) PES	0.78 OF 18	15 4 11 14 XSQ= 4.10 PHI= 0.305 XP = 0.0428
475	DRIFT TOWARD BEING THOSE WHERE EXHIBITIONISTIC DANCING IS STRONGLY OR MODERATELY EMPHASIZED (48) PES	0.72 OF 25	475	DRIFT TOWARD BEING THOSE WHERE EXHIBITIONISTIC DANCING IS NEGLIGIBLY EMPHASIZED (38) PES	0.59 OF 17	18 7 7 10 XSQ= 2.81 PHI= 0.259 XP = 0.0935

308 CULTURES WHERE AVERAGE SOCIALIZATION ANXIETY IS HIGH (22) W-C

308 CULTURES WHERE AVERAGE SOCIALIZATION ANXIETY IS LOW (18) W-C

BACKGROUND ON PAGE 138

BOTH SUBJECT AND PREDICATE

22 IN LEFT COLUMN

ALORESE, ARAPESH, ASHANTI, AZANDE, CHAGGA, CHIR-APACHE, DOBUANS, FON, HANO, KUTENAI, KWAKIUTL, LESU, MANUS, MAORI, NAVAHO, ONTONG-JAVA, RWALA, SAMOANS, SANPOIL, TANALA, TENINO, THONGA

18 IN RIGHT COLUMN

AINU, BALINESE, CHENCHU, COMANCHE, KURTATCHI, LAKHER, LEPCHA, MARQUESANS, PAPAGO, PUKAPUKA, SIRIONO, TETON, TIKOPIA, TROBRIAND, VENDA, WOGEO, YAGUA, YAKUT

360 EXCLUDED BECAUSE UNASCERTAINED

	Left column (high)		Right column (low)	Statistics
5	DRIFT MORE TOWARD BEING THOSE LOCATED OUTSIDE OF EAST EURASIA (330) — 0.95 OF 22	5	DRIFT LESS TOWARD BEING THOSE LOCATED OUTSIDE OF EAST EURASIA (330) — 0.72 OF 18	1 5 / 21 13 / XSQ= 2.57 / PHI= -0.253 / EP = 0.0734
82	IN ALL CASES ARE THOSE WHERE A CITY OR TOWN IS PRESENT, OR THE AVERAGE COMMUNITY SIZE IS FIFTY OR GREATER (178) — 1.00 OF 15	82	DRIFT LESS TOWARD BEING THOSE WHERE A CITY OR TOWN IS PRESENT, OR THE AVERAGE COMMUNITY SIZE IS FIFTY OR GREATER (178) — 0.75 OF 12	15 9 / 0 3 / XSQ= 2.07 / PHI= 0.277 / EP = 0.0752
97	TILT LESS TOWARD BEING THOSE WHERE THE HIERARCHY OF LOCAL JURISDICTION HAS THREE OR TWO LEVELS (273) GES,EA — 0.71 OF 21	97	IN ALL CASES ARE THOSE WHERE THE HIERARCHY OF LOCAL JURISDICTION HAS THREE OR TWO LEVELS (273) GES,EA — 1.00 OF 15	6 0 / 15 15 / XSQ= 3.29 / PHI= 0.302 / EP = 0.0304
149	DRIFT TOWARD BEING THOSE WHERE THE INCIDENCE OF THEFT IS HIGH (18) B-B-C — 0.64 OF 14	149	DRIFT TOWARD BEING THOSE WHERE THE INCIDENCE OF THEFT IS LOW (19) B-B-C — 0.75 OF 12	9 3 / 5 9 / XSQ= 2.59 / PHI= 0.315 / EP = 0.0618
181	IN ALL CASES ARE THOSE WHERE THE COMMUNITY IS OTHER THAN A DEME (337) — 1.00 OF 22	181	DRIFT LESS TOWARD BEING THOSE WHERE THE COMMUNITY IS OTHER THAN A DEME (337) — 0.83 OF 18	0 3 / 22 15 / XSQ= 1.93 / PHI= -0.219 / EP = 0.0826

213	TILT TOWARD BEING THOSE WHERE FIRST COUSIN MARRIAGE IS NOT PERMITTED (198)	0.82 OF 22	213	TILT TOWARD BEING THOSE WHERE FIRST COUSIN MARRIAGE IS PERMITTED (172)	0.50 OF 18	4 9 18 9 XSQ= 3.23 PHI= -0.284 EP = 0.0458
221	IN ALL CASES ARE THOSE WHERE MATRILATERAL CROSS-COUSIN MARRIAGE IS NOT PRESCRIBED OR PREFERRED (335)	1.00 OF 22	221	TILT LESS TOWARD BEING THOSE WHERE MATRILATERAL CROSS-COUSIN MARRIAGE IS NOT PRESCRIBED OR PREFERRED (335)	0.78 OF 18	0 4 22 14 XSQ= 3.24 PHI= -0.285 EP = 0.0335
302	TILT TOWARD BEING THOSE WHERE THE AVERAGE EARLY SATISFACTION POTENTIAL IS LOW (17) W-C	0.59 OF 22	302	TILT TOWARD BEING THOSE WHERE THE AVERAGE EARLY SATISFACTION POTENTIAL IS HIGH (23) W-C	0.78 OF 18	9 14 13 4 XSQ= 4.10 PHI= -0.320 EP = 0.0267
305	TEND TO BE THOSE WHERE THE EARLY SEXUAL SATISFACTION POTENTIAL IS LOW (24) W-C	0.77 OF 22	305	TEND TO BE THOSE WHERE THE EARLY SEXUAL SATISFACTION POTENTIAL IS HIGH (27) W-C	0.83 OF 18	5 15 17 3 XSQ= 12.22 PHI= -0.553 EP = 0.0003
309	TILT TOWARD BEING THOSE WHERE ORAL SOCIALIZATION ANXIETY IS HIGH (26) W-C	0.73 OF 22	309	TILT TOWARD BEING THOSE WHERE ORAL SOCIALIZATION ANXIETY IS LOW (27) W-C	0.72 OF 18	16 5 6 13 XSQ= 6.32 PHI= 0.397 EP = 0.0100
310	TEND TO BE THOSE WHERE ANAL SOCIALIZATION ANXIETY IS HIGH (22) W-C	0.82 OF 22	310	TEND TO BE THOSE WHERE ANAL SOCIALIZATION ANXIETY IS LOW (19) W-C	0.78 OF 18	18 4 4 14 XSQ= 11.90 PHI= 0.545 EP = 0.0003
311	TEND TO BE THOSE WHERE SEXUAL SOCIALIZATION ANXIETY IS HIGH (28) W-C	0.86 OF 22	311	TEND TO BE THOSE WHERE SEXUAL SOCIALIZATION ANXIETY IS LOW (23) W-C	0.72 OF 18	19 5 3 13 XSQ= 11.82 PHI= 0.544 EP = 0.0003
312	DRIFT TOWARD BEING THOSE WHERE DEPENDENCE SOCIALIZATION ANXIETY IS HIGH (24) W-C	0.68 OF 22	312	DRIFT TOWARD BEING THOSE WHERE DEPENDENCE SOCIALIZATION ANXIETY IS LOW (23) W-C	0.67 OF 18	15 6 7 12 XSQ= 3.52 PHI= 0.297 EP = 0.0550
313	TILT TOWARD BEING THOSE WHERE AGGRESSION SOCIALIZATION ANXIETY IS HIGH (26) W-C	0.73 OF 22	313	TILT TOWARD BEING THOSE WHERE AGGRESSION SOCIALIZATION ANXIETY IS LOW (28) W-C	0.67 OF 18	16 6 6 12 XSQ= 4.72 PHI= 0.343 EP = 0.0244

337	TILT TOWARD BEING THOSE 0.71 OF 17 WHERE THE CHILD'S INFERRED ANXIETY OVER NON-PERFORMANCE OF RESPONSIBLE BEHAVIOR IS HIGH (38) B-B-C	337	TILT TOWARD BEING THOSE 0.69 OF 16 WHERE THE CHILD'S INFERRED ANXIETY OVER NON-PERFORMANCE OF RESPONSIBLE BEHAVIOR IS LOW (35) B-B-C	12 5 5 11 XSQ= 3.65 PHI= 0.333 EP = 0.0381
350	TILT TOWARD BEING THOSE 0.73 OF 15 WHERE THE CHILD'S INFERRED ANXIETY OVER PERFORMANCE OF ACHIEVEMENT BEHAVIOR IS HIGH (34) B-B-C	350	TILT TOWARD BEING THOSE 0.70 OF 10 WHERE THE CHILD'S INFERRED ANXIETY OVER PERFORMANCE OF ACHIEVEMENT BEHAVIOR IS LOW (26) B-B-C	11 3 4 7 XSQ= 2.98 PHI= 0.345 EP = 0.0486
352	DRIFT TOWARD BEING THOSE 0.73 OF 15 WHERE THE TOTAL POSITIVE PRESSURE TOWARD DEVELOPING OBEDIENT BEHAVIOR IN THE CHILD IS HIGH (44) B-B-C	352	DRIFT TOWARD BEING THOSE 0.61 OF 18 WHERE THE TOTAL POSITIVE PRESSURE TOWARD DEVELOPING OBEDIENT BEHAVIOR IN THE CHILD IS LOW (28) B-B-C	11 7 4 11 XSQ= 2.65 PHI= 0.283 EP = 0.0801
353	LEAN TOWARD BEING THOSE 0.87 OF 15 WHERE THE CHILD'S INFERRED ANXIETY OVER NON-PERFORMANCE OF OBEDIENT BEHAVIOR IS HIGH (42) B-B-C	353	LEAN TOWARD BEING THOSE 0.67 OF 18 WHERE THE CHILD-S INFERRED ANXIETY OVER NON-PERFORMANCE OF OBEDIENT BEHAVIOR IS LOW (32) B-B-C	13 6 2 12 XSQ= 7.47 PHI= 0.476 EP = 0.0040
355	DRIFT TOWARD BEING THOSE 0.67 OF 15 WHERE THE CHILD'S INFERRED CONFLICT REGARDING OBEDIENT BEHAVIOR IS HIGH (35) B-B-C	355	DRIFT TOWARD BEING THOSE 0.67 OF 18 WHERE THE CHILD'S INFERRED CONFLICT REGARDING OBEDIENT BEHAVIOR IS LOW (38) B-B-C	10 6 5 12 XSQ= 2.43 PHI= 0.271 EP = 0.0844
373	TILT TOWARD BEING THOSE 0.60 OF 15 WHERE MALE INITIATION CEREMONIES AT PUBERTY ARE PRESENT (17) W-K-A	373	IN ALL CASES ARE THOSE 1.00 OF 7 WHERE MALE INITIATION CEREMONIES AT PUBERTY ARE ABSENT (27) W-K-A	9 0 6 7 XSQ= 4.84 PHI= 0.469 EP = 0.0167
385	DRIFT LESS TOWARD BEING THOSE 0.60 OF 15 WHERE SEXUAL EXPRESSION BY THE YOUNG IS SEMI-RESTRICTED OR PERMITTED (64) F-B	385	DRIFT MORE TOWARD BEING THOSE 0.93 OF 14 WHERE SEXUAL EXPRESSION BY THE YOUNG IS SEMI-RESTRICTED OR PERMITTED (64) F-B	6 1 9 13 XSQ= 2.66 PHI= 0.303 EP = 0.0801
391	TEND TO BE THOSE 0.63 OF 19 WHERE PREMARITAL SEX RELATIONS ARE STRONGLY PUNISHED AND IN FACT RARE, OR WEAKLY PUNISHED AND IN FACT NOT RARE (89) JTW,EA	391	IN ALL CASES ARE THOSE 1.00 OF 14 WHERE PREMARITAL SEX RELATIONS ARE PUNISHED ONLY IF PREGNANCY RESULTS, OR FREELY PERMITTED (90) JTW,EA	12 0 7 14 XSQ= 11.30 PHI= 0.585 EP = 0.0002
392	TILT TOWARD BEING THOSE 0.74 OF 19 WHERE PREMARITAL SEX RELATIONS ARE STRONGLY PUNISHED AND IN FACT RARE, OR WEAKLY PUNISHED AND IN FACT NOT RARE, OR PUNISHED ONLY IF PREGNANCY RESULTS (112) JTW,EA	392	TILT TOWARD BEING THOSE 0.64 OF 14 WHERE PREMARITAL SEX RELATIONS ARE FREELY PERMITTED (67) JTW,EA	14 5 5 9 XSQ= 3.33 PHI= 0.318 EP = 0.0397

393	TILT TOWARD BEING THOSE WHERE EXTRAMARITAL COITUS IS PUNISHED, RATHER THAN PERMITTED (43) F-B	0.73 OF 15	393	TILT TOWARD BEING THOSE WHERE EXTRAMARITAL COITUS IS PERMITTED, RATHER THAN PUNISHED (41) F-B	0.70 OF 10	11 3 4 7 XSQ= 2.98 PHI= 0.345 EP = 0.0486
398	LEAN TOWARD BEING THOSE WHERE THE INTENSITY OF SEX ANXIETY IS HIGH (16) WNS	0.80 OF 15	398	LEAN TOWARD BEING THOSE WHERE THE INTENSITY OF SEX ANXIETY IS LOW (16) WNS	0.82 OF 11	12 2 3 9 XSQ= 7.43 PHI= 0.535 EP = 0.0043
399	TILT TOWARD BEING THOSE WHERE INTENSITY OF CASTRATION ANXIETY IS HIGH (23) WNS	0.61 OF 18	399	TILT TOWARD BEING THOSE WHERE INTENSITY OF CASTRATION ANXIETY IS LOW (22) WNS	0.83 OF 12	11 2 7 10 XSQ= 4.12 PHI= 0.371 EP = 0.0256
403	TILT TOWARD BEING THOSE WHERE EXPLANATIONS OF ILLNESS OF AN ANAL NATURE ARE PRESENT (23) W-C	0.59 OF 22	403	TILT TOWARD BEING THOSE WHERE EXPLANATIONS OF ILLNESS OF AN ANAL NATURE ARE ABSENT (38) W-C	0.78 OF 18	13 4 9 14 XSQ= 4.10 PHI= 0.320 EP = 0.0267
447	TILT TOWARD BEING THOSE WHERE LOVE MAGIC IS PRESENT (20) S-R	0.92 OF 12	447	TILT TOWARD BEING THOSE WHERE LOVE MAGIC IS ABSENT (13) S-R	0.57 OF 14	11 6 1 8 XSQ= 4.82 PHI= 0.430 EP = 0.0145
459	TILT TOWARD BEING THOSE WHERE GAMES, IF PRESENT, INCLUDE GAMES OF CHANCE (82) R-A-B,EA	0.65 OF 17	459	TILT TOWARD BEING THOSE WHERE GAMES, IF PRESENT, DO NOT INCLUDE GAMES OF CHANCE (89) R-A-B,EA	0.79 OF 14	11 3 6 11 XSQ= 4.19 PHI= 0.368 EP = 0.0292
460	TILT TOWARD BEING THOSE WHERE GAMES, IF PRESENT, ARE NOT LIMITED TO GAMES OF SKILL ONLY (104) R-A-B,EA	0.76 OF 17	460	TILT TOWARD BEING THOSE WHERE GAMES, IF PRESENT, ARE LIMITED TO GAMES OF SKILL ONLY (67) R-A-B,EA	0.71 OF 14	4 10 13 4 XSQ= 5.31 PHI= -0.414 EP = 0.0122

309 CULTURES WHERE ORAL SOCIALIZATION ANXIETY IS HIGH (26) W-C	309 CULTURES WHERE ORAL SOCIALIZATION ANXIETY IS LOW (27) W-C

BACKGROUND ON PAGE 138

BOTH SUBJECT AND PREDICATE

26 IN LEFT COLUMN

ALORESE	ASHANTI	AZANDE	CHAGGA	DOBUANS	FON	KUTENAI	KWAKIUTL	LAMBA	LAPPS
LEPCHA	LESU	MANUS	MAORI	MARQUESANS	MASAI	NAVAHO	OMAHA	PUKAPUKA	RWALA
SAMOANS	SANPOIL	TAOS	THONGA	TROBRIAND	YAKUT				

27 IN RIGHT COLUMN

AINU	ANDAMANESE	ARAPESH	BALINESE	CHENCHU	CHIR-APACHE	COMANCHE	COPR ESKIMO	HANO	IFUGAO
JIVARO	KURTATCHI	LAKHER	ONTONG-JAVA	PAPAGO	SENIANG	SIRIONO	TANALA	TENINO	TETON
TIKOPIA	VENDA	WARRAU	WITOTO	WOGEO	YAGUA	YUKAGHIR			

347 EXCLUDED BECAUSE UNASCERTAINED

3	TILT LESS TOWARD BEING THOSE LOCATED OUTSIDE OF AFRICA (320)	0.73 OF 26	3	TILT MORE TOWARD BEING THOSE LOCATED OUTSIDE OF AFRICA (320)	0.96 OF 27	7 1 19 26 XSQ= 3.91 PHI= 0.272 XP = 0.0481
9	IN ALL CASES ARE THOSE LOCATED OUTSIDE OF SOUTH AMERICA (335)	1.00 OF 26	9	DRIFT LESS TOWARD BEING THOSE LOCATED OUTSIDE OF SOUTH AMERICA (335)	0.81 OF 27	0 5 26 22 XSQ= 3.37 PHI= -0.252 XP = 0.0664
62	TILT TOWARD BEING THOSE WHERE HUSBANDRY OF SOME KIND IS PRESENT (228)	0.77 OF 26	62	TILT TOWARD BEING THOSE WHERE HUSBANDRY OF ANY KIND IS ABSENT (172)	0.56 OF 27	20 12 6 15 XSQ= 4.56 PHI= 0.293 XP = 0.0327
71	TILT LESS TOWARD BEING THOSE WHERE METAL WORKING IS ABSENT (153)	0.57 OF 21	71	TILT MORE TOWARD BEING THOSE WHERE METAL WORKING IS ABSENT (153)	0.90 OF 20	9 2 12 18 XSQ= 4.08 PHI= 0.316 XP = 0.0433

82	TILT MORE TOWARD BEING THOSE WHERE A CITY OR TOWN IS PRESENT, OR THE AVERAGE COMMUNITY SIZE IS FIFTY OR GREATER (178)	0.90 OF 21	82	TILT LESS TOWARD BEING THOSE WHERE A CITY OR TOWN IS PRESENT, OR THE AVERAGE COMMUNITY SIZE IS FIFTY OR GREATER (178)	0.60 OF 15	19 9 2 6 XSQ= 3.10 PHI= 0.294 EP = 0.0461
86	TILT TOWARD BEING THOSE WHERE THE LEVEL OF POLITICAL INTEGRATION IS THE LARGE STATE, THE LITTLE STATE, OR THE MINIMAL STATE (148) GPM	0.59 OF 22	86	TILT TOWARD BEING THOSE WHERE THE LEVEL OF POLITICAL INTEGRATION IS THE AUTONOMOUS COMMUNITY, OR THE FAMILY (156) GPM	0.80 OF 20	13 4 9 16 XSQ= 5.12 PHI= 0.349 XP = 0.0236
96	TEND TO BE THOSE WHERE THE HIERARCHY OF NATIONAL JURISDICTION HAS FOUR, THREE, TWO OR ONE LEVEL (174) GES,EA	0.72 OF 25	96	TEND TO BE THOSE WHERE THE HIERARCHY OF NATIONAL JURISDICTION HAS NO LEVELS (156) GES,EA	0.79 OF 24	18 5 7 19 XSQ= 10.90 PHI= 0.472 XP = 0.0010
116	TILT TOWARD BEING THOSE WHERE OCCUPATIONAL SPECIALIZATION IS FULL-TIME, WHETHER OR NOT FOR SURPLUS PRODUCTION (20) JMH	0.67 OF 9	116	IN ALL CASES ARE THOSE WHERE OCCUPATIONAL SPECIALIZATION IS PART-TIME ONLY (34) JMH	1.00 OF 6	6 0 3 6 XSQ= 4.18 PHI= 0.528 EP = 0.0278
132	TILT TOWARD BEING THOSE WHERE ECONOMIC EXCHANGE INVOLVES THE USE OF MONEY (37) JMH	0.89 OF 9	132	TILT TOWARD BEING THOSE WHERE ECONOMIC EXCHANGE DOES NOT INVOLVE THE USE OF MONEY (17) JMH	0.83 OF 6	8 1 1 5 XSQ= 5.10 PHI= 0.583 EP = 0.0110
136	DRIFT TOWARD BEING THOSE WHERE FULL-TIME ENTREPRENEURS ARE PRESENT (18) JV	0.67 OF 9	136	DRIFT TOWARD BEING THOSE WHERE FULL-TIME ENTREPRENEURS ARE ABSENT (14) JV	0.86 OF 7	6 1 3 6 XSQ= 2.52 PHI= 0.397 EP = 0.0601
137	TILT TOWARD BEING THOSE WHERE INVIDIOUS DISPLAY OF WEALTH IS STRONGLY EMPHASIZED (37) PES	0.59 OF 22	137	TILT TOWARD BEING THOSE WHERE INVIDIOUS DISPLAY OF WEALTH IS MODERATELY, LITTLE, OR NEGATIVELY EMPHASIZED (52) PES	0.81 OF 21	13 4 9 17 XSQ= 5.63 PHI= 0.362 XP = 0.0177
144	TILT TOWARD BEING THOSE WHERE THE RATIO OF RESTITUTIVE TO REPRESSIVE SANCTIONS IS HIGH OR MEDIUM (27) WME	0.70 OF 10	144	TILT TOWARD BEING THOSE WHERE THE RATIO OF RESTITUTIVE TO REPRESSIVE SANCTIONS IS LOW (25) WME	0.86 OF 7	7 1 3 6 XSQ= 3.14 PHI= 0.430 EP = 0.0498
149	DRIFT TOWARD BEING THOSE WHERE THE INCIDENCE OF THEFT IS HIGH (18) B-B-C	0.60 OF 15	149	DRIFT TOWARD BEING THOSE WHERE THE INCIDENCE OF THEFT IS LOW (19) B-B-C	0.77 OF 13	9 3 6 10 XSQ= 2.52 PHI= 0.300 EP = 0.0671

No.	Statement	Prop.	N	No.	Statement	Prop.	N	Statistics
185	DRIFT MORE TOWARD BEING THOSE WHERE THE LARGEST NON-COGNATIC KIN GROUP IS THE MOEITY OR PHRATRY OR SIB (194)	0.94 OF	18	185	DRIFT LESS TOWARD BEING THOSE WHERE THE LARGEST NON-COGNATIC KIN GROUP IS THE MOEITY OR PHRATRY OR SIB (194)	0.64 OF	14	17 9 1 5 XSQ= 2.93 PHI= 0.303 EP = 0.0636
303	TILT TOWARD BEING THOSE WHERE THE EARLY ORAL SATISFACTION POTENTIAL IS LOW (25) W-C	0.62 OF	26	303	TILT TOWARD BEING THOSE WHERE THE EARLY ORAL SATISFACTION POTENTIAL IS HIGH (32) W-C	0.74 OF	27	10 20 16 7 XSQ= 5.47 PHI= -0.321 XP = 0.0194
308	TILT TOWARD BEING THOSE WHERE AVERAGE SOCIALIZATION ANXIETY IS HIGH (22) W-C	0.76 OF	21	308	TILT TOWARD BEING THOSE WHERE AVERAGE SOCIALIZATION ANXIETY IS LOW (18) W-C	0.68 OF	19	16 6 5 13 XSQ= 6.32 PHI= 0.397 EP = 0.0100
312	TILT TOWARD BEING THOSE WHERE DEPENDENCE SOCIALIZATION ANXIETY IS HIGH (24) W-C	0.71 OF	21	312	TILT TOWARD BEING THOSE WHERE DEPENDENCE SOCIALIZATION ANXIETY IS LOW (23) W-C	0.67 OF	24	15 8 6 16 XSQ= 5.07 PHI= 0.336 XP = 0.0243
317	LEAN TOWARD BEING THOSE WHERE DISPLAY OF AFFECTION TOWARD THE INFANT IS LOW (29) B-B-C	0.68 OF	19	317	LEAN TOWARD BEING THOSE WHERE DISPLAY OF AFFECTION TOWARD THE INFANT IS HIGH (39) B-B-C	0.82 OF	17	6 14 13 3 XSQ= 7.42 PHI= -0.454 EP = 0.0031
318	DRIFT TOWARD BEING THOSE WHERE THE OVERALL INDULGENCE OF THE INFANT IS LOW (31) B-B-C	0.65 OF	20	318	DRIFT TOWARD BEING THOSE WHERE THE OVERALL INDULGENCE OF THE INFANT IS HIGH (40) B-B-C	0.70 OF	20	7 14 13 6 XSQ= 3.61 PHI= -0.300 EP = 0.0562
320	TILT TOWARD BEING THOSE WHERE THE DEGREE OF REDUCTION OF THE INFANT'S DRIVES IS LOW (24) B-B-C	0.55 OF	20	320	TILT TOWARD BEING THOSE WHERE THE DEGREE OF REDUCTION OF THE INFANT'S DRIVES IS HIGH (45) B-B-C	0.79 OF	19	9 15 11 4 XSQ= 3.42 PHI= -0.296 EP = 0.0484
321	TILT TOWARD BEING THOSE WHERE THE IMMEDIACY OF REDUCTION OF THE INFANT'S DRIVES IS LOW (25) B-B-C	0.65 OF	20	321	TILT TOWARD BEING THOSE WHERE THE IMMEDIACY OF REDUCTION OF THE INFANT'S DRIVES IS HIGH (35) B-B-C	0.75 OF	16	7 12 13 4 XSQ= 4.21 PHI= -0.342 EP = 0.0228
322	TILT TOWARD BEING THOSE WHERE THE CONSISTENCY OF REDUCTION OF THE INFANT'S DRIVES IS LOW (32) B-B-C	0.74 OF	19	322	TILT TOWARD BEING THOSE WHERE THE CONSISTENCY OF REDUCTION OF THE INFANT'S DRIVES IS HIGH (27) B-B-C	0.63 OF	16	5 10 14 6 XSQ= 3.28 PHI= -0.306 EP = 0.0442

326	DRIFT TOWARD BEING THOSE 0.65 OF 20 WHERE THE INFERRED TRANSITION ANXIETY BETWEEN INFANCY AND CHILDHOOD IS HIGH (32) B-B-C	326	DRIFT TOWARD BEING THOSE 0.67 OF 18 WHERE THE INFERRED TRANSITION ANXIETY BETWEEN INFANCY AND CHILDHOOD IS LOW (35) B-B-C	13 6 7 12 XSQ= 2.64 PHI= 0.264 EP = 0.0624
334	TILT TOWARD BEING THOSE 0.65 OF 20 WHERE THE INDULGENCE OF THE CHILD IS LOW (38) B-B-C	334	TILT TOWARD BEING THOSE 0.76 OF 21 WHERE THE INDULGENCE OF THE CHILD IS HIGH (40) B-B-C	7 16 13 5 XSQ= 5.48 PHI= -0.366 XP = 0.0192
338	DRIFT TOWARD BEING THOSE 0.74 OF 19 WHERE THE CHILD'S INFERRED ANXIETY OVER PERFORMANCE OF RESPONSIBLE BEHAVIOR IS HIGH (44) B-B-C	338	DRIFT TOWARD BEING THOSE 0.56 OF 18 WHERE THE CHILD'S INFERRED ANXIETY OVER PERFORMANCE OF RESPONSIBLE BEHAVIOR IS LOW (29) B-B-C	14 8 5 10 XSQ= 2.18 PHI= 0.243 EP = 0.0991
353	TILT TOWARD BEING THOSE 0.79 OF 19 WHERE THE CHILD'S INFERRED ANXIETY OVER NON-PERFORMANCE OF OBEDIENT BEHAVIOR IS HIGH (42) B-B-C	353	TILT TOWARD BEING THOSE 0.58 OF 19 WHERE THE CHILD-S INFERRED ANXIETY OVER NON-PERFORMANCE OF OBEDIENT BEHAVIOR IS LOW (32) B-B-C	15 8 4 11 XSQ= 3.97 PHI= 0.323 EP = 0.0448
355	TILT TOWARD BEING THOSE 0.68 OF 19 WHERE THE CHILD'S INFERRED CONFLICT REGARDING OBEDIENT BEHAVIOR IS HIGH (35) B-B-C	355	TILT TOWARD BEING THOSE 0.68 OF 19 WHERE THE CHILD'S INFERRED CONFLICT REGARDING OBEDIENT BEHAVIOR IS LOW (38) B-B-C	13 6 6 13 XSQ= 3.79 PHI= 0.316 EP = 0.0294
377	DRIFT LESS TOWARD BEING THOSE 0.64 OF 25 WHERE MALE GENITAL MUTILATION IS ABSENT (242)	377	DRIFT MORE TOWARD BEING THOSE 0.91 OF 23 WHERE MALE GENITAL MUTILATION IS ABSENT (242)	9 2 16 21 XSQ= 3.63 PHI= 0.275 XP = 0.0568
398	DRIFT TOWARD BEING THOSE 0.69 OF 16 WHERE THE INTENSITY OF SEX ANXIETY IS HIGH (16) WNS	398	DRIFT TOWARD BEING THOSE 0.67 OF 15 WHERE THE INTENSITY OF SEX ANXIETY IS LOW (16) WNS	11 5 5 10 XSQ= 2.60 PHI= 0.290 EP = 0.0756
402	TILT TOWARD BEING THOSE 0.69 OF 26 WHERE EXPLANATIONS OF ILLNESS OF AN ORAL NATURE ARE PRESENT (31) W-C	402	TILT TOWARD BEING THOSE 0.63 OF 27 WHERE EXPLANATIONS OF ILLNESS OF AN ORAL NATURE ARE ABSENT (30) W-C	18 10 8 17 XSQ= 4.29 PHI= 0.285 XP = 0.0383
404	DRIFT LESS TOWARD BEING THOSE 0.54 OF 26 WHERE EXPLANATIONS OF ILLNESS OF A SEXUAL NATURE ARE ABSENT (42) W-C	404	DRIFT MORE TOWARD BEING THOSE 0.81 OF 27 WHERE EXPLANATIONS OF ILLNESS OF A SEXUAL NATURE ARE ABSENT (42) W-C	12 5 14 22 XSQ= 3.46 PHI= 0.256 XP = 0.0628

```
417  DRIFT TOWARD BEING THOSE          0.92 OF  12      417  DRIFT TOWARD BEING THOSE          0.50 OF   6          11     3
     WHERE WARFARE IS                                        WHERE WARFARE IS                                          1     3
     PREVALENT  (34) LWS                                     NOT PREVALENT  (9) LWS                           XSQ=     1.97
                                                                                                              PHI=    0.331
                                                                                                              EP =   0.0833

454  TILT TOWARD BEING THOSE           0.67 OF   9      454  TILT TOWARD BEING THOSE           0.88 OF   8           6     1
     WHERE THE OBJECTIVE OF THE INDIVIDUAL'S                 WHERE THE OBJECTIVE OF THE INDIVIDUAL'S                   3     7
     CONTACT WITH THE DIVINE                                 CONTACT WITH THE DIVINE                          XSQ=     3.14
     IS CONDUCIVE TO THE DEVELOPMENT OF THE                  IS NOT CONDUCIVE TO THE DEVELOPMENT OF THE       PHI=    0.430
     INDIVIDUAL'S NEED TO ACHIEVE  (18) DCM                  INDIVIDUAL'S NEED TO ACHIEVE  (18) DCM           EP =   0.0498

456  IN ALL CASES ARE THOSE            1.00 OF   9      456  TILT TOWARD BEING THOSE           0.50 OF   8           0     4
     WHERE THE INTERNALIZATION OF THE                        WHERE THE INTERNALIZATION OF THE                          9     4
     INDIVIDUAL'S CONTACT WITH THE DIVINE                    INDIVIDUAL'S CONTACT WITH THE DIVINE             XSQ=     3.43
     IS NOT CONDUCIVE TO THE DEVELOPMENT OF                  IS CONDUCIVE TO THE DEVELOPMENT OF               PHI=   -0.449
     THE INDIVIDUAL'S NEED TO ACHIEVE  (17) DCM              THE INDIVIDUAL'S NEED TO ACHIEVE  (19) DCM       EP =   0.0294

469  DRIFT TOWARD BEING THOSE          0.89 OF   9      469  DRIFT TOWARD BEING THOSE          0.67 OF   6           8     2
     WHERE CONTACT WITH OTHER CULTURES                       WHERE CONTACT WITH OTHER CULTURES                         1     4
     IS FREQUENT OR REGULAR, RATHER THAN                     IS IRREGULAR, RATHER THAN                        XSQ=     2.81
     IRREGULAR  (43) JMH                                     FREQUENT OR REGULAR  (11) JMH                    PHI=    0.433
                                                                                                              EP =   0.0889
```

```
310  CULTURES                                          310  CULTURES
     WHERE ANAL SOCIALIZATION ANXIETY                       WHERE ANAL SOCIALIZATION ANXIETY
     IS HIGH  (22) W-C                                      IS LOW  (19) W-C


BACKGROUND ON PAGE 138                                                        BOTH SUBJECT AND PREDICATE

     22  IN LEFT COLUMN

ARAPESH    ASHANTI    AZANDE     BALINESE   CHAGGA      CHIR-APACHE DOBUANS   FON        HANO       KUTENAI
LAKHER     LESU       MANUS      NAVAHO     ONTONG-JAVA PUKAPUKA    RWALA     SANPOIL    TANALA     TENINO
THONGA     TROBRIAND

     19  IN RIGHT COLUMN

AINU       ALORESE    CHENCHU    COMANCHE   KURTATCHI   KWAKIUTL    LEPCHA    MAORI      MARQUESANS PAPAGO
SAMOANS    SIRIONO    TETON      TIKOPIA    VENDA       WOGEO       YAGUA     YAKUT      YUKAGHIR

     359  EXCLUDED BECAUSE UNASCERTAINED

--------------------------------------------------------------------------------------------------------
 71  TILT LESS TOWARD BEING THOSE   0.53 OF  17       71  TILT MORE TOWARD BEING THOSE   0.93 OF  15        8   1
     WHERE METAL WORKING IS                               WHERE METAL WORKING IS                            9  14
     ABSENT  (153)                                        ABSENT  (153)                               XSQ=   4.59
                                                                                                      PHI=  0.379
                                                                                                      EP =  0.0179

 74  DRIFT TOWARD BEING THOSE       0.69 OF  16       74  DRIFT TOWARD BEING THOSE       0.63 OF  16       11   6
     WHERE POTTERY IS                                     WHERE POTTERY IS                                  5  10
     PRESENT  (145)                                       ABSENT  (93)                                XSQ=   2.01
                                                                                                      PHI=  0.250
                                                                                                      EP =  0.0938

 82  IN ALL CASES ARE THOSE         1.00 OF  15       82  TILT LESS TOWARD BEING THOSE   0.69 OF  13       15   9
     WHERE A CITY OR TOWN IS PRESENT, OR                  WHERE A CITY OR TOWN IS PRESENT, OR               0   4
     THE AVERAGE COMMUNITY SIZE IS                        THE AVERAGE COMMUNITY SIZE IS               XSQ=   3.16
     FIFTY OR GREATER  (178)                              FIFTY OR GREATER  (178)                     PHI=  0.336
                                                                                                      EP =  0.0349

179  TILT MORE TOWARD BEING THOSE   0.95 OF  22      179  TILT LESS TOWARD BEING THOSE   0.63 OF  19        1   7
     WHERE THE COMMUNITY IS OTHER THAN                    WHERE THE COMMUNITY IS OTHER THAN                21  12
     STRUCTURED ON A NON-CLAN BASIS AND                   STRUCTURED ON A NON-CLAN BASIS AND          XSQ=   4.87
     COMMONLY EXOGAMOUS  (340)                            COMMONLY EXOGAMOUS  (340)                   PHI= -0.345
                                                                                                      XP =  0.0273

180  DRIFT TOWARD BEING THOSE       0.77 OF  22      180  DRIFT TOWARD BEING THOSE       0.53 OF  19        5  10
     WHERE THE COMMUNITY IS                               WHERE THE COMMUNITY IS                           17   9
     COMMONLY NON-EXOGAMOUS, RATHER THAN                  COMMONLY EXOGAMOUS, RATHER THAN             XSQ=   2.75
     EXOGAMOUS  (258)                                     NON-EXOGAMOUS  (124)                        PHI= -0.259
                                                                                                      XP =  0.0975
```

260	DRIFT TCWARD BEING THCSE WHERE THE AGE OF MALES AT MARRIAGE IS TWENTY CR CVER (17) JKF	0.55 OF 11	260	DRIFT TOWARD BEING THOSE WHERE THE AGE CF MALES AT MARRIAGE IS LESS THAN TWENTY (38) JKH	0.89 OF 9	5 8 6 1 XSQ= 2.42 PHI= -0.348 EP = 0.0703
304	LEAN TCWARD BEING THCSE WHERE THE EARLY ANAL SATISFACTION PCTENTIAL IS LCW (22) W-C	0.77 OF 22	304	LEAN TOWARD BEING THOSE WHERE THE EARLY ANAL SATISFACTICN POTENTIAL IS HIGH (19) W-C	0.74 CF 19	5 14 17 5 XSQ= 8.70 PHI= -0.461 XP = 0.0032
305	DRIFT TCWARD BEING THCSE WHERE THE EARLY SEXUAL SATISFACTION PCTENTIAL IS LCW (24) W-C	0.64 OF 22	305	DRIFT TOWARD BEING THOSE WHERE THE EARLY SEXUAL SATISFACTION POTENTIAL IS HIGH (27) W-C	0.67 OF 18	8 12 14 6 XSQ= 2.53 PHI= -0.251 EP = 0.0679
308	TEND TC BE THCSE WHERE AVERAGE SCCIALIZATICN ANXIETY IS HIGH (22) W-C	0.82 OF 22	308	TEND TO BE THOSE WHERE AVERAGE SOCIALIZATICN ANXIETY IS LOW (18) W-C	0.78 CF 18	18 4 4 14 XSQ= 11.90 PHI= 0.545 EP = 0.0003
312	DRIFT TCWARD BEING THCSE WHERE DEPENDENCE SCCIALIZATION ANXIETY IS HIGH (24) W-C	0.68 OF 22	312	DRIFT TOWARD BEING THOSE WHERE DEPENDENCE SOCIALIZATICN ANXIETY IS LOW (23) W-C	0.67 OF 18	15 6 7 12 XSQ= 3.52 PHI= 0.297 EP = 0.0550
353	TILT TCWARC BEING THCSE WHERE THE CHILD'S INFERREC ANXIETY OVER NCN-PERFCRMANCE CF CBECIENT BEHAVIOR IS HIGH (42) B-B-C	0.80 OF 15	353	TILT TOWARD BEING THOSE WHERE THE CHILD-S INFERRED ANXIETY OVER NON-PERFORMANCE OF CBEDIENT BEHAVICR IS LOW (32) B-B-C	0.61 CF 18	12 7 3 11 XSQ= 4.10 PHI= 0.353 EP = 0.0329
385	TILT LESS TOWARC BEING THCSE WHERE SEXUAL EXPRESSICN BY THE YOUNG IS SEMI-RESTRICTED CR PERMITTED (64) F-B	0.57 OF 14	385	TILT MORE TOWARD BEING THCSE WHERE SEXUAL EXPRESSION BY THE YOUNG IS SEMI-RESTRICTED OR PERMITTED (64) F-B	0.94 OF 16	6 1 8 15 XSQ= 3.73 PHI= 0.353 EP = 0.0309
391	TILT TCWARD BEING THCSE WHERE PREMARITAL SEX RELATIONS ARE STRCNGLY PUNISHEC AND IN FACT RARE, OR WEAKLY PUNISHED ANC IN FACT NCT RARE (89) JTW,EA	0.56 OF 18	391	TILT TOWARD BEING THCSE WHERE PREMARITAL SEX RELATICNS ARE PUNISHED ONLY IF PREGNANCY RESULTS, CR FREELY PERMITTED (90) JTW,EA	0.87 CF 15	10 2 8 13 XSQ= 4.61 PHI= 0.374 EP = 0.0272
392	DRIFT TCWARD BEING THCSE WHERE PREMARITAL SEX RELATIONS ARE STRCNGLY PUNISHEC ANC IN FACT RARE, OR WEAKLY PUNISHEC ANC IN FACT NCT RARE, OR PUNISHED CNLY IF PREGNANCY RESULTS (112) JTW,EA	0.72 OF 18	392	DRIFT TOWARD BEING THOSE WHERE PREMARITAL SEX RELATICNS ARE FREELY PERMITTED (67) JTW,EA	0.60 OF 15	13 6 5 9 XSQ= 2.28 PHI= 0.263 EP = 0.0853

460	DRIFT TCWARD BEING THOSE WHERE GAMES, IF PRESENT, ARE NCT LIMITED TO GAMES CF SKILL CNLY (104) R-A-B,EA	0.71 OF 17	46C	DRIFT TOWARD BEING THOSE WHERE GAMES, IF PRESENT, ARE LIMITED TO GAMES OF SKILL ONLY (67) R-A-B,EA	0.64 OF 14	5 9 12 5 XSQ= 2.49 PHI= -0.284 EP = 0.0759

311 CULTURES WHERE SEXUAL SOCIALIZATION ANXIETY IS HIGH (28) W-C	311 CULTURES WHERE SEXUAL SOCIALIZATION ANXIETY IS LOW (23) W-C

BACKGROUND ON PAGE 138 — BOTH SUBJECT AND PREDICATE

28 IN LEFT COLUMN

ABIPON	ALORESE	ARAPESH	ASHANTI	AZANDE	CHAGGA	CHIR-APACHE	DOBUANS	FON	HANO
KURTATCHI	KUTENAI	KWAKIUTL	MANUS	NAVAHO	ONTONG-JAVA	PAPAGO	RIFFIANS	RWALA	SAMOANS
SANPOIL	TANALA	TENINO	TETON	TIV	VENDA	WAPISHANA	WOGEO		

23 IN RIGHT COLUMN

AINU	ANDAMANESE	BALINESE	CHENCHU	COMANCHE	IFUGAO	LAKHER	LAMBA	LEPCHA	LESU
MAORI	MARQUESANS	MARSHALLESE	MASAI	MURNGIN	PUKAPUKA	SIRIONO	THONGA	TIKOPIA	TROBRIAND
WITOTO	YAGUA	YAKUT							

349 EXCLUDED BECAUSE UNASCERTAINED

5	DRIFT MORE TOWARD BEING THOSE LOCATED OUTSIDE OF EAST EURASIA (330)	0.96 OF 28	5	DRIFT LESS TOWARD BEING THOSE LOCATED OUTSIDE OF EAST EURASIA (330)	0.74 OF 23	1 6 27 17 XSQ= 3.67 PHI= -0.268 XP = 0.0553
8	TILT LESS TOWARD BEING THOSE LOCATED OUTSIDE OF NORTH AMERICA (330)	0.68 OF 28	8	TILT MORE TOWARD BEING THOSE LOCATED OUTSIDE OF NORTH AMERICA (330)	0.96 OF 23	9 1 19 22 XSQ= 4.55 PHI= 0.299 XP = 0.0329
78	IN ALL CASES ARE THOSE WHERE THE WRITING SYSTEM IS ALPHABETIC-OR-PHONETIC, OR MNEMONIC, RATHER THAN BEING ABSENT (36) JMH	1.00 OF 7	78	TILT TOWARD BEING THOSE WHERE A WRITING SYSTEM IS ABSENT, RATHER THAN BEING PRESENT IN EITHER ALPHABETIC-OR-PHONETIC FORM OR MNEMONIC FORM (18) JMH	0.63 OF 8	7 3 0 5 XSQ= 4.05 PHI= 0.520 EP = 0.0256
81	TILT TOWARD BEING THOSE WHERE A CITY OR TOWN IS PRESENT, OR THE AVERAGE COMMUNITY SIZE IS 200 OR GREATER (89)	0.50 OF 18	81	TILT TOWARD BEING THOSE WHERE NO CITY OR TOWN IS PRESENT, AND THE AVERAGE COMMUNITY SIZE IS SMALLER THAN 200 (135)	0.87 OF 15	9 2 9 13 XSQ= 3.44 PHI= 0.323 EP = 0.0342

82	IN ALL CASES ARE THOSE WHERE A CITY OR TOWN IS PRESENT, OR THE AVERAGE COMMUNITY SIZE IS FIFTY OR GREATER (178)	1.00 OF	18	82	LEAN LESS TOWARD BEING THOSE WHERE A CITY OR TOWN IS PRESENT, OR THE AVERAGE COMMUNITY SIZE IS FIFTY OR GREATER (178)	0.60 OF	15	18 9 0 6 XSQ= 6.32 PHI= 0.438 EP = 0.0045
138	DRIFT TOWARD BEING THOSE WHERE SUPERORDINATE JUSTICE IS PRESENT (22) BBW	0.85 OF	13	138	DRIFT TOWARD BEING THOSE WHERE SUPERORDINATE JUSTICE IS ABSENT (18) BBW	0.55 OF	11	11 5 2 6 XSQ= 2.54 PHI= 0.325 EP = 0.0825
213	DRIFT TOWARD BEING THOSE WHERE FIRST COUSIN MARRIAGE IS NOT PERMITTED (198)	0.75 OF	28	213	DRIFT TOWARD BEING THOSE WHERE FIRST COUSIN MARRIAGE IS PERMITTED (172)	0.52 OF	23	7 12 21 11 XSQ= 2.91 PHI= -0.239 XP = 0.0880
278	IN ALL CASES ARE THOSE WHERE PROPERTY RIGHTS IN WOMEN ARE PRESENT (8) LWS	1.00 OF	2	278	IN ALL CASES ARE THOSE WHERE PROPERTY RIGHTS IN WOMEN ARE UNIMPORTANT OR ABSENT (14) LWS	1.00 OF	5	2 0 0 5 XSQ= 2.96 PHI= 0.650 EP = 0.0476
301	DRIFT TOWARD BEING THOSE WHERE THE POST-PARTUM SEX TABOO LASTS LONGER THAN ONE MONTH (96)	0.83 OF	18	301	DRIFT TOWARD BEING THOSE WHERE THE POST-PARTUM SEX TABOO LASTS ONE MONTH OR LESS (28)	0.50 OF	14	15 7 3 7 XSQ= 2.67 PHI= 0.289 EP = 0.0623
305	TEND TO BE THOSE WHERE THE EARLY SEXUAL SATISFACTION POTENTIAL IS LOW (24) W-C	0.74 OF	27	305	TEND TO BE THOSE WHERE THE EARLY SEXUAL SATISFACTION POTENTIAL IS HIGH (27) W-C	0.87 OF	23	7 20 20 3 XSQ= 16.25 PHI= -0.570 XP = 0.0001
308	TEND TO BE THOSE WHERE AVERAGE SOCIALIZATION ANXIETY IS HIGH (22) W-C	0.79 OF	24	308	TEND TO BE THOSE WHERE AVERAGE SOCIALIZATION ANXIETY IS LOW (18) W-C	0.81 OF	16	19 3 5 13 XSQ= 11.82 PHI= 0.544 EP = 0.0003
313	LEAN TOWARD BEING THOSE WHERE AGGRESSION SOCIALIZATION ANXIETY IS HIGH (26) W-C	0.69 OF	26	313	LEAN TOWARD BEING THOSE WHERE AGGRESSION SOCIALIZATION ANXIETY IS LOW (28) W-C	0.82 OF	22	18 4 8 18 XSQ= 10.54 PHI= 0.469 XP = 0.0012
314	TILT LESS TOWARD BEING THOSE WHERE THE INCIDENCE OF MOTHER-CHILD HOUSEHOLDS IS LOW (61) W-C,S	0.58 OF	19	314	TILT MORE TOWARD BEING THOSE WHERE THE INCIDENCE OF MOTHER-CHILD HOUSEHOLDS IS LOW (61) W-D,S	0.95 OF	19	8 1 11 18 XSQ= 5.24 PHI= 0.371 EP = 0.0188

315	IN ALL CASES ARE THOSE 1.00 OF 13 WHERE MOTHER AND NURSING CHILD CUSTOMARILY SLEEP IN THE SAME BED (37) W-D,S	315	DRIFT LESS TOWARD BEING THOSE 0.70 OF 10 WHERE MOTHER AND NURSING CHILD CUSTOMARILY SLEEP IN THE SAME BED (37) W-D,S	13 7 0 3 XSQ= 2.23 PHI= 0.311 EP = 0.0678
322	DRIFT TOWARD BEING THOSE 0.56 OF 18 WHERE THE CONSISTENCY OF REDUCTION OF THE INFANT'S DRIVES IS HIGH (27) B-B-C	322	DRIFT TOWARD BEING THOSE 0.75 OF 16 WHERE THE CONSISTENCY OF REDUCTION OF THE INFANT'S DRIVES IS LOW (32) B-B-C	10 4 8 12 XSQ= 2.13 PHI= 0.250 EP = 0.0921
323	DRIFT LESS TOWARD BEING THOSE 0.53 OF 19 WHERE THE CONSTANCY OF PRESENCE OF THE INFANT'S NURTURANT AGENT IS LOW (45) B-B-C	323	DRIFT MORE TOWARD BEING THOSE 0.80 OF 20 WHERE THE CONSTANCY OF PRESENCE OF THE INFANT'S NURTURANT AGENT IS LOW (45) B-B-C	9 4 10 16 XSQ= 2.17 PHI= 0.236 EP = 0.0958
350	TILT TOWARD BEING THOSE 0.76 OF 17 WHERE THE CHILD'S INFERRED ANXIETY OVER PERFORMANCE OF ACHIEVEMENT BEHAVIOR IS HIGH (34) B-B-C	350	TILT TOWARD BEING THOSE 0.73 OF 11 WHERE THE CHILD'S INFERRED ANXIETY OVER PERFORMANCE OF ACHIEVEMENT BEHAVIOR IS LOW (26) B-B-C	13 3 4 8 XSQ= 4.74 PHI= 0.412 EP = 0.0189
351	TILT TOWARD BEING THOSE 0.65 OF 17 WHERE THE CHILD'S INFERRED CONFLICT REGARDING ACHIEVEMENT BEHAVIOR IS HIGH (26) B-B-C	351	TILT TOWARD BEING THOSE 0.82 OF 11 WHERE THE CHILD'S INFERRED CONFLICT REGARDING ACHIEVEMENT BEHAVIOR IS LOW (34) B-B-C	11 2 6 9 XSQ= 4.09 PHI= 0.382 EP = 0.0238
352	DRIFT TOWARD BEING THOSE 0.72 OF 18 WHERE THE TOTAL POSITIVE PRESSURE TOWARD DEVELOPING OBEDIENT BEHAVIOR IN THE CHILD IS HIGH (44) B-B-C	352	DRIFT TOWARD BEING THOSE 0.60 OF 20 WHERE THE TOTAL POSITIVE PRESSURE TOWARD DEVELOPING OBEDIENT BEHAVIOR IN THE CHILD IS LOW (28) B-B-C	13 8 5 12 XSQ= 2.78 PHI= 0.271 EP = 0.0585
355	DRIFT TOWARD BEING THOSE 0.67 OF 18 WHERE THE CHILD'S INFERRED CONFLICT REGARDING OBEDIENT BEHAVIOR IS HIGH (35) B-B-C	355	DRIFT TOWARD BEING THOSE 0.65 OF 20 WHERE THE CHILD'S INFERRED CONFLICT REGARDING OBEDIENT BEHAVIOR IS LOW (38) B-B-C	12 7 6 13 XSQ= 2.64 PHI= 0.264 EP = 0.0624
386	DRIFT TOWARD BEING THOSE 0.69 OF 16 WHERE SEXUAL EXPRESSION BY THE YOUNG IS RESTRICTED OR SEMI-RESTRICTED (46) F-B	386	DRIFT TOWARD BEING THOSE 0.63 OF 19 WHERE SEXUAL EXPRESSION BY THE YOUNG IS PERMITTED (40) F-B	11 7 5 12 XSQ= 2.38 PHI= 0.261 EP = 0.0922
390	TILT LESS TOWARD BEING THOSE 0.65 OF 23 WHERE PREMARITAL SEX RELATIONS ARE WEAKLY PUNISHED AND IN FACT NOT RARE OR PUNISHED ONLY IF PREGNANCY RESULTS, OR FREELY PERMITTED (132) JTW,EA	390	IN ALL CASES ARE THOSE 1.00 OF 18 WHERE PREMARITAL SEX RELATIONS ARE WEAKLY PUNISHED AND IN FACT NOT RARE OR PUNISHED ONLY IF PREGNANCY RESULTS, OR FREELY PERMITTED (132) JTW,EA	8 0 15 18 XSQ= 5.72 PHI= 0.374 XP = 0.0168

```
391  TEND TO BE THOSE                 0.61 OF  23     391  TEND TO BE THOSE                 0.94 OF  18        14     1
     WHERE PREMARITAL SEX RELATIONS ARE                    WHERE PREMARITAL SEX RELATIONS ARE                      9    17
     STRONGLY PUNISHED AND IN FACT RARE, OR                PUN'SHED ONLY IF PREGNANCY RESULTS, OR          XSQ=    11.04
     WEAKLY PUNISHED AND                                   FREELY PERMITTED  (90) JTW,EA                   PHI=    0.519
     IN FACT NOT RARE  (89) JTW,EA                                                                         XP =   0.0009

392  TEND TO BE THOSE                 0.87 OF  23     392  TEND TO BE THOSE                 0.83 OF  18        20     3
     WHERE PREMARITAL SEX RELATIONS ARE                    WHERE PREMARITAL SEX RELATIONS ARE                      3    15
     STRONGLY PUNISHED AND IN FACT RARE, OR                FREELY PERMITTED  (67) JTW,EA                   XSQ=    17.50
     WEAKLY PUNISHED AND IN FACT NOT RARE, OR                                                              PHI=    0.653
     PUNISHED ONLY IF                                                                                      XP =   0.0000
     PREGNANCY RESULTS  (112) JTW,EA

393  DRIFT TOWARD BEING THOSE         0.76 OF  17     393  DRIFT TOWARD BEING THOSE         0.59 OF  17        13     7
     WHERE EXTRAMARITAL COITUS                             WHERE EXTRAMARITAL COITUS IS                            4    10
     IS PUNISHED, RATHER THAN                              PERMITTED, RATHER THAN                          XSQ=     3.04
     PERMITTED  (43) F-B                                   PUNISHED  (41) F-B                              PHI=    0.299
                                                                                                           EP =   0.0799

396  TILT LESS TOWARD BEING THOSE     0.53 OF  19     396  TILT MORE TOWARD BEING THOSE     0.88 OF  16         9     2
     WHERE THE STRENGTH OF MENSTRUAL TABOOS                WHERE THE STRENGTH OF MENSTRUAL TABOOS                 10    14
     IS LOW  (35) WNS                                      IS LOW  (35) WNS                                XSQ=     3.42
                                                                                                           PHI=    0.312
                                                                                                           EP =   0.0354

398  TEND TO BE THOSE                 0.87 OF  15     398  TEND TO BE THOSE                 0.80 OF  15        13     3
     WHERE THE INTENSITY OF SEX ANXIETY                    WHERE THE INTENSITY OF SEX ANXIETY                      2    12
     IS HIGH  (16) WNS                                     IS LOW  (16) WNS                                XSQ=    10.85
                                                                                                           PHI=    0.601
                                                                                                           EP =   0.0007

399  TILT TOWARD BEING THOSE          0.63 OF  19     399  TILT TOWARD BEING THOSE          0.80 OF  15        12     3
     WHERE INTENSITY OF CASTRATION ANXIETY                 WHERE INTENSITY OF CASTRATION ANXIETY                   7    12
     IS HIGH  (23) WNS                                     IS LOW  (22) WNS                                XSQ=     4.70
                                                                                                           PHI=    0.372
                                                                                                           EP =   0.0171

405  TILT TOWARD BEING THOSE          0.57 OF  28     405  TILT TOWARD BEING THOSE          0.78 OF  23        12    18
     WHERE EXPLANATIONS OF ILLNESS                         WHERE EXPLANATIONS OF ILLNESS                          16     5
     OF A DEPENDENCE NATURE                                OF A DEPENDENCE NATURE                          XSQ=     5.15
     ARE ABSENT  (27) W-C                                  ARE PRESENT  (34) W-C                           PHI=   -0.318
                                                                                                           XP =   0.0232

445  DRIFT TOWARD BEING THOSE         0.89 OF   9     445  DRIFT TOWARD BEING THOSE         0.58 OF  12         8     5
     WHERE SORCERY IS                                      WHERE SORCERY IS                                        1     7
     IMPORTANT  (26) EBW,DH                                UNIMPORTANT  (23) BBW,DH                        XSQ=     3.07
                                                                                                           PHI=    0.382
                                                                                                           EP =   0.0669

447  LEAN TOWARD BEING THOSE          0.93 OF  14     447  LEAN TOWARD BEING THOSE          0.63 OF  19        13     7
     WHERE LOVE MAGIC IS                                   WHERE LOVE MAGIC IS                                     1    12
     PRESENT  (20) S-R                                     ABSENT  (13) S-R                                XSQ=     8.38
                                                                                                           PHI=    0.504
                                                                                                           EP =   0.0014
```

459	LEAN TOWARD BEING THOSE WHERE GAMES, IF PRESENT, INCLUDE GAMES OF CHANCE (82) R-A-B,EA	0.57 OF 21	459	LEAN TOWARD BEING THOSE WHERE GAMES, IF PRESENT, DO NOT INCLUDE GAMES OF CHANCE (89) R-A-B,EA	0.89 OF 18	12 2 9 16 XSQ= 7.04 PHI= 0.425 EP = 0.0063
460	TILT TOWARD BEING THOSE WHERE GAMES, IF PRESENT, ARE NOT LIMITED TO GAMES OF SKILL ONLY (104) R-A-B,EA	0.71 OF 21	460	TILT TOWARD BEING THOSE WHERE GAMES, IF PRESENT, ARE LIMITED TO GAMES OF SKILL ONLY (67) R-A-B,EA	0.72 OF 18	6 13 15 5 XSQ= 5.75 PHI= -0.384 EP = 0.0104
476	DRIFT TOWARD BEING THOSE WHERE THE DEGREE OF INSOBRIETY IS MODERATE OR SLIGHT (18) CH	0.78 OF 9	476	DRIFT TOWARD BEING THOSE WHERE THE DEGREE OF INSOBRIETY IS STRONG (31) DH	0.67 OF 12	2 8 7 4 XSQ= 2.49 PHI= -0.344 EP = 0.0805

```
312 CULTURES                                         312 CULTURES
    WHERE DEPENDENCE SOCIALIZATION ANXIETY               WHERE DEPENDENCE SOCIALIZATION ANXIETY
    IS HIGH (24) W-C                                     IS LOW (23) W-C

BACKGROUND ON PAGE 138                                                    BOTH SUBJECT AND PREDICATE

     24  IN LEFT COLUMN

AINU        ALORESE     ASHANTI     AZANDE      BALINESE    CHIR-APACHE DOBUANS     DUSUN       IFUGAO      KUTENAI
KWAKIUTL    LAKHER      LESU        MAORI       NAVAHO      PUKAPUKA    RWALA       SAMOANS     SANPOIL     SENIANG
SIRIONO     TENINO      THONGA      TROBRIAND

     23  IN RIGHT COLUMN

ANDAMANESE  ARAPESH     CHAGGA      CHENCHU     COMANCHE    COPR ESKIMO FON         HANO        KURTATCHI   LEPCHA
MANUS       MARQUESANS  MARSHALLESE ONTONG-JAVA PAPAGO      TANALA      TETON       TIKOPIA     VENDA       WITOTO
WOGEO       YAGUA       YAKUT

     353  EXCLUDED BECAUSE UNASCERTAINED

308 DRIFT TOWARD BEING THOSE       0.71 OF 21    308 DRIFT TOWARD BEING THOSE       0.63 OF 19      15    7
    WHERE AVERAGE SOCIALIZATION ANXIETY              WHERE AVERAGE SOCIALIZATION ANXIETY             6   12
    IS HIGH (22) W-C                                 IS LOW (18) W-C                           XSQ=    3.52
                                                                                               PHI=   0.297
                                                                                               EP =  0.0550

309 TILT TOWARD BEING THOSE        0.65 OF 23    309 TILT TOWARD BEING THOSE        0.73 OF 22      15    6
    WHERE ORAL SOCIALIZATION ANXIETY                 WHERE ORAL SOCIALIZATION ANXIETY                8   16
    IS HIGH (26) W-C                                 IS LOW (27) W-C                           XSQ=    5.07
                                                                                               PHI=   0.336
                                                                                               XP =  0.0243

310 DRIFT TOWARD BEING THOSE       0.71 OF 21    310 DRIFT TOWARD BEING THOSE       0.63 OF 19      15    7
    WHERE ANAL SOCIALIZATION ANXIETY                 WHERE ANAL SOCIALIZATION ANXIETY                6   12
    IS HIGH (22) W-C                                 IS LOW (19) W-C                           XSQ=    3.52
                                                                                               PHI=   0.297
                                                                                               EP =  0.0550

318 TILT TOWARD BEING THOSE        0.69 OF 16    318 TILT TOWARD BEING THOSE        0.70 OF 20       5   14
    WHERE THE OVERALL INDULGENCE                     WHERE THE OVERALL INDULGENCE                   11    6
    OF THE INFANT                                    OF THE INFANT                             XSQ=    3.91
    IS LOW (31) B-B-C                                IS HIGH (40) B-B-C                        PHI=  -0.330
                                                                                               EP =  0.0425
```

No.		No.		
322	DRIFT TOWARD BEING THOSE 0.79 OF 14 WHERE THE CONSISTENCY OF REDUCTION OF THE INFANT'S DRIVES IS LOW (32) B-B-C	322	DRIFT TOWARD BEING THOSE 0.56 OF 18 WHERE THE CONSISTENCY OF REDUCTION OF THE INFANT'S DRIVES IS HIGH (27) B-B-C	3 10 11 8 XSQ= 2.52 PHI= -0.281 EP = 0.0751
323	DRIFT TOWARD BEING THOSE 0.81 OF 16 WHERE THE CONSTANCY OF PRESENCE OF THE INFANT'S NURTURANT AGENT IS LOW (45) B-B-C	323	DRIFT TOWARD BEING THOSE 0.50 OF 20 WHERE THE CONSTANCY OF PRESENCE OF THE INFANT'S NURTURANT AGENT IS HIGH (29) B-B-C	3 10 13 10 XSQ= 2.53 PHI= -0.265 EP = 0.0827
324	DRIFT TOWARD BEING THOSE 0.67 OF 15 WHERE THE PAIN INFLICTED ON THE INFANT BY THE NURTURANT AGENT IS HIGH (34) B-B-C	324	DRIFT TOWARD BEING THOSE 0.65 OF 20 WHERE THE PAIN INFLICTED ON THE INFANT BY THE NURTURANT AGENT IS LOW OR NEGLIGIBLE (32) B-B-C	10 7 5 13 XSQ= 2.29 PHI= 0.256 EP = 0.0922
325	DRIFT TOWARD BEING THOSE 0.81 OF 16 WHERE THE DEGREE OF DIFFUSION AMONG THE INFANT'S NURTURANT AGENTS IS HIGH (42) B-B-C	325	DRIFT TOWARD BEING THOSE 0.50 OF 20 WHERE THE DEGREE OF DIFFUSION AMONG THE INFANT'S NURTURANT AGENTS IS LOW (32) B-B-C	13 10 3 10 XSQ= 2.53 PHI= 0.265 EP = 0.0827
335	DRIFT TOWARD BEING THOSE 0.67 OF 18 WHERE INITIAL INDULGENCE OF DEPENDENCY IS LOW (18) WNS	335	DRIFT TOWARD BEING THOSE 0.67 OF 18 WHERE INITIAL INDULGENCE OF DEPENDENCY IS HIGH (20) WNS	6 12 12 6 XSQ= 2.78 PHI= -0.278 EP = 0.0564
342	TILT TOWARD BEING THOSE 0.77 OF 13 WHERE THE CHILD'S INFERRED ANXIETY OVER PERFORMANCE OF NURTURANT BEHAVIOR IS HIGH (18) B-B-C	342	TILT TOWARD BEING THOSE 0.73 OF 11 WHERE THE CHILD'S INFERRED ANXIETY OVER PERFORMANCE OF NURTURANT BEHAVIOR IS LOW (28) B-B-C	10 3 3 8 XSQ= 4.09 PHI= 0.413 EP = 0.0377
356	TILT TOWARD BEING THOSE 0.64 OF 14 WHERE ADOLESCENT PEER GROUPS OR PAIRS ARE PRESENT IN A SETTING OF COURTSHIP (29) JKH	356	TILT TOWARD BEING THOSE 0.88 OF 8 WHERE NEITHER ADOLESCENT PEER GROUPS NOR PAIRS ARE PRESENT IN A SETTING OF COURTSHIP (22) JKH	9 1 5 7 XSQ= 3.62 PHI= 0.405 EP = 0.0310
380	DRIFT TOWARD BEING THOSE 0.50 OF 14 WHERE SEGREGATION OF GIRLS AT MENARCHE IS ABSENT (20) F-B	380	DRIFT TOWARD BEING THOSE 0.89 OF 9 WHERE SEGREGATION OF GIRLS AT MENARCHE IS PRESENT (35) F-B	7 8 7 1 XSQ= 2.14 PHI= -0.305 EP = 0.0858
393	DRIFT TOWARD BEING THOSE 0.68 OF 19 WHERE EXTRAMARITAL COITUS IS PUNISHED, RATHER THAN PERMITTED (43) F-B	393	DRIFT TOWARD BEING THOSE 0.67 OF 12 WHERE EXTRAMARITAL COITUS IS PERMITTED, RATHER THAN PUNISHED (41) F-B	13 4 6 8 XSQ= 2.38 PHI= 0.277 EP = 0.0751

```
426  DRIFT TOWARD BEING THOSE         0.63 OF  19     426  DRIFT TOWARD BEING THOSE         0.70 OF  20         12    6
     WHERE A HIGH GOD IS                                   WHERE A HIGH GOD IS                                   7   14
     PRESENT  (156) GES,EA                                 ABSENT  (104) GES,EA                          XSQ=     3.08
                                                                                                         PHI=    0.281
                                                                                                         EP =   0.0562

473  DRIFT LESS TOWARD BEING THOSE  0.55 OF  20     473  DRIFT MORE TOWARD BEING THOSE  0.84 OF  19          9    3
     WHERE SENSITIVITY TO INSULT                           WHERE SENSITIVITY TO INSULT                          11   16
     IS MODERATE OR NEGLIGIBLE  (56) PES                   IS MODERATE OR NEGLIGIBLE  (56) PES           XSQ=     2.65
                                                                                                         PHI=    0.261
                                                                                                         EP =   0.0824
```

****

313 CULTURES WHERE AGGRESSION SOCIALIZATION ANXIETY IS HIGH (26) W-C	313 CULTURES WHERE AGGRESSION SOCIALIZATION ANXIETY IS LOW (28) W-C

BACKGROUND ON PAGE 138 BOTH SUBJECT AND PREDICATE

....

26 IN LEFT COLUMN

AINU	ALORESE	ARAPESH	ASHANTI	AZANDE	CHIR-APACHE	DOBUANS	FON	HANO	JIVARO
KUTENAI	KWAKIUTL	LEPCHA	MAORI	OMAHA	PAPAGO	RWALA	SAMOANS	SANPOIL	TANALA
TAOS	TENINO	TETON	VENDA	YAKUT	ZUNI				

28 IN RIGHT COLUMN

ABIPON	ANDAMANESE	BALINESE	CHAGGA	CHENCHU	COMANCHE	COPR ESKIMO	DUSUN	IFUGAO	KURTATCHI
LAKHER	LAMBA	LESU	MANUS	MARQUESANS	MARSHALLESE	MASAI	MURNGIN	NAVAHO	ONTONG-JAVA
PUKAPUKA	SIRIONO	THONGA	TIKOPIA	TIV	TROBRIAND	WOGEO	YAGUA		

346 EXCLUDED BECAUSE UNASCERTAINED

	High (26)			Low (28)			
6	TILT TOWARD BEING THOSE LOCATED OUTSIDE OF THE INSULAR PACIFIC (330)	0.81 OF 26	6	TILT TOWARD BEING THOSE LOCATED IN THE INSULAR PACIFIC (70)	0.50 OF 28	5 14 21 14 XSQ= 4.33 PHI= -0.283 XP = 0.0375
8	TILT LESS TOWARD BEING THOSE LOCATED OUTSIDE OF NORTH AMERICA (330)	0.58 OF 26	8	TILT MORE TOWARD BEING THOSE LOCATED OUTSIDE OF NORTH AMERICA (330)	0.89 OF 28	11 3 15 25 XSQ= 5.46 PHI= 0.318 XP = 0.0195
14	TEND TO BE THOSE WHERE THE LATITUDE IS THIRTY DEGREES OR GREATER (119)	0.58 OF 26	14	TEND TO BE THOSE WHERE THE LATITUDE IS LESS THAN THIRTY DEGREES (281)	0.89 OF 28	15 3 11 25 XSQ= 11.36 PHI= 0.459 XP = 0.0008
15	LEAN TOWARD BEING THOSE WHERE THE LATITUDE IS TWENTY DEGREES OR GREATER (183)	0.69 OF 26	15	LEAN TOWARD BEING THOSE WHERE THE LATITUDE IS LESS THAN TWENTY DEGREES (217)	0.79 OF 28	18 6 8 22 XSQ= 10.62 PHI= 0.443 XP = 0.0011

16	DRIFT TOWARD BEING THOSE WHERE THE LATITUDE IS TEN DEGREES OR GREATER (277)	0.77 OF 26	16	DRIFT TOWARD BEING THOSE WHERE THE LATITUDE IS LESS THAN TEN DEGREES (123)	0.50 OF 28	20 14 6 14 XSQ= 3.12 PHI= 0.240 XP = 0.0776
42	TILT TOWARD BEING THOSE WHERE THE NATURAL ENVIRONMENT IS OTHER THAN TROPICAL OR SUB-TROPICAL RAIN FOREST, OR MONSOON FOREST (244) FWM	0.73 OF 26	42	TILT TOWARD BEING THOSE WHERE THE NATURAL ENVIRONMENT IS TROPICAL OR SUB-TROPICAL RAIN FOREST, OR MONSOON FOREST (156) FWM	0.57 OF 28	7 16 19 12 XSQ= 3.88 PHI= -0.268 XP = 0.0490
73	TILT TOWARD BEING THOSE WHERE WEAVING IS PRESENT (118)	0.62 OF 21	73	TILT TOWARD BEING THOSE WHERE WEAVING IS ABSENT (130)	0.73 OF 22	13 6 8 16 XSQ= 3.92 PHI= 0.302 XP = 0.0478
82	IN ALL CASES ARE THOSE WHERE A CITY OR TOWN IS PRESENT, OR THE AVERAGE COMMUNITY SIZE IS FIFTY OR GREATER (178)	1.00 OF 16	82	TILT LESS TOWARD BEING THOSE WHERE A CITY OR TOWN IS PRESENT, OR THE AVERAGE COMMUNITY SIZE IS FIFTY OR GREATER (178)	0.65 OF 20	16 13 0 7 XSQ= 4.90 PHI= 0.369 EP = 0.0107
224	DRIFT TOWARD BEING THOSE WHERE COUSIN MARRIAGE IS PREFERENTIALLY OR PERMISSIVELY SYMMETRICAL, RATHER THAN EITHER PATRI- OR MATRILATERAL (106)	0.75 OF 8	224	DRIFT TOWARD BEING THOSE WHERE COUSIN MARRIAGE IS PREFERENTIALLY OR PERMISSIVELY EITHER PATRI- OR MATRILATERAL, RATHER THAN SYMMETRICAL (66)	0.78 OF 9	2 7 6 2 XSQ= 2.85 PHI= -0.410 EP = 0.0567
236	TILT TOWARD BEING THOSE WHERE THE FAMILY IS OF AN EXTENDED TYPE, RATHER THAN AN INDEPENDENT TYPE (213)	0.62 OF 26	236	TILT TOWARD BEING THOSE WHERE THE FAMILY IS OF AN INDEPENDENT TYPE, RATHER THAN AN EXTENDED TYPE (185)	0.71 OF 28	16 8 10 20 XSQ= 4.67 PHI= 0.294 XP = 0.0306
240	DRIFT TOWARD BEING THOSE WHERE THE FAMILY, IF EXTENDED, IS SMALL OR STEM, RATHER THAN LARGE (135)	0.69 OF 16	240	DRIFT TOWARD BEING THOSE WHERE THE FAMILY, IF EXTENDED, IS LARGE, RATHER THAN SMALL OR STEM (78)	0.75 OF 8	5 6 11 2 XSQ= 2.54 PHI= -0.325 EP = 0.0825
296	DRIFT TOWARD BEING THOSE WHERE INFANTICIDE IS PRESENT (18) BCA	0.71 OF 17	296	DRIFT TOWARD BEING THOSE WHERE INFANTICIDE IS ABSENT OR INFERRED ABSENT (15) BCA	0.63 OF 16	12 6 5 10 XSQ= 2.43 PHI= 0.271 EP = 0.0844
302	TILT TOWARD BEING THOSE WHERE THE AVERAGE EARLY SATISFACTION POTENTIAL IS LOW (17) W-C	0.59 OF 22	302	TILT TOWARD BEING THOSE WHERE THE AVERAGE EARLY SATISFACTION POTENTIAL IS HIGH (23) W-C	0.78 OF 18	9 14 13 4 XSQ= 4.10 PHI= -0.320 EP = 0.0267

305	TEND TO BE THOSE 0.73 OF 22 WHERE THE EARLY SEXUAL SATISFACTION POTENTIAL IS LOW (24) W-C	305	TEND TO BE THOSE 0.81 OF 26 WHERE THE EARLY SEXUAL SATISFACTION POTENTIAL IS HIGH (27) W-C	6 21 16 5 XSQ= 11.77 PHI= -0.495 XP = 0.0006
307	TEND TO BE THOSE 0.64 OF 25 WHERE THE EARLY AGGRESSION SATISFACTION POTENTIAL IS LOW (19) W-C	307	TEND TO BE THOSE 0.89 OF 27 WHERE THE EARLY AGGRESSION SATISFACTION POTENTIAL IS HIGH (33) W-C	9 24 16 3 XSQ= 13.46 PHI= -0.509 XP = 0.0002
308	TILT TOWARD BEING THOSE 0.73 OF 22 WHERE AVERAGE SOCIALIZATION ANXIETY IS HIGH (22) W-C	308	TILT TOWARD BEING THOSE 0.67 OF 18 WHERE AVERAGE SOCIALIZATION ANXIETY IS LOW (18) W-C	16 6 6 12 XSQ= 4.72 PHI= 0.343 EP = 0.0244
311	LEAN TOWARD BEING THOSE 0.82 OF 22 WHERE SEXUAL SOCIALIZATION ANXIETY IS HIGH (28) W-C	311	LEAN TOWARD BEING THOSE 0.69 OF 26 WHERE SEXUAL SOCIALIZATION ANXIETY IS LOW (23) W-C	18 8 4 18 XSQ= 10.54 PHI= 0.469 XP = 0.0012
322	DRIFT TOWARD BEING THOSE 0.61 OF 18 WHERE THE CONSISTENCY OF REDUCTION OF THE INFANT'S DRIVES IS HIGH (27) B-B-C	322	DRIFT TOWARD BEING THOSE 0.72 OF 18 WHERE THE CONSISTENCY OF REDUCTION OF THE INFANT'S DRIVES IS LOW (32) B-B-C	11 5 7 13 XSQ= 2.81 PHI= 0.280 EP = 0.0922
341	TILT TOWARD BEING THOSE 0.92 OF 12 WHERE THE CHILD'S INFERRED ANXIETY OVER NON-PERFORMANCE OF NURTURANT BEHAVIOR IS HIGH (30) B-B-C	341	TILT TOWARD BEING THOSE 0.54 OF 13 WHERE THE CHILD'S INFERRED ANXIETY OVER NON-PERFORMANCE OF NURTURANT BEHAVIOR IS LOW (16) B-B-C	11 6 1 7 XSQ= 4.03 PHI= 0.402 EP = 0.0302
350	DRIFT TOWARD BEING THOSE 0.72 OF 18 WHERE THE CHILD'S INFERRED ANXIETY OVER PERFORMANCE OF ACHIEVEMENT BEHAVIOR IS HIGH (34) B-B-C	350	DRIFT TOWARD BEING THOSE 0.62 OF 13 WHERE THE CHILD'S INFERRED ANXIETY OVER PERFORMANCE OF ACHIEVEMENT BEHAVIOR IS LOW (26) B-B-C	13 5 5 8 XSQ= 2.28 PHI= 0.271 EP = 0.0785
352	DRIFT TOWARD BEING THOSE 0.72 OF 18 WHERE THE TOTAL POSITIVE PRESSURE TOWARD DEVELOPING OBEDIENT BEHAVIOR IN THE CHILD IS HIGH (44) B-B-C	352	DRIFT TOWARD BEING THOSE 0.61 OF 23 WHERE THE TOTAL POSITIVE PRESSURE TOWARD DEVELOPING OBEDIENT BEHAVIOR IN THE CHILD IS LOW (28) B-B-C	13 9 5 14 XSQ= 3.22 PHI= 0.280 XP = 0.0729
353	TILT TOWARD BEING THOSE 0.83 OF 18 WHERE THE CHILD'S INFERRED ANXIETY OVER NON-PERFORMANCE OF OBEDIENT BEHAVIOR IS HIGH (42) B-B-C	353	TILT TOWARD BEING THOSE 0.57 OF 23 WHERE THE CHILD-S INFERRED ANXIETY OVER NON-PERFORMANCE OF OBEDIENT BEHAVIOR IS LOW (32) B-B-C	15 10 3 13 XSQ= 5.17 PHI= 0.355 XP = 0.0230

399	TILT TOWARD BEING THOSE WHERE INTENSITY OF CASTRATION ANXIETY IS HIGH (23) WNS	0.65 OF 17	399	TILT TOWARD BEING THOSE WHERE INTENSITY OF CASTRATION ANXIETY IS LOW (22) WNS	0.72 OF 18	11 5 6 13 XSQ= 3.43 PHI= 0.313 EP = 0.0437
426	TILT TOWARD BEING THOSE WHERE A HIGH GOD IS PRESENT (156) GES,EA	0.67 OF 21	426	TILT TOWARD BEING THOSE WHERE A HIGH GOD IS ABSENT (104) GES,EA	0.75 OF 24	14 6 7 18 XSQ= 6.28 PHI= 0.374 XP = 0.0122
435	DRIFT TOWARD BEING THOSE WHERE ABANDONMENT OF THE HOUSE OF THE DEAD IS NOT PRACTICED (19) LWS	0.88 OF 8	435	DRIFT TOWARD BEING THOSE WHERE ABANDONMENT OF THE HOUSE OF THE DEAD IS PRACTICED (12) LWS	0.75 OF 4	1 3 7 1 XSQ= 2.30 PHI= -0.437 EP = 0.0667
442	TILT TOWARD BEING THOSE WHERE FEAR OF ANIMAL SPIRITS IS HIGH (28) W-C	0.65 OF 26	442	TILT TOWARD BEING THOSE WHERE FEAR OF ANIMAL SPIRITS IS LOW (33) W-C	0.71 OF 28	17 8 9 20 XSQ= 5.94 PHI= 0.332 XP = 0.0148
447	TILT TOWARD BEING THOSE WHERE LOVE MAGIC IS PRESENT (20) S-R	0.83 OF 12	447	TILT TOWARD BEING THOSE WHERE LOVE MAGIC IS ABSENT (13) S-R	0.58 OF 19	10 8 2 11 XSQ= 3.58 PHI= 0.340 EP = 0.0317
459	LEAN TOWARD BEING THOSE WHERE GAMES, IF PRESENT, INCLUDE GAMES OF CHANCE (82) R-A-B,EA	0.70 OF 20	459	LEAN TOWARD BEING THOSE WHERE GAMES, IF PRESENT, DO NOT INCLUDE GAMES OF CHANCE (89) R-A-B,EA	0.81 OF 21	14 4 6 17 XSQ= 8.83 PHI= 0.464 XP = 0.0030
460	TILT TOWARD BEING THOSE WHERE GAMES, IF PRESENT, ARE NOT LIMITED TO GAMES OF SKILL ONLY (104) R-A-B,EA	0.80 OF 20	460	TILT TOWARD BEING THOSE WHERE GAMES, IF PRESENT, ARE LIMITED TO GAMES OF SKILL ONLY (67) R-A-B,EA	0.62 OF 21	4 13 16 8 XSQ= 5.79 PHI= -0.376 XP = 0.0162
474	DRIFT TOWARD BEING THOSE WHERE BOASTFULNESS IS MODERATE, NEGLIBIBLE, OR UNREPORTED (48) PES	0.71 OF 21	474	DRIFT TOWARD BEING THOSE WHERE BOASTFULNESS IS EXTREME (41) PES	0.58 OF 24	6 14 15 10 XSQ= 2.90 PHI= -0.254 XP = 0.0884
480	TILT TOWARD BEING THOSE WHERE COMPLEXITY OF ARTISTIC DESIGN IS HIGH (14) HB	0.67 OF 15	480	TILT TOWARD BEING THOSE WHERE COMPLEXITY OF ARTISTIC DESIGN IS LOW (15) HB	0.77 OF 13	10 3 5 10 XSQ= 3.71 PHI= 0.364 EP = 0.0296

314 CULTURES
WHERE THE INCIDENCE CF MOTHER-CHILD
HOUSEHOLDS IS HIGH (19) W-D,S

314 CULTURES
WHERE THE INCIDENCE CF MOTHER-CHILD
HOUSEHOLDS IS LOW (61) W-D,S

BACKGROUND ON PAGE 139

BOTH SUBJECT AND PREDICATE

19 IN LEFT COLUMN

ARAPESH	ASHANTI	AZANDE	BEMBA	FON	GANDA	KAPAUKU	KURTATCHI	MAGUZAWA	MENDE
MUNDURUCU	NUER	NYAKYUSA	TALLENSI	TANALA	THONGA	TIV	VENDA	YURCK	

61 IN RIGHT COLUMN

AINU	ALCRESE	ANDAMANESE	ARANDA	ARAUCANIANS	AYMARA	BALINESE	BHIL	CAGABA	CAMAYURA
CARIB	CHENCHU	CHIR-APACHE	COMANCHE	COPR ESKIMO	CUNA	DOBUANS	EGYPTIANS	GILYAK	HANO
IBAN	IFUGAC	JIVARO	KASKA	KAZAK	KORYAK	KUTENAI	KWAKIUTL	LAKHER	LAMBA
LAPPS	LEPCHA	MANUS	MAORI	MARQUESANS	MURNGIN	NAMA	NAMBICUARA	NAVAHO	OJIBWA
OMAHA	PAPAGO	PUKAPUKA	RIFFIANS	SAMOANS	SEMANG	SENIANG	SIRIONC	SIUAI	THAI
TIKCPIA	TIMBIRA	TROBRIAND	TRUKESE	TUBATULABAL	TUPINAMBA	TZELTAL	WITOTO	WOLEAIANS	YAGUA
ZUNI									

320 EXCLUDED BECAUSE UNASCERTAINED

3	TEND TO BE THOSE LOCATED IN AFRICA (80)	0.63 OF 19	3	TEND TO BE THOSE LOCATED OUTSIDE OF AFRICA (320)	0.97 OF 61	12 2 / 7 59	XSQ= 31.95 PHI= 0.632 XP = 0.
16	TILT TOWARD BEING THOSE WHERE THE LATITUDE IS LESS THAN TEN DEGREES (123)	0.63 OF 19	16	TILT TOWARD BEING THOSE WHERE THE LATITUDE IS TEN DEGREES OR GREATER (277)	0.72 OF 61	7 44 / 12 17	XSQ= 6.35 PHI= -0.282 XP = 0.0117
33	IN ALL CASES ARE THOSE WHERE THE NATURAL ENVIRONMENT IS OTHER THAN 'VERY HARSH,' I.E., DESERT, DESERT GRASSES AND SHRUBS, TUNDRA, OR HIGH PLATEAU STEPPE (341) FWM	1.00 OF 19	33	DRIFT LESS TOWARD BEING THOSE WHERE THE NATURAL ENVIRONMENT IS OTHER THAN 'VERY HARSH,' I.E., DESERT, DESERT GRASSES AND SHRUBS, TUNDRA, OR HIGH PLATEAU STEPPE (341) FWM	0.79 OF 61	0 13 / 19 48	XSQ= 3.40 PHI= -0.206 XP = 0.0654
46	DRIFT MORE TOWARD BEING THOSE OTHER THAN WHERE SETTLEMENTS ARE NON-FIXED AND MOVEMENT IS NOMADIC (260)	0.94 OF 18	46	DRIFT LESS TOWARD BEING THOSE OTHER THAN WHERE SETTLEMENTS ARE NON-FIXED AND MOVEMENT IS NOMADIC (260)	0.72 OF 57	1 16 / 17 41	XSQ= 2.78 PHI= -0.192 XP = 0.0957

No.		No.		
51	LEAN TOWARD BEING THOSE 0.89 OF 19 WHERE SUBSISTENCE IS PRIMARILY BY FOOD PRODUCTION -- I. E., AGRICULTURE OR HUSBANDRY -- RATHER THAN BY GATHERING (253)	51	LEAN TOWARD BEING THOSE 0.54 OF 61 WHERE SUBSISTENCE IS PRIMARILY BY FOOD GATHERING -- I. E., HUNTING, FISHING, OR COLLECTING -- RATHER THAN FOOD PRODUCTION (147)	17 28 2 33 XSQ= 9.48 PHI= 0.344 XP = 0.0021
71	LEAN TOWARD BEING THOSE 0.65 OF 17 WHERE METAL WORKING IS PRESENT (98)	71	LEAN TOWARD BEING THOSE 0.74 OF 50 WHERE METAL WORKING IS ABSENT (153)	11 13 6 37 XSQ= 6.67 PHI= 0.316 XP = 0.0098
85	TEND TO BE THOSE 0.50 OF 16 WHERE THE LEVEL OF POLITICAL INTEGRATION IS THE LARGE STATE, OR THE LITTLE STATE (70) GPM	85	TEND TO BE THOSE 0.92 OF 53 WHERE THE LEVEL OF POLITICAL INTEGRATION IS THE MINIMAL STATE, THE AUTONOMOUS COMMUNITY, OR THE FAMILY (234) GPM	8 4 8 49 XSQ= 12.60 PHI= 0.427 XP = 0.0004
86	LEAN TOWARD BEING THOSE 0.69 OF 16 WHERE THE LEVEL OF POLITICAL INTEGRATION IS THE LARGE STATE, THE LITTLE STATE, OR THE MINIMAL STATE (148) GPM	86	LEAN TOWARD BEING THOSE 0.72 OF 53 WHERE THE LEVEL OF POLITICAL INTEGRATION IS THE AUTONOMOUS COMMUNITY, OR THE FAMILY (156) GPM	11 15 5 38 XSQ= 6.93 PHI= 0.317 XP = 0.0085
95	LEAN LESS TOWARD BEING THOSE 0.56 OF 18 WHERE THE HIERARCHY OF NATIONAL JURISDICTION HAS ONE OR NO LEVELS (254) GES,EA	95	LEAN MORE TOWARD BEING THOSE 0.89 OF 56 WHERE THE HIERARCHY OF NATIONAL JURISDICTION HAS ONE OR NO LEVELS (254) GES,EA	8 6 10 50 XSQ= 8.02 PHI= 0.329 XP = 0.0046
102	DRIFT TOWARD BEING THOSE 0.74 OF 19 WHERE CLASS STRATIFICATION IS PRESENT (203)	102	DRIFT TOWARD BEING THOSE 0.55 OF 60 WHERE CLASS STRATIFICATION IS ABSENT (180)	14 27 5 33 XSQ= 3.68 PHI= 0.216 XP = 0.0552
106	DRIFT TOWARD BEING THOSE 0.79 OF 14 WHERE CLASS STRATIFICATION, IF PRESENT, IS BASED ON SOMETHING OTHER THAN WEALTH (126)	106	DRIFT TOWARD BEING THOSE 0.56 OF 27 WHERE CLASS STRATIFICATION, IF PRESENT, IS BASED ON WEALTH (77)	3 15 11 12 XSQ= 3.08 PHI= -0.274 XP = 0.0791
108	TILT TOWARD BEING THOSE 0.79 OF 14 WHERE CLASS STRATIFICATION, IF PRESENT, IS BASED ON A HEREDITARY ARISTOCRACY (74)	108	TILT TOWARD BEING THOSE 0.67 OF 27 WHERE CLASS STRATIFICATION, IF PRESENT, IS BASED ON SOMETHING OTHER THAN A HEREDITARY ARISTOCRACY (129)	11 9 3 18 XSQ= 5.85 PHI= 0.378 XP = 0.0156
110	TILT TOWARD BEING THOSE 0.68 OF 19 WHERE SLAVERY IS PRESENT (163)	110	TILT TOWARD BEING THOSE 0.65 OF 60 WHERE SLAVERY IS ABSENT (218)	13 21 6 39 XSQ= 5.28 PHI= 0.259 XP = 0.0215

129	TILT TCWARD BEING THCSE WHERE WEAVING IS MAINLY DCNE BY MALES (31)	0.71 OF 7	129	TILT TOWARD BEING THOSE WHERE WEAVING IS MAINLY DONE BY FEMALES (73)	0.77 OF 22	5 5 2 17 XSQ= 3.63 PHI= 0.354 EP = 0.0302
130	IN ALL CASES ARE THCSE WHERE LEATHER WCRKING IS MAINLY DCNE BY MALES (39)	1.00 OF 4	130	TILT TCWARD BEING THOSE WHERE LEATHER WORKING IS MAINLY DONE BY FEMALES (45)	0.65 OF 17	4 6 0 11 XSQ= 3.15 PHI= 0.387 EP = 0.0351
186	LEAN TCWARD BEING THCSE WHERE THE KIN GRCUP IS EXCLUSIVELY PATRILINEAL (150)	0.63 OF 19	186	LEAN TOWARD BEING THOSE WHERE THE KIN GRCUP IS OTHER THAN EXCLUSIVELY PATRILINEAL (250)	0.74 OF 61	12 16 7 45 XSQ= 7.14 PHI= 0.299 XP = 0.0076
188	LEAN MCRE TOWARC BEING THCSE WHERE THE KIN GRCUP IS CTHER THAN EXCLUSIVELY CCGNATIC (252)	0.95 OF 19	188	LEAN LESS TOWARD BEING THOSE WHERE THE KIN GROUP IS OTHER THAN EXCLUSIVELY CCGNATIC (252)	0.59 OF 61	1 25 18 36 XSQ= 6.88 PHI= -0.293 XP = 0.C087
192	DRIFT MCRE TCWARC BEING THCSE CTHER THAN WHERE THE CNLY KIN GROUP PRESENT IS A KINDREC CR ELSE BILATERAL DESCENT IS INFERREC (289)	0.95 OF 19	192	DRIFT LESS TOWARD BEING THCSE OTHER THAN WHERE THE ONLY KIN GRCUP PRESENT IS A KINDRED OR ELSE BILATERAL DESCENT IS INFERRED (289)	0.72 CF 61	1 17 18 44 XSQ= 3.05 PHI= -0.195 XP = 0.0808
242	IN ALL CASES ARE THCSE WHERE MARRIAGE IS COMMCNLY CR CCCASICNALLY PCLYGYNOUS, RATHER THAN MONCGAMCUS (314)	1.00 OF 19	242	TILT LESS TCWARD BEING THCSE WHERE MARRIAGE IS COMMONLY OR OCCASIONALLY PCLYGYNCUS, RATHER THAN MONCGAMOUS (314)	0.72 CF 60	19 43 0 17 XSQ= 5.28 PHI= 0.259 XP = 0.0215
243	TEND TC BE THCSE WHERE PCLYGYNY, IF PRESENT, HAS A HIGH INCICENCE (24) W-C,S	0.83 OF 18	243	TEND TO BE THOSE WHERE POLYGYNY, IF PRESENT, HAS A LOW INCIDENCE (36) W-D,S	0.78 CF 37	15 8 3 29 XSQ= 16.50 PHI= 0.548 XP = 0.0000
254	IN ALL CASES ARE THCSE WHERE HCUSEHCLD AUTHCRITY IS CN THE FATHER'S SICE, RATHER THAN THE MCTHER'S (9) CA	1.00 OF 4	254	DRIFT TOWARD BEING THOSE WHERE HOUSEHOLD AUTHORITY IS ON THE MOTHER'S SIDE, RATHER THAN THE FATHER'S (6) DA	0.67 OF 6	4 2 0 4 XSQ= 2.10 PHI= 0.458 EP = 0.0762
260	TILT TCWARD BEING THCSE WHERE THE AGE CF MALES AT MARRIAGE IS TWENTY CR CVER (17) JKH	0.60 OF 10	260	TILT TOWARD BEING THOSE WHERE THE AGE CF MALES AT MARRIAGE IS LESS THAN TWENTY (38) JKH	0.81 OF 26	4 21 6 5 XSQ= 3.90 PHI= -0.329 EP = 0.0390

263	LEAN MORE TOWARD BEING THOSE 0.89 OF 19 WHERE WIVES ARE OBTAINED BY RELATIVELY DIFFICULT MEANS, NAMELY BY BRIDE-PRICE, BRIDE-SERVICE, OR EXCHANGING A FEMALE RELATIVE (233)	263	LEAN LESS TOWARD BEING THOSE 0.51 OF 61 WHERE WIVES ARE OBTAINED BY RELATIVELY DIFFICULT MEANS, NAMELY BY BRIDE-PRICE, BRIDE-SERVICE, OR EXCHANGING A FEMALE RELATIVE (233)	17 31 2 30 XSQ= 7.48 PHI= 0.306 XP = 0.0062
304	IN ALL CASES ARE THOSE 1.00 OF 8 WHERE THE EARLY ANAL SATISFACTION POTENTIAL IS LOW (22) W-C	304	LEAN TOWARD BEING THOSE 0.57 OF 23 WHERE THE EARLY ANAL SATISFACTION POTENTIAL IS HIGH (19) W-C	0 13 8 10 XSQ= 5.64 PHI= -0.427 EP = 0.0096
311	TILT TOWARD BEING THOSE 0.89 OF 9 WHERE SEXUAL SOCIALIZATION ANXIETY IS HIGH (28) W-C	311	TILT TOWARD BEING THOSE 0.62 OF 29 WHERE SEXUAL SOCIALIZATION ANXIETY IS LOW (23) W-C	8 11 1 18 XSQ= 5.24 PHI= 0.371 EP = 0.0188
316	LEAN TOWARD BEING THOSE 0.80 OF 10 WHERE EXCLUSIVE MOTHER-SON SLEEPING ARRANGEMENTS LAST ONE YEAR OR LONGER (19) W-K-A	316	LEAN TOWARD BEING THOSE 0.73 OF 26 WHERE EXCLUSIVE MOTHER-SON SLEEPING ARRANGEMENTS LAST LESS THAN ONE YEAR (25) W-K-A	8 7 2 19 XSQ= 6.33 PHI= 0.419 EP = 0.0071
318	DRIFT TOWARD BEING THOSE 0.73 OF 11 WHERE THE OVERALL INDULGENCE OF THE INFANT IS LOW (31) B-B-C	318	DRIFT TOWARD BEING THOSE 0.63 OF 38 WHERE THE OVERALL INDULGENCE OF THE INFANT IS HIGH (40) B-B-C	3 24 8 14 XSQ= 3.11 PHI= -0.252 XP = 0.0779
324	TILT TOWARD BEING THOSE 0.82 OF 11 WHERE THE PAIN INFLICTED ON THE INFANT BY THE NURTURANT AGENT IS HIGH (34) B-B-C	324	TILT TOWARD BEING THOSE 0.59 OF 34 WHERE THE PAIN INFLICTED ON THE INFANT BY THE NURTURANT AGENT IS LOW OR NEGLIGIBLE (32) B-B-C	9 14 2 20 XSQ= 3.99 PHI= 0.298 XP = 0.0458
336	DRIFT TOWARD BEING THOSE 0.77 OF 13 WHERE THE TOTAL POSITIVE PRESSURE TOWARD DEVELOPING RESPONSIBLE BEHAVIOR IN THE CHILD IS HIGH (43) B-B-C	336	DRIFT TOWARD BEING THOSE 0.55 OF 38 WHERE THE TOTAL POSITIVE PRESSURE TOWARD DEVELOPING RESPONSIBLE BEHAVIOR IN THE CHILD IS LOW (32) B-B-C	10 17 3 21 XSQ= 2.84 PHI= 0.236 XP = 0.0920
337	TILT TOWARD BEING THOSE 0.77 OF 13 WHERE THE CHILD'S INFERRED ANXIETY OVER NON-PERFORMANCE OF RESPONSIBLE BEHAVIOR IS HIGH (38) B-B-C	337	TILT TOWARD BEING THOSE 0.64 OF 36 WHERE THE CHILD'S INFERRED ANXIETY OVER NON-PERFORMANCE OF RESPONSIBLE BEHAVIOR IS LOW (35) B-B-C	10 13 3 23 XSQ= 4.85 PHI= 0.315 XP = 0.0276
352	TILT TOWARD BEING THOSE 0.82 OF 11 WHERE THE TOTAL POSITIVE PRESSURE TOWARD DEVELOPING OBEDIENT BEHAVIOR IN THE CHILD IS HIGH (44) B-B-C	352	TILT TOWARD BEING THOSE 0.59 OF 37 WHERE THE TOTAL POSITIVE PRESSURE TOWARD DEVELOPING OBEDIENT BEHAVIOR IN THE CHILD IS LOW (28) B-B-C	9 15 2 22 XSQ= 4.25 PHI= 0.297 XP = 0.0393

```
353  DRIFT TOWARD BEING THOSE        0.82 OF  11     353  DRIFT TOWARD BEING THOSE        0.53 OF  38           9    18
     WHERE THE CHILD'S INFERRED ANXIETY OVER             WHERE THE CHILD-S INFERRED ANXIETY OVER                 2    20
     NON-PERFORMANCE OF OBEDIENT BEHAVIOR                NON-PERFORMANCE OF OBEDIENT BEHAVIOR          XSQ=        2.82
     IS HIGH   (42) B-B-C                                IS LOW   (32) B-B-C                           PHI=       0.240
                                                                                                        XP =      0.0932

365  TILT TOWARD BEING THOSE         0.88 OF   8     365  TILT TOWARD BEING THOSE         0.57 OF  21           7     9
     WHERE THE TIME SPENT IN                             WHERE THE TIME SPENT IN                                 1    12
     ADOLESCENT PEER GROUP ACTIVITY                      ADOLESCENT PEER GROUP ACTIVITY                XSQ=        3.04
     IS HIGH OR HIGH-MEDIUM  (30) JKH                    IS LOW-MEDIUM OR LOW   (15) JKH               PHI=       0.324
                                                                                                        EP =      0.0443

370  TEND TO BE THOSE                0.88 OF  16     370  TEND TO BE THOSE                0.73 OF  48          14    13
     WHERE THE SEGREGATION OF ADOLESCENT BOYS            WHERE THE SEGREGATION OF ADOLESCENT BOYS                2    35
     IS COMPLETE OR PARTIAL   (95)                       IS ABSENT   (148)                             XSQ=       15.57
                                                                                                        PHI=       0.493
                                                                                                        XP =      0.0001

386  IN ALL CASES ARE THOSE          1.00 OF   7     386  TILT TOWARD BEING THOSE         0.55 OF  38           7    17
     WHERE SEXUAL EXPRESSION BY THE YOUNG                WHERE SEXUAL EXPRESSION BY THE YOUNG                    0    21
     IS RESTRICTED OR                                    IS PERMITTED   (40) F-B                       XSQ=        5.20
     SEMI-RESTRICTED   (46) F-B                                                                        PHI=       0.340
                                                                                                        XP =      0.0226

399  TILT TOWARD BEING THOSE         0.82 OF  11     399  TILT TOWARD BEING THOSE         0.62 OF  26           9    10
     WHERE INTENSITY OF CASTRATION ANXIETY               WHERE INTENSITY OF CASTRATION ANXIETY                   2    16
     IS HIGH   (23) WNS                                  IS LOW   (22) WNS                             XSQ=        4.21
                                                                                                        PHI=       0.337
                                                                                                        EP =      0.0293

406  DRIFT TOWARD BEING THOSE        0.78 OF   9     406  DRIFT TOWARD BEING THOSE        0.63 OF  35           2    22
     WHERE EXPLANATIONS OF ILLNESS                       WHERE EXPLANATIONS OF ILLNESS                           7    13
     OF AN AGGRESSION NATURE                             OF AN AGGRESSION NATURE                       XSQ=        3.27
     ARE ABSENT   (33) W-C                               ARE PRESENT   (28) W-C                        PHI=      -0.273
                                                                                                        XP =      0.0706

440  DRIFT TOWARD BEING THOSE        0.78 OF   9     440  DRIFT TOWARD BEING THOSE        0.60 OF  35           2    21
     WHERE FEAR OF SPIRITS                               WHERE FEAR OF SPIRITS                                   7    14
     IS LOW   (29) W-C                                   IS HIGH   (32) W-C                            XSQ=        2.72
                                                                                                        PHI=      -0.249
                                                                                                        XP =      0.0990

447  IN ALL CASES ARE THOSE          1.00 OF   6     447  TILT TOWARD BEING THOSE         0.52 OF  23           6    11
     WHERE LOVE MAGIC IS                                 WHERE LOVE MAGIC IS                                     0    12
     PRESENT   (20) S-R                                  ABSENT   (13) S-R                             XSQ=        3.41
                                                                                                        PHI=       0.343
                                                                                                        EP =      0.0280

452  LEAN TOWARD BEING THOSE         0.82 OF  11     452  LEAN TOWARD BEING THOSE         0.74 OF  23           9     6
     WHERE TOTEMISM WITH FOOD TABOOS                     WHERE TOTEMISM WITH FOOD TABOOS                         2    17
     IS PRESENT   (19) WNS                               IS ABSENT   (24) WNS                          XSQ=        7.25
                                                                                                        PHI=       0.462
                                                                                                        EP =      0.0035
```

458	TEND TC BE THCSE WHERE GAMES, IF PRESENT, INCLUDE GAMES CF STRATEGY (52) R-A-B,EA	0.77 OF 13	458	TEND TO BE THOSE WHERE GAMES, IF PRESENT, DO NOT INCLUDE GAMES OF STRATEGY (119) R-A-B,EA	0.81 CF 42	10 8 3 34 XSQ= 12.59 PHI= 0.478 XP = 0.0004
460	TILT TOWARC BEING THOSE WHERE GAMES, IF PRESENT, ARE NCT LIMITED TO GAMES CF SKILL CNLY (104) R-A-B,EA	0.92 OF 13	46C	TILT TOWARD BEING THOSE WHERE GAMES, IF PRESENT, ARE LIMITED TO GAMES OF SKILL CNLY (67) R-A-B,EA	0.52 OF 42	1 22 12 20 XSQ= 6.42 PHI= -0.342 XP = 0.0113
476	DRIFT TCWARD BEING THCSE WHERE THE DEGREE OF INSOBRIETY IS MODERATE CR SLIGHT (18) CF	0.83 OF 6	476	DRIFT TOWARD BEING THOSE WHERE THE DEGREE OF INSCBRIETY IS STRONG (31) DH	0.68 OF 19	1 13 5 6 XSQ= 3.08 PHI= -0.351 EP = 0.0561

315 CULTURES WHERE MOTHER AND NURSING CHILD CUSTOMARILY SLEEP IN THE SAME BED (37) W-C,S	315 CULTURES WHERE MOTHER AND NURSING CHILD CUSTOMARILY SLEEP IN DIFFERENT BEDS (14) W-D,S

BACKGROUND ON PAGE 139 BOTH SUBJECT AND PREDICATE

37 IN LEFT COLUMN

ALORESE	ANDAMANESE	ARAPESH	ARAUCANIANS	ASHANTI	AYMARA	BHIL	CAMAYURA	CHENCHU	COPR ESKIMO
DOBUANS	EGYPTIANS	IFUGAO	KURTATCHI	LEPCHA	MAGUZAWA	MANUS	MENDE	NAMBICUARA	NAVAHO
PAPAGO	RIFFIANS	SAMOANS	SEMANG	SENIANG	SIRIONO	SIUAI	TALLENSI	TANALA	TARAHUMARA
TIV	TODA	TZELTAL	WITOTO	WOGEO	WOLEAIANS	YAGUA			

14 IN RIGHT COLUMN

AINU	COMANCHE	CUNA	GANDA	GILYAK	JIVARO	KAPAUKU	KASKA	KORYAK	LAPPS
OJIBWA	OMAHA	THAI	TROBRIAND						

349 EXCLUDED BECAUSE UNASCERTAINED

13	TEND TO BE THOSE WHERE THE LATITUDE IS LESS THAN FORTY DEGREES (329)	0.97 OF 37	13 TEND TO BE THOSE WHERE THE LATITUDE IS FORTY DEGREES OR GREATER (71)	0.50 OF 14	1 7 36 7 XSQ= 13.79 PHI= -0.520 XP = 0.0002
14	LEAN TOWARD BEING THOSE WHERE THE LATITUDE IS LESS THAN THIRTY DEGREES (281)	0.86 OF 37	14 LEAN TOWARD BEING THOSE WHERE THE LATITUDE IS THIRTY DEGREES OR GREATER (119)	0.57 OF 14	5 8 32 6 XSQ= 8.01 PHI= -0.396 XP = 0.0046
15	DRIFT TOWARD BEING THOSE WHERE THE LATITUDE IS LESS THAN TWENTY DEGREES (217)	0.73 OF 37	15 DRIFT TOWARD BEING THOSE WHERE THE LATITUDE IS TWENTY DEGREES OR GREATER (183)	0.57 OF 14	10 8 27 6 XSQ= 2.82 PHI= -0.235 XP = 0.0929
130	TILT TOWARD BEING THOSE WHERE LEATHER WORKING IS MAINLY DONE BY MALES (39)	0.78 OF 9	130 TILT TOWARD BEING THOSE WHERE LEATHER WORKING IS MAINLY DONE BY FEMALES (45)	0.86 OF 7	7 1 2 6 XSQ= 4.06 PHI= 0.504 EP = 0.0406

No.			No.			
241	IN ALL CASES ARE THOSE WHERE THE FAMILY, IF EXTENDED, IS LARGE OR SMALL, RATHER THAN STEM (187)	1.00 OF 19	241	DRIFT LESS TOWARD BEING THOSE WHERE THE FAMILY, IF EXTENDED, IS LARGE OR SMALL, RATHER THAN STEM (187)	0.78 OF 9	19 7 0 2 XSQ= 1.81 PHI= 0.255 EP = 0.0952
257	DRIFT TOWARD BEING THOSE WHERE THE SEVERITY OF SISTER AVOIDANCE IS LOW (17) WNS	0.92 OF 12	257	DRIFT TOWARD BEING THOSE WHERE THE SEVERITY OF SISTER AVOIDANCE IS HIGH (10) WNS	0.67 OF 3	1 2 11 1 XSQ= 2.11 PHI= -0.375 EP = 0.0813
311	DRIFT TOWARD BEING THOSE WHERE SEXUAL SOCIALIZATION ANXIETY IS HIGH (28) W-C	0.65 OF 20	311	IN ALL CASES ARE THOSE WHERE SEXUAL SOCIALIZATION ANXIETY IS LOW (23) W-C	1.00 OF 3	13 0 7 3 XSQ= 2.23 PHI= 0.311 EP = 0.0678
344	DRIFT TOWARD BEING THOSE WHERE THE TOTAL POSITIVE PRESSURE TOWARD DEVELOPING SELF-RELIANT BEHAVIOR IN THE CHILD IS LOW (40) B-B-C	0.62 OF 21	344	DRIFT TOWARD BEING THOSE WHERE THE TOTAL POSITIVE PRESSURE TOWARD DEVELOPING SELF-RELIANT BEHAVIOR IN THE CHILD IS HIGH (36) B-B-C	0.80 OF 10	8 8 13 2 XSQ= 3.23 PHI= -0.323 EP = 0.0538
346	DRIFT TOWARD BEING THOSE WHERE THE CHILD'S INFERRED ANXIETY OVER PERFORMANCE OF SELF-RELIANT BEHAVIOR IS HIGH (37) B-B-C	0.57 OF 21	346	DRIFT TOWARD BEING THOSE WHERE THE CHILD'S INFERRED ANXIETY OVER PERFORMANCE OF SELF-RELIANT BEHAVIOR IS LOW (39) B-B-C	0.80 OF 10	12 2 9 8 XSQ= 2.42 PHI= 0.280 EP = 0.0680
444	TILT TOWARD BEING THOSE WHERE THE USE OF DREAMS TO SEEK AND CONTROL SUPERNATURAL POWERS IS LOW (27) RGD	0.67 OF 18	444	TILT TOWARD BEING THOSE WHERE THE USE OF DREAMS TO SEEK AND CONTROL SUPERNATURAL POWERS IS HIGH (28) RGD	0.82 OF 11	6 9 12 2 XSQ= 4.63 PHI= -0.400 EP = 0.0209

316 CULTURES
WHERE EXCLUSIVE MOTHER-SON SLEEPING
ARRANGEMENTS LAST ONE YEAR
OR LONGER (19) W-K-A

316 CULTURES
WHERE EXCLUSIVE MOTHER-SON SLEEPING
ARRANGEMENTS LAST LESS THAN
ONE YEAR (25) W-K-A

BACKGROUND ON PAGE 139

BOTH SUBJECT AND PREDICATE

19 IN LEFT COLUMN

ASHANTI	AZANDE	CAGABA	CAMAYURA	CHAGGA	CHEYENNE	CHIR-APACHE	FON	GANDA	JIVARO
LESU	NUER	NYAKYUSA	SAMOANS	SIRIONO	THONGA	TIV	TROBRIAND	YAPESE	

25 IN RIGHT COLUMN

ALORESE	AMERICANS	ARAUCANIANS	BALINESE	COPR ESKIMO	EGYPTIANS	HANO	JAPANESE	KORYAK	KWAKIUTL
LAKHER	LAMBA	LAPPS	LEPCHA	MAORI	NAVAHO	OJIBWA	ONTONG-JAVA	PAPAGO	SERBS
TALLENSI	TANALA	TIMBIRA	TRUKESE	YAGUA					

356 EXCLUDED BECAUSE UNASCERTAINED

3	LEAN LESS TOWARD BEING THOSE LOCATED OUTSIDE OF AFRICA (320)	0.53 OF 19	3	LEAN MORE TOWARD BEING THOSE LOCATED OUTSIDE OF AFRICA (320)	0.92 OF 25	9 2 / 10 23 / XSQ= 6.95 / PHI= 0.397 / XP = 0.0084
13	IN ALL CASES ARE THOSE WHERE THE LATITUDE IS LESS THAN FORTY DEGREES (329)	1.00 OF 19	13	TILT LESS TOWARD BEING THOSE WHERE THE LATITUDE IS LESS THAN FORTY DEGREES (329)	0.72 OF 25	0 7 / 19 18 / XSQ= 4.41 / PHI= -0.316 / XP = 0.0358
14	TILT TOWARD BEING THOSE WHERE THE LATITUDE IS LESS THAN THIRTY DEGREES (281)	0.89 OF 19	14	TILT TOWARD BEING THOSE WHERE THE LATITUDE IS THIRTY DEGREES OR GREATER (119)	0.52 OF 25	2 13 / 17 12 / XSQ= 6.52 / PHI= -0.385 / XP = 0.0107
15	LEAN TOWARD BEING THOSE WHERE THE LATITUDE IS LESS THAN TWENTY DEGREES (217)	0.84 OF 19	15	LEAN TOWARD BEING THOSE WHERE THE LATITUDE IS TWENTY DEGREES OR GREATER (183)	0.68 OF 25	3 17 / 16 8 / XSQ= 9.86 / PHI= -0.473 / XP = 0.0017
16	TILT TOWARD BEING THOSE WHERE THE LATITUDE IS LESS THAN TEN DEGREES (123)	0.63 OF 19	16	TILT TOWARD BEING THOSE WHERE THE LATITUDE IS TEN DEGREES OR GREATER (277)	0.76 OF 25	7 19 / 12 6 / XSQ= 5.32 / PHI= -0.348 / XP = 0.0210

53	DRIFT TOWARD BEING THOSE 0.80 OF 15 WHERE FOOD PRODUCTION IS BY SIMPLE AGRICULTURE OR INCIPIENT FOOD PRODUCTION, RATHER THAN BY INTENSIVE AGRICULTURE (147)	53	DRIFT TOWARD BEING THOSE 0.56 OF 16 WHERE FOOD PRODUCTION IS BY INTENSIVE AGRICULTURE, RATHER THAN BY SIMPLE AGRICULTURE OR INCIPIENT FOOD PRODUCTION (91)	3 9 12 7 XSQ= 2.90 PHI= -0.306 EP = 0.0659
55	TILT TOWARD BEING THOSE 0.77 OF 13 WHERE FOOD PRODUCTION IS BY SIMPLE AGRICULTURE, RATHER THAN BY INTENSIVE AGRICULTURE (101)	55	TILT TOWARD BEING THOSE 0.75 OF 12 WHERE FOOD PRODUCTION IS BY INTENSIVE AGRICULTURE, RATHER THAN BY SIMPLE AGRICULTURE (91)	3 9 10 3 XSQ= 4.82 PHI= -0.439 EP = 0.0169
106	DRIFT MORE TOWARD BEING THOSE 0.90 OF 10 WHERE CLASS STRATIFICATION, IF PRESENT, IS BASED ON SOMETHING OTHER THAN WEALTH (126)	106	DRIFT LESS TOWARD BEING THOSE 0.56 OF 16 WHERE CLASS STRATIFICATION, IF PRESENT, IS BASED ON SOMETHING OTHER THAN WEALTH (126)	1 7 9 9 XSQ= 1.90 PHI= -0.270 EP = 0.0989
108	TILT TOWARD BEING THOSE 0.80 OF 10 WHERE CLASS STRATIFICATION, IF PRESENT, IS BASED ON A HEREDITARY ARISTOCRACY (74)	108	TILT TOWARD BEING THOSE 0.69 OF 16 WHERE CLASS STRATIFICATION, IF PRESENT, IS BASED ON SOMETHING OTHER THAN A HEREDITARY ARISTOCRACY (129)	8 5 2 11 XSQ= 4.06 PHI= 0.395 EP = 0.0414
127	LEAN TOWARD BEING THOSE 0.90 OF 10 WHERE THE FEMALES' CONTRIBUTION TO SUBSISTENCE IS HIGH (33) JKB	127	LEAN TOWARD BEING THOSE 0.76 OF 17 WHERE THE FEMALES' CONTRIBUTION TO SUBSISTENCE IS LOW (32) JKB	9 4 1 13 XSQ= 8.64 PHI= 0.566 EP = 0.0013
128	DRIFT TOWARD BEING THOSE 0.86 OF 7 WHERE, IF SUBSISTENCE IS PRIMARILY BY AGRICULTURE, THE WORK IS MAINLY DONE BY FEMALES (37)	128	DRIFT TOWARD BEING THOSE 0.80 OF 5 WHERE, IF SUBSISTENCE IS PRIMARILY BY AGRICULTURE, THE WORK IS MAINLY DONE BY MALES (40)	1 4 6 1 XSQ= 2.83 PHI= -0.486 EP = 0.0720
137	TILT TOWARD BEING THOSE 0.73 OF 15 WHERE INVIDIOUS DISPLAY OF WEALTH IS STRONGLY EMPHASIZED (37) PES	137	TILT TOWARD BEING THOSE 0.72 OF 18 WHERE INVIDIOUS DISPLAY OF WEALTH IS MODERATELY, LITTLE, OR NEGATIVELY EMPHASIZED (52) PES	11 5 4 13 XSQ= 5.10 PHI= 0.393 EP = 0.0149
240	TILT TOWARD BEING THOSE 0.64 OF 11 WHERE THE FAMILY, IF EXTENDED, IS LARGE, RATHER THAN SMALL OR STEM (78)	240	TILT TOWARD BEING THOSE 0.78 OF 18 WHERE THE FAMILY, IF EXTENDED, IS SMALL OR STEM, RATHER THAN LARGE (135)	7 4 4 14 XSQ= 3.37 PHI= 0.341 EP = 0.0482
242	TILT MORE TOWARD BEING THOSE 0.95 OF 19 WHERE MARRIAGE IS COMMONLY OR OCCASIONALLY POLYGYNOUS, RATHER THAN MONOGAMOUS (314)	242	TILT LESS TOWARD BEING THOSE 0.64 OF 25 WHERE MARRIAGE IS COMMONLY OR OCCASIONALLY POLYGYNOUS, RATHER THAN MONOGAMOUS (314)	18 16 1 9 XSQ= 4.19 PHI= 0.309 XP = 0.0407

243	TILT TOWARD BEING THOSE 0.60 OF 15 WHERE POLYGYNY, IF PRESENT, HAS A HIGH INCIDENCE (24) W-D,S	243	TILT TOWARD BEING THOSE 0.81 OF 16 WHERE POLYGYNY, IF PRESENT, HAS A LOW INCIDENCE (36) W-D,S	9 3 6 13 XSQ= 3.95 PHI= 0.357 EP = 0.0290
286	DRIFT TOWARD BEING THOSE 0.73 OF 11 WHERE THE NUMBER OF FOOD TABOOS DURING PREGNANCY IS HIGH (20) BCA	286	DRIFT TOWARD BEING THOSE 0.78 OF 9 WHERE THE NUMBER OF FOOD TABOOS DURING PREGNANCY IS LOW OR ABSENT (14) BCA	8 2 3 7 XSQ= 3.23 PHI= 0.402 EP = 0.0698
299	LEAN TOWARD BEING THOSE 0.60 OF 15 WHERE THE POST-PARTUM SEX TABOO LASTS LONGER THAN ONE YEAR (35)	299	LEAN TOWARD BEING THOSE 0.92 OF 13 WHERE THE POST-PARTUM SEX TABOO LASTS ONE YEAR OR LESS (89)	9 1 6 12 XSQ= 6.18 PHI= 0.470 EP = 0.0060
314	LEAN TOWARD BEING THOSE 0.53 OF 15 WHERE THE INCIDENCE OF MOTHER-CHILD HOUSEHOLDS IS HIGH (19) W-D,S	314	LEAN TOWARD BEING THOSE 0.90 OF 21 WHERE THE INCIDENCE OF MOTHER-CHILD HOUSEHOLDS IS LOW (61) W-D,S	8 2 7 19 XSQ= 6.33 PHI= 0.419 EP = 0.0071
368	DRIFT TOWARD BEING THOSE 0.67 OF 9 WHERE DISSOCIATION OF THE SEXES AT ADOLESCENCE IS HIGH OR MEDIUM (16) JKH	368	DRIFT TOWARD BEING THOSE 0.77 OF 13 WHERE DISSOCIATION OF THE SEXES AT ADOLESCENCE IS LOW (21) JKH	6 3 3 10 XSQ= 2.57 PHI= 0.342 EP = 0.0789
369	IN ALL CASES ARE THOSE 1.00 OF 17 WHERE DISSOCIATION OF THE SEXES AT ADOLESCENCE, OR CUSTOMS OF INITIATION AT ADOLESCENCE, ARE PRESENT (42) JKH	369	TEND TO BE THOSE 0.59 OF 17 WHERE BOTH DISSOCIATION OF THE SEXES AT ADOLESCENCE, AND CUSTOMS OF INITIATION AT ADOLESCENCE, ARE ABSENT (15) JKH	17 7 0 10 XSQ= 11.47 PHI= 0.581 EP = 0.0003
370	LEAN TOWARD BEING THOSE 0.65 OF 17 WHERE THE SEGREGATION OF ADOLESCENT BOYS IS COMPLETE OR PARTIAL (95)	370	LEAN TOWARD BEING THOSE 0.80 OF 20 WHERE THE SEGREGATION OF ADOLESCENT BOYS IS ABSENT (148)	11 4 6 16 XSQ= 5.88 PHI= 0.399 EP = 0.0084
373	LEAN TOWARD BEING THOSE 0.68 OF 19 WHERE MALE INITIATION CEREMONIES AT PUBERTY ARE PRESENT (17) W-K-A	373	LEAN TOWARD BEING THOSE 0.84 OF 25 WHERE MALE INITIATION CEREMONIES AT PUBERTY ARE ABSENT (27) W-K-A	13 4 6 21 XSQ= 10.40 PHI= 0.486 XP = 0.0013
377	DRIFT LESS TOWARD BEING THOSE 0.63 OF 19 WHERE MALE GENITAL MUTILATION IS ABSENT (242)	377	DRIFT MORE TOWARD BEING THOSE 0.91 OF 23 WHERE MALE GENITAL MUTILATION IS ABSENT (242)	7 2 12 21 XSQ= 3.37 PHI= 0.283 XP = 0.0665

382	TILT TOWARD BEING THOSE WHERE FEMALE INITIATION RITES ARE PRESENT (38) JKB	0.80 OF 10	382	TILT TOWARD BEING THOSE WHERE FEMALE INITIATION RITES ARE ABSENT (27) JKB	0.71 OF 17	8 5 2 12 XSQ= 4.59 PHI= 0.412 EP = 0.0183
385	DRIFT TOWARD BEING THOSE WHERE SEXUAL EXPRESSION BY THE YOUNG IS RESTRICTED (22) F-B	0.50 OF 12	385	DRIFT TOWARD BEING THOSE WHERE SEXUAL EXPRESSION BY THE YOUNG IS SEMI-RESTRICTED OR PERMITTED (64) F-B	0.86 OF 14	6 2 6 12 XSQ= 2.37 PHI= 0.302 EP = 0.0895
399	TILT TOWARD BEING THOSE WHERE INTENSITY OF CASTRATION ANXIETY IS HIGH (23) WNS	0.71 OF 14	399	TILT TOWARD BEING THOSE WHERE INTENSITY OF CASTRATION ANXIETY IS LOW (22) WNS	0.75 OF 16	10 4 4 12 XSQ= 4.74 PHI= 0.397 EP = 0.0261
406	DRIFT TOWARD BEING THOSE WHERE EXPLANATIONS OF ILLNESS OF AN AGGRESSION NATURE ARE ABSENT (33) W-C	0.58 OF 12	406	DRIFT TOWARD BEING THOSE WHERE EXPLANATIONS OF ILLNESS OF AN AGGRESSION NATURE ARE PRESENT (28) W-C	0.80 OF 15	5 12 7 3 XSQ= 2.72 PHI= -0.317 EP = 0.0568
419	TILT TOWARD BEING THOSE WHERE MILITARY GLORY IS STRONGLY OR MODERATELY EMPHASIZED (55) PES	0.87 OF 15	419	TILT TOWARD BEING THOSE WHERE MILITARY GLORY IS NEGLIGIBLY EMPHASIZED (31) PES	0.59 OF 17	13 7 2 10 XSQ= 5.23 PHI= 0.404 EP = 0.0118
420	LEAN TOWARD BEING THOSE WHERE BELLICOSITY IS EXTREME (41) PES	0.73 OF 15	420	LEAN TOWARD BEING THOSE WHERE BELLICOSITY IS MODERATE OR NEGLIGIBLE (46) PES	0.83 OF 18	11 3 4 15 XSQ= 8.56 PHI= 0.509 EP = 0.0016
427	TILT TOWARD BEING THOSE WHERE A HIGH GOD, IF PRESENT, IS INACTIVE, RATHER THAN ACTIVE (69) GES,EA	0.83 OF 12	427	TILT TOWARD BEING THOSE WHERE A HIGH GOD, IF PRESENT, IS ACTIVE, RATHER THAN INACTIVE (87) GES,EA	0.69 OF 13	2 9 10 4 XSQ= 5.03 PHI= -0.448 EP = 0.0154
445	IN ALL CASES ARE THOSE WHERE SORCERY IS IMPORTANT (26) BBW,DH	1.00 OF 6	445	DRIFT TOWARD BEING THOSE WHERE SORCERY IS UNIMPORTANT (23) BBW,DH	0.50 OF 8	6 4 0 4 XSQ= 2.11 PHI= 0.388 EP = 0.0849
452	DRIFT TOWARD BEING THOSE WHERE TOTEMISM WITH FOOD TABOOS IS PRESENT (19) WNS	0.75 OF 12	452	DRIFT TOWARD BEING THOSE WHERE TOTEMISM WITH FOOD TABOOS IS ABSENT (24) WNS	0.69 OF 16	9 5 3 11 XSQ= 3.65 PHI= 0.361 EP = 0.0542

472	LEAN TOWARC BEING THOSE WHERE THE COMPOSITE NARCISSISM INCEX IS HIGH (47) PES	0.94 OF 16	472	LEAN TOWARD BEING THOSE WHERE THE COMPOSITE NARCISSISM INDEX IS LOW (43) PES	0.61 OF 18	15	7
						1	11
					XSQ=		8.89
					PHI=		0.511
					EP =		0.0011

```
****************************************************************************************************

317  CULTURES                                        317  CULTURES
     WHERE DISPLAY OF AFFECTION TOWARD                    WHERE DISPLAY OF AFFECTION TOWARD
     THE INFANT IS HIGH  (39) B-B-C                       THE INFANT IS LOW  (29) B-B-C


BACKGROUND ON PAGE 140                                                    BOTH SUBJECT AND PREDICATE
....................................................................................................

     39   IN LEFT COLUMN

ANDAMANESE  ARAPESH    BALINESE    CHAGGA      CHENCHU     CHEYENNE    CHIR-APACHE CHUKCHEE    CROW        CUNA
HANO        JIVARO     KORYAK      KURTATCHI   LAU         LESU        MANUS       MAORI       MURNGIN     NUER
OMAHA       ONA        ONTONG-JAVA PAPAGO      SIRIONO     SOTHO       TALLENSI    TETON       TIKOPIA     TIMBIRA
TROBRIAND   TUPINAMBA  TURKANA     WINNEBAGO   WOGEO       WOLEAIANS   YAHGAN      YORUBA      ZUNI

     29   IN RIGHT COLUMN

AINU        ALORESE    ARANDA      ARAUCANIANS ASHANTI     AYMARA      AZANDE      CAMAYURA    COMANCHE    FON
GANDA       KASKA      KWAKIUTL    LEPCHA      MARQUESANS  MASAI       MBUNDU      NAVAHO      OJIBWA      PUKAPUKA
SAMOANS     SHERENTE   SWAZI       TANALA      TENETEHARA  THONGA      TRUKESE     WICHITA     YAKUT

     332  EXCLUDED BECAUSE UNASCERTAINED


----------------------------------------------------------------------------------------------------
 71  LEAN TOWARD BEING THOSE        0.87 OF  30        71  LEAN TOWARD BEING THOSE        0.54 OF  24              4   13
     WHERE METAL WORKING IS                                WHERE METAL WORKING IS                                 26   11
     ABSENT  (153)                                         PRESENT  (98)                                     XSQ=    8.50
                                                                                                             PHI=  -0.397
                                                                                                             XP =  0.0036

 85  DRIFT MORE TOWARD BEING THOSE  0.92 OF  36        85  DRIFT LESS TOWARD BEING THOSE  0.68 OF  22              3    7
     WHERE THE LEVEL OF POLITICAL INTEGRATION              WHERE THE LEVEL OF POLITICAL INTEGRATION               33   15
     IS THE MINIMAL STATE,                                 IS THE MINIMAL STATE,                             XSQ=    3.76
     THE AUTONOMOUS COMMUNITY, OR                          THE AUTONOMOUS COMMUNITY, OR                      PHI=  -0.255
     THE FAMILY  (234) GPM                                 THE FAMILY  (234) GPM                             XP =  0.0525

 96  TILT TOWARD BEING THOSE        0.64 OF  36        96  TILT TOWARD BEING THOSE        0.67 OF  27             13   18
     WHERE THE HIERARCHY                                   WHERE THE HIERARCHY                                    23    9
     OF NATIONAL JURISDICTION HAS                          OF NATIONAL JURISDICTION HAS                      XSQ=    4.61
     NO LEVELS  (156) GES,EA                               FOUR, THREE, TWO OR                               PHI=  -0.270
                                                           ONE LEVEL  (174) GES,EA                           XP =  0.0319

116  IN ALL CASES ARE THOSE         1.00 OF  16       116  LEAN TOWARD BEING THOSE        0.55 OF  11              0    6
     WHERE OCCUPATIONAL SPECIALIZATION IS                  WHERE OCCUPATIONAL SPECIALIZATION IS                   16    5
     PART-TIME ONLY  (34) JMH                              FULL-TIME, WHETHER OR NOT FOR                     XSQ=    8.29
                                                           SURPLUS PRODUCTION  (20) JMH                      PHI=  -0.554
                                                                                                             EP =  0.0016
```

137	DRIFT TOWARD BEING THOSE WHERE INVIDIOUS DISPLAY OF WEALTH IS MODERATELY, LITTLE, OR NEGATIVELY EMPHASIZED (52) PES	0.71 OF 28	137	DRIFT TOWARD BEING THOSE WHERE INVIDIOUS DISPLAY OF WEALTH IS STRONGLY EMPHASIZED (37) PES	0.59 OF 22	8 13 20 9 XSQ= 3.54 PHI= -0.266 XP = 0.0599
138	DRIFT TOWARD BEING THOSE WHERE SUPERORDINATE JUSTICE IS ABSENT (18) BBW	0.57 OF 14	138	DRIFT TOWARD BEING THOSE WHERE SUPERORDINATE JUSTICE IS PRESENT (22) BBW	0.88 OF 8	6 7 8 1 XSQ= 2.55 PHI= -0.341 EP = 0.0743
149	TILT TOWARD BEING THOSE WHERE THE INCIDENCE OF THEFT IS LOW (19) B-B-C	0.70 OF 20	149	TILT TOWARD BEING THOSE WHERE THE INCIDENCE OF THEFT IS HIGH (18) B-B-C	0.75 OF 16	6 12 14 4 XSQ= 5.51 PHI= -0.391 EP = 0.0176
286	TILT TOWARD BEING THOSE WHERE THE NUMBER OF FOOD TABOOS DURING PREGNANCY IS HIGH (20) BCA	0.77 OF 13	286	TILT TOWARD BEING THOSE WHERE THE NUMBER OF FOOD TABOOS DURING PREGNANCY IS LOW OR ABSENT (14) BCA	0.69 OF 13	10 4 3 9 XSQ= 3.87 PHI= 0.386 EP = 0.0472
306	DRIFT TOWARD BEING THOSE WHERE THE EARLY DEPENDENCE SATISFACTION POTENTIAL IS HIGH (28) W-C	0.74 OF 19	306	DRIFT TOWARD BEING THOSE WHERE THE EARLY DEPENDENCE SATISFACTION POTENTIAL IS LOW (24) W-C	0.60 OF 15	14 6 5 9 XSQ= 2.66 PHI= 0.280 EP = 0.0800
309	LEAN TOWARD BEING THOSE WHERE ORAL SOCIALIZATION ANXIETY IS LOW (27) W-C	0.70 OF 20	309	LEAN TOWARD BEING THOSE WHERE ORAL SOCIALIZATION ANXIETY IS HIGH (26) W-C	0.81 OF 16	6 13 14 3 XSQ= 7.42 PHI= -0.454 EP = 0.0031
318	TEND TO BE THOSE WHERE THE OVERALL INDULGENCE OF THE INFANT IS HIGH (40) B-B-C	0.84 OF 38	318	TEND TO BE THOSE WHERE THE OVERALL INDULGENCE OF THE INFANT IS LOW (31) B-B-C	0.75 OF 28	32 7 6 21 XSQ= 21.00 PHI= 0.564 XP = 0.0000
320	TEND TO BE THOSE WHERE THE DEGREE OF REDUCTION OF THE INFANT'S DRIVES IS HIGH (45) B-B-C	0.86 OF 37	320	TEND TO BE THOSE WHERE THE DEGREE OF REDUCTION OF THE INFANT'S DRIVES IS LOW (24) B-B-C	0.57 OF 28	32 12 5 16 XSQ= 11.95 PHI= 0.429 XP = 0.0005
321	TILT TOWARD BEING THOSE WHERE THE IMMEDIACY OF REDUCTION OF THE INFANT'S DRIVES IS HIGH (35) B-B-C	0.73 OF 33	321	TILT TOWARD BEING THOSE WHERE THE IMMEDIACY OF REDUCTION OF THE INFANT'S DRIVES IS LOW (25) B-B-C	0.62 OF 26	24 10 9 16 XSQ= 5.66 PHI= 0.310 XP = 0.0174

322	DRIFT TOWARD BEING THOSE 0.56 OF 32 WHERE THE CONSISTENCY OF REDUCTION OF THE INFANT'S DRIVES IS HIGH (27) B-B-C	322	DRIFT TOWARD BEING THOSE 0.69 OF 26 WHERE THE CONSISTENCY OF REDUCTION OF THE INFANT'S DRIVES IS LOW (32) B-B-C	18 8 14 18 XSQ= 2.81 PHI= 0.220 XP = 0.0939
324	TILT TOWARD BEING THOSE 0.63 OF 35 WHERE THE PAIN INFLICTED ON THE INFANT BY THE NURTURANT AGENT IS LOW OR NEGLIGIBLE (32) B-B-C	324	TILT TOWARD BEING THOSE 0.68 OF 28 WHERE THE PAIN INFLICTED ON THE INFANT BY THE NURTURANT AGENT IS HIGH (34) B-B-C	13 19 22 9 XSQ= 4.71 PHI= -0.273 XP = 0.0300
326	TILT TOWARD BEING THOSE 0.64 OF 33 WHERE THE INFERRED TRANSITION ANXIETY BETWEEN INFANCY AND CHILDHOOD IS LOW (35) B-B-C	326	TILT TOWARD BEING THOSE 0.68 OF 28 WHERE THE INFERRED TRANSITION ANXIETY BETWEEN INFANCY AND CHILDHOOD IS HIGH (32) B-B-C	12 19 21 9 XSQ= 4.82 PHI= -0.281 XP = 0.0282
330	DRIFT TOWARD BEING THOSE 0.61 OF 36 WHERE THE AGE OF THE INFANT AT TIME OF WEANING IS 2.5 YEARS OR HIGHER (34) B-B-C	330	DRIFT TOWARD BEING THOSE 0.67 OF 27 WHERE THE AGE OF THE INFANT AT TIME OF WEANING IS LOWER THAN 2.5 YEARS (36) B-B-C	22 9 14 18 XSQ= 3.72 PHI= 0.243 XP = 0.0539
334	TEND TO BE THOSE 0.77 OF 39 WHERE THE INDULGENCE OF THE CHILD IS HIGH (40) B-B-C	334	TEND TO BE THOSE 0.86 OF 29 WHERE THE INDULGENCE OF THE CHILD IS LOW (38) B-B-C	30 4 9 25 XSQ= 24.05 PHI= 0.595 XP = 0.0000
337	DRIFT TOWARD BEING THOSE 0.62 OF 37 WHERE THE CHILD'S INFERRED ANXIETY OVER NON-PERFORMANCE OF RESPONSIBLE BEHAVIOR IS LOW (35) B-B-C	337	DRIFT TOWARD BEING THOSE 0.64 OF 28 WHERE THE CHILD'S INFERRED ANXIETY OVER NON-PERFORMANCE OF RESPONSIBLE BEHAVIOR IS HIGH (38) B-B-C	14 18 23 10 XSQ= 3.47 PHI= -0.231 XP = 0.0627
338	LEAN TOWARD BEING THOSE 0.57 OF 37 WHERE THE CHILD'S INFERRED ANXIETY OVER PERFORMANCE OF RESPONSIBLE BEHAVIOR IS LOW (29) B-B-C	338	LEAN TOWARD BEING THOSE 0.82 OF 28 WHERE THE CHILD'S INFERRED ANXIETY OVER PERFORMANCE OF RESPONSIBLE BEHAVIOR IS HIGH (44) B-B-C	16 23 21 5 XSQ= 8.49 PHI= -0.361 XP = 0.0036
339	LEAN TOWARD BEING THOSE 0.73 OF 37 WHERE THE CHILD'S INFERRED CONFLICT REGARDING RESPONSIBLE BEHAVIOR IS LOW (42) B-B-C	339	LEAN TOWARD BEING THOSE 0.64 OF 28 WHERE THE CHILD'S INFERRED CONFLICT REGARDING RESPONSIBLE BEHAVIOR IS HIGH (31) B-B-C	10 18 27 10 XSQ= 7.57 PHI= -0.341 XP = 0.0059
341	DRIFT LESS TOWARD BEING THOSE 0.55 OF 22 WHERE THE CHILD'S INFERRED ANXIETY OVER NON-PERFORMANCE OF NURTURANT BEHAVIOR IS HIGH (30) B-B-C	341	DRIFT MORE TOWARD BEING THOSE 0.83 OF 18 WHERE THE CHILD'S INFERRED ANXIETY OVER NON-PERFORMANCE OF NURTURANT BEHAVIOR IS HIGH (30) B-B-C	12 15 10 3 XSQ= 2.54 PHI= -0.252 EP = 0.0896

No.		No.		
346	TILT TOWARD BEING THOSE 0.68 OF 38 WHERE THE CHILD'S INFERRED ANXIETY OVER PERFORMANCE OF SELF-RELIANT BEHAVIOR IS LOW (39) B-B-C	346	TILT TOWARD BEING THOSE 0.62 OF 29 WHERE THE CHILD'S INFERRED ANXIETY OVER PERFORMANCE OF SELF-RELIANT BEHAVIOR IS HIGH (37) B-B-C	12 18 26 11 XSQ= 5.01 PHI= -0.274 XP = 0.0252
347	DRIFT TOWARD BEING THOSE 0.66 OF 38 WHERE THE CHILD'S INFERRED CONFLICT REGARDING SELF-RELIANT BEHAVIOR IS LOW (39) B-B-C	347	DRIFT TOWARD BEING THOSE 0.59 OF 29 WHERE THE CHILD'S INFERRED CONFLICT REGARDING SELF-RELIANT BEHAVIOR IS HIGH (37) B-B-C	13 17 25 12 XSQ= 3.04 PHI= -0.213 XP = 0.0813
353	LEAN TOWARD BEING THOSE 0.64 OF 36 WHERE THE CHILD-S INFERRED ANXIETY OVER NON-PERFORMANCE OF OBEDIENT BEHAVIOR IS LOW (32) B-B-C	353	LEAN TOWARD BEING THOSE 0.79 OF 28 WHERE THE CHILD'S INFERRED ANXIETY OVER NON-PERFORMANCE OF OBEDIENT BEHAVIOR IS HIGH (42) B-B-C	13 22 23 6 XSQ= 9.81 PHI= -0.392 XP = 0.0017
354	TILT TOWARD BEING THOSE 0.64 OF 36 WHERE THE CHILD'S INFERRED ANXIETY OVER PERFORMANCE OF OBEDIENT BEHAVIOR IS LOW (37) B-B-C	354	TILT TOWARD BEING THOSE 0.67 OF 27 WHERE THE CHILD'S INFERRED ANXIETY OVER PERFORMANCE OF OBEDIENT BEHAVIOR IS HIGH (36) B-B-C	13 18 23 9 XSQ= 4.61 PHI= -0.270 XP = 0.0319
355	TILT TOWARD BEING THOSE 0.67 OF 36 WHERE THE CHILD'S INFERRED CONFLICT REGARDING OBEDIENT BEHAVIOR IS LOW (38) B-B-C	355	TILT TOWARD BEING THOSE 0.67 OF 27 WHERE THE CHILD'S INFERRED CONFLICT REGARDING OBEDIENT BEHAVIOR IS HIGH (35) B-B-C	12 18 24 9 XSQ= 5.60 PHI= -0.298 XP = 0.0179
368	TILT TOWARD BEING THOSE 0.69 OF 13 WHERE DISSOCIATION OF THE SEXES AT ADOLESCENCE IS HIGH OR MEDIUM (16) JKH	368	IN ALL CASES ARE THOSE 1.00 OF 5 WHERE DISSOCIATION OF THE SEXES AT ADOLESCENCE IS LOW (21) JKH	9 0 4 5 XSQ= 4.43 PHI= 0.496 EP = 0.0294
369	DRIFT MORE TOWARD BEING THOSE 0.89 OF 18 WHERE DISSOCIATION OF THE SEXES AT ADOLESCENCE, OR CUSTOMS OF INITIATION AT ADOLESCENCE, ARE PRESENT (42) JKH	369	DRIFT LESS TOWARD BEING THOSE 0.62 OF 13 WHERE DISSOCIATION OF THE SEXES AT ADOLESCENCE, OR CUSTOMS OF INITIATION AT ADOLESCENCE, ARE PRESENT (42) JKH	16 8 2 5 XSQ= 1.85 PHI= 0.245 EP = 0.0994
405	DRIFT TOWARD BEING THOSE 0.64 OF 22 WHERE EXPLANATIONS OF ILLNESS OF A DEPENDENCE NATURE ARE ABSENT (27) W-C	405	DRIFT TOWARD BEING THOSE 0.69 OF 16 WHERE EXPLANATIONS OF ILLNESS OF A DEPENDENCE NATURE ARE PRESENT (34) W-C	8 11 14 5 XSQ= 2.70 PHI= -0.267 EP = 0.0991
421	LEAN TOWARD BEING THOSE 0.79 OF 28 WHERE KILLING, TORTURING, OR MUTILATING OF THE ENEMY IS NEGLIGIBLY EMPHASIZED (47) PES	421	LEAN TOWARD BEING THOSE 0.67 OF 21 WHERE KILLING, TORTURING, OR MUTILATING OF THE ENEMY IS STRONGLY OR MODERATELY EMPHASIZED (37) PES	6 14 22 7 XSQ= 8.38 PHI= -0.414 XP = 0.0038

424	LEAN TOWARD BEING THOSE WHERE RELIGIOUS SPECIALISTS ARE PART-TIME, RATHER THAN FULL-TIME (33) JMH	0.94 OF 16	424	LEAN TOWARD BEING THOSE WHERE RELIGIOUS SPECIALISTS ARE FULL-TIME, RATHER THAN PART-TIME (21) JMH	0.64 OF 11	1 7 15 4 XSQ= 7.73 PHI= -0.535 EP = 0.0025
433	TILT TOWARD BEING THOSE WHERE BELIEF IN REINCARNATION IS ABSENT (28) GES	0.89 OF 9	433	TILT TOWARD BEING THOSE WHERE BELIEF IN REINCARNATION IS PRESENT (10) GES	0.63 OF 8	1 5 8 3 XSQ= 2.91 PHI= -0.413 EP = 0.0498
434	DRIFT TOWARD BEING THOSE WHERE ASCETICISM IN MOURNING BEHAVIOR IS LOW (30) JFG	0.57 OF 23	434	DRIFT TOWARD BEING THOSE WHERE ASCETICISM IN MOURNING BEHAVIOR IS HIGH (37) JFG	0.78 OF 18	10 14 13 4 XSQ= 3.58 PHI= -0.296 XP = 0.0584
441	LEAN TOWARD BEING THOSE WHERE FEAR OF HUMAN BEINGS IS HIGH (29) W-C	0.59 OF 22	441	LEAN TOWARD BEING THOSE WHERE FEAR OF HUMAN BEINGS IS LOW (32) W-C	0.88 OF 16	13 2 9 14 XSQ= 6.58 PHI= 0.416 EP = 0.0065
446	TILT TOWARD BEING THOSE WHERE WITCHCRAFT IS MODERATELY PRESENT OR ABSENT (24) GES	0.89 OF 9	446	TILT TOWARD BEING THOSE WHERE WITCHCRAFT IS SIGNIFICANTLY PRESENT (14) GES	0.63 OF 8	1 5 8 3 XSQ= 2.91 PHI= -0.413 EP = 0.0498
454	DRIFT TOWARD BEING THOSE WHERE THE OBJECTIVE OF THE INDIVIDUAL'S CONTACT WITH THE DIVINE IS NOT CONDUCIVE TO THE DEVELOPMENT OF THE INDIVIDUAL'S NEED TO ACHIEVE (18) DCM	0.67 OF 15	454	DRIFT TOWARD BEING THOSE WHERE THE OBJECTIVE OF THE INDIVIDUAL'S CONTACT WITH THE DIVINE IS CONDUCIVE TO THE DEVELOPMENT OF THE INDIVIDUAL'S NEED TO ACHIEVE (18) DCM	0.65 OF 17	5 11 10 6 XSQ= 2.01 PHI= -0.250 EP = 0.0938
458	DRIFT MORE TOWARD BEING THOSE WHERE GAMES, IF PRESENT, DO NOT INCLUDE GAMES OF STRATEGY (119) R-A-B,EA	0.88 OF 24	458	DRIFT LESS TOWARD BEING THOSE WHERE GAMES, IF PRESENT, DO NOT INCLUDE GAMES OF STRATEGY (119) R-A-B,EA	0.61 OF 23	3 9 21 14 XSQ= 3.09 PHI= -0.256 XP = 0.0787
469	DRIFT LESS TOWARD BEING THOSE WHERE CONTACT WITH OTHER CULTURES IS FREQUENT OR REGULAR, RATHER THAN IRREGULAR (43) JMH	0.69 OF 16	469	IN ALL CASES ARE THOSE WHERE CONTACT WITH OTHER CULTURES IS FREQUENT OR REGULAR, RATHER THAN IRREGULAR (43) JMH	1.00 OF 11	11 11 5 0 XSQ= 2.40 PHI= -0.298 EP = 0.0598
470	LEAN TOWARD BEING THOSE WHERE INNOVATIONS ARE ACCEPTED ONLY SELECTIVELY (33) JMH	0.94 OF 16	470	LEAN TOWARD BEING THOSE WHERE INNOVATIONS ARE GENERALLY ACCEPTED (21) JMH	0.55 OF 11	1 6 15 5 XSQ= 5.60 PHI= -0.455 EP = 0.0087

318 CULTURES WHERE THE OVERALL INDULGENCE OF THE INFANT IS HIGH (40) B-B-C	318 CULTURES WHERE THE OVERALL INDULGENCE OF THE INFANT IS LOW (31) B-B-C

BACKGROUND ON PAGE 140 — BOTH SUBJECT AND PREDICATE

40 IN LEFT COLUMN

ANDAMANESE	ARANDA	ARAPESH	ARAUCANIANS	CAMAYURA	CHENCHU	CHEYENNE	CHIR-APACHE	CHUKCHEE	COMANCHE
CROW	CUNA	HANO	JIVARO	KASKA	KURTATCHI	LAU	LEPCHA	LESU	MANUS
MAORI	NUER	OMAHA	ONA	ONTONG-JAVA	PAPAGO	SAMOANS	SOTHO	TETON	TIKOPIA
TIMBIRA	TROBRIAND	TUPINAMBA	TURKANA	WINNEBAGO	WOGEO	WOLEAIANS	YAGUA	YORUBA	ZUNI

31 IN RIGHT COLUMN

AINU	ALORESE	ASHANTI	AYMARA	AZANDE	BALINESE	CHAGGA	FON	GANDA	IFUGAO
KIKUYU	KORYAK	KWAKIUTL	LAMBA	MARQUESANS	MASAI	MBUNDU	NAVAHO	OJIBWA	PUKAPUKA
SIRIONO	SWAZI	TALLENSI	TANALA	TENETEHARA	THONGA	TRUKESE	VENDA	WICHITA	YAHGAN
YAKUT									

329 EXCLUDED BECAUSE UNASCERTAINED

	High (40)		Low (31)		Statistics
3	LEAN MORE TOWARD BEING THOSE LOCATED OUTSIDE OF AFRICA (320)	0.90 OF 40	LEAN LESS TOWARD BEING THOSE LOCATED OUTSIDE OF AFRICA (320)	0.58 OF 31	4 13 / 36 18 / XSQ= 8.11 / PHI= -0.338 / XP = 0.0044
51	TILT TOWARD BEING THOSE WHERE SUBSISTENCE IS PRIMARILY BY FOOD GATHERING -- I. E., HUNTING, FISHING, OR COLLECTING -- RATHER THAN FOOD PRODUCTION (147)	0.60 OF 40	TILT TOWARD BEING THOSE WHERE SUBSISTENCE IS PRIMARILY BY FOOD PRODUCTION -- I. E., AGRICULTURE OR HUSBANDRY -- RATHER THAN BY GATHERING (253)	0.71 OF 31	16 22 / 24 9 / XSQ= 5.55 / PHI= -0.279 / XP = 0.0185
54	DRIFT LESS TOWARD BEING THOSE WHERE FOOD PRODUCTION IS BY INTENSIVE OR SIMPLE AGRICULTURE, RATHER THAN BY INCIPIENT FOOD PRODUCTION (192)	0.63 OF 24	DRIFT MORE TOWARD BEING THOSE WHERE FOOD PRODUCTION IS BY INTENSIVE OR SIMPLE AGRICULTURE, RATHER THAN BY INCIPIENT FOOD PRODUCTION (192)	0.91 OF 22	15 20 / 9 2 / XSQ= 3.65 / PHI= -0.282 / XP = 0.0561
56	DRIFT LESS TOWARD BEING THOSE WHERE FOOD PRODUCTION IS BY SIMPLE AGRICULTURE, RATHER THAN BY INCIPIENT FOOD PRODUCTION (101)	0.53 OF 19	DRIFT MORE TOWARD BEING THOSE WHERE FOOD PRODUCTION IS BY SIMPLE AGRICULTURE, RATHER THAN BY INCIPIENT FOOD PRODUCTION (101)	0.86 OF 14	10 12 / 9 2 / XSQ= 2.62 / PHI= -0.282 / EP = 0.0674

71	TEND TO BE THOSE WHERE METAL WORKING IS ABSENT (153)	0.91 OF 33	71	TEND TO BE THOSE WHERE METAL WORKING IS PRESENT (98)	0.67 OF 24	3 16 30 8 XSQ= 18.22 PHI= -0.565 XP = 0.0000
85	TILT MORE TOWARD BEING THOSE WHERE THE LEVEL OF POLITICAL INTEGRATION IS THE MINIMAL STATE, THE AUTONOMOUS COMMUNITY, OR THE FAMILY (234) GPM	0.94 OF 35	85	TILT LESS TOWARD BEING THOSE WHERE THE LEVEL OF POLITICAL INTEGRATION IS THE MINIMAL STATE, THE AUTONOMOUS COMMUNITY, OR THE FAMILY (234) GPM	0.68 OF 25	2 8 33 17 XSQ= 5.49 PHI= -0.302 XP = 0.0192
96	TILT TOWARD BEING THOSE WHERE THE HIERARCHY OF NATIONAL JURISDICTION HAS NO LEVELS (156) GES,EA	0.65 OF 37	96	TILT TOWARD BEING THOSE WHERE THE HIERARCHY OF NATIONAL JURISDICTION HAS FOUR, THREE, TWO OR ONE LEVEL (174) GES,EA	0.69 OF 29	13 20 24 9 XSQ= 6.15 PHI= -0.305 XP = 0.0131
100	DRIFT LESS TOWARD BEING THOSE WHERE HIERARCHIES ARE MORE COMPLEX THAN THE 'SIMPLEST,' I. E., MORE COMPLEX THAN TWO LOCAL LEVELS WITH NO NATIONAL LEVELS (267) GES,EA	0.78 OF 37	100	DRIFT MORE TOWARD BEING THOSE WHERE HIERARCHIES ARE MORE COMPLEX THAN THE 'SIMPLEST,' I. E., MORE COMPLEX THAN TWO LOCAL LEVELS WITH NO NATIONAL LEVELS (267) GES,EA	0.97 OF 29	29 28 8 1 XSQ= 3.15 PHI= -0.218 XP = 0.0761
102	TILT TOWARD BEING THOSE WHERE CLASS STRATIFICATION IS ABSENT (180)	0.63 OF 40	102	TILT TOWARD BEING THOSE WHERE CLASS STRATIFICATION IS PRESENT (203)	0.65 OF 31	15 20 25 11 XSQ= 4.08 PHI= -0.240 XP = 0.0435
110	TILT TOWARD BEING THOSE WHERE SLAVERY IS ABSENT (218)	0.77 OF 40	110	TILT TOWARD BEING THOSE WHERE SLAVERY IS PRESENT (163)	0.52 OF 31	9 16 31 15 XSQ= 5.28 PHI= -0.273 XP = 0.0216
116	TILT MORE TOWARD BEING THOSE WHERE OCCUPATIONAL SPECIALIZATION IS PART-TIME ONLY (34) JMH	0.94 OF 16	116	TILT LESS TOWARD BEING THOSE WHERE OCCUPATIONAL SPECIALIZATION IS PART-TIME ONLY (34) JMH	0.55 OF 11	1 5 15 6 XSQ= 3.75 PHI= -0.373 EP = 0.0265
130	TILT TOWARD BEING THOSE WHERE LEATHER WORKING IS MAINLY DONE BY FEMALES (45)	0.90 OF 10	130	TILT TOWARD BEING THOSE WHERE LEATHER WORKING IS MAINLY DONE BY MALES (39)	0.64 OF 11	1 7 9 4 XSQ= 4.32 PHI= -0.453 EP = 0.0237
138	TILT TOWARD BEING THOSE WHERE SUPERORDINATE JUSTICE IS ABSENT (18) BBW	0.57 OF 14	138	TILT TOWARD BEING THOSE WHERE SUPERORDINATE JUSTICE IS PRESENT (22) BBW	0.90 OF 10	6 9 8 1 XSQ= 3.70 PHI= -0.393 EP = 0.0333

149	DRIFT TOWARD BEING THOSE 0.64 OF 22 WHERE THE INCIDENCE OF THEFT IS LOW (19) B-B-C	149	DRIFT TOWARD BEING THOSE 0.67 OF 15 WHERE THE INCIDENCE OF THEFT IS HIGH (18) B-B-C	8 10 14 5 XSQ= 2.18 PHI= -0.243 EP = 0.0991
175	DRIFT MORE TOWARD BEING THOSE 0.82 OF 40 WHERE THE COMMUNITY IS 'KIN-HETEROGENEOUS,' I. E. OTHER THAN A CLAN COMMUNITY OR A DEME (260)	175	DRIFT LESS TOWARD BEING THOSE 0.61 OF 31 WHERE THE COMMUNITY IS 'KIN-HETEROGENEOUS,' I. E. OTHER THAN A CLAN COMMUNITY OR A DEME (260)	7 12 33 19 XSQ= 3.00 PHI= -0.206 XP = 0.0833
183	LEAN LESS TOWARD BEING THOSE 0.68 OF 25 WHERE THE LARGEST NON-COGNATIC KIN GROUP IS SMALLER THAN A MOEITY, I. E., A PHRATRY OR SIB OR LINEAGE (218)	183	IN ALL CASES ARE THOSE 1.00 OF 23 WHERE THE LARGEST NON-COGNATIC KIN GROUP IS SMALLER THAN A MOEITY, I. E., A PHRATRY OR SIB OR LINEAGE (218)	8 0 17 23 XSQ= 6.68 PHI= 0.373 XP = 0.0098
184	TILT TOWARD BEING THOSE 0.52 OF 25 WHERE THE LARGEST NON-COGNATIC KIN GROUP IS THE MOEITY OR PHRATRY (77)	184	TILT TOWARD BEING THOSE 0.87 OF 23 WHERE THE LARGEST NON-COGNATIC KIN GROUP IS SMALLER THAN A PHRATRY, I. E. A SIB OR LINEAGE (175)	13 3 12 20 XSQ= 6.52 PHI= 0.369 XP = 0.0107
255	IN ALL CASES ARE THOSE 1.00 OF 10 WHERE GRANDPARENTAL AUTHORITY OVER PARENTS IS ABSENT (26) DA	255	TILT TOWARD BEING THOSE 0.60 OF 5 WHERE GRANDPARENTAL AUTHORITY OVER PARENTS IS PRESENT (7) DA	0 3 10 2 XSQ= 4.22 PHI= -0.530 EP = 0.0220
282	TILT TOWARD BEING THOSE 0.73 OF 15 WHERE THE STRENGTH OF DESIRE FOR CHILDREN IS LOW OR ABSENT (20) BCA	282	TILT TOWARD BEING THOSE 0.73 OF 15 WHERE THE STRENGTH OF DESIRE FOR CHILDREN IS HIGH (16) BCA	4 11 11 4 XSQ= 4.80 PHI= -0.400 EP = 0.0268
300	DRIFT TOWARD BEING THOSE 0.68 OF 19 WHERE THE POST-PARTUM SEX TABOO LASTS LONGER THAN SIX MONTHS (51)	300	DRIFT TOWARD BEING THOSE 0.62 OF 21 WHERE THE POST-PARTUM SEX TABOO LASTS SIX MONTHS OR LESS (73)	13 8 6 13 XSQ= 2.56 PHI= 0.253 EP = 0.0673
309	DRIFT TOWARD BEING THOSE 0.67 OF 21 WHERE ORAL SOCIALIZATION ANXIETY IS LOW (27) W-C	309	DRIFT TOWARD BEING THOSE 0.68 OF 19 WHERE ORAL SOCIALIZATION ANXIETY IS HIGH (26) W-C	7 13 14 6 XSQ= 3.61 PHI= -0.300 EP = 0.0562
312	TILT TOWARD BEING THOSE 0.74 OF 19 WHERE DEPENDENCE SOCIALIZATION ANXIETY IS LOW (23) W-C	312	TILT TOWARD BEING THOSE 0.65 OF 17 WHERE DEPENDENCE SOCIALIZATION ANXIETY IS HIGH (24) W-C	5 11 14 6 XSQ= 3.91 PHI= -0.330 EP = 0.0425

314	DRIFT MORE TOWARD BEING THOSE WHERE THE INCIDENCE OF MOTHER-CHILD HOUSEHOLDS IS LOW (61) W-D,S	0.89 OF 27	314	DRIFT LESS TOWARD BEING THOSE WHERE THE INCIDENCE OF MOTHER-CHILD HOUSEHOLDS IS LOW (61) W-D,S	0.64 OF 22	3 8 24 14 XSQ= 3.11 PHI= -0.252 XP = 0.0779
317	TEND TO BE THOSE WHERE DISPLAY OF AFFECTION TOWARD THE INFANT IS HIGH (39) B-B-C	0.82 OF 39	317	TEND TO BE THOSE WHERE DISPLAY OF AFFECTION TOWARD THE INFANT IS LOW (29) B-B-C	0.78 OF 27	32 6 7 21 XSQ= 21.00 PHI= 0.564 XP = 0.0000
319	LEAN TOWARD BEING THOSE WHERE PROTECTION OF THE INFANT FROM ENVIRONMENTAL DISCOMFORTS IS HIGH (35) B-B-C	0.71 OF 34	319	LEAN TOWARD BEING THOSE WHERE PROTECTION OF THE INFANT FROM ENVIRONMENTAL DISCOMFORTS IS LOW (30) B-B-C	0.67 OF 30	24 10 10 20 XSQ= 7.45 PHI= 0.341 XP = 0.0063
320	TEND TO BE THOSE WHERE THE DEGREE OF REDUCTION OF THE INFANT'S DRIVES IS HIGH (45) B-B-C	0.89 OF 38	320	TEND TO BE THOSE WHERE THE DEGREE OF REDUCTION OF THE INFANT'S DRIVES IS LOW (24) B-B-C	0.63 OF 30	34 11 4 19 XSQ= 18.59 PHI= 0.523 XP = 0.0000
321	LEAN TOWARD BEING THOSE WHERE THE IMMEDIACY OF REDUCTION OF THE INFANT'S DRIVES IS HIGH (35) B-B-C	0.76 OF 34	321	LEAN TOWARD BEING THOSE WHERE THE IMMEDIACY OF REDUCTION OF THE INFANT'S DRIVES IS LOW (25) B-B-C	0.65 OF 26	26 9 8 17 XSQ= 8.97 PHI= 0.387 XP = 0.0027
322	TEND TO BE THOSE WHERE THE CONSISTENCY OF REDUCTION OF THE INFANT'S DRIVES IS HIGH (27) B-B-C	0.70 OF 33	322	TEND TO BE THOSE WHERE THE CONSISTENCY OF REDUCTION OF THE INFANT'S DRIVES IS LOW (32) B-B-C	0.85 OF 26	23 4 10 22 XSQ= 15.16 PHI= 0.507 XP = 0.0001
324	TEND TO BE THOSE WHERE THE PAIN INFLICTED ON THE INFANT BY THE NURTURANT AGENT IS LOW OR NEGLIGIBLE (32) B-B-C	0.73 OF 37	324	TEND TO BE THOSE WHERE THE PAIN INFLICTED ON THE INFANT BY THE NURTURANT AGENT IS HIGH (34) B-B-C	0.83 OF 29	10 24 27 5 XSQ= 18.05 PHI= -0.523 XP = 0.0000
326	TILT TOWARD BEING THOSE WHERE THE INFERRED TRANSITION ANXIETY BETWEEN INFANCY AND CHILDHOOD IS LOW (35) B-B-C	0.66 OF 35	326	TILT TOWARD BEING THOSE WHERE THE INFERRED TRANSITION ANXIETY BETWEEN INFANCY AND CHILDHOOD IS HIGH (32) B-B-C	0.67 OF 30	12 20 23 10 XSQ= 5.54 PHI= -0.292 XP = 0.0186
334	TEND TO BE THOSE WHERE THE INDULGENCE OF THE CHILD IS HIGH (40) B-B-C	0.70 OF 40	334	TEND TO BE THOSE WHERE THE INDULGENCE OF THE CHILD IS LOW (38) B-B-C	0.74 OF 31	28 8 12 23 XSQ= 11.94 PHI= 0.410 XP = 0.0006

337	LEAN TOWARD BEING THOSE WHERE THE CHILD'S INFERRED ANXIETY OVER NON-PERFORMANCE OF RESPONSIBLE BEHAVIOR IS LOW (35) B-B-C	0.67 OF 39	337	LEAN TOWARD BEING THOSE WHERE THE CHILD'S INFERRED ANXIETY OVER NON-PERFORMANCE OF RESPONSIBLE BEHAVIOR IS HIGH (38) B-B-C	0.72 OF 29	13 21 26 8 XSQ= 8.66 PHI= -0.357 XP = 0.0033
339	LEAN TOWARD BEING THOSE WHERE THE CHILD'S INFERRED CONFLICT REGARDING RESPONSIBLE BEHAVIOR IS LOW (42) B-B-C	0.74 OF 39	339	LEAN TOWARD BEING THOSE WHERE THE CHILD'S INFERRED CONFLICT REGARDING RESPONSIBLE BEHAVIOR IS HIGH (31) B-B-C	0.66 OF 29	10 19 29 10 XSQ= 9.24 PHI= -0.369 XP = 0.0024
340	LEAN TOWARD BEING THOSE WHERE THE TOTAL POSITIVE PRESSURE TOWARD DEVELOPING NURTURANT BEHAVIOR IN THE CHILD IS HIGH (28) B-B-C	0.76 OF 25	340	LEAN TOWARD BEING THOSE WHERE THE TOTAL POSITIVE PRESSURE TOWARD DEVELOPING NURTURANT BEHAVIOR IN THE CHILD IS LOW (20) B-B-C	0.67 OF 21	19 7 6 14 XSQ= 6.81 PHI= 0.385 XP = 0.0091
342	TILT TOWARD BEING THOSE WHERE THE CHILD'S INFERRED ANXIETY OVER PERFORMANCE OF NURTURANT BEHAVIOR IS LOW (28) B-B-C	0.75 OF 24	342	TILT TOWARD BEING THOSE WHERE THE CHILD'S INFERRED ANXIETY OVER PERFORMANCE OF NURTURANT BEHAVIOR IS HIGH (18) B-B-C	0.60 OF 20	6 12 18 8 XSQ= 4.18 PHI= -0.308 XP = 0.0410
346	TILT TOWARD BEING THOSE WHERE THE CHILD'S INFERRED ANXIETY OVER PERFORMANCE OF SELF-RELIANT BEHAVIOR IS LOW (39) B-B-C	0.67 OF 39	346	TILT TOWARD BEING THOSE WHERE THE CHILD'S INFERRED ANXIETY OVER PERFORMANCE OF SELF-RELIANT BEHAVIOR IS HIGH (37) B-B-C	0.61 OF 31	13 19 26 12 XSQ= 4.37 PHI= -0.250 XP = 0.0365
347	TILT TOWARD BEING THOSE WHERE THE CHILD'S INFERRED CONFLICT REGARDING SELF-RELIANT BEHAVIOR IS LOW (39) B-B-C	0.69 OF 39	347	TILT TOWARD BEING THOSE WHERE THE CHILD'S INFERRED CONFLICT REGARDING SELF-RELIANT BEHAVIOR IS HIGH (37) B-B-C	0.65 OF 31	12 20 27 11 XSQ= 6.62 PHI= -0.308 XP = 0.0101
352	DRIFT TOWARD BEING THOSE WHERE THE TOTAL POSITIVE PRESSURE TOWARD DEVELOPING OBEDIENT BEHAVIOR IN THE CHILD IS LOW (28) B-B-C	0.51 OF 37	352	DRIFT TOWARD BEING THOSE WHERE THE TOTAL POSITIVE PRESSURE TOWARD DEVELOPING OBEDIENT BEHAVIOR IN THE CHILD IS HIGH (44) B-B-C	0.75 OF 28	18 21 19 7 XSQ= 3.58 PHI= -0.235 XP = 0.0585
353	LEAN TOWARD BEING THOSE WHERE THE CHILD-S INFERRED ANXIETY OVER NON-PERFORMANCE OF OBEDIENT BEHAVIOR IS LOW (32) B-B-C	0.62 OF 37	353	LEAN TOWARD BEING THOSE WHERE THE CHILD'S INFERRED ANXIETY OVER NON-PERFORMANCE OF OBEDIENT BEHAVIOR IS HIGH (42) B-B-C	0.77 OF 30	14 23 23 7 XSQ= 8.59 PHI= -0.358 XP = 0.0034
354	TILT TOWARD BEING THOSE WHERE THE CHILD'S INFERRED ANXIETY OVER PERFORMANCE OF OBEDIENT BEHAVIOR IS LOW (37) B-B-C	0.65 OF 37	354	TILT TOWARD BEING THOSE WHERE THE CHILD'S INFERRED ANXIETY OVER PERFORMANCE OF OBEDIENT BEHAVIOR IS HIGH (36) B-B-C	0.66 OF 29	13 19 24 10 XSQ= 4.85 PHI= -0.271 XP = 0.0276

No.			No.			
	WHERE THE CHILD'S INFERREC CONFLICT REGARDING CBECIENT BEHAVIOR IS LCW (38) B-B-C			WHERE THE CHILD'S INFERRED CONFLICT REGARDING OBEDIENT BEHAVIOR IS HIGH (35) B-B-C		24 11 XSQ= 3.72 PHI= -0.237 XP = 0.0539
405	LEAN TCWARC BEING THOSE WHERE EXPLANATICNS OF ILLNESS OF A DEPENDENCE NATURE ARE ABSENT (27) W-C	0.73 OF 22	405	LEAN TOWARD BEING THOSE WHERE EXPLANATIONS OF ILLNESS OF A DEPENDENCE NATURE ARE PRESENT (34) W-C	0.79 OF 19	6 15 16 4 XSQ= 8.93 PHI= -0.467 XP = 0.0028
425	DRIFT TCWARD BEING THCSE WHERE SUPERNATURALS ARE MAINLY BENEVCLENT, RATHER THAN AGGRESSIVE (16) L-T-W	0.57 OF 21	425	DRIFT TOWARD BEING THOSE WHERE SUPERNATURALS ARE MAINLY AGGRESSIVE, RATHER THAN BENEVOLENT (20) L-T-W	0.73 OF 15	12 4 9 11 XSQ= 2.17 PHI= 0.246 EP = 0.0958
438	TILT TOWARD BEING THOSE WHERE THIS-WCRLCLY FEARS CF HUMANS CR ANIMALS ARE GREATER THAN CTHER-WCRLCLY FEARS OF GHOSTS OR SPIRITS (17) W-C,JFG	0.50 OF 14	438	TILT TOWARD BEING THOSE WHERE OTHER-WORLDLY FEARS CF GHOSTS OR SPIRITS ARE GREATER THAN THIS-WORLDLY FEARS CF HUMANS OR ANIMALS (27) W-C,JFG	0.94 OF 17	7 16 7 1 XSQ= 5.67 PHI= -0.428 EP = 0.0109
455	LEAN TCWARC BEING THCSE WHERE THE MODE CF THE INDIVICUAL'S CCNTACT WITH THE DIVINE IS CCNDUCIVE TC THE DEVELOPMENT OF THE INDIVIDUAL'S NEEC TC ACHIEVE (17) CCM	0.72 OF 18	455	LEAN TOWARD BEING THOSE WHERE THE MODE OF THE INDIVIDUAL'S CONTACT WITH THE DIVINE IS NOT CONDUCIVE TO THE DEVELOPMENT OF THE INDIVIDUAL'S NEED TO ACHIEVE (19) DCM	0.81 OF 16	13 3 5 13 XSQ= 7.69 PHI= 0.476 EP = 0.0026
458	LEAN TOWARC BEING THOSE WHERE GAMES, IF PRESENT, DC NCT INCLUDE GAMES OF STRATEGY (119) R-A-B,EA	0.92 OF 26	458	LEAN TOWARD BEING THOSE WHERE GAMES, IF PRESENT, INCLUDE GAMES CF STRATEGY (52) R-A-B,EA	0.54 OF 24	2 13 24 11 XSQ= 10.72 PHI= -0.463 XP = 0.0011
460	TILT TCWARD BEING THOSE WHERE GAMES, IF PRESENT, ARE LIMITEC TO GAMES OF SKILL CNLY (67) R-A-B,EA	0.58 OF 26	460	TILT TOWARD BEING THOSE WHERE GAMES, IF PRESENT, ARE NOT LIMITED TO GAMES OF SKILL ONLY (104) R-A-B,EA	0.75 OF 24	15 6 11 18 XSQ= 4.22 PHI= 0.290 XP = 0.0401
473	TILT TOWARC BEING THOSE WHERE SENSITIVITY TO INSULT IS MCDERATE CR NEGLIGIBLE (56) PES	0.80 OF 30	473	TILT TOWARD BEING THOSE WHERE SENSITIVITY TO INSULT IS EXTREME (32) PES	0.50 OF 22	6 11 24 11 XSQ= 3.92 PHI= -0.274 XP = 0.0478
476	DRIFT TCWARD BEING THCSE WHERE THE DEGREE OF INSOBRIETY IS STRCNG (31) DH	0.73 OF 11	476	DRIFT TOWARD BEING THOSE WHERE THE DEGREE OF INSOBRIETY IS MODERATE OR SLIGHT (18) DH	0.69 OF 13	8 4 3 9 XSQ= 2.69 PHI= 0.334 EP = 0.0995

319 CULTURES WHERE PROTECTION OF THE INFANT FROM ENVIRONMENTAL DISCOMFORTS IS HIGH (35) B-B-C	319 CULTURES WHERE PROTECTION OF THE INFANT FROM ENVIRONMENTAL DISCOMFORTS IS LOW (30) B-B-C

BACKGROUND ON PAGE 140

BOTH SUBJECT AND PREDICATE

35 IN LEFT COLUMN

ARAUCANIANS	ASHANTI	BALINESE	CAMAYURA	CHAGGA	CHIR-APACHE	CHUKCHEE	COMANCHE	CROW	CUNA
HANO	JIVARO	KASKA	KWAKIUTL	LAU	LEPCHA	MANDAN	NAVAHO	NUER	OJIBWA
OMAHA	ONA	PAPAGO	PUKAPUKA	TANALA	TETON	TIKOPIA	TROBRIAND	TURKANA	WICHITA
WINNEBAGO	WOGEO	WOLEAIANS	YAHGAN	ZUNI					

30 IN RIGHT COLUMN

AINU	ALORESE	ARANDA	ARAPESH	AYMARA	AZANDE	CHENCHU	CHEYENNE	FON	GANDA
IFUGAO	KIKUYU	KORYAK	KURTATCHI	MANUS	MARQUESANS	MASAI	MBUNDU	SIRIONO	SOTHO
SWAZI	TALLENSI	TENETEHARA	THONGA	TRUKESE	TUPINAMBA	VENDA	YAGUA	YAKUT	YORUBA

335 EXCLUDED BECAUSE UNASCERTAINED

3	TILT MORE TOWARD BEING THOSE LOCATED OUTSIDE OF AFRICA (320)	0.89 OF 35	3	TILT LESS TOWARD BEING THOSE LOCATED OUTSIDE OF AFRICA (320)	0.60 OF 30	4 12 31 18 XSQ= 5.65 PHI= -0.295 XP = 0.0175
8	TEND LESS TO BE THOSE LOCATED OUTSIDE OF NORTH AMERICA (330)	0.57 OF 35	8	TEND MORE TO BE THOSE LOCATED OUTSIDE OF NORTH AMERICA (330)	0.97 OF 30	15 1 20 29 XSQ= 11.55 PHI= 0.422 XP = 0.0007
14	LEAN TOWARD BEING THOSE WHERE THE LATITUDE IS THIRTY DEGREES OR GREATER (119)	0.54 OF 35	14	LEAN TOWARD BEING THOSE WHERE THE LATITUDE IS LESS THAN THIRTY DEGREES (281)	0.87 OF 30	19 4 16 26 XSQ= 10.13 PHI= 0.395 XP = 0.0015
15	TILT TOWARD BEING THOSE WHERE THE LATITUDE IS TWENTY DEGREES OR GREATER (183)	0.60 OF 35	15	TILT TOWARD BEING THOSE WHERE THE LATITUDE IS LESS THAN TWENTY DEGREES (217)	0.70 OF 30	21 9 14 21 XSQ= 4.71 PHI= 0.269 XP = 0.0301

44	DRIFT LESS TOWARD BEING THOSE 0.52 OF 31 WHERE SETTLEMENTS ARE FIXED (222)	44	DRIFT MORE TOWARD BEING THOSE 0.77 OF 30 WHERE SETTLEMENTS ARE FIXED (222)	16 23 15 7 XSQ= 3.13 PHI= -0.227 XP = 0.0766
71	TILT TOWARD BEING THOSE 0.81 OF 26 WHERE METAL WORKING IS ABSENT (153)	71	TILT TOWARD BEING THOSE 0.52 OF 25 WHERE METAL WORKING IS PRESENT (98)	5 13 21 12 XSQ= 4.64 PHI= -0.302 XP = 0.0312
85	TILT MORE TOWARD BEING THOSE 0.93 OF 29 WHERE THE LEVEL OF POLITICAL INTEGRATION IS THE MINIMAL STATE, THE AUTONOMOUS COMMUNITY, OR THE FAMILY (234) GPM	85	TILT LESS TOWARD BEING THOSE 0.68 OF 25 WHERE THE LEVEL OF POLITICAL INTEGRATION IS THE MINIMAL STATE, THE AUTONOMOUS COMMUNITY, OR THE FAMILY (234) GPM	2 8 27 17 XSQ= 4.07 PHI= -0.274 XP = 0.0437
91	DRIFT TOWARD BEING THOSE 0.64 OF 11 WHERE SOCIETAL COMPLEXITY IS HIGH (18) F-W	91	DRIFT TOWARD BEING THOSE 0.80 OF 10 WHERE SOCIETAL COMPLEXITY IS LOW (22) F-W	7 2 4 8 XSQ= 2.49 PHI= 0.344 EP = 0.0805
94	IN ALL CASES ARE THOSE 1.00 OF 31 WHERE THE HIERARCHY OF NATIONAL JURISDICTION HAS TWO, ONE, OR NO LEVELS (296) GES,EA	94	DRIFT LESS TOWARD BEING THOSE 0.83 OF 29 WHERE THE HIERARCHY OF NATIONAL JURISDICTION HAS TWO, ONE, OR NO LEVELS (296) GES,EA	0 5 31 24 XSQ= 3.79 PHI= -0.251 XP = 0.0515
95	LEAN MORE TOWARD BEING THOSE 0.94 OF 31 WHERE THE HIERARCHY OF NATIONAL JURISDICTION HAS ONE OR NO LEVELS (254) GES,EA	95	LEAN LESS TOWARD BEING THOSE 0.59 OF 29 WHERE THE HIERARCHY OF NATIONAL JURISDICTION HAS ONE OR NO LEVELS (254) GES,EA	2 12 29 17 XSQ= 8.36 PHI= -0.373 XP = 0.0038
102	TILT TOWARD BEING THOSE 0.66 OF 35 WHERE CLASS STRATIFICATION IS ABSENT (180)	102	TILT TOWARD BEING THOSE 0.67 OF 30 WHERE CLASS STRATIFICATION IS PRESENT (203)	12 20 23 10 XSQ= 5.54 PHI= -0.292 XP = 0.0186
198	TILT LESS TOWARD BEING THOSE 0.69 OF 16 WHERE RULES FOR THE INHERITANCE OF REAL PROPERTY, IF PRESENT, FAVOR THE MALE HEIR OR LINE, RATHER THAN THE FEMALE (144)	198	IN ALL CASES ARE THOSE 1.00 OF 14 WHERE RULES FOR THE INHERITANCE OF REAL PROPERTY, IF PRESENT, FAVOR THE MALE HEIR OR LINE, RATHER THAN THE FEMALE (144)	11 14 5 0 XSQ= 3.24 PHI= -0.329 EP = 0.0447
236	DRIFT TOWARD BEING THOSE 0.71 OF 35 WHERE THE FAMILY IS OF AN EXTENDED TYPE, RATHER THAN AN INDEPENDENT TYPE (213)	236	DRIFT TOWARD BEING THOSE 0.53 OF 30 WHERE THE FAMILY IS OF AN INDEPENDENT TYPE, RATHER THAN AN EXTENDED TYPE (185)	25 14 10 16 XSQ= 3.16 PHI= 0.220 XP = 0.0755

240	LEAN TOWARD BEING THOSE WHERE THE FAMILY, IF EXTENDED, IS SMALL OR STEM, RATHER THAN LARGE (135)	0.72 OF 25	240	LEAN TOWARD BEING THOSE WHERE THE FAMILY, IF EXTENDED, IS LARGE, RATHER THAN SMALL OR STEM (78)	0.79 OF 14	7 11 18 3 XSQ= 7.31 PHI= -0.433 EP = 0.0033
243	TILT TOWARD BEING THOSE WHERE POLYGYNY, IF PRESENT, HAS A LOW INCIDENCE (36) W-D,S	0.72 OF 18	243	TILT TOWARD BEING THOSE WHERE POLYGYNY, IF PRESENT, HAS A HIGH INCIDENCE (24) W-D,S	0.67 OF 15	5 10 13 5 XSQ= 3.55 PHI= -0.328 EP = 0.0383
272	DRIFT TOWARD BEING THOSE WHERE THE DIVORCE RATE IS HIGH (29) CA	0.82 OF 11	272	DRIFT TOWARD BEING THOSE WHERE THE DIVORCE RATE IS LOW (28) CA	0.67 OF 9	9 3 2 6 XSQ= 3.04 PHI= 0.390 EP = 0.0648
277	TILT TOWARD BEING THOSE WHERE THE STATUS OF WOMEN IS NOT STRONGLY INFERIOR OR SUBJECTED (22) LWS	0.80 OF 10	277	IN ALL CASES ARE THOSE WHERE THE STATUS OF WOMEN IS INFERIOR OR SUBJECTED (14) LWS	1.00 OF 3	2 3 8 0 XSQ= 3.32 PHI= -0.505 EP = 0.0350
307	DRIFT TOWARD BEING THOSE WHERE THE EARLY AGGRESSION SATISFACTION POTENTIAL IS LOW (19) W-C	0.58 OF 19	307	DRIFT TOWARD BEING THOSE WHERE THE EARLY AGGRESSION SATISFACTION POTENTIAL IS HIGH (33) W-C	0.75 OF 16	8 12 11 4 XSQ= 2.61 PHI= -0.273 EP = 0.0866
318	LEAN TOWARD BEING THOSE WHERE THE OVERALL INDULGENCE OF THE INFANT IS HIGH (40) B-B-C	0.71 OF 34	318	LEAN TOWARD BEING THOSE WHERE THE OVERALL INDULGENCE OF THE INFANT IS LOW (31) B-B-C	0.67 OF 30	24 10 10 20 XSQ= 7.45 PHI= 0.341 XP = 0.0063
320	LEAN TOWARD BEING THOSE WHERE THE DEGREE OF REDUCTION OF THE INFANT'S DRIVES IS HIGH (45) B-B-C	0.82 OF 33	320	LEAN TOWARD BEING THOSE WHERE THE DEGREE OF REDUCTION OF THE INFANT'S DRIVES IS LOW (24) B-B-C	0.54 OF 28	27 13 6 15 XSQ= 6.91 PHI= 0.337 XP = 0.0086
322	TILT TOWARD BEING THOSE WHERE THE CONSISTENCY OF REDUCTION OF THE INFANT'S DRIVES IS HIGH (27) B-B-C	0.59 OF 29	322	TILT TOWARD BEING THOSE WHERE THE CONSISTENCY OF REDUCTION OF THE INFANT'S DRIVES IS LOW (32) B-B-C	0.78 OF 23	17 5 12 18 XSQ= 5.72 PHI= 0.332 XP = 0.0168
325	TILT TOWARD BEING THOSE WHERE THE DEGREE OF DIFFUSION AMONG THE INFANT'S NURTURANT AGENTS IS HIGH (42) B-B-C	0.71 OF 35	325	TILT TOWARD BEING THOSE WHERE THE DEGREE OF DIFFUSION AMONG THE INFANT'S NURTURANT AGENTS IS LOW (32) B-B-C	0.62 OF 29	25 11 10 18 XSQ= 5.93 PHI= 0.305 XP = 0.0149

```
339  DRIFT TOWARD BEING THOSE          0.69 OF  35      339  DRIFT TOWARD BEING THOSE          0.59 OF  29            11    17
     WHERE THE CHILD'S INFERRED CONFLICT                     WHERE THE CHILD'S INFERRED CONFLICT                       24    12
     REGARDING RESPONSIBLE BEHAVIOR                          REGARDING RESPONSIBLE BEHAVIOR                      XSQ=      3.72
     IS LOW  (42) B-B-C                                      IS HIGH  (31) B-B-C                                 PHI=   -0.241
                                                                                                                 XP =   0.0536

405  TILT TOWARD BEING THOSE           0.63 OF  19      405  TILT TOWARD BEING THOSE           0.75 OF  16             7    12
     WHERE EXPLANATIONS OF ILLNESS                           WHERE EXPLANATIONS OF ILLNESS                             12     4
     OF A DEPENDENCE NATURE                                  OF A DEPENDENCE NATURE                              XSQ=      3.67
     ARE ABSENT  (27) W-C                                    ARE PRESENT  (34) W-C                               PHI=   -0.324
                                                                                                                 EP =   0.0411

444  TILT TOWARD BEING THOSE           0.75 OF  16      444  TILT TOWARD BEING THOSE           0.73 OF  11            12     3
     WHERE THE USE OF DREAMS                                 WHERE THE USE OF DREAMS                                    4     8
     TO SEEK AND CONTROL SUPERNATURAL POWERS                 TO SEEK AND CONTROL SUPERNATURAL POWERS             XSQ=      4.24
     IS HIGH  (28) RGD                                       IS LOW  (27) RGD                                    PHI=    0.396
                                                                                                                 EP =   0.0220

471  DRIFT TOWARD BEING THOSE          0.63 OF   8      471  IN ALL CASES ARE THOSE            1.00 OF   4             5     0
     WHERE SECRET SOCIETIES ARE                              WHERE SECRET SOCIETIES ARE                                 3     4
     PRESENT  (9) LWS                                        UMIMPORTANT OR ABSENT  (14) LWS                     XSQ=      2.10
                                                                                                                 PHI=    0.418
                                                                                                                 EP =   0.0808
```

320 CULTURES WHERE THE DEGREE OF REDUCTION OF THE INFANT'S DRIVES IS HIGH (45) B-B-C	320 CULTURES WHERE THE DEGREE OF REDUCTION OF THE INFANT'S DRIVES IS LOW (24) B-B-C

BACKGROUND ON PAGE 140

BOTH SUBJECT AND PREDICATE

45 IN LEFT COLUMN

ANDAMANESE	ARANDA	ARAPESH	ASHANTI	CAMAYURA	CHENCHU	CHEYENNE	CHIR-APACHE	CHUKCHEE	COMANCHE
CROW	CUNA	HANO	KURTATCHI	KWAKIUTL	LAU	LEPCHA	MACRI	MASAI	NAVAHO
NUER	OJIBWA	OMAHA	ONA	ONTONG-JAVA	PAPAGO	SAMOANS	SIRIONO	SOTHO	TALLENSI
TANALA	TENETEHARA	TETON	TIKOPIA	TIMBIRA	TROBRIAND	TUPINAMBA	TURKANA	VENDA	WINNEBAGO
WOGEO	WOLEAIANS	YAHGAN	YORUBA	ZUNI					

24 IN RIGHT COLUMN

AINU	ALORESE	ARAUCANIANS	AYMARA	AZANDE	BALINESE	CHAGGA	FON	GANDA	IFUGAO
KASKA	KORYAK	LAKHER	LAMBA	LESU	MANUS	MARQUESANS	MBUNDU	PUKAPUKA	SWAZI
THONGA	TRUKESE	WICHITA	YAKUT						

331 EXCLUDED BECAUSE UNASCERTAINED

	High (45)		Low (24)		Statistics
8	DRIFT LESS TOWARD BEING THOSE 0.71 OF 45 LOCATED OUTSIDE OF NORTH AMERICA (330)	8	DRIFT MORE TOWARD BEING THOSE 0.92 OF 24 LOCATED OUTSIDE OF NORTH AMERICA (330)		13 2 32 22 XSQ= 2.77 PHI= 0.200 XP = 0.0959
44	TILT LESS TOWARD BEING THOSE 0.55 OF 42 WHERE SETTLEMENTS ARE FIXED (222)	44	TILT MORE TOWARD BEING THOSE 0.83 OF 23 WHERE SETTLEMENTS ARE FIXED (222)		23 19 19 4 XSQ= 3.90 PHI= -0.245 XP = 0.0484
46	DRIFT LESS TOWARD BEING THOSE 0.69 OF 42 OTHER THAN WHERE SETTLEMENTS ARE NON-FIXED AND MOVEMENT IS NOMADIC (260)	46	DRIFT MORE TOWARD BEING THOSE 0.91 OF 23 OTHER THAN WHERE SETTLEMENTS ARE NON-FIXED AND MOVEMENT IS NOMADIC (260)		13 2 29 21 XSQ= 2.99 PHI= 0.214 XP = 0.0839
51	DRIFT TOWARD BEING THOSE 0.56 OF 45 WHERE SUBSISTENCE IS PRIMARILY BY FOOD GATHERING -- I. E., HUNTING, FISHING, OR COLLECTING -- RATHER THAN FOOD PRODUCTION (147)	51	DRIFT TOWARD BEING THOSE 0.71 OF 24 WHERE SUBSISTENCE IS PRIMARILY BY FOOD PRODUCTION -- I. E., AGRICULTURE OR HUSBANDRY -- RATHER THAN BY GATHERING (253)		20 17 25 7 XSQ= 3.39 PHI= -0.222 XP = 0.0658

71	LEAN TOWARD BEING THOSE WHERE METAL WORKING IS ABSENT (153)	0.81 OF 36	71	LEAN TOWARD BEING THOSE WHERE METAL WORKING IS PRESENT (98)	0.63 OF 19	7 12 29 7 XSQ= 8.67 PHI= -0.397 XP = 0.0032
82	DRIFT LESS TOWARD BEING THOSE WHERE A CITY OR TOWN IS PRESENT, OR THE AVERAGE COMMUNITY SIZE IS FIFTY OR GREATER (178)	0.74 OF 31	82	IN ALL CASES ARE THOSE WHERE A CITY OR TOWN IS PRESENT, OR THE AVERAGE COMMUNITY SIZE IS FIFTY OR GREATER (178)	1.00 OF 18	23 18 8 0 XSQ= 3.82 PHI= -0.279 XP = 0.0505
85	TILT MORE TOWARD BEING THOSE WHERE THE LEVEL OF POLITICAL INTEGRATION IS THE MINIMAL STATE, THE AUTONOMOUS COMMUNITY, OR THE FAMILY (234) GPM	0.92 OF 37	85	TILT LESS TOWARD BEING THOSE WHERE THE LEVEL OF POLITICAL INTEGRATION IS THE MINIMAL STATE, THE AUTONOMOUS COMMUNITY, OR THE FAMILY (234) GPM	0.67 OF 21	3 7 34 14 XSQ= 4.34 PHI= -0.273 XP = 0.0373
95	DRIFT MORE TOWARD BEING THOSE WHERE THE HIERARCHY OF NATIONAL JURISDICTION HAS ONE OR NO LEVELS (254) GES,EA	0.83 OF 42	95	DRIFT LESS TOWARD BEING THOSE WHERE THE HIERARCHY OF NATIONAL JURISDICTION HAS ONE OR NO LEVELS (254) GES,EA	0.59 OF 22	7 9 35 13 XSQ= 3.32 PHI= -0.228 XP = 0.0682
97	DRIFT LESS TOWARD BEING THOSE WHERE THE HIERARCHY OF LOCAL JURISDICTION HAS THREE OR TWO LEVELS (273) GES,EA	0.76 OF 42	97	DRIFT MORE TOWARD BEING THOSE WHERE THE HIERARCHY OF LOCAL JURISDICTION HAS THREE OR TWO LEVELS (273) GES,EA	0.96 OF 23	10 1 32 22 XSQ= 2.74 PHI= 0.205 XP = 0.0979
102	TILT TOWARD BEING THOSE WHERE CLASS STRATIFICATION IS ABSENT (180)	0.60 OF 45	102	TILT TOWARD BEING THOSE WHERE CLASS STRATIFICATION IS PRESENT (203)	0.71 OF 24	18 17 27 7 XSQ= 4.78 PHI= -0.263 XP = 0.0287
132	DRIFT TOWARD BEING THOSE WHERE ECONOMIC EXCHANGE DOES NOT INVOLVE THE USE OF MONEY (17) JMH	0.53 OF 17	132	DRIFT TOWARD BEING THOSE WHERE ECONOMIC EXCHANGE INVOLVES THE USE OF MONEY (37) JMH	0.89 OF 9	8 8 9 1 XSQ= 2.76 PHI= -0.326 EP = 0.0873
133	TILT TOWARD BEING THOSE WHERE CONTRACTED DEBTS ARE MODERATELY PRESENT OR ABSENT (17) GES	0.67 OF 12	133	IN ALL CASES ARE THOSE WHERE CONTRACTED DEBTS ARE SIGNIFICANTLY PRESENT (17) GES	1.00 OF 5	4 5 8 0 XSQ= 3.90 PHI= -0.479 EP = 0.0294
137	LEAN TOWARD BEING THOSE WHERE INVIDIOUS DISPLAY OF WEALTH IS MODERATELY, LITTLE, OR NEGATIVELY EMPHASIZED (52) PES	0.71 OF 34	137	LEAN TOWARD BEING THOSE WHERE INVIDIOUS DISPLAY OF WEALTH IS STRONGLY EMPHASIZED (37) PES	0.72 OF 18	10 13 24 5 XSQ= 7.09 PHI= -0.369 XP = 0.0077

277	TILT TOWARD BEING THOSE 0.75 OF 12 WHERE THE STATUS OF WOMEN IS NOT STRONGLY INFERIOR OR SUBJECTED (22) LWS	277	IN ALL CASES ARE THOSE 1.00 OF 3 WHERE THE STATUS OF WOMEN IS INFERIOR OR SUBJECTED (14) LWS	3 3 9 0 XSQ= 2.93 PHI= -0.442 EP = 0.0440
280	IN ALL CASES ARE THOSE 1.00 OF 6 WHERE THE COMPOSITE FERTILITY LEVEL IS HIGH (13) MN	280	DRIFT TOWARD BEING THOSE 0.60 OF 5 WHERE THE COMPOSITE FERTILITY LEVEL IS LOW (12) MN	6 2 0 3 XSQ= 2.39 PHI= 0.466 EP = 0.0606
306	DRIFT TOWARD BEING THOSE 0.68 OF 22 WHERE THE EARLY DEPENDENCE SATISFACTION POTENTIAL IS HIGH (28) W-C	306	DRIFT TOWARD BEING THOSE 0.64 OF 14 WHERE THE EARLY DEPENDENCE SATISFACTION POTENTIAL IS LOW (24) W-C	15 5 7 9 XSQ= 2.46 PHI= 0.261 EP = 0.0874
309	TILT TOWARD BEING THOSE 0.63 OF 24 WHERE ORAL SOCIALIZATION ANXIETY IS LOW (27) W-C	309	TILT TOWARD BEING THOSE 0.73 OF 15 WHERE ORAL SOCIALIZATION ANXIETY IS HIGH (26) W-C	9 11 15 4 XSQ= 3.42 PHI= -0.296 EP = 0.0484
317	TEND TO BE THOSE 0.73 OF 44 WHERE DISPLAY OF AFFECTION TOWARD THE INFANT IS HIGH (39) B-B-C	317	TEND TO BE THOSE 0.76 OF 21 WHERE DISPLAY OF AFFECTION TOWARD THE INFANT IS LOW (29) B-B-C	32 5 12 16 XSQ= 11.95 PHI= 0.429 XP = 0.0005
318	TEND TO BE THOSE 0.76 OF 45 WHERE THE OVERALL INDULGENCE OF THE INFANT IS HIGH (40) B-B-C	318	TEND TO BE THOSE 0.83 OF 23 WHERE THE OVERALL INDULGENCE OF THE INFANT IS LOW (31) B-B-C	34 4 11 19 XSQ= 18.59 PHI= 0.523 XP = 0.0000
319	LEAN TOWARD BEING THOSE 0.67 OF 40 WHERE PROTECTION OF THE INFANT FROM ENVIRONMENTAL DISCOMFORTS IS HIGH (35) B-B-C	319	LEAN TOWARD BEING THOSE 0.71 OF 21 WHERE PROTECTION OF THE INFANT FROM ENVIRONMENTAL DISCOMFORTS IS LOW (30) B-B-C	27 6 13 15 XSQ= 6.91 PHI= 0.337 XP = 0.0086
321	LEAN TOWARD BEING THOSE 0.73 OF 41 WHERE THE IMMEDIACY OF REDUCTION OF THE INFANT'S DRIVES IS HIGH (35) B-B-C	321	LEAN TOWARD BEING THOSE 0.74 OF 19 WHERE THE IMMEDIACY OF REDUCTION OF THE INFANT'S DRIVES IS LOW (25) B-B-C	30 5 11 14 XSQ= 9.88 PHI= 0.406 XP = 0.0017
322	LEAN TOWARD BEING THOSE 0.60 OF 40 WHERE THE CONSISTENCY OF REDUCTION OF THE INFANT'S DRIVES IS HIGH (27) B-B-C	322	LEAN TOWARD BEING THOSE 0.84 OF 19 WHERE THE CONSISTENCY OF REDUCTION OF THE INFANT'S DRIVES IS LOW (32) B-B-C	24 3 16 16 XSQ= 8.44 PHI= 0.378 XP = 0.0037

No.	Statement	Proportion	No.	Statement	Proportion	Statistics
334	TILT TOWARD BEING THOSE WHERE THE INDULGENCE OF THE CHILD IS HIGH (40) B-B-C	0.60 OF 45	334	TILT TOWARD BEING THOSE WHERE THE INDULGENCE OF THE CHILD IS LOW (38) B-B-C	0.71 OF 24	27 7 18 17 XSQ= 4.78 PHI= 0.263 XP = 0.0287
335	DRIFT TOWARD BEING THOSE WHERE INITIAL INDULGENCE OF DEPENDENCY IS HIGH (20) WNS	0.68 OF 19	335	DRIFT TOWARD BEING THOSE WHERE INITIAL INDULGENCE OF DEPENDENCY IS LOW (18) WNS	0.73 OF 11	13 3 6 8 XSQ= 3.23 PHI= 0.328 EP = 0.0567
339	DRIFT TOWARD BEING THOSE WHERE THE CHILD'S INFERRED CONFLICT REGARDING RESPONSIBLE BEHAVIOR IS LOW (42) B-B-C	0.65 OF 43	339	DRIFT TOWARD BEING THOSE WHERE THE CHILD'S INFERRED CONFLICT REGARDING RESPONSIBLE BEHAVIOR IS HIGH (31) B-B-C	0.64 OF 22	15 14 28 8 XSQ= 3.78 PHI= -0.241 XP = 0.0520
340	DRIFT TOWARD BEING THOSE WHERE THE TOTAL POSITIVE PRESSURE TOWARD DEVELOPING NURTURANT BEHAVIOR IN THE CHILD IS HIGH (28) B-B-C	0.69 OF 29	340	DRIFT TOWARD BEING THOSE WHERE THE TOTAL POSITIVE PRESSURE TOWARD DEVELOPING NURTURANT BEHAVIOR IN THE CHILD IS LOW (20) B-B-C	0.67 OF 15	20 5 9 10 XSQ= 3.77 PHI= 0.293 XP = 0.0523
342	DRIFT TOWARD BEING THOSE WHERE THE CHILD'S INFERRED ANXIETY OVER PERFORMANCE OF NURTURANT BEHAVIOR IS LOW (28) B-B-C	0.68 OF 28	342	DRIFT TOWARD BEING THOSE WHERE THE CHILD'S INFERRED ANXIETY OVER PERFORMANCE OF NURTURANT BEHAVIOR IS HIGH (18) B-B-C	0.64 OF 14	9 9 19 5 XSQ= 2.73 PHI= -0.255 XP = 0.0982
347	TILT TOWARD BEING THOSE WHERE THE CHILD'S INFERRED CONFLICT REGARDING SELF-RELIANT BEHAVIOR IS LOW (39) B-B-C	0.64 OF 44	347	TILT TOWARD BEING THOSE WHERE THE CHILD'S INFERRED CONFLICT REGARDING SELF-RELIANT BEHAVIOR IS HIGH (37) B-B-C	0.65 OF 23	16 15 28 8 XSQ= 3.96 PHI= -0.243 XP = 0.0465
368	DRIFT TOWARD BEING THOSE WHERE DISSOCIATION OF THE SEXES AT ADOLESCENCE IS HIGH OR MEDIUM (16) JKH	0.62 OF 13	368	DRIFT TOWARD BEING THOSE WHERE DISSOCIATION OF THE SEXES AT ADOLESCENCE IS LOW (21) JKH	0.86 OF 7	8 1 5 6 XSQ= 2.42 PHI= 0.348 EP = 0.0703
393	TILT TOWARD BEING THOSE WHERE EXTRAMARITAL COITUS IS PERMITTED, RATHER THAN PUNISHED (41) F-B	0.65 OF 20	393	TILT TOWARD BEING THOSE WHERE EXTRAMARITAL COITUS IS PUNISHED, RATHER THAN PERMITTED (43) F-B	0.71 OF 17	7 12 13 5 XSQ= 3.34 PHI= -0.301 EP = 0.0489
402	DRIFT TOWARD BEING THOSE WHERE EXPLANATIONS OF ILLNESS OF AN ORAL NATURE ARE ABSENT (30) W-C	0.52 OF 25	402	DRIFT TOWARD BEING THOSE WHERE EXPLANATIONS OF ILLNESS OF AN ORAL NATURE ARE PRESENT (31) W-C	0.80 OF 15	12 12 13 3 XSQ= 2.78 PHI= -0.264 EP = 0.0556

```
405  TILT TOWARD BEING THOSE          0.60 OF  25      405  TILT TOWARD BEING THOSE          0.80 OF  15            10   12
     WHERE EXPLANATIONS OF ILLNESS                         WHERE EXPLANATIONS OF ILLNESS                           15    3
     OF A DEPENDENCE NATURE                                OF A DEPENDENCE NATURE                           XSQ=     4.55
     ARE ABSENT  (27) W-C                                  ARE PRESENT  (34) W-C                            PHI=   -0.337
                                                                                                            EP =   0.0217

424  LEAN TOWARD BEING THOSE          0.88 OF  17      424  LEAN TOWARD BEING THOSE          0.67 OF   9             2    6
     WHERE RELIGIOUS SPECIALISTS ARE                       WHERE RELIGIOUS SPECIALISTS ARE                         15    3
     PART-TIME, RATHER THAN                                FULL-TIME, RATHER THAN                           XSQ=     5.95
     FULL-TIME  (33) JMH                                   PART-TIME  (21) JMH                              PHI=   -0.478
                                                                                                            EP =   0.0077

458  DRIFT MORE TOWARD BEING THOSE    0.80 OF  30      458  DRIFT LESS TOWARD BEING THOSE    0.53 OF  19             6    9
     WHERE GAMES, IF PRESENT,                              WHERE GAMES, IF PRESENT,                                24   10
     DO NOT INCLUDE                                        DO NOT INCLUDE                                   XSQ=     2.91
     GAMES OF STRATEGY  (119) R-A-B,EA                     GAMES OF STRATEGY  (119) R-A-B,EA                PHI=   -0.244
                                                                                                            XP =   0.0878

470  TILT TOWARD BEING THOSE          0.88 OF  17      470  TILT TOWARD BEING THOSE          0.56 OF   9             2    5
     WHERE INNOVATIONS ARE                                 WHERE INNOVATIONS ARE                                   15    4
     ACCEPTED ONLY SELECTIVELY  (33) JMH                   GENERALLY ACCEPTED  (21) JMH                     XSQ=     3.73
                                                                                                            PHI=   -0.379
                                                                                                            EP =   0.0283

471  DRIFT TOWARD BEING THOSE         0.63 OF   8      471  IN ALL CASES ARE THOSE           1.00 OF   4             5    0
     WHERE SECRET SOCIETIES ARE                            WHERE SECRET SOCIETIES ARE                               3    4
     PRESENT  (9) LWS                                      UMIMPORTANT OR ABSENT  (14) LWS                  XSQ=     2.10
                                                                                                            PHI=    0.418
                                                                                                            EP =   0.0808
```

```
321  CULTURES                                  321  CULTURES
     WHERE THE IMMEDIACY OF REDUCTION               WHERE THE IMMEDIACY OF REDUCTION
     OF THE INFANT'S DRIVES                         OF THE INFANT'S DRIVES
     IS HIGH  (35) B-B-C                            IS LOW  (25) B-B-C

BACKGROUND ON PAGE 140                                        BOTH SUBJECT AND PREDICATE

     35  IN LEFT COLUMN

ANDAMANESE ARANDA     ARAPESH    CAMAYURA   CHENCHU    CHIR-APACHE HANO      KASKA      KURTATCHI  KWAKIUTL
LAMBA      LAU        LEPCHA     MANUS      MAORI      MBUNDU     NUER       ONTONG-JAVA PAPAGO    SAMOANS
SIRIONO    SOTHO      TALLENSI   TANALA     TENETEHARA TETON      TROBRIAND  TURKANA    WICHITA    WINNEBAGO
WOGEO      WOLEAIANS  YAHGAN     YORUBA     ZUNI

     25  IN RIGHT COLUMN

AINU       ALORESE    ASHANTI    AYMARA     AZANDE     BALINESE   CHAGGA     CHEYENNE   COMANCHE   CROW
FON        LESU       MARQUESANS MASAI      NAVAHO     OJIBWA     OMAHA      ONA        PUKAPUKA   SWAZI
THONGA     TIKOPIA    TIMBIRA    TRUKESE    YAKUT

     340  EXCLUDED BECAUSE UNASCERTAINED

------------------------------------------------------------------------------------------------------------
 96  LEAN TOWARD BEING THOSE       0.64 OF  33     96  LEAN TOWARD BEING THOSE       0.77 OF  22       12   17
     WHERE THE HIERARCHY                               WHERE THE HIERARCHY                             21    5
     OF NATIONAL JURISDICTION HAS                      OF NATIONAL JURISDICTION HAS               XSQ=    7.30
     NO LEVELS  (156) GES,EA                           FOUR, THREE, TWO OR                        PHI=  -0.364
                                                       ONE LEVEL  (174) GES,EA                    XP =  0.0069

137  DRIFT TOWARD BEING THOSE      0.71 OF  24    137  DRIFT TOWARD BEING THOSE      0.62 OF  21        7   13
     WHERE INVIDIOUS DISPLAY OF WEALTH                 WHERE INVIDIOUS DISPLAY OF WEALTH              17    8
     IS MODERATELY, LITTLE, OR                         IS STRONGLY EMPHASIZED  (37) PES           XSQ=    3.63
     NEGATIVELY EMPHASIZED  (52) PES                                                              PHI=  -0.284
                                                                                                  XP =  0.0569

282  TILT TOWARD BEING THOSE       0.82 OF  11    282  TILT TOWARD BEING THOSE       0.67 OF  15        2   10
     WHERE THE STRENGTH OF DESIRE FOR CHILDREN         WHERE THE STRENGTH OF DESIRE FOR CHILDREN       9    5
     IS LOW OR ABSENT  (20) BCA                        IS HIGH  (16) BCA                          XSQ=    4.21
                                                                                                  PHI=  -0.402
                                                                                                  EP =  0.0214

299  DRIFT LESS TOWARD BEING THOSE 0.55 OF  20    299  DRIFT MORE TOWARD BEING THOSE 0.86 OF  14        9    2
     WHERE THE POST-PARTUM SEX TABOO LASTS             WHERE THE POST-PARTUM SEX TABOO LASTS          11   12
     ONE YEAR OR LESS  (89)                            ONE YEAR OR LESS  (89)                     XSQ=    2.29
                                                                                                  PHI=   0.259
                                                                                                  EP =  0.0764
```

321/

```
303  TILT TOWARD BEING THOSE          0.68 OF  19     303  TILT TOWARD BEING THOSE          0.71 OF  17           13     5
     WHERE THE EARLY ORAL SATISFACTION                    WHERE THE EARLY ORAL SATISFACTION                      6    12
     POTENTIAL IS HIGH  (32) W-C                          POTENTIAL IS LOW  (25) W-C                     XSQ=       4.01
                                                                                                         PHI=      0.334
                                                                                                         EP =     0.0437

309  TILT TOWARD BEING THOSE          0.63 OF  19     309  TILT TOWARD BEING THOSE          0.76 OF  17            7    13
     WHERE ORAL SOCIALIZATION ANXIETY                     WHERE ORAL SOCIALIZATION ANXIETY                      12     4
     IS LOW  (27) W-C                                     IS HIGH  (26) W-C                              XSQ=       4.21
                                                                                                         PHI=     -0.342
                                                                                                         EP =     0.0228

317  TILT TOWARD BEING THOSE          0.71 OF  34     317  TILT TOWARD BEING THOSE          0.64 OF  25           24     9
     WHERE DISPLAY OF AFFECTION TOWARD                    WHERE DISPLAY OF AFFECTION TOWARD                     10    16
     THE INFANT IS HIGH  (39) B-B-C                       THE INFANT IS LOW  (29) B-B-C                  XSQ=       5.66
                                                                                                         PHI=      0.310
                                                                                                         XP =     0.0174

318  LEAN TOWARD BEING THOSE          0.74 OF  35     318  LEAN TOWARD BEING THOSE          0.68 OF  25           26     8
     WHERE THE OVERALL INDULGENCE                         WHERE THE OVERALL INDULGENCE                           9    17
     OF THE INFANT                                        OF THE INFANT                                  XSQ=       8.97
     IS HIGH  (40) B-B-C                                  IS LOW  (31) B-B-C                             PHI=      0.387
                                                                                                         XP =     0.0027

320  LEAN TOWARD BEING THOSE          0.86 OF  35     320  LEAN TOWARD BEING THOSE          0.56 OF  25           30    11
     WHERE THE DEGREE OF REDUCTION                        WHERE THE DEGREE OF REDUCTION                          5    14
     OF THE INFANT'S DRIVES                               OF THE INFANT'S DRIVES                         XSQ=       9.88
     IS HIGH  (45) B-B-C                                  IS LOW  (24) B-B-C                             PHI=      0.406
                                                                                                         XP =     0.0017

322  TEND TO BE THOSE                 0.68 OF  34     322  TEND TO BE THOSE                 0.84 OF  25           23     4
     WHERE THE CONSISTENCY OF REDUCTION                   WHERE THE CONSISTENCY OF REDUCTION                    11    21
     OF THE INFANT'S DRIVES                               OF THE INFANT'S DRIVES                         XSQ=      13.47
     IS HIGH  (27) B-B-C                                  IS LOW  (32) B-B-C                             PHI=      0.478
                                                                                                         XP =     0.0002

323  LEAN TOWARD BEING THOSE          0.57 OF  35     323  LEAN TOWARD BEING THOSE          0.84 OF  25           20     4
     WHERE THE CONSTANCY OF PRESENCE                      WHERE THE CONSTANCY OF PRESENCE                       15    21
     OF THE INFANT'S NURTURANT AGENT                      OF THE INFANT'S NURTURANT AGENT                XSQ=       8.64
     IS HIGH  (29) B-B-C                                  IS LOW  (45) B-B-C                             PHI=      0.380
                                                                                                         XP =     0.0033

324  DRIFT TOWARD BEING THOSE         0.62 OF  34     324  DRIFT TOWARD BEING THOSE         0.67 OF  24           13    16
     WHERE THE PAIN INFLICTED                             WHERE THE PAIN INFLICTED                              21     8
     ON THE INFANT BY THE NURTURANT AGENT                 ON THE INFANT BY THE NURTURANT AGENT           XSQ=       3.48
     IS LOW OR NEGLIGIBLE  (32) B-B-C                     IS HIGH  (34) B-B-C                            PHI=     -0.245
                                                                                                         XP =     0.0620

354  LEAN TOWARD BEING THOSE          0.63 OF  32     354  LEAN TOWARD BEING THOSE          0.78 OF  23           12    18
     WHERE THE CHILD'S INFERRED ANXIETY OVER              WHERE THE CHILD'S INFERRED ANXIETY OVER               20     5
     PERFORMANCE OF OBEDIENT BEHAVIOR                     PERFORMANCE OF OBEDIENT BEHAVIOR               XSQ=       7.40
     IS LOW  (37) B-B-C                                   IS HIGH  (36) B-B-C                            PHI=     -0.367
                                                                                                         XP =     0.0065
```

355	TILT TOWARD BEING THOSE 0.63 OF 32 WHERE THE CHILD'S INFERRED CONFLICT REGARDING OBEDIENT BEHAVIOR IS LOW (38) B-B-C	355	TILT TOWARD BEING THOSE 0.74 OF 23 WHERE THE CHILD'S INFERRED CONFLICT REGARDING OBEDIENT BEHAVIOR IS HIGH (35) B-B-C	12 17 20 6 XSQ= 5.73 PHI= -0.323 XP = 0.0167
365	DRIFT TOWARD BEING THOSE 0.60 OF 15 WHERE THE TIME SPENT IN ADOLESCENT PEER GROUP ACTIVITY IS LOW-MEDIUM OR LOW (15) JKH	365	DRIFT TOWARD BEING THOSE 0.86 OF 7 WHERE THE TIME SPENT IN ADOLESCENT PEER GROUP ACTIVITY IS HIGH OR HIGH-MEDIUM (30) JKH	6 6 9 1 XSQ= 2.39 PHI= -0.330 EP = 0.0743
377	DRIFT MORE TOWARD BEING THOSE 0.84 OF 32 WHERE MALE GENITAL MUTILATION IS ABSENT (242)	377	DRIFT LESS TOWARD BEING THOSE 0.61 OF 23 WHERE MALE GENITAL MUTILATION IS ABSENT (242)	5 9 27 14 XSQ= 2.76 PHI= -0.224 XP = 0.0969
393	DRIFT TOWARD BEING THOSE 0.77 OF 13 WHERE EXTRAMARITAL COITUS IS PERMITTED, RATHER THAN PUNISHED (41) F-B	393	DRIFT TOWARD BEING THOSE 0.61 OF 18 WHERE EXTRAMARITAL COITUS IS PUNISHED, RATHER THAN PERMITTED (43) F-B	3 11 10 7 XSQ= 3.01 PHI= -0.311 EP = 0.0669
421	TILT TOWARD BEING THOSE 0.78 OF 23 WHERE KILLING, TORTURING, OR MUTILATING OF THE ENEMY IS NEGLIGIBLY EMPHASIZED (47) PES	421	TILT TOWARD BEING THOSE 0.65 OF 20 WHERE KILLING, TORTURING, OR MUTILATING OF THE ENEMY IS STRONGLY OR MODERATELY EMPHASIZED (37) PES	5 13 18 7 XSQ= 6.54 PHI= -0.390 XP = 0.0105
456	TILT TOWARD BEING THOSE 0.73 OF 15 WHERE THE INTERNALIZATION OF THE INDIVIDUAL'S CONTACT WITH THE DIVINE IS CONDUCIVE TO THE DEVELOPMENT OF THE INDIVIDUAL'S NEED TO ACHIEVE (19) DCM	456	TILT TOWARD BEING THOSE 0.77 OF 13 WHERE THE INTERNALIZATION OF THE INDIVIDUAL'S CONTACT WITH THE DIVINE IS NOT CONDUCIVE TO THE DEVELOPMENT OF THE INDIVIDUAL'S NEED TO ACHIEVE (17) DCM	11 3 4 10 XSQ= 5.17 PHI= 0.430 EP = 0.0213
472	DRIFT TOWARD BEING THOSE 0.67 OF 24 WHERE THE COMPOSITE NARCISSISM INDEX IS LOW (43) PES	472	DRIFT TOWARD BEING THOSE 0.67 OF 21 WHERE THE COMPOSITE NARCISSISM INDEX IS HIGH (47) PES	8 14 16 7 XSQ= 3.74 PHI= -0.288 XP = 0.0533

322 CULTURES WHERE THE CONSISTENCY OF REDUCTION OF THE INFANT'S DRIVES IS HIGH (27) B-B-C	322 CULTURES WHERE THE CONSISTENCY OF REDUCTION OF THE INFANT'S DRIVES IS LOW (32) B-B-C

BACKGROUND ON PAGE 140 — BOTH SUBJECT AND PREDICATE

27 IN LEFT COLUMN

ANDAMANESE	ARANDA	ARAPESH	AZANDE	CAMAYURA	CHIR-APACHE	HANO	KASKA	LAMBA	LAU
LEPCHA	NUER	OMAHA	ONTONG-JAVA	PAPAGO	SAMOANS	TANALA	TENETEHARA	TETON	TIKOPIA
TIMBIRA	TURKANA	WINNEBAGO	WOGEO	WOLEAIANS	YORUBA	ZUNI			

32 IN RIGHT COLUMN

AINU	ALORESE	ASHANTI	AYMARA	BALINESE	CHAGGA	CHENCHU	CHEYENNE	COMANCHE	CROW
FON	KURTATCHI	KWAKIUTL	LESU	MANUS	MAORI	MARQUESANS	MASAI	MBUNDU	NAVAHO
OJIBWA	ONA	PUKAPUKA	SIRIONO	SOTHO	SWAZI	TALLENSI	THONGA	TRUKESE	WICHITA
YAHGAN	YAKUT								

341 EXCLUDED BECAUSE UNASCERTAINED

87	DRIFT LESS TOWARD BEING THOSE WHERE THE LEVEL OF POLITICAL INTEGRATION IS THE LARGE STATE, THE LITTLE STATE, THE MINIMAL STATE, OR THE AUTONOMOUS COMMUNITY (281) GPM	0.74 OF 23	87	DRIFT MORE TOWARD BEING THOSE WHERE THE LEVEL OF POLITICAL INTEGRATION IS THE LARGE STATE, THE LITTLE STATE, THE MINIMAL STATE, OR THE AUTONOMOUS COMMUNITY (281) GPM	0.96 OF 26	 XSQ= PHI= XP =	17 25 6 1 3.28 -0.259 0.0701
96	DRIFT TOWARD BEING THOSE WHERE THE HIERARCHY OF NATIONAL JURISDICTION HAS NO LEVELS (156) GES,EA	0.64 OF 25	96	DRIFT TOWARD BEING THOSE WHERE THE HIERARCHY OF NATIONAL JURISDICTION HAS FOUR, THREE, TWO OR ONE LEVEL (174) GES,EA	0.66 OF 29	 XSQ= PHI= XP =	9 19 16 10 3.58 -0.257 0.0586
132	DRIFT TOWARD BEING THOSE WHERE ECONOMIC EXCHANGE DOES NOT INVOLVE THE USE OF MONEY (17) JMH	0.67 OF 9	132	DRIFT TOWARD BEING THOSE WHERE ECONOMIC EXCHANGE INVOLVES THE USE OF MONEY (37) JMH	0.82 OF 11	 XSQ= PHI= EP =	3 9 6 2 3.04 -0.390 0.0648
137	TILT TOWARD BEING THOSE WHERE INVIDIOUS DISPLAY OF WEALTH IS MODERATELY, LITTLE, OR NEGATIVELY EMPHASIZED (52) PES	0.78 OF 18	137	TILT TOWARD BEING THOSE WHERE INVIDIOUS DISPLAY OF WEALTH IS STRONGLY EMPHASIZED (37) PES	0.58 OF 26	 XSQ= PHI= XP =	4 15 14 11 4.10 -0.305 0.0428

No.	Statement	Ratio	No.	Statement	Ratio	Statistics
183	TILT LESS TOWARD BEING THOSE WHERE THE LARGEST NON-COGNATIC KIN GROUP IS SMALLER THAN A MOEITY, I. E., A PHRATRY OR SIB OR LINEAGE (218)	0.63 OF 19	183	TILT MORE TOWARD BEING THOSE WHERE THE LARGEST NON-COGNATIC KIN GROUP IS SMALLER THAN A MOEITY, I. E., A PHRATRY OR SIB OR LINEAGE (218)	0.96 OF 23	7 1 12 22 XSQ= 5.17 PHI= 0.351 XP = 0.0229
309	TILT TOWARD BEING THOSE WHERE ORAL SOCIALIZATION ANXIETY IS LOW (27) W-C	0.67 OF 15	309	TILT TOWARD BEING THOSE WHERE ORAL SOCIALIZATION ANXIETY IS HIGH (26) W-C	0.70 OF 20	5 14 10 6 XSQ= 3.28 PHI= -0.306 EP = 0.0442
311	DRIFT TOWARD BEING THOSE WHERE SEXUAL SOCIALIZATION ANXIETY IS HIGH (28) W-C	0.71 OF 14	311	DRIFT TOWARD BEING THOSE WHERE SEXUAL SOCIALIZATION ANXIETY IS LOW (23) W-C	0.60 OF 20	10 8 4 12 XSQ= 2.13 PHI= 0.250 EP = 0.0921
312	DRIFT TOWARD BEING THOSE WHERE DEPENDENCE SOCIALIZATION ANXIETY IS LOW (23) W-C	0.77 OF 13	312	DRIFT TOWARD BEING THOSE WHERE DEPENDENCE SOCIALIZATION ANXIETY IS HIGH (24) W-C	0.58 OF 19	3 11 10 8 XSQ= 2.52 PHI= -0.281 EP = 0.0751
313	DRIFT TOWARD BEING THOSE WHERE AGGRESSION SOCIALIZATION ANXIETY IS HIGH (26) W-C	0.69 OF 16	313	DRIFT TOWARD BEING THOSE WHERE AGGRESSION SOCIALIZATION ANXIETY IS LOW (28) W-C	0.65 OF 20	11 7 5 13 XSQ= 2.81 PHI= 0.280 EP = 0.0922
317	DRIFT TOWARD BEING THOSE WHERE DISPLAY OF AFFECTION TOWARD THE INFANT IS HIGH (39) B-B-C	0.69 OF 26	317	DRIFT TOWARD BEING THOSE WHERE DISPLAY OF AFFECTION TOWARD THE INFANT IS LOW (29) B-B-C	0.56 OF 32	18 14 8 18 XSQ= 2.81 PHI= 0.220 XP = 0.0939
318	TEND TO BE THOSE WHERE THE OVERALL INDULGENCE OF THE INFANT IS HIGH (40) B-B-C	0.85 OF 27	318	TEND TO BE THOSE WHERE THE OVERALL INDULGENCE OF THE INFANT IS LOW (31) B-B-C	0.69 OF 32	23 10 4 22 XSQ= 15.16 PHI= 0.507 XP = 0.0001
319	TILT TOWARD BEING THOSE WHERE PROTECTION OF THE INFANT FROM ENVIRONMENTAL DISCOMFORTS IS HIGH (35) B-B-C	0.77 OF 22	319	TILT TOWARD BEING THOSE WHERE PROTECTION OF THE INFANT FROM ENVIRONMENTAL DISCOMFORTS IS LOW (30) B-B-C	0.60 OF 30	17 12 5 18 XSQ= 5.72 PHI= 0.332 XP = 0.0168
320	LEAN TOWARD BEING THOSE WHERE THE DEGREE OF REDUCTION OF THE INFANT'S DRIVES IS HIGH (45) B-B-C	0.89 OF 27	320	LEAN TOWARD BEING THOSE WHERE THE DEGREE OF REDUCTION OF THE INFANT'S DRIVES IS LOW (24) B-B-C	0.50 OF 32	24 16 3 16 XSQ= 8.44 PHI= 0.378 XP = 0.0037

321	TEND TO BE THOSE 0.85 OF 27 WHERE THE IMMEDIACY OF REDUCTION OF THE INFANT'S DRIVES IS HIGH (35) B-B-C	321	TEND TO BE THOSE 0.66 OF 32 WHERE THE IMMEDIACY OF REDUCTION OF THE INFANT'S DRIVES IS LOW (25) B-B-C	23 11 4 21 XSQ= 13.47 PHI= 0.478 XP = 0.0002
323	TEND TO BE THOSE 0.67 OF 27 WHERE THE CONSTANCY OF PRESENCE OF THE INFANT'S NURTURANT AGENT IS HIGH (29) B-B-C	323	TEND TO BE THOSE 0.81 OF 32 WHERE THE CONSTANCY OF PRESENCE OF THE INFANT'S NURTURANT AGENT IS LOW (45) B-B-C	18 6 9 26 XSQ= 12.02 PHI= 0.451 XP = 0.0005
324	TILT TOWARD BEING THOSE 0.68 OF 25 WHERE THE PAIN INFLICTED ON THE INFANT BY THE NURTURANT AGENT IS LOW OR NEGLIGIBLE (32) B-B-C	324	TILT TOWARD BEING THOSE 0.66 OF 32 WHERE THE PAIN INFLICTED ON THE INFANT BY THE NURTURANT AGENT IS HIGH (34) B-B-C	8 21 17 11 XSQ= 5.08 PHI= -0.298 XP = 0.0243
339	DRIFT TOWARD BEING THOSE 0.72 OF 25 WHERE THE CHILD'S INFERRED CONFLICT REGARDING RESPONSIBLE BEHAVIOR IS LOW (42) B-B-C	339	DRIFT TOWARD BEING THOSE 0.55 OF 31 WHERE THE CHILD'S INFERRED CONFLICT REGARDING RESPONSIBLE BEHAVIOR IS HIGH (31) B-B-C	7 17 18 14 XSQ= 3.05 PHI= -0.233 XP = 0.0808
344	TILT TOWARD BEING THOSE 0.73 OF 26 WHERE THE TOTAL POSITIVE PRESSURE TOWARD DEVELOPING SELF-RELIANT BEHAVIOR IN THE CHILD IS LOW (40) B-B-C	344	TILT TOWARD BEING THOSE 0.59 OF 32 WHERE THE TOTAL POSITIVE PRESSURE TOWARD DEVELOPING SELF-RELIANT BEHAVIOR IN THE CHILD IS HIGH (36) B-B-C	7 19 19 13 XSQ= 4.87 PHI= -0.290 XP = 0.0274
402	LEAN TOWARD BEING THOSE 0.69 OF 16 WHERE EXPLANATIONS OF ILLNESS OF AN ORAL NATURE ARE ABSENT (30) W-C	402	LEAN TOWARD BEING THOSE 0.85 OF 20 WHERE EXPLANATIONS OF ILLNESS OF AN ORAL NATURE ARE PRESENT (31) W-C	5 17 11 3 XSQ= 8.66 PHI= -0.491 EP = 0.0017
420	DRIFT MORE TOWARD BEING THOSE 0.83 OF 18 WHERE BELLICOSITY IS MODERATE OR NEGLIGIBLE (46) PES	420	DRIFT LESS TOWARD BEING THOSE 0.54 OF 24 WHERE BELLICOSITY IS MODERATE OR NEGLIGIBLE (46) PES	3 11 15 13 XSQ= 2.73 PHI= -0.255 XP = 0.0982
438	TILT TOWARD BEING THOSE 0.50 OF 10 WHERE THIS-WORLDLY FEARS OF HUMANS OR ANIMALS ARE GREATER THAN OTHER-WORLDLY FEARS OF GHOSTS OR SPIRITS (17) W-C,JFG	438	TILT TOWARD BEING THOSE 0.94 OF 16 WHERE OTHER-WORLDLY FEARS OF GHOSTS OR SPIRITS ARE GREATER THAN THIS-WORLDLY FEARS OF HUMANS OR ANIMALS (27) W-C,JFG	5 15 5 1 XSQ= 4.40 PHI= -0.411 EP = 0.0184
474	TILT TOWARD BEING THOSE 0.83 OF 18 WHERE BOASTFULNESS IS MODERATE, NEGLIBIBLE, OR UNREPORTED (48) PES	474	TILT TOWARD BEING THOSE 0.54 OF 26 WHERE BOASTFULNESS IS EXTREME (41) PES	3 14 15 12 XSQ= 4.73 PHI= -0.328 XP = 0.0296

323 CULTURES
WHERE THE CONSTANCY OF PRESENCE
OF THE INFANT'S NURTURANT AGENT
IS HIGH (29) B-B-C

323 CULTURES
WHERE THE CONSTANCY OF PRESENCE
OF THE INFANT'S NURTURANT AGENT
IS LOW (45) B-B-C

BACKGROUND ON PAGE 140

BOTH SUBJECT AND PREDICATE

29 IN LEFT COLUMN

ANDAMANESE	ARANDA	ARAPESH	AZANDE	CAMAYURA	FON	GANDA	JIVARO	KORYAK	LAU
LEPCHA	MANUS	NAVAHO	PAPAGO	SIRIONO	TANALA	TENETEHARA	TETON	TIMBIRA	TUPINAMBA
TURKANA	WICHITA	WINNEBAGO	WOGEO	WOLEAIANS	YAGUA	YAHGAN	YORUBA	ZUNI	

45 IN RIGHT COLUMN

AINU	ALORESE	ARAUCANIANS	ASHANTI	AYMARA	BALINESE	CHAGGA	CHENCHU	CHEYENNE	CHIR-APACHE
CHUKCHEE	COMANCHE	CROW	CUNA	HANO	IFUGAO	KASKA	KIKUYU	KURTATCHI	KWAKIUTL
LAMBA	LESU	MANDAN	MAORI	MARQUESANS	MASAI	MBUNDU	MURNGIN	NUER	OJIBWA
OMAHA	ONA	ONTONG-JAVA	PUKAPUKA	SAMOANS	SHERENTE	SOTHO	SWAZI	TALLENSI	THONGA
TIKOPIA	TROBRIAND	TRUKESE	VENDA	YAKUT					

326 EXCLUDED BECAUSE UNASCERTAINED

63	TILT TOWARD BEING THOSE WHERE HUSBANDRY, IF PRESENT, IS PRINCIPALLY IN THE FORM OF PIGS, SHEEP, OR GOATS, RATHER THAN BOVINE, EQUINE, CAMEL-LIKE, OR DEER-LIKE ANIMALS (74)	0.72 OF 18	63	TILT TOWARD BEING THOSE WHERE HUSBANDRY, IF PRESENT, IS PRINCIPALLY IN THE FORM OF BOVINE, EQUINE, CAMEL-LIKE, OR DEER-LIKE ANIMALS, RATHER THAN PIGS, SHEEP, OR GOATS (152)	0.63 OF 32	5 20 13 12 XSQ= 4.25 PHI= -0.292 XP = 0.0392
73	DRIFT TOWARD BEING THOSE WHERE WEAVING IS PRESENT (118)	0.57 OF 21	73	DRIFT TOWARD BEING THOSE WHERE WEAVING IS ABSENT (130)	0.71 OF 38	12 11 9 27 XSQ= 3.41 PHI= 0.241 XP = 0.0647
87	DRIFT LESS TOWARD BEING THOSE WHERE THE LEVEL OF POLITICAL INTEGRATION IS THE LARGE STATE, THE LITTLE STATE, THE MINIMAL STATE, OR THE AUTONOMOUS COMMUNITY (281) GPM	0.74 OF 27	87	DRIFT MORE TOWARD BEING THOSE WHERE THE LEVEL OF POLITICAL INTEGRATION IS THE LARGE STATE, THE LITTLE STATE, THE MINIMAL STATE, OR THE AUTONOMOUS COMMUNITY (281) GPM	0.94 OF 36	20 34 7 2 XSQ= 3.70 PHI= -0.242 XP = 0.0545
96	DRIFT TOWARD BEING THOSE WHERE THE HIERARCHY OF NATIONAL JURISDICTION HAS NO LEVELS (156) GES,EA	0.67 OF 27	96	DRIFT TOWARD BEING THOSE WHERE THE HIERARCHY OF NATIONAL JURISDICTION HAS FOUR, THREE, TWO OR ONE LEVEL (174) GES,EA	0.60 OF 42	9 25 18 17 XSQ= 3.52 PHI= -0.226 XP = 0.0605

100	DRIFT LESS TOWARD BEING THOSE 0.74 OF 27 WHERE HIERARCHIES ARE MORE COMPLEX THAN THE 'SIMPLEST,' I. E., MORE COMPLEX THAN TWO LOCAL LEVELS WITH NO NATIONAL LEVELS (267) GES,EA	100	DRIFT MORE TOWARD BEING THOSE 0.93 OF 42 WHERE HIERARCHIES ARE MORE COMPLEX THAN THE 'SIMPLEST,' I. E., MORE COMPLEX THAN TWO LOCAL LEVELS WITH NO NATIONAL LEVELS (267) GES,EA	20 39 7 3 XSQ= 3.29 PHI= -0.218 XP = 0.0699
132	TILT TOWARD BEING THOSE 0.70 OF 10 WHERE ECONOMIC EXCHANGE DOES NOT INVOLVE THE USE OF MONEY (17) JMH	132	TILT TOWARD BEING THOSE 0.72 OF 18 WHERE ECONOMIC EXCHANGE INVOLVES THE USE OF MONEY (37) JMH	3 13 7 5 XSQ= 3.11 PHI= -0.334 EP = 0.0497
135	DRIFT TOWARD BEING THOSE 0.67 OF 12 WHERE INDIVIDUAL OWNERSHIP OF ECONOMICALLY SIGNIFICANT PROPERTY IS NEGLIGIBLE OR ABSENT (14) GES	135	DRIFT TOWARD BEING THOSE 0.86 OF 7 WHERE INDIVIDUAL OWNERSHIP OF ECONOMICALLY SIGNIFICANT PROPERTY IS PRESENT (24) GES	4 6 8 1 XSQ= 2.99 PHI= -0.397 EP = 0.0573
141	TILT TOWARD BEING THOSE 0.80 OF 10 WHERE THE LEVEL OF SOCIAL SANCTION IS PUBLIC PROPERTY SANCTION OR PRIVATE SETTLEMENT, RATHER THAN PUBLIC CORPOREAL SANCTION (26) JMH	141	TILT TOWARD BEING THOSE 0.67 OF 18 WHERE THE LEVEL OF SOCIAL SANCTION IS PUBLIC CORPOREAL SANCTION, RATHER THAN PUBLIC PROPERTY SANCTION OR PRIVATE SETTLEMENT (28) JMH	2 12 8 6 XSQ= 3.89 PHI= -0.373 EP = 0.0461
142	TILT TOWARD BEING THOSE 0.70 OF 10 WHERE THE LEVEL OF SOCIAL SANCTION IS PRIVATE SETTLEMENT, RATHER THAN PUBLIC CORPOREAL SANCTION OR PUBLIC PROPERTY SETTLEMENT (16) JMH	142	TILT TOWARD BEING THOSE 0.83 OF 18 WHERE THE LEVEL OF SOCIAL SANCTION IS PUBLIC CORPOREAL SANCTION OR PUBLIC PROPERTY SANCTION, RATHER THAN PRIVATE SETTLEMENT (38) JMH	3 15 7 3 XSQ= 5.81 PHI= -0.456 EP = 0.0113
143	DRIFT TOWARD BEING THOSE 0.89 OF 9 WHERE THE RATIO OF RESTITUTIVE TO REPRESSIVE SANCTIONS IS MEDIUM OR LOW (32) WME	143	DRIFT TOWARD BEING THOSE 0.55 OF 11 WHERE THE RATIO OF RESTITUTIVE TO REPRESSIVE SANCTIONS IS HIGH (20) WME	1 6 8 5 XSQ= 2.42 PHI= -0.348 EP = 0.0703
144	DRIFT TOWARD BEING THOSE 0.78 OF 9 WHERE THE RATIO OF RESTITUTIVE TO REPRESSIVE SANCTIONS IS LOW (25) WME	144	DRIFT TOWARD BEING THOSE 0.64 OF 11 WHERE THE RATIO OF RESTITUTIVE TO REPRESSIVE SANCTIONS IS HIGH OR MEDIUM (27) WME	2 7 7 4 XSQ= 1.96 PHI= -0.313 EP = 0.0923
149	DRIFT TOWARD BEING THOSE 0.71 OF 14 WHERE THE INCIDENCE OF THEFT IS LOW (19) B-B-C	149	DRIFT TOWARD BEING THOSE 0.61 OF 23 WHERE THE INCIDENCE OF THEFT IS HIGH (18) B-B-C	4 14 10 9 XSQ= 2.46 PHI= -0.258 EP = 0.0911
224	TILT TOWARD BEING THOSE 0.88 OF 8 WHERE COUSIN MARRIAGE IS PREFERENTIALLY OR PERMISSIVELY SYMMETRICAL, RATHER THAN EITHER PATRI- OR MATRILATERAL (106)	224	TILT TOWARD BEING THOSE 0.58 OF 19 WHERE COUSIN MARRIAGE IS PREFERENTIALLY OR PERMISSIVELY EITHER PATRI- OR MATRILATERAL, RATHER THAN SYMMETRICAL (66)	1 11 7 8 XSQ= 3.04 PHI= -0.336 EP = 0.0433

No.	Subject	Proportion	No.	Relative	Proportion	Statistics
272	DRIFT TOWARD BEING THOSE WHERE THE DIVORCE RATE IS LOW (28) CA	0.67 OF 9	272	DRIFT TOWARD BEING THOSE WHERE THE DIVORCE RATE IS HIGH (29) CA	0.77 OF 13	3 10 6 3 XSQ= 2.57 PHI= -0.342 EP = 0.0789
279	DRIFT TOWARD BEING THOSE WHERE WIFE-LENDING OR WIFE-EXCHANGE IS PRESENT (10) LWS	0.75 OF 4	279	DRIFT TOWARD BEING THOSE WHERE WIFE-LENDING AND WIFE EXCHANGE ARE UNIMPORTANT OR ABSENT (19) LWS	0.88 OF 8	3 1 1 7 XSQ= 2.30 PHI= 0.437 EP = 0.0667
302	DRIFT TOWARD BEING THOSE WHERE THE AVERAGE EARLY SATISFACTION POTENTIAL IS HIGH (23) W-C	0.83 OF 12	302	DRIFT TOWARD BEING THOSE WHERE THE AVERAGE EARLY SATISFACTION POTENTIAL IS LOW (17) W-C	0.50 OF 22	10 11 2 11 XSQ= 2.38 PHI= 0.264 EP = 0.0750
303	TILT TOWARD BEING THOSE WHERE THE EARLY ORAL SATISFACTION POTENTIAL IS HIGH (32) W-C	0.79 OF 14	303	TILT TOWARD BEING THOSE WHERE THE EARLY ORAL SATISFACTION POTENTIAL IS LOW (25) W-C	0.63 OF 27	11 10 3 17 XSQ= 4.81 PHI= 0.343 XP = 0.0283
306	TILT TOWARD BEING THOSE WHERE THE EARLY DEPENDENCE SATISFACTION POTENTIAL IS HIGH (28) W-C	0.85 OF 13	306	TILT TOWARD BEING THOSE WHERE THE EARLY DEPENDENCE SATISFACTION POTENTIAL IS LOW (24) W-C	0.54 OF 24	11 11 2 13 XSQ= 3.78 PHI= 0.319 EP = 0.0353
311	DRIFT TOWARD BEING THOSE WHERE SEXUAL SOCIALIZATION ANXIETY IS HIGH (28) W-C	0.69 OF 13	311	DRIFT TOWARD BEING THOSE WHERE SEXUAL SOCIALIZATION ANXIETY IS LOW (23) W-C	0.62 OF 26	9 10 4 16 XSQ= 2.17 PHI= 0.236 EP = 0.0958
312	DRIFT TOWARD BEING THOSE WHERE DEPENDENCE SOCIALIZATION ANXIETY IS LOW (23) W-C	0.77 OF 13	312	DRIFT TOWARD BEING THOSE WHERE DEPENDENCE SOCIALIZATION ANXIETY IS HIGH (24) W-C	0.57 OF 23	3 13 10 10 XSQ= 2.53 PHI= -0.265 EP = 0.0827
321	LEAN TOWARD BEING THOSE WHERE THE IMMEDIACY OF REDUCTION OF THE INFANT'S DRIVES IS HIGH (35) B-B-C	0.83 OF 24	321	LEAN TOWARD BEING THOSE WHERE THE IMMEDIACY OF REDUCTION OF THE INFANT'S DRIVES IS LOW (25) B-B-C	0.58 OF 36	20 15 4 21 XSQ= 8.64 PHI= 0.380 XP = 0.0033
322	TEND TO BE THOSE WHERE THE CONSISTENCY OF REDUCTION OF THE INFANT'S DRIVES IS HIGH (27) B-B-C	0.75 OF 24	322	TEND TO BE THOSE WHERE THE CONSISTENCY OF REDUCTION OF THE INFANT'S DRIVES IS LOW (32) B-B-C	0.74 OF 35	18 9 6 26 XSQ= 12.02 PHI= 0.451 XP = 0.0005

No.		No.		
335	TILT TOWARD BEING THOSE 0.83 OF 12 WHERE INITIAL INDULGENCE OF DEPENDENCY IS HIGH (20) WNS	335	TILT TOWARD BEING THOSE 0.58 OF 19 WHERE INITIAL INDULGENCE OF DEPENDENCY IS LOW (18) WNS	10 8 2 11 XSQ= 3.58 PHI= 0.340 EP = 0.0317
336	DRIFT TOWARD BEING THOSE 0.57 OF 28 WHERE THE TOTAL POSITIVE PRESSURE TOWARD DEVELOPING RESPONSIBLE BEHAVIOR IN THE CHILD IS LOW (32) B-B-C	336	DRIFT TOWARD BEING THOSE 0.66 OF 44 WHERE THE TOTAL POSITIVE PRESSURE TOWARD DEVELOPING RESPONSIBLE BEHAVIOR IN THE CHILD IS HIGH (43) B-B-C	12 29 16 15 XSQ= 2.83 PHI= -0.198 XP = 0.0926
337	DRIFT TOWARD BEING THOSE 0.63 OF 27 WHERE THE CHILD'S INFERRED ANXIETY OVER NON-PERFORMANCE OF RESPONSIBLE BEHAVIOR IS LOW (35) B-B-C	337	DRIFT TOWARD BEING THOSE 0.60 OF 43 WHERE THE CHILD'S INFERRED ANXIETY OVER NON-PERFORMANCE OF RESPONSIBLE BEHAVIOR IS HIGH (38) B-B-C	10 26 17 17 XSQ= 2.77 PHI= -0.199 XP = 0.0962
344	TILT TOWARD BEING THOSE 0.71 OF 28 WHERE THE TOTAL POSITIVE PRESSURE TOWARD DEVELOPING SELF-RELIANT BEHAVIOR IN THE CHILD IS LOW (40) B-B-C	344	TILT TOWARD BEING THOSE 0.58 OF 45 WHERE THE TOTAL POSITIVE PRESSURE TOWARD DEVELOPING SELF-RELIANT BEHAVIOR IN THE CHILD IS HIGH (36) B-B-C	8 26 20 19 XSQ= 4.80 PHI= -0.256 XP = 0.0284
356	DRIFT TOWARD BEING THOSE 0.80 OF 10 WHERE NEITHER ADOLESCENT PEER GROUPS NOR PAIRS ARE PRESENT IN A SETTING OF COURTSHIP (22) JKH	356	DRIFT TOWARD BEING THOSE 0.62 OF 21 WHERE ADOLESCENT PEER GROUPS OR PAIRS ARE PRESENT IN A SETTING OF COURTSHIP (29) JKH	2 13 8 8 XSQ= 3.23 PHI= -0.323 EP = 0.0538
417	DRIFT TOWARD BEING THOSE 0.50 OF 6 WHERE WARFARE IS NOT PREVALENT (9) LWS	417	DRIFT TOWARD BEING THOSE 0.92 OF 12 WHERE WARFARE IS PREVALENT (34) LWS	3 11 3 1 XSQ= 1.97 PHI= -0.331 EP = 0.0833
419	TILT TOWARD BEING THOSE 0.60 OF 20 WHERE MILITARY GLORY IS NEGLIGIBLY EMPHASIZED (31) PES	419	TILT TOWARD BEING THOSE 0.72 OF 32 WHERE MILITARY GLORY IS STRONGLY OR MODERATELY EMPHASIZED (55) PES	8 23 12 9 XSQ= 3.95 PHI= -0.276 XP = 0.0467
420	DRIFT TOWARD BEING THOSE 0.79 OF 19 WHERE BELLICOSITY IS MODERATE OR NEGLIGIBLE (46) PES	420	DRIFT TOWARD BEING THOSE 0.50 OF 32 WHERE BELLICOSITY IS EXTREME (41) PES	4 16 15 16 XSQ= 3.06 PHI= -0.245 XP = 0.0800
435	TILT TOWARD BEING THOSE 0.83 OF 6 WHERE ABANDONMENT OF THE HOUSE OF THE DEAD IS PRACTICED (12) LWS	435	TILT TOWARD BEING THOSE 0.89 OF 9 WHERE ABANDONMENT OF THE HOUSE OF THE DEAD IS NOT PRACTICED (19) LWS	5 1 1 8 XSQ= 5.10 PHI= 0.583 EP = 0.0110

```
438  DRIFT LESS TOWARD BEING THOSE  0.55 OF  11     438  DRIFT MORE TOWARD BEING THOSE  0.86 OF  21          6    18
     WHERE OTHER-WORLDLY FEARS OF                        WHERE OTHER-WORLDLY FEARS OF                        5     3
     GHOSTS OR SPIRITS ARE GREATER THAN                  GHOSTS OR SPIRITS ARE GREATER THAN            XSQ=      2.26
     THIS-WORLDLY FEARS OF                               THIS-WORLDLY FEARS OF                         PHI=    -0.266
     HUMANS OR ANIMALS  (27) W-C,JFG                     HUMANS OR ANIMALS  (27) W-C,JFG               EP =    0.0877

460  DRIFT TOWARD BEING THOSE       0.60 OF  20     460  DRIFT TOWARD BEING THOSE       0.68 OF  31         12    10
     WHERE GAMES, IF PRESENT,                            WHERE GAMES, IF PRESENT,                            8    21
     ARE LIMITED TO                                      ARE NOT LIMITED TO                            XSQ=      2.77
     GAMES OF SKILL ONLY  (67) R-A-B,EA                  GAMES OF SKILL ONLY  (104) R-A-B,EA           PHI=     0.233
                                                                                                       XP =    0.0962

472  TILT TOWARD BEING THOSE        0.70 OF  20     472  TILT TOWARD BEING THOSE        0.62 OF  34          6    21
     WHERE THE COMPOSITE NARCISSISM INDEX                WHERE THE COMPOSITE NARCISSISM INDEX               14    13
     IS LOW  (43) PES                                    IS HIGH  (47) PES                             XSQ=      3.89
                                                                                                       PHI=    -0.268
                                                                                                       XP =    0.0485

473  DRIFT MORE TOWARD BEING THOSE  0.85 OF  20     473  DRIFT LESS TOWARD BEING THOSE  0.58 OF  33          3    14
     WHERE SENSITIVITY TO INSULT                         WHERE SENSITIVITY TO INSULT                        17    19
     IS MODERATE OR NEGLIGIBLE  (56) PES                 IS MODERATE OR NEGLIGIBLE  (56) PES           XSQ=      3.13
                                                                                                       PHI=    -0.243
                                                                                                       XP =    0.0768
```

324 CULTURES WHERE THE PAIN INFLICTED ON THE INFANT BY THE NURTURANT AGENT IS HIGH (34) B-B-C

324 CULTURES WHERE THE PAIN INFLICTED ON THE INFANT BY THE NURTURANT AGENT IS LOW OR NEGLIGIBLE (32) B-B-C

BACKGROUND ON PAGE 140 BOTH SUBJECT AND PREDICATE

34 IN LEFT COLUMN

AINU	ALORESE	ARANDA	ARAPESH	ARAUCANIANS	AZANDE	BALINESE	CHAGGA	CROW	CUNA
FON	GANDA	KIKUYU	KWAKIUTL	MAORI	MARQUESANS	MASAI	MBUNDU	NAVAHO	NUER
OJIBWA	ONA	PUKAPUKA	SIRIONO	SWAZI	TALLENSI	TANALA	TENETEHARA	THONGA	VENDA
WOLEAIANS	YAHGAN	YAKUT	YORUBA						

32 IN RIGHT COLUMN

ANDAMANESE	ASHANTI	AYMARA	CAMAYURA	CHENCHU	CHEYENNE	CHIR-APACHE	COMANCHE	HANO	KASKA
KORYAK	KURTATCHI	LAU	LEPCHA	LESU	MANUS	OMAHA	ONTONG-JAVA	PAPAGO	SAMOANS
SOTHO	TETON	TIKOPIA	TROBRIAND	TRUKESE	TUPINAMBA	TURKANA	WICHITA	WINNEBAGO	WOGEO
YAGUA	ZUNI								

334 EXCLUDED BECAUSE UNASCERTAINED

---

3 TILT LESS TOWARD BEING THOSE LOCATED OUTSIDE OF AFRICA (320) 0.62 OF 34

3 TILT MORE TOWARD BEING THOSE LOCATED OUTSIDE OF AFRICA (320) 0.91 OF 32

13 3
21 29
XSQ= 5.99
PHI= 0.301
XP = 0.0144

8 DRIFT MORE TOWARD BEING THOSE LOCATED OUTSIDE OF NORTH AMERICA (330) 0.88 OF 34

8 DRIFT LESS TOWARD BEING THOSE LOCATED OUTSIDE OF NORTH AMERICA (330) 0.66 OF 32

4 11
30 21
XSQ= 3.60
PHI= -0.233
XP = 0.0579

47 TILT TOWARD BEING THOSE WHERE, IF SETTLEMENTS ARE NON-FIXED, MOVEMENT IS NOMADIC, RATHER THAN NON-NOMADIC (72) 0.90 OF 10

47 TILT TOWARD BEING THOSE WHERE, IF SETTLEMENTS ARE NON-FIXED, MOVEMENT IS NON-NOMADIC, RATHER THAN NOMADIC (38) 0.58 OF 12

9 5
1 7
XSQ= 3.62
PHI= 0.405
EP = 0.0310

51 TILT TOWARD BEING THOSE WHERE SUBSISTENCE IS PRIMARILY BY FOOD PRODUCTION -- I. E., AGRICULTURE OR HUSBANDRY -- RATHER THAN BY GATHERING (253) 0.68 OF 34

51 TILT TOWARD BEING THOSE WHERE SUBSISTENCE IS PRIMARILY BY FOOD GATHERING -- I. E., HUNTING, FISHING, OR COLLECTING -- RATHER THAN FOOD PRODUCTION (147) 0.63 OF 32

23 12
11 20
XSQ= 4.87
PHI= 0.272
XP = 0.0274

No.	Statement	Prop.	No.	Statement	Prop.	Statistics
71	LEAN TCWARD BEING THOSE WHERE METAL WCRKING IS PRESENT (98)	0.50 OF 28	71	LEAN TOWARD BEING THOSE WHERE METAL WORKING IS ABSENT (153)	0.88 CF 25	14 3 / 14 22 / XSQ= 7.1C / PHI= 0.366 / XP = 0.0077
85	DRIFT LESS TCWARC BEING THOSE WHERE THE LEVEL CF POLITICAL INTEGRATICN IS THE MINIMAL STATE, THE AUTCNCMOUS CCMMUNITY, CR THE FAMILY (234) GPM	0.71 OF 28	85	DRIFT MORE TOWARD BEING THCSE WHERE THE LEVEL OF POLITICAL INTEGRATION IS THE MINIMAL STATE, THE AUTONOMOUS COMMUNITY, CR THE FAMILY (234) GPM	0.93 CF 27	8 2 / 20 25 / XSQ= 2.84 / PHI= 0.227 / XP = 0.092C
96	TILT TCWARD BEING THCSE WHERE THE HIERARCHY CF NATICNAL JURISDICTION HAS FCUR, THREE, TWC OR CNE LEVEL (174) GES,EA	0.67 OF 33	96	TILT TOWARD BEING THCSE WHERE THE HIERARCHY OF NATIONAL JURISDICTICN HAS NO LEVELS (156) GES,EA	0.64 OF 28	22 10 / 11 18 / XSQ= 4.64 / PHI= 0.276 / XP = 0.0312
110	TILT LESS TOWARC BEING THCSE WHERE SLAVERY IS ABSENT (218)	0.53 OF 34	110	TILT MORE TOWARD BEING THOSE WHERE SLAVERY IS ABSENT (218)	0.81 OF 32	16 6 / 18 26 / XSQ= 4.74 / PHI= 0.268 / XP = 0.0295
175	TILT LESS TOWARC BEING THCSE WHERE THE COMMUNITY IS 'KIN-HETERCGENECUS,' I. E. CTHER THAN A CLAN CCMMUNITY OR A CEME (260)	0.59 OF 34	175	TILT MORE TOWARD BEING THOSE WHERE THE COMMUNITY IS 'KIN-HETEROGENECUS,' I. E. OTHER THAN A CLAN COMMUNITY OR A DEME (260)	0.88 CF 32	14 4 / 20 28 / XSQ= 5.47 / PHI= 0.288 / XP = 0.0194
177	TILT LESS TOWARC BEING THCSE WHERE THE COMMUNITY IS CTHER THAN A SINGLE CLAN-CCMMUNITY ANC EXCGAMCUS (305)	0.71 OF 34	177	TILT MORE TOWARD BEING THOSE WHERE THE COMMUNITY IS CTHER THAN A SINGLE CLAN-COMMUNITY AND EXOGAMOUS (305)	0.94 OF 32	10 2 / 24 30 / XSQ= 4.49 / PHI= 0.261 / XP = 0.0341
182	DRIFT MORE TOWARD BEING THOSE CTHER THAN WHERE THE COMMUNITY IS STRUCTURED CN A NON-CLAN BASIS ANC AGAMCUS (256)	0.88 OF 34	182	DRIFT LESS TOWARD BEING THCSE OTHER THAN WHERE THE CCMMUNITY IS STRUCTURED ON A NON-CLAN BASIS AND AGAMOUS (256)	0.66 OF 32	4 11 / 30 21 / XSQ= 3.6C / PHI= -0.233 / XP = 0.0579
198	IN ALL CASES ARE THOSE WHERE RULES FCR THE INHERITANCE OF REAL PRCPERTY, IF PRESENT, FAVCR THE MALE HEIR CR LINE, RATHER THAN THE FEMALE (144)	1.00 OF 16	198	TILT LESS TOWARD BEING THOSE WHERE RULES FOR THE INHERITANCE OF REAL PROPERTY, IF PRESENT, FAVOR THE MALE HEIR CR LINE, RATHER THAN THE FEMALE (144)	0.71 CF 14	16 1C / 0 4 / XSQ= 3.09 / PHI= 0.321 / EP = 0.0365
204	DRIFT MORE TCWARC BEING THCSE WHERE MARITAL RESICENCE IS PATRILOCAL, VIRILOCAL, CR AVUNCULOCAL, RATHER THAN AMBILCCAL CR NECLCCAL (270)	0.93 OF 30	204	DRIFT LESS TOWARD BEING THCSE WHERE MARITAL RESIDENCE IS PATRILOCAL, VIRILOCAL, CR AVUNCULCCAL, RATHER THAN AMBILOCAL OR NECLOCAL (270)	0.73 CF 22	28 16 / 2 6 / XSQ= 2.71 / PHI= 0.228 / XP = 0.0998

209	TILT MORE TOWARD BEING THOSE 0.88 OF 32 WHERE MARITAL RESIDENCE IS PATRILOCAL, VIRILOCAL, OR AVUNCULOCAL, RATHER THAN MATRILOCAL OR UXORILOCAL (270)	209	TILT LESS TOWARD BEING THOSE 0.62 OF 26 WHERE MARITAL RESIDENCE IS PATRILOCAL, VIRILOCAL, OR AVUNCULOCAL, RATHER THAN MATRILOCAL OR UXORILOCAL (270)	28 16 4 10 XSQ= 3.96 PHI= 0.261 XP = 0.0467
242	DRIFT MORE TOWARD BEING THOSE 0.94 OF 33 WHERE MARRIAGE IS COMMONLY OR OCCASIONALLY POLYGYNOUS, RATHER THAN MONOGAMOUS (314)	242	DRIFT LESS TOWARD BEING THOSE 0.75 OF 32 WHERE MARRIAGE IS COMMONLY OR OCCASIONALLY POLYGYNOUS, RATHER THAN MONOGAMOUS (314)	31 24 2 8 XSQ= 3.14 PHI= 0.220 XP = 0.0764
243	LEAN TOWARD BEING THOSE 0.71 OF 17 WHERE POLYGYNY, IF PRESENT, HAS A HIGH INCIDENCE (24) W-C,S	243	LEAN TOWARD BEING THOSE 0.88 OF 17 WHERE POLYGYNY, IF PRESENT, HAS A LOW INCIDENCE (36) W-D,S	12 2 5 15 XSQ= 9.84 PHI= 0.538 EP = 0.0013
277	TILT TOWARD BEING THOSE 0.63 OF 8 WHERE THE STATUS OF WOMEN IS INFERIOR OR SUBJECTED (14) LWS	277	IN ALL CASES ARE THOSE 1.00 OF 6 WHERE THE STATUS OF WOMEN IS NOT STRONGLY INFERIOR OR SUBJECTED (22) LWS	5 0 3 6 XSQ= 3.43 PHI= 0.495 EP = 0.0310
282	LEAN TOWARD BEING THOSE 0.73 OF 15 WHERE THE STRENGTH OF DESIRE FOR CHILDREN IS HIGH (16) BCA	282	LEAN TOWARD BEING THOSE 0.85 OF 13 WHERE THE STRENGTH OF DESIRE FOR CHILDREN IS LOW OR ABSENT (20) BCA	11 2 4 11 XSQ= 7.22 PHI= 0.508 EP = 0.0032
299	LEAN TOWARD BEING THOSE 0.83 OF 24 WHERE THE POST-PARTUM SEX TABOO LASTS ONE YEAR OR LESS (89)	299	LEAN TOWARD BEING THOSE 0.67 OF 12 WHERE THE POST-PARTUM SEX TABOO LASTS LONGER THAN ONE YEAR (35)	4 8 20 4 XSQ= 6.89 PHI= -0.437 EP = 0.0067
312	DRIFT TOWARD BEING THOSE 0.59 OF 17 WHERE DEPENDENCE SOCIALIZATION ANXIETY IS HIGH (24) W-C	312	DRIFT TOWARD BEING THOSE 0.72 OF 18 WHERE DEPENDENCE SOCIALIZATION ANXIETY IS LOW (23) W-C	10 5 7 13 XSQ= 2.29 PHI= 0.256 EP = 0.0922
314	TILT LESS TOWARD BEING THOSE 0.61 OF 23 WHERE THE INCIDENCE OF MOTHER-CHILD HOUSEHOLDS IS LOW (61) W-C,S	314	TILT MORE TOWARD BEING THOSE 0.91 OF 22 WHERE THE INCIDENCE OF MOTHER-CHILD HOUSEHOLDS IS LOW (61) W-D,S	9 2 14 20 XSQ= 3.99 PHI= 0.298 XP = 0.0458
317	TILT TOWARD BEING THOSE 0.59 OF 32 WHERE DISPLAY OF AFFECTION TOWARD THE INFANT IS LOW (29) B-B-C	317	TILT TOWARD BEING THOSE 0.71 OF 31 WHERE DISPLAY OF AFFECTION TOWARD THE INFANT IS HIGH (39) B-B-C	13 22 19 9 XSQ= 4.71 PHI= -0.273 XP = 0.0300

318	TEND TO BE THOSE WHERE THE OVERALL INDULGENCE OF THE INFANT IS LOW (31) B-B-C	0.71 OF 34	318	TEND TO BE THOSE WHERE THE OVERALL INDULGENCE OF THE INFANT IS HIGH (40) B-B-C	0.84 OF 32	10 27 24 5 XSQ= 18.05 PHI= -0.523 XP = 0.0000
321	DRIFT TOWARD BEING THOSE WHERE THE IMMEDIACY OF REDUCTION OF THE INFANT'S DRIVES IS LOW (25) B-B-C	0.55 OF 29	321	DRIFT TOWARD BEING THOSE WHERE THE IMMEDIACY OF REDUCTION OF THE INFANT'S DRIVES IS HIGH (35) B-B-C	0.72 OF 29	13 21 16 8 XSQ= 3.48 PHI= -0.245 XP = 0.0620
322	TILT TOWARD BEING THOSE WHERE THE CONSISTENCY OF REDUCTION OF THE INFANT'S DRIVES IS LOW (32) B-B-C	0.72 OF 29	322	TILT TOWARD BEING THOSE WHERE THE CONSISTENCY OF REDUCTION OF THE INFANT'S DRIVES IS HIGH (27) B-B-C	0.61 OF 28	8 17 21 11 XSQ= 5.08 PHI= -0.298 XP = 0.0243
326	DRIFT TOWARD BEING THOSE WHERE THE INFERRED TRANSITION ANXIETY BETWEEN INFANCY AND CHILDHOOD IS HIGH (32) B-B-C	0.61 OF 33	326	DRIFT TOWARD BEING THOSE WHERE THE INFERRED TRANSITION ANXIETY BETWEEN INFANCY AND CHILDHOOD IS LOW (35) B-B-C	0.63 OF 30	20 11 13 19 XSQ= 2.71 PHI= 0.207 XP = 0.0998
340	TILT TOWARD BEING THOSE WHERE THE TOTAL POSITIVE PRESSURE TOWARD DEVELOPING NURTURANT BEHAVIOR IN THE CHILD IS LOW (20) B-B-C	0.61 OF 23	340	TILT TOWARD BEING THOSE WHERE THE TOTAL POSITIVE PRESSURE TOWARD DEVELOPING NURTURANT BEHAVIOR IN THE CHILD IS HIGH (28) B-B-C	0.73 OF 22	9 16 14 6 XSQ= 3.87 PHI= -0.293 XP = 0.0492
342	DRIFT TOWARD BEING THOSE WHERE THE CHILD'S INFERRED ANXIETY OVER PERFORMANCE OF NURTURANT BEHAVIOR IS HIGH (18) B-B-C	0.55 OF 22	342	DRIFT TOWARD BEING THOSE WHERE THE CHILD'S INFERRED ANXIETY OVER PERFORMANCE OF NURTURANT BEHAVIOR IS LOW (28) B-B-C	0.76 OF 21	12 5 10 16 XSQ= 3.06 PHI= 0.267 XP = 0.0804
356	TILT TOWARD BEING THOSE WHERE ADOLESCENT PEER GROUPS OR PAIRS ARE PRESENT IN A SETTING OF COURTSHIP (29) JKH	0.67 OF 15	356	TILT TOWARD BEING THOSE WHERE NEITHER ADOLESCENT PEER GROUPS NOR PAIRS ARE PRESENT IN A SETTING OF COURTSHIP (22) JKH	0.83 OF 12	10 2 5 10 XSQ= 4.88 PHI= 0.425 EP = 0.0185
405	LEAN TOWARD BEING THOSE WHERE EXPLANATIONS OF ILLNESS OF A DEPENDENCE NATURE ARE PRESENT (34) W-C	0.78 OF 18	405	LEAN TOWARD BEING THOSE WHERE EXPLANATIONS OF ILLNESS OF A DEPENDENCE NATURE ARE ABSENT (27) W-C	0.75 OF 20	14 5 4 15 XSQ= 8.55 PHI= 0.474 EP = 0.0029
425	DRIFT TOWARD BEING THOSE WHERE SUPERNATURALS ARE MAINLY AGGRESSIVE, RATHER THAN BENEVOLENT (20) L-T-W	0.73 OF 15	425	DRIFT TOWARD BEING THOSE WHERE SUPERNATURALS ARE MAINLY BENEVOLENT, RATHER THAN AGGRESSIVE (16) L-T-W	0.57 OF 21	4 12 11 9 XSQ= 2.17 PHI= -0.246 EP = 0.0958

426	DRIFT TCWARD BEING THCSE WHERE A HIGH GCC IS PRESENT (156) GES,EA	0.60 OF 3C	426	DRIFT TOWARD BEING THOSE WHERE A HIGH GCD IS ABSENT (104) GES,EA	0.67 OF 27	18 9 12 18 XSQ= 3.05 PHI= 0.231 XP = 0.0805
438	TILT MCRE TOWARC BEING THCSE WHERE CTHER-WCRLDLY FEARS CF GHCSTS CR SPIRITS ARE GREATER THAN THIS-WCRLDLY FEARS CF HUMANS CR ANIMALS (27) W-C,JFG	0.93 OF 15	438	TILT LESS TOWARD BEING THOSE WHERE OTHER-WORLDLY FEARS CF GHOSTS OR SPIRITS ARE GREATER THAN THIS-WORLDLY FEARS OF HUMANS OR ANIMALS (27) W-C,JFG	0.54 OF 13	14 7 1 6 XSQ= 3.88 PHI= 0.372 EP = 0.0286
458	LEAN LESS TOWARC BEING THCSE WHERE GAMES, IF PRESENT, DC NCT INCLUDE GAMES OF STRATEGY (119) R-A-B,EA	0.52 OF 25	458	LEAN MORE TOWARD BEING THOSE WHERE GAMES, IF PRESENT, DO NOT INCLUDE GAMES OF STRATEGY (119) R-A-B,EA	0.91 OF 22	12 2 13 20 XSQ= 6.71 PHI= 0.378 XP = 0.0096
471	DRIFT TCWARD BEING THCSE WHERE SECRET SCCIETIES ARE UMIMPCRTANT CR ABSENT (14) LWS	0.75 OF 8	471	IN ALL CASES ARE THOSE WHERE SECRET SOCIETIES ARE PRESENT (9) LWS	1.00 OF 3	2 3 6 C XSQ= 2.39 PHI= -0.466 EP = 0.0606
480	TILT TCWARD BEING THOSE WHERE CCMPLEXITY OF ARTISTIC CESIGN IS HIGH (14) HB	0.75 OF 12	48C	TILT TOWARD BEING THOSE WHERE COMPLEXITY OF ARTISTIC DESIGN IS LOW (15) HB	0.69 OF 13	9 4 3 9 XSQ= 3.28 PHI= 0.362 EP = 0.0472

```
325  CULTURES                                          325  CULTURES
     WHERE THE DEGREE OF DIFFUSION AMONG                    WHERE THE DEGREE OF DIFFUSION AMONG
     THE INFANT'S NURTURANT AGENTS                          THE INFANT'S NURTURANT AGENTS
     IS HIGH  (42) B-B-C                                    IS LOW  (32) B-B-C

BACKGROUND ON PAGE 140                                                        BOTH SUBJECT AND PREDICATE
..........................................................................................................

     42  IN LEFT COLUMN

ALORESE    ANDAMANESE  ARAPESH     ARAUCANIANS ASHANTI     BALINESE    CHIR-APACHE COMANCHE    CROW        CUNA
GANDA      HANO        IFUGAO      KIKUYU      KURTATCHI   KWAKIUTL    LAU         LEPCHA      LESU        MANDAN
MAORI      MARQUESANS  MASAI       MURNGIN     NAVAHO      NUER        NYAKYUSA    OMAHA       ONA         PAPAGO
PUKAPUKA   SAMOANS     TALLENSI    TETON       THONGA      TIKOPIA     TROBRIAND   TRUKESE     WICHITA     WOLEAIANS
YAHGAN     ZUNI

     32  IN RIGHT COLUMN

AINU       ARANDA      AYMARA      AZANDE      CAMAYURA    CHAGGA      CHENCHU     CHEYENNE    CHUKCHEE    FON
JIVARO     KASKA       LAMBA       MANUS       MBUNDU      OJIBWA      ONTONG-JAVA SHERENTE    SIRIONO     SOTHO
SWAZI      TANALA      TENETEHARA  TIMBIRA     TUPINAMBA   TURKANA     VENDA       WINNEBAGO   WOGEO       YAGUA
YAKUT      YORUBA

     326  EXCLUDED BECAUSE UNASCERTAINED

----------------------------------------------------------------------------------------------------------
  6  TILT LESS TOWARD BEING THOSE    0.62 OF  42      6  TILT MORE TOWARD BEING THOSE    0.88 OF  32       16     4
     LOCATED OUTSIDE OF                                  LOCATED OUTSIDE OF                                 26    28
     THE INSULAR PACIFIC  (330)                          THE INSULAR PACIFIC  (330)                    XSQ=     4.80
                                                                                                       PHI=    0.255
                                                                                                       XP =   0.0284

  9  DRIFT MORE TOWARD BEING THOSE   0.90 OF  42      9  DRIFT LESS TOWARD BEING THOSE   0.72 OF  32        4     9
     LOCATED OUTSIDE OF                                  LOCATED OUTSIDE OF                                 38    23
     SOUTH AMERICA  (335)                                SOUTH AMERICA  (335)                          XSQ=     3.15
                                                                                                       PHI=   -0.206
                                                                                                       XP =   0.0759

213  TEND TO BE THOSE                0.81 OF  42    213  TEND TO BE THOSE                0.59 OF  32        8    19
     WHERE FIRST COUSIN MARRIAGE IS                      WHERE FIRST COUSIN MARRIAGE IS                     34    13
     NOT PERMITTED  (198)                                PERMITTED  (172)                              XSQ=    11.07
                                                                                                       PHI=   -0.387
                                                                                                       XP =   0.0009

234  DRIFT TOWARD BEING THOSE        0.51 OF  39    234  DRIFT TOWARD BEING THOSE        0.75 OF  24       19    18
     WHERE THE COUSIN TERMINOLOGY IS                     WHERE THE COUSIN TERMINOLOGY IS                    20     6
     OF ESKIMO OR HAWAIIAN TYPE,                         OF CROW, OMAHA, OR IROQUOIS TYPE,             XSQ=     3.22
     RATHER THAN                                         RATHER THAN                                   PHI=   -0.226
     CROW, OMAHA, OR IROQUOIS TYPE  (170)                ESKIMO OR HAWAIIAN TYPE  (152)                XP =   0.0728
```

277	TILT TCWARD BEING THCSE WHERE THE STATUS OF WOMEN IS NCT STRCNGLY INFERIOR CR SUBJECTED (22) LWS	0.82 OF	11	277	TILT TOWARD BEING THCSE WHERE THE STATUS OF WOMEN IS INFERIOR OR SUBJECTED (14) LWS	0.80 CF	5	2 4 9 1 XSQ= 3.28 PHI= -0.453 EP = 0.0357
279	IN ALL CASES ARE THOSE WHERE WIFE-LENDING ANC WIFE EXCHANGE ARE UNIMPCRTANT CR ABSENT (19) LWS	1.00 OF	7	279	TILT TOWARD BEING THOSE WHERE WIFE-LENDING OR WIFE-EXCHANGE IS PRESENT (10) LWS	0.80 OF	5	0 4 7 1 XSQ= 5.19 PHI= -0.657 EP = 0.0101
296	TILT TCWARD BEING THCSE WHERE INFANTICICE IS ABSENT CR INFERREC ABSENT (15) BCA	0.68 OF	19	296	TILT TOWARD BEING THOSE WHERE INFANTICIDE IS PRESENT (18) BCA	0.89 CF	9	6 8 13 1 XSQ= 5.89 PHI= -0.459 EP = 0.0128
3C0	DRIFT TCWARD BEING THCSE WHERE THE FOST-PARTUM SEX TABCO LASTS LONGER THAN SIX MONTHS (51)	0.64 OF	25	3CC	DRIFT TOWARD BEING THOSE WHERE THE POST-PARTUM SEX TABOC LASTS SIX MONTHS OR LESS (73)	0.69 OF	16	16 5 9 11 XSQ= 2.98 PHI= 0.270 XP = 0.0843
312	DRIFT TCWARD BEING THCSE WHERE DEPENDENCE SCCIALIZATION ANXIETY IS HIGH (24) W-C	0.57 OF	23	312	DRIFT TOWARD BEING THOSE WHERE DEPENDENCE SOCIALIZATION ANXIETY IS LOW (23) W-C	0.77 CF	13	13 3 10 10 XSQ= 2.53 PHI= 0.265 EP = 0.0827
319	TILT TCWARD BEING THOSE WHERE PRCTECTICN OF THE INFANT FROM ENVIRCNMENTAL DISCOMFCRTS IS HIGH (35) B-B-C	0.69 OF	36	319	TILT TOWARD BEING THOSE WHERE PROTECTICN OF THE INFANT FROM ENVIRONMENTAL DISCCMFCRTS IS LOW (30) B-B-C	0.64 OF	28	25 10 11 18 XSQ= 5.93 PHI= 0.305 XP = 0.0149
366	TILT LESS TOWARC BEING THCSE WHERE DISSCCIATICN CF THE SEXES AT ADCLESCENCE IS MEDIUM CR LCW (41) JKH	0.59 OF	22	366	IN ALL CASES ARE THCSE WHERE DISSOCIATION CF THE SEXES AT ADOLESCENCE IS MEDIUM OR LCW (41) JKH	1.00 CF	13	9 0 13 13 XSQ= 5.18 PHI= 0.385 EP = 0.0131
471	TILT TCWARC BEING THCSE WHERE SECRET SCCIETIES ARE PRESENT (9) LWS	0.71 OF	7	471	IN ALL CASES ARE THCSE WHERE SECRET SOCIETIES ARE UMIMPORTANT OR ABSENT (14) LWS	1.00 OF	5	5 0 2 5 XSQ= 3.54 PHI= 0.543 EP = 0.0278

326 CULTURES WHERE THE INFERRED TRANSITION ANXIETY BETWEEN INFANCY AND CHILDHOOD IS HIGH (32) B-B-C	326 CULTURES WHERE THE INFERRED TRANSITION ANXIETY BETWEEN INFANCY AND CHILDHOOD IS LOW (35) B-B-C

BACKGROUND ON PAGE 140 BOTH SUBJECT AND PREDICATE

32 IN LEFT COLUMN

AINU	ALORESE	ARAPESH	ASHANTI	AYMARA	BALINESE	CHAGGA	CHENCHU	CROW	FON
GANDA	HANO	KASKA	KWAKIUTL	LAMBA	LAU	LEPCHA	MAORI	MASAI	MBUNDU
NAVAHO	OJIBWA	PUKAPUKA	SOTHO	SWAZI	TANALA	THONGA	TRUKESE	WINNEBAGO	WOLEAIANS
YAKUT	ZUNI								

35 IN RIGHT COLUMN

ARANDA	ARAUCANIANS	AZANDE	CAMAYURA	CHEYENNE	CHIR-APACHE	COMANCHE	CUNA	JIVARO	KIKUYU
KORYAK	KURTATCHI	LAKHER	LESU	MANUS	MARQUESANS	NUER	NYAKYUSA	OMAHA	ONA
ONTONG-JAVA	PAPAGO	SAMOANS	SIRIONO	TALLENSI	TENETEHARA	TETON	TROBRIAND	TUPINAMBA	TURKANA
VENDA	WICHITA	WOGEO	YAGUA	YAHGAN					

333 EXCLUDED BECAUSE UNASCERTAINED

9	TILT MORE TOWARD BEING THOSE LOCATED OUTSIDE OF SOUTH AMERICA (335)	0.97 OF 32	9	TILT LESS TOWARD BEING THOSE LOCATED OUTSIDE OF SOUTH AMERICA (335)	0.71 OF 35	1 10 31 25 XSQ= 6.14 PHI= -0.303 XP = 0.0132
71	TILT TOWARD BEING THOSE WHERE METAL WORKING IS PRESENT (98)	0.52 OF 23	71	TILT TOWARD BEING THOSE WHERE METAL WORKING IS ABSENT (153)	0.77 OF 31	12 7 11 24 XSQ= 3.86 PHI= 0.267 XP = 0.0496
84	TILT LESS TOWARD BEING THOSE WHERE THE LEVEL OF POLITICAL INTEGRATION IS THE LITTLE STATE, THE MINIMAL STATE, THE AUTONOMOUS COMMUNITY, OR THE FAMILY (262) GPM	0.80 OF 25	84	IN ALL CASES ARE THOSE WHERE THE LEVEL OF POLITICAL INTEGRATION IS THE LITTLE STATE, THE MINIMAL STATE, THE AUTONOMOUS COMMUNITY, OR THE FAMILY (262) GPM	1.00 OF 31	5 0 20 31 XSQ= 4.57 PHI= 0.286 XP = 0.0325
86	DRIFT TOWARD BEING THOSE WHERE THE LEVEL OF POLITICAL INTEGRATION IS THE LARGE STATE, THE LITTLE STATE, OR THE MINIMAL STATE (148) GPM	0.60 OF 25	86	DRIFT TOWARD BEING THOSE WHERE THE LEVEL OF POLITICAL INTEGRATION IS THE AUTONOMOUS COMMUNITY, OR THE FAMILY (156) GPM	0.68 OF 31	15 10 10 21 XSQ= 3.26 PHI= 0.241 XP = 0.0710

91	DRIFT TOWARD BEING THOSE WHERE SOCIETAL COMPLEXITY IS HIGH (18) F-W	0.67 OF 12	91	DRIFT TOWARD BEING THOSE WHERE SOCIETAL COMPLEXITY IS LOW (22) F-W	0.78 OF 9	8 2 4 7 XSQ= 2.49 PHI= 0.344 EP = 0.0805
94	DRIFT LESS TOWARD BEING THOSE WHERE THE HIERARCHY OF NATIONAL JURISDICTION HAS TWO, ONE, OR NO LEVELS (296) GES,EA	0.86 OF 29	94	IN ALL CASES ARE THOSE WHERE THE HIERARCHY OF NATIONAL JURISDICTION HAS TWO, ONE, OR NO LEVELS (296) GES,EA	1.00 OF 33	4 0 25 33 XSQ= 2.85 PHI= 0.214 XP = 0.0915
96	LEAN TOWARD BEING THOSE WHERE THE HIERARCHY OF NATIONAL JURISDICTION HAS FOUR, THREE, TWO OR ONE LEVEL (174) GES,EA	0.72 OF 29	96	LEAN TOWARD BEING THOSE WHERE THE HIERARCHY OF NATIONAL JURISDICTION HAS NO LEVELS (156) GES,EA	0.64 OF 33	21 12 8 21 XSQ= 6.67 PHI= 0.328 XP = 0.0098
132	DRIFT MORE TOWARD BEING THOSE WHERE ECONOMIC EXCHANGE INVOLVES THE USE OF MONEY (37) JMH	0.90 OF 10	132	DRIFT LESS TOWARD BEING THOSE WHERE ECONOMIC EXCHANGE INVOLVES THE USE OF MONEY (37) JMH	0.54 OF 13	9 7 1 6 XSQ= 1.99 PHI= 0.294 EP = 0.0886
188	LEAN MORE TOWARD BEING THOSE WHERE THE KIN GROUP IS OTHER THAN EXCLUSIVELY COGNATIC (252)	0.91 OF 32	188	LEAN LESS TOWARD BEING THOSE WHERE THE KIN GROUP IS OTHER THAN EXCLUSIVELY COGNATIC (252)	0.51 OF 35	3 17 29 18 XSQ= 10.46 PHI= -0.395 XP = 0.0012
192	IN ALL CASES ARE THOSE OTHER THAN WHERE THE ONLY KIN GROUP PRESENT IS A KINDRED OR ELSE BILATERAL DESCENT IS INFERRED (289)	1.00 OF 32	192	LEAN LESS ´ WARD BEING THOSE OTHER THAN WHERE THE ONLY KIN GROUP PRESENT IS A KINDRED OR ELSE BILATERAL DESCENT IS INFERRED (289)	0.69 OF 35	0 11 32 24 XSQ= 9.85 PHI= -0.383 XP = 0.0017
196	DRIFT MORE TOWARD BEING THOSE WHERE INDIVIDUAL RIGHTS IN REAL PROPERTY, AND RULES FOR INHERITANCE, ARE PRESENT (194)	0.81 OF 21	196	DRIFT LESS TOWARD BEING THOSE WHERE INDIVIDUAL RIGHTS IN REAL PROPERTY, AND RULES FOR INHERITANCE, ARE PRESENT (194)	0.52 OF 27	17 14 4 13 XSQ= 3.19 PHI= 0.258 XP = 0.0739
242	TILT LESS TOWARD BEING THOSE WHERE MARRIAGE IS COMMONLY OR OCCASIONALLY POLYGYNOUS, RATHER THAN MONOGAMOUS (314)	0.75 OF 32	242	TILT MORE TOWARD BEING THOSE WHERE MARRIAGE IS COMMONLY OR OCCASIONALLY POLYGYNOUS, RATHER THAN MONOGAMOUS (314)	0.97 OF 34	24 33 8 1 XSQ= 5.07 PHI= -0.277 XP = 0.0244
299	LEAN TOWARD BEING THOSE WHERE THE POST-PARTUM SEX TABOO LASTS ONE YEAR OR LESS (89)	0.89 OF 19	299	LEAN TOWARD BEING THOSE WHERE THE POST-PARTUM SEX TABOO LASTS LONGER THAN ONE YEAR (35)	0.58 OF 19	2 11 17 8 XSQ= 7.48 PHI= -0.444 EP = 0.0051

309	DRIFT TOWARD BEING THOSE 0.68 OF 19 WHERE ORAL SOCIALIZATION ANXIETY IS HIGH (26) W-C	309	DRIFT TOWARD BEING THOSE 0.63 OF 19 WHERE ORAL SOCIALIZATION ANXIETY IS LOW (27) W-C	13 7 6 12 XSQ= 2.64 PHI= 0.264 EP = 0.0624
317	TILT TOWARD BEING THOSE 0.61 OF 31 WHERE DISPLAY OF AFFECTION TOWARD THE INFANT IS LOW (29) B-B-C	317	TILT TOWARD BEING THOSE 0.70 OF 30 WHERE DISPLAY OF AFFECTION TOWARD THE INFANT IS HIGH (39) B-B-C	12 21 19 9 XSQ= 4.82 PHI= -0.281 XP = 0.0282
318	TILT TOWARD BEING THOSE 0.63 OF 32 WHERE THE OVERALL INDULGENCE OF THE INFANT IS LOW (31) B-B-C	318	TILT TOWARD BEING THOSE 0.70 OF 33 WHERE THE OVERALL INDULGENCE OF THE INFANT IS HIGH (40) B-B-C	12 23 20 10 XSQ= 5.54 PHI= -0.292 XP = 0.0186
324	DRIFT TOWARD BEING THOSE 0.65 OF 31 WHERE THE PAIN INFLICTED ON THE INFANT BY THE NURTURANT AGENT IS HIGH (34) B-B-C	324	DRIFT TOWARD BEING THOSE 0.59 OF 32 WHERE THE PAIN INFLICTED ON THE INFANT BY THE NURTURANT AGENT IS LOW OR NEGLIGIBLE (32) B-B-C	20 13 11 19 XSQ= 2.71 PHI= 0.207 XP = 0.0998
327	LEAN TOWARD BEING THOSE 0.69 OF 29 WHERE THE AGE OF THE INFANT AT TIME OF REDUCED CONTACT WITH MOTHER IS TWO YEARS OR LOWER (27) B-B-C	327	LEAN TOWARD BEING THOSE 0.73 OF 22 WHERE THE AGE OF THE INFANT AT TIME OF REDUCED CONTACT WITH MOTHER IS HIGHER THAN TWO YEARS (28) B-B-C	9 16 20 6 XSQ= 7.11 PHI= -0.373 XP = 0.0077
330	DRIFT TOWARD BEING THOSE 0.67 OF 30 WHERE THE AGE OF THE INFANT AT TIME OF WEANING IS LOWER THAN 2.5 YEARS (36) B-B-C	330	DRIFT TOWARD BEING THOSE 0.61 OF 33 WHERE THE AGE OF THE INFANT AT TIME OF WEANING IS 2.5 YEARS OR HIGHER (34) B-B-C	10 20 20 13 XSQ= 3.66 PHI= -0.241 XP = 0.0559
334	TEND TO BE THOSE 0.81 OF 32 WHERE THE INDULGENCE OF THE CHILD IS LOW (38) B-B-C	334	TEND TO BE THOSE 0.74 OF 35 WHERE THE INDULGENCE OF THE CHILD IS HIGH (40) B-B-C	6 26 26 9 XSQ= 18.50 PHI= -0.525 XP = 0.0000
337	TILT TOWARD BEING THOSE 0.65 OF 31 WHERE THE CHILD'S INFERRED ANXIETY OVER NON-PERFORMANCE OF RESPONSIBLE BEHAVIOR IS HIGH (38) B-B-C	337	TILT TOWARD BEING THOSE 0.64 OF 33 WHERE THE CHILD'S INFERRED ANXIETY OVER NON-PERFORMANCE OF RESPONSIBLE BEHAVIOR IS LOW (35) B-B-C	20 12 11 21 XSQ= 4.00 PHI= 0.250 XP = 0.0454
338	LEAN TOWARD BEING THOSE 0.81 OF 31 WHERE THE CHILD'S INFERRED ANXIETY OVER PERFORMANCE OF RESPONSIBLE BEHAVIOR IS HIGH (44) B-B-C	338	LEAN TOWARD BEING THOSE 0.61 OF 33 WHERE THE CHILD'S INFERRED ANXIETY OVER PERFORMANCE OF RESPONSIBLE BEHAVIOR IS LOW (29) B-B-C	25 13 6 20 XSQ= 9.63 PHI= 0.388 XP = 0.0019

339	TEND TO BE THOSE WHERE THE CHILD'S INFERRED CONFLICT REGARDING RESPONSIBLE BEHAVIOR IS HIGH (31) B-B-C	0.68 OF 31	339	TEND TO BE THOSE WHERE THE CHILD'S INFERRED CONFLICT REGARDING RESPONSIBLE BEHAVIOR IS LOW (42) B-B-C	0.82 OF 33	21 6 10 27 XSQ= 14.13 PHI= 0.470 XP = 0.0002
342	LEAN TOWARD BEING THOSE WHERE THE CHILD'S INFERRED ANXIETY OVER PERFORMANCE OF NURTURANT BEHAVIOR IS HIGH (18) B-B-C	0.62 OF 21	342	LEAN TOWARD BEING THOSE WHERE THE CHILD'S INFERRED ANXIETY OVER PERFORMANCE OF NURTURANT BEHAVIOR IS LOW (28) B-B-C	0.82 OF 22	13 4 8 18 XSQ= 6.86 PHI= 0.399 XP = 0.0088
345	TILT TOWARD BEING THOSE WHERE THE CHILD'S INFERRED ANXIETY OVER NON-PERFORMANCE OF SELF-RELIANT BEHAVIOR IS HIGH (37) B-B-C	0.66 OF 32	345	TILT TOWARD BEING THOSE WHERE THE CHILD'S INFERRED ANXIETY OVER NON-PERFORMANCE OF SELF-RELIANT BEHAVIOR IS LOW (39) B-B-C	0.65 OF 34	21 12 11 22 XSQ= 4.91 PHI= 0.273 XP = 0.0266
346	LEAN TOWARD BEING THOSE WHERE THE CHILD'S INFERRED ANXIETY OVER PERFORMANCE OF SELF-RELIANT BEHAVIOR IS HIGH (37) B-B-C	0.69 OF 32	346	LEAN TOWARD BEING THOSE WHERE THE CHILD'S INFERRED ANXIETY OVER PERFORMANCE OF SELF-RELIANT BEHAVIOR IS LOW (39) B-B-C	0.68 OF 34	22 11 10 23 XSQ= 7.34 PHI= 0.333 XP = 0.0067
347	LEAN TOWARD BEING THOSE WHERE THE CHILD'S INFERRED CONFLICT REGARDING SELF-RELIANT BEHAVIOR IS HIGH (37) B-B-C	0.72 OF 32	347	LEAN TOWARD BEING THOSE WHERE THE CHILD'S INFERRED CONFLICT REGARDING SELF-RELIANT BEHAVIOR IS LOW (39) B-B-C	0.71 OF 34	23 10 9 24 XSQ= 10.25 PHI= 0.394 XP = 0.0014
353	TEND TO BE THOSE WHERE THE CHILD'S INFERRED ANXIETY OVER NON-PERFORMANCE OF OBEDIENT BEHAVIOR IS HIGH (42) B-B-C	0.83 OF 30	353	TEND TO BE THOSE WHERE THE CHILD-S INFERRED ANXIETY OVER NON-PERFORMANCE OF OBEDIENT BEHAVIOR IS LOW (32) B-B-C	0.60 OF 35	25 14 5 21 XSQ= 10.90 PHI= 0.409 XP = 0.0010
354	TILT TOWARD BEING THOSE WHERE THE CHILD'S INFERRED ANXIETY OVER PERFORMANCE OF OBEDIENT BEHAVIOR IS HIGH (36) B-B-C	0.67 OF 30	354	TILT TOWARD BEING THOSE WHERE THE CHILD'S INFERRED ANXIETY OVER PERFORMANCE OF OBEDIENT BEHAVIOR IS LOW (37) B-B-C	0.65 OF 34	20 12 10 22 XSQ= 5.08 PHI= 0.282 XP = 0.0242
355	TILT TOWARD BEING THOSE WHERE THE CHILD'S INFERRED CONFLICT REGARDING OBEDIENT BEHAVIOR IS HIGH (35) B-B-C	0.67 OF 30	355	TILT TOWARD BEING THOSE WHERE THE CHILD'S INFERRED CONFLICT REGARDING OBEDIENT BEHAVIOR IS LOW (38) B-B-C	0.68 OF 34	20 11 10 23 XSQ= 6.20 PHI= 0.311 XP = 0.0128
403	DRIFT TOWARD BEING THOSE WHERE EXPLANATIONS OF ILLNESS OF AN ANAL NATURE ARE PRESENT (23) W-C	0.60 OF 20	403	DRIFT TOWARD BEING THOSE WHERE EXPLANATIONS OF ILLNESS OF AN ANAL NATURE ARE ABSENT (38) W-C	0.74 OF 19	12 5 8 14 XSQ= 3.23 PHI= 0.288 EP = 0.0536

427	DRIFT TOWARD BEING THOSE 0.75 OF 12 WHERE A HIGH GOD, IF PRESENT, IS INACTIVE, RATHER THAN ACTIVE (69) GES,EA	427 DRIFT TOWARD BEING THOSE 0.61 OF 18 WHERE A HIGH GOD, IF PRESENT, IS ACTIVE, RATHER THAN INACTIVE (87) GES,EA	3 11 9 7 XSQ= 2.46 PHI= -0.286 EP = 0.0717
455	DRIFT TOWARD BEING THOSE 0.75 OF 16 WHERE THE MODE OF THE INDIVIDUAL'S CONTACT WITH THE DIVINE IS NOT CONDUCIVE TO THE DEVELOPMENT OF THE INDIVIDUAL'S NEED TO ACHIEVE (19) DCM	455 DRIFT TOWARD BEING THOSE 0.63 OF 16 WHERE THE MODE OF THE INDIVIDUAL'S CONTACT WITH THE DIVINE IS CONDUCIVE TO THE DEVELOPMENT OF THE INDIVIDUAL'S NEED TO ACHIEVE (17) DCM	4 10 12 6 XSQ= 3.17 PHI= -0.315 EP = 0.0732
458	TILT TOWARD BEING THOSE 0.52 OF 23 WHERE GAMES, IF PRESENT, INCLUDE GAMES OF STRATEGY (52) R-A-B,EA	458 TILT TOWARD BEING THOSE 0.80 OF 25 WHERE GAMES, IF PRESENT, DO NOT INCLUDE GAMES OF STRATEGY (119) R-A-B,EA	12 5 11 20 XSQ= 4.11 PHI= 0.292 XP = 0.0427
460	DRIFT TOWARD BEING THOSE 0.78 OF 23 WHERE GAMES, IF PRESENT, ARE NOT LIMITED TO GAMES OF SKILL ONLY (104) R-A-B,EA	460 DRIFT TOWARD BEING THOSE 0.52 OF 25 WHERE GAMES, IF PRESENT, ARE LIMITED TO GAMES OF SKILL ONLY (67) R-A-B,EA	5 13 18 12 XSQ= 3.48 PHI= -0.269 XP = 0.0622
476	DRIFT TOWARD BEING THOSE 0.71 OF 14 WHERE THE DEGREE OF INSOBRIETY IS MODERATE OR SLIGHT (18) DH	476 DRIFT TOWARD BEING THOSE 0.75 OF 8 WHERE THE DEGREE OF INSOBRIETY IS STRONG (31) DH	4 6 10 2 XSQ= 2.75 PHI= -0.354 EP = 0.0743

327	CULTURES WHERE THE AGE OF THE INFANT AT TIME OF REDUCED CONTACT WITH MOTHER IS HIGHER THAN TWO YEARS (28) B-B-C	327	CULTURES WHERE THE AGE OF THE INFANT AT TIME OF REDUCED CONTACT WITH MOTHER IS TWO YEARS OR LOWER (27) B-B-C

BACKGROUND ON PAGE 141

BOTH SUBJECT AND PREDICATE

28 IN LEFT COLUMN

ANDAMANESE	ARAPESH	CAMAYURA	CHEYENNE	COMANCHE	IFUGAO	JIVARO	KORYAK	KWAKIUTL	LAMBA
LEPCHA	LESU	MACRI	NAVAHO	NUER	OJIBWA	OMAHA	ONTONG-JAVA	PAPAGO	SAMOANS
SIRIONO	SWAZI	TALLENSI	TENETEHARA	THONGA	WICHITA	YAHGAN	YORUBA		

27 IN RIGHT COLUMN

ALORESE	ASHANTI	AYMARA	BALINESE	CHAGGA	CHENCHU	CROW	FON	GANDA	HANO
KASKA	KIKUYU	KURTATCHI	LAU	MANUS	MASAI	MBUNDU	PUKAPUKA	SOTHO	TANALA
TIKOPIA	TRUKESE	TURKANA	WINNEBAGO	WOGEO	YAGUA	ZUNI			

345 EXCLUDED BECAUSE UNASCERTAINED

16	DRIFT TOWARD BEING THOSE WHERE THE LATITUDE IS TEN DEGREES OR GREATER (277)	0.75 OF 28	16	DRIFT TOWARD BEING THOSE WHERE THE LATITUDE IS LESS THAN TEN DEGREES (123)	0.52 OF 27	21 13 7 14 XSQ= 3.14 PHI= 0.239 XP = 0.0765
44	DRIFT LESS TOWARD BEING THOSE WHERE SETTLEMENTS ARE FIXED (222)	0.52 OF 27	44	DRIFT MORE TOWARD BEING THOSE WHERE SETTLEMENTS ARE FIXED (222)	0.80 OF 25	14 20 13 5 XSQ= 3.39 PHI= -0.255 XP = 0.0658
141	TILT TOWARD BEING THOSE WHERE THE LEVEL OF SOCIAL SANCTION IS PUBLIC PROPERTY SANCTION OR PRIVATE SETTLEMENT, RATHER THAN PUBLIC CORPOREAL SANCTION (26) JMH	0.70 OF 10	141	TILT TOWARD BEING THOSE WHERE THE LEVEL OF SOCIAL SANCTION IS PUBLIC CORPOREAL SANCTION, RATHER THAN PUBLIC PROPERTY SANCTION OR PRIVATE SETTLEMENT (28) JMH	0.86 OF 7	3 6 7 1 XSQ= 3.14 PHI= -0.430 EP = 0.0498
188	TEND TO BE THOSE WHERE THE KIN GROUP IS EXCLUSIVELY COGNATIC (148)	0.54 OF 28	188	TEND TO BE THOSE WHERE THE KIN GROUP IS OTHER THAN EXCLUSIVELY COGNATIC (252)	0.96 OF 27	15 1 13 26 XSQ= 14.24 PHI= 0.509 XP = 0.0002

192	LEAN LESS TOWARD BEING THOSE 0.71 OF 28 OTHER THAN WHERE THE ONLY KIN GROUP PRESENT IS A KINDRED OR ELSE BILATERAL DESCENT IS INFERRED (289)	192	IN ALL CASES ARE THOSE 1.00 OF 27 OTHER THAN WHERE THE ONLY KIN GROUP PRESENT IS A KINDRED OR ELSE BILATERAL DESCENT IS INFERRED (289)	8 0 20 27 XSQ= 6.88 PHI= 0.354 XP = 0.0087
204	DRIFT LESS TOWARD BEING THOSE 0.67 OF 21 WHERE MARITAL RESIDENCE IS PATRILOCAL, VIRILOCAL, OR AVUNCULOCAL, RATHER THAN AMBILOCAL OR NEOLOCAL (270)	204	DRIFT MORE TOWARD BEING THOSE 0.91 OF 23 WHERE MARITAL RESIDENCE IS PATRILOCAL, VIRILOCAL, OR AVUNCULOCAL, RATHER THAN AMBILOCAL OR NEOLOCAL (270)	14 21 7 2 XSQ= 2.72 PHI= -0.249 XP = 0.0990
234	TILT TOWARD BEING THOSE 0.62 OF 26 WHERE THE COUSIN TERMINOLOGY IS OF ESKIMO OR HAWAIIAN TYPE, RATHER THAN CROW, OMAHA, OR IROQUOIS TYPE (170)	234	TILT TOWARD BEING THOSE 0.77 OF 22 WHERE THE COUSIN TERMINOLOGY IS OF CROW, OMAHA, OR IROQUOIS TYPE, RATHER THAN ESKIMO OR HAWAIIAN TYPE (152)	10 17 16 5 XSQ= 5.80 PHI= -0.348 XP = 0.0160
236	TILT TOWARD BEING THOSE 0.75 OF 28 WHERE THE FAMILY IS OF AN EXTENDED TYPE, RATHER THAN AN INDEPENDENT TYPE (213)	236	TILT TOWARD BEING THOSE 0.59 OF 27 WHERE THE FAMILY IS OF AN INDEPENDENT TYPE, RATHER THAN AN EXTENDED TYPE (185)	21 11 7 16 XSQ= 5.30 PHI= 0.310 XP = 0.0214
242	DRIFT MORE TOWARD BEING THOSE 0.93 OF 28 WHERE MARRIAGE IS COMMONLY OR OCCASIONALLY POLYGYNOUS, RATHER THAN MONOGAMOUS (314)	242	DRIFT LESS TOWARD BEING THOSE 0.70 OF 27 WHERE MARRIAGE IS COMMONLY OR OCCASIONALLY POLYGYNOUS, RATHER THAN MONOGAMOUS (314)	26 19 2 8 XSQ= 3.28 PHI= 0.244 XP = 0.0700
326	LEAN TOWARD BEING THOSE 0.64 OF 25 WHERE THE INFERRED TRANSITION ANXIETY BETWEEN INFANCY AND CHILDHOOD IS LOW (35) B-B-C	326	LEAN TOWARD BEING THOSE 0.77 OF 26 WHERE THE INFERRED TRANSITION ANXIETY BETWEEN INFANCY AND CHILDHOOD IS HIGH (32) B-B-C	9 20 16 6 XSQ= 7.11 PHI= -0.373 XP = 0.0077
330	LEAN TOWARD BEING THOSE 0.67 OF 27 WHERE THE AGE OF THE INFANT AT TIME OF WEANING IS 2.5 YEARS OR HIGHER (34) B-B-C	330	LEAN TOWARD BEING THOSE 0.76 OF 25 WHERE THE AGE OF THE INFANT AT TIME OF WEANING IS LOWER THAN 2.5 YEARS (36) B-B-C	18 6 9 19 XSQ= 7.87 PHI= 0.389 XP = 0.0050
334	TILT TOWARD BEING THOSE 0.68 OF 28 WHERE THE INDULGENCE OF THE CHILD IS HIGH (40) B-B-C	334	TILT TOWARD BEING THOSE 0.67 OF 27 WHERE THE INDULGENCE OF THE CHILD IS LOW (38) B-B-C	19 9 9 18 XSQ= 5.25 PHI= 0.309 XP = 0.0220
341	TILT TOWARD BEING THOSE 0.85 OF 20 WHERE THE CHILD'S INFERRED ANXIETY OVER NON-PERFORMANCE OF NURTURANT BEHAVIOR IS HIGH (30) B-B-C	341	TILT TOWARD BEING THOSE 0.56 OF 18 WHERE THE CHILD'S INFERRED ANXIETY OVER NON-PERFORMANCE OF NURTURANT BEHAVIOR IS LOW (16) B-B-C	17 8 3 10 XSQ= 5.24 PHI= 0.371 EP = 0.0156

No.			No.			
346	DRIFT TOWARD BEING THOSE WHERE THE CHILD'S INFERRED ANXIETY OVER PERFORMANCE OF SELF-RELIANT BEHAVIOR IS LOW (39) B-B-C	0.67 OF 27	346	DRIFT TOWARD BEING THOSE WHERE THE CHILD'S INFERRED ANXIETY OVER PERFORMANCE OF SELF-RELIANT BEHAVIOR IS HIGH (37) B-B-C	0.63 OF 27	9 17 18 10 XSQ= 3.63 PHI= -0.259 XP = 0.0566
347	LEAN TOWARD BEING THOSE WHERE THE CHILD'S INFERRED CONFLICT REGARDING SELF-RELIANT BEHAVIOR IS LOW (39) B-B-C	0.70 OF 27	347	LEAN TOWARD BEING THOSE WHERE THE CHILD'S INFERRED CONFLICT REGARDING SELF-RELIANT BEHAVIOR IS HIGH (37) B-B-C	0.70 OF 27	8 19 19 8 XSQ= 7.41 PHI= -0.370 XP = 0.0065
402	DRIFT TOWARD BEING THOSE WHERE EXPLANATIONS OF ILLNESS OF AN ORAL NATURE ARE PRESENT (31) W-C	0.76 OF 17	402	DRIFT TOWARD BEING THOSE WHERE EXPLANATIONS OF ILLNESS OF AN ORAL NATURE ARE ABSENT (30) W-C	0.56 OF 16	13 7 4 9 XSQ= 2.45 PHI= 0.273 EP = 0.0799
446	IN ALL CASES ARE THOSE WHERE WITCHCRAFT IS MODERATELY PRESENT OR ABSENT (24) GES	1.00 OF 6	446	TILT TOWARD BEING THOSE WHERE WITCHCRAFT IS SIGNIFICANTLY PRESENT (14) GES	0.71 OF 7	0 5 6 2 XSQ= 4.27 PHI= -0.573 EP = 0.0210
458	TILT MORE TOWARD BEING THOSE WHERE GAMES, IF PRESENT, DO NOT INCLUDE GAMES OF STRATEGY (119) R-A-B,EA	0.88 OF 17	458	TILT LESS TOWARD BEING THOSE WHERE GAMES, IF PRESENT, DO NOT INCLUDE GAMES OF STRATEGY (119) R-A-B,EA	0.55 OF 20	2 9 15 11 XSQ= 3.40 PHI= -0.303 EP = 0.0365
476	TILT TOWARD BEING THOSE WHERE THE DEGREE OF INSOBRIETY IS STRONG (31) DH	0.78 OF 9	476	TILT TOWARD BEING THOSE WHERE THE DEGREE OF INSOBRIETY IS MODERATE OR SLIGHT (18) DH	0.88 OF 8	7 1 2 7 XSQ= 4.86 PHI= 0.535 EP = 0.0152

```
328 CULTURES                                          328 CULTURES
    WHERE THE AGE OF THE INFANT                           WHERE THE AGE OF THE INFANT
    AT THE ONSET OF SERIOUS SOCIALIZATION,                AT THE ONSET OF SERIOUS SOCIALIZATION,
    OTHER THAN WEANING,                                   OTHER THAN WEANING,
    IS HIGHER THAN TWO YEARS  (21) B-B-C                  IS TWO YEARS OR LOWER  (20) B-B-C

BACKGROUND ON PAGE 141                                                        BOTH SUBJECT AND PREDICATE

      21  IN LEFT COLUMN

ARAPESH     ARAUCANIANS AYMARA     BALINESE    CAMAYURA    CHAGGA     KASKA      LEPCHA      MBUNDU     OJIBWA
ONA         PAPAGO      SAMOANS    SIRIONO     SOTHO       SWAZI      TALLENSI   TENETEHARA  TRUKESE    WOGEO
WOLEAIANS

      20  IN RIGHT COLUMN

AINU        ALORESE     ASHANTI    COMANCHE    CROW        FON        GANDA      HANO        KWAKIUTL   LAU
LESU        MANUS       NAVAHO     ONTONG-JAVA PUKAPUKA    TANALA     VENDA      WICHITA     YORUBA     ZUNI

     359  EXCLUDED BECAUSE UNASCERTAINED

-------------------------------------------------------------------------------------------------------------
  9 TILT LESS TOWARD BEING THOSE   0.71 OF  21      9 IN ALL CASES ARE THOSE        1.00 OF  20          6    0
    LOCATED OUTSIDE OF                                LOCATED OUTSIDE OF                                15   20
    SOUTH AMERICA  (335)                              SOUTH AMERICA  (335)                         XSQ=   4.60
                                                                                                   PHI=  0.335
                                                                                                   XP = 0.0319

 45 TILT TOWARD BEING THOSE        0.57 OF  14     45 TILT TOWARD BEING THOSE       0.87 OF  15          6   13
    WHERE SETTLEMENTS, IF FIXED, ARE                  WHERE SETTLEMENTS, IF FIXED, ARE                   8    2
    NON-COMPACT, RATHER THAN                          COMPACT, RATHER THAN                         XSQ=   4.37
    COMPACT  (73)                                     NON-COMPACT  (149)                           PHI= -0.388
                                                                                                   EP = 0.0209

 80 IN ALL CASES ARE THOSE         1.00 OF  16     80 TILT LESS TOWARD BEING THOSE  0.71 OF  14          0    4
    WHERE NO CITY OR TOWN IS PRESENT  (185)           WHERE NO CITY OR TOWN IS PRESENT  (185)           16   10
                                                                                                   XSQ=   3.09
                                                                                                   PHI= -0.321
                                                                                                   EP = 0.0365

 96 DRIFT TOWARD BEING THOSE       0.63 OF  19     96 DRIFT TOWARD BEING THOSE      0.68 OF  19          7   13
    WHERE THE HIERARCHY                               WHERE THE HIERARCHY                               12    6
    OF NATIONAL JURISDICTION HAS                      OF NATIONAL JURISDICTION HAS                 XSQ=   2.64
    NO LEVELS  (156) GES,EA                           FOUR, THREE, TWO OR                          PHI= -0.264
                                                      ONE LEVEL  (174) GES,EA                      EP = 0.0624

198 IN ALL CASES ARE THOSE         1.00 OF  12    198 TILT LESS TOWARD BEING THOSE  0.57 OF   7         12    4
    WHERE RULES FOR THE INHERITANCE OF                WHERE RULES FOR THE INHERITANCE OF                 0    3
    REAL PROPERTY, IF PRESENT,                        REAL PROPERTY, IF PRESENT,                   XSQ=   3.31
    FAVOR THE MALE HEIR OR LINE, RATHER THAN          FAVOR THE MALE HEIR OR LINE, RATHER THAN     PHI=  0.417
    THE FEMALE  (144)                                 THE FEMALE  (144)                            EP = 0.0361
```

348	TILT TOWARD BEING THOSE 0.80 OF 20 WHERE THE TOTAL POSITIVE PRESSURE TOWARD DEVELOPING ACHIEVEMENT BEHAVIOR IN THE CHILD IS LOW (31) B-B-C	348	TILT TOWARD BEING THOSE 0.61 OF 18 WHERE THE TOTAL POSITIVE PRESSURE TOWARD DEVELOPING ACHIEVEMENT BEHAVIOR IN THE CHILD IS HIGH (32) B-B-C	4 11 16 7 XSQ= 5.09 PHI= -0.366 EP = 0.0189
349	TILT TOWARD BEING THOSE 0.68 OF 19 WHERE THE CHILD'S INFERRED ANXIETY OVER NON-PERFORMANCE OF ACHIEVEMENT BEHAVIOR IS LOW (28) B-B-C	349	TILT TOWARD BEING THOSE 0.72 OF 18 WHERE THE CHILD'S INFERRED ANXIETY OVER NON-PERFORMANCE OF ACHIEVEMENT BEHAVIOR IS HIGH (34) B-B-C	6 13 13 5 XSQ= 4.59 PHI= -0.352 EP = 0.0217
358	DRIFT LESS TOWARD BEING THOSE 0.56 OF 9 WHERE ADOLESCENT PEER GROUPS ARE PRESENT IN A SETTING OF WORK AND PUBLIC GATHERINGS AND LEISURE, OR OF PUBLIC GATHERINGS AND LEISURE, OR OF LEISURE ONLY (41) JKH	358	IN ALL CASES ARE THOSE 1.00 OF 8 WHERE ADOLESCENT PEER GROUPS ARE PRESENT IN A SETTING OF WORK AND PUBLIC GATHERINGS AND LEISURE, OR OF PUBLIC GATHERINGS AND LEISURE, OR OF LEISURE ONLY (41) JKH	5 8 4 0 XSQ= 2.51 PHI= -0.384 EP = 0.0824
391	TILT TOWARD BEING THOSE 0.85 OF 13 WHERE PREMARITAL SEX RELATIONS ARE PUNISHED ONLY IF PREGNANCY RESULTS, OR FREELY PERMITTED (90) JTW,EA	391	TILT TOWARD BEING THOSE 0.57 OF 14 WHERE PREMARITAL SEX RELATIONS ARE STRONGLY PUNISHED AND IN FACT RARE, OR WEAKLY PUNISHED AND IN FACT NOT RARE (89) JTW,EA	2 8 11 6 XSQ= 3.41 PHI= -0.355 EP = 0.0461
419	DRIFT TOWARD BEING THOSE 0.69 OF 13 WHERE MILITARY GLORY IS NEGLIGIBLY EMPHASIZED (31) PES	419	DRIFT TOWARD BEING THOSE 0.71 OF 17 WHERE MILITARY GLORY IS STRONGLY OR MODERATELY EMPHASIZED (55) PES	4 12 9 5 XSQ= 3.23 PHI= -0.328 EP = 0.0634
446	TILT TOWARD BEING THOSE 0.83 OF 6 WHERE WITCHCRAFT IS MODERATELY PRESENT OR ABSENT (24) GES	446	IN ALL CASES ARE THOSE 1.00 OF 3 WHERE WITCHCRAFT IS SIGNIFICANTLY PRESENT (14) GES	1 3 5 0 XSQ= 2.76 PHI= -0.553 EP = 0.0476

****

329 CULTURES
WHERE THE AGE AT TOILET TRAINING IS
TWO YEARS OR HIGHER (10) W-C

329 CULTURES
WHERE THE AGE AT TOILET TRAINING IS
LOWER THAN TWO YEARS (11) W-C

BACKGROUND ON PAGE 141

BOTH SUBJECT AND PREDICATE

....

10 IN LEFT COLUMN

BALINESE FON LEPCHA LESU MAORI NAVAHO SIRIONO TENINO TETON WOGEO

11 IN RIGHT COLUMN

ALORESE CHAGGA COMANCHE HANO KWAKIUTL MANUS MARQUESANS ONTONG-JAVA PAPAGO PUKAPUKA TANALA

379 EXCLUDED BECAUSE UNASCERTAINED

No.	Left column	Ratio	No.	Right column	Ratio	Statistics
184	DRIFT TOWARD BEING THOSE WHERE THE LARGEST NON-COGNATIC KIN GROUP IS THE MOIETY OR PHRATRY (77)	0.67 OF 6	184	IN ALL CASES ARE THOSE WHERE THE LARGEST NON-COGNATIC KIN GROUP IS SMALLER THAN A PHRATRY, I. E. A SIB OR LINEAGE (175)	1.00 OF 6	4 0 2 6 XSQ= 3.38 PHI= 0.530 EP = 0.0606
272	IN ALL CASES ARE THOSE WHERE THE DIVORCE RATE IS LOW (28) CA	1.00 OF 2	272	IN ALL CASES ARE THOSE WHERE THE DIVORCE RATE IS HIGH (29) CA	1.00 OF 4	0 4 2 0 XSQ= 2.34 PHI= -0.625 EP = 0.0667
302	DRIFT TOWARD BEING THOSE WHERE THE AVERAGE EARLY SATISFACTION POTENTIAL IS HIGH (23) W-C	0.90 OF 10	302	DRIFT TOWARD BEING THOSE WHERE THE AVERAGE EARLY SATISFACTION POTENTIAL IS LOW (17) W-C	0.55 OF 11	9 5 1 6 XSQ= 2.89 PHI= 0.371 EP = 0.0635
330	DRIFT TOWARD BEING THOSE WHERE THE AGE OF THE INFANT AT TIME OF WEANING IS 2.5 YEARS OR HIGHER (34) B-B-C	0.78 OF 9	330	DRIFT TOWARD BEING THOSE WHERE THE AGE OF THE INFANT AT TIME OF WEANING IS LOWER THAN 2.5 YEARS (36) B-B-C	0.70 OF 10	7 3 2 7 XSQ= 2.63 PHI= 0.372 EP = 0.0698
439	DRIFT TOWARD BEING THOSE WHERE FEAR OF GHOSTS IS LOW (31) W-C	0.60 OF 10	439	DRIFT TOWARD BEING THOSE WHERE FEAR OF GHOSTS IS HIGH (30) W-C	0.82 OF 11	4 9 6 2 XSQ= 2.31 PHI= -0.332 EP = 0.0805

```
*****************************************************************************************************************

330  CULTURES                                           330  CULTURES
     WHERE THE AGE OF THE INFANT                             WHERE THE AGE OF THE INFANT
     AT TIME OF WEANING                                      AT TIME OF WEANING
     IS 2.5 YEARS OR HIGHER  (34) B-B-C                      IS LOWER THAN 2.5 YEARS  (36) B-B-C


BACKGROUND ON PAGE 141                                                                   BOTH SUBJECT AND PREDICATE
.................................................................................................................

      34  IN LEFT COLUMN

AINU         ANDAMANESE  ARANDA      ARAPESH     BALINESE    CAMAYURA    CHEYENNE    CHUKCHEE    CUNA        JIVARO
KORYAK       KURTATCHI   KWAKIUTL    LAKHER      LEPCHA      LESU        MANUS       MBUNDU      MURNGIN     NAVAHO
NUER         NYAKYUSA    OJIBWA      OMAHA       ONTONG-JAVA SIRIONO     TALLENSI    TETON       THONGA      TURKANA
VENDA        WOGEO       WOLEAIANS   YORUBA

      36  IN RIGHT COLUMN

ALORESE      ARAUCANIANS ASHANTI     AYMARA      AZANDE      CHAGGA      CHIR-APACHE CROW        FON         GANDA
HANO         IFUGAO      KASKA       KIKUYU      LAMBA       LAU         MAORI       MARQUESANS  MASAI       ONA
PAPAGO       PUKAPUKA    SAMOANS     SHERENTE    SOTHO       SWAZI       TANALA      TENETEHARA  TIMBIRA     TROBRIAND
TRUKESE      WICHITA     WINNEBAGO   YAGUA       YAHGAN      ZUNI

      330  EXCLUDED BECAUSE UNASCERTAINED


-----------------------------------------------------------------------------------------------------------------
  5  DRIFT LESS TOWARD BEING THOSE  0.82 OF  34       5  DRIFT MORE TOWARD BEING THOSE  0.97 OF  36         6     1
     LOCATED OUTSIDE OF                                  LOCATED OUTSIDE OF                                28    35
     EAST EURASIA  (330)                                 EAST EURASIA  (330)                          XSQ=     2.80
                                                                                                      PHI=    0.200
                                                                                                      XP =   0.0941

242  DRIFT MORE TOWARD BEING THOSE  0.94 OF  34     242  DRIFT LESS TOWARD BEING THOSE  0.74 OF  35        32    26
     WHERE MARRIAGE IS                                   WHERE MARRIAGE IS                                  2     9
     COMMONLY OR OCCASIONALLY POLYGYNOUS,                COMMONLY OR OCCASIONALLY POLYGYNOUS,         XSQ=     3.69
     RATHER THAN MONOGAMOUS  (314)                       RATHER THAN MONOGAMOUS  (314)                PHI=    0.231
                                                                                                      XP =   0.0547

272  DRIFT TOWARD BEING THOSE       0.64 OF  11     272  DRIFT TOWARD BEING THOSE       0.78 OF   9         4     7
     WHERE THE DIVORCE RATE IS                           WHERE THE DIVORCE RATE IS                          7     2
     LOW  (28) CA                                        HIGH  (29) CA                                XSQ=     1.96
                                                                                                      PHI=   -0.313
                                                                                                      EP =   0.0923

286  DRIFT TOWARD BEING THOSE       0.79 OF  14     286  DRIFT TOWARD BEING THOSE       0.64 OF  14        11     5
     WHERE THE NUMBER OF FOOD TABOOS                     WHERE THE NUMBER OF FOOD TABOOS                    3     9
     DURING PREGNANCY                                    DURING PREGNANCY                             XSQ=     3.65
     IS HIGH  (20) BCA                                   IS LOW OR ABSENT  (14) BCA                   PHI=    0.361
                                                                                                      EP =   0.0542
```

302	DRIFT TCWARD BEING THCSE 0.81 OF 16 WHERE THE AVERAGE EARLY SATISFACTION PCTENTIAL IS HIGH (23) W-C	302	DRIFT TOWARD BEING THCSE 0.53 OF 15 WHERE THE AVERAGE EARLY SATISFACTICN POTENTIAL IS LOW (17) W-C	13 7 3 8 XSQ= 2.68 PHI= 0.294 EP = 0.0659
303	TILT TCWARD BEING THCSE 0.70 OF 20 WHERE THE EARLY CRAL SATISFACTION POTENTIAL IS HIGH (32) W-C	3C3	TILT TOWARD BEING THCSE 0.67 CF 18 WHERE THE EARLY ORAL SATISFACTICN POTENTIAL IS LCW (25) W-C	14 6 6 12 XSQ= 3.74 PHI= 0.314 EP = 0.0496
317	DRIFT TCWARD BEING THCSE 0.71 OF 31 WHERE DISPLAY CF AFFECTICN TOWARC THE INFANT IS HIGH (39) B-B-C	317	DRIFT TOWARD BEING THCSE 0.56 OF 32 WHERE DISPLAY OF AFFECTICN TCWARD THE INFANT IS LCW (29) B-B-C	22 14 9 18 XSQ= 3.72 PHI= 0.243 XP = 0.0539
326	DRIFT TCWARD BEING THCSE 0.67 OF 3C WHERE THE INFERRED TRANSITION ANXIETY BETWEEN INFANCY ANC CHILCHCOC IS LCW (35) B-B-C	326	DRIFT TOWARD BEING THCSE 0.61 CF 33 WHERE THE INFERRED TRANSITICN ANXIETY BETWEEN INFANCY AND CHILDHCCD IS HIGH (32) B-B-C	10 20 20 13 XSQ= 3.66 PHI= -0.241 XP = 0.0559
327	LEAN TCWARC BEING THOSE 0.75 OF 24 WHERE THE AGE OF THE INFANT AT TIME CF REDUCED CCNTACT WITH MOTHER IS HIGHER THAN TWC YEARS (28) B-B-C	327	LEAN TOWARD BEING THOSE 0.68 OF 28 WHERE THE AGE CF THE INFANT AT TIME OF REDUCED CCNTACT WITH MOTHER IS TWO YEARS OR LOWER (27) B-B-C	18 9 6 19 XSQ= 7.87 PHI= 0.389 XP = 0.0050
329	DRIFT TCWARD BEING THCSE 0.70 OF 1C WHERE THE AGE AT TCILET TRAINING IS TWC YEARS CR HIGHER (10) W-C	329	DRIFT TOWARD BEING THCSE 0.78 CF 9 WHERE THE AGE AT TOILET TRAINING IS LOWER THAN TWO YEARS (11) W-C	7 2 3 7 XSQ= 2.63 PHI= 0.372 EP = 0.0698
334	TILT TCWARC BEING THOSE 0.65 OF 34 WHERE THE INDULGENCE CF THE CHILD IS HIGH (40) B-B-C	334	TILT TOWARD BEING THOSE 0.64 OF 36 WHERE THE INDULGENCE OF THE CHILD IS LOW (38) B-B-C	22 13 12 23 XSQ= 4.63 PHI= 0.257 XP = 0.0314
343	LEAN TCWARD BEING THCSE 0.57 OF 23 WHERE THE CHILD'S INFERREC CONFLICT REGARDING NURTURANT BEHAVICR IS LCW (18) B-B-C	343	LEAN TOWARD BEING THOSE 0.86 CF 21 WHERE THE CHILD'S INFERRED CONFLICT REGARDING NURTURANT BEHAVICR IS HIGH (29) B-B-C	10 18 13 3 XSQ= 6.74 PHI= -0.391 XP = 0.0095
358	DRIFT LESS TCWARC BEING THCSE 0.68 OF 19 WHERE ADCLESCENT PEER GRCUPS ARE PRESENT IN A SETTING CF WCRK ANC PUBLIC GATHERINGS AND LEISURE, CR CF PUBLIC GATHERINGS ANC LEISURE, OR CF LEISURE CNLY (41) JKH	358	IN ALL CASES ARE THCSE 1.00 OF 13 WHERE ADOLESCENT PEER GRCUPS ARE PRESENT IN A SETTING OF WORK AND PUBLIC GATHERINGS AND LEISURE, OR OF PUBLIC GATHERINGS AND LEISURE, CR OF LEISURE CNLY (41) JKH	13 13 6 0 XSQ= 3.19 PHI= -0.316 EP = 0.0588

```
424  TILT TOWARD BEING THOSE          0.93 OF  15       424  TILT TOWARD BEING THOSE          0.56 OF   9              1     5
     WHERE RELIGIOUS SPECIALISTS ARE                         WHERE RELIGIOUS SPECIALISTS ARE                          14     4
     PART-TIME, RATHER THAN                                  FULL-TIME, RATHER THAN                            XSQ=     4.80
     FULL-TIME  (33) JMH                                     PART-TIME  (21) JMH                               PHI=   -0.447
                                                                                                               EP  =  0.0147

445  TILT TOWARD BEING THOSE          0.62 OF  13       445  TILT TOWARD BEING THOSE          0.82 OF  11              5     9
     WHERE SORCERY IS                                        WHERE SORCERY IS                                          8     2
     UNIMPORTANT  (23) BBW,DH                                IMPORTANT  (26) BBW,DH                            XSQ=     3.00
                                                                                                               PHI=   -0.353
                                                                                                               EP  =  0.0472
```

****

331 CULTURES WHERE THE AGE AT BEGINNING OF INDEPENDENCE TRAINING IS 3.8 YEARS OR HIGHER (16) W-C	331 CULTURES WHERE THE AGE AT BEGINNING OF INDEPENDENCE TRAINING IS LOWER THAN 3.8 YEARS (21) W-C

BACKGROUND ON PAGE 141 — BOTH SUBJECT AND PREDICATE

....

16 IN LEFT COLUMN

AINU, ARAPESH, AZANDE, CHAGGA, CHIR-APACHE, DOBUANS, DUSUN, FON, IFUGAO, KURTATCHI, LEPCHA, LESU, MARQUESANS, ONTONG-JAVA, TENINO, WOGEO

21 IN RIGHT COLUMN

ALORESE, BALINESE, CHENCHU, COMANCHE, HANO, KUTENAI, KWAKIUTL, MANUS, MAORI, NAVAHO, PAPAGO, PUKAPUKA, SAMOANS, SENIANG, SIRIONO, TANALA, TETON, THONGA, TIKOPIA, TROBRIAND, YAKUT

363 EXCLUDED BECAUSE UNASCERTAINED

16	TILT TOWARD BEING THOSE WHERE THE LATITUDE IS LESS THAN TEN DEGREES (123)	0.63 OF 16	16	TILT TOWARD BEING THOSE WHERE THE LATITUDE IS TEN DEGREES OR GREATER (277)	0.81 OF 21	6 17 10 4 XSQ= 5.56 PHI= -0.388 EP = 0.0152
45	LEAN TOWARD BEING THOSE WHERE SETTLEMENTS, IF FIXED, ARE NON-COMPACT, RATHER THAN COMPACT (73)	0.73 OF 11	45	LEAN TOWARD BEING THOSE WHERE SETTLEMENTS, IF FIXED, ARE COMPACT, RATHER THAN NON-COMPACT (149)	0.92 OF 12	3 11 8 1 XSQ= 7.47 PHI= -0.570 EP = 0.0028
87	TILT LESS TOWARD BEING THOSE WHERE THE LEVEL OF POLITICAL INTEGRATION IS THE LARGE STATE, THE LITTLE STATE, THE MINIMAL STATE, OR THE AUTONOMOUS COMMUNITY (281) GPM	0.69 OF 13	87	IN ALL CASES ARE THOSE WHERE THE LEVEL OF POLITICAL INTEGRATION IS THE LARGE STATE, THE LITTLE STATE, THE MINIMAL STATE, OR THE AUTONOMOUS COMMUNITY (281) GPM	1.00 OF 17	9 17 4 0 XSQ= 3.67 PHI= -0.350 EP = 0.0261
183	DRIFT LESS TOWARD BEING THOSE WHERE THE LARGEST NON-COGNATIC KIN GROUP IS SMALLER THAN A MOEITY, I. E., A PHRATRY OR SIB OR LINEAGE (218)	0.70 OF 10	183	IN ALL CASES ARE THOSE WHERE THE LARGEST NON-COGNATIC KIN GROUP IS SMALLER THAN A MOEITY, I. E., A PHRATRY OR SIB OR LINEAGE (218)	1.00 OF 13	3 0 7 13 XSQ= 2.23 PHI= 0.311 EP = 0.0678
243	DRIFT TOWARD BEING THOSE WHERE POLYGYNY, IF PRESENT, HAS A HIGH INCIDENCE (24) W-C,S	0.71 OF 7	243	DRIFT TOWARD BEING THOSE WHERE POLYGYNY, IF PRESENT, HAS A LOW INCIDENCE (36) W-D,S	0.80 OF 15	5 3 2 12 XSQ= 3.46 PHI= 0.397 EP = 0.0524

```
280  IN ALL CASES ARE THOSE           1.00 OF   2     280  IN ALL CASES ARE THOSE             1.00 OF   4            0      4
     WHERE THE COMPOSITE FERTILITY LEVEL                   WHERE THE COMPOSITE FERTILITY LEVEL                     2      0
     IS LOW   (12) MN                                      IS HIGH   (13) MN                                XSQ=     2.34
                                                                                                            PHI=   -0.625
                                                                                                            EP =   0.0667

285  DRIFT TOWARD BEING THOSE         0.73 OF  11     285  DRIFT TOWARD BEING THOSE           0.67 OF  12            8      4
     WHERE THE SEX TABOO DURING PREGNANCY                  WHERE THE SEX TABOO DURING PREGNANCY                    3      8
     IS PRESENT   (14) BCA                                 IS ABSENT OR INFERRED ABSENT   (17) BCA          XSQ=     2.17
                                                                                                            PHI=    0.307
                                                                                                            EP =   0.0995

296  DRIFT TOWARD BEING THOSE         0.75 OF  12     296  DRIFT TOWARD BEING THOSE           0.67 OF  12            9      4
     WHERE INFANTICIDE                                     WHERE INFANTICIDE                                       3      8
     IS PRESENT   (18) BCA                                 IS ABSENT OR INFERRED ABSENT   (15) BCA          XSQ=     2.69
                                                                                                            PHI=    0.334
                                                                                                            EP =   0.0995

332  TILT TOWARD BEING THOSE          0.73 OF  11     332  TILT TOWARD BEING THOSE            0.83 OF   6            8      1
     WHERE THE AGE AT BEGINNING                            WHERE THE AGE AT BEGINNING                              3      5
     OF MODESTY TRAINING IS                                OF MODESTY TRAINING IS                       XSQ=     2.91
     SIX YEARS OR HIGHER   (9) W-C                         LOWER THAN SIX YEARS   (8) W-C                   PHI=    0.413
                                                                                                            EP =   0.0498

349  DRIFT TOWARD BEING THOSE         0.67 OF   9     349  DRIFT TOWARD BEING THOSE           0.79 OF  14            3     11
     WHERE THE CHILD'S INFERRED ANXIETY OVER               WHERE THE CHILD'S INFERRED ANXIETY OVER                 6      3
     NON-PERFORMANCE OF ACHIEVEMENT BEHAVIOR               NON-PERFORMANCE OF ACHIEVEMENT BEHAVIOR      XSQ=     3.00
     IS LOW   (28) B-B-C                                   IS HIGH   (34) B-B-C                             PHI=   -0.361
                                                                                                            EP =   0.0771

356  TILT TOWARD BEING THOSE          0.88 OF   8     356  TILT TOWARD BEING THOSE            0.70 OF  10            1      7
     WHERE NEITHER ADOLESCENT PEER GROUPS                  WHERE ADOLESCENT PEER GROUPS                            7      3
     NOR PAIRS                                             OR PAIRS                                     XSQ=     3.85
     ARE PRESENT IN A SETTING OF                           ARE PRESENT IN A SETTING OF                  PHI=   -0.462
     COURTSHIP   (22) JKH                                  COURTSHIP   (29) JKH                         EP =   0.0248

397  DRIFT LESS TOWARD BEING THOSE    0.63 OF   8     397  IN ALL CASES ARE THOSE             1.00 OF  10            3      0
     WHERE SEX DISABILITY                                  WHERE SEX DISABILITY                                    5     10
     IS ABSENT   (42) JKH                                  IS ABSENT   (42) JKH                             XSQ=     2.20
                                                                                                            PHI=    0.350
                                                                                                            EP =   0.0686

426  DRIFT TOWARD BEING THOSE         0.79 OF  14     426  DRIFT TOWARD BEING THOSE           0.60 OF  15            3      9
     WHERE A HIGH GOD IS                                   WHERE A HIGH GOD IS                                    11      6
     ABSENT   (104) GES,EA                                 PRESENT   (156) GES,EA                           XSQ=     2.99
                                                                                                            PHI=   -0.321
                                                                                                            EP =   0.0604

427  IN ALL CASES ARE THOSE           1.00 OF   3     427  TILT TOWARD BEING THOSE            0.78 OF   9            3      2
     WHERE A HIGH GOD, IF PRESENT, IS                      WHERE A HIGH GOD, IF PRESENT, IS                        0      7
     ACTIVE, RATHER THAN                                   INACTIVE, RATHER THAN                        XSQ=     2.86
     INACTIVE   (87) GES,EA                                ACTIVE   (69) GES,EA                         PHI=    0.488
                                                                                                            EP =   0.0455
```

438	DRIFT LESS TOWARD BEING THOSE WHERE OTHER-WORLDLY FEARS OF GHOSTS OR SPIRITS ARE GREATER THAN THIS-WORLDLY FEARS OF HUMANS OR ANIMALS (27) W-C,JFG	0.55 OF 11	438	DRIFT MORE TOWARD BEING THOSE WHERE OTHER-WORLDLY FEARS OF GHOSTS OR SPIRITS ARE GREATER THAN THIS-WORLDLY FEARS OF HUMANS OR ANIMALS (27) W-C,JFG	0.87 OF 15	6 13 5 2 XSQ= 1.90 PHI= -0.270 EP = 0.0946
441	TILT TOWARD BEING THOSE WHERE FEAR OF HUMAN BEINGS IS HIGH (29) W-C	0.63 OF 16	441	TILT TOWARD BEING THOSE WHERE FEAR OF HUMAN BEINGS IS LOW (32) W-C	0.76 OF 21	10 5 6 16 XSQ= 4.15 PHI= 0.335 EP = 0.0409

332 CULTURES WHERE THE AGE AT BEGINNING OF MODESTY TRAINING IS SIX YEARS OR HIGHER (9) W-C

332 CULTURES WHERE THE AGE AT BEGINNING OF MODESTY TRAINING IS LOWER THAN SIX YEARS (8) W-C

BACKGROUND ON PAGE 141

BOTH SUBJECT AND PREDICATE

9 IN LEFT COLUMN

AINU DUSUN FON LEPCHA MARQUESANS ONTONG-JAVA SAMOANS TENINO WOGEO

8 IN RIGHT COLUMN

ALORESE ARAPESH CHIR-APACHE DOBUANS NAVAHO PAPAGO TANALA TIKOPIA

383 EXCLUDED BECAUSE UNASCERTAINED

36	IN ALL CASES ARE THOSE WHERE THE NATURAL ENVIRONMENT IS OTHER THAN 'VERY HARSH,' OR SUB-TROPICAL BUSH, OR TEMPERATE GRASSLAND (292) FWM	1.00 OF	9	36	DRIFT LESS TOWARD BEING THOSE WHERE THE NATURAL ENVIRONMENT IS OTHER THAN 'VERY HARSH,' OR SUB-TROPICAL BUSH, OR TEMPERATE GRASSLAND (292) FWM	0.63 OF	8	0 3 9 5	XSQ= 1.92 PHI= -0.336 EP = 0.0824
86	DRIFT TOWARD BEING THOSE WHERE THE LEVEL OF POLITICAL INTEGRATION IS THE LARGE STATE, THE LITTLE STATE, OR THE MINIMAL STATE (148) GPM	0.67 OF	6	86	DRIFT TOWARD BEING THOSE WHERE THE LEVEL OF POLITICAL INTEGRATION IS THE AUTONOMOUS COMMUNITY, OR THE FAMILY (156) GPM	0.88 OF	8	4 1 2 7	XSQ= 2.34 PHI= 0.409 EP = 0.0909
88	IN ALL CASES ARE THOSE WHERE, IF A HEADMANSHIP IS PRESENT, SUCCESSION IS HEREDITARY (165)	1.00 OF	8	88	TILT TOWARD BEING THOSE WHERE, IF A HEADMANSHIP IS PRESENT, SUCCESSION IS NON-HEREDITARY (106)	0.75 OF	4	0 3 8 1	XSQ= 4.50 PHI= -0.612 EP = 0.0182
331	TILT TOWARD BEING THOSE WHERE THE AGE AT BEGINNING OF INDEPENDENCE TRAINING IS 3.8 YEARS OR HIGHER (16) W-C	0.89 OF	9	331	TILT TOWARD BEING THOSE WHERE THE AGE AT BEGINNING OF INDEPENDENCE TRAINING IS LOWER THAN 3.8 YEARS (21) W-C	0.63 OF	8	8 3 1 5	XSQ= 2.91 PHI= 0.413 EP = 0.0498
403	DRIFT TOWARD BEING THOSE WHERE EXPLANATIONS OF ILLNESS OF AN ANAL NATURE ARE ABSENT (38) W-C	0.78 OF	9	403	DRIFT TOWARD BEING THOSE WHERE EXPLANATIONS OF ILLNESS OF AN ANAL NATURE ARE PRESENT (23) W-C	0.75 OF	8	2 6 7 2	XSQ= 2.85 PHI= -0.410 EP = 0.0567

332/

```
434  IN ALL CASES ARE THOSE          1.00 OF   4      434  DRIFT TOWARD BEING THOSE       0.67 OF   6          4    2
     WHERE ASCETICISM IN MOURNING BEHAVIOR                WHERE ASCETICISM IN MOURNING BEHAVIOR               0    4
     IS HIGH  (37) JFG                                    IS LOW  (30) JFG                              XSQ=   2.10
                                                                                                        PHI=  0.458
                                                                                                        EP =  0.0762
```

333	CULTURES WHERE THE AGE AT BEGINNING OF TRAINING IN HETEROSEXUAL PLAY INHIBITION IS EIGHT YEARS OR HIGHER (8) W-C	333	CULTURES WHERE THE AGE AT BEGINNING OF TRAINING IN HETEROSEXUAL PLAY INHIBITION IS LOWER THAN EIGHT YEARS (8) W-C

BACKGROUND ON PAGE 141

BOTH SUBJECT AND PREDICATE

8 IN LEFT COLUMN

BALINESE CHAGGA FON KURTATCHI LEPCHA LESU SAMOANS TROBRIAND

8 IN RIGHT COLUMN

ALORESE ARAPESH CHIR-APACHE HANO MANUS SIRIONO TENINO TETON

384 EXCLUDED BECAUSE UNASCERTAINED

8	IN ALL CASES ARE THOSE LOCATED OUTSIDE OF NORTH AMERICA (330)	1.00 OF 8	8	DRIFT TOWARD BEING THOSE LOCATED IN NORTH AMERICA (70)	0.50 OF 8	0 4 / 8 4 / XSQ= 3.00 / PHI= -0.433 / EP = 0.0769
14	IN ALL CASES ARE THOSE WHERE THE LATITUDE IS LESS THAN THIRTY DEGREES (281)	1.00 OF 8	14	DRIFT TOWARD BEING THOSE WHERE THE LATITUDE IS THIRTY DEGREES OR GREATER (119)	0.50 OF 8	0 4 / 8 4 / XSQ= 3.00 / PHI= -0.433 / EP = 0.0769
86	TILT TOWARD BEING THOSE WHERE THE LEVEL OF POLITICAL INTEGRATION IS THE LARGE STATE, THE LITTLE STATE, OR THE MINIMAL STATE (148) GPM	0.71 OF 7	86	IN ALL CASES ARE THOSE WHERE THE LEVEL OF POLITICAL INTEGRATION IS THE AUTONOMOUS COMMUNITY, OR THE FAMILY (156) GPM	1.00 OF 5	5 0 / 2 5 / XSQ= 3.54 / PHI= 0.543 / EP = 0.0278
106	TILT TOWARD BEING THOSE WHERE CLASS STRATIFICATION, IF PRESENT, IS BASED ON SOMETHING OTHER THAN WEALTH (126)	0.86 OF 7	106	IN ALL CASES ARE THOSE WHERE CLASS STRATIFICATION, IF PRESENT, IS BASED ON WEALTH (77)	1.00 OF 3	1 3 / 6 0 / XSQ= 3.35 / PHI= -0.579 / EP = 0.0333
108	TILT TOWARD BEING THOSE WHERE CLASS STRATIFICATION, IF PRESENT, IS BASED ON A HEREDITARY ARISTOCRACY (74)	0.86 OF 7	108	IN ALL CASES ARE THOSE WHERE CLASS STRATIFICATION, IF PRESENT, IS BASED ON SOMETHING OTHER THAN A HEREDITARY ARISTOCRACY (129)	1.00 OF 3	6 0 / 1 3 / XSQ= 3.35 / PHI= 0.579 / EP = 0.0333

185	IN ALL CASES ARE THOSE WHERE THE LARGEST NON-COGNATIC KIN GROUP IS THE MOEITY OR PHRATRY OR SIB (194)	1.00 OF	6	185	DRIFT TOWARD BEING THOSE WHERE THE LARGEST NON-COGNATIC KIN GROUP IS SMALLER THAN A SIB, I. E., THE LINEAGE (58)	0.60 OF	5	6 2 0 3 XSQ= 2.39 PHI= 0.466 EP = 0.0606
196	IN ALL CASES ARE THOSE WHERE INDIVIDUAL RIGHTS IN REAL PROPERTY, AND RULES FOR INHERITANCE, ARE PRESENT (194)	1.00 OF	4	196	DRIFT TOWARD BEING THOSE WHERE INDIVIDUAL RIGHTS IN REAL PROPERTY, OR RULES FOR INHERITANCE, ARE ABSENT (87)	0.71 OF	7	4 2 0 5 XSQ= 2.75 PHI= 0.500 EP = 0.0606
262	IN ALL CASES ARE THOSE WHERE WIVES ARE OBTAINED BY MEANS INVOLVING THE PRESENCE OF SOME CONSIDERATION (305)	1.00 OF	8	262	DRIFT TOWARD BEING THOSE WHERE WIVES ARE OBTAINED BY MEANS INVOLVING THE ABSENCE OF ANY CONSIDERATION (90)	0.50 OF	8	8 4 0 4 XSQ= 3.00 PHI= 0.433 EP = 0.0769
365	TILT TOWARD BEING THOSE WHERE THE TIME SPENT IN ADOLESCENT PEER GROUP ACTIVITY IS HIGH OR HIGH-MEDIUM (30) JKH	0.86 OF	7	365	IN ALL CASES ARE THOSE WHERE THE TIME SPENT IN ADOLESCENT PEER GROUP ACTIVITY IS LOW-MEDIUM OR LOW (15) JKH	1.00 OF	3	6 0 1 3 XSQ= 3.35 PHI= 0.579 EP = 0.0333
377	DRIFT TOWARD BEING THOSE WHERE MALE GENITAL MUTILATION IS PRESENT (83)	0.57 OF	7	377	IN ALL CASES ARE THOSE WHERE MALE GENITAL MUTILATION IS ABSENT (242)	1.00 OF	7	4 0 3 7 XSQ= 3.15 PHI= 0.474 EP = 0.0699
434	DRIFT TOWARD BEING THOSE WHERE ASCETICISM IN MOURNING BEHAVIOR IS HIGH (37) JFG	0.71 OF	7	434	IN ALL CASES ARE THOSE WHERE ASCETICISM IN MOURNING BEHAVIOR IS LOW (30) JFG	1.00 OF	4	5 0 2 4 XSQ= 2.75 PHI= 0.500 EP = 0.0606

334 CULTURES WHERE THE INDULGENCE OF THE CHILD IS HIGH (40) B-B-C

334 CULTURES WHERE THE INDULGENCE OF THE CHILD IS LOW (38) B-B-C

BACKGROUND ON PAGE 143

BOTH SUBJECT AND PREDICATE

40 IN LEFT COLUMN

ANDAMANESE	ARAPESH	BALINESE	CAMAYURA	CHENCHU	CHEYENNE	CHUKCHEE	COMANCHE	CROW	CUNA
HANO	IFUGAO	JIVARO	KIKUYU	KORYAK	LAKHER	LESU	MANDAN	MANUS	MAORI
MARQUESANS	MURNGIN	NUER	NYAKYUSA	OMAHA	ONA	ONTONG-JAVA	PAPAGO	SAMOANS	SIRIONO
TALLENSI	TETON	TIKOPIA	TIMBIRA	TROBRIAND	TUPINAMBA	WOGEO	YAGUA	YAHGAN	YORUBA

38 IN RIGHT COLUMN

AINU	ALORESE	ARANDA	ARAUCANIANS	ASHANTI	AYMARA	AZANDE	CHAGGA	CHIR-APACHE	FON
GANDA	KASKA	KURTATCHI	KWAKIUTL	LAMBA	LAU	LEPCHA	MASAI	MBUNDU	NAVAHO
OJIBWA	PUKAPUKA	SHERENTE	SOTHO	SWAZI	TANALA	TENETEHARA	THONGA	TIV	TRUKESE
TUCUNA	TURKANA	VENDA	WICHITA	WINNEBAGO	WOLEAIANS	YAKUT	ZUNI		

322 EXCLUDED BECAUSE UNASCERTAINED

3	TILT MORE TOWARD BEING THOSE LOCATED OUTSIDE OF AFRICA (320)	0.88 OF 40	3	TILT LESS TOWARD BEING THOSE LOCATED OUTSIDE OF AFRICA (320)	0.63 OF 38		5 14 35 24 XSQ= 5.02 PHI= -0.254 XP = 0.0251
51	DRIFT TOWARD BEING THOSE WHERE SUBSISTENCE IS PRIMARILY BY FOOD GATHERING -- I. E., HUNTING, FISHING, OR COLLECTING -- RATHER THAN FOOD PRODUCTION (147)	0.57 OF 40	51	DRIFT TOWARD BEING THOSE WHERE SUBSISTENCE IS PRIMARILY BY FOOD PRODUCTION -- I. E., AGRICULTURE OR HUSBANDRY -- RATHER THAN BY GATHERING (253)	0.66 OF 38		17 25 23 13 XSQ= 3.37 PHI= -0.208 XP = 0.0665
71	TILT TOWARD BEING THOSE WHERE METAL WORKING IS ABSENT (153)	0.80 OF 35	71	TILT TOWARD BEING THOSE WHERE METAL WORKING IS PRESENT (98)	0.54 OF 28		7 15 28 13 XSQ= 6.31 PHI= -0.316 XP = 0.0120
77	IN ALL CASES ARE THOSE WHERE THE WRITING SYSTEM IS MNEMONIC OR ABSENT, RATHER THAN BEING ALPHABETIC-OR-PHONETIC (39) JMH	1.00 OF 15	77	TILT LESS TOWARD BEING THOSE WHERE THE WRITING SYSTEM IS MNEMONIC OR ABSENT, RATHER THAN BEING ALPHABETIC-OR-PHONETIC (39) JMH	0.64 OF 14		0 5 15 9 XSQ= 4.21 PHI= -0.381 EP = 0.0169

85	TILT MORE TOWARD BEING THOSE WHERE THE LEVEL OF POLITICAL INTEGRATION IS THE MINIMAL STATE, THE AUTONOMOUS COMMUNITY, OR THE FAMILY (234) GPM	0.94 OF 36	85	TILT LESS TOWARD BEING THOSE WHERE THE LEVEL OF POLITICAL INTEGRATION IS THE MINIMAL STATE, THE AUTONOMOUS COMMUNITY, OR THE FAMILY (234) GPM	0.74 OF 31	2 8 34 23 XSQ= 3.90 PHI= -0.241 XP = 0.0482
88	DRIFT TOWARD BEING THOSE WHERE, IF A HEADMANSHIP IS PRESENT, SUCCESSION IS NON-HEREDITARY (106)	0.52 OF 29	88	DRIFT TOWARD BEING THOSE WHERE, IF A HEADMANSHIP IS PRESENT, SUCCESSION IS HEREDITARY (165)	0.73 OF 30	15 8 14 22 XSQ= 2.91 PHI= 0.222 XP = 0.0880
96	TILT TOWARD BEING THOSE WHERE THE HIERARCHY OF NATIONAL JURISDICTION HAS NO LEVELS (156) GES,EA	0.62 OF 37	96	TILT TOWARD BEING THOSE WHERE THE HIERARCHY OF NATIONAL JURISDICTION HAS FOUR, THREE, TWO OR ONE LEVEL (174) GES,EA	0.64 OF 36	14 23 23 13 XSQ= 3.97 PHI= -0.233 XP = 0.0464
116	TILT MORE TOWARD BEING THOSE WHERE OCCUPATIONAL SPECIALIZATION IS PART-TIME ONLY (34) JMH	0.93 OF 15	116	TILT LESS TOWARD BEING THOSE WHERE OCCUPATIONAL SPECIALIZATION IS PART-TIME ONLY (34) JMH	0.57 OF 14	1 6 14 8 XSQ= 3.39 PHI= -0.342 EP = 0.0352
128	DRIFT TOWARD BEING THOSE WHERE, IF SUBSISTENCE IS PRIMARILY BY AGRICULTURE, THE WORK IS MAINLY DONE BY MALES (40)	0.63 OF 8	128	DRIFT TOWARD BEING THOSE WHERE, IF SUBSISTENCE IS PRIMARILY BY AGRICULTURE, THE WORK IS MAINLY DONE BY FEMALES (37)	0.83 OF 12	5 2 3 10 XSQ= 2.65 PHI= 0.364 EP = 0.0623
132	LEAN TOWARD BEING THOSE WHERE ECONOMIC EXCHANGE DOES NOT INVOLVE THE USE OF MONEY (17) JMH	0.67 OF 15	132	LEAN TOWARD BEING THOSE WHERE ECONOMIC EXCHANGE INVOLVES THE USE OF MONEY (37) JMH	0.86 OF 14	5 12 10 2 XSQ= 6.17 PHI= -0.461 EP = 0.0078
142	DRIFT TOWARD BEING THOSE WHERE THE LEVEL OF SOCIAL SANCTION IS PRIVATE SETTLEMENT, RATHER THAN PUBLIC CORPOREAL SANCTION OR PUBLIC PROPERTY SETTLEMENT (16) JMH	0.53 OF 15	142	DRIFT TOWARD BEING THOSE WHERE THE LEVEL OF SOCIAL SANCTION IS PUBLIC CORPOREAL SANCTION OR PUBLIC PROPERTY SANCTION, RATHER THAN PRIVATE SETTLEMENT (38) JMH	0.86 OF 14	7 12 8 2 XSQ= 3.31 PHI= -0.338 EP = 0.0502
149	LEAN TOWARD BEING THOSE WHERE THE INCIDENCE OF THEFT IS LOW (19) B-B-C	0.74 OF 19	149	LEAN TOWARD BEING THOSE WHERE THE INCIDENCE OF THEFT IS HIGH (18) B-B-C	0.72 OF 18	5 13 14 5 XSQ= 6.07 PHI= -0.405 EP = 0.0086
152	DRIFT TOWARD BEING THOSE WHERE THE DIFFERENTIATION OF THE JURIDICAL AGENCY FROM THE MEDICAL AGENCY IS LOW (10) MJ	0.86 OF 7	152	IN ALL CASES ARE THOSE WHERE THE DIFFERENTIATION OF THE JURIDICAL AGENCY FROM THE MEDICAL AGENCY IS HIGH (10) MJ	1.00 OF 2	1 2 6 0 XSQ= 2.01 PHI= -0.472 EP = 0.0833

186	TILT MORE TOWARD BEING THOSE WHERE THE KIN GROUP IS OTHER THAN EXCLUSIVELY PATRILINEAL (250)	0.80 OF 40	186	TILT LESS TOWARD BEING THOSE WHERE THE KIN GROUP IS OTHER THAN EXCLUSIVELY PATRILINEAL (250)	0.53 OF 38	8 18 32 20 XSQ= 5.39 PHI= -0.263 XP = 0.0202
188	TEND LESS TO BE THOSE WHERE THE KIN GROUP IS OTHER THAN EXCLUSIVELY COGNATIC (252)	0.52 OF 40	188	TEND MORE TO BE THOSE WHERE THE KIN GROUP IS OTHER THAN EXCLUSIVELY COGNATIC (252)	0.89 OF 38	19 4 21 34 XSQ= 11.10 PHI= 0.377 XP = 0.0009
192	TILT LESS TOWARD BEING THOSE OTHER THAN WHERE THE ONLY KIN GROUP PRESENT IS A KINDRED OR ELSE BILATERAL DESCENT IS INFERRED (289)	0.72 OF 40	192	TILT MORE TOWARD BEING THOSE OTHER THAN WHERE THE ONLY KIN GROUP PRESENT IS A KINDRED OR ELSE BILATERAL DESCENT IS INFERRED (289)	0.92 OF 38	11 3 29 35 XSQ= 3.84 PHI= 0.222 XP = 0.0500
309	TILT TOWARD BEING THOSE WHERE ORAL SOCIALIZATION ANXIETY IS LOW (27) W-C	0.70 OF 23	309	TILT TOWARD BEING THOSE WHERE ORAL SOCIALIZATION ANXIETY IS HIGH (26) W-C	0.72 OF 18	7 13 16 5 XSQ= 5.48 PHI= -0.366 XP = 0.0192
317	TEND TO BE THOSE WHERE DISPLAY OF AFFECTION TOWARD THE INFANT IS HIGH (39) B-B-C	0.88 OF 34	317	TEND TO BE THOSE WHERE DISPLAY OF AFFECTION TOWARD THE INFANT IS LOW (29) B-B-C	0.74 OF 34	30 9 4 25 XSQ= 24.05 PHI= 0.595 XP = 0.0000
318	TEND TO BE THOSE WHERE THE OVERALL INDULGENCE OF THE INFANT IS HIGH (40) B-B-C	0.78 OF 36	318	TEND TO BE THOSE WHERE THE OVERALL INDULGENCE OF THE INFANT IS LOW (31) B-B-C	0.66 OF 35	28 12 8 23 XSQ= 11.94 PHI= 0.410 XP = 0.0006
320	TILT MORE TOWARD BEING THOSE WHERE THE DEGREE OF REDUCTION OF THE INFANT'S DRIVES IS HIGH (45) B-B-C	0.79 OF 34	320	TILT LESS TOWARD BEING THOSE WHERE THE DEGREE OF REDUCTION OF THE INFANT'S DRIVES IS HIGH (45) B-B-C	0.51 OF 35	27 18 7 17 XSQ= 4.78 PHI= 0.263 XP = 0.0287
326	TEND TO BE THOSE WHERE THE INFERRED TRANSITION ANXIETY BETWEEN INFANCY AND CHILDHOOD IS LOW (35) B-B-C	0.81 OF 32	326	TEND TO BE THOSE WHERE THE INFERRED TRANSITION ANXIETY BETWEEN INFANCY AND CHILDHOOD IS HIGH (32) B-B-C	0.74 OF 35	6 26 26 9 XSQ= 18.50 PHI= -0.525 XP = 0.0000
327	TILT TOWARD BEING THOSE WHERE THE AGE OF THE INFANT AT TIME OF REDUCED CONTACT WITH MOTHER IS HIGHER THAN TWO YEARS (28) B-B-C	0.68 OF 28	327	TILT TOWARD BEING THOSE WHERE THE AGE OF THE INFANT AT TIME OF REDUCED CONTACT WITH MOTHER IS TWO YEARS OR LOWER (27) B-B-C	0.67 OF 27	19 9 9 18 XSQ= 5.25 PHI= 0.309 XP = 0.0220

330	TILT TOWARD BEING THOSE 0.63 OF 35 WHERE THE AGE OF THE INFANT AT TIME OF WEANING IS 2.5 YEARS OR HIGHER (34) B-B-C	330	TILT TOWARD BEING THOSE 0.66 OF 35 WHERE THE AGE OF THE INFANT AT TIME OF WEANING IS LOWER THAN 2.5 YEARS (36) B-B-C	22 12 13 23	XSQ= 4.63 PHI= 0.257 XP = 0.0314
337	LEAN TOWARD BEING THOSE 0.68 OF 37 WHERE THE CHILD'S INFERRED ANXIETY OVER NON-PERFORMANCE OF RESPONSIBLE BEHAVIOR IS LOW (35) B-B-C	337	LEAN TOWARD BEING THOSE 0.72 OF 36 WHERE THE CHILD'S INFERRED ANXIETY OVER NON-PERFORMANCE OF RESPONSIBLE BEHAVIOR IS HIGH (38) B-B-C	12 26 25 10	XSQ= 10.04 PHI= -0.371 XP = 0.0015
338	TEND TO BE THOSE 0.68 OF 37 WHERE THE CHILD'S INFERRED ANXIETY OVER PERFORMANCE OF RESPONSIBLE BEHAVIOR IS LOW (29) B-B-C	338	TEND TO BE THOSE 0.89 OF 36 WHERE THE CHILD'S INFERRED ANXIETY OVER PERFORMANCE OF RESPONSIBLE BEHAVIOR IS HIGH (44) B-B-C	12 32 25 4	XSQ= 21.99 PHI= -0.549 XP = 0.0000
339	TEND TO BE THOSE 0.81 OF 37 WHERE THE CHILD'S INFERRED CONFLICT REGARDING RESPONSIBLE BEHAVIOR IS LOW (42) B-B-C	339	TEND TO BE THOSE 0.67 OF 36 WHERE THE CHILD'S INFERRED CONFLICT REGARDING RESPONSIBLE BEHAVIOR IS HIGH (31) B-B-C	7 24 30 12	XSQ= 15.13 PHI= -0.455 XP = 0.0001
345	LEAN TOWARD BEING THOSE 0.68 OF 38 WHERE THE CHILD'S INFERRED ANXIETY OVER NON-PERFORMANCE OF SELF-RELIANT BEHAVIOR IS LOW (39) B-B-C	345	LEAN TOWARD BEING THOSE 0.66 OF 38 WHERE THE CHILD'S INFERRED ANXIETY OVER NON-PERFORMANCE OF SELF-RELIANT BEHAVIOR IS HIGH (37) B-B-C	12 25 26 13	XSQ= 7.58 PHI= -0.316 XP = 0.0059
346	LEAN TOWARD BEING THOSE 0.71 OF 38 WHERE THE CHILD'S INFERRED ANXIETY OVER PERFORMANCE OF SELF-RELIANT BEHAVIOR IS LOW (39) B-B-C	346	LEAN TOWARD BEING THOSE 0.68 OF 38 WHERE THE CHILD'S INFERRED ANXIETY OVER PERFORMANCE OF SELF-RELIANT BEHAVIOR IS HIGH (37) B-B-C	11 26 27 12	XSQ= 10.32 PHI= -0.369 XP = 0.0013
347	TEND TO BE THOSE 0.76 OF 38 WHERE THE CHILD'S INFERRED CONFLICT REGARDING SELF-RELIANT BEHAVIOR IS LOW (39) B-B-C	347	TEND TO BE THOSE 0.74 OF 38 WHERE THE CHILD'S INFERRED CONFLICT REGARDING SELF-RELIANT BEHAVIOR IS HIGH (37) B-B-C	9 28 29 10	XSQ= 17.06 PHI= -0.474 XP = 0.0000
350	DRIFT TOWARD BEING THOSE 0.57 OF 30 WHERE THE CHILD'S INFERRED ANXIETY OVER PERFORMANCE OF ACHIEVEMENT BEHAVIOR IS LOW (26) B-B-C	350	DRIFT TOWARD BEING THOSE 0.70 OF 30 WHERE THE CHILD'S INFERRED ANXIETY OVER PERFORMANCE OF ACHIEVEMENT BEHAVIOR IS HIGH (34) B-B-C	13 21 17 9	XSQ= 3.33 PHI= -0.235 XP = 0.0682
353	TEND TO BE THOSE 0.70 OF 37 WHERE THE CHILD-S INFERRED ANXIETY OVER NON-PERFORMANCE OF OBEDIENT BEHAVIOR IS LOW (32) B-B-C	353	TEND TO BE THOSE 0.84 OF 37 WHERE THE CHILD'S INFERRED ANXIETY OVER NON-PERFORMANCE OF OBEDIENT BEHAVIOR IS HIGH (42) B-B-C	11 31 26 6	XSQ= 19.88 PHI= -0.518 XP = 0.0000

354	TEND TO BE THOSE WHERE THE CHILD'S INFERRED ANXIETY OVER PERFORMANCE OF OBEDIENT BEHAVIOR IS LOW (37) B-B-C	0.76 OF 37	354	TEND TO BE THOSE WHERE THE CHILD'S INFERRED ANXIETY OVER PERFORMANCE OF OBEDIENT BEHAVIOR IS HIGH (36) B-B-C	0.75 OF 36	9 27 28 9 XSQ= 16.77 PHI= -0.479 XP = 0.0000
355	TEND TO BE THOSE WHERE THE CHILD'S INFERRED CONFLICT REGARDING OBEDIENT BEHAVIOR IS LOW (38) B-B-C	0.78 OF 37	355	TEND TO BE THOSE WHERE THE CHILD'S INFERRED CONFLICT REGARDING OBEDIENT BEHAVIOR IS HIGH (35) B-B-C	0.75 OF 36	8 27 29 9 XSQ= 18.75 PHI= -0.507 XP = 0.0000
368	TILT TOWARD BEING THOSE WHERE DISSOCIATION OF THE SEXES AT ADOLESCENCE IS HIGH OR MEDIUM (16) JKH	0.64 OF 14	368	TILT TOWARD BEING THOSE WHERE DISSOCIATION OF THE SEXES AT ADOLESCENCE IS LOW (21) JKH	0.88 OF 8	9 1 5 7 XSQ= 3.62 PHI= 0.405 EP = 0.0310
398	DRIFT TOWARD BEING THOSE WHERE THE INTENSITY OF SEX ANXIETY IS LOW (16) WNS	0.71 OF 14	398	DRIFT TOWARD BEING THOSE WHERE THE INTENSITY OF SEX ANXIETY IS HIGH (16) WNS	0.67 OF 15	4 10 10 5 XSQ= 2.82 PHI= -0.312 EP = 0.0656
399	LEAN TOWARD BEING THOSE WHERE INTENSITY OF CASTRATION ANXIETY IS LOW (22) WNS	0.73 OF 22	399	LEAN TOWARD BEING THOSE WHERE INTENSITY OF CASTRATION ANXIETY IS HIGH (23) WNS	0.71 OF 21	6 15 16 6 XSQ= 6.71 PHI= -0.395 XP = 0.0096
402	DRIFT TOWARD BEING THOSE WHERE EXPLANATIONS OF ILLNESS OF AN ORAL NATURE ARE ABSENT (30) W-C	0.54 OF 24	402	DRIFT TOWARD BEING THOSE WHERE EXPLANATIONS OF ILLNESS OF AN ORAL NATURE ARE PRESENT (31) W-C	0.75 OF 20	11 15 13 5 XSQ= 2.73 PHI= -0.249 XP = 0.0986
403	TILT TOWARD BEING THOSE WHERE EXPLANATIONS OF ILLNESS OF AN ANAL NATURE ARE ABSENT (38) W-C	0.75 OF 24	403	TILT TOWARD BEING THOSE WHERE EXPLANATIONS OF ILLNESS OF AN ANAL NATURE ARE PRESENT (23) W-C	0.65 OF 20	6 13 18 7 XSQ= 5.58 PHI= -0.356 XP = 0.0182
421	LEAN TOWARD BEING THOSE WHERE KILLING, TORTURING, OR MUTILATING OF THE ENEMY IS NEGLIGIBLY EMPHASIZED (47) PES	0.76 OF 29	421	LEAN TOWARD BEING THOSE WHERE KILLING, TORTURING, OR MUTILATING OF THE ENEMY IS STRONGLY OR MODERATELY EMPHASIZED (37) PES	0.65 OF 26	7 17 22 9 XSQ= 7.88 PHI= -0.379 XP = 0.0050
425	DRIFT TOWARD BEING THOSE WHERE SUPERNATURALS ARE MAINLY BENEVOLENT, RATHER THAN AGGRESSIVE (16) L-T-W	0.61 OF 18	425	DRIFT TOWARD BEING THOSE WHERE SUPERNATURALS ARE MAINLY AGGRESSIVE, RATHER THAN BENEVOLENT (20) L-T-W	0.72 OF 18	11 5 7 13 XSQ= 2.81 PHI= 0.280 EP = 0.0922

433	IN ALL CASES ARE THCSE WHERE BELIEF IN REINCARNATION IS ABSENT (28) GES	1.00 OF 1C	433	TILT TOWARD BEING THOSE WHERE BELIEF IN REINCARNATICN IS PRESENT (10) GES	0.55 OF 11	0 6 10 5 XSQ= 5.20 PHI= -0.497 EP = 0.0124
446	DRIFT TCWARD BEING THCSE WHERE WITCHCRAFT IS MCDERATELY PRESENT OR ABSENT (24) GES	0.80 OF 10	446	DRIFT TOWARD BEING THOSE WHERE WITCHCRAFT IS SIGNIFICANTLY PRESENT (14) GES	0.64 CF 11	2 7 8 4 XSQ= 2.49 PHI= -0.344 EP = 0.0805
447	DRIFT TCWARD BEING THCSE WHERE LCVE MAGIC IS ABSENT (13) S-R	0.63 OF 16	447	DRIFT TOWARD BEING THOSE WHERE LOVE MAGIC IS PRESENT (20) S-R	0.77 OF 13	6 10 10 3 XSQ= 3.05 PHI= -0.325 EP = 0.0608
455	DRIFT TCWARD BEING THCSE WHERE THE MODE CF THE INCIVICUAL'S CCNTACT WITH THE DIVINE IS CCNDUCIVE TC THE CEVELCPMENT OF THE INDIVIDUAL'S NEED TC ACHIEVE (17) CCM	0.69 OF 13	455	DRIFT TOWARD BEING THOSE WHERE THE MODE OF THE INDIVIDUAL'S CONTACT WITH THE DIVINE IS NOT CONDUCIVE TC THE DEVELCPMENT OF THE INDIVIDUAL'S NEED TO ACHIEVE (19) DCM	0.65 CF 23	9 8 4 15 XSQ= 2.69 PHI= 0.274 EP = 0.0819
458	LEAN TCWARC BEING THCSE WHERE GAMES, IF PRESENT, DC NCT INCLUDE GAMES CF STRATEGY (119) R-A-B,EA	0.88 OF 25	458	LEAN TOWARD BEING THCSE WHERE GAMES, IF PRESENT, INCLUDE GAMES CF STRATEGY (52) R-A-B,EA	0.50 CF 30	3 15 22 15 XSQ= 7.30 PHI= -0.364 XP = 0.0069
460	TILT TCWARC BEING THCSE WHERE GAMES, IF PRESENT, ARE LIMITED TC GAMES CF SKILL CNLY (67) R-A-B,EA	0.60 OF 25	460	TILT TOWARD BEING THOSE WHERE GAMES, IF PRESENT, ARE NOT LIMITED TO GAMES OF SKILL CNLY (104) R-A-B,EA	0.73 CF 30	15 8 10 22 XSQ= 4.93 PHI= 0.299 XP = 0.0264
469	TILT LESS TOWARC BEINC THCSE WHERE CCNTACT WITH OTHER CULTURES IS FREQUENT CR REGULAR, RATHER THAN IRREGULAR (43) JMH	0.67 OF 15	469	IN ALL CASES ARE THCSE WHERE CONTACT WITH OTHER CULTURES IS FREQUENT OR REGULAR, RATHER THAN IRREGULAR (43) JMH	1.00 OF 14	10 14 5 C XSQ= 3.54 PHI= -0.350 EP = 0.0421
470	TILT TCWARC BEING THCSE WHERE INNCVATICNS ARE ACCEPTED CNLY SELECTIVELY (33) JMH	0.93 OF 15	470	TILT TOWARD BEING THOSE WHERE INNOVATICNS ARE GENERALLY ACCEPTED (21) JMH	0.50 OF 14	1 7 14 7 XSQ= 4.81 PHI= -0.407 EP = 0.0142
476	LEAN TCWARC BEING THCSE WHERE THE CEGREE OF INSCBRIETY IS STRCNG (31) DH	0.85 OF 13	476	LEAN TOWARD BEING THOSE WHERE THE DEGREE CF INSOBRIETY IS MODERATE OR SLIGHT (18) DH	0.79 OF 14	11 3 2 11 XSQ= 8.40 PHI= 0.558 EP = 0.0018

335 CULTURES WHERE INITIAL INDULGENCE OF DEPENDENCY IS HIGH (20) WAS	335 CULTURES WHERE INITIAL INDULGENCE OF DEPENDENCY IS LOW (18) WAS

BACKGROUND ON PAGE 143

BOTH SUBJECT AND PREDICATE

20 IN LEFT COLUMN

ANDAMANESE	ARAPESH	AZANDE	CHENCHU	COMANCHE	COPR ESKIMO	FON	KURTATCHI	LAPPS	MAORI
MURNGIN	NAVAHO	PAPAGO	PUKAPUKA	SIRIONO	TANALA	TROBRIAND	VENDA	WOGEO	YAGUA

18 IN RIGHT COLUMN

AINU	ALORESE	ASHANTI	BALINESE	DOBUANS	HANO	IFUGAO	KUTENAI	KWAKIUTL	LAKHER
LEPCHA	MANUS	MARQUESANS	SAMOANS	SENIANG	THONGA	TIKOPIA	WITOTO		

362 EXCLUDED BECAUSE UNASCERTAINED

36	DRIFT LESS TOWARD BEING THOSE WHERE THE NATURAL ENVIRONMENT IS OTHER THAN 'VERY HARSH,' OR SUB-TROPICAL BUSH, OR TEMPERATE GRASSLAND (292) FWM	0.60 OF 20	36	DRIFT MORE TOWARD BEING THOSE WHERE THE NATURAL ENVIRONMENT IS OTHER THAN 'VERY HARSH,' OR SUB-TROPICAL BUSH, OR TEMPERATE GRASSLAND (292) FWM	0.89 OF 18	8 2 / 12 16 / XSQ= 2.72 / PHI= 0.268 / EP = 0.0673
44	TILT LESS TOWARD BEING THOSE WHERE SETTLEMENTS ARE FIXED (222)	0.58 OF 19	44	TILT MORE TOWARD BEING THOSE WHERE SETTLEMENTS ARE FIXED (222)	0.94 OF 16	11 15 / 8 1 / XSQ= 4.12 / PHI= -0.343 / EP = 0.0221
82	TILT LESS TOWARD BEING THOSE WHERE A CITY OR TOWN IS PRESENT, OR THE AVERAGE COMMUNITY SIZE IS FIFTY OR GREATER (178)	0.56 OF 16	82	IN ALL CASES ARE THOSE WHERE A CITY OR TOWN IS PRESENT, OR THE AVERAGE COMMUNITY SIZE IS FIFTY OR GREATER (178)	1.00 OF 10	9 10 / 7 0 / XSQ= 3.97 / PHI= -0.391 / EP = 0.0227
102	DRIFT TOWARD BEING THOSE WHERE CLASS STRATIFICATION IS ABSENT (180)	0.60 OF 20	102	DRIFT TOWARD BEING THOSE WHERE CLASS STRATIFICATION IS PRESENT (203)	0.72 OF 18	8 13 / 12 5 / XSQ= 2.78 / PHI= -0.271 / EP = 0.0585
137	TILT TOWARD BEING THOSE WHERE INVIDIOUS DISPLAY OF WEALTH IS MODERATELY, LITTLE, OR NEGATIVELY EMPHASIZED (52) PES	0.80 OF 20	137	TILT TOWARD BEING THOSE WHERE INVIDIOUS DISPLAY OF WEALTH IS STRONGLY EMPHASIZED (37) PES	0.63 OF 16	4 10 / 16 6 / XSQ= 5.09 / PHI= -0.376 / EP = 0.0159

184	TILT TCWARD BEING THOSE 0.50 OF 14 WHERE THE LARGEST NCN-COGNATIC KIN GROUP IS THE MCEITY OR PHRATRY (77)	184	TILT TOWARD BEING THOSE 0.92 OF 12 WHERE THE LARGEST NON-CCGNATIC KIN GROUP IS SMALLER THAN A PHRATRY, I. E. A SIB OR LINEAGE (175)	7 1 7 11 XSQ= 3.49 PHI= 0.366 EP = 0.0357
243	TILT TCWARD BEING THOSE 0.56 OF 16 WHERE PCLYGYNY, IF PRESENT, HAS A HIGH INCIDENCE (24) W-C,S	243	TILT TOWARD BEING THOSE 0.90 OF 10 WHERE POLYGYNY, IF PRESENT, HAS A LOW INCIDENCE (36) W-D,S	9 1 7 9 XSQ= 3.78 PHI= 0.381 EP = 0.0367
302	LEAN TCWARD BEING THOSE 0.88 OF 16 WHERE THE AVERAGE EARLY SATISFACTION PCTENTIAL IS HIGH (23) W-C	302	LEAN TOWARD BEING THOSE 0.60 OF 15 WHERE THE AVERAGE EARLY SATISFACTICN POTENTIAL IS LOW (17) W-C	14 6 2 9 XSQ= 5.70 PHI= 0.429 EP = 0.0091
303	TILT TCWARD BEING THOSE 0.85 OF 20 WHERE THE EARLY CRAL SATISFACTION PCTENTIAL IS HIGH (32) W-C	303	TILT TOWARD BEING THOSE 0.56 OF 18 WHERE THE EARLY ORAL SATISFACTICN POTENTIAL IS LCW (25) W-C	17 8 3 10 XSQ= 5.24 PHI= 0.371 EP = 0.0156
306	IN ALL CASES ARE THCSE 1.00 OF 20 WHERE THE EARLY DEPENDENCE SATISFACTION PCTENTIAL IS HIGH (28) W-C	306	IN ALL CASES ARE THOSE 1.00 OF 18 WHERE THE EARLY DEPENDENCE SATISFACTION POTENTIAL IS LOW (24) W-C	20 0 0 18 XSQ= 34.09 PHI= 0.947 EP = 0.0000
312	DRIFT TCWARD BEING THOSE 0.67 OF 18 WHERE DEPENDENCE SCCIALIZATION ANXIETY IS LCW (23) W-C	312	DRIFT TOWARD BEING THOSE 0.67 OF 18 WHERE DEPENDENCE SOCIALIZATICN ANXIETY IS HIGH (24) W-C	6 12 12 6 XSQ= 2.78 PHI= -0.278 EP = 0.0564
320	DRIFT TCWARD BEING THCSE 0.81 OF 16 WHERE THE DEGREE OF REDUCTION OF THE INFANT'S CRIVES IS HIGH (45) B-B-C	320	DRIFT TOWARD BEING THOSE 0.57 OF 14 WHERE THE DEGREE OF REDUCTICN OF THE INFANT'S DRIVES IS LOW (24) B-B-C	13 6 3 8 XSQ= 3.23 PHI= 0.328 EP = 0.0567
323	TILT TCWARD BEING THOSE 0.56 OF 18 WHERE THE CONSTANCY OF PRESENCE CF THE INFANT'S NURTURANT AGENT IS HIGH (29) B-B-C	323	TILT TOWARD BEING THOSE 0.85 OF 13 WHERE THE CONSTANCY CF PRESENCE OF THE INFANT'S NURTURANT AGENT IS LOW (45) B-B-C	10 2 8 11 XSQ= 3.58 PHI= 0.340 EP = 0.0317
356	TILT TCWARD BEING THOSE 0.73 OF 11 WHERE NEITHER ACCLESCENT PEER GROUPS NCR PAIRS ARE PRESENT IN A SETTING CF CCURTSHIP (22) JKH	356	TILT TOWARD BEING THCSE 0.88 OF 8 WHERE ADOLESCENT PEER GRCUPS OR PAIRS ARE PRESENT IN A SETTING OF COURTSHIP (29) JKH	3 7 8 1 XSQ= 4.54 PHI= -0.489 EP = 0.0198

360	DRIFT TCWARD BEING THCSE WHERE ADCLESCENT PEER GROUPS ARE PRESENT CNLY IN A SETTING CF LEISURE, OR ELSE ARE ABSENT (23) JKH	0.88 OF 8	360	DRIFT TOWARD BEING THOSE WHERE ADOLESCENT PEER GRCUPS ARE PRESENT IN A SETTING OF WORK AND PUBLIC GATHERINGS AND LEISURE, OR AT LEAST OF PUBLIC GATHERINGS AND LEISURE (14) JKH	0.75 OF 4	1 3 7 1 XSQ= 2.30 PHI= -0.437 EP = 0.0667
368	DRIFT TCWARD BEING THCSE WHERE DISSCCIATICN CF THE SEXES AT ADCLESCENCE IS HIGH CR MEDIUM (16) JKH	0.67 OF 9	368	IN ALL CASES ARE THOSE WHERE DISSOCIATICN OF THE SEXES AT ADOLESCENCE IS LOW (21) JKH	1.00 OF 4	6 0 3 4 XSQ= 2.63 PHI= 0.450 EP = 0.0699
393	TILT TOWARD BEING THCSE WHERE EXTRAMARITAL COITUS IS PERMITTED, RATHER THAN PUNISHED (41) F-B	0.69 OF 13	393	TILT TOWARD BEING THOSE WHERE EXTRAMARITAL COITUS IS PUNISHED, RATHER THAN PERMITTED (43) F-B	0.77 OF 13	4 10 9 3 XSQ= 3.87 PHI= -0.386 EP = 0.0472
473	TILT TCWARD BEING THOSE WHERE SENSITIVITY TO INSULT IS MCDERATE CR NEGLIGIBLE (56) PES	0.85 OF 20	473	TILT TOWARD BEING THOSE WHERE SENSITIVITY TO INSULT IS EXTREME (32) PES	0.50 OF 16	3 8 17 8 XSQ= 3.61 PHI= -0.317 EP = 0.0335
479	DRIFT TCWARD BEING THCSE WHERE THE NEEC TC ACHIEVE, AS INFERRED FROM FCLKTALES, IS HIGH (18) JV	0.56 OF 9	479	IN ALL CASES ARE THCSE WHERE THE NEED TC ACHIEVE, AS INFERRED FROM FCLKTALES, IS LOW (18) JV	1.00 OF 5	5 0 4 5 XSQ= 2.24 PHI= 0.400 EP = 0.0859

336 CULTURES
WHERE THE TOTAL POSITIVE PRESSURE TOWARD
DEVELOPING RESPONSIBLE BEHAVIOR
IN THE CHILD
IS HIGH (43) B-B-C

336 CULTURES
WHERE THE TOTAL POSITIVE PRESSURE TOWARD
DEVELOPING RESPONSIBLE BEHAVIOR
IN THE CHILD
IS LOW (32) B-B-C

BACKGROUND ON PAGE 143

BOTH SUBJECT AND PREDICATE

43 IN LEFT COLUMN

AINU, ARAUCANIANS, ASHANTI, AYMARA, AZANDE, BALINESE, CHAGGA, CHENCHU, CHEYENNE, CHIR-APACHE, CHUKCHEE, CUNA, FON, GANDA, HANO, IFUGAO, KIKUYU, KURTATCHI, LAU, MANDAN, MASAI, MURNGIN, NAVAHO, NUER, NYAKYUSA, OJIBWA, ONTONG-JAVA, PAPAGO, SAMOANS, SOTHO, SWAZI, TALLENSI, TETON, THONGA, TIKOPIA, TUCUNA, TUPINAMBA, TURKANA, VENDA, WICHITA, YAGUA, YAKUT, YORUBA

32 IN RIGHT COLUMN

ALORESE, ARANDA, ARAPESH, CAMAYURA, COMANCHE, CROW, JIVARO, KASKA, KORYAK, KWAKIUTL, LAMBA, LEPCHA, LESU, MANUS, MAORI, MARQUESANS, MBUNDU, OMAHA, ONA, PUKAPUKA, SIRIONO, TANALA, TENETEHARA, TIMBIRA, TIV, TROBRIAND, TRUKESE, WINNEBAGO, WOGEO, WOLEAIANS, YAHGAN, ZUNI

325 EXCLUDED BECAUSE UNASCERTAINED

	High (left)			Low (right)		Statistics
3	TILT LESS TOWARD BEING THOSE LOCATED OUTSIDE OF AFRICA (320)	0.63 OF 43	3	TILT MORE TOWARD BEING THOSE LOCATED OUTSIDE OF AFRICA (320)	0.91 OF 32	16 3 / 27 29 / XSQ= 6.12 / PHI= 0.286 / XP = 0.0134
53	DRIFT LESS TOWARD BEING THOSE WHERE FOOD PRODUCTION IS BY SIMPLE AGRICULTURE OR INCIPIENT FOOD PRODUCTION, RATHER THAN BY INTENSIVE AGRICULTURE (147)	0.59 OF 29	53	DRIFT MORE TOWARD BEING THOSE WHERE FOOD PRODUCTION IS BY SIMPLE AGRICULTURE OR INCIPIENT FOOD PRODUCTION, RATHER THAN BY INTENSIVE AGRICULTURE (147)	0.85 OF 20	12 3 / 17 17 / XSQ= 2.74 / PHI= 0.236 / XP = 0.0982
55	DRIFT TOWARD BEING THOSE WHERE FOOD PRODUCTION IS BY INTENSIVE AGRICULTURE, RATHER THAN BY SIMPLE AGRICULTURE (91)	0.52 OF 23	55	DRIFT TOWARD BEING THOSE WHERE FOOD PRODUCTION IS BY SIMPLE AGRICULTURE, RATHER THAN BY INTENSIVE AGRICULTURE (101)	0.80 OF 15	12 3 / 11 12 / XSQ= 2.70 / PHI= 0.267 / EP = 0.0884
63	LEAN TOWARD BEING THOSE WHERE HUSBANDRY, IF PRESENT, IS PRINCIPALLY IN THE FORM OF BOVINE, EQUINE, CAMEL-LIKE, OR DEER-LIKE ANIMALS, RATHER THAN PIGS, SHEEP, OR GOATS (152)	0.68 OF 31	63	LEAN TOWARD BEING THOSE WHERE HUSBANDRY, IF PRESENT, IS PRINCIPALLY IN THE FORM OF PIGS, SHEEP, OR GOATS, RATHER THAN BOVINE, EQUINE, CAMEL-LIKE, OR DEER-LIKE ANIMALS (74)	0.76 OF 21	21 5 / 10 16 / XSQ= 7.99 / PHI= 0.392 / XP = 0.0047

No.				No.				
71	DRIFT LESS TOWARD BEING THOSE WHERE METAL WORKING IS ABSENT (153)	0.54 OF	35	71	DRIFT MORE TOWARD BEING THOSE WHERE METAL WORKING IS ABSENT (153)	0.81 OF	26	16 5 19 21 XSQ= 3.54 PHI= 0.241 XP = 0.0600
74	LEAN TOWARD BEING THOSE WHERE POTTERY IS PRESENT (145)	0.74 OF	34	74	LEAN TOWARD BEING THOSE WHERE POTTERY IS ABSENT (93)	0.70 OF	27	25 8 9 19 XSQ= 9.98 PHI= 0.404 XP = 0.0016
81	DRIFT LESS TOWARD BEING THOSE WHERE NO CITY OR TOWN IS PRESENT, AND THE AVERAGE COMMUNITY SIZE IS SMALLER THAN 200 (135)	0.55 OF	31	81	DRIFT MORE TOWARD BEING THOSE WHERE NO CITY OR TOWN IS PRESENT, AND THE AVERAGE COMMUNITY SIZE IS SMALLER THAN 200 (135)	0.83 OF	23	14 4 17 19 XSQ= 3.42 PHI= 0.252 XP = 0.0645
84	DRIFT LESS TOWARD BEING THOSE WHERE THE LEVEL OF POLITICAL INTEGRATION IS THE LITTLE STATE, THE MINIMAL STATE, THE AUTONOMOUS COMMUNITY, OR THE FAMILY (262) GPM	0.83 OF	35	84	IN ALL CASES ARE THOSE WHERE THE LEVEL OF POLITICAL INTEGRATION IS THE LITTLE STATE, THE MINIMAL STATE, THE AUTONOMOUS COMMUNITY, OR THE FAMILY (262) GPM	1.00 OF	29	6 0 29 29 XSQ= 3.65 PHI= 0.239 XP = 0.0560
85	TILT LESS TOWARD BEING THOSE WHERE THE LEVEL OF POLITICAL INTEGRATION IS THE MINIMAL STATE, THE AUTONOMOUS COMMUNITY, OR THE FAMILY (234) GPM	0.74 OF	35	85	TILT MORE TOWARD BEING THOSE WHERE THE LEVEL OF POLITICAL INTEGRATION IS THE MINIMAL STATE, THE AUTONOMOUS COMMUNITY, OR THE FAMILY (234) GPM	0.97 OF	29	9 1 26 28 XSQ= 4.39 PHI= 0.262 XP = 0.0361
95	TILT LESS TOWARD BEING THOSE WHERE THE HIERARCHY OF NATIONAL JURISDICTION HAS ONE OR NO LEVELS (254) GES,EA	0.65 OF	40	95	TILT MORE TOWARD BEING THOSE WHERE THE HIERARCHY OF NATIONAL JURISDICTION HAS ONE OR NO LEVELS (254) GES,EA	0.90 OF	30	14 3 26 27 XSQ= 4.55 PHI= 0.255 XP = 0.0330
102	TILT TOWARD BEING THOSE WHERE CLASS STRATIFICATION IS PRESENT (203)	0.58 OF	43	102	TILT TOWARD BEING THOSE WHERE CLASS STRATIFICATION IS ABSENT (180)	0.69 OF	32	25 10 18 22 XSQ= 4.30 PHI= 0.240 XP = 0.0380
118	DRIFT TOWARD BEING THOSE WHERE THE PERCENTAGE OF OCCUPATIONS THAT ARE SPECIALIZED IS HIGH OR MEDIUM (24) WME	0.55 OF	11	118	DRIFT TOWARD BEING THOSE WHERE THE PERCENTAGE OF OCCUPATIONS THAT ARE SPECIALIZED IS LOW (25) WME	0.89 OF	9	6 1 5 8 XSQ= 2.42 PHI= 0.348 EP = 0.0703
130	DRIFT TOWARD BEING THOSE WHERE LEATHER WORKING IS MAINLY DONE BY MALES (39)	0.54 OF	13	130	DRIFT TOWARD BEING THOSE WHERE LEATHER WORKING IS MAINLY DONE BY FEMALES (45)	0.88 OF	8	7 1 6 7 XSQ= 2.05 PHI= 0.312 EP = 0.0850

177	DRIFT LESS TOWARD BEING THOSE 0.71 OF 42 WHERE THE COMMUNITY IS OTHER THAN A SINGLE CLAN-COMMUNITY AND EXOGAMOUS (305)	177	DRIFT MORE TOWARD BEING THOSE 0.91 OF 32 WHERE THE COMMUNITY IS OTHER THAN A SINGLE CLAN-COMMUNITY AND EXOGAMOUS (305)	12 3 30 29 XSQ= 3.04 PHI= 0.203 XP = 0.0813
178	LEAN MORE TOWARD BEING THOSE 0.86 OF 42 WHERE THE COMMUNITY IS OTHER THAN SEGMENTED ON A CLAN BASIS AND NON-EXOGAMOUS (295)	178	LEAN LESS TOWARD BEING THOSE 0.53 OF 32 WHERE THE COMMUNITY IS OTHER THAN SEGMENTED ON A CLAN BASIS AND NON-EXOGAMOUS (295)	6 15 36 17 XSQ= 7.95 PHI= -0.328 XP = 0.0048
184	DRIFT TOWARD BEING THOSE 0.74 OF 31 WHERE THE LARGEST NON-COGNATIC KIN GROUP IS SMALLER THAN A PHRATRY, I. E. A SIB OR LINEAGE (175)	184	DRIFT TOWARD BEING THOSE 0.55 OF 22 WHERE THE LARGEST NON-COGNATIC KIN GROUP IS THE MOEITY OR PHRATRY (77)	8 12 23 10 XSQ= 3.38 PHI= -0.253 XP = 0.0659
186	TILT LESS TOWARD BEING THOSE 0.56 OF 43 WHERE THE KIN GROUP IS OTHER THAN EXCLUSIVELY PATRILINEAL (250)	186	TILT MORE TOWARD BEING THOSE 0.84 OF 32 WHERE THE KIN GROUP IS OTHER THAN EXCLUSIVELY PATRILINEAL (250)	19 5 24 27 XSQ= 5.63 PHI= 0.274 XP = 0.0177
187	TILT MORE TOWARD BEING THOSE 0.93 OF 42 WHERE THE KIN GROUP IS OTHER THAN EXCLUSIVELY MATRILINEAL (344)	187	TILT LESS TOWARD BEING THOSE 0.72 OF 32 WHERE THE KIN GROUP IS OTHER THAN EXCLUSIVELY MATRILINEAL (344)	3 9 39 23 XSQ= 4.44 PHI= -0.245 XP = 0.0351
190	TILT TOWARD BEING THOSE 0.86 OF 29 WHERE THE KIN GROUP IS PATRILINEAL OR DOUBLE-DESCENT, RATHER THAN MATRILINEAL (186)	190	TILT TOWARD BEING THOSE 0.50 OF 20 WHERE THE KIN GROUP IS MATRILINEAL, RATHER THAN PATRILINEAL OR DOUBLE-DESCENT (61)	25 10 4 10 XSQ= 5.93 PHI= 0.348 XP = 0.0149
240	DRIFT TOWARD BEING THOSE 0.63 OF 27 WHERE THE FAMILY, IF EXTENDED, IS SMALL OR STEM, RATHER THAN LARGE (135)	240	DRIFT TOWARD BEING THOSE 0.71 OF 17 WHERE THE FAMILY, IF EXTENDED, IS LARGE, RATHER THAN SMALL OR STEM (78)	10 12 17 5 XSQ= 3.45 PHI= -0.280 XP = 0.0632
282	DRIFT TOWARD BEING THOSE 0.65 OF 17 WHERE THE STRENGTH OF DESIRE FOR CHILDREN IS HIGH (16) BCA	282	DRIFT TOWARD BEING THOSE 0.71 OF 14 WHERE THE STRENGTH OF DESIRE FOR CHILDREN IS LOW OR ABSENT (20) BCA	11 4 6 10 XSQ= 2.70 PHI= 0.295 EP = 0.0732
314	DRIFT LESS TOWARD BEING THOSE 0.63 OF 27 WHERE THE INCIDENCE OF MOTHER-CHILD HOUSEHOLDS IS LOW (61) W-D,S	314	DRIFT MORE TOWARD BEING THOSE 0.88 OF 24 WHERE THE INCIDENCE OF MOTHER-CHILD HOUSEHOLDS IS LOW (61) W-D,S	10 3 17 21 XSQ= 2.84 PHI= 0.236 XP = 0.0920

323	DRIFT TOWARD BEING THOSE WHERE THE CONSTANCY OF PRESENCE OF THE INFANT'S NURTURANT AGENT IS LOW (45) B-B-C	0.71 OF 41	323	DRIFT TOWARD BEING THOSE WHERE THE CONSTANCY OF PRESENCE OF THE INFANT'S NURTURANT AGENT IS HIGH (29) B-B-C	0.52 OF 31	12 16 29 15 XSQ= 2.83 PHI= -0.198 XP = 0.0926
337	TEND TO BE THOSE WHERE THE CHILD'S INFERRED ANXIETY OVER NON-PERFORMANCE OF RESPONSIBLE BEHAVIOR IS HIGH (38) B-B-C	0.77 OF 43	337	TEND TO BE THOSE WHERE THE CHILD'S INFERRED ANXIETY OVER NON-PERFORMANCE OF RESPONSIBLE BEHAVIOR IS LOW (35) B-B-C	0.83 OF 30	33 5 10 25 XSQ= 23.21 PHI= 0.564 XP = 0.0000
339	LEAN TOWARD BEING THOSE WHERE THE CHILD'S INFERRED CONFLICT REGARDING RESPONSIBLE BEHAVIOR IS HIGH (31) B-B-C	0.58 OF 43	339	LEAN TOWARD BEING THOSE WHERE THE CHILD'S INFERRED CONFLICT REGARDING RESPONSIBLE BEHAVIOR IS LOW (42) B-B-C	0.80 OF 30	25 6 18 24 XSQ= 9.02 PHI= 0.351 XP = 0.0027
350	TILT TOWARD BEING THOSE WHERE THE CHILD'S INFERRED ANXIETY OVER PERFORMANCE OF ACHIEVEMENT BEHAVIOR IS HIGH (34) B-B-C	0.71 OF 34	350	TILT TOWARD BEING THOSE WHERE THE CHILD'S INFERRED ANXIETY OVER PERFORMANCE OF ACHIEVEMENT BEHAVIOR IS LOW (26) B-B-C	0.60 OF 25	24 10 10 15 XSQ= 4.34 PHI= 0.271 XP = 0.0373
352	TEND TO BE THOSE WHERE THE TOTAL POSITIVE PRESSURE TOWARD DEVELOPING OBEDIENT BEHAVIOR IN THE CHILD IS HIGH (44) B-B-C	0.79 OF 42	352	TEND TO BE THOSE WHERE THE TOTAL POSITIVE PRESSURE TOWARD DEVELOPING OBEDIENT BEHAVIOR IN THE CHILD IS LOW (28) B-B-C	0.64 OF 28	33 10 9 18 XSQ= 11.28 PHI= 0.401 XP = 0.0008
365	DRIFT TOWARD BEING THOSE WHERE THE TIME SPENT IN ADOLESCENT PEER GROUP ACTIVITY IS HIGH OR HIGH-MEDIUM (30) JKH	0.80 OF 15	365	DRIFT TOWARD BEING THOSE WHERE THE TIME SPENT IN ADOLESCENT PEER GROUP ACTIVITY IS LOW-MEDIUM OR LOW (15) JKH	0.58 OF 12	12 5 3 7 XSQ= 2.72 PHI= 0.317 EP = 0.0568
402	TILT TOWARD BEING THOSE WHERE EXPLANATIONS OF ILLNESS OF AN ORAL NATURE ARE ABSENT (30) W-C	0.57 OF 23	402	TILT TOWARD BEING THOSE WHERE EXPLANATIONS OF ILLNESS OF AN ORAL NATURE ARE PRESENT (31) W-C	0.79 OF 19	10 15 13 4 XSQ= 4.06 PHI= -0.311 XP = 0.0439
404	DRIFT TOWARD BEING THOSE WHERE EXPLANATIONS OF ILLNESS OF A SEXUAL NATURE ARE ABSENT (42) W-C	0.74 OF 23	404	DRIFT TOWARD BEING THOSE WHERE EXPLANATIONS OF ILLNESS OF A SEXUAL NATURE ARE PRESENT (19) W-C	0.58 OF 19	6 11 17 8 XSQ= 3.15 PHI= -0.274 XP = 0.0760
427	TILT TOWARD BEING THOSE WHERE A HIGH GOD, IF PRESENT, IS ACTIVE, RATHER THAN INACTIVE (87) GES,EA	0.61 OF 18	427	TILT TOWARD BEING THOSE WHERE A HIGH GOD, IF PRESENT, IS INACTIVE, RATHER THAN ACTIVE (69) GES,EA	0.79 OF 14	11 3 7 11 XSQ= 3.56 PHI= 0.333 EP = 0.0356

435	DRIFT TOWARD BEING THOSE 0.88 OF 8 WHERE ABANDONMENT OF THE HOUSE OF THE DEAD IS NOT PRACTICED (19) LWS	435	DRIFT TOWARD BEING THOSE 0.67 OF 6 WHERE ABANDONMENT OF THE HOUSE OF THE DEAD IS PRACTICED (12) LWS	1 4 7 2 XSQ= 2.34 PHI= -0.409 EP = 0.0909
459	TILT TOWARD BEING THOSE 0.58 OF 26 WHERE GAMES, IF PRESENT, INCLUDE GAMES OF CHANCE (82) R-A-B,EA	459	TILT TOWARD BEING THOSE 0.77 OF 26 WHERE GAMES, IF PRESENT, DO NOT INCLUDE GAMES OF CHANCE (89) R-A-B,EA	15 6 11 20 XSQ= 5.11 PHI= 0.314 XP = 0.0238
460	TILT TOWARD BEING THOSE 0.77 OF 26 WHERE GAMES, IF PRESENT, ARE NOT LIMITED TO GAMES OF SKILL ONLY (104) R-A-B,EA	460	TILT TOWARD BEING THOSE 0.58 OF 26 WHERE GAMES, IF PRESENT, ARE LIMITED TO GAMES OF SKILL ONLY (67) R-A-B,EA	6 15 20 11 XSQ= 5.11 PHI= -0.314 XP = 0.0238
480	DRIFT TOWARD BEING THOSE 0.65 OF 17 WHERE COMPLEXITY OF ARTISTIC DESIGN IS LOW (15) HB	480	DRIFT TOWARD BEING THOSE 0.78 OF 9 WHERE COMPLEXITY OF ARTISTIC DESIGN IS HIGH (14) HB	6 7 11 2 XSQ= 2.72 PHI= -0.323 EP = 0.0968

337 CULTURES WHERE THE CHILD'S INFERRED ANXIETY OVER NON-PERFORMANCE OF RESPONSIBLE BEHAVIOR IS HIGH (38) B-B-C	337 CULTURES WHERE THE CHILD'S INFERRED ANXIETY OVER NON-PERFORMANCE OF RESPONSIBLE BEHAVIOR IS LOW (35) B-B-C

BACKGROUND ON PAGE 143

BOTH SUBJECT AND PREDICATE

38 IN LEFT COLUMN

AINU	ALORESE	ASHANTI	AYMARA	AZANDE	CHAGGA	CHIR-APACHE	CHUKCHEE	FON	GANDA
HANO	IFUGAO	KIKUYU	KURTATCHI	KWAKIUTL	LAU	LEPCHA	MANDAN	MASAI	MBUNDU
MURNGIN	NAVAHO	NUER	NYAKYUSA	OJIBWA	ONTONG-JAVA	SAMOANS	SOTHO	SWAZI	TALLENSI
THONGA	TUCUNA	TURKANA	VENDA	WICHITA	WOLEAIANS	YAKUT	YORUBA		

35 IN RIGHT COLUMN

ARANDA	ARAPESH	ARAUCANIANS	BALINESE	CAMAYURA	CHENCHU	CHEYENNE	COMANCHE	CROW	CUNA
JIVARO	KASKA	KORYAK	LESU	MANUS	MAORI	MARQUESANS	OMAHA	ONA	PAPAGO
PUKAPUKA	TANALA	TENETEHARA	TETON	TIKOPIA	TIMBIRA	TIV	TROBRIAND	TRUKESE	TUPINAMBA
WINNEBAGO	WOGEO	YAGUA	YAHGAN	ZUNI					

327 EXCLUDED BECAUSE UNASCERTAINED

3	TEND LESS TO BE THOSE LOCATED OUTSIDE OF AFRICA (320)	0.55 OF 38	3	TEND MORE TO BE THOSE LOCATED OUTSIDE OF AFRICA (320)	0.97 OF 35	17 1 21 34 XSQ= 15.02 PHI= 0.454 XP = 0.0001
9	TILT MORE TOWARD BEING THOSE LOCATED OUTSIDE OF SOUTH AMERICA (335)	0.95 OF 38	9	TILT LESS TOWARD BEING THOSE LOCATED OUTSIDE OF SOUTH AMERICA (335)	0.71 OF 35	2 10 36 25 XSQ= 5.61 PHI= -0.277 XP = 0.0179
51	LEAN TOWARD BEING THOSE WHERE SUBSISTENCE IS PRIMARILY BY FOOD PRODUCTION -- I. E., AGRICULTURE OR HUSBANDRY -- RATHER THAN BY GATHERING (253)	0.71 OF 38	51	LEAN TOWARD BEING THOSE WHERE SUBSISTENCE IS PRIMARILY BY FOOD GATHERING -- I. E., HUNTING, FISHING, OR COLLECTING -- RATHER THAN FOOD PRODUCTION (147)	0.63 OF 35	27 13 11 22 XSQ= 7.14 PHI= 0.313 XP = 0.0075
62	DRIFT MORE TOWARD BEING THOSE WHERE HUSBANDRY OF SOME KIND IS PRESENT (228)	0.82 OF 38	62	DRIFT LESS TOWARD BEING THOSE WHERE HUSBANDRY OF SOME KIND IS PRESENT (228)	0.60 OF 35	31 21 7 14 XSQ= 3.15 PHI= 0.208 XP = 0.0757

63	LEAN TOWARD BEING THOSE WHERE HUSBANDRY, IF PRESENT, IS PRINCIPALLY IN THE FORM OF BOVINE, EQUINE, CAMEL-LIKE, OR DEER-LIKE ANIMALS, RATHER THAN PIGS, SHEEP, OR GOATS (152)	0.68 OF 31	63	LEAN TOWARD BEING THOSE WHERE HUSBANDRY, IF PRESENT, IS PRINCIPALLY IN THE FORM OF PIGS, SHEEP, OR GOATS, RATHER THAN BOVINE, EQUINE, CAMEL-LIKE, OR DEER-LIKE ANIMALS (74)	0.76 OF 21	21 5 10 16 XSQ= 7.99 PHI= 0.392 XP = 0.0047
71	LEAN TOWARD BEING THOSE WHERE METAL WORKING IS PRESENT (98)	0.53 OF 30	71	LEAN TOWARD BEING THOSE WHERE METAL WORKING IS ABSENT (153)	0.86 OF 29	16 4 14 25 XSQ= 8.60 PHI= 0.382 XP = 0.0034
74	DRIFT TOWARD BEING THOSE WHERE POTTERY IS PRESENT (145)	0.67 OF 30	74	DRIFT TOWARD BEING THOSE WHERE POTTERY IS ABSENT (93)	0.62 OF 29	20 11 10 18 XSQ= 3.80 PHI= 0.254 XP = 0.0513
85	LEAN LESS TOWARD BEING THOSE WHERE THE LEVEL OF POLITICAL INTEGRATION IS THE MINIMAL STATE, THE AUTONOMOUS COMMUNITY, OR THE FAMILY (234) GPM	0.69 OF 29	85	LEAN MORE TOWARD BEING THOSE WHERE THE LEVEL OF POLITICAL INTEGRATION IS THE MINIMAL STATE, THE AUTONOMOUS COMMUNITY, OR THE FAMILY (234) GPM	0.97 OF 33	9 1 20 32 XSQ= 7.00 PHI= 0.336 XP = 0.0082
95	TEND LESS TO BE THOSE WHERE THE HIERARCHY OF NATIONAL JURISDICTION HAS ONE OR NO LEVELS (254) GES,EA	0.57 OF 37	95	IN ALL CASES ARE THOSE WHERE THE HIERARCHY OF NATIONAL JURISDICTION HAS ONE OR NO LEVELS (254) GES,EA	1.00 OF 31	16 0 21 31 XSQ= 15.21 PHI= 0.473 XP = 0.0001
96	DRIFT TOWARD BEING THOSE WHERE THE HIERARCHY OF NATIONAL JURISDICTION HAS FOUR, THREE, TWO OR ONE LEVEL (174) GES,EA	0.62 OF 37	96	DRIFT TOWARD BEING THOSE WHERE THE HIERARCHY OF NATIONAL JURISDICTION HAS NO LEVELS (156) GES,EA	0.61 OF 31	23 12 14 19 XSQ= 2.83 PHI= 0.204 XP = 0.0923
102	TILT TOWARD BEING THOSE WHERE CLASS STRATIFICATION IS PRESENT (203)	0.63 OF 38	102	TILT TOWARD BEING THOSE WHERE CLASS STRATIFICATION IS ABSENT (180)	0.69 OF 35	24 11 14 24 XSQ= 6.13 PHI= 0.290 XP = 0.0133
130	DRIFT TOWARD BEING THOSE WHERE LEATHER WORKING IS MAINLY DONE BY MALES (39)	0.60 OF 10	130	DRIFT TOWARD BEING THOSE WHERE LEATHER WORKING IS MAINLY DONE BY FEMALES (45)	0.82 OF 11	6 2 4 9 XSQ= 2.31 PHI= 0.332 EP = 0.0805
143	DRIFT TOWARD BEING THOSE WHERE THE RATIO OF RESTITUTIVE TO REPRESSIVE SANCTIONS IS HIGH (20) WME	0.54 OF 13	143	DRIFT TOWARD BEING THOSE WHERE THE RATIO OF RESTITUTIVE TO REPRESSIVE SANCTIONS IS MEDIUM OR LOW (32) WME	0.89 OF 9	7 1 6 8 XSQ= 2.55 PHI= 0.341 EP = 0.0743

144	DRIFT TOWARD BEING THOSE WHERE THE RATIO OF RESTITUTIVE TO REPRESSIVE SANCTIONS IS HIGH OR MEDIUM (27) WME	0.62 OF 13	144	DRIFT TOWARD BEING THOSE WHERE THE RATIO OF RESTITUTIVE TO REPRESSIVE SANCTIONS IS LOW (25) WME	0.78 OF 9	8 2 5 7 XSQ= 1.92 PHI= 0.295 EP = 0.0991
149	LEAN TOWARD BEING THOSE WHERE THE INCIDENCE OF THEFT IS HIGH (18) B-B-C	0.76 OF 17	149	LEAN TOWARD BEING THOSE WHERE THE INCIDENCE OF THEFT IS LOW (19) B-B-C	0.72 OF 18	13 5 4 13 XSQ= 6.46 PHI= 0.430 EP = 0.0067
177	TILT LESS TOWARD BEING THOSE WHERE THE COMMUNITY IS OTHER THAN A SINGLE CLAN-COMMUNITY AND EXOGAMOUS (305)	0.68 OF 37	177	TILT MORE TOWARD BEING THOSE WHERE THE COMMUNITY IS OTHER THAN A SINGLE CLAN-COMMUNITY AND EXOGAMOUS (305)	0.91 OF 35	12 3 25 32 XSQ= 4.85 PHI= 0.259 XP = 0.0277
178	TILT MORE TOWARD BEING THOSE WHERE THE COMMUNITY IS OTHER THAN SEGMENTED ON A CLAN BASIS AND NON-EXOGAMOUS (295)	0.84 OF 37	178	TILT LESS TOWARD BEING THOSE WHERE THE COMMUNITY IS OTHER THAN SEGMENTED ON A CLAN BASIS AND NON-EXOGAMOUS (295)	0.60 OF 35	6 14 31 21 XSQ= 3.96 PHI= -0.234 XP = 0.0467
180	DRIFT TOWARD BEING THOSE WHERE THE COMMUNITY IS COMMONLY EXOGAMOUS, RATHER THAN NON-EXOGAMOUS (124)	0.51 OF 37	180	DRIFT TOWARD BEING THOSE WHERE THE COMMUNITY IS COMMONLY NON-EXOGAMOUS, RATHER THAN EXOGAMOUS (258)	0.71 OF 35	19 10 18 25 XSQ= 2.99 PHI= 0.204 XP = 0.0837
184	LEAN TOWARD BEING THOSE WHERE THE LARGEST NON-COGNATIC KIN GROUP IS SMALLER THAN A PHRATRY, I. E. A SIB OR LINEAGE (175)	0.77 OF 31	184	LEAN TOWARD BEING THOSE WHERE THE LARGEST NON-COGNATIC KIN GROUP IS THE MOEITY OR PHRATRY (77)	0.65 OF 20	7 13 24 7 XSQ= 7.48 PHI= -0.383 XP = 0.0062
186	TILT LESS TOWARD BEING THOSE WHERE THE KIN GROUP IS OTHER THAN EXCLUSIVELY PATRILINEAL (250)	0.55 OF 38	186	TILT MORE TOWARD BEING THOSE WHERE THE KIN GROUP IS OTHER THAN EXCLUSIVELY PATRILINEAL (250)	0.80 OF 35	17 7 21 28 XSQ= 3.99 PHI= 0.234 XP = 0.0457
188	TILT MORE TOWARD BEING THOSE WHERE THE KIN GROUP IS OTHER THAN EXCLUSIVELY COGNATIC (252)	0.82 OF 38	188	TILT LESS TOWARD BEING THOSE WHERE THE KIN GROUP IS OTHER THAN EXCLUSIVELY COGNATIC (252)	0.57 OF 35	7 15 31 20 XSQ= 4.07 PHI= -0.236 XP = 0.0436
240	TILT TOWARD BEING THOSE WHERE THE FAMILY, IF EXTENDED, IS SMALL OR STEM, RATHER THAN LARGE (135)	0.67 OF 24	240	TILT TOWARD BEING THOSE WHERE THE FAMILY, IF EXTENDED, IS LARGE, RATHER THAN SMALL OR STEM (78)	0.68 OF 19	8 13 16 6 XSQ= 3.92 PHI= -0.302 XP = 0.0478

302	TILT TCWARD BEING THOSE WHERE THE AVERAGE EARLY SATISFACTION PCTENTIAL IS LCW (17) W-C	0.59 OF 17	302	TILT TOWARD BEING THOSE WHERE THE AVERAGE EARLY SATISFACTICN POTENTIAL IS HIGH (23) W-C	0.81 CF 16	7 13 10 3 XSQ= 3.99 PHI= -0.348 EP = 0.0324
304	DRIFT TCWARD BEING THOSE WHERE THE EARLY ANAL SATISFACTION PCTENTIAL IS LCW (22) W-C	0.71 OF 17	304	DRIFT TOWARD BEING THOSE WHERE THE EARLY ANAL SATISFACTICN POTENTIAL IS HIGH (19) W-C	0.63 OF 16	5 10 12 6 XSQ= 2.43 PHI= -0.271 EP = 0.0844
306	DRIFT TCWARD BEING THCSE WHERE THE EARLY DEPENCENCE SATISFACTION PCTENTIAL IS LCW (24) W-C	0.58 OF 19	306	DRIFT TOWARD BEING THOSE WHERE THE EARLY DEPENDENCE SATISFACTION POTENTIAL IS HIGH (28) W-C	0.75 OF 16	8 12 11 4 XSQ= 2.61 PHI= -0.273 EP = 0.0866
308	TILT TCWARD BEING THOSE WHERE AVERAGE SCCIALIZATION ANXIETY IS HIGH (22) W-C	0.71 OF 17	308	TILT TOWARD BEING THOSE WHERE AVERAGE SCCIALIZATION ANXIETY IS LOW (18) W-C	0.69 OF 16	12 5 5 11 XSQ= 3.65 PHI= 0.333 EP = 0.0381
314	TILT LESS TOWARC BEING THCSE WHERE THE INCIDENCE CF MOTHER-CHILC HCUSEHCLDS IS LCW (61) W-C,S	0.57 OF 23	314	TILT MORE TOWARD BEING THCSE WHERE THE INCIDENCE CF MCTHER-CHILD HOUSEHOLDS IS LOW (61) W-D,S	0.88 OF 26	10 3 13 23 XSQ= 4.85 PHI= 0.315 XP = 0.0276
317	DRIFT TCWARD BEING THCSE WHERE DISPLAY CF AFFECTION TOWARD THE INFANT IS LCW (29) B-B-C	0.56 OF 32	317	DRIFT TOWARD BEING THOSE WHERE DISPLAY CF AFFECTICN TOWARD THE INFANT IS HIGH (39) B-B-C	0.70 OF 33	14 23 18 10 XSQ= 3.47 PHI= -0.231 XP = 0.0627
318	LEAN TCWARC BEING THCSE WHERE THE CVERALL INDULGENCE CF THE INFANT IS LCW (31) B-B-C	0.62 OF 34	318	LEAN TOWARD BEING THOSE WHERE THE OVERALL INDULGENCE OF THE INFANT IS HIGH (40) B-B-C	0.76 OF 34	13 26 21 8 XSQ= 8.66 PHI= -0.357 XP = 0.0033
323	DRIFT TCWARD BEING THCSE WHERE THE CONSTANCY CF PRESENCE OF THE INFANT'S NURTURANT AGENT IS LCW (45) B-B-C	0.72 OF 36	323	DRIFT TOWARD BEING THOSE WHERE THE CONSTANCY CF PRESENCE OF THE INFANT'S NURTURANT AGENT IS HIGH (29) B-B-C	0.50 OF 34	10 17 26 17 XSQ= 2.77 PHI= -0.199 XP = 0.0962
326	TILT TCWARC BEING THCSE WHERE THE INFERRED TRANSITION ANXIETY BETWEEN INFANCY ANC CHILCHCOC IS HIGH (32) B-B-C	0.63 OF 32	326	TILT TOWARD BEING THCSE WHERE THE INFERRED TRANSITICN ANXIETY BETWEEN INFANCY AND CHILDHCOD IS LOW (35) B-B-C	0.66 CF 32	20 11 12 21 XSQ= 4.00 PHI= 0.250 XP = 0.0454

334	LEAN TOWARD BEING THOSE 0.68 OF 38 WHERE THE INDULGENCE OF THE CHILD IS LOW (38) B-B-C	334	LEAN TOWARD BEING THOSE 0.71 OF 35 WHERE THE INDULGENCE OF THE CHILD IS HIGH (40) B-B-C	12 25 26 10 XSQ= 10.04 PHI= -0.371 XP = 0.0015
336	TEND TO BE THOSE 0.87 OF 38 WHERE THE TOTAL POSITIVE PRESSURE TOWARD DEVELOPING RESPONSIBLE BEHAVIOR IN THE CHILD IS HIGH (43) B-B-C	336	TEND TO BE THOSE 0.71 OF 35 WHERE THE TOTAL POSITIVE PRESSURE TOWARD DEVELOPING RESPONSIBLE BEHAVIOR IN THE CHILD IS LOW (32) B-B-C	33 10 5 25 XSQ= 23.21 PHI= 0.564 XP = 0.0000
338	TEND TO BE THOSE 0.82 OF 38 WHERE THE CHILD'S INFERRED ANXIETY OVER PERFORMANCE OF RESPONSIBLE BEHAVIOR IS HIGH (44) B-B-C	338	TEND TO BE THOSE 0.63 OF 35 WHERE THE CHILD'S INFERRED ANXIETY OVER PERFORMANCE OF RESPONSIBLE BEHAVIOR IS LOW (29) B-B-C	31 13 7 22 XSQ= 13.23 PHI= 0.426 XP = 0.0003
339	TEND TO BE THOSE 0.74 OF 38 WHERE THE CHILD'S INFERRED CONFLICT REGARDING RESPONSIBLE BEHAVIOR IS HIGH (31) B-B-C	339	TEND TO BE THOSE 0.91 OF 35 WHERE THE CHILD'S INFERRED CONFLICT REGARDING RESPONSIBLE BEHAVIOR IS LOW (42) B-B-C	28 3 10 32 XSQ= 29.01 PHI= 0.630 XP = 0.0000
345	TILT TOWARD BEING THOSE 0.61 OF 38 WHERE THE CHILD'S INFERRED ANXIETY OVER NON-PERFORMANCE OF SELF-RELIANT BEHAVIOR IS HIGH (37) B-B-C	345	TILT TOWARD BEING THOSE 0.66 OF 35 WHERE THE CHILD'S INFERRED ANXIETY OVER NON-PERFORMANCE OF SELF-RELIANT BEHAVIOR IS LOW (39) B-B-C	23 12 15 23 XSQ= 4.03 PHI= 0.235 XP = 0.0447
346	LEAN TOWARD BEING THOSE 0.66 OF 38 WHERE THE CHILD'S INFERRED ANXIETY OVER PERFORMANCE OF SELF-RELIANT BEHAVIOR IS HIGH (37) B-B-C	346	LEAN TOWARD BEING THOSE 0.69 OF 35 WHERE THE CHILD'S INFERRED ANXIETY OVER PERFORMANCE OF SELF-RELIANT BEHAVIOR IS LOW (39) B-B-C	25 11 13 24 XSQ= 7.29 PHI= 0.316 XP = 0.0069
347	LEAN TOWARD BEING THOSE 0.66 OF 38 WHERE THE CHILD'S INFERRED CONFLICT REGARDING SELF-RELIANT BEHAVIOR IS HIGH (37) B-B-C	347	LEAN TOWARD BEING THOSE 0.69 OF 35 WHERE THE CHILD'S INFERRED CONFLICT REGARDING SELF-RELIANT BEHAVIOR IS LOW (39) B-B-C	25 11 13 24 XSQ= 7.29 PHI= 0.316 XP = 0.0069
350	TILT TOWARD BEING THOSE 0.73 OF 30 WHERE THE CHILD'S INFERRED ANXIETY OVER PERFORMANCE OF ACHIEVEMENT BEHAVIOR IS HIGH (34) B-B-C	350	TILT TOWARD BEING THOSE 0.59 OF 29 WHERE THE CHILD'S INFERRED ANXIETY OVER PERFORMANCE OF ACHIEVEMENT BEHAVIOR IS LOW (26) B-B-C	22 12 8 17 XSQ= 4.93 PHI= 0.289 XP = 0.0264
351	TILT TOWARD BEING THOSE 0.60 OF 30 WHERE THE CHILD'S INFERRED CONFLICT REGARDING ACHIEVEMENT BEHAVIOR IS HIGH (26) B-B-C	351	TILT TOWARD BEING THOSE 0.72 OF 29 WHERE THE CHILD'S INFERRED CONFLICT REGARDING ACHIEVEMENT BEHAVIOR IS LOW (34) B-B-C	18 8 12 21 XSQ= 5.04 PHI= 0.292 XP = 0.0248

352	TILT TOWARD BEING THOSE 0.76 OF 37 WHERE THE TOTAL POSITIVE PRESSURE TOWARD DEVELOPING OBEDIENT BEHAVIOR IN THE CHILD IS HIGH (44) B-B-C	352	TILT TOWARD BEING THOSE 0.55 OF 31 WHERE THE TOTAL POSITIVE PRESSURE TOWARD DEVELOPING OBEDIENT BEHAVIOR IN THE CHILD IS LOW (28) B-B-C	28 14 9 17 XSQ= 5.42 PHI= 0.282 XP = 0.0199
353	TEND TO BE THOSE 0.78 OF 37 WHERE THE CHILD'S INFERRED ANXIETY OVER NON-PERFORMANCE OF OBEDIENT BEHAVIOR IS HIGH (42) B-B-C	353	TEND TO BE THOSE 0.70 OF 33 WHERE THE CHILD-S INFERRED ANXIETY OVER NON-PERFORMANCE OF OBEDIENT BEHAVIOR IS LOW (32) B-B-C	29 10 8 23 XSQ= 14.45 PHI= 0.454 XP = 0.0001
355	TILT TOWARD BEING THOSE 0.59 OF 37 WHERE THE CHILD'S INFERRED CONFLICT REGARDING OBEDIENT BEHAVIOR IS HIGH (35) B-B-C	355	TILT TOWARD BEING THOSE 0.69 OF 32 WHERE THE CHILD'S INFERRED CONFLICT REGARDING OBEDIENT BEHAVIOR IS LOW (38) B-B-C	22 10 15 22 XSQ= 4.42 PHI= 0.253 XP = 0.0356
393	DRIFT TOWARD BEING THOSE 0.68 OF 19 WHERE EXTRAMARITAL COITUS IS PUNISHED, RATHER THAN PERMITTED (43) F-B	393	DRIFT TOWARD BEING THOSE 0.67 OF 18 WHERE EXTRAMARITAL COITUS IS PERMITTED, RATHER THAN PUNISHED (41) F-B	13 6 6 12 XSQ= 3.26 PHI= 0.297 EP = 0.0502
399	DRIFT TOWARD BEING THOSE 0.65 OF 23 WHERE INTENSITY OF CASTRATION ANXIETY IS HIGH (23) WNS	399	DRIFT TOWARD BEING THOSE 0.71 OF 17 WHERE INTENSITY OF CASTRATION ANXIETY IS LOW (22) WNS	15 5 8 12 XSQ= 3.68 PHI= 0.303 EP = 0.0536
403	DRIFT TOWARD BEING THOSE 0.60 OF 20 WHERE EXPLANATIONS OF ILLNESS OF AN ANAL NATURE ARE PRESENT (23) W-C	403	DRIFT TOWARD BEING THOSE 0.70 OF 20 WHERE EXPLANATIONS OF ILLNESS OF AN ANAL NATURE ARE ABSENT (38) W-C	12 6 8 14 XSQ= 2.53 PHI= 0.251 EP = 0.0679
434	TILT TOWARD BEING THOSE 0.76 OF 21 WHERE ASCETICISM IN MOURNING BEHAVIOR IS HIGH (37) JFG	434	TILT TOWARD BEING THOSE 0.59 OF 22 WHERE ASCETICISM IN MOURNING BEHAVIOR IS LOW (30) JFG	16 9 5 13 XSQ= 4.14 PHI= 0.310 XP = 0.0419
435	DRIFT TOWARD BEING THOSE 0.88 OF 8 WHERE ABANDONMENT OF THE HOUSE OF THE DEAD IS NOT PRACTICED (19) LWS	435	DRIFT TOWARD BEING THOSE 0.67 OF 6 WHERE ABANDONMENT OF THE HOUSE OF THE DEAD IS PRACTICED (12) LWS	1 4 7 2 XSQ= 2.34 PHI= -0.409 EP = 0.0909
458	LEAN TOWARD BEING THOSE 0.52 OF 25 WHERE GAMES, IF PRESENT, INCLUDE GAMES OF STRATEGY (52) R-A-B,EA	458	LEAN TOWARD BEING THOSE 0.88 OF 25 WHERE GAMES, IF PRESENT, DO NOT INCLUDE GAMES OF STRATEGY (119) R-A-B,EA	13 3 12 22 XSQ= 7.44 PHI= 0.386 XP = 0.0064

337/

460	LEAN TOWARD BEING THOSE WHERE GAMES, IF PRESENT, ARE NOT LIMITED TO GAMES OF SKILL ONLY (104) R-A-B,EA	0.80 OF 25	460	LEAN TOWARD BEING THOSE WHERE GAMES, IF PRESENT, ARE LIMITED TO GAMES OF SKILL ONLY (67) R-A-B,EA	0.60 OF 25	5 15 20 10 XSQ= 6.75 PHI= -0.367 XP = 0.0094

****

338 CULTURES WHERE THE CHILD'S INFERRED ANXIETY OVER PERFORMANCE OF RESPONSIBLE BEHAVIOR IS HIGH (44) B-B-C	338 CULTURES WHERE THE CHILD'S INFERRED ANXIETY OVER PERFORMANCE OF RESPONSIBLE BEHAVIOR IS LOW (29) B-B-C

BACKGROUND ON PAGE 143 BOTH SUBJECT AND PREDICATE

44 IN LEFT COLUMN

AINU	ALORESE	ARANDA	ARAUCANIANS	ASHANTI	AYMARA	AZANDE	CHAGGA	CHUKCHEE	COMANCHE
FON	GANDA	HANO	IFUGAO	JIVARO	KASKA	KURTATCHI	KWAKIUTL	LAU	LEPCHA
MAORI	MASAI	MBUNDU	MURNGIN	NAVAHO	NYAKYUSA	OJIBWA	PAPAGO	SAMOANS	SOTHO
SWAZI	TENETEHARA	THONGA	TIV	TROBRIAND	TRUKESE	TUCUNA	TURKANA	VENDA	WINNEBAGO
WOLEAIANS	YAKUT	YORUBA	ZUNI						

29 IN RIGHT COLUMN

ARAPESH	BALINESE	CAMAYURA	CHENCHU	CHEYENNE	CHIR-APACHE	CROW	CUNA	KIKUYU	KORYAK
LESU	MANDAN	MANUS	MARQUESANS	NUER	OMAHA	ONA	ONTONG-JAVA	PUKAPUKA	TALLENSI
TANALA	TETON	TIKOPIA	TIMBIRA	TUPINAMBA	WICHITA	WOGEO	YAGUA	YAHGAN	

327 EXCLUDED BECAUSE UNASCERTAINED

3	TILT LESS TOWARD BEING THOSE LOCATED OUTSIDE OF AFRICA (320)	0.66 OF 44	3	TILT MORE TOWARD BEING THOSE LOCATED OUTSIDE OF AFRICA (320)	0.90 OF 29	15 3 29 26 XSQ= 4.10 PHI= 0.237 XP = 0.0428
44	DRIFT MORE TOWARD BEING THOSE WHERE SETTLEMENTS ARE FIXED (222)	0.76 OF 42	44	DRIFT LESS TOWARD BEING THOSE WHERE SETTLEMENTS ARE FIXED (222)	0.52 OF 27	32 14 10 13 XSQ= 3.35 PHI= 0.220 XP = 0.0670
71	TILT LESS TOWARD BEING THOSE WHERE METAL WORKING IS ABSENT (153)	0.53 OF 34	71	TILT MORE TOWARD BEING THOSE WHERE METAL WORKING IS ABSENT (153)	0.84 OF 25	16 4 18 21 XSQ= 4.89 PHI= 0.288 XP = 0.0270
73	DRIFT TOWARD BEING THOSE WHERE WEAVING IS PRESENT (118)	0.53 OF 36	73	DRIFT TOWARD BEING THOSE WHERE WEAVING IS ABSENT (130)	0.75 OF 24	19 6 17 18 XSQ= 3.50 PHI= 0.242 XP = 0.0614

85	TILT LESS TOWARD BEING THOSE WHERE THE LEVEL OF POLITICAL INTEGRATION IS THE MINIMAL STATE, THE AUTONOMOUS COMMUNITY, OR THE FAMILY (234) GPM	0.74 OF 35	85	TILT MORE TOWARD BEING THOSE WHERE THE LEVEL OF POLITICAL INTEGRATION IS THE MINIMAL STATE, THE AUTONOMOUS COMMUNITY, OR THE FAMILY (234) GPM	0.96 OF 27	9 1 26 26 XSQ= 3.95 PHI= 0.252 XP = 0.0468
88	DRIFT TOWARD BEING THOSE WHERE, IF A HEADMANSHIP IS PRESENT, SUCCESSION IS HEREDITARY (165)	0.70 OF 33	88	DRIFT TOWARD BEING THOSE WHERE, IF A HEADMANSHIP IS PRESENT, SUCCESSION IS NON-HEREDITARY (106)	0.57 OF 21	10 12 23 9 XSQ= 2.80 PHI= -0.228 XP = 0.0944
95	TEND LESS TO BE THOSE WHERE THE HIERARCHY OF NATIONAL JURISDICTION HAS ONE OR NO LEVELS (254) GES,EA	0.61 OF 41	95	IN ALL CASES ARE THOSE WHERE THE HIERARCHY OF NATIONAL JURISDICTION HAS ONE OR NO LEVELS (254) GES,EA	1.00 OF 27	16 0 25 27 XSQ= 11.70 PHI= 0.415 XP = 0.0006
139	LEAN TOWARD BEING THOSE WHERE SUPERORDINATE PUNISHMENT IS ABSENT (25) BBW	0.78 OF 18	139	LEAN TOWARD BEING THOSE WHERE SUPERORDINATE PUNISHMENT IS PRESENT (15) BBW	0.86 OF 7	4 6 14 1 XSQ= 6.03 PHI= -0.491 EP = 0.0068
149	TEND TO BE THOSE WHERE THE INCIDENCE OF THEFT IS HIGH (18) B-B-C	0.71 OF 24	149	TEND TO BE THOSE WHERE THE INCIDENCE OF THEFT IS LOW (19) B-B-C	0.91 OF 11	17 1 7 10 XSQ= 9.17 PHI= 0.512 EP = 0.0009
188	TILT MORE TOWARD BEING THOSE WHERE THE KIN GROUP IS OTHER THAN EXCLUSIVELY COGNATIC (252)	0.80 OF 44	188	TILT LESS TOWARD BEING THOSE WHERE THE KIN GROUP IS OTHER THAN EXCLUSIVELY COGNATIC (252)	0.55 OF 29	9 13 35 16 XSQ= 3.84 PHI= -0.229 XP = 0.0500
192	TILT MORE TOWARD BEING THOSE OTHER THAN WHERE THE ONLY KIN GROUP PRESENT IS A KINDRED OR ELSE BILATERAL DESCENT IS INFERRED (289)	0.91 OF 44	192	TILT LESS TOWARD BEING THOSE OTHER THAN WHERE THE ONLY KIN GROUP PRESENT IS A KINDRED OR ELSE BILATERAL DESCENT IS INFERRED (289)	0.69 OF 29	4 9 40 20 XSQ= 4.35 PHI= -0.244 XP = 0.0370
309	DRIFT TOWARD BEING THOSE WHERE ORAL SOCIALIZATION ANXIETY IS HIGH (26) W-C	0.64 OF 22	309	DRIFT TOWARD BEING THOSE WHERE ORAL SOCIALIZATION ANXIETY IS LOW (27) W-C	0.67 OF 15	14 5 8 10 XSQ= 2.18 PHI= 0.243 EP = 0.0991
317	LEAN TOWARD BEING THOSE WHERE DISPLAY OF AFFECTION TOWARD THE INFANT IS LOW (29) B-B-C	0.59 OF 39	317	LEAN TOWARD BEING THOSE WHERE DISPLAY OF AFFECTION TOWARD THE INFANT IS HIGH (39) B-B-C	0.81 OF 26	16 21 23 5 XSQ= 8.49 PHI= -0.361 XP = 0.0036

326	LEAN TOWARD BEING THOSE 0.66 OF 38 WHERE THE INFERRED TRANSITION ANXIETY BETWEEN INFANCY AND CHILDHOOD IS HIGH (32) B-B-C	326	LEAN TOWARD BEING THOSE 0.77 OF 26 WHERE THE INFERRED TRANSITION ANXIETY BETWEEN INFANCY AND CHILDHOOD IS LOW (35) B-B-C	25 6 13 20 XSQ= 9.63 PHI= 0.388 XP = 0.0019
334	TEND TO BE THOSE 0.73 OF 44 WHERE THE INDULGENCE OF THE CHILD IS LOW (38) B-B-C	334	TEND TO BE THOSE 0.86 OF 29 WHERE THE INDULGENCE OF THE CHILD IS HIGH (40) B-B-C	12 25 32 4 XSQ= 21.99 PHI= -0.549 XP = 0.0000
337	TEND TO BE THOSE 0.70 OF 44 WHERE THE CHILD'S INFERRED ANXIETY OVER NON-PERFORMANCE OF RESPONSIBLE BEHAVIOR IS HIGH (38) B-B-C	337	TEND TO BE THOSE 0.76 OF 29 WHERE THE CHILD'S INFERRED ANXIETY OVER NON-PERFORMANCE OF RESPONSIBLE BEHAVIOR IS LOW (35) B-B-C	31 7 13 22 XSQ= 13.23 PHI= 0.426 XP = 0.0003
339	TEND TO BE THOSE 0.66 OF 44 WHERE THE CHILD'S INFERRED CONFLICT REGARDING RESPONSIBLE BEHAVIOR IS HIGH (31) B-B-C	339	TEND TO BE THOSE 0.93 OF 29 WHERE THE CHILD'S INFERRED CONFLICT REGARDING RESPONSIBLE BEHAVIOR IS LOW (42) B-B-C	29 2 15 27 XSQ= 22.56 PHI= 0.556 XP = 0.0000
341	TILT TOWARD BEING THOSE 0.80 OF 25 WHERE THE CHILD'S INFERRED ANXIETY OVER NON-PERFORMANCE OF NURTURANT BEHAVIOR IS HIGH (30) B-B-C	341	TILT TOWARD BEING THOSE 0.52 OF 21 WHERE THE CHILD'S INFERRED ANXIETY OVER NON-PERFORMANCE OF NURTURANT BEHAVIOR IS LOW (16) B-B-C	20 10 5 11 XSQ= 3.94 PHI= 0.293 XP = 0.0470
344	DRIFT TOWARD BEING THOSE 0.57 OF 44 WHERE THE TOTAL POSITIVE PRESSURE TOWARD DEVELOPING SELF-RELIANT BEHAVIOR IN THE CHILD IS HIGH (36) B-B-C	344	DRIFT TOWARD BEING THOSE 0.69 OF 29 WHERE THE TOTAL POSITIVE PRESSURE TOWARD DEVELOPING SELF-RELIANT BEHAVIOR IN THE CHILD IS LOW (40) B-B-C	25 9 19 20 XSQ= 3.69 PHI= 0.225 XP = 0.0547
345	LEAN TOWARD BEING THOSE 0.64 OF 44 WHERE THE CHILD'S INFERRED ANXIETY OVER NON-PERFORMANCE OF SELF-RELIANT BEHAVIOR IS HIGH (37) B-B-C	345	LEAN TOWARD BEING THOSE 0.76 OF 29 WHERE THE CHILD'S INFERRED ANXIETY OVER NON-PERFORMANCE OF SELF-RELIANT BEHAVIOR IS LOW (39) B-B-C	28 7 16 22 XSQ= 9.40 PHI= 0.359 XP = 0.0022
346	LEAN TOWARD BEING THOSE 0.64 OF 44 WHERE THE CHILD'S INFERRED ANXIETY OVER PERFORMANCE OF SELF-RELIANT BEHAVIOR IS HIGH (37) B-B-C	346	LEAN TOWARD BEING THOSE 0.72 OF 29 WHERE THE CHILD'S INFERRED ANXIETY OVER PERFORMANCE OF SELF-RELIANT BEHAVIOR IS LOW (39) B-B-C	28 8 16 21 XSQ= 7.70 PHI= 0.325 XP = 0.0055
347	LEAN TOWARD BEING THOSE 0.64 OF 44 WHERE THE CHILD'S INFERRED CONFLICT REGARDING SELF-RELIANT BEHAVIOR IS HIGH (37) B-B-C	347	LEAN TOWARD BEING THOSE 0.72 OF 29 WHERE THE CHILD'S INFERRED CONFLICT REGARDING SELF-RELIANT BEHAVIOR IS LOW (39) B-B-C	28 8 16 21 XSQ= 7.70 PHI= 0.325 XP = 0.0055

349	DRIFT TOWARD BEING THOSE 0.67 OF 36 WHERE THE CHILD'S INFERRED ANXIETY OVER NON-PERFORMANCE OF ACHIEVEMENT BEHAVIOR IS HIGH (34) B-B-C	349	DRIFT TOWARD BEING THOSE 0.58 OF 24 WHERE THE CHILD'S INFERRED ANXIETY OVER NON-PERFORMANCE OF ACHIEVEMENT BEHAVIOR IS LOW (28) B-B-C	24 10 12 14 XSQ= 2.72 PHI= 0.213 XP = 0.0992
350	TILT TOWARD BEING THOSE 0.71 OF 35 WHERE THE CHILD'S INFERRED ANXIETY OVER PERFORMANCE OF ACHIEVEMENT BEHAVIOR IS HIGH (34) B-B-C	350	TILT TOWARD BEING THOSE 0.63 OF 24 WHERE THE CHILD'S INFERRED ANXIETY OVER PERFORMANCE OF ACHIEVEMENT BEHAVIOR IS LOW (26) B-B-C	25 9 10 15 XSQ= 5.39 PHI= 0.302 XP = 0.0202
351	TILT TOWARD BEING THOSE 0.57 OF 35 WHERE THE CHILD'S INFERRED CONFLICT REGARDING ACHIEVEMENT BEHAVIOR IS HIGH (26) B-B-C	351	TILT TOWARD BEING THOSE 0.75 OF 24 WHERE THE CHILD'S INFERRED CONFLICT REGARDING ACHIEVEMENT BEHAVIOR IS LOW (34) B-B-C	20 6 15 18 XSQ= 4.73 PHI= 0.283 XP = 0.0296
353	TILT TOWARD BEING THOSE 0.67 OF 43 WHERE THE CHILD'S INFERRED ANXIETY OVER NON-PERFORMANCE OF OBEDIENT BEHAVIOR IS HIGH (42) B-B-C	353	TILT TOWARD BEING THOSE 0.63 OF 27 WHERE THE CHILD-S INFERRED ANXIETY OVER NON-PERFORMANCE OF OBEDIENT BEHAVIOR IS LOW (32) B-B-C	29 10 14 17 XSQ= 5.04 PHI= 0.268 XP = 0.0247
354	TILT TOWARD BEING THOSE 0.57 OF 42 WHERE THE CHILD'S INFERRED ANXIETY OVER PERFORMANCE OF OBEDIENT BEHAVIOR IS HIGH (36) B-B-C	354	TILT TOWARD BEING THOSE 0.70 OF 27 WHERE THE CHILD'S INFERRED ANXIETY OVER PERFORMANCE OF OBEDIENT BEHAVIOR IS LOW (37) B-B-C	24 8 18 19 XSQ= 3.96 PHI= 0.239 XP = 0.0467
390	TILT MORE TOWARD BEING THOSE 0.91 OF 32 WHERE PREMARITAL SEX RELATIONS ARE WEAKLY PUNISHED AND IN FACT NOT RARE OR PUNISHED ONLY IF PREGNANCY RESULTS, OR FREELY PERMITTED (132) JTW,EA	390	TILT LESS TOWARD BEING THOSE 0.63 OF 19 WHERE PREMARITAL SEX RELATIONS ARE WEAKLY PUNISHED AND IN FACT NOT RARE OR PUNISHED ONLY IF PREGNANCY RESULTS, OR FREELY PERMITTED (132) JTW,EA	3 7 29 12 XSQ= 4.10 PHI= -0.283 XP = 0.0430
399	DRIFT TOWARD BEING THOSE 0.62 OF 26 WHERE INTENSITY OF CASTRATION ANXIETY IS HIGH (23) WNS	399	DRIFT TOWARD BEING THOSE 0.71 OF 14 WHERE INTENSITY OF CASTRATION ANXIETY IS LOW (22) WNS	16 4 10 10 XSQ= 2.75 PHI= 0.262 EP = 0.0958
406	DRIFT TOWARD BEING THOSE 0.60 OF 25 WHERE EXPLANATIONS OF ILLNESS OF AN AGGRESSION NATURE ARE PRESENT (28) W-C	406	DRIFT TOWARD BEING THOSE 0.73 OF 15 WHERE EXPLANATIONS OF ILLNESS OF AN AGGRESSION NATURE ARE ABSENT (33) W-C	15 4 10 11 XSQ= 2.95 PHI= 0.271 EP = 0.0550
419	TILT TOWARD BEING THOSE 0.76 OF 34 WHERE MILITARY GLORY IS STRONGLY OR MODERATELY EMPHASIZED (55) PES	419	TILT TOWARD BEING THOSE 0.61 OF 18 WHERE MILITARY GLORY IS NEGLIGIBLY EMPHASIZED (31) PES	26 7 8 11 XSQ= 5.64 PHI= 0.329 XP = 0.0176

421	TILT TOWARD BEING THOSE WHERE KILLING, TORTURING, OR MUTILATING OF THE ENEMY IS STRONGLY OR MODERATELY EMPHASIZED (37) PES	0.56 OF 34	421	TILT TOWARD BEING THOSE WHERE KILLING, TORTURING, OR MUTILATING OF THE ENEMY IS NEGLIGIBLY EMPHASIZED (47) PES	0.78 OF 18	19 4 15 14 XSQ= 4.13 PHI= 0.282 XP = 0.0422
433	TILT TOWARD BEING THOSE WHERE BELIEF IN REINCARNATION IS PRESENT (10) GES	0.50 OF 12	433	IN ALL CASES ARE THOSE WHERE BELIEF IN REINCARNATION IS ABSENT (28) GES	1.00 OF 9	6 0 6 9 XSQ= 4.09 PHI= 0.441 EP = 0.0186
434	DRIFT TOWARD BEING THOSE WHERE ASCETICISM IN MOURNING BEHAVIOR IS HIGH (37) JFG	0.69 OF 29	434	DRIFT TOWARD BEING THOSE WHERE ASCETICISM IN MOURNING BEHAVIOR IS LOW (30) JFG	0.64 OF 14	20 5 9 9 XSQ= 3.03 PHI= 0.266 XP = 0.0816
442	DRIFT TOWARD BEING THOSE WHERE FEAR OF ANIMAL SPIRITS IS HIGH (28) W-C	0.60 OF 25	442	DRIFT TOWARD BEING THOSE WHERE FEAR OF ANIMAL SPIRITS IS LOW (33) W-C	0.73 OF 15	15 4 10 11 XSQ= 2.95 PHI= 0.271 EP = 0.0550
445	LEAN TOWARD BEING THOSE WHERE SORCERY IS IMPORTANT (26) EBW,DH	0.74 OF 19	445	IN ALL CASES ARE THOSE WHERE SORCERY IS UNIMPORTANT (23) BBW,DH	1.00 OF 5	14 0 5 5 XSQ= 6.07 PHI= 0.503 EP = 0.0059
447	DRIFT TOWARD BEING THOSE WHERE LOVE MAGIC IS PRESENT (20) S-R	0.78 OF 18	447	DRIFT TOWARD BEING THOSE WHERE LOVE MAGIC IS ABSENT (13) S-R	0.71 OF 7	14 2 4 5 XSQ= 3.38 PHI= 0.367 EP = 0.0581
458	TILT LESS TOWARD BEING THOSE WHERE GAMES, IF PRESENT, DO NOT INCLUDE GAMES OF STRATEGY (119) R-A-B,EA	0.55 OF 31	458	TILT MORE TOWARD BEING THOSE WHERE GAMES, IF PRESENT, DO NOT INCLUDE GAMES OF STRATEGY (119) R-A-B,EA	0.89 OF 19	14 2 17 17 XSQ= 5.00 PHI= 0.316 XP = 0.0253
460	TILT TOWARD BEING THOSE WHERE GAMES, IF PRESENT, ARE NOT LIMITED TO GAMES OF SKILL ONLY (104) R-A-B,EA	0.74 OF 31	460	TILT TOWARD BEING THOSE WHERE GAMES, IF PRESENT, ARE LIMITED TO GAMES OF SKILL ONLY (67) R-A-B,EA	0.63 OF 19	8 12 23 7 XSQ= 5.38 PHI= -0.328 XP = 0.0204

339 CULTURES WHERE THE CHILD'S INFERRED CONFLICT REGARDING RESPONSIBLE BEHAVIOR IS HIGH (31) B-B-C	339 CULTURES WHERE THE CHILD'S INFERRED CONFLICT REGARDING RESPONSIBLE BEHAVIOR IS LOW (42) B-B-C

BACKGROUND ON PAGE 143 — BOTH SUBJECT AND PREDICATE

31 IN LEFT COLUMN

AINU	ALORESE	ASHANTI	AYMARA	AZANDE	CHAGGA	CHENCHU	CHUKCHEE	FON	GANDA
HANO	IFUGAO	KASKA	KORYAK	KURTATCHI	KWAKIUTL	LAU	LEPCHA	MASAI	MBUNDU
MURNGIN	NAVAHO	OJIBWA	SAMOANS	SOTHO	SWAZI	THONGA	TUCUNA	TURKANA	VENDA
YAKUT									

42 IN RIGHT COLUMN

ARANDA	ARAPESH	ARAUCANIANS	BALINESE	CAMAYURA	CHEYENNE	CHIR-APACHE	COMANCHE	CROW	CUNA
JIVARO	KIKUYU	LESU	MANDAN	MANUS	MAORI	MARQUESANS	NUER	NYAKYUSA	OMAHA
ONA	ONTONG-JAVA	PAPAGO	PUKAPUKA	TALLENSI	TANALA	TENETEHARA	TETON	TIKOPIA	TIMBIRA
TIV	TROBRIAND	TRUKESE	TUPINAMBA	WICHITA	WINNEBAGO	WOGEO	WOLEAIANS	YAGUA	YAHGAN
YORUBA	ZUNI								

327 EXCLUDED BECAUSE UNASCERTAINED

3	TILT LESS TOWARD BEING THOSE LOCATED OUTSIDE OF AFRICA (320)	0.61 OF 31	3	TILT MORE TOWARD BEING THOSE LOCATED OUTSIDE OF AFRICA (320)	0.86 OF 42	12 6 19 36 XSQ= 4.49 PHI= 0.248 XP = 0.0341
5	TILT LESS TOWARD BEING THOSE LOCATED OUTSIDE OF EAST EURASIA (330)	0.81 OF 31	5	TILT MORE TOWARD BEING THOSE LOCATED OUTSIDE OF EAST EURASIA (330)	0.98 OF 42	6 1 25 41 XSQ= 4.13 PHI= 0.238 XP = 0.0421
9	DRIFT MORE TOWARD BEING THOSE LOCATED OUTSIDE OF SOUTH AMERICA (335)	0.94 OF 31	9	DRIFT LESS TOWARD BEING THOSE LOCATED OUTSIDE OF SOUTH AMERICA (335)	0.76 OF 42	2 10 29 32 XSQ= 2.75 PHI= -0.194 XP = 0.0972
71	TILT TOWARD BEING THOSE WHERE METAL WORKING IS PRESENT (98)	0.54 OF 24	71	TILT TOWARD BEING THOSE WHERE METAL WORKING IS ABSENT (153)	0.80 OF 35	13 7 11 28 XSQ= 5.97 PHI= 0.318 XP = 0.0145

```
 85  LEAN LESS TOWARD BEING THOSE   0.65 OF  23     85  LEAN MORE TOWARD BEING THOSE   0.95 OF  39            8     2
     WHERE THE LEVEL OF POLITICAL INTEGRATION           WHERE THE LEVEL OF POLITICAL INTEGRATION            15    37
     IS THE MINIMAL STATE,                              IS THE MINIMAL STATE,                       XSQ=     7.34
     THE AUTONOMOUS COMMUNITY, OR                       THE AUTONOMOUS COMMUNITY, OR                PHI=    0.344
     THE FAMILY  (234) GPM                              THE FAMILY  (234) GPM                       XP =   0.0067

 95  TEND LESS TO BE THOSE          0.53 OF  30     95  TEND MORE TO BE THOSE          0.95 OF  38           14     2
     WHERE THE HIERARCHY                                WHERE THE HIERARCHY                                 16    36
     OF NATIONAL JURISDICTION HAS                       OF NATIONAL JURISDICTION HAS                XSQ=    13.75
     ONE OR NO LEVELS  (254) GES,EA                     ONE OR NO LEVELS  (254) GES,EA              PHI=    0.450
                                                                                                    XP =   0.0002

102  LEAN TOWARD BEING THOSE        0.68 OF  31    102  LEAN TOWARD BEING THOSE        0.67 OF  42           21    14
     WHERE CLASS STRATIFICATION IS                      WHERE CLASS STRATIFICATION IS                       10    28
     PRESENT  (203)                                     ABSENT  (180)                               XSQ=     7.14
                                                                                                    PHI=    0.313
                                                                                                    XP =   0.0075

128  DRIFT TOWARD BEING THOSE       0.90 OF  10    128  DRIFT TOWARD BEING THOSE       0.60 OF  10            1     6
     WHERE, IF SUBSISTENCE IS PRIMARILY BY              WHERE, IF SUBSISTENCE IS PRIMARILY BY                9     4
     AGRICULTURE, THE WORK IS                           AGRICULTURE, THE WORK IS                    XSQ=     3.52
     MAINLY DONE BY FEMALES  (37)                       MAINLY DONE BY MALES  (40)                  PHI=   -0.419
                                                                                                    EP =   0.0573

133  IN ALL CASES ARE THOSE         1.00 OF   5    133  TILT TOWARD BEING THOSE        0.67 OF  15            5     5
     WHERE CONTRACTED DEBTS ARE                         WHERE CONTRACTED DEBTS ARE                           0    10
     SIGNIFICANTLY PRESENT  (17) GES                    MODERATELY PRESENT OR ABSENT  (17) GES      XSQ=     4.27
                                                                                                    PHI=    0.462
                                                                                                    EP =   0.0325

149  LEAN TOWARD BEING THOSE        0.78 OF  18    149  LEAN TOWARD BEING THOSE        0.76 OF  17           14     4
     WHERE THE INCIDENCE OF THEFT                       WHERE THE INCIDENCE OF THEFT                         4    13
     IS HIGH  (18) B-B-C                                IS LOW  (19) B-B-C                          XSQ=     8.24
                                                                                                    PHI=    0.485
                                                                                                    EP =   0.0022

178  DRIFT MORE TOWARD BEING THOSE  0.84 OF  31    178  DRIFT LESS TOWARD BEING THOSE  0.63 OF  41            5    15
     WHERE THE COMMUNITY IS OTHER THAN                  WHERE THE COMMUNITY IS OTHER THAN                   26    26
     SEGMENTED ON A CLAN BASIS AND                      SEGMENTED ON A CLAN BASIS AND               XSQ=     2.73
     NON-EXOGAMOUS  (295)                               NON-EXOGAMOUS  (295)                        PHI=   -0.195
                                                                                                    XP =   0.0983

186  TILT LESS TOWARD BEING THOSE   0.52 OF  31    186  TILT MORE TOWARD BEING THOSE   0.79 OF  42           15     9
     WHERE THE KIN GROUP IS                             WHERE THE KIN GROUP IS                              16    33
     OTHER THAN                                         OTHER THAN                                  XSQ=     4.72
     EXCLUSIVELY PATRILINEAL  (250)                     EXCLUSIVELY PATRILINEAL  (250)              PHI=    0.254
                                                                                                    XP =   0.0299

188  TILT MORE TOWARD BEING THOSE   0.84 OF  31    188  TILT LESS TOWARD BEING THOSE   0.60 OF  42            5    17
     WHERE THE KIN GROUP IS                             WHERE THE KIN GROUP IS                              26    25
     OTHER THAN                                         OTHER THAN                                  XSQ=     3.93
     EXCLUSIVELY COGNATIC  (252)                        EXCLUSIVELY COGNATIC  (252)                 PHI=   -0.232
                                                                                                    XP =   0.0474
```

209	DRIFT MORE TOWARD BEING THOSE 0.89 OF 27 WHERE MARITAL RESIDENCE IS PATRILOCAL, VIRILOCAL, OR AVUNCULOCAL, RATHER THAN MATRILOCAL OR UXORILOCAL (270)	209	DRIFT LESS TOWARD BEING THOSE 0.68 OF 37 WHERE MARITAL RESIDENCE IS PATRILOCAL, VIRILOCAL, OR AVUNCULOCAL, RATHER THAN MATRILOCAL OR UXORILOCAL (270)	24 25 3 12 XSQ= 2.86 PHI= 0.211 XP = 0.0911
213	DRIFT LESS TOWARD BEING THOSE 0.52 OF 31 WHERE FIRST COUSIN MARRIAGE IS NOT PERMITTED (198)	213	DRIFT MORE TOWARD BEING THOSE 0.76 OF 42 WHERE FIRST COUSIN MARRIAGE IS NOT PERMITTED (198)	15 10 16 32 XSQ= 3.76 PHI= 0.227 XP = 0.0526
221	DRIFT LESS TOWARD BEING THOSE 0.84 OF 31 WHERE MATRILATERAL CROSS-COUSIN MARRIAGE IS NOT PRESCRIBED OR PREFERRED (335)	221	DRIFT MORE TOWARD BEING THOSE 0.98 OF 42 WHERE MATRILATERAL CROSS-COUSIN MARRIAGE IS NOT PRESCRIBED OR PREFERRED (335)	5 1 26 41 XSQ= 2.83 PHI= 0.197 XP = 0.0924
260	TILT TOWARD BEING THOSE 0.80 OF 15 WHERE THE AGE OF MALES AT MARRIAGE IS LESS THAN TWENTY (38) JKH	260	TILT TOWARD BEING THOSE 0.59 OF 17 WHERE THE AGE OF MALES AT MARRIAGE IS TWENTY OR OVER (17) JKH	12 7 3 10 XSQ= 3.50 PHI= 0.331 EP = 0.0359
282	DRIFT TOWARD BEING THOSE 0.67 OF 15 WHERE THE STRENGTH OF DESIRE FOR CHILDREN IS HIGH (16) BCA	282	DRIFT TOWARD BEING THOSE 0.69 OF 16 WHERE THE STRENGTH OF DESIRE FOR CHILDREN IS LOW OR ABSENT (20) BCA	10 5 5 11 XSQ= 2.60 PHI= 0.290 EP = 0.0756
317	LEAN TOWARD BEING THOSE 0.64 OF 28 WHERE DISPLAY OF AFFECTION TOWARD THE INFANT IS LOW (29) B-B-C	317	LEAN TOWARD BEING THOSE 0.73 OF 37 WHERE DISPLAY OF AFFECTION TOWARD THE INFANT IS HIGH (39) B-B-C	10 27 18 10 XSQ= 7.57 PHI= -0.341 XP = 0.0059
318	LEAN TOWARD BEING THOSE 0.66 OF 29 WHERE THE OVERALL INDULGENCE OF THE INFANT IS LOW (31) B-B-C	318	LEAN TOWARD BEING THOSE 0.74 OF 39 WHERE THE OVERALL INDULGENCE OF THE INFANT IS HIGH (40) B-B-C	10 29 19 10 XSQ= 9.24 PHI= -0.369 XP = 0.0024
319	DRIFT TOWARD BEING THOSE 0.61 OF 28 WHERE PROTECTION OF THE INFANT FROM ENVIRONMENTAL DISCOMFORTS IS LOW (30) B-B-C	319	DRIFT TOWARD BEING THOSE 0.67 OF 36 WHERE PROTECTION OF THE INFANT FROM ENVIRONMENTAL DISCOMFORTS IS HIGH (35) B-B-C	11 24 17 12 XSQ= 3.72 PHI= -0.241 XP = 0.0536
320	DRIFT LESS TOWARD BEING THOSE 0.52 OF 29 WHERE THE DEGREE OF REDUCTION OF THE INFANT'S DRIVES IS HIGH (45) B-B-C	320	DRIFT MORE TOWARD BEING THOSE 0.78 OF 36 WHERE THE DEGREE OF REDUCTION OF THE INFANT'S DRIVES IS HIGH (45) B-B-C	15 28 14 8 XSQ= 3.78 PHI= -0.241 XP = 0.0520

```
322  DRIFT TCWARD BEING THCSE          0.71 OF  24    322  DRIFT TOWARD BEING THOSE          0.56 OF  32          7    18
     WHERE THE CONSISTENCY CF REDUCTION                   WHERE THE CONSISTENCY OF REDUCTICN                    17    14
     CF THE INFANT'S CRIVES                               OF THE INFANT'S DRIVES                           XSQ=     3.05
     IS LCW   (32) B-B-C                                  IS HIGH   (27) B-B-C                             PHI=   -0.233
                                                                                                           XP =   0.0808

326  TEND TC BE THCSE                 0.78 OF  27    326  TEND TO BE THOSE                  0.73 OF  37         21    10
     WHERE THE INFERRED TRANSITION ANXIETY                WHERE THE INFERRED TRANSITICN ANXIETY                  6    27
     BETWEEN INFANCY ANC CHILCHCOC                        BETWEEN INFANCY AND CHILDHCCD                    XSQ=    14.13
     IS HIGH   (32) B-B-C                                 IS LOW   (35) B-B-C                              PHI=    0.470
                                                                                                           XP =   0.0002

334  TEND TC BE THCSE                 0.77 OF  31    334  TEND TO BE THOSE                  0.71 CF  42          7    30
     WHERE THE INDULGENCE OF THE CHILD                    WHERE THE INDULGENCE OF THE CHILD                     24    12
     IS LCW   (38) B-B-C                                  IS HIGH   (40) B-B-C                             XSQ=    15.13
                                                                                                           PHI=   -0.455
                                                                                                           XP =   0.0001

336  LEAN TOWARC BEING THOSE          0.81 OF  31    336  LEAN TOWARD BEING THOSE           0.57 CF  42         25    18
     WHERE THE TOTAL POSITIVE PRESSURE TOWARD             WHERE THE TOTAL POSITIVE PRESSURE TOWARC               6    24
     DEVELCPING RESPCNSIBLE BEHAVIOR                      DEVELOPING RESPONSIBLE BEHAVIOR                  XSQ=     9.02
     IN THE CHILD                                         IN THE CHILD                                     PHI=    0.351
     IS HIGH   (43) B-B-C                                 IS LOW   (32) B-B-C                              XP =   0.0027

337  TEND TC BE THCSE                 0.90 OF  31    337  TEND TO BE THOSE                  0.76 CF  42         28    10
     WHERE THE CHILD'S INFERREC ANXIETY OVER              WHERE THE CHILD'S INFERRED ANXIETY CVER                3    32
     NCN-PERFORMANCE OF RESPONSIBLE BEHAVIOR              NON-PERFORMANCE OF RESPONSIBLE BEHAVIOR          XSQ=    29.01
     IS HIGH   (38) B-B-C                                 IS LOW   (35) B-B-C                              PHI=    0.630
                                                                                                           XP =   0.0000

338  TEND TO BE THCSE                 0.94 OF  31    338  TEND TO BE THOSE                  0.64 CF  42         29    15
     WHERE THE CHILD'S INFERREC ANXIETY OVER              WHERE THE CHILD'S INFERRED ANXIETY OVER                2    27
     PERFCRMANCE CF RESPCNSIBLE BEHAVIOR                  PERFORMANCE OF RESPCNSIBLE BEHAVIOR              XSQ=    22.56
     IS HIGH   (44) B-B-C                                 IS LOW   (29) B-B-C                              PHI=    0.556
                                                                                                           XP =   0.0000

346  TILT TCWARC BEING THOSE          0.68 OF  31    346  TILT TOWARD BEING THCSE           0.64 OF  42         21    15
     WHERE THE CHILD'S INFERREC ANXIETY OVER              WHERE THE CHILD'S INFERRED ANXIETY CVER               10    27
     PERFORMANCE CF SELF-RELIANT BEHAVIOR                 PERFORMANCE OF SELF-RELIANT BEHAVIOR             XSQ=     6.09
     IS HIGH   (37) B-B-C                                 IS LOW   (39) B-B-C                              PHI=    0.289
                                                                                                           XP =   0.0136

347  TILT TCWARD BEING THOSE          0.68 OF  31    347  TILT TOWARD BEING THOSE           0.64 OF  42         21    15
     WHERE THE CHILD'S INFERREC CONFLICT                  WHERE THE CHILD'S INFERRED CCNFLICT                   10    27
     REGARDING SELF-RELIANT BEHAVIOR                      REGARDING SELF-RELIANT BEHAVIOR                  XSQ=     6.09
     IS HIGH   (37) B-B-C                                 IS LOW   (39) B-B-C                              PHI=    0.289
                                                                                                           XP =   0.0136

352  DRIFT MORE TCWARC BEING THCSE  0.76 OF  29      352  DRIFT LESS TCWARD BEING THCSE  0.51 CF  39            22    20
     WHERE THE TOTAL POSITIVE PRESSURE TOWARD             WHERE THE TOTAL POSITIVE PRESSURE TCWARC               7    19
     DEVELCPING OBEDIENT BEHAVICR                         DEVELOPING OBEDIENT BEHAVICR                     XSQ=     3.28
     IN THE CHILD                                         IN THE CHILD                                     PHI=    0.220
     IS HIGH   (44) B-B-C                                 IS HIGH   (44) B-B-C                             XP =   0.0702
```

353	LEAN TCWARD BEING THCSE 0.77 OF 30 WHERE THE CHILD'S INFERREC ANXIETY OVER NCN-PERFCRMANCE CF CBECIENT BEHAVIOR IS HIGH (42) B-B-C	353	LEAN TOWARD BEING THOSE 0.60 CF 40 WHERE THE CHILD-S INFERRED ANXIETY CVER NON-PERFORMANCE OF CBEDIENT BEHAVICR IS LOW (32) B-B-C	23 16 7 24 XSQ= 7.91 PHI= 0.336 XP = 0.0049
354	DRIFT TCWARD BEING THCSE 0.60 OF 30 WHERE THE CHILD'S INFERREC ANXIETY OVER PERFCRMANCE CF CBECIENT BEHAVIOR IS HIGH (36) B-B-C	354	DRIFT TOWARD BEING THOSE 0.64 CF 39 WHERE THE CHILD'S INFERRED ANXIETY OVER PERFORMANCE CF OBEDIENT BEHAVICR IS LOW (37) B-B-C	18 14 12 25 XSQ= 3.05 PHI= 0.210 XP = 0.0807
355	DRIFT TCWARD BEING THCSE 0.60 OF 30 WHERE THE CHILD'S INFERREC CONFLICT REGARDING CBEDIENT BEHAVICR IS HIGH (35) B-B-C	355	DRIFT TOWARD BEING THOSE 0.64 OF 39 WHERE THE CHILD'S INFERRED CCNFLICT REGARDING OBEDIENT BEHAVIOR IS LOW (38) B-B-C	18 14 12 25 XSQ= 3.05 PHI= 0.210 XP = 0.0807
428	DRIFT TCWARD BEING THCSE 0.88 OF 8 WHERE A HIGH GOC, IF PRESENT ANC ACTIVE, DCES NCT SUPPCRT HUMAN MORALITY, RATHER THAN SUPPCRTING IT (26) GES,EA	428	DRIFT TOWARD BEING THOSE 0.67 OF 6 WHERE A HIGH GCD, IF PRESENT AND ACTIVE, SUPPORTS HUMAN MORALITY, RATHER THAN NOT SUPPORTING IT (61) GES,EA	1 4 7 2 XSQ= 2.34 PHI= -0.409 EP = 0.0909
433	TILT TCWARC BEING THCSE 0.67 OF 6 WHERE BELIEF IN REINCARNATION IS PRESENT (10) GES	433	TILT TOWARD BEING THOSE 0.87 CF 15 WHERE BELIEF IN REINCARNATICN IS ABSENT (28) GES	4 2 2 13 XSQ= 3.65 PHI= 0.417 EP = 0.0307
434	TILT TCWARD BEING THOSE 0.77 OF 22 WHERE ASCETICISM IN MOURNING BEHAVIOR IS HIGH (37) JFG	434	TILT TOWARD BEING THOSE 0.62 OF 21 WHERE ASCETICISM IN MOURNING BEHAVIOR IS LOW (30) JFG	17 8 5 13 XSQ= 5.26 PHI= 0.350 XP = 0.0218
435	DRIFT TCWARD BEING THCSE 0.88 OF 8 WHERE ABANDONMENT CF THE HOUSE OF THE CEAD IS NCT PRACTICEC (19) LWS	435	DRIFT TOWARD BEING THOSE 0.67 CF 6 WHERE ABANDONMENT OF THE HCUSE OF THE DEAD IS PRACTICED (12) LWS	1 4 7 2 XSQ= 2.34 PHI= -0.409 EP = 0.0909
455	LEAN TOWARD BEING THOSE 0.76 OF 17 WHERE THE MODE CF THE INCIVICUAL'S CCNTACT WITH THE DIVINE IS NCT CCNCUCIVE TC THE CEVELOPMENT OF THE INDIVIDUAL'S NEEC TC ACHIEVE (19) DCM	455	LEAN TOWARD BEING THOSE 0.68 OF 19 WHERE THE MODE OF THE INDIVIDUAL'S CONTACT WITH THE DIVINE IS CONDUCIVE TC THE DEVELCPMENT CF THE INDIVIDUAL'S NEED TO ACHIEVE (17) DCM	4 13 13 6 XSQ= 5.57 PHI= -0.393 EP = 0.0096
456	DRIFT TCWARD BEING THCSE 0.65 OF 17 WHERE THE INTERNALIZATICN CF THE INDIVIDUAL'S CONTACT WITH THE CIVINE IS NCT CCNCUCIVE TC THE CEVELOPMENT OF THE INDIVICUAL'S NEEC TC ACHIEVE (17) DCM	456	DRIFT TOWARD BEING THCSE 0.68 CF 19 WHERE THE INTERNALIZATICN CF THE INDIVIDUAL'S CONTACT WITH THE DIVINE IS CONDUCIVE TC THE DEVELOPMENT CF THE INDIVIDUAL'S NEED TC ACHIEVE (19) CCM	6 13 11 6 XSQ= 2.73 PHI= -0.276 EP = 0.0933

```
********************************************************************************************************

340  CULTURES                                          340  CULTURES
     WHERE THE TOTAL POSITIVE PRESSURE TOWARD               WHERE THE TOTAL POSITIVE PRESSURE TOWARD
     DEVELOPING NURTURANT BEHAVIOR                          DEVELOPING NURTURANT BEHAVIOR
     IN THE CHILD                                           IN THE CHILD
     IS HIGH  (28) B-B-C                                    IS LOW  (20) B-B-C

BACKGROUND ON PAGE 143                                                         BOTH SUBJECT AND PREDICATE
........................................................................................................

    28  IN LEFT COLUMN

ARANDA     ARAPESH    ASHANTI    AYMARA     BALINESE   CAMAYURA   CHEYENNE   COMANCHE   CROW       IFUGAO
KASKA      LEPCHA     LESU       MANDAN     NAVAHO     NUER       NYAKYUSA   OJIBWA     OMAHA      ONA
PAPAGO     SAMOANS    SOTHO      TALLENSI   TETON      TIKOPIA    WINNEBAGO  YAGUA

    20  IN RIGHT COLUMN

ALORESE    CHAGGA     CHIR-APACHE HANO      KIKUYU     KWAKIUTL   MANUS      MAORI      MARQUESANS MBUNDU
PUKAPUKA   SIRIONO    SWAZI      THONGA     TRUKESE    VENDA      WICHITA    WOGEO      WOLEAIANS  YAHGAN

   352  EXCLUDED BECAUSE UNASCERTAINED

--------------------------------------------------------------------------------------------------------
 44  DRIFT TOWARD BEING THOSE       0.50 OF  24       44  DRIFT TOWARD BEING THOSE       0.80 OF  20          12    16
     WHERE SETTLEMENTS ARE NON-FIXED  (110)               WHERE SETTLEMENTS ARE FIXED  (222)                  12     4
                                                                                                        XSQ=    3.05
                                                                                                        PHI=  -0.263
                                                                                                        XP =  0.0810

 55  DRIFT TOWARD BEING THOSE       0.70 OF  10       55  DRIFT TOWARD BEING THOSE       0.69 OF  13           7     4
     WHERE FOOD PRODUCTION IS BY                          WHERE FOOD PRODUCTION IS BY                          3     9
     INTENSIVE AGRICULTURE, RATHER THAN BY                SIMPLE AGRICULTURE, RATHER THAN BY            XSQ=    2.09
     SIMPLE AGRICULTURE  (91)                             INTENSIVE AGRICULTURE  (101)                  PHI=   0.302
                                                                                                        EP =  0.0995

 56  TILT TOWARD BEING THOSE        0.63 OF   8       56  TILT TOWARD BEING THOSE        0.90 OF  10           3     9
     WHERE FOOD PRODUCTION IS BY                          WHERE FOOD PRODUCTION IS BY                          5     1
     INCIPIENT FOOD PRODUCTION, RATHER THAN BY            SIMPLE AGRICULTURE, RATHER THAN BY            XSQ=    3.40
     SIMPLE AGRICULTURE  (46)                             INCIPIENT FOOD PRODUCTION  (101)              PHI=  -0.435
                                                                                                        EP =  0.0430

 88  LEAN TOWARD BEING THOSE        0.58 OF  19       88  LEAN TOWARD BEING THOSE        0.93 OF  15          11     1
     WHERE, IF A HEADMANSHIP IS PRESENT,                  WHERE, IF A HEADMANSHIP IS PRESENT,                  8    14
     SUCCESSION IS NON-HEREDITARY  (106)                  SUCCESSION IS HEREDITARY  (165)               XSQ=    7.52
                                                                                                        PHI=   0.470
                                                                                                        EP =  0.0031

120  DRIFT TOWARD BEING THOSE       0.80 OF  10      120  DRIFT TOWARD BEING THOSE       0.75 OF   4           8     1
     WHERE THE CRAFT SPECIALIZATION SCORE                 WHERE THE CRAFT SPECIALIZATION SCORE                 2     3
     IS HIGH OR MEDIUM  (36) WME                          IS LOW  (17) WME                              XSQ=    1.75
                                                                                                        PHI=   0.354
                                                                                                        EP =  0.0949
```

135	TILT TOWARD BEING THOSE WHERE INDIVIDUAL OWNERSHIP OF ECONOMICALLY SIGNIFICANT PROPERTY IS PRESENT (24) GES	0.82 OF 11	135	IN ALL CASES ARE THOSE WHERE INDIVIDUAL OWNERSHIP OF ECONOMICALLY SIGNIFICANT PROPERTY IS NEGLIGIBLE OR ABSENT (14) GES	1.00 OF 3	9 0 2 3 XSQ= 3.77 PHI= 0.519 EP = 0.0275
176	DRIFT TOWARD BEING THOSE WHERE THE COMMUNITY IS OTHER THAN A CLAN-COMMUNITY OR A COMMUNITY STRUCTURED OR SEGMENTED ON A CLAN BASIS (213)	0.59 OF 27	176	DRIFT TOWARD BEING THOSE WHERE THE COMMUNITY IS A CLAN-COMMUNITY OR A COMMUNITY STRUCTURED OR SEGMENTED ON A CLAN BASIS (169)	0.70 OF 20	11 14 16 6 XSQ= 2.86 PHI= -0.247 XP = 0.0907
183	DRIFT LESS TOWARD BEING THOSE WHERE THE LARGEST NON-COGNATIC KIN GROUP IS SMALLER THAN A MOEITY, I. E., A PHRATRY OR SIB OR LINEAGE (218)	0.63 OF 19	183	DRIFT MORE TOWARD BEING THOSE WHERE THE LARGEST NON-COGNATIC KIN GROUP IS SMALLER THAN A MOEITY, I. E., A PHRATRY OR SIB OR LINEAGE (218)	0.93 OF 14	7 1 12 13 XSQ= 2.42 PHI= 0.271 EP = 0.0982
184	TILT LESS TOWARD BEING THOSE WHERE THE LARGEST NON-COGNATIC KIN GROUP IS SMALLER THAN A PHRATRY, I. E. A SIB OR LINEAGE (175)	0.53 OF 19	184	TILT MORE TOWARD BEING THOSE WHERE THE LARGEST NON-COGNATIC KIN GROUP IS SMALLER THAN A PHRATRY, I. E. A SIB OR LINEAGE (175)	0.93 OF 14	9 1 10 13 XSQ= 4.42 PHI= 0.366 EP = 0.0209
318	LEAN TOWARD BEING THOSE WHERE THE OVERALL INDULGENCE OF THE INFANT IS HIGH (40) B-B-C	0.73 OF 26	318	LEAN TOWARD BEING THOSE WHERE THE OVERALL INDULGENCE OF THE INFANT IS LOW (31) B-B-C	0.70 OF 20	19 6 7 14 XSQ= 6.81 PHI= 0.385 XP = 0.0091
320	DRIFT TOWARD BEING THOSE WHERE THE DEGREE OF REDUCTION OF THE INFANT'S DRIVES IS HIGH (45) B-B-C	0.80 OF 25	320	DRIFT TOWARD BEING THOSE WHERE THE DEGREE OF REDUCTION OF THE INFANT'S DRIVES IS LOW (24) B-B-C	0.53 OF 19	20 9 5 10 XSQ= 3.77 PHI= 0.293 XP = 0.0523
324	TILT TOWARD BEING THOSE WHERE THE PAIN INFLICTED ON THE INFANT BY THE NURTURANT AGENT IS LOW OR NEGLIGIBLE (32) B-B-C	0.64 OF 25	324	TILT TOWARD BEING THOSE WHERE THE PAIN INFLICTED ON THE INFANT BY THE NURTURANT AGENT IS HIGH (34) B-B-C	0.70 OF 20	9 14 16 6 XSQ= 3.87 PHI= -0.293 XP = 0.0492
372	DRIFT TOWARD BEING THOSE WHERE MALE INITIATION RITES ARE ABSENT (63) ASA	0.68 OF 22	372	DRIFT TOWARD BEING THOSE WHERE MALE INITIATION RITES ARE PRESENT (48) ASA	0.64 OF 14	7 9 15 5 XSQ= 2.46 PHI= -0.261 EP = 0.0874
385	TILT MORE TOWARD BEING THOSE WHERE SEXUAL EXPRESSION BY THE YOUNG IS SEMI-RESTRICTED OR PERMITTED (64) F-B	0.93 OF 15	385	TILT LESS TOWARD BEING THOSE WHERE SEXUAL EXPRESSION BY THE YOUNG IS SEMI-RESTRICTED OR PERMITTED (64) F-B	0.56 OF 16	1 7 14 9 XSQ= 3.79 PHI= -0.350 EP = 0.0373

405	TILT TOWARD BEING THOSE WHERE EXPLANATIONS OF ILLNESS OF A DEPENDENCE NATURE ARE ABSENT (27) W-C	0.71 OF 14	405	TILT TOWARD BEING THOSE WHERE EXPLANATIONS OF ILLNESS OF A DEPENDENCE NATURE ARE PRESENT (34) W-C	0.77 OF 13	4 10 10 3 XSQ= 4.52 PHI= -0.409 EP = 0.0213
425	DRIFT TOWARD BEING THOSE WHERE SUPERNATURALS ARE MAINLY BENEVOLENT, RATHER THAN AGGRESSIVE (16) L-T-W	0.63 OF 16	425	DRIFT TOWARD BEING THOSE WHERE SUPERNATURALS ARE MAINLY AGGRESSIVE, RATHER THAN BENEVOLENT (20) L-T-W	0.77 OF 13	10 3 6 10 XSQ= 3.05 PHI= 0.325 EP = 0.0608

341 CULTURES
WHERE THE CHILD'S INFERRED ANXIETY OVER
NON-PERFORMANCE OF NURTURANT BEHAVIOR
IS HIGH (30) B-B-C

341 CULTURES
WHERE THE CHILD'S INFERRED ANXIETY OVER
NON-PERFORMANCE OF NURTURANT BEHAVIOR
IS LOW (16) B-B-C

BACKGROUND ON PAGE 143

BOTH SUBJECT AND PREDICATE

30 IN LEFT COLUMN

ALORESE	ARANDA	ARAPESH	ASHANTI	AYMARA	CAMAYURA	CHAGGA	CHEYENNE	COMANCHE	IFUGAO
KASKA	KWAKIUTL	LEPCHA	LESU	MAORI	NAVAHO	NYAKYUSA	OJIBWA	OMAHA	ONA
PAPAGO	SAMCANS	SOTHO	SWAZI	TALLENSI	TETON	TRUKESE	VENDA	WICHITA	WOGEO

16 IN RIGHT COLUMN

BALINESE	CHIR-APACHE	CROW	KIKUYU	KURTATCHI	MANDAN	MANUS	MBUNDU	NUER	PUKAPUKA
THONGA	TIKOPIA	WINNEBAGO	WOLEAIANS	YAGUA	YAHGAN				

354 EXCLUDED BECAUSE UNASCERTAINED

73	TILT LESS TOWARD BEING THOSE WHERE WEAVING IS ABSENT (130)	0.54 OF 24	73	TILT MORE TOWARD BEING THOSE WHERE WEAVING IS ABSENT (130)	0.92 OF 13		11 1 13 12 XSQ= 3.99 PHI= 0.328 EP = 0.0272
78	DRIFT TOWARD BEING THOSE WHERE THE WRITING SYSTEM IS ALPHABETIC-OR-PHONETIC, OR MNEMONIC, RATHER THAN BEING ABSENT (36) JMH	0.86 OF 7	78	DRIFT TOWARD BEING THOSE WHERE A WRITING SYSTEM IS ABSENT, RATHER THAN BEING PRESENT IN EITHER ALPHABETIC-OR-PHONETIC FORM OR MNEMONIC FORM (18) JMH	0.67 OF 9		6 3 1 6 XSQ= 2.52 PHI= 0.397 EP = 0.0601
120	DRIFT TOWARD BEING THOSE WHERE THE CRAFT SPECIALIZATION SCORE IS HIGH OR MEDIUM (36) WME	0.80 OF 10	120	DRIFT TOWARD BEING THOSE WHERE THE CRAFT SPECIALIZATION SCORE IS LOW (17) WME	0.75 OF 4		8 1 2 3 XSQ= 1.75 PHI= 0.354 EP = 0.0949
133	DRIFT TOWARD BEING THOSE WHERE CONTRACTED DEBTS ARE SIGNIFICANTLY PRESENT (17) GES	0.57 OF 7	133	IN ALL CASES ARE THOSE WHERE CONTRACTED DEBTS ARE MODERATELY PRESENT OR ABSENT (17) GES	1.00 OF 5		4 0 3 5 XSQ= 2.10 PHI= 0.418 EP = 0.0808
137	DRIFT TOWARD BEING THOSE WHERE INVIDIOUS DISPLAY OF WEALTH IS STRONGLY EMPHASIZED (37) PES	0.64 OF 22	137	DRIFT TOWARD BEING THOSE WHERE INVIDIOUS DISPLAY OF WEALTH IS MODERATELY, LITTLE, OR NEGATIVELY EMPHASIZED (52) PES	0.75 OF 12		14 3 8 9 XSQ= 3.22 PHI= 0.308 EP = 0.0707

259	DRIFT TOWARD BEING THOSE 0.62 OF 13 WHERE THE SEVERITY OF MOTHER-IN-LAW AVOIDANCE IS LOW (20) WNS	259	DRIFT TOWARD BEING THOSE 0.86 OF 7 WHERE THE SEVERITY OF MOTHER-IN-LAW AVOIDANCE IS HIGH (26) WNS	5 6 8 1 XSQ= 2.42 PHI= -0.348 EP = 0.0703
313	TILT TOWARD BEING THOSE 0.65 OF 17 WHERE AGGRESSION SOCIALIZATION ANXIETY IS HIGH (26) W-C	313	TILT TOWARD BEING THOSE 0.88 OF 8 WHERE AGGRESSION SOCIALIZATION ANXIETY IS LOW (28) W-C	11 1 6 7 XSQ= 4.03 PHI= 0.402 EP = 0.0302
317	DRIFT TOWARD BEING THOSE 0.56 OF 27 WHERE DISPLAY OF AFFECTION TOWARD THE INFANT IS LOW (29) B-B-C	317	DRIFT TOWARD BEING THOSE 0.77 OF 13 WHERE DISPLAY OF AFFECTION TOWARD THE INFANT IS HIGH (39) B-B-C	12 10 15 3 XSQ= 2.54 PHI= -0.252 EP = 0.0896
327	TILT TOWARD BEING THOSE 0.68 OF 25 WHERE THE AGE OF THE INFANT AT TIME OF REDUCED CONTACT WITH MOTHER IS HIGHER THAN TWO YEARS (28) B-B-C	327	TILT TOWARD BEING THOSE 0.77 OF 13 WHERE THE AGE OF THE INFANT AT TIME OF REDUCED CONTACT WITH MOTHER IS TWO YEARS OR LOWER (27) B-B-C	17 3 8 10 XSQ= 5.24 PHI= 0.371 EP = 0.0156
338	TILT TOWARD BEING THOSE 0.67 OF 30 WHERE THE CHILD'S INFERRED ANXIETY OVER PERFORMANCE OF RESPONSIBLE BEHAVIOR IS HIGH (44) B-B-C	338	TILT TOWARD BEING THOSE 0.69 OF 16 WHERE THE CHILD'S INFERRED ANXIETY OVER PERFORMANCE OF RESPONSIBLE BEHAVIOR IS LOW (29) B-B-C	20 5 10 11 XSQ= 3.94 PHI= 0.293 XP = 0.0470
343	DRIFT TOWARD BEING THOSE 0.73 OF 30 WHERE THE CHILD'S INFERRED CONFLICT REGARDING NURTURANT BEHAVIOR IS HIGH (29) B-B-C	343	DRIFT TOWARD BEING THOSE 0.56 OF 16 WHERE THE CHILD'S INFERRED CONFLICT REGARDING NURTURANT BEHAVIOR IS LOW (18) B-B-C	22 7 8 9 XSQ= 2.75 PHI= 0.245 XP = 0.0971
405	DRIFT TOWARD BEING THOSE 0.65 OF 17 WHERE EXPLANATIONS OF ILLNESS OF A DEPENDENCE NATURE ARE ABSENT (27) W-C	405	DRIFT TOWARD BEING THOSE 0.75 OF 8 WHERE EXPLANATIONS OF ILLNESS OF A DEPENDENCE NATURE ARE PRESENT (34) W-C	6 6 11 2 XSQ= 2.03 PHI= -0.285 EP = 0.0968
443	DRIFT TOWARD BEING THOSE 0.53 OF 17 WHERE OVERALL FEAR OF OTHERS IS HIGH (31) W-C	443	DRIFT TOWARD BEING THOSE 0.88 OF 8 WHERE OVERALL FEAR OF OTHERS IS LOW (30) W-C	9 1 8 7 XSQ= 2.21 PHI= 0.298 EP = 0.0875
456	DRIFT TOWARD BEING THOSE 0.60 OF 15 WHERE THE INTERNALIZATION OF THE INDIVIDUAL'S CONTACT WITH THE DIVINE IS NOT CONDUCIVE TO THE DEVELOPMENT OF THE INDIVIDUAL'S NEED TO ACHIEVE (17) DCM	456	DRIFT TOWARD BEING THOSE 0.80 OF 10 WHERE THE INTERNALIZATION OF THE INDIVIDUAL'S CONTACT WITH THE DIVINE IS CONDUCIVE TO THE DEVELOPMENT OF THE INDIVIDUAL'S NEED TO ACHIEVE (19) DCM	6 8 9 2 XSQ= 2.44 PHI= -0.313 EP = 0.0992

342	CULTURES WHERE THE CHILD'S INFERRED ANXIETY OVER PERFORMANCE OF NURTURANT BEHAVIOR IS HIGH (18) B-B-C	342	CULTURES WHERE THE CHILD'S INFERRED ANXIETY OVER PERFORMANCE OF NURTURANT BEHAVIOR IS LOW (28) B-B-C

BACKGROUND ON PAGE 143 — BOTH SUBJECT AND PREDICATE

18 IN LEFT COLUMN

ALORESE, ARANDA, ARAPESH, ASHANTI, AYMARA, BALINESE, CHAGGA, CROW, IFUGAO, KWAKIUTL, MAORI, PUKAPUKA, SAMOANS, SIRIONO, SWAZI, THONGA, TRUKESE, WOGEO

28 IN RIGHT COLUMN

CAMAYURA, CHEYENNE, CHIR-APACHE, COMANCHE, KASKA, KIKUYU, LEPCHA, LESU, MANDAN, MANUS, MBUNDU, NAVAHO, NUER, NYAKYUSA, OJIBWA, OMAHA, ONA, PAPAGO, SOTHO, TALLENSI, TETON, TIKOPIA, VENDA, WICHITA, WINNEBAGO, WOLEAIANS, YAGUA, YAHGAN

354 EXCLUDED BECAUSE UNASCERTAINED

6	LEAN TOWARD BEING THOSE LOCATED IN THE INSULAR PACIFIC (70)	0.56 OF 18	6	LEAN TOWARD BEING THOSE LOCATED OUTSIDE OF THE INSULAR PACIFIC (330)	0.86 OF 28	10 4 / 8 24 / XSQ= 6.97 / PHI= 0.389 / XP = 0.0083
8	DRIFT MORE TOWARD BEING THOSE LOCATED OUTSIDE OF NORTH AMERICA (330)	0.89 OF 18	8	DRIFT LESS TOWARD BEING THOSE LOCATED OUTSIDE OF NORTH AMERICA (330)	0.57 OF 28	2 12 / 16 16 / XSQ= 3.82 / PHI= -0.288 / XP = 0.0505
14	TILT TOWARD BEING THOSE WHERE THE LATITUDE IS LESS THAN THIRTY DEGREES (281)	0.83 OF 18	14	TILT TOWARD BEING THOSE WHERE THE LATITUDE IS THIRTY DEGREES OR GREATER (119)	0.50 OF 28	3 14 / 15 14 / XSQ= 3.89 / PHI= -0.291 / XP = 0.0485
44	DRIFT TOWARD BEING THOSE WHERE SETTLEMENTS ARE FIXED (222)	0.82 OF 17	44	DRIFT TOWARD BEING THOSE WHERE SETTLEMENTS ARE NON-FIXED (110)	0.52 OF 25	14 12 / 3 13 / XSQ= 3.71 / PHI= 0.297 / XP = 0.0540
48	DRIFT TOWARD BEING THOSE WHERE THE FOOD SUPPLY IS SECURE, AND FOOD SHORTAGES ARE RARE OR OCCASIONAL (38) MGW	0.67 OF 15	48	DRIFT TOWARD BEING THOSE WHERE THE FOOD SUPPLY IS NOT SECURE, AND FOOD SHORTAGES ARE FREQUENT OR ANNUAL (41) MGW	0.65 OF 20	10 7 / 5 13 / XSQ= 2.29 / PHI= 0.256 / EP = 0.0922

55	DRIFT TOWARD BEING THOSE WHERE FOOD PRODUCTION IS BY SIMPLE AGRICULTURE, RATHER THAN BY INTENSIVE AGRICULTURE (101)	0.73 OF 11	55	DRIFT TOWARD BEING THOSE WHERE FOOD PRODUCTION IS BY INTENSIVE AGRICULTURE, RATHER THAN BY SIMPLE AGRICULTURE (91)	0.70 OF 10	3 7 8 3 XSQ= 2.31 PHI= -0.332 EP = 0.0861
56	TILT TOWARD BEING THOSE WHERE FOOD PRODUCTION IS BY SIMPLE AGRICULTURE, RATHER THAN BY INCIPIENT FOOD PRODUCTION (101)	0.89 OF 9	56	TILT TOWARD BEING THOSE WHERE FOOD PRODUCTION IS BY INCIPIENT FOOD PRODUCTION, RATHER THAN BY SIMPLE AGRICULTURE (46)	0.63 OF 8	8 3 1 5 XSQ= 2.91 PHI= 0.413 EP = 0.0498
63	DRIFT TOWARD BEING THOSE WHERE HUSBANDRY, IF PRESENT, IS PRINCIPALLY IN THE FORM OF PIGS, SHEEP, OR GOATS, RATHER THAN BOVINE, EQUINE, CAMEL-LIKE, OR DEER-LIKE ANIMALS (74)	0.62 OF 13	63	DRIFT TOWARD BEING THOSE WHERE HUSBANDRY, IF PRESENT, IS PRINCIPALLY IN THE FORM OF BOVINE, EQUINE, CAMEL-LIKE, OR DEER-LIKE ANIMALS, RATHER THAN PIGS, SHEEP, OR GOATS (152)	0.76 OF 17	5 13 8 4 XSQ= 2.99 PHI= -0.316 EP = 0.0610
88	TILT TOWARD BEING THOSE WHERE, IF A HEADMANSHIP IS PRESENT, SUCCESSION IS HEREDITARY (165)	0.86 OF 14	88	TILT TOWARD BEING THOSE WHERE, IF A HEADMANSHIP IS PRESENT, SUCCESSION IS NON-HEREDITARY (106)	0.53 OF 19	2 10 12 9 XSQ= 3.60 PHI= -0.330 EP = 0.0328
102	DRIFT TOWARD BEING THOSE WHERE CLASS STRATIFICATION IS PRESENT (203)	0.61 OF 18	102	DRIFT TOWARD BEING THOSE WHERE CLASS STRATIFICATION IS ABSENT (180)	0.71 OF 28	11 8 7 20 XSQ= 3.54 PHI= 0.277 XP = 0.0600
301	TILT LESS TOWARD BEING THOSE WHERE THE POST-PARTUM SEX TABOO LASTS LONGER THAN ONE MONTH (96)	0.58 OF 12	301	IN ALL CASES ARE THOSE WHERE THE POST-PARTUM SEX TABOO LASTS LONGER THAN ONE MONTH (96)	1.00 OF 11	7 11 5 0 XSQ= 3.66 PHI= -0.399 EP = 0.0373
312	TILT TOWARD BEING THOSE WHERE DEPENDENCE SOCIALIZATION ANXIETY IS HIGH (24) W-C	0.77 OF 13	312	TILT TOWARD BEING THOSE WHERE DEPENDENCE SOCIALIZATION ANXIETY IS LOW (23) W-C	0.73 OF 11	10 3 3 8 XSQ= 4.09 PHI= 0.413 EP = 0.0377
318	TILT TOWARD BEING THOSE WHERE THE OVERALL INDULGENCE OF THE INFANT IS LOW (31) B-B-C	0.67 OF 18	318	TILT TOWARD BEING THOSE WHERE THE OVERALL INDULGENCE OF THE INFANT IS HIGH (40) B-B-C	0.69 OF 26	6 18 12 8 XSQ= 4.18 PHI= -0.308 XP = 0.0410
320	DRIFT TOWARD BEING THOSE WHERE THE DEGREE OF REDUCTION OF THE INFANT'S DRIVES IS LOW (24) B-B-C	0.50 OF 18	320	DRIFT TOWARD BEING THOSE WHERE THE DEGREE OF REDUCTION OF THE INFANT'S DRIVES IS HIGH (45) B-B-C	0.79 OF 24	9 19 9 5 XSQ= 2.73 PHI= -0.255 XP = 0.0982

324	DRIFT TCWARD BEING THCSE 0.71 OF 17 WHERE THE PAIN INFLICTEC CN THE INFANT BY THE NURTURANT AGENT IS HIGH (34) B-B-C	324	DRIFT TOWARD BEING THOSE 0.62 OF 26 WHERE THE PAIN INFLICTED ON THE INFANT BY THE NURTURANT AGENT IS LOW OR NEGLIGIBLE (32) B-B-C	12 10 5 16 XSQ= 3.06 PHI= 0.267 XP = 0.0804
326	LEAN TCWARD BEING THCSE 0.76 OF 17 WHERE THE INFERRED TRANSITION ANXIETY BETWEEN INFANCY ANC CHILCHCOC IS HIGH (32) B-B-C	326	LEAN TOWARD BEING THOSE 0.69 OF 26 WHERE THE INFERRED TRANSITICN ANXIETY BETWEEN INFANCY AND CHILDHCCD IS LOW (35) B-B-C	13 8 4 18 XSQ= 6.86 PHI= 0.399 XP = 0.0088
343	TILT TCWARD BEING THCSE 0.83 OF 18 WHERE THE CHILD'S INFERREC CONFLICT REGARDING NURTURANT BEHAVICR IS HIGH (29) B-B-C	343	TILT TOWARD BEING THOSE 0.50 CF 28 WHERE THE CHILD'S INFERRED CCNFLICT REGARDING NURTURANT BEHAVICR IS LOW (18) B-B-C	15 14 3 14 XSQ= 3.89 PHI= 0.291 XP = 0.0485
354	LEAN TCWARD BEING THCSE 0.82 OF 17 WHERE THE CHILD'S INFERREC ANXIETY OVER PERFORMANCE CF CBECIENT BEHAVIOR IS HIGH (36) B-B-C	354	LEAN TOWARD BEING THOSE 0.64 OF 28 WHERE THE CHILD'S INFERRED ANXIETY OVER PERFORMANCE OF OBEDIENT BEHAVIOR IS LOW (37) B-B-C	14 10 3 18 XSQ= 7.47 PHI= 0.407 XP = 0.0063
355	TILT TCWARC BEING THOSE 0.76 OF 17 WHERE THE CHILD'S INFERREC CONFLICT REGARDING CBEDIENT BEHAVICR IS HIGH (35) B-B-C	355	TILT TOWARD BEING THOSE 0.64 CF 28 WHERE THE CHILD'S INFERRED CCNFLICT REGARDING OBEDIENT BEHAVIOR IS LOW (38) B-B-C	13 10 4 18 XSQ= 5.50 PHI= 0.349 XP = 0.0191
427	DRIFT TCWARD BEING THCSE 0.88 OF 8 WHERE A HIGH GCC, IF PRESENT, IS INACTIVE, RATHER THAN ACTIVE (69) GES,EA	427	DRIFT TOWARD BEING THOSE 0.60 OF 10 WHERE A HIGH GOD, IF PRESENT, IS ACTIVE, RATHER THAN INACTIVE (87) GES,EA	1 6 7 4 XSQ= 2.46 PHI= -0.369 EP = 0.0656
438	IN ALL CASES ARE THCSE 1.00 OF 10 WHERE CTHER-WCRLCLY FEARS OF GHCSTS CR SPIRITS ARE GREATER THAN THIS-WCRLDLY FEARS OF HUMANS CR ANIMALS (27) W-C,JFC	438	TILT TOWARD BEING THOSE 0.50 OF 8 WHERE THIS-WORLDLY FEARS OF HUMANS OR ANIMALS ARE GREATER THAN OTHER-WORLDLY FEARS OF GHOSTS OR SPIRITS (17) W-C,JFG	10 4 0 4 XSQ= 3.86 PHI= 0.463 EP = 0.0229
456	TILT TCWARD BEING THCSE 0.86 OF 7 WHERE THE INTERNALIZATICN CF THE INDIVIDUAL'S CONTACT WITH THE DIVINE IS NCT CCNDUCIVE TC THE DEVELOPMENT OF THE INDIVIDUAL'S NEEC TO ACHIEVE (17) DCM	456	TILT TOWARD BEING THOSE 0.71 OF 17 WHERE THE INTERNALIZATICN CF THE INDIVIDUAL'S CONTACT WITH THE DIVINE IS CONDUCIVE TO THE DEVELCPMENT OF THE INDIVIDUAL'S NEED TC ACHIEVE (19) CCM	1 12 6 5 XSQ= 4.27 PHI= -0.422 EP = 0.0233
480	TILT TCWARC BEING THOSE 0.67 OF 9 WHERE CCMPLEXITY CF ARTISTIC CESIGN IS HIGH (14) HB	480	IN ALL CASES ARE THCSE 1.00 OF 7 WHERE COMPLEXITY OF ARTISTIC DESIGN IS LOW (15) HB	6 0 3 7 XSQ= 4.89 PHI= 0.553 EP = 0.0114

343	CULTURES WHERE THE CHILD'S INFERREC CONFLICT REGARDING NURTURANT BEHAVIOR IS HIGH (29) B-B-C	343	CULTURES WHERE THE CHILD'S INFERRED CONFLICT REGARDING NURTURANT BEHAVIOR IS LOW (18) B-B-C

BACKGROUND ON PAGE 143 BOTH SUBJECT AND PREDICATE

29 IN LEFT COLUMN

ALORESE	ARANDA	ARAPESH	ASHANTI	AYMARA	BALINESE	CHAGGA	CHEYENNE	COMANCHE	CROW
IFUGAO	KASKA	MAORI	NAVAHO	NUER	NYAKYUSA	OMAHA	ONA	PAPAGO	PUKAPUKA
SAMOANS	SOTHO	SWAZI	TRUKESE	WICHITA	WINNEBAGO	WOGEO	WOLEAIANS	YAHGAN	

18 IN RIGHT COLUMN

CAMAYURA	CHIR-APACHE	KIKUYU	KURTATCHI	KWAKIUTL	LEPCHA	LESU	MANDAN	MANUS	MBUNDU
OJIBWA	SIRIONO	TALLENSI	TETON	THONGA	TIKOPIA	VENDA	YAGUA		

353 EXCLUDED BECAUSE UNASCERTAINED

36	DRIFT TOWARD BEING THOSE WHERE THE NATURAL ENVIRONMENT IS 'VERY HARSH,' OR SUB-TROPICAL BUSH, OR TEMPERATE GRASSLAND (108) FWM	0.52 OF 29	36	DRIFT TOWARD BEING THOSE WHERE THE NATURAL ENVIRONMENT IS OTHER THAN 'VERY HARSH,' OR SUB-TROPICAL BUSH, OR TEMPERATE GRASSLAND (292) FWM	0.78 OF 18	15 4 14 14 XSQ= 2.88 PHI= 0.248 XP = 0.0896
74	TILT TOWARD BEING THOSE WHERE POTTERY IS ABSENT (93)	0.67 OF 21	74	TILT TOWARD BEING THOSE WHERE POTTERY IS PRESENT (145)	0.69 OF 16	7 11 14 5 XSQ= 3.25 PHI= -0.296 EP = 0.0489
282	DRIFT TOWARD BEING THOSE WHERE THE STRENGTH OF DESIRE FOR CHILDREN IS HIGH (16) BCA	0.62 OF 13	282	DRIFT TOWARD BEING THOSE WHERE THE STRENGTH OF DESIRE FOR CHILDREN IS LOW OR ABSENT (20) BCA	0.78 OF 9	8 2 5 7 XSQ= 1.92 PHI= 0.295 EP = 0.0991
286	TILT TOWARD BEING THOSE WHERE THE NUMBER OF FOOD TABOOS DURING PREGNANCY IS LOW OR ABSENT (14) BCA	0.55 OF 11	286	IN ALL CASES ARE THOSE WHERE THE NUMBER OF FOOD TABOOS DURING PREGNANCY IS HIGH (20) BCA	1.00 OF 8	5 8 6 0 XSQ= 4.10 PHI= -0.465 EP = 0.0181
330	LEAN TOWARD BEING THOSE WHERE THE AGE OF THE INFANT AT TIME OF WEANING IS LOWER THAN 2.5 YEARS (36) B-B-C	0.64 OF 28	330	LEAN TOWARD BEING THOSE WHERE THE AGE OF THE INFANT AT TIME OF WEANING IS 2.5 YEARS OR HIGHER (34) B-B-C	0.81 OF 16	10 13 18 3 XSQ= 6.74 PHI= -0.391 XP = 0.0095

341	DRIFT TOWARD BEING THOSE WHERE THE CHILD'S INFERRED ANXIETY OVER NON-PERFORMANCE OF NURTURANT BEHAVIOR IS HIGH (30) B-B-C	0.76 OF 29	341	DRIFT TOWARD BEING THOSE WHERE THE CHILD'S INFERRED ANXIETY OVER NON-PERFORMANCE OF NURTURANT BEHAVIOR IS LOW (16) B-B-C	0.53 OF 17	22 8 / 7 9 / XSQ= 2.75 / PHI= 0.245 / XP = 0.0971
342	TILT TOWARD BEING THOSE WHERE THE CHILD'S INFERRED ANXIETY OVER PERFORMANCE OF NURTURANT BEHAVIOR IS HIGH (18) B-B-C	0.52 OF 29	342	TILT TOWARD BEING THOSE WHERE THE CHILD'S INFERRED ANXIETY OVER PERFORMANCE OF NURTURANT BEHAVIOR IS LOW (28) B-B-C	0.82 OF 17	15 3 / 14 14 / XSQ= 3.89 / PHI= 0.291 / XP = 0.0485
358	IN ALL CASES ARE THOSE WHERE ADOLESCENT PEER GROUPS ARE PRESENT IN A SETTING OF WORK AND PUBLIC GATHERINGS AND LEISURE, OR OF PUBLIC GATHERINGS AND LEISURE, OR OF LEISURE ONLY (41) JKH	1.00 OF 9	358	DRIFT LESS TOWARD BEING THOSE WHERE ADOLESCENT PEER GROUPS ARE PRESENT IN A SETTING OF WORK AND PUBLIC GATHERINGS AND LEISURE, OR OF PUBLIC GATHERINGS AND LEISURE, OR OF LEISURE ONLY (41) JKH	0.60 OF 10	9 6 / 0 4 / XSQ= 2.47 / PHI= 0.361 / EP = 0.0867
400	TILT TOWARD BEING THOSE WHERE HOMOSEXUAL ACTIVITY IS PERMITTED (36) F-B	0.69 OF 13	400	TILT TOWARD BEING THOSE WHERE HOMOSEXUAL ACTIVITY IS PROHIBITED (22) F-B	0.82 OF 11	4 9 / 9 2 / XSQ= 4.37 / PHI= -0.427 / EP = 0.0188
428	IN ALL CASES ARE THOSE WHERE A HIGH GOD, IF PRESENT AND ACTIVE, SUPPORTS HUMAN MORALITY, RATHER THAN NOT SUPPORTING IT (61) GES,EA	1.00 OF 4	428	IN ALL CASES ARE THOSE WHERE A HIGH GOD, IF PRESENT AND ACTIVE, DOES NOT SUPPORT HUMAN MORALITY, RATHER THAN SUPPORTING IT (26) GES,EA	1.00 OF 3	4 0 / 0 3 / XSQ= 3.51 / PHI= 0.708 / EP = 0.0286
438	IN ALL CASES ARE THOSE WHERE OTHER-WORLDLY FEARS OF GHOSTS OR SPIRITS ARE GREATER THAN THIS-WORLDLY FEARS OF HUMANS OR ANIMALS (27) W-C,JFG	1.00 OF 10	438	TILT LESS TOWARD BEING THOSE WHERE OTHER-WORLDLY FEARS OF GHOSTS OR SPIRITS ARE GREATER THAN THIS-WORLDLY FEARS OF HUMANS OR ANIMALS (27) W-C,JFG	0.56 OF 9	10 5 / 0 4 / XSQ= 3.27 / PHI= 0.415 / EP = 0.0325

****

344	CULTURES WHERE THE TOTAL POSITIVE PRESSURE TOWARD DEVELOPING SELF-RELIANT BEHAVIOR IN THE CHILD IS HIGH (36) B-B-C	344	CULTURES WHERE THE TOTAL POSITIVE PRESSURE TOWARD DEVELOPING SELF-RELIANT BEHAVIOR IN THE CHILD IS LOW (40) B-B-C

BACKGROUND ON PAGE 143 — BOTH SUBJECT AND PREDICATE

....

36 IN LEFT COLUMN

ALORESE	ARANDA	ARAUCANIANS	BALINESE	CHENCHU	CHEYENNE	CHIR-APACHE	CHUKCHEE	COMANCHE	CROW
CUNA	FON	GANDA	IFUGAO	JIVARO	KASKA	KURTATCHI	KWAKIUTL	LAMBA	MANUS
MAORI	MARQUESANS	MASAI	NYAKYUSA	OJIBWA	OMAHA	SIRIONO	SOTHO	SWAZI	THONGA
TIV	TROBRIAND	TRUKESE	TURKANA	VENDA	YORUBA				

40 IN RIGHT COLUMN

AINU	ARAPESH	ASHANTI	AYMARA	AZANDE	CAMAYURA	CHAGGA	HANO	KIKUYU	KORYAK
LAU	LEPCHA	LESU	MANDAN	MBUNDU	MURNGIN	NAVAHO	NUER	ONA	ONTONG-JAVA
PAPAGO	PUKAPUKA	SAMOANS	SHERENTE	TALLENSI	TANALA	TENETEHARA	TETON	TIKOPIA	TIMBIRA
TUCUNA	TUPINAMBA	WICHITA	WINNEBAGO	WOGEO	WOLEAIANS	YAGUA	YAHGAN	YAKUT	ZUNI

324 EXCLUDED BECAUSE UNASCERTAINED

	Left column		Right column	
47	DRIFT TOWARD BEING THOSE 0.83 OF 12 WHERE, IF SETTLEMENTS ARE NON-FIXED, MOVEMENT IS NOMADIC, RATHER THAN NON-NOMADIC (72)	47	DRIFT TOWARD BEING THOSE 0.58 OF 12 WHERE, IF SETTLEMENTS ARE NON-FIXED, MOVEMENT IS NON-NOMADIC, RATHER THAN NOMADIC (38)	10 5 2 7 XSQ= 2.84 PHI= 0.344 EP = 0.0894
94	DRIFT LESS TOWARD BEING THOSE 0.85 OF 34 WHERE THE HIERARCHY OF NATIONAL JURISDICTION HAS TWO, ONE, OR NO LEVELS (296) GES,EA	94	IN ALL CASES ARE THOSE 1.00 OF 37 WHERE THE HIERARCHY OF NATIONAL JURISDICTION HAS TWO, ONE, OR NO LEVELS (296) GES,EA	5 0 29 37 XSQ= 3.82 PHI= 0.232 XP = 0.0506
110	DRIFT LESS TOWARD BEING THOSE 0.53 OF 36 WHERE SLAVERY IS ABSENT (218)	110	DRIFT MORE TOWARD BEING THOSE 0.75 OF 40 WHERE SLAVERY IS ABSENT (218)	17 10 19 30 XSQ= 3.17 PHI= 0.204 XP = 0.0749
116	DRIFT MORE TOWARD BEING THOSE 0.92 OF 13 WHERE OCCUPATIONAL SPECIALIZATION IS PART-TIME ONLY (34) JMH	116	DRIFT LESS TOWARD BEING THOSE 0.60 OF 15 WHERE OCCUPATIONAL SPECIALIZATION IS PART-TIME ONLY (34) JMH	1 6 12 9 XSQ= 2.35 PHI= -0.289 EP = 0.0836

118	IN ALL CASES ARE THCSE 1.00 OF 9 WHERE THE PERCENTAGE CF OCCUPATIONS THAT ARE SPECIALIZED IS LCW (25) WME	118	LEAN TOWARD BEING THOSE 0.64 OF 11 WHERE THE PERCENTAGE OF OCCUPATICNS THAT ARE SPECIALIZED IS HIGH OR MEDIUM (24) WME	0 7 9 4 XSQ= 6.24 PHI= -0.558 EP = 0.0047
130	DRIFT TCWARD BEING THCSE 0.82 OF 11 WHERE LEATHER WCRKING IS MAINLY DONE BY FEMALES (45)	130	DRIFT TOWARD BEING THOSE 0.60 OF 10 WHERE LEATHER WORKING IS MAINLY DONE BY MALES (39)	2 6 9 4 XSQ= 2.31 PHI= -0.332 EP = 0.0805
137	DRIFT TCWARD BEING THCSE 0.57 OF 28 WHERE INVIDICUS DISPLAY OF WEALTH IS STRCNGLY EMPHASIZEC (37) PES	137	DRIFT TOWARD BEING THOSE 0.69 OF 26 WHERE INVIDIOUS DISPLAY CF WEALTH IS MODERATELY, LITTLE, CR NEGATIVELY EMPHASIZED (52) PES	16 8 12 18 XSQ= 2.80 PHI= 0.228 XP = 0.0940
201	DRIFT LESS TCWARC BEING THOSE 0.78 OF 36 WHERE MARITAL RESICENCE IS NCN-CPTICNAL, RATHER THAN AMBILCCAL CR NECLOCAL (334)	201	DRIFT MORE TOWARD BEING THCSE 0.95 CF 40 WHERE MARITAL RESIDENCE IS NON-OPTIONAL, RATHER THAN AMBILOCAL OR NECLOCAL (334)	28 38 8 2 XSQ= 3.53 PHI= -0.215 XP = 0.0604
204	DRIFT LESS TOWARC BEING THOSE 0.73 OF 3C WHERE MARITAL RESICENCE IS PATRILCCAL, VIRILOCAL, OR AVUNCULOCAL, RATHER THAN AMBILCCAL CR NECLOCAL (270)	204	DRIFT MORE TOWARD BEING THCSE 0.93 CF 30 WHERE MARITAL RESIDENCE IS PATRILOCAL, VIRILOCAL, CR AVUNCULOCAL, RATHER THAN AMBILOCAL OR NECLOCAL (270)	22 28 8 2 XSQ= 3.00 PHI= -0.224 XP = 0.0833
207	DRIFT TCWARD BEING THCSE 0.57 OF 14 WHERE MARITAL RESICENCE IS AMBILCCAL CR NECLOCAL, RATHER THAN MATRILCCAL OR UXCRILOCAL (64)	207	DRIFT TOWARD BEING THOSE 0.83 CF 12 WHERE MARITAL RESIDENCE IS MATRILOCAL OR UXORILOCAL, RATHER THAN AMBILOCAL OR NEOLOCAL (64)	6 10 8 2 XSQ= 2.93 PHI= -0.335 EP = 0.0511
295	DRIFT TCWARD BEING THCSE 0.78 OF 9 WHERE THE SEVERITY CF PUNISHMENT FOR ABCRTICN IS HIGH (11) BCA	295	DRIFT TOWARD BEING THOSE 0.70 OF 10 WHERE THE SEVERITY CF PUNISHMENT FOR ABORTION IS LOW OR ABSENT (12) BCA	7 3 2 7 XSQ= 2.63 PHI= 0.372 EP = 0.0698
315	DRIFT TCWARD BEING THCSE 0.50 OF 16 WHERE MCTHER ANC NURSING CHILC CUSTCMARILY SLEEP IN DIFFERENT BEDS (14) W-C,S	315	DRIFT TOWARD BEING THOSE 0.87 CF 15 WHERE MOTHER AND NURSING CHILD CUSTOMARILY SLEEP IN THE SAME BED (37) W-D,S	8 13 8 2 XSQ= 3.23 PHI= -0.323 EP = 0.0538
322	TILT TCWARC BEING THOSE 0.73 OF 26 WHERE THE CCNSISTENCY CF REDUCTION CF THE INFANT'S CRIVES IS LCW (32) B-B-C	322	TILT TOWARD BEING THOSE 0.59 OF 32 WHERE THE CONSISTENCY OF REDUCTICN OF THE INFANT'S DRIVES IS HIGH (27) B-B-C	7 19 19 13 XSQ= 4.87 PHI= -0.290 XP = 0.0274

323 TILT TOWARD BEING THOSE 0.76 OF 34 WHERE THE CONSTANCY OF PRESENCE OF THE INFANT'S NURTURANT AGENT IS LOW (45) B-B-C	323 TILT TOWARD BEING THOSE 0.51 OF 39 WHERE THE CONSTANCY OF PRESENCE OF THE INFANT'S NURTURANT AGENT IS HIGH (29) B-B-C	8 20 26 19 XSQ= 4.80 PHI= -0.256 XP = 0.0284
338 DRIFT TOWARD BEING THOSE 0.74 OF 34 WHERE THE CHILD'S INFERRED ANXIETY OVER PERFORMANCE OF RESPONSIBLE BEHAVIOR IS HIGH (44) B-B-C	338 DRIFT TOWARD BEING THOSE 0.51 OF 39 WHERE THE CHILD'S INFERRED ANXIETY OVER PERFORMANCE OF RESPONSIBLE BEHAVIOR IS LOW (29) B-B-C	25 19 9 20 XSQ= 3.69 PHI= 0.225 XP = 0.0547
345 TEND TO BE THOSE 0.75 OF 36 WHERE THE CHILD'S INFERRED ANXIETY OVER NON-PERFORMANCE OF SELF-RELIANT BEHAVIOR IS HIGH (37) B-B-C	345 TEND TO BE THOSE 0.75 OF 40 WHERE THE CHILD'S INFERRED ANXIETY OVER NON-PERFORMANCE OF SELF-RELIANT BEHAVIOR IS LOW (39) B-B-C	27 10 9 30 XSQ= 17.01 PHI= 0.473 XP = 0.0000
348 TILT TOWARD BEING THOSE 0.69 OF 29 WHERE THE TOTAL POSITIVE PRESSURE TOWARD DEVELOPING ACHIEVEMENT BEHAVIOR IN THE CHILD IS HIGH (32) B-B-C	348 TILT TOWARD BEING THOSE 0.65 OF 34 WHERE THE TOTAL POSITIVE PRESSURE TOWARD DEVELOPING ACHIEVEMENT BEHAVIOR IN THE CHILD IS LOW (31) B-B-C	20 12 9 22 XSQ= 5.82 PHI= 0.304 XP = 0.0159
349 TILT TOWARD BEING THOSE 0.72 OF 29 WHERE THE CHILD'S INFERRED ANXIETY OVER NON-PERFORMANCE OF ACHIEVEMENT BEHAVIOR IS HIGH (34) B-B-C	349 TILT TOWARD BEING THOSE 0.61 OF 33 WHERE THE CHILD'S INFERRED ANXIETY OVER NON-PERFORMANCE OF ACHIEVEMENT BEHAVIOR IS LOW (28) B-B-C	21 13 8 20 XSQ= 5.53 PHI= 0.299 XP = 0.0187
356 DRIFT TOWARD BEING THOSE 0.68 OF 19 WHERE ADOLESCENT PEER GROUPS OR PAIRS ARE PRESENT IN A SETTING OF COURTSHIP (29) JKH	356 DRIFT TOWARD BEING THOSE 0.69 OF 13 WHERE NEITHER ADOLESCENT PEER GROUPS NOR PAIRS ARE PRESENT IN A SETTING OF COURTSHIP (22) JKH	13 4 6 9 XSQ= 3.01 PHI= 0.307 EP = 0.0702
399 DRIFT TOWARD BEING THOSE 0.65 OF 23 WHERE INTENSITY OF CASTRATION ANXIETY IS HIGH (23) WNS	399 DRIFT TOWARD BEING THOSE 0.68 OF 19 WHERE INTENSITY OF CASTRATION ANXIETY IS LOW (22) WNS	15 6 8 13 XSQ= 3.46 PHI= 0.287 XP = 0.0629
400 TILT TOWARD BEING THOSE 0.67 OF 18 WHERE HOMOSEXUAL ACTIVITY IS PROHIBITED (22) F-B	400 TILT TOWARD BEING THOSE 0.78 OF 18 WHERE HOMOSEXUAL ACTIVITY IS PERMITTED (36) F-B	12 4 6 14 XSQ= 5.51 PHI= 0.391 EP = 0.0176
402 LEAN TOWARD BEING THOSE 0.86 OF 21 WHERE EXPLANATIONS OF ILLNESS OF AN ORAL NATURE ARE PRESENT (31) W-C	402 LEAN TOWARD BEING THOSE 0.67 OF 21 WHERE EXPLANATIONS OF ILLNESS OF AN ORAL NATURE ARE ABSENT (30) W-C	18 7 3 14 XSQ= 9.88 PHI= 0.485 XP = 0.0017

419	TILT TOWARD BEING THOSE WHERE MILITARY GLORY IS STRONGLY OR MODERATELY EMPHASIZED (55) PES	0.79 OF 28	419	TILT TOWARD BEING THOSE WHERE MILITARY GLORY IS NEGLIGIBLY EMPHASIZED (31) PES	0.56 OF 25	22 11 6 14 XSQ= 5.33 PHI= 0.317 XP = 0.0210
420	LEAN TOWARD BEING THOSE WHERE BELLICOSITY IS EXTREME (41) PES	0.59 OF 27	420	LEAN TOWARD BEING THOSE WHERE BELLICOSITY IS MODERATE OR NEGLIGIBLE (46) PES	0.80 OF 25	16 5 11 20 XSQ= 6.76 PHI= 0.361 XP = 0.0093
421	LEAN TOWARD BEING THOSE WHERE KILLING, TORTURING, OR MUTILATING OF THE ENEMY IS STRONGLY OR MODERATELY EMPHASIZED (37) PES	0.64 OF 28	421	LEAN TOWARD BEING THOSE WHERE KILLING, TORTURING, OR MUTILATING OF THE ENEMY IS NEGLIGIBLY EMPHASIZED (47) PES	0.80 OF 25	18 5 10 20 XSQ= 8.82 PHI= 0.408 XP = 0.0030
425	TILT TOWARD BEING THOSE WHERE SUPERNATURALS ARE MAINLY AGGRESSIVE, RATHER THAN BENEVOLENT (20) L-T-W	0.79 OF 14	425	TILT TOWARD BEING THOSE WHERE SUPERNATURALS ARE MAINLY BENEVOLENT, RATHER THAN AGGRESSIVE (16) L-T-W	0.62 OF 21	3 13 11 8 XSQ= 4.03 PHI= -0.340 EP = 0.0364
432	IN ALL CASES ARE THOSE WHERE AN ATTRACTIVE AFTERLIFE IS BELIEVED IN (27) LWS	1.00 OF 8	432	DRIFT TOWARD BEING THOSE WHERE AN ATTRACTIVE AFTERLIFE IS NOT BELIEVED IN (11) LWS	0.50 OF 6	8 3 0 3 XSQ= 2.55 PHI= 0.427 EP = 0.0549
455	DRIFT TOWARD BEING THOSE WHERE THE MODE OF THE INDIVIDUAL'S CONTACT WITH THE DIVINE IS CONDUCIVE TO THE DEVELOPMENT OF THE INDIVIDUAL'S NEED TO ACHIEVE (17) DCM	0.65 OF 17	455	DRIFT TOWARD BEING THOSE WHERE THE MODE OF THE INDIVIDUAL'S CONTACT WITH THE DIVINE IS NOT CONDUCIVE TO THE DEVELOPMENT OF THE INDIVIDUAL'S NEED TO ACHIEVE (19) DCM	0.68 OF 19	11 6 6 13 XSQ= 2.73 PHI= 0.276 EP = 0.0933
472	LEAN TOWARD BEING THOSE WHERE THE COMPOSITE NARCISSISM INDEX IS HIGH (47) PES	0.72 OF 29	472	LEAN TOWARD BEING THOSE WHERE THE COMPOSITE NARCISSISM INDEX IS LOW (43) PES	0.69 OF 26	21 8 8 18 XSQ= 7.94 PHI= 0.380 XP = 0.0048
474	TILT TOWARD BEING THOSE WHERE BOASTFULNESS IS EXTREME (41) PES	0.57 OF 28	474	TILT TOWARD BEING THOSE WHERE BOASTFULNESS IS MODERATE, NEGLIBIBLE, OR UNREPORTED (48) PES	0.77 OF 26	16 6 12 20 XSQ= 5.15 PHI= 0.309 XP = 0.0233
477	TILT TOWARD BEING THOSE WHERE ALCOHOLIC AGGRESSION IS STRONG (15) DH	0.71 OF 7	477	TILT TOWARD BEING THOSE WHERE ALCOHOLIC AGGRESSION IS MODERATE OR SLIGHT (19) DH	0.89 OF 9	5 1 2 8 XSQ= 3.81 PHI= 0.488 EP = 0.0350

345 CULTURES
WHERE THE CHILD'S INFERRED ANXIETY OVER
NON-PERFORMANCE OF SELF-RELIANT BEHAVIOR
IS HIGH (37) B-B-C

345 CULTURES
WHERE THE CHILD'S INFERRED ANXIETY OVER
NON-PERFORMANCE OF SELF-RELIANT BEHAVIOR
IS LOW (39) B-B-C

BACKGROUND ON PAGE 143

BOTH SUBJECT AND PREDICATE

37 IN LEFT COLUMN

AINU	ALORESE	ARANDA	ASHANTI	AYMARA	BALINESE	CHAGGA	CHIR-APACHE	CHUKCHEE	COMANCHE
CROW	FON	GANDA	JIVARO	KASKA	KURTATCHI	KWAKIUTL	LAMBA	MANDAN	MANUS
MAORI	NYAKYUSA	OJIBWA	OMAHA	SIRIONO	SOTHO	SWAZI	THONGA	TRUKESE	TUCUNA
TURKANA	VENDA	WICHITA	WINNEBAGO	WOLEAIANS	YORUBA	ZUNI			

39 IN RIGHT COLUMN

ARAPESH	ARAUCANIANS	AZANDE	CAMAYURA	CHENCHU	CHEYENNE	CUNA	HANO	IFUGAO	KIKUYU
KORYAK	LAU	LEPCHA	LESU	MARQUESANS	MASAI	MBUNDU	MURNGIN	NAVAHO	NUER
ONA	ONTONG-JAVA	PAPAGO	PUKAPUKA	SAMOANS	SHERENTE	TALLENSI	TANALA	TENETEHARA	TETON
TIKOPIA	TIMBIRA	TIV	TROBRIAND	TUPINAMBA	WOGEO	YAGUA	YAHGAN	YAKUT	

324 EXCLUDED BECAUSE UNASCERTAINED

---

80 DRIFT LESS TOWARD BEING THOSE 0.83 OF 23
WHERE NO CITY OR TOWN IS PRESENT (185)

80 IN ALL CASES ARE THOSE 1.00 OF 31
WHERE NO CITY OR TOWN IS PRESENT (185)

4	0
19	31
XSQ=	3.56
PHI=	0.257
XP =	0.0591

84 TILT LESS TOWARD BEING THOSE 0.81 OF 31
WHERE THE LEVEL OF POLITICAL INTEGRATION
IS THE LITTLE STATE, THE MINIMAL STATE,
THE AUTONOMOUS COMMUNITY, OR
THE FAMILY (262) GPM

84 IN ALL CASES ARE THOSE 1.00 OF 34
WHERE THE LEVEL OF POLITICAL INTEGRATION
IS THE LITTLE STATE, THE MINIMAL STATE,
THE AUTONOMOUS COMMUNITY, OR
THE FAMILY (262) GPM

6	0
25	34
XSQ=	5.12
PHI=	0.281
XP =	0.0236

94 TILT LESS TOWARD BEING THOSE 0.85 OF 33
WHERE THE HIERARCHY
OF NATIONAL JURISDICTION HAS
TWO, ONE, OR NO LEVELS (296) GES,EA

94 IN ALL CASES ARE THOSE 1.00 OF 38
WHERE THE HIERARCHY
OF NATIONAL JURISDICTION HAS
TWO, ONE, OR NO LEVELS (296) GES,EA

5	0
28	38
XSQ=	4.10
PHI=	0.240
XP =	0.0430

96 DRIFT TOWARD BEING THOSE 0.64 OF 33
WHERE THE HIERARCHY
OF NATIONAL JURISDICTION HAS
FOUR, THREE, TWO OR
ONE LEVEL (174) GES,EA

96 DRIFT TOWARD BEING THOSE 0.61 OF 38
WHERE THE HIERARCHY
OF NATIONAL JURISDICTION HAS
NO LEVELS (156) GES,EA

21	15
12	23
XSQ=	3.22
PHI=	0.213
XP =	0.0729

106	TILT TOWARD BEING THOSE 0.76 OF 17 WHERE CLASS STRATIFICATION, IF PRESENT, IS BASED ON SOMETHING OTHER THAN WEALTH (126)	106	TILT TOWARD BEING THOSE 0.61 OF 18 WHERE CLASS STRATIFICATION, IF PRESENT, IS BASED ON WEALTH (77)	4 11 13 7 XSQ= 3.62 PHI= -0.322 EP = 0.0409
108	DRIFT TOWARD BEING THOSE 0.71 OF 17 WHERE CLASS STRATIFICATION, IF PRESENT, IS BASED ON A HEREDITARY ARISTOCRACY (74)	108	DRIFT TOWARD BEING THOSE 0.61 OF 18 WHERE CLASS STRATIFICATION, IF PRESENT, IS BASED ON SOMETHING OTHER THAN A HEREDITARY ARISTOCRACY (129)	12 7 5 11 XSQ= 2.38 PHI= 0.261 EP = 0.0922
116	IN ALL CASES ARE THOSE 1.00 OF 12 WHERE OCCUPATIONAL SPECIALIZATION IS PART-TIME ONLY (34) JMH	116	TILT LESS TOWARD BEING THOSE 0.56 OF 16 WHERE OCCUPATIONAL SPECIALIZATION IS PART-TIME ONLY (34) JMH	0 7 12 9 XSQ= 4.86 PHI= -0.417 EP = 0.0103
148	LEAN TOWARD BEING THOSE 0.64 OF 14 WHERE THE INCIDENCE OF PERSONAL CRIME IS HIGH (12) B-B-C	148	LEAN TOWARD BEING THOSE 0.83 OF 18 WHERE THE INCIDENCE OF PERSONAL CRIME IS LOW (21) B-B-C	9 3 5 15 XSQ= 5.72 PHI= 0.423 EP = 0.0100
149	TILT TOWARD BEING THOSE 0.71 OF 17 WHERE THE INCIDENCE OF THEFT IS HIGH (18) B-B-C	149	TILT TOWARD BEING THOSE 0.68 OF 19 WHERE THE INCIDENCE OF THEFT IS LOW (19) B-B-C	12 6 5 13 XSQ= 4.01 PHI= 0.334 EP = 0.0437
192	DRIFT MORE TOWARD BEING THOSE 0.92 OF 37 OTHER THAN WHERE THE ONLY KIN GROUP PRESENT IS A KINDRED OR ELSE BILATERAL DESCENT IS INFERRED (289)	192	DRIFT LESS TOWARD BEING THOSE 0.74 OF 39 OTHER THAN WHERE THE ONLY KIN GROUP PRESENT IS A KINDRED OR ELSE BILATERAL DESCENT IS INFERRED (289)	3 10 34 29 XSQ= 2.97 PHI= -0.198 XP = 0.0847
260	DRIFT TOWARD BEING THOSE 0.80 OF 15 WHERE THE AGE OF MALES AT MARRIAGE IS LESS THAN TWENTY (38) JKH	260	DRIFT TOWARD BEING THOSE 0.53 OF 19 WHERE THE AGE OF MALES AT MARRIAGE IS TWENTY OR OVER (17) JKH	12 9 3 10 XSQ= 2.52 PHI= 0.272 EP = 0.0790
282	DRIFT TOWARD BEING THOSE 0.67 OF 15 WHERE THE STRENGTH OF DESIRE FOR CHILDREN IS HIGH (16) BCA	282	DRIFT TOWARD BEING THOSE 0.69 OF 16 WHERE THE STRENGTH OF DESIRE FOR CHILDREN IS LOW OR ABSENT (20) BCA	10 5 5 11 XSQ= 2.60 PHI= 0.290 EP = 0.0756
303	DRIFT TOWARD BEING THOSE 0.67 OF 18 WHERE THE EARLY ORAL SATISFACTION POTENTIAL IS LOW (25) W-C	303	DRIFT TOWARD BEING THOSE 0.64 OF 22 WHERE THE EARLY ORAL SATISFACTION POTENTIAL IS HIGH (32) W-C	6 14 12 8 XSQ= 2.53 PHI= -0.251 EP = 0.0679

326	TILT TOWARD BEING THOSE 0.64 OF 33 WHERE THE INFERRED TRANSITION ANXIETY BETWEEN INFANCY AND CHILDHOOD IS HIGH (32) B-B-C	326	TILT TOWARD BEING THOSE 0.67 OF 33 WHERE THE INFERRED TRANSITION ANXIETY BETWEEN INFANCY AND CHILDHOOD IS LOW (35) B-B-C	21 11 12 22 XSQ= 4.91 PHI= 0.273 XP = 0.0266
334	LEAN TOWARD BEING THOSE 0.68 OF 37 WHERE THE INDULGENCE OF THE CHILD IS LOW (38) B-B-C	334	LEAN TOWARD BEING THOSE 0.67 OF 39 WHERE THE INDULGENCE OF THE CHILD IS HIGH (40) B-B-C	12 26 25 13 XSQ= 7.58 PHI= -0.316 XP = 0.0059
337	TILT TOWARD BEING THOSE 0.66 OF 35 WHERE THE CHILD'S INFERRED ANXIETY OVER NON-PERFORMANCE OF RESPONSIBLE BEHAVIOR IS HIGH (38) B-B-C	337	TILT TOWARD BEING THOSE 0.61 OF 38 WHERE THE CHILD'S INFERRED ANXIETY OVER NON-PERFORMANCE OF RESPONSIBLE BEHAVIOR IS LOW (35) B-B-C	23 15 12 23 XSQ= 4.03 PHI= 0.235 XP = 0.0447
338	LEAN TOWARD BEING THOSE 0.80 OF 35 WHERE THE CHILD'S INFERRED ANXIETY OVER PERFORMANCE OF RESPONSIBLE BEHAVIOR IS HIGH (44) B-B-C	338	LEAN TOWARD BEING THOSE 0.58 OF 38 WHERE THE CHILD'S INFERRED ANXIETY OVER PERFORMANCE OF RESPONSIBLE BEHAVIOR IS LOW (29) B-B-C	28 16 7 22 XSQ= 9.40 PHI= 0.359 XP = 0.0022
344	TEND TO BE THOSE 0.73 OF 37 WHERE THE TOTAL POSITIVE PRESSURE TOWARD DEVELOPING SELF-RELIANT BEHAVIOR IN THE CHILD IS HIGH (36) B-B-C	344	TEND TO BE THOSE 0.77 OF 39 WHERE THE TOTAL POSITIVE PRESSURE TOWARD DEVELOPING SELF-RELIANT BEHAVIOR IN THE CHILD IS LOW (40) B-B-C	27 9 10 30 XSQ= 17.01 PHI= 0.473 XP = 0.0000
347	TILT TOWARD BEING THOSE 0.62 OF 37 WHERE THE CHILD'S INFERRED CONFLICT REGARDING SELF-RELIANT BEHAVIOR IS HIGH (37) B-B-C	347	TILT TOWARD BEING THOSE 0.64 OF 39 WHERE THE CHILD'S INFERRED CONFLICT REGARDING SELF-RELIANT BEHAVIOR IS LOW (39) B-B-C	23 14 14 25 XSQ= 4.24 PHI= 0.236 XP = 0.0394
349	TILT TOWARD BEING THOSE 0.69 OF 32 WHERE THE CHILD'S INFERRED ANXIETY OVER NON-PERFORMANCE OF ACHIEVEMENT BEHAVIOR IS HIGH (34) B-B-C	349	TILT TOWARD BEING THOSE 0.60 OF 30 WHERE THE CHILD'S INFERRED ANXIETY OVER NON-PERFORMANCE OF ACHIEVEMENT BEHAVIOR IS LOW (28) B-B-C	22 12 10 18 XSQ= 4.07 PHI= 0.256 XP = 0.0436
354	TEND TO BE THOSE 0.69 OF 36 WHERE THE CHILD'S INFERRED ANXIETY OVER PERFORMANCE OF OBEDIENT BEHAVIOR IS HIGH (36) B-B-C	354	TEND TO BE THOSE 0.72 OF 36 WHERE THE CHILD'S INFERRED ANXIETY OVER PERFORMANCE OF OBEDIENT BEHAVIOR IS LOW (37) B-B-C	25 10 11 26 XSQ= 10.90 PHI= 0.389 XP = 0.0010
355	DRIFT TOWARD BEING THOSE 0.58 OF 36 WHERE THE CHILD'S INFERRED CONFLICT REGARDING OBEDIENT BEHAVIOR IS HIGH (35) B-B-C	355	DRIFT TOWARD BEING THOSE 0.64 OF 36 WHERE THE CHILD'S INFERRED CONFLICT REGARDING OBEDIENT BEHAVIOR IS LOW (38) B-B-C	21 13 15 23 XSQ= 2.73 PHI= 0.195 XP = 0.0984

No.				No.				
386	DRIFT TOWARD BEING THOSE WHERE SEXUAL EXPRESSION BY THE YOUNG IS RESTRICTED OR SEMI-RESTRICTED (46) F-B	0.76 OF	25	386	DRIFT TOWARD BEING THOSE WHERE SEXUAL EXPRESSION BY THE YOUNG IS PERMITTED (40) F-B	0.55 OF	20	19 9 6 11 XSQ= 3.32 PHI= 0.272 XP = 0.0685
393	LEAN TOWARD BEING THOSE WHERE EXTRAMARITAL COITUS IS PUNISHED, RATHER THAN PERMITTED (43) F-B	0.76 OF	21	393	LEAN TOWARD BEING THOSE WHERE EXTRAMARITAL COITUS IS PERMITTED, RATHER THAN PUNISHED (41) F-B	0.78 OF	18	16 4 5 14 XSQ= 9.24 PHI= 0.487 EP = 0.0012
399	TEND TO BE THOSE WHERE INTENSITY OF CASTRATION ANXIETY IS HIGH (23) WNS	0.85 OF	20	399	TEND TO BE THOSE WHERE INTENSITY OF CASTRATION ANXIETY IS LOW (22) WNS	0.82 OF	22	17 4 3 18 XSQ= 16.13 PHI= 0.620 XP = 0.0001
402	TILT TOWARD BEING THOSE WHERE EXPLANATIONS OF ILLNESS OF AN ORAL NATURE ARE PRESENT (31) W-C	0.79 OF	19	402	TILT TOWARD BEING THOSE WHERE EXPLANATIONS OF ILLNESS OF AN ORAL NATURE ARE ABSENT (30) W-C	0.57 OF	23	15 10 4 13 XSQ= 4.06 PHI= 0.311 XP = 0.0439
419	DRIFT TOWARD BEING THOSE WHERE MILITARY GLORY IS STRONGLY OR MODERATELY EMPHASIZED (55) PES	0.77 OF	26	419	DRIFT TOWARD BEING THOSE WHERE MILITARY GLORY IS NEGLIGIBLY EMPHASIZED (31) PES	0.52 OF	27	20 13 6 14 XSQ= 3.52 PHI= 0.258 XP = 0.0605
421	TILT TOWARD BEING THOSE WHERE KILLING, TORTURING, OR MUTILATING OF THE ENEMY IS STRONGLY OR MODERATELY EMPHASIZED (37) PES	0.60 OF	25	421	TILT TOWARD BEING THOSE WHERE KILLING, TORTURING, OR MUTILATING OF THE ENEMY IS NEGLIGIBLY EMPHASIZED (47) PES	0.71 OF	28	15 8 10 20 XSQ= 4.11 PHI= 0.278 XP = 0.0427
424	DRIFT MORE TOWARD BEING THOSE WHERE RELIGIOUS SPECIALISTS ARE PART-TIME, RATHER THAN FULL-TIME (33) JMH	0.92 OF	12	424	DRIFT LESS TOWARD BEING THOSE WHERE RELIGIOUS SPECIALISTS ARE PART-TIME, RATHER THAN FULL-TIME (33) JMH	0.56 OF	16	1 7 11 9 XSQ= 2.66 PHI= -0.308 EP = 0.0882
425	TILT TOWARD BEING THOSE WHERE SUPERNATURALS ARE MAINLY AGGRESSIVE, RATHER THAN BENEVOLENT (20) L-T-W	0.76 OF	17	425	TILT TOWARD BEING THOSE WHERE SUPERNATURALS ARE MAINLY BENEVOLENT, RATHER THAN AGGRESSIVE (16) L-T-W	0.67 OF	18	4 12 13 6 XSQ= 4.93 PHI= -0.375 EP = 0.0176
432	IN ALL CASES ARE THOSE WHERE AN ATTRACTIVE AFTERLIFE IS BELIEVED IN (27) LWS	1.00 OF	8	432	DRIFT TOWARD BEING THOSE WHERE AN ATTRACTIVE AFTERLIFE IS NOT BELIEVED IN (11) LWS	0.50 OF	6	8 3 0 3 XSQ= 2.55 PHI= 0.427 EP = 0.0549

346 CULTURES WHERE THE CHILD'S INFERRED ANXIETY OVER PERFORMANCE OF SELF-RELIANT BEHAVIOR IS HIGH (37) B-B-C	346 CULTURES WHERE THE CHILD'S INFERRED ANXIETY OVER PERFORMANCE OF SELF-RELIANT BEHAVIOR IS LOW (39) B-B-C

BACKGROUND ON PAGE 143 BOTH SUBJECT AND PREDICATE

37 IN LEFT COLUMN

ALORESE	ARAUCANIANS	AYMARA	AZANDE	BALINESE	CAMAYURA	CHAGGA	CROW	HANO	KASKA
KIKUYU	KURTATCHI	LAMBA	LAU	LEPCHA	MANDAN	MARQUESANS	MASAI	MBUNDU	MURNGIN
NAVAHO	NYAKYUSA	OJIBWA	SAMOANS	SWAZI	TALLENSI	TANALA	THONGA	TIV	TRUKESE
TUCUNA	TURKANA	VENDA	WINNEBAGO	WOLEAIANS	YAKUT	ZUNI			

39 IN RIGHT COLUMN

AINU	ARANDA	ARAPESH	ASHANTI	CHENCHU	CHEYENNE	CHIR-APACHE	CHUKCHEE	COMANCHE	CUNA
FON	GANDA	IFUGAO	JIVARO	KORYAK	KWAKIUTL	LESU	MANUS	MAORI	NUER
OMAHA	ONA	ONTONG-JAVA	PAPAGO	PUKAPUKA	SHERENTE	SIRIONO	SOTHO	TENETEHARA	TETON
TIKOPIA	TIMBIRA	TROBRIAND	TUPINAMBA	WICHITA	WOGEO	YAGUA	YAHGAN	YORUBA	

324 EXCLUDED BECAUSE UNASCERTAINED

	Left column			Right column			Statistics
3	DRIFT LESS TOWARD BEING THOSE LOCATED OUTSIDE OF AFRICA (320)	0.65 OF 37	3	DRIFT MORE TOWARD BEING THOSE LOCATED OUTSIDE OF AFRICA (320)	0.85 OF 39		13 6 24 33 XSQ= 2.97 PHI= 0.198 XP = 0.0850
51	TILT TOWARD BEING THOSE WHERE SUBSISTENCE IS PRIMARILY BY FOOD PRODUCTION -- I. E., AGRICULTURE OR HUSBANDRY -- RATHER THAN BY GATHERING (253)	0.70 OF 37	51	TILT TOWARD BEING THOSE WHERE SUBSISTENCE IS PRIMARILY BY FOOD GATHERING -- I. E., HUNTING, FISHING, OR COLLECTING -- RATHER THAN FOOD PRODUCTION (147)	0.62 OF 39		26 15 11 24 XSQ= 6.51 PHI= 0.293 XP = 0.0108
53	DRIFT LESS TOWARD BEING THOSE WHERE FOOD PRODUCTION IS BY SIMPLE AGRICULTURE OR INCIPIENT FOOD PRODUCTION, RATHER THAN BY INTENSIVE AGRICULTURE (147)	0.59 OF 29	53	DRIFT MORE TOWARD BEING THOSE WHERE FOOD PRODUCTION IS BY SIMPLE AGRICULTURE OR INCIPIENT FOOD PRODUCTION, RATHER THAN BY INTENSIVE AGRICULTURE (147)	0.86 OF 21		12 3 17 18 XSQ= 3.07 PHI= 0.248 XP = 0.0800
71	TILT TOWARD BEING THOSE WHERE METAL WORKING IS PRESENT (98)	0.50 OF 30	71	TILT TOWARD BEING THOSE WHERE METAL WORKING IS ABSENT (153)	0.81 OF 31		15 6 15 25 XSQ= 5.06 PHI= 0.288 XP = 0.0245

77	DRIFT LESS TOWARD BEING THOSE 0.69 OF 16 WHERE THE WRITING SYSTEM IS MNEMONIC OR ABSENT, RATHER THAN BEING ALPHABETIC-OR-PHONETIC (39) JMH	77	IN ALL CASES ARE THOSE 1.00 OF 12 WHERE THE WRITING SYSTEM IS MNEMONIC OR ABSENT, RATHER THAN BEING ALPHABETIC-OR-PHONETIC (39) JMH	5 0 11 12 XSQ= 2.68 PHI= 0.310 EP = 0.0525
80	IN ALL CASES ARE THOSE 1.00 OF 30 WHERE NO CITY OR TOWN IS PRESENT (185)	80	DRIFT LESS TOWARD BEING THOSE 0.83 OF 24 WHERE NO CITY OR TOWN IS PRESENT (185)	0 4 30 20 XSQ= 3.24 PHI= -0.245 XP = 0.0717
95	DRIFT LESS TOWARD BEING THOSE 0.65 OF 34 WHERE THE HIERARCHY OF NATIONAL JURISDICTION HAS ONE OR NO LEVELS (254) GES,EA	95	DRIFT MORE TOWARD BEING THOSE 0.86 OF 37 WHERE THE HIERARCHY OF NATIONAL JURISDICTION HAS ONE OR NO LEVELS (254) GES,EA	12 5 22 32 XSQ= 3.50 PHI= 0.222 XP = 0.0615
132	TILT TOWARD BEING THOSE 0.81 OF 16 WHERE ECONOMIC EXCHANGE INVOLVES THE USE OF MONEY (37) JMH	132	TILT TOWARD BEING THOSE 0.67 OF 12 WHERE ECONOMIC EXCHANGE DOES NOT INVOLVE THE USE OF MONEY (17) JMH	13 4 3 8 XSQ= 4.74 PHI= 0.412 EP = 0.0189
142	LEAN TOWARD BEING THOSE 0.94 OF 16 WHERE THE LEVEL OF SOCIAL SANCTION IS PUBLIC CORPOREAL SANCTION OR PUBLIC PROPERTY SANCTION, RATHER THAN PRIVATE SETTLEMENT (38) JMH	142	LEAN TOWARD BEING THOSE 0.67 OF 12 WHERE THE LEVEL OF SOCIAL SANCTION IS PRIVATE SETTLEMENT, RATHER THAN PUBLIC CORPOREAL SANCTION OR PUBLIC PROPERTY SETTLEMENT (16) JMH	15 4 1 8 XSQ= 8.87 PHI= 0.563 EP = 0.0012
177	TILT LESS TOWARD BEING THOSE 0.67 OF 36 WHERE THE COMMUNITY IS OTHER THAN A SINGLE CLAN-COMMUNITY AND EXOGAMOUS (305)	177	TILT MORE TOWARD BEING THOSE 0.92 OF 39 WHERE THE COMMUNITY IS OTHER THAN A SINGLE CLAN-COMMUNITY AND EXOGAMOUS (305)	12 3 24 36 XSQ= 6.17 PHI= 0.287 XP = 0.0130
180	DRIFT TOWARD BEING THOSE 0.50 OF 36 WHERE THE COMMUNITY IS COMMONLY EXOGAMOUS, RATHER THAN NON-EXOGAMOUS (124)	180	DRIFT TOWARD BEING THOSE 0.72 OF 39 WHERE THE COMMUNITY IS COMMONLY NON-EXOGAMOUS, RATHER THAN EXOGAMOUS (258)	18 11 18 28 XSQ= 2.89 PHI= 0.196 XP = 0.0893
188	LEAN MORE TOWARD BEING THOSE 0.89 OF 37 WHERE THE KIN GROUP IS OTHER THAN EXCLUSIVELY COGNATIC (252)	188	LEAN LESS TOWARD BEING THOSE 0.54 OF 39 WHERE THE KIN GROUP IS OTHER THAN EXCLUSIVELY COGNATIC (252)	4 18 33 21 XSQ= 9.88 PHI= -0.360 XP = 0.0017
192	LEAN MORE TOWARD BEING THOSE 0.97 OF 37 OTHER THAN WHERE THE ONLY KIN GROUP PRESENT IS A KINDRED OR ELSE BILATERAL DESCENT IS INFERRED (289)	192	LEAN LESS TOWARD BEING THOSE 0.69 OF 39 OTHER THAN WHERE THE ONLY KIN GROUP PRESENT IS A KINDRED OR ELSE BILATERAL DESCENT IS INFERRED (289)	1 12 36 27 XSQ= 8.66 PHI= -0.338 XP = 0.0032

234	TILT TOWARD BEING THOSE WHERE THE COUSIN TERMINOLOGY IS OF CROW, OMAHA, OR IROQUOIS TYPE, RATHER THAN ESKIMO OR HAWAIIAN TYPE (152)	0.73 OF 33	234	TILT TOWARD BEING THOSE WHERE THE COUSIN TERMINOLOGY IS OF ESKIMO OR HAWAIIAN TYPE, RATHER THAN CROW, OMAHA, OR IROQUOIS TYPE (170)	0.56 OF 32	24 14 9 18 XSQ= 4.49 PHI= 0.263 XP = 0.0341
304	DRIFT TOWARD BEING THOSE WHERE THE EARLY ANAL SATISFACTION POTENTIAL IS LOW (22) W-C	0.71 OF 14	304	DRIFT TOWARD BEING THOSE WHERE THE EARLY ANAL SATISFACTION POTENTIAL IS HIGH (19) W-C	0.60 OF 20	4 12 10 8 XSQ= 2.13 PHI= -0.250 EP = 0.0921
315	DRIFT MORE TOWARD BEING THOSE WHERE MOTHER AND NURSING CHILD CUSTOMARILY SLEEP IN THE SAME BED (37) W-C,S	0.86 OF 14	315	DRIFT LESS TOWARD BEING THOSE WHERE MOTHER AND NURSING CHILD CUSTOMARILY SLEEP IN THE SAME BED (37) W-D,S	0.53 OF 17	12 9 2 8 XSQ= 2.42 PHI= 0.280 EP = 0.0680
317	TILT TOWARD BEING THOSE WHERE DISPLAY OF AFFECTION TOWARD THE INFANT IS LOW (29) B-B-C	0.60 OF 30	317	TILT TOWARD BEING THOSE WHERE DISPLAY OF AFFECTION TOWARD THE INFANT IS HIGH (39) B-B-C	0.70 OF 37	12 26 18 11 XSQ= 5.01 PHI= -0.274 XP = 0.0252
318	TILT TOWARD BEING THOSE WHERE THE OVERALL INDULGENCE OF THE INFANT IS LOW (31) B-B-C	0.59 OF 32	318	TILT TOWARD BEING THOSE WHERE THE OVERALL INDULGENCE OF THE INFANT IS HIGH (40) B-B-C	0.68 OF 38	13 26 19 12 XSQ= 4.37 PHI= -0.250 XP = 0.0365
326	LEAN TOWARD BEING THOSE WHERE THE INFERRED TRANSITION ANXIETY BETWEEN INFANCY AND CHILDHOOD IS HIGH (32) B-B-C	0.67 OF 33	326	LEAN TOWARD BEING THOSE WHERE THE INFERRED TRANSITION ANXIETY BETWEEN INFANCY AND CHILDHOOD IS LOW (35) B-B-C	0.70 OF 33	22 10 11 23 XSQ= 7.34 PHI= 0.333 XP = 0.0067
327	DRIFT TOWARD BEING THOSE WHERE THE AGE OF THE INFANT AT TIME OF REDUCED CONTACT WITH MOTHER IS TWO YEARS OR LOWER (27) B-B-C	0.65 OF 26	327	DRIFT TOWARD BEING THOSE WHERE THE AGE OF THE INFANT AT TIME OF REDUCED CONTACT WITH MOTHER IS HIGHER THAN TWO YEARS (28) B-B-C	0.64 OF 28	9 18 17 10 XSQ= 3.63 PHI= -0.259 XP = 0.0566
334	LEAN TOWARD BEING THOSE WHERE THE INDULGENCE OF THE CHILD IS LOW (38) B-B-C	0.70 OF 37	334	LEAN TOWARD BEING THOSE WHERE THE INDULGENCE OF THE CHILD IS HIGH (40) B-B-C	0.69 OF 39	11 27 26 12 XSQ= 10.32 PHI= -0.369 XP = 0.0013
337	LEAN TOWARD BEING THOSE WHERE THE CHILD'S INFERRED ANXIETY OVER NON-PERFORMANCE OF RESPONSIBLE BEHAVIOR IS HIGH (38) B-B-C	0.69 OF 36	337	LEAN TOWARD BEING THOSE WHERE THE CHILD'S INFERRED ANXIETY OVER NON-PERFORMANCE OF RESPONSIBLE BEHAVIOR IS LOW (35) B-B-C	0.65 OF 37	25 13 11 24 XSQ= 7.29 PHI= 0.316 XP = 0.0069

338	LEAN TOWARD BEING THOSE 0.78 OF 36 WHERE THE CHILD'S INFERRED ANXIETY OVER PERFORMANCE OF RESPONSIBLE BEHAVIOR IS HIGH (44) B-B-C	338	LEAN TOWARD BEING THOSE 0.57 OF 37 WHERE THE CHILD'S INFERRED ANXIETY CVER PERFORMANCE OF RESPCNSIBLE BEHAVICR IS LOW (29) B-B-C	28 16 8 21 XSQ= 7.70 PHI= 0.325 XP = 0.0055
339	TILT TOWARD BEING THOSE 0.58 OF 36 WHERE THE CHILD'S INFERRED CONFLICT REGARDING RESPCNSIBLE BEHAVIOR IS HIGH (31) B-B-C	339	TILT TOWARD BEING THOSE 0.73 OF 37 WHERE THE CHILD'S INFERRED CCNFLICT REGARDING RESPCNSIBLE BEHAVICR IS LOW (42) B-B-C	21 10 15 27 XSQ= 6.09 PHI= 0.289 XP = 0.0136
347	TEND TO BE THOSE 0.89 OF 37 WHERE THE CHILD'S INFERRED CONFLICT REGARDING SELF-RELIANT BEHAVIOR IS HIGH (37) B-B-C	347	TEND TO BE THCSE 0.90 CF 39 WHERE THE CHILD'S INFERRED CONFLICT REGARDING SELF-RELIANT BEHAVIOR IS LOW (39) B-B-C	33 4 4 35 XSQ= 44.24 PHI= 0.763 XP = 0.
350	TILT TOWARD BEING THOSE 0.72 OF 29 WHERE THE CHILD'S INFERRED ANXIETY OVER PERFORMANCE OF ACHIEVEMENT BEHAVIOR IS HIGH (34) B-B-C	350	TILT TOWARD BEING THOSE 0.58 OF 31 WHERE THE CHILD'S INFERRED ANXIETY OVER PERFORMANCE OF ACHIEVEMENT BEHAVICR IS LOW (26) B-B-C	21 13 8 18 XSQ= 4.49 PHI= 0.274 XP = 0.0340
351	TILT TOWARD BEING THOSE 0.62 OF 29 WHERE THE CHILD'S INFERRED CONFLICT REGARDING ACHIEVEMENT BEHAVIOR IS HIGH (26) B-B-C	351	TILT TOWARD BEING THOSE 0.74 OF 31 WHERE THE CHILD'S INFERRED CCNFLICT REGARDING ACHIEVEMENT BEHAVIOR IS LOW (34) B-B-C	18 8 11 23 XSQ= 6.61 PHI= 0.332 XP = 0.0101
353	LEAN TOWARD BEING THOSE 0.73 OF 37 WHERE THE CHILD'S INFERRED ANXIETY OVER NON-PERFORMANCE OF OBEDIENT BEHAVIOR IS HIGH (42) B-B-C	353	LEAN TOWARD BEING THOSE 0.61 OF 36 WHERE THE CHILD-S INFERRED ANXIETY OVER NON-PERFORMANCE OF OBEDIENT BEHAVICR IS LOW (32) B-B-C	27 14 10 22 XSQ= 7.28 PHI= 0.316 XP = 0.0070
377	DRIFT LESS TOWARD BEING THOSE 0.66 OF 35 WHERE MALE GENITAL MUTILATION IS ABSENT (242)	377	DRIFT MORE TOWARD BEING THCSE 0.86 OF 36 WHERE MALE GENITAL MUTILATICN IS ABSENT (242)	12 5 23 31 XSQ= 3.01 PHI= 0.206 XP = 0.0827
382	DRIFT TOWARD BEING THOSE 0.57 OF 14 WHERE FEMALE INITIATICN RITES ARE ABSENT (27) JKB	382	DRIFT TOWARD BEING THOSE 0.80 OF 15 WHERE FEMALE INITIATION RITES ARE PRESENT (38) JKB	6 12 8 3 XSQ= 2.81 PHI= -0.311 EP = 0.0604
391	TILT TOWARD BEING THOSE 0.80 OF 25 WHERE PREMARITAL SEX RELATIONS ARE PUNISHED ONLY IF PREGNANCY RESULTS, OR FREELY PERMITTED (90) JTW,EA	391	TILT TOWARD BEING THCSE 0.52 OF 27 WHERE PREMARITAL SEX RELATICNS ARE STRONGLY PUNISHED AND IN FACT RARE, OR WEAKLY PUNISHED AND IN FACT NOT RARE (89) JTW,EA	5 14 20 13 XSQ= 4.39 PHI= -0.291 XP = 0.0362

421	DRIFT TOWARD BEING THOSE 0.58 OF 26 WHERE KILLING, TORTURING, OR MUTILATING OF THE ENEMY IS STRONGLY OR MODERATELY EMPHASIZED (37) PES	421	DRIFT TOWARD BEING THOSE 0.70 OF 27 WHERE KILLING, TORTURING, OR MUTILATING OF THE ENEMY IS NEGLIGIBLY EMPHASIZED (47) PES	15 8 11 19 XSQ= 3.18 PHI= 0.245 XP = 0.0745
428	DRIFT TOWARD BEING THOSE 0.88 OF 8 WHERE A HIGH GOD, IF PRESENT AND ACTIVE, DOES NOT SUPPORT HUMAN MORALITY, RATHER THAN SUPPORTING IT (26) GES,EA	428	DRIFT TOWARD BEING THOSE 0.67 OF 6 WHERE A HIGH GOD, IF PRESENT AND ACTIVE, SUPPORTS HUMAN MORALITY, RATHER THAN NOT SUPPORTING IT (61) GES,EA	1 4 7 2 XSQ= 2.34 PHI= -0.409 EP = 0.0909
455	DRIFT TOWARD BEING THOSE 0.68 OF 19 WHERE THE MODE OF THE INDIVIDUAL'S CONTACT WITH THE DIVINE IS NOT CONDUCIVE TO THE DEVELOPMENT OF THE INDIVIDUAL'S NEED TO ACHIEVE (19) DCM	455	DRIFT TOWARD BEING THOSE 0.65 OF 17 WHERE THE MODE OF THE INDIVIDUAL'S CONTACT WITH THE DIVINE IS CONDUCIVE TO THE DEVELOPMENT OF THE INDIVIDUAL'S NEED TO ACHIEVE (17) DCM	6 11 13 6 XSQ= 2.73 PHI= -0.276 EP = 0.0933
458	LEAN TOWARD BEING THOSE 0.50 OF 28 WHERE GAMES, IF PRESENT, INCLUDE GAMES OF STRATEGY (52) R-A-B,EA	458	LEAN TOWARD BEING THOSE 0.88 OF 25 WHERE GAMES, IF PRESENT, DO NOT INCLUDE GAMES OF STRATEGY (119) R-A-B,EA	14 3 14 22 XSQ= 7.10 PHI= 0.366 XP = 0.0077
460	LEAN TOWARD BEING THOSE 0.79 OF 28 WHERE GAMES, IF PRESENT, ARE NOT LIMITED TO GAMES OF SKILL ONLY (104) R-A-B,EA	46C	LEAN TOWARD BEING THOSE 0.64 OF 25 WHERE GAMES, IF PRESENT, ARE LIMITED TO GAMES OF SKILL ONLY (67) R-A-B,EA	6 16 22 9 XSQ= 8.18 PHI= -0.393 XP = 0.0042
469	IN ALL CASES ARE THOSE 1.00 OF 16 WHERE CONTACT WITH OTHER CULTURES IS FREQUENT OR REGULAR, RATHER THAN IRREGULAR (43) JMH	469	LEAN LESS TOWARD BEING THOSE 0.58 OF 12 WHERE CONTACT WITH OTHER CULTURES IS FREQUENT OR REGULAR, RATHER THAN IRREGULAR (43) JMH	16 7 0 5 XSQ= 5.52 PHI= 0.444 EP = 0.0081
476	TEND TO BE THOSE 0.80 OF 15 WHERE THE DEGREE OF INSOBRIETY IS MODERATE OR SLIGHT (18) DH	476	TEND TO BE THOSE 0.90 OF 10 WHERE THE DEGREE OF INSOBRIETY IS STRONG (31) DH	3 9 12 1 XSQ= 9.14 PHI= -0.605 EP = 0.0010

347 CULTURES WHERE THE CHILD'S INFERRED CONFLICT REGARDING SELF-RELIANT BEHAVIOR IS HIGH (37) B-B-C	347 CULTURES WHERE THE CHILD'S INFERRED CONFLICT REGARDING SELF-RELIANT BEHAVIOR IS LOW (39) B-B-C

BACKGROUND ON PAGE 143

BOTH SUBJECT AND PREDICATE

37 IN LEFT COLUMN

ALORESE	ARAUCANIANS	AYMARA	AZANDE	BALINESE	CAMAYURA	CHAGGA	CROW	GANDA	HANO
KASKA	KIKUYU	KURTATCHI	LAMBA	LAU	MANDAN	MASAI	MBUNDU	MURNGIN	NAVAHO
NYAKYUSA	OJIBWA	SOTHO	SWAZI	TANALA	THONGA	TIV	TRUKESE	TUCUNA	TURKANA
VENDA	WICHITA	WINNEBAGO	WOLEAIANS	YAHGAN	YAKUT	ZUNI			

39 IN RIGHT COLUMN

AINU	ARANDA	ARAPESH	ASHANTI	CHENCHU	CHEYENNE	CHIR-APACHE	CHUKCHEE	COMANCHE	CUNA
FON	IFUGAO	JIVARO	KORYAK	KWAKIUTL	LEPCHA	LESU	MANUS	MAORI	MARQUESANS
NUER	OMAHA	ONA	ONTONG-JAVA	PAPAGO	PUKAPUKA	SAMOANS	SHERENTE	SIRIONO	TALLENSI
TENETEHARA	TETON	TIKOPIA	TIMBIRA	TROBRIAND	TUPINAMBA	WOGEO	YAGUA	YORUBA	

324 EXCLUDED BECAUSE UNASCERTAINED

3	TILT LESS TOWARD BEING THOSE LOCATED OUTSIDE OF AFRICA (320)	0.62 OF 37	3	TILT MORE TOWARD BEING THOSE LOCATED OUTSIDE OF AFRICA (320)	0.87 OF 39	14 5 23 34 XSQ= 5.07 PHI= 0.258 XP = 0.0243
51	TILT TOWARD BEING THOSE WHERE SUBSISTENCE IS PRIMARILY BY FOOD PRODUCTION -- I. E., AGRICULTURE OR HUSBANDRY -- RATHER THAN BY GATHERING (253)	0.68 OF 37	51	TILT TOWARD BEING THOSE WHERE SUBSISTENCE IS PRIMARILY BY FOOD GATHERING -- I. E., HUNTING, FISHING, OR COLLECTING -- RATHER THAN FOOD PRODUCTION (147)	0.59 OF 39	25 16 12 23 XSQ= 4.37 PHI= 0.240 XP = 0.0366
53	DRIFT LESS TOWARD BEING THOSE WHERE FOOD PRODUCTION IS BY SIMPLE AGRICULTURE OR INCIPIENT FOOD PRODUCTION, RATHER THAN BY INTENSIVE AGRICULTURE (147)	0.57 OF 28	53	DRIFT MORE TOWARD BEING THOSE WHERE FOOD PRODUCTION IS BY SIMPLE AGRICULTURE OR INCIPIENT FOOD PRODUCTION, RATHER THAN BY INTENSIVE AGRICULTURE (147)	0.86 OF 22	12 3 16 19 XSQ= 3.71 PHI= 0.273 XP = 0.0539
55	DRIFT TOWARD BEING THOSE WHERE FOOD PRODUCTION IS BY INTENSIVE AGRICULTURE, RATHER THAN BY SIMPLE AGRICULTURE (91)	0.52 OF 23	55	DRIFT TOWARD BEING THOSE WHERE FOOD PRODUCTION IS BY SIMPLE AGRICULTURE, RATHER THAN BY INTENSIVE AGRICULTURE (101)	0.80 OF 15	12 3 11 12 XSQ= 2.70 PHI= 0.267 EP = 0.0884

63	TILT TOWARD BEING THOSE 0.67 OF 27 WHERE HUSBANDRY, IF PRESENT, IS PRINCIPALLY IN THE FORM OF BOVINE, EQUINE, CAMEL-LIKE, OR DEER-LIKE ANIMALS, RATHER THAN PIGS, SHEEP, OR GOATS (152)	63	TILT TOWARD BEING THOSE 0.68 OF 25 WHERE HUSBANDRY, IF PRESENT, IS PRINCIPALLY IN THE FORM OF PIGS, SHEEP, OR GOATS, RATHER THAN BOVINE, EQUINE, CAMEL-LIKE, OR DEER-LIKE ANIMALS (74)	18 8 9 17 XSQ= 4.93 PHI= 0.308 XP = 0.0264
71	LEAN TOWARD BEING THOSE 0.54 OF 28 WHERE METAL WORKING IS PRESENT (98)	71	LEAN TOWARD BEING THOSE 0.82 OF 33 WHERE METAL WORKING IS ABSENT (153)	15 6 13 27 XSQ= 6.91 PHI= 0.337 XP = 0.0086
77	TILT LESS TOWARD BEING THOSE 0.64 OF 14 WHERE THE WRITING SYSTEM IS MNEMONIC OR ABSENT, RATHER THAN BEING ALPHABETIC-OR-PHONETIC (39) JMH	77	IN ALL CASES ARE THOSE 1.00 OF 14 WHERE THE WRITING SYSTEM IS MNEMONIC OR ABSENT, RATHER THAN BEING ALPHABETIC-OR-PHONETIC (39) JMH	5 0 9 14 XSQ= 3.90 PHI= 0.373 EP = 0.0407
95	TILT LESS TOWARD BEING THOSE 0.62 OF 34 WHERE THE HIERARCHY OF NATIONAL JURISDICTION HAS ONE OR NO LEVELS (254) GES,EA	95	TILT MORE TOWARD BEING THOSE 0.89 OF 37 WHERE THE HIERARCHY OF NATIONAL JURISDICTION HAS ONE OR NO LEVELS (254) GES,EA	13 4 21 33 XSQ= 5.89 PHI= 0.288 XP = 0.0152
141	DRIFT TOWARD BEING THOSE 0.71 OF 14 WHERE THE LEVEL OF SOCIAL SANCTION IS PUBLIC CORPOREAL SANCTION, RATHER THAN PUBLIC PROPERTY SANCTION OR PRIVATE SETTLEMENT (28) JMH	141	DRIFT TOWARD BEING THOSE 0.71 OF 14 WHERE THE LEVEL OF SOCIAL SANCTION IS PUBLIC PROPERTY SANCTION OR PRIVATE SETTLEMENT, RATHER THAN PUBLIC CORPOREAL SANCTION (26) JMH	10 4 4 10 XSQ= 3.57 PHI= 0.357 EP = 0.0570
142	TILT TOWARD BEING THOSE 0.93 OF 14 WHERE THE LEVEL OF SOCIAL SANCTION IS PUBLIC CORPOREAL SANCTION OR PUBLIC PROPERTY SANCTION, RATHER THAN PRIVATE SETTLEMENT (38) JMH	142	TILT TOWARD BEING THOSE 0.57 OF 14 WHERE THE LEVEL OF SOCIAL SANCTION IS PRIVATE SETTLEMENT, RATHER THAN PUBLIC CORPOREAL SANCTION OR PUBLIC PROPERTY SETTLEMENT (16) JMH	13 6 1 8 XSQ= 5.89 PHI= 0.459 EP = 0.0128
177	DRIFT LESS TOWARD BEING THOSE 0.69 OF 36 WHERE THE COMMUNITY IS OTHER THAN A SINGLE CLAN-COMMUNITY AND EXOGAMOUS (305)	177	DRIFT MORE TOWARD BEING THOSE 0.90 OF 39 WHERE THE COMMUNITY IS OTHER THAN A SINGLE CLAN-COMMUNITY AND EXOGAMOUS (305)	11 4 25 35 XSQ= 3.64 PHI= 0.220 XP = 0.0565
180	DRIFT TOWARD BEING THOSE 0.50 OF 36 WHERE THE COMMUNITY IS COMMONLY EXOGAMOUS, RATHER THAN NON-EXOGAMOUS (124)	18C	DRIFT TOWARD BEING THOSE 0.72 OF 39 WHERE THE COMMUNITY IS COMMONLY NON-EXOGAMOUS, RATHER THAN EXOGAMOUS (258)	18 11 18 28 XSQ= 2.89 PHI= 0.196 XP = 0.0893
188	LEAN MORE TOWARD BEING THOSE 0.89 OF 37 WHERE THE KIN GROUP IS OTHER THAN EXCLUSIVELY COGNATIC (252)	188	LEAN LESS TOWARD BEING THOSE 0.54 OF 39 WHERE THE KIN GROUP IS OTHER THAN EXCLUSIVELY COGNATIC (252)	4 18 33 21 XSQ= 9.88 PHI= -0.360 XP = 0.0017

192	TILT MORE TOWARD BEING THOSE 0.95 OF 37 OTHER THAN WHERE THE ONLY KIN GROUP PRESENT IS A KINDRED OR ELSE BILATERAL DESCENT IS INFERRED (289)	192	TILT LESS TOWARD BEING THOSE 0.72 OF 39 OTHER THAN WHERE THE ONLY KIN GROUP PRESENT IS A KINDRED OR ELSE BILATERAL DESCENT IS INFERRED (289)	2 11 35 28 XSQ= 5.45 PHI= -0.268 XP = 0.0196
234	LEAN TOWARD BEING THOSE 0.79 OF 33 WHERE THE COUSIN TERMINOLOGY IS OF CROW, OMAHA, OR IROQUOIS TYPE, RATHER THAN ESKIMO OR HAWAIIAN TYPE (152)	234	LEAN TOWARD BEING THOSE 0.63 OF 32 WHERE THE COUSIN TERMINOLOGY IS OF ESKIMO OR HAWAIIAN TYPE, RATHER THAN CROW, OMAHA, OR IROQUOIS TYPE (170)	26 12 7 20 XSQ= 9.77 PHI= 0.388 XP = 0.0018
259	TILT TOWARD BEING THOSE 0.85 OF 13 WHERE THE SEVERITY OF MOTHER-IN-LAW AVOIDANCE IS HIGH (26) WNS	259	TILT TOWARD BEING THOSE 0.65 OF 20 WHERE THE SEVERITY OF MOTHER-IN-LAW AVOIDANCE IS LOW (20) WNS	11 7 2 13 XSQ= 5.95 PHI= 0.425 EP = 0.0110
284	IN ALL CASES ARE THOSE 1.00 OF 4 WHERE CONTRACEPTION IS PRACTICED (10) CSF	284	DRIFT TOWARD BEING THOSE 0.75 OF 8 WHERE CONTRACEPTION IS NOT PRACTICED (7) CSF	4 2 0 6 XSQ= 3.38 PHI= 0.530 EP = 0.0606
317	DRIFT TOWARD BEING THOSE 0.57 OF 30 WHERE DISPLAY OF AFFECTION TOWARD THE INFANT IS LOW (29) B-B-C	317	DRIFT TOWARD BEING THOSE 0.68 OF 37 WHERE DISPLAY OF AFFECTION TOWARD THE INFANT IS HIGH (39) B-B-C	13 25 17 12 XSQ= 3.04 PHI= -0.213 XP = 0.0813
318	TILT TOWARD BEING THOSE 0.63 OF 32 WHERE THE OVERALL INDULGENCE OF THE INFANT IS LOW (31) B-B-C	318	TILT TOWARD BEING THOSE 0.71 OF 38 WHERE THE OVERALL INDULGENCE OF THE INFANT IS HIGH (40) B-B-C	12 27 20 11 XSQ= 6.62 PHI= -0.308 XP = 0.0101
320	TILT LESS TOWARD BEING THOSE 0.52 OF 31 WHERE THE DEGREE OF REDUCTION OF THE INFANT'S DRIVES IS HIGH (45) B-B-C	320	TILT MORE TOWARD BEING THOSE 0.78 OF 36 WHERE THE DEGREE OF REDUCTION OF THE INFANT'S DRIVES IS HIGH (45) B-B-C	16 28 15 8 XSQ= 3.96 PHI= -0.243 XP = 0.0465
326	LEAN TOWARD BEING THOSE 0.70 OF 33 WHERE THE INFERRED TRANSITION ANXIETY BETWEEN INFANCY AND CHILDHOOD IS HIGH (32) B-B-C	326	LEAN TOWARD BEING THOSE 0.73 OF 33 WHERE THE INFERRED TRANSITION ANXIETY BETWEEN INFANCY AND CHILDHOOD IS LOW (35) B-B-C	23 9 10 24 XSQ= 10.25 PHI= 0.394 XP = 0.0014
327	LEAN TOWARD BEING THOSE 0.70 OF 27 WHERE THE AGE OF THE INFANT AT TIME OF REDUCED CONTACT WITH MOTHER IS TWO YEARS OR LOWER (27) B-B-C	327	LEAN TOWARD BEING THOSE 0.70 OF 27 WHERE THE AGE OF THE INFANT AT TIME OF REDUCED CONTACT WITH MOTHER IS HIGHER THAN TWO YEARS (28) B-B-C	8 19 19 8 XSQ= 7.41 PHI= -0.370 XP = 0.0065

334	TEND TO BE THOSE 0.76 OF 37 WHERE THE INDULGENCE OF THE CHILD IS LOW (38) B-B-C	334	TEND TO BE THOSE 0.74 OF 39 WHERE THE INDULGENCE OF THE CHILD IS HIGH (40) B-B-C	9 29 28 10 XSQ= 17.06 PHI= -0.474 XP = 0.0000
337	LEAN TOWARD BEING THOSE 0.69 OF 36 WHERE THE CHILD'S INFERRED ANXIETY OVER NON-PERFORMANCE OF RESPONSIBLE BEHAVIOR IS HIGH (38) B-B-C	337	LEAN TOWARD BEING THOSE 0.65 OF 37 WHERE THE CHILD'S INFERRED ANXIETY OVER NON-PERFORMANCE OF RESPONSIBLE BEHAVIOR IS LOW (35) B-B-C	25 13 11 24 XSQ= 7.29 PHI= 0.316 XP = 0.0069
338	LEAN TOWARD BEING THOSE 0.78 OF 36 WHERE THE CHILD'S INFERRED ANXIETY OVER PERFORMANCE OF RESPONSIBLE BEHAVIOR IS HIGH (44) B-B-C	338	LEAN TOWARD BEING THOSE 0.57 OF 37 WHERE THE CHILD'S INFERRED ANXIETY OVER PERFORMANCE OF RESPONSIBLE BEHAVIOR IS LOW (29) B-B-C	28 16 8 21 XSQ= 7.70 PHI= 0.325 XP = 0.0055
339	TILT TOWARD BEING THOSE 0.58 OF 36 WHERE THE CHILD'S INFERRED CONFLICT REGARDING RESPONSIBLE BEHAVIOR IS HIGH (31) B-B-C	339	TILT TOWARD BEING THOSE 0.73 OF 37 WHERE THE CHILD'S INFERRED CONFLICT REGARDING RESPONSIBLE BEHAVIOR IS LOW (42) B-B-C	21 10 15 27 XSQ= 6.09 PHI= 0.289 XP = 0.0136
345	TILT TOWARD BEING THOSE 0.62 OF 37 WHERE THE CHILD'S INFERRED ANXIETY OVER NON-PERFORMANCE OF SELF-RELIANT BEHAVIOR IS HIGH (37) B-B-C	345	TILT TOWARD BEING THOSE 0.64 OF 39 WHERE THE CHILD'S INFERRED ANXIETY OVER NON-PERFORMANCE OF SELF-RELIANT BEHAVIOR IS LOW (39) B-B-C	23 14 14 25 XSQ= 4.24 PHI= 0.236 XP = 0.0394
346	TEND TO BE THOSE 0.89 OF 37 WHERE THE CHILD'S INFERRED ANXIETY OVER PERFORMANCE OF SELF-RELIANT BEHAVIOR IS HIGH (37) B-B-C	346	TEND TO BE THOSE 0.90 OF 39 WHERE THE CHILD'S INFERRED ANXIETY OVER PERFORMANCE OF SELF-RELIANT BEHAVIOR IS LOW (39) B-B-C	33 4 4 35 XSQ= 44.24 PHI= 0.763 XP = 0.
350	TILT TOWARD BEING THOSE 0.73 OF 30 WHERE THE CHILD'S INFERRED ANXIETY OVER PERFORMANCE OF ACHIEVEMENT BEHAVIOR IS HIGH (34) B-B-C	350	TILT TOWARD BEING THOSE 0.60 OF 30 WHERE THE CHILD'S INFERRED ANXIETY OVER PERFORMANCE OF ACHIEVEMENT BEHAVIOR IS LOW (26) B-B-C	22 12 8 18 XSQ= 5.50 PHI= 0.303 XP = 0.0190
351	TILT TOWARD BEING THOSE 0.60 OF 30 WHERE THE CHILD'S INFERRED CONFLICT REGARDING ACHIEVEMENT BEHAVIOR IS HIGH (26) B-B-C	351	TILT TOWARD BEING THOSE 0.73 OF 30 WHERE THE CHILD'S INFERRED CONFLICT REGARDING ACHIEVEMENT BEHAVIOR IS LOW (34) B-B-C	18 8 12 22 XSQ= 5.50 PHI= 0.303 XP = 0.0190
353	LEAN TOWARD BEING THOSE 0.73 OF 37 WHERE THE CHILD'S INFERRED ANXIETY OVER NON-PERFORMANCE OF OBEDIENT BEHAVIOR IS HIGH (42) B-B-C	353	LEAN TOWARD BEING THOSE 0.61 OF 36 WHERE THE CHILD-S INFERRED ANXIETY OVER NON-PERFORMANCE OF OBEDIENT BEHAVIOR IS LOW (32) B-B-C	27 14 10 22 XSQ= 7.28 PHI= 0.316 XP = 0.0070

354	TILT TCWARD BEING THOSE 0.62 OF 37 WHERE THE CHILD'S INFERREC ANXIETY OVER PERFCRMANCE CF CBECIENT BEHAVIOR IS HIGH (36) B-B-C	354	TILT TOWARD BEING THOSE 0.66 OF 35 WHERE THE CHILD'S INFERRED ANXIETY CVER PERFORMANCE OF OBEDIENT BEHAVIOR IS LOW (37) B-B-C	23 12 14 23 XSQ= 4.53 PHI= 0.251 XP = 0.0332
355	DRIFT TCWARD BEING THCSE 0.59 OF 37 WHERE THE CHILD'S INFERREC CONFLICT REGARCING CBEDIENT BEHAVICR IS HIGH (35) B-B-C	355	DRIFT TOWARD BEING THOSE 0.66 OF 35 WHERE THE CHILD'S INFERRED CONFLICT REGARDING OBEDIENT BEHAVIOR IS LOW (38) B-B-C	22 12 15 23 XSQ= 3.62 PHI= 0.224 XP = 0.0571
390	TILT MCRE TOWARC BEING THCSE 0.96 OF 23 WHERE PREMARITAL SEX RELATIONS ARE WEAKLY PUNISHED ANC IN FACT NCT RARE OR PUNISHED CNLY IF PREGNANCY RESULTS, OR FREELY PERMITTEC (132) JTW,EA	390	TILT LESS TOWARD BEING THOSE 0.69 OF 29 WHERE PREMARITAL SEX RELATICNS ARE WEAKLY PUNISHED AND IN FACT NOT RARE OR PUNISHED ONLY IF PREGNANCY RESULTS, OR FREELY PERMITTED (132) JTW,EA	1 9 22 20 XSQ= 4.29 PHI= -0.287 XP = 0.0384
421	DRIFT TCWARD BEING THCSE 0.58 OF 24 WHERE KILLING, TORTURING, CR MUTILATING CF THE ENEMY IS STRCNGLY CR MCDERATELY EMPHASIZED (37) PES	421	DRIFT TOWARD BEING THOSE 0.69 OF 29 WHERE KILLING, TORTURING, CR MUTILATING OF THE ENEMY IS NEGLIGIBLY EMPHASIZED (47) PES	14 9 10 20 XSQ= 2.95 PHI= 0.236 XP = 0.0859
446	DRIFT TCWARD BEING THCSE 0.64 OF 11 WHERE WITCHCRAFT IS SIGNIFICANTLY PRESENT (14) GES	446	DRIFT TOWARD BEING THOSE 0.80 OF 10 WHERE WITCHCRAFT IS MODERATELY PRESENT OR ABSENT (24) GES	7 2 4 8 XSQ= 2.49 PHI= 0.344 EP = 0.0805
453	TILT TCWARD BEING THOSE 0.53 OF 19 WHERE THE ROLE CF RELIGIOUS EXPERTS IS CCNDUCIVE TO THE DEVELCPMENT OF THE INDIVIDUAL'S NEED TO ACHIEVE (13) DCM	453	TILT TOWARD BEING THOSE 0.82 OF 17 WHERE THE ROLE OF RELIGIOUS EXPERTS IS NOT CONDUCIVE TO THE DEVELOPMENT OF THE INDIVIDUAL'S NEED TC ACHIEVE (23) DCM	10 3 9 14 XSQ= 3.36 PHI= 0.306 EP = 0.0411
458	TEND TC BE THCSE 0.58 OF 26 WHERE GAMES, IF PRESENT, INCLUDE GAMES CF STRATEGY (52) R-A-B,EA	458	TEND TO BE THOSE 0.93 OF 27 WHERE GAMES, IF PRESENT, DO NOT INCLUDE GAMES OF STRATEGY (119) R-A-B,EA	15 2 11 25 XSQ= 13.15 PHI= 0.498 XP = 0.0003
460	LEAN TOWARD BEING THOSE 0.81 OF 26 WHERE GAMES, IF PRESENT, ARE NCT LIMITED TO GAMES CF SKILL CNLY (104) R-A-B,EA	460	LEAN TOWARD BEING THOSE 0.63 OF 27 WHERE GAMES, IF PRESENT, ARE LIMITED TO GAMES OF SKILL ONLY (67) R-A-B,EA	5 17 21 10 XSQ= 8.71 PHI= -0.405 XP = 0.0032
469	IN ALL CASES ARE THOSE 1.00 OF 14 WHERE CCNTACT WITH CTHER CULTURES IS FREQUENT CR REGULAR, RATHER THAN IRREGULAR (43) JMH	469	TILT LESS TOWARD BEING THCSE 0.64 OF 14 WHERE CONTACT WITH OTHER CULTURES IS FREQUENT OR REGULAR, RATHER THAN IRREGULAR (43) JMH	14 9 0 5 XSQ= 3.90 PHI= 0.373 EP = 0.0407

347/

476	LEAN TCWARC BEING THOSE WHERE THE CEGREE OF INSOBRIETY IS MCDERATE CR SLIGHT (18) CH	0.79 OF 14	476	LEAN TOWARD BEING THOSE WHERE THE DEGREE OF INSOBRIETY IS STRONG (31) DH	0.82 OF 11	3 9 11 2 XSQ= 6.74 PHI= -0.519 EP = 0.0048

348 CULTURES WHERE THE TOTAL POSITIVE PRESSURE TOWARD DEVELCPING ACHIEVEMENT BEHAVIOR IN THE CHILD IS HIGH (32) B-B-C	348 CULTURES WHERE THE TOTAL POSITIVE PRESSURE TOWARC DEVELOPING ACHIEVEMENT BEHAVIOR IN THE CHILD IS LOW (31) B-B-C

BACKGROUND ON PAGE 143 — BCTH SUBJECT AND PREDICATE

32 IN LEFT CCLUMN

ARANDA	ARAUCANIANS	ASHANTI	CHAGGA	CHEYENNE	CHIR-APACHE	CHUKCHEE	COMANCHE	CROW	FON
GANDA	JIVARC	KIKUYU	KWAKIUTL	LAU	MANDAN	MANUS	MACRI	MASAI	NAVAHO
NYAKYUSA	CJIBWA	OMAHA	PAPAGO	PUKAPUKA	TETON	THCNGA	TIMBIRA	TIV	VENDA
WINNEBAGC	YAHGAN								

31 IN RIGHT CCLUMN

AINU	ARAPESH	AYMARA	AZANDE	BALINESE	CAMAYURA	CUNA	HANC	KASKA	KORYAK
LEPCHA	LESU	MBUNCU	MURNGIN	NUER	ONA	SAMOANS	SHERENTE	SIRICNO	SOTHO
SWAZI	TALLENSI	TANALA	TRUKESE	TURKANA	WICHITA	WOGEO	WOLEAIANS	YAGUA	YORUBA
ZUNI									

337 EXCLUCED BECAUSE UNASCERTAINEC

8	DRIFT LESS TOWARC BEING THCSE LCCATED CUTSIDE CF NCRTH AMERICA (330)	0.63 OF 32	8 DRIFT MORE TOWARD BEING THCSE LOCATED OUTSIDE OF NORTH AMERICA (330)	0.87 OF 31	12 4 20 27 XSQ= 3.81 PHI= 0.246 XP = 0.0508
14	TILT TCWARC BEING THOSE WHERE THE LATITUCE IS THIRTY DEGREES CR GREATER (119)	0.50 OF 32	14 TILT TOWARD BEING THOSE WHERE THE LATITUDE IS LESS THAN THIRTY DEGREES (281)	0.77 OF 31	16 7 16 24 XSQ= 3.99 PHI= 0.252 XP = 0.0457
15	DRIFT TCWARD BEING THCSE WHERE THE LATITUCE IS TWENTY DEGREES CR GREATER (183)	0.59 OF 32	15 DRIFT TOWARD BEING THOSE WHERE THE LATITUDE IS LESS THAN TWENTY DEGREES (217)	0.65 OF 31	19 11 13 20 XSQ= 2.71 PHI= 0.207 XP = 0.C998
36	DRIFT TCWARD BEING THCSE WHERE THE NATURAL ENVIRONMENT IS 'VERY HARSH,' CR SUB-TROPICAL BUSH, OR TEMPERATE GRASSLANC (108) FWM	0.53 OF 32	36 DRIFT TOWARD BEING THCSE WHERE THE NATURAL ENVIRCNMENT IS OTHER THAN 'VERY HARSH,' CR SUB-TRCPICAL BUSH, OR TEMPERATE GRASSLAND (292) FWM	0.74 OF 31	17 8 15 23 XSQ= 3.83 PHI= 0.247 XP = 0.0502

74	DRIFT TOWARD BEING THOSE WHERE POTTERY IS PRESENT (145)	0.68 OF 28	74	DRIFT TOWARD BEING THOSE WHERE POTTERY IS ABSENT (93)	0.64 OF 22	19 8 9 14 XSQ= 3.73 PHI= 0.273 XP = 0.0533
137	DRIFT TOWARD BEING THOSE WHERE INVIDIOUS DISPLAY OF WEALTH IS STRONGLY EMPHASIZED (37) PES	0.54 OF 26	137	DRIFT TOWARD BEING THOSE WHERE INVIDIOUS DISPLAY OF WEALTH IS MODERATELY, LITTLE, OR NEGATIVELY EMPHASIZED (52) PES	0.75 OF 20	14 5 12 15 XSQ= 2.78 PHI= 0.246 XP = 0.0954
148	LEAN TOWARD BEING THOSE WHERE THE INCIDENCE OF PERSONAL CRIME IS HIGH (12) B-B-C	0.64 OF 14	148	LEAN TOWARD BEING THOSE WHERE THE INCIDENCE OF PERSONAL CRIME IS LOW (21) B-B-C	0.92 OF 13	9 1 5 12 XSQ= 6.99 PHI= 0.509 EP = 0.0044
258	DRIFT TOWARD BEING THOSE WHERE THE SEVERITY OF SON'S WIFE AVOIDANCE IS HIGH (15) WNS	0.71 OF 14	258	IN ALL CASES ARE THOSE WHERE THE SEVERITY OF SON'S WIFE AVOIDANCE IS LOW (16) WNS	1.00 OF 3	10 0 4 3 XSQ= 2.67 PHI= 0.397 EP = 0.0515
259	DRIFT TOWARD BEING THOSE WHERE THE SEVERITY OF MOTHER-IN-LAW AVOIDANCE IS HIGH (26) WNS	0.76 OF 17	259	DRIFT TOWARD BEING THOSE WHERE THE SEVERITY OF MOTHER-IN-LAW AVOIDANCE IS LOW (20) WNS	0.63 OF 8	13 3 4 5 XSQ= 2.09 PHI= 0.289 EP = 0.0870
305	DRIFT TOWARD BEING THOSE WHERE THE EARLY SEXUAL SATISFACTION POTENTIAL IS LOW (24) W-C	0.69 OF 16	305	DRIFT TOWARD BEING THOSE WHERE THE EARLY SEXUAL SATISFACTION POTENTIAL IS HIGH (27) W-C	0.69 OF 13	5 9 11 4 XSQ= 2.76 PHI= -0.309 EP = 0.0656
328	TILT TOWARD BEING THOSE WHERE THE AGE OF THE INFANT AT THE ONSET OF SERIOUS SOCIALIZATION, OTHER THAN WEANING, IS TWO YEARS OR LOWER (20) B-B-C	0.73 OF 15	328	TILT TOWARD BEING THOSE WHERE THE AGE OF THE INFANT AT THE ONSET OF SERIOUS SOCIALIZATION, OTHER THAN WEANING, IS HIGHER THAN TWO YEARS (21) B-B-C	0.70 OF 23	4 16 11 7 XSQ= 5.09 PHI= -0.366 EP = 0.0189
344	TILT TOWARD BEING THOSE WHERE THE TOTAL POSITIVE PRESSURE TOWARD DEVELOPING SELF-RELIANT BEHAVIOR IN THE CHILD IS HIGH (36) B-B-C	0.63 OF 32	344	TILT TOWARD BEING THOSE WHERE THE TOTAL POSITIVE PRESSURE TOWARD DEVELOPING SELF-RELIANT BEHAVIOR IN THE CHILD IS LOW (40) B-B-C	0.71 OF 31	20 9 12 22 XSQ= 5.82 PHI= 0.304 XP = 0.0159
349	TEND TO BE THOSE WHERE THE CHILD'S INFERRED ANXIETY OVER NON-PERFORMANCE OF ACHIEVEMENT BEHAVIOR IS HIGH (34) B-B-C	0.94 OF 32	349	TEND TO BE THOSE WHERE THE CHILD'S INFERRED ANXIETY OVER NON-PERFORMANCE OF ACHIEVEMENT BEHAVIOR IS LOW (28) B-B-C	0.87 OF 30	30 4 2 26 XSQ= 37.25 PHI= 0.775 XP = 0.

350 LEAN TOWARD BEING THOSE 0.77 OF 31 WHERE THE CHILD'S INFERRED ANXIETY OVER PERFORMANCE OF ACHIEVEMENT BEHAVIOR IS HIGH (34) B-B-C	350 LEAN TOWARD BEING THOSE 0.66 OF 29 WHERE THE CHILD'S INFERRED ANXIETY OVER PERFORMANCE OF ACHIEVEMENT BEHAVIOR IS LOW (26) B-B-C	24 10 7 19 XSQ= 9.57 PHI= 0.399 XP = 0.0020
351 TILT TOWARD BEING THOSE 0.58 OF 31 WHERE THE CHILD'S INFERRED CONFLICT REGARDING ACHIEVEMENT BEHAVIOR IS HIGH (26) B-B-C	351 TILT TOWARD BEING THOSE 0.72 OF 29 WHERE THE CHILD'S INFERRED CONFLICT REGARDING ACHIEVEMENT BEHAVIOR IS LOW (34) B-B-C	18 8 13 21 XSQ= 4.49 PHI= 0.274 XP = 0.0340
358 DRIFT MORE TOWARD BEING THOSE 0.93 OF 15 WHERE ADOLESCENT PEER GROUPS ARE PRESENT IN A SETTING OF WORK AND PUBLIC GATHERINGS AND LEISURE, OR OF PUBLIC GATHERINGS AND LEISURE, OR OF LEISURE ONLY (41) JKH	358 DRIFT LESS TOWARD BEING THOSE 0.55 OF 11 WHERE ADOLESCENT PEER GROUPS ARE PRESENT IN A SETTING OF WORK AND PUBLIC GATHERINGS AND LEISURE, OR OF PUBLIC GATHERINGS AND LEISURE, OR OF LEISURE ONLY (41) JKH	14 6 1 5 XSQ= 3.42 PHI= 0.362 EP = 0.0538
382 TILT TOWARD BEING THOSE 0.85 OF 13 WHERE FEMALE INITIATION RITES ARE PRESENT (38) JKB	382 TILT TOWARD BEING THOSE 0.67 OF 12 WHERE FEMALE INITIATION RITES ARE ABSENT (27) JKB	11 4 2 8 XSQ= 4.87 PHI= 0.441 EP = 0.0154
386 DRIFT TOWARD BEING THOSE 0.80 OF 20 WHERE SEXUAL EXPRESSION BY THE YOUNG IS RESTRICTED OR SEMI-RESTRICTED (46) F-B	386 DRIFT TOWARD BEING THOSE 0.50 OF 16 WHERE SEXUAL EXPRESSION BY THE YOUNG IS PERMITTED (40) F-B	16 8 4 8 XSQ= 2.38 PHI= 0.257 EP = 0.0815
391 DRIFT TOWARD BEING THOSE 0.54 OF 24 WHERE PREMARITAL SEX RELATIONS ARE STRONGLY PUNISHED AND IN FACT RARE, OR WEAKLY PUNISHED AND IN FACT NOT RARE (89) JTW,EA	391 DRIFT TOWARD BEING THOSE 0.78 OF 18 WHERE PREMARITAL SEX RELATIONS ARE PUNISHED ONLY IF PREGNANCY RESULTS, OR FREELY PERMITTED (90) JTW,EA	13 4 11 14 XSQ= 3.13 PHI= 0.273 XP = 0.0768
398 DRIFT TOWARD BEING THOSE 0.73 OF 11 WHERE THE INTENSITY OF SEX ANXIETY IS HIGH (16) WNS	398 DRIFT TOWARD BEING THOSE 0.73 OF 11 WHERE THE INTENSITY OF SEX ANXIETY IS LOW (16) WNS	8 3 3 8 XSQ= 2.91 PHI= 0.364 EP = 0.0861
399 DRIFT TOWARD BEING THOSE 0.65 OF 20 WHERE INTENSITY OF CASTRATION ANXIETY IS HIGH (23) WNS	399 DRIFT TOWARD BEING THOSE 0.67 OF 15 WHERE INTENSITY OF CASTRATION ANXIETY IS LOW (22) WNS	13 5 7 10 XSQ= 2.29 PHI= 0.256 EP = 0.0922
402 TILT TOWARD BEING THOSE 0.78 OF 18 WHERE EXPLANATIONS OF ILLNESS OF AN ORAL NATURE ARE PRESENT (31) W-C	402 TILT TOWARD BEING THOSE 0.71 OF 14 WHERE EXPLANATIONS OF ILLNESS OF AN ORAL NATURE ARE ABSENT (30) W-C	14 4 4 10 XSQ= 5.88 PHI= 0.429 EP = 0.0110

```
419  TILT TOWARD BEING THOSE          0.78 OF  27     419  TILT TOWARD BEING THOSE          0.63 OF  19          21     7
     WHERE MILITARY GLORY                                  WHERE MILITARY GLORY                                     6    12
     IS STRONGLY OR                                        IS NEGLIGIBLY EMPHASIZED  (31) PES               XSQ=     6.22
     MODERATELY EMPHASIZED  (55) PES                                                                        PHI=    0.368
                                                                                                            XP =   0.0126

420  TILT TOWARD BEING THOSE          0.54 OF  24     420  TILT TOWARD BEING THOSE          0.85 OF  20          13     3
     WHERE BELLICOSITY                                     WHERE BELLICOSITY                                       11    17
     IS EXTREME  (41) PES                                  IS MODERATE OR NEGLIGIBLE  (46) PES              XSQ=     5.64
                                                                                                            PHI=    0.358
                                                                                                            XP =   0.0176

421  TILT TOWARD BEING THOSE          0.58 OF  26     421  TILT TOWARD BEING THOSE          0.80 OF  20          15     4
     WHERE KILLING, TORTURING, OR MUTILATING               WHERE KILLING, TORTURING, OR MUTILATING                 11    16
     OF THE ENEMY                                          OF THE ENEMY                                     XSQ=     5.16
     IS STRONGLY OR MODERATELY                             IS NEGLIGIBLY EMPHASIZED  (47) PES               PHI=    0.335
     EMPHASIZED  (37) PES                                                                                   XP =   0.0231

444  TILT TOWARD BEING THOSE          0.77 OF  13     444  TILT TOWARD BEING THOSE          0.73 OF  11          10     3
     WHERE THE USE OF DREAMS                               WHERE THE USE OF DREAMS                                  3     8
     TO SEEK AND CONTROL SUPERNATURAL POWERS               TO SEEK AND CONTROL SUPERNATURAL POWERS          XSQ=     4.09
     IS HIGH  (28) RGD                                     IS LOW  (27) RGD                                 PHI=    0.413
                                                                                                            EP =   0.0377

445  DRIFT TOWARD BEING THOSE         0.82 OF  11     445  DRIFT TOWARD BEING THOSE         0.60 OF  10           9     4
     WHERE SORCERY IS                                      WHERE SORCERY IS                                         2     6
     IMPORTANT  (26) BBW,DH                                UNIMPORTANT  (23) BBW,DH                         XSQ=     2.31
                                                                                                            PHI=    0.332
                                                                                                            EP =   0.0805

472  TILT TOWARD BEING THOSE          0.70 OF  27     472  TILT TOWARD BEING THOSE          0.70 OF  20          19     6
     WHERE THE COMPOSITE NARCISSISM INDEX                  WHERE THE COMPOSITE NARCISSISM INDEX                     8    14
     IS HIGH  (47) PES                                     IS LOW  (43) PES                                 XSQ=     5.99
                                                                                                            PHI=    0.357
                                                                                                            XP =   0.0144

474  TILT TOWARD BEING THOSE          0.58 OF  26     474  TILT TOWARD BEING THOSE          0.80 OF  20          15     4
     WHERE BOASTFULNESS IS EXTREME    (41) PES             WHERE BOASTFULNESS IS MODERATE,                         11    16
                                                           NEGLIBIBLE, OR UNREPORTED  (48) PES              XSQ=     5.16
                                                                                                            PHI=    0.335
                                                                                                            XP =   0.0231

475  DRIFT TOWARD BEING THOSE         0.78 OF  27     475  DRIFT TOWARD BEING THOSE         0.53 OF  19          21     9
     WHERE EXHIBITIONISTIC DANCING                         WHERE EXHIBITIONISTIC DANCING                            6    10
     IS STRONGLY OR MODERATELY                             IS NEGLIGIBLY EMPHASIZED  (38) PES               XSQ=     3.30
     EMPHASIZED  (48) PES                                                                                   PHI=    0.268
                                                                                                            XP =   0.0691

480  DRIFT TOWARD BEING THOSE         0.75 OF  12     480  DRIFT TOWARD BEING THOSE         0.75 OF   8           3     6
     WHERE COMPLEXITY OF ARTISTIC DESIGN                   WHERE COMPLEXITY OF ARTISTIC DESIGN                      9     2
     IS LOW  (15) HB                                       IS HIGH  (14) HB                                 XSQ=     3.04
                                                                                                            PHI=   -0.390
                                                                                                            EP =   0.0648
```

349 CULTURES
WHERE THE CHILD'S INFERRED ANXIETY OVER
NON-PERFORMANCE OF ACHIEVEMENT BEHAVIOR
IS HIGH (34) B-B-C

349 CULTURES
WHERE THE CHILD'S INFERRED ANXIETY OVER
NON-PERFORMANCE OF ACHIEVEMENT BEHAVIOR
IS LOW (28) B-B-C

BACKGROUND ON PAGE 143

BOTH SUBJECT AND PREDICATE

34 IN LEFT COLUMN

ARANDA	ARAUCANIANS	ASHANTI	CHAGGA	CHEYENNE	CHIR-APACHE	CHUKCHEE	COMANCHE	CROW	FON
GANDA	HANO	JIVARO	KIKUYU	KWAKIUTL	LAU	MANDAN	MANUS	MAORI	MASAI
NAVAHO	NYAKYUSA	OJIBWA	OMAHA	PAPAGO	PUKAPUKA	SAMOANS	SOTHO	TETON	THONGA
TIV	VENDA	WICHITA	WINNEBAGO						

28 IN RIGHT COLUMN

AINU	ARAPESH	AYMARA	AZANDE	BALINESE	CAMAYURA	CUNA	KASKA	KORYAK	LEPCHA
LESU	MBUNDU	MURNGIN	NUER	ONA	SHERENTE	SIRIONO	SWAZI	TALLENSI	TANALA
TIMBIRA	TRUKESE	TURKANA	WOGEO	YAGUA	YAHGAN	YORUBA	ZUNI		

338 EXCLUDED BECAUSE UNASCERTAINED

8	LEAN LESS TOWARD BEING THOSE LOCATED OUTSIDE OF NORTH AMERICA (330)	0.59 OF 34	8	LEAN MORE TOWARD BEING THOSE LOCATED OUTSIDE OF NORTH AMERICA (330)	0.93 OF 28	14 2 20 26 XSQ= 7.60 PHI= 0.350 XP = 0.0058
9	TILT MORE TOWARD BEING THOSE LOCATED OUTSIDE OF SOUTH AMERICA (335)	0.94 OF 34	9	TILT LESS TOWARD BEING THOSE LOCATED OUTSIDE OF SOUTH AMERICA (335)	0.68 OF 28	2 9 32 19 XSQ= 5.57 PHI= -0.300 XP = 0.0183
14	TILT TOWARD BEING THOSE WHERE THE LATITUDE IS THIRTY DEGREES OR GREATER (119)	0.50 OF 34	14	TILT TOWARD BEING THOSE WHERE THE LATITUDE IS LESS THAN THIRTY DEGREES (281)	0.79 OF 28	17 6 17 22 XSQ= 4.22 PHI= 0.261 XP = 0.0400
15	TILT TOWARD BEING THOSE WHERE THE LATITUDE IS TWENTY DEGREES OR GREATER (183)	0.62 OF 34	15	TILT TOWARD BEING THOSE WHERE THE LATITUDE IS LESS THAN TWENTY DEGREES (217)	0.68 OF 28	21 9 13 19 XSQ= 4.27 PHI= 0.263 XP = 0.0387

36	TILT TOWARD BEING THOSE WHERE THE NATURAL ENVIRONMENT IS 'VERY HARSH,' OR SUB-TROPICAL BUSH, OR TEMPERATE GRASSLAND (108) FWM	0.56 OF 34	36	TILT TOWARD BEING THOSE WHERE THE NATURAL ENVIRONMENT IS OTHER THAN 'VERY HARSH,' OR SUB-TROPICAL BUSH, OR TEMPERATE GRASSLAND (292) FWM	0.79 OF 28	19 6 15 22 XSQ= 6.21 PHI= 0.316 XP = 0.0127
74	TILT TOWARD BEING THOSE WHERE POTTERY IS PRESENT (145)	0.70 OF 27	74	TILT TOWARD BEING THOSE WHERE POTTERY IS ABSENT (93)	0.64 OF 22	19 8 8 14 XSQ= 4.38 PHI= 0.299 XP = 0.0365
86	DRIFT TOWARD BEING THOSE WHERE THE LEVEL OF POLITICAL INTEGRATION IS THE LARGE STATE, THE LITTLE STATE, OR THE MINIMAL STATE (148) GPM	0.61 OF 28	86	DRIFT TOWARD BEING THOSE WHERE THE LEVEL OF POLITICAL INTEGRATION IS THE AUTONOMOUS COMMUNITY, OR THE FAMILY (156) GPM	0.70 OF 23	17 7 11 16 XSQ= 3.51 PHI= 0.262 XP = 0.0610
96	LEAN TOWARD BEING THOSE WHERE THE HIERARCHY OF NATIONAL JURISDICTION HAS FOUR, THREE, TWO OR ONE LEVEL (174) GES,EA	0.68 OF 31	96	LEAN TOWARD BEING THOSE WHERE THE HIERARCHY OF NATIONAL JURISDICTION HAS NO LEVELS (156) GES,EA	0.73 OF 26	21 7 10 19 XSQ= 7.86 PHI= 0.371 XP = 0.0050
100	DRIFT MORE TOWARD BEING THOSE WHERE HIERARCHIES ARE MORE COMPLEX THAN THE 'SIMPLEST,' I. E., MORE COMPLEX THAN TWO LOCAL LEVELS WITH NO NATIONAL LEVELS (267) GES,EA	0.94 OF 31	100	DRIFT LESS TOWARD BEING THOSE WHERE HIERARCHIES ARE MORE COMPLEX THAN THE 'SIMPLEST,' I. E., MORE COMPLEX THAN TWO LOCAL LEVELS WITH NO NATIONAL LEVELS (267) GES,EA	0.73 OF 26	29 19 2 7 XSQ= 3.05 PHI= 0.231 XP = 0.0807
137	TILT TOWARD BEING THOSE WHERE INVIDIOUS DISPLAY OF WEALTH IS STRONGLY EMPHASIZED (37) PES	0.58 OF 26	137	TILT TOWARD BEING THOSE WHERE INVIDIOUS DISPLAY OF WEALTH IS MODERATELY, LITTLE, OR NEGATIVELY EMPHASIZED (52) PES	0.79 OF 19	15 4 11 15 XSQ= 4.63 PHI= 0.321 XP = 0.0314
148	TILT TOWARD BEING THOSE WHERE THE INCIDENCE OF PERSONAL CRIME IS HIGH (12) B-B-C	0.56 OF 16	148	TILT TOWARD BEING THOSE WHERE THE INCIDENCE OF PERSONAL CRIME IS LOW (21) B-B-C	0.91 OF 11	9 1 7 10 XSQ= 4.36 PHI= 0.402 EP = 0.0183
201	DRIFT LESS TOWARD BEING THOSE WHERE MARITAL RESIDENCE IS NON-OPTIONAL, RATHER THAN AMBILOCAL OR NEOLOCAL (334)	0.85 OF 34	201	IN ALL CASES ARE THOSE WHERE MARITAL RESIDENCE IS NON-OPTIONAL, RATHER THAN AMBILOCAL OR NEOLOCAL (334)	1.00 OF 28	29 28 5 0 XSQ= 2.71 PHI= -0.209 XP = 0.0994
272	DRIFT TOWARD BEING THOSE WHERE THE DIVORCE RATE IS HIGH (29) CA	0.80 OF 10	272	DRIFT TOWARD BEING THOSE WHERE THE DIVORCE RATE IS LOW (28) CA	0.75 OF 8	8 2 2 6 XSQ= 3.45 PHI= 0.437 EP = 0.0536

No.	Statement	No.	Statement	Statistics
305	LEAN TOWARD BEING THOSE 0.72 OF 18 WHERE THE EARLY SEXUAL SATISFACTION POTENTIAL IS LOW (24) W-C	305	LEAN TOWARD BEING THOSE 0.82 OF 11 WHERE THE EARLY SEXUAL SATISFACTION POTENTIAL IS HIGH (27) W-C	5 9 13 2 XSQ= 5.97 PHI= -0.454 EP = 0.0078
328	TILT TOWARD BEING THOSE 0.68 OF 19 WHERE THE AGE OF THE INFANT AT THE ONSET OF SERIOUS SOCIALIZATION, OTHER THAN WEANING, IS TWO YEARS OR LOWER (20) B-B-C	328	TILT TOWARD BEING THOSE 0.72 OF 18 WHERE THE AGE OF THE INFANT AT THE ONSET OF SERIOUS SOCIALIZATION, OTHER THAN WEANING, IS HIGHER THAN TWO YEARS (21) B-B-C	6 13 13 5 XSQ= 4.59 PHI= -0.352 EP = 0.0217
331	DRIFT TOWARD BEING THOSE 0.79 OF 14 WHERE THE AGE AT BEGINNING OF INDEPENDENCE TRAINING IS LOWER THAN 3.8 YEARS (21) W-C	331	DRIFT TOWARD BEING THOSE 0.67 OF 9 WHERE THE AGE AT BEGINNING OF INDEPENDENCE TRAINING IS 3.8 YEARS OR HIGHER (16) W-C	3 6 11 3 XSQ= 3.00 PHI= -0.361 EP = 0.0771
338	DRIFT TOWARD BEING THOSE 0.71 OF 34 WHERE THE CHILD'S INFERRED ANXIETY OVER PERFORMANCE OF RESPONSIBLE BEHAVIOR IS HIGH (44) B-B-C	338	DRIFT TOWARD BEING THOSE 0.54 OF 26 WHERE THE CHILD'S INFERRED ANXIETY OVER PERFORMANCE OF RESPONSIBLE BEHAVIOR IS LOW (29) B-B-C	24 12 10 14 XSQ= 2.72 PHI= 0.213 XP = 0.0992
344	TILT TOWARD BEING THOSE 0.62 OF 34 WHERE THE TOTAL POSITIVE PRESSURE TOWARD DEVELOPING SELF-RELIANT BEHAVIOR IN THE CHILD IS HIGH (36) B-B-C	344	TILT TOWARD BEING THOSE 0.71 OF 28 WHERE THE TOTAL POSITIVE PRESSURE TOWARD DEVELOPING SELF-RELIANT BEHAVIOR IN THE CHILD IS LOW (40) B-B-C	21 8 13 20 XSQ= 5.53 PHI= 0.299 XP = 0.0187
345	TILT TOWARD BEING THOSE 0.65 OF 34 WHERE THE CHILD'S INFERRED ANXIETY OVER NON-PERFORMANCE OF SELF-RELIANT BEHAVIOR IS HIGH (37) B-B-C	345	TILT TOWARD BEING THOSE 0.64 OF 28 WHERE THE CHILD'S INFERRED ANXIETY OVER NON-PERFORMANCE OF SELF-RELIANT BEHAVIOR IS LOW (39) B-B-C	22 10 12 18 XSQ= 4.07 PHI= 0.256 XP = 0.0436
348	TEND TO BE THOSE 0.88 OF 34 WHERE THE TOTAL POSITIVE PRESSURE TOWARD DEVELOPING ACHIEVEMENT BEHAVIOR IN THE CHILD IS HIGH (32) B-B-C	348	TEND TO BE THOSE 0.93 OF 28 WHERE THE TOTAL POSITIVE PRESSURE TOWARD DEVELOPING ACHIEVEMENT BEHAVIOR IN THE CHILD IS LOW (31) B-B-C	30 2 4 26 XSQ= 37.25 PHI= 0.775 XP = 0.
350	TEND TO BE THOSE 0.82 OF 33 WHERE THE CHILD'S INFERRED ANXIETY OVER PERFORMANCE OF ACHIEVEMENT BEHAVIOR IS HIGH (34) B-B-C	350	TEND TO BE THOSE 0.74 OF 27 WHERE THE CHILD'S INFERRED ANXIETY OVER PERFORMANCE OF ACHIEVEMENT BEHAVIOR IS LOW (26) B-B-C	27 7 6 20 XSQ= 16.68 PHI= 0.527 XP = 0.0000
351	LEAN TOWARD BEING THOSE 0.61 OF 33 WHERE THE CHILD'S INFERRED CONFLICT REGARDING ACHIEVEMENT BEHAVIOR IS HIGH (26) B-B-C	351	LEAN TOWARD BEING THOSE 0.78 OF 27 WHERE THE CHILD'S INFERRED CONFLICT REGARDING ACHIEVEMENT BEHAVIOR IS LOW (34) B-B-C	20 6 13 21 XSQ= 7.42 PHI= 0.352 XP = 0.0065

354	TILT TOWARD BEING THOSE 0.61 OF 33 WHERE THE CHILD'S INFERRED ANXIETY OVER PERFORMANCE OF OBEDIENT BEHAVIOR IS HIGH (36) B-B-C	354	TILT TOWARD BEING THOSE 0.69 OF 26 WHERE THE CHILD'S INFERRED ANXIETY OVER PERFORMANCE OF OBEDIENT BEHAVIOR IS LOW (37) B-B-C	20 8 13 18 XSQ= 4.06 PHI= 0.262 XP = 0.0438
355	TILT TOWARD BEING THOSE 0.61 OF 33 WHERE THE CHILD'S INFERRED CONFLICT REGARDING OBEDIENT BEHAVIOR IS HIGH (35) B-B-C	355	TILT TOWARD BEING THOSE 0.73 OF 26 WHERE THE CHILD'S INFERRED CONFLICT REGARDING OBEDIENT BEHAVIOR IS LOW (38) B-B-C	20 7 13 19 XSQ= 5.36 PHI= 0.301 XP = 0.0206
358	DRIFT MORE TOWARD BEING THOSE 0.93 OF 15 WHERE ADOLESCENT PEER GROUPS ARE PRESENT IN A SETTING OF WORK AND PUBLIC GATHERINGS AND LEISURE, OR OF PUBLIC GATHERINGS AND LEISURE, OR OF LEISURE ONLY (41) JKH	358	DRIFT LESS TOWARD BEING THOSE 0.55 OF 11 WHERE ADOLESCENT PEER GROUPS ARE PRESENT IN A SETTING OF WORK AND PUBLIC GATHERINGS AND LEISURE, OR OF PUBLIC GATHERINGS AND LEISURE, OR OF LEISURE ONLY (41) JKH	14 6 1 5 XSQ= 3.42 PHI= 0.362 EP = 0.0538
382	LEAN TOWARD BEING THOSE 0.92 OF 12 WHERE FEMALE INITIATION RITES ARE PRESENT (38) JKB	382	LEAN TOWARD BEING THOSE 0.75 OF 12 WHERE FEMALE INITIATION RITES ARE ABSENT (27) JKB	11 3 1 9 XSQ= 8.40 PHI= 0.592 EP = 0.0028
402	DRIFT TOWARD BEING THOSE 0.70 OF 20 WHERE EXPLANATIONS OF ILLNESS OF AN ORAL NATURE ARE PRESENT (31) W-C	402	DRIFT TOWARD BEING THOSE 0.67 OF 12 WHERE EXPLANATIONS OF ILLNESS OF AN ORAL NATURE ARE ABSENT (30) W-C	14 4 6 8 XSQ= 2.74 PHI= 0.293 EP = 0.0683
417	TILT TOWARD BEING THOSE 0.92 OF 13 WHERE WARFARE IS PREVALENT (34) LWS	417	IN ALL CASES ARE THOSE 1.00 OF 2 WHERE WARFARE IS NOT PREVALENT (9) LWS	12 0 1 2 XSQ= 4.36 PHI= 0.539 EP = 0.0286
419	LEAN TOWARD BEING THOSE 0.81 OF 26 WHERE MILITARY GLORY IS STRONGLY OR MODERATELY EMPHASIZED (55) PES	419	LEAN TOWARD BEING THOSE 0.63 OF 19 WHERE MILITARY GLORY IS NEGLIGIBLY EMPHASIZED (31) PES	21 7 5 12 XSQ= 7.24 PHI= 0.401 XP = 0.0071
420	TILT TOWARD BEING THOSE 0.54 OF 24 WHERE BELLICOSITY IS EXTREME (41) PES	420	TILT TOWARD BEING THOSE 0.84 OF 19 WHERE BELLICOSITY IS MODERATE OR NEGLIGIBLE (46) PES	13 3 11 16 XSQ= 5.14 PHI= 0.346 XP = 0.0233
421	TILT TOWARD BEING THOSE 0.58 OF 26 WHERE KILLING, TORTURING, OR MUTILATING OF THE ENEMY IS STRONGLY OR MODERATELY EMPHASIZED (37) PES	421	TILT TOWARD BEING THOSE 0.79 OF 19 WHERE KILLING, TORTURING, OR MUTILATING OF THE ENEMY IS NEGLIGIBLY EMPHASIZED (47) PES	15 4 11 15 XSQ= 4.63 PHI= 0.321 XP = 0.0314

437	TILT TOWARD BEING THOSE WHERE FEAR OF GHOSTS, SPIRITS, HUMANS OR ANIMALS IS HIGH (21) W-C,JFG	0.73 OF 15	437	TILT TOWARD BEING THOSE WHERE FEAR OF GHOSTS, SPIRITS, HUMANS OR ANIMALS IS LOW (23) W-C,JFG	0.70 OF 10	11 3 4 7 XSQ= 2.98 PHI= 0.345 EP = 0.0486
445	TILT TOWARD BEING THOSE WHERE SORCERY IS IMPORTANT (26) EBW,DH	0.83 OF 12	445	TILT TOWARD BEING THOSE WHERE SORCERY IS UNIMPORTANT (23) BBW,DH	0.67 OF 9	10 3 2 6 XSQ= 3.54 PHI= 0.410 EP = 0.0318
460	TILT TOWARD BEING THOSE WHERE GAMES, IF PRESENT, ARE NOT LIMITED TO GAMES OF SKILL ONLY (104) R-A-B,EA	0.80 OF 25	460	TILT TOWARD BEING THOSE WHERE GAMES, IF PRESENT, ARE LIMITED TO GAMES OF SKILL ONLY (67) R-A-B,EA	0.60 OF 20	5 12 20 8 XSQ= 5.96 PHI= -0.364 XP = 0.0147
472	LEAN TOWARD BEING THOSE WHERE THE COMPOSITE NARCISSISM INDEX IS HIGH (47) PES	0.74 OF 27	472	LEAN TOWARD BEING THOSE WHERE THE COMPOSITE NARCISSISM INDEX IS LOW (43) PES	0.74 OF 19	20 5 7 14 XSQ= 8.42 PHI= 0.428 XP = 0.0037
474	TILT TOWARD BEING THOSE WHERE BOASTFULNESS IS EXTREME (41) PES	0.58 OF 26	474	TILT TOWARD BEING THOSE WHERE BOASTFULNESS IS MODERATE, NEGLIBIBLE, OR UNREPORTED (48) PES	0.79 OF 19	15 4 11 15 XSQ= 4.63 PHI= 0.321 XP = 0.0314
475	TILT TOWARD BEING THOSE WHERE EXHIBITIONISTIC DANCING IS STRONGLY OR MODERATELY EMPHASIZED (48) PES	0.81 OF 27	475	TILT TOWARD BEING THOSE WHERE EXHIBITIONISTIC DANCING IS NEGLIGIBLY EMPHASIZED (38) PES	0.56 OF 18	22 8 5 10 XSQ= 5.10 PHI= 0.337 XP = 0.0239

350 CULTURES:
WHERE THE CHILD'S INFERRED ANXIETY OVER
PERFORMANCE OF ACHIEVEMENT BEHAVIOR
IS HIGH (34) B-B-C

350 CULTURES
WHERE THE CHILD'S INFERRED ANXIETY OVER
PERFORMANCE OF ACHIEVEMENT BEHAVIOR
IS LOW (26) B-B-C

BACKGROUND ON PAGE 143

BOTH SUBJECT AND PREDICATE

34 IN LEFT COLUMN

ARANDA	ARAUCANIANS	ASHANTI	AYMARA	AZANDE	CHAGGA	CHEYENNE	CHIR-APACHE	CHUKCHEE	CROW
GANDA	HANC	KIKUYU	KWAKIUTL	MANDAN	MAORI	MASAI	MBUNDU	NAVAHO	NYAKYUSA
OJIBWA	OMAHA	PAPAGO	SAMOANS	SWAZI	TANALA	TETON	THONGA	TIV	VENDA
WICHITA	WINNEBAGO	YORUBA	ZUNI						

26 IN RIGHT COLUMN

AINU	ARAPESH	BALINESE	CAMAYURA	COMANCHE	CUNA	FON	JIVARO	KASKA	KORYAK
LEPCHA	LESU	MANUS	MURNGIN	NUER	ONA	PUKAPUKA	SHERENTE	SOTHO	TALLENSI
TIMBIRA	TRUKESE	TURKANA	WOGEO	YAGUA	YAHGAN				

340 EXCLUDED BECAUSE UNASCERTAINED

	Left column			Right column			Statistics
6	DRIFT MORE TOWARD BEING THOSE LOCATED OUTSIDE OF THE INSULAR PACIFIC (330)	0.91 OF 34	6	DRIFT LESS TOWARD BEING THOSE LOCATED OUTSIDE OF THE INSULAR PACIFIC (330)	0.69 OF 26		3 8 / 31 18 / XSQ= 3.39 / PHI= -0.238 / XP = 0.0657
8	LEAN LESS TOWARD BEING THOSE LOCATED OUTSIDE OF NORTH AMERICA (330)	0.59 OF 34	8	LEAN MORE TOWARD BEING THOSE LOCATED OUTSIDE OF NORTH AMERICA (330)	0.92 OF 26		14 2 / 20 24 / XSQ= 6.82 / PHI= 0.337 / XP = 0.0090
9	TILT MORE TOWARD BEING THOSE LOCATED OUTSIDE OF SOUTH AMERICA (335)	0.94 OF 34	9	TILT LESS TOWARD BEING THOSE LOCATED OUTSIDE OF SOUTH AMERICA (335)	0.69 OF 26		2 8 / 32 18 / XSQ= 4.90 / PHI= -0.286 / XP = 0.0268
14	DRIFT TOWARD BEING THOSE WHERE THE LATITUDE IS THIRTY DEGREES OR GREATER (119)	0.50 OF 34	14	DRIFT TOWARD BEING THOSE WHERE THE LATITUDE IS LESS THAN THIRTY DEGREES (281)	0.77 OF 26		17 6 / 17 20 / XSQ= 3.45 / PHI= 0.240 / XP = 0.0632

15	TILT TOWARD BEING THOSE WHERE THE LATITUDE IS TWENTY DEGREES OR GREATER (183)	0.65 OF 34	15	TILT TOWARD BEING THOSE WHERE THE LATITUDE IS LESS THAN TWENTY DEGREES (217)	0.69 OF 26	22 8 12 18 XSQ= 5.50 PHI= 0.303 XP = 0.0190
16	DRIFT TOWARD BEING THOSE WHERE THE LATITUDE IS TEN DEGREES OR GREATER (277)	0.74 OF 34	16	DRIFT TOWARD BEING THOSE WHERE THE LATITUDE IS LESS THAN TEN DEGREES (123)	0.54 OF 26	25 12 9 14 XSQ= 3.58 PHI= 0.244 XP = 0.0583
36	TILT TOWARD BEING THOSE WHERE THE NATURAL ENVIRONMENT IS 'VERY HARSH,' OR SUB-TROPICAL BUSH, OR TEMPERATE GRASSLAND (108) FWM	0.56 OF 34	36	TILT TOWARD BEING THOSE WHERE THE NATURAL ENVIRONMENT IS OTHER THAN 'VERY HARSH,' OR SUB-TROPICAL BUSH, OR TEMPERATE GRASSLAND (292) FWM	0.77 OF 26	19 6 15 20 XSQ= 5.24 PHI= 0.296 XP = 0.0220
42	TILT MORE TOWARD BEING THOSE WHERE THE NATURAL ENVIRONMENT IS OTHER THAN TROPICAL OR SUB-TROPICAL RAIN FOREST, OR MONSOON FOREST (244) FWM	0.85 OF 34	42	TILT LESS TOWARD BEING THOSE WHERE THE NATURAL ENVIRONMENT IS OTHER THAN TROPICAL OR SUB-TROPICAL RAIN FOREST, OR MONSOON FOREST (244) FWM	0.54 OF 26	5 12 29 14 XSQ= 5.71 PHI= -0.309 XP = 0.0169
63	TILT TOWARD BEING THOSE WHERE HUSBANDRY, IF PRESENT, IS PRINCIPALLY IN THE FORM OF BOVINE, EQUINE, CAMEL-LIKE, OR DEER-LIKE ANIMALS, RATHER THAN PIGS, SHEEP, OR GOATS (152)	0.73 OF 26	63	TILT TOWARD BEING THOSE WHERE HUSBANDRY, IF PRESENT, IS PRINCIPALLY IN THE FORM OF PIGS, SHEEP, OR GOATS, RATHER THAN BOVINE, EQUINE, CAMEL-LIKE, OR DEER-LIKE ANIMALS (74)	0.69 OF 16	19 5 7 11 XSQ= 5.47 PHI= 0.361 XP = 0.0193
71	LEAN TOWARD BEING THOSE WHERE METAL WORKING IS PRESENT (98)	0.59 OF 27	71	LEAN TOWARD BEING THOSE WHERE METAL WORKING IS ABSENT (153)	0.86 OF 21	16 3 11 18 XSQ= 8.20 PHI= 0.413 XP = 0.0042
74	LEAN TOWARD BEING THOSE WHERE POTTERY IS PRESENT (145)	0.73 OF 26	74	LEAN TOWARD BEING THOSE WHERE POTTERY IS ABSENT (93)	0.71 OF 21	19 6 7 15 XSQ= 7.54 PHI= 0.401 XP = 0.0060
86	LEAN TOWARD BEING THOSE WHERE THE LEVEL OF POLITICAL INTEGRATION IS THE LARGE STATE, THE LITTLE STATE, OR THE MINIMAL STATE (148) GPM	0.67 OF 27	86	LEAN TOWARD BEING THOSE WHERE THE LEVEL OF POLITICAL INTEGRATION IS THE AUTONOMOUS COMMUNITY, OR THE FAMILY (156) GPM	0.77 OF 22	18 5 9 17 XSQ= 7.72 PHI= 0.397 XP = 0.0055
87	IN ALL CASES ARE THOSE WHERE THE LEVEL OF POLITICAL INTEGRATION IS THE LARGE STATE, THE LITTLE STATE, THE MINIMAL STATE, OR THE AUTONOMOUS COMMUNITY (281) GPM	1.00 OF 27	87	LEAN LESS TOWARD BEING THOSE WHERE THE LEVEL OF POLITICAL INTEGRATION IS THE LARGE STATE, THE LITTLE STATE, THE MINIMAL STATE, OR THE AUTONOMOUS COMMUNITY (281) GPM	0.68 OF 22	27 15 0 7 XSQ= 7.59 PHI= 0.394 XP = 0.0059

No.			No.			
96	TEND TO BE THOSE WHERE THE HIERARCHY OF NATIONAL JURISDICTION HAS FOUR, THREE, TWO OR ONE LEVEL (174) GES,EA	0.71 OF 31	96	TEND TO BE THOSE WHERE THE HIERARCHY OF NATIONAL JURISDICTION HAS NO LEVELS (156) GES,EA	0.79 OF 24	22 5 9 19 XSQ= 11.67 PHI= 0.461 XP = 0.0006
100	LEAN MORE TOWARD BEING THOSE WHERE HIERARCHIES ARE MORE COMPLEX THAN THE 'SIMPLEST,' I. E., MORE COMPLEX THAN TWO LOCAL LEVELS WITH NO NATIONAL LEVELS (267) GES,EA	0.97 OF 31	100	LEAN LESS TOWARD BEING THOSE WHERE HIERARCHIES ARE MORE COMPLEX THAN THE 'SIMPLEST,' I. E., MORE COMPLEX THAN TWO LOCAL LEVELS WITH NO NATIONAL LEVELS (267) GES,EA	0.67 OF 24	30 16 1 8 XSQ= 6.89 PHI= 0.354 XP = 0.0086
106	DRIFT TOWARD BEING THOSE WHERE CLASS STRATIFICATION, IF PRESENT, IS BASED ON SOMETHING OTHER THAN WEALTH (126)	0.76 OF 17	106	DRIFT TOWARD BEING THOSE WHERE CLASS STRATIFICATION, IF PRESENT, IS BASED ON WEALTH (77)	0.63 OF 8	4 5 13 3 XSQ= 2.09 PHI= -0.289 EP = 0.0870
149	DRIFT TOWARD BEING THOSE WHERE THE INCIDENCE OF THEFT IS HIGH (18) B-B-C	0.73 OF 15	149	DRIFT TOWARD BEING THOSE WHERE THE INCIDENCE OF THEFT IS LOW (19) B-B-C	0.69 OF 13	11 4 4 9 XSQ= 3.51 PHI= 0.354 EP = 0.0557
305	LEAN TOWARD BEING THOSE WHERE THE EARLY SEXUAL SATISFACTION POTENTIAL IS LOW (24) W-C	0.81 OF 16	305	LEAN TOWARD BEING THOSE WHERE THE EARLY SEXUAL SATISFACTION POTENTIAL IS HIGH (27) W-C	0.83 OF 12	3 10 13 2 XSQ= 9.05 PHI= -0.568 EP = 0.0016
308	TILT TOWARD BEING THOSE WHERE AVERAGE SOCIALIZATION ANXIETY IS HIGH (22) W-C	0.79 OF 14	308	TILT TOWARD BEING THOSE WHERE AVERAGE SOCIALIZATION ANXIETY IS LOW (18) W-C	0.64 OF 11	11 4 3 7 XSQ= 2.98 PHI= 0.345 EP = 0.0486
311	TILT TOWARD BEING THOSE WHERE SEXUAL SOCIALIZATION ANXIETY IS HIGH (28) W-C	0.81 OF 16	311	TILT TOWARD BEING THOSE WHERE SEXUAL SOCIALIZATION ANXIETY IS LOW (23) W-C	0.67 OF 12	13 4 3 8 XSQ= 4.74 PHI= 0.412 EP = 0.0189
313	DRIFT TOWARD BEING THOSE WHERE AGGRESSION SOCIALIZATION ANXIETY IS HIGH (26) W-C	0.72 OF 18	313	DRIFT TOWARD BEING THOSE WHERE AGGRESSION SOCIALIZATION ANXIETY IS LOW (28) W-C	0.62 OF 13	13 5 5 8 XSQ= 2.28 PHI= 0.271 EP = 0.0785
334	DRIFT TOWARD BEING THOSE WHERE THE INDULGENCE OF THE CHILD IS LOW (38) B-B-C	0.62 OF 34	334	DRIFT TOWARD BEING THOSE WHERE THE INDULGENCE OF THE CHILD IS HIGH (40) B-B-C	0.65 OF 26	13 17 21 9 XSQ= 3.33 PHI= -0.235 XP = 0.0682

336	TILT TOWARD BEING THOSE 0.71 OF 34 WHERE THE TOTAL POSITIVE PRESSURE TOWARD DEVELOPING RESPONSIBLE BEHAVIOR IN THE CHILD IS HIGH (43) B-B-C	336	TILT TOWARD BEING THOSE 0.60 OF 25 WHERE THE TOTAL POSITIVE PRESSURE TOWARD DEVELOPING RESPONSIBLE BEHAVIOR IN THE CHILD IS LOW (32) B-B-C	24 10 10 15 XSQ= 4.34 PHI= 0.271 XP = 0.0373
337	TILT TOWARD BEING THOSE 0.65 OF 34 WHERE THE CHILD'S INFERRED ANXIETY OVER NON-PERFORMANCE OF RESPONSIBLE BEHAVIOR IS HIGH (38) B-B-C	337	TILT TOWARD BEING THOSE 0.68 OF 25 WHERE THE CHILD'S INFERRED ANXIETY OVER NON-PERFORMANCE OF RESPONSIBLE BEHAVIOR IS LOW (35) B-B-C	22 8 12 17 XSQ= 4.93 PHI= 0.289 XP = 0.0264
338	TILT TOWARD BEING THOSE 0.74 OF 34 WHERE THE CHILD'S INFERRED ANXIETY OVER PERFORMANCE OF RESPONSIBLE BEHAVIOR IS HIGH (44) B-B-C	338	TILT TOWARD BEING THOSE 0.60 OF 25 WHERE THE CHILD'S INFERRED ANXIETY OVER PERFORMANCE OF RESPONSIBLE BEHAVIOR IS LOW (29) B-B-C	25 10 9 15 XSQ= 5.39 PHI= 0.302 XP = 0.0202
346	TILT TOWARD BEING THOSE 0.62 OF 34 WHERE THE CHILD'S INFERRED ANXIETY OVER PERFORMANCE OF SELF-RELIANT BEHAVIOR IS HIGH (37) B-B-C	346	TILT TOWARD BEING THOSE 0.69 OF 26 WHERE THE CHILD'S INFERRED ANXIETY OVER PERFORMANCE OF SELF-RELIANT BEHAVIOR IS LOW (39) B-B-C	21 8 13 18 XSQ= 4.49 PHI= 0.274 XP = 0.0340
347	TILT TOWARD BEING THOSE 0.65 OF 34 WHERE THE CHILD'S INFERRED CONFLICT REGARDING SELF-RELIANT BEHAVIOR IS HIGH (37) B-B-C	347	TILT TOWARD BEING THOSE 0.69 OF 26 WHERE THE CHILD'S INFERRED CONFLICT REGARDING SELF-RELIANT BEHAVIOR IS LOW (39) B-B-C	22 8 12 18 XSQ= 5.50 PHI= 0.303 XP = 0.0190
348	LEAN TOWARD BEING THOSE 0.71 OF 34 WHERE THE TOTAL POSITIVE PRESSURE TOWARD DEVELOPING ACHIEVEMENT BEHAVIOR IN THE CHILD IS HIGH (32) B-B-C	348	LEAN TOWARD BEING THOSE 0.73 OF 26 WHERE THE TOTAL POSITIVE PRESSURE TOWARD DEVELOPING ACHIEVEMENT BEHAVIOR IN THE CHILD IS LOW (31) B-B-C	24 7 10 19 XSQ= 9.57 PHI= 0.399 XP = 0.0020
349	TEND TO BE THOSE 0.79 OF 34 WHERE THE CHILD'S INFERRED ANXIETY OVER NON-PERFORMANCE OF ACHIEVEMENT BEHAVIOR IS HIGH (34) B-B-C	349	TEND TO BE THOSE 0.77 OF 26 WHERE THE CHILD'S INFERRED ANXIETY OVER NON-PERFORMANCE OF ACHIEVEMENT BEHAVIOR IS LOW (28) B-B-C	27 6 7 20 XSQ= 16.68 PHI= 0.527 XP = 0.0000
351	TEND TO BE THOSE 0.74 OF 34 WHERE THE CHILD'S INFERRED CONFLICT REGARDING ACHIEVEMENT BEHAVIOR IS HIGH (26) B-B-C	351	TEND TO BE THOSE 0.96 OF 26 WHERE THE CHILD'S INFERRED CONFLICT REGARDING ACHIEVEMENT BEHAVIOR IS LOW (34) B-B-C	25 1 9 25 XSQ= 26.37 PHI= 0.663 XP = 0.0000
352	LEAN TOWARD BEING THOSE 0.85 OF 34 WHERE THE TOTAL POSITIVE PRESSURE TOWARD DEVELOPING OBEDIENT BEHAVIOR IN THE CHILD IS HIGH (44) B-B-C	352	LEAN TOWARD BEING THOSE 0.59 OF 22 WHERE THE TOTAL POSITIVE PRESSURE TOWARD DEVELOPING OBEDIENT BEHAVIOR IN THE CHILD IS LOW (28) B-B-C	29 9 5 13 XSQ= 10.12 PHI= 0.425 XP = 0.0015

353	TILT TOWARD BEING THOSE 0.71 OF 34 WHERE THE CHILD'S INFERRED ANXIETY OVER NON-PERFORMANCE OF OBEDIENT BEHAVIOR IS HIGH (42) B-B-C	353	TILT TOWARD BEING THOSE 0.61 OF 23 WHERE THE CHILD-S INFERRED ANXIETY OVER NON-PERFORMANCE OF OBEDIENT BEHAVIOR IS LOW (32) B-B-C	24 9 10 14 XSQ= 4.35 PHI= 0.276 XP = 0.0369
354	TILT TOWARD BEING THOSE 0.59 OF 34 WHERE THE CHILD'S INFERRED ANXIETY OVER PERFORMANCE OF OBEDIENT BEHAVIOR IS HIGH (36) B-B-C	354	TILT TOWARD BEING THOSE 0.74 OF 23 WHERE THE CHILD'S INFERRED ANXIETY OVER PERFORMANCE OF OBEDIENT BEHAVIOR IS LOW (37) B-B-C	20 6 14 17 XSQ= 4.68 PHI= 0.287 XP = 0.0305
355	LEAN TOWARD BEING THOSE 0.62 OF 34 WHERE THE CHILD'S INFERRED CONFLICT REGARDING OBEDIENT BEHAVIOR IS HIGH (35) B-B-C	355	LEAN TOWARD BEING THOSE 0.78 OF 23 WHERE THE CHILD'S INFERRED CONFLICT REGARDING OBEDIENT BEHAVIOR IS LOW (38) B-B-C	21 5 13 18 XSQ= 7.32 PHI= 0.358 XP = 0.0068
358	IN ALL CASES ARE THOSE 1.00 OF 14 WHERE ADOLESCENT PEER GROUPS ARE PRESENT IN A SETTING OF WORK AND PUBLIC GATHERINGS AND LEISURE, OR OF PUBLIC GATHERINGS AND LEISURE, OR OF LEISURE ONLY (41) JKH	358	LEAN TOWARD BEING THOSE 0.50 OF 10 WHERE ADOLESCENT PEER GROUPS ARE ABSENT IN A SETTING OF WORK, AND OF PUBLIC GATHERINGS, AND OF LEISURE (11) JKH	14 5 0 5 XSQ= 6.07 PHI= 0.503 EP = 0.0059
400	DRIFT TOWARD BEING THOSE 0.78 OF 18 WHERE HOMOSEXUAL ACTIVITY IS PERMITTED (36) F-B	400	DRIFT TOWARD BEING THOSE 0.60 OF 10 WHERE HOMOSEXUAL ACTIVITY IS PROHIBITED (22) F-B	4 6 14 4 XSQ= 2.52 PHI= -0.300 EP = 0.0974
419	TILT TOWARD BEING THOSE 0.83 OF 24 WHERE MILITARY GLORY IS STRONGLY OR MODERATELY EMPHASIZED (55) PES	419	TILT TOWARD BEING THOSE 0.58 OF 19 WHERE MILITARY GLORY IS NEGLIGIBLY EMPHASIZED (31) PES	20 8 4 11 XSQ= 6.22 PHI= 0.380 XP = 0.0126
421	TILT TOWARD BEING THOSE 0.60 OF 25 WHERE KILLING, TORTURING, OR MUTILATING OF THE ENEMY IS STRONGLY OR MODERATELY EMPHASIZED (37) PES	421	TILT TOWARD BEING THOSE 0.78 OF 18 WHERE KILLING, TORTURING, OR MUTILATING OF THE ENEMY IS NEGLIGIBLY EMPHASIZED (47) PES	15 4 10 14 XSQ= 4.62 PHI= 0.328 XP = 0.0316
446	LEAN TOWARD BEING THOSE 0.89 OF 9 WHERE WITCHCRAFT IS SIGNIFICANTLY PRESENT (14) GES	446	LEAN TOWARD BEING THOSE 0.89 OF 9 WHERE WITCHCRAFT IS MODERATELY PRESENT OR ABSENT (24) GES	8 1 1 8 XSQ= 8.00 PHI= 0.667 EP = 0.0034
458	LEAN TOWARD BEING THOSE 0.50 OF 26 WHERE GAMES, IF PRESENT, INCLUDE GAMES OF STRATEGY (52) R-A-B,EA	458	LEAN TOWARD BEING THOSE 0.94 OF 17 WHERE GAMES, IF PRESENT, DO NOT INCLUDE GAMES OF STRATEGY (119) R-A-B,EA	13 1 13 16 XSQ= 7.21 PHI= 0.410 XP = 0.0072

```
459  TILT TCWARC BEING THOSE          0.62 OF  26      459  TILT TOWARD BEING THCSE          0.76 OF  17          16    4
     WHERE GAMES, IF PRESENT,                              WHERE GAMES, IF PRESENT,                                10   13
     INCLUCE GAMES CF CHANCE   (82) R-A-B,EA               DO NOT INCLUDE                                    XSQ=     4.54
                                                           GAMES OF CHANCE   (89) R-A-B,EA                   PHI=    0.325
                                                                                                             XP =   0.0331

460  TEND TC BE THCSE                0.92 OF  26      460  TEND TO BE THOSE                 0.76 CF  17           2   13
     WHERE GAMES, IF PRESENT,                              WHERE GAMES, IF PRESENT,                                24    4
     ARE NCT LIMITEC TC                                    ARE LIMITED TO                                    XSQ=    18.49
     GAMES CF SKILL CNLY   (104) R-A-B,EA                  GAMES OF SKILL ONLY   (67) R-A-B,EA               PHI=   -0.656
                                                                                                             XP =   0.0000

475  LEAN TCWARC BEING THCSE         0.88 OF  24      475  LEAN TOWARD BEING THCSE          0.58 OF  19          21    8
     WHERE EXHIBITICNISTIC CANCING                         WHERE EXHIBITICNISTIC DANCING                            3   11
     IS STRCNGLY CR MCDERATELY                             IS NEGLIGIBLY EMPHASIZED   (38) PES               XSQ=     7.99
     EMPHASIZEC   (48) PES                                                                                   PHI=    0.431
                                                                                                             XP =   0.0047
```

351 CULTURES
WHERE THE CHILD'S INFERRED CONFLICT
REGARDING ACHIEVEMENT BEHAVIOR
IS HIGH (26) B-B-C

351 CULTURES
WHERE THE CHILD'S INFERRED CONFLICT
REGARDING ACHIEVEMENT BEHAVIOR
IS LOW (34) B-B-C

BACKGROUND ON PAGE 143

BOTH SUBJECT AND PREDICATE

26 IN LEFT COLUMN

ARANDA	ASHANTI	AYMARA	AZANDE	CHIR-APACHE	CROW	GANDA	HANO	KIKUYU	KWAKIUTL
MANDAN	MBUNDU	MURNGIN	NAVAHO	NYAKYUSA	OJIBWA	OMAHA	PAPAGO	SAMOANS	SWAZI
TETON	THONGA	TIV	VENDA	WINNEBAGO	ZUNI				

34 IN RIGHT COLUMN

AINU	ARAPESH	ARAUCANIANS	BALINESE	CAMAYURA	CHAGGA	CHEYENNE	CHUKCHEE	COMANCHE	CUNA
FON	JIVARO	KASKA	KORYAK	LEPCHA	LESU	MANUS	MAORI	MASAI	NUER
ONA	PUKAPUKA	SHERENTE	SOTHO	TALLENSI	TANALA	TIMBIRA	TRUKESE	TURKANA	WICHITA
WOGEO	YAGUA	YAHGAN	YORUBA						

340 EXCLUDED BECAUSE UNASCERTAINED

	Left column			Right column		
8	LEAN LESS TOWARD BEING THOSE LOCATED OUTSIDE OF NORTH AMERICA (330)	0.54 OF 26	8	LEAN MORE TOWARD BEING THOSE LOCATED OUTSIDE OF NORTH AMERICA (330)	0.88 OF 34	12 4 14 30 XSQ= 7.24 PHI= 0.347 XP = 0.0071
9	TILT MORE TOWARD BEING THOSE LOCATED OUTSIDE OF SOUTH AMERICA (335)	0.96 OF 26	9	TILT LESS TOWARD BEING THOSE LOCATED OUTSIDE OF SOUTH AMERICA (335)	0.74 OF 34	1 9 25 25 XSQ= 3.92 PHI= -0.256 XP = 0.0476
16	DRIFT TOWARD BEING THOSE WHERE THE LATITUDE IS TEN DEGREES OR GREATER (277)	0.77 OF 26	16	DRIFT TOWARD BEING THOSE WHERE THE LATITUDE IS LESS THAN TEN DEGREES (123)	0.50 OF 34	20 17 6 17 XSQ= 3.45 PHI= 0.240 XP = 0.0632
42	DRIFT MORE TOWARD BEING THOSE WHERE THE NATURAL ENVIRONMENT IS OTHER THAN TROPICAL OR SUB-TROPICAL RAIN FOREST, OR MONSOON FOREST (244) FWM	0.85 OF 26	42	DRIFT LESS TOWARD BEING THOSE WHERE THE NATURAL ENVIRONMENT IS OTHER THAN TROPICAL OR SUB-TROPICAL RAIN FOREST, OR MONSOON FOREST (244) FWM	0.62 OF 34	4 13 22 21 XSQ= 2.75 PHI= -0.214 XP = 0.0974

74	TILT TOWARD BEING THOSE 0.75 OF 20 WHERE POTTERY IS PRESENT (145)	74	TILT TOWARD BEING THOSE 0.63 OF 27 WHERE POTTERY IS ABSENT (93)	15 10 5 17 XSQ= 5.21 PHI= 0.333 XP = 0.0224
87	IN ALL CASES ARE THOSE 1.00 OF 20 WHERE THE LEVEL OF POLITICAL INTEGRATION IS THE LARGE STATE, THE LITTLE STATE, THE MINIMAL STATE, OR THE AUTONOMOUS COMMUNITY (281) GPM	87	DRIFT LESS TOWARD BEING THOSE 0.76 OF 29 WHERE THE LEVEL OF POLITICAL INTEGRATION IS THE LARGE STATE, THE LITTLE STATE, THE MINIMAL STATE, OR THE AUTONOMOUS COMMUNITY (281) GPM	20 22 0 7 XSQ= 3.83 PHI= 0.280 XP = 0.0502
96	DRIFT TOWARD BEING THOSE 0.65 OF 23 WHERE THE HIERARCHY OF NATIONAL JURISDICTION HAS FOUR, THREE, TWO OR ONE LEVEL (174) GES,EA	96	DRIFT TOWARD BEING THOSE 0.63 OF 32 WHERE THE HIERARCHY OF NATIONAL JURISDICTION HAS NO LEVELS (156) GES,EA	15 12 8 20 XSQ= 3.08 PHI= 0.237 XP = 0.0793
108	DRIFT TOWARD BEING THOSE 0.82 OF 11 WHERE CLASS STRATIFICATION, IF PRESENT, IS BASED ON A HEREDITARY ARISTOCRACY (74)	108	DRIFT TOWARD BEING THOSE 0.57 OF 14 WHERE CLASS STRATIFICATION, IF PRESENT, IS BASED ON SOMETHING OTHER THAN A HEREDITARY ARISTOCRACY (129)	9 6 2 8 XSQ= 2.44 PHI= 0.313 EP = 0.0992
116	DRIFT TOWARD BEING THOSE 0.50 OF 10 WHERE OCCUPATIONAL SPECIALIZATION IS FULL-TIME, WHETHER OR NOT FOR SURPLUS PRODUCTION (20) JMH	116	DRIFT TOWARD BEING THOSE 0.91 OF 11 WHERE OCCUPATIONAL SPECIALIZATION IS PART-TIME ONLY (34) JMH	5 1 5 10 XSQ= 2.52 PHI= 0.347 EP = 0.0635
136	DRIFT TOWARD BEING THOSE 0.83 OF 12 WHERE FULL-TIME ENTREPRENEURS ARE PRESENT (18) JV	136	DRIFT TOWARD BEING THOSE 0.57 OF 14 WHERE FULL-TIME ENTREPRENEURS ARE ABSENT (14) JV	10 6 2 8 XSQ= 2.93 PHI= 0.335 EP = 0.0511
149	DRIFT TOWARD BEING THOSE 0.80 OF 10 WHERE THE INCIDENCE OF THEFT IS HIGH (18) B-B-C	149	DRIFT TOWARD BEING THOSE 0.61 OF 18 WHERE THE INCIDENCE OF THEFT IS LOW (19) B-B-C	8 7 2 11 XSQ= 2.87 PHI= 0.320 EP = 0.0546
198	TILT LESS TOWARD BEING THOSE 0.71 OF 14 WHERE RULES FOR THE INHERITANCE OF REAL PROPERTY, IF PRESENT, FAVOR THE MALE HEIR OR LINE, RATHER THAN THE FEMALE (144)	198	IN ALL CASES ARE THOSE 1.00 OF 15 WHERE RULES FOR THE INHERITANCE OF REAL PROPERTY, IF PRESENT, FAVOR THE MALE HEIR OR LINE, RATHER THAN THE FEMALE (144)	10 15 4 0 XSQ= 2.86 PHI= -0.314 EP = 0.0421
285	TILT TOWARD BEING THOSE 0.80 OF 10 WHERE THE SEX TABOO DURING PREGNANCY IS ABSENT OR INFERRED ABSENT (17) BCA	285	TILT TOWARD BEING THOSE 0.69 OF 13 WHERE THE SEX TABOO DURING PREGNANCY IS PRESENT (14) BCA	2 9 8 4 XSQ= 3.69 PHI= -0.401 EP = 0.0361

No.		No.		
305	LEAN TOWARD BEING THOSE 0.85 OF 13 WHERE THE EARLY SEXUAL SATISFACTION POTENTIAL IS LOW (24) W-C	305	LEAN TOWARD BEING THOSE 0.73 OF 15 WHERE THE EARLY SEXUAL SATISFACTION POTENTIAL IS HIGH (27) W-C	2 11 11 4 XSQ= 7.22 PHI= -0.508 EP = 0.0032
311	TILT TOWARD BEING THOSE 0.85 OF 13 WHERE SEXUAL SOCIALIZATION ANXIETY IS HIGH (28) W-C	311	TILT TOWARD BEING THOSE 0.60 OF 15 WHERE SEXUAL SOCIALIZATION ANXIETY IS LOW (23) W-C	11 6 2 9 XSQ= 4.09 PHI= 0.382 EP = 0.0238
337	TILT TOWARD BEING THOSE 0.69 OF 26 WHERE THE CHILD'S INFERRED ANXIETY OVER NON-PERFORMANCE OF RESPONSIBLE BEHAVIOR IS HIGH (38) B-B-C	337	TILT TOWARD BEING THOSE 0.64 OF 33 WHERE THE CHILD'S INFERRED ANXIETY OVER NON-PERFORMANCE OF RESPONSIBLE BEHAVIOR IS LOW (35) B-B-C	18 12 8 21 XSQ= 5.04 PHI= 0.292 XP = 0.0248
338	TILT TOWARD BEING THOSE 0.77 OF 26 WHERE THE CHILD'S INFERRED ANXIETY OVER PERFORMANCE OF RESPONSIBLE BEHAVIOR IS HIGH (44) B-B-C	338	TILT TOWARD BEING THOSE 0.55 OF 33 WHERE THE CHILD'S INFERRED ANXIETY OVER PERFORMANCE OF RESPONSIBLE BEHAVIOR IS LOW (29) B-B-C	20 15 6 18 XSQ= 4.73 PHI= 0.283 XP = 0.0296
346	TILT TOWARD BEING THOSE 0.69 OF 26 WHERE THE CHILD'S INFERRED ANXIETY OVER PERFORMANCE OF SELF-RELIANT BEHAVIOR IS HIGH (37) B-B-C	346	TILT TOWARD BEING THOSE 0.68 OF 34 WHERE THE CHILD'S INFERRED ANXIETY OVER PERFORMANCE OF SELF-RELIANT BEHAVIOR IS LOW (39) B-B-C	18 11 8 23 XSQ= 6.61 PHI= 0.332 XP = 0.0101
347	TILT TOWARD BEING THOSE 0.69 OF 26 WHERE THE CHILD'S INFERRED CONFLICT REGARDING SELF-RELIANT BEHAVIOR IS HIGH (37) B-B-C	347	TILT TOWARD BEING THOSE 0.65 OF 34 WHERE THE CHILD'S INFERRED CONFLICT REGARDING SELF-RELIANT BEHAVIOR IS LOW (39) B-B-C	18 12 8 22 XSQ= 5.50 PHI= 0.303 XP = 0.0190
348	TILT TOWARD BEING THOSE 0.69 OF 26 WHERE THE TOTAL POSITIVE PRESSURE TOWARD DEVELOPING ACHIEVEMENT BEHAVIOR IN THE CHILD IS HIGH (32) B-B-C	348	TILT TOWARD BEING THOSE 0.62 OF 34 WHERE THE TOTAL POSITIVE PRESSURE TOWARD DEVELOPING ACHIEVEMENT BEHAVIOR IN THE CHILD IS LOW (31) B-B-C	18 13 8 21 XSQ= 4.49 PHI= 0.274 XP = 0.0340
349	LEAN TOWARD BEING THOSE 0.77 OF 26 WHERE THE CHILD'S INFERRED ANXIETY OVER NON-PERFORMANCE OF ACHIEVEMENT BEHAVIOR IS HIGH (34) B-B-C	349	LEAN TOWARD BEING THOSE 0.62 OF 34 WHERE THE CHILD'S INFERRED ANXIETY OVER NON-PERFORMANCE OF ACHIEVEMENT BEHAVIOR IS LOW (28) B-B-C	20 13 6 21 XSQ= 7.42 PHI= 0.352 XP = 0.0065
350	TEND TO BE THOSE 0.96 OF 26 WHERE THE CHILD'S INFERRED ANXIETY OVER PERFORMANCE OF ACHIEVEMENT BEHAVIOR IS HIGH (34) B-B-C	350	TEND TO BE THOSE 0.74 OF 34 WHERE THE CHILD'S INFERRED ANXIETY OVER PERFORMANCE OF ACHIEVEMENT BEHAVIOR IS LOW (26) B-B-C	25 9 1 25 XSQ= 26.37 PHI= 0.663 XP = 0.0000

3517

No.		No.		
352	TILT MCRE TOWARC BEING THCSE 0.85 OF 26 WHERE THE TOTAL POSITIVE PRESSURE TOWARD DEVELCPING CBEDIENT BEHAVICR IN THE CHILD IS HIGH (44) B-B-C	352	TILT LESS TOWARD BEING THOSE 0.53 OF 30 WHERE THE TOTAL POSITIVE PRESSURE TOWARC DEVELOPING OBEDIENT BEHAVIOR IN THE CHILD IS HIGH (44) B-B-C	22 16 4 14 XSQ= 4.90 PHI= 0.296 XP = 0.0269
353	TILT TCWARD BEING THOSE 0.77 OF 26 WHERE THE CHILD'S INFERREC ANXIETY OVER NCN-PERFCRMANCE CF OBECIENT BEHAVIOR IS HIGH (42) B-B-C	353	TILT TOWARD BEING THOSE 0.58 OF 31 WHERE THE CHILD-S INFERRED ANXIETY OVER NON-PERFORMANCE OF OBEDIENT BEHAVIOR IS LOW (32) B-B-C	20 13 6 18 XSQ= 5.74 PHI= 0.317 XP = 0.0166
354	DRIFT TCWARD BEING THCSE 0.62 OF 26 WHERE THE CHILD'S INFERREC ANXIETY OVER PERFCRMANCE CF CBECIENT BEHAVIOR IS HIGH (36) B-B-C	354	DRIFT TOWARD BEING THOSE 0.68 OF 31 WHERE THE CHILD'S INFERRED ANXIETY OVER PERFORMANCE OF OBEDIENT BEHAVIOR IS LOW (37) B-B-C	16 10 10 21 XSQ= 3.78 PHI= 0.257 XP = 0.0519
355	TILT TCWARD BEING THOSE 0.65 OF 26 WHERE THE CHILD'S INFERREC CONFLICT REGARDING CBEDIENT BEHAVICR IS HIGH (35) B-B-C	355	TILT TOWARD BEING THOSE 0.71 OF 31 WHERE THE CHILD'S INFERRED CCNFLICT REGARDING OBEDIENT BEHAVIOR IS LOW (38) B-B-C	17 9 9 22 XSQ= 6.14 PHI= 0.328 XP = 0.0132
360	DRIFT TCWARD BEING THCSE 0.80 OF 5 WHERE ADCLESCENT PEER GROUPS ARE PRESENT IN A SETTING CF WORK AND PUBLIC GATHERINGS AND LEISURE, CR AT LEAST CF PUBLIC GATHERINGS ANC LEISURE (14) JKH	360	DRIFT TOWARD BEING THOSE 0.80 OF 10 WHERE ADOLESCENT PEER GRCUPS ARE PRESENT ONLY IN A SETTING OF LEISURE, OR ELSE ARE ABSENT (23) JKH	4 2 1 8 XSQ= 2.81 PHI= 0.433 EP = 0.0889
397	DRIFT LESS TCWARD BEING THOSE 0.58 OF 12 WHERE SEX DISABILITY IS ABSENT (42) JKH	397	DRIFT MORE TOWARD BEING THOSE 0.93 OF 15 WHERE SEX DISABILITY IS ABSENT (42) JKH	5 1 7 14 XSQ= 2.92 PHI= 0.329 EP = 0.0602
406	TILT TCWARD BEING THOSE 0.73 OF 15 WHERE EXPLANATICNS CF ILLNESS CF AN AGGRESSICN NATURE ARE PRESENT (28) W-C	406	TILT TOWARD BEING THOSE 0.69 OF 16 WHERE EXPLANATIONS OF ILLNESS OF AN AGGRESSION NATURE ARE ABSENT (33) W-C	11 5 4 11 XSQ= 3.93 PHI= 0.356 EP = 0.0320
421	DRIFT TCWARD BEING THCSE 0.63 OF 19 WHERE KILLING, TCRTURING, CR MUTILATING OF THE ENEMY IS STRONGLY CR MODERATELY EMPHASIZED (37) PES	421	DRIFT TOWARD BEING THOSE 0.71 OF 24 WHERE KILLING, TORTURING, OR MUTILATING OF THE ENEMY IS NEGLIGIBLY EMPHASIZED (47) PES	12 7 7 17 XSQ= 3.69 PHI= 0.293 XP = 0.0549
445	DRIFT TOWARD BEING THCSE 0.82 OF 11 WHERE SCRCERY IS IMPCRTANT (26) BBW,DH	445	DRIFT TOWARD BEING THOSE 0.60 OF 10 WHERE SORCERY IS UNIMPORTANT (23) BBW,DH	9 4 2 6 XSQ= 2.31 PHI= 0.332 EP = 0.0805

446	TILT TCWARD BEING THOSE WHERE WITCHCRAFT IS SIGNIFICANTLY PRESENT (14) GES	0.88 OF 8	446	TILT TOWARD BEING THOSE WHERE WITCHCRAFT IS MODERATELY PRESENT OR ABSENT (24) GES	0.80 OF 10	7 2 1 8 XSQ= 5.63 PHI= 0.559 EP = 0.0152
454	DRIFT TOWARD BEING THOSE WHERE THE CBJECTIVE OF THE INCIVICUAL'S CONTACT WITH THE DIVINE IS NCT CCNDUCIVE TC THE CEVELOPMENT OF THE INDIVIDUAL'S NEED TC ACHIEVE (18) DCM	0.67 OF 15	454	DRIFT TOWARD BEING THOSE WHERE THE OBJECTIVE OF THE INDIVIDUAL'S CONTACT WITH THE DIVINE IS CONDUCIVE TO THE DEVELCPMENT OF THE INDIVIDUAL'S NEED TO ACHIEVE (18) DCM	0.69 OF 16	5 11 10 5 XSQ= 2.60 PHI= -0.290 EP = 0.0756
458	TILT TOWARD BEING THOSE WHERE GAMES, IF PRESENT, INCLUDE GAMES OF STRATEGY (52) R-A-B,EA	0.53 OF 19	458	TILT TOWARD BEING THOSE WHERE GAMES, IF PRESENT, DO NOT INCLUDE GAMES OF STRATEGY (119) R-A-B,EA	0.83 OF 24	10 4 9 20 XSQ= 4.72 PHI= 0.331 XP = 0.0299
460	TEND TC BE THCSE WHERE GAMES, IF PRESENT, ARE NCT LIMITED TO GAMES CF SKILL CNLY (104) R-A-B,EA	0.95 OF 19	460	TEND TO BE THOSE WHERE GAMES, IF PRESENT, ARE LIMITED TO GAMES OF SKILL ONLY (67) R-A-B,EA	0.58 OF 24	1 14 18 10 XSQ= 10.92 PHI= -0.504 XP = 0.0010
471	TILT TCWARD BEING THOSE WHERE SECRET SOCIETIES ARE PRESENT (9) LWS	0.83 OF 6	471	IN ALL CASES ARE THOSE WHERE SECRET SOCIETIES ARE UMIMPORTANT OR ABSENT (14) LWS	1.00 OF 5	5 0 1 5 XSQ= 4.65 PHI= 0.650 EP = 0.0152
475	LEAN TOWARD BEING THOSE WHERE EXHIBITIONISTIC CANCING IS STRONGLY CR MCDERATELY EMPHASIZED (48) PES	0.95 OF 19	475	LEAN TOWARD BEING THOSE WHERE EXHIBITIONISTIC DANCING IS NEGLIGIBLY EMPHASIZED (38) PES	0.54 OF 24	18 11 1 13 XSQ= 9.43 PHI= 0.468 XP = 0.0021

352 CULTURES WHERE THE TOTAL POSITIVE PRESSURE TOWARD DEVELCPING OBEDIENT BEHAVICR IN THE CHILD IS HIGH (44) B-B-C	352 CULTURES WHERE THE TOTAL POSITIVE PRESSURE TOWARD DEVELOPING OBEDIENT BEHAVICR IN THE CHILD IS LOW (28) B-B-C	

BACKGROUND ON PAGE 143

BCTH SUBJECT AND PREDICATE

44 IN LEFT CCLUMN

AINU, ASHANTI, AYMARA, AZANDE, CHAGGA, CHENCHU, CHEYENNE, CHIR-APACHE, CHUKCHEE, CROW, CUNA, GANDA, HANC, KIKUYU, KWAKIUTL, LAMBA, LAU, LESU, MANCAN, MASAI, MBUNDU, NAVAHC, NYAKYUSA, OJIBWA, OMAHA, ONA, PAPAGO, SAMOANS, SHERENTE, SOTHO, SWAZI, TALLENSI, TANALA, TETON, THONGA, TIV, TUCUNA, TUPINAMBA, VENCA, WICHITA, YAGUA, YAHGAN, YAKUT, YORUBA

28 IN RIGHT CCLUMN

ALORESE, ARANDA, ARAUCANIANS, BALINESE, CAMAYURA, COMANCHE, IFUGAO, JIVARO, KASKA, KURTATCHI, LAKHER, LEPCHA, MANUS, MAORI, MARQUESANS, MURNGIN, NUER, ONTCNG-JAVA, PUKAPUKA, SIRIONO, TIKCPIA, TRCBRIANC, TRUKESE, TURKANA, WINNEBAGO, WOGEO, WOLEAIANS, ZUNI

328 EXCLUCED BECAUSE UNASCERTAINED

	Left column			Right column		
3	TILT LESS TOWARC BEING THCSE LOCATED CUTSIDE CF AFRICA (320)	0.64 OF 44	3	TILT MORE TOWARD BEING THOSE LOCATED OUTSIDE OF AFRICA (320)	0.93 OF 28	16 2 28 26 XSQ= 6.31 PHI= 0.296 XP = 0.0120
6	TEND TO BE THOSE LOCATED CUTSIDE OF THE INSULAR PACIFIC (330)	0.93 OF 44	6	TEND TO BE THOSE LOCATED IN THE INSULAR PACIFIC (70)	0.57 OF 28	3 16 41 12 XSQ= 19.79 PHI= -0.524 XP = 0.0000
36	TILT LESS TOWARC BEING THCSE WHERE THE NATURAL ENVIRONMENT IS CTHER THAN 'VERY HARSH,' OR SUB-TROPICAL BUSH, OR TEMPERATE GRASSLANC (292) FWM	0.55 OF 44	36	TILT MORE TOWARD BEING THOSE WHERE THE NATURAL ENVIRCNMENT IS OTHER THAN 'VERY HARSH,' OR SUB-TROPICAL BUSH, OR TEMPERATE GRASSLAND (292) FWM	0.82 OF 28	20 5 24 23 XSQ= 4.60 PHI= 0.253 XP = 0.0320
42	TILT TCWARD BEING THOSE WHERE THE NATURAL ENVIRONMENT IS CTHER THAN TROPICAL CR SUB-TRCPICAL RAIN FOREST, OR MONSCCN FCREST (244) FWM	0.73 OF 44	42	TILT TOWARD BEING THOSE WHERE THE NATURAL ENVIRCNMENT IS TROPICAL OR SUB-TRCPICAL RAIN FOREST, OR MONSOON FOREST (156) FWM	0.54 OF 28	12 15 32 13 XSQ= 3.99 PHI= -0.235 XP = 0.0458

63	LEAN TCWARD BEING THOSE WHERE HUSBANDRY, IF PRESENT, IS PRINCIPALLY IN THE FORM OF BOVINE, EQUINE, CAMEL-LIKE, OR DEER-LIKE ANIMALS, RATHER THAN PIGS, SHEEP, CR GOATS (152)	0.74 OF 31	63	LEAN TOWARD BEING THOSE WHERE HUSBANDRY, IF PRESENT, IS PRINCIPALLY IN THE FORM OF PIGS, SHEEP, OR GOATS, RATHER THAN BOVINE, EQUINE, CAMEL-LIKE, OR DEER-LIKE ANIMALS (74)	0.76 OF 17	23 4 8 13 XSQ= 9.49 PHI= 0.445 XP = 0.0021
71	LEAN LESS TOWARC BEING THCSE WHERE METAL WORKING IS ABSENT (153)	0.51 OF 37	71	LEAN MORE TOWARD BEING THOSE WHERE METAL WORKING IS ABSENT (153)	0.91 OF 22	18 2 19 20 XSQ= 7.95 PHI= 0.367 XP = 0.0048
74	LEAN TCWARD BEING THOSE WHERE PCTTERY IS PRESENT (145)	0.72 OF 36	74	LEAN TOWARD BEING THOSE WHERE POTTERY IS ABSENT (93)	0.70 OF 23	26 7 10 16 XSQ= 8.32 PHI= 0.376 XP = 0.0039
81	TILT LESS TOWARC BEING THCSE WHERE NO CITY OR TCWN IS PRESENT, AND THE AVERAGE COMMUNITY SIZE IS SMALLER THAN 200 (135)	0.53 OF 32	81	TILT MORE TOWARD BEING THOSE WHERE NO CITY OR TOWN IS PRESENT, AND THE AVERAGE COMMUNITY SIZE IS SMALLER THAN 200 (135)	0.89 OF 19	15 2 17 17 XSQ= 5.55 PHI= 0.330 XP = 0.0185
83	TILT LESS TOWARC BEING THOSE WHERE, WITH NC CITY ANC NC TOWN PRESENT, THE AVERAGE CCMMUNITY SIZE IS SMALLER THAN 200, RATHER THAN BETWEEN 200 AND 999 (135)	0.59 OF 29	83	TILT MORE TOWARD BEING THOSE WHERE, WITH NO CITY AND NO TOWN PRESENT, THE AVERAGE COMMUNITY SIZE IS SMALLER THAN 200, RATHER THAN BETWEEN 200 AND 999 (135)	0.94 OF 18	12 1 17 17 XSQ= 5.45 PHI= 0.340 XP = 0.0196
86	LEAN TCWARD BEING THCSE WHERE THE LEVEL CF POLITICAL INTEGRATION IS THE LARGE STATE, THE LITTLE STATE, OR THE MINIMAL STATE (148) GPM	0.61 OF 36	86	LEAN TOWARD BEING THOSE WHERE THE LEVEL OF POLITICAL INTEGRATION IS THE AUTONOMOUS COMMUNITY, OR THE FAMILY (156) GPM	0.76 OF 25	22 6 14 19 XSQ= 6.76 PHI= 0.333 XP = 0.0093
88	TILT TOWARD BEING THOSE WHERE, IF A HEADMANSHIP IS PRESENT, SUCCESSION IS NON-HEREDITARY (106)	0.52 OF 33	88	TILT TOWARD BEING THOSE WHERE, IF A HEADMANSHIP IS PRESENT, SUCCESSION IS HEREDITARY (165)	0.86 OF 22	17 3 16 19 XSQ= 6.63 PHI= 0.347 XP = 0.0100
96	TILT TCWARD BEING THOSE WHERE THE HIERARCHY OF NATIONAL JURISDICTION HAS FOUR, THREE, TWO OR ONE LEVEL (174) GES,EA	0.67 OF 42	96	TILT TOWARD BEING THOSE WHERE THE HIERARCHY OF NATIONAL JURISDICTION HAS NO LEVELS (156) GES,EA	0.68 OF 25	28 8 14 17 XSQ= 6.25 PHI= 0.305 XP = 0.0125
136	DRIFT TOWARD BEING THOSE WHERE FULL-TIME ENTREPRENEURS ARE PRESENT (18) JV	0.67 OF 21	136	DRIFT TOWARD BEING THOSE WHERE FULL-TIME ENTREPRENEURS ARE ABSENT (14) JV	0.75 OF 8	14 2 7 6 XSQ= 2.56 PHI= 0.297 EP = 0.0923

138	TILT TOWARD BEING THOSE WHERE SUPERORDINATE JUSTICE IS PRESENT (22) BBW	0.86 OF	14	138	TILT TOWARD BEING THOSE WHERE SUPERORDINATE JUSTICE IS ABSENT (18) BBW	0.67 OF	12	12 4 2 8 XSQ= 5.44 PHI= 0.457 EP = 0.0138
178	DRIFT MORE TOWARD BEING THOSE WHERE THE COMMUNITY IS OTHER THAN SEGMENTED ON A CLAN BASIS AND NON-EXOGAMOUS (295)	0.81 OF	43	178	DRIFT LESS TOWARD BEING THOSE WHERE THE COMMUNITY IS OTHER THAN SEGMENTED ON A CLAN BASIS AND NON-EXOGAMOUS (295)	0.61 OF	28	8 11 35 17 XSQ= 2.72 PHI= -0.196 XP = 0.0991
214	DRIFT MORE TOWARD BEING THOSE WHERE FIRST COUSIN MARRIAGE, IF PERMITTED, IS OTHER THAN UNILATERAL (144)	0.88 OF	17	214	DRIFT LESS TOWARD BEING THOSE WHERE FIRST COUSIN MARRIAGE, IF PERMITTED, IS OTHER THAN UNILATERAL (144)	0.55 OF	11	2 5 15 6 XSQ= 2.45 PHI= -0.296 EP = 0.0764
305	TILT TOWARD BEING THOSE WHERE THE EARLY SEXUAL SATISFACTION POTENTIAL IS LOW (24) W-C	0.57 OF	21	305	TILT TOWARD BEING THOSE WHERE THE EARLY SEXUAL SATISFACTION POTENTIAL IS HIGH (27) W-C	0.82 OF	17	9 14 12 3 XSQ= 4.59 PHI= -0.348 EP = 0.0202
307	TILT TOWARD BEING THOSE WHERE THE EARLY AGGRESSION SATISFACTION POTENTIAL IS LOW (19) W-C	0.50 OF	22	307	TILT TOWARD BEING THOSE WHERE THE EARLY AGGRESSION SATISFACTION POTENTIAL IS HIGH (33) W-C	0.84 OF	19	11 16 11 3 XSQ= 3.89 PHI= -0.308 XP = 0.0485
308	DRIFT TOWARD BEING THOSE WHERE AVERAGE SOCIALIZATION ANXIETY IS HIGH (22) W-C	0.61 OF	18	308	DRIFT TOWARD BEING THOSE WHERE AVERAGE SOCIALIZATION ANXIETY IS LOW (18) W-C	0.73 OF	15	11 4 7 11 XSQ= 2.65 PHI= 0.283 EP = 0.0801
311	DRIFT TOWARD BEING THOSE WHERE SEXUAL SOCIALIZATION ANXIETY IS HIGH (28) W-C	0.62 OF	21	311	DRIFT TOWARD BEING THOSE WHERE SEXUAL SOCIALIZATION ANXIETY IS LOW (23) W-C	0.71 OF	17	13 5 8 12 XSQ= 2.78 PHI= 0.271 EP = 0.0585
313	DRIFT TOWARD BEING THOSE WHERE AGGRESSION SOCIALIZATION ANXIETY IS HIGH (26) W-C	0.59 OF	22	313	DRIFT TOWARD BEING THOSE WHERE AGGRESSION SOCIALIZATION ANXIETY IS LOW (28) W-C	0.74 OF	19	13 5 9 14 XSQ= 3.22 PHI= 0.280 XP = 0.0729
314	TILT LESS TOWARD BEING THOSE WHERE THE INCIDENCE OF MOTHER-CHILD HOUSEHOLDS IS LOW (61) W-C,S	0.63 OF	24	314	TILT MORE TOWARD BEING THOSE WHERE THE INCIDENCE OF MOTHER-CHILD HOUSEHOLDS IS LOW (61) W-D,S	0.92 OF	24	9 2 15 22 XSQ= 4.25 PHI= 0.297 XP = 0.0393

318	DRIFT TOWARD BEING THCSE 0.54 OF 39 WHERE THE CVERALL INDULGENCE OF THE INFANT IS LOW (31) B-B-C	318	DRIFT TOWARD BEING THOSE 0.73 OF 26 WHERE THE OVERALL INDULGENCE OF THE INFANT IS HIGH (40) B-B-C	18 19 21 7 XSQ= 3.58 PHI= -0.235 XP = 0.0585
336	TEND TC BE THOSE 0.77 OF 43 WHERE THE TOTAL POSITIVE PRESSURE TOWARD DEVELCPING RESPCNSIBLE BEHAVIOR IN THE CHILD IS HIGH (43) B-B-C	336	TEND TO BE THOSE 0.67 OF 27 WHERE THE TOTAL POSITIVE PRESSURE TOWARD DEVELOPING RESPONSIBLE BEHAVIOR IN THE CHILD IS LOW (32) B-B-C	33 9 10 18 XSQ= 11.28 PHI= 0.401 XP = 0.0008
337	TILT TCWARD BEING THOSE 0.67 OF 42 WHERE THE CHILD'S INFERREC ANXIETY OVER NCN-PERFCRMANCE OF RESPCNSIBLE BEHAVIOR IS HIGH (38) B-B-C	337	TILT TOWARD BEING THOSE 0.65 OF 26 WHERE THE CHILD'S INFERRED ANXIETY OVER NON-PERFORMANCE OF RESPCNSIBLE BEHAVIOR IS LOW (35) B-B-C	28 9 14 17 XSQ= 5.42 PHI= 0.282 XP = 0.0199
339	DRIFT TCWARD BEING THOSE 0.52 OF 42 WHERE THE CHILD'S INFERREC CONFLICT REGARDING RESPCNSIBLE BEHAVIOR IS HIGH (31) B-B-C	339	DRIFT TOWARD BEING THOSE 0.73 OF 26 WHERE THE CHILD'S INFERRED CONFLICT REGARDING RESPONSIBLE BEHAVIOR IS LOW (42) B-B-C	22 7 20 19 XSQ= 3.28 PHI= 0.220 XP = 0.0702
350	LEAN TCWARD BEING THCSE 0.76 OF 38 WHERE THE CHILD'S INFERREC ANXIETY OVER PERFCRMANCE OF ACHIEVEMENT BEHAVIOR IS HIGH (34) B-B-C	350	LEAN TOWARD BEING THOSE 0.72 OF 18 WHERE THE CHILD'S INFERRED ANXIETY OVER PERFORMANCE OF ACHIEVEMENT BEHAVIOR IS LOW (26) B-B-C	29 5 9 13 XSQ= 10.12 PHI= 0.425 XP = 0.0015
351	TILT TCWARD BEING THOSE 0.58 OF 38 WHERE THE CHILD'S INFERREC CCNFLICT REGARDING ACHIEVEMENT BEHAVIOR IS HIGH (26) B-B-C	351	TILT TOWARD BEING THOSE 0.78 OF 18 WHERE THE CHILD'S INFERRED CONFLICT REGARDING ACHIEVEMENT BEHAVIOR IS LOW (34) B-B-C	22 4 16 14 XSQ= 4.90 PHI= 0.296 XP = 0.0269
353	LEAN TOWARD BEING THOSE 0.73 OF 44 WHERE THE CHILD'S INFERREC ANXIETY OVER NCN-PERFCRMANCE CF OBECIENT BEHAVIOR IS HIGH (42) B-B-C	353	LEAN TOWARD BEING THOSE 0.68 OF 28 WHERE THE CHILD-S INFERRED ANXIETY OVER NON-PERFORMANCE OF OBEDIENT BEHAVIOR IS LOW (32) B-B-C	32 9 12 19 XSQ= 9.90 PHI= 0.371 XP = 0.0017
358	DRIFT MORE TCWARC BEING THOSE 0.94 OF 16 WHERE ADOLESCENT PEER GROUPS ARE PRESENT IN A SETTING CF WORK AND PUBLIC GATHERINGS AND LEISURE, CR CF PUBLIC GATHERINGS ANC LEISURE, OR CF LEISURE ONLY (41) JKH	358	DRIFT LESS TOWARD BEING THCSE 0.64 OF 14 WHERE ADOLESCENT PEER GRCUPS ARE PRESENT IN A SETTING OF WORK AND PUBLIC GATHERINGS AND LEISURE, OR OF PUBLIC GATHERINGS AND LEISURE, OR OF LEISURE ONLY (41) JKH	15 9 1 5 XSQ= 2.42 PHI= 0.284 EP = 0.0725
366	DRIFT LESS TCWARC BEING THOSE 0.63 OF 19 WHERE DISSCCIATICN OF THE SEXES AT ADCLESCENCE IS MEDIUM CR LCW (41) JKH	366	DRIFT MORE TOWARD BEING THCSE 0.93 OF 15 WHERE DISSOCIATION OF THE SEXES AT ADOLESCENCE IS MEDIUM OR LOW (41) JKH	7 1 12 14 XSQ= 2.73 PHI= 0.283 EP = 0.0529

373	DRIFT TOWARD BEING THOSE WHERE MALE INITIATION CEREMONIES AT PUBERTY ARE PRESENT (17) W-K-A	0.55 OF	20	373	DRIFT TOWARD BEING THOSE WHERE MALE INITIATION CEREMONIES AT PUBERTY ARE ABSENT (27) W-K-A	0.77 OF	13	11 3 9 10 XSQ= 2.11 PHI= 0.253 EP = 0.0873
380	DRIFT TOWARD BEING THOSE WHERE SEGREGATION OF GIRLS AT MENARCHE IS PRESENT (35) F-B	0.81 OF	16	380	DRIFT TOWARD BEING THOSE WHERE SEGREGATION OF GIRLS AT MENARCHE IS ABSENT (20) F-B	0.56 OF	9	13 4 3 5 XSQ= 2.09 PHI= 0.289 EP = 0.0870
391	TILT LESS TOWARD BEING THOSE WHERE PREMARITAL SEX RELATIONS ARE PUNISHED ONLY IF PREGNANCY RESULTS, OR FREELY PERMITTED (90) JTW,EA	0.56 OF	32	391	TILT MORE TOWARD BEING THOSE WHERE PREMARITAL SEX RELATIONS ARE PUNISHED ONLY IF PREGNANCY RESULTS, OR FREELY PERMITTED (90) JTW,EA	0.89 OF	18	14 2 18 16 XSQ= 4.24 PHI= 0.291 XP = 0.0395
399	DRIFT TOWARD BEING THOSE WHERE INTENSITY OF CASTRATION ANXIETY IS HIGH (23) WNS	0.61 OF	23	399	DRIFT TOWARD BEING THOSE WHERE INTENSITY OF CASTRATION ANXIETY IS LOW (22) WNS	0.71 OF	17	14 5 9 12 XSQ= 2.72 PHI= 0.261 EP = 0.0624
400	TILT TOWARD BEING THOSE WHERE HOMOSEXUAL ACTIVITY IS PERMITTED (36) F-B	0.74 OF	19	400	TILT TOWARD BEING THOSE WHERE HOMOSEXUAL ACTIVITY IS PROHIBITED (22) F-B	0.73 OF	15	5 11 14 4 XSQ= 5.67 PHI= -0.408 EP = 0.0142
446	DRIFT TOWARD BEING THOSE WHERE WITCHCRAFT IS SIGNIFICANTLY PRESENT (14) GES	0.70 OF	10	446	DRIFT TOWARD BEING THOSE WHERE WITCHCRAFT IS MODERATELY PRESENT OR ABSENT (24) GES	0.78 OF	9	7 2 3 7 XSQ= 2.63 PHI= 0.372 EP = 0.0698
460	LEAN TOWARD BEING THOSE WHERE GAMES, IF PRESENT, ARE NOT LIMITED TO GAMES OF SKILL ONLY (104) R-A-B,EA	0.76 OF	33	460	LEAN TOWARD BEING THOSE WHERE GAMES, IF PRESENT, ARE LIMITED TO GAMES OF SKILL ONLY (67) R-A-B,EA	0.67 OF	18	8 12 25 6 XSQ= 7.10 PHI= -0.373 XP = 0.0077
475	DRIFT MORE TOWARD BEING THOSE WHERE EXHIBITIONISTIC DANCING IS STRONGLY OR MODERATELY EMPHASIZED (48) PES	0.79 OF	29	475	DRIFT LESS TOWARD BEING THOSE WHERE EXHIBITIONISTIC DANCING IS STRONGLY OR MODERATELY EMPHASIZED (48) PES	0.52 OF	23	23 12 6 11 XSQ= 3.15 PHI= 0.246 XP = 0.0760

****

353 CULTURES WHERE THE CHILD'S INFERRED ANXIETY OVER NON-PERFORMANCE OF OBEDIENT BEHAVIOR IS HIGH (42) B-B-C	353 CULTURES WHERE THE CHILD-S INFERRED ANXIETY OVER NON-PERFORMANCE OF OBEDIENT BEHAVIOR IS LOW (32) B-B-C

BACKGROUND ON PAGE 143 BOTH SUBJECT AND PREDICATE

....

42 IN LEFT COLUMN

AINU	ALORESE	ASHANTI	AYMARA	AZANDE	CHAGGA	CHIR-APACHE	CROW	GANDA	HANO
JIVARO	KASKA	KIKUYU	KWAKIUTL	LAKHER	LAMBA	LAU	LEPCHA	LESU	MASAI
MBUNDU	NAVAHO	NYAKYUSA	OJIBWA	OMAHA	ONTONG-JAVA	PUKAPUKA	SAMOANS	SHERENTE	SOTHO
SWAZI	TALLENSI	TANALA	TENETEHARA	THONGA	TIV	TUCUNA	VENDA	WICHITA	WOLEAIANS
YAKUT	ZUNI								

32 IN RIGHT COLUMN

ARANDA	ARAUCANIANS	BALINESE	CAMAYURA	CHENCHU	CHEYENNE	CHUKCHEE	COMANCHE	CUNA	IFUGAO
KORYAK	KURTATCHI	MANDAN	MANUS	MAORI	MARQUESANS	MURNGIN	NUER	ONA	PAPAGO
SIRIONO	TETON	TIKOPIA	TROBRIAND	TRUKESE	TUPINAMBA	TURKANA	WINNEBAGO	WOGEO	YAGUA
YAHGAN	YORUBA								

326 EXCLUDED BECAUSE UNASCERTAINED

3	TILT LESS TOWARD BEING THOSE LOCATED OUTSIDE OF AFRICA (320)	0.64 OF 42	3	TILT MORE TOWARD BEING THOSE LOCATED OUTSIDE OF AFRICA (320)	0.91 OF 32
					15 3 27 29 XSQ= 5.49 PHI= 0.272 XP = 0.0191
6	DRIFT MORE TOWARD BEING THOSE LOCATED OUTSIDE OF THE INSULAR PACIFIC (330)	0.83 OF 42	6	DRIFT LESS TOWARD BEING THOSE LOCATED OUTSIDE OF THE INSULAR PACIFIC (330)	0.63 OF 32
					7 12 35 20 XSQ= 3.11 PHI= -0.205 XP = 0.0778
44	TILT TOWARD BEING THOSE WHERE SETTLEMENTS ARE FIXED (222)	0.76 OF 42	44	TILT TOWARD BEING THOSE WHERE SETTLEMENTS ARE NON-FIXED (110)	0.50 OF 28
					32 14 10 14 XSQ= 4.02 PHI= 0.240 XP = 0.0450
51	LEAN TOWARD BEING THOSE WHERE SUBSISTENCE IS PRIMARILY BY FOOD PRODUCTION -- I. E., AGRICULTURE OR HUSBANDRY -- RATHER THAN BY GATHERING (253)	0.69 OF 42	51	LEAN TOWARD BEING THOSE WHERE SUBSISTENCE IS PRIMARILY BY FOOD GATHERING -- I. E., HUNTING, FISHING, OR COLLECTING -- RATHER THAN FOOD PRODUCTION (147)	0.66 OF 32
					29 11 13 21 XSQ= 7.45 PHI= 0.317 XP = 0.0063

54	TILT MORE TOWARD BEING THOSE WHERE FOOD PRODUCTION IS BY INTENSIVE OR SIMPLE AGRICULTURE, RATHER THAN BY INCIPIENT FOOD PRODUCTION (192)	0.88 OF 32	54	TILT LESS TOWARD BEING THOSE WHERE FOOD PRODUCTION IS BY INTENSIVE OR SIMPLE AGRICULTURE, RATHER THAN BY INCIPIENT FOOD PRODUCTION (192)	0.56 OF 16	28 9 4 7 XSQ= 4.26 PHI= 0.298 XP = 0.0390
56	DRIFT TOWARD BEING THOSE WHERE FOOD PRODUCTION IS BY SIMPLE AGRICULTURE, RATHER THAN BY INCIPIENT FOOD PRODUCTION (101)	0.80 OF 20	56	DRIFT TOWARD BEING THOSE WHERE FOOD PRODUCTION IS BY INCIPIENT FOOD PRODUCTION, RATHER THAN BY SIMPLE AGRICULTURE (46)	0.54 OF 13	16 6 4 7 XSQ= 2.68 PHI= 0.285 EP = 0.0645
62	TILT MORE TOWARD BEING THOSE WHERE HUSBANDRY OF SOME KIND IS PRESENT (228)	0.79 OF 42	62	TILT LESS TOWARD BEING THOSE WHERE HUSBANDRY OF SOME KIND IS PRESENT (228)	0.53 OF 32	33 17 9 15 XSQ= 4.27 PHI= 0.240 XP = 0.0388
71	LEAN TOWARD BEING THOSE WHERE METAL WORKING IS PRESENT (98)	0.52 OF 33	71	LEAN TOWARD BEING THOSE WHERE METAL WORKING IS ABSENT (153)	0.85 OF 27	17 4 16 23 XSQ= 7.25 PHI= 0.348 XP = 0.0071
81	TILT LESS TOWARD BEING THOSE WHERE NO CITY OR TOWN IS PRESENT, AND THE AVERAGE COMMUNITY SIZE IS SMALLER THAN 200 (135)	0.53 OF 30	81	TILT MORE TOWARD BEING THOSE WHERE NO CITY OR TOWN IS PRESENT, AND THE AVERAGE COMMUNITY SIZE IS SMALLER THAN 200 (135)	0.86 OF 22	14 3 16 19 XSQ= 4.88 PHI= 0.306 XP = 0.0271
82	TILT MORE TOWARD BEING THOSE WHERE A CITY OR TOWN IS PRESENT, OR THE AVERAGE COMMUNITY SIZE IS FIFTY OR GREATER (178)	0.93 OF 30	82	TILT LESS TOWARD BEING THOSE WHERE A CITY OR TOWN IS PRESENT, OR THE AVERAGE COMMUNITY SIZE IS FIFTY OR GREATER (178)	0.68 OF 22	28 15 2 7 XSQ= 3.99 PHI= 0.277 XP = 0.0458
83	TILT LESS TOWARD BEING THOSE WHERE, WITH NO CITY AND NO TOWN PRESENT, THE AVERAGE COMMUNITY SIZE IS SMALLER THAN 200, RATHER THAN BETWEEN 200 AND 999 (135)	0.59 OF 27	83	TILT MORE TOWARD BEING THOSE WHERE, WITH NO CITY AND NO TOWN PRESENT, THE AVERAGE COMMUNITY SIZE IS SMALLER THAN 200, RATHER THAN BETWEEN 200 AND 999 (135)	0.90 OF 21	11 2 16 19 XSQ= 4.36 PHI= 0.301 XP = 0.0369
86	DRIFT TOWARD BEING THOSE WHERE THE LEVEL OF POLITICAL INTEGRATION IS THE LARGE STATE, THE LITTLE STATE, OR THE MINIMAL STATE (148) GPM	0.56 OF 34	86	DRIFT TOWARD BEING THOSE WHERE THE LEVEL OF POLITICAL INTEGRATION IS THE AUTONOMOUS COMMUNITY, OR THE FAMILY (156) GPM	0.69 OF 29	19 9 15 20 XSQ= 2.97 PHI= 0.217 XP = 0.0847
96	TILT TOWARD BEING THOSE WHERE THE HIERARCHY OF NATIONAL JURISDICTION HAS FOUR, THREE, TWO OR ONE LEVEL (174) GES,EA	0.66 OF 41	96	TILT TOWARD BEING THOSE WHERE THE HIERARCHY OF NATIONAL JURISDICTION HAS NO LEVELS (156) GES,EA	0.68 OF 28	27 9 14 19 XSQ= 6.29 PHI= 0.302 XP = 0.0122

116	LEAN LESS TOWARD BEING THOSE 0.53 OF 15 WHERE OCCUPATIONAL SPECIALIZATION IS PART-TIME ONLY (34) JMH	116	IN ALL CASES ARE THOSE 1.00 OF 12 WHERE OCCUPATIONAL SPECIALIZATION IS PART-TIME ONLY (34) JMH	7 0 8 12 XSQ= 5.33 PHI= 0.444 EP = 0.0081
130	DRIFT TOWARD BEING THOSE 0.54 OF 13 WHERE LEATHER WORKING IS MAINLY DONE BY MALES (39)	130	DRIFT TOWARD BEING THOSE 0.88 OF 8 WHERE LEATHER WORKING IS MAINLY DONE BY FEMALES (45)	7 1 6 7 XSQ= 2.05 PHI= 0.312 EP = 0.0850
132	DRIFT TOWARD BEING THOSE 0.80 OF 15 WHERE ECONOMIC EXCHANGE INVOLVES THE USE OF MONEY (37) JMH	132	DRIFT TOWARD BEING THOSE 0.58 OF 12 WHERE ECONOMIC EXCHANGE DOES NOT INVOLVE THE USE OF MONEY (17) JMH	12 5 3 7 XSQ= 2.72 PHI= 0.317 EP = 0.0568
138	TILT TOWARD BEING THOSE 0.81 OF 16 WHERE SUPERORDINATE JUSTICE IS PRESENT (22) BBW	138	TILT TOWARD BEING THOSE 0.70 OF 10 WHERE SUPERORDINATE JUSTICE IS ABSENT (18) BBW	13 3 3 7 XSQ= 4.84 PHI= 0.431 EP = 0.0152
142	DRIFT TOWARD BEING THOSE 0.87 OF 15 WHERE THE LEVEL OF SOCIAL SANCTION IS PUBLIC CORPOREAL SANCTION OR PUBLIC PROPERTY SANCTION, RATHER THAN PRIVATE SETTLEMENT (38) JMH	142	DRIFT TOWARD BEING THOSE 0.50 OF 12 WHERE THE LEVEL OF SOCIAL SANCTION IS PRIVATE SETTLEMENT, RATHER THAN PUBLIC CORPOREAL SANCTION OR PUBLIC PROPERTY SETTLEMENT (16) JMH	13 6 2 6 XSQ= 2.72 PHI= 0.317 EP = 0.0870
186	DRIFT LESS TOWARD BEING THOSE 0.57 OF 42 WHERE THE KIN GROUP IS OTHER THAN EXCLUSIVELY PATRILINEAL (250)	186	DRIFT MORE TOWARD BEING THOSE 0.81 OF 32 WHERE THE KIN GROUP IS OTHER THAN EXCLUSIVELY PATRILINEAL (250)	18 6 24 26 XSQ= 3.78 PHI= 0.226 XP = 0.0519
188	TILT MORE TOWARD BEING THOSE 0.83 OF 42 WHERE THE KIN GROUP IS OTHER THAN EXCLUSIVELY COGNATIC (252)	188	TILT LESS TOWARD BEING THOSE 0.53 OF 32 WHERE THE KIN GROUP IS OTHER THAN EXCLUSIVELY COGNATIC (252)	7 15 35 17 XSQ= 6.55 PHI= -0.298 XP = 0.0105
192	TILT MORE TOWARD BEING THOSE 0.93 OF 42 OTHER THAN WHERE THE ONLY KIN GROUP PRESENT IS A KINDRED OR ELSE BILATERAL DESCENT IS INFERRED (289)	192	TILT LESS TOWARD BEING THOSE 0.69 OF 32 OTHER THAN WHERE THE ONLY KIN GROUP PRESENT IS A KINDRED OR ELSE BILATERAL DESCENT IS INFERRED (289)	3 10 39 22 XSQ= 5.72 PHI= -0.278 XP = 0.0168
302	TILT TOWARD BEING THOSE 0.53 OF 19 WHERE THE AVERAGE EARLY SATISFACTION POTENTIAL IS LOW (17) W-C	302	TILT TOWARD BEING THOSE 0.86 OF 14 WHERE THE AVERAGE EARLY SATISFACTION POTENTIAL IS HIGH (23) W-C	9 12 10 2 XSQ= 3.60 PHI= -0.330 EP = 0.0328

304	TILT TOWARD BEING THOSE WHERE THE EARLY ANAL SATISFACTION POTENTIAL IS LOW (22) W-C	0.68 OF 19	304	TILT TOWARD BEING THOSE WHERE THE EARLY ANAL SATISFACTION POTENTIAL IS HIGH (19) W-C	0.71 OF 14	6 10 13 4 XSQ= 3.65 PHI= -0.333 EP = 0.0366
307	LEAN TOWARD BEING THOSE WHERE THE EARLY AGGRESSION SATISFACTION POTENTIAL IS LOW (19) W-C	0.52 OF 25	307	LEAN TOWARD BEING THOSE WHERE THE EARLY AGGRESSION SATISFACTION POTENTIAL IS HIGH (33) W-C	0.94 OF 16	12 15 13 1 XSQ= 7.16 PHI= -0.418 XP = 0.0075
308	LEAN TOWARD BEING THOSE WHERE AVERAGE SOCIALIZATION ANXIETY IS HIGH (22) W-C	0.68 OF 19	308	LEAN TOWARD BEING THOSE WHERE AVERAGE SOCIALIZATION ANXIETY IS LOW (18) W-C	0.86 OF 14	13 2 6 12 XSQ= 7.47 PHI= 0.476 EP = 0.0040
309	TILT TOWARD BEING THOSE WHERE ORAL SOCIALIZATION ANXIETY IS HIGH (26) W-C	0.65 OF 23	309	TILT TOWARD BEING THOSE WHERE ORAL SOCIALIZATION ANXIETY IS LOW (27) W-C	0.73 OF 15	15 4 8 11 XSQ= 3.97 PHI= 0.323 EP = 0.0448
310	TILT TOWARD BEING THOSE WHERE ANAL SOCIALIZATION ANXIETY IS HIGH (22) W-C	0.63 OF 19	310	TILT TOWARD BEING THOSE WHERE ANAL SOCIALIZATION ANXIETY IS LOW (19) W-C	0.79 OF 14	12 3 7 11 XSQ= 4.10 PHI= 0.353 EP = 0.0329
313	TILT TOWARD BEING THOSE WHERE AGGRESSION SOCIALIZATION ANXIETY IS HIGH (26) W-C	0.60 OF 25	313	TILT TOWARD BEING THOSE WHERE AGGRESSION SOCIALIZATION ANXIETY IS LOW (28) W-C	0.81 OF 16	15 3 10 13 XSQ= 5.17 PHI= 0.355 XP = 0.0230
314	DRIFT LESS TOWARD BEING THOSE WHERE THE INCIDENCE OF MOTHER-CHILD HOUSEHOLDS IS LOW (61) W-C,S	0.67 OF 27	314	DRIFT MORE TOWARD BEING THOSE WHERE THE INCIDENCE OF MOTHER-CHILD HOUSEHOLDS IS LOW (61) W-D,S	0.91 OF 22	9 2 18 20 XSQ= 2.82 PHI= 0.240 XP = 0.0932
317	LEAN TOWARD BEING THOSE WHERE DISPLAY OF AFFECTION TOWARD THE INFANT IS LOW (29) B-B-C	0.63 OF 35	317	LEAN TOWARD BEING THOSE WHERE DISPLAY OF AFFECTION TOWARD THE INFANT IS HIGH (39) B-B-C	0.79 OF 29	13 23 22 6 XSQ= 9.81 PHI= -0.392 XP = 0.0017
318	LEAN TOWARD BEING THOSE WHERE THE OVERALL INDULGENCE OF THE INFANT IS LOW (31) B-B-C	0.62 OF 37	318	LEAN TOWARD BEING THOSE WHERE THE OVERALL INDULGENCE OF THE INFANT IS HIGH (40) B-B-C	0.77 OF 30	14 23 23 7 XSQ= 8.59 PHI= -0.358 XP = 0.0034

326	TEND TO BE THOSE 0.64 OF 39 WHERE THE INFERRED TRANSITION ANXIETY BETWEEN INFANCY AND CHILDHOOD IS HIGH (32) B-B-C	326	TEND TO BE THOSE 0.81 OF 26 WHERE THE INFERRED TRANSITION ANXIETY BETWEEN INFANCY AND CHILDHOOD IS LOW (35) B-B-C	25 5 14 21 XSQ= 10.90 PHI= 0.409 XP = 0.0010
334	TEND TO BE THOSE 0.74 OF 42 WHERE THE INDULGENCE OF THE CHILD IS LOW (38) B-B-C	334	TEND TO BE THOSE 0.81 OF 32 WHERE THE INDULGENCE OF THE CHILD IS HIGH (40) B-B-C	11 26 31 6 XSQ= 19.88 PHI= -0.518 XP = 0.0000
337	TEND TO BE THOSE 0.74 OF 39 WHERE THE CHILD'S INFERRED ANXIETY OVER NON-PERFORMANCE OF RESPONSIBLE BEHAVIOR IS HIGH (38) B-B-C	337	TEND TO BE THOSE 0.74 OF 31 WHERE THE CHILD'S INFERRED ANXIETY OVER NON-PERFORMANCE OF RESPONSIBLE BEHAVIOR IS LOW (35) B-B-C	29 8 10 23 XSQ= 14.45 PHI= 0.454 XP = 0.0001
338	TILT TOWARD BEING THOSE 0.74 OF 39 WHERE THE CHILD'S INFERRED ANXIETY OVER PERFORMANCE OF RESPONSIBLE BEHAVIOR IS HIGH (44) B-B-C	338	TILT TOWARD BEING THOSE 0.55 OF 31 WHERE THE CHILD'S INFERRED ANXIETY OVER PERFORMANCE OF RESPONSIBLE BEHAVIOR IS LOW (29) B-B-C	29 14 10 17 XSQ= 5.04 PHI= 0.268 XP = 0.0247
339	LEAN TOWARD BEING THOSE 0.59 OF 39 WHERE THE CHILD'S INFERRED CONFLICT REGARDING RESPONSIBLE BEHAVIOR IS HIGH (31) B-B-C	339	LEAN TOWARD BEING THOSE 0.77 OF 31 WHERE THE CHILD'S INFERRED CONFLICT REGARDING RESPONSIBLE BEHAVIOR IS LOW (42) B-B-C	23 7 16 24 XSQ= 7.91 PHI= 0.336 XP = 0.0049
346	LEAN TOWARD BEING THOSE 0.66 OF 41 WHERE THE CHILD'S INFERRED ANXIETY OVER PERFORMANCE OF SELF-RELIANT BEHAVIOR IS HIGH (37) B-B-C	346	LEAN TOWARD BEING THOSE 0.69 OF 32 WHERE THE CHILD'S INFERRED ANXIETY OVER PERFORMANCE OF SELF-RELIANT BEHAVIOR IS LOW (39) B-B-C	27 10 14 22 XSQ= 7.28 PHI= 0.316 XP = 0.0070
347	LEAN TOWARD BEING THOSE 0.66 OF 41 WHERE THE CHILD'S INFERRED CONFLICT REGARDING SELF-RELIANT BEHAVIOR IS HIGH (37) B-B-C	347	LEAN TOWARD BEING THOSE 0.69 OF 32 WHERE THE CHILD'S INFERRED CONFLICT REGARDING SELF-RELIANT BEHAVIOR IS LOW (39) B-B-C	27 10 14 22 XSQ= 7.28 PHI= 0.316 XP = 0.0070
350	TILT TOWARD BEING THOSE 0.73 OF 33 WHERE THE CHILD'S INFERRED ANXIETY OVER PERFORMANCE OF ACHIEVEMENT BEHAVIOR IS HIGH (34) B-B-C	350	TILT TOWARD BEING THOSE 0.58 OF 24 WHERE THE CHILD'S INFERRED ANXIETY OVER PERFORMANCE OF ACHIEVEMENT BEHAVIOR IS LOW (26) B-B-C	24 10 9 14 XSQ= 4.35 PHI= 0.276 XP = 0.0369
351	TILT TOWARD BEING THOSE 0.61 OF 33 WHERE THE CHILD'S INFERRED CONFLICT REGARDING ACHIEVEMENT BEHAVIOR IS HIGH (26) B-B-C	351	TILT TOWARD BEING THOSE 0.75 OF 24 WHERE THE CHILD'S INFERRED CONFLICT REGARDING ACHIEVEMENT BEHAVIOR IS LOW (34) B-B-C	20 6 13 18 XSQ= 5.74 PHI= 0.317 XP = 0.0166

352	LEAN TOWARD BEING THOSE 0.78 OF 41 WHERE THE TOTAL POSITIVE PRESSURE TOWARD DEVELOPING OBEDIENT BEHAVIOR IN THE CHILD IS HIGH (44) B-B-C	352	LEAN TOWARD BEING THOSE 0.61 OF 31 WHERE THE TOTAL POSITIVE PRESSURE TOWARD DEVELOPING OBEDIENT BEHAVIOR IN THE CHILD IS LOW (28) B-B-C	32 12 9 19 XSQ= 9.90 PHI= 0.371 XP = 0.0017
354	TEND TO BE THOSE 0.68 OF 41 WHERE THE CHILD'S INFERRED ANXIETY OVER PERFORMANCE OF OBEDIENT BEHAVIOR IS HIGH (36) B-B-C	354	TEND TO BE THOSE 0.75 OF 32 WHERE THE CHILD'S INFERRED ANXIETY OVER PERFORMANCE OF OBEDIENT BEHAVIOR IS LOW (37) B-B-C	28 8 13 24 XSQ= 11.80 PHI= 0.402 XP = 0.0006
355	TEND TO BE THOSE 0.73 OF 41 WHERE THE CHILD'S INFERRED CONFLICT REGARDING OBEDIENT BEHAVIOR IS HIGH (35) B-B-C	355	TEND TO BE THOSE 0.84 OF 32 WHERE THE CHILD'S INFERRED CONFLICT REGARDING OBEDIENT BEHAVIOR IS LOW (38) B-B-C	30 5 11 27 XSQ= 21.60 PHI= 0.544 XP = 0.0000
393	TILT TOWARD BEING THOSE 0.68 OF 25 WHERE EXTRAMARITAL COITUS IS PUNISHED, RATHER THAN PERMITTED (43) F-B	393	TILT TOWARD BEING THOSE 0.77 OF 13 WHERE EXTRAMARITAL COITUS IS PERMITTED, RATHER THAN PUNISHED (41) F-B	17 3 8 10 XSQ= 5.24 PHI= 0.371 EP = 0.0156
406	DRIFT TOWARD BEING THOSE 0.64 OF 25 WHERE EXPLANATIONS OF ILLNESS OF AN AGGRESSION NATURE ARE PRESENT (28) W-C	406	DRIFT TOWARD BEING THOSE 0.69 OF 16 WHERE EXPLANATIONS OF ILLNESS OF AN AGGRESSION NATURE ARE ABSENT (33) W-C	16 5 9 11 XSQ= 2.98 PHI= 0.270 XP = 0.0843
455	LEAN TOWARD BEING THOSE 0.71 OF 21 WHERE THE MODE OF THE INDIVIDUAL'S CONTACT WITH THE DIVINE IS NOT CONDUCIVE TO THE DEVELOPMENT OF THE INDIVIDUAL'S NEED TO ACHIEVE (19) DCM	455	LEAN TOWARD BEING THOSE 0.79 OF 14 WHERE THE MODE OF THE INDIVIDUAL'S CONTACT WITH THE DIVINE IS CONDUCIVE TO THE DEVELOPMENT OF THE INDIVIDUAL'S NEED TO ACHIEVE (17) DCM	6 11 15 3 XSQ= 6.52 PHI= -0.432 EP = 0.0059
458	TEND TO BE THOSE 0.52 OF 33 WHERE GAMES, IF PRESENT, INCLUDE GAMES OF STRATEGY (52) R-A-B,EA	458	IN ALL CASES ARE THOSE 1.00 OF 19 WHERE GAMES, IF PRESENT, DO NOT INCLUDE GAMES OF STRATEGY (119) R-A-B,EA	17 0 16 19 XSQ= 12.30 PHI= 0.486 XP = 0.0005
460	TEND TO BE THOSE 0.79 OF 33 WHERE GAMES, IF PRESENT, ARE NOT LIMITED TO GAMES OF SKILL ONLY (104) R-A-B,EA	460	TEND TO BE THOSE 0.74 OF 19 WHERE GAMES, IF PRESENT, ARE LIMITED TO GAMES OF SKILL ONLY (67) R-A-B,EA	7 14 26 5 XSQ= 11.70 PHI= -0.474 XP = 0.0006
471	DRIFT TOWARD BEING THOSE 0.71 OF 7 WHERE SECRET SOCIETIES ARE PRESENT (9) LWS	471	IN ALL CASES ARE THOSE 1.00 OF 4 WHERE SECRET SOCIETIES ARE UMIMPORTANT OR ABSENT (14) LWS	5 0 2 4 XSQ= 2.75 PHI= 0.500 EP = 0.0606

```
476  TILT TOWARD BEING THOSE             0.67 OF  18     476  TILT TOWARD BEING THOSE             0.88 OF   8            6    7
     WHERE THE DEGREE OF INSOBRIETY IS                        WHERE THE DEGREE OF INSOBRIETY IS                         12    1
     MODERATE OR SLIGHT  (18) DH                              STRONG  (31) DH                                    XSQ=     4.51
                                                                                                                 PHI=   -0.417
                                                                                                                 EP =   0.0302

479  DRIFT TOWARD BEING THOSE            0.62 OF  21     479  DRIFT TOWARD BEING THOSE            0.71 OF  14            8   10
     WHERE THE NEED TO ACHIEVE,                               WHERE THE NEED TO ACHIEVE,                                13    4
     AS INFERRED FROM FOLKTALES,                              AS INFERRED FROM FOLKTALES,                        XSQ=     2.52
     IS LOW  (18) JV                                          IS HIGH  (18) JV                                   PHI=   -0.268
                                                                                                                 EP =   0.0858
```

354 CULTURES
WHERE THE CHILD'S INFERRED ANXIETY OVER
PERFORMANCE OF OBEDIENT BEHAVIOR
IS HIGH (36) B-B-C

354 CULTURES
WHERE THE CHILD'S INFERRED ANXIETY OVER
PERFORMANCE OF OBEDIENT BEHAVIOR
IS LOW (37) B-B-C

BACKGROUND ON PAGE 143

BOTH SUBJECT AND PREDICATE

36 IN LEFT COLUMN

ALORESE	ARANDA	ASHANTI	AYMARA	AZANDE	BALINESE	CHAGGA	CHEYENNE	CHIR-APACHE	COMANCHE
CROW	GANDA	KURTATCHI	KWAKIUTL	LAKHER	LAMBA	LAU	MASAI	OJIBWA	OMAHA
PUKAPUKA	SAMOANS	SHERENTE	SIRIONO	SOTHO	SWAZI	THONGA	TIKOPIA	TIV	TRUKESE
TUCUNA	VENDA	WICHITA	WOLEAIANS	YAKUT	ZUNI				

37 IN RIGHT COLUMN

AINU	ARAUCANIANS	CAMAYURA	CHENCHU	CHUKCHEE	CUNA	HANO	IFUGAO	JIVARO	KASKA
KIKUYU	KORYAK	LEPCHA	LESU	MANDAN	MANUS	MAORI	MARQUESANS	MBUNDU	MURNGIN
NAVAHO	NUER	NYAKYUSA	ONA	ONTONG-JAVA	PAPAGO	TALLENSI	TANALA	TETON	TROBRIAND
TUPINAMBA	TURKANA	WINNEBAGO	WOGEO	YAGUA	YAHGAN	YORUBA			

327 EXCLUDED BECAUSE UNASCERTAINED

	High (36)			Low (37)		
54	DRIFT MORE TOWARD BEING THOSE WHERE FOOD PRODUCTION IS BY INTENSIVE OR SIMPLE AGRICULTURE, RATHER THAN BY INCIPIENT FOOD PRODUCTION (192)	0.91 OF 22	54	DRIFT LESS TOWARD BEING THOSE WHERE FOOD PRODUCTION IS BY INTENSIVE OR SIMPLE AGRICULTURE, RATHER THAN BY INCIPIENT FOOD PRODUCTION (192)	0.64 OF 25	20 16 / 2 9 / XSQ= 3.34 / PHI= 0.267 / XP = 0.0674
56	TILT TOWARD BEING THOSE WHERE FOOD PRODUCTION IS BY SIMPLE AGRICULTURE, RATHER THAN BY INCIPIENT FOOD PRODUCTION (101)	0.88 OF 16	56	TILT TOWARD BEING THOSE WHERE FOOD PRODUCTION IS BY INCIPIENT FOOD PRODUCTION, RATHER THAN BY SIMPLE AGRICULTURE (46)	0.56 OF 16	14 7 / 2 9 / XSQ= 4.99 / PHI= 0.395 / EP = 0.0233
86	TILT TOWARD BEING THOSE WHERE THE LEVEL OF POLITICAL INTEGRATION IS THE LARGE STATE, THE LITTLE STATE, OR THE MINIMAL STATE (148) GPM	0.60 OF 30	86	TILT TOWARD BEING THOSE WHERE THE LEVEL OF POLITICAL INTEGRATION IS THE AUTONOMOUS COMMUNITY, OR THE FAMILY (156) GPM	0.69 OF 32	18 10 / 12 22 / XSQ= 4.07 / PHI= 0.256 / XP = 0.0436
87	IN ALL CASES ARE THOSE WHERE THE LEVEL OF POLITICAL INTEGRATION IS THE LARGE STATE, THE LITTLE STATE, THE MINIMAL STATE, OR THE AUTONOMOUS COMMUNITY (281) GPM	1.00 OF 30	87	TILT LESS TOWARD BEING THOSE WHERE THE LEVEL OF POLITICAL INTEGRATION IS THE LARGE STATE, THE LITTLE STATE, THE MINIMAL STATE, OR THE AUTONOMOUS COMMUNITY (281) GPM	0.81 OF 32	30 26 / 0 6 / XSQ= 4.27 / PHI= 0.262 / XP = 0.0389

96	TEND TO BE THOSE WHERE THE HIERARCHY OF NATIONAL JURISDICTION HAS FOUR, THREE, TWO OR ONE LEVEL (174) GES,EA	0.76 OF 33	96	TEND TO BE THOSE WHERE THE HIERARCHY OF NATIONAL JURISDICTION HAS NO LEVELS (156) GES,EA	0.69 OF 35	25 11 8 24 XSQ= 11.68 PHI= 0.414 XP = 0.0006
106	TILT TOWARD BEING THOSE WHERE CLASS STRATIFICATION, IF PRESENT, IS BASED ON SOMETHING OTHER THAN WEALTH (126)	0.78 OF 18	106	TILT TOWARD BEING THOSE WHERE CLASS STRATIFICATION, IF PRESENT, IS BASED ON WEALTH (77)	0.65 OF 17	4 11 14 6 XSQ= 4.83 PHI= -0.371 EP = 0.0176
108	LEAN TOWARD BEING THOSE WHERE CLASS STRATIFICATION, IF PRESENT, IS BASED ON A HEREDITARY ARISTOCRACY (74)	0.78 OF 18	108	LEAN TOWARD BEING THOSE WHERE CLASS STRATIFICATION, IF PRESENT, IS BASED ON SOMETHING OTHER THAN A HEREDITARY ARISTOCRACY (129)	0.71 OF 17	14 5 4 12 XSQ= 6.41 PHI= 0.428 EP = 0.0067
127	DRIFT TOWARD BEING THOSE WHERE THE FEMALES' CONTRIBUTION TO SUBSISTENCE IS HIGH (33) JKB	0.79 OF 14	127	DRIFT TOWARD BEING THOSE WHERE THE FEMALES' CONTRIBUTION TO SUBSISTENCE IS LOW (32) JKB	0.62 OF 13	11 5 3 8 XSQ= 2.98 PHI= 0.332 EP = 0.0542
128	DRIFT TOWARD BEING THOSE WHERE, IF SUBSISTENCE IS PRIMARILY BY AGRICULTURE, THE WORK IS MAINLY DONE BY FEMALES (37)	0.89 OF 9	128	DRIFT TOWARD BEING THOSE WHERE, IF SUBSISTENCE IS PRIMARILY BY AGRICULTURE, THE WORK IS MAINLY DONE BY MALES (40)	0.60 OF 10	1 6 8 4 XSQ= 2.99 PHI= -0.397 EP = 0.0573
135	DRIFT TOWARD BEING THOSE WHERE INDIVIDUAL OWNERSHIP OF ECONOMICALLY SIGNIFICANT PROPERTY IS NEGLIGIBLE OR ABSENT (14) GES	0.71 OF 7	135	DRIFT TOWARD BEING THOSE WHERE INDIVIDUAL OWNERSHIP OF ECONOMICALLY SIGNIFICANT PROPERTY IS PRESENT (24) GES	0.75 OF 12	2 9 5 3 XSQ= 2.24 PHI= -0.343 EP = 0.0739
138	TILT TOWARD BEING THOSE WHERE SUPERORDINATE JUSTICE IS PRESENT (22) BBW	0.81 OF 16	138	TILT TOWARD BEING THOSE WHERE SUPERORDINATE JUSTICE IS ABSENT (18) BBW	0.70 OF 10	13 3 3 7 XSQ= 4.84 PHI= 0.431 EP = 0.0152
149	DRIFT TOWARD BEING THOSE WHERE THE INCIDENCE OF THEFT IS HIGH (18) B-B-C	0.67 OF 18	149	DRIFT TOWARD BEING THOSE WHERE THE INCIDENCE OF THEFT IS LOW (19) B-B-C	0.69 OF 16	12 5 6 11 XSQ= 2.95 PHI= 0.295 EP = 0.0844
317	TILT TOWARD BEING THOSE WHERE DISPLAY OF AFFECTION TOWARD THE INFANT IS LOW (29) B-B-C	0.58 OF 31	317	TILT TOWARD BEING THOSE WHERE DISPLAY OF AFFECTION TOWARD THE INFANT IS HIGH (39) B-B-C	0.72 OF 32	13 23 18 9 XSQ= 4.61 PHI= -0.270 XP = 0.0319

318 TILT TOWARD BEING THOSE 0.59 OF 32 WHERE THE OVERALL INDULGENCE OF THE INFANT IS LOW (31) B-B-C	318 TILT TOWARD BEING THOSE 0.71 OF 34 WHERE THE OVERALL INDULGENCE OF THE INFANT IS HIGH (40) B-B-C	13 24 19 10 XSQ= 4.85 PHI= -0.271 XP = 0.0276
321 LEAN TOWARD BEING THOSE 0.60 OF 30 WHERE THE IMMEDIACY OF REDUCTION OF THE INFANT'S DRIVES IS LOW (25) B-B-C	321 LEAN TOWARD BEING THOSE 0.80 OF 25 WHERE THE IMMEDIACY OF REDUCTION OF THE INFANT'S DRIVES IS HIGH (35) B-B-C	12 20 18 5 XSQ= 7.40 PHI= -0.367 XP = 0.0065
326 TILT TOWARD BEING THOSE 0.63 OF 32 WHERE THE INFERRED TRANSITION ANXIETY BETWEEN INFANCY AND CHILDHOOD IS HIGH (32) B-B-C	326 TILT TOWARD BEING THOSE 0.69 OF 32 WHERE THE INFERRED TRANSITION ANXIETY BETWEEN INFANCY AND CHILDHOOD IS LOW (35) B-B-C	20 10 12 22 XSQ= 5.08 PHI= 0.282 XP = 0.0242
334 TEND TO BE THOSE 0.75 OF 36 WHERE THE INDULGENCE OF THE CHILD IS LOW (38) B-B-C	334 TEND TO BE THOSE 0.76 OF 37 WHERE THE INDULGENCE OF THE CHILD IS HIGH (40) B-B-C	9 28 27 9 XSQ= 16.77 PHI= -0.479 XP = 0.0000
338 TILT TOWARD BEING THOSE 0.75 OF 32 WHERE THE CHILD'S INFERRED ANXIETY OVER PERFORMANCE OF RESPONSIBLE BEHAVIOR IS HIGH (44) B-B-C	338 TILT TOWARD BEING THOSE 0.51 OF 37 WHERE THE CHILD'S INFERRED ANXIETY OVER PERFORMANCE OF RESPONSIBLE BEHAVIOR IS LOW (29) B-B-C	24 18 8 19 XSQ= 3.96 PHI= 0.239 XP = 0.0467
339 DRIFT TOWARD BEING THOSE 0.56 OF 32 WHERE THE CHILD'S INFERRED CONFLICT REGARDING RESPONSIBLE BEHAVIOR IS HIGH (31) B-B-C	339 DRIFT TOWARD BEING THOSE 0.68 OF 37 WHERE THE CHILD'S INFERRED CONFLICT REGARDING RESPONSIBLE BEHAVIOR IS LOW (42) B-B-C	18 12 14 25 XSQ= 3.05 PHI= 0.210 XP = 0.0807
342 LEAN TOWARD BEING THOSE 0.58 OF 24 WHERE THE CHILD'S INFERRED ANXIETY OVER PERFORMANCE OF NURTURANT BEHAVIOR IS HIGH (18) B-B-C	342 LEAN TOWARD BEING THOSE 0.86 OF 21 WHERE THE CHILD'S INFERRED ANXIETY OVER PERFORMANCE OF NURTURANT BEHAVIOR IS LOW (28) B-B-C	14 3 10 18 XSQ= 7.47 PHI= 0.407 XP = 0.0063
345 TEND TO BE THOSE 0.71 OF 35 WHERE THE CHILD'S INFERRED ANXIETY OVER NON-PERFORMANCE OF SELF-RELIANT BEHAVIOR IS HIGH (37) B-B-C	345 TEND TO BE THOSE 0.70 OF 37 WHERE THE CHILD'S INFERRED ANXIETY OVER NON-PERFORMANCE OF SELF-RELIANT BEHAVIOR IS LOW (39) B-B-C	25 11 10 26 XSQ= 10.90 PHI= 0.389 XP = 0.0010
347 TILT TOWARD BEING THOSE 0.66 OF 35 WHERE THE CHILD'S INFERRED CONFLICT REGARDING SELF-RELIANT BEHAVIOR IS HIGH (37) B-B-C	347 TILT TOWARD BEING THOSE 0.62 OF 37 WHERE THE CHILD'S INFERRED CONFLICT REGARDING SELF-RELIANT BEHAVIOR IS LOW (39) B-B-C	23 14 12 23 XSQ= 4.53 PHI= 0.251 XP = 0.0332

349	TILT TOWARD BEING THOSE 0.71 OF 28 WHERE THE CHILD'S INFERRED ANXIETY OVER NON-PERFORMANCE OF ACHIEVEMENT BEHAVIOR IS HIGH (34) B-B-C	349	TILT TOWARD BEING THOSE 0.58 OF 31 WHERE THE CHILD'S INFERRED ANXIETY OVER NON-PERFORMANCE OF ACHIEVEMENT BEHAVIOR IS LOW (28) B-B-C	20 13 8 18 XSQ= 4.06 PHI= 0.262 XP = 0.0438
350	TILT TOWARD BEING THOSE 0.77 OF 26 WHERE THE CHILD'S INFERRED ANXIETY OVER PERFORMANCE OF ACHIEVEMENT BEHAVIOR IS HIGH (34) B-B-C	350	TILT TOWARD BEING THOSE 0.55 OF 31 WHERE THE CHILD'S INFERRED ANXIETY OVER PERFORMANCE OF ACHIEVEMENT BEHAVIOR IS LOW (26) B-B-C	20 14 6 17 XSQ= 4.68 PHI= 0.287 XP = 0.0305
351	DRIFT TOWARD BEING THOSE 0.62 OF 26 WHERE THE CHILD'S INFERRED CONFLICT REGARDING ACHIEVEMENT BEHAVIOR IS HIGH (26) B-B-C	351	DRIFT TOWARD BEING THOSE 0.68 OF 31 WHERE THE CHILD'S INFERRED CONFLICT REGARDING ACHIEVEMENT BEHAVIOR IS LOW (34) B-B-C	16 10 10 21 XSQ= 3.78 PHI= 0.257 XP = 0.0519
353	TEND TO BE THOSE 0.78 OF 36 WHERE THE CHILD'S INFERRED ANXIETY OVER NON-PERFORMANCE OF OBEDIENT BEHAVIOR IS HIGH (42) B-B-C	353	TEND TO BE THOSE 0.65 OF 37 WHERE THE CHILD-S INFERRED ANXIETY OVER NON-PERFORMANCE OF OBEDIENT BEHAVIOR IS LOW (32) B-B-C	28 13 8 24 XSQ= 11.80 PHI= 0.402 XP = 0.0006
355	TEND TO BE THOSE 0.89 OF 36 WHERE THE CHILD'S INFERRED CONFLICT REGARDING OBEDIENT BEHAVIOR IS HIGH (35) B-B-C	355	TEND TO BE THOSE 0.92 OF 37 WHERE THE CHILD'S INFERRED CONFLICT REGARDING OBEDIENT BEHAVIOR IS LOW (38) B-B-C	32 3 4 34 XSQ= 44.53 PHI= 0.781 XP = 0.
393	TILT TOWARD BEING THOSE 0.68 OF 22 WHERE EXTRAMARITAL COITUS IS PUNISHED, RATHER THAN PERMITTED (43) F-B	393	TILT TOWARD BEING THOSE 0.69 OF 16 WHERE EXTRAMARITAL COITUS IS PERMITTED, RATHER THAN PUNISHED (41) F-B	15 5 7 11 XSQ= 3.69 PHI= 0.312 EP = 0.0472
396	TILT TOWARD BEING THOSE 0.50 OF 20 WHERE THE STRENGTH OF MENSTRUAL TABOOS IS HIGH (18) WNS	396	TILT TOWARD BEING THOSE 0.90 OF 20 WHERE THE STRENGTH OF MENSTRUAL TABOOS IS LOW (35) WNS	10 2 10 18 XSQ= 5.83 PHI= 0.382 EP = 0.0138
399	TILT TOWARD BEING THOSE 0.70 OF 20 WHERE INTENSITY OF CASTRATION ANXIETY IS HIGH (23) WNS	399	TILT TOWARD BEING THOSE 0.75 OF 20 WHERE INTENSITY OF CASTRATION ANXIETY IS LOW (22) WNS	14 5 6 15 XSQ= 6.42 PHI= 0.401 EP = 0.0104
421	TILT TOWARD BEING THOSE 0.63 OF 27 WHERE KILLING, TORTURING, OR MUTILATING OF THE ENEMY IS STRONGLY OR MODERATELY EMPHASIZED (37) PES	421	TILT TOWARD BEING THOSE 0.75 OF 24 WHERE KILLING, TORTURING, OR MUTILATING OF THE ENEMY IS NEGLIGIBLY EMPHASIZED (47) PES	17 6 10 18 XSQ= 5.94 PHI= 0.341 XP = 0.0148

430	DRIFT TOWARD BEING THOSE 0.71 OF 7 WHERE SUPERNATURAL SANCTIONS FOR MORALITY, HAVING AN EFFECT ON AN INDIVIDUAL'S HEALTH, ARE ABSENT OR UNREPORTED (22) GES	430	DRIFT TOWARD BEING THOSE 0.75 OF 12 WHERE SUPERNATURAL SANCTIONS FOR MORALITY, HAVING AN EFFECT ON AN INDIVIDUAL'S HEALTH, ARE PRESENT (16) GES	2 9 5 3 XSQ= 2.24 PHI= -0.343 EP = 0.0739
437	DRIFT TOWARD BEING THOSE 0.65 OF 17 WHERE FEAR OF GHOSTS, SPIRITS, HUMANS OR ANIMALS IS LOW (23) W-C,JFG	437	DRIFT TOWARD BEING THOSE 0.67 OF 15 WHERE FEAR OF GHOSTS, SPIRITS, HUMANS OR ANIMALS IS HIGH (21) W-C,JFG	6 10 11 5 XSQ= 2.01 PHI= -0.250 EP = 0.0938
446	TILT TOWARD BEING THOSE 0.86 OF 7 WHERE WITCHCRAFT IS SIGNIFICANTLY PRESENT (14) GES	446	TILT TOWARD BEING THOSE 0.75 OF 12 WHERE WITCHCRAFT IS MODERATELY PRESENT OR ABSENT (24) GES	6 3 1 9 XSQ= 4.33 PHI= 0.477 EP = 0.0198
453	TILT TOWARD BEING THOSE 0.56 OF 18 WHERE THE ROLE OF RELIGIOUS EXPERTS IS CONDUCIVE TO THE DEVELOPMENT OF THE INDIVIDUAL'S NEED TO ACHIEVE (13) DCM	453	TILT TOWARD BEING THOSE 0.81 OF 16 WHERE THE ROLE OF RELIGIOUS EXPERTS IS NOT CONDUCIVE TO THE DEVELOPMENT OF THE INDIVIDUAL'S NEED TO ACHIEVE (23) DCM	10 3 8 13 XSQ= 3.43 PHI= 0.317 EP = 0.0386
458	DRIFT LESS TOWARD BEING THOSE 0.55 OF 29 WHERE GAMES, IF PRESENT, DO NOT INCLUDE GAMES OF STRATEGY (119) R-A-B,EA	458	DRIFT MORE TOWARD BEING THOSE 0.83 OF 23 WHERE GAMES, IF PRESENT, DO NOT INCLUDE GAMES OF STRATEGY (119) R-A-B,EA	13 4 16 19 XSQ= 3.23 PHI= 0.249 XP = 0.0723
460	DRIFT TOWARD BEING THOSE 0.72 OF 29 WHERE GAMES, IF PRESENT, ARE NOT LIMITED TO GAMES OF SKILL ONLY (104) R-A-B,EA	460	DRIFT TOWARD BEING THOSE 0.57 OF 23 WHERE GAMES, IF PRESENT, ARE LIMITED TO GAMES OF SKILL ONLY (67) R-A-B,EA	8 13 21 10 XSQ= 3.34 PHI= -0.253 XP = 0.0676

```
355  CULTURES                                        355  CULTURES
     WHERE THE CHILD'S INFERREC CONFLICT                  WHERE THE CHILD'S INFERRED CONFLICT
     REGARDING CBEDIENT BEHAVICR                          REGARDING OBEDIENT BEHAVIOR
     IS HIGH  (35) B-B-C                                  IS LOW  (38) B-B-C


BACKGROUND ON PAGE 143                                                       BOTH SUBJECT AND PREDICATE

      35  IN LEFT COLUMN

ALORESE     ARANDA      ASHANTI     AYMARA      AZANDE      CHAGGA      CHEYENNE    CHIR-APACHE CROW        GANDA
KWAKIUTL    LAKHER      LAMBA       LAU         MASAI       NAVAHO      OJIBWA      OMAHA       ONTONG-JAVA PUKAPUKA
SAMCANS     SHERENTE    SOTHO       SWAZI       THONGA      TIKOPIA     TIV         TRUKESE     TUCUNA      VENDA
WICHITA     WOGEO       WOLEAIANS   YAKUT       ZUNI

      38  IN RIGHT COLUMN

AINU        ARAUCANIANS BALINESE    CAMAYURA    CHENCHU     CHUKCHEE    COMANCHE    CUNA        HANC        IFUGAO
JIVARO      KASKA       KIKUYU      KORYAK      KURTATCHI   LEPCHA      LESU        MANDAN      MANUS       MAORI
MARQUESANS  MBUNDU      MURNGIN     NUER        NYAKYUSA    ONA         PAPAGO      SIRIONO     TALLENSI    TANALA
TETON       TROBRIAND   TUPINAMBA   TURKANA     WINNEBAGO   YAGUA       YAHGAN      YORUBA

     327  EXCLUDED BECAUSE UNASCERTAINED

-------------------------------------------------------------------------------------------------------------------
 56  DRIFT TOWARD BEING THOSE      0.82 OF  17       56  DRIFT TOWARD BEING THOSE      0.53 OF  15         14     7
     WHERE FOOD PRODUCTION IS BY                         WHERE FOOD PRODUCTION IS BY                        3     8
     SIMPLE AGRICULTURE, RATHER THAN BY                  INCIPIENT FOOD PRODUCTION, RATHER THAN BY      XSQ=     3.06
     INCIPIENT FOOD PRODUCTION  (101)                    SIMPLE AGRICULTURE  (46)                       PHI=    0.309
                                                                                                        EP =   0.0617

 96  LEAN TOWARD BEING THOSE       0.74 OF  34       96  LEAN TOWARD BEING THOSE       0.68 OF  34         25    11
     WHERE THE HIERARCHY                                 WHERE THE HIERARCHY                                9    23
     OF NATIONAL JURISDICTION HAS                        OF NATIONAL JURISDICTION HAS                   XSQ=     9.98
     FOUR, THREE, TWO OR                                 NO LEVELS  (156) GES,EA                        PHI=    0.383
     ONE LEVEL  (174) GES,EA                                                                            XP =   0.0016

108  DRIFT TOWARD BEING THOSE      0.71 OF  17      108  DRIFT TOWARD BEING THOSE      0.61 OF  18         12     7
     WHERE CLASS STRATIFICATION, IF PRESENT,             WHERE CLASS STRATIFICATION, IF PRESENT,            5    11
     IS BASED ON                                         IS BASED ON SOMETHING OTHER THAN               XSQ=     2.38
     A HEREDITARY ARISTOCRACY  (74)                      A HEREDITARY ARISTOCRACY  (129)                PHI=    0.261
                                                                                                        EP =   0.0922

116  TILT LESS TOWARD BEING THOSE  0.54 OF  13      116  TILT MORE TOWARD BEING THOSE  0.93 OF  14          6     1
     WHERE OCCUPATIONAL SPECIALIZATION IS                WHERE OCCUPATIONAL SPECIALIZATION IS               7    13
     PART-TIME ONLY  (34) JMH                            PART-TIME ONLY  (34) JMH                       XSQ=     3.50
                                                                                                        PHI=    0.360
                                                                                                        EP =   0.0329
```

135	DRIFT TOWARD BEING THOSE WHERE INDIVIDUAL OWNERSHIP OF ECONOMICALLY SIGNIFICANT PROPERTY IS NEGLIGIBLE OR ABSENT (14) GES	0.71 OF 7	135	DRIFT TOWARD BEING THOSE WHERE INDIVIDUAL OWNERSHIP OF ECONOMICALLY SIGNIFICANT PROPERTY IS PRESENT (24) GES	0.75 OF 12	2 9 5 3 XSQ= 2.24 PHI= -0.343 EP = 0.0739
137	DRIFT TOWARD BEING THOSE WHERE INVIDIOUS DISPLAY OF WEALTH IS STRONGLY EMPHASIZED (37) PES	0.62 OF 26	137	DRIFT TOWARD BEING THOSE WHERE INVIDIOUS DISPLAY OF WEALTH IS MODERATELY, LITTLE, OR NEGATIVELY EMPHASIZED (52) PES	0.69 OF 26	16 8 10 18 XSQ= 3.79 PHI= 0.270 XP = 0.0515
138	LEAN TOWARD BEING THOSE WHERE SUPERORDINATE JUSTICE IS PRESENT (22) BBW	0.87 OF 15	138	LEAN TOWARD BEING THOSE WHERE SUPERORDINATE JUSTICE IS ABSENT (18) BBW	0.73 OF 11	13 3 2 8 XSQ= 7.12 PHI= 0.523 EP = 0.0040
149	TILT TOWARD BEING THOSE WHERE THE INCIDENCE OF THEFT IS HIGH (18) B-B-C	0.73 OF 15	149	TILT TOWARD BEING THOSE WHERE THE INCIDENCE OF THEFT IS LOW (19) B-B-C	0.68 OF 19	11 6 4 13 XSQ= 4.29 PHI= 0.355 EP = 0.0366
152	IN ALL CASES ARE THOSE WHERE THE DIFFERENTIATION OF THE JURIDICAL AGENCY FROM THE MEDICAL AGENCY IS HIGH (10) MJ	1.00 OF 3	152	IN ALL CASES ARE THOSE WHERE THE DIFFERENTIATION OF THE JURIDICAL AGENCY FROM THE MEDICAL AGENCY IS LOW (10) MJ	1.00 OF 5	3 0 0 5 XSQ= 4.30 PHI= 0.733 EP = 0.0179
185	TILT MORE TOWARD BEING THOSE WHERE THE LARGEST NON-COGNATIC KIN GROUP IS THE MOEITY OR PHRATRY OR SIB (194)	0.93 OF 29	185	TILT LESS TOWARD BEING THOSE WHERE THE LARGEST NON-COGNATIC KIN GROUP IS THE MOEITY OR PHRATRY OR SIB (194)	0.65 OF 23	27 15 2 8 XSQ= 4.75 PHI= 0.302 XP = 0.0293
188	DRIFT MORE TOWARD BEING THOSE WHERE THE KIN GROUP IS OTHER THAN EXCLUSIVELY COGNATIC (252)	0.83 OF 35	188	DRIFT LESS TOWARD BEING THOSE WHERE THE KIN GROUP IS OTHER THAN EXCLUSIVELY COGNATIC (252)	0.61 OF 38	6 15 29 23 XSQ= 3.41 PHI= -0.216 XP = 0.0648
257	DRIFT TOWARD BEING THOSE WHERE THE SEVERITY OF SISTER AVOIDANCE IS HIGH (10) WNS	0.58 OF 12	257	DRIFT TOWARD BEING THOSE WHERE THE SEVERITY OF SISTER AVOIDANCE IS LOW (17) WNS	0.80 OF 10	7 2 5 8 XSQ= 1.92 PHI= 0.295 EP = 0.0991
258	TILT TOWARD BEING THOSE WHERE THE SEVERITY OF SON'S WIFE AVOIDANCE IS HIGH (15) WNS	0.80 OF 10	258	TILT TOWARD BEING THOSE WHERE THE SEVERITY OF SON'S WIFE AVOIDANCE IS LOW (16) WNS	0.67 OF 12	8 4 2 8 XSQ= 3.09 PHI= 0.375 EP = 0.0427

259	DRIFT TOWARD BEING THOSE WHERE THE SEVERITY OF MOTHER-IN-LAW AVOIDANCE IS HIGH (26) WNS	0.73 OF 15	259	DRIFT TOWARD BEING THOSE WHERE THE SEVERITY OF MOTHER-IN-LAW AVOIDANCE IS LOW (20) WNS	0.63 OF 16	11 6 4 10 XSQ= 2.70 PHI= 0.295 EP = 0.0732
308	DRIFT TOWARD BEING THOSE WHERE AVERAGE SOCIALIZATION ANXIETY IS HIGH (22) W-C	0.63 OF 16	308	DRIFT TOWARD BEING THOSE WHERE AVERAGE SOCIALIZATION ANXIETY IS LOW (18) W-C	0.71 OF 17	10 5 6 12 XSQ= 2.43 PHI= 0.271 EP = 0.0844
309	TILT TOWARD BEING THOSE WHERE ORAL SOCIALIZATION ANXIETY IS HIGH (26) W-C	0.68 OF 19	309	TILT TOWARD BEING THOSE WHERE ORAL SOCIALIZATION ANXIETY IS LOW (27) W-C	0.68 OF 19	13 6 6 13 XSQ= 3.79 PHI= 0.316 EP = 0.0294
311	DRIFT TOWARD BEING THOSE WHERE SEXUAL SOCIALIZATION ANXIETY IS HIGH (28) W-C	0.63 OF 19	311	DRIFT TOWARD BEING THOSE WHERE SEXUAL SOCIALIZATION ANXIETY IS LOW (23) W-C	0.68 OF 19	12 6 7 13 XSQ= 2.64 PHI= 0.264 EP = 0.0624
317	TILT TOWARD BEING THOSE WHERE DISPLAY OF AFFECTION TOWARD THE INFANT IS LOW (29) B-B-C	0.60 OF 30	317	TILT TOWARD BEING THOSE WHERE DISPLAY OF AFFECTION TOWARD THE INFANT IS HIGH (39) B-B-C	0.73 OF 33	12 24 18 9 XSQ= 5.60 PHI= -0.298 XP = 0.0179
318	DRIFT TOWARD BEING THOSE WHERE THE OVERALL INDULGENCE OF THE INFANT IS LOW (31) B-B-C	0.58 OF 31	318	DRIFT TOWARD BEING THOSE WHERE THE OVERALL INDULGENCE OF THE INFANT IS HIGH (40) B-B-C	0.69 OF 35	13 24 18 11 XSQ= 3.72 PHI= -0.237 XP = 0.0539
321	TILT TOWARD BEING THOSE WHERE THE IMMEDIACY OF REDUCTION OF THE INFANT'S DRIVES IS LOW (25) B-B-C	0.59 OF 29	321	TILT TOWARD BEING THOSE WHERE THE IMMEDIACY OF REDUCTION OF THE INFANT'S DRIVES IS HIGH (35) B-B-C	0.77 OF 26	12 20 17 6 XSQ= 5.73 PHI= -0.323 XP = 0.0167
326	TILT TOWARD BEING THOSE WHERE THE INFERRED TRANSITION ANXIETY BETWEEN INFANCY AND CHILDHOOD IS HIGH (32) B-B-C	0.65 OF 31	326	TILT TOWARD BEING THOSE WHERE THE INFERRED TRANSITION ANXIETY BETWEEN INFANCY AND CHILDHOOD IS LOW (35) B-B-C	0.70 OF 33	20 10 11 23 XSQ= 6.20 PHI= 0.311 XP = 0.0128
334	TEND TO BE THOSE WHERE THE INDULGENCE OF THE CHILD IS LOW (38) B-B-C	0.77 OF 35	334	TEND TO BE THOSE WHERE THE INDULGENCE OF THE CHILD IS HIGH (40) B-B-C	0.76 OF 38	8 29 27 9 XSQ= 18.75 PHI= -0.507 XP = 0.0000

337	TILT TOWARD BEING THOSE 0.69 OF 32 WHERE THE CHILD'S INFERRED ANXIETY OVER NON-PERFORMANCE OF RESPONSIBLE BEHAVIOR IS HIGH (38) B-B-C	337	TILT TOWARD BEING THOSE 0.59 OF 37 WHERE THE CHILD'S INFERRED ANXIETY OVER NON-PERFORMANCE OF RESPONSIBLE BEHAVIOR IS LOW (35) B-B-C	22 15 10 22 XSQ= 4.42 PHI= 0.253 XP = 0.0356
339	DRIFT TOWARD BEING THOSE 0.56 OF 32 WHERE THE CHILD'S INFERRED CONFLICT REGARDING RESPONSIBLE BEHAVIOR IS HIGH (31) B-B-C	339	DRIFT TOWARD BEING THOSE 0.68 OF 37 WHERE THE CHILD'S INFERRED CONFLICT REGARDING RESPONSIBLE BEHAVIOR IS LOW (42) B-B-C	18 12 14 25 XSQ= 3.05 PHI= 0.210 XP = 0.0807
342	TILT TOWARD BEING THOSE 0.57 OF 23 WHERE THE CHILD'S INFERRED ANXIETY OVER PERFORMANCE OF NURTURANT BEHAVIOR IS HIGH (18) B-B-C	342	TILT TOWARD BEING THOSE 0.82 OF 22 WHERE THE CHILD'S INFERRED ANXIETY OVER PERFORMANCE OF NURTURANT BEHAVIOR IS LOW (28) B-B-C	13 4 10 18 XSQ= 5.50 PHI= 0.349 XP = 0.0191
345	DRIFT TOWARD BEING THOSE 0.62 OF 34 WHERE THE CHILD'S INFERRED ANXIETY OVER NON-PERFORMANCE OF SELF-RELIANT BEHAVIOR IS HIGH (37) B-B-C	345	DRIFT TOWARD BEING THOSE 0.61 OF 38 WHERE THE CHILD'S INFERRED ANXIETY OVER NON-PERFORMANCE OF SELF-RELIANT BEHAVIOR IS LOW (39) B-B-C	21 15 13 23 XSQ= 2.73 PHI= 0.195 XP = 0.0984
347	DRIFT TOWARD BEING THOSE 0.65 OF 34 WHERE THE CHILD'S INFERRED CONFLICT REGARDING SELF-RELIANT BEHAVIOR IS HIGH (37) B-B-C	347	DRIFT TOWARD BEING THOSE 0.61 OF 38 WHERE THE CHILD'S INFERRED CONFLICT REGARDING SELF-RELIANT BEHAVIOR IS LOW (39) B-B-C	22 15 12 23 XSQ= 3.62 PHI= 0.224 XP = 0.0571
349	TILT TOWARD BEING THOSE 0.74 OF 27 WHERE THE CHILD'S INFERRED ANXIETY OVER NON-PERFORMANCE OF ACHIEVEMENT BEHAVIOR IS HIGH (34) B-B-C	349	TILT TOWARD BEING THOSE 0.59 OF 32 WHERE THE CHILD'S INFERRED ANXIETY OVER NON-PERFORMANCE OF ACHIEVEMENT BEHAVIOR IS LOW (28) B-B-C	20 13 7 19 XSQ= 5.36 PHI= 0.301 XP = 0.0206
350	LEAN TOWARD BEING THOSE 0.81 OF 26 WHERE THE CHILD'S INFERRED ANXIETY OVER PERFORMANCE OF ACHIEVEMENT BEHAVIOR IS HIGH (34) B-B-C	350	LEAN TOWARD BEING THOSE 0.58 OF 31 WHERE THE CHILD'S INFERRED ANXIETY OVER PERFORMANCE OF ACHIEVEMENT BEHAVIOR IS LOW (26) B-B-C	21 13 5 18 XSQ= 7.32 PHI= 0.358 XP = 0.0068
351	TILT TOWARD BEING THOSE 0.65 OF 26 WHERE THE CHILD'S INFERRED CONFLICT REGARDING ACHIEVEMENT BEHAVIOR IS HIGH (26) B-B-C	351	TILT TOWARD BEING THOSE 0.71 OF 31 WHERE THE CHILD'S INFERRED CONFLICT REGARDING ACHIEVEMENT BEHAVIOR IS LOW (34) B-B-C	17 9 9 22 XSQ= 6.14 PHI= 0.328 XP = 0.0132
353	TEND TO BE THOSE 0.86 OF 35 WHERE THE CHILD'S INFERRED ANXIETY OVER NON-PERFORMANCE OF OBEDIENT BEHAVIOR IS HIGH (42) B-B-C	353	TEND TO BE THOSE 0.71 OF 38 WHERE THE CHILD-S INFERRED ANXIETY OVER NON-PERFORMANCE OF OBEDIENT BEHAVIOR IS LOW (32) B-B-C	30 11 5 27 XSQ= 21.60 PHI= 0.544 XP = 0.0000

354	TEND TO BE THOSE 0.91 OF 35 WHERE THE CHILD'S INFERRED ANXIETY OVER PERFORMANCE OF OBEDIENT BEHAVIOR IS HIGH (36) B-B-C	354	TEND TO BE THOSE 0.89 OF 38 WHERE THE CHILD'S INFERRED ANXIETY OVER PERFORMANCE OF OBEDIENT BEHAVIOR IS LOW (37) B-B-C	32 4 3 34 XSQ= 44.53 PHI= 0.781 XP = 0.
358	IN ALL CASES ARE THOSE 1.00 OF 13 WHERE ADOLESCENT PEER GROUPS ARE PRESENT IN A SETTING OF WORK AND PUBLIC GATHERINGS AND LEISURE, OR OF PUBLIC GATHERINGS AND LEISURE, OR OF LEISURE ONLY (41) JKH	358	TILT LESS TOWARD BEING THOSE 0.65 OF 17 WHERE ADOLESCENT PEER GROUPS ARE PRESENT IN A SETTING OF WORK AND PUBLIC GATHERINGS AND LEISURE, OR OF PUBLIC GATHERINGS AND LEISURE, OR OF LEISURE ONLY (41) JKH	13 11 0 6 XSQ= 3.74 PHI= 0.353 EP = 0.0237
393	TILT TOWARD BEING THOSE 0.71 OF 21 WHERE EXTRAMARITAL COITUS IS PUNISHED, RATHER THAN PERMITTED (43) F-B	393	TILT TOWARD BEING THOSE 0.71 OF 17 WHERE EXTRAMARITAL COITUS IS PERMITTED, RATHER THAN PUNISHED (41) F-B	15 5 6 12 XSQ= 5.07 PHI= 0.365 EP = 0.0210
396	DRIFT LESS TOWARD BEING THOSE 0.55 OF 20 WHERE THE STRENGTH OF MENSTRUAL TABOOS IS LOW (35) WNS	396	DRIFT MORE TOWARD BEING THOSE 0.85 OF 20 WHERE THE STRENGTH OF MENSTRUAL TABOOS IS LOW (35) WNS	9 3 11 17 XSQ= 2.98 PHI= 0.273 EP = 0.0824
398	TILT TOWARD BEING THOSE 0.73 OF 11 WHERE THE INTENSITY OF SEX ANXIETY IS HIGH (16) WNS	398	TILT TOWARD BEING THOSE 0.75 OF 16 WHERE THE INTENSITY OF SEX ANXIETY IS LOW (16) WNS	8 4 3 12 XSQ= 4.24 PHI= 0.396 EP = 0.0220
399	DRIFT TOWARD BEING THOSE 0.65 OF 20 WHERE INTENSITY OF CASTRATION ANXIETY IS HIGH (23) WNS	399	DRIFT TOWARD BEING THOSE 0.70 OF 20 WHERE INTENSITY OF CASTRATION ANXIETY IS LOW (22) WNS	13 6 7 14 XSQ= 3.61 PHI= 0.300 EP = 0.0562
421	TILT TOWARD BEING THOSE 0.64 OF 25 WHERE KILLING, TORTURING, OR MUTILATING OF THE ENEMY IS STRONGLY OR MODERATELY EMPHASIZED (37) PES	421	TILT TOWARD BEING THOSE 0.73 OF 26 WHERE KILLING, TORTURING, OR MUTILATING OF THE ENEMY IS NEGLIGIBLY EMPHASIZED (47) PES	16 7 9 19 XSQ= 5.66 PHI= 0.333 XP = 0.0174
430	DRIFT TOWARD BEING THOSE 0.71 OF 7 WHERE SUPERNATURAL SANCTIONS FOR MORALITY, HAVING AN EFFECT ON AN INDIVIDUAL'S HEALTH, ARE ABSENT OR UNREPORTED (22) GES	430	DRIFT TOWARD BEING THOSE 0.75 OF 12 WHERE SUPERNATURAL SANCTIONS FOR MORALITY, HAVING AN EFFECT ON AN INDIVIDUAL'S HEALTH, ARE PRESENT (16) GES	2 9 5 3 XSQ= 2.24 PHI= -0.343 EP = 0.0739
446	TILT TOWARD BEING THOSE 0.86 OF 7 WHERE WITCHCRAFT IS SIGNIFICANTLY PRESENT (14) GES	446	TILT TOWARD BEING THOSE 0.75 OF 12 WHERE WITCHCRAFT IS MODERATELY PRESENT OR ABSENT (24) GES	6 3 1 9 XSQ= 4.33 PHI= 0.477 EP = 0.0198

```
456  DRIFT TCWARD BEING THOSE          0.65 OF  17     456  DRIFT TOWARD BEING THOSE          0.71 OF  17          6    12
     WHERE THE INTERNALIZATION CF THE                      WHERE THE INTERNALIZATION CF THE                       11     5
     INDIVIDUAL'S CONTACT WITH THE CIVINE                  INDIVIDUAL'S CONTACT WITH THE DIVINE            XSQ=     2.95
     IS NCT CONDUCIVE TC THE DEVELOPMENT OF                IS CONDUCIVE TO THE DEVELOPMENT OF              PHI=   -0.295
     THE INDIVIDUAL'S NEED TO ACHIEVE  (17) DCM            THE INDIVIDUAL'S NEED TO ACHIEVE  (19) DCM      EP =   0.0844

458  DRIFT LESS TCWARD BEING THOSE  0.55 OF  29           458  DRIFT MORE TOWARD BEING THOSE  0.83 OF  23          13     4
     WHERE GAMES, IF PRESENT,                              WHERE GAMES, IF PRESENT,                               16    19
     DC NOT INCLUDE                                        DO NOT INCLUDE                                  XSQ=     3.23
     GAMES OF STRATEGY  (119) R-A-B,EA                     GAMES OF STRATEGY  (119) R-A-B,EA               PHI=    0.249
                                                                                                           XP =   0.0723

459  DRIFT TCWARD BEING THOSE         0.52 OF  29         459  DRIFT TOWARD BEING THOSE          0.78 OF  23          15     5
     WHERE GAMES, IF PRESENT,                              WHERE GAMES, IF PRESENT,                               14    18
     INCLUDE GAMES CF CHANCE  (82) R-A-B,EA                DO NOT INCLUDE                                  XSQ=     3.69
                                                           GAMES OF CHANCE  (89) R-A-B,EA                  PHI=    0.266
                                                                                                           XP =   0.0548

460  TILT TCWARD BEING THOSE          0.76 OF  29         460  TILT TOWARD BEING THOSE           0.61 OF  23           7    14
     WHERE GAMES, IF PRESENT,                              WHERE GAMES, IF PRESENT,                               22     9
     ARE NCT LIMITED TO                                    ARE LIMITED TO                                  XSQ=     5.74
     GAMES OF SKILL CNLY  (104) R-A-B,EA                   GAMES OF SKILL CNLY  (67) R-A-B,EA              PHI=   -0.332
                                                                                                           XP =   0.0165

475  DRIFT MORE TOWARC BEING THOSE  0.81 OF  26           475  DRIFT LESS TOWARD BEING THOSE  0.54 OF  26          21    14
     WHERE EXHIBITIONISTIC CANCING                         WHERE EXHIBITIONISTIC DANCING                           5    12
     IS STRONGLY CR MCDERATELY                             IS STRONGLY OR MODERATELY                       XSQ=     3.15
     EMPHASIZED  (48) PES                                  EMPHASIZED  (48) PES                            PHI=    0.246
                                                                                                           XP =   0.0761
```

****

356	CULTURES WHERE ADOLESCENT PEER GROUPS OR PAIRS ARE PRESENT IN A SETTING OF COURTSHIP (29) JKH	356	CULTURES WHERE NEITHER ADOLESCENT PEER GROUPS NOR PAIRS ARE PRESENT IN A SETTING OF COURTSHIP (22) JKH

BACKGROUND ON PAGE 146 — BOTH SUBJECT AND PREDICATE

....

29 IN LEFT COLUMN

ALORESE	BALINESE	CARIB	CHUKCHEE	DIERI	GANDA	IFUGAO	IRISH	JUKUN	KACHIN
KAZAK	KWAKIUTL	LAKHER	MAORI	MASAI	MIAO	NUER	NYAKYUSA	ORAON	SAMOANS
SERBS	TALLENSI	THONGA	TIMBIRA	TIV	TROBRIAND	VENDA	WARRAU	YAKO	

22 IN RIGHT COLUMN

ABIPON	ANDAMANESE	ARAUCANIANS	AYMARA	AZANDE	CAGABA	CAMAYURA	CHEYENNE	CHIR-APACHE	EGYPTIANS
FON	JAPANESE	KURTATCHI	LEPCHA	LESU	MURNGIN	ONTONG-JAVA	PAPAGO	SANPOIL	SIRIONO
TANALA	YAPESE								

349 EXCLUDED BECAUSE UNASCERTAINED

3	DRIFT LESS TOWARD BEING THOSE LOCATED OUTSIDE OF AFRICA (320)	0.66 OF 29	3	DRIFT MORE TOWARD BEING THOSE LOCATED OUTSIDE OF AFRICA (320)	0.91 OF 22	 XSQ= PHI= XP =	10 2 19 20 3.18 0.250 0.0744
78	DRIFT TOWARD BEING THOSE WHERE A WRITING SYSTEM IS ABSENT, RATHER THAN BEING PRESENT IN EITHER ALPHABETIC-OR-PHONETIC FORM OR MNEMONIC FORM (18) JMH	0.78 OF 9	78	DRIFT TOWARD BEING THOSE WHERE THE WRITING SYSTEM IS ALPHABETIC-OR-PHONETIC, OR MNEMONIC, RATHER THAN BEING ABSENT (36) JMH	0.80 OF 5	 XSQ= PHI= EP =	2 4 7 1 2.34 -0.409 0.0909
96	DRIFT TOWARD BEING THOSE WHERE THE HIERARCHY OF NATIONAL JURISDICTION HAS FOUR, THREE, TWO OR ONE LEVEL (174) GES,EA	0.64 OF 28	96	DRIFT TOWARD BEING THOSE WHERE THE HIERARCHY OF NATIONAL JURISDICTION HAS NO LEVELS (156) GES,EA	0.67 OF 21	 XSQ= PHI= XP =	18 7 10 14 3.45 0.265 0.0634
118	TILT TOWARD BEING THOSE WHERE THE PERCENTAGE OF OCCUPATIONS THAT ARE SPECIALIZED IS LOW (25) WME	0.90 OF 10	118	TILT TOWARD BEING THOSE WHERE THE PERCENTAGE OF OCCUPATIONS THAT ARE SPECIALIZED IS HIGH OR MEDIUM (24) WME	0.75 OF 4	 XSQ= PHI= EP =	1 3 9 1 3.16 -0.475 0.0410

120	DRIFT TCWARD BEING THCSE WHERE THE CRAFT SPECIALIZATION SCORE IS LCW (17) WME	0.58 OF	12	120	IN ALL CASES ARE THOSE WHERE THE CRAFT SPECIALIZATION SCCRE IS HIGH OR MEDIUM (36) WME	1.00 OF	4	5 4 7 0 XSQ= 2.12 PHI= -0.364 EP = 0.0885
262	IN ALL CASES ARE THOSE WHERE WIVES ARE CBTAINEC BY MEANS INVCLVING THE PRESENCE CF SOME CCNSIDERATICN (305)	1.00 OF	29	262	LEAN LESS TOWARD BEING THOSE WHERE WIVES ARE OBTAINED BY MEANS INVOLVING THE PRESENCE OF SOME CONSIDERATION (305)	0.64 OF	22	29 14 0 8 XSQ= 9.91 PHI= 0.441 XP = 0.0016
306	TILT TCWARD BEING THCSE WHERE THE EARLY DEPENCENCE SATISFACTION POTENTIAL IS LCW (24) W-C	0.70 OF	10	306	TILT TOWARD BEING THOSE WHERE THE EARLY DEPENDENCE SATISFACTION POTENTIAL IS HIGH (28) W-C	0.79 OF	14	3 11 7 3 XSQ= 3.84 PHI= -0.400 EP = 0.0351
307	TILT TCWARD BEING THOSE WHERE THE EARLY AGGRESSION SATISFACTION PCTENTIAL IS HIGH (33) W-C	0.92 OF	12	307	TILT TOWARD BEING THOSE WHERE THE EARLY AGGRESSICN SATISFACTION POTENTIAL IS LOW (19) W-C	0.62 OF	13	11 5 1 8 XSQ= 5.53 PHI= 0.470 EP = 0.0112
312	TILT TCWARD BEING THOSE WHERE DEPENDENCE SCCIALIZATION ANXIETY IS HIGH (24) W-C	0.90 OF	10	312	TILT TOWARD BEING THOSE WHERE DEPENDENCE SOCIALIZATION ANXIETY IS LOW (23) W-C	0.58 OF	12	9 5 1 7 XSQ= 3.62 PHI= 0.405 EP = 0.0310
323	DRIFT TCWARD BEING THCSE WHERE THE CONSTANCY CF PRESENCE CF THE INFANT'S NURTURANT AGENT IS LCW (45) B-B-C	0.87 OF	15	323	DRIFT TOWARD BEING THOSE WHERE THE CONSTANCY CF PRESENCE OF THE INFANT'S NURTURANT AGENT IS HIGH (29) B-B-C	0.50 OF	16	2 8 13 8 XSQ= 3.23 PHI= -0.323 EP = 0.0538
324	TILT TCWARD BEING THCSE WHERE THE PAIN INFLICTEC CN THE INFANT BY THE NURTURANT AGENT IS HIGH (34) B-B-C	0.83 OF	12	324	TILT TOWARD BEING THOSE WHERE THE PAIN INFLICTED ON THE INFANT BY THE NURTURANT AGENT IS LOW OR NEGLIGIBLE (32) B-B-C	0.67 OF	15	10 5 2 10 XSQ= 4.88 PHI= 0.425 EP = 0.0185
331	TILT TCWARD BEING THOSE WHERE THE AGE AT BEGINNING OF INDEPENDENCE TRAINING IS LCWER THAN 3.8 YEARS (21) W-C	0.88 OF	8	331	TILT TOWARD BEING THOSE WHERE THE AGE AT BEGINNING OF INDEPENDENCE TRAINING IS 3.8 YEARS OR HIGHER (16) W-C	0.70 OF	10	1 7 7 3 XSQ= 3.85 PHI= -0.462 EP = 0.0248
335	TILT TCWARD BEING THCSE WHERE INITIAL INDULGENCE CF CEPENCENCY IS LCW (18) WNS	0.70 OF	10	335	TILT TOWARD BEING THOSE WHERE INITIAL INDULGENCE OF DEPENDENCY IS HIGH (20) WNS	0.89 OF	9	3 8 7 1 XSQ= 4.54 PHI= -0.489 EP = 0.0198

```
344  DRIFT TOWARD BEING THOSE          0.76 OF  17      344  DRIFT TOWARD BEING THOSE          0.60 OF  15          13    6
     WHERE THE TOTAL POSITIVE PRESSURE TOWARD                WHERE THE TOTAL POSITIVE PRESSURE TOWARD                4    9
     DEVELOPING SELF-RELIANT BEHAVIOR                        DEVELOPING SELF-RELIANT BEHAVIOR                 XSQ=     3.01
     IN THE CHILD                                            IN THE CHILD                                     PHI=    0.307
     IS HIGH  (36) B-B-C                                     IS LOW  (40) B-B-C                               EP =   0.0702

360  TILT TOWARD BEING THOSE           0.69 OF  16      360  TILT TOWARD BEING THOSE           0.81 OF  16          11    3
     WHERE ADOLESCENT PEER GROUPS ARE PRESENT                WHERE ADOLESCENT PEER GROUPS ARE PRESENT                5   13
     IN A SETTING OF WORK AND PUBLIC GATHERINGS              ONLY IN A SETTING OF LEISURE, OR ELSE            XSQ=     6.22
     AND LEISURE, OR AT LEAST OF                             ARE ABSENT  (23) JKH                             PHI=    0.441
     PUBLIC GATHERINGS AND LEISURE  (14) JKH                                                                  EP =   0.0113

397  DRIFT MORE TOWARD BEING THOSE  0.86 OF  29         397  DRIFT LESS TOWARD BEING THOSE  0.62 OF  21              4    8
     WHERE SEX DISABILITY                                    WHERE SEX DISABILITY                                   25   13
     IS ABSENT  (42) JKH                                     IS ABSENT  (42) JKH                              XSQ=     2.72
                                                                                                              PHI=   -0.233
                                                                                                              XP =   0.0989

436  IN ALL CASES ARE THOSE            1.00 OF   8      436  DRIFT TOWARD BEING THOSE          0.50 OF   4           8    2
     WHERE ACTIVE ANCESTRAL SPIRITS                          WHERE ACTIVE ANCESTRAL SPIRITS                          0    2
     ARE PRESENT  (27) GES                                   ARE ABSENT  (11) GES                             XSQ=     1.88
                                                                                                              PHI=    0.395
                                                                                                              EP =   0.0909

472  DRIFT TOWARD BEING THOSE          0.75 OF  20      472  DRIFT TOWARD BEING THOSE          0.56 OF  16          15    7
     WHERE THE COMPOSITE NARCISSISM INDEX                    WHERE THE COMPOSITE NARCISSISM INDEX                    5    9
     IS HIGH  (47) PES                                       IS LOW  (43) PES                                 XSQ=     2.46
                                                                                                              PHI=    0.261
                                                                                                              EP =   0.0874

473  TILT TOWARD BEING THOSE           0.55 OF  20      473  TILT TOWARD BEING THOSE           0.88 OF  16          11    2
     WHERE SENSITIVITY TO INSULT                             WHERE SENSITIVITY TO INSULT                             9   14
     IS EXTREME  (32) PES                                    IS MODERATE OR NEGLIGIBLE  (56) PES              XSQ=     5.24
                                                                                                              PHI=    0.381
                                                                                                              EP =   0.0140
```

357 CULTURES WHERE ADOLESCENT PEER GROUPS ARE PRESENT IN A SETTING OF COURTSHIP (23) JKH	357 CULTURES WHERE ADOLESCENT PEER GROUPS ARE ABSENT IN A SETTING OF COURTSHIP (28) JKH

BACKGROUND ON PAGE 146 SUBJECT ONLY

23 IN LEFT COLUMN

ALORESE	BALINESE	CARIB	CHUKCHEE	DIERI	GANDA	IFUGAO	IRISH	KACHIN	KAZAK
LAKHER	MAORI	MASAI	MIAO	NUER	NYAKYUSA	ORAON	SERBS	THONGA	TROBRIAND
VENDA	WARRAU	YAKO							

28 IN RIGHT COLUMN

ABIPON	ANDAMANESE	ARAUCANIANS	AYMARA	AZANDE	CAGABA	CAMAYURA	CHEYENNE	CHIR-APACHE	EGYPTIANS
FON	JAPANESE	JUKUN	KURTATCHI	KWAKIUTL	LEPCHA	LESU	MURNGIN	ONTONG-JAVA	PAPAGO
SAMOANS	SANPOIL	SIRIONO	TALLENSI	TANALA	TIMBIRA	TIV	YAPESE		

349 EXCLUDED BECAUSE UNASCERTAINED

8	IN ALL CASES ARE THOSE LOCATED OUTSIDE OF NORTH AMERICA (330)	1.00 OF 23	8	DRIFT LESS TOWARD BEING THOSE LOCATED OUTSIDE OF NORTH AMERICA (330)	0.82 OF 28	0 5 23 23 XSQ= 2.76 PHI= -0.233 XP = 0.0968
63	TILT TOWARD BEING THOSE WHERE HUSBANDRY, IF PRESENT, IS PRINCIPALLY IN THE FORM OF BOVINE, EQUINE, CAMEL-LIKE, OR DEER-LIKE ANIMALS, RATHER THAN PIGS, SHEEP, OR GOATS (152)	0.83 OF 18	63	TILT TOWARD BEING THOSE WHERE HUSBANDRY, IF PRESENT, IS PRINCIPALLY IN THE FORM OF PIGS, SHEEP, OR GOATS, RATHER THAN BOVINE, EQUINE, CAMEL-LIKE, OR DEER-LIKE ANIMALS (74)	0.53 OF 19	15 9 3 10 XSQ= 3.79 PHI= 0.320 EP = 0.0382
78	IN ALL CASES ARE THOSE WHERE A WRITING SYSTEM IS ABSENT, RATHER THAN BEING PRESENT IN EITHER ALPHABETIC-OR-PHONETIC FORM OR MNEMONIC FORM (18) JMH	1.00 OF 5	78	TILT TOWARD BEING THOSE WHERE THE WRITING SYSTEM IS ALPHABETIC-OR-PHONETIC, OR MNEMONIC, RATHER THAN BEING ABSENT (36) JMH	0.67 OF 9	0 6 5 3 XSQ= 3.43 PHI= -0.495 EP = 0.0310
96	DRIFT TOWARD BEING THOSE WHERE THE HIERARCHY OF NATIONAL JURISDICTION HAS FOUR, THREE, TWO OR ONE LEVEL (174) GES,EA	0.68 OF 22	96	DRIFT TOWARD BEING THOSE WHERE THE HIERARCHY OF NATIONAL JURISDICTION HAS NO LEVELS (156) GES,EA	0.63 OF 27	15 10 7 17 XSQ= 3.54 PHI= 0.269 XP = 0.0598

```
118  IN ALL CASES ARE THOSE          1.00 OF    7     118  DRIFT TOWARD BEING THOSE        0.57 OF    7          0      4
     WHERE THE PERCENTAGE OF OCCUPATIONS                   WHERE THE PERCENTAGE OF OCCUPATIONS                   7      3
     THAT ARE SPECIALIZED                                  THAT ARE SPECIALIZED                            XSQ=      3.15
     IS LOW  (25) WME                                      IS HIGH OR MEDIUM  (24) WME                     PHI=    -0.474
                                                                                                           EP =    0.0699

120  DRIFT TOWARD BEING THOSE        0.67 OF    9     120  DRIFT TOWARD BEING THOSE        0.86 OF    7          3      6
     WHERE THE CRAFT SPECIALIZATION SCORE                  WHERE THE CRAFT SPECIALIZATION SCORE                  6      1
     IS LOW  (17) WME                                      IS HIGH OR MEDIUM  (36) WME                     XSQ=      2.52
                                                                                                           PHI=    -0.397
                                                                                                           EP =    0.0601

209  DRIFT MORE TOWARD BEING THOSE  0.95 OF   19     209  DRIFT LESS TOWARD BEING THOSE  0.70 OF   23         18     16
     WHERE MARITAL RESIDENCE IS                            WHERE MARITAL RESIDENCE IS                            1      7
     PATRILOCAL, VIRILOCAL, OR AVUNCULOCAL,                PATRILOCAL, VIRILOCAL, OR AVUNCULOCAL,          XSQ=      2.80
     RATHER THAN                                           RATHER THAN                                     PHI=     0.258
     MATRILOCAL OR UXORILOCAL  (270)                       MATRILOCAL OR UXORILOCAL  (270)                 XP =    0.0943

258  DRIFT TOWARD BEING THOSE        0.75 OF    4     258  DRIFT TOWARD BEING THOSE        0.88 OF    8          3      1
     WHERE THE SEVERITY OF SON'S WIFE                      WHERE THE SEVERITY OF SON'S WIFE                      1      7
     AVOIDANCE IS HIGH  (15) WNS                           AVOIDANCE IS LOW  (16) WNS                      XSQ=      2.30
                                                                                                           PHI=     0.437
                                                                                                           EP =    0.0667

262  IN ALL CASES ARE THOSE          1.00 OF   23     262  TILT LESS TOWARD BEING THOSE   0.71 OF   28         23     20
     WHERE WIVES ARE OBTAINED BY                           WHERE WIVES ARE OBTAINED BY                           0      8
     MEANS INVOLVING THE PRESENCE                          MEANS INVOLVING THE PRESENCE                    XSQ=      5.78
     OF SOME CONSIDERATION  (305)                          OF SOME CONSIDERATION  (305)                    PHI=     0.337
                                                                                                           XP =    0.0162

282  DRIFT TOWARD BEING THOSE        0.67 OF    9     282  DRIFT TOWARD BEING THOSE        0.80 OF   10          6      2
     WHERE THE STRENGTH OF DESIRE FOR CHILDREN             WHERE THE STRENGTH OF DESIRE FOR CHILDREN             3      8
     IS HIGH  (16) BCA                                     IS LOW OR ABSENT  (20) BCA                      XSQ=      2.53
                                                                                                           PHI=     0.365
                                                                                                           EP =    0.0698

302  IN ALL CASES ARE THOSE          1.00 OF    7     302  TILT TOWARD BEING THOSE         0.54 OF   13          7      6
     WHERE THE AVERAGE EARLY SATISFACTION                  WHERE THE AVERAGE EARLY SATISFACTION                  0      7
     POTENTIAL IS HIGH  (23) W-C                           POTENTIAL IS LOW  (17) W-C                      XSQ=      3.67
                                                                                                           PHI=     0.429
                                                                                                           EP =    0.0233

307  IN ALL CASES ARE THOSE          1.00 OF    9     307  LEAN TOWARD BEING THOSE         0.56 OF   16          9      7
     WHERE THE EARLY AGGRESSION SATISFACTION               WHERE THE EARLY AGGRESSION SATISFACTION               0      9
     POTENTIAL IS HIGH  (33) W-C                           POTENTIAL IS LOW  (19) W-C                      XSQ=      5.66
                                                                                                           PHI=     0.476
                                                                                                           EP =    0.0078

311  TILT TOWARD BEING THOSE         0.78 OF    9     311  TILT TOWARD BEING THOSE         0.71 OF   17          2     12
     WHERE SEXUAL SOCIALIZATION ANXIETY                    WHERE SEXUAL SOCIALIZATION ANXIETY                    7      5
     IS LOW  (23) W-C                                      IS HIGH  (28) W-C                               XSQ=      3.76
                                                                                                           PHI=    -0.380
                                                                                                           EP =    0.0375
```

315	TILT TOWARD BEING THOSE 0.50 OF 4 WHERE MOTHER AND NURSING CHILD CUSTOMARILY SLEEP IN DIFFERENT BEDS (14) W-C,S	315	IN ALL CASES ARE THOSE 1.00 OF 13 WHERE MOTHER AND NURSING CHILD CUSTOMARILY SLEEP IN THE SAME BED (37) W-D,S	2 13 2 0 XSQ= 3.34 PHI= -0.443 EP = 0.0441
323	DRIFT MORE TOWARD BEING THOSE 0.91 OF 11 WHERE THE CONSTANCY OF PRESENCE OF THE INFANT'S NURTURANT AGENT IS LOW (45) B-B-C	323	DRIFT LESS TOWARD BEING THOSE 0.55 OF 20 WHERE THE CONSTANCY OF PRESENCE OF THE INFANT'S NURTURANT AGENT IS LOW (45) B-B-C	1 9 10 11 XSQ= 2.71 PHI= -0.295 EP = 0.0550
324	TILT TOWARD BEING THOSE 0.89 OF 9 WHERE THE PAIN INFLICTED ON THE INFANT BY THE NURTURANT AGENT IS HIGH (34) B-B-C	324	TILT TOWARD BEING THOSE 0.61 OF 18 WHERE THE PAIN INFLICTED ON THE INFANT BY THE NURTURANT AGENT IS LOW OR NEGLIGIBLE (32) B-B-C	8 7 1 11 XSQ= 4.22 PHI= 0.395 EP = 0.0192
344	LEAN TOWARD BEING THOSE 0.92 OF 12 WHERE THE TOTAL POSITIVE PRESSURE TOWARD DEVELOPING SELF-RELIANT BEHAVIOR IN THE CHILD IS HIGH (36) B-B-C	344	LEAN TOWARD BEING THOSE 0.60 OF 20 WHERE THE TOTAL POSITIVE PRESSURE TOWARD DEVELOPING SELF-RELIANT BEHAVIOR IN THE CHILD IS LOW (40) B-B-C	11 8 1 12 XSQ= 6.30 PHI= 0.444 EP = 0.0079
345	DRIFT TOWARD BEING THOSE 0.67 OF 12 WHERE THE CHILD'S INFERRED ANXIETY OVER NON-PERFORMANCE OF SELF-RELIANT BEHAVIOR IS HIGH (37) B-B-C	345	DRIFT TOWARD BEING THOSE 0.70 OF 20 WHERE THE CHILD'S INFERRED ANXIETY OVER NON-PERFORMANCE OF SELF-RELIANT BEHAVIOR IS LOW (39) B-B-C	8 6 4 14 XSQ= 2.74 PHI= 0.293 EP = 0.0683
360	TILT TOWARD BEING THOSE 0.73 OF 11 WHERE ADOLESCENT PEER GROUPS ARE PRESENT IN A SETTING OF WORK AND PUBLIC GATHERINGS AND LEISURE, OR AT LEAST OF PUBLIC GATHERINGS AND LEISURE (14) JKH	360	TILT TOWARD BEING THOSE 0.71 OF 21 WHERE ADOLESCENT PEER GROUPS ARE PRESENT ONLY IN A SETTING OF LEISURE, OR ELSE ARE ABSENT (23) JKH	8 6 3 15 XSQ= 4.07 PHI= 0.356 EP = 0.0265
419	DRIFT MORE TOWARD BEING THOSE 0.87 OF 15 WHERE MILITARY GLORY IS STRONGLY OR MODERATELY EMPHASIZED (55) PES	419	DRIFT LESS TOWARD BEING THOSE 0.55 OF 20 WHERE MILITARY GLORY IS STRONGLY OR MODERATELY EMPHASIZED (55) PES	13 11 2 9 XSQ= 2.65 PHI= 0.275 EP = 0.0693
420	TILT TOWARD BEING THOSE 0.79 OF 14 WHERE BELLICOSITY IS EXTREME (41) PES	420	TILT TOWARD BEING THOSE 0.62 OF 21 WHERE BELLICOSITY IS MODERATE OR NEGLIGIBLE (46) PES	11 8 3 13 XSQ= 4.03 PHI= 0.340 EP = 0.0364
438	DRIFT MORE TOWARD BEING THOSE 0.90 OF 10 WHERE OTHER-WORLDLY FEARS OF GHOSTS OR SPIRITS ARE GREATER THAN THIS-WORLDLY FEARS OF HUMANS OR ANIMALS (27) W-C,JFG	438	DRIFT LESS TOWARD BEING THOSE 0.53 OF 15 WHERE OTHER-WORLDLY FEARS OF GHOSTS OR SPIRITS ARE GREATER THAN THIS-WORLDLY FEARS OF HUMANS OR ANIMALS (27) W-C,JFG	9 8 1 7 XSQ= 2.21 PHI= 0.298 EP = 0.0875

```
450  DRIFT LESS TOWARD BEING THOSE  0.56 OF   9     450  DRIFT MORE TOWARD BEING THOSE  0.93 OF  14           5    13
     WHERE THE OBSERVATION OF FOOD TABOOS               WHERE THE OBSERVATION OF FOOD TABOOS                    4     1
     IS HIGH OR MEDIUM, RATHER THAN                     IS HIGH OR MEDIUM, RATHER THAN               XSQ=      2.56
     LOW  (60) JRL                                      LOW  (60) JRL                                PHI=    -0.333
                                                                                                     EP =    0.0562

458  DRIFT TOWARD BEING THOSE       0.60 OF  15     458  DRIFT TOWARD BEING THOSE       0.71 OF  24           9     7
     WHERE GAMES, IF PRESENT,                           WHERE GAMES, IF PRESENT,                                6    17
     INCLUDE GAMES OF STRATEGY  (52) R-A-B,EA           DO NOT INCLUDE                               XSQ=      2.46
                                                        GAMES OF STRATEGY  (119) R-A-B,EA            PHI=     0.251
                                                                                                     EP =    0.0944

472  DRIFT TOWARD BEING THOSE       0.80 OF  15     472  DRIFT TOWARD BEING THOSE       0.52 OF  21          12    10
     WHERE THE COMPOSITE NARCISSISM INDEX               WHERE THE COMPOSITE NARCISSISM INDEX                    3    11
     IS HIGH  (47) PES                                  IS LOW  (43) PES                             XSQ=      2.62
                                                                                                     PHI=     0.270
                                                                                                     EP =    0.0833

473  TILT TOWARD BEING THOSE        0.60 OF  15     473  TILT TOWARD BEING THOSE        0.81 OF  21           9     4
     WHERE SENSITIVITY TO INSULT                        WHERE SENSITIVITY TO INSULT                             6    17
     IS EXTREME  (32) PES                               IS MODERATE OR NEGLIGIBLE  (56) PES          XSQ=      4.71
                                                                                                     PHI=     0.362
                                                                                                     EP =    0.0168
```

358	CULTURES WHERE ADOLESCENT PEER GROUPS ARE PRESENT IN A SETTING OF WORK AND PUBLIC GATHERINGS AND LEISURE, OR OF PUBLIC GATHERINGS AND LEISURE, OR OF LEISURE ONLY (41) JKH	358	CULTURES WHERE ADOLESCENT PEER GROUPS ARE ABSENT IN A SETTING OF WORK, AND OF PUBLIC GATHERINGS, AND OF LEISURE (11) JKH

BACKGROUND ON PAGE 146

BOTH SUBJECT AND PREDICATE

41 IN LEFT COLUMN

ALORESE, ANDAMANESE, ARAUCANIANS, AYMARA, BALINESE, CARIB, CHEYENNE, CHIR-APACHE, CHUKCHEE, DIERI, EGYPTIANS, FON, JAPANESE, JUKUN, KACHIN, KAZAK, KURTATCHI, KWAKIUTL, LAKHER, LAMBA, LAU, LESU, MAORI, MIAO, NUER, NYAKYUSA, ONTONG-JAVA, ORAON, PAPAGO, RIFFIANS, SAMOANS, SANPOIL, SERBS, TANALA, THONGA, TIMBIRA, TIV, TROBRIAND, VENDA, YAKO, YAPESE

11 IN RIGHT COLUMN

ABIPON, CAGABA, CAMAYURA, COPR ESKIMO, CREEK, JIVARO, LEPCHA, MURNGIN, SIRIONO, TALLENSI, WARRAU

348 EXCLUDED BECAUSE UNASCERTAINED

9	LEAN TOWARD BEING THOSE LOCATED OUTSIDE OF SOUTH AMERICA (335)	0.90 OF 41	9	LEAN TOWARD BEING THOSE LOCATED IN SOUTH AMERICA (65)	0.55 OF 11	4 6 37 5 XSQ= 8.50 PHI= -0.404 XP = 0.0035
86	TILT TOWARD BEING THOSE WHERE THE LEVEL OF POLITICAL INTEGRATION IS THE LARGE STATE, THE LITTLE STATE, OR THE MINIMAL STATE (148) GPM	0.63 OF 35	86	TILT TOWARD BEING THOSE WHERE THE LEVEL OF POLITICAL INTEGRATION IS THE AUTONOMOUS COMMUNITY, OR THE FAMILY (156) GPM	0.89 OF 9	22 1 13 8 XSQ= 5.75 PHI= 0.361 XP = 0.0165
95	DRIFT LESS TOWARD BEING THOSE WHERE THE HIERARCHY OF NATIONAL JURISDICTION HAS ONE OR NO LEVELS (254) GES,EA	0.69 OF 39	95	IN ALL CASES ARE THOSE WHERE THE HIERARCHY OF NATIONAL JURISDICTION HAS ONE OR NO LEVELS (254) GES,EA	1.00 OF 11	12 0 27 11 XSQ= 2.93 PHI= 0.242 XP = 0.0871
96	LEAN TOWARD BEING THOSE WHERE THE HIERARCHY OF NATIONAL JURISDICTION HAS FOUR, THREE, TWO OR ONE LEVEL (174) GES,EA	0.62 OF 39	96	LEAN TOWARD BEING THOSE WHERE THE HIERARCHY OF NATIONAL JURISDICTION HAS NO LEVELS (156) GES,EA	0.91 OF 11	24 1 15 10 XSQ= 7.46 PHI= 0.386 XP = 0.0063

100	DRIFT MORE TOWARD BEING THOSE 0.92 OF 39 WHERE HIERARCHIES ARE MORE COMPLEX THAN THE 'SIMPLEST,' I. E., MORE COMPLEX THAN TWO LOCAL LEVELS WITH NO NATIONAL LEVELS (267) GES,EA	100	DRIFT LESS TOWARD BEING THOSE 0.64 OF 11 WHERE HIERARCHIES ARE MORE COMPLEX THAN THE 'SIMPLEST,' I. E., MORE COMPLEX THAN TWO LOCAL LEVELS WITH NO NATIONAL LEVELS (267) GES,EA	36 7 3 4 XSQ= 3.72 PHI= 0.273 XP = 0.0538
137	TILT LESS TOWARD BEING THOSE 0.54 OF 28 WHERE INVIDIOUS DISPLAY OF WEALTH IS MODERATELY, LITTLE, OR NEGATIVELY EMPHASIZED (52) PES	137	IN ALL CASES ARE THOSE 1.00 OF 8 WHERE INVIDIOUS DISPLAY OF WEALTH IS MODERATELY, LITTLE, OR NEGATIVELY EMPHASIZED (52) PES	13 0 15 8 XSQ= 3.98 PHI= 0.332 EP = 0.0319
240	DRIFT TOWARD BEING THOSE 0.67 OF 30 WHERE THE FAMILY, IF EXTENDED, IS SMALL OR STEM, RATHER THAN LARGE (135)	240	DRIFT TOWARD BEING THOSE 0.71 OF 7 WHERE THE FAMILY, IF EXTENDED, IS LARGE, RATHER THAN SMALL OR STEM (78)	10 5 20 2 XSQ= 2.02 PHI= -0.234 EP = 0.0953
328	DRIFT TOWARD BEING THOSE 0.62 OF 13 WHERE THE AGE OF THE INFANT AT THE ONSET OF SERIOUS SOCIALIZATION, OTHER THAN WEANING, IS TWO YEARS OR LOWER (20) B-B-C	328	IN ALL CASES ARE THOSE 1.00 OF 4 WHERE THE AGE OF THE INFANT AT THE ONSET OF SERIOUS SOCIALIZATION, OTHER THAN WEANING, IS HIGHER THAN TWO YEARS (21) B-B-C	5 4 8 0 XSQ= 2.51 PHI= -0.384 EP = 0.0824
330	DRIFT TOWARD BEING THOSE 0.50 OF 26 WHERE THE AGE OF THE INFANT AT TIME OF WEANING IS LOWER THAN 2.5 YEARS (36) B-B-C	330	IN ALL CASES ARE THOSE 1.00 OF 6 WHERE THE AGE OF THE INFANT AT TIME OF WEANING IS 2.5 YEARS OR HIGHER (34) B-B-C	13 6 13 0 XSQ= 3.19 PHI= -0.316 EP = 0.0588
343	DRIFT TOWARD BEING THOSE 0.60 OF 15 WHERE THE CHILD'S INFERRED CONFLICT REGARDING NURTURANT BEHAVIOR IS HIGH (29) B-B-C	343	IN ALL CASES ARE THOSE 1.00 OF 4 WHERE THE CHILD'S INFERRED CONFLICT REGARDING NURTURANT BEHAVIOR IS LOW (18) B-B-C	9 0 6 4 XSQ= 2.47 PHI= 0.361 EP = 0.0867
348	DRIFT TOWARD BEING THOSE 0.70 OF 20 WHERE THE TOTAL POSITIVE PRESSURE TOWARD DEVELOPING ACHIEVEMENT BEHAVIOR IN THE CHILD IS HIGH (32) B-B-C	348	DRIFT TOWARD BEING THOSE 0.83 OF 6 WHERE THE TOTAL POSITIVE PRESSURE TOWARD DEVELOPING ACHIEVEMENT BEHAVIOR IN THE CHILD IS LOW (31) B-B-C	14 1 6 5 XSQ= 3.42 PHI= 0.362 EP = 0.0538
349	DRIFT TOWARD BEING THOSE 0.70 OF 20 WHERE THE CHILD'S INFERRED ANXIETY OVER NON-PERFORMANCE OF ACHIEVEMENT BEHAVIOR IS HIGH (34) B-B-C	349	DRIFT TOWARD BEING THOSE 0.83 OF 6 WHERE THE CHILD'S INFERRED ANXIETY OVER NON-PERFORMANCE OF ACHIEVEMENT BEHAVIOR IS LOW (28) B-B-C	14 1 6 5 XSQ= 3.42 PHI= 0.362 EP = 0.0538
350	LEAN TOWARD BEING THOSE 0.74 OF 19 WHERE THE CHILD'S INFERRED ANXIETY OVER PERFORMANCE OF ACHIEVEMENT BEHAVIOR IS HIGH (34) B-B-C	350	IN ALL CASES ARE THOSE 1.00 OF 5 WHERE THE CHILD'S INFERRED ANXIETY OVER PERFORMANCE OF ACHIEVEMENT BEHAVIOR IS LOW (26) B-B-C	14 0 5 5 XSQ= 6.07 PHI= 0.503 EP = 0.0059

No.			No.			
352	DRIFT TOWARD BEING THOSE WHERE THE TOTAL POSITIVE PRESSURE TOWARD DEVELOPING OBEDIENT BEHAVIOR IN THE CHILD IS HIGH (44) B-B-C	0.63 OF 24	352	DRIFT TOWARD BEING THOSE WHERE THE TOTAL POSITIVE PRESSURE TOWARD DEVELOPING OBEDIENT BEHAVIOR IN THE CHILD IS LOW (28) B-B-C	0.83 OF 6	15 1 9 5 XSQ= 2.42 PHI= 0.284 EP = 0.0725
355	TILT TOWARD BEING THOSE WHERE THE CHILD'S INFERRED CONFLICT REGARDING OBEDIENT BEHAVIOR IS HIGH (35) B-B-C	0.54 OF 24	355	IN ALL CASES ARE THOSE WHERE THE CHILD'S INFERRED CONFLICT REGARDING OBEDIENT BEHAVIOR IS LOW (38) B-B-C	1.00 OF 6	13 0 11 6 XSQ= 3.74 PHI= 0.353 EP = 0.0237
365	TILT TOWARD BEING THOSE WHERE THE TIME SPENT IN ADOLESCENT PEER GROUP ACTIVITY IS HIGH OR HIGH-MEDIUM (30) JKH	0.75 OF 36	365	TILT TOWARD BEING THOSE WHERE THE TIME SPENT IN ADOLESCENT PEER GROUP ACTIVITY IS LOW-MEDIUM OR LOW (15) JKH	0.75 OF 8	27 2 9 6 XSQ= 5.23 PHI= 0.345 XP = 0.0222
395	DRIFT TOWARD BEING THOSE WHERE BELIEF IN THE UNCLEANNESS OF WOMEN IS UNIMPORTANT OR ABSENT (15) LWS	0.88 OF 8	395	IN ALL CASES ARE THOSE WHERE BELIEF IN THE UNCLEANNESS OF WOMEN IS PRESENT (18) LWS	1.00 OF 2	1 2 7 0 XSQ= 2.41 PHI= -0.491 EP = 0.0667
398	TILT TOWARD BEING THOSE WHERE THE INTENSITY OF SEX ANXIETY IS HIGH (16) WNS	0.64 OF 14	398	IN ALL CASES ARE THOSE WHERE THE INTENSITY OF SEX ANXIETY IS LOW (16) WNS	1.00 OF 5	9 0 5 5 XSQ= 3.80 PHI= 0.447 EP = 0.0325
458	TILT LESS TOWARD BEING THOSE WHERE GAMES, IF PRESENT, DO NOT INCLUDE GAMES OF STRATEGY (119) R-A-B,EA	0.58 OF 31	458	IN ALL CASES ARE THOSE WHERE GAMES, IF PRESENT, DO NOT INCLUDE GAMES OF STRATEGY (119) R-A-B,EA	1.00 OF 8	13 0 18 8 XSQ= 3.32 PHI= 0.292 EP = 0.0352
469	DRIFT TOWARD BEING THOSE WHERE CONTACT WITH OTHER CULTURES IS FREQUENT OR REGULAR, RATHER THAN IRREGULAR (43) JMH	0.91 OF 11	469	DRIFT TOWARD BEING THOSE WHERE CONTACT WITH OTHER CULTURES IS IRREGULAR, RATHER THAN FREQUENT OR REGULAR (11) JMH	0.60 OF 5	10 2 1 3 XSQ= 2.42 PHI= 0.389 EP = 0.0632
474	TILT TOWARD BEING THOSE WHERE BOASTFULNESS IS MODERATE, NEGLIBIBLE, OR UNREPORTED (48) PES	0.67 OF 27	474	TILT TOWARD BEING THOSE WHERE BOASTFULNESS IS EXTREME (41) PES	0.78 OF 9	9 7 18 2 XSQ= 3.75 PHI= -0.323 EP = 0.0491
475	TILT TOWARD BEING THOSE WHERE EXHIBITIONISTIC DANCING IS STRONGLY OR MODERATELY EMPHASIZED (48) PES	0.77 OF 26	475	TILT TOWARD BEING THOSE WHERE EXHIBITIONISTIC DANCING IS NEGLIGIBLY EMPHASIZED (38) PES	0.67 OF 9	20 3 6 6 XSQ= 3.87 PHI= 0.333 EP = 0.0378

359 CULTURES
WHERE ADOLESCENT PEER GROUPS ARE PRESENT
IN A SETTING CF WORK AND PUBLIC GATHERINGS
AND LEISURE, CR AT LEAST CF
PUBLIC GATHERINGS AND LEISURE (20) JKH
(INCLUDES SOME DOUBTFUL CODINGS)

359 CULTURES
WHERE ADOLESCENT PEER GROUPS ARE PRESENT
ONLY IN A SETTING OF LEISURE, OR ELSE
ARE ABSENT (32) JKH
(INCLUDES SOME DOUBTFUL CODINGS)

BACKGROUND ON PAGE 146

NEITHER SUBJECT NOR PREDICATE

20 IN LEFT CCLUMN

ARAUCANIANS	AYMARA	BALINESE	CHUKCHEE	JAPANESE	JUKUN	KWAKIUTL	LAKHER	MIAO	NUER
NYAKYUSA	CRAON	PAPAGO	SAMOANS	SERBS	TIV	TROBRIAND	VENDA	YAKO	YAPESE

32 IN RIGHT CCLUMN

ABIPON	ALCRESE	ANDAMANESE	CAGABA	CAMAYURA	CARIB	CHEYENNE	CHIR-APACHE	COPR ESKIMO	CREEK
DIERI	EGYPTIANS	FON	JIVARO	KACHIN	KAZAK	KURTATCHI	LAMBA	LAU	LEPCHA
LESU	MACRI	MURNGIN	ONTONG-JAVA	RIFFIANS	SANPOIL	SIRIONO	TALLENSI	TANALA	THONGA
TIMBIRA	WARRAU								

348 EXCLUDED BECAUSE UNASCERTAINEC

360	CULTURES WHERE ADOLESCENT PEER GROUPS ARE PRESENT IN A SETTING OF WORK AND PUBLIC GATHERINGS AND LEISURE, OR AT LEAST OF PUBLIC GATHERINGS AND LEISURE (14) JKH	360	CULTURES WHERE ADOLESCENT PEER GROUPS ARE PRESENT ONLY IN A SETTING OF LEISURE, OR ELSE ARE ABSENT (23) JKH

BACKGROUND ON PAGE 146 — BOTH SUBJECT AND PREDICATE

14 IN LEFT COLUMN

CHUKCHEE, JAPANESE, JUKUN, KWAKIUTL, LAKHER, MIAO, NUER, NYAKYUSA, ORAON, PAPAGO, SAMCANS, SERBS, YAKO, YAPESE

23 IN RIGHT COLUMN

ABIPON, ANDAMANESE, CAGABA, CAMAYURA, CHEYENNE, COPR ESKIMO, CREEK, DIERI, EGYPTIANS, JIVARO, KURTATCHI, LAMBA, LEPCHA, MAORI, MURNGIN, ONTONG-JAVA, RIFFIANS, SANPOIL, SIRIONO, TALLENSI, TANALA, TIMBIRA, WARRAU

363 EXCLUDED BECAUSE UNASCERTAINED

9	IN ALL CASES ARE THOSE LOCATED OUTSIDE OF SOUTH AMERICA (335)	1.00 OF 14	9	TILT LESS TOWARD BEING THOSE LOCATED OUTSIDE OF SOUTH AMERICA (335)	0.70 OF 23	0 7 14 16 XSQ= 3.46 PHI= -0.306 EP = 0.0309
51	TILT TOWARD BEING THOSE WHERE SUBSISTENCE IS PRIMARILY BY FOOD PRODUCTION -- I. E., AGRICULTURE OR HUSBANDRY -- RATHER THAN BY GATHERING (253)	0.79 OF 14	51	TILT TOWARD BEING THOSE WHERE SUBSISTENCE IS PRIMARILY BY FOOD GATHERING -- I. E., HUNTING, FISHING, OR COLLECTING -- RATHER THAN FOOD PRODUCTION (147)	0.61 OF 23	11 9 3 14 XSQ= 3.98 PHI= 0.328 EP = 0.0397
62	TILT TOWARD BEING THOSE WHERE HUSBANDRY OF SOME KIND IS PRESENT (228)	0.86 OF 14	62	TILT TOWARD BEING THOSE WHERE HUSBANDRY OF ANY KIND IS ABSENT (172)	0.52 OF 23	12 11 2 12 XSQ= 3.82 PHI= 0.321 EP = 0.0355
86	DRIFT TOWARD BEING THOSE WHERE THE LEVEL OF POLITICAL INTEGRATION IS THE LARGE STATE, THE LITTLE STATE, OR THE MINIMAL STATE (148) GPM	0.73 OF 11	86	DRIFT TOWARD BEING THOSE WHERE THE LEVEL OF POLITICAL INTEGRATION IS THE AUTONOMOUS COMMUNITY, OR THE FAMILY (156) GPM	0.65 OF 20	8 7 3 13 XSQ= 2.68 PHI= 0.294 EP = 0.0659
96	DRIFT TOWARD BEING THOSE WHERE THE HIERARCHY OF NATIONAL JURISDICTION HAS FOUR, THREE, TWO OR ONE LEVEL (174) GES,EA	0.64 OF 14	96	DRIFT TOWARD BEING THOSE WHERE THE HIERARCHY OF NATIONAL JURISDICTION HAS NO LEVELS (156) GES,EA	0.70 OF 23	9 7 5 16 XSQ= 2.80 PHI= 0.275 EP = 0.0857

100	IN ALL CASES ARE THOSE 1.00 OF 14 WHERE HIERARCHIES ARE MORE COMPLEX THAN THE 'SIMPLEST,' I. E., MORE COMPLEX THAN TWO LOCAL LEVELS WITH NO NATIONAL LEVELS (267) GES,EA	100	DRIFT LESS TOWARD BEING THOSE 0.74 OF 23 WHERE HIERARCHIES ARE MORE COMPLEX THAN THE 'SIMPLEST,' I. E., MORE COMPLEX THAN TWO LOCAL LEVELS WITH NO NATIONAL LEVELS (267) GES,EA	14 17 0 6 XSQ= 2.65 PHI= 0.268 EP = 0.0645
137	TILT TOWARD BEING THOSE 0.57 OF 7 WHERE INVIDIOUS DISPLAY OF WEALTH IS STRONGLY EMPHASIZED (37) PES	137	TILT TOWARD BEING THOSE 0.94 OF 16 WHERE INVIDIOUS DISPLAY OF WEALTH IS MODERATELY, LITTLE, OR NEGATIVELY EMPHASIZED (52) PES	4 1 3 15 XSQ= 4.72 PHI= 0.453 EP = 0.0173
184	IN ALL CASES ARE THOSE 1.00 OF 8 WHERE THE LARGEST NON-COGNATIC KIN GROUP IS SMALLER THAN A PHRATRY, I. E. A SIB OR LINEAGE (175)	184	DRIFT LESS TOWARD BEING THOSE 0.58 OF 12 WHERE THE LARGEST NON-COGNATIC KIN GROUP IS SMALLER THAN A PHRATRY, I. E. A SIB OR LINEAGE (175)	0 5 8 7 XSQ= 2.50 PHI= -0.354 EP = 0.0547
190	IN ALL CASES ARE THOSE 1.00 OF 8 WHERE THE KIN GROUP IS PATRILINEAL OR DOUBLE-DESCENT, RATHER THAN MATRILINEAL (186)	190	TILT TOWARD BEING THOSE 0.60 OF 10 WHERE THE KIN GROUP IS MATRILINEAL, RATHER THAN PATRILINEAL OR DOUBLE-DESCENT (61)	8 4 0 6 XSQ= 4.75 PHI= 0.514 EP = 0.0128
196	TILT TOWARD BEING THOSE 0.90 OF 10 WHERE INDIVIDUAL RIGHTS IN REAL PROPERTY, AND RULES FOR INHERITANCE, ARE PRESENT (194)	196	TILT TOWARD BEING THOSE 0.56 OF 16 WHERE INDIVIDUAL RIGHTS IN REAL PROPERTY, OR RULES FOR INHERITANCE, ARE ABSENT (87)	9 7 1 9 XSQ= 3.78 PHI= 0.381 EP = 0.0367
209	IN ALL CASES ARE THOSE 1.00 OF 11 WHERE MARITAL RESIDENCE IS PATRILOCAL, VIRILOCAL, OR AVUNCULOCAL, RATHER THAN MATRILOCAL OR UXORILOCAL (270)	209	TILT LESS TOWARD BEING THOSE 0.59 OF 17 WHERE MARITAL RESIDENCE IS PATRILOCAL, VIRILOCAL, OR AVUNCULOCAL, RATHER THAN MATRILOCAL OR UXORILOCAL (270)	11 10 0 7 XSQ= 4.04 PHI= 0.380 EP = 0.0233
240	TILT TOWARD BEING THOSE 0.83 OF 12 WHERE THE FAMILY, IF EXTENDED, IS SMALL OR STEM, RATHER THAN LARGE (135)	240	TILT TOWARD BEING THOSE 0.60 OF 15 WHERE THE FAMILY, IF EXTENDED, IS LARGE, RATHER THAN SMALL OR STEM (78)	2 9 10 6 XSQ= 3.55 PHI= -0.362 EP = 0.0473
306	DRIFT TOWARD BEING THOSE 0.75 OF 4 WHERE THE EARLY DEPENDENCE SATISFACTION POTENTIAL IS LOW (24) W-C	306	DRIFT TOWARD BEING THOSE 0.82 OF 11 WHERE THE EARLY DEPENDENCE SATISFACTION POTENTIAL IS HIGH (28) W-C	1 9 3 2 XSQ= 2.09 PHI= -0.373 EP = 0.0769
335	DRIFT TOWARD BEING THOSE 0.75 OF 4 WHERE INITIAL INDULGENCE OF DEPENDENCY IS LOW (18) WNS	335	DRIFT TOWARD BEING THOSE 0.88 OF 8 WHERE INITIAL INDULGENCE OF DEPENDENCY IS HIGH (20) WNS	1 7 3 1 XSQ= 2.30 PHI= -0.437 EP = 0.0667

351	DRIFT TOWARD BEING THOSE WHERE THE CHILD'S INFERRED CONFLICT REGARDING ACHIEVEMENT BEHAVIOR IS HIGH (26) B-B-C	0.67 OF	6	351	DRIFT TOWARD BEING THOSE WHERE THE CHILD'S INFERRED CONFLICT REGARDING ACHIEVEMENT BEHAVIOR IS LOW (34) B-B-C	0.89 OF	9	4 1 2 8 XSQ= 2.81 PHI= 0.433 EP = 0.0889
356	TILT TOWARD BEING THOSE WHERE ADOLESCENT PEER GROUPS OR PAIRS ARE PRESENT IN A SETTING OF COURTSHIP (29) JKH	0.79 OF	14	356	TILT TOWARD BEING THOSE WHERE NEITHER ADOLESCENT PEER GROUPS NOR PAIRS ARE PRESENT IN A SETTING OF COURTSHIP (22) JKH	0.72 OF	18	11 5 3 13 XSQ= 6.22 PHI= 0.441 EP = 0.0113
365	IN ALL CASES ARE THOSE WHERE THE TIME SPENT IN ADOLESCENT PEER GROUP ACTIVITY IS HIGH OR HIGH-MEDIUM (30) JKH	1.00 OF	13	365	TEND TO BE THOSE WHERE THE TIME SPENT IN ADOLESCENT PEER GROUP ACTIVITY IS LOW-MEDIUM OR LOW (15) JKH	0.58 OF	19	13 8 0 11 XSQ= 9.05 PHI= 0.532 EP = 0.0006
397	DRIFT MORE TOWARD BEING THOSE WHERE SEX DISABILITY IS ABSENT (42) JKH	0.93 OF	14	397	DRIFT LESS TOWARD BEING THOSE WHERE SEX DISABILITY IS ABSENT (42) JKH	0.59 OF	22	1 9 13 13 XSQ= 3.32 PHI= -0.304 EP = 0.0536
458	DRIFT TOWARD BEING THOSE WHERE GAMES, IF PRESENT, INCLUDE GAMES OF STRATEGY (52) R-A-B,EA	0.56 OF	9	458	DRIFT TOWARD BEING THOSE WHERE GAMES, IF PRESENT, DO NOT INCLUDE GAMES OF STRATEGY (119) R-A-B,EA	0.83 OF	18	5 3 4 15 XSQ= 2.69 PHI= 0.315 EP = 0.0721
460	IN ALL CASES ARE THOSE WHERE GAMES, IF PRESENT, ARE NOT LIMITED TO GAMES OF SKILL ONLY (104) R-A-B,EA	1.00 OF	9	460	LEAN TOWARD BEING THOSE WHERE GAMES, IF PRESENT, ARE LIMITED TO GAMES OF SKILL ONLY (67) R-A-B,EA	0.56 OF	18	0 10 9 8 XSQ= 5.74 PHI= -0.461 EP = 0.0088
475	DRIFT TOWARD BEING THOSE WHERE EXHIBITIONISTIC DANCING IS STRONGLY OR MODERATELY EMPHASIZED (48) PES	0.86 OF	7	475	DRIFT TOWARD BEING THOSE WHERE EXHIBITIONISTIC DANCING IS NEGLIGIBLY EMPHASIZED (38) PES	0.56 OF	16	6 7 1 9 XSQ= 1.99 PHI= 0.294 EP = 0.0886

****

361	CULTURES WHERE ADCLESCENT PEER GROUPS IN A WCRK SETTING ARE PRESENT (11) JKH	361	CULTURES WHERE ADOLESCENT PEER GRCUPS IN A WORK SETTING ARE ABSENT (40) JKH

BACKGROUND ON PAGE 146 SUBJECT ONLY

....

11 IN LEFT CCLUMN

DIERI	EGYPTIANS	FCN	GANCA	IFUGAO	JAPANESE	MASAI	MIAC	NUER	SAMOANS
TIV									

40 IN RIGHT CCLUMN

ABIPCN	ALCRESE	ANCAMANESE	ARAUCANIANS	AYMARA	AZANDE	BALINESE	CAGABA	CAMAYURA	CARIB
CHEYENNE	CHIR-APACHE	CHUKCHEE	COPR ESKIMO	CREEK	IRISH	JIVARO	JUKUN	KURTATCHI	LAKHER
LAMBA	LEPCHA	LESU	MAORI	NYAKYUSA	ONTONG-JAVA	ORACN	PAPAGC	RIFFIANS	SANPOIL
SERBS	SIRIONC	TALLENSI	TANALA	THONGA	TIMBIRA	TROBRIAND	VENDA	YAKC	YAPESE

349 EXCLUCED BECAUSE UNASCERTAINEC

84	TILT TCWARC BEING THCSE WHERE THE LEVEL CF PCLITICAL INTEGRATICN IS THE LARGE STATE (42) GPM	0.50 OF 8	84	TILT TOWARD BEING THOSE WHERE THE LEVEL CF PCLITICAL INTEGRATION IS THE LITTLE STATE, THE MINIMAL STATE, THE AUTONOMOUS COMMUNITY, CR THE FAMILY (262) GPM	0.91 OF 35	 XSQ= PHI= XP =	4 3 4 32 5.44 0.356 0.0197
95	DRIFT TCWARD BEING THCSE WHERE THE HIERARCHY CF NATICNAL JURISDICTICN HAS FCUR, THREE, CR TWC LEVELS (76) GES,EA	0.55 OF 11	95	DRIFT TOWARD BEING THOSE WHERE THE HIERARCHY OF NATIONAL JURISDICTION HAS ONE OR NO LEVELS (254) GES,EA	0.79 OF 38	 XSQ= PHI= XP =	6 8 5 30 3.19 0.255 0.0740
137	DRIFT TCWARD BEING THCSE WHERE INVICICUS DISPLAY OF WEALTH IS STRCNGLY EMPHASIZEC (37) PES	0.71 OF 7	137	DRIFT TOWARD BEING THOSE WHERE INVIDIOUS DISPLAY OF WEALTH IS MODERATELY, LITTLE, CR NEGATIVELY EMPHASIZED (52) PES	0.71 OF 28	 XSQ= PHI= EP =	5 8 2 2C 2.76 0.281 0.0754
302	IN ALL CASES ARE THCSE WHERE THE AVERAGE EARLY SATISFACTION POTENTIAL IS LCW (17) W-C	1.00 OF 2	302	DRIFT TOWARD BEING THOSE WHERE THE AVERAGE EARLY SATISFACTION POTENTIAL IS HIGH (23) W-C	0.76 CF 17	 XSQ= PHI= EP =	0 13 2 4 1.95 -0.320 0.0877

330	DRIFT TOWARD BEING THOSE WHERE THE AGE OF THE INFANT AT TIME OF WEANING IS LOWER THAN 2.5 YEARS (36) B-B-C	0.83 OF 6	330	DRIFT TOWARD BEING THOSE WHERE THE AGE OF THE INFANT AT TIME OF WEANING IS 2.5 YEARS OR HIGHER (34) B-B-C	0.59 OF 27	1 16 5 11 XSQ= 2.06 PHI= -0.250 EP = 0.0854
365	IN ALL CASES ARE THOSE WHERE THE TIME SPENT IN ADOLESCENT PEER GROUP ACTIVITY IS HIGH OR HIGH-MEDIUM (30) JKH	1.00 OF 8	365	DRIFT LESS TOWARD BEING THOSE WHERE THE TIME SPENT IN ADOLESCENT PEER GROUP ACTIVITY IS HIGH OR HIGH-MEDIUM (30) JKH	0.61 CF 36	8 22 0 14 XSQ= 2.95 PHI= 0.259 XP = 0.0861
368	IN ALL CASES ARE THOSE WHERE DISSOCIATION OF THE SEXES AT ADOLESCENCE IS LOW (21) JKH	1.00 OF 5	368	DRIFT TOWARD BEING THOSE WHERE DISSOCIATION OF THE SEXES AT ADOLESCENCE IS HIGH OR MEDIUM (16) JKH	0.52 OF 31	0 16 5 15 XSQ= 2.79 PHI= -0.278 EP = 0.0527
377	TILT TOWARD BEING THOSE WHERE MALE GENITAL MUTILATION IS PRESENT (83)	0.55 OF 11	377	TILT TOWARD BEING THOSE WHERE MALE GENITAL MUTILATION IS ABSENT (242)	0.87 CF 38	6 5 5 33 XSQ= 6.18 PHI= 0.355 XP = 0.0129
432	IN ALL CASES ARE THOSE WHERE AN ATTRACTIVE AFTERLIFE IS NOT BELIEVED IN (11) LWS	1.00 OF 2	432	IN ALL CASES ARE THOSE WHERE AN ATTRACTIVE AFTERLIFE IS BELIEVED IN (27) LWS	1.00 OF 7	0 7 2 0 XSQ= 4.14 PHI= -0.679 EP = 0.0278
458	TILT TOWARD BEING THOSE WHERE GAMES, IF PRESENT, INCLUDE GAMES OF STRATEGY (52) R-A-B,EA	0.75 OF 8	458	TILT TOWARD BEING THOSE WHERE GAMES, IF PRESENT, DO NOT INCLUDE GAMES OF STRATEGY (119) R-A-B,EA	0.68 OF 31	6 10 2 21 XSQ= 3.20 PHI= 0.286 EP = 0.0454
472	IN ALL CASES ARE THOSE WHERE THE COMPOSITE NARCISSISM INDEX IS HIGH (47) PES	1.00 OF 7	472	DRIFT LESS TOWARD BEING THOSE WHERE THE COMPOSITE NARCISSISM INDEX IS HIGH (47) PES	0.59 OF 29	7 17 0 12 XSQ= 2.68 PHI= 0.273 EP = 0.0704

362 CULTURES WHERE ADOLESCENT PEER GROUPS IN A SETTING OF PUBLIC GATHERINGS ARE PRESENT (21) JKH	362 CULTURES WHERE ADOLESCENT PEER GROUPS IN A SETTING OF PUBLIC GATHERINGS ARE ABSENT (30) JKH

BACKGROUND ON PAGE 146 — SUBJECT ONLY

21 IN LEFT COLUMN

ARAUCANIANS	AYMARA	BALINESE	CHUKCHEE	IRISH	JAPANESE	JUKUN	KWAKIUTL	LAKHER	MIAO
NUER	NYAKYUSA	ORAON	PAPAGO	SAMOANS	SERBS	TIV	TROBRIAND	VENDA	YAKO
YAPESE									

30 IN RIGHT COLUMN

ABIPON	ALORESE	ANDAMANESE	CAGABA	CAMAYURA	CARIB	CHEYENNE	CHIR-APACHE	COPR ESKIMO	CREEK
DIERI	EGYPTIANS	FON	JIVARO	KACHIN	KURTATCHI	LAMBA	LAU	LEPCHA	LESU
MAORI	MURNGIN	ONTONG-JAVA	RIFFIANS	SANPOIL	SIRIONO	TALLENSI	TANALA	TIMBIRA	WARRAU

349 EXCLUDED BECAUSE UNASCERTAINED

51	LEAN TOWARD BEING THOSE WHERE SUBSISTENCE IS PRIMARILY BY FOOD PRODUCTION -- I. E., AGRICULTURE OR HUSBANDRY -- RATHER THAN BY GATHERING (253)	0.86 OF 21	51	LEAN TOWARD BEING THOSE WHERE SUBSISTENCE IS PRIMARILY BY FOOD GATHERING -- I. E., HUNTING, FISHING, OR COLLECTING -- RATHER THAN FOOD PRODUCTION (147)	0.57 OF 30		18 13 / 3 17 / XSQ= 7.62 / PHI= 0.386 / XP = 0.0058
62	DRIFT MORE TOWARD BEING THOSE WHERE HUSBANDRY OF SOME KIND IS PRESENT (228)	0.86 OF 21	62	DRIFT LESS TOWARD BEING THOSE WHERE HUSBANDRY OF SOME KIND IS PRESENT (228)	0.57 OF 30		18 17 / 3 13 / XSQ= 3.59 / PHI= 0.265 / XP = 0.0583
71	DRIFT TOWARD BEING THOSE WHERE METAL WORKING IS PRESENT (98)	0.60 OF 15	71	DRIFT TOWARD BEING THOSE WHERE METAL WORKING IS ABSENT (153)	0.71 OF 28		9 8 / 6 20 / XSQ= 2.83 / PHI= 0.256 / XP = 0.0926
86	TILT TOWARD BEING THOSE WHERE THE LEVEL OF POLITICAL INTEGRATION IS THE LARGE STATE, THE LITTLE STATE, OR THE MINIMAL STATE (148) GPM	0.75 OF 16	86	TILT TOWARD BEING THOSE WHERE THE LEVEL OF POLITICAL INTEGRATION IS THE AUTONOMOUS COMMUNITY, OR THE FAMILY (156) GPM	0.63 OF 27		12 10 / 4 17 / XSQ= 4.37 / PHI= 0.319 / XP = 0.0365

```
 96  DRIFT TOWARD BEING THOSE         0.68 OF  19     96  DRIFT TOWARD BEING THOSE         0.63 OF  30         13    11
     WHERE THE HIERARCHY                                  WHERE THE HIERARCHY                                    6    19
     OF NATIONAL JURISDICTION HAS                         OF NATIONAL JURISDICTION HAS                     XSQ=     3.51
     FOUR, THREE, TWO OR                                  NO LEVELS  (156) GES,EA                          PHI=    0.268
     ONE LEVEL  (174) GES,EA                                                                               XP =   0.0610

100  IN ALL CASES ARE THOSE           1.00 OF  19    100  DRIFT LESS TOWARD BEING THOSE  0.77 OF  30         19    23
     WHERE HIERARCHIES ARE MORE COMPLEX THAN              WHERE HIERARCHIES ARE MORE COMPLEX THAN                0     7
     THE 'SIMPLEST,' I. E., MORE COMPLEX THAN             THE 'SIMPLEST,' I. E., MORE COMPLEX THAN         XSQ=     3.44
     TWO LOCAL LEVELS WITH                                TWO LOCAL LEVELS WITH                            PHI=    0.265
     NO NATIONAL LEVELS  (267) GES,EA                     NO NATIONAL LEVELS  (267) GES,EA                 XP =   0.0636

183  IN ALL CASES ARE THOSE           1.00 OF  13    183  DRIFT LESS TOWARD BEING THOSE  0.71 OF  17          0     5
     WHERE THE LARGEST NON-COGNATIC KIN GROUP             WHERE THE LARGEST NON-COGNATIC KIN GROUP              13    12
     IS SMALLER THAN A MOEITY, I. E.,                     IS SMALLER THAN A MOEITY, I. E.,                 XSQ=     2.71
     A PHRATRY OR SIB OR LINEAGE  (218)                   A PHRATRY OR SIB OR LINEAGE  (218)               PHI=   -0.301
                                                                                                           EP =   0.0525

185  DRIFT LESS TOWARD BEING THOSE  0.62 OF  13      185  DRIFT MORE TOWARD BEING THOSE  0.94 OF  17          8    16
     WHERE THE LARGEST NON-COGNATIC KIN GROUP             WHERE THE LARGEST NON-COGNATIC KIN GROUP               5     1
     IS THE MOEITY OR PHRATRY OR SIB  (194)               IS THE MOEITY OR PHRATRY OR SIB  (194)           XSQ=     3.06
                                                                                                           PHI=   -0.320
                                                                                                           EP =   0.0606

190  TILT MORE TOWARD BEING THOSE   0.92 OF  13      190  TILT LESS TOWARD BEING THOSE   0.53 OF  15         12     8
     WHERE THE KIN GROUP IS                               WHERE THE KIN GROUP IS                                 1     7
     PATRILINEAL OR DOUBLE-DESCENT,                       PATRILINEAL OR DOUBLE-DESCENT,                   XSQ=     3.45
     RATHER THAN MATRILINEAL  (186)                       RATHER THAN MATRILINEAL  (186)                   PHI=    0.351
                                                                                                           EP =   0.0377

196  DRIFT TOWARD BEING THOSE         0.81 OF  16    196  DRIFT TOWARD BEING THOSE         0.53 OF  19        13     9
     WHERE INDIVIDUAL RIGHTS IN REAL PROPERTY,            WHERE INDIVIDUAL RIGHTS IN REAL PROPERTY,              3    10
     AND RULES FOR INHERITANCE,                           OR RULES FOR INHERITANCE,                        XSQ=     2.94
     ARE PRESENT  (194)                                   ARE ABSENT  (87)                                 PHI=    0.290
                                                                                                           EP =   0.0776

209  IN ALL CASES ARE THOSE           1.00 OF  18    209  LEAN LESS TOWARD BEING THOSE   0.61 OF  23         18    14
     WHERE MARITAL RESIDENCE IS                           WHERE MARITAL RESIDENCE IS                             0     9
     PATRILOCAL, VIRILOCAL, OR AVUNCULOCAL,               PATRILOCAL, VIRILOCAL, OR AVUNCULOCAL,           XSQ=     6.88
     RATHER THAN                                          RATHER THAN                                      PHI=    0.410
     MATRILOCAL OR UXORILOCAL  (270)                      MATRILOCAL OR UXORILOCAL  (270)                  XP =   0.0087

236  DRIFT MORE TOWARD BEING THOSE  0.86 OF  21      236  DRIFT LESS TOWARD BEING THOSE  0.60 OF  30         18    18
     WHERE THE FAMILY IS                                  WHERE THE FAMILY IS                                    3    12
     OF AN EXTENDED TYPE, RATHER THAN                     OF AN EXTENDED TYPE, RATHER THAN                 XSQ=     2.79
     AN INDEPENDENT TYPE  (213)                           AN INDEPENDENT TYPE  (213)                       PHI=    0.234
                                                                                                           XP =   0.0947

323  DRIFT MORE TOWARD BEING THOSE  0.90 OF  10      323  DRIFT LESS TOWARD BEING THOSE  0.53 OF  19          1     9
     WHERE THE CONSTANCY OF PRESENCE                      WHERE THE CONSTANCY OF PRESENCE                        9    10
     OF THE INFANT'S NURTURANT AGENT                      OF THE INFANT'S NURTURANT AGENT                  XSQ=     2.56
     IS LOW  (45) B-B-C                                   IS LOW  (45) B-B-C                               PHI=   -0.297
                                                                                                           EP =   0.0976
```

331	IN ALL CASES ARE THOSE WHERE THE AGE AT BEGINNING OF INDEPENDENCE TRAINING IS LOWER THAN 3.8 YEARS (21) W-C	1.00 OF 5	331	TILT TOWARD BEING THOSE WHERE THE AGE AT BEGINNING OF INDEPENDENCE TRAINING IS 3.8 YEARS OR HIGHER (16) W-C	0.60 OF 10	0 6 5 4 XSQ= 2.81 PHI= -0.433 EP = 0.0440
350	TILT TOWARD BEING THOSE WHERE THE CHILD'S INFERRED ANXIETY OVER PERFORMANCE OF ACHIEVEMENT BEHAVIOR IS HIGH (34) B-B-C	0.82 OF 11	350	TILT TOWARD BEING THOSE WHERE THE CHILD'S INFERRED ANXIETY OVER PERFORMANCE OF ACHIEVEMENT BEHAVIOR IS LOW (26) B-B-C	0.67 OF 12	9 4 2 8 XSQ= 3.69 PHI= 0.401 EP = 0.0361
351	TILT TOWARD BEING THOSE WHERE THE CHILD'S INFERRED CONFLICT REGARDING ACHIEVEMENT BEHAVIOR IS HIGH (26) B-B-C	0.64 OF 11	351	TILT TOWARD BEING THOSE WHERE THE CHILD'S INFERRED CONFLICT REGARDING ACHIEVEMENT BEHAVIOR IS LOW (34) B-B-C	0.83 OF 12	7 2 4 10 XSQ= 3.53 PHI= 0.392 EP = 0.0361
356	TILT TOWARD BEING THOSE WHERE ADOLESCENT PEER GROUPS OR PAIRS ARE PRESENT IN A SETTING OF COURTSHIP (29) JKH	0.76 OF 21	356	TILT TOWARD BEING THOSE WHERE NEITHER ADOLESCENT PEER GROUPS NOR PAIRS ARE PRESENT IN A SETTING OF COURTSHIP (22) JKH	0.67 OF 24	16 8 5 16 XSQ= 6.63 PHI= 0.384 XP = 0.0100
365	IN ALL CASES ARE THOSE WHERE THE TIME SPENT IN ADOLESCENT PEER GROUP ACTIVITY IS HIGH OR HIGH-MEDIUM (30) JKH	1.00 OF 20	365	TEND TO BE THOSE WHERE THE TIME SPENT IN ADOLESCENT PEER GROUP ACTIVITY IS LOW-MEDIUM OR LOW (15) JKH	0.60 OF 25	20 10 0 15 XSQ= 15.40 PHI= 0.585 XP = 0.0001
426	DRIFT MORE TOWARD BEING THOSE WHERE A HIGH GOD IS PRESENT (156) GES,EA	0.86 OF 14	426	DRIFT LESS TOWARD BEING THOSE WHERE A HIGH GOD IS PRESENT (156) GES,EA	0.53 OF 30	12 16 2 14 XSQ= 3.04 PHI= 0.263 XP = 0.0813
427	DRIFT TOWARD BEING THOSE WHERE A HIGH GOD, IF PRESENT, IS ACTIVE, RATHER THAN INACTIVE (87) GES,EA	0.75 OF 12	427	DRIFT TOWARD BEING THOSE WHERE A HIGH GOD, IF PRESENT, IS INACTIVE, RATHER THAN ACTIVE (69) GES,EA	0.63 OF 16	9 6 3 10 XSQ= 2.52 PHI= 0.300 EP = 0.0671
442	TILT TOWARD BEING THOSE WHERE FEAR OF ANIMAL SPIRITS IS HIGH (28) W-C	0.88 OF 8	442	TILT TOWARD BEING THOSE WHERE FEAR OF ANIMAL SPIRITS IS LOW (33) W-C	0.58 OF 19	7 8 1 11 XSQ= 3.04 PHI= 0.336 EP = 0.0433
458	TILT TOWARD BEING THOSE WHERE GAMES, IF PRESENT, INCLUDE GAMES OF STRATEGY (52) R-A-B,EA	0.53 OF 15	458	TILT TOWARD BEING THOSE WHERE GAMES, IF PRESENT, DO NOT INCLUDE GAMES OF STRATEGY (119) R-A-B,EA	0.83 OF 23	8 4 7 19 XSQ= 3.89 PHI= 0.320 EP = 0.0326

459	DRIFT TOWARD BEING THOSE WHERE GAMES, IF PRESENT, INCLUDE GAMES OF CHANCE (82) R-A-B,EA	0.67 OF 15	459	DRIFT TOWARD BEING THOSE WHERE GAMES, IF PRESENT, DO NOT INCLUDE GAMES OF CHANCE (89) R-A-B,EA	0.65 OF 23	10 8 5 15 XSQ= 2.53 PHI= 0.258 EP = 0.0960
460	LEAN TOWARD BEING THOSE WHERE GAMES, IF PRESENT, ARE NOT LIMITED TO GAMES OF SKILL ONLY (104) R-A-B,EA	0.93 OF 15	460	LEAN TOWARD BEING THOSE WHERE GAMES, IF PRESENT, ARE LIMITED TO GAMES OF SKILL ONLY (67) R-A-B,EA	0.57 OF 23	1 13 14 10 XSQ= 7.67 PHI= -0.449 EP = 0.0021
470	DRIFT LESS TOWARD BEING THOSE WHERE INNOVATIONS ARE ACCEPTED ONLY SELECTIVELY (33) JMH	0.57 OF 7	470	IN ALL CASES ARE THOSE WHERE INNOVATIONS ARE ACCEPTED ONLY SELECTIVELY (33) JMH	1.00 OF 8	3 0 4 8 XSQ= 2.03 PHI= 0.367 EP = 0.0769
475	TILT TOWARD BEING THOSE WHERE EXHIBITIONISTIC DANCING IS STRONGLY OR MODERATELY EMPHASIZED (48) PES	0.92 OF 13	475	TILT TOWARD BEING THOSE WHERE EXHIBITIONISTIC DANCING IS NEGLIGIBLY EMPHASIZED (38) PES	0.52 OF 21	12 10 1 11 XSQ= 5.20 PHI= 0.391 EP = 0.0107
479	IN ALL CASES ARE THOSE WHERE THE NEED TO ACHIEVE, AS INFERRED FROM FOLKTALES, IS HIGH (18) JV	1.00 OF 4	479	IN ALL CASES ARE THOSE WHERE THE NEED TO ACHIEVE, AS INFERRED FROM FOLKTALES, IS LOW (18) JV	1.00 OF 3	4 0 0 3 XSQ= 3.51 PHI= 0.708 EP = 0.0286

363 CULTURES WHERE ADOLESCENT PEER GROUPS IN A LEISURE SETTING ARE PRESENT (44) JKH	363 CULTURES WHERE ADOLESCENT PEER GROUPS IN A LEISURE SETTING ARE ABSENT (11) JKH

BACKGROUND ON PAGE 146 SUBJECT ONLY

44 IN LEFT COLUMN

ALORESE	ANDAMANESE	ARAUCANIANS	AYMARA	BALINESE	CARIB	CHEYENNE	CHIR-APACHE	CHUKCHEE	DIERI
EGYPTIANS	FON	GANDA	IFUGAO	JAPANESE	JUKUN	KACHIN	KAZAK	KURTATCHI	KWAKIUTL
LAKHER	LAMBA	LAU	LESU	MAORI	MASAI	MIAO	NUER	NYAKYUSA	ONTONG-JAVA
ORAON	PAPAGO	RIFFIANS	SAMOANS	SANPOIL	SERBS	TANALA	THONGA	TIMBIRA	TIV
TROBRIAND	VENDA	YAKO	YAPESE						

11 IN RIGHT COLUMN

ABIPON	CAGABA	CAMAYURA	COPR ESKIMO	CREEK	JIVARO	LEPCHA	MURNGIN	SIRIONO	TALLENSI
WARRAU									

345 EXCLUDED BECAUSE UNASCERTAINED

	Left column			Right column		Statistics
9	LEAN TOWARD BEING THOSE LOCATED OUTSIDE OF SOUTH AMERICA (335)	0.91 OF 44	9	LEAN TOWARD BEING THOSE LOCATED IN SOUTH AMERICA (65)	0.55 OF 11	4 6 40 5 XSQ= 9.36 PHI= -0.412 XP = 0.0022
51	DRIFT TOWARD BEING THOSE WHERE SUBSISTENCE IS PRIMARILY BY FOOD PRODUCTION -- I. E., AGRICULTURE OR HUSBANDRY -- RATHER THAN BY GATHERING (253)	0.70 OF 44	51	DRIFT TOWARD BEING THOSE WHERE SUBSISTENCE IS PRIMARILY BY FOOD GATHERING -- I. E., HUNTING, FISHING, OR COLLECTING -- RATHER THAN FOOD PRODUCTION (147)	0.64 OF 11	31 4 13 7 XSQ= 3.07 PHI= 0.236 XP = 0.0798
62	DRIFT TOWARD BEING THOSE WHERE HUSBANDRY OF SOME KIND IS PRESENT (228)	0.77 OF 44	62	DRIFT TOWARD BEING THOSE WHERE HUSBANDRY OF ANY KIND IS ABSENT (172)	0.55 OF 11	34 5 10 6 XSQ= 2.91 PHI= 0.230 XP = 0.0878
86	TILT TOWARD BEING THOSE WHERE THE LEVEL OF POLITICAL INTEGRATION IS THE LARGE STATE, THE LITTLE STATE, OR THE MINIMAL STATE (148) GPM	0.62 OF 37	86	TILT TOWARD BEING THOSE WHERE THE LEVEL OF POLITICAL INTEGRATION IS THE AUTONOMOUS COMMUNITY, OR THE FAMILY (156) GPM	0.89 OF 9	23 1 14 8 XSQ= 5.65 PHI= 0.351 XP = 0.0174

96	LEAN TOWARD BEING THOSE WHERE THE HIERARCHY OF NATIONAL JURISDICTION HAS FOUR, THREE, TWO OR ONE LEVEL (174) GES,EA	0.62 OF 42	96	LEAN TOWARD BEING THOSE WHERE THE HIERARCHY OF NATIONAL JURISDICTION HAS NO LEVELS (156) GES,EA	0.91 OF 11	26 1 16 10 XSQ= 7.73 PHI= 0.382 XP = 0.0054
100	TILT MORE TOWARD BEING THOSE WHERE HIERARCHIES ARE MORE COMPLEX THAN THE 'SIMPLEST,' I. E., MORE COMPLEX THAN TWO LOCAL LEVELS WITH NO NATIONAL LEVELS (267) GES,EA	0.93 OF 42	100	TILT LESS TOWARD BEING THOSE WHERE HIERARCHIES ARE MORE COMPLEX THAN THE 'SIMPLEST,' I. E., MORE COMPLEX THAN TWO LOCAL LEVELS WITH NO NATIONAL LEVELS (267) GES,EA	0.64 OF 11	39 7 3 4 XSQ= 4.19 PHI= 0.281 XP = 0.0406
137	TILT LESS TOWARD BEING THOSE WHERE INVIDIOUS DISPLAY OF WEALTH IS MODERATELY, LITTLE, OR NEGATIVELY EMPHASIZED (52) PES	0.52 OF 31	137	IN ALL CASES ARE THOSE WHERE INVIDIOUS DISPLAY OF WEALTH IS MODERATELY, LITTLE, OR NEGATIVELY EMPHASIZED (52) PES	1.00 OF 8	15 0 16 8 XSQ= 4.41 PHI= 0.336 EP = 0.0146
240	DRIFT TOWARD BEING THOSE WHERE THE FAMILY, IF EXTENDED, IS SMALL OR STEM, RATHER THAN LARGE (135)	0.67 OF 30	240	DRIFT TOWARD BEING THOSE WHERE THE FAMILY, IF EXTENDED, IS LARGE, RATHER THAN SMALL OR STEM (78)	0.71 OF 7	10 5 20 2 XSQ= 2.02 PHI= -0.234 EP = 0.0953
328	DRIFT TOWARD BEING THOSE WHERE THE AGE OF THE INFANT AT THE ONSET OF SERIOUS SOCIALIZATION, OTHER THAN WEANING, IS TWO YEARS OR LOWER (20) B-B-C	0.64 OF 14	328	IN ALL CASES ARE THOSE WHERE THE AGE OF THE INFANT AT THE ONSET OF SERIOUS SOCIALIZATION, OTHER THAN WEANING, IS HIGHER THAN TWO YEARS (21) B-B-C	1.00 OF 4	5 4 9 0 XSQ= 2.89 PHI= -0.401 EP = 0.0824
330	TILT TOWARD BEING THOSE WHERE THE AGE OF THE INFANT AT TIME OF WEANING IS LOWER THAN 2.5 YEARS (36) B-B-C	0.55 OF 29	330	IN ALL CASES ARE THOSE WHERE THE AGE OF THE INFANT AT TIME OF WEANING IS 2.5 YEARS OR HIGHER (34) B-B-C	1.00 OF 6	13 6 16 0 XSQ= 4.08 PHI= -0.341 EP = 0.0216
343	DRIFT TOWARD BEING THOSE WHERE THE CHILD'S INFERRED CONFLICT REGARDING NURTURANT BEHAVIOR IS HIGH (29) B-B-C	0.63 OF 16	343	IN ALL CASES ARE THOSE WHERE THE CHILD'S INFERRED CONFLICT REGARDING NURTURANT BEHAVIOR IS LOW (18) B-B-C	1.00 OF 4	10 0 6 4 XSQ= 2.81 PHI= 0.375 EP = 0.0867
348	TILT TOWARD BEING THOSE WHERE THE TOTAL POSITIVE PRESSURE TOWARD DEVELOPING ACHIEVEMENT BEHAVIOR IN THE CHILD IS HIGH (32) B-B-C	0.73 OF 22	348	TILT TOWARD BEING THOSE WHERE THE TOTAL POSITIVE PRESSURE TOWARD DEVELOPING ACHIEVEMENT BEHAVIOR IN THE CHILD IS LOW (31) B-B-C	0.83 OF 6	16 1 6 5 XSQ= 4.08 PHI= 0.382 EP = 0.0221
349	TILT TOWARD BEING THOSE WHERE THE CHILD'S INFERRED ANXIETY OVER NON-PERFORMANCE OF ACHIEVEMENT BEHAVIOR IS HIGH (34) B-B-C	0.73 OF 22	349	TILT TOWARD BEING THOSE WHERE THE CHILD'S INFERRED ANXIETY OVER NON-PERFORMANCE OF ACHIEVEMENT BEHAVIOR IS LOW (28) B-B-C	0.83 OF 6	16 1 6 5 XSQ= 4.08 PHI= 0.382 EP = 0.0221

```
350  LEAN TOWARD BEING THOSE          0.76 OF  21    350  IN ALL CASES ARE THOSE           1.00 OF   5       16    0
     WHERE THE CHILD'S INFERRED ANXIETY OVER              WHERE THE CHILD'S INFERRED ANXIETY OVER               5    5
     PERFORMANCE OF ACHIEVEMENT BEHAVIOR                  PERFORMANCE OF ACHIEVEMENT BEHAVIOR           XSQ=     6.95
     IS HIGH  (34) B-B-C                                  IS LOW  (26) B-B-C                            PHI=     0.517
                                                                                                        EP =   0.0038

352  DRIFT TOWARD BEING THOSE         0.63 OF  27    352  DRIFT TOWARD BEING THOSE         0.83 OF   6       17    1
     WHERE THE TOTAL POSITIVE PRESSURE TOWARD             WHERE THE TOTAL POSITIVE PRESSURE TOWARD             10    5
     DEVELOPING OBEDIENT BEHAVIOR                         DEVELOPING OBEDIENT BEHAVIOR                  XSQ=     2.58
     IN THE CHILD                                         IN THE CHILD                                  PHI=     0.280
     IS HIGH  (44) B-B-C                                  IS LOW  (28) B-B-C                            EP =   0.0701

354  DRIFT TOWARD BEING THOSE         0.59 OF  27    354  DRIFT TOWARD BEING THOSE         0.83 OF   6       16    1
     WHERE THE CHILD'S INFERRED ANXIETY OVER              WHERE THE CHILD'S INFERRED ANXIETY OVER              11    5
     PERFORMANCE OF OBEDIENT BEHAVIOR                     PERFORMANCE OF OBEDIENT BEHAVIOR              XSQ=     2.06
     IS HIGH  (36) B-B-C                                  IS LOW  (37) B-B-C                            PHI=     0.250
                                                                                                        EP =   0.0854

355  TILT TOWARD BEING THOSE          0.56 OF  27    355  IN ALL CASES ARE THOSE           1.00 OF   6       15    0
     WHERE THE CHILD'S INFERRED CONFLICT                  WHERE THE CHILD'S INFERRED CONFLICT                  12    6
     REGARDING OBEDIENT BEHAVIOR                          REGARDING OBEDIENT BEHAVIOR                   XSQ=     4.08
     IS HIGH  (35) B-B-C                                  IS LOW  (38) B-B-C                            PHI=     0.351
                                                                                                        EP =   0.0213

365  TILT TOWARD BEING THOSE          0.75 OF  36    365  TILT TOWARD BEING THOSE          0.75 OF   8       27    2
     WHERE THE TIME SPENT IN                              WHERE THE TIME SPENT IN                               9    6
     ADOLESCENT PEER GROUP ACTIVITY                       ADOLESCENT PEER GROUP ACTIVITY                XSQ=     5.23
     IS HIGH OR HIGH-MEDIUM  (30) JKH                     IS LOW-MEDIUM OR LOW  (15) JKH                PHI=     0.345
                                                                                                        XP =   0.0222

395  DRIFT TOWARD BEING THOSE         0.88 OF   8    395  IN ALL CASES ARE THOSE           1.00 OF   2        1    2
     WHERE BELIEF IN                                      WHERE BELIEF IN                                       7    0
     THE UNCLEANNESS OF WOMEN IS                          THE UNCLEANNESS OF WOMEN IS                   XSQ=     2.41
     UNIMPORTANT OR ABSENT  (15) LWS                      PRESENT  (18) LWS                             PHI=   -0.491
                                                                                                        EP =   0.0667

398  TILT TOWARD BEING THOSE          0.60 OF  15    398  IN ALL CASES ARE THOSE           1.00 OF   5        9    0
     WHERE THE INTENSITY OF SEX ANXIETY                   WHERE THE INTENSITY OF SEX ANXIETY                    6    5
     IS HIGH  (16) WNS                                    IS LOW  (16) WNS                              XSQ=     3.30
                                                                                                        PHI=     0.406
                                                                                                        EP =   0.0379

458  TILT LESS TOWARD BEING THOSE     0.55 OF  33    458  IN ALL CASES ARE THOSE           1.00 OF   8       15    0
     WHERE GAMES, IF PRESENT,                             WHERE GAMES, IF PRESENT,                             18    8
     DO NOT INCLUDE                                       DO NOT INCLUDE                                XSQ=     3.94
     GAMES OF STRATEGY  (119) R-A-B,EA                    GAMES OF STRATEGY  (119) R-A-B,EA             PHI=     0.310
                                                                                                        XP =   0.0471

469  DRIFT TOWARD BEING THOSE         0.91 OF  11    469  DRIFT TOWARD BEING THOSE         0.60 OF   5       10    2
     WHERE CONTACT WITH OTHER CULTURES                    WHERE CONTACT WITH OTHER CULTURES                     1    3
     IS FREQUENT OR REGULAR, RATHER THAN                  IS IRREGULAR, RATHER THAN                     XSQ=     2.42
     IRREGULAR  (43) JMH                                  FREQUENT OR REGULAR  (11) JMH                 PHI=     0.389
                                                                                                        EP =   0.0632
```

474	DRIFT TCWARD BEING THCSE WHERE BCASTFULNESS IS MCDERATE, NEGLIBIBLE, CR UNREPCRTED (48) PES	0.63 OF 30	474	DRIFT TOWARD BEING THOSE WHERE BOASTFULNESS IS EXTREME (41) PES	0.78 OF 9		11 7 19 2
						XSQ= PHI= EP =	3.20 -0.286 0.0548
475	DRIFT TCWARD BEING THCSE WHERE EXHIBITICNISTIC CANCING IS STRCNGLY CR MCDERATELY EMPHASIZED (48) PES	0.72 OF 29	475	DRIFT TOWARD BEING THCSE WHERE EXHIBITICNISTIC DANCING IS NEGLIGIBLY EMPHASIZED (38) PES	0.67 OF 9		21 3 8 6
						XSQ= PHI= EP =	2.99 0.280 0.0516

364 CULTURES
WHERE THE TIME SPENT IN
ADOLESCENT PEER GROUP ACTIVITY
IS HIGH, RATHER THAN LOW (22) JKH

364 CULTURES
WHERE THE TIME SPENT IN
ADOLESCENT PEER GROUP ACTIVITY
IS LOW, RATHER THAN HIGH (6) JKH

BACKGROUND ON PAGE 146

SUBJECT ONLY

22 IN LEFT COLUMN

ARAUCANIANS AYMARA BALINESE CHEYENNE CREEK DIERI EGYPTIANS JAPANESE LAKHER MIAO
NUER NYAKYUSA ORAON PAPAGO SAMOANS SERBS TIMBIRA TIV TROBRIAND VENDA
YAKO YAPESE

6 IN RIGHT COLUMN

COPR ESKIMO JIVARO LEPCHA RIFFIANS SIRIONO TALLENSI

17 EXCLUDED BECAUSE AMBIGUOUS

ABIPON ALORESE ANDAMANESE CAMAYURA CARIB CHIR-APACHE CHUKCHEE FON IRISH JUKUN
KURTATCHI LAMBA LAU LESU MAORI SANPOIL TANALA

355 EXCLUDED BECAUSE UNASCERTAINED

	Left column			Right column			
42	DRIFT LESS TOWARD BEING THOSE WHERE THE NATURAL ENVIRONMENT IS OTHER THAN TROPICAL OR SUB-TROPICAL RAIN FOREST, OR MONSOON FOREST (244) FWM	0.55 OF 22	42	IN ALL CASES ARE THOSE WHERE THE NATURAL ENVIRONMENT IS OTHER THAN TROPICAL OR SUB-TROPICAL RAIN FOREST, OR MONSOON FOREST (244) FWM	1.00 OF 6	10 0 12 6 XSQ= 2.49 PHI= 0.298 EP = 0.0619
45	DRIFT TOWARD BEING THOSE WHERE SETTLEMENTS, IF FIXED, ARE COMPACT, RATHER THAN NON-COMPACT (149)	0.76 OF 17	45	DRIFT TOWARD BEING THOSE WHERE SETTLEMENTS, IF FIXED, ARE NON-COMPACT, RATHER THAN COMPACT (73)	0.75 OF 4	13 1 4 3 XSQ= 1.89 PHI= 0.300 EP = 0.0877
96	DRIFT TOWARD BEING THOSE WHERE THE HIERARCHY OF NATIONAL JURISDICTION HAS FOUR, THREE, TWO OR ONE LEVEL (174) GES,EA	0.70 OF 20	96	DRIFT TOWARD BEING THOSE WHERE THE HIERARCHY OF NATIONAL JURISDICTION HAS NO LEVELS (156) GES,EA	0.83 OF 6	14 1 6 5 XSQ= 3.42 PHI= 0.362 EP = 0.0538
106	TILT TOWARD BEING THOSE WHERE CLASS STRATIFICATION, IF PRESENT, IS BASED ON SOMETHING OTHER THAN WEALTH (126)	0.82 OF 11	106	IN ALL CASES ARE THOSE WHERE CLASS STRATIFICATION, IF PRESENT, IS BASED ON WEALTH (77)	1.00 OF 3	2 3 9 0 XSQ= 3.77 PHI= -0.519 EP = 0.0275

175	DRIFT TOWARD BEING THOSE WHERE THE COMMUNITY IS 'KIN-HETEROGENEOUS,' I. E. OTHER THAN A CLAN COMMUNITY OR A DEME (260)	0.77 OF 22	175	DRIFT TOWARD BEING THOSE WHERE THE COMMUNITY IS 'KIN-HOMOGENEOUS,' I. E. A CLAN COMMUNITY OR A DEME (122)	0.67 OF 6	5 4 17 2 XSQ= 2.40 PHI= -0.293 EP = 0.0638
323	DRIFT TOWARD BEING THOSE WHERE THE CONSTANCY OF PRESENCE OF THE INFANT'S NURTURANT AGENT IS LOW (45) B-B-C	0.80 OF 10	323	DRIFT TOWARD BEING THOSE WHERE THE CONSTANCY OF PRESENCE OF THE INFANT'S NURTURANT AGENT IS HIGH (29) B-B-C	0.75 OF 4	2 3 8 1 XSQ= 1.75 PHI= -0.354 EP = 0.0949
343	TILT TOWARD BEING THOSE WHERE THE CHILD'S INFERRED CONFLICT REGARDING NURTURANT BEHAVIOR IS HIGH (29) B-B-C	0.88 OF 8	343	IN ALL CASES ARE THOSE WHERE THE CHILD'S INFERRED CONFLICT REGARDING NURTURANT BEHAVIOR IS LOW (18) B-B-C	1.00 OF 3	7 0 1 3 XSQ= 3.93 PHI= 0.598 EP = 0.0242
350	DRIFT TOWARD BEING THOSE WHERE THE CHILD'S INFERRED ANXIETY OVER PERFORMANCE OF ACHIEVEMENT BEHAVIOR IS HIGH (34) B-B-C	0.73 OF 11	350	IN ALL CASES ARE THOSE WHERE THE CHILD'S INFERRED ANXIETY OVER PERFORMANCE OF ACHIEVEMENT BEHAVIOR IS LOW (26) B-B-C	1.00 OF 3	8 0 3 3 XSQ= 2.55 PHI= 0.427 EP = 0.0549
358	TEND TO BE THOSE WHERE ADOLESCENT PEER GROUPS ARE PRESENT IN A SETTING OF WORK AND PUBLIC GATHERINGS AND LEISURE, OR OF PUBLIC GATHERINGS AND LEISURE, OR OF LEISURE ONLY (41) JKH	0.95 OF 22	358	TEND TO BE THOSE WHERE ADOLESCENT PEER GROUPS ARE ABSENT IN A SETTING OF WORK, AND OF PUBLIC GATHERINGS, AND OF LEISURE (11) JKH	0.83 OF 6	21 1 1 5 XSQ= 13.02 PHI= 0.682 EP = 0.0004
360	TILT TOWARD BEING THOSE WHERE ADOLESCENT PEER GROUPS ARE PRESENT IN A SETTING OF WORK AND PUBLIC GATHERINGS AND LEISURE, OR AT LEAST OF PUBLIC GATHERINGS AND LEISURE (14) JKH	0.69 OF 16	360	IN ALL CASES ARE THOSE WHERE ADOLESCENT PEER GROUPS ARE PRESENT ONLY IN A SETTING OF LEISURE, OR ELSE ARE ABSENT (23) JKH	1.00 OF 6	11 0 5 6 XSQ= 5.73 PHI= 0.510 EP = 0.0124
370	DRIFT LESS TOWARD BEING THOSE WHERE THE SEGREGATION OF ADOLESCENT BOYS IS ABSENT (148)	0.53 OF 19	370	IN ALL CASES ARE THOSE WHERE THE SEGREGATION OF ADOLESCENT BOYS IS ABSENT (148)	1.00 OF 6	9 0 10 6 XSQ= 2.62 PHI= 0.324 EP = 0.0571
469	DRIFT TOWARD BEING THOSE WHERE CONTACT WITH OTHER CULTURES IS FREQUENT OR REGULAR, RATHER THAN IRREGULAR (43) JMH	0.88 OF 8	469	DRIFT TOWARD BEING THOSE WHERE CONTACT WITH OTHER CULTURES IS IRREGULAR, RATHER THAN FREQUENT OR REGULAR (11) JMH	0.75 OF 4	7 1 1 3 XSQ= 2.30 PHI= 0.437 EP = 0.0667

****

365 CULTURES WHERE THE TIME SPENT IN ADOLESCENT PEER GROUP ACTIVITY IS HIGH OR HIGH-MEDIUM (30) JKH	365 CULTURES WHERE THE TIME SPENT IN ADOLESCENT PEER GROUP ACTIVITY IS LOW-MEDIUM OR LOW (15) JKH

BACKGROUND ON PAGE 146

BOTH SUBJECT AND PREDICATE

....

30 IN LEFT COLUMN

ABIPON	ARAUCANIANS	AYMARA	BALINESE	CHEYENNE	CHUKCHEE	CREEK	DIERI	EGYPTIANS	FON
IRISH	JAPANESE	JUKUN	KURTATCHI	LAKHER	LESU	MIAO	NUER	NYAKYUSA	ORAON
PAPAGO	SAMCANS	SERBS	TANALA	TIMBIRA	TIV	TROBRIAND	VENDA	YAKO	YAPESE

15 IN RIGHT COLUMN

ALORESE	ANDAMANESE	CAMAYURA	CARIB	CHIR-APACHE	COPR ESKIMO	JIVARO	LAMBA	LAU	LEPCHA
MAORI	RIFFIANS	SANPOIL	SIRIONO	TALLENSI					

355 EXCLUDED BECAUSE UNASCERTAINED

	Left column			Right column		
62	TILT TOWARD BEING THOSE WHERE HUSBANDRY OF SOME KIND IS PRESENT (228)	0.87 OF 30	62	TILT TOWARD BEING THOSE WHERE HUSBANDRY OF ANY KIND IS ABSENT (172)	0.53 OF 15	26 7 4 8 XSQ= 6.26 PHI= 0.373 XP = 0.0123
71	DRIFT TOWARD BEING THOSE WHERE METAL WORKING IS PRESENT (98)	0.52 OF 25	71	DRIFT TOWARD BEING THOSE WHERE METAL WORKING IS ABSENT (153)	0.79 OF 14	13 3 12 11 XSQ= 2.32 PHI= 0.244 EP = 0.0930
81	DRIFT TOWARD BEING THOSE WHERE A CITY OR TOWN IS PRESENT, OR THE AVERAGE COMMUNITY SIZE IS 200 OR GREATER (89)	0.55 OF 20	81	DRIFT TOWARD BEING THOSE WHERE NO CITY OR TOWN IS PRESENT, AND THE AVERAGE COMMUNITY SIZE IS SMALLER THAN 200 (135)	0.82 OF 11	11 2 9 9 XSQ= 2.58 PHI= 0.289 EP = 0.0656
85	TILT LESS TOWARD BEING THOSE WHERE THE LEVEL OF POLITICAL INTEGRATION IS THE MINIMAL STATE, THE AUTONOMOUS COMMUNITY, OR THE FAMILY (234) GPM	0.69 OF 26	85	IN ALL CASES ARE THOSE WHERE THE LEVEL OF POLITICAL INTEGRATION IS THE MINIMAL STATE, THE AUTONOMOUS COMMUNITY, OR THE FAMILY (234) GPM	1.00 OF 12	8 0 18 12 XSQ= 3.01 PHI= 0.281 EP = 0.0385
86	DRIFT TOWARD BEING THOSE WHERE THE LEVEL OF POLITICAL INTEGRATION IS THE LARGE STATE, THE LITTLE STATE, OR THE MINIMAL STATE (148) GPM	0.65 OF 26	86	DRIFT TOWARD BEING THOSE WHERE THE LEVEL OF POLITICAL INTEGRATION IS THE AUTONOMOUS COMMUNITY, OR THE FAMILY (156) GPM	0.67 OF 12	17 4 9 8 XSQ= 2.24 PHI= 0.243 EP = 0.0873

106	LEAN TOWARD BEING THOSE WHERE CLASS STRATIFICATION, IF PRESENT, IS BASED ON SOMETHING OTHER THAN WEALTH (126)	0.83 OF 18	106	LEAN TOWARD BEING THOSE WHERE CLASS STRATIFICATION, IF PRESENT, IS BASED ON WEALTH (77)	0.83 OF 6	3 5 15 1 XSQ= 6.25 PHI= -0.510 EP = 0.0069
314	TILT LESS TOWARD BEING THOSE WHERE THE INCIDENCE OF MOTHER-CHILD HOUSEHOLDS IS LOW (61) W-D,S	0.56 OF 16	314	TILT MORE TOWARD BEING THOSE WHERE THE INCIDENCE OF MOTHER-CHILD HOUSEHOLDS IS LOW (61) W-D,S	0.92 OF 13	7 1 9 12 XSQ= 3.04 PHI= 0.324 EP = 0.0443
321	DRIFT TOWARD BEING THOSE WHERE THE IMMEDIACY OF REDUCTION OF THE INFANT'S DRIVES IS LOW (25) B-B-C	0.50 OF 12	321	DRIFT TOWARD BEING THOSE WHERE THE IMMEDIACY OF REDUCTION OF THE INFANT'S DRIVES IS HIGH (35) B-B-C	0.90 OF 10	6 9 6 1 XSQ= 2.39 PHI= -0.330 EP = 0.0743
333	IN ALL CASES ARE THOSE WHERE THE AGE AT BEGINNING OF TRAINING IN HETEROSEXUAL PLAY INHIBITION IS EIGHT YEARS OR HIGHER (8) W-C	1.00 OF 6	333	TILT TOWARD BEING THOSE WHERE THE AGE AT BEGINNING OF TRAINING IN HETEROSEXUAL PLAY INHIBITION IS LOWER THAN EIGHT YEARS (8) W-C	0.75 OF 4	6 1 0 3 XSQ= 3.35 PHI= 0.579 EP = 0.0333
336	DRIFT TOWARD BEING THOSE WHERE THE TOTAL POSITIVE PRESSURE TOWARD DEVELOPING RESPONSIBLE BEHAVIOR IN THE CHILD IS HIGH (43) B-B-C	0.71 OF 17	336	DRIFT TOWARD BEING THOSE WHERE THE TOTAL POSITIVE PRESSURE TOWARD DEVELOPING RESPONSIBLE BEHAVIOR IN THE CHILD IS LOW (32) B-B-C	0.70 OF 10	12 3 5 7 XSQ= 2.72 PHI= 0.317 EP = 0.0568
358	TILT MORE TOWARD BEING THOSE WHERE ADOLESCENT PEER GROUPS ARE PRESENT IN A SETTING OF WORK AND PUBLIC GATHERINGS AND LEISURE, OR OF PUBLIC GATHERINGS AND LEISURE, OR OF LEISURE ONLY (41) JKH	0.93 OF 29	358	TILT LESS TOWARD BEING THOSE WHERE ADOLESCENT PEER GROUPS ARE PRESENT IN A SETTING OF WORK AND PUBLIC GATHERINGS AND LEISURE, OR OF PUBLIC GATHERINGS AND LEISURE, OR OF LEISURE ONLY (41) JKH	0.60 OF 15	27 9 2 6 XSQ= 5.23 PHI= 0.345 XP = 0.0222
360	TEND TO BE THOSE WHERE ADOLESCENT PEER GROUPS ARE PRESENT IN A SETTING OF WORK AND PUBLIC GATHERINGS AND LEISURE, OR AT LEAST OF PUBLIC GATHERINGS AND LEISURE (14) JKH	0.62 OF 21	360	IN ALL CASES ARE THOSE WHERE ADOLESCENT PEER GROUPS ARE PRESENT ONLY IN A SETTING OF LEISURE, OR ELSE ARE ABSENT (23) JKH	1.00 OF 11	13 0 8 11 XSQ= 9.05 PHI= 0.532 EP = 0.0006
372	DRIFT TOWARD BEING THOSE WHERE MALE INITIATION RITES ARE PRESENT (48) ASA	0.53 OF 17	372	DRIFT TOWARD BEING THOSE WHERE MALE INITIATION RITES ARE ABSENT (63) ASA	0.85 OF 13	9 2 8 11 XSQ= 3.00 PHI= 0.316 EP = 0.0575
400	TILT TOWARD BEING THOSE WHERE HOMOSEXUAL ACTIVITY IS PERMITTED (36) F-B	0.58 OF 12	400	IN ALL CASES ARE THOSE WHERE HOMOSEXUAL ACTIVITY IS PROHIBITED (22) F-B	1.00 OF 5	5 5 7 0 XSQ= 2.84 PHI= -0.409 EP = 0.0441

402	DRIFT TCWARD BEING THOSE WHERE EXPLANATICNS OF ILLNESS OF AN CRAL NATURE ARE ABSENT (30) W-C	0.58 OF 12	402	DRIFT TOWARD BEING THOSE WHERE EXPLANATIONS OF ILLNESS OF AN ORAL NATURE ARE PRESENT (31) W-C	0.82 OF 11	5 9 7 2 XSQ= 2.38 PHI= -0.322 EP = 0.0894
405	TILT TCWARD BEING THOSE WHERE EXPLANATICNS CF ILLNESS CF A DEPENDENCE NATURE ARE ABSENT (27) W-C	0.67 OF 12	405	TILT TOWARD BEING THOSE WHERE EXPLANATICNS OF ILLNESS OF A DEPENDENCE NATURE ARE PRESENT (34) W-C	0.82 OF 11	4 9 8 2 XSQ= 3.69 PHI= -0.401 EP = 0.0361
406	TILT TCWARD BEING THOSE WHERE EXPLANATICNS CF ILLNESS OF AN AGGRESSICN NATURE ARE ABSENT (33) W-C	0.67 OF 12	406	TILT TOWARD BEING THOSE WHERE EXPLANATICNS OF ILLNESS OF AN AGGRESSION NATURE ARE PRESENT (28) W-C	0.82 OF 11	4 9 8 2 XSQ= 3.69 PHI= -0.401 EP = 0.0361
419	DRIFT TCWARD BEING THCSE WHERE MILITARY GLORY IS STRCNGLY CR MODERATELY EMPHASIZED (55) PES	0.74 OF 19	419	DRIFT TOWARD BEING THOSE WHERE MILITARY GLORY IS NEGLIGIBLY EMPHASIZED (31) PES	0.64 OF 11	14 4 5 7 XSQ= 2.64 PHI= 0.297 EP = 0.0626
452	DRIFT TOWARD BEING THCSE WHERE TOTEMISM WITH FCOD TABCCS IS PRESENT (19) WNS	0.58 OF 12	452	DRIFT TOWARD BEING THOSE WHERE TOTEMISM WITH FOOD TABCOS IS ABSENT (24) WNS	0.88 OF 8	7 1 5 7 XSQ= 2.51 PHI= 0.354 EP = 0.0697
458	TILT LESS TOWARC BEING THCSE WHERE GAMES, IF PRESENT, DC NCT INCLUDE GAMES OF STRATEGY (119) R-A-B,EA	0.54 OF 24	458	TILT MORE TOWARD BEING THOSE WHERE GAMES, IF PRESENT, DO NOT INCLUDE GAMES OF STRATEGY (119) R-A-B,EA	0.92 OF 12	11 1 13 11 XSQ= 3.52 PHI= 0.312 EP = 0.0307
460	DRIFT TCWARD BEING THCSE WHERE GAMES, IF PRESENT, ARE NCT LIMITED TO GAMES CF SKILL CNLY (104) R-A-B,EA	0.75 OF 24	460	DRIFT TOWARD BEING THOSE WHERE GAMES, IF PRESENT, ARE LIMITED TO GAMES OF SKILL ONLY (67) R-A-B,EA	0.58 OF 12	6 7 18 5 XSQ= 2.54 PHI= -0.266 EP = 0.0714
469	DRIFT TCWARD BEING THCSE WHERE CCNTACT WITH CTHER CULTURES IS FREQUENT CR REGULAR, RATHER THAN IRREGULAR (43) JMH	0.90 OF 10	469	DRIFT TOWARD BEING THOSE WHERE CONTACT WITH OTHER CULTURES IS IRREGULAR, RATHER THAN FREQUENT OR REGULAR (11) JMH	0.60 OF 5	9 2 1 3 XSQ= 2.09 PHI= 0.373 EP = 0.0769
475	DRIFT TCWARD BEING THOSE WHERE EXHIBITIONISTIC CANCING IS STRCNGLY CR MCDERATELY EMPHASIZED (48) PES	0.79 OF 19	475	DRIFT TOWARD BEING THOSE WHERE EXHIBITICNISTIC DANCING IS NEGLIGIBLY EMPHASIZED (38) PES	0.58 OF 12	15 5 4 7 XSQ= 2.99 PHI= 0.310 EP = 0.0564

366 CULTURES
WHERE DISSOCIATION OF THE SEXES
AT ADOLESCENCE
IS HIGH (16) JKH

366 CULTURES
WHERE DISSOCIATION OF THE SEXES
AT ADOLESCENCE
IS MEDIUM OR LOW (41) JKH

BACKGROUND ON PAGE 149

BOTH SUBJECT AND PREDICATE

16 IN LEFT COLUMN

ABIPON	ANDAMANESE	CARIB	EGYPTIANS	GANDA	LESU	MASAI	MURNGIN	NYAKYUSA	PAPAGO
RIFFIANS	SANPOIL	TALLENSI	THONGA	YAKO	YAPESE				

41 IN RIGHT COLUMN

ALORESE	ARAUCANIANS	AYMARA	AZANDE	BALINESE	CAGABA	CAMAYURA	CHEYENNE	CHIR-APACHE	CHUKCHEE
COPR ESKIMO	CREEK	DIERI	FON	IFUGAO	IRISH	JAPANESE	JIVARO	JUKUN	KACHIN
KAZAK	KURTATCHI	KWAKIUTL	LAKHER	LAMBA	LAU	LEPCHA	MAORI	MIAO	NUER
ONTONG-JAVA	CRAON	SAMOANS	SERBS	SIRIONO	TANALA	TIMBIRA	TIV	TROBRIAND	VENDA
WARRAU									

343 EXCLUDED BECAUSE UNASCERTAINED

	Left column		Right column		
98	DRIFT LESS TOWARD BEING THOSE WHERE THE HIERARCHY OF LOCAL JURISDICTION HAS FOUR OR THREE LEVELS (238) GES,EA	0.56 OF 16	DRIFT MORE TOWARD BEING THOSE WHERE THE HIERARCHY OF LOCAL JURISDICTION HAS FOUR OR THREE LEVELS (238) GES,EA	0.85 OF 40	9 34 7 6 XSQ= 3.81 PHI= -0.261 XP = 0.0510
284	IN ALL CASES ARE THOSE WHERE CONTRACEPTION IS PRACTICED (10) CSF	1.00 OF 5	DRIFT TOWARD BEING THOSE WHERE CONTRACEPTION IS NOT PRACTICED (7) CSF	0.57 OF 7	5 3 0 4 XSQ= 2.10 PHI= 0.418 EP = 0.0808
325	IN ALL CASES ARE THOSE WHERE THE DEGREE OF DIFFUSION AMONG THE INFANT'S NURTURANT AGENTS IS HIGH (42) B-B-C	1.00 OF 9	TILT TOWARD BEING THOSE WHERE THE DEGREE OF DIFFUSION AMONG THE INFANT'S NURTURANT AGENTS IS LOW (32) B-B-C	0.50 OF 26	9 13 0 13 XSQ= 5.18 PHI= 0.385 EP = 0.0131
352	DRIFT TOWARD BEING THOSE WHERE THE TOTAL POSITIVE PRESSURE TOWARD DEVELOPING OBEDIENT BEHAVIOR IN THE CHILD IS HIGH (44) B-B-C	0.88 OF 8	DRIFT TOWARD BEING THOSE WHERE THE TOTAL POSITIVE PRESSURE TOWARD DEVELOPING OBEDIENT BEHAVIOR IN THE CHILD IS LOW (28) B-B-C	0.54 OF 26	7 12 1 14 XSQ= 2.73 PHI= 0.283 EP = 0.0529

```
397  DRIFT LESS TOWARD BEING THOSE  0.56 OF  16     397  DRIFT MORE TOWARD BEING THOSE  0.82 OF  40           7     7
     WHERE SEX DISABILITY                                WHERE SEX DISABILITY                                 9    33
     IS ABSENT  (42) JKH                                 IS ABSENT  (42) JKH                            XSQ=      2.92
                                                                                                        PHI=     0.228
                                                                                                        XP =    0.0877

476  IN ALL CASES ARE THOSE         1.00 OF   7     476  TILT TOWARD BEING THOSE        0.57 OF  14           7     6
     WHERE THE DEGREE OF INSOBRIETY IS                   WHERE THE DEGREE OF INSOBRIETY IS                    0     8
     STRONG  (31) DH                                     MODERATE OR SLIGHT  (18) DH                    XSQ=      4.27
                                                                                                        PHI=     0.451
                                                                                                        EP =    0.0180

480  IN ALL CASES ARE THOSE         1.00 OF   5     480  LEAN TOWARD BEING THOSE        0.80 OF  10           0     8
     WHERE COMPLEXITY OF ARTISTIC DESIGN                 WHERE COMPLEXITY OF ARTISTIC DESIGN                  5     2
     IS LOW  (15) HB                                     IS HIGH  (14) HB                               XSQ=      5.66
                                                                                                        PHI=    -0.614
                                                                                                        EP =    0.0070
```

367 CULTURES
WHERE DISSCCIATICN CF THE SEXES
AT ADCLESCENCE
IS HIGH CR MEDIUM (28) JKH
(INCLUDES SOME CCUBTFUL CCCINGS)

367 CULTURES
WHERE DISSOCIATION OF THE SEXES
AT ADOLESCENCE
IS LOW (29) JKH
(INCLUDES SOME DOUBTFUL CODINGS)

BACKGROUND ON PAGE 149

NEITHER SUBJECT NOR PREDICATE

28 IN LEFT CCLUMN

ABIPCN	ANDAMANESE	CAMAYURA	CARIB	CHEYENNE	EGYPTIANS	GANDA	IRISH	JIVARO	JUKUN
KURTATCHI	KWAKIUTL	LAU	LESU	MAORI	MASAI	MURNGIN	NYAKYUSA	PAPAGO	RIFFIANS
SAMOANS	SANPCIL	SIRICNC	TALLENSI	THONGA	TROBRIAND	YAKC	YAPESE		

29 IN RIGHT CCLUMN

ALORESE	ARAUCANIANS	AYMARA	AZANDE	BALINESE	CAGABA	CHIR-APACHE	CHUKCHEE	COPR ESKIMO	CREEK
DIERI	FCN	IFUGAC	JAPANESE	KACHIN	KAZAK	LAKHER	LAMBA	LEPCHA	MIAO
NUER	CNTCNG-JAVA	ORACN	SERBS	TANALA	TIMBIRA	TIV	VENDA	WARRAU	

343 EXCLUCED BECAUSE UNASCERTAINEC

```
************************************************************************************************************

368  CULTURES                                            368  CULTURES
     WHERE DISSOCIATION OF THE SEXES                          WHERE DISSOCIATION OF THE SEXES
     AT ADOLESCENCE                                           AT ADOLESCENCE
     IS HIGH OR MEDIUM  (16) JKH                              IS LOW  (21) JKH


BACKGROUND ON PAGE 149                                                            BOTH SUBJECT AND PREDICATE
............................................................................................................

     16  IN LEFT COLUMN

ABIPON      ANDAMANESE  CARIB      CHEYENNE    JUKUN       KURTATCHI  LESU       MAORI      NYAKYUSA   PAPAGO
SANPOIL     SIRIONO     TALLENSI   TROBRIAND   YAKO        YAPESE

     21  IN RIGHT COLUMN

ALORESE     ARAUCANIANS CHIR-APACHE CHUKCHEE   COPR ESKIMO CREEK      DIERI      FON        IFUGAO     IRISH
JAPANESE    JIVARO      KAZAK      LAKHER      LAMBA       LEPCHA     MIAO       ORAON      SERBS      TANALA
TIMBIRA

     363  EXCLUDED BECAUSE UNASCERTAINED

------------------------------------------------------------------------------------------------------------
  5  DRIFT MORE TOWARD BEING THOSE  0.94 OF  16      5  DRIFT LESS TOWARD BEING THOSE  0.62 OF  21      1    8
     LOCATED OUTSIDE OF                                 LOCATED OUTSIDE OF                             15   13
     EAST EURASIA  (330)                                EAST EURASIA  (330)                      XSQ=     3.42
                                                                                                 PHI=   -0.304
                                                                                                 EP =   0.0501

 15  TILT TOWARD BEING THOSE        0.69 OF  16     15  TILT TOWARD BEING THOSE        0.71 OF  21      5   15
     WHERE THE LATITUDE IS                              WHERE THE LATITUDE IS                          11    6
     LESS THAN TWENTY DEGREES  (217)                    TWENTY DEGREES OR GREATER  (183)         XSQ=     4.40
                                                                                                 PHI=   -0.345
                                                                                                 EP =   0.0220

 16  DRIFT TOWARD BEING THOSE       0.50 OF  16     16  DRIFT TOWARD BEING THOSE       0.81 OF  21      8   17
     WHERE THE LATITUDE IS                              WHERE THE LATITUDE IS                           8    4
     LESS THAN TEN DEGREES  (123)                       TEN DEGREES OR GREATER  (277)            XSQ=     2.68
                                                                                                 PHI=   -0.269
                                                                                                 EP =   0.0768

 71  LEAN TOWARD BEING THOSE        0.86 OF  14     71  LEAN TOWARD BEING THOSE        0.65 OF  17      2   11
     WHERE METAL WORKING IS                             WHERE METAL WORKING IS                         12    6
     ABSENT  (153)                                      PRESENT  (98)                            XSQ=     6.08
                                                                                                 PHI=   -0.443
                                                                                                 EP =   0.0094

 84  IN ALL CASES ARE THOSE         1.00 OF  15     84  TILT LESS TOWARD BEING THOSE   0.72 OF  18      0    5
     WHERE THE LEVEL OF POLITICAL INTEGRATION           WHERE THE LEVEL OF POLITICAL INTEGRATION       15   13
     IS THE LITTLE STATE, THE MINIMAL STATE,            IS THE LITTLE STATE, THE MINIMAL STATE,  XSQ=     2.99
     THE AUTONOMOUS COMMUNITY, OR                       THE AUTONOMOUS COMMUNITY, OR             PHI=   -0.301
     THE FAMILY  (262) GPM                              THE FAMILY  (262) GPM                    EP =   0.0488
```

85	DRIFT MORE TOWARD BEING THOSE 0.93 OF 15 WHERE THE LEVEL OF POLITICAL INTEGRATION IS THE MINIMAL STATE, THE AUTONOMOUS COMMUNITY, OR THE FAMILY (234) GPM	85	DRIFT LESS TOWARD BEING THOSE 0.67 OF 18 WHERE THE LEVEL OF POLITICAL INTEGRATION IS THE MINIMAL STATE, THE AUTONOMOUS COMMUNITY, OR THE FAMILY (234) GPM	1 6 14 12 XSQ= 2.07 PHI= -0.250 EP = 0.0952
186	DRIFT MORE TOWARD BEING THOSE 0.94 OF 16 WHERE THE KIN GROUP IS OTHER THAN EXCLUSIVELY PATRILINEAL (250)	186	DRIFT LESS TOWARD BEING THOSE 0.62 OF 21 WHERE THE KIN GROUP IS OTHER THAN EXCLUSIVELY PATRILINEAL (250)	1 8 15 13 XSQ= 3.42 PHI= -0.304 EP = 0.0501
201	DRIFT LESS TOWARD BEING THOSE 0.56 OF 16 WHERE MARITAL RESIDENCE IS NON-OPTIONAL, RATHER THAN AMBILOCAL OR NEOLOCAL (334)	201	DRIFT MORE TOWARD BEING THOSE 0.86 OF 21 WHERE MARITAL RESIDENCE IS NON-OPTIONAL, RATHER THAN AMBILOCAL OR NEOLOCAL (334)	9 18 7 3 XSQ= 2.64 PHI= -0.267 EP = 0.0667
204	DRIFT TOWARD BEING THOSE 0.54 OF 13 WHERE MARITAL RESIDENCE IS AMBILOCAL OR NEOLOCAL, RATHER THAN PATRILOCAL, VIRILOCAL, OR AVUNCULOCAL (64)	204	DRIFT TOWARD BEING THOSE 0.83 OF 18 WHERE MARITAL RESIDENCE IS PATRILOCAL, VIRILOCAL, OR AVUNCULOCAL, RATHER THAN AMBILOCAL OR NEOLOCAL (270)	6 15 7 3 XSQ= 3.23 PHI= -0.323 EP = 0.0515
256	IN ALL CASES ARE THOSE 1.00 OF 7 WHERE GRANDPARENT AND GRANDCHILD ARE FRIENDLY EQUALS (25) CA	256	TILT TOWARD BEING THOSE 0.75 OF 4 WHERE GRANDPARENT AND GRANDCHILD ARE NOT FRIENDLY EQUALS (8) DA	7 1 0 3 XSQ= 3.93 PHI= 0.598 EP = 0.0242
299	DRIFT TOWARD BEING THOSE 0.60 OF 10 WHERE THE POST-PARTUM SEX TABOO LASTS LONGER THAN ONE YEAR (35)	299	DRIFT TOWARD BEING THOSE 0.82 OF 11 WHERE THE POST-PARTUM SEX TABOO LASTS ONE YEAR OR LESS (89)	6 2 4 9 XSQ= 2.31 PHI= 0.332 EP = 0.0805
306	TILT TOWARD BEING THOSE 0.89 OF 9 WHERE THE EARLY DEPENDENCE SATISFACTION POTENTIAL IS HIGH (28) W-C	306	TILT TOWARD BEING THOSE 0.63 OF 8 WHERE THE EARLY DEPENDENCE SATISFACTION POTENTIAL IS LOW (24) W-C	8 3 1 5 XSQ= 2.91 PHI= 0.413 EP = 0.0498
316	DRIFT TOWARD BEING THOSE 0.67 OF 9 WHERE EXCLUSIVE MOTHER-SON SLEEPING ARRANGEMENTS LAST ONE YEAR OR LONGER (19) W-K-A	316	DRIFT TOWARD BEING THOSE 0.77 OF 13 WHERE EXCLUSIVE MOTHER-SON SLEEPING ARRANGEMENTS LAST LESS THAN ONE YEAR (25) W-K-A	6 3 3 10 XSQ= 2.57 PHI= 0.342 EP = 0.0789
317	IN ALL CASES ARE THOSE 1.00 OF 9 WHERE DISPLAY OF AFFECTION TOWARD THE INFANT IS HIGH (39) B-B-C	317	TILT TOWARD BEING THOSE 0.56 OF 9 WHERE DISPLAY OF AFFECTION TOWARD THE INFANT IS LOW (29) B-B-C	9 4 0 5 XSQ= 4.43 PHI= 0.496 EP = 0.0294

320	DRIFT TOWARD BEING THOSE WHERE THE DEGREE OF REDUCTION OF THE INFANT'S DRIVES IS HIGH (45) B-B-C	0.89 OF 9	32C	DRIFT TOWARD BEING THOSE WHERE THE DEGREE OF REDUCTION OF THE INFANT'S DRIVES IS LOW (24) B-B-C	0.55 OF 11	8 5 1 6 XSQ= 2.42 PHI= 0.348 EP = 0.0703
334	TILT TOWARD BEING THOSE WHERE THE INDULGENCE OF THE CHILD IS HIGH (40) B-B-C	0.90 OF 10	334	TILT TOWARD BEING THOSE WHERE THE INDULGENCE OF THE CHILD IS LOW (38) B-B-C	0.58 OF 12	9 5 1 7 XSQ= 3.62 PHI= 0.405 EP = 0.0310
335	IN ALL CASES ARE THOSE WHERE INITIAL INDULGENCE OF DEPENDENCY IS HIGH (20) WNS	1.00 OF 6	335	DRIFT TOWARD BEING THOSE WHERE INITIAL INDULGENCE OF DEPENDENCY IS LOW (18) WNS	0.57 OF 7	6 3 0 4 XSQ= 2.63 PHI= 0.450 EP = 0.0699
382	TILT TOWARD BEING THOSE WHERE FEMALE INITIATION RITES ARE PRESENT (38) JKB	0.88 OF 8	382	TILT TOWARD BEING THOSE WHERE FEMALE INITIATION RITES ARE ABSENT (27) JKB	0.67 OF 12	7 4 1 8 XSQ= 3.71 PHI= 0.431 EP = 0.0281
405	DRIFT TOWARD BEING THOSE WHERE EXPLANATIONS OF ILLNESS OF A DEPENDENCE NATURE ARE ABSENT (27) W-C	0.67 OF 9	405	DRIFT TOWARD BEING THOSE WHERE EXPLANATIONS OF ILLNESS OF A DEPENDENCE NATURE ARE PRESENT (34) W-C	0.80 OF 10	3 8 6 2 XSQ= 2.53 PHI= -0.365 EP = 0.0698
406	DRIFT TOWARD BEING THOSE WHERE EXPLANATIONS OF ILLNESS OF AN AGGRESSION NATURE ARE ABSENT (33) W-C	0.67 OF 9	406	DRIFT TOWARD BEING THOSE WHERE EXPLANATIONS OF ILLNESS OF AN AGGRESSION NATURE ARE PRESENT (28) W-C	0.80 OF 10	3 8 6 2 XSQ= 2.53 PHI= -0.365 EP = 0.0698
458	DRIFT TOWARD BEING THOSE WHERE GAMES, IF PRESENT, DO NOT INCLUDE GAMES OF STRATEGY (119) R-A-B, EA	0.86 OF 14	458	DRIFT TOWARD BEING THOSE WHERE GAMES, IF PRESENT, INCLUDE GAMES OF STRATEGY (52) R-A-B, EA	0.50 OF 16	2 8 12 8 XSQ= 2.83 PHI= -0.307 EP = 0.0577
459	DRIFT TOWARD BEING THOSE WHERE GAMES, IF PRESENT, DO NOT INCLUDE GAMES OF CHANCE (89) R-A-B, EA	0.71 OF 14	459	DRIFT TOWARD BEING THOSE WHERE GAMES, IF PRESENT, INCLUDE GAMES OF CHANCE (82) R-A-B, EA	0.63 OF 16	4 10 10 6 XSQ= 2.22 PHI= -0.272 EP = 0.0813
460	DRIFT TOWARD BEING THOSE WHERE GAMES, IF PRESENT, ARE LIMITED TO GAMES OF SKILL ONLY (67) R-A-B, EA	0.57 OF 14	460	DRIFT TOWARD BEING THOSE WHERE GAMES, IF PRESENT, ARE NOT LIMITED TO GAMES OF SKILL ONLY (104) R-A-B, EA	0.81 OF 16	8 3 6 13 XSQ= 3.23 PHI= 0.328 EP = 0.0567

369 CULTURES
WHERE DISSOCIATION OF THE SEXES
AT ADOLESCENCE, OR
CUSTOMS OF INITIATION AT ADOLESCENCE,
ARE PRESENT (42) JKH

369 CULTURES
WHERE BOTH DISSOCIATION OF THE SEXES
AT ADOLESCENCE, AND
CUSTOMS OF INITIATION AT ADOLESCENCE,
ARE ABSENT (15) JKH

BACKGROUND ON PAGE 149

BOTH SUBJECT AND PREDICATE

42 IN LEFT COLUMN

ABIPON	ANDAMANESE	AZANDE	BALINESE	CAGABA	CAMAYURA	CARIB	CHEYENNE	CHIR-APACHE	CREEK
DIERI	EGYPTIANS	FON	GANDA	IRISH	JIVARO	JUKUN	KAZAK	KURTATCHI	KWAKIUTL
LAU	LESU	MAORI	MASAI	MURNGIN	NUER	NYAKYUSA	ORAON	PAPAGO	RIFFIANS
SAMOANS	SANPOIL	SIRIONO	TALLENSI	THONGA	TIMBIRA	TIV	TROBRIAND	VENDA	WARRAU
YAKO	YAPESE								

15 IN RIGHT COLUMN

ALORESE	ARAUCANIANS	AYMARA	CHUKCHEE	COPR ESKIMO	IFUGAO	JAPANESE	KACHIN	LAKHER	LAMBA
LEPCHA	MIAO	ONTONG-JAVA	SERBS	TANALA					

343 EXCLUDED BECAUSE UNASCERTAINED

5	LEAN MORE TOWARD BEING THOSE LOCATED OUTSIDE OF EAST EURASIA (330)	0.93 OF 42	5	LEAN LESS TOWARD BEING THOSE LOCATED OUTSIDE OF EAST EURASIA (330)	0.53 OF 15		3 7 39 8 XSQ= 9.36 PHI= -0.405 XP = 0.0022
16	DRIFT LESS TOWARD BEING THOSE WHERE THE LATITUDE IS TEN DEGREES OR GREATER (277)	0.57 OF 42	16	DRIFT MORE TOWARD BEING THOSE WHERE THE LATITUDE IS TEN DEGREES OR GREATER (277)	0.87 OF 15		24 13 18 2 XSQ= 3.03 PHI= -0.231 XP = 0.0816
53	DRIFT TOWARD BEING THOSE WHERE FOOD PRODUCTION IS BY SIMPLE AGRICULTURE OR INCIPIENT FOOD PRODUCTION, RATHER THAN BY INTENSIVE AGRICULTURE (147)	0.71 OF 28	53	DRIFT TOWARD BEING THOSE WHERE FOOD PRODUCTION IS BY INTENSIVE AGRICULTURE, RATHER THAN BY SIMPLE AGRICULTURE OR INCIPIENT FOOD PRODUCTION (91)	0.62 OF 13		8 8 20 5 XSQ= 2.79 PHI= -0.261 XP = 0.0950
71	TILT TOWARD BEING THOSE WHERE METAL WORKING IS ABSENT (153)	0.66 OF 35	71	TILT TOWARD BEING THOSE WHERE METAL WORKING IS PRESENT (98)	0.77 OF 13		12 10 23 3 XSQ= 5.33 PHI= -0.333 XP = 0.0210

106	DRIFT TOWARD BEING THOSE WHERE CLASS STRATIFICATION, IF PRESENT, IS BASED ON SOMETHING OTHER THAN WEALTH (126)	0.81 OF 21	106	DRIFT TOWARD BEING THOSE WHERE CLASS STRATIFICATION, IF PRESENT, IS BASED ON WEALTH (77)	0.58 OF 12	4 7 17 5 XSQ= 3.68 PHI= -0.334 EP = 0.0518
108	TILT TOWARD BEING THOSE WHERE CLASS STRATIFICATION, IF PRESENT, IS BASED ON A HEREDITARY ARISTOCRACY (74)	0.67 OF 21	108	TILT TOWARD BEING THOSE WHERE CLASS STRATIFICATION, IF PRESENT, IS BASED ON SOMETHING OTHER THAN A HEREDITARY ARISTOCRACY (129)	0.75 OF 12	14 3 7 9 XSQ= 3.77 PHI= 0.338 EP = 0.0324
184	TILT LESS TOWARD BEING THOSE WHERE THE LARGEST NON-COGNATIC KIN GROUP IS SMALLER THAN A PHRATRY, I. E. A SIB OR LINEAGE (175)	0.56 OF 25	184	IN ALL CASES ARE THOSE WHERE THE LARGEST NON-COGNATIC KIN GROUP IS SMALLER THAN A PHRATRY, I. E. A SIB OR LINEAGE (175)	1.00 OF 10	11 0 14 10 XSQ= 4.54 PHI= 0.360 EP = 0.0146
242	DRIFT MORE TOWARD BEING THOSE WHERE MARRIAGE IS COMMONLY OR OCCASIONALLY POLYGYNOUS, RATHER THAN MONOGAMOUS (314)	0.90 OF 42	242	DRIFT LESS TOWARD BEING THOSE WHERE MARRIAGE IS COMMONLY OR OCCASIONALLY POLYGYNOUS, RATHER THAN MONOGAMOUS (314)	0.67 OF 15	38 10 4 5 XSQ= 3.09 PHI= 0.233 XP = 0.0787
284	DRIFT TOWARD BEING THOSE WHERE CONTRACEPTION IS PRACTICED (10) CSF	0.80 OF 10	284	IN ALL CASES ARE THOSE WHERE CONTRACEPTION IS NOT PRACTICED (7) CSF	1.00 OF 2	8 0 2 2 XSQ= 1.88 PHI= 0.395 EP = 0.0909
299	TILT TOWARD BEING THOSE WHERE THE POST-PARTUM SEX TABOO LASTS LONGER THAN ONE YEAR (35)	0.50 OF 28	299	IN ALL CASES ARE THOSE WHERE THE POST-PARTUM SEX TABOO LASTS ONE YEAR OR LESS (89)	1.00 OF 6	14 0 14 6 XSQ= 3.24 PHI= 0.309 EP = 0.0311
316	TEND TO BE THOSE WHERE EXCLUSIVE MOTHER-SON SLEEPING ARRANGEMENTS LAST ONE YEAR OR LONGER (19) W-K-A	0.71 OF 24	316	IN ALL CASES ARE THOSE WHERE EXCLUSIVE MOTHER-SON SLEEPING ARRANGEMENTS LAST LESS THAN ONE YEAR (25) W-K-A	1.00 OF 10	17 0 7 10 XSQ= 11.47 PHI= 0.581 EP = 0.0003
317	DRIFT TOWARD BEING THOSE WHERE DISPLAY OF AFFECTION TOWARD THE INFANT IS HIGH (39) B-B-C	0.67 OF 24	317	DRIFT TOWARD BEING THOSE WHERE DISPLAY OF AFFECTION TOWARD THE INFANT IS LOW (29) B-B-C	0.71 OF 7	16 2 8 5 XSQ= 1.85 PHI= 0.245 EP = 0.0994
370	TILT TOWARD BEING THOSE WHERE THE SEGREGATION OF ADOLESCENT BOYS IS COMPLETE OR PARTIAL (95)	0.59 OF 34	370	TILT TOWARD BEING THOSE WHERE THE SEGREGATION OF ADOLESCENT BOYS IS ABSENT (148)	0.79 OF 14	20 3 14 11 XSQ= 4.16 PHI= 0.294 XP = 0.0414

372	LEAN TCWARD BEING THOSE WHERE MALE INITIATICN RITES ARE PRESENT (48) ASA	0.56 OF 27	372	IN ALL CASES ARE THOSE WHERE MALE INITIATION RITES ARE ABSENT (63) ASA	1.00 OF 10	15 0 12 10 XSQ= 7.18 PHI= 0.441 EP = 0.0022
373	LEAN TCWARD BEING THCSE WHERE MALE INITIATICN CEREMONIES AT PUBERTY ARE PRESENT (17) W-K-A	0.58 OF 24	373	IN ALL CASES ARE THOSE WHERE MALE INITIATION CEREMONIES AT PUBERTY ARE ABSENT (27) W-K-A	1.00 OF 10	14 0 10 10 XSQ= 7.65 PHI= 0.474 EP = 0.0017
382	TILT TCWARD BEING THOSE WHERE FEMALE INITIATICN RITES ARE PRESENT (38) JKB	0.65 OF 20	382	TILT TOWARD BEING THOSE WHERE FEMALE INITIATION RITES ARE ABSENT (27) JKB	0.88 OF 8	13 1 7 7 XSQ= 4.38 PHI= 0.395 EP = 0.0329
441	TILT TCWARD BEING THCSE WHERE FEAR OF HUMAN BEINGS IS HIGH (29) W-C	0.61 OF 23	441	TILT TOWARD BEING THOSE WHERE FEAR OF HUMAN BEINGS IS LOW (32) W-C	0.88 OF 8	14 1 9 7 XSQ= 3.79 PHI= 0.350 EP = 0.0373
449	TILT TCWARD BEING THOSE WHERE THE CBSERVATICN CF FCOD TABOOS IS HIGH, RATHER THAN MEDIUM CR LCW (25) JRL	0.70 OF 20	449	TILT TOWARD BEING THOSE WHERE THE OBSERVATICN OF FCOD TABCCS IS MEDIUM OR LOW, RATHER THAN HIGH (61) JRL	0.88 OF 8	14 1 6 7 XSQ= 5.46 PHI= 0.442 EP = 0.0108

370 CULTURES
WHERE THE SEGREGATION OF ACOLESCENT BOYS
IS CCMPLETE CR PARTIAL (95)

370 CULTURES
WHERE THE SEGREGATICN OF ADCLESCENT BOYS
IS ABSENT (148)

BACKGROUND ON PAGE 150

BOTH SUBJECT AND PREDICATE

95 IN LEFT CCLUMN

ABCR	ANDAMANESE	ARANCA	ASHANTI	AZANDE	BABWA	BARI	BEMBA	BHUIYA	BOZO
BUNLAP	CALLINAGC	CAMAYURA	CHERKESS	DIERI	DILLING	ELLICE	ENGA	EYAK	FON
FUTAJALCNKE	GANDA	GARC	GISU	GOND	GURE	HAIDA	HERERO	IFUGAO	ILA
INGASSANA	KAPAUKU	KARIERA	KATAB	KAZAK	KERAKI	KERALA	KHASI	KIKUYU	KISSI
KUBA	KUNG	KURTATCHI	LAKHER	LAMET	LANGO	LAU	LESU	LHOTA NAGA	LUO
MANUS	MASAI	MAYA	MBUNCU	MENDE	MONGO	MOSSI	MCTA	MUNCURUCU	MURNGIN
NAMA	NANDI	NDEMBU	NUER	NUNIVAK	NUPE	NYAKYUSA	ORACN	PAIWAN	PAWNEE
PURARI	PURUM	SAGACA	SENIANG	SHERENTE	SHILLUK	SOMALI	SWAZI	TANALA	TAPIRAPE
TENDA	THCNGA	TIMBIRA	TIWI	TOKELAU	TROBRIAND	TRUKESE	TSHIMSHIAN	TUCUNA	ULAWANS
VENDA	WANTOAT	WCGEC	YAPESE	YOMBE					

148 IN RIGHT CCLUMN

AINU	ALBANIANS	ALCRESE	AMBA	AMERICANS	APINAYE	ARAUCANIANS	ATSUGEWI	AYMARA	BAMBARA
BARABRA	BASSERI	BHIL	BIRIFOR	BLACK CARIB	BOERS	BRAZILIANS	BULGARIANS	BURUSHO	CAMBODIANS
CARIB	CAYAPA	CHENCHU	CHEROKEE	CHEYENNE	CHIR-APACHE	CHOCO	CHCROTI	CHORTI	CHUKCHEE
COCHITI	CCCRG	COPR ESKIMO	CREE	CUNA	CZECHS	DELAWARE	DIEGUENC	DUTCH	EGYPTIANS
FANG	FCX	GILYAK	GUAHIBO	HANO	HANUNOO	HASINAI	HAZARA	HUICHOL	HUTSUL
IBAN	INCA	IRISH	JAPANESE	JAVANESE	JEMEZ	JIVARO	KABYLE	KACHIN	KOHISTANI
KOL	KOREANS	KCRYAK	KUTENAI	LEPCHA	LOLO	MALAYS	MAM	MAMBILA	MANDAN
MANGAIANS	MARGI	MARICOPA	MARQUESANS	MARSHALLESE	MATACO	MATAKAM	MIAC	MIN CHINESE	MINCHIA
MISKITC	MNCNG GAR	MCNGUCR	MZAB	NAMBICUARA	NAVAHO	NICOBARESE	NURI	NYORO	OJIBWA
OKINAWANS	CMAHA	CNTCNG-JAVA	PALAUANS	PAPAGO	PARAUJANO	PUKAPUKA	RIFFIANS	ROMANS	RUNDI
RWALA	SAMCANS	SANPCIL	SANTAL	SARSI	SELUNG	SEMANG	SERBS	SHLUH	SINHALESE
SIRICNC	SUBANUN	SYRIANS	TAGBANUA	TALAMANCA	TALLENSI	TACS	TAREUMIUT	TEHUELCHE	TENETEHARA
TENINC	TERA	TERENA	THAI	TIKOPIA	TIV	TODA	TCLCWA	TORAJA	TOTONAC
TRISTAN	TUCANC	TUNEBO	TWANA	VEDDA	WALLOONS	WARRAU	WASHO	WICHITA	WITOTO
WOLEAIANS	WCLCF	YAGUA	YAKUT	YORUBA	YUKAGHIR	YUKI	ZUNI		

157 EXCLUCED BECAUSE UNASCERTAINEC

3 TEND LESS TO BE THCSE LCCATED CUTSIDE CF AFRICA (320) — 0.59 OF 95

3 TEND MORE TO BE THOSE LOCATED OUTSIDE OF AFRICA (320) — 0.92 OF 148

39	12
56	136

XSQ= 35.91
PHI= 0.384
XP = 0.

4	LEAN MORE TOWARD BEING THOSE LOCATED OUTSIDE OF THE CIRCUM-MEDITERRANEAN (355)	0.98 OF 95	4	LEAN LESS TOWARD BEING THOSE LOCATED OUTSIDE OF THE CIRCUM-MEDITERRANEAN (355)	0.84 OF 148	2 23 93 125 XSQ= 9.91 PHI= -0.202 XP = 0.0016
6	TEND LESS TO BE THOSE LOCATED OUTSIDE OF THE INSULAR PACIFIC (330)	0.72 OF 95	6	TEND MORE TO BE THOSE LOCATED OUTSIDE OF THE INSULAR PACIFIC (330)	0.89 OF 148	27 16 68 132 XSQ= 11.14 PHI= 0.214 XP = 0.0008
8	TEND MORE TO BE THOSE LOCATED OUTSIDE OF NORTH AMERICA (330)	0.95 OF 95	8	TEND LESS TO BE THOSE LOCATED OUTSIDE OF NORTH AMERICA (330)	0.78 OF 148	5 33 90 115 XSQ= 11.47 PHI= -0.217 XP = 0.0007
9	TILT MORE TOWARD BEING THOSE LOCATED OUTSIDE OF SOUTH AMERICA (335)	0.92 OF 95	9	TILT LESS TOWARD BEING THOSE LOCATED OUTSIDE OF SOUTH AMERICA (335)	0.81 OF 148	8 28 87 120 XSQ= 4.26 PHI= -0.132 XP = 0.0391
15	TEND TO BE THOSE WHERE THE LATITUDE IS LESS THAN TWENTY DEGREES (217)	0.71 OF 95	15	TEND TO BE THOSE WHERE THE LATITUDE IS TWENTY DEGREES OR GREATER (183)	0.56 OF 148	28 83 67 65 XSQ= 15.45 PHI= -0.252 XP = 0.0001
33	DRIFT MORE TOWARD BEING THOSE WHERE THE NATURAL ENVIRONMENT IS OTHER THAN 'VERY HARSH,' I.E., DESERT, DESERT GRASSES AND SHRUBS, TUNDRA, OR HIGH PLATEAU STEPPE (341) FWM	0.91 OF 95	33	DRIFT LESS TOWARD BEING THOSE WHERE THE NATURAL ENVIRONMENT IS OTHER THAN 'VERY HARSH,' I.E., DESERT, DESERT GRASSES AND SHRUBS, TUNDRA, OR HIGH PLATEAU STEPPE (341) FWM	0.81 OF 148	9 28 86 120 XSQ= 3.30 PHI= -0.117 XP = 0.0693
36	TILT MORE TOWARD BEING THOSE WHERE THE NATURAL ENVIRONMENT IS OTHER THAN 'VERY HARSH,' OR SUB-TROPICAL BUSH, OR TEMPERATE GRASSLAND (292) FWM	0.84 OF 95	36	TILT LESS TOWARD BEING THOSE WHERE THE NATURAL ENVIRONMENT IS OTHER THAN 'VERY HARSH,' OR SUB-TROPICAL BUSH, OR TEMPERATE GRASSLAND (292) FWM	0.72 OF 148	15 42 80 106 XSQ= 4.43 PHI= -0.135 XP = 0.0353
42	TILT TOWARD BEING THOSE WHERE THE NATURAL ENVIRONMENT IS TROPICAL OR SUB-TROPICAL RAIN FOREST, OR MONSOON FOREST (156) FWM	0.53 OF 95	42	TILT TOWARD BEING THOSE WHERE THE NATURAL ENVIRONMENT IS OTHER THAN TROPICAL OR SUB-TROPICAL RAIN FOREST, OR MONSOON FOREST (244) FWM	0.65 OF 148	50 52 45 96 XSQ= 6.57 PHI= 0.164 XP = 0.0104
53	TEND TO BE THOSE WHERE FOOD PRODUCTION IS BY SIMPLE AGRICULTURE OR INCIPIENT FOOD PRODUCTION, RATHER THAN BY INTENSIVE AGRICULTURE (147)	0.77 OF 71	53	TEND TO BE THOSE WHERE FOOD PRODUCTION IS BY INTENSIVE AGRICULTURE, RATHER THAN BY SIMPLE AGRICULTURE OR INCIPIENT FOOD PRODUCTION (91)	0.52 OF 106	16 55 55 51 XSQ= 14.05 PHI= -0.282 XP = 0.0002

55	TEND TO BE THOSE WHERE FOOD PRODUCTION IS BY SIMPLE AGRICULTURE, RATHER THAN BY INTENSIVE AGRICULTURE (101)	0.75 OF 63	55	TEND TO BE THOSE WHERE FOOD PRODUCTION IS BY INTENSIVE AGRICULTURE, RATHER THAN BY SIMPLE AGRICULTURE (91)	0.60 OF 91	16 55 47 36 XSQ= 17.01 PHI= -0.332 XP = 0.0000
63	TILT LESS TOWARD BEING THOSE WHERE HUSBANDRY, IF PRESENT, IS PRINCIPALLY IN THE FORM OF BOVINE, EQUINE, CAMEL-LIKE, OR DEER-LIKE ANIMALS, RATHER THAN PIGS, SHEEP, OR GOATS (152)	0.55 OF 73	63	TILT MORE TOWARD BEING THOSE WHERE HUSBANDRY, IF PRESENT, IS PRINCIPALLY IN THE FORM OF BOVINE, EQUINE, CAMEL-LIKE, OR DEER-LIKE ANIMALS, RATHER THAN PIGS, SHEEP, OR GOATS (152)	0.73 OF 107	40 78 33 29 XSQ= 5.52 PHI= -0.175 XP = 0.0188
73	TILT TOWARD BEING THOSE WHERE WEAVING IS ABSENT (130)	0.60 OF 75	73	TILT TOWARD BEING THOSE WHERE WEAVING IS PRESENT (118)	0.57 OF 110	30 63 45 47 XSQ= 4.65 PHI= -0.159 XP = 0.0310
74	TILT LESS TOWARD BEING THOSE WHERE POTTERY IS PRESENT (145)	0.52 OF 73	74	TILT MORE TOWARD BEING THOSE WHERE POTTERY IS PRESENT (145)	0.70 OF 103	38 72 35 31 XSQ= 5.07 PHI= -0.170 XP = 0.0243
77	IN ALL CASES ARE THOSE WHERE THE WRITING SYSTEM IS MNEMONIC OR ABSENT, RATHER THAN BEING ALPHABETIC-OR-PHONETIC (39) JMH	1.00 OF 12	77	DRIFT LESS TOWARD BEING THOSE WHERE THE WRITING SYSTEM IS MNEMONIC OR ABSENT, RATHER THAN BEING ALPHABETIC-OR-PHONETIC (39) JMH	0.67 OF 30	0 10 12 20 XSQ= 3.57 PHI= -0.292 XP = 0.0587
79	LEAN MORE TOWARD BEING THOSE WHERE NO CITY IS PRESENT (201)	0.98 OF 66	79	LEAN LESS TOWARD BEING THOSE WHERE NO CITY IS PRESENT (201)	0.81 OF 107	1 20 65 87 XSQ= 9.74 PHI= -0.237 XP = 0.0018
80	TILT MORE TOWARD BEING THOSE WHERE NO CITY OR TOWN IS PRESENT (185)	0.91 OF 66	80	TILT LESS TOWARD BEING THOSE WHERE NO CITY OR TOWN IS PRESENT (185)	0.76 OF 107	6 26 60 81 XSQ= 5.29 PHI= -0.175 XP = 0.0214
81	TILT MORE TOWARD BEING THOSE WHERE NO CITY OR TOWN IS PRESENT, AND THE AVERAGE COMMUNITY SIZE IS SMALLER THAN 200 (135)	0.71 OF 66	81	TILT LESS TOWARD BEING THOSE WHERE NO CITY OR TOWN IS PRESENT, AND THE AVERAGE COMMUNITY SIZE IS SMALLER THAN 200 (135)	0.51 OF 107	19 52 47 55 XSQ= 5.83 PHI= -0.184 XP = 0.0158
88	LEAN TOWARD BEING THOSE WHERE, IF A HEADMANSHIP IS PRESENT, SUCCESSION IS HEREDITARY (165)	0.73 OF 67	88	LEAN TOWARD BEING THOSE WHERE, IF A HEADMANSHIP IS PRESENT, SUCCESSION IS NON-HEREDITARY (106)	0.50 OF 100	18 50 49 50 XSQ= 7.96 PHI= -0.218 XP = 0.0048

90	TILT LESS TOWARD BEING THOSE 0.69 OF 49 WHERE, IF A HEREDITARY HEADMANSHIP IS PRESENT, SUCCESSION IS PATRILINEAL, RATHER THAN MATRILINEAL (127)	90	TILT MORE TOWARD BEING THOSE 0.88 OF 90 WHERE, IF A HEREDITARY HEADMANSHIP IS PRESENT, SUCCESSION IS PATRILINEAL, RATHER THAN MATRILINEAL (127)	34 44 15 6 XSQ= 4.08 PHI= -0.203 XP = 0.0435
94	TILT MORE TOWARD BEING THOSE 0.96 OF 95 WHERE THE HIERARCHY OF NATIONAL JURISDICTION HAS TWO, ONE, OR NO LEVELS (296) GES,EA	94	TILT LESS TOWARD BEING THOSE 0.87 OF 145 WHERE THE HIERARCHY OF NATIONAL JURISDICTION HAS TWO, ONE, OR NO LEVELS (296) GES,EA	4 19 91 126 XSQ= 4.26 PHI= -0.133 XP = 0.0390
107	LEAN MORE TOWARD BEING THOSE 0.89 OF 55 WHERE CLASS STRATIFICATION, IF PRESENT, IS BASED ON SOMETHING OTHER THAN OCCUPATIONAL STATUS (160)	107	LEAN LESS TOWARD BEING THOSE 0.66 OF 73 WHERE CLASS STRATIFICATION, IF PRESENT, IS BASED ON SOMETHING OTHER THAN OCCUPATIONAL STATUS (160)	6 25 49 48 XSQ= 8.08 PHI= -0.251 XP = 0.0045
108	TILT LESS TOWARD BEING THOSE 0.56 OF 55 WHERE CLASS STRATIFICATION, IF PRESENT, IS BASED ON SOMETHING OTHER THAN A HEREDITARY ARISTOCRACY (129)	108	TILT MORE TOWARD BEING THOSE 0.77 OF 73 WHERE CLASS STRATIFICATION, IF PRESENT, IS BASED ON SOMETHING OTHER THAN A HEREDITARY ARISTOCRACY (129)	24 17 31 56 XSQ= 5.07 PHI= 0.199 XP = 0.0244
128	LEAN TOWARD BEING THOSE 0.73 OF 26 WHERE, IF SUBSISTENCE IS PRIMARILY BY AGRICULTURE, THE WORK IS MAINLY DONE BY FEMALES (37)	128	LEAN TOWARD BEING THOSE 0.66 OF 38 WHERE, IF SUBSISTENCE IS PRIMARILY BY AGRICULTURE, THE WORK IS MAINLY DONE BY MALES (40)	7 25 19 13 XSQ= 7.84 PHI= -0.350 XP = 0.0051
139	DRIFT TOWARD BEING THOSE 0.80 OF 15 WHERE SUPERORDINATE PUNISHMENT IS ABSENT (25) BBW	139	DRIFT TOWARD BEING THOSE 0.53 OF 17 WHERE SUPERORDINATE PUNISHMENT IS PRESENT (15) BBW	3 9 12 8 XSQ= 2.42 PHI= -0.275 EP = 0.0759
176	TEND TO BE THOSE 0.62 OF 94 WHERE THE COMMUNITY IS A CLAN-COMMUNITY OR A COMMUNITY STRUCTURED OR SEGMENTED ON A CLAN BASIS (169)	176	TEND TO BE THOSE 0.63 OF 145 WHERE THE COMMUNITY IS OTHER THAN A CLAN-COMMUNITY OR A COMMUNITY STRUCTURED OR SEGMENTED ON A CLAN BASIS (213)	58 53 36 92 XSQ= 13.51 PHI= 0.238 XP = 0.0002
177	LEAN LESS TOWARD BEING THOSE 0.69 OF 94 WHERE THE COMMUNITY IS OTHER THAN A SINGLE CLAN-COMMUNITY AND EXOGAMOUS (305)	177	LEAN MORE TOWARD BEING THOSE 0.86 OF 145 WHERE THE COMMUNITY IS OTHER THAN A SINGLE CLAN-COMMUNITY AND EXOGAMOUS (305)	29 21 65 124 XSQ= 8.27 PHI= 0.186 XP = 0.0040
180	DRIFT LESS TOWARD BEING THOSE 0.60 OF 94 WHERE THE COMMUNITY IS COMMONLY NON-EXOGAMOUS, RATHER THAN EXOGAMOUS (258)	180	DRIFT MORE TOWARD BEING THOSE 0.72 OF 145 WHERE THE COMMUNITY IS COMMONLY NON-EXOGAMOUS, RATHER THAN EXOGAMOUS (258)	38 40 56 105 XSQ= 3.71 PHI= 0.125 XP = 0.0540

181	TILT MORE TOWARD BEING THOSE 0.95 OF 94 WHERE THE COMMUNITY IS OTHER THAN A DEME (337)	181	TILT LESS TOWARD BEING THOSE 0.84 OF 145 WHERE THE COMMUNITY IS OTHER THAN A DEME (337)	5 23 89 122 XSQ= 5.15 PHI= -0.147 XP = 0.0232
183	LEAN LESS TOWARD BEING THOSE 0.77 OF 83 WHERE THE LARGEST NON-COGNATIC KIN GROUP IS SMALLER THAN A MOEITY, I. E., A PHRATRY OR SIB OR LINEAGE (218)	183	LEAN MORE TOWARD BEING THOSE 0.94 OF 77 WHERE THE LARGEST NON-COGNATIC KIN GROUP IS SMALLER THAN A MOEITY, I. E., A PHRATRY OR SIB OR LINEAGE (218)	19 5 64 72 XSQ= 7.19 PHI= 0.212 XP = 0.0073
184	TILT LESS TOWARD BEING THOSE 0.61 OF 83 WHERE THE LARGEST NON-COGNATIC KIN GROUP IS SMALLER THAN A PHRATRY, I. E. A SIB OR LINEAGE (175)	184	TILT MORE TOWARD BEING THOSE 0.78 OF 77 WHERE THE LARGEST NON-COGNATIC KIN GROUP IS SMALLER THAN A PHRATRY, I. E. A SIB OR LINEAGE (175)	32 17 51 60 XSQ= 4.36 PHI= 0.165 XP = 0.0368
186	LEAN LESS TOWARD BEING THOSE 0.52 OF 95 WHERE THE KIN GROUP IS OTHER THAN EXCLUSIVELY PATRILINEAL (250)	186	LEAN MORE TOWARD BEING THOSE 0.70 OF 148 WHERE THE KIN GROUP IS OTHER THAN EXCLUSIVELY PATRILINEAL (250)	46 45 49 103 XSQ= 7.27 PHI= 0.173 XP = 0.0070
187	TILT LESS TOWARD BEING THOSE 0.79 OF 95 WHERE THE KIN GROUP IS OTHER THAN EXCLUSIVELY MATRILINEAL (344)	187	TILT MORE TOWARD BEING THOSE 0.90 OF 147 WHERE THE KIN GROUP IS OTHER THAN EXCLUSIVELY MATRILINEAL (344)	20 14 75 133 XSQ= 5.43 PHI= 0.150 XP = 0.0198
188	TEND MORE TO BE THOSE 0.87 OF 95 WHERE THE KIN GROUP IS OTHER THAN EXCLUSIVELY COGNATIC (252)	188	TEND LESS TO BE THOSE 0.52 OF 148 WHERE THE KIN GROUP IS OTHER THAN EXCLUSIVELY COGNATIC (252)	12 71 83 77 XSQ= 30.58 PHI= -0.355 XP = 0.
192	TEND MORE TO BE THOSE 0.95 OF 95 OTHER THAN WHERE THE ONLY KIN GROUP PRESENT IS A KINDRED OR ELSE BILATERAL DESCENT IS INFERRED (289)	192	TEND LESS TO BE THOSE 0.58 OF 148 OTHER THAN WHERE THE ONLY KIN GROUP PRESENT IS A KINDRED OR ELSE BILATERAL DESCENT IS INFERRED (289)	5 62 90 86 XSQ= 37.06 PHI= -0.391 XP = 0.
197	TILT MORE TOWARD BEING THOSE 0.94 OF 53 WHERE RULES FOR THE INHERITANCE OF REAL PROPERTY, IF PRESENT, FAVOR EITHER THE MALE HEIR OR LINE, OR THE FEMALE HEIR OR LINE (165)	197	TILT LESS TOWARD BEING THOSE 0.80 OF 74 WHERE RULES FOR THE INHERITANCE OF REAL PROPERTY, IF PRESENT, FAVOR EITHER THE MALE HEIR OR LINE, OR THE FEMALE HEIR OR LINE (165)	50 59 3 15 XSQ= 4.28 PHI= 0.184 XP = 0.0385
201	TILT MORE TOWARD BEING THOSE 0.92 OF 95 WHERE MARITAL RESIDENCE IS NON-OPTIONAL, RATHER THAN AMBILOCAL OR NEOLOCAL (334)	201	TILT LESS TOWARD BEING THOSE 0.80 OF 148 WHERE MARITAL RESIDENCE IS NON-OPTIONAL, RATHER THAN AMBILOCAL OR NEOLOCAL (334)	87 118 8 30 XSQ= 5.29 PHI= 0.148 XP = 0.0214

204	LEAN MORE TOWARD BEING THOSE 0.91 OF 85 WHERE MARITAL RESIDENCE IS PATRILOCAL, VIRILOCAL, OR AVUNCULOCAL, RATHER THAN AMBILOCAL OR NEOLOCAL (270)	204 LEAN LESS TOWARD BEING THOSE 0.74 OF 117 WHERE MARITAL RESIDENCE IS PATRILOCAL, VIRILOCAL, OR AVUNCULOCAL, RATHER THAN AMBILOCAL OR NEOLOCAL (270)	77 87 8 30 XSQ= 7.46 PHI= 0.192 XP = 0.0063
209	TILT MORE TOWARD BEING THOSE 0.89 OF 87 WHERE MARITAL RESIDENCE IS PATRILOCAL, VIRILOCAL, OR AVUNCULOCAL, RATHER THAN MATRILOCAL OR UXORILOCAL (270)	209 TILT LESS TOWARD BEING THOSE 0.74 OF 118 WHERE MARITAL RESIDENCE IS PATRILOCAL, VIRILOCAL, OR AVUNCULOCAL, RATHER THAN MATRILOCAL OR UXORILOCAL (270)	77 87 10 31 XSQ= 5.94 PHI= 0.170 XP = 0.0148
214	TILT LESS TOWARD BEING THOSE 0.71 OF 45 WHERE FIRST COUSIN MARRIAGE, IF PERMITTED, IS OTHER THAN UNILATERAL (144)	214 TILT MORE TOWARD BEING THOSE 0.90 OF 59 WHERE FIRST COUSIN MARRIAGE, IF PERMITTED, IS OTHER THAN UNILATERAL (144)	13 6 32 53 XSQ= 4.80 PHI= 0.215 XP = 0.0284
234	TEND TO BE THOSE 0.71 OF 78 WHERE THE COUSIN TERMINOLOGY IS OF CROW, OMAHA, OR IROQUOIS TYPE, RATHER THAN ESKIMO OR HAWAIIAN TYPE (152)	234 TEND TO BE THOSE 0.68 OF 121 WHERE THE COUSIN TERMINOLOGY IS OF ESKIMO OR HAWAIIAN TYPE, RATHER THAN CROW, OMAHA, OR IROQUOIS TYPE (170)	55 39 23 82 XSQ= 26.37 PHI= 0.364 XP = 0.0000
236	TILT TOWARD BEING THOSE 0.51 OF 95 WHERE THE FAMILY IS OF AN INDEPENDENT TYPE, RATHER THAN AN EXTENDED TYPE (185)	236 TILT TOWARD BEING THOSE 0.63 OF 147 WHERE THE FAMILY IS OF AN EXTENDED TYPE, RATHER THAN AN INDEPENDENT TYPE (213)	47 93 48 54 XSQ= 3.95 PHI= -0.128 XP = 0.0468
242	LEAN MORE TOWARD BEING THOSE 0.88 OF 95 WHERE MARRIAGE IS COMMONLY OR OCCASIONALLY POLYGYNOUS, RATHER THAN MONOGAMOUS (314)	242 LEAN LESS TOWARD BEING THOSE 0.72 OF 145 WHERE MARRIAGE IS COMMONLY OR OCCASIONALLY POLYGYNOUS, RATHER THAN MONOGAMOUS (314)	84 105 11 40 XSQ= 7.86 PHI= 0.181 XP = 0.0051
243	DRIFT TOWARD BEING THOSE 0.60 OF 25 WHERE POLYGYNY, IF PRESENT, HAS A HIGH INCIDENCE (24) W-C,S	243 DRIFT TOWARD BEING THOSE 0.68 OF 25 WHERE POLYGYNY, IF PRESENT, HAS A LOW INCIDENCE (36) W-D,S	15 8 10 17 XSQ= 2.90 PHI= 0.241 XP = 0.0887
256	DRIFT TOWARD BEING THOSE 0.50 OF 12 WHERE GRANDPARENT AND GRANDCHILD ARE NOT FRIENDLY EQUALS (8) DA	256 DRIFT TOWARD BEING THOSE 0.92 OF 12 WHERE GRANDPARENT AND GRANDCHILD ARE FRIENDLY EQUALS (25) DA	6 11 6 1 XSQ= 3.23 PHI= -0.367 EP = 0.0686
259	TILT TOWARD BEING THOSE 0.78 OF 18 WHERE THE SEVERITY OF MOTHER-IN-LAW AVOIDANCE IS HIGH (26) WNS	259 TILT TOWARD BEING THOSE 0.61 OF 23 WHERE THE SEVERITY OF MOTHER-IN-LAW AVOIDANCE IS LOW (20) WNS	14 9 4 14 XSQ= 4.66 PHI= 0.337 XP = 0.0310

262	LEAN MORE TOWARD BEING THOSE WHERE WIVES ARE OBTAINED BY MEANS INVOLVING THE PRESENCE OF SOME CONSIDERATION (305)	0.88 OF 95	262	LEAN LESS TOWARD BEING THOSE WHERE WIVES ARE OBTAINED BY MEANS INVOLVING THE PRESENCE OF SOME CONSIDERATION (305)	0.72 OF 148	84 106 11 42 XSQ= 8.62 PHI= 0.188 XP = 0.0033
263	TEND TO BE THOSE WHERE WIVES ARE OBTAINED BY RELATIVELY DIFFICULT MEANS, NAMELY BY BRIDE-PRICE, BRIDE-SERVICE, OR EXCHANGING A FEMALE RELATIVE (233)	0.77 OF 95	263	TEND TO BE THOSE WHERE WIVES ARE OBTAINED BY RELATIVELY EASY MEANS, NAMELY BY TOKEN BRIDE-PRICE, GIFT EXCHANGE, ABSENCE OF ANY CONSIDERATION, OR RECEIPT OF DOWRY (162)	0.51 OF 148	73 72 22 76 XSQ= 17.96 PHI= 0.272 XP = 0.0000
277	TILT TOWARD BEING THOSE WHERE THE STATUS OF WOMEN IS NOT STRONGLY INFERIOR OR SUBJECTED (22) LWS	0.90 OF 10	277	TILT TOWARD BEING THOSE WHERE THE STATUS OF WOMEN IS INFERIOR OR SUBJECTED (14) LWS	0.50 OF 18	1 9 9 9 XSQ= 2.91 PHI= -0.322 EP = 0.0484
280	TILT TOWARD BEING THOSE WHERE THE COMPOSITE FERTILITY LEVEL IS LOW (12) MN	0.75 OF 12	280	TILT TOWARD BEING THOSE WHERE THE COMPOSITE FERTILITY LEVEL IS HIGH (13) MN	0.88 OF 8	3 7 9 1 XSQ= 5.21 PHI= -0.510 EP = 0.0198
304	TILT TOWARD BEING THOSE WHERE THE EARLY ANAL SATISFACTION POTENTIAL IS LOW (22) W-C	0.83 OF 12	304	TILT TOWARD BEING THOSE WHERE THE EARLY ANAL SATISFACTION POTENTIAL IS HIGH (19) W-C	0.62 OF 21	2 13 10 8 XSQ= 4.61 PHI= -0.374 EP = 0.0272
314	TEND TO BE THOSE WHERE THE INCIDENCE OF MOTHER-CHILD HOUSEHOLDS IS HIGH (19) W-D,S	0.52 OF 27	314	TEND TO BE THOSE WHERE THE INCIDENCE OF MOTHER-CHILD HOUSEHOLDS IS LOW (61) W-D,S	0.95 OF 37	14 2 13 35 XSQ= 15.57 PHI= 0.493 XP = 0.0001
316	LEAN TOWARD BEING THOSE WHERE EXCLUSIVE MOTHER-SON SLEEPING ARRANGEMENTS LAST ONE YEAR OR LONGER (19) W-K-A	0.73 OF 15	316	LEAN TOWARD BEING THOSE WHERE EXCLUSIVE MOTHER-SON SLEEPING ARRANGEMENTS LAST LESS THAN ONE YEAR (25) W-K-A	0.73 OF 22	11 6 4 16 XSQ= 5.88 PHI= 0.399 EP = 0.0084
369	TILT MORE TOWARD BEING THOSE WHERE DISSOCIATION OF THE SEXES AT ADOLESCENCE, OR CUSTOMS OF INITIATION AT ADOLESCENCE, ARE PRESENT (42) JKH	0.87 OF 23	369	TILT LESS TOWARD BEING THOSE WHERE DISSOCIATION OF THE SEXES AT ADOLESCENCE, OR CUSTOMS OF INITIATION AT ADOLESCENCE, ARE PRESENT (42) JKH	0.56 OF 25	20 14 3 11 XSQ= 4.16 PHI= 0.294 XP = 0.0414
372	LEAN TOWARD BEING THOSE WHERE MALE INITIATION RITES ARE PRESENT (48) ASA	0.63 OF 46	372	LEAN TOWARD BEING THOSE WHERE MALE INITIATION RITES ARE ABSENT (63) ASA	0.69 OF 42	29 13 17 29 XSQ= 7.82 PHI= 0.298 XP = 0.0052

377	LEAN LESS TOWARD BEING THOSE WHERE MALE GENITAL MUTILATION IS ABSENT (242)	0.65 OF 93	377	LEAN MORE TOWARD BEING THOSE WHERE MALE GENITAL MUTILATION IS ABSENT (242)	0.83 OF 144	 XSQ= PHI= XP =	33 25 60 119 9.08 0.196 0.0026
391	TILT TOWARD BEING THOSE WHERE PREMARITAL SEX RELATIONS ARE PUNISHED ONLY IF PREGNANCY RESULTS, OR FREELY PERMITTED (90) JTW,EA	0.65 OF 46	391	TILT TOWARD BEING THOSE WHERE PREMARITAL SEX RELATIONS ARE STRONGLY PUNISHED AND IN FACT RARE, OR WEAKLY PUNISHED AND IN FACT NOT RARE (89) JTW,EA	0.57 OF 89	 XSQ= PHI= XP =	16 51 30 38 5.28 -0.198 0.0215
406	DRIFT TOWARD BEING THOSE WHERE EXPLANATIONS OF ILLNESS OF AN AGGRESSION NATURE ARE ABSENT (33) W-C	0.71 OF 17	406	DRIFT TOWARD BEING THOSE WHERE EXPLANATIONS OF ILLNESS OF AN AGGRESSION NATURE ARE PRESENT (28) W-C	0.61 OF 31	 XSQ= PHI= XP =	5 19 12 12 3.28 -0.261 0.0702
420	TILT TOWARD BEING THOSE WHERE BELLICOSITY IS EXTREME (41) PES	0.68 OF 28	420	TILT TOWARD BEING THOSE WHERE BELLICOSITY IS MODERATE OR NEGLIGIBLE (46) PES	0.66 OF 41	 XSQ= PHI= XP =	19 14 9 27 6.29 0.302 0.0122
427	LEAN TOWARD BEING THOSE WHERE A HIGH GOD, IF PRESENT, IS INACTIVE, RATHER THAN ACTIVE (69) GES,EA	0.62 OF 42	427	LEAN TOWARD BEING THOSE WHERE A HIGH GOD, IF PRESENT, IS ACTIVE, RATHER THAN INACTIVE (87) GES,EA	0.65 OF 75	 XSQ= PHI= XP =	16 49 26 26 7.02 -0.245 0.0080
432	TILT TOWARD BEING THOSE WHERE AN ATTRACTIVE AFTERLIFE IS NOT BELIEVED IN (11) LWS	0.50 OF 12	432	TILT TOWARD BEING THOSE WHERE AN ATTRACTIVE AFTERLIFE IS BELIEVED IN (27) LWS	0.88 OF 17	 XSQ= PHI= EP =	6 15 6 2 3.41 -0.343 0.0382
434	DRIFT TOWARD BEING THOSE WHERE ASCETICISM IN MOURNING BEHAVIOR IS HIGH (37) JFG	0.71 OF 24	434	DRIFT TOWARD BEING THOSE WHERE ASCETICISM IN MOURNING BEHAVIOR IS LOW (30) JFG	0.58 OF 31	 XSQ= PHI= XP =	17 13 7 18 3.47 0.251 0.0627
438	DRIFT TOWARD BEING THOSE WHERE OTHER-WORLDLY FEARS OF GHOSTS OR SPIRITS ARE GREATER THAN THIS-WORLDLY FEARS OF HUMANS OR ANIMALS (27) W-C,JFG	0.80 OF 15	438	DRIFT TOWARD BEING THOSE WHERE THIS-WORLDLY FEARS OF HUMANS OR ANIMALS ARE GREATER THAN OTHER-WORLDLY FEARS OF GHOSTS OR SPIRITS (17) W-C,JFG	0.52 OF 21	 XSQ= PHI= EP =	12 10 3 11 2.62 0.270 0.0833
459	TEND TO BE THOSE WHERE GAMES, IF PRESENT, DO NOT INCLUDE GAMES OF CHANCE (89) R-A-B,EA	0.76 OF 54	459	TEND TO BE THOSE WHERE GAMES, IF PRESENT, INCLUDE GAMES OF CHANCE (82) R-A-B,EA	0.62 OF 77	 XSQ= PHI= XP =	13 48 41 29 17.17 -0.362 0.0000

370/

460	TILT TOWARD BEING THOSE WHERE GAMES, IF PRESENT, ARE LIMITED TO GAMES OF SKILL ONLY (67) R-A-B, EA	0.54 OF 54	460	TILT TOWARD BEING THOSE WHERE GAMES, IF PRESENT, ARE NOT LIMITED TO GAMES OF SKILL ONLY (104) R-A-B, EA	0.70 OF 77	29 23 25 54 XSQ= 6.57 PHI= 0.224 XP = 0.0104

371 CULTURES
WHERE ADOLESCENT BOYS ARE
SEGREGATED AND RESIDE WITH
A GROUP OF PEERS (41)

371 CULTURES
OTHER THAN WHERE ADOLESCENT BOYS ARE
SEGREGATED AND RESIDE WITH
A GROUP OF PEERS (202)

BACKGROUND ON PAGE 150 — SUBJECT ONLY

41 IN LEFT COLUMN

ABOR	ANDAMANESE	BHUIYA	BOZO	BUNLAP	CALLINAGO	ELLICE	GOND	KERAKI	KHASI
KIKUYU	KURTATCHI	LAMET	LANGO	LAU	LESU	LHOTA NAGA	MASAI	MAYA	MENDE
MOSSI	MOTA	MUNDURUCU	MURNGIN	NANDI	NYAKYUSA	ORAON	PURARI	SENIANG	SHERENTE
SOMALI	TAPIRAPE	TENDA	TOKELAU	TROBRIAND	TRUKESE	ULAWANS	VENDA	WANTOAT	WOGEO
YAPESE									

202 IN RIGHT COLUMN

AINU	ALBANIANS	ALORESE	AMBA	AMERICANS	APINAYE	ARANDA	ARAUCANIANS	ASHANTI	ATSUGEWI
AYMARA	AZANDE	BABWA	BAMBARA	BARABRA	BARI	BASSERI	BEMBA	BHIL	BIRIFOR
BLACK CARIB	BOERS	BRAZILIANS	BULGARIANS	BURUSHO	CAMAYURA	CAMBODIANS	CARIB	CAYAPA	CHENCHU
CHERKESS	CHEROKEE	CHEYENNE	CHIR-APACHE	CHOCO	CHOROTI	CHORTI	CHUKCHEE	COCHITI	COORG
COPR ESKIMO	CREE	CUNA	CZECHS	DELAWARE	DIEGUENO	DIERI	DILLING	DUTCH	EGYPTIANS
ENGA	EYAK	FANG	FON	FOX	FUTAJALONKE	GANDA	GARO	GILYAK	GISU
GUAHIBO	GURE	HAIDA	HANO	HANUNOO	HASINAI	HAZARA	HERERO	HUICHOL	HUTSUL
IBAN	IFUGAO	ILA	INCA	INGASSANA	IRISH	JAPANESE	JAVANESE	JEMEZ	JIVARO
KABYLE	KACHIN	KAPAUKU	KARIERA	KATAB	KAZAK	KERALA	KISSI	KOHISTANI	KOL
KOREANS	KORYAK	KUBA	KUNG	KUTENAI	LAKHER	LEPCHA	LOLO	LUO	MALAYS
MAM	MAMBILA	MANDAN	MANGAIANS	MANUS	MARGI	MARICOPA	MARQUESANS	MARSHALLESE	MATACO
MATAKAM	MBUNDU	MIAO	MIN CHINESE	MINCHIA	MISKITO	MNONG GAR	MONGO	MONGUOR	MZAB
NAMA	NAMBICUARA	NAVAHO	NDEMBU	NICOBARESE	NUER	NUNIVAK	NUPE	NURI	NYORO
OJIBWA	OKINAWANS	OMAHA	ONTONG-JAVA	PAIWAN	PALAUANS	PAPAGO	PARAUJANO	PAWNEE	PUKAPUKA
PURUM	RIFFIANS	ROMANS	RUNDI	RWALA	SAGADA	SAMOANS	SANPOIL	SANTAL	SARSI
SELUNG	SEMANG	SERPS	SHILLUK	SHLUH	SINHALESE	SIRIONO	SUBANUN	SWAZI	SYRIANS
TAGBANUA	TALAMANCA	TALLENSI	TANALA	TAOS	TAREUMIUT	TEHUELCHE	TENETEHARA	TENINO	TERA
TERENA	THAI	THONGA	TIKOPIA	TIMBIRA	TIV	TIWI	TODA	TOLOWA	TORAJA
TOTONAC	TRISTAN	TSHIMSHIAN	TUCANO	TUCUNA	TUNEBO	TWANA	VEDDA	WALLOONS	WARRAU
WASHO	WICHITA	WITOTO	WOLEAIANS	WOLOF	YAGUA	YAKUT	YOMBE	YORUBA	YUKAGHIR
YUKI	ZUNI								

157 EXCLUDED BECAUSE UNASCERTAINED

---

6 TEND LESS TO BE THOSE LOCATED OUTSIDE OF THE INSULAR PACIFIC (330) — 0.59 OF 41

6 TEND MORE TO BE THOSE LOCATED OUTSIDE OF THE INSULAR PACIFIC (330) — 0.87 OF 202

17	26
24	176

XSQ= 17.22
PHI= 0.266
XP = 0.0000

```
 8  IN ALL CASES ARE THOSE           1.00 OF  41     8  LEAN LESS TOWARD BEING THOSE   0.81 OF 202        0   38
    LOCATED OUTSIDE OF                                 LOCATED OUTSIDE OF                                41  164
    NORTH AMERICA  (330)                               NORTH AMERICA  (330)                       XSQ=     7.77
                                                                                                  PHI=   -0.179
                                                                                                  XP =   0.0053

14  IN ALL CASES ARE THOSE           1.00 OF  41    14  TEND LESS TO BE THOSE          0.65 OF 202        0   71
    WHERE THE LATITUDE IS                              WHERE THE LATITUDE IS                             41  131
    LESS THAN THIRTY DEGREES  (281)                    LESS THAN THIRTY DEGREES  (281)            XSQ=    18.70
                                                                                                  PHI=   -0.277
                                                                                                  XP =   0.0000

15  TEND TO BE THOSE                 0.80 OF  41    15  TEND TO BE THOSE               0.51 OF 202        8  103
    WHERE THE LATITUDE IS                              WHERE THE LATITUDE IS                             33   99
    LESS THAN TWENTY DEGREES  (217)                    TWENTY DEGREES OR GREATER  (183)           XSQ=    12.37
                                                                                                  PHI=   -0.226
                                                                                                  XP =   0.0004

33  DRIFT MORE TOWARD BEING THOSE  0.95 OF  41      33  DRIFT LESS TOWARD BEING THOSE  0.83 OF 202        2   35
    WHERE THE NATURAL ENVIRONMENT IS                   WHERE THE NATURAL ENVIRONMENT IS                  39  167
    OTHER THAN 'VERY HARSH,' I.E., DESERT,             OTHER THAN 'VERY HARSH,' I.E., DESERT,     XSQ=     3.18
    DESERT GRASSES AND SHRUBS, TUNDRA, OR              DESERT GRASSES AND SHRUBS, TUNDRA, OR      PHI=   -0.114
    HIGH PLATEAU STEPPE  (341) FWM                     HIGH PLATEAU STEPPE  (341) FWM             XP =   0.0744

36  TILT MORE TOWARD BEING THOSE   0.90 OF  41      36  TILT LESS TOWARD BEING THOSE   0.74 OF 202        4   53
    WHERE THE NATURAL ENVIRONMENT IS                   WHERE THE NATURAL ENVIRONMENT IS                  37  149
    OTHER THAN                                         OTHER THAN                                 XSQ=     4.28
    'VERY HARSH,' OR SUB-TROPICAL BUSH, OR             'VERY HARSH,' OR SUB-TROPICAL BUSH, OR     PHI=   -0.133
    TEMPERATE GRASSLAND  (292) FWM                     TEMPERATE GRASSLAND  (292) FWM             XP =   0.0386

42  TEND TO BE THOSE                 0.71 OF  41    42  TEND TO BE THOSE               0.64 OF 202       29   73
    WHERE THE NATURAL ENVIRONMENT IS                   WHERE THE NATURAL ENVIRONMENT IS                  12  129
    TROPICAL OR SUB-TROPICAL RAIN FOREST, OR           OTHER THAN                                 XSQ=    15.36
    MONSOON FOREST  (156) FWM                          TROPICAL OR SUB-TROPICAL RAIN FOREST, OR   PHI=    0.251
                                                       MONSOON FOREST  (244) FWM                  XP =   0.0001

53  TILT MORE TOWARD BEING THOSE   0.81 OF  31      53  TILT LESS TOWARD BEING THOSE   0.55 OF 146        6   65
    WHERE FOOD PRODUCTION IS BY                        WHERE FOOD PRODUCTION IS BY                       25   81
    SIMPLE AGRICULTURE OR                              SIMPLE AGRICULTURE OR                      XSQ=     5.73
    INCIPIENT FOOD PRODUCTION, RATHER THAN BY          INCIPIENT FOOD PRODUCTION, RATHER THAN BY  PHI=   -0.180
    INTENSIVE AGRICULTURE  (147)                       INTENSIVE AGRICULTURE  (147)               XP =   0.0166

55  TILT TOWARD BEING THOSE          0.77 OF  26    55  TILT TOWARD BEING THOSE        0.51 OF 128        6   65
    WHERE FOOD PRODUCTION IS BY                        WHERE FOOD PRODUCTION IS BY                       20   63
    SIMPLE AGRICULTURE, RATHER THAN BY                 INTENSIVE AGRICULTURE, RATHER THAN BY      XSQ=     5.61
    INTENSIVE AGRICULTURE  (101)                       SIMPLE AGRICULTURE  (91)                   PHI=   -0.191
                                                                                                  XP =   0.0179

63  TILT TOWARD BEING THOSE          0.53 OF  32    63  TILT TOWARD BEING THOSE        0.70 OF 148       15  103
    WHERE HUSBANDRY, IF PRESENT,                       WHERE HUSBANDRY, IF PRESENT,                      17   45
    IS PRINCIPALLY IN THE FORM OF                      IS PRINCIPALLY IN THE FORM OF              XSQ=     5.05
    PIGS, SHEEP, OR GOATS, RATHER THAN                 BOVINE, EQUINE, CAMEL-LIKE, OR DEER-LIKE   PHI=   -0.168
    BOVINE, EQUINE, CAMEL-LIKE, OR DEER-LIKE           ANIMALS, RATHER THAN                       XP =   0.0246
    ANIMALS  (74)                                      PIGS, SHEEP, OR GOATS  (152)
```

79	IN ALL CASES ARE THOSE 1.00 OF 28 WHERE NO CITY IS PRESENT (201)	79	DRIFT LESS TOWARD BEING THOSE 0.86 OF 145 WHERE NO CITY IS PRESENT (201)	0 21 28 124 XSQ= 3.36 PHI= -0.139 XP = 0.0669
81	TILT MORE TOWARD BEING THOSE 0.79 OF 28 WHERE NO CITY OR TOWN IS PRESENT, AND THE AVERAGE COMMUNITY SIZE IS SMALLER THAN 200 (135)	81	TILT LESS TOWARD BEING THOSE 0.55 OF 145 WHERE NO CITY OR TOWN IS PRESENT, AND THE AVERAGE COMMUNITY SIZE IS SMALLER THAN 200 (135)	6 65 22 80 XSQ= 4.39 PHI= -0.159 XP = 0.0362
84	TILT MORE TOWARD BEING THOSE 0.97 OF 33 WHERE THE LEVEL OF POLITICAL INTEGRATION IS THE LITTLE STATE, THE MINIMAL STATE, THE AUTONOMOUS COMMUNITY, OR THE FAMILY (262) GPM	84	TILT LESS TOWARD BEING THOSE 0.81 OF 150 WHERE THE LEVEL OF POLITICAL INTEGRATION IS THE LITTLE STATE, THE MINIMAL STATE, THE AUTONOMOUS COMMUNITY, OR THE FAMILY (262) GPM	1 29 32 121 XSQ= 4.12 PHI= -0.150 XP = 0.0423
85	DRIFT MORE TOWARD BEING THOSE 0.91 OF 33 WHERE THE LEVEL OF POLITICAL INTEGRATION IS THE MINIMAL STATE, THE AUTONOMOUS COMMUNITY, OR THE FAMILY (234) GPM	85	DRIFT LESS TOWARD BEING THOSE 0.73 OF 150 WHERE THE LEVEL OF POLITICAL INTEGRATION IS THE MINIMAL STATE, THE AUTONOMOUS COMMUNITY, OR THE FAMILY (234) GPM	3 40 30 110 XSQ= 3.72 PHI= -0.143 XP = 0.0537
94	IN ALL CASES ARE THOSE 1.00 OF 41 WHERE THE HIERARCHY OF NATIONAL JURISDICTION HAS TWO, ONE, OR NO LEVELS (296) GES,EA	94	TILT LESS TOWARD BEING THOSE 0.88 OF 199 WHERE THE HIERARCHY OF NATIONAL JURISDICTION HAS TWO, ONE, OR NO LEVELS (296) GES,EA	0 23 41 176 XSQ= 3.99 PHI= -0.129 XP = 0.0457
152	IN ALL CASES ARE THOSE 1.00 OF 5 WHERE THE DIFFERENTIATION OF THE JURIDICAL AGENCY FROM THE MEDICAL AGENCY IS LOW (10) MJ	152	TILT TOWARD BEING THOSE 0.60 OF 10 WHERE THE DIFFERENTIATION OF THE JURIDICAL AGENCY FROM THE MEDICAL AGENCY IS HIGH (10) MJ	0 6 5 4 XSQ= 2.81 PHI= -0.433 EP = 0.0440
176	LEAN TOWARD BEING THOSE 0.67 OF 40 WHERE THE COMMUNITY IS A CLAN-COMMUNITY OR A COMMUNITY STRUCTURED OR SEGMENTED ON A CLAN BASIS (169)	176	LEAN TOWARD BEING THOSE 0.58 OF 199 WHERE THE COMMUNITY IS OTHER THAN A CLAN-COMMUNITY OR A COMMUNITY STRUCTURED OR SEGMENTED ON A CLAN BASIS (213)	27 84 13 115 XSQ= 7.58 PHI= 0.178 XP = 0.0059
178	LEAN LESS TOWARD BEING THOSE 0.57 OF 40 WHERE THE COMMUNITY IS OTHER THAN SEGMENTED ON A CLAN BASIS AND NON-EXOGAMOUS (295)	178	LEAN MORE TOWARD BEING THOSE 0.79 OF 199 WHERE THE COMMUNITY IS OTHER THAN SEGMENTED ON A CLAN BASIS AND NON-EXOGAMOUS (295)	17 41 23 158 XSQ= 7.54 PHI= 0.178 XP = 0.0060
183	TILT LESS TOWARD BEING THOSE 0.72 OF 36 WHERE THE LARGEST NON-COGNATIC KIN GROUP IS SMALLER THAN A MOEITY, I. E., A PHRATRY OR SIB OR LINEAGE (218)	183	TILT MORE TOWARD BEING THOSE 0.89 OF 124 WHERE THE LARGEST NON-COGNATIC KIN GROUP IS SMALLER THAN A MOEITY, I. E., A PHRATRY OR SIB OR LINEAGE (218)	10 14 26 110 XSQ= 4.73 PHI= 0.172 XP = 0.0297

Left	Right	Statistics
184 DRIFT LESS TOWARD BEING THOSE 0.56 OF 36 WHERE THE LARGEST NON-COGNATIC KIN GROUP IS SMALLER THAN A PHRATRY, I. E. A SIB OR LINEAGE (175)	184 DRIFT MORE TOWARD BEING THOSE 0.73 OF 124 WHERE THE LARGEST NON-COGNATIC KIN GROUP IS SMALLER THAN A PHRATRY, I. E. A SIB OR LINEAGE (175)	16 33 20 91 XSQ= 3.38 PHI= 0.145 XP = 0.0661
188 LEAN MORE TOWARD BEING THOSE 0.88 OF 41 WHERE THE KIN GROUP IS OTHER THAN EXCLUSIVELY COGNATIC (252)	188 LEAN LESS TOWARD BEING THOSE 0.61 OF 202 WHERE THE KIN GROUP IS OTHER THAN EXCLUSIVELY COGNATIC (252)	5 78 36 124 XSQ= 9.44 PHI= -0.197 XP = 0.0021
192 TEND MORE TO BE THOSE 0.95 OF 41 OTHER THAN WHERE THE ONLY KIN GROUP PRESENT IS A KINDRED OR ELSE BILATERAL DESCENT IS INFERRED (289)	192 TEND LESS TO BE THOSE 0.68 OF 202 OTHER THAN WHERE THE ONLY KIN GROUP PRESENT IS A KINDRED OR ELSE BILATERAL DESCENT IS INFERRED (289)	2 65 39 137 XSQ= 11.39 PHI= -0.216 XP = 0.0007
214 TEND LESS TO BE THOSE 0.53 OF 19 WHERE FIRST COUSIN MARRIAGE, IF PERMITTED, IS OTHER THAN UNILATERAL (144)	214 TEND MORE TO BE THOSE 0.88 OF 85 WHERE FIRST COUSIN MARRIAGE, IF PERMITTED, IS OTHER THAN UNILATERAL (144)	9 10 10 75 XSQ= 10.91 PHI= 0.324 XP = 0.0010
234 LEAN TOWARD BEING THOSE 0.71 OF 35 WHERE THE COUSIN TERMINOLOGY IS OF CROW, OMAHA, OR IROQUOIS TYPE, RATHER THAN ESKIMO OR HAWAIIAN TYPE (152)	234 LEAN TOWARD BEING THOSE 0.58 OF 164 WHERE THE COUSIN TERMINOLOGY IS OF ESKIMO OR HAWAIIAN TYPE, RATHER THAN CROW, OMAHA, OR IROQUOIS TYPE (170)	25 69 10 95 XSQ= 8.83 PHI= 0.211 XP = 0.0030
236 TILT TOWARD BEING THOSE 0.59 OF 41 WHERE THE FAMILY IS OF AN INDEPENDENT TYPE, RATHER THAN AN EXTENDED TYPE (185)	236 TILT TOWARD BEING THOSE 0.61 OF 201 WHERE THE FAMILY IS OF AN EXTENDED TYPE, RATHER THAN AN INDEPENDENT TYPE (213)	17 123 24 78 XSQ= 4.66 PHI= -0.139 XP = 0.0309
240 DRIFT TOWARD BEING THOSE 0.59 OF 17 WHERE THE FAMILY, IF EXTENDED, IS LARGE, RATHER THAN SMALL OR STEM (78)	240 DRIFT TOWARD BEING THOSE 0.67 OF 123 WHERE THE FAMILY, IF EXTENDED, IS SMALL OR STEM, RATHER THAN LARGE (135)	10 40 7 83 XSQ= 3.43 PHI= 0.156 XP = 0.0641
263 DRIFT MORE TOWARD BEING THOSE 0.73 OF 41 WHERE WIVES ARE OBTAINED BY RELATIVELY DIFFICULT MEANS, NAMELY BY BRIDE-PRICE, BRIDE-SERVICE, OR EXCHANGING A FEMALE RELATIVE (233)	263 DRIFT LESS TOWARD BEING THOSE 0.57 OF 202 WHERE WIVES ARE OBTAINED BY RELATIVELY DIFFICULT MEANS, NAMELY BY BRIDE-PRICE, BRIDE-SERVICE, OR EXCHANGING A FEMALE RELATIVE (233)	30 115 11 87 XSQ= 3.09 PHI= 0.113 XP = 0.0787
300 TILT TOWARD BEING THOSE 0.68 OF 19 WHERE THE POST-PARTUM SEX TABOO LASTS LONGER THAN SIX MONTHS (51)	300 TILT TOWARD BEING THOSE 0.63 OF 76 WHERE THE POST-PARTUM SEX TABOO LASTS SIX MONTHS OR LESS (73)	13 28 6 48 XSQ= 4.96 PHI= 0.228 XP = 0.0260

```
302  IN ALL CASES ARE THCSE           1.00 OF   5     302  DRIFT TOWARD BEING THOSE          0.52 OF  27              5   13
     WHERE THE AVERAGE EARLY SATISFACTION                  WHERE THE AVERAGE EARLY SATISFACTICN                       0   14
     POTENTIAL IS HIGH  (23) W-C                           POTENTIAL IS LOW  (17) W-C                            XSQ=     2.74
                                                                                                                  PHI=    0.293
                                                                                                                  EP =   0.0525

306  TILT TCWARC BEING THOSE          0.88 OF   8     306  TILT TOWARD BEING THOSE           0.59 OF  32              7   13
     WHERE THE EARLY DEPENCENCE SATISFACTION               WHERE THE EARLY DEPENDENCE SATISFACTION                    1   19
     POTENTIAL IS HIGH  (28) W-C                           POTENTIAL IS LCW  (24) W-C                            XSQ=     3.91
                                                                                                                  PHI=    0.312
                                                                                                                  EP =   0.0436

313  DRIFT TCWARD BEING THCSE         0.88 OF   8     313  DRIFT TOWARD BEING THOSE          0.57 CF  35              1   20
     WHERE AGGRESSICN SCCIALIZATION ANXIETY                WHERE AGGRESSION SOCIALIZATION ANXIETY                     7   15
     IS LCW  (28) W-C                                      IS HIGH  (26) W-C                                     XSQ=     3.56
                                                                                                                  PHI=   -0.288
                                                                                                                  XP =   0.0592

335  DRIFT TCWARD REING THCSE         0.86 OF   7     335  DRIFT TOWARD BEING THOSE          0.58 OF  24              6   10
     WHERE INITIAL INCULGENCE CF CEPENCENCY                WHERE INITIAL INDULGENCE CF DEPENDENCY                     1   14
     IS HIGH  (20) WNS                                     IS LOW  (18) WNS                                      XSQ=     2.63
                                                                                                                  PHI=    0.291
                                                                                                                  EP =   0.0829

366  DRIFT TCWARD BEING THCSE         0.55 OF  11     366  DRIFT TOWARD BEING THOSE          0.78 CF  37              6    8
     WHERE DISSCCIATICN CF THE SEXES                       WHERE DISSOCIATION OF THE SEXES                            5   29
     AT ADCLESCENCE                                        AT ADOLESCENCE                                        XSQ=     3.00
     IS HIGH  (16) JKH                                     IS MEDIUM OR LCW  (41) JKH                            PHI=    0.250
                                                                                                                  XP =   0.0834

368  LEAN TCWARC BEING THOSE          0.86 OF   7     368  LEAN TOWARD BEING THCSE           0.75 OF  24              6    6
     WHERE DISSCCIATICN CF THE SEXES                       WHERE DISSOCIATION OF THE SEXES                            1   18
     AT ADCLESCENCE                                        AT ADOLESCENCE                                        XSQ=     6.06
     IS HIGH CR MEDIUM  (16) JKH                           IS LOW  (21) JKH                                      PHI=    0.442
                                                                                                                  EP =   0.0070

369  IN ALL CASES ARE THCSE           1.00 OF  11     369  TILT LESS TOWARD BEING THOSE      0.62 CF  37             11   23
     WHERE DISSCCIATICN CF THE SEXES                       WHERE DISSOCIATION CF THE SEXES                            0   14
     AT ADCLESCENCE, OR                                    AT ADOLESCENCE, OR                                    XSQ=     4.19
     CUSTCMS CF INITIATICN AT ACOLESCENCE,                 CUSTOMS OF INITIATION AT ADCLESCENCE,                 PHI=    0.295
     ARE PRESENT  (42) JKH                                 ARE PRESENT  (42) JKH                                 XP =   0.0407

372  TILT TCWARC BEING THOSE          0.73 OF  22     372  TILT TOWARD BEING THOSE           0.61 OF  66             16   26
     WHERE MALE INITIATICN RITES ARE                       WHERE MALE INITIATICN RITES ARE                            6   40
     PRESENT  (48) ASA                                     ABSENT  (63) ASA                                      XSQ=     6.07
                                                                                                                  PHI=    0.263
                                                                                                                  XP =   0.0137

391  LEAN TCWARD BEING THCSE          0.84 OF  19     391  LEAN TOWARD BEING THOSE           0.55 CF 116              3   64
     WHERE PREMARITAL SEX RELATIONS ARE                    WHERE PREMARITAL SEX RELATICNS ARE                        16   52
     PUNISHED CNLY IF PREGNANCY RESULTS, OR                STRONGLY PUNISHED AND IN FACT RARE, OR                XSQ=     8.62
     FREELY PERMITTEC  (90) JTW,EA                         WEAKLY PUNISHED AND                                   PHI=   -0.253
                                                           IN FACT NOT RARE  (89) JTW,EA                         XP =   0.0033
```

```
392  TILT TOWARD BEING THOSE          0.63 OF  19    392  TILT TOWARD BEING THOSE          0.70 OF 116          7   81
     WHERE PREMARITAL SEX RELATIONS ARE                  WHERE PREMARITAL SEX RELATIONS ARE                   12   35
     FREELY PERMITTED  (67) JTW,EA                       STRONGLY PUNISHED AND IN FACT RARE, OR        XSQ=     6.44
                                                         WEAKLY PUNISHED AND IN FACT NOT RARE, OR      PHI=   -0.218
                                                         PUNISHED ONLY IF                              XP =   0.0111
                                                         PREGNANCY RESULTS  (112) JTW,EA

425  IN ALL CASES ARE THOSE           1.00 OF   5    425  DRIFT TOWARD BEING THOSE         0.50 OF  24           0   12
     WHERE SUPERNATURALS ARE MAINLY                      WHERE SUPERNATURALS ARE MAINLY                        5   12
     AGGRESSIVE, RATHER THAN                             BENEVOLENT, RATHER THAN                       XSQ=     2.45
     BENEVOLENT  (20) L-T-W                              AGGRESSIVE  (16) L-T-W                        PHI=   -0.291
                                                                                                       EP =   0.0588

434  DRIFT TOWARD BEING THOSE         0.82 OF  11    434  DRIFT TOWARD BEING THOSE         0.52 OF  44           9   21
     WHERE ASCETICISM IN MOURNING BEHAVIOR               WHERE ASCETICISM IN MOURNING BEHAVIOR                 2   23
     IS HIGH  (37) JFG                                   IS LOW  (30) JFG                              XSQ=     2.86
                                                                                                       PHI=    0.228
                                                                                                       XP =   0.0905

441  DRIFT TOWARD BEING THOSE         0.78 OF   9    441  DRIFT TOWARD BEING THOSE         0.64 OF  39           7   14
     WHERE FEAR OF HUMAN BEINGS                          WHERE FEAR OF HUMAN BEINGS                            2   25
     IS HIGH  (29) W-C                                   IS LOW  (32) W-C                              XSQ=     3.65
                                                                                                       PHI=    0.276
                                                                                                       XP =   0.0561

459  LEAN TOWARD BEING THOSE          0.82 OF  28    459  LEAN TOWARD BEING THOSE          0.54 OF 103           5   56
     WHERE GAMES, IF PRESENT,                            WHERE GAMES, IF PRESENT,                             23   47
     DO NOT INCLUDE                                      INCLUDE GAMES OF CHANCE  (82) R-A-B,EA        XSQ=    10.37
     GAMES OF CHANCE  (89) R-A-B,EA                                                                    PHI=   -0.281
                                                                                                       XP =   0.0013

460  LEAN TOWARD BEING THOSE          0.64 OF  28    460  LEAN TOWARD BEING THOSE          0.67 OF 103          18   34
     WHERE GAMES, IF PRESENT,                            WHERE GAMES, IF PRESENT,                             10   69
     ARE LIMITED TO                                      ARE NOT LIMITED TO                            XSQ=     7.74
     GAMES OF SKILL ONLY  (67) R-A-B,EA                  GAMES OF SKILL ONLY  (104) R-A-B,EA           PHI=    0.243
                                                                                                       XP =   0.0054
```

372 CULTURES
WHERE MALE INITIATION RITES ARE
PRESENT (48) ASA

372 CULTURES
WHERE MALE INITIATION RITES ARE
ABSENT (63) ASA

BACKGROUND ON PAGE 150

BOTH SUBJECT AND PREDICATE

48 IN LEFT COLUMN

ANDAMANESE	APINAYE	ARANDA	ARAPESH	ATSUGEWI	AZANDE	BALINESE	BARI	CALLINAGO	DIERI
DOROBO	FON	HANO	ILA	INCA	INGASSANA	JUKUN	KARIERA	KERAKI	KURTATCHI
LANGO	LAU	LESU	MANUS	MARGI	MARQUESANS	MASAI	MENDE	MURNGIN	NAMA
NAMBICUARA	NANDI	NYORO	ONA	PUKAPUKA	SAMOANS	SENIANG	SWAZI	TAOS	THONGA
TIKOPIA	TIMBIRA	TOKELAU	TRUKESE	VENDA	WOGEO	YAO	ZUNI		

63 IN RIGHT COLUMN

ALORESE	AMERICANS	ARAUCANIANS	ASHANTI	AWEIKOMA	AYMARA	BATAK	BHUIYA	CARIB	CAYAPA
CHENCHU	CHEROKEE	CHEYENNE	CHIR-APACHE	COMANCHE	COPR ESKIMO	CREEK	CROW	CUNA	DOBUANS
EYAK	FOX	GANDA	GOND	HAIDA	HAVASUPAI	HO	IFUGAO	KASKA	KATAB
KERALA	KIOW-APACHE	KUTENAI	LAKHER	LAMBA	LEPCHA	LHOTA NAGA	MAORI	MARICOPA	MARSHALLESE
MATACO	MBUNDU	MOTA	NAVAHO	OJIBWA	ONTONG-JAVA	PAPAGO	RIFFIANS	RWALA	SANPOIL
SHERENTE	SHILLUK	SIRIONO	TALLENSI	TANALA	TETON	TROBRIAND	TUPINAMBA	VEDDA	WAPISHANA
WINNEBAGO	YAGUA	YARURO							

289 EXCLUDED BECAUSE UNASCERTAINED

	Present (48)			Absent (63)			
3	LEAN LESS TOWARD BEING THOSE LOCATED OUTSIDE OF AFRICA (320)	0.63 OF 48	3	LEAN MORE TOWARD BEING THOSE LOCATED OUTSIDE OF AFRICA (320)	0.89 OF 63	18 7 30 56 XSQ= 9.41 PHI= 0.291 XP = 0.0022
5	TILT MORE TOWARD BEING THOSE LOCATED OUTSIDE OF EAST EURASIA (330)	0.98 OF 48	5	TILT LESS TOWARD BEING THOSE LOCATED OUTSIDE OF EAST EURASIA (330)	0.84 OF 63	1 10 47 53 XSQ= 4.36 PHI= -0.198 XP = 0.0368
6	LEAN LESS TOWARD BEING THOSE LOCATED OUTSIDE OF THE INSULAR PACIFIC (330)	0.60 OF 48	6	LEAN MORE TOWARD BEING THOSE LOCATED OUTSIDE OF THE INSULAR PACIFIC (330)	0.86 OF 63	19 9 29 54 XSQ= 7.95 PHI= 0.268 XP = 0.0048

8	LEAN MORE TOWARD BEING THOSE LOCATED OUTSIDE OF NORTH AMERICA (330)	0.92 OF 48	8	LEAN LESS TOWARD BEING THOSE LOCATED OUTSIDE OF NORTH AMERICA (330)	0.67 OF 63	4 21 44 42 XSQ= 8.38 PHI= -0.275 XP = 0.0038
15	LEAN TOWARD BEING THOSE WHERE THE LATITUDE IS LESS THAN TWENTY DEGREES (217)	0.75 OF 48	15	LEAN TOWARD BEING THOSE WHERE THE LATITUDE IS TWENTY DEGREES OR GREATER (183)	0.56 OF 63	12 35 36 28 XSQ= 9.20 PHI= -0.288 XP = 0.0024
54	DRIFT MORE TOWARD BEING THOSE WHERE FOOD PRODUCTION IS BY INTENSIVE OR SIMPLE AGRICULTURE, RATHER THAN BY INCIPIENT FOOD PRODUCTION (192)	0.88 OF 32	54	DRIFT LESS TOWARD BEING THOSE WHERE FOOD PRODUCTION IS BY INTENSIVE OR SIMPLE AGRICULTURE, RATHER THAN BY INCIPIENT FOOD PRODUCTION (192)	0.66 OF 38	28 25 4 13 XSQ= 3.35 PHI= 0.219 XP = 0.0672
56	TILT MORE TOWARD BEING THOSE WHERE FOOD PRODUCTION IS BY SIMPLE AGRICULTURE, RATHER THAN BY INCIPIENT FOOD PRODUCTION (101)	0.83 OF 23	56	TILT LESS TOWARD BEING THOSE WHERE FOOD PRODUCTION IS BY SIMPLE AGRICULTURE, RATHER THAN BY INCIPIENT FOOD PRODUCTION (101)	0.52 OF 27	19 14 4 13 XSQ= 3.95 PHI= 0.281 XP = 0.0467
73	TILT MORE TOWARD BEING THOSE WHERE WEAVING IS ABSENT (130)	0.82 OF 38	73	TILT LESS TOWARD BEING THOSE WHERE WEAVING IS ABSENT (130)	0.54 OF 50	7 23 31 27 XSQ= 6.13 PHI= -0.264 XP = 0.0133
127	LEAN TOWARD BEING THOSE WHERE THE FEMALES' CONTRIBUTION TO SUBSISTENCE IS HIGH (33) JKB	0.92 OF 13	127	LEAN TOWARD BEING THOSE WHERE THE FEMALES' CONTRIBUTION TO SUBSISTENCE IS LOW (32) JKB	0.59 OF 22	12 9 1 13 XSQ= 6.98 PHI= 0.447 EP = 0.0039
128	DRIFT TOWARD BEING THOSE WHERE, IF SUBSISTENCE IS PRIMARILY BY AGRICULTURE, THE WORK IS MAINLY DONE BY FEMALES (37)	0.73 OF 15	128	DRIFT TOWARD BEING THOSE WHERE, IF SUBSISTENCE IS PRIMARILY BY AGRICULTURE, THE WORK IS MAINLY DONE BY MALES (40)	0.67 OF 12	4 8 11 4 XSQ= 2.85 PHI= -0.325 EP = 0.0574
135	DRIFT TOWARD BEING THOSE WHERE INDIVIDUAL OWNERSHIP OF ECONOMICALLY SIGNIFICANT PROPERTY IS NEGLIGIBLE OR ABSENT (14) GES	0.75 OF 8	135	DRIFT TOWARD BEING THOSE WHERE INDIVIDUAL OWNERSHIP OF ECONOMICALLY SIGNIFICANT PROPERTY IS PRESENT (24) GES	0.75 OF 12	2 9 6 3 XSQ= 3.04 PHI= -0.390 EP = 0.0648
176	DRIFT TOWARD BEING THOSE WHERE THE COMMUNITY IS A CLAN-COMMUNITY OR A COMMUNITY STRUCTURED OR SEGMENTED ON A CLAN BASIS (169)	0.60 OF 48	176	DRIFT TOWARD BEING THOSE WHERE THE COMMUNITY IS OTHER THAN A CLAN-COMMUNITY OR A COMMUNITY STRUCTURED OR SEGMENTED ON A CLAN BASIS (213)	0.59 OF 63	29 26 19 37 XSQ= 3.27 PHI= 0.172 XP = 0.0707

340 DRIFT TOWARD BEING THOSE 0.56 OF 16 WHERE THE TOTAL POSITIVE PRESSURE TOWARD DEVELOPING NURTURANT BEHAVIOR IN THE CHILD IS LOW (20) B-B-C	340 DRIFT TOWARD BEING THOSE 0.75 OF 20 WHERE THE TOTAL POSITIVE PRESSURE TOWARD DEVELOPING NURTURANT BEHAVIOR IN THE CHILD IS HIGH (28) B-B-C	7 15 9 5 XSQ= 2.46 PHI= -0.261 EP = 0.0874
365 DRIFT TOWARD BEING THOSE 0.82 OF 11 WHERE THE TIME SPENT IN ADOLESCENT PEER GROUP ACTIVITY IS HIGH OR HIGH-MEDIUM (30) JKH	365 DRIFT TOWARD BEING THOSE 0.58 OF 19 WHERE THE TIME SPENT IN ADOLESCENT PEER GROUP ACTIVITY IS LOW-MEDIUM OR LOW (15) JKH	9 8 2 11 XSQ= 3.00 PHI= 0.316 EP = 0.0575
369 IN ALL CASES ARE THOSE 1.00 OF 15 WHERE DISSOCIATION OF THE SEXES AT ADOLESCENCE, OR CUSTOMS OF INITIATION AT ADOLESCENCE, ARE PRESENT (42) JKH	369 LEAN LESS TOWARD BEING THOSE 0.55 OF 22 WHERE DISSOCIATION OF THE SEXES AT ADOLESCENCE, OR CUSTOMS OF INITIATION AT ADOLESCENCE, ARE PRESENT (42) JKH	15 12 0 10 XSQ= 7.18 PHI= 0.441 EP = 0.0022
370 LEAN TOWARD BEING THOSE 0.69 OF 42 WHERE THE SEGREGATION OF ADOLESCENT BOYS IS COMPLETE OR PARTIAL (95)	370 LEAN TOWARD BEING THOSE 0.63 OF 46 WHERE THE SEGREGATION OF ADOLESCENT BOYS IS ABSENT (148)	29 17 13 29 XSQ= 7.82 PHI= 0.298 XP = 0.0052
373 LEAN TOWARD BEING THOSE 0.78 OF 9 WHERE MALE INITIATION CEREMONIES AT PUBERTY ARE PRESENT (17) W-K-A	373 LEAN TOWARD BEING THOSE 0.86 OF 21 WHERE MALE INITIATION CEREMONIES AT PUBERTY ARE ABSENT (27) W-K-A	7 3 2 18 XSQ= 8.75 PHI= 0.540 EP = 0.0017
377 TEND LESS TO BE THOSE 0.60 OF 47 WHERE MALE GENITAL MUTILATION IS ABSENT (242)	377 TEND MORE TO BE THOSE 0.95 OF 55 WHERE MALE GENITAL MUTILATION IS ABSENT (242)	19 3 28 52 XSQ= 16.31 PHI= 0.400 XP = 0.0001
380 TILT LESS TOWARD BEING THOSE 0.55 OF 20 WHERE SEGREGATION OF GIRLS AT MENARCHE IS PRESENT (35) F-B	380 TILT MORE TOWARD BEING THOSE 0.89 OF 18 WHERE SEGREGATION OF GIRLS AT MENARCHE IS PRESENT (35) F-B	11 16 9 2 XSQ= 3.77 PHI= -0.315 EP = 0.0327
400 DRIFT TOWARD BEING THOSE 0.68 OF 19 WHERE HOMOSEXUAL ACTIVITY IS PERMITTED (36) F-B	400 DRIFT TOWARD BEING THOSE 0.64 OF 22 WHERE HOMOSEXUAL ACTIVITY IS PROHIBITED (22) F-B	6 14 13 8 XSQ= 3.01 PHI= -0.271 XP = 0.0828
430 DRIFT TOWARD BEING THOSE 0.88 OF 8 WHERE SUPERNATURAL SANCTIONS FOR MORALITY, HAVING AN EFFECT ON AN INDIVIDUAL'S HEALTH, ARE ABSENT OR UNREPORTED (22) GES	430 DRIFT TOWARD BEING THOSE 0.58 OF 12 WHERE SUPERNATURAL SANCTIONS FOR MORALITY, HAVING AN EFFECT ON AN INDIVIDUAL'S HEALTH, ARE PRESENT (16) GES	1 7 7 5 XSQ= 2.51 PHI= -0.354 EP = 0.0697

No.	Left	Ratio	No.	Right	Ratio	Statistics
440	LEAN TOWARD BEING THOSE WHERE FEAR OF SPIRITS IS LOW (29) W-C	0.76 OF 21	440	LEAN TOWARD BEING THOSE WHERE FEAR OF SPIRITS IS HIGH (32) W-C	0.69 OF 26	5 18 / 16 8 / XSQ= 7.86 / PHI= -0.409 / XP = 0.0051
449	DRIFT TOWARD BEING THOSE WHERE THE OBSERVATION OF FOOD TABOOS IS HIGH, RATHER THAN MEDIUM OR LOW (25) JRL	0.63 OF 16	449	DRIFT TOWARD BEING THOSE WHERE THE OBSERVATION OF FOOD TABOOS IS MEDIUM OR LOW, RATHER THAN HIGH (61) JRL	0.70 OF 27	10 8 / 6 19 / XSQ= 3.21 / PHI= 0.273 / XP = 0.0731
456	TILT TOWARD BEING THOSE WHERE THE INTERNALIZATION OF THE INDIVIDUAL'S CONTACT WITH THE DIVINE IS NOT CONDUCIVE TO THE DEVELOPMENT OF THE INDIVIDUAL'S NEED TO ACHIEVE (17) DCM	0.89 OF 9	456	TILT TOWARD BEING THOSE WHERE THE INTERNALIZATION OF THE INDIVIDUAL'S CONTACT WITH THE DIVINE IS CONDUCIVE TO THE DEVELOPMENT OF THE INDIVIDUAL'S NEED TO ACHIEVE (19) DCM	0.67 OF 15	1 10 / 8 5 / XSQ= 4.93 / PHI= -0.453 / EP = 0.0131
458	DRIFT LESS TOWARD BEING THOSE WHERE GAMES, IF PRESENT, DO NOT INCLUDE GAMES OF STRATEGY (119) R-A-B,EA	0.61 OF 33	458	DRIFT MORE TOWARD BEING THOSE WHERE GAMES, IF PRESENT, DO NOT INCLUDE GAMES OF STRATEGY (119) R-A-B,EA	0.82 OF 38	13 7 / 20 31 / XSQ= 2.87 / PHI= 0.201 / XP = 0.0901
480	DRIFT TOWARD BEING THOSE WHERE COMPLEXITY OF ARTISTIC DESIGN IS HIGH (14) HB	0.64 OF 11	480	DRIFT TOWARD BEING THOSE WHERE COMPLEXITY OF ARTISTIC DESIGN IS LOW (15) HB	0.77 OF 13	7 3 / 4 10 / XSQ= 2.54 / PHI= 0.325 / EP = 0.0953

```
373  CULTURES                                          373  CULTURES
     WHERE MALE INITIATION CEREMONIES                       WHERE MALE INITIATION CEREMONIES
     AT PUBERTY ARE PRESENT  (17) W-K-A                     AT PUBERTY ARE ABSENT  (27) W-K-A


BACKGROUND ON PAGE 151                                                        BOTH SUBJECT AND PREDICATE
.......................................................................................................

      17  IN LEFT COLUMN

AZANDE      CAGABA      CAMAYURA    CHAGGA      CHEYENNE    CHIR-APACHE FON         HANO        JIVARO      KWAKIUTL
LESU        NUER        OJIBWA      SAMOANS     THONGA      TIMBIRA     TIV

      27  IN RIGHT COLUMN

ALORESE     AMERICANS   ARAUCANIANS ASHANTI     BALINESE    COPR ESKIMO EGYPTIANS   GANDA       JAPANESE    KORYAK
LAKHER      LAMBA       LAPPS       LEPCHA      MAORI       NAVAHO      NYAKYUSA    CNTCNG-JAVA PAPAGO      SERBS
SIRIONO     TALLENSI    TANALA      TROBRIAND   TRUKESE     YAGUA       YAPESE

     356  EXCLUDED BECAUSE UNASCERTAINED

-------------------------------------------------------------------------------------------------------
 53  DRIFT TOWARD BEING THOSE      0.83 OF  12       53  DRIFT TOWARD BEING THOSE      0.53 OF  19          2   10
     WHERE FOOD PRODUCTION IS BY                          WHERE FOOD PRODUCTION IS BY                      10    9
     SIMPLE AGRICULTURE OR                                INTENSIVE AGRICULTURE, RATHER THAN BY     XSQ=     2.64
     INCIPIENT FOOD PRODUCTION, RATHER THAN BY            SIMPLE AGRICULTURE OR                     PHI=   -0.292
     INTENSIVE AGRICULTURE  (147)                         INCIPIENT FOOD PRODUCTION  (91)           EP  =  0.0652

 55  DRIFT TOWARD BEING THOSE      0.78 OF   9       55  DRIFT TOWARD BEING THOSE      0.63 OF  16          2   10
     WHERE FOOD PRODUCTION IS BY                          WHERE FOOD PRODUCTION IS BY                       7    6
     SIMPLE AGRICULTURE, RATHER THAN BY                   INTENSIVE AGRICULTURE, RATHER THAN BY     XSQ=     2.30
     INTENSIVE AGRICULTURE  (101)                         SIMPLE AGRICULTURE  (91)                  PHI=   -0.304
                                                                                                    EP  =  0.0968

108  DRIFT TOWARD BEING THOSE      0.86 OF   7      108  DRIFT TOWARD BEING THOSE      0.63 OF  19          6    7
     WHERE CLASS STRATIFICATION, IF PRESENT,              WHERE CLASS STRATIFICATION, IF PRESENT,           1   12
     IS BASED ON                                          IS BASED ON SOMETHING OTHER THAN          XSQ=     3.13
     A HEREDITARY ARISTOCRACY  (74)                       A HEREDITARY ARISTOCRACY  (129)           PHI=    0.347
                                                                                                    EP  =  0.0730

110  DRIFT TOWARD BEING THOSE      0.76 OF  17      110  DRIFT TOWARD BEING THOSE      0.56 OF  27          4   15
     WHERE SLAVERY IS ABSENT  (218)                       WHERE SLAVERY IS PRESENT  (163)                  13   12
                                                                                                    XSQ=     3.15
                                                                                                    PHI=   -0.268
                                                                                                    XP  =  0.0758

127  TEND TO BE THOSE              0.91 OF  11      127  TEND TO BE THOSE              0.81 OF  16         10    3
     WHERE THE FEMALES' CONTRIBUTION                      WHERE THE FEMALES' CONTRIBUTION                   1   13
     TO SUBSISTENCE                                       TO SUBSISTENCE                            XSQ=    10.86
     IS HIGH  (33) JKB                                    IS LOW  (32) JKB                          PHI=    0.634
                                                                                                    EP  =  0.0003
```

128	IN ALL CASES ARE THOSE WHERE, IF SUBSISTENCE IS PRIMARILY BY AGRICULTURE, THE WORK IS MAINLY DONE BY FEMALES (37)	1.00 OF 4	128	DRIFT TOWARD BEING THOSE WHERE, IF SUBSISTENCE IS PRIMARILY BY AGRICULTURE, THE WORK IS MAINLY DONE BY MALES (40)	0.63 OF 8	0 5 4 3 XSQ= 2.10 PHI= -0.418 EP = 0.0808
196	DRIFT LESS TOWARD BEING THOSE WHERE INDIVIDUAL RIGHTS IN REAL PROPERTY, AND RULES FOR INHERITANCE, ARE PRESENT (194)	0.54 OF 13	196	DRIFT MORE TOWARD BEING THOSE WHERE INDIVIDUAL RIGHTS IN REAL PROPERTY, AND RULES FOR INHERITANCE, ARE PRESENT (194)	0.86 OF 21	7 18 6 3 XSQ= 2.71 PHI= -0.282 EP = 0.0565
224	IN ALL CASES ARE THOSE WHERE COUSIN MARRIAGE IS PREFERENTIALLY OR PERMISSIVELY SYMMETRICAL, RATHER THAN EITHER PATRI- OR MATRILATERAL (106)	1.00 OF 4	224	DRIFT TOWARD BEING THOSE WHERE COUSIN MARRIAGE IS PREFERENTIALLY OR PERMISSIVELY EITHER PATRI- OR MATRILATERAL, RATHER THAN SYMMETRICAL (66)	0.64 OF 11	0 7 4 4 XSQ= 2.56 PHI= -0.413 EP = 0.0769
296	DRIFT TOWARD BEING THOSE WHERE INFANTICIDE IS PRESENT (18) BCA	0.75 OF 8	296	DRIFT TOWARD BEING THOSE WHERE INFANTICIDE IS ABSENT OR INFERRED ABSENT (15) BCA	0.80 OF 10	6 2 2 8 XSQ= 3.45 PHI= 0.437 EP = 0.0536
299	TILT TOWARD BEING THOSE WHERE THE POST-PARTUM SEX TABOO LASTS LONGER THAN ONE YEAR (35)	0.58 OF 12	299	TILT TOWARD BEING THOSE WHERE THE POST-PARTUM SEX TABOO LASTS ONE YEAR OR LESS (89)	0.81 OF 16	7 3 5 13 XSQ= 3.11 PHI= 0.334 EP = 0.0497
301	IN ALL CASES ARE THOSE WHERE THE POST-PARTUM SEX TABOO LASTS LONGER THAN ONE MONTH (96)	1.00 OF 12	301	DRIFT LESS TOWARD BEING THOSE WHERE THE POST-PARTUM SEX TABOO LASTS LONGER THAN ONE MONTH (96)	0.69 OF 16	12 11 0 5 XSQ= 2.68 PHI= 0.310 EP = 0.0525
302	DRIFT TOWARD BEING THOSE WHERE THE AVERAGE EARLY SATISFACTION POTENTIAL IS LOW (17) W-C	0.67 OF 9	302	DRIFT TOWARD BEING THOSE WHERE THE AVERAGE EARLY SATISFACTION POTENTIAL IS HIGH (23) W-C	0.77 OF 13	3 10 6 3 XSQ= 2.57 PHI= -0.342 EP = 0.0789
303	DRIFT TOWARD BEING THOSE WHERE THE EARLY ORAL SATISFACTION POTENTIAL IS LOW (25) W-C	0.80 OF 10	303	DRIFT TOWARD BEING THOSE WHERE THE EARLY ORAL SATISFACTION POTENTIAL IS HIGH (32) W-C	0.63 OF 16	2 10 8 6 XSQ= 2.93 PHI= -0.335 EP = 0.0511
308	IN ALL CASES ARE THOSE WHERE AVERAGE SOCIALIZATION ANXIETY IS HIGH (22) W-C	1.00 OF 9	308	TILT TOWARD BEING THOSE WHERE AVERAGE SOCIALIZATION ANXIETY IS LOW (18) W-C	0.54 OF 13	9 6 0 7 XSQ= 4.84 PHI= 0.469 EP = 0.0167

373/

316	LEAN TOWARD BEING THOSE 0.76 OF 17 WHERE EXCLUSIVE MOTHER-SON SLEEPING ARRANGEMENTS LAST ONE YEAR OR LONGER (19) W-K-A	316	LEAN TOWARD BEING THOSE 0.78 OF 27 WHERE EXCLUSIVE MOTHER-SON SLEEPING ARRANGEMENTS LAST LESS THAN ONE YEAR (25) W-K-A	13 6 4 21 XSQ= 10.40 PHI= 0.486 XP = 0.0013
352	DRIFT TOWARD BEING THOSE 0.79 OF 14 WHERE THE TOTAL POSITIVE PRESSURE TOWARD DEVELOPING OBEDIENT BEHAVIOR IN THE CHILD IS HIGH (44) B-B-C	352	DRIFT TOWARD BEING THOSE 0.53 OF 19 WHERE THE TOTAL POSITIVE PRESSURE TOWARD DEVELOPING OBEDIENT BEHAVIOR IN THE CHILD IS LOW (28) B-B-C	11 9 3 10 XSQ= 2.11 PHI= 0.253 EP = 0.0873
369	IN ALL CASES ARE THOSE 1.00 OF 14 WHERE DISSOCIATION OF THE SEXES AT ADOLESCENCE, OR CUSTOMS OF INITIATION AT ADOLESCENCE, ARE PRESENT (42) JKH	369	LEAN TOWARD BEING THOSE 0.50 OF 20 WHERE BOTH DISSOCIATION OF THE SEXES AT ADOLESCENCE, AND CUSTOMS OF INITIATION AT ADOLESCENCE, ARE ABSENT (15) JKH	14 10 0 10 XSQ= 7.65 PHI= 0.474 EP = 0.0017
372	LEAN TOWARD BEING THOSE 0.70 OF 10 WHERE MALE INITIATION RITES ARE PRESENT (48) ASA	372	LEAN TOWARD BEING THOSE 0.90 OF 20 WHERE MALE INITIATION RITES ARE ABSENT (63) ASA	7 2 3 18 XSQ= 8.75 PHI= 0.540 EP = 0.0017
377	TILT LESS TOWARD BEING THOSE 0.59 OF 17 WHERE MALE GENITAL MUTILATION IS ABSENT (242)	377	TILT MORE TOWARD BEING THOSE 0.92 OF 25 WHERE MALE GENITAL MUTILATION IS ABSENT (242)	7 2 10 23 XSQ= 4.79 PHI= 0.338 XP = 0.0286
382	DRIFT TOWARD BEING THOSE 0.73 OF 11 WHERE FEMALE INITIATION RITES ARE PRESENT (38) JKB	382	DRIFT TOWARD BEING THOSE 0.69 OF 16 WHERE FEMALE INITIATION RITES ARE ABSENT (27) JKB	8 5 3 11 XSQ= 2.98 PHI= 0.332 EP = 0.0542
399	DRIFT TOWARD BEING THOSE 0.69 OF 13 WHERE INTENSITY OF CASTRATION ANXIETY IS HIGH (23) WNS	399	DRIFT TOWARD BEING THOSE 0.71 OF 17 WHERE INTENSITY OF CASTRATION ANXIETY IS LOW (22) WNS	9 5 4 12 XSQ= 3.23 PHI= 0.328 EP = 0.0634
441	TILT TOWARD BEING THOSE 0.73 OF 11 WHERE FEAR OF HUMAN BEINGS IS HIGH (29) W-C	441	TILT TOWARD BEING THOSE 0.75 OF 16 WHERE FEAR OF HUMAN BEINGS IS LOW (32) W-C	8 4 3 12 XSQ= 4.24 PHI= 0.396 EP = 0.0220
445	IN ALL CASES ARE THOSE 1.00 OF 6 WHERE SORCERY IS IMPORTANT (26) EBW,DH	445	DRIFT TOWARD BEING THOSE 0.50 OF 8 WHERE SORCERY IS UNIMPORTANT (23) BBW,DH	6 4 0 4 XSQ= 2.11 PHI= 0.388 EP = 0.0849

373/

```
449  IN ALL CASES ARE THCSE            1.00 OF    8        449  TILT TOWARD BEING THCSE            0.56 OF    9             8     4
     WHERE THE CBSERVATICN CF FCOD TABOOS                       WHERE THE OBSERVATICN OF FCCD TABCCS                      0     5
     IS HIGH, RATHER THAN                                       IS MEDIUM OR LOW, RATHER THAN                      XSQ=     3.90
     MEDIUM CR LOW  (25) JRL                                    HIGH  (61) JRL                                     PHI=    0.479
                                                                                                                   EP =   0.0294

453  DRIFT TCWARD BEING THCSE          0.67 OF    6        453  IN ALL CASES ARE THOSE             1.00 OF    6             4     0
     WHERE THE ROLE CF RELIGIOUS EXPERTS                        WHERE THE ROLE OF RELIGIOUS EXPERTS                       2     6
     IS CCNDUCIVE TC THE CEVELCPMENT OF THE                     IS NOT CONDUCIVE TO THE DEVELCPMENT CF THE         XSQ=     3.38
     INDIVIDUAL'S NEED TC ACHIEVE  (13) DCM                     INDIVIDUAL'S NEED TC ACHIEVE  (23) DCM             PHI=    0.530
                                                                                                                   EP =   0.0606

472  TILT TCWARD BEING THOSE           0.87 OF   15        472  TILT TOWARD BEING THOSE            0.53 OF   19            13     9
     WHERE THE COMPCSITE NARCISSISM INCEX                       WHERE THE COMPOSITE NARCISSISM INDEX                      2    10
     IS HIGH  (47) PES                                          IS LOW  (43) PES                                   XSQ=     4.08
                                                                                                                   PHI=    0.346
                                                                                                                   EP =   0.0297
```

374 CULTURES WHERE MALE PUBERTY RITES ARE PRESENT (43) F-B	374 CULTURES WHERE MALE PUBERTY RITES ARE ABSENT (18) F-B

BACKGROUND ON PAGE 151 NEITHER SUBJECT NOR PREDICATE

43 IN LEFT COLUMN

AINU	ALORESE	ANDAMANESE	APINAYE	ARANDA	AZANDE	BALINESE	CHAGGA	CREEK	DELAWARE
DIERI	DUSUN	FON	GILBERTESE	HANO	ILA	JIVARO	JUKUN	KERAKI	KURTATCHI
LANGO	LESU	MARSHALLESE	MASAI	MBUNDU	NAMA	NANDI	PONAPEANS	PUKAPUKA	PURARI
SEMINOLE	SENIANG	SHERENTE	SWAZI	TANALA	TAOS	THONGA	TIKOPIA	TOKELAU	VENDA
WOGEO	WOLOF	ZUNI							

18 IN RIGHT COLUMN

CARIB	CAYAPA	COPR ESKIMO	CUNA	GOAJIRO	GOND	HUICHOL	KAZAK	KIOW-APACHE	LAKHER
LAPPS	LEPCHA	MARICOPA	NASKAPI	SIRIONO	TARAHUMARA	TEHUELCHE	TRUKESE		

339 EXCLUDED BECAUSE UNASCERTAINED

```
****************************************************************************************************

375  CULTURES                                            375  CULTURES
     WHERE IMPORTANT SECRETS                                  WHERE IMPORTANT SECRETS
     ASSOCIATED WITH MALE INITIATION RITES                    ASSOCIATED WITH MALE INITIATION RITES
     ARE PRESENT  (12) ASA                                    ARE ABSENT  (11) ASA


BACKGROUND ON PAGE 151                                                                    SUBJECT ONLY
....................................................................................................

       12   IN LEFT COLUMN

ARAPESH    AZANDE     CHAGGA     HANO       KURTATCHI  LESU       MURNGIN    TAOS       THONGA     VENDA
WOGEO      ZUNI

       11   IN RIGHT COLUMN

ANDAMANESE BALINESE   FON        JIVARO     MANUS      MARQUESANS MASAI      PUKAPUKA   SAMOANS    TIKOPIA
TIV

       26   EXCLUDED BECAUSE IRRELEVANT

ALORESE    ASHANTI    CHENCHU    CHIR-APACHE COMANCHE  COPR ESKIMO DOBUANS   IFUGAO     KUTENAI    LAKHER
LAMBA      LEPCHA     MAORI      MARSHALLESE NAVAHO    ONTONG-JAVA PAPAGO    RIFFIANS   RWALA      SANPOIL
SIRIONO    TANALA     TETON      TROBRIAND   WAPISHANA YAGUA

      351   EXCLUDED BECAUSE UNASCERTAINED


----------------------------------------------------------------------------------------------------
 15  TILT LESS TOWARD BEING THOSE   0.58 OF  12      15  IN ALL CASES ARE THOSE        1.00 OF  11          5    0
     WHERE THE LATITUDE IS                               WHERE THE LATITUDE IS                              7   11
     LESS THAN TWENTY DEGREES  (217)                     LESS THAN TWENTY DEGREES  (217)              XSQ=    3.66
                                                                                                      PHI=   0.399
                                                                                                      EP =  0.0373

 42  DRIFT TOWARD BEING THOSE       0.67 OF  12      42  DRIFT TOWARD BEING THOSE      0.73 OF  11          4    8
     WHERE THE NATURAL ENVIRONMENT IS                    WHERE THE NATURAL ENVIRONMENT IS                   8    3
     OTHER THAN                                          TROPICAL OR SUB-TROPICAL RAIN FOREST, OR     XSQ=    2.17
     TROPICAL OR SUB-TROPICAL RAIN FOREST, OR            MONSOON FOREST  (156) FWM                    PHI=  -0.307
     MONSOON FOREST  (244) FWM                                                                        EP =  0.0995

 55  DRIFT TOWARD BEING THOSE       0.50 OF  10      55  IN ALL CASES ARE THOSE        1.00 OF   6          5    0
     WHERE FOOD PRODUCTION IS BY                         WHERE FOOD PRODUCTION IS BY                        5    6
     INTENSIVE AGRICULTURE, RATHER THAN BY               SIMPLE AGRICULTURE, RATHER THAN BY           XSQ=    2.35
     SIMPLE AGRICULTURE  (91)                            INTENSIVE AGRICULTURE  (101)                 PHI=   0.383
                                                                                                      EP =  0.0934

188  DRIFT MORE TOWARD BEING THOSE  0.92 OF  12     188  DRIFT LESS TOWARD BEING THOSE 0.55 OF  11          1    5
     WHERE THE KIN GROUP IS                              WHERE THE KIN GROUP IS                            11    6
     OTHER THAN                                          OTHER THAN                                   XSQ=    2.40
     EXCLUSIVELY COGNATIC  (252)                         EXCLUSIVELY COGNATIC  (252)                  PHI=  -0.323
                                                                                                      EP =  0.0686
```

234	LEAN TOWARD BEING THOSE 0.90 OF 10 WHERE THE COUSIN TERMINOLOGY IS OF CROW, OMAHA, OR IROQUOIS TYPE, RATHER THAN ESKIMO OR HAWAIIAN TYPE (152)	234	LEAN TOWARD BEING THOSE 0.88 OF 8 WHERE THE COUSIN TERMINOLOGY IS OF ESKIMO OR HAWAIIAN TYPE, RATHER THAN CROW, OMAHA, OR IROQUOIS TYPE (170)	9 1 1 7 XSQ= 7.90 PHI= 0.662 EP = 0.0029
243	IN ALL CASES ARE THOSE 1.00 OF 7 WHERE POLYGYNY, IF PRESENT, HAS A HIGH INCIDENCE (24) W-C,S	243	DRIFT TOWARD BEING THOSE 0.57 OF 7 WHERE POLYGYNY, IF PRESENT, HAS A LOW INCIDENCE (36) W-D,S	7 3 0 4 XSQ= 3.15 PHI= 0.474 EP = 0.0699
344	DRIFT TOWARD BEING THOSE 0.73 OF 11 WHERE THE TOTAL POSITIVE PRESSURE TOWARD DEVELOPING SELF-RELIANT BEHAVIOR IN THE CHILD IS LOW (40) B-B-C	344	DRIFT TOWARD BEING THOSE 0.70 OF 10 WHERE THE TOTAL POSITIVE PRESSURE TOWARD DEVELOPING SELF-RELIANT BEHAVIOR IN THE CHILD IS HIGH (36) B-B-C	3 7 8 3 XSQ= 2.31 PHI= -0.332 EP = 0.0861
347	DRIFT TOWARD BEING THOSE 0.73 OF 11 WHERE THE CHILD'S INFERRED CONFLICT REGARDING SELF-RELIANT BEHAVIOR IS HIGH (37) B-B-C	347	DRIFT TOWARD BEING THOSE 0.70 OF 10 WHERE THE CHILD'S INFERRED CONFLICT REGARDING SELF-RELIANT BEHAVIOR IS LOW (39) B-B-C	8 3 3 7 XSQ= 2.31 PHI= 0.332 EP = 0.0861
349	DRIFT TOWARD BEING THOSE 0.60 OF 10 WHERE THE CHILD'S INFERRED ANXIETY OVER NON-PERFORMANCE OF ACHIEVEMENT BEHAVIOR IS LOW (28) B-B-C	349	DRIFT TOWARD BEING THOSE 0.88 OF 8 WHERE THE CHILD'S INFERRED ANXIETY OVER NON-PERFORMANCE OF ACHIEVEMENT BEHAVIOR IS HIGH (34) B-B-C	4 7 6 1 XSQ= 2.46 PHI= -0.369 EP = 0.0656
380	IN ALL CASES ARE THOSE 1.00 OF 4 WHERE SEGREGATION OF GIRLS AT MENARCHE IS PRESENT (35) F-B	380	DRIFT TOWARD BEING THOSE 0.63 OF 8 WHERE SEGREGATION OF GIRLS AT MENARCHE IS ABSENT (20) F-B	4 3 0 5 XSQ= 2.10 PHI= 0.418 EP = 0.0808
392	DRIFT TOWARD BEING THOSE 0.88 OF 8 WHERE PREMARITAL SEX RELATIONS ARE STRONGLY PUNISHED AND IN FACT RARE, OR WEAKLY PUNISHED AND IN FACT NOT RARE, OR PUNISHED ONLY IF PREGNANCY RESULTS (112) JTW,EA	392	DRIFT TOWARD BEING THOSE 0.60 OF 10 WHERE PREMARITAL SEX RELATIONS ARE FREELY PERMITTED (67) JTW,EA	7 4 1 6 XSQ= 2.46 PHI= 0.369 EP = 0.0656
402	DRIFT TOWARD BEING THOSE 0.67 OF 12 WHERE EXPLANATIONS OF ILLNESS OF AN ORAL NATURE ARE ABSENT (30) W-C	402	DRIFT TOWARD BEING THOSE 0.73 OF 11 WHERE EXPLANATIONS OF ILLNESS OF AN ORAL NATURE ARE PRESENT (31) W-C	4 8 8 3 XSQ= 2.17 PHI= -0.307 EP = 0.0995
440	DRIFT TOWARD BEING THOSE 0.83 OF 12 WHERE FEAR OF SPIRITS IS LOW (29) W-C	440	DRIFT TOWARD BEING THOSE 0.55 OF 11 WHERE FEAR OF SPIRITS IS HIGH (32) W-C	2 6 10 5 XSQ= 2.15 PHI= -0.306 EP = 0.0894

```
441  TEND TO BE THOSE               0.92 OF  12     441  TEND TO BE THOSE               0.82 OF  11          11     2
     WHERE FEAR OF HUMAN BEINGS                          WHERE FEAR OF HUMAN BEINGS                          1     9
     IS HIGH  (29) W-C                                   IS LOW  (32) W-C                              XSQ=     9.80
                                                                                                       PHI=    0.653
                                                                                                       EP =   0.0006

445  IN ALL CASES ARE THOSE         1.00 OF   7     445  TILT TOWARD BEING THOSE        0.60 OF   5           7     2
     WHERE SORCERY IS                                    WHERE SORCERY IS                                    0     3
     IMPORTANT  (26) EBW,DH                              UNIMPORTANT  (23) BBW,DH                      XSQ=     2.86
                                                                                                       PHI=    0.488
                                                                                                       EP =   0.0455

447  TILT TOWARD BEING THOSE        0.88 OF   8     447  TILT TOWARD BEING THOSE        0.86 OF   7           7     1
     WHERE LOVE MAGIC IS                                 WHERE LOVE MAGIC IS                                 1     6
     PRESENT  (20) S-R                                   ABSENT  (13) S-R                              XSQ=     5.37
                                                                                                       PHI=    0.598
                                                                                                       EP =   0.0101
```

376	CULTURES WHERE ORDEALS OF CONSIDERABLE SEVERITY ASSOCIATED WITH MALE INITIATION RITES ARE PRESENT (9) ASA	376	CULTURES WHERE ORDEALS OF CONSIDERABLE SEVERITY ASSOCIATED WITH MALE INITIATION RITES ARE ABSENT (13) ASA

BACKGROUND ON PAGE 151

SUBJECT ONLY

9 IN LEFT COLUMN

ARAPESH AZANDE CHAGGA HANO JIVARO KURTATCHI THONGA VENDA ZUNI

13 IN RIGHT COLUMN

ANDAMANESE BALINESE FON MANUS MARQUESANS MASAI MURNGIN PUKAPUKA SAMOANS TAOS
TIKOPIA TIV WOGEO

26 EXCLUDED BECAUSE IRRELEVANT

ALORESE ASHANTI CHENCHU CHIR-APACHE COMANCHE COPR ESKIMO DOBUANS IFUGAO KUTENAI LAKHER
LAMBA LEPCHA MAORI MARSHALLESE NAVAHO ONTONG-JAVA PAPAGO RIFFIANS RWALA SANPOIL
SIRIONO TANALA TETON TROBRIAND WAPISHANA YAGUA

352 EXCLUDED BECAUSE UNASCERTAINED

6	DRIFT TOWARD BEING THOSE LOCATED OUTSIDE OF THE INSULAR PACIFIC (330)	0.78 OF 9	6	DRIFT TOWARD BEING THOSE LOCATED IN THE INSULAR PACIFIC (70)	0.62 OF 13	2 8 7 5	XSQ= PHI= EP =	1.92 -0.295 0.0991
36	TILT TOWARD BEING THOSE WHERE THE NATURAL ENVIRONMENT IS 'VERY HARSH,' OR SUB-TROPICAL BUSH, OR TEMPERATE GRASSLAND (108) FWM	0.67 OF 9	36	TILT TOWARD BEING THOSE WHERE THE NATURAL ENVIRONMENT IS OTHER THAN 'VERY HARSH,' OR SUB-TROPICAL BUSH, OR TEMPERATE GRASSLAND (292) FWM	0.85 OF 13	6 2 3 11	XSQ= PHI= EP =	4.03 0.428 0.0260
42	DRIFT TOWARD BEING THOSE WHERE THE NATURAL ENVIRONMENT IS OTHER THAN TROPICAL OR SUB-TROPICAL RAIN FOREST, OR MONSOON FOREST (244) FWM	0.78 OF 9	42	DRIFT TOWARD BEING THOSE WHERE THE NATURAL ENVIRONMENT IS TROPICAL OR SUB-TROPICAL RAIN FOREST, OR MONSOON FOREST (156) FWM	0.69 OF 13	2 9 7 4	XSQ= PHI= EP =	3.01 -0.370 0.0805
74	IN ALL CASES ARE THOSE WHERE POTTERY IS PRESENT (145)	1.00 OF 5	74	TILT TOWARD BEING THOSE WHERE POTTERY IS ABSENT (93)	0.58 OF 12	5 5 0 7	XSQ= PHI= EP =	2.84 0.409 0.0441

```
234  IN ALL CASES ARE THOSE            1.00 OF   7    234  LEAN TOWARD BEING THOSE           0.80 OF  10             7     2
     WHERE THE COUSIN TERMINOLOGY IS                       WHERE THE COUSIN TERMINOLOGY IS                             0     8
     OF CROW, OMAHA, OR IROQUOIS TYPE,                     OF ESKIMO OR HAWAIIAN TYPE,                           XSQ=     7.61
     RATHER THAN                                           RATHER THAN                                           PHI=    0.669
     ESKIMO OR HAWAIIAN TYPE  (152)                        CROW, OMAHA, OR IROQUOIS TYPE  (170)                  EP =   0.0023

243  IN ALL CASES ARE THOSE            1.00 OF   6    243  DRIFT TOWARD BEING THOSE          0.50 OF   8             6     4
     WHERE POLYGYNY, IF PRESENT,                           WHERE POLYGYNY, IF PRESENT,                                 0     4
     HAS A HIGH INCIDENCE  (24) W-C,S                      HAS A LOW INCIDENCE  (36) W-D,S                       XSQ=     2.11
                                                                                                                 PHI=    0.388
                                                                                                                 EP =   0.0849

263  DRIFT TOWARD BEING THOSE          0.78 OF   9    263  DRIFT TOWARD BEING THOSE          0.69 OF  13             7     4
     WHERE WIVES ARE OBTAINED BY                           WHERE WIVES ARE OBTAINED                                    2     9
     RELATIVELY DIFFICULT MEANS, NAMELY BY                 BY RELATIVELY EASY MEANS, NAMELY BY                   XSQ=     3.01
     BRIDE-PRICE, BRIDE-SERVICE, OR                        TOKEN BRIDE-PRICE, GIFT EXCHANGE,                     PHI=    0.370
     EXCHANGING A FEMALE RELATIVE  (233)                   ABSENCE OF ANY CONSIDERATION, OR                      EP =   0.0805
                                                           RECEIPT OF DOWRY  (162)

313  DRIFT TOWARD BEING THOSE          0.67 OF   9    313  DRIFT TOWARD BEING THOSE          0.77 OF  13             6     3
     WHERE AGGRESSION SOCIALIZATION ANXIETY                WHERE AGGRESSION SOCIALIZATION ANXIETY                      3    10
     IS HIGH  (26) W-C                                     IS LOW  (28) W-C                                      XSQ=     2.57
                                                                                                                 PHI=    0.342
                                                                                                                 EP =   0.0789

338  DRIFT TOWARD BEING THOSE          0.89 OF   9    338  DRIFT TOWARD BEING THOSE          0.55 OF  11             8     5
     WHERE THE CHILD'S INFERRED ANXIETY OVER               WHERE THE CHILD'S INFERRED ANXIETY OVER                     1     6
     PERFORMANCE OF RESPONSIBLE BEHAVIOR                   PERFORMANCE OF RESPONSIBLE BEHAVIOR                   XSQ=     2.42
     IS HIGH  (44) B-B-C                                   IS LOW  (29) B-B-C                                    PHI=    0.348
                                                                                                                 EP =   0.0703

347  DRIFT TOWARD BEING THOSE          0.78 OF   9    347  DRIFT TOWARD BEING THOSE          0.64 OF  11             7     4
     WHERE THE CHILD'S INFERRED CONFLICT                   WHERE THE CHILD'S INFERRED CONFLICT                         2     7
     REGARDING SELF-RELIANT BEHAVIOR                       REGARDING SELF-RELIANT BEHAVIOR                       XSQ=     1.96
     IS HIGH  (37) B-B-C                                   IS LOW  (39) B-B-C                                    PHI=    0.313
                                                                                                                 EP =   0.0923

353  DRIFT TOWARD BEING THOSE          0.88 OF   8    353  DRIFT TOWARD BEING THOSE          0.60 OF  10             7     4
     WHERE THE CHILD'S INFERRED ANXIETY OVER               WHERE THE CHILD-S INFERRED ANXIETY OVER                     1     6
     NON-PERFORMANCE OF OBEDIENT BEHAVIOR                  NON-PERFORMANCE OF OBEDIENT BEHAVIOR                  XSQ=     2.46
     IS HIGH  (42) B-B-C                                   IS LOW  (32) B-B-C                                    PHI=    0.369
                                                                                                                 EP =   0.0656

441  TILT TOWARD BEING THOSE           0.89 OF   9    441  TILT TOWARD BEING THOSE           0.69 OF  13             8     4
     WHERE FEAR OF HUMAN BEINGS                            WHERE FEAR OF HUMAN BEINGS                                  1     9
     IS HIGH  (29) W-C                                     IS LOW  (32) W-C                                      XSQ=     5.09
                                                                                                                 PHI=    0.481
                                                                                                                 EP =   0.0115

445  IN ALL CASES ARE THOSE            1.00 OF   7    445  TILT TOWARD BEING THOSE           0.60 OF   5             7     2
     WHERE SORCERY IS                                      WHERE SORCERY IS                                            0     3
     IMPORTANT  (26) BBW,DH                                UNIMPORTANT  (23) BBW,DH                              XSQ=     2.86
                                                                                                                 PHI=    0.488
                                                                                                                 EP =   0.0455
```

```
447  IN ALL CASES ARE THOSE          1.00 OF   6        447  LEAN TOWARD BEING THOSE         0.88 OF   8           6     1
     WHERE LOVE MAGIC IS                                     WHERE LOVE MAGIC IS                                    0     7
     PRESENT  (20) S-R                                       ABSENT  (13) S-R                                 XSQ=     7.29
                                                                                                              PHI=    0.722
                                                                                                              EP =   0.0047

458  TILT TOWARD BEING THOSE         0.83 OF   6        458  TILT TOWARD BEING THOSE         0.73 OF  11           5     3
     WHERE GAMES, IF PRESENT,                                WHERE GAMES, IF PRESENT,                               1     8
     INCLUDE GAMES OF STRATEGY  (52) R-A-B,EA                DO NOT INCLUDE                                   XSQ=     2.91
                                                             GAMES OF STRATEGY  (119) R-A-B,EA                PHI=    0.413
                                                                                                              EP =   0.0498

459  TILT TOWARD BEING THOSE         0.83 OF   6        459  TILT TOWARD BEING THOSE         0.73 OF  11           5     3
     WHERE GAMES, IF PRESENT,                                WHERE GAMES, IF PRESENT,                               1     8
     INCLUDE GAMES OF CHANCE  (82) R-A-B,EA                  DO NOT INCLUDE                                   XSQ=     2.91
                                                             GAMES OF CHANCE  (89) R-A-B,EA                   PHI=    0.413
                                                                                                              EP =   0.0498
```

377 CULTURES
WHERE MALE GENITAL MUTILATION
IS PRESENT (83)

377 CULTURES
WHERE MALE GENITAL MUTILATION
IS ABSENT (242)

BACKGROUND ON PAGE 151

BOTH SUBJECT AND PREDICATE

83 IN LEFT COLUMN

ARANDA	AZANDE	BAMBARA	BAMILEKE	BANDA	BARABRA	BASSERI	BAYA	BEJA	BOZO
BUNLAP	BURUSHO	CHAGGA	CHERKESS	DAGUR	DIERI	DILLING	DOGON	DOROBO	EGYPTIANS
FANG	FON	FUTAJALONKE	GISU	GURE	HAZARA	HEBREWS	HERERO	INGASSANA	IRAQW
JAVANESE	KABYLE	KAZAK	KIKUYU	KISSI	KOHISTANI	KPE	KUBA	LAU	LESU
MACASSARESE	MALAYS	MAMVU	MANGAIANS	MARQUESANS	MASAI	MENDE	MERINA	MONGO	MOSSI
MURINBATA	MURNGIN	MZAB	NANDI	NUPE	PAEZ	PATHAN	REGEIBAT	RIFFIANS	RWALA
SAMOANS	SANDAWE	SHLUH	SIWANS	SOMALI	SONGHAI	SWAZI	SYRIANS	TANALA	TEDA
TENDA	TERA	THONGA	TIGRINYA	TIKOPIA	TIV	TOKELAU	TOTONAC	TURKMEN	WOLOF
YAO	YOMBE	YORUBA							

242 IN RIGHT COLUMN

ABIPON	ABOR	AINU	AKHA	ALACALUF	ALBANIANS	ALORESE	AMBA	AMERICANS	ANDAMANESE
APINAYE	ARAPESH	ARAUCANIANS	ASHANTI	ATAYAL	ATSUGEWI	AWEIKOMA	AYMARA	AZTEC	BABWA
BACAIRI	BARI	BEMBA	BHIL	BHUIYA	BIRIFOR	BLACK CARIB	BOERS	BORORO	BOTOCUDO
BRAZILIANS	CADUVEC	CAGABA	CALLINAGO	CAMAYURA	CAMBODIANS	CARIB	CAYAPA	CHAMACOCO	CHENCHU
CHEROKEE	CHEYENNE	CHIBCHA	CHIR-APACHE	CHIRIGUANO	CHOCO	CHOROTI	CHORTI	CHUKCHEE	COCHITI
COORG	COPR ESKIMO	CREE	CREEK	CROW	CUNA	CZECHS	DARD	DELAWARE	DIEGUENO
DUTCH	ENGA	EYAK	FOX	GANDA	GARO	GILYAK	GOAJIRO	GOND	GROS VENTRE
GUAHIBO	GUATO	HAIDA	HANO	HANUNOO	HASINAI	HAVASUPAI	HUICHOL	HUKUNDIKA	HURON
HUTSUL	IBAN	IFUGAO	ILA	INCA	INGALIK	IRISH	JAPANESE	JEMEZ	JIVARO
JUKUN	KACHIN	KAPAUKU	KARIERA	KASKA	KATAB	KERAKI	KERALA	KHALKA	KHASI
KOL	KOREANS	KORYAK	KUNG	KURTATCHI	KUTENAI	KWAKIUTL	LAKHER	LAMBA	LAMET
LANGO	LAPPS	LEPCHA	LHOTA NAGA	LOLO	LOZI	LUO	MAM	MANDAN	MANIHIKI
MANUS	MACRI	MARGI	MARICOPA	MARSHALLESE	MATACO	MATAKAM	MAYA	MBUNDU	MBUTI
MIAMI	MIAO	MIN CHINESE	MINCHIA	MISKITO	MIWOK	MNONG GAR	MONGUOR	MOTA	MOTILON
MUNDURUCU	NABESNA	NAMA	NAMBICUARA	NATCHEZ	NAVAHO	NICOBARESE	NOMLAKI	NUER	NUNIVAK
NYAKYUSA	NYORO	OJIBWA	OKINAWANS	OMAHA	ONA	ORAON	PAIWAN	PALAUANS	PAPAGO
PARAUJANO	PAWNEE	PONAPEANS	PUKAPUKA	PURARI	PURUM	ROMANS	RUNDI	SAGADA	SAMOYED
SANPOIL	SANTAL	SARSI	SELUNG	SEMANG	SENIANG	SERBS	SHERENTE	SHILLUK	SINHALESE
SIRIONO	SIUAI	SOTHO	SUBANUN	TAGBANUA	TALAMANCA	TALLENSI	TAOS	TAPIRAPE	TARAHUMARA
TAREUMIUT	TEHUELCHE	TENETEHARA	TENINO	TERENA	TESO	THAI	TIMBIRA	TIMUCUA	TIWI
TODA	TOLOWA	TORAJA	TRISTAN	TROBRIAND	TRUKESE	TRUMAI	TSHIMSHIAN	TUBATULABAL	TUCANO
TUCUNA	TUNEBO	TUPINAMBA	TURKANA	TWANA	ULAWANS	UTE	VEDDA	VENDA	WAICA
WALLOONS	WANTOAT	WAPISHANA	WARRAU	WASHO	WICHITA	WIKMUNKAN	WITOTO	WOGEO	WOLEAIANS
YABARANA	YAGUA	YAHGAN	YAKO	YAKUT	YAPESE	YARURO	YOKUTS	YUKAGHIR	YUKI
YUROK	ZUNI								

75 EXCLUDED BECAUSE UNASCERTAINED

3	TEND LESS TC BE THCSE LOCATED CUTSIDE CF AFRICA (320)	0.57 OF 83	3	TEND MORE TO BE THOSE LOCATED OUTSIDE OF AFRICA (320)	0.87 OF 242	36 31 47 211 XSQ= 33.43 PHI= 0.321 XP = 0.
4	TEND LESS TO BE THCSE LCCATED CUTSIDE CF THE CIRCUM-MEDITERRANEAN (355)	0.76 OF 83	4	TEND MORE TO BE THOSE LOCATED OUTSIDE OF THE CIRCUM-MEDITERRANEAN (355)	0.95 CF 242	20 13 63 229 XSQ= 21.74 PHI= 0.259 XP = 0.0000
8	TEND MCRE TO BE THCSE LOCATED CUTSIDE CF NCRTH AMERICA (330)	0.99 OF 83	8	TEND LESS TO BE THOSE LOCATED OUTSIDE OF NORTH AMERICA (330)	0.76 OF 242	1 58 82 184 XSQ= 20.05 PHI= -0.248 XP = 0.0000
9	TEND MCRE TC BE THCSE LOCATED CUTSIDE OF SCUTH AMERICA (335)	0.99 OF 83	9	TEND LESS TO BE THOSE LOCATED OUTSIDE OF SOUTH AMERICA (335)	0.76 CF 242	1 58 82 184 XSQ= 20.05 PHI= -0.248 XP = 0.0000
12	IN ALL CASES ARE THOSE WHERE THE LATITUDE IS LESS THAN FIFTY DEGREES (367)	1.00 OF 83	12	LEAN LESS TOWARD BEING THOSE WHERE THE LATITUDE IS LESS THAN FIFTY DEGREES (367)	0.88 OF 242	0 29 83 213 XSQ= 9.50 PHI= -0.171 XP = 0.0021
15	TILT TCWARD BEING THCSE WHERE THE LATITUDE IS LESS THAN TWENTY DEGREES (217)	0.64 OF 83	15	TILT TOWARD BEING THOSE WHERE THE LATITUDE IS TWENTY DEGREES OR GREATER (183)	0.51 CF 242	30 123 53 119 XSQ= 4.77 PHI= -0.121 XP = 0.0289
44	TILT MORE TOWARC BEING THCSE WHERE SETTLEMENTS ARE FIXEC (222)	0.77 OF 83	44	TILT LESS TOWARD BEING THOSE WHERE SETTLEMENTS ARE FIXED (222)	0.63 OF 241	64 152 19 89 XSQ= 4.86 PHI= 0.122 XP = 0.0275
51	TEND MCRE TO BE THCSE WHERE SUBSISTENCE IS PRIMARILY BY FCCD PRODUCTICN -- I. E., AGRICULTURE OR HUSBANCRY -- RATHER THAN BY GATHERING (253)	0.89 OF 83	51	TEND LESS TO BE THOSE WHERE SUBSISTENCE IS PRIMARILY BY FOOD PRODUCTION -- I. E., AGRICULTURE OR HUSBANDRY -- RATHER THAN BY GATHERING (253)	0.52 OF 242	74 127 9 115 XSQ= 33.70 PHI= 0.322 XP = 0.
53	TILT TCWARD BEING THOSE WHERE FCCD PRCDUCTICN IS BY INTENSIVE AGRICULTURE, RATHER THAN BY SIMPLE AGRICULTURE CR INCIPIENT FCCD PRCDUCTICN (91)	0.51 OF 67	53	TILT TOWARD BEING THOSE WHERE FOOD PRODUCTICN IS BY SIMPLE AGRICULTURE CR INCIPIENT FOOD PRODUCTION, RATHER THAN BY INTENSIVE AGRICULTURE (147)	0.67 OF 159	34 53 33 106 XSQ= 5.32 PHI= 0.153 XP = 0.0210

56	TEND MORE TO BE THOSE 0.97 OF 33 WHERE FOOD PRODUCTION IS BY SIMPLE AGRICULTURE, RATHER THAN BY INCIPIENT FOOD PRODUCTION (101)	56	TEND LESS TO BE THOSE 0.64 OF 106 WHERE FOOD PRODUCTION IS BY SIMPLE AGRICULTURE, RATHER THAN BY INCIPIENT FOOD PRODUCTION (101)	32 68 1 38 XSQ= 11.85 PHI= 0.292 XP = 0.0006
62	TEND MORE TO BE THOSE 0.84 OF 83 WHERE HUSBANDRY OF SOME KIND IS PRESENT (228)	62	TEND LESS TO BE THOSE 0.62 OF 242 WHERE HUSBANDRY OF SOME KIND IS PRESENT (228)	70 149 13 93 XSQ= 13.56 PHI= 0.204 XP = 0.0002
71	TEND TO BE THOSE 0.73 OF 52 WHERE METAL WORKING IS PRESENT (98)	71	TEND TO BE THOSE 0.69 OF 186 WHERE METAL WORKING IS ABSENT (153)	38 57 14 129 XSQ= 28.76 PHI= 0.348 XP = 0.0000
86	TEND TO BE THOSE 0.71 OF 62 WHERE THE LEVEL OF POLITICAL INTEGRATION IS THE LARGE STATE, THE LITTLE STATE, OR THE MINIMAL STATE (148) GPM	86	TEND TO BE THOSE 0.61 OF 191 WHERE THE LEVEL OF POLITICAL INTEGRATION IS THE AUTONOMOUS COMMUNITY, OR THE FAMILY (156) GPM	44 74 18 117 XSQ= 18.26 PHI= 0.269 XP = 0.0000
90	DRIFT MORE TOWARD BEING THOSE 0.91 OF 34 WHERE, IF A HEREDITARY HEADMANSHIP IS PRESENT, SUCCESSION IS PATRILINEAL, RATHER THAN MATRILINEAL (127)	90	DRIFT LESS TOWARD BEING THOSE 0.74 OF 103 WHERE, IF A HEREDITARY HEADMANSHIP IS PRESENT, SUCCESSION IS PATRILINEAL, RATHER THAN MATRILINEAL (127)	31 76 3 27 XSQ= 3.56 PHI= 0.161 XP = 0.0592
96	TEND TO BE THOSE 0.77 OF 83 WHERE THE HIERARCHY OF NATIONAL JURISDICTION HAS FOUR, THREE, TWO OR ONE LEVEL (174) GES,EA	96	TEND TO BE THOSE 0.56 OF 239 WHERE THE HIERARCHY OF NATIONAL JURISDICTION HAS NO LEVELS (156) GES,EA	64 104 19 135 XSQ= 26.53 PHI= 0.287 XP = 0.0000
97	LEAN LESS TOWARD BEING THOSE 0.71 OF 83 WHERE THE HIERARCHY OF LOCAL JURISDICTION HAS THREE OR TWO LEVELS (273) GES,EA	97	LEAN MORE TOWARD BEING THOSE 0.87 OF 240 WHERE THE HIERARCHY OF LOCAL JURISDICTION HAS THREE OR TWO LEVELS (273) GES,EA	24 32 59 208 XSQ= 9.39 PHI= 0.170 XP = 0.0022
98	LEAN MORE TOWARD BEING THOSE 0.84 OF 83 WHERE THE HIERARCHY OF LOCAL JURISDICTION HAS FOUR OR THREE LEVELS (238) GES,EA	98	LEAN LESS TOWARD BEING THOSE 0.67 OF 240 WHERE THE HIERARCHY OF LOCAL JURISDICTION HAS FOUR OR THREE LEVELS (238) GES,EA	70 161 13 79 XSQ= 8.19 PHI= 0.159 XP = 0.0042
100	LEAN MORE TOWARD BEING THOSE 0.93 OF 83 WHERE HIERARCHIES ARE MORE COMPLEX THAN THE 'SIMPLEST,' I. E., MORE COMPLEX THAN TWO LOCAL LEVELS WITH NO NATIONAL LEVELS (267) GES,EA	100	LEAN LESS TOWARD BEING THOSE 0.76 OF 239 WHERE HIERARCHIES ARE MORE COMPLEX THAN THE 'SIMPLEST,' I. E., MORE COMPLEX THAN TWO LOCAL LEVELS WITH NO NATIONAL LEVELS (267) GES,EA	77 182 6 57 XSQ= 9.78 PHI= 0.174 XP = 0.0018

102	LEAN TOWARD BEING THOSE WHERE CLASS STRATIFICATION IS PRESENT (203)	0.67 OF 79	102	LEAN TOWARD BEING THOSE WHERE CLASS STRATIFICATION IS ABSENT (180)	0.53 OF 237	53 112 26 125 XSQ= 8.56 PHI= 0.165 XP = 0.0034
106	DRIFT MORE TOWARD BEING THOSE WHERE CLASS STRATIFICATION, IF PRESENT, IS BASED ON SOMETHING OTHER THAN WEALTH (126)	0.70 OF 53	106	DRIFT LESS TOWARD BEING THOSE WHERE CLASS STRATIFICATION, IF PRESENT, IS BASED ON SOMETHING OTHER THAN WEALTH (126)	0.54 OF 112	16 51 37 61 XSQ= 2.91 PHI= -0.133 XP = 0.0883
109	TEND LESS TO BE THOSE WHERE CASTES ARE ABSENT (317)	0.67 OF 73	109	TEND MORE TO BE THOSE WHERE CASTES ARE ABSENT (317)	0.92 OF 231	24 18 49 213 XSQ= 27.24 PHI= 0.299 XP = 0.0000
110	TEND TO BE THOSE WHERE SLAVERY IS PRESENT (163)	0.62 OF 79	110	TEND TO BE THOSE WHERE SLAVERY IS ABSENT (218)	0.66 OF 235	49 80 30 155 XSQ= 17.99 PHI= 0.239 XP = 0.0000
120	DRIFT MORE TOWARD BEING THOSE WHERE THE CRAFT SPECIALIZATION SCORE IS HIGH OR MEDIUM (36) WME	0.92 OF 13	120	DRIFT LESS TOWARD BEING THOSE WHERE THE CRAFT SPECIALIZATION SCORE IS HIGH OR MEDIUM (36) WME	0.58 OF 38	12 22 1 16 XSQ= 3.73 PHI= 0.270 XP = 0.0535
129	TEND TO BE THOSE WHERE WEAVING IS MAINLY DONE BY MALES (31)	0.62 OF 26	129	TEND TO BE THOSE WHERE WEAVING IS MAINLY DONE BY FEMALES (73)	0.84 OF 74	16 12 10 62 XSQ= 17.42 PHI= 0.417 XP = 0.0000
130	LEAN TOWARD BEING THOSE WHERE LEATHER WORKING IS MAINLY DONE BY MALES (39)	0.81 OF 16	130	LEAN TOWARD BEING THOSE WHERE LEATHER WORKING IS MAINLY DONE BY FEMALES (45)	0.62 OF 65	13 25 3 40 XSQ= 7.80 PHI= 0.310 XP = 0.0052
149	DRIFT TOWARD BEING THOSE WHERE THE INCIDENCE OF THEFT IS HIGH (18) B-B-C	0.78 OF 9	149	DRIFT TOWARD BEING THOSE WHERE THE INCIDENCE OF THEFT IS LOW (19) B-B-C	0.62 OF 26	7 10 2 16 XSQ= 2.71 PHI= 0.278 EP = 0.0599
175	TILT LESS TOWARD BEING THOSE WHERE THE COMMUNITY IS 'KIN-HETEROGENEOUS,' I. E. OTHER THAN A CLAN COMMUNITY OR A DEME (260)	0.57 OF 77	175	TILT MORE TOWARD BEING THOSE WHERE THE COMMUNITY IS 'KIN-HETEROGENEOUS,' I. E. OTHER THAN A CLAN COMMUNITY OR A DEME (260)	0.72 OF 235	33 65 44 170 XSQ= 5.53 PHI= 0.133 XP = 0.0187

176	TEND TO BE THOSE WHERE THE COMMUNITY IS A CLAN-COMMUNITY OR A COMMUNITY STRUCTURED OR SEGMENTED ON A CLAN BASIS (169)	0.66 OF 77	176	TEND TO BE THOSE WHERE THE COMMUNITY IS OTHER THAN A CLAN-COMMUNITY OR A COMMUNITY STRUCTURED OR SEGMENTED ON A CLAN BASIS (213)	0.63 OF 235	51 87 26 148 XSQ= 18.90 PHI= 0.246 XP = 0.0000
177	TEND LESS TO BE THOSE WHERE THE COMMUNITY IS OTHER THAN A SINGLE CLAN-COMMUNITY AND EXOGAMOUS (305)	0.65 OF 77	177	TEND MORE TO BE THOSE WHERE THE COMMUNITY IS OTHER THAN A SINGLE CLAN-COMMUNITY AND EXOGAMOUS (305)	0.85 OF 235	27 36 50 199 XSQ= 12.83 PHI= 0.203 XP = 0.0003
179	TILT MORE TOWARD BEING THOSE WHERE THE COMMUNITY IS OTHER THAN STRUCTURED ON A NON-CLAN BASIS AND COMMONLY EXOGAMOUS (340)	0.95 OF 77	179	TILT LESS TOWARD BEING THOSE WHERE THE COMMUNITY IS OTHER THAN STRUCTURED ON A NON-CLAN BASIS AND COMMONLY EXOGAMOUS (340)	0.85 OF 235	4 35 73 200 XSQ= 4.14 PHI= -0.115 XP = 0.0419
180	DRIFT LESS TOWARD BEING THOSE WHERE THE COMMUNITY IS COMMONLY NON-EXOGAMOUS, RATHER THAN EXOGAMOUS (258)	0.57 OF 77	180	DRIFT MORE TOWARD BEING THOSE WHERE THE COMMUNITY IS COMMONLY NON-EXOGAMOUS, RATHER THAN EXOGAMOUS (258)	0.69 OF 235	33 73 44 162 XSQ= 3.09 PHI= 0.100 XP = 0.0788
182	TILT MORE TOWARD BEING THOSE OTHER THAN WHERE THE COMMUNITY IS STRUCTURED ON A NON-CLAN BASIS AND AGAMOUS (256)	0.79 OF 77	182	TILT LESS TOWARD BEING THOSE OTHER THAN WHERE THE COMMUNITY IS STRUCTURED ON A NON-CLAN BASIS AND AGAMOUS (256)	0.64 OF 235	16 84 61 151 XSQ= 5.30 PHI= -0.130 XP = 0.0214
183	DRIFT MORE TOWARD BEING THOSE WHERE THE LARGEST NON-COGNATIC KIN GROUP IS SMALLER THAN A MOEITY, I. E., A PHRATRY OR SIB OR LINEAGE (218)	0.92 OF 73	183	DRIFT LESS TOWARD BEING THOSE WHERE THE LARGEST NON-COGNATIC KIN GROUP IS SMALLER THAN A MOEITY, I. E., A PHRATRY OR SIB OR LINEAGE (218)	0.81 OF 135	6 26 67 109 XSQ= 3.63 PHI= -0.132 XP = 0.0568
186	TEND TO BE THOSE WHERE THE KIN GROUP IS EXCLUSIVELY PATRILINEAL (150)	0.63 OF 83	186	TEND TO BE THOSE WHERE THE KIN GROUP IS OTHER THAN EXCLUSIVELY PATRILINEAL (250)	0.71 OF 242	52 69 31 173 XSQ= 29.38 PHI= 0.301 XP = 0.0000
188	TEND MORE TO BE THOSE WHERE THE KIN GROUP IS OTHER THAN EXCLUSIVELY COGNATIC (252)	0.88 OF 83	188	TEND LESS TO BE THOSE WHERE THE KIN GROUP IS OTHER THAN EXCLUSIVELY COGNATIC (252)	0.56 OF 242	10 107 73 135 XSQ= 26.38 PHI= -0.285 XP = 0.0000
190	TEND MORE TO BE THOSE WHERE THE KIN GROUP IS PATRILINEAL OR DOUBLE-DESCENT, RATHER THAN MATRILINEAL (186)	0.90 OF 71	190	TEND LESS TO BE THOSE WHERE THE KIN GROUP IS PATRILINEAL OR DOUBLE-DESCENT, RATHER THAN MATRILINEAL (186)	0.67 OF 132	64 89 7 43 XSQ= 11.64 PHI= 0.239 XP = 0.0006

192	TEND MORE TO BE THOSE 0.94 OF 83 OTHER THAN WHERE THE ONLY KIN GROUP PRESENT IS A KINDRED OR ELSE BILATERAL DESCENT IS INFERRED (289)	192	TEND LESS TO BE THOSE 0.64 OF 242 OTHER THAN WHERE THE ONLY KIN GROUP PRESENT IS A KINDRED OR ELSE BILATERAL DESCENT IS INFERRED (289)	5 86 78 156 XSQ= 25.26 PHI= -0.279 XP = 0.0000
196	TILT MORE TOWARD BEING THOSE 0.79 OF 62 WHERE INDIVIDUAL RIGHTS IN REAL PROPERTY, AND RULES FOR INHERITANCE, ARE PRESENT (194)	196	TILT LESS TOWARD BEING THOSE 0.63 OF 175 WHERE INDIVIDUAL RIGHTS IN REAL PROPERTY, AND RULES FOR INHERITANCE, ARE PRESENT (194)	49 111 13 64 XSQ= 4.40 PHI= 0.136 XP = 0.0360
198	DRIFT MORE TOWARD BEING THOSE 0.96 OF 46 WHERE RULES FOR THE INHERITANCE OF REAL PROPERTY, IF PRESENT, FAVOR THE MALE HEIR OR LINE, RATHER THAN THE FEMALE (144)	198	DRIFT LESS TOWARD BEING THOSE 0.83 OF 93 WHERE RULES FOR THE INHERITANCE OF REAL PROPERTY, IF PRESENT, FAVOR THE MALE HEIR OR LINE, RATHER THAN THE FEMALE (144)	44 77 2 16 XSQ= 3.44 PHI= 0.157 XP = 0.0635
201	LEAN MORE TOWARD BEING THOSE 0.95 OF 83 WHERE MARITAL RESIDENCE IS NON-OPTIONAL, RATHER THAN AMBILOCAL OR NEOLOCAL (334)	201	LEAN LESS TOWARD BEING THOSE 0.80 OF 241 WHERE MARITAL RESIDENCE IS NON-OPTIONAL, RATHER THAN AMBILOCAL OR NEOLOCAL (334)	79 194 4 47 XSQ= 8.96 PHI= 0.166 XP = 0.0028
204	TEND MORE TO BE THOSE 0.95 OF 79 WHERE MARITAL RESIDENCE IS PATRILOCAL, VIRILOCAL, OR AVUNCULOCAL, RATHER THAN AMBILOCAL OR NEOLOCAL (270)	204	TEND LESS TO BE THOSE 0.75 OF 189 WHERE MARITAL RESIDENCE IS PATRILOCAL, VIRILOCAL, OR AVUNCULOCAL, RATHER THAN AMBILOCAL OR NEOLOCAL (270)	75 142 4 47 XSQ= 12.93 PHI= 0.220 XP = 0.0003
209	TEND MORE TO BE THOSE 0.95 OF 79 WHERE MARITAL RESIDENCE IS PATRILOCAL, VIRILOCAL, OR AVUNCULOCAL, RATHER THAN MATRILOCAL OR UXORILOCAL (270)	209	TEND LESS TO BE THOSE 0.73 OF 194 WHERE MARITAL RESIDENCE IS PATRILOCAL, VIRILOCAL, OR AVUNCULOCAL, RATHER THAN MATRILOCAL OR UXORILOCAL (270)	75 142 4 52 XSQ= 14.97 PHI= 0.234 XP = 0.0001
210	TEND MORE TO BE THOSE 0.97 OF 64 WHERE MARITAL RESIDENCE IS PATRILOCAL, RATHER THAN MATRILOCAL (169)	210	TEND LESS TO BE THOSE 0.75 OF 102 WHERE MARITAL RESIDENCE IS PATRILOCAL, RATHER THAN MATRILOCAL (169)	62 77 2 25 XSQ= 11.68 PHI= 0.265 XP = 0.0006
225	TILT TOWARD BEING THOSE 0.63 OF 16 WHERE COUSIN MARRIAGE IS PREFERENTIALLY OR PERMISSIVELY PATRILATERAL, RATHER THAN MATRILATERAL (23)	225	TILT TOWARD BEING THOSE 0.75 OF 36 WHERE COUSIN MARRIAGE IS PREFERENTIALLY OR PERMISSIVELY MATRILATERAL, RATHER THAN PATRILATERAL (43)	10 9 6 27 XSQ= 5.20 PHI= 0.316 XP = 0.0226
241	DRIFT MORE TOWARD BEING THOSE 0.98 OF 42 WHERE THE FAMILY, IF EXTENDED, IS LARGE OR SMALL, RATHER THAN STEM (187)	241	DRIFT LESS TOWARD BEING THOSE 0.85 OF 130 WHERE THE FAMILY, IF EXTENDED, IS LARGE OR SMALL, RATHER THAN STEM (187)	41 111 1 19 XSQ= 3.51 PHI= 0.143 XP = 0.0610

242	LEAN MORE TOWARD BEING THOSE WHERE MARRIAGE IS COMMONLY OR OCCASIONALLY POLYGYNOUS, RATHER THAN MONOGAMOUS (314)	0.93 OF 81	242	LEAN LESS TOWARD BEING THOSE WHERE MARRIAGE IS COMMONLY OR OCCASIONALLY POLYGYNOUS, RATHER THAN MONOGAMOUS (314)	0.77 OF 241	75 186 6 55 XSQ= 8.40 PHI= 0.162 XP = 0.0037
243	DRIFT TOWARD BEING THOSE WHERE POLYGYNY, IF PRESENT, HAS A HIGH INCIDENCE (24) W-D,S	0.64 OF 14	243	DRIFT TOWARD BEING THOSE WHERE POLYGYNY, IF PRESENT, HAS A LOW INCIDENCE (36) W-D,S	0.66 OF 44	9 15 5 29 XSQ= 2.84 PHI= 0.221 XP = 0.0917
254	IN ALL CASES ARE THOSE WHERE HOUSEHOLD AUTHORITY IS ON THE FATHER'S SIDE, RATHER THAN THE MOTHER'S (9) DA	1.00 OF 4	254	DRIFT TOWARD BEING THOSE WHERE HOUSEHOLD AUTHORITY IS ON THE MOTHER'S SIDE, RATHER THAN THE FATHER'S (6) DA	0.67 OF 9	4 3 0 6 XSQ= 2.63 PHI= 0.450 EP = 0.0699
262	TEND MORE TO BE THOSE WHERE WIVES ARE OBTAINED BY MEANS INVOLVING THE PRESENCE OF SOME CONSIDERATION (305)	0.94 OF 82	262	TEND LESS TO BE THOSE WHERE WIVES ARE OBTAINED BY MEANS INVOLVING THE PRESENCE OF SOME CONSIDERATION (305)	0.72 OF 240	77 172 5 68 XSQ= 15.99 PHI= 0.223 XP = 0.0001
263	TEND MORE TO BE THOSE WHERE WIVES ARE OBTAINED BY RELATIVELY DIFFICULT MEANS, NAMELY BY BRIDE-PRICE, BRIDE-SERVICE, OR EXCHANGING A FEMALE RELATIVE (233)	0.82 OF 82	263	TEND LESS TO BE THOSE WHERE WIVES ARE OBTAINED BY RELATIVELY DIFFICULT MEANS, NAMELY BY BRIDE-PRICE, BRIDE-SERVICE, OR EXCHANGING A FEMALE RELATIVE (233)	0.52 OF 240	67 126 15 114 XSQ= 20.51 PHI= 0.252 XP = 0.0000
279	DRIFT TOWARD BEING THOSE WHERE WIFE-LENDING OR WIFE-EXCHANGE IS PRESENT (10) LWS	0.63 OF 8	279	DRIFT TOWARD BEING THOSE WHERE WIFE-LENDING AND WIFE EXCHANGE ARE UNIMPORTANT OR ABSENT (19) LWS	0.75 OF 20	5 5 3 15 XSQ= 2.06 PHI= 0.271 EP = 0.0913
296	DRIFT TOWARD BEING THOSE WHERE INFANTICIDE IS PRESENT (18) BCA	0.86 OF 7	296	DRIFT TOWARD BEING THOSE WHERE INFANTICIDE IS ABSENT OR INFERRED ABSENT (15) BCA	0.57 OF 23	6 10 1 13 XSQ= 2.34 PHI= 0.279 EP = 0.0860
299	DRIFT LESS TOWARD BEING THOSE WHERE THE POST-PARTUM SEX TABOO LASTS ONE YEAR OR LESS (89)	0.58 OF 36	299	DRIFT MORE TOWARD BEING THOSE WHERE THE POST-PARTUM SEX TABOO LASTS ONE YEAR OR LESS (89)	0.77 OF 88	15 20 21 68 XSQ= 3.64 PHI= 0.171 XP = 0.0565
302	DRIFT TOWARD BEING THOSE WHERE THE AVERAGE EARLY SATISFACTION POTENTIAL IS LOW (17) W-C	0.70 OF 10	302	DRIFT TOWARD BEING THOSE WHERE THE AVERAGE EARLY SATISFACTION POTENTIAL IS HIGH (23) W-C	0.68 OF 25	3 17 7 8 XSQ= 2.80 PHI= -0.283 EP = 0.0619

309	DRIFT TCWARD BEING THCSE WHERE CRAL SCCIALIZATICN ANXIETY IS HIGH (26) W-C	0.82 OF 11	309	DRIFT TOWARD BEING THOSE WHERE ORAL SOCIALIZATICN ANXIETY IS LOW (27) W-C	0.57 OF 37	9 16 2 21 XSQ= 3.63 PHI= 0.275 XP = 0.0568
316	DRIFT TCWARD BEING THOSE WHERE EXCLUSIVE MOTHER-SCN SLEEPING ARRANGEMENTS LAST CNE YEAR CR LCNGER (19) W-K-A	0.78 OF 9	316	DRIFT TOWARD BEING THOSE WHERE EXCLUSIVE MOTHER-SCN SLEEPING ARRANGEMENTS LAST LESS THAN ONE YEAR (25) W-K-A	0.64 OF 33	7 12 2 21 XSQ= 3.37 PHI= 0.283 XP = 0.0665
321	DRIFT TCWARD BEING THCSE WHERE THE IMMEDIACY CF REDUCTION OF THE INFANT'S DRIVES IS LCW (25) B-B-C	0.64 OF 14	321	DRIFT TOWARD BEING THOSE WHERE THE IMMEDIACY OF REDUCTION OF THE INFANT'S DRIVES IS HIGH (35) B-B-C	0.66 CF 41	5 27 9 14 XSQ= 2.76 PHI= -0.224 XP = 0.0969
333	IN ALL CASES ARE THOSE WHERE THE AGE AT BEGINNING CF TRAINING IN HETERCSEXUAL PLAY INHIBITION IS EIGHT YEARS CR HIGHER (8) W-C	1.00 OF 4	333	DRIFT TOWARD BEING THOSE WHERE THE AGE AT BEGINNING OF TRAINING IN HETEROSEXUAL PLAY INHIBITICN IS LOWER THAN EIGHT YEARS (8) W-C	0.70 OF 10	4 3 0 7 XSQ= 3.15 PHI= 0.474 EP = 0.0699
346	DRIFT TCWARD BEING THCSE WHERE THE CHILD'S INFERRED ANXIETY OVER PERFCRMANCE CF SELF-RELIANT BEHAVIOR IS HIGH (37) B-B-C	0.71 OF 17	346	DRIFT TOWARD BEING THOSE WHERE THE CHILD'S INFERRED ANXIETY OVER PERFORMANCE OF SELF-RELIANT BEHAVIOR IS LOW (39) B-B-C	0.57 OF 54	12 23 5 31 XSQ= 3.01 PHI= 0.206 XP = 0.0827
370	LEAN TCWARD BEING THOSE WHERE THE SEGREGATION CF ACOLESCENT BOYS IS CCMPLETE CR PARTIAL (95)	0.57 OF 58	37C	LEAN TOWARD BEING THOSE WHERE THE SEGREGATION OF ADCLESCENT BOYS IS ABSENT (148)	0.66 CF 179	33 60 25 119 XSQ= 9.08 PHI= 0.196 XP = 0.0026
372	TEND TC BE THCSE WHERE MALE INITIATICN RITES ARE PRESENT (48) ASA	0.86 OF 22	372	TEND TO BE THOSE WHERE MALE INITIATICN RITES ARE ABSENT (63) ASA	0.65 CF 80	19 28 3 52 XSQ= 16.31 PHI= 0.400 XP = 0.0001
373	TILT TCWARD BEING THCSE WHERE MALE INITIATION CEREMONIES AT PUBERTY ARE PRESENT (17) W-K-A	0.78 OF 9	373	TILT TOWARD BEING THOSE WHERE MALE INITIATION CEREMONIES AT PUBERTY ARE ABSENT (27) W-K-A	0.70 CF 33	7 10 2 23 XSQ= 4.79 PHI= 0.338 XP = 0.0286
426	TEND MCRE TO BE THCSE WHERE A HIGH GCC IS PRESENT (156) GES,EA	0.78 OF 68	426	TEND LESS TO BE THOSE WHERE A HIGH GOD IS PRESENT (156) GES,EA	0.54 OF 189	53 102 15 87 XSQ= 11.03 PHI= 0.207 XP = 0.0009

427	DRIFT TOWARD BEING THOSE 0.66 OF 53 WHERE A HIGH GOD, IF PRESENT, IS ACTIVE, RATHER THAN INACTIVE (87) GES,EA	427	DRIFT TOWARD BEING THOSE 0.50 OF 102 WHERE A HIGH GOD, IF PRESENT, IS INACTIVE, RATHER THAN ACTIVE (69) GES,EA	35 51 18 51 XSQ= 3.01 PHI= 0.139 XP = 0.0827
428	TEND MORE TO BE THOSE 0.91 OF 35 WHERE A HIGH GOD, IF PRESENT AND ACTIVE, SUPPORTS HUMAN MORALITY, RATHER THAN NOT SUPPORTING IT (61) GES,EA	428	TEND LESS TO BE THOSE 0.55 OF 51 WHERE A HIGH GOD, IF PRESENT AND ACTIVE, SUPPORTS HUMAN MORALITY, RATHER THAN NOT SUPPORTING IT (61) GES,EA	32 28 3 23 XSQ= 11.45 PHI= 0.365 XP = 0.0007
451	IN ALL CASES ARE THOSE 1.00 OF 5 WHERE TOTEMISM IS PRESENT (15) LWS	451	TILT TOWARD BEING THOSE 0.57 OF 21 WHERE TOTEMISM IS UNIMPORTANT OR ABSENT (12) LWS	5 9 0 12 XSQ= 3.26 PHI= 0.354 EP = 0.0425
458	TEND TO BE THOSE 0.63 OF 32 WHERE GAMES, IF PRESENT, INCLUDE GAMES OF STRATEGY (52) R-A-B,EA	458	TEND TO BE THOSE 0.78 OF 136 WHERE GAMES, IF PRESENT, DO NOT INCLUDE GAMES OF STRATEGY (119) R-A-B,EA	20 30 12 106 XSQ= 18.38 PHI= 0.331 XP = 0.0000
472	DRIFT TOWARD BEING THOSE 0.71 OF 21 WHERE THE COMPOSITE NARCISSISM INDEX IS HIGH (47) PES	472	DRIFT TOWARD BEING THOSE 0.54 OF 65 WHERE THE COMPOSITE NARCISSISM INDEX IS LOW (43) PES	15 30 6 35 XSQ= 3.11 PHI= 0.190 XP = 0.0776
475	TILT TOWARD BEING THOSE 0.82 OF 17 WHERE EXHIBITIONISTIC DANCING IS STRONGLY OR MODERATELY EMPHASIZED (48) PES	475	TILT TOWARD BEING THOSE 0.51 OF 65 WHERE EXHIBITIONISTIC DANCING IS NEGLIGIBLY EMPHASIZED (38) PES	14 32 3 33 XSQ= 4.73 PHI= 0.240 XP = 0.0296

378 CULTURES WHERE MALE GENITAL MUTILATION, IF PRESENT, OCCURS IN LATE CHILDHOOD OR EARLIER (38)

378 CULTURES WHERE MALE GENITAL MUTILATION, IF PRESENT, OCCURS IN ADOLESCENCE OR LATER (29)

BACKGROUND ON PAGE 151

SUBJECT ONLY

38 IN LEFT COLUMN

AZANDE	BARABRA	BASSERI	BAYA	BEJA	BUNLAP	DIERI	EGYPTIANS	KAZAK	KOHISTANI
KPE	KUBA	LESU	MACASSARESE	MERINA	MONGO	MOSSI	MURNGIN	MZAB	NUPE
PAEZ	PATHAN	RIFFIANS	RWALA	SAMOANS	SANDAWE	SIWANS	SOMALI	SONGHAI	SYRIANS
TANALA	TENDA	TERA	TIGRINYA	TIV	WOLOF	YAO	YORUBA		

29 IN RIGHT COLUMN

ARANDA	BAMBARA	BAMILEKE	BANDA	BOZO	CHAGGA	DILLING	DOGON	DOROBO	FANG
FON	FUTAJALONKE	GISU	JAVANESE	KIKUYU	KISSI	LAU	MAMVU	MANGAIANS	MARQUESANS
MASAI	MENDE	MURINBATA	NANDI	SWAZI	TEDA	THONGA	TIKOPIA	TOKELAU	

16 EXCLUDED BECAUSE AMBIGUOUS

BURUSHO	CHERKESS	DAGUR	GURE	HAZARA	HEBREWS	HERERO	INGASSANA	IRAQW	KABYLE
MALAYS	REGEIBAT	SHLUH	TOTONAC	TURKMEN	YOMBE				

242 EXCLUDED BECAUSE IRRELEVANT (SEE RIGHT COLUMN, PARAGRAPH 377)

75 EXCLUDED BECAUSE UNASCERTAINED

3	LEAN TOWARD BEING THOSE LOCATED OUTSIDE OF AFRICA (320)	0.68 OF 38	3	LEAN TOWARD BEING THOSE LOCATED IN AFRICA (80)	0.69 OF 29	12 20 26 9 XSQ= 7.78 PHI= -0.341 XP = 0.0053
4	LEAN LESS TOWARD BEING THOSE LOCATED OUTSIDE OF THE CIRCUM-MEDITERRANEAN (355)	0.66 OF 38	4	LEAN MORE TOWARD BEING THOSE LOCATED OUTSIDE OF THE CIRCUM-MEDITERRANEAN (355)	0.97 OF 29	13 1 25 28 XSQ= 7.65 PHI= 0.338 XP = 0.0057
5	DRIFT LESS TOWARD BEING THOSE LOCATED OUTSIDE OF EAST EURASIA (330)	0.84 OF 38	5	IN ALL CASES ARE THOSE LOCATED OUTSIDE OF EAST EURASIA (330)	1.00 OF 29	6 0 32 29 XSQ= 3.28 PHI= 0.221 XP = 0.0702

14	TILT LESS TOWARD BEING THOSE WHERE THE LATITUDE IS LESS THAN THIRTY DEGREES (281)	0.79 OF 38	14 IN ALL CASES ARE THOSE WHERE THE LATITUDE IS LESS THAN THIRTY DEGREES (281) 1.00 OF 29	8 0 30 29 XSQ= 5.08 PHI= 0.275 XP = 0.0243
73	TEND TO BE THOSE WHERE WEAVING IS PRESENT (118)	0.81 OF 27	73 TEND TO BE THOSE WHERE WEAVING IS ABSENT (130) 0.76 OF 21	22 5 5 16 XSQ= 13.71 PHI= 0.534 XP = 0.0002
110	DRIFT TOWARD BEING THOSE WHERE SLAVERY IS PRESENT (163)	0.69 OF 36	110 DRIFT TOWARD BEING THOSE WHERE SLAVERY IS ABSENT (218) 0.55 OF 29	25 13 11 16 XSQ= 3.06 PHI= 0.217 XP = 0.0803
116	IN ALL CASES ARE THOSE WHERE OCCUPATIONAL SPECIALIZATION IS FULL-TIME, WHETHER OR NOT FOR SURPLUS PRODUCTION (20) JMH	1.00 OF 4	116 IN ALL CASES ARE THOSE WHERE OCCUPATIONAL SPECIALIZATION IS PART-TIME ONLY (34) JMH 1.00 OF 4	4 0 0 4 XSQ= 4.50 PHI= 0.750 EP = 0.0286
180	DRIFT TOWARD BEING THOSE WHERE THE COMMUNITY IS COMMONLY NON-EXOGAMOUS, RATHER THAN EXOGAMOUS (258)	0.68 OF 37	180 DRIFT TOWARD BEING THOSE WHERE THE COMMUNITY IS COMMONLY EXOGAMOUS, RATHER THAN NON-EXOGAMOUS (124) 0.57 OF 28	12 16 25 12 XSQ= 3.03 PHI= -0.216 XP = 0.0820
225	TILT TOWARD BEING THOSE WHERE COUSIN MARRIAGE IS PREFERENTIALLY OR PERMISSIVELY PATRILATERAL, RATHER THAN MATRILATERAL (23)	0.78 OF 9	225 IN ALL CASES ARE THOSE WHERE COUSIN MARRIAGE IS PREFERENTIALLY OR PERMISSIVELY MATRILATERAL, RATHER THAN PATRILATERAL (43) 1.00 OF 3	7 0 2 3 XSQ= 2.86 PHI= 0.488 EP = 0.0455
348	TILT TOWARD BEING THOSE WHERE THE TOTAL POSITIVE PRESSURE TOWARD DEVELOPING ACHIEVEMENT BEHAVIOR IN THE CHILD IS LOW (31) B-B-C	0.86 OF 7	348 TILT TOWARD BEING THOSE WHERE THE TOTAL POSITIVE PRESSURE TOWARD DEVELOPING ACHIEVEMENT BEHAVIOR IN THE CHILD IS HIGH (32) B-B-C 0.88 OF 8	1 7 6 1 XSQ= 5.37 PHI= -0.598 EP = 0.0101
349	TILT TOWARD BEING THOSE WHERE THE CHILD'S INFERRED ANXIETY OVER NON-PERFORMANCE OF ACHIEVEMENT BEHAVIOR IS LOW (28) B-B-C	0.71 OF 7	349 TILT TOWARD BEING THOSE WHERE THE CHILD'S INFERRED ANXIETY OVER NON-PERFORMANCE OF ACHIEVEMENT BEHAVIOR IS HIGH (34) B-B-C 0.88 OF 8	2 7 5 1 XSQ= 3.23 PHI= -0.464 EP = 0.0406
372	DRIFT LESS TOWARD BEING THOSE WHERE MALE INITIATION RITES ARE PRESENT (48) ASA	0.67 OF 9	372 IN ALL CASES ARE THOSE WHERE MALE INITIATION RITES ARE PRESENT (48) ASA 1.00 OF 12	6 12 3 0 XSQ= 2.34 PHI= -0.334 EP = 0.0632

406	TILT TCWARD BEING THCSE WHERE EXPLANATICNS CF ILLNESS CF AN AGGRESSICN NATURE ARE PRESENT (28) W-C	0.63 OF 8	406	IN ALL CASES ARE THOSE WHERE EXPLANATIONS OF ILLNESS OF AN AGGRESSICN NATURE ARE ABSENT (33) W-C	1.00 OF 6	5 0 3 6 XSQ= 3.43 PHI= 0.495 EP = 0.0310
426	TILT MORE TOWARC BEING THCSE WHERE A HIGH GCC IS PRESENT (156) GES,EA	0.85 OF 34	426	TILT LESS TOWARD BEING THOSE WHERE A HIGH GCD IS PRESENT (156) GES,EA	0.57 OF 23	29 13 5 10 XSQ= 4.47 PHI= 0.280 XP = 0.0345
434	LEAN TCWARC BEING THCSE WHERE ASCETICISM IN MOURNING BEHAVIOR IS LCW (30) JFG	0.83 OF 6	434	IN ALL CASES ARE THOSE WHERE ASCETICISM IN MOURNING BEHAVIOR IS HIGH (37) JFG	1.00 CF 7	1 7 5 0 XSQ= 6.29 PHI= -0.695 EP = 0.0047

379 CULTURES
WHERE SEVERE GENITAL OPERATIONS
ASSOCIATED WITH MALE INITIATION RITES
ARE PRESENT (14) ASA

379 CULTURES
WHERE SEVERE GENITAL OPERATIONS
ASSOCIATED WITH MALE INITIATION RITES
ARE ABSENT (9) ASA

BACKGROUND ON PAGE 152

SUBJECT ONLY

14 IN LEFT COLUMN

ARAPESH	AZANDE	CHAGGA	FON	LESU	MARQUESANS	MASAI	MURNGIN	SAMOANS	THONGA
TIKOPIA	TIV	VENDA	WOGEO						

9 IN RIGHT COLUMN

ANDAMANESE	BALINESE	HANO	JIVARO	KURTATCHI	MANUS	PUKAPUKA	TAOS	ZUNI

26 EXCLUDED BECAUSE IRRELEVANT

ALORESE	ASHANTI	CHENCHU	CHIR-APACHE	COMANCHE	COPR ESKIMO	DOBUANS	IFUGAO	KUTENAI	LAKHER
LAMBA	LEPCHA	MAORI	MARSHALLESE	NAVAHO	ONTONG-JAVA	PAPAGO	RIFFIANS	RWALA	SANPOIL
SIRIONO	TANALA	TETON	TROBRIAND	WAPISHANA	YAGUA				

351 EXCLUDED BECAUSE UNASCERTAINED

3	TILT TOWARD BEING THOSE LOCATED IN AFRICA (80)	0.50 OF 14	3	IN ALL CASES ARE THOSE LOCATED OUTSIDE OF AFRICA (320)	1.00 OF 9	7 0 7 9 XSQ= 4.32 PHI= 0.434 EP = 0.0189
8	IN ALL CASES ARE THOSE LOCATED OUTSIDE OF NORTH AMERICA (330)	1.00 OF 14	8	TILT LESS TOWARD BEING THOSE LOCATED OUTSIDE OF NORTH AMERICA (330)	0.67 OF 9	0 3 14 6 XSQ= 2.83 PHI= -0.351 EP = 0.0474
14	IN ALL CASES ARE THOSE WHERE THE LATITUDE IS LESS THAN THIRTY DEGREES (281)	1.00 OF 14	14	TILT LESS TOWARD BEING THOSE WHERE THE LATITUDE IS LESS THAN THIRTY DEGREES (281)	0.67 OF 9	0 3 14 6 XSQ= 2.83 PHI= -0.351 EP = 0.0474
33	DRIFT MORE TOWARD BEING THOSE WHERE THE NATURAL ENVIRONMENT IS OTHER THAN 'VERY HARSH,' I.E., DESERT, DESERT GRASSES AND SHRUBS, TUNDRA, OR HIGH PLATEAU STEPPE (341) FWM	0.93 OF 14	33	DRIFT LESS TOWARD BEING THOSE WHERE THE NATURAL ENVIRONMENT IS OTHER THAN 'VERY HARSH,' I.E., DESERT, DESERT GRASSES AND SHRUBS, TUNDRA, OR HIGH PLATEAU STEPPE (341) FWM	0.56 OF 9	1 4 13 5 XSQ= 2.56 PHI= -0.333 EP = 0.0562

No.	Statement	Proportion	N	No.	Statement	Proportion	N	Statistics
86	DRIFT TOWARD BEING THOSE WHERE THE LEVEL OF POLITICAL INTEGRATION IS THE LARGE STATE, THE LITTLE STATE, OR THE MINIMAL STATE (148) GPM	0.58 OF	12	86	DRIFT TOWARD BEING THOSE WHERE THE LEVEL OF POLITICAL INTEGRATION IS THE AUTONOMOUS COMMUNITY, OR THE FAMILY (156) GPM	0.88 OF	8	7 1 5 7 XSQ= 2.51 PHI= 0.354 EP = 0.0697
88	TILT TOWARD BEING THOSE WHERE, IF A HEADMANSHIP IS PRESENT, SUCCESSION IS HEREDITARY (165)	0.91 OF	11	88	TILT TOWARD BEING THOSE WHERE, IF A HEADMANSHIP IS PRESENT, SUCCESSION IS NON-HEREDITARY (106)	0.57 OF	7	1 4 10 3 XSQ= 2.82 PHI= -0.396 EP = 0.0474
95	DRIFT LESS TOWARD BEING THOSE WHERE THE HIERARCHY OF NATIONAL JURISDICTION HAS ONE OR NO LEVELS (254) GES,EA	0.57 OF	14	95	IN ALL CASES ARE THOSE WHERE THE HIERARCHY OF NATIONAL JURISDICTION HAS ONE OR NO LEVELS (254) GES,EA	1.00 OF	8	6 0 8 8 XSQ= 2.80 PHI= 0.357 EP = 0.0511
96	TILT TOWARD BEING THOSE WHERE THE HIERARCHY OF NATIONAL JURISDICTION HAS FOUR, THREE, TWO OR ONE LEVEL (174) GES,EA	0.71 OF	14	96	TILT TOWARD BEING THOSE WHERE THE HIERARCHY OF NATIONAL JURISDICTION HAS NO LEVELS (156) GES,EA	0.88 OF	8	10 1 4 7 XSQ= 4.91 PHI= 0.472 EP = 0.0237
137	DRIFT TOWARD BEING THOSE WHERE INVIDIOUS DISPLAY OF WEALTH IS STRONGLY EMPHASIZED (37) PES	0.57 OF	14	137	DRIFT TOWARD BEING THOSE WHERE INVIDIOUS DISPLAY OF WEALTH IS MODERATELY, LITTLE, OR NEGATIVELY EMPHASIZED (52) PES	0.86 OF	7	8 1 6 6 XSQ= 1.97 PHI= 0.306 EP = 0.0873
142	IN ALL CASES ARE THOSE WHERE THE LEVEL OF SOCIAL SANCTION IS PUBLIC CORPOREAL SANCTION OR PUBLIC PROPERTY SANCTION, RATHER THAN PRIVATE SETTLEMENT (38) JMH	1.00 OF	6	142	TILT TOWARD BEING THOSE WHERE THE LEVEL OF SOCIAL SANCTION IS PRIVATE SETTLEMENT, RATHER THAN PUBLIC CORPOREAL SANCTION OR PUBLIC PROPERTY SETTLEMENT (16) JMH	0.75 OF	4	6 1 0 3 XSQ= 3.35 PHI= 0.579 EP = 0.0333
149	TILT TOWARD BEING THOSE WHERE THE INCIDENCE OF THEFT IS HIGH (18) B-B-C	0.75 OF	8	149	TILT TOWARD BEING THOSE WHERE THE INCIDENCE OF THEFT IS LOW (19) B-B-C	0.86 OF	7	6 1 2 6 XSQ= 3.36 PHI= 0.473 EP = 0.0406
181	IN ALL CASES ARE THOSE WHERE THE COMMUNITY IS OTHER THAN A DEME (337)	1.00 OF	14	181	TILT LESS TOWARD BEING THOSE WHERE THE COMMUNITY IS OTHER THAN A DEME (337)	0.67 OF	9	0 3 14 6 XSQ= 2.83 PHI= -0.351 EP = 0.0474
185	IN ALL CASES ARE THOSE WHERE THE LARGEST NON-COGNATIC KIN GROUP IS THE MOEITY OR PHRATRY OR SIB (194)	1.00 OF	12	185	DRIFT LESS TOWARD BEING THOSE WHERE THE LARGEST NON-COGNATIC KIN GROUP IS THE MOEITY OR PHRATRY OR SIB (194)	0.60 OF	5	12 3 0 2 XSQ= 2.27 PHI= 0.365 EP = 0.0735

186	TILT LESS TOWARC BEING THCSE WHERE THE KIN GRCUP IS CTHER THAN EXCLUSIVELY PATRILINEAL (250)	0.57 OF 14	186	IN ALL CASES ARE THOSE WHERE THE KIN GROUP IS OTHER THAN EXCLUSIVELY PATRILINEAL (250)	1.00 OF 9	6 0 8 9 XSQ= 3.23 PHI= 0.375 EP = 0.0481
190	TILT TCWARD BEING THOSE WHERE THE KIN GRCUP IS PATRILINEAL CR CCUBLE-CESCENT, RATHER THAN MATRILINEAL (186)	0.92 OF 12	19C	TILT TOWARD BEING THOSE WHERE THE KIN GROUP IS MATRILINEAL, RATHER THAN PATRILINEAL OR DOUBLE-DESCENT (61)	0.75 OF 4	11 1 1 3 XSQ= 4.00 PHI= 0.500 EP = 0.0269
198	IN ALL CASES ARE THOSE WHERE RULES FCR THE INHERITANCE OF REAL PROPERTY, IF PRESENT, FAVCR THE MALE HEIR CR LINE, RATHER THAN THE FEMALE (144)	1.00 OF 7	198	IN ALL CASES ARE THOSE WHERE RULES FOR THE INHERITANCE OF REAL PROPERTY, IF PRESENT, FAVOR THE FEMALE HEIR OR LINE, RATHER THAN THE MALE (21)	1.00 OF 2	7 0 0 2 XSQ= 4.14 PHI= 0.679 EP = 0.0278
242	IN ALL CASES ARE THOSE WHERE MARRIAGE IS COMMCNLY CR CCCASICNALLY PCLYGYNOUS, RATHER THAN MCNCGAMCUS (314)	1.00 OF 13	242	LEAN TOWARD BEING THOSE WHERE MARRIAGE IS MCNOGAMOUS, RATHER THAN COMMONLY OR OCCASIONALLY POLYGYNOUS (81)	0.56 OF 9	13 4 0 5 XSQ= 6.45 PHI= 0.541 EP = 0.0048
285	DRIFT TOWARD BEING THCSE WHERE THE SEX TABOC DURING PREGNANCY IS PRESENT (14) BCA	0.60 OF 10	285	IN ALL CASES ARE THOSE WHERE THE SEX TABOO DURING PREGNANCY IS ABSENT OR INFERRED ABSENT (17) BCA	1.00 OF 4	6 0 4 4 XSQ= 2.11 PHI= 0.388 EP = 0.0849
296	TILT TCWARD BEING THOSE WHERE INFANTICICE IS PRESENT (18) BCA	0.89 OF 9	296	TILT TOWARD BEING THOSE WHERE INFANTICIDE IS ABSENT OR INFERRED ABSENT (15) BCA	0.83 OF 6	8 1 1 5 XSQ= 5.10 PHI= 0.583 EP = 0.0110
314	DRIFT TOWARD BEING THCSE WHERE THE INCIDENCE CF MOTHER-CHILC HCUSEHCLDS IS HIGH (19) W-D,S	0.60 OF 10	314	DRIFT TOWARD BEING THOSE WHERE THE INCIDENCE OF MOTHER-CHILD HOUSEHOLDS IS LOW (61) W-D,S	0.88 OF 8	6 1 4 7 XSQ= 2.46 PHI= 0.369 EP = 0.0656
316	IN ALL CASES ARE THOSE WHERE EXCLUSIVE MOTHER-SCN SLEEPING ARRANGEMENTS LAST CNE YEAR CR LCNGER (19) W-K-A	1.00 OF 7	316	DRIFT TOWARD BEING THOSE WHERE EXCLUSIVE MOTHER-SCN SLEEPING ARRANGEMENTS LAST LESS THAN ONE YEAR (25) W-K-A	0.67 CF 3	7 1 0 2 XSQ= 2.41 PHI= 0.491 EP = 0.0667
341	DRIFT TCWARD BEING THCSE WHERE THE CHILD'S INFERREC ANXIETY OVER NCN-PERFCRMANCE OF NURTURANT BEHAVIOR IS HIGH (30) B-B-C	0.75 OF 8	341	IN ALL CASES ARE THOSE WHERE THE CHILD'S INFERRED ANXIETY OVER NON-PERFORMANCE OF NURTURANT BEHAVICR IS LOW (16) B-B-C	1.00 OF 4	6 0 2 4 XSQ= 3.38 PHI= 0.530 EP = 0.0606

No.	Description	Prop.	N	No.	Description	Prop.	N	Statistics
352	DRIFT TCWARD BEING THCSE WHERE THE TOTAL POSITIVE PRESSURE TOWARD DEVELCPING OBEDIENT BEHAVICR IN THE CHILD IS HIGH (44) B-B-C	0.67 OF	12	352	DRIFT TOWARD BEING THOSE WHERE THE TOTAL POSITIVE PRESSURE TOWARD DEVELOPING OBEDIENT BEHAVICR IN THE CHILD IS LOW (28) B-B-C	0.86 OF	7	8 1 4 6 XSQ= 2.99 PHI= 0.397 EP = 0.0573
355	DRIFT TCWARD BEING THOSE WHERE THE CHILD'S INFERREC CONFLICT REGARDING CBEDIENT BEHAVICR IS HIGH (35) B-B-C	0.75 OF	12	355	DRIFT TOWARD BEING THOSE WHERE THE CHILD'S INFERRED CONFLICT REGARDING OBEDIENT BEHAVIOR IS LOW (38) B-B-C	0.71 OF	7	9 2 3 5 XSQ= 2.24 PHI= 0.343 EP = 0.0739
377	LEAN TCWARD BEING THCSE WHERE MALE GENITAL MUTILATION IS PRESENT (83)	0.79 OF	14	377	IN ALL CASES ARE THOSE WHERE MALE GENITAL MUTILATICN IS ABSENT (242)	1.00 OF	8	11 0 3 8 XSQ= 9.63 PHI= 0.661 EP = 0.0010
452	IN ALL CASES ARE THOSE WHERE TCTEMISM WITH FCOC TABOOS IS PRESENT (19) WNS	1.00 OF	6	452	DRIFT TOWARD BEING THOSE WHERE TOTEMISM WITH FOOD TABCOS IS ABSENT (24) WNS	0.60 OF	5	6 2 0 3 XSQ= 2.39 PHI= 0.466 EP = 0.0606
472	DRIFT TCWARD BEING THCSE WHERE THE COMPOSITE NARCISSISM INCEX IS HIGH (47) PES	0.79 OF	14	472	DRIFT TOWARD BEING THOSE WHERE THE COMPOSITE NARCISSISM INDEX IS LOW (43) PES	0.63 CF	8	11 3 3 5 XSQ= 2.15 PHI= 0.312 EP = 0.0815

380 CULTURES
WHERE SEGREGATION OF GIRLS AT MENARCHE
IS PRESENT (35) F-B

380 CULTURES
WHERE SEGREGATION OF GIRLS AT MENARCHE
IS ABSENT (20) F-B

BACKGROUND ON PAGE 153

BOTH SUBJECT AND PREDICATE

35 IN LEFT COLUMN

ANDAMANESE	ASHANTI	CARIB	CHAGGA	CHEYENNE	CHIR-APACHE	CREE	CUNA	FON	FOX
GOAJIRO	HANC	HAVASUPAI	ILA	KUTENAI	KWAKIUTL	LAMBA	MANUS	MARICOPA	MARSHALLESE
MATACO	MBUNDU	NAMA	NANDI	NAVAHO	PAPAGO	SWAZI	TEHUELCHE	THONGA	TOLOWA
TROBRIAND	TRUKESE	WOGEO	WOLOF	YAPESE					

20 IN RIGHT COLUMN

ABIPON	AINU	ALORESE	APINAYE	ARANDA	BALINESE	CHOROTI	DIERI	DUSUN	KIOW-APACHE
LANGO	LIFU	PALAUANS	PUKAPUKA	SAMOANS	SENIANG	TIKOPIA	TIV	TODA	WARRAU

345 EXCLUDED BECAUSE UNASCERTAINED

	Left column			Right column		
6	LEAN TOWARD BEING THOSE LOCATED OUTSIDE OF THE INSULAR PACIFIC (330)	0.83 OF 35	6	LEAN TOWARD BEING THOSE LOCATED IN THE INSULAR PACIFIC (70)	0.55 OF 20	6 11 29 9 XSQ= 6.86 PHI= -0.353 XP = 0.0088
8	TILT LESS TOWARD BEING THOSE LOCATED OUTSIDE OF NORTH AMERICA (330)	0.66 OF 35	8	TILT MORE TOWARD BEING THOSE LOCATED OUTSIDE OF NORTH AMERICA (330)	0.95 OF 20	12 1 23 19 XSQ= 4.53 PHI= 0.287 XP = 0.0332
14	DRIFT LESS TOWARD BEING THOSE WHERE THE LATITUDE IS LESS THAN THIRTY DEGREES (281)	0.63 OF 35	14	DRIFT MORE TOWARD BEING THOSE WHERE THE LATITUDE IS LESS THAN THIRTY DEGREES (281)	0.90 OF 20	13 2 22 18 XSQ= 3.46 PHI= 0.251 XP = 0.0629
62	DRIFT TOWARD BEING THOSE WHERE HUSBANDRY OF SOME KIND IS PRESENT (228)	0.74 OF 35	62	DRIFT TOWARD BEING THOSE WHERE HUSBANDRY OF ANY KIND IS ABSENT (172)	0.55 OF 20	26 9 9 11 XSQ= 3.54 PHI= 0.254 XP = 0.0600

71	DRIFT LESS TCWARD BEING THCSE WHERE METAL WORKING IS ABSENT (153)	0.61 OF 31	71	DRIFT MORE TOWARD BEING THCSE WHERE METAL WORKING IS ABSENT (153)	0.93 OF 14	12 1 19 13 XSQ= 3.27 PHI= 0.269 XP = 0.0707
74	LEAN TCWARD BEING THCSE WHERE PCTTERY IS PRESENT (145)	0.82 OF 28	74	LEAN TOWARD BEING THOSE WHERE POTTERY IS ABSENT (93)	0.73 OF 15	23 4 5 11 XSQ= 10.60 PHI= 0.497 XP = 0.0011
136	DRIFT TCWARD BEING THCSE WHERE FULL-TIME ENTREPRENEURS ARE PRESENT (18) JV	0.86 OF 7	136	IN ALL CASES ARE THOSE WHERE FULL-TIME ENTREPRENEURS ARE ABSENT (14) JV	1.00 OF 2	6 0 1 2 XSQ= 2.01 PHI= 0.472 EP = 0.0833
234	TILT TCWARD BEING THCSE WHERE THE COUSIN TERMINCLCGY IS CF CRCW, CMAHA, CR IRCQUCIS TYPE, RATHER THAN ESKIMC CR HAWAIIAN TYPE (152)	0.71 OF 31	234	TILT TOWARD BEING THOSE WHERE THE COUSIN TERMINCLOGY IS OF ESKIMO OR HAWAIIAN TYPE, RATHER THAN CROW, OMAHA, OR IROQUOIS TYPE (170)	0.68 OF 19	22 6 9 13 XSQ= 5.90 PHI= 0.344 XP = 0.0151
312	DRIFT TCWARD BEING THCSE WHERE DEPENDENCE SCCIALIZATION ANXIETY IS LCW (23) W-C	0.53 OF 15	312	DRIFT TOWARD BEING THOSE WHERE DEPENDENCE SOCIALIZATICN ANXIETY IS HIGH (24) W-C	0.88 OF 8	7 7 8 1 XSQ= 2.14 PHI= -0.305 EP = 0.0858
352	DRIFT TCWARD BEING THCSE WHERE THE TOTAL PCSITIVE PRESSURE TOWARD DEVELCPING CBEDIENT BEHAVICR IN THE CHILD IS HIGH (44) B-B-C	0.76 OF 17	352	DRIFT TOWARD BEING THOSE WHERE THE TOTAL PCSITIVE PRESSURE TOWARC DEVELOPING OBEDIENT BEHAVICR IN THE CHILD IS LOW (28) B-B-C	0.63 CF 8	13 3 4 5 XSQ= 2.09 PHI= 0.289 EP = 0.0870
372	TILT TCWARC BEING THCSE WHERE MALE INITIATICN RITES ARE ABSENT (63) ASA	0.59 OF 27	372	TILT TOWARD BEING THOSE WHERE MALE INITIATION RITES ARE PRESENT (48) ASA	0.82 OF 11	11 9 16 2 XSQ= 3.77 PHI= -0.315 EP = 0.0327
382	IN ALL CASES ARE THCSE WHERE FEMALE INITIATICN RITES ARE PRESENT (38) JKB	1.00 OF 13	382	LEAN TOWARD BEING THOSE WHERE FEMALE INITIATION RITES ARE ABSENT (27) JKB	0.57 CF 7	13 3 0 4 XSQ= 6.06 PHI= 0.550 EP = 0.0072
437	DRIFT TCWARD BEING THCSE WHERE FEAR CF GHCSTS, SPIRITS, HUMANS OR ANIMALS IS HIGH (21) W-C,JFG	0.62 OF 13	437	DRIFT TOWARD BEING THOSE WHERE FEAR OF GHOSTS, SPIRITS, HUMANS OR ANIMALS IS LOW (23) W-C,JFG	0.78 CF 9	8 2 5 7 XSQ= 1.92 PHI= 0.295 EP = 0.0991

451	DRIFT TOWARD BEING THOSE WHERE TOTEMISM IS UNIMPORTANT OR ABSENT (12) LWS	0.57 OF 7	451	IN ALL CASES ARE THOSE WHERE TOTEMISM IS PRESENT (15) LWS	1.00 OF 5	3 5 4 0 XSQ= 2.10 PHI= -0.418 EP = 0.0808
459	TILT TOWARD BEING THOSE WHERE GAMES, IF PRESENT, INCLUDE GAMES OF CHANCE (82) R-A-B,EA	0.61 OF 28	459	TILT TOWARD BEING THOSE WHERE GAMES, IF PRESENT, DO NOT INCLUDE GAMES OF CHANCE (89) R-A-B,EA	0.79 OF 14	17 3 11 11 XSQ= 4.31 PHI= 0.320 XP = 0.0379
460	TILT TOWARD BEING THOSE WHERE GAMES, IF PRESENT, ARE NOT LIMITED TO GAMES OF SKILL ONLY (104) R-A-B,EA	0.75 OF 28	460	TILT TOWARD BEING THOSE WHERE GAMES, IF PRESENT, ARE LIMITED TO GAMES OF SKILL ONLY (67) R-A-B,EA	0.71 OF 14	7 10 21 4 XSQ= 6.53 PHI= -0.394 XP = 0.0106
480	DRIFT TOWARD BEING THOSE WHERE COMPLEXITY OF ARTISTIC DESIGN IS LOW (15) HB	0.64 OF 11	480	IN ALL CASES ARE THOSE WHERE COMPLEXITY OF ARTISTIC DESIGN IS HIGH (14) HB	1.00 OF 4	4 4 7 0 XSQ= 2.56 PHI= -0.413 EP = 0.0769

382 CULTURES WHERE FEMALE INITIATION RITES ARE PRESENT (38) JKB	382 CULTURES WHERE FEMALE INITIATION RITES ARE ABSENT (27) JKB

BACKGROUND ON PAGE 153

BOTH SUBJECT AND PREDICATE

38 IN LEFT COLUMN

ANDAMANESE	ARANDA	BEMBA	BURMESE	CAGABA	CARIB	CHAMACOCO	CHEYENNE	CHIR-APACHE	CHOROTI
CUNA	FON	GANDA	GOAJIRO	JIVARO	KURTATCHI	LAMBA	LESU	MENDE	MOSSI
MUNDURUCU	NAMA	NAMBICUARA	NASKAPI	NAVAHO	OJIBWA	PAPAGO	PUKAPUKA	SANPOIL	TEDA
TEHUELCHE	THAI	THONGA	TUBATULABAL	TUPINAMBA	WOLEAIANS	YAGUA	YUROK		

27 IN RIGHT COLUMN

AINU	ALORESE	AMERICANS	ARAUCANIANS	AYMARA	AZANDE	BALINESE	BHIL	BULGARIANS	CAYAPA
COPR ESKIMO	DILLING	EGYPTIANS	JAPANESE	KAZAK	KHASI	LAPPS	LEPCHA	MAGUZAWA	NUER
RWALA	SAMOYED	SOMALI	TALLENSI	TANALA	TIMBIRA	TODA			

335 EXCLUDED BECAUSE UNASCERTAINED

4	TILT MORE TOWARD BEING THOSE LOCATED OUTSIDE OF THE CIRCUM-MEDITERRANEAN (355)	0.97 OF 38	4	TILT LESS TOWARD BEING THOSE LOCATED OUTSIDE OF THE CIRCUM-MEDITERRANEAN (355)	0.74 OF 27	1 7 37 20	XSQ= 5.92 PHI= -0.302 XP = 0.0149
5	TILT MORE TOWARD BEING THOSE LOCATED OUTSIDE OF EAST EURASIA (330)	0.92 OF 38	5	TILT LESS TOWARD BEING THOSE LOCATED OUTSIDE OF EAST EURASIA (330)	0.67 OF 27	3 9 35 18	XSQ= 5.20 PHI= -0.283 XP = 0.0226
8	DRIFT LESS TOWARD BEING THOSE LOCATED OUTSIDE OF NORTH AMERICA (330)	0.76 OF 38	8	DRIFT MORE TOWARD BEING THOSE LOCATED OUTSIDE OF NORTH AMERICA (330)	0.96 OF 27	9 1 29 26	XSQ= 3.43 PHI= 0.230 XP = 0.0641
51	LEAN TOWARD BEING THOSE WHERE SUBSISTENCE IS PRIMARILY BY FOOD GATHERING -- I. E., HUNTING, FISHING, OR COLLECTING -- RATHER THAN FOOD PRODUCTION (147)	0.55 OF 38	51	LEAN TOWARD BEING THOSE WHERE SUBSISTENCE IS PRIMARILY BY FOOD PRODUCTION -- I. E., AGRICULTURE OR HUSBANDRY -- RATHER THAN BY GATHERING (253)	0.81 OF 27	17 22 21 5	XSQ= 7.41 PHI= -0.338 XP = 0.0065

53	TILT TOWARD BEING THOSE WHERE FOOD PRODUCTION IS BY SIMPLE AGRICULTURE OR INCIPIENT FOOD PRODUCTION, RATHER THAN BY INTENSIVE AGRICULTURE (147)	0.82 OF 22	53	TILT TOWARD BEING THOSE WHERE FOOD PRODUCTION IS BY INTENSIVE AGRICULTURE, RATHER THAN BY SIMPLE AGRICULTURE OR INCIPIENT FOOD PRODUCTION (91)	0.59 OF 17	4 10 18 7 XSQ= 5.23 PHI= -0.366 EP = 0.0172
55	TILT TOWARD BEING THOSE WHERE FOOD PRODUCTION IS BY SIMPLE AGRICULTURE, RATHER THAN BY INTENSIVE AGRICULTURE (101)	0.73 OF 15	55	TILT TOWARD BEING THOSE WHERE FOOD PRODUCTION IS BY INTENSIVE AGRICULTURE, RATHER THAN BY SIMPLE AGRICULTURE (91)	0.71 OF 14	4 10 11 4 XSQ= 4.16 PHI= -0.379 EP = 0.0268
62	DRIFT LESS TOWARD BEING THOSE WHERE HUSBANDRY OF SOME KIND IS PRESENT (228)	0.55 OF 38	62	DRIFT MORE TOWARD BEING THOSE WHERE HUSBANDRY OF SOME KIND IS PRESENT (228)	0.81 OF 27	21 22 17 5 XSQ= 3.75 PHI= -0.240 XP = 0.0529
63	TILT TOWARD BEING THOSE WHERE HUSBANDRY, IF PRESENT, IS PRINCIPALLY IN THE FORM OF PIGS, SHEEP, OR GOATS, RATHER THAN BOVINE, EQUINE, CAMEL-LIKE, OR DEER-LIKE ANIMALS (74)	0.52 OF 21	63	TILT TOWARD BEING THOSE WHERE HUSBANDRY, IF PRESENT, IS PRINCIPALLY IN THE FORM OF BOVINE, EQUINE, CAMEL-LIKE, OR DEER-LIKE ANIMALS, RATHER THAN PIGS, SHEEP, OR GOATS (152)	0.82 OF 22	10 18 11 4 XSQ= 4.13 PHI= -0.310 XP = 0.0422
71	DRIFT TOWARD BEING THOSE WHERE METAL WORKING IS ABSENT (153)	0.69 OF 35	71	DRIFT TOWARD BEING THOSE WHERE METAL WORKING IS PRESENT (98)	0.62 OF 21	11 13 24 8 XSQ= 3.81 PHI= -0.261 XP = 0.0509
74	TILT TOWARD BEING THOSE WHERE POTTERY IS PRESENT (145)	0.80 OF 35	74	TILT TOWARD BEING THOSE WHERE POTTERY IS ABSENT (93)	0.52 OF 21	28 10 7 11 XSQ= 4.91 PHI= 0.296 XP = 0.0267
85	DRIFT MORE TOWARD BEING THOSE WHERE THE LEVEL OF POLITICAL INTEGRATION IS THE MINIMAL STATE, THE AUTONOMOUS COMMUNITY, OR THE FAMILY (234) GPM	0.78 OF 36	85	DRIFT LESS TOWARD BEING THOSE WHERE THE LEVEL OF POLITICAL INTEGRATION IS THE MINIMAL STATE, THE AUTONOMOUS COMMUNITY, OR THE FAMILY (234) GPM	0.52 OF 21	8 10 28 11 XSQ= 2.87 PHI= -0.224 XP = 0.0902
97	DRIFT MORE TOWARD BEING THOSE WHERE THE HIERARCHY OF LOCAL JURISDICTION HAS THREE OR TWO LEVELS (273) GES,EA	0.94 OF 36	97	DRIFT LESS TOWARD BEING THOSE WHERE THE HIERARCHY OF LOCAL JURISDICTION HAS THREE OR TWO LEVELS (273) GES,EA	0.76 OF 25	2 6 34 19 XSQ= 2.93 PHI= -0.219 XP = 0.0867
102	TILT TOWARD BEING THOSE WHERE CLASS STRATIFICATION IS ABSENT (180)	0.57 OF 37	102	TILT TOWARD BEING THOSE WHERE CLASS STRATIFICATION IS PRESENT (203)	0.74 OF 27	16 20 21 7 XSQ= 4.84 PHI= -0.275 XP = 0.0278

109	TILT MCRE TOWARC BEING THCSE WHERE CASTES ARE AESENT (317)	0.95 OF	37	109	TILT LESS TOWARD BEING THCSE WHERE CASTES ARE ABSENT (317)	0.72 CF	25	2 7 35 18 XSQ= 4.45 PHI= -0.268 XP = 0.0349
118	DRIFT TCWARD BEING THCSE WHERE THE PERCENTAGE CF OCCUPATIONS THAT ARE SPECIALIZEC IS LCW (25) WME	0.73 OF	11	118	DRIFT TOWARD BEING THOSE WHERE THE PERCENTAGE OF OCCUPATICNS THAT ARE SPECIALIZED IS HIGH OR MEDIUM (24) WME	0.67 OF	12	3 8 8 4 XSQ= 2.17 PHI= -0.307 EP = 0.0995
138	TILT TCWARC BEING THCSE WHERE SUPERORDINATE JUSTICE IS ABSENT (18) BBW	0.67 OF	9	138	TILT TOWARD BEING THCSE WHERE SUPERORDINATE JUSTICE IS PRESENT (22) BBW	0.88 OF	8	3 7 6 1 XSQ= 3.14 PHI= -0.430 EP = 0.0498
143	TILT TCWARD BEING THOSE WHERE THE RATIC CF RESTITUTIVE TC REPRESSIVE SANCTICNS IS MEDIUM CR LCW (32) WME	0.90 OF	1C	143	TILT TOWARD BEING THOSE WHERE THE RATIO OF RESTITUTIVE TO REPRESSIVE SANCTICNS IS HIGH (20) WME	0.53 CF	15	1 8 9 7 XSQ= 3.19 PHI= -0.357 EP = 0.0405
144	TILT TCWARC BEING THOSE WHERE THE RATIC CF RESTITUTIVE TC REPRESSIVE SANCTIONS IS LCW (25) WME	0.80 OF	10	144	TILT TOWARD BEING THOSE WHERE THE RATIO OF RESTITUTIVE TO REPRESSIVE SANCTICNS IS HIGH OR MEDIUM (27) WME	0.73 CF	15	2 11 8 4 XSQ= 4.87 PHI= -0.441 EP = 0.0154
147	IN ALL CASES ARE THCSE WHERE CCDIFIED LAWS ARE UNIMPCRTANT CR ABSENT (13) LWS	1.00 OF	2	147	IN ALL CASES ARE THOSE WHERE CODIFIED LAWS ARE PRESENT (20) LWS	1.00 CF	6	0 6 2 0 XSQ= 3.56 PHI= -0.667 EP = 0.0357
182	DRIFT LESS TCWARD BEING THCSE CTHER THAN WHERE THE COMMUNITY IS STRUCTURED ON A NCN-CLAN BASIS ANC AGAMOUS (256)	0.53 OF	38	182	DRIFT MORE TOWARD BEING THCSE OTHER THAN WHERE THE COMMUNITY IS STRUCTURED ON A NON-CLAN BASIS AND AGAMOUS (256)	0.78 OF	27	18 6 20 21 XSQ= 3.27 PHI= 0.224 XP = 0.0704
186	TILT TCWARD BEING THOSE WHERE THE KIN GRCUP IS CTHER THAN EXCLUSIVELY PATRILINEAL (250)	0.76 OF	38	186	TILT TOWARD BEING THOSE WHERE THE KIN GRCUP IS EXCLUSIVELY PATRILINEAL (150)	0.52 OF	27	9 14 29 13 XSQ= 4.31 PHI= -0.258 XP = 0.0378
188	DRIFT TCWARD BEING THCSE WHERE THE KIN GRCUP IS EXCLUSIVELY COGNATIC (148)	0.50 OF	38	188	DRIFT TOWARD BEING THCSE WHERE THE KIN GROUP IS OTHER THAN EXCLUSIVELY COGNATIC (252)	0.74 CF	27	19 7 19 20 XSQ= 2.87 PHI= 0.210 XP = 0.0900

196	TILT TOWARD BEING THOSE 0.58 OF 24 WHERE INDIVIDUAL RIGHTS IN REAL PROPERTY, OR RULES FOR INHERITANCE, ARE ABSENT (87)	196	TILT TOWARD BEING THOSE 0.77 OF 22 WHERE INDIVIDUAL RIGHTS IN REAL PROPERTY, AND RULES FOR INHERITANCE, ARE PRESENT (194)	10 17 14 5 XSQ= 4.62 PHI= -0.317 XP = 0.0315
209	TILT LESS TOWARD BEING THOSE 0.63 OF 32 WHERE MARITAL RESIDENCE IS PATRILOCAL, VIRILOCAL, OR AVUNCULOCAL, RATHER THAN MATRILOCAL OR UXORILOCAL (270)	209	TILT MORE TOWARD BEING THOSE 0.92 OF 25 WHERE MARITAL RESIDENCE IS PATRILOCAL, VIRILOCAL, OR AVUNCULOCAL, RATHER THAN MATRILOCAL OR UXORILOCAL (270)	20 23 12 2 XSQ= 5.10 PHI= -0.299 XP = 0.0240
224	DRIFT MORE TOWARD BEING THOSE 0.88 OF 16 WHERE COUSIN MARRIAGE IS PREFERENTIALLY OR PERMISSIVELY SYMMETRICAL, RATHER THAN EITHER PATRI- OR MATRILATERAL (106)	224	DRIFT LESS TOWARD BEING THOSE 0.54 OF 13 WHERE COUSIN MARRIAGE IS PREFERENTIALLY OR PERMISSIVELY SYMMETRICAL, RATHER THAN EITHER PATRI- OR MATRILATERAL (106)	2 6 14 7 XSQ= 2.56 PHI= -0.297 EP = 0.0923
240	DRIFT LESS TOWARD BEING THOSE 0.56 OF 18 WHERE THE FAMILY, IF EXTENDED, IS SMALL OR STEM, RATHER THAN LARGE (135)	240	DRIFT MORE TOWARD BEING THOSE 0.84 OF 19 WHERE THE FAMILY, IF EXTENDED, IS SMALL OR STEM, RATHER THAN LARGE (135)	8 3 10 16 XSQ= 2.39 PHI= 0.254 EP = 0.0789
316	TILT TOWARD BEING THOSE 0.62 OF 13 WHERE EXCLUSIVE MOTHER-SON SLEEPING ARRANGEMENTS LAST ONE YEAR OR LONGER (19) W-K-A	316	TILT TOWARD BEING THOSE 0.86 OF 14 WHERE EXCLUSIVE MOTHER-SON SLEEPING ARRANGEMENTS LAST LESS THAN ONE YEAR (25) W-K-A	8 2 5 12 XSQ= 4.59 PHI= 0.412 EP = 0.0183
346	DRIFT TOWARD BEING THOSE 0.67 OF 18 WHERE THE CHILD'S INFERRED ANXIETY OVER PERFORMANCE OF SELF-RELIANT BEHAVIOR IS LOW (39) B-B-C	346	DRIFT TOWARD BEING THOSE 0.73 OF 11 WHERE THE CHILD'S INFERRED ANXIETY OVER PERFORMANCE OF SELF-RELIANT BEHAVIOR IS HIGH (37) B-B-C	6 8 12 3 XSQ= 2.81 PHI= -0.311 EP = 0.0604
348	TILT TOWARD BEING THOSE 0.73 OF 15 WHERE THE TOTAL POSITIVE PRESSURE TOWARD DEVELOPING ACHIEVEMENT BEHAVIOR IN THE CHILD IS HIGH (32) B-B-C	348	TILT TOWARD BEING THOSE 0.80 OF 10 WHERE THE TOTAL POSITIVE PRESSURE TOWARD DEVELOPING ACHIEVEMENT BEHAVIOR IN THE CHILD IS LOW (31) B-B-C	11 2 4 8 XSQ= 4.87 PHI= 0.441 EP = 0.0154
349	LEAN TOWARD BEING THOSE 0.79 OF 14 WHERE THE CHILD'S INFERRED ANXIETY OVER NON-PERFORMANCE OF ACHIEVEMENT BEHAVIOR IS HIGH (34) B-B-C	349	LEAN TOWARD BEING THOSE 0.90 OF 10 WHERE THE CHILD'S INFERRED ANXIETY OVER NON-PERFORMANCE OF ACHIEVEMENT BEHAVIOR IS LOW (28) B-B-C	11 1 3 9 XSQ= 8.40 PHI= 0.592 EP = 0.0028
368	TILT TOWARD BEING THOSE 0.64 OF 11 WHERE DISSOCIATION OF THE SEXES AT ADOLESCENCE IS HIGH OR MEDIUM (16) JKH	368	TILT TOWARD BEING THOSE 0.89 OF 9 WHERE DISSOCIATION OF THE SEXES AT ADOLESCENCE IS LOW (21) JKH	7 1 4 8 XSQ= 3.71 PHI= 0.431 EP = 0.0281

369	TILT TOWARD BEING THOSE 0.93 OF 14 WHERE DISSOCIATION OF THE SEXES AT ADOLESCENCE, OR CUSTOMS OF INITIATION AT ADOLESCENCE, ARE PRESENT (42) JKH	369	TILT TOWARD BEING THOSE 0.50 OF 14 WHERE BOTH DISSOCIATION OF THE SEXES AT ADOLESCENCE, AND CUSTOMS OF INITIATION AT ADOLESCENCE, ARE ABSENT (15) JKH	13 7 1 7 XSQ= 4.38 PHI= 0.395 EP = 0.0329
373	DRIFT TOWARD BEING THOSE 0.62 OF 13 WHERE MALE INITIATION CEREMONIES AT PUBERTY ARE PRESENT (17) W-K-A	373	DRIFT TOWARD BEING THOSE 0.79 OF 14 WHERE MALE INITIATION CEREMONIES AT PUBERTY ARE ABSENT (27) W-K-A	8 3 5 11 XSQ= 2.98 PHI= 0.332 EP = 0.0542
380	LEAN TOWARD BEING THOSE 0.81 OF 16 WHERE SEGREGATION OF GIRLS AT MENARCHE IS PRESENT (35) F-B	380	IN ALL CASES ARE THOSE 1.00 OF 4 WHERE SEGREGATION OF GIRLS AT MENARCHE IS ABSENT (20) F-B	13 0 3 4 XSQ= 6.06 PHI= 0.550 EP = 0.0072
385	TILT LESS TOWARD BEING THOSE 0.65 OF 20 WHERE SEXUAL EXPRESSION BY THE YOUNG IS SEMI-RESTRICTED OR PERMITTED (64) F-B	385	IN ALL CASES ARE THOSE 1.00 OF 11 WHERE SEXUAL EXPRESSION BY THE YOUNG IS SEMI-RESTRICTED OR PERMITTED (64) F-B	7 0 13 11 XSQ= 3.17 PHI= 0.320 EP = 0.0331
386	DRIFT TOWARD BEING THOSE 0.65 OF 20 WHERE SEXUAL EXPRESSION BY THE YOUNG IS RESTRICTED OR SEMI-RESTRICTED (46) F-B	386	DRIFT TOWARD BEING THOSE 0.73 OF 11 WHERE SEXUAL EXPRESSION BY THE YOUNG IS PERMITTED (40) F-B	13 3 7 8 XSQ= 2.68 PHI= 0.294 EP = 0.0659
396	LEAN TOWARD BEING THOSE 0.63 OF 16 WHERE THE STRENGTH OF MENSTRUAL TABOOS IS HIGH (18) WNS	396	LEAN TOWARD BEING THOSE 0.92 OF 13 WHERE THE STRENGTH OF MENSTRUAL TABOOS IS LOW (35) WNS	10 1 6 12 XSQ= 6.97 PHI= 0.490 EP = 0.0057
397	TILT LESS TOWARD BEING THOSE 0.54 OF 13 WHERE SEX DISABILITY IS ABSENT (42) JKH	397	TILT MORE TOWARD BEING THOSE 0.93 OF 14 WHERE SEX DISABILITY IS ABSENT (42) JKH	6 1 7 13 XSQ= 3.50 PHI= 0.360 EP = 0.0329
402	DRIFT TOWARD BEING THOSE 0.77 OF 13 WHERE EXPLANATIONS OF ILLNESS OF AN ORAL NATURE ARE PRESENT (31) W-C	402	DRIFT TOWARD BEING THOSE 0.67 OF 9 WHERE EXPLANATIONS OF ILLNESS OF AN ORAL NATURE ARE ABSENT (30) W-C	10 3 3 6 XSQ= 2.57 PHI= 0.342 EP = 0.0789
405	LEAN TOWARD BEING THOSE 0.62 OF 13 WHERE EXPLANATIONS OF ILLNESS OF A DEPENDENCE NATURE ARE ABSENT (27) W-C	405	IN ALL CASES ARE THOSE 1.00 OF 9 WHERE EXPLANATIONS OF ILLNESS OF A DEPENDENCE NATURE ARE PRESENT (34) W-C	5 9 8 0 XSQ= 6.25 PHI= -0.533 EP = 0.0055

```
424  TILT TOWARD BEING THOSE          0.88 OF  16     424  TILT TOWARD BEING THOSE          0.58 OF  12          2    7
     WHERE RELIGIOUS SPECIALISTS ARE                      WHERE RELIGIOUS SPECIALISTS ARE                          14    5
     PART-TIME, RATHER THAN                               FULL-TIME, RATHER THAN                             XSQ=     4.67
     FULL-TIME  (33) JMH                                  PART-TIME  (21) JMH                                PHI=   -0.408
                                                                                                             EP =   0.0166

427  TILT TOWARD BEING THOSE          0.61 OF  18     427  TILT TOWARD BEING THOSE          0.82 OF  17          7   14
     WHERE A HIGH GOD, IF PRESENT, IS                     WHERE A HIGH GOD, IF PRESENT, IS                         11    3
     INACTIVE, RATHER THAN                                ACTIVE, RATHER THAN                                XSQ=     5.19
     ACTIVE  (69) GES,EA                                  INACTIVE  (87) GES,EA                              PHI=   -0.385
                                                                                                             EP =   0.0153

429  TILT TOWARD BEING THOSE          0.63 OF   8     429  TILT TOWARD BEING THOSE          0.89 OF   9          3    8
     WHERE SUPERNATURAL SANCTIONS FOR MORALITY            WHERE SUPERNATURAL SANCTIONS FOR MORALITY                 5    1
     ARE ABSENT OR UNREPORTED  (9) GES                    ARE PRESENT  (28) GES                              XSQ=     2.91
                                                                                                             PHI=   -0.413
                                                                                                             EP =   0.0498

430  IN ALL CASES ARE THOSE           1.00 OF   8     430  TILT TOWARD BEING THOSE          0.60 OF  10          0    6
     WHERE SUPERNATURAL SANCTIONS FOR MORALITY,           WHERE SUPERNATURAL SANCTIONS FOR MORALITY,                8    4
     HAVING AN EFFECT ON                                  HAVING AN EFFECT ON                                XSQ=     4.75
     AN INDIVIDUAL'S HEALTH,                              AN INDIVIDUAL'S HEALTH,                            PHI=   -0.514
     ARE ABSENT OR UNREPORTED  (22) GES                   ARE PRESENT  (16) GES                              EP =   0.0128

445  DRIFT TOWARD BEING THOSE         0.62 OF  13     445  DRIFT TOWARD BEING THOSE         0.80 OF  10          8    2
     WHERE SORCERY IS                                     WHERE SORCERY IS                                          5    8
     IMPORTANT  (26) EBW,DH                               UNIMPORTANT  (23) BBW,DH                           XSQ=     2.46
                                                                                                             PHI=    0.327
                                                                                                             EP =   0.0903

476  TILT TOWARD BEING THOSE          0.92 OF  13     476  TILT TOWARD BEING THOSE          0.60 OF  10         12    4
     WHERE THE DEGREE OF INSOBRIETY IS                    WHERE THE DEGREE OF INSOBRIETY IS                         1    6
     STRONG  (31) DH                                      MODERATE OR SLIGHT  (18) DH                        XSQ=     5.04
                                                                                                             PHI=    0.468
                                                                                                             EP =   0.0186

480  TILT TOWARD BEING THOSE          0.86 OF   7     480  IN ALL CASES ARE THOSE           1.00 OF   4          1    4
     WHERE COMPLEXITY OF ARTISTIC DESIGN                  WHERE COMPLEXITY OF ARTISTIC DESIGN                       6    0
     IS LOW  (15) HB                                      IS HIGH  (14) HB                                   XSQ=     4.48
                                                                                                             PHI=   -0.638
                                                                                                             EP =   0.0152
```

383 CULTURES
WHERE FEMALE INITIATION RITES, IF PRESENT,
ARE PAINFUL (9) JKB

383 CULTURES
WHERE FEMALE INITIATION RITES, IF PRESENT,
ARE NOT PAINFUL (29) JKB

BACKGROUND ON PAGE 153

SUBJECT ONLY

9 IN LEFT COLUMN

ARANDA	CHAMACOCO	CHOROTI	FON	MENDE	MOSSI	MUNDURUCU	THONGA	TUPINAMBA

29 IN RIGHT COLUMN

ANDAMANESE	BEMBA	BURMESE	CAGABA	CARIB	CHEYENNE	CHIR-APACHE	CUNA	GANDA	GOAJIRO
JIVARO	KURTATCHI	LAMBA	LESU	NAMA	NAMBICUARA	NASKAPI	NAVAHO	OJIBWA	PAPAGO
PUKAPUKA	SANPOIL	TEDA	TEHUELCHE	THAI	TUBATULABAL	WOLEAIANS	YAGUA	YUROK	

27 EXCLUDED BECAUSE IRRELEVANT (SEE RIGHT COLUMN, PARAGRAPH 382)

335 EXCLUDED BECAUSE UNASCERTAINED

3	DRIFT LESS TOWARD BEING THOSE LOCATED OUTSIDE OF AFRICA (320)	0.56 OF	9	3	DRIFT MORE TOWARD BEING THOSE LOCATED OUTSIDE OF AFRICA (320)	0.86 OF	29	4 4 5 25 XSQ= 2.26 PHI= 0.244 EP = 0.0713
8	IN ALL CASES ARE THOSE LOCATED OUTSIDE OF NORTH AMERICA (330)	1.00 OF	9	8	DRIFT LESS TOWARD BEING THOSE LOCATED OUTSIDE OF NORTH AMERICA (330)	0.69 OF	29	0 9 9 20 XSQ= 2.14 PHI= -0.238 EP = 0.0818
14	IN ALL CASES ARE THOSE WHERE THE LATITUDE IS LESS THAN THIRTY DEGREES (281)	1.00 OF	9	14	DRIFT LESS TOWARD BEING THOSE WHERE THE LATITUDE IS LESS THAN THIRTY DEGREES (281)	0.66 OF	29	0 10 9 19 XSQ= 2.62 PHI= -0.263 EP = 0.0785
88	IN ALL CASES ARE THOSE WHERE, IF A HEADMANSHIP IS PRESENT, SUCCESSION IS HEREDITARY (165)	1.00 OF	5	88	TILT TOWARD BEING THOSE WHERE, IF A HEADMANSHIP IS PRESENT, SUCCESSION IS NON-HEREDITARY (106)	0.58 OF	26	0 15 5 11 XSQ= 3.52 PHI= -0.337 EP = 0.0434

97	DRIFT LESS TOWARD BEING THOSE WHERE THE HIERARCHY OF LOCAL JURISDICTION HAS THREE OR TWO LEVELS (273) GES,EA	0.78 OF	9	97	IN ALL CASES ARE THOSE WHERE THE HIERARCHY OF LOCAL JURISDICTION HAS THREE OR TWO LEVELS (273) GES,EA	1.00 OF	27	2 0 7 27 XSQ= 2.82 PHI= 0.280 EP = 0.0571
149	IN ALL CASES ARE THOSE WHERE THE INCIDENCE OF THEFT IS HIGH (18) B-B-C	1.00 OF	2	149	DRIFT TOWARD BEING THOSE WHERE THE INCIDENCE OF THEFT IS LOW (19) B-B-C	0.82 OF	11	2 2 0 9 XSQ= 2.17 PHI= 0.409 EP = 0.0769
176	DRIFT TOWARD BEING THOSE WHERE THE COMMUNITY IS A CLAN-COMMUNITY OR A COMMUNITY STRUCTURED OR SEGMENTED ON A CLAN BASIS (169)	0.56 OF	9	176	DRIFT TOWARD BEING THOSE WHERE THE COMMUNITY IS OTHER THAN A CLAN-COMMUNITY OR A COMMUNITY STRUCTURED OR SEGMENTED ON A CLAN BASIS (213)	0.79 OF	29	5 6 4 23 XSQ= 2.54 PHI= 0.259 EP = 0.0875
186	TILT TOWARD BEING THOSE WHERE THE KIN GROUP IS EXCLUSIVELY PATRILINEAL (150)	0.56 OF	9	186	TILT TOWARD BEING THOSE WHERE THE KIN GROUP IS OTHER THAN EXCLUSIVELY PATRILINEAL (250)	0.86 OF	29	5 4 4 25 XSQ= 4.52 PHI= 0.345 EP = 0.0203
190	IN ALL CASES ARE THOSE WHERE THE KIN GROUP IS PATRILINEAL OR DOUBLE-DESCENT, RATHER THAN MATRILINEAL (186)	1.00 OF	6	190	TILT TOWARD BEING THOSE WHERE THE KIN GROUP IS MATRILINEAL, RATHER THAN PATRILINEAL OR DOUBLE-DESCENT (61)	0.58 OF	12	6 5 0 7 XSQ= 3.54 PHI= 0.443 EP = 0.0377
263	IN ALL CASES ARE THOSE WHERE WIVES ARE OBTAINED BY RELATIVELY DIFFICULT MEANS, NAMELY BY BRIDE-PRICE, BRIDE-SERVICE, OR EXCHANGING A FEMALE RELATIVE (233)	1.00 OF	9	263	TILT LESS TOWARD BEING THOSE WHERE WIVES ARE OBTAINED BY RELATIVELY DIFFICULT MEANS, NAMELY BY BRIDE-PRICE, BRIDE-SERVICE, OR EXCHANGING A FEMALE RELATIVE (233)	0.52 OF	29	9 15 0 14 XSQ= 4.96 PHI= 0.361 EP = 0.0143
314	TILT TOWARD BEING THOSE WHERE THE INCIDENCE OF MOTHER-CHILD HOUSEHOLDS IS HIGH (19) W-D,S	0.67 OF	6	314	TILT TOWARD BEING THOSE WHERE THE INCIDENCE OF MOTHER-CHILD HOUSEHOLDS IS LOW (61) W-D,S	0.81 OF	21	4 4 2 17 XSQ= 3.05 PHI= 0.336 EP = 0.0441
319	IN ALL CASES ARE THOSE WHERE PROTECTION OF THE INFANT FROM ENVIRONMENTAL DISCOMFORTS IS LOW (30) B-B-C	1.00 OF	4	319	DRIFT TOWARD BEING THOSE WHERE PROTECTION OF THE INFANT FROM ENVIRONMENTAL DISCOMFORTS IS HIGH (35) B-B-C	0.67 OF	12	0 8 4 4 XSQ= 3.00 PHI= -0.433 EP = 0.0769
342	IN ALL CASES ARE THOSE WHERE THE CHILD'S INFERRED ANXIETY OVER PERFORMANCE OF NURTURANT BEHAVIOR IS HIGH (18) B-B-C	1.00 OF	2	342	DRIFT TOWARD BEING THOSE WHERE THE CHILD'S INFERRED ANXIETY OVER PERFORMANCE OF NURTURANT BEHAVIOR IS LOW (28) B-B-C	0.89 OF	9	2 1 0 8 XSQ= 2.81 PHI= 0.505 EP = 0.0545

370	TILT TOWARD BEING THOSE WHERE THE SEGREGATION OF ADOLESCENT BOYS IS COMPLETE OR PARTIAL (95)	0.86 OF 7	370	TILT TOWARD BEING THOSE WHERE THE SEGREGATION OF ADOLESCENT BOYS IS ABSENT (148)	0.71 OF 21		6 6 1 15 XSQ= 4.86 PHI= 0.417 EP = 0.0228
377	LEAN TOWARD BEING THOSE WHERE MALE GENITAL MUTILATION IS PRESENT (83)	0.56 OF 9	377	LEAN TOWARD BEING THOSE WHERE MALE GENITAL MUTILATION IS ABSENT (242)	0.93 OF 27		5 2 4 25 XSQ= 7.15 PHI= 0.446 EP = 0.0056
385	TILT TOWARD BEING THOSE WHERE SEXUAL EXPRESSION BY THE YOUNG IS RESTRICTED (22) F-B	0.80 OF 5	385	TILT TOWARD BEING THOSE WHERE SEXUAL EXPRESSION BY THE YOUNG IS SEMI-RESTRICTED OR PERMITTED (64) F-B	0.80 OF 15		4 3 1 12 XSQ= 3.59 PHI= 0.424 EP = 0.0307
421	IN ALL CASES ARE THOSE WHERE KILLING, TORTURING, OR MUTILATING OF THE ENEMY IS STRONGLY OR MODERATELY EMPHASIZED (37) PES	1.00 OF 3	421	DRIFT TOWARD BEING THOSE WHERE KILLING, TORTURING, OR MUTILATING OF THE ENEMY IS NEGLIGIBLY EMPHASIZED (47) PES	0.65 OF 17		3 6 0 11 XSQ= 2.10 PHI= 0.324 EP = 0.0737

****

385 CULTURES
WHERE SEXUAL EXPRESSICN BY THE YOUNG
IS RESTRICTED (22) F-B

385 CULTURES
WHERE SEXUAL EXPRESSION BY THE YOUNG
IS SEMI-RESTRICTED OR
PERMITTED (64) F-B

BACKGROUND ON PAGE 153 PREDICATE ONLY

....

22 IN LEFT CCLUMN

APINAYE	ASHANTI	CHAGGA	CHIR-APACHE	CHOROTI	CHUKCHEE	CUNA	FCN	JUKUN	LAMBA
MANUS	MASAI	MATACO	MURNGIN	PENOBSCOT	SENIANG	SIRIONO	SWAZI	THONGA	TRUKESE
TUPINAMBA	WOLOF								

64 IN RIGHT CCLUMN

AINU	ALORESE	ANDAMANESE	ARANDA	AYMARA	AZANDE	BALINESE	CARIB	COPR ESKIMO	CREE
CREEK	CROW	DOBUANS	DUSUN	GANDA	GILYAK	GOAJIRO	GOND	HANO	HAVASUPAI
HUICHOL	IFUGAO	ILA	KAZAK	KIOW-APACHE	KURTATCHI	KUTENAI	KWAKIUTL	LANGO	LAPPS
LEPCHA	LESU	MANDAN	MAORI	MARQUESANS	MARSHALLESE	MBUNDU	NAMA	NANDI	NASKAPI
NATCHEZ	OJIBWA	OMAHA	PALAUANS	PAPAGO	PONAPEANS	PUKAPUKA	PURARI	SAMOANS	SEMINOLE
TAOS	TARAHUMARA	TIKOPIA	TIMBIRA	TODA	TOKELAU	TROBRIAND	VENDA	WOGEO	YAGUA
YAKUT	YAPESE	YARURO	YUKAGHIR						

314 EXCLUDED BECAUSE UNASCERTAINED

----

386 CULTURES
WHERE SEXUAL EXPRESSION BY THE YOUNG
IS RESTRICTED OR
SEMI-RESTRICTED (46) F-B

386 CULTURES
WHERE SEXUAL EXPRESSION BY THE YOUNG
IS PERMITTED (40) F-B

BACKGROUND ON PAGE 154

BOTH SUBJECT AND PREDICATE

46 IN LEFT COLUMN

ALORESE	ANDAMANESE	APINAYE	ARANDA	ASHANTI	AZANDE	CHAGGA	CHIR-APACHE	CHOROTI	CHUKCHEE
CREEK	CROW	CUNA	DUSUN	FON	GANDA	HAVASUPAI	HUICHOL	JUKUN	KIOW-APACHE
KURTATCHI	KUTENAI	LAMBA	LANGO	MANDAN	MANUS	MASAI	MATACO	MBUNDU	MURNGIN
OMAHA	PAPAGO	PENOBSCOT	PURARI	SEMINOLE	SENIANG	SIRIONO	SWAZI	THONGA	TIMBIRA
TOKELAU	TRUKESE	TUPINAMBA	VENDA	WOLOF	YAGUA				

40 IN RIGHT COLUMN

AINU	AYMARA	BALINESE	CARIB	COPR ESKIMO	CREE	DOBUANS	GILYAK	GOAJIRO	GOND
HANO	IFUGAO	ILA	KAZAK	KWAKIUTL	LAPPS	LEPCHA	LESU	MAORI	MARQUESANS
MARSHALLESE	NAMA	NANDI	NASKAPI	NATCHEZ	OJIBWA	PALAUANS	PONAPEANS	PUKAPUKA	SAMOANS
TAOS	TARAHUMARA	TIKOPIA	TODA	TROBRIAND	WOGEO	YAKUT	YAPESE	YARURO	YUKAGHIR

314 EXCLUDED BECAUSE UNASCERTAINED

3	TILT LESS TOWARD BEING THOSE LOCATED OUTSIDE OF AFRICA (320)	0.72 OF 46	3	TILT MORE TOWARD BEING THOSE LOCATED OUTSIDE OF AFRICA (320)	0.92 OF 40		13 3 33 37 XSQ= 4.80 PHI= 0.236 XP = 0.0285
5	DRIFT MORE TOWARD BEING THOSE LOCATED OUTSIDE OF EAST EURASIA (330)	0.96 OF 46	5	DRIFT LESS TOWARD BEING THOSE LOCATED OUTSIDE OF EAST EURASIA (330)	0.80 OF 40		2 8 44 32 XSQ= 3.69 PHI= -0.207 XP = 0.0547
12	TILT MORE TOWARD BEING THOSE WHERE THE LATITUDE IS LESS THAN FIFTY DEGREES (367)	0.96 OF 46	12	TILT LESS TOWARD BEING THOSE WHERE THE LATITUDE IS LESS THAN FIFTY DEGREES (367)	0.77 OF 40		2 9 44 31 XSQ= 4.80 PHI= -0.236 XP = 0.0285
74	TILT TOWARD BEING THOSE WHERE POTTERY IS PRESENT (145)	0.68 OF 38	74	TILT TOWARD BEING THOSE WHERE POTTERY IS ABSENT (93)	0.58 OF 31		26 13 12 18 XSQ= 3.86 PHI= 0.236 XP = 0.0496

116	DRIFT MORE TOWARD BEING THOSE 0.87 OF 15 WHERE OCCUPATIONAL SPECIALIZATION IS PART-TIME ONLY (34) JMH	116	DRIFT LESS TOWARD BEING THOSE 0.55 OF 11 WHERE OCCUPATIONAL SPECIALIZATION IS PART-TIME ONLY (34) JMH	2 5 13 6 XSQ= 1.90 PHI= -0.270 EP = 0.0946
131	DRIFT LESS TOWARD BEING THOSE 0.70 OF 23 WHERE THE CONSTRUCTION OF PERMANENT HOUSES OR THE ERECTION OF TEMPORARY DWELLINGS IS MAINLY DONE BY MALES (136)	131	DRIFT MORE TOWARD BEING THOSE 0.96 OF 23 WHERE THE CONSTRUCTION OF PERMANENT HOUSES OR THE ERECTION OF TEMPORARY DWELLINGS IS MAINLY DONE BY MALES (136)	16 22 7 1 XSQ= 3.78 PHI= -0.287 XP = 0.0518
142	DRIFT LESS TOWARD BEING THOSE 0.53 OF 15 WHERE THE LEVEL OF SOCIAL SANCTION IS PUBLIC CORPOREAL SANCTION OR PUBLIC PROPERTY SANCTION, RATHER THAN PRIVATE SETTLEMENT (38) JMH	142	DRIFT MORE TOWARD BEING THOSE 0.91 OF 11 WHERE THE LEVEL OF SOCIAL SANCTION IS PUBLIC CORPOREAL SANCTION OR PUBLIC PROPERTY SANCTION, RATHER THAN PRIVATE SETTLEMENT (38) JMH	8 10 7 1 XSQ= 2.63 PHI= -0.318 EP = 0.0838
209	DRIFT LESS TOWARD BEING THOSE 0.63 OF 38 WHERE MARITAL RESIDENCE IS PATRILOCAL, VIRILOCAL, OR AVUNCULOCAL, RATHER THAN MATRILOCAL OR UXORILOCAL (270)	209	DRIFT MORE TOWARD BEING THOSE 0.84 OF 31 WHERE MARITAL RESIDENCE IS PATRILOCAL, VIRILOCAL, OR AVUNCULOCAL, RATHER THAN MATRILOCAL OR UXORILOCAL (270)	24 26 14 5 XSQ= 2.71 PHI= -0.198 XP = 0.1000
225	IN ALL CASES ARE THOSE 1.00 OF 6 WHERE COUSIN MARRIAGE IS PREFERENTIALLY OR PERMISSIVELY MATRILATERAL, RATHER THAN PATRILATERAL (43)	225	TILT TOWARD BEING THOSE 0.75 OF 4 WHERE COUSIN MARRIAGE IS PREFERENTIALLY OR PERMISSIVELY PATRILATERAL, RATHER THAN MATRILATERAL (23)	0 3 6 1 XSQ= 3.35 PHI= -0.579 EP = 0.0333
243	TILT LESS TOWARD BEING THOSE 0.53 OF 19 WHERE POLYGYNY, IF PRESENT, HAS A LOW INCIDENCE (36) W-D,S	243	TILT MORE TOWARD BEING THOSE 0.93 OF 15 WHERE POLYGYNY, IF PRESENT, HAS A LOW INCIDENCE (36) W-D,S	9 1 10 14 XSQ= 4.87 PHI= 0.379 EP = 0.0204
259	DRIFT TOWARD BEING THOSE 0.69 OF 16 WHERE THE SEVERITY OF MOTHER-IN-LAW AVOIDANCE IS HIGH (26) WNS	259	DRIFT TOWARD BEING THOSE 0.75 OF 12 WHERE THE SEVERITY OF MOTHER-IN-LAW AVOIDANCE IS LOW (20) WNS	11 3 5 9 XSQ= 3.65 PHI= 0.361 EP = 0.0542
263	DRIFT TOWARD BEING THOSE 0.63 OF 46 WHERE WIVES ARE OBTAINED BY RELATIVELY DIFFICULT MEANS, NAMELY BY BRIDE-PRICE, BRIDE-SERVICE, OR EXCHANGING A FEMALE RELATIVE (233)	263	DRIFT TOWARD BEING THOSE 0.57 OF 40 WHERE WIVES ARE OBTAINED BY RELATIVELY EASY MEANS, NAMELY BY TOKEN BRIDE-PRICE, GIFT EXCHANGE, ABSENCE OF ANY CONSIDERATION, OR RECEIPT OF DOWRY (162)	29 17 17 23 XSQ= 2.85 PHI= 0.182 XP = 0.0913
295	DRIFT TOWARD BEING THOSE 0.64 OF 11 WHERE THE SEVERITY OF PUNISHMENT FOR ABORTION IS HIGH (11) BCA	295	DRIFT TOWARD BEING THOSE 0.80 OF 10 WHERE THE SEVERITY OF PUNISHMENT FOR ABORTION IS LOW OR ABSENT (12) BCA	7 2 4 8 XSQ= 2.49 PHI= 0.344 EP = 0.0805

311	DRIFT TOWARD BEING THOSE 0.61 OF 18 WHERE SEXUAL SOCIALIZATION ANXIETY IS HIGH (28) W-C	311	DRIFT TOWARD BEING THOSE 0.71 OF 17 WHERE SEXUAL SOCIALIZATION ANXIETY IS LOW (23) W-C	11 5 7 12 XSQ= 2.38 PHI= 0.261 EP = 0.0922
314	TILT LESS TOWARD BEING THOSE 0.71 OF 24 WHERE THE INCIDENCE OF MOTHER-CHILD HOUSEHOLDS IS LOW (61) W-D,S	314	IN ALL CASES ARE THOSE 1.00 OF 21 WHERE THE INCIDENCE OF MOTHER-CHILD HOUSEHOLDS IS LOW (61) W-D,S	7 0 17 21 XSQ= 5.20 PHI= 0.340 XP = 0.0226
345	DRIFT TOWARD BEING THOSE 0.68 OF 28 WHERE THE CHILD'S INFERRED ANXIETY OVER NON-PERFORMANCE OF SELF-RELIANT BEHAVIOR IS HIGH (37) B-B-C	345	DRIFT TOWARD BEING THOSE 0.65 OF 17 WHERE THE CHILD'S INFERRED ANXIETY OVER NON-PERFORMANCE OF SELF-RELIANT BEHAVIOR IS LOW (39) B-B-C	19 6 9 11 XSQ= 3.32 PHI= 0.272 XP = 0.0685
348	DRIFT TOWARD BEING THOSE 0.67 OF 24 WHERE THE TOTAL POSITIVE PRESSURE TOWARD DEVELOPING ACHIEVEMENT BEHAVIOR IN THE CHILD IS HIGH (32) B-B-C	348	DRIFT TOWARD BEING THOSE 0.67 OF 12 WHERE THE TOTAL POSITIVE PRESSURE TOWARD DEVELOPING ACHIEVEMENT BEHAVIOR IN THE CHILD IS LOW (31) B-B-C	16 4 8 8 XSQ= 2.38 PHI= 0.257 EP = 0.0815
382	DRIFT TOWARD BEING THOSE 0.81 OF 16 WHERE FEMALE INITIATION RITES ARE PRESENT (38) JKB	382	DRIFT TOWARD BEING THOSE 0.53 OF 15 WHERE FEMALE INITIATION RITES ARE ABSENT (27) JKB	13 7 3 8 XSQ= 2.68 PHI= 0.294 EP = 0.0659
392	DRIFT TOWARD BEING THOSE 0.59 OF 27 WHERE PREMARITAL SEX RELATIONS ARE STRONGLY PUNISHED AND IN FACT RARE, OR WEAKLY PUNISHED AND IN FACT NOT RARE, OR PUNISHED ONLY IF PREGNANCY RESULTS (112) JTW,EA	392	DRIFT TOWARD BEING THOSE 0.66 OF 32 WHERE PREMARITAL SEX RELATIONS ARE FREELY PERMITTED (67) JTW,EA	16 11 11 21 XSQ= 2.72 PHI= 0.215 XP = 0.0991
393	TILT TOWARD BEING THOSE 0.61 OF 36 WHERE EXTRAMARITAL COITUS IS PUNISHED, RATHER THAN PERMITTED (43) F-B	393	TILT TOWARD BEING THOSE 0.72 OF 25 WHERE EXTRAMARITAL COITUS IS PERMITTED, RATHER THAN PUNISHED (41) F-B	22 7 14 18 XSQ= 5.23 PHI= 0.293 XP = 0.0222
397	DRIFT LESS TOWARD BEING THOSE 0.72 OF 18 WHERE SEX DISABILITY IS ABSENT (42) JKH	397	IN ALL CASES ARE THOSE 1.00 OF 13 WHERE SEX DISABILITY IS ABSENT (42) JKH	5 0 13 13 XSQ= 2.50 PHI= 0.284 EP = 0.0580
398	DRIFT TOWARD BEING THOSE 0.67 OF 15 WHERE THE INTENSITY OF SEX ANXIETY IS HIGH (16) WNS	398	DRIFT TOWARD BEING THOSE 0.78 OF 9 WHERE THE INTENSITY OF SEX ANXIETY IS LOW (16) WNS	10 2 5 7 XSQ= 2.84 PHI= 0.344 EP = 0.0894

399	DRIFT TOWARD BEING THOSE 0.69 OF 16 WHERE INTENSITY OF CASTRATION ANXIETY IS HIGH (23) WNS	399	DRIFT TOWARD BEING THOSE 0.71 OF 14 WHERE INTENSITY OF CASTRATION ANXIETY IS LOW (22) WNS	11 4 5 10 XSQ= 3.35 PHI= 0.334 EP = 0.0656
421	DRIFT TOWARD BEING THOSE 0.54 OF 24 WHERE KILLING, TORTURING, OR MUTILATING OF THE ENEMY IS STRONGLY OR MODERATELY EMPHASIZED (37) PES	421	DRIFT TOWARD BEING THOSE 0.77 OF 22 WHERE KILLING, TORTURING, OR MUTILATING OF THE ENEMY IS NEGLIGIBLY EMPHASIZED (47) PES	13 5 11 17 XSQ= 3.53 PHI= 0.277 XP = 0.0601
424	TILT TOWARD BEING THOSE 0.87 OF 15 WHERE RELIGIOUS SPECIALISTS ARE PART-TIME, RATHER THAN FULL-TIME (33) JMH	424	TILT TOWARD BEING THOSE 0.55 OF 11 WHERE RELIGIOUS SPECIALISTS ARE FULL-TIME, RATHER THAN PART-TIME (21) JMH	2 6 13 5 XSQ= 3.31 PHI= -0.357 EP = 0.0384
429	DRIFT TOWARD BEING THOSE 0.50 OF 6 WHERE SUPERNATURAL SANCTIONS FOR MORALITY ARE ABSENT OR UNREPORTED (9) GES	429	IN ALL CASES ARE THOSE 1.00 OF 8 WHERE SUPERNATURAL SANCTIONS FOR MORALITY ARE PRESENT (28) GES	3 8 3 0 XSQ= 2.55 PHI= -0.427 EP = 0.0549
443	DRIFT TOWARD BEING THOSE 0.71 OF 21 WHERE OVERALL FEAR OF OTHERS IS LOW (30) W-C	443	DRIFT TOWARD BEING THOSE 0.62 OF 21 WHERE OVERALL FEAR OF OTHERS IS HIGH (31) W-C	6 13 15 8 XSQ= 3.46 PHI= -0.287 XP = 0.0629
455	TILT TOWARD BEING THOSE 0.60 OF 15 WHERE THE MODE OF THE INDIVIDUAL'S CONTACT WITH THE DIVINE IS CONDUCIVE TO THE DEVELOPMENT OF THE INDIVIDUAL'S NEED TO ACHIEVE (17) DCM	455	IN ALL CASES ARE THOSE 1.00 OF 5 WHERE THE MODE OF THE INDIVIDUAL'S CONTACT WITH THE DIVINE IS NOT CONDUCIVE TO THE DEVELOPMENT OF THE INDIVIDUAL'S NEED TO ACHIEVE (19) DCM	9 0 6 5 XSQ= 3.30 PHI= 0.406 EP = 0.0379
460	DRIFT TOWARD BEING THOSE 0.71 OF 31 WHERE GAMES, IF PRESENT, ARE NOT LIMITED TO GAMES OF SKILL ONLY (104) R-A-B,EA	460	DRIFT TOWARD BEING THOSE 0.56 OF 27 WHERE GAMES, IF PRESENT, ARE LIMITED TO GAMES OF SKILL ONLY (67) R-A-B,EA	9 15 22 12 XSQ= 3.16 PHI= -0.234 XP = 0.0753
478	DRIFT TOWARD BEING THOSE 0.83 OF 6 WHERE THE ABANDONMENT OR KILLING OF OLD PEOPLE IS UNIMPORTANT OR ABSENT (12) LWS	478	DRIFT TOWARD BEING THOSE 0.83 OF 6 WHERE THE ABANDONMENT OR KILLING OF OLD PEOPLE IS PRESENT (12) LWS	1 5 5 1 XSQ= 3.00 PHI= -0.500 EP = 0.0801
479	TILT TOWARD BEING THOSE 0.67 OF 15 WHERE THE NEED TO ACHIEVE, AS INFERRED FROM FOLKTALES, IS HIGH (18) JV	479	IN ALL CASES ARE THOSE 1.00 OF 5 WHERE THE NEED TO ACHIEVE, AS INFERRED FROM FOLKTALES, IS LOW (18) JV	10 0 5 5 XSQ= 4.27 PHI= 0.462 EP = 0.0325

386/

```
480  LEAN TOWARD BEING THOSE          0.82 OF  11       480  LEAN TOWARD BEING THOSE          0.82 OF  11           2     9
     WHERE COMPLEXITY OF ARTISTIC DESIGN                        WHERE COMPLEXITY OF ARTISTIC DESIGN                   9     2
     IS LOW  (15) HB                                            IS HIGH  (14) HB                               XSQ=     6.55
                                                                                                               PHI=   -0.545
                                                                                                               EP =   0.0089
```

387 CULTURES
WHERE PREMARITAL CCITUS IS
FCRBIDDEN (19) CSF

387 CULTURES
WHERE PREMARITAL CCITUS IS
NOT FORBIDDEN (17) CSF

BACKGROUND ON PAGE 154

NEITHER SUBJECT NOR PREDICATE

19 IN LEFT CCLUMN

ANDAMANESE	ASHANTI	CREEK	CROW	KAZAK	KURTATCHI	KWAKIUTL	MACRI	MBUNDU	MURNGIN
NAMA	RIFFIANS	SANPCIL	TARAHUMARA	TIV	TUBATULABAL	WITCTO	YAKUT	YURCK	

17 IN RIGHT CCLUMN

AINU	ARANDA	CARIB	DOBUANS	IFUGAO	LANGO	LEPCHA	LESU	MASAI	PUKAPUKA
THONGA	TIKCPIA	TCCA	TROBRIANC	TUPINAMBA	VENDA	YUKAGHIR			

364 EXCLUCED BECAUSE UNASCERTAINEC

388 CULTURES
WHERE PREMARITAL CCITUS IS
PRESENT (24) CSF

388 CULTURES
WHERE PREMARITAL CCITUS IS
ABSENT OR RARE (8) CSF

BACKGROUND ON PAGE 154

NEITHER SUBJECT NOR PREDICATE

24 IN LEFT CCLUMN

ANDAMANESE	ARANDA	CREEK	CROW	DOBUANS	IFUGAO	KURTATCHI	KWAKIUTL	LANGC	LEPCHA
LESU	MACRI	MASAI	MURNGIN	PUKAPUKA	SANPOIL	TARAHUMARA	THCNGA	TIKCPIA	TOCA
TROBRIAND	TUBATULABAL	VENCA	YUKAGHIR						

8 IN RIGHT CCLUMN

ASHANTI	MBUNDU	NAMA	RIFFIANS	TIV	WITOTO	YAKUT	YURCK

368 EXCLUCED BECAUSE UNASCERTAINEC

389 CULTURES
WHERE PREMARITAL SEX RELATIONS ARE
STRONGLY PUNISHEC AND
IN FACT RARE, RATHER THAN
FREELY PERMITTEC (47) JTW,EA

389 CULTURES
WHERE PREMARITAL SEX RELATICNS ARE
FREELY PERMITTED, RATHER THAN
STRONGLY PUNISHED AND
IN FACT RARE (67) JTW,EA

BACKGROUND ON PAGE 154

SUBJECT ONLY

47 IN LEFT CCLUMN

ABIPCN, ALBANIANS, ASHANTI, ATSUGEWI, BASSERI, BURUSHO, CAMBODIANS, CHEYENNE, CHIR-APACHE, COORG, CUNA, EGYPTIANS, ENGA, FON, GILBERTESE, HAZARA, HEBREWS, INCA, IRISH, JAPANESE, JAVANESE, KHEVSUR, KIKUYU, KORYAK, KWAKIUTL, LUO, MAM, MAMVU, MANUS, MINCHIA, MZAB, NUPE, CNA, PURUM, RUNDI, RWALA, SANTAL, SARSI, SERBS, SHLUH, TEDA, TENINC, THAI, TOLOWA, TWANA, ULAWANS, VIETNAMESE

67 IN RIGHT CCLUMN

ABOR, AINU, AKHA, AMBA, ANDAMANESE, AWEIKOMA, BATAK, BHUIYA, BORCRO, CARIB, CHENCHU, CHIBCHA, CHCROTI, CHUKCHEE, DELAWARE, DOBUANS, ELLICE, FANG, FUTAJALONKE, GONC, HAWAIIANS, HUTSUL, IFUGAO, ILA, JIVARO, KASKA, LAMET, LEPCHA, LOLC, MAGUZAWA, MANIHIKI, MACRI, MARQUESANS, MARSHALLESE, MASAI, MATACO, MENTAWEI, MERINA, MONGC, NATCHEZ, NICCBARESE, CJIBWA, PALAUANS, PARAUJANO, PONAPEANS, PUKAPUKA, RAROIANS, SAGADA, SAMCANS, SINHALESE, SIRIONC, TANALA, TARAHUMARA, TAREUMIUT, TENDA, THONGA, TODA, TOKELAU, TROBRIAND, TRUKESE, TRUMAI, TUPINAMBA, WOLEAIANS, YABARANA, YAGUA, YAKUT, YAPESE

88 EXCLUCED BECAUSE IRRELEVANT

ALORESE, AMERICANS, APINAYE, ARANCA, ARAPESH, ARAUCANIANS, AYMARA, AZANDE, AZTEC, BARI, BAYA, BEMBA, BHIL, BOTOCUCO, BRAZILIANS, CALLINAGO, CHAGGA, COPR ESKIMO, CREEK, DUTCH, GANDA, GARC, GILYAK, GISU, GOAJIRO, GROS VENTRE, HAIDA, HANC, IBAN, INGALIK, KACHIN, KAPAUKU, KAZAK, KERAKI, KIOW-APACHE, KOREANS, KUNG, KURTATCHI, KUTENAI, LAKHER, LAPPS, LAU, LUBA, MACASSARESE, MANGAIANS, MISKITO, MONGUOR, MUNDURUCU, MURNGIN, NABESNA, NAMA, NAMBICUARA, NAVAHO, NOMLAKI, NYAKYUSA, OKINAWANS, OMAHA, RIFFIANS, SAMCYEC, SANPOIL, SEMANG, SHILLUK, SIUAI, SOMALI, SONGHAI, TALAMANCA, TALLENSI, TACS, TAPIRAPE, TEHUELCHE, TERENA, TIKCPIA, TIMBIRA, TIV, TIWI, TRISTAN, TUBATULABAL, TUCUNA, UTE, VECCA, VENDA, WITCTC, WCGEC, WOLOF, YAHGAN, YAO, YORUBA, YUKI

198 EXCLUCED BECAUSE UNASCERTAINEC

---

4 LEAN LESS TOWARC BEING THCSE 0.79 OF 47
LCCATED CUTSIDE CF
THE CIRCUM-MEDITERRANEAN (355)

4 LEAN MORE TOWARD BEING THOSE 0.97 OF 67
LOCATED OUTSIDE OF
THE CIRCUM-MEDITERRANEAN (355)

10	2
37	65

XSQ= 7.97
PHI= 0.264
XP = 0.0048

6	TILT MORE TOWARD BEING THOSE LOCATED OUTSIDE OF THE INSULAR PACIFIC (330)	0.89 OF 47	6	TILT LESS TOWARD BEING THOSE LOCATED OUTSIDE OF THE INSULAR PACIFIC (330)	0.69 OF 67	5 21 42 46 XSQ= 5.60 PHI= -0.222 XP = 0.0179
15	TILT TOWARD BEING THOSE WHERE THE LATITUDE IS TWENTY DEGREES OR GREATER (183)	0.60 OF 47	15	TILT TOWARD BEING THOSE WHERE THE LATITUDE IS LESS THAN TWENTY DEGREES (217)	0.64 OF 67	28 24 19 43 XSQ= 5.36 PHI= 0.217 XP = 0.0206
42	TILT TOWARD BEING THOSE WHERE THE NATURAL ENVIRONMENT IS OTHER THAN TROPICAL OR SUB-TROPICAL RAIN FOREST, OR MONSOON FOREST (244) FWM	0.68 OF 47	42	TILT TOWARD BEING THOSE WHERE THE NATURAL ENVIRONMENT IS TROPICAL OR SUB-TROPICAL RAIN FOREST, OR MONSOON FOREST (156) FWM	0.55 OF 67	15 37 32 30 XSQ= 5.15 PHI= -0.212 XP = 0.0233
53	TEND TO BE THOSE WHERE FOOD PRODUCTION IS BY INTENSIVE AGRICULTURE, RATHER THAN BY SIMPLE AGRICULTURE OR INCIPIENT FOOD PRODUCTION (91)	0.71 OF 31	53	TEND TO BE THOSE WHERE FOOD PRODUCTION IS BY SIMPLE AGRICULTURE OR INCIPIENT FOOD PRODUCTION, RATHER THAN BY INTENSIVE AGRICULTURE (147)	0.76 OF 42	22 10 9 32 XSQ= 14.25 PHI= 0.442 XP = 0.0002
54	IN ALL CASES ARE THOSE WHERE FOOD PRODUCTION IS BY INTENSIVE OR SIMPLE AGRICULTURE, RATHER THAN BY INCIPIENT FOOD PRODUCTION (192)	1.00 OF 31	54	LEAN LESS TOWARD BEING THOSE WHERE FOOD PRODUCTION IS BY INTENSIVE OR SIMPLE AGRICULTURE, RATHER THAN BY INCIPIENT FOOD PRODUCTION (192)	0.76 OF 42	31 32 0 10 XSQ= 6.66 PHI= 0.302 XP = 0.0099
55	LEAN TOWARD BEING THOSE WHERE FOOD PRODUCTION IS BY INTENSIVE AGRICULTURE, RATHER THAN BY SIMPLE AGRICULTURE (91)	0.71 OF 31	55	LEAN TOWARD BEING THOSE WHERE FOOD PRODUCTION IS BY SIMPLE AGRICULTURE, RATHER THAN BY INTENSIVE AGRICULTURE (101)	0.69 OF 32	22 10 9 22 XSQ= 8.41 PHI= 0.365 XP = 0.0037
62	TILT MORE TOWARD BEING THOSE WHERE HUSBANDRY OF SOME KIND IS PRESENT (228)	0.83 OF 47	62	TILT LESS TOWARD BEING THOSE WHERE HUSBANDRY OF SOME KIND IS PRESENT (228)	0.61 OF 67	39 41 8 26 XSQ= 5.27 PHI= 0.215 XP = 0.0217
63	DRIFT MORE TOWARD BEING THOSE WHERE HUSBANDRY, IF PRESENT, IS PRINCIPALLY IN THE FORM OF BOVINE, EQUINE, CAMEL-LIKE, OR DEER-LIKE ANIMALS, RATHER THAN PIGS, SHEEP, OR GOATS (152)	0.72 OF 39	63	DRIFT LESS TOWARD BEING THOSE WHERE HUSBANDRY, IF PRESENT, IS PRINCIPALLY IN THE FORM OF BOVINE, EQUINE, CAMEL-LIKE, OR DEER-LIKE ANIMALS, RATHER THAN PIGS, SHEEP, OR GOATS (152)	0.51 OF 41	28 21 11 20 XSQ= 2.75 PHI= 0.185 XP = 0.0972
71	LEAN TOWARD BEING THOSE WHERE METAL WORKING IS PRESENT (98)	0.57 OF 35	71	LEAN TOWARD BEING THOSE WHERE METAL WORKING IS ABSENT (153)	0.74 OF 54	20 14 15 40 XSQ= 7.49 PHI= 0.290 XP = 0.0062

81	TEND TC BE THCSE WHERE A CITY CR TOWN IS PRESENT, OR THE AVERAGE COPPUNITY SIZE IS 200 CR GREATER (89)	0.62 OF 34	81	TEND TO BE THOSE WHERE NO CITY OR TOWN IS PRESENT, AND THE AVERAGE COPPUNITY SIZE IS SMALLER THAN 200 (135)	0.80 OF 46	21 9 / 13 37 / XSQ= 13.11 / PHI= 0.405 / XP = 0.0003
82	IN ALL CASES ARE THCSE WHERE A CITY CR TOWN IS PRESENT, OR THE AVERAGE COPPUNITY SIZE IS FIFTY CR GREATER (178)	1.00 OF 34	82	LEAN LESS TOWARD BEING THOSE WHERE A CITY OR TOWN IS PRESENT, OR THE AVERAGE COPPUNITY SIZE IS FIFTY OR GREATER (178)	0.70 OF 46	34 32 / 0 14 / XSQ= 10.52 / PHI= 0.363 / XP = 0.0012
83	TILT LESS TOWARC BEING THCSE WHERE, WITH NC CITY ANC NC TOWN PRESENT, THE AVERAGE COPPUNITY SIZE IS SPALLER THAN 200, RATHER THAN BETWEEN 200 AND 599 (135)	0.62 OF 21	83	TILT MORE TOWARD BEING THOSE WHERE, WITH NO CITY AND NO TCWN PRESENT, THE AVERAGE COPPUNITY SIZE IS SMALLER THAN 200, RATHER THAN BETWEEN 200 AND 999 (135)	0.90 OF 41	8 4 / 13 37 / XSQ= 5.44 / PHI= 0.296 / XP = 0.0196
86	TILT TCWARD BEING THCSE WHERE THE LEVEL OF POLITICAL INTEGRATICN IS THE LARGE STATE, THE LITTLE STATE, OR THE PINIMAL STATE (148) GPM	0.68 OF 34	86	TILT TOWARD BEING THOSE WHERE THE LEVEL OF PCLITICAL INTEGRATION IS THE AUTONOMOUS COPPUNITY, OR THE FAMILY (156) GPM	0.61 OF 56	23 22 / 11 34 / XSQ= 5.72 / PHI= 0.252 / XP = 0.0168
87	IN ALL CASES ARE THOSE WHERE THE LEVEL OF POLITICAL INTEGRATION IS THE LARGE STATE, THE LITTLE STATE, THE PINIPAL STATE, CR THE AUTCNCPOUS COPPUNITY (281) GPM	1.00 OF 34	87	DRIFT LESS TOWARD BEING THCSE WHERE THE LEVEL OF PCLITICAL INTEGRATION IS THE LARGE STATE, THE LITTLE STATE, THE MINIMAL STATE, OR THE AUTONOMOUS COMMUNITY (281) GPM	0.88 OF 56	34 49 / 0 7 / XSQ= 3.03 / PHI= 0.183 / XP = 0.0817
88	LEAN TCWARD BEING THCSE WHERE, IF A HEACPANSHIP IS PRESENT, SUCCESSION IS NCN-HEREDITARY (106)	0.61 OF 33	88	LEAN TOWARD BEING THOSE WHERE, IF A HEADPANSHIP IS PRESENT, SUCCESSION IS HEREDITARY (165)	0.73 OF 48	20 13 / 13 35 / XSQ= 7.77 / PHI= 0.310 / XP = 0.0053
90	IN ALL CASES ARE THCSE WHERE, IF A HEREDITARY HEACMANSHIP IS PRESENT, SUCCESSICN IS PATRILINEAL, RATHER THAN MATRILINEAL (127)	1.00 OF 13	90	TILT LESS TOWARD BEING THOSE WHERE, IF A HEREDITARY HEADPANSHIP IS PRESENT, SUCCESSICN IS PATRILINEAL, RATHER THAN MATRILINEAL (127)	0.63 OF 35	13 22 / 0 13 / XSQ= 4.87 / PHI= 0.319 / XP = 0.0273
91	IN ALL CASES ARE THCSE WHERE SCCIETAL CCPPLEXITY IS HIGH (18) F-W	1.00 OF 4	91	TILT TOWARD BEING THOSE WHERE SOCIETAL COMPLEXITY IS LOW (22) F-W	0.82 OF 11	4 2 / 0 9 / XSQ= 5.13 / PHI= 0.585 / EP = 0.0110
94	LEAN LESS TOWARC BEING THCSE WHERE THE HIERARCHY OF NATICNAL JURISDICTICN HAS TWC, CNE, CR NC LEVELS (296) GES,EA	0.78 OF 45	94	LEAN MORE TOWARD BEING THOSE WHERE THE HIERARCHY OF NATIONAL JURISDICTICN HAS TWO, ONE, OR NO LEVELS (296) GES,EA	0.97 OF 61	10 2 / 35 59 / XSQ= 7.47 / PHI= 0.265 / XP = 0.0063

102	TILT MORE TOWARD BEING THOSE WHERE CLASS STRATIFICATION IS PRESENT (203)	0.76 OF 46	102	TILT LESS TOWARD BEING THOSE WHERE CLASS STRATIFICATION IS PRESENT (203)	0.51 OF 65	35 33 11 32 XSQ= 6.25 PHI= 0.237 XP = 0.0124
107	TEND LESS TO BE THOSE WHERE CLASS STRATIFICATION, IF PRESENT, IS BASED ON SOMETHING OTHER THAN OCCUPATIONAL STATUS (160)	0.60 OF 35	107	IN ALL CASES ARE THOSE WHERE CLASS STRATIFICATION, IF PRESENT, IS BASED ON SOMETHING OTHER THAN OCCUPATIONAL STATUS (160)	1.00 OF 33	14 0 21 33 XSQ= 14.27 PHI= 0.458 XP = 0.0002
108	LEAN TOWARD BEING THOSE WHERE CLASS STRATIFICATION, IF PRESENT, IS BASED ON SOMETHING OTHER THAN A HEREDITARY ARISTOCRACY (129)	0.86 OF 35	108	LEAN TOWARD BEING THOSE WHERE CLASS STRATIFICATION, IF PRESENT, IS BASED ON A HEREDITARY ARISTOCRACY (74)	0.52 OF 33	5 17 30 16 XSQ= 9.12 PHI= -0.366 XP = 0.0025
110	TILT TOWARD BEING THOSE WHERE SLAVERY IS PRESENT (163)	0.51 OF 45	110	TILT TOWARD BEING THOSE WHERE SLAVERY IS ABSENT (218)	0.73 OF 66	23 18 22 48 XSQ= 5.54 PHI= 0.223 XP = 0.0185
118	IN ALL CASES ARE THOSE WHERE THE PERCENTAGE OF OCCUPATIONS THAT ARE SPECIALIZED IS HIGH OR MEDIUM (24) WME	1.00 OF 4	118	TILT TOWARD BEING THOSE WHERE THE PERCENTAGE OF OCCUPATIONS THAT ARE SPECIALIZED IS LOW (25) WME	0.69 OF 13	4 4 0 9 XSQ= 3.43 PHI= 0.449 EP = 0.0294
127	DRIFT TOWARD BEING THOSE WHERE THE FEMALES' CONTRIBUTION TO SUBSISTENCE IS LOW (32) JKB	0.78 OF 9	127	DRIFT TOWARD BEING THOSE WHERE THE FEMALES' CONTRIBUTION TO SUBSISTENCE IS HIGH (33) JKB	0.67 OF 15	2 10 7 5 XSQ= 2.84 PHI= -0.344 EP = 0.0894
138	IN ALL CASES ARE THOSE WHERE SUPERORDINATE JUSTICE IS PRESENT (22) BBW	1.00 OF 4	138	DRIFT TOWARD BEING THOSE WHERE SUPERORDINATE JUSTICE IS ABSENT (18) BBW	0.62 OF 13	4 5 0 8 XSQ= 2.51 PHI= 0.384 EP = 0.0824
139	DRIFT TOWARD BEING THOSE WHERE SUPERORDINATE PUNISHMENT IS PRESENT (15) BBW	0.75 OF 4	139	DRIFT TOWARD BEING THOSE WHERE SUPERORDINATE PUNISHMENT IS ABSENT (25) BBW	0.77 OF 13	3 3 1 10 XSQ= 1.70 PHI= 0.316 EP = 0.0987
186	TILT TOWARD BEING THOSE WHERE THE KIN GROUP IS EXCLUSIVELY PATRILINEAL (150)	0.51 OF 47	186	TILT TOWARD BEING THOSE WHERE THE KIN GROUP IS OTHER THAN EXCLUSIVELY PATRILINEAL (250)	0.70 OF 67	24 20 23 47 XSQ= 4.39 PHI= 0.196 XP = 0.0362

187	IN ALL CASES ARE THOSE WHERE THE KIN GROUP IS OTHER THAN EXCLUSIVELY MATRILINEAL (344)	1.00 OF 47	187	TILT LESS TOWARD BEING THOSE WHERE THE KIN GROUP IS OTHER THAN EXCLUSIVELY MATRILINEAL (344)	0.86 OF 66	0 9 47 57 XSQ= 5.23 PHI= -0.215 XP = 0.0222
190	IN ALL CASES ARE THOSE WHERE THE KIN GROUP IS PATRILINEAL OR DOUBLE-DESCENT, RATHER THAN MATRILINEAL (186)	1.00 OF 28	190	LEAN LESS TOWARD BEING THOSE WHERE THE KIN GROUP IS PATRILINEAL OR DOUBLE-DESCENT, RATHER THAN MATRILINEAL (186)	0.65 OF 34	28 22 0 12 XSQ= 10.10 PHI= 0.404 XP = 0.0015
198	DRIFT MORE TOWARD BEING THOSE WHERE RULES FOR THE INHERITANCE OF REAL PROPERTY, IF PRESENT, FAVOR THE MALE HEIR OR LINE, RATHER THAN THE FEMALE (144)	0.96 OF 24	198	DRIFT LESS TOWARD BEING THOSE WHERE RULES FOR THE INHERITANCE OF REAL PROPERTY, IF PRESENT, FAVOR THE MALE HEIR OR LINE, RATHER THAN THE FEMALE (144)	0.73 OF 26	23 19 1 7 XSQ= 3.26 PHI= 0.256 XP = 0.0708
201	LEAN MORE TOWARD BEING THOSE WHERE MARITAL RESIDENCE IS NON-OPTIONAL, RATHER THAN AMBILOCAL OR NEOLOCAL (334)	0.96 OF 47	201	LEAN LESS TOWARD BEING THOSE WHERE MARITAL RESIDENCE IS NON-OPTIONAL, RATHER THAN AMBILOCAL OR NEOLOCAL (334)	0.75 OF 67	45 50 2 17 XSQ= 7.41 PHI= 0.255 XP = 0.0065
204	LEAN MORE TOWARD BEING THOSE WHERE MARITAL RESIDENCE IS PATRILOCAL, VIRILOCAL, OR AVUNCULOCAL, RATHER THAN AMBILOCAL OR NEOLOCAL (270)	0.95 OF 42	204	LEAN LESS TOWARD BEING THOSE WHERE MARITAL RESIDENCE IS PATRILOCAL, VIRILOCAL, OR AVUNCULOCAL, RATHER THAN AMBILOCAL OR NEOLOCAL (270)	0.69 OF 55	40 38 2 17 XSQ= 8.74 PHI= 0.300 XP = 0.0031
210	IN ALL CASES ARE THOSE WHERE MARITAL RESIDENCE IS PATRILOCAL, RATHER THAN MATRILOCAL (169)	1.00 OF 27	210	TILT LESS TOWARD BEING THOSE WHERE MARITAL RESIDENCE IS PATRILOCAL, RATHER THAN MATRILOCAL (169)	0.77 OF 26	27 20 0 6 XSQ= 4.92 PHI= 0.305 XP = 0.0266
234	LEAN TOWARD BEING THOSE WHERE THE COUSIN TERMINOLOGY IS OF ESKIMO OR HAWAIIAN TYPE, RATHER THAN CROW, OMAHA, OR IROQUOIS TYPE (170)	0.82 OF 33	234	LEAN TOWARD BEING THOSE WHERE THE COUSIN TERMINOLOGY IS OF CROW, OMAHA, OR IROQUOIS TYPE, RATHER THAN ESKIMO OR HAWAIIAN TYPE (152)	0.53 OF 57	6 30 27 27 XSQ= 8.95 PHI= -0.315 XP = 0.0028
240	LEAN TOWARD BEING THOSE WHERE THE FAMILY, IF EXTENDED, IS SMALL OR STEM, RATHER THAN LARGE (135)	0.83 OF 29	240	LEAN TOWARD BEING THOSE WHERE THE FAMILY, IF EXTENDED, IS LARGE, RATHER THAN SMALL OR STEM (78)	0.53 OF 34	5 18 24 16 XSQ= 7.13 PHI= -0.337 XP = 0.0076
262	TILT MORE TOWARD BEING THOSE WHERE WIVES ARE OBTAINED BY MEANS INVOLVING THE PRESENCE OF SOME CONSIDERATION (305)	0.91 OF 47	262	TILT LESS TOWARD BEING THOSE WHERE WIVES ARE OBTAINED BY MEANS INVOLVING THE PRESENCE OF SOME CONSIDERATION (305)	0.72 OF 67	43 48 4 19 XSQ= 5.58 PHI= 0.221 XP = 0.0182

278	IN ALL CASES ARE THOSE 1.00 OF 4 WHERE PROPERTY RIGHTS IN WOMEN ARE PRESENT (8) LWS	278	IN ALL CASES ARE THOSE 1.00 OF 5 WHERE PROPERTY RIGHTS IN WOMEN ARE UNIMPORTANT OR ABSENT (14) LWS	4 0 0 5 XSQ= 5.41 PHI= 0.775 EP = 0.0079
301	TILT MORE TOWARD BEING THOSE 0.90 OF 20 WHERE THE POST-PARTUM SEX TABOO LASTS LONGER THAN ONE MONTH (96)	301	TILT LESS TOWARD BEING THOSE 0.57 OF 30 WHERE THE POST-PARTUM SEX TABOO LASTS LONGER THAN ONE MONTH (96)	18 17 2 13 XSQ= 4.86 PHI= 0.312 XP = 0.0275
305	IN ALL CASES ARE THOSE 1.00 OF 8 WHERE THE EARLY SEXUAL SATISFACTION POTENTIAL IS LOW (24) W-C	305	LEAN TOWARD BEING THOSE 0.72 OF 18 WHERE THE EARLY SEXUAL SATISFACTION POTENTIAL IS HIGH (27) W-C	0 13 8 5 XSQ= 8.85 PHI= -0.583 EP = 0.0016
308	IN ALL CASES ARE THOSE 1.00 OF 7 WHERE AVERAGE SOCIALIZATION ANXIETY IS HIGH (22) W-C	308	LEAN TOWARD BEING THOSE 0.64 OF 14 WHERE AVERAGE SOCIALIZATION ANXIETY IS LOW (18) W-C	7 5 0 9 XSQ= 5.47 PHI= 0.510 EP = 0.0071
310	DRIFT TOWARD BEING THOSE 0.86 OF 7 WHERE ANAL SOCIALIZATION ANXIETY IS HIGH (22) W-C	310	DRIFT TOWARD BEING THOSE 0.64 OF 14 WHERE ANAL SOCIALIZATION ANXIETY IS LOW (19) W-C	6 5 1 9 XSQ= 2.89 PHI= 0.371 EP = 0.0635
311	IN ALL CASES ARE THOSE 1.00 OF 8 WHERE SEXUAL SOCIALIZATION ANXIETY IS HIGH (28) W-C	311	TEND TO BE THOSE 0.83 OF 18 WHERE SEXUAL SOCIALIZATION ANXIETY IS LOW (23) W-C	8 3 0 15 XSQ= 12.53 PHI= 0.694 EP = 0.0001
338	DRIFT TOWARD BEING THOSE 0.70 OF 10 WHERE THE CHILD'S INFERRED ANXIETY OVER PERFORMANCE OF RESPONSIBLE BEHAVIOR IS LOW (29) B-B-C	338	DRIFT TOWARD BEING THOSE 0.71 OF 21 WHERE THE CHILD'S INFERRED ANXIETY OVER PERFORMANCE OF RESPONSIBLE BEHAVIOR IS HIGH (44) B-B-C	3 15 7 6 XSQ= 3.23 PHI= -0.323 EP = 0.0515
346	TILT TOWARD BEING THOSE 0.90 OF 10 WHERE THE CHILD'S INFERRED ANXIETY OVER PERFORMANCE OF SELF-RELIANT BEHAVIOR IS LOW (39) B-B-C	346	TILT TOWARD BEING THOSE 0.50 OF 22 WHERE THE CHILD'S INFERRED ANXIETY OVER PERFORMANCE OF SELF-RELIANT BEHAVIOR IS HIGH (37) B-B-C	1 11 9 11 XSQ= 3.14 PHI= -0.313 EP = 0.0496
352	DRIFT TOWARD BEING THOSE 0.88 OF 8 WHERE THE TOTAL POSITIVE PRESSURE TOWARD DEVELOPING OBEDIENT BEHAVIOR IN THE CHILD IS HIGH (44) B-B-C	352	DRIFT TOWARD BEING THOSE 0.50 OF 22 WHERE THE TOTAL POSITIVE PRESSURE TOWARD DEVELOPING OBEDIENT BEHAVIOR IN THE CHILD IS LOW (28) B-B-C	7 11 1 11 XSQ= 2.05 PHI= 0.262 EP = 0.0994

385	TILT TOWARD BEING THOSE WHERE SEXUAL EXPRESSION BY THE YOUNG IS RESTRICTED (22) F-B	0.83 OF	6	385	TILT TOWARD BEING THOSE WHERE SEXUAL EXPRESSION BY THE YOUNG IS SEMI-RESTRICTED OR PERMITTED (64) F-B	0.75 OF	32	5 8 1 24 XSQ= 5.27 PHI= 0.372 EP = 0.0123
386	DRIFT TOWARD BEING THOSE WHERE SEXUAL EXPRESSION BY THE YOUNG IS RESTRICTED OR SEMI-RESTRICTED (46) F-B	0.83 OF	6	386	DRIFT TOWARD BEING THOSE WHERE SEXUAL EXPRESSION BY THE YOUNG IS PERMITTED (40) F-B	0.66 OF	32	5 11 1 21 XSQ= 3.16 PHI= 0.288 EP = 0.0647
393	TILT TOWARD BEING THOSE WHERE EXTRAMARITAL COITUS IS PUNISHED, RATHER THAN PERMITTED (43) F-B	0.78 OF	9	393	TILT TOWARD BEING THOSE WHERE EXTRAMARITAL COITUS IS PERMITTED, RATHER THAN PUNISHED (41) F-B	0.65 OF	26	7 9 2 17 XSQ= 3.43 PHI= 0.313 EP = 0.0498
397	LEAN TOWARD BEING THOSE WHERE SEX DISABILITY IS PRESENT (14) JKH	0.56 OF	9	397	IN ALL CASES ARE THOSE WHERE SEX DISABILITY IS ABSENT (42) JKH	1.00 OF	14	5 0 4 14 XSQ= 6.94 PHI= 0.549 EP = 0.0037
398	IN ALL CASES ARE THOSE WHERE THE INTENSITY OF SEX ANXIETY IS HIGH (16) WNS	1.00 OF	5	398	IN ALL CASES ARE THOSE WHERE THE INTENSITY OF SEX ANXIETY IS LOW (16) WNS	1.00 OF	11	5 0 0 11 XSQ= 11.68 PHI= 0.855 EP = 0.0002
399	IN ALL CASES ARE THOSE WHERE INTENSITY OF CASTRATION ANXIETY IS HIGH (23) WNS	1.00 OF	7	399	LEAN TOWARD BEING THOSE WHERE INTENSITY OF CASTRATION ANXIETY IS LOW (22) WNS	0.63 OF	16	7 6 0 10 XSQ= 5.41 PHI= 0.485 EP = 0.0075
404	TILT TOWARD BEING THOSE WHERE EXPLANATIONS OF ILLNESS OF A SEXUAL NATURE ARE PRESENT (19) W-C	0.63 OF	8	404	TILT TOWARD BEING THOSE WHERE EXPLANATIONS OF ILLNESS OF A SEXUAL NATURE ARE ABSENT (42) W-C	0.84 OF	19	5 3 3 16 XSQ= 3.86 PHI= 0.378 EP = 0.0267
420	TILT TOWARD BEING THOSE WHERE BELLICOSITY IS EXTREME (41) PES	0.75 OF	12	420	TILT TOWARD BEING THOSE WHERE BELLICOSITY IS MODERATE OR NEGLIGIBLE (46) PES	0.64 OF	25	9 9 3 16 XSQ= 3.50 PHI= 0.308 EP = 0.0382
421	DRIFT TOWARD BEING THOSE WHERE KILLING, TORTURING, OR MUTILATING OF THE ENEMY IS STRONGLY OR MODERATELY EMPHASIZED (37) PES	0.73 OF	11	421	DRIFT TOWARD BEING THOSE WHERE KILLING, TORTURING, OR MUTILATING OF THE ENEMY IS NEGLIGIBLY EMPHASIZED (47) PES	0.67 OF	24	8 8 3 16 XSQ= 3.26 PHI= 0.305 EP = 0.0652

426	DRIFT TOWARD BEING THOSE WHERE A HIGH GOD IS PRESENT (156) GES,EA	0.68 OF 38	426	DRIFT TOWARD BEING THOSE WHERE A HIGH GOD IS ABSENT (104) GES,EA	0.53 OF 51	26 24 12 27 XSQ= 3.22 PHI= 0.190 XP = 0.0729
427	TILT TOWARD BEING THOSE WHERE A HIGH GOD, IF PRESENT, IS ACTIVE, RATHER THAN INACTIVE (87) GES,EA	0.73 OF 26	427	TILT TOWARD BEING THOSE WHERE A HIGH GOD, IF PRESENT, IS INACTIVE, RATHER THAN ACTIVE (69) GES,EA	0.67 OF 24	19 8 7 16 XSQ= 6.42 PHI= 0.358 XP = 0.0113
428	TILT TOWARD BEING THOSE WHERE A HIGH GOD, IF PRESENT AND ACTIVE, SUPPORTS HUMAN MORALITY, RATHER THAN NOT SUPPORTING IT (61) GES,EA	0.89 OF 19	428	TILT TOWARD BEING THOSE WHERE A HIGH GOD, IF PRESENT AND ACTIVE, DOES NOT SUPPORT HUMAN MORALITY, RATHER THAN SUPPORTING IT (26) GES,EA	0.63 OF 8	17 3 2 5 XSQ= 5.44 PHI= 0.449 EP = 0.0114
450	LEAN TOWARD BEING THOSE WHERE THE OBSERVATION OF FOOD TABOOS IS LOW, RATHER THAN HIGH OR MEDIUM (26) JRL	0.67 OF 9	450	LEAN TOWARD BEING THOSE WHERE THE OBSERVATION OF FOOD TABOOS IS HIGH OR MEDIUM, RATHER THAN LOW (60) JRL	0.92 OF 24	3 22 6 2 XSQ= 9.16 PHI= -0.527 EP = 0.0017
458	TILT TOWARD BEING THOSE WHERE GAMES, IF PRESENT, INCLUDE GAMES OF STRATEGY (52) R-A-B,EA	0.52 OF 29	458	TILT TOWARD BEING THOSE WHERE GAMES, IF PRESENT, DO NOT INCLUDE GAMES OF STRATEGY (119) R-A-B,EA	0.79 OF 39	15 8 14 31 XSQ= 5.91 PHI= 0.295 XP = 0.0150
459	DRIFT TOWARD BEING THOSE WHERE GAMES, IF PRESENT, INCLUDE GAMES OF CHANCE (82) R-A-B,EA	0.59 OF 29	459	DRIFT TOWARD BEING THOSE WHERE GAMES, IF PRESENT, DO NOT INCLUDE GAMES OF CHANCE (89) R-A-B,EA	0.67 OF 39	17 13 12 26 XSQ= 3.35 PHI= 0.222 XP = 0.0672
460	LEAN TOWARD BEING THOSE WHERE GAMES, IF PRESENT, ARE NOT LIMITED TO GAMES OF SKILL ONLY (104) R-A-B,EA	0.79 OF 29	460	LEAN TOWARD BEING THOSE WHERE GAMES, IF PRESENT, ARE LIMITED TO GAMES OF SKILL ONLY (67) R-A-B,EA	0.56 OF 39	6 22 23 17 XSQ= 7.35 PHI= -0.329 XP = 0.0067
468	DRIFT TOWARD BEING THOSE WHERE CONTACT WITH OTHER CULTURES IS FREQUENT, RATHER THAN REGULAR OR IRREGULAR (17) JMH	0.67 OF 6	468	DRIFT TOWARD BEING THOSE WHERE CONTACT WITH OTHER CULTURES IS REGULAR OR IRREGULAR, RATHER THAN FREQUENT (37) JMH	0.81 OF 16	4 3 2 13 XSQ= 2.67 PHI= 0.349 EP = 0.0536
472	TILT TOWARD BEING THOSE WHERE THE COMPOSITE NARCISSISM INDEX IS HIGH (47) PES	0.77 OF 13	472	TILT TOWARD BEING THOSE WHERE THE COMPOSITE NARCISSISM INDEX IS LOW (43) PES	0.60 OF 25	10 10 3 15 XSQ= 3.31 PHI= 0.295 EP = 0.0434

****

390 CULTURES WHERE PREMARITAL SEX RELATIONS ARE STRONGLY PUNISHED AND IN FACT RARE (47) JTW,EA	390 CULTURES WHERE PREMARITAL SEX RELATIONS ARE WEAKLY PUNISHED AND IN FACT NOT RARE OR PUNISHED ONLY IF PREGNANCY RESULTS, OR FREELY PERMITTED (132) JTW,EA

BACKGROUND ON PAGE 154 — BOTH SUBJECT AND PREDICATE

....

47 IN LEFT COLUMN

ABIPON	ALBANIANS	ASHANTI	ATSUGEWI	BASSERI	BURUSHO	CAMBODIANS	CHEYENNE	CHIR-APACHE	COORG
CUNA	EGYPTIANS	ENGA	FON	GILBERTESE	HAZARA	HEBREWS	INCA	IRISH	JAPANESE
JAVANESE	KHEVSUR	KIKUYU	KORYAK	KWAKIUTL	LUO	MAM	MAMVU	MANUS	MINCHIA
MZAB	NUPE	ONA	PURUM	RUNDI	RWALA	SANTAL	SARSI	SERBS	SHLUH
TEDA	TENINO	THAI	TOLOWA	TWANA	ULAWANS	VIETNAMESE			

132 IN RIGHT COLUMN

ABOR	AINU	AKHA	ALORESE	AMBA	AMERICANS	ANDAMANESE	ARAUCANIANS	AWEIKOMA	AYMARA
AZANDE	AZTEC	BARI	BATAK	BAYA	BHIL	BHUIYA	BORORO	BRAZILIANS	CARIB
CHAGGA	CHENCHU	CHIBCHA	CHOROTI	CHUKCHEE	DELAWARE	DOBUANS	ELLICE	FANG	FUTAJALONKE
GANDA	GARO	GILYAK	GISU	GOAJIRO	GOND	HAIDA	HANO	HAWAIIANS	HUTSUL
IBAN	IFUGAO	ILA	INGALIK	JIVARO	KACHIN	KAPAUKU	KASKA	KAZAK	KIOW-APACHE
KOREANS	KURTATCHI	KUTENAI	LAKHER	LAMET	LAPPS	LAU	LEPCHA	LOLO	MACASSARESE
MAGUZAWA	MANGAIANS	MANIHIKI	MAORI	MARQUESANS	MARSHALLESE	MASAI	MATACO	MENTAWEI	MERINA
MONGO	MONGUOR	NAMA	NATCHEZ	NAVAHO	NICOBARESE	NOMLAKI	OJIBWA	OKINAWANS	OMAHA
PALAUANS	PARAUJANO	PONAPEANS	PUKAPUKA	RAROIANS	RIFFIANS	SAGADA	SAMOANS	SANPOIL	SEMANG
SHILLUK	SINHALESE	SIRIONO	SIUAI	SOMALI	SONGHAI	TALAMANCA	TALLENSI	TANALA	TAOS
TARAHUMARA	TAREUMIUT	TEHUELCHE	TENDA	THONGA	TIKOPIA	TIMBIRA	TIV	TODA	TOKELAU
TRISTAN	TROBRIAND	TRUKESE	TRUMAI	TUBATULABAL	TUCUNA	TUPINAMBA	UTE	VEDDA	VENDA
WITOTO	WOGEO	WOLEAIANS	WOLOF	YABARANA	YAGUA	YAHGAN	YAKUT	YAO	YAPESE
YORUBA	YUKI								

23 EXCLUDED BECAUSE IRRELEVANT

APINAYE	ARANDA	ARAPESH	BEMBA	BOTOCUDO	CALLINAGO	COPR ESKIMO	CREEK	DUTCH	GROS VENTRE
KERAKI	KUNG	LUBA	MISKITO	MUNDURUCU	MURNGIN	NABESNA	NAMBICUARA	NYAKYUSA	SAMOYED
TAPIRAPE	TERENA	TIWI							

198 EXCLUDED BECAUSE UNASCERTAINED

----

4 TILT LESS TOWARD BEING THOSE 0.79 OF 47 LOCATED OUTSIDE OF THE CIRCUM-MEDITERRANEAN (355)	4 TILT MORE TOWARD BEING THOSE 0.92 OF 132 LOCATED OUTSIDE OF THE CIRCUM-MEDITERRANEAN (355)		10 10
			37 122
		XSQ=	5.25
		PHI=	0.171
		XP =	0.0220

6	DRIFT MCRE TCWARC BEING THCSE 0.89 OF 47 LCCATED CUTSIDE CF THE INSULAR PACIFIC (330)	6	DRIFT LESS TOWARD BEING THOSE 0.77 OF 132 LOCATED OUTSIDE OF THE INSULAR PACIFIC (330)	5 31 42 101 XSQ= 2.81 PHI= -0.125 XP = 0.0939
15	DRIFT TCWARD BEING THCSE 0.60 OF 47 WHERE THE LATITUDE IS TWENTY DEGREES CR GREATER (183)	15	DRIFT TOWARD BEING THOSE 0.57 CF 132 WHERE THE LATITUDE IS LESS THAN TWENTY DEGREES (217)	28 57 19 75 XSQ= 3.11 PHI= 0.132 XP = 0.0780
53	TEND TC BE THCSE 0.71 OF 31 WHERE FCCD PRCDUCTION IS BY INTENSIVE AGRICULTURE, RATHER THAN BY SIMPLE AGRICULTURE CR INCIPIENT FCCD PRODUCTICN (91)	53	TEND TO BE THOSE 0.69 OF 86 WHERE FOOD PRODUCTION IS BY SIMPLE AGRICULTURE OR INCIPIENT FOOD PRODUCTICN, RATHER THAN BY INTENSIVE AGRICULTURE (147)	22 27 9 59 XSQ= 13.08 PHI= 0.334 XP = 0.0003
54	IN ALL CASES ARE THCSE 1.00 OF 31 WHERE FCCD PRCDUCTICN IS BY INTENSIVE CR SIMPLE AGRICULTURE, RATHER THAN BY INCIPIENT FCCD PRCDUCTICN (192)	54	TILT LESS TOWARD BEING THCSE 0.81 OF 86 WHERE FOOD PRODUCTICN IS BY INTENSIVE OR SIMPLE AGRICULTURE, RATHER THAN BY INCIPIENT FOOD PRODUCTICN (192)	31 70 0 16 XSQ= 5.20 PHI= 0.211 XP = 0.0226
55	LEAN TCWARC BEING THOSE 0.71 OF 31 WHERE FCCD PRCDUCTION IS BY INTENSIVE AGRICULTURE, RATHER THAN BY SIMPLE AGRICULTURE (91)	55	LEAN TOWARD BEING THOSE 0.61 OF 70 WHERE FOOD PRODUCTION IS BY SIMPLE AGRICULTURE, RATHER THAN BY INTENSIVE AGRICULTURE (101)	22 27 9 43 XSQ= 7.78 PHI= 0.277 XP = 0.0053
62	DRIFT MCRE TCWARC BEING THCSE 0.83 OF 47 WHERE HUSBANDRY CF SOME KIND IS PRESENT (228)	62	DRIFT LESS TOWARD BEING THCSE 0.67 OF 132 WHERE HUSBANDRY OF SOME KIND IS PRESENT (228)	39 88 8 44 XSQ= 3.72 PHI= 0.144 XP = 0.0538
81	LEAN TCWARC BEING THOSE 0.62 OF 34 WHERE A CITY CR TOWN IS PRESENT, OR THE AVERAGE COMMUNITY SIZE IS 200 CR GREATER (89)	81	LEAN TOWARD BEING THOSE 0.70 OF 97 WHERE NO CITY OR TOWN IS PRESENT, AND THE AVERAGE COMMUNITY SIZE IS SMALLER THAN 200 (135)	21 29 13 68 XSQ= 9.53 PHI= 0.270 XP = 0.0020
82	IN ALL CASES ARE THCSE 1.00 OF 34 WHERE A CITY CR TOWN IS PRESENT, CR THE AVERAGE COMMUNITY SIZE IS FIFTY CR GREATER (178)	82	LEAN LESS TOWARD BEING THOSE 0.78 OF 97 WHERE A CITY OR TOWN IS PRESENT, OR THE AVERAGE COMMUNITY SIZE IS FIFTY OR GREATER (178)	34 76 0 21 XSQ= 7.23 PHI= 0.235 XP = 0.0072
83	DRIFT LESS TCWARC BEING THCSE 0.62 OF 21 WHERE, WITH NC CITY AND NC TOWN PRESENT, THE AVERAGE COMMUNITY SIZE IS SMALLER THAN 200, RATHER THAN BETWEEN 200 AND 999 (135)	83	DRIFT MORE TOWARD BEING THCSE 0.82 OF 83 WHERE, WITH NO CITY AND NO TOWN PRESENT, THE AVERAGE COMMUNITY SIZE IS SMALLER THAN 200, RATHER THAN BETWEEN 200 AND 999 (135)	8 15 13 68 XSQ= 2.83 PHI= 0.165 XP = 0.0928

86	TILT TOWARD BEING THOSE 0.68 OF 34 WHERE THE LEVEL OF POLITICAL INTEGRATION IS THE LARGE STATE, THE LITTLE STATE, OR THE MINIMAL STATE (148) GPM	86	TILT TOWARD BEING THOSE 0.56 OF 110 WHERE THE LEVEL OF POLITICAL INTEGRATION IS THE AUTONOMOUS COMMUNITY, OR THE FAMILY (156) GPM	23 48 11 62 XSQ= 5.07 PHI= 0.188 XP = 0.0244
87	IN ALL CASES ARE THOSE 1.00 OF 34 WHERE THE LEVEL OF POLITICAL INTEGRATION IS THE LARGE STATE, THE LITTLE STATE, THE MINIMAL STATE, OR THE AUTONOMOUS COMMUNITY (281) GPM	87	DRIFT LESS TOWARD BEING THOSE 0.89 OF 110 WHERE THE LEVEL OF POLITICAL INTEGRATION IS THE LARGE STATE, THE LITTLE STATE, THE MINIMAL STATE, OR THE AUTONOMOUS COMMUNITY (281) GPM	34 98 0 12 XSQ= 2.74 PHI= 0.138 XP = 0.0976
88	LEAN TOWARD BEING THOSE 0.61 OF 33 WHERE, IF A HEADMANSHIP IS PRESENT, SUCCESSION IS NON-HEREDITARY (106)	88	LEAN TOWARD BEING THOSE 0.71 OF 97 WHERE, IF A HEADMANSHIP IS PRESENT, SUCCESSION IS HEREDITARY (165)	20 28 13 69 XSQ= 9.33 PHI= 0.268 XP = 0.0023
90	IN ALL CASES ARE THOSE 1.00 OF 13 WHERE, IF A HEREDITARY HEADMANSHIP IS PRESENT, SUCCESSION IS PATRILINEAL, RATHER THAN MATRILINEAL (127)	9C	DRIFT LESS TOWARD BEING THOSE 0.74 OF 69 WHERE, IF A HEREDITARY HEADMANSHIP IS PRESENT, SUCCESSION IS PATRILINEAL, RATHER THAN MATRILINEAL (127)	13 51 0 18 XSQ= 2.96 PHI= 0.19C XP = 0.0856
91	IN ALL CASES ARE THOSE 1.00 OF 4 WHERE SOCIETAL COMPLEXITY IS HIGH (18) F-W	91	TILT TOWARD BEING THOSE 0.63 OF 24 WHERE SOCIETAL COMPLEXITY IS LOW (22) F-W	4 9 0 15 XSQ= 3.16 PHI= 0.336 EP = 0.0349
94	TILT LESS TOWARD BEING THOSE 0.78 OF 45 WHERE THE HIERARCHY OF NATIONAL JURISDICTION HAS TWO, ONE, OR NO LEVELS (296) GES,EA	94	TILT MORE TOWARD BEING THOSE 0.93 OF 124 WHERE THE HIERARCHY OF NATIONAL JURISDICTION HAS TWO, ONE, OR NO LEVELS (296) GES,EA	10 9 35 115 XSQ= 5.99 PHI= 0.188 XP = 0.0144
102	TILT MORE TOWARD BEING THOSE 0.76 OF 46 WHERE CLASS STRATIFICATION IS PRESENT (203)	102	TILT LESS TOWARD BEING THOSE 0.57 OF 130 WHERE CLASS STRATIFICATION IS PRESENT (203)	35 74 11 56 XSQ= 4.51 PHI= 0.160 XP = 0.0337
107	LEAN LESS TOWARD BEING THOSE 0.60 OF 35 WHERE CLASS STRATIFICATION, IF PRESENT, IS BASED ON SOMETHING OTHER THAN OCCUPATIONAL STATUS (160)	107	LEAN MORE TOWARD BEING THOSE 0.88 OF 74 WHERE CLASS STRATIFICATION, IF PRESENT, IS BASED ON SOMETHING OTHER THAN OCCUPATIONAL STATUS (160)	14 9 21 65 XSQ= 9.45 PHI= 0.294 XP = 0.0021
108	LEAN MORE TOWARD BEING THOSE 0.86 OF 35 WHERE CLASS STRATIFICATION, IF PRESENT, IS BASED ON SOMETHING OTHER THAN A HEREDITARY ARISTOCRACY (129)	108	LEAN LESS TOWARD BEING THOSE 0.58 OF 74 WHERE CLASS STRATIFICATION, IF PRESENT, IS BASED ON SOMETHING OTHER THAN A HEREDITARY ARISTOCRACY (129)	5 31 30 43 XSQ= 6.99 PHI= -0.253 XP = 0.0082

127	DRIFT TOWARD BEING THOSE WHERE THE FEMALES' CONTRIBUTION TO SUBSISTENCE IS LOW (32) JKB	0.78 OF 9	127	DRIFT TOWARD BEING THOSE WHERE THE FEMALES' CONTRIBUTION TO SUBSISTENCE IS HIGH (33) JKB	0.62 OF 34	2 21 7 13 XSQ= 3.02 PHI= -0.265 XP = 0.0820
136	IN ALL CASES ARE THOSE WHERE FULL-TIME ENTREPRENEURS ARE PRESENT (18) JV	1.00 OF 4	136	DRIFT TOWARD BEING THOSE WHERE FULL-TIME ENTREPRENEURS ARE ABSENT (14) JV	0.58 OF 19	4 8 0 11 XSQ= 2.42 PHI= 0.324 EP = 0.0932
186	DRIFT TOWARD BEING THOSE WHERE THE KIN GROUP IS EXCLUSIVELY PATRILINEAL (150)	0.51 OF 47	186	DRIFT TOWARD BEING THOSE WHERE THE KIN GROUP IS OTHER THAN EXCLUSIVELY PATRILINEAL (250)	0.64 OF 132	24 47 23 85 XSQ= 2.84 PHI= 0.126 XP = 0.0917
187	IN ALL CASES ARE THOSE WHERE THE KIN GROUP IS OTHER THAN EXCLUSIVELY MATRILINEAL (344)	1.00 OF 47	187	TILT LESS TOWARD BEING THOSE WHERE THE KIN GROUP IS OTHER THAN EXCLUSIVELY MATRILINEAL (344)	0.85 OF 131	0 19 47 112 XSQ= 6.19 PHI= -0.186 XP = 0.0129
190	IN ALL CASES ARE THOSE WHERE THE KIN GROUP IS PATRILINEAL OR DOUBLE-DESCENT, RATHER THAN MATRILINEAL (186)	1.00 OF 28	190	LEAN LESS TOWARD BEING THOSE WHERE THE KIN GROUP IS PATRILINEAL OR DOUBLE-DESCENT, RATHER THAN MATRILINEAL (186)	0.71 OF 79	28 56 0 23 XSQ= 8.73 PHI= 0.286 XP = 0.0031
201	TILT MORE TOWARD BEING THOSE WHERE MARITAL RESIDENCE IS NON-OPTIONAL, RATHER THAN AMBILOCAL OR NEOLOCAL (334)	0.96 OF 47	201	TILT LESS TOWARD BEING THOSE WHERE MARITAL RESIDENCE IS NON-OPTIONAL, RATHER THAN AMBILOCAL OR NEOLOCAL (334)	0.80 OF 132	45 105 2 27 XSQ= 5.56 PHI= 0.176 XP = 0.0184
204	TILT MORE TOWARD BEING THOSE WHERE MARITAL RESIDENCE IS PATRILOCAL, VIRILOCAL, OR AVUNCULOCAL, RATHER THAN AMBILOCAL OR NEOLOCAL (270)	0.95 OF 42	204	TILT LESS TOWARD BEING THOSE WHERE MARITAL RESIDENCE IS PATRILOCAL, VIRILOCAL, OR AVUNCULOCAL, RATHER THAN AMBILOCAL OR NEOLOCAL (270)	0.76 OF 111	40 84 2 27 XSQ= 6.37 PHI= 0.204 XP = 0.0116
210	IN ALL CASES ARE THOSE WHERE MARITAL RESIDENCE IS PATRILOCAL, RATHER THAN MATRILOCAL (169)	1.00 OF 27	210	TILT LESS TOWARD BEING THOSE WHERE MARITAL RESIDENCE IS PATRILOCAL, RATHER THAN MATRILOCAL (169)	0.79 OF 63	27 50 0 13 XSQ= 4.95 PHI= 0.235 XP = 0.0261
234	LEAN MORE TOWARD BEING THOSE WHERE THE COUSIN TERMINOLOGY IS OF ESKIMO OR HAWAIIAN TYPE, RATHER THAN CROW, OMAHA, OR IROQUOIS TYPE (170)	0.82 OF 33	234	LEAN LESS TOWARD BEING THOSE WHERE THE COUSIN TERMINOLOGY IS OF ESKIMO OR HAWAIIAN TYPE, RATHER THAN CROW, OMAHA, OR IROQUOIS TYPE (170)	0.50 OF 113	6 56 27 57 XSQ= 9.05 PHI= -0.249 XP = 0.0026

240	TILT MORE TOWARD BEING THOSE WHERE THE FAMILY, IF EXTENDED, IS SMALL OR STEM, RATHER THAN LARGE (135)	0.83 OF 29	240	TILT LESS TOWARD BEING THOSE WHERE THE FAMILY, IF EXTENDED, IS SMALL OR STEM, RATHER THAN LARGE (135)	0.58 OF 65	5 27 / 24 38 / XSQ= 4.25 / PHI= -0.213 / XP = 0.0393
262	TILT MORE TOWARD BEING THOSE WHERE WIVES ARE OBTAINED BY MEANS INVOLVING THE PRESENCE OF SOME CONSIDERATION (305)	0.91 OF 47	262	TILT LESS TOWARD BEING THOSE WHERE WIVES ARE OBTAINED BY MEANS INVOLVING THE PRESENCE OF SOME CONSIDERATION (305)	0.73 OF 132	43 97 / 4 35 / XSQ= 5.58 / PHI= 0.177 / XP = 0.0182
278	IN ALL CASES ARE THOSE WHERE PROPERTY RIGHTS IN WOMEN ARE PRESENT (8) LWS	1.00 OF 4	278	TILT TOWARD BEING THOSE WHERE PROPERTY RIGHTS IN WOMEN ARE UNIMPORTANT OR ABSENT (14) LWS	0.71 OF 14	4 4 / 0 10 / XSQ= 3.86 / PHI= 0.463 / EP = 0.0229
305	IN ALL CASES ARE THOSE WHERE THE EARLY SEXUAL SATISFACTION POTENTIAL IS LOW (24) W-C	1.00 OF 8	305	TEND TO BE THOSE WHERE THE EARLY SEXUAL SATISFACTION POTENTIAL IS HIGH (27) W-C	0.66 OF 32	0 21 / 8 11 / XSQ= 8.58 / PHI= -0.463 / EP = 0.0010
308	IN ALL CASES ARE THOSE WHERE AVERAGE SOCIALIZATION ANXIETY IS HIGH (22) W-C	1.00 OF 7	308	TILT TOWARD BEING THOSE WHERE AVERAGE SOCIALIZATION ANXIETY IS LOW (18) W-C	0.54 OF 26	7 12 / 0 14 / XSQ= 4.53 / PHI= 0.370 / EP = 0.0126
310	DRIFT TOWARD BEING THOSE WHERE ANAL SOCIALIZATION ANXIETY IS HIGH (22) W-C	0.86 OF 7	310	DRIFT TOWARD BEING THOSE WHERE ANAL SOCIALIZATION ANXIETY IS LOW (19) W-C	0.54 OF 26	6 12 / 1 14 / XSQ= 2.07 / PHI= 0.250 / EP = 0.0952
311	IN ALL CASES ARE THOSE WHERE SEXUAL SOCIALIZATION ANXIETY IS HIGH (28) W-C	1.00 OF 8	311	TILT TOWARD BEING THOSE WHERE SEXUAL SOCIALIZATION ANXIETY IS LOW (23) W-C	0.55 OF 33	8 15 / 0 18 / XSQ= 5.72 / PHI= 0.374 / XP = 0.0168
338	TILT TOWARD BEING THOSE WHERE THE CHILD'S INFERRED ANXIETY OVER PERFORMANCE OF RESPONSIBLE BEHAVIOR IS LOW (29) B-B-C	0.70 OF 10	338	TILT TOWARD BEING THOSE WHERE THE CHILD'S INFERRED ANXIETY OVER PERFORMANCE OF RESPONSIBLE BEHAVIOR IS HIGH (44) B-B-C	0.71 OF 41	3 29 / 7 12 / XSQ= 4.10 / PHI= -0.283 / XP = 0.0430
346	TILT TOWARD BEING THOSE WHERE THE CHILD'S INFERRED ANXIETY OVER PERFORMANCE OF SELF-RELIANT BEHAVIOR IS LOW (39) B-B-C	0.90 OF 10	346	TILT TOWARD BEING THOSE WHERE THE CHILD'S INFERRED ANXIETY OVER PERFORMANCE OF SELF-RELIANT BEHAVIOR IS HIGH (37) B-B-C	0.57 OF 42	1 24 / 9 18 / XSQ= 5.43 / PHI= -0.323 / XP = 0.0198

No.				No.					
347	TILT TOWARD BEING THOSE WHERE THE CHILD'S INFERRED CONFLICT REGARDING SELF-RELIANT BEHAVIOR IS LOW (39) B-B-C	0.90 OF	10	347	TILT TOWARD BEING THOSE WHERE THE CHILD'S INFERRED CONFLICT REGARDING SELF-RELIANT BEHAVIOR IS HIGH (37) B-B-C	0.52 OF	42	 XSQ= PHI= XP =	1 22 9 20 4.29 -0.287 0.0384
385	LEAN TOWARD BEING THOSE WHERE SEXUAL EXPRESSION BY THE YOUNG IS RESTRICTED (22) F-B	0.83 OF	6	385	LEAN TOWARD BEING THOSE WHERE SEXUAL EXPRESSION BY THE YOUNG IS SEMI-RESTRICTED OR PERMITTED (64) F-B	0.81 OF	53	 XSQ= PHI= XP =	5 10 1 43 8.66 0.383 0.0033
397	TILT TOWARD BEING THOSE WHERE SEX DISABILITY IS PRESENT (14) JKH	0.56 OF	9	397	TILT TOWARD BEING THOSE WHERE SEX DISABILITY IS ABSENT (42) JKH	0.83 OF	30	 XSQ= PHI= EP =	5 5 4 25 3.64 0.306 0.0321
398	IN ALL CASES ARE THOSE WHERE THE INTENSITY OF SEX ANXIETY IS HIGH (16) WNS	1.00 OF	5	398	TILT TOWARD BEING THOSE WHERE THE INTENSITY OF SEX ANXIETY IS LOW (16) WNS	0.65 OF	20	 XSQ= PHI= EP =	5 7 0 13 4.42 0.420 0.0149
399	IN ALL CASES ARE THOSE WHERE INTENSITY OF CASTRATION ANXIETY IS HIGH (23) WNS	1.00 OF	7	399	LEAN TOWARD BEING THOSE WHERE INTENSITY OF CASTRATION ANXIETY IS LOW (22) WNS	0.57 OF	30	 XSQ= PHI= EP =	7 13 0 17 5.23 0.376 0.0094
404	DRIFT TOWARD BEING THOSE WHERE EXPLANATIONS OF ILLNESS OF A SEXUAL NATURE ARE PRESENT (19) W-C	0.63 OF	8	404	DRIFT TOWARD BEING THOSE WHERE EXPLANATIONS OF ILLNESS OF A SEXUAL NATURE ARE ABSENT (42) W-C	0.76 OF	37	 XSQ= PHI= XP =	5 9 3 28 2.87 0.252 0.0903
420	DRIFT TOWARD BEING THOSE WHERE BELLICOSITY IS EXTREME (41) PES	0.75 OF	12	420	DRIFT TOWARD BEING THOSE WHERE BELLICOSITY IS MODERATE OR NEGLIGIBLE (46) PES	0.58 OF	55	 XSQ= PHI= XP =	9 23 3 32 3.12 0.216 0.0774
427	DRIFT TOWARD BEING THOSE WHERE A HIGH GOD, IF PRESENT, IS ACTIVE, RATHER THAN INACTIVE (87) GES,EA	0.73 OF	26	427	DRIFT TOWARD BEING THOSE WHERE A HIGH GOD, IF PRESENT, IS INACTIVE, RATHER THAN ACTIVE (69) GES,EA	0.51 OF	63	 XSQ= PHI= XP =	19 31 7 32 3.35 0.194 0.0674
428	TILT MORE TOWARD BEING THOSE WHERE A HIGH GOD, IF PRESENT AND ACTIVE, SUPPORTS HUMAN MORALITY, RATHER THAN NOT SUPPORTING IT (61) GES,EA	0.89 OF	19	428	TILT LESS TOWARD BEING THOSE WHERE A HIGH GOD, IF PRESENT AND ACTIVE, SUPPORTS HUMAN MORALITY, RATHER THAN NOT SUPPORTING IT (61) GES,EA	0.52 OF	31	 XSQ= PHI= XP =	17 16 2 15 5.93 0.344 0.0149

450	LEAN TOWARD BEING THOSE 0.67 OF 9 WHERE THE OBSERVATION OF FOOD TABOOS IS LOW, RATHER THAN HIGH OR MEDIUM (26) JRL	450	LEAN TOWARD BEING THOSE 0.81 OF 52 WHERE THE OBSERVATION OF FOOD TABOOS IS HIGH OR MEDIUM, RATHER THAN LOW (60) JRL	3 42 6 10 XSQ= 6.64 PHI= -0.330 XP = 0.0100
458	TILT TOWARD BEING THOSE 0.52 OF 29 WHERE GAMES, IF PRESENT, INCLUDE GAMES OF STRATEGY (52) R-A-B,EA	458	TILT TOWARD BEING THOSE 0.72 OF 83 WHERE GAMES, IF PRESENT, DO NOT INCLUDE GAMES OF STRATEGY (119) R-A-B,EA	15 23 14 60 XSQ= 4.51 PHI= 0.201 XP = 0.0337
460	TILT MORE TOWARD BEING THOSE 0.79 OF 29 WHERE GAMES, IF PRESENT, ARE NOT LIMITED TO GAMES OF SKILL ONLY (104) R-A-B,EA	460	TILT LESS TOWARD BEING THOSE 0.54 OF 83 WHERE GAMES, IF PRESENT, ARE NOT LIMITED TO GAMES OF SKILL ONLY (104) R-A-B,EA	6 38 23 45 XSQ= 4.67 PHI= -0.204 XP = 0.0307
468	TILT TOWARD BEING THOSE 0.67 OF 6 WHERE CONTACT WITH OTHER CULTURES IS FREQUENT, RATHER THAN REGULAR OR IRREGULAR (17) JMH	468	TILT TOWARD BEING THOSE 0.81 OF 31 WHERE CONTACT WITH OTHER CULTURES IS REGULAR OR IRREGULAR, RATHER THAN FREQUENT (37) JMH	4 6 2 25 XSQ= 3.56 PHI= 0.310 EP = 0.0347
472	DRIFT TOWARD BEING THOSE 0.77 OF 13 WHERE THE COMPOSITE NARCISSISM INDEX IS HIGH (47) PES	472	DRIFT TOWARD BEING THOSE 0.56 OF 57 WHERE THE COMPOSITE NARCISSISM INDEX IS LOW (43) PES	10 25 3 32 XSQ= 3.40 PHI= 0.220 XP = 0.0652

391 CULTURES
WHERE PREMARITAL SEX RELATIONS ARE
STRONGLY PUNISHED AND IN FACT RARE, OR
WEAKLY PUNISHED AND
IN FACT NOT RARE (89) JTW,EA

391 CULTURES
WHERE PREMARITAL SEX RELATIONS ARE
PUNISHED ONLY IF PREGNANCY RESULTS, OR
FREELY PERMITTED (90) JTW,EA

BACKGROUND ON PAGE 154

BOTH SUBJECT AND PREDICATE

89 IN LEFT COLUMN

ABIPON	ALBANIANS	ALORESE	AMERICANS	ASHANTI	ATSUGEWI	AZTEC	BARI	BASSERI	BAYA
BHIL	BRAZILIANS	BURUSHO	CAMBODIANS	CHAGGA	CHEYENNE	CHIR-APACHE	COORG	CUNA	EGYPTIANS
ENGA	FON	GANDA	GILBERTESE	GILYAK	GOAJIRO	HAZARA	HEBREWS	IBAN	INCA
INGALIK	IRISH	JAPANESE	JAVANESE	KAZAK	KHEVSUR	KIKUYU	KIOW-APACHE	KOREANS	KORYAK
KUTENAI	KWAKIUTL	LUO	MACASSARESE	MAM	MAMVU	MANGAIANS	MANUS	MINCHIA	MZAB
NAVAHO	NOMLAKI	NUPE	OKINAWANS	OMAHA	ONA	PURUM	RIFFIANS	RUNDI	RWALA
SANPOIL	SANTAL	SARSI	SEMANG	SERBS	SHILLUK	SHLUH	SIUAI	SOMALI	SONGHAI
TEDA	TEHUELCHE	TENINO	THAI	TIMBIRA	TOLOWA	TRISTAN	TUBATULABAL	TUCUNA	TWANA
ULAWANS	UTE	VEDDA	VIETNAMESE	WITOTO	WOLOF	YAHGAN	YORUBA	YUKI	

90 IN RIGHT COLUMN

ABOR	AINU	AKHA	AMBA	ANDAMANESE	ARAUCANIANS	AWEIKOMA	AYMARA	AZANDE	BATAK
BHUIYA	BORORO	CARIB	CHENCHU	CHIBCHA	CHOROTI	CHUKCHEE	DELAWARE	DOBUANS	ELLICE
FANG	FUTAJALONKE	GARO	GISU	GOND	HAIDA	HANO	HAWAIIANS	HUTSUL	IFUGAO
ILA	JIVARO	KACHIN	KAPAUKU	KASKA	KURTATCHI	LAKHER	LAMET	LAPPS	LAU
LEPCHA	LOLO	MAGUZAWA	MANIHIKI	MAORI	MARQUESANS	MARSHALLESE	MASAI	MATACO	MENTAWEI
MERINA	MONGO	MONGUOR	NAMA	NATCHEZ	NICOBARESE	OJIBWA	PALAUANS	PARAUJANO	PONAPEANS
PUKAPUKA	RARCIANS	SAGADA	SAMOANS	SINHALESE	SIRIONO	TALAMANCA	TALLENSI	TANALA	TAOS
TARAHUMARA	TAREUMIUT	TENDA	THONGA	TIKOPIA	TIV	TODA	TOKELAU	TROBRIAND	TRUKESE
TRUMAI	TUPINAMBA	VENDA	WOGEO	WOLEAIANS	YABARANA	YAGUA	YAKUT	YAO	YAPESE

23 EXCLUDED BECAUSE IRRELEVANT (SEE 'IRRELEVANT,' PARAGRAPH 390)

198 EXCLUDED BECAUSE UNASCERTAINED

---

4 LEAN LESS TOWARD BEING THOSE LOCATED OUTSIDE OF THE CIRCUM-MEDITERRANEAN (355)	0.81 OF 89	4 LEAN MORE TOWARD BEING THOSE LOCATED OUTSIDE OF THE CIRCUM-MEDITERRANEAN (355)	0.97 OF 90	17 3 72 87 XSQ= 9.68 PHI= 0.233 XP = 0.0019
6 LEAN MORE TOWARD BEING THOSE LOCATED OUTSIDE OF THE INSULAR PACIFIC (330)	0.89 OF 89	6 LEAN LESS TOWARD BEING THOSE LOCATED OUTSIDE OF THE INSULAR PACIFIC (330)	0.71 OF 90	10 26 79 64 XSQ= 7.62 PHI= -0.206 XP = 0.0058

8	DRIFT LESS TOWARD BEING THOSE LOCATED OUTSIDE OF NORTH AMERICA (330)	0.79 OF 89	8	DRIFT MORE TOWARD BEING THOSE LOCATED OUTSIDE OF NORTH AMERICA (330)	0.90 OF 90	19 9 70 81 XSQ= 3.55 PHI= 0.141 XP = 0.0596
15	TILT TOWARD BEING THOSE WHERE THE LATITUDE IS TWENTY DEGREES OR GREATER (183)	0.56 OF 89	15	TILT TOWARD BEING THOSE WHERE THE LATITUDE IS LESS THAN TWENTY DEGREES (217)	0.61 OF 90	50 35 39 55 XSQ= 4.69 PHI= 0.162 XP = 0.0303
42	TILT TOWARD BEING THOSE WHERE THE NATURAL ENVIRONMENT IS OTHER THAN TROPICAL OR SUB-TROPICAL RAIN FOREST, OR MONSOON FOREST (244) FWM	0.66 OF 89	42	TILT TOWARD BEING THOSE WHERE THE NATURAL ENVIRONMENT IS TROPICAL OR SUB-TROPICAL RAIN FOREST, OR MONSOON FOREST (156) FWM	0.50 OF 90	30 45 59 45 XSQ= 4.23 PHI= -0.154 XP = 0.0396
44	DRIFT LESS TOWARD BEING THOSE WHERE SETTLEMENTS ARE FIXED (222)	0.64 OF 86	44	DRIFT MORE TOWARD BEING THOSE WHERE SETTLEMENTS ARE FIXED (222)	0.78 OF 85	55 66 31 19 XSQ= 3.24 PHI= -0.138 XP = 0.0718
46	DRIFT LESS TOWARD BEING THOSE OTHER THAN WHERE SETTLEMENTS ARE NON-FIXED AND MOVEMENT IS NOMADIC (260)	0.73 OF 86	46	DRIFT MORE TOWARD BEING THOSE OTHER THAN WHERE SETTLEMENTS ARE NON-FIXED AND MOVEMENT IS NOMADIC (260)	0.86 OF 85	23 12 63 73 XSQ= 3.45 PHI= 0.142 XP = 0.0634
53	LEAN TOWARD BEING THOSE WHERE FOOD PRODUCTION IS BY INTENSIVE AGRICULTURE, RATHER THAN BY SIMPLE AGRICULTURE OR INCIPIENT FOOD PRODUCTION (91)	0.58 OF 55	53	LEAN TOWARD BEING THOSE WHERE FOOD PRODUCTION IS BY SIMPLE AGRICULTURE OR INCIPIENT FOOD PRODUCTION, RATHER THAN BY INTENSIVE AGRICULTURE (147)	0.73 OF 62	32 17 23 45 XSQ= 10.10 PHI= 0.294 XP = 0.0015
55	LEAN TOWARD BEING THOSE WHERE FOOD PRODUCTION IS BY INTENSIVE AGRICULTURE, RATHER THAN BY SIMPLE AGRICULTURE (91)	0.64 OF 50	55	LEAN TOWARD BEING THOSE WHERE FOOD PRODUCTION IS BY SIMPLE AGRICULTURE, RATHER THAN BY INTENSIVE AGRICULTURE (101)	0.67 OF 51	32 17 18 34 XSQ= 8.32 PHI= 0.287 XP = 0.0039
63	DRIFT MORE TOWARD BEING THOSE WHERE HUSBANDRY, IF PRESENT, IS PRINCIPALLY IN THE FORM OF BOVINE, EQUINE, CAMEL-LIKE, OR DEER-LIKE ANIMALS, RATHER THAN PIGS, SHEEP, OR GOATS (152)	0.73 OF 67	63	DRIFT LESS TOWARD BEING THOSE WHERE HUSBANDRY, IF PRESENT, IS PRINCIPALLY IN THE FORM OF BOVINE, EQUINE, CAMEL-LIKE, OR DEER-LIKE ANIMALS, RATHER THAN PIGS, SHEEP, OR GOATS (152)	0.55 OF 60	49 33 18 27 XSQ= 3.79 PHI= 0.173 XP = 0.0515
71	LEAN TOWARD BEING THOSE WHERE METAL WORKING IS PRESENT (98)	0.56 OF 73	71	LEAN TOWARD BEING THOSE WHERE METAL WORKING IS ABSENT (153)	0.67 OF 75	41 25 32 50 XSQ= 6.91 PHI= 0.216 XP = 0.0086

81	LEAN TOWARD BEING THOSE WHERE A CITY OR TOWN IS PRESENT, OR THE AVERAGE COMMUNITY SIZE IS 200 OR GREATER (89)	0.51 OF 67	81	LEAN TOWARD BEING THOSE WHERE NO CITY OR TOWN IS PRESENT, AND THE AVERAGE COMMUNITY SIZE IS SMALLER THAN 200 (135)	0.75 OF 64	34 16 33 48 XSQ= 8.14 PHI= 0.249 XP = 0.0043
84	TEND LESS TO BE THOSE WHERE THE LEVEL OF POLITICAL INTEGRATION IS THE LITTLE STATE, THE MINIMAL STATE, THE AUTONOMOUS COMMUNITY, OR THE FAMILY (262) GPM	0.70 OF 70	84	TEND MORE TO BE THOSE WHERE THE LEVEL OF POLITICAL INTEGRATION IS THE LITTLE STATE, THE MINIMAL STATE, THE AUTONOMOUS COMMUNITY, OR THE FAMILY (262) GPM	0.95 OF 74	21 4 49 70 XSQ= 13.50 PHI= 0.306 XP = 0.0002
85	TEND LESS TO BE THOSE WHERE THE LEVEL OF POLITICAL INTEGRATION IS THE MINIMAL STATE, THE AUTONOMOUS COMMUNITY, OR THE FAMILY (234) GPM	0.63 OF 70	85	TEND MORE TO BE THOSE WHERE THE LEVEL OF POLITICAL INTEGRATION IS THE MINIMAL STATE, THE AUTONOMOUS COMMUNITY, OR THE FAMILY (234) GPM	0.88 OF 74	26 9 44 65 XSQ= 10.88 PHI= 0.275 XP = 0.0010
88	LEAN TOWARD BEING THOSE WHERE, IF A HEADMANSHIP IS PRESENT, SUCCESSION IS NON-HEREDITARY (106)	0.50 OF 64	88	LEAN TOWARD BEING THOSE WHERE, IF A HEADMANSHIP IS PRESENT, SUCCESSION IS HEREDITARY (165)	0.76 OF 66	32 16 32 50 XSQ= 8.18 PHI= 0.251 XP = 0.0042
90	LEAN MORE TOWARD BEING THOSE WHERE, IF A HEREDITARY HEADMANSHIP IS PRESENT, SUCCESSION IS PATRILINEAL, RATHER THAN MATRILINEAL (127)	0.97 OF 32	90	LEAN LESS TOWARD BEING THOSE WHERE, IF A HEREDITARY HEADMANSHIP IS PRESENT, SUCCESSION IS PATRILINEAL, RATHER THAN MATRILINEAL (127)	0.66 OF 50	31 33 1 17 XSQ= 9.13 PHI= 0.334 XP = 0.0025
91	TILT TOWARD BEING THOSE WHERE SOCIETAL COMPLEXITY IS HIGH (18) F-W	0.80 OF 10	91	TILT TOWARD BEING THOSE WHERE SOCIETAL COMPLEXITY IS LOW (22) F-W	0.72 OF 18	8 5 2 13 XSQ= 5.11 PHI= 0.427 EP = 0.0163
94	TEND LESS TO BE THOSE WHERE THE HIERARCHY OF NATIONAL JURISDICTION HAS TWO, ONE, OR NO LEVELS (296) GES,EA	0.80 OF 86	94	TEND MORE TO BE THOSE WHERE THE HIERARCHY OF NATIONAL JURISDICTION HAS TWO, ONE, OR NO LEVELS (296) GES,EA	0.98 OF 83	17 2 69 81 XSQ= 11.07 PHI= 0.256 XP = 0.0009
95	TILT LESS TOWARD BEING THOSE WHERE THE HIERARCHY OF NATIONAL JURISDICTION HAS ONE OR NO LEVELS. (254) GES,EA	0.66 OF 86	95	TILT MORE TOWARD BEING THOSE WHERE THE HIERARCHY OF NATIONAL JURISDICTION HAS ONE OR NO LEVELS (254) GES,EA	0.82 OF 83	29 15 57 68 XSQ= 4.59 PHI= 0.165 XP = 0.0322
107	TEND LESS TO BE THOSE WHERE CLASS STRATIFICATION, IF PRESENT, IS BASED ON SOMETHING OTHER THAN OCCUPATIONAL STATUS (160)	0.61 OF 59	107	IN ALL CASES ARE THOSE WHERE CLASS STRATIFICATION, IF PRESENT, IS BASED ON SOMETHING OTHER THAN OCCUPATIONAL STATUS (160)	1.00 OF 50	23 0 36 50 XSQ= 22.42 PHI= 0.454 XP = 0.0000

108	LEAN TOWARD BEING THOSE 0.81 OF 59 WHERE CLASS STRATIFICATION, IF PRESENT, IS BASED ON SOMETHING OTHER THAN A HEREDITARY ARISTOCRACY (129)	108	LEAN TOWARD BEING THOSE 0.50 OF 50 WHERE CLASS STRATIFICATION, IF PRESENT, IS BASED ON A HEREDITARY ARISTOCRACY (74)	11 25 48 25 XSQ= 10.65 PHI= -0.313 XP = 0.0011
110	TILT LESS TOWARD BEING THOSE 0.51 OF 87 WHERE SLAVERY IS ABSENT (218)	110	TILT MORE TOWARD BEING THOSE 0.66 OF 89 WHERE SLAVERY IS ABSENT (218)	43 30 44 59 XSQ= 3.85 PHI= 0.148 XP = 0.0496
131	TILT LESS TOWARD BEING THOSE 0.79 OF 47 WHERE THE CONSTRUCTION OF PERMANENT HOUSES OR THE ERECTION OF TEMPORARY DWELLINGS IS MAINLY DONE BY MALES (136)	131	TILT MORE TOWARD BEING THOSE 0.94 OF 54 WHERE THE CONSTRUCTION OF PERMANENT HOUSES OR THE ERECTION OF TEMPORARY DWELLINGS IS MAINLY DONE BY MALES (136)	37 51 10 3 XSQ= 4.22 PHI= -0.205 XP = 0.0398
138	DRIFT TOWARD BEING THOSE 0.89 OF 9 WHERE SUPERORDINATE JUSTICE IS PRESENT (22) BBW	138	DRIFT TOWARD BEING THOSE 0.50 OF 18 WHERE SUPERORDINATE JUSTICE IS ABSENT (18) BBW	8 9 1 9 XSQ= 2.40 PHI= 0.298 EP = 0.0912
152	DRIFT TOWARD BEING THOSE 0.86 OF 7 WHERE THE DIFFERENTIATION OF THE JURIDICAL AGENCY FROM THE MEDICAL AGENCY IS HIGH (10) MJ	152	DRIFT TOWARD BEING THOSE 0.80 OF 5 WHERE THE DIFFERENTIATION OF THE JURIDICAL AGENCY FROM THE MEDICAL AGENCY IS LOW (10) MJ	6 1 1 4 XSQ= 2.83 PHI= 0.486 EP = 0.0720
179	DRIFT LESS TOWARD BEING THOSE 0.82 OF 88 WHERE THE COMMUNITY IS OTHER THAN STRUCTURED ON A NON-CLAN BASIS AND COMMONLY EXOGAMOUS (340)	179	DRIFT MORE TOWARD BEING THOSE 0.92 OF 87 WHERE THE COMMUNITY IS OTHER THAN STRUCTURED ON A NON-CLAN BASIS AND COMMONLY EXOGAMOUS (340)	16 7 72 80 XSQ= 3.10 PHI= 0.133 XP = 0.0783
187	DRIFT MORE TOWARD BEING THOSE 0.94 OF 89 WHERE THE KIN GROUP IS OTHER THAN EXCLUSIVELY MATRILINEAL (344)	187	DRIFT LESS TOWARD BEING THOSE 0.84 OF 89 WHERE THE KIN GROUP IS OTHER THAN EXCLUSIVELY MATRILINEAL (344)	5 14 84 75 XSQ= 3.77 PHI= -0.146 XP = 0.0522
190	LEAN MORE TOWARD BEING THOSE 0.91 OF 53 WHERE THE KIN GROUP IS PATRILINEAL OR DOUBLE-DESCENT, RATHER THAN MATRILINEAL (186)	190	LEAN LESS TOWARD BEING THOSE 0.67 OF 54 WHERE THE KIN GROUP IS PATRILINEAL OR DOUBLE-DESCENT, RATHER THAN MATRILINEAL (186)	48 36 5 18 XSQ= 7.69 PHI= 0.268 XP = 0.0055
192	DRIFT LESS TOWARD BEING THOSE 0.66 OF 89 OTHER THAN WHERE THE ONLY KIN GROUP PRESENT IS A KINDRED OR ELSE BILATERAL DESCENT IS INFERRED (289)	192	DRIFT MORE TOWARD BEING THOSE 0.79 OF 90 OTHER THAN WHERE THE ONLY KIN GROUP PRESENT IS A KINDRED OR ELSE BILATERAL DESCENT IS INFERRED (289)	30 19 59 71 XSQ= 2.97 PHI= 0.129 XP = 0.0850

198	TILT MORE TOWARD BEING THOSE 0.95 OF 41 WHERE RULES FOR THE INHERITANCE OF REAL PROPERTY, IF PRESENT, FAVOR THE MALE HEIR OR LINE, RATHER THAN THE FEMALE (144)	198	TILT LESS TOWARD BEING THOSE 0.75 OF 40 WHERE RULES FOR THE INHERITANCE OF REAL PROPERTY, IF PRESENT, FAVOR THE MALE HEIR OR LINE, RATHER THAN THE FEMALE (144)	39 30 2 10 XSQ= 5.00 PHI= 0.248 XP = 0.0254
204	DRIFT MORE TOWARD BEING THOSE 0.87 OF 79 WHERE MARITAL RESIDENCE IS PATRILOCAL, VIRILOCAL, OR AVUNCULOCAL, RATHER THAN AMBILOCAL OR NEOLOCAL (270)	204	DRIFT LESS TOWARD BEING THOSE 0.74 OF 74 WHERE MARITAL RESIDENCE IS PATRILOCAL, VIRILOCAL, OR AVUNCULOCAL, RATHER THAN AMBILOCAL OR NEOLOCAL (270)	69 55 10 19 XSQ= 3.41 PHI= 0.149 XP = 0.0648
210	TILT MORE TOWARD BEING THOSE 0.94 OF 47 WHERE MARITAL RESIDENCE IS PATRILOCAL, RATHER THAN MATRILOCAL (169)	210	TILT LESS TOWARD BEING THOSE 0.77 OF 43 WHERE MARITAL RESIDENCE IS PATRILOCAL, RATHER THAN MATRILOCAL (169)	44 33 3 10 XSQ= 3.90 PHI= 0.208 XP = 0.0483
213	DRIFT TOWARD BEING THOSE 0.63 OF 84 WHERE FIRST COUSIN MARRIAGE IS NOT PERMITTED (198)	213	DRIFT TOWARD BEING THOSE 0.51 OF 86 WHERE FIRST COUSIN MARRIAGE IS PERMITTED (172)	31 44 53 42 XSQ= 2.95 PHI= -0.132 XP = 0.0859
220	TILT MORE TOWARD BEING THOSE 0.85 OF 84 WHERE FIRST COUSIN MARRIAGE IN SOME FORM OR OTHER IS NOT PRESCRIBED OR PREFERRED (273)	220	TILT LESS TOWARD BEING THOSE 0.67 OF 86 WHERE FIRST COUSIN MARRIAGE IN SOME FORM OR OTHER IS NOT PRESCRIBED OR PREFERRED (273)	13 28 71 58 XSQ= 5.87 PHI= -0.186 XP = 0.0154
221	DRIFT MORE TOWARD BEING THOSE 0.95 OF 84 WHERE MATRILATERAL CROSS-COUSIN MARRIAGE IS NOT PRESCRIBED OR PREFERRED (335)	221	DRIFT LESS TOWARD BEING THOSE 0.86 OF 86 WHERE MATRILATERAL CROSS-COUSIN MARRIAGE IS NOT PRESCRIBED OR PREFERRED (335)	4 12 80 74 XSQ= 3.20 PHI= -0.137 XP = 0.0736
234	LEAN TOWARD BEING THOSE 0.72 OF 68 WHERE THE COUSIN TERMINOLOGY IS OF ESKIMO OR HAWAIIAN TYPE, RATHER THAN CROW, OMAHA, OR IROQUOIS TYPE (170)	234	LEAN TOWARD BEING THOSE 0.55 OF 78 WHERE THE COUSIN TERMINOLOGY IS OF CROW, OMAHA, OR IROQUOIS TYPE, RATHER THAN ESKIMO OR HAWAIIAN TYPE (152)	19 43 49 35 XSQ= 9.91 PHI= -0.260 XP = 0.0016
240	LEAN TOWARD BEING THOSE 0.83 OF 46 WHERE THE FAMILY, IF EXTENDED, IS SMALL OR STEM, RATHER THAN LARGE (135)	240	LEAN TOWARD BEING THOSE 0.50 OF 48 WHERE THE FAMILY, IF EXTENDED, IS LARGE, RATHER THAN SMALL OR STEM (78)	8 24 38 24 XSQ= 9.72 PHI= -0.322 XP = 0.0018
262	DRIFT MORE TOWARD BEING THOSE 0.84 OF 89 WHERE WIVES ARE OBTAINED BY MEANS INVOLVING THE PRESENCE OF SOME CONSIDERATION (305)	262	DRIFT LESS TOWARD BEING THOSE 0.72 OF 90 WHERE WIVES ARE OBTAINED BY MEANS INVOLVING THE PRESENCE OF SOME CONSIDERATION (305)	75 65 14 25 XSQ= 3.14 PHI= 0.132 XP = 0.0765

279	DRIFT TOWARD BEING THOSE WHERE WIFE-LENDING AND WIFE EXCHANGE ARE UNIMPORTANT OR ABSENT (19) LWS	0.85 OF 13	279	DRIFT TOWARD BEING THOSE WHERE WIFE-LENDING OR WIFE-EXCHANGE IS PRESENT (10) LWS	0.56 OF 9	2 5 11 4 XSQ= 2.32 PHI= -0.325 EP = 0.0743
301	DRIFT MORE TOWARD BEING THOSE WHERE THE POST-PARTUM SEX TABOO LASTS LONGER THAN ONE MONTH (96)	0.86 OF 43	301	DRIFT LESS TOWARD BEING THOSE WHERE THE POST-PARTUM SEX TABOO LASTS LONGER THAN ONE MONTH (96)	0.67 OF 42	37 28 6 14 XSQ= 3.42 PHI= 0.201 XP = 0.0643
305	LEAN TOWARD BEING THOSE WHERE THE EARLY SEXUAL SATISFACTION POTENTIAL IS LOW (24) W-C	0.79 OF 14	305	LEAN TOWARD BEING THOSE WHERE THE EARLY SEXUAL SATISFACTION POTENTIAL IS HIGH (27) W-C	0.69 OF 26	3 18 11 8 XSQ= 6.53 PHI= -0.404 EP = 0.0072
308	IN ALL CASES ARE THOSE WHERE AVERAGE SOCIALIZATION ANXIETY IS HIGH (22) W-C	1.00 OF 12	308	TEND TO BE THOSE WHERE AVERAGE SOCIALIZATION ANXIETY IS LOW (18) W-C	0.67 OF 21	12 7 0 14 XSQ= 11.30 PHI= 0.585 EP = 0.0002
310	TILT TOWARD BEING THOSE WHERE ANAL SOCIALIZATION ANXIETY IS HIGH (22) W-C	0.83 OF 12	310	TILT TOWARD BEING THOSE WHERE ANAL SOCIALIZATION ANXIETY IS LOW (19) W-C	0.62 OF 21	10 8 2 13 XSQ= 4.61 PHI= 0.374 EP = 0.0272
311	TEND TO BE THOSE WHERE SEXUAL SOCIALIZATION ANXIETY IS HIGH (28) W-C	0.93 OF 15	311	TEND TO BE THOSE WHERE SEXUAL SOCIALIZATION ANXIETY IS LOW (23) W-C	0.65 OF 26	14 9 1 17 XSQ= 11.04 PHI= 0.519 XP = 0.0009
328	TILT TOWARD BEING THOSE WHERE THE AGE OF THE INFANT AT THE ONSET OF SERIOUS SOCIALIZATION, OTHER THAN WEANING, IS TWO YEARS OR LOWER (20) B-B-C	0.80 OF 10	328	TILT TOWARD BEING THOSE WHERE THE AGE OF THE INFANT AT THE ONSET OF SERIOUS SOCIALIZATION, OTHER THAN WEANING, IS HIGHER THAN TWO YEARS (21) B-B-C	0.65 OF 17	2 11 8 6 XSQ= 3.41 PHI= -0.355 EP = 0.0461
346	TILT TOWARD BEING THOSE WHERE THE CHILD'S INFERRED ANXIETY OVER PERFORMANCE OF SELF-RELIANT BEHAVIOR IS LOW (39) B-B-C	0.74 OF 19	346	TILT TOWARD BEING THOSE WHERE THE CHILD'S INFERRED ANXIETY OVER PERFORMANCE OF SELF-RELIANT BEHAVIOR IS HIGH (37) B-B-C	0.61 OF 33	5 20 14 13 XSQ= 4.39 PHI= -0.291 XP = 0.0362
348	DRIFT TOWARD BEING THOSE WHERE THE TOTAL POSITIVE PRESSURE TOWARD DEVELOPING ACHIEVEMENT BEHAVIOR IN THE CHILD IS HIGH (32) B-B-C	0.76 OF 17	348	DRIFT TOWARD BEING THOSE WHERE THE TOTAL POSITIVE PRESSURE TOWARD DEVELOPING ACHIEVEMENT BEHAVIOR IN THE CHILD IS LOW (31) B-B-C	0.56 OF 25	13 11 4 14 XSQ= 3.13 PHI= 0.273 XP = 0.0768

352	TILT MORE TOWARD BEING THOSE 0.88 OF 16 WHERE THE TOTAL POSITIVE PRESSURE TOWARD DEVELOPING OBEDIENT BEHAVIOR IN THE CHILD IS HIGH (44) B-B-C	352	TILT LESS TOWARD BEING THOSE 0.53 OF 34 WHERE THE TOTAL POSITIVE PRESSURE TOWARD DEVELOPING OBEDIENT BEHAVIOR IN THE CHILD IS HIGH (44) B-B-C	14 18 2 16 XSQ= 4.24 PHI= 0.291 XP = 0.0395
370	TILT MORE TOWARD BEING THOSE 0.76 OF 67 WHERE THE SEGREGATION OF ADOLESCENT BOYS IS ABSENT (148)	370	TILT LESS TOWARD BEING THOSE 0.56 OF 68 WHERE THE SEGREGATION OF ADOLESCENT BOYS IS ABSENT (148)	16 30 51 38 XSQ= 5.28 PHI= -0.198 XP = 0.0215
386	LEAN TOWARD BEING THOSE 0.76 OF 17 WHERE SEXUAL EXPRESSION BY THE YOUNG IS RESTRICTED OR SEMI-RESTRICTED (46) F-B	386	LEAN TOWARD BEING THOSE 0.67 OF 42 WHERE SEXUAL EXPRESSION BY THE YOUNG IS PERMITTED (40) F-B	13 14 4 28 XSQ= 7.42 PHI= 0.355 XP = 0.0065
393	TILT TOWARD BEING THOSE 0.78 OF 23 WHERE EXTRAMARITAL COITUS IS PUNISHED, RATHER THAN PERMITTED (43) F-B	393	TILT TOWARD BEING THOSE 0.57 OF 35 WHERE EXTRAMARITAL COITUS IS PERMITTED, RATHER THAN PUNISHED (41) F-B	18 15 5 20 XSQ= 5.72 PHI= 0.314 XP = 0.0167
397	LEAN TOWARD BEING THOSE 0.53 OF 15 WHERE SEX DISABILITY IS PRESENT (14) JKH	397	LEAN TOWARD BEING THOSE 0.92 OF 24 WHERE SEX DISABILITY IS ABSENT (42) JKH	8 2 7 22 XSQ= 7.59 PHI= 0.441 EP = 0.0030
398	IN ALL CASES ARE THOSE 1.00 OF 10 WHERE THE INTENSITY OF SEX ANXIETY IS HIGH (16) WNS	398	TEND TO BE THOSE 0.87 OF 15 WHERE THE INTENSITY OF SEX ANXIETY IS LOW (16) WNS	10 2 0 13 XSQ= 14.75 PHI= 0.768 EP = 0.0000
399	TILT TOWARD BEING THOSE 0.83 OF 12 WHERE INTENSITY OF CASTRATION ANXIETY IS HIGH (23) WNS	399	TILT TOWARD BEING THOSE 0.60 OF 25 WHERE INTENSITY OF CASTRATION ANXIETY IS LOW (22) WNS	10 10 2 15 XSQ= 4.51 PHI= 0.349 EP = 0.0173
404	DRIFT TOWARD BEING THOSE 0.50 OF 16 WHERE EXPLANATIONS OF ILLNESS OF A SEXUAL NATURE ARE PRESENT (19) W-C	404	DRIFT TOWARD BEING THOSE 0.79 OF 29 WHERE EXPLANATIONS OF ILLNESS OF A SEXUAL NATURE ARE ABSENT (42) W-C	8 6 8 23 XSQ= 2.88 PHI= 0.253 XP = 0.0898
426	TILT MORE TOWARD BEING THOSE 0.68 OF 78 WHERE A HIGH GOD IS PRESENT (156) GES,EA	426	TILT LESS TOWARD BEING THOSE 0.51 OF 71 WHERE A HIGH GOD IS PRESENT (156) GES,EA	53 36 25 35 XSQ= 3.91 PHI= 0.162 XP = 0.0481

428	LEAN TOWARD BEING THOSE 0.79 OF 34 WHERE A HIGH GOD, IF PRESENT AND ACTIVE, SUPPORTS HUMAN MORALITY, RATHER THAN NOT SUPPORTING IT (61) GES,EA	428	LEAN TOWARD BEING THOSE 0.63 OF 16 WHERE A HIGH GOD, IF PRESENT AND ACTIVE, DOES NOT SUPPORT HUMAN MORALITY, RATHER THAN SUPPORTING IT (26) GES,EA	27 6 7 10 XSQ= 6.75 PHI= 0.367 XP = 0.0094
447	IN ALL CASES ARE THOSE 1.00 OF 7 WHERE LOVE MAGIC IS PRESENT (20) S-R	447	TILT TOWARD BEING THOSE 0.53 OF 19 WHERE LOVE MAGIC IS ABSENT (13) S-R	7 9 0 10 XSQ= 3.97 PHI= 0.391 EP = 0.0227
450	TEND TO BE THOSE 0.50 OF 26 WHERE THE OBSERVATION OF FOOD TABOOS IS LOW, RATHER THAN HIGH OR MEDIUM (26) JRL	450	TEND TO BE THOSE 0.91 OF 35 WHERE THE OBSERVATION OF FOOD TABOOS IS HIGH OR MEDIUM, RATHER THAN LOW (60) JRL	13 32 13 3 XSQ= 11.18 PHI= -0.428 XP = 0.0008
451	DRIFT TOWARD BEING THOSE 0.70 OF 10 WHERE TOTEMISM IS UNIMPORTANT OR ABSENT (12) LWS	451	DRIFT TOWARD BEING THOSE 0.73 OF 11 WHERE TOTEMISM IS PRESENT (15) LWS	3 8 7 3 XSQ= 2.31 PHI= -0.332 EP = 0.0861
458	DRIFT LESS TOWARD BEING THOSE 0.58 OF 57 WHERE GAMES, IF PRESENT, DO NOT INCLUDE GAMES OF STRATEGY (119) R-A-B,EA	458	DRIFT MORE TOWARD BEING THOSE 0.75 OF 55 WHERE GAMES, IF PRESENT, DO NOT INCLUDE GAMES OF STRATEGY (119) R-A-B,EA	24 14 33 41 XSQ= 2.76 PHI= 0.157 XP = 0.0967
459	DRIFT TOWARD BEING THOSE 0.56 OF 57 WHERE GAMES, IF PRESENT, INCLUDE GAMES OF CHANCE (82) R-A-B,EA	459	DRIFT TOWARD BEING THOSE 0.62 OF 55 WHERE GAMES, IF PRESENT, DO NOT INCLUDE GAMES OF CHANCE (89) R-A-B,EA	32 21 25 34 XSQ= 2.94 PHI= 0.162 XP = 0.0866
460	DRIFT MORE TOWARD BEING THOSE 0.70 OF 57 WHERE GAMES, IF PRESENT, ARE NOT LIMITED TO GAMES OF SKILL ONLY (104) R-A-B,EA	460	DRIFT LESS TOWARD BEING THOSE 0.51 OF 55 WHERE GAMES, IF PRESENT, ARE NOT LIMITED TO GAMES OF SKILL ONLY (104) R-A-B,EA	17 27 40 28 XSQ= 3.59 PHI= -0.179 XP = 0.0583
478	DRIFT TOWARD BEING THOSE 0.78 OF 9 WHERE THE ABANDONMENT OR KILLING OF OLD PEOPLE IS UNIMPORTANT OR ABSENT (12) LWS	478	DRIFT TOWARD BEING THOSE 0.78 OF 9 WHERE THE ABANDONMENT OR KILLING OF OLD PEOPLE IS PRESENT (12) LWS	2 7 7 2 XSQ= 3.56 PHI= -0.444 EP = 0.0567

****

392 CULTURES WHERE PREMARITAL SEX RELATIONS ARE STRONGLY PUNISHED AND IN FACT RARE, OR WEAKLY PUNISHED AND IN FACT NOT RARE, OR PUNISHED ONLY IF PREGNANCY RESULTS (112) JTW,EA	392 CULTURES WHERE PREMARITAL SEX RELATIONS ARE FREELY PERMITTED (67) JTW,EA

BACKGROUND ON PAGE 154 BOTH SUBJECT AND PREDICATE

....

112 IN LEFT COLUMN

ABIPON	ALBANIANS	ALORESE	AMERICANS	ARAUCANIANS	ASHANTI	ATSUGEWI	AYMARA	AZANDE	AZTEC
BARI	BASSERI	BAYA	BHIL	BRAZILIANS	BURUSHO	CAMBODIANS	CHAGGA	CHEYENNE	CHIR-APACHE
COORG	CUNA	EGYPTIANS	ENGA	FON	GANDA	GARO	GILBERTESE	GILYAK	GISU
GOAJIRO	HAIDA	HANO	HAZARA	HEBREWS	IBAN	INCA	INGALIK	IRISH	JAPANESE
JAVANESE	KACHIN	KAPAUKU	KAZAK	KHEVSUR	KIKUYU	KIOW-APACHE	KOREANS	KORYAK	KURTATCHI
KUTENAI	KWAKIUTL	LAKHER	LAPPS	LAU	LUO	MACASSARESE	MAM	MAMVU	MANGAIANS
MANUS	MINCHIA	MONGUOR	MZAB	NAMA	NAVAHO	NOMLAKI	NUPE	OKINAWANS	OMAHA
ONA	PURUM	RIFFIANS	RUNDI	RWALA	SANPOIL	SANTAL	SARSI	SEMANG	SERBS
SHILLUK	SHLUH	SIUAI	SOMALI	SONGHAI	TALAMANCA	TALLENSI	TAOS	TEDA	TEHUELCHE
TENINO	THAI	TIKOPIA	TIMBIRA	TIV	TOLOWA	TRISTAN	TUBATULABAL	TUCUNA	TWANA
ULAWANS	UTE	VEDDA	VENDA	VIETNAMESE	WITOTO	WOGEO	WOLOF	YAHGAN	YAO
YORUBA	YUKI								

67 IN RIGHT COLUMN

ABOR	AINU	AKHA	AMBA	ANDAMANESE	AWEIKOMA	BATAK	BHUIYA	BORORO	CARIB
CHENCHU	CHIBCHA	CHOROTI	CHUKCHEE	DELAWARE	DOBUANS	ELLICE	FANG	FUTAJALONKE	GOND
HAWAIIANS	HUTSUL	IFUGAO	ILA	JIVARO	KASKA	LAMET	LEPCHA	LOLO	MAGUZAWA
MANIHIKI	MAORI	MARQUESANS	MARSHALLESE	MASAI	MATACO	MENTAWEI	MERINA	MONGO	NATCHEZ
NICOBARESE	OJIBWA	PALAUANS	PARAUJANO	PONAPEANS	PUKAPUKA	RAROIANS	SAGADA	SAMOANS	SINHALESE
SIRIONO	TANALA	TARAHUMARA	TAREUMIUT	TENDA	THONGA	TODA	TOKELAU	TROBRIAND	TRUKESE
TRUMAI	TUPINAMBA	WOLEAIANS	YABARANA	YAGUA	YAKUT	YAPESE			

23 EXCLUDED BECAUSE IRRELEVANT (SEE 'IRRELEVANT,' PARAGRAPH 390)

198 EXCLUDED BECAUSE UNASCERTAINED

4	TILT LESS TOWARD BEING THOSE 0.84 OF 112 LOCATED OUTSIDE OF THE CIRCUM-MEDITERRANEAN (355)	4	TILT MORE TOWARD BEING THOSE 0.97 OF 67 LOCATED OUTSIDE OF THE CIRCUM-MEDITERRANEAN (355)	18 2 94 65 XSQ= 5.98 PHI= 0.183 XP = 0.0145
6	LEAN MORE TOWARD BEING THOSE 0.87 OF 112 LOCATED OUTSIDE OF THE INSULAR PACIFIC (330)	6	LEAN LESS TOWARD BEING THOSE 0.69 OF 67 LOCATED OUTSIDE OF THE INSULAR PACIFIC (330)	15 21 97 46 XSQ= 7.33 PHI= -0.202 XP = 0.0068

8 DRIFT LESS TOWARD BEING THOSE 0.80 OF 112 LOCATED OUTSIDE OF NORTH AMERICA (330)	8 DRIFT MORE TOWARD BEING THOSE 0.91 OF 67 LOCATED OUTSIDE OF NORTH AMERICA (330)	22 6 90 61 XSQ= 2.86 PHI= 0.126 XP = 0.0906
15 TILT TOWARD BEING THOSE 0.54 OF 112 WHERE THE LATITUDE IS TWENTY DEGREES OR GREATER (183)	15 TILT TOWARD BEING THOSE 0.64 OF 67 WHERE THE LATITUDE IS LESS THAN TWENTY DEGREES (217)	61 24 51 43 XSQ= 5.12 PHI= 0.169 XP = 0.0237
33 DRIFT LESS TOWARD BEING THOSE 0.81 OF 112 WHERE THE NATURAL ENVIRONMENT IS OTHER THAN 'VERY HARSH,' I.E., DESERT, DESERT GRASSES AND SHRUBS, TUNDRA, OR HIGH PLATEAU STEPPE (341) FWM	33 DRIFT MORE TOWARD BEING THOSE 0.93 OF 67 WHERE THE NATURAL ENVIRONMENT IS OTHER THAN 'VERY HARSH,' I.E., DESERT, DESERT GRASSES AND SHRUBS, TUNDRA, OR HIGH PLATEAU STEPPE (341) FWM	21 5 91 62 XSQ= 3.44 PHI= 0.139 XP = 0.0636
42 LEAN TOWARD BEING THOSE 0.66 OF 112 WHERE THE NATURAL ENVIRONMENT IS OTHER THAN TROPICAL OR SUB-TROPICAL RAIN FOREST, OR MONSOON FOREST (244) FWM	42 LEAN TOWARD BEING THOSE 0.55 OF 67 WHERE THE NATURAL ENVIRONMENT IS TROPICAL OR SUB-TROPICAL RAIN FOREST, OR MONSOON FOREST (156) FWM	38 37 74 30 XSQ= 6.96 PHI= -0.197 XP = 0.0083
48 DRIFT TOWARD BEING THOSE 0.59 OF 32 WHERE THE FOOD SUPPLY IS NOT SECURE, AND FOOD SHORTAGES ARE FREQUENT OR ANNUAL (41) MGW	48 DRIFT TOWARD BEING THOSE 0.68 OF 22 WHERE THE FOOD SUPPLY IS SECURE, AND FOOD SHORTAGES ARE RARE OR OCCASIONAL (38) MGW	13 15 19 7 XSQ= 2.94 PHI= -0.233 XP = 0.0865
53 LEAN TOWARD BEING THOSE 0.52 OF 75 WHERE FOOD PRODUCTION IS BY INTENSIVE AGRICULTURE, RATHER THAN BY SIMPLE AGRICULTURE OR INCIPIENT FOOD PRODUCTION (91)	53 LEAN TOWARD BEING THOSE 0.76 OF 42 WHERE FOOD PRODUCTION IS BY SIMPLE AGRICULTURE OR INCIPIENT FOOD PRODUCTION, RATHER THAN BY INTENSIVE AGRICULTURE (147)	39 10 36 32 XSQ= 7.67 PHI= 0.256 XP = 0.0056
55 TILT TOWARD BEING THOSE 0.57 OF 69 WHERE FOOD PRODUCTION IS BY INTENSIVE AGRICULTURE, RATHER THAN BY SIMPLE AGRICULTURE (91)	55 TILT TOWARD BEING THOSE 0.69 OF 32 WHERE FOOD PRODUCTION IS BY SIMPLE AGRICULTURE, RATHER THAN BY INTENSIVE AGRICULTURE (101)	39 10 30 22 XSQ= 4.62 PHI= 0.214 XP = 0.0315
62 TILT MORE TOWARD BEING THOSE 0.77 OF 112 WHERE HUSBANDRY OF SOME KIND IS PRESENT (228)	62 TILT LESS TOWARD BEING THOSE 0.61 OF 67 WHERE HUSBANDRY OF SOME KIND IS PRESENT (228)	86 41 26 26 XSQ= 4.22 PHI= 0.153 XP = 0.0400
63 TILT MORE TOWARD BEING THOSE 0.71 OF 86 WHERE HUSBANDRY, IF PRESENT, IS PRINCIPALLY IN THE FORM OF BOVINE, EQUINE, CAMEL-LIKE, OR DEER-LIKE ANIMALS, RATHER THAN PIGS, SHEEP, OR GOATS (152)	63 TILT LESS TOWARD BEING THOSE 0.51 OF 41 WHERE HUSBANDRY, IF PRESENT, IS PRINCIPALLY IN THE FORM OF BOVINE, EQUINE, CAMEL-LIKE, OR DEER-LIKE ANIMALS, RATHER THAN PIGS, SHEEP, OR GOATS (152)	61 21 25 20 XSQ= 3.89 PHI= 0.175 XP = 0.0485

71	TEND TO BE THOSE WHERE METAL WORKING IS PRESENT (98)	0.55 OF 94	71	TEND TO BE THOSE WHERE METAL WORKING IS ABSENT (153)	0.74 OF 54	52 14 42 40	XSQ= 10.83 PHI= 0.271 XP = 0.0010
74	DRIFT MORE TOWARD BEING THOSE WHERE POTTERY IS PRESENT (145)	0.68 OF 91	74	DRIFT LESS TOWARD BEING THOSE WHERE POTTERY IS PRESENT (145)	0.52 OF 54	62 28 29 26	XSQ= 3.15 PHI= 0.148 XP = 0.0757
79	TILT LESS TOWARD BEING THOSE WHERE NO CITY IS PRESENT (201)	0.84 OF 85	79	TILT MORE TOWARD BEING THOSE WHERE NO CITY IS PRESENT (201)	0.98 OF 46	14 1 71 45	XSQ= 4.69 PHI= 0.189 XP = 0.0303
80	TILT LESS TOWARD BEING THOSE WHERE NO CITY OR TOWN IS PRESENT (185)	0.75 OF 85	80	TILT MORE TOWARD BEING THOSE WHERE NO CITY OR TOWN IS PRESENT (185)	0.91 OF 46	21 4 64 42	XSQ= 3.97 PHI= 0.174 XP = 0.0463
81	LEAN LESS TOWARD BEING THOSE WHERE NO CITY OR TOWN IS PRESENT, AND THE AVERAGE COMMUNITY SIZE IS SMALLER THAN 200 (135)	0.52 OF 85	81	LEAN MORE TOWARD BEING THOSE WHERE NO CITY OR TOWN IS PRESENT, AND THE AVERAGE COMMUNITY SIZE IS SMALLER THAN 200 (135)	0.80 OF 46	41 9 44 37	XSQ= 9.22 PHI= 0.265 XP = 0.0024
82	LEAN MORE TOWARD BEING THOSE WHERE A CITY OR TOWN IS PRESENT, OR THE AVERAGE COMMUNITY SIZE IS FIFTY OR GREATER (178)	0.92 OF 85	82	LEAN LESS TOWARD BEING THOSE WHERE A CITY OR TOWN IS PRESENT, OR THE AVERAGE COMMUNITY SIZE IS FIFTY OR GREATER (178)	0.70 OF 46	78 32 7 14	XSQ= 9.34 PHI= 0.267 XP = 0.0022
83	TILT LESS TOWARD BEING THOSE WHERE, WITH NO CITY AND NO TOWN PRESENT, THE AVERAGE COMMUNITY SIZE IS SMALLER THAN 200, RATHER THAN BETWEEN 200 AND 999 (135)	0.70 OF 63	83	TILT MORE TOWARD BEING THOSE WHERE, WITH NO CITY AND NO TOWN PRESENT, THE AVERAGE COMMUNITY SIZE IS SMALLER THAN 200, RATHER THAN BETWEEN 200 AND 999 (135)	0.90 OF 41	19 4 44 37	XSQ= 4.88 PHI= 0.217 XP = 0.0272
86	DRIFT TOWARD BEING THOSE WHERE THE LEVEL OF POLITICAL INTEGRATION IS THE LARGE STATE, THE LITTLE STATE, OR THE MINIMAL STATE (148) GPM	0.56 OF 88	86	DRIFT TOWARD BEING THOSE WHERE THE LEVEL OF POLITICAL INTEGRATION IS THE AUTONOMOUS COMMUNITY, OR THE FAMILY (156) GPM	0.61 OF 56	49 22 39 34	XSQ= 3.05 PHI= 0.146 XP = 0.0805
90	LEAN MORE TOWARD BEING THOSE WHERE, IF A HEREDITARY HEADMANSHIP IS PRESENT, SUCCESSION IS PATRILINEAL, RATHER THAN MATRILINEAL (127)	0.89 OF 47	90	LEAN LESS TOWARD BEING THOSE WHERE, IF A HEREDITARY HEADMANSHIP IS PRESENT, SUCCESSION IS PATRILINEAL, RATHER THAN MATRILINEAL (127)	0.63 OF 35	42 22 5 13	XSQ= 6.75 PHI= 0.287 XP = 0.0094

91	TILT TOWARD BEING THOSE WHERE SOCIETAL COMPLEXITY IS HIGH (18) F-W	0.65 OF 17	91	TILT TOWARD BEING THOSE WHERE SOCIETAL COMPLEXITY IS LOW (22) F-W	0.82 OF 11	11 2 6 9 XSQ= 4.09 PHI= 0.382 EP = 0.0238
94	TILT LESS TOWARD BEING THOSE WHERE THE HIERARCHY OF NATIONAL JURISDICTION HAS TWO, ONE, OR NO LEVELS (296) GES,EA	0.84 OF 108	94	TILT MORE TOWARD BEING THOSE WHERE THE HIERARCHY OF NATIONAL JURISDICTION HAS TWO, ONE, OR NO LEVELS (296) GES,EA	0.97 OF 61	17 2 91 59 XSQ= 4.88 PHI= 0.170 XP = 0.0271
102	TILT MORE TOWARD BEING THOSE WHERE CLASS STRATIFICATION IS PRESENT (203)	0.68 OF 111	102	TILT LESS TOWARD BEING THOSE WHERE CLASS STRATIFICATION IS PRESENT (203)	0.51 OF 65	76 33 35 32 XSQ= 4.72 PHI= 0.164 XP = 0.0298
107	TEND LESS TO BE THOSE WHERE CLASS STRATIFICATION, IF PRESENT, IS BASED ON SOMETHING OTHER THAN OCCUPATIONAL STATUS (160)	0.70 OF 76	107	IN ALL CASES ARE THOSE WHERE CLASS STRATIFICATION, IF PRESENT, IS BASED ON SOMETHING OTHER THAN OCCUPATIONAL STATUS (160)	1.00 OF 33	23 0 53 33 XSQ= 10.91 PHI= 0.316 XP = 0.0010
108	TILT TOWARD BEING THOSE WHERE CLASS STRATIFICATION, IF PRESENT, IS BASED ON SOMETHING OTHER THAN A HEREDITARY ARISTOCRACY (129)	0.75 OF 76	108	TILT TOWARD BEING THOSE WHERE CLASS STRATIFICATION, IF PRESENT, IS BASED ON A HEREDITARY ARISTOCRACY (74)	0.52 OF 33	19 17 57 16 XSQ= 6.16 PHI= -0.238 XP = 0.0130
110	LEAN TOWARD BEING THOSE WHERE SLAVERY IS PRESENT (163)	0.50 OF 110	110	LEAN TOWARD BEING THOSE WHERE SLAVERY IS ABSENT (218)	0.73 OF 66	55 18 55 48 XSQ= 7.87 PHI= 0.211 XP = 0.0050
118	TILT TOWARD BEING THOSE WHERE THE PERCENTAGE OF OCCUPATIONS THAT ARE SPECIALIZED IS HIGH OR MEDIUM (24) WME	0.70 OF 23	118	TILT TOWARD BEING THOSE WHERE THE PERCENTAGE OF OCCUPATIONS THAT ARE SPECIALIZED IS LOW (25) WME	0.69 OF 13	16 4 7 9 XSQ= 3.61 PHI= 0.317 EP = 0.0379
138	TILT TOWARD BEING THOSE WHERE SUPERORDINATE JUSTICE IS PRESENT (22) BBW	0.86 OF 14	138	TILT TOWARD BEING THOSE WHERE SUPERORDINATE JUSTICE IS ABSENT (18) BBW	0.62 OF 13	12 5 2 8 XSQ= 4.59 PHI= 0.412 EP = 0.0183
141	TILT TOWARD BEING THOSE WHERE THE LEVEL OF SOCIAL SANCTION IS PUBLIC CORPOREAL SANCTION, RATHER THAN PUBLIC PROPERTY SANCTION OR PRIVATE SETTLEMENT (28) JMH	0.67 OF 21	141	TILT TOWARD BEING THOSE WHERE THE LEVEL OF SOCIAL SANCTION IS PUBLIC PROPERTY SANCTION OR PRIVATE SETTLEMENT, RATHER THAN PUBLIC CORPOREAL SANCTION (26) JMH	0.69 OF 16	14 5 7 11 XSQ= 3.25 PHI= 0.296 EP = 0.0489

148 DRIFT TOWARD BEING THCSE 0.62 OF 13 WHERE THE INCIDENCE OF PERSONAL CRIME IS HIGH (12) B-B-C	148 DRIFT TOWARD BEING THOSE 0.80 OF 15 WHERE THE INCIDENCE OF PERSCNAL CRIME IS LOW (21) B-B-C	8 3 5 12 XSQ= 3.45 PHI= 0.351 EP = 0.0510
149 DRIFT TOWARD BEING THCSE 0.71 OF 14 WHERE THE INCIDENCE CF THEFT IS HIGH (18) B-B-C	149 DRIFT TOWARD BEING THOSE 0.65 CF 17 WHERE THE INCIDENCE OF THEFT IS LOW (19) B-B-C	10 6 4 11 XSQ= 2.70 PHI= 0.295 EP = 0.0732
180 DRIFT LESS TOWARC BEING THCSE 0.58 OF 110 WHERE THE COMMUNITY IS COMMCNLY NCN-EXCGAMCUS, RATHER THAN EXCGAMCUS (258)	180 DRIFT MORE TOWARD BEING THCSE 0.74 OF 65 WHERE THE COMMUNITY IS COMMONLY NON-EXOGAMOUS, RATHER THAN EXOGAMOUS (258)	46 17 64 48 XSQ= 3.70 PHI= 0.145 XP = 0.0545
186 DRIFT LESS TCWARC BEING THCSE 0.54 OF 112 WHERE THE KIN GRCUP IS CTHER THAN EXCLUSIVELY PATRILINEAL (250)	186 DRIFT MORE TOWARD BEING THCSE 0.70 OF 67 WHERE THE KIN GROUP IS OTHER THAN EXCLUSIVELY PATRILINEAL (250)	51 20 61 47 XSQ= 3.68 PHI= 0.143 XP = 0.0551
190 TILT MORE TOWARC BEING THCSE 0.85 OF 73 WHERE THE KIN GRCUP IS PATRILINEAL CR DCUBLE-DESCENT, RATHER THAN MATRILINEAL (186)	190 TILT LESS TOWARD BEING THOSE 0.65 OF 34 WHERE THE KIN GROUP IS PATRILINEAL OR DOUBLE-DESCENT, RATHER THAN MATRILINEAL (186)	62 22 11 12 XSQ= 4.49 PHI= 0.205 XP = 0.0341
198 DRIFT MCRE TCWARC BEING THCSE 0.91 OF 55 WHERE RULES FCR THE INHERITANCE OF REAL PRCPERTY, IF PRESENT, FAVOR THE MALE HEIR OR LINE, RATHER THAN THE FEMALE (144)	198 DRIFT LESS TOWARD BEING THCSE 0.73 OF 26 WHERE RULES FOR THE INHERITANCE CF REAL PROPERTY, IF PRESENT, FAVOR THE MALE HEIR OR LINE, RATHER THAN THE FEMALE (144)	50 19 5 7 XSQ= 3.15 PHI= 0.197 XP = 0.0760
201 TILT MCRE TCWARC BEING THOSE 0.89 OF 112 WHERE MARITAL RESICENCE IS NCN-CPTICNAL, RATHER THAN AMBILCCAL CR NECLOCAL (334)	201 TILT LESS TOWARD BEING THOSE 0.75 OF 67 WHERE MARITAL RESIDENCE IS NON-OPTIONAL, RATHER THAN AMBILOCAL OR NEOLOCAL (334)	100 50 12 17 XSQ= 5.60 PHI= 0.177 XP = 0.0180
204 LEAN MORE TCWARC BEING THCSE 0.88 OF 98 WHERE MARITAL RESICENCE IS PATRILOCAL, VIRILOCAL, OR AVUNCULOCAL, RATHER THAN AMBILCCAL CR NECLOCAL (270)	204 LEAN LESS TOWARD BEING THOSE 0.69 OF 55 WHERE MARITAL RÉSIDENCE IS PATRILOCAL, VIRILCCAL, OR AVUNCULOCAL, RATHER THAN AMBILOCAL OR NECLOCAL (270)	86 38 12 17 XSQ= 6.82 PHI= 0.211 XP = 0.0090
213 DRIFT TCWARD BEING THCSE 0.62 OF 107 WHERE FIRST CCUSIN MARRIAGE IS NCT PERMITTED (198)	213 DRIFT TOWARD BEING THCSE 0.54 OF 63 WHERE FIRST COUSIN MARRIAGE IS PERMITTED (172)	41 34 66 29 XSQ= 3.33 PHI= -0.140 XP = 0.0680

234	DRIFT TOWARD BEING THOSE 0.64 OF 89 WHERE THE COUSIN TERMINOLOGY IS OF ESKIMO OR HAWAIIAN TYPE, RATHER THAN CROW, OMAHA, OR IROQUOIS TYPE (170)	234	DRIFT TOWARD BEING THOSE 0.53 OF 57 WHERE THE COUSIN TERMINOLOGY IS OF CROW, OMAHA, OR IROQUOIS TYPE, RATHER THAN ESKIMO OR HAWAIIAN TYPE (152)	32 30 57 27 XSQ= 3.30 PHI= -0.150 XP = 0.0692
240	LEAN TOWARD BEING THOSE 0.77 OF 60 WHERE THE FAMILY, IF EXTENDED, IS SMALL OR STEM, RATHER THAN LARGE (135)	240	LEAN TOWARD BEING THOSE 0.53 OF 34 WHERE THE FAMILY, IF EXTENDED, IS LARGE, RATHER THAN SMALL OR STEM (78)	14 18 46 16 XSQ= 7.21 PHI= -0.277 XP = 0.0073
259	TILT TOWARD BEING THOSE 0.64 OF 22 WHERE THE SEVERITY OF MOTHER-IN-LAW AVOIDANCE IS HIGH (26) WNS	259	TILT TOWARD BEING THOSE 0.82 OF 11 WHERE THE SEVERITY OF MOTHER-IN-LAW AVOIDANCE IS LOW (20) WNS	14 2 8 9 XSQ= 4.38 PHI= 0.364 EP = 0.0255
278	TILT TOWARD BEING THOSE 0.62 OF 13 WHERE PROPERTY RIGHTS IN WOMEN ARE PRESENT (8) LWS	278	IN ALL CASES ARE THOSE 1.00 OF 5 WHERE PROPERTY RIGHTS IN WOMEN ARE UNIMPORTANT OR ABSENT (14) LWS	8 0 5 5 XSQ= 3.33 PHI= 0.430 EP = 0.0359
301	LEAN MORE TOWARD BEING THOSE 0.87 OF 55 WHERE THE POST-PARTUM SEX TABOO LASTS LONGER THAN ONE MONTH (96)	301	LEAN LESS TOWARD BEING THOSE 0.57 OF 30 WHERE THE POST-PARTUM SEX TABOO LASTS LONGER THAN ONE MONTH (96)	48 17 7 13 XSQ= 8.48 PHI= 0.316 XP = 0.0036
305	TILT TOWARD BEING THOSE 0.64 OF 22 WHERE THE EARLY SEXUAL SATISFACTION POTENTIAL IS LOW (24) W-C	305	TILT TOWARD BEING THOSE 0.72 OF 18 WHERE THE EARLY SEXUAL SATISFACTION POTENTIAL IS HIGH (27) W-C	8 13 14 5 XSQ= 3.77 PHI= -0.307 EP = 0.0309
308	TILT TOWARD BEING THOSE 0.74 OF 19 WHERE AVERAGE SOCIALIZATION ANXIETY IS HIGH (22) W-C	308	TILT TOWARD BEING THOSE 0.64 OF 14 WHERE AVERAGE SOCIALIZATION ANXIETY IS LOW (18) W-C	14 5 5 9 XSQ= 3.33 PHI= 0.318 EP = 0.0397
310	DRIFT TOWARD BEING THOSE 0.68 OF 19 WHERE ANAL SOCIALIZATION ANXIETY IS HIGH (22) W-C	310	DRIFT TOWARD BEING THOSE 0.64 OF 14 WHERE ANAL SOCIALIZATION ANXIETY IS LOW (19) W-C	13 5 6 9 XSQ= 2.28 PHI= 0.263 EP = 0.0853
311	TEND TO BE THOSE 0.87 OF 23 WHERE SEXUAL SOCIALIZATION ANXIETY IS HIGH (28) W-C	311	TEND TO BE THOSE 0.83 OF 18 WHERE SEXUAL SOCIALIZATION ANXIETY IS LOW (23) W-C	20 3 3 15 XSQ= 17.50 PHI= 0.653 XP = 0.0000

386	DRIFT TOWARD BEING THOSE WHERE SEXUAL EXPRESSION BY THE YOUNG IS RESTRICTED OR SEMI-RESTRICTED (46) F-B	0.59 OF 27	386	DRIFT TOWARD BEING THOSE WHERE SEXUAL EXPRESSION BY THE YOUNG IS PERMITTED (40) F-B	0.66 OF 32	16 11 11 21 XSQ= 2.72 PHI= 0.215 XP = 0.0991
393	LEAN TOWARD BEING THOSE WHERE EXTRAMARITAL COITUS IS PUNISHED, RATHER THAN PERMITTED (43) F-B	0.75 OF 32	393	LEAN TOWARD BEING THOSE WHERE EXTRAMARITAL COITUS IS PERMITTED, RATHER THAN PUNISHED (41) F-B	0.65 OF 26	24 9 8 17 XSQ= 7.96 PHI= 0.371 XP = 0.0048
397	LEAN LESS TOWARD BEING THOSE WHERE SEX DISABILITY IS ABSENT (42) JKH	0.60 OF 25	397	IN ALL CASES ARE THOSE WHERE SEX DISABILITY IS ABSENT (42) JKH	1.00 OF 14	10 0 15 14 XSQ= 5.58 PHI= 0.378 EP = 0.0066
398	TEND TO BE THOSE WHERE THE INTENSITY OF SEX ANXIETY IS HIGH (16) WNS	0.86 OF 14	398	IN ALL CASES ARE THOSE WHERE THE INTENSITY OF SEX ANXIETY IS LOW (16) WNS	1.00 OF 11	12 0 2 11 XSQ= 14.86 PHI= 0.771 EP = 0.0000
426	TILT TOWARD BEING THOSE WHERE A HIGH GOD IS PRESENT (156) GES,EA	0.66 OF 98	426	TILT TOWARD BEING THOSE WHERE A HIGH GOD IS ABSENT (104) GES,EA	0.53 OF 51	65 24 33 27 XSQ= 4.41 PHI= 0.172 XP = 0.0358
427	TILT TOWARD BEING THOSE WHERE A HIGH GOD, IF PRESENT, IS ACTIVE, RATHER THAN INACTIVE (87) GES,EA	0.65 OF 65	427	TILT TOWARD BEING THOSE WHERE A HIGH GOD, IF PRESENT, IS INACTIVE, RATHER THAN ACTIVE (69) GES,EA	0.67 OF 24	42 8 23 16 XSQ= 5.75 PHI= 0.254 XP = 0.0164
441	DRIFT TOWARD BEING THOSE WHERE FEAR OF HUMAN BEINGS IS HIGH (29) W-C	0.65 OF 26	441	DRIFT TOWARD BEING THOSE WHERE FEAR OF HUMAN BEINGS IS LOW (32) W-C	0.68 OF 19	17 6 9 13 XSQ= 3.76 PHI= 0.289 XP = 0.0525
447	TILT TOWARD BEING THOSE WHERE LOVE MAGIC IS PRESENT (20) S-R	0.85 OF 13	447	TILT TOWARD BEING THOSE WHERE LOVE MAGIC IS ABSENT (13) S-R	0.62 OF 13	11 5 2 8 XSQ= 4.06 PHI= 0.395 EP = 0.0414
450	TILT LESS TOWARD BEING THOSE WHERE THE OBSERVATION OF FOOD TABOOS IS HIGH OR MEDIUM, RATHER THAN LOW (60) JRL	0.62 OF 37	450	TILT MORE TOWARD BEING THOSE WHERE THE OBSERVATION OF FOOD TABOOS IS HIGH OR MEDIUM, RATHER THAN LOW (60) JRL	0.92 OF 24	23 22 14 2 XSQ= 5.11 PHI= -0.290 XP = 0.0237

458	TILT LESS TOWARD BEING THOSE WHERE GAMES, IF PRESENT, DO NOT INCLUDE GAMES OF STRATEGY (119) R-A-B,EA	0.59 OF 73	458	TILT MORE TOWARD BEING THOSE WHERE GAMES, IF PRESENT, DO NOT INCLUDE GAMES OF STRATEGY (119) R-A-B,EA	0.79 OF 39	30 8 43 31 XSQ= 3.93 PHI= 0.187 XP = 0.0474
459	TILT TOWARD BEING THOSE WHERE GAMES, IF PRESENT, INCLUDE GAMES OF CHANCE (82) R-A-B,EA	0.55 OF 73	459	TILT TOWARD BEING THOSE WHERE GAMES, IF PRESENT, DO NOT INCLUDE GAMES OF CHANCE (89) R-A-B,EA	0.67 OF 39	40 13 33 26 XSQ= 3.88 PHI= 0.186 XP = 0.0490
460	TILT TOWARD BEING THOSE WHERE GAMES, IF PRESENT, ARE NOT LIMITED TO GAMES OF SKILL ONLY (104) R-A-B,EA	0.70 OF 73	460	TILT TOWARD BEING THOSE WHERE GAMES, IF PRESENT, ARE LIMITED TO GAMES OF SKILL ONLY (67) R-A-B,EA	0.56 OF 39	22 22 51 17 XSQ= 6.30 PHI= -0.237 XP = 0.0121
475	TILT TOWARD BEING THOSE WHERE EXHIBITIONISTIC DANCING IS STRONGLY OR MODERATELY EMPHASIZED (48) PES	0.67 OF 42	475	TILT TOWARD BEING THOSE WHERE EXHIBITIONISTIC DANCING IS NEGLIGIBLY EMPHASIZED (38) PES	0.63 OF 24	28 9 14 15 XSQ= 4.16 PHI= 0.251 XP = 0.0415

393 CLLTURES
WHERE EXTRAMARITAL COITUS
IS PUNISHED, RATHER THAN
PERMITTED (43) F-B

393 CULTURES
WHERE EXTRAMARITAL COITUS IS
PERMITTED, RATHER THAN
PUNISHED (41) F-B

BACKGROUND ON PAGE 155 — BOTH SUBJECT AND PREDICATE

43 IN LEFT CCLUMN

ABIPCN	AINU	ALCRESE	ASHANTI	AYMARA	AZANDE	CHAGGA	CHIR-APACHE	CREEK	CROW
DOBUANS	FON	GANDA	GILBERTESE	IFUGAO	JIVARO	JUKUN	KAZAK	KHASI	KUTENAI
LAKHER	LAMBA	LANGC	MAORI	MARICOPA	MATACO	OMAHA	PENOBSCOT	RIFFIANS	RWALA
SEMANG	SENIANG	SWAZI	TAOS	TEHUELCHE	THONGA	TIV	TOKELAU	TOLOWA	TUPINAMBA
VEDDA	VENDA	WITCTC							

41 IN RIGHT CCLUMN

APINAYE	ARANDA	CHENCHU	CHEYENNE	CHOROTI	CHUKCHEE	COPR ESKIMO	CREE	DIERI	DUSUN
GILYAK	HANC	ILA	KERAKI	KIOW-APACHE	LAPPS	LEPCHA	LESU	LHOTA NAGA	MARQUESANS
MARSHALLESE	MASAI	MBUNDU	MURNGIN	NAMA	NANDI	NASKAPI	NATCHEZ	PAPAGO	PONAPEANS
PUKAPUKA	PURARI	SIRICNC	TANALA	TARAHUMARA	TENDA	TENINO	TIMBIRA	TROBRIAND	TRUKESE
ZUNI									

316 EXCLUCED BECAUSE UNASCERTAINEC

12	DRIFT MORE TOWARD BEING THOSE WHERE THE LATITUDE IS LESS THAN FIFTY DEGREES (367)	0.98 OF 43	12	DRIFT LESS TOWARD BEING THOSE WHERE THE LATITUDE IS LESS THAN FIFTY DEGREES (367)	0.85 OF 41		1 6 42 35 XSQ= 2.71 PHI= -0.180 XP = 0.0999
73	DRIFT TOWARD BEING THOSE WHERE WEAVING IS PRESENT (118)	0.56 OF 36	73	DRIFT TOWARD BEING THOSE WHERE WEAVING IS ABSENT (130)	0.69 OF 36		20 11 16 25 XSQ= 3.63 PHI= 0.224 XP = 0.0569
74	TILT TOWARD BEING THOSE WHERE POTTERY IS PRESENT (145)	0.71 OF 35	74	TILT TOWARD BEING THOSE WHERE POTTERY IS ABSENT (93)	0.61 OF 36		25 14 10 22 XSQ= 6.33 PHI= 0.299 XP = 0.0119
78	DRIFT TOWARD BEING THOSE WHERE THE WRITING SYSTEM IS ALPHABETIC-OR-PHONETIC, OR MNEMONIC, RATHER THAN BEING ABSENT (36) JMH	0.73 OF 11	78	DRIFT TOWARD BEING THOSE WHERE A WRITING SYSTEM IS ABSENT, RATHER THAN BEING PRESENT IN EITHER ALPHABETIC-OR-PHONETIC FORM OR MNEMONIC FORM (18) JMH	0.73 OF 11		8 3 3 8 XSQ= 2.91 PHI= 0.364 EP = 0.0861

80	DRIFT LESS TOWARD BEING THOSE 0.84 OF 25 WHERE NO CITY OR TOWN IS PRESENT (185)	80	IN ALL CASES ARE THOSE 1.00 OF 31 WHERE NO CITY OR TOWN IS PRESENT (185)	4 0 21 31 XSQ= 3.20 PHI= 0.239 XP = 0.0736
82	TILT MORE TOWARD BEING THOSE 0.92 OF 25 WHERE A CITY OR TOWN IS PRESENT, OR THE AVERAGE COMMUNITY SIZE IS FIFTY OR GREATER (178)	82	TILT LESS TOWARD BEING THOSE 0.65 OF 31 WHERE A CITY OR TOWN IS PRESENT, OR THE AVERAGE COMMUNITY SIZE IS FIFTY OR GREATER (178)	23 20 2 11 XSQ= 4.42 PHI= 0.281 XP = 0.0354
85	TILT LESS TOWARD BEING THOSE 0.77 OF 39 WHERE THE LEVEL OF POLITICAL INTEGRATION IS THE MINIMAL STATE, THE AUTONOMOUS COMMUNITY, OR THE FAMILY (234) GPM	85	TILT MORE TOWARD BEING THOSE 0.97 OF 32 WHERE THE LEVEL OF POLITICAL INTEGRATION IS THE MINIMAL STATE, THE AUTONOMOUS COMMUNITY, OR THE FAMILY (234) GPM	9 1 30 31 XSQ= 4.25 PHI= 0.245 XP = 0.0392
96	TILT TOWARD BEING THOSE 0.64 OF 39 WHERE THE HIERARCHY OF NATIONAL JURISDICTION HAS FOUR, THREE, TWO OR ONE LEVEL (174) GES,EA	96	TILT TOWARD BEING THOSE 0.63 OF 38 WHERE THE HIERARCHY OF NATIONAL JURISDICTION HAS NO LEVELS (156) GES,EA	25 14 14 24 XSQ= 4.68 PHI= 0.247 XP = 0.0305
110	LEAN TOWARD BEING THOSE 0.53 OF 43 WHERE SLAVERY IS PRESENT (163)	110	LEAN TOWARD BEING THOSE 0.82 OF 40 WHERE SLAVERY IS ABSENT (218)	23 7 20 33 XSQ= 10.12 PHI= 0.349 XP = 0.0015
133	IN ALL CASES ARE THOSE 1.00 OF 5 WHERE CONTRACTED DEBTS ARE SIGNIFICANTLY PRESENT (17) GES	133	TILT TOWARD BEING THOSE 0.67 OF 9 WHERE CONTRACTED DEBTS ARE MODERATELY PRESENT OR ABSENT (17) GES	5 3 0 6 XSQ= 3.43 PHI= 0.495 EP = 0.0310
137	DRIFT TOWARD BEING THOSE 0.50 OF 24 WHERE INVIDIOUS DISPLAY OF WEALTH IS STRONGLY EMPHASIZED (37) PES	137	DRIFT TOWARD BEING THOSE 0.80 OF 20 WHERE INVIDIOUS DISPLAY OF WEALTH IS MODERATELY, LITTLE, OR NEGATIVELY EMPHASIZED (52) PES	12 4 12 16 XSQ= 3.05 PHI= 0.263 XP = 0.0810
148	TILT TOWARD BEING THOSE 0.63 OF 8 WHERE THE INCIDENCE OF PERSONAL CRIME IS HIGH (12) B-B-C	148	TILT TOWARD BEING THOSE 0.92 OF 12 WHERE THE INCIDENCE OF PERSONAL CRIME IS LOW (21) B-B-C	5 1 3 11 XSQ= 4.38 PHI= 0.468 EP = 0.0181
149	LEAN TOWARD BEING THOSE 0.88 OF 8 WHERE THE INCIDENCE OF THEFT IS HIGH (18) B-B-C	149	LEAN TOWARD BEING THOSE 0.77 OF 13 WHERE THE INCIDENCE OF THEFT IS LOW (19) B-B-C	7 3 1 10 XSQ= 5.86 PHI= 0.528 EP = 0.0075

175	DRIFT LESS TOWARD BEING THOSE 0.60 OF 43 WHERE THE COMMUNITY IS 'KIN-HETEROGENEOUS,' I. E. OTHER THAN A CLAN COMMUNITY OR A DEME (260)	175	DRIFT MORE TOWARD BEING THOSE 0.80 OF 41 WHERE THE COMMUNITY IS 'KIN-HETEROGENEOUS,' I. E. OTHER THAN A CLAN COMMUNITY OR A DEME (260)	17 8 26 33 XSQ= 3.12 PHI= 0.193 XP = 0.0771
178	DRIFT MORE TOWARD BEING THOSE 0.86 OF 43 WHERE THE COMMUNITY IS OTHER THAN SEGMENTED ON A CLAN BASIS AND NON-EXOGAMOUS (295)	178	DRIFT LESS TOWARD BEING THOSE 0.66 OF 41 WHERE THE COMMUNITY IS OTHER THAN SEGMENTED ON A CLAN BASIS AND NON-EXOGAMOUS (295)	6 14 37 27 XSQ= 3.67 PHI= -0.209 XP = 0.0554
183	DRIFT MORE TOWARD BEING THOSE 0.93 OF 28 WHERE THE LARGEST NON-COGNATIC KIN GROUP IS SMALLER THAN A MOEITY, I. E., A PHRATRY OR SIB OR LINEAGE (218)	183	DRIFT LESS TOWARD BEING THOSE 0.70 OF 27 WHERE THE LARGEST NON-COGNATIC KIN GROUP IS SMALLER THAN A MOEITY, I. E., A PHRATRY OR SIB OR LINEAGE (218)	2 8 26 19 XSQ= 3.28 PHI= -0.244 XP = 0.0700
190	DRIFT MORE TOWARD BEING THOSE 0.78 OF 27 WHERE THE KIN GROUP IS PATRILINEAL OR DOUBLE-DESCENT, RATHER THAN MATRILINEAL (186)	190	DRIFT LESS TOWARD BEING THOSE 0.52 OF 25 WHERE THE KIN GROUP IS PATRILINEAL OR DOUBLE-DESCENT, RATHER THAN MATRILINEAL (186)	21 13 6 12 XSQ= 2.76 PHI= 0.230 XP = 0.0968
207	DRIFT TOWARD BEING THOSE 0.59 OF 17 WHERE MARITAL RESIDENCE IS AMBILOCAL OR NEOLOCAL, RATHER THAN MATRILOCAL OR UXORILOCAL (64)	207	DRIFT TOWARD BEING THOSE 0.73 OF 15 WHERE MARITAL RESIDENCE IS MATRILOCAL OR UXORILOCAL, RATHER THAN AMBILOCAL OR NEOLOCAL (64)	7 11 10 4 XSQ= 2.17 PHI= -0.260 EP = 0.0870
214	IN ALL CASES ARE THOSE 1.00 OF 16 WHERE FIRST COUSIN MARRIAGE, IF PERMITTED, IS OTHER THAN UNILATERAL (144)	214	TILT LESS TOWARD BEING THOSE 0.68 OF 19 WHERE FIRST COUSIN MARRIAGE, IF PERMITTED, IS OTHER THAN UNILATERAL (144)	0 6 16 13 XSQ= 4.08 PHI= -0.341 EP = 0.0216
258	TILT TOWARD BEING THOSE 0.60 OF 10 WHERE THE SEVERITY OF SON'S WIFE AVOIDANCE IS HIGH (15) WNS	258	IN ALL CASES ARE THOSE 1.00 OF 7 WHERE THE SEVERITY OF SON'S WIFE AVOIDANCE IS LOW (16) WNS	6 0 4 7 XSQ= 4.13 PHI= 0.493 EP = 0.0175
282	TILT TOWARD BEING THOSE 0.65 OF 17 WHERE THE STRENGTH OF DESIRE FOR CHILDREN IS HIGH (16) BCA	282	TILT TOWARD BEING THOSE 0.80 OF 10 WHERE THE STRENGTH OF DESIRE FOR CHILDREN IS LOW OR ABSENT (20) BCA	11 2 6 8 XSQ= 3.41 PHI= 0.355 EP = 0.0461
295	TILT TOWARD BEING THOSE 0.70 OF 10 WHERE THE SEVERITY OF PUNISHMENT FOR ABORTION IS HIGH (11) BCA	295	TILT TOWARD BEING THOSE 0.86 OF 7 WHERE THE SEVERITY OF PUNISHMENT FOR ABORTION IS LOW OR ABSENT (12) BCA	7 1 3 6 XSQ= 3.14 PHI= 0.430 EP = 0.0498

301	DRIFT MORE TOWARD BEING THOSE 0.82 OF 22 WHERE THE POST-PARTUM SEX TABOO LASTS LONGER THAN ONE MONTH (96)	301	DRIFT LESS TOWARD BEING THOSE 0.52 OF 21 WHERE THE POST-PARTUM SEX TABOO LASTS LONGER THAN ONE MONTH (96)	18 11 4 10 XSQ= 3.01 PHI= 0.264 XP = 0.0830
305	DRIFT TOWARD BEING THOSE 0.65 OF 20 WHERE THE EARLY SEXUAL SATISFACTION POTENTIAL IS LOW (24) W-C	305	DRIFT TOWARD BEING THOSE 0.71 OF 14 WHERE THE EARLY SEXUAL SATISFACTION POTENTIAL IS HIGH (27) W-C	7 10 13 4 XSQ= 3.04 PHI= -0.299 EP = 0.0799
306	LEAN TOWARD BEING THOSE 0.74 OF 19 WHERE THE EARLY DEPENDENCE SATISFACTION POTENTIAL IS LOW (24) W-C	306	LEAN TOWARD BEING THOSE 0.75 OF 16 WHERE THE EARLY DEPENDENCE SATISFACTION POTENTIAL IS HIGH (28) W-C	5 12 14 4 XSQ= 6.41 PHI= -0.428 EP = 0.0067
308	TILT TOWARD BEING THOSE 0.79 OF 14 WHERE AVERAGE SOCIALIZATION ANXIETY IS HIGH (22) W-C	308	TILT TOWARD BEING THOSE 0.64 OF 11 WHERE AVERAGE SOCIALIZATION ANXIETY IS LOW (18) W-C	11 4 3 7 XSQ= 2.98 PHI= 0.345 EP = 0.0486
311	DRIFT TOWARD BEING THOSE 0.65 OF 20 WHERE SEXUAL SOCIALIZATION ANXIETY IS HIGH (28) W-C	311	DRIFT TOWARD BEING THOSE 0.71 OF 14 WHERE SEXUAL SOCIALIZATION ANXIETY IS LOW (23) W-C	13 4 7 10 XSQ= 3.04 PHI= 0.299 EP = 0.0799
312	DRIFT TOWARD BEING THOSE 0.76 OF 17 WHERE DEPENDENCE SOCIALIZATION ANXIETY IS HIGH (24) W-C	312	DRIFT TOWARD BEING THOSE 0.57 OF 14 WHERE DEPENDENCE SOCIALIZATION ANXIETY IS LOW (23) W-C	13 6 4 8 XSQ= 2.38 PHI= 0.277 EP = 0.0751
320	TILT TOWARD BEING THOSE 0.63 OF 19 WHERE THE DEGREE OF REDUCTION OF THE INFANT'S DRIVES IS LOW (24) B-B-C	320	TILT TOWARD BEING THOSE 0.72 OF 18 WHERE THE DEGREE OF REDUCTION OF THE INFANT'S DRIVES IS HIGH (45) B-B-C	7 13 12 5 XSQ= 3.34 PHI= -0.301 EP = 0.0489
321	DRIFT TOWARD BEING THOSE 0.79 OF 14 WHERE THE IMMEDIACY OF REDUCTION OF THE INFANT'S DRIVES IS LOW (25) B-B-C	321	DRIFT TOWARD BEING THOSE 0.59 OF 17 WHERE THE IMMEDIACY OF REDUCTION OF THE INFANT'S DRIVES IS HIGH (35) B-B-C	3 10 11 7 XSQ= 3.01 PHI= -0.311 EP = 0.0669
335	TILT TOWARD BEING THOSE 0.71 OF 14 WHERE INITIAL INDULGENCE OF DEPENDENCY IS LOW (18) WNS	335	TILT TOWARD BEING THOSE 0.75 OF 12 WHERE INITIAL INDULGENCE OF DEPENDENCY IS HIGH (20) WNS	4 9 10 3 XSQ= 3.87 PHI= -0.386 EP = 0.0472

No.				No.				
337	DRIFT TOWARD BEING THOSE WHERE THE CHILD'S INFERRED ANXIETY OVER NON-PERFORMANCE OF RESPONSIBLE BEHAVIOR IS HIGH (38) B-B-C	0.68 OF	19	337	DRIFT TOWARD BEING THOSE WHERE THE CHILD'S INFERRED ANXIETY OVER NON-PERFORMANCE OF RESPONSIBLE BEHAVIOR IS LOW (35) B-B-C	0.67 OF	18	13 6 6 12 XSQ= 3.26 PHI= 0.297 EP = 0.0502
345	LEAN TOWARD BEING THOSE WHERE THE CHILD'S INFERRED ANXIETY OVER NON-PERFORMANCE OF SELF-RELIANT BEHAVIOR IS HIGH (37) B-B-C	0.80 OF	20	345	LEAN TOWARD BEING THOSE WHERE THE CHILD'S INFERRED ANXIETY OVER NON-PERFORMANCE OF SELF-RELIANT BEHAVIOR IS LOW (39) B-B-C	0.74 OF	19	16 5 4 14 XSQ= 9.24 PHI= 0.487 EP = 0.0012
353	TILT TOWARD BEING THOSE WHERE THE CHILD'S INFERRED ANXIETY OVER NON-PERFORMANCE OF OBEDIENT BEHAVIOR IS HIGH (42) B-B-C	0.85 OF	20	353	TILT TOWARD BEING THOSE WHERE THE CHILD-S INFERRED ANXIETY OVER NON-PERFORMANCE OF OBEDIENT BEHAVIOR IS LOW (32) B-B-C	0.56 OF	18	17 8 3 10 XSQ= 5.24 PHI= 0.371 EP = 0.0156
354	TILT TOWARD BEING THOSE WHERE THE CHILD'S INFERRED ANXIETY OVER PERFORMANCE OF OBEDIENT BEHAVIOR IS HIGH (36) B-B-C	0.75 OF	20	354	TILT TOWARD BEING THOSE WHERE THE CHILD'S INFERRED ANXIETY OVER PERFORMANCE OF OBEDIENT BEHAVIOR IS LOW (37) B-B-C	0.61 OF	18	15 7 5 11 XSQ= 3.69 PHI= 0.312 EP = 0.0472
355	TILT TOWARD BEING THOSE WHERE THE CHILD'S INFERRED CONFLICT REGARDING OBEDIENT BEHAVIOR IS HIGH (35) B-B-C	0.75 OF	20	355	TILT TOWARD BEING THOSE WHERE THE CHILD'S INFERRED CONFLICT REGARDING OBEDIENT BEHAVIOR IS LOW (38) B-B-C	0.67 OF	18	15 6 5 12 XSQ= 5.07 PHI= 0.365 EP = 0.0210
386	TILT TOWARD BEING THOSE WHERE SEXUAL EXPRESSION BY THE YOUNG IS RESTRICTED OR SEMI-RESTRICTED (46) F-B	0.76 OF	29	386	TILT TOWARD BEING THOSE WHERE SEXUAL EXPRESSION BY THE YOUNG IS PERMITTED (40) F-B	0.56 OF	32	22 14 7 18 XSQ= 5.23 PHI= 0.293 XP = 0.0222
391	TILT TOWARD BEING THOSE WHERE PREMARITAL SEX RELATIONS ARE STRONGLY PUNISHED AND IN FACT RARE, OR WEAKLY PUNISHED AND IN FACT NOT RARE (89) JTW,EA	0.55 OF	33	391	TILT TOWARD BEING THOSE WHERE PREMARITAL SEX RELATIONS ARE PUNISHED ONLY IF PREGNANCY RESULTS, OR FREELY PERMITTED (90) JTW,EA	0.80 OF	25	18 5 15 20 XSQ= 5.72 PHI= 0.314 XP = 0.0167
392	LEAN TOWARD BEING THOSE WHERE PREMARITAL SEX RELATIONS ARE STRONGLY PUNISHED AND IN FACT RARE, OR WEAKLY PUNISHED AND IN FACT NOT RARE, OR PUNISHED ONLY IF PREGNANCY RESULTS (112) JTW,EA	0.73 OF	33	392	LEAN TOWARD BEING THOSE WHERE PREMARITAL SEX RELATIONS ARE FREELY PERMITTED (67) JTW,EA	0.68 OF	25	24 8 9 17 XSQ= 7.96 PHI= 0.371 XP = 0.0048
398	TILT TOWARD BEING THOSE WHERE THE INTENSITY OF SEX ANXIETY IS HIGH (16) WNS	0.67 OF	12	398	TILT TOWARD BEING THOSE WHERE THE INTENSITY OF SEX ANXIETY IS LOW (16) WNS	0.83 OF	12	8 2 4 10 XSQ= 4.29 PHI= 0.423 EP = 0.0361

399	TEND TO BE THOSE WHERE INTENSITY OF CASTRATION ANXIETY IS HIGH (23) WNS	0.87 OF 15	399	TEND TO BE THOSE WHERE INTENSITY OF CASTRATION ANXIETY IS LOW (22) WNS	0.87 OF 15	13 2 2 13	XSQ= 13.33 PHI= 0.667 EP = 0.0001
419	LEAN TOWARD BEING THOSE WHERE MILITARY GLORY IS STRONGLY OR MODERATELY EMPHASIZED (55) PES	0.92 OF 25	419	LEAN TOWARD BEING THOSE WHERE MILITARY GLORY IS NEGLIGIBLY EMPHASIZED (31) PES	0.56 OF 18	23 8 2 10	XSQ= 9.52 PHI= 0.470 XP = 0.0020
420	LEAN TOWARD BEING THOSE WHERE BELLICOSITY IS EXTREME (41) PES	0.83 OF 23	420	LEAN TOWARD BEING THOSE WHERE BELLICOSITY IS MODERATE OR NEGLIGIBLE (46) PES	0.70 OF 20	19 6 4 14	XSQ= 10.10 PHI= 0.485 XP = 0.0015
421	LEAN TOWARD BEING THOSE WHERE KILLING, TORTURING, OR MUTILATING OF THE ENEMY IS STRONGLY OR MODERATELY EMPHASIZED (37) PES	0.78 OF 23	421	LEAN TOWARD BEING THOSE WHERE KILLING, TORTURING, OR MUTILATING OF THE ENEMY IS NEGLIGIBLY EMPHASIZED (47) PES	0.74 OF 19	18 5 5 14	XSQ= 9.33 PHI= 0.471 XP = 0.0023
425	TILT TOWARD BEING THOSE WHERE SUPERNATURALS ARE MAINLY AGGRESSIVE, RATHER THAN BENEVOLENT (20) L-T-W	0.89 OF 9	425	TILT TOWARD BEING THOSE WHERE SUPERNATURALS ARE MAINLY BENEVOLENT, RATHER THAN AGGRESSIVE (16) L-T-W	0.70 OF 10	1 7 8 3	XSQ= 4.54 PHI= -0.489 EP = 0.0198
447	DRIFT TOWARD BEING THOSE WHERE LOVE MAGIC IS PRESENT (20) S-R	0.79 OF 14	447	DRIFT TOWARD BEING THOSE WHERE LOVE MAGIC IS ABSENT (13) S-R	0.63 OF 8	11 3 3 5	XSQ= 2.15 PHI= 0.312 EP = 0.0815
450	TILT LESS TOWARD BEING THOSE WHERE THE OBSERVATION OF FOOD TABOOS IS HIGH OR MEDIUM, RATHER THAN LOW (60) JRL	0.65 OF 17	450	IN ALL CASES ARE THOSE WHERE THE OBSERVATION OF FOOD TABOOS IS HIGH OR MEDIUM, RATHER THAN LOW (60) JRL	1.00 OF 14	11 14 6 0	XSQ= 4.07 PHI= -0.363 EP = 0.0209
460	DRIFT TOWARD BEING THOSE WHERE GAMES, IF PRESENT, ARE NOT LIMITED TO GAMES OF SKILL ONLY (104) R-A-B,EA	0.74 OF 31	460	DRIFT TOWARD BEING THOSE WHERE GAMES, IF PRESENT, ARE LIMITED TO GAMES OF SKILL ONLY (67) R-A-B,EA	0.50 OF 30	8 15 23 15	XSQ= 2.84 PHI= -0.216 XP = 0.0920

394 CULTURES
WHERE EXTRAMARITAL CCITUS IS
PRESENT (16) CSF

394 CULTURES
WHERE EXTRAMARITAL COITUS IS
ABSENT (8) CSF

BACKGROUND ON PAGE 155

SUBJECT ONLY

16 IN LEFT CCLUMN

ASHANTI	IFUGAC	KAZAK	KURTATCHI	KWAKIUTL	LEPCHA	LESU	MACRI	MASAI	MBUNDU
MURNGIN	SENIANG	TANALA	TIKOPIA	TODA	YAKUT				

8 IN RIGHT CCLUMN

AINU	ANDAMANESE	APINAYE	CROW	CUNA	JIVARO	RIFFIANS	THCNGA

376 EXCLUDED RECAUSE UNASCERTAINEC

	Present (16)				Absent (8)			
6	DRIFT LESS TCWARC BEING THCSE LOCATED CUTSIDE CF THE INSULAR PACIFIC (330)	0.56 OF	16	6	IN ALL CASES ARE THOSE LOCATED OUTSIDE OF THE INSULAR PACIFIC (330)	1.00 OF	8	7 0 / 9 8 / XSQ= 3.05 / PHI= 0.357 / EP = 0.0538
9	IN ALL CASES ARE THCSE LOCATED CUTSIDE CF SCUTH AMERICA (335)	1.00 OF	16	9	TILT LESS TOWARD BEING THOSE LOCATED OUTSIDE OF SOUTH AMERICA (335)	0.63 OF	8	0 3 / 16 5 / XSQ= 3.86 / PHI= -0.401 / EP = 0.0277
110	DRIFT TCWARD BEING THCSE WHERE SLAVERY IS PRESENT (163)	0.56 OF	16	11C	DRIFT TOWARD BEING THCSE WHERE SLAVERY IS ABSENT (218)	0.88 OF	8	9 1 / 7 7 / XSQ= 2.59 / PHI= 0.329 / EP = 0.0791
181	IN ALL CASES ARE THCSE WHERE THE COMMUNITY IS CTHER THAN A DEME (337)	1.00 OF	16	181	TILT LESS TOWARD BEING THOSE WHERE THE COMMUNITY IS CTHER THAN A DEME (337)	0.63 OF	8	0 3 / 16 5 / XSQ= 3.86 / PHI= -0.401 / EP = 0.0277
240	TILT TCWARD BEING THCSE WHERE THE FAMILY, IF EXTENCED, IS SMALL CR STEM, RATHER THAN LARGE (135)	0.86 OF	7	24C	TILT TOWARD BEING THOSE WHERE THE FAMILY, IF EXTENDED, IS LARGE, RATHER THAN SMALL OR STEM (78)	0.83 OF	6	1 5 / 6 1 / XSQ= 3.73 / PHI= -0.536 / EP = 0.0291

243	DRIFT TCWARD BEING THCSE WHERE PCLYGYNY, IF PRESENT, HAS A LCW INCIDENCE (36) W-C,S	0.70 OF 10	243	IN ALL CASES ARE THOSE WHERE POLYGYNY, IF PRESENT, HAS A HIGH INCIDENCE (24) W-D,S	1.00 OF 3	3 3 7 0 XSQ= 2.17 PHI= -0.408 EP = 0.0699
315	IN ALL CASES ARE THCSE WHERE MCTHER ANC NURSING CHILC CUSTOMARILY SLEEP IN THE SAME BED (37) W-C,S	1.00 OF 7	315	TILT TOWARD BEING THOSE WHERE MOTHER AND NURSING CHILD CUSTOMARILY SLEEP IN DIFFERENT BEDS (14) W-D,S	0.60 CF 5	7 2 0 3 XSQ= 2.86 PHI= 0.488 EP = 0.0455
424	TILT TCWARD BEING THOSE WHERE RELIGICUS SPECIALISTS ARE FULL-TIME, RATHER THAN PART-TIME (21) JMH	0.80 OF 5	424	IN ALL CASES ARE THCSE WHERE RELIGIOUS SPECIALISTS ARE PART-TIME, RATHER THAN FULL-TIME (33) JMH	1.00 OF 5	4 0 1 5 XSQ= 3.75 PHI= 0.612 EP = 0.0476
455	IN ALL CASES ARE THCSE WHERE THE MODE CF THE INCIVICUAL'S CCNTACT WITH THE DIVINE IS NCT CCNCUCIVE TC THE CEVELOPMENT OF THE INDIVIDUAL'S NEEC TC ACHIEVE (19) CCM	1.00 OF 5	455	TILT TOWARD BEING THOSE WHERE THE MODE OF THE INDIVIDUAL'S CONTACT WITH THE DIVINE IS CONDUCIVE TC THE DEVELCPMENT CF THE INDIVIDUAL'S NEED TO ACHIEVE (17) DCM	0.75 CF 4	0 3 5 1 XSQ= 2.76 PHI= -0.553 EP = 0.0476
476	TILT TCWARC BEING THOSE WHERE THE CEGREE CF INSCBRIETY IS MCDERATE CR SLIGHT (18) CH	0.64 OF 11	476	IN ALL CASES ARE THCSE WHERE THE DEGREE OF INSCBRIETY IS STRONG (31) DH	1.00 CF 6	4 6 7 0 XSQ= 4.13 PHI= -0.493 EP = 0.0175

	Left column		Right column	
395	CULTURES WHERE BELIEF IN THE UNCLEANNESS OF WOMEN IS PRESENT (18) LWS	395	CULTURES WHERE BELIEF IN THE UNCLEANNESS OF WOMEN IS UNIMPORTANT OR ABSENT (15) LWS	

BACKGROUND ON PAGE 155 BOTH SUBJECT AND PREDICATE

18 IN LEFT COLUMN

ALBANIANS ARANDA ASHANTI CREEK HAIDA HEBREWS JIVARO LANGO LAPPS MAORI
NAMA OMAHA TODA VEDDA WITOTO YAHGAN YAKUT YUKAGHIR

15 IN RIGHT COLUMN

ANDAMANESE ARAUCANIANS AZTEC CHUKCHEE CROW DIERI HANO IBAN KAZAK KUNG
NAVAHO RWALA SAMOANS SEMANG TROBRIAND

367 EXCLUDED BECAUSE UNASCERTAINED

	Left column			Right column		Statistics
175	DRIFT LESS TOWARD BEING THOSE WHERE THE COMMUNITY IS 'KIN-HETEROGENEOUS,' I. E. OTHER THAN A CLAN COMMUNITY OR A DEME (260)	0.53 OF 17	175	DRIFT MORE TOWARD BEING THOSE WHERE THE COMMUNITY IS 'KIN-HETEROGENEOUS,' I. E. OTHER THAN A CLAN COMMUNITY OR A DEME (260)	0.87 OF 15	8 2 9 13 XSQ= 2.80 PHI= 0.296 EP = 0.0605
214	IN ALL CASES ARE THOSE WHERE FIRST COUSIN MARRIAGE, IF PERMITTED, IS OTHER THAN UNILATERAL (144)	1.00 OF 10	214	DRIFT TOWARD BEING THOSE WHERE FIRST COUSIN MARRIAGE, IF PERMITTED, IS UNILATERAL (28)	0.50 OF 4	0 2 10 2 XSQ= 2.46 PHI= -0.420 EP = 0.0659
358	DRIFT TOWARD BEING THOSE WHERE ADOLESCENT PEER GROUPS ARE ABSENT IN A SETTING OF WORK, AND OF PUBLIC GATHERINGS, AND OF LEISURE (11) JKH	0.67 OF 3	358	IN ALL CASES ARE THOSE WHERE ADOLESCENT PEER GROUPS ARE PRESENT IN A SETTING OF WORK AND PUBLIC GATHERINGS AND LEISURE, OR OF PUBLIC GATHERINGS AND LEISURE, OR OF LEISURE ONLY (41) JKH	1.00 OF 7	1 7 2 0 XSQ= 2.41 PHI= -0.491 EP = 0.0667
403	DRIFT TOWARD BEING THOSE WHERE EXPLANATIONS OF ILLNESS OF AN ANAL NATURE ARE ABSENT (38) W-C	0.88 OF 8	403	DRIFT TOWARD BEING THOSE WHERE EXPLANATIONS OF ILLNESS OF AN ANAL NATURE ARE PRESENT (23) W-C	0.67 OF 6	1 4 7 2 XSQ= 2.34 PHI= -0.409 EP = 0.0909
431	IN ALL CASES ARE THOSE WHERE SUPERNATURAL SANCTIONS FOR MORALITY, HAVING AN EFFECT ON AN INDIVIDUAL'S AFTERLIFE, ARE ABSENT OR UNREPORTED (25) GES	1.00 OF 4	431	IN ALL CASES ARE THOSE WHERE SUPERNATURAL SANCTIONS FOR MORALITY, HAVING AN EFFECT ON AN INDIVIDUAL'S AFTER LIFE, ARE PRESENT (10) GES	1.00 OF 2	0 2 4 0 XSQ= 2.34 PHI= -0.625 EP = 0.0667

```
395/

475  TEND TC BE THCSE                  0.86 OF  14      475  TEND TO BE THOSE                 0.90 CF  10          2     9
     WHERE EXHIBITICNISTIC CANCING                            WHERE EXHIBITICNISTIC DANCING                          12     1
     IS NEGLIGIBLY EMPHASIZEC  (38) PES                       IS STRONGLY OR MODERATELY                         XSQ=   10.59
                                                              EMPHASIZED  (48) PES                               PHI=  -0.664
                                                                                                                 EP =  0.0005
```

396 CULTURES
WHERE THE STRENGTH OF MENSTRUAL TABOOS
IS HIGH (18) WAS

396 CULTURES
WHERE THE STRENGTH OF MENSTRUAL TABOOS
IS LOW (35) WAS

BACKGROUND ON PAGE 156

BOTH SUBJECT AND PREDICATE

18 IN LEFT COLUMN

ARAPESH	ASHANTI	BALINESE	CHEYENNE	FON	GANDA	GOND	KURTATCHI	KWAKIUTL	LAMBA
NAMA	OJIBWA	PAPAGO	SANPOIL	TIV	WARRAU	WOGEO	WOLEAIANS		

35 IN RIGHT COLUMN

AINU	ALORESE	ARAUCANIANS	AYMARA	AZANDE	CHENCHU	CHIR-APACHE	CHUKCHEE	COPR ESKIMO	GROS VENTRE
HANO	JIVARO	KAZAK	LAKHER	LEPCHA	LESU	MANUS	MAORI	MARQUESANS	MASAI
MURNGIN	NAVAHO	NYAKYUSA	ONTONG-JAVA	PUKAPUKA	RWALA	SAMOANS	SIRIONO	TALLENSI	TANALA
TARAHUMARA	THONGA	TIMBIRA	TROBRIAND	WITOTO					

347 EXCLUDED BECAUSE UNASCERTAINED

	Left column		Right column	Statistics
55	DRIFT MORE TOWARD BEING THOSE 0.90 OF 10 WHERE FOOD PRODUCTION IS BY SIMPLE AGRICULTURE, RATHER THAN BY INTENSIVE AGRICULTURE (101)	55	DRIFT LESS TOWARD BEING THOSE 0.53 OF 17 WHERE FOOD PRODUCTION IS BY SIMPLE AGRICULTURE, RATHER THAN BY INTENSIVE AGRICULTURE (101)	1 8 9 9 XSQ= 2.40 PHI= -0.298 EP = 0.0912
78	IN ALL CASES ARE THOSE 1.00 OF 5 WHERE THE WRITING SYSTEM IS ALPHABETIC-OR-PHONETIC, OR MNEMONIC, RATHER THAN BEING ABSENT (36) JMH	78	TILT TOWARD BEING THOSE 0.57 OF 14 WHERE A WRITING SYSTEM IS ABSENT, RATHER THAN BEING PRESENT IN EITHER ALPHABETIC-OR-PHONETIC FORM OR MNEMONIC FORM (18) JMH	5 6 0 8 XSQ= 2.87 PHI= 0.389 EP = 0.0445
80	TILT LESS TOWARD BEING THOSE 0.75 OF 12 WHERE NO CITY OR TOWN IS PRESENT (185)	80	IN ALL CASES ARE THOSE 1.00 OF 26 WHERE NO CITY OR TOWN IS PRESENT (185)	3 0 9 26 XSQ= 4.04 PHI= 0.326 EP = 0.0261
84	DRIFT LESS TOWARD BEING THOSE 0.75 OF 16 WHERE THE LEVEL OF POLITICAL INTEGRATION IS THE LITTLE STATE, THE MINIMAL STATE, THE AUTONOMOUS COMMUNITY, OR THE FAMILY (262) GPM	84	DRIFT MORE TOWARD BEING THOSE 0.97 OF 29 WHERE THE LEVEL OF POLITICAL INTEGRATION IS THE LITTLE STATE, THE MINIMAL STATE, THE AUTONOMOUS COMMUNITY, OR THE FAMILY (262) GPM	4 1 12 28 XSQ= 2.91 PHI= 0.254 XP = 0.0879

No.	Statement	Ratio	No.	Statement	Ratio	Statistics
138	DRIFT TCWARD BEING THCSE WHERE SUPERORDINATE JUSTICE IS PRESENT (22) BBW	0.89 OF 9	138	DRIFT TOWARD BEING THOSE WHERE SUPERORDINATE JUSTICE IS ABSENT (18) BBW	0.53 OF 15	8 7 1 8 XSQ= 2.67 PHI= 0.333 EP = 0.0803
26C	DRIFT TCWARD BEING THCSE WHERE THE AGE CF MALES AT MARRIAGE IS LESS THAN TWENTY (38) JKH	0.90 OF 10	260	DRIFT TOWARD BEING THOSE WHERE THE AGE OF MALES AT MARRIAGE IS TWENTY OR OVER (17) JKH	0.50 OF 24	9 12 1 12 XSQ= 3.24 PHI= 0.309 EP = 0.0514
311	TILT TCWARD BEING THCSE WHERE SEXUAL SCCIALIZATION ANXIETY IS HIGH (28) W-C	0.82 OF 11	311	TILT TOWARD BEING THOSE WHERE SEXUAL SOCIALIZATION ANXIETY IS LOW (23) W-C	0.58 OF 24	9 10 2 14 XSQ= 3.42 PHI= 0.312 EP = 0.0354
354	TILT TCWARD BEING THCSE WHERE THE CHILD'S INFERREC ANXIETY OVER PERFORMANCE CF CBECIENT BEHAVIOR IS HIGH (36) B-B-C	0.83 OF 12	354	TILT TOWARD BEING THOSE WHERE THE CHILD'S INFERRED ANXIETY OVER PERFORMANCE OF OBEDIENT BEHAVIOR IS LOW (37) B-B-C	0.64 OF 28	10 10 2 18 XSQ= 5.83 PHI= 0.382 EP = 0.0138
355	TILT TOWARD BEING THCSE WHERE THE CHILC'S INFERREC CONFLICT REGARDING CBECIENT BEFAVICR IS HIGH (35) B-B-C	0.75 OF 12	355	TILT TOWARD BEING THOSE WHERE THE CHILD'S INFERRED CCNFLICT REGARDING OBEDIENT BEHAVIOR IS LOW (38) B-B-C	0.61 OF 28	9 11 3 17 XSQ= 2.98 PHI= 0.273 EP = 0.0481
382	LEAN TCWARC BEING THCSE WHERE FEMALE INITIATICN RITES ARE PRESENT (38) JKB	0.91 OF 11	382	LEAN TOWARD BEING THOSE WHERE FEMALE INITIATICN RITES ARE ABSENT (27) JKB	0.67 OF 18	10 6 1 12 XSQ= 6.97 PHI= 0.490 EP = 0.0057
397	TILT TCWARD BEING THCSE WHERE SEX CISABILITY IS PRESENT (14) JKH	0.55 OF 11	397	TILT TOWARD BEING THOSE WHERE SEX DISABILITY IS ABSENT (42) JKH	0.83 OF 24	6 4 5 20 XSQ= 3.61 PHI= 0.321 EP = 0.0413
398	TILT TCWARD BEING THOSE WHERE THE INTENSITY CF SEX ANXIETY IS HIGH (16) WNS	0.89 OF 9	398	TILT TOWARD BEING THOSE WHERE THE INTENSITY OF SEX ANXIETY IS LOW (16) WNS	0.67 OF 21	8 7 1 14 XSQ= 5.71 PHI= 0.436 EP = 0.0142
399	TILT TCWARD BEING THOSE WHERE INTENSITY CF CASTRATION ANXIETY IS HIGH (23) WNS	0.80 OF 15	399	TILT TOWARD BEING THOSE WHERE INTENSITY OF CASTRATICN ANXIETY IS LOW (22) WNS	0.63 OF 30	12 11 3 19 XSQ= 5.88 PHI= 0.361 XP = 0.0153

```
405  TILT TOWARD BEING THOSE          0.67 OF  12      405  TILT TOWARD BEING THOSE          0.73 OF  26           4   19
     WHERE EXPLANATIONS OF ILLNESS                          WHERE EXPLANATIONS OF ILLNESS                          8    7
     OF A DEPENDENCE NATURE                                 OF A DEPENDENCE NATURE                          XSQ=    3.89
     ARE ABSENT  (27) W-C                                   ARE PRESENT  (34) W-C                           PHI=  -0.320
                                                                                                            EP =  0.0326
```

****

397 CULTURES WHERE SEX DISABILITY IS PRESENT (14) JKH	397 CULTURES WHERE SEX DISABILITY IS ABSENT (42) JKH

BACKGROUND ON PAGE 156 — BOTH SUBJECT AND PREDICATE

....

14 IN LEFT COLUMN

ABIPON	CHEYENNE	CHIR-APACHE	EGYPTIANS	GANDA	IRISH	KURTATCHI	LAMBA	MURNGIN	NYAKYUSA
ONTONG-JAVA	RIFFIANS	SANPOIL	TIV						

42 IN RIGHT COLUMN

ALORESE	ANDAMANESE	ARAUCANIANS	AYMARA	AZANDE	BALINESE	CAMAYURA	CARIB	CHUKCHEE	COPR ESKIMO
CREEK	DIERI	FON	IFUGAO	JAPANESE	JIVARO	JUKUN	KACHIN	KAZAK	KWAKIUTL
LAKHER	LAU	LEPCHA	LESU	MAORI	MASAI	MIAO	NUER	ORAON	PAPAGO
SAMOANS	SERBS	SIRIONO	TALLENSI	TANALA	THONGA	TIMBIRA	TROBRIAND	VENDA	WARRAU
YAKO	YAPESE								

344 EXCLUDED BECAUSE UNASCERTAINED

	Present (14)		Absent (42)	Statistics
4	DRIFT LESS TOWARD BEING THOSE 0.79 OF 14 LOCATED OUTSIDE OF THE CIRCUM-MEDITERRANEAN (355)	4	DRIFT MORE TOWARD BEING THOSE 0.98 OF 42 LOCATED OUTSIDE OF THE CIRCUM-MEDITERRANEAN (355)	3 1 11 41 XSQ= 3.23 PHI= 0.240 XP = 0.0723
80	DRIFT LESS TOWARD BEING THOSE 0.56 OF 9 WHERE NO CITY OR TOWN IS PRESENT (185)	80	DRIFT MORE TOWARD BEING THOSE 0.87 OF 31 WHERE NO CITY OR TOWN IS PRESENT (185)	4 4 5 27 XSQ= 2.59 PHI= 0.254 EP = 0.0594
131	DRIFT LESS TOWARD BEING THOSE 0.63 OF 8 WHERE THE CONSTRUCTION OF PERMANENT HOUSES OR THE ERECTION OF TEMPORARY DWELLINGS IS MAINLY DONE BY MALES (136)	131	DRIFT MORE TOWARD BEING THOSE 0.93 OF 27 WHERE THE CONSTRUCTION OF PERMANENT HOUSES OR THE ERECTION OF TEMPORARY DWELLINGS IS MAINLY DONE BY MALES (136)	5 25 3 2 XSQ= 2.44 PHI= -0.264 EP = 0.0665
178	IN ALL CASES ARE THOSE 1.00 OF 14 WHERE THE COMMUNITY IS OTHER THAN SEGMENTED ON A CLAN BASIS AND NON-EXOGAMOUS (295)	178	TILT LESS TOWARD BEING THOSE 0.64 OF 42 WHERE THE COMMUNITY IS OTHER THAN SEGMENTED ON A CLAN BASIS AND NON-EXOGAMOUS (295)	0 15 14 27 XSQ= 5.13 PHI= -0.303 XP = 0.0235

259	DRIFT TCWARD BEING THCSE WHERE THE SEVERITY CF MOTHER-IN-LAW AVCIDANCE IS HICH (26) WNS	0.88 OF 8	259	DRIFT TOWARD BEING THOSE WHERE THE SEVERITY OF MOTHER-IN-LAW AVOIDANCE IS LCW (20) WNS	0.56 OF 16	 XSQ= PHI= EP =	7 1 2.59 0.329 0.0791	7 9
331	IN ALL CASES ARE THOSE WHERE THE AGE AT BEGINNING OF INDEPENDENCE TRAINING IS 3.8 YEARS CR HIGHER (16) W-C	1.00 OF 3	331	DRIFT TOWARD BEING THOSE WHERE THE AGE AT BEGINNING OF INDEPENDENCE TRAINING IS LOWER THAN 3.8 YEARS (21) W-C	0.67 OF 15	 XSQ= PHI= EP =	3 0 2.20 0.350 0.0686	5 10
351	DRIFT TCWARD BEING THCSE WHERE THE CHILD'S INFERREC CONFLICT REGARDING ACHIEVEMENT BEHAVIOR IS HIGH (26) B-B-C	0.83 OF 6	351	DRIFT TOWARD BEING THOSE WHERE THE CHILD'S INFERRED CONFLICT REGARDING ACHIEVEMENT BEHAVICR IS LOW (34) B-B-C	0.67 OF 21	 XSQ= PHI= EP =	5 1 2.92 0.329 0.0602	7 14
356	DRIFT TCWARD BEING THCSE WHERE NEITHER ADCLESCENT PEER GROUPS NCR PAIRS ARE PRESENT IN A SETTING CF CCURTSHIP (22) JKH	0.67 OF 12	356	DRIFT TOWARD BEING THOSE WHERE ADOLESCENT PEER GRCUPS OR PAIRS ARE PRESENT IN A SETTING OF COURTSHIP (29) JKH	0.66 OF 38	 XSQ= PHI= XP =	4 8 2.72 -0.233 0.0989	25 13
360	DRIFT TCWARD BEING THCSE WHERE ADCLESCENT PEER GROUPS ARE PRESENT CNLY IN A SETTING CF LEISURE, OR ELSE ARE ABSENT (23) JKH	0.90 OF 10	360	DRIFT TOWARD BEING THOSE WHERE ADOLESCENT PEER GRCUPS ARE PRESENT IN A SETTING OF WORK AND PUBLIC GATHERINGS AND LEISURE, OR AT LEAST OF PUBLIC GATHERINGS AND LEISURE (14) JKH	0.50 OF 26	 XSQ= PHI= EP =	1 9 3.32 -0.304 0.0536	13 13
366	DRIFT TCWARD BEING THCSE WHERE DISSCCIATICN CF THE SEXES AT ADCLESCENCE IS HIGH (16) JKH	0.50 OF 14	366	DRIFT TOWARD BEING THCSE WHERE DISSOCIATICN OF THE SEXES AT ADOLESCENCE IS MEDIUM OR LCW (41) JKH	0.79 OF 42	 XSQ= PHI= XP =	7 7 2.92 0.228 0.0877	9 33
382	TILT TCWARD BEING THCSE WHERE FEMALE INITIATICN RITES ARE PRESENT (38) JKB	0.86 OF 7	382	TILT TOWARD BEING THCSE WHERE FEMALE INITIATION RITES ARE ABSENT (27) JKB	0.65 OF 20	 XSQ= PHI= EP =	6 1 3.50 0.360 0.0329	7 13
386	IN ALL CASES ARE THCSE WHERE SEXUAL EXPRESSICN BY THE YOUNG IS RESTRICTED CR SEMI-RESTRICTED (46) F-B	1.00 OF 5	386	DRIFT TOWARD BEING THCSE WHERE SEXUAL EXPRESSICN BY THE YOUNG IS PERMITTED (40) F-B	0.50 OF 26	 XSQ= PHI= EP =	5 0 2.50 0.284 0.0580	13 13
390	TILT TCWARD BEING THCSE WHERE PREMARITAL SEX RELATIONS ARE STRCNGLY PUNISHED AND IN FACT RARE (47) JTW,EA	0.50 OF 10	390	TILT TOWARD BEING THOSE WHERE PREMARITAL SEX RELATICNS ARE WEAKLY PUNISHED AND IN FACT NOT RARE OR PUNISHED ONLY IF PREGNANCY RESULTS, OR FREELY PERMITTED (132) JTW,EA	0.86 OF 29	 XSQ= PHI= EP =	5 5 3.64 0.306 0.0321	4 25

391	LEAN TOWARD BEING THOSE WHERE PREMARITAL SEX RELATIONS ARE STRONGLY PUNISHED AND IN FACT RARE, OR WEAKLY PUNISHED AND IN FACT NOT RARE (89) JTW,EA	0.80 OF 10	391	LEAN TOWARD BEING THOSE WHERE PREMARITAL SEX RELATIONS ARE PUNISHED ONLY IF PREGNANCY RESULTS, OR FREELY PERMITTED (90) JTW,EA	0.76 OF 29	8 7 2 22 XSQ= 7.59 PHI= 0.441 EP = 0.0030
392	IN ALL CASES ARE THOSE WHERE PREMARITAL SEX RELATIONS ARE STRONGLY PUNISHED AND IN FACT RARE, OR WEAKLY PUNISHED AND IN FACT NOT RARE, OR PUNISHED ONLY IF PREGNANCY RESULTS (112) JTW,EA	1.00 OF 10	392	LEAN LESS TOWARD BEING THOSE WHERE PREMARITAL SEX RELATIONS ARE STRONGLY PUNISHED AND IN FACT RARE, OR WEAKLY PUNISHED AND IN FACT NOT RARE, OR PUNISHED ONLY IF PREGNANCY RESULTS (112) JTW,EA	0.52 OF 29	10 15 0 14 XSQ= 5.58 PHI= 0.378 EP = 0.0066
396	TILT TOWARD BEING THOSE WHERE THE STRENGTH OF MENSTRUAL TABOOS IS HIGH (18) WNS	0.60 OF 10	396	TILT TOWARD BEING THOSE WHERE THE STRENGTH OF MENSTRUAL TABOOS IS LOW (35) WNS	0.80 OF 25	6 5 4 20 XSQ= 3.61 PHI= 0.321 EP = 0.0413
399	DRIFT TOWARD BEING THOSE WHERE INTENSITY OF CASTRATION ANXIETY IS HIGH (23) WNS	0.80 OF 10	399	DRIFT TOWARD BEING THOSE WHERE INTENSITY OF CASTRATION ANXIETY IS LOW (22) WNS	0.64 OF 22	8 8 2 14 XSQ= 3.64 PHI= 0.337 EP = 0.0538
420	DRIFT TOWARD BEING THOSE WHERE BELLICOSITY IS EXTREME (41) PES	0.80 OF 10	420	DRIFT TOWARD BEING THOSE WHERE BELLICOSITY IS MODERATE OR NEGLIGIBLE (46) PES	0.53 OF 30	8 14 2 16 XSQ= 2.15 PHI= 0.232 EP = 0.0823
441	DRIFT TOWARD BEING THOSE WHERE FEAR OF HUMAN BEINGS IS HIGH (29) W-C	0.78 OF 9	441	DRIFT TOWARD BEING THOSE WHERE FEAR OF HUMAN BEINGS IS LOW (32) W-C	0.64 OF 22	7 8 2 14 XSQ= 2.88 PHI= 0.305 EP = 0.0538
446	IN ALL CASES ARE THOSE WHERE WITCHCRAFT IS SIGNIFICANTLY PRESENT (14) GES	1.00 OF 3	446	DRIFT TOWARD BEING THOSE WHERE WITCHCRAFT IS MODERATELY PRESENT OR ABSENT (24) GES	0.70 OF 10	3 3 0 7 XSQ= 2.17 PHI= 0.408 EP = 0.0699

398 CULTURES WHERE THE INTENSITY OF SEX ANXIETY IS HIGH (16) WNS

398 CULTURES WHERE THE INTENSITY OF SEX ANXIETY IS LOW (16) WNS

BACKGROUND ON PAGE 156

BOTH SUBJECT AND PREDICATE

16 IN LEFT COLUMN

ALORESE, ARAPESH, ASHANTI, AZANDE, CHAGGA, CHIR-APACHE, FON, KURTATCHI, KWAKIUTL, LAMBA, LESU, MANUS, NAVAHO, PAPAGO, SANPOIL, WITOTO

16 IN RIGHT COLUMN

AINU, BALINESE, CHENCHU, COPR ESKIMO, HANO, JIVARO, LAKHER, LEPCHA, MARQUESANS, MASAI, MURNGIN, SIRIONO, TANALA, THONGA, TROBRIAND, YAGUA

368 EXCLUDED BECAUSE UNASCERTAINED

	Left column			Right column		Statistics
5	IN ALL CASES ARE THOSE LOCATED OUTSIDE OF EAST EURASIA (330)	1.00 OF 16	5	TILT LESS TOWARD BEING THOSE LOCATED OUTSIDE OF EAST EURASIA (330)	0.69 OF 16	0 5 16 11 XSQ= 3.79 PHI= -0.344 EP = 0.0434
63	DRIFT TOWARD BEING THOSE WHERE HUSBANDRY, IF PRESENT, IS PRINCIPALLY IN THE FORM OF PIGS, SHEEP, OR GOATS, RATHER THAN BOVINE, EQUINE, CAMEL-LIKE, OR DEER-LIKE ANIMALS (74)	0.80 OF 10	63	DRIFT TOWARD BEING THOSE WHERE HUSBANDRY, IF PRESENT, IS PRINCIPALLY IN THE FORM OF BOVINE, EQUINE, CAMEL-LIKE, OR DEER-LIKE ANIMALS, RATHER THAN PIGS, SHEEP, OR GOATS (152)	0.70 OF 10	2 7 8 3 XSQ= 3.23 PHI= -0.402 EP = 0.0698
74	TILT TOWARD BEING THOSE WHERE POTTERY IS PRESENT (145)	0.85 OF 13	74	TILT TOWARD BEING THOSE WHERE POTTERY IS ABSENT (93)	0.57 OF 14	11 6 2 8 XSQ= 3.41 PHI= 0.355 EP = 0.0461
78	IN ALL CASES ARE THOSE WHERE THE WRITING SYSTEM IS ALPHABETIC-OR-PHONETIC, OR MNEMONIC, RATHER THAN BEING ABSENT (36) JMH	1.00 OF 4	78	TILT TOWARD BEING THOSE WHERE A WRITING SYSTEM IS ABSENT, RATHER THAN BEING PRESENT IN EITHER ALPHABETIC-OR-PHONETIC FORM OR MNEMONIC FORM (18) JMH	0.80 OF 5	4 1 0 4 XSQ= 2.98 PHI= 0.575 EP = 0.0476
81	DRIFT TOWARD BEING THOSE WHERE A CITY OR TOWN IS PRESENT, OR THE AVERAGE COMMUNITY SIZE IS 200 OR GREATER (89)	0.50 OF 10	81	DRIFT TOWARD BEING THOSE WHERE NO CITY OR TOWN IS PRESENT, AND THE AVERAGE COMMUNITY SIZE IS SMALLER THAN 200 (135)	0.92 OF 12	5 1 5 11 XSQ= 2.90 PHI= 0.363 EP = 0.0557

82	IN ALL CASES ARE THOSE WHERE A CITY OR TOWN IS PRESENT, OR THE AVERAGE COMMUNITY SIZE IS FIFTY OR GREATER (178)	1.00 OF	10	82	TILT TOWARD BEING THOSE WHERE NO CITY OR TOWN IS PRESENT, AND THE AVERAGE COMMUNITY SIZE IS SMALLER THAN FIFTY (46)	0.50 OF	12	10 6 0 6 XSQ= 4.59 PHI= 0.457 EP = 0.0152
118	DRIFT TOWARD BEING THOSE WHERE THE PERCENTAGE OF OCCUPATIONS THAT ARE SPECIALIZED IS HIGH OR MEDIUM (24) WME	0.80 OF	5	118	DRIFT TOWARD BEING THOSE WHERE THE PERCENTAGE OF OCCUPATIONS THAT ARE SPECIALIZED IS LOW (25) WME	0.83 OF	6	4 1 1 5 XSQ= 2.23 PHI= 0.450 EP = 0.0801
148	DRIFT TOWARD BEING THOSE WHERE THE INCIDENCE OF PERSONAL CRIME IS HIGH (12) B-B-C	0.64 OF	11	148	DRIFT TOWARD BEING THOSE WHERE THE INCIDENCE OF PERSONAL CRIME IS LOW (21) B-B-C	0.88 OF	8	7 1 4 7 XSQ= 3.09 PHI= 0.403 EP = 0.0587
149	TILT TOWARD BEING THOSE WHERE THE INCIDENCE OF THEFT IS HIGH (18) B-B-C	0.64 OF	11	149	TILT TOWARD BEING THOSE WHERE THE INCIDENCE OF THEFT IS LOW (19) B-B-C	0.90 OF	10	7 1 4 9 XSQ= 4.32 PHI= 0.453 EP = 0.0237
152	IN ALL CASES ARE THOSE WHERE THE DIFFERENTIATION OF THE JURIDICAL AGENCY FROM THE MEDICAL AGENCY IS HIGH (10) MJ	1.00 OF	2	152	IN ALL CASES ARE THOSE WHERE THE DIFFERENTIATION OF THE JURIDICAL AGENCY FROM THE MEDICAL AGENCY IS LOW (10) MJ	1.00 OF	4	2 0 0 4 XSQ= 2.34 PHI= 0.625 EP = 0.0667
213	DRIFT TOWARD BEING THOSE WHERE FIRST COUSIN MARRIAGE IS NOT PERMITTED (198)	0.75 OF	16	213	DRIFT TOWARD BEING THOSE WHERE FIRST COUSIN MARRIAGE IS PERMITTED (172)	0.63 OF	16	4 10 12 6 XSQ= 3.17 PHI= -0.315 EP = 0.0732
242	IN ALL CASES ARE THOSE WHERE MARRIAGE IS COMMONLY OR OCCASIONALLY POLYGYNOUS, RATHER THAN MONOGAMOUS (314)	1.00 OF	16	242	TILT LESS TOWARD BEING THOSE WHERE MARRIAGE IS COMMONLY OR OCCASIONALLY POLYGYNOUS, RATHER THAN MONOGAMOUS (314)	0.73 OF	15	16 11 0 4 XSQ= 2.81 PHI= 0.301 EP = 0.0434
256	DRIFT TOWARD BEING THOSE WHERE GRANDPARENT AND GRANDCHILD ARE FRIENDLY EQUALS (25) DA	0.86 OF	7	256	IN ALL CASES ARE THOSE WHERE GRANDPARENT AND GRANDCHILD ARE NOT FRIENDLY EQUALS (8) DA	1.00 OF	2	6 0 1 2 XSQ= 2.01 PHI= 0.472 EP = 0.0833
305	DRIFT TOWARD BEING THOSE WHERE THE EARLY SEXUAL SATISFACTION POTENTIAL IS LOW (24) W-C	0.56 OF	16	305	DRIFT TOWARD BEING THOSE WHERE THE EARLY SEXUAL SATISFACTION POTENTIAL IS HIGH (27) W-C	0.79 OF	14	7 11 9 3 XSQ= 2.46 PHI= -0.286 EP = 0.0717

308	LEAN TOWARD BEING THOSE 0.86 OF 14 WHERE AVERAGE SOCIALIZATION ANXIETY IS HIGH (22) W-C	308	LEAN TOWARD BEING THOSE 0.75 OF 12 WHERE AVERAGE SOCIALIZATION ANXIETY IS LOW (18) W-C	12 3 2 9 XSQ= 7.43 PHI= 0.535 EP = 0.0043
309	DRIFT TOWARD BEING THOSE 0.69 OF 16 WHERE ORAL SOCIALIZATION ANXIETY IS HIGH (26) W-C	309	DRIFT TOWARD BEING THOSE 0.67 OF 15 WHERE ORAL SOCIALIZATION ANXIETY IS LOW (27) W-C	11 5 5 10 XSQ= 2.60 PHI= 0.290 EP = 0.0756
311	TEND TO BE THOSE 0.81 OF 16 WHERE SEXUAL SOCIALIZATION ANXIETY IS HIGH (28) W-C	311	TEND TO BE THOSE 0.86 OF 14 WHERE SEXUAL SOCIALIZATION ANXIETY IS LOW (23) W-C	13 2 3 12 XSQ= 10.85 PHI= 0.601 EP = 0.0007
334	DRIFT TOWARD BEING THOSE 0.71 OF 14 WHERE THE INDULGENCE OF THE CHILD IS LOW (38) B-B-C	334	DRIFT TOWARD BEING THOSE 0.67 OF 15 WHERE THE INDULGENCE OF THE CHILD IS HIGH (40) B-B-C	4 10 10 5 XSQ= 2.82 PHI= -0.312 EP = 0.0656
348	DRIFT TOWARD BEING THOSE 0.73 OF 11 WHERE THE TOTAL POSITIVE PRESSURE TOWARD DEVELOPING ACHIEVEMENT BEHAVIOR IN THE CHILD IS HIGH (32) B-B-C	348	DRIFT TOWARD BEING THOSE 0.73 OF 11 WHERE THE TOTAL POSITIVE PRESSURE TOWARD DEVELOPING ACHIEVEMENT BEHAVIOR IN THE CHILD IS LOW (31) B-B-C	8 3 3 8 XSQ= 2.91 PHI= 0.364 EP = 0.0861
355	TILT TOWARD BEING THOSE 0.67 OF 12 WHERE THE CHILD'S INFERRED CONFLICT REGARDING OBEDIENT BEHAVIOR IS HIGH (35) B-B-C	355	TILT TOWARD BEING THOSE 0.80 OF 15 WHERE THE CHILD'S INFERRED CONFLICT REGARDING OBEDIENT BEHAVIOR IS LOW (38) B-B-C	8 3 4 12 XSQ= 4.24 PHI= 0.396 EP = 0.0220
358	IN ALL CASES ARE THOSE 1.00 OF 9 WHERE ADOLESCENT PEER GROUPS ARE PRESENT IN A SETTING OF WORK AND PUBLIC GATHERINGS AND LEISURE, OR OF PUBLIC GATHERINGS AND LEISURE, OR OF LEISURE ONLY (41) JKH	358	TILT TOWARD BEING THOSE 0.50 OF 10 WHERE ADOLESCENT PEER GROUPS ARE ABSENT IN A SETTING OF WORK, AND OF PUBLIC GATHERINGS, AND OF LEISURE (11) JKH	9 5 0 5 XSQ= 3.80 PHI= 0.447 EP = 0.0325
386	DRIFT TOWARD BEING THOSE 0.83 OF 12 WHERE SEXUAL EXPRESSION BY THE YOUNG IS RESTRICTED OR SEMI-RESTRICTED (46) F-B	386	DRIFT TOWARD BEING THOSE 0.58 OF 12 WHERE SEXUAL EXPRESSION BY THE YOUNG IS PERMITTED (40) F-B	10 5 2 7 XSQ= 2.84 PHI= 0.344 EP = 0.0894
391	TEND TO BE THOSE 0.83 OF 12 WHERE PREMARITAL SEX RELATIONS ARE STRONGLY PUNISHED AND IN FACT RARE, OR WEAKLY PUNISHED AND IN FACT NOT RARE (89) JTW,EA	391	IN ALL CASES ARE THOSE 1.00 OF 13 WHERE PREMARITAL SEX RELATIONS ARE PUNISHED ONLY IF PREGNANCY RESULTS, OR FREELY PERMITTED (90) JTW,EA	10 0 2 13 XSQ= 14.75 PHI= 0.768 EP = 0.0000

No.	Left	Prop.	No.	Right	Prop.	Statistics
392	IN ALL CASES ARE THCSE WHERE PREMARITAL SEX RELATIONS ARE STRCNGLY PUNISHED AND IN FACT RARE, OR WEAKLY PUNISHED ANC IN FACT NCT RARE, OR PUNISHED CNLY IF PREGNANCY RESULTS (112) JTW,EA	1.00 OF 12	392	TEND TO BE THOSE WHERE PREMARITAL SEX RELATICNS ARE FREELY PERMITTED (67) JTW,EA	0.85 OF 13	12 2 / 0 11 / XSQ= 14.86 / PHI= 0.771 / EP = 0.0000
393	TILT TCWARD BEING THCSE WHERE EXTRAMARITAL CCITUS IS PUNISHED, RATHER THAN PERMITTED (43) F-B	0.80 OF 10	393	TILT TOWARD BEING THCSE WHERE EXTRAMARITAL COITUS IS PERMITTED, RATHER THAN PUNISHED (41) F-B	0.71 CF 14	8 4 / 2 10 / XSQ= 4.29 / PHI= 0.423 / EP = 0.0361
396	TILT TCWARD BEING THOSE WHERE THE STRENGTH OF MENSTRUAL TABOOS IS HIGH (18) WNS	0.53 OF 15	396	TILT TOWARD BEING THOSE WHERE THE STRENGTH OF MENSTRUAL TABOOS IS LOW (35) WNS	0.93 OF 15	8 1 / 7 14 / XSQ= 5.71 / PHI= 0.436 / EP = 0.0142
399	LEAN TOWARC BEING THCSE WHERE INTENSITY CF CASTRATION ANXIETY IS HIGH (23) WNS	0.79 OF 14	399	LEAN TOWARD BEING THCSE WHERE INTENSITY OF CASTRATICN ANXIETY IS LOW (22) WNS	0.79 CF 14	11 3 / 3 11 / XSQ= 7.00 / PHI= 0.500 / EP = 0.0070
404	TEND TO BE THOSE WHERE EXPLANATICNS CF ILLNESS CF A SEXUAL NATURE ARE PRESENT (19) W-C	0.69 OF 16	404	TEND TO BE THOSE WHERE EXPLANATICNS OF ILLNESS OF A SEXUAL NATURE ARE ABSENT (42) W-C	0.94 CF 16	11 1 / 5 15 / XSQ= 10.80 / PHI= 0.581 / EP = 0.0006
439	DRIFT TCWARD BEING THCSE WHERE FEAR OF GHCSTS IS HIGH (30) W-C	0.69 OF 16	439	DRIFT TOWARD BEING THCSE WHERE FEAR OF GHOSTS IS LOW (31) W-C	0.69 OF 16	11 5 / 5 11 / XSQ= 3.13 / PHI= 0.312 / EP = 0.0756
445	IN ALL CASES ARE THCSE WHERE SCRCERY IS IMPCRTANT (26) BBW,CH	1.00 OF 5	445	TILT TOWARD BEING THOSE WHERE SORCERY IS UNIMPORTANT (23) BBW,DH	0.60 OF 10	5 4 / 0 6 / XSQ= 2.81 / PHI= 0.433 / EP = 0.0440
447	TILT TCWARC BEING THCSE WHERE LOVE MAGIC IS PRESENT (20) S-R	0.92 OF 12	447	TILT TOWARD BEING THOSE WHERE LOVE MAGIC IS ABSENT (13) S-R	0.67 CF 9	11 3 / 1 6 / XSQ= 5.47 / PHI= 0.510 / EP = 0.0158
459	DRIFT TCWARD BEING THCSE WHERE GAMES, IF PRESENT, INCLUDE GAMES CF CHANCE (82) R-A-B,EA	0.57 OF 14	459	DRIFT TOWARD BEING THOSE WHERE GAMES, IF PRESENT, DO NOT INCLUDE GAMES OF CHANCE (89) R-A-B,EA	0.82 CF 11	8 2 / 6 9 / XSQ= 2.44 / PHI= 0.313 / EP = 0.0992

399 CULTURES
WHERE INTENSITY OF CASTRATION ANXIETY
IS HIGH (23) WNS

399 CULTURES
WHERE INTENSITY OF CASTRATION ANXIETY
IS LOW (22) WNS

BACKGROUND ON PAGE 156

BOTH SUBJECT AND PREDICATE

23 IN LEFT COLUMN

AINU	ALORESE	ARAPESH	ASHANTI	AYMARA	AZANDE	CHEYENNE	CHIR-APACHE	CHUKCHEE	FON
GANDA	JIVARO	KURTATCHI	KWAKIUTL	LAMBA	MANUS	NYAKYUSA	OJIBWA	RWALA	SANPOIL
THONGA	TIV	WOLEAIANS							

22 IN RIGHT COLUMN

ARAUCANIANS	BALINESE	CHENCHU	HANO	LAKHER	LEPCHA	LESU	MAORI	MARQUESANS	MASAI
MURNGIN	NAVAHO	ONTONG-JAVA	PAPAGO	PUKAPUKA	SAMOANS	SIRIONO	TALLENSI	TANALA	TIMBIRA
TROBRIAND	WOGEO								

355 EXCLUDED BECAUSE UNASCERTAINED

	Left column				Right column			
3	DRIFT LESS TOWARD BEING THOSE LOCATED OUTSIDE OF AFRICA (320)	0.65 OF	23	3	DRIFT MORE TOWARD BEING THOSE LOCATED OUTSIDE OF AFRICA (320)	0.91 OF	22	8 2 15 20 XSQ= 2.94 PHI= 0.255 XP = 0.0866
13	DRIFT LESS TOWARD BEING THOSE WHERE THE LATITUDE IS LESS THAN FORTY DEGREES (329)	0.78 OF	23	13	IN ALL CASES ARE THOSE WHERE THE LATITUDE IS LESS THAN FORTY DEGREES (329)	1.00 OF	22	5 0 18 22 XSQ= 3.40 PHI= 0.275 XP = 0.0650
47	IN ALL CASES ARE THOSE WHERE, IF SETTLEMENTS ARE NON-FIXED, MOVEMENT IS NOMADIC, RATHER THAN NON-NOMADIC (72)	1.00 OF	6	47	DRIFT TOWARD BEING THOSE WHERE, IF SETTLEMENTS ARE NON-FIXED, MOVEMENT IS NON-NOMADIC, RATHER THAN NOMADIC (38)	0.57 OF	7	6 3 0 4 XSQ= 2.63 PHI= 0.450 EP = 0.0699
56	DRIFT MORE TOWARD BEING THOSE WHERE FOOD PRODUCTION IS BY SIMPLE AGRICULTURE, RATHER THAN BY INCIPIENT FOOD PRODUCTION (101)	0.92 OF	12	56	DRIFT LESS TOWARD BEING THOSE WHERE FOOD PRODUCTION IS BY SIMPLE AGRICULTURE, RATHER THAN BY INCIPIENT FOOD PRODUCTION (101)	0.55 OF	11	11 6 1 5 XSQ= 2.40 PHI= 0.323 EP = 0.0686

74	LEAN TOWARD BEING THOSE WHERE POTTERY IS PRESENT (145)	0.80 OF 20	74	LEAN TOWARD BEING THOSE WHERE POTTERY IS ABSENT (93)	0.65 OF 20	16 7 4 13 XSQ= 6.55 PHI= 0.405 EP = 0.0095
85	DRIFT LESS TOWARD BEING THOSE WHERE THE LEVEL OF POLITICAL INTEGRATION IS THE MINIMAL STATE, THE AUTONOMOUS COMMUNITY, OR THE FAMILY (234) GPM	0.68 OF 19	85	DRIFT MORE TOWARD BEING THOSE WHERE THE LEVEL OF POLITICAL INTEGRATION IS THE MINIMAL STATE, THE AUTONOMOUS COMMUNITY, OR THE FAMILY (234) GPM	0.95 OF 19	6 1 13 18 XSQ= 2.80 PHI= 0.272 EP = 0.0897
91	TILT TOWARD BEING THOSE WHERE SOCIETAL COMPLEXITY IS LOW (22) F-W	0.88 OF 8	91	TILT TOWARD BEING THOSE WHERE SOCIETAL COMPLEXITY IS HIGH (18) F-W	0.71 OF 7	1 5 7 2 XSQ= 3.23 PHI= -0.464 EP = 0.0406
96	DRIFT TOWARD BEING THOSE WHERE THE HIERARCHY OF NATIONAL JURISDICTION HAS FOUR, THREE, TWO OR ONE LEVEL (174) GES,EA	0.68 OF 22	96	DRIFT TOWARD BEING THOSE WHERE THE HIERARCHY OF NATIONAL JURISDICTION HAS NO LEVELS (156) GES,EA	0.62 OF 21	15 8 7 13 XSQ= 2.79 PHI= 0.255 XP = 0.0946
97	TILT MORE TOWARD BEING THOSE WHERE THE HIERARCHY OF LOCAL JURISDICTION HAS THREE OR TWO LEVELS (273) GES,EA	0.91 OF 23	97	TILT LESS TOWARD BEING THOSE WHERE THE HIERARCHY OF LOCAL JURISDICTION HAS THREE OR TWO LEVELS (273) GES,EA	0.62 OF 21	2 8 21 13 XSQ= 3.86 PHI= -0.296 XP = 0.0495
128	DRIFT TOWARD BEING THOSE WHERE, IF SUBSISTENCE IS PRIMARILY BY AGRICULTURE, THE WORK IS MAINLY DONE BY FEMALES (37)	0.88 OF 8	128	DRIFT TOWARD BEING THOSE WHERE, IF SUBSISTENCE IS PRIMARILY BY AGRICULTURE, THE WORK IS MAINLY DONE BY MALES (40)	0.75 OF 4	1 3 7 1 XSQ= 2.30 PHI= -0.437 EP = 0.0667
148	DRIFT TOWARD BEING THOSE WHERE THE INCIDENCE OF PERSONAL CRIME IS HIGH (12) B-B-C	0.58 OF 12	148	DRIFT TOWARD BEING THOSE WHERE THE INCIDENCE OF PERSONAL CRIME IS LOW (21) B-B-C	0.82 OF 11	7 2 5 9 XSQ= 2.38 PHI= 0.322 EP = 0.0894
178	DRIFT MORE TOWARD BEING THOSE WHERE THE COMMUNITY IS OTHER THAN SEGMENTED ON A CLAN BASIS AND NON-EXOGAMOUS (295)	0.83 OF 23	178	DRIFT LESS TOWARD BEING THOSE WHERE THE COMMUNITY IS OTHER THAN SEGMENTED ON A CLAN BASIS AND NON-EXOGAMOUS (295)	0.55 OF 22	4 10 19 12 XSQ= 2.93 PHI= -0.255 XP = 0.0872
187	DRIFT MORE TOWARD BEING THOSE WHERE THE KIN GROUP IS OTHER THAN EXCLUSIVELY MATRILINEAL (344)	0.95 OF 22	187	DRIFT LESS TOWARD BEING THOSE WHERE THE KIN GROUP IS OTHER THAN EXCLUSIVELY MATRILINEAL (344)	0.73 OF 22	1 6 21 16 XSQ= 2.72 PHI= -0.249 XP = 0.0992

214	IN ALL CASES ARE THOSE WHERE FIRST COUSIN MARRIAGE, IF PERMITTED, IS OTHER THAN UNILATERAL (144)	1.00 OF 8	214	DRIFT LESS TOWARD BEING THOSE WHERE FIRST COUSIN MARRIAGE, IF PERMITTED, IS OTHER THAN UNILATERAL (144)	0.56 OF 9	0 4 8 5 XSQ= 2.51 PHI= -0.384 EP = 0.0824
224	DRIFT TOWARD BEING THOSE WHERE COUSIN MARRIAGE IS PREFERENTIALLY OR PERMISSIVELY SYMMETRICAL, RATHER THAN EITHER PATRI- OR MATRILATERAL (106)	0.75 OF 8	224	DRIFT TOWARD BEING THOSE WHERE COUSIN MARRIAGE IS PREFERENTIALLY OR PERMISSIVELY EITHER PATRI- OR MATRILATERAL, RATHER THAN SYMMETRICAL (66)	0.78 OF 9	2 7 6 2 XSQ= 2.85 PHI= -0.410 EP = 0.0567
296	DRIFT TOWARD BEING THOSE WHERE INFANTICIDE IS PRESENT (18) BCA	0.73 OF 11	296	DRIFT TOWARD BEING THOSE WHERE INFANTICIDE IS ABSENT OR INFERRED ABSENT (15) BCA	0.69 OF 13	8 4 3 9 XSQ= 2.69 PHI= 0.334 EP = 0.0995
308	TILT TOWARD BEING THOSE WHERE AVERAGE SOCIALIZATION ANXIETY IS HIGH (22) W-C	0.85 OF 13	308	TILT TOWARD BEING THOSE WHERE AVERAGE SOCIALIZATION ANXIETY IS LOW (18) W-C	0.59 OF 17	11 7 2 10 XSQ= 4.12 PHI= 0.371 EP = 0.0256
311	TILT TOWARD BEING THOSE WHERE SEXUAL SOCIALIZATION ANXIETY IS HIGH (28) W-C	0.80 OF 15	311	TILT TOWARD BEING THOSE WHERE SEXUAL SOCIALIZATION ANXIETY IS LOW (23) W-C	0.63 OF 19	12 7 3 12 XSQ= 4.70 PHI= 0.372 EP = 0.0171
313	TILT TOWARD BEING THOSE WHERE AGGRESSION SOCIALIZATION ANXIETY IS HIGH (26) W-C	0.69 OF 16	313	TILT TOWARD BEING THOSE WHERE AGGRESSION SOCIALIZATION ANXIETY IS LOW (28) W-C	0.68 OF 19	11 6 5 13 XSQ= 3.43 PHI= 0.313 EP = 0.0437
314	TILT LESS TOWARD BEING THOSE WHERE THE INCIDENCE OF MOTHER-CHILD HOUSEHOLDS IS LOW (61) W-C,S	0.53 OF 19	314	TILT MORE TOWARD BEING THOSE WHERE THE INCIDENCE OF MOTHER-CHILD HOUSEHOLDS IS LOW (61) W-D,S	0.89 OF 18	9 2 10 16 XSQ= 4.21 PHI= 0.337 EP = 0.0293
316	TILT TOWARD BEING THOSE WHERE EXCLUSIVE MOTHER-SON SLEEPING ARRANGEMENTS LAST ONE YEAR OR LONGER. (19) W-K-A	0.71 OF 14	316	TILT TOWARD BEING THOSE WHERE EXCLUSIVE MOTHER-SON SLEEPING ARRANGEMENTS LAST LESS THAN ONE YEAR (25) W-K-A	0.75 OF 16	10 4 4 12 XSQ= 4.74 PHI= 0.397 EP = 0.0261
334	LEAN TOWARD BEING THOSE WHERE THE INDULGENCE OF THE CHILD IS LOW (38) B-B-C	0.71 OF 21	334	LEAN TOWARD BEING THOSE WHERE THE INDULGENCE OF THE CHILD IS HIGH (40) B-B-C	0.73 OF 22	6 16 15 6 XSQ= 6.71 PHI= -0.395 XP = 0.0096

```
337 DRIFT TOWARD BEING THOSE        0.75 OF  20    337 DRIFT TOWARD BEING THOSE        0.60 OF  20           15    8
    WHERE THE CHILD'S INFERRED ANXIETY OVER            WHERE THE CHILD'S INFERRED ANXIETY OVER                5   12
    NON-PERFORMANCE OF RESPONSIBLE BEHAVIOR            NON-PERFORMANCE OF RESPONSIBLE BEHAVIOR         XSQ=     3.68
    IS HIGH  (38) B-B-C                                IS LOW  (35) B-B-C                              PHI=    0.303
                                                                                                       EP =   0.0536

338 DRIFT TOWARD BEING THOSE        0.80 OF  20    338 DRIFT TOWARD BEING THOSE        0.50 OF  20           16   10
    WHERE THE CHILD'S INFERRED ANXIETY OVER            WHERE THE CHILD'S INFERRED ANXIETY OVER                4   10
    PERFORMANCE OF RESPONSIBLE BEHAVIOR                PERFORMANCE OF RESPONSIBLE BEHAVIOR             XSQ=     2.75
    IS HIGH  (44) B-B-C                                IS LOW  (29) B-B-C                              PHI=    0.262
                                                                                                       EP =   0.0958

344 DRIFT TOWARD BEING THOSE        0.71 OF  21    344 DRIFT TOWARD BEING THOSE        0.62 OF  21           15    8
    WHERE THE TOTAL POSITIVE PRESSURE TOWARD           WHERE THE TOTAL POSITIVE PRESSURE TOWARD               6   13
    DEVELOPING SELF-RELIANT BEHAVIOR                   DEVELOPING SELF-RELIANT BEHAVIOR                XSQ=     3.46
    IN THE CHILD                                       IN THE CHILD                                    PHI=    0.287
    IS HIGH  (36) B-B-C                                IS LOW  (40) B-B-C                              XP =   0.0629

345 TEND TO BE THOSE                0.81 OF  21    345 TEND TO BE THOSE                0.86 OF  21           17    3
    WHERE THE CHILD'S INFERRED ANXIETY OVER            WHERE THE CHILD'S INFERRED ANXIETY OVER                4   18
    NON-PERFORMANCE OF SELF-RELIANT BEHAVIOR           NON-PERFORMANCE OF SELF-RELIANT BEHAVIOR        XSQ=    16.13
    IS HIGH  (37) B-B-C                                IS LOW  (39) B-B-C                              PHI=    0.620
                                                                                                       XP =   0.0001

348 DRIFT TOWARD BEING THOSE        0.72 OF  18    348 DRIFT TOWARD BEING THOSE        0.59 OF  17           13    7
    WHERE THE TOTAL POSITIVE PRESSURE TOWARD           WHERE THE TOTAL POSITIVE PRESSURE TOWARD               5   10
    DEVELOPING ACHIEVEMENT BEHAVIOR                    DEVELOPING ACHIEVEMENT BEHAVIOR                 XSQ=     2.29
    IN THE CHILD                                       IN THE CHILD                                    PHI=    0.256
    IS HIGH  (32) B-B-C                                IS LOW  (31) B-B-C                              EP =   0.0922

352 DRIFT TOWARD BEING THOSE        0.74 OF  19    352 DRIFT TOWARD BEING THOSE        0.57 OF  21           14    9
    WHERE THE TOTAL POSITIVE PRESSURE TOWARD           WHERE THE TOTAL POSITIVE PRESSURE TOWARD               5   12
    DEVELOPING OBEDIENT BEHAVIOR                       DEVELOPING OBEDIENT BEHAVIOR                    XSQ=     2.72
    IN THE CHILD                                       IN THE CHILD                                    PHI=    0.261
    IS HIGH  (44) B-B-C                                IS LOW  (28) B-B-C                              EP =   0.0624

354 TILT TOWARD BEING THOSE         0.74 OF  19    354 TILT TOWARD BEING THOSE         0.71 OF  21           14    6
    WHERE THE CHILD'S INFERRED ANXIETY OVER            WHERE THE CHILD'S INFERRED ANXIETY OVER                5   15
    PERFORMANCE OF OBEDIENT BEHAVIOR                   PERFORMANCE OF OBEDIENT BEHAVIOR                XSQ=     6.42
    IS HIGH  (36) B-B-C                                IS LOW  (37) B-B-C                              PHI=    0.401
                                                                                                       EP =   0.0104

355 DRIFT TOWARD BEING THOSE        0.68 OF  19    355 DRIFT TOWARD BEING THOSE        0.67 OF  21           13    7
    WHERE THE CHILD'S INFERRED CONFLICT                WHERE THE CHILD'S INFERRED CONFLICT                    6   14
    REGARDING OBEDIENT BEHAVIOR                        REGARDING OBEDIENT BEHAVIOR                     XSQ=     3.61
    IS HIGH  (35) B-B-C                                IS LOW  (38) B-B-C                              PHI=    0.300
                                                                                                       EP =   0.0562

373 DRIFT TOWARD BEING THOSE        0.64 OF  14    373 DRIFT TOWARD BEING THOSE        0.75 OF  16            9    4
    WHERE MALE INITIATION CEREMONIES                   WHERE MALE INITIATION CEREMONIES                       5   12
    AT PUBERTY ARE PRESENT  (17) W-K-A                 AT PUBERTY ARE ABSENT  (27) W-K-A               XSQ=     3.23
                                                                                                       PHI=    0.328
                                                                                                       EP =   0.0634
```

386	DRIFT TOWARD BEING THOSE WHERE SEXUAL EXPRESSION BY THE YOUNG IS RESTRICTED OR SEMI-RESTRICTED (46) F-B	0.73 OF 15	386	DRIFT TOWARD BEING THOSE WHERE SEXUAL EXPRESSION BY THE YOUNG IS PERMITTED (40) F-B	0.67 OF 15	11 5 4 10 XSQ= 3.35 PHI= 0.334 EP = 0.0656
390	LEAN LESS TOWARD BEING THOSE WHERE PREMARITAL SEX RELATIONS ARE WEAKLY PUNISHED AND IN FACT NOT RARE OR PUNISHED ONLY IF PREGNANCY RESULTS, OR FREELY PERMITTED (132) JTW,EA	0.65 OF 20	390	IN ALL CASES ARE THOSE WHERE PREMARITAL SEX RELATIONS ARE WEAKLY PUNISHED AND IN FACT NOT RARE OR PUNISHED ONLY IF PREGNANCY RESULTS, OR FREELY PERMITTED (132) JTW,EA	1.00 OF 17	7 0 13 17 XSQ= 5.23 PHI= 0.376 EP = 0.0094
391	TILT TOWARD BEING THOSE WHERE PREMARITAL SEX RELATIONS ARE STRONGLY PUNISHED AND IN FACT RARE, OR WEAKLY PUNISHED AND IN FACT NOT RARE (89) JTW,EA	0.50 OF 20	391	TILT TOWARD BEING THOSE WHERE PREMARITAL SEX RELATIONS ARE PUNISHED ONLY IF PREGNANCY RESULTS, OR FREELY PERMITTED (90) JTW,EA	0.88 OF 17	10 2 10 15 XSQ= 4.51 PHI= 0.349 EP = 0.0173
393	TEND TO BE THOSE WHERE EXTRAMARITAL COITUS IS PUNISHED, RATHER THAN PERMITTED (43) F-B	0.87 OF 15	393	TEND TO BE THOSE WHERE EXTRAMARITAL COITUS IS PERMITTED, RATHER THAN PUNISHED (41) F-B	0.87 OF 15	13 2 2 13 XSQ= 13.33 PHI= 0.667 EP = 0.0001
396	TILT TOWARD BEING THOSE WHERE THE STRENGTH OF MENSTRUAL TABOOS IS HIGH (18) WNS	0.52 OF 23	396	TILT TOWARD BEING THOSE WHERE THE STRENGTH OF MENSTRUAL TABOOS IS LOW (35) WNS	0.86 OF 22	12 3 11 19 XSQ= 5.88 PHI= 0.361 XP = 0.0153
397	DRIFT TOWARD BEING THOSE WHERE SEX DISABILITY IS PRESENT (14) JKH	0.50 OF 16	397	DRIFT TOWARD BEING THOSE WHERE SEX DISABILITY IS ABSENT (42) JKH	0.88 OF 16	8 2 8 14 XSQ= 3.64 PHI= 0.337 EP = 0.0538
398	LEAN TOWARD BEING THOSE WHERE THE INTENSITY OF SEX ANXIETY IS HIGH (16) WNS	0.79 OF 14	398	LEAN TOWARD BEING THOSE WHERE THE INTENSITY OF SEX ANXIETY IS LOW (16) WNS	0.79 OF 14	11 3 3 11 XSQ= 7.00 PHI= 0.500 EP = 0.0070
404	TILT TOWARD BEING THOSE WHERE EXPLANATIONS OF ILLNESS OF A SEXUAL NATURE ARE PRESENT (19) W-C	0.69 OF 16	404	TILT TOWARD BEING THOSE WHERE EXPLANATIONS OF ILLNESS OF A SEXUAL NATURE ARE ABSENT (42) W-C	0.74 OF 19	11 5 5 14 XSQ= 4.71 PHI= 0.367 EP = 0.0185
419	TILT TOWARD BEING THOSE WHERE MILITARY GLORY IS STRONGLY OR MODERATELY EMPHASIZED (55) PES	0.77 OF 22	419	TILT TOWARD BEING THOSE WHERE MILITARY GLORY IS NEGLIGIBLY EMPHASIZED (31) PES	0.58 OF 19	17 8 5 11 XSQ= 3.92 PHI= 0.309 XP = 0.0476

421	TILT TOWARD BEING THOSE WHERE KILLING, TORTURING, OR MUTILATING OF THE ENEMY IS STRONGLY OR MODERATELY EMPHASIZED (37) PES	0.60 OF 20	421	TILT TOWARD BEING THOSE WHERE KILLING, TORTURING, OR MUTILATING OF THE ENEMY IS NEGLIGIBLY EMPHASIZED (47) PES	0.76 OF 21	12 5 8 16 XSQ= 4.14 PHI= 0.318 XP = 0.0419
447	TILT TOWARD BEING THOSE WHERE LOVE MAGIC IS PRESENT (20) S-R	0.90 OF 10	447	TILT TOWARD BEING THOSE WHERE LOVE MAGIC IS ABSENT (13) S-R	0.62 OF 13	9 5 1 8 XSQ= 4.33 PHI= 0.434 EP = 0.0288
458	DRIFT LESS TOWARD BEING THOSE WHERE GAMES, IF PRESENT, DO NOT INCLUDE GAMES OF STRATEGY (119) R-A-B,EA	0.53 OF 19	458	DRIFT MORE TOWARD BEING THOSE WHERE GAMES, IF PRESENT, DO NOT INCLUDE GAMES OF STRATEGY (119) R-A-B,EA	0.82 OF 17	9 3 10 14 XSQ= 2.35 PHI= 0.256 EP = 0.0830
460	DRIFT TOWARD BEING THOSE WHERE GAMES, IF PRESENT, ARE NOT LIMITED TO GAMES OF SKILL ONLY (104) R-A-B,EA	0.79 OF 19	460	DRIFT TOWARD BEING THOSE WHERE GAMES, IF PRESENT, ARE LIMITED TO GAMES OF SKILL ONLY (67) R-A-B,EA	0.53 OF 17	4 9 15 8 XSQ= 2.69 PHI= -0.274 EP = 0.0819

400 CULTURES WHERE HOMOSEXUAL ACTIVITY IS PROHIBITED (22) F-B

400 CULTURES WHERE HOMOSEXUAL ACTIVITY IS PERMITTED (36) F-B

BACKGROUND ON PAGE 156

BOTH SUBJECT AND PREDICATE

22 IN LEFT COLUMN

ALORESE	BALINESE	CHIR-APACHE	CUNA	GOAJIRO	IFUGAO	KURTATCHI	KWAKIUTL	LAKHER	LEPCHA
MANUS	MARSHALLESE	MBUNDU	OJIBWA	RWALA	SANPOIL	SIRIONO	TIKOPIA	TIMBIRA	TROBRIAND
TRUKESE	YARURO								

36 IN RIGHT COLUMN

ARANDA	AYMARA	AZANDE	CHUKCHEE	CREEK	CROW	FON	HANO	ILA	KERAKI
KORYAK	LANGO	MANDAN	MARICOPA	NAMA	NASKAPI	NATCHEZ	NAVAHO	OMAHA	PALAUANS
PAPAGO	PUKAPUKA	SAMOANS	SEMINOLE	SIWANS	TANALA	TENDA	THONGA	TUBATULABAL	TUPINAMBA
WITOTO	WOGEO	WOLOF	YAKUT	YUROK	ZUNI				

342 EXCLUDED BECAUSE UNASCERTAINED

	Left column		Right column	Statistics
6	DRIFT LESS TOWARD BEING THOSE 0.59 OF 22 LOCATED OUTSIDE OF THE INSULAR PACIFIC (330)	6	DRIFT MORE TOWARD BEING THOSE 0.83 OF 36 LOCATED OUTSIDE OF THE INSULAR PACIFIC (330)	9 6 13 30 XSQ= 3.02 PHI= 0.228 XP = 0.0824
15	DRIFT TOWARD BEING THOSE 0.68 OF 22 WHERE THE LATITUDE IS LESS THAN TWENTY DEGREES (217)	15	DRIFT TOWARD BEING THOSE 0.61 OF 36 WHERE THE LATITUDE IS TWENTY DEGREES OR GREATER (183)	7 22 15 14 XSQ= 3.59 PHI= -0.249 XP = 0.0582
42	DRIFT TOWARD BEING THOSE 0.50 OF 22 WHERE THE NATURAL ENVIRONMENT IS TROPICAL OR SUB-TROPICAL RAIN FOREST, OR MONSOON FOREST (156) FWM	42	DRIFT TOWARD BEING THOSE 0.75 OF 36 WHERE THE NATURAL ENVIRONMENT IS OTHER THAN TROPICAL OR SUB-TROPICAL RAIN FOREST, OR MONSOON FOREST (244) FWM	11 9 11 27 XSQ= 2.75 PHI= 0.218 XP = 0.0971
45	DRIFT LESS TOWARD BEING THOSE 0.67 OF 15 WHERE SETTLEMENTS, IF FIXED, ARE COMPACT, RATHER THAN NON-COMPACT (149)	45	DRIFT MORE TOWARD BEING THOSE 0.95 OF 20 WHERE SETTLEMENTS, IF FIXED, ARE COMPACT, RATHER THAN NON-COMPACT (149)	10 19 5 1 XSQ= 3.05 PHI= -0.295 EP = 0.0640

47	IN ALL CASES ARE THOSE 1.00 OF 6 WHERE, IF SETTLEMENTS ARE NON-FIXED, MOVEMENT IS NOMADIC, RATHER THAN NON-NOMADIC (72)	47	TILT TOWARD BEING THOSE 0.57 OF 14 WHERE, IF SETTLEMENTS ARE NON-FIXED, MOVEMENT IS NON-NOMADIC, RATHER THAN NOMADIC (38)	6 6 0 8 XSQ= 3.58 PHI= 0.423 EP = 0.0419
71	DRIFT MORE TOWARD BEING THOSE 0.83 OF 18 WHERE METAL WORKING IS ABSENT (153)	71	DRIFT LESS TOWARD BEING THOSE 0.55 OF 31 WHERE METAL WORKING IS ABSENT (153)	3 14 15 17 XSQ= 2.92 PHI= -0.244 XP = 0.0875
129	IN ALL CASES ARE THOSE 1.00 OF 8 WHERE WEAVING IS MAINLY DONE BY FEMALES (73)	129	DRIFT LESS TOWARD BEING THOSE 0.57 OF 14 WHERE WEAVING IS MAINLY DONE BY FEMALES (73)	0 6 8 8 XSQ= 2.80 PHI= -0.357 EP = 0.0511
186	TILT MORE TOWARD BEING THOSE 0.91 OF 22 WHERE THE KIN GROUP IS OTHER THAN EXCLUSIVELY PATRILINEAL (250)	186	TILT LESS TOWARD BEING THOSE 0.64 OF 36 WHERE THE KIN GROUP IS OTHER THAN EXCLUSIVELY PATRILINEAL (250)	2 13 20 23 XSQ= 3.89 PHI= -0.259 XP = 0.0487
221	DRIFT LESS TOWARD BEING THOSE 0.86 OF 22 WHERE MATRILATERAL CROSS-COUSIN MARRIAGE IS NOT PRESCRIBED OR PREFERRED (335)	221	IN ALL CASES ARE THOSE 1.00 OF 36 WHERE MATRILATERAL CROSS-COUSIN MARRIAGE IS NOT PRESCRIBED OR PREFERRED (335)	3 0 19 36 XSQ= 2.77 PHI= 0.219 XP = 0.0960
224	TILT TOWARD BEING THOSE 0.60 OF 10 WHERE COUSIN MARRIAGE IS PREFERENTIALLY OR PERMISSIVELY EITHER PATRI- OR MATRILATERAL, RATHER THAN SYMMETRICAL (66)	224	TILT TOWARD BEING THOSE 0.86 OF 14 WHERE COUSIN MARRIAGE IS PREFERENTIALLY OR PERMISSIVELY SYMMETRICAL, RATHER THAN EITHER PATRI- OR MATRILATERAL (106)	6 2 4 12 XSQ= 3.62 PHI= 0.388 EP = 0.0324
255	IN ALL CASES ARE THOSE 1.00 OF 6 WHERE GRANDPARENTAL AUTHORITY OVER PARENTS IS ABSENT (26) DA	255	DRIFT TOWARD BEING THOSE 0.60 OF 5 WHERE GRANDPARENTAL AUTHORITY OVER PARENTS IS PRESENT (7) DA	0 3 6 2 XSQ= 2.39 PHI= -0.466 EP = 0.0606
305	TILT TOWARD BEING THOSE 0.73 OF 15 WHERE THE EARLY SEXUAL SATISFACTION POTENTIAL IS HIGH (27) W-C	305	TILT TOWARD BEING THOSE 0.75 OF 12 WHERE THE EARLY SEXUAL SATISFACTION POTENTIAL IS LOW (24) W-C	11 3 4 9 XSQ= 4.45 PHI= 0.406 EP = 0.0213
343	TILT TOWARD BEING THOSE 0.69 OF 13 WHERE THE CHILD'S INFERRED CONFLICT REGARDING NURTURANT BEHAVIOR IS LOW (18) B-B-C	343	TILT TOWARD BEING THOSE 0.82 OF 11 WHERE THE CHILD'S INFERRED CONFLICT REGARDING NURTURANT BEHAVIOR IS HIGH (29) B-B-C	4 9 9 2 XSQ= 4.37 PHI= -0.427 EP = 0.0188

344	TILT TCWARC BEING THCSE 0.75 OF 16 WHERE THE TOTAL POSITIVE PRESSURE TOWARD DEVELCPING SELF-RELIANT BEHAVIOR IN THE CHILD IS HIGH (36) B-B-C	344	TILT TOWARD BEING THOSE 0.70 OF 20 WHERE THE TOTAL POSITIVE PRESSURE TOWARC DEVELOPING SELF-RELIANT BEHAVICR IN THE CHILD IS LOW (40) B-B-C	12 6 4 14 XSQ= 5.51 PHI= 0.391 EP = 0.0176
350	DRIFT TCWARD BEING THOSE 0.60 OF 10 WHERE THE CHILD'S INFERREC ANXIETY OVER PERFCRMANCE CF ACHIEVEMENT BEHAVIOR IS LCW (26) B-B-C	350	DRIFT TOWARD BEING THCSE 0.78 OF 18 WHERE THE CHILD'S INFERRED ANXIETY OVER PERFORMANCE OF ACHIEVEMENT BEHAVIOR IS HIGH (34) B-B-C	4 14 6 4 XSQ= 2.52 PHI= -0.300 EP = 0.0974
352	TILT TCWARC BEING THCSE 0.69 OF 16 WHERE THE TOTAL POSITIVE PRESSURE TOWARD DEVELCPING CBEDIENT BEHAVICR IN THE CHILD IS LCW (28) B-B-C	352	TILT TOWARD BEING THOSE 0.78 CF 18 WHERE THE TOTAL POSITIVE PRESSURE TCWARC DEVELOPING OBEDIENT BEHAVICR IN THE CHILD IS HIGH (44) B-B-C	5 14 11 4 XSQ= 5.67 PHI= -0.408 EP = 0.0142
365	TILT TCWARD BEING THOSE 0.50 OF 10 WHERE THE TIME SPENT IN ADCLESCENT PEER GRCUP ACTIVITY IS LCW-MEDIUM CR LCW (15) JKH	365	IN ALL CASES ARE THCSE 1.00 OF 7 WHERE THE TIME SPENT IN ADOLESCENT PEER GROUP ACTIVITY IS HIGH OR HIGH-MEDIUM (30) JKH	5 7 5 0 XSQ= 2.84 PHI= -0.409 EP = 0.0441
372	DRIFT TCWARD BEING THCSE 0.70 OF 20 WHERE MALE INITIATICN RITES ARE ABSENT (63) ASA	372	DRIFT TOWARD BEING THOSE 0.62 CF 21 WHERE MALE INITIATICN RITES ARE PRESENT (48) ASA	6 13 14 8 XSQ= 3.01 PHI= -0.271 XP = 0.0828
405	TILT TCWARC BEING THOSE 0.87 OF 15 WHERE EXPLANATICNS OF ILLNESS CF A DEPENDENCE NATURE ARE PRESENT (34) W-C	405	TILT TOWARD BEING THOSE 0.57 OF 14 WHERE EXPLANATICNS OF ILLNESS OF A DEPENDENCE NATURE ARE ABSENT (27) W-C	13 6 2 8 XSQ= 4.37 PHI= 0.388 EP = 0.0209
445	DRIFT TCWARD BEING THCSE 0.86 OF 7 WHERE SCRCERY IS UNIMPCRTANT (23) BBW,DH	445	DRIFT TOWARD BEING THCSE 0.56 CF 16 WHERE SORCERY IS IMPORTANT (26) BBW,DH	1 9 6 7 XSQ= 1.99 PHI= -0.294 EP = 0.0886
446	IN ALL CASES ARE THOSE 1.00 OF 4 WHERE WITCHCRAFT IS MCDERATELY PRESENT CR ABSENT (24) GES	446	IN ALL CASES ARE THCSE 1.00 OF 7 WHERE WITCHCRAFT IS SIGNIFICANTLY PRESENT (14) GES	0 7 4 0 XSQ= 7.10 PHI= -0.804 EP = 0.0030
459	TILT TCWARC BEING THCSE 0.75 OF 16 WHERE GAMES, IF PRESENT, DC NCT INCLUDE GAMES CF CHANCE (89) R-A-B,EA	459	TILT TOWARD BEING THOSE 0.64 OF 28 WHERE GAMES, IF PRESENT, INCLUDE GAMES OF CHANCE (82) R-A-B,EA	4 18 12 10 XSQ= 4.81 PHI= -0.331 XP = 0.0283

400/

```
460  TILT TCWARC BEING THCSE         0.63 OF  16       46C  TILT TOWARD BEING THOSE         0.75 OF  28          10     7
     WHERE GAMES, IF PRESENT,                               WHERE GAMES, IF PRESENT,                                   6    21
     ARE LIMITED TC                                         ARE NOT LIMITED TO                                   XSQ=     4.56
     GAMES CF SKILL CNLY  (67) R-A-B,EA                     GAMES OF SKILL CNLY  (104) R-A-B,EA                  PHI=    0.322
                                                                                                                 XP =   0.0327
```

401 CULTURES WHERE THE INCIDENCE OF VENEREAL DISEASE IS HIGH (10) MN	401 CULTURES WHERE THE INCIDENCE OF VENEREAL DISEASE IS LOW (9) MN

BACKGROUND ON PAGE 156

NEITHER SUBJECT NOR PREDICATE

10 IN LEFT COLUMN

ASHANTI DUSUN GANDA LESU MASAI MONGO NGONI NUPE TODA YAPESE

9 IN RIGHT COLUMN

ALORESE HAVASUPAI KAPAUKU NAVAHO OJIBWA PURARI SINHALESE TALLENSI TIKOPIA

381 EXCLUDED BECAUSE UNASCERTAINED

402 CULTURES WHERE EXPLANATIONS OF ILLNESS OF AN ORAL NATURE ARE PRESENT (31) W-C

402 CULTURES WHERE EXPLANATIONS OF ILLNESS OF AN ORAL NATURE ARE ABSENT (30) W-C

BACKGROUND ON PAGE 157

BOTH SUBJECT AND PREDICATE

31 IN LEFT COLUMN

AINU	ALORESE	ANDAMANESE	CHAGGA	CHIR-APACHE	COMANCHE	DOBUANS	FON	IFUGAO	JIVARO
KURTATCHI	KWAKIUTL	LAMBA	LEPCHA	LESU	MANUS	MAORI	MARQUESANS	MASAI	NAVAHO
OMAHA	PUKAPUKA	RIFFIANS	SENIANG	SIRIONO	THONGA	TIV	TROBRIAND	WAPISHANA	WITOTO
YAKUT									

30 IN RIGHT COLUMN

ABIPON	ARAPESH	ASHANTI	AZANDE	BALINESE	CHENCHU	COPR ESKIMO	DUSUN	HANO	KUTENAI
LAKHER	LAPPS	MARSHALLESE	MURNGIN	ONTONG-JAVA	PAPAGO	RWALA	SAMOANS	SANPOIL	TANALA
TAOS	TENINO	TETON	TIKOPIA	VENDA	WARRAU	WOGEO	YAGUA	YUKAGHIR	ZUNI

339 EXCLUDED BECAUSE UNASCERTAINED

	Left column				Right column			Statistics
118	DRIFT TOWARD BEING THOSE WHERE THE PERCENTAGE OF OCCUPATIONS THAT ARE SPECIALIZED IS LOW (25) WME	0.80 OF 10	118	DRIFT TOWARD BEING THOSE WHERE THE PERCENTAGE OF OCCUPATIONS THAT ARE SPECIALIZED IS HIGH OR MEDIUM (24) WME	0.71 OF 7			2 5 / 8 2 / XSQ= 2.62 / PHI= -0.393 / EP = 0.0584
127	LEAN TOWARD BEING THOSE WHERE THE FEMALES' CONTRIBUTION TO SUBSISTENCE IS HIGH (33) JKB	0.77 OF 13	127	LEAN TOWARD BEING THOSE WHERE THE FEMALES' CONTRIBUTION TO SUBSISTENCE IS LOW (32) JKB	0.89 OF 9			10 1 / 3 8 / XSQ= 6.77 / PHI= 0.555 / EP = 0.0075
137	TILT TOWARD BEING THOSE WHERE INVIDIOUS DISPLAY OF WEALTH IS STRONGLY EMPHASIZED (37) PES	0.54 OF 26	137	TILT TOWARD BEING THOSE WHERE INVIDIOUS DISPLAY OF WEALTH IS MODERATELY, LITTLE, OR NEGATIVELY EMPHASIZED (52) PES	0.82 OF 22			14 4 / 12 18 / XSQ= 5.03 / PHI= 0.324 / XP = 0.0248
139	TILT TOWARD BEING THOSE WHERE SUPERORDINATE PUNISHMENT IS ABSENT (25) BBW	0.80 OF 15	139	TILT TOWARD BEING THOSE WHERE SUPERORDINATE PUNISHMENT IS PRESENT (15) BBW	0.67 OF 12			3 8 / 12 4 / XSQ= 4.24 / PHI= -0.396 / EP = 0.0220

No.	Statement	Proportion	No.	Statement	Proportion	Statistics
143	DRIFT TCWARD BEING THCSE WHERE THE RATIC CF RESTITUTIVE TC REPRESSIVE SANCTIONS IS HIGH (20) WME	0.64 OF 11	143	DRIFT TOWARD BEING THOSE WHERE THE RATIO OF RESTITUTIVE TO REPRESSIVE SANCTICNS IS MEDIUM OR LOW (32) WME	0.88 OF 8	7 1 4 7 XSQ= 3.09 PHI= 0.403 EP = 0.0587
144	DRIFT TCWARD BEING THCSE WHERE THE RATIC CF RESTITUTIVE TC REPRESSIVE SANCTICNS IS HIGH CR MEDIUM (27) WME	0.73 OF 11	144	DRIFT TOWARD BEING THOSE WHERE THE RATIC OF RESTITUTIVE TO REPRESSIVE SANCTICNS IS LOW (25) WME	0.75 OF 8	8 2 3 6 XSQ= 2.53 PHI= 0.365 EP = 0.0698
192	TILT MORE TOWARC BEINC THCSE CTHER THAN WHERE THE CNLY KIN GROUP PRESENT IS A KINCREC CR ELSE BILATERAL DESCENT IS INFERREC (289)	0.87 OF 31	192	TILT LESS TOWARD BEING THOSE OTHER THAN WHERE THE ONLY KIN GRCUP PRESENT IS A KINDRED CR ELSE BILATERAL DESCENT IS INFERRED (289)	0.60 OF 30	4 12 27 18 XSQ= 4.47 PHI= -0.271 XP = 0.0345
278	IN ALL CASES ARE THOSE WHERE PRCPERTY RIGHTS IN WOMEN ARE UNIMPCRTANT CR ABSENT (14) LWS	1.00 OF 5	278	IN ALL CASES ARE THOSE WHERE PROPERTY RIGHTS IN WCMEN ARE PRESENT (8) LWS	1.00 CF 2	0 2 5 0 XSQ= 2.96 PHI= -0.650 EP = 0.0476
309	TILT TCWARC BEING THCSE WHERE CRAL SCCIALIZATICN ANXIETY IS HIGH (26) W-C	0.64 OF 28	309	TILT TOWARD BEING THOSE WHERE ORAL SOCIALIZATICN ANXIETY IS LOW (27) W-C	0.68 OF 25	18 8 10 17 XSQ= 4.29 PHI= 0.285 XP = 0.0383
320	DRIFT TCWARD BEING THOSE WHERE THE DEGREE OF REDUCTION CF THE INFANT'S CRIVES IS LCW (24) B-B-C	0.50 OF 24	32C	DRIFT TOWARD BEING THOSE WHERE THE DEGREE OF REDUCTICN OF THE INFANT'S DRIVES IS HIGH (45) B-B-C	0.81 OF 16	12 13 12 3 XSQ= 2.78 PHI= -0.264 EP = 0.0556
322	LEAN TCWARC BEING THCSE WHERE THE CCNSISTENCY CF REDUCTION CF THE INFANT'S CRIVES IS LCW (32) B-B-C	0.77 OF 22	322	LEAN TOWARD BEING THOSE WHERE THE CONSISTENCY OF REDUCTION OF THE INFANT'S DRIVES IS HIGH (27) B-B-C	0.79 CF 14	5 11 17 3 XSQ= 8.66 PHI= -0.491 EP = 0.0017
327	DRIFT TCWARD BEING THCSE WHERE THE AGE CF THE INFANT AT TIME CF REDUCED CCNTACT WITH MOTHER IS HIGHER THAN TWO YEARS (28) B-B-C	0.65 OF 20	327	DRIFT TOWARD BEING THOSE WHERE THE AGE CF THE INFANT AT TIME OF REDUCED CONTACT WITH MCTHER IS TWO YEARS OR LOWER (27) B-B-C	0.69 OF 13	13 4 7 9 XSQ= 2.45 PHI= 0.273 EP = 0.0799
334	DRIFT TCWARD BEING THCSE WHERE THE INDULGENCE CF THE CHILD IS LCW (38) B-B-C	0.58 OF 26	334	DRIFT TOWARD BEING THOSE WHERE THE INDULGENCE OF THE CHILD IS HIGH (40) B-B-C	0.72 OF 18	11 13 15 5 XSQ= 2.73 PHI= -0.249 XP = 0.0986

No.	Statement	Proportion	No.	Statement	Proportion	Statistics
336	TILT TOWARD BEING THOSE WHERE THE TOTAL POSITIVE PRESSURE TOWARD DEVELOPING RESPONSIBLE BEHAVIOR IN THE CHILD IS LOW (32) B-B-C	0.60 OF 25	336	TILT TOWARD BEING THOSE WHERE THE TOTAL POSITIVE PRESSURE TOWARD DEVELOPING RESPONSIBLE BEHAVIOR IN THE CHILD IS HIGH (43) B-B-C	0.76 OF 17	10 13 15 4 XSQ= 4.06 PHI= -0.311 XP = 0.0439
344	LEAN TOWARD BEING THOSE WHERE THE TOTAL POSITIVE PRESSURE TOWARD DEVELOPING SELF-RELIANT BEHAVIOR IN THE CHILD IS HIGH (36) B-B-C	0.72 OF 25	344	LEAN TOWARD BEING THOSE WHERE THE TOTAL POSITIVE PRESSURE TOWARD DEVELOPING SELF-RELIANT BEHAVIOR IN THE CHILD IS LOW (40) B-B-C	0.82 OF 17	18 3 7 14 XSQ= 9.88 PHI= 0.485 XP = 0.0017
345	TILT TOWARD BEING THOSE WHERE THE CHILD'S INFERRED ANXIETY OVER NON-PERFORMANCE OF SELF-RELIANT BEHAVIOR IS HIGH (37) B-B-C	0.60 OF 25	345	TILT TOWARD BEING THOSE WHERE THE CHILD'S INFERRED ANXIETY OVER NON-PERFORMANCE OF SELF-RELIANT BEHAVIOR IS LOW (39) B-B-C	0.76 OF 17	15 4 10 13 XSQ= 4.06 PHI= 0.311 XP = 0.0439
348	TILT TOWARD BEING THOSE WHERE THE TOTAL POSITIVE PRESSURE TOWARD DEVELOPING ACHIEVEMENT BEHAVIOR IN THE CHILD IS HIGH (32) B-B-C	0.78 OF 18	348	TILT TOWARD BEING THOSE WHERE THE TOTAL POSITIVE PRESSURE TOWARD DEVELOPING ACHIEVEMENT BEHAVIOR IN THE CHILD IS LOW (31) B-B-C	0.71 OF 14	14 4 4 10 XSQ= 5.88 PHI= 0.429 EP = 0.0110
349	DRIFT TOWARD BEING THOSE WHERE THE CHILD'S INFERRED ANXIETY OVER NON-PERFORMANCE OF ACHIEVEMENT BEHAVIOR IS HIGH (34) B-B-C	0.78 OF 18	349	DRIFT TOWARD BEING THOSE WHERE THE CHILD'S INFERRED ANXIETY OVER NON-PERFORMANCE OF ACHIEVEMENT BEHAVIOR IS LOW (28) B-B-C	0.57 OF 14	14 6 4 8 XSQ= 2.74 PHI= 0.293 EP = 0.0683
365	DRIFT TOWARD BEING THOSE WHERE THE TIME SPENT IN ADOLESCENT PEER GROUP ACTIVITY IS LOW-MEDIUM OR LOW (15) JKH	0.64 OF 14	365	DRIFT TOWARD BEING THOSE WHERE THE TIME SPENT IN ADOLESCENT PEER GROUP ACTIVITY IS HIGH OR HIGH-MEDIUM (30) JKH	0.78 OF 9	5 7 9 2 XSQ= 2.38 PHI= -0.322 EP = 0.0894
382	DRIFT TOWARD BEING THOSE WHERE FEMALE INITIATION RITES ARE PRESENT (38) JKB	0.77 OF 13	382	DRIFT TOWARD BEING THOSE WHERE FEMALE INITIATION RITES ARE ABSENT (27) JKB	0.67 OF 9	10 3 3 6 XSQ= 2.57 PHI= 0.342 EP = 0.0789
403	TILT TOWARD BEING THOSE WHERE EXPLANATIONS OF ILLNESS OF AN ANAL NATURE ARE PRESENT (23) W-C	0.55 OF 31	403	TILT TOWARD BEING THOSE WHERE EXPLANATIONS OF ILLNESS OF AN ANAL NATURE ARE ABSENT (38) W-C	0.80 OF 30	17 6 14 24 XSQ= 6.46 PHI= 0.326 XP = 0.0110
404	TILT LESS TOWARD BEING THOSE WHERE EXPLANATIONS OF ILLNESS OF A SEXUAL NATURE ARE ABSENT (42) W-C	0.55 OF 31	404	TILT MORE TOWARD BEING THOSE WHERE EXPLANATIONS OF ILLNESS OF A SEXUAL NATURE ARE ABSENT (42) W-C	0.83 OF 30	14 5 17 25 XSQ= 4.52 PHI= 0.272 XP = 0.0335

424	TILT TCWARC BEING THOSE WHERE RELIGICUS SPECIALISTS ARE PART-TIME, RATHER THAN FULL-TIME (33) JMH	0.82 OF 11	424	TILT TOWARD BEING THOSE WHERE RELIGIOUS SPECIALISTS ARE FULL-TIME, RATHER THAN PART-TIME (21) JMH	0.83 OF 6	 XSQ= PHI= EP =	2 5 9 1 4.38 -0.508 0.0345
425	TEND TC BE THCSE WHERE SUPERNATURALS ARE MAINLY AGGRESSIVE, RATHER THAN BENEVCLENT (20) L-T-W	0.88 OF 16	425	TEND TO BE THOSE WHERE SUPERNATURALS ARE MAINLY BENEVOLENT, RATHER THAN AGGRESSIVE (16) L-T-W	0.77 CF 13	 XSQ= PHI= EP =	2 10 14 3 9.76 -0.580 0.0007
427	TILT TCWARC BEING THOSE WHERE A HIGH GOC, IF PRESENT, IS INACTIVE, RATHER THAN ACTIVE (69) GES,EA	0.75 OF 12	427	TILT TOWARD BEING THOSE WHERE A HIGH GOD, IF PRESENT, IS ACTIVE, RATHER THAN INACTIVE (87) GES,EA	0.75 OF 12	 XSQ= PHI= EP =	3 9 9 3 4.17 -0.417 0.0391
434	DRIFT TCWARD BEING THCSE WHERE ASCETICISM IN MOURNING BEHAVIOR IS HIGH (37) JFG	0.64 OF 25	434	DRIFT TOWARD BEING THOSE WHERE ASCETICISM IN MOURNING BEHAVIOR IS LOW (30) JFG	0.71 CF 17	 XSQ= PHI= XP =	16 5 9 12 3.56 0.291 0.0593
440	DRIFT TCWARD BEING THCSE WHERE FEAR OF SPIRITS IS HIGH (32) W-C	0.65 OF 31	44C	DRIFT TOWARD BEING THOSE WHERE FEAR OF SPIRITS IS LOW (29) W-C	0.60 OF 30	 XSQ= PHI= XP =	20 12 11 18 2.76 0.213 0.0968

403 CULTURES
WHERE EXPLANATICNS CF ILLNESS
OF AN ANAL NATURE
ARE PRESENT (23) W-C

403 CULTURES
WHERE EXPLANATICNS OF ILLNESS
OF AN ANAL NATURE
ARE ABSENT (38) W-C

BACKGROUND ON PAGE 157

BCTH SUBJECT AND PREDICATE

23 IN LEFT CCLUMN

AINU	ALCRESE	ARAPESH	ASHANTI	CHAGGA	CHIR-APACHE	DOBUANS	HANC	KURTATCHI	KWAKIUTL
LAMBA	LEPCHA	LESU	MANUS	MASAI	MURNGIN	NAVAHO	RIFFIANS	RWALA	SENIANG
TANALA	TIV	TRCBRIAND							

38 IN RIGHT CCLUMN

ABIPON	ANDAMANESE	AZANDE	BALINESE	CHENCHU	COMANCHE	COPR ESKIMO	DUSUN	FON	IFUGAO
JIVARC	KUTENAI	LAKHER	LAPPS	MAORI	MARQUESANS	MARSHALLESE	OMAHA	ONTCNG-JAVA	PAPAGO
PUKAPUKA	SAMCANS	SANPCIL	SIRIONO	TAOS	TENINO	TETON	THCNGA	TIKCPIA	VENCA
WAPISHANA	WARRAU	WITCTO	WOGEO	YAGUA	YAKUT	YUKAGHIR	ZUNI		

339 EXCLUDED BECAUSE UNASCERTAINEC

	Left column			Right column		Statistics
9	IN ALL CASES ARE THCSE LCCATED CUTSIDE CF SOUTH AMERICA (335)	1.00 OF 23	9	DRIFT LESS TOWARD BEING THCSE LOCATED OUTSIDE OF SOUTH AMERICA (335)	0.82 OF 38	0 7 23 31 XSQ= 3.14 PHI= -0.227 XP = 0.0762
62	DRIFT TCWARD BEING THCSE WHERE HUSBANDRY CF SOME KIND IS PRESENT (228)	0.78 OF 23	62	DRIFT TOWARD BEING THOSE WHERE HUSBANDRY OF ANY KIND IS ABSENT (172)	0.50 OF 38	18 19 5 19 XSQ= 3.68 PHI= 0.246 XP = 0.0549
71	DRIFT LESS TCWARC BEING THCSE WHERE METAL WORKING IS ABSENT (153)	0.53 OF 17	71	DRIFT MORE TOWARD BEING THCSE WHERE METAL WORKING IS ABSENT (153)	0.83 OF 29	8 5 9 24 XSQ= 3.34 PHI= 0.270 XP = 0.0674
90	DRIFT LESS TCWARC BEING THCSE WHERE, IF A HEREDITARY HEACMANSHIP IS PRESENT, SUCCESSICN IS PATRILINEAL, RATHER THAN MATRILINEAL (127)	0.67 OF 9	90	DRIFT MORE TOWARD BEING THCSE WHERE, IF A HEREDITARY HEADMANSHIP IS PRESENT, SUCCESSICN IS PATRILINEAL, RATHER THAN MATRILINEAL (127)	0.95 OF 19	6 18 3 1 XSQ= 1.97 PHI= -0.265 EP = 0.0841

91	TILT TCWARC BEING THOSE WHERE SCCIETAL CCMPLEXITY IS HIGH (18) F-W	0.86 OF 7	91	TILT TOWARD BEING THOSE WHERE SOCIETAL COMPLEXITY IS LOW (22) F-W	0.71 CF 14	6 4 1 10 XSQ= 4.03 PHI= 0.438 EP = 0.0237
132	IN ALL CASES ARE THCSE WHERE ECCNCMIC EXCHANGE INVCLVES THE USE CF MCNEY (37) JMH	1.00 OF 6	132	TILT TOWARD BEING THOSE WHERE ECONOMIC EXCHANGE DOES NOT INVOLVE THE USE OF MONEY (17) JMH	0.55 CF 11	6 5 0 6 XSQ= 2.95 PHI= 0.417 EP = 0.0427
135	IN ALL CASES ARE THCSE WHERE INDIVIDUAL OWNERSHIP OF ECCNOMICALLY SIGNIFICANT PROPERTY IS PRESENT (24) GES	1.00 OF 5	135	TILT TOWARD BEING THOSE WHERE INDIVIDUAL OWNERSHIP CF ECONOMICALLY SIGNIFICANT PROPERTY IS NEGLIGIBLE OR ABSENT (14) GES	0.83 CF 6	5 1 0 5 XSQ= 4.65 PHI= 0.650 EP = 0.0152
187	TILT LESS TCWARC BEING THCSE WHERE THE KIN GRCUP IS OTHER THAN EXCLUSIVELY MATRILINEAL (344)	0.73 OF 22	187	TILT MORE TOWARD BEING THOSE WHERE THE KIN GROUP IS OTHER THAN EXCLUSIVELY MATRILINEAL (344)	0.95 CF 38	6 2 16 36 XSQ= 4.09 PHI= 0.261 XP = 0.0431
188	TEND TO BE THCSE WHERE THE KIN GRCUP IS CTHER THAN EXCLUSIVELY CCGNATIC (252)	0.91 OF 23	188	TEND TO BE THOSE WHERE THE KIN GROUP IS EXCLUSIVELY COGNATIC (148)	0.58 OF 38	2 22 21 16 XSQ= 12.54 PHI= -0.453 XP = 0.0004
192	LEAN MCRE TOWARC BEING THCSE CTHER THAN WHERE THE CNLY KIN GROUP PRESENT IS A KINCREC CR ELSE BILATERAL CESCENT IS INFERREC (289)	0.96 OF 23	192	LEAN LESS TOWARD BEING THCSE OTHER THAN WHERE THE CNLY KIN GRCUP PRESENT IS A KINDRED CR ELSE BILATERAL DESCENT IS INFERRED (289)	0.61 CF 38	1 15 22 23 XSQ= 7.41 PHI= -0.349 XP = 0.0065
234	TILT TCWARD BEING THOSE WHERE THE COUSIN TERMINCLCGY IS CF CRCW, CMAHA, CR IRCCUOIS TYPE, RATHER THAN ESKIMC CR HAWAIIAN TYPE (152)	0.71 OF 17	234	TILT TOWARD BEING THOSE WHERE THE COUSIN TERMINCLCGY IS OF ESKIMO OR HAWAIIAN TYPE, RATHER THAN CROW, OMAHA, OR IRCQUOIS TYPE (170)	0.65 CF 31	12 11 5 20 XSQ= 4.11 PHI= 0.292 XP = 0.0427
240	TILT TCWARD BEING THCSE WHERE THE FAMILY, IF EXTENCEC, IS SMALL OR STEM, RATHER THAN LARGE (135)	0.80 OF 10	24C	TILT TOWARD BEING THOSE WHERE THE FAMILY, IF EXTENDED, IS LARGE, RATHER THAN SMALL OR STEM (78)	0.65 CF 17	2 11 8 6 XSQ= 3.41 PHI= -0.355 EP = 0.0461
259	DRIFT TCWARD BEING THCSE WHERE THE SEVERITY CF MCTHER-IN-LAW AVCIDANCE IS HIGH (26) WNS	0.62 OF 13	259	DRIFT TOWARD BEING THOSE WHERE THE SEVERITY CF MCTHER-IN-LAW AVOIDANCE IS LOW (20) WNS	0.79 CF 14	8 3 5 11 XSQ= 2.98 PHI= 0.332 EP = 0.0542

285	DRIFT TOWARD BEING THOSE 0.63 OF 16 WHERE THE SEX TABOO DURING PREGNANCY IS PRESENT (14) BCA	285	DRIFT TOWARD BEING THOSE 0.73 OF 15 WHERE THE SEX TABOO DURING PREGNANCY IS ABSENT OR INFERRED ABSENT (17) BCA	10 4 6 11 XSQ= 2.70 PHI= 0.295 EP = 0.0732
307	DRIFT TOWARD BEING THOSE 0.52 OF 21 WHERE THE EARLY AGGRESSION SATISFACTION POTENTIAL IS LOW (19) W-C	307	DRIFT TOWARD BEING THOSE 0.74 OF 31 WHERE THE EARLY AGGRESSION SATISFACTION POTENTIAL IS HIGH (33) W-C	10 23 11 8 XSQ= 2.75 PHI= -0.230 XP = 0.0971
308	TILT TOWARD BEING THOSE 0.76 OF 17 WHERE AVERAGE SOCIALIZATION ANXIETY IS HIGH (22) W-C	308	TILT TOWARD BEING THOSE 0.61 OF 23 WHERE AVERAGE SOCIALIZATION ANXIETY IS LOW (18) W-C	13 9 4 14 XSQ= 4.10 PHI= 0.320 EP = 0.0267
326	DRIFT TOWARD BEING THOSE 0.71 OF 17 WHERE THE INFERRED TRANSITION ANXIETY BETWEEN INFANCY AND CHILDHOOD IS HIGH (32) B-B-C	326	DRIFT TOWARD BEING THOSE 0.64 OF 22 WHERE THE INFERRED TRANSITION ANXIETY BETWEEN INFANCY AND CHILDHOOD IS LOW (35) B-B-C	12 8 5 14 XSQ= 3.23 PHI= 0.288 EP = 0.0536
332	DRIFT TOWARD BEING THOSE 0.75 OF 8 WHERE THE AGE AT BEGINNING OF MODESTY TRAINING IS LOWER THAN SIX YEARS (8) W-C	332	DRIFT TOWARD BEING THOSE 0.78 OF 9 WHERE THE AGE AT BEGINNING OF MODESTY TRAINING IS SIX YEARS OR HIGHER (9) W-C	2 7 6 2 XSQ= 2.85 PHI= -0.410 EP = 0.0567
334	TILT TOWARD BEING THOSE 0.68 OF 19 WHERE THE INDULGENCE OF THE CHILD IS LOW (38) B-B-C	334	TILT TOWARD BEING THOSE 0.72 OF 25 WHERE THE INDULGENCE OF THE CHILD IS HIGH (40) B-B-C	6 18 13 7 XSQ= 5.58 PHI= -0.356 XP = 0.0182
385	TILT LESS TOWARD BEING THOSE 0.53 OF 17 WHERE SEXUAL EXPRESSION BY THE YOUNG IS SEMI-RESTRICTED OR PERMITTED (64) F-B	385	TILT MORE TOWARD BEING THOSE 0.88 OF 25 WHERE SEXUAL EXPRESSION BY THE YOUNG IS SEMI-RESTRICTED OR PERMITTED (64) F-B	8 3 9 22 XSQ= 4.75 PHI= 0.336 XP = 0.0293
395	DRIFT TOWARD BEING THOSE 0.80 OF 5 WHERE BELIEF IN THE UNCLEANNESS OF WOMEN IS UNIMPORTANT OR ABSENT (15) LWS	395	DRIFT TOWARD BEING THOSE 0.78 OF 9 WHERE BELIEF IN THE UNCLEANNESS OF WOMEN IS PRESENT (18) LWS	1 7 4 2 XSQ= 2.34 PHI= -0.409 EP = 0.0909
402	TILT TOWARD BEING THOSE 0.74 OF 23 WHERE EXPLANATIONS OF ILLNESS OF AN ORAL NATURE ARE PRESENT (31) W-C	402	TILT TOWARD BEING THOSE 0.63 OF 38 WHERE EXPLANATIONS OF ILLNESS OF AN ORAL NATURE ARE ABSENT (30) W-C	17 14 6 24 XSQ= 6.46 PHI= 0.326 XP = 0.0110

403/

```
404  TILT TOWARD BEING THOSE          0.52 OF  23     404  TILT TOWARD BEING THOSE          0.82 OF  38          12     7
     WHERE EXPLANATIONS OF ILLNESS                        WHERE EXPLANATIONS OF ILLNESS                         11    31
     OF A SEXUAL NATURE                                   OF A SEXUAL NATURE                            XSQ=      6.12
     ARE PRESENT  (19) W-C                                ARE ABSENT  (42) W-C                          PHI=     0.317
                                                                                                        XP =    0.0134

444  TILT TOWARD BEING THOSE          0.75 OF   8     444  TILT TOWARD BEING THOSE          0.79 OF  14           2    11
     WHERE THE USE OF DREAMS                              WHERE THE USE OF DREAMS                                6     3
     TO SEEK AND CONTROL SUPERNATURAL POWERS              TO SEEK AND CONTROL SUPERNATURAL POWERS       XSQ=      4.03
     IS LOW  (27) RGD                                     IS HIGH  (28) RGD                             PHI=    -0.428
                                                                                                        EP =    0.0260

447  TILT TOWARD BEING THOSE          0.86 OF  14     447  TILT TOWARD BEING THOSE          0.58 OF  19          12     8
     WHERE LOVE MAGIC IS                                  WHERE LOVE MAGIC IS                                    2    11
     PRESENT  (20) S-R                                    ABSENT  (13) S-R                              XSQ=      4.72
                                                                                                        PHI=     0.378
                                                                                                        EP =    0.0151

455  TILT TOWARD BEING THOSE          0.89 OF   9     455  TILT TOWARD BEING THOSE          0.63 OF   8           1     5
     WHERE THE MODE OF THE INDIVIDUAL'S                   WHERE THE MODE OF THE INDIVIDUAL'S                     8     3
     CONTACT WITH THE DIVINE                              CONTACT WITH THE DIVINE                       XSQ=      2.91
     IS NOT CONDUCIVE TO THE DEVELOPMENT OF THE           IS CONDUCIVE TO THE DEVELOPMENT OF THE        PHI=    -0.413
     INDIVIDUAL'S NEED TO ACHIEVE  (19) DCM               INDIVIDUAL'S NEED TO ACHIEVE  (17) DCM        EP =    0.0498

474  DRIFT TOWARD BEING THOSE         0.71 OF  21     474  DRIFT TOWARD BEING THOSE         0.57 OF  28           6    16
     WHERE BOASTFULNESS IS MODERATE,                      WHERE BOASTFULNESS IS EXTREME  (41) PES               15    12
     NEGLIBIBLE, OR UNREPORTED  (48) PES                                                                XSQ=      2.89
                                                                                                        PHI=    -0.243
                                                                                                        XP =    0.0892
```

****

404 CULTURES WHERE EXPLANATIONS OF ILLNESS OF A SEXUAL NATURE ARE PRESENT (19) W-C	404 CULTURES WHERE EXPLANATIONS OF ILLNESS OF A SEXUAL NATURE ARE ABSENT (42) W-C

BACKGROUND ON PAGE 157 BOTH SUBJECT AND PREDICATE

....

19 IN LEFT COLUMN

ALORESE ARAPESH AZANDE CHIR-APACHE FON KURTATCHI KWAKIUTL LAMBA LEPCHA LESU
MANUS MACRI OMAHA PAPAGO PUKAPUKA RIFFIANS RWALA TETON TIV

42 IN RIGHT COLUMN

ABIPON AINU ANDAMANESE ASHANTI BALINESE CHAGGA CHENCHU COMANCHE COPR ESKIMO DOBUANS
DUSUN HANO IFUGAO JIVARO KUTENAI LAKHER LAPPS MARQUESANS MARSHALLESE MASAI
MURNGIN NAVAHO ONTONG-JAVA SAMOANS SANPOIL SENIANG SIRIONO TANALA TAOS TENINO
THONGA TIKOPIA TROBRIAND VENDA WAPISHANA WARRAU WITOTO WOGEO YAGUA YAKUT
YUKAGHIR ZUNI

339 EXCLUDED BECAUSE UNASCERTAINED

	Left column			Right column			
73	DRIFT TOWARD BEING THOSE WHERE WEAVING IS PRESENT (118)	0.67 OF 15	73	DRIFT TOWARD BEING THOSE WHERE WEAVING IS ABSENT (130)	0.68 OF 31		10 10 5 21 XSQ= 3.57 PHI= 0.279 XP = 0.0588
82	IN ALL CASES ARE THOSE WHERE A CITY OR TOWN IS PRESENT, OR THE AVERAGE COMMUNITY SIZE IS FIFTY OR GREATER (178)	1.00 OF 12	82	TILT LESS TOWARD BEING THOSE WHERE A CITY OR TOWN IS PRESENT, OR THE AVERAGE COMMUNITY SIZE IS FIFTY OR GREATER (178)	0.68 OF 28		12 19 0 9 XSQ= 3.30 PHI= 0.287 EP = 0.0375
98	DRIFT MORE TOWARD BEING THOSE WHERE THE HIERARCHY OF LOCAL JURISDICTION HAS FOUR OR THREE LEVELS (238) GES,EA	0.89 OF 18	98	DRIFT LESS TOWARD BEING THOSE WHERE THE HIERARCHY OF LOCAL JURISDICTION HAS FOUR OR THREE LEVELS (238) GES,EA	0.63 OF 38		16 24 2 14 XSQ= 2.80 PHI= 0.224 XP = 0.0941
127	DRIFT TOWARD BEING THOSE WHERE THE FEMALES' CONTRIBUTION TO SUBSISTENCE IS HIGH (33) JKB	0.73 OF 11	127	DRIFT TOWARD BEING THOSE WHERE THE FEMALES' CONTRIBUTION TO SUBSISTENCE IS LOW (32) JKB	0.73 OF 11		8 3 3 8 XSQ= 2.91 PHI= 0.364 EP = 0.0861

No.		No.		
242	DRIFT MORE TCWARC BEING THCSE 0.95 OF 19 WHERE MARRIAGE IS COMMCNLY CR CCCASICNALLY PCLYGYNOUS, RATHER THAN MCNCGAMCUS (314)	242	DRIFT LESS TOWARD BEING THCSE 0.71 OF 41 WHERE MARRIAGE IS COMMONLY OR OCCASIONALLY PCLYGYNCUS, RATHER THAN MONCGAMCUS (314)	18 29 1 12 XSQ= 3.11 PHI= 0.228 XP = 0.0779
259	DRIFT TCWARD BEING THCSE 0.64 OF 11 WHERE THE SEVERITY CF MCTHER-IN-LAW AVCIDANCE IS HIGH (26) WNS	259	DRIFT TOWARD BEING THOSE 0.75 CF 16 WHERE THE SEVERITY CF MCTHER-IN-LAW AVOIDANCE IS LOW (20) WNS	7 4 4 12 XSQ= 2.59 PHI= 0.310 EP = 0.0608
300	DRIFT TCWARD BEING THCSE 0.69 OF 13 WHERE THE POST-PARTUM SEX TABCO LASTS LCNGER THAN SIX MONTHS (51)	300	DRIFT TOWARD BEING THOSE 0.64 OF 22 WHERE THE POST-PARTUM SEX TABOO LASTS SIX MONTHS OR LESS (73)	9 8 4 14 XSQ= 2.34 PHI= 0.259 EP = 0.0858
309	DRIFT TCWARD BEING THCSE 0.71 OF 17 WHERE CRAL SCCIALIZATICN ANXIETY IS HIGH (26) W-C	309	DRIFT TOWARD BEING THOSE 0.61 OF 36 WHERE ORAL SOCIALIZATICN ANXIETY IS LOW (27) W-C	12 14 5 22 XSQ= 3.46 PHI= 0.256 XP = 0.0628
336	DRIFT TCWARD BEING THCSE 0.65 OF 17 WHERE THE TOTAL PCSITIVE PRESSURE TOWARD DEVELCPING RESPCNSIBLE BEHAVIOR IN THE CHILD IS LCW (32) B-B-C	336	DRIFT TOWARD BEING THOSE 0.68 OF 25 WHERE THE TOTAL PCSITIVE PRESSURE TOWARD DEVELOPING RESPONSIBLE BEHAVIOR IN THE CHILD IS HIGH (43) B-B-C	6 17 11 8 XSQ= 3.15 PHI= -0.274 XP = 0.0760
391	DRIFT TCWARD BEING THCSE 0.57 OF 14 WHERE PREMARITAL SEX RELATIONS ARE STRCNGLY PUNISHEC AND IN FACT RARE, OR WEAKLY PUNISHED ANC IN FACT NCT RARE (89) JTW,EA	391	DRIFT TOWARD BEING THOSE 0.74 OF 31 WHERE PREMARITAL SEX RELATICNS ARE PUNISHED ONLY IF PREGNANCY RESULTS, OR FREELY PERMITTED (90) JTW,EA	8 8 6 23 XSQ= 2.88 PHI= 0.253 XP = 0.0898
398	TEND TC BE THCSE 0.92 OF 12 WHERE THE INTENSITY CF SEX ANXIETY IS HIGH (16) WNS	398	TEND TO BE THOSE 0.75 CF 20 WHERE THE INTENSITY OF SEX ANXIETY IS LOW (16) WNS	11 5 1 15 XSQ= 10.80 PHI= 0.581 EP = 0.0006
399	TILT TCWARD BEING THCSE 0.69 OF 16 WHERE INTENSITY CF CASTRATION ANXIETY IS HIGH (23) WNS	399	TILT TOWARD BEING THOSE 0.74 OF 19 WHERE INTENSITY OF CASTRATICN ANXIETY IS LOW (22) WNS	11 5 5 14 XSQ= 4.71 PHI= 0.367 EP = 0.0185
402	TILT TCWARD BEING THCSE 0.74 OF 19 WHERE EXPLANATICNS CF ILLNESS CF AN CRAL NATURE ARE PRESENT (31) W-C	402	TILT TOWARD BEING THOSE 0.60 OF 42 WHERE EXPLANATICNS OF ILLNESS OF AN ORAL NATURE ARE ABSENT (30) W-C	14 17 5 25 XSQ= 4.52 PHI= 0.272 XP = 0.0335

```
403  TILT TOWARD BEING THOSE          0.63 OF  19    403  TILT TOWARD BEING THOSE          0.74 OF  42          12    11
     WHERE EXPLANATIONS OF ILLNESS                        WHERE EXPLANATIONS OF ILLNESS                            7    31
     OF AN ANAL NATURE                                    OF AN ANAL NATURE                                  XSQ=     6.12
     ARE PRESENT  (23) W-C                                ARE ABSENT  (38) W-C                               PHI=    0.317
                                                                                                             XP =   0.0134

447  DRIFT TOWARD BEING THOSE         0.83 OF  12    447  DRIFT TOWARD BEING THOSE         0.52 OF  21          10    10
     WHERE LOVE MAGIC IS                                  WHERE LOVE MAGIC IS                                      2    11
     PRESENT  (20) S-R                                    ABSENT  (13) S-R                                   XSQ=     2.72
                                                                                                             PHI=    0.287
                                                                                                             EP =   0.0672
```

405 CULTURES
WHERE EXPLANATICNS CF ILLNESS
CF A DEPENCENCE NATURE
ARE PRESENT (34) W-C

405 CULTURES
WHERE EXPLANATICNS OF ILLNESS
OF A DEPENDENCE NATURE
ARE ABSENT (27) W-C

BACKGROUND ON PAGE 157

BCTH SUBJECT AND PREDICATE

34 IN LEFT CCLUMN

AINU	ALCRESE	AZANCE	BALINESE	CHENCHU	CHIR-APACHE	COPR ESKIMO	DUSUN	IFUGAO	KWAKIUTL
LAKHER	LAMBA	LAPPS	LEPCHA	MANUS	MAORI	MARQUESANS	MARSHALLESE	MASAI	MURNGIN
PUKAPUKA	RIFFIANS	RWALA	SANPOIL	SIRIONO	TANALA	TENINO	THCNGA	TIKCPIA	VENCA
WAPISHANA	WITCTC	YAKUT	YUKAGHIR						

27 IN RIGHT CCLUMN

ABIPCN	ANDAMANESE	ARAPESH	ASHANTI	CHAGGA	COMANCHE	DOBUANS	FCN	HANC	JIVARO
KURTATCHI	KUTENAI	LESU	NAVAHO	OMAHA	ONTONG-JAVA	PAPAGO	SAMOANS	SENIANG	TAOS
TETCN	TIV	TRCBRIAND	WARRAU	WOGEO	YAGUA	ZUNI			

339 EXCLUCED BECAUSE UNASCERTAINEC

47	DRIFT TCWARD BEING THCSE 0.83 OF 12 WHERE, IF SETTLEMENTS ARE NON-FIXEC, MOVEMENT IS NCMADIC, RATHER THAN NCN-NCMADIC (72)	47	DRIFT TOWARD BEING THOSE 0.63 OF 8 WHERE, IF SETTLEMENTS ARE NCN-FIXED, MOVEMENT IS NON-NOMADIC, RATHER THAN NOMADIC (38)	10 3 2 5 XSQ= 2.65 PHI= 0.364 EP = 0.0623
63	DRIFT TCWARD BEING THCSE 0.67 OF 18 WHERE HUSBANDRY, IF PRESENT, IS PRINCIPALLY IN THE FORM OF BOVINE, ECUINE, CAMEL-LIKE, OR DEER-LIKE ANIMALS, RATHER THAN PIGS, SHEEP, CR GCATS (152)	63	DRIFT TOWARD BEING THOSE 0.68 CF 19 WHERE HUSBANDRY, IF PRESENT, IS PRINCIPALLY IN THE FCRM OF PIGS, SHEEP, OR GOATS, RATHER THAN BOVINE, EQUINE, CAMEL-LIKE, CR DEER-LIKE ANIMALS (74)	12 6 6 13 XSQ= 3.26 PHI= 0.297 EP = 0.0502
81	TILT TCWARD BEING THOSE 0.83 OF 23 WHERE NC CITY CR TCWN IS PRESENT, AND THE AVERAGE COMMUNITY SIZE IS SMALLER THAN 200 (135)	81	TILT TOWARD BEING THOSE 0.53 OF 17 WHERE A CITY OR TOWN IS PRESENT, OR THE AVERAGE COMMUNITY SIZE IS 20C OR GREATER (89)	4 9 19 8 XSQ= 4.13 PHI= -0.321 EP = 0.0383
88	TILT TCWARC BEING THOSE 0.79 OF 24 WHERE, IF A HEACMANSHIP IS PRESENT, SUCCESSICN IS HERECITARY (165)	88	TILT TOWARD BEING THOSE 0.59 OF 22 WHERE, IF A HEADMANSHIP IS PRESENT, SUCCESSION IS NCN-HEREDITARY (106)	5 13 19 9 XSQ= 5.54 PHI= -0.347 XP = 0.0186

```
102  DRIFT TCWARD BEING THCSE          0.62 OF  34     102  DRIFT TOWARD BEING THOSE          0.67 CF  27        21    9
     WHERE CLASS STRATIFICATICN IS                          WHERE CLASS STRATIFICATICN IS                          13   18
     PRESENT  (203)                                         ABSENT  (180)                                     XSQ=     3.80
                                                                                                              PHI=    0.249
                                                                                                              XP =   0.0514

129  DRIFT TCWARD BEING THCSE          0.80 OF  1C     129  DRIFT TOWARD BEING THOSE          0.67 OF   9         2    6
     WHERE WEAVING IS                                       WHERE WEAVING IS                                        8    3
     MAINLY DCNE BY FEMALES  (73)                           MAINLY DONE BY MALES  (31)                        XSQ=     2.53
                                                                                                              PHI=   -0.365
                                                                                                              EP =   0.0698

184  TILT TCWARD BEING THCSE           0.81 OF  21     184  TILT TOWARD BEING THOSE           0.63 CF  16         4   10
     WHERE THE LARGEST NCN-CCGNATIC KIN GROUP               WHERE THE LARGEST NON-CCGNATIC KIN GROUP              17    6
     IS SMALLER THAN A PHRATRY, I. E.                       IS THE MOEITY OR PHRATRY  (77)                    XSQ=     5.56
     A SIB CR LINEAGE  (175)                                                                                  PHI=   -0.388
                                                                                                              EP =   0.0152

198  IN ALL CASES ARE THCSE            1.00 OF  1C     198  TILT LESS TOWARD BEING THOSE  0.55 OF  11            10    6
     WHERE RULES FCR THE INHERITANCE OF                     WHERE RULES FCR THE INHERITANCE CF                      0    5
     REAL PRCPERTY, IF PRESENT,                             REAL PROPERTY, IF PRESENT,                        XSQ=     3.72
     FAVCR THE MALE HEIR CR LINE, RATHER THAN               FAVOR THE MALE HEIR OR LINE, RATHER THAN          PHI=    0.421
     THE FEMALE  (144)                                      THE FEMALE  (144)                                 EP =   0.0351

213  TILT LESS TOWARC BEING THCSE  0.53 OF  34         213  TILT MORE TOWARD BEING THCSE  0.85 CF  26            16    4
     WHERE FIRST CCUSIN MARRIAGE IS                         WHERE FIRST COUSIN MARRIAGE IS                        18   22
     NCT PERMITTED  (198)                                   NOT PERMITTED  (198)                              XSQ=     5.30
                                                                                                              PHI=    0.297
                                                                                                              XP =   0.0213

220  TILT LESS TOWARC BEINC THCSE  0.68 OF  34         22C  TILT MORE TOWARD BEING THCSE  0.96 OF  26            11    1
     WHERE FIRST CCUSIN MARRIACE                            WHERE FIRST COUSIN MARRIAGE                           23   25
     IN SCME FCRM CR CTHER                                  IN SOME FORM OR CTHER                             XSQ=     5.81
     IS NCT PRESCRIBEC CR PREFERREC  (273)                  IS NOT PRESCRIBED CR PREFERRED  (273)             PHI=    0.311
                                                                                                              XP =   0.0160

221  DRIFT LESS TCWARC BEING THCSE 0.82 OF  34         221  IN ALL CASES ARE THCSE            1.00 CF  26         6    0
     WHERE MATRILATERAL CRCSS-CCUSIN MARRIAGE               WHERE MATRILATERAL CROSS-CCUSIN MARRIAGE              28   26
     IS NCT PRESCRIBEC CR PREFERREC  (335)                  IS NOT PRESCRIBED CR PREFERRED  (335)             XSQ=     3.33
                                                                                                              PHI=    0.235
                                                                                                              XP =   0.0682

299  TILT TCWARD BEING THOSE           0.85 OF  2C     299  TILT TOWARD BEING THOSE           0.53 OF  15         3    8
     WHERE THE POST-PARTUM SEX TABCO LASTS                  WHERE THE POST-PARTUM SEX TABOO LASTS                 17    7
     CNE YEAR CR LESS  (89)                                 LONGER THAN ONE YEAR  (35)                        XSQ=     4.20
                                                                                                              PHI=   -0.346
                                                                                                              EP =   0.0271

300  TILT TCWARD BEING THCSE           0.70 OF  20     30C  TILT TOWARD BEING THOSE           0.73 CF  15         6   11
     WHERE THE POST-PARTUM SEX TABOO LASTS                  WHERE THE POST-PARTUM SEX TABCC LASTS                 14    4
     SIX MCNTHS OR LESS  (73)                               LONGER THAN SIX MONTHS  (51)                      XSQ=     4.83
                                                                                                              PHI=   -0.371
                                                                                                              EP =   0.0176
```

307	DRIFT TOWARD BEING THOSE WHERE THE EARLY AGGRESSION SATISFACTION POTENTIAL IS HIGH (33) W-C	0.76 OF 29	307	DRIFT TOWARD BEING THOSE WHERE THE EARLY AGGRESSION SATISFACTION POTENTIAL IS LOW (19) W-C	0.52 OF 23	22 11 7 12 XSQ= 3.22 PHI= 0.249 XP = 0.0726
311	TILT TOWARD BEING THOSE WHERE SEXUAL SOCIALIZATION ANXIETY IS LOW (23) W-C	0.60 OF 30	311	TILT TOWARD BEING THOSE WHERE SEXUAL SOCIALIZATION ANXIETY IS HIGH (28) W-C	0.76 OF 21	12 16 18 5 XSQ= 5.15 PHI= -0.318 XP = 0.0232
317	DRIFT TOWARD BEING THOSE WHERE DISPLAY OF AFFECTION TOWARD THE INFANT IS LOW (29) B-B-C	0.58 OF 19	317	DRIFT TOWARD BEING THOSE WHERE DISPLAY OF AFFECTION TOWARD THE INFANT IS HIGH (39) B-B-C	0.74 OF 19	8 14 11 5 XSQ= 2.70 PHI= -0.267 EP = 0.0991
318	LEAN TOWARD BEING THOSE WHERE THE OVERALL INDULGENCE OF THE INFANT IS LOW (31) B-B-C	0.71 OF 21	318	LEAN TOWARD BEING THOSE WHERE THE OVERALL INDULGENCE OF THE INFANT IS HIGH (40) B-B-C	0.80 OF 20	6 16 15 4 XSQ= 8.93 PHI= -0.467 XP = 0.0028
319	TILT TOWARD BEING THOSE WHERE PROTECTION OF THE INFANT FROM ENVIRONMENTAL DISCOMFORTS IS LOW (30) B-B-C	0.63 OF 19	319	TILT TOWARD BEING THOSE WHERE PROTECTION OF THE INFANT FROM ENVIRONMENTAL DISCOMFORTS IS HIGH (35) B-B-C	0.75 OF 16	7 12 12 4 XSQ= 3.67 PHI= -0.324 EP = 0.0411
320	TILT TOWARD BEING THOSE WHERE THE DEGREE OF REDUCTION OF THE INFANT'S DRIVES IS LOW (24) B-B-C	0.55 OF 22	320	TILT TOWARD BEING THOSE WHERE THE DEGREE OF REDUCTION OF THE INFANT'S DRIVES IS HIGH (45) B-B-C	0.83 OF 18	10 15 12 3 XSQ= 4.55 PHI= -0.337 EP = 0.0217
324	LEAN TOWARD BEING THOSE WHERE THE PAIN INFLICTED ON THE INFANT BY THE NURTURANT AGENT IS HIGH (34) B-B-C	0.74 OF 19	324	LEAN TOWARD BEING THOSE WHERE THE PAIN INFLICTED ON THE INFANT BY THE NURTURANT AGENT IS LOW OR NEGLIGIBLE (32) B-B-C	0.79 OF 19	14 4 5 15 XSQ= 8.55 PHI= 0.474 EP = 0.0029
340	TILT TOWARD BEING THOSE WHERE THE TOTAL POSITIVE PRESSURE TOWARD DEVELOPING NURTURANT BEHAVIOR IN THE CHILD IS LOW (20) B-B-C	0.71 OF 14	340	TILT TOWARD BEING THOSE WHERE THE TOTAL POSITIVE PRESSURE TOWARD DEVELOPING NURTURANT BEHAVIOR IN THE CHILD IS HIGH (28) B-B-C	0.77 OF 13	4 10 10 3 XSQ= 4.52 PHI= -0.409 EP = 0.0213
341	DRIFT TOWARD BEING THOSE WHERE THE CHILD'S INFERRED ANXIETY OVER NON-PERFORMANCE OF NURTURANT BEHAVIOR IS LOW (16) B-B-C	0.50 OF 12	341	DRIFT TOWARD BEING THOSE WHERE THE CHILD'S INFERRED ANXIETY OVER NON-PERFORMANCE OF NURTURANT BEHAVIOR IS HIGH (30) B-B-C	0.85 OF 13	6 11 6 2 XSQ= 2.03 PHI= -0.285 EP = 0.0968

```
365  TILT TOWARD BEING THOSE          0.69 OF  13   365  TILT TOWARD BEING THOSE          0.80 OF  10          4     8
     WHERE THE TIME SPENT IN                             WHERE THE TIME SPENT IN                                9     2
     ADOLESCENT PEER GROUP ACTIVITY                      ADOLESCENT PEER GROUP ACTIVITY                XSQ=    3.69
     IS LOW-MEDIUM OR LOW  (15) JKH                      IS HIGH OR HIGH-MEDIUM  (30) JKH               PHI=  -0.401
                                                                                                        EP =  0.0361

368  DRIFT TOWARD BEING THOSE         0.73 OF  11   368  DRIFT TOWARD BEING THOSE         0.75 OF   8          3     6
     WHERE DISSOCIATION OF THE SEXES                     WHERE DISSOCIATION OF THE SEXES                        8     2
     AT ADOLESCENCE                                      AT ADOLESCENCE                                 XSQ=    2.53
     IS LOW  (21) JKH                                    IS HIGH OR MEDIUM  (16) JKH                    PHI=  -0.365
                                                                                                        EP =  0.0698

382  LEAN TOWARD BEING THOSE          0.64 OF  14   382  IN ALL CASES ARE THOSE           1.00 OF   8          5     8
     WHERE FEMALE INITIATION RITES                       WHERE FEMALE INITIATION RITES                          9     0
     ARE ABSENT  (27) JKB                                ARE PRESENT  (38) JKB                          XSQ=    6.25
                                                                                                        PHI=  -0.533
                                                                                                        EP =  0.0055

396  TILT TOWARD BEING THOSE          0.83 OF  23   396  TILT TOWARD BEING THOSE          0.53 OF  15          4     8
     WHERE THE STRENGTH OF MENSTRUAL TABOOS              WHERE THE STRENGTH OF MENSTRUAL TABOOS                19     7
     IS LOW  (35) WNS                                    IS HIGH  (18) WNS                              XSQ=    3.89
                                                                                                        PHI=  -0.320
                                                                                                        EP =  0.0326

400  TILT TOWARD BEING THOSE          0.68 OF  19   400  TILT TOWARD BEING THOSE          0.80 OF  10         13     2
     WHERE HOMOSEXUAL ACTIVITY                           WHERE HOMOSEXUAL ACTIVITY                              6     8
     IS PROHIBITED  (22) F-B                             IS PERMITTED  (36) F-B                         XSQ=    4.37
                                                                                                        PHI=   0.388
                                                                                                        EP =  0.0209

424  TILT TOWARD BEING THOSE          0.67 OF   9   424  TILT TOWARD BEING THOSE          0.88 OF   8          6     1
     WHERE RELIGIOUS SPECIALISTS ARE                     WHERE RELIGIOUS SPECIALISTS ARE                        3     7
     FULL-TIME, RATHER THAN                              PART-TIME, RATHER THAN                         XSQ=    3.14
     PART-TIME  (21) JMH                                 FULL-TIME  (33) JMH                            PHI=   0.430
                                                                                                        EP =  0.0498

426  TILT TOWARD BEING THOSE          0.64 OF  28   426  TILT TOWARD BEING THOSE          0.71 OF  21         18     6
     WHERE A HIGH GOD IS                                 WHERE A HIGH GOD IS                                   10    15
     PRESENT  (156) GES,EA                               ABSENT  (104) GES,EA                           XSQ=    4.78
                                                                                                        PHI=   0.312
                                                                                                        XP =  0.0288

430  DRIFT TOWARD BEING THOSE         0.83 OF   6   430  DRIFT TOWARD BEING THOSE         0.80 OF   5          5     1
     WHERE SUPERNATURAL SANCTIONS FOR MORALITY,          WHERE SUPERNATURAL SANCTIONS FOR MORALITY,             1     4
     HAVING AN EFFECT ON                                 HAVING AN EFFECT ON                            XSQ=    2.23
     AN INDIVIDUAL'S HEALTH,                             AN INDIVIDUAL'S HEALTH,                        PHI=   0.450
     ARE PRESENT  (16) GES                               ARE ABSENT OR UNREPORTED  (22) GES             EP =  0.0801

447  DRIFT TOWARD BEING THOSE         0.52 OF  21   447  DRIFT TOWARD BEING THOSE         0.83 OF  12         10    10
     WHERE LOVE MAGIC IS                                 WHERE LOVE MAGIC IS                                   11     2
     ABSENT  (13) S-R                                    PRESENT  (20) S-R                              XSQ=    2.72
                                                                                                        PHI=  -0.287
                                                                                                        EP =  0.0672
```

```
452  TILT TOWARD BEING THOSE          0.69 OF  13     452  TILT TOWARD BEING THOSE          0.77 OF  13            4    10
     WHERE TOTEMISM WITH FOOD TABOOS                       WHERE TOTEMISM WITH FOOD TABOOS                         9     3
     IS ABSENT  (24) WNS                                   IS PRESENT  (19) WNS                             XSQ=     3.87
                                                                                                            PHI=   -0.386
                                                                                                            EP =   0.0472

478  IN ALL CASES ARE THOSE           1.00 OF   4     478  TILT TOWARD BEING THOSE          0.80 OF   5            4     1
     WHERE THE ABANDONMENT OR KILLING OF                   WHERE THE ABANDONMENT OR KILLING OF                     0     4
     OLD PEOPLE IS                                         OLD PEOPLE IS                                    XSQ=     2.98
     PRESENT  (12) LWS                                     UNIMPORTANT OR ABSENT  (12) LWS                  PHI=    0.575
                                                                                                            EP =   0.0476
```

****

406 CULTURES WHERE EXPLANATIONS OF ILLNESS OF AN AGGRESSION NATURE ARE PRESENT (28) W-C	406 CULTURES WHERE EXPLANATIONS OF ILLNESS OF AN AGGRESSION NATURE ARE ABSENT (33) W-C

BACKGROUND ON PAGE 157

BOTH SUBJECT AND PREDICATE

....

28 IN LEFT COLUMN

ALORESE	AZANDE	CHIR-APACHE	COPR ESKIMO	HANO	IFUGAO	JIVARO	KWAKIUTL	LAKHER	LAMBA
LAPPS	LEPCHA	MACRI	MURNGIN	NAVAHO	OMAHA	PAPAGO	PUKAPUKA	RIFFIANS	SAMOANS
SANPOIL	SENIANG	TAOS	TIV	WARRAU	YAGUA	YAKUT	ZUNI		

33 IN RIGHT COLUMN

ABIPON	AINU	ANDAMANESE	ARAPESH	ASHANTI	BALINESE	CHAGGA	CHENCHU	COMANCHE	CUBUANS
DUSUN	FON	KURTATCHI	KUTENAI	LESU	MANUS	MARQUESANS	MARSHALLESE	MASAI	ONTONG-JAVA
RWALA	SIRIONO	TANALA	TENINO	TETON	THONGA	TIKOPIA	TROBRIAND	VENDA	WAPISHANA
WITOTO	WOGEO	YUKAGHIR							

339 EXCLUDED BECAUSE UNASCERTAINED

8	DRIFT LESS TOWARD BEING THOSE 0.64 OF 28 LOCATED OUTSIDE OF NORTH AMERICA (330)	8	DRIFT MORE TOWARD BEING THOSE 0.88 OF 33 LOCATED OUTSIDE OF NORTH AMERICA (330)	10 4 18 29 XSQ= 3.53 PHI= 0.240 XP = 0.0604
14	TILT TOWARD BEING THOSE 0.50 OF 28 WHERE THE LATITUDE IS THIRTY DEGREES OR GREATER (119)	14	TILT TOWARD BEING THOSE 0.79 OF 33 WHERE THE LATITUDE IS LESS THAN THIRTY DEGREES (281)	14 7 14 26 XSQ= 4.36 PHI= 0.267 XP = 0.0368
16	TILT TOWARD BEING THOSE 0.79 OF 28 WHERE THE LATITUDE IS TEN DEGREES OR GREATER (277)	16	TILT TOWARD BEING THOSE 0.52 OF 33 WHERE THE LATITUDE IS LESS THAN TEN DEGREES (123)	22 16 6 17 XSQ= 4.63 PHI= 0.275 XP = 0.0315
33	DRIFT LESS TOWARD BEING THOSE 0.68 OF 28 WHERE THE NATURAL ENVIRONMENT IS OTHER THAN 'VERY HARSH,' I.E., DESERT, DESERT GRASSES AND SHRUBS, TUNDRA, OR HIGH PLATEAU STEPPE (341) FWM	33	DRIFT MORE TOWARD BEING THOSE 0.91 OF 33 WHERE THE NATURAL ENVIRONMENT IS OTHER THAN 'VERY HARSH,' I.E., DESERT, DESERT GRASSES AND SHRUBS, TUNDRA, OR HIGH PLATEAU STEPPE (341) FWM	9 3 19 30 XSQ= 3.74 PHI= 0.248 XP = 0.0531

No.		No.		
42	DRIFT TOWARD BEING THOSE 0.71 OF 28 WHERE THE NATURAL ENVIRONMENT IS OTHER THAN TROPICAL OR SUB-TROPICAL RAIN FOREST, OR MONSOON FOREST (244) FWM	42	DRIFT TOWARD BEING THOSE 0.55 OF 33 WHERE THE NATURAL ENVIRONMENT IS TROPICAL OR SUB-TROPICAL RAIN FOREST, OR MONSOON FOREST (156) FWM	8 18 20 15 XSQ= 3.18 PHI= -0.228 XP = 0.0744
116	DRIFT TOWARD BEING THOSE 0.75 OF 8 WHERE OCCUPATIONAL SPECIALIZATION IS FULL-TIME, WHETHER OR NOT FOR SURPLUS PRODUCTION (20) JMH	116	DRIFT TOWARD BEING THOSE 0.78 OF 9 WHERE OCCUPATIONAL SPECIALIZATION IS PART-TIME ONLY (34) JMH	6 2 2 7 XSQ= 2.85 PHI= 0.410 EP = 0.0567
234	DRIFT TOWARD BEING THOSE 0.68 OF 22 WHERE THE COUSIN TERMINOLOGY IS OF ESKIMO OR HAWAIIAN TYPE, RATHER THAN CROW, OMAHA, OR IROQUOIS TYPE (170)	234	DRIFT TOWARD BEING THOSE 0.62 OF 26 WHERE THE COUSIN TERMINOLOGY IS OF CROW, OMAHA, OR IROQUOIS TYPE, RATHER THAN ESKIMO OR HAWAIIAN TYPE (152)	7 16 15 10 XSQ= 3.11 PHI= -0.255 XP = 0.0778
285	TILT TOWARD BEING THOSE 0.80 OF 15 WHERE THE SEX TABOO DURING PREGNANCY IS ABSENT OR INFERRED ABSENT (17) BCA	285	TILT TOWARD BEING THOSE 0.69 OF 16 WHERE THE SEX TABOO DURING PREGNANCY IS PRESENT (14) BCA	3 11 12 5 XSQ= 5.59 PHI= -0.425 EP = 0.0113
314	DRIFT MORE TOWARD BEING THOSE 0.92 OF 24 WHERE THE INCIDENCE OF MOTHER-CHILD HOUSEHOLDS IS LOW (61) W-D,S	314	DRIFT LESS TOWARD BEING THOSE 0.65 OF 20 WHERE THE INCIDENCE OF MOTHER-CHILD HOUSEHOLDS IS LOW (61) W-D,S	2 7 22 13 XSQ= 3.27 PHI= -0.273 XP = 0.0706
316	DRIFT TOWARD BEING THOSE 0.71 OF 17 WHERE EXCLUSIVE MOTHER-SON SLEEPING ARRANGEMENTS LAST LESS THAN ONE YEAR (25) W-K-A	316	DRIFT TOWARD BEING THOSE 0.70 OF 10 WHERE EXCLUSIVE MOTHER-SON SLEEPING ARRANGEMENTS LAST ONE YEAR OR LONGER (19) W-K-A	5 7 12 3 XSQ= 2.72 PHI= -0.317 EP = 0.0568
338	DRIFT TOWARD BEING THOSE 0.79 OF 19 WHERE THE CHILD'S INFERRED ANXIETY OVER PERFORMANCE OF RESPONSIBLE BEHAVIOR IS HIGH (44) B-B-C	338	DRIFT TOWARD BEING THOSE 0.52 OF 21 WHERE THE CHILD'S INFERRED ANXIETY OVER PERFORMANCE OF RESPONSIBLE BEHAVIOR IS LOW (29) B-B-C	15 10 4 11 XSQ= 2.95 PHI= 0.271 EP = 0.0550
351	TILT TOWARD BEING THOSE 0.69 OF 16 WHERE THE CHILD'S INFERRED CONFLICT REGARDING ACHIEVEMENT BEHAVIOR IS HIGH (26) B-B-C	351	TILT TOWARD BEING THOSE 0.73 OF 15 WHERE THE CHILD'S INFERRED CONFLICT REGARDING ACHIEVEMENT BEHAVIOR IS LOW (34) B-B-C	11 4 5 11 XSQ= 3.93 PHI= 0.356 EP = 0.0320
353	DRIFT TOWARD BEING THOSE 0.76 OF 21 WHERE THE CHILD'S INFERRED ANXIETY OVER NON-PERFORMANCE OF OBEDIENT BEHAVIOR IS HIGH (42) B-B-C	353	DRIFT TOWARD BEING THOSE 0.55 OF 20 WHERE THE CHILD-S INFERRED ANXIETY OVER NON-PERFORMANCE OF OBEDIENT BEHAVIOR IS LOW (32) B-B-C	16 9 5 11 XSQ= 2.98 PHI= 0.270 XP = 0.0843

365	TILT TCWARD BEING THOSE WHERE THE TIME SPENT IN ADCLESCENT PEER GRCUP ACTIVITY IS LCW-MEDIUM CR LCW (15) JKH	0.69 OF 13	365	TILT TOWARD BEING THOSE WHERE THE TIME SPENT IN ADOLESCENT PEER GROUP ACTIVITY IS HIGH OR HIGH-MEDIUM (30) JKH	0.80 CF 10	4 8 9 2 XSQ= 3.69 PHI= -0.401 EP = 0.0361
368	DRIFT TCWARD BEING THCSE WHERE DISSCCIATICN CF THE SEXES AT ADCLESCENCE IS LCW (21) JKH	0.73 OF 11	368	DRIFT TOWARD BEING THCSE WHERE DISSOCIATION OF THE SEXES AT ADOLESCENCE IS HIGH OR MEDIUM (16) JKH	0.75 OF 8	3 6 8 2 XSQ= 2.53 PHI= -0.365 EP = 0.0698
370	DRIFT TCWARD BEING THCSE WHERE THE SEGREGATICN CF ADOLESCENT BOYS IS ABSENT (148)	0.79 OF 24	37C	DRIFT TOWARD BEING THOSE WHERE THE SEGREGATION OF ADCLESCENT BOYS IS COMPLETE OR PARTIAL (95)	0.50 CF 24	5 12 19 12 XSQ= 3.28 PHI= -0.261 XP = 0.0702
426	TILT TCWARD BEING THOSE WHERE A HIGH GCC IS PRESENT (156) GES,EA	0.67 OF 24	426	TILT TOWARD BEING THOSE WHERE A HIGH GCD IS ABSENT (104) GES,EA	0.68 OF 25	16 8 8 17 XSQ= 4.58 PHI= 0.306 XP = 0.0323
432	DRIFT LESS TCWARC BEING THCSE WHERE AN ATTRACTIVE AFTERLIFE IS BELIEVED IN (27) LWS	0.57 OF 7	432	IN ALL CASES ARE THOSE WHERE AN ATTRACTIVE AFTERLIFE IS BELIEVED IN (27) LWS	1.00 CF 9	4 9 3 0 XSQ= 2.35 PHI= -0.383 EP = 0.0625
452	DRIFT TCWARD BEING THCSE WHERE TCTEMISM WITH FCCC TABOOS IS ABSENT (24) WNS	0.64 OF 14	452	DRIFT TOWARD BEING THOSE WHERE TOTEMISM WITH FCCD TABCOS IS PRESENT (19) WNS	0.75 OF 12	5 9 9 3 XSQ= 2.59 PHI= -0.315 EP = 0.0618
459	DRIFT TCWARD BEING THCSE WHERE GAMES, IF PRESENT, INCLUDE GAMES CF CHANCE (82) R-A-B,EA	0.55 OF 22	459	DRIFT TOWARD BEING THCSE WHERE GAMES, IF PRESENT, DO NOT INCLUDE GAMES OF CHANCE (89) R-A-B,EA	0.75 CF 24	12 6 10 18 XSQ= 3.06 PHI= 0.258 XP = 0.0804
460	DRIFT TCWARD BEING THCSE WHERE GAMES, IF PRESENT, ARE NCT LIMITED TO GAMES CF SKILL CNLY (104) R-A-B,EA	0.68 OF 22	46C	DRIFT TOWARD BEING THCSE WHERE GAMES, IF PRESENT, ARE LIMITED TO GAMES OF SKILL ONLY (67) R-A-B,EA	0.63 OF 24	7 15 15 9 XSQ= 3.19 PHI= -0.263 XP = 0.0742

407 CULTURES
WHERE PERFORMANCE THERAPIES
OF AN ORAL NATURE
ARE PRESENT (37) W-C

407 CULTURES
WHERE PERFORMANCE THERAPIES
OF AN ORAL NATURE
ARE ABSENT (17) W-C

BACKGROUND ON PAGE 157

SUBJECT ONLY

37 IN LEFT COLUMN

ABIPON	AINU	ANDAMANESE	AZANDE	BALINESE	CHAGGA	CHENCHU	CHIR-APACHE	COPR ESKIMO	DUSUN
FON	HANO	JIVARO	KURTATCHI	KWAKIUTL	LAKHER	LAMBA	LAPPS	LEPCHA	LESU
MAORI	MARSHALLESE	MURNGIN	OMAHA	PAPAGO	PUKAPUKA	RIFFIANS	RWALA	SANPOIL	SIRIONO
TANALA	TAOS	TENINO	TETON	THONGA	WITOTO	ZUNI			

17 IN RIGHT COLUMN

ALORESE	ARAPESH	COMANCHE	DOBUANS	IFUGAO	MANUS	MARQUESANS	MASAI	NAVAHO	ONTONG-JAVA
SENIANG	TIKOPIA	TROBRIAND	WARRAU	WOGEO	YAGUA	YAKUT			

346 EXCLUDED BECAUSE UNASCERTAINED

---

6 LEAN TOWARD BEING THOSE LOCATED OUTSIDE OF THE INSULAR PACIFIC (330) — 0.78 OF 37

6 LEAN TOWARD BEING THOSE LOCATED IN THE INSULAR PACIFIC (70) — 0.65 OF 17

8 11
29 6
XSQ= 7.69
PHI= -0.377
XP = 0.0056

15 TILT TOWARD BEING THOSE WHERE THE LATITUDE IS TWENTY DEGREES OR GREATER (183) — 0.57 OF 37

15 TILT TOWARD BEING THOSE WHERE THE LATITUDE IS LESS THAN TWENTY DEGREES (217) — 0.82 OF 17

21 3
16 14
XSQ= 5.72
PHI= 0.325
XP = 0.0168

16 DRIFT TOWARD BEING THOSE WHERE THE LATITUDE IS TEN DEGREES OR GREATER (277) — 0.73 OF 37

16 DRIFT TOWARD BEING THOSE WHERE THE LATITUDE IS LESS THAN TEN DEGREES (123) — 0.59 OF 17

27 7
10 10
XSQ= 3.78
PHI= 0.265
XP = 0.0519

36 DRIFT LESS TOWARD BEING THOSE WHERE THE NATURAL ENVIRONMENT IS OTHER THAN 'VERY HARSH,' OR SUB-TROPICAL BUSH, OR TEMPERATE GRASSLAND (292) FWM — 0.54 OF 37

36 DRIFT MORE TOWARD BEING THOSE WHERE THE NATURAL ENVIRONMENT IS OTHER THAN 'VERY HARSH,' OR SUB-TROPICAL BUSH, OR TEMPERATE GRASSLAND (292) FWM — 0.82 OF 17

17 3
20 14
XSQ= 2.88
PHI= 0.231
XP = 0.0898

42	LEAN TOWARD BEING THOSE WHERE THE NATURAL ENVIRONMENT IS OTHER THAN TROPICAL OR SUB-TROPICAL RAIN FOREST, OR MONSOON FOREST (244) FWM	0.70 OF 37	42	LEAN TOWARD BEING THOSE WHERE THE NATURAL ENVIRONMENT IS TROPICAL OR SUB-TROPICAL RAIN FOREST, OR MONSOON FOREST (156) FWM	0.76 OF 17	11 13 26 4 XSQ= 8.50 PHI= -0.397 XP = 0.0036
63	TILT TOWARD BEING THOSE WHERE HUSBANDRY, IF PRESENT, IS PRINCIPALLY IN THE FORM OF BOVINE, EQUINE, CAMEL-LIKE, OR DEER-LIKE ANIMALS, RATHER THAN PIGS, SHEEP, OR GOATS (152)	0.67 OF 21	63	TILT TOWARD BEING THOSE WHERE HUSBANDRY, IF PRESENT, IS PRINCIPALLY IN THE FORM OF PIGS, SHEEP, OR GOATS, RATHER THAN BOVINE, EQUINE, CAMEL-LIKE, OR DEER-LIKE ANIMALS (74)	0.82 OF 11	14 2 7 9 XSQ= 4.99 PHI= 0.395 EP = 0.0233
137	TILT TOWARD BEING THOSE WHERE INVIDIOUS DISPLAY OF WEALTH IS MODERATELY, LITTLE, OR NEGATIVELY EMPHASIZED (52) PES	0.79 OF 29	137	TILT TOWARD BEING THOSE WHERE INVIDIOUS DISPLAY OF WEALTH IS STRONGLY EMPHASIZED (37) PES	0.60 OF 15	6 9 23 6 XSQ= 5.16 PHI= -0.343 XP = 0.0231
285	TILT TOWARD BEING THOSE WHERE THE SEX TABOO DURING PREGNANCY IS ABSENT OR INFERRED ABSENT (17) BCA	0.70 OF 20	285	TILT TOWARD BEING THOSE WHERE THE SEX TABOO DURING PREGNANCY IS PRESENT (14) BCA	0.88 OF 8	6 7 14 1 XSQ= 5.46 PHI= -0.442 EP = 0.0108
345	TILT TOWARD BEING THOSE WHERE THE CHILD'S INFERRED ANXIETY OVER NON-PERFORMANCE OF SELF-RELIANT BEHAVIOR IS HIGH (37) B-B-C	0.58 OF 24	345	TILT TOWARD BEING THOSE WHERE THE CHILD'S INFERRED ANXIETY OVER NON-PERFORMANCE OF SELF-RELIANT BEHAVIOR IS LOW (39) B-B-C	0.79 OF 14	14 3 10 11 XSQ= 3.49 PHI= 0.303 EP = 0.0432
356	DRIFT TOWARD BEING THOSE WHERE NEITHER ADOLESCENT PEER GROUPS NOR PAIRS ARE PRESENT IN A SETTING OF COURTSHIP (22) JKH	0.72 OF 18	356	DRIFT TOWARD BEING THOSE WHERE ADOLESCENT PEER GROUPS OR PAIRS ARE PRESENT IN A SETTING OF COURTSHIP (29) JKH	0.83 OF 6	5 5 13 1 XSQ= 3.66 PHI= -0.390 EP = 0.0501

```
408  CULTURES                                        408  CULTURES
     WHERE PERFCRMANCE THERAPIES                          WHERE PERFORMANCE THERAPIES
     OF AN ANAL NATURE                                    OF AN ANAL NATURE
     ARE PRESENT  (22) W-C                                ARE ABSENT  (32) W-C
```

BACKGROUND ON PAGE 157

SUBJECT ONLY

```
   22  IN LEFT CCLUMN

ABIPCN      AINU         ANCAMANESE  AZANCE    CHIR-APACHE HANO       JIVARO       KWAKIUTL    LAPPS      LESU
MAORI       MARSHALLESE  MASAI       MURNGIN   NAVAHO      OMAHA      PAPAGO       PUKAPUKA    RWALA      SANPOIL
THONGA      WITCTC

   32  IN RIGHT CCLUMN

ALORESE     ARAPESH      BALINESE    CHACGA    CHENCHU     COMANCHE   COPR ESKIMO  DCBUANS     DUSUN      FON
IFUGAO      KURTATCHI    LAKHER      LAMBA     LEPCHA      MANUS      MARQUESANS   CNTCNG-JAVA RIFFIANS   SENIANG
SIRICNC     TANALA       TACS        TENINO    TETON       TIKOPIA    TROBRIAND    WARRAU      WOGEO      YAGUA
YAKUT       ZUNI

  346  EXCLUCED BECAUSE UNASCERTAINEC
```

```
33  TILT LESS TOWARC BEING THCSE   0.64 OF  22     33  TILT MORE TOWARD BEING THCSE   0.91 OF  32           8    3
    WHERE THE NATURAL ENVIRCNMENT IS                   WHERE THE NATURAL ENVIRCNMENT IS                    14   29
    CTHER THAN 'VERY HARSH,' I.E., DESERT,             OTHER THAN 'VERY HARSH,' I.E., DESERT,       XSQ=    4.31
    DESERT GRASSES AND SHRUBS, TUNCRA, OR              DESERT GRASSES AND SHRUBS, TUNDRA, OR        PHI=   0.282
    HIGH PLATEAU STEPPE  (341) FWM                     HIGH PLATEAU STEPPE  (341) FWM               XP =  0.0379

36  TILT TCWARC BEING THCSE        0.59 OF  22     36  TILT TOWARD BEING THCSE        0.78 CF  32          13    7
    WHERE THE NATURAL ENVIRONMENT IS                   WHERE THE NATURAL ENVIRONMENT IS                     9   25
    'VERY HARSH,' CR SUB-TRCPICAL BUSH, OR             OTHER THAN                                   XSQ=    6.23
    TEMPERATE GRASSLANC  (108) FWM                     'VERY HARSH,' OR SUB-TRCPICAL BUSH, CR       PHI=   0.340
                                                       TEMPERATE GRASSLAND  (292) FWM               XP =  0.0126

42  TILT TCWARD BEING THOSE        0.77 OF  22     42  TILT TOWARD BEING THOSE        0.59 OF  32           5   19
    WHERE THE NATURAL ENVIRONMENT IS                   WHERE THE NATURAL ENVIRCNMENT IS                    17   13
    CTHER THAN                                         TROPICAL OR SUB-TROPICAL RAIN FOREST, OR     XSQ=    5.68
    TRCPICAL CR SUB-TRCPICAL RAIN FOREST, OR           MONSOON FOREST  (156) FWM                    PHI=  -0.324
    MCNSCCN FCREST  (244) FWM                                                                       XP =  0.0171

46  DRIFT LESS TCWARC BEING THCSE  0.64 OF  22     46  DRIFT MORE TOWARD BEING THCSE  0.89 CF  27           8    3
    CTHER THAN WHERE SETTLEMENTS ARE                   OTHER THAN WHERE SETTLEMENTS ARE                    14   24
    NCN-FIXED AND MCVEMENT IS                          NON-FIXED AND MOVEMENT IS                    XSQ=    3.11
    NOMADIC  (260)                                     NOMADIC  (260)                               PHI=   0.252
                                                                                                    XP =  0.0779
```

54	TILT LESS TOWARD BEING THOSE 0.55 OF 11 WHERE FOOD PRODUCTION IS BY INTENSIVE OR SIMPLE AGRICULTURE, RATHER THAN BY INCIPIENT FOOD PRODUCTION (192)	54	TILT MORE TOWARD BEING THOSE 0.94 OF 18 WHERE FOOD PRODUCTION IS BY INTENSIVE OR SIMPLE AGRICULTURE, RATHER THAN BY INCIPIENT FOOD PRODUCTION (192)	6 17 5 1 XSQ= 4.42 PHI= -0.390 EP = 0.0185
56	DRIFT TOWARD BEING THOSE 0.50 OF 10 WHERE FOOD PRODUCTION IS BY INCIPIENT FOOD PRODUCTION, RATHER THAN BY SIMPLE AGRICULTURE (46)	56	DRIFT TOWARD BEING THOSE 0.91 OF 11 WHERE FOOD PRODUCTION IS BY SIMPLE AGRICULTURE, RATHER THAN BY INCIPIENT FOOD PRODUCTION (101)	5 10 5 1 XSQ= 2.52 PHI= -0.347 EP = 0.0635
131	TILT LESS TOWARD BEING THOSE 0.71 OF 14 WHERE THE CONSTRUCTION OF PERMANENT HOUSES OR THE ERECTION OF TEMPORARY DWELLINGS IS MAINLY DONE BY MALES (136)	131	IN ALL CASES ARE THOSE 1.00 OF 16 WHERE THE CONSTRUCTION OF PERMANENT HOUSES OR THE ERECTION OF TEMPORARY DWELLINGS IS MAINLY DONE BY MALES (136)	10 16 4 0 XSQ= 3.09 PHI= -0.321 EP = 0.0365
137	DRIFT MORE TOWARD BEING THOSE 0.84 OF 19 WHERE INVIDIOUS DISPLAY OF WEALTH IS MODERATELY, LITTLE, OR NEGATIVELY EMPHASIZED (52) PES	137	DRIFT LESS TOWARD BEING THOSE 0.52 OF 25 WHERE INVIDIOUS DISPLAY OF WEALTH IS MODERATELY, LITTLE, OR NEGATIVELY EMPHASIZED (52) PES	3 12 16 13 XSQ= 3.65 PHI= -0.288 XP = 0.0559
139	DRIFT TOWARD BEING THOSE 0.89 OF 9 WHERE SUPERORDINATE PUNISHMENT IS ABSENT (25) BBW	139	DRIFT TOWARD BEING THOSE 0.50 OF 14 WHERE SUPERORDINATE PUNISHMENT IS PRESENT (15) BBW	1 7 8 7 XSQ= 2.14 PHI= -0.305 EP = 0.0858
285	DRIFT TOWARD BEING THOSE 0.73 OF 15 WHERE THE SEX TABOO DURING PREGNANCY IS ABSENT OR INFERRED ABSENT (17) BCA	285	DRIFT TOWARD BEING THOSE 0.69 OF 13 WHERE THE SEX TABOO DURING PREGNANCY IS PRESENT (14) BCA	4 9 11 4 XSQ= 3.51 PHI= -0.354 EP = 0.0557
307	TILT TOWARD BEING THOSE 0.58 OF 19 WHERE THE EARLY AGGRESSION SATISFACTION POTENTIAL IS LOW (19) W-C	307	TILT TOWARD BEING THOSE 0.75 OF 28 WHERE THE EARLY AGGRESSION SATISFACTION POTENTIAL IS HIGH (33) W-C	8 21 11 7 XSQ= 3.88 PHI= -0.287 XP = 0.0487
308	TILT TOWARD BEING THOSE 0.77 OF 13 WHERE AVERAGE SOCIALIZATION ANXIETY IS HIGH (22) W-C	308	TILT TOWARD BEING THOSE 0.61 OF 23 WHERE AVERAGE SOCIALIZATION ANXIETY IS LOW (18) W-C	10 9 3 14 XSQ= 3.36 PHI= 0.306 EP = 0.0411
312	DRIFT TOWARD BEING THOSE 0.69 OF 16 WHERE DEPENDENCE SOCIALIZATION ANXIETY IS HIGH (24) W-C	312	DRIFT TOWARD BEING THOSE 0.63 OF 27 WHERE DEPENDENCE SOCIALIZATION ANXIETY IS LOW (23) W-C	11 10 5 17 XSQ= 2.87 PHI= 0.259 XP = 0.0900

No.				No.				
315	DRIFT TOWARD BEING THOSE WHERE MOTHER AND NURSING CHILD CUSTOMARILY SLEEP IN DIFFERENT BEDS (14) W-C,S	0.50 OF	8	315	DRIFT TOWARD BEING THOSE WHERE MOTHER AND NURSING CHILD CUSTOMARILY SLEEP IN THE SAME BED (37) W-D,S	0.88 OF	17	4 15 4 2 XSQ= 2.52 PHI= -0.317 EP = 0.0593
325	DRIFT MORE TOWARD BEING THOSE WHERE THE DEGREE OF DIFFUSION AMONG THE INFANT'S NURTURANT AGENTS IS HIGH (42) B-B-C	0.81 OF	16	325	DRIFT LESS TOWARD BEING THOSE WHERE THE DEGREE OF DIFFUSION AMONG THE INFANT'S NURTURANT AGENTS IS HIGH (42) B-B-C	0.52 OF	23	13 12 3 11 XSQ= 2.32 PHI= 0.244 EP = 0.0930
327	DRIFT TOWARD BEING THOSE WHERE THE AGE OF THE INFANT AT TIME OF REDUCED CONTACT WITH MOTHER IS HIGHER THAN TWO YEARS (28) B-B-C	0.75 OF	12	327	DRIFT TOWARD BEING THOSE WHERE THE AGE OF THE INFANT AT TIME OF REDUCED CONTACT WITH MOTHER IS TWO YEARS OR LOWER (27) B-B-C	0.63 OF	19	9 7 3 12 XSQ= 2.90 PHI= 0.306 EP = 0.0659
351	TILT TOWARD BEING THOSE WHERE THE CHILD'S INFERRED CONFLICT REGARDING ACHIEVEMENT BEHAVIOR IS HIGH (26) B-B-C	0.60 OF	15	351	TILT TOWARD BEING THOSE WHERE THE CHILD'S INFERRED CONFLICT REGARDING ACHIEVEMENT BEHAVIOR IS LOW (34) B-B-C	0.83 OF	12	9 2 6 10 XSQ= 3.55 PHI= 0.362 EP = 0.0473
352	TILT TOWARD BEING THOSE WHERE THE TOTAL POSITIVE PRESSURE TOWARD DEVELOPING OBEDIENT BEHAVIOR IN THE CHILD IS HIGH (44) B-B-C	0.73 OF	15	352	TILT TOWARD BEING THOSE WHERE THE TOTAL POSITIVE PRESSURE TOWARD DEVELOPING OBEDIENT BEHAVIOR IN THE CHILD IS LOW (28) B-B-C	0.68 OF	22	11 7 4 15 XSQ= 4.60 PHI= 0.353 EP = 0.0201
353	TILT TOWARD BEING THOSE WHERE THE CHILD'S INFERRED ANXIETY OVER NON-PERFORMANCE OF OBEDIENT BEHAVIOR IS HIGH (42) B-B-C	0.80 OF	15	353	TILT TOWARD BEING THOSE WHERE THE CHILD-S INFERRED ANXIETY OVER NON-PERFORMANCE OF OBEDIENT BEHAVIOR IS LOW (32) B-B-C	0.59 OF	22	12 9 3 13 XSQ= 4.07 PHI= 0.332 EP = 0.0235
366	LEAN TOWARD BEING THOSE WHERE DISSOCIATION OF THE SEXES AT ADOLESCENCE IS HIGH (16) JKH	0.62 OF	13	366	LEAN TOWARD BEING THOSE WHERE DISSOCIATION OF THE SEXES AT ADOLESCENCE IS MEDIUM OR LOW (41) JKH	0.93 OF	15	8 1 5 14 XSQ= 7.26 PHI= 0.509 EP = 0.0036
368	DRIFT TOWARD BEING THOSE WHERE DISSOCIATION OF THE SEXES AT ADOLESCENCE IS HIGH OR MEDIUM (16) JKH	0.75 OF	8	368	DRIFT TOWARD BEING THOSE WHERE DISSOCIATION OF THE SEXES AT ADOLESCENCE IS LOW (21) JKH	0.73 OF	11	6 3 2 8 XSQ= 2.53 PHI= 0.365 EP = 0.0698
369	IN ALL CASES ARE THOSE WHERE DISSOCIATION OF THE SEXES AT ADOLESCENCE, OR CUSTOMS OF INITIATION AT ADOLESCENCE, ARE PRESENT (42) JKH	1.00 OF	13	369	LEAN TOWARD BEING THOSE WHERE BOTH DISSOCIATION OF THE SEXES AT ADOLESCENCE, AND CUSTOMS OF INITIATION AT ADOLESCENCE, ARE ABSENT (15) JKH	0.53 OF	15	13 7 0 8 XSQ= 7.27 PHI= 0.510 EP = 0.0025

373	TILT TCWARC BEING THOSE WHERE MALE INITIATICN CEREMONIES AT PUBERTY ARE PRESENT (17) W-K-A	0.64 OF 11	373	TILT TOWARD BEING THOSE WHERE MALE INITIATICN CEREMCNIES AT PUBERTY ARE ABSENT (27) W-K-A	0.85 OF 13	7 2 4 11 XSQ= 4.04 PHI= 0.410 EP = 0.0327
437	DRIFT TCWARD BEING THCSE WHERE FEAR OF GHOSTS, SPIRITS, HUMANS CR ANIMALS IS HIGH (21) W-C,JFG	0.71 OF 17	437	DRIFT TOWARD BEING THOSE WHERE FEAR OF GHOSTS, SPIRITS, HUMANS OR ANIMALS IS LOW (23) W-C,JFG	0.60 CF 20	12 8 5 12 XSQ= 2.34 PHI= 0.251 EP = 0.0994
444	IN ALL CASES ARE THOSE WHERE THE USE OF DREAMS TC SEEK AND CCNTROL SUPERNATURAL POWERS IS HIGH (28) RGD	1.00 OF 8	444	TILT TOWARD BEING THOSE WHERE THE USE CF DREAMS TO SEEK AND CONTROL SUPERNATURAL POWERS IS LOW (27) RGD	0.55 OF 11	8 5 0 6 XSQ= 4.10 PHI= 0.465 EP = 0.0181
476	TILT TCWARD BEING THCSE WHERE THE DEGREE OF INSOBRIETY IS STRCNG (31) DH	0.83 OF 12	476	TILT TOWARD BEING THOSE WHERE THE DEGREE OF INSCBRIETY IS MODERATE OR SLIGHT (18) DH	0.70 CF 10	10 3 2 7 XSQ= 4.40 PHI= 0.447 EP = 0.0274

409 CULTURES
WHERE PERFORMANCE THERAPIES
OF A DEPENDENCE NATURE
ARE PRESENT (28) W-C

409 CULTURES
WHERE PERFORMANCE THERAPIES
OF A DEPENDENCE NATURE
ARE ABSENT (26) W-C

BACKGROUND ON PAGE 157 — SUBJECT ONLY

28 IN LEFT COLUMN

AINU	BALINESE	CHAGGA	CHIR-APACHE	DUSUN
LAPPS	LEPCHA	LESU	MANUS	MAORI
SENIANG	TAOS	TETON	TIKOPIA	WARRAU
FON	HANO	IFUGAO	KURTATCHI	KWAKIUTL
MARSHALLESE	NAVAHO	ONTONG-JAVA	PUKAPUKA	RWALA
WITOTO	YAKUT	ZUNI		

26 IN RIGHT COLUMN

ABIPON	ALORESE	ANDAMANESE	ARAPESH	AZANDE
LAKHER	LAMBA	MARQUESANS	MASAI	MURNGIN
TANALA	TENINO	THONGA	TROBRIAND	WOGEO
CHENCHU	COMANCHE	COPPER ESKIMO	DOBUANS	JIVARO
OMAHA	PAPAGO	RIFFIANS	SANPOIL	SIRIONO
YAGUA				

346 EXCLUDED BECAUSE UNASCERTAINED

---

55 DRIFT TOWARD BEING THOSE 0.55 OF 11
WHERE FOOD PRODUCTION IS BY
INTENSIVE AGRICULTURE, RATHER THAN BY
SIMPLE AGRICULTURE (91)

55 DRIFT TOWARD BEING THOSE 0.83 OF 12
WHERE FOOD PRODUCTION IS BY
SIMPLE AGRICULTURE, RATHER THAN BY
INTENSIVE AGRICULTURE (101)

6 2
5 10
XSQ= 2.15
PHI= 0.306
EP = 0.0894

56 DRIFT TOWARD BEING THOSE 0.50 OF 10
WHERE FOOD PRODUCTION IS BY
INCIPIENT FOOD PRODUCTION, RATHER THAN BY
SIMPLE AGRICULTURE (46)

56 DRIFT TOWARD BEING THOSE 0.91 OF 11
WHERE FOOD PRODUCTION IS BY
SIMPLE AGRICULTURE, RATHER THAN BY
INCIPIENT FOOD PRODUCTION (101)

5 10
5 1
XSQ= 2.52
PHI= -0.347
EP = 0.0635

77 DRIFT TOWARD BEING THOSE 0.50 OF 8
WHERE THE WRITING SYSTEM IS
ALPHABETIC-OR-PHONETIC, RATHER THAN BEING
MNEMONIC OR ABSENT (15) JMH

77 IN ALL CASES ARE THOSE 1.00 OF 7
WHERE THE WRITING SYSTEM IS
MNEMONIC OR ABSENT, RATHER THAN BEING
ALPHABETIC-OR-PHONETIC (39) JMH

4 0
4 7
XSQ= 2.56
PHI= 0.413
EP = 0.0769

81 TILT LESS TOWARD BEING THOSE 0.53 OF 17
WHERE NO CITY OR TOWN IS PRESENT, AND
THE AVERAGE COMMUNITY SIZE IS
SMALLER THAN 200 (135)

81 TILT MORE TOWARD BEING THOSE 0.89 OF 18
WHERE NO CITY OR TOWN IS PRESENT, AND
THE AVERAGE COMMUNITY SIZE IS
SMALLER THAN 200 (135)

8 2
9 16
XSQ= 3.91
PHI= 0.334
EP = 0.0275

No.				No.				
82	TILT MORE TOWARD BEING THOSE WHERE A CITY OR TOWN IS PRESENT, OR THE AVERAGE COMMUNITY SIZE IS FIFTY OR GREATER (178)	0.94 OF	17	82	TILT LESS TOWARD BEING THOSE WHERE A CITY OR TOWN IS PRESENT, OR THE AVERAGE COMMUNITY SIZE IS FIFTY OR GREATER (178)	0.61 OF	18	16 11 1 7 XSQ= 3.69 PHI= 0.325 EP = 0.0408
83	TILT LESS TOWARD BEING THOSE WHERE, WITH NO CITY AND NO TOWN PRESENT, THE AVERAGE COMMUNITY SIZE IS SMALLER THAN 200, RATHER THAN BETWEEN 200 AND 999 (135)	0.60 OF	15	83	TILT MORE TOWARD BEING THOSE WHERE, WITH NO CITY AND NO TOWN PRESENT, THE AVERAGE COMMUNITY SIZE IS SMALLER THAN 200, RATHER THAN BETWEEN 200 AND 999 (135)	0.94 OF	17	6 1 9 16 XSQ= 3.61 PHI= 0.336 EP = 0.0330
91	TILT TOWARD BEING THOSE WHERE SOCIETAL COMPLEXITY IS HIGH (18) F-W	0.70 OF	10	91	TILT TOWARD BEING THOSE WHERE SOCIETAL COMPLEXITY IS LOW (22) F-W	0.89 OF	9	7 1 3 8 XSQ= 4.54 PHI= 0.489 EP = 0.0198
132	TILT TOWARD BEING THOSE WHERE ECONOMIC EXCHANGE INVOLVES THE USE OF MONEY (37) JMH	0.88 OF	8	132	TILT TOWARD BEING THOSE WHERE ECONOMIC EXCHANGE DOES NOT INVOLVE THE USE OF MONEY (17) JMH	0.71 OF	7	7 2 1 5 XSQ= 3.23 PHI= 0.464 EP = 0.0406
207	DRIFT TOWARD BEING THOSE WHERE MARITAL RESIDENCE IS MATRILOCAL OR UXORILOCAL, RATHER THAN AMBILOCAL OR NEOLOCAL (64)	0.58 OF	12	207	DRIFT TOWARD BEING THOSE WHERE MARITAL RESIDENCE IS AMBILOCAL OR NEOLOCAL, RATHER THAN MATRILOCAL OR UXORILOCAL (64)	0.89 OF	9	7 1 5 8 XSQ= 3.07 PHI= 0.382 EP = 0.0669
221	IN ALL CASES ARE THOSE WHERE MATRILATERAL CROSS-COUSIN MARRIAGE IS NOT PRESCRIBED OR PREFERRED (335)	1.00 OF	27	221	DRIFT LESS TOWARD BEING THOSE WHERE MATRILATERAL CROSS-COUSIN MARRIAGE IS NOT PRESCRIBED OR PREFERRED (335)	0.81 OF	26	0 5 27 21 XSQ= 3.70 PHI= -0.264 XP = 0.0543
295	TILT TOWARD BEING THOSE WHERE THE SEVERITY OF PUNISHMENT FOR ABORTION IS LOW OR ABSENT (12) BCA	0.77 OF	13	295	TILT TOWARD BEING THOSE WHERE THE SEVERITY OF PUNISHMENT FOR ABORTION IS HIGH (11) BCA	0.75 OF	8	3 6 10 2 XSQ= 3.54 PHI= -0.410 EP = 0.0318
302	DRIFT TOWARD BEING THOSE WHERE THE AVERAGE EARLY SATISFACTION POTENTIAL IS LOW (17) W-C	0.53 OF	19	302	DRIFT TOWARD BEING THOSE WHERE THE AVERAGE EARLY SATISFACTION POTENTIAL IS HIGH (23) W-C	0.76 OF	17	9 13 10 4 XSQ= 2.09 PHI= -0.241 EP = 0.0967
306	DRIFT TOWARD BEING THOSE WHERE THE EARLY DEPENDENCE SATISFACTION POTENTIAL IS LOW (24) W-C	0.58 OF	26	306	DRIFT TOWARD BEING THOSE WHERE THE EARLY DEPENDENCE SATISFACTION POTENTIAL IS HIGH (28) W-C	0.71 OF	21	11 15 15 6 XSQ= 2.89 PHI= -0.248 XP = 0.0889

335	DRIFT TOWARD BEING THOSE 0.63 OF 16 WHERE INITIAL INDULGENCE OF DEPENDENCY IS LOW (18) WNS	DRIFT TOWARD BEING THOSE 0.72 OF 18 WHERE INITIAL INDULGENCE OF DEPENDENCY IS HIGH (20) WNS	6 13 10 5 XSQ= 2.85 PHI= -0.290 EP = 0.0824
366	TILT MORE TOWARD BEING THOSE 0.91 OF 11 WHERE DISSOCIATION OF THE SEXES AT ADOLESCENCE IS MEDIUM OR LOW (41) JKH	TILT LESS TOWARD BEING THOSE 0.53 OF 17 WHERE DISSOCIATION OF THE SEXES AT ADOLESCENCE IS MEDIUM OR LOW (41) JKH	1 8 10 9 XSQ= 2.84 PHI= -0.319 EP = 0.0491
386	TILT TOWARD BEING THOSE 0.67 OF 21 WHERE SEXUAL EXPRESSION BY THE YOUNG IS PERMITTED (40) F-B	TILT TOWARD BEING THOSE 0.69 OF 16 WHERE SEXUAL EXPRESSION BY THE YOUNG IS RESTRICTED OR SEMI-RESTRICTED (46) F-B	7 11 14 5 XSQ= 3.25 PHI= -0.296 EP = 0.0489
398	DRIFT TOWARD BEING THOSE 0.69 OF 13 WHERE THE INTENSITY OF SEX ANXIETY IS HIGH (16) WNS	DRIFT TOWARD BEING THOSE 0.67 OF 18 WHERE THE INTENSITY OF SEX ANXIETY IS LOW (16) WNS	9 6 4 12 XSQ= 2.59 PHI= 0.289 EP = 0.0732
435	DRIFT TOWARD BEING THOSE 0.86 OF 7 WHERE ABANDONMENT OF THE HOUSE OF THE DEAD IS NOT PRACTICED (19) LWS	DRIFT TOWARD BEING THOSE 0.75 OF 4 WHERE ABANDONMENT OF THE HOUSE OF THE DEAD IS PRACTICED (12) LWS	1 3 6 1 XSQ= 1.86 PHI= -0.411 EP = 0.0879
478	IN ALL CASES ARE THOSE 1.00 OF 4 WHERE THE ABANDONMENT OR KILLING OF OLD PEOPLE IS PRESENT (12) LWS	IN ALL CASES ARE THOSE 1.00 OF 3 WHERE THE ABANDONMENT OR KILLING OF OLD PEOPLE IS UNIMPORTANT OR ABSENT (12) LWS	4 0 0 3 XSQ= 3.51 PHI= 0.708 EP = 0.0286

410 CULTURES
WHERE PERFORMANCE THERAPIES
OF AN AGGRESSION NATURE
ARE PRESENT (31) W-C

410 CULTURES
WHERE PERFORMANCE THERAPIES
OF AN AGGRESSION NATURE
ARE ABSENT (23) W-C

BACKGROUND ON PAGE 157

SUBJECT ONLY

31 IN LEFT COLUMN

AINU	ANDAMANESE	AZANDE	CHAGGA	CHIR-APACHE	COMANCHE	COPR ESKIMO	DUSUN	FON	JIVARO
KWAKIUTL	LAMBA	LAPPS	LEPCHA	LESU	MAORI	MARSHALLESE	MURNGIN	NAVAHO	ONTONG-JAVA
PUKAPUKA	RIFFIANS	RWALA	SANPOIL	SIRIONO	TANALA	TAOS	THONGA	TIKOPIA	WITOTO
YAKUT									

23 IN RIGHT COLUMN

ABIPON	ALORESE	ARAPESH	BALINESE	CHENCHU	DOBUANS	HANO	IFUGAO	KURTATCHI	LAKHER
MANUS	MARQUESANS	MASAI	OMAHA	PAPAGO	SENIANG	TENINO	TETON	TROBRIAND	WARRAU
WOGEO	YAGUA	ZUNI							

346 EXCLUDED BECAUSE UNASCERTAINED

	Left column		Right column	Statistics
42	DRIFT TOWARD BEING THOSE 0.68 OF 31 WHERE THE NATURAL ENVIRONMENT IS OTHER THAN TROPICAL OR SUB-TROPICAL RAIN FOREST, OR MONSOON FOREST (244) FWM	42	DRIFT TOWARD BEING THOSE 0.61 OF 23 WHERE THE NATURAL ENVIRONMENT IS TROPICAL OR SUB-TROPICAL RAIN FOREST, OR MONSOON FOREST (156) FWM	10 14 21 9 XSQ= 3.30 PHI= -0.247 XP = 0.0695
47	TILT TOWARD BEING THOSE 0.82 OF 11 WHERE, IF SETTLEMENTS ARE NON-FIXED, MOVEMENT IS NOMADIC, RATHER THAN NON-NOMADIC (72)	47	TILT TOWARD BEING THOSE 0.71 OF 7 WHERE, IF SETTLEMENTS ARE NON-FIXED, MOVEMENT IS NON-NOMADIC, RATHER THAN NOMADIC (38)	9 2 2 5 XSQ= 3.11 PHI= 0.416 EP = 0.0491
149	DRIFT TOWARD BEING THOSE 0.53 OF 17 WHERE THE INCIDENCE OF THEFT IS HIGH (18) B-B-C	149	DRIFT TOWARD BEING THOSE 0.89 OF 9 WHERE THE INCIDENCE OF THEFT IS LOW (19) B-B-C	9 1 8 8 XSQ= 2.76 PHI= 0.326 EP = 0.0873
198	IN ALL CASES ARE THOSE 1.00 OF 9 WHERE RULES FOR THE INHERITANCE OF REAL PROPERTY, IF PRESENT, FAVOR THE MALE HEIR OR LINE, RATHER THAN THE FEMALE (144)	198	DRIFT LESS TOWARD BEING THOSE 0.64 OF 11 WHERE RULES FOR THE INHERITANCE OF REAL PROPERTY, IF PRESENT, FAVOR THE MALE HEIR OR LINE, RATHER THAN THE FEMALE (144)	9 7 0 4 XSQ= 2.13 PHI= 0.327 EP = 0.0941

272	LEAN TOWARD BEING THOSE WHERE THE DIVORCE RATE IS LOW (28) CA	0.83 OF 6	272	IN ALL CASES ARE THOSE WHERE THE DIVORCE RATE IS HIGH (29) CA	1.00 OF 7	1 7 5 0 XSQ= 6.29 PHI= -0.695 EP = 0.0047
296	DRIFT TOWARD BEING THOSE WHERE INFANTICIDE IS PRESENT (18) BCA	0.68 OF 19	296	DRIFT TOWARD BEING THOSE WHERE INFANTICIDE IS ABSENT OR INFERRED ABSENT (15) BCA	0.67 OF 12	13 4 6 8 XSQ= 2.38 PHI= 0.277 EP = 0.0751
300	DRIFT TOWARD BEING THOSE WHERE THE POST-PARTUM SEX TABOO LASTS SIX MONTHS OR LESS (73)	0.67 OF 21	3CC	DRIFT TOWARD BEING THOSE WHERE THE POST-PARTUM SEX TABOO LASTS LONGER THAN SIX MONTHS (51)	0.73 OF 11	7 8 14 3 XSQ= 3.06 PHI= -0.309 EP = 0.0617
302	TILT TOWARD BEING THOSE WHERE THE AVERAGE EARLY SATISFACTION POTENTIAL IS LOW (17) W-C	0.55 OF 2C	302	TILT TOWARD BEING THOSE WHERE THE AVERAGE EARLY SATISFACTION POTENTIAL IS HIGH (23) W-C	0.81 OF 16	9 13 11 3 XSQ= 3.51 PHI= -0.312 EP = 0.0407
317	DRIFT TOWARD BEING THOSE WHERE DISPLAY OF AFFECTION TOWARD THE INFANT IS LOW (29) B-B-C	0.52 OF 21	317	DRIFT TOWARD BEING THOSE WHERE DISPLAY OF AFFECTION TOWARD THE INFANT IS HIGH (39) B-B-C	0.80 OF 15	10 12 11 3 XSQ= 2.62 PHI= -0.270 EP = 0.0833
324	DRIFT TOWARD BEING THOSE WHERE THE PAIN INFLICTED ON THE INFANT BY THE NURTURANT AGENT IS HIGH (34) B-B-C	0.63 OF 19	324	DRIFT TOWARD BEING THOSE WHERE THE PAIN INFLICTED ON THE INFANT BY THE NURTURANT AGENT IS LOW OR NEGLIGIBLE (32) B-B-C	0.69 OF 16	12 5 7 11 XSQ= 2.38 PHI= 0.261 EP = 0.0922
327	TILT TOWARD BEING THOSE WHERE THE AGE OF THE INFANT AT TIME OF REDUCED CONTACT WITH MOTHER IS HIGHER THAN TWO YEARS (28) B-B-C	0.71 OF 17	327	TILT TOWARD BEING THOSE WHERE THE AGE OF THE INFANT AT TIME OF REDUCED CONTACT WITH MOTHER IS TWO YEARS OR LOWER (27) B-B-C	0.71 OF 14	12 4 5 10 XSQ= 3.88 PHI= 0.354 EP = 0.0320
334	TILT TOWARD BEING THOSE WHERE THE INDULGENCE OF THE CHILD IS LOW (38) B-B-C	0.59 OF 22	334	TILT TOWARD BEING THOSE WHERE THE INDULGENCE OF THE CHILD IS HIGH (40) B-B-C	0.78 OF 18	9 14 13 4 XSQ= 4.10 PHI= -0.320 EP = 0.0267
337	DRIFT TOWARD BEING THOSE WHERE THE CHILD'S INFERRED ANXIETY OVER NON-PERFORMANCE OF RESPONSIBLE BEHAVIOR IS HIGH (38) B-B-C	0.63 OF 19	337	DRIFT TOWARD BEING THOSE WHERE THE CHILD'S INFERRED ANXIETY OVER NON-PERFORMANCE OF RESPONSIBLE BEHAVIOR IS LOW (35) B-B-C	0.71 OF 17	12 5 7 12 XSQ= 2.86 PHI= 0.282 EP = 0.0543

353	TILT TOWARD BEING THOSE WHERE THE CHILD'S INFERRED ANXIETY OVER NON-PERFORMANCE OF OBEDIENT BEHAVIOR IS HIGH (42) B-B-C	0.75 OF 20	353	TILT TOWARD BEING THOSE WHERE THE CHILD-S INFERRED ANXIETY OVER NON-PERFORMANCE OF OBEDIENT BEHAVIOR IS LOW (32) B-B-C	0.65 OF 17	15 6 5 11 XSQ= 4.40 PHI= 0.345 EP = 0.0220
356	TILT TOWARD BEING THOSE WHERE NEITHER ADOLESCENT PEER GROUPS NOR PAIRS ARE PRESENT IN A SETTING OF COURTSHIP (22) JKH	0.79 OF 14	356	TILT TOWARD BEING THOSE WHERE ADOLESCENT PEER GROUPS OR PAIRS ARE PRESENT IN A SETTING OF COURTSHIP (29) JKH	0.70 OF 10	3 7 11 3 XSQ= 3.84 PHI= -0.400 EP = 0.0351
365	TILT TOWARD BEING THOSE WHERE THE TIME SPENT IN ADOLESCENT PEER GROUP ACTIVITY IS LOW-MEDIUM OR LOW (15) JKH	0.77 OF 13	365	TILT TOWARD BEING THOSE WHERE THE TIME SPENT IN ADOLESCENT PEER GROUP ACTIVITY IS HIGH OR HIGH-MEDIUM (30) JKH	0.86 OF 7	3 6 10 1 XSQ= 4.90 PHI= -0.495 EP = 0.0166
377	DRIFT LESS TOWARD BEING THOSE WHERE MALE GENITAL MUTILATION IS ABSENT (242)	0.64 OF 28	377	DRIFT MORE TOWARD BEING THOSE WHERE MALE GENITAL MUTILATION IS ABSENT (242)	0.90 OF 20	10 2 18 18 XSQ= 2.86 PHI= 0.244 XP = 0.0910
405	TILT TOWARD BEING THOSE WHERE EXPLANATIONS OF ILLNESS OF A DEPENDENCE NATURE ARE PRESENT (34) W-C	0.71 OF 31	405	TILT TOWARD BEING THOSE WHERE EXPLANATIONS OF ILLNESS OF A DEPENDENCE NATURE ARE ABSENT (27) W-C	0.61 OF 23	22 9 9 14 XSQ= 4.25 PHI= 0.281 XP = 0.0393
430	IN ALL CASES ARE THOSE WHERE SUPERNATURAL SANCTIONS FOR MORALITY, HAVING AN EFFECT ON AN INDIVIDUAL'S HEALTH, ARE PRESENT (16) GES	1.00 OF 4	430	TILT TOWARD BEING THOSE WHERE SUPERNATURAL SANCTIONS FOR MORALITY, HAVING AN EFFECT ON AN INDIVIDUAL'S HEALTH, ARE ABSENT OR UNREPORTED (22) GES	0.83 OF 6	4 1 0 5 XSQ= 3.75 PHI= 0.612 EP = 0.0476

	Left column		Right column
411	CULTURES WHERE AVOIDANCE THERAPIES OF AN ORAL NATURE ARE PRESENT (36) W-C	411	CULTURES WHERE AVOIDANCE THERAPIES OF AN ORAL NATURE ARE ABSENT (18) W-C

BACKGROUND ON PAGE 157

SUBJECT ONLY

36 IN LEFT COLUMN

ABIPON	AINU	ALORESE	ANDAMANESE	ARAPESH	AZANDE	CHAGGA	CHENCHU	CHIR-APACHE	COPR ESKIMO
FON	HANO	JIVARO	KURTATCHI	KWAKIUTL	LAKHER	LAMBA	LAPPS	LEPCHA	LESU
MAORI	MARSHALLESE	MASAI	MURNGIN	NAVAHO	OMAHA	PAPAGO	PUKAPUKA	SANPOIL	SENIANG
TAOS	THONGA	WARRAU	WITOTO	YAGUA	ZUNI				

18 IN RIGHT COLUMN

BALINESE	COMANCHE	COBUANS	DUSUN	IFUGAO	MANUS	MARQUESANS	ONTONG-JAVA	RIFFIANS	RWALA
SIRIONO	TANALA	TENINO	TETON	TIKOPIA	TROBRIAND	WOGEO	YAKUT		

346 EXCLUDED BECAUSE UNASCERTAINED

	Left column			Right column		Statistics
6	DRIFT TOWARD BEING THOSE LOCATED OUTSIDE OF THE INSULAR PACIFIC (330)	0.75 OF 36	6	DRIFT TOWARD BEING THOSE LOCATED IN THE INSULAR PACIFIC (70)	0.56 OF 18	9 10 27 8 XSQ= 3.66 PHI= -0.260 XP = 0.0556
36	DRIFT LESS TOWARD BEING THOSE WHERE THE NATURAL ENVIRONMENT IS OTHER THAN 'VERY HARSH,' OR SUB-TROPICAL BUSH, OR TEMPERATE GRASSLAND (292) FWM	0.53 OF 36	36	DRIFT MORE TOWARD BEING THOSE WHERE THE NATURAL ENVIRONMENT IS OTHER THAN 'VERY HARSH,' OR SUB-TROPICAL BUSH, OR TEMPERATE GRASSLAND (292) FWM	0.83 OF 18	17 3 19 15 XSQ= 3.58 PHI= 0.258 XP = 0.0584
98	DRIFT LESS TOWARD BEING THOSE WHERE THE HIERARCHY OF LOCAL JURISDICTION HAS FOUR OR THREE LEVELS (238) GES,EA	0.61 OF 36	98	DRIFT MORE TOWARD BEING THOSE WHERE THE HIERARCHY OF LOCAL JURISDICTION HAS FOUR OR THREE LEVELS (238) GES,EA	0.92 OF 13	22 12 14 1 XSQ= 3.03 PHI= -0.249 XP = 0.0817
99	DRIFT TOWARD BEING THOSE WHERE, WITH NATIONAL HIERARCHY ABSENT, THE HIERARCHY OF LOCAL JURISDICTION HAS TWO LEVELS (63) GES,EA	0.50 OF 22	99	IN ALL CASES ARE THOSE WHERE, WITH NATIONAL HIERARCHY ABSENT, THE HIERARCHY OF LOCAL JURISDICTION HAS FOUR OR THREE LEVELS (93) GES,EA	1.00 OF 6	11 6 11 0 XSQ= 3.07 PHI= -0.331 EP = 0.0549

No.	Subject	Ratio	No.	Predicate	Ratio	Statistics
100	DRIFT LESS TOWARD BEING THOSE WHERE HIERARCHIES ARE MORE COMPLEX THAN THE 'SIMPLEST,' I. E., MORE COMPLEX THAN TWO LOCAL LEVELS WITH NO NATIONAL LEVELS (267) GES,EA	0.69 OF 36	100	IN ALL CASES ARE THOSE WHERE HIERARCHIES ARE MORE COMPLEX THAN THE 'SIMPLEST,' I. E., MORE COMPLEX THAN TWO LOCAL LEVELS WITH NO NATIONAL LEVELS (267) GES,EA	1.00 OF 13	25 13 11 0 XSQ= 3.52 PHI= -0.268 XP = 0.0607
102	TILT TOWARD BEING THOSE WHERE CLASS STRATIFICATION IS ABSENT (180)	0.61 OF 36	102	TILT TOWARD BEING THOSE WHERE CLASS STRATIFICATION IS PRESENT (203)	0.72 OF 18	14 13 22 5 XSQ= 4.08 PHI= -0.275 XP = 0.0433
137	DRIFT TOWARD BEING THOSE WHERE INVIDIOUS DISPLAY OF WEALTH IS MODERATELY, LITTLE, OR NEGATIVELY EMPHASIZED (52) PES	0.77 OF 30	137	DRIFT TOWARD BEING THOSE WHERE INVIDIOUS DISPLAY OF WEALTH IS STRONGLY EMPHASIZED (37) PES	0.57 OF 14	7 8 23 6 XSQ= 3.47 PHI= -0.281 XP = 0.0626
139	DRIFT TOWARD BEING THOSE WHERE SUPERORDINATE PUNISHMENT IS ABSENT (25) BBW	0.80 OF 15	139	DRIFT TOWARD BEING THOSE WHERE SUPERORDINATE PUNISHMENT IS PRESENT (15) BBW	0.63 OF 8	3 5 12 3 XSQ= 2.49 PHI= -0.329 EP = 0.0713
263	DRIFT TOWARD BEING THOSE WHERE WIVES ARE OBTAINED BY RELATIVELY DIFFICULT MEANS, NAMELY BY BRIDE-PRICE, BRIDE-SERVICE, OR EXCHANGING A FEMALE RELATIVE (233)	0.58 OF 36	263	DRIFT TOWARD BEING THOSE WHERE WIVES ARE OBTAINED BY RELATIVELY EASY MEANS, NAMELY BY TOKEN BRIDE-PRICE, GIFT EXCHANGE, ABSENCE OF ANY CONSIDERATION, OR RECEIPT OF DOWRY (162)	0.72 OF 18	21 5 15 13 XSQ= 3.35 PHI= 0.249 XP = 0.0673
285	DRIFT TOWARD BEING THOSE WHERE THE SEX TABOO DURING PREGNANCY IS ABSENT OR INFERRED ABSENT (17) BCA	0.64 OF 22	285	DRIFT TOWARD BEING THOSE WHERE THE SEX TABOO DURING PREGNANCY IS PRESENT (14) BCA	0.83 OF 6	8 5 14 1 XSQ= 2.51 PHI= -0.299 EP = 0.0691
307	DRIFT TOWARD BEING THOSE WHERE THE EARLY AGGRESSION SATISFACTION POTENTIAL IS LOW (19) W-C	0.50 OF 30	307	DRIFT TOWARD BEING THOSE WHERE THE EARLY AGGRESSION SATISFACTION POTENTIAL IS HIGH (33) W-C	0.82 OF 17	15 14 15 3 XSQ= 3.53 PHI= -0.274 XP = 0.0601
326	DRIFT TOWARD BEING THOSE WHERE THE INFERRED TRANSITION ANXIETY BETWEEN INFANCY AND CHILDHOOD IS HIGH (32) B-B-C	0.64 OF 25	326	DRIFT TOWARD BEING THOSE WHERE THE INFERRED TRANSITION ANXIETY BETWEEN INFANCY AND CHILDHOOD IS LOW (35) B-B-C	0.73 OF 11	16 3 9 8 XSQ= 2.79 PHI= 0.278 EP = 0.0704
334	TILT TOWARD BEING THOSE WHERE THE INDULGENCE OF THE CHILD IS LOW (38) B-B-C	0.56 OF 27	334	TILT TOWARD BEING THOSE WHERE THE INDULGENCE OF THE CHILD IS HIGH (40) B-B-C	0.85 OF 13	12 11 15 2 XSQ= 4.27 PHI= -0.327 EP = 0.0204

337	DRIFT TOWARD BEING THOSE 0.58 OF 24 WHERE THE CHILD'S INFERRED ANXIETY OVER NON-PERFORMANCE OF RESPONSIBLE BEHAVIOR IS HIGH (38) B-B-C	337	DRIFT TOWARD BEING THOSE 0.75 OF 12 WHERE THE CHILD'S INFERRED ANXIETY OVER NON-PERFORMANCE OF RESPONSIBLE BEHAVIOR IS LOW (35) B-B-C	14 3 10 9 XSQ= 2.35 PHI= 0.256 EP = 0.0830
338	DRIFT TOWARD BEING THOSE 0.71 OF 24 WHERE THE CHILD'S INFERRED ANXIETY OVER PERFORMANCE OF RESPONSIBLE BEHAVIOR IS HIGH (44) B-B-C	338	DRIFT TOWARD BEING THOSE 0.67 OF 12 WHERE THE CHILD'S INFERRED ANXIETY OVER PERFORMANCE OF RESPONSIBLE BEHAVIOR IS LOW (29) B-B-C	17 4 7 8 XSQ= 3.21 PHI= 0.299 EP = 0.0707
339	TILT TOWARD BEING THOSE 0.58 OF 24 WHERE THE CHILD'S INFERRED CONFLICT REGARDING RESPONSIBLE BEHAVIOR IS HIGH (31) B-B-C	339	TILT TOWARD BEING THOSE 0.83 OF 12 WHERE THE CHILD'S INFERRED CONFLICT REGARDING RESPONSIBLE BEHAVIOR IS LOW (42) B-B-C	14 2 10 10 XSQ= 4.06 PHI= 0.336 EP = 0.0317
352	TILT TOWARD BEING THOSE 0.63 OF 24 WHERE THE TOTAL POSITIVE PRESSURE TOWARD DEVELOPING OBEDIENT BEHAVIOR IN THE CHILD IS HIGH (44) B-B-C	352	TILT TOWARD BEING THOSE 0.77 OF 13 WHERE THE TOTAL POSITIVE PRESSURE TOWARD DEVELOPING OBEDIENT BEHAVIOR IN THE CHILD IS LOW (28) B-B-C	15 3 9 10 XSQ= 3.79 PHI= 0.320 EP = 0.0382
353	LEAN TOWARD BEING THOSE 0.75 OF 24 WHERE THE CHILD'S INFERRED ANXIETY OVER NON-PERFORMANCE OF OBEDIENT BEHAVIOR IS HIGH (42) B-B-C	353	LEAN TOWARD BEING THOSE 0.77 OF 13 WHERE THE CHILD-S INFERRED ANXIETY OVER NON-PERFORMANCE OF OBEDIENT BEHAVIOR IS LOW (32) B-B-C	18 3 6 10 XSQ= 7.27 PHI= 0.443 EP = 0.0046
382	DRIFT TOWARD BEING THOSE 0.68 OF 19 WHERE FEMALE INITIATION RITES ARE PRESENT (38) JKB	382	IN ALL CASES ARE THOSE 1.00 OF 3 WHERE FEMALE INITIATION RITES ARE ABSENT (27) JKB	13 0 6 3 XSQ= 2.59 PHI= 0.343 EP = 0.0545
406	LEAN TOWARD BEING THOSE 0.64 OF 36 WHERE EXPLANATIONS OF ILLNESS OF AN AGGRESSION NATURE ARE PRESENT (28) W-C	406	LEAN TOWARD BEING THOSE 0.83 OF 18 WHERE EXPLANATIONS OF ILLNESS OF AN AGGRESSION NATURE ARE ABSENT (33) W-C	23 3 13 15 XSQ= 8.91 PHI= 0.406 XP = 0.0028

412 CULTURES WHERE AVOIDANCE THERAPIES OF AN ANAL NATURE ARE PRESENT (31) W-C

412 CULTURES WHERE AVOIDANCE THERAPIES OF AN ANAL NATURE ARE ABSENT (23) W-C

BACKGROUND ON PAGE 157

SUBJECT ONLY

31 IN LEFT COLUMN

ABIPON	AINU	ALORESE	ANDAMANESE	AZANDE	BALINESE	CHAGGA	DOBUANS	DUSUN	FON
HANO	JIVARO	KWAKIUTL	LAMBA	LAPPS	LEPCHA	LESU	MANUS	MAORI	MARSHALLESE
MASAI	MURNGIN	NAVAHO	OMAHA	ONTONG-JAVA	PUKAPUKA	SANPOIL	TAOS	THONGA	TIKOPIA
ZUNI									

23 IN RIGHT COLUMN

ARAPESH	CHENCHU	CHIR-APACHE	COMANCHE	COPR ESKIMO	IFUGAO	KURTATCHI	LAKHER	MARQUESANS	PAPAGO
RIFFIANS	RWALA	SENIANG	SIRIONO	TANALA	TENINO	TETON	TROBRIAND	WARRAU	WITOTO
WOGEO	YAGUA	YAKUT							

346 EXCLUDED BECAUSE UNASCERTAINED

	Left column			Right column			Statistics
3	DRIFT LESS TOWARD BEING THOSE LOCATED OUTSIDE OF AFRICA (320)	0.81 OF 31	3	IN ALL CASES ARE THOSE LOCATED OUTSIDE OF AFRICA (320)	1.00 OF 23		6 0 25 23 XSQ= 3.24 PHI= 0.245 XP = 0.0719
282	DRIFT TOWARD BEING THOSE WHERE THE STRENGTH OF DESIRE FOR CHILDREN IS HIGH (16) BCA	0.57 OF 21	282	DRIFT TOWARD BEING THOSE WHERE THE STRENGTH OF DESIRE FOR CHILDREN IS LOW OR ABSENT (20) BCA	0.82 OF 11		12 2 9 9 XSQ= 3.01 PHI= 0.307 EP = 0.0608
303	TILT TOWARD BEING THOSE WHERE THE EARLY ORAL SATISFACTION POTENTIAL IS LOW (25) W-C	0.62 OF 29	303	TILT TOWARD BEING THOSE WHERE THE EARLY ORAL SATISFACTION POTENTIAL IS HIGH (32) W-C	0.77 OF 22		11 17 18 5 XSQ= 6.31 PHI= -0.352 XP = 0.0120
308	TILT TOWARD BEING THOSE WHERE AVERAGE SOCIALIZATION ANXIETY IS HIGH (22) W-C	0.74 OF 19	308	TILT TOWARD BEING THOSE WHERE AVERAGE SOCIALIZATION ANXIETY IS LOW (18) W-C	0.71 OF 17		14 5 5 12 XSQ= 5.39 PHI= 0.387 EP = 0.0180

309	TEND TO BE THOSE 0.73 OF 26 WHERE ORAL SOCIALIZATION ANXIETY IS HIGH (26) W-C	309	TEND TO BE THOSE 0.82 OF 22 WHERE ORAL SOCIALIZATION ANXIETY IS LOW (27) W-C	19 4 7 18 XSQ= 12.27 PHI= 0.506 XP = 0.0005
321	DRIFT TOWARD BEING THOSE 0.59 OF 22 WHERE THE IMMEDIACY OF REDUCTION OF THE INFANT'S DRIVES IS LOW (25) B-B-C	321	DRIFT TOWARD BEING THOSE 0.77 OF 13 WHERE THE IMMEDIACY OF REDUCTION OF THE INFANT'S DRIVES IS HIGH (35) B-B-C	9 10 13 3 XSQ= 2.94 PHI= -0.290 EP = 0.0776
326	TILT TOWARD BEING THOSE 0.71 OF 21 WHERE THE INFERRED TRANSITION ANXIETY BETWEEN INFANCY AND CHILDHOOD IS HIGH (32) B-B-C	326	TILT TOWARD BEING THOSE 0.73 OF 15 WHERE THE INFERRED TRANSITION ANXIETY BETWEEN INFANCY AND CHILDHOOD IS LOW (35) B-B-C	15 4 6 11 XSQ= 5.35 PHI= 0.386 EP = 0.0166
337	DRIFT TOWARD BEING THOSE 0.59 OF 22 WHERE THE CHILD'S INFERRED ANXIETY OVER NON-PERFORMANCE OF RESPONSIBLE BEHAVIOR IS HIGH (38) B-B-C	337	DRIFT TOWARD BEING THOSE 0.71 OF 14 WHERE THE CHILD'S INFERRED ANXIETY OVER NON-PERFORMANCE OF RESPONSIBLE BEHAVIOR IS LOW (35) B-B-C	13 4 9 10 XSQ= 2.09 PHI= 0.241 EP = 0.0967
353	LEAN TOWARD BEING THOSE 0.77 OF 22 WHERE THE CHILD'S INFERRED ANXIETY OVER NON-PERFORMANCE OF OBEDIENT BEHAVIOR IS HIGH (42) B-B-C	353	LEAN TOWARD BEING THOSE 0.73 OF 15 WHERE THE CHILD-S INFERRED ANXIETY OVER NON-PERFORMANCE OF OBEDIENT BEHAVIOR IS LOW (32) B-B-C	17 4 5 11 XSQ= 7.36 PHI= 0.446 EP = 0.0059
355	DRIFT TOWARD BEING THOSE 0.59 OF 22 WHERE THE CHILD'S INFERRED CONFLICT REGARDING OBEDIENT BEHAVIOR IS HIGH (35) B-B-C	355	DRIFT TOWARD BEING THOSE 0.73 OF 15 WHERE THE CHILD'S INFERRED CONFLICT REGARDING OBEDIENT BEHAVIOR IS LOW (38) B-B-C	13 4 9 11 XSQ= 2.58 PHI= 0.264 EP = 0.0924
372	DRIFT TOWARD BEING THOSE 0.61 OF 23 WHERE MALE INITIATION RITES ARE PRESENT (48) ASA	372	DRIFT TOWARD BEING THOSE 0.74 OF 19 WHERE MALE INITIATION RITES ARE ABSENT (63) ASA	14 5 9 14 XSQ= 3.72 PHI= 0.297 XP = 0.0539
428	DRIFT TOWARD BEING THOSE 0.75 OF 4 WHERE A HIGH GOD, IF PRESENT AND ACTIVE, DOES NOT SUPPORT HUMAN MORALITY, RATHER THAN SUPPORTING IT (26) GES,EA	428	DRIFT TOWARD BEING THOSE 0.86 OF 7 WHERE A HIGH GOD, IF PRESENT AND ACTIVE, SUPPORTS HUMAN MORALITY, RATHER THAN NOT SUPPORTING IT (61) GES,EA	1 6 3 1 XSQ= 1.86 PHI= -0.411 EP = 0.0879
456	IN ALL CASES ARE THOSE 1.00 OF 8 WHERE THE INTERNALIZATION OF THE INDIVIDUAL'S CONTACT WITH THE DIVINE IS NOT CONDUCIVE TO THE DEVELOPMENT OF THE INDIVIDUAL'S NEED TO ACHIEVE (17) DCM	456	TILT TOWARD BEING THOSE 0.57 OF 7 WHERE THE INTERNALIZATION OF THE INDIVIDUAL'S CONTACT WITH THE DIVINE IS CONDUCIVE TO THE DEVELOPMENT OF THE INDIVIDUAL'S NEED TO ACHIEVE (19) DCM	0 4 8 3 XSQ= 3.65 PHI= -0.494 EP = 0.0256

413 CULTURES WHERE AVOIDANCE THERAPIES OF A SEXUAL NATURE ARE PRESENT (13) W-C

413 CULTURES WHERE AVOIDANCE THERAPIES OF A SEXUAL NATURE ARE ABSENT (41) W-C

BACKGROUND ON PAGE 157

SUBJECT ONLY

13 IN LEFT COLUMN

FON	HANC	IFUGAO	JIVARO	LESU	MANUS	MARSHALLESE	NAVAHO	RIFFIANS	RWALA
SENIANG	THONGA	WITOTO							

41 IN RIGHT COLUMN

ABIPON	AINU	ALORESE	ANDAMANESE	ARAPESH	AZANDE	BALINESE	CHAGGA	CHENCHU	CHIR-APACHE
COMANCHE	COPR ESKIMO	DOBUANS	DUSUN	KURTATCHI	KWAKIUTL	LAKHER	LAMBA	LAPPS	LEPCHA
MAORI	MARQUESANS	MASAI	MURNGIN	OMAHA	ONTONG-JAVA	PAPAGO	PUKAPUKA	SANPOIL	SIRIONO
TANALA	TAOS	TENINO	TETON	TIKOPIA	TROBRIAND	WARRAU	WOGEO	YAGUA	YAKUT
ZUNI									

346 EXCLUDED BECAUSE UNASCERTAINED

	Present (13)			Absent (41)			
62	TILT TOWARD BEING THOSE WHERE HUSBANDRY OF SOME KIND IS PRESENT (228)	0.92 OF 13	62	TILT TOWARD BEING THOSE WHERE HUSBANDRY OF ANY KIND IS ABSENT (172)	0.51 OF 41	12 20 1 21 XSQ= 6.05 PHI= 0.335 XP = 0.0139
77	DRIFT TOWARD BEING THOSE WHERE THE WRITING SYSTEM IS ALPHABETIC-OR-PHONETIC, RATHER THAN BEING MNEMONIC OR ABSENT (15) JMH	0.60 OF 5	77	DRIFT TOWARD BEING THOSE WHERE THE WRITING SYSTEM IS MNEMONIC OR ABSENT, RATHER THAN BEING ALPHABETIC-OR-PHONETIC (39) JMH	0.90 OF 10	3 1 2 9 XSQ= 2.09 PHI= 0.373 EP = 0.0769
80	DRIFT LESS TOWARD BEING THOSE WHERE NO CITY OR TOWN IS PRESENT (185)	0.78 OF 9	80	IN ALL CASES ARE THOSE WHERE NO CITY OR TOWN IS PRESENT (185)	1.00 OF 26	2 0 7 26 XSQ= 2.70 PHI= 0.278 EP = 0.0605
81	DRIFT TOWARD BEING THOSE WHERE A CITY OR TOWN IS PRESENT, OR THE AVERAGE COMMUNITY SIZE IS 200 OR GREATER (89)	0.56 OF 9	81	DRIFT TOWARD BEING THOSE WHERE NO CITY OR TOWN IS PRESENT, AND THE AVERAGE COMMUNITY SIZE IS SMALLER THAN 200 (135)	0.81 OF 26	5 5 4 21 XSQ= 2.73 PHI= 0.279 EP = 0.0814

82	IN ALL CASES ARE THOSE WHERE A CITY OR TOWN IS PRESENT, OR THE AVERAGE COMMUNITY SIZE IS FIFTY OR GREATER (178)	1.00 OF 9	82	DRIFT LESS TOWARD BEING THOSE WHERE A CITY OR TOWN IS PRESENT, OR THE AVERAGE COMMUNITY SIZE IS FIFTY OR GREATER (178)	0.69 OF 26	 XSQ= PHI= EP =	9 18 0 8 2.06 0.242 0.0815
176	TILT TOWARD BEING THOSE WHERE THE COMMUNITY IS A CLAN-COMMUNITY OR A COMMUNITY STRUCTURED OR SEGMENTED ON A CLAN BASIS (169)	0.77 OF 13	176	TILT TOWARD BEING THOSE WHERE THE COMMUNITY IS OTHER THAN A CLAN-COMMUNITY OR A COMMUNITY STRUCTURED OR SEGMENTED ON A CLAN BASIS (213)	0.66 OF 41	 XSQ= PHI= XP =	10 14 3 27 5.68 0.324 0.0171
177	DRIFT LESS TOWARD BEING THOSE WHERE THE COMMUNITY IS OTHER THAN A SINGLE CLAN-COMMUNITY AND EXOGAMOUS (305)	0.62 OF 13	177	DRIFT MORE TOWARD BEING THOSE WHERE THE COMMUNITY IS OTHER THAN A SINGLE CLAN-COMMUNITY AND EXOGAMOUS (305)	0.88 OF 41	 XSQ= PHI= XP =	5 5 8 36 2.94 0.233 0.0864
234	DRIFT TOWARD BEING THOSE WHERE THE COUSIN TERMINOLOGY IS OF CROW, OMAHA, OR IROQUOIS TYPE, RATHER THAN ESKIMO OR HAWAIIAN TYPE (152)	0.86 OF 7	234	DRIFT TOWARD BEING THOSE WHERE THE COUSIN TERMINOLOGY IS OF ESKIMO OR HAWAIIAN TYPE, RATHER THAN CROW, OMAHA, OR IROQUOIS TYPE (170)	0.58 OF 36	 XSQ= PHI= XP =	6 15 1 21 2.96 0.262 0.0854
279	TILT TOWARD BEING THOSE WHERE WIFE-LENDING OR WIFE-EXCHANGE IS PRESENT (10) LWS	0.75 OF 4	279	IN ALL CASES ARE THOSE WHERE WIFE-LENDING AND WIFE EXCHANGE ARE UNIMPORTANT OR ABSENT (19) LWS	1.00 OF 5	 XSQ= PHI= EP =	3 0 1 5 2.76 0.553 0.0476
305	TILT TOWARD BEING THOSE WHERE THE EARLY SEXUAL SATISFACTION POTENTIAL IS LOW (24) W-C	0.73 OF 11	305	TILT TOWARD BEING THOSE WHERE THE EARLY SEXUAL SATISFACTION POTENTIAL IS HIGH (27) W-C	0.68 OF 34	 XSQ= PHI= XP =	3 23 8 11 4.02 -0.299 0.0449
306	DRIFT TOWARD BEING THOSE WHERE THE EARLY DEPENDENCE SATISFACTION POTENTIAL IS LOW (24) W-C	0.73 OF 11	306	DRIFT TOWARD BEING THOSE WHERE THE EARLY DEPENDENCE SATISFACTION POTENTIAL IS HIGH (28) W-C	0.64 OF 36	 XSQ= PHI= XP =	3 23 8 13 3.21 -0.261 0.0732
308	IN ALL CASES ARE THOSE WHERE AVERAGE SOCIALIZATION ANXIETY IS HIGH (22) W-C	1.00 OF 7	308	LEAN TOWARD BEING THOSE WHERE AVERAGE SOCIALIZATION ANXIETY IS LOW (18) W-C	0.59 OF 29	 XSQ= PHI= EP =	7 12 0 17 5.60 0.394 0.0084
310	IN ALL CASES ARE THOSE WHERE ANAL SOCIALIZATION ANXIETY IS HIGH (22) W-C	1.00 OF 7	310	TILT TOWARD BEING THOSE WHERE ANAL SOCIALIZATION ANXIETY IS LOW (19) W-C	0.55 OF 29	 XSQ= PHI= EP =	7 13 0 16 4.90 0.369 0.0107

```
320  DRIFT TOWARD BEING THOSE          0.71 OF   7       320  DRIFT TOWARD BEING THOSE          0.67 OF  30            2    20
     WHERE THE DEGREE OF REDUCTION                            WHERE THE DEGREE OF REDUCTION                              5    10
     OF THE INFANT'S DRIVES                                   OF THE INFANT'S DRIVES                             XSQ=     2.02
     IS LOW   (24) B-B-C                                      IS HIGH   (45) B-B-C                               PHI=   -0.234
                                                                                                                  EP =   0.0953

354  DRIFT TOWARD BEING THOSE          0.86 OF   7       354  DRIFT TOWARD BEING THOSE          0.57 OF  30            1    17
     WHERE THE CHILD'S INFERRED ANXIETY OVER                  WHERE THE CHILD'S INFERRED ANXIETY OVER                    6    13
     PERFORMANCE OF OBEDIENT BEHAVIOR                         PERFORMANCE OF OBEDIENT BEHAVIOR                   XSQ=     2.56
     IS LOW   (37) B-B-C                                      IS HIGH   (36) B-B-C                               PHI=   -0.263
                                                                                                                  EP =   0.0897

373  TILT TOWARD BEING THOSE           0.83 OF   6       373  TILT TOWARD BEING THOSE           0.78 OF  18            5     4
     WHERE MALE INITIATION CEREMONIES                         WHERE MALE INITIATION CEREMONIES                           1    14
     AT PUBERTY ARE PRESENT   (17) W-K-A                      AT PUBERTY ARE ABSENT   (27) W-K-A                 XSQ=     4.80
                                                                                                                 PHI=    0.447
                                                                                                                  EP =   0.0147

445  IN ALL CASES ARE THOSE            1.00 OF   4       445  DRIFT TOWARD BEING THOSE          0.56 OF  18            4     8
     WHERE SORCERY IS                                         WHERE SORCERY IS                                           0    10
     IMPORTANT   (26) EBW,DH                                  UNIMPORTANT   (23) BBW,DH                          XSQ=     2.14
                                                                                                                 PHI=    0.312
                                                                                                                  EP =   0.0964

477  IN ALL CASES ARE THOSE            1.00 OF   3       477  DRIFT TOWARD BEING THOSE          0.73 OF  11            3     3
     WHERE ALCOHOLIC AGGRESSION IS                            WHERE ALCOHOLIC AGGRESSION IS                              0     8
     STRONG   (15) DH                                         MODERATE OR SLIGHT   (19) DH                       XSQ=     2.55
                                                                                                                 PHI=    0.427
                                                                                                                  EP =   0.0549
```

414	CULTURES WHERE AVOIDANCE THERAPIES OF A DEPENDENCE NATURE ARE PRESENT (23) W-C	414	CULTURES WHERE AVOIDANCE THERAPIES OF A DEPENDENCE NATURE ARE ABSENT (31) W-C

BACKGROUND ON PAGE 157 — SUBJECT ONLY

23 IN LEFT COLUMN

ALORESE, AZANDE, BALINESE, COPR ESKIMO, DUSUN, JIVARO, KWAKIUTL, LAKHER, LAMBA, LESU, MAORI, MARSHALLESE, MASAI, NAVAHO, OMAHA, ONTONG-JAVA, RWALA, SIRIONO, TAOS, WARRAU, WITOTO, YAKUT, ZUNI

31 IN RIGHT COLUMN

ABIPON, AINU, ANDAMANESE, ARAPESH, CHAGGA, CHENCHU, CHIR-APACHE, COMANCHE, DOBUANS, FON, HANO, IFUGAO, KURTATCHI, LAPPS, LEPCHA, MANUS, MARQUESANS, MURNGIN, PAPAGO, PUKAPUKA, RIFFIANS, SANPOIL, SENIANG, TANALA, TENINO, TETON, THONGA, TIKOPIA, TROBRIAND, WOGEO, YAGUA

346 EXCLUDED BECAUSE UNASCERTAINED

	Left column			Right column		Statistics
54	DRIFT LESS TOWARD BEING THOSE WHERE FOOD PRODUCTION IS BY INTENSIVE OR SIMPLE AGRICULTURE, RATHER THAN BY INCIPIENT FOOD PRODUCTION (192)	0.62 OF 13	54	DRIFT MORE TOWARD BEING THOSE WHERE FOOD PRODUCTION IS BY INTENSIVE OR SIMPLE AGRICULTURE, RATHER THAN BY INCIPIENT FOOD PRODUCTION (192)	0.94 OF 16	8 15 5 1 XSQ= 2.78 PHI= -0.310 EP = 0.0638
73	DRIFT TOWARD BEING THOSE WHERE WEAVING IS PRESENT (118)	0.61 OF 18	73	DRIFT TOWARD BEING THOSE WHERE WEAVING IS ABSENT (130)	0.70 OF 23	11 7 7 16 XSQ= 2.71 PHI= 0.257 XP = 0.0995
77	DRIFT TOWARD BEING THOSE WHERE THE WRITING SYSTEM IS ALPHABETIC-OR-PHONETIC, RATHER THAN BEING MNEMONIC OR ABSENT (15) JMH	0.50 OF 8	77	IN ALL CASES ARE THOSE WHERE THE WRITING SYSTEM IS MNEMONIC OR ABSENT, RATHER THAN BEING ALPHABETIC-OR-PHONETIC (39) JMH	1.00 OF 7	4 0 4 7 XSQ= 2.56 PHI= 0.413 EP = 0.0769
110	TILT TOWARD BEING THOSE WHERE SLAVERY IS PRESENT (163)	0.52 OF 23	110	TILT TOWARD BEING THOSE WHERE SLAVERY IS ABSENT (218)	0.77 OF 31	12 7 11 24 XSQ= 3.86 PHI= 0.267 XP = 0.0496

136	IN ALL CASES ARE THOSE WHERE FULL-TIME ENTREPRENEURS ARE PRESENT (18) JV	1.00 OF 3	136	DRIFT TOWARD BEING THOSE WHERE FULL-TIME ENTREPRENEURS ARE ABSENT (14) JV	0.73 OF 11	3 3 0 8 XSQ= 2.55 PHI= 0.427 EP = 0.0549
148	DRIFT TOWARD BEING THOSE WHERE THE INCIDENCE OF PERSONAL CRIME IS HIGH (12) B-B-C	0.71 OF 7	148	DRIFT TOWARD BEING THOSE WHERE THE INCIDENCE OF PERSONAL CRIME IS LOW (21) B-B-C	0.71 OF 17	5 5 2 12 XSQ= 2.08 PHI= 0.294 EP = 0.0850
209	DRIFT LESS TOWARD BEING THOSE WHERE MARITAL RESIDENCE IS PATRILOCAL, VIRILOCAL, OR AVUNCULOCAL, RATHER THAN MATRILOCAL OR UXORILOCAL (270)	0.65 OF 17	209	DRIFT MORE TOWARD BEING THOSE WHERE MARITAL RESIDENCE IS PATRILOCAL, VIRILOCAL, OR AVUNCULOCAL, RATHER THAN MATRILOCAL OR UXORILOCAL (270)	0.92 OF 24	11 22 6 2 XSQ= 3.05 PHI= -0.273 XP = 0.0808
210	TILT LESS TOWARD BEING THOSE WHERE MARITAL RESIDENCE IS PATRILOCAL, RATHER THAN MATRILOCAL (169)	0.56 OF 9	210	TILT MORE TOWARD BEING THOSE WHERE MARITAL RESIDENCE IS PATRILOCAL, RATHER THAN MATRILOCAL (169)	0.93 OF 15	5 14 4 1 XSQ= 2.85 PHI= -0.344 EP = 0.0474
303	TILT TOWARD BEING THOSE WHERE THE EARLY ORAL SATISFACTION POTENTIAL IS LOW (25) W-C	0.64 OF 22	303	TILT TOWARD BEING THOSE WHERE THE EARLY ORAL SATISFACTION POTENTIAL IS HIGH (32) W-C	0.69 OF 29	8 20 14 9 XSQ= 4.13 PHI= -0.285 XP = 0.0420
312	DRIFT TOWARD BEING THOSE WHERE DEPENDENCE SOCIALIZATION ANXIETY IS HIGH (24) W-C	0.69 OF 16	312	DRIFT TOWARD BEING THOSE WHERE DEPENDENCE SOCIALIZATION ANXIETY IS LOW (23) W-C	0.63 OF 27	11 10 5 17 XSQ= 2.87 PHI= 0.259 XP = 0.0900
324	DRIFT TOWARD BEING THOSE WHERE THE PAIN INFLICTED ON THE INFANT BY THE NURTURANT AGENT IS HIGH (34) B-B-C	0.69 OF 13	324	DRIFT TOWARD BEING THOSE WHERE THE PAIN INFLICTED ON THE INFANT BY THE NURTURANT AGENT IS LOW OR NEGLIGIBLE (32) B-B-C	0.64 OF 22	9 8 4 14 XSQ= 2.34 PHI= 0.259 EP = 0.0858
353	TILT TOWARD BEING THOSE WHERE THE CHILD'S INFERRED ANXIETY OVER NON-PERFORMANCE OF OBEDIENT BEHAVIOR IS HIGH (42) B-B-C	0.81 OF 16	353	TILT TOWARD BEING THOSE WHERE THE CHILD-S INFERRED ANXIETY OVER NON-PERFORMANCE OF OBEDIENT BEHAVIOR IS LOW (32) B-B-C	0.62 OF 21	13 8 3 13 XSQ= 5.24 PHI= 0.376 EP = 0.0178
354	TILT TOWARD BEING THOSE WHERE THE CHILD'S INFERRED ANXIETY OVER PERFORMANCE OF OBEDIENT BEHAVIOR IS HIGH (36) B-B-C	0.69 OF 16	354	TILT TOWARD BEING THOSE WHERE THE CHILD'S INFERRED ANXIETY OVER PERFORMANCE OF OBEDIENT BEHAVIOR IS LOW (37) B-B-C	0.67 OF 21	11 7 5 14 XSQ= 3.25 PHI= 0.296 EP = 0.0489

355	TILT TOWARD BEING THOSE 0.69 OF 16 WHERE THE CHILD'S INFERRED CONFLICT REGARDING OBEDIENT BEHAVIOR IS HIGH (35) B-B-C	355	TILT TOWARD BEING THOSE 0.71 OF 21 WHERE THE CHILD'S INFERRED CONFLICT REGARDING OBEDIENT BEHAVIOR IS LOW (38) B-B-C		11 6 5 15 XSQ= 4.40 PHI= 0.345 EP = 0.0220
356	DRIFT TOWARD BEING THOSE 0.64 OF 11 WHERE ADOLESCENT PEER GROUPS OR PAIRS ARE PRESENT IN A SETTING OF COURTSHIP (29) JKH	356	DRIFT TOWARD BEING THOSE 0.77 OF 13 WHERE NEITHER ADOLESCENT PEER GROUPS NOR PAIRS ARE PRESENT IN A SETTING OF COURTSHIP (22) JKH		7 3 4 10 XSQ= 2.54 PHI= 0.325 EP = 0.0953
417	IN ALL CASES ARE THOSE 1.00 OF 8 WHERE WARFARE IS PREVALENT (34) LWS	417	DRIFT LESS TOWARD BEING THOSE 0.57 OF 7 WHERE WARFARE IS PREVALENT (34) LWS		8 4 0 3 XSQ= 2.03 PHI= 0.367 EP = 0.0769
434	LEAN TOWARD BEING THOSE 0.80 OF 15 WHERE ASCETICISM IN MOURNING BEHAVIOR IS LOW (30) JFG	434	LEAN TOWARD BEING THOSE 0.73 OF 22 WHERE ASCETICISM IN MOURNING BEHAVIOR IS HIGH (37) JFG		3 16 12 6 XSQ= 7.93 PHI= -0.463 EP = 0.0025
479	IN ALL CASES ARE THOSE 1.00 OF 3 WHERE THE NEED TO ACHIEVE, AS INFERRED FROM FOLKTALES, IS HIGH (18) JV	479	TILT TOWARD BEING THOSE 0.85 OF 13 WHERE THE NEED TO ACHIEVE, AS INFERRED FROM FOLKTALES, IS LOW (18) JV		3 2 0 11 XSQ= 4.66 PHI= 0.540 EP = 0.0179

```
415  CULTURES                                     415  CULTURES
     WHERE AVOIDANCE THERAPIES                         WHERE AVOIDANCE THERAPIES
     OF AN AGGRESSION NATURE                           OF AN AGGRESSION NATURE
     ARE PRESENT  (25) W-C                             ARE ABSENT  (29) W-C

BACKGROUND ON PAGE 157                                                               SUBJECT ONLY

     25  IN LEFT COLUMN

AINU        ALORESE     BALINESE    CHAGGA      CHENCHU     COPR ESKIMO DUSUN       FON         IFUGAO      KWAKIUTL
LAKHER      LAMBA       LAPPS       LEPCHA      MANUS       NAVAHO      OMAHA       PAPAGO      RWALA       TANALA
TAOS        TETON       TIKOPIA     WARRAU      YAKUT

     29  IN RIGHT COLUMN

ABIPON      ANDAMANESE  ARAPESH     AZANDE      CHIR-APACHE COMANCHE    DOBUANS     HANO        JIVARO      KURTATCHI
LESU        MAORI       MARQUESANS  MARSHALLESE MASAI       MURNGIN     ONTONG-JAVA PUKAPUKA    RIFFIANS    SANPOIL
SENIANG     SIRIONO     TENINO      THONGA      TROBRIAND   WITOTO      WOGEO       YAGUA       ZUNI

     346  EXCLUDED BECAUSE UNASCERTAINED

-----------------------------------------------------------------------------------------------------------------
 5  DRIFT LESS TOWARD BEING THOSE  0.76 OF  25      5  DRIFT MORE TOWARD BEING THOSE  0.97 OF  29           6     1
    LOCATED OUTSIDE OF                                 LOCATED OUTSIDE OF                                  19    28
    EAST EURASIA  (330)                                EAST EURASIA  (330)                          XSQ=      3.37
                                                                                                    PHI=     0.250
                                                                                                    XP =    0.0664

12  DRIFT LESS TOWARD BEING THOSE  0.84 OF  25     12  IN ALL CASES ARE THOSE         1.00 OF  29           4     0
    WHERE THE LATITUDE IS                              WHERE THE LATITUDE IS                               21    29
    LESS THAN FIFTY DEGREES  (367)                     LESS THAN FIFTY DEGREES  (367)               XSQ=      2.95
                                                                                                    PHI=     0.234
                                                                                                    XP =    0.0859

13  DRIFT LESS TOWARD BEING THOSE  0.72 OF  25     13  DRIFT MORE TOWARD BEING THOSE  0.93 OF  29           7     2
    WHERE THE LATITUDE IS                              WHERE THE LATITUDE IS                               18    27
    LESS THAN FORTY DEGREES  (329)                     LESS THAN FORTY DEGREES  (329)               XSQ=      2.92
                                                                                                    PHI=     0.233
                                                                                                    XP =    0.0875

73  TILT TOWARD BEING THOSE        0.69 OF  16     73  TILT TOWARD BEING THOSE        0.72 OF  25          11     7
    WHERE WEAVING IS                                   WHERE WEAVING IS                                     5    18
    PRESENT  (118)                                     ABSENT  (130)                                XSQ=      5.03
                                                                                                    PHI=     0.350
                                                                                                    XP =    0.0249
```

No.	Left	Ratio	No.	Right	Ratio	Table / Statistics
110	TILT TOWARD BEING THOSE WHERE SLAVERY IS PRESENT (163)	0.52 OF 25	110	TILT TOWARD BEING THOSE WHERE SLAVERY IS ABSENT (218)	0.79 OF 29	13 6 / 12 23 / XSQ= 4.48 / PHI= 0.288 / XP = 0.0343
127	TILT TOWARD BEING THOSE WHERE THE FEMALES' CONTRIBUTION TO SUBSISTENCE IS LOW (32) JKB	0.75 OF 12	127	TILT TOWARD BEING THOSE WHERE THE FEMALES' CONTRIBUTION TO SUBSISTENCE IS HIGH (33) JKB	0.80 OF 10	3 8 / 9 2 / XSQ= 4.58 / PHI= -0.456 / EP = 0.0300
138	DRIFT TOWARD BEING THOSE WHERE SUPERORDINATE JUSTICE IS PRESENT (22) BBW	0.78 OF 9	138	DRIFT TOWARD BEING THOSE WHERE SUPERORDINATE JUSTICE IS ABSENT (18) BBW	0.64 OF 14	7 5 / 2 9 / XSQ= 2.38 / PHI= 0.322 / EP = 0.0894
176	TILT TOWARD BEING THOSE WHERE THE COMMUNITY IS OTHER THAN A CLAN-COMMUNITY OR A COMMUNITY STRUCTURED OR SEGMENTED ON A CLAN BASIS (213)	0.72 OF 25	176	TILT TOWARD BEING THOSE WHERE THE COMMUNITY IS A CLAN-COMMUNITY OR A COMMUNITY STRUCTURED OR SEGMENTED ON A CLAN BASIS (169)	0.59 OF 29	7 17 / 18 12 / XSQ= 3.93 / PHI= -0.270 / XP = 0.0473
198	IN ALL CASES ARE THOSE WHERE RULES FOR THE INHERITANCE OF REAL PROPERTY, IF PRESENT, FAVOR THE MALE HEIR OR LINE, RATHER THAN THE FEMALE (144)	1.00 OF 10	198	DRIFT LESS TOWARD BEING THOSE WHERE RULES FOR THE INHERITANCE OF REAL PROPERTY, IF PRESENT, FAVOR THE MALE HEIR OR LINE, RATHER THAN THE FEMALE (144)	0.60 OF 10	10 6 / 0 4 / XSQ= 2.81 / PHI= 0.375 / EP = 0.0867
214	IN ALL CASES ARE THOSE WHERE FIRST COUSIN MARRIAGE, IF PERMITTED, IS OTHER THAN UNILATERAL (144)	1.00 OF 9	214	DRIFT LESS TOWARD BEING THOSE WHERE FIRST COUSIN MARRIAGE, IF PERMITTED, IS OTHER THAN UNILATERAL (144)	0.63 OF 8	0 3 / 9 5 / XSQ= 1.92 / PHI= -0.336 / EP = 0.0824
240	TILT TOWARD BEING THOSE WHERE THE FAMILY, IF EXTENDED, IS SMALL OR STEM, RATHER THAN LARGE (135)	0.89 OF 9	240	TILT TOWARD BEING THOSE WHERE THE FAMILY, IF EXTENDED, IS LARGE, RATHER THAN SMALL OR STEM (78)	0.69 OF 13	1 9 / 8 4 / XSQ= 5.09 / PHI= -0.481 / EP = 0.0115
243	DRIFT TOWARD BEING THOSE WHERE POLYGYNY, IF PRESENT, HAS A LOW INCIDENCE (36) W-C,S	0.82 OF 11	243	DRIFT TOWARD BEING THOSE WHERE POLYGYNY, IF PRESENT, HAS A HIGH INCIDENCE (24) W-D,S	0.60 OF 15	2 9 / 9 6 / XSQ= 2.99 / PHI= -0.339 / EP = 0.0506
258	TILT TOWARD BEING THOSE WHERE THE SEVERITY OF SON'S WIFE AVOIDANCE IS HIGH (15) WNS	0.60 OF 10	258	IN ALL CASES ARE THOSE WHERE THE SEVERITY OF SON'S WIFE AVOIDANCE IS LOW (16) WNS	1.00 OF 8	6 0 / 4 8 / XSQ= 4.75 / PHI= 0.514 / EP = 0.0128

260	TILT TOWARD BEING THOSE WHERE THE AGE OF MALES AT MARRIAGE IS LESS THAN TWENTY (38) JKH	0.92 OF 12	260	TILT TOWARD BEING THOSE WHERE THE AGE OF MALES AT MARRIAGE IS TWENTY OR OVER (17) JKH	0.50 OF 16	11 8 1 8 XSQ= 3.71 PHI= 0.364 EP = 0.0390
284	IN ALL CASES ARE THOSE WHERE CONTRACEPTION IS NOT PRACTICED (7) CSF	1.00 OF 4	284	TILT TOWARD BEING THOSE WHERE CONTRACEPTION IS PRACTICED (10) CSF	0.88 OF 8	0 7 4 1 XSQ= 5.19 PHI= -0.657 EP = 0.0101
299	IN ALL CASES ARE THOSE WHERE THE POST-PARTUM SEX TABOO LASTS ONE YEAR OR LESS (89)	1.00 OF 12	299	TILT LESS TOWARD BEING THOSE WHERE THE POST-PARTUM SEX TABOO LASTS ONE YEAR OR LESS (89)	0.55 OF 20	0 9 12 11 XSQ= 5.45 PHI= -0.413 EP = 0.0117
300	DRIFT TOWARD BEING THOSE WHERE THE POST-PARTUM SEX TABOO LASTS SIX MONTHS OR LESS (73)	0.75 OF 12	300	DRIFT TOWARD BEING THOSE WHERE THE POST-PARTUM SEX TABOO LASTS LONGER THAN SIX MONTHS (51)	0.60 OF 20	3 12 9 8 XSQ= 2.42 PHI= -0.275 EP = 0.0759
316	TILT TOWARD BEING THOSE WHERE EXCLUSIVE MOTHER-SON SLEEPING ARRANGEMENTS LAST LESS THAN ONE YEAR (25) W-K-A	0.85 OF 13	316	TILT TOWARD BEING THOSE WHERE EXCLUSIVE MOTHER-SON SLEEPING ARRANGEMENTS LAST ONE YEAR OR LONGER (19) W-K-A	0.64 OF 11	2 7 11 4 XSQ= 4.04 PHI= -0.410 EP = 0.0327
326	DRIFT TOWARD BEING THOSE WHERE THE INFERRED TRANSITION ANXIETY BETWEEN INFANCY AND CHILDHOOD IS HIGH (32) B-B-C	0.71 OF 17	326	DRIFT TOWARD BEING THOSE WHERE THE INFERRED TRANSITION ANXIETY BETWEEN INFANCY AND CHILDHOOD IS LOW (35) B-B-C	0.63 OF 19	12 7 5 12 XSQ= 2.86 PHI= 0.282 EP = 0.0543
360	DRIFT LESS TOWARD BEING THOSE WHERE ADOLESCENT PEER GROUPS ARE PRESENT ONLY IN A SETTING OF LEISURE, OR ELSE ARE ABSENT (23) JKH	0.63 OF 8	360	IN ALL CASES ARE THOSE WHERE ADOLESCENT PEER GROUPS ARE PRESENT ONLY IN A SETTING OF LEISURE, OR ELSE ARE ABSENT (23) JKH	1.00 OF 10	3 0 5 10 XSQ= 2.20 PHI= 0.350 EP = 0.0686
366	TILT TOWARD BEING THOSE WHERE DISSOCIATION OF THE SEXES AT ADOLESCENCE IS MEDIUM OR LOW (41) JKH	0.92 OF 12	366	TILT TOWARD BEING THOSE WHERE DISSOCIATION OF THE SEXES AT ADOLESCENCE IS HIGH (16) JKH	0.50 OF 16	1 8 11 8 XSQ= 3.71 PHI= -0.364 EP = 0.0390
368	LEAN TOWARD BEING THOSE WHERE DISSOCIATION OF THE SEXES AT ADOLESCENCE IS LOW (21) JKH	0.89 OF 9	368	LEAN TOWARD BEING THOSE WHERE DISSOCIATION OF THE SEXES AT ADOLESCENCE IS HIGH OR MEDIUM (16) JKH	0.80 OF 10	1 8 8 2 XSQ= 6.47 PHI= -0.583 EP = 0.0055

369	LEAN TOWARD BEING THOSE WHERE BOTH DISSOCIATION OF THE SEXES AT ADOLESCENCE, AND CUSTOMS OF INITIATION AT ADOLESCENCE, ARE ABSENT (15) JKH	0.58 OF 12	369	LEAN TOWARD BEING THOSE WHERE DISSOCIATION OF THE SEXES AT ADOLESCENCE, OR CUSTOMS OF INITIATION AT ADOLESCENCE, ARE PRESENT (42) JKH	0.94 OF 16	5 15 7 1 XSQ= 6.74 PHI= -0.491 EP = 0.0084
382	TILT TOWARD BEING THOSE WHERE FEMALE INITIATION RITES ARE ABSENT (27) JKB	0.67 OF 12	382	TILT TOWARD BEING THOSE WHERE FEMALE INITIATION RITES ARE PRESENT (38) JKB	0.90 OF 10	4 9 8 1 XSQ= 5.09 PHI= -0.481 EP = 0.0115
397	DRIFT MORE TOWARD BEING THOSE WHERE SEX DISABILITY IS ABSENT (42) JKH	0.92 OF 12	397	DRIFT LESS TOWARD BEING THOSE WHERE SEX DISABILITY IS ABSENT (42) JKH	0.56 OF 16	1 7 11 9 XSQ= 2.66 PHI= -0.308 EP = 0.0882
430	IN ALL CASES ARE THOSE WHERE SUPERNATURAL SANCTIONS FOR MORALITY, HAVING AN EFFECT ON AN INDIVIDUAL'S HEALTH, ARE PRESENT (16) GES	1.00 OF 4	430	TILT TOWARD BEING THOSE WHERE SUPERNATURAL SANCTIONS FOR MORALITY, HAVING AN EFFECT ON AN INDIVIDUAL'S HEALTH, ARE ABSENT OR UNREPORTED (22) GES	0.83 OF 6	4 1 0 5 XSQ= 3.75 PHI= 0.612 EP = 0.0476
438	DRIFT TOWARD BEING THOSE WHERE OTHER-WORLDLY FEARS OF GHOSTS OR SPIRITS ARE GREATER THAN THIS-WORLDLY FEARS OF HUMANS OR ANIMALS (27) W-C,JFG	0.82 OF 17	438	DRIFT TOWARD BEING THOSE WHERE THIS-WORLDLY FEARS OF HUMANS OR ANIMALS ARE GREATER THAN OTHER-WORLDLY FEARS OF GHOSTS OR SPIRITS (17) W-C,JFG	0.50 OF 20	14 10 3 10 XSQ= 2.92 PHI= 0.281 EP = 0.0823
441	LEAN TOWARD BEING THOSE WHERE FEAR OF HUMAN BEINGS IS LOW (32) W-C	0.76 OF 25	441	LEAN TOWARD BEING THOSE WHERE FEAR OF HUMAN BEINGS IS HIGH (29) W-C	0.69 OF 29	6 20 19 9 XSQ= 9.15 PHI= -0.412 XP = 0.0025
445	TILT TOWARD BEING THOSE WHERE SORCERY IS UNIMPORTANT (23) BBW,DH	0.67 OF 12	445	TILT TOWARD BEING THOSE WHERE SORCERY IS IMPORTANT (26) BBW,DH	0.80 OF 10	4 8 8 2 XSQ= 3.09 PHI= -0.375 EP = 0.0427
453	IN ALL CASES ARE THOSE WHERE THE ROLE OF RELIGIOUS EXPERTS IS NOT CONDUCIVE TO THE DEVELOPMENT OF THE INDIVIDUAL'S NEED TO ACHIEVE (23) DCM	1.00 OF 6	453	TILT TOWARD BEING THOSE WHERE THE ROLE OF RELIGIOUS EXPERTS IS CONDUCIVE TO THE DEVELOPMENT OF THE INDIVIDUAL'S NEED TO ACHIEVE (13) DCM	0.56 OF 9	0 5 6 4 XSQ= 2.81 PHI= -0.433 EP = 0.0440
477	DRIFT TOWARD BEING THOSE WHERE ALCOHOLIC AGGRESSION IS MODERATE OR SLIGHT (19) DH	0.78 OF 9	477	DRIFT TOWARD BEING THOSE WHERE ALCOHOLIC AGGRESSION IS STRONG (15) DH	0.80 OF 5	2 4 7 1 XSQ= 2.34 PHI= -0.409 EP = 0.0909

416 CULTURES
WHERE THE THREAT FROM ARMED ATTACK
BY ALIEN SOCIETIES
IS CONSIDERABLE (10) GES

416 CULTURES
WHERE THE THREAT FROM ARMED ATTACK
BY ALIEN SOCIETIES
IS LIMITED OR NEGLIGIBLE (26) GES

BACKGROUND ON PAGE 160

NEITHER SUBJECT NOR PREDICATE

10 IN LEFT COLUMN

AZANDE IFUGAO KAREN MARQUESANS NANDI TANALA TIMBIRA TIV TRUMAI YUROK

26 IN RIGHT COLUMN

ARANDA ARAPESH AYMARA AZTEC BEMBA COPR ESKIMO CUNA DOBUANS GANDA HEBREWS
IBAN KASKA LEPCHA LOZI MIAO NAMA NUER NYAKYUSA ROMANS SAMOYED
TALLENSI TODA WINNEBAGO WOLEAIANS YAGUA YOKUTS

364 EXCLUDED BECAUSE UNASCERTAINED

417 CULTURES WHERE WARFARE IS PREVALENT (34) LWS	417 CULTURES WHERE WARFARE IS NOT PREVALENT (9) LWS

BACKGROUND ON PAGE 160 — BOTH SUBJECT AND PREDICATE

34 IN LEFT CCLUMN

ABIPCN	ALBANIANS	ARAUCANIANS	ASHANTI	AZTEC	CHUKCHEE	CREEK	CRCW	DIERI	FANG
FON	HAIDA	HANC	HEBREWS	IBAN	INCA	JIVARC	KAZAK	KUNG	KUTENAI
KWAKIUTL	LANGO	MACRI	MOTA	NAMA	NAVAHO	OMAHA	RWALA	SAMCANS	SERI
SHILLUK	TRCBRIANC	WITCTO	YAKUT						

9 IN RIGHT CCLUMN

AINU	ANDAMANESE	ARANCA	LAPPS	SEMANG	TODA	VEDDA	YAHGAN	YUKAGHIR

357 EXCLUCED BECAUSE UNASCERTAINEC

	Left column			Right column		Statistics
5	TEND TC BE THCSE LCCATED CUTSICE OF EAST EURASIA (330)	0.91 OF 34	5	TEND TO BE THOSE LOCATED IN EAST EURASIA (70)	0.67 OF 9	3 6 / 31 3 / XSQ= 11.10 / PHI= -0.508 / XP = 0.0009
44	TILT TCWARC BEING THCSE WHERE SETTLEMENTS ARE FIXEC (222)	0.64 OF 33	44	TILT TOWARD BEING THOSE WHERE SETTLEMENTS ARE NCN-FIXED (110)	0.89 CF 9	21 1 / 12 8 / XSQ= 5.86 / PHI= 0.373 / XP = 0.0155
46	TILT TCWARC BEING THCSE CTHER THAN WHERE SETTLEMENTS ARE NCN-FIXED AND MCVEMENT IS NCMADIC (260)	0.70 OF 33	46	TILT TOWARD BEING THOSE WHERE SETTLEMENTS ARE NON-FIXED AND MOVEMENT IS NOMADIC (72)	0.78 OF 9	10 7 / 23 2 / XSQ= 4.79 / PHI= -0.338 / XP = 0.0286
62	TILT TCWARC BEING THCSE WHERE HUSBANDRY CF SCME KIND IS PRESENT. (228)	0.74 OF 34	62	TILT TOWARD BEING THOSE WHERE HUSBANDRY OF ANY KIND IS ABSENT (172)	0.78 CF 9	25 2 / 9 7 / XSQ= 5.97 / PHI= 0.373 / XP = 0.0145
71	TILT TCWARC BEING THCSE WHERE METAL WCRKING IS PRESENT (98)	0.55 OF 29	71	IN ALL CASES ARE THCSE WHERE METAL WORKING IS ABSENT (153)	1.00 OF 7	16 0 / 13 7 / XSQ= 4.90 / PHI= 0.369 / EP = 0.0107

```
 73  TILT TOWARD BEING THOSE          0.60 OF  30     73  TILT TOWARD BEING THOSE          0.86 OF   7         18     1
     WHERE WEAVING IS                                    WHERE WEAVING IS                                      12     6
     PRESENT  (118)                                      ABSENT  (130)                                  XSQ=      3.09
                                                                                                        PHI=     0.289
                                                                                                        EP  =   0.0422

 74  DRIFT TOWARD BEING THOSE         0.70 OF  27     74  DRIFT TOWARD BEING THOSE         0.71 OF   7         19     2
     WHERE POTTERY IS                                    WHERE POTTERY IS                                       8     5
     PRESENT  (145)                                      ABSENT  (93)                                   XSQ=      2.53
                                                                                                        PHI=     0.273
                                                                                                        EP  =   0.0789

 82  TEND TO BE THOSE                 0.86 OF  22     82  IN ALL CASES ARE THOSE           1.00 OF   8         19     0
     WHERE A CITY OR TOWN IS PRESENT, OR                 WHERE NO CITY OR TOWN IS PRESENT, AND                  3     8
     THE AVERAGE COMMUNITY SIZE IS                       THE AVERAGE COMMUNITY SIZE IS                  XSQ=     15.31
     FIFTY OR GREATER  (178)                             SMALLER THAN FIFTY  (46)                       PHI=     0.714
                                                                                                        EP  =   0.0000

 86  TILT TOWARD BEING THOSE          0.53 OF  32     86  IN ALL CASES ARE THOSE           1.00 OF   8         17     0
     WHERE THE LEVEL OF POLITICAL INTEGRATION            WHERE THE LEVEL OF POLITICAL INTEGRATION              15     8
     IS THE LARGE STATE, THE LITTLE STATE,               IS THE AUTONOMOUS COMMUNITY, OR                XSQ=      5.38
     OR THE MINIMAL STATE  (148) GPM                     THE FAMILY  (156) GPM                          PHI=     0.367
                                                                                                        EP  =   0.0125

100  TILT TOWARD BEING THOSE          0.88 OF  33    100  TILT TOWARD BEING THOSE          0.56 OF   9         29     4
     WHERE HIERARCHIES ARE MORE COMPLEX THAN             WHERE HIERARCHIES ARE THE 'SIMPLEST'                   4     5
     THE 'SIMPLEST,' I. E., MORE COMPLEX THAN            I. E., WHERE THERE ARE ONLY                    XSQ=      5.55
     TWO LOCAL LEVELS WITH                               TWO LOCAL LEVELS WITH                          PHI=     0.364
     NO NATIONAL LEVELS  (267) GES,EA                    NO NATIONAL LEVELS  (63) GES,EA                XP  =   0.0184

102  TILT TOWARD BEING THOSE          0.62 OF  34    102  TILT TOWARD BEING THOSE          0.89 OF   9         21     1
     WHERE CLASS STRATIFICATION IS                       WHERE CLASS STRATIFICATION IS                         13     8
     PRESENT  (203)                                      ABSENT  (180)                                  XSQ=      5.42
                                                                                                        PHI=     0.355
                                                                                                        XP  =   0.0199

110  TILT TOWARD BEING THOSE          0.59 OF  34    110  TILT TOWARD BEING THOSE          0.89 OF   9         20     1
     WHERE SLAVERY IS PRESENT  (163)                     WHERE SLAVERY IS ABSENT  (218)                        14     8
                                                                                                        XSQ=      4.71
                                                                                                        PHI=     0.331
                                                                                                        XP  =   0.0299

131  DRIFT TOWARD BEING THOSE         0.78 OF  18    131  DRIFT TOWARD BEING THOSE         0.75 OF   4         14     1
     WHERE THE CONSTRUCTION OF PERMANENT HOUSES          WHERE THE CONSTRUCTION OF PERMANENT HOUSES             4     3
     OR THE ERECTION OF TEMPORARY DWELLINGS              OR THE ERECTION OF TEMPORARY DWELLINGS         XSQ=      2.12
     IS MAINLY DONE BY MALES  (136)                      IS MAINLY DONE BY FEMALES  (21)                PHI=     0.311
                                                                                                        EP  =   0.0766

137  DRIFT LESS TOWARD BEING THOSE 0.56 OF  25       137  IN ALL CASES ARE THOSE           1.00 OF   6         11     0
     WHERE INVIDIOUS DISPLAY OF WEALTH                   WHERE INVIDIOUS DISPLAY OF WEALTH                     14     6
     IS MODERATELY, LITTLE, OR                           IS MODERATELY, LITTLE, OR                      XSQ=      2.40
     NEGATIVELY EMPHASIZED  (52) PES                     NEGATIVELY EMPHASIZED  (52) PES                PHI=     0.278
                                                                                                        EP  =   0.0658
```

No.	Statement	Proportion	N	No.	Statement	Proportion	N	Statistics
141	DRIFT TOWARD BEING THOSE WHERE THE LEVEL OF SOCIAL SANCTION IS PUBLIC CORPOREAL SANCTION, RATHER THAN PUBLIC PROPERTY SANCTION OR PRIVATE SETTLEMENT (28) JMH	0.69 OF	13	141	IN ALL CASES ARE THOSE WHERE THE LEVEL OF SOCIAL SANCTION IS PUBLIC PROPERTY SANCTION OR PRIVATE SETTLEMENT, RATHER THAN PUBLIC CORPOREAL SANCTION (26) JMH	1.00 OF	3	9 0 4 3 XSQ= 2.35 PHI= 0.383 EP = 0.0625
180	DRIFT TOWARD BEING THOSE WHERE THE COMMUNITY IS COMMONLY NON-EXOGAMOUS, RATHER THAN EXOGAMOUS (258)	0.64 OF	33	180	DRIFT TOWARD BEING THOSE WHERE THE COMMUNITY IS COMMONLY EXOGAMOUS, RATHER THAN NON-EXOGAMOUS (124)	0.78 OF	9	12 7 21 2 XSQ= 3.37 PHI= -0.283 XP = 0.0665
192	DRIFT TOWARD BEING THOSE OTHER THAN WHERE THE ONLY KIN GROUP PRESENT IS A KINDRED OR ELSE BILATERAL DESCENT IS INFERRED (289)	0.79 OF	34	192	DRIFT TOWARD BEING THOSE WHERE THE ONLY KIN GROUP PRESENT IS A KINDRED OR ELSE BILATERAL DESCENT IS INFERRED (111)	0.56 OF	9	7 5 27 4 XSQ= 2.76 PHI= -0.253 XP = 0.0966
262	DRIFT MORE TOWARD BEING THOSE WHERE WIVES ARE OBTAINED BY MEANS INVOLVING THE PRESENCE OF SOME CONSIDERATION (305)	0.88 OF	34	262	DRIFT LESS TOWARD BEING THOSE WHERE WIVES ARE OBTAINED BY MEANS INVOLVING THE PRESENCE OF SOME CONSIDERATION (305)	0.56 OF	9	30 5 4 4 XSQ= 3.09 PHI= 0.268 XP = 0.0786
300	TILT TOWARD BEING THOSE WHERE THE POST-PARTUM SEX TABOO LASTS LONGER THAN SIX MONTHS (51)	0.58 OF	19	300	IN ALL CASES ARE THOSE WHERE THE POST-PARTUM SEX TABOO LASTS SIX MONTHS OR LESS (73)	1.00 OF	6	11 0 8 6 XSQ= 4.08 PHI= 0.404 EP = 0.0196
305	DRIFT TOWARD BEING THOSE WHERE THE EARLY SEXUAL SATISFACTION POTENTIAL IS LOW (24) W-C	0.85 OF	13	305	IN ALL CASES ARE THOSE WHERE THE EARLY SEXUAL SATISFACTION POTENTIAL IS HIGH (27) W-C	1.00 OF	2	2 2 11 0 XSQ= 2.76 PHI= -0.429 EP = 0.0571
309	DRIFT TOWARD BEING THOSE WHERE ORAL SOCIALIZATION ANXIETY IS HIGH (26) W-C	0.79 OF	14	309	DRIFT TOWARD BEING THOSE WHERE ORAL SOCIALIZATION ANXIETY IS LOW (27) W-C	0.75 OF	4	11 1 3 3 XSQ= 1.97 PHI= 0.331 EP = 0.0833
323	DRIFT TOWARD BEING THOSE WHERE THE CONSTANCY OF PRESENCE OF THE INFANT'S NURTURANT AGENT IS LOW (45) B-B-C	0.79 OF	14	323	DRIFT TOWARD BEING THOSE WHERE THE CONSTANCY OF PRESENCE OF THE INFANT'S NURTURANT AGENT IS HIGH (29) B-B-C	0.75 OF	4	3 3 11 1 XSQ= 1.97 PHI= -0.331 EP = 0.0833
349	IN ALL CASES ARE THOSE WHERE THE CHILD'S INFERRED ANXIETY OVER NON-PERFORMANCE OF ACHIEVEMENT BEHAVIOR IS HIGH (34) B-B-C	1.00 OF	12	349	TILT TOWARD BEING THOSE WHERE THE CHILD'S INFERRED ANXIETY OVER NON-PERFORMANCE OF ACHIEVEMENT BEHAVIOR IS LOW (28) B-B-C	0.67 OF	3	12 1 0 2 XSQ= 4.36 PHI= 0.539 EP = 0.0286

```
419  TEND TO BE THOSE                0.96 OF  25     419  TEND TO BE THOSE                  0.83 OF   6          24     1
     WHERE MILITARY GLORY                                 WHERE MILITARY GLORY                                    1     5
     IS STRONGLY OR                                       IS NEGLIGIBLY EMPHASIZED  (31) PES            XSQ=   14.76
     MODERATELY EMPHASIZED  (55) PES                                                                    PHI=   0.690
                                                                                                        EP =   0.0002

420  TEND TO BE THOSE                0.81 OF  26     420  IN ALL CASES ARE THOSE            1.00 OF   6          21     0
     WHERE BELLICOSITY                                    WHERE BELLICOSITY                                       5     6
     IS EXTREME  (41) PES                                 IS MODERATE OR NEGLIGIBLE  (46) PES           XSQ=   10.74
                                                                                                        PHI=   0.579
                                                                                                        EP =   0.0005

421  DRIFT TOWARD BEING THOSE        0.70 OF  23     421  DRIFT TOWARD BEING THOSE          0.83 OF   6          16     1
     WHERE KILLING, TORTURING, OR MUTILATING              WHERE KILLING, TORTURING, OR MUTILATING                 7     5
     OF THE ENEMY                                         OF THE ENEMY                                  XSQ=    3.53
     IS STRONGLY OR MODERATELY                            IS NEGLIGIBLY EMPHASIZED  (47) PES            PHI=   0.349
     EMPHASIZED  (37) PES                                                                               EP =   0.0563

459  LEAN TOWARD BEING THOSE         0.57 OF  28     459  IN ALL CASES ARE THOSE            1.00 OF   7          16     0
     WHERE GAMES, IF PRESENT,                             WHERE GAMES, IF PRESENT,                               12     7
     INCLUDE GAMES OF CHANCE  (82) R-A-B,EA               DO NOT INCLUDE                                XSQ=    5.25
                                                          GAMES OF CHANCE  (89) R-A-B,EA                PHI=   0.387
                                                                                                        EP =   0.0092

460  LEAN TOWARD BEING THOSE         0.64 OF  28     460  IN ALL CASES ARE THOSE            1.00 OF   7          10     7
     WHERE GAMES, IF PRESENT,                             WHERE GAMES, IF PRESENT,                               18     0
     ARE NOT LIMITED TO                                   ARE LIMITED TO                                XSQ=    6.87
     GAMES OF SKILL ONLY  (104) R-A-B,EA                  GAMES OF SKILL ONLY  (67) R-A-B,EA            PHI=  -0.443
                                                                                                        EP =   0.0029

472  LEAN TOWARD BEING THOSE         0.69 OF  26     472  IN ALL CASES ARE THOSE            1.00 OF   6          18     0
     WHERE THE COMPOSITE NARCISSISM INDEX                 WHERE THE COMPOSITE NARCISSISM INDEX                    8     6
     IS HIGH  (47) PES                                    IS LOW  (43) PES                              XSQ=    6.89
                                                                                                        PHI=   0.464
                                                                                                        EP =   0.0033

474  LEAN TOWARD BEING THOSE         0.69 OF  26     474  IN ALL CASES ARE THOSE            1.00 OF   6          18     0
     WHERE BOASTFULNESS IS EXTREME  (41) PES              WHERE BOASTFULNESS IS MODERATE,                         8     6
                                                          NEGLIBIBLE, OR UNREPORTED  (48) PES           XSQ=    6.89
                                                                                                        PHI=   0.464
                                                                                                        EP =   0.0033
```

418 CULTURES WHERE WARFARE IS COMMON OR CHRONIC (8) CH	418 CULTURES WHERE WARFARE IS RARE OR INFREQUENT (24) DH

BACKGROUND ON PAGE 160 — NEITHER SUBJECT NOR PREDICATE

8 IN LEFT COLUMN

ABIPON CREEK GOAJIRO JIVARO MARICOPA MURNGIN PAPAGO TUPINAMBA

24 IN RIGHT COLUMN

AINU ANDAMANESE APINAYE BALINESE CARIB CAYAPA CHOROTI CHUKCHEE CUNA GOND
HANO HUICHOL KAZAK KHALKA LAMBA LEPCHA NASKAPI SAMOYED TANALA TARAHUMARA
TEHUELCHE TODA YAKUT ZUNI

368 EXCLUDED BECAUSE UNASCERTAINED

419	CULTURES WHERE MILITARY GLORY IS STRONGLY OR MODERATELY EMPHASIZED (55) PES	419	CULTURES WHERE MILITARY GLORY IS NEGLIGIBLY EMPHASIZED (31) PES

BACKGROUND ON PAGE 160

BOTH SUBJECT AND PREDICATE

55 IN LEFT COLUMN

ABIPON	AINU	ALBANIANS	ARAUCANIANS	ASHANTI	AZANDE	AZTEC	BEMBA	BHIL	CHAGGA
CHEYENNE	CHIR-APACHE	CHUKCHEE	COMANCHE	CREEK	CROW	DOBUANS	FON	GANDA	HAIDA
HEBREWS	IBAN	IFUGAO	INCA	JIVARO	KASKA	KAZAK	KURTATCHI	KWAKIUTL	LAKHER
LANGO	MANUS	MAORI	MASAI	MURNGIN	NAMA	NAVAHO	NUER	NYAKYUSA	OJIBWA
RIFFIANS	RWALA	SOMALI	TANALA	TAPIRAPE	THONGA	TIKOPIA	TIV	TROBRIAND	VENDA
WARRAU	WITOTO	WOLOF	YAKUT	ZUNI					

31 IN RIGHT COLUMN

ALORESE	AMERICANS	ANDAMANESE	ARANDA	ARAPESH	AYMARA	BALINESE	CHENCHU	CUNA	CZECHS
GOND	HANO	KOREANS	LAPPS	LAU	LEPCHA	LESU	PAPAGO	PUKAPUKA	SANPOIL
SIRIONO	TALLENSI	TIMBIRA	TODA	TRUMAI	VIETNAMESE	WOGEO	WOLEAIANS	YAGUA	YAHGAN
YUROK									

314 EXCLUDED BECAUSE UNASCERTAINED

3	TILT LESS TOWARD BEING THOSE LOCATED OUTSIDE OF AFRICA (320)	0.75 OF 55	3	TILT MORE TOWARD BEING THOSE LOCATED OUTSIDE OF AFRICA (320)	0.97 OF 31	14 1 41 30 XSQ= 5.35 PHI= 0.249 XP = 0.0208
71	LEAN TOWARD BEING THOSE WHERE METAL WORKING IS PRESENT (98)	0.57 OF 47	71	LEAN TOWARD BEING THOSE WHERE METAL WORKING IS ABSENT (153)	0.80 OF 25	27 5 20 20 XSQ= 7.81 PHI= 0.329 XP = 0.0052
82	DRIFT MORE TOWARD BEING THOSE WHERE A CITY OR TOWN IS PRESENT, OR THE AVERAGE COMMUNITY SIZE IS FIFTY OR GREATER (178)	0.87 OF 39	82	DRIFT LESS TOWARD BEING THOSE WHERE A CITY OR TOWN IS PRESENT, OR THE AVERAGE COMMUNITY SIZE IS FIFTY OR GREATER (178)	0.64 OF 28	34 18 5 10 XSQ= 3.69 PHI= 0.235 XP = 0.0548
86	TILT TOWARD BEING THOSE WHERE THE LEVEL OF POLITICAL INTEGRATION IS THE LARGE STATE, THE LITTLE STATE, OR THE MINIMAL STATE (148) GPM	0.56 OF 48	86	TILT TOWARD BEING THOSE WHERE THE LEVEL OF POLITICAL INTEGRATION IS THE AUTONOMOUS COMMUNITY, OR THE FAMILY (156) GPM	0.70 OF 27	27 8 21 19 XSQ= 3.91 PHI= 0.228 XP = 0.0480

96	TILT TCWARD BEING THOSE WHERE THE HIERARCHY OF NATICNAL JURISDICTICN HAS FCUR, THREE, TWC OR CNE LEVEL (174) GES,EA	0.64 OF 53	96	TILT TOWARD BEING THOSE WHERE THE HIERARCHY OF NATIONAL JURISDICTICN HAS NO LEVELS (156) GES,EA	0.62 OF 29	34 11 19 18 XSQ= 4.20 PHI= 0.226 XP = 0.0404
108	LEAN TCWARD BEING THOSE WHERE CLASS STRATIFICATICN, IF PRESENT, IS BASED CN A HEREDITARY ARISTCCRACY (74)	0.55 OF 33	108	LEAN TOWARD BEING THOSE WHERE CLASS STRATIFICATICN, IF PRESENT, IS BASED ON SOMETHING OTHER THAN A HEREDITARY ARISTOCRACY (129)	0.93 OF 14	18 1 15 13 XSQ= 7.31 PHI= 0.394 XP = 0.0069
110	DRIFT TCWARD BEING THCSE WHERE SLAVERY IS PRESENT (163)	0.53 OF 55	110	DRIFT TOWARD BEING THOSE WHERE SLAVERY IS ABSENT (218)	0.71 CF 31	29 9 26 22 XSQ= 3.60 PHI= 0.205 XP = 0.0576
137	DRIFT LESS TCWARC BEING THOSE WHERE INVIDICUS DISPLAY CF WEALTH IS MCDERATELY, LITTLE, CR NEGATIVELY EMPHASIZEC (52) PES	0.52 OF 54	137	DRIFT MORE TOWARD BEING THCSE WHERE INVIDIOUS DISPLAY OF WEALTH IS MODERATELY, LITTLE, CR NEGATIVELY EMPHASIZED (52) PES	0.74 OF 31	26 8 28 23 XSQ= 3.22 PHI= 0.195 XP = 0.0728
141	TILT TCWARD BEING THCSE WHERE THE LEVEL CF SCCIAL SANCTION IS PUBLIC CCRPCREAL SANCTION, RATHER THAN PUBLIC PRCPERTY SANCTICN CR PRIVATE SETTLEMENT (28) JMH	0.73 OF 22	141	TILT TOWARD BEING THOSE WHERE THE LEVEL OF SOCIAL SANCTICN IS PUBLIC PROPERTY SANCTICN OR PRIVATE SETTLEMENT, RATHER THAN PUBLIC CORPOREAL SANCTICN (26) JMH	0.75 CF 12	16 3 6 9 XSQ= 5.37 PHI= 0.397 EP = 0.0120
148	TEND TC BE THCSE WHERE THE INCIDENCE OF PERSONAL CRIME IS HIGH (12) B-B-C	0.63 OF 19	148	IN ALL CASES ARE THCSE WHERE THE INCIDENCE CF PERSCNAL CRIME IS LOW (21) B-B-C	1.00 OF 11	12 0 7 11 XSQ= 9.10 PHI= 0.551 EP = 0.0006
149	LEAN TCWARC BEING THCSE WHERE THE INCIDENCE CF THEFT IS HIGH (18) B-B-C	0.68 OF 19	149	LEAN TOWARD BEING THCSE WHERE THE INCIDENCE OF THEFT IS LOW (19) B-B-C	0.87 CF 15	13 2 6 13 XSQ= 8.20 PHI= 0.491 EP = 0.0019
242	LEAN MCRE TOWARC BEING THCSE WHERE MARRIAGE IS COMMCNLY CR CCCASICNALLY PCLYGYNOUS, RATHER THAN MCNCGAMCUS (314)	0.87 OF 55	242	LEAN LESS TOWARD BEING THOSE WHERE MARRIAGE IS COMMONLY OR OCCASICNALLY PCLYGYNOUS, RATHER THAN MONOGAMOUS (314)	0.60 OF 30	48 18 7 12 XSQ= 6.82 PHI= 0.283 XP = 0.0090
258	TILT TCWARC BEING THCSE WHERE THE SEVERITY CF SCN'S WIFE AVCIDANCE IS HIGH (15) WNS	0.67 OF 15	258	TILT TOWARD BEING THOSE WHERE THE SEVERITY OF SCN'S WIFE AVOIDANCE IS LCW (16) WNS	0.88 CF 8	10 1 5 7 XSQ= 4.16 PHI= 0.425 EP = 0.0272

259	TILT TOWARD BEING THOSE 0.71 OF 24 WHERE THE SEVERITY OF MOTHER-IN-LAW AVOIDANCE IS HIGH (26) WNS	259	TILT TOWARD BEING THOSE 0.73 OF 11 WHERE THE SEVERITY OF MOTHER-IN-LAW AVOIDANCE IS LOW (20) WNS	17 3 7 8	XSQ= 4.20 PHI= 0.346 EP = 0.0271
262	DRIFT MORE TOWARD BEING THOSE 0.87 OF 55 WHERE WIVES ARE OBTAINED BY MEANS INVOLVING THE PRESENCE OF SOME CONSIDERATION (305)	262	DRIFT LESS TOWARD BEING THOSE 0.68 OF 31 WHERE WIVES ARE OBTAINED BY MEANS INVOLVING THE PRESENCE OF SOME CONSIDERATION (305)	48 21 7 10	XSQ= 3.62 PHI= 0.205 XP = 0.0572
263	DRIFT TOWARD BEING THOSE 0.62 OF 55 WHERE WIVES ARE OBTAINED BY RELATIVELY DIFFICULT MEANS, NAMELY BY BRIDE-PRICE, BRIDE-SERVICE, OR EXCHANGING A FEMALE RELATIVE (233)	263	DRIFT TOWARD BEING THOSE 0.61 OF 31 WHERE WIVES ARE OBTAINED BY RELATIVELY EASY MEANS, NAMELY BY TOKEN BRIDE-PRICE, GIFT EXCHANGE, ABSENCE OF ANY CONSIDERATION, OR RECEIPT OF DOWRY (162)	34 12 21 19	XSQ= 3.38 PHI= 0.198 XP = 0.0661
301	DRIFT MORE TOWARD BEING THOSE 0.85 OF 34 WHERE THE POST-PARTUM SEX TABOO LASTS LONGER THAN ONE MONTH (96)	301	DRIFT LESS TOWARD BEING THOSE 0.58 OF 19 WHERE THE POST-PARTUM SEX TABOO LASTS LONGER THAN ONE MONTH (96)	29 11 5 8	XSQ= 3.57 PHI= 0.260 XP = 0.0587
302	DRIFT TOWARD BEING THOSE 0.52 OF 21 WHERE THE AVERAGE EARLY SATISFACTION POTENTIAL IS LOW (17) W-C	302	DRIFT TOWARD BEING THOSE 0.85 OF 13 WHERE THE AVERAGE EARLY SATISFACTION POTENTIAL IS HIGH (23) W-C	10 11 11 2	XSQ= 3.22 PHI= -0.308 EP = 0.0672
305	TILT TOWARD BEING THOSE 0.56 OF 27 WHERE THE EARLY SEXUAL SATISFACTION POTENTIAL IS LOW (24) W-C	305	TILT TOWARD BEING THOSE 0.86 OF 14 WHERE THE EARLY SEXUAL SATISFACTION POTENTIAL IS HIGH (27) W-C	12 12 15 2	XSQ= 4.88 PHI= -0.345 XP = 0.0272
316	TILT TOWARD BEING THOSE 0.65 OF 20 WHERE EXCLUSIVE MOTHER-SON SLEEPING ARRANGEMENTS LAST ONE YEAR OR LONGER (19) W-K-A	316	TILT TOWARD BEING THOSE 0.83 OF 12 WHERE EXCLUSIVE MOTHER-SON SLEEPING ARRANGEMENTS LAST LESS THAN ONE YEAR (25) W-K-A	13 2 7 10	XSQ= 5.23 PHI= 0.404 EP = 0.0118
323	TILT TOWARD BEING THOSE 0.74 OF 31 WHERE THE CONSTANCY OF PRESENCE OF THE INFANT'S NURTURANT AGENT IS LOW (45) B-B-C	323	TILT TOWARD BEING THOSE 0.57 OF 21 WHERE THE CONSTANCY OF PRESENCE OF THE INFANT'S NURTURANT AGENT IS HIGH (29) B-B-C	8 12 23 9	XSQ= 3.95 PHI= -0.276 XP = 0.0467
328	DRIFT TOWARD BEING THOSE 0.75 OF 16 WHERE THE AGE OF THE INFANT AT THE ONSET OF SERIOUS SOCIALIZATION, OTHER THAN WEANING, IS TWO YEARS OR LOWER (20) B-B-C	328	DRIFT TOWARD BEING THOSE 0.64 OF 14 WHERE THE AGE OF THE INFANT AT THE ONSET OF SERIOUS SOCIALIZATION, OTHER THAN WEANING, IS HIGHER THAN TWO YEARS (21) B-B-C	4 9 12 5	XSQ= 3.23 PHI= -0.328 EP = 0.0634

338	TILT TOWARD BEING THOSE 0.79 OF 33 WHERE THE CHILD'S INFERRED ANXIETY OVER PERFORMANCE OF RESPONSIBLE BEHAVIOR IS HIGH (44) B-B-C	338	TILT TOWARD BEING THOSE 0.58 OF 19 WHERE THE CHILD'S INFERRED ANXIETY OVER PERFORMANCE OF RESPONSIBLE BEHAVIOR IS LOW (29) B-B-C	26 8 7 11 XSQ= 5.64 PHI= 0.329 XP = 0.0176
344	TILT TOWARD BEING THOSE 0.67 OF 33 WHERE THE TOTAL POSITIVE PRESSURE TOWARD DEVELOPING SELF-RELIANT BEHAVIOR IN THE CHILD IS HIGH (36) B-B-C	344	TILT TOWARD BEING THOSE 0.70 OF 20 WHERE THE TOTAL POSITIVE PRESSURE TOWARD DEVELOPING SELF-RELIANT BEHAVIOR IN THE CHILD IS LOW (40) B-B-C	22 6 11 14 XSQ= 5.33 PHI= 0.317 XP = 0.0210
345	DRIFT TOWARD BEING THOSE 0.61 OF 33 WHERE THE CHILD'S INFERRED ANXIETY OVER NON-PERFORMANCE OF SELF-RELIANT BEHAVIOR IS HIGH (37) B-B-C	345	DRIFT TOWARD BEING THOSE 0.70 OF 20 WHERE THE CHILD'S INFERRED ANXIETY OVER NON-PERFORMANCE OF SELF-RELIANT BEHAVIOR IS LOW (39) B-B-C	20 6 13 14 XSQ= 3.52 PHI= 0.258 XP = 0.0605
348	TILT TOWARD BEING THOSE 0.75 OF 28 WHERE THE TOTAL POSITIVE PRESSURE TOWARD DEVELOPING ACHIEVEMENT BEHAVIOR IN THE CHILD IS HIGH (32) B-B-C	348	TILT TOWARD BEING THOSE 0.67 OF 18 WHERE THE TOTAL POSITIVE PRESSURE TOWARD DEVELOPING ACHIEVEMENT BEHAVIOR IN THE CHILD IS LOW (31) B-B-C	21 6 7 12 XSQ= 6.22 PHI= 0.368 XP = 0.0126
349	LEAN TOWARD BEING THOSE 0.75 OF 28 WHERE THE CHILD'S INFERRED ANXIETY OVER NON-PERFORMANCE OF ACHIEVEMENT BEHAVIOR IS HIGH (34) B-B-C	349	LEAN TOWARD BEING THOSE 0.71 OF 17 WHERE THE CHILD'S INFERRED ANXIETY OVER NON-PERFORMANCE OF ACHIEVEMENT BEHAVIOR IS LOW (28) B-B-C	21 5 7 12 XSQ= 7.24 PHI= 0.401 XP = 0.0071
350	TILT TOWARD BEING THOSE 0.71 OF 28 WHERE THE CHILD'S INFERRED ANXIETY OVER PERFORMANCE OF ACHIEVEMENT BEHAVIOR IS HIGH (34) B-B-C	350	TILT TOWARD BEING THOSE 0.73 OF 15 WHERE THE CHILD'S INFERRED ANXIETY OVER PERFORMANCE OF ACHIEVEMENT BEHAVIOR IS LOW (26) B-B-C	20 4 8 11 XSQ= 6.22 PHI= 0.380 XP = 0.0126
365	DRIFT TOWARD BEING THOSE 0.78 OF 18 WHERE THE TIME SPENT IN ADOLESCENT PEER GROUP ACTIVITY IS HIGH OR HIGH-MEDIUM (30) JKH	365	DRIFT TOWARD BEING THOSE 0.58 OF 12 WHERE THE TIME SPENT IN ADOLESCENT PEER GROUP ACTIVITY IS LOW-MEDIUM OR LOW (15) JKH	14 5 4 7 XSQ= 2.64 PHI= 0.297 EP = 0.0626
393	LEAN TOWARD BEING THOSE 0.74 OF 31 WHERE EXTRAMARITAL COITUS IS PUNISHED, RATHER THAN PERMITTED (43) F-B	393	LEAN TOWARD BEING THOSE 0.83 OF 12 WHERE EXTRAMARITAL COITUS IS PERMITTED, RATHER THAN PUNISHED (41) F-B	23 2 8 10 XSQ= 9.52 PHI= 0.470 XP = 0.0020
399	TILT TOWARD BEING THOSE 0.68 OF 25 WHERE INTENSITY OF CASTRATION ANXIETY IS HIGH (23) WNS	399	TILT TOWARD BEING THOSE 0.69 OF 16 WHERE INTENSITY OF CASTRATION ANXIETY IS LOW (22) WNS	17 5 8 11 XSQ= 3.92 PHI= 0.309 XP = 0.0476

417	TEND TO BE THOSE WHERE WARFARE IS PREVALENT (34) LWS	0.96 OF 25	417	TEND TO BE THOSE WHERE WARFARE IS NOT PREVALENT (9) LWS	0.83 OF 6	24 1 1 5 XSQ= 14.76 PHI= 0.690 EP = 0.0002
420	TEND TO BE THOSE WHERE BELLICOSITY IS EXTREME (41) PES	0.77 OF 52	420	IN ALL CASES ARE THOSE WHERE BELLICOSITY IS MODERATE OR NEGLIGIBLE (46) PES	1.00 OF 31	40 0 12 31 XSQ= 43.00 PHI= 0.720 XP = 0.
421	TEND TO BE THOSE WHERE KILLING, TORTURING, OR MUTILATING OF THE ENEMY IS STRONGLY OR MODERATELY EMPHASIZED (37) PES	0.67 OF 49	421	TEND TO BE THOSE WHERE KILLING, TORTURING, OR MUTILATING OF THE ENEMY IS NEGLIGIBLY EMPHASIZED (47) PES	0.90 OF 31	33 3 16 28 XSQ= 23.24 PHI= 0.539 XP = 0.0000
429	TILT TOWARD BEING THOSE WHERE SUPERNATURAL SANCTIONS FOR MORALITY ARE PRESENT (28) GES	0.93 OF 15	429	TILT TOWARD BEING THOSE WHERE SUPERNATURAL SANCTIONS FOR MORALITY ARE ABSENT OR UNREPORTED (9) GES	0.50 OF 12	14 6 1 6 XSQ= 4.46 PHI= 0.406 EP = 0.0237
430	DRIFT TOWARD BEING THOSE WHERE SUPERNATURAL SANCTIONS FOR MORALITY, HAVING AN EFFECT ON AN INDIVIDUAL'S HEALTH, ARE PRESENT (16) GES	0.60 OF 15	430	DRIFT TOWARD BEING THOSE WHERE SUPERNATURAL SANCTIONS FOR MORALITY, HAVING AN EFFECT ON AN INDIVIDUAL'S HEALTH, ARE ABSENT OR UNREPORTED (22) GES	0.77 OF 13	9 3 6 10 XSQ= 2.52 PHI= 0.300 EP = 0.0671
458	DRIFT LESS TOWARD BEING THOSE WHERE GAMES, IF PRESENT, DO NOT INCLUDE GAMES OF STRATEGY (119) R-A-B,EA	0.52 OF 44	458	DRIFT MORE TOWARD BEING THOSE WHERE GAMES, IF PRESENT, DO NOT INCLUDE GAMES OF STRATEGY (119) R-A-B,EA	0.79 OF 24	21 5 23 19 XSQ= 3.69 PHI= 0.233 XP = 0.0549
460	TILT TOWARD BEING THOSE WHERE GAMES, IF PRESENT, ARE NOT LIMITED TO GAMES OF SKILL ONLY (104) R-A-B,EA	0.70 OF 44	460	TILT TOWARD BEING THOSE WHERE GAMES, IF PRESENT, ARE LIMITED TO GAMES OF SKILL ONLY (67) R-A-B,EA	0.58 OF 24	13 14 31 10 XSQ= 4.24 PHI= -0.250 XP = 0.0395
472	TEND TO BE THOSE WHERE THE COMPOSITE NARCISSISM INDEX IS HIGH (47) PES	0.69 OF 55	472	TEND TO BE THOSE WHERE THE COMPOSITE NARCISSISM INDEX IS LOW (43) PES	0.84 OF 31	38 5 17 26 XSQ= 20.18 PHI= 0.484 XP = 0.0000
473	TILT LESS TOWARD BEING THOSE WHERE SENSITIVITY TO INSULT IS MODERATE OR NEGLIGIBLE (56) PES	0.56 OF 54	473	TILT MORE TOWARD BEING THOSE WHERE SENSITIVITY TO INSULT IS MODERATE OR NEGLIGIBLE (56) PES	0.83 OF 30	24 5 30 25 XSQ= 5.41 PHI= 0.254 XP = 0.0200

419/

474	TEND TO BE THOSE WHERE BOASTFULNESS IS EXTREME	0.63 OF 54 (41) PES	474	TEND TO BE THOSE WHERE BOASTFULNESS IS MODERATE, NEGLIBIBLE, OR UNREPORTED	0.81 OF 31 (48) PES	34 6 20 25 XSQ= 13.33 PHI= 0.396 XP = 0.0003

420 CULTURES WHERE BELLICOSITY IS EXTREME (41) PES

420 CULTURES WHERE BELLICOSITY IS MODERATE OR NEGLIGIBLE (46) PES

BACKGROUND ON PAGE 161

BOTH SUBJECT AND PREDICATE

41 IN LEFT COLUMN

ABIPON	ALBANIANS	ARAUCANIANS	ASHANTI	AZANDE	AZTEC	BEMBA	BHIL	CHEYENNE	CHIR-APACHE
COMANCHE	CREEK	CROW	DOBUANS	FON	GANDA	HAIDA	HEBREWS	IBAN	IFUGAO
INCA	JIVARO	KAZAK	KURTATCHI	LAKHER	LANGO	MAORI	MARQUESANS	MASAI	MURNGIN
NAMA	NUER	NYAKYUSA	RIFFIANS	RWALA	SOMALI	THONGA	TROBRIAND	WARRAU	WITOTO
YAKUT									

46 IN RIGHT COLUMN

AINU	ALORESE	AMERICANS	ANDAMANESE	ARANDA	ARAPESH	AYMARA	BALINESE	CHENCHU	CHUKCHEE
COPR ESKIMO	CUNA	CZECHS	GOND	HANO	KASKA	KOREANS	KWAKIUTL	LAPPS	LAU
LEPCHA	LESU	NAVAHO	OJIBWA	PAPAGO	PUKAPUKA	SAMOANS	SANPOIL	SIRIONO	SIWANS
TALLENSI	TANALA	TAPIRAPE	TIKOPIA	TIMBIRA	TIV	TODA	TRUMAI	VIETNAMESE	WOGEO
WOLEAIANS	WOLOF	YAGUA	YAHGAN	YUROK	ZUNI				

313 EXCLUDED BECAUSE UNASCERTAINED

3	LEAN LESS TOWARD BEING THOSE LOCATED OUTSIDE OF AFRICA (320)	0.73 OF 41	3	LEAN MORE TOWARD BEING THOSE LOCATED OUTSIDE OF AFRICA (320)	0.96 OF 46	11 2 30 44 XSQ= 6.94 PHI= 0.282 XP = 0.0084
71	LEAN TOWARD BEING THOSE WHERE METAL WORKING IS PRESENT (98)	0.61 OF 36	71	LEAN TOWARD BEING THOSE WHERE METAL WORKING IS ABSENT (153)	0.74 OF 38	22 10 14 28 XSQ= 7.76 PHI= 0.324 XP = 0.0054
74	DRIFT TOWARD BEING THOSE WHERE POTTERY IS PRESENT (145)	0.71 OF 34	74	DRIFT TOWARD BEING THOSE WHERE POTTERY IS ABSENT (93)	0.54 OF 39	24 18 10 21 XSQ= 3.49 PHI= 0.219 XP = 0.0616
82	DRIFT MORE TOWARD BEING THOSE WHERE A CITY OR TOWN IS PRESENT, OR THE AVERAGE COMMUNITY SIZE IS FIFTY OR GREATER (178)	0.89 OF 27	82	DRIFT LESS TOWARD BEING THOSE WHERE A CITY OR TOWN IS PRESENT, OR THE AVERAGE COMMUNITY SIZE IS FIFTY OR GREATER (178)	0.68 OF 41	24 28 3 13 XSQ= 2.78 PHI= 0.202 XP = 0.0955

86	TILT TOWARD BEING THOSE 0.65 OF 37 WHERE THE LEVEL OF POLITICAL INTEGRATION IS THE LARGE STATE, THE LITTLE STATE, OR THE MINIMAL STATE (148) GPM	86	TILT TOWARD BEING THOSE 0.67 OF 39 WHERE THE LEVEL OF POLITICAL INTEGRATION IS THE AUTONOMOUS COMMUNITY, OR THE FAMILY (156) GPM	24 13 13 26 XSQ= 6.35 PHI= 0.289 XP = 0.0118
96	DRIFT TOWARD BEING THOSE 0.67 OF 39 WHERE THE HIERARCHY OF NATIONAL JURISDICTION HAS FOUR, THREE, TWO OR ONE LEVEL (174) GES,EA	96	DRIFT TOWARD BEING THOSE 0.57 OF 44 WHERE THE HIERARCHY OF NATIONAL JURISDICTION HAS NO LEVELS (156) GES,EA	26 19 13 25 XSQ= 3.70 PHI= 0.211 XP = 0.0545
108	DRIFT TOWARD BEING THOSE 0.54 OF 26 WHERE CLASS STRATIFICATION, IF PRESENT, IS BASED ON A HEREDITARY ARISTOCRACY (74)	108	DRIFT TOWARD BEING THOSE 0.76 OF 21 WHERE CLASS STRATIFICATION, IF PRESENT, IS BASED ON SOMETHING OTHER THAN A HEREDITARY ARISTOCRACY (129)	14 5 12 16 XSQ= 3.19 PHI= 0.261 XP = 0.0739
131	DRIFT LESS TOWARD BEING THOSE 0.74 OF 27 WHERE THE CONSTRUCTION OF PERMANENT HOUSES OR THE ERECTION OF TEMPORARY DWELLINGS IS MAINLY DONE BY MALES (136)	131	DRIFT MORE TOWARD BEING THOSE 0.94 OF 31 WHERE THE CONSTRUCTION OF PERMANENT HOUSES OR THE ERECTION OF TEMPORARY DWELLINGS IS MAINLY DONE BY MALES (136)	20 29 7 2 XSQ= 2.82 PHI= -0.221 XP = 0.0930
141	DRIFT TOWARD BEING THOSE 0.73 OF 15 WHERE THE LEVEL OF SOCIAL SANCTION IS PUBLIC CORPOREAL SANCTION, RATHER THAN PUBLIC PROPERTY SANCTION OR PRIVATE SETTLEMENT (28) JMH	141	DRIFT TOWARD BEING THOSE 0.60 OF 20 WHERE THE LEVEL OF SOCIAL SANCTION IS PUBLIC PROPERTY SANCTION OR PRIVATE SETTLEMENT, RATHER THAN PUBLIC CORPOREAL SANCTION (26) JMH	11 8 4 12 XSQ= 2.61 PHI= 0.273 FP = 0.0866
242	TILT MORE TOWARD BEING THOSE 0.90 OF 40 WHERE MARRIAGE IS COMMONLY OR OCCASIONALLY POLYGYNOUS, RATHER THAN MONOGAMOUS (314)	242	TILT LESS TOWARD BEING THOSE 0.64 OF 45 WHERE MARRIAGE IS COMMONLY OR OCCASIONALLY POLYGYNOUS, RATHER THAN MONOGAMOUS (314)	36 29 4 16 XSQ= 6.33 PHI= 0.273 XP = 0.0119
262	DRIFT MORE TOWARD BEING THOSE 0.90 OF 41 WHERE WIVES ARE OBTAINED BY MEANS INVOLVING THE PRESENCE OF SOME CONSIDERATION (305)	262	DRIFT LESS TOWARD BEING THOSE 0.72 OF 46 WHERE WIVES ARE OBTAINED BY MEANS INVOLVING THE PRESENCE OF SOME CONSIDERATION (305)	37 33 4 13 XSQ= 3.62 PHI= 0.204 XP = 0.0572
263	TILT TOWARD BEING THOSE 0.66 OF 41 WHERE WIVES ARE OBTAINED BY RELATIVELY DIFFICULT MEANS, NAMELY BY BRIDE-PRICE, BRIDE-SERVICE, OR EXCHANGING A FEMALE RELATIVE (233)	263	TILT TOWARD BEING THOSE 0.59 OF 46 WHERE WIVES ARE OBTAINED BY RELATIVELY EASY MEANS, NAMELY BY TOKEN BRIDE-PRICE, GIFT EXCHANGE, ABSENCE OF ANY CONSIDERATION, OR RECEIPT OF DOWRY (162)	27 19 14 27 XSQ= 4.30 PHI= 0.222 XP = 0.0380
316	LEAN TOWARD BEING THOSE 0.79 OF 14 WHERE EXCLUSIVE MOTHER-SON SLEEPING ARRANGEMENTS LAST ONE YEAR OR LONGER (19) W-K-A	316	LEAN TOWARD BEING THOSE 0.79 OF 19 WHERE EXCLUSIVE MOTHER-SON SLEEPING ARRANGEMENTS LAST LESS THAN ONE YEAR (25) W-K-A	11 4 3 15 XSQ= 8.56 PHI= 0.509 EP = 0.0016

```
322  DRIFT TOWARD BEING THOSE         0.79 OF  14     322  DRIFT TOWARD BEING THOSE         0.54 OF  28        3    15
     WHERE THE CONSISTENCY OF REDUCTION                    WHERE THE CONSISTENCY OF REDUCTION                 11    13
     OF THE INFANT'S DRIVES                                OF THE INFANT'S DRIVES                       XSQ=     2.73
     IS LOW   (32) B-B-C                                   IS HIGH   (27) B-B-C                         PHI=   -0.255
                                                                                                        XP =   0.0982

323  DRIFT MORE TOWARD BEING THOSE  0.80 OF  20      323  DRIFT LESS TOWARD BEING THOSE  0.52 OF  31          4    15
     WHERE THE CONSTANCY OF PRESENCE                       WHERE THE CONSTANCY OF PRESENCE                    16    16
     OF THE INFANT'S NURTURANT AGENT                       OF THE INFANT'S NURTURANT AGENT              XSQ=     3.06
     IS LOW   (45) B-B-C                                   IS LOW   (45) B-B-C                          PHI=   -0.245
                                                                                                        XP =   0.0800

344  LEAN TOWARD BEING THOSE          0.76 OF  21     344  LEAN TOWARD BEING THOSE          0.65 OF  31        16    11
     WHERE THE TOTAL POSITIVE PRESSURE TOWARD              WHERE THE TOTAL POSITIVE PRESSURE TOWARD            5    20
     DEVELOPING SELF-RELIANT BEHAVIOR                      DEVELOPING SELF-RELIANT BEHAVIOR             XSQ=     6.76
     IN THE CHILD                                          IN THE CHILD                                 PHI=    0.361
     IS HIGH   (36) B-B-C                                  IS LOW   (40) B-B-C                          XP =   0.0093

348  TILT TOWARD BEING THOSE          0.81 OF  16     348  TILT TOWARD BEING THOSE          0.61 OF  28        13    11
     WHERE THE TOTAL POSITIVE PRESSURE TOWARD              WHERE THE TOTAL POSITIVE PRESSURE TOWARD            3    17
     DEVELOPING ACHIEVEMENT BEHAVIOR                       DEVELOPING ACHIEVEMENT BEHAVIOR              XSQ=     5.64
     IN THE CHILD                                          IN THE CHILD                                 PHI=    0.358
     IS HIGH   (32) B-B-C                                  IS LOW   (31) B-B-C                          XP =   0.0176

349  TILT TOWARD BEING THOSE          0.81 OF  16     349  TILT TOWARD BEING THOSE          0.59 OF  27        13    11
     WHERE THE CHILD'S INFERRED ANXIETY OVER               WHERE THE CHILD'S INFERRED ANXIETY OVER             3    16
     NON-PERFORMANCE OF ACHIEVEMENT BEHAVIOR               NON-PERFORMANCE OF ACHIEVEMENT BEHAVIOR      XSQ=     5.14
     IS HIGH   (34) B-B-C                                  IS LOW   (28) B-B-C                          PHI=    0.346
                                                                                                        XP =   0.0233

370  TILT TOWARD BEING THOSE          0.58 OF  33     370  TILT TOWARD BEING THOSE          0.75 OF  36        19     9
     WHERE THE SEGREGATION OF ADOLESCENT BOYS              WHERE THE SEGREGATION OF ADOLESCENT BOYS           14    27
     IS COMPLETE OR PARTIAL   (95)                         IS ABSENT   (148)                            XSQ=     6.29
                                                                                                        PHI=    0.302
                                                                                                        XP =   0.0122

390  DRIFT LESS TOWARD BEING THOSE  0.72 OF  32      390  DRIFT MORE TOWARD BEING THOSE  0.91 OF  35          9     3
     WHERE PREMARITAL SEX RELATIONS ARE                    WHERE PREMARITAL SEX RELATIONS ARE                 23    32
     WEAKLY PUNISHED AND IN FACT NOT RARE OR               WEAKLY PUNISHED AND IN FACT NOT RARE OR      XSQ=     3.12
     PUNISHED ONLY IF PREGNANCY RESULTS, OR                PUNISHED ONLY IF PREGNANCY RESULTS, OR       PHI=    0.216
     FREELY PERMITTED   (132) JTW,EA                       FREELY PERMITTED   (132) JTW,EA              XP =   0.0774

393  LEAN TOWARD BEING THOSE          0.76 OF  25     393  LEAN TOWARD BEING THOSE          0.78 OF  18        19     4
     WHERE EXTRAMARITAL COITUS                             WHERE EXTRAMARITAL COITUS IS                        6    14
     IS PUNISHED, RATHER THAN                              PERMITTED, RATHER THAN                       XSQ=    10.10
     PERMITTED   (43) F-B                                  PUNISHED   (41) F-B                          PHI=    0.485
                                                                                                        XP =   0.0015

397  DRIFT LESS TOWARD BEING THOSE  0.64 OF  22      397  DRIFT MORE TOWARD BEING THOSE  0.89 OF  18          8     2
     WHERE SEX DISABILITY                                  WHERE SEX DISABILITY                               14    16
     IS ABSENT   (42) JKH                                  IS ABSENT   (42) JKH                         XSQ=     2.15
                                                                                                        PHI=    0.232
                                                                                                        EP =   0.0823
```

417	IN ALL CASES ARE THCSE 1.00 OF 21 WHERE WARFARE IS PREVALENT (34) LWS	417	TEND TO BE THOSE 0.55 OF 11 WHERE WARFARE IS NOT PREVALENT (9) LWS	21 5 0 6 XSQ= 10.74 PHI= 0.579 EP = 0.0005
419	IN ALL CASES ARE THCSE 1.00 OF 40 WHERE MILITARY GLCRY IS STRONGLY CR MCDERATELY EMPHASIZED (55) PES	419	TEND TO BE THOSE 0.72 OF 43 WHERE MILITARY GLORY IS NEGLIGIBLY EMPHASIZED (31) PES	40 12 0 31 XSQ= 43.00 PHI= 0.720 XP = 0.
421	TEND TC BE THCSE 0.78 OF 36 WHERE KILLING, TCRTURING, CR MUTILATINC CF THE ENEMY IS STRONGLY CR MCDERATELY EMPHASIZED (37) PES	421	TEND TO BE THOSE 0.83 CF 46 WHERE KILLING, TORTURING, CR MUTILATING OF THE ENEMY IS NEGLIGIBLY EMPHASIZED (47) PES	28 8 8 38 XSQ= 27.50 PHI= 0.579 XP = 0.0000
453	DRIFT TCWARD BEING THCSE 0.64 OF 11 WHERE THE RCLE CF RELIGIOUS EXPERTS IS CCNDUCIVE TC THE DEVELOPMENT OF THE INDIVIDUAL'S NEED TC ACHIEVE (13) DCM	453	DRIFT TOWARD BEING THOSE 0.75 CF 12 WHERE THE ROLE CF RELIGICUS EXPERTS IS NOT CONDUCIVE TO THE DEVELCPMENT OF THE INDIVIDUAL'S NEED TO ACHIEVE (23) DCM	7 3 4 9 XSQ= 2.09 PHI= 0.302 EP = 0.0995
458	DRIFT LESS TOWARD BEING THOSE 0.52 OF 31 WHERE GAMES, IF PRESENT, DC NCT INCLUDE GAMES CF STRATEGY (119) R-A-B,EA	458	DRIFT MORE TOWARD BEING THCSE 0.74 OF 38 WHERE GAMES, IF PRESENT, DO NOT INCLUDE GAMES OF STRATEGY (119) R-A-B,EA	15 10 16 28 XSQ= 2.71 PHI= 0.198 XP = 0.0999
472	TEND TC BE THCSE 0.76 OF 41 WHERE THE COMPCSITE NARCISSISM INCEX IS HIGH (47) PES	472	TEND TO BE THOSE 0.70 CF 46 WHERE THE COMPOSITE NARCISSISM INDEX IS LOW (43) PES	31 14 10 32 XSQ= 15.95 PHI= 0.428 XP = 0.0001
473	TILT TCWARC BEING THOSE 0.50 OF 40 WHERE SENSITIVITY TC INSULT IS EXTREME (32) PES	473	TILT TOWARD BEING THOSE 0.76 OF 45 WHERE SENSITIVITY TO INSULT IS MODERATE OR NEGLIGIBLE (56) PES	20 11 20 34 XSQ= 4.92 PHI= 0.241 XP = 0.0266
474	TEND TC BE THCSE 0.67 OF 40 WHERE BCASTFULNESS IS EXTREME (41) PES	474	TEND TO BE THOSE 0.72 CF 46 WHERE BOASTFULNESS IS MCDERATE, NEGLIBIBLE, OR UNREPORTED (48) PES	27 13 13 33 XSQ= 11.71 PHI= 0.369 XP = 0.0006

****

421 CULTURES WHERE KILLING, TORTURING, OR MUTILATING OF THE ENEMY IS STRONGLY OR MODERATELY EMPHASIZED (37) PES	421 CULTURES WHERE KILLING, TORTURING, OR MUTILATING OF THE ENEMY IS NEGLIGIBLY EMPHASIZED (47) PES

BACKGROUND ON PAGE 161 BOTH SUBJECT AND PREDICATE

....

37 IN LEFT COLUMN

ABIPON	ALBANIANS	ALORESE	ARANDA	ARAUCANIANS	ASHANTI	AYMARA	AZANDE	AZTEC	CHEYENNE
CHIR-APACHE	COMANCHE	CREEK	CROW	DOBUANS	FON	HAIDA	HEBREWS	IBAN	IFUGAO
INCA	JIVARO	KASKA	KURTATCHI	LAKHER	LANGO	MARQUESANS	MASAI	NAVAHO	OJIBWA
SOMALI	THONGA	TIV	VENDA	WARRAU	WITOTO	ZUNI			

47 IN RIGHT COLUMN

AINU	AMERICANS	ANDAMANESE	ARAPESH	BALINESE	BEMBA	CHAGGA	CHENCHU	CHUKCHEE	COPR ESKIMO
CUNA	CZECHS	GANDA	GOND	HANO	KAZAK	KOREANS	KWAKIUTL	LAPPS	LAU
LEPCHA	LESU	MAORI	MURNGIN	NUER	NYAKYUSA	PAPAGO	PUKAPUKA	SAMOANS	SANPOIL
SIRIONO	SIWANS	TALLENSI	TANALA	TAPIRAPE	TIKOPIA	TIMBIRA	TODA	TROBRIAND	TRUMAI
VIETNAMESE	WOGEO	WOLEAIANS	WOLOF	YAGUA	YAHGAN	YUROK			

316 EXCLUDED BECAUSE UNASCERTAINED

5	TILT MORE TOWARD BEING THOSE LOCATED OUTSIDE OF EAST EURASIA (330)	0.97 OF 37	5	TILT LESS TOWARD BEING THOSE LOCATED OUTSIDE OF EAST EURASIA (330)	0.77 OF 47	1 11 36 36 XSQ= 5.65 PHI= -0.259 XP = 0.0174
8	DRIFT LESS TOWARD BEING THOSE LOCATED OUTSIDE OF NORTH AMERICA (330)	0.70 OF 37	8	DRIFT MORE TOWARD BEING THOSE LOCATED OUTSIDE OF NORTH AMERICA (330)	0.87 OF 47	11 6 26 41 XSQ= 2.71 PHI= 0.180 XP = 0.0994
71	DRIFT TOWARD BEING THOSE WHERE METAL WORKING IS PRESENT (98)	0.53 OF 30	71	DRIFT TOWARD BEING THOSE WHERE METAL WORKING IS ABSENT (153)	0.72 OF 40	16 11 14 29 XSQ= 3.80 PHI= 0.233 XP = 0.0513
78	DRIFT MORE TOWARD BEING THOSE WHERE THE WRITING SYSTEM IS ALPHABETIC-OR-PHONETIC, OR MNEMONIC, RATHER THAN BEING ABSENT (36) JMH	0.86 OF 14	78	DRIFT LESS TOWARD BEING THOSE WHERE THE WRITING SYSTEM IS ALPHABETIC-OR-PHONETIC, OR MNEMONIC, RATHER THAN BEING ABSENT (36) JMH	0.53 OF 19	12 10 2 9 XSQ= 2.62 PHI= 0.282 EP = 0.0674

No.			No.			
127	DRIFT TOWARD BEING THOSE WHERE THE FEMALES' CONTRIBUTION TO SUBSISTENCE IS HIGH (33) JKB	0.71 OF 14	127	DRIFT TOWARD BEING THOSE WHERE THE FEMALES' CONTRIBUTION TO SUBSISTENCE IS LOW (32) JKB	0.61 OF 23	10 9 4 14 XSQ= 2.46 PHI= 0.258 EP = 0.0911
133	LEAN TOWARD BEING THOSE WHERE CONTRACTED DEBTS ARE SIGNIFICANTLY PRESENT (17) GES	0.91 OF 11	133	LEAN TOWARD BEING THOSE WHERE CONTRACTED DEBTS ARE MODERATELY PRESENT OR ABSENT (17) GES	0.63 OF 16	10 6 1 10 XSQ= 5.65 PHI= 0.457 EP = 0.0076
149	TILT TOWARD BEING THOSE WHERE THE INCIDENCE OF THEFT IS HIGH (18) B-B-C	0.82 OF 11	149	TILT TOWARD BEING THOSE WHERE THE INCIDENCE OF THEFT IS LOW (19) B-B-C	0.68 OF 22	9 7 2 15 XSQ= 5.47 PHI= 0.407 EP = 0.0104
295	TILT TOWARD BEING THOSE WHERE THE SEVERITY OF PUNISHMENT FOR ABORTION IS HIGH (11) BCA	0.80 OF 10	295	TILT TOWARD BEING THOSE WHERE THE SEVERITY OF PUNISHMENT FOR ABORTION IS LOW OR ABSENT (12) BCA	0.73 OF 11	8 3 2 8 XSQ= 3.92 PHI= 0.432 EP = 0.0300
306	DRIFT TOWARD BEING THOSE WHERE THE EARLY DEPENDENCE SATISFACTION POTENTIAL IS LOW (24) W-C	0.63 OF 16	306	DRIFT TOWARD BEING THOSE WHERE THE EARLY DEPENDENCE SATISFACTION POTENTIAL IS HIGH (28) W-C	0.71 OF 24	6 17 10 7 XSQ= 3.11 PHI= -0.279 EP = 0.0531
317	LEAN TOWARD BEING THOSE WHERE DISPLAY OF AFFECTION TOWARD THE INFANT IS LOW (29) B-B-C	0.70 OF 20	317	LEAN TOWARD BEING THOSE WHERE DISPLAY OF AFFECTION TOWARD THE INFANT IS HIGH (39) B-B-C	0.76 OF 29	6 22 14 7 XSQ= 8.38 PHI= -0.414 XP = 0.0038
321	TILT TOWARD BEING THOSE WHERE THE IMMEDIACY OF REDUCTION OF THE INFANT'S DRIVES IS LOW (25) B-B-C	0.72 OF 18	321	TILT TOWARD BEING THOSE WHERE THE IMMEDIACY OF REDUCTION OF THE INFANT'S DRIVES IS HIGH (35) B-B-C	0.72 OF 25	5 18 13 7 XSQ= 6.54 PHI= -0.390 XP = 0.0105
334	LEAN TOWARD BEING THOSE WHERE THE INDULGENCE OF THE CHILD IS LOW (38) B-B-C	0.71 OF 24	334	LEAN TOWARD BEING THOSE WHERE THE INDULGENCE OF THE CHILD IS HIGH (40) B-B-C	0.71 OF 31	7 22 17 9 XSQ= 7.88 PHI= -0.379 XP = 0.0050
338	TILT MORE TOWARD BEING THOSE WHERE THE CHILD'S INFERRED ANXIETY OVER PERFORMANCE OF RESPONSIBLE BEHAVIOR IS HIGH (44) B-B-C	0.83 OF 23	338	TILT LESS TOWARD BEING THOSE WHERE THE CHILD'S INFERRED ANXIETY OVER PERFORMANCE OF RESPONSIBLE BEHAVIOR IS HIGH (44) B-B-C	0.52 OF 29	19 15 4 14 XSQ= 4.13 PHI= 0.282 XP = 0.0422

344	LEAN TOWARD BEING THOSE 0.78 OF 23 WHERE THE TOTAL POSITIVE PRESSURE TOWARD DEVELOPING SELF-RELIANT BEHAVIOR IN THE CHILD IS HIGH (36) B-B-C	344	LEAN TOWARD BEING THOSE 0.67 OF 30 WHERE THE TOTAL POSITIVE PRESSURE TOWARD DEVELOPING SELF-RELIANT BEHAVIOR IN THE CHILD IS LOW (40) B-B-C	18 10 5 20 XSQ= 8.82 PHI= 0.408 XP = 0.0030
345	TILT TOWARD BEING THOSE 0.65 OF 23 WHERE THE CHILD'S INFERRED ANXIETY OVER NON-PERFORMANCE OF SELF-RELIANT BEHAVIOR IS HIGH (37) B-B-C	345	TILT TOWARD BEING THOSE 0.67 OF 30 WHERE THE CHILD'S INFERRED ANXIETY OVER NON-PERFORMANCE OF SELF-RELIANT BEHAVIOR IS LOW (39) B-B-C	15 10 8 20 XSQ= 4.11 PHI= 0.278 XP = 0.0427
346	DRIFT TOWARD BEING THOSE 0.65 OF 23 WHERE THE CHILD'S INFERRED ANXIETY OVER PERFORMANCE OF SELF-RELIANT BEHAVIOR IS HIGH (37) B-B-C	346	DRIFT TOWARD BEING THOSE 0.63 OF 30 WHERE THE CHILD'S INFERRED ANXIETY OVER PERFORMANCE OF SELF-RELIANT BEHAVIOR IS LOW (39) B-B-C	15 11 8 19 XSQ= 3.18 PHI= 0.245 XP = 0.0745
347	DRIFT TOWARD BEING THOSE 0.61 OF 23 WHERE THE CHILD'S INFERRED CONFLICT REGARDING SELF-RELIANT BEHAVIOR IS HIGH (37) B-B-C	347	DRIFT TOWARD BEING THOSE 0.67 OF 30 WHERE THE CHILD'S INFERRED CONFLICT REGARDING SELF-RELIANT BEHAVIOR IS LOW (39) B-B-C	14 10 9 20 XSQ= 2.95 PHI= 0.236 XP = 0.0859
348	TILT TOWARD BEING THOSE 0.79 OF 19 WHERE THE TOTAL POSITIVE PRESSURE TOWARD DEVELOPING ACHIEVEMENT BEHAVIOR IN THE CHILD IS HIGH (32) B-B-C	348	TILT TOWARD BEING THOSE 0.59 OF 27 WHERE THE TOTAL POSITIVE PRESSURE TOWARD DEVELOPING ACHIEVEMENT BEHAVIOR IN THE CHILD IS LOW (31) B-B-C	15 11 4 16 XSQ= 5.16 PHI= 0.335 XP = 0.0231
349	TILT TOWARD BEING THOSE 0.79 OF 19 WHERE THE CHILD'S INFERRED ANXIETY OVER NON-PERFORMANCE OF ACHIEVEMENT BEHAVIOR IS HIGH (34) B-B-C	349	TILT TOWARD BEING THOSE 0.58 OF 26 WHERE THE CHILD'S INFERRED ANXIETY OVER NON-PERFORMANCE OF ACHIEVEMENT BEHAVIOR IS LOW (28) B-B-C	15 11 4 15 XSQ= 4.63 PHI= 0.321 XP = 0.0314
350	TILT TOWARD BEING THOSE 0.79 OF 19 WHERE THE CHILD'S INFERRED ANXIETY OVER PERFORMANCE OF ACHIEVEMENT BEHAVIOR IS HIGH (34) B-B-C	350	TILT TOWARD BEING THOSE 0.58 OF 24 WHERE THE CHILD'S INFERRED ANXIETY OVER PERFORMANCE OF ACHIEVEMENT BEHAVIOR IS LOW (26) B-B-C	15 10 4 14 XSQ= 4.62 PHI= 0.328 XP = 0.0316
351	DRIFT TOWARD BEING THOSE 0.63 OF 19 WHERE THE CHILD'S INFERRED CONFLICT REGARDING ACHIEVEMENT BEHAVIOR IS HIGH (26) B-B-C	351	DRIFT TOWARD BEING THOSE 0.71 OF 24 WHERE THE CHILD'S INFERRED CONFLICT REGARDING ACHIEVEMENT BEHAVIOR IS LOW (34) B-B-C	12 7 7 17 XSQ= 3.69 PHI= 0.293 XP = 0.0549
354	TILT TOWARD BEING THOSE 0.74 OF 23 WHERE THE CHILD'S INFERRED ANXIETY OVER PERFORMANCE OF OBEDIENT BEHAVIOR IS HIGH (36) B-B-C	354	TILT TOWARD BEING THOSE 0.64 OF 28 WHERE THE CHILD'S INFERRED ANXIETY OVER PERFORMANCE OF OBEDIENT BEHAVIOR IS LOW (37) B-B-C	17 10 6 18 XSQ= 5.94 PHI= 0.341 XP = 0.0148

No.				No.				
355	TILT TOWARD BEING THOSE WHERE THE CHILD'S INFERRED CONFLICT REGARDING OBEDIENT BEHAVIOR IS HIGH (35) B-B-C	0.70 OF	23	355	TILT TOWARD BEING THOSE WHERE THE CHILD'S INFERRED CONFLICT REGARDING OBEDIENT BEHAVIOR IS LOW (38) B-B-C	0.68 OF	28	16 9 7 19 XSQ= 5.66 PHI= 0.333 XP = 0.0174
386	DRIFT TOWARD BEING THOSE WHERE SEXUAL EXPRESSION BY THE YOUNG IS RESTRICTED OR SEMI-RESTRICTED (46) F-B	0.72 OF	18	386	DRIFT TOWARD BEING THOSE WHERE SEXUAL EXPRESSION BY THE YOUNG IS PERMITTED (40) F-B	0.61 OF	28	13 11 5 17 XSQ= 3.53 PHI= 0.277 XP = 0.0601
393	LEAN TOWARD BEING THOSE WHERE EXTRAMARITAL COITUS IS PUNISHED, RATHER THAN PERMITTED (43) F-B	0.78 OF	23	393	LEAN TOWARD BEING THOSE WHERE EXTRAMARITAL COITUS IS PERMITTED, RATHER THAN PUNISHED (41) F-B	0.74 OF	19	18 5 5 14 XSQ= 9.33 PHI= 0.471 XP = 0.0023
399	TILT TOWARD BEING THOSE WHERE INTENSITY OF CASTRATION ANXIETY IS HIGH (23) WNS	0.71 OF	17	399	TILT TOWARD BEING THOSE WHERE INTENSITY OF CASTRATION ANXIETY IS LOW (22) WNS	0.67 OF	24	12 8 5 16 XSQ= 4.14 PHI= 0.318 XP = 0.0419
417	DRIFT MORE TOWARD BEING THOSE WHERE WARFARE IS PREVALENT (34) LWS	0.94 OF	17	417	DRIFT LESS TOWARD BEING THOSE WHERE WARFARE IS PREVALENT (34) LWS	0.58 OF	12	16 7 1 5 XSQ= 3.53 PHI= 0.349 EP = 0.0563
419	TEND TO BE THOSE WHERE MILITARY GLORY IS STRONGLY OR MODERATELY EMPHASIZED (55) PES	0.92 OF	36	419	TEND TO BE THOSE WHERE MILITARY GLORY IS NEGLIGIBLY EMPHASIZED (31) PES	0.64 OF	44	33 16 3 28 XSQ= 23.24 PHI= 0.539 XP = 0.0000
420	TEND TO BE THOSE WHERE BELLICOSITY IS EXTREME (41) PES	0.78 OF	36	420	TEND TO BE THOSE WHERE BELLICOSITY IS MODERATE OR NEGLIGIBLE (46) PES	0.83 OF	46	28 8 8 38 XSQ= 27.50 PHI= 0.579 XP = 0.0000
460	DRIFT MORE TOWARD BEING THOSE WHERE GAMES, IF PRESENT, ARE NOT LIMITED TO GAMES OF SKILL ONLY (104) R-A-B,EA	0.76 OF	29	460	DRIFT LESS TOWARD BEING THOSE WHERE GAMES, IF PRESENT, ARE NOT LIMITED TO GAMES OF SKILL ONLY (104) R-A-B,EA	0.53 OF	38	7 18 22 20 XSQ= 2.87 PHI= -0.207 XP = 0.0904
472	TILT TOWARD BEING THOSE WHERE THE COMPOSITE NARCISSISM INDEX IS HIGH (47) PES	0.70 OF	37	472	TILT TOWARD BEING THOSE WHERE THE COMPOSITE NARCISSISM INDEX IS LOW (43) PES	0.60 OF	47	26 19 11 28 XSQ= 6.26 PHI= 0.273 XP = 0.0123

421/

474	TEND TC BE THCSE	0.70 OF 37	474	TEND TO BE THOSE	0.70 CF 46		26 14
	WHERE BCASTFULNESS IS EXTREME	(41) PES		WHERE BOASTFULNESS IS MCDERATE,			11 32
				NEGLIBIBLE, OR UNREPORTED (48) PES		XSQ=	11.49
						PHI=	0.372
						XP =	0.0007

422 CULTURES WHERE CANNIBALISM IS PRESENT (6) LWS

422 CULTURES WHERE CANNIBALISM IS UNIMPORTANT OR ABSENT (21) LWS

BACKGROUND ON PAGE 162

SUBJECT ONLY

6 IN LEFT COLUMN

ARANDA AZTEC DIERI FANG MAORI WITOTO

21 IN RIGHT COLUMN

AINU ANDAMANESE ARAUCANIANS ASHANTI CHUKCHEE HAIDA HANO IBAN JIVARO KUNG
KWAKIUTL LANGO MOTA OMAHA SAMOANS SEMANG TROBRIAND VEDDA YAHGAN YAKUT
YUKAGHIR

373 EXCLUDED BECAUSE UNASCERTAINED

277	TILT TOWARD BEING THOSE WHERE THE STATUS OF WOMEN IS INFERIOR OR SUBJECTED (14) LWS	0.80 OF 5	277	TILT TOWARD BEING THOSE WHERE THE STATUS OF WOMEN IS NOT STRONGLY INFERIOR OR SUBJECTED (22) LWS	0.79 OF 19	4 4 1 15 XSQ= 3.82 PHI= 0.399 EP = 0.0277
377	TILT TOWARD BEING THOSE WHERE MALE GENITAL MUTILATION IS PRESENT (83)	0.50 OF 6	377	TILT TOWARD BEING THOSE WHERE MALE GENITAL MUTILATION IS ABSENT (242)	0.95 OF 21	3 1 3 20 XSQ= 4.41 PHI= 0.404 EP = 0.0248

```
******************************************************************************************************

423  CULTURES                                             423  CULTURES
     WHERE AN ORGANIZED PRIESTHOOD                             WHERE AN ORGANIZED PRIESTHOOD
     IS PRESENT  (13) LWS                                      IS UNIMPORTANT OR ABSENT  (21) LWS


BACKGROUND ON PAGE 162                                                                    SUBJECT ONLY
......................................................................................................

     13  IN LEFT COLUMN

ALBANIANS  ARANDA      ASHANTI   AZTEC     CREEK     FON       HEBREWS   INCA       MAORI     NAMA
OMAHA      SAMCANS     TCCA

     21  IN RIGHT COLUMN

AINU       ARAUCANIANS CHUKCHEE  CROW      DIERI     HAIDA     HANC      IBAN       JIVARO    KAZAK
KUNG       KWAKIUTL    LANGC     MOTA      NAVAHO    SEMANG    SHILLUK   TRCBRIAND  VECCA     WITOTO
YAKUT

    366  EXCLUDED BECAUSE UNASCERTAINED

------------------------------------------------------------------------------------------------------
 80  TILT LESS TOWARD BEING THOSE   0.64 OF  11     80  IN ALL CASES ARE THOSE        1.00 OF  13          4     0
     WHERE NO CITY OR TOWN IS PRESENT  (185)            WHERE NO CITY OR TOWN IS PRESENT  (185)            7    13
                                                                                               XSQ=     3.36
                                                                                               PHI=    0.374
                                                                                               EP =   0.0311

 86  LEAN TOWARD BEING THOSE        0.85 OF  13     86  LEAN TOWARD BEING THOSE       0.72 OF  18         11     5
     WHERE THE LEVEL OF POLITICAL INTEGRATION           WHERE THE LEVEL OF POLITICAL INTEGRATION           2    13
     IS THE LARGE STATE, THE LITTLE STATE,              IS THE AUTONOMOUS COMMUNITY, OR        XSQ=     7.62
     OR THE MINIMAL STATE  (148) GPM                    THE FAMILY  (156) GPM                  PHI=    0.496
                                                                                               EP =   0.0032

 95  TILT TOWARD BEING THOSE        0.54 OF  13     95  TILT TOWARD BEING THOSE       0.90 OF  21          7     2
     WHERE THE HIERARCHY                                WHERE THE HIERARCHY                                6    19
     OF NATIONAL JURISDICTION HAS                       OF NATIONAL JURISDICTION HAS           XSQ=     5.99
     FOUR, THREE, OR TWO LEVELS  (76) GES,EA            ONE OR NO LEVELS  (254) GES,EA         PHI=    0.420
                                                                                               EP =   0.0130

 96  LEAN TOWARD BEING THOSE        0.92 OF  13     96  LEAN TOWARD BEING THOSE       0.67 OF  21         12     7
     WHERE THE HIERARCHY                                WHERE THE HIERARCHY                                1    14
     OF NATIONAL JURISDICTION HAS                       OF NATIONAL JURISDICTION HAS           XSQ=     9.06
     FOUR, THREE, TWO OR                                NO LEVELS  (156) GES,EA                PHI=    0.516
     ONE LEVEL  (174) GES,EA                                                                   EP =   0.0011

118  TILT TOWARD BEING THOSE        0.83 OF   6    118  IN ALL CASES ARE THOSE        1.00 OF   4          5     0
     WHERE THE PERCENTAGE OF OCCUPATIONS                WHERE THE PERCENTAGE OF OCCUPATIONS                1     4
     THAT ARE SPECIALIZED                               THAT ARE SPECIALIZED                   XSQ=     3.75
     IS HIGH OR MEDIUM  (24) WME                        IS LOW  (25) WME                       PHI=    0.612
                                                                                               EP =   0.0476
```

147	DRIFT MORE TOWARD BEING THOSE WHERE CODIFIED LAWS ARE PRESENT (20) LWS	0.90 OF 10	147	DRIFT LESS TOWARD BEING THOSE WHERE CODIFIED LAWS ARE PRESENT (20) LWS	0.56 OF 16	9 9 1 7 XSQ= 1.90 PHI= 0.270 EP = 0.0989
187	DRIFT MORE TOWARD BEING THOSE WHERE THE KIN GROUP IS OTHER THAN EXCLUSIVELY MATRILINEAL (344)	0.92 OF 13	187	DRIFT LESS TOWARD BEING THOSE WHERE THE KIN GROUP IS OTHER THAN EXCLUSIVELY MATRILINEAL (344)	0.60 OF 20	1 8 12 12 XSQ= 2.68 PHI= -0.285 EP = 0.0560
190	TILT TOWARD BEING THOSE WHERE THE KIN GROUP IS PATRILINEAL OR DOUBLE-DESCENT, RATHER THAN MATRILINEAL (186)	0.89 OF 9	190	TILT TOWARD BEING THOSE WHERE THE KIN GROUP IS MATRILINEAL, RATHER THAN PATRILINEAL OR DOUBLE-DESCENT (61)	0.57 OF 14	8 6 1 8 XSQ= 3.13 PHI= 0.369 EP = 0.0397
277	TILT TOWARD BEING THOSE WHERE THE STATUS OF WOMEN IS INFERIOR OR SUBJECTED (14) LWS	0.64 OF 11	277	TILT TOWARD BEING THOSE WHERE THE STATUS OF WOMEN IS NOT STRONGLY INFERIOR OR SUBJECTED (22) LWS	0.78 OF 18	7 4 4 14 XSQ= 3.37 PHI= 0.341 EP = 0.0482
278	LEAN TOWARD BEING THOSE WHERE PROPERTY RIGHTS IN WOMEN ARE PRESENT (8) LWS	0.83 OF 6	278	LEAN TOWARD BEING THOSE WHERE PROPERTY RIGHTS IN WOMEN ARE UNIMPORTANT OR ABSENT (14) LWS	0.85 OF 13	5 2 1 11 XSQ= 5.49 PHI= 0.537 EP = 0.0095
347	IN ALL CASES ARE THOSE WHERE THE CHILD'S INFERRED CONFLICT REGARDING SELF-RELIANT BEHAVIOR IS LOW (39) B-B-C	1.00 OF 6	347	DRIFT TOWARD BEING THOSE WHERE THE CHILD'S INFERRED CONFLICT REGARDING SELF-RELIANT BEHAVIOR IS HIGH (37) B-B-C	0.50 OF 10	0 5 6 5 XSQ= 2.35 PHI= -0.383 EP = 0.0934
390	TILT LESS TOWARD BEING THOSE WHERE PREMARITAL SEX RELATIONS ARE WEAKLY PUNISHED AND IN FACT NOT RARE OR PUNISHED ONLY IF PREGNANCY RESULTS, OR FREELY PERMITTED (132) JTW,EA	0.55 OF 11	390	TILT MORE TOWARD BEING THOSE WHERE PREMARITAL SEX RELATIONS ARE WEAKLY PUNISHED AND IN FACT NOT RARE OR PUNISHED ONLY IF PREGNANCY RESULTS, OR FREELY PERMITTED (132) JTW,EA	0.94 OF 16	5 1 6 15 XSQ= 3.75 PHI= 0.373 EP = 0.0265
395	TILT TOWARD BEING THOSE WHERE BELIEF IN THE UNCLEANNESS OF WOMEN IS PRESENT (18) LWS	0.82 OF 11	395	TILT TOWARD BEING THOSE WHERE BELIEF IN THE UNCLEANNESS OF WOMEN IS UNIMPORTANT OR ABSENT (15) LWS	0.65 OF 17	9 6 2 11 XSQ= 4.09 PHI= 0.382 EP = 0.0238
396	DRIFT TOWARD BEING THOSE WHERE THE STRENGTH OF MENSTRUAL TABOOS IS HIGH (18) WNS	0.60 OF 5	396	DRIFT TOWARD BEING THOSE WHERE THE STRENGTH OF MENSTRUAL TABOOS IS LOW (35) WNS	0.90 OF 10	3 1 2 9 XSQ= 2.09 PHI= 0.373 EP = 0.0769

423/

```
440  TILT TCWARD BEING THCSE          0.80 OF   5     440  TILT TOWARD BEING THOSE          0.88 OF   8          1     7
     WHERE FEAR OF SPIRITS                                WHERE FEAR OF SPIRITS                                  4     1
     IS LCW   (29) W-C                                    IS HIGH  (32) W-C                              XSQ=     3.41
                                                                                                         PHI=   -0.512
                                                                                                         EP =   0.0319

442  TILT TOWARD BEING THCSE          0.60 OF   5     442  IN ALL CASES ARE THOSE           1.00 CF   8          2     8
     WHERE FEAR OF ANIMAL SPIRITS                         WHERE FEAR OF ANIMAL SPIRITS                           3     0
     IS LCW   (33) W-C                                    IS HIGH  (28) W-C                              XSQ=     3.32
                                                                                                         PHI=   -0.505
                                                                                                         EP =   0.0350

443  TILT TCWARD BEING THCSE          0.60 OF   5     443  IN ALL CASES ARE THOSE           1.00 OF   8          2     8
     WHERE CVERALL FEAR CF CTHERS                         WHERE OVERALL FEAR OF OTHERS                           3     0
     IS LCW   (30) W-C                                    IS HIGH  (31) W-C                              XSQ=     3.32
                                                                                                         PHI=   -0.505
                                                                                                         EP =   0.0350

444  DRIFT TCWARD BEING THCSE         0.75 OF   4     444  DRIFT TOWARD BEING THOSE         0.88 CF   8          1     7
     WHERE THE USE CF DREAMS                              WHERE THE USE OF DREAMS                                3     1
     TC SEEK AND CCNTRCL SUPERNATURAL POWERS              TO SEEK AND CONTRCL SUPERNATURAL PCWERS        XSQ=     2.30
     IS LCW   (27) RGC                                    IS HIGH  (28) RGD                              PHI=   -0.437
                                                                                                         EP =   0.0667

458  TILT TCWARD BEING THCSE          0.50 OF  12     458  TILT TOWARD BEING THOSE          0.88 CF  16          6     2
     WHERE GAMES, IF PRESENT,                             WHERE GAMES, IF PRESENT,                               6    14
     INCLUDE GAMES CF STRATEGY  (52) R-A-B,EA             DO NOT INCLUDE                                 XSQ=     3.07
                                                          GAMES OF STRATEGY  (119) R-A-B,EA              PHI=    0.331
                                                                                                         EP =   0.0441
```

424	CULTURES WHERE RELIGIOUS SPECIALISTS ARE FULL-TIME, RATHER THAN PART-TIME (21) JMH	424	CULTURES WHERE RELIGIOUS SPECIALISTS ARE PART-TIME, RATHER THAN FULL-TIME (33) JMH	

BACKGROUND ON PAGE 163 — BOTH SUBJECT AND PREDICATE

21 IN LEFT COLUMN

ARAUCANIANS, AZANDE, AZTEC, BULGARIANS, BURMESE, BURUSHO, CAMBODIANS, CAYAPA, DARD, KASKA, KHASI, KOREANS, MARSHALLESE, MBUNDU, PUKAPUKA, RWALA, SAMOANS, TIKOPIA, TODA, VIETNAMESE, YAKUT

33 IN RIGHT COLUMN

ANDAMANESE, ARANDA, BEMBA, CHAGGA, CHUKCHEE, COPR ESKIMO, CREEK, CROW, CUNA, GILYAK, IBAN, JIVARO, KAREN, KORYAK, KURTATCHI, LOLO, MANDAN, MIAO, NAMA, NAVAHO, NUER, OJIBWA, SAMOYED, SIRIONO, TALLENSI, TEHUELCHE, THONGA, TIMBIRA, TIV, TROBRIAND, TUPINAMBA, WOLEAIANS, YUROK

346 EXCLUDED BECAUSE UNASCERTAINED

51	TILT TOWARD BEING THOSE WHERE SUBSISTENCE IS PRIMARILY BY FOOD PRODUCTION -- I. E., AGRICULTURE OR HUSBANDRY -- RATHER THAN BY GATHERING (253)	0.86 OF 21	51	TILT TOWARD BEING THOSE WHERE SUBSISTENCE IS PRIMARILY BY FOOD GATHERING -- I. E., HUNTING, FISHING, OR COLLECTING -- RATHER THAN FOOD PRODUCTION (147)	0.52 OF 33	18 16 3 17 XSQ= 6.11 PHI= 0.337 XP = 0.0134
77	LEAN TOWARD BEING THOSE WHERE THE WRITING SYSTEM IS ALPHABETIC-OR-PHONETIC, RATHER THAN BEING MNEMONIC OR ABSENT (15) JMH	0.52 OF 21	77	LEAN TOWARD BEING THOSE WHERE THE WRITING SYSTEM IS MNEMONIC OR ABSENT, RATHER THAN BEING ALPHABETIC-OR-PHONETIC (39) JMH	0.88 OF 33	11 4 10 29 XSQ= 8.46 PHI= 0.396 XP = 0.0036
80	TILT LESS TOWARD BEING THOSE WHERE NO CITY OR TOWN IS PRESENT (185)	0.74 OF 19	80	IN ALL CASES ARE THOSE WHERE NO CITY OR TOWN IS PRESENT (185)	1.00 OF 26	5 0 14 26 XSQ= 5.26 PHI= 0.342 XP = 0.0218
81	DRIFT TOWARD BEING THOSE WHERE A CITY OR TOWN IS PRESENT, OR THE AVERAGE COMMUNITY SIZE IS 200 OR GREATER (89)	0.53 OF 19	81	DRIFT TOWARD BEING THOSE WHERE NO CITY OR TOWN IS PRESENT, AND THE AVERAGE COMMUNITY SIZE IS SMALLER THAN 200 (135)	0.77 OF 26	10 6 9 20 XSQ= 2.99 PHI= 0.258 XP = 0.0836

85	TEND TO BE THOSE 0.60 OF 20 WHERE THE LEVEL OF POLITICAL INTEGRATION IS THE LARGE STATE, OR THE LITTLE STATE (70) GPM	85	TEND TO BE THOSE 0.90 OF 30 WHERE THE LEVEL OF POLITICAL INTEGRATION IS THE MINIMAL STATE, THE AUTONOMOUS COMMUNITY, OR THE FAMILY (234) GPM	12 3 8 27 XSQ= 12.00 PHI= 0.490 XP = 0.0005
86	TILT TOWARD BEING THOSE 0.70 OF 20 WHERE THE LEVEL OF POLITICAL INTEGRATION IS THE LARGE STATE, THE LITTLE STATE, OR THE MINIMAL STATE (148) GPM	86	TILT TOWARD BEING THOSE 0.67 OF 30 WHERE THE LEVEL OF POLITICAL INTEGRATION IS THE AUTONOMOUS COMMUNITY, OR THE FAMILY (156) GPM	14 10 6 20 XSQ= 5.08 PHI= 0.319 XP = 0.0242
94	DRIFT LESS TOWARD BEING THOSE 0.85 OF 20 WHERE THE HIERARCHY OF NATIONAL JURISDICTION HAS TWO, ONE, OR NO LEVELS (296) GES,EA	94	IN ALL CASES ARE THOSE 1.00 OF 32 WHERE THE HIERARCHY OF NATIONAL JURISDICTION HAS TWO, ONE, OR NO LEVELS (296) GES,EA	3 0 17 32 XSQ= 2.71 PHI= 0.228 XP = 0.0998
95	TEND TO BE THOSE 0.50 OF 20 WHERE THE HIERARCHY OF NATIONAL JURISDICTION HAS FOUR, THREE, OR TWO LEVELS (76) GES,EA	95	TEND TO BE THOSE 0.94 OF 32 WHERE THE HIERARCHY OF NATIONAL JURISDICTION HAS ONE OR NO LEVELS (254) GES,EA	10 2 10 30 XSQ= 10.92 PHI= 0.458 XP = 0.0010
96	LEAN TOWARD BEING THOSE 0.85 OF 20 WHERE THE HIERARCHY OF NATIONAL JURISDICTION HAS FOUR, THREE, TWO OR ONE LEVEL (174) GES,EA	96	LEAN TOWARD BEING THOSE 0.56 OF 32 WHERE THE HIERARCHY OF NATIONAL JURISDICTION HAS NO LEVELS (156) GES,EA	17 14 3 18 XSQ= 7.07 PHI= 0.369 XP = 0.0078
102	TILT TOWARD BEING THOSE 0.81 OF 21 WHERE CLASS STRATIFICATION IS PRESENT (203)	102	TILT TOWARD BEING THOSE 0.55 OF 33 WHERE CLASS STRATIFICATION IS ABSENT (180)	17 15 4 18 XSQ= 5.31 PHI= 0.314 XP = 0.0212
106	TILT TOWARD BEING THOSE 0.82 OF 17 WHERE CLASS STRATIFICATION, IF PRESENT, IS BASED ON SOMETHING OTHER THAN WEALTH (126)	106	TILT TOWARD BEING THOSE 0.60 OF 15 WHERE CLASS STRATIFICATION, IF PRESENT, IS BASED ON WEALTH (77)	3 9 14 6 XSQ= 4.43 PHI= -0.372 EP = 0.0269
107	LEAN LESS TOWARD BEING THOSE 0.53 OF 17 WHERE CLASS STRATIFICATION, IF PRESENT, IS BASED ON SOMETHING OTHER THAN OCCUPATIONAL STATUS (160)	107	IN ALL CASES ARE THOSE 1.00 OF 15 WHERE CLASS STRATIFICATION, IF PRESENT, IS BASED ON SOMETHING OTHER THAN OCCUPATIONAL STATUS (160)	8 0 9 15 XSQ= 7.07 PHI= 0.470 EP = 0.0029
116	TEND TO BE THOSE 0.81 OF 21 WHERE OCCUPATIONAL SPECIALIZATION IS FULL-TIME, WHETHER OR NOT FOR SURPLUS PRODUCTION (20) JMH	116	TEND TO BE THOSE 0.91 OF 33 WHERE OCCUPATIONAL SPECIALIZATION IS PART-TIME ONLY (34) JMH	17 3 4 30 XSQ= 25.42 PHI= 0.686 XP = 0.0000

118	TILT TOWARD BEING THOSE 0.83 OF 6 WHERE THE PERCENTAGE OF OCCUPATIONS THAT ARE SPECIALIZED IS HIGH OR MEDIUM (24) WME	118	TILT TOWARD BEING THOSE 0.77 OF 13 WHERE THE PERCENTAGE OF OCCUPATIONS THAT ARE SPECIALIZED IS LOW (25) WME	5 3 1 10 XSQ= 3.89 PHI= 0.453 EP = 0.0408
132	TILT MORE TOWARD BEING THOSE 0.90 OF 21 WHERE ECONOMIC EXCHANGE INVOLVES THE USE OF MONEY (37) JMH	132	TILT LESS TOWARD BEING THOSE 0.55 OF 33 WHERE ECONOMIC EXCHANGE INVOLVES THE USE OF MONEY (37) JMH	19 18 2 15 XSQ= 6.11 PHI= 0.336 XP = 0.0135
133	IN ALL CASES ARE THOSE 1.00 OF 4 WHERE CONTRACTED DEBTS ARE SIGNIFICANTLY PRESENT (17) GES	133	DRIFT TOWARD BEING THOSE 0.67 OF 12 WHERE CONTRACTED DEBTS ARE MODERATELY PRESENT OR ABSENT (17) GES	4 4 0 8 XSQ= 3.00 PHI= 0.433 EP = 0.0769
138	IN ALL CASES ARE THOSE 1.00 OF 4 WHERE SUPERORDINATE JUSTICE IS PRESENT (22) BBW	138	DRIFT TOWARD BEING THOSE 0.70 OF 10 WHERE SUPERORDINATE JUSTICE IS ABSENT (18) BBW	4 3 0 7 XSQ= 3.15 PHI= 0.474 EP = 0.0699
139	TILT TOWARD BEING THOSE 0.75 OF 4 WHERE SUPERORDINATE PUNISHMENT IS PRESENT (15) BBW	139	TILT TOWARD BEING THOSE 0.90 OF 10 WHERE SUPERORDINATE PUNISHMENT IS ABSENT (25) BBW	3 1 1 9 XSQ= 3.16 PHI= 0.475 EP = 0.0410
141	TILT TOWARD BEING THOSE 0.71 OF 21 WHERE THE LEVEL OF SOCIAL SANCTION IS PUBLIC CORPOREAL SANCTION, RATHER THAN PUBLIC PROPERTY SANCTION OR PRIVATE SETTLEMENT (28) JMH	141	TILT TOWARD BEING THOSE 0.61 OF 33 WHERE THE LEVEL OF SOCIAL SANCTION IS PUBLIC PROPERTY SANCTION OR PRIVATE SETTLEMENT, RATHER THAN PUBLIC CORPOREAL SANCTION (26) JMH	15 13 6 20 XSQ= 4.07 PHI= 0.275 XP = 0.0437
163	IN ALL CASES ARE THOSE 1.00 OF 3 WHERE THE EMPHASIS ON INDIVIDUAL VOLITION AS THE CAUSE OF CRIME IS HIGH (7) MJ	163	IN ALL CASES ARE THOSE 1.00 OF 6 WHERE THE EMPHASIS ON INDIVIDUAL VOLITION AS THE CAUSE OF CRIME IS LOW (10) MJ	3 0 0 6 XSQ= 5.06 PHI= 0.750 EP = 0.0119
196	DRIFT TOWARD BEING THOSE 0.80 OF 15 WHERE INDIVIDUAL RIGHTS IN REAL PROPERTY, AND RULES FOR INHERITANCE, ARE PRESENT (194)	196	DRIFT TOWARD BEING THOSE 0.52 OF 23 WHERE INDIVIDUAL RIGHTS IN REAL PROPERTY, OR RULES FOR INHERITANCE, ARE ABSENT (87)	12 11 3 12 XSQ= 2.70 PHI= 0.267 EP = 0.0884
263	DRIFT TOWARD BEING THOSE 0.67 OF 21 WHERE WIVES ARE OBTAINED BY RELATIVELY EASY MEANS, NAMELY BY TOKEN BRIDE-PRICE, GIFT EXCHANGE, ABSENCE OF ANY CONSIDERATION, OR RECEIPT OF DOWRY (162)	263	DRIFT TOWARD BEING THOSE 0.61 OF 33 WHERE WIVES ARE OBTAINED BY RELATIVELY DIFFICULT MEANS, NAMELY BY BRIDE-PRICE, BRIDE-SERVICE, OR EXCHANGING A FEMALE RELATIVE (233)	7 20 14 13 XSQ= 2.81 PHI= -0.228 XP = 0.0940

306	TILT TOWARD BEING THOSE WHERE THE EARLY DEPENDENCE SATISFACTION POTENTIAL IS LOW (24) W-C	0.71 OF 7	306	TILT TOWARD BEING THOSE WHERE THE EARLY DEPENDENCE SATISFACTION POTENTIAL IS HIGH (28) W-C	0.88 OF 8	2 7 5 1 XSQ= 3.23 PHI= -0.464 EP = 0.0406
317	LEAN TOWARD BEING THOSE WHERE DISPLAY OF AFFECTION TOWARD THE INFANT IS LOW (29) B-B-C	0.88 OF 8	317	LEAN TOWARD BEING THOSE WHERE DISPLAY OF AFFECTION TOWARD THE INFANT IS HIGH (39) B-B-C	0.79 OF 19	1 15 7 4 XSQ= 7.73 PHI= -0.535 EP = 0.0025
320	LEAN TOWARD BEING THOSE WHERE THE DEGREE OF REDUCTION OF THE INFANT'S DRIVES IS LOW (24) B-B-C	0.75 OF 8	320	LEAN TOWARD BEING THOSE WHERE THE DEGREE OF REDUCTION OF THE INFANT'S DRIVES IS HIGH (45) B-B-C	0.83 OF 18	2 15 6 3 XSQ= 5.95 PHI= -0.478 EP = 0.0077
330	TILT TOWARD BEING THOSE WHERE THE AGE OF THE INFANT AT TIME OF WEANING IS LOWER THAN 2.5 YEARS (36) B-B-C	0.83 OF 6	330	TILT TOWARD BEING THOSE WHERE THE AGE OF THE INFANT AT TIME OF WEANING IS 2.5 YEARS OR HIGHER (34) B-B-C	0.78 OF 18	1 14 5 4 XSQ= 4.80 PHI= -0.447 EP = 0.0147
345	DRIFT TOWARD BEING THOSE WHERE THE CHILD'S INFERRED ANXIETY OVER NON-PERFORMANCE OF SELF-RELIANT BEHAVIOR IS LOW (39) B-B-C	0.88 OF 8	345	DRIFT TOWARD BEING THOSE WHERE THE CHILD'S INFERRED ANXIETY OVER NON-PERFORMANCE OF SELF-RELIANT BEHAVIOR IS HIGH (37) B-B-C	0.55 OF 20	1 11 7 9 XSQ= 2.66 PHI= -0.308 EP = 0.0882
382	TILT TOWARD BEING THOSE WHERE FEMALE INITIATION RITES ARE ABSENT (27) JKB	0.78 OF 9	382	TILT TOWARD BEING THOSE WHERE FEMALE INITIATION RITES ARE PRESENT (38) JKB	0.74 OF 19	2 14 7 5 XSQ= 4.67 PHI= -0.408 EP = 0.0166
386	TILT TOWARD BEING THOSE WHERE SEXUAL EXPRESSION BY THE YOUNG IS PERMITTED (40) F-B	0.75 OF 8	386	TILT TOWARD BEING THOSE WHERE SEXUAL EXPRESSION BY THE YOUNG IS RESTRICTED OR SEMI-RESTRICTED (46) F-B	0.72 OF 18	2 13 6 5 XSQ= 3.31 PHI= -0.357 EP = 0.0384
402	TILT TOWARD BEING THOSE WHERE EXPLANATIONS OF ILLNESS OF AN ORAL NATURE ARE ABSENT (30) W-C	0.71 OF 7	402	TILT TOWARD BEING THOSE WHERE EXPLANATIONS OF ILLNESS OF AN ORAL NATURE ARE PRESENT (31) W-C	0.90 OF 10	2 9 5 1 XSQ= 4.38 PHI= -0.508 EP = 0.0345
405	TILT TOWARD BEING THOSE WHERE EXPLANATIONS OF ILLNESS OF A DEPENDENCE NATURE ARE PRESENT (34) W-C	0.86 OF 7	405	TILT TOWARD BEING THOSE WHERE EXPLANATIONS OF ILLNESS OF A DEPENDENCE NATURE ARE ABSENT (27) W-C	0.70 OF 10	6 3 1 7 XSQ= 3.14 PHI= 0.430 EP = 0.0498

```
425  IN ALL CASES ARE THOSE             1.00 OF   4     425  TILT TOWARD BEING THOSE           0.88 OF   8          4    1
     WHERE SUPERNATURALS ARE MAINLY                          WHERE SUPERNATURALS ARE MAINLY                         0    7
     BENEVOLENT, RATHER THAN                                 AGGRESSIVE, RATHER THAN                          XSQ=      5.19
     AGGRESSIVE  (16) L-T-W                                  BENEVOLENT  (20) L-T-W                           PHI=     0.657
                                                                                                              EP =    0.0101

433  DRIFT TOWARD BEING THOSE           0.75 OF   4     433  DRIFT TOWARD BEING THOSE          0.80 OF  15          3    3
     WHERE BELIEF IN REINCARNATION                           WHERE BELIEF IN REINCARNATION                          1   12
     IS PRESENT  (10) GES                                    IS ABSENT  (28) GES                              XSQ=      2.24
                                                                                                              PHI=     0.344
                                                                                                              EP =    0.0709

435  IN ALL CASES ARE THOSE             1.00 OF   4     435  DRIFT TOWARD BEING THOSE          0.60 OF  10          0    6
     WHERE ABANDONMENT OF THE HOUSE OF THE DEAD              WHERE ABANDONMENT OF THE HOUSE OF THE DEAD             4    4
     IS NOT PRACTICED  (19) LWS                              IS PRACTICED  (12) LWS                           XSQ=      2.11
                                                                                                              PHI=    -0.388
                                                                                                              EP =    0.0849

468  TILT TOWARD BEING THOSE            0.52 OF  21     468  TILT TOWARD BEING THOSE           0.82 OF  33         11    6
     WHERE CONTACT WITH OTHER CULTURES                       WHERE CONTACT WITH OTHER CULTURES                     10   27
     IS FREQUENT, RATHER THAN                                IS REGULAR OR IRREGULAR, RATHER THAN             XSQ=      5.46
     REGULAR OR IRREGULAR  (17) JMH                          FREQUENT  (37) JMH                               PHI=     0.318
                                                                                                              XP =    0.0194

470  TILT TOWARD BEING THOSE            0.62 OF  21     470  TILT TOWARD BEING THOSE           0.76 OF  33         13    8
     WHERE INNOVATIONS ARE                                   WHERE INNOVATIONS ARE                                  8   25
     GENERALLY ACCEPTED  (21) JMH                            ACCEPTED ONLY SELECTIVELY  (33) JMH              XSQ=      6.16
                                                                                                              PHI=     0.338
                                                                                                              XP =    0.0131
```

425 CULTURES WHERE SUPERNATURALS ARE MAINLY BENEVOLENT, RATHER THAN AGGRESSIVE (16) L-T-W	425 CULTURES WHERE SUPERNATURALS ARE MAINLY AGGRESSIVE, RATHER THAN BENEVOLENT (20) L-T-W

BACKGROUND ON PAGE 163 — BOTH SUBJECT AND PREDICATE

16 IN LEFT COLUMN

ARAPESH	ASHANTI	CHENCHU	CHEYENNE	COMANCHE	HANO	MBUNDU	ONTONG-JAVA	PAPAGO	PUKAPUKA
SAMOANS	TALLENSI	TETON	TIKOPIA	WINNEBAGO	ZUNI				

20 IN RIGHT COLUMN

ALORESE	ANDAMANESE	AYMARA	CHAGGA	CHIR-APACHE	FON	KURTATCHI	KWAKIUTL	LEPCHA	LESU
MANUS	MAORI	NAVAHO	OJIBWA	SIRIONO	TENETEHARA	THONGA	VENDA	WOGEO	YAGUA

364 EXCLUDED BECAUSE UNASCERTAINED

97 LEAN LESS TOWARD BEING THOSE WHERE THE HIERARCHY OF LOCAL JURISDICTION HAS THREE OR TWO LEVELS (273) GES,EA	0.54 OF 13	97 LEAN MORE TOWARD BEING THOSE WHERE THE HIERARCHY OF LOCAL JURISDICTION HAS THREE OR TWO LEVELS (273) GES,EA	0.95 OF 20	6 1 7 19 XSQ= 5.71 PHI= 0.416 EP = 0.0084
127 DRIFT TOWARD BEING THOSE WHERE THE FEMALES' CONTRIBUTION TO SUBSISTENCE IS LOW (32) JKB	0.75 OF 4	127 DRIFT TOWARD BEING THOSE WHERE THE FEMALES' CONTRIBUTION TO SUBSISTENCE IS HIGH (33) JKB	0.83 OF 12	1 10 3 2 XSQ= 2.42 PHI= -0.389 EP = 0.0632
259 TILT TOWARD BEING THOSE WHERE THE SEVERITY OF MOTHER-IN-LAW AVOIDANCE IS LOW (20) WNS	0.89 OF 9	259 TILT TOWARD BEING THOSE WHERE THE SEVERITY OF MOTHER-IN-LAW AVOIDANCE IS HIGH (26) WNS	0.64 OF 11	1 7 8 4 XSQ= 3.71 PHI= -0.431 EP = 0.0281
301 DRIFT TOWARD BEING THOSE WHERE THE POST-PARTUM SEX TABOO LASTS ONE MONTH OR LESS (28)	0.50 OF 6	301 DRIFT TOWARD BEING THOSE WHERE THE POST-PARTUM SEX TABOO LASTS LONGER THAN ONE MONTH (96)	0.92 OF 13	3 12 3 1 XSQ= 2.24 PHI= -0.344 EP = 0.0709
318 DRIFT TOWARD BEING THOSE WHERE THE OVERALL INDULGENCE OF THE INFANT IS HIGH (40) B-B-C	0.75 OF 16	318 DRIFT TOWARD BEING THOSE WHERE THE OVERALL INDULGENCE OF THE INFANT IS LOW (31) B-B-C	0.55 OF 20	12 9 4 11 XSQ= 2.17 PHI= 0.246 EP = 0.0958

324	DRIFT TOWARD BEING THOSE 0.75 OF 16 WHERE THE PAIN INFLICTED ON THE INFANT BY THE NURTURANT AGENT IS LOW OR NEGLIGIBLE (32) B-B-C	324	DRIFT TOWARD BEING THOSE 0.55 OF 20 WHERE THE PAIN INFLICTED ON THE INFANT BY THE NURTURANT AGENT IS HIGH (34) B-B-C	4 11 12 9 XSQ= 2.17 PHI= -0.246 EP = 0.0958
334	DRIFT TOWARD BEING THOSE 0.69 OF 16 WHERE THE INDULGENCE OF THE CHILD IS HIGH (40) B-B-C	334	DRIFT TOWARD BEING THOSE 0.65 OF 20 WHERE THE INDULGENCE OF THE CHILD IS LOW (38) B-B-C	11 7 5 13 XSQ= 2.81 PHI= 0.280 EP = 0.0922
340	DRIFT TOWARD BEING THOSE 0.77 OF 13 WHERE THE TOTAL POSITIVE PRESSURE TOWARD DEVELOPING NURTURANT BEHAVIOR IN THE CHILD IS HIGH (28) B-B-C	340	DRIFT TOWARD BEING THOSE 0.63 OF 16 WHERE THE TOTAL POSITIVE PRESSURE TOWARD DEVELOPING NURTURANT BEHAVIOR IN THE CHILD IS LOW (20) B-B-C	10 6 3 10 XSQ= 3.05 PHI= 0.325 EP = 0.0608
344	TILT TOWARD BEING THOSE 0.81 OF 16 WHERE THE TOTAL POSITIVE PRESSURE TOWARD DEVELOPING SELF-RELIANT BEHAVIOR IN THE CHILD IS LOW (40) B-B-C	344	TILT TOWARD BEING THOSE 0.58 OF 19 WHERE THE TOTAL POSITIVE PRESSURE TOWARD DEVELOPING SELF-RELIANT BEHAVIOR IN THE CHILD IS HIGH (36) B-B-C	3 11 13 8 XSQ= 4.03 PHI= -0.340 EP = 0.0364
345	TILT TOWARD BEING THOSE 0.75 OF 16 WHERE THE CHILD'S INFERRED ANXIETY OVER NON-PERFORMANCE OF SELF-RELIANT BEHAVIOR IS LOW (39) B-B-C	345	TILT TOWARD BEING THOSE 0.68 OF 19 WHERE THE CHILD'S INFERRED ANXIETY OVER NON-PERFORMANCE OF SELF-RELIANT BEHAVIOR IS HIGH (37) B-B-C	4 13 12 6 XSQ= 4.93 PHI= -0.375 EP = 0.0176
393	TILT TOWARD BEING THOSE 0.88 OF 8 WHERE EXTRAMARITAL COITUS IS PERMITTED, RATHER THAN PUNISHED (41) F-B	393	TILT TOWARD BEING THOSE 0.73 OF 11 WHERE EXTRAMARITAL COITUS IS PUNISHED, RATHER THAN PERMITTED (43) F-B	1 8 7 3 XSQ= 4.54 PHI= -0.489 EP = 0.0198
402	TEND TO BE THOSE 0.83 OF 12 WHERE EXPLANATIONS OF ILLNESS OF AN ORAL NATURE ARE ABSENT (30) W-C	402	TEND TO BE THOSE 0.82 OF 17 WHERE EXPLANATIONS OF ILLNESS OF AN ORAL NATURE ARE PRESENT (31) W-C	2 14 10 3 XSQ= 9.76 PHI= -0.580 EP = 0.0007
424	TILT TOWARD BEING THOSE 0.80 OF 5 WHERE RELIGIOUS SPECIALISTS ARE FULL-TIME, RATHER THAN PART-TIME (21) JMH	424	IN ALL CASES ARE THOSE 1.00 OF 7 WHERE RELIGIOUS SPECIALISTS ARE PART-TIME, RATHER THAN FULL-TIME (33) JMH	4 0 1 7 XSQ= 5.19 PHI= 0.657 EP = 0.0101
452	IN ALL CASES ARE THOSE 1.00 OF 6 WHERE TOTEMISM WITH FOOD TABOOS IS PRESENT (19) WNS	452	LEAN TOWARD BEING THOSE 0.73 OF 11 WHERE TOTEMISM WITH FOOD TABOOS IS ABSENT (24) WNS	6 3 0 8 XSQ= 5.58 PHI= 0.573 EP = 0.0090

```
**************************************************************************************************

426  CULTURES                                          426  CULTURES
     WHERE A HIGH GOD IS                                    WHERE A HIGH GOD IS
     PRESENT  (156) GES,EA                                  ABSENT  (104) GES,EA


BACKGROUND ON PAGE 163                                                  BOTH SUBJECT AND PREDICATE
..................................................................................................

     156  IN LEFT COLUMN

ALBANIANS     ALORESE      AMERICANS     APINAYE       ARAUCANIANS ASHANTI     AYMARA      AZANDE      AZTEC        BAMBARA
BAMILEKE      BARABRA      BARI          BASSERI       BEJA        BEMBA       BHIL        BHUIYA      BIRIFOR      BLACK CARIB
BOERS         BOZO         BRAZILIANS    BULGARIANS    BURUSHO     CAGABA      CALLINAGO   CAMAYURA    CARIB        CHAMACOCO
CHERKESS      CHOCO        CHORTI        CHUKCHEE      CREEK       CUNA        CZECHS      DAGUR       DELAWARE     DUTCH
EGYPTIANS     FANG         FOX           FUTAJALONKE   GANDA       GARO        GILYAK      GISU        GOAJIRO      GOND
GROS VENTRE   GURE         HASINAI       HAZARA        HEBREWS     HURON       HUTSUL      ILA         INCA         INGALIK
IRISH         JAVANESE     JIVARO        KABYLE        KACHIN      KAPAUKU     KATAB       KAZAK       KHASI        KIKUYU
KOHISTANI     KORYAK       KPE           KUBA          KUNG        LAKHER      LAMBA       LANGO       LAPPS        LEPCHA
LOZI          LUO          MACASSARESE   MALAYS        MAM         MAMVU       MAORI       MATAKAM     MBUNDU       MBUTI
MENDE         MIAMI        MISKITO       MONGO         MOSSI       MZAB        NANDI       NATCHEZ     NOMLAKI      NUER
NUPE          NYAKYUSA     NYORO         ONA           PAPAGO      PARAUJANO   PATHAN      PUKAPUKA    REGEIBAT     RIFFIANS
RUNDI         RWALA        SAMOANS       SAMOYED       SANDAWE     SANPOIL     SANTAL      SEMANG      SERBS        SHILLUK
SHLUH         SIRIONO      SIWANS        SOMALI        SONGHAI     SYRIANS     TALAMANCA   TANALA      TARAHUMARA   TEDA
TEHUELCHE     TENDA        TENINO        TERENA        TESO        THONGA      TIGRINYA    TIV         TIWI         TRISTAN
TUCANO        TUNEBO       TUPINAMBA     TURKANA       TURKMEN     UTE         VENDA       WALLOONS    WANTOAT      WARRAU
WITOTO        WOLOF        YAHGAN        YAKUT         YORUBA      YUKI

     104  IN RIGHT COLUMN

ABIPON        ABOR         AINU          ALACALUF      AMBA        ANDAMANESE  ARANDA      ARAPESH     ATAYAL       ATSUGEWI
AWEIKOMA      BACAIRI      BORORO        BUNLAP        CAYAPA      CHAGGA      CHENCHU     CHEYENNE    CHIR-APACHE  CHOROTI
COCHITI       COORG        COPR ESKIMO   CREE          CROW        DARD        DIEGUENO    DIERI       DOROBO       EYAK
FON           HAIDA        HAWAIIANS     HUKUNDIKA     IBAN        IFUGAO      KASKA       KERAKI      KOREANS      KURTATCHI
KUTENAI       LAU          LESU          LHOTA NAGA    LOLO        MANGAIANS   MANIHIKI    MANUS       MARICOPA     MARQUESANS
MARSHALLESE   MATACO       MNONG GAR     MOTA          MUNDURUCU   MURINBATA   MURNGIN     NARESNA     NAMA         NAMBICUARA
NAVAHO        NUNIVAK      OKINAWANS     OMAHA         ONTONG-JAVA PAIWAN      PALAUANS    PONAPEANS   PURUM        ROMANS
SAGADA        SHERENTE     SIUAI         SOTHO         SWAZI       TALLENSI    TAPIRAPE    TAREUMIUT   TENETEHARA   THAI
TIKOPIA       TIMBIRA      TIMUCUA       TOCA          TOLOWA      TROBRIAND   TRUKESE     TRUMAI      TSHIMSHIAN   TUBATULABAL
TUCUNA        TWANA        ULAWANS       VEDDA         WASHO       WOGEO       WOLEAIANS   YABARANA    YAGUA        YAKO
YAO           YOKUTS       YUROK         ZUNI

     140  EXCLUDED BECAUSE UNASCERTAINED

--------------------------------------------------------------------------------------------------
  3  TEND LESS TO BE THOSE         0.71 OF 156        3  TEND MORE TO BE THOSE       0.90 OF 104      45    10
     LOCATED OUTSIDE OF                                  LOCATED OUTSIDE OF                          111    94
     AFRICA  (320)                                       AFRICA  (320)                             XSQ=  12.71
                                                                                                   PHI=  0.221
                                                                                                   XP =  0.0004
```

4	TEND LESS TO BE THOSE LOCATED OUTSIDE OF THE CIRCUM-MEDITERRANEAN (355)	0.80 OF 156	4	TEND MORE TO BE THOSE LOCATED OUTSIDE OF THE CIRCUM-MEDITERRANEAN (355)	0.99 OF 104	31 1 125 103 XSQ= 18.96 PHI= 0.270 XP = 0.0000
6	TEND MORE TO BE THOSE LOCATED OUTSIDE OF THE INSULAR PACIFIC (330)	0.94 OF 156	6	TEND LESS TO BE THOSE LOCATED OUTSIDE OF THE INSULAR PACIFIC (330)	0.69 OF 104	9 32 147 72 XSQ= 27.51 PHI= -0.325 XP = 0.0000
8	LEAN MORE TOWARD BEING THOSE LOCATED OUTSIDE OF NORTH AMERICA (330)	0.89 OF 156	8	LEAN LESS TOWARD BEING THOSE LOCATED OUTSIDE OF NORTH AMERICA (330)	0.73 OF 104	17 28 139 76 XSQ= 10.11 PHI= -0.197 XP = 0.0015
42	LEAN MORE TOWARD BEING THOSE WHERE THE NATURAL ENVIRONMENT IS OTHER THAN TROPICAL OR SUB-TROPICAL RAIN FOREST, OR MONSOON FOREST (244) FWM	0.71 OF 156	42	LEAN LESS TOWARD BEING THOSE WHERE THE NATURAL ENVIRONMENT IS OTHER THAN TROPICAL OR SUB-TROPICAL RAIN FOREST, OR MONSOON FOREST (244) FWM	0.52 OF 104	46 50 110 54 XSQ= 8.48 PHI= -0.181 XP = 0.0036
44	DRIFT MORE TOWARD BEING THOSE WHERE SETTLEMENTS ARE FIXED (222)	0.69 OF 156	44	DRIFT LESS TOWARD BEING THOSE WHERE SETTLEMENTS ARE FIXED (222)	0.58 OF 103	108 60 48 43 XSQ= 2.82 PHI= 0.104 XP = 0.0933
51	TEND TO BE THOSE WHERE SUBSISTENCE IS PRIMARILY BY FOOD PRODUCTION -- I. E., AGRICULTURE OR HUSBANDRY -- RATHER THAN BY GATHERING (253)	0.71 OF 156	51	TEND TO BE THOSE WHERE SUBSISTENCE IS PRIMARILY BY FOOD GATHERING -- I. E., HUNTING, FISHING, OR COLLECTING -- RATHER THAN FOOD PRODUCTION (147)	0.58 OF 104	110 44 46 60 XSQ= 19.41 PHI= 0.273 XP = 0.0000
53	TILT LESS TOWARD BEING THOSE WHERE FOOD PRODUCTION IS BY SIMPLE AGRICULTURE OR INCIPIENT FOOD PRODUCTION, RATHER THAN BY INTENSIVE AGRICULTURE (147)	0.58 OF 123	53	TILT MORE TOWARD BEING THOSE WHERE FOOD PRODUCTION IS BY SIMPLE AGRICULTURE OR INCIPIENT FOOD PRODUCTION, RATHER THAN BY INTENSIVE AGRICULTURE (147)	0.75 OF 55	52 14 71 41 XSQ= 3.92 PHI= 0.148 XP = 0.0478
55	DRIFT TOWARD BEING THOSE WHERE FOOD PRODUCTION IS BY INTENSIVE AGRICULTURE, RATHER THAN BY SIMPLE AGRICULTURE (91)	0.52 OF 100	55	DRIFT TOWARD BEING THOSE WHERE FOOD PRODUCTION IS BY SIMPLE AGRICULTURE, RATHER THAN BY INTENSIVE AGRICULTURE (101)	0.67 OF 43	52 14 48 29 XSQ= 3.82 PHI= 0.164 XP = 0.0505
62	LEAN MORE TOWARD BEING THOSE WHERE HUSBANDRY OF SOME KIND IS PRESENT (228)	0.75 OF 156	62	LEAN LESS TOWARD BEING THOSE WHERE HUSBANDRY OF SOME KIND IS PRESENT (228)	0.55 OF 104	117 57 39 47 XSQ= 10.60 PHI= 0.202 XP = 0.0011

63	TEND TO BE THOSE WHERE HUSBANDRY, IF PRESENT, IS PRINCIPALLY IN THE FORM OF BOVINE, EQUINE, CAMEL-LIKE, OR DEER-LIKE ANIMALS, RATHER THAN PIGS, SHEEP, OR GOATS (152)	0.75 OF 117	63	TEND TO BE THOSE WHERE HUSBANDRY, IF PRESENT, IS PRINCIPALLY IN THE FORM OF PIGS, SHEEP, OR GOATS, RATHER THAN BOVINE, EQUINE, CAMEL-LIKE, OR DEER-LIKE ANIMALS (74)	0.54 OF 57	88 26 29 31 XSQ= 13.58 PHI= 0.279 XP = 0.0002
71	TEND TO BE THOSE WHERE METAL WORKING IS PRESENT (98)	0.56 OF 124	71	TEND TO BE THOSE WHERE METAL WORKING IS ABSENT (153)	0.82 OF 87	70 16 54 71 XSQ= 29.12 PHI= 0.371 XP = 0.0000
73	TILT TOWARD BEING THOSE WHERE WEAVING IS PRESENT (118)	0.56 OF 123	73	TILT TOWARD BEING THOSE WHERE WEAVING IS ABSENT (130)	0.60 OF 86	69 34 54 52 XSQ= 4.91 PHI= 0.153 XP = 0.0267
74	TEND TO BE THOSE WHERE POTTERY IS PRESENT (145)	0.74 OF 122	74	TEND TO BE THOSE WHERE POTTERY IS ABSENT (93)	0.51 OF 84	90 41 32 43 XSQ= 12.33 PHI= 0.245 XP = 0.0004
80	TILT LESS TOWARD BEING THOSE WHERE NO CITY OR TOWN IS PRESENT (185)	0.79 OF 107	80	TILT MORE TOWARD BEING THOSE WHERE NO CITY OR TOWN IS PRESENT (185)	0.92 OF 75	23 6 84 69 XSQ= 5.03 PHI= 0.166 XP = 0.0249
81	LEAN LESS TOWARD BEING THOSE WHERE NO CITY OR TOWN IS PRESENT, AND THE AVERAGE COMMUNITY SIZE IS SMALLER THAN 200 (135)	0.55 OF 107	81	LEAN MORE TOWARD BEING THOSE WHERE NO CITY OR TOWN IS PRESENT, AND THE AVERAGE COMMUNITY SIZE IS SMALLER THAN 200 (135)	0.76 OF 75	48 18 59 57 XSQ= 7.42 PHI= 0.202 XP = 0.0064
82	TEND MORE TO BE THOSE WHERE A CITY OR TOWN IS PRESENT, OR THE AVERAGE COMMUNITY SIZE IS FIFTY OR GREATER (178)	0.90 OF 107	82	TEND LESS TO BE THOSE WHERE A CITY OR TOWN IS PRESENT, OR THE AVERAGE COMMUNITY SIZE IS FIFTY OR GREATER (178)	0.67 OF 75	96 50 11 25 XSQ= 13.35 PHI= 0.271 XP = 0.0003
86	TEND TO BE THOSE WHERE THE LEVEL OF POLITICAL INTEGRATION IS THE LARGE STATE, THE LITTLE STATE, OR THE MINIMAL STATE (148) GPM	0.60 OF 117	86	TEND TO BE THOSE WHERE THE LEVEL OF POLITICAL INTEGRATION IS THE AUTONOMOUS COMMUNITY, OR THE FAMILY (156) GPM	0.73 OF 85	70 23 47 62 XSQ= 19.98 PHI= 0.315 XP = 0.0000
96	TEND TO BE THOSE WHERE THE HIERARCHY OF NATIONAL JURISDICTION HAS FOUR, THREE, TWO OR ONE LEVEL (174) GES,EA	0.63 OF 154	96	TEND TO BE THOSE WHERE THE HIERARCHY OF NATIONAL JURISDICTION HAS NO LEVELS (156) GES,EA	0.65 OF 103	97 36 57 67 XSQ= 18.32 PHI= 0.267 XP = 0.0000

97	TILT LESS TOWARD BEING THOSE WHERE THE HIERARCHY OF LOCAL JURISDICTION HAS THREE OR TWO LEVELS (273) GES,EA	0.79 OF 155	97	TILT MORE TOWARD BEING THOSE WHERE THE HIERARCHY OF LOCAL JURISDICTION HAS THREE OR TWO LEVELS (273) GES,EA	0.89 OF 103	33 11 122 92 XSQ= 4.20 PHI= 0.128 XP = 0.0403
102	LEAN TOWARD BEING THOSE WHERE CLASS STRATIFICATION IS PRESENT (203)	0.63 OF 154	102	LEAN TOWARD BEING THOSE WHERE CLASS STRATIFICATION IS ABSENT (180)	0.54 OF 103	97 47 57 56 XSQ= 6.86 PHI= 0.163 XP = 0.0088
107	TILT LESS TOWARD BEING THOSE WHERE CLASS STRATIFICATION, IF PRESENT, IS BASED ON SOMETHING OTHER THAN OCCUPATIONAL STATUS (160)	0.73 OF 97	107	TILT MORE TOWARD BEING THOSE WHERE CLASS STRATIFICATION, IF PRESENT, IS BASED ON SOMETHING OTHER THAN OCCUPATIONAL STATUS (160)	0.91 OF 47	26 4 71 43 XSQ= 5.36 PHI= 0.193 XP = 0.0206
108	TILT MORE TOWARD BEING THOSE WHERE CLASS STRATIFICATION, IF PRESENT, IS BASED ON SOMETHING OTHER THAN A HEREDITARY ARISTOCRACY (129)	0.72 OF 97	108	TILT LESS TOWARD BEING THOSE WHERE CLASS STRATIFICATION, IF PRESENT, IS BASED ON SOMETHING OTHER THAN A HEREDITARY ARISTOCRACY (129)	0.53 OF 47	27 22 70 25 XSQ= 4.27 PHI= -0.172 XP = 0.0389
109	TEND LESS TO BE THOSE WHERE CASTES ARE ABSENT (317)	0.80 OF 142	109	TEND MORE TO BE THOSE WHERE CASTES ARE ABSENT (317)	0.96 OF 102	29 4 113 98 XSQ= 12.44 PHI= 0.226 XP = 0.0004
110	TEND TO BE THOSE WHERE SLAVERY IS PRESENT (163)	0.52 OF 151	110	TEND TO BE THOSE WHERE SLAVERY IS ABSENT (218)	0.73 OF 100	78 27 73 73 XSQ= 14.03 PHI= 0.236 XP = 0.0002
129	TILT LESS TOWARD BEING THOSE WHERE WEAVING IS MAINLY DONE BY FEMALES (73)	0.62 OF 58	129	TILT MORE TOWARD BEING THOSE WHERE WEAVING IS MAINLY DONE BY FEMALES (73)	0.85 OF 33	22 5 36 28 XSQ= 4.20 PHI= 0.215 XP = 0.0405
184	TEND TO BE THOSE WHERE THE LARGEST NON-COGNATIC KIN GROUP IS SMALLER THAN A PHRATRY, I. E. A SIB OR LINEAGE (175)	0.77 OF 105	184	TEND TO BE THOSE WHERE THE LARGEST NON-COGNATIC KIN GROUP IS THE MOEITY OR PHRATRY (77)	0.52 OF 66	24 34 81 32 XSQ= 13.60 PHI= -0.282 XP = 0.0002
186	LEAN LESS TOWARD BEING THOSE WHERE THE KIN GROUP IS OTHER THAN EXCLUSIVELY PATRILINEAL (250)	0.55 OF 156	186	LEAN MORE TOWARD BEING THOSE WHERE THE KIN GROUP IS OTHER THAN EXCLUSIVELY PATRILINEAL (250)	0.72 OF 104	70 29 86 75 XSQ= 6.93 PHI= 0.163 XP = 0.0085

187	TILT MORE TOWARD BEING THOSE WHERE THE KIN GROUP IS OTHER THAN EXCLUSIVELY MATRILINEAL (344)	0.90 OF 156	187	TILT LESS TOWARD BEING THOSE WHERE THE KIN GROUP IS OTHER THAN EXCLUSIVELY MATRILINEAL (344)	0.79 OF 103	15 22 141 81 XSQ= 6.06 PHI= -0.153 XP = 0.0138
190	TEND MORE TO BE THOSE WHERE THE KIN GROUP IS PATRILINEAL OR DOUBLE-DESCENT, RATHER THAN MATRILINEAL (186)	0.84 OF 103	190	TEND LESS TO BE THOSE WHERE THE KIN GROUP IS PATRILINEAL OR DOUBLE-DESCENT, RATHER THAN MATRILINEAL (186)	0.59 OF 64	87 38 16 26 XSQ= 11.90 PHI= 0.267 XP = 0.0006
197	DRIFT MORE TOWARD BEING THOSE WHERE RULES FOR THE INHERITANCE OF REAL PROPERTY, IF PRESENT, FAVOR EITHER THE MALE HEIR OR LINE, OR THE FEMALE HEIR OR LINE (165)	0.91 OF 80	197	DRIFT LESS TOWARD BEING THOSE WHERE RULES FOR THE INHERITANCE OF REAL PROPERTY, IF PRESENT, FAVOR EITHER THE MALE HEIR OR LINE, OR THE FEMALE HEIR OR LINE (165)	0.78 OF 45	73 35 7 10 XSQ= 3.38 PHI= 0.164 XP = 0.0662
198	TILT MORE TOWARD BEING THOSE WHERE RULES FOR THE INHERITANCE OF REAL PROPERTY, IF PRESENT, FAVOR THE MALE HEIR OR LINE, RATHER THAN THE FEMALE (144)	0.92 OF 73	198	TILT LESS TOWARD BEING THOSE WHERE RULES FOR THE INHERITANCE OF REAL PROPERTY, IF PRESENT, FAVOR THE MALE HEIR OR LINE, RATHER THAN THE FEMALE (144)	0.74 OF 35	67 26 6 9 XSQ= 4.68 PHI= 0.208 XP = 0.0305
209	TILT MORE TOWARD BEING THOSE WHERE MARITAL RESIDENCE IS PATRILOCAL, VIRILOCAL, OR AVUNCULOCAL, RATHER THAN MATRILOCAL OR UXORILOCAL (270)	0.87 OF 134	209	TILT LESS TOWARD BEING THOSE WHERE MARITAL RESIDENCE IS PATRILOCAL, VIRILOCAL, OR AVUNCULOCAL, RATHER THAN MATRILOCAL OR UXORILOCAL (270)	0.72 OF 85	116 61 18 24 XSQ= 6.43 PHI= 0.171 XP = 0.0112
210	TILT MORE TOWARD BEING THOSE WHERE MARITAL RESIDENCE IS PATRILOCAL, RATHER THAN MATRILOCAL (169)	0.90 OF 89	210	TILT LESS TOWARD BEING THOSE WHERE MARITAL RESIDENCE IS PATRILOCAL, RATHER THAN MATRILOCAL (169)	0.72 OF 47	80 34 9 13 XSQ= 5.75 PHI= 0.206 XP = 0.0165
234	TILT TOWARD BEING THOSE WHERE THE COUSIN TERMINOLOGY IS OF ESKIMO OR HAWAIIAN TYPE, RATHER THAN CROW, OMAHA, OR IROQUOIS TYPE (170)	0.58 OF 116	234	TILT TOWARD BEING THOSE WHERE THE COUSIN TERMINOLOGY IS OF CROW, OMAHA, OR IROQUOIS TYPE, RATHER THAN ESKIMO OR HAWAIIAN TYPE (152)	0.57 OF 93	49 53 67 40 XSQ= 3.92 PHI= -0.137 XP = 0.0476
236	DRIFT TOWARD BEING THOSE WHERE THE FAMILY IS OF AN EXTENDED TYPE, RATHER THAN AN INDEPENDENT TYPE (213)	0.58 OF 156	236	DRIFT TOWARD BEING THOSE WHERE THE FAMILY IS OF AN INDEPENDENT TYPE, RATHER THAN AN EXTENDED TYPE (185)	0.54 OF 104	90 48 66 56 XSQ= 2.89 PHI= 0.105 XP = 0.0892
262	LEAN MORE TOWARD BEING THOSE WHERE WIVES ARE OBTAINED BY MEANS INVOLVING THE PRESENCE OF SOME CONSIDERATION (305)	0.86 OF 156	262	LEAN LESS TOWARD BEING THOSE WHERE WIVES ARE OBTAINED BY MEANS INVOLVING THE PRESENCE OF SOME CONSIDERATION (305)	0.69 OF 102	134 70 22 32 XSQ= 10.10 PHI= 0.198 XP = 0.0015

263	LEAN TOWARD BEING THOSE 0.67 OF 156 WHERE WIVES ARE OBTAINED BY RELATIVELY DIFFICULT MEANS, NAMELY BY BRIDE-PRICE, BRIDE-SERVICE, OR EXCHANGING A FEMALE RELATIVE (233)	263	LEAN TOWARD BEING THOSE 0.53 OF 102 WHERE WIVES ARE OBTAINED BY RELATIVELY EASY MEANS, NAMELY BY TOKEN BRIDE-PRICE, GIFT EXCHANGE, ABSENCE OF ANY CONSIDERATION, OR RECEIPT OF DOWRY (162)	104 48 52 54 XSQ= 9.00 PHI= 0.187 XP = 0.0027
285	LEAN TOWARD BEING THOSE 0.80 OF 15 WHERE THE SEX TABOO DURING PREGNANCY IS ABSENT OR INFERRED ABSENT (17) BCA	285	LEAN TOWARD BEING THOSE 0.75 OF 12 WHERE THE SEX TABOO DURING PREGNANCY IS PRESENT (14) BCA	3 9 12 3 XSQ= 6.09 PHI= -0.475 EP = 0.0071
312	DRIFT TOWARD BEING THOSE 0.67 OF 18 WHERE DEPENDENCE SOCIALIZATION ANXIETY IS HIGH (24) W-C	312	DRIFT TOWARD BEING THOSE 0.67 OF 21 WHERE DEPENDENCE SOCIALIZATION ANXIETY IS LOW (23) W-C	12 7 6 14 XSQ= 3.08 PHI= 0.281 EP = 0.0562
313	TILT TOWARD BEING THOSE 0.70 OF 20 WHERE AGGRESSION SOCIALIZATION ANXIETY IS HIGH (26) W-C	313	TILT TOWARD BEING THOSE 0.72 OF 25 WHERE AGGRESSION SOCIALIZATION ANXIETY IS LOW (28) W-C	14 7 6 18 XSQ= 6.28 PHI= 0.374 XP = 0.0122
324	DRIFT TOWARD BEING THOSE 0.67 OF 27 WHERE THE PAIN INFLICTED ON THE INFANT BY THE NURTURANT AGENT IS HIGH (34) B-B-C	324	DRIFT TOWARD BEING THOSE 0.60 OF 30 WHERE THE PAIN INFLICTED ON THE INFANT BY THE NURTURANT AGENT IS LOW OR NEGLIGIBLE (32) B-B-C	18 12 9 18 XSQ= 3.05 PHI= 0.231 XP = 0.0805
331	DRIFT TOWARD BEING THOSE 0.75 OF 12 WHERE THE AGE AT BEGINNING OF INDEPENDENCE TRAINING IS LOWER THAN 3.8 YEARS (21) W-C	331	DRIFT TOWARD BEING THOSE 0.65 OF 17 WHERE THE AGE AT BEGINNING OF INDEPENDENCE TRAINING IS 3.8 YEARS OR HIGHER (16) W-C	3 11 9 6 XSQ= 2.99 PHI= -0.321 EP = 0.0604
377	TEND LESS TO BE THOSE 0.66 OF 155 WHERE MALE GENITAL MUTILATION IS ABSENT (242)	377	TEND MORE TO BE THOSE 0.85 OF 102 WHERE MALE GENITAL MUTILATION IS ABSENT (242)	53 15 102 87 XSQ= 11.03 PHI= 0.207 XP = 0.0009
391	TILT TOWARD BEING THOSE 0.60 OF 89 WHERE PREMARITAL SEX RELATIONS ARE STRONGLY PUNISHED AND IN FACT RARE, OR WEAKLY PUNISHED AND IN FACT NOT RARE (89) JTW,EA	391	TILT TOWARD BEING THOSE 0.58 OF 60 WHERE PREMARITAL SEX RELATIONS ARE PUNISHED ONLY IF PREGNANCY RESULTS, OR FREELY PERMITTED (90) JTW,EA	53 25 36 35 XSQ= 3.91 PHI= 0.162 XP = 0.0481
405	TILT TOWARD BEING THOSE 0.75 OF 24 WHERE EXPLANATIONS OF ILLNESS OF A DEPENDENCE NATURE ARE PRESENT (34) W-C	405	TILT TOWARD BEING THOSE 0.60 OF 25 WHERE EXPLANATIONS OF ILLNESS OF A DEPENDENCE NATURE ARE ABSENT (27) W-C	18 10 6 15 XSQ= 4.78 PHI= 0.312 XP = 0.0288

```
406  TILT TCWARD BEING THOSE          0.67 OF  24     406  TILT TOWARD BEING THOSE          0.68 OF  25          16     8
     WHERE EXPLANATICNS CF ILLNESS                         WHERE EXPLANATIONS CF ILLNESS                              8    17
     CF AN AGGRESSICN NATURE                               OF AN AGGRESSION NATURE                              XSQ=     4.58
     ARE PRESENT  (28) W-C                                 ARE ABSENT  (33) W-C                                 PHI=    0.306
                                                                                                                XP =   0.0323

434  DRIFT TCWARD BEING THCSE         0.59 OF  29     434  DRIFT TOWARD BEING THOSE         0.69 OF  29          12    20
     WHERE ASCETICISM IN MOURNING BEHAVIOR                 WHERE ASCETICISM IN MOURNING BEHAVIOR                     17     9
     IS LCW  (30) JFG                                      IS HIGH  (37) JFG                                    XSQ=     3.42
                                                                                                                PHI=   -0.243
                                                                                                                XP =   0.0646

442  TILT TOWARD BEING THOSE          0.63 OF  24     442  TILT TOWARD BEING THOSE          0.72 OF  25          15     7
     WHERE FEAR OF ANIMAL SPIRITS                          WHERE FEAR OF ANIMAL SPIRITS                               9    18
     IS HIGH  (28) W-C                                     IS LOW  (33) W-C                                     XSQ=     4.58
                                                                                                                PHI=    0.306
                                                                                                                XP =   0.0324

454  DRIFT TCWARD BEING THCSE         0.71 OF  14     454  DRIFT TOWARD BEING THCSE         0.67 OF  15          10     5
     WHERE THE CBJECTIVE OF THE INCIVICUAL'S               WHERE THE OBJECTIVE OF THE INDIVIDUAL'S                    4    10
     CCNTACT WITH THE DIVINE                               CONTACT WITH THE DIVINE                              XSQ=     2.82
     IS CCNDUCIVE TC THE DEVELCPMENT OF THE                IS NOT CONDUCIVE TO THE DEVELOPMENT CF THE           PHI=    0.312
     INDIVIDUAL'S NEED TC ACHIEVE  (18) DCM                INDIVIDUAL'S NEED TC ACHIEVE  (18) DCM               EP =   0.0656

458  TEND LESS TO BE THCSE            0.55 OF  80     458  TEND MORE TO BE THOSE            0.85 CF  74          36    11
     WHERE GAMES, IF PRESENT,                              WHERE GAMES, IF PRESENT,                                  44    63
     DC NCT INCLUDE                                        DO NOT INCLUDE                                       XSQ=    15.07
     GAMES CF STRATEGY  (119) R-A-B,EA                     GAMES OF STRATEGY  (119) R-A-B,EA                    PHI=    0.313
                                                                                                                XP =   0.0001

479  DRIFT TCWARD BEING THCSE         0.64 OF  14     479  DRIFT TOWARD BEING THCSE         0.73 OF  15           9     4
     WHERE THE NEED TC ACHIEVE,                            WHERE THE NEED TO ACHIEVE,                                 5    11
     AS INFERRED FRCM FCLKTALES,                           AS INFERRED FROM FCLKTALES,                          XSQ=     2.76
     IS HIGH  (18) JV                                      IS LOW  (18) JV                                      PHI=    0.309
                                                                                                                EP =   0.0656
```

427 CULTURES
WHERE A HIGH GOD, IF PRESENT, IS
ACTIVE, RATHER THAN
INACTIVE (87) GES,EA

427 CULTURES
WHERE A HIGH GOD, IF PRESENT, IS
INACTIVE, RATHER THAN
ACTIVE (69) GES,EA

BACKGROUND ON PAGE 163

BOTH SUBJECT AND PREDICATE

87 IN LEFT COLUMN

ALBANIANS	AMERICANS	ARAUCANIANS	AYMARA	AZANDE	AZTEC	BAMBARA	BARABRA	BASSERI	BEJA
BEMBA	BHIL	BLACK CARIB	BOERS	BOZO	BRAZILIANS	BULGARIANS	BURUSHO	CHAMACOCO	CHERKESS
CHUKCHEE	CUNA	CZECHS	DAGUR	DELAWARE	DUTCH	EGYPTIANS	FOX	FUTAJALONKE	GOAJIRO
GOND	GROS VENTRE	HASINAI	HAZARA	HEBREWS	HUTSUL	IRISH	JAVANESE	KABYLE	KACHIN
KATAB	KAZAK	KIKUYU	KOHISTANI	KORYAK	KUNG	LAKHER	LANGO	LAPPS	LEPCHA
MACASSARESE	MALAYS	MAM	MBUTI	MIAMI	MISKITO	MZAB	NUER	NUPE	PAPAGO
PATHAN	REGEIBAT	RIFFIANS	RWALA	SAMOYED	SANPOIL	SEMANG	SERBS	SHLUH	SIWANS
SOMALI	SONGHAI	SYRIANS	TALAMANCA	TARAHUMARA	TEDA	TENINO	TIGRINYA	TRISTAN	TURKANA
TURKMEN	VENDA	WALLOONS	WARRAU	WOLOF	YAHGAN	YAKUT			

69 IN RIGHT COLUMN

ALORESE	APINAYE	ASHANTI	BAMILEKE	BARI	BHUIYA	BIRIFOR	CAGABA	CALLINAGO	CAMAYURA
CARIB	CHOCO	CHORTI	CREEK	FANG	GANDA	GARO	GILYAK	GISU	GURE
HURON	ILA	INCA	INGALIK	JIVARO	KAPAUKU	KHASI	KPE	KUBA	LAMBA
LOZI	LUO	MAMVU	MAORI	MATAKAM	MBUNDU	MENDE	MONGO	MOSSI	NANDI
NATCHEZ	NOMLAKI	NYAKYUSA	NYORO	ONA	PARAUJANO	PUKAPUKA	RUNDI	SAMOANS	SANDAWE
SANTAL	SHILLUK	SIRIONO	TANALA	TEHUELCHE	TENDA	TERENA	TESO	THONGA	TIV
TIWI	TUCANO	TUNEBO	TUPINAMBA	UTE	WANTOAT	WITOTO	YORUBA	YUKI	

104 EXCLUDED BECAUSE IRRELEVANT (SEE RIGHT COLUMN, PARAGRAPH 426)

140 EXCLUDED BECAUSE UNASCERTAINED

3	TEND MORE TO BE THOSE LOCATED OUTSIDE OF AFRICA (320)	0.84 OF 87	3	TEND LESS TO BE THOSE LOCATED OUTSIDE OF AFRICA (320)	0.55 OF 69	14 31 73 38 XSQ= 14.22 PHI= -0.302 XP = 0.0002
4	TEND LESS TO BE THOSE LOCATED OUTSIDE OF THE CIRCUM-MEDITERRANEAN (355)	0.64 OF 87	4	IN ALL CASES ARE THOSE LOCATED OUTSIDE OF THE CIRCUM-MEDITERRANEAN (355)	1.00 OF 69	31 0 56 69 XSQ= 28.49 PHI= 0.427 XP = 0.0000

5	TILT LESS TOWARD BEING THOSE 0.78 OF 87 LOCATED OUTSIDE OF EAST EURASIA (330)	5	TILT MORE TOWARD BEING THOSE 0.91 OF 69 LOCATED OUTSIDE OF EAST EURASIA (330)	19 6 68 63 XSQ= 4.01 PHI= 0.160 XP = 0.0452
6	DRIFT MORE TOWARD BEING THOSE 0.98 OF 87 LOCATED OUTSIDE OF THE INSULAR PACIFIC (330)	6	DRIFT LESS TOWARD BEING THOSE 0.90 OF 69 LOCATED OUTSIDE OF THE INSULAR PACIFIC (330)	2 7 85 62 XSQ= 3.03 PHI= -0.139 XP = 0.0815
9	DRIFT MORE TOWARD BEING THOSE 0.87 OF 87 LOCATED OUTSIDE OF SOUTH AMERICA (335)	9	DRIFT LESS TOWARD BEING THOSE 0.74 OF 69 LOCATED OUTSIDE OF SOUTH AMERICA (335)	11 18 76 51 XSQ= 3.75 PHI= -0.155 XP = 0.0528
15	TEND TO BE THOSE 0.66 OF 87 WHERE THE LATITUDE IS TWENTY DEGREES OR GREATER (183)	15	TEND TO BE THOSE 0.74 OF 69 WHERE THE LATITUDE IS LESS THAN TWENTY DEGREES (217)	57 18 30 51 XSQ= 22.41 PHI= 0.379 XP = 0.0000
33	TILT LESS TOWARD BEING THOSE 0.79 OF 87 WHERE THE NATURAL ENVIRONMENT IS OTHER THAN 'VERY HARSH,' I.E., DESERT, DESERT GRASSES AND SHRUBS, TUNDRA, OR HIGH PLATEAU STEPPE (341) FWM	33	TILT MORE TOWARD BEING THOSE 0.93 OF 69 WHERE THE NATURAL ENVIRONMENT IS OTHER THAN 'VERY HARSH,' I.E., DESERT, DESERT GRASSES AND SHRUBS, TUNDRA, OR HIGH PLATEAU STEPPE (341) FWM	18 5 69 64 XSQ= 4.51 PHI= 0.170 XP = 0.0336
36	DRIFT LESS TOWARD BEING THOSE 0.68 OF 87 WHERE THE NATURAL ENVIRONMENT IS OTHER THAN 'VERY HARSH,' OR SUB-TROPICAL BUSH, OR TEMPERATE GRASSLAND (292) FWM	36	DRIFT MORE TOWARD BEING THOSE 0.83 OF 69 WHERE THE NATURAL ENVIRONMENT IS OTHER THAN 'VERY HARSH,' OR SUB-TROPICAL BUSH, OR TEMPERATE GRASSLAND (292) FWM	28 12 59 57 XSQ= 3.67 PHI= 0.153 XP = 0.0552
42	TEND MORE TO BE THOSE 0.85 OF 87 WHERE THE NATURAL ENVIRONMENT IS OTHER THAN TROPICAL OR SUB-TROPICAL RAIN FOREST, OR MONSOON FOREST (244) FWM	42	TEND LESS TO BE THOSE 0.52 OF 69 WHERE THE NATURAL ENVIRONMENT IS OTHER THAN TROPICAL OR SUB-TROPICAL RAIN FOREST, OR MONSOON FOREST (244) FWM	13 33 74 36 XSQ= 18.46 PHI= -0.344 XP = 0.0000
44	TILT LESS TOWARD BEING THOSE 0.62 OF 87 WHERE SETTLEMENTS ARE FIXED (222)	44	TILT MORE TOWARD BEING THOSE 0.78 OF 69 WHERE SETTLEMENTS ARE FIXED (222)	54 54 33 15 XSQ= 4.01 PHI= -0.160 XP = 0.0453
46	DRIFT LESS TOWARD BEING THOSE 0.75 OF 87 OTHER THAN WHERE SETTLEMENTS ARE NON-FIXED AND MOVEMENT IS NOMADIC (260)	46	DRIFT MORE TOWARD BEING THOSE 0.88 OF 69 OTHER THAN WHERE SETTLEMENTS ARE NON-FIXED AND MOVEMENT IS NOMADIC (260)	22 8 65 61 XSQ= 3.81 PHI= 0.156 XP = 0.0511

48	DRIFT TOWARD BEING THOSE 0.78 OF 18 WHERE THE FOOD SUPPLY IS NOT SECURE, AND FOOD SHORTAGES ARE FREQUENT OR ANNUAL (41) MGW	48	DRIFT TOWARD BEING THOSE 0.53 OF 19 WHERE THE FOOD SUPPLY IS SECURE, AND FOOD SHORTAGES ARE RARE OR OCCASIONAL (38) MGW	4 10 14 9 XSQ= 2.46 PHI= -0.258 EP = 0.0911
53	TEND TO BE THOSE 0.63 OF 65 WHERE FOOD PRODUCTION IS BY INTENSIVE AGRICULTURE, RATHER THAN BY SIMPLE AGRICULTURE OR INCIPIENT FOOD PRODUCTION (91)	53	TEND TO BE THOSE 0.81 OF 58 WHERE FOOD PRODUCTION IS BY SIMPLE AGRICULTURE OR INCIPIENT FOOD PRODUCTION, RATHER THAN BY INTENSIVE AGRICULTURE (147)	41 11 24 47 XSQ= 22.67 PHI= 0.429 XP = 0.0000
55	TEND TO BE THOSE 0.76 OF 54 WHERE FOOD PRODUCTION IS BY INTENSIVE AGRICULTURE, RATHER THAN BY SIMPLE AGRICULTURE (91)	55	TEND TO BE THOSE 0.76 OF 46 WHERE FOOD PRODUCTION IS BY SIMPLE AGRICULTURE, RATHER THAN BY INTENSIVE AGRICULTURE (101)	41 11 13 35 XSQ= 24.88 PHI= 0.499 XP = 0.0000
63	LEAN MORE TOWARD BEING THOSE 0.86 OF 70 WHERE HUSBANDRY, IF PRESENT, IS PRINCIPALLY IN THE FORM OF BOVINE, EQUINE, CAMEL-LIKE, OR DEER-LIKE ANIMALS, RATHER THAN PIGS, SHEEP, OR GOATS (152)	63	LEAN LESS TOWARD BEING THOSE 0.60 OF 47 WHERE HUSBANDRY, IF PRESENT, IS PRINCIPALLY IN THE FORM OF BOVINE, EQUINE, CAMEL-LIKE, OR DEER-LIKE ANIMALS, RATHER THAN PIGS, SHEEP, OR GOATS (152)	60 28 10 19 XSQ= 8.95 PHI= 0.277 XP = 0.0028
77	TILT LESS TOWARD BEING THOSE 0.54 OF 13 WHERE THE WRITING SYSTEM IS MNEMONIC OR ABSENT, RATHER THAN BEING ALPHABETIC-OR-PHONETIC (39) JMH	77	IN ALL CASES ARE THOSE 1.00 OF 12 WHERE THE WRITING SYSTEM IS MNEMONIC OR ABSENT, RATHER THAN BEING ALPHABETIC-OR-PHONETIC (39) JMH	6 0 7 12 XSQ= 4.98 PHI= 0.446 EP = 0.0149
81	DRIFT TOWARD BEING THOSE 0.53 OF 64 WHERE A CITY OR TOWN IS PRESENT, OR THE AVERAGE COMMUNITY SIZE IS 200 OR GREATER (89)	81	DRIFT TOWARD BEING THOSE 0.67 OF 43 WHERE NO CITY OR TOWN IS PRESENT, AND THE AVERAGE COMMUNITY SIZE IS SMALLER THAN 200 (135)	34 14 30 29 XSQ= 3.61 PHI= 0.184 XP = 0.0576
86	TILT TOWARD BEING THOSE 0.71 OF 62 WHERE THE LEVEL OF POLITICAL INTEGRATION IS THE LARGE STATE, THE LITTLE STATE, OR THE MINIMAL STATE (148) GPM	86	TILT TOWARD BEING THOSE 0.53 OF 55 WHERE THE LEVEL OF POLITICAL INTEGRATION IS THE AUTONOMOUS COMMUNITY, OR THE FAMILY (156) GPM	44 26 18 29 XSQ= 5.86 PHI= 0.224 XP = 0.0155
88	DRIFT LESS TOWARD BEING THOSE 0.52 OF 54 WHERE, IF A HEADMANSHIP IS PRESENT, SUCCESSION IS HEREDITARY (165)	88	DRIFT MORE TOWARD BEING THOSE 0.71 OF 55 WHERE, IF A HEADMANSHIP IS PRESENT, SUCCESSION IS HEREDITARY (165)	26 16 28 39 XSQ= 3.41 PHI= 0.177 XP = 0.0647
95	DRIFT LESS TOWARD BEING THOSE 0.60 OF 85 WHERE THE HIERARCHY OF NATIONAL JURISDICTION HAS ONE OR NO LEVELS (254) GES,EA	95	DRIFT MORE TOWARD BEING THOSE 0.75 OF 69 WHERE THE HIERARCHY OF NATIONAL JURISDICTION HAS ONE OR NO LEVELS (254) GES,EA	34 17 51 52 XSQ= 3.39 PHI= 0.148 XP = 0.0654

98	DRIFT MORE TOWARD BEING THOSE 0.78 OF 86 WHERE THE HIERARCHY OF LOCAL JURISDICTION HAS FOUR OR THREE LEVELS (238) GES,EA	98	DRIFT LESS TOWARD BEING THOSE 0.64 OF 69 WHERE THE HIERARCHY OF LOCAL JURISDICTION HAS FOUR OR THREE LEVELS (238) GES,EA	67 44 19 25 XSQ= 3.10 PHI= 0.141 XP = 0.0782
102	TILT MORE TOWARD BEING THOSE 0.72 OF 86 WHERE CLASS STRATIFICATION IS PRESENT (203)	102	TILT LESS TOWARD BEING THOSE 0.51 OF 68 WHERE CLASS STRATIFICATION IS PRESENT (203)	62 35 24 33 XSQ= 6.07 PHI= 0.199 XP = 0.0137
109	TILT LESS TOWARD BEING THOSE 0.72 OF 76 WHERE CASTES ARE ABSENT (317)	109	TILT MORE TOWARD BEING THOSE 0.88 OF 66 WHERE CASTES ARE ABSENT (317)	21 8 55 58 XSQ= 4.32 PHI= 0.174 XP = 0.0377
118	TILT TOWARD BEING THOSE 0.75 OF 16 WHERE THE PERCENTAGE OF OCCUPATIONS THAT ARE SPECIALIZED IS HIGH OR MEDIUM (24) WME	118	TILT TOWARD BEING THOSE 0.80 OF 10 WHERE THE PERCENTAGE OF OCCUPATIONS THAT ARE SPECIALIZED IS LOW (25) WME	12 2 4 8 XSQ= 5.44 PHI= 0.457 EP = 0.0138
128	LEAN TOWARD BEING THOSE 0.75 OF 24 WHERE, IF SUBSISTENCE IS PRIMARILY BY AGRICULTURE, THE WORK IS MAINLY DONE BY MALES (40)	128	LEAN TOWARD BEING THOSE 0.77 OF 22 WHERE, IF SUBSISTENCE IS PRIMARILY BY AGRICULTURE, THE WORK IS MAINLY DONE BY FEMALES (37)	18 5 6 17 XSQ= 10.54 PHI= 0.479 XP = 0.0012
141	TILT TOWARD BEING THOSE 0.62 OF 13 WHERE THE LEVEL OF SOCIAL SANCTION IS PUBLIC CORPOREAL SANCTION, RATHER THAN PUBLIC PROPERTY SANCTION OR PRIVATE SETTLEMENT (28) JMH	141	TILT TOWARD BEING THOSE 0.83 OF 12 WHERE THE LEVEL OF SOCIAL SANCTION IS PUBLIC PROPERTY SANCTION OR PRIVATE SETTLEMENT, RATHER THAN PUBLIC CORPOREAL SANCTION (26) JMH	8 2 5 10 XSQ= 3.53 PHI= 0.376 EP = 0.0414
144	TILT TOWARD BEING THOSE 0.80 OF 20 WHERE THE RATIO OF RESTITUTIVE TO REPRESSIVE SANCTIONS IS HIGH OR MEDIUM (27) WME	144	TILT TOWARD BEING THOSE 0.70 OF 10 WHERE THE RATIO OF RESTITUTIVE TO REPRESSIVE SANCTIONS IS LOW (25) WME	16 3 4 7 XSQ= 5.19 PHI= 0.416 EP = 0.0147
176	TILT TOWARD BEING THOSE 0.63 OF 82 WHERE THE COMMUNITY IS OTHER THAN A CLAN-COMMUNITY OR A COMMUNITY STRUCTURED OR SEGMENTED ON A CLAN BASIS (213)	176	TILT TOWARD BEING THOSE 0.57 OF 69 WHERE THE COMMUNITY IS A CLAN-COMMUNITY OR A COMMUNITY STRUCTURED OR SEGMENTED ON A CLAN BASIS (169)	30 39 52 30 XSQ= 5.23 PHI= -0.186 XP = 0.0223
184	DRIFT LESS TOWARD BEING THOSE 0.70 OF 56 WHERE THE LARGEST NON-COGNATIC KIN GROUP IS SMALLER THAN A PHRATRY, I. E. A SIB OR LINEAGE (175)	184	DRIFT MORE TOWARD BEING THOSE 0.86 OF 49 WHERE THE LARGEST NON-COGNATIC KIN GROUP IS SMALLER THAN A PHRATRY, I. E. A SIB OR LINEAGE (175)	17 7 39 42 XSQ= 2.97 PHI= 0.168 XP = 0.0848

186	DRIFT TOWARD BEING THOSE WHERE THE KIN GROUP IS EXCLUSIVELY PATRILINEAL (150)	0.52 OF 87	186	DRIFT TOWARD BEING THOSE WHERE THE KIN GROUP IS OTHER THAN EXCLUSIVELY PATRILINEAL (250)	0.64 OF 69	45 25 42 44 XSQ= 3.13 PHI= 0.142 XP = 0.0767
187	LEAN MORE TOWARD BEING THOSE WHERE THE KIN GROUP IS OTHER THAN EXCLUSIVELY MATRILINEAL (344)	0.97 OF 87	187	LEAN LESS TOWARD BEING THOSE WHERE THE KIN GROUP IS OTHER THAN EXCLUSIVELY MATRILINEAL (344)	0.83 OF 69	3 12 84 57 XSQ= 7.08 PHI= -0.213 XP = 0.0078
190	TILT MORE TOWARD BEING THOSE WHERE THE KIN GROUP IS PATRILINEAL OR DOUBLE-DESCENT, RATHER THAN MATRILINEAL (186)	0.93 OF 56	190	TILT LESS TOWARD BEING THOSE WHERE THE KIN GROUP IS PATRILINEAL OR DOUBLE-DESCENT, RATHER THAN MATRILINEAL (186)	0.74 OF 47	52 35 4 12 XSQ= 5.26 PHI= 0.226 XP = 0.0218
192	DRIFT LESS TOWARD BEING THOSE OTHER THAN WHERE THE ONLY KIN GROUP PRESENT IS A KINDRED OR ELSE BILATERAL DESCENT IS INFERRED (289)	0.68 OF 87	192	DRIFT MORE TOWARD BEING THOSE OTHER THAN WHERE THE ONLY KIN GROUP PRESENT IS A KINDRED OR ELSE BILATERAL DESCENT IS INFERRED (289)	0.81 OF 69	28 13 59 56 XSQ= 2.88 PHI= 0.136 XP = 0.0896
196	TILT MORE TOWARD BEING THOSE WHERE INDIVIDUAL RIGHTS IN REAL PROPERTY, AND RULES FOR INHERITANCE, ARE PRESENT (194)	0.79 OF 67	196	TILT LESS TOWARD BEING THOSE WHERE INDIVIDUAL RIGHTS IN REAL PROPERTY, AND RULES FOR INHERITANCE, ARE PRESENT (194)	0.57 OF 47	53 27 14 20 XSQ= 5.20 PHI= 0.214 XP = 0.0226
210	DRIFT MORE TOWARD BEING THOSE WHERE MARITAL RESIDENCE IS PATRILOCAL, RATHER THAN MATRILOCAL (169)	0.96 OF 51	210	DRIFT LESS TOWARD BEING THOSE WHERE MARITAL RESIDENCE IS PATRILOCAL, RATHER THAN MATRILOCAL (169)	0.82 OF 38	49 31 2 7 XSQ= 3.57 PHI= 0.200 XP = 0.0589
214	TILT MORE TOWARD BEING THOSE WHERE FIRST COUSIN MARRIAGE, IF PERMITTED, IS OTHER THAN UNILATERAL (144)	0.95 OF 39	214	TILT LESS TOWARD BEING THOSE WHERE FIRST COUSIN MARRIAGE, IF PERMITTED, IS OTHER THAN UNILATERAL (144)	0.74 OF 27	2 7 37 20 XSQ= 4.23 PHI= -0.253 XP = 0.0398
234	TILT TOWARD BEING THOSE WHERE THE COUSIN TERMINOLOGY IS OF ESKIMO OR HAWAIIAN TYPE, RATHER THAN CROW, OMAHA, OR IROQUOIS TYPE (170)	0.68 OF 60	234	TILT TOWARD BEING THOSE WHERE THE COUSIN TERMINOLOGY IS OF CROW, OMAHA, OR IROQUOIS TYPE, RATHER THAN ESKIMO OR HAWAIIAN TYPE (152)	0.54 OF 56	19 30 41 26 XSQ= 4.83 PHI= -0.204 XP = 0.0279
240	LEAN TOWARD BEING THOSE WHERE THE FAMILY, IF EXTENDED, IS SMALL OR STEM, RATHER THAN LARGE (135)	0.73 OF 55	240	LEAN TOWARD BEING THOSE WHERE THE FAMILY, IF EXTENDED, IS LARGE, RATHER THAN SMALL OR STEM (78)	0.57 OF 35	15 20 40 15 XSQ= 6.82 PHI= -0.275 XP = 0.0090

300	DRIFT TCWARD BEING THCSE 0.74 OF 31 WHERE THE POST-PARTUM SEX TABCO LASTS SIX MCNTHS CR LESS (73)	300	DRIFT TOWARD BEING THOSE 0.52 OF 33 WHERE THE POST-PARTUM SEX TABCO LASTS LONGER THAN SIX MONTHS (51)	8 17 23 16 XSQ= 3.42 PHI= -0.231 XP = 0.0643
316	TILT TCWARD BEING THCSE 0.82 OF 11 WHERE EXCLUSIVE MOTHER-SON SLEEPING ARRANGEMENTS LAST LESS THAN CNE YEAR (25) W-K-A	316	TILT TOWARD BEING THOSE 0.71 CF 14 WHERE EXCLUSIVE MOTHER-SON SLEEPING ARRANGEMENTS LAST CNE YEAR OR LONGER (19) W-K-A	2 10 9 4 XSQ= 5.03 PHI= -0.448 EP = 0.0154
326	DRIFT TCWARD BEING THCSE 0.79 OF 14 WHERE THE INFERRED TRANSITION ANXIETY BETWEEN INFANCY ANC CHILCHCOC IS LCW (35) B-B-C	326	DRIFT TOWARD BEING THOSE 0.56 OF 16 WHERE THE INFERRED TRANSITICN ANXIETY BETWEEN INFANCY AND CHILDHCCD IS HIGH (32) B-B-C	3 9 11 7 XSQ= 2.46 PHI= -0.286 EP = 0.0717
331	TILT TCWARD BEING THCSE 0.60 OF 5 WHERE THE AGE AT BEGINNINC CF INDEPENDENCE TRAINING IS 3.8 YEARS CR HIGHER (16) W-C	331	IN ALL CASES ARE THOSE 1.00 CF 7 WHERE THE AGE AT BEGINNING OF INDEPENDENCE TRAINING IS LOWER THAN 3.8 YEARS (21) W-C	3 0 2 7 XSQ= 2.86 PHI= 0.488 EP = 0.0455
336	TILT TCWARC REING THOSE 0.79 OF 14 WHERE THE TOTAL POSITIVE PRESSURE TOWARD DEVELCPING RESPCNSIBLE BEHAVIOR IN THE CHILD IS HIGH (43) B-B-C	336	TILT TOWARD BEING THOSE 0.61 CF 18 WHERE THE TOTAL POSITIVE PRESSURE TOWARC DEVELOPING RESPONSIBLE BEHAVIOR IN THE CHILD IS LOW (32) B-B-C	11 7 3 11 XSQ= 3.56 PHI= 0.333 EP = 0.0356
342	DRIFT TCWARD BEING THCSE 0.86 OF 7 WHERE THE CHILD'S INFERREC ANXIETY OVER PERFCRMANCE CF NURTURANT BEHAVIOR IS LCW (28) B-B-C	342	DRIFT TOWARD BEING THOSE 0.64 CF 11 WHERE THE CHILD'S INFERRED ANXIETY OVER PERFORMANCE OF NURTURANT BEHAVICR IS HIGH (18) B-B-C	1 7 6 4 XSQ= 2.46 PHI= -0.369 EP = 0.0656
370	LEAN TOWARD BEING THOSE 0.75 OF 65 WHERE THE SEGREGATICN CF ACOLESCENT BOYS IS ABSENT (148)	37C	LEAN TOWARD BEING THOSE 0.50 OF 52 WHERE THE SEGREGATION CF ADCLESCENT BOYS IS COMPLETE CR PARTIAL (95)	16 26 49 26 XSQ= 7.02 PHI= -0.245 XP = 0.0080
377	DRIFT LESS TCWARC BEING THCSE 0.59 OF 86 WHERE MALE GENITAL MUTILATION IS ABSENT (242)	377	DRIFT MORE TOWARD BEING THCSE 0.74 CF 69 WHERE MALE GENITAL MUTILATICN IS ABSENT (242)	35 18 51 51 XSQ= 3.01 PHI= 0.139 XP = 0.0827
382	TILT TOWARC BEING THOSE 0.67 OF 21 WHERE FEMALE INITIATICN RITES ARE ABSENT (27) JKB	382	TILT TOWARD BEING THOSE 0.79 OF 14 WHERE FEMALE INITIATION RITES ARE PRESENT (38) JKB	7 11 14 3 XSQ= 5.19 PHI= -0.385 EP = 0.0153

390	DRIFT LESS TOWARD BEING THOSE WHERE PREMARITAL SEX RELATIONS ARE WEAKLY PUNISHED AND IN FACT NOT RARE OR PUNISHED ONLY IF PREGNANCY RESULTS, OR FREELY PERMITTED (132) JTW,EA	0.62 OF 50	390	DRIFT MORE TOWARD BEING THOSE WHERE PREMARITAL SEX RELATIONS ARE WEAKLY PUNISHED AND IN FACT NOT RARE OR PUNISHED ONLY IF PREGNANCY RESULTS, OR FREELY PERMITTED (132) JTW,EA	0.82 OF 39	19 7 31 32 XSQ= 3.35 PHI= 0.194 XP = 0.0674
392	TILT MORE TOWARD BEING THOSE WHERE PREMARITAL SEX RELATIONS ARE STRONGLY PUNISHED AND IN FACT RARE, OR WEAKLY PUNISHED AND IN FACT NOT RARE, OR PUNISHED ONLY IF PREGNANCY RESULTS (112) JTW,EA	0.84 OF 50	392	TILT LESS TOWARD BEING THOSE WHERE PREMARITAL SEX RELATIONS ARE STRONGLY PUNISHED AND IN FACT RARE, OR WEAKLY PUNISHED AND IN FACT NOT RARE, OR PUNISHED ONLY IF PREGNANCY RESULTS (112) JTW,EA	0.59 OF 39	42 23 8 16 XSQ= 5.75 PHI= 0.254 XP = 0.0164
402	TILT TOWARD BEING THOSE WHERE EXPLANATIONS OF ILLNESS OF AN ORAL NATURE ARE ABSENT (30) W-C	0.75 OF 12	402	TILT TOWARD BEING THOSE WHERE EXPLANATIONS OF ILLNESS OF AN ORAL NATURE ARE PRESENT (31) W-C	0.75 OF 12	3 9 9 3 XSQ= 4.17 PHI= -0.417 EP = 0.0391
436	DRIFT TOWARD BEING THOSE WHERE ACTIVE ANCESTRAL SPIRITS ARE ABSENT (11) GES	0.50 OF 10	436	IN ALL CASES ARE THOSE WHERE ACTIVE ANCESTRAL SPIRITS ARE PRESENT (27) GES	1.00 OF 6	5 6 5 0 XSQ= 2.35 PHI= -0.383 EP = 0.0934
442	DRIFT TOWARD BEING THOSE WHERE FEAR OF ANIMAL SPIRITS IS HIGH (28) W-C	0.83 OF 12	442	DRIFT TOWARD BEING THOSE WHERE FEAR OF ANIMAL SPIRITS IS LOW (33) W-C	0.58 OF 12	10 5 2 7 XSQ= 2.84 PHI= 0.344 EP = 0.0894
444	DRIFT TOWARD BEING THOSE WHERE THE USE OF DREAMS TO SEEK AND CONTROL SUPERNATURAL POWERS IS HIGH (28) RGD	0.69 OF 16	444	DRIFT TOWARD BEING THOSE WHERE THE USE OF DREAMS TO SEEK AND CONTROL SUPERNATURAL POWERS IS LOW (27) RGD	0.67 OF 15	11 5 5 10 XSQ= 2.60 PHI= 0.290 EP = 0.0756
446	TILT TOWARD BEING THOSE WHERE WITCHCRAFT IS MODERATELY PRESENT OR ABSENT (24) GES	0.80 OF 10	446	TILT TOWARD BEING THOSE WHERE WITCHCRAFT IS SIGNIFICANTLY PRESENT (14) GES	0.83 OF 6	2 5 8 1 XSQ= 3.81 PHI= -0.488 EP = 0.0350
450	TILT TOWARD BEING THOSE WHERE THE OBSERVATION OF FOOD TABOOS IS LOW, RATHER THAN HIGH OR MEDIUM (26) JRL	0.50 OF 28	450	TILT TOWARD BEING THOSE WHERE THE OBSERVATION OF FOOD TABOOS IS HIGH OR MEDIUM, RATHER THAN LOW (60) JRL	0.82 OF 22	14 18 14 4 XSQ= 4.12 PHI= -0.287 XP = 0.0424
459	TILT TOWARD BEING THOSE WHERE GAMES, IF PRESENT, INCLUDE GAMES OF CHANCE (82) R-A-B,EA	0.57 OF 42	459	TILT TOWARD BEING THOSE WHERE GAMES, IF PRESENT, DO NOT INCLUDE GAMES OF CHANCE (89) R-A-B,EA	0.71 OF 38	24 11 18 27 XSQ= 5.35 PHI= 0.259 XP = 0.0207

471	IN ALL CASES ARE THOSE WHERE SECRET SOCIETIES ARE UNIMPCRTANT CR ABSENT (14) LWS	1.00 OF 6	471	IN ALL CASES ARE THOSE WHERE SECRET SOCIETIES ARE PRESENT (9) LWS	1.00 OF 2	0 2 6 0 XSQ= 3.56 PHI= -0.667 EP = 0.0357
474	DRIFT TCWARD BEING THCSE WHERE BCASTFULNESS IS MCDERATE, NEGLIBIBLE, CR UNREPCRTEC (48) PES	0.63 OF 30	474	DRIFT TOWARD BEING THCSE WHERE BOASTFULNESS IS EXTREME	0.71 CF 14 (41) PES	11 10 19 4 XSQ= 3.34 PHI= -0.275 XP = 0.0678

428 CULTURES
WHERE A HIGH GOD, IF PRESENT AND ACTIVE,
SUPPORTS HUMAN MORALITY, RATHER THAN
NOT SUPPORTING IT (61) GES,EA

428 CULTURES
WHERE A HIGH GOD, IF PRESENT AND ACTIVE,
DOES NOT SUPPORT HUMAN MORALITY,
RATHER THAN SUPPORTING IT (26) GES,EA

BACKGROUND ON PAGE 163

BOTH SUBJECT AND PREDICATE

61 IN LEFT COLUMN

ALBANIANS	AMERICANS	AYMARA	BARABRA	BASSERI	BEJA	BLACK CARIB	BOERS	BOZO	BRAZILIANS
BULGARIANS	BURUSHO	CHERKESS	CUNA	CZECHS	DAGUR	DUTCH	EGYPTIANS	FOX	FUTAJALONKE
GROS VENTRE	HASINAI	HAZARA	HEBREWS	HUTSUL	IRISH	JAVANESE	KABYLE	KAZAK	KOHISTANI
LAKHER	LAPPS	MACASSARESE	MALAYS	MAM	MBUTI	MISKITO	MZAB	NUER	NUPE
PAPAGO	PATHAN	REGEIBAT	RIFFIANS	RWALA	SERBS	SHLUH	SIWANS	SOMALI	SONGHAI
SYRIANS	TARAHUMARA	TEDA	TENINO	TIGRINYA	TRISTAN	TURKMEN	WALLOONS	WARRAU	WOLOF
YAHGAN									

26 IN RIGHT COLUMN

ARAUCANIANS	AZANDE	AZTEC	BAMBARA	BEMBA	BHIL	CHAMACOCO	CHUKCHEE	DELAWARE	GOAJIRO
GOND	KACHIN	KATAB	KIKUYU	KORYAK	KUNG	LANGO	LEPCHA	MIAMI	SAMOYED
SANPOIL	SEMANG	TALAMANCA	TURKANA	VENDA	YAKUT				

173 EXCLUDED BECAUSE IRRELEVANT

ABIPON	ABOR	AINU	ALACALUF	ALORESE	AMBA	ANDAMANESE	APINAYE	ARANDA	ARAPESH
ASHANTI	ATAYAL	ATSUGEWI	AWEIKOMA	BACAIRI	BAMILEKE	BARI	BHUIYA	BIRIFOR	BORORO
BUNLAP	CAGABA	CALLINAGO	CAMAYURA	CARIB	CAYAPA	CHAGGA	CHENCHU	CHEYENNE	CHIR-APACHE
CHOCO	CHOROTI	CHORTI	COCHITI	COORG	COPR ESKIMO	CREE	CREEK	CROW	DARD
DIEGUENO	DIERI	DOROBO	EYAK	FANG	FON	GANDA	GARO	GILYAK	GISU
GURE	HAIDA	HAWAIIANS	HUKUNDIKA	HURON	IBAN	IFUGAO	ILA	INCA	INGALIK
JIVARO	KAPAUKU	KASKA	KERAKI	KHASI	KOREANS	KPE	KUBA	KURTATCHI	KUTENAI
LAMBA	LAU	LESU	LHOTA NAGA	LOLO	LOZI	LUO	MAMVU	MANGAIANS	MANIHIKI
MANUS	MACRI	MARICOPA	MARQUESANS	MARSHALLESE	MATACO	MATAKAM	MBUNDU	MENDE	MNONG GAR
MONGO	MOSSI	MOTA	MUNDURUCU	MURINBATA	MURNGIN	NABESNA	NAMA	NAMBICUARA	NANDI
NATCHEZ	NAVAHO	NOMLAKI	NUNIVAK	NYAKYUSA	NYORO	OKINAWANS	OMAHA	ONA	ONTONG-JAVA
PAIWAN	PALAUANS	PARAUJANO	PONAPEANS	PUKAPUKA	PURUM	ROMANS	RUNDI	SAGADA	SAMOANS
SANDAWE	SANTAL	SHERENTE	SHILLUK	SIRIONO	SIUAI	SOTHO	SWAZI	TALLENSI	TANALA
TAPIRAPE	TAREUMIUT	TEHUELCHE	TENDA	TENETEHARA	TERENA	TESO	THAI	THONGA	TIKOPIA
TIMBIRA	TIMUCUA	TIV	TIWI	TODA	TOLOWA	TROBRIAND	TRUKESE	TRUMAI	TSHIMSHIAN
TUBATULABAL	TUCANO	TUCUNA	TUNEBO	TUPINAMBA	TWANA	ULAWANS	UTE	VEDDA	WANTOAT
WASHO	WITOTO	WOGEO	WOLEAIANS	YABARANA	YAGUA	YAKO	YAO	YOKUTS	YORUBA
YUKI	YUROK	ZUNI							

140 EXCLUDED BECAUSE UNASCERTAINED

3	LEAN MORE TOWARD BEING THOSE 0.92 OF 61 LOCATED OUTSIDE OF AFRICA (320)	3	LEAN LESS TOWARD BEING THOSE 0.65 OF 26 LOCATED OUTSIDE OF AFRICA (320)	5 9 56 17 XSQ= 7.57 PHI= -0.295 XP = 0.0059
4	TEND TO BE THOSE 0.51 OF 61 LOCATED IN THE CIRCUM-MEDITERRANEAN (45)	4	IN ALL CASES ARE THOSE 1.00 OF 26 LOCATED OUTSIDE OF THE CIRCUM-MEDITERRANEAN (355)	31 0 30 26 XSQ= 18.37 PHI= 0.460 XP = 0.0000
14	DRIFT TOWARD BEING THOSE 0.54 OF 61 WHERE THE LATITUDE IS THIRTY DEGREES OR GREATER (119)	14	DRIFT TOWARD BEING THOSE 0.69 OF 26 WHERE THE LATITUDE IS LESS THAN THIRTY DEGREES (281)	33 8 28 18 XSQ= 3.10 PHI= 0.189 XP = 0.0783
51	TILT MORE TOWARD BEING THOSE 0.82 OF 61 WHERE SUBSISTENCE IS PRIMARILY BY FOOD PRODUCTION -- I. E., AGRICULTURE OR HUSBANDRY -- RATHER THAN BY GATHERING (253)	51	TILT LESS TOWARD BEING THOSE 0.54 OF 26 WHERE SUBSISTENCE IS PRIMARILY BY FOOD PRODUCTION -- I. E., AGRICULTURE OR HUSBANDRY -- RATHER THAN BY GATHERING (253)	50 14 11 12 XSQ= 6.04 PHI= 0.263 XP = 0.0140
53	LEAN TOWARD BEING THOSE 0.76 OF 45 WHERE FOOD PRODUCTION IS BY INTENSIVE AGRICULTURE, RATHER THAN BY SIMPLE AGRICULTURE OR INCIPIENT FOOD PRODUCTION (91)	53	LEAN TOWARD BEING THOSE 0.65 OF 20 WHERE FOOD PRODUCTION IS BY SIMPLE AGRICULTURE OR INCIPIENT FOOD PRODUCTION, RATHER THAN BY INTENSIVE AGRICULTURE (147)	34 7 11 13 XSQ= 8.11 PHI= 0.353 XP = 0.0044
55	DRIFT MORE TOWARD BEING THOSE 0.83 OF 41 WHERE FOOD PRODUCTION IS BY INTENSIVE AGRICULTURE, RATHER THAN BY SIMPLE AGRICULTURE (91)	55	DRIFT LESS TOWARD BEING THOSE 0.54 OF 13 WHERE FOOD PRODUCTION IS BY INTENSIVE AGRICULTURE, RATHER THAN BY SIMPLE AGRICULTURE (91)	34 7 7 6 XSQ= 3.11 PHI= 0.240 XP = 0.0776
63	TILT MORE TOWARD BEING THOSE 0.92 OF 52 WHERE HUSBANDRY, IF PRESENT, IS PRINCIPALLY IN THE FORM OF BOVINE, EQUINE, CAMEL-LIKE, OR DEER-LIKE ANIMALS, RATHER THAN PIGS, SHEEP, OR GOATS (152)	63	TILT LESS TOWARD BEING THOSE 0.67 OF 18 WHERE HUSBANDRY, IF PRESENT, IS PRINCIPALLY IN THE FORM OF BOVINE, EQUINE, CAMEL-LIKE, OR DEER-LIKE ANIMALS, RATHER THAN PIGS, SHEEP, OR GOATS (152)	48 12 4 6 XSQ= 5.24 PHI= 0.274 XP = 0.0221
73	TILT TOWARD BEING THOSE 0.74 OF 39 WHERE WEAVING IS PRESENT (118)	73	TILT TOWARD BEING THOSE 0.55 OF 22 WHERE WEAVING IS ABSENT (130)	29 10 10 12 XSQ= 3.92 PHI= 0.253 XP = 0.0477
81	TILT TOWARD BEING THOSE 0.66 OF 41 WHERE A CITY OR TOWN IS PRESENT, OR THE AVERAGE COMMUNITY SIZE IS 200 OR GREATER (89)	81	TILT TOWARD BEING THOSE 0.70 OF 23 WHERE NO CITY OR TOWN IS PRESENT, AND THE AVERAGE COMMUNITY SIZE IS SMALLER THAN 200 (135)	27 7 14 16 XSQ= 6.07 PHI= 0.308 XP = 0.0138

85	TILT TOWARD BEING THOSE 0.50 OF 42 WHERE THE LEVEL OF POLITICAL INTEGRATION IS THE LARGE STATE, OR THE LITTLE STATE (70) GPM	85	TILT TOWARD BEING THOSE 0.80 OF 20 WHERE THE LEVEL OF POLITICAL INTEGRATION IS THE MINIMAL STATE, THE AUTONOMOUS COMMUNITY, OR THE FAMILY (234) GPM	21 4 21 16 XSQ= 3.90 PHI= 0.251 XP = 0.0484
86	LEAN TOWARD BEING THOSE 0.83 OF 42 WHERE THE LEVEL OF POLITICAL INTEGRATION IS THE LARGE STATE, THE LITTLE STATE, OR THE MINIMAL STATE (148) GPM	86	LEAN TOWARD BEING THOSE 0.55 OF 20 WHERE THE LEVEL OF POLITICAL INTEGRATION IS THE AUTONOMOUS COMMUNITY, OR THE FAMILY (156) GPM	35 9 7 11 XSQ= 7.89 PHI= 0.357 XP = 0.0050
88	LEAN TOWARD BEING THOSE 0.67 OF 33 WHERE, IF A HEADMANSHIP IS PRESENT, SUCCESSION IS NON-HEREDITARY (106)	88	LEAN TOWARD BEING THOSE 0.81 OF 21 WHERE, IF A HEADMANSHIP IS PRESENT, SUCCESSION IS HEREDITARY (165)	22 4 11 17 XSQ= 9.83 PHI= 0.427 XP = 0.0017
94	LEAN LESS TOWARD BEING THOSE 0.73 OF 59 WHERE THE HIERARCHY OF NATIONAL JURISDICTION HAS TWO, ONE, OR NO LEVELS (296) GES,EA	94	IN ALL CASES ARE THOSE 1.00 OF 26 WHERE THE HIERARCHY OF NATIONAL JURISDICTION HAS TWO, ONE, OR NO LEVELS (296) GES,EA	16 0 43 26 XSQ= 7.00 PHI= 0.287 XP = 0.0081
96	LEAN TOWARD BEING THOSE 0.76 OF 59 WHERE THE HIERARCHY OF NATIONAL JURISDICTION HAS FOUR, THREE, TWO OR ONE LEVEL (174) GES,EA	96	LEAN TOWARD BEING THOSE 0.58 OF 26 WHERE THE HIERARCHY OF NATIONAL JURISDICTION HAS NO LEVELS (156) GES,EA	45 11 14 15 XSQ= 7.81 PHI= 0.303 XP = 0.0052
107	TILT LESS TOWARD BEING THOSE 0.59 OF 44 WHERE CLASS STRATIFICATION, IF PRESENT, IS BASED ON SOMETHING OTHER THAN OCCUPATIONAL STATUS (160)	107	TILT MORE TOWARD BEING THOSE 0.89 OF 18 WHERE CLASS STRATIFICATION, IF PRESENT, IS BASED ON SOMETHING OTHER THAN OCCUPATIONAL STATUS (160)	18 2 26 16 XSQ= 3.92 PHI= 0.251 XP = 0.0478
109	TILT LESS TOWARD BEING THOSE 0.63 OF 52 WHERE CASTES ARE ABSENT (317)	109	TILT MORE TOWARD BEING THOSE 0.92 OF 24 WHERE CASTES ARE ABSENT (317)	19 2 33 22 XSQ= 5.20 PHI= 0.262 XP = 0.0226
181	DRIFT LESS TOWARD BEING THOSE 0.84 OF 58 WHERE THE COMMUNITY IS OTHER THAN A DEME (337)	181	IN ALL CASES ARE THOSE 1.00 OF 24 WHERE THE COMMUNITY IS OTHER THAN A DEME (337)	9 0 49 24 XSQ= 2.75 PHI= 0.183 XP = 0.0975
187	IN ALL CASES ARE THOSE 1.00 OF 61 WHERE THE KIN GROUP IS OTHER THAN EXCLUSIVELY MATRILINEAL (344)	187	TILT LESS TOWARD BEING THOSE 0.88 OF 26 WHERE THE KIN GROUP IS OTHER THAN EXCLUSIVELY MATRILINEAL (344)	0 3 61 23 XSQ= 4.24 PHI= -0.221 XP = 0.0396

190	IN ALL CASES ARE THOSE WHERE THE KIN GROUP IS PATRILINEAL OR DOUBLE-DESCENT, RATHER THAN MATRILINEAL (186)	1.00 OF 37	190	TILT LESS TOWARD BEING THOSE WHERE THE KIN GROUP IS PATRILINEAL OR DOUBLE-DESCENT, RATHER THAN MATRILINEAL (186)	0.79 OF 19	37 15 0 4 XSQ= 5.51 PHI= 0.314 XP = 0.0189
198	IN ALL CASES ARE THOSE WHERE RULES FOR THE INHERITANCE OF REAL PROPERTY, IF PRESENT, FAVOR THE MALE HEIR OR LINE, RATHER THAN THE FEMALE (144)	1.00 OF 32	198	TILT LESS TOWARD BEING THOSE WHERE RULES FOR THE INHERITANCE OF REAL PROPERTY, IF PRESENT, FAVOR THE MALE HEIR OR LINE, RATHER THAN THE FEMALE (144)	0.80 OF 15	32 12 0 3 XSQ= 3.90 PHI= 0.288 XP = 0.0483
214	IN ALL CASES ARE THOSE WHERE FIRST COUSIN MARRIAGE, IF PERMITTED, IS OTHER THAN UNILATERAL (144)	1.00 OF 29	214	DRIFT LESS TOWARD BEING THOSE WHERE FIRST COUSIN MARRIAGE, IF PERMITTED, IS OTHER THAN UNILATERAL (144)	0.80 OF 10	0 2 29 8 XSQ= 2.69 PHI= -0.263 EP = 0.0607
225	LEAN TOWARD BEING THOSE WHERE COUSIN MARRIAGE IS PREFERENTIALLY OR PERMISSIVELY PATRILATERAL, RATHER THAN MATRILATERAL (23)	0.75 OF 12	225	IN ALL CASES ARE THOSE WHERE COUSIN MARRIAGE IS PREFERENTIALLY OR PERMISSIVELY MATRILATERAL, RATHER THAN PATRILATERAL (43)	1.00 OF 5	9 0 3 5 XSQ= 5.24 PHI= 0.555 EP = 0.0090
234	DRIFT TOWARD BEING THOSE WHERE THE COUSIN TERMINOLOGY IS OF ESKIMO OR HAWAIIAN TYPE, RATHER THAN CROW, OMAHA, OR IROQUOIS TYPE (170)	0.77 OF 40	234	DRIFT TOWARD BEING THOSE WHERE THE COUSIN TERMINOLOGY IS OF CROW, OMAHA, OR IROQUOIS TYPE, RATHER THAN ESKIMO OR HAWAIIAN TYPE (152)	0.50 OF 20	9 10 31 10 XSQ= 3.48 PHI= -0.241 XP = 0.0623
242	TILT LESS TOWARD BEING THOSE WHERE MARRIAGE IS COMMONLY OR OCCASIONALLY POLYGYNOUS, RATHER THAN MONOGAMOUS (314)	0.70 OF 61	242	TILT MORE TOWARD BEING THOSE WHERE MARRIAGE IS COMMONLY OR OCCASIONALLY POLYGYNOUS, RATHER THAN MONOGAMOUS (314)	0.96 OF 26	43 25 18 1 XSQ= 5.61 PHI= -0.254 XP = 0.0179
278	IN ALL CASES ARE THOSE WHERE PROPERTY RIGHTS IN WOMEN ARE PRESENT (8) LWS	1.00 OF 4	278	DRIFT TOWARD BEING THOSE WHERE PROPERTY RIGHTS IN WOMEN ARE UNIMPORTANT OR ABSENT (14) LWS	0.71 OF 7	4 2 0 5 XSQ= 2.75 PHI= 0.500 EP = 0.0606
339	DRIFT TOWARD BEING THOSE WHERE THE CHILD'S INFERRED CONFLICT REGARDING RESPONSIBLE BEHAVIOR IS LOW (42) B-B-C	0.80 OF 5	339	DRIFT TOWARD BEING THOSE WHERE THE CHILD'S INFERRED CONFLICT REGARDING RESPONSIBLE BEHAVIOR IS HIGH (31) B-B-C	0.78 OF 9	1 7 4 2 XSQ= 2.34 PHI= -0.409 EP = 0.0909
343	IN ALL CASES ARE THOSE WHERE THE CHILD'S INFERRED CONFLICT REGARDING NURTURANT BEHAVIOR IS HIGH (29) B-B-C	1.00 OF 4	343	IN ALL CASES ARE THOSE WHERE THE CHILD'S INFERRED CONFLICT REGARDING NURTURANT BEHAVIOR IS LOW (18) B-B-C	1.00 OF 3	4 0 0 3 XSQ= 3.51 PHI= 0.708 EP = 0.0286

346	DRIFT TOWARD BEING THOSE WHERE THE CHILD'S INFERRED ANXIETY OVER PERFORMANCE OF SELF-RELIANT BEHAVIOR IS LOW (39) B-B-C	0.80 OF 5	346	DRIFT TOWARD BEING THOSE WHERE THE CHILD'S INFERRED ANXIETY OVER PERFORMANCE OF SELF-RELIANT BEHAVIOR IS HIGH (37) B-B-C	0.78 OF 9	1 7 4 2 XSQ= 2.34 PHI= -0.409 EP = 0.0909
377	TEND TO BE THOSE WHERE MALE GENITAL MUTILATION IS PRESENT (83)	0.53 OF 60	377	TEND TO BE THOSE WHERE MALE GENITAL MUTILATION IS ABSENT (242)	0.88 OF 26	32 3 28 23 XSQ= 11.45 PHI= 0.365 XP = 0.0007
390	TILT TOWARD BEING THOSE WHERE PREMARITAL SEX RELATIONS ARE STRONGLY PUNISHED AND IN FACT RARE (47) JTW,EA	0.52 OF 33	390	TILT TOWARD BEING THOSE WHERE PREMARITAL SEX RELATIONS ARE WEAKLY PUNISHED AND IN FACT NOT RARE OR PUNISHED ONLY IF PREGNANCY RESULTS, OR FREELY PERMITTED (132) JTW,EA	0.88 OF 17	17 2 16 15 XSQ= 5.93 PHI= 0.344 XP = 0.0149
391	LEAN TOWARD BEING THOSE WHERE PREMARITAL SEX RELATIONS ARE STRONGLY PUNISHED AND IN FACT RARE, OR WEAKLY PUNISHED AND IN FACT NOT RARE (89) JTW,EA	0.82 OF 33	391	LEAN TOWARD BEING THOSE WHERE PREMARITAL SEX RELATIONS ARE PUNISHED ONLY IF PREGNANCY RESULTS, OR FREELY PERMITTED (90) JTW,EA	0.59 OF 17	27 7 6 10 XSQ= 6.75 PHI= 0.367 XP = 0.0094
450	LEAN TOWARD BEING THOSE WHERE THE OBSERVATION OF FOOD TABOOS IS LOW, RATHER THAN HIGH OR MEDIUM (26) JRL	0.75 OF 16	450	LEAN TOWARD BEING THOSE WHERE THE OBSERVATION OF FOOD TABOOS IS HIGH OR MEDIUM, RATHER THAN LOW (60) JRL	0.83 OF 12	4 10 12 2 XSQ= 7.15 PHI= -0.505 EP = 0.0063

429 CULTURES
WHERE SUPERNATURAL SANCTIONS FOR MORALITY
ARE PRESENT (28) GES

429 CULTURES
WHERE SUPERNATURAL SANCTIONS FOR MORALITY
ARE ABSENT OR UNREPORTED (9) GES

BACKGROUND ON PAGE 164

BOTH SUBJECT AND PREDICATE

28 IN LEFT COLUMN

ARAPESH	AYMARA	AZANDE	AZTEC	COPR ESKIMO	CUNA	DOBUANS	GANDA	HEBREWS	IBAN
IFUGAO	KAREN	KASKA	LEPCHA	MARQUESANS	MIAO	NAMA	NANDI	NUER	NYAKYUSA
ROMANS	SAMOYED	TALLENSI	TANALA	TIV	WINNEBAGO	YAHGAN	ZUNI		

9 IN RIGHT COLUMN

ARANDA	BEMBA	LOZI	TIMBIRA	TRUMAI	WOLEAIANS	YAGUA	YOKUTS	YUROK

363 EXCLUDED BECAUSE UNASCERTAINED

45	DRIFT TOWARD BEING THOSE WHERE SETTLEMENTS, IF FIXED, ARE NON-COMPACT, RATHER THAN COMPACT (73)	0.53 OF 19	45	IN ALL CASES ARE THOSE WHERE SETTLEMENTS, IF FIXED, ARE COMPACT, RATHER THAN NON-COMPACT (149)	1.00 OF 5	9 5 10 0 XSQ= 2.61 PHI= -0.330 EP = 0.0530
51	LEAN TOWARD BEING THOSE WHERE SUBSISTENCE IS PRIMARILY BY FOOD PRODUCTION -- I. E., AGRICULTURE OR HUSBANDRY -- RATHER THAN BY GATHERING (253)	0.79 OF 28	51	LEAN TOWARD BEING THOSE WHERE SUBSISTENCE IS PRIMARILY BY FOOD GATHERING -- I. E., HUNTING, FISHING, OR COLLECTING -- RATHER THAN FOOD PRODUCTION (147)	0.78 OF 9	22 2 6 7 XSQ= 7.18 PHI= 0.440 EP = 0.0041
53	TILT TOWARD BEING THOSE WHERE FOOD PRODUCTION IS BY INTENSIVE AGRICULTURE, RATHER THAN BY SIMPLE AGRICULTURE OR INCIPIENT FOOD PRODUCTION (91)	0.59 OF 22	53	IN ALL CASES ARE THOSE WHERE FOOD PRODUCTION IS BY SIMPLE AGRICULTURE OR INCIPIENT FOOD PRODUCTION, RATHER THAN BY INTENSIVE AGRICULTURE (147)	1.00 OF 5	13 0 9 5 XSQ= 3.58 PHI= 0.364 EP = 0.0407
54	DRIFT TOWARD BEING THOSE WHERE FOOD PRODUCTION IS BY INTENSIVE OR SIMPLE AGRICULTURE, RATHER THAN BY INCIPIENT FOOD PRODUCTION (192)	0.86 OF 22	54	DRIFT TOWARD BEING THOSE WHERE FOOD PRODUCTION IS BY INCIPIENT FOOD PRODUCTION, RATHER THAN BY INTENSIVE OR SIMPLE AGRICULTURE (46)	0.60 OF 5	19 2 3 3 XSQ= 2.74 PHI= 0.319 EP = 0.0560
81	DRIFT LESS TOWARD BEING THOSE WHERE NO CITY OR TOWN IS PRESENT, AND THE AVERAGE COMMUNITY SIZE IS SMALLER THAN 200 (135)	0.63 OF 19	81	IN ALL CASES ARE THOSE WHERE NO CITY OR TOWN IS PRESENT, AND THE AVERAGE COMMUNITY SIZE IS SMALLER THAN 200 (135)	1.00 OF 8	7 0 12 8 XSQ= 2.29 PHI= 0.291 EP = 0.0681

133	TILT TOWARD BEING THOSE WHERE CONTRACTED DEBTS ARE SIGNIFICANTLY PRESENT (17) GES	0.60 OF 25	133	TILT TOWARD BEING THOSE WHERE CONTRACTED DEBTS ARE MODERATELY PRESENT OR ABSENT (17) GES	0.88 OF 8	15 1 10 7 XSQ= 3.74 PHI= 0.337 EP = 0.0391
135	DRIFT TOWARD BEING THOSE WHERE INDIVIDUAL OWNERSHIP OF ECONOMICALLY SIGNIFICANT PROPERTY IS PRESENT (24) GES	0.71 OF 28	135	DRIFT TOWARD BEING THOSE WHERE INDIVIDUAL OWNERSHIP OF ECONOMICALLY SIGNIFICANT PROPERTY IS NEGLIGIBLE OR ABSENT (14) GES	0.67 OF 9	20 3 8 6 XSQ= 2.74 PHI= 0.272 EP = 0.0569
141	TILT TOWARD BEING THOSE WHERE THE LEVEL OF SOCIAL SANCTION IS PUBLIC CORPOREAL SANCTION, RATHER THAN PUBLIC PROPERTY SANCTION OR PRIVATE SETTLEMENT (28) JMH	0.69 OF 13	141	IN ALL CASES ARE THOSE WHERE THE LEVEL OF SOCIAL SANCTION IS PUBLIC PROPERTY SANCTION OR PRIVATE SETTLEMENT, RATHER THAN PUBLIC CORPOREAL SANCTION (26) JMH	1.00 OF 5	9 0 4 5 XSQ= 4.43 PHI= 0.496 EP = 0.0294
142	LEAN TOWARD BEING THOSE WHERE THE LEVEL OF SOCIAL SANCTION IS PUBLIC CORPOREAL SANCTION OR PUBLIC PROPERTY SANCTION, RATHER THAN PRIVATE SETTLEMENT (38) JMH	0.92 OF 13	142	LEAN TOWARD BEING THOSE WHERE THE LEVEL OF SOCIAL SANCTION IS PRIVATE SETTLEMENT, RATHER THAN PUBLIC CORPOREAL SANCTION OR PUBLIC PROPERTY SETTLEMENT (16) JMH	0.80 OF 5	12 1 1 4 XSQ= 6.15 PHI= 0.585 EP = 0.0077
196	TILT TOWARD BEING THOSE WHERE INDIVIDUAL RIGHTS IN REAL PROPERTY, AND RULES FOR INHERITANCE, ARE PRESENT (194)	0.81 OF 21	196	TILT TOWARD BEING THOSE WHERE INDIVIDUAL RIGHTS IN REAL PROPERTY, OR RULES FOR INHERITANCE, ARE ABSENT (87)	0.71 OF 7	17 2 4 5 XSQ= 4.42 PHI= 0.397 EP = 0.0196
382	TILT TOWARD BEING THOSE WHERE FEMALE INITIATION RITES ARE ABSENT (27) JKB	0.73 OF 11	382	TILT TOWARD BEING THOSE WHERE FEMALE INITIATION RITES ARE PRESENT (38) JKB	0.83 OF 6	3 5 8 1 XSQ= 2.91 PHI= -0.413 EP = 0.0498
386	DRIFT TOWARD BEING THOSE WHERE SEXUAL EXPRESSION BY THE YOUNG IS PERMITTED (40) F-B	0.73 OF 11	386	IN ALL CASES ARE THOSE WHERE SEXUAL EXPRESSION BY THE YOUNG IS RESTRICTED OR SEMI-RESTRICTED (46) F-B	1.00 OF 3	3 3 8 0 XSQ= 2.55 PHI= -0.427 EP = 0.0549
419	TILT TOWARD BEING THOSE WHERE MILITARY GLORY IS STRONGLY OR MODERATELY EMPHASIZED (55) PES	0.70 OF 20	419	TILT TOWARD BEING THOSE WHERE MILITARY GLORY IS NEGLIGIBLY EMPHASIZED (31) PES	0.86 OF 7	14 1 6 6 XSQ= 4.46 PHI= 0.406 EP = 0.0237

430 CULTURES
WHERE SUPERNATURAL SANCTIONS FOR MORALITY,
HAVING AN EFFECT ON
AN INDIVIDUAL'S HEALTH,
ARE PRESENT (16) GES

430 CULTURES
WHERE SUPERNATURAL SANCTIONS FOR MORALITY,
HAVING AN EFFECT ON
AN INDIVIDUAL'S HEALTH,
ARE ABSENT OR UNREPORTED (22) GES

BACKGROUND ON PAGE 164

BOTH SUBJECT AND PREDICATE

16 IN LEFT COLUMN

AZANDE, COPR ESKIMO, HEBREWS, IBAN, IFUGAO, KASKA, LEPCHA, MIAO, NUER, NYAKYUSA, ROMANS, TALLENSI, TANALA, TIV, WINNEBAGO, YAHGAN

22 IN RIGHT COLUMN

ARANDA, ARAPESH, AYMARA, AZTEC, BEMBA, CUNA, DOBUANS, GANDA, KAREN, LOZI, MARQUESANS, NAMA, NANDI, SAMOYED, TIMBIRA, TODA, TRUMAI, WOLEAIANS, YAGUA, YOKUTS, YUROK, ZUNI

362 EXCLUDED BECAUSE UNASCERTAINED

15	DRIFT TOWARD BEING THOSE WHERE THE LATITUDE IS TWENTY DEGREES OR GREATER (183)	0.56 OF 16	15	DRIFT TOWARD BEING THOSE WHERE THE LATITUDE IS LESS THAN TWENTY DEGREES (217)	0.73 OF 22	9 6 / 7 16 / XSQ= 2.16 / PHI= 0.238 / EP = 0.0987
135	DRIFT TOWARD BEING THOSE WHERE INDIVIDUAL OWNERSHIP OF ECONOMICALLY SIGNIFICANT PROPERTY IS PRESENT (24) GES	0.81 OF 16	135	DRIFT TOWARD BEING THOSE WHERE INDIVIDUAL OWNERSHIP OF ECONOMICALLY SIGNIFICANT PROPERTY IS NEGLIGIBLE OR ABSENT (14) GES	0.50 OF 22	13 11 / 3 11 / XSQ= 2.66 / PHI= 0.265 / EP = 0.0877
138	DRIFT TOWARD BEING THOSE WHERE SUPERORDINATE JUSTICE IS PRESENT (22) BBW	0.67 OF 6	138	IN ALL CASES ARE THOSE WHERE SUPERORDINATE JUSTICE IS ABSENT (18) BBW	1.00 OF 4	4 0 / 2 4 / XSQ= 2.10 / PHI= 0.458 / EP = 0.0762
240	DRIFT TOWARD BEING THOSE WHERE THE FAMILY, IF EXTENDED, IS SMALL OR STEM, RATHER THAN LARGE (135)	0.80 OF 10	240	DRIFT TOWARD BEING THOSE WHERE THE FAMILY, IF EXTENDED, IS LARGE, RATHER THAN SMALL OR STEM (78)	0.67 OF 9	2 6 / 8 3 / XSQ= 2.53 / PHI= -0.365 / EP = 0.0698
263	TILT TOWARD BEING THOSE WHERE WIVES ARE OBTAINED BY RELATIVELY DIFFICULT MEANS, NAMELY BY BRIDE-PRICE, BRIDE-SERVICE, OR EXCHANGING A FEMALE RELATIVE (233)	0.80 OF 15	263	TILT TOWARD BEING THOSE WHERE WIVES ARE OBTAINED BY RELATIVELY EASY MEANS, NAMELY BY TOKEN BRIDE-PRICE, GIFT EXCHANGE, ABSENCE OF ANY CONSIDERATION, OR RECEIPT OF DOWRY (162)	0.55 OF 22	12 10 / 3 12 / XSQ= 3.10 / PHI= 0.289 / EP = 0.0471

272	TILT TCWARD BEING THCSE WHERE THE DIVCRCE RATE IS LOW (28) CA	0.80 OF 5	272	TILT TOWARD BEING THOSE WHERE THE DIVORCE RATE IS HIGH (29) CA	0.88 CF 8	1 7 4 1 XSQ= 3.41 PHI= -0.512 EP = 0.0319
299	TILT TCWARD BEING THCSE WHERE THE POST-PARTUM SEX TABCO LASTS LCNGER THAN CNE YEAR (35)	0.57 OF 7	299	TILT TOWARD BEING THOSE WHERE THE POST-PARTUM SEX TABOO LASTS ONE YEAR OR LESS (89)	0.92 OF 12	4 1 3 11 XSQ= 3.21 PHI= 0.411 EP = 0.0379
303	IN ALL CASES ARE THCSE WHERE THE EARLY CRAL SATISFACTION POTENTIAL IS HIGH (32) W-C	1.00 OF 5	303	TILT TOWARD BEING THOSE WHERE THE EARLY ORAL SATISFACTICN POTENTIAL IS LOW (25) W-C	0.75 OF 4	5 1 0 3 XSQ= 2.76 PHI= 0.553 EP = 0.0476
354	DRIFT TCWARD BEING THCSE WHERE THE CHILD'S INFERREC ANXIETY OVER PERFORMANCE CF CBECIENT BEHAVIOR IS LCW (37) B-B-C	0.82 OF 11	354	DRIFT TOWARD BEING THOSE WHERE THE CHILD'S INFERRED ANXIETY OVER PERFORMANCE OF OBEDIENT BEHAVIOR IS HIGH (36) B-B-C	0.63 CF 8	2 5 9 3 XSQ= 2.24 PHI= -0.343 EP = 0.0739
355	DRIFT TCWARD BEING THCSE WHERE THE CHILD'S INFERREC CONFLICT REGARDING CBECIENT BEHAVICR IS LCW (38) B-B-C	0.82 OF 11	355	DRIFT TOWARD BEING THOSE WHERE THE CHILD'S INFERRED CCNFLICT REGARDING OBEDIENT BEHAVIOR IS HIGH (35) B-B-C	0.63 OF 8	2 5 9 3 XSQ= 2.24 PHI= -0.343 EP = 0.0739
372	DRIFT TCWARD BEING THCSE WHERE MALE INITIATICN RITES ARE ABSENT (63) ASA	0.88 OF 8	372	DRIFT TOWARD BEING THOSE WHERE MALE INITIATION RITES ARE PRESENT (48) ASA	0.58 CF 12	1 7 7 5 XSQ= 2.51 PHI= -0.354 EP = 0.0697
382	IN ALL CASES ARE THCSE WHERE FEMALE INITIATICN RITES ARE ABSENT (27) JKB	1.00 OF 6	382	TILT TOWARD BEING THOSE WHERE FEMALE INITIATION RITES ARE PRESENT (38) JKB	0.67 CF 12	0 8 6 4 XSQ= 4.75 PHI= -0.514 EP = 0.0128
405	DRIFT TCWARD BEING THCSE WHERE EXPLANATICNS CF ILLNESS CF A DEPENDENCE NATURE ARE PRESENT (34) W-C	0.83 OF 6	405	DRIFT TOWARD BEING THOSE WHERE EXPLANATIONS OF ILLNESS OF A DEPENDENCE NATURE ARE ABSENT (27) W-C	0.80 CF 5	5 1 1 4 XSQ= 2.23 PHI= 0.450 EP = 0.0801
419	DRIFT TCWARD BEING THCSE WHERE MILITARY GLORY IS STRCNGLY CR MODERATELY EMPHASIZED (55) PES	0.75 OF 12	419	DRIFT TOWARD BEING THOSE WHERE MILITARY GLORY IS NEGLIGIBLY EMPHASIZED (31) PES	0.63 CF 16	9 6 3 10 XSQ= 2.52 PHI= 0.300 EP = 0.0671

```
430/

474  TILT TOWARD BEING THOSE          0.58 OF  12        474  TILT TOWARD BEING THOSE         0.82 OF  17              7    3
     WHERE BOASTFULNESS IS EXTREME  (41) PES                   WHERE BOASTFULNESS IS MODERATE,                            5   14
                                                               NEGLIBIBLE, OR UNREPORTED  (48)  PES           XSQ=     3.51
                                                                                                              PHI=    0.348
                                                                                                              EP =   0.0460
```

431 CULTURES
WHERE SUPERNATURAL SANCTIONS FOR MORALITY,
HAVING AN EFFECT ON
AN INDIVIDUAL'S AFTER LIFE,
ARE PRESENT (10) GES

431 CULTURES
WHERE SUPERNATURAL SANCTIONS FOR MORALITY,
HAVING AN EFFECT ON
AN INDIVIDUAL'S AFTERLIFE,
ARE ABSENT OR UNREPORTED (25) GES

BACKGROUND ON PAGE 164

BOTH SUBJECT AND PREDICATE

10 IN LEFT COLUMN

AZTEC	CUNA	GANDA	IBAN	KAREN	LEPCHA	MARQUESANS	MIAO	TANALA	WINNEBAGO

25 IN RIGHT COLUMN

ARANDA	ARAPESH	AYMARA	AZANDE	BEMBA	COPR ESKIMO	DOBUANS	IFUGAO	KASKA	LOZI
NAMA	NANDI	NUER	NYAKYUSA	TALLENSI	TIMBIRA	TIV	TODA	TRUMAI	WOLEAIANS
YAGUA	YAHGAN	YOKUTS	YUROK	ZUNI					

365 EXCLUDED BECAUSE UNASCERTAINED

5	TILT LESS TOWARD BEING THOSE LOCATED OUTSIDE OF EAST EURASIA (330)	0.60 OF 10	5	TILT MORE TOWARD BEING THOSE LOCATED OUTSIDE OF EAST EURASIA (330)	0.96 OF 25		4 1 6 24 XSQ= 4.91 PHI= 0.374 EP = 0.0169
36	IN ALL CASES ARE THOSE WHERE THE NATURAL ENVIRONMENT IS OTHER THAN 'VERY HARSH,' OR SUB-TROPICAL BUSH, OR TEMPERATE GRASSLAND (292) FWM	1.00 OF 10	36	DRIFT LESS TOWARD BEING THOSE WHERE THE NATURAL ENVIRONMENT IS OTHER THAN 'VERY HARSH,' OR SUB-TROPICAL BUSH, OR TEMPERATE GRASSLAND (292) FWM	0.68 OF 25		0 8 10 17 XSQ= 2.53 PHI= -0.269 EP = 0.0734
42	DRIFT TOWARD BEING THOSE WHERE THE NATURAL ENVIRONMENT IS TROPICAL OR SUB-TROPICAL RAIN FOREST, OR MONSOON FOREST (156) FWM	0.70 OF 10	42	DRIFT TOWARD BEING THOSE WHERE THE NATURAL ENVIRONMENT IS OTHER THAN TROPICAL OR SUB-TROPICAL RAIN FOREST, OR MONSOON FOREST (244) FWM	0.72 OF 25		7 7 3 18 XSQ= 3.65 PHI= 0.323 EP = 0.0529
44	IN ALL CASES ARE THOSE WHERE SETTLEMENTS ARE FIXED (222)	1.00 OF 8	44	TILT LESS TOWARD BEING THOSE WHERE SETTLEMENTS ARE FIXED (222)	0.58 OF 24		8 14 0 10 XSQ= 3.10 PHI= 0.311 EP = 0.0353
73	TILT TOWARD BEING THOSE WHERE WEAVING IS PRESENT (118)	0.75 OF 8	73	TILT TOWARD BEING THOSE WHERE WEAVING IS ABSENT (130)	0.71 OF 21		6 6 2 15 XSQ= 3.41 PHI= 0.343 EP = 0.0382

```
 80  TILT LESS TOWARD BEING THOSE   0.67 OF   6      80  IN ALL CASES ARE THOSE          1.00 OF  20            2     0
     WHERE NO CITY OR TOWN IS PRESENT  (185)             WHERE NO CITY OR TOWN IS PRESENT  (185)                4    20
                                                                                                       XSQ=      3.29
                                                                                                       PHI=     0.356
                                                                                                       EP =    0.0462

 86  TILT TOWARD BEING THOSE        0.75 OF   8      86  TILT TOWARD BEING THOSE         0.71 OF  21            6     6
     WHERE THE LEVEL OF POLITICAL INTEGRATION            WHERE THE LEVEL OF POLITICAL INTEGRATION               2    15
     IS THE LARGE STATE, THE LITTLE STATE,               IS THE AUTONOMOUS COMMUNITY, OR              XSQ=      3.41
     OR THE MINIMAL STATE  (148) GPM                     THE FAMILY  (156) GPM                        PHI=     0.343
                                                                                                       EP =    0.0382

 91  IN ALL CASES ARE THOSE         1.00 OF   2      91  IN ALL CASES ARE THOSE          1.00 OF   7            2     0
     WHERE SOCIETAL COMPLEXITY                           WHERE SOCIETAL COMPLEXITY                              0     7
     IS HIGH  (18) F-W                                   IS LOW  (22) F-W                             XSQ=      4.14
                                                                                                       PHI=     0.679
                                                                                                       EP =    0.0278

139  IN ALL CASES ARE THOSE         1.00 OF   2     139  IN ALL CASES ARE THOSE          1.00 OF   8            2     0
     WHERE SUPERORDINATE PUNISHMENT IS                   WHERE SUPERORDINATE PUNISHMENT IS                      0     8
     PRESENT  (15) BBW                                   ABSENT  (25) BBW                             XSQ=      4.73
                                                                                                       PHI=     0.687
                                                                                                       EP =    0.0222

177  IN ALL CASES ARE THOSE         1.00 OF  10     177  DRIFT LESS TOWARD BEING THOSE   0.68 OF  25            0     8
     WHERE THE COMMUNITY IS OTHER THAN                   WHERE THE COMMUNITY IS OTHER THAN                     10    17
     A SINGLE CLAN-COMMUNITY AND                         A SINGLE CLAN-COMMUNITY AND                  XSQ=      2.53
     EXOGAMOUS  (305)                                    EXOGAMOUS  (305)                             PHI=    -0.269
                                                                                                       EP =    0.0734

196  IN ALL CASES ARE THOSE         1.00 OF   7     196  TILT LESS TOWARD BEING THOSE    0.52 OF  21            7    11
     WHERE INDIVIDUAL RIGHTS IN REAL PROPERTY,           WHERE INDIVIDUAL RIGHTS IN REAL PROPERTY,              0    10
     AND RULES FOR INHERITANCE,                          AND RULES FOR INHERITANCE,                   XSQ=      3.32
     ARE PRESENT  (194)                                  ARE PRESENT  (194)                           PHI=     0.344
                                                                                                       EP =    0.0302

395  IN ALL CASES ARE THOSE         1.00 OF   2     395  IN ALL CASES ARE THOSE          1.00 OF   4            0     4
     WHERE BELIEF IN                                     WHERE BELIEF IN                                        2     0
     THE UNCLEANNESS OF WOMEN IS                         THE UNCLEANNESS OF WOMEN IS                  XSQ=      2.34
     UNIMPORTANT OR ABSENT  (15) LWS                     PRESENT  (18) LWS                            PHI=    -0.625
                                                                                                       EP =    0.0667

436  DRIFT TOWARD BEING THOSE       0.50 OF  10     436  DRIFT TOWARD BEING THOSE        0.84 OF  25            5    21
     WHERE ACTIVE ANCESTRAL SPIRITS                      WHERE ACTIVE ANCESTRAL SPIRITS                         5     4
     ARE ABSENT  (11) GES                                ARE PRESENT  (27) GES                        XSQ=      2.73
                                                                                                       PHI=    -0.279
                                                                                                       EP =    0.0814

441  IN ALL CASES ARE THOSE         1.00 OF   3     441  TILT TOWARD BEING THOSE         0.88 OF   8            0     7
     WHERE FEAR OF HUMAN BEINGS                          WHERE FEAR OF HUMAN BEINGS                             3     1
     IS LOW  (32) W-C                                    IS HIGH  (29) W-C                            XSQ=      3.93
                                                                                                       PHI=    -0.598
                                                                                                       EP =    0.0242
```

445	IN ALL CASES ARE THOSE WHERE SORCERY IS UNIMPORTANT (23) BBW,DH	1.00 OF	3	445	IN ALL CASES ARE THOSE WHERE SORCERY IS IMPORTANT (26) BBW,DH	1.00 OF	6	 XSQ= PHI= EP =	0 6 3 0 5.06 -0.750 0.0119
449	DRIFT TOWARD BEING THOSE WHERE THE OBSERVATION OF FOOD TABOOS IS MEDIUM OR LOW, RATHER THAN HIGH (61) JRL	0.86 OF	7	449	DRIFT TOWARD BEING THOSE WHERE THE OBSERVATION OF FOOD TABOOS IS HIGH, RATHER THAN MEDIUM OR LOW (25) JRL	0.57 OF	14	 XSQ= PHI= EP =	1 8 6 6 1.97 -0.306 0.0873
468	DRIFT TOWARD BEING THOSE WHERE CONTACT WITH OTHER CULTURES IS FREQUENT, RATHER THAN REGULAR OR IRREGULAR (17) JMH	0.60 OF	5	468	DRIFT TOWARD BEING THOSE WHERE CONTACT WITH OTHER CULTURES IS REGULAR OR IRREGULAR, RATHER THAN FREQUENT (37) JMH	0.85 OF	13	 XSQ= PHI= EP =	3 2 2 11 1.70 0.308 0.0987

****

432 CULTURES WHERE AN ATTRACTIVE AFTERLIFE IS BELIEVED IN (27) LWS	432 CULTURES WHERE AN ATTRACTIVE AFTERLIFE IS NOT BELIEVED IN (11) LWS

BACKGROUND ON PAGE 164 — BOTH SUBJECT AND PREDICATE

27 IN LEFT COLUMN

ABIPON	AINU	ANDAMANESE	ARANDA	ARAUCANIANS	ASHANTI	AZTEC	CHUKCHEE	CREEK	CROW
HEBREWS	IBAN	INCA	JIVARO	KAZAK	KUTENAI	KWAKIUTL	NAMA	NAVAHO	OMAHA
RWALA	SEMANG	TODA	TROBRIAND	VEDDA	WITOTO	YUKAGHIR			

11 IN RIGHT COLUMN

DIERI	HAIDA	KUNG	LANGO	LAPPS	MOTA	SAMOANS	SERI	SHILLUK	YAHGAN
YAKUT									

362 EXCLUDED BECAUSE UNASCERTAINED

No.	Left column		No.	Right column		Statistics
74	TILT TOWARD BEING THOSE WHERE POTTERY IS PRESENT (145)	0.73 OF 22	74	TILT TOWARD BEING THOSE WHERE POTTERY IS ABSENT (93)	0.75 OF 8	16 2 6 6 XSQ= 3.76 PHI= 0.354 EP = 0.0342
120	IN ALL CASES ARE THOSE WHERE THE CRAFT SPECIALIZATION SCORE IS HIGH OR MEDIUM (36) WME	1.00 OF 9	120	TILT TOWARD BEING THOSE WHERE THE CRAFT SPECIALIZATION SCORE IS LOW (17) WME	0.67 OF 3	9 1 0 2 XSQ= 3.20 PHI= 0.516 EP = 0.0455
278	DRIFT TOWARD BEING THOSE WHERE PROPERTY RIGHTS IN WOMEN ARE PRESENT (8) LWS	0.50 OF 14	278	IN ALL CASES ARE THOSE WHERE PROPERTY RIGHTS IN WOMEN ARE UNIMPORTANT OR ABSENT (14) LWS	1.00 OF 6	7 0 7 6 XSQ= 2.68 PHI= 0.366 EP = 0.0515
344	DRIFT TOWARD BEING THOSE WHERE THE TOTAL POSITIVE PRESSURE TOWARD DEVELOPING SELF-RELIANT BEHAVIOR IN THE CHILD IS HIGH (36) B-B-C	0.73 OF 11	344	IN ALL CASES ARE THOSE WHERE THE TOTAL POSITIVE PRESSURE TOWARD DEVELOPING SELF-RELIANT BEHAVIOR IN THE CHILD IS LOW (40) B-B-C	1.00 OF 3	8 0 3 3 XSQ= 2.55 PHI= 0.427 EP = 0.0549
345	DRIFT TOWARD BEING THOSE WHERE THE CHILD'S INFERRED ANXIETY OVER NON-PERFORMANCE OF SELF-RELIANT BEHAVIOR IS HIGH (37) B-B-C	0.73 OF 11	345	IN ALL CASES ARE THOSE WHERE THE CHILD'S INFERRED ANXIETY OVER NON-PERFORMANCE OF SELF-RELIANT BEHAVIOR IS LOW (39) B-B-C	1.00 OF 3	8 0 3 3 XSQ= 2.55 PHI= 0.427 EP = 0.0549

```
370  TILT TCWARD BEING THCSE          0.71 OF  21        37C  TILT TOWARD BEING THOSE         0.75 CF   8           6     6
     WHERE THE SEGREGATICN CF ADOLESCENT BOYS                WHERE THE SEGREGATICN OF ADCLESCENT BOYS            15     2
     IS ABSENT  (148)                                        IS COMPLETE OR PARTIAL  (95)                   XSQ=      3.41
                                                                                                            PHI=    -0.343
                                                                                                            EP =    0.0382

406  DRIFT TCWARD BEING THCSE         0.69 OF  13        406  IN ALL CASES ARE THCSE          1.00 CF   3           4     3
     WHERE EXPLANATICNS CF ILLNESS                           WHERE EXPLANATICNS OF ILLNESS                        9     0
     CF AN AGGRESSICN NATURE                                 OF AN AGGRESSICN NATURE                        XSQ=      2.35
     ARE ABSENT  (33) W-C                                    ARE PRESENT  (28) W-C                          PHI=    -0.383
                                                                                                            EP =    0.0625

478  DRIFT TCWARD BEING THCSE         0.67 OF  15        478  DRIFT TOWARD BEING THOSE        0.78 CF   9           5     7
     WHERE THE ABANDCNMENT CR KILLING OF                     WHERE THE ABANDCNMENT OR KILLING CF                 10     2
     CLD PECPLE IS                                           OLD PEOPLE IS                                  XSQ=      2.84
     UNIMPCRTANT CR ABSENT  (12) LWS                         PRESENT  (12) LWS                              PHI=    -0.344
                                                                                                            EP =    0.0894
```

```
****************************************************************************************************

433  CULTURES                                          433  CULTURES
     WHERE BELIEF IN REINCARNATION                          WHERE BELIEF IN REINCARNATICN
     IS PRESENT  (10) GES                                   IS ABSENT  (28) GES


BACKGROUND ON PAGE 164                                                    BCTH SUBJECT AND PREDICATE
....................................................................................................

     10  IN LEFT CCLUMN

ARANDA      AZANDE      GANCA      KAREN      KASKA       LEPCHA     MIAC       NANDI      TODA       WINNEBAGO

     28  IN RIGHT CCLUMN

ARAPESH     AYMARA      AZTEC      BEMBA      COPR ESKIMO CUNA       DOBUANS    HEBREWS    IBAN       IFUGAO
LOZI        MARQUESANS  NAMA       NUER       NYAKYUSA    ROMANS     SAMCYED    TALLENSI   TANALA     TIMBIRA
TIV         TRUMAI      WCLEAIANS  YAGUA      YAHGAN      YOKUTS     YURCK      ZUNI

    362  EXCLUCED BECAUSE UNASCERTAINEC

----------------------------------------------------------------------------------------------------
  5  TILT LESS TOWARC BEING THCSE    0.60 OF  10      5  TILT MORE TOWARD BEING THOSE   0.93 OF  28          4   2
     LOCATED CUTSIDE CF                                  LOCATED OUTSIDE OF                                  6  26
     EAST EURASIA  (330)                                 EAST EURASIA  (330)                         XSQ=     3.77
                                                                                                     PHI=    0.315
                                                                                                     EP =   0.0314

 45  IN ALL CASES ARE THOSE          1.00 OF   5     45  LEAN TOWARD BEING THOSE        0.74 OF  19          0  14
     WHERE SETTLEMENTS, IF FIXEC, ARE                    WHERE SETTLEMENTS, IF FIXED, ARE                    5   5
     NCN-CCMPACT, RATHER THAN                            COMPACT, RATHER THAN                        XSQ=     6.07
     CCMPACT  (73)                                       NON-COMPACT  (149)                          PHI=   -0.503
                                                                                                     EP =   0.0059

 63  IN ALL CASES ARE THOSE          1.00 OF   5     63  DRIFT TOWARD BEING THOSE       0.50 OF  20          5  10
     WHERE HUSBANDRY, IF PRESENT,                        WHERE HUSBANDRY, IF PRESENT,                        0  10
     IS PRINCIPALLY IN THE FORM OF                       IS PRINCIPALLY IN THE FCRM OF               XSQ=     2.34
     BOVINE, ECUINE, CAMEL-LIKE, OR DEER-LIKE            PIGS, SHEEP, OR GOATS, RATHER THAN          PHI=    0.306
     ANIMALS, RATHER THAN                                BOVINE, EQUINE, CAMEL-LIKE, CR DEER-LIKE    EP =   0.0613
     PIGS, SHEEP, CR GCATS  (152)                        ANIMALS  (74)

118  DRIFT TCWARD BEING THCSE        0.75 OF   4    118  DRIFT TOWARD BEING THOSE       0.83 OF  12          3   2
     WHERE THE PERCENTAGE CF OCCUPATIONS                 WHERE THE PERCENTAGE OF CCCUPATICNS                 1  10
     THAT ARE SPECIALIZED                                THAT ARE SPECIALIZED                        XSQ=     2.42
     IS HIGH CR MEDIUM  (24) WME                         IS LOW  (25) WME                            PHI=    0.389
                                                                                                     EP =   0.0632

188  IN ALL CASES ARE THCSE          1.00 OF  10    188  TILT LESS TOWARD BEING THOSE   0.61 CF  28          0  11
     WHERE THE KIN GRCUP IS                              WHERE THE KIN GROUP IS                             10  17
     CTHER THAN                                          OTHER THAN                                  XSQ=     3.78
     EXCLUSIVELY COGNATIC  (252)                         EXCLUSIVELY COGNATIC  (252)                 PHI=   -0.316
                                                                                                     EP =   0.0200
```

4337

```
192  IN ALL CASES ARE THCSE          1.00 OF  10     192  DRIFT LESS TOWARD BEING THCSE  0.71 OF  28            0    8
     OTHER THAN WHERE THE CNLY KIN GROUP                 OTHER THAN WHERE THE ONLY KIN GRCUP                   10   20
     PRESENT IS A KINCRED CR ELSE                        PRESENT IS A KINDRED OR ELSE                   XSQ=     2.10
     BILATERAL DESCENT IS INFERREC  (289)                BILATERAL DESCENT IS INFERRED  (289)           PHI=   -0.235
                                                                                                        EP =   0.0821

201  IN ALL CASES ARE THCSE          1.00 OF  10     201  DRIFT LESS TOWARD BEING THCSE  0.71 OF  28           10   20
     WHERE MARITAL RESICENCE IS                          WHERE MARITAL RESIDENCE IS                             0    8
     NCN-CPTICNAL, RATHER THAN                           NON-OPTIONAL, RATHER THAN                      XSQ=     2.10
     AMBILCCAL CR NECLOCAL  (334)                        AMBILOCAL OR NECLOCAL  (334)                   PHI=    0.235
                                                                                                        EP =   0.0821

279  IN ALL CASES ARE THCSE          1.00 OF   2     279  IN ALL CASES ARE THCSE         1.00 OF   4            2    0
     WHERE WIFE-LENDING CR                               WHERE WIFE-LENDING AND                                 0    4
     WIFE-EXCHANGE IS                                    WIFE EXCHANGE ARE                              XSQ=     2.34
     PRESENT  (10) LWS                                   UNIMPORTANT OR ABSENT  (19) LWS                PHI=    0.625
                                                                                                        EP =   0.0667

317  TILT TCWARD BEING THOSE         0.83 OF   6     317  TILT TOWARD BEING THOSE        0.73 OF  11            1    8
     WHERE DISPLAY CF AFFECTICN TOWARD                   WHERE DISPLAY OF AFFECTICN TOWARD                      5    3
     THE INFANT IS LCW  (29) B-B-C                       THE INFANT IS HIGH  (39) B-B-C                 XSQ=     2.91
                                                                                                        PHI=   -0.413
                                                                                                        EP =   0.0498

334  IN ALL CASES ARE THCSE          1.00 OF   6     334  TILT TOWARD BEING THOSE        0.67 OF  15            0   10
     WHERE THE INDULGENCE CF THE CHILD                   WHERE THE INDULGENCE OF THE CHILD                      6    5
     IS LCW  (38) B-B-C                                  IS HIGH  (40) B-B-C                            XSQ=     5.20
                                                                                                        PHI=   -0.497
                                                                                                        EP =   0.0124

338  IN ALL CASES ARE THCSE          1.00 OF   6     338  TILT TOWARD BEING THOSE        0.60 OF  15            6    6
     WHERE THE CHILD'S INFERREC ANXIETY OVER             WHERE THE CHILD'S INFERRED ANXIETY OVER                0    9
     PERFCRMANCE CF RESPCNSIBLE BEHAVIOR                 PERFORMANCE OF RESPCNSIBLE BEHAVICR            XSQ=     4.09
     IS HIGH  (44) B-B-C                                 IS LOW  (29) B-B-C                             PHI=    0.441
                                                                                                        EP =   0.0186

339  TILT TCWARC BEING THOSE         0.67 OF   6     339  TILT TOWARD BEING THOSE        0.87 CF  15            4    2
     WHERE THE CHILD'S INFERREC CONFLICT                 WHERE THE CHILD'S INFERRED CONFLICT                    2   13
     REGARDING RESPCNSIBLE BEHAVIOR                      REGARDING RESPONSIBLE BEHAVIOR                 XSQ=     3.65
     IS HIGH  (31) B-B-C                                 IS LOW  (42) B-B-C                             PHI=    0.417
                                                                                                        EP =   0.0307

424  DRIFT TCWARD BEING THCSE        0.50 OF   6     424  DRIFT TOWARD BEING THOSE       0.92 OF  13            3    1
     WHERE RELIGICUS SPECIALISTS ARE                     WHERE RELIGIOUS SPECIALISTS ARE                        3   12
     FULL-TIME, RATHER THAN                              PART-TIME, RATHER THAN                         XSQ=     2.24
     PART-TIME  (21) JMH                                 FULL-TIME  (33) JMH                            PHI=    0.344
                                                                                                        EP =   0.0709
```

434 CULTURES
WHERE ASCETICISM IN MOURNING BEHAVIOR
IS HIGH (37) JFG

434 CULTURES
WHERE ASCETICISM IN MOURNING BEHAVIOR
IS LOW (30) JFG

BACKGROUND ON PAGE 164

BOTH SUBJECT AND PREDICATE

37 IN LEFT COLUMN

ABIPON	AINU	ANDAMANESE	APINAYE	ARANDA	ASHANTI	AYMARA	CHAGGA	CHEYENNE	CHOROTI
CROW	DOBUANS	FON	GANDA	IFUGAO	JIVARO	JUKUN	KASKA	KURTATCHI	KWAKIUTL
LANGO	LAU	LEPCHA	MARQUESANS	MATACO	MBUNDU	MURNGIN	NAVAHO	PUKAPUKA	SANPOIL
SENIANG	THONGA	TIMBIRA	TODA	TOKELAU	TROBRIAND	VENDA			

30 IN RIGHT COLUMN

ALORESE	ARAUCANIANS	AZANDE	BALINESE	CHENCHU	CHIR-APACHE	CHUKCHEE	CUNA	GOND	HANO
ILA	KAZAK	KUTENAI	LAKHER	LAMBA	LESU	MAORI	MARICOPA	OMAHA	PALAUANS
PAPAGO	SIRIONO	TANALA	TAOS	TIV	TUPINAMBA	WAPISHANA	WARRAU	YAGUA	ZUNI

333 EXCLUDED BECAUSE UNASCERTAINED

87	TILT LESS TOWARD BEING THOSE 0.81 OF 31 WHERE THE LEVEL OF POLITICAL INTEGRATION IS THE LARGE STATE, THE LITTLE STATE, THE MINIMAL STATE, OR THE AUTONOMOUS COMMUNITY (281) GPM	87	IN ALL CASES ARE THOSE 1.00 OF 29 WHERE THE LEVEL OF POLITICAL INTEGRATION IS THE LARGE STATE, THE LITTLE STATE, THE MINIMAL STATE, OR THE AUTONOMOUS COMMUNITY (281) GPM	25 29 6 0 XSQ= 4.27 PHI= -0.267 XP = 0.0388
88	DRIFT TOWARD BEING THOSE 0.76 OF 29 WHERE, IF A HEADMANSHIP IS PRESENT, SUCCESSION IS HEREDITARY (165)	88	DRIFT TOWARD BEING THOSE 0.52 OF 23 WHERE, IF A HEADMANSHIP IS PRESENT, SUCCESSION IS NON-HEREDITARY (106)	7 12 22 11 XSQ= 3.22 PHI= -0.249 XP = 0.0726
98	DRIFT LESS TOWARD BEING THOSE 0.64 OF 36 WHERE THE HIERARCHY OF LOCAL JURISDICTION HAS FOUR OR THREE LEVELS (238) GES,EA	98	DRIFT MORE TOWARD BEING THOSE 0.86 OF 29 WHERE THE HIERARCHY OF LOCAL JURISDICTION HAS FOUR OR THREE LEVELS (238) GES,EA	23 25 13 4 XSQ= 3.07 PHI= -0.217 XP = 0.0799
99	DRIFT TOWARD BEING THOSE 0.50 OF 18 WHERE, WITH NATIONAL HIERARCHY ABSENT, THE HIERARCHY OF LOCAL JURISDICTION HAS TWO LEVELS (63) GES,EA	99	DRIFT TOWARD BEING THOSE 0.85 OF 13 WHERE, WITH NATIONAL HIERARCHY ABSENT, THE HIERARCHY OF LOCAL JURISDICTION HAS FOUR OR THREE LEVELS (93) GES,EA	9 11 9 2 XSQ= 2.58 PHI= -0.289 EP = 0.0656

100	DRIFT LESS TOWARD BEING THOSE 0.74 OF 35 WHERE HIERARCHIES ARE MORE COMPLEX THAN THE 'SIMPLEST,' I. E., MORE COMPLEX THAN TWO LOCAL LEVELS WITH NO NATIONAL LEVELS (267) GES,EA	100	DRIFT MORE TOWARD BEING THOSE 0.93 OF 29 WHERE HIERARCHIES ARE MORE COMPLEX THAN THE 'SIMPLEST,' I. E., MORE COMPLEX THAN TWO LOCAL LEVELS WITH NO NATIONAL LEVELS (267) GES,EA	26 27 9 2 XSQ= 2.73 PHI= -0.207 XP = 0.0982
137	TILT TOWARD BEING THOSE 0.52 OF 29 WHERE INVIDIOUS DISPLAY OF WEALTH IS STRONGLY EMPHASIZED (37) PES	137	TILT TOWARD BEING THOSE 0.81 OF 21 WHERE INVIDIOUS DISPLAY OF WEALTH IS MODERATELY, LITTLE, OR NEGATIVELY EMPHASIZED (52) PES	15 4 14 17 XSQ= 4.22 PHI= 0.291 XP = 0.0399
149	DRIFT TOWARD BEING THOSE 0.65 OF 17 WHERE THE INCIDENCE OF THEFT IS HIGH (18) B-B-C	149	DRIFT TOWARD BEING THOSE 0.75 OF 12 WHERE THE INCIDENCE OF THEFT IS LOW (19) B-B-C	11 3 6 9 XSQ= 2.99 PHI= 0.321 EP = 0.0604
180	DRIFT LESS TOWARD BEING THOSE 0.54 OF 37 WHERE THE COMMUNITY IS COMMONLY NON-EXOGAMOUS, RATHER THAN EXOGAMOUS (258)	180	DRIFT MORE TOWARD BEING THOSE 0.77 OF 30 WHERE THE COMMUNITY IS COMMONLY NON-EXOGAMOUS, RATHER THAN EXOGAMOUS (258)	17 7 20 23 XSQ= 2.77 PHI= 0.203 XP = 0.0962
317	DRIFT TOWARD BEING THOSE 0.58 OF 24 WHERE DISPLAY OF AFFECTION TOWARD THE INFANT IS LOW (29) B-B-C	317	DRIFT TOWARD BEING THOSE 0.76 OF 17 WHERE DISPLAY OF AFFECTION TOWARD THE INFANT IS HIGH (39) B-B-C	10 13 14 4 XSQ= 3.58 PHI= -0.296 XP = 0.0584
332	DRIFT TOWARD BEING THOSE 0.67 OF 6 WHERE THE AGE AT BEGINNING OF MODESTY TRAINING IS SIX YEARS OR HIGHER (9) W-C	332	IN ALL CASES ARE THOSE 1.00 OF 4 WHERE THE AGE AT BEGINNING OF MODESTY TRAINING IS LOWER THAN SIX YEARS (8) W-C	4 0 2 4 XSQ= 2.10 PHI= 0.458 EP = 0.0762
333	IN ALL CASES ARE THOSE 1.00 OF 5 WHERE THE AGE AT BEGINNING OF TRAINING IN HETEROSEXUAL PLAY INHIBITION IS EIGHT YEARS OR HIGHER (8) W-C	333	DRIFT TOWARD BEING THOSE 0.67 OF 6 WHERE THE AGE AT BEGINNING OF TRAINING IN HETEROSEXUAL PLAY INHIBITION IS LOWER THAN EIGHT YEARS (8) W-C	5 2 0 4 XSQ= 2.75 PHI= 0.500 EP = 0.0606
337	TILT TOWARD BEING THOSE 0.64 OF 25 WHERE THE CHILD'S INFERRED ANXIETY OVER NON-PERFORMANCE OF RESPONSIBLE BEHAVIOR IS HIGH (38) B-B-C	337	TILT TOWARD BEING THOSE 0.72 OF 18 WHERE THE CHILD'S INFERRED ANXIETY OVER NON-PERFORMANCE OF RESPONSIBLE BEHAVIOR IS LOW (35) B-B-C	16 5 9 13 XSQ= 4.14 PHI= 0.310 XP = 0.0419
338	DRIFT TOWARD BEING THOSE 0.80 OF 25 WHERE THE CHILD'S INFERRED ANXIETY OVER PERFORMANCE OF RESPONSIBLE BEHAVIOR IS HIGH (44) B-B-C	338	DRIFT TOWARD BEING THOSE 0.50 OF 18 WHERE THE CHILD'S INFERRED ANXIETY OVER PERFORMANCE OF RESPONSIBLE BEHAVIOR IS LOW (29) B-B-C	20 9 5 9 XSQ= 3.03 PHI= 0.266 XP = 0.0816

339	TILT TOWARD BEING THOSE 0.68 OF 25 WHERE THE CHILD'S INFERRED CONFLICT REGARDING RESPONSIBLE BEHAVIOR IS HIGH (31) B-B-C	339	TILT TOWARD BEING THOSE 0.72 OF 18 WHERE THE CHILD'S INFERRED CONFLICT REGARDING RESPONSIBLE BEHAVIOR IS LOW (42) B-B-C	 XSQ= PHI= XP =	17 5 8 13 5.26 0.350 0.0218
370	DRIFT TOWARD BEING THOSE 0.57 OF 30 WHERE THE SEGREGATION OF ADOLESCENT BOYS IS COMPLETE OR PARTIAL (95)	370	DRIFT TOWARD BEING THOSE 0.72 OF 25 WHERE THE SEGREGATION OF ADOLESCENT BOYS IS ABSENT (148)	 XSQ= PHI= XP =	17 7 13 18 3.47 0.251 0.0627
402	DRIFT TOWARD BEING THOSE 0.76 OF 21 WHERE EXPLANATIONS OF ILLNESS OF AN ORAL NATURE ARE PRESENT (31) W-C	402	DRIFT TOWARD BEING THOSE 0.57 OF 21 WHERE EXPLANATIONS OF ILLNESS OF AN ORAL NATURE ARE ABSENT (30) W-C	 XSQ= PHI= XP =	16 9 5 12 3.56 0.291 0.0593
426	DRIFT TOWARD BEING THOSE 0.63 OF 32 WHERE A HIGH GOD IS ABSENT (104) GES,EA	426	DRIFT TOWARD BEING THOSE 0.65 OF 26 WHERE A HIGH GOD IS PRESENT (156) GES,EA	 XSQ= PHI= XP =	12 17 20 9 3.42 -0.243 0.0646
437	TILT TOWARD BEING THOSE 0.67 OF 21 WHERE FEAR OF GHOSTS, SPIRITS, HUMANS OR ANIMALS IS HIGH (21) W-C,JFG	437	TILT TOWARD BEING THOSE 0.70 OF 23 WHERE FEAR OF GHOSTS, SPIRITS, HUMANS OR ANIMALS IS LOW (23) W-C,JFG	 XSQ= PHI= XP =	14 7 7 16 4.42 0.317 0.0356
455	LEAN TOWARD BEING THOSE 0.73 OF 15 WHERE THE MODE OF THE INDIVIDUAL'S CONTACT WITH THE DIVINE IS NOT CONDUCIVE TO THE DEVELOPMENT OF THE INDIVIDUAL'S NEED TO ACHIEVE (19) DCM	455	IN ALL CASES ARE THOSE 1.00 OF 6 WHERE THE MODE OF THE INDIVIDUAL'S CONTACT WITH THE DIVINE IS CONDUCIVE TO THE DEVELOPMENT OF THE INDIVIDUAL'S NEED TO ACHIEVE (17) DCM	 XSQ= PHI= EP =	4 6 11 0 6.53 -0.558 0.0039

****

435 CULTURES
WHERE ABANDONMENT OF THE HOUSE OF THE DEAD
IS PRACTICED (12) LWS

435 CULTURES
WHERE ABANDONMENT OF THE HOUSE OF THE DEAD
IS NOT PRACTICED (19) LWS

BACKGROUND ON PAGE 165 | BOTH SUBJECT AND PREDICATE

....

12 IN LEFT COLUMN

ABIPON	ANDAMANESE	ARANDA	CROW	DIERI	JIVARO	KUNG	LANGO	NAMA	NAVAHO
VEDDA	YAHGAN								

19 IN RIGHT COLUMN

AINU	ASHANTI	AZTEC	CHUKCHEE	CREEK	FANG	FON	HANO	HEBREWS	IBAN
MAORI	MOTA	SAMOANS	SEMANG	SHILLUK	TODA	TROBRIAND	WITOTO	YAKUT	

369 EXCLUDED BECAUSE UNASCERTAINED

33	TILT TOWARD BEING THOSE 0.58 OF 12 WHERE THE NATURAL ENVIRONMENT IS 'VERY HARSH,' I.E., DESERT, DESERT GRASSES AND SHRUBS, TUNDRA, OR HIGH PLATEAU STEPPE (59) FWM	33	TILT TOWARD BEING THOSE 0.89 OF 19 WHERE THE NATURAL ENVIRONMENT IS OTHER THAN 'VERY HARSH,' I.E., DESERT, DESERT GRASSES AND SHRUBS, TUNDRA, OR HIGH PLATEAU STEPPE (341) FWM	7 2 5 17 XSQ= 6.00 PHI= 0.440 EP = 0.0118
36	LEAN TOWARD BEING THOSE 0.75 OF 12 WHERE THE NATURAL ENVIRONMENT IS 'VERY HARSH,' OR SUB-TROPICAL BUSH, OR TEMPERATE GRASSLAND (108) FWM	36	LEAN TOWARD BEING THOSE 0.79 OF 19 WHERE THE NATURAL ENVIRONMENT IS OTHER THAN 'VERY HARSH,' OR SUB-TROPICAL BUSH, OR TEMPERATE GRASSLAND (292) FWM	9 4 3 15 XSQ= 6.71 PHI= 0.465 EP = 0.0075
44	LEAN TOWARD BEING THOSE 0.83 OF 12 WHERE SETTLEMENTS ARE NON-FIXED (110)	44	LEAN TOWARD BEING THOSE 0.79 OF 19 WHERE SETTLEMENTS ARE FIXED (222)	2 15 10 4 XSQ= 9.14 PHI= -0.543 EP = 0.0011
46	LEAN TOWARD BEING THOSE 0.75 OF 12 WHERE SETTLEMENTS ARE NON-FIXED AND MOVEMENT IS NOMADIC (72)	46	LEAN TOWARD BEING THOSE 0.84 OF 19 OTHER THAN WHERE SETTLEMENTS ARE NON-FIXED AND MOVEMENT IS NOMADIC (260)	9 3 3 16 XSQ= 8.52 PHI= 0.524 EP = 0.0019
51	TILT TOWARD BEING THOSE 0.83 OF 12 WHERE SUBSISTENCE IS PRIMARILY BY FOOD GATHERING -- I. E., HUNTING, FISHING, OR COLLECTING -- RATHER THAN FOOD PRODUCTION (147)	51	TILT TOWARD BEING THOSE 0.63 OF 19 WHERE SUBSISTENCE IS PRIMARILY BY FOOD PRODUCTION -- I. E., AGRICULTURE OR HUSBANDRY -- RATHER THAN BY GATHERING (253)	2 12 10 7 XSQ= 4.68 PHI= -0.389 EP = 0.0245

82	DRIFT TOWARD BEING THCSE WHERE NO CITY CR TCWN IS PRESENT, AND THE AVERAGE CCMMUNITY SIZE IS SMALLER THAN FIFTY (46)	0.67 OF 9	82	DRIFT TOWARD BEING THOSE WHERE A CITY OR TOWN IS PRESENT, OR THE AVERAGE COMMUNITY SIZE IS FIFTY OR GREATER (178)	0.77 OF 13	3 10 6 3 XSQ= 2.57 PHI= -0.342 EP = 0.0789
85	IN ALL CASES ARE THCSE WHERE THE LEVEL CF PCLITICAL INTEGRATION IS THE MINIMAL STATE, THE AUTCNCMOUS CCMMUNITY, CR THE FAMILY (234) GPM	1.00 OF 12	85	TILT LESS TCWARD BEING THCSE WHERE THE LEVEL OF PCLITICAL INTEGRATION IS THE MINIMAL STATE, THE AUTONOMOUS COMMUNITY, CR THE FAMILY (234) GPM	0.59 OF 17	0 7 12 10 XSQ= 4.46 PHI= -0.392 EP = 0.0230
86	DRIFT TCWARD BEING THCSE WHERE THE LEVEL CF POLITICAL INTEGRATICN IS THE AUTCNCMOUS COMMUNITY, OR THE FAMILY (156) GPM	0.83 OF 12	86	DRIFT TOWARD BEING THOSE WHERE THE LEVEL OF POLITICAL INTEGRATION IS THE LARGE STATE, THE LITTLE STATE, OR THE MINIMAL STATE (148) GPM	0.59 OF 17	2 10 10 7 XSQ= 3.56 PHI= -0.350 EP = 0.0535
95	IN ALL CASES ARE THCSE WHERE THE HIERARCHY OF NATICNAL JURISDICTICN HAS CNE CR NC LEVELS (254) GES,EA	1.00 OF 12	95	DRIFT LESS TOWARD BEING THCSE WHERE THE HIERARCHY OF NATIONAL JURISDICTION HAS ONE OR NO LEVELS (254) GES,EA	0.68 CF 19	0 6 12 13 XSQ= 2.89 PHI= -0.306 EP = 0.0585
96	TILT TCWARC BEING THCSE WHERE THE HIERARCHY CF NATICNAL JURISDICTICN HAS NC LEVELS (156) GES,EA	0.83 OF 12	96	TILT TOWARD BEING THOSE WHERE THE HIERARCHY OF NATIONAL JURISDICTICN HAS FOUR, THREE, TWC OR ONE LEVEL (174) GES,EA	0.63 OF 19	2 12 10 7 XSQ= 4.68 PHI= -0.389 EP = 0.0245
98	LEAN TCWARC BEING THOSE WHERE THE HIERARCHY CF LCCAL JURISDICTICN HAS TWC LEVELS (93) GES,EA	0.67 OF 12	98	LEAN TOWARD BEING THOSE WHERE THE HIERARCHY OF LOCAL JURISDICTION HAS FOUR OR THREE LEVELS (238) GES,EA	0.84 OF 19	4 16 8 3 XSQ= 6.24 PHI= -0.449 EP = 0.0070
100	TILT TCWARD BEING THCSE WHERE HIERARCHIES ARE THE 'SIMPLEST' I. E., WHERE THERE ARE CNLY TWC LCCAL LEVELS WITH NC NATICNAL LEVELS (63) GES,EA	0.50 OF 12	100	TILT TOWARD BEING THOSE WHERE HIERARCHIES ARE MORE COMPLEX THAN THE 'SIMPLEST,' I. E., MORE COMPLEX THAN TWO LOCAL LEVELS WITH NO NATIONAL LEVELS (267) GES,EA	0.89 OF 19	6 17 6 2 XSQ= 4.10 PHI= -0.364 EP = 0.0316
102	DRIFT TCWARD BEING THCSE WHERE CLASS STRATIFICATICN IS ABSENT (180)	0.75 OF 12	102	DRIFT TOWARD BEING THOSE WHERE CLASS STRATIFICATICN IS PRESENT (203)	0.63 CF 19	3 12 9 7 XSQ= 2.90 PHI= -0.306 EP = 0.0659
131	TILT TCWARD BEING THCSE WHERE THE CCNSTRUCTION CF PERMANENT HOUSES CR THE ERECTICN CF TEMPCRARY CWELLINGS IS MAINLY DCNE BY FEMALES (21)	0.67 OF 6	131	TILT TOWARD BEING THOSE WHERE THE CONSTRUCTICN CF PERMANENT HOUSES OR THE ERECTION OF TEMPCRARY DWELLINGS IS MAINLY DONE BY MALES (136)	0.90 CF 10	2 9 4 1 XSQ= 3.28 PHI= -0.453 EP = 0.0357

132	TILT TOWARD BEING THOSE WHERE ECONOMIC EXCHANGE DOES NOT INVOLVE THE USE OF MONEY (17) JMH	0.83 OF 6	132	TILT TOWARD BEING THOSE WHERE ECONOMIC EXCHANGE INVOLVES THE USE OF MONEY (37) JMH	0.88 OF 8	 XSQ= PHI= EP =	1 7 5 1 4.43 -0.562 0.0256
133	IN ALL CASES ARE THOSE WHERE CONTRACTED DEBTS ARE MODERATELY PRESENT OR ABSENT (17) GES	1.00 OF 3	133	IN ALL CASES ARE THOSE WHERE CONTRACTED DEBTS ARE SIGNIFICANTLY PRESENT (17) GES	1.00 OF 4	 XSQ= PHI= EP =	0 4 3 0 3.51 -0.708 0.0286
137	DRIFT TOWARD BEING THOSE WHERE INVIDIOUS DISPLAY OF WEALTH IS MODERATELY, LITTLE, OR NEGATIVELY EMPHASIZED (52) PES	0.88 OF 8	137	DRIFT TOWARD BEING THOSE WHERE INVIDIOUS DISPLAY OF WEALTH IS STRONGLY EMPHASIZED (37) PES	0.53 OF 15	 XSQ= PHI= EP =	1 8 7 7 2.14 -0.305 0.0858
143	IN ALL CASES ARE THOSE WHERE THE RATIO OF RESTITUTIVE TO REPRESSIVE SANCTIONS IS MEDIUM OR LOW (32) WME	1.00 OF 4	143	DRIFT TOWARD BEING THOSE WHERE THE RATIO OF RESTITUTIVE TO REPRESSIVE SANCTIONS IS HIGH (20) WME	0.67 OF 6	 XSQ= PHI= EP =	0 4 4 2 2.10 -0.458 0.0762
144	IN ALL CASES ARE THOSE WHERE THE RATIO OF RESTITUTIVE TO REPRESSIVE SANCTIONS IS LOW (25) WME	1.00 OF 4	144	DRIFT TOWARD BEING THOSE WHERE THE RATIO OF RESTITUTIVE TO REPRESSIVE SANCTIONS IS HIGH OR MEDIUM (27) WME	0.67 OF 6	 XSQ= PHI= EP =	0 4 4 2 2.10 -0.458 0.0762
147	TILT TOWARD BEING THOSE WHERE CODIFIED LAWS ARE UNIMPORTANT OR ABSENT (13) LWS	0.75 OF 8	147	TILT TOWARD BEING THOSE WHERE CODIFIED LAWS ARE PRESENT (20) LWS	0.73 OF 15	 XSQ= PHI= EP =	2 11 6 4 3.19 -0.372 0.0393
176	DRIFT TOWARD BEING THOSE WHERE THE COMMUNITY IS OTHER THAN A CLAN-COMMUNITY OR A COMMUNITY STRUCTURED OR SEGMENTED ON A CLAN BASIS (213)	0.75 OF 12	176	DRIFT TOWARD BEING THOSE WHERE THE COMMUNITY IS A CLAN-COMMUNITY OR A COMMUNITY STRUCTURED OR SEGMENTED ON A CLAN BASIS (169)	0.67 OF 18	 XSQ= PHI= EP =	3 12 9 6 3.47 -0.340 0.0604
178	IN ALL CASES ARE THOSE WHERE THE COMMUNITY IS OTHER THAN SEGMENTED ON A CLAN BASIS AND NON-EXOGAMOUS (295)	1.00 OF 12	178	LEAN LESS TOWARD BEING THOSE WHERE THE COMMUNITY IS OTHER THAN SEGMENTED ON A CLAN BASIS AND NON-EXOGAMOUS (295)	0.56 OF 18	 XSQ= PHI= EP =	0 8 12 10 5.18 -0.415 0.0100
196	DRIFT TOWARD BEING THOSE WHERE INDIVIDUAL RIGHTS IN REAL PROPERTY, OR RULES FOR INHERITANCE, ARE ABSENT (87)	0.78 OF 9	196	DRIFT TOWARD BEING THOSE WHERE INDIVIDUAL RIGHTS IN REAL PROPERTY, AND RULES FOR INHERITANCE, ARE PRESENT (194)	0.64 OF 14	 XSQ= PHI= EP =	2 9 7 5 2.38 -0.322 0.0894

259	IN ALL CASES ARE THOSE WHERE THE SEVERITY OF MOTHER-IN-LAW AVOIDANCE IS HIGH (26) WNS	1.00 OF 4	259	TILT TOWARD BEING THOSE WHERE THE SEVERITY OF MOTHER-IN-LAW AVOIDANCE IS LOW (20) WNS	0.86 OF 7	4 1 0 6 XSQ= 4.48 PHI= 0.638 EP = 0.0152
277	DRIFT TOWARD BEING THOSE WHERE THE STATUS OF WOMEN IS NOT STRONGLY INFERIOR OR SUBJECTED (22) LWS	0.89 OF 9	277	DRIFT TOWARD BEING THOSE WHERE THE STATUS OF WOMEN IS INFERIOR OR SUBJECTED (14) LWS	0.53 OF 17	1 9 8 8 XSQ= 2.76 PHI= -0.326 EP = 0.0873
313	DRIFT TOWARD BEING THOSE WHERE AGGRESSION SOCIALIZATION ANXIETY IS LOW (28) W-C	0.75 OF 4	313	DRIFT TOWARD BEING THOSE WHERE AGGRESSION SOCIALIZATION ANXIETY IS HIGH (26) W-C	0.88 OF 8	1 7 3 1 XSQ= 2.30 PHI= -0.437 EP = 0.0667
323	TILT TOWARD BEING THOSE WHERE THE CONSTANCY OF PRESENCE OF THE INFANT'S NURTURANT AGENT IS HIGH (29) B-B-C	0.83 OF 6	323	TILT TOWARD BEING THOSE WHERE THE CONSTANCY OF PRESENCE OF THE INFANT'S NURTURANT AGENT IS LOW (45) B-B-C	0.89 OF 9	5 1 1 8 XSQ= 5.10 PHI= 0.583 EP = 0.0110
336	DRIFT TOWARD BEING THOSE WHERE THE TOTAL POSITIVE PRESSURE TOWARD DEVELOPING RESPONSIBLE BEHAVIOR IN THE CHILD IS LOW (32) B-B-C	0.80 OF 5	336	DRIFT TOWARD BEING THOSE WHERE THE TOTAL POSITIVE PRESSURE TOWARD DEVELOPING RESPONSIBLE BEHAVIOR IN THE CHILD IS HIGH (43) B-B-C	0.78 OF 9	1 7 4 2 XSQ= 2.34 PHI= -0.409 EP = 0.0909
337	DRIFT TOWARD BEING THOSE WHERE THE CHILD'S INFERRED ANXIETY OVER NON-PERFORMANCE OF RESPONSIBLE BEHAVIOR IS LOW (35) B-B-C	0.80 OF 5	337	DRIFT TOWARD BEING THOSE WHERE THE CHILD'S INFERRED ANXIETY OVER NON-PERFORMANCE OF RESPONSIBLE BEHAVIOR IS HIGH (38) B-B-C	0.78 OF 9	1 7 4 2 XSQ= 2.34 PHI= -0.409 EP = 0.0909
339	DRIFT TOWARD BEING THOSE WHERE THE CHILD'S INFERRED CONFLICT REGARDING RESPONSIBLE BEHAVIOR IS LOW (42) B-B-C	0.80 OF 5	339	DRIFT TOWARD BEING THOSE WHERE THE CHILD'S INFERRED CONFLICT REGARDING RESPONSIBLE BEHAVIOR IS HIGH (31) B-B-C	0.78 OF 9	1 7 4 2 XSQ= 2.34 PHI= -0.409 EP = 0.0909
424	IN ALL CASES ARE THOSE WHERE RELIGIOUS SPECIALISTS ARE PART-TIME, RATHER THAN FULL-TIME (33) JMH	1.00 OF 6	424	DRIFT TOWARD BEING THOSE WHERE RELIGIOUS SPECIALISTS ARE FULL-TIME, RATHER THAN PART-TIME (21) JMH	0.50 OF 8	0 4 6 4 XSQ= 2.11 PHI= -0.388 EP = 0.0849
452	DRIFT TOWARD BEING THOSE WHERE TOTEMISM WITH FOOD TABOOS IS ABSENT (24) WNS	0.80 OF 5	452	DRIFT TOWARD BEING THOSE WHERE TOTEMISM WITH FOOD TABOOS IS PRESENT (19) WNS	0.86 OF 7	1 6 4 1 XSQ= 2.83 PHI= -0.486 EP = 0.0720

4357

```
480  IN ALL CASES ARE THOSE          1.00 OF   2        480  DRIFT TOWARD BEING THOSE       0.88 OF   8          0    7
     WHERE COMPLEXITY OF ARTISTIC DESIGN                     WHERE COMPLEXITY OF ARTISTIC DESIGN                   2    1
     IS LOW  (15) HB                                         IS HIGH  (14) HB                                XSQ=    2.41
                                                                                                             PHI=  -0.491
                                                                                                             EP =  0.0667
```

```
************************************************************************************************************

436  CULTURES                                               436  CULTURES
     WHERE ACTIVE ANCESTRAL SPIRITS                              WHERE ACTIVE ANCESTRAL SPIRITS
     ARE PRESENT  (27) GES                                       ARE ABSENT  (11) GES


BACKGROUND ON PAGE 165                                                             BOTH SUBJECT AND PREDICATE
............................................................................................................

      27  IN LEFT COLUMN

ARANDA      ARAPESH     AYMARA      BEMBA       COPR ESKIMO DOBUANS     GANDA       HEBREWS     IFUGAO      KAREN
KASKA       LOZI        MARQUESANS  MIAO        NAMA        NANDI       NUER        NYAKYUSA    TALLENSI    TANALA
TIMBIRA     TIV         WOLEAIANS   YAGUA       YAHGAN      YOKUTS      ZUNI

      11  IN RIGHT COLUMN

AZANDE      AZTEC       CUNA        IBAN        LEPCHA      ROMANS      SAMOYED     TODA        TRUMAI      WINNEBAGO
YUROK

     362  EXCLUDED BECAUSE UNASCERTAINED

------------------------------------------------------------------------------------------------------------
 78  TILT TOWARD BEING THOSE         0.50 OF  12         78  IN ALL CASES ARE THOSE          1.00 OF   7           6     7
     WHERE A WRITING SYSTEM IS                               WHERE THE WRITING SYSTEM IS                           6     0
     ABSENT, RATHER THAN BEING PRESENT IN                    ALPHABETIC-OR-PHONETIC, OR MNEMONIC,            XSQ=     3.06
     EITHER ALPHABETIC-OR-PHONETIC FORM OR                   RATHER THAN BEING ABSENT  (36) JMH              PHI=   -0.402
     MNEMONIC FORM  (18) JMH                                                                                 EP =   0.0436

 79  IN ALL CASES ARE THOSE          1.00 OF  19         79  DRIFT LESS TOWARD BEING THOSE  0.78 OF   9            0     2
     WHERE NO CITY IS PRESENT  (201)                         WHERE NO CITY IS PRESENT  (201)                      19     7
                                                                                                             XSQ=     1.81
                                                                                                             PHI=   -0.255
                                                                                                             EP =   0.0952

 98  TILT LESS TOWARD BEING THOSE    0.56 OF  25         98  IN ALL CASES ARE THOSE          1.00 OF   9           14     9
     WHERE THE HIERARCHY                                     WHERE THE HIERARCHY                                  11     0
     OF LOCAL JURISDICTION HAS                               OF LOCAL JURISDICTION HAS                       XSQ=     4.02
     FOUR OR THREE LEVELS  (238) GES,EA                      FOUR OR THREE LEVELS  (238) GES,EA              PHI=   -0.344
                                                                                                             EP =   0.0172

110  DRIFT TOWARD BEING THOSE        0.63 OF  27        110  DRIFT TOWARD BEING THOSE        0.73 OF  11          10     8
     WHERE SLAVERY IS ABSENT  (218)                          WHERE SLAVERY IS PRESENT  (163)                      17     3
                                                                                                             XSQ=     2.69
                                                                                                             PHI=   -0.266
                                                                                                             EP =   0.0741

116  TILT TOWARD BEING THOSE         0.92 OF  12        116  TILT TOWARD BEING THOSE         0.57 OF   7           1     4
     WHERE OCCUPATIONAL SPECIALIZATION IS                    WHERE OCCUPATIONAL SPECIALIZATION IS                 11     3
     PART-TIME ONLY  (34) JMH                                FULL-TIME, WHETHER OR NOT FOR                   XSQ=     3.21
                                                             SURPLUS PRODUCTION  (20) JMH                    PHI=   -0.411
                                                                                                             EP =   0.0379
```

133	DRIFT TCWARD BEING THCSE 0.63 OF 24 WHERE CCNTRACTEC DEBTS ARE MODERATELY PRESENT OR ABSENT (17) GES	133	DRIFT TOWARD BEING THCSE 0.80 CF 10 WHERE CONTRACTED DEBTS ARE SIGNIFICANTLY PRESENT (17) GES	9 8 15 2 XSQ= 3.54 PHI= -0.323 EP = 0.0570
188	TILT TCWARD BEING THCSE 0.81 OF 27 WHERE THE KIN GRCUP IS CTHER THAN EXCLUSIVELY CCGNATIC (252)	188	TILT TOWARD BEING THOSE 0.55 CF 11 WHERE THE KIN GRCUP IS EXCLUSIVELY CCGNATIC (148)	5 6 22 5 XSQ= 3.34 PHI= -0.296 EP = 0.0471
356	DRIFT TCWARD BEING THCSE 0.80 OF 10 WHERE ADCLESCENT PEER CRCUPS CR PAIRS ARE PRESENT IN A SETTING CF CCURTSHIP (29) JKH	356	IN ALL CASES ARE THCSE 1.00 CF 2 WHERE NEITHER ADCLESCENT PEER GRCUPS NOR PAIRS ARE PRESENT IN A SETTING CF COURTSHIP (22) JKH	8 0 2 2 XSQ= 1.88 PHI= 0.395 EP = 0.0909
427	DRIFT TCWARD BEING THCSE 0.55 OF 11 WHERE A HIGH GCC, IF PRESENT, IS INACTIVE, RATHER THAN ACTIVE (69) GES,EA	427	IN ALL CASES ARE THCSE 1.00 CF 5 WHERE A HIGH GCD, IF PRESENT, IS ACTIVE, RATHER THAN INACTIVE (87) GES,EA	5 5 6 0 XSQ= 2.35 PHI= -0.383 EP = 0.0934
431	DRIFT TCWARD BEING THCSE 0.81 OF 26 WHERE SUPERNATURAL SANCTICNS FOR MORALITY, HAVING AN EFFECT CN AN INDIVIDUAL'S AFTERLIFE, ARE ABSENT OR UNREPCRTEC (25) GES	431	DRIFT TOWARD BEING THCSE 0.56 CF 9 WHERE SUPERNATURAL SANCTIONS FOR MORALITY, HAVING AN EFFECT ON AN INDIVIDUAL'S AFTER LIFE, ARE PRESENT (10) GES	5 5 21 4 XSQ= 2.73 PHI= -0.279 EP = 0.0814

****

437	CULTURES WHERE FEAR OF GHOSTS, SPIRITS, HUMANS OR ANIMALS IS HIGH (21) W-C,JFG	437	CULTURES WHERE FEAR OF GHOSTS, SPIRITS, HUMANS OR ANIMALS IS LOW (23) W-C,JFG

BACKGROUND ON PAGE 165 — BOTH SUBJECT AND PREDICATE

....

21 IN LEFT COLUMN

AINU	ANDAMANESE	CHAGGA	CHIR-APACHE	DOBUANS	FON	HANO	IFUGAO	JIVARO	KWAKIUTL
LAKHER	MAORI	MARQUESANS	MURNGIN	NAVAHO	OMAHA	PAPAGO	SANPOIL	SENIANG	TANALA
VENDA									

23 IN RIGHT COLUMN

ABIPON	ALORESE	ASHANTI	AZANDE	BALINESE	CHENCHU	KAZAK	KURTATCHI	KUTENAI	LAMBA
LEPCHA	LESU	PALAUANS	PUKAPUKA	SIRIONO	TAOS	THONGA	TIV	TROBRIAND	WAPISHANA
WARRAU	YAGUA	ZUNI							

356 EXCLUDED BECAUSE UNASCERTAINED

16	TILT TOWARD BEING THOSE WHERE THE LATITUDE IS TEN DEGREES OR GREATER (277)	0.81 OF 21	16	TILT TOWARD BEING THOSE WHERE THE LATITUDE IS LESS THAN TEN DEGREES (123)	0.52 OF 23	17 11 4 12 XSQ= 3.87 PHI= 0.297 XP = 0.0491
87	TILT LESS TOWARD BEING THOSE WHERE THE LEVEL OF POLITICAL INTEGRATION IS THE LARGE STATE, THE LITTLE STATE, THE MINIMAL STATE, OR THE AUTONOMOUS COMMUNITY (281) GPM	0.75 OF 16	87	IN ALL CASES ARE THOSE WHERE THE LEVEL OF POLITICAL INTEGRATION IS THE LARGE STATE, THE LITTLE STATE, THE MINIMAL STATE, OR THE AUTONOMOUS COMMUNITY (281) GPM	1.00 OF 22	12 22 4 0 XSQ= 3.78 PHI= -0.315 EP = 0.0247
90	IN ALL CASES ARE THOSE WHERE, IF A HEREDITARY HEADMANSHIP IS PRESENT, SUCCESSION IS PATRILINEAL, RATHER THAN MATRILINEAL (127)	1.00 OF 11	90	DRIFT LESS TOWARD BEING THOSE WHERE, IF A HEREDITARY HEADMANSHIP IS PRESENT, SUCCESSION IS PATRILINEAL, RATHER THAN MATRILINEAL (127)	0.64 OF 11	11 7 0 4 XSQ= 2.75 PHI= 0.354 EP = 0.0902
263	TILT TOWARD BEING THOSE WHERE WIVES ARE OBTAINED BY RELATIVELY EASY MEANS, NAMELY BY TOKEN BRIDE-PRICE, GIFT EXCHANGE, ABSENCE OF ANY CONSIDERATION, OR RECEIPT OF DOWRY (162)	0.62 OF 21	263	TILT TOWARD BEING THOSE WHERE WIVES ARE OBTAINED BY RELATIVELY DIFFICULT MEANS, NAMELY BY BRIDE-PRICE, BRIDE-SERVICE, OR EXCHANGING A FEMALE RELATIVE (233)	0.74 OF 23	8 17 13 6 XSQ= 4.37 PHI= -0.315 XP = 0.0365

296	TILT TOWARD BEING THOSE WHERE INFANTICIDE IS PRESENT (18) BCA	0.61 OF 18	296	TILT TOWARD BEING THOSE WHERE INFANTICIDE IS ABSENT OR INFERRED ABSENT (15) BCA	0.89 OF 9	11 1 7 8 XSQ= 4.22 PHI= 0.395 EP = 0.0192
302	LEAN TOWARD BEING THOSE WHERE THE AVERAGE EARLY SATISFACTION POTENTIAL IS LOW (17) W-C	0.67 OF 15	302	LEAN TOWARD BEING THOSE WHERE THE AVERAGE EARLY SATISFACTION POTENTIAL IS HIGH (23) W-C	0.86 OF 14	5 12 10 2 XSQ= 6.17 PHI= -0.461 EP = 0.0078
307	TILT TOWARD BEING THOSE WHERE THE EARLY AGGRESSION SATISFACTION POTENTIAL IS LOW (19) W-C	0.65 OF 20	307	TILT TOWARD BEING THOSE WHERE THE EARLY AGGRESSION SATISFACTION POTENTIAL IS HIGH (33) W-C	0.76 OF 17	7 13 13 4 XSQ= 4.80 PHI= -0.360 EP = 0.0202
349	TILT TOWARD BEING THOSE WHERE THE CHILD'S INFERRED ANXIETY OVER NON-PERFORMANCE OF ACHIEVEMENT BEHAVIOR IS HIGH (34) B-B-C	0.79 OF 14	349	TILT TOWARD BEING THOSE WHERE THE CHILD'S INFERRED ANXIETY OVER NON-PERFORMANCE OF ACHIEVEMENT BEHAVIOR IS LOW (28) B-B-C	0.64 OF 11	11 4 3 7 XSQ= 2.98 PHI= 0.345 EP = 0.0486
380	DRIFT TOWARD BEING THOSE WHERE SEGREGATION OF GIRLS AT MENARCHE IS PRESENT (35) F-B	0.80 OF 10	380	DRIFT TOWARD BEING THOSE WHERE SEGREGATION OF GIRLS AT MENARCHE IS ABSENT (20) F-B	0.58 OF 12	8 5 2 7 XSQ= 1.92 PHI= 0.295 EP = 0.0991
434	TILT TOWARD BEING THOSE WHERE ASCETICISM IN MOURNING BEHAVIOR IS HIGH (37) JFG	0.67 OF 21	434	TILT TOWARD BEING THOSE WHERE ASCETICISM IN MOURNING BEHAVIOR IS LOW (30) JFG	0.70 OF 23	14 7 7 16 XSQ= 4.42 PHI= 0.317 XP = 0.0356
439	LEAN TOWARD BEING THOSE WHERE FEAR OF GHOSTS IS HIGH (30) W-C	0.71 OF 21	439	LEAN TOWARD BEING THOSE WHERE FEAR OF GHOSTS IS LOW (31) W-C	0.81 OF 21	15 4 6 17 XSQ= 9.61 PHI= 0.478 XP = 0.0019
440	TILT TOWARD BEING THOSE WHERE FEAR OF SPIRITS IS HIGH (32) W-C	0.71 OF 21	440	TILT TOWARD BEING THOSE WHERE FEAR OF SPIRITS IS LOW (29) W-C	0.67 OF 21	15 7 6 14 XSQ= 4.68 PHI= 0.334 XP = 0.0306
443	TEND TO BE THOSE WHERE OVERALL FEAR OF OTHERS IS HIGH (31) W-C	0.86 OF 21	443	TEND TO BE THOSE WHERE OVERALL FEAR OF OTHERS IS LOW (30) W-C	0.81 OF 21	18 4 3 17 XSQ= 16.13 PHI= 0.620 XP = 0.0001

437/

453	IN ALL CASES ARE THOSE WHERE THE ROLE OF RELIGIOUS EXPERTS IS NOT CONDUCIVE TO THE DEVELOPMENT OF THE INDIVIDUAL'S NEED TO ACHIEVE (23) DCM	1.00 OF 7	453	DRIFT TOWARD BEING THOSE. WHERE THE ROLE OF RELIGIOUS EXPERTS IS CONDUCIVE TO THE DEVELOPMENT OF THE INDIVIDUAL'S NEED TO ACHIEVE (13) DCM	0.50 OF 6		0 3 7 3 XSQ= 2.17 PHI= -0.408 EP = 0.0699
476	TILT TOWARD BEING THOSE WHERE THE DEGREE OF INSOBRIETY IS STRONG (31) DH	0.69 OF 13	476	TILT TOWARD BEING THOSE WHERE THE DEGREE OF INSOBRIETY IS MODERATE OR SLIGHT (18) DH	0.80 OF 10		9 2 4 8 XSQ= 3.69 PHI= 0.401 EP = 0.0361

```
438  CULTURES                                          438  CULTURES
     WHERE OTHER-WORLDLY FEARS OF                           WHERE THIS-WORLDLY FEARS OF
     GHOSTS OR SPIRITS ARE GREATER THAN                     HUMANS OR ANIMALS ARE GREATER THAN
     THIS-WORLDLY FEARS OF                                  OTHER-WORLDLY FEARS OF
     HUMANS OR ANIMALS  (27) W-C,JFG                        GHOSTS OR SPIRITS  (17) W-C,JFG

BACKGROUND ON PAGE 165                                                          BOTH SUBJECT AND PREDICATE
..........................................................................................................

     27  IN LEFT COLUMN

AINU       ALORESE    ANDAMANESE  ASHANTI   BALINESE    CHAGGA    CHENCHU   FON      IFUGAO   KAZAK
KURTATCHI  KWAKIUTL   LAMBA       MAORI     MARQUESANS  MURNGIN   NAVAHO    OMAHA    PAPAGO   PUKAPUKA
SENIANG    SIRIONO    TANALA      THONGA    TROBRIAND   VENDA     WARRAU

     17  IN RIGHT COLUMN

ABIPON     AZANDE     CHIR-APACHE DOBUANS   HANO        JIVARO    KUTENAI   LAKHER   LEPCHA   LESU
PALAUANS   SANPOIL    TAOS        TIV       WAPISHANA   YAGUA     ZUNI

    356  EXCLUDED BECAUSE UNASCERTAINED

----------------------------------------------------------------------------------------------------------
260  DRIFT TOWARD BEING THOSE       0.83 OF  18     260  DRIFT TOWARD BEING THOSE      0.56 OF   9          15    4
     WHERE THE AGE OF MALES AT MARRIAGE                  WHERE THE AGE OF MALES AT MARRIAGE                  3    5
     IS LESS THAN TWENTY  (38) JKH                       IS TWENTY OR OVER  (17) JKH                   XSQ=     2.69
                                                                                                       PHI=    0.315
                                                                                                       EP =   0.0721

282  DRIFT TOWARD BEING THOSE       0.61 OF  18     282  DRIFT TOWARD BEING THOSE      0.82 OF  11          11    2
     WHERE THE STRENGTH OF DESIRE FOR CHILDREN           WHERE THE STRENGTH OF DESIRE FOR CHILDREN           7    9
     IS HIGH  (16) BCA                                   IS LOW OR ABSENT  (20) BCA                    XSQ=     3.50
                                                                                                       PHI=    0.347
                                                                                                       EP =   0.0524

299  LEAN TOWARD BEING THOSE        0.89 OF  18     299  LEAN TOWARD BEING THOSE       0.75 OF   8           2    6
     WHERE THE POST-PARTUM SEX TABOO LASTS               WHERE THE POST-PARTUM SEX TABOO LASTS              16    2
     ONE YEAR OR LESS  (89)                              LONGER THAN ONE YEAR  (35)                    XSQ=     7.83
                                                                                                       PHI=   -0.549
                                                                                                       EP =   0.0028

300  LEAN TOWARD BEING THOSE        0.72 OF  18     300  LEAN TOWARD BEING THOSE       0.88 OF   8           5    7
     WHERE THE POST-PARTUM SEX TABOO LASTS               WHERE THE POST-PARTUM SEX TABOO LASTS              13    1
     SIX MONTHS OR LESS  (73)                            LONGER THAN SIX MONTHS  (51)                  XSQ=     5.73
                                                                                                       PHI=   -0.469
                                                                                                       EP =   0.0093

318  TILT TOWARD BEING THOSE        0.70 OF  23     318  TILT TOWARD BEING THOSE       0.88 OF   8           7    7
     WHERE THE OVERALL INDULGENCE                        WHERE THE OVERALL INDULGENCE                       16    1
     OF THE INFANT                                       OF THE INFANT                                 XSQ=     5.67
     IS LOW  (31) B-B-C                                  IS HIGH  (40) B-B-C                           PHI=   -0.428
                                                                                                       EP =   0.0109
```

322	TILT TOWARD BEING THOSE WHERE THE CONSISTENCY OF REDUCTION OF THE INFANT'S DRIVES IS LOW (32) B-B-C	0.75 OF 20	322	TILT TOWARD BEING THOSE WHERE THE CONSISTENCY OF REDUCTION OF THE INFANT'S DRIVES IS HIGH (27) B-B-C	0.83 OF 6	5 5 15 1 XSQ= 4.40 PHI= -0.411 EP = 0.0184
323	DRIFT TOWARD BEING THOSE WHERE THE CONSTANCY OF PRESENCE OF THE INFANT'S NURTURANT AGENT IS LOW (45) B-B-C	0.75 OF 24	323	DRIFT TOWARD BEING THOSE WHERE THE CONSTANCY OF PRESENCE OF THE INFANT'S NURTURANT AGENT IS HIGH (29) B-B-C	0.63 OF 8	6 5 18 3 XSQ= 2.26 PHI= -0.266 EP = 0.0877
324	TILT TOWARD BEING THOSE WHERE THE PAIN INFLICTED ON THE INFANT BY THE NURTURANT AGENT IS HIGH (34) B-B-C	0.67 OF 21	324	TILT TOWARD BEING THOSE WHERE THE PAIN INFLICTED ON THE INFANT BY THE NURTURANT AGENT IS LOW OR NEGLIGIBLE (32) B-B-C	0.86 OF 7	14 1 7 6 XSQ= 3.88 PHI= 0.372 EP = 0.0286
331	DRIFT TOWARD BEING THOSE WHERE THE AGE AT BEGINNING OF INDEPENDENCE TRAINING IS LOWER THAN 3.8 YEARS (21) W-C	0.68 OF 19	331	DRIFT TOWARD BEING THOSE WHERE THE AGE AT BEGINNING OF INDEPENDENCE TRAINING IS 3.8 YEARS OR HIGHER (16) W-C	0.71 OF 7	6 5 13 2 XSQ= 1.90 PHI= -0.270 EP = 0.0946
342	TILT TOWARD BEING THOSE WHERE THE CHILD'S INFERRED ANXIETY OVER PERFORMANCE OF NURTURANT BEHAVIOR IS HIGH (18) B-B-C	0.71 OF 14	342	IN ALL CASES ARE THOSE WHERE THE CHILD'S INFERRED ANXIETY OVER PERFORMANCE OF NURTURANT BEHAVIOR IS LOW (28) B-B-C	1.00 OF 4	10 0 4 4 XSQ= 3.86 PHI= 0.463 EP = 0.0229
343	TILT TOWARD BEING THOSE WHERE THE CHILD'S INFERRED CONFLICT REGARDING NURTURANT BEHAVIOR IS HIGH (29) B-B-C	0.67 OF 15	343	IN ALL CASES ARE THOSE WHERE THE CHILD'S INFERRED CONFLICT REGARDING NURTURANT BEHAVIOR IS LOW (18) B-B-C	1.00 OF 4	10 0 5 4 XSQ= 3.27 PHI= 0.415 EP = 0.0325
370	DRIFT TOWARD BEING THOSE WHERE THE SEGREGATION OF ADOLESCENT BOYS IS COMPLETE OR PARTIAL (95)	0.55 OF 22	370	DRIFT TOWARD BEING THOSE WHERE THE SEGREGATION OF ADOLESCENT BOYS IS ABSENT (148)	0.79 OF 14	12 3 10 11 XSQ= 2.62 PHI= 0.270 EP = 0.0833
439	TEND TO BE THOSE WHERE FEAR OF GHOSTS IS HIGH (30) W-C	0.69 OF 26	439	TEND TO BE THOSE WHERE FEAR OF GHOSTS IS LOW (31) W-C	0.94 OF 16	18 1 8 15 XSQ= 13.42 PHI= 0.565 XP = 0.0002
441	TILT TOWARD BEING THOSE WHERE FEAR OF HUMAN BEINGS IS LOW (32) W-C	0.62 OF 26	441	TILT TOWARD BEING THOSE WHERE FEAR OF HUMAN BEINGS IS HIGH (29) W-C	0.81 OF 16	10 13 16 3 XSQ= 5.69 PHI= -0.368 XP = 0.0170

439 CULTURES WHERE FEAR OF GHOSTS IS HIGH (30) W-C

439 CULTURES WHERE FEAR OF GHOSTS IS LOW (31) W-C

BACKGROUND ON PAGE 165

BOTH SUBJECT AND PREDICATE

30 IN LEFT COLUMN

ALORESE	ANDAMANESE	ARAPESH	CHAGGA	CHENCHU	CHIR-APACHE	COPR ESKIMO	DUSUN	FON	IFUGAO
KWAKIUTL	LAMBA	LAPPS	MANUS	MAORI	MARQUESANS	MARSHALLESE	MURNGIN	NAVAHO	OMAHA
ONTONG-JAVA	PAPAGO	PUKAPUKA	SAMOANS	SENIANG	TANALA	TIKOPIA	VENDA	WITOTO	WOGEO

31 IN RIGHT COLUMN

ABIPON	AINU	ASHANTI	AZANDE	BALINESE	COMANCHE	DOBUANS	HANO	JIVARO	KURTATCHI
KUTENAI	LAKHER	LEPCHA	LESU	MASAI	RIFFIANS	RWALA	SANPOIL	SIRIONO	TAOS
TENINO	TETON	THONGA	TIV	TROBRIAND	WAPISHANA	WARRAU	YAGUA	YAKUT	YUKAGHIR
ZUNI									

339 EXCLUDED BECAUSE UNASCERTAINED

---

6 TILT TOWARD BEING THOSE LOCATED IN THE INSULAR PACIFIC (70) — 0.50 OF 30

6 TILT TOWARD BEING THOSE LOCATED OUTSIDE OF THE INSULAR PACIFIC (330) — 0.84 OF 31

15	5
15	26
XSQ=	6.47
PHI=	0.326
XP =	0.0109

42 DRIFT TOWARD BEING THOSE WHERE THE NATURAL ENVIRONMENT IS TROPICAL OR SUB-TROPICAL RAIN FOREST, OR MONSOON FOREST (156) FWM — 0.57 OF 30

42 DRIFT TOWARD BEING THOSE WHERE THE NATURAL ENVIRONMENT IS OTHER THAN TROPICAL OR SUB-TROPICAL RAIN FOREST, OR MONSOON FOREST (244) FWM — 0.71 OF 31

17	9
13	22
XSQ=	3.70
PHI=	0.246
XP =	0.0545

74 DRIFT TOWARD BEING THOSE WHERE POTTERY IS ABSENT (93) — 0.58 OF 24

74 DRIFT TOWARD BEING THOSE WHERE POTTERY IS PRESENT (145) — 0.73 OF 22

10	16
14	6
XSQ=	3.33
PHI=	-0.269
XP =	0.0680

85 DRIFT MORE TOWARD BEING THOSE WHERE THE LEVEL OF POLITICAL INTEGRATION IS THE MINIMAL STATE, THE AUTONOMOUS COMMUNITY, OR THE FAMILY (234) GPM — 0.96 OF 26

85 DRIFT LESS TOWARD BEING THOSE WHERE THE LEVEL OF POLITICAL INTEGRATION IS THE MINIMAL STATE, THE AUTONOMOUS COMMUNITY, OR THE FAMILY (234) GPM — 0.74 OF 23

1	6
25	17
XSQ=	3.28
PHI=	-0.259
XP =	0.0701

198	IN ALL CASES ARE THCSE 1.00 OF 11 WHERE RULES FCR THE INHERITANCE OF REAL PRCPERTY, IF PRESENT, FAVCR THE MALE HEIR CR LINE, RATHER THAN THE FEMALE (144)	198	TILT TOWARD BEING THOSE 0.50 OF 10 WHERE RULES FOR THE INHERITANCE CF REAL PROPERTY, IF PRESENT, FAVOR THE FEMALE HEIR OR LINE, RATHER THAN THE MALE (21)	11 5 0 5 XSQ= 4.73 PHI= 0.474 EP = 0.0124
260	DRIFT TCWARD BEING THCSE 0.87 OF 15 WHERE THE AGE CF MALES AT MARRIAGE IS LESS THAN TWENTY (38) JKH	260	DRIFT TOWARD BEING THOSE 0.50 OF 16 WHERE THE AGE CF MALES AT MARRIAGE IS TWENTY OR OVER (17) JKH	13 8 2 8 XSQ= 3.23 PHI= 0.323 EP = 0.0538
329	DRIFT TCWARD BEING THCSE 0.69 OF 13 WHERE THE AGE AT TCILET TRAINING IS LCWER THAN TWC YEARS (11) W-C	329	DRIFT TOWARD BEING THOSE 0.75 CF 8 WHERE THE AGE AT TOILET TRAINING IS TWO YEARS OR HIGHER (10) W-C	4 6 9 2 XSQ= 2.31 PHI= -0.332 EP = 0.0805
398	DRIFT TCWARD BEING THCSE 0.69 OF 16 WHERE THE INTENSITY CF SEX ANXIETY IS HIGH (16) WNS	398	DRIFT TOWARD BEING THOSE 0.69 OF 16 WHERE THE INTENSITY OF SEX ANXIETY IS LOW (16) WNS	11 5 5 11 XSQ= 3.13 PHI= 0.312 EP = 0.0756
437	LEAN TCWARD BEING THCSE 0.79 OF 19 WHERE FEAR OF GHCSTS, SPIRITS, HUMANS CR ANIMALS IS HIGH (21) W-C,JFG	437	LEAN TOWARD BEING THOSE 0.74 OF 23 WHERE FEAR OF GHOSTS, SPIRITS, HUMANS OR ANIMALS IS LOW (23) W-C,JFG	15 6 4 17 XSQ= 9.61 PHI= 0.478 XP = 0.0019
438	TEND TC BE THCSE 0.95 OF 19 WHERE CTHER-WCRLDLY FEARS CF GHCSTS CR SPIRITS ARE GREATER THAN THIS-WCRLDLY FEARS CF HUMANS CR ANIMALS (27) W-C,JFG	438	TEND TO BE THOSE 0.65 OF 23 WHERE THIS-WORLDLY FEARS CF HUMANS OR ANIMALS ARE GREATER THAN OTHER-WORLDLY FEARS OF GHOSTS OR SPIRITS (17) W-C,JFG	18 8 1 15 XSQ= 13.42 PHI= 0.565 XP = 0.0002
446	DRIFT TCWARD BEING THCSE 0.80 OF 5 WHERE WITCHCRAFT IS MCDERATELY PRESENT CR ABSENT (24) GES	446	DRIFT TOWARD BEING THOSE 0.83 CF 6 WHERE WITCHCRAFT IS SIGNIFICANTLY PRESENT (14) GES	1 5 4 1 XSQ= 2.23 PHI= -0.450 EP = 0.0801
453	IN ALL CASES ARE THCSE 1.00 OF 8 WHERE THE ROLE CF RELIGICUS EXPERTS IS NCT CCNDUCIVE TC THE DEVELOPMENT OF THE INDIVIDUAL'S NEED TC ACHIEVE (23) DCM	453	TILT TOWARD BEING THOSE 0.56 OF 9 WHERE THE RCLE CF RELIGICUS EXPERTS IS CONDUCIVE TO THE DEVELCPMENT CF THE INDIVIDUAL'S NEED TO ACHIEVE (13) DCM	0 5 8 4 XSQ= 3.90 PHI= -0.479 EP = 0.0294

440	CULTURES WHERE FEAR OF SPIRITS IS HIGH (32) W-C	440	CULTURES WHERE FEAR OF SPIRITS IS LOW (29) W-C

BACKGROUND ON PAGE 165 — BOTH SUBJECT AND PREDICATE

32 IN LEFT COLUMN

AINU	ALORESE	ANDAMANESE	BALINESE	CHAGGA	CHIR-APACHE	DOBUANS	DUSUN	HANO	IFUGAO
JIVARO	LAKHER	LAMBA	LAPPS	MANUS	MAORI	MARQUESANS	MARSHALLESE	NAVAHO	ONTONG-JAVA
PAPAGO	RIFFIANS	SANPOIL	SIRIONO	TANALA	TETON	TIV	TROBRIAND	WAPISHANA	WITOTO
YAKUT	YUKAGHIR								

29 IN RIGHT COLUMN

ABIPON	ARAPESH	ASHANTI	AZANDE	CHENCHU	COMANCHE	COPR ESKIMO	FON	KURTATCHI	KUTENAI
KWAKIUTL	LEPCHA	LESU	MASAI	MURNGIN	OMAHA	PUKAPUKA	RWALA	SAMOANS	SENIANG
TAOS	TENINO	THONGA	TIKOPIA	VENDA	WARRAU	WOGEO	YAGUA	ZUNI	

339 EXCLUDED BECAUSE UNASCERTAINED

56	DRIFT LESS TOWARD BEING THOSE WHERE FOOD PRODUCTION IS BY SIMPLE AGRICULTURE, RATHER THAN BY INCIPIENT FOOD PRODUCTION (101)	0.57 OF 14	56	DRIFT MORE TOWARD BEING THOSE WHERE FOOD PRODUCTION IS BY SIMPLE AGRICULTURE, RATHER THAN BY INCIPIENT FOOD PRODUCTION (101)	0.91 OF 11	8 10 6 1 XSQ= 2.01 PHI= -0.284 EP = 0.0900
73	DRIFT TOWARD BEING THOSE WHERE WEAVING IS PRESENT (118)	0.60 OF 20	73	DRIFT TOWARD BEING THOSE WHERE WEAVING IS ABSENT (130)	0.69 OF 26	12 8 8 18 XSQ= 2.83 PHI= 0.248 XP = 0.0925
130	DRIFT TOWARD BEING THOSE WHERE LEATHER WORKING IS MAINLY DONE BY MALES (39)	0.67 OF 6	130	IN ALL CASES ARE THOSE WHERE LEATHER WORKING IS MAINLY DONE BY FEMALES (45)	1.00 OF 6	4 0 2 6 XSQ= 3.38 PHI= 0.530 EP = 0.0606
143	DRIFT TOWARD BEING THOSE WHERE THE RATIO OF RESTITUTIVE TO REPRESSIVE SANCTIONS IS HIGH (20) WME	0.64 OF 11	143	DRIFT TOWARD BEING THOSE WHERE THE RATIO OF RESTITUTIVE TO REPRESSIVE SANCTIONS IS MEDIUM OR LOW (32) WME	0.88 OF 8	7 1 4 7 XSQ= 3.09 PHI= 0.403 EP = 0.0587

149	DRIFT TOWARD BEING THOSE WHERE THE INCIDENCE OF THEFT IS LOW (19) B-B-C	0.77 OF 13	149	DRIFT TOWARD BEING THOSE WHERE THE INCIDENCE OF THEFT IS HIGH (18) B-B-C	0.60 OF 15	3 9 10 6 XSQ= 2.52 PHI= -0.300 EP = 0.0671
183	IN ALL CASES ARE THOSE WHERE THE LARGEST NON-COGNATIC KIN GROUP IS SMALLER THAN A MOEITY, I. E., A PHRATRY OR SIB OR LINEAGE (218)	1.00 OF 17	183	TILT LESS TOWARD BEING THOSE WHERE THE LARGEST NON-COGNATIC KIN GROUP IS SMALLER THAN A MOEITY, I. E., A PHRATRY OR SIB OR LINEAGE (218)	0.75 OF 20	0 5 17 15 XSQ= 3.01 PHI= -0.285 EP = 0.0498
185	DRIFT LESS TOWARD BEING THOSE WHERE THE LARGEST NON-COGNATIC KIN GROUP IS THE MOEITY OR PHRATRY OR SIB (194)	0.71 OF 17	185	DRIFT MORE TOWARD BEING THOSE WHERE THE LARGEST NON-COGNATIC KIN GROUP IS THE MOEITY OR PHRATRY OR SIB (194)	0.95 OF 20	12 19 5 1 XSQ= 2.43 PHI= -0.256 EP = 0.0752
190	DRIFT LESS TOWARD BEING THOSE WHERE THE KIN GROUP IS PATRILINEAL OR DOUBLE-DESCENT, RATHER THAN MATRILINEAL (186)	0.53 OF 15	190	DRIFT MORE TOWARD BEING THOSE WHERE THE KIN GROUP IS PATRILINEAL OR DOUBLE-DESCENT, RATHER THAN MATRILINEAL (186)	0.84 OF 19	8 16 7 3 XSQ= 2.51 PHI= -0.271 EP = 0.0680
254	IN ALL CASES ARE THOSE WHERE HOUSEHOLD AUTHORITY IS ON THE MOTHER'S SIDE, RATHER THAN THE FATHER'S (6) DA	1.00 OF 4	254	IN ALL CASES ARE THOSE WHERE HOUSEHOLD AUTHORITY IS ON THE FATHER'S SIDE, RATHER THAN THE MOTHER'S (9) DA	1.00 OF 6	0 6 4 0 XSQ= 6.27 PHI= -0.792 EP = 0.0048
278	IN ALL CASES ARE THOSE WHERE PROPERTY RIGHTS IN WOMEN ARE UNIMPORTANT OR ABSENT (14) LWS	1.00 OF 5	278	IN ALL CASES ARE THOSE WHERE PROPERTY RIGHTS IN WOMEN ARE PRESENT (8) LWS	1.00 OF 2	0 2 5 0 XSQ= 2.96 PHI= -0.650 EP = 0.0476
314	DRIFT MORE TOWARD BEING THOSE WHERE THE INCIDENCE OF MOTHER-CHILD HOUSEHOLDS IS LOW (61) W-D,S	0.91 OF 23	314	DRIFT LESS TOWARD BEING THOSE WHERE THE INCIDENCE OF MOTHER-CHILD HOUSEHOLDS IS LOW (61) W-D,S	0.67 OF 21	2 7 21 14 XSQ= 2.72 PHI= -0.249 XP = 0.0990
372	LEAN TOWARD BEING THOSE WHERE MALE INITIATION RITES ARE ABSENT (63) ASA	0.78 OF 23	372	LEAN TOWARD BEING THOSE WHERE MALE INITIATION RITES ARE PRESENT (48) ASA	0.67 OF 24	5 16 18 8 XSQ= 7.86 PHI= -0.409 XP = 0.0051
402	DRIFT TOWARD BEING THOSE WHERE EXPLANATIONS OF ILLNESS OF AN ORAL NATURE ARE PRESENT (31) W-C	0.63 OF 32	402	DRIFT TOWARD BEING THOSE WHERE EXPLANATIONS OF ILLNESS OF AN ORAL NATURE ARE ABSENT (30) W-C	0.62 OF 29	20 11 12 18 XSQ= 2.76 PHI= 0.213 XP = 0.0968

```
437  TILT TCWARD BEING THCSE          0.68 OF  22    437  TILT TOWARD BEING THOSE          0.70 OF  20          15     6
     WHERE FEAR OF GHCSTS, SPIRITS,                      WHERE FEAR OF GHOSTS, SPIRITS,                         7    14
     HUMANS CR ANIMALS                                   HUMANS OR ANIMALS                               XSQ=      4.68
     IS HIGH  (21) W-C,JFG                               IS LOW  (23) W-C,JFG                            PHI=     0.334
                                                                                                         XP =    0.0306

443  LEAN TCWARD BEING THCSE          0.69 OF  32    443  LEAN TOWARD BEING THOSE          0.69 OF  29          22     9
     WHERE CVERALL FEAR CF CTHERS                        WHERE OVERALL FEAR CF OTHERS                          10    20
     IS HIGH  (31) W-C                                   IS LOW  (30) W-C                                XSQ=      7.22
                                                                                                         PHI=     0.344
                                                                                                         XP =    0.0072

453  IN ALL CASES ARE THCSE           1.00 OF   7    453  TILT TOWARD BEING THOSE          0.50 OF  10           0     5
     WHERE THE ROLE CF RELIGICUS EXPERTS                 WHERE THE ROLE OF RELIGICUS EXPERTS                    7     5
     IS NCT CCNDUCIVE TC THE CEVELOPMENT OF THE          IS CONDUCIVE TC THE DEVELCPMENT OF THE          XSQ=      2.84
     INDIVIDUAL'S NEED TC ACHIEVE  (23) CCM              INDIVIDUAL'S NEED TC ACHIEVE  (13) DCM          PHI=    -0.409
                                                                                                         EP =    0.0441
```

****

441 CULTURES WHERE FEAR OF HUMAN BEINGS IS HIGH (29) W-C	441 CULTURES WHERE FEAR OF HUMAN BEINGS IS LOW (32) W-C

BACKGROUND ON PAGE 165 — BOTH SUBJECT AND PREDICATE

29 IN LEFT COLUMN

ABIPON	ARAPESH	AZANDE	CHAGGA	CHIR-APACHE	DOBUANS	HANO	IFUGAO	JIVARO	KURTATCHI
KWAKIUTL	LAPPS	LESU	MAORI	MURNGIN	OMAHA	RIFFIANS	SANPOIL	SENIANG	TAOS
TENINO	TIV	TROBRIAND	VENDA	WAPISHANA	WITOTO	WOGEO	YAGUA	ZUNI	

32 IN RIGHT COLUMN

AINU	ALORESE	ANDAMANESE	ASHANTI	BALINESE	CHENCHU	COMANCHE	COPR ESKIMO	DUSUN	FON
KUTENAI	LAKHER	LAMBA	LEPCHA	MANUS	MARQUESANS	MARSHALLESE	MASAI	NAVAHO	ONTONG-JAVA
PAPAGO	PUKAPUKA	RWALA	SAMOANS	SIRIONO	TANALA	TETON	THONGA	TIKOPIA	WARRAU
YAKUT	YUKAGHIR								

339 EXCLUDED BECAUSE UNASCERTAINED

	High (29)			Low (32)			Statistics
5	IN ALL CASES ARE THOSE LOCATED OUTSIDE OF EAST EURASIA (330)	1.00 OF 29	5	TILT LESS TOWARD BEING THOSE LOCATED OUTSIDE OF EAST EURASIA (330)	0.75 OF 32		0 8 / 29 24 / XSQ= 6.29 / PHI= -0.321 / XP = 0.0121
81	DRIFT LESS TOWARD BEING THOSE WHERE NO CITY OR TOWN IS PRESENT, AND THE AVERAGE COMMUNITY SIZE IS SMALLER THAN 200 (135)	0.53 OF 19	81	DRIFT MORE TOWARD BEING THOSE WHERE NO CITY OR TOWN IS PRESENT, AND THE AVERAGE COMMUNITY SIZE IS SMALLER THAN 200 (135)	0.81 OF 21		9 4 / 10 17 / XSQ= 2.47 / PHI= 0.249 / EP = 0.0915
83	DRIFT LESS TOWARD BEING THOSE WHERE, WITH NO CITY AND NO TOWN PRESENT, THE AVERAGE COMMUNITY SIZE IS SMALLER THAN 200, RATHER THAN BETWEEN 200 AND 999 (135)	0.59 OF 17	83	DRIFT MORE TOWARD BEING THOSE WHERE, WITH NO CITY AND NO TOWN PRESENT, THE AVERAGE COMMUNITY SIZE IS SMALLER THAN 200, RATHER THAN BETWEEN 200 AND 999 (135)	0.89 OF 19		7 2 / 10 17 / XSQ= 3.01 / PHI= 0.289 / EP = 0.0551
96	DRIFT TOWARD BEING THOSE WHERE THE HIERARCHY OF NATIONAL JURISDICTION HAS NO LEVELS (156) GES,EA	0.68 OF 28	96	DRIFT TOWARD BEING THOSE WHERE THE HIERARCHY OF NATIONAL JURISDICTION HAS FOUR, THREE, TWO OR ONE LEVEL (174) GES,EA	0.61 OF 28		9 17 / 19 11 / XSQ= 3.52 / PHI= -0.251 / XP = 0.0607

100	TILT LESS TOWARD BEING THOSE 0.68 OF 28 WHERE HIERARCHIES ARE MORE COMPLEX THAN THE 'SIMPLEST,' I. E., MORE COMPLEX THAN TWO LOCAL LEVELS WITH NO NATIONAL LEVELS (267) GES,EA	100	TILT MORE TOWARD BEING THOSE 0.93 OF 28 WHERE HIERARCHIES ARE MORE COMPLEX THAN THE 'SIMPLEST,' I. E., MORE COMPLEX THAN TWO LOCAL LEVELS WITH NO NATIONAL LEVELS (267) GES,EA	19 26 9 2 XSQ= 4.07 PHI= -0.270 XP = 0.0436
138	TILT TOWARD BEING THOSE 0.59 OF 17 WHERE SUPERORDINATE JUSTICE IS ABSENT (18) BBW	138	TILT TOWARD BEING THOSE 0.90 OF 10 WHERE SUPERORDINATE JUSTICE IS PRESENT (22) BBW	7 9 10 1 XSQ= 4.36 PHI= -0.402 EP = 0.0183
139	LEAN TOWARD BEING THOSE 0.82 OF 17 WHERE SUPERORDINATE PUNISHMENT IS ABSENT (25) BBW	139	LEAN TOWARD BEING THOSE 0.80 OF 10 WHERE SUPERORDINATE PUNISHMENT IS PRESENT (15) BBW	3 8 14 2 XSQ= 7.72 PHI= -0.535 EP = 0.0034
176	DRIFT TOWARD BEING THOSE 0.59 OF 29 WHERE THE COMMUNITY IS A CLAN-COMMUNITY OR A COMMUNITY STRUCTURED OR SEGMENTED ON A CLAN BASIS (169)	176	DRIFT TOWARD BEING THOSE 0.69 OF 32 WHERE THE COMMUNITY IS OTHER THAN A CLAN-COMMUNITY OR A COMMUNITY STRUCTURED OR SEGMENTED ON A CLAN BASIS (213)	17 10 12 22 XSQ= 3.58 PHI= 0.242 XP = 0.0586
183	TILT LESS TOWARD BEING THOSE 0.72 OF 18 WHERE THE LARGEST NON-COGNATIC KIN GROUP IS SMALLER THAN A MOEITY, I. E., A PHRATRY OR SIB OR LINEAGE (218)	183	IN ALL CASES ARE THOSE 1.00 OF 19 WHERE THE LARGEST NON-COGNATIC KIN GROUP IS SMALLER THAN A MOEITY, I. E., A PHRATRY OR SIB OR LINEAGE (218)	5 0 13 19 XSQ= 3.96 PHI= 0.327 EP = 0.0197
243	TILT TOWARD BEING THOSE 0.64 OF 14 WHERE POLYGYNY, IF PRESENT, HAS A HIGH INCIDENCE (24) W-D,S	243	TILT TOWARD BEING THOSE 0.76 OF 17 WHERE POLYGYNY, IF PRESENT, HAS A LOW INCIDENCE (36) W-D,S	9 4 5 13 XSQ= 3.70 PHI= 0.345 EP = 0.0325
286	TILT TOWARD BEING THOSE 0.81 OF 16 WHERE THE NUMBER OF FOOD TABOOS DURING PREGNANCY IS HIGH (20) BCA	286	TILT TOWARD BEING THOSE 0.61 OF 18 WHERE THE NUMBER OF FOOD TABOOS DURING PREGNANCY IS LOW OR ABSENT (14) BCA	13 7 3 11 XSQ= 4.65 PHI= 0.370 EP = 0.0173
299	LEAN TOWARD BEING THOSE 0.56 OF 18 WHERE THE POST-PARTUM SEX TABOO LASTS LONGER THAN ONE YEAR (35)	299	LEAN TOWARD BEING THOSE 0.94 OF 17 WHERE THE POST-PARTUM SEX TABOO LASTS ONE YEAR OR LESS (89)	10 1 8 16 XSQ= 7.84 PHI= 0.473 EP = 0.0027
300	LEAN TOWARD BEING THOSE 0.72 OF 18 WHERE THE POST-PARTUM SEX TABOO LASTS LONGER THAN SIX MONTHS (51)	300	LEAN TOWARD BEING THOSE 0.76 OF 17 WHERE THE POST-PARTUM SEX TABOO LASTS SIX MONTHS OR LESS (73)	13 4 5 13 XSQ= 6.46 PHI= 0.430 EP = 0.0067

317	LEAN TOWARD BEING THOSE 0.87 OF 15 WHERE DISPLAY OF AFFECTION TOWARD THE INFANT IS HIGH (39) B-B-C	317	LEAN TOWARD BEING THOSE 0.61 OF 23 WHERE DISPLAY OF AFFECTION TOWARD THE INFANT IS LOW (29) B-B-C	13 9 2 14 XSQ= 6.58 PHI= 0.416 EP = 0.0065
331	TILT TOWARD BEING THOSE 0.67 OF 15 WHERE THE AGE AT BEGINNING OF INDEPENDENCE TRAINING IS 3.8 YEARS OR HIGHER (16) W-C	331	TILT TOWARD BEING THOSE 0.73 OF 22 WHERE THE AGE AT BEGINNING OF INDEPENDENCE TRAINING IS LOWER THAN 3.8 YEARS (21) W-C	10 6 5 16 XSQ= 4.15 PHI= 0.335 EP = 0.0409
369	TILT MORE TOWARD BEING THOSE 0.93 OF 15 WHERE DISSOCIATION OF THE SEXES AT ADOLESCENCE, OR CUSTOMS OF INITIATION AT ADOLESCENCE, ARE PRESENT (42) JKH	369	TILT LESS TOWARD BEING THOSE 0.56 OF 16 WHERE DISSOCIATION OF THE SEXES AT ADOLESCENCE, OR CUSTOMS OF INITIATION AT ADOLESCENCE, ARE PRESENT (42) JKH	14 9 1 7 XSQ= 3.79 PHI= 0.350 EP = 0.0373
373	TILT TOWARD BEING THOSE 0.67 OF 12 WHERE MALE INITIATION CEREMONIES AT PUBERTY ARE PRESENT (17) W-K-A	373	TILT TOWARD BEING THOSE 0.80 OF 15 WHERE MALE INITIATION CEREMONIES AT PUBERTY ARE ABSENT (27) W-K-A	8 3 4 12 XSQ= 4.24 PHI= 0.396 EP = 0.0220
392	DRIFT TOWARD BEING THOSE 0.74 OF 23 WHERE PREMARITAL SEX RELATIONS ARE STRONGLY PUNISHED AND IN FACT RARE, OR WEAKLY PUNISHED AND IN FACT NOT RARE, OR PUNISHED ONLY IF PREGNANCY RESULTS (112) JTW,EA	392	DRIFT TOWARD BEING THOSE 0.59 OF 22 WHERE PREMARITAL SEX RELATIONS ARE FREELY PERMITTED (67) JTW,EA	17 9 6 13 XSQ= 3.76 PHI= 0.289 XP = 0.0525
397	DRIFT LESS TOWARD BEING THOSE 0.53 OF 15 WHERE SEX DISABILITY IS ABSENT (42) JKH	397	DRIFT MORE TOWARD BEING THOSE 0.88 OF 16 WHERE SEX DISABILITY IS ABSENT (42) JKH	7 2 8 14 XSQ= 2.88 PHI= 0.305 EP = 0.0538
431	IN ALL CASES ARE THOSE 1.00 OF 7 WHERE SUPERNATURAL SANCTIONS FOR MORALITY, HAVING AN EFFECT ON AN INDIVIDUAL'S AFTERLIFE, ARE ABSENT OR UNREPORTED (25) GES	431	TILT TOWARD BEING THOSE 0.75 OF 4 WHERE SUPERNATURAL SANCTIONS FOR MORALITY, HAVING AN EFFECT ON AN INDIVIDUAL'S AFTER LIFE, ARE PRESENT (10) GES	0 3 7 1 XSQ= 3.93 PHI= -0.598 EP = 0.0242
438	TILT TOWARD BEING THOSE 0.57 OF 23 WHERE THIS-WORLDLY FEARS OF HUMANS OR ANIMALS ARE GREATER THAN OTHER-WORLDLY FEARS OF GHOSTS OR SPIRITS (17) W-C,JFG	438	TILT TOWARD BEING THOSE 0.84 OF 19 WHERE OTHER-WORLDLY FEARS OF GHOSTS OR SPIRITS ARE GREATER THAN THIS-WORLDLY FEARS OF HUMANS OR ANIMALS (27) W-C,JFG	10 16 13 3 XSQ= 5.69 PHI= -0.368 XP = 0.0170
443	TEND TO BE THOSE 0.79 OF 29 WHERE OVERALL FEAR OF OTHERS IS HIGH (31) W-C	443	TEND TO BE THOSE 0.75 OF 32 WHERE OVERALL FEAR OF OTHERS IS LOW (30) W-C	23 8 6 24 XSQ= 15.85 PHI= 0.510 XP = 0.0001

445	LEAN TCWARD BEING THCSE WHERE SCRCERY IS IMPCRTANT (26) EBW,CH	0.92 OF 12	445	LEAN TOWARD BEING THOSE WHERE SORCERY IS UNIMPORTANT (23) BBW,DH	0.69 CF 13	11 4 1 9 XSQ= 7.27 PHI= 0.539 EP = 0.0036
447	LEAN TCWARD BEING THOSE WHERE LCVE MAGIC IS PRESENT (20) S-R	0.88 OF 16	447	LEAN TOWARD BEING THCSE WHERE LOVE MAGIC IS ABSENT (13) S-R	0.65 OF 17	14 6 2 11 XSQ= 7.35 PHI= 0.472 EP = 0.0039
471	IN ALL CASES ARE THCSE WHERE SECRET SCCIETIES ARE PRESENT (9) LWS	1.00 OF 3	471	TILT TOWARD BEING THOSE WHERE SECRET SOCIETIES ARE UMIMPORTANT OR ABSENT (14) LWS	0.83 CF 6	3 1 0 5 XSQ= 2.76 PHI= 0.553 EP = 0.0476

442 CULTURES
WHERE FEAR OF ANIMAL SPIRITS
IS HIGH (28) W-C

442 CULTURES
WHERE FEAR OF ANIMAL SPIRITS
IS LOW (33) W-C

BACKGROUND ON PAGE 165

BOTH SUBJECT AND PREDICATE

28 IN LEFT COLUMN

AINU	ARAPESH	AZANDE	BALINESE	CHIR-APACHE	COMANCHE	DOBUANS	FON	HANO	JIVARO
KWAKIUTL	LAKHER	LAPPS	LEPCHA	MAORI	NAVAHO	PAPAGO	RIFFIANS	SANPOIL	SIRIONO
TAOS	TENINO	TIKOPIA	TIV	TROBRIAND	VENDA	WITOTO	YAKUT		

33 IN RIGHT COLUMN

ABIPON	ALORESE	ANDAMANESE	ASHANTI	CHAGGA	CHENCHU	COPR ESKIMO	DUSUN	IFUGAO	KURTATCHI
KUTENAI	LAMBA	LESU	MANUS	MARQUESANS	MARSHALLESE	MASAI	MURNGIN	OMAHA	ONTONG-JAVA
PUKAPUKA	RWALA	SAMOANS	SENIANG	TANALA	TETON	THONGA	WAPISHANA	WARRAU	WOGEO
YAGUA	YUKAGHIR	ZUNI							

339 EXCLUDED BECAUSE UNASCERTAINED

14	TILT TOWARD BEING THOSE WHERE THE LATITUDE IS THIRTY DEGREES OR GREATER (119)	0.50 OF 28	14	TILT TOWARD BEING THOSE WHERE THE LATITUDE IS LESS THAN THIRTY DEGREES (281)	0.79 OF 33 14 7 14 26 XSQ= 4.36 PHI= 0.267 XP = 0.0368
15	TILT TOWARD BEING THOSE WHERE THE LATITUDE IS TWENTY DEGREES OR GREATER (183)	0.61 OF 28	15	TILT TOWARD BEING THOSE WHERE THE LATITUDE IS LESS THAN TWENTY DEGREES (217)	0.70 OF 33 17 10 11 23 XSQ= 4.51 PHI= 0.272 XP = 0.0336
42	DRIFT TOWARD BEING THOSE WHERE THE NATURAL ENVIRONMENT IS OTHER THAN TROPICAL OR SUB-TROPICAL RAIN FOREST, OR MONSOON FOREST (244) FWM	0.71 OF 28	42	DRIFT TOWARD BEING THOSE WHERE THE NATURAL ENVIRONMENT IS TROPICAL OR SUB-TROPICAL RAIN FOREST, OR MONSOON FOREST (156) FWM	0.55 OF 33 8 18 20 15 XSQ= 3.18 PHI= -0.228 XP = 0.0744
73	TILT TOWARD BEING THOSE WHERE WEAVING IS PRESENT (118)	0.61 OF 23	73	TILT TOWARD BEING THOSE WHERE WEAVING IS ABSENT (130)	0.74 OF 23 14 6 9 17 XSQ= 4.33 PHI= 0.307 XP = 0.0373

74	DRIFT TCWARD BEING THCSE WHERE POTTERY IS PRESENT (145)	0.73 OF 22	74	DRIFT TOWARD BEING THOSE WHERE POTTERY IS ABSENT (93)	0.58 OF 24	16 10 6 14 XSQ= 3.33 PHI= 0.269 XP = 0.0680
81	TILT TCWARD BEING THOSE WHERE A CITY OR TOWN IS PRESENT, OR THE AVERAGE COMMUNITY SIZE IS 200 CR GREATER (89)	0.56 OF 16	81	TILT TOWARD BEING THOSE WHERE NO CITY OR TOWN IS PRESENT, AND THE AVERAGE COMMUNITY SIZE IS SMALLER THAN 200 (135)	0.83 OF 24	9 4 7 20 XSQ= 5.17 PHI= 0.360 EP = 0.0154
83	TILT TCWARD BEING THCSE WHERE, WITH NC CITY ANC NC TOWN PRESENT, THE AVERAGE COMMUNITY SIZE IS BETWEEN 200 AND 999, RATHER THAN SMALLER THAN 200 (45)	0.50 OF 14	83	TILT TOWARD BEING THOSE WHERE, WITH NO CITY AND NO TOWN PRESENT, THE AVERAGE COMMUNITY SIZE IS SMALLER THAN 200, RATHER THAN BETWEEN 200 AND 999 (135)	0.91 OF 22	7 2 7 20 XSQ= 5.61 PHI= 0.395 EP = 0.0144
197	IN ALL CASES ARE THCSE WHERE RULES FCR THE INHERITANCE OF REAL PRCPERTY, IF PRESENT, FAVCR EITHER THE MALE HEIR OR LINE, CR THE FEMALE HEIR CR LINE (165)	1.00 OF 13	197	DRIFT LESS TOWARD BEING THCSE WHERE RULES FOR THE INHERITANCE CF REAL PROPERTY, IF PRESENT, FAVOR EITHER THE MALE HEIR CR LINE, OR THE FEMALE HEIR OR LINE (165)	0.73 OF 11	13 8 0 3 XSQ= 1.94 PHI= 0.284 EP = 0.0815
236	LEAN TCWARD BEING THCSE WHERE THE FAMILY IS OF AN EXTENDED TYPE, RATHER THAN AN INDEPENDENT TYPE (213)	0.64 OF 28	236	LEAN TOWARD BEING THOSE WHERE THE FAMILY IS OF AN INDEPENDENT TYPE, RATHER THAN AN EXTENDED TYPE (185)	0.73 CF 33	18 9 10 24 XSQ= 6.98 PHI= 0.338 XP = 0.0083
263	TILT TCWARD BEING THCSE WHERE WIVES ARE CBTAINEC BY RELATIVELY EASY MEANS, NAMELY BY TOKEN BRIDE-PRICE, GIFT EXCHANGE, ABSENCE CF ANY CCNSICERATICN, OR RECEIPT CF DCWRY (162)	0.68 OF 28	263	TILT TOWARD BEING THOSE WHERE WIVES ARE OBTAINED BY RELATIVELY DIFFICULT MEANS, NAMELY BY BRIDE-PRICE, BRIDE-SERVICE, CR EXCHANGING A FEMALE RELATIVE (233)	0.67 CF 33	9 22 19 11 XSQ= 5.91 PHI= -0.311 XP = 0.0151
272	DRIFT TCWARD BEING THCSE WHERE THE DIVCRCE RATE IS LCW (28) CA	0.67 OF 6	272	DRIFT TOWARD BEING THOSE WHERE THE DIVORCE RATE IS HIGH (29) CA	0.88 OF 8	2 7 4 1 XSQ= 2.34 PHI= -0.409 EP = 0.0909
285	DRIFT TCWARD BEING THCSE WHERE THE SEX TABCC DURING PREGNANCY IS ABSENT CR INFERREC ABSENT (17) BCA	0.68 OF 19	285	DRIFT TOWARD BEING THOSE WHERE THE SEX TABOO DURING PREGNANCY IS PRESENT (14) BCA	0.67 CF 12	6 8 13 4 XSQ= 2.38 PHI= -0.277 EP = 0.0751
307	TILT TCWARC BEING THOSE WHERE THE EARLY AGGRESSICN SATISFACTICN PCTENTIAL IS LCW (19) W-C	0.54 OF 24	307	TILT TOWARD BEING THOSE WHERE THE EARLY AGGRESSICN SATISFACTION POTENTIAL IS HIGH (33) W-C	0.79 OF 28	11 22 13 6 XSQ= 4.64 PHI= -0.299 XP = 0.0311

No.	Left item	Proportion	No.	Right item	Proportion	Statistics
313	TILT TOWARD BEING THOSE WHERE AGGRESSION SOCIALIZATION ANXIETY IS HIGH (26) W-C	0.68 OF 25	313	TILT TOWARD BEING THOSE WHERE AGGRESSION SOCIALIZATION ANXIETY IS LOW (28) W-C	0.69 OF 29	17 9 8 20 XSQ= 5.94 PHI= 0.332 XP = 0.0148
338	DRIFT TOWARD BEING THOSE WHERE THE CHILD'S INFERRED ANXIETY OVER PERFORMANCE OF RESPONSIBLE BEHAVIOR IS HIGH (44) B-B-C	0.79 OF 19	338	DRIFT TOWARD BEING THOSE WHERE THE CHILD'S INFERRED ANXIETY OVER PERFORMANCE OF RESPONSIBLE BEHAVIOR IS LOW (29) B-B-C	0.52 OF 21	15 10 4 11 XSQ= 2.95 PHI= 0.271 EP = 0.0550
426	TILT TOWARD BEING THOSE WHERE A HIGH GOD IS PRESENT (156) GES,EA	0.68 OF 22	426	TILT TOWARD BEING THOSE WHERE A HIGH GOD IS ABSENT (104) GES,EA	0.67 OF 27	15 9 7 18 XSQ= 4.58 PHI= 0.306 XP = 0.0324
427	DRIFT TOWARD BEING THOSE WHERE A HIGH GOD, IF PRESENT, IS ACTIVE, RATHER THAN INACTIVE (87) GES,EA	0.67 OF 15	427	DRIFT TOWARD BEING THOSE WHERE A HIGH GOD, IF PRESENT, IS INACTIVE, RATHER THAN ACTIVE (69) GES,EA	0.78 OF 9	10 2 5 7 XSQ= 2.84 PHI= 0.344 EP = 0.0894
443	LEAN TOWARD BEING THOSE WHERE OVERALL FEAR OF OTHERS IS HIGH (31) W-C	0.71 OF 28	443	LEAN TOWARD BEING THOSE WHERE OVERALL FEAR OF OTHERS IS LOW (30) W-C	0.67 OF 33	20 11 8 22 XSQ= 7.34 PHI= 0.347 XP = 0.0068
447	DRIFT TOWARD BEING THOSE WHERE LOVE MAGIC IS PRESENT (20) S-R	0.75 OF 20	447	DRIFT TOWARD BEING THOSE WHERE LOVE MAGIC IS ABSENT (13) S-R	0.62 OF 13	15 5 5 8 XSQ= 3.01 PHI= 0.302 EP = 0.0673
480	DRIFT TOWARD BEING THOSE WHERE COMPLEXITY OF ARTISTIC DESIGN IS HIGH (14) HB	0.69 OF 13	480	DRIFT TOWARD BEING THOSE WHERE COMPLEXITY OF ARTISTIC DESIGN IS LOW (15) HB	0.73 OF 15	9 4 4 11 XSQ= 3.51 PHI= 0.354 EP = 0.0557

443	CULTURES WHERE CVERALL FEAR CF CTHERS IS HIGH (31) W-C	443	CULTURES WHERE OVERALL FEAR OF OTHERS IS LOW (30) W-C

BACKGROUND ON PAGE 165 — BCTH SUBJECT AND PREDICATE

31 IN LEFT CCLUMN

AINU, ARAPESH, CHAGGA, CHIR-APACHE, DOBUANS, HANO, IFUGAO, JIVARC, KWAKIUTL, LAKHER, LAPPS, MACRI, MARQUESANS, MARSHALLESE, MURNGIN, NAVAHO, OMAHA, CNTCNG-JAVA, RIFFIANS, SANPOIL, SENIANG, TANALA, TACS, TENINO, TIV, TROBRIAND, VENDA, WAPISHANA, WITOTO, WOGEO, YAKUT

30 IN RIGHT CCLUMN

ABIPCN, ALCRESE, ANCAMANESE, ASHANTI, AZANDE, BALINESE, CHENCHU, COMANCHE, COPR ESKIMO, DUSUN, FON, KURTATCHI, KUTENAI, LAMBA, LEPCHA, LESU, MANUS, MASAI, PAPAGC, PUKAPUKA, RWALA, SAMCANS, SIRICNC, TETON, THONGA, TIKOPIA, WARRAU, YAGUA, YUKAGHIR, ZUNI

339 EXCLUDED BECAUSE UNASCERTAINEC

	Left column		Right column	Statistics
83	DRIFT LESS TCWARC BEING THCSE 0.59 OF 17 WHERE, WITH NC CITY ANC NC TOWN PRESENT, THE AVERAGE COMMUNITY SIZE IS SMALLER THAN 200, RATHER THAN BETWEEN 200 AND 999 (135)	83	DRIFT MORE TOWARD BEING THCSE 0.89 CF 19 WHERE, WITH NO CITY AND NO TCWN PRESENT, THE AVERAGE COMMUNITY SIZE IS SMALLER THAN 200, RATHER THAN BETWEEN 200 AND 999 (135)	7 2 10 17 XSQ= 3.01 PHI= 0.289 EP = 0.0551
95	TILT MORE TOWARC BEING THCSE 0.93 OF 30 WHERE THE HIERARCHY OF NATICNAL JURISDICTICN HAS CNE CR NC LEVELS (254) GES,EA	95	TILT LESS TOWARD BEING THCSE 0.69 CF 26 WHERE THE HIERARCHY OF NATIONAL JURISDICTION HAS ONE OR NO LEVELS (254) GES,EA	2 8 28 18 XSQ= 4.00 PHI= -0.267 XP = 0.0456
128	DRIFT TCWARD BEING THCSE 0.67 OF 6 WHERE, IF SUBSISTENCE IS PRIMARILY BY AGRICULTURE, THE WCRK IS MAINLY DCNE BY MALES (40)	128	IN ALL CASES ARE THOSE 1.00 CF 6 WHERE, IF SUBSISTENCE IS PRIMARILY BY AGRICULTURE, THE WORK IS MAINLY DONE BY FEMALES (37)	4 0 2 6 XSQ= 3.38 PHI= 0.530 EP = 0.0606
135	DRIFT TCWARD BEING THOSE 0.83 OF 6 WHERE INDIVIDUAL OWNERSHIP OF ECCNCMICALLY SIGNIFICANT PROPERTY IS PRESENT (24) GES	135	DRIFT TOWARD BEING THOSE 0.80 OF 5 WHERE INDIVIDUAL OWNERSHIP CF ECONOMICALLY SIGNIFICANT PRCPERTY IS NEGLIGIBLE CR ABSENT (14) GES	5 1 1 4 XSQ= 2.23 PHI= 0.450 EP = 0.0801

243	DRIFT TOWARD BEING THOSE WHERE POLYGYNY, IF PRESENT, HAS A HIGH INCIDENCE (24) W-C,S	0.62 OF 13	243	DRIFT TOWARD BEING THOSE WHERE POLYGYNY, IF PRESENT, HAS A LOW INCIDENCE (36) W-D,S	0.72 OF 18	 XSQ= PHI= EP =	8 5 5 13 2.28 0.271 0.0785
263	TILT TOWARD BEING THOSE WHERE WIVES ARE OBTAINED BY RELATIVELY EASY MEANS, NAMELY BY TOKEN BRIDE-PRICE, GIFT EXCHANGE, ABSENCE OF ANY CONSIDERATION, OR RECEIPT OF DOWRY (162)	0.65 OF 31	263	TILT TOWARD BEING THOSE WHERE WIVES ARE OBTAINED BY RELATIVELY DIFFICULT MEANS, NAMELY BY BRIDE-PRICE, BRIDE-SERVICE, OR EXCHANGING A FEMALE RELATIVE (233)	0.67 OF 30	 XSQ= PHI= XP =	11 20 20 10 4.75 -0.279 0.0293
296	DRIFT TOWARD BEING THOSE WHERE INFANTICIDE IS PRESENT (18) BCA	0.68 OF 19	296	DRIFT TOWARD BEING THOSE WHERE INFANTICIDE IS ABSENT OR INFERRED ABSENT (15) BCA	0.64 OF 14	 XSQ= PHI= EP =	13 5 6 9 2.28 0.263 0.0853
341	DRIFT MORE TOWARD BEING THOSE WHERE THE CHILD'S INFERRED ANXIETY OVER NON-PERFORMANCE OF NURTURANT BEHAVIOR IS HIGH (30) B-B-C	0.90 OF 10	341	DRIFT LESS TOWARD BEING THOSE WHERE THE CHILD'S INFERRED ANXIETY OVER NON-PERFORMANCE OF NURTURANT BEHAVIOR IS HIGH (30) B-B-C	0.53 OF 15	 XSQ= PHI= EP =	9 8 1 7 2.21 0.298 0.0875
386	DRIFT TOWARD BEING THOSE WHERE SEXUAL EXPRESSION BY THE YOUNG IS PERMITTED (40) F-B	0.68 OF 19	386	DRIFT TOWARD BEING THOSE WHERE SEXUAL EXPRESSION BY THE YOUNG IS RESTRICTED OR SEMI-RESTRICTED (46) F-B	0.65 OF 23	 XSQ= PHI= XP =	6 15 13 8 3.46 -0.287 0.0629
437	TEND TO BE THOSE WHERE FEAR OF GHOSTS, SPIRITS, HUMANS OR ANIMALS IS HIGH (21) W-C,JFG	0.82 OF 22	437	TEND TO BE THOSE WHERE FEAR OF GHOSTS, SPIRITS, HUMANS OR ANIMALS IS LOW (23) W-C,JFG	0.85 OF 20	 XSQ= PHI= XP =	18 3 4 17 16.13 0.620 0.0001
440	LEAN TOWARD BEING THOSE WHERE FEAR OF SPIRITS IS HIGH (32) W-C	0.71 OF 31	440	LEAN TOWARD BEING THOSE WHERE FEAR OF SPIRITS IS LOW (29) W-C	0.67 OF 30	 XSQ= PHI= XP =	22 10 9 20 7.22 0.344 0.0072
441	TEND TO BE THOSE WHERE FEAR OF HUMAN BEINGS IS HIGH (29) W-C	0.74 OF 31	441	TEND TO BE THOSE WHERE FEAR OF HUMAN BEINGS IS LOW (32) W-C	0.80 OF 30	 XSQ= PHI= XP =	23 6 8 24 15.85 0.510 0.0001
442	LEAN TOWARD BEING THOSE WHERE FEAR OF ANIMAL SPIRITS IS HIGH (28) W-C	0.65 OF 31	442	LEAN TOWARD BEING THOSE WHERE FEAR OF ANIMAL SPIRITS IS LOW (33) W-C	0.73 OF 30	 XSQ= PHI= XP =	20 8 11 22 7.34 0.347 0.0068

443/

```
453  IN ALL CASES ARE THOSE             1.00 OF    7      453  TILT TOWARD BEING THOSE          0.50 OF  10              0     5
     WHERE THE ROLE OF RELIGIOUS EXPERTS                         WHERE THE ROLE OF RELIGIOUS EXPERTS                          7     5
     IS NOT CONDUCIVE TO THE DEVELOPMENT OF THE                  IS CONDUCIVE TO THE DEVELOPMENT OF THE               XSQ=      2.84
     INDIVIDUAL'S NEED TO ACHIEVE  (23) DCM                      INDIVIDUAL'S NEED TO ACHIEVE  (13) DCM               PHI=    -0.409
                                                                                                                     EP =    0.0441
```

****

444	CULTURES WHERE THE USE CF DREAMS TC SEEK AND CCNTRCL SUPERNATURAL POWERS IS HIGH (28) RGD	444	CULTURES WHERE THE USE OF DREAMS TO SEEK AND CONTRCL SUPERNATURAL PCWERS IS LOW (27) RGD

BACKGROUND ON PAGE 166

BCTH SUBJECT AND PREDICATE

....

28 IN LEFT CCLUMN

ANDAMANESE	ARAUCANIANS	AZANDE	BEMBA	CHUKCHEE	COMANCHE	COPR ESKIMO	CRCW	CUNA	FANG
IFUGAO	JIVARO	KAPAUKU	KASKA	LAPPS	MUNDURUCU	NASKAPI	NYAKYUSA	OJIBWA	OMAHA
PAPAGO	PUKAPUKA	RWALA	SEMANG	TROBRIAND	WOLOF	YAKUT	YARURO		

27 IN RIGHT CCLUMN

ASHANTI	AYMARA	BHIL	BURMESE	CALLINAGO	GANDA	IBAN	KAREN	KURTATCHI	LEPCHA
MARQUESANS	MATACO	MINCHIA	MOSSI	NAMA	RIFFIANS	SAMOANS	SIRIONO	SOMALI	TALLENSI
TANALA	THAI	TIV	TUBATULABAL	TUPINAMBA	WOLEAIANS	YORUBA			

345 EXCLUDED BECAUSE UNASCERTAINED

8	TILT LESS TOWARD BEING THOSE LOCATED OUTSIDE OF NORTH AMERICA (330)	0.71 OF 28	8	TILT MORE TOWARD BEING THOSE LOCATED OUTSIDE OF NORTH AMERICA (330)	0.96 OF 27	8 1 20 26 XSQ= 4.53 PHI= 0.287 XP = 0.0334
13	LEAN LESS TOWARD BEING THOSE WHERE THE LATITUDE IS LESS THAN FORTY DEGREES (329)	0.68 OF 28	13	IN ALL CASES ARE THOSE WHERE THE LATITUDE IS LESS THAN FORTY DEGREES (329)	1.00 OF 27	9 0 19 27 XSQ= 8.16 PHI= 0.385 XP = 0.0043
14	LEAN LESS TOWARD BEING THOSE WHERE THE LATITUDE IS LESS THAN THIRTY DEGREES (281)	0.54 OF 28	14	LEAN MORE TOWARD BEING THOSE WHERE THE LATITUDE IS LESS THAN THIRTY DEGREES (281)	0.93 OF 27	13 2 15 25 XSQ= 8.68 PHI= 0.397 XP = 0.0032
44	TILT TOWARD BEING THOSE WHERE SETTLEMENTS ARE NON-FIXED (110)	0.58 OF 26	44	TILT TOWARD BEING THOSE WHERE SETTLEMENTS ARE FIXED (222)	0.80 OF 25	11 20 15 5 XSQ= 6.10 PHI= -0.346 XP = 0.0135

```
 53  DRIFT MORE TOWARD BEING THOSE  0.82 OF  17    53  DRIFT LESS TOWARD BEING THOSE  0.55 OF  20          3    9
     WHERE FOOD PRODUCTION IS BY                       WHERE FOOD PRODUCTION IS BY                            14   11
     SIMPLE AGRICULTURE OR                             SIMPLE AGRICULTURE OR                           XSQ=     2.01
     INCIPIENT FOOD PRODUCTION, RATHER THAN BY         INCIPIENT FOOD PRODUCTION, RATHER THAN BY       PHI=   -0.233
     INTENSIVE AGRICULTURE  (147)                      INTENSIVE AGRICULTURE  (147)                    EP =   0.0939

 81  IN ALL CASES ARE THOSE         1.00 OF  22    81  TEND LESS TO BE THOSE          0.52 OF  23          0   11
     WHERE NO CITY OR TOWN IS PRESENT, AND             WHERE NO CITY OR TOWN IS PRESENT, AND                  22   12
     THE AVERAGE COMMUNITY SIZE IS                     THE AVERAGE COMMUNITY SIZE IS                   XSQ=    11.46
     SMALLER THAN 200  (135)                           SMALLER THAN 200  (135)                         PHI=   -0.505
                                                                                                       XP =   0.0007

 87  DRIFT LESS TOWARD BEING THOSE  0.80 OF  25    87  IN ALL CASES ARE THOSE         1.00 OF  23         20   23
     WHERE THE LEVEL OF POLITICAL INTEGRATION          WHERE THE LEVEL OF POLITICAL INTEGRATION                5    0
     IS THE LARGE STATE, THE LITTLE STATE,             IS THE LARGE STATE, THE LITTLE STATE,           XSQ=     3.22
     THE MINIMAL STATE, OR                             THE MINIMAL STATE, OR                           PHI=   -0.259
     THE AUTONOMOUS COMMUNITY  (281) GPM               THE AUTONOMOUS COMMUNITY  (281) GPM             XP =   0.0730

 97  TILT MORE TOWARD BEING THOSE   0.96 OF  26    97  TILT LESS TOWARD BEING THOSE   0.68 OF  25          1    8
     WHERE THE HIERARCHY                               WHERE THE HIERARCHY                                    25   17
     OF LOCAL JURISDICTION HAS                         OF LOCAL JURISDICTION HAS                       XSQ=     5.15
     THREE OR TWO LEVELS  (273) GES,EA                 THREE OR TWO LEVELS  (273) GES,EA               PHI=   -0.318
                                                                                                       XP =   0.0233

100  DRIFT LESS TOWARD BEING THOSE  0.73 OF  26   100  DRIFT MORE TOWARD BEING THOSE  0.96 OF  24         19   23
     WHERE HIERARCHIES ARE MORE COMPLEX THAN           WHERE HIERARCHIES ARE MORE COMPLEX THAN                 7    1
     THE 'SIMPLEST,' I. E., MORE COMPLEX THAN          THE 'SIMPLEST,' I. E., MORE COMPLEX THAN        XSQ=     3.26
     TWO LOCAL LEVELS WITH                             TWO LOCAL LEVELS WITH                           PHI=   -0.256
     NO NATIONAL LEVELS  (267) GES,EA                  NO NATIONAL LEVELS  (267) GES,EA                XP =   0.0708

102  DRIFT TOWARD BEING THOSE       0.54 OF  28   102  DRIFT TOWARD BEING THOSE       0.74 OF  27         13   20
     WHERE CLASS STRATIFICATION IS                     WHERE CLASS STRATIFICATION IS                          15    7
     ABSENT  (180)                                     PRESENT  (203)                                  XSQ=     3.30
                                                                                                       PHI=   -0.245
                                                                                                       XP =   0.0692

118  DRIFT TOWARD BEING THOSE       0.69 OF  13   118  DRIFT TOWARD BEING THOSE       0.70 OF  10          4    7
     WHERE THE PERCENTAGE OF OCCUPATIONS               WHERE THE PERCENTAGE OF OCCUPATIONS                     9    3
     THAT ARE SPECIALIZED                              THAT ARE SPECIALIZED                            XSQ=     2.09
     IS LOW  (25) WME                                  IS HIGH OR MEDIUM  (24) WME                     PHI=   -0.302
                                                                                                       EP =   0.0995

120  TILT LESS TOWARD BEING THOSE   0.62 OF  13   120  IN ALL CASES ARE THOSE         1.00 OF  11          8   11
     WHERE THE CRAFT SPECIALIZATION SCORE              WHERE THE CRAFT SPECIALIZATION SCORE                    5    0
     IS HIGH OR MEDIUM  (36) WME                       IS HIGH OR MEDIUM  (36) WME                     XSQ=     3.27
                                                                                                       PHI=   -0.369
                                                                                                       EP =   0.0411

130  LEAN TOWARD BEING THOSE        0.83 OF  12   130  LEAN TOWARD BEING THOSE        0.80 OF  10          2    8
     WHERE LEATHER WORKING IS                          WHERE LEATHER WORKING IS                               10    2
     MAINLY DONE BY FEMALES  (45)                      MAINLY DONE BY MALES  (39)                      XSQ=     6.45
                                                                                                       PHI=   -0.542
                                                                                                       EP =   0.0083
```

152	DRIFT TOWARD BEING THOSE WHERE THE DIFFERENTIATION OF THE JURIDICAL AGENCY FROM THE MEDICAL AGENCY IS LOW (10) MJ	0.86 OF 7	152	DRIFT TOWARD BEING THOSE WHERE THE DIFFERENTIATION OF THE JURIDICAL AGENCY FROM THE MEDICAL AGENCY IS HIGH (10) MJ	0.75 OF 4	1 3 6 1 XSQ= 1.86 PHI= -0.411 EP = 0.0879
163	IN ALL CASES ARE THOSE WHERE THE EMPHASIS ON INDIVIDUAL VOLITION AS THE CAUSE OF CRIME IS LOW (10) MJ	1.00 OF 5	163	TILT TOWARD BEING THOSE WHERE THE EMPHASIS ON INDIVIDUAL VOLITION AS THE CAUSE OF CRIME IS HIGH (7) MJ	0.75 OF 4	0 3 5 1 XSQ= 2.76 PHI= -0.553 EP = 0.0476
183	DRIFT LESS TOWARD BEING THOSE WHERE THE LARGEST NON-COGNATIC KIN GROUP IS SMALLER THAN A MOEITY, I. E., A PHRATRY OR SIB OR LINEAGE (218)	0.81 OF 16	183	IN ALL CASES ARE THOSE WHERE THE LARGEST NON-COGNATIC KIN GROUP IS SMALLER THAN A MOEITY, I. E., A PHRATRY OR SIB OR LINEAGE (218)	1.00 OF 19	3 0 13 19 XSQ= 1.87 PHI= 0.231 EP = 0.0856
184	TILT TOWARD BEING THOSE WHERE THE LARGEST NON-COGNATIC KIN GROUP IS THE MOEITY OR PHRATRY (77)	0.50 OF 16	184	TILT TOWARD BEING THOSE WHERE THE LARGEST NON-COGNATIC KIN GROUP IS SMALLER THAN A PHRATRY, I. E. A SIB OR LINEAGE (175)	0.89 OF 19	8 2 8 17 XSQ= 4.84 PHI= 0.372 EP = 0.0218
255	IN ALL CASES ARE THOSE WHERE GRANDPARENTAL AUTHORITY OVER PARENTS IS ABSENT (26) DA	1.00 OF 5	255	DRIFT TOWARD BEING THOSE WHERE GRANDPARENTAL AUTHORITY OVER PARENTS IS PRESENT (7) DA	0.67 OF 6	0 4 5 2 XSQ= 2.75 PHI= -0.500 EP = 0.0606
272	TILT TOWARD BEING THOSE WHERE THE DIVORCE RATE IS HIGH (29) CA	0.79 OF 14	272	TILT TOWARD BEING THOSE WHERE THE DIVORCE RATE IS LOW (28) CA	0.75 OF 12	11 3 3 9 XSQ= 5.46 PHI= 0.458 EP = 0.0162
315	TILT TOWARD BEING THOSE WHERE MOTHER AND NURSING CHILD CUSTOMARILY SLEEP IN DIFFERENT BEDS (14) W-D,S	0.60 OF 15	315	TILT TOWARD BEING THOSE WHERE MOTHER AND NURSING CHILD CUSTOMARILY SLEEP IN THE SAME BED (37) W-D,S	0.86 OF 14	6 12 9 2 XSQ= 4.63 PHI= -0.400 EP = 0.0209
319	TILT TOWARD BEING THOSE WHERE PROTECTION OF THE INFANT FROM ENVIRONMENTAL DISCOMFORTS IS HIGH (35) B-B-C	0.80 OF 15	319	TILT TOWARD BEING THOSE WHERE PROTECTION OF THE INFANT FROM ENVIRONMENTAL DISCOMFORTS IS LOW (30) B-B-C	0.67 OF 12	12 4 3 8 XSQ= 4.24 PHI= 0.396 EP = 0.0220
348	TILT TOWARD BEING THOSE WHERE THE TOTAL POSITIVE PRESSURE TOWARD DEVELOPING ACHIEVEMENT BEHAVIOR IN THE CHILD IS HIGH (32) B-B-C	0.77 OF 13	348	TILT TOWARD BEING THOSE WHERE THE TOTAL POSITIVE PRESSURE TOWARD DEVELOPING ACHIEVEMENT BEHAVIOR IN THE CHILD IS LOW (31) B-B-C	0.73 OF 11	10 3 3 8 XSQ= 4.09 PHI= 0.413 EP = 0.0377

```
403  TILT TCWARD BEING THCSE          0.85 OF  13        403  TILT TOWARD BEING THOSE          0.67 OF   9              2     6
     WHERE EXPLANATICNS CF ILLNESS                           WHERE EXPLANATIONS OF ILLNESS                              11     3
     OF AN ANAL NATURE                                       OF AN ANAL NATURE                                  XSQ=     4.03
     ARE ABSENT  (38) W-C                                    ARE PRESENT  (23) W-C                              PHI=   -0.428
                                                                                                                EP =   0.0260

427  DRIFT TOWARD BEING THCSE         0.69 OF  16        427  DRIFT TOWARD BEING THOSE         0.67 OF  15             11     5
     WHERE A HIGH GCC, IF PRESENT, IS                        WHERE A HIGH GOD, IF PRESENT, IS                            5    10
     ACTIVE, RATHER THAN                                     INACTIVE, RATHER THAN                              XSQ=     2.60
     INACTIVE  (87) GES,EA                                   ACTIVE  (69) GES,EA                                PHI=    0.290
                                                                                                                EP =   0.0756
```

445 CULTURES
WHERE SORCERY IS
IMPORTANT (26) EBW,DH

445 CULTURES
WHERE SORCERY IS
UNIMPORTANT (23) BBW,DH

BACKGROUND ON PAGE 166

BOTH SUBJECT AND PREDICATE

26 IN LEFT COLUMN

ABIPON	ASHANTI	AZANDE	CARIB	CHAGGA	CHOROTI	CHUKCHEE	CREEK	GOND	HANO
HUICHOL	IFUGAO	JIVARO	LAMBA	MAORI	MURNGIN	NAMA	PAPAGO	TARAHUMARA	TEHUELCHE
THONGA	TIV	TODA	VENDA	WOLOF	ZUNI				

23 IN RIGHT COLUMN

AINU	ANDAMANESE	APINAYE	BALINESE	CAYAPA	CUNA	DUSUN	GOAJIRO	KAZAK	KHALKA
KHASI	LAKHER	LANGO	LEPCHA	MARICOPA	MASAI	MBUNDU	NASKAPI	OMAHA	SAMOYED
TANALA	TUPINAMBA	YAKUT							

351 EXCLUDED BECAUSE UNASCERTAINED

	Left column			Right column			
5	TILT MORE TOWARD BEING THOSE LOCATED OUTSIDE OF EAST EURASIA (330)	0.88 OF 26	5	TILT LESS TOWARD BEING THOSE LOCATED OUTSIDE OF EAST EURASIA (330)	0.57 OF 23	3 10 23 13 XSQ= 4.85 PHI= -0.315 XP = 0.0276
13	DRIFT MORE TOWARD BEING THOSE WHERE THE LATITUDE IS LESS THAN FORTY DEGREES (329)	0.92 OF 26	13	DRIFT LESS TOWARD BEING THOSE WHERE THE LATITUDE IS LESS THAN FORTY DEGREES (329)	0.70 OF 23	2 7 24 16 XSQ= 2.83 PHI= -0.240 XP = 0.0925
36	DRIFT TOWARD BEING THOSE WHERE THE NATURAL ENVIRONMENT IS 'VERY HARSH,' OR SUB-TROPICAL BUSH, OR TEMPERATE GRASSLAND (108) FWM	0.62 OF 26	36	DRIFT TOWARD BEING THOSE WHERE THE NATURAL ENVIRONMENT IS OTHER THAN 'VERY HARSH,' OR SUB-TROPICAL BUSH, OR TEMPERATE GRASSLAND (292) FWM	0.70 OF 23	16 7 10 16 XSQ= 3.57 PHI= 0.270 XP = 0.0587
42	TILT MORE TOWARD BEING THOSE WHERE THE NATURAL ENVIRONMENT IS OTHER THAN TROPICAL OR SUB-TROPICAL RAIN FOREST, OR MONSOON FOREST (244) FWM	0.88 OF 26	42	TILT LESS TOWARD BEING THOSE WHERE THE NATURAL ENVIRONMENT IS OTHER THAN TROPICAL OR SUB-TROPICAL RAIN FOREST, OR MONSOON FOREST (244) FWM	0.57 OF 23	3 10 23 13 XSQ= 4.85 PHI= -0.315 XP = 0.0276

148	TILT TOWARD BEING THOSE WHERE THE INCIDENCE OF PERSONAL CRIME IS HIGH (12) B-B-C	0.67 OF 9	148	IN ALL CASES ARE THOSE WHERE THE INCIDENCE OF PERSONAL CRIME IS LOW (21) B-B-C	1.00 OF 6	6 0 3 6 XSQ= 4.18 PHI= 0.528 EP = 0.0278
149	DRIFT TOWARD BEING THOSE WHERE THE INCIDENCE OF THEFT IS HIGH (18) B-B-C	0.67 OF 9	149	DRIFT TOWARD BEING THOSE WHERE THE INCIDENCE OF THEFT IS LOW (19) B-B-C	0.86 OF 7	6 1 3 6 XSQ= 2.52 PHI= 0.397 EP = 0.0601
305	DRIFT TOWARD BEING THOSE WHERE THE EARLY SEXUAL SATISFACTION POTENTIAL IS LOW (24) W-C	0.62 OF 13	305	DRIFT TOWARD BEING THOSE WHERE THE EARLY SEXUAL SATISFACTION POTENTIAL IS HIGH (27) W-C	0.88 OF 8	5 7 8 1 XSQ= 3.07 PHI= -0.382 EP = 0.0669
311	DRIFT TOWARD BEING THOSE WHERE SEXUAL SOCIALIZATION ANXIETY IS HIGH (28) W-C	0.62 OF 13	311	DRIFT TOWARD BEING THOSE WHERE SEXUAL SOCIALIZATION ANXIETY IS LOW (23) W-C	0.88 OF 8	8 1 5 7 XSQ= 3.07 PHI= 0.382 EP = 0.0669
316	DRIFT TOWARD BEING THOSE WHERE EXCLUSIVE MOTHER-SON SLEEPING ARRANGEMENTS LAST ONE YEAR OR LONGER (19) W-K-A	0.60 OF 10	316	IN ALL CASES ARE THOSE WHERE EXCLUSIVE MOTHER-SON SLEEPING ARRANGEMENTS LAST LESS THAN ONE YEAR (25) W-K-A	1.00 OF 4	6 0 4 4 XSQ= 2.11 PHI= 0.388 EP = 0.0849
330	TILT TOWARD BEING THOSE WHERE THE AGE OF THE INFANT AT TIME OF WEANING IS LOWER THAN 2.5 YEARS (36) B-B-C	0.64 OF 14	330	TILT TOWARD BEING THOSE WHERE THE AGE OF THE INFANT AT TIME OF WEANING IS 2.5 YEARS OR HIGHER (34) B-B-C	0.80 OF 10	5 8 9 2 XSQ= 3.00 PHI= -0.353 EP = 0.0472
338	IN ALL CASES ARE THOSE WHERE THE CHILD'S INFERRED ANXIETY OVER PERFORMANCE OF RESPONSIBLE BEHAVIOR IS HIGH (44) B-B-C	1.00 OF 14	338	LEAN TOWARD BEING THOSE WHERE THE CHILD'S INFERRED ANXIETY OVER PERFORMANCE OF RESPONSIBLE BEHAVIOR IS LOW (29) B-B-C	0.50 OF 10	14 5 0 5 XSQ= 6.07 PHI= 0.503 EP = 0.0059
348	DRIFT TOWARD BEING THOSE WHERE THE TOTAL POSITIVE PRESSURE TOWARD DEVELOPING ACHIEVEMENT BEHAVIOR IN THE CHILD IS HIGH (32) B-B-C	0.69 OF 13	348	DRIFT TOWARD BEING THOSE WHERE THE TOTAL POSITIVE PRESSURE TOWARD DEVELOPING ACHIEVEMENT BEHAVIOR IN THE CHILD IS LOW (31) B-B-C	0.75 OF 8	9 2 4 6 XSQ= 2.31 PHI= 0.332 EP = 0.0805
349	TILT TOWARD BEING THOSE WHERE THE CHILD'S INFERRED ANXIETY OVER NON-PERFORMANCE OF ACHIEVEMENT BEHAVIOR IS HIGH (34) B-B-C	0.77 OF 13	349	TILT TOWARD BEING THOSE WHERE THE CHILD'S INFERRED ANXIETY OVER NON-PERFORMANCE OF ACHIEVEMENT BEHAVIOR IS LOW (28) B-B-C	0.75 OF 8	10 2 3 6 XSQ= 3.54 PHI= 0.410 EP = 0.0318

351	DRIFT TOWARD BEING THOSE WHERE THE CHILD'S INFERRED CONFLICT REGARDING ACHIEVEMENT BEHAVIOR IS HIGH (26) B-B-C	0.69 OF 13	351	DRIFT TOWARD BEING THOSE WHERE THE CHILD'S INFERRED CONFLICT REGARDING ACHIEVEMENT BEHAVIOR IS LOW (34) B-B-C	0.75 OF 8	9 2 4 6 XSQ= 2.31 PHI= 0.332 EP = 0.0805
373	DRIFT TOWARD BEING THOSE WHERE MALE INITIATION CEREMONIES AT PUBERTY ARE PRESENT (17) W-K-A	0.60 OF 10	373	IN ALL CASES ARE THOSE WHERE MALE INITIATION CEREMONIES AT PUBERTY ARE ABSENT (27) W-K-A	1.00 OF 4	6 0 4 4 XSQ= 2.11 PHI= 0.388 EP = 0.0849
382	DRIFT TOWARD BEING THOSE WHERE FEMALE INITIATION RITES ARE PRESENT (38) JKB	0.80 OF 10	382	DRIFT TOWARD BEING THOSE WHERE FEMALE INITIATION RITES ARE ABSENT (27) JKB	0.62 OF 13	8 5 2 8 XSQ= 2.46 PHI= 0.327 EP = 0.0903
398	TILT TOWARD BEING THOSE WHERE THE INTENSITY OF SEX ANXIETY IS HIGH (16) WNS	0.56 OF 9	398	IN ALL CASES ARE THOSE WHERE THE INTENSITY OF SEX ANXIETY IS LOW (16) WNS	1.00 OF 6	5 0 4 6 XSQ= 2.81 PHI= 0.433 EP = 0.0440
400	DRIFT MORE TOWARD BEING THOSE WHERE HOMOSEXUAL ACTIVITY IS PERMITTED (36) F-B	0.90 OF 10	400	DRIFT LESS TOWARD BEING THOSE WHERE HOMOSEXUAL ACTIVITY IS PERMITTED (36) F-B	0.54 OF 13	1 6 9 7 XSQ= 1.99 PHI= -0.294 EP = 0.0886
431	IN ALL CASES ARE THOSE WHERE SUPERNATURAL SANCTIONS FOR MORALITY, HAVING AN EFFECT ON AN INDIVIDUAL'S AFTERLIFE, ARE ABSENT OR UNREPORTED (25) GES	1.00 OF 6	431	IN ALL CASES ARE THOSE WHERE SUPERNATURAL SANCTIONS FOR MORALITY, HAVING AN EFFECT ON AN INDIVIDUAL'S AFTER LIFE, ARE PRESENT (10) GES	1.00 OF 3	0 3 6 0 XSQ= 5.06 PHI= -0.750 EP = 0.0119
441	LEAN TOWARD BEING THOSE WHERE FEAR OF HUMAN BEINGS IS HIGH (29) W-C	0.73 OF 15	441	LEAN TOWARD BEING THOSE WHERE FEAR OF HUMAN BEINGS IS LOW (32) W-C	0.90 OF 10	11 1 4 9 XSQ= 7.27 PHI= 0.539 EP = 0.0036
449	TILT TOWARD BEING THOSE WHERE THE OBSERVATION OF FOOD TABOOS IS HIGH, RATHER THAN MEDIUM OR LOW (25) JRL	0.50 OF 14	449	TILT TOWARD BEING THOSE WHERE THE OBSERVATION OF FOOD TABOOS IS MEDIUM OR LOW, RATHER THAN HIGH (61) JRL	0.91 OF 11	7 1 7 10 XSQ= 3.04 PHI= 0.349 EP = 0.0421
459	DRIFT TOWARD BEING THOSE WHERE GAMES, IF PRESENT, INCLUDE GAMES OF CHANCE (82) R-A-B,EA	0.65 OF 20	459	DRIFT TOWARD BEING THOSE WHERE GAMES, IF PRESENT, DO NOT INCLUDE GAMES OF CHANCE (89) R-A-B,EA	0.71 OF 14	13 4 7 10 XSQ= 3.04 PHI= 0.299 EP = 0.0799

446	CULTURES WHERE WITCHCRAFT IS SIGNIFICANTLY PRESENT (14) GES	446	CULTURES WHERE WITCHCRAFT IS MODERATELY PRESENT OR ABSENT (24) GES

BACKGROUND ON PAGE 167

BOTH SUBJECT AND PREDICATE

14 IN LEFT COLUMN

ARANDA AYMARA AZANDE DOBUANS GANDA LOZI NAMA NYAKYUSA TANALA TIV
YAGUA YOKUTS YUROK ZUNI

24 IN RIGHT COLUMN

ARAPESH AZTEC BEMBA COPR ESKIMO CUNA HEBREWS IBAN IFUGAO KAREN KASKA
LEPCHA MARQUESANS MIAO NANDI NUER ROMANS SAMOYED TALLENSI TIMBIRA TODA
TRUMAI WINNEBAGO WOLEAIANS YAHGAN

362 EXCLUDED BECAUSE UNASCERTAINED

	Left column			Right column		Statistics
74	DRIFT TOWARD BEING THOSE WHERE POTTERY IS PRESENT (145)	0.75 OF 12	74	DRIFT TOWARD BEING THOSE WHERE POTTERY IS ABSENT (93)	0.69 OF 16	9 5 / 3 11 / XSQ= 3.65 / PHI= 0.361 / EP = 0.0542
129	DRIFT TOWARD BEING THOSE WHERE WEAVING IS MAINLY DONE BY MALES (31)	0.67 OF 3	129	IN ALL CASES ARE THOSE WHERE WEAVING IS MAINLY DONE BY FEMALES (73)	1.00 OF 7	2 0 / 1 7 / XSQ= 2.41 / PHI= 0.491 / EP = 0.0667
144	DRIFT TOWARD BEING THOSE WHERE THE RATIO OF RESTITUTIVE TO REPRESSIVE SANCTIONS IS LOW (25) WME	0.78 OF 9	144	DRIFT TOWARD BEING THOSE WHERE THE RATIO OF RESTITUTIVE TO REPRESSIVE SANCTIONS IS HIGH OR MEDIUM (27) WME	0.78 OF 9	2 7 / 7 2 / XSQ= 3.56 / PHI= -0.444 / EP = 0.0567
180	TILT TOWARD BEING THOSE WHERE THE COMMUNITY IS COMMONLY EXOGAMOUS, RATHER THAN NON-EXOGAMOUS (124)	0.64 OF 14	180	TILT TOWARD BEING THOSE WHERE THE COMMUNITY IS COMMONLY NON-EXOGAMOUS, RATHER THAN EXOGAMOUS (258)	0.74 OF 23	9 6 / 5 17 / XSQ= 3.80 / PHI= 0.321 / EP = 0.0379
213	DRIFT MORE TOWARD BEING THOSE WHERE FIRST COUSIN MARRIAGE IS NOT PERMITTED (198)	0.86 OF 14	213	DRIFT LESS TOWARD BEING THOSE WHERE FIRST COUSIN MARRIAGE IS NOT PERMITTED (198)	0.57 OF 23	2 10 / 12 13 / XSQ= 2.18 / PHI= -0.243 / EP = 0.0836

317	TILT TOWARD BEING THOSE 0.83 OF WHERE DISPLAY OF AFFECTION TOWARD THE INFANT IS LOW (29) B-B-C	6	317	TILT TOWARD BEING THOSE 0.73 OF WHERE DISPLAY OF AFFECTION TOWARD THE INFANT IS HIGH (39) B-B-C	11	1 8 5 3 XSQ= 2.91 PHI= -0.413 EP = 0.0498
327	IN ALL CASES ARE THOSE 1.00 OF WHERE THE AGE OF THE INFANT AT TIME OF REDUCED CONTACT WITH MOTHER IS TWO YEARS OR LOWER (27) B-B-C	5	327	TILT TOWARD BEING THOSE 0.75 OF WHERE THE AGE OF THE INFANT AT TIME OF REDUCED CONTACT WITH MOTHER IS HIGHER THAN TWO YEARS (28) B-B-C	8	0 6 5 2 XSQ= 4.27 PHI= -0.573 EP = 0.0210
328	TILT TOWARD BEING THOSE 0.75 OF WHERE THE AGE OF THE INFANT AT THE ONSET OF SERIOUS SOCIALIZATION, OTHER THAN WEANING, IS TWO YEARS OR LOWER (20) B-B-C	4	328	IN ALL CASES ARE THOSE 1.00 OF WHERE THE AGE OF THE INFANT AT THE ONSET OF SERIOUS SOCIALIZATION, OTHER THAN WEANING, IS HIGHER THAN TWO YEARS (21) B-B-C	5	1 5 3 0 XSQ= 2.76 PHI= -0.553 EP = 0.0476
334	DRIFT TOWARD BEING THOSE 0.78 OF WHERE THE INDULGENCE OF THE CHILD IS LOW (38) B-B-C	9	334	DRIFT TOWARD BEING THOSE 0.67 OF WHERE THE INDULGENCE OF THE CHILD IS HIGH (40) B-B-C	12	2 8 7 4 XSQ= 2.49 PHI= -0.344 EP = 0.0805
347	DRIFT TOWARD BEING THOSE 0.78 OF WHERE THE CHILD'S INFERRED CONFLICT REGARDING SELF-RELIANT BEHAVIOR IS HIGH (37) B-B-C	9	347	DRIFT TOWARD BEING THOSE 0.67 OF WHERE THE CHILD'S INFERRED CONFLICT REGARDING SELF-RELIANT BEHAVIOR IS LOW (39) B-B-C	12	7 4 2 8 XSQ= 2.49 PHI= 0.344 EP = 0.0805
350	LEAN TOWARD BEING THOSE 0.89 OF WHERE THE CHILD'S INFERRED ANXIETY OVER PERFORMANCE OF ACHIEVEMENT BEHAVIOR IS HIGH (34) B-B-C	9	350	LEAN TOWARD BEING THOSE 0.89 OF WHERE THE CHILD'S INFERRED ANXIETY OVER PERFORMANCE OF ACHIEVEMENT BEHAVIOR IS LOW (26) B-B-C	9	8 1 1 8 XSQ= 8.00 PHI= 0.667 EP = 0.0034
351	TILT TOWARD BEING THOSE 0.78 OF WHERE THE CHILD'S INFERRED CONFLICT REGARDING ACHIEVEMENT BEHAVIOR IS HIGH (26) B-B-C	9	351	TILT TOWARD BEING THOSE 0.89 OF WHERE THE CHILD'S INFERRED CONFLICT REGARDING ACHIEVEMENT BEHAVIOR IS LOW (34) B-B-C	9	7 1 2 8 XSQ= 5.63 PHI= 0.559 EP = 0.0152
352	DRIFT TOWARD BEING THOSE 0.78 OF WHERE THE TOTAL POSITIVE PRESSURE TOWARD DEVELOPING OBEDIENT BEHAVIOR IN THE CHILD IS HIGH (44) B-B-C	9	352	DRIFT TOWARD BEING THOSE 0.70 OF WHERE THE TOTAL POSITIVE PRESSURE TOWARD DEVELOPING OBEDIENT BEHAVIOR IN THE CHILD IS LOW (28) B-B-C	10	7 3 2 7 XSQ= 2.63 PHI= 0.372 EP = 0.0698
354	TILT TOWARD BEING THOSE 0.67 OF WHERE THE CHILD'S INFERRED ANXIETY OVER PERFORMANCE OF OBEDIENT BEHAVIOR IS HIGH (36) B-B-C	9	354	TILT TOWARD BEING THOSE 0.90 OF WHERE THE CHILD'S INFERRED ANXIETY OVER PERFORMANCE OF OBEDIENT BEHAVIOR IS LOW (37) B-B-C	10	6 1 3 9 XSQ= 4.33 PHI= 0.477 EP = 0.0198

355	TILT TOWARD BEING THOSE WHERE THE CHILD'S INFERRED CONFLICT REGARDING OBEDIENT BEHAVIOR IS HIGH (35) B-B-C	0.67 OF	9	355	TILT TOWARD BEING THOSE WHERE THE CHILD'S INFERRED CONFLICT REGARDING OBEDIENT BEHAVIOR IS LOW (38) B-B-C	0.90 OF	10	6 1 3 9 XSQ= 4.33 PHI= 0.477 EP = 0.0198
397	DRIFT TOWARD BEING THOSE WHERE SEX DISABILITY IS PRESENT (14) JKH	0.50 OF	6	397	IN ALL CASES ARE THOSE WHERE SEX DISABILITY IS ABSENT (42) JKH	1.00 OF	7	3 0 3 7 XSQ= 2.17 PHI= 0.408 EP = 0.0699
400	IN ALL CASES ARE THOSE WHERE HOMOSEXUAL ACTIVITY IS PERMITTED (36) F-B	1.00 OF	7	400	IN ALL CASES ARE THOSE WHERE HOMOSEXUAL ACTIVITY IS PROHIBITED (22) F-B	1.00 OF	4	0 4 7 0 XSQ= 7.10 PHI= -0.804 EP = 0.0030
427	TILT TOWARD BEING THOSE WHERE A HIGH GOD, IF PRESENT, IS INACTIVE, RATHER THAN ACTIVE (69) GES,EA	0.71 OF	7	427	TILT TOWARD BEING THOSE WHERE A HIGH GOD, IF PRESENT, IS ACTIVE, RATHER THAN INACTIVE (87) GES,EA	0.89 OF	9	2 8 5 1 XSQ= 3.81 PHI= -0.488 EP = 0.0350
439	DRIFT TOWARD BEING THOSE WHERE FEAR OF GHOSTS IS LOW (31) W-C	0.83 OF	6	439	DRIFT TOWARD BEING THOSE WHERE FEAR OF GHOSTS IS HIGH (30) W-C	0.80 OF	5	1 4 5 1 XSQ= 2.23 PHI= -0.450 EP = 0.0801
458	DRIFT TOWARD BEING THOSE WHERE GAMES, IF PRESENT, INCLUDE GAMES OF STRATEGY (52) R-A-B,EA	0.58 OF	12	458	DRIFT TOWARD BEING THOSE WHERE GAMES, IF PRESENT, DO NOT INCLUDE GAMES OF STRATEGY (119) R-A-B,EA	0.83 OF	12	7 2 5 10 XSQ= 2.84 PHI= 0.344 EP = 0.0894
460	DRIFT TOWARD BEING THOSE WHERE GAMES, IF PRESENT, ARE NOT LIMITED TO GAMES OF SKILL ONLY (104) R-A-B,EA	0.83 OF	12	460	DRIFT TOWARD BEING THOSE WHERE GAMES, IF PRESENT, ARE LIMITED TO GAMES OF SKILL ONLY (67) R-A-B,EA	0.58 OF	12	2 7 10 5 XSQ= 2.84 PHI= -0.344 EP = 0.0894

****

447 CULTURES WHERE LOVE MAGIC IS PRESENT (20) S-R	447 CULTURES WHERE LOVE MAGIC IS ABSENT (13) S-R

BACKGROUND ON PAGE 167 — BOTH SUBJECT AND PREDICATE

....

20 IN LEFT COLUMN

AINU, ALORESE, ARAPESH, AZANDE, CHAGGA, COMANCHE, DOBUANS, KURTATCHI, KWAKIUTL, LESU, MAORI, NAVAHO, PAPAGO, RIFFIANS, SANPOIL, THONGA, TIV, TROBRIAND, VENDA, WITOTO

13 IN RIGHT COLUMN

ANDAMANESE, BALINESE, CHENCHU, IFUGAO, LAKHER, LAMBA, MARQUESANS, MURNGIN, PUKAPUKA, SAMOANS, SIRIONO, TIKOPIA, YAKUT

367 EXCLUDED BECAUSE UNASCERTAINED

	Left column			Right column		
8	DRIFT LESS TOWARD BEING THOSE LOCATED OUTSIDE OF NORTH AMERICA (330)	0.75 OF 20	8	IN ALL CASES ARE THOSE LOCATED OUTSIDE OF NORTH AMERICA (330)	1.00 OF 13	5 0 15 13 XSQ= 2.13 PHI= 0.254 EP = 0.0707
15	DRIFT TOWARD BEING THOSE WHERE THE LATITUDE IS TWENTY DEGREES OR GREATER (183)	0.50 OF 20	15	DRIFT TOWARD BEING THOSE WHERE THE LATITUDE IS LESS THAN TWENTY DEGREES (217)	0.85 OF 13	10 2 10 11 XSQ= 2.72 PHI= 0.287 EP = 0.0672
36	DRIFT LESS TOWARD BEING THOSE WHERE THE NATURAL ENVIRONMENT IS OTHER THAN 'VERY HARSH,' OR SUB-TROPICAL BUSH, OR TEMPERATE GRASSLAND (292) FWM	0.60 OF 20	36	DRIFT MORE TOWARD BEING THOSE WHERE THE NATURAL ENVIRONMENT IS OTHER THAN 'VERY HARSH,' OR SUB-TROPICAL BUSH, OR TEMPERATE GRASSLAND (292) FWM	0.92 OF 13	8 1 12 12 XSQ= 2.68 PHI= 0.285 EP = 0.0560
81	DRIFT TOWARD BEING THOSE WHERE A CITY OR TOWN IS PRESENT, OR THE AVERAGE COMMUNITY SIZE IS 200 OF GREATER (89)	0.50 OF 12	81	DRIFT TOWARD BEING THOSE WHERE NO CITY OR TOWN IS PRESENT, AND THE AVERAGE COMMUNITY SIZE IS SMALLER THAN 200 (135)	0.90 OF 10	6 1 6 9 XSQ= 2.39 PHI= 0.330 EP = 0.0743
82	IN ALL CASES ARE THOSE WHERE A CITY OR TOWN IS PRESENT, OR THE AVERAGE COMMUNITY SIZE IS FIFTY OR GREATER (178)	1.00 OF 12	82	TILT LESS TOWARD BEING THOSE WHERE A CITY OR TOWN IS PRESENT, OR THE AVERAGE COMMUNITY SIZE IS FIFTY OR GREATER (178)	0.60 OF 10	12 6 0 4 XSQ= 3.49 PHI= 0.398 EP = 0.0287

142	IN ALL CASES ARE THOSE WHERE THE LEVEL OF SOCIAL SANCTION IS PUBLIC CORPOREAL SANCTION OR PUBLIC PROPERTY SANCTION, RATHER THAN PRIVATE SETTLEMENT (38) JMH	1.00 OF 7	142	DRIFT TOWARD BEING THOSE WHERE THE LEVEL OF SOCIAL SANCTION IS PRIVATE SETTLEMENT, RATHER THAN PUBLIC CORPOREAL SANCTION OR PUBLIC PROPERTY SETTLEMENT (16) JMH	0.50 OF 6	7 3 0 3 XSQ= 2.17 PHI= 0.408 EP = 0.0699
213	DRIFT TOWARD BEING THOSE WHERE FIRST COUSIN MARRIAGE IS NOT PERMITTED (198)	0.75 OF 20	213	DRIFT TOWARD BEING THOSE WHERE FIRST COUSIN MARRIAGE IS PERMITTED (172)	0.62 OF 13	5 8 15 5 XSQ= 3.01 PHI= -0.302 EP = 0.0673
220	LEAN TOWARD BEING THOSE WHERE FIRST COUSIN MARRIAGE IN SOME FORM OR OTHER IS NOT PRESCRIBED OR PREFERRED (273)	0.95 OF 20	220	LEAN TOWARD BEING THOSE WHERE FIRST COUSIN MARRIAGE IN SOME FORM OR OTHER IS PRESCRIBED OR PREFERRED (97)	0.54 OF 13	1 7 19 6 XSQ= 7.75 PHI= -0.485 EP = 0.0026
221	TILT MORE TOWARD BEING THOSE WHERE MATRILATERAL CROSS-COUSIN MARRIAGE IS NOT PRESCRIBED OR PREFERRED (335)	0.95 OF 20	221	TILT LESS TOWARD BEING THOSE WHERE MATRILATERAL CROSS-COUSIN MARRIAGE IS NOT PRESCRIBED OR PREFERRED (335)	0.62 OF 13	1 5 19 8 XSQ= 3.89 PHI= -0.344 EP = 0.0248
242	DRIFT MORE TOWARD BEING THOSE WHERE MARRIAGE IS COMMONLY OR OCCASIONALLY POLYGYNOUS, RATHER THAN MONOGAMOUS (314)	0.95 OF 20	242	DRIFT LESS TOWARD BEING THOSE WHERE MARRIAGE IS COMMONLY OR OCCASIONALLY POLYGYNOUS, RATHER THAN MONOGAMOUS (314)	0.67 OF 12	19 8 1 4 XSQ= 2.67 PHI= 0.289 EP = 0.0531
296	DRIFT TOWARD BEING THOSE WHERE INFANTICIDE IS PRESENT (18) BCA	0.64 OF 14	296	DRIFT TOWARD BEING THOSE WHERE INFANTICIDE IS ABSENT OR INFERRED ABSENT (15) BCA	0.86 OF 7	9 1 5 6 XSQ= 2.89 PHI= 0.371 EP = 0.0635
300	DRIFT TOWARD BEING THOSE WHERE THE POST-PARTUM SEX TABOO LASTS LONGER THAN SIX MONTHS (51)	0.60 OF 15	300	DRIFT TOWARD BEING THOSE WHERE THE POST-PARTUM SEX TABOO LASTS SIX MONTHS OR LESS (73)	0.86 OF 7	9 1 6 6 XSQ= 2.39 PHI= 0.330 EP = 0.0743
301	TEND TO BE THOSE WHERE THE POST-PARTUM SEX TABOO LASTS LONGER THAN ONE MONTH (96)	0.93 OF 15	301	TEND TO BE THOSE WHERE THE POST-PARTUM SEX TABOO LASTS ONE MONTH OR LESS (28)	0.86 OF 7	14 1 1 6 XSQ= 10.34 PHI= 0.686 EP = 0.0006
305	TILT LESS TOWARD BEING THOSE WHERE THE EARLY SEXUAL SATISFACTION POTENTIAL IS HIGH (27) W-C	0.53 OF 19	305	TILT MORE TOWARD BEING THOSE WHERE THE EARLY SEXUAL SATISFACTION POTENTIAL IS HIGH (27) W-C	0.92 OF 13	10 12 9 1 XSQ= 3.96 PHI= -0.352 EP = 0.0237

```
308  TILT TOWARD BEING THOSE          0.65 OF  17     308  TILT TOWARD BEING THOSE          0.89 OF   9          11     1
     WHERE AVERAGE SOCIALIZATION ANXIETY                  WHERE AVERAGE SOCIALIZATION ANXIETY                   6     8
     IS HIGH  (22) W-C                                    IS LOW  (18) W-C                                 XSQ=     4.82
                                                                                                           PHI=    0.430
                                                                                                           EP =   0.0145

311  LEAN TOWARD BEING THOSE          0.65 OF  20     311  LEAN TOWARD BEING THOSE          0.92 OF  13          13     1
     WHERE SEXUAL SOCIALIZATION ANXIETY                   WHERE SEXUAL SOCIALIZATION ANXIETY                    7    12
     IS HIGH  (28) W-C                                    IS LOW  (23) W-C                                 XSQ=     8.38
                                                                                                           PHI=    0.504
                                                                                                           EP =   0.0014

313  TILT TOWARD BEING THOSE          0.56 OF  18     313  TILT TOWARD BEING THOSE          0.85 OF  13          10     2
     WHERE AGGRESSION SOCIALIZATION ANXIETY               WHERE AGGRESSION SOCIALIZATION ANXIETY                8    11
     IS HIGH  (26) W-C                                    IS LOW  (28) W-C                                 XSQ=     3.58
                                                                                                           PHI=    0.340
                                                                                                           EP =   0.0317

314  TILT LESS TOWARD BEING THOSE     0.65 OF  17     314  IN ALL CASES ARE THOSE           1.00 OF  12           6     0
     WHERE THE INCIDENCE OF MOTHER-CHILD                  WHERE THE INCIDENCE OF MOTHER-CHILD                  11    12
     HOUSEHOLDS IS LOW  (61) W-C,S                        HOUSEHOLDS IS LOW  (61) W-D,S                    XSQ=     3.41
                                                                                                           PHI=    0.343
                                                                                                           EP =   0.0280

334  DRIFT TOWARD BEING THOSE         0.63 OF  16     334  DRIFT TOWARD BEING THOSE         0.77 OF  13           6    10
     WHERE THE INDULGENCE OF THE CHILD                    WHERE THE INDULGENCE OF THE CHILD                    10     3
     IS LOW  (38) B-B-C                                   IS HIGH  (40) B-B-C                              XSQ=     3.05
                                                                                                           PHI=   -0.325
                                                                                                           EP =   0.0608

338  DRIFT TOWARD BEING THOSE         0.88 OF  16     338  DRIFT TOWARD BEING THOSE         0.56 OF   9          14     4
     WHERE THE CHILD'S INFERRED ANXIETY OVER              WHERE THE CHILD'S INFERRED ANXIETY OVER               2     5
     PERFORMANCE OF RESPONSIBLE BEHAVIOR                  PERFORMANCE OF RESPONSIBLE BEHAVIOR              XSQ=     3.38
     IS HIGH  (44) B-B-C                                  IS LOW  (29) B-B-C                               PHI=    0.367
                                                                                                           EP =   0.0581

391  TILT LESS TOWARD BEING THOSE     0.56 OF  16     391  IN ALL CASES ARE THOSE           1.00 OF  10           7     0
     WHERE PREMARITAL SEX RELATIONS ARE                   WHERE PREMARITAL SEX RELATIONS ARE                    9    10
     PUNISHED ONLY IF PREGNANCY RESULTS, OR               PUNISHED ONLY IF PREGNANCY RESULTS, OR           XSQ=     3.97
     FREELY PERMITTED  (90) JTW,EA                        FREELY PERMITTED  (90) JTW,EA                    PHI=    0.391
                                                                                                           EP =   0.0227

392  TILT TOWARD BEING THOSE          0.69 OF  16     392  TILT TOWARD BEING THOSE          0.80 OF  10          11     2
     WHERE PREMARITAL SEX RELATIONS ARE                   WHERE PREMARITAL SEX RELATIONS ARE                    5     8
     STRONGLY PUNISHED AND IN FACT RARE, OR               FREELY PERMITTED  (67) JTW,EA                    XSQ=     4.06
     WEAKLY PUNISHED AND IN FACT NOT RARE, OR                                                              PHI=    0.395
     PUNISHED ONLY IF                                                                                      EP =   0.0414
     PREGNANCY RESULTS  (112) JTW,EA

393  DRIFT TOWARD BEING THOSE         0.79 OF  14     393  DRIFT TOWARD BEING THOSE         0.63 OF   8          11     3
     WHERE EXTRAMARITAL COITUS                            WHERE EXTRAMARITAL COITUS IS                          3     5
     IS PUNISHED, RATHER THAN                             PERMITTED, RATHER THAN                           XSQ=     2.15
     PERMITTED  (43) F-B                                  PUNISHED  (41) F-B                               PHI=    0.312
                                                                                                           EP =   0.0815
```

398	TILT TOWARD BEING THOSE WHERE THE INTENSITY OF SEX ANXIETY IS HIGH (16) WNS	0.79 OF 14	398	TILT TOWARD BEING THOSE WHERE THE INTENSITY OF SEX ANXIETY IS LOW (16) WNS	0.86 OF 7	11 1 3 6 XSQ= 5.47 PHI= 0.510 EP = 0.0158
399	TILT TOWARD BEING THOSE WHERE INTENSITY OF CASTRATION ANXIETY IS HIGH (23) WNS	0.64 OF 14	399	TILT TOWARD BEING THOSE WHERE INTENSITY OF CASTRATION ANXIETY IS LOW (22) WNS	0.89 OF 9	9 1 5 8 XSQ= 4.33 PHI= 0.434 EP = 0.0288
403	TILT TOWARD BEING THOSE WHERE EXPLANATIONS OF ILLNESS OF AN ANAL NATURE ARE PRESENT (23) W-C	0.60 OF 20	403	TILT TOWARD BEING THOSE WHERE EXPLANATIONS OF ILLNESS OF AN ANAL NATURE ARE ABSENT (38) W-C	0.85 OF 13	12 2 8 11 XSQ= 4.72 PHI= 0.378 EP = 0.0151
404	DRIFT TOWARD BEING THOSE WHERE EXPLANATIONS OF ILLNESS OF A SEXUAL NATURE ARE PRESENT (19) W-C	0.50 OF 20	404	DRIFT TOWARD BEING THOSE WHERE EXPLANATIONS OF ILLNESS OF A SEXUAL NATURE ARE ABSENT (42) W-C	0.85 OF 13	10 2 10 11 XSQ= 2.72 PHI= 0.287 EP = 0.0672
405	DRIFT TOWARD BEING THOSE WHERE EXPLANATIONS OF ILLNESS OF A DEPENDENCE NATURE ARE ABSENT (27) W-C	0.50 OF 20	405	DRIFT TOWARD BEING THOSE WHERE EXPLANATIONS OF ILLNESS OF A DEPENDENCE NATURE ARE PRESENT (34) W-C	0.85 OF 13	10 11 10 2 XSQ= 2.72 PHI= -0.287 EP = 0.0672
441	LEAN TOWARD BEING THOSE WHERE FEAR OF HUMAN BEINGS IS HIGH (29) W-C	0.70 OF 20	441	LEAN TOWARD BEING THOSE WHERE FEAR OF HUMAN BEINGS IS LOW (32) W-C	0.85 OF 13	14 2 6 11 XSQ= 7.35 PHI= 0.472 EP = 0.0039
442	DRIFT TOWARD BEING THOSE WHERE FEAR OF ANIMAL SPIRITS IS HIGH (28) W-C	0.75 OF 20	442	DRIFT TOWARD BEING THOSE WHERE FEAR OF ANIMAL SPIRITS IS LOW (33) W-C	0.62 OF 13	15 5 5 8 XSQ= 3.01 PHI= 0.302 EP = 0.0673

448	CULTURES WHERE THE CBSERVATION OF FCOD TABOOS IS HIGH, RATHER THAN LCW (25) JRL	448	CULTURES WHERE THE OBSERVATION OF FCOD TABCCS IS LOW, RATHER THAN HIGH (26) JRL

BACKGROUND ON PAGE 167 — SUBJECT ONLY

25 IN LEFT CCLUMN

ANDAMANESE, AZANDE, CALLINAGO, CREEK, FANG, IFUGAO, JIVARO, KASKA, KURTATCHI, LAU,
LUO, MARQUESANS, NAVAHO, NUER, OJIBWA, PAPAGO, RUNDI, SAMOANS, TALLENSI, THONGA,
TIKOPIA, TIMBIRA, TIV, TROBRIAND, WOLEAIANS

26 IN RIGHT CCLUMN

AYMARA, BAMBARA, BURUSHO, CARIB, CAYAPA, CUNA, CZECHS, DARD, IRISH, KAZAK,
KHASI, KOREANS, LOLO, MACASSARESE, MALAYS, MENDE, MIAO, MUNDURUCU, NUPE, RWALA,
SEMANG, SOMALI, TEHUELCHE, THAI, TIBETANS, WOLOF

35 EXCLUDED BECAUSE IRRELEVANT

ARANDA, ARAUCANIANS, AWEIKOMA, AZTEC, BEMBA, BHIL, CHUKCHEE, COMANCHE, COPR ESKIMO, CROW,
GOND, IBAN, KAPAUKU, KIKUYU, LEPCHA, MANDAN, MATACO, MBUNDU, MISKITO, MONGO,
MOSSI, NAMA, NAMBICUARA, NASKAPI, OMAHA, PUKAPUKA, RIFFIANS, SANPOIL, SIRIONO, TANALA,
TODA, TUBATULABAL, TUPINAMBA, WOGEO, YORUBA

314 EXCLUDED BECAUSE UNASCERTAINED

	Left column			Right column		
4	IN ALL CASES ARE THOSE LOCATED OUTSIDE OF THE CIRCUM-MEDITERRANEAN (355)	1.00 OF 25	4	DRIFT LESS TOWARD BEING THOSE LOCATED OUTSIDE OF THE CIRCUM-MEDITERRANEAN (355)	0.81 OF 26	0 5 25 21 XSQ= 3.38 PHI= -0.257 XP = 0.0661
5	LEAN MORE TOWARD BEING THOSE LOCATED OUTSIDE OF EAST EURASIA (330)	0.96 OF 25	5	LEAN LESS TOWARD BEING THOSE LOCATED OUTSIDE OF EAST EURASIA (330)	0.58 OF 26	1 11 24 15 XSQ= 8.37 PHI= -0.405 XP = 0.0038
6	TILT LESS TOWARD BEING THOSE LOCATED OUTSIDE OF THE INSULAR PACIFIC (330)	0.68 OF 25	6	TILT MORE TOWARD BEING THOSE LOCATED OUTSIDE OF THE INSULAR PACIFIC (330)	0.96 OF 26	8 1 17 25 XSQ= 5.15 PHI= 0.318 XP = 0.0233

8	DRIFT LESS TOWARD BEING THOSE 0.80 OF 25 LOCATED OUTSIDE OF NORTH AMERICA (330)	8	IN ALL CASES ARE THOSE 1.00 OF 26 LOCATED OUTSIDE OF NORTH AMERICA (330)	5 0 20 26 XSQ= 3.73 PHI= 0.270 XP = 0.0536
53	TILT TOWARD BEING THOSE 0.79 OF 19 WHERE FOOD PRODUCTION IS BY SIMPLE AGRICULTURE OR INCIPIENT FOOD PRODUCTION, RATHER THAN BY INTENSIVE AGRICULTURE (147)	53	TILT TOWARD BEING THOSE 0.60 OF 20 WHERE FOOD PRODUCTION IS BY INTENSIVE AGRICULTURE, RATHER THAN BY SIMPLE AGRICULTURE OR INCIPIENT FOOD PRODUCTION (91)	4 12 15 8 XSQ= 4.61 PHI= -0.344 EP = 0.0225
55	TILT TOWARD BEING THOSE 0.73 OF 15 WHERE FOOD PRODUCTION IS BY SIMPLE AGRICULTURE, RATHER THAN BY INTENSIVE AGRICULTURE (101)	55	TILT TOWARD BEING THOSE 0.67 OF 18 WHERE FOOD PRODUCTION IS BY INTENSIVE AGRICULTURE, RATHER THAN BY SIMPLE AGRICULTURE (91)	4 12 11 6 XSQ= 3.76 PHI= -0.338 EP = 0.0366
63	LEAN TOWARD BEING THOSE 0.71 OF 17 WHERE HUSBANDRY, IF PRESENT, IS PRINCIPALLY IN THE FORM OF PIGS, SHEEP, OR GOATS, RATHER THAN BOVINE, EQUINE, CAMEL-LIKE, OR DEER-LIKE ANIMALS (74)	63	LEAN TOWARD BEING THOSE 0.82 OF 22 WHERE HUSBANDRY, IF PRESENT, IS PRINCIPALLY IN THE FORM OF BOVINE, EQUINE, CAMEL-LIKE, OR DEER-LIKE ANIMALS, RATHER THAN PIGS, SHEEP, OR GOATS (152)	5 18 12 4 XSQ= 8.83 PHI= -0.476 EP = 0.0025
71	TILT TOWARD BEING THOSE 0.63 OF 24 WHERE METAL WORKING IS ABSENT (153)	71	TILT TOWARD BEING THOSE 0.78 OF 23 WHERE METAL WORKING IS PRESENT (98)	9 18 15 5 XSQ= 6.40 PHI= -0.369 XP = 0.0114
73	TEND TO BE THOSE 0.67 OF 24 WHERE WEAVING IS ABSENT (130)	73	TEND TO BE THOSE 0.96 OF 23 WHERE WEAVING IS PRESENT (118)	8 22 16 1 XSQ= 17.15 PHI= -0.604 XP = 0.0000
80	IN ALL CASES ARE THOSE 1.00 OF 20 WHERE NO CITY OR TOWN IS PRESENT (185)	8C	DRIFT LESS TOWARD BEING THOSE 0.78 OF 23 WHERE NO CITY OR TOWN IS PRESENT (185)	0 5 20 18 XSQ= 3.03 PHI= -0.266 XP = 0.0816
84	IN ALL CASES ARE THOSE 1.00 OF 23 WHERE THE LEVEL OF POLITICAL INTEGRATION IS THE LITTLE STATE, THE MINIMAL STATE, THE AUTONOMOUS COMMUNITY, OR THE FAMILY (262) GPM	84	LEAN LESS TOWARD BEING THOSE 0.64 OF 22 WHERE THE LEVEL OF POLITICAL INTEGRATION IS THE LITTLE STATE, THE MINIMAL STATE, THE AUTONOMOUS COMMUNITY, OR THE FAMILY (262) GPM	0 8 23 14 XSQ= 7.84 PHI= -0.417 XP = 0.0051
85	LEAN TOWARD BEING THOSE 0.87 OF 23 WHERE THE LEVEL OF POLITICAL INTEGRATION IS THE MINIMAL STATE, THE AUTONOMOUS COMMUNITY, OR THE FAMILY (234) GPM	85	LEAN TOWARD BEING THOSE 0.64 OF 22 WHERE THE LEVEL OF POLITICAL INTEGRATION IS THE LARGE STATE, OR THE LITTLE STATE (70) GPM	3 14 20 8 XSQ= 10.19 PHI= -0.476 XP = 0.0014

No.		No.		
86	TILT TOWARD BEING THOSE 0.65 OF 23 WHERE THE LEVEL OF POLITICAL INTEGRATION IS THE AUTONOMOUS COMMUNITY, OR THE FAMILY (156) GPM	86	TILT TOWARD BEING THOSE 0.73 OF 22 WHERE THE LEVEL OF POLITICAL INTEGRATION IS THE LARGE STATE, THE LITTLE STATE, OR THE MINIMAL STATE (148) GPM	8 16 15 6 XSQ= 5.07 PHI= -0.336 XP = 0.0243
107	TILT TOWARD BEING THOSE 0.92 OF 13 WHERE CLASS STRATIFICATION, IF PRESENT, IS BASED ON SOMETHING OTHER THAN OCCUPATIONAL STATUS (160)	107	TILT TOWARD BEING THOSE 0.50 OF 20 WHERE CLASS STRATIFICATION, IF PRESENT, IS BASED ON OCCUPATIONAL STATUS (43)	1 10 12 10 XSQ= 4.59 PHI= -0.373 EP = 0.0216
110	TILT TOWARD BEING THOSE 0.72 OF 25 WHERE SLAVERY IS ABSENT (218)	110	TILT TOWARD BEING THOSE 0.63 OF 24 WHERE SLAVERY IS PRESENT (163)	7 15 18 9 XSQ= 4.58 PHI= -0.306 XP = 0.0324
187	DRIFT LESS TOWARD BEING THOSE 0.76 OF 25 WHERE THE KIN GROUP IS OTHER THAN EXCLUSIVELY MATRILINEAL (344)	187	DRIFT MORE TOWARD BEING THOSE 0.96 OF 26 WHERE THE KIN GROUP IS OTHER THAN EXCLUSIVELY MATRILINEAL (344)	6 1 19 25 XSQ= 2.84 PHI= 0.236 XP = 0.0922
190	TILT LESS TOWARD BEING THOSE 0.56 OF 18 WHERE THE KIN GROUP IS PATRILINEAL OR DOUBLE-DESCENT, RATHER THAN MATRILINEAL (186)	190	TILT MORE TOWARD BEING THOSE 0.94 OF 16 WHERE THE KIN GROUP IS PATRILINEAL OR DOUBLE-DESCENT, RATHER THAN MATRILINEAL (186)	10 15 8 1 XSQ= 4.54 PHI= -0.365 EP = 0.0189
210	DRIFT LESS TOWARD BEING THOSE 0.58 OF 12 WHERE MARITAL RESIDENCE IS PATRILOCAL, RATHER THAN MATRILOCAL (169)	210	DRIFT MORE TOWARD BEING THOSE 0.93 OF 15 WHERE MARITAL RESIDENCE IS PATRILOCAL, RATHER THAN MATRILOCAL (169)	7 14 5 1 XSQ= 2.92 PHI= -0.329 EP = 0.0602
234	TILT TOWARD BEING THOSE 0.57 OF 21 WHERE THE COUSIN TERMINOLOGY IS OF CROW, OMAHA, OR IROQUOIS TYPE, RATHER THAN ESKIMO OR HAWAIIAN TYPE (152)	234	TILT TOWARD BEING THOSE 0.81 OF 21 WHERE THE COUSIN TERMINOLOGY IS OF ESKIMO OR HAWAIIAN TYPE, RATHER THAN CROW, OMAHA, OR IROQUOIS TYPE (170)	12 4 9 17 XSQ= 4.95 PHI= 0.343 XP = 0.0261
390	DRIFT MORE TOWARD BEING THOSE 0.90 OF 21 WHERE PREMARITAL SEX RELATIONS ARE WEAKLY PUNISHED AND IN FACT NOT RARE OR PUNISHED ONLY IF PREGNANCY RESULTS, OR FREELY PERMITTED (132) JTW,EA	390	DRIFT LESS TOWARD BEING THOSE 0.63 OF 16 WHERE PREMARITAL SEX RELATIONS ARE WEAKLY PUNISHED AND IN FACT NOT RARE OR PUNISHED ONLY IF PREGNANCY RESULTS, OR FREELY PERMITTED (132) JTW,EA	2 6 19 10 XSQ= 2.71 PHI= -0.270 EP = 0.0554
391	TEND TO BE THOSE 0.81 OF 21 WHERE PREMARITAL SEX RELATIONS ARE PUNISHED ONLY IF PREGNANCY RESULTS, OR FREELY PERMITTED (90) JTW,EA	391	TEND TO BE THOSE 0.81 OF 16 WHERE PREMARITAL SEX RELATIONS ARE STRONGLY PUNISHED AND IN FACT RARE, OR WEAKLY PUNISHED AND IN FACT NOT RARE (89) JTW,EA	4 13 17 3 XSQ= 11.75 PHI= -0.564 EP = 0.0002

```
392  TILT TOWARD BEING THOSE          0.52 OF  21      392  TILT TOWARD BEING THOSE          0.88 OF  16            10   14
     WHERE PREMARITAL SEX RELATIONS ARE                     WHERE PREMARITAL SEX RELATIONS ARE                      11    2
     FREELY PERMITTED  (67) JTW,EA                          STRONGLY PUNISHED AND IN FACT RARE, OR         XSQ=     4.71
                                                            WEAKLY PUNISHED AND IN FACT NOT RARE, OR       PHI=   -0.357
                                                            PUNISHED ONLY IF                               EP =   0.0165
                                                            PREGNANCY RESULTS  (112) JTW,EA

427  LEAN TOWARD BEING THOSE          0.75 OF  12      427  LEAN TOWARD BEING THOSE          0.78 OF  18             3   14
     WHERE A HIGH GOD, IF PRESENT, IS                       WHERE A HIGH GOD, IF PRESENT, IS                         9    4
     INACTIVE, RATHER THAN                                  ACTIVE, RATHER THAN                            XSQ=     6.16
     ACTIVE  (69) GES,EA                                    INACTIVE  (87) GES,EA                          PHI=   -0.453
                                                                                                           EP =   0.0080

468  LEAN TOWARD BEING THOSE          0.88 OF  17      468  LEAN TOWARD BEING THOSE          0.70 OF  10             2    7
     WHERE CONTACT WITH OTHER CULTURES                      WHERE CONTACT WITH OTHER CULTURES                       15    3
     IS REGULAR OR IRREGULAR, RATHER THAN                   IS FREQUENT, RATHER THAN                       XSQ=     7.17
     FREQUENT  (37) JMH                                     REGULAR OR IRREGULAR  (17) JMH                 PHI=   -0.515
                                                                                                           EP =   0.0036

470  TILT TOWARD BEING THOSE          0.76 OF  17      470  TILT TOWARD BEING THOSE          0.70 OF  10             4    7
     WHERE INNOVATIONS ARE                                  WHERE INNOVATIONS ARE                                   13    3
     ACCEPTED ONLY SELECTIVELY  (33) JMH                    GENERALLY ACCEPTED  (21) JMH                   XSQ=     3.87
                                                                                                           PHI=   -0.379
                                                                                                           EP =   0.0402
```

449 CULTURES WHERE THE OBSERVATION OF FOOD TABOOS IS HIGH, RATHER THAN MEDIUM OR LOW (25) JRL	449 CULTURES WHERE THE OBSERVATION OF FOOD TABOOS IS MEDIUM OR LOW, RATHER THAN HIGH (61) JRL

BACKGROUND ON PAGE 167 PREDICATE ONLY

25 IN LEFT COLUMN

ANDAMANESE	AZANDE	CALLINAGO	CREEK	FANG	IFUGAO	JIVARO	KASKA	KURTATCHI	LAU
LUO	MARQUESANS	NAVAHO	NUER	OJIBWA	PAPAGO	RUNDI	SAMOANS	TALLENSI	THONGA
TIKOPIA	TIMBIRA	TIV	TROBRIAND	WOLEAIANS					

61 IN RIGHT COLUMN

ARANDA	ARAUCANIANS	AWEIKOMA	AYMARA	AZTEC	BAMBARA	BEMBA	BHIL	BURUSHO	CARIB
CAYAPA	CHUKCHEE	COMANCHE	COPR ESKIMO	CROW	CUNA	CZECHS	DARD	GOND	IBAN
IRISH	KAPAUKU	KAZAK	KHASI	KIKUYU	KOREANS	LEPCHA	LOLO	MACASSARESE	MALAYS
MANDAN	MATACO	MBUNDU	MENDE	MIAO	MISKITO	MONGO	MOSSI	MUNDURUCU	NAMA
NAMBICUARA	NASKAPI	NUPE	OMAHA	PUKAPUKA	RIFFIANS	RWALA	SANPOIL	SEMANG	SIRIONO
SOMALI	TANALA	TEHUELCHE	THAI	TIBETANS	TODA	TUBATULABAL	TUPINAMBA	WOGEO	WOLOF
YORUBA									

314 EXCLUDED BECAUSE UNASCERTAINED

450 CULTURES
WHERE THE OBSERVATION OF FOOD TABOOS
IS HIGH OR MEDIUM, RATHER THAN
LOW (60) JRL

450 CULTURES
WHERE THE OBSERVATION OF FOOD TABOOS
IS LOW, RATHER THAN
HIGH OR MEDIUM (26) JRL

BACKGROUND ON PAGE 167

PREDICATE ONLY

60 IN LEFT COLUMN

ANDAMANESE ARANDA ARAUCANIANS AWEIKOMA AZANDE AZTEC BEMBA BHIL CALLINAGO CHUKCHEE
COMANCHE COPR ESKIMO CREEK CROW FANG GOND IBAN IFUGAO JIVARO KAPAUKU
KASKA KIKUYU KURTATCHI LAU LEPCHA LUO MANDAN MARQUESANS MATACO MBUNDU
MISKITO MONGO MOSSI NAMA NAMBICUARA NASKAPI NAVAHO NUER OJIBWA OMAHA
PAPAGO PUKAPUKA RIFFIANS RUNDI SAMOANS SANPOIL SIRIONO TALLENSI TANALA THONGA
TIKOPIA TIMBIRA TIV TODA TROBRIAND TUBATULABAL TUPINAMBA WOGEO WOLEAIANS YORUBA

26 IN RIGHT COLUMN

AYMARA BAMBARA BURUSHO CARIB CAYAPA CUNA CZECHS DARD IRISH KAZAK
KHASI KOREANS LOLO MACASSARESE MALAYS MENDE MIAO MUNDURUCU NUPE RWALA
SEMANG SOMALI TEHUELCHE THAI TIBETANS WOLOF

314 EXCLUDED BECAUSE UNASCERTAINED

```
451  CULTURES                                          451  CULTURES
     WHERE TOTEMISM IS                                      WHERE TOTEMISM IS
     PRESENT  (15) LWS                                      UNIMPORTANT OR ABSENT  (12) LWS


BACKGROUND ON PAGE 167                                                     BOTH SUBJECT AND PREDICATE

     15  IN LEFT COLUMN

AINU       ARANDA     ARAUCANIANS CREEK    DIERI      FANG       FON        HAIDA      HANO       OMAHA
SAMOANS    SERI       SHILLUK     TODA     TROBRIAND

     12  IN RIGHT COLUMN

IBAN       JIVARO     KUNG        KUTENAI  KWAKIUTL   LAPPS      MOTA       NAMA       NAVAHO     SEMANG
WITOTO     YAHGAN

    373  EXCLUDED BECAUSE UNASCERTAINED

----------------------------------------------------------------------------------------------------------
 46  DRIFT TOWARD BEING THOSE        0.86 OF  14     46  DRIFT TOWARD BEING THOSE        0.50 OF  12          2     6
     OTHER THAN WHERE SETTLEMENTS ARE                    WHERE SETTLEMENTS ARE                               12     6
     NON-FIXED AND MOVEMENT IS                           NON-FIXED AND MOVEMENT IS                   XSQ=      2.37
     NOMADIC  (260)                                      NOMADIC  (72)                               PHI=    -0.302
                                                                                                     EP =    0.0895

 86  DRIFT LESS TOWARD BEING THOSE  0.54 OF  13     86  DRIFT MORE TOWARD BEING THOSE  0.91 OF  11            6     1
     WHERE THE LEVEL OF POLITICAL INTEGRATION            WHERE THE LEVEL OF POLITICAL INTEGRATION             7    10
     IS THE AUTONOMOUS COMMUNITY, OR                     IS THE AUTONOMOUS COMMUNITY, OR             XSQ=      2.37
     THE FAMILY  (156) GPM                               THE FAMILY  (156) GPM                       PHI=     0.314
                                                                                                     EP =    0.0778

 87  IN ALL CASES ARE THOSE          1.00 OF  13     87  DRIFT LESS TOWARD BEING THOSE  0.73 OF  11          13     8
     WHERE THE LEVEL OF POLITICAL INTEGRATION            WHERE THE LEVEL OF POLITICAL INTEGRATION             0     3
     IS THE LARGE STATE, THE LITTLE STATE,               IS THE LARGE STATE, THE LITTLE STATE,       XSQ=      1.94
     THE MINIMAL STATE, OR                               THE MINIMAL STATE, OR                       PHI=     0.284
     THE AUTONOMOUS COMMUNITY  (281) GPM                 THE AUTONOMOUS COMMUNITY  (281) GPM         EP =    0.0815

147  TILT TOWARD BEING THOSE         0.77 OF  13    147  TILT TOWARD BEING THOSE         0.75 OF   8          10     2
     WHERE CODIFIED LAWS ARE                             WHERE CODIFIED LAWS ARE                              3     6
     PRESENT  (20) LWS                                   UNIMPORTANT OR ABSENT  (13) LWS             XSQ=      3.54
                                                                                                     PHI=     0.410
                                                                                                     EP =    0.0318

148  IN ALL CASES ARE THOSE          1.00 OF   4    148  IN ALL CASES ARE THOSE          1.00 OF   3           0     3
     WHERE THE INCIDENCE OF PERSONAL CRIME               WHERE THE INCIDENCE OF PERSONAL CRIME                4     0
     IS LOW  (21) B-B-C                                  IS HIGH  (12) B-B-C                         XSQ=      3.51
                                                                                                     PHI=    -0.708
                                                                                                     EP =    0.0286
```

176	TILT TOWARD BEING THOSE WHERE THE COMMUNITY IS A CLAN-COMMUNITY OR A COMMUNITY STRUCTURED OR SEGMENTED ON A CLAN BASIS (169)	0.73 OF	15	176	TILT TOWARD BEING THOSE WHERE THE COMMUNITY IS OTHER THAN A CLAN-COMMUNITY OR A COMMUNITY STRUCTURED OR SEGMENTED ON A CLAN BASIS (213)	0.75 OF	12	11 3 4 9 XSQ= 4.45 PHI= 0.406 EP = 0.0213
178	TILT LESS TOWARD BEING THOSE WHERE THE COMMUNITY IS OTHER THAN SEGMENTED ON A CLAN BASIS AND NON-EXOGAMOUS (295)	0.53 OF	15	178	TILT MORE TOWARD BEING THOSE WHERE THE COMMUNITY IS OTHER THAN SEGMENTED ON A CLAN BASIS AND NON-EXOGAMOUS (295)	0.92 OF	12	7 1 8 11 XSQ= 3.04 PHI= 0.336 EP = 0.0433
179	DRIFT MORE TOWARD BEING THOSE WHERE THE COMMUNITY IS OTHER THAN STRUCTURED ON A NON-CLAN BASIS AND COMMONLY EXOGAMOUS (340)	0.93 OF	15	179	DRIFT LESS TOWARD BEING THOSE WHERE THE COMMUNITY IS OTHER THAN STRUCTURED ON A NON-CLAN BASIS AND COMMONLY EXOGAMOUS (340)	0.58 OF	12	1 5 14 7 XSQ= 2.92 PHI= -0.329 EP = 0.0602
188	LEAN TOWARD BEING THOSE WHERE THE KIN GROUP IS OTHER THAN EXCLUSIVELY COGNATIC (252)	0.87 OF	15	188	LEAN TOWARD BEING THOSE WHERE THE KIN GROUP IS EXCLUSIVELY COGNATIC (148)	0.67 OF	12	2 8 13 4 XSQ= 6.01 PHI= -0.472 EP = 0.0069
192	TILT TOWARD BEING THOSE OTHER THAN WHERE THE ONLY KIN GROUP PRESENT IS A KINDRED OR ELSE BILATERAL DESCENT IS INFERRED (289)	0.93 OF	15	192	TILT TOWARD BEING THOSE WHERE THE ONLY KIN GROUP PRESENT IS A KINDRED OR ELSE BILATERAL DESCENT IS INFERRED (111)	0.50 OF	12	1 6 14 6 XSQ= 4.46 PHI= -0.406 EP = 0.0237
234	TILT TOWARD BEING THOSE WHERE THE COUSIN TERMINOLOGY IS OF CROW, OMAHA, OR IROQUOIS TYPE, RATHER THAN ESKIMO OR HAWAIIAN TYPE (152)	0.83 OF	12	234	TILT TOWARD BEING THOSE WHERE THE COUSIN TERMINOLOGY IS OF ESKIMO OR HAWAIIAN TYPE, RATHER THAN CROW, OMAHA, OR IROQUOIS TYPE (170)	0.70 OF	10	10 3 2 7 XSQ= 4.40 PHI= 0.447 EP = 0.0274
277	DRIFT LESS TOWARD BEING THOSE WHERE THE STATUS OF WOMEN IS NOT STRONGLY INFERIOR OR SUBJECTED (22) LWS	0.54 OF	13	277	DRIFT MORE TOWARD BEING THOSE WHERE THE STATUS OF WOMEN IS NOT STRONGLY INFERIOR OR SUBJECTED (22) LWS	0.91 OF	11	6 1 7 10 XSQ= 2.37 PHI= 0.314 EP = 0.0778
377	TILT LESS TOWARD BEING THOSE WHERE MALE GENITAL MUTILATION IS ABSENT (242)	0.64 OF	14	377	IN ALL CASES ARE THOSE WHERE MALE GENITAL MUTILATION IS ABSENT (242)	1.00 OF	12	5 0 9 12 XSQ= 3.26 PHI= 0.354 EP = 0.0425
380	DRIFT TOWARD BEING THOSE WHERE SEGREGATION OF GIRLS AT MENARCHE IS ABSENT (20) F-B	0.63 OF	8	380	IN ALL CASES ARE THOSE WHERE SEGREGATION OF GIRLS AT MENARCHE IS PRESENT (35) F-B	1.00 OF	4	3 4 5 0 XSQ= 2.10 PHI= -0.418 EP = 0.0808

```
391  DRIFT TOWARD BEING THOSE        0.73 OF  11      391  DRIFT TOWARD BEING THOSE        0.70 OF  10           3     7
     WHERE PREMARITAL SEX RELATIONS ARE                    WHERE PREMARITAL SEX RELATICNS ARE                      8     3
     PUNISHED CNLY IF PREGNANCY RESULTS, OR                STRONGLY PUNISHED AND IN FACT RARE, OR          XSQ=     2.31
     FREELY PERMITTED  (90) JTW,EA                         WEAKLY PUNISHED AND                             PHI=   -0.332
                                                           IN FACT NOT RARE  (89) JTW,EA                   EP  =  0.0861

452  IN ALL CASES ARE THOSE          1.00 OF   5      452  IN ALL CASES ARE THOSE          1.00 OF   5           5     0
     WHERE TOTEMISM WITH FOOD TABOOS                       WHERE TOTEMISM WITH FOOD TABOOS                         0     5
     IS PRESENT  (19) WNS                                  IS ABSENT  (24) WNS                             XSQ=     6.40
                                                                                                           PHI=    0.800
                                                                                                           EP  =  0.0079

469  IN ALL CASES ARE THOSE          1.00 OF   6      469  TILT TOWARD BEING THOSE         0.75 OF   4           6     1
     WHERE CONTACT WITH CTHER CULTURES                     WHERE CONTACT WITH OTHER CULTURES                       0     3
     IS FREQUENT OR REGULAR, RATHER THAN                   IS IRREGULAR, RATHER THAN                       XSQ=     3.35
     IRREGULAR  (43) JMH                                   FREQUENT OR REGULAR  (11) JMH                   PHI=    0.579
                                                                                                           EP  =  0.0333
```

452 CULTURES
WHERE TOTEMISM WITH FOOD TABOOS
IS PRESENT (19) WNS

452 CULTURES
WHERE TOTEMISM WITH FOOD TABOOS
IS ABSENT (24) WNS

BACKGROUND ON PAGE 167

BOTH SUBJECT AND PREDICATE

19 IN LEFT COLUMN

AINU	ARAPESH	ASHANTI	AZANDE	CAGABA	CHAGGA	FON	GANDA	GOND	HANO
KURTATCHI	LAKHER	LANGO	ONTONG-JAVA	SAMOANS	TALLENSI	TANALA	TIV	TROBRIAND	

24 IN RIGHT COLUMN

ALORESE	AYMARA	BALINESE	CHIR-APACHE	COPR ESKIMO	EGYPTIANS	JIVARO	KAZAK	KORYAK	LAPPS
LAU	LEPCHA	MANUS	MAORI	MENDE	NAMA	NAVAHO	NYAKYUSA	TARAHUMARA	TIMBIRA
TURKANA	YAGUA	YAHGAN	YUKAGHIR						

357 EXCLUDED BECAUSE UNASCERTAINED

	Left column (19)		Right column (24)	Statistics
14	DRIFT MORE TOWARD BEING THOSE 0.89 OF 19 WHERE THE LATITUDE IS LESS THAN THIRTY DEGREES (281)	14	DRIFT LESS TOWARD BEING THOSE 0.63 OF 24 WHERE THE LATITUDE IS LESS THAN THIRTY DEGREES (281)	2 9 / 17 15 / XSQ= 2.76 / PHI= -0.253 / XP = 0.0967
33	TILT MORE TOWARD BEING THOSE 0.95 OF 19 WHERE THE NATURAL ENVIRONMENT IS OTHER THAN 'VERY HARSH,' I.E., DESERT, DESERT GRASSES AND SHRUBS, TUNDRA, OR HIGH PLATEAU STEPPE (341) FWM	33	TILT LESS TOWARD BEING THOSE 0.58 OF 24 WHERE THE NATURAL ENVIRONMENT IS OTHER THAN 'VERY HARSH,' I.E., DESERT, DESERT GRASSES AND SHRUBS, TUNDRA, OR HIGH PLATEAU STEPPE (341) FWM	1 10 / 18 14 / XSQ= 5.59 / PHI= -0.361 / XP = 0.0180
36	TILT TOWARD BEING THOSE 0.84 OF 19 WHERE THE NATURAL ENVIRONMENT IS OTHER THAN 'VERY HARSH,' OR SUB-TROPICAL BUSH, OR TEMPERATE GRASSLAND (292) FWM	36	TILT TOWARD BEING THOSE 0.50 OF 24 WHERE THE NATURAL ENVIRONMENT IS 'VERY HARSH,' OR SUB-TROPICAL BUSH, OR TEMPERATE GRASSLAND (108) FWM	3 12 / 16 12 / XSQ= 4.06 / PHI= -0.307 / XP = 0.0439
44	TILT MORE TOWARD BEING THOSE 0.95 OF 19 WHERE SETTLEMENTS ARE FIXED (222)	44	TILT LESS TOWARD BEING THOSE 0.57 OF 23 WHERE SETTLEMENTS ARE FIXED (222)	18 13 / 1 10 / XSQ= 6.01 / PHI= 0.378 / XP = 0.0142
46	IN ALL CASES ARE THOSE 1.00 OF 19 OTHER THAN WHERE SETTLEMENTS ARE NON-FIXED AND MOVEMENT IS NOMADIC (260)	46	TILT LESS TOWARD BEING THOSE 0.65 OF 23 OTHER THAN WHERE SETTLEMENTS ARE NON-FIXED AND MOVEMENT IS NOMADIC (260)	0 8 / 19 15 / XSQ= 6.06 / PHI= -0.380 / XP = 0.0138

51	TILT TOWARD BEING THOSE 0.89 OF 19 WHERE SUBSISTENCE IS PRIMARILY BY FOOD PRODUCTION -- I. E., AGRICULTURE OR HUSBANDRY -- RATHER THAN BY GATHERING (253)	51	TILT TOWARD BEING THOSE 0.50 OF 24 WHERE SUBSISTENCE IS PRIMARILY BY FOOD GATHERING -- I. E., HUNTING, FISHING, OR COLLECTING -- RATHER THAN FOOD PRODUCTION (147)	17 12 2 12 XSQ= 5.83 PHI= 0.368 XP = 0.0157
54	IN ALL CASES ARE THOSE 1.00 OF 17 WHERE FOOD PRODUCTION IS BY INTENSIVE OR SIMPLE AGRICULTURE, RATHER THAN BY INCIPIENT FOOD PRODUCTION (192)	54	TILT LESS TOWARD BEING THOSE 0.64 OF 14 WHERE FOOD PRODUCTION IS BY INTENSIVE OR SIMPLE AGRICULTURE, RATHER THAN BY INCIPIENT FOOD PRODUCTION (192)	17 9 0 5 XSQ= 4.84 PHI= 0.395 EP = 0.0118
56	IN ALL CASES ARE THOSE 1.00 OF 12 WHERE FOOD PRODUCTION IS BY SIMPLE AGRICULTURE, RATHER THAN BY INCIPIENT FOOD PRODUCTION (101)	56	LEAN TOWARD BEING THOSE 0.56 OF 9 WHERE FOOD PRODUCTION IS BY INCIPIENT FOOD PRODUCTION, RATHER THAN BY SIMPLE AGRICULTURE (46)	12 4 0 5 XSQ= 5.96 PHI= 0.533 EP = 0.0062
82	IN ALL CASES ARE THOSE 1.00 OF 14 WHERE A CITY OR TOWN IS PRESENT, OR THE AVERAGE COMMUNITY SIZE IS FIFTY OR GREATER (178)	82	DRIFT LESS TOWARD BEING THOSE 0.72 OF 18 WHERE A CITY OR TOWN IS PRESENT, OR THE AVERAGE COMMUNITY SIZE IS FIFTY OR GREATER (178)	14 13 0 5 XSQ= 2.74 PHI= 0.293 EP = 0.0525
88	DRIFT TOWARD BEING THOSE 0.75 OF 16 WHERE, IF A HEADMANSHIP IS PRESENT, SUCCESSION IS HEREDITARY (165)	88	DRIFT TOWARD BEING THOSE 0.64 OF 14 WHERE, IF A HEADMANSHIP IS PRESENT, SUCCESSION IS NON-HEREDITARY (106)	4 9 12 5 XSQ= 3.23 PHI= -0.328 EP = 0.0634
100	DRIFT MORE TOWARD BEING THOSE 0.95 OF 19 WHERE HIERARCHIES ARE MORE COMPLEX THAN THE 'SIMPLEST,' I. E., MORE COMPLEX THAN TWO LOCAL LEVELS WITH NO NATIONAL LEVELS (267) GES,EA	100	DRIFT LESS TOWARD BEING THOSE 0.68 OF 22 WHERE HIERARCHIES ARE MORE COMPLEX THAN THE 'SIMPLEST,' I. E., MORE COMPLEX THAN TWO LOCAL LEVELS WITH NO NATIONAL LEVELS (267) GES,EA	18 15 1 7 XSQ= 3.04 PHI= 0.272 XP = 0.0811
108	DRIFT TOWARD BEING THOSE 0.67 OF 15 WHERE CLASS STRATIFICATION, IF PRESENT, IS BASED ON A HEREDITARY ARISTOCRACY (74)	108	DRIFT TOWARD BEING THOSE 0.71 OF 14 WHERE CLASS STRATIFICATION, IF PRESENT, IS BASED ON SOMETHING OTHER THAN A HEREDITARY ARISTOCRACY (129)	10 4 5 10 XSQ= 2.82 PHI= 0.312 EP = 0.0656
142	IN ALL CASES ARE THOSE 1.00 OF 7 WHERE THE LEVEL OF SOCIAL SANCTION IS PUBLIC CORPOREAL SANCTION OR PUBLIC PROPERTY SANCTION, RATHER THAN PRIVATE SETTLEMENT (38) JMH	142	DRIFT TOWARD BEING THOSE 0.50 OF 6 WHERE THE LEVEL OF SOCIAL SANCTION IS PRIVATE SETTLEMENT, RATHER THAN PUBLIC CORPOREAL SANCTION OR PUBLIC PROPERTY SETTLEMENT (16) JMH	7 3 0 3 XSQ= 2.17 PHI= 0.408 EP = 0.0699
196	TILT TOWARD BEING THOSE 0.87 OF 15 WHERE INDIVIDUAL RIGHTS IN REAL PROPERTY, AND RULES FOR INHERITANCE, ARE PRESENT (194)	196	TILT TOWARD BEING THOSE 0.53 OF 19 WHERE INDIVIDUAL RIGHTS IN REAL PROPERTY, OR RULES FOR INHERITANCE, ARE ABSENT (87)	13 9 2 10 XSQ= 4.08 PHI= 0.346 EP = 0.0297

No.		No.		
234	DRIFT TOWARD BEING THOSE 0.67 OF 15 WHERE THE COUSIN TERMINOLOGY IS OF CROW, OMAHA, OR IROQUOIS TYPE, RATHER THAN ESKIMO OR HAWAIIAN TYPE (152)	234	DRIFT TOWARD BEING THOSE 0.67 OF 18 WHERE THE COUSIN TERMINOLOGY IS OF ESKIMO OR HAWAIIAN TYPE, RATHER THAN CROW, OMAHA, OR IROQUOIS TYPE (170)	10 6 5 12 XSQ= 2.43 PHI= 0.271 EP = 0.0844
243	LEAN TOWARD BEING THOSE 0.67 OF 12 WHERE POLYGYNY, IF PRESENT, HAS A HIGH INCIDENCE (24) W-C,S	243	LEAN TOWARD BEING THOSE 0.84 OF 19 WHERE POLYGYNY, IF PRESENT, HAS A LOW INCIDENCE (36) W-D,S	8 3 4 16 XSQ= 6.24 PHI= 0.449 EP = 0.0070
302	DRIFT TOWARD BEING THOSE 0.62 OF 13 WHERE THE AVERAGE EARLY SATISFACTION POTENTIAL IS LOW (17) W-C	302	DRIFT TOWARD BEING THOSE 0.88 OF 8 WHERE THE AVERAGE EARLY SATISFACTION POTENTIAL IS HIGH (23) W-C	5 7 8 1 XSQ= 3.07 PHI= -0.382 EP = 0.0669
314	LEAN TOWARD BEING THOSE 0.60 OF 15 WHERE THE INCIDENCE OF MOTHER-CHILD HOUSEHOLDS IS HIGH (19) W-D,S	314	LEAN TOWARD BEING THOSE 0.89 OF 19 WHERE THE INCIDENCE OF MOTHER-CHILD HOUSEHOLDS IS LOW (61) W-D,S	9 2 6 17 XSQ= 7.25 PHI= 0.462 EP = 0.0035
316	DRIFT TOWARD BEING THOSE 0.64 OF 14 WHERE EXCLUSIVE MOTHER-SON SLEEPING ARRANGEMENTS LAST ONE YEAR OR LONGER (19) W-K-A	316	DRIFT TOWARD BEING THOSE 0.79 OF 14 WHERE EXCLUSIVE MOTHER-SON SLEEPING ARRANGEMENTS LAST LESS THAN ONE YEAR (25) W-K-A	9 3 5 11 XSQ= 3.65 PHI= 0.361 EP = 0.0542
365	DRIFT TOWARD BEING THOSE 0.88 OF 8 WHERE THE TIME SPENT IN ADOLESCENT PEER GROUP ACTIVITY IS HIGH OR HIGH-MEDIUM (30) JKH	365	DRIFT TOWARD BEING THOSE 0.58 OF 12 WHERE THE TIME SPENT IN ADOLESCENT PEER GROUP ACTIVITY IS LOW-MEDIUM OR LOW (15) JKH	7 5 1 7 XSQ= 2.51 PHI= 0.354 EP = 0.0697
405	TILT TOWARD BEING THOSE 0.71 OF 14 WHERE EXPLANATIONS OF ILLNESS OF A DEPENDENCE NATURE ARE ABSENT (27) W-C	405	TILT TOWARD BEING THOSE 0.75 OF 12 WHERE EXPLANATIONS OF ILLNESS OF A DEPENDENCE NATURE ARE PRESENT (34) W-C	4 9 10 3 XSQ= 3.87 PHI= -0.386 EP = 0.0472
406	DRIFT TOWARD BEING THOSE 0.64 OF 14 WHERE EXPLANATIONS OF ILLNESS OF AN AGGRESSION NATURE ARE ABSENT. (33) W-C	406	DRIFT TOWARD BEING THOSE 0.75 OF 12 WHERE EXPLANATIONS OF ILLNESS OF AN AGGRESSION NATURE ARE PRESENT (28) W-C	5 9 9 3 XSQ= 2.59 PHI= -0.315 EP = 0.0618
425	LEAN TOWARD BEING THOSE 0.67 OF 9 WHERE SUPERNATURALS ARE MAINLY BENEVOLENT, RATHER THAN AGGRESSIVE (16) L-T-W	425	IN ALL CASES ARE THOSE 1.00 OF 8 WHERE SUPERNATURALS ARE MAINLY AGGRESSIVE, RATHER THAN BENEVOLENT (20) L-T-W	6 0 3 8 XSQ= 5.58 PHI= 0.573 EP = 0.0090

```
435  DRIFT TOWARD BEING THOSE        0.86 OF   7     435  DRIFT TOWARD BEING THOSE        0.80 OF   5           1     4
     WHERE ABANDONMENT OF THE HOUSE OF THE DEAD           WHERE ABANDONMENT OF THE HOUSE OF THE DEAD            6     1
     IS NOT PRACTICED  (19) LWS                           IS PRACTICED  (12) LWS                        XSQ=     2.83
                                                                                                        PHI=   -0.486
                                                                                                        EP =   0.0720

451  IN ALL CASES ARE THOSE          1.00 OF   5     451  IN ALL CASES ARE THOSE          1.00 OF   5           5     0
     WHERE TOTEMISM IS                                    WHERE TOTEMISM IS                                     0     5
     PRESENT  (15) LWS                                    UNIMPORTANT OR ABSENT  (12) LWS               XSQ=     6.40
                                                                                                        PHI=    0.800
                                                                                                        EP =   0.0079

469  IN ALL CASES ARE THOSE          1.00 OF   7     469  DRIFT TOWARD BEING THOSE        0.50 OF   6           7     3
     WHERE CONTACT WITH OTHER CULTURES                    WHERE CONTACT WITH OTHER CULTURES                     0     3
     IS FREQUENT OR REGULAR, RATHER THAN                  IS IRREGULAR, RATHER THAN                     XSQ=     2.17
     IRREGULAR  (43) JMH                                  FREQUENT OR REGULAR  (11) JMH                 PHI=    0.408
                                                                                                        EP =   0.0699
```

453	CULTURES WHERE THE ROLE OF RELIGIOUS EXPERTS IS CONDUCIVE TO THE DEVELOPMENT OF THE INDIVIDUAL'S NEED TO ACHIEVE (13) DCM	453	CULTURES WHERE THE ROLE OF RELIGIOUS EXPERTS IS NOT CONDUCIVE TO THE DEVELOPMENT OF THE INDIVIDUAL'S NEED TO ACHIEVE (23) DCM

BACKGROUND ON PAGE 168

BOTH SUBJECT AND PREDICATE

13 IN LEFT COLUMN

AZANDE CHEYENNE COMANCHE CROW CUNA KURTATCHI MANDAN MASAI OJIBWA THONGA
WICHITA WINNEBAGO WOLEAIANS

23 IN RIGHT COLUMN

AINU ARANDA ARAPESH ARAUCANIANS ASHANTI CHAGGA CHIR-APACHE CHUKCHEE KASKA KIKUYU
KORYAK LEPCHA MARQUESANS MBUNDU NAVAHO PAPAGO PUKAPUKA SOTHO TENETEHARA TETON
TUCUNA VENDA YORUBA

364 EXCLUDED BECAUSE UNASCERTAINED

	Left column			Right column		Statistics
8	DRIFT TOWARD BEING THOSE LOCATED IN NORTH AMERICA (70)	0.54 OF 13	8	DRIFT TOWARD BEING THOSE LOCATED OUTSIDE OF NORTH AMERICA (330)	0.78 OF 23	7 5 6 18 XSQ= 2.54 PHI= 0.266 EP = 0.0714
81	IN ALL CASES ARE THOSE WHERE NO CITY OR TOWN IS PRESENT, AND THE AVERAGE COMMUNITY SIZE IS SMALLER THAN 200 (135)	1.00 OF 7	81	DRIFT LESS TOWARD BEING THOSE WHERE NO CITY OR TOWN IS PRESENT, AND THE AVERAGE COMMUNITY SIZE IS SMALLER THAN 200 (135)	0.53 OF 17	0 8 7 9 XSQ= 3.05 PHI= -0.357 EP = 0.0538
86	DRIFT TOWARD BEING THOSE WHERE THE LEVEL OF POLITICAL INTEGRATION IS THE LARGE STATE, THE LITTLE STATE, OR THE MINIMAL STATE (148) GPM	0.73 OF 11	86	DRIFT TOWARD BEING THOSE WHERE THE LEVEL OF POLITICAL INTEGRATION IS THE AUTONOMOUS COMMUNITY, OR THE FAMILY (156) GPM	0.68 OF 19	8 6 3 13 XSQ= 3.23 PHI= 0.328 EP = 0.0567
96	LEAN TOWARD BEING THOSE WHERE THE HIERARCHY OF NATIONAL JURISDICTION HAS FOUR, THREE, TWO OR ONE LEVEL (174) GES,EA	0.91 OF 11	96	LEAN TOWARD BEING THOSE WHERE THE HIERARCHY OF NATIONAL JURISDICTION HAS NO LEVELS (156) GES,EA	0.59 OF 22	10 9 1 13 XSQ= 5.60 PHI= 0.412 EP = 0.0089
201	TILT LESS TOWARD BEING THOSE WHERE MARITAL RESIDENCE IS NON-OPTIONAL, RATHER THAN AMBILOCAL OR NEOLOCAL (334)	0.77 OF 13	201	IN ALL CASES ARE THOSE WHERE MARITAL RESIDENCE IS NON-OPTIONAL, RATHER THAN AMBILOCAL OR NEOLOCAL (334)	1.00 OF 23	10 23 3 0 XSQ= 3.16 PHI= -0.296 EP = 0.0401

204	TILT LESS TOWARC BEING THOSE WHERE MARITAL RESICENCE IS PATRILOCAL, VIRILOCAL, OR AVUNCULOCAL, RATHER THAN AMBILOCAL OR NECLOCAL (270)	0.67 OF	9	204	IN ALL CASES ARE THOSE WHERE MARITAL RESIDENCE IS PATRILOCAL, VIRILOCAL, OR AVUNCULOCAL, RATHER THAN AMBILOCAL OR NEOLOCAL (270)	1.00 OF	19	6 19 3 0 XSQ= 4.04 PHI= -0.380 EP = 0.0256
220	IN ALL CASES ARE THOSE WHERE FIRST CCUSIN MARRIACE IN SOME FORM OR OTHER IS NOT PRESCRIBED OR PREFERRED (273)	1.00 OF	13	220	TILT LESS TOWARD BEING THOSE WHERE FIRST COUSIN MARRIAGE IN SOME FORM OR OTHER IS NOT PRESCRIBED OR PREFERRED (273)	0.70 OF	23	0 7 13 16 XSQ= 3.16 PHI= -0.296 EP = 0.0343
284	IN ALL CASES ARE THOSE WHERE CONTRACEPTION IS PRACTICED (10) CSF	1.00 OF	4	284	IN ALL CASES ARE THOSE WHERE CONTRACEPTION IS NOT PRACTICED (7) CSF	1.00 OF	3	4 0 0 3 XSQ= 3.51 PHI= 0.708 EP = 0.0286
300	DRIFT TOWARD BEING THOSE WHERE THE POST-PARTUM SEX TABOO LASTS LONGER THAN SIX MONTHS (51)	0.71 OF	7	300	DRIFT TOWARD BEING THOSE WHERE THE POST-PARTUM SEX TABOO LASTS SIX MONTHS OR LESS (73)	0.73 OF	15	5 4 2 11 XSQ= 2.32 PHI= 0.325 EP = 0.0743
307	IN ALL CASES ARE THOSE WHERE THE EARLY AGGRESSION SATISFACTION POTENTIAL IS HIGH (33) W-C	1.00 OF	5	307	TILT TOWARD BEING THOSE WHERE THE EARLY AGGRESSION SATISFACTION POTENTIAL IS LOW (19) W-C	0.58 OF	12	5 5 0 7 XSQ= 2.84 PHI= 0.409 EP = 0.0441
347	TILT TOWARD BEING THOSE WHERE THE CHILD'S INFERREC CONFLICT REGARDING SELF-RELIANT BEHAVIOR IS HIGH (37) B-B-C	0.77 OF	13	347	TILT TOWARD BEING THOSE WHERE THE CHILD'S INFERRED CONFLICT REGARDING SELF-RELIANT BEHAVIOR IS LOW (39) B-B-C	0.61 OF	23	10 9 3 14 XSQ= 3.36 PHI= 0.306 EP = 0.0411
354	TILT TOWARD BEING THOSE WHERE THE CHILD'S INFERREC ANXIETY OVER PERFORMANCE CF CBECIENT BEHAVIOR IS HIGH (36) B-B-C	0.77 OF	13	354	TILT TOWARD BEING THOSE WHERE THE CHILD'S INFERRED ANXIETY OVER PERFORMANCE OF OBEDIENT BEHAVIOR IS LOW (37) B-B-C	0.62 OF	21	10 8 3 13 XSQ= 3.43 PHI= 0.317 EP = 0.0386
373	IN ALL CASES ARE THOSE WHERE MALE INITIATICN CEREMONIES AT PUBERTY ARE PRESENT (17) W-K-A	1.00 OF	4	373	DRIFT TOWARD BEING THOSE WHERE MALE INITIATION CEREMONIES AT PUBERTY ARE ABSENT (27) W-K-A	0.75 OF	8	4 2 0 6 XSQ= 3.38 PHI= 0.530 EP = 0.0606
420	DRIFT TOWARD BEING THOSE WHERE BELLICOSITY IS EXTREME (41) PES	0.70 OF	10	420	DRIFT TOWARD BEING THOSE WHFRE BELLICOSITY IS MODERATE OR NEGLIGIBLE (46) PES	0.69 OF	13	7 4 3 9 XSQ= 2.09 PHI= 0.302 EP = 0.0995

437	IN ALL CASES ARE THOSE WHERE FEAR OF GHCSTS, SPIRITS, HUMANS OR ANIMALS IS LCW (23) W-C,JFG	1.00 OF 3	437	DRIFT TOWARD BEING THOSE WHERE FEAR OF GHOSTS, SPIRITS, HUMANS OR ANIMALS IS HIGH (21) W-C,JFG	0.70 OF 10	0 7 3 3 XSQ= 2.17 PHI= -0.408 EP = 0.0699
439	IN ALL CASES ARE THOSE WHERE FEAR OF GHOSTS IS LCW (31) W-C	1.00 OF 5	439	TILT TOWARD BEING THOSE WHERE FEAR OF GHOSTS IS HIGH (30) W-C	0.67 OF 12	0 8 5 4 XSQ= 3.90 PHI= -0.479 EP = 0.0294
440	IN ALL CASES ARE THOSE WHERE FEAR OF SPIRITS IS LCW (29) W-C	1.00 OF 5	440	TILT TOWARD BEING THOSE WHERE FEAR OF SPIRITS IS HIGH (32) W-C	0.58 OF 12	0 7 5 5 XSQ= 2.84 PHI= -0.409 EP = 0.0441
443	IN ALL CASES ARE THOSE WHERE OVERALL FEAR OF CTHERS IS LCW (30) W-C	1.00 OF 5	443	TILT TOWARD BEING THOSE WHERE OVERALL FEAR OF OTHERS IS HIGH (31) W-C	0.58 OF 12	0 7 5 5 XSQ= 2.84 PHI= -0.409 EP = 0.0441
455	DRIFT TOWARD BEING THCSE WHERE THE MODE CF THE INDIVIDUAL'S CONTACT WITH THE DIVINE IS CONDUCIVE TO THE DEVELCPMENT OF THE INDIVIDUAL'S NEED TO ACHIEVE (17) DCM	0.69 OF 13	455	DRIFT TOWARD BEING THOSE WHERE THE MODE OF THE INDIVIDUAL'S CONTACT WITH THE DIVINE IS NOT CONDUCIVE TO THE DEVELOPMENT OF THE INDIVIDUAL'S NEED TO ACHIEVE (19) DCM	0.65 OF 23	9 8 4 15 XSQ= 2.69 PHI= 0.274 EP = 0.0819
474	TILT TOWARD BEING THOSE WHERE BCASTFULNESS IS EXTREME (41) PES	0.70 OF 10	474	TILT TOWARD BEING THOSE WHERE BOASTFULNESS IS MODERATE, NEGLIBIBLE, OR UNREPORTED (48) PES	0.80 OF 15	7 3 3 12 XSQ= 4.34 PHI= 0.417 EP = 0.0344
479	DRIFT TOWARD BEING THOSE WHERE THE NEED TO ACHIEVE, AS INFERRED FROM FOLKTALES, IS HIGH (18) JV	0.75 OF 12	479	DRIFT TOWARD BEING THOSE WHERE THE NEED TO ACHIEVE, AS INFERRED FROM FOLKTALES, IS LOW (18) JV	0.61 OF 23	9 9 3 14 XSQ= 2.75 PHI= 0.280 EP = 0.0750

	Left		Right	
454	CULTURES WHERE THE OBJECTIVE OF THE INDIVIDUAL'S CONTACT WITH THE DIVINE IS CONDUCIVE TO THE DEVELOPMENT OF THE INDIVIDUAL'S NEED TO ACHIEVE (18) DCM	454	CULTURES WHERE THE OBJECTIVE OF THE INDIVIDUAL'S CONTACT WITH THE DIVINE IS NOT CONDUCIVE TO THE DEVELOPMENT OF THE INDIVIDUAL'S NEED TO ACHIEVE (18) DCM	

BACKGROUND ON PAGE 168

BOTH SUBJECT AND PREDICATE

18 IN LEFT COLUMN

ARANDA, ASHANTI, AZANDE, CHAGGA, CHUKCHEE, COMANCHE, CUNA, KASKA, KIKUYU, KORYAK, LEPCHA, MASAI, MBUNDU, PUKAPUKA, TENETEHARA, TUCUNA, WICHITA, YORUBA

18 IN RIGHT COLUMN

AINU, ARAPESH, ARAUCANIANS, CHEYENNE, CHIR-APACHE, CROW, KURTATCHI, MANDAN, MARQUESANS, NAVAHO, OJIBWA, PAPAGO, SOTHO, TETON, THONGA, VENDA, WINNEBAGO, WOLEAIANS

364 EXCLUDED BECAUSE UNASCERTAINED

	Left column			Right column		Statistics
8	DRIFT TOWARD BEING THOSE LOCATED OUTSIDE OF NORTH AMERICA (330)	0.83 OF 18	8	DRIFT TOWARD BEING THOSE LOCATED IN NORTH AMERICA (70)	0.50 OF 18	3 9 15 9 XSQ= 3.12 PHI= -0.295 EP = 0.0750
14	DRIFT TOWARD BEING THOSE WHERE THE LATITUDE IS LESS THAN THIRTY DEGREES (281)	0.72 OF 18	14	DRIFT TOWARD BEING THOSE WHERE THE LATITUDE IS THIRTY DEGREES OR GREATER (119)	0.61 OF 18	5 11 13 7 XSQ= 2.81 PHI= -0.280 EP = 0.0922
15	TILT TOWARD BEING THOSE WHERE THE LATITUDE IS LESS THAN TWENTY DEGREES (217)	0.61 OF 18	15	TILT TOWARD BEING THOSE WHERE THE LATITUDE IS TWENTY DEGREES OR GREATER (183)	0.78 OF 18	7 14 11 4 XSQ= 4.11 PHI= -0.338 EP = 0.0409
110	DRIFT TOWARD BEING THOSE WHERE SLAVERY IS PRESENT (163)	0.50 OF 18	110	DRIFT TOWARD BEING THOSE WHERE SLAVERY IS ABSENT (218)	0.83 OF 18	9 3 9 15 XSQ= 3.12 PHI= 0.295 EP = 0.0750
259	IN ALL CASES ARE THOSE WHERE THE SEVERITY OF MOTHER-IN-LAW AVOIDANCE IS LOW (20) WNS	1.00 OF 3	259	TILT TOWARD BEING THOSE WHERE THE SEVERITY OF MOTHER-IN-LAW AVOIDANCE IS HIGH (26) WNS	0.80 OF 10	0 8 3 2 XSQ= 3.32 PHI= -0.505 EP = 0.0350

262	TILT MORE TOWARD BEING THOSE WHERE WIVES ARE OBTAINED BY MEANS INVOLVING THE PRESENCE OF SOME CONSIDERATION (305) 0.94 OF 18	262	TILT LESS TOWARD BEING THOSE WHERE WIVES ARE OBTAINED BY MEANS INVOLVING THE PRESENCE OF SOME CONSIDERATION (305) 0.59 OF 17	17 10 1 7	XSQ= 4.43 PHI= 0.356 EP = 0.0178
263	LEAN TOWARD BEING THOSE WHERE WIVES ARE OBTAINED BY RELATIVELY DIFFICULT MEANS, NAMELY BY BRIDE-PRICE, BRIDE-SERVICE, OR EXCHANGING A FEMALE RELATIVE (233) 0.89 OF 18	263	LEAN TOWARD BEING THOSE WHERE WIVES ARE OBTAINED BY RELATIVELY EASY MEANS, NAMELY BY TOKEN BRIDE-PRICE, GIFT EXCHANGE, ABSENCE OF ANY CONSIDERATION, OR RECEIPT OF DOWRY (162) 0.65 OF 17	16 6 2 11	XSQ= 8.58 PHI= 0.495 EP = 0.0016
272	DRIFT TOWARD BEING THOSE WHERE THE DIVORCE RATE IS LOW (28) CA 0.67 OF 9	272	IN ALL CASES ARE THOSE WHERE THE DIVORCE RATE IS HIGH (29) CA 1.00 OF 4	3 4 6 0	XSQ= 2.63 PHI= -0.450 EP = 0.0699
309	TILT TOWARD BEING THOSE WHERE ORAL SOCIALIZATION ANXIETY IS HIGH (26) W-C 0.86 OF 7	309	TILT TOWARD BEING THOSE WHERE ORAL SOCIALIZATION ANXIETY IS LOW (27) W-C 0.70 OF 10	6 3 1 7	XSQ= 3.14 PHI= 0.430 EP = 0.0498
351	DRIFT TOWARD BEING THOSE WHERE THE CHILD'S INFERRED CONFLICT REGARDING ACHIEVEMENT BEHAVIOR IS LOW (34) B-B-C 0.69 OF 16	351	DRIFT TOWARD BEING THOSE WHERE THE CHILD'S INFERRED CONFLICT REGARDING ACHIEVEMENT BEHAVIOR IS HIGH (26) B-B-C 0.67 OF 15	5 10 11 5	XSQ= 2.60 PHI= -0.290 EP = 0.0756
426	DRIFT TOWARD BEING THOSE WHERE A HIGH GOD IS PRESENT (156) GES,EA 0.67 OF 15	426	DRIFT TOWARD BEING THOSE WHERE A HIGH GOD IS ABSENT (104) GES,EA 0.71 OF 14	10 4 5 10	XSQ= 2.82 PHI= 0.312 EP = 0.0656
449	TILT TOWARD BEING THOSE WHERE THE OBSERVATION OF FOOD TABOOS IS MEDIUM OR LOW, RATHER THAN HIGH (61) JRL 0.82 OF 11	449	TILT TOWARD BEING THOSE WHERE THE OBSERVATION OF FOOD TABOOS IS HIGH, RATHER THAN MEDIUM OR LOW (25) JRL 0.70 OF 10	2 7 9 3	XSQ= 3.82 PHI= -0.427 EP = 0.0300

455 CULTURES WHERE THE MODE OF THE INDIVIDUAL'S CONTACT WITH THE DIVINE IS CONDUCIVE TO THE DEVELOPMENT OF THE INDIVIDUAL'S NEED TO ACHIEVE (17) DCM	455 CULTURES WHERE THE MODE OF THE INDIVIDUAL'S CONTACT WITH THE DIVINE IS NOT CONDUCIVE TO THE DEVELOPMENT OF THE INDIVIDUAL'S NEED TO ACHIEVE (19) DCM

BACKGROUND ON PAGE 168

BOTH SUBJECT AND PREDICATE

17 IN LEFT COLUMN

ARANDA, ARAUCANIANS, AZANDE, CHEYENNE, CHIR-APACHE, CHUKCHEE, COMANCHE, CROW, CUNA, MANDAN, PAPAGO, SOTHO, TETON, THONGA, WICHITA, WINNEBAGO, YORUBA

19 IN RIGHT COLUMN

AINU, ARAPESH, ASHANTI, CHAGGA, KASKA, KIKUYU, KORYAK, KURTATCHI, LEPCHA, MARQUESANS, MASAI, MBUNDU, NAVAHO, OJIBWA, PUKAPUKA, TENETEHARA, TUCUNA, VENDA, WOLEAIANS

364 EXCLUDED BECAUSE UNASCERTAINED

	Left column			Right column		Statistics
8	TILT TOWARD BEING THOSE LOCATED IN NORTH AMERICA (70)	0.53 OF 17	8	TILT TOWARD BEING THOSE LOCATED OUTSIDE OF NORTH AMERICA (330)	0.84 OF 19	9 3 8 16 XSQ= 4.03 PHI= 0.334 EP = 0.0328
14	TILT TOWARD BEING THOSE WHERE THE LATITUDE IS THIRTY DEGREES OR GREATER (119)	0.65 OF 17	14	TILT TOWARD BEING THOSE WHERE THE LATITUDE IS LESS THAN THIRTY DEGREES (281)	0.74 OF 19	11 5 6 14 XSQ= 3.91 PHI= 0.330 EP = 0.0425
15	LEAN TOWARD BEING THOSE WHERE THE LATITUDE IS TWENTY DEGREES OR GREATER (183)	0.82 OF 17	15	LEAN TOWARD BEING THOSE WHERE THE LATITUDE IS LESS THAN TWENTY DEGREES (217)	0.63 OF 19	14 7 3 12 XSQ= 5.89 PHI= 0.404 EP = 0.0080
16	TILT TOWARD BEING THOSE WHERE THE LATITUDE IS TEN DEGREES OR GREATER (277)	0.82 OF 17	16	TILT TOWARD BEING THOSE WHERE THE LATITUDE IS LESS THAN TEN DEGREES (123)	0.53 OF 19	14 9 3 10 XSQ= 3.36 PHI= 0.306 EP = 0.0411
36	TILT TOWARD BEING THOSE WHERE THE NATURAL ENVIRONMENT IS 'VERY HARSH,' OR SUB-TROPICAL BUSH, OR TEMPERATE GRASSLAND (108) FWM	0.65 OF 17	36	TILT TOWARD BEING THOSE WHERE THE NATURAL ENVIRONMENT IS OTHER THAN 'VERY HARSH,' OR SUB-TROPICAL BUSH, OR TEMPERATE GRASSLAND (292) FWM	0.74 OF 19	11 5 6 14 XSQ= 3.91 PHI= 0.330 EP = 0.0425

42	TILT MORE TOWARD BEING THOSE 0.94 OF 17 WHERE THE NATURAL ENVIRONMENT IS OTHER THAN TROPICAL OR SUB-TROPICAL RAIN FOREST, OR MONSOON FOREST (244) FWM	42	TILT LESS TOWARD BEING THOSE 0.58 OF 19 WHERE THE NATURAL ENVIRONMENT IS OTHER THAN TROPICAL OR SUB-TROPICAL RAIN FOREST, OR MONSOON FOREST (244) FWM	1 8 16 11 XSQ= 4.50 PHI= -0.353 EP = 0.0198
86	DRIFT TOWARD BEING THOSE 0.67 OF 15 WHERE THE LEVEL OF POLITICAL INTEGRATION IS THE LARGE STATE, THE LITTLE STATE, OR THE MINIMAL STATE (148) GPM	86	DRIFT TOWARD BEING THOSE 0.73 OF 15 WHERE THE LEVEL OF POLITICAL INTEGRATION IS THE AUTONOMOUS COMMUNITY, OR THE FAMILY (156) GPM	10 4 5 11 XSQ= 3.35 PHI= 0.334 EP = 0.0656
131	DRIFT LESS TOWARD BEING THOSE 0.56 OF 9 WHERE THE CONSTRUCTION OF PERMANENT HOUSES OR THE ERECTION OF TEMPORARY DWELLINGS IS MAINLY DONE BY MALES (136)	131	IN ALL CASES ARE THOSE 1.00 OF 9 WHERE THE CONSTRUCTION OF PERMANENT HOUSES OR THE ERECTION OF TEMPORARY DWELLINGS IS MAINLY DONE BY MALES (136)	5 9 4 0 XSQ= 2.89 PHI= -0.401 EP = 0.0824
132	LEAN TOWARD BEING THOSE 0.63 OF 8 WHERE ECONOMIC EXCHANGE DOES NOT INVOLVE THE USE OF MONEY (17) JMH	132	IN ALL CASES ARE THOSE 1.00 OF 9 WHERE ECONOMIC EXCHANGE INVOLVES THE USE OF MONEY (37) JMH	3 9 5 0 XSQ= 5.24 PHI= -0.555 EP = 0.0090
188	DRIFT LESS TOWARD BEING THOSE 0.53 OF 17 WHERE THE KIN GROUP IS OTHER THAN EXCLUSIVELY COGNATIC (252)	188	DRIFT MORE TOWARD BEING THOSE 0.84 OF 19 WHERE THE KIN GROUP IS OTHER THAN EXCLUSIVELY COGNATIC (252)	8 3 9 16 XSQ= 2.79 PHI= 0.278 EP = 0.0704
196	DRIFT TOWARD BEING THOSE 0.64 OF 14 WHERE INDIVIDUAL RIGHTS IN REAL PROPERTY, OR RULES FOR INHERITANCE, ARE ABSENT (87)	196	DRIFT TOWARD BEING THOSE 0.77 OF 13 WHERE INDIVIDUAL RIGHTS IN REAL PROPERTY, AND RULES FOR INHERITANCE, ARE PRESENT (194)	5 10 9 3 XSQ= 3.12 PHI= -0.340 EP = 0.0542
305	TILT TOWARD BEING THOSE 0.83 OF 6 WHERE THE EARLY SEXUAL SATISFACTION POTENTIAL IS LOW (24) W-C	305	TILT TOWARD BEING THOSE 0.73 OF 11 WHERE THE EARLY SEXUAL SATISFACTION POTENTIAL IS HIGH (27) W-C	1 8 5 3 XSQ= 2.91 PHI= -0.413 EP = 0.0498
317	DRIFT TOWARD BEING THOSE 0.63 OF 16 WHERE DISPLAY OF AFFECTION TOWARD THE INFANT IS HIGH (39) B-B-C	317	DRIFT TOWARD BEING THOSE 0.69 OF 16 WHERE DISPLAY OF AFFECTION TOWARD THE INFANT IS LOW (29) B-B-C	10 5 6 11 XSQ= 2.01 PHI= 0.250 EP = 0.0938
318	LEAN TOWARD BEING THOSE 0.81 OF 16 WHERE THE OVERALL INDULGENCE OF THE INFANT IS HIGH (40) B-B-C	318	LEAN TOWARD BEING THOSE 0.72 OF 18 WHERE THE OVERALL INDULGENCE OF THE INFANT IS LOW (31) B-B-C	13 5 3 13 XSQ= 7.69 PHI= 0.476 EP = 0.0026

326	DRIFT TOWARD BEING THOSE 0.71 OF 14 WHERE THE INFERRED TRANSITION ANXIETY BETWEEN INFANCY AND CHILDHOOD IS LOW (35) B-B-C	326	DRIFT TOWARD BEING THOSE 0.67 OF 18 WHERE THE INFERRED TRANSITION ANXIETY BETWEEN INFANCY AND CHILDHOOD IS HIGH (32) B-B-C	4 12 10 6 XSQ= 3.17 PHI= -0.315 EP = 0.0732
334	DRIFT TOWARD BEING THOSE 0.53 OF 17 WHERE THE INDULGENCE OF THE CHILD IS HIGH (40) B-B-C	334	DRIFT TOWARD BEING THOSE 0.79 OF 19 WHERE THE INDULGENCE OF THE CHILD IS LOW (38) B-B-C	9 4 8 15 XSQ= 2.69 PHI= 0.274 EP = 0.0819
339	LEAN TOWARD BEING THOSE 0.76 OF 17 WHERE THE CHILD'S INFERRED CONFLICT REGARDING RESPONSIBLE BEHAVIOR IS LOW (42) B-B-C	339	LEAN TOWARD BEING THOSE 0.68 OF 19 WHERE THE CHILD'S INFERRED CONFLICT REGARDING RESPONSIBLE BEHAVIOR IS HIGH (31) B-B-C	4 13 13 6 XSQ= 5.57 PHI= -0.393 EP = 0.0096
344	DRIFT TOWARD BEING THOSE 0.65 OF 17 WHERE THE TOTAL POSITIVE PRESSURE TOWARD DEVELOPING SELF-RELIANT BEHAVIOR IN THE CHILD IS HIGH (36) B-B-C	344	DRIFT TOWARD BEING THOSE 0.68 OF 19 WHERE THE TOTAL POSITIVE PRESSURE TOWARD DEVELOPING SELF-RELIANT BEHAVIOR IN THE CHILD IS LOW (40) B-B-C	11 6 6 13 XSQ= 2.73 PHI= 0.276 EP = 0.0933
346	DRIFT TOWARD BEING THOSE 0.65 OF 17 WHERE THE CHILD'S INFERRED ANXIETY OVER PERFORMANCE OF SELF-RELIANT BEHAVIOR IS LOW (39) B-B-C	346	DRIFT TOWARD BEING THOSE 0.68 OF 19 WHERE THE CHILD'S INFERRED ANXIETY OVER PERFORMANCE OF SELF-RELIANT BEHAVIOR IS HIGH (37) B-B-C	6 13 11 6 XSQ= 2.73 PHI= -0.276 EP = 0.0933
353	LEAN TOWARD BEING THOSE 0.65 OF 17 WHERE THE CHILD-S INFERRED ANXIETY OVER NON-PERFORMANCE OF OBEDIENT BEHAVIOR IS LOW (32) B-B-C	353	LEAN TOWARD BEING THOSE 0.83 OF 18 WHERE THE CHILD'S INFERRED ANXIETY OVER NON-PERFORMANCE OF OBEDIENT BEHAVIOR IS HIGH (42) B-B-C	6 15 11 3 XSQ= 6.52 PHI= -0.432 EP = 0.0059
386	IN ALL CASES ARE THOSE 1.00 OF 9 WHERE SEXUAL EXPRESSION BY THE YOUNG IS RESTRICTED OR SEMI-RESTRICTED (46) F-B	386	TILT LESS TOWARD BEING THOSE 0.55 OF 11 WHERE SEXUAL EXPRESSION BY THE YOUNG IS RESTRICTED OR SEMI-RESTRICTED (46) F-B	9 6 0 5 XSQ= 3.30 PHI= 0.406 EP = 0.0379
403	TILT TOWARD BEING THOSE 0.83 OF 6 WHERE EXPLANATIONS OF ILLNESS OF AN ANAL NATURE ARE ABSENT (38) W-C	403	TILT TOWARD BEING THOSE 0.73 OF 11 WHERE EXPLANATIONS OF ILLNESS OF AN ANAL NATURE ARE PRESENT (23) W-C	1 8 5 3 XSQ= 2.91 PHI= -0.413 EP = 0.0498
434	LEAN TOWARD BEING THOSE 0.60 OF 10 WHERE ASCETICISM IN MOURNING BEHAVIOR IS LOW (30) JFG	434	IN ALL CASES ARE THOSE 1.00 OF 11 WHERE ASCETICISM IN MOURNING BEHAVIOR IS HIGH (37) JFG	4 11 6 0 XSQ= 6.53 PHI= -0.558 EP = 0.0039

```
453  DRIFT TOWARD BEING THOSE          0.53 OF  17     453  DRIFT TOWARD BEING THOSE            0.79 OF  19            9     4
     WHERE THE ROLE CF RELIGIOUS EXPERTS                    WHERE THE ROLE OF RELIGIOUS EXPERTS                        8    15
     IS CONDUCIVE TO THE DEVELCPMENT OF THE                 IS NOT CONDUCIVE TO THE DEVELCPMENT OF THE        XSQ=      2.69
     INDIVIDUAL'S NEED TO ACHIEVE  (13) DCM                 INDIVIDUAL'S NEED TO ACHIEVE  (23) DCM            PHI=     0.274
                                                                                                              EP =    0.0819

459  LEAN TOWARD BEING THOSE           0.89 OF   9     459  LEAN TOWARD BEING THOSE             0.75 OF  16            8     4
     WHERE GAMES, IF PRESENT,                               WHERE GAMES, IF PRESENT,                                   1    12
     INCLUDE GAMES OF CHANCE  (82) R-A-B,EA                 DO NOT INCLUDE                                    XSQ=      7.03
                                                            GAMES OF CHANCE  (89) R-A-B,EA                    PHI=     0.530
                                                                                                              EP =    0.0036

479  TILT TOWARD BEING THOSE           0.75 OF  16     479  TILT TOWARD BEING THOSE             0.68 OF  19           12     6
     WHERE THE NEED TO ACHIEVE,                             WHERE THE NEED TO ACHIEVE,                                 4    13
     AS INFERRED FROM FCLKTALES,                            AS INFERRED FROM FOLKTALES,                       XSQ=      4.93
     IS HIGH  (18) JV                                       IS LOW  (18) JV                                   PHI=     0.375
                                                                                                              EP =    0.0176
```

	Left column		Right column
456	CULTURES WHERE THE INTERNALIZATION OF THE INDIVIDUAL'S CONTACT WITH THE DIVINE IS CONDUCIVE TO THE DEVELOPMENT OF THE INDIVIDUAL'S NEED TO ACHIEVE (19) DCM	456	CULTURES WHERE THE INTERNALIZATION OF THE INDIVIDUAL'S CONTACT WITH THE DIVINE IS NOT CONDUCIVE TO THE DEVELOPMENT OF THE INDIVIDUAL'S NEED TO ACHIEVE (17) DCM

BACKGROUND ON PAGE 168

BOTH SUBJECT AND PREDICATE

19 IN LEFT COLUMN

ARAUCANIANS	CHIR-APACHE	COMANCHE	CROW	CUNA	KASKA	KIKUYU	KORYAK	KURTATCHI	MANDAN
MBUNDU	OJIBWA	PAPAGO	SOTHO	TENETEHARA	WICHITA	WINNEBAGO	WOLEAIANS	YORUBA	

17 IN RIGHT COLUMN

AINU	ARANDA	ARAPESH	ASHANTI	AZANDE	CHAGGA	CHEYENNE	CHUKCHEE	LEPCHA	MARQUESANS
MASAI	NAVAHO	PUKAPUKA	TETON	THONGA	TUCUNA	VENDA			

364 EXCLUDED BECAUSE UNASCERTAINED

	Left column			Right column		Statistics
8	DRIFT LESS TOWARD BEING THOSE LOCATED OUTSIDE OF NORTH AMERICA (330)	0.53 OF 19	8	DRIFT MORE TOWARD BEING THOSE LOCATED OUTSIDE OF NORTH AMERICA (330)	0.82 OF 17	9 3 10 14 XSQ= 2.35 PHI= 0.256 EP = 0.0830
204	DRIFT LESS TOWARD BEING THOSE WHERE MARITAL RESIDENCE IS PATRILOCAL, VIRILOCAL, OR AVUNCULOCAL, RATHER THAN AMBILOCAL OR NEOLOCAL (270)	0.77 OF 13	204	IN ALL CASES ARE THOSE WHERE MARITAL RESIDENCE IS PATRILOCAL, VIRILOCAL, OR AVUNCULOCAL, RATHER THAN AMBILOCAL OR NEOLOCAL (270)	1.00 OF 15	10 15 3 0 XSQ= 1.84 PHI= -0.256 EP = 0.0873
282	IN ALL CASES ARE THOSE WHERE THE STRENGTH OF DESIRE FOR CHILDREN IS LOW OR ABSENT (20) BCA	1.00 OF 4	282	TILT TOWARD BEING THOSE WHERE THE STRENGTH OF DESIRE FOR CHILDREN IS HIGH (16) BCA	0.82 OF 11	0 9 4 2 XSQ= 5.13 PHI= -0.585 EP = 0.0110
309	IN ALL CASES ARE THOSE WHERE ORAL SOCIALIZATION ANXIETY IS LOW (27) W-C	1.00 OF 4	309	TILT TOWARD BEING THOSE WHERE ORAL SOCIALIZATION ANXIETY IS HIGH (26) W-C	0.69 OF 13	0 9 4 4 XSQ= 3.43 PHI= -0.449 EP = 0.0294
321	TILT TOWARD BEING THOSE WHERE THE IMMEDIACY OF REDUCTION OF THE INFANT'S DRIVES IS HIGH (35) B-B-C	0.79 OF 14	321	TILT TOWARD BEING THOSE WHERE THE IMMEDIACY OF REDUCTION OF THE INFANT'S DRIVES IS LOW (25) B-B-C	0.71 OF 14	11 4 3 10 XSQ= 5.17 PHI= 0.430 EP = 0.0213

```
339  DRIFT TOWARD BEING THOSE        0.68 OF  19    339  DRIFT TOWARD BEING THOSE        0.65 OF  17          6   11
     WHERE THE CHILD'S INFERRED CONFLICT                 WHERE THE CHILD'S INFERRED CONFLICT                 13    6
     REGARDING RESPONSIBLE BEHAVIOR                      REGARDING RESPONSIBLE BEHAVIOR                XSQ=     2.73
     IS LOW  (42) B-B-C                                  IS HIGH  (31) B-B-C                           PHI=   -0.276
                                                                                                       EP =   0.0933

341  DRIFT TOWARD BEING THOSE        0.57 OF  14    341  DRIFT TOWARD BEING THOSE        0.82 OF  11          6    9
     WHERE THE CHILD'S INFERRED ANXIETY OVER             WHERE THE CHILD'S INFERRED ANXIETY OVER              8    2
     NON-PERFORMANCE OF NURTURANT BEHAVIOR               NON-PERFORMANCE OF NURTURANT BEHAVIOR         XSQ=     2.44
     IS LOW  (16) B-B-C                                  IS HIGH  (30) B-B-C                           PHI=   -0.313
                                                                                                       EP =   0.0992

342  TILT TOWARD BEING THOSE         0.92 OF  13    342  TILT TOWARD BEING THOSE         0.55 OF  11          1    6
     WHERE THE CHILD'S INFERRED ANXIETY OVER             WHERE THE CHILD'S INFERRED ANXIETY OVER             12    5
     PERFORMANCE OF NURTURANT BEHAVIOR                   PERFORMANCE OF NURTURANT BEHAVIOR             XSQ=     4.27
     IS LOW  (28) B-B-C                                  IS HIGH  (18) B-B-C                           PHI=   -0.422
                                                                                                       EP =   0.0233

355  DRIFT TOWARD BEING THOSE        0.67 OF  18    355  DRIFT TOWARD BEING THOSE        0.69 OF  16          6   11
     WHERE THE CHILD'S INFERRED CONFLICT                 WHERE THE CHILD'S INFERRED CONFLICT                 12    5
     REGARDING OBEDIENT BEHAVIOR                         REGARDING OBEDIENT BEHAVIOR                   XSQ=     2.95
     IS LOW  (38) B-B-C                                  IS HIGH  (35) B-B-C                           PHI=   -0.295
                                                                                                       EP =   0.0844

372  TILT TOWARD BEING THOSE         0.91 OF  11    372  TILT TOWARD BEING THOSE         0.62 OF  13          1    8
     WHERE MALE INITIATION RITES ARE                     WHERE MALE INITIATION RITES ARE                     10    5
     ABSENT  (63) ASA                                    PRESENT  (48) ASA                             XSQ=     4.93
                                                                                                       PHI=   -0.453
                                                                                                       EP =   0.0131
```

457 CULTURES WHERE GAMES OF SOME KIND ARE PRESENT (171) R-A-B,EA

457 CULTURES WHERE NO GAMES OF ANY KIND ARE PRESENT (18) R-A-B,EA

BACKGROUND ON PAGE 169 — SUBJECT ONLY

171 IN LEFT COLUMN

ABIPON	ABOR	AINU	ALBANIANS	AMERICANS	ANDAMANESE	APINAYE	ARANDA	ARAUCANIANS	ASHANTI
ATSUGEWI	AYMARA	AZANDE	AZTEC	BACAIRI	BASSERI	BHIL	BHUIYA	BORORO	BUNLAP
BURUSHO	CADUVEO	CAMAYURA	CARIB	CHAGGA	CHEROKEE	CHEYENNE	CHIR-APACHE	CHIRIGUANO	CHOROTI
CHUKCHEE	COORG	COPR ESKIMO	CREE	CREEK	CROW	CZECHS	DARD	DIEGUENO	DIERI
EGYPTIANS	ELLICE	EYAK	FANG	FON	GANDA	GOAJIRO	GROS VENTRE	HAIDA	HASINAI
HAWAIIANS	HUKUNDIKA	HURON	HUTSUL	IBAN	ILA	INCA	INGALIK	IRISH	JAPANESE
JEMEZ	JUKUN	KASKA	KAZAK	KERAKI	KHASI	KIKUYU	KOREANS	KORYAK	KUBA
KUNG	KURTATCHI	KUTENAI	KWAKIUTL	LAKHER	LAMBA	LAPPS	LAU	LEPCHA	LESU
LHOTA NAGA	LUO	MACASSARESE	MANGAIANS	MANIHIKI	MANUS	MAORI	MARICOPA	MARQUESANS	MARSHALLESE
MASAI	MATACO	MAYA	MBUNDU	MENDE	MIAMI	MIN CHINESE	MISKITO	MIWOK	MOSSI
MOTA	NABESNA	NAMA	NATCHEZ	NAVAHO	NICOBARESE	NOMLAKI	NUNIVAK	NYAKYUSA	NYORO
OKINAWANS	OMAHA	ONA	PAIWAN	PALAUANS	PAPAGO	PUKAPUKA	RUNDI	RWALA	SAGADA
SAMOANS	SANPOIL	SEMANG	SENIANG	SERBS	SHERENTE	SIRIONO	SIWANS	SOMALI	SYRIANS
TALLENSI	TANALA	TAOS	TAPIRAPE	TARAHUMARA	TAREUMIUT	TEHUELCHE	TENINO	THAI	THONGA
TIKOPIA	TIMBIRA	TIV	TIWI	TODA	TOLOWA	TROBRIAND	TRUKESE	TRUMAI	TUCUNA
TWANA	ULAWANS	UTE	VENDA	VIETNAMESE	WANTOAT	WAPISHANA	WARRAU	WASHO	WITOTO
WOGEO	WOLEAIANS	WOLOF	YAGUA	YAHGAN	YAKUT	YAO	YOKUTS	YUKI	YUROK
ZUNI									

18 IN RIGHT COLUMN

ALACALUF	CAGABA	CAYAPA	CHENCHU	CHORTI	CUNA	GARO	HUICHOL	JIVARO	KATAB
MURNGIN	PAEZ	TALAMANCA	TENETEHARA	TUCANO	TUPINAMBA	VEDDA	YARURO		

211 EXCLUDED BECAUSE UNASCERTAINED

9	TEND TO BE THOSE LOCATED OUTSIDE OF SOUTH AMERICA (335)	0.83 OF 171	9	TEND TO BE THOSE LOCATED IN SOUTH AMERICA (65)	0.67 OF 18
					29 12 142 6 XSQ= 20.85 PHI= -0.332 XP = 0.0000
15	LEAN TOWARD BEING THOSE WHERE THE LATITUDE IS TWENTY DEGREES OR GREATER (183)	0.54 OF 171	15	LEAN TOWARD BEING THOSE WHERE THE LATITUDE IS LESS THAN TWENTY DEGREES (217)	0.83 OF 18
					93 3 78 15 XSQ= 7.82 PHI= 0.203 XP = 0.0052

16	TILT TOWARD BEING THOSE WHERE THE LATITUDE IS TEN DEGREES OR GREATER (277)	0.75 OF 171	16	TILT TOWARD BEING THOSE WHERE THE LATITUDE IS LESS THAN TEN DEGREES (123)	0.56 OF 18	128 8 43 10 XSQ= 6.03 PHI= 0.179 XP = 0.0140
55	DRIFT TOWARD BEING THOSE WHERE FOOD PRODUCTION IS BY INTENSIVE AGRICULTURE, RATHER THAN BY SIMPLE AGRICULTURE (91)	0.50 OF 80	55	DRIFT TOWARD BEING THOSE WHERE FOOD PRODUCTION IS BY SIMPLE AGRICULTURE, RATHER THAN BY INTENSIVE AGRICULTURE (101)	0.82 OF 11	40 2 40 9 XSQ= 2.76 PHI= 0.174 XP = 0.0965
63	TILT TOWARD BEING THOSE WHERE HUSBANDRY, IF PRESENT, IS PRINCIPALLY IN THE FORM OF BOVINE, EQUINE, CAMEL-LIKE, OR DEER-LIKE ANIMALS, RATHER THAN PIGS, SHEEP, OR GOATS (152)	0.64 OF 106	63	TILT TOWARD BEING THOSE WHERE HUSBANDRY, IF PRESENT, IS PRINCIPALLY IN THE FORM OF PIGS, SHEEP, OR GOATS, RATHER THAN BOVINE, EQUINE, CAMEL-LIKE, OR DEER-LIKE ANIMALS (74)	0.75 OF 12	68 3 38 9 XSQ= 5.36 PHI= 0.213 XP = 0.0206
71	TILT LESS TOWARD BEING THOSE WHERE METAL WORKING IS ABSENT (153)	0.60 OF 153	71	TILT MORE TOWARD BEING THOSE WHERE METAL WORKING IS ABSENT (153)	0.94 OF 16	61 1 92 15 XSQ= 5.68 PHI= 0.183 XP = 0.0172
85	DRIFT LESS TOWARD BEING THOSE WHERE THE LEVEL OF POLITICAL INTEGRATION IS THE MINIMAL STATE, THE AUTONOMOUS COMMUNITY, OR THE FAMILY (234) GPM	0.76 OF 143	85	IN ALL CASES ARE THOSE WHERE THE LEVEL OF POLITICAL INTEGRATION IS THE MINIMAL STATE, THE AUTONOMOUS COMMUNITY, OR THE FAMILY (234) GPM	1.00 OF 15	34 0 109 15 XSQ= 3.25 PHI= 0.143 XP = 0.0716
95	TILT LESS TOWARD BEING THOSE WHERE THE HIERARCHY OF NATIONAL JURISDICTION HAS ONE OR NO LEVELS (254) GES,EA	0.75 OF 169	95	IN ALL CASES ARE THOSE WHERE THE HIERARCHY OF NATIONAL JURISDICTION HAS ONE OR NO LEVELS (254) GES,EA	1.00 OF 18	42 0 127 18 XSQ= 4.43 PHI= 0.154 XP = 0.0353
96	DRIFT TOWARD BEING THOSE WHERE THE HIERARCHY OF NATIONAL JURISDICTION HAS FOUR, THREE, TWO OR ONE LEVEL (174) GES,EA	0.51 OF 169	96	DRIFT TOWARD BEING THOSE WHERE THE HIERARCHY OF NATIONAL JURISDICTION HAS NO LEVELS (156) GES,EA	0.72 OF 18	87 5 82 13 XSQ= 2.77 PHI= 0.122 XP = 0.0961
102	TILT TOWARD BEING THOSE WHERE CLASS STRATIFICATION IS PRESENT (203)	0.58 OF 168	102	TILT TOWARD BEING THOSE WHERE CLASS STRATIFICATION IS ABSENT (180)	0.71 OF 17	97 5 71 12 XSQ= 3.93 PHI= 0.146 XP = 0.0475
106	TILT TOWARD BEING THOSE WHERE CLASS STRATIFICATION, IF PRESENT, IS BASED ON SOMETHING OTHER THAN WEALTH (126)	0.59 OF 97	106	IN ALL CASES ARE THOSE WHERE CLASS STRATIFICATION, IF PRESENT, IS BASED ON WEALTH (77)	1.00 OF 5	40 5 57 0 XSQ= 4.49 PHI= -0.210 XP = 0.0341

175	TILT TOWARD BEING THOSE 0.73 OF 168 WHERE THE COMMUNITY IS 'KIN-HETEROGENEOUS,' I. E. OTHER THAN A CLAN COMMUNITY OR A DEME (260)	175	TILT TOWARD BEING THOSE 0.56 OF 16 WHERE THE COMMUNITY IS 'KIN-HOMOGENEOUS,' I. E. A CLAN COMMUNITY OR A DEME (122)	46 9 122 7 XSQ= 4.51 PHI= -0.157 XP = 0.0336
178	DRIFT LESS TOWARD BEING THOSE 0.76 OF 168 WHERE THE COMMUNITY IS OTHER THAN SEGMENTED ON A CLAN BASIS AND NON-EXOGAMOUS (295)	178	IN ALL CASES ARE THOSE 1.00 OF 16 WHERE THE COMMUNITY IS OTHER THAN SEGMENTED ON A CLAN BASIS AND NON-EXOGAMOUS (295)	41 0 127 16 XSQ= 3.71 PHI= 0.142 XP = 0.0540
181	TILT MORE TOWARD BEING THOSE 0.90 OF 168 WHERE THE COMMUNITY IS OTHER THAN A DEME (337)	181	TILT LESS TOWARD BEING THOSE 0.69 OF 16 WHERE THE COMMUNITY IS OTHER THAN A DEME (337)	16 5 152 11 XSQ= 4.84 PHI= -0.162 XP = 0.0278
204	DRIFT TOWARD BEING THOSE 0.81 OF 144 WHERE MARITAL RESIDENCE IS PATRILOCAL, VIRILOCAL, OR AVUNCULOCAL, RATHER THAN AMBILOCAL OR NEOLOCAL (270)	204	DRIFT TOWARD BEING THOSE 0.50 OF 10 WHERE MARITAL RESIDENCE IS AMBILOCAL OR NEOLOCAL, RATHER THAN PATRILOCAL, VIRILOCAL, OR AVUNCULOCAL (64)	116 5 28 5 XSQ= 3.53 PHI= 0.151 XP = 0.0603
209	LEAN TOWARD BEING THOSE 0.81 OF 143 WHERE MARITAL RESIDENCE IS PATRILOCAL, VIRILOCAL, OR AVUNCULOCAL, RATHER THAN MATRILOCAL OR UXORILOCAL (270)	209	LEAN TOWARD BEING THOSE 0.62 OF 13 WHERE MARITAL RESIDENCE IS MATRILOCAL OR UXORILOCAL, RATHER THAN PATRILOCAL, VIRILOCAL, OR AVUNCULOCAL (64)	116 5 27 8 XSQ= 10.13 PHI= 0.255 XP = 0.0015
220	DRIFT MORE TOWARD BEING THOSE 0.80 OF 167 WHERE FIRST COUSIN MARRIAGE IN SOME FORM OR OTHER IS NOT PRESCRIBED OR PREFERRED (273)	220	DRIFT LESS TOWARD BEING THOSE 0.59 OF 17 WHERE FIRST COUSIN MARRIAGE IN SOME FORM OR OTHER IS NOT PRESCRIBED OR PREFERRED (273)	34 7 133 10 XSQ= 2.75 PHI= -0.122 XP = 0.0971
354	DRIFT TOWARD BEING THOSE 0.56 OF 52 WHERE THE CHILD'S INFERRED ANXIETY OVER PERFORMANCE OF OBEDIENT BEHAVIOR IS HIGH (36) B-B-C	354	IN ALL CASES ARE THOSE 1.00 OF 5 WHERE THE CHILD'S INFERRED ANXIETY OVER PERFORMANCE OF OBEDIENT BEHAVIOR IS LOW (37) B-B-C	29 0 23 5 XSQ= 3.66 PHI= 0.254 XP = 0.0556
355	DRIFT TOWARD BEING THOSE 0.56 OF 52 WHERE THE CHILD'S INFERRED CONFLICT REGARDING OBEDIENT BEHAVIOR IS HIGH (35) B-B-C	355	IN ALL CASES ARE THOSE 1.00 OF 5 WHERE THE CHILD'S INFERRED CONFLICT REGARDING OBEDIENT BEHAVIOR IS LOW (38) B-B-C	29 0 23 5 XSQ= 3.66 PHI= 0.254 XP = 0.0556
358	TILT TOWARD BEING THOSE 0.79 OF 39 WHERE ADOLESCENT PEER GROUPS ARE PRESENT IN A SETTING OF WORK AND PUBLIC GATHERINGS AND LEISURE, OR OF PUBLIC GATHERINGS AND LEISURE, OR OF LEISURE ONLY (41) JKH	358	IN ALL CASES ARE THOSE 1.00 OF 3 WHERE ADOLESCENT PEER GROUPS ARE ABSENT IN A SETTING OF WORK, AND OF PUBLIC GATHERINGS, AND OF LEISURE (11) JKH	31 0 8 3 XSQ= 5.46 PHI= 0.360 XP = 0.0195

457/

```
476  DRIFT LESS TOWARD BEING THOSE  0.59 OF  34     476  IN ALL CASES ARE THOSE        1.00 OF   6          20     6
     WHERE THE DEGREE OF INSOBRIETY IS                    WHERE THE DEGREE OF INSOBRIETY IS                 14     0
     STRCNG  (31) DH                                      STRONG  (31) DH                                XSQ=    2.21
                                                                                                         PHI=  -0.235
                                                                                                         EP =  0.0743
```

458 CULTURES WHERE GAMES, IF PRESENT, INCLUDE GAMES OF STRATEGY (52) R-A-B,EA

458 CULTURES WHERE GAMES, IF PRESENT, DO NOT INCLUDE GAMES OF STRATEGY (119) R-A-B,EA

BACKGROUND ON PAGE 169

BOTH SUBJECT AND PREDICATE

52 IN LEFT COLUMN

ALBANIANS	AMERICANS	ASHANTI	AZANDE	AZTEC	BASSERI	BURUSHO	CHAGGA	CZECHS	DARD
EGYPTIANS	FON	GANDA	HAWAIIANS	ILA	INCA	IRISH	JAPANESE	JUKUN	KAZAK
KIKUYU	KOREANS	KUBA	LAKHER	LAMBA	LUO	MASAI	MBUNDU	MENDE	MIN CHINESE
MOSSI	NAMA	NYAKYUSA	NYORO	OKINAWANS	RUNDI	SERBS	SIWANS	SOMALI	SYRIANS
TANALA	TARAHUMARA	THAI	THONGA	TIV	VENDA	VIETNAMESE	WOLEAIANS	WOLOF	YAKUT
YAO	ZUNI								

119 IN RIGHT COLUMN

ABIPON	ABOR	AINU	ANDAMANESE	APINAYE	ARANDA	ARAUCANIANS	ATSUGEWI	AYMARA	BACAIRI
BHIL	BHUIYA	BORORO	BUNLAP	CADUVEO	CAMAYURA	CARIB	CHEROKEE	CHEYENNE	CHIR-APACHE
CHIRIGUANO	CHOROTI	CHUKCHEE	COORG	COPR ESKIMO	CREE	CREEK	CROW	DIEGUENO	DIERI
ELLICE	EYAK	FANG	GOAJIRO	GROS VENTRE	HAIDA	HASINAI	HUKUNDIKA	HURON	HUTSUL
IBAN	INGALIK	JEMEZ	KASKA	KERAKI	KHASI	KORYAK	KUNG	KURTATCHI	KUTENAI
KWAKIUTL	LAPPS	LAU	LEPCHA	LESU	LHOTA NAGA	MACASSARESE	MANGAIANS	MANIHIKI	MANUS
MAORI	MARICOPA	MARQUESANS	MARSHALLESE	MATACO	MAYA	MIAMI	MISKITO	MIWOK	MOTA
NABESNA	NATCHEZ	NAVAHO	NICOBARESE	NOMLAKI	NUNIVAK	OMAHA	ONA	PAIWAN	PALAUANS
PAPAGO	PUKAPUKA	RWALA	SAGADA	SAMOANS	SANPOIL	SEMANG	SENIANG	SHERENTE	SIRIONO
TALLENSI	TACS	TAPIRAPE	TAREUMIUT	TEHUELCHE	TENINO	TIKOPIA	TIMBIRA	TIWI	TODA
TOLOWA	TROBRIAND	TRUKESE	TRUMAI	TUCUNA	TWANA	ULAWANS	UTE	WANTOAT	WAPISHANA
WARRAU	WASHO	WITOTO	WOGEO	YAGUA	YAHGAN	YOKUTS	YUKI	YUROK	

18 EXCLUDED BECAUSE IRRELEVANT (SEE RIGHT COLUMN, PARAGRAPH 457)

211 EXCLUDED BECAUSE UNASCERTAINED

3	TEND LESS TO BE THOSE LOCATED OUTSIDE OF AFRICA (320)	0.56 OF 52	3 TEND MORE TO BE THOSE LOCATED OUTSIDE OF AFRICA (320)	0.97 OF 119	23 3 29 116 XSQ= 45.65 PHI= 0.517 XP = 0.
4	TEND LESS TO BE THOSE LOCATED OUTSIDE OF THE CIRCUM-MEDITERRANEAN (355)	0.81 OF 52	4 TEND MORE TO BE THOSE LOCATED OUTSIDE OF THE CIRCUM-MEDITERRANEAN (355)	0.97 OF 119	10 3 42 116 XSQ= 12.10 PHI= 0.266 XP = 0.0005

5	DRIFT LESS TOWARD BEING THOSE LOCATED OUTSIDE OF EAST EURASIA (330)	0.75 OF 52	5	DRIFT MORE TOWARD BEING THOSE LOCATED OUTSIDE OF EAST EURASIA (330)	0.88 OF 119	13 14 39 105 XSQ= 3.82 PHI= 0.150 XP = 0.0505
6	LEAN MORE TOWARD BEING THOSE LOCATED OUTSIDE OF THE INSULAR PACIFIC (330)	0.96 OF 52	6	LEAN LESS TOWARD BEING THOSE LOCATED OUTSIDE OF THE INSULAR PACIFIC (330)	0.75 OF 119	2 30 50 89 XSQ= 9.50 PHI= -0.236 XP = 0.0021
8	TEND MORE TO BE THOSE LOCATED OUTSIDE OF NORTH AMERICA (330)	0.94 OF 52	8	TEND LESS TO BE THOSE LOCATED OUTSIDE OF NORTH AMERICA (330)	0.66 OF 119	3 41 49 78 XSQ= 14.12 PHI= -0.287 XP = 0.0002
9	LEAN MORE TOWARD BEING THOSE LOCATED OUTSIDE OF SOUTH AMERICA (335)	0.98 OF 52	9	LEAN LESS TOWARD BEING THOSE LOCATED OUTSIDE OF SOUTH AMERICA (335)	0.76 OF 119	1 28 51 91 XSQ= 10.51 PHI= -0.248 XP = 0.0012
13	DRIFT MORE TOWARD BEING THOSE WHERE THE LATITUDE IS LESS THAN FORTY DEGREES (329)	0.87 OF 52	13	DRIFT LESS TOWARD BEING THOSE WHERE THE LATITUDE IS LESS THAN FORTY DEGREES (329)	0.73 OF 119	7 32 45 87 XSQ= 2.98 PHI= -0.132 XP = 0.0841
14	DRIFT MORE TOWARD BEING THOSE WHERE THE LATITUDE IS LESS THAN THIRTY DEGREES (281)	0.73 OF 52	14	DRIFT LESS TOWARD BEING THOSE WHERE THE LATITUDE IS LESS THAN THIRTY DEGREES (281)	0.56 OF 119	14 52 38 67 XSQ= 3.62 PHI= -0.145 XP = 0.0572
44	LEAN MORE TOWARD BEING THOSE WHERE SETTLEMENTS ARE FIXED (222)	0.81 OF 52	44	LEAN LESS TOWARD BEING THOSE WHERE SETTLEMENTS ARE FIXED (222)	0.56 OF 118	42 66 10 52 XSQ= 8.57 PHI= 0.224 XP = 0.0034
46	TILT MORE TOWARD BEING THOSE OTHER THAN WHERE SETTLEMENTS ARE NON-FIXED AND MOVEMENT IS NOMADIC (260)	0.88 OF 52	46	TILT LESS TOWARD BEING THOSE OTHER THAN WHERE SETTLEMENTS ARE NON-FIXED AND MOVEMENT IS NOMADIC (260)	0.70 OF 118	6 35 46 83 XSQ= 5.52 PHI= -0.180 XP = 0.0187
51	TEND TO BE THOSE WHERE SUBSISTENCE IS PRIMARILY BY FOOD PRODUCTION -- I. E., AGRICULTURE OR HUSBANDRY -- RATHER THAN BY GATHERING (253)	0.94 OF 52	51	TEND TO BE THOSE WHERE SUBSISTENCE IS PRIMARILY BY FOOD GATHERING -- I. E., HUNTING, FISHING, OR COLLECTING -- RATHER THAN FOOD PRODUCTION (147)	0.67 OF 119	49 39 3 80 XSQ= 52.29 PHI= 0.553 XP = 0.

No.	Statement	Proportion	No.	Statement	Proportion	Statistics
53	TEND TO BE THOSE WHERE FOOD PRODUCTION IS BY INTENSIVE AGRICULTURE, RATHER THAN BY SIMPLE AGRICULTURE OR INCIPIENT FOOD PRODUCTION (91)	0.64 OF 47	53	TEND TO BE THOSE WHERE FOOD PRODUCTION IS BY SIMPLE AGRICULTURE OR INCIPIENT FOOD PRODUCTION, RATHER THAN BY INTENSIVE AGRICULTURE (147)	0.83 OF 58	30 10 17 48 XSQ= 21.96 PHI= 0.457 XP = 0.0000
55	LEAN TOWARD BEING THOSE WHERE FOOD PRODUCTION IS BY INTENSIVE AGRICULTURE, RATHER THAN BY SIMPLE AGRICULTURE (91)	0.67 OF 45	55	LEAN TOWARD BEING THOSE WHERE FOOD PRODUCTION IS BY SIMPLE AGRICULTURE, RATHER THAN BY INTENSIVE AGRICULTURE (101)	0.71 OF 35	30 10 15 25 XSQ= 9.96 PHI= 0.353 XP = 0.0016
56	TILT MORE TOWARD BEING THOSE WHERE FOOD PRODUCTION IS BY SIMPLE AGRICULTURE, RATHER THAN BY INCIPIENT FOOD PRODUCTION (101)	0.88 OF 17	56	TILT LESS TOWARD BEING THOSE WHERE FOOD PRODUCTION IS BY SIMPLE AGRICULTURE, RATHER THAN BY INCIPIENT FOOD PRODUCTION (101)	0.52 OF 48	15 25 2 23 XSQ= 5.49 PHI= 0.291 XP = 0.0191
62	TEND TO BE THOSE WHERE HUSBANDRY OF SOME KIND IS PRESENT (228)	0.92 OF 52	62	TEND TO BE THOSE WHERE HUSBANDRY OF ANY KIND IS ABSENT (172)	0.51 OF 119	48 58 4 61 XSQ= 27.33 PHI= 0.400 XP = 0.0000
63	LEAN MORE TOWARD BEING THOSE WHERE HUSBANDRY, IF PRESENT, IS PRINCIPALLY IN THE FORM OF BOVINE, EQUINE, CAMEL-LIKE, OR DEER-LIKE ANIMALS, RATHER THAN PIGS, SHEEP, OR GOATS (152)	0.79 OF 48	63	LEAN LESS TOWARD BEING THOSE WHERE HUSBANDRY, IF PRESENT, IS PRINCIPALLY IN THE FORM OF BOVINE, EQUINE, CAMEL-LIKE, OR DEER-LIKE ANIMALS, RATHER THAN PIGS, SHEEP, OR GOATS (152)	0.52 OF 58	38 30 10 28 XSQ= 7.45 PHI= 0.265 XP = 0.0063
71	TEND TO BE THOSE WHERE METAL WORKING IS PRESENT (98)	0.91 OF 44	71	TEND TO BE THOSE WHERE METAL WORKING IS ABSENT (153)	0.81 OF 109	40 21 4 88 XSQ= 64.16 PHI= 0.648 XP = 0.
73	TEND TO BE THOSE WHERE WEAVING IS PRESENT (118)	0.70 OF 44	73	TEND TO BE THOSE WHERE WEAVING IS ABSENT (130)	0.62 OF 107	31 41 13 66 XSQ= 11.65 PHI= 0.278 XP = 0.0006
74	LEAN MORE TOWARD BEING THOSE WHERE POTTERY IS PRESENT (145)	0.80 OF 44	74	LEAN LESS TOWARD BEING THOSE WHERE POTTERY IS PRESENT (145)	0.53 OF 106	35 56 9 50 XSQ= 8.21 PHI= 0.234 XP = 0.0042
79	TEND LESS TO BE THOSE WHERE NO CITY IS PRESENT (201)	0.72 OF 46	79	IN ALL CASES ARE THOSE WHERE NO CITY IS PRESENT (201)	1.00 OF 81	13 0 33 81 XSQ= 22.52 PHI= 0.421 XP = 0.0000

81	TEND TO BE THOSE 0.70 OF 46 WHERE A CITY OR TOWN IS PRESENT, OR THE AVERAGE COMMUNITY SIZE IS 200 OR GREATER (89)	81	TEND TO BE THOSE 0.80 OF 81 WHERE NO CITY OR TOWN IS PRESENT, AND THE AVERAGE COMMUNITY SIZE IS SMALLER THAN 200 (135)	32 16 14 65 XSQ= 28.88 PHI= 0.477 XP = 0.0000
83	LEAN LESS TOWARD BEING THOSE 0.54 OF 26 WHERE, WITH NO CITY AND NO TOWN PRESENT, THE AVERAGE COMMUNITY SIZE IS SMALLER THAN 200, RATHER THAN BETWEEN 200 AND 999 (135)	83	LEAN MORE TOWARD BEING THOSE 0.83 OF 78 WHERE, WITH NO CITY AND NO TOWN PRESENT, THE AVERAGE COMMUNITY SIZE IS SMALLER THAN 200, RATHER THAN BETWEEN 200 AND 999 (135)	12 13 14 65 XSQ= 7.74 PHI= 0.273 XP = 0.0054
85	TEND TO BE THOSE 0.64 OF 45 WHERE THE LEVEL OF POLITICAL INTEGRATION IS THE LARGE STATE, OR THE LITTLE STATE (70) GPM	85	TEND TO BE THOSE 0.95 OF 98 WHERE THE LEVEL OF POLITICAL INTEGRATION IS THE MINIMAL STATE, THE AUTONOMOUS COMMUNITY, OR THE FAMILY (234) GPM	29 5 16 93 XSQ= 56.69 PHI= 0.630 XP = 0.
86	TEND TO BE THOSE 0.87 OF 45 WHERE THE LEVEL OF POLITICAL INTEGRATION IS THE LARGE STATE, THE LITTLE STATE, OR THE MINIMAL STATE (148) GPM	86	TEND TO BE THOSE 0.70 OF 98 WHERE THE LEVEL OF POLITICAL INTEGRATION IS THE AUTONOMOUS COMMUNITY, OR THE FAMILY (156) GPM	39 29 6 69 XSQ= 38.02 PHI= 0.516 XP = 0.
95	TEND TO BE THOSE 0.67 OF 52 WHERE THE HIERARCHY OF NATIONAL JURISDICTION HAS FOUR, THREE, OR TWO LEVELS (76) GES,EA	95	TEND TO BE THOSE 0.94 OF 117 WHERE THE HIERARCHY OF NATIONAL JURISDICTION HAS ONE OR NO LEVELS (254) GES,EA	35 7 17 110 XSQ= 69.25 PHI= 0.640 XP = 0.
96	TEND TO BE THOSE 0.90 OF 52 WHERE THE HIERARCHY OF NATIONAL JURISDICTION HAS FOUR, THREE, TWO OR ONE LEVEL (174) GES,EA	96	TEND TO BE THOSE 0.66 OF 117 WHERE THE HIERARCHY OF NATIONAL JURISDICTION HAS NO LEVELS (156) GES,EA	47 40 5 77 XSQ= 43.29 PHI= 0.506 XP = 0.
100	TEND MORE TO BE THOSE 0.98 OF 52 WHERE HIERARCHIES ARE MORE COMPLEX THAN THE 'SIMPLEST,' I. E., MORE COMPLEX THAN TWO LOCAL LEVELS WITH NO NATIONAL LEVELS (267) GES,EA	100	TEND LESS TO BE THOSE 0.73 OF 117 WHERE HIERARCHIES ARE MORE COMPLEX THAN THE 'SIMPLEST,' I. E., MORE COMPLEX THAN TWO LOCAL LEVELS WITH NO NATIONAL LEVELS (267) GES,EA	51 85 1 32 XSQ= 13.24 PHI= 0.280 XP = 0.0003
102	TEND TO BE THOSE 0.85 OF 52 WHERE CLASS STRATIFICATION IS PRESENT (203)	102	TEND TO BE THOSE 0.54 OF 116 WHERE CLASS STRATIFICATION IS ABSENT (180)	44 53 8 63 XSQ= 20.73 PHI= 0.351 XP = 0.0000
106	TEND TO BE THOSE 0.80 OF 44 WHERE CLASS STRATIFICATION, IF PRESENT, IS BASED ON SOMETHING OTHER THAN WEALTH (126)	106	TEND TO BE THOSE 0.58 OF 53 WHERE CLASS STRATIFICATION, IF PRESENT, IS BASED ON WEALTH (77)	9 31 35 22 XSQ= 12.83 PHI= -0.364 XP = 0.0003

107	LEAN LESS TOWARD BEING THOSE WHERE CLASS STRATIFICATION, IF PRESENT, IS BASED ON SOMETHING OTHER THAN OCCUPATIONAL STATUS (160)	0.64 OF 44	107	LEAN MORE TOWARD BEING THOSE WHERE CLASS STRATIFICATION, IF PRESENT, IS BASED ON SOMETHING OTHER THAN OCCUPATIONAL STATUS (160)	0.92 OF 53	16 4 28 49 XSQ= 10.50 PHI= 0.329 XP = 0.0012
109	TEND LESS TO BE THOSE WHERE CASTES ARE ABSENT (317)	0.75 OF 48	109	TEND MORE TO BE THOSE WHERE CASTES ARE ABSENT (317)	0.96 OF 115	12 5 36 110 XSQ= 13.33 PHI= 0.286 XP = 0.0003
110	TEND TO BE THOSE WHERE SLAVERY IS PRESENT (163)	0.62 OF 50	110	TEND TO BE THOSE WHERE SLAVERY IS ABSENT (218)	0.74 OF 116	31 30 19 86 XSQ= 18.11 PHI= 0.330 XP = 0.0000
116	TILT TOWARD BEING THOSE WHERE OCCUPATIONAL SPECIALIZATION IS FULL-TIME, WHETHER OR NOT FOR SURPLUS PRODUCTION (20) JMH	0.69 OF 13	116	TILT TOWARD BEING THOSE WHERE OCCUPATIONAL SPECIALIZATION IS PART-TIME ONLY (34) JMH	0.72 OF 25	9 7 4 18 XSQ= 4.39 PHI= 0.340 EP = 0.0356
129	TEND TO BE THOSE WHERE WEAVING IS MAINLY DONE BY MALES (31)	0.50 OF 26	129	TEND TO BE THOSE WHERE WEAVING IS MAINLY DONE BY FEMALES (73)	0.92 OF 39	13 3 13 36 XSQ= 12.85 PHI= 0.445 XP = 0.0003
130	LEAN TOWARD BEING THOSE WHERE LEATHER WORKING IS MAINLY DONE BY MALES (39)	0.79 OF 14	130	LEAN TOWARD BEING THOSE WHERE LEATHER WORKING IS MAINLY DONE BY FEMALES (45)	0.69 OF 45	11 14 3 31 XSQ= 8.00 PHI= 0.368 XP = 0.0047
138	LEAN TOWARD BEING THOSE WHERE SUPERORDINATE JUSTICE IS PRESENT (22) BBW	0.91 OF 11	138	LEAN TOWARD BEING THOSE WHERE SUPERORDINATE JUSTICE IS ABSENT (18) BBW	0.61 OF 18	10 7 1 11 XSQ= 5.62 PHI= 0.440 EP = 0.0080
141	DRIFT TOWARD BEING THOSE WHERE THE LEVEL OF SOCIAL SANCTION IS PUBLIC CORPOREAL SANCTION, RATHER THAN PUBLIC PROPERTY SANCTION OR PRIVATE SETTLEMENT (28) JMH	0.77 OF 13	141	DRIFT TOWARD BEING THOSE WHERE THE LEVEL OF SOCIAL SANCTION IS PUBLIC PROPERTY SANCTION OR PRIVATE SETTLEMENT, RATHER THAN PUBLIC CORPOREAL SANCTION (26) JMH	0.56 OF 25	10 11 3 14 XSQ= 2.54 PHI= 0.258 EP = 0.0863
142	IN ALL CASES ARE THOSE WHERE THE LEVEL OF SOCIAL SANCTION IS PUBLIC CORPOREAL SANCTION OR PUBLIC PROPERTY SANCTION, RATHER THAN PRIVATE SETTLEMENT (38) JMH	1.00 OF 13	142	LEAN LESS TOWARD BEING THOSE WHERE THE LEVEL OF SOCIAL SANCTION IS PUBLIC CORPOREAL SANCTION OR PUBLIC PROPERTY SANCTION, RATHER THAN PRIVATE SETTLEMENT (38) JMH	0.60 OF 25	13 15 0 10 XSQ= 5.15 PHI= 0.368 EP = 0.0078

183	IN ALL CASES ARE THOSE 1.00 OF 42 WHERE THE LARGEST NON-COGNATIC KIN GROUP IS SMALLER THAN A MOEITY, I. E., A PHRATRY OR SIB OR LINEAGE (218)	183	TEND LESS TO BE THOSE 0.66 OF 61 WHERE THE LARGEST NON-COGNATIC KIN GROUP IS SMALLER THAN A MOEITY, I. E., A PHRATRY OR SIB OR LINEAGE (218)	0 21 42 40 XSQ= 16.10 PHI= -0.395 XP = 0.0001
184	LEAN MORE TOWARD BEING THOSE 0.81 OF 42 WHERE THE LARGEST NON-COGNATIC KIN GROUP IS SMALLER THAN A PHRATRY, I. E. A SIB OR LINEAGE (175)	184	LEAN LESS TOWARD BEING THOSE 0.51 OF 61 WHERE THE LARGEST NON-COGNATIC KIN GROUP IS SMALLER THAN A PHRATRY, I. E. A SIB OR LINEAGE (175)	8 30 34 31 XSQ= 8.45 PHI= -0.286 XP = 0.0037
186	TEND TO BE THOSE 0.54 OF 52 WHERE THE KIN GROUP IS EXCLUSIVELY PATRILINEAL (150)	186	TEND TO BE THOSE 0.78 OF 119 WHERE THE KIN GROUP IS OTHER THAN EXCLUSIVELY PATRILINEAL (250)	28 26 24 93 XSQ= 15.70 PHI= 0.303 XP = 0.0001
188	TEND MORE TO BE THOSE 0.81 OF 52 WHERE THE KIN GROUP IS OTHER THAN EXCLUSIVELY COGNATIC (252)	188	TEND LESS TO BE THOSE 0.51 OF 119 WHERE THE KIN GROUP IS OTHER THAN EXCLUSIVELY COGNATIC (252)	10 58 42 61 XSQ= 11.95 PHI= -0.264 XP = 0.0005
190	LEAN MORE TOWARD BEING THOSE 0.88 OF 41 WHERE THE KIN GROUP IS PATRILINEAL OR DOUBLE-DESCENT, RATHER THAN MATRILINEAL (186)	190	LEAN LESS TOWARD BEING THOSE 0.57 OF 58 WHERE THE KIN GROUP IS PATRILINEAL OR DOUBLE-DESCENT, RATHER THAN MATRILINEAL (186)	36 33 5 25 XSQ= 9.45 PHI= 0.309 XP = 0.0021
192	LEAN MORE TOWARD BEING THOSE 0.87 OF 52 OTHER THAN WHERE THE ONLY KIN GROUP PRESENT IS A KINDRED OR ELSE BILATERAL DESCENT IS INFERRED (289)	192	LEAN LESS TOWARD BEING THOSE 0.64 OF 119 OTHER THAN WHERE THE ONLY KIN GROUP PRESENT IS A KINDRED OR ELSE BILATERAL DESCENT IS INFERRED (289)	7 43 45 76 XSQ= 7.93 PHI= -0.215 XP = 0.0049
196	LEAN TOWARD BEING THOSE 0.76 OF 45 WHERE INDIVIDUAL RIGHTS IN REAL PROPERTY, AND RULES FOR INHERITANCE, ARE PRESENT (194)	196	LEAN TOWARD BEING THOSE 0.54 OF 79 WHERE INDIVIDUAL RIGHTS IN REAL PROPERTY, OR RULES FOR INHERITANCE, ARE ABSENT (87)	34 36 11 43 XSQ= 9.30 PHI= 0.274 XP = 0.0023
209	TILT MORE TOWARD BEING THOSE 0.93 OF 45 WHERE MARITAL RESIDENCE IS PATRILOCAL, VIRILOCAL, OR AVUNCULOCAL, RATHER THAN MATRILOCAL OR UXORILOCAL (270)	209	TILT LESS TOWARD BEING THOSE 0.76 OF 98 WHERE MARITAL RESIDENCE IS PATRILOCAL, VIRILOCAL, OR AVUNCULOCAL, RATHER THAN MATRILOCAL OR UXORILOCAL (270)	42 74 3 24 XSQ= 5.29 PHI= 0.192 XP = 0.0215
210	TILT MORE TOWARD BEING THOSE 0.94 OF 33 WHERE MARITAL RESIDENCE IS PATRILOCAL, RATHER THAN MATRILOCAL (169)	210	TILT LESS TOWARD BEING THOSE 0.72 OF 43 WHERE MARITAL RESIDENCE IS PATRILOCAL, RATHER THAN MATRILOCAL (169)	31 31 2 12 XSQ= 4.57 PHI= 0.245 XP = 0.0326

No.	Left statement	No.	Right statement	Statistics
220	DRIFT LESS TOWARD BEING THOSE 0.71 OF 51 WHERE FIRST COUSIN MARRIAGE IN SOME FORM OR OTHER IS NOT PRESCRIBED OR PREFERRED (273)	220	DRIFT MORE TOWARD BEING THOSE 0.84 OF 116 WHERE FIRST COUSIN MARRIAGE IN SOME FORM OR OTHER IS NOT PRESCRIBED OR PREFERRED (273)	15 19 36 97 XSQ= 2.95 PHI= 0.133 XP = 0.0858
221	DRIFT LESS TOWARD BEING THOSE 0.88 OF 51 WHERE MATRILATERAL CROSS-COUSIN MARRIAGE IS NOT PRESCRIBED OR PREFERRED (335)	221	DRIFT MORE TOWARD BEING THOSE 0.97 OF 116 WHERE MATRILATERAL CROSS-COUSIN MARRIAGE IS NOT PRESCRIBED OR PREFERRED (335)	6 4 45 112 XSQ= 3.00 PHI= 0.134 XP = 0.0832
236	DRIFT TOWARD BEING THOSE 0.65 OF 52 WHERE THE FAMILY IS OF AN EXTENDED TYPE, RATHER THAN AN INDEPENDENT TYPE (213)	236	DRIFT TOWARD BEING THOSE 0.50 OF 119 WHERE THE FAMILY IS OF AN INDEPENDENT TYPE, RATHER THAN AN EXTENDED TYPE (185)	34 59 18 60 XSQ= 3.03 PHI= 0.133 XP = 0.0815
243	DRIFT TOWARD BEING THOSE 0.56 OF 16 WHERE POLYGYNY, IF PRESENT, HAS A HIGH INCIDENCE (24) W-D,S	243	DRIFT TOWARD BEING THOSE 0.74 OF 27 WHERE POLYGYNY, IF PRESENT, HAS A LOW INCIDENCE (36) W-D,S	9 7 7 20 XSQ= 2.76 PHI= 0.253 XP = 0.0965
262	TILT MORE TOWARD BEING THOSE 0.87 OF 52 WHERE WIVES ARE OBTAINED BY MEANS INVOLVING THE PRESENCE OF SOME CONSIDERATION (305)	262	TILT LESS TOWARD BEING THOSE 0.69 OF 119 WHERE WIVES ARE OBTAINED BY MEANS INVOLVING THE PRESENCE OF SOME CONSIDERATION (305)	45 82 7 37 XSQ= 5.00 PHI= 0.171 XP = 0.0254
263	TILT TOWARD BEING THOSE 0.63 OF 52 WHERE WIVES ARE OBTAINED BY RELATIVELY DIFFICULT MEANS, NAMELY BY BRIDE-PRICE, BRIDE-SERVICE, OR EXCHANGING A FEMALE RELATIVE (233)	263	TILT TOWARD BEING THOSE 0.57 OF 119 WHERE WIVES ARE OBTAINED BY RELATIVELY EASY MEANS, NAMELY BY TOKEN BRIDE-PRICE, GIFT EXCHANGE, ABSENCE OF ANY CONSIDERATION, OR RECEIPT OF DOWRY (162)	33 51 19 68 XSQ= 5.35 PHI= 0.177 XP = 0.0207
278	TILT TOWARD BEING THOSE 0.83 OF 6 WHERE PROPERTY RIGHTS IN WOMEN ARE PRESENT (8) LWS	278	TILT TOWARD BEING THOSE 0.82 OF 11 WHERE PROPERTY RIGHTS IN WOMEN ARE UNIMPORTANT OR ABSENT (14) LWS	5 2 1 9 XSQ= 4.38 PHI= 0.508 EP = 0.0345
282	TILT TOWARD BEING THOSE 0.70 OF 10 WHERE THE STRENGTH OF DESIRE FOR CHILDREN IS HIGH (16) BCA	282	TILT TOWARD BEING THOSE 0.76 OF 17 WHERE THE STRENGTH OF DESIRE FOR CHILDREN IS LOW OR ABSENT (20) BCA	7 4 3 13 XSQ= 3.87 PHI= 0.379 EP = 0.0402
295	TILT TOWARD BEING THOSE 0.83 OF 6 WHERE THE SEVERITY OF PUNISHMENT FOR ABORTION IS HIGH (11) BCA	295	TILT TOWARD BEING THOSE 0.73 OF 11 WHERE THE SEVERITY OF PUNISHMENT FOR ABORTION IS LOW OR ABSENT (12) BCA	5 3 1 8 XSQ= 2.91 PHI= 0.413 EP = 0.0498

```
304  TILT TOWARD BEING THOSE          0.89 OF   9     304  TILT TOWARD BEING THOSE          0.64 OF  22          1   14
     WHERE THE EARLY ANAL SATISFACTION                    WHERE THE EARLY ANAL SATISFACTION                    8    8
     POTENTIAL IS LOW  (22) W-C                           POTENTIAL IS HIGH  (19) W-C                 XSQ=      5.11
                                                                                                      PHI=    -0.406
                                                                                                      EP =    0.0155

314  TEND TO BE THOSE                 0.56 OF  18     314  TEND TO BE THOSE                 0.92 OF  37         10    3
     WHERE THE INCIDENCE OF MOTHER-CHILD                  WHERE THE INCIDENCE OF MOTHER-CHILD                  8   34
     HOUSEHOLDS IS HIGH  (19) W-D,S                       HOUSEHOLDS IS LOW  (61) W-D,S               XSQ=     12.59
                                                                                                      PHI=     0.478
                                                                                                      XP =    0.0004

317  DRIFT TOWARD BEING THOSE         0.75 OF  12     317  DRIFT TOWARD BEING THOSE         0.60 OF  35          3   21
     WHERE DISPLAY OF AFFECTION TOWARD                    WHERE DISPLAY OF AFFECTION TOWARD                    9   14
     THE INFANT IS LOW  (29) B-B-C                        THE INFANT IS HIGH  (39) B-B-C              XSQ=      3.09
                                                                                                      PHI=    -0.256
                                                                                                      XP =    0.0787

318  LEAN TOWARD BEING THOSE          0.87 OF  15     318  LEAN TOWARD BEING THOSE          0.69 OF  35          2   24
     WHERE THE OVERALL INDULGENCE                         WHERE THE OVERALL INDULGENCE                        13   11
     OF THE INFANT                                        OF THE INFANT                               XSQ=     10.72
     IS LOW  (31) B-B-C                                   IS HIGH  (40) B-B-C                         PHI=    -0.463
                                                                                                      XP =    0.0011

320  DRIFT TOWARD BEING THOSE         0.60 OF  15     320  DRIFT TOWARD BEING THOSE         0.71 OF  34          6   24
     WHERE THE DEGREE OF REDUCTION                        WHERE THE DEGREE OF REDUCTION                        9   10
     OF THE INFANT'S DRIVES                               OF THE INFANT'S DRIVES                      XSQ=      2.91
     IS LOW  (24) B-B-C                                   IS HIGH  (45) B-B-C                         PHI=    -0.244
                                                                                                      XP =    0.0878

324  LEAN TOWARD BEING THOSE          0.86 OF  14     324  LEAN TOWARD BEING THOSE          0.61 OF  33         12   13
     WHERE THE PAIN INFLICTED                             WHERE THE PAIN INFLICTED                             2   20
     ON THE INFANT BY THE NURTURANT AGENT                 ON THE INFANT BY THE NURTURANT AGENT        XSQ=      6.71
     IS HIGH  (34) B-B-C                                  IS LOW OR NEGLIGIBLE  (32) B-B-C            PHI=     0.378
                                                                                                      XP =    0.0096

326  TILT TOWARD BEING THOSE          0.71 OF  17     326  TILT TOWARD BEING THOSE          0.65 OF  31         12   11
     WHERE THE INFERRED TRANSITION ANXIETY                WHERE THE INFERRED TRANSITION ANXIETY                5   20
     BETWEEN INFANCY AND CHILDHOOD                        BETWEEN INFANCY AND CHILDHOOD               XSQ=      4.11
     IS HIGH  (32) B-B-C                                  IS LOW  (35) B-B-C                          PHI=     0.292
                                                                                                      XP =    0.0427

327  TILT TOWARD BEING THOSE          0.82 OF  11     327  TILT TOWARD BEING THOSE          0.58 OF  26          2   15
     WHERE THE AGE OF THE INFANT                          WHERE THE AGE OF THE INFANT                          9   11
     AT TIME OF REDUCED CONTACT WITH MOTHER               AT TIME OF REDUCED CONTACT WITH MOTHER      XSQ=      3.40
     IS TWO YEARS OR LOWER  (27) B-B-C                    IS HIGHER THAN TWO YEARS  (28) B-B-C        PHI=    -0.303
                                                                                                      EP =    0.0365

334  LEAN TOWARD BEING THOSE          0.83 OF  18     334  LEAN TOWARD BEING THOSE          0.59 OF  37          3   22
     WHERE THE INDULGENCE OF THE CHILD                    WHERE THE INDULGENCE OF THE CHILD                   15   15
     IS LOW  (38) B-B-C                                   IS HIGH  (40) B-B-C                         XSQ=      7.30
                                                                                                      PHI=    -0.364
                                                                                                      XP =    0.0069
```

337	LEAN TOWARD BEING THOSE WHERE THE CHILD'S INFERRED ANXIETY OVER NON-PERFORMANCE OF RESPONSIBLE BEHAVIOR IS HIGH (38) B-B-C	0.81 OF	16	337	LEAN TOWARD BEING THOSE WHERE THE CHILD'S INFERRED ANXIETY OVER NON-PERFORMANCE OF RESPONSIBLE BEHAVIOR IS LOW (35) B-B-C	0.65 OF	34	13 12 3 22 XSQ= 7.44 PHI= 0.386 XP = 0.0064
338	TILT TOWARD BEING THOSE WHERE THE CHILD'S INFERRED ANXIETY OVER PERFORMANCE OF RESPONSIBLE BEHAVIOR IS HIGH (44) B-B-C	0.88 OF	16	338	TILT TOWARD BEING THOSE WHERE THE CHILD'S INFERRED ANXIETY OVER PERFORMANCE OF RESPONSIBLE BEHAVIOR IS LOW (29) B-B-C	0.50 OF	34	14 17 2 17 XSQ= 5.00 PHI= 0.316 XP = 0.0253
346	LEAN TOWARD BEING THOSE WHERE THE CHILD'S INFERRED ANXIETY OVER PERFORMANCE OF SELF-RELIANT BEHAVIOR IS HIGH (37) B-B-C	0.82 OF	17	346	LEAN TOWARD BEING THOSE WHERE THE CHILD'S INFERRED ANXIETY OVER PERFORMANCE OF SELF-RELIANT BEHAVIOR IS LOW (39) B-B-C	0.61 OF	36	14 14 3 22 XSQ= 7.10 PHI= 0.366 XP = 0.0077
347	TEND TO BE THOSE WHERE THE CHILD'S INFERRED CONFLICT REGARDING SELF-RELIANT BEHAVIOR IS HIGH (37) B-B-C	0.88 OF	17	347	TEND TO BE THOSE WHERE THE CHILD'S INFERRED CONFLICT REGARDING SELF-RELIANT BEHAVIOR IS LOW (39) B-B-C	0.69 OF	36	15 11 2 25 XSQ= 13.15 PHI= 0.498 XP = 0.0003
350	LEAN TOWARD BEING THOSE WHERE THE CHILD'S INFERRED ANXIETY OVER PERFORMANCE OF ACHIEVEMENT BEHAVIOR IS HIGH (34) B-B-C	0.93 OF	14	350	LEAN TOWARD BEING THOSE WHERE THE CHILD'S INFERRED ANXIETY OVER PERFORMANCE OF ACHIEVEMENT BEHAVIOR IS LOW (26) B-B-C	0.55 OF	29	13 13 1 16 XSQ= 7.21 PHI= 0.410 XP = 0.0072
351	TILT TOWARD BEING THOSE WHERE THE CHILD'S INFERRED CONFLICT REGARDING ACHIEVEMENT BEHAVIOR IS HIGH (26) B-B-C	0.71 OF	14	351	TILT TOWARD BEING THOSE WHERE THE CHILD'S INFERRED CONFLICT REGARDING ACHIEVEMENT BEHAVIOR IS LOW (34) B-B-C	0.69 OF	29	10 9 4 20 XSQ= 4.72 PHI= 0.331 XP = 0.0299
353	IN ALL CASES ARE THOSE WHERE THE CHILD'S INFERRED ANXIETY OVER NON-PERFORMANCE OF OBEDIENT BEHAVIOR IS HIGH (42) B-B-C	1.00 OF	17	353	TEND TO BE THOSE WHERE THE CHILD-S INFERRED ANXIETY OVER NON-PERFORMANCE OF OBEDIENT BEHAVIOR IS LOW (32) B-B-C	0.54 OF	35	17 16 0 19 XSQ= 12.30 PHI= 0.486 XP = 0.0005
354	DRIFT TOWARD BEING THOSE WHERE THE CHILD'S INFERRED ANXIETY OVER PERFORMANCE OF OBEDIENT BEHAVIOR IS HIGH (36) B-B-C	0.76 OF	17	354	DRIFT TOWARD BEING THOSE WHERE THE CHILD'S INFERRED ANXIETY OVER PERFORMANCE OF OBEDIENT BEHAVIOR IS LOW (37) B-B-C	0.54 OF	35	13 16 4 19 XSQ= 3.23 PHI= 0.249 XP = 0.0723
355	DRIFT TOWARD BEING THOSE WHERE THE CHILD'S INFERRED CONFLICT REGARDING OBEDIENT BEHAVIOR IS HIGH (35) B-B-C	0.76 OF	17	355	DRIFT TOWARD BEING THOSE WHERE THE CHILD'S INFERRED CONFLICT REGARDING OBEDIENT BEHAVIOR IS LOW (38) B-B-C	0.54 OF	35	13 16 4 19 XSQ= 3.23 PHI= 0.249 XP = 0.0723

358	IN ALL CASES ARE THOSE 1.00 OF 13 WHERE ADOLESCENT PEER GROUPS ARE PRESENT IN A SETTING OF WORK AND PUBLIC GATHERINGS AND LEISURE, OR OF PUBLIC GATHERINGS AND LEISURE, OR OF LEISURE ONLY (41) JKH	358	TILT LESS TOWARD BEING THOSE 0.69 OF 26 WHERE ADOLESCENT PEER GROUPS ARE PRESENT IN A SETTING OF WORK AND PUBLIC GATHERINGS AND LEISURE, OR OF PUBLIC GATHERINGS AND LEISURE, OR OF LEISURE ONLY (41) JKH	13 18 0 8 XSQ= 3.32 PHI= 0.292 EP = 0.0352
360	DRIFT TOWARD BEING THOSE 0.63 OF 8 WHERE ADOLESCENT PEER GROUPS ARE PRESENT IN A SETTING OF WORK AND PUBLIC GATHERINGS AND LEISURE, OR AT LEAST OF PUBLIC GATHERINGS AND LEISURE (14) JKH	360	DRIFT TOWARD BEING THOSE 0.79 OF 19 WHERE ADOLESCENT PEER GROUPS ARE PRESENT ONLY IN A SETTING OF LEISURE, OR ELSE ARE ABSENT (23) JKH	5 4 3 15 XSQ= 2.69 PHI= 0.315 EP = 0.0721
365	TILT MORE TOWARD BEING THOSE 0.92 OF 12 WHERE THE TIME SPENT IN ADOLESCENT PEER GROUP ACTIVITY IS HIGH OR HIGH-MEDIUM (30) JKH	365	TILT LESS TOWARD BEING THOSE 0.54 OF 24 WHERE THE TIME SPENT IN ADOLESCENT PEER GROUP ACTIVITY IS HIGH OR HIGH-MEDIUM (30) JKH	11 13 1 11 XSQ= 3.52 PHI= 0.312 EP = 0.0307
368	DRIFT TOWARD BEING THOSE 0.80 OF 10 WHERE DISSOCIATION OF THE SEXES AT ADOLESCENCE IS LOW (21) JKH	368	DRIFT TOWARD BEING THOSE 0.60 OF 20 WHERE DISSOCIATION OF THE SEXES AT ADOLESCENCE IS HIGH OR MEDIUM (16) JKH	2 12 8 8 XSQ= 2.83 PHI= -0.307 EP = 0.0577
372	DRIFT TOWARD BEING THOSE 0.65 OF 20 WHERE MALE INITIATION RITES ARE PRESENT (48) ASA	372	DRIFT TOWARD BEING THOSE 0.61 OF 51 WHERE MALE INITIATION RITES ARE ABSENT (63) ASA	13 20 7 31 XSQ= 2.87 PHI= 0.201 XP = 0.0901
377	TEND LESS TO BE THOSE 0.60 OF 50 WHERE MALE GENITAL MUTILATION IS ABSENT (242)	377	TEND MORE TO BE THOSE 0.90 OF 118 WHERE MALE GENITAL MUTILATION IS ABSENT (242)	20 12 30 106 XSQ= 18.38 PHI= 0.331 XP = 0.0000
391	DRIFT TOWARD BEING THOSE 0.63 OF 38 WHERE PREMARITAL SEX RELATIONS ARE STRONGLY PUNISHED AND IN FACT RARE, OR WEAKLY PUNISHED AND IN FACT NOT RARE (89) JTW,EA	391	DRIFT TOWARD BEING THOSE 0.55 OF 74 WHERE PREMARITAL SEX RELATIONS ARE PUNISHED ONLY IF PREGNANCY RESULTS, OR FREELY PERMITTED (90) JTW,EA	24 33 14 41 XSQ= 2.76 PHI= 0.157 XP = 0.0967
399	DRIFT TOWARD BEING THOSE 0.75 OF 12 WHERE INTENSITY OF CASTRATION ANXIETY IS HIGH (23) WNS	399	DRIFT TOWARD BEING THOSE 0.58 OF 24 WHERE INTENSITY OF CASTRATION ANXIETY IS LOW (22) WNS	9 10 3 14 XSQ= 2.35 PHI= 0.256 EP = 0.0830
419	DRIFT MORE TOWARD BEING THOSE 0.81 OF 26 WHERE MILITARY GLORY IS STRONGLY OR MODERATELY EMPHASIZED (55) PES	419	DRIFT LESS TOWARD BEING THOSE 0.55 OF 42 WHERE MILITARY GLORY IS STRONGLY OR MODERATELY EMPHASIZED (55) PES	21 23 5 19 XSQ= 3.69 PHI= 0.233 XP = 0.0549

420	DRIFT TOWARD BEING THOSE WHERE BELLICOSITY IS EXTREME (41) PES	0.60 OF 25	420	DRIFT TOWARD BEING THOSE WHERE BELLICOSITY IS MODERATE OR NEGLIGIBLE (46) PES	0.64 OF 44	15 16 10 28 XSQ= 2.71 PHI= 0.198 XP = 0.0999
426	TEND TO BE THOSE WHERE A HIGH GOD IS PRESENT (156) GES,EA	0.77 OF 47	426	TEND TO BE THOSE WHERE A HIGH GOD IS ABSENT (104) GES,EA	0.59 OF 107	36 44 11 63 XSQ= 15.07 PHI= 0.313 XP = 0.0001
446	DRIFT TOWARD BEING THOSE WHERE WITCHCRAFT IS SIGNIFICANTLY PRESENT (14) GES	0.78 OF 9	446	DRIFT TOWARD BEING THOSE WHERE WITCHCRAFT IS MODERATELY PRESENT OR ABSENT (24) GES	0.67 OF 15	7 5 2 10 XSQ= 2.84 PHI= 0.344 EP = 0.0894
450	DRIFT LESS TOWARD BEING THOSE WHERE THE OBSERVATION OF FOOD TABOOS IS HIGH OR MEDIUM, RATHER THAN LOW (60) JRL	0.55 OF 22	450	DRIFT MORE TOWARD BEING THOSE WHERE THE OBSERVATION OF FOOD TABOOS IS HIGH OR MEDIUM, RATHER THAN LOW (60) JRL	0.81 OF 37	12 30 10 7 XSQ= 3.53 PHI= -0.245 XP = 0.0602
468	TEND TO BE THOSE WHERE CONTACT WITH OTHER CULTURES IS FREQUENT, RATHER THAN REGULAR OR IRREGULAR (17) JMH	0.62 OF 13	468	TEND TO BE THOSE WHERE CONTACT WITH OTHER CULTURES IS REGULAR OR IRREGULAR, RATHER THAN FREQUENT (37) JMH	0.92 OF 25	8 2 5 23 XSQ= 10.03 PHI= 0.514 EP = 0.0009
470	TILT TOWARD BEING THOSE WHERE INNOVATIONS ARE GENERALLY ACCEPTED (21) JMH	0.62 OF 13	470	TILT TOWARD BEING THOSE WHERE INNOVATIONS ARE ACCEPTED ONLY SELECTIVELY (33) JMH	0.80 OF 25	8 5 5 20 XSQ= 4.84 PHI= 0.357 EP = 0.0279
476	TILT TOWARD BEING THOSE WHERE THE DEGREE OF INSOBRIETY IS MODERATE OR SLIGHT (18) CF	0.65 OF 17	476	TILT TOWARD BEING THOSE WHERE THE DEGREE OF INSOBRIETY IS STRONG (31) DH	0.82 OF 17	6 14 11 3 XSQ= 5.95 PHI= -0.418 EP = 0.0134

459 CULTURES
WHERE GAMES, IF PRESENT,
INCLUDE GAMES OF CHANCE (82) R-A-B,EA

459 CULTURES
WHERE GAMES, IF PRESENT,
DO NOT INCLUDE
GAMES OF CHANCE (89) R-A-B,EA

BACKGROUND ON PAGE 169

BOTH SUBJECT AND PREDICATE

82 IN LEFT COLUMN

AMERICANS	ARAUCANIANS	ATSUGEWI	AYMARA	AZANDE	AZTEC	BASSERI	CHAGGA	CHEROKEE	CHEYENNE
CHIR-APACHE	CHIRIGUANO	CHOROTI	CHUKCHEE	COPR ESKIMO	CREE	CREEK	CROW	CZECHS	DARD
DIEGUENO	EGYPTIANS	EYAK	FON	GROS VENTRE	HAIDA	HASINAI	HAWAIIANS	HUKUNDIKA	HURON
HUTSUL	INCA	IRISH	JAPANESE	JEMEZ	KASKA	KAZAK	KOREANS	KUBA	KUTENAI
KWAKIUTL	MARICOPA	MATACO	MAYA	MENDE	MIAMI	MIN CHINESE	MIWOK	NABESNA	NAMA
NAVAHO	NOMLAKI	OKINAWANS	OMAHA	PALAUANS	PAPAGO	SAMOANS	SANPOIL	SERBS	SYRIANS
TALLENSI	TAOS	TARAHUMARA	TAREUMIUT	TEHUELCHE	TENINO	THAI	THONGA	TOLOWA	TRUKESE
TWANA	ULAWANS	UTE	VENDA	VIETNAMESE	WASHO	WOLOF	YAKUT	YOKUTS	YUKI
YUROK	ZUNI								

89 IN RIGHT COLUMN

ABIPON	ABOR	AINU	ALBANIANS	ANDAMANESE	APINAYE	ARANDA	ASHANTI	BACAIRI	BHIL
BHUIYA	BORORO	BUNLAP	BURUSHO	CADUVEO	CAMAYURA	CARIB	COORG	DIERI	ELLICE
FANG	GANDA	GOAJIRO	IBAN	ILA	INGALIK	JUKUN	KERAKI	KHASI	KIKUYU
KORYAK	KUNG	KURTATCHI	LAKHER	LAMBA	LAPPS	LAU	LEPCHA	LESU	LHOTA NAGA
LUO	MACASSARESE	MANGAIANS	MANIHIKI	MANUS	MAORI	MARQUESANS	MARSHALLESE	MASAI	MBUNDU
MISKITO	MOSSI	MOTA	NATCHEZ	NICOBARESE	NUNIVAK	NYAKYUSA	NYORO	ONA	PAIWAN
PUKAPUKA	RUNDI	RWALA	SAGADA	SEMANG	SENIANG	SHERENTE	SIRIONO	SIWANS	SOMALI
TANALA	TAPIRAPE	TIKOPIA	TIMBIRA	TIV	TIWI	TODA	TROBRIAND	TRUMAI	TUCUNA
WANTOAT	WAPISHANA	WARRAU	WITOTO	WOGEO	WOLEAIANS	YAGUA	YAHGAN	YAO	

18 EXCLUDED BECAUSE IRRELEVANT

ALACALUF	CAGABA	CAYAPA	CHENCHU	CHORTI	CUNA	GARO	HUICHOL	JIVARO	KATAB
MURNGIN	PAEZ	TALAMANCA	TENETEHARA	TUCANO	TUPINAMBA	VEDDA	YARURO		

211 EXCLUDED BECAUSE UNASCERTAINED

6	TEND MORE TO BE THOSE LOCATED OUTSIDE OF THE INSULAR PACIFIC (330)	0.94 OF 82	6	TEND LESS TO BE THOSE LOCATED OUTSIDE OF THE INSULAR PACIFIC (330)	0.70 OF 89	5 27 77 62 XSQ= 14.93 PHI= -0.295 XP = 0.0001
8	TEND TO BE THOSE LOCATED IN NORTH AMERICA (70)	0.50 OF 82	8	TEND TO BE THOSE LOCATED OUTSIDE OF NORTH AMERICA (330)	0.97 OF 89	41 3 41 86 XSQ= 46.15 PHI= 0.519 XP = 0.

9	TILT MORE TOWARD BEING THOSE LOCATED OUTSIDE OF SOUTH AMERICA (335)	0.90 OF 82	9	TILT LESS TOWARD BEING THOSE LOCATED OUTSIDE OF SOUTH AMERICA (335)	0.76 OF 89	8 21 74 68 XSQ= 4.86 PHI= -0.169 XP = 0.0274
14	TEND TO BE THOSE WHERE THE LATITUDE IS THIRTY DEGREES OR GREATER (119)	0.66 OF 82	14	TEND TO BE THOSE WHERE THE LATITUDE IS LESS THAN THIRTY DEGREES (281)	0.87 OF 89	54 12 28 77 XSQ= 47.21 PHI= 0.525 XP = 0.
15	TEND TO BE THOSE WHERE THE LATITUDE IS TWENTY DEGREES OR GREATER (183)	0.79 OF 82	15	TEND TO BE THOSE WHERE THE LATITUDE IS LESS THAN TWENTY DEGREES (217)	0.69 OF 89	65 28 17 61 XSQ= 37.42 PHI= 0.468 XP = 0.
36	LEAN LESS TOWARD BEING THOSE WHERE THE NATURAL ENVIRONMENT IS OTHER THAN 'VERY HARSH,' OR SUB-TROPICAL BUSH, OR TEMPERATE GRASSLAND (292) FWM	0.57 OF 82	36	LEAN MORE TOWARD BEING THOSE WHERE THE NATURAL ENVIRONMENT IS OTHER THAN 'VERY HARSH,' OR SUB-TROPICAL BUSH, OR TEMPERATE GRASSLAND (292) FWM	0.81 OF 89	35 17 47 72 XSQ= 10.13 PHI= 0.243 XP = 0.0015
42	TEND TO BE THOSE WHERE THE NATURAL ENVIRONMENT IS OTHER THAN TROPICAL OR SUB-TROPICAL RAIN FOREST, OR MONSOON FOREST (244) FWM	0.84 OF 82	42	TEND TO BE THOSE WHERE THE NATURAL ENVIRONMENT IS TROPICAL OR SUB-TROPICAL RAIN FOREST, OR MONSOON FOREST (156) FWM	0.56 OF 89	13 50 69 39 XSQ= 28.12 PHI= -0.406 XP = 0.0000
44	DRIFT LESS TOWARD BEING THOSE WHERE SETTLEMENTS ARE FIXED (222)	0.56 OF 81	44	DRIFT MORE TOWARD BEING THOSE WHERE SETTLEMENTS ARE FIXED (222)	0.71 OF 89	45 63 36 26 XSQ= 3.61 PHI= -0.146 XP = 0.0573
48	LEAN TOWARD BEING THOSE WHERE THE FOOD SUPPLY IS NOT SECURE, AND FOOD SHORTAGES ARE FREQUENT OR ANNUAL (41) MGW	0.77 OF 26	48	LEAN TOWARD BEING THOSE WHERE THE FOOD SUPPLY IS SECURE, AND FOOD SHORTAGES ARE RARE OR OCCASIONAL (38) MGW	0.66 OF 29	6 19 20 10 XSQ= 8.32 PHI= -0.389 XP = 0.0039
53	LEAN TOWARD BEING THOSE WHERE FOOD PRODUCTION IS BY INTENSIVE AGRICULTURE, RATHER THAN BY SIMPLE AGRICULTURE OR INCIPIENT FOOD PRODUCTION (91)	0.54 OF 46	53	LEAN TOWARD BEING THOSE WHERE FOOD PRODUCTION IS BY SIMPLE AGRICULTURE OR INCIPIENT FOOD PRODUCTION, RATHER THAN BY INTENSIVE AGRICULTURE (147)	0.75 OF 59	25 15 21 44 XSQ= 7.98 PHI= 0.276 XP = 0.0047
55	LEAN TOWARD BEING THOSE WHERE FOOD PRODUCTION IS BY INTENSIVE AGRICULTURE, RATHER THAN BY SIMPLE AGRICULTURE (91)	0.69 OF 36	55	LEAN TOWARD BEING THOSE WHERE FOOD PRODUCTION IS BY SIMPLE AGRICULTURE, RATHER THAN BY INTENSIVE AGRICULTURE (101)	0.66 OF 44	25 15 11 29 XSQ= 8.54 PHI= 0.327 XP = 0.0035

	Left		Right	Statistics
63	DRIFT MORE TOWARD BEING THOSE 0.73 OF 49 WHERE HUSBANDRY, IF PRESENT, IS PRINCIPALLY IN THE FORM OF BOVINE, EQUINE, CAMEL-LIKE, OR DEER-LIKE ANIMALS, RATHER THAN PIGS, SHEEP, OR GOATS (152)	63	DRIFT LESS TOWARD BEING THOSE 0.56 OF 57 WHERE HUSBANDRY, IF PRESENT, IS PRINCIPALLY IN THE FORM OF BOVINE, EQUINE, CAMEL-LIKE, OR DEER-LIKE ANIMALS, RATHER THAN PIGS, SHEEP, OR GOATS (152)	36 32 13 25 XSQ= 2.73 PHI= 0.160 XP = 0.0986
73	DRIFT TOWARD BEING THOSE 0.55 OF 74 WHERE WEAVING IS PRESENT (118)	73	DRIFT TOWARD BEING THOSE 0.60 OF 77 WHERE WEAVING IS ABSENT (130)	41 31 33 46 XSQ= 2.89 PHI= 0.138 XP = 0.0892
79	TEND LESS TO BE THOSE 0.79 OF 62 WHERE NO CITY IS PRESENT (201)	79	IN ALL CASES ARE THOSE 1.00 OF 65 WHERE NO CITY IS PRESENT (201)	13 0 49 65 XSQ= 12.99 PHI= 0.320 XP = 0.0003
81	LEAN TOWARD BEING THOSE 0.52 OF 62 WHERE A CITY OR TOWN IS PRESENT, OR THE AVERAGE COMMUNITY SIZE IS 200 OR GREATER (89)	81	LEAN TOWARD BEING THOSE 0.75 OF 65 WHERE NO CITY OR TOWN IS PRESENT, AND THE AVERAGE COMMUNITY SIZE IS SMALLER THAN 200 (135)	32 16 30 49 XSQ= 8.72 PHI= 0.262 XP = 0.0031
84	TILT LESS TOWARD BEING THOSE 0.79 OF 67 WHERE THE LEVEL OF POLITICAL INTEGRATION IS THE LITTLE STATE, THE MINIMAL STATE, THE AUTONOMOUS COMMUNITY, OR THE FAMILY (262) GPM	84	TILT MORE TOWARD BEING THOSE 0.93 OF 76 WHERE THE LEVEL OF POLITICAL INTEGRATION IS THE LITTLE STATE, THE MINIMAL STATE, THE AUTONOMOUS COMMUNITY, OR THE FAMILY (262) GPM	14 5 53 71 XSQ= 5.15 PHI= 0.190 XP = 0.0232
85	LEAN LESS TOWARD BEING THOSE 0.66 OF 67 WHERE THE LEVEL OF POLITICAL INTEGRATION IS THE MINIMAL STATE, THE AUTONOMOUS COMMUNITY, OR THE FAMILY (234) GPM	85	LEAN MORE TOWARD BEING THOSE 0.86 OF 76 WHERE THE LEVEL OF POLITICAL INTEGRATION IS THE MINIMAL STATE, THE AUTONOMOUS COMMUNITY, OR THE FAMILY (234) GPM	23 11 44 65 XSQ= 6.69 PHI= 0.216 XP = 0.0097
88	TILT LESS TOWARD BEING THOSE 0.54 OF 63 WHERE, IF A HEADMANSHIP IS PRESENT, SUCCESSION IS HEREDITARY (165)	88	TILT MORE TOWARD BEING THOSE 0.74 OF 65 WHERE, IF A HEADMANSHIP IS PRESENT, SUCCESSION IS HEREDITARY (165)	29 17 34 48 XSQ= 4.66 PHI= 0.191 XP = 0.0308
94	DRIFT LESS TOWARD BEING THOSE 0.86 OF 80 WHERE THE HIERARCHY OF NATIONAL JURISDICTION HAS TWO, ONE, OR NO LEVELS (296) GES,EA	94	DRIFT MORE TOWARD BEING THOSE 0.96 OF 89 WHERE THE HIERARCHY OF NATIONAL JURISDICTION HAS TWO, ONE, OR NO LEVELS (296) GES,EA	11 4 69 85 XSQ= 3.39 PHI= 0.142 XP = 0.0655
95	LEAN LESS TOWARD BEING THOSE 0.65 OF 80 WHERE THE HIERARCHY OF NATIONAL JURISDICTION HAS ONE OR NO LEVELS (254) GES,EA	95	LEAN MORE TOWARD BEING THOSE 0.84 OF 89 WHERE THE HIERARCHY OF NATIONAL JURISDICTION HAS ONE OR NO LEVELS (254) GES,EA	28 14 52 75 XSQ= 7.38 PHI= 0.209 XP = 0.0066

No.	Left		No.	Right		Statistics
149	TILT TOWARD BEING THOSE WHERE THE INCIDENCE OF THEFT IS HIGH (18) B-B-C	0.79 OF 14	149	TILT TOWARD BEING THOSE WHERE THE INCIDENCE OF THEFT IS LOW (19) B-B-C	0.63 OF 16	11 6 3 10 XSQ= 3.59 PHI= 0.346 EP = 0.0329
192	TILT LESS TOWARD BEING THOSE OTHER THAN WHERE THE ONLY KIN GROUP PRESENT IS A KINDRED OR ELSE BILATERAL DESCENT IS INFERRED (289)	0.62 OF 82	192	TILT MORE TOWARD BEING THOSE OTHER THAN WHERE THE ONLY KIN GROUP PRESENT IS A KINDRED OR ELSE BILATERAL DESCENT IS INFERRED (289)	0.79 OF 89	31 19 51 70 XSQ= 4.82 PHI= 0.168 XP = 0.0281
213	DRIFT MORE TOWARD BEING THOSE WHERE FIRST COUSIN MARRIAGE IS NOT PERMITTED (198)	0.69 OF 80	213	DRIFT LESS TOWARD BEING THOSE WHERE FIRST COUSIN MARRIAGE IS NOT PERMITTED (198)	0.53 OF 87	25 41 55 46 XSQ= 3.76 PHI= -0.150 XP = 0.0526
220	DRIFT MORE TOWARD BEING THOSE WHERE FIRST COUSIN MARRIAGE IN SOME FORM OR OTHER IS NOT PRESCRIBED OR PREFERRED (273)	0.86 OF 80	220	DRIFT LESS TOWARD BEING THOSE WHERE FIRST COUSIN MARRIAGE IN SOME FORM OR OTHER IS NOT PRESCRIBED OR PREFERRED (273)	0.74 OF 87	11 23 69 64 XSQ= 3.39 PHI= -0.143 XP = 0.0655
234	TILT TOWARD BEING THOSE WHERE THE COUSIN TERMINOLOGY IS OF ESKIMO OR HAWAIIAN TYPE, RATHER THAN CROW, OMAHA, OR IROQUOIS TYPE (170)	0.64 OF 73	234	TILT TOWARD BEING THOSE WHERE THE COUSIN TERMINOLOGY IS OF CROW, OMAHA, OR IROQUOIS TYPE, RATHER THAN ESKIMO OR HAWAIIAN TYPE (152)	0.58 OF 76	26 44 47 32 XSQ= 6.55 PHI= -0.210 XP = 0.0105
241	DRIFT LESS TOWARD BEING THOSE WHERE THE FAMILY, IF EXTENDED, IS LARGE OR SMALL, RATHER THAN STEM (187)	0.82 OF 50	241	DRIFT MORE TOWARD BEING THOSE WHERE THE FAMILY, IF EXTENDED, IS LARGE OR SMALL, RATHER THAN STEM (187)	0.95 OF 43	41 41 9 2 XSQ= 2.77 PHI= -0.173 XP = 0.0958
263	DRIFT TOWARD BEING THOSE WHERE WIVES ARE OBTAINED BY RELATIVELY EASY MEANS, NAMELY BY TOKEN BRIDE-PRICE, GIFT EXCHANGE, ABSENCE OF ANY CONSIDERATION, OR RECEIPT OF DOWRY (162)	0.59 OF 82	263	DRIFT TOWARD BEING THOSE WHERE WIVES ARE OBTAINED BY RELATIVELY DIFFICULT MEANS, NAMELY BY BRIDE-PRICE, BRIDE-SERVICE, OR EXCHANGING A FEMALE RELATIVE (233)	0.56 OF 89	34 50 48 39 XSQ= 3.13 PHI= -0.135 XP = 0.0767
282	DRIFT TOWARD BEING THOSE WHERE THE STRENGTH OF DESIRE FOR CHILDREN IS HIGH (16) BCA	0.64 OF 11	282	DRIFT TOWARD BEING THOSE WHERE THE STRENGTH OF DESIRE FOR CHILDREN IS LOW OR ABSENT (20) BCA	0.75 OF 16	7 4 4 12 XSQ= 2.59 PHI= 0.310 EP = 0.0608
305	TILT TOWARD BEING THOSE WHERE THE EARLY SEXUAL SATISFACTION POTENTIAL IS LOW (24) W-C	0.79 OF 14	305	TILT TOWARD BEING THOSE WHERE THE EARLY SEXUAL SATISFACTION POTENTIAL IS HIGH (27) W-C	0.65 OF 26	3 17 11 9 XSQ= 5.38 PHI= -0.367 EP = 0.0187

308	TILT TOWARD BEING THOSE 0.79 OF 14 WHERE AVERAGE SOCIALIZATION ANXIETY IS HIGH (22) W-C	308	TILT TOWARD BEING THOSE 0.65 OF 17 WHERE AVERAGE SOCIALIZATION ANXIETY IS LOW (18) W-C	11 6 3 11 XSQ= 4.19 PHI= 0.368 EP = 0.0292
311	LEAN TOWARD BEING THOSE 0.86 OF 14 WHERE SEXUAL SOCIALIZATION ANXIETY IS HIGH (28) W-C	311	LEAN TOWARD BEING THOSE 0.64 OF 25 WHERE SEXUAL SOCIALIZATION ANXIETY IS LOW (23) W-C	12 9 2 16 XSQ= 7.04 PHI= 0.425 EP = 0.0063
313	LEAN TOWARD BEING THOSE 0.78 OF 18 WHERE AGGRESSION SOCIALIZATION ANXIETY IS HIGH (26) W-C	313	LEAN TOWARD BEING THOSE 0.74 OF 23 WHERE AGGRESSION SOCIALIZATION ANXIETY IS LOW (28) W-C	14 6 4 17 XSQ= 8.83 PHI= 0.464 XP = 0.0030
336	TILT TOWARD BEING THOSE 0.71 OF 21 WHERE THE TOTAL POSITIVE PRESSURE TOWARD DEVELOPING RESPONSIBLE BEHAVIOR IN THE CHILD IS HIGH (43) B-B-C	336	TILT TOWARD BEING THOSE 0.65 OF 31 WHERE THE TOTAL POSITIVE PRESSURE TOWARD DEVELOPING RESPONSIBLE BEHAVIOR IN THE CHILD IS LOW (32) B-B-C	15 11 6 20 XSQ= 5.11 PHI= 0.314 XP = 0.0238
350	TILT TOWARD BEING THOSE 0.80 OF 20 WHERE THE CHILD'S INFERRED ANXIETY OVER PERFORMANCE OF ACHIEVEMENT BEHAVIOR IS HIGH (34) B-B-C	350	TILT TOWARD BEING THOSE 0.57 OF 23 WHERE THE CHILD'S INFERRED ANXIETY OVER PERFORMANCE OF ACHIEVEMENT BEHAVIOR IS LOW (26) B-B-C	16 10 4 13 XSQ= 4.54 PHI= 0.325 XP = 0.0331
355	DRIFT TOWARD BEING THOSE 0.75 OF 20 WHERE THE CHILD'S INFERRED CONFLICT REGARDING OBEDIENT BEHAVIOR IS HIGH (35) B-B-C	355	DRIFT TOWARD BEING THOSE 0.56 OF 32 WHERE THE CHILD'S INFERRED CONFLICT REGARDING OBEDIENT BEHAVIOR IS LOW (38) B-B-C	15 14 5 18 XSQ= 3.69 PHI= 0.266 XP = 0.0548
368	DRIFT TOWARD BEING THOSE 0.71 OF 14 WHERE DISSOCIATION OF THE SEXES AT ADOLESCENCE IS LOW (21) JKH	368	DRIFT TOWARD BEING THOSE 0.63 OF 16 WHERE DISSOCIATION OF THE SEXES AT ADOLESCENCE IS HIGH OR MEDIUM (16) JKH	4 10 10 6 XSQ= 2.22 PHI= -0.272 EP = 0.0813
370	TEND TO BE THOSE 0.79 OF 61 WHERE THE SEGREGATION OF ADOLESCENT BOYS IS ABSENT (148)	370	TEND TO BE THOSE 0.59 OF 70 WHERE THE SEGREGATION OF ADOLESCENT BOYS IS COMPLETE OR PARTIAL (95)	13 41 48 29 XSQ= 17.17 PHI= -0.362 XP = 0.0000
380	TILT TOWARD BEING THOSE 0.85 OF 20 WHERE SEGREGATION OF GIRLS AT MENARCHE IS PRESENT (35) F-B	380	TILT TOWARD BEING THOSE 0.50 OF 22 WHERE SEGREGATION OF GIRLS AT MENARCHE IS ABSENT (20) F-B	17 11 3 11 XSQ= 4.31 PHI= 0.320 XP = 0.0379

No.	Statement	Proportion	N	No.	Statement	Proportion	N	Statistics
391	DRIFT TOWARD BEING THOSE WHERE PREMARITAL SEX RELATIONS ARE STRONGLY PUNISHED AND IN FACT RARE, OR WEAKLY PUNISHED ANC IN FACT NCT RARE (89) JTW,EA	0.60 OF	53	391	DRIFT TOWARD BEING THOSE WHERE PREMARITAL SEX RELATIONS ARE PUNISHED ONLY IF PREGNANCY RESULTS, OR FREELY PERMITTED (90) JTW,EA	0.58 OF	59	32 25 21 34 XSQ= 2.94 PHI= 0.162 XP = 0.0866
398	DRIFT TOWARD BEING THOSE WHERE THE INTENSITY OF SEX ANXIETY IS HIGH (16) WNS	0.80 OF	10	398	DRIFT TOWARD BEING THOSE WHERE THE INTENSITY OF SEX ANXIETY IS LOW (16) WNS	0.60 OF	15	8 6 2 9 XSQ= 2.44 PHI= 0.313 EP = 0.0992
400	TILT TOWARD BEING THOSE WHERE HOMCSEXUAL ACTIVITY IS PERMITTED (36) F-B	0.82 OF	22	400	TILT TOWARD BEING THOSE WHERE HOMOSEXUAL ACTIVITY IS PROHIBITED (22) F-B	0.55 OF	22	4 12 18 10 XSQ= 4.81 PHI= -0.331 XP = 0.0283
406	DRIFT TOWARD BEING THOSE WHERE EXPLANATIONS OF ILLNESS OF AN AGGRESSICN NATURE ARE PRESENT (28) W-C	0.67 OF	18	406	DRIFT TOWARD BEING THOSE WHERE EXPLANATIONS OF ILLNESS OF AN AGGRESSION NATURE ARE ABSENT (33) W-C	0.64 OF	28	12 10 6 18 XSQ= 3.06 PHI= 0.258 XP = 0.0804
417	IN ALL CASES ARE THOSE WHERE WARFARE IS PREVALENT (34) LWS	1.00 OF	16	417	LEAN LESS TOWARD BEING THOSE WHERE WARFARE IS PREVALENT (34) LWS	0.63 OF	19	16 12 0 7 XSQ= 5.25 PHI= 0.387 EP = 0.0092
427	TILT TOWARD BEING THOSE WHERE A HIGH GOD, IF PRESENT, IS ACTIVE, RATHER THAN INACTIVE (87) GES,EA	0.69 OF	35	427	TILT TOWARD BEING THOSE WHERE A HIGH GOD, IF PRESENT, IS INACTIVE, RATHER THAN ACTIVE (69) GES,EA	0.60 OF	45	24 18 11 27 XSQ= 5.35 PHI= 0.259 XP = 0.0207
445	DRIFT TOWARD BEING THCSE WHERE SORCERY IS IMPORTANT (26) BBW,DH	0.76 OF	17	445	DRIFT TOWARD BEING THOSE WHERE SORCERY IS UNIMPORTANT (23) BBW,DH	0.59 OF	17	13 7 4 10 XSQ= 3.04 PHI= 0.299 EP = 0.0799
455	LEAN TOWARD BEING THOSE WHERE THE MODE CF THE INDIVICUAL'S CONTACT WITH THE DIVINE IS CONDUCIVE TO THE DEVELOPMENT OF THE INDIVIDUAL'S NEED TO ACHIEVE (17) DCM	0.67 OF	12	455	LEAN TOWARD BEING THOSE WHERE THE MODE OF THE INDIVIDUAL'S CONTACT WITH THE DIVINE IS NOT CONDUCIVE TO THE DEVELOPMENT OF THE INDIVIDUAL'S NEED TO ACHIEVE (19) DCM	0.92 OF	13	8 1 4 12 XSQ= 7.03 PHI= 0.530 EP = 0.0036

460 CULTURES
WHERE GAMES, IF PRESENT,
ARE LIMITED TO
GAMES OF SKILL ONLY (67) R-A-B,EA

460 CULTURES
WHERE GAMES, IF PRESENT,
ARE NOT LIMITED TO
GAMES OF SKILL ONLY (104) R-A-B,EA

BACKGROUND ON PAGE 169

BOTH SUBJECT AND PREDICATE

67 IN LEFT COLUMN

ABIPON	ABOR	AINU	ANDAMANESE	APINAYE	ARANDA	BACAIRI	BHIL	BHUIYA	BORORO
BUNLAP	CADUVEO	CAMAYURA	CARIB	COORG	DIERI	ELLICE	FANG	GOAJIRO	IBAN
INGALIK	KERAKI	KHASI	KORYAK	KUNG	KURTATCHI	LAPPS	LAU	LEPCHA	LESU
LHOTA NAGA	MACASSARESE	MANGAIANS	MANIHIKI	MANUS	MAORI	MARQUESANS	MARSHALLESE	MISKITO	MOTA
NATCHEZ	NICOBARESE	NUNIVAK	ONA	PAIWAN	PUKAPUKA	RWALA	SAGADA	SEMANG	SENIANG
SHERENTE	SIRIONO	TAPIRAPE	TIKOPIA	TIMBIRA	TIWI	TODA	TROBRIAND	TRUMAI	TUCUNA
WANTOAT	WAPISHANA	WARRAU	WITOTO	WOGEO	YAGUA	YAHGAN			

104 IN RIGHT COLUMN

ALBANIANS	AMERICANS	ARAUCANIANS	ASHANTI	ATSUGEWI	AYMARA	AZANDE	AZTEC	BASSERI	BURUSHO
CHAGGA	CHEROKEE	CHEYENNE	CHIR-APACHE	CHIRIGUANO	CHOROTI	CHUKCHEE	COPR ESKIMO	CREE	CREEK
CROW	CZECHS	DARD	DIEGUENO	EGYPTIANS	EYAK	FON	GANDA	GROS VENTRE	HAIDA
HASINAI	HAWAIIANS	HUKUNDIKA	HURON	HUTSUL	ILA	INCA	IRISH	JAPANESE	JEMEZ
JUKUN	KASKA	KAZAK	KIKUYU	KOREANS	KUBA	KUTENAI	KWAKIUTL	LAKHER	LAMBA
LUO	MARICOPA	MASAI	MATACO	MAYA	MBUNDU	MENDE	MIAMI	MIN CHINESE	MIWOK
MOSSI	NABESNA	NAMA	NAVAHO	NOMLAKI	NYAKYUSA	NYORO	OKINAWANS	OMAHA	PALAUANS
PAPAGO	RUNDI	SAMOANS	SANPOIL	SERBS	SIWANS	SOMALI	SYRIANS	TALLENSI	TANALA
TAOS	TARAHUMARA	TAREUMIUT	TEHUELCHE	TENINO	THAI	THONGA	TIV	TOLOWA	TRUKESE
TWANA	ULAWANS	UTE	VENDA	VIETNAMESE	WASHO	WOLEAIANS	WOLOF	YAKUT	YAO
YOKUTS	YUKI	YURCK	ZUNI						

18 EXCLUDED BECAUSE IRRELEVANT

ALACALUF	CAGABA	CAYAPA	CHENCHU	CHORTI	CUNA	GARO	HUICHOL	JIVARO	KATAB
MURNGIN	PAEZ	TALAMANCA	TENETEHARA	TUCANO	TUPINAMBA	VEDDA	YARURO		

211 EXCLUDED BECAUSE UNASCERTAINED

---

3 TEND MORE TO BE THOSE LOCATED OUTSIDE OF AFRICA (320) — 0.97 OF 67

3 TEND LESS TO BE THOSE LOCATED OUTSIDE OF AFRICA (320) — 0.77 OF 104

2	24
65	80

XSQ= 11.25
PHI= -0.256
XP = 0.0008

6 TEND LESS TO BE THOSE LOCATED OUTSIDE OF THE INSULAR PACIFIC (330) — 0.61 OF 67

6 TEND MORE TO BE THOSE LOCATED OUTSIDE OF THE INSULAR PACIFIC (330) — 0.94 OF 104

26	6
41	98

XSQ= 27.11
PHI= 0.398
XP = 0.0000

No.	Statement	Proportion	No.	Statement	Proportion	Statistics
8	TEND MORE TO BE THOSE LOCATED OUTSIDE OF NORTH AMERICA (330)	0.96 OF 67	8	TEND LESS TO BE THOSE LOCATED OUTSIDE OF NORTH AMERICA (330)	0.61 OF 104	3 41 64 63 XSQ= 24.24 PHI= -0.377 XP = 0.0000
9	TEND LESS TO BE THOSE LOCATED OUTSIDE OF SOUTH AMERICA (335)	0.69 OF 67	9	TEND MORE TO BE THOSE LOCATED OUTSIDE OF SOUTH AMERICA (335)	0.92 OF 104	21 8 46 96 XSQ= 14.55 PHI= 0.292 XP = 0.0001
14	TEND TO BE THOSE WHERE THE LATITUDE IS LESS THAN THIRTY DEGREES (281)	0.85 OF 67	14	TEND TO BE THOSE WHERE THE LATITUDE IS THIRTY DEGREES OR GREATER (119)	0.54 OF 104	10 56 57 48 XSQ= 24.43 PHI= -0.378 XP = 0.0000
15	TEND TO BE THOSE WHERE THE LATITUDE IS LESS THAN TWENTY DEGREES (217)	0.66 OF 67	15	TEND TO BE THOSE WHERE THE LATITUDE IS TWENTY DEGREES OR GREATER (183)	0.67 OF 104	23 70 44 34 XSQ= 16.56 PHI= -0.311 XP = 0.0000
36	TILT MORE TOWARD BEING THOSE WHERE THE NATURAL ENVIRONMENT IS OTHER THAN 'VERY HARSH,' OR SUB-TROPICAL BUSH, OR TEMPERATE GRASSLAND (292) FWM	0.81 OF 67	36	TILT LESS TOWARD BEING THOSE WHERE THE NATURAL ENVIRONMENT IS OTHER THAN 'VERY HARSH,' OR SUB-TROPICAL BUSH, OR TEMPERATE GRASSLAND (292) FWM	0.63 OF 104	13 39 54 65 XSQ= 5.48 PHI= -0.179 XP = 0.0192
42	TEND TO BE THOSE WHERE THE NATURAL ENVIRONMENT IS TROPICAL OR SUB-TROPICAL RAIN FOREST, OR MONSOON FOREST (156) FWM	0.66 OF 67	42	TEND TO BE THOSE WHERE THE NATURAL ENVIRONMENT IS OTHER THAN TROPICAL OR SUB-TROPICAL RAIN FOREST, OR MONSOON FOREST (244) FWM	0.82 OF 104	44 19 23 85 XSQ= 37.34 PHI= 0.467 XP = 0.
51	DRIFT TOWARD BEING THOSE WHERE SUBSISTENCE IS PRIMARILY BY FOOD GATHERING -- I. E., HUNTING, FISHING, OR COLLECTING -- RATHER THAN FOOD PRODUCTION (147)	0.58 OF 67	51	DRIFT TOWARD BEING THOSE WHERE SUBSISTENCE IS PRIMARILY BY FOOD PRODUCTION -- I. E., AGRICULTURE OR HUSBANDRY -- RATHER THAN BY GATHERING (253)	0.58 OF 104	28 60 39 44 XSQ= 3.51 PHI= -0.143 XP = 0.0609
53	TEND TO BE THOSE WHERE FOOD PRODUCTION IS BY SIMPLE AGRICULTURE OR INCIPIENT FOOD PRODUCTION, RATHER THAN BY INTENSIVE AGRICULTURE (147)	0.90 OF 39	53	TEND TO BE THOSE WHERE FOOD PRODUCTION IS BY INTENSIVE AGRICULTURE, RATHER THAN BY SIMPLE AGRICULTURE OR INCIPIENT FOOD PRODUCTION (91)	0.55 OF 66	4 36 35 30 XSQ= 18.56 PHI= -0.420 XP = 0.0000
55	TEND TO BE THOSE WHERE FOOD PRODUCTION IS BY SIMPLE AGRICULTURE, RATHER THAN BY INTENSIVE AGRICULTURE (101)	0.83 OF 24	55	TEND TO BE THOSE WHERE FOOD PRODUCTION IS BY INTENSIVE AGRICULTURE, RATHER THAN BY SIMPLE AGRICULTURE (91)	0.64 OF 56	4 36 20 20 XSQ= 13.39 PHI= -0.409 XP = 0.0003

63	LEAN TOWARD BEING THOSE WHERE HUSBANDRY, IF PRESENT, IS PRINCIPALLY IN THE FORM OF PIGS, SHEEP, OR GOATS, RATHER THAN BOVINE, EQUINE, CAMEL-LIKE, OR DEER-LIKE ANIMALS (74)	0.57 OF 37	63	LEAN TOWARD BEING THOSE WHERE HUSBANDRY, IF PRESENT, IS PRINCIPALLY IN THE FORM OF BOVINE, EQUINE, CAMEL-LIKE, OR DEER-LIKE ANIMALS, RATHER THAN PIGS, SHEEP, OR GOATS (152)	0.75 OF 69	16 52 21 17 XSQ= 9.45 PHI= -0.299 XP = 0.0021
71	TEND TO BE THOSE WHERE METAL WORKING IS ABSENT (153)	0.80 OF 59	71	TEND TO BE THOSE WHERE METAL WORKING IS PRESENT (98)	0.52 OF 94	12 49 47 45 XSQ= 13.98 PHI= -0.302 XP = 0.0002
73	TILT TOWARD BEING THOSE WHERE WEAVING IS ABSENT (130)	0.65 OF 57	73	TILT TOWARD BEING THOSE WHERE WEAVING IS PRESENT (118)	0.55 OF 94	20 52 37 42 XSQ= 5.04 PHI= -0.183 XP = 0.0248
74	LEAN TOWARD BEING THOSE WHERE POTTERY IS ABSENT (93)	0.54 OF 56	74	LEAN TOWARD BEING THOSE WHERE POTTERY IS PRESENT (145)	0.69 OF 94	26 65 30 29 XSQ= 6.67 PHI= -0.211 XP = 0.0098
80	IN ALL CASES ARE THOSE WHERE NO CITY OR TOWN IS PRESENT (185)	1.00 OF 47	80	TEND LESS TO BE THOSE WHERE NO CITY OR TOWN IS PRESENT (185)	0.75 OF 80	0 20 47 60 XSQ= 12.13 PHI= -0.309 XP = 0.0005
81	TEND TO BE THOSE WHERE NO CITY OR TOWN IS PRESENT, AND THE AVERAGE COMMUNITY SIZE IS SMALLER THAN 200 (135)	0.89 OF 47	81	TEND TO BE THOSE WHERE A CITY OR TOWN IS PRESENT, OR THE AVERAGE COMMUNITY SIZE IS 200 OR GREATER (89)	0.54 OF 80	5 43 42 37 XSQ= 21.61 PHI= -0.412 XP = 0.0000
83	LEAN MORE TOWARD BEING THOSE WHERE, WITH NO CITY AND NO TOWN PRESENT, THE AVERAGE COMMUNITY SIZE IS SMALLER THAN 200, RATHER THAN BETWEEN 200 AND 999 (135)	0.91 OF 46	83	LEAN LESS TOWARD BEING THOSE WHERE, WITH NO CITY AND NO TOWN PRESENT, THE AVERAGE COMMUNITY SIZE IS SMALLER THAN 200, RATHER THAN BETWEEN 200 AND 999 (135)	0.64 OF 58	4 21 42 37 XSQ= 9.18 PHI= -0.297 XP = 0.0024
86	TEND TO BE THOSE WHERE THE LEVEL OF POLITICAL INTEGRATION IS THE AUTONOMOUS COMMUNITY, OR THE FAMILY (156) GPM	0.73 OF 56	86	TEND TO BE THOSE WHERE THE LEVEL OF POLITICAL INTEGRATION IS THE LARGE STATE, THE LITTLE STATE, OR THE MINIMAL STATE (148) GPM	0.61 OF 87	15 53 41 34 XSQ= 14.58 PHI= -0.319 XP = 0.0001
88	DRIFT MORE TOWARD BEING THOSE WHERE, IF A HEADMANSHIP IS PRESENT, SUCCESSION IS HEREDITARY (165)	0.76 OF 49	88	DRIFT LESS TOWARD BEING THOSE WHERE, IF A HEADMANSHIP IS PRESENT, SUCCESSION IS HEREDITARY (165)	0.57 OF 79	12 34 37 45 XSQ= 3.75 PHI= -0.171 XP = 0.0528

No.		Proportion	No.		Proportion	Statistics
96	TEND TO BE THOSE WHERE THE HIERARCHY OF NATIONAL JURISDICTION HAS NO LEVELS (156) GES,EA	0.66 OF 67	96	TEND TO BE THOSE WHERE THE HIERARCHY OF NATIONAL JURISDICTION HAS FOUR, THREE, TWO OR ONE LEVEL (174) GES,EA	0.63 OF 102	23 64 44 38 XSQ= 11.96 PHI= -0.266 XP = 0.0005
102	DRIFT TOWARD BEING THOSE WHERE CLASS STRATIFICATION IS ABSENT (180)	0.52 OF 65	102	DRIFT TOWARD BEING THOSE WHERE CLASS STRATIFICATION IS PRESENT (203)	0.64 OF 103	31 66 34 37 XSQ= 3.74 PHI= -0.149 XP = 0.0532
110	TEND MORE TO BE THOSE WHERE SLAVERY IS ABSENT (218)	0.80 OF 65	110	TEND LESS TO BE THOSE WHERE SLAVERY IS ABSENT (218)	0.52 OF 101	13 48 52 53 XSQ= 11.73 PHI= -0.266 XP = 0.0006
129	IN ALL CASES ARE THOSE WHERE WEAVING IS MAINLY DONE BY FEMALES (73)	1.00 OF 19	129	LEAN LESS TOWARD BEING THOSE WHERE WEAVING IS MAINLY DONE BY FEMALES (73)	0.65 OF 46	0 16 19 30 XSQ= 6.99 PHI= -0.328 XP = 0.0082
138	LEAN TOWARD BEING THOSE WHERE SUPERORDINATE JUSTICE IS ABSENT (18) BBW	0.80 OF 10	138	LEAN TOWARD BEING THOSE WHERE SUPERORDINATE JUSTICE IS PRESENT (22) BBW	0.79 OF 19	2 15 8 4 XSQ= 7.11 PHI= -0.495 EP = 0.0045
141	DRIFT TOWARD BEING THOSE WHERE THE LEVEL OF SOCIAL SANCTION IS PUBLIC PROPERTY SANCTION OR PRIVATE SETTLEMENT, RATHER THAN PUBLIC CORPOREAL SANCTION (26) JMH	0.64 OF 14	141	DRIFT TOWARD BEING THOSE WHERE THE LEVEL OF SOCIAL SANCTION IS PUBLIC CORPOREAL SANCTION, RATHER THAN PUBLIC PROPERTY SANCTION OR PRIVATE SETTLEMENT (28) JMH	0.67 OF 24	5 16 9 8 XSQ= 2.29 PHI= -0.245 EP = 0.0943
142	TILT TOWARD BEING THOSE WHERE THE LEVEL OF SOCIAL SANCTION IS PRIVATE SETTLEMENT, RATHER THAN PUBLIC CORPOREAL SANCTION OR PUBLIC PROPERTY SETTLEMENT (16) JMH	0.50 OF 14	142	TILT TOWARD BEING THOSE WHERE THE LEVEL OF SOCIAL SANCTION IS PUBLIC CORPOREAL SANCTION OR PUBLIC PROPERTY SANCTION, RATHER THAN PRIVATE SETTLEMENT (38) JMH	0.88 OF 24	7 21 7 3 XSQ= 4.62 PHI= -0.349 EP = 0.0207
149	DRIFT TOWARD BEING THOSE WHERE THE INCIDENCE OF THEFT IS LOW (19) B-B-C	0.67 OF 12	149	DRIFT TOWARD BEING THOSE WHERE THE INCIDENCE OF THEFT IS HIGH (18) B-B-C	0.72 OF 18	4 13 8 5 XSQ= 2.99 PHI= -0.316 EP = 0.0610
184	TILT TOWARD BEING THOSE WHERE THE LARGEST NON-COGNATIC KIN GROUP IS THE MOEITY OR PHRATRY (77)	0.51 OF 37	184	TILT TOWARD BEING THOSE WHERE THE LARGEST NON-COGNATIC KIN GROUP IS SMALLER THAN A PHRATRY, I. E. A SIB OR LINEAGE (175)	0.71 OF 66	19 19 18 47 XSQ= 4.26 PHI= 0.203 XP = 0.0390

186	TILT MORE TOWARD BEING THOSE WHERE THE KIN GROUP IS OTHER THAN EXCLUSIVELY PATRILINEAL (250)	0.79 OF 67	186	TILT LESS TOWARD BEING THOSE WHERE THE KIN GROUP IS OTHER THAN EXCLUSIVELY PATRILINEAL (250)	0.62 OF 104	14 40 53 64 XSQ= 5.03 PHI= -0.172 XP = 0.0248
224	DRIFT MORE TOWARD BEING THOSE WHERE COUSIN MARRIAGE IS PREFERENTIALLY OR PERMISSIVELY SYMMETRICAL, RATHER THAN EITHER PATRI- OR MATRILATERAL (106)	0.77 OF 31	224	DRIFT LESS TOWARD BEING THOSE WHERE COUSIN MARRIAGE IS PREFERENTIALLY OR PERMISSIVELY SYMMETRICAL, RATHER THAN EITHER PATRI- OR MATRILATERAL (106)	0.54 OF 35	7 16 24 19 XSQ= 2.92 PHI= -0.210 XP = 0.0873
236	DRIFT TOWARD BEING THOSE WHERE THE FAMILY IS OF AN INDEPENDENT TYPE, RATHER THAN AN EXTENDED TYPE (185)	0.55 OF 67	236	DRIFT TOWARD BEING THOSE WHERE THE FAMILY IS OF AN EXTENDED TYPE, RATHER THAN AN INDEPENDENT TYPE (213)	0.61 OF 104	30 63 37 41 XSQ= 3.49 PHI= -0.143 XP = 0.0618
278	TILT TOWARD BEING THOSE WHERE PROPERTY RIGHTS IN WOMEN ARE UNIMPORTANT OR ABSENT (14) LWS	0.89 OF 9	278	TILT TOWARD BEING THOSE WHERE PROPERTY RIGHTS IN WOMEN ARE PRESENT (8) LWS	0.75 OF 8	1 6 8 2 XSQ= 4.74 PHI= -0.528 EP = 0.0152
295	TILT TOWARD BEING THOSE WHERE THE SEVERITY OF PUNISHMENT FOR ABORTION IS LOW OR ABSENT (12) BCA	0.86 OF 7	295	TILT TOWARD BEING THOSE WHERE THE SEVERITY OF PUNISHMENT FOR ABORTION IS HIGH (11) BCA	0.70 OF 10	1 7 6 3 XSQ= 3.14 PHI= -0.430 EP = 0.0498
308	TILT TOWARD BEING THOSE WHERE AVERAGE SOCIALIZATION ANXIETY IS LOW (18) W-C	0.71 OF 14	308	TILT TOWARD BEING THOSE WHERE AVERAGE SOCIALIZATION ANXIETY IS HIGH (22) W-C	0.76 OF 17	4 13 10 4 XSQ= 5.31 PHI= -0.414 EP = 0.0122
310	DRIFT TOWARD BEING THOSE WHERE ANAL SOCIALIZATION ANXIETY IS LOW (19) W-C	0.64 OF 14	310	DRIFT TOWARD BEING THOSE WHERE ANAL SOCIALIZATION ANXIETY IS HIGH (22) W-C	0.71 OF 17	5 12 9 5 XSQ= 2.49 PHI= -0.284 EP = 0.0759
311	TILT TOWARD BEING THOSE WHERE SEXUAL SOCIALIZATION ANXIETY IS LOW (23) W-C	0.68 OF 19	311	TILT TOWARD BEING THOSE WHERE SEXUAL SOCIALIZATION ANXIETY IS HIGH (28) W-C	0.75 OF 20	6 15 13 5 XSQ= 5.75 PHI= -0.384 EP = 0.0104
313	TILT TOWARD BEING THOSE WHERE AGGRESSION SOCIALIZATION ANXIETY IS LOW (28) W-C	0.76 OF 17	313	TILT TOWARD BEING THOSE WHERE AGGRESSION SOCIALIZATION ANXIETY IS HIGH (26) W-C	0.67 OF 24	4 16 13 8 XSQ= 5.79 PHI= -0.376 XP = 0.0162

314	TILT MORE TOWARD BEING THOSE 0.96 OF 23 WHERE THE INCIDENCE OF MOTHER-CHILD HOUSEHOLDS IS LOW (61) W-D,S	314	TILT LESS TOWARD BEING THOSE 0.63 OF 32 WHERE THE INCIDENCE OF MOTHER-CHILD HOUSEHOLDS IS LOW (61) W-D,S	1 12 22 20 XSQ= 6.42 PHI= -0.342 XP = 0.0113
318	TILT TOWARD BEING THOSE 0.71 OF 21 WHERE THE OVERALL INDULGENCE OF THE INFANT IS HIGH (40) B-B-C	318	TILT TOWARD BEING THOSE 0.62 OF 29 WHERE THE OVERALL INDULGENCE OF THE INFANT IS LOW (31) B-B-C	15 11 6 18 XSQ= 4.22 PHI= 0.290 XP = 0.0401
323	DRIFT TOWARD BEING THOSE 0.55 OF 22 WHERE THE CONSTANCY OF PRESENCE OF THE INFANT'S NURTURANT AGENT IS HIGH (29) B-B-C	323	DRIFT TOWARD BEING THOSE 0.72 OF 29 WHERE THE CONSTANCY OF PRESENCE OF THE INFANT'S NURTURANT AGENT IS LOW (45) B-B-C	12 8 10 21 XSQ= 2.77 PHI= 0.233 XP = 0.0962
326	DRIFT TOWARD BEING THOSE 0.72 OF 18 WHERE THE INFERRED TRANSITION ANXIETY BETWEEN INFANCY AND CHILDHOOD IS LOW (35) B-B-C	326	DRIFT TOWARD BEING THOSE 0.60 OF 30 WHERE THE INFERRED TRANSITION ANXIETY BETWEEN INFANCY AND CHILDHOOD IS HIGH (32) B-B-C	5 18 13 12 XSQ= 3.48 PHI= -0.269 XP = 0.0622
334	TILT TOWARD BEING THOSE 0.65 OF 23 WHERE THE INDULGENCE OF THE CHILD IS HIGH (40) B-B-C	334	TILT TOWARD BEING THOSE 0.69 OF 32 WHERE THE INDULGENCE OF THE CHILD IS LOW (38) B-B-C	15 10 8 22 XSQ= 4.93 PHI= 0.299 XP = 0.0264
336	TILT TOWARD BEING THOSE 0.71 OF 21 WHERE THE TOTAL POSITIVE PRESSURE TOWARD DEVELOPING RESPONSIBLE BEHAVIOR IN THE CHILD IS LOW (32) B-B-C	336	TILT TOWARD BEING THOSE 0.65 OF 31 WHERE THE TOTAL POSITIVE PRESSURE TOWARD DEVELOPING RESPONSIBLE BEHAVIOR IN THE CHILD IS HIGH (43) B-B-C	6 20 15 11 XSQ= 5.11 PHI= -0.314 XP = 0.0238
337	LEAN TOWARD BEING THOSE 0.75 OF 20 WHERE THE CHILD'S INFERRED ANXIETY OVER NON-PERFORMANCE OF RESPONSIBLE BEHAVIOR IS LOW (35) B-B-C	337	LEAN TOWARD BEING THOSE 0.67 OF 30 WHERE THE CHILD'S INFERRED ANXIETY OVER NON-PERFORMANCE OF RESPONSIBLE BEHAVIOR IS HIGH (38) B-B-C	5 20 15 10 XSQ= 6.75 PHI= -0.367 XP = 0.0094
338	TILT TOWARD BEING THOSE 0.60 OF 20 WHERE THE CHILD'S INFERRED ANXIETY OVER PERFORMANCE OF RESPONSIBLE BEHAVIOR IS LOW (29) B-B-C	338	TILT TOWARD BEING THOSE 0.77 OF 30 WHERE THE CHILD'S INFERRED ANXIETY OVER PERFORMANCE OF RESPONSIBLE BEHAVIOR IS HIGH (44) B-B-C	8 23 12 7 XSQ= 5.38 PHI= -0.328 XP = 0.0204
346	LEAN TOWARD BEING THOSE 0.73 OF 22 WHERE THE CHILD'S INFERRED ANXIETY OVER PERFORMANCE OF SELF-RELIANT BEHAVIOR IS LOW (39) B-B-C	346	LEAN TOWARD BEING THOSE 0.71 OF 31 WHERE THE CHILD'S INFERRED ANXIETY OVER PERFORMANCE OF SELF-RELIANT BEHAVIOR IS HIGH (37) B-B-C	6 22 16 9 XSQ= 8.18 PHI= -0.393 XP = 0.0042

347	LEAN TOWARD BEING THOSE 0.77 OF 22 WHERE THE CHILD'S INFERRED CONFLICT REGARDING SELF-RELIANT BEHAVIOR IS LOW (39) B-B-C	347	LEAN TOWARD BEING THOSE 0.68 OF 31 WHERE THE CHILD'S INFERRED CONFLICT REGARDING SELF-RELIANT BEHAVIOR IS HIGH (37) B-B-C	5 21 17 10 XSQ= 8.71 PHI= -0.405 XP = 0.0032
349	TILT TOWARD BEING THOSE 0.71 OF 17 WHERE THE CHILD'S INFERRED ANXIETY OVER NON-PERFORMANCE OF ACHIEVEMENT BEHAVIOR IS LOW (28) B-B-C	349	TILT TOWARD BEING THOSE 0.71 OF 28 WHERE THE CHILD'S INFERRED ANXIETY OVER NON-PERFORMANCE OF ACHIEVEMENT BEHAVIOR IS HIGH (34) B-B-C	5 20 12 8 XSQ= 5.96 PHI= -0.364 XP = 0.0147
350	TEND TO BE THOSE 0.87 OF 15 WHERE THE CHILD'S INFERRED ANXIETY OVER PERFORMANCE OF ACHIEVEMENT BEHAVIOR IS LOW (26) B-B-C	350	TEND TO BE THOSE 0.86 OF 28 WHERE THE CHILD'S INFERRED ANXIETY OVER PERFORMANCE OF ACHIEVEMENT BEHAVIOR IS HIGH (34) B-B-C	2 24 13 4 XSQ= 18.49 PHI= -0.656 XP = 0.0000
351	TEND TO BE THOSE 0.93 OF 15 WHERE THE CHILD'S INFERRED CONFLICT REGARDING ACHIEVEMENT BEHAVIOR IS LOW (34) B-B-C	351	TEND TO BE THOSE 0.64 OF 28 WHERE THE CHILD'S INFERRED CONFLICT REGARDING ACHIEVEMENT BEHAVIOR IS HIGH (26) B-B-C	1 18 14 10 XSQ= 10.92 PHI= -0.504 XP = 0.0010
352	LEAN TOWARD BEING THOSE 0.60 OF 20 WHERE THE TOTAL POSITIVE PRESSURE TOWARD DEVELOPING OBEDIENT BEHAVIOR IN THE CHILD IS LOW (28) B-B-C	352	LEAN TOWARD BEING THOSE 0.81 OF 31 WHERE THE TOTAL POSITIVE PRESSURE TOWARD DEVELOPING OBEDIENT BEHAVIOR IN THE CHILD IS HIGH (44) B-B-C	8 25 12 6 XSQ= 7.10 PHI= -0.373 XP = 0.0077
353	TEND TO BE THOSE 0.67 OF 21 WHERE THE CHILD-S INFERRED ANXIETY OVER NON-PERFORMANCE OF OBEDIENT BEHAVIOR IS LOW (32) B-B-C	353	TEND TO BE THOSE 0.84 OF 31 WHERE THE CHILD'S INFERRED ANXIETY OVER NON-PERFORMANCE OF OBEDIENT BEHAVIOR IS HIGH (42) B-B-C	7 26 14 5 XSQ= 11.70 PHI= -0.474 XP = 0.0006
354	DRIFT TOWARD BEING THOSE 0.62 OF 21 WHERE THE CHILD'S INFERRED ANXIETY OVER PERFORMANCE OF OBEDIENT BEHAVIOR IS LOW (37) B-B-C	354	DRIFT TOWARD BEING THOSE 0.68 OF 31 WHERE THE CHILD'S INFERRED ANXIETY OVER PERFORMANCE OF OBEDIENT BEHAVIOR IS HIGH (36) B-B-C	8 21 13 10 XSQ= 3.34 PHI= -0.253 XP = 0.0676
355	TILT TOWARD BEING THOSE 0.67 OF 21 WHERE THE CHILD'S INFERRED CONFLICT REGARDING OBEDIENT BEHAVIOR IS LOW (38) B-B-C	355	TILT TOWARD BEING THOSE 0.71 OF 31 WHERE THE CHILD'S INFERRED CONFLICT REGARDING OBEDIENT BEHAVIOR IS HIGH (35) B-B-C	7 22 14 9 XSQ= 5.74 PHI= -0.332 XP = 0.0165
360	IN ALL CASES ARE THOSE 1.00 OF 10 WHERE ADOLESCENT PEER GROUPS ARE PRESENT ONLY IN A SETTING OF LEISURE, OR ELSE ARE ABSENT (23) JKH	360	LEAN TOWARD BEING THOSE 0.53 OF 17 WHERE ADOLESCENT PEER GROUPS ARE PRESENT IN A SETTING OF WORK AND PUBLIC GATHERINGS AND LEISURE, OR AT LEAST OF PUBLIC GATHERINGS AND LEISURE (14) JKH	0 9 10 8 XSQ= 5.74 PHI= -0.461 EP = 0.0088

365	DRIFT TOWARD BEING THCSE WHERE THE TIME SPENT IN ADCLESCENT PEER GRCUP ACTIVITY IS LCW-MEDIUM OR LCW (15) JKH	0.54 OF 13	365	DRIFT TOWARD BEING THOSE WHERE THE TIME SPENT IN ADOLESCENT PEER GROUP ACTIVITY IS HIGH OR HIGH-MEDIUM (30) JKH	0.78 OF 23	6 18 7 5 XSQ= 2.54 PHI= -0.266 EP = 0.0714
368	DRIFT TOWARD BEING THCSE WHERE DISSCCIATION OF THE SEXES AT ADCLESCENCE IS HIGH OR MEDIUM (16) JKH	0.73 OF 11	368	DRIFT TOWARD BEING THOSE WHERE DISSOCIATION OF THE SEXES AT ADOLESCENCE IS LOW (21) JKH	0.68 OF 19	8 6 3 13 XSQ= 3.23 PHI= 0.328 EP = 0.0567
370	TILT TOWARD BEING THOSE WHERE THE SEGREGATION CF ADOLESCENT BOYS IS COMPLETE CR PARTIAL (95)	0.56 OF 52	370	TILT TOWARD BEING THOSE WHERE THE SEGREGATION OF ADCLESCENT BOYS IS ABSENT (148)	0.68 OF 79	29 25 23 54 XSQ= 6.57 PHI= 0.224 XP = 0.0104
380	TILT TOWARD BEING THOSE WHERE SEGREGATICN CF GIRLS AT MENARCHE IS ABSENT (20) F-B	0.59 OF 17	380	TILT TOWARD BEING THOSE WHERE SEGREGATION OF GIRLS AT MENARCHE IS PRESENT (35) F-B	0.84 OF 25	7 21 10 4 XSQ= 6.53 PHI= -0.394 XP = 0.0106
386	DRIFT TOWARD BEING THOSE WHERE SEXUAL EXPRESSICN BY THE YOUNG IS PERMITTED (40) F-B	0.63 OF 24	386	DRIFT TOWARD BEING THOSE WHERE SEXUAL EXPRESSION BY THE YOUNG IS RESTRICTED OR SEMI-RESTRICTED (46) F-B	0.65 OF 34	9 22 15 12 XSQ= 3.16 PHI= -0.234 XP = 0.0753
391	DRIFT TCWARD BEING THCSE WHERE PREMARITAL SEX RELATIONS ARE PUNISHED CNLY IF PREGNANCY RESULTS, OR FREELY PERMITTEC (90) JTW,EA	0.61 OF 44	391	DRIFT TOWARD BEING THOSE WHERE PREMARITAL SEX RELATIONS ARE STRONGLY PUNISHED AND IN FACT RARE, OR WEAKLY PUNISHED AND IN FACT NOT RARE (89) JTW,EA	0.59 OF 68	17 40 27 28 XSQ= 3.59 PHI= -0.179 XP = 0.0583
392	TILT TOWARC BEING THOSE WHERE PREMARITAL SEX RELATIONS ARE FREELY PERMITTED (67) JTW,EA	0.50 OF 44	392	TILT TOWARD BEING THOSE WHERE PREMARITAL SEX RELATICNS ARE STRONGLY PUNISHED AND IN FACT RARE, OR WEAKLY PUNISHED AND IN FACT NOT RARE, OR PUNISHED ONLY IF PREGNANCY RESULTS (112) JTW,EA	0.75 OF 68	22 51 22 17 XSQ= 6.30 PHI= -0.237 XP = 0.0121
393	DRIFT TOWARD BEING THOSE WHERE EXTRAMARITAL COITUS IS PERMITTED, RATHER THAN PUNISHED (41) F-B	0.65 OF 23	393	DRIFT TOWARD BEING THOSE WHERE EXTRAMARITAL COITUS IS PUNISHED, RATHER THAN PERMITTED (43) F-B	0.61 OF 38	8 23 15 15 XSQ= 2.84 PHI= -0.216 XP = 0.0920
399	DRIFT TOWARD BEING THOSE WHERE INTENSITY OF CASTRATION ANXIETY IS LCW (22) WNS	0.69 OF 13	399	DRIFT TOWARD BEING THOSE WHERE INTENSITY OF CASTRATION ANXIETY IS HIGH (23) WNS	0.65 OF 23	4 15 9 8 XSQ= 2.69 PHI= -0.274 EP = 0.0819

```
400  TILT TOWARD BEING THOSE          0.59 OF  17     400  TILT TOWARD BEING THOSE          0.78 OF  27          10     6
     WHERE HOMOSEXUAL ACTIVITY                             WHERE HOMOSEXUAL ACTIVITY                                   7    21
     IS PROHIBITED  (22) F-B                               IS PERMITTED  (36) F-B                             XSQ=      4.56
                                                                                                              PHI=     0.322
                                                                                                              XP  =   0.0327

406  DRIFT TOWARD BEING THOSE         0.68 OF  22     406  DRIFT TOWARD BEING THOSE         0.63 OF  24           7    15
     WHERE EXPLANATIONS OF ILLNESS                         WHERE EXPLANATIONS OF ILLNESS                              15     9
     OF AN AGGRESSION NATURE                               OF AN AGGRESSION NATURE                            XSQ=      3.19
     ARE ABSENT  (33) W-C                                  ARE PRESENT  (28) W-C                              PHI=    -0.263
                                                                                                              XP  =   0.0742

417  LEAN LESS TOWARD BEING THOSE     0.59 OF  17     417  IN ALL CASES ARE THOSE           1.00 OF  18          10    18
     WHERE WARFARE IS                                      WHERE WARFARE IS                                            7     0
     PREVALENT  (34) LWS                                   PREVALENT  (34) LWS                                XSQ=      6.87
                                                                                                              PHI=    -0.443
                                                                                                              EP  =   0.0029

419  TILT TOWARD BEING THOSE          0.52 OF  27     419  TILT TOWARD BEING THOSE          0.76 OF  41          13    31
     WHERE MILITARY GLORY                                  WHERE MILITARY GLORY                                       14    10
     IS NEGLIGIBLY EMPHASIZED  (31) PES                    IS STRONGLY OR                                     XSQ=      4.24
                                                           MODERATELY EMPHASIZED  (55) PES                    PHI=    -0.250
                                                                                                              XP  =   0.0395

421  DRIFT TOWARD BEING THOSE         0.72 OF  25     421  DRIFT TOWARD BEING THOSE         0.52 OF  42           7    22
     WHERE KILLING, TORTURING, OR MUTILATING               WHERE KILLING, TORTURING, OR MUTILATING                    18    20
     OF THE ENEMY                                          OF THE ENEMY                                       XSQ=      2.87
     IS NEGLIGIBLY EMPHASIZED  (47) PES                    IS STRONGLY OR MODERATELY                          PHI=    -0.207
                                                           EMPHASIZED  (37) PES                               XP  =   0.0904

446  DRIFT TOWARD BEING THOSE         0.78 OF   9     446  DRIFT TOWARD BEING THOSE         0.67 OF  15           2    10
     WHERE WITCHCRAFT                                      WHERE WITCHCRAFT                                            7     5
     IS MODERATELY PRESENT OR                              IS SIGNIFICANTLY PRESENT  (14) GES                 XSQ=      2.84
     ABSENT  (24) GES                                                                                         PHI=    -0.344
                                                                                                              EP  =   0.0894

470  DRIFT MORE TOWARD BEING THOSE    0.86 OF  14     470  DRIFT LESS TOWARD BEING THOSE    0.54 OF  24           2    11
     WHERE INNOVATIONS ARE                                 WHERE INNOVATIONS ARE                                      12    13
     ACCEPTED ONLY SELECTIVELY  (33) JMH                   ACCEPTED ONLY SELECTIVELY  (33) JMH                XSQ=      2.63
                                                                                                              PHI=    -0.263
                                                                                                              EP  =   0.0773

472  TILT TOWARD BEING THOSE          0.64 OF  28     472  TILT TOWARD BEING THOSE          0.64 OF  44          10    28
     WHERE THE COMPOSITE NARCISSISM INDEX                  WHERE THE COMPOSITE NARCISSISM INDEX                       18    16
     IS LOW  (43) PES                                      IS HIGH  (47) PES                                  XSQ=      4.29
                                                                                                              PHI=    -0.244
                                                                                                              XP  =   0.0383
```

461 CULTURES
WHERE GAMES OF STRATEGY, RATHER THAN
CHANCE, ARE PRESENT (22) R-A-B,EA

461 CULTURES
WHERE GAMES OF CHANCE, RATHER THAN
STRATEGY, ARE PRESENT (52) R-A-B,EA

BACKGROUND ON PAGE 169

SUBJECT ONLY

22 IN LEFT COLUMN

ALBANIANS	ASHANTI	BURUSHO	GANDA	ILA	JUKUN	KIKUYU	LAKHER	LAMBA	LUO
MASAI	MBUNDU	MOSSI	NYAKYUSA	NYORO	RUNDI	SIWANS	SOMALI	TANALA	TIV
WOLEAIANS	YAO								

52 IN RIGHT COLUMN

ARAUCANIANS	ATSUGEWI	AYMARA	CHEROKEE	CHEYENNE	CHIR-APACHE	CHIRIGUANO	CHOROTI	CHUKCHEE	COPR ESKIMO
CREE	CREEK	CROW	DIEGUENO	EYAK	GROS VENTRE	HAIDA	HASINAI	HUKUNDIKA	HURON
HUTSUL	JEMEZ	KASKA	KUTENAI	KWAKIUTL	MARICOPA	MATACO	MAYA	MIAMI	MIWOK
NABESNA	NAVAHO	NOMLAKI	OMAHA	PALAUANS	PAPAGO	SAMOANS	SANPOIL	TALLENSI	TAOS
TAREUMIUT	TEHUELCHE	TENINO	TOLOWA	TRUKESE	TWANA	ULAWANS	UTE	WASHO	YOKUTS
YUKI	YUROK								

30 EXCLUDED BECAUSE AMBIGUOUS

AMERICANS	AZANDE	AZTEC	BASSERI	CHAGGA	CZECHS	DARD	EGYPTIANS	FON	HAWAIIANS
INCA	IRISH	JAPANESE	KAZAK	KOREANS	KUBA	MENDE	MIN CHINESE	NAMA	OKINAWANS
SERBS	SYRIANS	TARAHUMARA	THAI	THONGA	VENDA	VIETNAMESE	WOLOF	YAKUT	ZUNI

85 EXCLUDED BECAUSE IRRELEVANT

ABIPON	ABOR	AINU	ALACALUF	ANDAMANESE	APINAYE	ARANDA	BACAIRI	BHIL	BHUIYA
BORORO	BUNLAP	CADUVEO	CAGABA	CAMAYURA	CARIB	CAYAPA	CHENCHU	CHORTI	COORG
CUNA	DIERI	ELLICE	FANG	GARO	GOAJIRO	HUICHOL	IBAN	INGALIK	JIVARO
KATAB	KERAKI	KHASI	KORYAK	KUNG	KURTATCHI	LAPPS	LAU	LEPCHA	LESU
LHOTA NAGA	MACASSARESE	MANGAIANS	MANIHIKI	MANUS	MAORI	MARQUESANS	MARSHALLESE	MISKITO	MOTA
MURNGIN	NATCHEZ	NICOBARESE	NUNIVAK	ONA	PAEZ	PAIWAN	PUKAPUKA	RWALA	SAGADA
SEMANG	SENIANG	SHERENTE	SIRIONO	TALAMANCA	TAPIRAPE	TENETEHARA	TIKOPIA	TIMBIRA	TIWI
TODA	TROBRIAND	TRUMAI	TUCANO	TUCUNA	TUPINAMBA	VEDDA	WANTOAT	WAPISHANA	WARRAU
WITOTO	WOGEO	YAGUA	YAHGAN	YARURO					

211 EXCLUDED BECAUSE UNASCERTAINED

---

3 TEND TO BE THOSE LOCATED IN AFRICA (80) — 0.68 OF 22

3 TEND TO BE THOSE LOCATED OUTSIDE OF AFRICA (320) — 0.98 OF 52

15	1
7	51

XSQ= 36.23
PHI= 0.700
XP = 0.

8	IN ALL CASES ARE THOSE LOCATED OUTSIDE OF NORTH AMERICA (330)	1.00 OF 22	8	TEND TO BE THOSE LOCATED IN NORTH AMERICA (70)	0.73 OF 52	0 38 22 14 XSQ= 30.19 PHI= -0.639 XP = 0.0000
12	IN ALL CASES ARE THOSE WHERE THE LATITUDE IS LESS THAN FIFTY DEGREES (367)	1.00 OF 22	12	DRIFT LESS TOWARD BEING THOSE WHERE THE LATITUDE IS LESS THAN FIFTY DEGREES (367)	0.81 OF 52	0 10 22 42 XSQ= 3.38 PHI= -0.214 XP = 0.0658
14	TEND TO BE THOSE WHERE THE LATITUDE IS LESS THAN THIRTY DEGREES (281)	0.91 OF 22	14	TEND TO BE THOSE WHERE THE LATITUDE IS THIRTY DEGREES OR GREATER (119)	0.81 OF 52	2 42 20 10 XSQ= 30.04 PHI= -0.637 XP = 0.0000
15	TEND TO BE THOSE WHERE THE LATITUDE IS LESS THAN TWENTY DEGREES (217)	0.77 OF 22	15	TEND TO BE THOSE WHERE THE LATITUDE IS TWENTY DEGREES OR GREATER (183)	0.87 OF 52	5 45 17 7 XSQ= 25.89 PHI= -0.591 XP = 0.0000
16	TEND TO BE THOSE WHERE THE LATITUDE IS LESS THAN TEN DEGREES (123)	0.55 OF 22	16	TEND TO BE THOSE WHERE THE LATITUDE IS TEN DEGREES OR GREATER (277)	0.96 OF 52	10 50 12 2 XSQ= 22.71 PHI= -0.554 XP = 0.0000
36	TILT MORE TOWARD BEING THOSE WHERE THE NATURAL ENVIRONMENT IS OTHER THAN 'VERY HARSH,' OR SUB-TROPICAL BUSH, OR TEMPERATE GRASSLAND (292) FWM	0.82 OF 22	36	TILT LESS TOWARD BEING THOSE WHERE THE NATURAL ENVIRONMENT IS OTHER THAN 'VERY HARSH,' OR SUB-TROPICAL BUSH, OR TEMPERATE GRASSLAND (292) FWM	0.52 OF 52	4 25 18 27 XSQ= 4.61 PHI= -0.250 XP = 0.0318
44	LEAN TOWARD BEING THOSE WHERE SETTLEMENTS ARE FIXED (222)	0.86 OF 22	44	LEAN TOWARD BEING THOSE WHERE SETTLEMENTS ARE NON-FIXED (110)	0.57 OF 51	19 22 3 29 XSQ= 9.98 PHI= 0.370 XP = 0.0016
46	TILT MORE TOWARD BEING THOSE OTHER THAN WHERE SETTLEMENTS ARE NON-FIXED AND MOVEMENT IS NOMADIC (260)	0.91 OF 22	46	TILT LESS TOWARD BEING THOSE OTHER THAN WHERE SETTLEMENTS ARE NON-FIXED AND MOVEMENT IS NOMADIC (260)	0.63 OF 51	2 19 20 32 XSQ= 4.65 PHI= -0.253 XP = 0.0310
51	IN ALL CASES ARE THOSE WHERE SUBSISTENCE IS PRIMARILY BY FOOD PRODUCTION -- I. E., AGRICULTURE OR HUSBANDRY -- RATHER THAN BY GATHERING (253)	1.00 OF 22	51	TEND TO BE THOSE WHERE SUBSISTENCE IS PRIMARILY BY FOOD GATHERING -- I. E., HUNTING, FISHING, OR COLLECTING -- RATHER THAN FOOD PRODUCTION (147)	0.79 OF 52	22 11 0 41 XSQ= 35.77 PHI= 0.695 XP = 0.

54	IN ALL CASES ARE THOSE WHERE FOOD PRODUCTION IS BY INTENSIVE OR SIMPLE AGRICULTURE, RATHER THAN BY INCIPIENT FOOD PRODUCTION (192)	1.00 OF 20	54	LEAN LESS TOWARD BEING THOSE WHERE FOOD PRODUCTION IS BY INTENSIVE OR SIMPLE AGRICULTURE, RATHER THAN BY INCIPIENT FOOD PRODUCTION (192)	0.58 OF 19	20 11 0 8 XSQ= 8.17 PHI= 0.458 EP = 0.0012
56	IN ALL CASES ARE THOSE WHERE FOOD PRODUCTION IS BY SIMPLE AGRICULTURE, RATHER THAN BY INCIPIENT FOOD PRODUCTION (101)	1.00 OF 9	56	LEAN TOWARD BEING THOSE WHERE FOOD PRODUCTION IS BY INCIPIENT FOOD PRODUCTION, RATHER THAN BY SIMPLE AGRICULTURE (46)	0.62 OF 13	9 5 0 8 XSQ= 6.25 PHI= 0.533 EP = 0.0055
62	TEND TO BE THOSE WHERE HUSBANDRY OF SOME KIND IS PRESENT (228)	0.91 OF 22	62	TEND TO BE THOSE WHERE HUSBANDRY OF ANY KIND IS ABSENT (172)	0.60 OF 52	20 21 2 31 XSQ= 13.99 PHI= 0.435 XP = 0.0002
71	TEND TO BE THOSE WHERE METAL WORKING IS PRESENT (98)	0.90 OF 21	71	TEND TO BE THOSE WHERE METAL WORKING IS ABSENT (153)	0.82 OF 50	19 9 2 41 XSQ= 29.56 PHI= 0.645 XP = 0.0000
81	DRIFT TOWARD BEING THOSE WHERE A CITY OR TOWN IS PRESENT, OR THE AVERAGE COMMUNITY SIZE IS 200 OR GREATER (89)	0.61 OF 18	81	DRIFT TOWARD BEING THOSE WHERE NO CITY OR TOWN IS PRESENT, AND THE AVERAGE COMMUNITY SIZE IS SMALLER THAN 200 (135)	0.68 OF 34	11 11 7 23 XSQ= 2.90 PHI= 0.236 XP = 0.0888
84	TILT LESS TOWARD BEING THOSE WHERE THE LEVEL OF POLITICAL INTEGRATION IS THE LITTLE STATE, THE MINIMAL STATE, THE AUTONOMOUS COMMUNITY, OR THE FAMILY (262) GPM	0.80 OF 20	84	IN ALL CASES ARE THOSE WHERE THE LEVEL OF POLITICAL INTEGRATION IS THE LITTLE STATE, THE MINIMAL STATE, THE AUTONOMOUS COMMUNITY, OR THE FAMILY (262) GPM	1.00 OF 42	4 0 16 42 XSQ= 5.97 PHI= 0.310 XP = 0.0145
86	LEAN TOWARD BEING THOSE WHERE THE LEVEL OF POLITICAL INTEGRATION IS THE LARGE STATE, THE LITTLE STATE, OR THE MINIMAL STATE (148) GPM	0.80 OF 20	86	LEAN TOWARD BEING THOSE WHERE THE LEVEL OF POLITICAL INTEGRATION IS THE AUTONOMOUS COMMUNITY, OR THE FAMILY (156) GPM	0.67 OF 42	16 14 4 28 XSQ= 10.02 PHI= 0.402 XP = 0.0015
94	TILT LESS TOWARD BEING THOSE WHERE THE HIERARCHY OF NATIONAL JURISDICTION HAS TWO, ONE, OR NO LEVELS (296) GES,EA	0.86 OF 22	94	IN ALL CASES ARE THOSE WHERE THE HIERARCHY OF NATIONAL JURISDICTION HAS TWO, ONE, OR NO LEVELS (296) GES,EA	1.00 OF 50	3 0 19 50 XSQ= 4.11 PHI= 0.239 XP = 0.0426
95	TEND TO BE THOSE WHERE THE HIERARCHY OF NATIONAL JURISDICTION HAS FOUR, THREE, OR TWO LEVELS (76) GES,EA	0.50 OF 22	95	TEND TO BE THOSE WHERE THE HIERARCHY OF NATIONAL JURISDICTION HAS ONE OR NO LEVELS (254) GES,EA	0.92 OF 50	11 4 11 46 XSQ= 13.89 PHI= 0.439 XP = 0.0002

```
 96  TEND TC BE THCSE                 0.86 OF  22     96  TEND TO BE THOSE                 0.66 OF  50        19    17
     WHERE THE HIERARCHY                                   WHERE THE HIERARCHY                                   3    33
     OF NATICNAL JURISDICTION HAS                          OF NATIONAL JURISDICTION HAS                    XSQ=   14.73
     FOUR, THREE, TWC OR                                   NO LEVELS  (156) GES,EA                         PHI=   0.452
     CNE LEVEL  (174) GES,EA                                                                               XP =  0.0001

 97  TILT LESS TOWARD BEING THOSE     0.68 OF  22     97  TILT MORE TOWARD BEING THOSE     0.90 OF  51         7     5
     WHERE THE HIERARCHY                                   WHERE THE HIERARCHY                                  15    46
     OF LCCAL JURISDICTION HAS                             OF LOCAL JURISDICTION HAS                       XSQ=    3.94
     THREE OR TWO LEVELS  (273) GES,EA                     THREE OR TWO LEVELS  (273) GES,EA               PHI=   0.232
                                                                                                           XP =  0.0472

100  IN ALL CASES ARE THOSE           1.00 OF  22    100  TILT LESS TOWARD BEING THOSE     0.70 OF  50        22    35
     WHERE HIERARCHIES ARE MORE COMPLEX THAN               WHERE HIERARCHIES ARE MORE COMPLEX THAN              0    15
     THE 'SIMPLEST,' I. E., MORE COMPLEX THAN              THE 'SIMPLEST,' I. E., MORE COMPLEX THAN        XSQ=    6.62
     TWC LCCAL LEVELS WITH                                 TWO LOCAL LEVELS WITH                           PHI=   0.303
     NO NATICNAL LEVELS  (267) GES,EA                      NO NATIONAL LEVELS  (267) GES,EA                XP =  0.0101

102  DRIFT TOWARD BEING THOSE         0.68 OF  22    102  DRIFT TOWARD BEING THOSE         0.57 OF  51        15    22
     WHERE CLASS STRATIFICATION IS                         WHERE CLASS STRATIFICATION IS                         7    29
     PRESENT  (203)                                        ABSENT  (180)                                   XSQ=    2.92
                                                                                                           PHI=   0.200
                                                                                                           XP =  0.0875

106  TILT TCWARD BEING THOSE          0.67 OF  15    106  TILT TOWARD BEING THOSE          0.73 OF  22         5    16
     WHERE CLASS STRATIFICATION, IF PRESENT,               WHERE CLASS STRATIFICATION, IF PRESENT,              10     6
     IS BASED CN SOMETHING OTHER THAN                      IS BASED ON WEALTH  (77)                        XSQ=    4.15
     WEALTH  (126)                                                                                         PHI=  -0.335
                                                                                                           EP =  0.0409

109  LEAN LESS TOWARD BEING THOSE     0.75 OF  20    109  IN ALL CASES ARE THOSE           1.00 OF  52         5     0
     WHERE CASTES ARE ABSENT  (317)                        WHERE CASTES ARE ABSENT  (317)                       15    52
                                                                                                           XSQ=   10.37
                                                                                                           PHI=   0.379
                                                                                                           XP =  0.0013

110  LEAN TCWARD BEING THCSE          0.76 OF  21    110  LEAN TOWARD BEING THOSE          0.67 OF  51        16    17
     WHERE SLAVERY IS PRESENT  (163)                       WHERE SLAVERY IS ABSENT  (218)                        5    34
                                                                                                           XSQ=    9.35
                                                                                                           PHI=   0.360
                                                                                                           XP =  0.0022

116  DRIFT TOWARD BEING THOSE         0.75 OF   4    116  DRIFT TOWARD BEING THOSE         0.82 OF  11         3     2
     WHERE OCCUPATIONAL SPECIALIZATION IS                  WHERE OCCUPATIONAL SPECIALIZATION IS                  1     9
     FULL-TIME, WHETHER OR NOT FOR                         PART-TIME ONLY  (34) JMH                        XSQ=    2.09
     SURPLUS PRODUCTION  (20) JMH                                                                          PHI=   0.373
                                                                                                           EP =  0.0769

128  TILT TCWARD BEING THOSE          0.75 OF   8    128  TILT TOWARD BEING THOSE          0.88 OF   8         2     7
     WHERE, IF SUBSISTENCE IS PRIMARILY BY                 WHERE, IF SUBSISTENCE IS PRIMARILY BY                 6     1
     AGRICULTURE, THE WCRK IS                              AGRICULTURE, THE WORK IS                        XSQ=    4.06
     MAINLY DCNE BY FEMALES  (37)                          MAINLY DONE BY MALES  (40)                      PHI=  -0.504
                                                                                                           EP =  0.0406
```

129	DRIFT TOWARD BEING THOSE WHERE WEAVING IS MAINLY DONE BY MALES (31)	0.50 OF 10	129	DRIFT TOWARD BEING THOSE WHERE WEAVING IS MAINLY DONE BY FEMALES (73)	0.85 OF 20	5 3 5 17 XSQ= 2.58 PHI= 0.293 EP = 0.0778
130	LEAN TOWARD BEING THOSE WHERE LEATHER WORKING IS MAINLY DONE BY MALES (39)	0.89 OF 9	130	LEAN TOWARD BEING THOSE WHERE LEATHER WORKING IS MAINLY DONE BY FEMALES (45)	0.67 OF 36	8 12 1 24 XSQ= 6.89 PHI= 0.391 XP = 0.0087
183	IN ALL CASES ARE THOSE WHERE THE LARGEST NON-COGNATIC KIN GROUP IS SMALLER THAN A MOEITY, I. E., A PHRATRY OR SIB OR LINEAGE (218)	1.00 OF 21	183	TILT LESS TOWARD BEING THOSE WHERE THE LARGEST NON-COGNATIC KIN GROUP IS SMALLER THAN A MOEITY, I. E., A PHRATRY OR SIB OR LINEAGE (218)	0.71 OF 24	0 7 21 17 XSQ= 5.20 PHI= -0.340 XP = 0.0226
184	TILT MORE TOWARD BEING THOSE WHERE THE LARGEST NON-COGNATIC KIN GROUP IS SMALLER THAN A PHRATRY, I. E. A SIB OR LINEAGE (175)	0.90 OF 21	184	TILT LESS TOWARD BEING THOSE WHERE THE LARGEST NON-COGNATIC KIN GROUP IS SMALLER THAN A PHRATRY, I. E. A SIB OR LINEAGE (175)	0.54 OF 24	2 11 19 13 XSQ= 5.53 PHI= -0.351 XP = 0.0187
186	TILT TOWARD BEING THOSE WHERE THE KIN GROUP IS EXCLUSIVELY PATRILINEAL (150)	0.55 OF 22	186	TILT TOWARD BEING THOSE WHERE THE KIN GROUP IS OTHER THAN EXCLUSIVELY PATRILINEAL (250)	0.77 OF 52	12 12 10 40 XSQ= 5.62 PHI= 0.276 XP = 0.0177
188	TEND TO BE THOSE WHERE THE KIN GROUP IS OTHER THAN EXCLUSIVELY COGNATIC (252)	0.95 OF 22	188	TEND TO BE THOSE WHERE THE KIN GROUP IS EXCLUSIVELY COGNATIC (148)	0.54 OF 52	1 28 21 24 XSQ= 13.77 PHI= -0.431 XP = 0.0002
190	TILT TOWARD BEING THOSE WHERE THE KIN GROUP IS PATRILINEAL OR DOUBLE-DESCENT, RATHER THAN MATRILINEAL (186)	0.85 OF 20	190	TILT TOWARD BEING THOSE WHERE THE KIN GROUP IS MATRILINEAL, RATHER THAN PATRILINEAL OR DOUBLE-DESCENT (61)	0.52 OF 23	17 11 3 12 XSQ= 4.97 PHI= 0.340 XP = 0.0257
192	IN ALL CASES ARE THOSE OTHER THAN WHERE THE ONLY KIN GROUP PRESENT IS A KINDRED OR ELSE BILATERAL DESCENT IS INFERRED (289)	1.00 OF 22	192	TEND LESS TO BE THOSE OTHER THAN WHERE THE ONLY KIN GROUP PRESENT IS A KINDRED OR ELSE BILATERAL DESCENT IS INFERRED (289)	0.54 OF 52	0 24 22 28 XSQ= 13.00 PHI= -0.419 XP = 0.0003
196	LEAN TOWARD BEING THOSE WHERE INDIVIDUAL RIGHTS IN REAL PROPERTY, AND RULES FOR INHERITANCE, ARE PRESENT (194)	0.88 OF 17	196	LEAN TOWARD BEING THOSE WHERE INDIVIDUAL RIGHTS IN REAL PROPERTY, OR RULES FOR INHERITANCE, ARE ABSENT (87)	0.58 OF 38	15 16 2 22 XSQ= 8.37 PHI= 0.390 XP = 0.0038

209	DRIFT MORE TOWARD BEING THOSE WHERE MARITAL RESIDENCE IS PATRILOCAL, VIRILOCAL, OR AVUNCULOCAL, RATHER THAN MATRILOCAL OR UXORILOCAL (270)	0.94 OF	18	209	DRIFT LESS TOWARD BEING THOSE WHERE MARITAL RESIDENCE IS PATRILOCAL, VIRILOCAL, OR AVUNCULOCAL, RATHER THAN MATRILOCAL OR UXORILOCAL (270)	0.71 OF	41	17 29 1 12 XSQ= 2.83 PHI= 0.219 XP = 0.0925
210	DRIFT MORE TOWARD BEING THOSE WHERE MARITAL RESIDENCE IS PATRILOCAL, RATHER THAN MATRILOCAL (169)	0.93 OF	14	210	DRIFT LESS TOWARD BEING THOSE WHERE MARITAL RESIDENCE IS PATRILOCAL, RATHER THAN MATRILOCAL (169)	0.60 OF	15	13 9 1 6 XSQ= 2.66 PHI= 0.303 EP = 0.0801
213	DRIFT LESS TOWARD BEING THOSE WHERE FIRST COUSIN MARRIAGE IS NOT PERMITTED (198)	0.55 OF	22	213	DRIFT MORE TOWARD BEING THOSE WHERE FIRST COUSIN MARRIAGE IS NOT PERMITTED (198)	0.78 OF	51	10 11 12 40 XSQ= 3.19 PHI= 0.209 XP = 0.0740
220	LEAN LESS TOWARD BEING THOSE WHERE FIRST COUSIN MARRIAGE IN SOME FORM OR OTHER IS NOT PRESCRIBED OR PREFERRED (273)	0.59 OF	22	220	LEAN MORE TOWARD BEING THOSE WHERE FIRST COUSIN MARRIAGE IN SOME FORM OR OTHER IS NOT PRESCRIBED OR PREFERRED (273)	0.90 OF	51	9 5 13 46 XSQ= 7.69 PHI= 0.325 XP = 0.0055
234	DRIFT TOWARD BEING THOSE WHERE THE COUSIN TERMINOLOGY IS OF CROW, OMAHA, OR IROQUOIS TYPE, RATHER THAN ESKIMO OR HAWAIIAN TYPE (152)	0.67 OF	18	234	DRIFT TOWARD BEING THOSE WHERE THE COUSIN TERMINOLOGY IS OF ESKIMO OR HAWAIIAN TYPE, RATHER THAN CROW, OMAHA, OR IROQUOIS TYPE (170)	0.60 OF	50	12 20 6 30 XSQ= 2.78 PHI= 0.202 XP = 0.0953
262	DRIFT MORE TOWARD BEING THOSE WHERE WIVES ARE OBTAINED BY MEANS INVOLVING THE PRESENCE OF SOME CONSIDERATION (305)	0.91 OF	22	262	DRIFT LESS TOWARD BEING THOSE WHERE WIVES ARE OBTAINED BY MEANS INVOLVING THE PRESENCE OF SOME CONSIDERATION (305)	0.67 OF	52	20 35 2 17 XSQ= 3.36 PHI= 0.213 XP = 0.0668
263	LEAN TOWARD BEING THOSE WHERE WIVES ARE OBTAINED BY RELATIVELY DIFFICULT MEANS, NAMELY BY BRIDE-PRICE, BRIDE-SERVICE, OR EXCHANGING A FEMALE RELATIVE (233)	0.77 OF	22	263	LEAN TOWARD BEING THOSE WHERE WIVES ARE OBTAINED BY RELATIVELY EASY MEANS, NAMELY BY TOKEN BRIDE-PRICE, GIFT EXCHANGE, ABSENCE OF ANY CONSIDERATION, OR RECEIPT OF DOWRY (162)	0.65 OF	52	17 18 5 34 XSQ= 9.64 PHI= 0.361 XP = 0.0019
305	DRIFT TOWARD BEING THOSE WHERE THE EARLY SEXUAL SATISFACTION POTENTIAL IS HIGH (27) W-C	0.67 OF	6	305	DRIFT TOWARD BEING THOSE WHERE THE EARLY SEXUAL SATISFACTION POTENTIAL IS LOW (24) W-C	0.88 OF	8	4 1 2 7 XSQ= 2.34 PHI= 0.409 EP = 0.0909
311	DRIFT TOWARD BEING THOSE WHERE SEXUAL SOCIALIZATION ANXIETY IS LOW (23) W-C	0.50 OF	6	311	IN ALL CASES ARE THOSE WHERE SEXUAL SOCIALIZATION ANXIETY IS HIGH (28) W-C	1.00 OF	8	3 8 3 0 XSQ= 2.55 PHI= -0.427 EP = 0.0549

314	DRIFT TOWARD BEING THOSE WHERE THE INCIDENCE OF MOTHER-CHILD HOUSEHOLDS IS HIGH (19) W-D,S	0.63 OF 8	314	DRIFT TOWARD BEING THOSE WHERE THE INCIDENCE OF MOTHER-CHILD HOUSEHOLDS IS LOW (61) W-D,S	0.86 OF 14	5 2 3 12 XSQ= 3.46 PHI= 0.397 EP = 0.0524
318	TILT TOWARD BEING THOSE WHERE THE OVERALL INDULGENCE OF THE INFANT IS LOW (31) B-B-C	0.88 OF 8	318	TILT TOWARD BEING THOSE WHERE THE OVERALL INDULGENCE OF THE INFANT IS HIGH (40) B-B-C	0.64 OF 14	1 9 7 5 XSQ= 3.62 PHI= -0.405 EP = 0.0310
324	DRIFT TOWARD BEING THOSE WHERE THE PAIN INFLICTED ON THE INFANT BY THE NURTURANT AGENT IS HIGH (34) B-B-C	0.86 OF 7	324	DRIFT TOWARD BEING THOSE WHERE THE PAIN INFLICTED ON THE INFANT BY THE NURTURANT AGENT IS LOW OR NEGLIGIBLE (32) B-B-C	0.62 OF 13	6 5 1 8 XSQ= 2.42 PHI= 0.348 EP = 0.0703
327	DRIFT TOWARD BEING THOSE WHERE THE AGE OF THE INFANT AT TIME OF REDUCED CONTACT WITH MOTHER IS TWO YEARS OR LOWER (27) B-B-C	0.86 OF 7	327	DRIFT TOWARD BEING THOSE WHERE THE AGE OF THE INFANT AT TIME OF REDUCED CONTACT WITH MOTHER IS HIGHER THAN TWO YEARS (28) B-B-C	0.64 OF 11	1 7 6 4 XSQ= 2.46 PHI= -0.369 EP = 0.0656
347	TILT TOWARD BEING THOSE WHERE THE CHILD'S INFERRED CONFLICT REGARDING SELF-RELIANT BEHAVIOR IS HIGH (37) B-B-C	0.90 OF 10	347	TILT TOWARD BEING THOSE WHERE THE CHILD'S INFERRED CONFLICT REGARDING SELF-RELIANT BEHAVIOR IS LOW (39) B-B-C	0.57 OF 14	9 6 1 8 XSQ= 3.70 PHI= 0.393 EP = 0.0333
353	IN ALL CASES ARE THOSE WHERE THE CHILD'S INFERRED ANXIETY OVER NON-PERFORMANCE OF OBEDIENT BEHAVIOR IS HIGH (42) B-B-C	1.00 OF 11	353	TILT LESS TOWARD BEING THOSE WHERE THE CHILD'S INFERRED ANXIETY OVER NON-PERFORMANCE OF OBEDIENT BEHAVIOR IS HIGH (42) B-B-C	0.64 OF 14	11 9 0 5 XSQ= 2.93 PHI= 0.342 EP = 0.0464
370	TEND TO BE THOSE WHERE THE SEGREGATION OF ADOLESCENT BOYS IS COMPLETE OR PARTIAL (95)	0.67 OF 18	370	TEND TO BE THOSE WHERE THE SEGREGATION OF ADOLESCENT BOYS IS ABSENT (148)	0.86 OF 37	12 5 6 32 XSQ= 13.63 PHI= 0.498 XP = 0.0002
377	TEND LESS TO BE THOSE WHERE MALE GENITAL MUTILATION IS ABSENT (242)	0.59 OF 22	377	TEND MORE TO BE THOSE WHERE MALE GENITAL MUTILATION IS ABSENT (242)	0.98 OF 52	9 1 13 51 XSQ= 16.91 PHI= 0.478 XP = 0.0000
403	TILT TOWARD BEING THOSE WHERE EXPLANATIONS OF ILLNESS OF AN ANAL NATURE ARE PRESENT (23) W-C	0.83 OF 6	403	TILT TOWARD BEING THOSE WHERE EXPLANATIONS OF ILLNESS OF AN ANAL NATURE ARE ABSENT (38) W-C	0.73 OF 11	5 3 1 8 XSQ= 2.91 PHI= 0.413 EP = 0.0498

426	TEND TO BE THCSE WHERE A HIGH GOC IS PRESENT (156) GES,EA	0.90 OF 20	426	TEND TO BE THOSE WHERE A HIGH GOD IS ABSENT (104) GES,EA	0.62 OF 45	18 17 2 28 XSQ= 13.17 PHI= 0.450 XP = 0.0003
444	DRIFT TCWARD BEING THCSE WHERE THE USE OF DREAMS TO SEEK AND CCNTROL SUPERNATURAL POWERS IS LCW (27) RGC	0.88 OF 8	444	DRIFT TOWARD BEING THOSE WHERE THE USE OF DREAMS TO SEEK AND CONTROL SUPERNATURAL POWERS IS HIGH (28) RGD	0.64 OF 11	1 7 7 4 XSQ= 3.09 PHI= -0.403 EP = 0.0587
455	IN ALL CASES ARE THOSE WHERE THE MODE CF THE INCIVIDUAL'S CCNTACT WITH THE DIVINE IS NCT CONDUCIVE TC THE DEVELOPMENT OF THE INDIVIDUAL'S NEED TO ACHIEVE (19) DCM	1.00 OF 5	455	TILT TOWARD BEING THOSE WHERE THE MODE OF THE INDIVIDUAL'S CONTACT WITH THE DIVINE IS CONDUCIVE TO THE DEVELOPMENT OF THE INDIVIDUAL'S NEED TO ACHIEVE (17) DCM	0.75 OF 8	0 6 5 2 XSQ= 4.27 PHI= -0.573 EP = 0.0210
468	LEAN TOWARD BEING THOSE WHERE CONTACT WITH OTHER CULTURES IS FREQUENT, RATHER THAN REGULAR CR IRREGULAR (17) JMH	0.75 OF 4	468	IN ALL CASES ARE THOSE WHERE CONTACT WITH OTHER CULTURES IS REGULAR OR IRREGULAR, RATHER THAN FREQUENT (37) JMH	1.00 OF 11	3 0 1 11 XSQ= 6.16 PHI= 0.641 EP = 0.0088

462 CULTURES
WHERE GAMES OF
STRATEGY, CHANCE, AND SKILL -- RATHER THAN
SKILL ONLY -- ARE PRESENT (30) R-A-B,EA

462 CULTURES
WHERE GAMES OF
SKILL ONLY -- RATHER THAN
STRATEGY, CHANCE, AND SKILL --
ARE PRESENT (67) R-A-B,EA

BACKGROUND ON PAGE 169

SUBJECT ONLY

30 IN LEFT COLUMN

AMERICANS	AZANDE	AZTEC	BASSERI	CHAGGA	CZECHS	DARD	EGYPTIANS	FON	HAWAIIANS
INCA	IRISH	JAPANESE	KAZAK	KOREANS	KUBA	MENDE	MIN CHINESE	NAMA	OKINAWANS
SERBS	SYRIANS	TARAHUMARA	THAI	THONGA	VENDA	VIETNAMESE	WOLOF	YAKUT	ŻUNI

67 IN RIGHT COLUMN

ABIPON	ABOR	AINU	ANDAMANESE	APINAYE	ARANDA	BACAIRI	BHIL	BHUIYA	BORORO
BUNLAP	CADUVEO	CAMAYURA	CARIB	COORG	DIERI	ELLICE	FANG	GOAJIRO	IBAN
INGALIK	KERAKI	KHASI	KORYAK	KUNG	KURTATCHI	LAPPS	LAU	LEPCHA	LESU
LHOTA NAGA	MACASSARESE	MANGAIANS	MANIHIKI	MANUS	MAORI	MARQUESANS	MARSHALLESE	MISKITO	MOTA
NATCHEZ	NICOBARESE	NUNIVAK	ONA	PAIWAN	PUKAPUKA	RWALA	SAGADA	SEMANG	SENIANG
SHERENTE	SIRIONO	TAPIRAPE	TIKOPIA	TIMBIRA	TIWI	TODA	TROBRIAND	TRUMAI	TUCUNA
WANTOAT	WAPISHANA	WARRAU	WITOTO	WOGEO	YAGUA	YAHGAN			

92 EXCLUDED BECAUSE IRRELEVANT

ALACALUF	ALBANIANS	ARAUCANIANS	ASHANTI	ATSUGEWI	AYMARA	BURUSHO	CAGABA	CAYAPA	CHENCHU
CHEROKEE	CHEYENNE	CHIR-APACHE	CHIRIGUANO	CHOROTI	CHORTI	CHUKCHEE	COPR ESKIMO	CREE	CREEK
CROW	CUNA	DIEGUENO	EYAK	GANDA	GARO	GROS VENTRE	HAIDA	HASINAI	HUICHOL
HUKUNDIKA	HURON	HUTSUL	ILA	JEMEZ	JIVARO	JUKUN	KASKA	KATAB	KIKUYU
KUTENAI	KWAKIUTL	LAKHER	LAMBA	LUO	MARICOPA	MASAI	MATACO	MAYA	MBUNDU
MIAMI	MIWOK	MOSSI	MURNGIN	NABESNA	NAVAHO	NOMLAKI	NYAKYUSA	NYORO	OMAHA
PAEZ	PALAUANS	PAPAGO	RUNDI	SAMOANS	SANPOIL	SIWANS	SOMALI	TALAMANCA	TALLENSI
TANALA	TAOS	TAREUMIUT	TEHUELCHE	TENETEHARA	TENINO	TIV	TOLOWA	TRUKESE	TUCANO
TUPINAMBA	TWANA	ULAWANS	UTE	VEDDA	WASHO	WOLEAIANS	YAO	YARURO	YOKUTS
YUKI	YUROK								

211 EXCLUDED BECAUSE UNASCERTAINED

3 LEAN LESS TOWARD BEING THOSE LOCATED OUTSIDE OF AFRICA (320) 0.73 OF 30

3 LEAN MORE TOWARD BEING THOSE LOCATED OUTSIDE OF AFRICA (320) 0.97 OF 67

8	2
22	65
XSQ=	10.14
PHI=	0.323
XP =	0.0015

4 LEAN LESS TOWARD BEING THOSE LOCATED OUTSIDE OF THE CIRCUM-MEDITERRANEAN (355) 0.77 OF 30

4 LEAN MORE TOWARD BEING THOSE LOCATED OUTSIDE OF THE CIRCUM-MEDITERRANEAN (355) 0.97 OF 67

7	2
23	65
XSQ=	7.92
PHI=	0.286
XP =	0.0049

6	TEND MORE TO BE THCSE LOCATED OUTSIDE OF THE INSULAR PACIFIC (330)	0.97 OF 30	6	TEND LESS TO BE THOSE LOCATED OUTSIDE OF THE INSULAR PACIFIC (330)	0.61 OF 67	1 26 29 41 XSQ= 11.27 PHI= -0.341 XP = 0.0008
9	LEAN MORE TOWARC BEING THOSE LOCATED OUTSIDE OF SOUTH AMERICA (335)	0.97 OF 30	9	LEAN LESS TOWARD BEING THOSE LOCATED OUTSIDE OF SOUTH AMERICA (335)	0.69 OF 67	1 21 29 46 XSQ= 7.74 PHI= -0.283 XP = 0.0054
15	LEAN TOWARD BEING THOSE WHERE THE LATITUDE IS TWENTY DEGREES CR GREATER (183)	0.67 OF 30	15	LEAN TOWARD BEING THOSE WHERE THE LATITUDE IS LESS THAN TWENTY DEGREES (217)	0.66 OF 67	20 23 10 44 XSQ= 7.52 PHI= 0.278 XP = 0.0061
42	TEND TO BE THOSE WHERE THE NATURAL ENVIRONMENT IS OTHER THAN TRCPICAL CR SUB-TRCPICAL RAIN FOREST, OR MONSCCN FOREST (244) FWM	0.73 OF 30	42	TEND TO BE THOSE WHERE THE NATURAL ENVIRONMENT IS TROPICAL OR SUB-TROPICAL RAIN FOREST, OR MONSOON FOREST (156) FWM	0.66 OF 67	8 44 22 23 XSQ= 11.16 PHI= -0.339 XP = 0.0008
48	LEAN TOWARD BEING THOSE WHERE THE FOOD SUPPLY IS NOT SECURE, AND FCOD SHORTAGES ARE FREQUENT OR ANNUAL (41) MGW	0.90 OF 10	48	LEAN TOWARD BEING THOSE WHERE THE FOOD SUPPLY IS SECURE, AND FOOD SHORTAGES ARE RARE OR OCCASIONAL (38) MGW	0.63 OF 19	1 12 9 7 XSQ= 5.49 PHI= -0.435 EP = 0.0084
51	TEND TO BE THOSE WHERE SUBSISTENCE IS PRIMARILY BY FCOD PRODUCTION -- I. E., AGRICULTURE OR HUSBANDRY -- RATHER THAN BY GATHERING (253)	0.90 OF 30	51	TEND TO BE THOSE WHERE SUBSISTENCE IS PRIMARILY BY FOOD GATHERING -- I. E., HUNTING, FISHING, OR COLLECTING -- RATHER THAN FOOD PRODUCTION (147)	0.58 OF 67	27 28 3 39 XSQ= 17.70 PHI= 0.427 XP = 0.0000
53	TEND TO BE THOSE WHERE FCOD PRODUCTICN IS BY INTENSIVE AGRICULTURE, RATHER THAN BY SIMPLE AGRICULTURE OR INCIPIENT FOOD PRODUCTICN (91)	0.70 OF 27	53	TEND TO BE THOSE WHERE FOOD PRODUCTION IS BY SIMPLE AGRICULTURE OR INCIPIENT FOOD PRODUCTION, RATHER THAN BY INTENSIVE AGRICULTURE (147)	0.90 OF 39	19 4 8 35 XSQ= 22.82 PHI= 0.588 XP = 0.0000
55	TEND TO BE THOSE WHERE FCOD PRODUCTION IS BY INTENSIVE AGRICULTURE, RATHER THAN BY SIMPLE AGRICULTURE (91)	0.76 OF 25	55	TEND TO BE THOSE WHERE FOOD PRODUCTION IS BY SIMPLE AGRICULTURE, RATHER THAN BY INTENSIVE AGRICULTURE (101)	0.83 OF 24	19 4 6 20 XSQ= 15.01 PHI= 0.553 XP = 0.0001
62	TEND MORE TO BE THCSE WHERE HUSBANDRY OF SOME KIND IS PRESENT (228)	0.93 OF 30	62	TEND LESS TO BE THOSE WHERE HUSBANDRY OF SOME KIND IS PRESENT (228)	0.55 OF 67	28 37 2 30 XSQ= 11.94 PHI= 0.351 XP = 0.0005

63	LEAN TOWARD BEING THOSE WHERE HUSBANDRY, IF PRESENT, IS PRINCIPALLY IN THE FORM OF BOVINE, EQUINE, CAMEL-LIKE, OR DEER-LIKE ANIMALS, RATHER THAN PIGS, SHEEP, OR GOATS (152)	0.79 OF 28	63	LEAN TOWARD BEING THOSE WHERE HUSBANDRY, IF PRESENT, IS PRINCIPALLY IN THE FORM OF PIGS, SHEEP, OR GOATS, RATHER THAN BOVINE, EQUINE, CAMEL-LIKE, OR DEER-LIKE ANIMALS (74)	0.57 OF 37	22 16 6 21 XSQ= 6.80 PHI= 0.323 XP = 0.0091
71	TEND TO BE THOSE WHERE METAL WORKING IS PRESENT (98)	0.91 OF 23	71	TEND TO BE THOSE WHERE METAL WORKING IS ABSENT (153)	0.80 OF 59	21 12 2 47 XSQ= 31.77 PHI= 0.622 XP = 0.
73	TEND TO BE THOSE WHERE WEAVING IS PRESENT (118)	0.83 OF 24	73	TEND TO BE THOSE WHERE WEAVING IS ABSENT (130)	0.65 OF 57	20 20 4 37 XSQ= 13.86 PHI= 0.414 XP = 0.0002
74	TILT TOWARD BEING THOSE WHERE POTTERY IS PRESENT (145)	0.78 OF 23	74	TILT TOWARD BEING THOSE WHERE POTTERY IS ABSENT (93)	0.54 OF 56	18 26 5 30 XSQ= 5.47 PHI= 0.263 XP = 0.0194
80	TEND TO BE THOSE WHERE A CITY OR TOWN IS PRESENT (39)	0.54 OF 28	80	IN ALL CASES ARE THOSE WHERE NO CITY OR TOWN IS PRESENT (185)	1.00 OF 47	15 0 13 47 XSQ= 28.21 PHI= 0.613 XP = 0.0000
81	TEND TO BE THOSE WHERE A CITY OR TOWN IS PRESENT, OR THE AVERAGE COMMUNITY SIZE IS 200 OR GREATER (89)	0.75 OF 28	81	TEND TO BE THOSE WHERE NO CITY OR TOWN IS PRESENT, AND THE AVERAGE COMMUNITY SIZE IS SMALLER THAN 200 (135)	0.89 OF 47	21 5 7 42 XSQ= 29.31 PHI= 0.625 XP = 0.0000
82	IN ALL CASES ARE THOSE WHERE A CITY OR TOWN IS PRESENT, OR THE AVERAGE COMMUNITY SIZE IS FIFTY OR GREATER (178)	1.00 OF 28	82	LEAN LESS TOWARD BEING THOSE WHERE A CITY OR TOWN IS PRESENT, OR THE AVERAGE COMMUNITY SIZE IS FIFTY OR GREATER (178)	0.68 OF 47	28 32 0 15 XSQ= 9.26 PHI= 0.351 XP = 0.0023
83	TILT LESS TOWARD BEING THOSE WHERE, WITH NO CITY AND NO TOWN PRESENT, THE AVERAGE COMMUNITY SIZE IS SMALLER THAN 200, RATHER THAN BETWEEN 200 AND 999 (135)	0.58 OF 12	83	TILT MORE TOWARD BEING THOSE WHERE, WITH NO CITY AND NO TOWN PRESENT, THE AVERAGE COMMUNITY SIZE IS SMALLER THAN 200, RATHER THAN BETWEEN 200 AND 999 (135)	0.91 OF 46	5 4 7 42 XSQ= 5.58 PHI= 0.310 XP = 0.0182
84	TEND TO BE THOSE WHERE THE LEVEL OF POLITICAL INTEGRATION IS THE LARGE STATE (42) GPM	0.56 OF 25	84	TEND TO BE THOSE WHERE THE LEVEL OF POLITICAL INTEGRATION IS THE LITTLE STATE, THE MINIMAL STATE, THE AUTONOMOUS COMMUNITY, OR THE FAMILY (262) GPM	0.98 OF 56	14 1 11 55 XSQ= 30.17 PHI= 0.610 XP = 0.0000

No.			No.			
85	TEND TO BE THOSE WHERE THE LEVEL OF POLITICAL INTEGRATION IS THE LARGE STATE, OR THE LITTLE STATE (70) GPM	0.84 OF 25	85	TEND TO BE THOSE WHERE THE LEVEL OF POLITICAL INTEGRATION IS THE MINIMAL STATE, THE AUTONOMOUS COMMUNITY, OR THE FAMILY (234) GPM	0.95 OF 56	21 3 4 53 XSQ= 47.57 PHI= 0.766 XP = 0.
86	TEND TO BE THOSE WHERE THE LEVEL OF POLITICAL INTEGRATION IS THE LARGE STATE, THE LITTLE STATE, OR THE MINIMAL STATE (148) GPM	0.92 OF 25	86	TEND TO BE THOSE WHERE THE LEVEL OF POLITICAL INTEGRATION IS THE AUTONOMOUS COMMUNITY, OR THE FAMILY (156) GPM	0.73 OF 56	23 15 2 41 XSQ= 26.95 PHI= 0.577 XP = 0.0000
88	LEAN TOWARD BEING THOSE WHERE, IF A HEADMANSHIP IS PRESENT, SUCCESSION IS NCN-HEREDITARY (106)	0.58 OF 24	88	LEAN TOWARD BEING THOSE WHERE, IF A HEADMANSHIP IS PRESENT, SUCCESSION IS HEREDITARY (165)	0.76 OF 49	14 12 10 37 XSQ= 6.64 PHI= 0.302 XP = 0.0100
95	TEND TO BE THOSE WHERE THE HIERARCHY OF NATIONAL JURISDICTION HAS FOUR, THREE, OR TWC LEVELS (76) GES,EA	0.80 OF 30	95	TEND TO BE THOSE WHERE THE HIERARCHY OF NATIONAL JURISDICTION HAS ONE OR NO LEVELS (254) GES,EA	0.96 OF 67	24 3 6 64 XSQ= 55.14 PHI= 0.754 XP = 0.
96	TEND TO BE THOSE WHERE THE HIERARCHY OF NATIONAL JURISDICTION HAS FOUR, THREE, TWC OR ONE LEVEL (174) GES,EA	0.93 OF 30	96	TEND TO BE THOSE WHERE THE HIERARCHY OF NATIONAL JURISDICTION HAS NO LEVELS (156) GES,EA	0.66 OF 67	28 23 2 44 XSQ= 26.62 PHI= 0.524 XP = 0.0000
100	TILT MORE TOWARD BEING THOSE WHERE HIERARCHIES ARE MORE COMPLEX THAN THE 'SIMPLEST,' I. E., MORE COMPLEX THAN TWO LCCAL LEVELS WITH NO NATIONAL LEVELS (267) GES,EA	0.97 OF 30	100	TILT LESS TOWARD BEING THOSE WHERE HIERARCHIES ARE MORE COMPLEX THAN THE 'SIMPLEST,' I. E., MORE COMPLEX THAN TWO LOCAL LEVELS WITH NO NATIONAL LEVELS (267) GES,EA	0.75 OF 67	29 50 1 17 XSQ= 5.28 PHI= 0.233 XP = 0.0216
102	TEND TO BE THOSE WHERE CLASS STRATIFICATION IS PRESENT (203)	0.97 OF 30	102	TEND TO BE THOSE WHERE CLASS STRATIFICATION IS ABSENT (180)	0.52 OF 65	29 31 1 34 XSQ= 19.11 PHI= 0.448 XP = 0.0000
106	LEAN MORE TOWARD BEING THOSE WHERE CLASS STRATIFICATION, IF PRESENT, IS BASED CN SOMETHING OTHER THAN WEALTH (126)	0.86 OF 29	106	LEAN LESS TOWARD BEING THOSE WHERE CLASS STRATIFICATION, IF PRESENT, IS BASED ON SOMETHING OTHER THAN WEALTH (126)	0.52 OF 31	4 15 25 16 XSQ= 6.76 PHI= -0.336 XP = 0.0093
107	LEAN LESS TOWARD BEING THOSE WHERE CLASS STRATIFICATION, IF PRESENT, IS BASED CN SOMETHING OTHER THAN OCCUPATIONAL STATUS (160)	0.55 OF 29	107	LEAN MORE TOWARD BEING THOSE WHERE CLASS STRATIFICATION, IF PRESENT, IS BASED ON SOMETHING OTHER THAN OCCUPATIONAL STATUS (160)	0.90 OF 31	13 3 16 28 XSQ= 7.75 PHI= 0.360 XP = 0.0054

109	DRIFT LESS TOWARD BEING THOSE WHERE CASTES ARE ABSENT (317)	0.75 OF 28	109	DRIFT MORE TOWARD BEING THOSE WHERE CASTES ARE ABSENT (317)	0.92 OF 63	7 5 21 58 XSQ= 3.55 PHI= 0.198 XP = 0.0595
110	LEAN TOWARD BEING THOSE WHERE SLAVERY IS PRESENT (163)	0.52 OF 29	110	LEAN TOWARD BEING THOSE WHERE SLAVERY IS ABSENT (218)	0.80 OF 65	15 13 14 52 XSQ= 8.19 PHI= 0.295 XP = 0.0042
129	TEND TO BE THOSE WHERE WEAVING IS MAINLY DONE BY MALES (31)	0.50 OF 16	129	IN ALL CASES ARE THOSE WHERE WEAVING IS MAINLY DONE BY FEMALES (73)	1.00 OF 19	8 0 8 19 XSQ= 9.64 PHI= 0.525 EP = 0.0005
138	TILT TOWARD BEING THOSE WHERE SUPERORDINATE JUSTICE IS PRESENT (22) BBW	0.83 OF 6	138	TILT TOWARD BEING THOSE WHERE SUPERORDINATE JUSTICE IS ABSENT (18) BBW	0.80 OF 10	5 2 1 8 XSQ= 3.81 PHI= 0.488 EP = 0.0350
141	TILT TOWARD BEING THOSE WHERE THE LEVEL OF SOCIAL SANCTION IS PUBLIC CORPOREAL SANCTION, RATHER THAN PUBLIC PROPERTY SANCTION OR PRIVATE SETTLEMENT (28) JMH	0.89 OF 9	141	TILT TOWARD BEING THOSE WHERE THE LEVEL OF SOCIAL SANCTION IS PUBLIC PROPERTY SANCTION OR PRIVATE SETTLEMENT, RATHER THAN PUBLIC CORPOREAL SANCTION (26) JMH	0.64 OF 14	8 5 1 9 XSQ= 4.33 PHI= 0.434 EP = 0.0288
142	IN ALL CASES ARE THOSE WHERE THE LEVEL OF SOCIAL SANCTION IS PUBLIC CORPOREAL SANCTION OR PUBLIC PROPERTY SANCTION, RATHER THAN PRIVATE SETTLEMENT (38) JMH	1.00 OF 9	142	TILT TOWARD BEING THOSE WHERE THE LEVEL OF SOCIAL SANCTION IS PRIVATE SETTLEMENT, RATHER THAN PUBLIC CORPOREAL SANCTION OR PUBLIC PROPERTY SETTLEMENT (16) JMH	0.50 OF 14	9 7 0 7 XSQ= 4.32 PHI= 0.434 EP = 0.0189
183	IN ALL CASES ARE THOSE WHERE THE LARGEST NON-COGNATIC KIN GROUP IS SMALLER THAN A MOEITY, I. E., A PHRATRY OR SIB OR LINEAGE (218)	1.00 OF 21	183	LEAN LESS TOWARD BEING THOSE WHERE THE LARGEST NON-COGNATIC KIN GROUP IS SMALLER THAN A MOEITY, I. E., A PHRATRY OR SIB OR LINEAGE (218)	0.62 OF 37	0 14 21 23 XSQ= 8.51 PHI= -0.383 XP = 0.0035
186	LEAN TOWARD BEING THOSE WHERE THE KIN GROUP IS EXCLUSIVELY PATRILINEAL (150)	0.53 OF 30	186	LEAN TOWARD BEING THOSE WHERE THE KIN GROUP IS OTHER THAN EXCLUSIVELY PATRILINEAL (250)	0.79 OF 67	16 14 14 53 XSQ= 8.74 PHI= 0.300 XP = 0.0031
190	DRIFT MORE TOWARD BEING THOSE WHERE THE KIN GROUP IS PATRILINEAL OR DOUBLE-DESCENT, RATHER THAN MATRILINEAL (186)	0.90 OF 21	190	DRIFT LESS TOWARD BEING THOSE WHERE THE KIN GROUP IS PATRILINEAL OR DOUBLE-DESCENT, RATHER THAN MATRILINEAL (186)	0.63 OF 35	19 22 2 13 XSQ= 3.79 PHI= 0.260 XP = 0.0514

234	TILT TOWARD BEING THOSE WHERE THE COUSIN TERMINOLOGY IS OF ESKIMO OR HAWAIIAN TYPE, RATHER THAN CROW, OMAHA, OR IROQUOIS TYPE (170)	0.74 OF 23	234	TILT TOWARD BEING THOSE WHERE THE COUSIN TERMINOLOGY IS OF CROW, OMAHA, OR IROQUOIS TYPE, RATHER THAN ESKIMO OR HAWAIIAN TYPE (152)	0.55 OF 58	6 32 17 26 XSQ= 4.49 PHI= -0.235 XP = 0.0341
236	TILT TOWARD BEING THOSE WHERE THE FAMILY IS OF AN EXTENDED TYPE, RATHER THAN AN INDEPENDENT TYPE (213)	0.70 OF 30	236	TILT TOWARD BEING THOSE WHERE THE FAMILY IS OF AN INDEPENDENT TYPE, RATHER THAN AN EXTENDED TYPE (185)	0.55 OF 67	21 30 9 37 XSQ= 4.32 PHI= 0.211 XP = 0.0376
241	DRIFT LESS TOWARD BEING THOSE WHERE THE FAMILY, IF EXTENDED, IS LARGE OR SMALL, RATHER THAN STEM (187)	0.71 OF 21	241	DRIFT MORE TOWARD BEING THOSE WHERE THE FAMILY, IF EXTENDED, IS LARGE OR SMALL, RATHER THAN STEM (187)	0.93 OF 30	15 28 6 2 XSQ= 2.98 PHI= -0.242 XP = 0.0844
278	DRIFT TOWARD BEING THOSE WHERE PROPERTY RIGHTS IN WOMEN ARE PRESENT (8) LWS	0.75 OF 4	278	DRIFT TOWARD BEING THOSE WHERE PROPERTY RIGHTS IN WOMEN ARE UNIMPORTANT OR ABSENT (14) LWS	0.89 OF 9	3 1 1 8 XSQ= 2.73 PHI= 0.458 EP = 0.0517
282	IN ALL CASES ARE THOSE WHERE THE STRENGTH OF DESIRE FOR CHILDREN IS HIGH (16) BCA	1.00 OF 5	282	LEAN TOWARD BEING THOSE WHERE THE STRENGTH OF DESIRE FOR CHILDREN IS LOW OR ABSENT (20) BCA	0.82 OF 11	5 2 0 9 XSQ= 6.32 PHI= 0.629 EP = 0.0048
295	DRIFT TOWARD BEING THOSE WHERE THE SEVERITY OF PUNISHMENT FOR ABORTION IS HIGH (11) BCA	0.75 OF 4	295	DRIFT TOWARD BEING THOSE WHERE THE SEVERITY OF PUNISHMENT FOR ABORTION IS LOW OR ABSENT (12) BCA	0.86 OF 7	3 1 1 6 XSQ= 1.86 PHI= 0.411 EP = 0.0879
313	DRIFT TOWARD BEING THOSE WHERE AGGRESSION SOCIALIZATION ANXIETY IS HIGH (26) W-C	0.71 OF 7	313	DRIFT TOWARD BEING THOSE WHERE AGGRESSION SOCIALIZATION ANXIETY IS LOW (28) W-C	0.76 OF 17	5 4 2 13 XSQ= 3.03 PHI= 0.355 EP = 0.0606
314	LEAN TOWARD BEING THOSE WHERE THE INCIDENCE OF MOTHER-CHILD HOUSEHOLDS IS HIGH (19) W-D,S	0.50 OF 10	314	LEAN TOWARD BEING THOSE WHERE THE INCIDENCE OF MOTHER-CHILD HOUSEHOLDS IS LOW (61) W-D,S	0.96 OF 23	5 1 5 22 XSQ= 6.94 PHI= 0.458 EP = 0.0054
318	TILT TOWARD BEING THOSE WHERE THE OVERALL INDULGENCE OF THE INFANT IS LOW (31) B-B-C	0.86 OF 7	318	TILT TOWARD BEING THOSE WHERE THE OVERALL INDULGENCE OF THE INFANT IS HIGH (40) B-B-C	0.71 OF 21	1 15 6 6 XSQ= 4.86 PHI= -0.417 EP = 0.0228

320	DRIFT TOWARD BEING THOSE WHERE THE DEGREE OF REDUCTION OF THE INFANT'S DRIVES IS LOW (24) B-B-C	0.71 OF 7	320	DRIFT TOWARD BEING THOSE WHERE THE DEGREE OF REDUCTION OF THE INFANT'S DRIVES IS HIGH (45) B-B-C	0.70 OF 20	2 14 5 6 XSQ= 2.17 PHI= -0.283 EP = 0.0840
321	DRIFT TOWARD BEING THOSE WHERE THE IMMEDIACY OF REDUCTION OF THE INFANT'S DRIVES IS LOW (25) B-B-C	0.83 OF 6	321	DRIFT TOWARD BEING THOSE WHERE THE IMMEDIACY OF REDUCTION OF THE INFANT'S DRIVES IS HIGH (35) B-B-C	0.63 OF 19	1 12 5 7 XSQ= 2.31 PHI= -0.304 EP = 0.0730
324	DRIFT TOWARD BEING THOSE WHERE THE PAIN INFLICTED ON THE INFANT BY THE NURTURANT AGENT IS HIGH (34) B-B-C	0.86 OF 7	324	DRIFT TOWARD BEING THOSE WHERE THE PAIN INFLICTED ON THE INFANT BY THE NURTURANT AGENT IS LOW OR NEGLIGIBLE (32) B-B-C	0.60 OF 20	6 8 1 12 XSQ= 2.70 PHI= 0.316 EP = 0.0768
326	DRIFT TOWARD BEING THOSE WHERE THE INFERRED TRANSITION ANXIETY BETWEEN INFANCY AND CHILDHOOD IS HIGH (32) B-B-C	0.71 OF 7	326	DRIFT TOWARD BEING THOSE WHERE THE INFERRED TRANSITION ANXIETY BETWEEN INFANCY AND CHILDHOOD IS LOW (35) B-B-C	0.72 OF 18	5 5 2 13 XSQ= 2.39 PHI= 0.309 EP = 0.0752
334	IN ALL CASES ARE THOSE WHERE THE INDULGENCE OF THE CHILD IS LOW (38) B-B-C	1.00 OF 7	334	LEAN TOWARD BEING THOSE WHERE THE INDULGENCE OF THE CHILD IS HIGH (40) B-B-C	0.65 OF 23	0 15 7 8 XSQ= 6.71 PHI= -0.473 EP = 0.0063
336	TILT TOWARD BEING THOSE WHERE THE TOTAL POSITIVE PRESSURE TOWARD DEVELOPING RESPONSIBLE BEHAVIOR IN THE CHILD IS HIGH (43) B-B-C	0.86 OF 7	336	TILT TOWARD BEING THOSE WHERE THE TOTAL POSITIVE PRESSURE TOWARD DEVELOPING RESPONSIBLE BEHAVIOR IN THE CHILD IS LOW (32) B-B-C	0.71 OF 21	6 6 1 15 XSQ= 4.86 PHI= 0.417 EP = 0.0228
337	LEAN TOWARD BEING THOSE WHERE THE CHILD'S INFERRED ANXIETY OVER NON-PERFORMANCE OF RESPONSIBLE BEHAVIOR IS HIGH (38) B-B-C	0.86 OF 7	337	LEAN TOWARD BEING THOSE WHERE THE CHILD'S INFERRED ANXIETY OVER NON-PERFORMANCE OF RESPONSIBLE BEHAVIOR IS LOW (35) B-B-C	0.75 OF 20	6 5 1 15 XSQ= 5.60 PHI= 0.455 EP = 0.0087
338	IN ALL CASES ARE THOSE WHERE THE CHILD'S INFERRED ANXIETY OVER PERFORMANCE OF RESPONSIBLE BEHAVIOR IS HIGH (44) B-B-C	1.00 OF 7	338	LEAN TOWARD BEING THOSE WHERE THE CHILD'S INFERRED ANXIETY OVER PERFORMANCE OF RESPONSIBLE BEHAVIOR IS LOW (29) B-B-C	0.60 OF 20	7 8 0 12 XSQ= 5.33 PHI= 0.444 EP = 0.0081
339	TILT TOWARD BEING THOSE WHERE THE CHILD'S INFERRED CONFLICT REGARDING RESPONSIBLE BEHAVIOR IS HIGH (31) B-B-C	0.86 OF 7	339	TILT TOWARD BEING THOSE WHERE THE CHILD'S INFERRED CONFLICT REGARDING RESPONSIBLE BEHAVIOR IS LOW (42) B-B-C	0.70 OF 20	6 6 1 14 XSQ= 4.46 PHI= 0.406 EP = 0.0237

345	DRIFT TCWARD BEING THOSE 0.71 OF 7 WHERE THE CHILD'S INFERREC ANXIETY OVER NCN-PERFORMANCE OF SELF-RELIANT BEHAVIOR IS HIGH (37) B-B-C	345	DRIFT TOWARD BEING THOSE 0.68 OF 22 WHERE THE CHILD'S INFERRED ANXIETY OVER NON-PERFORMANCE OF SELF-RELIANT BEHAVIOR IS LOW (39) B-B-C	5 7 2 15 XSQ= 2.00 PHI= 0.262 EP = 0.0920
346	TILT TCWARD BEING THOSE 0.86 OF 7 WHERE THE CHILD'S INFERREC ANXIETY OVER PERFCRMANCE CF SELF-RELIANT BEHAVIOR IS HIGH (37) B-B-C	346	TILT TOWARD BEING THOSE 0.73 OF 22 WHERE THE CHILD'S INFERRED ANXIETY OVER PERFORMANCE OF SELF-RELIANT BEHAVIOR IS LOW (39) B-B-C	6 6 1 16 XSQ= 5.26 PHI= 0.426 EP = 0.0106
347	LEAN TOWARD BEING THOSE 0.86 OF 7 WHERE THE CHILD'S INFERREC CONFLICT REGARDING SELF-RELIANT BEHAVIOR IS HIGH (37) B-B-C	347	LEAN TOWARD BEING THOSE 0.77 OF 22 WHERE THE CHILD'S INFERRED CONFLICT REGARDING SELF-RELIANT BEHAVIOR IS LOW (39) B-B-C	6 5 1 17 XSQ= 6.47 PHI= 0.472 EP = 0.0055
350	LEAN TCWARD BEING THOSE 0.83 OF 6 WHERE THE CHILD'S INFERREC ANXIETY OVER PERFCRMANCE OF ACHIEVEMENT BEHAVIOR IS HIGH (34) B-B-C	350	LEAN TOWARD BEING THOSE 0.87 OF 15 WHERE THE CHILD'S INFERRED ANXIETY OVER PERFORMANCE OF ACHIEVEMENT BEHAVIOR IS LOW (26) B-B-C	5 2 1 13 XSQ= 6.56 PHI= 0.559 EP = 0.0055
351	TILT TCWARD BEING THOSE 0.67 OF 6 WHERE THE CHILD'S INFERREC CONFLICT REGARDING ACHIEVEMENT BEHAVIOR IS HIGH (26) B-B-C	351	TILT TOWARD BEING THOSE 0.93 OF 15 WHERE THE CHILD'S INFERRED CONFLICT REGARDING ACHIEVEMENT BEHAVIOR IS LOW (34) B-B-C	4 1 2 14 XSQ= 5.52 PHI= 0.513 EP = 0.0114
353	IN ALL CASES ARE THOSE 1.00 OF 6 WHERE THE CHILD'S INFERREC ANXIETY OVER NCN-PERFORMANCE CF OBEDIENT BEHAVIOR IS HIGH (42) B-B-C	353	LEAN TOWARD BEING THOSE 0.67 OF 21 WHERE THE CHILD-S INFERRED ANXIETY OVER NON-PERFORMANCE OF OBEDIENT BEHAVIOR IS LOW (32) B-B-C	6 7 0 14 XSQ= 5.85 PHI= 0.466 EP = 0.0058
354	IN ALL CASES ARE THOSE 1.00 OF 6 WHERE THE CHILD'S INFERREC ANXIETY OVER PERFCRMANCE CF CBEDIENT BEHAVIOR IS HIGH (36) B-B-C	354	TILT TOWARD BEING THOSE 0.62 OF 21 WHERE THE CHILD'S INFERRED ANXIETY OVER PERFORMANCE OF OBEDIENT BEHAVICR IS LOW (37) B-B-C	6 8 0 13 XSQ= 4.90 PHI= 0.426 EP = 0.0159
355	IN ALL CASES ARE THCSE 1.00 OF 6 WHERE THE CHILD'S INFERREC CONFLICT REGARDING CBEDIENT BEHAVICR IS HIGH (35) B-B-C	355	LEAN TOWARD BEING THOSE 0.67 OF 21 WHERE THE CHILD'S INFERRED CONFLICT REGARDING OBEDIENT BEHAVIOR IS LOW (38) B-B-C	6 7 0 14 XSQ= 5.85 PHI= 0.466 EP = 0.0058
360	TILT TCWARD BEING THOSE 0.67 OF 3 WHERE ADOLESCENT PEER GRCUPS ARE PRESENT IN A SETTING OF WORK AND PUBLIC GATHERINGS AND LEISURE, CR AT LEAST CF PUBLIC GATHERINGS AND LEISURE (14) JKH	360	IN ALL CASES ARE THOSE 1.00 OF 10 WHERE ADOLESCENT PEER GRCUPS ARE PRESENT ONLY IN A SETTING CF LEISURE, OR ELSE ARE ABSENT (23) JKH	2 0 1 10 XSQ= 3.59 PHI= 0.525 EP = 0.0385

365	IN ALL CASES ARE THOSE WHERE THE TIME SPENT IN ADOLESCENT PEER GRCUP ACTIVITY IS HIGH OR HIGH-MEDIUM (30) JKH	1.00 OF 6	365	TILT TOWARD BEING THOSE WHERE THE TIME SPENT IN ADOLESCENT PEER GROUP ACTIVITY IS LOW-MEDIUM OR LOW (15) JKH	0.54 OF 13	6 6 0 7 XSQ= 3.06 PHI= 0.402 EP = 0.0436
368	IN ALL CASES ARE THOSE WHERE DISSCCIATION OF THE SEXES AT ADCLESCENCE IS LOW (21) JKH	1.00 OF 5	368	TILT TOWARD BEING THOSE WHERE DISSOCIATION OF THE SEXES AT ADOLESCENCE IS HIGH OR MEDIUM (16) JKH	0.73 OF 11	0 8 5 3 XSQ= 4.65 PHI= -0.539 EP = 0.0256
377	TILT LESS TOWARD BEING THOSE WHERE MALE GENITAL MUTILATION IS ABSENT (242)	0.61 OF 28	377	TILT MORE TOWARD BEING THOSE WHERE MALE GENITAL MUTILATION IS ABSENT (242)	0.83 OF 66	11 11 17 55 XSQ= 4.42 PHI= 0.217 XP = 0.0355
380	IN ALL CASES ARE THOSE WHERE SEGREGATICN CF GIRLS AT MENARCHE IS PRESENT (35) F-B	1.00 OF 5	380	TILT TOWARD BEING THOSE WHERE SEGREGATION OF GIRLS AT MENARCHE IS ABSENT (20) F-B	0.59 OF 17	5 7 0 10 XSQ= 3.28 PHI= 0.386 EP = 0.0396
391	TILT TOWARD BEING THOSE WHERE PREMARITAL SEX RELATIONS ARE STRONGLY PUNISHED AND IN FACT RARE, OR WEAKLY PUNISHED AND IN FACT NCT RARE (89) JTW,EA	0.70 OF 23	391	TILT TOWARD BEING THOSE WHERE PREMARITAL SEX RELATIONS ARE PUNISHED ONLY IF PREGNANCY RESULTS, OR FREELY PERMITTED (90) JTW,EA	0.61 OF 44	16 17 7 27 XSQ= 4.61 PHI= 0.262 XP = 0.0318
392	TILT TOWARD BEING THOSE WHERE PREMARITAL SEX RELATIONS ARE STRONGLY PUNISHED AND IN FACT RARE, OR WEAKLY PUNISHED AND IN FACT NCT RARE, OR PUNISHED CNLY IF PREGNANCY RESULTS (112) JTW,EA	0.83 OF 23	392	TILT TOWARD BEING THOSE WHERE PREMARITAL SEX RELATICNS ARE FREELY PERMITTED (67) JTW,EA	0.50 OF 44	19 22 4 22 XSQ= 5.46 PHI= 0.285 XP = 0.0195
399	IN ALL CASES ARE THOSE WHERE INTENSITY OF CASTRATION ANXIETY IS HIGH (23) WNS	1.00 OF 3	399	DRIFT TOWARD BEING THOSE WHERE INTENSITY OF CASTRATION ANXIETY IS LOW (22) WNS	0.69 OF 13	3 4 0 9 XSQ= 2.35 PHI= 0.383 EP = 0.0625
400	IN ALL CASES ARE THOSE WHERE HOMCSEXUAL ACTIVITY IS PERMITTED (36) F-B	1.00 OF 7	400	TILT TOWARD BEING THOSE WHERE HOMOSEXUAL ACTIVITY IS PROHIBITED (22) F-B	0.59 OF 17	0 10 7 7 XSQ= 4.85 PHI= -0.449 EP = 0.0188
426	DRIFT TOWARD BEING THOSE WHERE A HIGH GOD IS PRESENT (156) GES,EA	0.67 OF 27	426	DRIFT TOWARD BEING THOSE WHERE A HIGH GOD IS ABSENT (104) GES,EA	0.56 OF 62	18 27 9 35 XSQ= 3.15 PHI= 0.188 XP = 0.0759

427	DRIFT TOWARD BEING THOSE WHERE A HIGH GOD, IF PRESENT, IS ACTIVE, RATHER THAN INACTIVE (87) GES,EA	0.78 OF	18	427	DRIFT TOWARD BEING THOSE WHERE A HIGH GOD, IF PRESENT, IS INACTIVE, RATHER THAN ACTIVE (69) GES,EA	0.56 OF	27	14 12 4 15 XSQ= 3.65 PHI= 0.285 XP = 0.0562
450	TILT TOWARD BEING THOSE WHERE THE OBSERVATION OF FCOD TABOOS IS LCW, RATHER THAN HIGH CR MEDIUM (26) JRL	0.67 OF	12	450	TILT TOWARD BEING THOSE WHERE THE OBSERVATION OF FOOD TABOOS IS HIGH OR MEDIUM, RATHER THAN LOW (60) JRL	0.77 OF	22	4 17 8 5 XSQ= 4.62 PHI= -0.369 EP = 0.0248
468	DRIFT TOWARD BEING THOSE WHERE CONTACT WITH OTHER CULTURES IS FREQUENT, RATHER THAN REGULAR OR IRREGULAR (17) JMH	0.56 OF	9	468	DRIFT TOWARD BEING THOSE WHERE CONTACT WITH OTHER CULTURES IS REGULAR OR IRREGULAR, RATHER THAN FREQUENT (37) JMH	0.86 OF	14	5 2 4 12 XSQ= 2.67 PHI= 0.341 EP = 0.0657
470	TILT TOWARD BEING THOSE WHERE INNCVATIONS ARE GENERALLY ACCEPTED (21) JMH	0.67 OF	9	470	TILT TOWARD BEING THOSE WHERE INNOVATIONS ARE ACCEPTED ONLY SELECTIVELY (33) JMH	0.86 OF	14	6 2 3 12 XSQ= 4.52 PHI= 0.443 EP = 0.0228

463 CULTURES WHERE GAMES OF STRATEGY, CHANCE, AND SKILL -- RATHER THAN STRATEGY AND SKILL ONLY -- ARE PRESENT (30) R-A-B,EA	463 CULTURES WHERE GAMES OF STRATEGY AND SKILL ONLY -- RATHER THAN STRATEGY, CHANCE, AND SKILL -- ARE PRESENT (19) R-A-B,EA

BACKGROUND ON PAGE 169

SUBJECT ONLY

30 IN LEFT COLUMN

AMERICANS	AZANDE	AZTEC	BASSERI	CHAGGA	CZECHS	DARD	EGYPTIANS	FON	HAWAIIANS
INCA	IRISH	JAPANESE	KAZAK	KOREANS	KUBA	MENDE	MIN CHINESE	NAMA	OKINAWANS
SERBS	SYRIANS	TARAHUMARA	THAI	THONGA	VENDA	VIETNAMESE	WOLOF	YAKUT	ZUNI

19 IN RIGHT COLUMN

ALBANIANS	ASHANTI	BURUSHO	GANDA	ILA	JUKUN	KIKUYU	LAKHER	LAMBA	LUO
MASAI	MBUNDU	NYAKYUSA	NYORO	RUNDI	TANALA	TIV	WOLEAIANS	YAO	

140 EXCLUDED BECAUSE IRRELEVANT

ABIPON	ABOR	AINU	ALACALUF	ANDAMANESE	APINAYE	ARANDA	ARAUCANIANS	ATSUGEWI	AYMARA
BACAIRI	BHIL	BHUIYA	BORORO	BUNLAP	CADUVEO	CAGABA	CAMAYURA	CARIB	CAYAPA
CHENCHU	CHEROKEE	CHEYENNE	CHIR-APACHE	CHIRIGUANO	CHOROTI	CHORTI	CHUKCHEE	COORG	COPR ESKIMO
CREE	CREEK	CROW	CUNA	DIEGUENO	DIERI	ELLICE	EYAK	FANG	GARO
GOAJIRO	GROS VENTRE	HAIDA	HASINAI	HUICHOL	HUKUNDIKA	HURON	HUTSUL	IBAN	INGALIK
JEMEZ	JIVARO	KASKA	KATAB	KERAKI	KHASI	KORYAK	KUNG	KURTATCHI	KUTENAI
KWAKIUTL	LAPPS	LAU	LEPCHA	LESU	LHOTA NAGA	MACASSARESE	MANGAIANS	MANIHIKI	MANUS
MAORI	MARICOPA	MARQUESANS	MARSHALLESE	MATACO	MAYA	MIAMI	MISKITO	MIWOK	MOSSI
MOTA	MURNGIN	NABESNA	NATCHEZ	NAVAHO	NICOBARESE	NOMLAKI	NUNIVAK	OMAHA	ONA
PAEZ	PAIWAN	PALAUANS	PAPAGO	PUKAPUKA	RWALA	SAGADA	SAMOANS	SANPOIL	SEMANG
SENIANG	SHERENTE	SIRIONO	SIWANS	SOMALI	TALAMANCA	TALLENSI	TAOS	TAPIRAPE	TAREUMIUT
TEHUELCHE	TENETEHARA	TENINO	TIKOPIA	TIMBIRA	TIWI	TODA	TOLOWA	TROBRIAND	TRUKESE
TRUMAI	TUCANO	TUCUNA	TUPINAMBA	TWANA	ULAWANS	UTE	VEDDA	WANTOAT	WAPISHANA
WARRAU	WASHO	WITOTO	WOGEO	YAGUA	YAHGAN	YARURO	YOKUTS	YUKI	YUROK

211 EXCLUDED BECAUSE UNASCERTAINED

3	LEAN TOWARD BEING THOSE LOCATED OUTSIDE OF AFRICA (320)	0.73 OF 30	3	LEAN TOWARD BEING THOSE LOCATED IN AFRICA (80)	0.74 OF 19	8 14 22 5 XSQ= 8.58 PHI= -0.418 XP = 0.0034
15	LEAN TOWARD BEING THOSE WHERE THE LATITUDE IS TWENTY DEGREES OR GREATER (183)	0.67 OF 30	15	LEAN TOWARD BEING THOSE WHERE THE LATITUDE IS LESS THAN TWENTY DEGREES (217)	0.79 OF 19	20 4 10 15 XSQ= 7.95 PHI= 0.403 XP = 0.0048

16	LEAN TOWARD BEING THOSE 0.83 OF 30 WHERE THE LATITUDE IS TEN DEGREES OR GREATER (277)	16	LEAN TOWARD BEING THOSE 0.58 OF 19 WHERE THE LATITUDE IS LESS THAN TEN DEGREES (123)	25 8 5 11 XSQ= 7.21 PHI= 0.384 XP = 0.0072
48	TILT TOWARD BEING THOSE 0.90 OF 10 WHERE THE FOOD SUPPLY IS NOT SECURE, AND FOOD SHORTAGES ARE FREQUENT OR ANNUAL (41) MGW	48	TILT TOWARD BEING THOSE 0.70 OF 10 WHERE THE FOOD SUPPLY IS SECURE, AND FOOD SHORTAGES ARE RARE OR OCCASIONAL (38) MGW	1 7 9 3 XSQ= 5.21 PHI= -0.510 EP = 0.0198
73	TILT TOWARD BEING THOSE 0.83 OF 24 WHERE WEAVING IS PRESENT (118)	73	TILT TOWARD BEING THOSE 0.53 OF 17 WHERE WEAVING IS ABSENT (130)	20 8 4 9 XSQ= 4.49 PHI= 0.331 XP = 0.0341
79	LEAN LESS TOWARD BEING THOSE 0.54 OF 28 WHERE NO CITY IS PRESENT (201)	79	IN ALL CASES ARE THOSE 1.00 OF 15 WHERE NO CITY IS PRESENT (201)	13 0 15 15 XSQ= 7.90 PHI= 0.429 XP = 0.0049
80	TILT TOWARD BEING THOSE 0.54 OF 28 WHERE A CITY OR TOWN IS PRESENT (39)	80	TILT TOWARD BEING THOSE 0.87 OF 15 WHERE NO CITY OR TOWN IS PRESENT (185)	15 2 13 13 XSQ= 5.04 PHI= 0.342 XP = 0.0248
84	TILT TOWARD BEING THOSE 0.56 OF 25 WHERE THE LEVEL OF POLITICAL INTEGRATION IS THE LARGE STATE (42) GPM	84	TILT TOWARD BEING THOSE 0.82 OF 17 WHERE THE LEVEL OF POLITICAL INTEGRATION IS THE LITTLE STATE, THE MINIMAL STATE, THE AUTONOMOUS COMMUNITY, OR THE FAMILY (262) GPM	14 3 11 14 XSQ= 4.69 PHI= 0.334 XP = 0.0304
85	LEAN TOWARD BEING THOSE 0.84 OF 25 WHERE THE LEVEL OF POLITICAL INTEGRATION IS THE LARGE STATE, OR THE LITTLE STATE (70) GPM	85	LEAN TOWARD BEING THOSE 0.65 OF 17 WHERE THE LEVEL OF POLITICAL INTEGRATION IS THE MINIMAL STATE, THE AUTONOMOUS COMMUNITY, OR THE FAMILY (234) GPM	21 6 4 11 XSQ= 8.44 PHI= 0.448 XP = 0.0037
88	DRIFT TOWARD BEING THOSE 0.58 OF 24 WHERE, IF A HEADMANSHIP IS PRESENT, SUCCESSION IS NON-HEREDITARY (106)	88	DRIFT TOWARD BEING THOSE 0.73 OF 15 WHERE, IF A HEADMANSHIP IS PRESENT, SUCCESSION IS HEREDITARY (165)	14 4 10 11 XSQ= 2.56 PHI= 0.256 EP = 0.0978
90	IN ALL CASES ARE THOSE 1.00 OF 10 WHERE, IF A HEREDITARY HEADMANSHIP IS PRESENT, SUCCESSION IS PATRILINEAL, RATHER THAN MATRILINEAL (127)	90	DRIFT LESS TOWARD BEING THOSE 0.64 OF 11 WHERE, IF A HEREDITARY HEADMANSHIP IS PRESENT, SUCCESSION IS PATRILINEAL, RATHER THAN MATRILINEAL (127)	10 7 0 4 XSQ= 2.44 PHI= 0.341 EP = 0.0902

95	TILT TOWARD BEING THOSE 0.80 OF 30 WHERE THE HIERARCHY OF NATIONAL JURISDICTION HAS FOUR, THREE, OR TWO LEVELS (76) GES,EA	95	TILT TOWARD BEING THOSE 0.53 OF 19 WHERE THE HIERARCHY OF NATIONAL JURISDICTION HAS ONE OR NO LEVELS (254) GES,EA	24 9 6 10 XSQ= 4.25 PHI= 0.294 XP = 0.0393
102	LEAN MORE TOWARD BEING THOSE 0.97 OF 30 WHERE CLASS STRATIFICATION IS PRESENT (203)	102	LEAN LESS TOWARD BEING THOSE 0.63 OF 19 WHERE CLASS STRATIFICATION IS PRESENT (203)	29 12 1 7 XSQ= 7.27 PHI= 0.385 XP = 0.0070
184	DRIFT LESS TOWARD BEING THOSE 0.71 OF 21 WHERE THE LARGEST NON-COGNATIC KIN GROUP IS SMALLER THAN A PHRATRY, I. E. A SIB OR LINEAGE (175)	184	DRIFT MORE TOWARD BEING THOSE 0.94 OF 18 WHERE THE LARGEST NON-COGNATIC KIN GROUP IS SMALLER THAN A PHRATRY, I. E. A SIB OR LINEAGE (175)	6 1 15 17 XSQ= 2.10 PHI= 0.232 EP = 0.0985
188	DRIFT LESS TOWARD BEING THOSE 0.70 OF 30 WHERE THE KIN GROUP IS OTHER THAN EXCLUSIVELY COGNATIC (252)	188	DRIFT MORE TOWARD BEING THOSE 0.95 OF 19 WHERE THE KIN GROUP IS OTHER THAN EXCLUSIVELY COGNATIC (252)	9 1 21 18 XSQ= 2.99 PHI= 0.247 XP = 0.0837
192	DRIFT LESS TOWARD BEING THOSE 0.77 OF 30 OTHER THAN WHERE THE ONLY KIN GROUP PRESENT IS A KINDRED OR ELSE BILATERAL DESCENT IS INFERRED (289)	192	IN ALL CASES ARE THOSE 1.00 OF 19 OTHER THAN WHERE THE ONLY KIN GROUP PRESENT IS A KINDRED OR ELSE BILATERAL DESCENT IS INFERRED (289)	7 0 23 19 XSQ= 3.44 PHI= 0.265 XP = 0.0636
234	LEAN TOWARD BEING THOSE 0.74 OF 23 WHERE THE COUSIN TERMINOLOGY IS OF ESKIMO OR HAWAIIAN TYPE, RATHER THAN CROW, OMAHA, OR IROQUOIS TYPE (170)	234	LEAN TOWARD BEING THOSE 0.71 OF 17 WHERE THE COUSIN TERMINOLOGY IS OF CROW, OMAHA, OR IROQUOIS TYPE, RATHER THAN ESKIMO OR HAWAIIAN TYPE (152)	6 12 17 5 XSQ= 6.13 PHI= -0.391 EP = 0.0095
242	DRIFT LESS TOWARD BEING THOSE 0.70 OF 30 WHERE MARRIAGE IS COMMONLY OR OCCASIONALLY POLYGYNOUS, RATHER THAN MONOGAMOUS (314)	242	DRIFT MORE TOWARD BEING THOSE 0.95 OF 19 WHERE MARRIAGE IS COMMONLY OR OCCASIONALLY POLYGYNOUS, RATHER THAN MONOGAMOUS (314)	21 18 9 1 XSQ= 2.99 PHI= -0.247 XP = 0.0837
372	DRIFT TOWARD BEING THOSE 0.89 OF 9 WHERE MALE INITIATION RITES ARE PRESENT (48) ASA	372	DRIFT TOWARD BEING THOSE 0.55 OF 11 WHERE MALE INITIATION RITES ARE ABSENT (63) ASA	8 5 1 6 XSQ= 2.42 PHI= 0.348 EP = 0.0703
403	TILT TOWARD BEING THOSE 0.86 OF 7 WHERE EXPLANATIONS OF ILLNESS OF AN ANAL NATURE ARE ABSENT (38) W-C	403	TILT TOWARD BEING THOSE 0.83 OF 6 WHERE EXPLANATIONS OF ILLNESS OF AN ANAL NATURE ARE PRESENT (23) W-C	1 5 6 1 XSQ= 3.73 PHI= -0.536 EP = 0.0291

427	LEAN TCWARD BEING THOSE WHERE A HIGH GCC, IF PRESENT, IS ACTIVE, RATHER THAN INACTIVE (87) GES,EA	0.78 OF 18	427	LEAN TOWARD BEING THOSE WHERE A HIGH GOD, IF PRESENT, IS INACTIVE, RATHER THAN ACTIVE (69) GES,EA	0.73 OF 15	14 4 4 11 XSQ= 6.68 PHI= 0.450 EP = 0.0053
450	TILT TOWARD BEING THOSE WHERE THE CBSERVATION CF FCOD TABOOS IS LCW, RATHER THAN HIGH CR MEDIUM (26) JRL	0.67 OF 12	450	TILT TOWARD BEING THOSE WHERE THE OBSERVATION OF FCOD TABOOS IS HIGH OR MEDIUM, RATHER THAN LOW (60) JRL	0.88 OF 8	4 7 8 1 XSQ= 3.71 PHI= -0.431 EP = 0.0281

464 CULTURES
WHERE GAMES OF
STRATEGY, CHANCE, AND SKILL -- RATHER THAN
CHANCE AND SKILL ONLY --
ARE PRESENT (30) R-A-B,EA

464 CULTURES
WHERE GAMES OF
CHANCE AND SKILL ONLY -- RATHER THAN
STRATEGY, CHANCE, AND SKILL --
ARE PRESENT (51) R-A-B,EA

BACKGROUND ON PAGE 169

SUBJECT ONLY

30 IN LEFT CCLUMN

AMERICANS	AZANDE	AZTEC	BASSERI	CHAGGA	CZECHS	DARD	EGYPTIANS	FON	HAWAIIANS
INCA	IRISH	JAPANESE	KAZAK	KOREANS	KUBA	MENDE	MIN CHINESE	NAMA	OKINAWANS
SERBS	SYRIANS	TARAHUMARA	THAI	THONGA	VENDA	VIETNAMESE	WOLOF	YAKUT	ZUNI

51 IN RIGHT CCLUMN

ARAUCANIANS	ATSUGEWI	AYMARA	CHEROKEE	CHEYENNE	CHIR-APACHE	CHIRIGUANO	CHCROTI	CHUKCHEE	COPR ESKIMO
CREE	CREEK	CRCW	DIEGUENO	EYAK	GROS VENTRE	HAIDA	HASINAI	HUKUNDIKA	HURON
JEMEZ	KASKA	KUTENAI	KWAKIUTL	MARICOPA	MATACO	MAYA	MIAMI	MIWCK	NABESNA
NAVAHO	NCMLAKI	OMAHA	PALAUANS	PAPAGO	SAMOANS	SANPOIL	TALLENSI	TAOS	TAREUMIUT
TEHUELCHE	TENINC	TCLOWA	TRUKESE	TWANA	ULAWANS	UTE	WASHO	YOKUTS	YUKI
YURCK									

108 EXCLUDED BECAUSE IRRELEVANT

ABIPCN	ABCR	AINU	ALACALUF	ALBANIANS	ANDAMANESE	APINAYE	ARANDA	ASHANTI	BACAIRI
BHIL	BHUIYA	BORCRC	BUNLAP	BURUSHO	CADUVEO	CAGABA	CAMAYURA	CARIB	CAYAPA
CHENCHU	CHCRTI	CCCRG	CUNA	DIERI	ELLICE	FANG	GANDA	GARO	GOAJIRO
HUICHCL	HUTSUL	IBAN	ILA	INGALIK	JIVARO	JUKUN	KATAB	KERAKI	KHASI
KIKUYU	KORYAK	KUNG	KURTATCHI	LAKHER	LAMBA	LAPPS	LAU	LEPCHA	LESU
LHOTA NAGA	LUC	MACASSARESE	MANGAIANS	MANIHIKI	MANUS	MAORI	MARQUESANS	MARSHALLESE	MASAI
MBUNDU	MISKITO	MOSSI	MOTA	MURNGIN	NATCHEZ	NICCBARESE	NUNIVAK	NYAKYUSA	NYORO
ONA	PAEZ	PAIWAN	PUKAPUKA	RUNDI	RWALA	SAGADA	SEMANG	SENIANG	SHERENTE
SIRIONO	SIWANS	SOMALI	TALAMANCA	TANALA	TAPIRAPE	TENETEHARA	TIKOPIA	TIMBIRA	TIV
TIWI	TODA	TRCBRIAND	TRUMAI	TUCANO	TUCUNA	TUPINAMBA	VEDDA	WANTOAT	WAPISHANA
WARRAU	WITCTC	WCGEC	WOLEAIANS	YAGUA	YAHGAN	YAO	YARURO		

211 EXCLUDED BECAUSE UNASCERTAINEC

---

3 LEAN LESS TOWARD BEING THCSE 0.73 OF 30
LCCATED OUTSIDE OF
AFRICA (320)

3 LEAN MORE TOWARD BEING THOSE 0.98 OF 51
LOCATED OUTSIDE OF
AFRICA (320)

8	1
22	50
XSQ=	9.31
PHI=	0.339
XP =	0.0023

4 LEAN LESS TOWARC BEING THCSE 0.77 OF 30
LOCATED OUTSIDE OF
THE CIRCUM-MEDITERRANEAN (355)

4 IN ALL CASES ARE THOSE 1.00 OF 51
LOCATED OUTSIDE OF
THE CIRCUM-MEDITERRANEAN (355)

7	0
23	51
XSQ=	10.24
PHI=	0.356
XP =	0.0014

5	TEND LESS TO BE THOSE LOCATED OUTSIDE OF EAST EURASIA (330)	0.67 OF 30	5	TEND MORE TO BE THOSE LOCATED OUTSIDE OF EAST EURASIA (330)	0.98 OF 51	10 1 20 50 XSQ= 13.28 PHI= 0.405 XP = 0.0003
8	TEND TO BE THOSE LOCATED OUTSIDE OF NORTH AMERICA (330)	0.90 OF 30	8	TEND TO BE THOSE LOCATED IN NORTH AMERICA (70)	0.75 OF 51	3 38 27 13 XSQ= 28.92 PHI= -0.598 XP = 0.0000
14	TEND TO BE THOSE WHERE THE LATITUDE IS LESS THAN THIRTY DEGREES (281)	0.60 OF 30	14	TEND TO BE THOSE WHERE THE LATITUDE IS THIRTY DEGREES OR GREATER (119)	0.80 OF 51	12 41 18 10 XSQ= 11.90 PHI= -0.383 XP = 0.0006
42	DRIFT LESS TOWARD BEING THOSE WHERE THE NATURAL ENVIRONMENT IS OTHER THAN TROPICAL OR SUB-TROPICAL RAIN FOREST, OR MONSOON FOREST (244) FWM	0.73 OF 30	42	DRIFT MORE TOWARD BEING THOSE WHERE THE NATURAL ENVIRONMENT IS OTHER THAN TROPICAL OR SUB-TROPICAL RAIN FOREST, OR MONSOON FOREST (244) FWM	0.90 OF 51	8 5 22 46 XSQ= 2.83 PHI= 0.187 XP = 0.0923
44	LEAN TOWARD BEING THOSE WHERE SETTLEMENTS ARE FIXED (222)	0.77 OF 30	44	LEAN TOWARD BEING THOSE WHERE SETTLEMENTS ARE NON-FIXED (110)	0.58 OF 50	23 21 7 29 XSQ= 7.76 PHI= 0.311 XP = 0.0053
46	TILT MORE TOWARD BEING THOSE OTHER THAN WHERE SETTLEMENTS ARE NON-FIXED AND MOVEMENT IS NOMADIC (260)	0.87 OF 30	46	TILT LESS TOWARD BEING THOSE OTHER THAN WHERE SETTLEMENTS ARE NON-FIXED AND MOVEMENT IS NOMADIC (260)	0.62 OF 50	4 19 26 31 XSQ= 4.43 PHI= -0.235 XP = 0.0353
51	TEND TO BE THOSE WHERE SUBSISTENCE IS PRIMARILY BY FOOD PRODUCTION -- I. E., AGRICULTURE OR HUSBANDRY -- RATHER THAN BY GATHERING (253)	0.90 OF 30	51	TEND TO BE THOSE WHERE SUBSISTENCE IS PRIMARILY BY FOOD GATHERING -- I. E., HUNTING, FISHING, OR COLLECTING -- RATHER THAN FOOD PRODUCTION (147)	0.80 OF 51	27 10 3 41 XSQ= 34.94 PHI= 0.657 XP = 0.
53	TILT TOWARD BEING THOSE WHERE FOOD PRODUCTION IS BY INTENSIVE AGRICULTURE, RATHER THAN BY SIMPLE AGRICULTURE OR INCIPIENT FOOD PRODUCTION (91)	0.70 OF 27	53	TILT TOWARD BEING THOSE WHERE FOOD PRODUCTION IS BY SIMPLE AGRICULTURE OR INCIPIENT FOOD PRODUCTION, RATHER THAN BY INTENSIVE AGRICULTURE (147)	0.72 OF 18	19 5 8 13 XSQ= 6.25 PHI= 0.373 XP = 0.0124
62	TEND TO BE THOSE WHERE HUSBANDRY OF SOME KIND IS PRESENT (228)	0.93 OF 30	62	TEND TO BE THOSE WHERE HUSBANDRY OF ANY KIND IS ABSENT (172)	0.61 OF 51	28 20 2 31 XSQ= 20.73 PHI= 0.506 XP = 0.0000

71	TEND TO BE THOSE WHERE METAL WORKING IS PRESENT (98)	0.91 OF 23	71	TEND TO BE THOSE WHERE METAL WORKING IS ABSENT (153)	0.84 OF 49	21 8 2 41 XSQ= 33.53 PHI= 0.682 XP = 0.
73	LEAN TOWARD BEING THOSE WHERE WEAVING IS PRESENT (118)	0.83 OF 24	73	LEAN TOWARD BEING THOSE WHERE WEAVING IS ABSENT (130)	0.59 OF 49	20 20 4 29 XSQ= 10.10 PHI= 0.372 XP = 0.0015
79	TEND LESS TO BE THCSE WHERE NO CITY IS PRESENT (201)	0.54 OF 28	79	IN ALL CASES ARE THOSE WHERE NO CITY IS PRESENT (201)	1.00 OF 33	13 0 15 33 XSQ= 16.80 PHI= 0.525 XP = 0.0000
80	TEND TO BE THOSE WHERE A CITY OR TOWN IS PRESENT (39)	0.54 OF 28	80	TEND TO BE THOSE WHERE NO CITY OR TOWN IS PRESENT (185)	0.97 OF 33	15 1 13 32 XSQ= 17.47 PHI= 0.535 XP = 0.0000
81	LEAN TOWARD BEING THOSE WHERE A CITY OR TOWN IS PRESENT, OR THE AVERAGE COMMUNITY SIZE IS 200 OR GREATER (89)	0.75 OF 28	81	LEAN TOWARD BEING THOSE WHERE NO CITY OR TOWN IS PRESENT, AND THE AVERAGE COMMUNITY SIZE IS SMALLER THAN 200 (135)	0.70 OF 33	21 10 7 23 XSQ= 10.39 PHI= 0.413 XP = 0.0013
82	IN ALL CASES ARE THOSE WHERE A CITY OR TOWN IS PRESENT, OR THE AVERAGE COMMUNITY SIZE IS FIFTY OR GREATER (178)	1.00 OF 28	82	TILT LESS TOWARD BEING THOSE WHERE A CITY OR TOWN IS PRESENT, OR THE AVERAGE COMMUNITY SIZE IS FIFTY OR GREATER (178)	0.79 OF 33	28 26 0 7 XSQ= 4.78 PHI= 0.280 XP = 0.0287
84	TEND TO BE THOSE WHERE THE LEVEL OF POLITICAL INTEGRATION IS THE LARGE STATE (42) GPM	0.56 OF 25	84	IN ALL CASES ARE THOSE WHERE THE LEVEL OF POLITICAL INTEGRATION IS THE LITTLE STATE, THE MINIMAL STATE, THE AUTONOMOUS COMMUNITY, OR THE FAMILY (262) GPM	1.00 OF 42	14 0 11 42 XSQ= 26.44 PHI= 0.628 XP = 0.0000
85	TEND TO BE THOSE WHERE THE LEVEL OF POLITICAL INTEGRATION IS THE LARGE STATE, OR THE LITTLE STATE (70) GPM	0.84 OF 25	85	TEND TO BE THOSE WHERE THE LEVEL OF POLITICAL INTEGRATION IS THE MINIMAL STATE, THE AUTONOMOUS COMMUNITY, OR THE FAMILY (234) GPM	0.95 OF 42	21 2 4 40 XSQ= 40.20 PHI= 0.775 XP = 0.
86	TEND TO BE THOSE WHERE THE LEVEL OF POLITICAL INTEGRATION IS THE LARGE STATE, THE LITTLE STATE, OR THE MINIMAL STATE (148) GPM	0.92 OF 25	86	TEND TO BE THOSE WHERE THE LEVEL OF POLITICAL INTEGRATION IS THE AUTONOMOUS COMMUNITY, OR THE FAMILY (156) GPM	0.67 OF 42	23 14 2 28 XSQ= 19.51 PHI= 0.540 XP = 0.0000

No.		Proportion	No.		Proportion	Statistics
94	TEND LESS TO BE THOSE WHERE THE HIERARCHY OF NATIONAL JURISDICTION HAS TWO, ONE, OR NO LEVELS (296) GES,EA	0.63 OF 30	94	IN ALL CASES ARE THOSE WHERE THE HIERARCHY OF NATIONAL JURISDICTION HAS TWO, ONE, OR NO LEVELS (296) GES,EA	1.00 OF 50	11 0 19 50 XSQ= 18.28 PHI= 0.478 XP = 0.0000
95	TEND TO BE THOSE WHERE THE HIERARCHY OF NATIONAL JURISDICTION HAS FOUR, THREE, OR TWO LEVELS (76) GES,EA	0.80 OF 30	95	TEND TO BE THOSE WHERE THE HIERARCHY OF NATIONAL JURISDICTION HAS ONE OR NO LEVELS (254) GES,EA	0.92 OF 50	24 4 6 46 XSQ= 39.62 PHI= 0.704 XP = 0.
96	TEND TO BE THOSE WHERE THE HIERARCHY OF NATIONAL JURISDICTION HAS FOUR, THREE, TWO OR ONE LEVEL (174) GES,EA	0.93 OF 30	96	TEND TO BE THOSE WHERE THE HIERARCHY OF NATIONAL JURISDICTION HAS NO LEVELS (156) GES,EA	0.66 OF 50	28 17 2 33 XSQ= 24.47 PHI= 0.553 XP = 0.0000
100	LEAN MORE TOWARD BEING THOSE WHERE HIERARCHIES ARE MORE COMPLEX THAN THE 'SIMPLEST,' I. E., MORE COMPLEX THAN TWO LOCAL LEVELS WITH NO NATIONAL LEVELS (267) GES,EA	0.97 OF 30	100	LEAN LESS TOWARD BEING THOSE WHERE HIERARCHIES ARE MORE COMPLEX THAN THE 'SIMPLEST,' I. E., MORE COMPLEX THAN TWO LOCAL LEVELS WITH NO NATIONAL LEVELS (267) GES,EA	0.70 OF 50	29 35 1 15 XSQ= 6.75 PHI= 0.290 XP = 0.0094
102	TEND TO BE THOSE WHERE CLASS STRATIFICATION IS PRESENT (203)	0.97 OF 30	102	TEND TO BE THOSE WHERE CLASS STRATIFICATION IS ABSENT (180)	0 58 OF 50	29 21 1 29 XSQ= 21.63 PHI= 0.520 XP = 0.0000
106	TEND TO BE THOSE WHERE CLASS STRATIFICATION, IF PRESENT, IS BASED ON SOMETHING OTHER THAN WEALTH (126)	0.86 OF 29	106	TEND TO BE THOSE WHERE CLASS STRATIFICATION, IF PRESENT, IS BASED ON WEALTH (77)	0.71 OF 21	4 15 25 6 XSQ= 14.81 PHI= -0.544 XP = 0.0001
107	LEAN LESS TOWARD BEING THOSE WHERE CLASS STRATIFICATION, IF PRESENT, IS BASED ON SOMETHING OTHER THAN OCCUPATIONAL STATUS (160)	0.55 OF 29	107	LEAN MORE TOWARD BEING THOSE WHERE CLASS STRATIFICATION, IF PRESENT, IS BASED ON SOMETHING OTHER THAN OCCUPATIONAL STATUS (160)	0.95 OF 21	13 1 16 20 XSQ= 7.81 PHI= 0.395 XP = 0.0052
109	TEND LESS TO BE THOSE WHERE CASTES ARE ABSENT (317)	0.75 OF 28	109	IN ALL CASES ARE THOSE WHERE CASTES ARE ABSENT (317)	1.00 OF 51	7 0 21 51 XSQ= 11.07 PHI= 0.374 XP = 0.0009
116	DRIFT TOWARD BEING THOSE WHERE OCCUPATIONAL SPECIALIZATION IS FULL-TIME, WHETHER OR NOT FOR SURPLUS PRODUCTION (20) JMH	0.67 OF 9	116	DRIFT TOWARD BEING THOSE WHERE OCCUPATIONAL SPECIALIZATION IS PART-TIME ONLY (34) JMH	0.82 OF 11	6 2 3 9 XSQ= 3.04 PHI= 0.390 EP = 0.0648

129	DRIFT TOWARD BEING THCSE WHERE WEAVING IS MAINLY DONE BY MALES (31)	0.50 OF 16	129	DRIFT TOWARD BEING THOSE WHERE WEAVING IS MAINLY DONE BY FEMALES (73)	0.84 OF 19	8 3 8 16 XSQ= 3.26 PHI= 0.305 EP = 0.0652
179	DRIFT MORE TOWARC BEING THOSE WHERE THE COMMUNITY IS OTHER THAN STRUCTURED ON A NON-CLAN BASIS ANC COMMONLY EXOGAMOUS (340)	0.97 OF 30	179	DRIFT LESS TOWARD BEING THOSE WHERE THE COMMUNITY IS OTHER THAN STRUCTURED ON A NON-CLAN BASIS AND COMMONLY EXOGAMOUS (340)	0.80 OF 50	1 10 29 40 XSQ= 3.10 PHI= -0.197 XP = 0.0783
183	IN ALL CASES ARE THOSE WHERE THE LARGEST NON-COGNATIC KIN GROUP IS SMALLER THAN A MOEITY, I. E., A PHRATRY OR SIB OR LINEAGE (218)	1.00 OF 21	183	TILT LESS TOWARD BEING THOSE WHERE THE LARGEST NON-COGNATIC KIN GROUP IS SMALLER THAN A MOEITY, I. E., A PHRATRY OR SIB OR LINEAGE (218)	0.71 OF 24	0 7 21 17 XSQ= 5.20 PHI= -0.340 XP = 0.0226
186	TILT TOWARD BEING THOSE WHERE THE KIN GROUP IS EXCLUSIVELY PATRILINEAL (150)	0.53 OF 30	186	TILT TOWARD BEING THOSE WHERE THE KIN GROUP IS OTHER THAN EXCLUSIVELY PATRILINEAL (250)	0.76 OF 51	16 12 14 39 XSQ= 6.16 PHI= 0.276 XP = 0.0131
188	DRIFT TOWARD BEING THOSE WHERE THE KIN GROUP IS OTHER THAN EXCLUSIVELY COGNATIC (252)	0.70 OF 30	188	DRIFT TOWARD BEING THOSE WHERE THE KIN GROUP IS EXCLUSIVELY COGNATIC (148)	0.53 OF 51	9 27 21 24 XSQ= 3.15 PHI= -0.197 XP = 0.0759
190	LEAN TOWARD BEING THOSE WHERE THE KIN GROUP IS PATRILINEAL OR DOUBLE-DESCENT, RATHER THAN MATRILINEAL (186)	0.90 OF 21	190	LEAN TOWARD BEING THOSE WHERE THE KIN GROUP IS MATRILINEAL, RATHER THAN PATRILINEAL OR DOUBLE-DESCENT (61)	0.52 OF 23	19 11 2 12 XSQ= 7.34 PHI= 0.409 XP = 0.0067
192	DRIFT MORE TOWARD BEING THOSE OTHER THAN WHERE THE ONLY KIN GROUP PRESENT IS A KINDRED OR ELSE BILATERAL DESCENT IS INFERRED (289)	0.77 OF 30	192	DRIFT LESS TOWARD BEING THOSE OTHER THAN WHERE THE ONLY KIN GROUP PRESENT IS A KINDRED OR ELSE BILATERAL DESCENT IS INFERRED (289)	0.55 OF 51	7 23 23 28 XSQ= 2.96 PHI= -0.191 XP = 0.0853
196	DRIFT TOWARD BEING THOSE WHERE INDIVIDUAL RIGHTS IN REAL PROPERTY, AND RULES FOR INHERITANCE, ARE PRESENT (194)	0.68 OF 28	196	DRIFT TOWARD BEING THOSE WHERE INDIVIDUAL RIGHTS IN REAL PROPERTY, OR RULES FOR INHERITANCE, ARE ABSENT (87)	0.59 OF 37	19 15 9 22 XSQ= 3.74 PHI= 0.240 XP = 0.0533
209	DRIFT MORE TOWARD BEING THOSE WHERE MARITAL RESIDENCE IS PATRILOCAL, VIRILOCAL, OR AVUNCULOCAL, RATHER THAN MATRILOCAL OR UXORILOCAL (270)	0.93 OF 27	209	DRIFT LESS TOWARD BEING THOSE WHERE MARITAL RESIDENCE IS PATRILOCAL, VIRILOCAL, OR AVUNCULOCAL, RATHER THAN MATRILOCAL OR UXORILOCAL (270)	0.71 OF 41	25 29 2 12 XSQ= 3.52 PHI= 0.227 XP = 0.0608

210	TILT MORE TOWARD BEING THOSE WHERE MARITAL RESIDENCE IS PATRILOCAL, RATHER THAN MATRILOCAL (169)	0.95 OF 19	210	TILT LESS TOWARD BEING THOSE WHERE MARITAL RESIDENCE IS PATRILOCAL, RATHER THAN MATRILOCAL (169)	0.60 OF 15	18 9 1 6 XSQ= 4.24 PHI= 0.353 EP = 0.0282
213	TILT LESS TOWARD BEING THOSE WHERE FIRST COUSIN MARRIAGE IS NOT PERMITTED (198)	0.52 OF 29	213	TILT MORE TOWARD BEING THOSE WHERE FIRST COUSIN MARRIAGE IS NOT PERMITTED (198)	0.78 OF 51	14 11 15 40 XSQ= 4.96 PHI= 0.249 XP = 0.0260
272	TILT TOWARD BEING THOSE WHERE THE DIVORCE RATE IS LOW (28) CA	0.75 OF 8	272	IN ALL CASES ARE THOSE WHERE THE DIVORCE RATE IS HIGH (29) CA	1.00 OF 5	2 5 6 0 XSQ= 4.27 PHI= -0.573 EP = 0.0210
282	IN ALL CASES ARE THOSE WHERE THE STRENGTH OF DESIRE FOR CHILDREN IS HIGH (16) BCA	1.00 OF 5	282	DRIFT TOWARD BEING THOSE WHERE THE STRENGTH OF DESIRE FOR CHILDREN IS LOW OR ABSENT (20) BCA	0.67 OF 6	5 2 0 4 XSQ= 2.75 PHI= 0.500 EP = 0.0606
314	DRIFT TOWARD BEING THOSE WHERE THE INCIDENCE OF MOTHER-CHILD HOUSEHOLDS IS HIGH (19) W-D,S	0.50 OF 10	314	DRIFT TOWARD BEING THOSE WHERE THE INCIDENCE OF MOTHER-CHILD HOUSEHOLDS IS LOW (61) W-D,S	0.86 OF 14	5 2 5 12 XSQ= 2.08 PHI= 0.294 EP = 0.0850
318	DRIFT TOWARD BEING THOSE WHERE THE OVERALL INDULGENCE OF THE INFANT IS LOW (31) B-B-C	0.86 OF 7	318	DRIFT TOWARD BEING THOSE WHERE THE OVERALL INDULGENCE OF THE INFANT IS HIGH (40) B-B-C	0.64 OF 14	1 9 6 5 XSQ= 2.89 PHI= -0.371 EP = 0.0635
324	DRIFT TOWARD BEING THOSE WHERE THE PAIN INFLICTED ON THE INFANT BY THE NURTURANT AGENT IS HIGH (34) B-B-C	0.86 OF 7	324	DRIFT TOWARD BEING THOSE WHERE THE PAIN INFLICTED ON THE INFANT BY THE NURTURANT AGENT IS LOW OR NEGLIGIBLE (32) B-B-C	0.62 OF 13	6 5 1 8 XSQ= 2.42 PHI= 0.348 EP = 0.0703
334	IN ALL CASES ARE THOSE WHERE THE INDULGENCE OF THE CHILD IS LOW (38) B-B-C	1.00 OF 7	334	TILT TOWARD BEING THOSE WHERE THE INDULGENCE OF THE CHILD IS HIGH (40) B-B-C	0.50 OF 14	0 7 7 7 XSQ= 3.24 PHI= -0.393 EP = 0.0468
339	DRIFT TOWARD BEING THOSE WHERE THE CHILD'S INFERRED CONFLICT REGARDING RESPONSIBLE BEHAVIOR IS HIGH (31) B-B-C	0.86 OF 7	339	DRIFT TOWARD BEING THOSE WHERE THE CHILD'S INFERRED CONFLICT REGARDING RESPONSIBLE BEHAVIOR IS LOW (42) B-B-C	0.57 OF 14	6 6 1 8 XSQ= 1.97 PHI= 0.306 EP = 0.0873

340	IN ALL CASES ARE THOSE 1.00 OF 3 WHERE THE TOTAL POSITIVE PRESSURE TOWARD DEVELCPING NURTURANT BEHAVIOR IN THE CHILD IS LOW (20) B-B-C	340	TILT TOWARD BEING THOSE 0.75 OF 12 WHERE THE TOTAL POSITIVE PRESSURE TOWARD DEVELOPING NURTURANT BEHAVIOR IN THE CHILD IS HIGH (28) B-B-C	0 9 3 3 XSQ= 2.93 PHI= -0.442 EP = 0.0440
347	DRIFT TOWARD BEING THOSE 0.86 OF 7 WHERE THE CHILD'S INFERREC CONFLICT REGARDING SELF-RELIANT BEHAVIOR IS HIGH (37) B-B-C	347	DRIFT TOWARD BEING THOSE 0.57 OF 14 WHERE THE CHILD'S INFERRED CONFLICT REGARDING SELF-RELIANT BEHAVIOR IS LOW (39) B-B-C	6 6 1 8 XSQ= 1.97 PHI= 0.306 EP = 0.0873
372	TEND TO BE THOSE 0.89 OF 9 WHERE MALE INITIATION RITES ARE PRESENT (48) ASA	372	TEND TO BE THOSE 0.82 OF 22 WHERE MALE INITIATION RITES ARE ABSENT (63) ASA	8 4 1 18 XSQ= 10.64 PHI= 0.586 EP = 0.0005
377	TEND LESS TO BE THCSE 0.61 OF 28 WHERE MALE GENITAL MUTILATION IS ABSENT (242)	377	TEND MORE TO BE THOSE 0.98 OF 51 WHERE MALE GENITAL MUTILATION IS ABSENT (242)	11 1 17 50 XSQ= 16.76 PHI= 0.461 XP = 0.0000
426	TILT TOWARD BEING THOSE 0.67 OF 27 WHERE A HIGH GOC IS PRESENT (156) GES,EA	426	TILT TOWARD BEING THOSE 0.64 OF 44 WHERE A HIGH GOD IS ABSENT (104) GES,EA	18 16 9 28 XSQ= 5.00 PHI= 0.265 XP = 0.0253
450	LEAN TOWARD BEING THOSE 0.67 OF 12 WHERE THE CBSERVATION OF FCOD TABOOS IS LOW, RATHER THAN HIGH CR MEDIUM (26) JRL	450	LEAN TOWARD BEING THOSE 0.87 OF 15 WHERE THE OBSERVATION OF FCOD TABOOS IS HIGH OR MEDIUM, RATHER THAN LOW (60) JRL	4 13 8 2 XSQ= 6.01 PHI= -0.472 EP = 0.0069
456	IN ALL CASES ARE THOSE 1.00 OF 4 WHERE THE INTERNALIZATION OF THE INDIVIDUAL'S CONTACT WITH THE DIVINE IS NOT CONDUCIVE TO THE DEVELOPMENT OF THE INDIVIDUAL'S NEED TO ACHIEVE (17) DCM	456	DRIFT TOWARD BEING THOSE 0.63 OF 8 WHERE THE INTERNALIZATION OF THE INDIVIDUAL'S CONTACT WITH THE DIVINE IS CONDUCIVE TO THE DEVELOPMENT OF THE INDIVIDUAL'S NEED TC ACHIEVE (19) DCM	0 5 4 3 XSQ= 2.10 PHI= -0.418 EP = 0.0808
468	LEAN TOWARD BEING THOSE 0.56 OF 9 WHERE CONTACT WITH OTHER CULTURES IS FREQUENT, RATHER THAN REGULAR OR IRREGULAR (17) JMH	468	IN ALL CASES ARE THOSE 1.00 OF 11 WHERE CONTACT WITH OTHER CULTURES IS REGULAR OR IRREGULAR, RATHER THAN FREQUENT (37) JMH	5 0 4 11 XSQ= 5.45 PHI= 0.522 EP = 0.0081

465 CULTURES
WHERE GAMES OF
STRATEGY, CHANCE, AND SKILL -- RATHER THAN
NO GAMES AT ALL --
ARE PRESENT (30) R-A-B,EA

465 CULTURES
WHERE NO GAMES AT ALL -- RATHER THAN
GAMES OF STRATEGY, CHANCE, AND SKILL --
ARE PRESENT (18) R-A-B,EA

BACKGROUND ON PAGE 169

SUBJECT ONLY

30 IN LEFT COLUMN

AMERICANS AZANDE AZTEC BASSERI CHAGGA CZECHS DARD EGYPTIANS FON HAWAIIANS
INCA IRISH JAPANESE KAZAK KOREANS KUBA MENDE MIN CHINESE NAMA OKINAWANS
SERBS SYRIANS TARAHUMARA THAI THONGA VENDA VIETNAMESE WOLOF YAKUT ZUNI

18 IN RIGHT COLUMN

ALACALUF CAGABA CAYAPA CHENCHU CHORTI CUNA GARO HUICHOL JIVARO KATAB
MURNGIN PAEZ TALAMANCA TENETEHARA TUCANO TUPINAMBA VEDDA YARURO

141 EXCLUDED BECAUSE IRRELEVANT

ABIPON ABCR AINU ALBANIANS ANDAMANESE APINAYE ARANDA ARAUCANIANS ASHANTI ATSUGEWI
AYMARA BACAIRI BHIL BHUIYA BORORO BUNLAP BURUSHO CADUVEO CAMAYURA CARIB
CHEROKEE CHEYENNE CHIR-APACHE CHIRIGUANO CHOROTI CHUKCHEE COORG COPR ESKIMO CREE CREEK
CROW DIEGUENO DIERI ELLICE EYAK FANG GANDA GOAJIRO GROS VENTRE HAIDA
HASINAI HUKUNDIKA HURON HUTSUL IBAN ILA INGALIK JEMEZ JUKUN KASKA
KERAKI KHASI KIKUYU KORYAK KUNG KURTATCHI KUTENAI KWAKIUTL LAKHER LAMBA
LAPPS LAU LEPCHA LESU LHOTA NAGA LUO MACASSARESE MANGAIANS MANIHIKI MANUS
MAORI MARICOPA MARQUESANS MARSHALLESE MASAI MATACO MAYA MBUNDU MIAMI MISKITO
MIWOK MOSSI MOTA NABESNA NATCHEZ NAVAHO NICOBARESE NOMLAKI NUNIVAK NYAKYUSA
NYORO OMAHA ONA PAIWAN PALAUANS PAPAGO PUKAPUKA RUNDI RWALA SAGADA
SAMOANS SANPOIL SEMANG SENIANG SHERENTE SIRIONO SIWANS SOMALI TALLENSI TANALA
TAOS TAPIRAPE TAREUMIUT TEHUELCHE TENINO TIKOPIA TIMBIRA TIV TIWI TODA
TOLOWA TROBRIAND TRUKESE TRUMAI TUCUNA TWANA ULAWANS UTE WANTOAT WAPISHANA
WARRAU WASHO WITOTO WOGEO WOLEAIANS YAGUA YAHGAN YAO YOKUTS YUKI
YUROK

211 EXCLUDED BECAUSE UNASCERTAINED

---

4 DRIFT LESS TOWARD BEING THOSE LOCATED OUTSIDE OF THE CIRCUM-MEDITERRANEAN (355) 0.77 OF 30

4 IN ALL CASES ARE THOSE LOCATED OUTSIDE OF THE CIRCUM-MEDITERRANEAN (355) 1.00 OF 18

7	0
23	18
XSQ=	3.22
PHI=	0.259
XP =	0.0726

9 TEND TO BE THOSE LOCATED OUTSIDE OF SOUTH AMERICA (335) 0.97 OF 30

9 TEND TO BE THOSE LOCATED IN SOUTH AMERICA (65) 0.67 OF 18

1	12
29	6
XSQ=	19.76
PHI=	-0.642
XP =	0.0000

15	LEAN TOWARD BEING THOSE WHERE THE LATITUDE IS TWENTY DEGREES OR GREATER (183)	0.67 OF 30	15	LEAN TOWARD BEING THOSE WHERE THE LATITUDE IS LESS THAN TWENTY DEGREES (217)	0.83 OF 18	20 3 10 15 XSQ= 9.36 PHI= 0.441 XP = 0.0022
16	TILT TOWARD BEING THOSE WHERE THE LATITUDE IS TEN DEGREES OR GREATER (277)	0.83 OF 30	16	TILT TOWARD BEING THOSE WHERE THE LATITUDE IS LESS THAN TEN DEGREES (123)	0.56 OF 18	25 8 5 10 XSQ= 6.21 PHI= 0.360 XP = 0.0127
42	DRIFT TOWARD BEING THOSE WHERE THE NATURAL ENVIRONMENT IS OTHER THAN TROPICAL OR SUB-TROPICAL RAIN FOREST, OR MONSOON FOREST (244) FWM	0.73 OF 30	42	DRIFT TOWARD BEING THOSE WHERE THE NATURAL ENVIRONMENT IS TROPICAL OR SUB-TROPICAL RAIN FOREST, OR MONSOON FOREST (156) FWM	0.56 OF 18	8 10 22 8 XSQ= 2.87 PHI= -0.244 XP = 0.0903
51	TILT MORE TOWARD BEING THOSE WHERE SUBSISTENCE IS PRIMARILY BY FOOD PRODUCTION -- I. E., AGRICULTURE OR HUSBANDRY -- RATHER THAN BY GATHERING (253)	0.90 OF 30	51	TILT LESS TOWARD BEING THOSE WHERE SUBSISTENCE IS PRIMARILY BY FOOD PRODUCTION -- I. E., AGRICULTURE OR HUSBANDRY -- RATHER THAN BY GATHERING (253)	0.61 OF 18	27 11 3 7 XSQ= 4.08 PHI= 0.291 XP = 0.0435
53	LEAN TOWARD BEING THOSE WHERE FOOD PRODUCTION IS BY INTENSIVE AGRICULTURE, RATHER THAN BY SIMPLE AGRICULTURE OR INCIPIENT FOOD PRODUCTION (91)	0.70 OF 27	53	LEAN TOWARD BEING THOSE WHERE FOOD PRODUCTION IS BY SIMPLE AGRICULTURE OR INCIPIENT FOOD PRODUCTION, RATHER THAN BY INTENSIVE AGRICULTURE (147)	0.86 OF 14	19 2 8 12 XSQ= 9.47 PHI= 0.481 XP = 0.0021
55	LEAN TOWARD BEING THOSE WHERE FOOD PRODUCTION IS BY INTENSIVE AGRICULTURE, RATHER THAN BY SIMPLE AGRICULTURE (91)	0.76 OF 25	55	LEAN TOWARD BEING THOSE WHERE FOOD PRODUCTION IS BY SIMPLE AGRICULTURE, RATHER THAN BY INTENSIVE AGRICULTURE (101)	0.82 OF 11	19 2 6 9 XSQ= 8.26 PHI= 0.479 EP = 0.0024
62	TILT MORE TOWARD BEING THOSE WHERE HUSBANDRY OF SOME KIND IS PRESENT (228)	0.93 OF 30	62	TILT LESS TOWARD BEING THOSE WHERE HUSBANDRY OF SOME KIND IS PRESENT (228)	0.67 OF 18	28 12 2 6 XSQ= 4.00 PHI= 0.289 XP = 0.0455
63	LEAN TOWARD BEING THOSE WHERE HUSBANDRY, IF PRESENT, IS PRINCIPALLY IN THE FORM OF BOVINE, EQUINE, CAMEL-LIKE, OR DEER-LIKE ANIMALS, RATHER THAN PIGS, SHEEP, OR GOATS (152)	0.79 OF 28	63	LEAN TOWARD BEING THOSE WHERE HUSBANDRY, IF PRESENT, IS PRINCIPALLY IN THE FORM OF PIGS, SHEEP, OR GOATS, RATHER THAN BOVINE, EQUINE, CAMEL-LIKE, OR DEER-LIKE ANIMALS (74)	0.75 OF 12	22 3 6 9 XSQ= 8.13 PHI= 0.451 EP = 0.0032
71	TEND TO BE THOSE WHERE METAL WORKING IS PRESENT (98)	0.91 OF 23	71	TEND TO BE THOSE WHERE METAL WORKING IS ABSENT (153)	0.94 OF 16	21 1 2 15 XSQ= 24.41 PHI= 0.791 EP = 0.0000

```
 80  LEAN TOWARD BEING THOSE          0.54 OF  28     80  IN ALL CASES ARE THOSE           1.00 OF  10        15     0
     WHERE A CITY OR TOWN IS PRESENT  (39)                WHERE NO CITY OR TOWN IS PRESENT  (185)            13    10
                                                                                                     XSQ=      6.75
                                                                                                     PHI=     0.421
                                                                                                     EP =    0.0027

 81  DRIFT TOWARD BEING THOSE         0.75 OF  28     81  DRIFT TOWARD BEING THOSE         0.60 OF  10        21     4
     WHERE A CITY OR TOWN IS PRESENT, OR                  WHERE NO CITY OR TOWN IS PRESENT, AND               7     6
     THE AVERAGE COMMUNITY SIZE IS                        THE AVERAGE COMMUNITY SIZE IS              XSQ=      2.61
     200 OR GREATER  (89)                                 SMALLER THAN 200  (135)                    PHI=     0.262
                                                                                                     EP =    0.0620

 82  IN ALL CASES ARE THOSE           1.00 OF  28     82  LEAN LESS TOWARD BEING THOSE     0.60 OF  10        28     6
     WHERE A CITY OR TOWN IS PRESENT, OR                  WHERE A CITY OR TOWN IS PRESENT, OR                 0     4
     THE AVERAGE COMMUNITY SIZE IS                        THE AVERAGE COMMUNITY SIZE IS              XSQ=      8.63
     FIFTY OR GREATER  (178)                              FIFTY OR GREATER  (178)                    PHI=     0.477
                                                                                                     EP =    0.0028

 85  TEND TO BE THOSE                 0.84 OF  25     85  IN ALL CASES ARE THOSE           1.00 OF  15        21     0
     WHERE THE LEVEL OF POLITICAL INTEGRATION             WHERE THE LEVEL OF POLITICAL INTEGRATION            4    15
     IS THE LARGE STATE, OR                               IS THE MINIMAL STATE,                      XSQ=     23.26
     THE LITTLE STATE  (70) GPM                           THE AUTONOMOUS COMMUNITY, OR               PHI=     0.763
                                                          THE FAMILY  (234) GPM                      EP =    0.0000

 86  TEND TO BE THOSE                 0.92 OF  25     86  TEND TO BE THOSE                 0.73 OF  15        23     4
     WHERE THE LEVEL OF POLITICAL INTEGRATION             WHERE THE LEVEL OF POLITICAL INTEGRATION            2    11
     IS THE LARGE STATE, THE LITTLE STATE,                IS THE AUTONOMOUS COMMUNITY, OR            XSQ=     15.38
     OR THE MINIMAL STATE  (148) GPM                      THE FAMILY  (156) GPM                      PHI=     0.620
                                                                                                     EP =    0.0000

 95  TEND TO BE THOSE                 0.80 OF  30     95  IN ALL CASES ARE THOSE           1.00 OF  18        24     0
     WHERE THE HIERARCHY                                  WHERE THE HIERARCHY                                 6    18
     OF NATIONAL JURISDICTION HAS                         OF NATIONAL JURISDICTION HAS               XSQ=     25.69
     FOUR, THREE, OR TWO LEVELS  (76) GES,EA              ONE OR NO LEVELS  (254) GES,EA             PHI=     0.732
                                                                                                     XP =    0.0000

 96  TEND TO BE THOSE                 0.93 OF  30     96  TEND TO BE THOSE                 0.72 OF  18        28     5
     WHERE THE HIERARCHY                                  WHERE THE HIERARCHY                                 2    13
     OF NATIONAL JURISDICTION HAS                         OF NATIONAL JURISDICTION HAS               XSQ=     19.56
     FOUR, THREE, TWO OR                                  NO LEVELS  (156) GES,EA                    PHI=     0.638
     ONE LEVEL  (174) GES,EA                                                                         XP =    0.0000

100  TILT MORE TOWARD BEING THOSE     0.97 OF  30    100  TILT LESS TOWARD BEING THOSE     0.67 OF  18        29    12
     WHERE HIERARCHIES ARE MORE COMPLEX THAN              WHERE HIERARCHIES ARE MORE COMPLEX THAN             1     6
     THE 'SIMPLEST,' I. E., MORE COMPLEX THAN             THE 'SIMPLEST,' I. E., MORE COMPLEX THAN   XSQ=      5.90
     TWO LOCAL LEVELS WITH                                TWO LOCAL LEVELS WITH                      PHI=     0.351
     NO NATIONAL LEVELS  (267) GES,EA                     NO NATIONAL LEVELS  (267) GES,EA           XP =    0.0152

102  TEND TO BE THOSE                 0.97 OF  30    102  TEND TO BE THOSE                 0.71 OF  17        29     5
     WHERE CLASS STRATIFICATION IS                        WHERE CLASS STRATIFICATION IS                       1    12
     PRESENT  (203)                                       ABSENT  (180)                              XSQ=     21.28
                                                                                                     PHI=     0.673
                                                                                                     XP =    0.0000
```

106	TEND TO BE THOSE WHERE CLASS STRATIFICATION, IF PRESENT, IS BASED ON SOMETHING OTHER THAN WEALTH (126)	0.86 OF	29	106	IN ALL CASES ARE THOSE WHERE CLASS STRATIFICATION, IF PRESENT, IS BASED ON WEALTH (77)	1.00 OF	5	4 5 25 0 XSQ= 12.16 PHI= -0.598 EP = 0.0005
109	DRIFT LESS TOWARD BEING THOSE WHERE CASTES ARE ABSENT (317)	0.75 OF	28	109	IN ALL CASES ARE THOSE WHERE CASTES ARE ABSENT (317)	1.00 OF	18	7 0 21 18 XSQ= 3.55 PHI= 0.278 XP = 0.0597
110	DRIFT TOWARD BEING THOSE WHERE SLAVERY IS PRESENT (163)	0.52 OF	29	110	DRIFT TOWARD BEING THOSE WHERE SLAVERY IS ABSENT (218)	0.78 OF	18	15 4 14 14 XSQ= 2.88 PHI= 0.248 XP = 0.0896
116	DRIFT TOWARD BEING THOSE WHERE OCCUPATIONAL SPECIALIZATION IS FULL-TIME, WHETHER OR NOT FOR SURPLUS PRODUCTION (20) JMH	0.67 OF	9	116	IN ALL CASES ARE THOSE WHERE OCCUPATIONAL SPECIALIZATION IS PART-TIME ONLY (34) JMH	1.00 OF	4	6 0 3 4 XSQ= 2.63 PHI= 0.450 EP = 0.0699
142	IN ALL CASES ARE THOSE WHERE THE LEVEL OF SOCIAL SANCTION IS PUBLIC CORPOREAL SANCTION OR PUBLIC PROPERTY SANCTION, RATHER THAN PRIVATE SETTLEMENT (38) JMH	1.00 OF	9	142	DRIFT TOWARD BEING THOSE WHERE THE LEVEL OF SOCIAL SANCTION IS PRIVATE SETTLEMENT, RATHER THAN PUBLIC CORPOREAL SANCTION OR PUBLIC PROPERTY SETTLEMENT (16) JMH	0.50 OF	4	9 2 0 2 XSQ= 2.17 PHI= 0.409 EP = 0.0769
178	DRIFT LESS TOWARD BEING THOSE WHERE THE COMMUNITY IS OTHER THAN SEGMENTED ON A CLAN BASIS AND NON-EXOGAMOUS (295)	0.73 OF	30	178	IN ALL CASES ARE THOSE WHERE THE COMMUNITY IS OTHER THAN SEGMENTED ON A CLAN BASIS AND NON-EXOGAMOUS (295)	1.00 OF	16	8 0 22 16 XSQ= 3.48 PHI= 0.275 XP = 0.0623
183	IN ALL CASES ARE THOSE WHERE THE LARGEST NON-COGNATIC KIN GROUP IS SMALLER THAN A MOEITY, I. E., A PHRATRY OR SIB OR LINEAGE (218)	1.00 OF	21	183	TILT LESS TOWARD BEING THOSE WHERE THE LARGEST NON-COGNATIC KIN GROUP IS SMALLER THAN A MOEITY, I. E., A PHRATRY OR SIB OR LINEAGE (218)	0.57 OF	7	0 3 21 4 XSQ= 6.10 PHI= -0.467 EP = 0.0107
186	TILT TOWARD BEING THOSE WHERE THE KIN GROUP IS EXCLUSIVELY PATRILINEAL (150)	0.53 OF	30	186	TILT TOWARD BEING THOSE WHERE THE KIN GROUP IS OTHER THAN EXCLUSIVELY PATRILINEAL (250)	0.83 OF	18	16 3 14 15 XSQ= 4.88 PHI= 0.319 XP = 0.0271
188	DRIFT TOWARD BEING THOSE WHERE THE KIN GROUP IS OTHER THAN EXCLUSIVELY COGNATIC (252)	0.70 OF	30	188	DRIFT TOWARD BEING THOSE WHERE THE KIN GROUP IS EXCLUSIVELY COGNATIC (148)	0.61 OF	18	9 11 21 7 XSQ= 3.29 PHI= -0.262 XP = 0.0696

190	DRIFT MORE TOWARD BEING THOSE WHERE THE KIN GROUP IS PATRILINEAL OR DOUBLE-DESCENT, RATHER THAN MATRILINEAL (186)	0.90 OF	21	190	DRIFT LESS TOWARD BEING THOSE WHERE THE KIN GROUP IS PATRILINEAL OR DOUBLE-DESCENT, RATHER THAN MATRILINEAL (186)	0.57 OF	7	19 4 2 3 XSQ= 2.03 PHI= 0.269 EP = 0.0825
204	TILT TOWARD BEING THOSE WHERE MARITAL RESIDENCE IS PATRILOCAL, VIRILOCAL, OR AVUNCULOCAL, RATHER THAN AMBILOCAL OR NEOLOCAL (270)	0.89 OF	28	204	TILT TOWARD BEING THOSE WHERE MARITAL RESIDENCE IS AMBILOCAL OR NEOLOCAL, RATHER THAN PATRILOCAL, VIRILOCAL, OR AVUNCULOCAL (64)	0.50 OF	10	25 5 3 5 XSQ= 4.68 PHI= 0.351 EP = 0.0186
209	TEND TO BE THOSE WHERE MARITAL RESIDENCE IS PATRILOCAL, VIRILOCAL, OR AVUNCULOCAL, RATHER THAN MATRILOCAL OR UXORILOCAL (270)	0.93 OF	27	209	TEND TO BE THOSE WHERE MARITAL RESIDENCE IS MATRILOCAL OR UXORILOCAL, RATHER THAN PATRILOCAL, VIRILOCAL, OR AVUNCULOCAL (64)	0.62 OF	13	25 5 2 8 XSQ= 10.98 PHI= 0.524 EP = 0.0006
210	TILT TOWARD BEING THOSE WHERE MARITAL RESIDENCE IS PATRILOCAL, RATHER THAN MATRILOCAL (169)	0.95 OF	19	210	TILT TOWARD BEING THOSE WHERE MARITAL RESIDENCE IS MATRILOCAL, RATHER THAN PATRILOCAL (31)	0.50 OF	6	18 3 1 3 XSQ= 3.87 PHI= 0.393 EP = 0.0312
314	DRIFT TOWARD BEING THOSE WHERE THE INCIDENCE OF MOTHER-CHILD HOUSEHOLDS IS HIGH (19) W-D,S	0.50 OF	10	314	IN ALL CASES ARE THOSE WHERE THE INCIDENCE OF MOTHER-CHILD HOUSEHOLDS IS LOW (61) W-D,S	1.00 OF	6	5 0 5 6 XSQ= 2.35 PHI= 0.383 EP = 0.0934
318	DRIFT TOWARD BEING THOSE WHERE THE OVERALL INDULGENCE OF THE INFANT IS LOW (31) B-B-C	0.86 OF	7	318	DRIFT TOWARD BEING THOSE WHERE THE OVERALL INDULGENCE OF THE INFANT IS HIGH (40) B-B-C	0.80 OF	5	1 4 6 1 XSQ= 2.83 PHI= -0.486 EP = 0.0720
320	DRIFT TOWARD BEING THOSE WHERE THE DEGREE OF REDUCTION OF THE INFANT'S DRIVES IS LOW (24) B-B-C	0.71 OF	7	320	IN ALL CASES ARE THOSE WHERE THE DEGREE OF REDUCTION OF THE INFANT'S DRIVES IS HIGH (45) B-B-C	1.00 OF	4	2 4 5 0 XSQ= 2.75 PHI= -0.500 EP = 0.0606
334	IN ALL CASES ARE THOSE WHERE THE INDULGENCE OF THE CHILD IS LOW (38) B-B-C	1.00 OF	7	334	LEAN TOWARD BEING THOSE WHERE THE INDULGENCE OF THE CHILD IS HIGH (40) B-B-C	0.83 OF	6	0 5 7 1 XSQ= 6.29 PHI= -0.695 EP = 0.0047
337	TILT TOWARD BEING THOSE WHERE THE CHILD'S INFERRED ANXIETY OVER NON-PERFORMANCE OF RESPONSIBLE BEHAVIOR IS HIGH (38) B-B-C	0.86 OF	7	337	TILT TOWARD BEING THOSE WHERE THE CHILD'S INFERRED ANXIETY OVER NON-PERFORMANCE OF RESPONSIBLE BEHAVIOR IS LOW (35) B-B-C	0.83 OF	6	6 1 1 5 XSQ= 3.73 PHI= 0.536 EP = 0.0291

338	IN ALL CASES ARE THOSE 1.00 OF 7 WHERE THE CHILD'S INFERRED ANXIETY OVER PERFORMANCE OF RESPONSIBLE BEHAVIOR IS HIGH (44) B-B-C	338	DRIFT TOWARD BEING THOSE 0.50 OF 6 WHERE THE CHILD'S INFERRED ANXIETY OVER PERFORMANCE OF RESPONSIBLE BEHAVIOR IS LOW (29) B-B-C	7 3 0 3 XSQ= 2.17 PHI= 0.408 EP = 0.0699
346	TILT TOWARD BEING THOSE 0.86 OF 7 WHERE THE CHILD'S INFERRED ANXIETY OVER PERFORMANCE OF SELF-RELIANT BEHAVIOR IS HIGH (37) B-B-C	346	TILT TOWARD BEING THOSE 0.83 OF 6 WHERE THE CHILD'S INFERRED ANXIETY OVER PERFORMANCE OF SELF-RELIANT BEHAVIOR IS LOW (39) B-B-C	6 1 1 5 XSQ= 3.73 PHI= 0.536 EP = 0.0291
347	TILT TOWARD BEING THOSE 0.86 OF 7 WHERE THE CHILD'S INFERRED CONFLICT REGARDING SELF-RELIANT BEHAVIOR IS HIGH (37) B-B-C	347	TILT TOWARD BEING THOSE 0.83 OF 6 WHERE THE CHILD'S INFERRED CONFLICT REGARDING SELF-RELIANT BEHAVIOR IS LOW (39) B-B-C	6 1 1 5 XSQ= 3.73 PHI= 0.536 EP = 0.0291
350	TILT TOWARD BEING THOSE 0.83 OF 6 WHERE THE CHILD'S INFERRED ANXIETY OVER PERFORMANCE OF ACHIEVEMENT BEHAVIOR IS HIGH (34) B-B-C	350	IN ALL CASES ARE THOSE 1.00 OF 3 WHERE THE CHILD'S INFERRED ANXIETY OVER PERFORMANCE OF ACHIEVEMENT BEHAVIOR IS LOW (26) B-B-C	5 0 1 3 XSQ= 2.76 PHI= 0.553 EP = 0.0476
353	IN ALL CASES ARE THOSE 1.00 OF 6 WHERE THE CHILD'S INFERRED ANXIETY OVER NON-PERFORMANCE OF OBEDIENT BEHAVIOR IS HIGH (42) B-B-C	353	DRIFT TOWARD BEING THOSE 0.67 OF 6 WHERE THE CHILD-S INFERRED ANXIETY OVER NON-PERFORMANCE OF OBEDIENT BEHAVIOR IS LOW (32) B-B-C	6 2 0 4 XSQ= 3.38 PHI= 0.530 EP = 0.0606
354	IN ALL CASES ARE THOSE 1.00 OF 6 WHERE THE CHILD'S INFERRED ANXIETY OVER PERFORMANCE OF OBEDIENT BEHAVIOR IS HIGH (36) B-B-C	354	IN ALL CASES ARE THOSE 1.00 OF 5 WHERE THE CHILD'S INFERRED ANXIETY OVER PERFORMANCE OF OBEDIENT BEHAVIOR IS LOW (37) B-B-C	6 0 0 5 XSQ= 7.34 PHI= 0.817 EP = 0.0022
355	IN ALL CASES ARE THOSE 1.00 OF 6 WHERE THE CHILD'S INFERRED CONFLICT REGARDING OBEDIENT BEHAVIOR IS HIGH (35) B-B-C	355	IN ALL CASES ARE THOSE 1.00 OF 5 WHERE THE CHILD'S INFERRED CONFLICT REGARDING OBEDIENT BEHAVIOR IS LOW (38) B-B-C	6 0 0 5 XSQ= 7.34 PHI= 0.817 EP = 0.0022
358	IN ALL CASES ARE THOSE 1.00 OF 7 WHERE ADOLESCENT PEER GROUPS ARE PRESENT IN A SETTING OF WORK AND PUBLIC GATHERINGS AND LEISURE, OR OF PUBLIC GATHERINGS AND LEISURE, OR OF LEISURE ONLY (41) JKH	358	IN ALL CASES ARE THOSE 1.00 OF 3 WHERE ADOLESCENT PEER GROUPS ARE ABSENT IN A SETTING OF WORK, AND OF PUBLIC GATHERINGS, AND OF LEISURE (11) JKH	7 0 0 3 XSQ= 5.80 PHI= 0.762 EP = 0.0083
372	LEAN TOWARD BEING THOSE 0.89 OF 9 WHERE MALE INITIATION RITES ARE PRESENT (48) ASA	372	LEAN TOWARD BEING THOSE 0.88 OF 8 WHERE MALE INITIATION RITES ARE ABSENT (63) ASA	8 1 1 7 XSQ= 7.09 PHI= 0.646 EP = 0.0034

No.	Statement	Ratio	N	No.	Statement	Ratio	N	Statistics
377	DRIFT LESS TOWARD BEING THOSE WHERE MALE GENITAL MUTILATION IS ABSENT (242)	0.61 OF	28	377	DRIFT MORE TOWARD BEING THOSE WHERE MALE GENITAL MUTILATION IS ABSENT (242)	0.89 OF	18	11 2 17 16 XSQ= 3.01 PHI= 0.256 XP = 0.0826
391	DRIFT TOWARD BEING THOSE WHERE PREMARITAL SEX RELATIONS ARE STRONGLY PUNISHED AND IN FACT RARE, OR WEAKLY PUNISHED AND IN FACT NOT RARE (89) JTW,EA	0.70 OF	23	391	DRIFT TOWARD BEING THOSE WHERE PREMARITAL SEX RELATIONS ARE PUNISHED ONLY IF PREGNANCY RESULTS, OR FREELY PERMITTED (90) JTW,EA	0.71 OF	7	16 2 7 5 XSQ= 2.24 PHI= 0.273 EP = 0.0837
400	IN ALL CASES ARE THOSE WHERE HOMOSEXUAL ACTIVITY IS PERMITTED (36) F-B	1.00 OF	7	400	DRIFT TOWARD BEING THOSE WHERE HOMOSEXUAL ACTIVITY IS PROHIBITED (22) F-B	0.67 OF	3	0 2 7 1 XSQ= 2.41 PHI= -0.491 EP = 0.0667
427	TILT TOWARD BEING THOSE WHERE A HIGH GOD, IF PRESENT, IS ACTIVE, RATHER THAN INACTIVE (87) GES,EA	0.78 OF	18	427	TILT TOWARD BEING THOSE WHERE A HIGH GOD, IF PRESENT, IS INACTIVE, RATHER THAN ACTIVE (69) GES,EA	0.67 OF	9	14 3 4 6 XSQ= 3.36 PHI= 0.353 EP = 0.0393
456	IN ALL CASES ARE THOSE WHERE THE INTERNALIZATION OF THE INDIVIDUAL'S CONTACT WITH THE DIVINE IS NOT CONDUCIVE TO THE DEVELOPMENT OF THE INDIVIDUAL'S NEED TO ACHIEVE (17) DCM	1.00 OF	4	456	IN ALL CASES ARE THOSE WHERE THE INTERNALIZATION OF THE INDIVIDUAL'S CONTACT WITH THE DIVINE IS CONDUCIVE TO THE DEVELOPMENT OF THE INDIVIDUAL'S NEED TO ACHIEVE (19) DCM	1.00 OF	2	0 2 4 0 XSQ= 2.34 PHI= -0.625 EP = 0.0667
476	TILT TOWARD BEING THOSE WHERE THE DEGREE OF INSOBRIETY IS MODERATE OR SLIGHT (18) DH	0.60 OF	10	476	IN ALL CASES ARE THOSE WHERE THE DEGREE OF INSOBRIETY IS STRONG (31) DH	1.00 OF	6	4 6 6 0 XSQ= 3.48 PHI= -0.467 EP = 0.0338

466 CULTURES
WHERE, IF GAMES ARE PRESENT BUT
GAMES OF STRATEGY ABSENT, GAMES INCLUDE
THOSE OF BOTH CHANCE AND SKILL,
RATHER THAN
SKILL ONLY (51) R-A-B, EA

466 CULTURES
WHERE, IF GAMES ARE PRESENT BUT
GAMES OF STRATEGY ABSENT, GAMES INCLUDE
THOSE OF SKILL ONLY
RATHER THAN
BOTH CHANCE AND SKILL (67) R-A-B, EA

BACKGROUND ON PAGE 169

SUBJECT ONLY

51 IN LEFT COLUMN

ARAUCANIANS ATSUGEWI AYMARA CHEROKEE CHEYENNE CHIR-APACHE CHIRIGUANO CHOROTI CHUKCHEE COPR ESKIMO
CREE CREEK CROW DIEGUENO EYAK GROS VENTRE HAIDA HASINAI HUKUNDIKA HURON
JEMEZ KASKA KUTENAI KWAKIUTL MARICOPA MATACO MAYA MIAMI MIWOK NABESNA
NAVAHO NOMLAKI OMAHA PALAUANS PAPAGO SAMOANS SANPOIL TALLENSI TAOS TAREUMIUT
TEHUELCHE TENINO TOLOWA TRUKESE TWANA ULAWANS UTE WASHO YOKUTS YUKI
YUROK

67 IN RIGHT COLUMN

ABIPON ABOR AINU ANDAMANESE APINAYE ARANDA BACAIRI BHIL BHUIYA BORORO
BUNLAP CADUVEO CAMAYURA CARIB COORG DIERI ELLICE FANG GOAJIRO IBAN
INGALIK KERAKI KHASI KORYAK KUNG KURTATCHI LAPPS LAU LEPCHA LESU
LHOTA NAGA MACASSARESE MANGAIANS MANIHIKI MANUS MAORI MARQUESANS MARSHALLESE MISKITO MOTA
NATCHEZ NICOBARESE NUNIVAK ONA PAIWAN PUKAPUKA RWALA SAGADA SEMANG SENIANG
SHERENTE SIRIONO TAPIRAPE TIKOPIA TIMBIRA TIWI TODA TROBRIAND TRUMAI TUCUNA
WANTOAT WAPISHANA WARRAU WITOTO WOGEO YAGUA YAHGAN

71 EXCLUDED BECAUSE IRRELEVANT

ALACALUF ALBANIANS AMERICANS ASHANTI AZANDE AZTEC BASSERI BURUSHO CAGABA CAYAPA
CHAGGA CHENCHU CHORTI CUNA CZECHS DARD EGYPTIANS FON GANDA GARO
HAWAIIANS HUICHOL HUTSUL ILA INCA IRISH JAPANESE JIVARO JUKUN KATAB
KAZAK KIKUYU KOREANS KUBA LAKHER LAMBA LUO MASAI MBUNDU MENDE
MIN CHINESE MOSSI MURNGIN NAMA NYAKYUSA NYORO OKINAWANS PAEZ RUNDI SERBS
SIWANS SOMALI SYRIANS TALAMANCA TANALA TARAHUMARA TENETEHARA THAI THONGA TIV
TUCANO TUPINAMBA VEDDA VENDA VIETNAMESE WOLEAIANS WOLOF YAKUT YAO YARURO
ZUNI

211 EXCLUDED BECAUSE UNASCERTAINED

5 LEAN MORE TOWARD BEING THOSE 0.98 OF 51
LOCATED OUTSIDE OF
EAST EURASIA (330)

5 LEAN LESS TOWARD BEING THOSE 0.81 OF 67
LOCATED OUTSIDE OF
EAST EURASIA (330)

1	13
50	54

XSQ= 6.84
PHI= -0.241
XP = 0.0089

6	TEND MORE TO BE THOSE LOCATED OUTSIDE OF THE INSULAR PACIFIC (330)	0.92 OF 51	6	TEND LESS TO BE THOSE LOCATED OUTSIDE OF THE INSULAR PACIFIC (330)	0.61 OF 67	4 26 47 41 XSQ= 13.05 PHI= -0.333 XP = 0.0003
8	TEND TO BE THOSE LOCATED IN NORTH AMERICA (70)	0.75 OF 51	8	TEND TO BE THOSE LOCATED OUTSIDE OF NORTH AMERICA (330)	0.96 OF 67	38 3 13 64 XSQ= 59.59 PHI= 0.711 XP = 0.
9	TILT MORE TOWARD BEING THOSE LOCATED OUTSIDE OF SOUTH AMERICA (335)	0.86 OF 51	9	TILT LESS TOWARD BEING THOSE LOCATED OUTSIDE OF SOUTH AMERICA (335)	0.69 OF 67	7 21 44 46 XSQ= 4.04 PHI= -0.185 XP = 0.0444
14	TEND TO BE THOSE WHERE THE LATITUDE IS THIRTY DEGREES OR GREATER (119)	0.80 OF 51	14	TEND TO BE THOSE WHERE THE LATITUDE IS LESS THAN THIRTY DEGREES (281)	0.85 OF 67	41 10 10 57 XSQ= 47.94 PHI= 0.637 XP = 0.
15	TEND TO BE THOSE WHERE THE LATITUDE IS TWENTY DEGREES OR GREATER (183)	0.86 OF 51	15	TEND TO BE THOSE WHERE THE LATITUDE IS LESS THAN TWENTY DEGREES (217)	0.66 OF 67	44 23 7 44 XSQ= 29.76 PHI= 0.502 XP = 0.0000
36	LEAN LESS TOWARD BEING THOSE WHERE THE NATURAL ENVIRONMENT IS OTHER THAN 'VERY HARSH,' OR SUB-TROPICAL BUSH, OR TEMPERATE GRASSLAND (292) FWM	0.51 OF 51	36	LEAN MORE TOWARD BEING THOSE WHERE THE NATURAL ENVIRONMENT IS OTHER THAN 'VERY HARSH,' OR SUB-TROPICAL BUSH, OR TEMPERATE GRASSLAND (292) FWM	0.81 OF 67	25 13 26 54 XSQ= 10.32 PHI= 0.296 XP = 0.0013
42	TEND TO BE THOSE WHERE THE NATURAL ENVIRONMENT IS OTHER THAN TROPICAL OR SUB-TROPICAL RAIN FOREST, OR MONSOON FOREST (244) FWM	0.90 OF 51	42	TEND TO BE THOSE WHERE THE NATURAL ENVIRONMENT IS TROPICAL OR SUB-TROPICAL RAIN FOREST, OR MONSOON FOREST (156) FWM	0.66 OF 67	5 44 46 23 XSQ= 34.96 PHI= -0.544 XP = 0.
44	TILT TOWARD BEING THOSE WHERE SETTLEMENTS ARE NON-FIXED (110)	0.58 OF 50	44	TILT TOWARD BEING THOSE WHERE SETTLEMENTS ARE FIXED (222)	0.66 OF 67	21 44 29 23 XSQ= 5.57 PHI= -0.218 XP = 0.0182
48	DRIFT TOWARD BEING THOSE WHERE THE FOOD SUPPLY IS NOT SECURE, AND FOOD SHORTAGES ARE FREQUENT OR ANNUAL (41) MGW	0.69 OF 16	48	DRIFT TOWARD BEING THOSE WHERE THE FOOD SUPPLY IS SECURE, AND FOOD SHORTAGES ARE RARE OR OCCASIONAL (38) MGW	0.63 OF 19	5 12 11 7 XSQ= 2.38 PHI= -0.261 EP = 0.0922

51	TILT MORE TOWARD BEING THOSE WHERE SUBSISTENCE IS PRIMARILY BY FOOD GATHERING -- I. E., HUNTING, FISHING, OR COLLECTING -- RATHER THAN FOOD PRODUCTION (147)	0.80 OF 51	51	TILT LESS TOWARD BEING THOSE WHERE SUBSISTENCE IS PRIMARILY BY FOOD GATHERING -- I. E., HUNTING, FISHING, OR COLLECTING -- RATHER THAN FOOD PRODUCTION (147)	0.58 OF 67	10 28 41 39 XSQ= 5.55 PHI= -0.217 XP = 0.0185
55	DRIFT TOWARD BEING THOSE WHERE FOOD PRODUCTION IS BY INTENSIVE AGRICULTURE, RATHER THAN BY SIMPLE AGRICULTURE (91)	0.50 OF 10	55	DRIFT TOWARD BEING THOSE WHERE FOOD PRODUCTION IS BY SIMPLE AGRICULTURE, RATHER THAN BY INTENSIVE AGRICULTURE (101)	0.83 OF 24	5 4 5 20 XSQ= 2.50 PHI= 0.271 EP = 0.0847
81	DRIFT LESS TOWARD BEING THOSE WHERE NO CITY OR TOWN IS PRESENT, AND THE AVERAGE COMMUNITY SIZE IS SMALLER THAN 200 (135)	0.70 OF 33	81	DRIFT MORE TOWARD BEING THOSE WHERE NO CITY OR TOWN IS PRESENT, AND THE AVERAGE COMMUNITY SIZE IS SMALLER THAN 200 (135)	0.89 OF 47	10 5 23 42 XSQ= 3.72 PHI= 0.215 XP = 0.0539
83	DRIFT LESS TOWARD BEING THOSE WHERE, WITH NO CITY AND NO TOWN PRESENT, THE AVERAGE COMMUNITY SIZE IS SMALLER THAN 200, RATHER THAN BETWEEN 200 AND 999 (135)	0.72 OF 32	83	DRIFT MORE TOWARD BEING THOSE WHERE, WITH NO CITY AND NO TOWN PRESENT, THE AVERAGE COMMUNITY SIZE IS SMALLER THAN 200, RATHER THAN BETWEEN 200 AND 999 (135)	0.91 OF 46	9 4 23 42 XSQ= 3.83 PHI= 0.221 XP = 0.0505
127	DRIFT TOWARD BEING THOSE WHERE THE FEMALES' CONTRIBUTION TO SUBSISTENCE IS LOW (32) JKB	0.75 OF 12	127	DRIFT TOWARD BEING THOSE WHERE THE FEMALES' CONTRIBUTION TO SUBSISTENCE IS HIGH (33) JKB	0.63 OF 16	3 10 9 6 XSQ= 2.52 PHI= -0.300 EP = 0.0671
149	DRIFT TOWARD BEING THOSE WHERE THE INCIDENCE OF THEFT IS HIGH (18) B-B-C	0.78 OF 9	149	DRIFT TOWARD BEING THOSE WHERE THE INCIDENCE OF THEFT IS LOW (19) B-B-C	0.67 OF 12	7 4 2 8 XSQ= 2.49 PHI= 0.344 EP = 0.0805
192	DRIFT LESS TOWARD BEING THOSE OTHER THAN WHERE THE ONLY KIN GROUP PRESENT IS A KINDRED OR ELSE BILATERAL DESCENT IS INFERRED (289)	0.55 OF 51	192	DRIFT MORE TOWARD BEING THOSE OTHER THAN WHERE THE ONLY KIN GROUP PRESENT IS A KINDRED OR ELSE BILATERAL DESCENT IS INFERRED (289)	0.72 OF 67	23 19 28 48 XSQ= 2.85 PHI= 0.155 XP = 0.0915
213	LEAN MORE TOWARD BEING THOSE WHERE FIRST COUSIN MARRIAGE IS NOT PERMITTED (198)	0.78 OF 51	213	LEAN LESS TOWARD BEING THOSE WHERE FIRST COUSIN MARRIAGE IS NOT PERMITTED (198)	0.52 OF 65	11 31 40 34 XSQ= 7.35 PHI= -0.252 XP = 0.0067
272	IN ALL CASES ARE THOSE WHERE THE DIVORCE RATE IS HIGH (29) CA	1.00 OF 5	272	DRIFT TOWARD BEING THOSE WHERE THE DIVORCE RATE IS LOW (28) CA	0.53 OF 15	5 7 0 8 XSQ= 2.50 PHI= 0.354 EP = 0.0547

305	TILT TOWARD BEING THOSE WHERE THE EARLY SEXUAL SATISFACTION POTENTIAL IS LOW (24) W-C	0.88 OF 8	305	TILT TOWARD BEING THOSE WHERE THE EARLY SEXUAL SATISFACTION POTENTIAL IS HIGH (27) W-C	0.65 OF 20	1 13 7 7 XSQ= 4.38 PHI= -0.395 EP = 0.0329
308	TILT TOWARD BEING THOSE WHERE AVERAGE SOCIALIZATION ANXIETY IS HIGH (22) W-C	0.88 OF 8	308	TILT TOWARD BEING THOSE WHERE AVERAGE SOCIALIZATION ANXIETY IS LOW (18) W-C	0.71 OF 14	7 4 1 10 XSQ= 4.91 PHI= 0.472 EP = 0.0237
311	IN ALL CASES ARE THOSE WHERE SEXUAL SOCIALIZATION ANXIETY IS HIGH (28) W-C	1.00 OF 8	311	LEAN TOWARD BEING THOSE WHERE SEXUAL SOCIALIZATION ANXIETY IS LOW (23) W-C	0.68 OF 19	8 6 0 13 XSQ= 7.99 PHI= 0.544 EP = 0.0019
313	LEAN TOWARD BEING THOSE WHERE AGGRESSION SOCIALIZATION ANXIETY IS HIGH (26) W-C	0.82 OF 11	313	LEAN TOWARD BEING THOSE WHERE AGGRESSION SOCIALIZATION ANXIETY IS LOW (28) W-C	0.76 OF 17	9 4 2 13 XSQ= 6.93 PHI= 0.497 EP = 0.0056
323	TILT TOWARD BEING THOSE WHERE THE CONSTANCY OF PRESENCE OF THE INFANT'S NURTURANT AGENT IS LOW (45) B-B-C	0.86 OF 14	323	TILT TOWARD BEING THOSE WHERE THE CONSTANCY OF PRESENCE OF THE INFANT'S NURTURANT AGENT IS HIGH (29) B-B-C	0.55 OF 22	2 12 12 10 XSQ= 4.26 PHI= -0.344 EP = 0.0334
336	DRIFT TOWARD BEING THOSE WHERE THE TOTAL POSITIVE PRESSURE TOWARD DEVELOPING RESPONSIBLE BEHAVIOR IN THE CHILD IS HIGH (43) B-B-C	0.64 OF 14	336	DRIFT TOWARD BEING THOSE WHERE THE TOTAL POSITIVE PRESSURE TOWARD DEVELOPING RESPONSIBLE BEHAVIOR IN THE CHILD IS LOW (32) B-B-C	0.71 OF 21	9 6 5 15 XSQ= 3.04 PHI= 0.295 EP = 0.0796
344	DRIFT TOWARD BEING THOSE WHERE THE TOTAL POSITIVE PRESSURE TOWARD DEVELOPING SELF-RELIANT BEHAVIOR IN THE CHILD IS HIGH (36) B-B-C	0.64 OF 14	344	DRIFT TOWARD BEING THOSE WHERE THE TOTAL POSITIVE PRESSURE TOWARD DEVELOPING SELF-RELIANT BEHAVIOR IN THE CHILD IS LOW (40) B-B-C	0.68 OF 22	9 7 5 15 XSQ= 2.46 PHI= 0.261 EP = 0.0874
346	DRIFT TOWARD BEING THOSE WHERE THE CHILD'S INFERRED ANXIETY OVER PERFORMANCE OF SELF-RELIANT BEHAVIOR IS HIGH (37) B-B-C	0.57 OF 14	346	DRIFT TOWARD BEING THOSE WHERE THE CHILD'S INFERRED ANXIETY OVER PERFORMANCE OF SELF-RELIANT BEHAVIOR IS LOW (39) B-B-C	0.73 OF 22	8 6 6 16 XSQ= 2.08 PHI= 0.240 EP = 0.0924
349	TILT TOWARD BEING THOSE WHERE THE CHILD'S INFERRED ANXIETY OVER NON-PERFORMANCE OF ACHIEVEMENT BEHAVIOR IS HIGH (34) B-B-C	0.71 OF 14	349	TILT TOWARD BEING THOSE WHERE THE CHILD'S INFERRED ANXIETY OVER NON-PERFORMANCE OF ACHIEVEMENT BEHAVIOR IS LOW (28) B-B-C	0.71 OF 17	10 5 4 12 XSQ= 3.88 PHI= 0.354 EP = 0.0320

350 TEND TO BÉ THOSE 0.79 OF 14 WHERE THE CHILD'S INFERRED ANXIETY OVER PERFORMANCE OF ACHIEVEMENT BEHAVIOR IS HIGH (34) B-B-C	350 TEND TO BE THOSE 0.87 OF 15 WHERE THE CHILD'S INFERRED ANXIETY OVER PERFORMANCE OF ACHIEVEMENT BEHAVIOR IS LOW (26) B-B-C	11 2 3 13 XSQ= 9.96 PHI= 0.586 EP = 0.0007
351 LEAN TOWARD BEING THOSE 0.57 OF 14 WHERE THE CHILD'S INFERRED CONFLICT REGARDING ACHIEVEMENT BEHAVIOR IS HIGH (26) B-B-C	351 LEAN TOWARD BEING THOSE 0.93 OF 15 WHERE THE CHILD'S INFERRED CONFLICT REGARDING ACHIEVEMENT BEHAVIOR IS LOW (34) B-B-C	8 1 6 14 XSQ= 6.42 PHI= 0.471 EP = 0.0052
352 TILT TOWARD BEING THOSE 0.79 OF 14 WHERE THE TOTAL POSITIVE PRESSURE TOWARD DEVELOPING OBEDIENT BEHAVIOR IN THE CHILD IS HIGH (44) B-B-C	352 TILT TOWARD BEING THOSE 0.60 OF 20 WHERE THE TOTAL POSITIVE PRESSURE TOWARD DEVELOPING OBEDIENT BEHAVIOR IN THE CHILD IS LOW (28) B-B-C	11 8 3 12 XSQ= 3.53 PHI= 0.322 EP = 0.0382
353 DRIFT TOWARD BEING THOSE 0.64 OF 14 WHERE THE CHILD'S INFERRED ANXIETY OVER NON-PERFORMANCE OF OBEDIENT BEHAVIOR IS HIGH (42) B-B-C	353 DRIFT TOWARD BEING THOSE 0.67 OF 21 WHERE THE CHILD-S INFERRED ANXIETY OVER NON-PERFORMANCE OF OBEDIENT BEHAVIOR IS LOW (32) B-B-C	9 7 5 14 XSQ= 2.12 PHI= 0.246 EP = 0.0937
355 DRIFT TOWARD BEING THOSE 0.64 OF 14 WHERE THE CHILD'S INFERRED CONFLICT REGARDING OBEDIENT BEHAVIOR IS HIGH (35) B-B-C	355 DRIFT TOWARD BEING THOSE 0.67 OF 21 WHERE THE CHILD'S INFERRED CONFLICT REGARDING OBEDIENT BEHAVIOR IS LOW (38) B-B-C	9 7 5 14 XSQ= 2.12 PHI= 0.246 EP = 0.0937
360 TILT LESS TOWARD BEING THOSE 0.56 OF 9 WHERE ADOLESCENT PEER GROUPS ARE PRESENT ONLY IN A SETTING OF LEISURE, OR ELSE ARE ABSENT (23) JKH	360 IN ALL CASES ARE THOSE 1.00 OF 10 WHERE ADOLESCENT PEER GROUPS ARE PRESENT ONLY IN A SETTING OF LEISURE, OR ELSE ARE ABSENT (23) JKH	4 0 5 10 XSQ= 3.27 PHI= 0.415 EP = 0.0325
370 TEND TO BE THOSE 0.86 OF 36 WHERE THE SEGREGATION OF ADOLESCENT BOYS IS ABSENT (148)	370 TEND TO BE THOSE 0.56 OF 52 WHERE THE SEGREGATION OF ADOLESCENT BOYS IS COMPLETE OR PARTIAL (95)	5 29 31 23 XSQ= 14.02 PHI= -0.399 XP = 0.0002
372 TILT TOWARD BEING THOSE 0.82 OF 22 WHERE MALE INITIATION RITES ARE ABSENT (63) ASA	372 TILT TOWARD BEING THOSE 0.55 OF 29 WHERE MALE INITIATION RITES ARE PRESENT (48) ASA	4 16 18 13 XSQ= 5.71 PHI= -0.335 XP = 0.0168
377 TILT MORE TOWARD BEING THOSE 0.98 OF 51 WHERE MALE GENITAL MUTILATION IS ABSENT (242)	377 TILT LESS TOWARD BEING THOSE 0.83 OF 66 WHERE MALE GENITAL MUTILATION IS ABSENT (242)	1 11 50 55 XSQ= 5.26 PHI= -0.212 XP = 0.0219

380	TILT TOWARD BEING THOSE WHERE SEGREGATICN CF GIRLS AT MENARCHE IS PRESENT (35) F-B	0.80 OF 15	380	TILT TOWARD BEING THOSE WHERE SEGREGATION OF GIRLS AT MENARCHE IS ABSENT (20) F-B	0.59 OF 17	12 7 3 10 XSQ= 3.50 PHI= 0.331 EP = 0.0359
392	DRIFT TOWARD BEING THOSE WHERE PREMARITAL SEX RELATIONS ARE STRONGLY PUNISHED AND IN FACT RARE, OR WEAKLY PUNISHED AND IN FACT NOT RARE, OR PUNISHED CNLY IF PREGNANCY RESULTS (112) JTW,EA	0.72 OF 29	392	DRIFT TOWARD BEING THOSE WHERE PREMARITAL SEX RELATIONS ARE FREELY PERMITTED (67) JTW,EA	0.50 OF 44	21 22 8 22 XSQ= 2.76 PHI= 0.194 XP = 0.0966
400	DRIFT TOWARD BEING THOSE WHERE HOMCSEXUAL ACTIVITY IS PERMITTED (36) F-B	0.73 OF 15	400	DRIFT TOWARD BEING THOSE WHERE HOMOSEXUAL ACTIVITY IS PROHIBITED (22) F-B	0.59 OF 17	4 10 11 7 XSQ= 2.17 PHI= -0.260 EP = 0.0870
406	TILT TOWARD BEING THOSE WHERE EXPLANATICNS OF ILLNESS OF AN AGGRESSION NATURE ARE PRESENT (28) W-C	0.82 OF 11	406	TILT TOWARD BEING THOSE WHERE EXPLANATIONS OF ILLNESS OF AN AGGRESSION NATURE ARE ABSENT (33) W-C	0.68 OF 22	9 7 2 15 XSQ= 5.47 PHI= 0.407 EP = 0.0104
417	IN ALL CASES ARE THOSE WHERE WARFARE IS PREVALENT (34) LWS	1.00 OF 10	417	TILT LESS TOWARD BEING THOSE WHERE WARFARE IS PREVALENT (34) LWS	0.59 OF 17	10 10 0 7 XSQ= 3.62 PHI= 0.366 EP = 0.0261
455	TILT TOWARD BEING THOSE WHERE THE MODE CF THE INDIVIDUAL'S CONTACT WITH THE DIVINE IS CONDUCIVE TO THE DEVELCPMENT OF THE INDIVIDUAL'S NEED TO ACHIEVE (17) DCM	0.75 OF 8	455	TILT TOWARD BEING THOSE WHERE THE MODE OF THE INDIVIDUAL'S CONTACT WITH THE DIVINE IS NOT CONDUCIVE TO THE DEVELOPMENT OF THE INDIVIDUAL'S NEED TO ACHIEVE (19) DCM	0.88 OF 8	6 1 2 7 XSQ= 4.06 PHI= 0.504 EP = 0.0406
475	DRIFT TOWARD BEING THOSE WHERE EXHIBITIONISTIC DANCING IS STRONGLY OR MODERATELY EMPHASIZED (48) PES	0.76 OF 17	475	DRIFT TOWARD BEING THOSE WHERE EXHIBITIONISTIC DANCING IS NEGLIGIBLY EMPHASIZED (38) PES	0.56 OF 27	13 12 4 15 XSQ= 3.15 PHI= 0.268 XP = 0.0758

467 CULTURES
WHERE CONTACT WITH OTHER CULTURES
IS FREQUENT, RATHER THAN
IRREGULAR (17) JMH

467 CULTURES
WHERE CONTACT WITH OTHER CULTURES
IS IRREGULAR, RATHER THAN
FREQUENT (11) JMH

BACKGROUND ON PAGE 171

SUBJECT ONLY

17 IN LEFT COLUMN

AZTEC	BULGARIANS	BURMESE	BURUSHO	CAMBODIANS	CUNA	DARD	KHASI	KOREANS	LOLO
MBUNDU	MIAC	SAMOYED	THONGA	TIV	TODA	VIETNAMESE			

11 IN RIGHT COLUMN

COPR ESKIMO	GILYAK	IBAN	JIVARO	NAMA	NUER	RWALA	SIRIONO	TIKOPIA	TUPINAMBA
YUROK									

26 EXCLUDED BECAUSE IRRELEVANT

ANDAMANESE	ARANDA	ARAUCANIANS	AZANDE	BEMBA	CAYAPA	CHAGGA	CHUKCHEE	CREEK	CROW
KAREN	KASKA	KORYAK	KURTATCHI	MANDAN	MARSHALLESE	NAVAHO	OJIBWA	PUKAPUKA	SAMOANS
TALLENSI	TEHUELCHE	TIMBIRA	TROBRIAND	WOLEAIANS	YAKUT				

346 EXCLUDED BECAUSE UNASCERTAINED

5	LEAN TOWARD BEING THOSE LOCATED IN EAST EURASIA (70)	0.65 OF 17	5	LEAN TOWARD BEING THOSE LOCATED OUTSIDE OF EAST EURASIA (330)	0.91 OF 11	11 1 6 10 XSQ= 6.32 PHI= 0.475 EP = 0.0060
44	DRIFT TOWARD BEING THOSE WHERE SETTLEMENTS ARE FIXED (222)	0.81 OF 16	44	DRIFT TOWARD BEING THOSE WHERE SETTLEMENTS ARE NON-FIXED (110)	0.55 OF 11	13 5 3 6 XSQ= 2.32 PHI= 0.293 EP = 0.0969
46	LEAN TOWARD BEING THOSE OTHER THAN WHERE SETTLEMENTS ARE NON-FIXED AND MOVEMENT IS NOMADIC (260)	0.94 OF 16	46	LEAN TOWARD BEING THOSE WHERE SETTLEMENTS ARE NON-FIXED AND MOVEMENT IS NOMADIC (72)	0.55 OF 11	1 6 15 5 XSQ= 5.60 PHI= -0.455 EP = 0.0087
47	DRIFT TOWARD BEING THOSE WHERE, IF SETTLEMENTS ARE NON-FIXED, MOVEMENT IS NON-NOMADIC, RATHER THAN NOMADIC (38)	0.67 OF 3	47	IN ALL CASES ARE THOSE WHERE, IF SETTLEMENTS ARE NON-FIXED, MOVEMENT IS NOMADIC, RATHER THAN NON-NOMADIC (72)	1.00 OF 6	1 6 2 0 XSQ= 2.01 PHI= -0.472 EP = 0.0833

51	LEAN TOWARD BEING THOSE 0.94 OF 17 WHERE SUBSISTENCE IS PRIMARILY BY FOOD PRODUCTION -- I. E., AGRICULTURE OR HUSBANDRY -- RATHER THAN BY GATHERING (253)	51	LEAN TOWARD BEING THOSE 0.64 OF 11 WHERE SUBSISTENCE IS PRIMARILY BY FOOD GATHERING -- I. E., HUNTING, FISHING, OR COLLECTING -- RATHER THAN FOOD PRODUCTION (147)	16 4 1 7 XSQ= 8.27 PHI= 0.543 EP = 0.0019
53	DRIFT TOWARD BEING THOSE 0.60 OF 15 WHERE FOOD PRODUCTION IS BY INTENSIVE AGRICULTURE, RATHER THAN BY SIMPLE AGRICULTURE OR INCIPIENT FOOD PRODUCTION (91)	53	IN ALL CASES ARE THOSE 1.00 OF 4 WHERE FOOD PRODUCTION IS BY SIMPLE AGRICULTURE OR INCIPIENT FOOD PRODUCTION, RATHER THAN BY INTENSIVE AGRICULTURE (147)	9 0 6 4 XSQ= 2.47 PHI= 0.361 EP = 0.0867
54	DRIFT TOWARD BEING THOSE 0.93 OF 15 WHERE FOOD PRODUCTION IS BY INTENSIVE OR SIMPLE AGRICULTURE, RATHER THAN BY INCIPIENT FOOD PRODUCTION (192)	54	DRIFT TOWARD BEING THOSE 0.50 OF 4 WHERE FOOD PRODUCTION IS BY INCIPIENT FOOD PRODUCTION, RATHER THAN BY INTENSIVE OR SIMPLE AGRICULTURE (46)	14 2 1 2 XSQ= 1.80 PHI= 0.307 EP = 0.0970
62	TILT TOWARD BEING THOSE 0.88 OF 17 WHERE HUSBANDRY OF SOME KIND IS PRESENT (228)	62	TILT TOWARD BEING THOSE 0.55 OF 11 WHERE HUSBANDRY OF ANY KIND IS ABSENT (172)	15 5 2 6 XSQ= 4.08 PHI= 0.382 EP = 0.0299
71	DRIFT TOWARD BEING THOSE 0.77 OF 13 WHERE METAL WORKING IS PRESENT (98)	71	DRIFT TOWARD BEING THOSE 0.64 OF 11 WHERE METAL WORKING IS ABSENT (153)	10 4 3 7 XSQ= 2.54 PHI= 0.325 EP = 0.0953
77	TILT LESS TOWARD BEING THOSE 0.53 OF 17 WHERE THE WRITING SYSTEM IS MNEMONIC OR ABSENT, RATHER THAN BEING ALPHABETIC-OR-PHONETIC (39) JMH	77	TILT MORE TOWARD BEING THOSE 0.91 OF 11 WHERE THE WRITING SYSTEM IS MNEMONIC OR ABSENT, RATHER THAN BEING ALPHABETIC-OR-PHONETIC (39) JMH	8 1 9 10 XSQ= 2.84 PHI= 0.319 EP = 0.0491
84	DRIFT LESS TOWARD BEING THOSE 0.63 OF 16 WHERE THE LEVEL OF POLITICAL INTEGRATION IS THE LITTLE STATE, THE MINIMAL STATE, THE AUTONOMOUS COMMUNITY, OR THE FAMILY (262) GPM	84	IN ALL CASES ARE THOSE 1.00 OF 9 WHERE THE LEVEL OF POLITICAL INTEGRATION IS THE LITTLE STATE, THE MINIMAL STATE, THE AUTONOMOUS COMMUNITY, OR THE FAMILY (262) GPM	6 0 10 9 XSQ= 2.62 PHI= 0.324 EP = 0.0571
85	TILT TOWARD BEING THOSE 0.63 OF 16 WHERE THE LEVEL OF POLITICAL INTEGRATION IS THE LARGE STATE, OR THE LITTLE STATE (70) GPM	85	TILT TOWARD BEING THOSE 0.89 OF 9 WHERE THE LEVEL OF POLITICAL INTEGRATION IS THE MINIMAL STATE, THE AUTONOMOUS COMMUNITY, OR THE FAMILY (234) GPM	10 1 6 8 XSQ= 4.26 PHI= 0.413 EP = 0.0330
86	LEAN TOWARD BEING THOSE 0.81 OF 16 WHERE THE LEVEL OF POLITICAL INTEGRATION IS THE LARGE STATE, THE LITTLE STATE, OR THE MINIMAL STATE (148) GPM	86	LEAN TOWARD BEING THOSE 0.78 OF 9 WHERE THE LEVEL OF POLITICAL INTEGRATION IS THE AUTONOMOUS COMMUNITY, OR THE FAMILY (156) GPM	13 2 3 7 XSQ= 6.08 PHI= 0.493 EP = 0.0090

87	IN ALL CASES ARE THOSE WHERE THE LEVEL OF POLITICAL INTEGRATION IS THE LARGE STATE, THE LITTLE STATE, THE MINIMAL STATE, OR THE AUTONOMOUS COMMUNITY (281) GPM	1.00 OF 16	87	TILT LESS TOWARD BEING THOSE WHERE THE LEVEL OF POLITICAL INTEGRATION IS THE LARGE STATE, THE LITTLE STATE, THE MINIMAL STATE, OR THE AUTONOMOUS COMMUNITY (281) GPM	0.67 OF 9	16 6 0 3 XSQ= 3.32 PHI= 0.364 EP = 0.0365
91	TILT TOWARD BEING THOSE WHERE SOCIETAL COMPLEXITY IS HIGH (18) F-W	0.80 OF 5	91	IN ALL CASES ARE THOSE WHERE SOCIETAL COMPLEXITY IS LOW (22) F-W	1.00 OF 6	4 0 1 6 XSQ= 4.48 PHI= 0.638 EP = 0.0152
95	LEAN TOWARD BEING THOSE WHERE THE HIERARCHY OF NATIONAL JURISDICTION HAS FOUR, THREE, OR TWO LEVELS (76) GES,EA	0.50 OF 16	95	IN ALL CASES ARE THOSE WHERE THE HIERARCHY OF NATIONAL JURISDICTION HAS ONE OR NO LEVELS (254) GES,EA	1.00 OF 11	8 0 8 11 XSQ= 5.60 PHI= 0.455 EP = 0.0082
96	TILT TOWARD BEING THOSE WHERE THE HIERARCHY OF NATIONAL JURISDICTION HAS FOUR, THREE, TWO OR ONE LEVEL (174) GES,EA	0.88 OF 16	96	TILT TOWARD BEING THOSE WHERE THE HIERARCHY OF NATIONAL JURISDICTION HAS NO LEVELS (156) GES,EA	0.64 OF 11	14 4 2 7 XSQ= 5.54 PHI= 0.453 EP = 0.0115
100	IN ALL CASES ARE THOSE WHERE HIERARCHIES ARE MORE COMPLEX THAN THE 'SIMPLEST,' I. E., MORE COMPLEX THAN TWO LOCAL LEVELS WITH NO NATIONAL LEVELS (267) GES,EA	1.00 OF 16	100	DRIFT LESS TOWARD BEING THOSE WHERE HIERARCHIES ARE MORE COMPLEX THAN THE 'SIMPLEST,' I. E., MORE COMPLEX THAN TWO LOCAL LEVELS WITH NO NATIONAL LEVELS (267) GES,EA	0.73 OF 11	16 8 0 3 XSQ= 2.54 PHI= 0.306 EP = 0.0564
102	DRIFT TOWARD BEING THOSE WHERE CLASS STRATIFICATION IS PRESENT (203)	0.82 OF 17	102	DRIFT TOWARD BEING THOSE WHERE CLASS STRATIFICATION IS ABSENT (180)	0.55 OF 11	14 5 3 6 XSQ= 2.65 PHI= 0.308 EP = 0.0946
106	TILT TOWARD BEING THOSE WHERE CLASS STRATIFICATION, IF PRESENT, IS BASED ON SOMETHING OTHER THAN WEALTH (126)	0.86 OF 14	106	TILT TOWARD BEING THOSE WHERE CLASS STRATIFICATION, IF PRESENT, IS BASED ON WEALTH (77)	0.80 OF 5	2 4 12 1 XSQ= 4.64 PHI= -0.494 EP = 0.0173
107	TILT TOWARD BEING THOSE WHERE CLASS STRATIFICATION, IF PRESENT, IS BASED ON OCCUPATIONAL STATUS (43)	0.57 OF 14	107	IN ALL CASES ARE THOSE WHERE CLASS STRATIFICATION, IF PRESENT, IS BASED ON SOMETHING OTHER THAN OCCUPATIONAL STATUS (160)	1.00 OF 5	8 0 6 5 XSQ= 2.87 PHI= 0.389 EP = 0.0445
116	LEAN TOWARD BEING THOSE WHERE OCCUPATIONAL SPECIALIZATION IS FULL-TIME, WHETHER OR NOT FOR SURPLUS PRODUCTION (20) JMH	0.76 OF 17	116	LEAN TOWARD BEING THOSE WHERE OCCUPATIONAL SPECIALIZATION IS PART-TIME ONLY (34) JMH	0.91 OF 11	13 1 4 10 XSQ= 9.58 PHI= 0.585 EP = 0.0013

132	IN ALL CASES ARE THOSE 1.00 OF 17 WHERE ECONOMIC EXCHANGE INVOLVES THE USE OF MONEY (37) JMH	132	TEND TO BE THOSE 0.73 OF 11 WHERE ECONOMIC EXCHANGE DOES NOT INVOLVE THE USE OF MONEY (17) JMH	17 3 0 8 XSQ= 13.93 PHI= 0.705 EP = 0.0001
142	DRIFT MORE TOWARD BEING THOSE 0.88 OF 17 WHERE THE LEVEL OF SOCIAL SANCTION IS PUBLIC CORPOREAL SANCTION OR PUBLIC PROPERTY SANCTION, RATHER THAN PRIVATE SETTLEMENT (38) JMH	142	DRIFT LESS TOWARD BEING THOSE 0.55 OF 11 WHERE THE LEVEL OF SOCIAL SANCTION IS PUBLIC CORPOREAL SANCTION OR PUBLIC PROPERTY SANCTION, RATHER THAN PRIVATE SETTLEMENT (38) JMH	15 6 2 5 XSQ= 2.45 PHI= 0.296 EP = 0.0764
196	DRIFT TOWARD BEING THOSE 0.79 OF 14 WHERE INDIVIDUAL RIGHTS IN REAL PROPERTY, AND RULES FOR INHERITANCE, ARE PRESENT (194)	196	DRIFT TOWARD BEING THOSE 0.63 OF 8 WHERE INDIVIDUAL RIGHTS IN REAL PROPERTY, OR RULES FOR INHERITANCE, ARE ABSENT (87)	11 3 3 5 XSQ= 2.15 PHI= 0.312 EP = 0.0815
334	TILT TOWARD BEING THOSE 0.75 OF 4 WHERE THE INDULGENCE OF THE CHILD IS LOW (38) B-B-C	334	IN ALL CASES ARE THOSE 1.00 OF 5 WHERE THE INDULGENCE OF THE CHILD IS HIGH (40) B-B-C	1 5 3 0 XSQ= 2.76 PHI= -0.553 EP = 0.0476
346	TILT TOWARD BEING THOSE 0.75 OF 4 WHERE THE CHILD'S INFERRED ANXIETY OVER PERFORMANCE OF SELF-RELIANT BEHAVIOR IS HIGH (37) B-B-C	346	IN ALL CASES ARE THOSE 1.00 OF 5 WHERE THE CHILD'S INFERRED ANXIETY OVER PERFORMANCE OF SELF-RELIANT BEHAVIOR IS LOW (39) B-B-C	3 0 1 5 XSQ= 2.76 PHI= 0.553 EP = 0.0476
347	TILT TOWARD BEING THOSE 0.75 OF 4 WHERE THE CHILD'S INFERRED CONFLICT REGARDING SELF-RELIANT BEHAVIOR IS HIGH (37) B-B-C	347	IN ALL CASES ARE THOSE 1.00 OF 5 WHERE THE CHILD'S INFERRED CONFLICT REGARDING SELF-RELIANT BEHAVIOR IS LOW (39) B-B-C	3 0 1 5 XSQ= 2.76 PHI= 0.553 EP = 0.0476
352	IN ALL CASES ARE THOSE 1.00 OF 4 WHERE THE TOTAL POSITIVE PRESSURE TOWARD DEVELOPING OBEDIENT BEHAVIOR IN THE CHILD IS HIGH (44) B-B-C	352	TILT TOWARD BEING THOSE 0.80 OF 5 WHERE THE TOTAL POSITIVE PRESSURE TOWARD DEVELOPING OBEDIENT BEHAVIOR IN THE CHILD IS LOW (28) B-B-C	4 1 0 4 XSQ= 2.98 PHI= 0.575 EP = 0.0476
424	TILT TOWARD BEING THOSE 0.65 OF 17 WHERE RELIGIOUS SPECIALISTS ARE FULL-TIME, RATHER THAN PART-TIME (21) JMH	424	TILT TOWARD BEING THOSE 0.82 OF 11 WHERE RELIGIOUS SPECIALISTS ARE PART-TIME, RATHER THAN FULL-TIME (33) JMH	11 2 6 9 XSQ= 4.09 PHI= 0.382 EP = 0.0238
450	DRIFT TOWARD BEING THOSE 0.58 OF 12 WHERE THE OBSERVATION OF FOOD TABOOS IS LOW, RATHER THAN HIGH OR MEDIUM (26) JRL	450	DRIFT TOWARD BEING THOSE 0.89 OF 9 WHERE THE OBSERVATION OF FOOD TABOOS IS HIGH OR MEDIUM, RATHER THAN LOW (60) JRL	5 8 7 1 XSQ= 3.07 PHI= -0.382 EP = 0.0669

```
458  TILT TOWARD BEING THOSE          0.80 OF  10     458  TILT TOWARD BEING THOSE          0.86 OF   7           8     1
     WHERE GAMES, IF PRESENT,                              WHERE GAMES, IF PRESENT,                                2     6
     INCLUDE GAMES OF STRATEGY  (52) R-A-B,EA              DO NOT INCLUDE                                    XSQ=     4.74
                                                           GAMES OF STRATEGY  (119) R-A-B,EA                 PHI=    0.528
                                                                                                             EP =   0.0152

470  TEND TO BE THOSE                 0.76 OF  17     470  IN ALL CASES ARE THOSE           1.00 OF  11          13     0
     WHERE INNCVATIONS ARE                                 WHERE INNOVATIONS ARE                                4    11
     GENERALLY ACCEPTED  (21) JMH                          ACCEPTED ONLY SELECTIVELY  (33) JMH               XSQ=    12.78
                                                                                                             PHI=    0.676
                                                                                                             EP =   0.0001
```

468 CULTURES
WHERE CONTACT WITH OTHER CULTURES
IS FREQUENT, RATHER THAN
REGULAR OR IRREGULAR (17) JMH

468 CULTURES
WHERE CONTACT WITH OTHER CULTURES
IS REGULAR OR IRREGULAR, RATHER THAN
FREQUENT (37) JMH

BACKGROUND ON PAGE 171

PREDICATE ONLY

17 IN LEFT COLUMN

AZTEC BULGARIANS BURMESE BURUSHO CAMBODIANS CUNA DARD KHASI KOREANS LOLO
MBUNDU MIAO SAMOYED THONGA TIV TODA VIETNAMESE

37 IN RIGHT COLUMN

ANDAMANESE ARANDA ARAUCANIANS AZANDE BEMBA CAYAPA CHAGGA CHUKCHEE COPR ESKIMO CREEK
CROW GILYAK IBAN JIVARO KAREN KASKA KORYAK KURTATCHI MANDAN MARSHALLESE
NAMA NAVAHO NUER OJIBWA PUKAPUKA RWALA SAMOANS SIRIONO TALLENSI TEHUELCHE
TIKOPIA TIMBIRA TROBRIAND TUPINAMBA WOLEAIANS YAKUT YUROK

346 EXCLUDED BECAUSE UNASCERTAINED

469 CULTURES
WHERE CCNTACT WITH CTHER CULTURES
IS FREQUENT OR REGULAR, RATHER THAN
IRREGULAR (43) JMH

469 CULTURES
WHERE CONTACT WITH OTHER CULTURES
IS IRREGULAR, RATHER THAN
FREQUENT OR REGULAR (11) JMH

BACKGROUND ON PAGE 171

PREDICATE ONLY

43 IN LEFT COLUMN

ANDAMANESE	ARANDA	ARAUCANIANS	AZANDE	AZTEC	BEMBA	BULGARIANS	BURMESE	BURUSHO	CAMBODIANS
CAYAPA	CHAGGA	CHUKCHEE	CREEK	CROW	CUNA	DARD	KAREN	KASKA	KHASI
KOREANS	KORYAK	KURTATCHI	LOLO	MANDAN	MARSHALLESE	MBUNDU	MIAO	NAVAHO	OJIBWA
PUKAPUKA	SAMCANS	SAMOYEC	TALLENSI	TEHUELCHE	THONGA	TIMBIRA	TIV	TODA	TROBRIAND
VIETNAMESE	WOLEAIANS	YAKUT							

11 IN RIGHT CCLUMN

COPR ESKIMO	GILYAK	IBAN	JIVARO	NAMA	NUER	RWALA	SIRIONC	TIKOPIA	TUPINAMBA
YUROK									

346 EXCLUDED BECAUSE UNASCERTAINED

470	CULTURES WHERE INNOVATIONS ARE GENERALLY ACCEPTED (21) JMH	470	CULTURES WHERE INNOVATIONS ARE ACCEPTED ONLY SELECTIVELY (33) JMH

BACKGROUND ON PAGE 171 — BOTH SUBJECT AND PREDICATE

21 IN LEFT COLUMN

ARAUCANIANS AZTEC BEMBA BURMESE BURUSHO CAMBODIANS CAYAPA CUNA DARD KASKA
KOREANS LOLO MARSHALLESE MIAO NAVAHO PUKAPUKA SAMOYED THONGA TIV VIETNAMESE
YAKUT

33 IN RIGHT COLUMN

ANDAMANESE ARANDA AZANDE BULGARIANS CHAGGA CHUKCHEE COPR ESKIMO CREEK CROW GILYAK
IBAN JIVARO KAREN KHASI KORYAK KURTATCHI MANDAN MBUNDU NAMA NUER
OJIBWA RWALA SAMOANS SIRIONO TALLENSI TEHUELCHE TIKOPIA TIMBIRA TODA TROBRIAND
TUPINAMBA WOLEAIANS YUROK

346 EXCLUDED BECAUSE UNASCERTAINED

No.	Left column		No.	Right column		Statistics
5	DRIFT LESS TOWARD BEING THOSE LOCATED OUTSIDE OF EAST EURASIA (330)	0.52 OF 21	5	DRIFT MORE TOWARD BEING THOSE LOCATED OUTSIDE OF EAST EURASIA (330)	0.79 OF 33	10 7 11 26 XSQ= 3.01 PHI= 0.236 XP = 0.0825
51	DRIFT MORE TOWARD BEING THOSE WHERE SUBSISTENCE IS PRIMARILY BY FOOD PRODUCTION -- I. E., AGRICULTURE OR HUSBANDRY -- RATHER THAN BY GATHERING (253)	0.81 OF 21	51	DRIFT LESS TOWARD BEING THOSE WHERE SUBSISTENCE IS PRIMARILY BY FOOD PRODUCTION -- I. E., AGRICULTURE OR HUSBANDRY -- RATHER THAN BY GATHERING (253)	0.52 OF 33	17 17 4 16 XSQ= 3.59 PHI= 0.258 XP = 0.0581
73	DRIFT TOWARD BEING THOSE WHERE WEAVING IS PRESENT (118)	0.67 OF 18	73	DRIFT TOWARD BEING THOSE WHERE WEAVING IS ABSENT (130)	0.65 OF 31	12 11 6 20 XSQ= 3.28 PHI= 0.259 XP = 0.0700
77	TEND TO BE THOSE WHERE THE WRITING SYSTEM IS ALPHABETIC-OR-PHONETIC, RATHER THAN BEING MNEMONIC OR ABSENT (15) JMH	0.57 OF 21	77	TEND TO BE THOSE WHERE THE WRITING SYSTEM IS MNEMONIC OR ABSENT, RATHER THAN BEING ALPHABETIC-OR-PHONETIC (39) JMH	0.91 OF 33	12 3 9 30 XSQ= 12.47 PHI= 0.481 XP = 0.0004

85	TILT TOWARD BEING THOSE 0.53 OF 19 WHERE THE LEVEL OF POLITICAL INTEGRATION IS THE LARGE STATE, OR THE LITTLE STATE (70) GPM	85	TILT TOWARD BEING THOSE 0.84 OF 31 WHERE THE LEVEL OF POLITICAL INTEGRATION IS THE MINIMAL STATE, THE AUTONOMOUS COMMUNITY, OR THE FAMILY (234) GPM	10 5 9 26 XSQ= 5.84 PHI= 0.342 XP = 0.0157
95	DRIFT LESS TOWARD BEING THOSE 0.60 OF 20 WHERE THE HIERARCHY OF NATIONAL JURISDICTION HAS ONE OR NO LEVELS (254) GES,EA	95	DRIFT MORE TOWARD BEING THOSE 0.88 OF 32 WHERE THE HIERARCHY OF NATIONAL JURISDICTION HAS ONE OR NO LEVELS (254) GES,EA	8 4 12 28 XSQ= 3.81 PHI= 0.271 XP = 0.0510
110	DRIFT TOWARD BEING THOSE 0.63 OF 19 WHERE SLAVERY IS PRESENT (163)	110	DRIFT TOWARD BEING THOSE 0.67 OF 33 WHERE SLAVERY IS ABSENT (218)	12 11 7 22 XSQ= 3.22 PHI= 0.249 XP = 0.0726
116	LEAN TOWARD BEING THOSE 0.62 OF 21 WHERE OCCUPATIONAL SPECIALIZATION IS FULL-TIME, WHETHER OR NOT FOR SURPLUS PRODUCTION (20) JMH	116	LEAN TOWARD BEING THOSE 0.79 OF 33 WHERE OCCUPATIONAL SPECIALIZATION IS PART-TIME ONLY (34) JMH	13 7 8 26 XSQ= 7.45 PHI= 0.371 XP = 0.0063
132	LEAN MORE TOWARD BEING THOSE 0.95 OF 21 WHERE ECONOMIC EXCHANGE INVOLVES THE USE OF MONEY (37) JMH	132	LEAN LESS TOWARD BEING THOSE 0.52 OF 33 WHERE ECONOMIC EXCHANGE INVOLVES THE USE OF MONEY (37) JMH	20 17 1 16 XSQ= 9.44 PHI= 0.418 XP = 0.0021
141	TILT TOWARD BEING THOSE 0.71 OF 21 WHERE THE LEVEL OF SOCIAL SANCTION IS PUBLIC CORPOREAL SANCTION, RATHER THAN PUBLIC PROPERTY SANCTION OR PRIVATE SETTLEMENT (28) JMH	141	TILT TOWARD BEING THOSE 0.61 OF 33 WHERE THE LEVEL OF SOCIAL SANCTION IS PUBLIC PROPERTY SANCTION OR PRIVATE SETTLEMENT, RATHER THAN PUBLIC CORPOREAL SANCTION (26) JMH	15 13 6 20 XSQ= 4.07 PHI= 0.275 XP = 0.0437
152	IN ALL CASES ARE THOSE 1.00 OF 4 WHERE THE DIFFERENTIATION OF THE JURIDICAL AGENCY FROM THE MEDICAL AGENCY IS HIGH (10) MJ	152	TILT TOWARD BEING THOSE 0.83 OF 6 WHERE THE DIFFERENTIATION OF THE JURIDICAL AGENCY FROM THE MEDICAL AGENCY IS LOW (10) MJ	4 1 0 5 XSQ= 3.75 PHI= 0.612 EP = 0.0476
186	DRIFT LESS TOWARD BEING THOSE 0.57 OF 21 WHERE THE KIN GROUP IS OTHER THAN EXCLUSIVELY PATRILINEAL (250)	186	DRIFT MORE TOWARD BEING THOSE 0.82 OF 33 WHERE THE KIN GROUP IS OTHER THAN EXCLUSIVELY PATRILINEAL (250)	9 6 12 27 XSQ= 2.76 PHI= 0.226 XP = 0.0965
317	LEAN TOWARD BEING THOSE 0.86 OF 7 WHERE DISPLAY OF AFFECTION TOWARD THE INFANT IS LOW (29) B-B-C	317	LEAN TOWARD BEING THOSE 0.75 OF 20 WHERE DISPLAY OF AFFECTION TOWARD THE INFANT IS HIGH (39) B-B-C	1 15 6 5 XSQ= 5.60 PHI= -0.455 EP = 0.0087

No.			No.			
320	TILT TOWARD BEING THOSE WHERE THE DEGREE OF REDUCTION OF THE INFANT'S DRIVES IS LOW (24) B-B-C	0.71 OF 7	320	TILT TOWARD BEING THOSE WHERE THE DEGREE OF REDUCTION OF THE INFANT'S DRIVES IS HIGH (45) B-B-C	0.79 OF 19	2 15 5 4 XSQ= 3.73 PHI= -0.379 EP = 0.0283
334	TILT TOWARD BEING THOSE WHERE THE INDULGENCE OF THE CHILD IS LOW (38) B-B-C	0.88 OF 8	334	TILT TOWARD BEING THOSE WHERE THE INDULGENCE OF THE CHILD IS HIGH (40) B-B-C	0.67 OF 21	1 14 7 7 XSQ= 4.81 PHI= -0.407 EP = 0.0142
424	TILT TOWARD BEING THOSE WHERE RELIGIOUS SPECIALISTS ARE FULL-TIME, RATHER THAN PART-TIME (21) JMH	0.62 OF 21	424	TILT TOWARD BEING THOSE WHERE RELIGIOUS SPECIALISTS ARE PART-TIME, RATHER THAN FULL-TIME (33) JMH	0.76 OF 33	13 8 8 25 XSQ= 6.16 PHI= 0.338 XP = 0.0131
450	TILT LESS TOWARD BEING THOSE WHERE THE OBSERVATION OF FOOD TABOOS IS HIGH OR MEDIUM, RATHER THAN LOW (60) JRL	0.53 OF 15	450	TILT MORE TOWARD BEING THOSE WHERE THE OBSERVATION OF FOOD TABOOS IS HIGH OR MEDIUM, RATHER THAN LOW (60) JRL	0.89 OF 27	8 24 7 3 XSQ= 4.90 PHI= -0.342 XP = 0.0268
458	TILT TOWARD BEING THOSE WHERE GAMES, IF PRESENT, INCLUDE GAMES OF STRATEGY (52) R-A-B,EA	0.62 OF 13	458	TILT TOWARD BEING THOSE WHERE GAMES, IF PRESENT, DO NOT INCLUDE GAMES OF STRATEGY (119) R-A-B,EA	0.80 OF 25	8 5 5 20 XSQ= 4.84 PHI= 0.357 EP = 0.0279
460	DRIFT MORE TOWARD BEING THOSE WHERE GAMES, IF PRESENT, ARE NOT LIMITED TO GAMES OF SKILL ONLY (104) R-A-B,EA	0.85 OF 13	460	DRIFT LESS TOWARD BEING THOSE WHERE GAMES, IF PRESENT, ARE NOT LIMITED TO GAMES OF SKILL ONLY (104) R-A-B,EA	0.52 OF 25	2 12 11 13 XSQ= 2.63 PHI= -0.263 EP = 0.0773
468	TEND TO BE THOSE WHERE CONTACT WITH OTHER CULTURES IS FREQUENT, RATHER THAN REGULAR OR IRREGULAR (17) JMH	0.62 OF 21	468	TEND TO BE THOSE WHERE CONTACT WITH OTHER CULTURES IS REGULAR OR IRREGULAR, RATHER THAN FREQUENT (37) JMH	0.88 OF 33	13 4 8 29 XSQ= 12.53 PHI= 0.482 XP = 0.0004
469	IN ALL CASES ARE THOSE WHERE CONTACT WITH OTHER CULTURES IS FREQUENT OR REGULAR, RATHER THAN IRREGULAR (43) JMH	1.00 OF 21	469	LEAN LESS TOWARD BEING THOSE WHERE CONTACT WITH OTHER CULTURES IS FREQUENT OR REGULAR, RATHER THAN IRREGULAR (43) JMH	0.67 OF 33	21 22 0 11 XSQ= 6.86 PHI= 0.356 XP = 0.0088

471 CULTURES
WHERE SECRET SOCIETIES ARE
PRESENT (9) LWS

471 CULTURES
WHERE SECRET SOCIETIES ARE
UMIMPORTANT OR ABSENT (14) LWS

BACKGROUND ON PAGE 172

BOTH SUBJECT AND PREDICATE

9 IN LEFT COLUMN

ASHANTI CROW DIERI FANG HAIDA HANO KWAKIUTL MOTA OMAHA

14 IN RIGHT COLUMN

AINU ARANDA ARAUCANIANS AZTEC CHUKCHEE FON IBAN KUNG KUTENAI SERI
VEDDA YAHGAN YAKUT YUKAGHIR

377 EXCLUDED BECAUSE UNASCERTAINED

46	DRIFT TOWARD BEING THOSE OTHER THAN WHERE SETTLEMENTS ARE NON-FIXED AND MOVEMENT IS NOMADIC (260)	0.78 OF 9	46	DRIFT TOWARD BEING THOSE WHERE SETTLEMENTS ARE NON-FIXED AND MOVEMENT IS NOMADIC (72)	0.62 OF 13	2 8 7 5 XSQ= 1.92 PHI= -0.295 EP = 0.0991
187	TILT TOWARD BEING THOSE WHERE THE KIN GROUP IS EXCLUSIVELY MATRILINEAL (55)	0.56 OF 9	187	TILT TOWARD BEING THOSE WHERE THE KIN GROUP IS OTHER THAN EXCLUSIVELY MATRILINEAL (344)	0.92 OF 13	5 1 4 12 XSQ= 3.97 PHI= 0.425 EP = 0.0461
188	TILT TOWARD BEING THOSE WHERE THE KIN GROUP IS OTHER THAN EXCLUSIVELY COGNATIC (252)	0.89 OF 9	188	TILT TOWARD BEING THOSE WHERE THE KIN GROUP IS EXCLUSIVELY COGNATIC (148)	0.57 OF 14	1 8 8 6 XSQ= 3.13 PHI= -0.369 EP = 0.0397
192	IN ALL CASES ARE THOSE OTHER THAN WHERE THE ONLY KIN GROUP PRESENT IS A KINDRED OR ELSE BILATERAL DESCENT IS INFERRED (289)	1.00 OF 9	192	TILT TOWARD BEING THOSE WHERE THE ONLY KIN GROUP PRESENT IS A KINDRED OR ELSE BILATERAL DESCENT IS INFERRED (111)	0.50 OF 14	0 7 9 7 XSQ= 4.32 PHI= -0.434 EP = 0.0189
198	TILT TOWARD BEING THOSE WHERE RULES FOR THE INHERITANCE OF REAL PROPERTY, IF PRESENT, FAVOR THE FEMALE HEIR OR LINE, RATHER THAN THE MALE (21)	0.80 OF 5	198	IN ALL CASES ARE THOSE WHERE RULES FOR THE INHERITANCE OF REAL PROPERTY, IF PRESENT, FAVOR THE MALE HEIR OR LINE, RATHER THAN THE FEMALE (144)	1.00 OF 4	1 4 4 0 XSQ= 2.98 PHI= -0.575 EP = 0.0476

234	TILT TOWARD BEING THOSE WHERE THE COUSIN TERMINOLCGY IS OF CRCW, CMAHA, OR IRCQUOIS TYPE, RATHER THAN ESKIMC OR HAWAIIAN TYPE (152)	0.88 OF	8	234	TILT TOWARD BEING THOSE WHERE THE COUSIN TERMINOLOGY IS OF ESKIMO OR HAWAIIAN TYPE, RATHER THAN CROW, OMAHA, OR IROQUOIS TYPE (170)	0.70 OF	10	7 3 1 7 XSQ= 3.85 PHI= 0.462 EP = 0.0248
319	IN ALL CASES ARE THOSE WHERE PROTECTION OF THE INFANT FROM ENVIRONMENTAL DISCOMFORTS IS HIGH (35) B-B-C	1.00 OF	5	319	DRIFT TOWARD BEING THOSE WHERE PROTECTION OF THE INFANT FROM ENVIRONMENTAL DISCOMFORTS IS LOW (30) B-B-C	0.57 OF	7	5 3 0 4 XSQ= 2.10 PHI= 0.418 EP = 0.0808
320	IN ALL CASES ARE THOSE WHERE THE DEGREE OF REDUCTION OF THE INFANT'S DRIVES IS HIGH (45) B-B-C	1.00 OF	5	320	DRIFT TOWARD BEING THOSE WHERE THE DEGREE OF REDUCTION OF THE INFANT'S DRIVES IS LOW (24) B-B-C	0.57 OF	7	5 3 0 4 XSQ= 2.10 PHI= 0.418 EP = 0.0808
324	DRIFT TOWARD BEING THOSE WHERE THE PAIN INFLICTED ON THE INFANT BY THE NURTURANT AGENT IS LOW OR NEGLIGIBLE (32) B-B-C	0.60 OF	5	324	IN ALL CASES ARE THOSE WHERE THE PAIN INFLICTED ON THE INFANT BY THE NURTURANT AGENT IS HIGH (34) B-B-C	1.00 OF	6	2 6 3 0 XSQ= 2.39 PHI= -0.466 EP = 0.0606
325	IN ALL CASES ARE THOSE WHERE THE DEGREE OF DIFFUSION AMONG THE INFANT'S NURTURANT AGENTS IS HIGH (42) B-B-C	1.00 OF	5	325	TILT TOWARD BEING THOSE WHERE THE DEGREE OF DIFFUSION AMONG THE INFANT'S NURTURANT AGENTS IS LOW (32) B-B-C	0.71 OF	7	5 2 0 5 XSQ= 3.54 PHI= 0.543 EP = 0.0278
351	IN ALL CASES ARE THOSE WHERE THE CHILD'S INFERRED CONFLICT REGARDING ACHIEVEMENT BEHAVIOR IS HIGH (26) B-B-C	1.00 OF	5	351	TILT TOWARD BEING THOSE WHERE THE CHILD'S INFERRED CONFLICT REGARDING ACHIEVEMENT BEHAVIOR IS LOW (34) B-B-C	0.83 OF	6	5 1 0 5 XSQ= 4.65 PHI= 0.650 EP = 0.0152
353	IN ALL CASES ARE THOSE WHERE THE CHILD'S INFERRED ANXIETY OVER NON-PERFORMANCE OF OBEDIENT BEHAVIOR IS HIGH (42) B-B-C	1.00 OF	5	353	DRIFT TOWARD BEING THOSE WHERE THE CHILD-S INFERRED ANXIETY OVER NON-PERFORMANCE OF OBEDIENT BEHAVIOR IS LOW (32) B-B-C	0.67 OF	6	5 2 0 4 XSQ= 2.75 PHI= 0.500 EP = 0.0606
427	IN ALL CASES ARE THOSE WHERE A HIGH GOD, IF PRESENT, IS INACTIVE, RATHER THAN ACTIVE (69) GES,EA	1.00 OF	2	427	IN ALL CASES ARE THOSE WHERE A HIGH GOD, IF PRESENT, IS ACTIVE, RATHER THAN INACTIVE (87) GES,EA	1.00 OF	6	0 6 2 0 XSQ= 3.56 PHI= -0.667 EP = 0.0357
441	TILT TOWARD BEING THOSE WHERE FEAR OF HUMAN BEINGS IS HIGH (29) W-C	0.75 OF	4	441	IN ALL CASES ARE THOSE WHERE FEAR OF HUMAN BEINGS IS LOW (32) W-C	1.00 OF	5	3 0 1 5 XSQ= 2.76 PHI= 0.553 EP = 0.0476

****

472 CULTURES
WHERE THE COMPOSITE NARCISSISM INCEX
IS HIGH (47) PES

472 CULTURES
WHERE THE COMPOSITE NARCISSISM INDEX
IS LOW (43) PES

BACKGROUND ON PAGE 172

BOTH SUBJECT AND PREDICATE

47 IN LEFT COLUMN

ABIPON	ALBANIANS	ARAUCANIANS	ASHANTI	AZANDE	AZTEC	BALINESE	BEMBA	CHAGGA	CHEYENNE
CHIR-APACHE	CHUKCHEE	COMANCHE	COPR ESKIMO	CREEK	CROW	FON	GANDA	HAICA	HEBREWS
IBAN	IFUGAO	INCA	JIVARO	KOREANS	KWAKIUTL	LAKHER	LESU	MANUS	MAORI
MARQUESANS	MASAI	NUER	NYAKYUSA	OJIBWA	RIFFIANS	SAMOANS	SIWANS	SOMALI	THONGA
TIKOPIA	TIV	TRCBRIAND	WARRAU	WOGEO	WOLOF	YUROK			

43 IN RIGHT CCLUMN

AINU	ALCRESE	AMERICANS	ANDAMANESE	ARANDA	ARAPESH	AYMARA	BHIL	CHENCHU	CUNA
CZECHS	DOBUANS	GOND	HANO	KASKA	KAZAK	KURTATCHI	LANGO	LAPPS	LAU
LEPCHA	MURNGIN	NAMA	NAVAHO	PAPAGO	PUKAPUKA	RWALA	SANPOIL	SIRIONO	TALLENSI
TANALA	TAPIRAPE	TIMBIRA	TODA	TRUMAI	VENDA	VIETNAMESE	WITOTO	WOLEAIANS	YAGUA
YAHGAN	YAKUT	ZUNI							

310 EXCLUDED BECAUSE UNASCERTAINEC

---

5 TILT MORE TOWARD BEING THOSE 0.94 OF 47
LOCATED OUTSIDE OF
EAST EURASIA (330)

5 TILT LESS TOWARD BEING THOSE 0.74 OF 43
LOCATED OUTSIDE OF
EAST EURASIA (330)

3 11
44 32
XSQ= 4.92
PHI= -0.234
XP = 0.0265

16 DRIFT LESS TOWARD BEING THOSE 0.60 OF 47
WHERE THE LATITUDE IS
TEN DEGREES OR GREATER (277)

16 DRIFT MORE TOWARD BEING THOSE 0.79 OF 43
WHERE THE LATITUDE IS
TEN DEGREES OR GREATER (277)

28 34
19 9
XSQ= 3.12
PHI= -0.186
XP = 0.0771

86 LEAN TOWARD BEING THOSE 0.64 OF 42
WHERE THE LEVEL OF POLITICAL INTEGRATION
IS THE LARGE STATE, THE LITTLE STATE,
OR THE MINIMAL STATE (148) GPM

86 LEAN TOWARD BEING THOSE 0.69 OF 36
WHERE THE LEVEL OF POLITICAL INTEGRATION
IS THE AUTONOMOUS COMMUNITY, OR
THE FAMILY (156) GPM

27 11
15 25
XSQ= 7.53
PHI= 0.311
XP = 0.0061

89 DRIFT TOWARD BEING THOSE 0.54 OF 13
WHERE, IF A NON-HEREDITARY HEADMANSHIP
IS PRESENT, SUCCESSION IS BY MEANS
OTHER THAN CONSENSUS (43)

89 DRIFT TOWARD BEING THOSE 0.83 OF 12
WHERE, IF A NON-HEREDITARY HEADMANSHIP
IS PRESENT, SUCCESSION IS
BY CONSENSUS (63)

6 10
7 2
XSQ= 2.30
PHI= -0.304
EP = 0.0968

96	DRIFT TOWARD BEING THOSE WHERE THE HIERARCHY OF NATIONAL JURISDICTION HAS FOUR, THREE, TWO OR ONE LEVEL (174) GES,EA	0.64 OF 45	96	DRIFT TOWARD BEING THOSE WHERE THE HIERARCHY OF NATIONAL JURISDICTION HAS NO LEVELS (156) GES,EA	0.56 OF 41	29 18 16 23 XSQ= 2.87 PHI= 0.183 XP = 0.0902
100	DRIFT MORE TOWARD BEING THOSE WHERE HIERARCHIES ARE MORE COMPLEX THAN THE 'SIMPLEST,' I. E., MORE COMPLEX THAN TWO LOCAL LEVELS WITH NO NATIONAL LEVELS (267) GES,EA	0.93 OF 45	100	DRIFT LESS TOWARD BEING THOSE WHERE HIERARCHIES ARE MORE COMPLEX THAN THE 'SIMPLEST,' I. E., MORE COMPLEX THAN TWO LOCAL LEVELS WITH NO NATIONAL LEVELS (267) GES,EA	0.78 OF 41	42 32 3 9 XSQ= 3.00 PHI= 0.187 XP = 0.0833
106	DRIFT TOWARD BEING THOSE WHERE CLASS STRATIFICATION, IF PRESENT, IS BASED ON SOMETHING OTHER THAN WEALTH (126)	0.70 OF 30	106	DRIFT TOWARD BEING THOSE WHERE CLASS STRATIFICATION, IF PRESENT, IS BASED ON WEALTH (77)	0.60 OF 20	9 12 21 8 XSQ= 3.29 PHI= -0.256 XP = 0.0698
108	TILT TOWARD BEING THOSE WHERE CLASS STRATIFICATION, IF PRESENT, IS BASED ON A HEREDITARY ARISTOCRACY (74)	0.57 OF 30	108	TILT TOWARD BEING THOSE WHERE CLASS STRATIFICATION, IF PRESENT, IS BASED ON SOMETHING OTHER THAN A HEREDITARY ARISTOCRACY (129)	0.80 OF 20	17 4 13 16 XSQ= 5.20 PHI= 0.323 XP = 0.0225
110	DRIFT TOWARD BEING THOSE WHERE SLAVERY IS PRESENT (163)	0.53 OF 47	110	DRIFT TOWARD BEING THOSE WHERE SLAVERY IS ABSENT (218)	0.67 OF 43	25 14 22 29 XSQ= 3.10 PHI= 0.186 XP = 0.0784
136	TILT TOWARD BEING THOSE WHERE FULL-TIME ENTREPRENEURS ARE PRESENT (18) JV	0.80 OF 10	136	TILT TOWARD BEING THOSE WHERE FULL-TIME ENTREPRENEURS ARE ABSENT (14) JV	0.75 OF 12	8 3 2 9 XSQ= 4.58 PHI= 0.456 EP = 0.0300
137	TEND TO BE THOSE WHERE INVIDIOUS DISPLAY OF WEALTH IS STRONGLY EMPHASIZED (37) PES	0.63 OF 46	137	TEND TO BE THOSE WHERE INVIDIOUS DISPLAY OF WEALTH IS MODERATELY, LITTLE, OR NEGATIVELY EMPHASIZED (52) PES	0.81 OF 43	29 8 17 35 XSQ= 16.29 PHI= 0.428 XP = 0.0001
148	LEAN TOWARD BEING THOSE WHERE THE INCIDENCE OF PERSONAL CRIME IS HIGH (12) B-B-C	0.63 OF 16	148	LEAN TOWARD BEING THOSE WHERE THE INCIDENCE OF PERSONAL CRIME IS LOW (21) B-B-C	0.87 OF 15	10 2 6 13 XSQ= 5.95 PHI= 0.438 EP = 0.0091
149	TILT TOWARD BEING THOSE WHERE THE INCIDENCE OF THEFT IS HIGH (18) B-B-C	0.65 OF 17	149	TILT TOWARD BEING THOSE WHERE THE INCIDENCE OF THEFT IS LOW (19) B-B-C	0.72 OF 18	11 5 6 13 XSQ= 3.43 PHI= 0.313 EP = 0.0437

242	TILT MORE TOWARD BEING THOSE 0.89 OF 46 WHERE MARRIAGE IS COMMONLY OR OCCASIONALLY POLYGYNOUS, RATHER THAN MONOGAMOUS (314)	242	TILT LESS TOWARD BEING THOSE 0.64 OF 42 WHERE MARRIAGE IS COMMONLY OR OCCASIONALLY POLYGYNOUS, RATHER THAN MONOGAMOUS (314)	41 27 5 15 XSQ= 6.37 PHI= 0.269 XP = 0.0116
258	TILT TOWARD BEING THOSE 0.69 OF 13 WHERE THE SEVERITY OF SON'S WIFE AVOIDANCE IS HIGH (15) WNS	258	TILT TOWARD BEING THOSE 0.82 OF 11 WHERE THE SEVERITY OF SON'S WIFE AVOIDANCE IS LOW (16) WNS	9 2 4 9 XSQ= 4.37 PHI= 0.427 EP = 0.0188
260	TILT LESS TOWARD BEING THOSE 0.52 OF 25 WHERE THE AGE OF MALES AT MARRIAGE IS LESS THAN TWENTY (38) JKH	260	TILT MORE TOWARD BEING THOSE 0.87 OF 15 WHERE THE AGE OF MALES AT MARRIAGE IS LESS THAN TWENTY (38) JKH	13 13 12 2 XSQ= 3.55 PHI= -0.298 EP = 0.0403
300	DRIFT TOWARD BEING THOSE 0.61 OF 28 WHERE THE POST-PARTUM SEX TABOO LASTS LONGER THAN SIX MONTHS (51)	300	DRIFT TOWARD BEING THOSE 0.67 OF 27 WHERE THE POST-PARTUM SEX TABOO LASTS SIX MONTHS OR LESS (73)	17 9 11 18 XSQ= 3.11 PHI= 0.238 XP = 0.0779
307	DRIFT TOWARD BEING THOSE 0.74 OF 23 WHERE THE EARLY AGGRESSION SATISFACTION POTENTIAL IS HIGH (33) W-C	307	DRIFT TOWARD BEING THOSE 0.57 OF 21 WHERE THE EARLY AGGRESSION SATISFACTION POTENTIAL IS LOW (19) W-C	17 9 6 12 XSQ= 3.19 PHI= 0.269 XP = 0.0741
316	LEAN TOWARD BEING THOSE 0.68 OF 22 WHERE EXCLUSIVE MOTHER-SON SLEEPING ARRANGEMENTS LAST ONE YEAR OR LONGER (19) W-K-A	316	LEAN TOWARD BEING THOSE 0.92 OF 12 WHERE EXCLUSIVE MOTHER-SON SLEEPING ARRANGEMENTS LAST LESS THAN ONE YEAR (25) W-K-A	15 1 7 11 XSQ= 8.89 PHI= 0.511 EP = 0.0011
321	DRIFT TOWARD BEING THOSE 0.64 OF 22 WHERE THE IMMEDIACY OF REDUCTION OF THE INFANT'S DRIVES IS LOW (25) B-B-C	321	DRIFT TOWARD BEING THOSE 0.70 OF 23 WHERE THE IMMEDIACY OF REDUCTION OF THE INFANT'S DRIVES IS HIGH (35) B-B-C	8 16 14 7 XSQ= 3.74 PHI= -0.288 XP = 0.0533
323	TILT TOWARD BEING THOSE 0.78 OF 27 WHERE THE CONSTANCY OF PRESENCE OF THE INFANT'S NURTURANT AGENT IS LOW (45) B-B-C	323	TILT TOWARD BEING THOSE 0.52 OF 27 WHERE THE CONSTANCY OF PRESENCE OF THE INFANT'S NURTURANT AGENT IS HIGH (29) B-B-C	6 14 21 13 XSQ= 3.89 PHI= -0.268 XP = 0.0485
344	LEAN TOWARD BEING THOSE 0.72 OF 29 WHERE THE TOTAL POSITIVE PRESSURE TOWARD DEVELOPING SELF-RELIANT BEHAVIOR IN THE CHILD IS HIGH (36) B-B-C	344	LEAN TOWARD BEING THOSE 0.69 OF 26 WHERE THE TOTAL POSITIVE PRESSURE TOWARD DEVELOPING SELF-RELIANT BEHAVIOR IN THE CHILD IS LOW (40) B-B-C	21 8 8 18 XSQ= 7.94 PHI= 0.380 XP = 0.0048

348	TILT TOWARD BEING THOSE 0.76 OF 25 WHERE THE TOTAL POSITIVE PRESSURE TOWARD DEVELOPING ACHIEVEMENT BEHAVIOR IN THE CHILD IS HIGH (32) B-B-C	348	TILT TOWARD BEING THOSE 0.64 OF 22 WHERE THE TOTAL POSITIVE PRESSURE TOWARD DEVELOPING ACHIEVEMENT BEHAVIOR IN THE CHILD IS LOW (31) B-B-C	19 8 6 14 XSQ= 5.99 PHI= 0.357 XP = 0.0144
349	LEAN TOWARD BEING THOSE 0.80 OF 25 WHERE THE CHILD'S INFERREC ANXIETY OVER NCN-PERFORMANCE OF ACHIEVEMENT BEHAVIOR IS HIGH (34) B-B-C	349	LEAN TOWARD BEING THOSE 0.67 OF 21 WHERE THE CHILD'S INFERRED ANXIETY OVER NON-PERFORMANCE OF ACHIEVEMENT BEHAVIOR IS LOW (28) B-B-C	20 7 5 14 XSQ= 8.42 PHI= 0.428 XP = 0.0037
356	DRIFT TOWARD BEING THOSE 0.68 OF 22 WHERE ADOLESCENT PEER GROUPS OR PAIRS ARE PRESENT IN A SETTING CF COURTSHIP (29) JKH	356	DRIFT TOWARD BEING THOSE 0.64 OF 14 WHERE NEITHER ADOLESCENT PEER GROUPS NOR PAIRS ARE PRESENT IN A SETTING OF COURTSHIP (22) JKH	15 5 7 9 XSQ= 2.46 PHI= 0.261 EP = 0.0874
373	TILT TOWARD BEING THOSE 0.59 OF 22 WHERE MALE INITIATION CEREMONIES AT PUBERTY ARE PRESENT (17) W-K-A	373	TILT TOWARD BEING THOSE 0.83 OF 12 WHERE MALE INITIATION CEREMONIES AT PUBERTY ARE ABSENT (27) W-K-A	13 2 9 10 XSQ= 4.08 PHI= 0.346 EP = 0.0297
377	DRIFT LESS TOWARD BEING THOSE 0.67 OF 45 WHERE MALE GENITAL MUTILATION IS ABSENT (242)	377	DRIFT MORE TOWARD BEING THOSE 0.85 OF 41 WHERE MALE GENITAL MUTILATION IS ABSENT (242)	15 6 30 35 XSQ= 3.11 PHI= 0.190 XP = 0.0776
390	DRIFT LESS TOWARD BEING THOSE 0.71 OF 35 WHERE PREMARITAL SEX RELATIONS ARE WEAKLY PUNISHED ANC IN FACT NOT RARE OR PUNISHED CNLY IF PREGNANCY RESULTS, OR FREELY PERMITTEC (132) JTW,EA	390	DRIFT MORE TOWARD BEING THOSE 0.91 OF 35 WHERE PREMARITAL SEX RELATIONS ARE WEAKLY PUNISHED AND IN FACT NOT RARE OR PUNISHED ONLY IF PREGNANCY RESULTS, OR FREELY PERMITTED (132) JTW,EA	10 3 25 32 XSQ= 3.40 PHI= 0.220 XP = 0.0652
417	IN ALL CASES ARE THCSE 1.00 OF 18 WHERE WARFARE IS PREVALENT (34) LWS	417	LEAN LESS TOWARD BEING THOSE 0.57 OF 14 WHERE WARFARE IS PREVALENT (34) LWS	18 8 0 6 XSQ= 6.89 PHI= 0.464 EP = 0.0033
419	TEND TO BE THOSE 0.88 OF 43 WHERE MILITARY GLORY IS STRONGLY OR MODERATELY EMPHASIZED (55) PES	419	TEND TO BE THOSE 0.60 OF 43 WHERE MILITARY GLORY IS NEGLIGIBLY EMPHASIZED (31) PES	38 17 5 26 XSQ= 20.18 PHI= 0.484 XP = 0.0000
420	TEND TO BE THOSE 0.69 OF 45 WHERE BELLICOSITY IS EXTREME (41) PES	420	TEND TO BE THOSE 0.76 OF 42 WHERE BELLICOSITY IS MODERATE OR NEGLIGIBLE (46) PES	31 10 14 32 XSQ= 15.95 PHI= 0.428 XP = 0.0001

421	TILT TOWARD BEING THOSE WHERE KILLING, TORTURING, OR MUTILATING OF THE ENEMY IS STRONGLY OR MODERATELY EMPHASIZED (37) PES	0.58 OF 45	421	TILT TOWARD BEING THOSE WHERE KILLING, TORTURING, OR MUTILATING OF THE ENEMY IS NEGLIGIBLY EMPHASIZED (47) PES	0.72 OF 39	26 11 19 28 XSQ= 6.26 PHI= 0.273 XP = 0.0123
460	TILT TOWARD BEING THOSE WHERE GAMES, IF PRESENT, ARE NOT LIMITED TO GAMES OF SKILL ONLY (104) R-A-B,EA	0.74 OF 38	460	TILT TOWARD BEING THOSE WHERE GAMES, IF PRESENT, ARE LIMITED TO GAMES OF SKILL ONLY (67) R-A-B,EA	0.53 OF 34	10 18 28 16 XSQ= 4.29 PHI= -0.244 XP = 0.0383
473	TEND TO BE THOSE WHERE SENSITIVITY TO INSULT IS EXTREME (32) PES	0.62 OF 47	473	TEND TO BE THOSE WHERE SENSITIVITY TO INSULT IS MODERATE OR NEGLIGIBLE (56) PES	0.93 OF 41	29 3 18 38 XSQ= 25.69 PHI= 0.540 XP = 0.0000
474	TEND TO BE THOSE WHERE BOASTFULNESS IS EXTREME (41) PES	0.74 OF 46	474	TEND TO BE THOSE WHERE BOASTFULNESS IS MODERATE, NEGLIBIBLE, OR UNREPORTED (48) PES	0.84 OF 43	34 7 12 36 XSQ= 27.44 PHI= 0.555 XP = 0.0000
475	TILT TOWARD BEING THOSE WHERE EXHIBITIONISTIC DANCING IS STRONGLY OR MODERATELY EMPHASIZED (48) PES	0.70 OF 46	475	TILT TOWARD BEING THOSE WHERE EXHIBITIONISTIC DANCING IS NEGLIGIBLY EMPHASIZED (38) PES	0.60 OF 40	32 16 14 24 XSQ= 6.43 PHI= 0.273 XP = 0.0112

473	CULTURES WHERE SENSITIVITY TO INSULT IS EXTREME (32) PES	473	CULTURES WHERE SENSITIVITY TO INSULT IS MODERATE OR NEGLIGIBLE (56) PES

BACKGROUND ON PAGE 173 — BOTH SUBJECT AND PREDICATE

32 IN LEFT COLUMN

ABIPON	ALBANIANS	ALCRESE	ASHANTI	AZANDE	AZTEC	BALINESE	BEMBA	BHIL	CHAGGA
HAIDA	HEBREWS	IFUGAO	JIVARO	KOREANS	KWAKIUTL	MAORI	MARQUESANS	MASAI	NUER
NYAKYUSA	OJIBWA	RIFFIANS	SAMOANS	SIWANS	SOMALI	TIKOPIA	TROBRIAND	WARRAU	WOLOF
YAHGAN	YURCK								

56 IN RIGHT COLUMN

AINU	AMERICANS	ANDAMANESE	ARANDA	ARAPESH	ARAUCANIANS	AYMARA	CHENCHU	CHEYENNE	CHIR-APACHE
CHUKCHEE	COMANCHE	COPR ESKIMO	CREEK	CROW	CUNA	CZECHS	DOBUANS	FON	GANDA
GOND	HANC	IBAN	INCA	KASKA	KAZAK	KURTATCHI	LAKHER	LANGO	LAPPS
LAU	LEPCHA	LESU	MANUS	MURNGIN	NAMA	NAVAHO	PAPAGO	PUKAPUKA	RWALA
SANPCIL	SIRIONO	TALLENSI	TANALA	TAPIRAPE	THONGA	TIMBIRA	TIV	TODA	VENDA
VIETNAMESE	WITCTC	WOGEC	WOLEAIANS	YAGUA	ZUNI				

312 EXCLUDED BECAUSE UNASCERTAINED

86	DRIFT TOWARD BEING THOSE WHERE THE LEVEL OF POLITICAL INTEGRATION IS THE LARGE STATE, THE LITTLE STATE, OR THE MINIMAL STATE (148) GPM	0.64 OF 28	86	DRIFT TOWARD BEING THOSE WHERE THE LEVEL OF POLITICAL INTEGRATION IS THE AUTONOMOUS COMMUNITY, OR THE FAMILY (156) GPM	0.60 OF 48	18 19 10 29 XSQ= 3.39 PHI= 0.211 XP = 0.0657
94	IN ALL CASES ARE THOSE WHERE THE HIERARCHY OF NATIONAL JURISDICTION HAS TWO, ONE, OR NO LEVELS (296) GES,EA	1.00 OF 31	94	DRIFT LESS TOWARD BEING THOSE WHERE THE HIERARCHY OF NATIONAL JURISDICTION HAS TWO, ONE, OR NO LEVELS (296) GES,EA	0.87 OF 53	0 7 31 46 XSQ= 2.90 PHI= -0.186 XP = 0.0883
96	TILT TOWARD BEING THOSE WHERE THE HIERARCHY OF NATIONAL JURISDICTION HAS FOUR, THREE, TWO OR ONE LEVEL (174) GES,EA	0.71 OF 31	96	TILT TOWARD BEING THOSE WHERE THE HIERARCHY OF NATIONAL JURISDICTION HAS NO LEVELS (156) GES,EA	0.55 OF 53	22 24 9 29 XSQ= 4.22 PHI= 0.224 XP = 0.0399
102	TILT TOWARD BEING THOSE WHERE CLASS STRATIFICATION IS PRESENT (203)	0.75 OF 32	102	TILT TOWARD BEING THOSE WHERE CLASS STRATIFICATION IS ABSENT (180)	0.55 OF 56	24 25 8 31 XSQ= 6.42 PHI= 0.270 XP = 0.0113

109	LEAN LESS TOWARD BEING THOSE WHERE CASTES ARE ABSENT (317)	0.73 OF 30	109	LEAN MORE TOWARD BEING THOSE WHERE CASTES ARE ABSENT (317)	0.98 OF 54	8 1 22 53 XSQ= 9.96 PHI= 0.344 XP = 0.0016
110	DRIFT TOWARD BEING THOSE WHERE SLAVERY IS PRESENT (163)	0.56 OF 32	110	DRIFT TOWARD BEING THOSE WHERE SLAVERY IS ABSENT (218)	0.66 OF 56	18 19 14 37 XSQ= 3.30 PHI= 0.194 XP = 0.0694
137	TILT TOWARD BEING THOSE WHERE INVIDIOUS DISPLAY OF WEALTH IS STRONGLY EMPHASIZED (37) PES	0.58 OF 31	137	TILT TOWARD BEING THOSE WHERE INVIDIOUS DISPLAY OF WEALTH IS MODERATELY, LITTLE, OR NEGATIVELY EMPHASIZED (52) PES	0.68 OF 56	18 18 13 38 XSQ= 4.51 PHI= 0.228 XP = 0.0337
148	TILT TOWARD BEING THOSE WHERE THE INCIDENCE OF PERSONAL CRIME IS HIGH (12) B-B-C	0.78 OF 9	148	TILT TOWARD BEING THOSE WHERE THE INCIDENCE OF PERSONAL CRIME IS LOW (21) B-B-C	0.76 OF 21	7 5 2 16 XSQ= 5.56 PHI= 0.431 EP = 0.0125
196	LEAN TOWARD BEING THOSE WHERE INDIVIDUAL RIGHTS IN REAL PROPERTY, AND RULES FOR INHERITANCE, ARE PRESENT (194)	0.91 OF 23	196	LEAN TOWARD BEING THOSE WHERE INDIVIDUAL RIGHTS IN REAL PROPERTY, OR RULES FOR INHERITANCE, ARE ABSENT (87)	0.52 OF 44	21 21 2 23 XSQ= 10.47 PHI= 0.395 XP = 0.0012
207	DRIFT TOWARD BEING THOSE WHERE MARITAL RESIDENCE IS AMBILOCAL OR NEOLOCAL, RATHER THAN MATRILOCAL OR UXORILOCAL (64)	0.86 OF 7	207	DRIFT TOWARD BEING THOSE WHERE MARITAL RESIDENCE IS MATRILOCAL OR UXORILOCAL, RATHER THAN AMBILOCAL OR NEOLOCAL (64)	0.57 OF 21	1 12 6 9 XSQ= 2.35 PHI= -0.289 EP = 0.0836
209	TILT MORE TOWARD BEING THOSE WHERE MARITAL RESIDENCE IS PATRILOCAL, VIRILOCAL, OR AVUNCULOCAL, RATHER THAN MATRILOCAL OR UXORILOCAL (270)	0.96 OF 26	209	TILT LESS TOWARD BEING THOSE WHERE MARITAL RESIDENCE IS PATRILOCAL, VIRILOCAL, OR AVUNCULOCAL, RATHER THAN MATRILOCAL OR UXORILOCAL (270)	0.74 OF 47	25 35 1 12 XSQ= 4.00 PHI= 0.234 XP = 0.0455
225	DRIFT TOWARD BEING THOSE WHERE COUSIN MARRIAGE IS PREFERENTIALLY OR PERMISSIVELY PATRILATERAL, RATHER THAN MATRILATERAL (23)	0.75 OF 4	225	DRIFT TOWARD BEING THOSE WHERE COUSIN MARRIAGE IS PREFERENTIALLY OR PERMISSIVELY MATRILATERAL, RATHER THAN PATRILATERAL (43)	0.88 OF 8	3 1 1 7 XSQ= 2.30 PHI= 0.437 EP = 0.0667
234	DRIFT TOWARD BEING THOSE WHERE THE COUSIN TERMINOLOGY IS OF ESKIMO OR HAWAIIAN TYPE, RATHER THAN CROW, OMAHA, OR IROQUOIS TYPE (170)	0.71 OF 24	234	DRIFT TOWARD BEING THOSE WHERE THE COUSIN TERMINOLOGY IS OF CROW, OMAHA, OR IROQUOIS TYPE, RATHER THAN ESKIMO OR HAWAIIAN TYPE (152)	0.55 OF 49	7 27 17 22 XSQ= 3.37 PHI= -0.215 XP = 0.0662

242	TILT MORE TOWARD BEING THOSE 0.94 OF 31 WHERE MARRIAGE IS COMMONLY OR OCCASIONALLY POLYGYNOUS, RATHER THAN MONOGAMOUS (314)	242	TILT LESS TOWARD BEING THOSE 0.67 OF 55 WHERE MARRIAGE IS COMMONLY OR OCCASIONALLY POLYGYNOUS, RATHER THAN MONOGAMOUS (314)	29 37 2 18 XSQ= 6.27 PHI= 0.270 XP = 0.0123
258	DRIFT TOWARD BEING THOSE 0.75 OF 8 WHERE THE SEVERITY OF SON'S WIFE AVOIDANCE IS HIGH (15) WNS	258	DRIFT TOWARD BEING THOSE 0.69 OF 16 WHERE THE SEVERITY OF SON'S WIFE AVOIDANCE IS LOW (16) WNS	6 5 2 11 XSQ= 2.54 PHI= 0.325 EP = 0.0825
262	TILT MORE TOWARD BEING THOSE 0.94 OF 32 WHERE WIVES ARE OBTAINED BY MEANS INVOLVING THE PRESENCE OF SOME CONSIDERATION (305)	262	TILT LESS TOWARD BEING THOSE 0.73 OF 56 WHERE WIVES ARE OBTAINED BY MEANS INVOLVING THE PRESENCE OF SOME CONSIDERATION (305)	30 41 2 15 XSQ= 4.27 PHI= 0.220 XP = 0.0388
263	DRIFT TOWARD BEING THOSE 0.69 OF 32 WHERE WIVES ARE OBTAINED BY RELATIVELY DIFFICULT MEANS, NAMELY BY BRIDE-PRICE, BRIDE-SERVICE, OR EXCHANGING A FEMALE RELATIVE (233)	263	DRIFT TOWARD BEING THOSE 0.54 OF 56 WHERE WIVES ARE OBTAINED BY RELATIVELY EASY MEANS, NAMELY BY TOKEN BRIDE-PRICE, GIFT EXCHANGE, ABSENCE OF ANY CONSIDERATION, OR RECEIPT OF DOWRY (162)	22 26 10 30 XSQ= 3.24 PHI= 0.192 XP = 0.0718
282	DRIFT TOWARD BEING THOSE 0.67 OF 12 WHERE THE STRENGTH OF DESIRE FOR CHILDREN IS HIGH (16) BCA	282	DRIFT TOWARD BEING THOSE 0.70 OF 20 WHERE THE STRENGTH OF DESIRE FOR CHILDREN IS LOW OR ABSENT (20) BCA	8 6 4 14 XSQ= 2.74 PHI= 0.293 EP = 0.0683
303	LEAN TOWARD BEING THOSE 0.73 OF 15 WHERE THE EARLY ORAL SATISFACTION POTENTIAL IS LOW (25) W-C	303	LEAN TOWARD BEING THOSE 0.72 OF 29 WHERE THE EARLY ORAL SATISFACTION POTENTIAL IS HIGH (32) W-C	4 21 11 8 XSQ= 6.67 PHI= -0.389 XP = 0.0098
306	DRIFT TOWARD BEING THOSE 0.69 OF 13 WHERE THE EARLY DEPENDENCE SATISFACTION POTENTIAL IS LOW (24) W-C	306	DRIFT TOWARD BEING THOSE 0.66 OF 29 WHERE THE EARLY DEPENDENCE SATISFACTION POTENTIAL IS HIGH (28) W-C	4 19 9 10 XSQ= 3.08 PHI= -0.271 XP = 0.0790
312	DRIFT TOWARD BEING THOSE 0.75 OF 12 WHERE DEPENDENCE SOCIALIZATION ANXIETY IS HIGH (24) W-C	312	DRIFT TOWARD BEING THOSE 0.59 OF 27 WHERE DEPENDENCE SOCIALIZATION ANXIETY IS LOW (23) W-C	9 11 3 16 XSQ= 2.65 PHI= 0.261 EP = 0.0824
318	TILT TOWARD BEING THOSE 0.65 OF 17 WHERE THE OVERALL INDULGENCE OF THE INFANT IS LOW (31) B-B-C	318	TILT TOWARD BEING THOSE 0.69 OF 35 WHERE THE OVERALL INDULGENCE OF THE INFANT IS HIGH (40) B-B-C	6 24 11 11 XSQ= 3.92 PHI= -0.274 XP = 0.0478

323	DRIFT MORE TOWARD BEING THOSE WHERE THE CONSTANCY OF PRESENCE OF THE INFANT'S NURTURANT AGENT IS LOW (45) B-B-C	0.82 OF 17	323	DRIFT LESS TOWARD BEING. THOSE WHERE THE CONSTANCY OF PRESENCE OF THE INFANT'S NURTURANT AGENT IS LOW (45) B-B-C	0.53 OF 36	3 17 14 19 XSQ= 3.13 PHI= -0.243 XP = 0.0768
335	TILT TOWARD BEING THOSE WHERE INITIAL INDULGENCE OF DEPENDENCY IS LOW (18) WNS	0.73 OF 11	335	TILT TOWARD BEING THOSE WHERE INITIAL INDULGENCE OF DEPENDENCY IS HIGH (20) WNS	0.68 OF 25	3 17 8 8 XSQ= 3.61 PHI= -0.317 EP = 0.0335
356	TILT TOWARD BEING THOSE WHERE ADOLESCENT PEER GROUPS OR PAIRS ARE PRESENT IN A SETTING OF COURTSHIP (29) JKH	0.85 OF 13	356	TILT TOWARD BEING THOSE WHERE NEITHER ADOLESCENT PEER GROUPS NOR PAIRS ARE PRESENT IN A SETTING OF COURTSHIP (22) JKH	0.61 OF 23	11 9 2 14 XSQ= 5.24 PHI= 0.381 EP = 0.0140
419	TILT MORE TOWARD BEING THOSE WHERE MILITARY GLORY IS STRONGLY OR MODERATELY EMPHASIZED (55) PES	0.83 OF 29	419	TILT LESS TOWARD BEING THOSE WHERE MILITARY GLORY IS STRONGLY OR MODERATELY EMPHASIZED (55) PES	0.55 OF 55	24 30 5 25 XSQ= 5.41 PHI= 0.254 XP = 0.0200
420	TILT TOWARD BEING THOSE WHERE BELLICOSITY IS EXTREME (41) PES	0.65 OF 31	420	TILT TOWARD BEING THOSE WHERE BELLICOSITY IS MODERATE OR NEGLIGIBLE (46) PES	0.63 OF 54	20 20 11 34 XSQ= 4.92 PHI= 0.241 XP = 0.0266
472	TEND TO BE THOSE WHERE THE COMPOSITE NARCISSISM INDEX IS HIGH (47) PES	0.91 OF 32	472	TEND TO BE THOSE WHERE THE COMPOSITE NARCISSISM INDEX IS LOW (43) PES	0.68 OF 56	29 18 3 38 XSQ= 25.69 PHI= 0.540 XP = 0.0000
474	TILT TOWARD BEING THOSE WHERE BOASTFULNESS IS EXTREME (41) PES	0.65 OF 31	474	TILT TOWARD BEING THOSE WHERE BOASTFULNESS IS MODERATE, NEGLIBIBLE, OR UNREPORTED (48) PES	0.64 OF 56	20 20 11 36 XSQ= 5.56 PHI= 0.253 XP = 0.0184

474 CULTURES
WHERE BOASTFULNESS IS EXTREME (41) PES

474 CULTURES
WHERE BOASTFULNESS IS MODERATE,
NEGLIBIBLE, OR UNREPORTED (48) PES

BACKGROUND ON PAGE 174 BOTH SUBJECT AND PREDICATE

41 IN LEFT COLUMN

ABIPCN	ALBANIANS	ARAUCANIANS	ASHANTI	AZANDE	AZTEC	BEMBA	CHEYENNE	COMANCHE	COPR ESKIMO
CREEK	CRCW	FCN	HAICA	HEBREWS	IBAN	IFUGAO	INCA	JIVARO	KOREANS
KWAKIUTL	LAKHER	LANGO	MANUS	MAORI	MASAI	OJIBWA	PUKAPUKA	SIRIONO	SOMALI
TALLENSI	TAPIRAPE	THCNGA	TIKOPIA	TIV	TROBRIAND	TRUMAI	WARRAU	WITOTO	WOGEO
WOLOF									

48 IN RIGHT COLUMN

AINU	ALCRESE	AMERICANS	ANDAMANESE	ARANDA	ARAPESH	AYMARA	BALINESE	BHIL	CHAGGA
CHENCHU	CHIR-APACHE	CHUKCHEE	CUNA	CZECHS	DOBUANS	GANDA	GOND	HANO	KASKA
KAZAK	KURTATCHI	LAPPS	LAU	LEPCHA	LESU	MARQUESANS	MURNGIN	NAMA	NAVAHO
NUER	PAPAGC	RIFFIANS	RWALA	SAMOANS	SANPOIL	SIWANS	TANALA	TIMBIRA	TODA
VENDA	VIETNAMESE	WCLEAIANS	YACUA	YAHGAN	YAKUT	YUROK	ZUNI		

311 EXCLUDED BECAUSE UNASCERTAINED

5	TILT MORE TOWARD BEING THOSE LOCATED OUTSIDE OF EAST EURASIA (330)	0.95 OF 41	5	TILT LESS TOWARD BEING THOSE LOCATED OUTSIDE OF EAST EURASIA (330)	0.75 OF 48	2 12 39 36 XSQ= 5.32 PHI= -0.245 XP = 0.0211
73	DRIFT TOWARD BEING THOSE WHERE WEAVING IS PRESENT (118)	0.61 OF 36	73	DRIFT TOWARD BEING THOSE WHERE WEAVING IS ABSENT (130)	0.63 OF 40	22 15 14 25 XSQ= 3.34 PHI= 0.210 XP = 0.0678
110	TILT TOWARD BEING THOSE WHERE SLAVERY IS PRESENT (163)	0.56 OF 41	110	TILT TOWARD BEING THOSE WHERE SLAVERY IS ABSENT (218)	0.69 OF 48	23 15 18 33 XSQ= 4.61 PHI= 0.228 XP = 0.0318
137	TILT TOWARD BEING THOSE WHERE INVIDIOUS DISPLAY OF WEALTH IS STRONGLY EMPHASIZED (37) PES	0.55 OF 40	137	TILT TOWARD BEING THOSE WHERE INVIDIOUS DISPLAY OF WEALTH IS MODERATELY, LITTLE, OR NEGATIVELY EMPHASIZED (52) PES	0.71 OF 48	22 14 18 34 XSQ= 5.00 PHI= 0.238 XP = 0.0253

144	DRIFT TOWARD BEING THCSE WHERE THE RATIO OF RESTITUTIVE TO REPRESSIVE SANCTIONS IS LOW (25) WME	0.59 OF	17	144	DRIFT TOWARD BEING THOSE WHERE THE RATIO OF RESTITUTIVE TO REPRESSIVE SANCTIONS IS HIGH OR MEDIUM (27) WME	0.73 OF	22	7 16 10 6 XSQ= 2.75 PHI= -0.266 EP = 0.0586
148	DRIFT TOWARD BEING THCSE WHERE THE INCIDENCE CF PERSONAL CRIME IS HIGH (12) B-B-C	0.62 OF	13	148	DRIFT TOWARD BEING THOSE WHERE THE INCIDENCE OF PERSONAL CRIME IS LOW (21) B-B-C	0.78 OF	18	8 4 5 14 XSQ= 3.40 PHI= 0.331 EP = 0.0596
260	TILT TOWARD BEING THOSE WHERE THE AGE OF MALES AT MARRIAGE IS TWENTY CR OVER (17) JKH	0.53 OF	19	260	TILT TOWARD BEING THOSE WHERE THE AGE OF MALES AT MARRIAGE IS LESS THAN TWENTY (38) JKH	0.85 OF	20	9 17 10 3 XSQ= 4.63 PHI= -0.345 EP = 0.0187
280	IN ALL CASES ARE THOSE WHERE THE COMPOSITE FERTILITY LEVEL IS HIGH (13) MN	1.00 OF	7	280	TILT TOWARD BEING THOSE WHERE THE COMPOSITE FERTILITY LEVEL IS LOW (12) MN	0.60 OF	5	7 2 0 3 XSQ= 2.86 PHI= 0.488 EP = 0.0455
300	DRIFT TOWARD BEING THCSE WHERE THE POST-PARTUM SEX TABOO LASTS LONGER THAN SIX MONTHS (51)	0.63 OF	24	300	DRIFT TOWARD BEING THOSE WHERE THE POST-PARTUM SEX TABOO LASTS SIX MONTHS OR LESS (73)	0.65 OF	31	15 11 9 20 XSQ= 2.95 PHI= 0.232 XP = 0.0858
307	TILT TOWARD BEING THOSE WHERE THE EARLY AGGRESSION SATISFACTION POTENTIAL IS HIGH (33) W-C	0.79 OF	19	307	TILT TOWARD BEING THOSE WHERE THE EARLY AGGRESSION SATISFACTION POTENTIAL IS LOW (19) W-C	0.56 OF	25	15 11 4 14 XSQ= 4.10 PHI= 0.305 XP = 0.0428
313	DRIFT TOWARD BEING THCSE WHERE AGGRESSION SCCIALIZATION ANXIETY IS LOW (28) W-C	0.70 OF	20	313	DRIFT TOWARD BEING THOSE WHERE AGGRESSION SOCIALIZATION ANXIETY IS HIGH (26) W-C	0.60 OF	25	6 15 14 10 XSQ= 2.90 PHI= -0.254 XP = 0.0884
322	TILT TOWARD BEING THOSE WHERE THE CONSISTENCY CF REDUCTION OF THE INFANT'S DRIVES IS LOW (32) B-B-C	0.82 OF	17	322	TILT TOWARD BEING THOSE WHERE THE CONSISTENCY OF REDUCTION OF THE INFANT'S DRIVES IS HIGH (27) B-B-C	0.56 OF	27	3 15 14 12 XSQ= 4.73 PHI= -0.328 XP = 0.0296
344	TILT TOWARD BEING THOSE WHERE THE TOTAL POSITIVE PRESSURE TOWARD DEVELOPING SELF-RELIANT BEHAVIOR IN THE CHILD IS HIGH (36) B-B-C	0.73 OF	22	344	TILT TOWARD BEING THOSE WHERE THE TOTAL POSITIVE PRESSURE TOWARD DEVELOPING SELF-RELIANT BEHAVIOR IN THE CHILD IS LOW (40) B-B-C	0.63 OF	32	16 12 6 20 XSQ= 5.15 PHI= 0.309 XP = 0.0233

No.		No.		
348	TILT TOWARD BEING THOSE 0.79 OF 19 WHERE THE TOTAL POSITIVE PRESSURE TOWARD DEVELOPING ACHIEVEMENT BEHAVIOR IN THE CHILD IS HIGH (32) B-B-C	348	TILT TOWARD BEING THOSE 0.59 OF 27 WHERE THE TOTAL POSITIVE PRESSURE TOWARD DEVELOPING ACHIEVEMENT BEHAVIOR IN THE CHILD IS LOW (31) B-B-C	15 11 4 16 XSQ= 5.16 PHI= 0.335 XP = 0.0231
349	TILT TOWARD BEING THOSE 0.79 OF 19 WHERE THE CHILD'S INFERRED ANXIETY OVER NON-PERFORMANCE OF ACHIEVEMENT BEHAVIOR IS HIGH (34) B-B-C	349	TILT TOWARD BEING THOSE 0.58 OF 26 WHERE THE CHILD'S INFERRED ANXIETY OVER NON-PERFORMANCE OF ACHIEVEMENT BEHAVIOR IS LOW (28) B-B-C	15 11 4 15 XSQ= 4.63 PHI= 0.321 XP = 0.0314
358	TILT LESS TOWARD BEING THOSE 0.56 OF 16 WHERE ADOLESCENT PEER GROUPS ARE PRESENT IN A SETTING OF WORK AND PUBLIC GATHERINGS AND LEISURE, OR OF PUBLIC GATHERINGS AND LEISURE, OR OF LEISURE ONLY (41) JKH	358	TILT MORE TOWARD BEING THOSE 0.90 OF 20 WHERE ADOLESCENT PEER GROUPS ARE PRESENT IN A SETTING OF WORK AND PUBLIC GATHERINGS AND LEISURE, OR OF PUBLIC GATHERINGS AND LEISURE, OR OF LEISURE ONLY (41) JKH	9 18 7 2 XSQ= 3.75 PHI= -0.323 EP = 0.0491
403	DRIFT TOWARD BEING THOSE 0.73 OF 22 WHERE EXPLANATIONS OF ILLNESS OF AN ANAL NATURE ARE ABSENT (38) W-C	403	DRIFT TOWARD BEING THOSE 0.56 OF 27 WHERE EXPLANATIONS OF ILLNESS OF AN ANAL NATURE ARE PRESENT (23) W-C	6 15 16 12 XSQ= 2.89 PHI= -0.243 XP = 0.0892
417	IN ALL CASES ARE THOSE 1.00 OF 18 WHERE WARFARE IS PREVALENT (34) LWS	417	LEAN LESS TOWARD BEING THOSE 0.57 OF 14 WHERE WARFARE IS PREVALENT (34) LWS	18 8 0 6 XSQ= 6.89 PHI= 0.464 EP = 0.0033
419	TEND TO BE THOSE 0.85 OF 40 WHERE MILITARY GLORY IS STRONGLY OR MODERATELY EMPHASIZED (55) PES	419	TEND TO BE THOSE 0.56 OF 45 WHERE MILITARY GLORY IS NEGLIGIBLY EMPHASIZED (31) PES	34 20 6 25 XSQ= 13.33 PHI= 0.396 XP = 0.0003
420	TEND TO BE THOSE 0.67 OF 40 WHERE BELLICOSITY IS EXTREME (41) PES	420	TEND TO BE THOSE 0.72 OF 46 WHERE BELLICOSITY IS MODERATE OR NEGLIGIBLE (46) PES	27 13 13 33 XSQ= 11.71 PHI= 0.369 XP = 0.0006
421	TEND TO BE THOSE 0.65 OF 40 WHERE KILLING, TORTURING, OR MUTILATING OF THE ENEMY IS STRONGLY OR MODERATELY EMPHASIZED (37) PES	421	TEND TO BE THOSE 0.74 OF 43 WHERE KILLING, TORTURING, OR MUTILATING OF THE ENEMY IS NEGLIGIBLY EMPHASIZED (47) PES	26 11 14 32 XSQ= 11.49 PHI= 0.372 XP = 0.0007
427	DRIFT LESS TOWARD BEING THOSE 0.52 OF 21 WHERE A HIGH GOD, IF PRESENT, IS ACTIVE, RATHER THAN INACTIVE (87) GES,EA	427	DRIFT MORE TOWARD BEING THOSE 0.83 OF 23 WHERE A HIGH GOD, IF PRESENT, IS ACTIVE, RATHER THAN INACTIVE (87) GES,EA	11 19 10 4 XSQ= 3.34 PHI= -0.275 XP = 0.0678

430	TILT TOWARD BEING THOSE 0.70 OF 10 WHERE SUPERNATURAL SANCTIONS FOR MORALITY, HAVING AN EFFECT ON AN INDIVIDUAL'S HEALTH, ARE PRESENT (16) GES	430	TILT TOWARD BEING THOSE 0.74 OF 19 WHERE SUPERNATURAL SANCTIONS FOR MORALITY, HAVING AN EFFECT ON AN INDIVIDUAL'S HEALTH, ARE ABSENT OR UNREPORTED (22) GES	7 5 3 14 XSQ= 3.51 PHI= 0.348 EP = 0.0460
453	TILT TOWARD BEING THOSE 0.70 OF 10 WHERE THE ROLE OF RELIGIOUS EXPERTS IS CONDUCIVE TO THE DEVELOPMENT OF THE INDIVIDUAL'S NEED TO ACHIEVE (13) DCM	453	TILT TOWARD BEING THOSE 0.80 OF 15 WHERE THE ROLE OF RELIGIOUS EXPERTS IS NOT CONDUCIVE TO THE DEVELOPMENT OF THE INDIVIDUAL'S NEED TO ACHIEVE (23) DCM	7 3 3 12 XSQ= 4.34 PHI= 0.417 EP = 0.0344
472	TEND TO BE THOSE 0.83 OF 41 WHERE THE COMPOSITE NARCISSISM INDEX IS HIGH (47) PES	472	TEND TO BE THOSE 0.75 OF 48 WHERE THE COMPOSITE NARCISSISM INDEX IS LOW (43) PES	34 12 7 36 XSQ= 27.44 PHI= 0.555 XP = 0.0000
473	TILT TOWARD BEING THOSE 0.50 OF 40 WHERE SENSITIVITY TO INSULT IS EXTREME (32) PES	473	TILT TOWARD BEING THOSE 0.77 OF 47 WHERE SENSITIVITY TO INSULT IS MODERATE OR NEGLIGIBLE (56) PES	20 11 20 36 XSQ= 5.56 PHI= 0.253 XP = 0.0184
477	DRIFT TOWARD BEING THOSE 0.67 OF 9 WHERE ALCOHOLIC AGGRESSION IS STRONG (15) DH	477	DRIFT TOWARD BEING THOSE 0.80 OF 10 WHERE ALCOHOLIC AGGRESSION IS MODERATE OR SLIGHT (19) DH	6 2 3 8 XSQ= 2.53 PHI= 0.365 EP = 0.0698
478	TILT TOWARD BEING THOSE 0.75 OF 8 WHERE THE ABANDONMENT OR KILLING OF OLD PEOPLE IS UNIMPORTANT OR ABSENT (12) LWS	478	TILT TOWARD BEING THOSE 0.88 OF 8 WHERE THE ABANDONMENT OR KILLING OF OLD PEOPLE IS PRESENT (12) LWS	2 7 6 1 XSQ= 4.06 PHI= -0.504 EP = 0.0406

475 CULTURES
WHERE EXHIBITIONISTIC DANCING
IS STRONGLY OR MODERATELY
EMPHASIZED (48) PES

475 CULTURES
WHERE EXHIBITIONISTIC DANCING
IS NEGLIGIBLY EMPHASIZED (38) PES

BACKGROUND ON PAGE 175

BOTH SUBJECT AND PREDICATE

48 IN LEFT COLUMN

AMERICANS	ARANDA	ARAUCANIANS	ASHANTI	AYMARA	AZANDE	AZTEC	BALINESE	BEMBA	CHAGGA
CHENCHU	CHEYENNE	CHIR-APACHE	CHUKCHEE	COPR ESKIMO	CROW	GANDA	GOND	HANO	IBAN
KOREANS	KURTATCHI	KWAKIUTL	LAKHER	LAU	LESU	MANUS	MARQUESANS	MURNGIN	NAVAHO
NYAKYUSA	OJIBWA	PAPAGO	PUKAPUKA	RIFFIANS	SAMOANS	SIWANS	TALLENSI	THONGA	TIKOPIA
TIMBIRA	TIV	TROBRIAND	VENDA	VIETNAMESE	WOGEO	WOLOF	YUROK		

38 IN RIGHT COLUMN

ABIPON	AINU	ALBANIANS	ALORESE	ANDAMANESE	ARAPESH	BHIL	COMANCHE	CREEK	CUNA
CZECHS	DOBUANS	FON	HAIDA	IFUGAO	INCA	JIVARO	KASKA	LANGO	LAPPS
LEPCHA	MAORI	MASAI	NAMA	NUER	SANPOIL	SIRIONO	SOMALI	TAPIRAPE	TODA
TRUMAI	WARRAU	WITOTO	WOLEAIANS	YAGUA	YAHGAN	YAKUT	ZUNI		

314 EXCLUDED BECAUSE UNASCERTAINED

	Left column			Right column		
9	TILT MORE TOWARD BEING THOSE LOCATED OUTSIDE OF SOUTH AMERICA (335)	0.94 OF 48	9	TILT LESS TOWARD BEING THOSE LOCATED OUTSIDE OF SOUTH AMERICA (335)	0.71 OF 38	3 11 45 27 XSQ= 6.44 PHI= -0.274 XP = 0.0112
54	DRIFT MORE TOWARD BEING THOSE WHERE FOOD PRODUCTION IS BY INTENSIVE OR SIMPLE AGRICULTURE, RATHER THAN BY INCIPIENT FOOD PRODUCTION (192)	0.86 OF 35	54	DRIFT LESS TOWARD BEING THOSE WHERE FOOD PRODUCTION IS BY INTENSIVE OR SIMPLE AGRICULTURE, RATHER THAN BY INCIPIENT FOOD PRODUCTION (192)	0.62 OF 21	30 13 5 8 XSQ= 2.95 PHI= 0.229 XP = 0.0861
56	DRIFT TOWARD BEING THOSE WHERE FOOD PRODUCTION IS BY SIMPLE AGRICULTURE, RATHER THAN BY INCIPIENT FOOD PRODUCTION (101)	0.76 OF 21	56	DRIFT TOWARD BEING THOSE WHERE FOOD PRODUCTION IS BY INCIPIENT FOOD PRODUCTION, RATHER THAN BY SIMPLE AGRICULTURE (46)	0.53 OF 15	16 7 5 8 XSQ= 2.15 PHI= 0.244 EP = 0.0895
62	DRIFT MORE TOWARD BEING THOSE WHERE HUSBANDRY OF SOME KIND IS PRESENT (228)	0.77 OF 48	62	DRIFT LESS TOWARD BEING THOSE WHERE HUSBANDRY OF SOME KIND IS PRESENT (228)	0.58 OF 38	37 22 11 16 XSQ= 2.79 PHI= 0.180 XP = 0.0949

86	DRIFT TOWARD BEING THOSE 0.56 OF 43 WHERE THE LEVEL OF POLITICAL INTEGRATION IS THE LARGE STATE, THE LITTLE STATE, OR THE MINIMAL STATE (148) GPM	86	DRIFT TOWARD BEING THOSE 0.68 OF 31 WHERE THE LEVEL OF POLITICAL INTEGRATION IS THE AUTONOMOUS COMMUNITY, OR THE FAMILY (156) GPM	24 10 19 21 XSQ= 3.13 PHI= 0.206 XP = 0.0768
99	DRIFT MORE TOWARD BEING THOSE 0.84 OF 19 WHERE, WITH NATIONAL HIERARCHY ABSENT, THE HIERARCHY OF LOCAL JURISDICTION HAS FOUR OR THREE LEVELS (93) GES,EA	99	DRIFT LESS TOWARD BEING THOSE 0.55 OF 20 WHERE, WITH NATIONAL HIERARCHY ABSENT, THE HIERARCHY OF LOCAL JURISDICTION HAS FOUR OR THREE LEVELS (93) GES,EA	16 11 3 9 XSQ= 2.65 PHI= 0.261 EP = 0.0824
100	TILT MORE TOWARD BEING THOSE 0.93 OF 46 WHERE HIERARCHIES ARE MORE COMPLEX THAN THE 'SIMPLEST,' I. E., MORE COMPLEX THAN TWO LOCAL LEVELS WITH NO NATIONAL LEVELS (267) GES,EA	100	TILT LESS TOWARD BEING THOSE 0.75 OF 36 WHERE HIERARCHIES ARE MORE COMPLEX THAN THE 'SIMPLEST,' I. E., MORE COMPLEX THAN TWO LOCAL LEVELS WITH NO NATIONAL LEVELS (267) GES,EA	43 27 3 9 XSQ= 4.14 PHI= 0.225 XP = 0.0419
102	DRIFT TOWARD BEING THOSE 0.63 OF 48 WHERE CLASS STRATIFICATION IS PRESENT (203)	102	DRIFT TOWARD BEING THOSE 0.58 OF 38 WHERE CLASS STRATIFICATION IS ABSENT (180)	30 16 18 22 XSQ= 2.77 PHI= 0.180 XP = 0.0958
137	LEAN TOWARD BEING THOSE 0.56 OF 48 WHERE INVIDIOUS DISPLAY OF WEALTH IS STRONGLY EMPHASIZED (37) PES	137	LEAN TOWARD BEING THOSE 0.76 OF 37 WHERE INVIDIOUS DISPLAY OF WEALTH IS MODERATELY, LITTLE, OR NEGATIVELY EMPHASIZED (52) PES	27 9 21 28 XSQ= 7.46 PHI= 0.296 XP = 0.0063
143	TILT TOWARD BEING THOSE 0.73 OF 22 WHERE THE RATIO OF RESTITUTIVE TO REPRESSIVE SANCTIONS IS MEDIUM OR LOW (32) WME	143	TILT TOWARD BEING THOSE 0.67 OF 15 WHERE THE RATIO OF RESTITUTIVE TO REPRESSIVE SANCTIONS IS HIGH (20) WME	6 10 16 5 XSQ= 4.15 PHI= -0.335 EP = 0.0409
258	DRIFT TOWARD BEING THOSE 0.59 OF 17 WHERE THE SEVERITY OF SON'S WIFE AVOIDANCE IS HIGH (15) WNS	258	DRIFT TOWARD BEING THOSE 0.86 OF 7 WHERE THE SEVERITY OF SON'S WIFE AVOIDANCE IS LOW (16) WNS	10 1 7 6 XSQ= 2.37 PHI= 0.314 EP = 0.0778
307	DRIFT TOWARD BEING THOSE 0.72 OF 25 WHERE THE EARLY AGGRESSION SATISFACTION POTENTIAL IS HIGH (33) W-C	307	DRIFT TOWARD BEING THOSE 0.59 OF 17 WHERE THE EARLY AGGRESSION SATISFACTION POTENTIAL IS LOW (19) W-C	18 7 7 10 XSQ= 2.81 PHI= 0.259 XP = 0.0935
348	DRIFT TOWARD BEING THOSE 0.70 OF 30 WHERE THE TOTAL POSITIVE PRESSURE TOWARD DEVELOPING ACHIEVEMENT BEHAVIOR IN THE CHILD IS HIGH (32) B-B-C	348	DRIFT TOWARD BEING THOSE 0.63 OF 16 WHERE THE TOTAL POSITIVE PRESSURE TOWARD DEVELOPING ACHIEVEMENT BEHAVIOR IN THE CHILD IS LOW (31) B-B-C	21 6 9 10 XSQ= 3.30 PHI= 0.268 XP = 0.0691

349	TILT TOWARD BEING THOSE 0.73 OF 30 WHERE THE CHILD'S INFERREC ANXIETY OVER NON-PERFORMANCE OF ACHIEVEMENT BEHAVIOR IS HIGH (34) B-B-C	349	TILT TOWARD BEING THOSE 0.67 OF 15 WHERE THE CHILD'S INFERRED ANXIETY OVER NON-PERFORMANCE OF ACHIEVEMENT BEHAVIOR IS LOW (28) B-B-C	22 5 8 10 XSQ= 5.10 PHI= 0.337 XP = 0.0239
350	LEAN TOWARD BEING THOSE 0.72 OF 29 WHERE THE CHILD'S INFERREC ANXIETY OVER PERFORMANCE OF ACHIEVEMENT BEHAVIOR IS HIGH (34) B-B-C	350	LEAN TOWARD BEING THOSE 0.79 OF 14 WHERE THE CHILD'S INFERRED ANXIETY OVER PERFORMANCE OF ACHIEVEMENT BEHAVIOR IS LOW (26) B-B-C	21 3 8 11 XSQ= 7.99 PHI= 0.431 XP = 0.0047
351	LEAN TOWARD BEING THOSE 0.62 OF 29 WHERE THE CHILD'S INFERREC CONFLICT REGARDING ACHIEVEMENT BEHAVIOR IS HIGH (26) B-B-C	351	LEAN TOWARD BEING THOSE 0.93 OF 14 WHERE THE CHILD'S INFERRED CONFLICT REGARDING ACHIEVEMENT BEHAVIOR IS LOW (34) B-B-C	18 1 11 13 XSQ= 9.43 PHI= 0.468 XP = 0.0021
352	DRIFT TOWARD BEING THOSE 0.66 OF 35 WHERE THE TOTAL POSITIVE PRESSURE TOWARD DEVELOPING OBEDIENT BEHAVICR IN THE CHILD IS HIGH (44) B-B-C	352	DRIFT TOWARD BEING THOSE 0.65 OF 17 WHERE THE TOTAL POSITIVE PRESSURE TOWARD DEVELOPING OBEDIENT BEHAVIOR IN THE CHILD IS LOW (28) B-B-C	23 6 12 11 XSQ= 3.15 PHI= 0.246 XP = 0.0760
355	DRIFT TCWARD BEING THOSE 0.60 OF 35 WHERE THE CHILD'S INFERREC CONFLICT REGARDING CBEDIENT BEHAVICR IS HIGH (35) B-B-C	355	DRIFT TOWARD BEING THOSE 0.71 OF 17 WHERE THE CHILD'S INFERRED CONFLICT REGARDING OBEDIENT BEHAVIOR IS LOW (38) B-B-C	21 5 14 12 XSQ= 3.15 PHI= 0.246 XP = 0.0761
358	TILT TOWARD BEING THOSE 0.87 OF 23 WHERE ADOLESCENT PEER GROUPS ARE PRESENT IN A SETTING OF WORK AND PUBLIC GATHERINGS AND LEISURE, CR OF PUBLIC GATHERINGS AND LEISURE, OR OF LEISURE CNLY (41) JKH	358	TILT TOWARD BEING THOSE 0.50 OF 12 WHERE ADOLESCENT PEER GROUPS ARE ABSENT IN A SETTING OF WORK, AND OF PUBLIC GATHERINGS, AND CF LEISURE (11) JKH	20 6 3 6 XSQ= 3.87 PHI= 0.333 EP = 0.0378
360	DRIFT LESS TCWARD BEING THOSE 0.54 OF 13 WHERE ADOLESCENT PEER GROUPS ARE PRESENT CNLY IN A SETTING CF LEISURE, OR ELSE ARE ABSENT (23) JKH	360	DRIFT MORE TOWARD BEING THCSE 0.90 OF 10 WHERE ADOLESCENT PEER GROUPS ARE PRESENT ONLY IN A SETTING OF LEISURE, OR ELSE ARE ABSENT (23) JKH	6 1 7 9 XSQ= 1.99 PHI= 0.294 EP = 0.0886
365	DRIFT TOWARD BEING THOSE 0.75 OF 20 WHERE THE TIME SPENT IN ADCLESCENT PEER GRCUP ACTIVITY IS HICH OR HIGH-MECIUM (30) JKH	365	DRIFT TOWARD BEING THOSE 0.64 OF 11 WHERE THE TIME SPENT IN ADOLESCENT PEER GROUP ACTIVITY IS LOW-MEDIUM OR LOW (15) JKH	15 4 5 7 XSQ= 2.99 PHI= 0.310 EP = 0.0564
377	TILT LESS TOWARD BEING THOSE 0.70 OF 46 WHERE MALE GENITAL MUTILATION IS ABSENT (242)	377	TILT MORE TOWARD BEING THOSE 0.92 OF 36 WHERE MALE GENITAL MUTILATION IS ABSENT (242)	14 3 32 33 XSQ= 4.73 PHI= 0.240 XP = 0.0296

392	TILT TOWARD BEING THOSE WHERE PREMARITAL SEX RELATIONS ARE STRONGLY PUNISHEC AND IN FACT RARE, OR WEAKLY PUNISHED AND IN FACT NOT RARE, OR PUNISHED CNLY IF PREGNANCY RESULTS (112) JTW,EA	0.76 OF 37	392	TILT TOWARD BEING THOSE WHERE PREMARITAL SEX RELATIONS ARE FREELY PERMITTED (67) JTW,EA	0.52 OF 29	28 14 9 15 XSQ= 4.16 PHI= 0.251 XP = 0.0415
395	TEND TO BE THOSE WHERE BELIEF IN THE UNCLEANNESS OF WOMEN IS UNIMPCRTANT OR ABSENT (15) LWS	0.82 OF 11	395	TEND TO BE THOSE WHERE BELIEF IN THE UNCLEANNESS OF WOMEN IS PRESENT (18) LWS	0.92 OF 13	2 12 9 1 XSQ= 10.59 PHI= -0.664 EP = 0.0005
472	TILT TOWARD BEING THOSE WHERE THE COMPOSITE NARCISSISM INCEX IS HIGH (47) PES	0.67 OF 48	472	TILT TOWARD BEING THOSE WHERE THE COMPOSITE NARCISSISM INDEX IS LOW (43) PES	0.63 OF 38	32 14 16 24 XSQ= 6.43 PHI= 0.273 XP = 0.0112

476 CULTURES
WHERE THE DEGREE OF INSOBRIETY IS
STRONG (31) DH

476 CULTURES
WHERE THE DEGREE OF INSOBRIETY IS
MODERATE OR SLIGHT (18) DH

BACKGROUND ON PAGE 175

BOTH SUBJECT AND PREDICATE

31 IN LEFT COLUMN

ABIPON	AINU	ANDAMANESE	APINAYE	CARIB	CAYAPA	CHOROTI	CHUKCHEE	CREEK	CUNA
DUSUN	GOAJIRO	HUICHOL	IFUGAO	JIVARO	KHALKA	KHASI	LAKHER	MAORI	MASAI
MURNGIN	NAMA	NASKAPI	OMAHA	PAPAGO	SAMOYED	TARAHUMARA	TEHUELCHE	THONGA	TUPINAMBA
WOLOF									

18 IN RIGHT COLUMN

ASHANTI	AZANDE	BALINESE	CHAGGA	GOND	HANO	KAZAK	LAMBA	LANGO	LEPCHA
MARICOPA	MBUNDU	TANALA	TIV	TODA	VENDA	YAKUT	ZUNI		

351 EXCLUDED BECAUSE UNASCERTAINED

	Left column		Right column		Statistics
3	TILT MORE TOWARD BEING THOSE LOCATED OUTSIDE OF AFRICA (320)	0.90 OF 31	TILT LESS TOWARD BEING THOSE LOCATED OUTSIDE OF AFRICA (320)	0.56 OF 18	3 8 28 10 XSQ= 6.04 PHI= -0.351 XP = 0.0140
9	TILT LESS TOWARD BEING THOSE LOCATED OUTSIDE OF SOUTH AMERICA (335)	0.68 OF 31	IN ALL CASES ARE THOSE LOCATED OUTSIDE OF SOUTH AMERICA (335)	1.00 OF 18	10 0 21 18 XSQ= 5.44 PHI= 0.333 XP = 0.0196
44	DRIFT LESS TOWARD BEING THOSE WHERE SETTLEMENTS ARE FIXED (222)	0.52 OF 29	DRIFT MORE TOWARD BEING THOSE WHERE SETTLEMENTS ARE FIXED (222)	0.82 OF 17	15 14 14 3 XSQ= 3.10 PHI= -0.260 XP = 0.0783
51	LEAN TOWARD BEING THOSE WHERE SUBSISTENCE IS PRIMARILY BY FOOD GATHERING -- I. E., HUNTING, FISHING, OR COLLECTING -- RATHER THAN FOOD PRODUCTION (147)	0.55 OF 31	LEAN TOWARD BEING THOSE WHERE SUBSISTENCE IS PRIMARILY BY FOOD PRODUCTION -- I. E., AGRICULTURE OR HUSBANDRY -- RATHER THAN BY GATHERING (253)	0.89 OF 18	14 16 17 2 XSQ= 7.42 PHI= -0.389 XP = 0.0064

53	TILT MORE TOWARD BEING THOSE 0.89 OF 19 WHERE FOOD PRODUCTION IS BY SIMPLE AGRICULTURE OR INCIPIENT FOOD PRODUCTION, RATHER THAN BY INTENSIVE AGRICULTURE (147)	53	TILT LESS TOWARD BEING THOSE 0.57 OF 14 WHERE FOOD PRODUCTION IS BY SIMPLE AGRICULTURE OR INCIPIENT FOOD PRODUCTION, RATHER THAN BY INTENSIVE AGRICULTURE (147)	2 6 17 8 XSQ= 3.00 PHI= -0.301 EP = 0.0473
54	TILT LESS TOWARD BEING THOSE 0.53 OF 19 WHERE FOOD PRODUCTION IS BY INTENSIVE OR SIMPLE AGRICULTURE, RATHER THAN BY INCIPIENT FOOD PRODUCTION (192)	54	TILT MORE TOWARD BEING THOSE 0.93 OF 14 WHERE FOOD PRODUCTION IS BY INTENSIVE OR SIMPLE AGRICULTURE, RATHER THAN BY INCIPIENT FOOD PRODUCTION (192)	10 13 9 1 XSQ= 4.42 PHI= -0.366 EP = 0.0209
56	DRIFT TOWARD BEING THOSE 0.53 OF 17 WHERE FOOD PRODUCTION IS BY INCIPIENT FOOD PRODUCTION, RATHER THAN BY SIMPLE AGRICULTURE (46)	56	DRIFT TOWARD BEING THOSE 0.88 OF 8 WHERE FOOD PRODUCTION IS BY SIMPLE AGRICULTURE, RATHER THAN BY INCIPIENT FOOD PRODUCTION (101)	8 7 9 1 XSQ= 2.21 PHI= -0.298 EP = 0.0875
82	TILT LESS TOWARD BEING THOSE 0.59 OF 22 WHERE A CITY OR TOWN IS PRESENT, OR THE AVERAGE COMMUNITY SIZE IS FIFTY OR GREATER (178)	82	TILT MORE TOWARD BEING THOSE 0.94 OF 16 WHERE A CITY OR TOWN IS PRESENT, OR THE AVERAGE COMMUNITY SIZE IS FIFTY OR GREATER (178)	13 15 9 1 XSQ= 4.09 PHI= -0.328 EP = 0.0250
86	TILT TOWARD BEING THOSE 0.61 OF 28 WHERE THE LEVEL OF POLITICAL INTEGRATION IS THE AUTONOMOUS COMMUNITY, OR THE FAMILY (156) GPM	86	TILT TOWARD BEING THOSE 0.80 OF 15 WHERE THE LEVEL OF POLITICAL INTEGRATION IS THE LARGE STATE, THE LITTLE STATE, OR THE MINIMAL STATE (148) GPM	11 12 17 3 XSQ= 4.97 PHI= -0.340 XP = 0.0257
91	DRIFT TOWARD BEING THOSE 0.75 OF 12 WHERE SOCIETAL COMPLEXITY IS LOW (22) F-W	91	DRIFT TOWARD BEING THOSE 0.70 OF 10 WHERE SOCIETAL COMPLEXITY IS HIGH (18) F-W	3 7 9 3 XSQ= 2.82 PHI= -0.358 EP = 0.0836
96	DRIFT TOWARD BEING THOSE 0.55 OF 29 WHERE THE HIERARCHY OF NATIONAL JURISDICTION HAS NO LEVELS (156) GES,EA	96	DRIFT TOWARD BEING THOSE 0.76 OF 17 WHERE THE HIERARCHY OF NATIONAL JURISDICTION HAS FOUR, THREE, TWO OR ONE LEVEL (174) GES,EA	13 13 16 4 XSQ= 3.17 PHI= -0.263 XP = 0.0748
100	TILT LESS TOWARD BEING THOSE 0.72 OF 29 WHERE HIERARCHIES ARE MORE COMPLEX THAN THE 'SIMPLEST,' I. E., MORE COMPLEX THAN TWO LOCAL LEVELS WITH NO NATIONAL LEVELS (267) GES,EA	100	IN ALL CASES ARE THOSE 1.00 OF 17 WHERE HIERARCHIES ARE MORE COMPLEX THAN THE 'SIMPLEST,' I. E., MORE COMPLEX THAN TWO LOCAL LEVELS WITH NO NATIONAL LEVELS (267) GES,EA	21 17 8 0 XSQ= 3.92 PHI= -0.292 XP = 0.0477
108	DRIFT TOWARD BEING THOSE 0.71 OF 17 WHERE CLASS STRATIFICATION, IF PRESENT, IS BASED ON SOMETHING OTHER THAN A HEREDITARY ARISTOCRACY (129)	108	DRIFT TOWARD BEING THOSE 0.67 OF 12 WHERE CLASS STRATIFICATION, IF PRESENT, IS BASED ON A HEREDITARY ARISTOCRACY (74)	5 8 12 4 XSQ= 2.58 PHI= -0.299 EP = 0.0667

No.	Left description	Prop.	No.	Right description	Prop.	Statistics
116	TILT TOWARD BEING THOSE WHERE OCCUPATIONAL SPECIALIZATION IS PART-TIME ONLY (34) JMH	0.83 OF 12	116	TILT TOWARD BEING THOSE WHERE OCCUPATIONAL SPECIALIZATION IS FULL-TIME, WHETHER OR NOT FOR SURPLUS PRODUCTION (20) JMH	0.83 OF 6	2 5 10 1 XSQ= 4.94 PHI= -0.524 EP = 0.0128
129	DRIFT TOWARD BEING THOSE WHERE WEAVING IS MAINLY DONE BY FEMALES (73)	0.83 OF 18	129	DRIFT TOWARD BEING THOSE WHERE WEAVING IS MAINLY DONE BY MALES (31)	0.63 OF 8	3 5 15 3 XSQ= 3.52 PHI= -0.368 EP = 0.0601
138	TILT TOWARD BEING THOSE WHERE SUPERORDINATE JUSTICE IS ABSENT (18) BBW	0.75 OF 8	138	TILT TOWARD BEING THOSE WHERE SUPERORDINATE JUSTICE IS PRESENT (22) BBW	0.85 OF 13	2 11 6 2 XSQ= 5.15 PHI= -0.495 EP = 0.0176
147	DRIFT TOWARD BEING THOSE WHERE CODIFIED LAWS ARE UNIMPORTANT OR ABSENT (13) LWS	0.57 OF 7	147	IN ALL CASES ARE THOSE WHERE CODIFIED LAWS ARE PRESENT (20) LWS	1.00 OF 5	3 5 4 0 XSQ= 2.10 PHI= -0.418 EP = 0.0808
176	TILT TOWARD BEING THOSE WHERE THE COMMUNITY IS OTHER THAN A CLAN-COMMUNITY OR A COMMUNITY STRUCTURED OR SEGMENTED ON A CLAN BASIS (213)	0.74 OF 31	176	TILT TOWARD BEING THOSE WHERE THE COMMUNITY IS A CLAN-COMMUNITY OR A COMMUNITY STRUCTURED OR SEGMENTED ON A CLAN BASIS (169)	0.61 OF 18	8 11 23 7 XSQ= 4.58 PHI= -0.306 XP = 0.0323
177	DRIFT MORE TOWARD BEING THOSE WHERE THE COMMUNITY IS OTHER THAN A SINGLE CLAN-COMMUNITY AND EXOGAMOUS (305)	0.87 OF 31	177	DRIFT LESS TOWARD BEING THOSE WHERE THE COMMUNITY IS OTHER THAN A SINGLE CLAN-COMMUNITY AND EXOGAMOUS (305)	0.61 OF 18	4 7 27 11 XSQ= 3.05 PHI= -0.250 XP = 0.0807
183	TILT LESS TOWARD BEING THOSE WHERE THE LARGEST NON-COGNATIC KIN GROUP IS SMALLER THAN A MOEITY, I. E., A PHRATRY OR SIB OR LINEAGE (218)	0.71 OF 14	183	IN ALL CASES ARE THOSE WHERE THE LARGEST NON-COGNATIC KIN GROUP IS SMALLER THAN A MOEITY, I. E., A PHRATRY OR SIB OR LINEAGE (218)	1.00 OF 17	4 0 10 17 XSQ= 3.32 PHI= 0.327 EP = 0.0318
186	DRIFT TOWARD BEING THOSE WHERE THE KIN GROUP IS OTHER THAN EXCLUSIVELY PATRILINEAL (250)	0.81 OF 31	186	DRIFT TOWARD BEING THOSE WHERE THE KIN GROUP IS EXCLUSIVELY PATRILINEAL (150)	0.50 OF 18	6 9 25 9 XSQ= 3.70 PHI= -0.275 XP = 0.0546
188	LEAN TOWARD BEING THOSE WHERE THE KIN GROUP IS EXCLUSIVELY COGNATIC (148)	0.55 OF 31	188	LEAN TOWARD BEING THOSE WHERE THE KIN GROUP IS OTHER THAN EXCLUSIVELY COGNATIC (252)	0.94 OF 18	17 1 14 17 XSQ= 9.88 PHI= 0.449 XP = 0.0017

192	LEAN LESS TOWARD BEING THOSE OTHER THAN WHERE THE ONLY KIN GROUP PRESENT IS A KINDRED OR ELSE BILATERAL DESCENT IS INFERRED (289)	0.55 OF	31	192	IN ALL CASES ARE THOSE OTHER THAN WHERE THE ONLY KIN GROUP PRESENT IS A KINDRED OR ELSE BILATERAL DESCENT IS INFERRED (289)	1.00 OF	18	14 0 17 18 XSQ= 9.28 PHI= 0.435 XP = 0.0023
272	DRIFT TOWARD BEING THOSE WHERE THE DIVORCE RATE IS HIGH (29) CA	0.80 OF	10	272	DRIFT TOWARD BEING THOSE WHERE THE DIVORCE RATE IS LOW (28) CA	0.71 OF	7	8 2 2 5 XSQ= 2.62 PHI= 0.393 EP = 0.0584
304	DRIFT TOWARD BEING THOSE WHERE THE EARLY ANAL SATISFACTION POTENTIAL IS HIGH (19) W-C	0.60 OF	5	304	DRIFT TOWARD BEING THOSE WHERE THE EARLY ANAL SATISFACTION POTENTIAL IS LOW (22) W-C	0.89 OF	9	3 1 2 8 XSQ= 1.75 PHI= 0.354 EP = 0.0949
311	DRIFT TOWARD BEING THOSE WHERE SEXUAL SOCIALIZATION ANXIETY IS LOW (23) W-C	0.80 OF	10	311	DRIFT TOWARD BEING THOSE WHERE SEXUAL SOCIALIZATION ANXIETY IS HIGH (28) W-C	0.64 OF	11	2 7 8 4 XSQ= 2.49 PHI= -0.344 EP = 0.0805
314	DRIFT MORE TOWARD BEING THOSE WHERE THE INCIDENCE OF MOTHER-CHILD HOUSEHOLDS IS LOW (61) W-C,S	0.93 OF	14	314	DRIFT LESS TOWARD BEING THOSE WHERE THE INCIDENCE OF MOTHER-CHILD HOUSEHOLDS IS LOW (61) W-D,S	0.55 OF	11	1 5 13 6 XSQ= 3.08 PHI= -0.351 EP = 0.0561
318	DRIFT TOWARD BEING THOSE WHERE THE OVERALL INDULGENCE OF THE INFANT IS HIGH (40) B-B-C	0.67 OF	12	318	DRIFT TOWARD BEING THOSE WHERE THE OVERALL INDULGENCE OF THE INFANT IS LOW (31) B-B-C	0.75 OF	12	8 3 4 9 XSQ= 2.69 PHI= 0.334 EP = 0.0995
326	DRIFT TOWARD BEING THOSE WHERE THE INFERRED TRANSITION ANXIETY BETWEEN INFANCY AND CHILDHOOD IS LOW (35) B-B-C	0.60 OF	10	326	DRIFT TOWARD BEING THOSE WHERE THE INFERRED TRANSITION ANXIETY BETWEEN INFANCY AND CHILDHOOD IS HIGH (32) B-B-C	0.83 OF	12	4 10 6 2 XSQ= 2.75 PHI= -0.354 EP = 0.0743
327	TILT TOWARD BEING THOSE WHERE THE AGE OF THE INFANT AT TIME OF REDUCED CONTACT WITH MOTHER IS HIGHER THAN TWO YEARS (28) B-B-C	0.88 OF	8	327	TILT TOWARD BEING THOSE WHERE THE AGE OF THE INFANT AT TIME OF REDUCED CONTACT WITH MOTHER IS TWO YEARS OR LOWER (27) B-B-C	0.78 OF	9	7 2 1 7 XSQ= 4.86 PHI= 0.535 EP = 0.0152
334	LEAN TOWARD BEING THOSE WHERE THE INDULGENCE OF THE CHILD IS HIGH (40) B-B-C	0.79 OF	14	334	LEAN TOWARD BEING THOSE WHERE THE INDULGENCE OF THE CHILD IS LOW (38) B-B-C	0.85 OF	13	11 2 3 11 XSQ= 8.40 PHI= 0.558 EP = 0.0018

346	TEND TO BE THOSE 0.75 OF 12 WHERE THE CHILD'S INFERREC ANXIETY OVER PERFORMANCE CF SELF-RELIANT BEHAVIOR IS LCW (39) B-B-C	346	TEND TO BE THOSE 0.92 OF 13 WHERE THE CHILD'S INFERRED ANXIETY OVER PERFORMANCE OF SELF-RELIANT BEHAVIOR IS HIGH (37) B-B-C	3 12 9 1 XSQ= 9.14 PHI= -0.605 EP = 0.0010
347	LEAN TOWARD BEING THOSE 0.75 OF 12 WHERE THE CHILD'S INFERREC CONFLICT REGARDING SELF-RELIANT BEHAVIOR IS LCW (39) B-B-C	347	LEAN TOWARD BEING THOSE 0.85 OF 13 WHERE THE CHILD'S INFERRED CONFLICT REGARDING SELF-RELIANT BEHAVIOR IS HIGH (37) B-B-C	3 11 9 2 XSQ= 6.74 PHI= -0.519 EP = 0.0048
353	TILT TOWARD BEING THOSE 0.54 OF 13 WHERE THE CHILD-S INFERREC ANXIETY OVER NCN-PERFORMANCE CF CBECIENT BEHAVIOR IS LCW (32) B-B-C	353	TILT TOWARD BEING THOSE 0.92 OF 13 WHERE THE CHILD'S INFERRED ANXIETY OVER NON-PERFORMANCE OF OBEDIENT BEHAVIOR IS HIGH (42) B-B-C	6 12 7 1 XSQ= 4.51 PHI= -0.417 EP = 0.0302
366	TILT TOWARD BEING THCSE 0.54 OF 13 WHERE DISSCCIATION CF THE SEXES AT ADCLESCENCE IS HIGH (16) JKH	366	IN ALL CASES ARE THOSE 1.00 OF 8 WHERE DISSOCIATION OF THE SEXES AT ADOLESCENCE IS MEDIUM OR LOW (41) JKH	7 0 6 8 XSQ= 4.27 PHI= 0.451 EP = 0.0180
382	TILT TOWARD BEING THOSE 0.75 OF 16 WHERE FEMALE INITIATICN RITES ARE PRESENT (38) JKB	382	TILT TOWARD BEING THOSE 0.86 OF 7 WHERE FEMALE INITIATION RITES ARE ABSENT (27) JKB	12 1 4 6 XSQ= 5.04 PHI= 0.468 EP = 0.0186
437	TILT TCWARD BEING THOSE 0.82 OF 11 WHERE FEAR OF GHOSTS, SPIRITS, HUMANS CR ANIMALS IS HIGH (21) W-C,JFG	437	TILT TOWARD BEING THOSE 0.67 OF 12 WHERE FEAR OF GHOSTS, SPIRITS, HUMANS OR ANIMALS IS LOW (23) W-C,JFG	9 4 2 8 XSQ= 3.69 PHI= 0.401 EP = 0.0361
458	TILT TCWARD BEING THOSE 0.70 OF 20 WHERE GAMES, IF PRESENT, DO NCT INCLUDE GAMES OF STRATEGY (119) R-A-B,EA	458	TILT TOWARD BEING THOSE 0.79 OF 14 WHERE GAMES, IF PRESENT, INCLUDE GAMES OF STRATEGY (52) R-A-B,EA	6 11 14 3 XSQ= 5.95 PHI= -0.418 EP = 0.0134
477	TILT TCWARD BEING THCSE 0.56 OF 25 WHERE ALCCHOLIC AGGRESSION IS STRCNG (15) DH	477	TILT TOWARD BEING THOSE 0.89 CF 9 WHERE ALCOHOLIC AGGRESSION IS MODERATE OR SLIGHT (19) DH	14 1 11 8 XSQ= 3.74 PHI= 0.332 EP = 0.0258
480	DRIFT TOWARD BEING THOSE 0.78 OF 9 WHERE COMPLEXITY OF ARTISTIC CESIGN IS LCW (15) HB	480	DRIFT TOWARD BEING THOSE 0.80 OF 5 WHERE COMPLEXITY OF ARTISTIC DESIGN IS HIGH (14) HB	2 4 7 1 XSQ= 2.34 PHI= -0.409 EP = 0.0909

```
477  CULTURES                                     477  CULTURES
     WHERE ALCOHOLIC AGGRESSION IS                     WHERE ALCOHOLIC AGGRESSION IS
     STRONG  (15) DH                                   MODERATE OR SLIGHT  (19) DH


BACKGROUND ON PAGE 175                                                     BOTH SUBJECT AND PREDICATE

       15  IN LEFT COLUMN

ABIPON    CARIB     CAYAPA     CHUKCHEE  GOAJIRO   HUICHOL   IFUGAO      JIVARO      KHALKA    LANGO
MURNGIN   OMAHA     TEHUELCHE  THONGA    WOLOF

       19  IN RIGHT COLUMN

AINU      APINAYE   ASHANTI    AZANDE    CHAGGA    CHOROTI   CUNA        DUSUN       GOND      LAKHER
LEPCHA    MARICOPA  NASKAPI    PAPAGO    SAMOYED   TANALA    TARAHUMARA  TUPINAMBA   VENDA

      366  EXCLUDED BECAUSE UNASCERTAINED

-------------------------------------------------------------------------------------------------------
 44  DRIFT TOWARD BEING THOSE       0.53 OF  15    44  DRIFT TOWARD BEING THOSE       0.82 OF  17        7    14
     WHERE SETTLEMENTS ARE NON-FIXED  (110)            WHERE SETTLEMENTS ARE FIXED  (222)                8     3
                                                                                                  XSQ=     3.06
                                                                                                  PHI=   -0.309
                                                                                                  EP =   0.0617

 46  TILT LESS TOWARD BEING THOSE   0.60 OF  15    46  TILT MORE TOWARD BEING THOSE   0.94 OF  17        6     1
     OTHER THAN WHERE SETTLEMENTS ARE                  OTHER THAN WHERE SETTLEMENTS ARE                  9    16
     NON-FIXED AND MOVEMENT IS                         NON-FIXED AND MOVEMENT IS                  XSQ=     3.61
     NOMADIC  (260)                                    NOMADIC  (260)                             PHI=    0.336
                                                                                                  EP =   0.0330

 62  DRIFT MORE TOWARD BEING THOSE  0.87 OF  15    62  DRIFT LESS TOWARD BEING THOSE  0.53 OF  19       13    10
     WHERE HUSBANDRY OF SOME KIND                      WHERE HUSBANDRY OF SOME KIND                      2     9
     IS PRESENT  (228)                                 IS PRESENT  (228)                          XSQ=     3.02
                                                                                                  PHI=    0.298
                                                                                                  EP =   0.0640

 78  TILT TOWARD BEING THOSE        0.80 OF   5    78  IN ALL CASES ARE THOSE         1.00 OF   5        1     5
     WHERE A WRITING SYSTEM IS                         WHERE THE WRITING SYSTEM IS                       4     0
     ABSENT, RATHER THAN BEING PRESENT IN              ALPHABETIC-OR-PHONETIC, OR MNEMONIC,       XSQ=     3.75
     EITHER ALPHABETIC-OR-PHONETIC FORM OR             RATHER THAN BEING ABSENT  (36) JMH         PHI=   -0.612
     MNEMONIC FORM  (18) JMH                                                                      EP =   0.0476

 91  IN ALL CASES ARE THOSE         1.00 OF   5    91  DRIFT TOWARD BEING THOSE       0.63 OF   8        0     5
     WHERE SOCIETAL COMPLEXITY                         WHERE SOCIETAL COMPLEXITY                         5     3
     IS LOW  (22) F-W                                  IS HIGH  (18) F-W                          XSQ=     2.78
                                                                                                  PHI=   -0.462
                                                                                                  EP =   0.0754
```

96	TILT TCWARD BEING THOSE WHERE THE HIERARCHY OF NATICNAL JURISDICTICN HAS NO LEVELS (156) GES,EA	0.73 OF 15	96	TILT TOWARD BEING THOSE WHERE THE HIERARCHY OF NATIONAL JURISDICTION HAS FOUR, THREE, TWO OR ONE LEVEL (174) GES,EA	0.65 OF 17	4 11 11 6 XSQ= 3.23 PHI= -0.318 EP = 0.0416
138	LEAN TOWARD BEING THOSE WHERE SUPERORDINATE JUSTICE IS ABSENT (18) BBW	0.86 OF 7	138	IN ALL CASES ARE THOSE WHERE SUPERORDINATE JUSTICE IS PRESENT (22) BBW	1.00 OF 7	1 7 6 0 XSQ= 7.29 PHI= -0.722 EP = 0.0047
201	DRIFT LESS TCWARC BEING THOSE WHERE MARITAL RESIDENCE IS NON-OPTIONAL, RATHER THAN AMBILCCAL OR NECLOCAL (334)	0.67 OF 15	201	DRIFT MORE TOWARD BEING THCSE WHERE MARITAL RESIDENCE IS NON-OPTIONAL, RATHER THAN AMBILOCAL OR NEOLOCAL (334)	0.95 OF 19	10 18 5 1 XSQ= 2.82 PHI= -0.288 EP = 0.0663
207	IN ALL CASES ARE THOSE WHERE MARITAL RESICENCE IS AMBILCCAL CR NECLOCAL, RATHER THAN MATRILOCAL OR UXCRILOCAL (64)	1.00 OF 5	207	TILT TOWARD BEING THOSE WHERE MARITAL RESIDENCE IS MATRILOCAL OR UXORILOCAL, RATHER THAN AMBILOCAL OR NEOLOCAL (64)	0.80 OF 5	0 4 5 1 XSQ= 3.75 PHI= -0.612 EP = 0.0476
241	DRIFT LESS TCWARC BEING THOSE WHERE THE FAMILY, IF EXTENCEC, IS LARGE OR SMALL, RATHER THAN STEM (187)	0.67 OF 9	241	IN ALL CASES ARE THOSE WHERE THE FAMILY, IF EXTENDED, IS LARGE OR SMALL, RATHER THAN STEM (187)	1.00 OF 11	6 11 3 0 XSQ= 2.10 PHI= -0.324 EP = 0.0737
259	TILT TOWARD BEING THOSE WHERE THE SEVERITY OF MOTHER-IN-LAW AVCIDANCE IS HIGH (26) WNS	0.80 OF 5	259	IN ALL CASES ARE THOSE WHERE THE SEVERITY OF MOTHER-IN-LAW AVOIDANCE IS LOW (20) WNS	1.00 OF 4	4 0 1 4 XSQ= 2.98 PHI= 0.575 EP = 0.0476
344	TILT TCWARD BEING THOSE WHERE THE TOTAL POSITIVE PRESSURE TOWARD DEVELCPING SELF-RELIANT BEHAVIOR IN THE CHILD IS HIGH (36) B-B-C	0.83 OF 6	344	TILT TOWARD BEING THOSE WHERE THE TOTAL POSITIVE PRESSURE TOWARD DEVELOPING SELF-RELIANT BEHAVIOR IN THE CHILD IS LOW (40) B-B-C	0.80 OF 10	5 2 1 8 XSQ= 3.81 PHI= 0.488 EP = 0.0350
474	DRIFT TCWARD BEING THOSE WHERE BOASTFULNESS IS EXTREME (41) PES	0.75 OF 8	474	DRIFT TOWARD BEING THOSE WHERE BOASTFULNESS IS MODERATE, NEGLIBIBLE, OR UNREPORTED (48) PES	0.73 OF 11	6 3 2 8 XSQ= 2.53 PHI= 0.365 EP = 0.0698
476	TILT MORE TOWARC BEING THCSE WHERE THE DEGREE OF INSOBRIETY IS STRONG (31) DH	0.93 OF 15	476	TILT LESS TOWARD BEING THOSE WHERE THE DEGREE OF INSOBRIETY IS STRONG (31) DH	0.58 OF 19	14 11 1 8 XSQ= 3.74 PHI= 0.332 EP = 0.0258

478 CULTURES WHERE THE ABANDONMENT OR KILLING OF OLD PEOPLE IS PRESENT (12) LWS	478 CULTURES WHERE THE ABANDONMENT OR KILLING OF OLD PEOPLE IS UNIMPORTANT OR ABSENT (12) LWS	

BACKGROUND ON PAGE 176 — BOTH SUBJECT AND PREDICATE

12 IN LEFT COLUMN

AINU ARAUCANIANS CHUKCHEE KUNG LAPPS MOTA NAMA SAMOANS SERI WITOTO
YAHGAN YAKUT

12 IN RIGHT COLUMN

ANDAMANESE AZTEC CREEK DIERI HEBREWS IBAN KUTENAI LANGO OMAHA SEMANG
TROBRIAND VEDDA

376 EXCLUDED BECAUSE UNASCERTAINED

Left column	Right column	Statistics
33 DRIFT TOWARD BEING THOSE 0.50 OF 12 WHERE THE NATURAL ENVIRONMENT IS 'VERY HARSH,' I.E., DESERT, DESERT GRASSES AND SHRUBS, TUNDRA, OR HIGH PLATEAU STEPPE (59) FWM	33 DRIFT TOWARD BEING THOSE 0.92 OF 12 WHERE THE NATURAL ENVIRONMENT IS OTHER THAN 'VERY HARSH,' I.E., DESERT, DESERT GRASSES AND SHRUBS, TUNDRA, OR HIGH PLATEAU STEPPE (341) FWM	6 1 6 11 XSQ= 3.23 PHI= 0.367 EP = 0.0686
185 DRIFT TOWARD BEING THOSE 0.50 OF 6 WHERE THE LARGEST NON-COGNATIC KIN GROUP IS SMALLER THAN A SIB, I. E., THE LINEAGE (58)	185 IN ALL CASES ARE THOSE 1.00 OF 7 WHERE THE LARGEST NON-COGNATIC KIN GROUP IS THE MOEITY OR PHRATRY OR SIB (194)	3 7 3 0 XSQ= 2.17 PHI= -0.408 EP = 0.0699
386 DRIFT TOWARD BEING THOSE 0.83 OF 6 WHERE SEXUAL EXPRESSION BY THE YOUNG IS PERMITTED (40) F-B	386 DRIFT TOWARD BEING THOSE 0.83 OF 6 WHERE SEXUAL EXPRESSION BY THE YOUNG IS RESTRICTED OR SEMI-RESTRICTED (46) F-B	1 5 5 1 XSQ= 3.00 PHI= -0.500 EP = 0.0801
391 DRIFT TOWARD BEING THOSE 0.78 OF 9 WHERE PREMARITAL SEX RELATIONS ARE PUNISHED ONLY IF PREGNANCY RESULTS, OR FREELY PERMITTED (90) JTW,EA	391 DRIFT TOWARD BEING THOSE 0.78 OF 9 WHERE PREMARITAL SEX RELATIONS ARE STRONGLY PUNISHED AND IN FACT RARE, OR WEAKLY PUNISHED AND IN FACT NOT RARE (89) JTW,EA	2 7 7 2 XSQ= 3.56 PHI= -0.444 EP = 0.0567
405 TILT TOWARD BEING THOSE 0.80 OF 5 WHERE EXPLANATIONS OF ILLNESS OF A DEPENDENCE NATURE ARE PRESENT (34) W-C	405 IN ALL CASES ARE THOSE 1.00 OF 4 WHERE EXPLANATIONS OF ILLNESS OF A DEPENDENCE NATURE ARE ABSENT (27) W-C	4 0 1 4 XSQ= 2.98 PHI= 0.575 EP = 0.0476

432	DRIFT TOWARD BEING THOSE WHERE AN ATTRACTIVE AFTERLIFE IS NCT BELIEVED IN (11) LWS	0.58 OF 12	432	DRIFT TOWARD BEING THOSE WHERE AN ATTRACTIVE AFTERLIFE IS BELIEVED IN (27) LWS	0.83 OF 12	5 10 7 2 XSQ= 2.84 PHI= -0.344 EP = 0.0894
474	TILT TOWARD BEING THOSE WHERE BOASTFULNESS IS MODERATE, NEGLIBIBLE, CR UNREPORTED (48) PES	0.78 OF 9	474	TILT TOWARD BEING THOSE WHERE BOASTFULNESS IS EXTREME (41) PES	0.86 OF 7	2 6 7 1 XSQ= 4.06 PHI= -0.504 EP = 0.0406

479 CULTURES WHERE THE NEED TO ACHIEVE, AS INFERRED FROM FOLKTALES, IS HIGH (18) JV	479 CULTURES WHERE THE NEED TO ACHIEVE, AS INFERRED FROM FOLKTALES, IS LOW (18) JV

BACKGROUND ON PAGE 176 — BOTH SUBJECT AND PREDICATE

18 IN LEFT COLUMN

ARANDA ARAUCANIANS AZANDE CHUKCHEE COMANCHE CROW CUNA KORYAK MANDAN MASAI
MBUNDU NAVAHO PAPAGO VENDA WICHITA WINNEBAGO WOLEAIANS YORUBA

18 IN RIGHT COLUMN

AINU ARAPESH ASHANTI CHAGGA CHENCHU CHIR-APACHE KASKA KIKUYU KURTATCHI LEPCHA
MARQUESANS OJIBWA PUKAPUKA SOTHO TENETEHARA TETON THONGA TUCUNA

364 EXCLUDED BECAUSE UNASCERTAINED

	Left column			Right column			Statistics
33	DRIFT LESS TOWARD BEING THOSE WHERE THE NATURAL ENVIRONMENT IS OTHER THAN 'VERY HARSH,' I.E., DESERT, DESERT GRASSES AND SHRUBS, TUNDRA, OR HIGH PLATEAU STEPPE (341) FWM	0.67 OF 18	33	DRIFT MORE TOWARD BEING THOSE WHERE THE NATURAL ENVIRONMENT IS OTHER THAN 'VERY HARSH,' I.E., DESERT, DESERT GRASSES AND SHRUBS, TUNDRA, OR HIGH PLATEAU STEPPE (341) FWM	0.94 OF 18	6 1 / 12 17 / XSQ= 2.84 / PHI= 0.281 / EP = 0.0877
44	DRIFT TOWARD BEING THOSE WHERE SETTLEMENTS ARE NON-FIXED (110)	0.56 OF 16	44	DRIFT TOWARD BEING THOSE WHERE SETTLEMENTS ARE FIXED (222)	0.76 OF 17	7 13 / 9 4 / XSQ= 2.45 / PHI= -0.273 / EP = 0.0799
54	DRIFT LESS TOWARD BEING THOSE WHERE FOOD PRODUCTION IS BY INTENSIVE OR SIMPLE AGRICULTURE, RATHER THAN BY INCIPIENT FOOD PRODUCTION (192)	0.69 OF 13	54	IN ALL CASES ARE THOSE WHERE FOOD PRODUCTION IS BY INTENSIVE OR SIMPLE AGRICULTURE, RATHER THAN BY INCIPIENT FOOD PRODUCTION (192)	1.00 OF 11	9 11 / 4 0 / XSQ= 2.15 / PHI= -0.299 / EP = 0.0983
110	TILT TOWARD BEING THOSE WHERE SLAVERY IS PRESENT (163)	0.56 OF 18	110	TILT TOWARD BEING THOSE WHERE SLAVERY IS ABSENT (218)	0.89 OF 18	10 2 / 8 16 / XSQ= 6.12 / PHI= 0.412 / EP = 0.0116
136	DRIFT TOWARD BEING THOSE WHERE FULL-TIME ENTREPRENEURS ARE PRESENT (18) JV	0.73 OF 15	136	DRIFT TOWARD BEING THOSE WHERE FULL-TIME ENTREPRENEURS ARE ABSENT (14) JV	0.59 OF 17	11 7 / 4 10 / XSQ= 2.17 / PHI= 0.260 / EP = 0.0870

180	DRIFT TOWARD BEING THOSE 0.82 OF 17 WHERE THE COMMUNITY IS COMMONLY NON-EXOGAMOUS, RATHER THAN EXOGAMOUS (258)	180	DRIFT TOWARD BEING THOSE 0.50 OF 18 WHERE THE COMMUNITY IS COMMONLY EXOGAMOUS, RATHER THAN NON-EXOGAMOUS (124)	3 9 14 9 XSQ= 2.75 PHI= -0.280 EP = 0.0750
286	TILT TOWARD BEING THOSE 0.83 OF 6 WHERE THE NUMBER OF FOOD TABOOS DURING PREGNANCY IS LOW OR ABSENT (14) BCA	286	TILT TOWARD BEING THOSE 0.78 OF 9 WHERE THE NUMBER OF FOOD TABOOS DURING PREGNANCY IS HIGH (20) BCA	1 7 5 2 XSQ= 3.23 PHI= -0.464 EP = 0.0406
335	IN ALL CASES ARE THOSE 1.00 OF 5 WHERE INITIAL INDULGENCE OF DEPENDENCY IS HIGH (20) WNS	335	DRIFT TOWARD BEING THOSE 0.56 OF 9 WHERE INITIAL INDULGENCE OF DEPENDENCY IS LOW (18) WNS	5 4 0 5 XSQ= 2.24 PHI= 0.400 EP = 0.0859
353	DRIFT TOWARD BEING THOSE 0.56 OF 18 WHERE THE CHILD-S INFERRED ANXIETY OVER NON-PERFORMANCE OF OBEDIENT BEHAVIOR IS LOW (32) B-B-C	353	DRIFT TOWARD BEING THOSE 0.76 OF 17 WHERE THE CHILD'S INFERRED ANXIETY OVER NON-PERFORMANCE OF OBEDIENT BEHAVIOR IS HIGH (42) B-B-C	8 13 10 4 XSQ= 2.52 PHI= -0.268 EP = 0.0858
386	IN ALL CASES ARE THOSE 1.00 OF 10 WHERE SEXUAL EXPRESSION BY THE YOUNG IS RESTRICTED OR SEMI-RESTRICTED (46) F-B	386	TILT TOWARD BEING THOSE 0.50 OF 10 WHERE SEXUAL EXPRESSION BY THE YOUNG IS PERMITTED (40) F-B	10 5 0 5 XSQ= 4.27 PHI= 0.462 EP = 0.0325
426	DRIFT TOWARD BEING THOSE 0.69 OF 13 WHERE A HIGH GOD IS PRESENT (156) GES,EA	426	DRIFT TOWARD BEING THOSE 0.69 OF 16 WHERE A HIGH GOD IS ABSENT (104) GES,EA	9 5 4 11 XSQ= 2.76 PHI= 0.309 EP = 0.0656
453	DRIFT TOWARD BEING THOSE 0.50 OF 18 WHERE THE ROLE OF RELIGIOUS EXPERTS IS CONDUCIVE TO THE DEVELOPMENT OF THE INDIVIDUAL'S NEED TO ACHIEVE (13) DCM	453	DRIFT TOWARD BEING THOSE 0.82 OF 17 WHERE THE ROLE OF RELIGIOUS EXPERTS IS NOT CONDUCIVE TO THE DEVELOPMENT OF THE INDIVIDUAL'S NEED TO ACHIEVE (23) DCM	9 3 9 14 XSQ= 2.75 PHI= 0.280 EP = 0.0750
455	TILT TOWARD BEING THOSE 0.67 OF 18 WHERE THE MODE OF THE INDIVIDUAL'S CONTACT WITH THE DIVINE IS CONDUCIVE TO THE DEVELOPMENT OF THE INDIVIDUAL'S NEED TO ACHIEVE (17) DCM	455	TILT TOWARD BEING THOSE 0.76 OF 17 WHERE THE MODE OF THE INDIVIDUAL'S CONTACT WITH THE DIVINE IS NOT CONDUCIVE TO THE DEVELOPMENT OF THE INDIVIDUAL'S NEED TO ACHIEVE (19) DCM	12 4 6 13 XSQ= 4.93 PHI= 0.375 EP = 0.0176

****

480 CULTURES WHERE COMPLEXITY OF ARTISTIC CESIGN IS HIGH (14) HB	480 CULTURES WHERE COMPLEXITY OF ARTISTIC DESIGN IS LOW (15) HB

BACKGROUND ON PAGE 176 BOTH SUBJECT AND PREDICATE

14 IN LEFT COLUMN

AINU ALCRESE ARAPESH BALINESE FON HANO JAPANESE KWAKIUTL MAORI MARQUESANS
SAMOANS TRCBRIANC YAKUT ZUNI

15 IN RIGHT COLUMN

ANDAMANESE ASHANTI CHENCHU CHIR-APACHE COMANCHE IFUGAO MARSHALLESE MASAI MURNGIN NAVAHO
OMAHA PAPAGC TETCN THONGA YAGUA

371 EXCLUDED BECAUSE UNASCERTAINEC

36	DRIFT TOWARD BEING THOSE WHERE THE NATURAL ENVIRONMENT IS OTHER THAN 'VERY HARSH,' OR SUB-TROPICAL BUSH, OR TEMPERATE GRASSLAND (292) FWM	0.79 OF 14	36	DRIFT TOWARD BEING THOSE WHERE THE NATURAL ENVIRONMENT IS 'VERY HARSH,' OR SUB-TROPICAL BUSH, OR TEMPERATE GRASSLAND (108) FWM	0.60 OF 15	3 9 11 6	XSQ= 2.99 PHI= -0.321 EP = 0.0604
44	TILT TOWARD BEING THOSE WHERE SETTLEMENTS ARE FIXEC (222)	0.92 OF 13	44	TILT TOWARD BEING THOSE WHERE SETTLEMENTS ARE NON-FIXED (110)	0.62 OF 13	12 5 1 8	XSQ= 6.12 PHI= 0.485 EP = 0.0112
48	DRIFT TOWARD BEING THOSE WHERE THE FOOD SUPPLY IS SECURE, AND FOOD SHORTAGES ARE RARE OR OCCASIONAL (38) MGW	0.78 OF 9	48	DRIFT TOWARD BEING THOSE WHERE THE FOOD SUPPLY IS NOT SECURE, AND FOOD SHORTAGES ARE FREQUENT OR ANNUAL (41) MGW	0.73 OF 11	7 3 2 8	XSQ= 3.23 PHI= 0.402 EP = 0.0698
51	DRIFT TOWARD BEING THOSE WHERE SUBSISTENCE IS PRIMARILY BY FOOD PRODUCTION -- I. E., AGRICULTURE OR HUSBANDRY -- RATHER THAN BY GATHERING (253)	0.71 OF 14	51	DRIFT TOWARD BEING THOSE WHERE SUBSISTENCE IS PRIMARILY BY FOOD GATHERING -- I. E., HUNTING, FISHING, OR COLLECTING -- RATHER THAN FOOD PRODUCTION (147)	0.67 OF 15	10 5 4 10	XSQ= 2.82 PHI= 0.312 EP = 0.0656
82	IN ALL CASES ARE THOSE WHERE A CITY OR TOWN IS PRESENT, OR THE AVERAGE COMMUNITY SIZE IS FIFTY OR GREATER (178)	1.00 OF 9	82	TILT TOWARD BEING THOSE WHERE NO CITY OR TOWN IS PRESENT, AND THE AVERAGE COMMUNITY SIZE IS SMALLER THAN FIFTY (46)	0.50 OF 10	9 5 0 5	XSQ= 3.80 PHI= 0.447 EP = 0.0325

86	DRIFT TOWARD BEING THOSE 0.73 OF 11 WHERE THE LEVEL OF POLITICAL INTEGRATION IS THE LARGE STATE, THE LITTLE STATE, OR THE MINIMAL STATE (148) GPM	86	DRIFT TOWARD BEING THOSE 0.73 OF 11 WHERE THE LEVEL OF POLITICAL INTEGRATION IS THE AUTONOMOUS COMMUNITY, OR THE FAMILY (156) GPM	8 3 3 8 XSQ= 2.91 PHI= 0.364 EP = 0.0861
88	TILT TOWARD BEING THOSE 0.73 OF 11 WHERE, IF A HEADMANSHIP IS PRESENT, SUCCESSION IS HEREDITARY (165)	88	TILT TOWARD BEING THOSE 0.75 OF 12 WHERE, IF A HEADMANSHIP IS PRESENT, SUCCESSION IS NON-HEREDITARY (106)	3 9 8 3 XSQ= 3.50 PHI= -0.390 EP = 0.0391
102	TILT TOWARD BEING THOSE 0.71 OF 14 WHERE CLASS STRATIFICATION IS PRESENT (203)	102	TILT TOWARD BEING THOSE 0.73 OF 15 WHERE CLASS STRATIFICATION IS ABSENT (180)	10 4 4 11 XSQ= 4.16 PHI= 0.379 EP = 0.0268
178	DRIFT TOWARD BEING THOSE 0.50 OF 14 WHERE THE COMMUNITY IS SEGMENTED ON A CLAN BASIS AND NON-EXOGAMOUS (87)	178	DRIFT TOWARD BEING THOSE 0.87 OF 15 WHERE THE COMMUNITY IS OTHER THAN SEGMENTED ON A CLAN BASIS AND NON-EXOGAMOUS (295)	7 2 7 13 XSQ= 3.00 PHI= 0.321 EP = 0.0502
196	DRIFT TOWARD BEING THOSE 0.89 OF 9 WHERE INDIVIDUAL RIGHTS IN REAL PROPERTY, AND RULES FOR INHERITANCE, ARE PRESENT (194)	196	DRIFT TOWARD BEING THOSE 0.58 OF 12 WHERE INDIVIDUAL RIGHTS IN REAL PROPERTY, OR RULES FOR INHERITANCE, ARE ABSENT (87)	8 5 1 7 XSQ= 3.07 PHI= 0.382 EP = 0.0669
303	TILT TOWARD BEING THOSE 0.83 OF 12 WHERE THE EARLY ORAL SATISFACTION POTENTIAL IS LOW (25) W-C	303	TILT TOWARD BEING THOSE 0.60 OF 15 WHERE THE EARLY ORAL SATISFACTION POTENTIAL IS HIGH (32) W-C	2 9 10 6 XSQ= 3.55 PHI= -0.362 EP = 0.0473
313	TILT TOWARD BEING THOSE 0.77 OF 13 WHERE AGGRESSION SOCIALIZATION ANXIETY IS HIGH (26) W-C	313	TILT TOWARD BEING THOSE 0.67 OF 15 WHERE AGGRESSION SOCIALIZATION ANXIETY IS LOW (28) W-C	10 5 3 10 XSQ= 3.71 PHI= 0.364 EP = 0.0296
324	TILT TOWARD BEING THOSE 0.69 OF 13 WHERE THE PAIN INFLICTED ON THE INFANT BY THE NURTURANT AGENT IS HIGH (34) B-B-C	324	TILT TOWARD BEING THOSE 0.75 OF 12 WHERE THE PAIN INFLICTED ON THE INFANT BY THE NURTURANT AGENT IS LOW OR NEGLIGIBLE (32) B-B-C	9 3 4 9 XSQ= 3.28 PHI= 0.362 EP = 0.0472
336	DRIFT TOWARD BEING THOSE 0.54 OF 13 WHERE THE TOTAL POSITIVE PRESSURE TOWARD DEVELOPING RESPONSIBLE BEHAVIOR IN THE CHILD IS LOW (32) B-B-C	336	DRIFT TOWARD BEING THOSE 0.85 OF 13 WHERE THE TOTAL POSITIVE PRESSURE TOWARD DEVELOPING RESPONSIBLE BEHAVIOR IN THE CHILD IS HIGH (43) B-B-C	6 11 7 2 XSQ= 2.72 PHI= -0.323 EP = 0.0968

No.	Subject	Ratio	No.	Related attribute	Ratio	Statistics
342	IN ALL CASES ARE THOSE WHERE THE CHILD'S INFERRED ANXIETY OVER PERFORMANCE OF NURTURANT BEHAVIOR IS HIGH (18) B-B-C	1.00 OF 6	342	TILT TOWARD BEING THOSE WHERE THE CHILD'S INFERRED ANXIETY OVER PERFORMANCE OF NURTURANT BEHAVIOR IS LOW (28) B-B-C	0.70 OF 10	6 3 0 7 XSQ= 4.89 PHI= 0.553 EP = 0.0114
348	DRIFT TOWARD BEING THOSE WHERE THE TOTAL POSITIVE PRESSURE TOWARD DEVELOPING ACHIEVEMENT BEHAVIOR IN THE CHILD IS LOW (31) B-B-C	0.67 OF 9	348	DRIFT TOWARD BEING THOSE WHERE THE TOTAL POSITIVE PRESSURE TOWARD DEVELOPING ACHIEVEMENT BEHAVIOR IN THE CHILD IS HIGH (32) B-B-C	0.82 OF 11	3 9 6 2 XSQ= 3.04 PHI= -0.390 EP = 0.0648
366	IN ALL CASES ARE THOSE WHERE DISSOCIATION OF THE SEXES AT ADOLESCENCE IS MEDIUM OR LOW (41) JKH	1.00 OF 8	366	LEAN TOWARD BEING THOSE WHERE DISSOCIATION OF THE SEXES AT ADOLESCENCE IS HIGH (16) JKH	0.71 OF 7	0 5 8 2 XSQ= 5.66 PHI= -0.614 EP = 0.0070
372	DRIFT TOWARD BEING THOSE WHERE MALE INITIATION RITES ARE PRESENT (48) ASA	0.70 OF 10	372	DRIFT TOWARD BEING THOSE WHERE MALE INITIATION RITES ARE ABSENT (63) ASA	0.71 OF 14	7 4 3 10 XSQ= 2.54 PHI= 0.325 EP = 0.0953
380	DRIFT TOWARD BEING THOSE WHERE SEGREGATION OF GIRLS AT MENARCHE IS ABSENT (20) F-B	0.50 OF 8	380	IN ALL CASES ARE THOSE WHERE SEGREGATION OF GIRLS AT MENARCHE IS PRESENT (35) F-B	1.00 OF 7	4 7 4 0 XSQ= 2.56 PHI= -0.413 EP = 0.0769
382	TILT TOWARD BEING THOSE WHERE FEMALE INITIATION RITES ARE ABSENT (27) JKB	0.80 OF 5	382	IN ALL CASES ARE THOSE WHERE FEMALE INITIATION RITES ARE PRESENT (38) JKB	1.00 OF 6	1 6 4 0 XSQ= 4.48 PHI= -0.638 EP = 0.0152
386	LEAN TOWARD BEING THOSE WHERE SEXUAL EXPRESSION BY THE YOUNG IS PERMITTED (40) F-B	0.82 OF 11	386	LEAN TOWARD BEING THOSE WHERE SEXUAL EXPRESSION BY THE YOUNG IS RESTRICTED OR SEMI-RESTRICTED (46) F-B	0.82 OF 11	2 9 9 2 XSQ= 6.55 PHI= -0.545 EP = 0.0089
435	IN ALL CASES ARE THOSE WHERE ABANDONMENT OF THE HOUSE OF THE DEAD IS NOT PRACTICED (19) LWS	1.00 OF 7	435	DRIFT TOWARD BEING THOSE WHERE ABANDONMENT OF THE HOUSE OF THE DEAD IS PRACTICED (12) LWS	0.67 OF 3	0 2 7 1 XSQ= 2.41 PHI= -0.491 EP = 0.0667
442	DRIFT TOWARD BEING THOSE WHERE FEAR OF ANIMAL SPIRITS IS HIGH (28) W-C	0.69 OF 13	442	DRIFT TOWARD BEING THOSE WHERE FEAR OF ANIMAL SPIRITS IS LOW (33) W-C	0.73 OF 15	9 4 4 11 XSQ= 3.51 PHI= 0.354 EP = 0.0557

480/

```
476  DRIFT TOWARD BEING THOSE        0.67 OF   6        476  DRIFT TOWARD BEING THOSE        0.88 OF   8            2     7
     WHERE THE DEGRFE OF INSOBRIETY IS                          WHERE THE DEGREE OF INSOBRIETY IS                       4     1
     MODERATE CR SLIGHT   (18) CH                               STRONG   (31) DH                                  XSQ=     2.34
                                                                                                                  PHI=   -0.409
                                                                                                                  EP =   0.0909
```

481 CULTURES
WHERE THE PRINCIPAL ETHNOGRAPHERS
HAVE BEEN AMERICAN (113)

481 CULTURES
WHERE THE PRINCIPAL ETHNOGRAPHERS
HAVE BEEN OTHER THAN AMERICAN (275)

BACKGROUND ON PAGE 177

BOTH SUBJECT AND PREDICATE

113 IN LEFT COLUMN

AMBA	AMERICANS	ARAPESH	ATSUGEWI	AWEIKOMA	AYMARA	BACAIRI	BRAZILIANS	BULGARIANS	BURYAT
CADUVEO	CAMAYURA	CAMBA	CARIB	CHEROKEE	CHEYENNE	CHIR-APACHE	CHORTI	COMANCHE	CREE
CREEK	DAGUR	DELAWARE	DIEGUENO	DUTCH	EYAK	FOX	GILBERTESE	GROS VENTRE	HAIDA
HANO	HANUNCO	HASINAI	HAVASUPAI	HAZARA	HUKUNDIKA	HURON	IFUGAO	INCA	INGALIK
IRISH	JAPANESE	JEMEZ	KALMYK	KASKA	KAZAK	KHALKA	KIOW-APACHE	KOL	KOREANS
KUTENAI	LAKALAI	LESU	MAGUZAWA	MAM	MANDAN	MARICOPA	MARQUESANS	MARSHALLESE	MAZATECO
MBUGWE	MIAMI	MIN CHINESE	MIWOK	MONGUOR	NABESNA	NASKAPI	NAVAHO	NOMLAKI	NUNIVAK
OMAHA	PALAUANS	PAPAGO	PAWNEE	PENOBSCOT	POPOLUCA	SANPOIL	SARAMACCA	SEMINOLE	SERBS
SERI	SIRIONO	SIUAI	SUBANUN	SYRIANS	TAGBANUA	TALAMANCA	TANALA	TAOS	TARAHUMARA
TAREUMIUT	TENINO	TERENA	TETON	TIMUCUA	TOKELAU	TOLOWA	TRUKESE	TRUMAI	TSHIMSHIAN
TUBATULABAL	TUCANO	TWANA	UTE	WALLOONS	WAPISHANA	WICHITA	WOLEAIANS	YARURO	YOKUTS
YUKI	YUROK	ZUNI							

275 IN RIGHT COLUMN

12 EXCLUDED BECAUSE UNASCERTAINED

3	TEND MORE TO BE THOSE LOCATED OUTSIDE OF AFRICA (320)	0.98 OF 113	3	TEND LESS TO BE THOSE LOCATED OUTSIDE OF AFRICA (320)	0.73 OF 275	2 74 111 201 XSQ= 30.56 PHI= -0.281 XP = 0.
5	TILT MORE TOWARD BEING THOSE LOCATED OUTSIDE OF EAST EURASIA (330)	0.90 OF 113	5	TILT LESS TOWARD BEING THOSE LOCATED OUTSIDE OF EAST EURASIA (330)	0.80 OF 275	11 56 102 219 XSQ= 5.61 PHI= -0.120 XP = 0.0178
8	TEND TO BE THOSE LOCATED IN NORTH AMERICA (70)	0.50 OF 113	8	TEND TO BE THOSE LOCATED OUTSIDE OF NORTH AMERICA (330)	0.95 OF 275	57 13 56 262 XSQ= 110.13 PHI= 0.533 XP = 0.

14	TEND TO BE THOSE 0.59 OF 113 WHERE THE LATITUDE IS THIRTY DEGREES OR GREATER (119)	14	TEND TO BE THOSE 0.82 OF 275 WHERE THE LATITUDE IS LESS THAN THIRTY DEGREES (281)	67 49 46 226 XSQ= 63.77 PHI= 0.405 XP = 0.
15	TEND TO BE THOSE 0.69 OF 113 WHERE THE LATITUDE IS TWENTY DEGREES OR GREATER (183)	15	TEND TO BE THOSE 0.64 OF 275 WHERE THE LATITUDE IS LESS THAN TWENTY DEGREES (217)	78 100 35 175 XSQ= 33.11 PHI= 0.292 XP = 0.
33	DRIFT LESS TOWARD BEING THOSE 0.81 OF 113 WHERE THE NATURAL ENVIRONMENT IS OTHER THAN 'VERY HARSH,' I.E., DESERT, DESERT GRASSES AND SHRUBS, TUNDRA, OR HIGH PLATEAU STEPPE (341) FWM	33	DRIFT MORE TOWARD BEING THOSE 0.88 OF 275 WHERE THE NATURAL ENVIRONMENT IS OTHER THAN 'VERY HARSH,' I.E., DESERT, DESERT GRASSES AND SHRUBS, TUNDRA, OR HIGH PLATEAU STEPPE (341) FWM	22 33 91 242 XSQ= 3.08 PHI= 0.089 XP = 0.0791
36	TILT LESS TOWARD BEING THOSE 0.65 OF 113 WHERE THE NATURAL ENVIRONMENT IS OTHER THAN 'VERY HARSH,' OR SUB-TROPICAL BUSH, OR TEMPERATE GRASSLAND (292) FWM	36	TILT MORE TOWARD BEING THOSE 0.77 OF 275 WHERE THE NATURAL ENVIRONMENT IS OTHER THAN 'VERY HARSH,' OR SUB-TROPICAL BUSH, OR TEMPERATE GRASSLAND (292) FWM	39 63 74 212 XSQ= 4.98 PHI= 0.113 XP = 0.0256
42	LEAN MORE TOWARD BEING THOSE 0.73 OF 113 WHERE THE NATURAL ENVIRONMENT IS OTHER THAN TROPICAL OR SUB-TROPICAL RAIN FOREST, OR MONSOON FOREST (244) FWM	42	LEAN LESS TOWARD BEING THOSE 0.55 OF 275 WHERE THE NATURAL ENVIRONMENT IS OTHER THAN TROPICAL OR SUB-TROPICAL RAIN FOREST, OR MONSOON FOREST (244) FWM	31 123 82 152 XSQ= 9.30 PHI= -0.155 XP = 0.0023
44	TILT LESS TOWARD BEING THOSE 0.57 OF 95 WHERE SETTLEMENTS ARE FIXED (222)	44	TILT MORE TOWARD BEING THOSE 0.72 OF 229 WHERE SETTLEMENTS ARE FIXED (222)	54 165 41 64 XSQ= 6.41 PHI= -0.141 XP = 0.0113
47	DRIFT LESS TOWARD BEING THOSE 0.54 OF 41 WHERE, IF SETTLEMENTS ARE NON-FIXED, MOVEMENT IS NOMADIC, RATHER THAN NON-NOMADIC (72)	47	DRIFT MORE TOWARD BEING THOSE 0.72 OF 64 WHERE, IF SETTLEMENTS ARE NON-FIXED, MOVEMENT IS NOMADIC, RATHER THAN NON-NOMADIC (72)	22 46 19 18 XSQ= 2.88 PHI= -0.166 XP = 0.0897
51	TEND TO BE THOSE 0.56 OF 113 WHERE SUBSISTENCE IS PRIMARILY BY FOOD GATHERING -- I. E., HUNTING, FISHING, OR COLLECTING -- RATHER THAN FOOD PRODUCTION (147)	51	TEND TO BE THOSE 0.70 OF 275 WHERE SUBSISTENCE IS PRIMARILY BY FOOD PRODUCTION -- I. E., AGRICULTURE OR HUSBANDRY -- RATHER THAN BY GATHERING (253)	50 193 63 82 XSQ= 21.92 PHI= -0.238 XP = 0.0000
54	TEND LESS TO BE THOSE 0.65 OF 62 WHERE FOOD PRODUCTION IS BY INTENSIVE OR SIMPLE AGRICULTURE, RATHER THAN BY INCIPIENT FOOD PRODUCTION (192)	54	TEND MORE TO BE THOSE 0.87 OF 171 WHERE FOOD PRODUCTION IS BY INTENSIVE OR SIMPLE AGRICULTURE, RATHER THAN BY INCIPIENT FOOD PRODUCTION (192)	40 148 22 23 XSQ= 12.80 PHI= -0.234 XP = 0.0003

55	TILT TOWARD BEING THOSE WHERE FOOD PRODUCTION IS BY INTENSIVE AGRICULTURE, RATHER THAN BY SIMPLE AGRICULTURE (91)	0.63 OF 40	55	TILT TOWARD BEING THOSE WHERE FOOD PRODUCTION IS BY SIMPLE AGRICULTURE, RATHER THAN BY INTENSIVE AGRICULTURE (101)	0.57 OF 148	25 63 15 85 XSQ= 4.26 PHI= 0.150 XP = 0.0391
56	TEND TO BE THOSE WHERE FOOD PRODUCTION IS BY INCIPIENT FOOD PRODUCTION, RATHER THAN BY SIMPLE AGRICULTURE (46)	0.59 OF 37	56	TEND TO BE THOSE WHERE FOOD PRODUCTION IS BY SIMPLE AGRICULTURE, RATHER THAN BY INCIPIENT FOOD PRODUCTION (101)	0.79 OF 108	15 85 22 23 XSQ= 17.01 PHI= -0.343 XP = 0.0000
62	DRIFT TOWARD BEING THOSE WHERE HUSBANDRY OF ANY KIND IS ABSENT (172)	0.50 OF 113	62	DRIFT TOWARD BEING THOSE WHERE HUSBANDRY OF SOME KIND IS PRESENT (228)	0.60 OF 275	56 165 57 110 XSQ= 3.15 PHI= -0.090 XP = 0.0760
71	TEND MORE TO BE THOSE WHERE METAL WORKING IS ABSENT (153)	0.80 OF 75	71	TEND LESS TO BE THOSE WHERE METAL WORKING IS ABSENT (153)	0.54 OF 173	15 80 60 93 XSQ= 14.16 PHI= -0.239 XP = 0.0002
77	TILT TOWARD BEING THOSE WHERE THE WRITING SYSTEM IS ALPHABETIC-OR-PHONETIC, RATHER THAN BEING MNEMONIC OR ABSENT (15) JMH	0.60 OF 10	77	TILT TOWARD BEING THOSE WHERE THE WRITING SYSTEM IS MNEMONIC OR ABSENT, RATHER THAN BEING ALPHABETIC-OR-PHONETIC (39) JMH	0.79 OF 43	6 9 4 34 XSQ= 4.33 PHI= 0.286 XP = 0.0375
79	TILT LESS TOWARD BEING THOSE WHERE NO CITY IS PRESENT (201)	0.81 OF 58	79	TILT MORE TOWARD BEING THOSE WHERE NO CITY IS PRESENT (201)	0.93 OF 163	11 12 47 151 XSQ= 5.00 PHI= 0.150 XP = 0.0254
85	DRIFT MORE TOWARD BEING THOSE WHERE THE LEVEL OF POLITICAL INTEGRATION IS THE MINIMAL STATE, THE AUTONOMOUS COMMUNITY, OR THE FAMILY (234) GPM	0.84 OF 86	85	DRIFT LESS TOWARD BEING THOSE WHERE THE LEVEL OF POLITICAL INTEGRATION IS THE MINIMAL STATE, THE AUTONOMOUS COMMUNITY, OR THE FAMILY (234) GPM	0.74 OF 210	14 55 72 155 XSQ= 2.82 PHI= -0.098 XP = 0.0930
88	DRIFT LESS TOWARD BEING THOSE WHERE, IF A HEADMANSHIP IS PRESENT, SUCCESSION IS HEREDITARY (165)	0.53 OF 78	88	DRIFT MORE TOWARD BEING THOSE WHERE, IF A HEADMANSHIP IS PRESENT, SUCCESSION IS HEREDITARY (165)	0.65 OF 189	37 67 41 122 XSQ= 2.85 PHI= 0.103 XP = 0.0913
102	DRIFT TOWARD BEING THOSE WHERE CLASS STRATIFICATION IS ABSENT (180)	0.54 OF 111	102	DRIFT TOWARD BEING THOSE WHERE CLASS STRATIFICATION IS PRESENT (203)	0.57 OF 260	51 148 60 112 XSQ= 3.34 PHI= -0.095 XP = 0.0676

109	LEAN MORE TOWARD BEING THOSE 0.95 OF 106 WHERE CASTES ARE ABSENT (317)	109	LEAN LESS TOWARD BEING THOSE 0.83 OF 253 WHERE CASTES ARE ABSENT (317)	5 44 101 209 XSQ= 9.13 PHI= -0.160 XP = 0.0025
110	TEND TO BE THOSE 0.73 OF 110 WHERE SLAVERY IS ABSENT (218)	110	TEND TO BE THOSE 0.50 OF 260 WHERE SLAVERY IS PRESENT (163)	30 130 80 130 XSQ= 15.35 PHI= -0.204 XP = 0.0001
128	DRIFT TOWARD BEING THOSE 0.79 OF 14 WHERE, IF SUBSISTENCE IS PRIMARILY BY AGRICULTURE, THE WORK IS MAINLY DONE BY MALES (40)	128	DRIFT TOWARD BEING THOSE 0.52 OF 61 WHERE, IF SUBSISTENCE IS PRIMARILY BY AGRICULTURE, THE WORK IS MAINLY DONE BY FEMALES (37)	11 29 3 32 XSQ= 3.25 PHI= 0.208 XP = 0.0716
129	DRIFT MORE TOWARD BEING THOSE 0.86 OF 29 WHERE WEAVING IS MAINLY DONE BY FEMALES (73)	129	DRIFT LESS TOWARD BEING THOSE 0.65 OF 74 WHERE WEAVING IS MAINLY DONE BY FEMALES (73)	4 26 25 48 XSQ= 3.62 PHI= -0.188 XP = 0.0570
176	TILT MORE TOWARD BEING THOSE 0.65 OF 108 WHERE THE COMMUNITY IS OTHER THAN A CLAN-COMMUNITY OR A COMMUNITY STRUCTURED OR SEGMENTED ON A CLAN BASIS (213)	176	TILT LESS TOWARD BEING THOSE 0.52 OF 262 WHERE THE COMMUNITY IS OTHER THAN A CLAN-COMMUNITY OR A COMMUNITY STRUCTURED OR SEGMENTED ON A CLAN BASIS (213)	38 127 70 135 XSQ= 4.94 PHI= -0.116 XP = 0.0262
177	TILT MORE TOWARD BEING THOSE 0.87 OF 108 WHERE THE COMMUNITY IS OTHER THAN A SINGLE CLAN-COMMUNITY AND EXOGAMOUS (305)	177	TILT LESS TOWARD BEING THOSE 0.77 OF 262 WHERE THE COMMUNITY IS OTHER THAN A SINGLE CLAN-COMMUNITY AND EXOGAMOUS (305)	14 61 94 201 XSQ= 4.42 PHI= -0.109 XP = 0.0355
180	TILT MORE TOWARD BEING THOSE 0.77 OF 108 WHERE THE COMMUNITY IS COMMONLY NON-EXOGAMOUS, RATHER THAN EXOGAMOUS (258)	180	TILT LESS TOWARD BEING THOSE 0.64 OF 262 WHERE THE COMMUNITY IS COMMONLY NON-EXOGAMOUS, RATHER THAN EXOGAMOUS (258)	25 95 83 167 XSQ= 5.42 PHI= -0.121 XP = 0.0200
182	TILT LESS TOWARD BEING THOSE 0.59 OF 108 OTHER THAN WHERE THE COMMUNITY IS STRUCTURED ON A NON-CLAN BASIS AND AGAMOUS (256)	182	TILT MORE TOWARD BEING THOSE 0.71 OF 262 OTHER THAN WHERE THE COMMUNITY IS STRUCTURED ON A NON-CLAN BASIS AND AGAMOUS (256)	44 77 64 185 XSQ= 3.98 PHI= 0.104 XP = 0.0461
184	DRIFT LESS TOWARD BEING THOSE 0.58 OF 55 WHERE THE LARGEST NON-COGNATIC KIN GROUP IS SMALLER THAN A PHRATRY, I. E. A SIB OR LINEAGE (175)	184	DRIFT MORE TOWARD BEING THOSE 0.73 OF 187 WHERE THE LARGEST NON-COGNATIC KIN GROUP IS SMALLER THAN A PHRATRY, I. E. A SIB OR LINEAGE (175)	23 51 32 136 XSQ= 3.58 PHI= 0.122 XP = 0.0585

186	TEND MORE TO BE THOSE WHERE THE KIN GROUP IS OTHER THAN EXCLUSIVELY PATRILINEAL (250)	0.78 OF 113	186	TEND LESS TO BE THOSE WHERE THE KIN GROUP IS OTHER THAN EXCLUSIVELY PATRILINEAL (250)	0.57 OF 275	25 118 88 157 XSQ= 13.99 PHI= -0.190 XP = 0.0002
187	TILT LESS TOWARD BEING THOSE WHERE THE KIN GROUP IS OTHER THAN EXCLUSIVELY MATRILINEAL (344)	0.80 OF 113	187	TILT MORE TOWARD BEING THOSE WHERE THE KIN GROUP IS OTHER THAN EXCLUSIVELY MATRILINEAL (344)	0.89 OF 274	23 30 90 244 XSQ= 5.22 PHI= 0.116 XP = 0.0224
188	TEND TO BE THOSE WHERE THE KIN GROUP IS EXCLUSIVELY COGNATIC (148)	0.51 OF 113	188	TEND TO BE THOSE WHERE THE KIN GROUP IS OTHER THAN EXCLUSIVELY COGNATIC (252)	0.68 OF 275	58 88 55 187 XSQ= 11.94 PHI= 0.175 XP = 0.0006
190	TEND TO BE THOSE WHERE THE KIN GROUP IS MATRILINEAL, RATHER THAN PATRILINEAL OR DOUBLE-DESCENT (61)	0.50 OF 54	190	TEND TO BE THOSE WHERE THE KIN GROUP IS PATRILINEAL OR DOUBLE-DESCENT, RATHER THAN MATRILINEAL (186)	0.83 OF 183	27 151 27 32 XSQ= 21.87 PHI= -0.304 XP = 0.0000
192	TEND LESS TO BE THOSE OTHER THAN WHERE THE ONLY KIN GROUP PRESENT IS A KINDRED OR ELSE BILATERAL DESCENT IS INFERRED (289)	0.58 OF 113	192	TEND MORE TO BE THOSE OTHER THAN WHERE THE ONLY KIN GROUP PRESENT IS A KINDRED OR ELSE BILATERAL DESCENT IS INFERRED (289)	0.77 OF 275	47 62 66 213 XSQ= 13.46 PHI= 0.186 XP = 0.0002
196	TILT LESS TOWARD BEING THOSE WHERE INDIVIDUAL RIGHTS IN REAL PROPERTY, AND RULES FOR INHERITANCE, ARE PRESENT (194)	0.57 OF 81	196	TILT MORE TOWARD BEING THOSE WHERE INDIVIDUAL RIGHTS IN REAL PROPERTY, AND RULES FOR INHERITANCE, ARE PRESENT (194)	0.73 OF 192	46 140 35 52 XSQ= 6.10 PHI= -0.149 XP = 0.0135
198	LEAN LESS TOWARD BEING THOSE WHERE RULES FOR THE INHERITANCE OF REAL PROPERTY, IF PRESENT, FAVOR THE MALE HEIR OR LINE, RATHER THAN THE FEMALE (144)	0.72 OF 36	198	LEAN MORE TOWARD BEING THOSE WHERE RULES FOR THE INHERITANCE OF REAL PROPERTY, IF PRESENT, FAVOR THE MALE HEIR OR LINE, RATHER THAN THE FEMALE (144)	0.92 OF 121	26 111 10 10 XSQ= 7.83 PHI= -0.223 XP = 0.0051
201	DRIFT LESS TOWARD BEING THOSE WHERE MARITAL RESIDENCE IS NON-OPTIONAL, RATHER THAN AMBILOCAL OR NEOLOCAL (334)	0.78 OF 113	201	DRIFT MORE TOWARD BEING THOSE WHERE MARITAL RESIDENCE IS NON-OPTIONAL, RATHER THAN AMBILOCAL OR NEOLOCAL (334)	0.86 OF 273	88 235 25 38 XSQ= 3.36 PHI= -0.093 XP = 0.0668
204	TILT LESS TOWARD BEING THOSE WHERE MARITAL RESIDENCE IS PATRILOCAL, VIRILOCAL, OR AVUNCULOCAL, RATHER THAN AMBILOCAL OR NEOLOCAL (270)	0.71 OF 85	204	TILT MORE TOWARD BEING THOSE WHERE MARITAL RESIDENCE IS PATRILOCAL, VIRILOCAL, OR AVUNCULOCAL, RATHER THAN AMBILOCAL OR NEOLOCAL (270)	0.84 OF 238	60 200 25 38 XSQ= 6.38 PHI= -0.141 XP = 0.0115

209	LEAN LESS TOWARD BEING THOSE WHERE MARITAL RESIDENCE IS PATRILOCAL, VIRILOCAL, OR AVUNCULOCAL, RATHER THAN MATRILOCAL OR UXORILOCAL (270)	0.68 OF 88	209	LEAN MORE TOWARD BEING THOSE WHERE MARITAL RESIDENCE IS PATRILOCAL, VIRILOCAL, OR AVUNCULOCAL, RATHER THAN MATRILOCAL OR UXORILOCAL (270)	0.85 OF 235	60 200 28 35 XSQ= 10.63 PHI= -0.181 XP = 0.0011
210	TEND LESS TO BE THOSE WHERE MARITAL RESIDENCE IS PATRILOCAL, RATHER THAN MATRILOCAL (169)	0.62 OF 42	210	TEND MORE TO BE THOSE WHERE MARITAL RESIDENCE IS PATRILOCAL, RATHER THAN MATRILOCAL (169)	0.91 OF 149	26 135 16 14 XSQ= 18.27 PHI= -0.309 XP = 0.0000
213	LEAN TOWARD BEING THOSE WHERE FIRST COUSIN MARRIAGE IS NOT PERMITTED (198)	0.66 OF 107	213	LEAN TOWARD BEING THOSE WHERE FIRST COUSIN MARRIAGE IS PERMITTED (172)	0.52 OF 252	36 131 71 121 XSQ= 9.43 PHI= -0.162 XP = 0.0021
220	TILT MORE TOWARD BEING THOSE WHERE FIRST COUSIN MARRIAGE IN SOME FORM OR OTHER IS NOT PRESCRIBED OR PREFERRED (273)	0.81 OF 107	220	TILT LESS TOWARD BEING THOSE WHERE FIRST COUSIN MARRIAGE IN SOME FORM OR OTHER IS NOT PRESCRIBED OR PREFERRED (273)	0.70 OF 252	20 75 87 177 XSQ= 4.18 PHI= -0.108 XP = 0.0409
221	DRIFT MORE TOWARD BEING THOSE WHERE MATRILATERAL CROSS-COUSIN MARRIAGE IS NOT PRESCRIBED OR PREFERRED (335)	0.95 OF 107	221	DRIFT LESS TOWARD BEING THOSE WHERE MATRILATERAL CROSS-COUSIN MARRIAGE IS NOT PRESCRIBED OR PREFERRED (335)	0.88 OF 252	5 30 102 222 XSQ= 3.68 PHI= -0.101 XP = 0.0551
242	TILT LESS TOWARD BEING THOSE WHERE MARRIAGE IS COMMONLY OR OCCASIONALLY POLYGYNOUS, RATHER THAN MONOGAMOUS (314)	0.72 OF 112	242	TILT MORE TOWARD BEING THOSE WHERE MARRIAGE IS COMMONLY OR OCCASIONALLY POLYGYNOUS, RATHER THAN MONOGAMOUS (314)	0.82 OF 271	81 223 31 48 XSQ= 4.22 PHI= -0.105 XP = 0.0400
254	TILT TOWARD BEING THOSE WHERE HOUSEHOLD AUTHORITY IS ON THE MOTHER'S SIDE, RATHER THAN THE FATHER'S (6) DA	0.71 OF 7	254	TILT TOWARD BEING THOSE WHERE HOUSEHOLD AUTHORITY IS ON THE FATHER'S SIDE, RATHER THAN THE MOTHER'S (9) DA	0.88 OF 8	2 7 5 1 XSQ= 3.23 PHI= -0.464 EP = 0.0406
257	TILT TOWARD BEING THOSE WHERE THE SEVERITY OF SISTER AVOIDANCE IS LOW (17) WNS	0.85 OF 13	257	TILT TOWARD BEING THOSE WHERE THE SEVERITY OF SISTER AVOIDANCE IS HIGH (10) WNS	0.57 OF 14	2 8 11 6 XSQ= 3.41 PHI= -0.355 EP = 0.0461
258	TILT TOWARD BEING THOSE WHERE THE SEVERITY OF SON'S WIFE AVOIDANCE IS LOW (16) WNS	0.77 OF 13	258	TILT TOWARD BEING THOSE WHERE THE SEVERITY OF SON'S WIFE AVOIDANCE IS HIGH (15) WNS	0.67 OF 18	3 12 10 6 XSQ= 4.13 PHI= -0.365 EP = 0.0290

262	TEND LESS TO BE THCSE 0.62 OF 112 WHERE WIVES ARE OBTAINED BY MEANS INVOLVING THE PRESENCE OF SOME CCNSIDERATION (305)	262	TEND MORE TO BE THOSE 0.84 OF 271 WHERE WIVES ARE OBTAINED BY MEANS INVOLVING THE PRESENCE OF SOME CONSIDERATION (305)	69 227 43 44 XSQ= 20.92 PHI= -0.234 XP = 0.0000
263	TEND TO BE THOSE 0.57 OF 112 WHERE WIVES ARE OBTAINED BY RELATIVELY EASY MEANS, NAMELY BY TOKEN BRIDE-PRICE, GIFT EXCHANGE, ABSENCE OF ANY CCNSIDERATICN, OR RECEIPT OF DOWRY (162)	263	TEND TO BE THOSE 0.65 OF 271 WHERE WIVES ARE OBTAINED BY RELATIVELY DIFFICULT MEANS, NAMELY BY BRIDE-PRICE, BRIDE-SERVICE, OR EXCHANGING A FEMALE RELATIVE (233)	48 177 64 94 XSQ= 15.58 PHI= -0.202 XP = 0.0001
307	DRIFT TOWARD BEING THOSE 0.56 OF 18 WHERE THE EARLY AGGRESSION SATISFACTION POTENTIAL IS LOW (19) W-C	307	DRIFT TOWARD BEING THOSE 0.74 OF 34 WHERE THE EARLY AGGRESSION SATISFACTION POTENTIAL IS HIGH (33) W-C	8 25 10 9 XSQ= 3.13 PHI= -0.245 XP = 0.0768
324	TILT TOWARD BEING THOSE 0.70 OF 20 WHERE THE PAIN INFLICTEC CN THE INFANT BY THE NURTURANT AGENT IS LCW OR NEGLIGIBLE (32) B-B-C	324	TILT TOWARD BEING THOSE 0.62 OF 45 WHERE THE PAIN INFLICTED ON THE INFANT BY THE NURTURANT AGENT IS HIGH (34) B-B-C	6 28 14 17 XSQ= 4.54 PHI= -0.264 XP = 0.0330
333	TILT TOWARD BEING THOSE 0.86 OF 7 WHERE THE AGE AT BEGINNING OF TRAINING IN HETERCSEXUAL PLAY INHIBITION IS LOWER THAN EIGHT YEARS (8) W-C	333	TILT TOWARD BEING THOSE 0.78 OF 9 WHERE THE AGE AT BEGINNING OF TRAINING IN HETEROSEXUAL PLAY INHIBITION IS EIGHT YEARS OR HIGHER (8) W-C	1 7 6 2 XSQ= 4.06 PHI= -0.504 EP = 0.0406
339	DRIFT MORE TOWARD BEING THOSE 0.76 OF 21 WHERE THE CHILD'S INFERREC CONFLICT REGARDING RESPONSIBLE BEHAVIOR IS LOW (42) B-B-C	339	DRIFT LESS TOWARD BEING THCSE 0.51 OF 51 WHERE THE CHILD'S INFERRED CONFLICT REGARDING RESPONSIBLE BEHAVIOR IS LOW (42) B-B-C	5 25 16 26 XSQ= 2.92 PHI= -0.201 XP = 0.0874
356	DRIFT TOWARD BEING THOSE 0.67 OF 15 WHERE NEITHER ADOLESCENT PEER GROUPS NOR PAIRS ARE PRESENT IN A SETTING OF COURTSHIP (22) JKH	356	DRIFT TOWARD BEING THOSE 0.67 OF 36 WHERE ADOLESCENT PEER GROUPS OR PAIRS ARE PRESENT IN A SETTING OF COURTSHIP (29) JKH	5 24 10 12 XSQ= 3.53 PHI= -0.263 XP = 0.0601
370	TEND MORE TO BE THCSE 0.83 OF 69 WHERE THE SEGREGATION OF ADOLESCENT BOYS IS ABSENT (148)	370	TEND LESS TO BE THOSE 0.53 OF 170 WHERE THE SEGREGATION OF ADOLESCENT BOYS IS ABSENT (148)	12 80 57 90 XSQ= 17.01 PHI= -0.267 XP = 0.0000
372	TILT TOWARD BEING THOSE 0.73 OF 37 WHERE MALE INITIATION RITES ARE ABSENT (63) ASA	372	TILT TOWARD BEING THOSE 0.51 OF 73 WHERE MALE INITIATION RITES ARE PRESENT (48) ASA	10 37 27 36 XSQ= 4.69 PHI= -0.207 XP = 0.0303

377	TEND MORE TO BE THCSE 0.92 OF 95 WHERE MALE GENITAL MUTILATION IS ABSENT (242)	377	TEND LESS TO BE THOSE 0.68 OF 222 WHERE MALE GENITAL MUTILATION IS ABSENT (242)	8 71 87 151 XSQ= 18.50 PHI= -0.242 XP = 0.0000
380	TILT MORE TOWARC BEING THCSE 0.88 OF 16 WHERE SEGREGATICN CF GIRLS AT MENARCHE IS PRESENT (35) F-B	380	TILT LESS TOWARD BEING THOSE 0.53 OF 38 WHERE SEGREGATION OF GIRLS AT MENARCHE IS PRESENT (35) F-B	14 20 2 18 XSQ= 4.47 PHI= 0.288 XP = 0.0345
426	TILT TCWARD BEING THCSE 0.51 OF 75 WHERE A HIGH GOC IS ABSENT (104) GES,EA	426	TILT TOWARD BEING THOSE 0.64 OF 179 WHERE A HIGH GOD IS PRESENT (156) GES,EA	37 114 38 65 XSQ= 3.94 PHI= -0.125 XP = 0.0471
434	DRIFT TOWARD BEING THCSE 0.64 OF 22 WHERE ASCETICISM IN MOURNING BEHAVIOR IS LCW (30) JFG	434	DRIFT TOWARD BEING THOSE 0.64 OF 45 WHERE ASCETICISM IN MOURNING BEHAVIOR IS HIGH (37) JFG	8 29 14 16 XSQ= 3.64 PHI= -0.233 XP = 0.0562
454	DRIFT TCWARD BEING THCSE 0.75 OF 12 WHERE THE CBJECTIVE CF THE INDIVICUAL'S CONTACT WITH THE DIVINE IS NOT CCNDUCIVE TC THE DEVELOPMENT OF THE INDIVIDUAL'S NEED TO ACHIEVE (18) DCM	454	DRIFT TOWARD BEING THOSE 0.63 OF 24 WHERE THE OBJECTIVE OF THE INDIVIDUAL'S CONTACT WITH THE DIVINE IS CONDUCIVE TO THE DEVELCPMENT OF THE INDIVIDUAL'S NEED TO ACHIEVE (18) DCM	3 15 9 9 XSQ= 3.12 PHI= -0.295 EP = 0.0750
458	DRIFT MORE TCWARD BEING THOSE 0.7° OF 62 WHERE GAMES, IF PRESENT, DO NCT INCLUDE GAMES OF STRATEGY (119) R-A-B,EA	458	DRIFT LESS TOWARD BEING THOSE 0.64 OF 107 WHERE GAMES, IF PRESENT, DO NOT INCLUDE GAMES OF STRATEGY (119) R-A-B,EA	13 38 49 69 XSQ= 3.28 PHI= -0.139 XP = 0.0701
459	TEND TO BE THOSE 0.77 OF 62 WHERE GAMES, IF PRESENT, INCLUDE GAMES OF CHANCE (82) R-A-B,EA	459	TEND TO BE THOSE 0.69 OF 107 WHERE GAMES, IF PRESENT, DO NOT INCLUDE GAMES OF CHANCE (89) R-A-B,EA	48 33 14 74 XSQ= 32.28 PHI= 0.437 XP = 0.
460	TEND TO BE THOSE 0.81 OF 62 WHERE GAMES, IF PRESENT, ARE NCT LIMITED TO GAMES OF SKILL CNLY (104) R-A-B,EA	460	TEND TO BE THOSE 0.50 OF 107 WHERE GAMES, IF PRESENT, ARE LIMITED TO GAMES OF SKILL ONLY (67) R-A-B,EA	12 54 50 53 XSQ= 14.68 PHI= -0.295 XP = 0.0001
473	DRIFT MORE TOWARD BEING THOSE 0.79 OF 24 WHERE SENSITIVITY TO INSULT IS MODERATE OR NEGLIGIBLE (56) PES	473	DRIFT LESS TOWARD BEING THCSE 0.57 OF 63 WHERE SENSITIVITY TO INSULT IS MODERATE OR NEGLIGIBLE (56) PES	5 27 19 36 XSQ= 2.74 PHI= -0.177 XP = 0.0979

481/

487 DRIFT MORE TOWARD BEING THOSE 0.94 OF 85
ABOUT WHICH THE PRINCIPAL ETHNOGRAPHIES
WERE PUBLISHED IN 1930 OR AFTER (227)

487 DRIFT LESS TOWARD BEING THOSE 0.85 OF 167
ABOUT WHICH THE PRINCIPAL ETHNOGRAPHIES
WERE PUBLISHED IN 1930 OR AFTER (227)

	5	25
	80	142
XSQ=		3.61
PHI=		-0.120
XP =		0.0574

482 CULTURES WHERE THE PRINCIPAL ETHNOGRAPHERS HAVE BEEN BRITISH (52)

482 CULTURES WHERE THE PRINCIPAL ETHNOGRAPHERS HAVE BEEN OTHER THAN BRITISH (336)

BACKGROUND ON PAGE 177

BOTH SUBJECT AND PREDICATE

52 IN LEFT COLUMN

ANDAMANESE	ARANDA	ASHANTI	BARI	BEMBA	BURUSHO	DIERI	DOBUANS	DOROBO	ELLICE
GISU	GOND	GURE	IBAN	INGASSANA	JUKUN	KACHIN	KATAB	KERAKI	KERALA
KURTATCHI	LAMBA	LANGO	LEPCHA	LHOTA NAGA	LIFU	LOZI	MANGAIANS	MANIHIKI	MARGI
MBUNDU	MENDE	MINCHIA	MOTA	NGONI	NUER	NYAKYUSA	NYORO	ONTONG-JAVA	SENIANG
SWAZI	TALLENSI	TAMIL	TERA	TESO	TIKOPIA	ULAWANS	VEDDA	WIKMUNKAN	WOGEO
YAKO	YAO								

336 IN RIGHT COLUMN

12 EXCLUDED BECAUSE UNASCERTAINED

	British (52)		Other than British (336)			
3	TEND LESS TO BE THOSE LOCATED OUTSIDE OF AFRICA (320)	0.54 OF 52	TEND MORE TO BE THOSE LOCATED OUTSIDE OF AFRICA (320)	0.85 OF 336	24 52 28 284	XSQ= 24.99 PHI= 0.254 XP = 0.0000
4	DRIFT MORE TOWARD BEING THOSE LOCATED OUTSIDE OF THE CIRCUM-MEDITERRANEAN (355)	0.98 OF 52	DRIFT LESS TOWARD BEING THOSE LOCATED OUTSIDE OF THE CIRCUM-MEDITERRANEAN (355)	0.88 OF 336	1 40 51 296	XSQ= 3.75 PHI= -0.098 XP = 0.0528
6	LEAN LESS TOWARD BEING THOSE LOCATED OUTSIDE OF THE INSULAR PACIFIC (330)	0.67 OF 52	LEAN MORE TOWARD BEING THOSE LOCATED OUTSIDE OF THE INSULAR PACIFIC (330)	0.85 OF 336	17 52 35 284	XSQ= 7.99 PHI= 0.143 XP = 0.0047
8	IN ALL CASES ARE THOSE LOCATED OUTSIDE OF NORTH AMERICA (330)	1.00 OF 52	TEND LESS TO BE THOSE LOCATED OUTSIDE OF NORTH AMERICA (330)	0.79 OF 336	0 70 52 266	XSQ= 11.85 PHI= -0.175 XP = 0.0006

9	IN ALL CASES ARE THOSE LOCATED OUTSIDE OF SOUTH AMERICA (335)	1.00 OF 52	9	LEAN LESS TOWARD BEING THOSE LOCATED OUTSIDE OF SOUTH AMERICA (335)	0.81 OF 336	0 65 52 271 XSQ= 10.74 PHI= -0.166 XP = 0.0011
13	IN ALL CASES ARE THOSE WHERE THE LATITUDE IS LESS THAN FORTY DEGREES (329) .	1.00 OF 52	13	TEND LESS TO BE THOSE WHERE THE LATITUDE IS LESS THAN FORTY DEGREES (329)	0.79 OF 336	0 69 52 267 XSQ= 11.62 PHI= -0.173 XP = 0.0007
14	TEND MORE TO BE THOSE WHERE THE LATITUDE IS LESS THAN THIRTY DEGREES (281)	0.98 OF 52	14	TEND LESS TO BE THOSE WHERE THE LATITUDE IS LESS THAN THIRTY DEGREES (281)	0.66 OF 336	1 115 51 221 XSQ= 20.91 PHI= -0.232 XP = 0.0000
15	TEND MORE TO BE THOSE WHERE THE LATITUDE IS LESS THAN TWENTY DEGREES (217)	0.79 OF 52	15	TEND LESS TO BE THOSE WHERE THE LATITUDE IS LESS THAN TWENTY DEGREES (217)	0.50 OF 336	11 167 41 169 XSQ= 13.65 PHI= -0.188 XP = 0.0002
33	DRIFT MORE TOWARD BEING THOSE WHERE THE NATURAL ENVIRONMENT IS OTHER THAN 'VERY HARSH,' I.E., DESERT, DESERT GRASSES AND SHRUBS, TUNDRA, OR HIGH PLATEAU STEPPE (341) FWM	0.94 OF 52	33	DRIFT LESS TOWARD BEING THOSE WHERE THE NATURAL ENVIRONMENT IS OTHER THAN 'VERY HARSH,' I.E., DESERT, DESERT GRASSES AND SHRUBS, TUNDRA, OR HIGH PLATEAU STEPPE (341) FWM	0.85 OF 336	3 52 49 284 XSQ= 2.74 PHI= -0.084 XP = 0.0981
36	TILT MORE TOWARD BEING THOSE WHERE THE NATURAL ENVIRONMENT IS OTHER THAN 'VERY HARSH,' OR SUB-TROPICAL BUSH, OR TEMPERATE GRASSLAND (292) FWM	0.88 OF 52	36	TILT LESS TOWARD BEING THOSE WHERE THE NATURAL ENVIRONMENT IS OTHER THAN 'VERY HARSH,' OR SUB-TROPICAL BUSH, OR TEMPERATE GRASSLAND (292) FWM	0.71 OF 336	6 96 46 240 XSQ= 5.89 PHI= -0.123 XP = 0.0152
51	TILT MORE TOWARD BEING THOSE WHERE SUBSISTENCE IS PRIMARILY BY FOOD PRODUCTION -- I. E., AGRICULTURE OR HUSBANDRY -- RATHER THAN BY GATHERING (253)	0.79 OF 52	51	TILT LESS TOWARD BEING THOSE WHERE SUBSISTENCE IS PRIMARILY BY FOOD PRODUCTION -- I. E., AGRICULTURE OR HUSBANDRY -- RATHER THAN BY GATHERING (253)	0.60 OF 336	41 202 11 134 XSQ= 5.97 PHI= 0.124 XP = 0.0145
54	TILT MORE TOWARD BEING THOSE WHERE FOOD PRODUCTION IS BY INTENSIVE OR SIMPLE AGRICULTURE, RATHER THAN BY INCIPIENT FOOD PRODUCTION (192)	0.97 OF 37	54	TILT LESS TOWARD BEING THOSE WHERE FOOD PRODUCTION IS BY INTENSIVE OR SIMPLE AGRICULTURE, RATHER THAN BY INCIPIENT FOOD PRODUCTION (192)	0.78 OF 196	36 152 1 44 XSQ= 6.57 PHI= 0.168 XP = 0.0104
55	TILT TOWARD BEING THOSE WHERE FOOD PRODUCTION IS BY SIMPLE AGRICULTURE, RATHER THAN BY INTENSIVE AGRICULTURE (101)	0.72 OF 36	55	TILT TOWARD BEING THOSE WHERE FOOD PRODUCTION IS BY INTENSIVE AGRICULTURE, RATHER THAN BY SIMPLE AGRICULTURE (91)	0.51 OF 152	10 78 26 74 XSQ= 5.57 PHI= -0.172 XP = 0.0183

56	LEAN MORE TOWARD BEING THOSE WHERE FOOD PRODUCTION IS BY SIMPLE AGRICULTURE, RATHER THAN BY INCIPIENT FOOD PRODUCTION (101)	0.96 OF 27	56	LEAN LESS TOWARD BEING THOSE WHERE FOOD PRODUCTION IS BY SIMPLE AGRICULTURE, RATHER THAN BY INCIPIENT FOOD PRODUCTION (101)	0.63 OF 118	26 74 / 1 44 / XSQ= 10.06 / PHI= 0.263 / XP = 0.0015
62	DRIFT MORE TOWARD BEING THOSE WHERE HUSBANDRY OF SOME KIND IS PRESENT (228)	0.69 OF 52	62	DRIFT LESS TOWARD BEING THOSE WHERE HUSBANDRY OF SOME KIND IS PRESENT (228)	0.55 OF 336	36 185 / 16 151 / XSQ= 3.13 / PHI= 0.090 / XP = 0.0767
73	LEAN TOWARD BEING THOSE WHERE WEAVING IS ABSENT (130)	0.77 OF 35	73	LEAN TOWARD BEING THOSE WHERE WEAVING IS PRESENT (118)	0.51 OF 210	8 108 / 27 102 / XSQ= 8.71 / PHI= -0.189 / XP = 0.0032
77	IN ALL CASES ARE THOSE WHERE THE WRITING SYSTEM IS MNEMONIC OR ABSENT, RATHER THAN BEING ALPHABETIC-OR-PHONETIC (39) JMH	1.00 OF 10	77	DRIFT LESS TOWARD BEING THOSE WHERE THE WRITING SYSTEM IS MNEMONIC OR ABSENT, RATHER THAN BEING ALPHABETIC-OR-PHONETIC (39) JMH	0.65 OF 43	0 15 / 10 28 / XSQ= 3.30 / PHI= -0.249 / XP = 0.0694
88	DRIFT MORE TOWARD BEING THOSE WHERE, IF A HEADMANSHIP IS PRESENT, SUCCESSION IS HEREDITARY (165)	0.76 OF 38	88	DRIFT LESS TOWARD BEING THOSE WHERE, IF A HEADMANSHIP IS PRESENT, SUCCESSION IS HEREDITARY (165)	0.59 OF 229	9 95 / 29 134 / XSQ= 3.63 / PHI= -0.117 / XP = 0.0569
97	TILT LESS TOWARD BEING THOSE WHERE THE HIERARCHY OF LOCAL JURISDICTION HAS THREE OR TWO LEVELS (273) GES,EA	0.69 OF 48	97	TILT MORE TOWARD BEING THOSE WHERE THE HIERARCHY OF LOCAL JURISDICTION HAS THREE OR TWO LEVELS (273) GES,EA	0.84 OF 275	15 43 / 33 232 / XSQ= 5.74 / PHI= 0.133 / XP = 0.0165
108	TILT TOWARD BEING THOSE WHERE CLASS STRATIFICATION, IF PRESENT, IS BASED ON A HEREDITARY ARISTOCRACY (74)	0.55 OF 31	108	TILT TOWARD BEING THOSE WHERE CLASS STRATIFICATION, IF PRESENT, IS BASED ON SOMETHING OTHER THAN A HEREDITARY ARISTOCRACY (129)	0.67 OF 168	17 56 / 14 112 / XSQ= 4.33 / PHI= 0.147 / XP = 0.0375
130	IN ALL CASES ARE THOSE WHERE LEATHER WORKING IS MAINLY DONE BY MALES (39)	1.00 OF 4	130	DRIFT TOWARD BEING THOSE WHERE LEATHER WORKING IS MAINLY DONE BY FEMALES (45)	0.56 OF 79	4 35 / 0 44 / XSQ= 2.77 / PHI= 0.183 / XP = 0.0961
176	DRIFT TOWARD BEING THOSE WHERE THE COMMUNITY IS A CLAN-COMMUNITY OR A COMMUNITY STRUCTURED OR SEGMENTED ON A CLAN BASIS (169)	0.57 OF 51	176	DRIFT TOWARD BEING THOSE WHERE THE COMMUNITY IS OTHER THAN A CLAN-COMMUNITY OR A COMMUNITY STRUCTURED OR SEGMENTED ON A CLAN BASIS (213)	0.57 OF 319	29 136 / 22 183 / XSQ= 3.05 / PHI= 0.091 / XP = 0.0807

177	DRIFT LESS TOWARD BEING THOSE 0.69 OF 51 WHERE THE COMMUNITY IS OTHER THAN A SINGLE CLAN-COMMUNITY AND EXOGAMOUS (305)	177	DRIFT MORE TOWARD BEING THOSE 0.82 OF 319 WHERE THE COMMUNITY IS OTHER THAN A SINGLE CLAN-COMMUNITY AND EXOGAMOUS (305)	16 59 35 260 XSQ= 3.75 PHI= 0.101 XP = 0.0528
180	DRIFT LESS TOWARD BEING THOSE 0.55 OF 51 WHERE THE COMMUNITY IS COMMONLY NON-EXOGAMOUS, RATHER THAN EXOGAMOUS (258)	180	DRIFT MORE TOWARD BEING THOSE 0.70 OF 319 WHERE THE COMMUNITY IS COMMONLY NON-EXOGAMOUS, RATHER THAN EXOGAMOUS (258)	23 97 28 222 XSQ= 3.69 PHI= 0.100 XP = 0.0549
188	TILT MORE TOWARD BEING THOSE 0.79 OF 52 WHERE THE KIN GROUP IS OTHER THAN EXCLUSIVELY COGNATIC (252)	188	TILT LESS TOWARD BEING THOSE 0.60 OF 336 WHERE THE KIN GROUP IS OTHER THAN EXCLUSIVELY COGNATIC (252)	11 135 41 201 XSQ= 6.16 PHI= -0.126 XP = 0.0131
192	TEND MORE TO BE THOSE 0.94 OF 52 OTHER THAN WHERE THE ONLY KIN GROUP PRESENT IS A KINDRED OR ELSE BILATERAL DESCENT IS INFERRED (289)	192	TEND LESS TO BE THOSE 0.68 OF 336 OTHER THAN WHERE THE ONLY KIN GROUP PRESENT IS A KINDRED OR ELSE BILATERAL DESCENT IS INFERRED (289)	3 106 49 230 XSQ= 13.56 PHI= -0.187 XP = 0.0002
196	LEAN MORE TOWARD BEING THOSE 0.89 OF 36 WHERE INDIVIDUAL RIGHTS IN REAL PROPERTY, AND RULES FOR INHERITANCE, ARE PRESENT (194)	196	LEAN LESS TOWARD BEING THOSE 0.65 OF 237 WHERE INDIVIDUAL RIGHTS IN REAL PROPERTY, AND RULES FOR INHERITANCE, ARE PRESENT (194)	32 154 4 83 XSQ= 7.16 PHI= 0.162 XP = 0.0074
209	TILT MORE TOWARD BEING THOSE 0.93 OF 43 WHERE MARITAL RESIDENCE IS PATRILOCAL, VIRILOCAL, OR AVUNCULOCAL, RATHER THAN MATRILOCAL OR UXORILOCAL (270)	209	TILT LESS TOWARD BEING THOSE 0.79 OF 280 WHERE MARITAL RESIDENCE IS PATRILOCAL, VIRILOCAL, OR AVUNCULOCAL, RATHER THAN MATRILOCAL OR UXORILOCAL (270)	40 220 3 60 XSQ= 4.08 PHI= 0.112 XP = 0.0434
299	TILT TOWARD BEING THOSE 0.53 OF 17 WHERE THE POST-PARTUM SEX TABOO LASTS LONGER THAN ONE YEAR (35)	299	TILT TOWARD BEING THOSE 0.76 OF 103 WHERE THE POST-PARTUM SEX TABOO LASTS ONE YEAR OR LESS (89)	9 25 8 78 XSQ= 4.58 PHI= 0.195 XP = 0.0324
314	DRIFT LESS TOWARD BEING THOSE 0.53 OF 15 WHERE THE INCIDENCE OF MOTHER-CHILD HOUSEHOLDS IS LOW (61) W-C,S	314	DRIFT MORE TOWARD BEING THOSE 0.81 OF 64 WHERE THE INCIDENCE OF MOTHER-CHILD HOUSEHOLDS IS LOW (61) W-D,S	7 12 8 52 XSQ= 3.77 PHI= 0.218 XP = 0.0522
330	TILT TOWARD BEING THOSE 0.77 OF 13 WHERE THE AGE OF THE INFANT AT TIME OF WEANING IS 2.5 YEARS OR HIGHER (34) B-B-C	330	TILT TOWARD BEING THOSE 0.59 OF 56 WHERE THE AGE OF THE INFANT AT TIME OF WEANING IS LOWER THAN 2.5 YEARS (36) B-B-C	10 23 3 33 XSQ= 4.09 PHI= 0.244 XP = 0.0431

370	TEND TO BE THOSE 0.67 OF 39 WHERE THE SEGREGATION OF ACOLESCENT BOYS IS COMPLETE CR PARTIAL (95)	370	TEND TO BE THOSE 0.67 OF 200 WHERE THE SEGREGATION OF ADOLESCENT BOYS IS ABSENT (148)	26 66 13 134 XSQ= 14.23 PHI= 0.244 XP = 0.0002
372	DRIFT TCWARD BEING THCSE 0.58 OF 31 WHERE MALE INITIATION RITES ARE PRESENT (48) ASA	372	DRIFT TOWARD BEING THOSE 0.63 OF 79 WHERE MALE INITIATION RITES ARE ABSENT (63) ASA	18 29 13 50 XSQ= 3.32 PHI= 0.174 XP = 0.0683
428	TILT TOWARD BEING THOSE 0.75 OF 8 WHERE A HIGH GOD, IF PRESENT AND ACTIVE, DOES NOT SUPPORT HUMAN MORALITY, RATHER THAN SUPPORTING IT (26) GES,EA	428	TILT TOWARD BEING THOSE 0.75 OF 76 WHERE A HIGH GOD, IF PRESENT AND ACTIVE, SUPPORTS HUMAN MORALITY, RATHER THAN NOT SUPPORTING IT (61) GES,EA	2 57 6 19 XSQ= 6.43 PHI= -0.277 XP = 0.0112
434	DRIFT TCWARD BEING THCSE 0.83 OF 12 WHERE ASCETICISM IN MOURNING BEHAVIOR IS HIGH (37) JFG	434	DRIFT TOWARD BEING THOSE 0.51 OF 55 WHERE ASCETICISM IN MOURNING BEHAVIOR IS LOW (30) JFG	10 27 2 28 XSQ= 3.39 PHI= 0.225 XP = 0.0656
459	TEND TO BE THOSE 0.88 OF 26 WHERE GAMES, IF PRESENT, DO NOT INCLUDE GAMES OF CHANCE (89) R-A-B,EA	459	TEND TO BE THOSE 0.55 OF 143 WHERE GAMES, IF PRESENT, INCLUDE GAMES OF CHANCE (82) R-A-B,EA	3 78 23 65 XSQ= 14.63 PHI= -0.294 XP = 0.0001
460	DRIFT TCWARD BEING THCSE 0.58 OF 26 WHERE GAMES, IF PRESENT, ARE LIMITED TO GAMES OF SKILL CNLY (67) R-A-B,EA	460	DRIFT TOWARD BEING THOSE 0.64 OF 143 WHERE GAMES, IF PRESENT, ARE NOT LIMITED TO GAMES OF SKILL ONLY (104) R-A-B,EA	15 51 11 92 XSQ= 3.61 PHI= 0.146 XP = 0.0575
476	TILT TCWARD BEING THOSE 0.86 OF 7 WHERE THE DEGREE OF INSOBRIETY IS MODERATE CR SLIGHT (18) DH	476	TILT TOWARD BEING THOSE 0.71 OF 42 WHERE THE DEGREE OF INSOBRIETY IS STRONG (31) DH	1 30 6 12 XSQ= 6.15 PHI= -0.354 XP = 0.0131
488	DRIFT MORE TCWARD BEING THOSE 0.87 OF 30 ABOUT WHICH THE PRINCIPAL ETHNOGRAPHIES WERE PUBLISHED BEFCRE 1950 (185)	488	DRIFT LESS TOWARD BEING THOSE 0.69 OF 220 ABOUT WHICH THE PRINCIPAL ETHNOGRAPHIES WERE PUBLISHED BEFORE 1950 (185)	26 152 4 68 XSQ= 3.17 PHI= 0.113 XP = 0.0752

483	CULTURES WHERE THE PRINCIPAL ETHNOGRAPHERS HAVE BEEN AMERICAN, RATHER THAN BRITISH (113)	483	CULTURES WHERE THE PRINCIPAL ETHNOGRAPHERS HAVE BEEN BRITISH, RATHER THAN AMERICAN (52)

BACKGROUND ON PAGE 177 — BOTH SUBJECT AND PREDICATE

113 IN LEFT COLUMN (SEE LEFT COLUMN, PARAGRAPH 481)

52 IN RIGHT COLUMN (SEE LEFT COLUMN, PARAGRAPH 482)

223 EXCLUDED BECAUSE IRRELEVANT

12 EXCLUDED BECAUSE UNASCERTAINED

3	TEND MORE TO BE THOSE LOCATED OUTSIDE OF AFRICA (320)	0.98 OF 113	3	TEND LESS TO BE THOSE LOCATED OUTSIDE OF AFRICA (320)	0.54 OF 52	2 24 111 28 XSQ= 49.56 PHI= -0.548 XP = 0.
6	LEAN MORE TOWARD BEING THOSE LOCATED OUTSIDE OF THE INSULAR PACIFIC (330)	0.87 OF 113	6	LEAN LESS TOWARD BEING THOSE LOCATED OUTSIDE OF THE INSULAR PACIFIC (330)	0.67 OF 52	15 17 98 35 XSQ= 7.39 PHI= -0.212 XP = 0.0066
8	TEND TO BE THOSE LOCATED IN NORTH AMERICA (70)	0.50 OF 113	8	IN ALL CASES ARE THOSE LOCATED OUTSIDE OF NORTH AMERICA (330)	1.00 OF 52	57 0 56 52 XSQ= 37.87 PHI= 0.479 XP = 0.
9	LEAN LESS TOWARD BEING THOSE LOCATED OUTSIDE OF SOUTH AMERICA (335)	0.84 OF 113	9	IN ALL CASES ARE THOSE LOCATED OUTSIDE OF SOUTH AMERICA (335)	1.00 OF 52	18 0 95 52 XSQ= 7.73 PHI= 0.216 XP = 0.0054
13	TEND LESS TO BE THOSE WHERE THE LATITUDE IS LESS THAN FORTY DEGREES (329)	0.65 OF 113	13	IN ALL CASES ARE THOSE WHERE THE LATITUDE IS LESS THAN FORTY DEGREES (329)	1.00 OF 52	40 0 73 52 XSQ= 22.41 PHI= 0.369 XP = 0.0000

14	TEND TO BE THOSE WHERE THE LATITUDE IS THIRTY DEGREES OR GREATER (119)	0.59 OF 113	14	TEND TO BE THOSE WHERE THE LATITUDE IS LESS THAN THIRTY DEGREES (281)	0.98 OF 52	67 1 46 51 XSQ= 46.04 PHI= 0.528 XP = 0.
15	TEND TO BE THOSE WHERE THE LATITUDE IS TWENTY DEGREES OR GREATER (183)	0.69 OF 113	15	TEND TO BE THOSE WHERE THE LATITUDE IS LESS THAN TWENTY DEGREES (217)	0.79 OF 52	78 11 35 41 XSQ= 30.95 PHI= 0.433 XP = 0.
33	TILT LESS TOWARD BEING THOSE WHERE THE NATURAL ENVIRONMENT IS OTHER THAN 'VERY HARSH,' I.E., DESERT, DESERT GRASSES AND SHRUBS, TUNDRA, OR HIGH PLATEAU STEPPE (341) FWM	0.81 OF 113	33	TILT MORE TOWARD BEING THOSE WHERE THE NATURAL ENVIRONMENT IS OTHER THAN 'VERY HARSH,' I.E., DESERT, DESERT GRASSES AND SHRUBS, TUNDRA, OR HIGH PLATEAU STEPPE (341) FWM	0.94 OF 52	22 3 91 49 XSQ= 4.19 PHI= 0.159 XP = 0.0407
36	LEAN LESS TOWARD BEING THOSE WHERE THE NATURAL ENVIRONMENT IS OTHER THAN 'VERY HARSH,' OR SUB-TROPICAL BUSH, OR TEMPERATE GRASSLAND (292) FWM	0.65 OF 113	36	LEAN MORE TOWARD BEING THOSE WHERE THE NATURAL ENVIRONMENT IS OTHER THAN 'VERY HARSH,' OR SUB-TROPICAL BUSH, OR TEMPERATE GRASSLAND (292) FWM	0.88 OF 52	39 6 74 46 XSQ= 8.35 PHI= 0.225 XP = 0.0038
42	DRIFT MORE TOWARD BEING THOSE WHERE THE NATURAL ENVIRONMENT IS OTHER THAN TROPICAL OR SUB-TROPICAL RAIN FOREST, OR MONSOON FOREST (244) FWM	0.73 OF 113	42	DRIFT LESS TOWARD BEING THOSE WHERE THE NATURAL ENVIRONMENT IS OTHER THAN TROPICAL OR SUB-TROPICAL RAIN FOREST, OR MONSOON FOREST (244) FWM	0.56 OF 52	31 23 82 29 XSQ= 3.83 PHI= -0.152 XP = 0.0503
44	TILT LESS TOWARD BEING THOSE WHERE SETTLEMENTS ARE FIXED (222)	0.57 OF 95	44	TILT MORE TOWARD BEING THOSE WHERE SETTLEMENTS ARE FIXED (222)	0.77 OF 48	54 37 41 11 XSQ= 4.81 PHI= -0.183 XP = 0.0284
51	TEND TO BE THOSE WHERE SUBSISTENCE IS PRIMARILY BY FOOD GATHERING -- I. E., HUNTING, FISHING, OR COLLECTING -- RATHER THAN FOOD PRODUCTION (147)	0.56 OF 113	51	TEND TO BE THOSE WHERE SUBSISTENCE IS PRIMARILY BY FOOD PRODUCTION -- I. E., AGRICULTURE OR HUSBANDRY -- RATHER THAN BY GATHERING (253)	0.79 OF 52	50 41 63 11 XSQ= 15.86 PHI= -0.310 XP = 0.0001
54	TEND LESS TO BE THOSE WHERE FOOD PRODUCTION IS BY INTENSIVE OR SIMPLE AGRICULTURE, RATHER THAN BY INCIPIENT FOOD PRODUCTION (192)	0.65 OF 62	54	TEND MORE TO BE THOSE WHERE FOOD PRODUCTION IS BY INTENSIVE OR SIMPLE AGRICULTURE, RATHER THAN BY INCIPIENT FOOD PRODUCTION (192)	0.97 OF 37	40 36 22 1 XSQ= 12.18 PHI= -0.351 XP = 0.0005
55	LEAN TOWARD BEING THOSE WHERE FOOD PRODUCTION IS BY INTENSIVE AGRICULTURE, RATHER THAN BY SIMPLE AGRICULTURE (91)	0.63 OF 40	55	LEAN TOWARD BEING THOSE WHERE FOOD PRODUCTION IS BY SIMPLE AGRICULTURE, RATHER THAN BY INTENSIVE AGRICULTURE (101)	0.72 OF 36	25 10 15 26 XSQ= 7.85 PHI= 0.321 XP = 0.0051

56	TEND TO BE THOSE WHERE FOOD PRODUCTION IS BY INCIPIENT FOOD PRODUCTION, RATHER THAN BY SIMPLE AGRICULTURE (46)	0.59 OF 37	56	TEND TO BE THOSE WHERE FOOD PRODUCTION IS BY SIMPLE AGRICULTURE, RATHER THAN BY INCIPIENT FOOD PRODUCTION (101)	0.96 OF 27	15 26 22 1 XSQ= 18.72 PHI= -0.541 XP = 0.0000
62	TILT TOWARD BEING THOSE WHERE HUSBANDRY OF ANY KIND IS ABSENT (172)	0.50 OF 113	62	TILT TOWARD BEING THOSE WHERE HUSBANDRY OF SOME KIND IS PRESENT (228)	0.69 OF 52	56 36 57 16 XSQ= 4.82 PHI= -0.171 XP = 0.0282
71	LEAN MORE TOWARD BEING THOSE WHERE METAL WORKING IS ABSENT (153)	0.80 OF 75	71	LEAN LESS TOWARD BEING THOSE WHERE METAL WORKING IS ABSENT (153)	0.54 OF 37	15 17 60 20 XSQ= 6.95 PHI= -0.249 XP = 0.0084
73	TILT LESS TOWARD BEING THOSE WHERE WEAVING IS ABSENT (130)	0.54 OF 76	73	TILT MORE TOWARD BEING THOSE WHERE WEAVING IS ABSENT (130)	0.77 OF 35	35 8 41 27 XSQ= 4.50 PHI= 0.201 XP = 0.0339
77	TILT TOWARD BEING THOSE WHERE THE WRITING SYSTEM IS ALPHABETIC-OR-PHONETIC, RATHER THAN BEING MNEMONIC OR ABSENT (15) JMH	0.60 OF 10	77	IN ALL CASES ARE THOSE WHERE THE WRITING SYSTEM IS MNEMONIC OR ABSENT, RATHER THAN BEING ALPHABETIC-OR-PHONETIC (39) JMH	1.00 OF 10	6 0 4 10 XSQ= 5.95 PHI= 0.546 EP = 0.0108
79	DRIFT LESS TOWARD BEING THOSE WHERE NO CITY IS PRESENT (201)	0.81 OF 58	79	DRIFT MORE TOWARD BEING THOSE WHERE NO CITY IS PRESENT (201)	0.97 OF 30	11 1 47 29 XSQ= 2.88 PHI= 0.181 XP = 0.0895
88	TILT LESS TOWARD BEING THOSE WHERE, IF A HEADMANSHIP IS PRESENT, SUCCESSION IS HEREDITARY (165)	0.53 OF 78	88	TILT MORE TOWARD BEING THOSE WHERE, IF A HEADMANSHIP IS PRESENT, SUCCESSION IS HEREDITARY (165)	0.76 OF 38	37 9 41 29 XSQ= 5.07 PHI= 0.209 XP = 0.0243
97	TILT MORE TOWARD BEING THOSE WHERE THE HIERARCHY OF LOCAL JURISDICTION HAS THREE OR TWO LEVELS (273) GES,EA	0.88 OF 96	97	TILT LESS TOWARD BEING THOSE WHERE THE HIERARCHY OF LOCAL JURISDICTION HAS THREE OR TWO LEVELS (273) GES,EA	0.69 OF 48	12 15 84 33 XSQ= 6.21 PHI= -0.208 XP = 0.0127
108	DRIFT TOWARD BEING THOSE WHERE CLASS STRATIFICATION, IF PRESENT, IS BASED ON SOMETHING OTHER THAN A HEREDITARY ARISTOCRACY (129)	0.69 OF 51	108	DRIFT TOWARD BEING THOSE WHERE CLASS STRATIFICATION, IF PRESENT, IS BASED ON A HEREDITARY ARISTOCRACY (74)	0.55 OF 31	16 17 35 14 XSQ= 3.49 PHI= -0.206 XP = 0.0616

110	TILT MORE TOWARD BEING THOSE 0.73 OF 110 WHERE SLAVERY IS ABSENT (218)	110	TILT LESS TOWARD BEING THOSE 0.51 OF 51 WHERE SLAVERY IS ABSENT (218)	30 25 80 26 XSQ= 6.39 PHI= -0.199 XP = 0.0115
128	DRIFT TOWARD BEING THOSE 0.79 OF 14 WHERE, IF SUBSISTENCE IS PRIMARILY BY AGRICULTURE, THE WORK IS MAINLY DONE BY MALES (40)	128	DRIFT TOWARD BEING THOSE 0.62 OF 13 WHERE, IF SUBSISTENCE IS PRIMARILY BY AGRICULTURE, THE WORK IS MAINLY DONE BY FEMALES (37)	11 5 3 8 XSQ= 2.98 PHI= 0.332 EP = 0.0542
129	TILT TOWARD BEING THOSE 0.86 OF 29 WHERE WEAVING IS MAINLY DONE BY FEMALES (73)	129	TILT TOWARD BEING THOSE 0.57 OF 7 WHERE WEAVING IS MAINLY DONE BY MALES (31)	4 4 25 3 XSQ= 3.88 PHI= -0.328 EP = 0.0301
130	DRIFT TOWARD BEING THOSE 0.62 OF 37 WHERE LEATHER WORKING IS MAINLY DONE BY FEMALES (45)	130	IN ALL CASES ARE THOSE 1.00 OF 4 WHERE LEATHER WORKING IS MAINLY DONE BY MALES (39)	14 4 23 0 XSQ= 3.42 PHI= -0.289 XP = 0.0644
176	TILT TOWARD BEING THOSE 0.65 OF 108 WHERE THE COMMUNITY IS OTHER THAN A CLAN-COMMUNITY OR A COMMUNITY STRUCTURED OR SEGMENTED ON A CLAN BASIS (213)	176	TILT TOWARD BEING THOSE 0.57 OF 51 WHERE THE COMMUNITY IS A CLAN-COMMUNITY OR A COMMUNITY STRUCTURED OR SEGMENTED ON A CLAN BASIS (169)	38 29 70 22 XSQ= 5.82 PHI= -0.191 XP = 0.0159
177	TILT MORE TOWARD BEING THOSE 0.87 OF 108 WHERE THE COMMUNITY IS OTHER THAN A SINGLE CLAN-COMMUNITY AND EXOGAMOUS (305)	177	TILT LESS TOWARD BEING THOSE 0.69 OF 51 WHERE THE COMMUNITY IS OTHER THAN A SINGLE CLAN-COMMUNITY AND EXOGAMOUS (305)	14 16 94 35 XSQ= 6.51 PHI= -0.202 XP = 0.0107
180	LEAN MORE TOWARD BEING THOSE 0.77 OF 108 WHERE THE COMMUNITY IS COMMONLY NON-EXOGAMOUS, RATHER THAN EXOGAMOUS (258)	180	LEAN LESS TOWARD BEING THOSE 0.55 OF 51 WHERE THE COMMUNITY IS COMMONLY NON-EXOGAMOUS, RATHER THAN EXOGAMOUS (258)	25 23 83 28 XSQ= 6.91 PHI= -0.209 XP = 0.0086
182	DRIFT LESS TOWARD BEING THOSE 0.59 OF 108 OTHER THAN WHERE THE COMMUNITY IS STRUCTURED ON A NON-CLAN BASIS AND AGAMOUS (256)	182	DRIFT MORE TOWARD BEING THOSE 0.75 OF 51 OTHER THAN WHERE THE COMMUNITY IS STRUCTURED ON A NON-CLAN BASIS AND AGAMOUS (256)	44 13 64 38 XSQ= 2.87 PHI= 0.134 XP = 0.0902
184	DRIFT LESS TOWARD BEING THOSE 0.58 OF 55 WHERE THE LARGEST NON-COGNATIC KIN GROUP IS SMALLER THAN A PHRATRY, I. E. A SIB OR LINEAGE (175)	184	DRIFT MORE TOWARD BEING THOSE 0.78 OF 41 WHERE THE LARGEST NON-COGNATIC KIN GROUP IS SMALLER THAN A PHRATRY, I. E. A SIB OR LINEAGE (175)	23 9 32 32 XSQ= 3.33 PHI= 0.186 XP = 0.0682

186	LEAN MORE TOWARD BEING THOSE WHERE THE KIN GROUP IS OTHER THAN EXCLUSIVELY PATRILINEAL (250)	0.78 OF 113	186	LEAN LESS TOWARD BEING THOSE WHERE THE KIN GROUP IS OTHER THAN EXCLUSIVELY PATRILINEAL (250)	0.54 OF 52	25 24 88 28 XSQ= 8.73 PHI= -0.230 XP = 0.0031
188	TEND TO BE THOSE WHERE THE KIN GROUP IS EXCLUSIVELY COGNATIC (148)	0.51 OF 113	188	TEND TO BE THOSE WHERE THE KIN GROUP IS OTHER THAN EXCLUSIVELY COGNATIC (252)	0.79 OF 52	58 11 55 41 XSQ= 12.11 PHI= 0.271 XP = 0.0005
190	TILT TOWARD BEING THOSE WHERE THE KIN GROUP IS MATRILINEAL, RATHER THAN PATRILINEAL OR DOUBLE-DESCENT (61)	0.50 OF 54	190	TILT TOWARD BEING THOSE WHERE THE KIN GROUP IS PATRILINEAL OR DOUBLE-DESCENT, RATHER THAN MATRILINEAL (186)	0.75 OF 40	27 30 27 10 XSQ= 5.02 PHI= -0.231 XP = 0.0251
192	TEND LESS TO BE THOSE OTHER THAN WHERE THE ONLY KIN GROUP PRESENT IS A KINDRED OR ELSE BILATERAL DESCENT IS INFERRED (289)	0.58 OF 113	192	TEND MORE TO BE THOSE OTHER THAN WHERE THE ONLY KIN GROUP PRESENT IS A KINDRED OR ELSE BILATERAL DESCENT IS INFERRED (289)	0.94 OF 52	47 3 66 49 XSQ= 19.98 PHI= 0.348 XP = 0.0000
196	LEAN LESS TOWARD BEING THOSE WHERE INDIVIDUAL RIGHTS IN REAL PROPERTY, AND RULES FOR INHERITANCE, ARE PRESENT (194)	0.57 OF 81	196	LEAN MORE TOWARD BEING THOSE WHERE INDIVIDUAL RIGHTS IN REAL PROPERTY, AND RULES FOR INHERITANCE, ARE PRESENT (194)	0.89 OF 36	46 32 35 4 XSQ= 10.16 PHI= -0.295 XP = 0.0014
209	LEAN LESS TOWARD BEING THOSE WHERE MARITAL RESIDENCE IS PATRILOCAL, VIRILOCAL, OR AVUNCULOCAL, RATHER THAN MATRILOCAL OR UXORILOCAL (270)	0.68 OF 88	209	LEAN MORE TOWARD BEING THOSE WHERE MARITAL RESIDENCE IS PATRILOCAL, VIRILOCAL, OR AVUNCULOCAL, RATHER THAN MATRILOCAL OR UXORILOCAL (270)	0.93 OF 43	60 40 28 3 XSQ= 8.54 PHI= -0.255 XP = 0.0035
210	LEAN LESS TOWARD BEING THOSE WHERE MARITAL RESIDENCE IS PATRILOCAL, RATHER THAN MATRILOCAL (169)	0.62 OF 42	210	LEAN MORE TOWARD BEING THOSE WHERE MARITAL RESIDENCE IS PATRILOCAL, RATHER THAN MATRILOCAL (169)	0.93 OF 30	26 28 16 2 XSQ= 7.62 PHI= -0.325 XP = 0.0058
221	DRIFT MORE TOWARD BEING THOSE WHERE MATRILATERAL CROSS-COUSIN MARRIAGE IS NOT PRESCRIBED OR PREFERRED (335)	0.95 OF 107	221	DRIFT LESS TOWARD BEING THOSE WHERE MATRILATERAL CROSS-COUSIN MARRIAGE IS NOT PRESCRIBED OR PREFERRED (335)	0.87 OF 52	5 7 102 45 XSQ= 2.72 PHI= -0.131 XP = 0.0993
242	TILT LESS TOWARD BEING THOSE WHERE MARRIAGE IS COMMONLY OR OCCASIONALLY POLYGYNOUS, RATHER THAN MONOGAMOUS (314)	0.72 OF 112	242	TILT MORE TOWARD BEING THOSE WHERE MARRIAGE IS COMMONLY OR OCCASIONALLY POLYGYNOUS, RATHER THAN MONOGAMOUS (314)	0.88 OF 52	81 46 31 6 XSQ= 4.41 PHI= -0.164 XP = 0.0357

243	DRIFT TOWARD BEING THOSE WHERE POLYGYNY, IF PRESENT, HAS A LOW INCIDENCE (36) W-D,S	0.80 OF 15	243	DRIFT TOWARD BEING THOSE WHERE POLYGYNY, IF PRESENT, HAS A HIGH INCIDENCE (24) W-D,S	0.62 OF 13	3 8 12 5 XSQ= 3.45 PHI= -0.351 EP = 0.0510
262	LEAN LESS TOWARD BEING THOSE WHERE WIVES ARE OBTAINED BY MEANS INVOLVING THE PRESENCE OF SOME CONSIDERATION (305)	0.62 OF 112	262	LEAN MORE TOWARD BEING THOSE WHERE WIVES ARE OBTAINED BY MEANS INVOLVING THE PRESENCE OF SOME CONSIDERATION (305)	0.87 OF 52	69 45 43 7 XSQ= 9.27 PHI= -0.238 XP = 0.0023
263	TILT TOWARD BEING THOSE WHERE WIVES ARE OBTAINED BY RELATIVELY EASY MEANS, NAMELY BY TOKEN BRIDE-PRICE, GIFT EXCHANGE, ABSENCE OF ANY CONSIDERATION, OR RECEIPT OF DOWRY (162)	0.57 OF 112	263	TILT TOWARD BEING THOSE WHERE WIVES ARE OBTAINED BY RELATIVELY DIFFICULT MEANS, NAMELY BY BRIDE-PRICE, BRIDE-SERVICE, OR EXCHANGING A FEMALE RELATIVE (233)	0.65 OF 52	48 34 64 18 XSQ= 6.34 PHI= -0.197 XP = 0.0118
299	DRIFT TOWARD BEING THOSE WHERE THE POST-PARTUM SEX TABOO LASTS ONE YEAR OR LESS (89)	0.79 OF 29	299	DRIFT TOWARD BEING THOSE WHERE THE POST-PARTUM SEX TABOO LASTS LONGER THAN ONE YEAR (35)	0.53 OF 17	6 9 23 8 XSQ= 3.71 PHI= -0.284 XP = 0.0540
314	DRIFT MORE TOWARD BEING THOSE WHERE THE INCIDENCE OF MOTHER-CHILD HOUSEHOLDS IS LOW (61) W-D,S	0.83 OF 24	314	DRIFT LESS TOWARD BEING THOSE WHERE THE INCIDENCE OF MOTHER-CHILD HOUSEHOLDS IS LOW (61) W-D,S	0.53 OF 15	4 7 20 8 XSQ= 2.75 PHI= -0.266 EP = 0.0685
330	DRIFT TOWARD BEING THOSE WHERE THE AGE OF THE INFANT AT TIME OF WEANING IS LOWER THAN 2.5 YEARS (36) B-B-C	0.55 OF 20	330	DRIFT TOWARD BEING THOSE WHERE THE AGE OF THE INFANT AT TIME OF WEANING IS 2.5 YEARS OR HIGHER (34) B-B-C	0.77 OF 13	9 10 11 3 XSQ= 2.11 PHI= -0.253 EP = 0.0873
333	DRIFT TOWARD BEING THOSE WHERE THE AGE AT BEGINNING OF TRAINING IN HETEROSEXUAL PLAY INHIBITION IS LOWER THAN EIGHT YEARS (8) W-C	0.86 OF 7	333	IN ALL CASES ARE THOSE WHERE THE AGE AT BEGINNING OF TRAINING IN HETEROSEXUAL PLAY INHIBITION IS EIGHT YEARS OR HIGHER (8) W-C	1.00 OF 2	1 2 6 0 XSQ= 2.01 PHI= -0.472 EP = 0.0833
337	DRIFT TOWARD BEING THOSE WHERE THE CHILD'S INFERRED ANXIETY OVER NON-PERFORMANCE OF RESPONSIBLE BEHAVIOR IS LOW (35) B-B-C	0.62 OF 21	337	DRIFT TOWARD BEING THOSE WHERE THE CHILD'S INFERRED ANXIETY OVER NON-PERFORMANCE OF RESPONSIBLE BEHAVIOR IS HIGH (38) B-B-C	0.75 OF 12	8 9 13 3 XSQ= 2.82 PHI= -0.292 EP = 0.0707
370	TEND TO BE THOSE WHERE THE SEGREGATION OF ADOLESCENT BOYS IS ABSENT (148)	0.83 OF 69	370	TEND TO BE THOSE WHERE THE SEGREGATION OF ADOLESCENT BOYS IS COMPLETE OR PARTIAL (95)	0.67 OF 39	12 26 57 13 XSQ= 24.41 PHI= -0.475 XP = 0.0000

No.	Left	Proportion	No.	Right	Proportion	Statistics
372	TILT TOWARD BEING THOSE WHERE MALE INITIATION RITES ARE ABSENT (63) ASA	0.73 OF 37	372	TILT TOWARD BEING THOSE WHERE MALE INITIATION RITES ARE PRESENT (48) ASA	0.58 OF 31	10 18 27 13 XSQ= 5.49 PHI= -0.284 XP = 0.0191
377	LEAN MORE TOWARD BEING THOSE WHERE MALE GENITAL MUTILATION IS ABSENT (242)	0.92 OF 95	377	LEAN LESS TOWARD BEING THOSE WHERE MALE GENITAL MUTILATION IS ABSENT (242)	0.72 OF 46	8 13 87 33 XSQ= 8.12 PHI= -0.240 XP = 0.0044
380	TILT TOWARD BEING THOSE WHERE SEGREGATION OF GIRLS AT MENARCHE IS PRESENT (35) F-B	0.88 OF 16	380	TILT TOWARD BEING THOSE WHERE SEGREGATION OF GIRLS AT MENARCHE IS ABSENT (20) F-B	0.50 OF 12	14 6 2 6 XSQ= 3.07 PHI= 0.331 EP = 0.0441
417	IN ALL CASES ARE THOSE WHERE WARFARE IS PREVALENT (34) LWS	1.00 OF 9	417	DRIFT LESS TOWARD BEING THOSE WHERE WARFARE IS PREVALENT (34) LWS	0.63 OF 8	9 5 0 3 XSQ= 1.92 PHI= 0.336 EP = 0.0824
428	LEAN TOWARD BEING THOSE WHERE A HIGH GOD, IF PRESENT AND ACTIVE, SUPPORTS HUMAN MORALITY, RATHER THAN NOT SUPPORTING IT (61) GES,EA	0.83 OF 23	428	LEAN TOWARD BEING THOSE WHERE A HIGH GOD, IF PRESENT AND ACTIVE, DOES NOT SUPPORT HUMAN MORALITY, RATHER THAN SUPPORTING IT (26) GES,EA	0.75 OF 8	19 2 4 6 XSQ= 6.57 PHI= 0.460 EP = 0.0059
434	TILT TOWARD BEING THOSE WHERE ASCETICISM IN MOURNING BEHAVIOR IS LOW (30) JFG	0.64 OF 22	434	TILT TOWARD BEING THOSE WHERE ASCETICISM IN MOURNING BEHAVIOR IS HIGH (37) JFG	0.83 OF 12	8 10 14 2 XSQ= 5.12 PHI= -0.388 EP = 0.0129
459	TEND TO BE THOSE WHERE GAMES, IF PRESENT, INCLUDE GAMES OF CHANCE (82) R-A-B,EA	0.77 OF 62	459	TEND TO BE THOSE WHERE GAMES, IF PRESENT, DO NOT INCLUDE GAMES OF CHANCE (89) R-A-B,EA	0.88 OF 26	48 3 14 23 XSQ= 29.98 PHI= 0.584 XP = 0.0000
460	TEND TO BE THOSE WHERE GAMES, IF PRESENT, ARE NOT LIMITED TO GAMES OF SKILL ONLY (104) R-A-B,EA	0.81 OF 62	460	TEND TO BE THOSE WHERE GAMES, IF PRESENT, ARE LIMITED TO GAMES OF SKILL ONLY (67) R-A-B,EA	0.58 OF 26	12 15 50 11 XSQ= 10.92 PHI= -0.352 XP = 0.0010
476	DRIFT TOWARD BEING THOSE WHERE THE DEGREE OF INSOBRIETY IS STRONG (31) DH	0.62 OF 13	476	DRIFT TOWARD BEING THOSE WHERE THE DEGREE OF INSOBRIETY IS MODERATE OR SLIGHT (18) DH	0.86 OF 7	8 1 5 6 XSQ= 2.42 PHI= 0.348 EP = 0.0703

483/

488 DRIFT LESS TOWARD BEING THOSE 0.66 OF 89 ABOUT WHICH THE PRINCIPAL ETHNOGRAPHIES WERE PUBLISHED BEFORE 1950 (185)

488 DRIFT MORE TOWARD BEING THOSE 0.87 OF 30 ABOUT WHICH THE PRINCIPAL ETHNOGRAPHIES WERE PUBLISHED BEFORE 1950 (185)

	59	26
	30	4
XSQ=	3.62	
PHI=	-0.174	
XP =	0.0571	

484 CULTURES WHERE THE PRINCIPAL ETHNOGRAPHERS HAVE BEEN GERMAN (18)

484 CULTURES WHERE THE PRINCIPAL ETHNOGRAPHERS HAVE BEEN OTHER THAN GERMAN (370)

BACKGROUND ON PAGE 177

SUBJECT ONLY

18 IN LEFT COLUMN

ABIPON	AKHA	BERGDAMA	CARINYA	CHENCHU	GUAHIBO	GUATO	HERERO	ONA	PALIKUR
PARAUJANO	SHERENTE	TIMBIRA	TUCUNA	WANTOAT	WUTE	YABARANA	YAHGAN		

370 IN RIGHT COLUMN

12 EXCLUDED BECAUSE UNASCERTAINED

	German (18)			Other than German (370)		Statistics
8	IN ALL CASES ARE THOSE LOCATED OUTSIDE OF NORTH AMERICA (330)	1.00 OF 18	8	DRIFT LESS TOWARD BEING THOSE LOCATED OUTSIDE OF NORTH AMERICA (330)	0.81 OF 370	0 70 18 300 XSQ= 2.97 PHI= -0.088 XP = 0.0846
9	TEND TO BE THOSE LOCATED IN SOUTH AMERICA (65)	0.67 OF 18	9	TEND TO BE THOSE LOCATED OUTSIDE OF SOUTH AMERICA (335)	0.86 OF 370	12 53 6 317 XSQ= 30.07 PHI= 0.278 XP = 0.0000
46	DRIFT LESS TOWARD BEING THOSE OTHER THAN WHERE SETTLEMENTS ARE NON-FIXED AND MOVEMENT IS NOMADIC (260)	0.57 OF 14	46	DRIFT MORE TOWARD BEING THOSE OTHER THAN WHERE SETTLEMENTS ARE NON-FIXED AND MOVEMENT IS NOMADIC (260)	0.80 OF 310	6 62 8 248 XSQ= 2.95 PHI= 0.095 XP = 0.0856
51	LEAN TOWARD BEING THOSE WHERE SUBSISTENCE IS PRIMARILY BY FOOD GATHERING -- I. E., HUNTING, FISHING, OR COLLECTING -- RATHER THAN FOOD PRODUCTION (147)	0.72 OF 18	51	LEAN TOWARD BEING THOSE WHERE SUBSISTENCE IS PRIMARILY BY FOOD PRODUCTION -- I. E., AGRICULTURE OR HUSBANDRY -- RATHER THAN BY GATHERING (253)	0.64 OF 370	5 238 13 132 XSQ= 8.30 PHI= -0.146 XP = 0.0040
54	TILT TOWARD BEING THOSE WHERE FOOD PRODUCTION IS BY INCIPIENT FOOD PRODUCTION, RATHER THAN BY INTENSIVE OR SIMPLE AGRICULTURE (46)	0.67 OF 6	54	TILT TOWARD BEING THOSE WHERE FOOD PRODUCTION IS BY INTENSIVE OR SIMPLE AGRICULTURE, RATHER THAN BY INCIPIENT FOOD PRODUCTION (192)	0.82 OF 227	2 186 4 41 XSQ= 6.02 PHI= -0.161 XP = 0.0142

62	DRIFT TOWARD BEING THOSE WHERE HUSBANDRY OF ANY KIND IS ABSENT (172)	0.67 OF 18	62	DRIFT TOWARD BEING THOSE WHERE HUSBANDRY OF SOME KIND IS PRESENT (228)	0.58 OF 370	6 215 12 155 XSQ= 3.35 PHI= -0.093 XP = 0.0674
71	IN ALL CASES ARE THOSE WHERE METAL WORKING IS ABSENT (153)	1.00 OF 10	71	TILT LESS TOWARD BEING THOSE WHERE METAL WORKING IS ABSENT (153)	0.60 OF 238	0 95 10 143 XSQ= 4.89 PHI= -0.140 XP = 0.0270
81	IN ALL CASES ARE THOSE WHERE NO CITY OR TOWN IS PRESENT, AND THE AVERAGE COMMUNITY SIZE IS SMALLER THAN 200 (135)	1.00 OF 8	81	TILT LESS TOWARD BEING THOSE WHERE NO CITY OR TOWN IS PRESENT, AND THE AVERAGE COMMUNITY SIZE IS SMALLER THAN 200 (135)	0.59 OF 213	0 88 8 125 XSQ= 3.90 PHI= -0.133 XP = 0.0482
82	DRIFT TOWARD BEING THOSE WHERE NO CITY OR TOWN IS PRESENT, AND THE AVERAGE COMMUNITY SIZE IS SMALLER THAN FIFTY (46)	0.50 OF 8	82	DRIFT TOWARD BEING THOSE WHERE A CITY OR TOWN IS PRESENT, OR THE AVERAGE COMMUNITY SIZE IS FIFTY OR GREATER (178)	0.81 OF 213	4 172 4 41 XSQ= 2.80 PHI= -0.113 XP = 0.0943
85	IN ALL CASES ARE THOSE WHERE THE LEVEL OF POLITICAL INTEGRATION IS THE MINIMAL STATE, THE AUTONOMOUS COMMUNITY, OR THE FAMILY (234) GPM	1.00 OF 14	85	DRIFT LESS TOWARD BEING THOSE WHERE THE LEVEL OF POLITICAL INTEGRATION IS THE MINIMAL STATE, THE AUTONOMOUS COMMUNITY, OR THE FAMILY (234) GPM	0.76 OF 282	0 69 14 213 XSQ= 3.20 PHI= -0.104 XP = 0.0735
86	TILT TOWARD BEING THOSE WHERE THE LEVEL OF POLITICAL INTEGRATION IS THE AUTONOMOUS COMMUNITY, OR THE FAMILY (156) GPM	0.86 OF 14	86	TILT TOWARD BEING THOSE WHERE THE LEVEL OF POLITICAL INTEGRATION IS THE LARGE STATE, THE LITTLE STATE, OR THE MINIMAL STATE (148) GPM	0.50 OF 282	2 141 12 141 XSQ= 5.46 PHI= -0.136 XP = 0.0195
95	IN ALL CASES ARE THOSE WHERE THE HIERARCHY OF NATIONAL JURISDICTION HAS ONE OR NO LEVELS (254) GES,EA	1.00 OF 14	95	DRIFT LESS TOWARD BEING THOSE WHERE THE HIERARCHY OF NATIONAL JURISDICTION HAS ONE OR NO LEVELS (254) GES,EA	0.76 OF 308	0 75 14 233 XSQ= 3.19 PHI= -0.099 XP = 0.0743
96	LEAN TOWARD BEING THOSE WHERE THE HIERARCHY OF NATIONAL JURISDICTION HAS NO LEVELS (156) GES,EA	0.93 OF 14	96	LEAN TOWARD BEING THOSE WHERE THE HIERARCHY OF NATIONAL JURISDICTION HAS FOUR, THREE, TWO OR ONE LEVEL (174) GES,EA	0.55 OF 308	1 168 13 140 XSQ= 10.24 PHI= -0.178 XP = 0.0014
98	LEAN TOWARD BEING THOSE WHERE THE HIERARCHY OF LOCAL JURISDICTION HAS TWO LEVELS (93) GES,EA	0.64 OF 14	98	LEAN TOWARD BEING THOSE WHERE THE HIERARCHY OF LOCAL JURISDICTION HAS FOUR OR THREE LEVELS (238) GES,EA	0.74 OF 309	5 229 9 80 XSQ= 8.06 PHI= -0.158 XP = 0.0045

100	TEND TO BE THOSE 0.57 OF 14 WHERE HIERARCHIES ARE THE 'SIMPLEST' I. E., WHERE THERE ARE ONLY TWO LOCAL LEVELS WITH NO NATIONAL LEVELS (63) GES,EA	100	TEND TO BE THOSE 0.83 OF 308 WHERE HIERARCHIES ARE MORE COMPLEX THAN THE 'SIMPLEST,' I. E., MORE COMPLEX THAN TWO LOCAL LEVELS WITH NO NATIONAL LEVELS (267) GES,EA	6 256 8 52 XSQ= 11.78 PHI= -0.191 XP = 0.0006
102	LEAN TOWARD BEING THOSE 0.82 OF 17 WHERE CLASS STRATIFICATION IS ABSENT (180)	102	LEAN TOWARD BEING THOSE 0.55 OF 354 WHERE CLASS STRATIFICATION IS PRESENT (203)	3 196 14 158 XSQ= 7.83 PHI= -0.145 XP = 0.0051
179	LEAN LESS TOWARD BEING THOSE 0.63 OF 16 WHERE THE COMMUNITY IS OTHER THAN STRUCTURED ON A NON-CLAN BASIS AND COMMONLY EXOGAMOUS (340)	179	LEAN MORE TOWARD BEING THOSE 0.90 OF 354 WHERE THE COMMUNITY IS OTHER THAN STRUCTURED ON A NON-CLAN BASIS AND COMMONLY EXOGAMOUS (340)	6 34 10 320 XSQ= 9.63 PHI= 0.161 XP = 0.0019
184	DRIFT TOWARD BEING THOSE 0.60 OF 10 WHERE THE LARGEST NON-COGNATIC KIN GROUP IS THE MOEITY OR PHRATRY (77)	184	DRIFT TOWARD BEING THOSE 0.71 OF 232 WHERE THE LARGEST NON-COGNATIC KIN GROUP IS SMALLER THAN A PHRATRY, I. E. A SIB OR LINEAGE (175)	6 68 4 164 XSQ= 2.93 PHI= 0.110 XP = 0.0869
196	TILT TOWARD BEING THOSE 0.67 OF 12 WHERE INDIVIDUAL RIGHTS IN REAL PROPERTY, OR RULES FOR INHERITANCE, ARE ABSENT (87)	196	TILT TOWARD BEING THOSE 0.70 OF 261 WHERE INDIVIDUAL RIGHTS IN REAL PROPERTY, AND RULES FOR INHERITANCE, ARE PRESENT (194)	4 182 8 79 XSQ= 5.42 PHI= -0.141 XP = 0.0199
236	TILT TOWARD BEING THOSE 0.78 OF 18 WHERE THE FAMILY IS OF AN INDEPENDENT TYPE, RATHER THAN AN EXTENDED TYPE (185)	236	TILT TOWARD BEING THOSE 0.56 OF 368 WHERE THE FAMILY IS OF AN EXTENDED TYPE, RATHER THAN AN INDEPENDENT TYPE (213)	4 206 14 162 XSQ= 6.58 PHI= -0.131 XP = 0.0103
349	IN ALL CASES ARE THOSE 1.00 OF 4 WHERE THE CHILD'S INFERRED ANXIETY OVER NON-PERFORMANCE OF ACHIEVEMENT BEHAVIOR IS LOW (28) B-B-C	349	DRIFT TOWARD BEING THOSE 0.60 OF 57 WHERE THE CHILD'S INFERRED ANXIETY OVER NON-PERFORMANCE OF ACHIEVEMENT BEHAVIOR IS HIGH (34) B-B-C	0 34 4 23 XSQ= 3.24 PHI= -0.231 XP = 0.0717
350	IN ALL CASES ARE THOSE 1.00 OF 4 WHERE THE CHILD'S INFERRED ANXIETY OVER PERFORMANCE OF ACHIEVEMENT BEHAVIOR IS LOW (26) B-B-C	350	DRIFT TOWARD BEING THOSE 0.62 OF 55 WHERE THE CHILD'S INFERRED ANXIETY OVER PERFORMANCE OF ACHIEVEMENT BEHAVIOR IS HIGH (34) B-B-C	0 34 4 21 XSQ= 3.58 PHI= -0.246 XP = 0.0585
459	IN ALL CASES ARE THOSE 1.00 OF 7 WHERE GAMES, IF PRESENT, DO NOT INCLUDE GAMES OF CHANCE (89) R-A-B,EA	459	TILT TOWARD BEING THOSE 0.50 OF 162 WHERE GAMES, IF PRESENT, INCLUDE GAMES OF CHANCE (82) R-A-B,EA	0 81 7 81 XSQ= 4.87 PHI= -0.170 XP = 0.0274

484/

```
460  IN ALL CASES ARE THOSE          1.00 OF   7      460  LEAN TOWARD BEING THOSE         0.64 OF 162           7   59
     WHERE GAMES, IF PRESENT,                              WHERE GAMES, IF PRESENT,                                0  103
     ARE LIMITED TO                                        ARE NOT LIMITED TO                               XSQ=    8.88
     GAMES OF SKILL CNLY  (67) R-A-B,EA                    GAMES OF SKILL ONLY  (104) R-A-B,EA              PHI=   0.229
                                                                                                            XP =  0.0029
```

485 CULTURES WHERE THE PRINCIPAL ETHNOGRAPHERS HAVE BEEN FRENCH (12)

485 CULTURES WHERE THE PRINCIPAL ETHNOGRAPHERS HAVE BEEN OTHER THAN FRENCH (376)

BACKGROUND ON PAGE 177

SUBJECT ONLY

12 IN LEFT COLUMN

AJIE BAMBARA BANDA BASQUES BOZO DOGON FUTAJALONKE KABYLE KISSI MNONG GAR
MZAB NYANEKA

376 IN RIGHT COLUMN

12 EXCLUDED BECAUSE UNASCERTAINED

	Left column			Right column		
3	LEAN TOWARD BEING THOSE LOCATED IN AFRICA (80)	0.58 OF 12	3	LEAN TOWARD BEING THOSE LOCATED OUTSIDE OF AFRICA (320)	0.82 OF 376	7 69 5 307 XSQ= 9.40 PHI= 0.156 XP = 0.0022
51	DRIFT MORE TOWARD BEING THOSE WHERE SUBSISTENCE IS PRIMARILY BY FOOD PRODUCTION -- I. E., AGRICULTURE OR HUSBANDRY -- RATHER THAN BY GATHERING (253)	0.92 OF 12	51	DRIFT LESS TOWARD BEING THOSE WHERE SUBSISTENCE IS PRIMARILY BY FOOD PRODUCTION -- I. E., AGRICULTURE OR HUSBANDRY -- RATHER THAN BY GATHERING (253)	0.62 OF 376	11 232 1 144 XSQ= 3.27 PHI= 0.092 XP = 0.0704
97	TEND TO BE THOSE WHERE THE HIERARCHY OF LOCAL JURISDICTION HAS FOUR LEVELS (58) GES,EA	0.67 OF 9	97	TEND TO BE THOSE WHERE THE HIERARCHY OF LOCAL JURISDICTION HAS THREE OR TWO LEVELS (273) GES,EA	0.83 OF 314	6 52 3 262 XSQ= 11.70 PHI= 0.190 XP = 0.0006
109	LEAN LESS TOWARD BEING THOSE WHERE CASTES ARE ABSENT (317)	0.55 OF 11	109	LEAN MORE TOWARD BEING THOSE WHERE CASTES ARE ABSENT (317)	0.87 OF 348	5 44 6 304 XSQ= 7.15 PHI= 0.141 XP = 0.0075
110	TILT TOWARD BEING THOSE WHERE SLAVERY IS PRESENT (163)	0.83 OF 12	110	TILT TOWARD BEING THOSE WHERE SLAVERY IS ABSENT (218)	0.58 OF 358	10 150 2 208 XSQ= 6.52 PHI= 0.133 XP = 0.0107

176	LEAN TOWARD BEING THOSE WHERE THE COMMUNITY IS A CLAN-COMMUNITY OR A COMMUNITY STRUCTURED OR SEGMENTED ON A CLAN BASIS (169)	0.91 OF 11	176	LEAN TOWARD BEING THOSE WHERE THE COMMUNITY IS OTHER THAN A CLAN-COMMUNITY OR A COMMUNITY STRUCTURED OR SEGMENTED ON A CLAN BASIS (213)	0.57 OF 359	10 155 1 204 XSQ= 8.01 PHI= 0.147 XP = 0.0047
186	TILT TOWARD BEING THOSE WHERE THE KIN GROUP IS EXCLUSIVELY PATRILINEAL (150)	0.75 OF 12	186	TILT TOWARD BEING THOSE WHERE THE KIN GROUP IS OTHER THAN EXCLUSIVELY PATRILINEAL (250)	0.64 OF 376	9 134 3 242 XSQ= 6.14 PHI= 0.126 XP = 0.0132
188	DRIFT MORE TOWARD BEING THOSE WHERE THE KIN GROUP IS OTHER THAN EXCLUSIVELY COGNATIC (252)	0.92 OF 12	188	DRIFT LESS TOWARD BEING THOSE WHERE THE KIN GROUP IS OTHER THAN EXCLUSIVELY COGNATIC (252)	0.61 OF 376	1 145 11 231 XSQ= 3.33 PHI= -0.093 XP = 0.0680
196	IN ALL CASES ARE THOSE WHERE INDIVIDUAL RIGHTS IN REAL PROPERTY, AND RULES FOR INHERITANCE, ARE PRESENT (194)	1.00 OF 9	196	DRIFT LESS TOWARD BEING THOSE WHERE INDIVIDUAL RIGHTS IN REAL PROPERTY, AND RULES FOR INHERITANCE, ARE PRESENT (194)	0.67 OF 264	9 177 0 87 XSQ= 2.97 PHI= 0.104 XP = 0.0849
213	DRIFT TOWARD BEING THOSE WHERE FIRST COUSIN MARRIAGE IS PERMITTED (172)	0.80 OF 10	213	DRIFT TOWARD BEING THOSE WHERE FIRST COUSIN MARRIAGE IS NOT PERMITTED (198)	0.54 OF 349	8 159 2 190 XSQ= 3.35 PHI= 0.097 XP = 0.0670
221	DRIFT LESS TOWARD BEING THOSE WHERE MATRILATERAL CROSS-COUSIN MARRIAGE IS NOT PRESCRIBED OR PREFERRED (335)	0.70 OF 10	221	DRIFT MORE TOWARD BEING THOSE WHERE MATRILATERAL CROSS-COUSIN MARRIAGE IS NOT PRESCRIBED OR PREFERRED (335)	0.91 OF 349	3 32 7 317 XSQ= 2.72 PHI= 0.087 XP = 0.0992
377	TEND TO BE THOSE WHERE MALE GENITAL MUTILATION IS PRESENT (83)	0.89 OF 9	377	TEND TO BE THOSE WHERE MALE GENITAL MUTILATION IS ABSENT (242)	0.77 OF 308	8 71 1 237 XSQ= 16.89 PHI= 0.231 XP = 0.0000

486 CULTURES
ABOUT WHICH THE PRINCIPAL ETHNOGRAPHIES
WERE PUBLISHED BEFCRE 1930, RATHER THAN
IN 1950 OR AFTER (32)

486 CULTURES
ABOUT WHICH THE PRINCIPAL ETHNOGRAPHIES
WERE PUBLISHED IN 1950 OR AFTER,
RATHER THAN BEFORE 1930 (72)

BACKGROUND ON PAGE 178

SUBJECT ONLY

32 IN LEFT CCLUMN

ABIPCN	ARANDA	BABWA	CHERKESS	CHUKCHEE	DARD	GARO	GISU	HAVASUPAI	HERERO
KAREN	KORYAK	LHOTA NAGA	LIFU	MANCHU	MERINA	MIN CHINESE	MOTA	MZAB	NICOBARESE
OMAHA	PALIKUR	ROTINESE	SELUNG	TALAMANCA	THONGA	TORAJA	ULAWANS	VEDCA	WAPISHANA
WUTE	YUKAGHIR								

72 IN RIGHT CCLUMN

AMBA	AMERICANS	ARYANS	BAJUN	BASSERI	BELU	BLACK CARIB	BRAZILIANS	BURYAT	CAMAYURA
CAMBA	CARINYA	CHINANTEC	CREE	CZECHS	DAGUR	EGYPTIANS	ENGA	GILBERTESE	GUAHIBO
HANO	HANUNCO	IRAQW	JAVANESE	KAPAUKU	KERALA	KHALKA	KOHISTANI	KOREANS	KUMYK
LAKALAI	LAMET	LOLC	MACASSARESE	MIAO	MNONG GAR	MONGUOR	MURINBATA	NABESNA	NGONI
NOMLAKI	NYARO	OJIBWA	OKINAWANS	ORAON	PALAUANS	PATHAN	PORTUGUESE	RARCIANS	REGEIBAT
SAGADA	SERBS	SIRICNC	SIUAI	SUBANUN	SYRIANS	TAGBANUA	TAMIL	TAREUMIUT	TEDA
TESO	TRUKESE	TRUMAI	TUCUNA	WAICA	WALLOONS	WANTOAT	WOLEAIANS	WOLOF	YABARANA
YARURO	YORUBA								

284 EXCLUDED BECAUSE IRRELEVANT

ABOR	AINU	AJIE	AKHA	ALACALUF	ALBANIANS	ALORESE	ANDAMANESE	APINAYE	ARAPESH
ARAUCANIANS	ASHANTI	ATSUGEWI	AWEIKOMA	AYMARA	AZANDE	AZTEC	BACAIRI	BALINESE	BAMBARA
BAMILEKE	BANDA	BARABRA	BARI	BASQUES	BATAK	BAYA	BEJA	BEMBA	BENGALI
BERGDAMA	BETE	BHIL	BHUIYA	BIRIFOR	BOERS	BORORO	BOTOCUDO	BOZO	BUDUMA
BULGARIANS	BUNLAP	BURMESE	BURUSHO	CADUVEO	CAGABA	CALLINAGO	CAMBODIANS	CARAJA	CARIB
CAYAPA	CHAGGA	CHAMACCCO	CHENCHU	CHEREMIS	CHEROKEE	CHEYENNE	CHIR-APACHE	CHIRIGUANO	CHOCO
CHOROTI	CHCRTI	COCHITI	COMANCHE	COORG	COPR ESKIMO	CREEK	CROW	CUNA	DELAWARE
DIEGUENO	DIERI	DILLING	DOBUANS	DOGON	DOROBO	DUTCH	ELLICE	EYAK	FANG
FON	FOX	FUTAJALONKE	GANDA	GILYAK	GOAJIRO	GOND	GROS VENTRE	GUATO	GURE
HAIDA	HASANIA	HASINAI	HAZARA	HEBREWS	HEHE	HO	HUICHOL	HUKUNDIKA	HURON
HUTSUL	IBAN	ICELANDERS	IFUGAO	INCA	INGALIK	INGASSANA	IRISH	JAPANESE	JEMEZ
JIVARO	JUKUN	KABYLE	KACHIN	KARIERA	KASKA	KATAB	KAZAK	KERAKI	KET
KHASI	KHEVSUR	KIKUYU	KIOW-APACHE	KISSI	KOL	KPE	KUBA	KUNG	KURTATCHI
KUTENAI	KWAKIUTL	LAKHER	LAMBA	LANGO	LAPPS	LAU	LEPCHA	LESU	LOZI
LUBA	LUC	MAGUZAWA	MALAYS	MAM	MAMBILA	MAMVU	MANDAN	MANGAIANS	MANIHIKI
MANUS	MACRI	MARGI	MARICOPA	MARQUESANS	MARSHALLESE	MASAI	MATACO	MATAKAM	MAYA
MAZATECO	MBUNDU	MBUTI	MENDE	MENTAWEI	MIAMI	MINANGKABAU	MINCHIA	MISKITO	MIWOK
MONGO	MOSSI	MOTILON	MUNDURUCU	MURNGIN	NAMA	NAMBICUARA	NANDI	NASKAPI	NATCHEZ
NAVAHO	NDEMBU	NUER	NUNIVAK	NUPE	NURI	NYAKYUSA	NYANEKA	NYORO	ONA
ONTONG-JAVA	PAEZ	PAPAGO	PARAUJANO	PAWNEE	PENDE	PENOBSCOT	PONAPEANS	POPCLUCA	PUKAPUKA
PURARI	PURUM	RIFFIANS	ROMANS	ROTUMANS	RUNDI	RWALA	SAMOANS	SAMOYED	SANPOIL

SANTAL	SARAMACCA	SARSI	SEMANG	SEMINOLE	SENIANG	SERI	SHERENTE	SHILLUK	SHLUH
SIMBOESE	SINHALESE	SIWANS	SOMALI	SONGHAI	SOTHO	SWAZI	TALLENSI	TANALA	TANIMBARESE
TAOS	TAPIRAPE	TARAHUMARA	TEHUELCHE	TENDA	TENETEHARA	TENINO	TERENA	TETON	THAI
TIBETANS	TIGRINYA	TIKOPIA	TIMBIRA	TIMUCUA	TIV	TIWI	TODA	TOKELAU	TOLOWA
TOTONAC	TRISTAN	TROBRIAND	TSHIMSHIAN	TUBATULABAL	TUCANO	TUNEBO	TUPINAMBA	TURKANA	TURKMEN
TWANA	TZELTAL	UTE	VENDA	VIETNAMESE	WAROPEN	WARRAU	WASHO	WICHITA	WIKMUNKAN
WINNEBAGO	WITOTO	WOGEO	YAGUA	YAHGAN	YAKO	YAKUT	YAO	YAPESE	YOKUTS
YOMBE	YUKI	YUROK	ZUNI						

12 EXCLUDED BECAUSE UNASCERTAINED

84	TILT MORE TOWARD BEING THOSE 0.96 OF 28 WHERE THE LEVEL OF POLITICAL INTEGRATION IS THE LITTLE STATE, THE MINIMAL STATE, THE AUTONOMOUS COMMUNITY, OR THE FAMILY (262) GPM	84	TILT LESS TOWARD BEING THOSE 0.74 OF 39 WHERE THE LEVEL OF POLITICAL INTEGRATION IS THE LITTLE STATE, THE MINIMAL STATE, THE AUTONOMOUS COMMUNITY, OR THE FAMILY (262) GPM	1 10 27 29 XSQ= 4.29 PHI= -0.253 XP = 0.0384
85	DRIFT MORE TOWARD BEING THOSE 0.89 OF 28 WHERE THE LEVEL OF POLITICAL INTEGRATION IS THE MINIMAL STATE, THE AUTONOMOUS COMMUNITY, OR THE FAMILY (234) GPM	85	DRIFT LESS TOWARD BEING THOSE 0.67 OF 39 WHERE THE LEVEL OF POLITICAL INTEGRATION IS THE MINIMAL STATE, THE AUTONOMOUS COMMUNITY, OR THE FAMILY (234) GPM	3 13 25 26 XSQ= 3.43 PHI= -0.226 XP = 0.0641
107	TILT MORE TOWARD BEING THOSE 0.95 OF 20 WHERE CLASS STRATIFICATION, IF PRESENT, IS BASED ON SOMETHING OTHER THAN OCCUPATIONAL STATUS (160)	107	TILT LESS TOWARD BEING THOSE 0.62 OF 39 WHERE CLASS STRATIFICATION, IF PRESENT, IS BASED ON SOMETHING OTHER THAN OCCUPATIONAL STATUS (160)	1 15 19 24 XSQ= 5.89 PHI= -0.316 XP = 0.0152
109	DRIFT MORE TOWARD BEING THOSE 0.94 OF 31 WHERE CASTES ARE ABSENT (317)	109	DRIFT LESS TOWARD BEING THOSE 0.75 OF 64 WHERE CASTES ARE ABSENT (317)	2 16 29 48 XSQ= 3.55 PHI= -0.193 XP = 0.0596
110	LEAN TOWARD BEING THOSE 0.65 OF 31 WHERE SLAVERY IS PRESENT (163)	110	LEAN TOWARD BEING THOSE 0.66 OF 67 WHERE SLAVERY IS ABSENT (218)	20 23 11 44 XSQ= 6.67 PHI= 0.261 XP = 0.0098
130	IN ALL CASES ARE THOSE 1.00 OF 4 WHERE LEATHER WORKING IS MAINLY DONE BY FEMALES (45)	130	DRIFT TOWARD BEING THOSE 0.60 OF 10 WHERE LEATHER WORKING IS MAINLY DONE BY MALES (39)	0 6 4 4 XSQ= 2.11 PHI= -0.388 EP = 0.0849
183	DRIFT LESS TOWARD BEING THOSE 0.77 OF 22 WHERE THE LARGEST NON-COGNATIC KIN GROUP IS SMALLER THAN A MOEITY, I. E., A PHRATRY OR SIB OR LINEAGE (218)	183	DRIFT MORE TOWARD BEING THOSE 0.96 OF 46 WHERE THE LARGEST NON-COGNATIC KIN GROUP IS SMALLER THAN A MOEITY, I. E., A PHRATRY OR SIB OR LINEAGE (218)	5 2 17 44 XSQ= 3.64 PHI= 0.231 XP = 0.0566

260	DRIFT TOWARD BEING THOSE WHERE THE AGE OF MALES AT MARRIAGE IS TWENTY OR OVER (17) JKH	0.67 OF 3	260	IN ALL CASES ARE THOSE WHERE THE AGE OF MALES AT MARRIAGE IS LESS THAN TWENTY (38) JKH	1.00 OF 6	1 6 2 0 XSQ= 2.01 PHI= -0.472 EP = 0.0833
348	DRIFT TOWARD BEING THOSE WHERE THE TOTAL POSITIVE PRESSURE TOWARD DEVELOPING ACHIEVEMENT BEHAVIOR IN THE CHILD IS HIGH (32) B-B-C	0.80 OF 5	348	DRIFT TOWARD BEING THOSE WHERE THE TOTAL POSITIVE PRESSURE TOWARD DEVELOPING ACHIEVEMENT BEHAVIOR IN THE CHILD IS LOW (31) B-B-C	0.86 OF 7	4 1 1 6 XSQ= 2.83 PHI= 0.486 EP = 0.0720
400	IN ALL CASES ARE THOSE WHERE HOMOSEXUAL ACTIVITY IS PERMITTED (36) F-B	1.00 OF 5	400	DRIFT TOWARD BEING THOSE WHERE HOMOSEXUAL ACTIVITY IS PROHIBITED (22) F-B	0.57 OF 7	0 4 5 3 XSQ= 2.10 PHI= -0.418 EP = 0.0808
420	DRIFT TOWARD BEING THOSE WHERE BELLICOSITY IS EXTREME (41) PES	0.50 OF 4	420	IN ALL CASES ARE THOSE WHERE BELLICOSITY IS MODERATE OR NEGLIGIBLE (46) PES	1.00 OF 9	2 0 2 9 XSQ= 2.17 PHI= 0.409 EP = 0.0769
421	DRIFT TOWARD BEING THOSE WHERE KILLING, TORTURING, OR MUTILATING OF THE ENEMY IS STRONGLY OR MODERATELY EMPHASIZED (37) PES	0.75 OF 4	421	DRIFT TOWARD BEING THOSE WHERE KILLING, TORTURING, OR MUTILATING OF THE ENEMY IS NEGLIGIBLY EMPHASIZED (47) PES	0.89 OF 9	3 1 1 8 XSQ= 2.73 PHI= 0.458 EP = 0.0517
428	LEAN TOWARD BEING THOSE WHERE A HIGH GOD, IF PRESENT AND ACTIVE, DOES NOT SUPPORT HUMAN MORALITY, RATHER THAN SUPPORTING IT (26) GES,EA	0.60 OF 5	428	IN ALL CASES ARE THOSE WHERE A HIGH GOD, IF PRESENT AND ACTIVE, SUPPORTS HUMAN MORALITY, RATHER THAN NOT SUPPORTING IT (61) GES,EA	1.00 OF 17	2 17 3 0 XSQ= 7.27 PHI= -0.575 EP = 0.0065
442	IN ALL CASES ARE THOSE WHERE FEAR OF ANIMAL SPIRITS IS LOW (33) W-C	1.00 OF 5	442	IN ALL CASES ARE THOSE WHERE FEAR OF ANIMAL SPIRITS IS HIGH (28) W-C	1.00 OF 2	0 2 5 0 XSQ= 2.96 PHI= -0.650 EP = 0.0476
481	TILT MORE TOWARD BEING THOSE WHERE THE PRINCIPAL ETHNOGRAPHERS HAVE BEEN OTHER THAN AMERICAN (275)	0.83 OF 30	481	TILT LESS TOWARD BEING THOSE WHERE THE PRINCIPAL ETHNOGRAPHERS HAVE BEEN OTHER THAN AMERICAN (275)	0.58 OF 72	5 30 25 42 XSQ= 4.82 PHI= -0.217 XP = 0.0282
482	TILT LESS TOWARD BEING THOSE WHERE THE PRINCIPAL ETHNOGRAPHERS HAVE BEEN OTHER THAN BRITISH (336)	0.77 OF 30	482	TILT MORE TOWARD BEING THOSE WHERE THE PRINCIPAL ETHNOGRAPHERS HAVE BEEN OTHER THAN BRITISH (336)	0.94 OF 72	7 4 23 68 XSQ= 5.23 PHI= 0.226 XP = 0.0222

```
483  LEAN TOWARD BEING THOSE          0.58 OF  12      483  LEAN TOWARD BEING THOSE          0.88 OF  34           5    30
     WHERE THE PRINCIPAL ETHNOGRAPHERS                        WHERE THE PRINCIPAL ETHNOGRAPHERS                           7     4
     HAVE BEEN BRITISH,                                       HAVE BEEN AMERICAN,                                  XSQ=     8.17
     RATHER THAN AMERICAN  (52)                               RATHER THAN BRITISH  (113)                           PHI=   -0.421
                                                                                                                   XP =   0.0043
```

****

487 CULTURES
ABOUT WHICH THE PRINCIPAL ETHNOGRAPHIES
WERE PUBLISHED BEFCRE 1930 (32)

487 CULTURES
ABOUT WHICH THE PRINCIPAL ETHNCGRAPHIES
WERE PUBLISHED IN 1930 OR AFTER (227)

BACKGROUND ON PAGE 178

BOTH SUBJECT AND PREDICATE

....

32 IN LEFT CCLUMN

ABIPCN	ARANDA	BABWA	CHERKESS	CHUKCHEE	DARD	GARO	GISU	HAVASUPAI	HERERO
KAREN	KORYAK	LHOTA NAGA	LIFU	MANCHU	MERINA	MIN CHINESE	MOTA	MZAB	NICOBARESE
OMAHA	PALIKUR	ROTINESE	SELUNG	TALAMANCA	THONGA	TORAJA	ULAWANS	VEDCA	WAPISHANA
WUTE	YUKAGHIR								

227 IN RIGHT CCLUMN

AJIE	AKHA	ALORESE	AMBA	AMERICANS	APINAYE	ARAPESH	ARAUCANIANS	ARYANS	ATSUGEWI
AWEIKOMA	AYMARA	AZTEC	BACAIRI	BAJUN	BALINESE	BAMILEKE	BANDA	BASSERI	BEJA
BELU	BEMBA	BENGALI	BERGDAMA	BETE	BHUIYA	BIRIFOR	BLACK CARIB	BORORO	BOZO
BRAZILIANS	BULGARIANS	BURUSHO	BURYAT	CADUVEO	CAGABA	CALLINAGO	CAMAYURA	CAMBA	CARAJA
CARIB	CARINYA	CHENCHU	CHEROKEE	CHINANTEC	CHIR-APACHE	CHOCO	CHORTI	COMANCHE	COORG
CREE	CUNA	CZECHS	DAGUR	DILLING	DOBUANS	DOROBO	DUTCH	EGYPTIANS	ELLICE
ENGA	EYAK	FOX	GILBERTESE	GOAJIRO	GOND	GUAHIBO	GURE	HANO	HANUNOO
HASANIA	HAZARA	HUKUNDIKA	HURON	INCA	INGALIK	IRAQW	IRISH	JAPANESE	JAVANESE
JIVARO	JUKUN	KACHIN	KAPAUKU	KASKA	KATAB	KAZAK	KERAKI	KERALA	KET
KHALKA	KHEVSUR	KIKUYU	KIOW-APACHE	KOHISTANI	KOL	KOREANS	KUMYK	KUNG	KURTATCHI
KWAKIUTL	LAKALAI	LAKHER	LAMBA	LAMET	LAPPS	LEPCHA	LESU	LOLC	LOZI
LUBA	MACASSARESE	MAGUZAWA	MALAYS	MAM	MAMBILA	MANGAIANS	MANIHIKI	MANUS	MARGI
MARICOPA	MARSHALLESE	MATAKAM	MAZATECO	MBUNDU	MENDE	MIAO	MINCHIA	MISKITO	MNONG GAR
MONGO	MONGUCR	MOTILON	MUNDURUCU	MURINBATA	MURNGIN	NABESNA	NAMBICUARA	NDEMBU	NGONI
NOMLAKI	NUER	NUNIVAK	NUPE	NYAKYUSA	NYANEKA	NYARO	OJIBWA	OKINAWANS	ONA
ONTONG-JAVA	ORACN	PALAUANS	PAPAGO	PATHAN	PAWNEE	PENOBSCOT	PONAPEANS	POPCLUCA	PORTUGUESE
PUKAPUKA	PURUM	RAROIANS	REGEIBAT	SAGADA	SAMOANS	SANPOIL	SANTAL	SARSI	SEMINOLE
SENIANG	SERBS	SHERENTE	SIRIONO	SIUAI	SOMALI	SONGHAI	SUBANUN	SWAZI	SYRIANS
TAGBANUA	TALLENSI	TAMIL	TANALA	TANIMBARESE	TAOS	TAPIRAPE	TAREUMIUT	TEDA	TENETEHARA
TENINO	TERENA	TESO	THAI	TIKOPIA	TIMBIRA	TIV	TIWI	TOKELAU	TOLOWA
TRISTAN	TRUKESE	TRUMAI	TSHIMSHIAN	TUCANO	TUCUNA	TWANA	TZELTAL	UTE	VENDA
VIETNAMESE	WAICA	WALLOONS	WANTOAT	WAROPEN	WIKMUNKAN	WOGEO	WOLEAIANS	WOLCF	YABARANA
YAGUA	YAHGAN	YAKC	YAKUT	YARURO	YORUBA	YUKI			

129 EXCLUDED BECAUSE IRRELEVANT

ABOR	AINU	ALACALUF	ALBANIANS	ANDAMANESE	ASHANTI	AZANDE	BAMBARA	BARABRA	BARI
BASQUES	BATAK	BAYA	BHIL	BOERS	BOTOCUDO	BUDUMA	BUNLAP	BURMESE	CAMBODIANS
CAYAPA	CHAGGA	CHAMACCCO	CHEREMIS	CHEYENNE	CHIRIGUANO	CHOROTI	COCHITI	COPR ESKIMO	CREEK
CROW	DELAWARE	DIEGUENC	DIERI	DOGON	FANG	FON	FUTAJALONKE	GANCA	GILYAK
GROS VENTRE	GUATO	HAICA	HASINAI	HEBREWS	HEHE	HO	HUICHOL	HUTSUL	IBAN
ICELANDERS	IFUGAO	INGASSANA	JEMEZ	KABYLE	KARIERA	KHASI	KISSI	KPE	KUBA

KUTENAI	LANGO	LAU	LUO	MAMVU	MANDAN	MAORI	MARQUESANS	MASAI	MATACO
MAYA	MBUTI	MENTAWEI	MIAMI	MINANGKABAU	MIWOK	MOSSI	NAMA	NANDI	NASKAPI
NATCHEZ	NAVAHO	NURI	NYORO	PAEZ	PARAUJANO	PENDE	PURARI	RIFFIANS	ROMANS
ROTUMANS	RUNDI	RWALA	SAMOYED	SARAMACCA	SEMANG	SERI	SHILLUK	SHLUH	SIMBOESE
SINHALESE	SIWANS	SOTHO	TARAHUMARA	TEHUELCHE	TENDA	TETON	TIBETANS	TIGRINYA	TIMUCUA
TODA	TOTCNAC	TRCBRIAND	TUBATULABAL	TUNEBO	TUPINAMBA	TURKANA	TURKMEN	WARRAU	WASHO
WICHITA	WINNEBAGC	WITCTO	YAO	YAPESE	YOKUTS	YOMBE	YUROK	ZUNI	

12 EXCLUDED BECAUSE UNASCERTAINED

5	LEAN LESS TOWARD BEING THOSE LOCATED OUTSIDE OF EAST EURASIA (330)	0.59 OF 32	5	LEAN MORE TOWARD BEING THOSE LOCATED OUTSIDE OF EAST EURASIA (330)	0.82 OF 227	13 40 19 187 XSQ= 7.76 PHI= 0.173 XP = 0.0053
97	DRIFT MORE TOWARD BEING THOSE WHERE THE HIERARCHY OF LOCAL JURISDICTION HAS THREE OR TWO LEVELS (273) GES,EA	0.96 OF 26	97	DRIFT LESS TOWARD BEING THOSE WHERE THE HIERARCHY OF LOCAL JURISDICTION HAS THREE OR TWO LEVELS (273) GES,EA	0.78 OF 190	1 41 25 149 XSQ= 3.53 PHI= -0.128 XP = 0.0603
107	DRIFT MORE TOWARD BEING THOSE WHERE CLASS STRATIFICATION, IF PRESENT, IS BASED ON SOMETHING OTHER THAN OCCUPATIONAL STATUS (160)	0.95 OF 20	107	DRIFT LESS TOWARD BEING THOSE WHERE CLASS STRATIFICATION, IF PRESENT, IS BASED ON SOMETHING OTHER THAN OCCUPATIONAL STATUS (160)	0.73 OF 112	1 30 19 82 XSQ= 3.35 PHI= -0.159 XP = 0.0671
110	TILT TOWARD BEING THOSE WHERE SLAVERY IS PRESENT (163)	0.65 OF 31	110	TILT TOWARD BEING THOSE WHERE SLAVERY IS ABSENT (218)	0.61 OF 217	20 84 11 133 XSQ= 6.40 PHI= 0.161 XP = 0.0114
282	IN ALL CASES ARE THOSE WHERE THE STRENGTH OF DESIRE FOR CHILDREN IS HIGH (16) BCA	1.00 OF 2	282	DRIFT TOWARD BEING THOSE WHERE THE STRENGTH OF DESIRE FOR CHILDREN IS LOW OR ABSENT (20) BCA	0.82 OF 22	2 4 0 18 XSQ= 2.91 PHI= 0.348 EP = 0.0543
301	DRIFT TOWARD BEING THOSE WHERE THE POST-PARTUM SEX TABOO LASTS ONE MONTH OR LESS (28)	0.67 OF 6	301	DRIFT TOWARD BEING THOSE WHERE THE POST-PARTUM SEX TABOO LASTS LONGER THAN ONE MONTH (96)	0.76 OF 72	2 55 4 17 XSQ= 3.26 PHI= -0.204 XP = 0.0710
305	IN ALL CASES ARE THOSE WHERE THE EARLY SEXUAL SATISFACTION POTENTIAL IS LOW (24) W-C	1.00 OF 3	305	DRIFT TOWARD BEING THOSE WHERE THE EARLY SEXUAL SATISFACTION POTENTIAL IS HIGH (27) W-C	0.63 OF 32	0 20 3 12 XSQ= 2.20 PHI= -0.250 EP = 0.0695

```
315  IN ALL CASES ARE THOSE          1.00 OF   2     315  DRIFT TOWARD BEING THOSE        0.76 OF  34          0   26
     WHERE MOTHER AND NURSING CHILC                      WHERE MOTHER AND NURSING CHILD                       2    8
     CUSTOMARILY SLEEP IN                                CUSTOMARILY SLEEP IN                          XSQ=      2.35
     DIFFERENT BEDS  (14) W-C,S                          THE SAME BED  (37) W-D,S                      PHI=    -0.256
                                                                                                       EP =    0.0714

400  IN ALL CASES ARE THOSE          1.00 OF   5     400  TILT TOWARD BEING THOSE         0.59 OF  32          0   19
     WHERE HOMCSEXUAL ACTIVITY                           WHERE HOMOSEXUAL ACTIVITY                            5   13
     IS PERMITTED  (36) F-B                              IS PROHIBITED  (22) F-B                       XSQ=      3.96
                                                                                                       PHI=    -0.327
                                                                                                       EP =    0.0197

433  IN ALL CASES ARE THOSE          1.00 OF   2     433  TILT TOWARD BEING THOSE         0.85 OF  20          2    3
     WHERE BELIEF IN REINCARNATION                       WHERE BELIEF IN REINCARNATION                        0   17
     IS PRESENT  (10) GES                                IS ABSENT  (28) GES                           XSQ=      3.42
                                                                                                       PHI=     0.394
                                                                                                       EP =    0.0433

442  IN ALL CASES ARE THCSE          1.00 OF   5     442  TILT TOWARD BEING THOSE         0.57 OF  35          0   20
     WHERE FEAR OF ANIMAL SPIRITS                        WHERE FEAR OF ANIMAL SPIRITS                         5   15
     IS LCW  (33) W-C                                    IS HIGH  (28) W-C                             XSQ=      3.66
                                                                                                       PHI=    -0.302
                                                                                                       EP =    0.0471

477  IN ALL CASES ARE THOSE          1.00 OF   4     477  DRIFT TOWARD BEING THOSE        0.60 OF  15          4    6
     WHERE ALCOHOLIC AGGRESSION IS                       WHERE ALCOHOLIC AGGRESSION IS                        0    9
     STRCNG  (15) DH                                     MODERATE OR SLIGHT  (19) DH                   XSQ=      2.47
                                                                                                       PHI=     0.361
                                                                                                       EP =    0.0867

481  DRIFT MORE TOWARD BEING THOSE 0.83 OF  30     481  DRIFT LESS TOWARD BEING THOSE  0.64 OF 222          5   80
     WHERE THE PRINCIPAL ETHNOGRAPHERS                   WHERE THE PRINCIPAL ETHNOGRAPHERS                   25  142
     HAVE BEEN CTHER THAN AMERICAN  (275)                HAVE BEEN OTHER THAN AMERICAN  (275)          XSQ=      3.61
                                                                                                       PHI=    -0.120
                                                                                                       XP =    0.0574
```

488 CULTURES
ABOUT WHICH THE PRINCIPAL ETHNOGRAPHIES
WERE PUBLISHED BEFORE 1950 (185)

488 CULTURES
ABOUT WHICH THE PRINCIPAL ETHNOGRAPHIES
WERE PUBLISHED IN 1950 OR AFTER (72)

BACKGROUND ON PAGE 178

BOTH SUBJECT AND PREDICATE

185 IN LEFT COLUMN

ABIPON	AJIE	AKHA	ALACALUF	ALORESE	ANDAMANESE	ARANDA	ARAPESH	AWEIKOMA	BABWA
BASQUES	BAYA	BEJA	BERGDAMA	BHUIYA	BOERS	BOTOCUDO	BOZO	BUDUMA	BULGARIANS
BURUSHO	CADUVEO	CARIB	CAYAPA	CHAGGA	CHAMACOCO	CHENCHU	CHERKESS	CHEROKEE	CHIR-APACHE
CHIRIGUANO	CHOROTI	CHORTI	CHUKCHEE	COCHITI	COMANCHE	COPR ESKIMO	CREEK	CROW	CUNA
DARD	DIEGUENO	DILLING	DOBUANS	DUTCH	ELLICE	EYAK	FON	FOX	FUTAJALONKE
GARO	GILYAK	GISU	GOND	GUATO	HAIDA	HASANIA	HAVASUPAI	HEHE	HERERO
HO	HUKUNDIKA	HUTSUL	ICELANDERS	IFUGAO	INCA	INGASSANA	IRISH	JEMEZ	JIVARO
JUKUN	KABYLE	KAREN	KAZAK	KERAKI	KET	KHASI	KHEVSUR	KIOW-APACHE	KOL
KORYAK	KURTATCHI	KUTENAI	LANGO	LAU	LEPCHA	LESU	LHOTA NAGA	LIFU	LUBA
MAGUZAWA	MAM	MANCHU	MANGAIANS	MANIHIKI	MANUS	MAORI	MARGI	MARICOPA	MARQUESANS
MARSHALLESE	MASAI	MATACO	MAYA	MAZATECO	MERINA	MIAMI	MIN CHINESE	MINCHIA	MISKITO
MIWOK	MONGO	MOTA	MOTILON	MZAB	NAMA	NASKAPI	NATCHEZ	NAVAHO	NICOBARESE
NUNIVAK	NYANEKA	OMAHA	ONA	ONTONG-JAVA	PALIKUR	PAPAGO	PENOBSCOT	PONAPEANS	POPOLUCA
PUKAPUKA	RIFFIANS	ROMANS	ROTINESE	ROTUMANS	RWALA	SANPOIL	SARAMACCA	SELUNG	SEMANG
SEMINOLE	SENIANG	SHERENTE	SHLUH	SIWANS	TALAMANCA	TANALA	TANIMBARESE	TAOS	TAPIRAPE
TARAHUMARA	TEHUELCHE	TENETEHARA	TERENA	TETON	THONGA	TIKOPIA	TIMBIRA	TIMUCUA	TODA
TOKELAU	TOLOWA	TORAJA	TRISTAN	TUBATULABAL	TUPINAMBA	TZELTAL	ULAWANS	UTE	VEDDA
VENDA	VIETNAMESE	WAPISHANA	WAROPEN	WINNEBAGO	WITOTO	WOGEO	WUTE	YAGUA	YAHGAN
YAKUT	YOKUTS	YOMBE	YUKAGHIR	YUKI					

72 IN RIGHT COLUMN

AMBA	AMERICANS	ARYANS	BAJUN	BASSERI	BELU	BLACK CARIB	BRAZILIANS	BURYAT	CAMAYURA
CAMBA	CARINYA	CHINANTEC	CREE	CZECHS	DAGUR	EGYPTIANS	ENGA	GILBERTESE	GUAHIBO
HANO	HANUNOO	IRAQW	JAVANESE	KAPAUKU	KERALA	KHALKA	KOHISTANI	KOREANS	KUMYK
LAKALAI	LAMET	LOLO	MACASSARESE	MIAO	MNONG GAR	MONGUOR	MURINBATA	NABESNA	NGONI
NOMLAKI	NYARO	OJIBWA	OKINAWANS	ORAON	PALAUANS	PATHAN	PORTUGUESE	RAROIANS	REGEIBAT
SAGADA	SERBS	SIRIONO	SIUAI	SUBANUN	SYRIANS	TAGBANUA	TAMIL	TAREUMIUT	TEDA
TESO	TRUKESE	TRUMAI	TUCUNA	WAICA	WALLOONS	WANTOAT	WOLEAIANS	WOLOF	YABARANA
YARURO	YORUBA								

131 EXCLUDED BECAUSE IRRELEVANT

ABOR	AINU	ALBANIANS	APINAYE	ARAUCANIANS	ASHANTI	ATSUGEWI	AYMARA	AZANDE	AZTEC
BACAIRI	BALINESE	BAMBARA	BAMILEKE	BANDA	BARABRA	BARI	BATAK	BEMBA	BENGALI
BETE	BHIL	BIRIFOR	BORORO	BUNLAP	BURMESE	CAGABA	CALLINAGO	CAMBODIANS	CARAJA
CHEREMIS	CHEYENNE	CHOCO	COORG	DELAWARE	DIERI	DOGON	DOROBO	FANG	GANDA
GOAJIRO	GROS VENTRE	GURE	HASINAI	HAZARA	HEBREWS	HUICHOL	HURON	IBAN	INGALIK
JAPANESE	KACHIN	KARIERA	KASKA	KATAB	KIKUYU	KISSI	KPE	KUBA	KUNG

KWAKIUTL	LAKHER	LAMBA	LAPPS	LOZI	LUO	MALAYS	MAMBILA	MAMVU	MANDAN
MATAKAM	MBUNDU	MBUTI	MENDE	MENTAWEI	MINANGKABAU	MOSSI	MUNDURUCU	MURNGIN	NAMBICUARA
NANDI	NDEMBU	NUER	NUPE	NURI	NYAKYUSA	NYORO	PAEZ	PARAUJANO	PAWNEE
PENDE	PURARI	PURUM	RUNDI	SAMOANS	SAMOYED	SANTAL	SARSI	SERI	SHILLUK
SIMBOESE	SINHALESE	SOMALI	SONGHAI	SOTHO	SWAZI	TALLENSI	TENDA	TENINO	THAI
TIBETANS	TIGRINYA	TIV	TIWI	TOTONAC	TROBRIAND	TSHIMSHIAN	TUCANO	TUNEBO	TURKANA
TURKMEN	TWANA	WARRAU	WASHO	WICHITA	WIKMUNKAN	YAKO	YAO	YAPESE	YUROK
ZUNI									

12 EXCLUDED BECAUSE UNASCERTAINEC

8	TILT LESS TOWARD BEING THOSE LOCATED OUTSIDE OF NORTH AMERICA (330)	0.78 OF 185	8	TILT MORE TOWARD BEING THOSE LOCATED OUTSIDE OF NORTH AMERICA (330)	0.90 OF 72	40 7 145 65 XSQ= 4.15 PHI= 0.127 XP = 0.0417
36	DRIFT LESS TOWARD BEING THOSE WHERE THE NATURAL ENVIRONMENT IS OTHER THAN 'VERY HARSH,' OR SUB-TROPICAL BUSH, OR TEMPERATE GRASSLANC (292) FWM	0.68 OF 185	36	DRIFT MORE TOWARD BEING THOSE WHERE THE NATURAL ENVIRONMENT IS OTHER THAN 'VERY HARSH,' OR SUB-TROPICAL BUSH, OR TEMPERATE GRASSLAND (292) FWM	0.79 OF 72	60 15 125 57 XSQ= 2.84 PHI= 0.105 XP = 0.0922
51	LEAN LESS TOWARD BEING THOSE WHERE SUBSISTENCE IS PRIMARILY BY FOOD PRODUCTION -- I. E., AGRICULTURE OR HUSBANDRY -- RATHER THAN BY GATHERING (253)	0.54 OF 185	51	LEAN MORE TOWARD BEING THOSE WHERE SUBSISTENCE IS PRIMARILY BY FOOD PRODUCTION -- I. E., AGRICULTURE OR HUSBANDRY -- RATHER THAN BY GATHERING (253)	0.74 OF 72	99 53 86 19 XSQ= 7.85 PHI= -0.175 XP = 0.0051
53	TILT TOWARD BEING THOSE WHERE FOOD PRODUCTION IS BY SIMPLE AGRICULTURE OR INCIPIENT FOOD PRODUCTION, RATHER THAN BY INTENSIVE AGRICULTURE (147)	0.69 OF 101	53	TILT TOWARD BEING THOSE WHERE FOOD PRODUCTION IS BY INTENSIVE AGRICULTURE, RATHER THAN BY SIMPLE AGRICULTURE OR INCIPIENT FOOD PRODUCTION (91)	0.52 OF 44	31 23 70 21 XSQ= 5.22 PHI= -0.190 XP = 0.0224
71	TILT MORE TOWARD BEING THOSE WHERE METAL WORKING IS ABSENT (153)	0.75 OF 110	71	TILT LESS TOWARD BEING THOSE WHERE METAL WORKING IS ABSENT (153)	0.53 OF 45	27 21 83 24 XSQ= 6.31 PHI= -0.202 XP = 0.0120
79	LEAN MORE TOWARD BEING THOSE WHERE NO CITY IS PRESENT (201)	0.94 OF 95	79	LEAN LESS TOWARD BEING THOSE WHERE NO CITY IS PRESENT (201)	0.73 OF 44	6 12 89 32 XSQ= 9.93 PHI= -0.267 XP = 0.0016
80	DRIFT MORE TOWARD BEING THOSE WHERE NO CITY OR TOWN IS PRESENT (185)	0.86 OF 95	80	DRIFT LESS TOWARD BEING THOSE WHERE NO CITY OR TOWN IS PRESENT (185)	0.73 OF 44	13 12 82 32 XSQ= 2.90 PHI= -0.144 XP = 0.0886

84	LEAN MORE TOWARD BEING THOSE 0.92 OF 158 WHERE THE LEVEL OF POLITICAL INTEGRATION IS THE LITTLE STATE, THE MINIMAL STATE, THE AUTONOMOUS COMMUNITY, OR THE FAMILY (262) GPM	84	LEAN LESS TOWARD BEING THOSE 0.74 OF 39 WHERE THE LEVEL OF POLITICAL INTEGRATION IS THE LITTLE STATE, THE MINIMAL STATE, THE AUTONOMOUS COMMUNITY, OR THE FAMILY (262) GPM	12 10 146 29 XSQ= 8.53 PHI= -0.208 XP = 0.0035
85	TILT MORE TOWARD BEING THOSE 0.83 OF 158 WHERE THE LEVEL OF POLITICAL INTEGRATION IS THE MINIMAL STATE, THE AUTONOMOUS COMMUNITY, OR THE FAMILY (234) GPM	85	TILT LESS TOWARD BEING THOSE 0.67 OF 39 WHERE THE LEVEL OF POLITICAL INTEGRATION IS THE MINIMAL STATE, THE AUTONOMOUS COMMUNITY, OR THE FAMILY (234) GPM	27 13 131 26 XSQ= 4.15 PHI= -0.145 XP = 0.0417
94	LEAN MORE TOWARD BEING THOSE 0.94 OF 149 WHERE THE HIERARCHY OF NATIONAL JURISDICTION HAS TWO, ONE, OR NO LEVELS (296) GES,EA	94	LEAN LESS TOWARD BEING THOSE 0.79 OF 57 WHERE THE HIERARCHY OF NATIONAL JURISDICTION HAS TWO, ONE, OR NO LEVELS (296) GES,EA	9 12 140 45 XSQ= 8.58 PHI= -0.204 XP = 0.0034
95	LEAN MORE TOWARD BEING THOSE 0.85 OF 149 WHERE THE HIERARCHY OF NATIONAL JURISDICTION HAS ONE OR NO LEVELS (254) GES,EA	95	LEAN LESS TOWARD BEING THOSE 0.67 OF 57 WHERE THE HIERARCHY OF NATIONAL JURISDICTION HAS ONE OR NO LEVELS (254) GES,EA	23 19 126 38 XSQ= 7.07 PHI= -0.185 XP = 0.0078
107	LEAN MORE TOWARD BEING THOSE 0.86 OF 86 WHERE CLASS STRATIFICATION, IF PRESENT, IS BASED ON SOMETHING OTHER THAN OCCUPATIONAL STATUS (160)	107	LEAN LESS TOWARD BEING THOSE 0.62 OF 39 WHERE CLASS STRATIFICATION, IF PRESENT, IS BASED ON SOMETHING OTHER THAN OCCUPATIONAL STATUS (160)	12 15 74 24 XSQ= 8.12 PHI= -0.255 XP = 0.0044
109	LEAN MORE TOWARD BEING THOSE 0.92 OF 172 WHERE CASTES ARE ABSENT (317)	109	LEAN LESS TOWARD BEING THOSE 0.75 OF 64 WHERE CASTES ARE ABSENT (317)	14 16 158 48 XSQ= 10.48 PHI= -0.211 XP = 0.0012
131	DRIFT LESS TOWARD BEING THOSE 0.83 OF 70 WHERE THE CONSTRUCTION OF PERMANENT HOUSES OR THE ERECTION OF TEMPORARY DWELLINGS IS MAINLY DONE BY MALES (136)	131	DRIFT MORE TOWARD BEING THOSE 0.97 OF 33 WHERE THE CONSTRUCTION OF PERMANENT HOUSES OR THE ERECTION OF TEMPORARY DWELLINGS IS MAINLY DONE BY MALES (136)	58 32 12 1 XSQ= 2.87 PHI= -0.167 XP = 0.0902
163	DRIFT TOWARD BEING THOSE 0.86 OF 7 WHERE THE EMPHASIS ON INDIVIDUAL VOLITION AS THE CAUSE OF CRIME IS LOW (10) MJ	163	IN ALL CASES ARE THOSE 1.00 OF 2 WHERE THE EMPHASIS ON INDIVIDUAL VOLITION AS THE CAUSE OF CRIME IS HIGH (7) MJ	1 2 6 0 XSQ= 2.01 PHI= -0.472 EP = 0.0833
178	DRIFT MORE TOWARD BEING THOSE 0.81 OF 174 WHERE THE COMMUNITY IS OTHER THAN SEGMENTED ON A CLAN BASIS AND NON-EXOGAMOUS (295)	178	DRIFT LESS TOWARD BEING THOSE 0.70 OF 71 WHERE THE COMMUNITY IS OTHER THAN SEGMENTED ON A CLAN BASIS AND NON-EXOGAMOUS (295)	33 21 141 50 XSQ= 2.72 PHI= -0.105 XP = 0.0993

183	DRIFT LESS TOWARD BEING THOSE 0.84 OF 108 WHERE THE LARGEST NON-COGNATIC KIN GROUP IS SMALLER THAN A MOEITY, I. E., A PHRATRY OR SIB OR LINEAGE (218)	183	DRIFT MORE TOWARD BEING THOSE 0.96 OF 46 WHERE THE LARGEST NON-COGNATIC KIN GROUP IS SMALLER THAN A MOEITY, I. E., A PHRATRY OR SIB OR LINEAGE (218)	17 2 91 44 XSQ= 2.89 PHI= 0.137 XP = 0.0891
196	TILT LESS TOWARD BEING THOSE 0.60 OF 128 WHERE INDIVIDUAL RIGHTS IN REAL PROPERTY, AND RULES FOR INHERITANCE, ARE PRESENT (194)	196	TILT MORE TOWARD BEING THOSE 0.80 OF 49 WHERE INDIVIDUAL RIGHTS IN REAL PROPERTY, AND RULES FOR INHERITANCE, ARE PRESENT (194)	77 39 51 10 XSQ= 5.10 PHI= -0.170 XP = 0.0240
213	DRIFT TOWARD BEING THOSE 0.58 OF 167 WHERE FIRST COUSIN MARRIAGE IS NOT PERMITTED (198)	213	DRIFT TOWARD BEING THOSE 0.55 OF 65 WHERE FIRST COUSIN MARRIAGE IS PERMITTED (172)	70 36 97 29 XSQ= 2.90 PHI= -0.112 XP = 0.0886
220	LEAN MORE TOWARD BEING THOSE 0.81 OF 167 WHERE FIRST COUSIN MARRIAGE IN SOME FORM OR OTHER IS NOT PRESCRIBED OR PREFERRED (273)	220	LEAN LESS TOWARD BEING THOSE 0.62 OF 65 WHERE FIRST COUSIN MARRIAGE IN SOME FORM OR OTHER IS NOT PRESCRIBED OR PREFERRED (273)	32 25 135 40 XSQ= 8.39 PHI= -0.190 XP = 0.0038
241	LEAN MORE TOWARD BEING THOSE 0.92 OF 92 WHERE THE FAMILY, IF EXTENDED, IS LARGE OR SMALL, RATHER THAN STEM (187)	241	LEAN LESS TOWARD BEING THOSE 0.73 OF 37 WHERE THE FAMILY, IF EXTENDED, IS LARGE OR SMALL, RATHER THAN STEM (187)	85 27 7 10 XSQ= 7.08 PHI= 0.234 XP = 0.0078
346	DRIFT TOWARD BEING THOSE 0.67 OF 42 WHERE THE CHILD'S INFERRED ANXIETY OVER PERFORMANCE OF SELF-RELIANT BEHAVIOR IS LOW (39) B-B-C	346	DRIFT TOWARD BEING THOSE 0.75 OF 8 WHERE THE CHILD'S INFERRED ANXIETY OVER PERFORMANCE OF SELF-RELIANT BEHAVIOR IS HIGH (37) B-B-C	14 6 28 2 XSQ= 3.28 PHI= -0.256 XP = 0.0701
347	DRIFT TOWARD BEING THOSE 0.69 OF 42 WHERE THE CHILD'S INFERRED CONFLICT REGARDING SELF-RELIANT BEHAVIOR IS LOW (39) B-B-C	347	DRIFT TOWARD BEING THOSE 0.75 OF 8 WHERE THE CHILD'S INFERRED CONFLICT REGARDING SELF-RELIANT BEHAVIOR IS HIGH (37) B-B-C	13 6 29 2 XSQ= 3.82 PHI= -0.276 XP = 0.0506
348	TILT TOWARD BEING THOSE 0.69 OF 32 WHERE THE TOTAL POSITIVE PRESSURE TOWARD DEVELOPING ACHIEVEMENT BEHAVIOR IN THE CHILD IS HIGH (32) B-B-C	348	TILT TOWARD BEING THOSE 0.86 OF 7 WHERE THE TOTAL POSITIVE PRESSURE TOWARD DEVELOPING ACHIEVEMENT BEHAVIOR IN THE CHILD IS LOW (31) B-B-C	22 1 10 6 XSQ= 4.97 PHI= 0.357 EP = 0.0127
419	DRIFT TOWARD BEING THOSE 0.61 OF 49 WHERE MILITARY GLORY IS STRONGLY OR MODERATELY EMPHASIZED (55) PES	419	DRIFT TOWARD BEING THOSE 0.78 OF 9 WHERE MILITARY GLORY IS NEGLIGIBLY EMPHASIZED (31) PES	30 2 19 7 XSQ= 3.23 PHI= 0.236 XP = 0.0722

420	TILT LESS TOWARD BEING THOSE 0.53 OF 49 WHERE BELLICOSITY IS MODERATE OR NEGLIGIBLE (46) PES	420	IN ALL CASES ARE THOSE 1.00 OF 9 WHERE BELLICOSITY IS MODERATE OR NEGLIGIBLE (46) PES	23 0 26 9 XSQ= 5.18 PHI= 0.299 XP = 0.0229
428	TILT LESS TOWARD BEING THOSE 0.68 OF 37 WHERE A HIGH GOD, IF PRESENT AND ACTIVE, SUPPORTS HUMAN MORALITY, RATHER THAN NOT SUPPORTING IT (61) GES,EA	428	IN ALL CASES ARE THOSE 1.00 OF 17 WHERE A HIGH GOD, IF PRESENT AND ACTIVE, SUPPORTS HUMAN MORALITY, RATHER THAN NOT SUPPORTING IT (61) GES,EA	25 17 12 0 XSQ= 5.34 PHI= -0.314 XP = 0.0209
458	TILT MORE TOWARD BEING THOSE 0.80 OF 90 WHERE GAMES, IF PRESENT, DO NOT INCLUDE GAMES OF STRATEGY (119) R-A-B,EA	458	TILT LESS TOWARD BEING THOSE 0.57 OF 23 WHERE GAMES, IF PRESENT, DO NOT INCLUDE GAMES OF STRATEGY (119) R-A-B,EA	18 10 72 13 XSQ= 4.23 PHI= -0.194 XP = 0.0397
482	DRIFT LESS TOWARD BEING THOSE 0.85 OF 178 WHERE THE PRINCIPAL ETHNOGRAPHERS HAVE BEEN OTHER THAN BRITISH (336)	482	DRIFT MORE TOWARD BEING THOSE 0.94 OF 72 WHERE THE PRINCIPAL ETHNOGRAPHERS HAVE BEEN OTHER THAN BRITISH (336)	26 4 152 68 XSQ= 3.17 PHI= 0.113 XP = 0.0752
483	DRIFT LESS TOWARD BEING THOSE 0.69 OF 85 WHERE THE PRINCIPAL ETHNOGRAPHERS HAVE BEEN AMERICAN, RATHER THAN BRITISH (113)	483	DRIFT MORE TOWARD BEING THOSE 0.88 OF 34 WHERE THE PRINCIPAL ETHNOGRAPHERS HAVE BEEN AMERICAN, RATHER THAN BRITISH (113)	59 30 26 4 XSQ= 3.62 PHI= -0.174 XP = 0.0571

489 CULTURES
INCLUDED IN CHARLES ACKERMAN'S
STUDY OF DIVORCE (57)

489 CULTURES
NOT INCLUDED IN CHARLES ACKERMAN'S
STUDY OF DIVORCE (343)

SUBJECT ONLY, F.C. 1-488 AND 527-536
BOTH SUBJECT AND PREDICATE, F.C. 489-526

BACKGROUND ON PAGE 180

57 IN LEFT COLUMN

ABIPON	ALORESE	ANDAMANESE	ATAYAL	AWEIKOMA	AZANDE	AZTEC	BEMBA	BHIL	BURMESE
CALLINAGO	CAYAPA	CHUKCHEE	COMANCHE	CUNA	FANG	GOND	IBAN	IFUGAO	ILA
INCA	KAZAK	KHASI	KIKUYU	KORYAK	LAU	LEPCHA	LOLO	LOZI	MACASSARESE
MAGUZAWA	MANDAN	MARQUESANS	MBUNDU	MUNDURUCU	NAMBICUARA	NYAKYUSA	OJIBWA	OMAHA	PAPAGO
PAWNEE	SAMCANS	SEMANG	SIRIONO	SIWANS	SOMALI	TARAHUMARA	THAI	TIKOPIA	TODA
TUBATULABAL	VEDDA	VIETNAMESE	YAO	YORUBA	YUROK	ZUNI			

343 IN RIGHT COLUMN

	Included (57)		Not included (343)	
5	DRIFT LESS TOWARD BEING THOSE 0.74 OF 57 LOCATED OUTSIDE OF EAST EURASIA (330)	5	DRIFT MORE TOWARD BEING THOSE 0.84 OF 343 LOCATED OUTSIDE OF EAST EURASIA (330)	15 55 42 288 XSQ= 2.90 PHI= 0.085 XP = 0.0885
81	TILT MORE TOWARD BEING THOSE 0.75 OF 48 WHERE NO CITY OR TOWN IS PRESENT, AND THE AVERAGE COMMUNITY SIZE IS SMALLER THAN 200 (135)	81	TILT LESS TOWARD BEING THOSE 0.56 OF 176 WHERE NO CITY OR TOWN IS PRESENT, AND THE AVERAGE COMMUNITY SIZE IS SMALLER THAN 200 (135)	12 77 36 99 XSQ= 4.78 PHI= -0.146 XP = 0.0288
83	DRIFT MORE TOWARD BEING THOSE 0.88 OF 41 WHERE, WITH NO CITY AND NO TOWN PRESENT, THE AVERAGE COMMUNITY SIZE IS SMALLER THAN 200, RATHER THAN BETWEEN 200 AND 999 (135)	83	DRIFT LESS TOWARD BEING THOSE 0.71 OF 139 WHERE, WITH NO CITY AND NO TOWN PRESENT, THE AVERAGE COMMUNITY SIZE IS SMALLER THAN 200, RATHER THAN BETWEEN 200 AND 999 (135)	5 40 36 99 XSQ= 3.80 PHI= -0.145 XP = 0.0512
98	DRIFT MORE TOWARD BEING THOSE 0.83 OF 54 WHERE THE HIERARCHY OF LOCAL JURISDICTION HAS FOUR OR THREE LEVELS (238) GES,EA	98	DRIFT LESS TOWARD BEING THOSE 0.70 OF 277 WHERE THE HIERARCHY OF LOCAL JURISDICTION HAS FOUR OR THREE LEVELS (238) GES,EA	45 193 9 84 XSQ= 3.52 PHI= 0.103 XP = 0.0605
99	DRIFT MORE TOWARD BEING THOSE 0.78 OF 23 WHERE, WITH NATIONAL HIERARCHY ABSENT, THE HIERARCHY OF LOCAL JURISDICTION HAS FOUR OR THREE LEVELS (93) GES,EA	99	DRIFT LESS TOWARD BEING THOSE 0.56 OF 133 WHERE, WITH NATIONAL HIERARCHY ABSENT, THE HIERARCHY OF LOCAL JURISDICTION HAS FOUR OR THREE LEVELS (93) GES,EA	18 75 5 58 XSQ= 3.04 PHI= 0.140 XP = 0.0812

100	DRIFT MORE TOWARD BEING THOSE 0.91 OF 54 WHERE HIERARCHIES ARE MORE COMPLEX THAN THE 'SIMPLEST,' I. E., MORE COMPLEX THAN TWO LOCAL LEVELS WITH NO NATIONAL LEVELS (267) GES,EA	DRIFT LESS TOWARD BEING THOSE 0.79 OF 276 WHERE HIERARCHIES ARE MORE COMPLEX THAN THE 'SIMPLEST,' I. E., MORE COMPLEX THAN TWO LOCAL LEVELS WITH NO NATIONAL LEVELS (267) GES,EA	49 218 5 58 XSQ= 3.32 PHI= 0.100 XP = 0.0686
110	TILT TOWARD BEING THOSE 0.56 OF 57 WHERE SLAVERY IS PRESENT (163)	TILT TOWARD BEING THOSE 0.60 OF 324 WHERE SLAVERY IS ABSENT (218)	32 131 25 193 XSQ= 4.27 PHI= 0.106 XP = 0.0389
133	TILT TOWARD BEING THOSE 0.83 OF 12 WHERE CONTRACTED DEBTS ARE SIGNIFICANTLY PRESENT (17) GES	TILT TOWARD BEING THOSE 0.68 OF 22 WHERE CONTRACTED DEBTS ARE MODERATELY PRESENT OR ABSENT (17) GES	10 7 2 15 XSQ= 6.31 PHI= 0.431 EP = 0.0104
136	LEAN TOWARD BEING THOSE 0.91 OF 11 WHERE FULL-TIME ENTREPRENEURS ARE PRESENT (18) JV	LEAN TOWARD BEING THOSE 0.62 OF 21 WHERE FULL-TIME ENTREPRENEURS ARE ABSENT (14) JV	10 8 1 13 XSQ= 6.18 PHI= 0.439 EP = 0.0075
186	DRIFT MORE TOWARD BEING THOSE 0.74 OF 57 WHERE THE KIN GROUP IS OTHER THAN EXCLUSIVELY PATRILINEAL (250)	DRIFT LESS TOWARD BEING THOSE 0.61 OF 343 WHERE THE KIN GROUP IS OTHER THAN EXCLUSIVELY PATRILINEAL (250)	15 135 42 208 XSQ= 3.01 PHI= -0.087 XP = 0.0826
210	TILT LESS TOWARD BEING THOSE 0.67 OF 24 WHERE MARITAL RESIDENCE IS PATRILOCAL, RATHER THAN MATRILOCAL (169)	TILT MORE TOWARD BEING THOSE 0.87 OF 176 WHERE MARITAL RESIDENCE IS PATRILOCAL, RATHER THAN MATRILOCAL (169)	16 153 8 23 XSQ= 5.17 PHI= -0.161 XP = 0.0230
259	DRIFT TOWARD BEING THOSE 0.65 OF 17 WHERE THE SEVERITY OF MOTHER-IN-LAW AVOIDANCE IS LOW (20) WNS	DRIFT TOWARD BEING THOSE 0.69 OF 29 WHERE THE SEVERITY OF MOTHER-IN-LAW AVOIDANCE IS HIGH (26) WNS	6 20 11 9 XSQ= 3.67 PHI= -0.282 XP = 0.0554
310	TILT TOWARD BEING THOSE 0.89 OF 9 WHERE ANAL SOCIALIZATION ANXIETY IS LOW (19) W-C	TILT TOWARD BEING THOSE 0.66 OF 32 WHERE ANAL SOCIALIZATION ANXIETY IS HIGH (22) W-C	1 21 8 11 XSQ= 6.35 PHI= -0.393 XP = 0.0118
334	DRIFT TOWARD BEING THOSE 0.70 OF 23 WHERE THE INDULGENCE OF THE CHILD IS HIGH (40) B-B-C	DRIFT TOWARD BEING THOSE 0.56 OF 55 WHERE THE INDULGENCE OF THE CHILD IS LOW (38) B-B-C	16 24 7 31 XSQ= 3.39 PHI= 0.208 XP = 0.0657

403	DRIFT MORE TOWARD BEING THOSE WHERE EXPLANATICNS OF ILLNESS OF AN ANAL NATURE ARE ABSENT (38) W-C	0.86 OF 14	403	DRIFT LESS TOWARD BEING THCSE WHERE EXPLANATIONS OF ILLNESS OF AN ANAL NATURE ARE ABSENT (38) W-C	0.55 OF 47	2 21 12 26 XSQ= 3.05 PHI= -0.224 XP = 0.0809
428	LEAN TOWARD BEING THOSE WHERE A HIGH GOD, IF PRESENT AND ACTIVE, DOES NOT SUPPORT HUMAN MORALITY, RATHER THAN SUPPORTING IT (26) GES,EA	0.59 OF 17	428	LEAN TOWARD BEING THOSE WHERE A HIGH GOD, IF PRESENT AND ACTIVE, SUPPORTS HUMAN MORALITY, RATHER THAN NOT SUPPORTING IT (61) GES,EA	0.77 OF 70	7 54 10 16 XSQ= 6.81 PHI= -0.280 XP = 0.0090
432	DRIFT MCRE TOWARC BEING THOSE WHERE AN ATTRACTIVE AFTERLIFE IS BELIEVED IN (27) LWS	0.92 OF 12	432	DRIFT LESS TOWARD BEING THCSE WHERE AN ATTRACTIVE AFTERLIFE IS BELIEVED IN (27) LWS	0.62 OF 26	11 16 1 10 XSQ= 2.31 PHI= 0.246 EP = 0.0704
436	TILT TOWARD BEING THOSE WHERE ACTIVE ANCESTRAL SPIRITS ARE ABSENT (11) GES	0.54 OF 13	436	TILT TOWARD BEING THOSE WHERE ACTIVE ANCESTRAL SPIRITS ARE PRESENT (27) GES	0.84 OF 25	6 21 7 4 XSQ= 4.26 PHI= -0.335 EP = 0.0244
443	TILT TOWARD BEING THOSE WHERE OVERALL FEAR CF CTHERS IS LCW (30) W-C	0.79 OF 14	443	TILT TOWARD BEING THOSE WHERE OVERALL FEAR OF OTHERS IS HIGH (31) W-C	0.60 OF 47	3 28 11 19 XSQ= 4.85 PHI= -0.282 XP = 0.0277
473	DRIFT TOWARD BEING THOSE WHERE SENSITIVITY TO INSULT IS EXTREME (32) PES	0.50 OF 30	473	DRIFT TOWARD BEING THOSE WHERE SENSITIVITY TO INSULT IS MODERATE OR NEGLIGIBLE (56) PES	0.71 OF 58	15 17 15 41 XSQ= 2.82 PHI= 0.179 XP = 0.0932
490	LEAN LESS TOWARD BEING THCSE NOT INCLUDED IN ALBERT S. ANTHONY'S SAMPLE ON MALE INITIATION RITES (287)	0.56 OF 57	490	LEAN MORE TOWARD BEING THOSE NOT INCLUDED IN ALBERT S. ANTHONY'S SAMPLE ON MALE INITIATION RITES (287)	0.74 OF 343	25 88 32 255 XSQ= 7.12 PHI= 0.133 XP = 0.0076
492	DRIFT LESS TOWARD BEING THOSE NOT INCLUDED IN BARBARA CHARTIER AYRES' STUDY OF FEMALE INITIATION RITES (361)	0.82 OF 57	492	DRIFT MORE TOWARD BEING THCSE NOT INCLUDED IN BARBARA CHARTIER AYRES' STUDY OF FEMALE INITIATION RITES (361)	0.92 OF 343	10 29 47 314 XSQ= 3.61 PHI= 0.095 XP = 0.0573
493	TEND LESS TO BE THCSE NOT INCLUDED IN BACCN, BARRY, AND CHILC'S STUDY OF CHILD REARING (322)	0.60 OF 57	493	TEND MORE TO BE THOSE NOT INCLUDED IN BACON, BARRY, AND CHILD'S STUDY OF CHILD REARING (322)	0.84 CF 343	23 55 34 288 XSQ= 16.89 PHI= 0.206 XP = 0.0000

494	TILT LESS TOWARD BEING THCSE 0.84 OF 57 NOT INCLUDED IN HERBERT M. BARRY III'S STUDY OF ART (371)	494	TILT MORE TOWARD BEING THOSE 0.94 OF 343 NOT INCLUDED IN HERBERT M. BARRY III'S STUDY OF ART (371)	9 20 48 323 XSQ= 5.80 PHI= 0.120 XP = 0.0160
495	TEND LESS TO BE THCSE 0.63 OF 57 NOT INCLUDED IN JUCITH K. BROWN'S STUDY OF FEMALE INITIATICN RITES (335)	495	TEND MORE TO BE THOSE 0.87 OF 343 NOT INCLUDED IN JUDITH K. BROWN'S STUDY OF FEMALE INITIATION RITES (335)	21 44 36 299 XSQ= 18.98 PHI= 0.218 XP = 0.0000
496	TEND LESS TO BE THCSE 0.54 OF 57 NOT INCLUDED IN ROY G. D'ANDRADE'S STUDY OF DREAMS (345)	496	TEND MORE TO BE THOSE 0.92 OF 343 NOT INCLUDED IN ROY G. D'ANDRADE'S STUDY OF DREAMS (345)	26 29 31 314 XSQ= 53.82 PHI= 0.367 XP = 0.
497	TEND LESS TO BE THCSE 0.60 OF 57 NOT INCLUDED IN WILLIAM M. EVAN'S STUDY OF LAW (339)	497	TEND MORE TO BE THOSE 0.89 OF 343 NOT INCLUDED IN WILLIAM M. EVAN'S STUDY OF LAW (339)	23 38 34 305 XSQ= 30.18 PHI= 0.275 XP = 0.0000
498	LEAN LESS TOWARD BEING THCSE 0.74 OF 57 NOT INCLUDED IN C. S. FORC'S STUDY OF SEX (349)	498	LEAN MORE TOWARD BEING THOSE 0.90 OF 343 NOT INCLUDED IN C. S. FORD'S STUDY OF SEX (349)	15 36 42 307 XSQ= 9.62 PHI= 0.155 XP = 0.0019
499	LEAN LESS TOWARD BEING THOSE 0.63 OF 57 NOT INCLUDED IN FORD AND BEACH'S SAMPLE ON SEXUAL EXPRESSICN BY THE YOUNG (314)	499	LEAN MORE TOWARD BEING THOSE 0.81 OF 343 NOT INCLUDED IN FORD AND BEACH'S SAMPLE ON SEXUAL EXPRESSION BY THE YOUNG (314)	21 65 36 278 XSQ= 8.24 PHI= 0.144 XP = 0.0041
500	LEAN LESS TOWARD BEING THOSE 0.77 OF 57 NOT INCLUDED IN FREEMAN ANC WINCH'S STUDY OF SOCIETAL COMPLEXITY (360)	500	LEAN MORE TOWARD BEING THOSE 0.92 OF 343 NOT INCLUDED IN FREEMAN AND WINCH'S STUDY OF SOCIETAL COMPLEXITY (360)	13 27 44 316 XSQ= 10.51 PHI= 0.162 XP = 0.0012
501	TEND LESS TO BE THCSE 0.67 OF 57 NOT INCLUDED IN JOAN FRIENCLY GOODMAN'S STUDY OF ASCETIC MOURNING BEHAVIOR (333)	501	TEND MORE TO BE THOSE 0.86 OF 343 NOT INCLUDED IN JOAN FRIENDLY GOODMAN'S STUDY OF ASCETIC MOURNING BEHAVIOR (333)	19 48 38 295 XSQ= 11.76 PHI= 0.171 XP = 0.0006
502	DRIFT LESS TOWARD BEING THOSE 0.77 OF 57 NOT INCLUDED IN JOHN K. HARLEY'S STUDY OF ADOLESCENT PEER GROUPS (343)	502	DRIFT MORE TOWARD BEING THOSE 0.87 OF 343 NOT INCLUDED IN JOHN K. HARLEY'S STUDY OF ADOLESCENT PEER GROUPS (343)	13 44 44 299 XSQ= 3.21 PHI= 0.090 XP = 0.0733

503	TEND LESS TO BE THCSE 0.63 OF 57 NOT INCLUDED IN JOHN M. HICKMAN'S STUDY OF THE FOLK-URBAN CCNTINUUM (346)	503	TEND MORE TO BE THOSE 0.90 OF 343 NOT INCLUDED IN JOHN M. HICKMAN'S STUDY OF THE FOLK-URBAN CONTINUUM (346)	21 33 36 310 XSQ= 28.73 PHI= 0.268 XP = 0.0000
504	TEND LESS TO BE THCSE 0.70 OF 57 NOT INCLUDED IN DONALC HORTON'S STUDY OF ALCHCLISM (351)	504	TEND MORE TO BE THOSE 0.91 CF 343 NOT INCLUDED IN DONALD HORTCN'S STUDY OF ALCHOLISM (351)	17 32 40 311 XSQ= 17.24 PHI= 0.208 XP = 0.0000
505	TEND LESS TO BE THCSE 0.84 OF 57 NOT INCLUDED IN MERRILL JACKSON'S STUDY OF CRIMINAL LAW AND MEDICINE (380)	505	TEND MORE TO BE THOSE 0.97 OF 343 NOT INCLUDED IN MERRILL JACKSON'S STUDY OF CRIMINAL LAW AND MEDICINE (380)	9 11 48 332 XSQ= 13.75 PHI= 0.185 XP = 0.0002
506	LEAN LESS TOWARD BEING THCSE 0.81 OF 57 NOT INCLUDED IN LAMBERT, TRIANDIS, AND WOLF'S STUDY OF SUPERNATURAL BEINCS (364)	506	LEAN MORE TOWARD BEING THOSE 0.93 OF 343 NOT INCLUDED IN LAMBERT, TRIANDIS, AND WOLF'S STUDY OF SUPERNATURAL BEINGS (364)	11 25 46 318 XSQ= 7.20 PHI= 0.134 XP = 0.0073
507	TEND TO BE THCSE 0.68 OF 57 INCLUDED IN JAMES R. LEARY'S STUDY OF FCOD TABOCS (86)	507	TEND TO BE THOSE 0.86 OF 343 NOT INCLUDED IN JAMES R. LEARY'S STUDY OF FOOD TABOOS (314)	39 47 18 296 XSQ= 83.50 PHI= 0.457 XP = 0.
508	TEND LESS TO BE THCSE 0.75 OF 57 NOT INCLUDED IN CAVID C. MCCLELLANC'S STUDY OF ACHIEVEMENT MOTIVATION (360)	508	TEND MORE TO BE THOSE 0.92 OF 343 NOT INCLUDED IN DAVID C. MCCLELLAND'S STUDY OF ACHIEVEMENT MOTIVATION (360)	14 26 43 317 XSQ= 13.83 PHI= 0.186 XP = 0.0002
510	TILT LESS TOWARD BEING THCSE 0.88 OF 57 NOT INCLUDED IN RACUL NARRCLL'S STUDY OF SCCIETAL COMPLEXITY (380)	510	TILT MORE TOWARD BEING THOSE 0.96 OF 343 NOT INCLUDED IN RAOUL NARRCLL'S STUDY OF SOCIETAL COMPLEXITY (380)	7 13 50 330 XSQ= 5.74 PHI= 0.120 XP = 0.0166
511	LEAN TOWARD BEING THCSE 0.67 OF 57 INCLUDED IN ROBERTS, ARTH ANC BUSH'S SAMPLE ON GAMES, AS MCDIFIED BY THE ETHNOGRAPHIC ATLAS (189)	511	LEAN TOWARD BEING THOSE 0.56 CF 343 NOT INCLUDED IN ROBERTS, ARTH AND BUSH'S SAMPLE ON GAMES, AS MODIFIED BY THE ETHNOGRAPHIC ATLAS (211)	38 151 19 192 XSQ= 9.17 PHI= 0.151 XP = 0.0025
512	TILT LESS TOWARD BEING THCSE 0.82 OF 57 NOT INCLUDED IN SHIRLEY ANC ROMNEY'S STUDY OF LCVE MAGIC (367)	512	TILT MORE TOWARD BEING THOSE 0.93 OF 343 NOT INCLUDED IN SHIRLEY AND ROMNEY'S STUDY OF LOVE MAGIC (367)	10 23 47 320 XSQ= 6.22 PHI= 0.125 XP = 0.0126

No.		No.		
513	LEAN LESS TOWARD BEING THOSE 0.77 OF 57 NOT INCLUDED IN LEO W. SIMMONS' STUDY OF THE TREATMENT OF THE AGED (357)	513	LEAN MORE TOWARD BEING THOSE 0.91 OF 343 NOT INCLUDED IN LEO W. SIMMONS' STUDY OF THE TREATMENT OF THE AGED (357)	13 30 44 313 XSQ= 8.66 PHI= 0.147 XP = 0.0033
514	TEND TO BE THOSE 0.53 OF 57 INCLUDED IN PHILIP E. SLATER'S STUDY OF NARCISSISM (90)	514	TEND TO BE THOSE 0.83 OF 343 NOT INCLUDED IN PHILIP E. SLATER'S STUDY OF NARCISSISM (310)	30 60 27 283 XSQ= 32.62 PHI= 0.286 XP = 0.
515	TEND LESS TO BE THOSE 0.68 OF 57 NOT INCLUDED IN WILLIAM N. STEPHENS' SAMPLE ON AVOIDANCE RELATIONSHIPS (348)	515	TEND MORE TO BE THOSE 0.90 OF 343 NOT INCLUDED IN WILLIAM N. STEPHENS' SAMPLE ON AVOIDANCE RELATIONSHIPS (348)	18 34 39 309 XSQ= 18.42 PHI= 0.215 XP = 0.0000
516	TILT MORE TOWARD BEING THOSE 0.95 OF 57 INCLUDED IN GUY E. SWANSON'S SAMPLE ON LOCAL JURISDICTION, AS MODIFIED BY THE ETHNOGRAPHIC ATLAS (331)	516	TILT LESS TOWARD BEING THOSE 0.81 OF 343 INCLUDED IN GUY E. SWANSON'S SAMPLE ON LOCAL JURISDICTION, AS MODIFIED BY THE ETHNOGRAPHIC ATLAS (331)	54 277 3 66 XSQ= 5.75 PHI= 0.120 XP = 0.0165
517	TEND MORE TO BE THOSE 0.88 OF 57 INCLUDED IN GUY E. SWANSON'S SAMPLE ON HIGH GODS, AS MODIFIED BY THE ETHNOGRAPHIC ATLAS (260)	517	TEND LESS TO BE THOSE 0.61 OF 343 INCLUDED IN GUY E. SWANSON'S SAMPLE ON HIGH GODS, AS MODIFIED BY THE ETHNOGRAPHIC ATLAS (260)	50 210 7 133 XSQ= 13.94 PHI= 0.187 XP = 0.0002
518	TEND TO BE THOSE 0.56 OF 57 INCLUDED IN STANLEY H. UDY, JR.'S STUDY OF WORK ORGANIZATION (105)	518	TEND TO BE THOSE 0.79 OF 343 NOT INCLUDED IN STANLEY H. UDY, JR.'S STUDY OF WORK ORGANIZATION (295)	32 73 25 270 XSQ= 28.90 PHI= 0.269 XP = 0.0000
519	TEND LESS TO BE THOSE 0.77 OF 57 NOT INCLUDED IN JOSEPH VEROFF'S STUDY OF ACHIEVEMENT MOTIVATION AS REVEALED IN FOLKTALES (364)	519	TEND MORE TO BE THOSE 0.93 OF 343 NOT INCLUDED IN JOSEPH VEROFF'S STUDY OF ACHIEVEMENT MOTIVATION AS REVEALED IN FOLKTALES (364)	13 23 44 320 XSQ= 13.57 PHI= 0.184 XP = 0.0002
520	TILT LESS TOWARD BEING THOSE 0.81 OF 57 NOT INCLUDED IN BEATRICE BLYTH WHITING'S STUDY OF SORCERY (360)	520	TILT MORE TOWARD BEING THOSE 0.92 OF 343 NOT INCLUDED IN BEATRICE BLYTH WHITING'S STUDY OF SORCERY (360)	11 29 46 314 XSQ= 5.24 PHI= 0.114 XP = 0.0221
522	LEAN LESS TOWARD BEING THOSE 0.65 OF 57 NOT INCLUDED IN MARJORIE GRANT WHITING'S STUDY OF DIET (318)	522	LEAN MORE TOWARD BEING THOSE 0.82 OF 343 NOT INCLUDED IN MARJORIE GRANT WHITING'S STUDY OF DIET (318)	20 62 37 281 XSQ= 7.67 PHI= 0.138 XP = 0.0056

489/

523	DRIFT LESS TOWARD BEING THOSE 0.75 OF 57 NOT INCLUDED IN WHITING AND CHILD'S STUDY OF CHILD TRAINING AND PERSONALITY (339)	523	DRIFT MORE TOWARD BEING THOSE 0.86 OF 343 NOT INCLUDED IN WHITING AND CHILD'S STUDY OF CHILD TRAINING AND PERSONALITY (339)	14 47 43 296 XSQ= 3.66 PHI= 0.096 XP = 0.0558

490 CULTURES
INCLUDED IN ALBERT S. ANTHONY'S
SAMPLE ON MALE INITIATION RITES (113)

490 CULTURES
NOT INCLUDED IN ALBERT S. ANTHONY'S
SAMPLE ON MALE INITIATION RITES (287)

BACKGROUND ON PAGE 180

SUBJECT ONLY, F.C. 1-480 AND 527-536
BOTH SUBJECT AND PREDICATE, F.C. 481-526

113 IN LEFT COLUMN

ALORESE	AMERICANS	ANDAMANESE	APINAYE	ARANDA	ARAPESH	ARAUCANIANS	ASHANTI	ATSUGEWI	AWEIKOMA
AYMARA	AZANDE	BALINESE	BARI	BATAK	BHUIYA	BUNLAP	CALLINAGO	CARIB	CAYAPA
CHENCHU	CHEROKEE	CHEYENNE	CHIR-APACHE	COCHITI	COMANCHE	COPR ESKIMO	CREEK	CROW	CUNA
DIERI	DOBUANS	DOROBO	EYAK	FON	FOX	GANDA	GOND	HAIDA	HANO
HAVASUPAI	HO	IFUGAO	ILA	INCA	INGASSANA	JUKUN	KARIERA	KASKA	KATAB
KERAKI	KERALA	KIOW-APACHE	KURTATCHI	KUTENAI	LAKHER	LAMBA	LANGO	LAU	LEPCHA
LESU	LHOTA NAGA	MANUS	MAORI	MARGI	MARICOPA	MARQUESANS	MARSHALLESE	MASAI	MATACO
MBUNDU	MENDE	MOTA	MURNGIN	NAMA	NAMBICUARA	NANDI	NAVAHO	NYORO	OJIBWA
ONA	ONTONG-JAVA	PAPAGO	PUKAPUKA	RIFFIANS	RWALA	SAMOANS	SANPOIL	SENIANG	SHERENTE
SHILLUK	SIRIONO	SWAZI	TALLENSI	TANALA	TAOS	TETON	THONGA	TIKOPIA	TIMBIRA
TOKELAU	TROBRIAND	TRUKESE	TUPINAMBA	VEDDA	VENDA	WAPISHANA	WINNEBAGO	WOGEO	YAGUA
YAO	YARURO	ZUNI							

287 IN RIGHT COLUMN

	Left column			Right column		
4	LEAN MORE TOWARD BEING THOSE LOCATED OUTSIDE OF THE CIRCUM-MEDITERRANEAN (355)	0.97 OF 113	4	LEAN LESS TOWARD BEING THOSE LOCATED OUTSIDE OF THE CIRCUM-MEDITERRANEAN (355)	0.85 OF 287	3 42 110 245 XSQ= 10.48 PHI= -0.162 XP = 0.0012
5	TILT MORE TOWARD BEING THOSE LOCATED OUTSIDE OF EAST EURASIA (330)	0.90 OF 113	5	TILT LESS TOWARD BEING THOSE LOCATED OUTSIDE OF EAST EURASIA (330)	0.79 OF 287	11 59 102 228 XSQ= 5.85 PHI= -0.121 XP = 0.0156
6	TILT LESS TOWARD BEING THOSE LOCATED OUTSIDE OF THE INSULAR PACIFIC (330)	0.74 OF 113	6	TILT MORE TOWARD BEING THOSE LOCATED OUTSIDE OF THE INSULAR PACIFIC (330)	0.86 OF 287	29 41 84 246 XSQ= 6.50 PHI= 0.128 XP = 0.0108
8	DRIFT LESS TOWARD BEING THOSE LOCATED OUTSIDE OF NORTH AMERICA (330)	0.77 OF 113	8	DRIFT MORE TOWARD BEING THOSE LOCATED OUTSIDE OF NORTH AMERICA (330)	0.85 OF 287	26 44 87 243 XSQ= 2.80 PHI= 0.084 XP = 0.0943

51	TILT LESS TOWARD BEING THOSE 0.54 OF 113 WHERE SUBSISTENCE IS PRIMARILY BY FOOD PRODUCTION -- I. E., AGRICULTURE OR HUSBANDRY -- RATHER THAN BY GATHERING (253)	51	TILT MORE TOWARD BEING THOSE 0.67 OF 287 WHERE SUBSISTENCE IS PRIMARILY BY FOOD PRODUCTION -- I. E., AGRICULTURE OR HUSBANDRY -- RATHER THAN BY GATHERING (253)	61 192 52 95 XSQ= 5.28 PHI= -0.115 XP = 0.0216
53	DRIFT MORE TOWARD BEING THOSE 0.71 OF 72 WHERE FOOD PRODUCTION IS BY SIMPLE AGRICULTURE OR INCIPIENT FOOD PRODUCTION, RATHER THAN BY INTENSIVE AGRICULTURE (147)	53	DRIFT LESS TOWARD BEING THOSE 0.58 OF 166 WHERE FOOD PRODUCTION IS BY SIMPLE AGRICULTURE OR INCIPIENT FOOD PRODUCTION, RATHER THAN BY INTENSIVE AGRICULTURE (147)	21 70 51 96 XSQ= 3.07 PHI= -0.113 XP = 0.0800
63	LEAN LESS TOWARD BEING THOSE 0.52 OF 67 WHERE HUSBANDRY, IF PRESENT, IS PRINCIPALLY IN THE FORM OF BOVINE, EQUINE, CAMEL-LIKE, OR DEER-LIKE ANIMALS, RATHER THAN PIGS, SHEEP, OR GOATS (152)	63	LEAN MORE TOWARD BEING THOSE 0.74 OF 159 WHERE HUSBANDRY, IF PRESENT, IS PRINCIPALLY IN THE FORM OF BOVINE, EQUINE, CAMEL-LIKE, OR DEER-LIKE ANIMALS, RATHER THAN PIGS, SHEEP, OR GOATS (152)	35 117 32 42 XSQ= 8.81 PHI= -0.197 XP = 0.0030
73	LEAN TOWARD BEING THOSE 0.66 OF 88 WHERE WEAVING IS ABSENT (130)	73	LEAN TOWARD BEING THOSE 0.55 OF 160 WHERE WEAVING IS PRESENT (118)	30 88 58 72 XSQ= 9.13 PHI= -0.192 XP = 0.0025
79	LEAN MORE TOWARD BEING THOSE 0.97 OF 79 WHERE NO CITY IS PRESENT (201)	79	LEAN LESS TOWARD BEING THOSE 0.86 OF 145 WHERE NO CITY IS PRESENT (201)	2 21 77 124 XSQ= 6.68 PHI= -0.173 XP = 0.0097
80	TILT MORE TOWARD BEING THOSE 0.91 OF 79 WHERE NO CITY OR TOWN IS PRESENT (185)	80	TILT LESS TOWARD BEING THOSE 0.78 OF 145 WHERE NO CITY OR TOWN IS PRESENT (185)	7 32 72 113 XSQ= 5.32 PHI= -0.154 XP = 0.0211
102	DRIFT TOWARD BEING THOSE 0.55 OF 111 WHERE CLASS STRATIFICATION IS ABSENT (180)	102	DRIFT TOWARD BEING THOSE 0.56 OF 272 WHERE CLASS STRATIFICATION IS PRESENT (203)	50 153 61 119 XSQ= 3.54 PHI= -0.096 XP = 0.0600
107	TILT MORE TOWARD BEING THOSE 0.92 OF 50 WHERE CLASS STRATIFICATION, IF PRESENT, IS BASED ON SOMETHING OTHER THAN OCCUPATIONAL STATUS (160)	107	TILT LESS TOWARD BEING THOSE 0.75 OF 153 WHERE CLASS STRATIFICATION, IF PRESENT, IS BASED ON SOMETHING OTHER THAN OCCUPATIONAL STATUS (160)	4 39 46 114 XSQ= 5.90 PHI= -0.170 XP = 0.0152
109	TILT MORE TOWARD BEING THOSE 0.94 OF 108 WHERE CASTES ARE ABSENT (317)	109	TILT LESS TOWARD BEING THOSE 0.83 OF 260 WHERE CASTES ARE ABSENT (317)	7 44 101 216 XSQ= 6.12 PHI= -0.129 XP = 0.0134

110	TILT MORE TOWARD BEING THOSE 0.67 OF 111 WHERE SLAVERY IS ABSENT (218)	110	TILT LESS TOWARD BEING THOSE 0.53 OF 270 WHERE SLAVERY IS ABSENT (218)	37 126 74 144 XSQ= 5.18 PHI= -0.117 XP = 0.0228
139	DRIFT LESS TOWARD BEING THOSE 0.53 OF 30 WHERE SUPERORDINATE PUNISHMENT IS ABSENT (25) BBW	139	DRIFT MORE TOWARD BEING THOSE 0.90 OF 10 WHERE SUPERORDINATE PUNISHMENT IS ABSENT (25) BBW	14 1 16 9 XSQ= 2.88 PHI= 0.268 EP = 0.0599
143	TILT TOWARD BEING THOSE 0.77 OF 26 WHERE THE RATIO OF RESTITUTIVE TO REPRESSIVE SANCTIONS IS MEDIUM OR LOW (32) WME	143	TILT TOWARD BEING THOSE 0.54 OF 26 WHERE THE RATIO OF RESTITUTIVE TO REPRESSIVE SANCTIONS IS HIGH (20) WME	6 14 20 12 XSQ= 3.98 PHI= -0.277 XP = 0.0460
144	DRIFT TOWARD BEING THOSE 0.62 OF 26 WHERE THE RATIO OF RESTITUTIVE TO REPRESSIVE SANCTIONS IS LOW (25) WME	144	DRIFT TOWARD BEING THOSE 0.65 OF 26 WHERE THE RATIO OF RESTITUTIVE TO REPRESSIVE SANCTIONS IS HIGH OR MEDIUM (27) WME	10 17 16 9 XSQ= 2.77 PHI= -0.231 XP = 0.0958
148	TILT TOWARD BEING THOSE 0.71 OF 28 WHERE THE INCIDENCE OF PERSONAL CRIME IS LOW (21) B-B-C	148	TILT TOWARD BEING THOSE 0.80 OF 5 WHERE THE INCIDENCE OF PERSONAL CRIME IS HIGH (12) B-B-C	8 4 20 1 XSQ= 2.88 PHI= -0.295 EP = 0.0471
183	LEAN LESS TOWARD BEING THOSE 0.77 OF 79 WHERE THE LARGEST NON-COGNATIC KIN GROUP IS SMALLER THAN A MOEITY, I. E., A PHRATRY OR SIB OR LINEAGE (218)	183	LEAN MORE TOWARD BEING THOSE 0.91 OF 173 WHERE THE LARGEST NON-COGNATIC KIN GROUP IS SMALLER THAN A MOEITY, I. E., A PHRATRY OR SIB OR LINEAGE (218)	18 16 61 157 XSQ= 7.39 PHI= 0.171 XP = 0.0065
185	DRIFT MORE TOWARD BEING THOSE 0.85 OF 79 WHERE THE LARGEST NON-COGNATIC KIN GROUP IS THE MOEITY OR PHRATRY OR SIB (194)	185	DRIFT LESS TOWARD BEING THOSE 0.73 OF 173 WHERE THE LARGEST NON-COGNATIC KIN GROUP IS THE MOEITY OR PHRATRY OR SIB (194)	67 127 12 46 XSQ= 3.36 PHI= 0.115 XP = 0.0668
187	TILT LESS TOWARD BEING THOSE 0.79 OF 113 WHERE THE KIN GROUP IS OTHER THAN EXCLUSIVELY MATRILINEAL (344)	187	TILT MORE TOWARD BEING THOSE 0.89 OF 286 WHERE THE KIN GROUP IS OTHER THAN EXCLUSIVELY MATRILINEAL (344)	24 31 89 255 XSQ= 6.52 PHI= 0.128 XP = 0.0107
188	DRIFT MORE TOWARD BEING THOSE 0.70 OF 113 WHERE THE KIN GROUP IS OTHER THAN EXCLUSIVELY COGNATIC (252)	188	DRIFT LESS TOWARD BEING THOSE 0.60 OF 287 WHERE THE KIN GROUP IS OTHER THAN EXCLUSIVELY COGNATIC (252)	34 114 79 173 XSQ= 2.83 PHI= -0.084 XP = 0.0927

190	TILT LESS TOWARD BEING THOSE 0.66 OF 76 WHERE THE KIN GROUP IS PATRILINEAL OR DOUBLE-DESCENT, RATHER THAN MATRILINEAL (186)	190	TILT MORE TOWARD BEING THOSE 0.80 OF 171 WHERE THE KIN GROUP IS PATRILINEAL OR DOUBLE-DESCENT, RATHER THAN MATRILINEAL (186)	50 136 26 35 XSQ= 4.63 PHI= -0.137 XP = 0.0314
192	DRIFT MORE TOWARD BEING THOSE 0.80 OF 113 OTHER THAN WHERE THE ONLY KIN GROUP PRESENT IS A KINDRED OR ELSE BILATERAL DESCENT IS INFERRED (289)	192	DRIFT LESS TOWARD BEING THOSE 0.69 OF 287 OTHER THAN WHERE THE ONLY KIN GROUP PRESENT IS A KINDRED OR ELSE BILATERAL DESCENT IS INFERRED (289)	23 88 90 199 XSQ= 3.80 PHI= -0.097 XP = 0.0513
209	DRIFT LESS TOWARD BEING THOSE 0.74 OF 94 WHERE MARITAL RESIDENCE IS PATRILOCAL, VIRILOCAL, OR AVUNCULOCAL, RATHER THAN MATRILOCAL OR UXORILOCAL (270)	209	DRIFT MORE TOWARD BEING THOSE 0.83 OF 240 WHERE MARITAL RESIDENCE IS PATRILOCAL, VIRILOCAL, OR AVUNCULOCAL, RATHER THAN MATRILOCAL OR UXORILOCAL (270)	70 200 24 40 XSQ= 2.88 PHI= -0.093 XP = 0.0898
210	TILT LESS TOWARD BEING THOSE 0.75 OF 60 WHERE MARITAL RESIDENCE IS PATRILOCAL, RATHER THAN MATRILOCAL (169)	210	TILT MORE TOWARD BEING THOSE 0.89 OF 140 WHERE MARITAL RESIDENCE IS PATRILOCAL, RATHER THAN MATRILOCAL (169)	45 124 15 16 XSQ= 4.92 PHI= -0.157 XP = 0.0266
214	DRIFT LESS TOWARD BEING THOSE 0.75 OF 48 WHERE FIRST COUSIN MARRIAGE, IF PERMITTED, IS OTHER THAN UNILATERAL (144)	214	DRIFT MORE TOWARD BEING THOSE 0.87 OF 124 WHERE FIRST COUSIN MARRIAGE, IF PERMITTED, IS OTHER THAN UNILATERAL (144)	12 16 36 108 XSQ= 2.88 PHI= 0.129 XP = 0.0896
234	TEND TO BE THOSE 0.63 OF 103 WHERE THE COUSIN TERMINOLOGY IS OF CROW, OMAHA, OR IROQUOIS TYPE, RATHER THAN ESKIMO OR HAWAIIAN TYPE (152)	234	TEND TO BE THOSE 0.60 OF 219 WHERE THE COUSIN TERMINOLOGY IS OF ESKIMO OR HAWAIIAN TYPE, RATHER THAN CROW, OMAHA, OR IROQUOIS TYPE (170)	65 87 38 132 XSQ= 14.44 PHI= 0.212 XP = 0.0001
240	TILT TOWARD BEING THOSE 0.50 OF 58 WHERE THE FAMILY, IF EXTENDED, IS LARGE, RATHER THAN SMALL OR STEM (78)	240	TILT TOWARD BEING THOSE 0.68 OF 155 WHERE THE FAMILY, IF EXTENDED, IS SMALL OR STEM, RATHER THAN LARGE (135)	29 49 29 106 XSQ= 5.38 PHI= 0.159 XP = 0.0204
280	TILT TOWARD BEING THOSE 0.71 OF 14 WHERE THE COMPOSITE FERTILITY LEVEL IS HIGH (13) MN	280	TILT TOWARD BEING THOSE 0.73 OF 11 WHERE THE COMPOSITE FERTILITY LEVEL IS LOW (12) MN	10 3 4 8 XSQ= 3.21 PHI= 0.358 EP = 0.0472
301	TILT LESS TOWARD BEING THOSE 0.67 OF 55 WHERE THE POST-PARTUM SEX TABOO LASTS LONGER THAN ONE MONTH (96)	301	TILT MORE TOWARD BEING THOSE 0.86 OF 69 WHERE THE POST-PARTUM SEX TABOO LASTS LONGER THAN ONE MONTH (96)	37 59 18 10 XSQ= 4.82 PHI= -0.197 XP = 0.0281

360	TILT TOWARD BEING THOSE 0.81 OF 21 WHERE ADOLESCENT PEER GROUPS ARE PRESENT CNLY IN A SETTING CF LEISURE, OR ELSE ARE ABSENT (23) JKH	360	TILT TOWARD BEING THOSE 0.63 OF 16 WHERE ADOLESCENT PEER GROUPS ARE PRESENT IN A SETTING OF WORK AND PUBLIC GATHERINGS AND LEISURE, OR AT LEAST OF PUBLIC GATHERINGS AND LEISURE (14) JKH	4 10 17 6 XSQ= 5.56 PHI= -0.388 EP = 0.0152
365	DRIFT LESS TOWARC BEING THOSE 0.57 OF 30 WHERE THE TIME SPENT IN ADOLESCENT PEER GRCUP ACTIVITY IS HIGH CR HIGH-MEDIUM (30) JKH	365	DRIFT MORE TOWARD BEING THCSE 0.87 OF 15 WHERE THE TIME SPENT IN ADOLESCENT PEER GROUP ACTIVITY IS HIGH OR HIGH-MEDIUM (30) JKH	17 13 13 2 XSQ= 2.81 PHI= -0.250 XP = 0.0935
370	LEAN TOWARD BEING THOSE 0.52 OF 90 WHERE THE SEGREGATION OF ADOLESCENT BOYS IS COMPLETE CR PARTIAL (95)	370	LEAN TOWARD BEING THOSE 0.69 OF 153 WHERE THE SEGREGATION OF ADCLESCENT BOYS IS ABSENT (148)	47 48 43 105 XSQ= 9.49 PHI= 0.198 XP = 0.0021
391	LEAN TOWARD BEING THOSE 0.66 OF 65 WHERE PREMARITAL SEX RELATIONS ARE PUNISHED CNLY IF PREGNANCY RESULTS, OR FREELY PERMITTED (90) JTW,EA	391	LEAN TOWARD BEING THOSE 0.59 OF 114 WHERE PREMARITAL SEX RELATIONS ARE STRONGLY PUNISHED AND IN FACT RARE, OR WEAKLY PUNISHED AND IN FACT NOT RARE (89) JTW,EA	22 67 43 47 XSQ= 9.32 PHI= -0.228 XP = 0.0023
399	TILT TOWARD BEING THOSE 0.58 OF 38 WHERE INTENSITY OF CASTRATION ANXIETY IS LCW (22) WNS	399	IN ALL CASES ARE THOSE 1.00 OF 7 WHERE INTENSITY OF CASTRATICN ANXIETY IS HIGH (23) WNS	16 7 22 0 XSQ= 5.78 PHI= -0.358 XP = 0.0162
400	TILT LESS TOWARD BEING THCSE 0.51 OF 41 WHERE HOMCSEXUAL ACTIVITY IS PERMITTED (36) F-B	400	TILT MORE TOWARD BEING THOSE 0.88 OF 17 WHERE HOMOSEXUAL ACTIVITY IS PERMITTED (36) F-B	20 2 21 15 XSQ= 5.51 PHI= 0.308 XP = 0.0189
426	TEND TO BE THOSE 0.54 OF 90 WHERE A HIGH GOD IS ABSENT (104) GES,EA	426	TEND TO BE THOSE 0.68 OF 170 WHERE A HIGH GOD IS PRESENT (156) GES,EA	41 115 49 55 XSQ= 11.06 PHI= -0.206 XP = 0.0009
427	TILT TOWARD BEING THOSE 0.61 OF 41 WHERE A HIGH GOD, IF PRESENT, IS INACTIVE, RATHER THAN ACTIVE (69) GES,EA	427	TILT TOWARD BEING THOSE 0.62 OF 115 WHERE A HIGH GOD, IF PRESENT, IS ACTIVE, RATHER THAN INACTIVE (87) GES,EA	16 71 25 44 XSQ= 5.43 PHI= -0.187 XP = 0.0197
449	TILT LESS TOWARD BEING THOSE 0.58 OF 43 WHERE THE CBSERVATION OF FCOD TABOOS IS MEDIUM CR LOW, RATHER THAN HIGH (61) JRL	449	TILT MORE TOWARD BEING THOSE 0.84 OF 43 WHERE THE OBSERVATION OF FCOD TABOOS IS MEDIUM OR LOW, RATHER THAN HIGH (61) JRL	18 7 25 36 XSQ= 5.64 PHI= 0.256 XP = 0.0176

450	LEAN MORE TOWARD BEING THOSE 0.86 OF 43 WHERE THE OBSERVATION OF FOOD TABOOS IS HIGH OR MEDIUM, RATHER THAN LOW (60) JRL	450	LEAN LESS TOWARD BEING THOSE 0.53 OF 43 WHERE THE OBSERVATION OF FOOD TABOOS IS HIGH OR MEDIUM, RATHER THAN LOW (60) JRL	37 23 6 20 XSQ= 9.32 PHI= 0.329 XP = 0.0023
468	LEAN TOWARD BEING THOSE 0.88 OF 26 WHERE CONTACT WITH OTHER CULTURES IS REGULAR OR IRREGULAR, RATHER THAN FREQUENT (37) JMH	468	LEAN TOWARD BEING THOSE 0.50 OF 28 WHERE CONTACT WITH OTHER CULTURES IS FREQUENT, RATHER THAN REGULAR OR IRREGULAR (17) JMH	3 14 23 14 XSQ= 7.55 PHI= -0.374 XP = 0.0060
473	LEAN TOWARD BEING THOSE 0.76 OF 58 WHERE SENSITIVITY TO INSULT IS MODERATE OR NEGLIGIBLE (56) PES	473	LEAN TOWARD BEING THOSE 0.60 OF 30 WHERE SENSITIVITY TO INSULT IS EXTREME (32) PES	14 18 44 12 XSQ= 9.49 PHI= -0.328 XP = 0.0021
482	TEND LESS TO BE THCSE 0.72 OF 112 WHERE THE PRINCIPAL ETHNOGRAPHERS HAVE BEEN OTHER THAN BRITISH (336)	482	TEND MORE TO BE THOSE 0.92 OF 276 WHERE THE PRINCIPAL ETHNOGRAPHERS HAVE BEEN OTHER THAN BRITISH (336)	31 21 81 255 XSQ= 25.95 PHI= 0.259 XP = 0.0000
483	LEAN LESS TOWARD BEING THOSE 0.54 OF 68 WHERE THE PRINCIPAL ETHNOGRAPHERS HAVE BEEN AMERICAN, RATHER THAN BRITISH (113)	483	LEAN MORE TOWARD BEING THOSE 0.78 OF 97 WHERE THE PRINCIPAL ETHNOGRAPHERS HAVE BEEN AMERICAN, RATHER THAN BRITISH (113)	37 76 31 21 XSQ= 9.53 PHI= -0.240 XP = 0.0020
488	TEND MORE TO BE THCSE 0.91 OF 79 ABOUT WHICH THE PRINCIPAL ETHNOGRAPHIES WERE PUBLISHED BEFCRE 1950 (185)	488	TEND LESS TO BE THOSE 0.63 OF 178 ABOUT WHICH THE PRINCIPAL ETHNOGRAPHIES WERE PUBLISHED BEFORE 1950 (185)	72 113 7 65 XSQ= 19.40 PHI= 0.275 XP = 0.0000
489	LEAN LESS TOWARD BEING THOSE 0.78 OF 113 NOT INCLUDED IN CHARLES ACKERMAN'S STUDY OF DIVORCE (343)	489	LEAN MORE TOWARD BEING THOSE 0.89 OF 287 NOT INCLUDED IN CHARLES ACKERMAN'S STUDY OF DIVORCE (343)	25 32 88 255 XSQ= 7.12 PHI= 0.133 XP = 0.0076
491	TEND LESS TO BE THCSE 0.66 OF 113 NOT INCLUDED IN DORRIAN APPLE'S STUDY OF GRANDPARENTHOOD (352)	491	TEND MORE TO BE THOSE 0.97 OF 287 NOT INCLUDED IN DORRIAN APPLE'S STUDY OF GRANDPARENTHOOD (352)	38 10 75 277 XSQ= 66.94 PHI= 0.409 XP = 0.
492	TEND LESS TO BE THCSE 0.72 OF 113 NOT INCLUDED IN BARBARA CHARTIER AYRES' STUDY OF FEMALE INITIATION RITES (361)	492	TEND MORE TO BE THOSE 0.98 OF 287 NOT INCLUDED IN BARBARA CHARTIER AYRES' STUDY OF FEMALE INITIATION RITES (361)	32 7 81 280 XSQ= 58.80 PHI= 0.383 XP = 0.

493	TEND LESS TO BE THCSE 0.50 OF 113 NCT INCLUDED IN BACCN, BARRY, AND CHILD'S STUDY OF CHILD REARING (322)	493	TEND MORE TO BE THOSE 0.92 OF 287 NOT INCLUDED IN BACON, BARRY, AND CHILD'S STUDY OF CHILD REARING (322)	56 22 57 265 XSQ= 87.99 PHI= 0.469 XP = 0.
494	TEND LESS TO BE THCSE 0.79 OF 113 NCT INCLUDED IN HERBERT M. BARRY III'S STUDY OF ART (371)	494	TEND MORE TO BE THOSE 0.98 OF 287 NOT INCLUDED IN HERBERT M. BARRY III'S STUDY OF ART (371)	24 5 89 282 XSQ= 42.98 PHI= 0.328 XP = 0.
495	TEND LESS TO BE THCSE 0.69 OF 113 NOT INCLUDED IN JUDITH K. BROWN'S STUDY OF FEMALE INITIATION RITES (335)	495	TEND MORE TO BE THOSE 0.90 OF 287 NOT INCLUDED IN JUDITH K. BROWN'S STUDY OF FEMALE INITIATION RITES (335)	35 30 78 257 XSQ= 23.60 PHI= 0.243 XP = 0.0000
496	TEND LESS TO BE THCSE 0.73 OF 113 NOT INCLUDED IN ROY G. D'ANDRADE'S STUDY OF DREAMS (345)	496	TEND MORE TO BE THOSE 0.91 OF 287 NOT INCLUDED IN ROY G. D'ANDRADE'S STUDY OF DREAMS (345)	30 25 83 262 XSQ= 20.28 PHI= 0.225 XP = 0.0000
497	TEND LESS TO BE THCSE 0.73 OF 113 NOT INCLUDED IN WILLIAM M. EVAN'S STUDY OF LAW (339)	497	TEND MORE TO BE THOSE 0.90 OF 287 NOT INCLUDED IN WILLIAM M. EVAN'S STUDY OF LAW (339)	31 30 82 257 XSQ= 16.80 PHI= 0.205 XP = 0.0000
498	TEND LESS TO BE THCSE 0.69 OF 113 NOT INCLUDED IN C. S. FORC'S STUDY OF SEX (349)	498	TEND MORE TO BE THOSE 0.94 OF 287 NOT INCLUDED IN C. S. FORD'S STUDY OF SEX (349)	35 16 78 271 XSQ= 44.76 PHI= 0.335 XP = 0.
499	TEND TO BE THOSE 0.52 OF 113 INCLUDED IN FORD AND BEACH'S SAMPLE ON SEXUAL EXPRESSICN BY THE YCUNG (86)	499	TEND TO BE THOSE 0.91 OF 287 NOT INCLUDED IN FORD AND BEACH'S SAMPLE ON SEXUAL EXPRESSION BY THE YOUNG (314)	59 27 54 260 XSQ= 85.50 PHI= 0.462 XP = 0.
500	TEND LESS TO BE THCSE 0.77 OF 113 NOT INCLUDED IN FREEMAN ANC WINCH'S STUDY OF SOCIETAL CCMPLEXITY (360)	500	TEND MORE TO BE THOSE 0.95 OF 287 NOT INCLUDED IN FREEMAN AND WINCH'S STUDY OF SOCIETAL COMPLEXITY (360)	26 14 87 273 XSQ= 27.63 PHI= 0.263 XP = 0.0000
501	TEND LESS TO BE THCSE 0.52 OF 113 NOT INCLUDED IN JOAN FRIENDLY GOOCMAN'S STUDY OF ASCETIC MCURNING BEHAVIOR (333)	501	TEND MORE TO BE THOSE 0.95 OF 287 NOT INCLUDED IN JOAN FRIENDLY GCODMAN'S STUDY OF ASCETIC MOURNING BEHAVIOR (333)	54 13 59 274 XSQ= 105.72 PHI= 0.514 XP = 0.

No.		No.		
502	TEND LESS TO BE THCSE 0.67 OF 113 NCT INCLUDED IN JOHN K. HARLEY'S STUDY OF ADOLESCENT PEER GROUPS (343)	502	TEND MORE TO BE THOSE 0.93 OF 287 NOT INCLUDED IN JOHN K. HARLEY'S STUDY OF ADOLESCENT PEER GROUPS (343)	37 20 76 267 XSQ= 42.00 PHI= 0.324 XP = 0.
503	TEND LESS TO BE THCSE 0.77 OF 113 NOT INCLUDED IN JOHN M. HICKMAN'S STUDY OF THE FOLK-URBAN CCNTINUUM (346)	503	TEND MORE TO BE THOSE 0.90 OF 287 NOT INCLUDED IN JOHN M. HICKMAN'S STUDY OF THE FOLK-URBAN CONTINUUM (346)	26 28 87 259 XSQ= 11.09 PHI= 0.166 XP = 0.0009
504	TEND LESS TO BE THCSE 0.75 OF 113 NOT INCLUDED IN DONALD HORTON'S STUDY OF ALCHOLISM (351)	504	TEND MORE TO BE THOSE 0.93 OF 287 NOT INCLUDED IN DONALD HORTON'S STUDY OF ALCHOLISM (351)	28 21 85 266 XSQ= 21.40 PHI= 0.231 XP = 0.0000
506	TEND LESS TO BE THCSE 0.71 OF 113 NOT INCLUDED IN LAMBERT, TRIANDIS, AND WOLF'S STUDY OF SUPERNATURAL BEINGS (364)	506	TEND MORE TO BE THOSE 0.99 OF 287 NOT INCLUDED IN LAMBERT, TRIANDIS, AND WOLF'S STUDY OF SUPERNATURAL BEINGS (364)	33 3 80 284 XSQ= 75.09 PHI= 0.433 XP = 0.
507	TEND LESS TO BE THCSE 0.62 OF 113 NOT INCLUDED IN JAMES R. LEARY'S STUDY OF FCOD TABOCS (314)	507	TEND MORE TO BE THOSE 0.85 OF 287 NOT INCLUDED IN JAMES R. LEARY'S STUDY OF FOOD TABOOS (314)	43 43 70 244 XSQ= 24.22 PHI= 0.246 XP = 0.0000
508	TEND LESS TO BE THCSE 0.76 OF 113 NOT INCLUDED IN DAVID C. MCCLELLAND'S STUDY OF ACHIEVEMENT MCTIVATION (360)	508	TEND MORE TO BE THOSE 0.95 OF 287 NOT INCLUDED IN DAVID C. MCCLELLAND'S STUDY OF ACHIEVEMENT MOTIVATION (360)	27 13 86 274 XSQ= 31.66 PHI= 0.281 XP = 0.
509	LEAN LESS TOWARD BEING THCSE 0.88 OF 113 NOT INCLUDED IN MONI NAG'S STUDY OF FERTILITY (375)	509	LEAN MORE TOWARD BEING THOSE 0.96 OF 287 NOT INCLUDED IN MONI NAG'S STUDY OF FERTILITY (375)	14 11 99 276 XSQ= 8.72 PHI= 0.148 XP = 0.0031
510	TEND LESS TO BE THCSE 0.88 OF 113 NOT INCLUDED IN RACUL NARRCLL'S STUDY CF SOCIETAL COMPLEXITY (380)	510	TEND MORE TO BE THOSE 0.98 OF 287 NOT INCLUDED IN RAOUL NARRCLL'S STUDY OF SOCIETAL COMPLEXITY (380)	13 7 100 280 XSQ= 12.18 PHI= 0.175 XP = 0.0005
511	TEND TO BE THCSE 0.71 OF 113 INCLUDED IN RCBERTS, ARTH AND BUSH'S SAMPLE ON GAMES, AS MODIFIED BY THE ETHNOGRAPHIC ATLAS (189)	511	TEND TO BE THOSE 0.62 OF 287 NOT INCLUDED IN ROBERTS, ARTH AND BUSH'S SAMPLE ON GAMES, AS MODIFIED BY THE ETHNOGRAPHIC ATLAS (211)	80 109 33 178 XSQ= 33.73 PHI= 0.290 XP = 0.

512	TEND LESS TO BE THCSE 0.76 OF 113 NOT INCLUDED IN SHIRLEY ANC ROMNEY'S STUDY OF LCVE MAGIC (367)	512	TEND MORE TO BE THOSE 0.98 OF 287 NOT INCLUDED IN SHIRLEY AND ROMNEY'S STUDY OF LOVE MAGIC (367)	27 6 86 281 XSQ= 48.08 PHI= 0.347 XP = 0.
513	TEND LESS TO BE THCSE 0.81 OF 113 NOT INCLUDED IN LEC W. SIMMONS' STUDY OF THE TREATMENT OF THE AGEC (357)	513	TEND MORE TO BE THOSE 0.93 OF 287 NOT INCLUDED IN LEO W. SIMMONS' STUDY OF THE TREATMENT OF THE AGED (357)	22 21 91 266 XSQ= 11.24 PHI= 0.168 XP = 0.0008
514	TEND TO BE THOSE 0.51 OF 113 INCLUDED IN PHILIP E. SLATER'S STUDY OF NARCISSISM (90)	514	TEND TO BE THOSE 0.89 OF 287 NOT INCLUDED IN PHILIP E. SLATER'S STUDY OF NARCISSISM (310)	58 32 55 255 XSQ= 72.77 PHI= 0.427 XP = 0.
515	TEND LESS TO BE THCSE 0.65 OF 113 NOT INCLUDED IN WILLIAM N. STEPHENS' SAMPLE CN AVCIDANCE RELATIONSHIPS (348)	515	TEND MORE TO BE THOSE 0.95 OF 287 NOT INCLUDED IN WILLIAM N. STEPHENS' SAMPLE ON AVOIDANCE RELATICNSHIPS (348)	39 13 74 274 XSQ= 61.82 PHI= 0.393 XP = 0.
516	LEAN MORE TOWARC BEING THOSE 0.93 OF 113 INCLUDED IN GUY E. SWANSON'S SAMPLE ON LOCAL JURISCICTION, AS MODIFIED BY THE ETHNOGRAPHIC ATLAS (331)	516	LEAN LESS TOWARD BEING THCSE 0.79 OF 287 INCLUDED IN GUY E. SWANSON'S SAMPLE ON LOCAL JURISDICTICN, AS MODIFIED BY THE ETHNOGRAPHIC ATLAS (331)	105 226 8 61 XSQ= 10.44 PHI= 0.162 XP = 0.0012
517	TEND MORE TO BE THCSE 0.80 OF 113 INCLUDED IN GUY E. SWANSON'S SAMPLE CN HIGH GODS, AS MCDIFIED BY THE ETHNOGRAPHIC ATLAS (260)	517	TEND LESS TO BE THOSE 0.59 OF 287 INCLUDED IN GUY E. SWANSON'S SAMPLE ON HIGH GODS, AS MODIFIED BY THE ETHNOGRAPHIC ATLAS (260)	90 170 23 117 XSQ= 13.97 PHI= 0.187 XP = 0.0002
518	TEND LESS TO BE THCSE 0.54 OF 113 NOT INCLUDED IN STANLEY H. UDY, JR.'S STUDY OF WCRK ORGANIZATION (295)	518	TEND MORE TO BE THOSE 0.82 OF 287 NOT INCLUDED IN STANLEY H. UDY, JR.'S STUDY OF WORK ORGANIZATION (295)	52 53 61 234 XSQ= 30.38 PHI= 0.276 XP = 0.
519	TEND LESS TO BE THCSE 0.79 OF 113 NOT INCLUDED IN JOSEPH VERCFF'S STUDY CF ACHIEVEMENT MOTIVATION AS REVEALED IN FCLKTALES (364)	519	TEND MORE TO BE THOSE 0.96 OF 287 NOT INCLUDED IN JOSEPH VEROFF'S STUDY OF ACHIEVEMENT MOTIVATION AS REVEALED IN FOLKTALES (364)	24 12 89 275 XSQ= 26.76 PHI= 0.259 XP = 0.0000
520	TEND LESS TO BE THCSE 0.73 OF 113 NOT INCLUDED IN BEATRICE BLYTH WHITING'S STUDY OF SCRCERY (360)	520	TEND MORE TC BE THOSE 0.97 CF 287 NOT INCLUDED IN BEATRICE BLYTH WHITING'S STUDY OF SORCERY (360)	30 10 83 277 XSQ= 45.39 PHI= 0.337 XP = 0.

```
522  TEND TO BE THOSE                  0.50 OF 113     522  TEND TO BE THOSE                  0.91 OF 287          57   25
     INCLUDED IN                                            NOT INCLUDED IN                                          56  262
     MARJCRIE GRANT WHITING'S                               MARJORIE GRANT WHITING'S                           XSQ=   84.10
     STUDY OF DIET  (82)                                    STUDY OF DIET  (318)                               PHI=   0.459
                                                                                                               XP =  0.

523  TEND LESS TO BE THCSE             0.58 OF 113     523  TEND MORE TO BE THOSE             0.95 OF 287          47   14
     NCT INCLUDED IN WHITING AND CHILD'S                    NOT INCLUDED IN WHITING AND CHILD'S                      66  273
     STUDY OF CHILD TRAINING                                STUDY OF CHILD TRAINING                            XSQ=   81.75
     AND PERSONALITY  (339)                                 AND PERSONALITY  (339)                             PHI=   0.452
                                                                                                               XP =  0.

524  TEND LESS TO BE THCSE             0.73 OF 113     524  TEND MORE TO BE THOSE             0.95 OF 287          30   14
     NOT INCLUDED IN                                        NOT INCLUDED IN                                          83  273
     WHITING, KLUCKHCHN, ANC ANTHONY'S                      WHITING, KLUCKHOHN, AND ANTHONY'S                  XSQ=   36.71
     STUDY OF MALE INITIATICN CEREMONIES  (356)             STUDY OF MALE INITIATION CEREMONIES  (356)         PHI=   0.303
                                                                                                               XP =  0.
```

491 CULTURES INCLUDED IN DORRIAN APPLE'S STUDY OF GRANDPARENTHOOD (48)

491 CULTURES NOT INCLUDED IN DORRIAN APPLE'S STUDY OF GRANDPARENTHOOD (352)

BACKGROUND ON PAGE 180

SUBJECT ONLY, F.C. 1-480 AND 527-536
BOTH SUBJECT AND PREDICATE, F.C. 481-526

48 IN LEFT COLUMN

ARAPESH	ASHANTI	ATSUGEWI	AZANDE	BHUIYA	BURMESE	CHEROKEE	CHEYENNE	CHIR-APACHE	COMANCHE
DILLING	FON	FOX	HAIDA	HANO	HEHE	JUKUN	KASKA	KATAB	KIOW-APACHE
KOREANS	KURTATCHI	LAKHER	LESU	LOZI	MANUS	MARSHALLESE	MURNGIN	NAMA	NAVAHO
NYAKYUSA	OJIBWA	ONTONG-JAVA	PAPAGO	SANPOIL	SARAMACCA	SEMINOLE	SHILLUK	SWAZI	TALLENSI
TANALA	TARAHUMARA	THONGA	TIKOPIA	TIMBIRA	TRUKESE	VENDA	WOLEAIANS		

352 IN RIGHT COLUMN

No.	Left column (48)	Proportion	No.	Right column (352)	Proportion	Statistics
3	DRIFT LESS TOWARD BEING THOSE LOCATED OUTSIDE OF AFRICA (320)	0.69 OF 48	3	DRIFT MORE TOWARD BEING THOSE LOCATED OUTSIDE OF AFRICA (320)	0.82 OF 352	15 65 33 287 XSQ= 3.55 PHI= 0.094 XP = 0.0595
4	IN ALL CASES ARE THOSE LOCATED OUTSIDE OF THE CIRCUM-MEDITERRANEAN (355)	1.00 OF 48	4	TILT LESS TOWARD BEING THOSE LOCATED OUTSIDE OF THE CIRCUM-MEDITERRANEAN (355)	0.87 OF 352	0 45 48 307 XSQ= 5.69 PHI= -0.119 XP = 0.0170
8	LEAN LESS TOWARD BEING THOSE LOCATED OUTSIDE OF NORTH AMERICA (330)	0.67 OF 48	8	LEAN MORE TOWARD BEING THOSE LOCATED OUTSIDE OF NORTH AMERICA (330)	0.85 OF 352	16 54 32 298 XSQ= 8.27 PHI= 0.144 XP = 0.0040
9	TILT MORE TOWARD BEING THOSE LOCATED OUTSIDE OF SOUTH AMERICA (335)	0.96 OF 48	9	TILT LESS TOWARD BEING THOSE LOCATED OUTSIDE OF SOUTH AMERICA (335)	0.82 OF 352	2 63 46 289 XSQ= 4.89 PHI= -0.111 XP = 0.0271
82	DRIFT MORE TOWARD BEING THOSE WHERE A CITY OR TOWN IS PRESENT, OR THE AVERAGE COMMUNITY SIZE IS FIFTY OR GREATER (178)	0.93 OF 29	82	DRIFT LESS TOWARD BEING THOSE WHERE A CITY OR TOWN IS PRESENT, OR THE AVERAGE COMMUNITY SIZE IS FIFTY OR GREATER (178)	0.77 OF 195	27 151 2 44 XSQ= 2.90 PHI= 0.114 XP = 0.0887

108	LEAN TOWARD BEING THOSE WHERE CLASS STRATIFICATION, IF PRESENT, IS BASED ON A HEREDITARY ARISTOCRACY (74)	0.63 OF 24	108	LEAN TOWARD BEING THOSE WHERE CLASS STRATIFICATION, IF PRESENT, IS BASED ON SOMETHING OTHER THAN A HEREDITARY ARISTOCRACY (129)	0.67 OF 179	15 59 9 120 XSQ= 6.75 PHI= 0.182 XP = 0.0094
109	TILT MORE TOWARD BEING THOSE WHERE CASTES ARE ABSENT (317)	0.98 OF 46	109	TILT LESS TOWARD BEING THOSE WHERE CASTES ARE ABSENT (317)	0.84 OF 322	1 50 45 272 XSQ= 4.95 PHI= -0.116 XP = 0.0262
139	DRIFT TOWARD BEING THOSE WHERE SUPERORDINATE PUNISHMENT IS PRESENT (15) BBW	0.64 OF 11	139	DRIFT TOWARD BEING THOSE WHERE SUPERORDINATE PUNISHMENT IS ABSENT (25) BBW	0.72 OF 29	7 8 4 21 XSQ= 3.02 PHI= 0.275 EP = 0.0654
142	DRIFT MORE TOWARD BEING THOSE WHERE THE LEVEL OF SOCIAL SANCTION IS PUBLIC CORPOREAL SANCTION OR PUBLIC PROPERTY SANCTION, RATHER THAN PRIVATE SETTLEMENT (38) JMH	0.93 OF 14	142	DRIFT LESS TOWARD BEING THOSE WHERE THE LEVEL OF SOCIAL SANCTION IS PUBLIC CORPOREAL SANCTION OR PUBLIC PROPERTY SANCTION, RATHER THAN PRIVATE SETTLEMENT (38) JMH	0.63 OF 40	13 25 1 15 XSQ= 3.24 PHI= 0.245 XP = 0.0717
144	DRIFT TOWARD BEING THOSE WHERE THE RATIO OF RESTITUTIVE TO REPRESSIVE SANCTIONS IS LOW (25) WME	0.75 OF 12	144	DRIFT TOWARD BEING THOSE WHERE THE RATIO OF RESTITUTIVE TO REPRESSIVE SANCTIONS IS HIGH OR MEDIUM (27) WME	0.60 OF 40	3 24 9 16 XSQ= 3.24 PHI= -0.249 XP = 0.0720
178	DRIFT LESS TOWARD BEING THOSE WHERE THE COMMUNITY IS OTHER THAN SEGMENTED ON A CLAN BASIS AND NON-EXOGAMOUS (295)	0.67 OF 48	178	DRIFT MORE TOWARD BEING THOSE WHERE THE COMMUNITY IS OTHER THAN SEGMENTED ON A CLAN BASIS AND NON-EXOGAMOUS (295)	0.79 OF 334	16 71 32 263 XSQ= 2.83 PHI= 0.086 XP = 0.0927
188	DRIFT MORE TOWARD BEING THOSE WHERE THE KIN GROUP IS OTHER THAN EXCLUSIVELY COGNATIC (252)	0.75 OF 48	188	DRIFT LESS TOWARD BEING THOSE WHERE THE KIN GROUP IS OTHER THAN EXCLUSIVELY COGNATIC (252)	0.61 OF 352	12 136 36 216 XSQ= 2.81 PHI= -0.084 XP = 0.0937
190	DRIFT LESS TOWARD BEING THOSE WHERE THE KIN GROUP IS PATRILINEAL OR DOUBLE-DESCENT, RATHER THAN MATRILINEAL (186)	0.62 OF 34	190	DRIFT MORE TOWARD BEING THOSE WHERE THE KIN GROUP IS PATRILINEAL OR DOUBLE-DESCENT, RATHER THAN MATRILINEAL (186)	0.77 OF 213	21 165 13 48 XSQ= 3.09 PHI= -0.112 XP = 0.0789
192	DRIFT MORE TOWARD BEING THOSE OTHER THAN WHERE THE ONLY KIN GROUP PRESENT IS A KINDRED OR ELSE BILATERAL DESCENT IS INFERRED (289)	0.83 OF 48	192	DRIFT LESS TOWARD BEING THOSE OTHER THAN WHERE THE ONLY KIN GROUP PRESENT IS A KINDRED OR ELSE BILATERAL DESCENT IS INFERRED (289)	0.71 OF 352	8 103 40 249 XSQ= 2.74 PHI= -0.083 XP = 0.0977

209	TILT LESS TOWARD BEING THCSE WHERE MARITAL RESICENCE IS PATRILCCAL, VIRILOCAL, OR AVUNCULOCAL, RATHER THAN MATRILOCAL OR UXCRILOCAL (270)	0.67 OF 40	209	TILT MORE TOWARD BEING THOSE WHERE MARITAL RESIDENCE IS PATRILOCAL, VIRILOCAL, OR AVUNCULOCAL, RATHER THAN MATRILOCAL OR UXORILOCAL (270)	0.83 OF 294	27 243 13 51 XSQ= 4.29 PHI= -0.113 XP = 0.0384
210	TILT LESS TOWARD BEING THOSE WHERE MARITAL RESIDENCE IS PATRILOCAL, RATHER THAN MATRILOCAL (169)	0.69 OF 26	210	TILT MORE TOWARD BEING THOSE WHERE MARITAL RESIDENCE IS PATRILOCAL, RATHER THAN MATRILOCAL (169)	0.87 OF 174	18 151 8 23 XSQ= 4.06 PHI= -0.143 XP = 0.0438
277	IN ALL CASES ARE THOSE WHERE THE STATUS OF WOMEN IS NOT STRONGLY INFERICR OR SUBJECTED (22) LWS	1.00 OF 6	277	DRIFT LESS TOWARD BEING THCSE WHERE THE STATUS OF WOMEN IS NOT STRONGLY INFERIOR OR SUBJECTED (22) LWS	0.53 OF 30	0 14 6 16 XSQ= 2.83 PHI= -0.280 EP = 0.0625
280	TILT TOWARD BEING THCSE WHERE THE COMPOSITE FERTILITY LEVEL IS HIGH (13) MN	0.88 OF 8	280	TILT TOWARD BEING THOSE WHERE THE COMPOSITE FERTILITY LEVEL IS LOW (12) MN	0.65 OF 17	7 6 1 11 XSQ= 4.03 PHI= 0.402 EP = 0.0302
286	DRIFT TCWARD BEING THOSE WHERE THE NUMBER OF FCCC TABOOS DURING PREGNANCY IS LCW OR ABSENT (14) BCA	0.59 OF 17	286	DRIFT TOWARD BEING THOSE WHERE THE NUMBER OF FOOD TABOOS DURING PREGNANCY IS HIGH (20) BCA	0.76 OF 17	7 13 10 4 XSQ= 3.04 PHI= -0.299 EP = 0.0799
304	TILT TOWARD BEING THCSE WHERE THE EARLY ANAL SATISFACTION POTENTIAL IS LOW (22) W-C	0.74 OF 19	304	TILT TOWARD BEING THOSE WHERE THE EARLY ANAL SATISFACTION POTENTIAL IS HIGH (19) W-C	0.64 OF 22	5 14 14 8 XSQ= 4.31 PHI= -0.324 XP = 0.0379
310	TILT TOWARD BEING THOSE WHERE ANAL SOCIALIZATION ANXIETY IS HIGH (22) W-C	0.74 OF 19	310	TILT TOWARD BEING THOSE WHERE ANAL SOCIALIZATION ANXIETY IS LOW (19) W-C	0.64 OF 22	14 8 5 14 XSQ= 4.31 PHI= 0.324 XP = 0.0379
314	TILT LESS TOWARC BEING THOSE WHERE THE INCIDENCE OF MOTHER-CHILC HOUSEHOLDS IS LCW (61) W-C,S	0.60 OF 25	314	TILT MORE TOWARD BEING THOSE WHERE THE INCIDENCE OF MOTHER-CHILD HOUSEHOLDS IS LOW (61) W-D,S	0.84 OF 55	10 9 15 46 XSQ= 4.08 PHI= 0.226 XP = 0.0435
332	DRIFT TOWARD BEING THCSE WHERE THE AGE AT BEGINNING OF MODESTY TRAINING IS LOWER THAN SIX YEARS (8) W-C	0.75 OF 8	332	DRIFT TOWARD BEING THOSE WHERE THE AGE AT BEGINNING OF MODESTY TRAINING IS SIX YEARS OR HIGHER (9) W-C	0.78 OF 9	2 7 6 2 XSQ= 2.85 PHI= -0.410 EP = 0.0567

370	TILT TOWARD BEING THOSE 0.57 OF 37 WHERE THE SEGREGATION CF ACOLESCENT BOYS IS COMPLETE OR PARTIAL (95)	370	TILT TOWARD BEING THOSE 0.64 OF 206 WHERE THE SEGREGATION OF ADCLESCENT BOYS IS ABSENT (148)	21 74 16 132 XSQ= 4.88 PHI= 0.142 XP = 0.0272
380	TILT MORE TOWARD BEING THOSE 0.88 OF 16 WHERE SEGREGATICN CF GIRLS AT MENARCHE IS PRESENT (35) F-B	380	TILT LESS TOWARD BEING THOSE 0.54 OF 39 WHERE SEGREGATION OF GIRLS AT MENARCHE IS PRESENT (35) F-B	14 21 2 18 XSQ= 4.19 PHI= 0.276 XP = 0.0406
398	DRIFT TOWARD BEING THOSE 0.69 OF 16 WHERE THE INTENSITY OF SEX ANXIETY IS HIGH (16) WNS	398	DRIFT TOWARD BEING THOSE 0.69 OF 16 WHERE THE INTENSITY OF SEX ANXIETY IS LOW (16) WNS	11 5 5 11 XSQ= 3.13 PHI= 0.312 EP = 0.0756
426	TILT TOWARD BEING THOSE 0.59 OF 37 WHERE A HIGH GOD IS ABSENT (104) GES,EA	426	TILT TOWARD BEING THOSE 0.63 OF 223 WHERE A HIGH GOD IS PRESENT (156) GES,EA	15 141 22 82 XSQ= 5.89 PHI= -0.151 XP = 0.0152
445	DRIFT TOWARD BEING THOSE 0.82 OF 11 WHERE SORCERY IS IMPORTANT (26) BBW,DH	445	DRIFT TOWARD BEING THOSE 0.55 OF 38 WHERE SORCERY IS UNIMPORTANT (23) BBW,DH	9 17 2 21 XSQ= 3.34 PHI= 0.261 XP = 0.0677
449	TEND TO BE THOSE 0.69 OF 16 WHERE THE OBSERVATION OF FCOD TABOOS IS HIGH, RATHER THAN MEDIUM OR LOW (25) JRL	449	TEND TO BE THOSE 0.80 OF 70 WHERE THE OBSERVATION OF FOOD TABOOS IS MEDIUM OR LOW, RATHER THAN HIGH (61) JRL	11 14 5 56 XSQ= 12.74 PHI= 0.385 XP = 0.0004
454	DRIFT TOWARD BEING THOSE 0.71 OF 14 WHERE THE CBJECTIVE OF THE INCIVICUAL'S CONTACT WITH THE DIVINE IS NOT CONDUCIVE TC THE DEVELOPMENT OF THE INDIVIDUAL'S NEED TO ACHIEVE (18) DCM	454	DRIFT TOWARD BEING THOSE 0.64 OF 22 WHERE THE OBJECTIVE OF THE INDIVIDUAL'S CONTACT WITH THE DIVINE IS CONDUCIVE TO THE DEVELOPMENT OF THE INDIVIDUAL'S NEED TO ACHIEVE (18) DCM	4 14 10 8 XSQ= 2.92 PHI= -0.285 EP = 0.0858
460	DRIFT MORE TOWARD BEING THOSE 0.77 OF 31 WHERE GAMES, IF PRESENT, ARE NCT LIMITED TO GAMES OF SKILL CNLY (104) R-A-B,EA	460	DRIFT LESS TOWARD BEING THOSE 0.57 OF 140 WHERE GAMES, IF PRESENT, ARE NOT LIMITED TO GAMES OF SKILL ONLY (104) R-A-B,EA	7 60 24 80 XSQ= 3.57 PHI= -0.144 XP = 0.0589
475	DRIFT TOWARD BEING THOSE 0.71 OF 28 WHERE EXHIBITIONISTIC DANCING IS STRONGLY OR MODERATELY EMPHASIZED (48) PES	475	DRIFT TOWARD BEING THOSE 0.52 OF 58 WHERE EXHIBITIONISTIC DANCING IS NEGLIGIBLY EMPHASIZED (38) PES	20 28 8 30 XSQ= 3.22 PHI= 0.193 XP = 0.0728

481	LEAN LESS TOWARD BEING THOSE 0.51 OF 47 WHERE THE PRINCIPAL ETHNOGRAPHERS HAVE BEEN OTHER THAN AMERICAN (275)	481	LEAN MORE TOWARD BEING THOSE 0.74 OF 341 WHERE THE PRINCIPAL ETHNOGRAPHERS HAVE BEEN OTHER THAN AMERICAN (275)	23 90 24 251 XSQ= 9.11 PHI= 0.153 XP = 0.0025
488	DRIFT MORE TOWARD BEING THOSE 0.85 OF 34 ABOUT WHICH THE PRINCIPAL ETHNOGRAPHIES WERE PUBLISHED BEFORE 1950 (185)	488	DRIFT LESS TOWARD BEING THOSE 0.70 OF 223 ABOUT WHICH THE PRINCIPAL ETHNOGRAPHIES WERE PUBLISHED BEFORE 1950 (185)	29 156 5 67 XSQ= 2.72 PHI= 0.103 XP = 0.0989
490	TEND TO BE THOSE 0.79 OF 48 INCLUDED IN ALBERT S. ANTHONY'S SAMPLE ON MALE INITIATION RITES (113)	490	TEND TO BE THOSE 0.79 OF 352 NOT INCLUDED IN ALBERT S. ANTHONY'S SAMPLE ON MALE INITIATION RITES (287)	38 75 10 277 XSQ= 66.94 PHI= 0.409 XP = 0.
492	TEND LESS TO BE THOSE 0.63 OF 48 NOT INCLUDED IN BARBARA CHARTIER AYRES' STUDY OF FEMALE INITIATION RITES (361)	492	TEND MORE TO BE THOSE 0.94 OF 352 NOT INCLUDED IN BARBARA CHARTIER AYRES' STUDY OF FEMALE INITIATION RITES (361)	18 21 30 331 XSQ= 44.22 PHI= 0.332 XP = 0.
493	TEND TO BE THOSE 0.58 OF 48 INCLUDED IN BACON, BARRY, AND CHILD'S STUDY OF CHILD REARING (78)	493	TEND TO BE THOSE 0.86 OF 352 NOT INCLUDED IN BACON, BARRY, AND CHILD'S STUDY OF CHILD REARING (322)	28 50 20 302 XSQ= 49.63 PHI= 0.352 XP = 0.
494	TEND LESS TO BE THOSE 0.77 OF 48 NOT INCLUDED IN HERBERT M. BARRY III'S STUDY OF ART (371)	494	TEND MORE TO BE THOSE 0.95 OF 352 NOT INCLUDED IN HERBERT M. BARRY III'S STUDY OF ART (371)	11 18 37 334 XSQ= 17.35 PHI= 0.208 XP = 0.0000
495	TEND LESS TO BE THOSE 0.63 OF 48 NOT INCLUDED IN JUDITH K. BROWN'S STUDY OF FEMALE INITIATION RITES (335)	495	TEND MORE TO BE THOSE 0.87 OF 352 NOT INCLUDED IN JUDITH K. BROWN'S STUDY OF FEMALE INITIATION RITES (335)	18 47 30 305 XSQ= 16.37 PHI= 0.202 XP = 0.0001
496	LEAN LESS TOWARD BEING THOSE 0.73 OF 48 NOT INCLUDED IN ROY G. D'ANDRADE'S STUDY OF DREAMS (345)	496	LEAN MORE TOWARD BEING THOSE 0.88 OF 352 NOT INCLUDED IN ROY G. D'ANDRADE'S STUDY OF DREAMS (345)	13 42 35 310 XSQ= 6.95 PHI= 0.132 XP = 0.0084
497	LEAN LESS TOWARD BEING THOSE 0.69 OF 48 NOT INCLUDED IN WILLIAM M. EVAN'S STUDY OF LAW (339)	497	LEAN MORE TOWARD BEING THOSE 0.87 OF 352 NOT INCLUDED IN WILLIAM M. EVAN'S STUDY OF LAW (339)	15 46 33 306 XSQ= 9.44 PHI= 0.154 XP = 0.0021

498	TEND LESS TO BE THCSE 0.71 OF 48 NOT INCLUDED IN C. S. FORC'S STUDY OF SEX (349)	498	TEND MORE TO BE THOSE 0.89 OF 352 NOT INCLUDED IN C. S. FORD'S STUDY OF SEX (349)	14 37 34 315 XSQ= 11.59 PHI= 0.170 XP = 0.0007
499	TEND LESS TO BE THCSE 0.52 OF 48 NOT INCLUDED IN FORD AND BEACH'S SAMPLE ON SEXUAL EXPRESSICN BY THE YOUNG (314)	499	TEND MORE TO BE THOSE 0.82 OF 352 NOT INCLUDED IN FORD AND BEACH'S SAMPLE ON SEXUAL EXPRESSION BY THE YOUNG (314)	23 63 25 289 XSQ= 20.81 PHI= 0.228 XP = 0.0000
500	TEND LESS TO BE THCSE 0.75 OF 48 NOT INCLUDED IN FREEMAN ANC WINCH'S STUDY OF SCCIETAL CCMPLEXITY (360)	500	TEND MORE TO BE THOSE 0.92 OF 352 NOT INCLUDED IN FREEMAN AND WINCH'S STUDY OF SOCIETAL COMPLEXITY (360)	12 28 36 324 XSQ= 11.81 PHI= 0.172 XP = 0.0006
501	TEND LESS TO BE THCSE 0.60 OF 48 NOT INCLUDED IN JOAN FRIENDLY GOODMAN'S STUDY OF ASCETIC MCURNING BEHAVIOR (333)	501	TEND MORE TO BE THOSE 0.86 OF 352 NOT INCLUDED IN JOAN FRIENDLY GOODMAN'S STUDY OF ASCETIC MOURNING BEHAVIOR (333)	19 48 29 304 XSQ= 18.58 PHI= 0.215 XP = 0.0000
502	TEND LESS TO BE THCSE 0.63 OF 48 NOT INCLUDED IN JOHN K. HARLEY'S STUDY OF ADOLESCENT PEER GROUPS (343)	502	TEND MORE TO BE THOSE 0.89 OF 352 NOT INCLUDED IN JOHN K. HARLEY'S STUDY OF ADOLESCENT PEER GROUPS (343)	18 39 30 313 XSQ= 22.02 PHI= 0.235 XP = 0.0000
503	LEAN LESS TOWARD BEING THCSE 0.71 OF 48 NOT INCLUDED IN JOHN M. HICKMAN'S STUDY OF THE FOLK-URBAN CCNTINUUM (346)	503	LEAN MORE TOWARD BEING THOSE 0.89 OF 352 NOT INCLUDED IN JOHN M. HICKMAN'S STUDY OF THE FOLK-URBAN CONTINUUM (346)	14 40 34 312 XSQ= 9.99 PHI= 0.158 XP = 0.0016
504	TILT LESS TOWARD BEING THOSE 0.77 OF 48 NOT INCLUDED IN DONALD HORTON'S STUDY OF ALCHOLISM (351)	504	TILT MORE TOWARD BEING THOSE 0.89 OF 352 NOT INCLUDED IN DONALD HORTON'S STUDY OF ALCHOLISM (351)	11 38 37 314 XSQ= 4.70 PHI= 0.108 XP = 0.0301
506	TEND LESS TO BE THCSE 0.63 OF 48 NOT INCLUDED IN LAMBERT, TRIANDIS, AND WOLF'S STUDY OF SUPERNATURAL BEINGS (364)	506	TEND MORE TO BE THOSE 0.95 OF 352 NOT INCLUDED IN LAMBERT, TRIANDIS, AND WOLF'S STUDY OF SUPERNATURAL BEINGS (364)	18 18 30 334 XSQ= 50.21 PHI= 0.354 XP = 0.
507	DRIFT LESS TOWARD BEING THOSE 0.67 OF 48 NOT INCLUDED IN JAMES R. LEARY'S STUDY OF FCOD TABOCS (314)	507	DRIFT MORE TOWARD BEING THOSE 0.80 OF 352 NOT INCLUDED IN JAMES R. LEARY'S STUDY OF FOOD TABOOS (314)	16 70 32 282 XSQ= 3.76 PHI= 0.097 XP = 0.0524

508	TEND LESS TO BE THCSE 0.69 OF 48 NCT INCLUDED IN DAVID C. MCCLELLAND'S STUDY OF ACHIEVEMENT MOTIVATION (360)	508	TEND MORE TO BE THOSE 0.93 OF 352 NOT INCLUDED IN DAVID C. MCCLELLAND'S STUDY OF ACHIEVEMENT MOTIVATION (360)	15 25 33 327 XSQ= 24.75 PHI= 0.249 XP = 0.0000
509	LEAN LESS TOWARD BEING THCSE 0.83 OF 48 NCT INCLUDED IN MONI NAG'S STUDY OF FERTILITY (375)	509	LEAN MORE TOWARD BEING THOSE 0.95 OF 352 NOT INCLUDED IN MONI NAG'S STUDY OF FERTILITY (375)	8 17 40 335 XSQ= 8.18 PHI= 0.143 XP = 0.0042
510	TILT LESS TOWARD BEING THCSE 0.88 OF 48 NOT INCLUDED IN RACUL NARRCLL'S STUDY OF SCCIETAL CCMPLEXITY (380)	510	TILT MORE TOWARD BEING THOSE 0.96 OF 352 NOT INCLUDED IN RAOUL NARRCLL'S STUDY OF SOCIETAL COMPLEXITY (380)	6 14 42 338 XSQ= 4.79 PHI= 0.109 XP = 0.0286
511	LEAN TOWARD BEING THOSE 0.69 OF 48 INCLUDED IN ROBERTS, ARTH AND BUSH'S SAMPLE CN GAMES, AS MCDIFIED BY THE ETHNOGRAPHIC ATLAS (189)	511	LEAN TOWARD BEING THOSE 0.56 OF 352 NOT INCLUDED IN ROBERTS, ARTH AND BUSH'S SAMPLE ON GAMES, AS MODIFIED BY THE ETHNOGRAPHIC ATLAS (211)	33 156 15 196 XSQ= 9.16 PHI= 0.151 XP = 0.0025
512	TEND LESS TO BE THCSE 0.73 OF 48 NOT INCLUDED IN SHIRLEY ANC ROMNEY'S STUDY OF LCVE MAGIC (367)	512	TEND MORE TO BE THOSE 0.94 OF 352 NOT INCLUDED IN SHIRLEY AND ROMNEY'S STUDY OF LOVE MAGIC (367)	13 20 35 332 XSQ= 22.81 PHI= 0.239 XP = 0.0000
514	TEND TO BE THOSE 0.60 OF 48 INCLUDED IN PHILIP E. SLATER'S STUDY OF NARCISSISM (90)	514	TEND TO BE THOSE 0.83 OF 352 NOT INCLUDED IN PHILIP E. SLATER'S STUDY OF NARCISSISM (310)	29 61 19 291 XSQ= 42.53 PHI= 0.326 XP = 0.
515	TEND TO BE THOSE 0.52 OF 48 INCLUDED IN WILLIAM N. STEPHENS' SAMPLE ON AVCIDANCE RELATIONSHIPS (52)	515	TEND TO BE THOSE 0.92 OF 352 NOT INCLUDED IN WILLIAM N. STEPHENS' SAMPLE ON AVOIDANCE RELATIONSHIPS (348)	25 27 23 325 XSQ= 69.79 PHI= 0.418 XP = 0.
517	DRIFT MORE TOWARD BEING THOSE 0.77 OF 48 INCLUDED IN GUY E. SWANSON'S SAMPLE ON HIGH GODS, AS MODIFIED BY THE ETHNOGRAPHIC ATLAS (260)	517	DRIFT LESS TOWARD BEING THOSE 0.63 OF 352 INCLUDED IN GUY E. SWANSON'S SAMPLE ON HIGH GODS, AS MODIFIED BY THE ETHNOGRAPHIC ATLAS (260)	37 223 11 129 XSQ= 2.92 PHI= 0.085 XP = 0.0873
518	LEAN LESS TOWARD BEING THOSE 0.56 OF 48 NOT INCLUDED IN STANLEY H. UDY, JR.'S STUDY OF WORK ORGANIZATION (295)	518	LEAN MORE TOWARD BEING THOSE 0.76 OF 352 NOT INCLUDED IN STANLEY H. UDY, JR.'S STUDY OF WORK ORGANIZATION (295)	21 84 27 268 XSQ= 7.63 PHI= 0.138 XP = 0.0057

519	TEND LESS TO BE THOSE NOT INCLUDED IN JOSEPH VEROFF'S STUDY OF ACHIEVEMENT MOTIVATION AS REVEALED IN FOLKTALES (364)	0.73 OF 48	519	TEND MORE TO BE THOSE NOT INCLUDED IN JOSEPH VEROFF'S STUDY OF ACHIEVEMENT MOTIVATION AS REVEALED IN FOLKTALES (364)	0.93 OF 352	13 23 35 329 XSQ= 19.34 PHI= 0.220 XP = 0.0000
520	LEAN LESS TOWARD BEING THOSE NOT INCLUDED IN BEATRICE BLYTH WHITING'S STUDY OF SORCERY (360)	0.77 OF 48	520	LEAN MORE TOWARD BEING THOSE NOT INCLUDED IN BEATRICE BLYTH WHITING'S STUDY OF SORCERY (360)	0.92 OF 352	11 29 37 323 XSQ= 8.55 PHI= 0.146 XP = 0.0035
522	TEND TO BE THOSE INCLUDED IN MARJORIE GRANT WHITING'S STUDY OF DIET (82)	0.54 OF 48	522	TEND TO BE THOSE NOT INCLUDED IN MARJORIE GRANT WHITING'S STUDY OF DIET (318)	0.84 OF 352	26 56 22 296 XSQ= 35.62 PHI= 0.298 XP = 0.
523	TEND LESS TO BE THOSE NOT INCLUDED IN WHITING AND CHILD'S STUDY OF CHILD TRAINING AND PERSONALITY (339)	0.56 OF 48	523	TEND MORE TO BE THOSE NOT INCLUDED IN WHITING AND CHILD'S STUDY OF CHILD TRAINING AND PERSONALITY (339)	0.89 OF 352	21 40 27 312 XSQ= 31.82 PHI= 0.282 XP = 0.
524	TEND LESS TO BE THOSE NOT INCLUDED IN WHITING, KLUCKHOHN, AND ANTHONY'S STUDY OF MALE INITIATION CEREMONIES (356)	0.63 OF 48	524	TEND MORE TO BE THOSE NOT INCLUDED IN WHITING, KLUCKHOHN, AND ANTHONY'S STUDY OF MALE INITIATION CEREMONIES (356)	0.93 OF 352	18 26 30 326 XSQ= 36.11 PHI= 0.300 XP = 0.

492 CULTURES
INCLUDED IN BARBARA CHARTIER AYRES' STUDY OF FEMALE INITIATION RITES (39)

492 CULTURES
NOT INCLUDED IN BARBARA CHARTIER AYRES' STUDY OF FEMALE INITIATION RITES (361)

BACKGROUND ON PAGE 180

SUBJECT ONLY, F.C. 1-480 AND 527-536
BOTH SUBJECT AND PREDICATE, F.C. 481-526

39 IN LEFT COLUMN

AINU	ALCRESE	ANDAMANESE	ARAPESH	ASHANTI	AZANDE	BALINESE	CHAGGA	CHIR-APACHE	COMANCHE
DOBUANS	DUSUN	FON	HANO	IFUGAO	JIVARO	KURTATCHI	KUTENAI	KWAKIUTL	LAKHER
LEPCHA	LESU	MAORI	MARSHALLESE	MASAI	NAVAHO	OMAHA	PAPAGO	PUKAPUKA	SANPOIL
SIRIONO	TANALA	THONGA	TIKOPIA	TIV	TROBRIAND	VENDA	WOGEO	YAGUA	

361 IN RIGHT COLUMN

No.	Left column (39)	Ratio	No.	Right column (361)	Ratio	Statistics
4	IN ALL CASES ARE THOSE LOCATED OUTSIDE OF THE CIRCUM-MEDITERRANEAN (355)	1.00 OF 39	4	TILT LESS TOWARD BEING THOSE LOCATED OUTSIDE OF THE CIRCUM-MEDITERRANEAN (355)	0.88 OF 361	0 45 / 39 316 / XSQ= 4.30 / PHI= -0.104 / XP = 0.0381
6	LEAN LESS TOWARD BEING THOSE LOCATED OUTSIDE OF THE INSULAR PACIFIC (330)	0.64 OF 39	6	LEAN MORE TOWARD BEING THOSE LOCATED OUTSIDE OF THE INSULAR PACIFIC (330)	0.84 OF 361	14 56 / 25 305 / XSQ= 8.77 / PHI= 0.148 / XP = 0.0031
16	DRIFT LESS TOWARD BEING THOSE WHERE THE LATITUDE IS TEN DEGREES OR GREATER (277)	0.56 OF 39	16	DRIFT MORE TOWARD BEING THOSE WHERE THE LATITUDE IS TEN DEGREES OR GREATER (277)	0.71 OF 361	22 255 / 17 106 / XSQ= 2.71 / PHI= -0.082 / XP = 0.0997
63	TILT TOWARD BEING THOSE WHERE HUSBANDRY, IF PRESENT, IS PRINCIPALLY IN THE FORM OF PIGS, SHEEP, OR GOATS, RATHER THAN BOVINE, EQUINE, CAMEL-LIKE, OR DEER-LIKE ANIMALS (74)	0.56 OF 25	63	TILT TOWARD BEING THOSE WHERE HUSBANDRY, IF PRESENT, IS PRINCIPALLY IN THE FORM OF BOVINE, EQUINE, CAMEL-LIKE, OR DEER-LIKE ANIMALS, RATHER THAN PIGS, SHEEP, OR GOATS (152)	0.70 OF 201	11 141 / 14 60 / XSQ= 5.77 / PHI= -0.160 / XP = 0.0163
87	TILT LESS TOWARD BEING THOSE WHERE THE LEVEL OF POLITICAL INTEGRATION IS THE LARGE STATE, THE LITTLE STATE, THE MINIMAL STATE, OR THE AUTONOMOUS COMMUNITY (281) GPM	0.80 OF 30	87	TILT MORE TOWARD BEING THOSE WHERE THE LEVEL OF POLITICAL INTEGRATION IS THE LARGE STATE, THE LITTLE STATE, THE MINIMAL STATE, OR THE AUTONOMOUS COMMUNITY (281) GPM	0.94 OF 274	24 257 / 6 17 / XSQ= 5.52 / PHI= -0.135 / XP = 0.0188

107	IN ALL CASES ARE THOSE WHERE CLASS STRATIFICATION, IF PRESENT, IS BASED ON SOMETHING OTHER THAN OCCUPATIONAL STATUS (160)	1.00 OF 19	107	TILT LESS TOWARD BEING THOSE WHERE CLASS STRATIFICATION, IF PRESENT, IS BASED ON SOMETHING OTHER THAN OCCUPATIONAL STATUS (160)	0.77 OF 184	0 43 19 141 XSQ= 4.32 PHI= -0.146 XP = 0.0377
108	TEND TO BE THOSE WHERE CLASS STRATIFICATION, IF PRESENT, IS BASED ON A HEREDITARY ARISTOCRACY (74)	0.79 OF 19	108	TEND TO BE THOSE WHERE CLASS STRATIFICATION, IF PRESENT, IS BASED ON SOMETHING OTHER THAN A HEREDITARY ARISTOCRACY (129)	0.68 OF 184	15 59 4 125 XSQ= 14.38 PHI= 0.266 XP = 0.0001
128	TILT TOWARD BEING THOSE WHERE, IF SUBSISTENCE IS PRIMARILY BY AGRICULTURE, THE WORK IS MAINLY DONE BY FEMALES (37)	0.89 OF 9	128	TILT TOWARD BEING THOSE WHERE, IF SUBSISTENCE IS PRIMARILY BY AGRICULTURE, THE WORK IS MAINLY DONE BY MALES (40)	0.57 OF 68	1 39 8 29 XSQ= 5.08 PHI= -0.257 XP = 0.0242
213	TILT MORE TOWARD BEING THOSE WHERE FIRST COUSIN MARRIAGE IS NOT PERMITTED (198)	0.72 OF 39	213	TILT LESS TOWARD BEING THOSE WHERE FIRST COUSIN MARRIAGE IS NOT PERMITTED (198)	0.51 OF 331	11 161 28 170 XSQ= 5.06 PHI= -0.117 XP = 0.0244
257	DRIFT TOWARD BEING THOSE WHERE THE SEVERITY OF SISTER AVOIDANCE IS LOW (17) WNS	0.80 OF 15	257	DRIFT TOWARD BEING THOSE WHERE THE SEVERITY OF SISTER AVOIDANCE IS HIGH (10) WNS	0.58 OF 12	3 7 12 5 XSQ= 2.72 PHI= -0.317 EP = 0.0568
259	TILT TOWARD BEING THOSE WHERE THE SEVERITY OF MOTHER-IN-LAW AVOIDANCE IS LOW (20) WNS	0.65 OF 20	259	TILT TOWARD BEING THOSE WHERE THE SEVERITY OF MOTHER-IN-LAW AVOIDANCE IS HIGH (26) WNS	0.73 OF 26	7 19 13 7 XSQ= 5.21 PHI= -0.337 XP = 0.0225
263	DRIFT TOWARD BEING THOSE WHERE WIVES ARE OBTAINED BY RELATIVELY EASY MEANS, NAMELY BY TOKEN BRIDE-PRICE, GIFT EXCHANGE, ABSENCE OF ANY CONSIDERATION, OR RECEIPT OF DOWRY (162)	0.56 OF 39	263	DRIFT TOWARD BEING THOSE WHERE WIVES ARE OBTAINED BY RELATIVELY DIFFICULT MEANS, NAMELY BY BRIDE-PRICE, BRIDE-SERVICE, OR EXCHANGING A FEMALE RELATIVE (233)	0.61 OF 356	17 216 22 140 XSQ= 3.56 PHI= -0.095 XP = 0.0590
300	DRIFT TOWARD BEING THOSE WHERE THE POST-PARTUM SEX TABOO LASTS LONGER THAN SIX MONTHS (51)	0.58 OF 24	300	DRIFT TOWARD BEING THOSE WHERE THE POST-PARTUM SEX TABOO LASTS SIX MONTHS OR LESS (73)	0.63 OF 100	14 37 10 63 XSQ= 2.81 PHI= 0.151 XP = 0.0937
332	DRIFT TOWARD BEING THOSE WHERE THE AGE AT BEGINNING OF MODESTY TRAINING IS LOWER THAN SIX YEARS (8) W-C	0.62 OF 13	332	IN ALL CASES ARE THOSE WHERE THE AGE AT BEGINNING OF MODESTY TRAINING IS SIX YEARS OR HIGHER (9) W-C	1.00 OF 4	5 4 8 0 XSQ= 2.51 PHI= -0.384 EP = 0.0824

342	DRIFT TOWARD BEING THCSE 0.55 OF 22 WHERE THE CHILD'S INFERREC ANXIETY OVER PERFORMANCE OF NURTURANT BEHAVIOR IS HIGH (18) B-B-C	342	DRIFT TOWARD BEING THOSE 0.75 OF 24 WHERE THE CHILD'S INFERRED ANXIETY OVER PERFORMANCE OF NURTURANT BEHAVIOR IS LOW (28) B-B-C	12 6 10 18 XSQ= 3.06 PHI= 0.258 XP = 0.0804
391	TILT TOWARD BEING THOSE 0.70 OF 33 WHERE PREMARITAL SEX RELATIONS ARE PUNISHED CNLY IF PREGNANCY RESULTS, OR FREELY PERMITTEC (90) JTW,EA	391	TILT TOWARD BEING THOSE 0.54 OF 146 WHERE PREMARITAL SEX RELATICNS ARE STRONGLY PUNISHED AND IN FACT RARE, OR WEAKLY PUNISHED AND IN FACT NOT RARE (89) JTW,EA	10 79 23 67 XSQ= 5.19 PHI= -0.170 XP = 0.0228
400	TILT TOWARD BEING THOSE 0.57 OF 23 WHERE HOMCSEXUAL ACTIVITY IS PRCHIBITED (22) F-B	400	TILT TOWARD BEING THOSE 0.74 OF 35 WHERE HOMOSEXUAL ACTIVITY IS PERMITTED (36) F-B	13 9 10 26 XSQ= 4.36 PHI= 0.274 XP = 0.0367
425	TILT TOWARD BEING THOSE 0.70 OF 23 WHERE SUPERNATURALS ARE MAINLY AGGRESSIVE, RATHER THAN BENEVCLENT (20) L-T-W	425	TILT TOWARD BEING THOSE 0.69 OF 13 WHERE SUPERNATURALS ARE MAINLY BENEVOLENT, RATHER THAN AGGRESSIVE (16) L-T-W	7 9 16 4 XSQ= 3.61 PHI= -0.317 EP = 0.0379
432	IN ALL CASES ARE THCSE 1.00 OF 9 WHERE AN ATTRACTIVE AFTERLIFE IS BELIEVED IN (27) LWS	432	TILT LESS TOWARD BEING THOSE 0.62 OF 29 WHERE AN ATTRACTIVE AFTERLIFE IS BELIEVED IN (27) LWS	9 18 0 11 XSQ= 3.14 PHI= 0.287 EP = 0.0378
442	DRIFT TOWARD BEING THOSE 0.56 OF 39 WHERE FEAR OF ANIMAL SPIRITS IS HIGH (28) W-C	442	DRIFT TOWARD BEING THOSE 0.73 OF 22 WHERE FEAR OF ANIMAL SPIRITS IS LOW (33) W-C	22 6 17 16 XSQ= 3.71 PHI= 0.247 XP = 0.0542
447	TILT TOWARD BEING THOSE 0.72 OF 25 WHERE LOVE MAGIC IS PRESENT (20) S-R	447	TILT TOWARD BEING THOSE 0.75 OF 8 WHERE LOVE MAGIC IS ABSENT (13) S-R	18 2 7 6 XSQ= 3.81 PHI= 0.340 EP = 0.0351
449	LEAN TOWARD BEING THOSE 0.58 OF 19 WHERE THE CBSERVATION OF FCOD TABOOS IS HIGH, RATHER THAN MEDIUM OR LOW (25) JRL	449	LEAN TOWARD BEING THOSE 0.79 OF 67 WHERE THE OBSERVATION OF FCOD TABOOS IS MEDIUM OR LOW, RATHER THAN HIGH (61) JRL	11 14 8 53 XSQ= 8.11 PHI= 0.307 XP = 0.0044
450	IN ALL CASES ARE THCSE 1.00 OF 19 WHERE THE CBSERVATION CF FCOD TABOOS IS HIGH OR MEDIUM, RATHER THAN LOW (60) JRL	450	LEAN LESS TOWARD BEING THOSE 0.61 OF 67 WHERE THE OBSERVATION OF FOOD TABOOS IS HIGH OR MEDIUM, RATHER THAN LOW (60) JRL	19 41 0 26 XSQ= 8.81 PHI= 0.320 XP = 0.0030

No.		No.		Statistics
456	TILT TOWARD BEING THOSE 0.73 OF 15 WHERE THE INTERNALIZATION OF THE INDIVIDUAL'S CONTACT WITH THE DIVINE IS NOT CONDUCIVE TO THE DEVELOPMENT OF THE INDIVIDUAL'S NEED TO ACHIEVE (17) DCM	456	TILT TOWARD BEING THOSE 0.71 OF 21 WHERE THE INTERNALIZATION OF THE INDIVIDUAL'S CONTACT WITH THE DIVINE IS CONDUCIVE TO THE DEVELOPMENT OF THE INDIVIDUAL'S NEED TO ACHIEVE (19) DCM	4 15 11 6 XSQ= 5.35 PHI= -0.386 EP = 0.0166
488	TILT MORE TOWARD BEING THOSE 0.93 OF 30 ABOUT WHICH THE PRINCIPAL ETHNOGRAPHIES WERE PUBLISHED BEFORE 1950 (185)	488	TILT LESS TOWARD BEING THOSE 0.69 OF 227 ABOUT WHICH THE PRINCIPAL ETHNOGRAPHIES WERE PUBLISHED BEFORE 1950 (185)	28 157 2 70 XSQ= 6.52 PHI= 0.159 XP = 0.0106
489	DRIFT LESS TOWARD BEING THOSE 0.74 OF 39 NOT INCLUDED IN CHARLES ACKERMAN'S STUDY OF DIVORCE (343)	489	DRIFT MORE TOWARD BEING THOSE 0.87 OF 361 NOT INCLUDED IN CHARLES ACKERMAN'S STUDY OF DIVORCE (343)	10 47 29 314 XSQ= 3.61 PHI= 0.095 XP = 0.0573
490	TEND TO BE THOSE 0.82 OF 39 INCLUDED IN ALBERT S. ANTHONY'S SAMPLE ON MALE INITIATION RITES (113)	490	TEND TO BE THOSE 0.78 OF 361 NOT INCLUDED IN ALBERT S. ANTHONY'S SAMPLE ON MALE INITIATION RITES (287)	32 81 7 280 XSQ= 58.80 PHI= 0.383 XP = 0.
491	TEND LESS TO BE THOSE 0.54 OF 39 NOT INCLUDED IN DORRIAN APPLE'S STUDY OF GRANDPARENTHOOD (352)	491	TEND MORE TO BE THOSE 0.92 OF 361 NOT INCLUDED IN DORRIAN APPLE'S STUDY OF GRANDPARENTHOOD (352)	18 30 21 331 XSQ= 44.22 PHI= 0.332 XP = 0.
493	TEND TO BE THOSE 0.87 OF 39 INCLUDED IN BACON, BARRY, AND CHILD'S STUDY OF CHILD REARING (78)	493	TEND TO BE THOSE 0.88 OF 361 NOT INCLUDED IN BACON, BARRY, AND CHILD'S STUDY OF CHILD REARING (322)	34 44 5 317 XSQ= 121.36 PHI= 0.551 XP = 0.
494	TEND TO BE THOSE 0.54 OF 39 INCLUDED IN HERBERT M. BARRY III'S STUDY OF ART (29)	494	TEND TO BE THOSE 0.98 OF 361 NOT INCLUDED IN HERBERT M. BARRY III'S STUDY OF ART (371)	21 8 18 353 XSQ= 131.96 PHI= 0.574 XP = 0.
495	TEND LESS TO BE THOSE 0.54 OF 39 NOT INCLUDED IN JUDITH K. BROWN'S STUDY OF FEMALE INITIATION RITES (335)	495	TEND MORE TO BE THOSE 0.87 OF 361 NOT INCLUDED IN JUDITH K. BROWN'S STUDY OF FEMALE INITIATION RITES (335)	18 47 21 314 XSQ= 26.01 PHI= 0.255 XP = 0.0000
496	TEND LESS TO BE THOSE 0.62 OF 39 NOT INCLUDED IN ROY G. D'ANDRADE'S STUDY OF DREAMS (345)	496	TEND MORE TO BE THOSE 0.89 OF 361 NOT INCLUDED IN ROY G. D'ANDRADE'S STUDY OF DREAMS (345)	15 40 24 321 XSQ= 20.00 PHI= 0.224 XP = 0.0000

No.			No.			Statistics
497	TEND LESS TO BE THOSE NOT INCLUDED IN WILLIAM M. EVAN'S STUDY OF LAW (339)	0.62 OF 39	497	TEND MORE TO BE THOSE NOT INCLUDED IN WILLIAM M. EVAN'S STUDY OF LAW (339)	0.87 OF 361	15 46 24 315 XSQ= 16.08 PHI= 0.200 XP = 0.0001
498	TEND TO BE THOSE INCLUDED IN C. S. FORD'S STUDY OF SEX (51)	0.62 OF 39	498	TEND TO BE THOSE NOT INCLUDED IN C. S. FORD'S STUDY OF SEX (349)	0.93 OF 361	24 27 15 334 XSQ= 87.67 PHI= 0.468 XP = 0.
499	TEND TO BE THOSE INCLUDED IN FORD AND BEACH'S SAMPLE ON SEXUAL EXPRESSION BY THE YOUNG (86)	0.79 OF 39	499	TEND TO BE THOSE NOT INCLUDED IN FORD AND BEACH'S SAMPLE ON SEXUAL EXPRESSION BY THE YOUNG (314)	0.85 OF 361	31 55 8 306 XSQ= 82.33 PHI= 0.454 XP = 0.
500	TEND LESS TO BE THOSE NOT INCLUDED IN FREEMAN AND WINCH'S STUDY OF SOCIETAL COMPLEXITY (360)	0.56 OF 39	500	TEND MORE TO BE THOSE NOT INCLUDED IN FREEMAN AND WINCH'S STUDY OF SOCIETAL COMPLEXITY (360)	0.94 OF 361	17 23 22 338 XSQ= 50.12 PHI= 0.354 XP = 0.
501	TEND TO BE THOSE INCLUDED IN JOAN FRIENDLY GOODMAN'S STUDY OF ASCETIC MOURNING BEHAVIOR (67)	0.82 OF 39	501	TEND TO BE THOSE NOT INCLUDED IN JOAN FRIENDLY GOODMAN'S STUDY OF ASCETIC MOURNING BEHAVIOR (333)	0.90 OF 361	32 35 7 326 XSQ= 127.01 PHI= 0.563 XP = 0.
502	TEND TO BE THOSE INCLUDED IN JOHN K. HARLEY'S STUDY OF ADOLESCENT PEER GROUPS (57)	0.59 OF 39	502	TEND TO BE THOSE NOT INCLUDED IN JOHN K. HARLEY'S STUDY OF ADOLESCENT PEER GROUPS (343)	0.91 OF 361	23 34 16 327 XSQ= 66.74 PHI= 0.408 XP = 0.
503	TEND LESS TO BE THOSE NOT INCLUDED IN JOHN M. HICKMAN'S STUDY OF THE FOLK-URBAN CONTINUUM (346)	0.67 OF 39	503	TEND MORE TO BE THOSE NOT INCLUDED IN JOHN M. HICKMAN'S STUDY OF THE FOLK-URBAN CONTINUUM (346)	0.89 OF 361	13 41 26 320 XSQ= 12.74 PHI= 0.178 XP = 0.0004
504	TEND TO BE THOSE INCLUDED IN DONALD HORTON'S STUDY OF ALCOHOLISM (49)	0.51 OF 39	504	TEND TO BE THOSE NOT INCLUDED IN DONALD HORTON'S STUDY OF ALCHOLISM (351)	0.92 OF 361	20 29 19 332 XSQ= 57.29 PHI= 0.378 XP = 0.
505	TILT LESS TOWARD BEING THOSE NOT INCLUDED IN MERRILL JACKSON'S STUDY OF CRIMINAL LAW AND MEDICINE (380)	0.87 OF 39	505	TILT MORE TOWARD BEING THOSE NOT INCLUDED IN MERRILL JACKSON'S STUDY OF CRIMINAL LAW AND MEDICINE (380)	0.96 OF 361	5 15 34 346 XSQ= 3.89 PHI= 0.099 XP = 0.0486

506	TEND TO BE THOSE INCLUDED IN LAMBERT, TRIANDIS, AND WOLF'S STUDY OF SUPERNATURAL BEINGS (36)	0.59 OF 39	506	TEND TO BE THOSE NOT INCLUDED IN LAMBERT, TRIANDIS, AND WOLF'S STUDY OF SUPERNATURAL BEINGS (364)	0.96 OF 361	23 13 16 348 XSQ= 125.10 PHI= 0.559 XP = 0.
507	TEND LESS TO BE THOSE NOT INCLUDED IN JAMES R. LEARY'S STUDY OF FOOD TABOOS (314)	0.51 OF 39	507	TEND MORE TO BE THOSE NOT INCLUDED IN JAMES R. LEARY'S STUDY OF FOOD TABOOS (314)	0.81 OF 361	19 67 20 294 XSQ= 17.22 PHI= 0.208 XP = 0.0000
508	TEND LESS TO BE THOSE NOT INCLUDED IN DAVID C. MCCLELLAND'S STUDY OF ACHIEVEMENT MOTIVATION (360)	0.56 OF 39	508	TEND MORE TO BE THOSE NOT INCLUDED IN DAVID C. MCCLELLAND'S STUDY OF ACHIEVEMENT MOTIVATION (360)	0.94 OF 361	17 23 22 338 XSQ= 50.12 PHI= 0.354 XP = 0.
509	TEND LESS TO BE THOSE NOT INCLUDED IN MONI NAG'S STUDY OF FERTILITY (375)	0.79 OF 39	509	TEND MORE TO BE THOSE NOT INCLUDED IN MONI NAG'S STUDY OF FERTILITY (375)	0.95 OF 361	8 17 31 344 XSQ= 12.43 PHI= 0.176 XP = 0.0004
510	TEND LESS TO BE THOSE NOT INCLUDED IN RAOUL NARROLL'S STUDY OF SOCIETAL COMPLEXITY (380)	0.82 OF 39	510	TEND MORE TO BE THOSE NOT INCLUDED IN RAOUL NARROLL'S STUDY OF SOCIETAL COMPLEXITY (380)	0.96 OF 361	7 13 32 348 XSQ= 12.38 PHI= 0.176 XP = 0.0004
511	TEND TO BE THOSE INCLUDED IN ROBERTS, ARTH AND BUSH'S SAMPLE ON GAMES, AS MODIFIED BY THE ETHNOGRAPHIC ATLAS (189)	0.79 OF 39	511	TEND TO BE THOSE NOT INCLUDED IN ROBERTS, ARTH AND BUSH'S SAMPLE ON GAMES, AS MODIFIED BY THE ETHNOGRAPHIC ATLAS (211)	0.56 OF 361	31 158 8 203 XSQ= 16.61 PHI= 0.204 XP = 0.0000
512	TEND TO BE THOSE INCLUDED IN SHIRLEY AND ROMNEY'S STUDY OF LOVE MAGIC (33)	0.64 OF 39	512	TEND TO BE THOSE NOT INCLUDED IN SHIRLEY AND ROMNEY'S STUDY OF LOVE MAGIC (367)	0.98 OF 361	25 8 14 353 XSQ= 170.01 PHI= 0.652 XP = 0.
513	TEND LESS TO BE THOSE NOT INCLUDED IN LEO W. SIMMONS' STUDY OF THE TREATMENT OF THE AGED (357)	0.69 OF 39	513	TEND MORE TO BE THOSE NOT INCLUDED IN LEO W. SIMMONS' STUDY OF THE TREATMENT OF THE AGED (357)	0.91 OF 361	12 31 27 330 XSQ= 15.81 PHI= 0.199 XP = 0.0001
514	TEND TO BE THOSE INCLUDED IN PHILIP E. SLATER'S STUDY OF NARCISSISM (90)	0.90 OF 39	514	TEND TO BE THOSE NOT INCLUDED IN PHILIP E. SLATER'S STUDY OF NARCISSISM (310)	0.85 OF 361	35 55 4 306 XSQ= 107.82 PHI= 0.519 XP = 0.

515	TEND TO BE THOSE INCLUDED IN WILLIAM N. STEPHENS' SAMPLE ON AVOIDANCE RELATIONSHIPS (52)	0.59 OF 39	515	TEND TO BE THOSE NOT INCLUDED IN WILLIAM N. STEPHENS' SAMPLE ON AVOIDANCE RELATIONSHIPS (348)	0.92 OF 361	23 29 16 332 XSQ= 76.32 PHI= 0.437 XP = 0.
517	TILT MORE TOWARD BEING THOSE INCLUDED IN GUY E. SWANSON'S SAMPLE ON HIGH GODS, AS MODIFIED BY THE ETHNOGRAPHIC ATLAS (260)	0.82 OF 39	517	TILT LESS TOWARD BEING THOSE INCLUDED IN GUY E. SWANSON'S SAMPLE ON HIGH GODS, AS MODIFIED BY THE ETHNOGRAPHIC ATLAS (260)	0.63 OF 361	32 228 7 133 XSQ= 4.72 PHI= 0.109 XP = 0.0298
518	TEND TO BE THOSE INCLUDED IN STANLEY H. UDY, JR.'S STUDY OF WORK ORGANIZATION (105)	0.59 OF 39	518	TEND TO BE THOSE NOT INCLUDED IN STANLEY H. UDY, JR.'S STUDY OF WORK ORGANIZATION (295)	0.77 OF 361	23 82 16 279 XSQ= 22.07 PHI= 0.235 XP = 0.0000
519	TEND LESS TO BE THOSE NOT INCLUDED IN JOSEPH VEROFF'S STUDY OF ACHIEVEMENT MOTIVATION AS REVEALED IN FOLKTALES (364)	0.62 OF 39	519	TEND MORE TO BE THOSE NOT INCLUDED IN JOSEPH VEROFF'S STUDY OF ACHIEVEMENT MOTIVATION AS REVEALED IN FOLKTALES (364)	0.94 OF 361	15 21 24 340 XSQ= 41.90 PHI= 0.324 XP = 0.
520	TEND LESS TO BE THOSE NOT INCLUDED IN BEATRICE BLYTH WHITING'S STUDY OF SORCERY (360)	0.51 OF 39	520	TEND MORE TO BE THOSE NOT INCLUDED IN BEATRICE BLYTH WHITING'S STUDY OF SORCERY (360)	0.94 OF 361	19 21 20 340 XSQ= 67.29 PHI= 0.410 XP = 0.
522	TEND TO BE THOSE INCLUDED IN MARJORIE GRANT WHITING'S STUDY OF DIET (82)	0.77 OF 39	522	TEND TO BE THOSE NOT INCLUDED IN MARJORIE GRANT WHITING'S STUDY OF DIET (318)	0.86 OF 361	30 52 9 309 XSQ= 80.62 PHI= 0.449 XP = 0.
523	IN ALL CASES ARE THOSE INCLUDED IN WHITING AND CHILD'S STUDY OF CHILD TRAINING AND PERSONALITY (61)	1.00 OF 39	523	TEND TO BE THOSE NOT INCLUDED IN WHITING AND CHILD'S STUDY OF CHILD TRAINING AND PERSONALITY (339)	0.94 OF 361	39 22 0 339 XSQ= 232.94 PHI= 0.763 XP = 0.
524	TEND TO BE THOSE INCLUDED IN WHITING, KLUCKHOHN, AND ANTHONY'S STUDY OF MALE INITIATION CEREMONIES (44)	0.56 OF 39	524	TEND TO BE THOSE NOT INCLUDED IN WHITING, KLUCKHOHN, AND ANTHONY'S STUDY OF MALE INITIATION CEREMONIES (356)	0.94 OF 361	22 22 17 339 XSQ= 85.95 PHI= 0.464 XP = 0.

493 CULTURES INCLUDED IN BACON, BARRY, AND CHILD'S STUDY OF CHILD REARING (78)

493 CULTURES NOT INCLUDED IN BACON, BARRY, AND CHILD'S STUDY OF CHILD REARING (322)

BACKGROUND ON PAGE 180

SUBJECT ONLY, F.C. 1-480 AND 527-536
BOTH SUBJECT AND PREDICATE, F.C. 481-526

78 IN LEFT COLUMN

AINU	ALORESE	ANDAMANESE	ARANDA	ARAPESH	ARAUCANIANS	ASHANTI	AYMARA	AZANDE	BALINESE
CAMAYURA	CHAGGA	CHENCHU	CHEYENNE	CHIR-APACHE	CHUKCHEE	COMANCHE	CROW	CUNA	FON
GANDA	HANO	IFUGAO	JIVARO	KASKA	KIKUYU	KORYAK	KURTATCHI	KWAKIUTL	LAKHER
LAMBA	LAU	LEPCHA	LESU	MANDAN	MANUS	MAORI	MARQUESANS	MASAI	MBUNDU
MURNGIN	NAVAHO	NUER	NYAKYUSA	OJIBWA	OMAHA	ONA	ONTONG-JAVA	PAPAGO	PUKAPUKA
SAMOANS	SHERENTE	SIRIONO	SOTHO	SWAZI	TALLENSI	TANALA	TENETEHARA	TETON	THONGA
TIKOPIA	TIMBIRA	TIV	TROBRIAND	TRUKESE	TUCUNA	TUPINAMBA	TURKANA	VENDA	WICHITA
WINNEBAGO	WOGEO	WOLEAIANS	YAGUA	YAHGAN	YAKUT	YORUBA	ZUNI		

322 IN RIGHT COLUMN

	Left column (78)			Right column (322)		Statistics
4	IN ALL CASES ARE THOSE LOCATED OUTSIDE OF THE CIRCUM-MEDITERRANEAN (355)	1.00 OF 78	4	TEND LESS TO BE THOSE LOCATED OUTSIDE OF THE CIRCUM-MEDITERRANEAN (355)	0.86 OF 322	0 45 78 277 XSQ= 10.92 PHI= -0.165 XP = 0.0010
6	DRIFT LESS TOWARD BEING THOSE LOCATED OUTSIDE OF THE INSULAR PACIFIC (330)	0.74 OF 78	6	DRIFT MORE TOWARD BEING THOSE LOCATED OUTSIDE OF THE INSULAR PACIFIC (330)	0.84 OF 322	20 50 58 272 XSQ= 3.78 PHI= 0.097 XP = 0.0520
16	TILT LESS TOWARD BEING THOSE WHERE THE LATITUDE IS TEN DEGREES OR GREATER (277)	0.59 OF 78	16	TILT MORE TOWARD BEING THOSE WHERE THE LATITUDE IS TEN DEGREES OR GREATER (277)	0.72 OF 322	46 231 32 91 XSQ= 4.22 PHI= -0.103 XP = 0.0399
51	DRIFT LESS TOWARD BEING THOSE WHERE SUBSISTENCE IS PRIMARILY BY FOOD PRODUCTION -- I. E., AGRICULTURE OR HUSBANDRY -- RATHER THAN BY GATHERING (253)	0.54 OF 78	51	DRIFT MORE TOWARD BEING THOSE WHERE SUBSISTENCE IS PRIMARILY BY FOOD PRODUCTION -- I. E., AGRICULTURE OR HUSBANDRY -- RATHER THAN BY GATHERING (253)	0.66 OF 322	42 211 36 111 XSQ= 3.20 PHI= -0.089 XP = 0.0736
62	TILT MORE TOWARD BEING THOSE WHERE HUSBANDRY OF SOME KIND IS PRESENT (228)	0.68 OF 78	62	TILT LESS TOWARD BEING THOSE WHERE HUSBANDRY OF SOME KIND IS PRESENT (228)	0.54 OF 322	53 175 25 147 XSQ= 4.20 PHI= 0.102 XP = 0.0404

```
 63  LEAN LESS TOWARD BEING THOSE     0.51 OF  53      63  LEAN MORE TOWARD BEING THOSE     0.72 OF 173         27  125
     WHERE HUSBANDRY, IF PRESENT,                         WHERE HUSBANDRY, IF PRESENT,                             26   48
     IS PRINCIPALLY IN THE FORM OF                        IS PRINCIPALLY IN THE FORM OF                      XSQ=     7.43
     BOVINE, EQUINE, CAMEL-LIKE, OR DEER-LIKE             BOVINE, EQUINE, CAMEL-LIKE, OR DEER-LIKE           PHI=   -0.181
     ANIMALS, RATHER THAN                                 ANIMALS, RATHER THAN                               XP =   0.0064
     PIGS, SHEEP, OR GOATS  (152)                         PIGS, SHEEP, OR GOATS  (152)

 79  TILT MORE TOWARD BEING THOSE     0.98 OF  55      79  TILT LESS TOWARD BEING THOSE     0.87 OF 169          1   22
     WHERE NO CITY IS PRESENT  (201)                      WHERE NO CITY IS PRESENT  (201)                          54  147
                                                                                                             XSQ=     4.50
                                                                                                             PHI=   -0.142
                                                                                                             XP =   0.0339

 80  TILT MORE TOWARD BEING THOSE     0.93 OF  55      80  TILT LESS TOWARD BEING THOSE     0.79 OF 169          4   35
     WHERE NO CITY OR TOWN IS PRESENT  (185)              WHERE NO CITY OR TOWN IS PRESENT  (185)                  51  134
                                                                                                             XSQ=     4.32
                                                                                                             PHI=   -0.139
                                                                                                             XP =   0.0377

 87  DRIFT LESS TOWARD BEING THOSE    0.87 OF  67      87  DRIFT MORE TOWARD BEING THOSE    0.94 OF 237         58  223
     WHERE THE LEVEL OF POLITICAL INTEGRATION             WHERE THE LEVEL OF POLITICAL INTEGRATION                  9   14
     IS THE LARGE STATE, THE LITTLE STATE,                IS THE LARGE STATE, THE LITTLE STATE,              XSQ=     3.22
     THE MINIMAL STATE, OR                                THE MINIMAL STATE, OR                              PHI=   -0.103
     THE AUTONOMOUS COMMUNITY  (281) GPM                  THE AUTONOMOUS COMMUNITY  (281) GPM                XP =   0.0726

107  LEAN MORE TOWARD BEING THOSE     0.97 OF  36     107  LEAN LESS TOWARD BEING THOSE     0.75 OF 167          1   42
     WHERE CLASS STRATIFICATION, IF PRESENT,              WHERE CLASS STRATIFICATION, IF PRESENT,                  35  125
     IS BASED ON SOMETHING OTHER THAN                     IS BASED ON SOMETHING OTHER THAN                   XSQ=     7.59
     OCCUPATIONAL STATUS  (160)                           OCCUPATIONAL STATUS  (160)                         PHI=   -0.193
                                                                                                             XP =   0.0059

108  TILT TOWARD BEING THOSE          0.56 OF  36     108  TILT TOWARD BEING THOSE          0.68 OF 167         20   54
     WHERE CLASS STRATIFICATION, IF PRESENT,              WHERE CLASS STRATIFICATION, IF PRESENT,                  16  113
     IS BASED ON                                          IS BASED ON SOMETHING OTHER THAN                   XSQ=     5.93
     A HEREDITARY ARISTOCRACY  (74)                       A HEREDITARY ARISTOCRACY  (129)                    PHI=    0.171
                                                                                                             XP =   0.0149

109  LEAN MORE TOWARD BEING THOSE     0.96 OF  77     109  LEAN LESS TOWARD BEING THOSE     0.84 OF 291          3   48
     WHERE CASTES ARE ABSENT  (317)                       WHERE CASTES ARE ABSENT  (317)                           74  243
                                                                                                             XSQ=     7.07
                                                                                                             PHI=   -0.139
                                                                                                             XP =   0.0078

116  DRIFT TOWARD BEING THOSE         0.76 OF  29     116  DRIFT TOWARD BEING THOSE         0.52 OF  25          7   13
     WHERE OCCUPATIONAL SPECIALIZATION IS                 WHERE OCCUPATIONAL SPECIALIZATION IS                     22   12
     PART-TIME ONLY  (34) JMH                             FULL-TIME, WHETHER OR NOT FOR                      XSQ=     3.35
                                                          SURPLUS PRODUCTION  (20) JMH                       PHI=   -0.249
                                                                                                             XP =   0.0670

183  DRIFT LESS TOWARD BEING THOSE    0.78 OF  55     183  DRIFT MORE TOWARD BEING THOSE    0.89 OF 197         12   22
     WHERE THE LARGEST NON-COGNATIC KIN GROUP             WHERE THE LARGEST NON-COGNATIC KIN GROUP                 43  175
     IS SMALLER THAN A MOEITY, I. E.,                     IS SMALLER THAN A MOEITY, I. E.,                   XSQ=     3.32
     A PHRATRY OR SIB OR LINEAGE  (218)                   A PHRATRY OR SIB OR LINEAGE  (218)                 PHI=    0.115
                                                                                                             XP =   0.0686
```

192	TILT MORE TOWARC BEING THCSE 0.82 OF 78 OTHER THAN WHERE THE CNLY KIN GROUP PRESENT IS A KINDRED CR ELSE BILATERAL DESCENT IS INFERRED (289)	192	TILT LESS TOWARD BEING THOSE 0.70 OF 322 OTHER THAN WHERE THE ONLY KIN GROUP PRESENT IS A KINDRED OR ELSE BILATERAL DESCENT IS INFERRED (289)	14 97 64 225 XSQ= 4.06 PHI= -0.101 XP = 0.0440
197	DRIFT MORE TCWARD BEING THOSE 0.97 OF 34 WHERE RULES FOR THE INHERITANCE OF REAL PRCPERTY, IF PRESENT, FAVOR EITHER THE MALE HEIR OR LINE, OR THE FEMALE HEIR CR LINE (165)	197	DRIFT LESS TOWARD BEING THOSE 0.82 OF 160 WHERE RULES FOR THE INHERITANCE OF REAL PROPERTY, IF PRESENT, FAVOR EITHER THE MALE HEIR OR LINE, OR THE FEMALE HEIR OR LINE (165)	33 132 1 28 XSQ= 3.60 PHI= 0.136 XP = 0.0578
213	DRIFT MORE TOWARC BEING THOSE 0.63 OF 78 WHERE FIRST CCUSIN MARRIAGE IS NOT PERMITTED (198)	213	DRIFT LESS TOWARD BEING THOSE 0.51 OF 292 WHERE FIRST COUSIN MARRIAGE IS NOT PERMITTED (198)	29 143 49 149 XSQ= 2.98 PHI= -0.090 XP = 0.0841
234	DRIFT TOWARD BEING THCSE 0.58 OF 67 WHERE THE COUSIN TERMINOLOGY IS OF CRCW, CMAHA, OR IROQUOIS TYPE, RATHER THAN ESKIMC CR HAWAIIAN TYPE (152)	234	DRIFT TOWARD BEING THOSE 0.56 CF 255 WHERE THE COUSIN TERMINOLOGY IS OF ESKIMO OR HAWAIIAN TYPE, RATHER THAN CROW, OMAHA, OR IRCQUOIS TYPE (170)	39 113 28 142 XSQ= 3.57 PHI= 0.105 XP = 0.0588
240	DRIFT TCWARD BEING THCSE 0.50 OF 44 WHERE THE FAMILY, IF EXTENCED, IS LARGE, RATHER THAN SMALL OR STEM (78)	240	DRIFT TOWARD BEING THOSE 0.67 OF 169 WHERE THE FAMILY, IF EXTENDED, IS SMALL OR STEM, RATHER THAN LARGE (135)	22 56 22 113 XSQ= 3.58 PHI= 0.130 XP = 0.0584
300	DRIFT TCWARD BEING THCSE 0.53 OF 43 WHERE THE POST-PARTUM SEX TABOO LASTS LONGER THAN SIX MONTHS (51)	300	DRIFT TOWARD BEING THOSE 0.65 OF 81 WHERE THE POST-PARTUM SEX TABOO LASTS SIX MONTHS OR LESS (73)	23 28 20 53 XSQ= 3.41 PHI= 0.166 XP = 0.0649
305	TILT TOWARD BEING THOSE 0.61 OF 41 WHERE THE EARLY SEXUAL SATISFACTION POTENTIAL IS HIGH (27) W-C	305	TILT TOWARD BEING THOSE 0.80 OF 10 WHERE THE EARLY SEXUAL SATISFACTION POTENTIAL IS LOW (24) W-C	25 2 16 8 XSQ= 3.90 PHI= 0.276 XP = 0.0483
308	DRIFT TOWARD BEING THCSE 0.51 OF 35 WHERE AVERAGE SCCIALIZATICN ANXIETY IS LOW (18) W-C	308	IN ALL CASES ARE THOSE 1.00 OF 5 WHERE AVERAGE SOCIALIZATION ANXIETY IS HIGH (22) W-C	17 5 18 0 XSQ= 2.83 PHI= -0.266 EP = 0.0530
386	DRIFT TOWARD BEING THOSE 0.63 OF 46 WHERE SEXUAL EXPRESSICN BY THE YOUNG IS RESTRICTED OR SEMI-RESTRICTED (46) F-B	386	DRIFT TOWARD BEING THOSE 0.57 OF 40 WHERE SEXUAL EXPRESSION BY THE YOUNG IS PERMITTED (40) F-B	29 17 17 23 XSQ= 2.85 PHI= 0.182 XP = 0.0913

391	TILT TOWARD BEING THOSE WHERE PREMARITAL SEX RELATIONS ARE PUNISHED ONLY IF PREGNANCY RESULTS, OR FREELY PERMITTED (90) JTW,EA	0.65 OF 54	391	TILT TOWARD BEING THOSE WHERE PREMARITAL SEX RELATIONS ARE STRONGLY PUNISHED AND IN FACT RARE, OR WEAKLY PUNISHED AND IN FACT NOT RARE (89) JTW,EA	0.56 OF 125	19 70 35 55 XSQ= 5.73 PHI= -0.179 XP = 0.0167
402	DRIFT TOWARD BEING THOSE WHERE EXPLANATIONS OF ILLNESS OF AN ORAL NATURE ARE PRESENT (31) W-C	0.59 OF 44	402	DRIFT TOWARD BEING THOSE WHERE EXPLANATIONS OF ILLNESS OF AN ORAL NATURE ARE ABSENT (30) W-C	0.71 OF 17	26 5 18 12 XSQ= 3.22 PHI= 0.230 XP = 0.0729
404	DRIFT LESS TOWARD BEING THOSE WHERE EXPLANATIONS OF ILLNESS OF A SEXUAL NATURE ARE ABSENT (42) W-C	0.61 OF 44	404	DRIFT MORE TOWARD BEING THOSE WHERE EXPLANATIONS OF ILLNESS OF A SEXUAL NATURE ARE ABSENT (42) W-C	0.88 OF 17	17 2 27 15 XSQ= 2.97 PHI= 0.221 XP = 0.0848
426	TILT TOWARD BEING THOSE WHERE A HIGH GOD IS ABSENT (104) GES,EA	0.51 OF 68	426	TILT TOWARD BEING THOSE WHERE A HIGH GOD IS PRESENT (156) GES,EA	0.64 OF 192	33 123 35 69 XSQ= 4.42 PHI= -0.130 XP = 0.0355
428	TILT TOWARD BEING THOSE WHERE A HIGH GOD, IF PRESENT AND ACTIVE, DOES NOT SUPPORT HUMAN MORALITY, RATHER THAN SUPPORTING IT (26) GES,EA	0.60 OF 15	428	TILT TOWARD BEING THOSE WHERE A HIGH GOD, IF PRESENT AND ACTIVE, SUPPORTS HUMAN MORALITY, RATHER THAN NOT SUPPORTING IT (61) GES,EA	0.76 OF 72	6 55 9 17 XSQ= 6.20 PHI= -0.267 XP = 0.0127
438	DRIFT TOWARD BEING THOSE WHERE OTHER-WORLDLY FEARS OF GHOSTS OR SPIRITS ARE GREATER THAN THIS-WORLDLY FEARS OF HUMANS OR ANIMALS (27) W-C,JFG	0.71 OF 34	438	DRIFT TOWARD BEING THOSE WHERE THIS-WORLDLY FEARS OF HUMANS OR ANIMALS ARE GREATER THAN OTHER-WORLDLY FEARS OF GHOSTS OR SPIRITS (17) W-C,JFG	0.70 OF 10	24 3 10 7 XSQ= 3.79 PHI= 0.294 XP = 0.0514
449	TEND TO BE THOSE WHERE THE OBSERVATION OF FOOD TABOOS IS HIGH, RATHER THAN MEDIUM OR LOW (25) JRL	0.53 OF 38	449	TEND TO BE THOSE WHERE THE OBSERVATION OF FOOD TABOOS IS MEDIUM OR LOW, RATHER THAN HIGH (61) JRL	0.90 OF 48	20 5 18 43 XSQ= 16.34 PHI= 0.436 XP = 0.0001
450	TEND TO BE THOSE WHERE THE OBSERVATION OF FOOD TABOOS IS HIGH OR MEDIUM, RATHER THAN LOW (60) JRL	0.95 OF 38	450	TEND TO BE THOSE WHERE THE OBSERVATION OF FOOD TABOOS IS LOW, RATHER THAN HIGH OR MEDIUM (26) JRL	0.50 OF 48	36 24 2 24 XSQ= 18.06 PHI= 0.458 XP = 0.0000
468	LEAN TOWARD BEING THOSE WHERE CONTACT WITH OTHER CULTURES IS REGULAR OR IRREGULAR, RATHER THAN FREQUENT (37) JMH	0.86 OF 29	468	LEAN TOWARD BEING THOSE WHERE CONTACT WITH OTHER CULTURES IS FREQUENT, RATHER THAN REGULAR OR IRREGULAR (17) JMH	0.52 OF 25	4 13 25 12 XSQ= 7.40 PHI= -0.370 XP = 0.0065

475	DRIFT TOWARD BEING THOSE WHERE EXHIBITIONISTIC DANCING IS STRONGLY OR MODERATELY EMPHASIZED (48) PES	0.64 OF 56	475	DRIFT TOWARD BEING THOSE WHERE EXHIBITIONISTIC DANCING IS NEGLIGIBLY EMPHASIZED (38) PES	0.60 OF 30	36 12 20 18 XSQ= 3.74 PHI= 0.209 XP = 0.0532
488	TILT MORE TOWARD BEING THOSE ABOUT WHICH THE PRINCIPAL ETHNOGRAPHIES WERE PUBLISHED BEFORE 1950 (185)	0.84 OF 51	488	TILT LESS TOWARD BEING THOSE ABOUT WHICH THE PRINCIPAL ETHNOGRAPHIES WERE PUBLISHED BEFORE 1950 (185)	0.69 OF 206	43 142 8 64 XSQ= 4.06 PHI= 0.126 XP = 0.0438
489	TEND LESS TO BE THOSE NOT INCLUDED IN CHARLES ACKERMAN'S STUDY OF DIVORCE (343)	0.71 OF 78	489	TEND MORE TO BE THOSE NOT INCLUDED IN CHARLES ACKERMAN'S STUDY OF DIVORCE (343)	0.89 OF 322	23 34 55 288 XSQ= 16.89 PHI= 0.206 XP = 0.0000
490	TEND TO BE THOSE INCLUDED IN ALBERT S. ANTHONY'S SAMPLE ON MALE INITIATION RITES (113)	0.72 OF 78	490	TEND TO BE THOSE NOT INCLUDED IN ALBERT S. ANTHONY'S SAMPLE ON MALE INITIATION RITES (287)	0.82 OF 322	56 57 22 265 XSQ= 87.99 PHI= 0.469 XP = 0.
491	TEND LESS TO BE THOSE NOT INCLUDED IN DORRIAN APPLE'S STUDY OF GRANDPARENTHOOD (352)	0.64 OF 78	491	TEND MORE TO BE THOSE NOT INCLUDED IN DORRIAN APPLE'S STUDY OF GRANDPARENTHOOD (352)	0.94 OF 322	28 20 50 302 XSQ= 49.63 PHI= 0.352 XP = 0.
492	TEND LESS TO BE THOSE NOT INCLUDED IN BARBARA CHARTIER AYRES' STUDY OF FEMALE INITIATION RITES (361)	0.56 OF 78	492	TEND MORE TO BE THOSE NOT INCLUDED IN BARBARA CHARTIER AYRES' STUDY OF FEMALE INITIATION RITES (361)	0.98 OF 322	34 5 44 317 XSQ= 121.36 PHI= 0.551 XP = 0.
494	TEND LESS TO BE THOSE NOT INCLUDED IN HERBERT M. BARRY III'S STUDY OF ART (371)	0.65 OF 78	494	TEND MORE TO BE THOSE NOT INCLUDED IN HERBERT M. BARRY III'S STUDY OF ART (371)	0.99 OF 322	27 2 51 320 XSQ= 102.91 PHI= 0.507 XP = 0.
495	TEND LESS TO BE THOSE NOT INCLUDED IN JUDITH K. BROWN'S STUDY OF FEMALE INITIATION RITES (335)	0.62 OF 78	495	TEND MORE TO BE THOSE NOT INCLUDED IN JUDITH K. BROWN'S STUDY OF FEMALE INITIATION RITES (335)	0.89 OF 322	30 35 48 287 XSQ= 33.13 PHI= 0.288 XP = 0.
496	TEND LESS TO BE THOSE NOT INCLUDED IN ROY G. D'ANDRADE'S STUDY OF DREAMS (345)	0.60 OF 78	496	TEND MORE TO BE THOSE NOT INCLUDED IN ROY G. D'ANDRADE'S STUDY OF DREAMS (345)	0.93 OF 322	31 24 47 298 XSQ= 52.51 PHI= 0.362 XP = 0.

497	TEND LESS TO BE THCSE NOT INCLUDED IN WILLIAM M. EVAN'S STUDY OF LAW (339)	0.67 OF 78	497	TEND MORE TO BE THOSE NOT INCLUDED IN WILLIAM M. EVAN'S STUDY OF LAW (339)	0.89 OF 322	26 35 52 287 XSQ= 22.81 PHI= 0.239 XP = 0.0000
498	TEND LESS TO BE THCSE NOT INCLUDED IN C. S. FORC'S STUDY OF SEX (349)	0.62 OF 78	498	TEND MORE TO BE THOSE NOT INCLUDED IN C. S. FORD'S STUDY OF SEX (349)	0.93 OF 322	30 21 48 301 XSQ= 54.75 PHI= 0.370 XP = 0.
499	TEND TO BE THOSE INCLUDED IN FORD AND BEACH'S SAMPLE ON SEXUAL EXPRESSICN BY THE YCUNG (86)	0.59 OF 78	499	TEND TO BE THOSE NOT INCLUDED IN FORD AND BEACH'S SAMPLE ON SEXUAL EXPRESSION BY THE YOUNG (314)	0.88 OF 322	46 40 32 282 XSQ= 77.89 PHI= 0.441 XP = 0.
500	TEND LESS TO BE THCSE NOT INCLUDED IN FREEMAN ANC WINCH'S STUDY OF SOCIETAL CCMPLEXITY (360)	0.69 OF 78	500	TEND MORE TO BE THOSE NOT INCLUDED IN FREEMAN AND WINCH'S STUDY OF SOCIETAL COMPLEXITY (360)	0.95 OF 322	24 16 54 306 XSQ= 43.62 PHI= 0.330 XP = 0.
501	TEND TO BE THCSE INCLUDED IN JOAN FRIENDLY GOODMAN'S STUDY OF ASCETIC MCURNING BEHAVIOR (67)	0.60 OF 78	501	TEND TO BE THOSE NOT INCLUDED IN JOAN FRIENDLY GOODMAN'S STUDY OF ASCETIC MOURNING BEHAVIOR (333)	0.94 OF 322	47 20 31 302 XSQ= 127.68 PHI= 0.565 XP = 0.
502	TEND LESS TO BE THCSE NOT INCLUDED IN JOHN K. HARLEY'S STUDY OF ADOLESCENT PEER GROUPS (343)	0.53 OF 78	502	TEND MORE TO BE THOSE NOT INCLUDED IN JOHN K. HARLEY'S STUDY OF ADOLESCENT PEER GROUPS (343)	0.94 OF 322	37 20 41 302 XSQ= 83.99 PHI= 0.458 XP = 0.
503	TEND LESS TO BE THCSE NOT INCLUDED IN JOHN M. HICKMAN'S STUDY OF THE FOLK-URBAN CONTINUUM (346)	0.63 OF 78	503	TEND MORE TO BE THOSE NOT INCLUDED IN JOHN M. HICKMAN'S STUDY OF THE FOLK-URBAN CONTINUUM (346)	0.92 OF 322	29 25 49 297 XSQ= 44.04 PHI= 0.332 XP = 0.
504	TEND LESS TO BE THCSE NOT INCLUDED IN DONALC HORTON'S STUDY OF ALCHOLISM (351)	0.67 OF 78	504	TEND MORE TO BE THOSE NOT INCLUDED IN DONALD HORTCN'S STUDY OF ALCHOLISM (351)	0.93 OF 322	26 23 52 299 XSQ= 37.67 PHI= 0.307 XP = 0.
505	LEAN LESS TOWARC BEING THOSE NOT INCLUDED IN MERRILL JACKSON'S STUDY OF CRIMINAL LAW AND MEDICINE (380)	0.88 OF 78	505	LEAN MORE TOWARD BEING THOSE NOT INCLUDED IN MERRILL JACKSON'S STUDY OF CRIMINAL LAW AND MEDICINE (380)	0.97 OF 322	9 11 69 311 XSQ= 7.09 PHI= 0.133 XP = 0.0077

506	TEND LESS TO BE THCSE NOT INCLUDED IN LAMBERT, TRIANDIS, AND WOLF'S STUDY OF SUPERNATURAL BEINGS (364)	0.54 OF 78	506	IN ALL CASES ARE THOSE NOT INCLUDED IN LAMBERT, TRIANDIS, AND WOLF'S STUDY OF SUPERNATURAL BEINGS (364)	1.00 OF 322	36 0 / 42 322 / XSQ= 157.73 / PHI= 0.628 / XP = 0.
507	TEND LESS TO BE THCSE NOT INCLUDED IN JAMES R. LEARY'S STUDY OF FCOD TABOCS (314)	0.51 OF 78	507	TEND MORE TO BE THOSE NOT INCLUDED IN JAMES R. LEARY'S STUDY OF FOOD TABOOS (314)	0.85 OF 322	38 48 / 40 274 / XSQ= 40.55 / PHI= 0.318 / XP = 0.
508	TEND TC BE THOSE INCLUDED IN DAVID C. MCCLELLAND'S STUDY OF ACHIEVEMENT MOTIVATION (40)	0.51 OF 78	508	IN ALL CASES ARE THOSE NOT INCLUDED IN DAVID C. MCCLELLAND'S STUDY OF ACHIEVEMENT MOTIVATION (360)	1.00 OF 322	40 0 / 38 322 / XSQ= 177.82 / PHI= 0.667 / XP = 0.
509	LEAN LESS TOWARC BEING THCSE NOT INCLUDED IN MONI NAG'S STUDY OF FERTILITY (375)	0.86 OF 78	509	LEAN MORE TOWARD BEING THOSE NOT INCLUDED IN MONI NAG'S STUDY OF FERTILITY (375)	0.96 OF 322	11 14 / 67 308 / XSQ= 8.60 / PHI= 0.147 / XP = 0.0034
510	TEND LESS TO BE THCSE NOT INCLUDED IN RACUL NARRCLL'S STUDY OF SCCIETAL COMPLEXITY (380)	0.82 OF 78	510	TEND MORE TO BE THOSE NOT INCLUDED IN RAOUL NARRCLL'S STUDY OF SOCIETAL COMPLEXITY (380)	0.98 OF 322	14 6 / 64 316 / XSQ= 30.90 / PHI= 0.278 / XP = 0.
511	TEND TO BE THOSE INCLUDED IN ROBERTS, ARTH AND BUSH'S SAMPLE ON GAMES, AS MCCIFIED BY THE ETHNOGRAPHIC ATLAS (189)	0.78 OF 78	511	TEND TO BE THOSE NOT INCLUDED IN ROBERTS, ARTH AND BUSH'S SAMPLE ON GAMES, AS MODIFIED BY THE ETHNOGRAPHIC ATLAS (211)	0.60 OF 322	61 128 / 17 194 / XSQ= 35.72 / PHI= 0.299 / XP = 0.
512	TEND LESS TO BE THCSE NOT INCLUDED IN SHIRLEY AND ROMNEY'S STUDY OF LCVE MAGIC (367)	0.63 OF 78	512	TEND MORE TO BE THOSE NOT INCLUDED IN SHIRLEY AND ROMNEY'S STUDY OF LOVE MAGIC (367)	0.99 OF 322	29 4 / 49 318 / XSQ= 102.44 / PHI= 0.506 / XP = 0.
513	TEND LESS TO BE THCSE NOT INCLUDED IN LEC W. SIMMONS' STUDY CF THE TREATMENT CF THE AGEC (357)	0.77 OF 78	513	TEND MORE TO BE THOSE NOT INCLUDED IN LEO W. SIMMONS' STUDY OF THE TREATMENT OF THE AGED (357)	0.92 OF 322	18 25 / 60 297 / XSQ= 13.79 / PHI= 0.186 / XP = 0.0002
514	TEND TO BE THOSE INCLUDED IN PHILIP E. SLATER'S STUDY OF NARCISSISM (90)	0.73 OF 78	514	TEND TO BE THOSE NOT INCLUDED IN PHILIP E. SLATER'S STUDY OF NARCISSISM (310)	0.90 OF 322	57 33 / 21 289 / XSQ= 138.56 / PHI= 0.589 / XP = 0.

515	TEND TO BE THOSE 0.50 OF 78 INCLUDED IN WILLIAM N. STEPHENS' SAMPLE ON AVOIDANCE RELATIONSHIPS (52)	515	TEND TO BE THOSE 0.96 OF 322 NOT INCLUDED IN WILLIAM N. STEPHENS' SAMPLE ON AVOIDANCE RELATIONSHIPS (348)	39 13 39 309 XSQ= 113.26 PHI= 0.532 XP = 0.
516	LEAN MORE TOWARD BEING THOSE 0.95 OF 78 INCLUDED IN GUY E. SWANSON'S SAMPLE ON LOCAL JURISDICTION, AS MODIFIED BY THE ETHNOGRAPHIC ATLAS (331)	516	LEAN LESS TOWARD BEING THOSE 0.80 OF 322 INCLUDED IN GUY E. SWANSON'S SAMPLE ON LOCAL JURISDICTION, AS MODIFIED BY THE ETHNOGRAPHIC ATLAS (331)	74 257 4 65 XSQ= 8.95 PHI= 0.150 XP = 0.0028
517	TEND MORE TO BE THOSE 0.87 OF 78 INCLUDED IN GUY E. SWANSON'S SAMPLE ON HIGH GODS, AS MODIFIED BY THE ETHNOGRAPHIC ATLAS (260)	517	TEND LESS TO BE THOSE 0.60 OF 322 INCLUDED IN GUY E. SWANSON'S SAMPLE ON HIGH GODS, AS MODIFIED BY THE ETHNOGRAPHIC ATLAS (260)	68 192 10 130 XSQ= 19.76 PHI= 0.222 XP = 0.0000
518	TEND TO BE THOSE 0.56 OF 78 INCLUDED IN STANLEY H. UDY, JR.'S STUDY OF WORK ORGANIZATION (105)	518	TEND TO BE THOSE 0.81 OF 322 NOT INCLUDED IN STANLEY H. UDY, JR.'S STUDY OF WORK ORGANIZATION (295)	44 61 34 261 XSQ= 43.61 PHI= 0.330 XP = 0.
519	TEND LESS TO BE THOSE 0.54 OF 78 NOT INCLUDED IN JOSEPH VEROFF'S STUDY OF ACHIEVEMENT MOTIVATION AS REVEALED IN FOLKTALES (364)	519	IN ALL CASES ARE THOSE 1.00 OF 322 NOT INCLUDED IN JOSEPH VEROFF'S STUDY OF ACHIEVEMENT MOTIVATION AS REVEALED IN FOLKTALES (364)	36 0 42 322 XSQ= 157.73 PHI= 0.628 XP = 0.
522	TEND TO BE THOSE 0.76 OF 78 INCLUDED IN MARJORIE GRANT WHITING'S STUDY OF DIET (82)	522	TEND TO BE THOSE 0.93 OF 322 NOT INCLUDED IN MARJORIE GRANT WHITING'S STUDY OF DIET (318)	59 23 19 299 XSQ= 176.59 PHI= 0.664 XP = 0.
523	TEND TO BE THOSE 0.56 OF 78 INCLUDED IN WHITING AND CHILD'S STUDY OF CHILD TRAINING AND PERSONALITY (61)	523	TEND TO BE THOSE 0.95 OF 322 NOT INCLUDED IN WHITING AND CHILD'S STUDY OF CHILD TRAINING AND PERSONALITY (339)	44 17 34 305 XSQ= 123.09 PHI= 0.555 XP = 0.
524	TEND LESS TO BE THOSE 0.54 OF 78 NOT INCLUDED IN WHITING, KLUCKHOHN, AND ANTHONY'S STUDY OF MALE INITIATION CEREMONIES (356)	524	TEND MORE TO BE THOSE 0.98 OF 322 NOT INCLUDED IN WHITING, KLUCKHOHN, AND ANTHONY'S STUDY OF MALE INITIATION CEREMONIES (356)	36 8 42 314 XSQ= 117.89 PHI= 0.543 XP = 0.

```
****************************************************************************************************

494  CULTURES                                          494  CULTURES
     INCLUDED IN HERBERT M. BARRY III'S                     NOT INCLUDED IN HERBERT M. BARRY III'S
     STUDY OF ART  (29)                                     STUDY OF ART  (371)


                                                            SUBJECT ONLY, F.C. 1-480 AND 527-536
BACKGROUND ON PAGE 180                                  BOTH SUBJECT AND PREDICATE, F.C. 481-526
....................................................................................................

     29  IN LEFT COLUMN

AINU        ALCRESE    ANCAMANESE  ARAPESH    ASHANTI   BALINESE    CHENCHU       CHIR-APACHE COMANCHE  FON
HANO        IFUGAO     JAPANESE    KWAKIUTL   MAORI     MARQUESANS  MARSHALLESE   MASAI       MURNGIN   NAVAHO
OMAHA       PAPAGO     SAMOANS     TETON      THONGA    TROBRIAND   YAGUA         YAKUT       ZUNI

     371  IN RIGHT COLUMN

----------------------------------------------------------------------------------------------------
  4  IN ALL CASES ARE THOSE        1.00 OF  29      4  DRIFT LESS TOWARD BEING THOSE  0.88 OF 371        0   45
     LOCATED OUTSIDE OF                                LOCATED OUTSIDE OF                               29  326
     THE CIRCUM-MEDITERRANEAN  (355)                   THE CIRCUM-MEDITERRANEAN  (355)              XSQ=    2.84
                                                                                                    PHI=  -0.084
                                                                                                    XP =  0.0918

  6  TILT LESS TOWARD BEING THOSE  0.66 OF  29      6  TILT MORE TOWARD BEING THOSE   0.84 OF 371       10   60
     LOCATED OUTSIDE OF                                LOCATED OUTSIDE OF                               19  311
     THE INSULAR PACIFIC  (330)                        THE INSULAR PACIFIC  (330)                   XSQ=    5.04
                                                                                                    PHI=   0.112
                                                                                                    XP =  0.0247

  8  DRIFT LESS TOWARD BEING THOSE 0.69 OF  29      8  DRIFT MORE TOWARD BEING THOSE  0.84 OF 371        9   61
     LOCATED OUTSIDE OF                                LOCATED OUTSIDE OF                               20  310
     NORTH AMERICA  (330)                              NORTH AMERICA  (330)                         XSQ=    3.02
                                                                                                    PHI=   0.087
                                                                                                    XP =  0.0822

  9  DRIFT MORE TOWARD BEING THOSE 0.97 OF  29      9  DRIFT LESS TOWARD BEING THOSE  0.83 OF 371        1   64
     LOCATED OUTSIDE OF                                LOCATED OUTSIDE OF                               28  307
     SOUTH AMERICA  (335)                              SOUTH AMERICA  (335)                         XSQ=    2.82
                                                                                                    PHI=  -0.084
                                                                                                    XP =  0.0931

 63  TILT TOWARD BEING THOSE       0.58 OF  19     63  TILT TOWARD BEING THOSE        0.70 OF 207        8  144
     WHERE HUSBANDRY, IF PRESENT,                      WHERE HUSBANDRY, IF PRESENT,                     11   63
     IS PRINCIPALLY IN THE FORM OF                     IS PRINCIPALLY IN THE FORM OF                XSQ=    4.78
     PIGS, SHEEP, OR GOATS, RATHER THAN                BOVINE, EQUINE, CAMEL-LIKE, OR DEER-LIKE     PHI=  -0.145
     BOVINE, EQUINE, CAMEL-LIKE, OR DEER-LIKE          ANIMALS, RATHER THAN                         XP =  0.0288
     ANIMALS  (74)                                     PIGS, SHEEP, OR GOATS  (152)
```

108	TILT TOWARD BEING THOSE WHERE CLASS STRATIFICATION, IF PRESENT, IS BASED ON A HEREDITARY ARISTOCRACY (74)	0.71 OF 14	108	TILT TOWARD BEING THOSE WHERE CLASS STRATIFICATION, IF PRESENT, IS BASED ON SOMETHING OTHER THAN A HEREDITARY ARISTOCRACY (129)	0.66 OF 189	10 64 4 125 XSQ= 6.40 PHI= 0.178 XP = 0.0114
184	DRIFT TOWARD BEING THOSE WHERE THE LARGEST NON-COGNATIC KIN GROUP IS THE MOEITY OR PHRATRY (77)	0.53 OF 17	184	DRIFT TOWARD BEING THOSE WHERE THE LARGEST NON-COGNATIC KIN GROUP IS SMALLER THAN A PHRATRY, I. E. A SIB OR LINEAGE (175)	0.71 OF 235	9 68 8 167 XSQ= 3.25 PHI= 0.114 XP = 0.0715
198	DRIFT LESS TOWARD BEING THOSE WHERE RULES FOR THE INHERITANCE OF REAL PROPERTY, IF PRESENT, FAVOR THE MALE HEIR OR LINE, RATHER THAN THE FEMALE (144)	0.67 OF 12	198	DRIFT MORE TOWARD BEING THOSE WHERE RULES FOR THE INHERITANCE OF REAL PROPERTY, IF PRESENT, FAVOR THE MALE HEIR OR LINE, RATHER THAN THE FEMALE (144)	0.89 OF 153	8 136 4 17 XSQ= 3.15 PHI= -0.138 XP = 0.0760
259	TILT TOWARD BEING THOSE WHERE THE SEVERITY OF MOTHER-IN-LAW AVOIDANCE IS LOW (20) WNS	0.71 OF 17	259	TILT TOWARD BEING THOSE WHERE THE SEVERITY OF MOTHER-IN-LAW AVOIDANCE IS HIGH (26) WNS	0.72 OF 29	5 21 12 8 XSQ= 6.41 PHI= -0.373 XP = 0.0114
263	TILT TOWARD BEING THOSE WHERE WIVES ARE OBTAINED BY RELATIVELY EASY MEANS, NAMELY BY TOKEN BRIDE-PRICE, GIFT EXCHANGE, ABSENCE OF ANY CONSIDERATION, OR RECEIPT OF DOWRY (162)	0.62 OF 29	263	TILT TOWARD BEING THOSE WHERE WIVES ARE OBTAINED BY RELATIVELY DIFFICULT MEANS, NAMELY BY BRIDE-PRICE, BRIDE-SERVICE, OR EXCHANGING A FEMALE RELATIVE (233)	0.61 OF 366	11 222 18 144 XSQ= 4.84 PHI= -0.111 XP = 0.0279
272	TILT TOWARD BEING THOSE WHERE THE DIVORCE RATE IS HIGH (29) CA	0.89 OF 9	272	TILT TOWARD BEING THOSE WHERE THE DIVORCE RATE IS LOW (28) CA	0.56 OF 48	8 21 1 27 XSQ= 4.50 PHI= 0.281 XP = 0.0338
280	IN ALL CASES ARE THOSE WHERE THE COMPOSITE FERTILITY LEVEL IS HIGH (13) MN	1.00 OF 5	280	TILT TOWARD BEING THOSE WHERE THE COMPOSITE FERTILITY LEVEL IS LOW (12) MN	0.60 OF 20	5 8 0 12 XSQ= 3.62 PHI= 0.380 EP = 0.0391
286	TILT TOWARD BEING THOSE WHERE THE NUMBER OF FOOD TABOOS DURING PREGNANCY IS LOW OR ABSENT (14) BCA	0.61 OF 18	286	TILT TOWARD BEING THOSE WHERE THE NUMBER OF FOOD TABOOS DURING PREGNANCY IS HIGH (20) BCA	0.81 OF 16	7 13 11 3 XSQ= 4.65 PHI= -0.370 EP = 0.0173
303	DRIFT TOWARD BEING THOSE WHERE THE EARLY ORAL SATISFACTION POTENTIAL IS LOW (25) W-C	0.59 OF 27	303	DRIFT TOWARD BEING THOSE WHERE THE EARLY ORAL SATISFACTION POTENTIAL IS HIGH (32) W-C	0.70 OF 30	11 21 16 9 XSQ= 3.82 PHI= -0.259 XP = 0.0505

325	LEAN TOWARD BEING THOSE WHERE THE DEGREE OF DIFFUSION AMONG THE INFANT'S NURTURANT AGENTS IS HIGH (42) B-B-C	0.81 OF 27	325	LEAN TOWARD BEING THOSE WHERE THE DEGREE OF DIFFUSION AMONG THE INFANT'S NURTURANT AGENTS IS LOW (32) B-B-C	0.57 OF 47	22 20 5 27 XSQ= 9.06 PHI= 0.350 XP = 0.0026
392	TILT TOWARD BEING THOSE WHERE PREMARITAL SEX RELATIONS ARE FREELY PERMITTED (67) JTW,EA	0.59 OF 22	392	TILT TOWARD BEING THOSE WHERE PREMARITAL SEX RELATIONS ARE STRONGLY PUNISHED AND IN FACT RARE, OR WEAKLY PUNISHED AND IN FACT NOT RARE, OR PUNISHED ONLY IF PREGNANCY RESULTS (112) JTW,EA	0.66 OF 157	9 103 13 54 XSQ= 4.03 PHI= -0.150 XP = 0.0448
426	LEAN TOWARD BEING THOSE WHERE A HIGH GOD IS ABSENT (104) GES,EA	0.68 OF 22	426	LEAN TOWARD BEING THOSE WHERE A HIGH GOD IS PRESENT (156) GES,EA	0.63 OF 238	7 149 15 89 XSQ= 6.72 PHI= -0.161 XP = 0.0095
438	TILT TOWARD BEING THOSE WHERE OTHER-WORLDLY FEARS OF GHOSTS OR SPIRITS ARE GREATER THAN THIS-WORLDLY FEARS OF HUMANS OR ANIMALS (27) W-C,JFG	0.81 OF 21	438	TILT TOWARD BEING THOSE WHERE THIS-WORLDLY FEARS OF HUMANS OR ANIMALS ARE GREATER THAN OTHER-WORLDLY FEARS OF GHOSTS OR SPIRITS (17) W-C,JFG	0.57 OF 23	17 10 4 13 XSQ= 5.02 PHI= 0.338 XP = 0.0251
449	TEND TO BE THOSE WHERE THE OBSERVATION OF FOOD TABOOS IS HIGH, RATHER THAN MEDIUM OR LOW (25) JRL	0.80 OF 10	449	TEND TO BE THOSE WHERE THE OBSERVATION OF FOOD TABOOS IS MEDIUM OR LOW, RATHER THAN HIGH (61) JRL	0.78 OF 76	8 17 2 59 XSQ= 11.58 PHI= 0.367 XP = 0.0007
450	IN ALL CASES ARE THOSE WHERE THE OBSERVATION OF FOOD TABOOS IS HIGH OR MEDIUM, RATHER THAN LOW (60) JRL	1.00 OF 10	450	DRIFT LESS TOWARD BEING THOSE WHERE THE OBSERVATION OF FOOD TABOOS IS HIGH OR MEDIUM, RATHER THAN LOW (60) JRL	0.66 OF 76	10 50 0 26 XSQ= 3.42 PHI= 0.199 XP = 0.0646
456	DRIFT TOWARD BEING THOSE WHERE THE INTERNALIZATION OF THE INDIVIDUAL'S CONTACT WITH THE DIVINE IS NOT CONDUCIVE TO THE DEVELOPMENT OF THE INDIVIDUAL'S NEED TO ACHIEVE (17) DCM	0.73 OF 11	456	DRIFT TOWARD BEING THOSE WHERE THE INTERNALIZATION OF THE INDIVIDUAL'S CONTACT WITH THE DIVINE IS CONDUCIVE TO THE DEVELOPMENT OF THE INDIVIDUAL'S NEED TO ACHIEVE (19) DCM	0.64 OF 25	3 16 8 9 XSQ= 2.79 PHI= -0.278 EP = 0.0704
481	DRIFT LESS TOWARD BEING THOSE WHERE THE PRINCIPAL ETHNOGRAPHERS HAVE BEEN OTHER THAN AMERICAN (275)	0.55 OF 29	481	DRIFT MORE TOWARD BEING THOSE WHERE THE PRINCIPAL ETHNOGRAPHERS HAVE BEEN OTHER THAN AMERICAN (275)	0.72 OF 359	13 100 16 259 XSQ= 2.97 PHI= 0.087 XP = 0.0850
488	TILT MORE TOWARD BEING THOSE ABOUT WHICH THE PRINCIPAL ETHNOGRAPHIES WERE PUBLISHED BEFORE 1950 (185)	0.95 OF 20	488	TILT LESS TOWARD BEING THOSE ABOUT WHICH THE PRINCIPAL ETHNOGRAPHIES WERE PUBLISHED BEFORE 1950 (185)	0.70 OF 237	19 166 1 71 XSQ= 4.53 PHI= 0.133 XP = 0.0334

489	TILT LESS TOWARD BEING THCSE NOT INCLUDED IN CHARLES ACKERMAN'S STUDY OF DIVORCE (343)	0.69 OF 29	489	TILT MORE TOWARD BEING THOSE NOT INCLUDED IN CHARLES ACKERMAN'S STUDY OF DIVORCE (343)	0.87 OF 371	9 48 20 323 XSQ= 5.80 PHI= 0.120 XP = 0.0160
490	TEND TC BE THOSE INCLUDED IN ALBERT S. ANTHONY'S SAMPLE ON MALE INITIATION RITES (113)	0.83 OF 29	490	TEND TO BE THOSE NOT INCLUDED IN ALBERT S. ANTHONY'S SAMPLE ON MALE INITIATION RITES (287)	0.76 OF 371	24 89 5 282 XSQ= 42.98 PHI= 0.328 XP = 0.
491	TEND LESS TO BE THCSE NOT INCLUDED IN DORRIAN APPLE'S STUDY CF GRANDPARENTHCCC (352)	0.62 OF 29	491	TEND MORE TO BE THOSE NOT INCLUDED IN DORRIAN APPLE'S STUDY OF GRANDPARENTHOOD (352)	0.90 OF 371	11 37 18 334 XSQ= 17.35 PHI= 0.208 XP = 0.0000
492	TEND TC BE THOSE INCLUDED IN BARBARA CHARTIER AYRES' STUDY OF FEMALE INITIATION RITES (39)	0.72 OF 29	492	TEND TO BE THOSE NOT INCLUDED IN BARBARA CHARTIER AYRES' STUDY OF FEMALE INITIATION RITES (361)	0.95 OF 371	21 18 8 353 XSQ= 131.96 PHI= 0.574 XP = 0.
493	TEND TO BE THOSE INCLUDED IN BACCN, BARRY, AND CHILC'S STUDY CF CHILD REARING (78)	0.93 OF 29	493	TEND TO BE THOSE NOT INCLUDED IN BACON, BARRY, AND CHILD'S STUDY OF CHILD REARING (322)	0.86 OF 371	27 51 2 320 XSQ= 102.91 PHI= 0.507 XP = 0.
495	LEAN LESS TOWARD BEING THCSE NOT INCLUDED IN JUCITH K. BROWN'S STUDY OF FEMALE INITIATION RITES (335)	0.62 OF 29	495	LEAN MORE TOWARD BEING THOSE NOT INCLUDED IN JUDITH K. BROWN'S STUDY OF FEMALE INITIATICN RITES (335)	0.85 OF 371	11 54 18 317 XSQ= 9.15 PHI= 0.151 XP = 0.0025
496	LEAN LESS TOWARC BEING THOSE NOT INCLUDED IN ROY G. C'ANDRADE'S STUDY CF DREAMS (345)	0.66 OF 29	496	LEAN MORE TOWARD BEING THOSE NOT INCLUDED IN ROY G. D'ANDRADE'S STUDY OF DREAMS (345)	0.88 OF 371	10 45 19 326 XSQ= 9.53 PHI= 0.154 XP = 0.0020
497	TILT LESS TOWARC BEING THCSE NCT INCLUDED IN WILLIAM M. EVAN'S STUDY CF LAW (339)	0.69 OF 29	497	TILT MORE TOWARD BEING THCSE NOT INCLUDED IN WILLIAM M. EVAN'S STUDY OF LAW (339)	0.86 OF 371	9 52 20 319 XSQ= 4.78 PHI= 0.109 XP = 0.0287
498	TEND LESS TO BE THCSE NOT INCLUDED IN C. S. FORC'S STUDY OF SEX (349)	0.55 OF 29	498	TEND MORE TO BE THOSE NOT INCLUDED IN C. S. FORD'S STUDY OF SEX (349)	0.90 OF 371	13 38 16 333 XSQ= 25.90 PHI= 0.254 XP = 0.0000

499	TEND TO BE THOSE INCLUDED IN FORD AND BEACH'S SAMPLE ON SEXUAL EXPRESSION BY THE YOUNG (86)	0.76 OF 29	499	TEND TO BE THOSE NOT INCLUDED IN FORD AND BEACH'S SAMPLE ON SEXUAL EXPRESSION BY THE YOUNG (314)	0.83 OF 371	22 64 7 307 XSQ= 51.33 PHI= 0.358 XP = 0.
500	TEND LESS TO BE THOSE NOT INCLUDED IN FREEMAN AND WINCH'S STUDY OF SOCIETAL COMPLEXITY (360)	0.69 OF 29	500	TEND MORE TO BE THOSE NOT INCLUDED IN FREEMAN AND WINCH'S STUDY OF SOCIETAL COMPLEXITY (360)	0.92 OF 371	9 31 20 340 XSQ= 12.95 PHI= 0.180 XP = 0.0003
501	TEND TO BE THOSE INCLUDED IN JOAN FRIENDLY GOODMAN'S STUDY OF ASCETIC MOURNING BEHAVIOR (67)	0.72 OF 29	501	TEND TO BE THOSE NOT INCLUDED IN JOAN FRIENDLY GOODMAN'S STUDY OF ASCETIC MOURNING BEHAVIOR (333)	0.88 OF 371	21 46 8 325 XSQ= 65.24 PHI= 0.404 XP = 0.
502	TEND TO BE THOSE INCLUDED IN JOHN K. HARLEY'S STUDY OF ADOLESCENT PEER GROUPS (57)	0.52 OF 29	502	TEND TO BE THOSE NOT INCLUDED IN JOHN K. HARLEY'S STUDY OF ADOLESCENT PEER GROUPS (343)	0.89 OF 371	15 42 14 329 XSQ= 32.70 PHI= 0.286 XP = 0.
504	TEND LESS TO BE THOSE NOT INCLUDED IN DONALD HORTON'S STUDY OF ALCHOLISM (351)	0.55 OF 29	504	TEND MORE TO BE THOSE NOT INCLUDED IN DONALD HORTON'S STUDY OF ALCHOLISM (351)	0.90 OF 371	13 36 16 335 XSQ= 27.69 PHI= 0.263 XP = 0.0000
505	TEND LESS TO BE THOSE NOT INCLUDED IN MERRILL JACKSON'S STUDY OF CRIMINAL LAW AND MEDICINE (380)	0.79 OF 29	505	TEND MORE TO BE THOSE NOT INCLUDED IN MERRILL JACKSON'S STUDY OF CRIMINAL LAW AND MEDICINE (380)	0.96 OF 371	6 14 23 357 XSQ= 12.84 PHI= 0.179 XP = 0.0003
506	TEND TO BE THOSE INCLUDED IN LAMBERT, TRIANDIS, AND WOLF'S STUDY OF SUPERNATURAL BEINGS (36)	0.62 OF 29	506	TEND TO BE THOSE NOT INCLUDED IN LAMBERT, TRIANDIS, AND WOLF'S STUDY OF SUPERNATURAL BEINGS (364)	0.95 OF 371	18 18 11 353 XSQ= 100.65 PHI= 0.502 XP = 0.
508	TEND TO BE THOSE INCLUDED IN DAVID C. MCCLELLAND'S STUDY OF ACHIEVEMENT MOTIVATION (40)	0.52 OF 29	508	TEND TO BE THOSE NOT INCLUDED IN DAVID C. MCCLELLAND'S STUDY OF ACHIEVEMENT MOTIVATION (360)	0.93 OF 371	15 25 14 346 XSQ= 55.59 PHI= 0.373 XP = 0.
509	TILT LESS TOWARD BEING THOSE NOT INCLUDED IN MONI NAG'S STUDY OF FERTILITY (375)	0.83 OF 29	509	TILT MORE TOWARD BEING THOSE NOT INCLUDED IN MONI NAG'S STUDY OF FERTILITY (375)	0.95 OF 371	5 20 24 351 XSQ= 4.58 PHI= 0.107 XP = 0.0323

No.			No.			
510	LEAN LESS TOWARD BEING THOSE NOT INCLUDED IN RACUL NARRCLL'S STUDY OF SCCIETAL CCMPLEXITY (380)	0.83 OF 29	510	LEAN MORE TOWARD BEING THOSE NOT INCLUDED IN RAOUL NARROLL'S STUDY OF SOCIETAL COMPLEXITY (380)	0.96 OF 371	5 15 24 356 XSQ= 7.28 PHI= 0.135 XP = 0.0070
511	LEAN TOWARD BEING THOSE INCLUDED IN ROBERTS, ARTH AND BUSH'S SAMPLE ON GAMES, AS MCDIFIED BY THE ETHNOGRAPHIC ATLAS (189)	0.76 OF 29	511	LEAN TOWARD BEING THOSE NOT INCLUDED IN ROBERTS, ARTH AND BUSH'S SAMPLE ON GAMES, AS MODIFIED BY THE ETHNOGRAPHIC ATLAS (211)	0.55 OF 371	22 167 7 204 XSQ= 9.07 PHI= 0.151 XP = 0.0026
512	TEND TO BE THOSE INCLUDED IN SHIRLEY AND RCMNEY'S STUDY OF LCVE MAGIC (33)	0.62 OF 29	512	TEND TO BE THOSE NOT INCLUDED IN SHIRLEY AND ROMNEY'S STUDY OF LOVE MAGIC (367)	0.96 OF 371	18 15 11 356 XSQ= 112.10 PHI= 0.529 XP = 0.
513	TEND LESS TO BE THCSE NOT INCLUDED IN LEC W. SIMMONS' STUDY OF THE TREATMENT OF THE AGEC (357)	0.59 OF 29	513	TEND MORE TO BE THOSE NOT INCLUDED IN LEO W. SIMMCNS' STUDY OF THE TREATMENT OF THE AGED (357)	0.92 OF 371	12 31 17 340 XSQ= 27.23 PHI= 0.261 XP = 0.0000
514	TEND TO BE THOSE INCLUDED IN PHILIP E. SLATER'S STUDY OF NARCISSISM (90)	0.86 OF 29	514	TEND TO BE THOSE NOT INCLUDED IN PHILIP E. SLATER'S STUDY OF NARCISSISM (310)	0.82 OF 371	25 65 4 306 XSQ= 68.89 PHI= 0.415 XP = 0.
515	TEND TO BE THOSE INCLUDED IN WILLIAM N. STEPHENS' SAMPLE ON AVOIDANCE RELATICNSHIPS (52)	0.62 OF 29	515	TEND TO BE THOSE NOT INCLUDED IN WILLIAM N. STEPHENS' SAMPLE ON AVOIDANCE RELATIONSHIPS (348)	0.91 OF 371	18 34 11 337 XSQ= 61.97 PHI= 0.394 XP = 0.
518	TEND TO BE THOSE INCLUDED IN STANLEY H. UDY, JR.'S STUDY OF WCRK ORGANIZATICN (105)	0.55 OF 29	518	TEND TO BE THOSE NOT INCLUDED IN STANLEY H. UDY, JR.'S STUDY OF WORK ORGANIZATION (295)	0.76 OF 371	16 89 13 282 XSQ= 11.95 PHI= 0.173 XP = 0.0005
519	TEND LESS TO BE THCSE NOT INCLUDED IN JOSEPH VERCFF'S STUDY OF ACHIEVEMENT MCTIVATICN AS REVEALED IN FCLKTALES (364)	0.59 OF 29	519	TEND MORE TO BE THOSE NOT INCLUDED IN JOSEPH VERCFF'S STUDY OF ACHIEVEMENT MOTIVATION AS REVEALED IN FOLKTALES (364)	0.94 OF 371	12 24 17 347 XSQ= 35.88 PHI= 0.299 XP = 0.
520	TEND LESS TO BE THCSE NOT INCLUDED IN BEATRICE BLYTH WHITING'S STUDY OF SCRCERY (360)	0.62 OF 29	520	TEND MORE TO BE THOSE NOT INCLUDED IN BEATRICE BLYTH WHITING'S STUDY OF SORCERY (360)	0.92 OF 371	11 29 18 342 XSQ= 23.86 PHI= 0.244 XP = 0.0000

```
522  TEND TO BE THOSE               0.69 OF  29    522  TEND TO BE THOSE               0.83 OF 371          20   62
     INCLUDED IN                                         NOT INCLUDED IN                                       9  309
     MARJCRIE GRANT WHITING'S                            MARJORIE GRANT WHITING'S                       XSQ=   41.91
     STUDY OF DIET  (82)                                 STUDY OF DIET  (318)                           PHI=   0.324
                                                                                                        XP =  0.

523  TEND TC BE THCSE               0.97 OF  29    523  TEND TO BE THOSE               0.91 OF 371          28   33
     INCLUDED IN WHITING ANC CHILD'S                     NOT INCLUDED IN WHITING AND CHILD'S                   1  338
     STUDY OF CHILD TRAINING                             STUDY OF CHILD TRAINING                        XSQ= 153.20
     AND PERSCNALITY  (61)                               AND PERSONALITY  (339)                         PHI=   0.619
                                                                                                        XP =  0.

524  TEND TO BE THOSE               0.52 OF  29    524  TEND TC BE THOSE               0.92 OF 371          15   29
     INCLUDED IN                                         NOT INCLUDED IN                                      14  342
     WHITING, KLUCKHCHN, ANC ANTHONY'S                   WHITING, KLUCKHOHN, AND ANTHCNY'S              XSQ=   48.58
     STUDY OF MALE INITIATICN CEREMONIES  (44)           STUDY OF MALE INITIATION CEREMONIES  (356)     PHI=   0.348
                                                                                                        XP =  0.
```

495 CULTURES
INCLUDED IN JUDITH K. BROWN'S
STUDY OF FEMALE INITIATION RITES (65)

495 CULTURES
NOT INCLUDED IN JUDITH K. BROWN'S
STUDY OF FEMALE INITIATION RITES (335)

BACKGROUND ON PAGE 180

SUBJECT ONLY, F.C. 1-480 AND 527-536
BOTH SUBJECT AND PREDICATE, F.C. 481-526

65 IN LEFT COLUMN

AINU	ALORESE	AMERICANS	ANDAMANESE	ARANDA
BHIL	BULGARIANS	BURMESE	CAGABA	CARIB
COPR ESKIMO	CUNA	DILLING	EGYPTIANS	FON
KHASI	KURTATCHI	LAMBA	LAPPS	LEPCHA
NAMA	NAMBICUARA	NASKAPI	NAVAHO	NUER
SANPOIL	SOMALI	TALLENSI	TANALA	TEDA
TUBATULABAL	TUPINAMBA	WOLEAIANS	YAGUA	YUROK

ARAUCANIANS	AYMARA	AZANDE	BALINESE	BEMBA
CAYAPA	CHAMACOCO	CHEYENNE	CHIR-APACHE	CHOROTI
GANDA	GOAJIRO	JAPANESE	JIVARO	KAZAK
LESU	MAGUZAWA	MENDE	MOSSI	MUNDURUCU
OJIBWA	PAPAGO	PUKAPUKA	RWALA	SAMOYED
TEHUELCHE	THAI	THONGA	TIMBIRA	TODA

335 IN RIGHT COLUMN

9 DRIFT LESS TOWARD BEING THOSE 0.75 OF 65
LOCATED OUTSIDE OF
SOUTH AMERICA (335)

9 DRIFT MORE TOWARD BEING THOSE 0.85 OF 335
LOCATED OUTSIDE OF
SOUTH AMERICA (335)

16 49
49 286
XSQ= 3.29
PHI= 0.091
XP = 0.0697

33 DRIFT LESS TOWARD BEING THOSE 0.77 OF 65
WHERE THE NATURAL ENVIRONMENT IS
OTHER THAN 'VERY HARSH,' I.E., DESERT,
DESERT GRASSES AND SHRUBS, TUNDRA, OR
HIGH PLATEAU STEPPE (341) FWM

33 DRIFT MORE TOWARD BEING THOSE 0.87 OF 335
WHERE THE NATURAL ENVIRONMENT IS
OTHER THAN 'VERY HARSH,' I.E., DESERT,
DESERT GRASSES AND SHRUBS, TUNDRA, OR
HIGH PLATEAU STEPPE (341) FWM

15 44
50 291
XSQ= 3.53
PHI= 0.094
XP = 0.0604

46 TILT LESS TOWARD BEING THOSE 0.67 OF 61
OTHER THAN WHERE SETTLEMENTS ARE
NON-FIXED AND MOVEMENT IS
NOMADIC (260)

46 TILT MORE TOWARD BEING THOSE 0.81 OF 271
OTHER THAN WHERE SETTLEMENTS ARE
NON-FIXED AND MOVEMENT IS
NOMADIC (260)

20 52
41 219
XSQ= 4.65
PHI= 0.118
XP = 0.0310

82 DRIFT LESS TOWARD BEING THOSE 0.70 OF 50
WHERE A CITY OR TOWN IS PRESENT, OR
THE AVERAGE COMMUNITY SIZE IS
FIFTY OR GREATER (178)

82 DRIFT MORE TOWARD BEING THOSE 0.82 OF 174
WHERE A CITY OR TOWN IS PRESENT, OR
THE AVERAGE COMMUNITY SIZE IS
FIFTY OR GREATER (178)

35 143
15 31
XSQ= 2.83
PHI= -0.112
XP = 0.0928

84 TILT LESS TOWARD BEING THOSE 0.77 OF 57
WHERE THE LEVEL OF POLITICAL INTEGRATION
IS THE LITTLE STATE, THE MINIMAL STATE,
THE AUTONOMOUS COMMUNITY, OR
THE FAMILY (262) GPM

84 TILT MORE TOWARD BEING THOSE 0.88 OF 247
WHERE THE LEVEL OF POLITICAL INTEGRATION
IS THE LITTLE STATE, THE MINIMAL STATE,
THE AUTONOMOUS COMMUNITY, OR
THE FAMILY (262) GPM

13 29
44 218
XSQ= 3.88
PHI= 0.113
XP = 0.0489

91	TILT TOWARD BEING THOSE WHERE SOCIETAL COMPLEXITY IS LOW (22) F-W	0.74 OF 19	91	TILT TOWARD BEING THOSE WHERE SOCIETAL COMPLEXITY IS HIGH (18) F-W	0.62 OF 21	5 13 14 8 XSQ= 3.77 PHI= -0.307 EP = 0.0309
137	TILT TOWARD BEING THOSE WHERE INVIDIOUS DISPLAY OF WEALTH IS MODERATELY, LITTLE, OR NEGATIVELY EMPHASIZED (52) PES	0.72 OF 39	137	TILT TOWARD BEING THOSE WHERE INVIDIOUS DISPLAY OF WEALTH IS STRONGLY EMPHASIZED (37) PES	0.52 OF 50	11 26 28 24 XSQ= 4.17 PHI= -0.217 XP = 0.0410
176	DRIFT MORE TOWARD BEING THOSE WHERE THE COMMUNITY IS OTHER THAN A CLAN-COMMUNITY OR A COMMUNITY STRUCTURED OR SEGMENTED ON A CLAN BASIS (213)	0.66 OF 65	176	DRIFT LESS TOWARD BEING THOSE WHERE THE COMMUNITY IS OTHER THAN A CLAN-COMMUNITY OR A COMMUNITY STRUCTURED OR SEGMENTED ON A CLAN BASIS (213)	0.54 OF 317	22 147 43 170 XSQ= 2.94 PHI= -0.088 XP = 0.0863
279	TILT TOWARD BEING THOSE WHERE WIFE-LENDING OR WIFE-EXCHANGE IS PRESENT (10) LWS	0.83 OF 6	279	TILT TOWARD BEING THOSE WHERE WIFE-LENDING AND WIFE EXCHANGE ARE UNIMPORTANT OR ABSENT (19) LWS	0.78 OF 23	5 5 1 18 XSQ= 5.50 PHI= 0.435 EP = 0.0105
307	DRIFT TOWARD BEING THOSE WHERE THE EARLY AGGRESSION SATISFACTION POTENTIAL IS LOW (19) W-C	0.52 OF 21	307	DRIFT TOWARD BEING THOSE WHERE THE EARLY AGGRESSION SATISFACTION POTENTIAL IS HIGH (33) W-C	0.74 OF 31	10 23 11 8 XSQ= 2.75 PHI= -0.230 XP = 0.0971
356	LEAN TOWARD BEING THOSE WHERE NEITHER ADOLESCENT PEER GROUPS NOR PAIRS ARE PRESENT IN A SETTING OF COURTSHIP (22) JKH	0.64 OF 25	356	LEAN TOWARD BEING THOSE WHERE ADOLESCENT PEER GROUPS OR PAIRS ARE PRESENT IN A SETTING OF COURTSHIP (29) JKH	0.77 OF 26	9 20 16 6 XSQ= 7.11 PHI= -0.373 XP = 0.0077
360	TILT TOWARD BEING THOSE WHERE ADOLESCENT PEER GROUPS ARE PRESENT ONLY IN A SETTING OF LEISURE, OR ELSE ARE ABSENT (23) JKH	0.81 OF 16	360	TILT TOWARD BEING THOSE WHERE ADOLESCENT PEER GROUPS ARE PRESENT IN A SETTING OF WORK AND PUBLIC GATHERINGS AND LEISURE, OR AT LEAST OF PUBLIC GATHERINGS AND LEISURE (14) JKH	0.52 OF 21	3 11 13 10 XSQ= 3.05 PHI= -0.287 EP = 0.0475
404	TILT TOWARD BEING THOSE WHERE EXPLANATIONS OF ILLNESS OF A SEXUAL NATURE ARE PRESENT (19) W-C	0.50 OF 22	404	TILT TOWARD BEING THOSE WHERE EXPLANATIONS OF ILLNESS OF A SEXUAL NATURE ARE ABSENT (42) W-C	0.79 OF 39	11 8 11 31 XSQ= 4.41 PHI= 0.269 XP = 0.0357
417	DRIFT LESS TOWARD BEING THOSE WHERE WARFARE IS PREVALENT (34) LWS	0.58 OF 12	417	DRIFT MORE TOWARD BEING THOSE WHERE WARFARE IS PREVALENT (34) LWS	0.87 OF 31	7 27 5 4 XSQ= 2.76 PHI= -0.253 XP = 0.0966

419	TILT LESS TOWARD BEING THOSE WHERE MILITARY GLORY IS STRONGLY OR MODERATELY EMPHASIZED (55) PES	0.51 OF 39	419	TILT MORE TOWARD BEING THOSE WHERE MILITARY GLORY IS STRONGLY OR MODERATELY EMPHASIZED (55) PES	0.74 OF 47	20 35 / 19 12 / XSQ= 4.02 / PHI= -0.216 / XP = 0.0451
425	TILT TOWARD BEING THOSE WHERE SUPERNATURALS ARE MAINLY AGGRESSIVE, RATHER THAN BENEVOLENT (20) L-T-W	0.75 OF 16	425	TILT TOWARD BEING THOSE WHERE SUPERNATURALS ARE MAINLY BENEVOLENT, RATHER THAN AGGRESSIVE (16) L-T-W	0.60 OF 20	4 12 / 12 8 / XSQ= 3.11 / PHI= -0.294 / EP = 0.0485
443	TILT TOWARD BEING THOSE WHERE OVERALL FEAR OF OTHERS IS LOW (30) W-C	0.68 OF 22	443	TILT TOWARD BEING THOSE WHERE OVERALL FEAR OF OTHERS IS HIGH (31) W-C	0.62 OF 39	7 24 / 15 15 / XSQ= 3.85 / PHI= -0.251 / XP = 0.0497
472	DRIFT TOWARD BEING THOSE WHERE THE COMPOSITE NARCISSISM INDEX IS LOW (43) PES	0.60 OF 40	472	DRIFT TOWARD BEING THOSE WHERE THE COMPOSITE NARCISSISM INDEX IS HIGH (47) PES	0.62 OF 50	16 31 / 24 19 / XSQ= 3.47 / PHI= -0.196 / XP = 0.0623
473	DRIFT MORE TOWARD BEING THOSE WHERE SENSITIVITY TO INSULT IS MODERATE OR NEGLIGIBLE (56) PES	0.75 OF 40	473	DRIFT LESS TOWARD BEING THOSE WHERE SENSITIVITY TO INSULT IS MODERATE OR NEGLIGIBLE (56) PES	0.54 OF 48	10 22 / 30 26 / XSQ= 3.24 / PHI= -0.192 / XP = 0.0718
474	TILT TOWARD BEING THOSE WHERE BOASTFULNESS IS MODERATE, NEGLIBIBLE, OR UNREPORTED (48) PES	0.70 OF 40	474	TILT TOWARD BEING THOSE WHERE BOASTFULNESS IS EXTREME (41) PES	0.59 OF 49	12 29 / 28 20 / XSQ= 6.42 / PHI= -0.269 / XP = 0.0113
488	TILT MORE TOWARD BEING THOSE ABOUT WHICH THE PRINCIPAL ETHNOGRAPHIES WERE PUBLISHED BEFORE 1950 (185)	0.88 OF 40	488	TILT LESS TOWARD BEING THOSE ABOUT WHICH THE PRINCIPAL ETHNOGRAPHIES WERE PUBLISHED BEFORE 1950 (185)	0.69 OF 217	35 150 / 5 67 / XSQ= 4.78 / PHI= 0.136 / XP = 0.0288
489	TEND LESS TO BE THOSE NOT INCLUDED IN CHARLES ACKERMAN'S STUDY OF DIVORCE (343)	0.68 OF 65	489	TEND MORE TO BE THOSE NOT INCLUDED IN CHARLES ACKERMAN'S STUDY OF DIVORCE (343)	0.89 OF 335	21 36 / 44 299 / XSQ= 18.98 / PHI= 0.218 / XP = 0.0000
490	TEND TO BE THOSE INCLUDED IN ALBERT S. ANTHONY'S SAMPLE ON MALE INITIATION RITES (113)	0.54 OF 65	490	TEND TO BE THOSE NOT INCLUDED IN ALBERT S. ANTHONY'S SAMPLE ON MALE INITIATION RITES (287)	0.77 OF 335	35 78 / 30 257 / XSQ= 23.60 / PHI= 0.243 / XP = 0.0000

491	TEND LESS TO BE THCSE NOT INCLUDED IN DORRIAN APPLE'S STUDY OF GRANDPARENTHCCD (352)	0.72 OF 65	491	TEND MORE TO BE THOSE NOT INCLUDED IN DORRIAN APPLE'S STUDY OF GRANDPARENTHOOD (352)	0.91 OF 335	18 30 47 305 XSQ= 16.37 PHI= 0.202 XP = 0.0001
492	TEND LESS TO BE THCSE NOT INCLUDED IN BARBARA CHARTIER AYRES' STUDY OF FEMALE INITIATION RITES (361)	0.72 OF 65	492	TEND MORE TO BE THOSE NOT INCLUDED IN BARBARA CHARTIER AYRES' STUDY OF FEMALE INITIATION RITES (361)	0.94 OF 335	18 21 47 314 XSQ= 26.01 PHI= 0.255 XP = 0.0000
493	TEND LESS TO BE THCSE NOT INCLUDED IN BACCN, BARRY, AND CHILC'S STUDY OF CHILD REARING (322)	0.54 OF 65	493	TEND MORE TO BE THOSE NOT INCLUDED IN BACON, BARRY, AND CHILD'S STUDY OF CHILD REARING (322)	0.86 OF 335	30 48 35 287 XSQ= 33.13 PHI= 0.288 XP = 0.
494	LEAN LESS TOWARD BEING THCSE NOT INCLUDED IN HERBERT M. BARRY III'S STUDY OF ART (371)	0.83 OF 65	494	LEAN MORE TOWARD BEING THOSE NOT INCLUDED IN HERBERT M. BARRY III'S STUDY OF ART (371)	0.95 OF 335	11 18 54 317 XSQ= 9.15 PHI= 0.151 XP = 0.0025
496	TEND LESS TO BE THCSE NOT INCLUDED IN ROY G. D'ANDRADE'S STUDY OF DREAMS (345)	0.55 OF 65	496	TEND MORE TO BE THOSE NOT INCLUDED IN ROY G. D'ANDRADE'S STUDY OF DREAMS (345)	0.92 OF 335	29 26 36 309 XSQ= 59.28 PHI= 0.385 XP = 0.
497	TEND LESS TO BE THCSE NOT INCLUDED IN WILLIAM M. EVAN'S STUDY OF LAW (339)	0.57 OF 65	497	TEND MORE TO BE THOSE NOT INCLUDED IN WILLIAM M. EVAN'S STUDY OF LAW (339)	0.90 OF 335	28 33 37 302 XSQ= 43.96 PHI= 0.332 XP = 0.
498	TEND LESS TO BE THCSE NOT INCLUDED IN C. S. FORC'S STUDY OF SEX (349)	0.65 OF 65	498	TEND MORE TO BE THOSE NOT INCLUDED IN C. S. FORD'S STUDY OF SEX (349)	0.92 OF 335	23 28 42 307 XSQ= 33.36 PHI= 0.289 XP = 0.
499	TEND LESS TO BE THCSE NOT INCLUDED IN FORC AND BEACH'S SAMPLE CN SEXUAL EXPRESSICN BY THE YCUNG (314)	0.52 OF 65	499	TEND MORE TO BE THOSE NOT INCLUDED IN FORD AND BEACH'S SAMPLE ON SEXUAL EXPRESSION BY THE YOUNG (314)	0.84 OF 335	31 55 34 280 XSQ= 29.72 PHI= 0.273 XP = 0.0000
500	TEND LESS TO BE THCSE NOT INCLUDED IN FREEMAN ANC WINCH'S STUDY OF SCCIETAL COMPLEXITY (360)	0.71 OF 65	500	TEND MORE TO BE THOSE NOT INCLUDED IN FREEMAN AND WINCH'S STUDY OF SOCIETAL COMPLEXITY (360)	0.94 OF 335	19 21 46 314 XSQ= 29.39 PHI= 0.271 XP = 0.0000

501	TEND LESS TO BE THCSE 0.54 OF 65 NOT INCLUDED IN JOAN FRIENCLY GOOCMAN'S STUDY OF ASCETIC MCURNING BEHAVIOR (333)	501	TEND MORE TO BE THOSE 0.89 OF 335 NOT INCLUDED IN JOAN FRIENDLY GOODMAN'S STUDY OF ASCETIC MOURNING BEHAVIOR (333)	30 37 35 298 XSQ= 45.64 PHI= 0.338 XP = 0.
502	TEND LESS TO BE THCSE 0.57 OF 65 NOT INCLUDED IN JOHN K. HARLEY'S STUDY OF ACOLESCENT PEER CROUPS (343)	502	TEND MORE TO BE THOSE 0.91 OF 335 NOT INCLUDED IN JOHN K. HARLEY'S STUDY OF ADOLESCENT PEER GROUPS (343)	28 29 37 306 XSQ= 50.00 PHI= 0.354 XP = 0.
503	TEND LESS TO BE THCSE 0.57 OF 65 NOT INCLUDED IN JOHN M. HICKMAN'S STUDY OF THE FOLK-URBAN CCNTINUUM (346)	503	TEND MORE TO BE THOSE 0.92 OF 335 NOT INCLUDED IN JOHN M. HICKMAN'S STUDY OF THE FOLK-URBAN CONTINUUM (346)	28 26 37 309 XSQ= 55.16 PHI= 0.371 XP = 0.
504	TEND LESS TO BE THCSE 0.65 OF 65 NOT INCLUDED IN DONALC HORTON'S STUDY OF ALCHOLISM (351)	504	TEND MORE TO BE THOSE 0.92 OF 335 NOT INCLUDED IN DCNALD HORTCN'S STUDY OF ALCHOLISM (351)	23 26 42 309 XSQ= 36.12 PHI= 0.300 XP = 0.
505	TEND LESS TO BE THCSE 0.85 OF 65 NOT INCLUDED IN MERRILL JACKSON'S STUDY OF CRIMINAL LAW ANC MEDICINE (380)	505	TEND MORE TO BE THCSE 0.97 OF 335 NOT INCLUDED IN MERRILL JACKSON'S STUDY OF CRIMINAL LAW AND MEDICINE (380)	10 10 55 325 XSQ= 15.11 PHI= 0.194 XP = 0.0001
506	TEND LESS TO BE THCSE 0.75 OF 65 NOT INCLUDED IN LAMBERT, TRIANDIS, AND WCLF'S STUDY OF SUPERNATURAL BEINCS (364)	506	TEND MORE TO BE THOSE 0.94 OF 335 NOT INCLUDED IN LAMBERT, TRIANDIS, AND WCLF'S STUDY OF SUPERNATURAL BEINGS (364)	16 20 49 315 XSQ= 20.89 PHI= 0.229 XP = 0.0000
507	TEND TO BE THOSE 0.62 OF 65 INCLUDED IN JAMES R. LEARY'S STUDY OF FCOD TABOCS (86)	507	TEND TO BE THOSE 0.86 OF 335 NOT INCLUDED IN JAMES R. LEARY'S STUDY OF FOOD TABOOS (314)	40 46 25 289 XSQ= 70.91 PHI= 0.421 XP = 0.
508	TEND LESS TO BE THCSE 0.77 OF 65 NOT INCLUDED IN DAVID C. MCCLELLANC'S STUDY OF ACHIEVEMENT MCTIVATION (360)	508	TEND MORE TO BE THOSE 0.93 OF 335 NOT INCLUDED IN DAVID C. MCCLELLAND'S STUDY OF ACHIEVEMENT MOTIVATION (360)	15 25 50 310 XSQ= 13.06 PHI= 0.181 XP = 0.0003
509	TILT LESS TOWARC BEING THCSE 0.86 OF 65 NCT INCLUDED IN MONI NAG'S STUDY OF FERTILITY (375)	509	TILT MORE TOWARD BEING THOSE 0.95 OF 335 NOT INCLUDED IN MONI NAG'S STUDY OF FERTILITY (375)	9 16 56 319 XSQ= 6.17 PHI= 0.124 XP = 0.0130

No.			No.			
510	TEND LESS TO BE THOSE NOT INCLUDED IN RAOUL NARROLL'S STUDY OF SOCIETAL COMPLEXITY (380)	0.85 OF 65	510	TEND MORE TO BE THOSE NOT INCLUDED IN RAOUL NARROLL'S STUDY OF SOCIETAL COMPLEXITY (380)	0.97 OF 335	10 10 55 325 XSQ= 15.11 PHI= 0.194 XP = 0.0001
511	TEND TO BE THOSE INCLUDED IN ROBERTS, ARTH AND BUSH'S SAMPLE ON GAMES, AS MODIFIED BY THE ETHNOGRAPHIC ATLAS (189)	0.75 OF 65	511	TEND TO BE THOSE NOT INCLUDED IN ROBERTS, ARTH AND BUSH'S SAMPLE ON GAMES, AS MODIFIED BY THE ETHNOGRAPHIC ATLAS (211)	0.58 OF 335	49 140 16 195 XSQ= 23.32 PHI= 0.241 XP = 0.0000
512	TEND LESS TO BE THOSE NOT INCLUDED IN SHIRLEY AND ROMNEY'S STUDY OF LOVE MAGIC (367)	0.80 OF 65	512	TEND MORE TO BE THOSE NOT INCLUDED IN SHIRLEY AND ROMNEY'S STUDY OF LOVE MAGIC (367)	0.94 OF 335	13 20 52 315 XSQ= 12.36 PHI= 0.176 XP = 0.0004
513	TILT LESS TOWARD BEING THOSE NOT INCLUDED IN LEO W. SIMMONS' STUDY OF THE TREATMENT OF THE AGED (357)	0.82 OF 65	513	TILT MORE TOWARD BEING THOSE NOT INCLUDED IN LEO W. SIMMONS' STUDY OF THE TREATMENT OF THE AGED (357)	0.91 OF 335	12 31 53 304 XSQ= 3.90 PHI= 0.099 XP = 0.0483
514	TEND TO BE THOSE INCLUDED IN PHILIP E. SLATER'S STUDY OF NARCISSISM (90)	0.62 OF 65	514	TEND TO BE THOSE NOT INCLUDED IN PHILIP E. SLATER'S STUDY OF NARCISSISM (310)	0.85 OF 335	40 50 25 285 XSQ= 65.18 PHI= 0.404 XP = 0.
515	TEND LESS TO BE THOSE NOT INCLUDED IN WILLIAM N. STEPHENS' SAMPLE ON AVOIDANCE RELATIONSHIPS (348)	0.68 OF 65	515	TEND MORE TO BE THOSE NOT INCLUDED IN WILLIAM N. STEPHENS' SAMPLE ON AVOIDANCE RELATIONSHIPS (348)	0.91 OF 335	21 31 44 304 XSQ= 23.58 PHI= 0.243 XP = 0.0000
516	TILT MORE TOWARD BEING THOSE INCLUDED IN GUY E. SWANSON'S SAMPLE ON LOCAL JURISDICTION, AS MODIFIED BY THE ETHNOGRAPHIC ATLAS (331)	0.94 OF 65	516	TILT LESS TOWARD BEING THOSE INCLUDED IN GUY E. SWANSON'S SAMPLE ON LOCAL JURISDICTION, AS MODIFIED BY THE ETHNOGRAPHIC ATLAS (331)	0.81 OF 335	61 270 4 65 XSQ= 5.80 PHI= 0.120 XP = 0.0160
517	TEND MORE TO BE THOSE INCLUDED IN GUY E. SWANSON'S SAMPLE ON HIGH GODS, AS MODIFIED BY THE ETHNOGRAPHIC ATLAS (260)	0.89 OF 65	517	TEND LESS TO BE THOSE INCLUDED IN GUY E. SWANSON'S SAMPLE ON HIGH GODS, AS MODIFIED BY THE ETHNOGRAPHIC ATLAS (260)	0.60 OF 335	58 202 7 133 XSQ= 18.78 PHI= 0.217 XP = 0.0000
518	TEND TO BE THOSE INCLUDED IN STANLEY H. UDY, JR.'S STUDY OF WORK ORGANIZATION (105)	0.54 OF 65	518	TEND TO BE THOSE NOT INCLUDED IN STANLEY H. UDY, JR.'S STUDY OF WORK ORGANIZATION (295)	0.79 OF 335	35 70 30 265 XSQ= 28.85 PHI= 0.269 XP = 0.0000

519	TEND LESS TO BE THOSE NOT INCLUDED IN JOSEPH VEROFF'S STUDY OF ACHIEVEMENT MOTIVATION AS REVEALED IN FOLKTALES (364)	0.78 OF 65	519	TEND MORE TO BE THOSE NOT INCLUDED IN JOSEPH VEROFF'S STUDY OF ACHIEVEMENT MOTIVATION AS REVEALED IN FOLKTALES (364)	0.93 OF 335	14 22 51 313 XSQ= 13.13 PHI= 0.181 XP = 0.0003
520	TEND LESS TO BE THOSE NOT INCLUDED IN BEATRICE BLYTH WHITING'S STUDY OF SORCERY (360)	0.74 OF 65	520	TEND MORE TO BE THOSE NOT INCLUDED IN BEATRICE BLYTH WHITING'S STUDY OF SORCERY (360)	0.93 OF 335	17 23 48 312 XSQ= 20.41 PHI= 0.226 XP = 0.0000
522	TEND TO BE THOSE INCLUDED IN MARJORIE GRANT WHITING'S STUDY OF DIET (82)	0.60 OF 65	522	TEND TO BE THOSE NOT INCLUDED IN MARJORIE GRANT WHITING'S STUDY OF DIET (318)	0.87 OF 335	39 43 26 292 XSQ= 71.44 PHI= 0.423 XP = 0.
523	TEND LESS TO BE THOSE NOT INCLUDED IN WHITING AND CHILD'S STUDY OF CHILD TRAINING AND PERSONALITY (339)	0.66 OF 65	523	TEND MORE TO BE THOSE NOT INCLUDED IN WHITING AND CHILD'S STUDY OF CHILD TRAINING AND PERSONALITY (339)	0.88 OF 335	22 39 43 296 XSQ= 19.08 PHI= 0.218 XP = 0.0000
524	TEND LESS TO BE THOSE NOT INCLUDED IN WHITING, KLUCKHOHN, AND ANTHONY'S STUDY OF MALE INITIATION CEREMONIES (356)	0.58 OF 65	524	TEND MORE TO BE THOSE NOT INCLUDED IN WHITING, KLUCKHOHN, AND ANTHONY'S STUDY OF MALE INITIATION CEREMONIES (356)	0.95 OF 335	27 17 38 318 XSQ= 70.26 PHI= 0.419 XP = 0.

496 CULTURES INCLUDED IN ROY G. D'ANDRADE'S STUDY OF DREAMS (55)

496 CULTURES NOT INCLUDED IN ROY G. D'ANDRADE'S STUDY OF DREAMS (345)

BACKGROUND ON PAGE 180

SUBJECT ONLY, F.C. 1-480 AND 527-536
BOTH SUBJECT AND PREDICATE, F.C. 481-526

55 IN LEFT COLUMN

ANDAMANESE	ARAUCANIANS	ASHANTI	AYMARA	AZANDE	BEMBA	BHIL	BURMESE	CALLINAGO	CHUKCHEE
COMANCHE	COPR ESKIMO	CRCW	CUNA	FANG	GANDA	IBAN	IFUGAO	JIVARO	KAPAUKU
KAREN	KASKA	KURTATCHI	LAPPS	LEPCHA	MARQUESANS	MATACO	MINCHIA	MOSSI	MUNDURUCU
NAMA	NASKAPI	NYAKYUSA	OJIBWA	OMAHA	PAPAGO	PUKAPUKA	RIFFIANS	RWALA	SAMOANS
SEMANG	SIRIONO	SOMALI	TALLENSI	TANALA	THAI	TIV	TROBRIAND	TUBATULABAL	TUPINAMBA
WOLEAIANS	WCLCF	YAKUT	YARURO	YORUBA					

345 IN RIGHT CCLUMN

	Included (55)			Not included (345)		
62	TILT MORE TOWARD BEING THOSE WHERE HUSBANDRY OF SOME KIND IS PRESENT (228)	0.71 OF 55	62	TILT LESS TOWARD BEING THOSE WHERE HUSBANDRY OF SOME KIND IS PRESENT (228)	0.55 OF 345	39 189 / 16 156 / XSQ= 4.40 / PHI= 0.105 / XP = 0.0360
63	TILT LESS TOWARD BEING THOSE WHERE HUSBANDRY, IF PRESENT, IS PRINCIPALLY IN THE FORM OF BOVINE, EQUINE, CAMEL-LIKE, OR DEER-LIKE ANIMALS, RATHER THAN PIGS, SHEEP, OR GOATS (152)	0.51 OF 39	63	TILT MORE TOWARD BEING THOSE WHERE HUSBANDRY, IF PRESENT, IS PRINCIPALLY IN THE FORM OF BOVINE, EQUINE, CAMEL-LIKE, OR DEER-LIKE ANIMALS, RATHER THAN PIGS, SHEEP, OR GOATS (152)	0.71 OF 187	20 132 / 19 55 / XSQ= 4.62 / PHI= -0.143 / XP = 0.0316
81	TILT MORE TOWARD BEING THOSE WHERE NO CITY OR TOWN IS PRESENT, AND THE AVERAGE COMMUNITY SIZE IS SMALLER THAN 200 (135)	0.76 OF 45	81	TILT LESS TOWARD BEING THOSE WHERE NO CITY OR TOWN IS PRESENT, AND THE AVERAGE COMMUNITY SIZE IS SMALLER THAN 200 (135)	0.56 OF 179	11 78 / 34 101 / XSQ= 4.73 / PHI= -0.145 / XP = 0.0297
83	DRIFT MORE TOWARD BEING THOSE WHERE, WITH NO CITY AND NO TOWN PRESENT, THE AVERAGE COMMUNITY SIZE IS SMALLER THAN 200, RATHER THAN BETWEEN 200 AND 999 (135)	0.87 OF 39	83	DRIFT LESS TOWARD BEING THOSE WHERE, WITH NO CITY AND NO TOWN PRESENT, THE AVERAGE COMMUNITY SIZE IS SMALLER THAN 200, RATHER THAN BETWEEN 200 AND 999 (135)	0.72 OF 141	5 40 / 34 101 / XSQ= 3.15 / PHI= -0.132 / XP = 0.0758
91	TILT TOWARD BEING THOSE WHERE SOCIETAL COMPLEXITY IS LOW (22) F-W	0.74 OF 19	91	TILT TOWARD BEING THOSE WHERE SOCIETAL COMPLEXITY IS HIGH (18) F-W	0.62 OF 21	5 13 / 14 8 / XSQ= 3.77 / PHI= -0.307 / EP = 0.0309

No.	Subject		No.	Predicate		Statistics
243	DRIFT TOWARD BEING THOSE WHERE POLYGYNY, IF PRESENT, HAS A HIGH INCIDENCE (24) W-D,S	0.56 OF 25	243	DRIFT TOWARD BEING THOSE WHERE POLYGYNY, IF PRESENT, HAS A LOW INCIDENCE (36) W-D,S	0.71 OF 35	14 10 11 25 XSQ= 3.50 PHI= 0.242 XP = 0.0614
296	LEAN TOWARD BEING THOSE WHERE INFANTICIDE IS ABSENT OR INFERRED ABSENT (15) BCA	0.77 OF 13	296	LEAN TOWARD BEING THOSE WHERE INFANTICIDE IS PRESENT (18) BCA	0.75 OF 20	3 15 10 5 XSQ= 6.60 PHI= -0.447 EP = 0.0052
372	DRIFT MORE TOWARD BEING THOSE WHERE MALE INITIATION RITES ARE ABSENT (63) ASA	0.73 OF 30	372	DRIFT LESS TOWARD BEING THOSE WHERE MALE INITIATION RITES ARE ABSENT (63) ASA	0.51 OF 81	8 40 22 41 XSQ= 3.72 PHI= -0.183 XP = 0.0536
391	DRIFT TOWARD BEING THOSE WHERE PREMARITAL SEX RELATIONS ARE PUNISHED ONLY IF PREGNANCY RESULTS, OR FREELY PERMITTED (90) JTW,EA	0.64 OF 42	391	DRIFT TOWARD BEING THOSE WHERE PREMARITAL SEX RELATIONS ARE STRONGLY PUNISHED AND IN FACT RARE, OR WEAKLY PUNISHED AND IN FACT NOT RARE (89) JTW,EA	0.54 OF 137	15 74 27 63 XSQ= 3.61 PHI= -0.142 XP = 0.0576
450	TILT MORE TOWARD BEING THOSE WHERE THE OBSERVATION OF FOOD TABOOS IS HIGH OR MEDIUM, RATHER THAN LOW (60) JRL	0.83 OF 46	450	TILT LESS TOWARD BEING THOSE WHERE THE OBSERVATION OF FOOD TABOOS IS HIGH OR MEDIUM, RATHER THAN LOW (60) JRL	0.55 OF 40	38 22 8 18 XSQ= 6.48 PHI= 0.274 XP = 0.0109
468	LEAN TOWARD BEING THOSE WHERE CONTACT WITH OTHER CULTURES IS REGULAR OR IRREGULAR, RATHER THAN FREQUENT (37) JMH	0.88 OF 26	468	LEAN TOWARD BEING THOSE WHERE CONTACT WITH OTHER CULTURES IS FREQUENT, RATHER THAN REGULAR OR IRREGULAR (17) JMH	0.50 OF 28	3 14 23 14 XSQ= 7.55 PHI= -0.374 XP = 0.0060
489	TEND LESS TO BE THOSE NOT INCLUDED IN CHARLES ACKERMAN'S STUDY OF DIVORCE (343)	0.53 OF 55	489	TEND MORE TO BE THOSE NOT INCLUDED IN CHARLES ACKERMAN'S STUDY OF DIVORCE (343)	0.91 OF 345	26 31 29 314 XSQ= 53.82 PHI= 0.367 XP = 0.
490	TEND TO BE THOSE INCLUDED IN ALBERT S. ANTHONY'S SAMPLE ON MALE INITIATION RITES (113)	0.55 OF 55	490	TEND TO BE THOSE NOT INCLUDED IN ALBERT S. ANTHONY'S SAMPLE ON MALE INITIATION RITES (287)	0.76 OF 345	30 83 25 262 XSQ= 20.28 PHI= 0.225 XP = 0.0000
491	LEAN LESS TOWARD BEING THOSE NOT INCLUDED IN DORRIAN APPLE'S STUDY OF GRANDPARENTHOOD (352)	0.76 OF 55	491	LEAN MORE TOWARD BEING THOSE NOT INCLUDED IN DORRIAN APPLE'S STUDY OF GRANDPARENTHOOD (352)	0.90 OF 345	13 35 42 310 XSQ= 6.95 PHI= 0.132 XP = 0.0084

492	TEND LESS TO BE THCSE 0.73 OF 55 NOT INCLUDED IN BARBARA CHARTIER AYRES' STUDY OF FEMALE INITIATION RITES (361)	492	TEND MORE TO BE THOSE 0.93 OF 345 NOT INCLUDED IN BARBARA CHARTIER AYRES' STUDY OF FEMALE INITIATION RITES (361)	15 24 40 321 XSQ= 20.00 PHI= 0.224 XP = 0.0000
493	TEND TO BE THOSE 0.56 OF 55 INCLUDED IN BACCN, BARRY, AND CHILC'S STUDY OF CHILD REARING (78)	493	TEND TO BE THOSE 0.86 OF 345 NOT INCLUDED IN BACON, BARRY, AND CHILD'S STUDY OF CHILD REARING (322)	31 47 24 298 XSQ= 52.51 PHI= 0.362 XP = 0.
494	LEAN LESS TOWARC BEING THOSE 0.82 OF 55 NOT INCLUDED IN HERBERT M. BARRY III'S STUDY OF ART (371)	494	LEAN MORE TOWARD BEING THOSE 0.94 OF 345 NOT INCLUDED IN HERBERT M. BARRY III'S STUDY OF ART (371)	10 19 45 326 XSQ= 9.53 PHI= 0.154 XP = 0.0020
495	TEND TO BE THOSE 0.53 OF 55 INCLUDED IN JUDITH K. BROWN'S STUDY OF FEMALE INITIATION RITES (65)	495	TEND TO BE THOSE 0.90 OF 345 NOT INCLUDED IN JUDITH K. BROWN'S STUDY OF FEMALE INITIATICN RITES (335)	29 36 26 309 XSQ= 59.28 PHI= 0.385 XP = 0.
497	TEND LESS TO BE THCSE 0.51 OF 55 NOT INCLUDED IN WILLIAM M. EVAN'S STUDY OF LAW (339)	497	TEND MORE TO BE THOSE 0.90 OF 345 NOT INCLUDED IN WILLIAM M. EVAN'S STUDY OF LAW (339)	27 34 28 311 XSQ= 53.51 PHI= 0.366 XP = 0.
498	TEND LESS TO BE THCSE 0.62 OF 55 NOT INCLUDED IN C. S. FORC'S STUDY OF SEX (349)	498	TEND MORE TO BE THOSE 0.91 OF 345 NOT INCLUDED IN C. S. FORD'S STUDY OF SEX (349)	21 30 34 315 XSQ= 34.47 PHI= 0.294 XP = 0.
499	TEND TO BE THOSE 0.51 OF 55 INCLUDED IN FORD AND BEACH'S SAMPLE ON SEXUAL EXPRESSICN BY THE YOUNG (86)	499	TEND TO BE THOSE 0.83 OF 345 NOT INCLUDED IN FORD AND BEACH'S SAMPLE ON SEXUAL EXPRESSION BY THE YOUNG (314)	28 58 27 287 XSQ= 30.69 PHI= 0.277 XP = 0.
500	TEND LESS TO BE THCSE 0.65 OF 55 NOT INCLUDED IN FREEMAN ANC WINCH'S STUDY OF SCCIETAL CCMPLEXITY (360)	500	TEND MORE TO BE THOSE 0.94 OF 345 NOT INCLUDED IN FREEMAN AND WINCH'S STUDY OF SOCIETAL COMPLEXITY (360)	19 21 36 324 XSQ= 39.58 PHI= 0.315 XP = 0.
501	TEND LESS TO BE THCSE 0.56 OF 55 NOT INCLUDED IN JOAN FRIENCLY GOODMAN'S STUDY OF ASCETIC MOURNING BEHAVIOR (333)	501	TEND MORE TO BE THOSE 0.88 OF 345 NOT INCLUDED IN JOAN FRIENDLY GOODMAN'S STUDY OF ASCETIC MOURNING BEHAVIOR (333)	24 43 31 302 XSQ= 30.86 PHI= 0.278 XP = 0.

No.		No.		
502	TEND LESS TO BE THCSE 0.64 OF 55 NCT INCLUDED IN JOHN K. HARLEY'S STUDY OF ADOLESCENT PEER GROUPS (343)	502	TEND MORE TC BE THOSE 0.89 OF 345 NOT INCLUDED IN JOHN K. HARLEY'S STUDY OF ADOLESCENT PEER GRCUPS (343)	20 37 35 308 XSQ= 23.46 PHI= 0.242 XP = 0.0000
503	TEND LESS TO BE THCSE 0.53 OF 55 NOT INCLUDED IN JOHN M. HICKMAN'S STUDY OF THE FOLK-URBAN CCNTINUUM (346)	503	TEND MORE TO BE THOSE 0.92 OF 345 NOT INCLUDED IN JOHN M. HICKMAN'S STUDY OF THE FOLK-URBAN CONTINUUM (346)	26 28 29 317 XSQ= 58.98 PHI= 0.384 XP = 0.
504	TEND LESS TO BE THCSE 0.71 OF 55 NOT INCLUDED IN DONALD HORTON'S STUDY OF ALCHOLISM (351)	504	TEND MORE TO BE THOSE 0.90 OF 345 NOT INCLUDED IN DONALD HORTCN'S STUDY OF ALCHOLISM (351)	16 33 39 312 XSQ= 15.06 PHI= 0.194 XP = 0.0001
505	TEND LESS TO BE THCSE 0.80 OF 55 NOT INCLUDED IN MERRILL JACKSON'S STUDY OF CRIMINAL LAW AND MEDICINE (380)	505	TEND MORE TO BE THOSE 0.97 OF 345 NOT INCLUDED IN MERRILL JACKSON'S STUDY OF CRIMINAL LAW AND MEDICINE (380)	11 9 44 336 XSQ= 26.66 PHI= 0.258 XP = 0.0000
506	TEND LESS TO BE THCSE 0.78 OF 55 NCT INCLUDED IN LAMBERT, TRIANDIS, AND WOLF'S STUDY OF SUPERNATURAL BEINGS (364)	506	TEND MORE TO BE THOSE 0.93 OF 345 NOT INCLUDED IN LAMBERT, TRIANDIS, AND WOLF'S STUDY OF SUPERNATURAL BEINGS (364)	12 24 43 321 XSQ= 11.04 PHI= 0.166 XP = 0.0009
507	TEND TO BE THOSE 0.84 OF 55 INCLUDED IN JAMES R. LEARY'S STUDY OF FCOD TABOCS (86)	507	TEND TO BE THOSE 0.88 OF 345 NOT INCLUDED IN JAMES R. LEARY'S STUDY OF FOOD TABOOS (314)	46 40 9 305 XSQ= 141.64 PHI= 0.595 XP = 0.
508	TEND LESS TO BE THCSE 0.71 OF 55 NOT INCLUDED IN DAVID C. MCCLELLAND'S STUDY OF ACHIEVEMENT MCTIVATION (360)	508	TEND MORE TO BE THOSE 0.93 OF 345 NOT INCLUDED IN DAVID C. MCCLELLAND'S STUDY OF ACHIEVEMENT MOTIVATION (360)	16 24 39 321 XSQ= 23.42 PHI= 0.242 XP = 0.0000
511	TEND TO BE THOSE 0.75 OF 55 INCLUDED IN ROBERTS, ARTH AND BUSH'S SAMPLE ON GAMES, AS MODIFIED BY THE ETHNOGRAPHIC ATLAS (189)	511	TEND TO BE THOSE 0.57 OF 345 NOT INCLUDED IN ROBERTS, ARTH AND BUSH'S SAMPLE ON GAMES, AS MODIFIED BY THE ETHNOGRAPHIC ATLAS (211)	41 148 14 197 XSQ= 17.81 PHI= 0.211 XP = 0.0000
512	TEND LESS TO BE THCSE 0.75 OF 55 NOT INCLUDED IN SHIRLEY AND ROMNEY'S STUDY OF LOVE MAGIC (367)	512	TEND MORE TO BE THOSE 0.94 OF 345 NOT INCLUDED IN SHIRLEY AND ROMNEY'S STUDY OF LOVE MAGIC (367)	14 19 41 326 XSQ= 22.37 PHI= 0.236 XP = 0.0000

513	TEND LESS TO BE THCSE 0.71 OF 55 NOT INCLUDED IN LEC W. SIMMONS' STUDY OF THE TREATMENT OF THE AGED (357)	513	TEND MORE TO BE THOSE 0.92 OF 345 NOT INCLUDED IN LEO W. SIMMONS' STUDY OF THE TREATMENT OF THE AGED (357)	16 27 39 318 XSQ= 20.20 PHI= 0.225 XP = 0.0000
514	TEND TO BE THOSE 0.69 OF 55 INCLUDED IN PHILIP E. SLATER'S STUDY OF NARCISSISM (90)	514	TEND TO BE THOSE 0.85 OF 345 NOT INCLUDED IN PHILIP E. SLATER'S STUDY OF NARCISSISM (310)	38 52 17 293 XSQ= 76.31 PHI= 0.437 XP = 0.
515	TEND LESS TO BE THCSE 0.56 OF 55 NOT INCLUDED IN WILLIAM N. STEPHENS' SAMPLE CN AVOIDANCE RELATICNSHIPS (348)	515	TEND MORE TO BE THOSE 0.92 OF 345 NOT INCLUDED IN WILLIAM N. STEPHENS' SAMPLE ON AVOIDANCE RELATIONSHIPS (348)	24 28 31 317 XSQ= 49.83 PHI= 0.353 XP = 0.
516	DRIFT MORE TOWARD BEING THOSE 0.93 OF 55 INCLUDED IN GUY E. SWANSON'S SAMPLE ON LOCAL JURISDICTICN, AS MODIFIED BY THE ETHNOGRAPHIC ATLAS (331)	516	DRIFT LESS TOWARD BEING THOSE 0.81 OF 345 INCLUDED IN GUY E. SWANSON'S SAMPLE ON LOCAL JURISDICTION, AS MODIFIED BY THE ETHNOGRAPHIC ATLAS (331)	51 280 4 65 XSQ= 3.67 PHI= 0.096 XP = 0.0553
517	TEND MORE TO BE THCSE 0.87 OF 55 INCLUDED IN GUY E. SWANSON'S SAMPLE ON HIGH GODS, AS MODIFIED BY THE ETHNOGRAPHIC ATLAS (260)	517	TEND LESS TO BE THOSE 0.61 OF 345 INCLUDED IN GUY E. SWANSON'S SAMPLE ON HIGH GODS, AS MODIFIED BY THE ETHNOGRAPHIC ATLAS (260)	48 212 7 133 XSQ= 12.79 PHI= 0.179 XP = 0.0003
518	TEND TO BE THOSE 0.64 OF 55 INCLUDED IN STANLEY H. UDY, JR.'S STUDY OF WCRK ORGANIZATION (105)	518	TEND TO BE THOSE 0.80 OF 345 NOT INCLUDED IN STANLEY H. UDY, JR.'S STUDY OF WORK ORGANIZATION (295)	35 70 20 275 XSQ= 43.83 PHI= 0.331 XP = 0.
519	TEND LESS TO BE THCSE 0.71 OF 55 NOT INCLUDED IN JOSEPH VEROFF'S STUDY OF ACHIEVEMENT MOTIVATION AS REVEALED IN FOLKTALES (364)	519	TEND MORE TO BE THOSE 0.94 OF 345 NOT INCLUDED IN JOSEPH VEROFF'S STUDY OF ACHIEVEMENT MOTIVATION AS REVEALED IN FOLKTALES (364)	16 20 39 325 XSQ= 28.65 PHI= 0.268 XP = 0.0000
520	TEND LESS TO BE THCSE 0.75 OF 55 NOT INCLUDED IN BEATRICE BLYTH WHITING'S STUDY OF SORCERY (360)	520	TEND MORE TO BE THOSE 0.92 OF 345 NOT INCLUDED IN BEATRICE BLYTH WHITING'S STUDY OF SORCERY (360)	14 26 41 319 XSQ= 14.99 PHI= 0.194 XP = 0.0001
522	TEND TO BE THOSE 0.51 OF 55 INCLUDED IN MARJORIE GRANT WHITING'S STUDY OF DIET (82)	522	TEND TO BE THOSE 0.84 OF 345 NOT INCLUDED IN MARJORIE GRANT WHITING'S STUDY OF DIET (318)	28 54 27 291 XSQ= 34.05 PHI= 0.292 XP = 0.

523	TEND LESS TO BE THCSE NOT INCLUDED IN WHITING AND CHILD'S STUDY OF CHILD TRAINING AND PERSONALITY (339)	0.60 OF 55	523	TEND MORE TO BE THOSE NOT INCLUDED IN WHITING AND CHILD'S STUDY OF CHILD TRAINING AND PERSONALITY (339)	0.89 OF 345	22 39 33 306 XSQ= 28.04 PHI= 0.265 XP = 0.0000
524	TEND LESS TO BE THCSE NOT INCLUDED IN WHITING, KLUCKHCHN, AND ANTHONY'S STUDY OF MALE INITIATION CEREMONIES (356)	0.69 OF 55	524	TEND MORE TO BE THOSE NOT INCLUDED IN WHITING, KLUCKHOHN, AND ANTHONY'S STUDY OF MALE INITIATION CEREMONIES (356)	0.92 OF 345	17 27 38 318 XSQ= 23.51 PHI= 0.242 XP = 0.0000

497 CULTURES INCLUDED IN WILLIAM M. EVAN'S STUDY OF LAW (61)	497 CULTURES NOT INCLUDED IN WILLIAM M. EVAN'S STUDY OF LAW (339)

BACKGROUND ON PAGE 180

SUBJECT ONLY, F.C. 1-480 AND 527-536
BOTH SUBJECT AND PREDICATE, F.C. 481-526

61 IN LEFT COLUMN

ALBANIANS	ALCRESE	ARANDA	ASHANTI	AZANDE	BHIL	CARIB	CHAGGA	CHEYENNE	COORG
COPR ESKIMO	CZECHS	DARD	GANDA	GOAJIRO	GOND	HANO	HAVASUPAI	IBAN	IFUGAO
INCA	JIVARO	KACHIN	KAPAUKU	KAZAK	KOREANS	LAPPS	LEPCHA	MAGUZAWA	MAORI
MATACO	MISKITO	MUNDURUCU	NAMA	NAMBICUARA	NUER	NYAKYUSA	OJIBWA	PAPAGO	RIFFIANS
RWALA	SEMANG	SENIANG	SIWANS	SOMALI	TALLENSI	TANALA	THONGA	TIKOPIA	TIMBIRA
TIV	TODA	TROBRIAND	TRUKESE	VIETNAMESE	WOLOF	YAHGAN	YAKUT	YAO	YOKUTS
YUROK									

339 IN RIGHT COLUMN

33	DRIFT LESS TOWARD BEING THOSE 0.77 OF 61 WHERE THE NATURAL ENVIRONMENT IS OTHER THAN 'VERY HARSH,' I.E., DESERT, DESERT GRASSES AND SHRUBS, TUNDRA, OR HIGH PLATEAU STEPPE (341) FWM	33	DRIFT MORE TOWARD BEING THOSE 0.87 OF 339 WHERE THE NATURAL ENVIRONMENT IS OTHER THAN 'VERY HARSH,' I.E., DESERT, DESERT GRASSES AND SHRUBS, TUNDRA, OR HIGH PLATEAU STEPPE (341) FWM	 XSQ= PHI= XP =	14 45 47 294 3.12 0.088 0.0774
36	DRIFT LESS TOWARD BEING THOSE 0.62 OF 61 WHERE THE NATURAL ENVIRONMENT IS OTHER THAN 'VERY HARSH,' OR SUB-TROPICAL BUSH, OR TEMPERATE GRASSLAND (292) FWM	36	DRIFT MORE TOWARD BEING THOSE 0.75 OF 339 WHERE THE NATURAL ENVIRONMENT IS OTHER THAN 'VERY HARSH,' OR SUB-TROPICAL BUSH, OR TEMPERATE GRASSLAND (292) FWM	 XSQ= PHI= XP =	23 85 38 254 3.57 0.094 0.0589
62	TILT MORE TOWARD BEING THOSE 0.72 OF 61 WHERE HUSBANDRY OF SOME KIND IS PRESENT (228)	62	TILT LESS TOWARD BEING THOSE 0.54 OF 339 WHERE HUSBANDRY OF SOME KIND IS PRESENT (228)	 XSQ= PHI= XP =	44 184 17 155 6.01 0.123 0.0142
177	DRIFT LESS TOWARD BEING THOSE 0.70 OF 61 WHERE THE COMMUNITY IS OTHER THAN A SINGLE CLAN-COMMUNITY AND EXOGAMOUS (305)	177	DRIFT MORE TOWARD BEING THOSE 0.82 OF 321 WHERE THE COMMUNITY IS OTHER THAN A SINGLE CLAN-COMMUNITY AND EXOGAMOUS (305)	 XSQ= PHI= XP =	18 59 43 262 3.28 0.093 0.0700
179	LEAN LESS TOWARD BEING THOSE 0.79 OF 61 WHERE THE COMMUNITY IS OTHER THAN STRUCTURED ON A NON-CLAN BASIS AND COMMONLY EXOGAMOUS (340)	179	LEAN MORE TOWARD BEING THOSE 0.91 OF 321 WHERE THE COMMUNITY IS OTHER THAN STRUCTURED ON A NON-CLAN BASIS AND COMMONLY EXOGAMOUS (340)	 XSQ= PHI= XP =	13 29 48 292 6.69 0.132 0.0097

180	TEND TO BE THOSE 0.52 OF 61 WHERE THE COMMUNITY IS COMMONLY EXOGAMOUS, RATHER THAN NON-EXOGAMOUS (124)	180	TEND TO BE THOSE 0.71 OF 321 WHERE THE COMMUNITY IS COMMONLY NON-EXOGAMOUS, RATHER THAN EXOGAMOUS (258)	32 92 29 229 XSQ= 12.18 PHI= 0.179 XP = 0.0005
185	TILT MORE TOWARD BEING THOSE 0.91 OF 43 WHERE THE LARGEST NON-COGNATIC KIN GROUP IS THE MOEITY OR PHRATRY OR SIB (194)	185	TILT LESS TOWARD BEING THOSE 0.74 OF 209 WHERE THE LARGEST NON-COGNATIC KIN GROUP IS THE MOEITY OR PHRATRY OR SIB (194)	39 155 4 54 XSQ= 4.61 PHI= 0.135 XP = 0.0318
224	DRIFT MORE TOWARD BEING THOSE 0.79 OF 24 WHERE COUSIN MARRIAGE IS PREFERENTIALLY OR PERMISSIVELY SYMMETRICAL, RATHER THAN EITHER PATRI- OR MATRILATERAL (106)	224	DRIFT LESS TOWARD BEING THOSE 0.59 OF 148 WHERE COUSIN MARRIAGE IS PREFERENTIALLY OR PERMISSIVELY SYMMETRICAL, RATHER THAN EITHER PATRI- OR MATRILATERAL (106)	5 61 19 87 XSQ= 2.82 PHI= -0.128 XP = 0.0932
236	DRIFT MORE TOWARD BEING THOSE 0.66 OF 61 WHERE THE FAMILY IS OF AN EXTENDED TYPE, RATHER THAN AN INDEPENDENT TYPE (213)	236	DRIFT LESS TOWARD BEING THOSE 0.51 OF 337 WHERE THE FAMILY IS OF AN EXTENDED TYPE, RATHER THAN AN INDEPENDENT TYPE (213)	40 173 21 164 XSQ= 3.66 PHI= 0.096 XP = 0.0559
255	DRIFT LESS TOWARD BEING THOSE 0.58 OF 12 WHERE GRANDPARENTAL AUTHORITY OVER PARENTS IS ABSENT (26) DA	255	DRIFT MORE TOWARD BEING THOSE 0.90 OF 21 WHERE GRANDPARENTAL AUTHORITY OVER PARENTS IS ABSENT (26) DA	5 2 7 19 XSQ= 2.99 PHI= 0.301 EP = 0.0709
280	TILT TOWARD BEING THOSE 0.75 OF 12 WHERE THE COMPOSITE FERTILITY LEVEL IS HIGH (13) MN	280	TILT TOWARD BEING THOSE 0.69 OF 13 WHERE THE COMPOSITE FERTILITY LEVEL IS LOW (12) MN	9 4 3 9 XSQ= 3.28 PHI= 0.362 EP = 0.0472
314	DRIFT LESS TOWARD BEING THOSE 0.65 OF 37 WHERE THE INCIDENCE OF MOTHER-CHILD HOUSEHOLDS IS LOW (61) W-D,S	314	DRIFT MORE TOWARD BEING THOSE 0.86 OF 43 WHERE THE INCIDENCE OF MOTHER-CHILD HOUSEHOLDS IS LOW (61) W-D,S	13 6 24 37 XSQ= 3.83 PHI= 0.219 XP = 0.0504
390	DRIFT MORE TOWARD BEING THOSE 0.85 OF 46 WHERE PREMARITAL SEX RELATIONS ARE WEAKLY PUNISHED AND IN FACT NOT RARE OR PUNISHED ONLY IF PREGNANCY RESULTS, OR FREELY PERMITTED (132) JTW,EA	390	DRIFT LESS TOWARD BEING THOSE 0.70 OF 133 WHERE PREMARITAL SEX RELATIONS ARE WEAKLY PUNISHED AND IN FACT NOT RARE OR PUNISHED ONLY IF PREGNANCY RESULTS, OR FREELY PERMITTED (132) JTW,EA	7 40 39 93 XSQ= 3.17 PHI= -0.133 XP = 0.0751
406	TILT TOWARD BEING THOSE 0.67 OF 21 WHERE EXPLANATIONS OF ILLNESS OF AN AGGRESSION NATURE ARE PRESENT (28) W-C	406	TILT TOWARD BEING THOSE 0.65 OF 40 WHERE EXPLANATIONS OF ILLNESS OF AN AGGRESSION NATURE ARE ABSENT (33) W-C	14 14 7 26 XSQ= 4.36 PHI= 0.267 XP = 0.0368

430	TILT TOWARD BEING THOSE 0.61 OF 18 WHERE SUPERNATURAL SANCTIONS FOR MORALITY, HAVING AN EFFECT ON AN INDIVIDUAL'S HEALTH, ARE PRESENT (16) GES	430	TILT TOWARD BEING THOSE 0.75 OF 20 WHERE SUPERNATURAL SANCTIONS FOR MORALITY, HAVING AN EFFECT ON AN INDIVIDUAL'S HEALTH, ARE ABSENT OR UNREPORTED (22) GES	11 5 7 15 XSQ= 3.69 PHI= 0.312 EP = 0.0472
445	TILT TOWARD BEING THOSE 0.75 OF 20 WHERE SORCERY IS IMPORTANT (26) BBW,DH	445	TILT TOWARD BEING THOSE 0.62 OF 29 WHERE SORCERY IS UNIMPORTANT (23) BBW,DH	15 11 5 18 XSQ= 5.13 PHI= 0.323 XP = 0.0236
456	DRIFT TOWARD BEING THOSE 0.78 OF 9 WHERE THE INTERNALIZATION OF THE INDIVIDUAL'S CONTACT WITH THE DIVINE IS NOT CONDUCIVE TO THE DEVELOPMENT OF THE INDIVIDUAL'S NEED TO ACHIEVE (17) DCM	456	DRIFT TOWARD BEING THOSE 0.63 OF 27 WHERE THE INTERNALIZATION OF THE INDIVIDUAL'S CONTACT WITH THE DIVINE IS CONDUCIVE TO THE DEVELOPMENT OF THE INDIVIDUAL'S NEED TO ACHIEVE (19) DCM	2 17 7 10 XSQ= 3.01 PHI= -0.289 EP = 0.0551
458	TILT LESS TOWARD BEING THOSE 0.55 OF 47 WHERE GAMES, IF PRESENT, DO NOT INCLUDE GAMES OF STRATEGY (119) R-A-B,EA	458	TILT MORE TOWARD BEING THOSE 0.75 OF 124 WHERE GAMES, IF PRESENT, DO NOT INCLUDE GAMES OF STRATEGY (119) R-A-B,EA	21 31 26 93 XSQ= 5.34 PHI= 0.177 XP = 0.0208
469	TILT LESS TOWARD BEING THOSE 0.64 OF 22 WHERE CONTACT WITH OTHER CULTURES IS FREQUENT OR REGULAR, RATHER THAN IRREGULAR (43) JMH	469	TILT MORE TOWARD BEING THOSE 0.91 OF 32 WHERE CONTACT WITH OTHER CULTURES IS FREQUENT OR REGULAR, RATHER THAN IRREGULAR (43) JMH	14 29 8 3 XSQ= 4.31 PHI= -0.282 XP = 0.0379
473	TILT LESS TOWARD BEING THOSE 0.51 OF 43 WHERE SENSITIVITY TO INSULT IS MODERATE OR NEGLIGIBLE (56) PES	473	TILT MORE TOWARD BEING THOSE 0.76 OF 45 WHERE SENSITIVITY TO INSULT IS MODERATE OR NEGLIGIBLE (56) PES	21 11 22 34 XSQ= 4.65 PHI= 0.230 XP = 0.0311
476	DRIFT TOWARD BEING THOSE 0.55 OF 20 WHERE THE DEGREE OF INSOBRIETY IS MODERATE OR SLIGHT (18) DH	476	DRIFT TOWARD BEING THOSE 0.76 OF 29 WHERE THE DEGREE OF INSOBRIETY IS STRONG (31) DH	9 22 11 7 XSQ= 3.61 PHI= -0.272 XP = 0.0573
489	TEND LESS TO BE THOSE 0.62 OF 61 NOT INCLUDED IN CHARLES ACKERMAN'S STUDY OF DIVORCE (343)	489	TEND MORE TO BE THOSE 0.90 OF 339 NOT INCLUDED IN CHARLES ACKERMAN'S STUDY OF DIVORCE (343)	23 34 38 305 XSQ= 30.18 PHI= 0.275 XP = 0.0000
490	TEND TO BE THOSE 0.51 OF 61 INCLUDED IN ALBERT S. ANTHONY'S SAMPLE ON MALE INITIATION RITES (113)	490	TEND TO BE THOSE 0.76 OF 339 NOT INCLUDED IN ALBERT S. ANTHONY'S SAMPLE ON MALE INITIATION RITES (287)	31 82 30 257 XSQ= 16.80 PHI= 0.205 XP = 0.0000

491	LEAN LESS TOWARD BEING THOSE 0.75 OF 61 NOT INCLUDED IN DORRIAN APPLE'S STUDY OF GRANDPARENTHCCD (352)	491	LEAN MORE TOWARD BEING THOSE 0.90 OF 339 NOT INCLUDED IN DORRIAN APPLE'S STUDY OF GRANDPARENTHOOD (352)	15 33 46 306 XSQ= 9.44 PHI= 0.154 XP = 0.0021
492	TEND LESS TO BE THCSE 0.75 OF 61 NOT INCLUDED IN BARBARA CHARTIER AYRES' STUDY OF FEMALE INITIATION RITES (361)	492	TEND MORE TO BE THOSE 0.93 OF 339 NOT INCLUDED IN BARBARA CHARTIER AYRES' STUDY OF FEMALE INITIATION RITES (361)	15 24 46 315 XSQ= 16.08 PHI= 0.200 XP = 0.0001
493	TEND LESS TO BE THCSE 0.57 OF 61 NOT INCLUDED IN BACON, BARRY, AND CHILD'S STUDY OF CHILD REARING (322)	493	TEND MORE TO BE THOSE 0.85 OF 339 NOT INCLUDED IN BACON, BARRY, AND CHILD'S STUDY OF CHILD REARING (322)	26 52 35 287 XSQ= 22.81 PHI= 0.239 XP = 0.0000
494	TILT LESS TOWARD BEING THCSE 0.85 OF 61 NOT INCLUDED IN HERBERT M. BARRY III'S STUDY OF ART (371)	494	TILT MORE TOWARD BEING THOSE 0.94 OF 339 NOT INCLUDED IN HERBERT M. BARRY III'S STUDY OF ART (371)	9 20 52 319 XSQ= 4.78 PHI= 0.109 XP = 0.0287
495	TEND LESS TO BE THCSE 0.54 OF 61 NOT INCLUDED IN JUDITH K. BROWN'S STUDY OF FEMALE INITIATION RITES (335)	495	TEND MORE TO BE THOSE 0.89 OF 339 NOT INCLUDED IN JUDITH K. BROWN'S STUDY OF FEMALE INITIATICN RITES (335)	28 37 33 302 XSQ= 43.96 PHI= 0.332 XP = 0.
496	TEND LESS TO BE THCSE 0.56 OF 61 NOT INCLUDED IN ROY G. D'ANDRADE'S STUDY OF DREAMS (345)	496	TEND MORE TO BE THOSE 0.92 OF 339 NOT INCLUDED IN ROY G. D'ANDRADE'S STUDY OF DREAMS (345)	27 28 34 311 XSQ= 53.51 PHI= 0.366 XP = 0.
498	TEND LESS TO BE THCSE 0.62 OF 61 NOT INCLUDED IN C. S. FORD'S STUDY OF SEX (349)	498	TEND MORE TO BE THOSE 0.92 OF 339 NOT INCLUDED IN C. S. FORD'S STUDY OF SEX (349)	23 28 38 311 XSQ= 37.69 PHI= 0.307 XP = 0.
499	TEND LESS TO BE THCSE 0.51 OF 61 NOT INCLUDED IN FORD AND BEACH'S SAMPLE ON SEXUAL EXPRESSICN BY THE YOUNG (314)	499	TEND MORE TO BE THOSE 0.83 OF 339 NOT INCLUDED IN FORD AND BEACH'S SAMPLE ON SEXUAL EXPRESSION BY THE YOUNG (314)	30 56 31 283 XSQ= 30.77 PHI= 0.277 XP = 0.
500	TEND LESS TO BE THCSE 0.66 OF 61 NOT INCLUDED IN FREEMAN AND WINCH'S STUDY OF SOCIETAL COMPLEXITY (360)	500	TEND MORE TO BE THOSE 0.94 OF 339 NOT INCLUDED IN FREEMAN AND WINCH'S STUDY OF SOCIETAL COMPLEXITY (360)	21 19 40 320 XSQ= 44.57 PHI= 0.334 XP = 0.

501	TEND LESS TO BE THOSE 0.62 OF 61 NOT INCLUDED IN JOAN FRIENDLY GOODMAN'S STUDY OF ASCETIC MOURNING BEHAVIOR (333)	501	TEND MORE TO BE THOSE 0.87 OF 339 NOT INCLUDED IN JOAN FRIENDLY GOODMAN'S STUDY OF ASCETIC MOURNING BEHAVIOR (333)	23 44 38 295 XSQ= 20.93 PHI= 0.229 XP = 0.0000
502	TEND LESS TO BE THOSE 0.64 OF 61 NOT INCLUDED IN JOHN K. HARLEY'S STUDY OF ADOLESCENT PEER GROUPS (343)	502	TEND MORE TO BE THOSE 0.90 OF 339 NOT INCLUDED IN JOHN K. HARLEY'S STUDY OF ADOLESCENT PEER GROUPS (343)	22 35 39 304 XSQ= 25.97 PHI= 0.255 XP = 0.0000
503	TEND LESS TO BE THOSE 0.64 OF 61 NOT INCLUDED IN JOHN M. HICKMAN'S STUDY OF THE FOLK-URBAN CONTINUUM (346)	503	TEND MORE TO BE THOSE 0.91 OF 339 NOT INCLUDED IN JOHN M. HICKMAN'S STUDY OF THE FOLK-URBAN CONTINUUM (346)	22 32 39 307 XSQ= 29.15 PHI= 0.270 XP = 0.0000
504	TEND LESS TO BE THOSE 0.67 OF 61 NOT INCLUDED IN DONALD HORTON'S STUDY OF ALCHOLISM (351)	504	TEND MORE TO BE THOSE 0.91 OF 339 NOT INCLUDED IN DONALD HORTON'S STUDY OF ALCHOLISM (351)	20 29 41 310 XSQ= 26.03 PHI= 0.255 XP = 0.0000
506	LEAN LESS TOWARD BEING THOSE 0.80 OF 61 NOT INCLUDED IN LAMBERT, TRIANDIS, AND WOLF'S STUDY OF SUPERNATURAL BEINGS (364)	506	LEAN MORE TOWARD BEING THOSE 0.93 OF 339 NOT INCLUDED IN LAMBERT, TRIANDIS, AND WOLF'S STUDY OF SUPERNATURAL BEINGS (364)	12 24 49 315 XSQ= 8.53 PHI= 0.146 XP = 0.0035
507	TEND TO BE THOSE 0.59 OF 61 INCLUDED IN JAMES R. LEARY'S STUDY OF FOOD TABOOS (86)	507	TEND TO BE THOSE 0.85 OF 339 NOT INCLUDED IN JAMES R. LEARY'S STUDY OF FOOD TABOOS (314)	36 50 25 289 XSQ= 57.43 PHI= 0.379 XP = 0.
509	TEND LESS TO BE THOSE 0.80 OF 61 NOT INCLUDED IN MONI NAG'S STUDY OF FERTILITY (375)	509	TEND MORE TO BE THOSE 0.96 OF 339 NOT INCLUDED IN MONI NAG'S STUDY OF FERTILITY (375)	12 13 49 326 XSQ= 19.51 PHI= 0.221 XP = 0.0000
510	TEND LESS TO BE THOSE 0.85 OF 61 NOT INCLUDED IN RAOUL NAROLL'S STUDY OF SOCIETAL COMPLEXITY (380)	510	TEND MORE TO BE THOSE 0.97 OF 339 NOT INCLUDED IN RAOUL NAROLL'S STUDY OF SOCIETAL COMPLEXITY (380)	9 11 52 328 XSQ= 12.10 PHI= 0.174 XP = 0.0005
511	TEND TO BE THOSE 0.79 OF 61 INCLUDED IN ROBERTS, ARTH AND BUSH'S SAMPLE ON GAMES, AS MODIFIED BY THE ETHNOGRAPHIC ATLAS (189)	511	TEND TO BE THOSE 0.58 OF 339 NOT INCLUDED IN ROBERTS, ARTH AND BUSH'S SAMPLE ON GAMES, AS MODIFIED BY THE ETHNOGRAPHIC ATLAS (211)	48 141 13 198 XSQ= 27.07 PHI= 0.260 XP = 0.0000

512	LEAN LESS TOWARC BEING THCSE NOT INCLUDED IN SHIRLEY ANC ROMNEY'S STUDY OF LOVE MAGIC (367)	0.80 OF 61	512	LEAN MORE TOWARD BEING THOSE NOT INCLUDED IN SHIRLEY AND ROMNEY'S STUDY OF LOVE MAGIC (367)	0.94 OF 339	12 21 49 318 XSQ= 10.69 PHI= 0.163 XP = 0.0011
513	TEND LESS TO BE THCSE NOT INCLUDED IN LEC W. SIMMONS' STUDY OF THE TREATMENT OF THE AGEC (357)	0.72 OF 61	513	TEND MORE TO BE THOSE NOT INCLUDED IN LEO W. SIMMONS' STUDY OF THE TREATMENT OF THE AGED (357)	0.92 OF 339	17 26 44 313 XSQ= 19.93 PHI= 0.223 XP = 0.0000
514	TEND TO BE THOSE INCLUDED IN PHILIP E. SLATER'S STUDY OF NARCISSISM (90)	0.72 OF 61	514	TEND TO BE THOSE NOT INCLUDED IN PHILIP E. SLATER'S STUDY OF NARCISSISM (310)	0.86 OF 339	44 46 17 293 XSQ= 98.34 PHI= 0.496 XP = 0.
515	TEND LESS TO BE THCSE NOT INCLUDED IN WILLIAM N. STEPHENS' SAMPLE ON AVOIDANCE RELATIONSHIPS (348)	0.64 OF 61	515	TEND MORE TO BE THOSE NOT INCLUDED IN WILLIAM N. STEPHENS' SAMPLE ON AVOIDANCE RELATIONSHIPS (348)	0.91 OF 339	22 30 39 309 XSQ= 31.49 PHI= 0.281 XP = 0.
516	TEND MORE TO BE THCSE INCLUDED IN GUY E. SWANSON'S SAMPLE ON LOCAL JURISDICTION, AS MODIFIED BY THE ETHNOGRAPHIC ATLAS (331)	0.98 OF 61	516	TEND LESS TO BE THOSE INCLUDED IN GUY E. SWANSON'S SAMPLE ON LOCAL JURISDICTICN, AS MODIFIED BY THE ETHNOGRAPHIC ATLAS (331)	0.80 OF 339	60 271 1 68 XSQ= 11.03 PHI= 0.166 XP = 0.0009
517	TEND MORE TO BE THCSE INCLUDED IN GUY E. SWANSCN'S SAMPLE CN HIGH GODS, AS MODIFIED BY THE ETHNOGRAPHIC ATLAS (260)	0.90 OF 61	517	TEND LESS TO BE THOSE INCLUDED IN GUY E. SWANSCN'S SAMPLE ON HIGH GODS, AS MODIFIED BY THE ETHNOGRAPHIC ATLAS (260)	0.60 OF 339	55 205 6 134 XSQ= 18.75 PHI= 0.217 XP = 0.0000
518	TEND TO BE THOSE INCLUDED IN STANLEY H. UDY, JR.'S STUDY OF WCRK ORGANIZATION (105)	0.56 OF 61	518	TEND TO BE THOSE NOT INCLUDED IN STANLEY H. UDY, JR.'S STUDY OF WORK ORGANIZATION (295)	0.79 OF 339	34 71 27 268 XSQ= 30.56 PHI= 0.276 XP = 0.
520	TEND LESS TO BE THCSE NCT INCLUDED IN BEATRICE BLYTH WHITING'S STUDY OF SCRCERY (360)	0.69 OF 61	520	TEND MORE TO BE THOSE NOT INCLUDED IN BEATRICE BLYTH WHITING'S STUDY OF SORCERY (360)	0.94 OF 339	19 21 42 318 XSQ= 33.05 PHI= 0.287 XP = 0.
522	TEND LESS TO BE THCSE NCT INCLUDED IN MARJORIE GRANT WHITING'S STUDY OF DIET (318)	0.52 OF 61	522	TEND MORE TO BE THOSE NOT INCLUDED IN MARJORIE GRANT WHITING'S STUDY OF DIET (318)	0.84 OF 339	29 53 32 286 XSQ= 30.37 PHI= 0.276 XP = 0.

523	TEND LESS TO BE THCSE NOT INCLUDED IN WHITING AND CHILD'S STUDY OF CHILD TRAINING AND PERSCNALITY (339)	0.66 OF 61	523	TEND MORE TO BE THOSE NOT INCLUDED IN WHITING AND CHILD'S STUDY OF CHILD TRAINING AND PERSONALITY (339)	0.88 OF 339	21 40 40 299 XSQ= 18.77 PHI= 0.217 XP = 0.0000
524	TEND LESS TO BE THCSE NOT INCLUDED IN WHITING, KLUCKHCHN, ANC ANTHONY'S STUDY OF MALE INITIATICN CEREMONIES (356)	0.62 OF 61	524	TEND MORE TO BE THOSE NOT INCLUDED IN WHITING, KLUCKHOHN, AND ANTHONY'S STUDY OF MALE INITIATION CEREMONIES (356)	0.94 OF 339	23 21 38 318 XSQ= 49.26 PHI= 0.351 XP = 0.

498 CULTURES
INCLUDED IN C. S. FORD'S
STUDY OF SEX (51)

498 CULTURES
NOT INCLUDED IN C. S. FORD'S
STUDY OF SEX (349)

BACKGROUND ON PAGE 180

SUBJECT ONLY, F.C. 1-480 AND 527-536
BOTH SUBJECT AND PREDICATE, F.C. 481-526

51 IN LEFT COLUMN

AINU	ANDAMANESE	APINAYE	ARANDA	ASHANTI	AZANDE	CARIB	CHOROTI	CHUKCHEE	COPR ESKIMO
CREEK	CROW	CUNA	DOBUANS	GOND	HANO	IFUGAO	JIVARO	KAZAK	KURTATCHI
KWAKIUTL	LAKHER	LANGO	LEPCHA	LESU	MAORI	MARICOPA	MASAI	MBUNDU	MURNGIN
NAMA	OMAHA	PUKAPUKA	RIFFIANS	SAMOYED	SANPOIL	SENIANG	TANALA	TARAHUMARA	THONGA
TIKOPIA	TIV	TOCA	TROBRIAND	TUBATULABAL	TUPINAMBA	VENDA	WITOTO	YAKUT	YUKAGHIR
YUROK									

349 IN RIGHT COLUMN

No.	Left column (51)		No.	Right column (349)		Statistics
4	TILT MORE TOWARD BEING THOSE LOCATED OUTSIDE OF THE CIRCUM-MEDITERRANEAN (355)	0.98 OF 51	4	TILT LESS TOWARD BEING THOSE LOCATED OUTSIDE OF THE CIRCUM-MEDITERRANEAN (355)	0.87 OF 349	1 44 50 305 XSQ= 4.04 PHI= -0.101 XP = 0.0444
11	TILT LESS TOWARD BEING THOSE WHERE THE LATITUDE IS LESS THAN SIXTY DEGREES (385)	0.90 OF 51	11	TILT MORE TOWARD BEING THOSE WHERE THE LATITUDE IS LESS THAN SIXTY DEGREES (385)	0.97 OF 349	5 10 46 339 XSQ= 4.17 PHI= 0.102 XP = 0.0412
36	TILT LESS TOWARD BEING THOSE WHERE THE NATURAL ENVIRONMENT IS OTHER THAN 'VERY HARSH,' OR SUB-TROPICAL BUSH, OR TEMPERATE GRASSLAND (292) FWM	0.59 OF 51	36	TILT MORE TOWARD BEING THOSE WHERE THE NATURAL ENVIRONMENT IS OTHER THAN 'VERY HARSH,' OR SUB-TROPICAL BUSH, OR TEMPERATE GRASSLAND (292) FWM	0.75 OF 349	21 87 30 262 XSQ= 5.16 PHI= 0.114 XP = 0.0231
51	TILT TOWARD BEING THOSE WHERE SUBSISTENCE IS PRIMARILY BY FOOD GATHERING -- I. E., HUNTING, FISHING, OR COLLECTING -- RATHER THAN FOOD PRODUCTION (147)	0.51 OF 51	51	TILT TOWARD BEING THOSE WHERE SUBSISTENCE IS PRIMARILY BY FOOD PRODUCTION -- I. E., AGRICULTURE OR HUSBANDRY -- RATHER THAN BY GATHERING (253)	0.65 OF 349	25 228 26 121 XSQ= 4.41 PHI= -0.105 XP = 0.0356
53	DRIFT MORE TOWARD BEING THOSE WHERE FOOD PRODUCTION IS BY SIMPLE AGRICULTURE OR INCIPIENT FOOD PRODUCTION, RATHER THAN BY INTENSIVE AGRICULTURE (147)	0.78 OF 32	53	DRIFT LESS TOWARD BEING THOSE WHERE FOOD PRODUCTION IS BY SIMPLE AGRICULTURE OR INCIPIENT FOOD PRODUCTION, RATHER THAN BY INTENSIVE AGRICULTURE (147)	0.59 OF 206	7 84 25 122 XSQ= 3.43 PHI= -0.120 XP = 0.0641

54	TILT LESS TOWARD BEING THOSE 0.66 OF 32 WHERE FOOD PRODUCTION IS BY INTENSIVE OR SIMPLE AGRICULTURE, RATHER THAN BY INCIPIENT FOOD PRODUCTION (192)	54	TILT MORE TOWARD BEING THOSE 0.83 OF 206 WHERE FOOD PRODUCTION IS BY INTENSIVE OR SIMPLE AGRICULTURE, RATHER THAN BY INCIPIENT FOOD PRODUCTION (192)	21 171 11 35 XSQ= 4.31 PHI= -0.135 XP = 0.0379
77	TILT MORE TOWARD BEING THOSE 0.91 OF 22 WHERE THE WRITING SYSTEM IS MNEMONIC OR ABSENT, RATHER THAN BEING ALPHABETIC-OR-PHONETIC (39) JMH	77	TILT LESS TOWARD BEING THOSE 0.59 OF 32 WHERE THE WRITING SYSTEM IS MNEMONIC OR ABSENT, RATHER THAN BEING ALPHABETIC-OR-PHONETIC (39) JMH	2 13 20 19 XSQ= 4.99 PHI= -0.304 XP = 0.0256
79	IN ALL CASES ARE THOSE 1.00 OF 41 WHERE NO CITY IS PRESENT (201)	79	TILT LESS TOWARD BEING THOSE 0.87 OF 183 WHERE NO CITY IS PRESENT (201)	0 23 41 160 XSQ= 4.46 PHI= -0.141 XP = 0.0347
80	TILT MORE TOWARD BEING THOSE 0.95 OF 41 WHERE NO CITY OR TOWN IS PRESENT (185)	80	TILT LESS TOWARD BEING THOSE 0.80 OF 183 WHERE NO CITY OR TOWN IS PRESENT (185)	2 37 39 146 XSQ= 4.47 PHI= -0.141 XP = 0.0346
81	TILT MORE TOWARD BEING THOSE 0.76 OF 41 WHERE NO CITY OR TOWN IS PRESENT, AND THE AVERAGE COMMUNITY SIZE IS SMALLER THAN 200 (135)	81	TILT LESS TOWARD BEING THOSE 0.57 OF 183 WHERE NO CITY OR TOWN IS PRESENT, AND THE AVERAGE COMMUNITY SIZE IS SMALLER THAN 200 (135)	10 79 31 104 XSQ= 4.18 PHI= -0.137 XP = 0.0409
82	DRIFT LESS TOWARD BEING THOSE 0.68 OF 41 WHERE A CITY OR TOWN IS PRESENT, OR THE AVERAGE COMMUNITY SIZE IS FIFTY OR GREATER (178)	82	DRIFT MORE TOWARD BEING THOSE 0.82 OF 183 WHERE A CITY OR TOWN IS PRESENT, OR THE AVERAGE COMMUNITY SIZE IS FIFTY OR GREATER (178)	28 150 13 33 XSQ= 3.05 PHI= -0.117 XP = 0.0809
94	DRIFT MORE TOWARD BEING THOSE 0.98 OF 50 WHERE THE HIERARCHY OF NATIONAL JURISDICTION HAS TWO, ONE, OR NO LEVELS (296) GES,EA	94	DRIFT LESS TOWARD BEING THOSE 0.88 OF 280 WHERE THE HIERARCHY OF NATIONAL JURISDICTION HAS TWO, ONE, OR NO LEVELS (296) GES,EA	1 33 49 247 XSQ= 3.40 PHI= -0.102 XP = 0.0652
107	IN ALL CASES ARE THOSE 1.00 OF 27 WHERE CLASS STRATIFICATION, IF PRESENT, IS BASED ON SOMETHING OTHER THAN OCCUPATIONAL STATUS (160)	107	LEAN LESS TOWARD BEING THOSE 0.76 OF 176 WHERE CLASS STRATIFICATION, IF PRESENT, IS BASED ON SOMETHING OTHER THAN OCCUPATIONAL STATUS (160)	0 43 27 133 XSQ= 6.97 PHI= -0.185 XP = 0.0083
109	DRIFT MORE TOWARD BEING THOSE 0.96 OF 49 WHERE CASTES ARE ABSENT (317)	109	DRIFT LESS TOWARD BEING THOSE 0.85 OF 319 WHERE CASTES ARE ABSENT (317)	2 49 47 270 XSQ= 3.63 PHI= -0.099 XP = 0.0567

No.	Left		No.	Right		Statistics
118	DRIFT TOWARD BEING THOSE WHERE THE PERCENTAGE OF OCCUPATIONS THAT ARE SPECIALIZED IS LOW (25) WME	0.68 OF 19	118	DRIFT TOWARD BEING THOSE WHERE THE PERCENTAGE OF OCCUPATIONS THAT ARE SPECIALIZED IS HIGH OR MEDIUM (24) WME	0.60 OF 30	6 18 13 12 XSQ= 2.71 PHI= -0.235 XP = 0.0998
139	DRIFT TOWARD BEING THOSE WHERE SUPERORDINATE PUNISHMENT IS ABSENT (25) BBW	0.72 OF 29	139	DRIFT TOWARD BEING THOSE WHERE SUPERORDINATE PUNISHMENT IS PRESENT (15) BBW	0.64 OF 11	8 7 21 4 XSQ= 3.02 PHI= -0.275 EP = 0.0654
152	IN ALL CASES ARE THOSE WHERE THE DIFFERENTIATION OF THE JURIDICAL AGENCY FROM THE MEDICAL AGENCY IS LOW (10) MJ	1.00 OF 6	152	TILT TOWARD BEING THOSE WHERE THE DIFFERENTIATION OF THE JURIDICAL AGENCY FROM THE MEDICAL AGENCY IS HIGH (10) MJ	0.71 OF 14	0 10 6 4 XSQ= 5.95 PHI= -0.546 EP = 0.0108
163	IN ALL CASES ARE THOSE WHERE THE EMPHASIS ON INDIVIDUAL VOLITION AS THE CAUSE OF CRIME IS LOW (10) MJ	1.00 OF 5	163	TILT TOWARD BEING THOSE WHERE THE EMPHASIS ON INDIVIDUAL VOLITION AS THE CAUSE OF CRIME IS HIGH (7) MJ	0.58 OF 12	0 7 5 5 XSQ= 2.84 PHI= -0.409 EP = 0.0441
196	LEAN TOWARD BEING THOSE WHERE INDIVIDUAL RIGHTS IN REAL PROPERTY, OR RULES FOR INHERITANCE, ARE ABSENT (87)	0.51 OF 35	196	LEAN TOWARD BEING THOSE WHERE INDIVIDUAL RIGHTS IN REAL PROPERTY, AND RULES FOR INHERITANCE, ARE PRESENT (194)	0.72 OF 246	17 177 18 69 XSQ= 6.78 PHI= -0.155 XP = 0.0092
234	DRIFT TOWARD BEING THOSE WHERE THE COUSIN TERMINOLOGY IS OF CROW, OMAHA, OR IROQUOIS TYPE, RATHER THAN ESKIMO OR HAWAIIAN TYPE (152)	0.61 OF 41	234	DRIFT TOWARD BEING THOSE WHERE THE COUSIN TERMINOLOGY IS OF ESKIMO OR HAWAIIAN TYPE, RATHER THAN CROW, OMAHA, OR IROQUOIS TYPE (170)	0.55 OF 281	25 127 16 154 XSQ= 2.97 PHI= 0.096 XP = 0.0848
262	TILT MORE TOWARD BEING THOSE WHERE WIVES ARE OBTAINED BY MEANS INVOLVING THE PRESENCE OF SOME CONSIDERATION (305)	0.92 OF 51	262	TILT LESS TOWARD BEING THOSE WHERE WIVES ARE OBTAINED BY MEANS INVOLVING THE PRESENCE OF SOME CONSIDERATION (305)	0.75 OF 344	47 258 4 86 XSQ= 6.49 PHI= 0.128 XP = 0.0109
301	LEAN LESS TOWARD BEING THOSE WHERE THE POST-PARTUM SEX TABOO LASTS LONGER THAN ONE MONTH (96)	0.57 OF 28	301	LEAN MORE TOWARD BEING THOSE WHERE THE POST-PARTUM SEX TABOO LASTS LONGER THAN ONE MONTH (96)	0.83 OF 96	16 80 12 16 XSQ= 7.07 PHI= -0.239 XP = 0.0078
304	DRIFT TOWARD BEING THOSE WHERE THE EARLY ANAL SATISFACTION POTENTIAL IS LOW (22) W-C	0.70 OF 20	304	DRIFT TOWARD BEING THOSE WHERE THE EARLY ANAL SATISFACTION POTENTIAL IS HIGH (19) W-C	0.62 OF 21	6 13 14 8 XSQ= 3.01 PHI= -0.271 XP = 0.0828

323	DRIFT MORE TOWARD BEING THOSE 0.75 OF 28 WHERE THE CONSTANCY OF PRESENCE OF THE INFANT'S NURTURANT AGENT IS LOW (45) B-B-C	323	DRIFT LESS TOWARD BEING THOSE 0.52 OF 46 WHERE THE CONSTANCY OF PRESENCE OF THE INFANT'S NURTURANT AGENT IS LOW (45) B-B-C	7 22 21 24 XSQ= 2.91 PHI= -0.198 XP = 0.0881
328	TILT TOWARD BEING THOSE 0.82 OF 11 WHERE THE AGE OF THE INFANT AT THE ONSET OF SERIOUS SOCIALIZATION, OTHER THAN WEANING, IS TWO YEARS OR LOWER (20) B-B-C	328	TILT TOWARD BEING THOSE 0.63 OF 30 WHERE THE AGE OF THE INFANT AT THE ONSET OF SERIOUS SOCIALIZATION, OTHER THAN WEANING, IS HIGHER THAN TWO YEARS (21) B-B-C	2 19 9 11 XSQ= 4.88 PHI= -0.345 XP = 0.0271
391	LEAN TOWARD BEING THOSE 0.76 OF 37 WHERE PREMARITAL SEX RELATIONS ARE PUNISHED ONLY IF PREGNANCY RESULTS, OR FREELY PERMITTED (90) JTW,EA	391	LEAN TOWARD BEING THOSE 0.56 OF 142 WHERE PREMARITAL SEX RELATIONS ARE STRONGLY PUNISHED AND IN FACT RARE, OR WEAKLY PUNISHED AND IN FACT NOT RARE (89) JTW,EA	9 80 28 62 XSQ= 10.79 PHI= -0.245 XP = 0.0010
392	TILT TOWARD BEING THOSE 0.54 OF 37 WHERE PREMARITAL SEX RELATIONS ARE FREELY PERMITTED (67) JTW,EA	392	TILT TOWARD BEING THOSE 0.67 OF 142 WHERE PREMARITAL SEX RELATIONS ARE STRONGLY PUNISHED AND IN FACT RARE, OR WEAKLY PUNISHED AND IN FACT NOT RARE, OR PUNISHED ONLY IF PREGNANCY RESULTS (112) JTW,EA	17 95 20 47 XSQ= 4.65 PHI= -0.161 XP = 0.0311
402	DRIFT TOWARD BEING THOSE 0.65 OF 31 WHERE EXPLANATIONS OF ILLNESS OF AN ORAL NATURE ARE PRESENT (31) W-C	402	DRIFT TOWARD BEING THOSE 0.63 OF 30 WHERE EXPLANATIONS OF ILLNESS OF AN ORAL NATURE ARE ABSENT (30) W-C	20 11 11 19 XSQ= 3.68 PHI= 0.246 XP = 0.0550
428	LEAN TOWARD BEING THOSE 0.64 OF 14 WHERE A HIGH GOD, IF PRESENT AND ACTIVE, DOES NOT SUPPORT HUMAN MORALITY, RATHER THAN SUPPORTING IT (26) GES,EA	428	LEAN TOWARD BEING THOSE 0.77 OF 73 WHERE A HIGH GOD, IF PRESENT AND ACTIVE, SUPPORTS HUMAN MORALITY, RATHER THAN NOT SUPPORTING IT (61) GES,EA	5 56 9 17 XSQ= 7.57 PHI= -0.295 XP = 0.0059
432	TILT MORE TOWARD BEING THOSE 0.89 OF 18 WHERE AN ATTRACTIVE AFTERLIFE IS BELIEVED IN (27) LWS	432	TILT LESS TOWARD BEING THOSE 0.55 OF 20 WHERE AN ATTRACTIVE AFTERLIFE IS BELIEVED IN (27) LWS	16 11 2 9 XSQ= 3.77 PHI= 0.315 EP = 0.0327
450	LEAN MORE TOWARD BEING THOSE 0.90 OF 29 WHERE THE OBSERVATION OF FOOD TABOOS IS HIGH OR MEDIUM, RATHER THAN LOW (60) JRL	450	LEAN LESS TOWARD BEING THOSE 0.60 OF 57 WHERE THE OBSERVATION OF FOOD TABOOS IS HIGH OR MEDIUM, RATHER THAN LOW (60) JRL	26 34 3 23 XSQ= 6.84 PHI= 0.282 XP = 0.0089
456	TILT TOWARD BEING THOSE 0.71 OF 14 WHERE THE INTERNALIZATION OF THE INDIVIDUAL'S CONTACT WITH THE DIVINE IS NOT CONDUCIVE TO THE DEVELOPMENT OF THE INDIVIDUAL'S NEED TO ACHIEVE (17) DCM	456	TILT TOWARD BEING THOSE 0.68 OF 22 WHERE THE INTERNALIZATION OF THE INDIVIDUAL'S CONTACT WITH THE DIVINE IS CONDUCIVE TO THE DEVELOPMENT OF THE INDIVIDUAL'S NEED TO ACHIEVE (19) DCM	4 15 10 7 XSQ= 3.91 PHI= -0.330 EP = 0.0388

No.			No.			
488	TEND MORE TO BE THOSE ABOUT WHICH THE PRINCIPAL ETHNOGRAPHIES WERE PUBLISHED BEFORE 1950 (185)	0.97 OF 39	488	TEND LESS TO BE THOSE ABOUT WHICH THE PRINCIPAL ETHNOGRAPHIES WERE PUBLISHED BEFORE 1950 (185)	0.67 OF 218	38 147 1 71 XSQ= 13.32 PHI= 0.228 XP = 0.0003
489	LEAN LESS TOWARD BEING THOSE NOT INCLUDED IN CHARLES ACKERMAN'S STUDY OF DIVORCE (343)	0.71 OF 51	489	LEAN MORE TOWARD BEING THOSE NOT INCLUDED IN CHARLES ACKERMAN'S STUDY OF DIVORCE (343)	0.88 OF 349	15 42 36 307 XSQ= 9.62 PHI= 0.155 XP = 0.0019
490	TEND TO BE THOSE INCLUDED IN ALBERT S. ANTHONY'S SAMPLE ON MALE INITIATION RITES (113)	0.69 OF 51	490	TEND TO BE THOSE NOT INCLUDED IN ALBERT S. ANTHONY'S SAMPLE ON MALE INITIATION RITES (287)	0.78 OF 349	35 78 16 271 XSQ= 44.76 PHI= 0.335 XP = 0.
491	TEND LESS TO BE THOSE NOT INCLUDED IN DORRIAN APPLE'S STUDY OF GRANDPARENTHOOD (352)	0.73 OF 51	491	TEND MORE TO BE THOSE NOT INCLUDED IN DORRIAN APPLE'S STUDY OF GRANDPARENTHOOD (352)	0.90 OF 349	14 34 37 315 XSQ= 11.59 PHI= 0.170 XP = 0.0007
492	TEND LESS TO BE THOSE NOT INCLUDED IN BARBARA CHARTIER AYRES' STUDY OF FEMALE INITIATION RITES (361)	0.53 OF 51	492	TEND MORE TO BE THOSE NOT INCLUDED IN BARBARA CHARTIER AYRES' STUDY OF FEMALE INITIATION RITES (361)	0.96 OF 349	24 15 27 334 XSQ= 87.67 PHI= 0.468 XP = 0.
493	TEND TO BE THOSE INCLUDED IN BACON, BARRY, AND CHILD'S STUDY OF CHILD REARING (78)	0.59 OF 51	493	TEND TO BE THOSE NOT INCLUDED IN BACON, BARRY, AND CHILD'S STUDY OF CHILD REARING (322)	0.86 OF 349	30 48 21 301 XSQ= 54.75 PHI= 0.370 XP = 0.
494	TEND LESS TO BE THOSE NOT INCLUDED IN HERBERT M. BARRY III'S STUDY OF ART (371)	0.75 OF 51	494	TEND MORE TO BE THOSE NOT INCLUDED IN HERBERT M. BARRY III'S STUDY OF ART (371)	0.95 OF 349	13 16 38 333 XSQ= 25.90 PHI= 0.254 XP = 0.0000
495	TEND LESS TO BE THOSE NOT INCLUDED IN JUDITH K. BROWN'S STUDY OF FEMALE INITIATION RITES (335)	0.55 OF 51	495	TEND MORE TO BE THOSE NOT INCLUDED IN JUDITH K. BROWN'S STUDY OF FEMALE INITIATION RITES (335)	0.88 OF 349	23 42 28 307 XSQ= 33.36 PHI= 0.289 XP = 0.
496	TEND LESS TO BE THOSE NOT INCLUDED IN ROY G. D'ANDRADE'S STUDY OF DREAMS (345)	0.59 OF 51	496	TEND MORE TO BE THOSE NOT INCLUDED IN ROY G. D'ANDRADE'S STUDY OF DREAMS (345)	0.90 OF 349	21 34 30 315 XSQ= 34.47 PHI= 0.294 XP = 0.

497	TEND LESS TO BE THOSE NOT INCLUDED IN WILLIAM M. EVAN'S STUDY OF LAW (339)	0.55 OF 51	497	TEND MORE TO BE THOSE NOT INCLUDED IN WILLIAM M. EVAN'S STUDY OF LAW (339)	0.89 OF 349	23 38 28 311 XSQ= 37.69 PHI= 0.307 XP = 0.
499	TEND TO BE THOSE INCLUDED IN FORD AND BEACH'S SAMPLE ON SEXUAL EXPRESSION BY THE YOUNG (86)	0.78 OF 51	499	TEND TO BE THOSE NOT INCLUDED IN FORD AND BEACH'S SAMPLE ON SEXUAL EXPRESSION BY THE YOUNG (314)	0.87 OF 349	40 46 11 303 XSQ= 108.42 PHI= 0.521 XP = 0.
500	TEND TO BE THOSE INCLUDED IN FREEMAN AND WINCH'S STUDY OF SOCIETAL COMPLEXITY (40)	0.51 OF 51	500	TEND TO BE THOSE NOT INCLUDED IN FREEMAN AND WINCH'S STUDY OF SOCIETAL COMPLEXITY (360)	0.96 OF 349	26 14 25 335 XSQ= 103.92 PHI= 0.510 XP = 0.
501	TEND TO BE THOSE INCLUDED IN JOAN FRIENDLY GOODMAN'S STUDY OF ASCETIC MOURNING BEHAVIOR (67)	0.73 OF 51	501	TEND TO BE THOSE NOT INCLUDED IN JOAN FRIENDLY GOODMAN'S STUDY OF ASCETIC MOURNING BEHAVIOR (333)	0.91 OF 349	37 30 14 319 XSQ= 125.97 PHI= 0.561 XP = 0.
502	TEND LESS TO BE THOSE NOT INCLUDED IN JOHN K. HARLEY'S STUDY OF ADOLESCENT PEER GROUPS (343)	0.53 OF 51	502	TEND MORE TO BE THOSE NOT INCLUDED IN JOHN K. HARLEY'S STUDY OF ADOLESCENT PEER GROUPS (343)	0.91 OF 349	24 33 27 316 XSQ= 48.46 PHI= 0.348 XP = 0.
503	TEND LESS TO BE THOSE NOT INCLUDED IN JOHN M. HICKMAN'S STUDY OF THE FOLK-URBAN CONTINUUM (346)	0.57 OF 51	503	TEND MORE TO BE THOSE NOT INCLUDED IN JOHN M. HICKMAN'S STUDY OF THE FOLK-URBAN CONTINUUM (346)	0.91 OF 349	22 32 29 317 XSQ= 41.11 PHI= 0.321 XP = 0.
504	TEND TO BE THOSE INCLUDED IN DONALD HORTON'S STUDY OF ALCCHOLISM (49)	0.65 OF 51	504	TEND TO BE THOSE NOT INCLUDED IN DONALD HORTON'S STUDY OF ALCHOLISM (351)	0.95 OF 349	33 16 18 333 XSQ= 144.09 PHI= 0.600 XP = 0.
505	TILT LESS TOWARD BEING THOSE NOT INCLUDED IN MERRILL JACKSON'S STUDY OF CRIMINAL LAW AND MEDICINE (380)	0.88 OF 51	505	TILT MORE TOWARD BEING THOSE NOT INCLUDED IN MERRILL JACKSON'S STUDY OF CRIMINAL LAW AND MEDICINE (380)	0.96 OF 349	6 14 45 335 XSQ= 4.12 PHI= 0.101 XP = 0.0424
506	TEND LESS TO BE THOSE NOT INCLUDED IN LAMBERT, TRIANDIS, AND WOLF'S STUDY OF SUPERNATURAL BEINGS (364)	0.75 OF 51	506	TEND MORE TO BE THOSE NOT INCLUDED IN LAMBERT, TRIANDIS, AND WOLF'S STUDY OF SUPERNATURAL BEINGS (364)	0.93 OF 349	13 23 38 326 XSQ= 17.17 PHI= 0.207 XP = 0.0000

507	TEND TO BE THOSE 0.57 OF 51 INCLUDED IN JAMES R. LEARY'S STUDY OF FOOD TABOOS (86)	507	TEND TO BE THOSE 0.84 OF 349 NOT INCLUDED IN JAMES R. LEARY'S STUDY OF FOOD TABOOS (314)	29 57 22 292 XSQ= 40.94 PHI= 0.320 XP = 0.
508	TEND LESS TO BE THOSE 0.69 OF 51 NOT INCLUDED IN DAVID C. MCCLELLAND'S STUDY OF ACHIEVEMENT MOTIVATION (360)	508	TEND MORE TO BE THOSE 0.93 OF 349 NOT INCLUDED IN DAVID C. MCCLELLAND'S STUDY OF ACHIEVEMENT MOTIVATION (360)	16 24 35 325 XSQ= 27.01 PHI= 0.260 XP = 0.0000
509	TILT LESS TOWARD BEING THOSE 0.86 OF 51 NOT INCLUDED IN MONI NAG'S STUDY OF FERTILITY (375)	509	TILT MORE TOWARD BEING THOSE 0.95 OF 349 NOT INCLUDED IN MONI NAG'S STUDY OF FERTILITY (375)	7 18 44 331 XSQ= 4.21 PHI= 0.103 XP = 0.0402
510	TEND LESS TO BE THOSE 0.82 OF 51 NOT INCLUDED IN RAOUL NARROLL'S STUDY OF SOCIETAL COMPLEXITY (380)	510	TEND MORE TO BE THOSE 0.97 OF 349 NOT INCLUDED IN RAOUL NARROLL'S STUDY OF SOCIETAL COMPLEXITY (380)	9 11 42 338 XSQ= 16.75 PHI= 0.205 XP = 0.0000
511	TEND TO BE THOSE 0.82 OF 51 INCLUDED IN ROBERTS, ARTH AND BUSH'S SAMPLE ON GAMES, AS MODIFIED BY THE ETHNOGRAPHIC ATLAS (189)	511	TEND TO BE THOSE 0.58 OF 349 NOT INCLUDED IN ROBERTS, ARTH AND BUSH'S SAMPLE ON GAMES, AS MODIFIED BY THE ETHNOGRAPHIC ATLAS (211)	42 147 9 202 XSQ= 27.31 PHI= 0.261 XP = 0.0000
512	TEND LESS TO BE THOSE 0.59 OF 51 NOT INCLUDED IN SHIRLEY AND ROMNEY'S STUDY OF LOVE MAGIC (367)	512	TEND MORE TO BE THOSE 0.97 OF 349 NOT INCLUDED IN SHIRLEY AND ROMNEY'S STUDY OF LOVE MAGIC (367)	21 12 30 337 XSQ= 78.81 PHI= 0.444 XP = 0.
513	TEND LESS TO BE THOSE 0.61 OF 51 NOT INCLUDED IN LEO W. SIMMONS' STUDY OF THE TREATMENT OF THE AGED (357)	513	TEND MORE TO BE THOSE 0.93 OF 349 NOT INCLUDED IN LEO W. SIMMONS' STUDY OF THE TREATMENT OF THE AGED (357)	20 23 31 326 XSQ= 46.02 PHI= 0.339 XP = 0.
514	TEND TO BE THOSE 0.76 OF 51 INCLUDED IN PHILIP E. SLATER'S STUDY OF NARCISSISM (90)	514	TEND TO BE THOSE 0.85 OF 349 NOT INCLUDED IN PHILIP E. SLATER'S STUDY OF NARCISSISM (310)	39 51 12 298 XSQ= 94.13 PHI= 0.485 XP = 0.
515	TEND LESS TO BE THOSE 0.65 OF 51 NOT INCLUDED IN WILLIAM N. STEPHENS' SAMPLE ON AVOIDANCE RELATIONSHIPS (348)	515	TEND MORE TO BE THOSE 0.90 OF 349 NOT INCLUDED IN WILLIAM N. STEPHENS' SAMPLE ON AVOIDANCE RELATIONSHIPS (348)	18 34 33 315 XSQ= 23.48 PHI= 0.242 XP = 0.0000

516	LEAN MORE TOWARD BEING THOSE INCLUDED IN GUY E. SWANSON'S SAMPLE ON LOCAL JURISDICTION, AS MODIFIED BY THE ETHNOGRAPHIC ATLAS (331)	0.98 OF 51	516	LEAN LESS TOWARD BEING THOSE INCLUDED IN GUY E. SWANSON'S SAMPLE ON LOCAL JURISDICTION, AS MODIFIED BY THE ETHNOGRAPHIC ATLAS (331)	0.81 OF 349	50 281 1 68 XSQ= 8.38 PHI= 0.145 XP = 0.0038
517	TEND MORE TO BE THOSE INCLUDED IN GUY E. SWANSON'S SAMPLE ON HIGH GODS, AS MODIFIED BY THE ETHNOGRAPHIC ATLAS (260)	0.88 OF 51	517	TEND LESS TO BE THOSE INCLUDED IN GUY E. SWANSON'S SAMPLE ON HIGH GODS, AS MODIFIED BY THE ETHNOGRAPHIC ATLAS (260)	0.62 OF 349	45 215 6 134 XSQ= 12.73 PHI= 0.178 XP = 0.0004
518	TEND TO BE THOSE INCLUDED IN STANLEY H. UDY, JR.'S STUDY OF WORK ORGANIZATION (105)	0.65 OF 51	518	TEND TO BE THOSE NOT INCLUDED IN STANLEY H. UDY, JR.'S STUDY OF WORK ORGANIZATION (295)	0.79 OF 349	33 72 18 277 XSQ= 42.40 PHI= 0.326 XP = 0.
519	TEND LESS TO BE THOSE NOT INCLUDED IN JOSEPH VEROFF'S STUDY OF ACHIEVEMENT MOTIVATION AS REVEALED IN FOLKTALES (364)	0.73 OF 51	519	TEND MORE TO BE THOSE NOT INCLUDED IN JOSEPH VEROFF'S STUDY OF ACHIEVEMENT MOTIVATION AS REVEALED IN FOLKTALES (364)	0.94 OF 349	14 22 37 327 XSQ= 21.78 PHI= 0.233 XP = 0.0000
520	TEND TO BE THOSE INCLUDED IN BEATRICE BLYTH WHITING'S STUDY OF SORCERY (40)	0.57 OF 51	520	TEND TO BE THOSE NOT INCLUDED IN BEATRICE BLYTH WHITING'S STUDY OF SORCERY (360)	0.97 OF 349	29 11 22 338 XSQ= 136.73 PHI= 0.585 XP = 0.
522	TEND TO BE THOSE INCLUDED IN MARJORIE GRANT WHITING'S STUDY OF DIET (82)	0.59 OF 51	522	TEND TO BE THOSE NOT INCLUDED IN MARJORIE GRANT WHITING'S STUDY OF DIET (318)	0.85 OF 349	30 52 21 297 XSQ= 50.02 PHI= 0.354 XP = 0.
523	TEND TO BE THOSE INCLUDED IN WHITING AND CHILD'S STUDY OF CHILD TRAINING AND PERSONALITY (61)	0.61 OF 51	523	TEND TO BE THOSE NOT INCLUDED IN WHITING AND CHILD'S STUDY OF CHILD TRAINING AND PERSONALITY (339)	0.91 OF 349	31 30 20 319 XSQ= 89.78 PHI= 0.474 XP = 0.
524	TEND LESS TO BE THOSE NOT INCLUDED IN WHITING, KLUCKHOHN, AND ANTHONY'S STUDY OF MALE INITIATION CEREMONIES (356)	0.73 OF 51	524	TEND MORE TO BE THOSE NOT INCLUDED IN WHITING, KLUCKHOHN, AND ANTHONY'S STUDY OF MALE INITIATION CEREMONIES (356)	0.91 OF 349	14 30 37 319 XSQ= 14.29 PHI= 0.189 XP = 0.0002

499 CULTURES
INCLUDED IN FORD AND BEACH'S
SAMPLE ON SEXUAL EXPRESSION
BY THE YOUNG (86)

499 CULTURES
NOT INCLUDED IN FORD AND BEACH'S
SAMPLE ON SEXUAL EXPRESSION
BY THE YOUNG (314)

BACKGROUND ON PAGE 180

SUBJECT ONLY, F.C. 1-480 AND 527-536
BOTH SUBJECT AND PREDICATE, F.C. 481-526

86 IN LEFT COLUMN

AINU	ALORESE	ANDAMANESE	APINAYE	ARANDA	ASHANTI	AYMARA	AZANDE	BALINESE	CARIB
CHAGGA	CHIR-APACHE	CHOROTI	CHUKCHEE	COPR ESKIMO	CREE	CREEK	CROW	CUNA	DOBUANS
DUSUN	FON	GANDA	GILYAK	GOAJIRO	GOND	HANO	HAVASUPAI	HUICHOL	IFUGAO
ILA	JUKUN	KAZAK	KIOW-APACHE	KURTATCHI	KUTENAI	KWAKIUTL	LAMBA	LANGO	LAPPS
LEPCHA	LESU	MANDAN	MANUS	MAORI	MARQUESANS	MARSHALLESE	MASAI	MATACO	MBUNDU
MURNGIN	NAMA	NANDI	NASKAPI	NATCHEZ	OJIBWA	OMAHA	PALAUANS	PAPAGO	PENOBSCOT
PONAPEANS	PUKAPUKA	PURARI	SAMOANS	SEMINOLE	SENIANG	SIRIONO	SWAZI	TAOS	TARAHUMARA
THONGA	TIKOPIA	TIMBIRA	TODA	TOKELAU	TROBRIAND	TRUKESE	TUPINAMBA	VENDA	WOGEO
WOLOF	YAGUA	YAKUT	YAPESE	YARURO	YUKAGHIR				

314 IN RIGHT COLUMN

4	LEAN MORE TOWARD BEING THOSE LOCATED OUTSIDE OF THE CIRCUM-MEDITERRANEAN (355)	0.98 OF 86	4	LEAN LESS TOWARD BEING THOSE LOCATED OUTSIDE OF THE CIRCUM-MEDITERRANEAN (355)	0.86 OF 314	2 43 / 84 271 / XSQ= 7.64 / PHI= -0.138 / XP = 0.0057
6	LEAN LESS TOWARD BEING THOSE LOCATED OUTSIDE OF THE INSULAR PACIFIC (330)	0.71 OF 86	6	LEAN MORE TOWARD BEING THOSE LOCATED OUTSIDE OF THE INSULAR PACIFIC (330)	0.86 OF 314	25 45 / 61 269 / XSQ= 9.16 / PHI= 0.151 / XP = 0.0025
8	DRIFT LESS TOWARD BEING THOSE LOCATED OUTSIDE OF NORTH AMERICA (330)	0.76 OF 86	8	DRIFT MORE TOWARD BEING THOSE LOCATED OUTSIDE OF NORTH AMERICA (330)	0.84 OF 314	21 49 / 65 265 / XSQ= 3.05 / PHI= 0.087 / XP = 0.0809
51	TILT LESS TOWARD BEING THOSE WHERE SUBSISTENCE IS PRIMARILY BY FOOD PRODUCTION -- I. E., AGRICULTURE OR HUSBANDRY -- RATHER THAN BY GATHERING (253)	0.53 OF 86	51	TILT MORE TOWARD BEING THOSE WHERE SUBSISTENCE IS PRIMARILY BY FOOD PRODUCTION -- I. E., AGRICULTURE OR HUSBANDRY -- RATHER THAN BY GATHERING (253)	0.66 OF 314	46 207 / 40 107 / XSQ= 3.97 / PHI= -0.100 / XP = 0.0463

53	LEAN MORE TOWARD BEING THOSE 0.78 OF 51 WHERE FOOD PRODUCTION IS BY SIMPLE AGRICULTURE OR INCIPIENT FOOD PRODUCTION, RATHER THAN BY INTENSIVE AGRICULTURE (147)	53	LEAN LESS TOWARD BEING THOSE 0.57 OF 187 WHERE FOOD PRODUCTION IS BY SIMPLE AGRICULTURE OR INCIPIENT FOOD PRODUCTION, RATHER THAN BY INTENSIVE AGRICULTURE (147)	11 80 40 107 XSQ= 6.76 PHI= -0.169 XP = 0.0093
55	TILT TOWARD BEING THOSE 0.70 OF 37 WHERE FOOD PRODUCTION IS BY SIMPLE AGRICULTURE, RATHER THAN BY INTENSIVE AGRICULTURE (101)	55	TILT TOWARD BEING THOSE 0.52 OF 155 WHERE FOOD PRODUCTION IS BY INTENSIVE AGRICULTURE, RATHER THAN BY SIMPLE AGRICULTURE (91)	11 80 26 75 XSQ= 4.89 PHI= -0.160 XP = 0.0270
63	TILT LESS TOWARD BEING THOSE 0.54 OF 54 WHERE HUSBANDRY, IF PRESENT, IS PRINCIPALLY IN THE FORM OF BOVINE, EQUINE, CAMEL-LIKE, OR DEER-LIKE ANIMALS, RATHER THAN PIGS, SHEEP, OR GOATS (152)	63	TILT MORE TOWARD BEING THOSE 0.72 OF 172 WHERE HUSBANDRY, IF PRESENT, IS PRINCIPALLY IN THE FORM OF BOVINE, EQUINE, CAMEL-LIKE, OR DEER-LIKE ANIMALS, RATHER THAN PIGS, SHEEP, OR GOATS (152)	29 123 25 49 XSQ= 5.14 PHI= -0.151 XP = 0.0234
71	TILT MORE TOWARD BEING THOSE 0.72 OF 68 WHERE METAL WORKING IS ABSENT (153)	71	TILT LESS TOWARD BEING THOSE 0.57 OF 183 WHERE METAL WORKING IS ABSENT (153)	19 79 49 104 XSQ= 4.21 PHI= -0.130 XP = 0.0401
77	LEAN MORE TOWARD BEING THOSE 0.92 OF 26 WHERE THE WRITING SYSTEM IS MNEMONIC OR ABSENT, RATHER THAN BEING ALPHABETIC-OR-PHONETIC (39) JMH	77	LEAN LESS TOWARD BEING THOSE 0.54 OF 28 WHERE THE WRITING SYSTEM IS MNEMONIC OR ABSENT, RATHER THAN BEING ALPHABETIC-OR-PHONETIC (39) JMH	2 13 24 15 XSQ= 8.24 PHI= -0.391 XP = 0.0041
79	IN ALL CASES ARE THOSE 1.00 OF 59 WHERE NO CITY IS PRESENT (201)	79	LEAN LESS TOWARD BEING THOSE 0.86 OF 165 WHERE NO CITY IS PRESENT (201)	0 23 59 142 XSQ= 7.71 PHI= -0.186 XP = 0.0055
80	LEAN MORE TOWARD BEING THOSE 0.95 OF 59 WHERE NO CITY OR TOWN IS PRESENT (185)	80	LEAN LESS TOWARD BEING THOSE 0.78 OF 165 WHERE NO CITY OR TOWN IS PRESENT (185)	3 36 56 129 XSQ= 7.34 PHI= -0.181 XP = 0.0067
81	DRIFT MORE TOWARD BEING THOSE 0.71 OF 59 WHERE NO CITY OR TOWN IS PRESENT, AND THE AVERAGE COMMUNITY SIZE IS SMALLER THAN 200 (135)	81	DRIFT LESS TOWARD BEING THOSE 0.56 OF 165 WHERE NO CITY OR TOWN IS PRESENT, AND THE AVERAGE COMMUNITY SIZE IS SMALLER THAN 200 (135)	17 72 42 93 XSQ= 3.39 PHI= -0.123 XP = 0.0655
107	LEAN MORE TOWARD BEING THOSE 0.98 OF 44 WHERE CLASS STRATIFICATION, IF PRESENT, IS BASED ON SOMETHING OTHER THAN OCCUPATIONAL STATUS (160)	107	LEAN LESS TOWARD BEING THOSE 0.74 OF 159 WHERE CLASS STRATIFICATION, IF PRESENT, IS BASED ON SOMETHING OTHER THAN OCCUPATIONAL STATUS (160)	1 42 43 117 XSQ= 10.63 PHI= -0.229 XP = 0.0011

108	DRIFT TOWARD BEING THOSE WHERE CLASS STRATIFICATION, IF PRESENT, IS BASED ON A HEREDITARY ARISTOCRACY (74)	0.50 OF 44	108	DRIFT TOWARD BEING THOSE WHERE CLASS STRATIFICATION, IF PRESENT, IS BASED ON SOMETHING OTHER THAN A HEREDITARY ARISTOCRACY (129)	0.67 OF 159	22 52 22 107 XSQ= 3.74 PHI= 0.136 XP = 0.0533
109	TILT MORE TOWARD BEING THOSE WHERE CASTES ARE ABSENT (317)	0.94 OF 84	109	TILT LESS TOWARD BEING THOSE WHERE CASTES ARE ABSENT (317)	0.84 OF 284	5 46 79 238 XSQ= 4.87 PHI= -0.115 XP = 0.0273
110	TILT MORE TOWARD BEING THOSE WHERE SLAVERY IS ABSENT (218)	0.69 OF 85	110	TILT LESS TOWARD BEING THOSE WHERE SLAVERY IS ABSENT (218)	0.54 OF 296	26 137 59 159 XSQ= 6.02 PHI= -0.126 XP = 0.0141
127	LEAN TOWARD BEING THOSE WHERE THE FEMALES' CONTRIBUTION TO SUBSISTENCE IS HIGH (33) JKB	0.71 OF 31	127	LEAN TOWARD BEING THOSE WHERE THE FEMALES' CONTRIBUTION TO SUBSISTENCE IS LOW (32) JKB	0.68 OF 34	22 11 9 23 XSQ= 8.19 PHI= 0.355 XP = 0.0042
128	TILT TOWARD BEING THOSE WHERE, IF SUBSISTENCE IS PRIMARILY BY AGRICULTURE, THE WORK IS MAINLY DONE BY FEMALES (37)	0.68 OF 22	128	TILT TOWARD BEING THOSE WHERE, IF SUBSISTENCE IS PRIMARILY BY AGRICULTURE, THE WORK IS MAINLY DONE BY MALES (40)	0.60 OF 55	7 33 15 22 XSQ= 3.93 PHI= -0.226 XP = 0.0473
130	TILT TOWARD BEING THOSE WHERE LEATHER WORKING IS MAINLY DONE BY FEMALES (45)	0.74 OF 23	130	TILT TOWARD BEING THOSE WHERE LEATHER WORKING IS MAINLY DONE BY MALES (39)	0.54 OF 61	6 33 17 28 XSQ= 4.20 PHI= -0.224 XP = 0.0404
132	TILT TOWARD BEING THOSE WHERE ECONOMIC EXCHANGE DOES NOT INVOLVE THE USE OF MONEY (17) JMH	0.50 OF 26	132	TILT TOWARD BEING THOSE WHERE ECONOMIC EXCHANGE INVOLVES THE USE OF MONEY (37) JMH	0.86 OF 28	13 24 13 4 XSQ= 6.40 PHI= -0.344 XP = 0.0114
186	LEAN MORE TOWARD BEING THOSE WHERE THE KIN GROUP IS OTHER THAN EXCLUSIVELY PATRILINEAL (250)	0.78 OF 86	186	LEAN LESS TOWARD BEING THOSE WHERE THE KIN GROUP IS OTHER THAN EXCLUSIVELY PATRILINEAL (250)	0.58 OF 314	19 131 67 183 XSQ= 10.27 PHI= -0.160 XP = 0.0013
190	DRIFT LESS TOWARD BEING THOSE WHERE THE KIN GROUP IS PATRILINEAL OR DOUBLE-DESCENT, RATHER THAN MATRILINEAL (186)	0.65 OF 52	190	DRIFT MORE TOWARD BEING THOSE WHERE THE KIN GROUP IS PATRILINEAL OR DOUBLE-DESCENT, RATHER THAN MATRILINEAL (186)	0.78 OF 195	34 152 18 43 XSQ= 2.84 PHI= -0.107 XP = 0.0918

209	DRIFT LESS TOWARD BEING THOSE 0.72 OF 69 WHERE MARITAL RESIDENCE IS PATRILOCAL, VIRILOCAL, OR AVUNCULOCAL, RATHER THAN MATRILOCAL OR UXORILOCAL (270)	209	DRIFT MORE TOWARD BEING THOSE 0.83 OF 265 WHERE MARITAL RESIDENCE IS PATRILOCAL, VIRILOCAL, OR AVUNCULOCAL, RATHER THAN MATRILOCAL OR UXORILOCAL (270)	50 220 19 45 XSQ= 3.29 PHI= -0.099 XP = 0.0699
210	DRIFT LESS TOWARD BEING THOSE 0.74 OF 38 WHERE MARITAL RESIDENCE IS PATRILOCAL, RATHER THAN MATRILOCAL (169)	210	DRIFT MORE TOWARD BEING THOSE 0.87 OF 162 WHERE MARITAL RESIDENCE IS PATRILOCAL, RATHER THAN MATRILOCAL (169)	28 141 10 21 XSQ= 3.23 PHI= -0.127 XP = 0.0722
213	DRIFT MORE TOWARD BEING THOSE 0.63 OF 86 WHERE FIRST COUSIN MARRIAGE IS NOT PERMITTED (198)	213	DRIFT LESS TOWARD BEING THOSE 0.51 OF 284 WHERE FIRST COUSIN MARRIAGE IS NOT PERMITTED (198)	32 140 54 144 XSQ= 3.41 PHI= -0.096 XP = 0.0650
234	TILT TOWARD BEING THOSE 0.58 OF 76 WHERE THE COUSIN TERMINOLOGY IS OF CROW, OMAHA, OR IROQUOIS TYPE, RATHER THAN ESKIMO OR HAWAIIAN TYPE (152)	234	TILT TOWARD BEING THOSE 0.56 OF 246 WHERE THE COUSIN TERMINOLOGY IS OF ESKIMO OR HAWAIIAN TYPE, RATHER THAN CROW, OMAHA, OR IROQUOIS TYPE (170)	44 108 32 138 XSQ= 4.02 PHI= 0.112 XP = 0.0450
243	DRIFT TOWARD BEING THOSE 0.71 OF 34 WHERE POLYGYNY, IF PRESENT, HAS A LOW INCIDENCE (36) W-D,S	243	DRIFT TOWARD BEING THOSE 0.54 OF 26 WHERE POLYGYNY, IF PRESENT, HAS A HIGH INCIDENCE (24) W-D,S	10 14 24 12 XSQ= 2.72 PHI= -0.213 XP = 0.0992
301	DRIFT LESS TOWARD BEING THOSE 0.66 OF 41 WHERE THE POST-PARTUM SEX TABOO LASTS LONGER THAN ONE MONTH (96)	301	DRIFT MORE TOWARD BEING THOSE 0.83 OF 83 WHERE THE POST-PARTUM SEX TABOO LASTS LONGER THAN ONE MONTH (96)	27 69 14 14 XSQ= 3.75 PHI= -0.174 XP = 0.0528
303	TILT TOWARD BEING THOSE 0.55 OF 42 WHERE THE EARLY ORAL SATISFACTION POTENTIAL IS LOW (25) W-C	303	TILT TOWARD BEING THOSE 0.87 OF 15 WHERE THE EARLY ORAL SATISFACTION POTENTIAL IS HIGH (32) W-C	19 13 23 2 XSQ= 6.11 PHI= -0.327 XP = 0.0134
309	TILT TOWARD BEING THOSE 0.59 OF 39 WHERE ORAL SOCIALIZATION ANXIETY IS HIGH (26) W-C	309	TILT TOWARD BEING THOSE 0.79 OF 14 WHERE ORAL SOCIALIZATION ANXIETY IS LOW (27) W-C	23 3 16 11 XSQ= 4.41 PHI= 0.288 XP = 0.0358
311	DRIFT TOWARD BEING THOSE 0.54 OF 35 WHERE SEXUAL SOCIALIZATION ANXIETY IS LOW (23) W-C	311	DRIFT TOWARD BEING THOSE 0.75 OF 16 WHERE SEXUAL SOCIALIZATION ANXIETY IS HIGH (28) W-C	16 12 19 4 XSQ= 2.71 PHI= -0.231 XP = 0.0996

314	DRIFT MORE TOWARD BEING THOSE 0.84 OF 45 WHERE THE INCIDENCE OF MOTHER-CHILD HOUSEHOLDS IS LOW (61) W-D,S	DRIFT LESS TOWARD BEING THOSE 0.66 OF 35 WHERE THE INCIDENCE OF MOTHER-CHILD HOUSEHOLDS IS LOW (61) W-D,S	7 12 38 23 XSQ= 2.85 PHI= -0.189 XP = 0.0914
320	DRIFT LESS TOWARD BEING THOSE 0.56 OF 43 WHERE THE DEGREE OF REDUCTION OF THE INFANT'S DRIVES IS HIGH (45) B-B-C	DRIFT MORE TOWARD BEING THOSE 0.81 OF 26 WHERE THE DEGREE OF REDUCTION OF THE INFANT'S DRIVES IS HIGH (45) B-B-C	24 21 19 5 XSQ= 3.42 PHI= -0.223 XP = 0.0646
321	LEAN TOWARD BEING THOSE 0.57 OF 37 WHERE THE IMMEDIACY OF REDUCTION OF THE INFANT'S DRIVES IS LOW (25) B-B-C	LEAN TOWARD BEING THOSE 0.83 OF 23 WHERE THE IMMEDIACY OF REDUCTION OF THE INFANT'S DRIVES IS HIGH (35) B-B-C	16 19 21 4 XSQ= 7.50 PHI= -0.353 XP = 0.0062
323	TILT TOWARD BEING THOSE 0.72 OF 46 WHERE THE CONSTANCY OF PRESENCE OF THE INFANT'S NURTURANT AGENT IS LOW (45) B-B-C	TILT TOWARD BEING THOSE 0.57 OF 28 WHERE THE CONSTANCY OF PRESENCE OF THE INFANT'S NURTURANT AGENT IS HIGH (29) B-B-C	13 16 33 12 XSQ= 4.94 PHI= -0.258 XP = 0.0262
339	TILT TOWARD BEING THOSE 0.53 OF 43 WHERE THE CHILD'S INFERRED CONFLICT REGARDING RESPONSIBLE BEHAVIOR IS HIGH (31) B-B-C	TILT TOWARD BEING THOSE 0.73 OF 30 WHERE THE CHILD'S INFERRED CONFLICT REGARDING RESPONSIBLE BEHAVIOR IS LOW (42) B-B-C	23 8 20 22 XSQ= 4.16 PHI= 0.239 XP = 0.0413
342	LEAN TOWARD BEING THOSE 0.59 OF 29 WHERE THE CHILD'S INFERRED ANXIETY OVER PERFORMANCE OF NURTURANT BEHAVIOR IS HIGH (18) B-B-C	LEAN TOWARD BEING THOSE 0.94 OF 17 WHERE THE CHILD'S INFERRED ANXIETY OVER PERFORMANCE OF NURTURANT BEHAVIOR IS LOW (28) B-B-C	17 1 12 16 XSQ= 10.40 PHI= 0.475 XP = 0.0013
351	DRIFT TOWARD BEING THOSE 0.54 OF 35 WHERE THE CHILD'S INFERRED CONFLICT REGARDING ACHIEVEMENT BEHAVIOR IS HIGH (25) B-B-C	DRIFT TOWARD BEING THOSE 0.72 OF 25 WHERE THE CHILD'S INFERRED CONFLICT REGARDING ACHIEVEMENT BEHAVIOR IS LOW (34) B-B-C	19 7 16 18 XSQ= 3.10 PHI= 0.227 XP = 0.0782
391	TEND TO BE THOSE 0.71 OF 59 WHERE PREMARITAL SEX RELATIONS ARE PUNISHED ONLY IF PREGNANCY RESULTS, OR FREELY PERMITTED (90) JTW,EA	TEND TO BE THOSE 0.60 OF 120 WHERE PREMARITAL SEX RELATIONS ARE STRONGLY PUNISHED AND IN FACT RARE, OR WEAKLY PUNISHED AND IN FACT NOT RARE (89) JTW,EA	17 72 42 48 XSQ= 14.17 PHI= -0.281 XP = 0.0002
392	LEAN TOWARD BEING THOSE 0.54 OF 59 WHERE PREMARITAL SEX RELATIONS ARE FREELY PERMITTED (67) JTW,EA	LEAN TOWARD BEING THOSE 0.71 OF 120 WHERE PREMARITAL SEX RELATIONS ARE STRONGLY PUNISHED AND IN FACT RARE, OR WEAKLY PUNISHED AND IN FACT NOT RARE, OR PUNISHED ONLY IF PREGNANCY RESULTS (112) JTW,EA	27 85 32 35 XSQ= 9.57 PHI= -0.231 XP = 0.0020

425	LEAN TOWARD BEING THOSE 0.72 OF 25 WHERE SUPERNATURALS ARE MAINLY AGGRESSIVE, RATHER THAN BENEVOLENT (20) L-T-W	425	LEAN TOWARD BEING THOSE 0.82 OF 11 WHERE SUPERNATURALS ARE MAINLY BENEVOLENT, RATHER THAN AGGRESSIVE (16) L-T-W	7 9 18 2 XSQ= 6.91 PHI= -0.438 EP = 0.0042
428	DRIFT TOWARD BEING THOSE 0.53 OF 15 WHERE A HIGH GOD, IF PRESENT AND ACTIVE, DOES NOT SUPPORT HUMAN MORALITY, RATHER THAN SUPPORTING IT (26) GES,EA	428	DRIFT TOWARD BEING THOSE 0.75 OF 72 WHERE A HIGH GOD, IF PRESENT AND ACTIVE, SUPPORTS HUMAN MORALITY, RATHER THAN NOT SUPPORTING IT (61) GES,EA	7 54 8 18 XSQ= 3.50 PHI= -0.201 XP = 0.0614
450	TILT MORE TOWARD BEING THOSE 0.86 OF 35 WHERE THE OBSERVATION OF FOOD TABOOS IS HIGH OR MEDIUM, RATHER THAN LOW (60) JRL	450	TILT LESS TOWARD BEING THOSE 0.59 OF 51 WHERE THE OBSERVATION OF FOOD TABOOS IS HIGH OR MEDIUM, RATHER THAN LOW (60) JRL	30 30 5 21 XSQ= 5.90 PHI= 0.262 XP = 0.0152
468	TILT MORE TOWARD BEING THOSE 0.85 OF 26 WHERE CONTACT WITH OTHER CULTURES IS REGULAR OR IRREGULAR, RATHER THAN FREQUENT (37) JMH	468	TILT LESS TOWARD BEING THOSE 0.54 OF 28 WHERE CONTACT WITH OTHER CULTURES IS REGULAR OR IRREGULAR, RATHER THAN FREQUENT (37) JMH	4 13 22 15 XSQ= 4.67 PHI= -0.294 XP = 0.0307
470	LEAN TOWARD BEING THOSE 0.81 OF 26 WHERE INNOVATIONS ARE ACCEPTED ONLY SELECTIVELY (33) JMH	470	LEAN TOWARD BEING THOSE 0.57 OF 28 WHERE INNOVATIONS ARE GENERALLY ACCEPTED (21) JMH	5 16 21 12 XSQ= 6.64 PHI= -0.351 XP = 0.0100
488	LEAN MORE TOWARD BEING THOSE 0.87 OF 63 ABOUT WHICH THE PRINCIPAL ETHNOGRAPHIES WERE PUBLISHED BEFORE 1950 (185)	488	LEAN LESS TOWARD BEING THOSE 0.67 OF 194 ABOUT WHICH THE PRINCIPAL ETHNOGRAPHIES WERE PUBLISHED BEFORE 1950 (185)	55 130 8 64 XSQ= 8.73 PHI= 0.184 XP = 0.0031
489	LEAN LESS TOWARD BEING THOSE 0.76 OF 86 NOT INCLUDED IN CHARLES ACKERMAN'S STUDY OF DIVORCE (343)	489	LEAN MORE TOWARD BEING THOSE 0.89 OF 314 NOT INCLUDED IN CHARLES ACKERMAN'S STUDY OF DIVORCE (343)	21 36 65 278 XSQ= 8.24 PHI= 0.144 XP = 0.0041
490	TEND TO BE THOSE 0.69 OF 86 INCLUDED IN ALBERT S. ANTHONY'S SAMPLE ON MALE INITIATION RITES (113)	490	TEND TO BE THOSE 0.83 OF 314 NOT INCLUDED IN ALBERT S. ANTHONY'S SAMPLE ON MALE INITIATION RITES (287)	59 54 27 260 XSQ= 85.50 PHI= 0.462 XP = 0.
491	TEND LESS TO BE THOSE 0.73 OF 86 NOT INCLUDED IN DORRIAN APPLE'S STUDY OF GRANDPARENTHOOD (352)	491	TEND MORE TO BE THOSE 0.92 OF 314 NOT INCLUDED IN DORRIAN APPLE'S STUDY OF GRANDPARENTHOOD (352)	23 25 63 289 XSQ= 20.81 PHI= 0.228 XP = 0.0000

499/

492	TEND LESS TO BE THCSE NOT INCLUDED IN BARBARA CHARTIER AYRES' STUDY OF FEMALE INITIATION RITES (361)	0.64 OF 86	492	TEND MORE TO BE THOSE NOT INCLUDED IN BARBARA CHARTIER AYRES' STUDY OF FEMALE INITIATION RITES (361)	0.97 OF 314	31 8 55 306 XSQ= 82.33 PHI= 0.454 XP = 0.
493	TEND TO BE THOSE INCLUDED IN BACCN, BARRY, AND CHILD'S STUDY OF CHILD REARING (78)	0.53 OF 86	493	TEND TO BE THOSE NOT INCLUDED IN BACON, BARRY, AND CHILD'S STUDY OF CHILD REARING (322)	0.90 OF 314	46 32 40 282 XSQ= 77.89 PHI= 0.441 XP = 0.
494	TEND LESS TO BE THCSE NCT INCLUDED IN HERBERT M. BARRY III'S STUDY OF ART (371)	0.74 OF 86	494	TEND MORE TO BE THOSE NOT INCLUDED IN HERBERT M. BARRY III'S STUDY OF ART (371)	0.98 OF 314	22 7 64 307 XSQ= 51.33 PHI= 0.358 XP = 0.
495	TEND LESS TO BE THCSE NOT INCLUDED IN JUDITH K. BROWN'S STUDY OF FEMALE INITIATION RITES (335)	0.64 OF 86	495	TEND MORE TO BE THOSE NOT INCLUDED IN JUDITH K. BROWN'S STUDY OF FEMALE INITIATION RITES (335)	0.89 OF 314	31 34 55 280 XSQ= 29.72 PHI= 0.273 XP = 0.0000
496	TEND LESS TO BE THCSE NOT INCLUDED IN ROY G. D'ANDRADE'S STUDY OF DREAMS (345)	0.67 OF 86	496	TEND MORE TO BE THOSE NOT INCLUDED IN ROY G. D'ANDRADE'S STUDY OF DREAMS (345)	0.91 OF 314	28 27 58 287 XSQ= 30.69 PHI= 0.277 XP = 0.
497	TEND LESS TO BE THCSE NOT INCLUDED IN WILLIAM M. EVAN'S STUDY OF LAW (339)	0.65 OF 86	497	TEND MORE TO BE THOSE NOT INCLUDED IN WILLIAM M. EVAN'S STUDY OF LAW (339)	0.90 OF 314	30 31 56 283 XSQ= 30.77 PHI= 0.277 XP = 0.
498	TEND LESS TO BE THCSE NOT INCLUDED IN C. S. FORC'S STUDY OF SEX (349)	0.53 OF 86	498	TEND MORE TO BE THOSE NOT INCLUDED IN C. S. FORD'S STUDY OF SEX (349)	0.96 OF 314	40 11 46 303 XSQ= 108.42 PHI= 0.521 XP = 0.
500	TEND LESS TO BE THCSE NOT INCLUDED IN FREEMAN ANC WINCH'S STUDY OF SCCIETAL COMPLEXITY (360)	0.70 OF 86	500	TEND MORE TO BE THOSE NOT INCLUDED IN FREEMAN AND WINCH'S STUDY OF SOCIETAL COMPLEXITY (360)	0.96 OF 314	26 14 60 300 XSQ= 47.01 PHI= 0.343 XP = 0.
501	TEND TO BE THOSE INCLUDED IN JOAN FRIENCLY GOODMAN'S STUDY OF ASCETIC MCURNING BEHAVIOR (67)	0.59 OF 86	501	TEND TO BE THOSE NOT INCLUDED IN JOAN FRIENDLY GOODMAN'S STUDY OF ASCETIC MOURNING BEHAVIOR (333)	0.95 OF 314	51 16 35 298 XSQ= 138.40 PHI= 0.588 XP = 0.

502	TEND LESS TO BE THCSE 0.64 OF 86 NOT INCLUDED IN JOHN K. HARLEY'S STUDY OF ADOLESCENT PEER GROUPS (343)	502	TEND MORE TO BE THOSE 0.92 OF 314 NOT INCLUDED IN JOHN K. HARLEY'S STUDY OF ADOLESCENT PEER GROUPS (343)	 XSQ= PHI= XP =	31 26 55 288 40.35 0.318 0.
503	TEND LESS TO BE THCSE 0.70 OF 86 NOT INCLUDED IN JOHN M. HICKMAN'S STUDY OF THE FOLK-URBAN CONTINUUM (346)	503	TEND MORE TO BE THOSE 0.91 OF 314 NOT INCLUDED IN JOHN M. HICKMAN'S STUDY OF THE FOLK-URBAN CONTINUUM (346)	 XSQ= PHI= XP =	26 28 60 286 24.47 0.247 0.0000
504	TEND LESS TO BE THCSE 0.58 OF 86 NOT INCLUDED IN DONALC HORTON'S STUDY OF ALCHOLISM (351)	504	TEND MORE TO BE THOSE 0.96 OF 314 NOT INCLUDED IN DONALD HORTON'S STUDY OF ALCHOLISM (351)	 XSQ= PHI= XP =	36 13 50 301 85.88 0.463 0.
506	TEND LESS TO BE THCSE 0.71 OF 86 NOT INCLUDED IN LAMBERT, TRIANDIS, AND WOLF'S STUDY OF SUPERNATURAL BEINGS (364)	506	TEND MORE TO BE THOSE 0.96 OF 314 NOT INCLUDED IN LAMBERT, TRIANDIS, AND WOLF'S STUDY OF SUPERNATURAL BEINGS (364)	 XSQ= PHI= XP =	25 11 61 303 50.80 0.356 0.
507	TEND LESS TO BE THCSE 0.59 OF 86 NOT INCLUDED IN JAMES R. LEARY'S STUDY OF FCOD TABOCS (314)	507	TEND MORE TO BE THOSE 0.84 OF 314 NOT INCLUDED IN JAMES R. LEARY'S STUDY OF FOOD TABOOS (314)	 XSQ= PHI= XP =	35 51 51 263 22.50 0.237 0.0000
508	TEND LESS TO BE THCSE 0.74 OF 86 NOT INCLUDED IN DAVID C. MCCLELLAND'S STUDY OF ACHIEVEMENT MOTIVATION (360)	508	TEND MORE TO BE THOSE 0.94 OF 314 NOT INCLUDED IN DAVID C. MCCLELLAND'S STUDY OF ACHIEVEMENT MOTIVATION (360)	 XSQ= PHI= XP =	22 18 64 296 27.39 0.262 0.0000
509	TEND LESS TO BE THCSE 0.84 OF 86 NOT INCLUDED IN MONI NAG'S STUDY OF FERTILITY (375)	509	TEND MORE TO BE THOSE 0.96 OF 314 NOT INCLUDED IN MONI NAG'S STUDY OF FERTILITY (375)	 XSQ= PHI= XP =	14 11 72 303 16.69 0.204 0.0000
510	TEND LESS TO BE THCSE 0.85 OF 86 NOT INCLUDED IN RACUL NARRCLL'S STUDY OF SCCIETAL COMPLEXITY (380)	510	TEND MORE TO BE THOSE 0.98 OF 314 NOT INCLUDED IN RAOUL NARROLL'S STUDY OF SOCIETAL COMPLEXITY (380)	 XSQ= PHI= XP =	13 7 73 307 20.97 0.229 0.0000
511	TEND TO BE THOSE 0.73 OF 86 INCLUDED IN ROBERTS, ARTH AND BUSH'S SAMPLE ON GAMES, AS MODIFIED BY THE ETHNOGRAPHIC ATLAS (189)	511	TEND TO BE THOSE 0.60 OF 314 NOT INCLUDED IN ROBERTS, ARTH AND BUSH'S SAMPLE ON GAMES, AS MODIFIED BY THE ETHNOGRAPHIC ATLAS (211)	 XSQ= PHI= XP =	63 126 23 188 28.41 0.267 0.0000

```
512  TEND LESS TO BE THCSE            0.72 OF  86     512  TEND MORE TO BE THOSE           0.97 OF 314          24    9
     NOT INCLUDED IN SHIRLEY AND ROMNEY'S                  NOT INCLUDED IN SHIRLEY AND ROMNEY'S                 62  305
     STUDY OF LCVE MAGIC  (367)                            STUDY OF LOVE MAGIC  (367)                   XSQ=    52.67
                                                                                                        PHI=    0.363
                                                                                                        XP =   0.

513  TEND LESS TO BE THCSE            0.74 OF  86     513  TEND MORE TO BE THOSE           0.93 OF 314          22   21
     NOT INCLUDED IN LEC W. SIMMONS'                       NOT INCLUDED IN LEO W. SIMMONS'                      64  293
     STUDY OF THE TREATMENT OF THE AGEC  (357)             STUDY OF THE TREATMENT OF THE AGED  (357)    XSQ=    23.19
                                                                                                        PHI=    0.241
                                                                                                        XP =   0.0000

514  TEND TO BE THOSE                 0.57 OF  86     514  TEND TO BE THOSE                0.87 OF 314          49   41
     INCLUDED IN PHILIP E. SLATER'S                        NOT INCLUDED IN PHILIP E. SLATER'S                   37  273
     STUDY CF NARCISSISM  (90)                             STUDY OF NARCISSISM  (310)                   XSQ=    72.18
                                                                                                        PHI=    0.425
                                                                                                        XP =   0.

515  TEND LESS TO BE THCSE            0.64 OF  86     515  TEND MORE TO BE THOSE           0.93 OF 314          31   21
     NOT INCLUDED IN WILLIAM N. STEPHENS'                  NOT INCLUDED IN WILLIAM N. STEPHENS'                 55  293
     SAMPLE CN AVOIDANCE RELATICNSHIPS  (348)              SAMPLE ON AVOIDANCE RELATIONSHIPS  (348)     XSQ=    48.89
                                                                                                        PHI=    0.350
                                                                                                        XP =   0.

516  TILT MORE TOWARC BEING THCSE     0.92 OF  86     516  TILT LESS TOWARD BEING THOSE    0.80 OF 314          79  252
     INCLUDED IN GUY E. SWANSCN'S                          INCLUDED IN GUY E. SWANSON'S                          7   62
     SAMPLE CN LOCAL JURISCICTICN, AS MODIFIED             SAMPLE ON LOCAL JURISDICTICN, AS MODIFIED    XSQ=     5.58
     BY THE ETHNOGRAPHIC ATLAS  (331)                      BY THE ETHNOGRAPHIC ATLAS  (331)             PHI=    0.118
                                                                                                        XP =   0.0181

517  DRIFT MORE TCWARC BEING THOSE    0.74 OF  86     517  DRIFT LESS TOWARD BEING THCSE   0.62 OF 314          64  196
     INCLUDED IN GUY E. SWANSON'S                          INCLUDED IN GUY E. SWANSON'S                         22  118
     SAMPLE ON HIGH GODS, AS MODIFIED                      SAMPLE ON HIGH GODS, AS MODIFIED             XSQ=     3.76
     BY THE ETHNOGRAPHIC ATLAS  (260)                      BY THE ETHNOGRAPHIC ATLAS  (260)             PHI=    0.097
                                                                                                        XP =   0.0525

518  TEND TO BE THOSE                 0.52 OF  86     518  TEND TO BE THOSE                0.81 OF 314          45   60
     INCLUDED IN STANLEY H. UDY, JR.'S                     NOT INCLUDED IN STANLEY H. UDY, JR.'S                41  254
     STUDY OF WCRK ORGANIZATION  (105)                     STUDY OF WORK ORGANIZATICN  (295)            XSQ=    36.78
                                                                                                        PHI=    0.303
                                                                                                        XP =   0.

519  TEND LESS TO BE THCSE            0.77 OF  86     519  TEND MORE TO BE THOSE           0.95 OF 314          20   16
     NCT INCLUDED IN JOSEPH VEROFF'S                       NOT INCLUDED IN JOSEPH VEROFF'S                      66  298
     STUDY OF ACHIEVEMENT MOTIVATION AS                    STUDY OF ACHIEVEMENT MOTIVATION AS           XSQ=    25.01
     REVEALED IN FCLKTALES  (364)                          REVEALED IN FOLKTALES  (364)                 PHI=    0.250
                                                                                                        XP =   0.0000

520  TEND LESS TO BE THCSE            0.70 OF  86     520  TEND MORE TO BE THOSE           0.96 OF 314          26   14
     NCT INCLUDED IN                                       NOT INCLUDED IN                                      60  300
     BEATRICE BLYTH WHITING'S                              BEATRICE BLYTH WHITING'S                     XSQ=    47.01
     STUDY OF SCRCERY  (360)                               STUDY OF SORCERY  (360)                      PHI=    0.343
                                                                                                        XP =   0.
```

522	TEND TO BE THOSE INCLUDED IN MARJORIE GRANT WHITING'S STUDY OF DIET (82)	0.52 OF 86	522	TEND TO BE THOSE NOT INCLUDED IN MARJORIE GRANT WHITING'S STUDY OF DIET (318)	0.88 OF 314	45 37 41 277 XSQ= 65.62 PHI= 0.405 XP = 0.
523	TEND LESS TO BE THOSE NOT INCLUDED IN WHITING AND CHILD'S STUDY OF CHILD TRAINING AND PERSONALITY (339)	0.51 OF 86	523	TEND MORE TO BE THOSE NOT INCLUDED IN WHITING AND CHILD'S STUDY OF CHILD TRAINING AND PERSONALITY (339)	0.94 OF 314	42 19 44 295 XSQ= 92.34 PHI= 0.480 XP = 0.
524	TEND LESS TO BE THOSE NOT INCLUDED IN WHITING, KLUCKHOHN, AND ANTHONY'S STUDY OF MALE INITIATION CEREMONIES (356)	0.70 OF 86	524	TEND MORE TO BE THOSE NOT INCLUDED IN WHITING, KLUCKHOHN, AND ANTHONY'S STUDY OF MALE INITIATION CEREMONIES (356)	0.94 OF 314	26 18 60 296 XSQ= 38.93 PHI= 0.312 XP = 0.

500 CULTURES
INCLUDED IN FREEMAN AND WINCH'S
STUDY OF SOCIETAL COMPLEXITY (40)

500 CULTURES
NOT INCLUDED IN FREEMAN AND WINCH'S
STUDY OF SOCIETAL COMPLEXITY (360)

BACKGROUND ON PAGE 180

SUBJECT ONLY, F.C. 1-480 AND 527-536
BOTH SUBJECT AND PREDICATE, F.C. 481-526

40 IN LEFT COLUMN

ANDAMANESE	ARANDA	ASHANTI	AZANDE	BALINESE	CAYAPA	CHAGGA	CHUKCHEE	COPR ESKIMO	CREEK
CROW	CUNA	CZECHS	HANO	HEBREWS	IFUGAO	JIVARO	KAZAK	KOREANS	KURTATCHI
LAKHER	LAPPS	LEPCHA	MAORI	MBUNDU	NAMA	NAVAHO	RIFFIANS	ROMANS	SANPOIL
SIRIONO	SIWANS	THONGA	TUPINAMBA	VENDA	VIETNAMESE	WOLEAIANS	YAKUT	YARURO	YUROK

360 IN RIGHT COLUMN

15	DRIFT TOWARD BEING THOSE WHERE THE LATITUDE IS TWENTY DEGREES OR GREATER (183) — 0.60 OF 40	15	DRIFT TOWARD BEING THOSE WHERE THE LATITUDE IS LESS THAN TWENTY DEGREES (217) — 0.56 OF 360	24 159 16 201 XSQ= 3.03 PHI= 0.087 XP = 0.0819
47	DRIFT MORE TOWARD BEING THOSE WHERE, IF SETTLEMENTS ARE NON-FIXED, MOVEMENT IS NOMADIC, RATHER THAN NON-NOMADIC (72) — 0.92 OF 12	47	DRIFT LESS TOWARD BEING THOSE WHERE, IF SETTLEMENTS ARE NON-FIXED, MOVEMENT IS NOMADIC, RATHER THAN NON-NOMADIC (72) — 0.62 OF 98	11 61 1 37 XSQ= 2.90 PHI= 0.162 XP = 0.0889
62	DRIFT MORE TOWARD BEING THOSE WHERE HUSBANDRY OF SOME KIND IS PRESENT (228) — 0.72 OF 40	62	DRIFT LESS TOWARD BEING THOSE WHERE HUSBANDRY OF SOME KIND IS PRESENT (228) — 0.55 OF 360	29 199 11 161 XSQ= 3.68 PHI= 0.096 XP = 0.0550
85	DRIFT LESS TOWARD BEING THOSE WHERE THE LEVEL OF POLITICAL INTEGRATION IS THE MINIMAL STATE, THE AUTONOMOUS COMMUNITY, OR THE FAMILY (234) GPM — 0.63 OF 35	85	DRIFT MORE TOWARD BEING THOSE WHERE THE LEVEL OF POLITICAL INTEGRATION IS THE MINIMAL STATE, THE AUTONOMOUS COMMUNITY, OR THE FAMILY (234) GPM — 0.79 OF 269	13 57 22 212 XSQ= 3.59 PHI= 0.109 XP = 0.0580
102	DRIFT MORE TOWARD BEING THOSE WHERE CLASS STRATIFICATION IS PRESENT (203) — 0.67 OF 40	102	DRIFT LESS TOWARD BEING THOSE WHERE CLASS STRATIFICATION IS PRESENT (203) — 0.51 OF 343	27 176 13 167 XSQ= 3.15 PHI= 0.091 XP = 0.0761

148	DRIFT TOWARD BEING THOSE 0.53 OF 15 WHERE THE INCIDENCE OF PERSONAL CRIME IS HIGH (12) B-B-C	148	DRIFT TOWARD BEING THOSE 0.78 OF 18 WHERE THE INCIDENCE OF PERSONAL CRIME IS LOW (21) B-B-C	8 4 7 14 XSQ= 2.21 PHI= 0.259 EP = 0.0827
236	DRIFT MORE TOWARD BEING THOSE 0.67 OF 40 WHERE THE FAMILY IS OF AN EXTENDED TYPE, RATHER THAN AN INDEPENDENT TYPE (213)	236	DRIFT LESS TOWARD BEING THOSE 0.52 OF 358 WHERE THE FAMILY IS OF AN EXTENDED TYPE, RATHER THAN AN INDEPENDENT TYPE (213)	27 186 13 172 XSQ= 2.90 PHI= 0.085 XP = 0.0887
282	TILT TOWARD BEING THOSE 0.71 OF 14 WHERE THE STRENGTH OF DESIRE FOR CHILDREN IS HIGH (16) BCA	282	TILT TOWARD BEING THOSE 0.73 OF 22 WHERE THE STRENGTH OF DESIRE FOR CHILDREN IS LOW OR ABSENT (20) BCA	10 6 4 16 XSQ= 5.09 PHI= 0.376 EP = 0.0159
285	TILT TOWARD BEING THOSE 0.80 OF 15 WHERE THE SEX TABOO DURING PREGNANCY IS ABSENT OR INFERRED ABSENT (17) BCA	285	TILT TOWARD BEING THOSE 0.69 OF 16 WHERE THE SEX TABOO DURING PREGNANCY IS PRESENT (14) BCA	3 11 12 5 XSQ= 5.59 PHI= -0.425 EP = 0.0113
296	TILT TOWARD BEING THOSE 0.65 OF 17 WHERE INFANTICIDE IS ABSENT OR INFERRED ABSENT (15) BCA	296	TILT TOWARD BEING THOSE 0.75 OF 16 WHERE INFANTICIDE IS PRESENT (18) BCA	6 12 11 4 XSQ= 3.76 PHI= -0.338 EP = 0.0366
324	DRIFT TOWARD BEING THOSE 0.70 OF 20 WHERE THE PAIN INFLICTED ON THE INFANT BY THE NURTURANT AGENT IS HIGH (34) B-B-C	324	DRIFT TOWARD BEING THOSE 0.57 OF 46 WHERE THE PAIN INFLICTED ON THE INFANT BY THE NURTURANT AGENT IS LOW OR NEGLIGIBLE (32) B-B-C	14 20 6 26 XSQ= 2.94 PHI= 0.211 XP = 0.0866
330	TILT TOWARD BEING THOSE 0.68 OF 22 WHERE THE AGE OF THE INFANT AT TIME OF WEANING IS 2.5 YEARS OR HIGHER (34) B-B-C	330	TILT TOWARD BEING THOSE 0.60 OF 48 WHERE THE AGE OF THE INFANT AT TIME OF WEANING IS LOWER THAN 2.5 YEARS (36) B-B-C	15 19 7 29 XSQ= 3.86 PHI= 0.235 XP = 0.0494
338	TILT MORE TOWARD BEING THOSE 0.81 OF 21 WHERE THE CHILD'S INFERRED ANXIETY OVER PERFORMANCE OF RESPONSIBLE BEHAVIOR IS HIGH (44) B-B-C	338	TILT LESS TOWARD BEING THOSE 0.52 OF 52 WHERE THE CHILD'S INFERRED ANXIETY OVER PERFORMANCE OF RESPONSIBLE BEHAVIOR IS HIGH (44) B-B-C	17 27 4 25 XSQ= 4.12 PHI= 0.238 XP = 0.0423
339	DRIFT TOWARD BEING THOSE 0.62 OF 21 WHERE THE CHILD'S INFERRED CONFLICT REGARDING RESPONSIBLE BEHAVIOR IS HIGH (31) B-B-C	339	DRIFT TOWARD BEING THOSE 0.65 OF 52 WHERE THE CHILD'S INFERRED CONFLICT REGARDING RESPONSIBLE BEHAVIOR IS LOW (42) B-B-C	13 18 8 34 XSQ= 3.51 PHI= 0.219 XP = 0.0610

342	TILT TOWARD BEING THOSE 0.64 OF 14 WHERE THE CHILD'S INFERRED ANXIETY OVER PERFORMANCE OF NURTURANT BEHAVIOR IS HIGH (18) B-B-C	342	TILT TOWARD BEING THOSE 0.72 OF 32 WHERE THE CHILD'S INFERRED ANXIETY OVER PERFORMANCE OF NURTURANT BEHAVIOR IS LOW (28) B-B-C	9 9 5 23 XSQ= 3.94 PHI= 0.293 XP = 0.0473
360	DRIFT MORE TOWARD BEING THOSE 0.83 OF 12 WHERE ADOLESCENT PEER GROUPS ARE PRESENT ONLY IN A SETTING OF LEISURE, OR ELSE ARE ABSENT (23) JKH	360	DRIFT LESS TOWARD BEING THOSE 0.52 OF 25 WHERE ADOLESCENT PEER GROUPS ARE PRESENT ONLY IN A SETTING OF LEISURE, OR ELSE ARE ABSENT (23) JKH	2 12 10 13 XSQ= 2.18 PHI= -0.243 EP = 0.0836
365	DRIFT TOWARD BEING THOSE 0.57 OF 14 WHERE THE TIME SPENT IN ADOLESCENT PEER GROUP ACTIVITY IS LOW-MEDIUM OR LOW (15) JKH	365	DRIFT TOWARD BEING THOSE 0.77 OF 31 WHERE THE TIME SPENT IN ADOLESCENT PEER GROUP ACTIVITY IS HIGH OR HIGH-MEDIUM (30) JKH	6 24 8 7 XSQ= 3.75 PHI= -0.289 XP = 0.0529
442	TILT TOWARD BEING THOSE 0.67 OF 21 WHERE FEAR OF ANIMAL SPIRITS IS HIGH (28) W-C	442	TILT TOWARD BEING THOSE 0.65 OF 40 WHERE FEAR OF ANIMAL SPIRITS IS LOW (33) W-C	14 14 7 26 XSQ= 4.36 PHI= 0.267 XP = 0.0368
458	TILT TOWARD BEING THOSE 0.52 OF 29 WHERE GAMES, IF PRESENT, INCLUDE GAMES OF STRATEGY (52) R-A-B,EA	458	TILT TOWARD BEING THOSE 0.74 OF 142 WHERE GAMES, IF PRESENT, DO NOT INCLUDE GAMES OF STRATEGY (119) R-A-B,EA	15 37 14 105 XSQ= 6.33 PHI= 0.192 XP = 0.0118
489	LEAN LESS TOWARD BEING THOSE 0.67 OF 40 NOT INCLUDED IN CHARLES ACKERMAN'S STUDY OF DIVORCE (343)	489	LEAN MORE TOWARD BEING THOSE 0.88 OF 360 NOT INCLUDED IN CHARLES ACKERMAN'S STUDY OF DIVORCE (343)	13 44 27 316 XSQ= 10.51 PHI= 0.162 XP = 0.0012
490	TEND TO BE THOSE 0.65 OF 40 INCLUDED IN ALBERT S. ANTHONY'S SAMPLE ON MALE INITIATION RITES (113)	490	TEND TO BE THOSE 0.76 OF 360 NOT INCLUDED IN ALBERT S. ANTHONY'S SAMPLE ON MALE INITIATION RITES (287)	26 87 14 273 XSQ= 27.63 PHI= 0.263 XP = 0.0000
491	TEND LESS TO BE THOSE 0.70 OF 40 NOT INCLUDED IN DORRIAN APPLE'S STUDY OF GRANDPARENTHOOD (352)	491	TEND MORE TO BE THOSE 0.90 OF 360 NOT INCLUDED IN DORRIAN APPLE'S STUDY OF GRANDPARENTHOOD (352)	12 36 28 324 XSQ= 11.81 PHI= 0.172 XP = 0.0006
492	TEND LESS TO BE THOSE 0.57 OF 40 NOT INCLUDED IN BARBARA CHARTIER AYRES' STUDY OF FEMALE INITIATION RITES (361)	492	TEND MORE TO BE THOSE 0.94 OF 360 NOT INCLUDED IN BARBARA CHARTIER AYRES' STUDY OF FEMALE INITIATION RITES (361)	17 22 23 338 XSQ= 50.12 PHI= 0.354 XP = 0.

No.	Statement	Ratio	No.	Statement	Ratio	Statistics
493	TEND TO BE THCSE INCLUDED IN BACCN, BARRY, AND CHILD'S STUDY OF CHILD REARING (78)	0.60 OF 40	493	TEND TO BE THOSE NOT INCLUDED IN BACON, BARRY, AND CHILD'S STUDY OF CHILD REARING (322)	0.85 OF 360	24 54 16 306 XSQ= 43.62 PHI= 0.330 XP = 0.
494	TEND LESS TO BE THCSE NOT INCLUDED IN HERBERT M. BARRY III'S STUDY OF ART (371)	0.77 OF 40	494	TEND MORE TO BE THOSE NOT INCLUDED IN HERBERT M. BARRY III'S STUDY OF ART (371)	0.94 OF 360	9 20 31 340 XSQ= 12.95 PHI= 0.180 XP = 0.0003
495	TEND LESS TO BE THCSE NOT INCLUDED IN JUDITH K. BROWN'S STUDY OF FEMALE INITIATION RITES (335)	0.52 OF 40	495	TEND MORE TO BE THOSE NOT INCLUDED IN JUDITH K. BROWN'S STUDY OF FEMALE INITIATION RITES (335)	0.87 OF 360	19 46 21 314 XSQ= 29.39 PHI= 0.271 XP = 0.0000
496	TEND LESS TO BE THCSE NOT INCLUDED IN ROY G. D'ANDRADE'S STUDY OF DREAMS (345)	0.52 OF 40	496	TEND MORE TO BE THOSE NOT INCLUDED IN ROY G. D'ANDRADE'S STUDY OF DREAMS (345)	0.90 OF 360	19 36 21 324 XSQ= 39.58 PHI= 0.315 XP = 0.
497	TEND TO BE THCSE INCLUDED IN WILLIAM M. EVAN'S STUDY OF LAW (61)	0.52 OF 40	497	TEND TO BE THOSE NOT INCLUDED IN WILLIAM M. EVAN'S STUDY OF LAW (339)	0.89 OF 360	21 40 19 320 XSQ= 44.57 PHI= 0.334 XP = 0.
498	TEND TO BE THOSE INCLUDED IN C. S. FCRD'S STUDY OF SEX (51)	0.65 OF 40	498	TEND TO BE THOSE NOT INCLUDED IN C. S. FORD'S STUDY OF SEX (349)	0.93 OF 360	26 25 14 335 XSQ= 103.92 PHI= 0.510 XP = 0.
499	TEND TO BE THOSE INCLUDED IN FORD AND BEACH'S SAMPLE ON SEXUAL EXPRESSION BY THE YOUNG (86)	0.65 OF 40	499	TEND TO BE THOSE NOT INCLUDED IN FORD AND BEACH'S SAMPLE ON SEXUAL EXPRESSION BY THE YOUNG (314)	0.83 OF 360	26 60 14 300 XSQ= 47.01 PHI= 0.343 XP = 0.
501	TEND TO BE THOSE INCLUDED IN JOAN FRIENDLY GOODMAN'S STUDY OF ASCETIC MOURNING BEHAVIOR (67)	0.60 OF 40	501	TEND TO BE THOSE NOT INCLUDED IN JOAN FRIENDLY GOODMAN'S STUDY OF ASCETIC MOURNING BEHAVIOR (333)	0.88 OF 360	24 43 16 317 XSQ= 56.22 PHI= 0.375 XP = 0.
502	TEND LESS TO BE THCSE NOT INCLUDED IN JOHN K. HARLEY'S STUDY OF ADOLESCENT PEER GROUPS (343)	0.55 OF 40	502	TEND MORE TO BE THOSE NOT INCLUDED IN JOHN K. HARLEY'S STUDY OF ADOLESCENT PEER GROUPS (343)	0.89 OF 360	18 39 22 321 XSQ= 31.65 PHI= 0.281 XP = 0.

503	TEND TO BE THOSE 0.57 OF 40 INCLUDED IN JOHN M. HICKMAN'S STUDY OF THE FOLK-URBAN CONTINUUM (54)	503	TEND TO BE THOSE 0.91 OF 360 NOT INCLUDED IN JOHN M. HICKMAN'S STUDY OF THE FOLK-URBAN CONTINUUM (346)	23 31 17 329 XSQ= 69.56 PHI= 0.417 XP = 0.
504	TEND TO BE THOSE 0.52 OF 40 INCLUDED IN DONALD HORTON'S STUDY OF ALCOHOLISM (49)	504	TEND TO BE THOSE 0.92 OF 360 NOT INCLUDED IN DONALD HORTON'S STUDY OF ALCHOLISM (351)	21 28 19 332 XSQ= 62.89 PHI= 0.397 XP = 0.
505	LEAN LESS TOWARD BEING THOSE 0.85 OF 40 NOT INCLUDED IN MERRILL JACKSON'S STUDY OF CRIMINAL LAW AND MEDICINE (380)	505	LEAN MORE TOWARD BEING THOSE 0.96 OF 360 NOT INCLUDED IN MERRILL JACKSON'S STUDY OF CRIMINAL LAW AND MEDICINE (380)	6 14 34 346 XSQ= 7.16 PHI= 0.134 XP = 0.0074
506	TEND LESS TO BE THOSE 0.70 OF 40 NOT INCLUDED IN LAMBERT, TRIANDIS, AND WOLF'S STUDY OF SUPERNATURAL BEINGS (364)	506	TEND MORE TO BE THOSE 0.93 OF 360 NOT INCLUDED IN LAMBERT, TRIANDIS, AND WOLF'S STUDY OF SUPERNATURAL BEINGS (364)	12 24 28 336 XSQ= 21.17 PHI= 0.230 XP = 0.0000
507	TEND TO BE THOSE 0.63 OF 40 INCLUDED IN JAMES R. LEARY'S STUDY OF FOOD TABOOS (86)	507	TEND TO BE THOSE 0.83 OF 360 NOT INCLUDED IN JAMES R. LEARY'S STUDY OF FOOD TABOOS (314)	25 61 15 299 XSQ= 41.61 PHI= 0.323 XP = 0.
508	TEND LESS TO BE THOSE 0.63 OF 40 NOT INCLUDED IN DAVID C. MCCLELLAND'S STUDY OF ACHIEVEMENT MOTIVATION (360)	508	TEND MORE TO BE THOSE 0.93 OF 360 NOT INCLUDED IN DAVID C. MCCLELLAND'S STUDY OF ACHIEVEMENT MOTIVATION (360)	15 25 25 335 XSQ= 34.03 PHI= 0.292 XP = 0.
510	DRIFT LESS TOWARD BEING THOSE 0.88 OF 40 NOT INCLUDED IN RAOUL NARROLL'S STUDY OF SOCIETAL COMPLEXITY (380)	510	DRIFT MORE TOWARD BEING THOSE 0.96 OF 360 NOT INCLUDED IN RAOUL NARROLL'S STUDY OF SOCIETAL COMPLEXITY (380)	5 15 35 345 XSQ= 3.65 PHI= 0.096 XP = 0.0559
511	TEND TO BE THOSE 0.85 OF 40 INCLUDED IN ROBERTS, ARTH AND BUSH'S SAMPLE ON GAMES, AS MODIFIED BY THE ETHNOGRAPHIC ATLAS (189)	511	TEND TO BE THOSE 0.57 OF 360 NOT INCLUDED IN ROBERTS, ARTH AND BUSH'S SAMPLE ON GAMES, AS MODIFIED BY THE ETHNOGRAPHIC ATLAS (211)	34 155 6 205 XSQ= 23.76 PHI= 0.244 XP = 0.0000
512	TEND LESS TO BE THOSE 0.63 OF 40 NOT INCLUDED IN SHIRLEY AND ROMNEY'S STUDY OF LOVE MAGIC (367)	512	TEND MORE TO BE THOSE 0.95 OF 360 NOT INCLUDED IN SHIRLEY AND ROMNEY'S STUDY OF LOVE MAGIC (367)	15 18 25 342 XSQ= 46.03 PHI= 0.339 XP = 0.

513	TEND LESS TO BE THOSE NOT INCLUDED IN LEO W. SIMMONS' STUDY OF THE TREATMENT OF THE AGED (357)	0.63 OF 40	513	TEND MORE TO BE THOSE NOT INCLUDED IN LEO W. SIMMONS' STUDY OF THE TREATMENT OF THE AGED (357)	0.92 OF 360	15 28 25 332 XSQ= 30.12 PHI= 0.274 XP = 0.0000
514	TEND TO BE THOSE INCLUDED IN PHILIP E. SLATER'S STUDY OF NARCISSISM (90)	0.88 OF 40	514	TEND TO BE THOSE NOT INCLUDED IN PHILIP E. SLATER'S STUDY OF NARCISSISM (310)	0.85 OF 360	35 55 5 305 XSQ= 103.58 PHI= 0.509 XP = 0.
515	LEAN LESS TOWARD BEING THOSE NOT INCLUDED IN WILLIAM N. STEPHENS' SAMPLE ON AVOIDANCE RELATIONSHIPS (348)	0.70 OF 40	515	LEAN MORE TOWARD BEING THOSE NOT INCLUDED IN WILLIAM N. STEPHENS' SAMPLE ON AVOIDANCE RELATIONSHIPS (348)	0.89 OF 360	12 40 28 320 XSQ= 9.75 PHI= 0.156 XP = 0.0018
516	DRIFT MORE TOWARD BEING THOSE INCLUDED IN GUY E. SWANSON'S SAMPLE ON LOCAL JURISDICTION, AS MODIFIED BY THE ETHNOGRAPHIC ATLAS (331)	0.95 OF 40	516	DRIFT LESS TOWARD BEING THOSE INCLUDED IN GUY E. SWANSON'S SAMPLE ON LOCAL JURISDICTION, AS MODIFIED BY THE ETHNOGRAPHIC ATLAS (331)	0.81 OF 360	38 293 2 67 XSQ= 3.77 PHI= 0.097 XP = 0.0523
517	TEND MORE TO BE THOSE INCLUDED IN GUY E. SWANSON'S SAMPLE ON HIGH GODS, AS MODIFIED BY THE ETHNOGRAPHIC ATLAS (260)	0.90 OF 40	517	TEND LESS TO BE THOSE INCLUDED IN GUY E. SWANSON'S SAMPLE ON HIGH GODS, AS MODIFIED BY THE ETHNOGRAPHIC ATLAS (260)	0.62 OF 360	36 224 4 136 XSQ= 11.02 PHI= 0.166 XP = 0.0009
518	TEND TO BE THOSE INCLUDED IN STANLEY H. UDY, JR.'S STUDY OF WORK ORGANIZATION (105)	0.67 OF 40	518	TEND TO BE THOSE NOT INCLUDED IN STANLEY H. UDY, JR.'S STUDY OF WORK ORGANIZATION (295)	0.78 OF 360	27 78 13 282 XSQ= 36.73 PHI= 0.303 XP = 0.
519	TEND LESS TO BE THOSE NOT INCLUDED IN JOSEPH VEROFF'S STUDY OF ACHIEVEMENT MOTIVATION AS REVEALED IN FOLKTALES (364)	0.65 OF 40	519	TEND MORE TO BE THOSE NOT INCLUDED IN JOSEPH VEROFF'S STUDY OF ACHIEVEMENT MOTIVATION AS REVEALED IN FOLKTALES (364)	0.94 OF 360	14 22 26 338 XSQ= 33.24 PHI= 0.288 XP = 0.
520	TEND LESS TO BE THOSE NOT INCLUDED IN BEATRICE BLYTH WHITING'S STUDY OF SORCERY (360)	0.52 OF 40	520	TEND MORE TO BE THOSE NOT INCLUDED IN BEATRICE BLYTH WHITING'S STUDY OF SORCERY (360)	0.94 OF 360	19 21 21 339 XSQ= 64.89 PHI= 0.403 XP = 0.
522	TEND TO BE THOSE INCLUDED IN MARJORIE GRANT WHITING'S STUDY OF DIET (82)	0.63 OF 40	522	TEND TO BE THOSE NOT INCLUDED IN MARJORIE GRANT WHITING'S STUDY OF DIET (318)	0.84 OF 360	25 57 15 303 XSQ= 45.28 PHI= 0.336 XP = 0.

523	TEND TO BE THOSE INCLUDED IN WHITING ANC CHILD'S STUDY OF CHILD TRAINING AND PERSCNALITY (61)	0.52 OF 40	523	TEND TO BE THOSE NOT INCLUDED IN WHITING AND CHILD'S STUDY OF CHILD TRAINING AND PERSONALITY (339)	0.89 OF 360	21 40 19 320 XSQ= 44.57 PHI= 0.334 XP = 0.
524	TEND LESS TO BE THCSE NOT INCLUDED IN WHITING, KLUCKHCHN, ANC ANTHONY'S STUDY OF MALE INITIATICN CEREMONIES (356)	0.65 OF 40	524	TEND MORE TO BE THOSE NOT INCLUDED IN WHITING, KLUCKHOHN, AND ANTHONY'S STUDY OF MALE INITIATICN CEREMONIES (356)	0.92 OF 360	14 30 26 330 XSQ= 23.50 PHI= 0.242 XP = 0.0000

```
501  CULTURES                                                  501  CULTURES
     INCLUDED IN JOAN FRIENDLY GOODMAN'S                            NOT INCLUDED IN JOAN FRIENDLY GOODMAN'S
     STUDY OF ASCETIC MOURNING BEHAVIOR  (67)                       STUDY OF
                                                                    ASCETIC MOURNING BEHAVIOR  (333)

                                                                         SUBJECT ONLY, F.C. 1-480 AND 527-536
BACKGROUND ON PAGE 180                                              BOTH SUBJECT AND PREDICATE, F.C. 481-526

      67  IN LEFT COLUMN

ABIPON      AINU        ALCRESE     ANDAMANESE  APINAYE     ARANDA      ARAUCANIANS ASHANTI     AYMARA      AZANDE
BALINESE    CHAGGA      CHENCHU     CHEYENNE    CHIR-APACHE CHOROTI     CHUKCHEE    CROW        CUNA        DOBUANS
FON         GANDA       GOND        HANO        IFUGAO      ILA         JIVARO      JUKUN       KASKA       KAZAK
KURTATCHI   KUTENAI     KWAKIUTL    LAKHER      LAMBA       LANGO       LAU         LEPCHA      LESU        MAORI
MARICOPA    MARQUESANS  MATACO      MBUNDU      MURNGIN     NAVAHO      OMAHA       PALAUANS    PAPAGO      PUKAPUKA
SANPOIL     SENIANG     SIRIONO     TANALA      TAOS        THONGA      TIMBIRA     TIV         TODA        TOKELAU
TROBRIAND   TUPINAMBA   VENDA       WAPISHANA   WARRAU      YAGUA       ZUNI

     333  IN RIGHT COLUMN

-----------------------------------------------------------------------------------------------------------------------
  4  IN ALL CASES ARE THOSE          1.00 OF  67      4  LEAN LESS TOWARD BEING THOSE   0.86 OF 333          0    45
     LOCATED OUTSIDE OF                                  LOCATED OUTSIDE OF                                  67   288
     THE CIRCUM-MEDITERRANEAN  (355)                     THE CIRCUM-MEDITERRANEAN  (355)               XSQ=      8.89
                                                                                                       PHI=    -0.149
                                                                                                       XP =    0.0029

 36  TILT LESS TOWARD BEING THOSE    0.61 OF  67     36  TILT MORE TOWARD BEING THOSE   0.75 OF 333         26    82
     WHERE THE NATURAL ENVIRONMENT IS                    WHERE THE NATURAL ENVIRONMENT IS                    41   251
     OTHER THAN                                          OTHER THAN                                    XSQ=      4.99
     'VERY HARSH,' OR SUB-TROPICAL BUSH, OR              'VERY HARSH,' OR SUB-TROPICAL BUSH, OR        PHI=     0.112
     TEMPERATE GRASSLAND  (292) FWM                      TEMPERATE GRASSLAND  (292) FWM                XP =    0.0254

 62  DRIFT MORE TOWARD BEING THOSE   0.67 OF  67     62  DRIFT LESS TOWARD BEING THOSE  0.55 OF 333         45   183
     WHERE HUSBANDRY OF SOME KIND                        WHERE HUSBANDRY OF SOME KIND                        22   150
     IS PRESENT  (228)                                   IS PRESENT  (228)                             XSQ=      2.91
                                                                                                       PHI=     0.085
                                                                                                       XP =    0.0879

 63  TILT LESS TOWARD BEING THOSE    0.51 OF  45     63  TILT MORE TOWARD BEING THOSE   0.71 OF 181         23   129
     WHERE HUSBANDRY, IF PRESENT,                        WHERE HUSBANDRY, IF PRESENT,                        22    52
     IS PRINCIPALLY IN THE FORM OF                       IS PRINCIPALLY IN THE FORM OF                 XSQ=      5.77
     BOVINE, EQUINE, CAMEL-LIKE, OR DEER-LIKE            BOVINE, EQUINE, CAMEL-LIKE, OR DEER-LIKE      PHI=    -0.160
     ANIMALS, RATHER THAN                                ANIMALS, RATHER THAN                          XP =    0.0163
     PIGS, SHEEP, OR GOATS  (152)                        PIGS, SHEEP, OR GOATS  (152)

 79  IN ALL CASES ARE THOSE          1.00 OF  48     79  TILT LESS TOWARD BEING THOSE   0.87 OF 176          0    23
     WHERE NO CITY IS PRESENT  (201)                     WHERE NO CITY IS PRESENT  (201)                     48   153
                                                                                                       XSQ=      5.64
                                                                                                       PHI=    -0.159
                                                                                                       XP =    0.0175
```

80	TILT MORE TOWARD BEING THOSE 0.94 OF 48 WHERE NO CITY OR TOWN IS PRESENT (185)	80	TILT LESS TOWARD BEING THOSE 0.80 OF 176 WHERE NO CITY OR TOWN IS PRESENT (185)	3 36 45 140 XSQ= 4.35 PHI= -0.139 XP = 0.0370
107	IN ALL CASES ARE THOSE 1.00 OF 33 WHERE CLASS STRATIFICATION, IF PRESENT, IS BASED ON SOMETHING OTHER THAN OCCUPATIONAL STATUS (160)	107	LEAN LESS TOWARD BEING THOSE 0.75 OF 170 WHERE CLASS STRATIFICATION, IF PRESENT, IS BASED ON SOMETHING OTHER THAN OCCUPATIONAL STATUS (160)	0 43 33 127 XSQ= 9.13 PHI= -0.212 XP = 0.0025
108	LEAN TOWARD BEING THOSE 0.61 OF 33 WHERE CLASS STRATIFICATION, IF PRESENT, IS BASED ON A HEREDITARY ARISTOCRACY (74)	108	LEAN TOWARD BEING THOSE 0.68 OF 170 WHERE CLASS STRATIFICATION, IF PRESENT, IS BASED ON SOMETHING OTHER THAN A HEREDITARY ARISTOCRACY (129)	20 54 13 116 XSQ= 8.72 PHI= 0.207 XP = 0.0032
109	LEAN MORE TOWARD BEING THOSE 0.98 OF 65 WHERE CASTES ARE ABSENT (317)	109	LEAN LESS TOWARD BEING THOSE 0.83 OF 303 WHERE CASTES ARE ABSENT (317)	1 50 64 253 XSQ= 8.82 PHI= -0.155 XP = 0.0030
128	DRIFT TOWARD BEING THOSE 0.71 OF 17 WHERE, IF SUBSISTENCE IS PRIMARILY BY AGRICULTURE, THE WORK IS MAINLY DONE BY FEMALES (37)	128	DRIFT TOWARD BEING THOSE 0.58 OF 60 WHERE, IF SUBSISTENCE IS PRIMARILY BY AGRICULTURE, THE WORK IS MAINLY DONE BY MALES (40)	5 35 12 25 XSQ= 3.36 PHI= -0.209 XP = 0.0670
133	TILT TOWARD BEING THOSE 0.73 OF 15 WHERE CONTRACTED DEBTS ARE SIGNIFICANTLY PRESENT (17) GES	133	TILT TOWARD BEING THOSE 0.63 OF 19 WHERE CONTRACTED DEBTS ARE MODERATELY PRESENT OR ABSENT (17) GES	11 6 4 13 XSQ= 4.29 PHI= 0.355 EP = 0.0366
184	DRIFT LESS TOWARD BEING THOSE 0.57 OF 44 WHERE THE LARGEST NON-COGNATIC KIN GROUP IS SMALLER THAN A PHRATRY, I. E. A SIB OR LINEAGE (175)	184	DRIFT MORE TOWARD BEING THOSE 0.72 OF 208 WHERE THE LARGEST NON-COGNATIC KIN GROUP IS SMALLER THAN A PHRATRY, I. E. A SIB OR LINEAGE (175)	19 58 25 150 XSQ= 3.32 PHI= 0.115 XP = 0.0686
196	TILT LESS TOWARD BEING THOSE 0.53 OF 45 WHERE INDIVIDUAL RIGHTS IN REAL PROPERTY, AND RULES FOR INHERITANCE, ARE PRESENT (194)	196	TILT MORE TOWARD BEING THOSE 0.72 OF 236 WHERE INDIVIDUAL RIGHTS IN REAL PROPERTY, AND RULES FOR INHERITANCE, ARE PRESENT (194)	24 170 21 66 XSQ= 5.34 PHI= -0.138 XP = 0.0208
198	TILT LESS TOWARD BEING THOSE 0.71 OF 21 WHERE RULES FOR THE INHERITANCE OF REAL PROPERTY, IF PRESENT, FAVOR THE MALE HEIR OR LINE, RATHER THAN THE FEMALE (144)	198	TILT MORE TOWARD BEING THOSE 0.90 OF 144 WHERE RULES FOR THE INHERITANCE OF REAL PROPERTY, IF PRESENT, FAVOR THE MALE HEIR OR LINE, RATHER THAN THE FEMALE (144)	15 129 6 15 XSQ= 3.93 PHI= -0.154 XP = 0.0475

209	DRIFT LESS TOWARD BEING THOSE 0.71 OF 55 WHERE MARITAL RESIDENCE IS PATRILOCAL, VIRILOCAL, OR AVUNCULOCAL, RATHER THAN MATRILOCAL OR UXORILOCAL (270)	209	DRIFT MORE TOWARD BEING THOSE 0.83 OF 279 WHERE MARITAL RESIDENCE IS PATRILOCAL, VIRILOCAL, OR AVUNCULOCAL, RATHER THAN MATRILOCAL OR UXORILOCAL (270)	39 231 16 48 XSQ= 3.46 PHI= -0.102 XP = 0.0629
210	DRIFT LESS TOWARD BEING THOSE 0.72 OF 29 WHERE MARITAL RESIDENCE IS PATRILOCAL, RATHER THAN MATRILOCAL (169)	210	DRIFT MORE TOWARD BEING THOSE 0.87 OF 171 WHERE MARITAL RESIDENCE IS PATRILOCAL, RATHER THAN MATRILOCAL (169)	21 148 8 23 XSQ= 2.78 PHI= -0.118 XP = 0.0954
234	DRIFT TOWARD BEING THOSE 0.58 OF 60 WHERE THE COUSIN TERMINOLOGY IS OF CROW, OMAHA, OR IROQUOIS TYPE, RATHER THAN ESKIMO OR HAWAIIAN TYPE (152)	234	DRIFT TOWARD BEING THOSE 0.55 OF 262 WHERE THE COUSIN TERMINOLOGY IS OF ESKIMO OR HAWAIIAN TYPE, RATHER THAN CROW, OMAHA, OR IROQUOIS TYPE (170)	35 117 25 145 XSQ= 3.14 PHI= 0.099 XP = 0.0766
296	TILT TOWARD BEING THOSE 0.56 OF 27 WHERE INFANTICIDE IS ABSENT OR INFERRED ABSENT (15) BCA	296	IN ALL CASES ARE THOSE 1.00 OF 6 WHERE INFANTICIDE IS PRESENT (18) BCA	12 6 15 0 XSQ= 4.08 PHI= -0.351 EP = 0.0213
301	TILT LESS TOWARD BEING THOSE 0.63 OF 38 WHERE THE POST-PARTUM SEX TABOO LASTS LONGER THAN ONE MONTH (96)	301	TILT MORE TOWARD BEING THOSE 0.84 OF 86 WHERE THE POST-PARTUM SEX TABOO LASTS LONGER THAN ONE MONTH (96)	24 72 14 14 XSQ= 5.25 PHI= -0.206 XP = 0.0219
307	DRIFT LESS TOWARD BEING THOSE 0.54 OF 37 WHERE THE EARLY AGGRESSION SATISFACTION POTENTIAL IS HIGH (33) W-C	307	DRIFT MORE TOWARD BEING THOSE 0.87 OF 15 WHERE THE EARLY AGGRESSION SATISFACTION POTENTIAL IS HIGH (33) W-C	20 13 17 2 XSQ= 3.59 PHI= -0.263 XP = 0.0581
312	TILT TOWARD BEING THOSE 0.63 OF 32 WHERE DEPENDENCE SOCIALIZATION ANXIETY IS HIGH (24) W-C	312	TILT TOWARD BEING THOSE 0.73 OF 15 WHERE DEPENDENCE SOCIALIZATION ANXIETY IS LOW (23) W-C	20 4 12 11 XSQ= 3.91 PHI= 0.288 XP = 0.0479
328	DRIFT TOWARD BEING THOSE 0.63 OF 24 WHERE THE AGE OF THE INFANT AT THE ONSET OF SERIOUS SOCIALIZATION, OTHER THAN WEANING, IS TWO YEARS OR LOWER (20) B-B-C	328	DRIFT TOWARD BEING THOSE 0.71 OF 17 WHERE THE AGE OF THE INFANT AT THE ONSET OF SERIOUS SOCIALIZATION, OTHER THAN WEANING, IS HIGHER THAN TWO YEARS (21) B-B-C	9 12 15 5 XSQ= 3.14 PHI= -0.277 XP = 0.0765
342	DRIFT TOWARD BEING THOSE 0.54 OF 24 WHERE THE CHILD'S INFERRED ANXIETY OVER PERFORMANCE OF NURTURANT BEHAVIOR IS HIGH (18) B-B-C	342	DRIFT TOWARD BEING THOSE 0.77 OF 22 WHERE THE CHILD'S INFERRED ANXIETY OVER PERFORMANCE OF NURTURANT BEHAVIOR IS LOW (28) B-B-C	13 5 11 17 XSQ= 3.53 PHI= 0.277 XP = 0.0601

No.		No.		
344	DRIFT TOWARD BEING THOSE 0.58 OF 45 WHERE THE TOTAL POSITIVE PRESSURE TOWARD DEVELOPING SELF-RELIANT BEHAVIOR IN THE CHILD IS HIGH (36) B-B-C	344	DRIFT TOWARD BEING THOSE 0.68 OF 31 WHERE THE TOTAL POSITIVE PRESSURE TOWARD DEVELOPING SELF-RELIANT BEHAVIOR IN THE CHILD IS LOW (40) B-B-C	26 10 19 21 XSQ= 3.83 PHI= 0.224 XP = 0.0505
386	DRIFT TOWARD BEING THOSE 0.63 OF 51 WHERE SEXUAL EXPRESSION BY THE YOUNG IS RESTRICTED OR SEMI-RESTRICTED (46) F-B	386	DRIFT TOWARD BEING THOSE 0.60 OF 35 WHERE SEXUAL EXPRESSION BY THE YOUNG IS PERMITTED (40) F-B	32 14 19 21 XSQ= 3.45 PHI= 0.200 XP = 0.0632
391	LEAN TOWARD BEING THOSE 0.69 OF 51 WHERE PREMARITAL SEX RELATIONS ARE PUNISHED ONLY IF PREGNANCY RESULTS, OR FREELY PERMITTED (90) JTW,EA	391	LEAN TOWARD BEING THOSE 0.57 OF 128 WHERE PREMARITAL SEX RELATIONS ARE STRONGLY PUNISHED AND IN FACT RARE, OR WEAKLY PUNISHED AND IN FACT NOT RARE (89) JTW,EA	16 73 35 55 XSQ= 8.61 PHI= -0.219 XP = 0.0034
393	TILT TOWARD BEING THOSE 0.61 OF 51 WHERE EXTRAMARITAL COITUS IS PUNISHED, RATHER THAN PERMITTED (43) F-B	393	TILT TOWARD BEING THOSE 0.64 OF 33 WHERE EXTRAMARITAL COITUS IS PERMITTED, RATHER THAN PUNISHED (41) F-B	31 12 20 21 XSQ= 3.85 PHI= 0.214 XP = 0.0496
402	DRIFT TOWARD BEING THOSE 0.60 OF 42 WHERE EXPLANATIONS OF ILLNESS OF AN ORAL NATURE ARE PRESENT (31) W-C	402	DRIFT TOWARD BEING THOSE 0.68 OF 19 WHERE EXPLANATIONS OF ILLNESS OF AN ORAL NATURE ARE ABSENT (30) W-C	25 6 17 13 XSQ= 3.05 PHI= 0.223 XP = 0.0809
406	DRIFT TOWARD BEING THOSE 0.55 OF 42 WHERE EXPLANATIONS OF ILLNESS OF AN AGGRESSION NATURE ARE PRESENT (28) W-C	406	DRIFT TOWARD BEING THOSE 0.74 OF 19 WHERE EXPLANATIONS OF ILLNESS OF AN AGGRESSION NATURE ARE ABSENT (33) W-C	23 5 19 14 XSQ= 3.19 PHI= 0.229 XP = 0.0739
425	DRIFT TOWARD BEING THOSE 0.67 OF 24 WHERE SUPERNATURALS ARE MAINLY AGGRESSIVE, RATHER THAN BENEVOLENT (20) L-T-W	425	DRIFT TOWARD BEING THOSE 0.67 OF 12 WHERE SUPERNATURALS ARE MAINLY BENEVOLENT, RATHER THAN AGGRESSIVE (16) L-T-W	8 8 16 4 XSQ= 2.38 PHI= -0.257 EP = 0.0815
428	TILT TOWARD BEING THOSE 0.57 OF 14 WHERE A HIGH GOD, IF PRESENT AND ACTIVE, DOES NOT SUPPORT HUMAN MORALITY, RATHER THAN SUPPORTING IT (26) GES,EA	428	TILT TOWARD BEING THOSE 0.75 OF 73 WHERE A HIGH GOD, IF PRESENT AND ACTIVE, SUPPORTS HUMAN MORALITY, RATHER THAN NOT SUPPORTING IT (61) GES,EA	6 55 8 18 XSQ= 4.47 PHI= -0.227 XP = 0.0345
432	LEAN MORE TOWARD BEING THOSE 0.94 OF 17 WHERE AN ATTRACTIVE AFTERLIFE IS BELIEVED IN (27) LWS	432	LEAN LESS TOWARD BEING THOSE 0.52 OF 21 WHERE AN ATTRACTIVE AFTERLIFE IS BELIEVED IN (27) LWS	16 11 1 10 XSQ= 6.06 PHI= 0.399 EP = 0.0099

No.		No.		
446	TILT TOWARD BEING THOSE 0.56 OF 16 WHERE WITCHCRAFT IS SIGNIFICANTLY PRESENT (14) GES	446	TILT TOWARD BEING THOSE 0.77 OF 22 WHERE WITCHCRAFT IS MODERATELY PRESENT OR ABSENT (24) GES	9 5 7 17 XSQ= 3.15 PHI= 0.288 EP = 0.0468
449	TILT LESS TOWARD BEING THCSE 0.56 OF 32 WHERE THE CBSERVATICN OF FCOD TABOOS IS MEDIUM CR LOW, RATHER THAN HIGH (61) JRL	449	TILT MORE TOWARD BEING THOSE 0.80 OF 54 WHERE THE OBSERVATION OF FCOD TABCOS IS MEDIUM OR LOW, RATHER THAN HIGH (61) JRL	14 11 18 43 XSQ= 4.25 PHI= 0.222 XP = 0.0392
450	LEAN MORE TOWARD BEING THOSE 0.91 OF 32 WHERE THE CBSERVATION CF FCOD TABOOS IS HIGH CR MEDIUM, RATHER THAN LOW (60) JRL	450	LEAN LESS TOWARD BEING THOSE 0.57 OF 54 WHERE THE OBSERVATION OF FCOD TABCOS IS HIGH OR MEDIUM, RATHER THAN LOW (60) JRL	29 31 3 23 XSQ= 9.00 PHI= 0.323 XP = 0.0027
456	TILT TOWARD BEING THOSE 0.62 OF 21 WHERE THE INTERNALIZATICN OF THE INDIVIDUAL'S CONTACT WITH THE DIVINE IS NCT CONCUCIVE TC THE CEVELOPMENT OF THE INDIVIDUAL'S NEED TC ACHIEVE (17) DCM	456	TILT TOWARD BEING THOSE 0.73 OF 15 WHERE THE INTERNALIZATICN OF THE INDIVIDUAL'S CONTACT WITH THE DIVINE IS CONDUCIVE TO THE DEVELOPMENT OF THE INDIVIDUAL'S NEED TO ACHIEVE (19) DCM	8 11 13 4 XSQ= 3.06 PHI= -0.292 EP = 0.0489
473	TILT TOWARD BEING THOSE 0.75 OF 51 WHERE SENSITIVITY TO INSULT IS MODERATE CR NEGLIGIBLE (56) PES	473	TILT TOWARD BEING THOSE 0.51 OF 37 WHERE SENSITIVITY TO INSULT IS EXTREME (32) PES	13 19 38 18 XSQ= 5.13 PHI= -0.241 XP = 0.0235
474	DRIFT TOWARD BEING THCSE 0.63 OF 51 WHERE BOASTFULNESS IS MODERATE, NEGLIBIBLE, OR UNREPORTED (48) PES	474	DRIFT TOWARD BEING THOSE 0.58 OF 38 WHERE BOASTFULNESS IS EXTREME (41) PES	19 22 32 16 XSQ= 2.95 PHI= -0.182 XP = 0.0859
476	LEAN TOWARD BEING THOSE 0.52 OF 33 WHERE THE DEGREE OF INSCBRIETY IS MODERATE CR SLIGHT (18) CH	476	LEAN TOWARD BEING THOSE 0.94 OF 16 WHERE THE DEGREE OF INSOBRIETY IS STRONG (31) DH	16 15 17 1 XSQ= 7.65 PHI= -0.395 XP = 0.0057
488	TEND MORE TO BE THCSE 0.94 OF 47 ABCUT WHICH THE PRINCIPAL ETHNOGRAPHIES WERE PUBLISHED BEFCRE 1950 (185)	488	TEND LESS TO BE THOSE 0.67 OF 210 ABOUT WHICH THE PRINCIPAL ETHNOGRAPHIES WERE PUBLISHED BEFORE 1950 (185)	44 141 3 69 XSQ= 12.07 PHI= 0.217 XP = 0.0005
489	TEND LESS TO BE THCSE 0.72 OF 67 NOT INCLUDED IN CHARLES ACKERMAN'S STUDY OF DIVORCE (343)	489	TEND MORE TO BE THOSE 0.89 OF 333 NOT INCLUDED IN CHARLES ACKERMAN'S STUDY OF DIVORCE (343)	19 38 48 295 XSQ= 11.76 PHI= 0.171 XP = 0.0006

No.			No.			
490	TEND TO BE THOSE INCLUDED IN ALBERT S. ANTHONY'S SAMPLE ON MALE INITIATION RITES (113)	0.81 OF 67	490	TEND TO BE THOSE NOT INCLUDED IN ALBERT S. ANTHONY'S SAMPLE ON MALE INITIATION RITES (287)	0.82 OF 333	54 59 13 274 XSQ= 105.72 PHI= 0.514 XP = 0.
491	TEND LESS TO BE THOSE NOT INCLUDED IN DORRIAN APPLE'S STUDY OF GRANDPARENTHOOD (352)	0.72 OF 67	491	TEND MORE TO BE THOSE NOT INCLUDED IN DORRIAN APPLE'S STUDY OF GRANDPARENTHOOD (352)	0.91 OF 333	19 29 48 304 XSQ= 18.58 PHI= 0.215 XP = 0.0000
492	TEND LESS TO BE THOSE NOT INCLUDED IN BARBARA CHARTIER AYRES' STUDY OF FEMALE INITIATION RITES (361)	0.52 OF 67	492	TEND MORE TO BE THOSE NOT INCLUDED IN BARBARA CHARTIER AYRES' STUDY OF FEMALE INITIATION RITES (361)	0.98 OF 333	32 7 35 326 XSQ= 127.01 PHI= 0.563 XP = 0.
493	TEND TO BE THOSE INCLUDED IN BACON, BARRY, AND CHILD'S STUDY OF CHILD REARING (78)	0.70 OF 67	493	TEND TO BE THOSE NOT INCLUDED IN BACON, BARRY, AND CHILD'S STUDY OF CHILD REARING (322)	0.91 OF 333	47 31 20 302 XSQ= 127.68 PHI= 0.565 XP = 0.
494	TEND LESS TO BE THOSE NOT INCLUDED IN HERBERT M. BARRY III'S STUDY OF ART (371)	0.69 OF 67	494	TEND MORE TO BE THOSE NOT INCLUDED IN HERBERT M. BARRY III'S STUDY OF ART (371)	0.98 OF 333	21 8 46 325 XSQ= 65.24 PHI= 0.404 XP = 0.
495	TEND LESS TO BE THOSE NOT INCLUDED IN JUDITH K. BROWN'S STUDY OF FEMALE INITIATION RITES (335)	0.55 OF 67	495	TEND MORE TO BE THOSE NOT INCLUDED IN JUDITH K. BROWN'S STUDY OF FEMALE INITIATION RITES (335)	0.89 OF 333	30 35 37 298 XSQ= 45.64 PHI= 0.338 XP = 0.
496	TEND LESS TO BE THOSE NOT INCLUDED IN ROY G. D'ANDRADE'S STUDY OF DREAMS (345)	0.64 OF 67	496	TEND MORE TO BE THOSE NOT INCLUDED IN ROY G. D'ANDRADE'S STUDY OF DREAMS (345)	0.91 OF 333	24 31 43 302 XSQ= 30.86 PHI= 0.278 XP = 0.
497	TEND LESS TO BE THOSE NOT INCLUDED IN WILLIAM M. EVAN'S STUDY OF LAW (339)	0.66 OF 67	497	TEND MORE TO BE THOSE NOT INCLUDED IN WILLIAM M. EVAN'S STUDY OF LAW (339)	0.89 OF 333	23 38 44 295 XSQ= 20.93 PHI= 0.229 XP = 0.0000
498	TEND TO BE THOSE INCLUDED IN C. S. FORD'S STUDY OF SEX (51)	0.55 OF 67	498	TEND TO BE THOSE NOT INCLUDED IN C. S. FORD'S STUDY OF SEX (349)	0.96 OF 333	37 14 30 319 XSQ= 125.97 PHI= 0.561 XP = 0.

499	TEND TO BE THOSE INCLUDED IN FORD AND BEACH'S SAMPLE ON SEXUAL EXPRESSION BY THE YOUNG (86)	0.76 OF 67	499	TEND TO BE THOSE NOT INCLUDED IN FORD AND BEACH'S SAMPLE ON SEXUAL EXPRESSION BY THE YOUNG (314)	0.89 OF 333	51 35 16 298 XSQ= 138.40 PHI= 0.588 XP = 0.
500	TEND LESS TO BE THOSE NOT INCLUDED IN FREEMAN AND WINCH'S STUDY OF SOCIETAL COMPLEXITY (360)	0.64 OF 67	500	TEND MORE TO BE THOSE NOT INCLUDED IN FREEMAN AND WINCH'S STUDY OF SOCIETAL COMPLEXITY (360)	0.95 OF 333	24 16 43 317 XSQ= 56.22 PHI= 0.375 XP = 0.
502	TEND TO BE THOSE INCLUDED IN JOHN K. HARLEY'S STUDY OF ADOLESCENT PEER GROUPS (57)	0.52 OF 67	502	TEND TO BE THOSE NOT INCLUDED IN JOHN K. HARLEY'S STUDY OF ADOLESCENT PEER GROUPS (343)	0.93 OF 333	35 22 32 311 XSQ= 91.35 PHI= 0.478 XP = 0.
503	TEND LESS TO BE THOSE NOT INCLUDED IN JOHN M. HICKMAN'S STUDY OF THE FOLK-URBAN CONTINUUM (346)	0.69 OF 67	503	TEND MORE TO BE THOSE NOT INCLUDED IN JOHN M. HICKMAN'S STUDY OF THE FOLK-URBAN CONTINUUM (346)	0.90 OF 333	21 33 46 300 XSQ= 20.15 PHI= 0.224 XP = 0.0000
504	TEND LESS TO BE THOSE NOT INCLUDED IN DONALD HORTON'S STUDY OF ALCHOLISM (351)	0.51 OF 67	504	TEND MORE TO BE THOSE NOT INCLUDED IN DONALD HORTON'S STUDY OF ALCHOLISM (351)	0.95 OF 333	33 16 34 317 XSQ= 98.42 PHI= 0.496 XP = 0.
506	TEND LESS TO BE THOSE NOT INCLUDED IN LAMBERT, TRIANDIS, AND WOLF'S STUDY OF SUPERNATURAL BEINGS (364)	0.64 OF 67	506	TEND MORE TO BE THOSE NOT INCLUDED IN LAMBERT, TRIANDIS, AND WOLF'S STUDY OF SUPERNATURAL BEINGS (364)	0.96 OF 333	24 12 43 321 XSQ= 66.81 PHI= 0.409 XP = 0.
507	TEND LESS TO BE THOSE NOT INCLUDED IN JAMES R. LEARY'S STUDY OF FOOD TABOOS (314)	0.52 OF 67	507	TEND MORE TO BE THOSE NOT INCLUDED IN JAMES R. LEARY'S STUDY OF FOOD TABOOS (314)	0.84 OF 333	32 54 35 279 XSQ= 31.04 PHI= 0.279 XP = 0.
508	TEND LESS TO BE THOSE NOT INCLUDED IN DAVID C. MCCLELLAND'S STUDY OF ACHIEVEMENT MOTIVATION (360)	0.63 OF 67	508	TEND MORE TO BE THOSE NOT INCLUDED IN DAVID C. MCCLELLAND'S STUDY OF ACHIEVEMENT MOTIVATION (360)	0.95 OF 333	25 15 42 318 XSQ= 63.12 PHI= 0.397 XP = 0.
509	DRIFT LESS TOWARD BEING THOSE NOT INCLUDED IN MONI NAG'S STUDY OF FERTILITY (375)	0.88 OF 67	509	DRIFT MORE TOWARD BEING THOSE NOT INCLUDED IN MONI NAG'S STUDY OF FERTILITY (375)	0.95 OF 333	8 17 59 316 XSQ= 3.36 PHI= 0.092 XP = 0.0669

```
510  TEND LESS TO BE THCSE             0.85 OF   67     510  TEND MORE TO BE THOSE             0.97 OF 333         10   10
     NCT INCLUDED IN RACUL NARRCLL'S                         NOT INCLUDED IN RAOUL NARROLL'S                        57  323
     STUDY OF SCCIETAL COMPLEXITY  (380)                     STUDY OF SOCIETAL COMPLEXITY  (380)              XSQ=    14.28
                                                                                                               PHI=    0.189
                                                                                                               XP =   0.0002

511  TEND TO BE THOSE                  0.88 OF   67     511  TEND TO BE THOSE                  0.61 OF 333         59  130
     INCLUDED IN RCBERTS, ARTH AND BUSH'S                    NOT INCLUDED IN ROBERTS, ARTH AND BUSH'S                8  203
     SAMPLE ON GAMES, AS MCDIFIED                            SAMPLE ON GAMES, AS MODIFIED                     XSQ=    51.83
     BY THE ETHNOGRAPHIC ATLAS  (189)                        BY THE ETHNOGRAPHIC ATLAS  (211)                 PHI=    0.360
                                                                                                               XP =   0.

512  TEND LESS TO BE THCSE             0.61 OF   67     512  TEND MORE TO BE THOSE             0.98 OF 333         26    7
     NOT INCLUDED IN SHIRLEY AND ROMNEY'S                    NOT INCLUDED IN SHIRLEY AND ROMNEY'S                   41  326
     STUDY OF LCVE MAGIC  (367)                              STUDY OF LOVE MAGIC  (367)                       XSQ=    94.48
                                                                                                               PHI=    0.486
                                                                                                               XP =   0.

513  TEND LESS TO BE THCSE             0.70 OF   67     513  TEND MORE TO BE THOSE             0.93 OF 333         20   23
     NOT INCLUDED IN LEC W. SIMMONS'                         NOT INCLUDED IN LEO W. SIMMONS'                        47  310
     STUDY OF THE TREATMENT OF THE AGED  (357)               STUDY OF THE TREATMENT OF THE AGED  (357)        XSQ=    28.26
                                                                                                               PHI=    0.266
                                                                                                               XP =   0.0000

514  TEND TO BE THOSE                  0.76 OF   67     514  TEND TO BE THOSE                  0.88 OF 333         51   39
     INCLUDED IN PHILIP E. SLATER'S                          NOT INCLUDED IN PHILIP E. SLATER'S                     16  294
     STUDY OF NARCISSISM  (90)                               STUDY OF NARCISSISM  (310)                       XSQ=   129.03
                                                                                                               PHI=    0.568
                                                                                                               XP =   0.

515  TEND LESS TO BE THCSE             0.54 OF   67     515  TEND MORE TO BE THOSE             0.94 OF 333         31   21
     NOT INCLUDED IN WILLIAM N. STEPHENS'                    NOT INCLUDED IN WILLIAM N. STEPHENS'                   36  312
     SAMPLE ON AVOIDANCE RELATIONSHIPS  (348)                SAMPLE ON AVOIDANCE RELATIONSHIPS  (348)         XSQ=    75.26
                                                                                                               PHI=    0.434
                                                                                                               XP =   0.

516  LEAN MORE TOWARD BEING THCSE      0.97 OF   67     516  LEAN LESS TOWARD BEING THOSE      0.80 OF 333         65  266
     INCLUDED IN GUY E. SWANSON'S                            INCLUDED IN GUY E. SWANSON'S                            2   67
     SAMPLE ON LOCAL JURISDICTION, AS MODIFIED               SAMPLE ON LOCAL JURISDICTION, AS MODIFIED        XSQ=    10.30
     BY THE ETHNOGRAPHIC ATLAS  (331)                        BY THE ETHNOGRAPHIC ATLAS  (331)                 PHI=    0.160
                                                                                                               XP =   0.0013

517  TEND MORE TO BE THCSE             0.87 OF   67     517  TEND LESS TO BE THOSE             0.61 OF 333         58  202
     INCLUDED IN GUY E. SWANSON'S                            INCLUDED IN GUY E. SWANSON'S                            9  131
     SAMPLE CN HIGH GCDS, AS MCDIFIED                        SAMPLE ON HIGH GODS, AS MODIFIED                 XSQ=    15.34
     BY THE ETHNOGRAPHIC ATLAS  (260)                        BY THE ETHNOGRAPHIC ATLAS  (260)                 PHI=    0.196
                                                                                                               XP =   0.0001

518  TEND TO BE THOSE                  0.60 OF   67     518  TEND TO BE THOSE                  0.80 OF 333         40   65
     INCLUDED IN STANLEY H. UDY, JR.'S                       NOT INCLUDED IN STANLEY H. UDY, JR.'S                  27  268
     STUDY OF WCRK ORGANIZATION  (105)                       STUDY OF WORK ORGANIZATION  (295)                XSQ=    44.47
                                                                                                               PHI=    0.333
                                                                                                               XP =   0.
```

519	TEND LESS TO BE THCSE NOT INCLUDED IN JOSEPH VEROFF'S STUDY OF ACHIEVEMENT MOTIVATION AS REVEALED IN FOLKTALES (364)	0.69 OF 67	519	TEND MORE TO BE THOSE NOT INCLUDED IN JOSEPH VEROFF'S STUDY OF ACHIEVEMENT MOTIVATION AS REVEALED IN FOLKTALES (364)	0.95 OF 333	21 15 46 318 XSQ= 45.83 PHI= 0.339 XP = 0.
520	TEND LESS TO BE THCSE NOT INCLUDED IN BEATRICE BLYTH WHITING'S STUDY OF SCRCERY (360)	0.60 OF 67	520	TEND MORE TO BE THOSE NOT INCLUDED IN BEATRICE BLYTH WHITING'S STUDY OF SORCERY (360)	0.96 OF 333	27 13 40 320 XSQ= 78.10 PHI= 0.442 XP = 0.
521	TEND TO BE THOSE INCLUDED IN JOHN W. M. WHITING'S STUDY OF SCCIALIZATION PRCCESS AND PERSCNALITY (47)	0.52 OF 67	521	TEND TO BE THOSE NOT INCLUDED IN JOHN W. M. WHITING'S STUDY OF SOCIALIZATION PROCESS AND PERSONALITY (353)	0.96 OF 333	35 12 32 321 XSQ= 122.59 PHI= 0.554 XP = 0.
522	TEND TO BE THOSE INCLUDED IN MARJORIE GRANT WHITING'S STUDY OF DIET (82)	0.69 OF 67	522	TEND TO BE THOSE NOT INCLUDED IN MARJORIE GRANT WHITING'S STUDY OF DIET (318)	0.89 OF 333	46 36 21 297 XSQ= 111.00 PHI= 0.527 XP = 0.
523	TEND TO BE THOSE INCLUDED IN WHITING AND CHILD'S STUDY OF CHILD TRAINING AND PERSONALITY (61)	0.63 OF 67	523	TEND TO BE THOSE NOT INCLUDED IN WHITING AND CHILD'S STUDY OF CHILD TRAINING AND PERSONALITY (339)	0.94 OF 333	42 19 25 314 XSQ= 135.75 PHI= 0.583 XP = 0.
524	TEND LESS TO BE THCSE NOT INCLUDED IN WHITING, KLUCKHOHN, AND ANTHONY'S STUDY OF MALE INITIATICN CEREMONIES (356)	0.60 OF 67	524	TEND MORE TO BE THOSE NOT INCLUDED IN WHITING, KLUCKHOHN, AND ANTHONY'S STUDY OF MALE INITIATION CEREMONIES (356)	0.95 OF 333	27 17 40 316 XSQ= 67.02 PHI= 0.409 XP = 0.

502 CULTURES
INCLUDED IN JOHN K. HARLEY'S
STUDY OF ADOLESCENT PEER GROUPS (57)

502 CULTURES
NOT INCLUDED IN JOHN K. HARLEY'S
STUDY OF ADOLESCENT PEER GROUPS (343)

BACKGROUND ON PAGE 180

SUBJECT ONLY, F.C. 1-480 AND 527-536
BOTH SUBJECT AND PREDICATE, F.C. 481-526

57 IN LEFT COLUMN

ABIPON	ALORESE	ANDAMANESE	ARAUCANIANS	AYMARA	AZANDE	BALINESE	CAGABA	CAMAYURA	CARIB
CHEYENNE	CHIR-APACHE	CHUKCHEE	COPR ESKIMO	CREEK	DIERI	EGYPTIANS	FON	GANDA	IFUGAO
IRISH	JAPANESE	JIVARO	JUKUN	KACHIN	KAZAK	KURTATCHI	KWAKIUTL	LAKHER	LAMBA
LAU	LEPCHA	LESU	MAORI	MASAI	MIAO	MURNGIN	NUER	NYAKYUSA	ONTONG-JAVA
ORAON	PAPAGO	RIFFIANS	SAMOANS	SANPOIL	SERBS	SIRIONO	TALLENSI	TANALA	THONGA
TIMBIRA	TIV	TROBRIAND	VENDA	WARRAU	YAKO	YAPESE			

343 IN RIGHT COLUMN

---

62 TILT MORE TOWARD BEING THOSE 0.70 OF 57
WHERE HUSBANDRY OF SOME KIND
IS PRESENT (228)

62 TILT LESS TOWARD BEING THOSE 0.55 OF 343
WHERE HUSBANDRY OF SOME KIND
IS PRESENT (228)

40 188
17 155
XSQ= 4.10
PHI= 0.101
XP = 0.0428

78 DRIFT TOWARD BEING THOSE 0.53 OF 17
WHERE A WRITING SYSTEM IS
ABSENT, RATHER THAN BEING PRESENT IN
EITHER ALPHABETIC-OR-PHONETIC FORM OR
MNEMONIC FORM (18) JMH

78 DRIFT TOWARD BEING THOSE 0.76 OF 37
WHERE THE WRITING SYSTEM IS
ALPHABETIC-OR-PHONETIC, OR MNEMONIC,
RATHER THAN BEING ABSENT (36) JMH

8 28
9 9
XSQ= 3.10
PHI= -0.240
XP = 0.0782

97 DRIFT LESS TOWARD BEING THOSE 0.73 OF 56
WHERE THE HIERARCHY
OF LOCAL JURISDICTION HAS
THREE OR TWO LEVELS (273) GES,EA

97 DRIFT MORE TOWARD BEING THOSE 0.84 OF 275
WHERE THE HIERARCHY
OF LOCAL JURISDICTION HAS
THREE OR TWO LEVELS (273) GES,EA

15 43
41 232
XSQ= 3.27
PHI= 0.099
XP = 0.0707

108 DRIFT TOWARD BEING THOSE 0.52 OF 33
WHERE CLASS STRATIFICATION, IF PRESENT,
IS BASED ON
A HEREDITARY ARISTOCRACY (74)

108 DRIFT TOWARD BEING THOSE 0.66 OF 170
WHERE CLASS STRATIFICATION, IF PRESENT,
IS BASED ON SOMETHING OTHER THAN
A HEREDITARY ARISTOCRACY (129)

17 57
16 113
XSQ= 3.12
PHI= 0.124
XP = 0.0773

116 DRIFT MORE TOWARD BEING THOSE 0.82 OF 17
WHERE OCCUPATIONAL SPECIALIZATION IS
PART-TIME ONLY (34) JMH

116 DRIFT LESS TOWARD BEING THOSE 0.54 OF 37
WHERE OCCUPATIONAL SPECIALIZATION IS
PART-TIME ONLY (34) JMH

3 17
14 20
XSQ= 2.88
PHI= -0.231
XP = 0.0898

118	TILT TOWARD BEING THOSE 0.75 OF 16 WHERE THE PERCENTAGE OF OCCUPATIONS THAT ARE SPECIALIZED IS LOW (25) WME	118	TILT TOWARD BEING THOSE 0.61 OF 33 WHERE THE PERCENTAGE OF OCCUPATIONS THAT ARE SPECIALIZED IS HIGH OR MEDIUM (24) WME	4 20 12 13 XSQ= 4.13 PHI= -0.290 XP = 0.0420
197	IN ALL CASES ARE THOSE 1.00 OF 25 WHERE RULES FOR THE INHERITANCE OF REAL PROPERTY, IF PRESENT, FAVOR EITHER THE MALE HEIR OR LINE, OR THE FEMALE HEIR OR LINE (165)	197	DRIFT LESS TOWARD BEING THOSE 0.83 OF 169 WHERE RULES FOR THE INHERITANCE OF REAL PROPERTY, IF PRESENT, FAVOR EITHER THE MALE HEIR OR LINE, OR THE FEMALE HEIR OR LINE (165)	25 140 0 29 XSQ= 3.78 PHI= 0.140 XP = 0.0517
236	TILT MORE TOWARD BEING THOSE 0.67 OF 57 WHERE THE FAMILY IS OF AN EXTENDED TYPE, RATHER THAN AN INDEPENDENT TYPE (213)	236	TILT LESS TOWARD BEING THOSE 0.51 OF 341 WHERE THE FAMILY IS OF AN EXTENDED TYPE, RATHER THAN AN INDEPENDENT TYPE (213)	38 175 19 166 XSQ= 4.03 PHI= 0.101 XP = 0.0448
254	IN ALL CASES ARE THOSE 1.00 OF 5 WHERE HOUSEHOLD AUTHORITY IS ON THE FATHER'S SIDE, RATHER THAN THE MOTHER'S (9) CA	254	TILT TOWARD BEING THOSE 0.60 OF 10 WHERE HOUSEHOLD AUTHORITY IS ON THE MOTHER'S SIDE, RATHER THAN THE FATHER'S (6) DA	5 4 0 6 XSQ= 2.81 PHI= 0.433 EP = 0.0440
257	DRIFT TOWARD BEING THOSE 0.58 OF 12 WHERE THE SEVERITY OF SISTER AVOIDANCE IS HIGH (10) WNS	257	DRIFT TOWARD BEING THOSE 0.80 OF 15 WHERE THE SEVERITY OF SISTER AVOIDANCE IS LOW (17) WNS	7 3 5 12 XSQ= 2.72 PHI= 0.317 EP = 0.0568
295	TILT TOWARD BEING THOSE 0.69 OF 13 WHERE THE SEVERITY OF PUNISHMENT FOR ABORTION IS HIGH (11) BCA	295	TILT TOWARD BEING THOSE 0.80 OF 10 WHERE THE SEVERITY OF PUNISHMENT FOR ABORTION IS LOW OR ABSENT (12) BCA	9 2 4 8 XSQ= 3.69 PHI= 0.401 EP = 0.0361
300	TILT TOWARD BEING THOSE 0.59 OF 34 WHERE THE POST-PARTUM SEX TABOO LASTS LONGER THAN SIX MONTHS (51)	300	TILT TOWARD BEING THOSE 0.66 OF 90 WHERE THE POST-PARTUM SEX TABOO LASTS SIX MONTHS OR LESS (73)	20 31 14 59 XSQ= 5.09 PHI= 0.203 XP = 0.0240
304	DRIFT TOWARD BEING THOSE 0.70 OF 20 WHERE THE EARLY ANAL SATISFACTION POTENTIAL IS LOW (22) W-C	304	DRIFT TOWARD BEING THOSE 0.62 OF 21 WHERE THE EARLY ANAL SATISFACTION POTENTIAL IS HIGH (19) W-C	6 13 14 8 XSQ= 3.01 PHI= -0.271 XP = 0.0828
327	DRIFT TOWARD BEING THOSE 0.65 OF 26 WHERE THE AGE OF THE INFANT AT TIME OF REDUCED CONTACT WITH MOTHER IS HIGHER THAN TWO YEARS (28) B-B-C	327	DRIFT TOWARD BEING THOSE 0.62 OF 29 WHERE THE AGE OF THE INFANT AT TIME OF REDUCED CONTACT WITH MOTHER IS TWO YEARS OR LOWER (27) B-B-C	17 11 9 18 XSQ= 3.11 PHI= 0.238 XP = 0.0779

344	DRIFT TCWARD BEING THCSE 0.60 OF 35 WHERE THE TOTAL POSITIVE PRESSURE TOWARD DEVELCPING SELF-RELIANT BEFAVIOR IN THE CHILD IS HIGH (36) B-B-C	344	DRIFT TOWARD BEING THOSE 0.63 OF 41 WHERE THE TOTAL POSITIVE PRESSURE TOWARD DEVELOPING SELF-RELIANT BEHAVIOR IN THE CHILD IS LOW (40) B-B-C	21 15 14 26 XSQ= 3.27 PHI= 0.207 XP = 0.0707
400	TILT TOWARD BEING THOSE 0.57 OF 21 WHERE HOMCSEXUAL ACTIVITY IS PRCHIBITED (22) F-B	400	TILT TOWARD BEING THOSE 0.73 OF 37 WHERE HOMOSEXUAL ACTIVITY IS PERMITTED (36) F-B	12 10 9 27 XSQ= 3.96 PHI= 0.261 XP = 0.0466
406	DRIFT TCWARD BEING THCSE 0.58 OF 31 WHERE EXPLANATICNS CF ILLNESS OF AN AGGRESSION NATURE ARE PRESENT (28) W-C	406	DRIFT TOWARD BEING THOSE 0.67 OF 30 WHERE EXPLANATIONS OF ILLNESS OF AN AGGRESSION NATURE ARE ABSENT (33) W-C	18 10 13 20 XSQ= 2.83 PHI= 0.215 XP = 0.0928
424	DRIFT MORE TOWARD BEING THOSE 0.82 OF 17 WHERE RELIGIOUS SPECIALISTS ARE PART-TIME, RATHER THAN FULL-TIME (33) JMH	424	DRIFT LESS TOWARD BEING THCSE 0.51 OF 37 WHERE RELIGIOUS SPECIALISTS ARE PART-TIME, RATHER THAN FULL-TIME (33) JMH	3 18 14 19 XSQ= 3.50 PHI= -0.254 XP = 0.0615
425	DRIFT TOWARD BEING THCSE 0.72 OF 18 WHERE SUPERNATURALS ARE MAINLY AGGRESSIVE, RATHER THAN BENEVCLENT (20) L-T-W	425	DRIFT TOWARD BEING THOSE 0.61 OF 18 WHERE SUPERNATURALS ARE MAINLY BENEVOLENT, RATHER THAN AGGRESSIVE (16) L-T-W	5 11 13 7 XSQ= 2.81 PHI= -0.280 EP = 0.0922
430	LEAN TOWARD BEING THOSE 0.77 OF 13 WHERE SUPERNATURAL SANCTICNS FOR MORALITY, HAVING AN EFFECT ON AN INDIVIDUAL'S HEALTH, ARE PRESENT (16) GES	430	LEAN TOWARD BEING THOSE 0.76 OF 25 WHERE SUPERNATURAL SANCTIONS FOR MORALITY, HAVING AN EFFECT ON AN INDIVIDUAL'S HEALTH, ARE ABSENT OR UNREPORTED (22) GES	10 6 3 19 XSQ= 7.78 PHI= 0.452 EP = 0.0045
449	LEAN TOWARD BEING THOSE 0.54 OF 28 WHERE THE CBSERVATICN CF FCOD TABOOS IS HIGH, RATHER THAN MEDIUM OR LOW (25) JRL	449	LEAN TOWARD BEING THOSE 0.83 OF 58 WHERE THE OBSERVATION OF FCOD TABOOS IS MEDIUM OR LOW, RATHER THAN HIGH (61) JRL	15 10 13 48 XSQ= 10.39 PHI= 0.348 XP = 0.0013
472	DRIFT TOWARD BEING THOSE 0.63 OF 41 WHERE THE COMPOSITE NARCISSISM INDEX IS HIGH (47) PES	472	DRIFT TOWARD BEING THOSE 0.57 OF 49 WHERE THE COMPOSITE NARCISSISM INDEX IS LOW (43) PES	26 21 15 28 XSQ= 3.00 PHI= 0.183 XP = 0.0832
489	DRIFT LESS TOWARD BEING THOSE 0.77 OF 57 NOT INCLUDED IN CHARLES ACKERMAN'S STUDY OF DIVORCE (343)	489	DRIFT MORE TOWARD BEING THCSE 0.87 OF 343 NOT INCLUDED IN CHARLES ACKERMAN'S STUDY OF DIVORCE (343)	13 44 44 299 XSQ= 3.21 PHI= 0.090 XP = 0.0733

```
490  TEND TO BE THOSE                     0.65 OF  57     490  TEND TO BE THOSE                     0.78 OF 343          37   76
     INCLUDED IN ALBERT S. ANTHONY'S                           NOT INCLUDED IN ALBERT S. ANTHONY'S                         20  267
     SAMPLE ON MALE INITIATION RITES  (113)                    SAMPLE ON MALE INITIATION RITES  (287)               XSQ=   42.00
                                                                                                                    PHI=   0.324
                                                                                                                    XP =  0.

491  TEND LESS TO BE THOSE                0.68 OF  57     491  TEND MORE TO BE THOSE                0.91 OF 343          18   30
     NOT INCLUDED IN DORRIAN APPLE'S                           NOT INCLUDED IN DORRIAN APPLE'S                             39  313
     STUDY OF GRANDPARENTHOOD  (352)                           STUDY OF GRANDPARENTHOOD  (352)                      XSQ=   22.02
                                                                                                                    PHI=   0.235
                                                                                                                    XP =  0.0000

492  TEND LESS TO BE THOSE                0.60 OF  57     492  TEND MORE TO BE THOSE                0.95 OF 343          23   16
     NOT INCLUDED IN BARBARA CHARTIER AYRES'                   NOT INCLUDED IN BARBARA CHARTIER AYRES'                     34  327
     STUDY OF FEMALE INITIATION RITES  (361)                   STUDY OF FEMALE INITIATION RITES  (361)              XSQ=   66.74
                                                                                                                    PHI=   0.408
                                                                                                                    XP =  0.

493  TEND TO BE THOSE                     0.65 OF  57     493  TEND TO BE THOSE                     0.88 OF 343          37   41
     INCLUDED IN                                               NOT INCLUDED IN                                             20  302
     BACON, BARRY, AND CHILD'S                                 BACON, BARRY, AND CHILD'S                            XSQ=   83.99
     STUDY OF CHILD REARING  (78)                              STUDY OF CHILD REARING  (322)                        PHI=   0.458
                                                                                                                    XP =  0.

494  TEND LESS TO BE THOSE                0.74 OF  57     494  TEND MORE TO BE THOSE                0.96 OF 343          15   14
     NOT INCLUDED IN HERBERT M. BARRY III'S                    NOT INCLUDED IN HERBERT M. BARRY III'S                      42  329
     STUDY OF ART  (371)                                       STUDY OF ART  (371)                                  XSQ=   32.70
                                                                                                                    PHI=   0.286
                                                                                                                    XP =  0.

495  TEND LESS TO BE THOSE                0.51 OF  57     495  TEND MORE TO BE THOSE                0.89 OF 343          28   37
     NOT INCLUDED IN JUDITH K. BROWN'S                         NOT INCLUDED IN JUDITH K. BROWN'S                           29  306
     STUDY OF FEMALE INITIATION RITES  (335)                   STUDY OF FEMALE INITIATION RITES  (335)              XSQ=   50.00
                                                                                                                    PHI=   0.354
                                                                                                                    XP =  0.

496  TEND LESS TO BE THOSE                0.65 OF  57     496  TEND MORE TO BE THOSE                0.90 OF 343          20   35
     NOT INCLUDED IN ROY G. D'ANDRADE'S                        NOT INCLUDED IN ROY G. D'ANDRADE'S                          37  308
     STUDY OF DREAMS  (345)                                    STUDY OF DREAMS  (345)                               XSQ=   23.46
                                                                                                                    PHI=   0.242
                                                                                                                    XP =  0.0000

497  TEND LESS TO BE THOSE                0.61 OF  57     497  TEND MORE TO BE THOSE                0.89 OF 343          22   39
     NOT INCLUDED IN WILLIAM M. EVAN'S                         NOT INCLUDED IN WILLIAM M. EVAN'S                           35  304
     STUDY OF LAW  (339)                                       STUDY OF LAW  (339)                                  XSQ=   25.97
                                                                                                                    PHI=   0.255
                                                                                                                    XP =  0.0000

498  TEND LESS TO BE THOSE                0.58 OF  57     498  TEND MORE TO BE THOSE                0.92 OF 343          24   27
     NOT INCLUDED IN C. S. FORD'S                              NOT INCLUDED IN C. S. FORD'S                                33  316
     STUDY OF SEX  (349)                                       STUDY OF SEX  (349)                                  XSQ=   48.46
                                                                                                                    PHI=   0.348
                                                                                                                    XP =  0.
```

499	TEND TO BE THOSE INCLUDED IN FORD AND BEACH'S SAMPLE ON SEXUAL EXPRESSION BY THE YOUNG (86)	0.54 OF 57	499	TEND TO BE THOSE NOT INCLUDED IN FORD AND BEACH'S SAMPLE ON SEXUAL EXPRESSION BY THE YOUNG (314)	0.84 OF 343	31 55 26 288 XSQ= 40.35 PHI= 0.318 XP = 0.
500	TEND LESS TO BE THOSE NOT INCLUDED IN FREEMAN AND WINCH'S STUDY OF SOCIETAL COMPLEXITY (360)	0.68 OF 57	500	TEND MORE TO BE THOSE NOT INCLUDED IN FREEMAN AND WINCH'S STUDY OF SOCIETAL COMPLEXITY (360)	0.94 OF 343	18 22 39 321 XSQ= 31.65 PHI= 0.281 XP = 0.
501	TEND TO BE THOSE INCLUDED IN JOAN FRIENDLY GOODMAN'S STUDY OF ASCETIC MOURNING BEHAVIOR (67)	0.61 OF 57	501	TEND TO BE THOSE NOT INCLUDED IN JOAN FRIENDLY GOODMAN'S STUDY OF ASCETIC MOURNING BEHAVIOR (333)	0.91 OF 343	35 32 22 311 XSQ= 91.35 PHI= 0.478 XP = 0.
503	TEND LESS TO BE THOSE NOT INCLUDED IN JOHN M. HICKMAN'S STUDY OF THE FOLK-URBAN CONTINUUM (346)	0.70 OF 57	503	TEND MORE TO BE THOSE NOT INCLUDED IN JOHN M. HICKMAN'S STUDY OF THE FOLK-URBAN CONTINUUM (346)	0.89 OF 343	17 37 40 306 XSQ= 13.58 PHI= 0.184 XP = 0.0002
504	TEND LESS TO BE THOSE NOT INCLUDED IN DONALD HORTON'S STUDY OF ALCHOLISM (351)	0.63 OF 57	504	TEND MORE TO BE THOSE NOT INCLUDED IN DONALD HORTON'S STUDY OF ALCHOLISM (351)	0.92 OF 343	21 28 36 315 XSQ= 34.78 PHI= 0.295 XP = 0.
505	TILT LESS TOWARD BEING THOSE NOT INCLUDED IN MERRILL JACKSON'S STUDY OF CRIMINAL LAW AND MEDICINE (380)	0.88 OF 57	505	TILT MORE TOWARD BEING THOSE NOT INCLUDED IN MERRILL JACKSON'S STUDY OF CRIMINAL LAW AND MEDICINE (380)	0.96 OF 343	7 13 50 330 XSQ= 5.74 PHI= 0.120 XP = 0.0166
506	TEND LESS TO BE THOSE NOT INCLUDED IN LAMBERT, TRIANDIS, AND WOLF'S STUDY OF SUPERNATURAL BEINGS (364)	0.68 OF 57	506	TEND MORE TO BE THOSE NOT INCLUDED IN LAMBERT, TRIANDIS, AND WOLF'S STUDY OF SUPERNATURAL BEINGS (364)	0.95 OF 343	18 18 39 325 XSQ= 38.22 PHI= 0.309 XP = 0.
507	TEND LESS TO BE THOSE NOT INCLUDED IN JAMES R. LEARY'S STUDY OF FOOD TABOOS (314)	0.51 OF 57	507	TEND MORE TO BE THOSE NOT INCLUDED IN JAMES R. LEARY'S STUDY OF FOOD TABOOS (314)	0.83 OF 343	28 58 29 285 XSQ= 28.17 PHI= 0.265 XP = 0.0000
508	LEAN LESS TOWARD BEING THOSE NOT INCLUDED IN DAVID C. MCCLELLAND'S STUDY OF ACHIEVEMENT MOTIVATION (360)	0.79 OF 57	508	LEAN MORE TOWARD BEING THOSE NOT INCLUDED IN DAVID C. MCCLELLAND'S STUDY OF ACHIEVEMENT MOTIVATION (360)	0.92 OF 343	12 28 45 315 XSQ= 7.65 PHI= 0.138 XP = 0.0057

509	TILT LESS TOWARD BEING THOSE 0.86 OF 57 NOT INCLUDED IN MONI NAG'S STUDY OF FERTILITY (375)	509	TILT MORE TOWARD BEING THOSE 0.95 OF 343 NOT INCLUDED IN MONI NAG'S STUDY OF FERTILITY (375)	8 17 49 326 XSQ= 5.41 PHI= 0.116 XP = 0.0200
510	DRIFT LESS TOWARD BEING THOSE 0.89 OF 57 NOT INCLUDED IN RAOUL NARROLL'S STUDY OF SOCIETAL COMPLEXITY (380)	510	DRIFT MORE TOWARD BEING THOSE 0.96 OF 343 NOT INCLUDED IN RAOUL NARROLL'S STUDY OF SOCIETAL COMPLEXITY (380)	6 14 51 329 XSQ= 3.02 PHI= 0.087 XP = 0.0820
511	TEND TO BE THOSE 0.81 OF 57 INCLUDED IN ROBERTS, ARTH AND BUSH'S SAMPLE ON GAMES, AS MODIFIED BY THE ETHNOGRAPHIC ATLAS (189)	511	TEND TO BE THOSE 0.58 OF 343 NOT INCLUDED IN ROBERTS, ARTH AND BUSH'S SAMPLE ON GAMES, AS MODIFIED BY THE ETHNOGRAPHIC ATLAS (211)	46 143 11 200 XSQ= 28.30 PHI= 0.266 XP = 0.0000
512	TEND LESS TO BE THOSE 0.63 OF 57 NOT INCLUDED IN SHIRLEY AND ROMNEY'S STUDY OF LOVE MAGIC (367)	512	TEND MORE TO BE THOSE 0.97 OF 343 NOT INCLUDED IN SHIRLEY AND ROMNEY'S STUDY OF LOVE MAGIC (367)	21 12 36 331 XSQ= 67.45 PHI= 0.411 XP = 0.
513	LEAN LESS TOWARD BEING THOSE 0.77 OF 57 NOT INCLUDED IN LEO W. SIMMONS' STUDY OF THE TREATMENT OF THE AGED (357)	513	LEAN MORE TOWARD BEING THOSE 0.91 OF 343 NOT INCLUDED IN LEO W. SIMMONS' STUDY OF THE TREATMENT OF THE AGED (357)	13 30 44 313 XSQ= 8.66 PHI= 0.147 XP = 0.0033
514	TEND TO BE THOSE 0.72 OF 57 INCLUDED IN PHILIP E. SLATER'S STUDY OF NARCISSISM (90)	514	TEND TO BE THOSE 0.86 OF 343 NOT INCLUDED IN PHILIP E. SLATER'S STUDY OF NARCISSISM (310)	41 49 16 294 XSQ= 89.86 PHI= 0.474 XP = 0.
515	TEND LESS TO BE THOSE 0.54 OF 57 NOT INCLUDED IN WILLIAM N. STEPHENS' SAMPLE ON AVOIDANCE RELATIONSHIPS (348)	515	TEND MORE TO BE THOSE 0.92 OF 343 NOT INCLUDED IN WILLIAM N. STEPHENS' SAMPLE ON AVOIDANCE RELATIONSHIPS (348)	26 26 31 317 XSQ= 59.20 PHI= 0.385 XP = 0.
516	LEAN MORE TOWARD BEING THOSE 0.98 OF 57 INCLUDED IN GUY E. SWANSON'S SAMPLE ON LOCAL JURISDICTION, AS MODIFIED BY THE ETHNOGRAPHIC ATLAS (331)	516	LEAN LESS TOWARD BEING THOSE 0.80 OF 343 INCLUDED IN GUY E. SWANSON'S SAMPLE ON LOCAL JURISDICTION, AS MODIFIED BY THE ETHNOGRAPHIC ATLAS (331)	56 275 1 68 XSQ= 9.95 PHI= 0.158 XP = 0.0016
517	TEND MORE TO BE THOSE 0.86 OF 57 INCLUDED IN GUY E. SWANSON'S SAMPLE ON HIGH GODS, AS MODIFIED BY THE ETHNOGRAPHIC ATLAS (260)	517	TEND LESS TO BE THOSE 0.62 OF 343 INCLUDED IN GUY E. SWANSON'S SAMPLE ON HIGH GODS, AS MODIFIED BY THE ETHNOGRAPHIC ATLAS (260)	49 211 8 132 XSQ= 11.79 PHI= 0.172 XP = 0.0006

518	TEND TO BE THOSE 0.53 OF 57 INCLUDED IN STANLEY H. UDY, JR.'S STUDY OF WCRK ORGANIZATICN (105)	518	TEND TO BE THOSE 0.78 OF 343 NOT INCLUDED IN STANLEY H. UDY, JR.'S STUDY OF WORK ORGANIZATION (295)	30 75 27 268 XSQ= 22.33 PHI= 0.236 XP = 0.0000
519	TILT LESS TOWARD BEING THCSE 0.82 OF 57 NOT INCLUDED IN JOSEPH VEROFF'S STUDY OF ACHIEVEMENT MOTIVATION AS REVEALED IN FCLKTALES (364)	519	TILT MORE TOWARD BEING THOSE 0.92 OF 343 NOT INCLUDED IN JOSEPH VERCFF'S STUDY OF ACHIEVEMENT MOTIVATION AS REVEALED IN FOLKTALES (364)	10 26 47 317 XSQ= 4.77 PHI= 0.109 XP = 0.0290
520	TEND LESS TO BE THCSE 0.53 OF 57 NOT INCLUDED IN BEATRICE BLYTH WHITING'S STUDY OF SCRCERY (360)	520	TEND MORE TO BE THOSE 0.96 OF 343 NOT INCLUDED IN BEATRICE BLYTH WHITING'S STUDY OF SORCERY (360)	27 13 30 330 XSQ= 98.35 PHI= 0.496 XP = 0.
521	TEND LESS TO BE THCSE 0.60 OF 57 NOT INCLUDED IN JOHN W. M. WHITING'S STUDY OF SCCIALIZATION PROCESS AND PERSCNALITY (353)	521	TEND MORE TO BE THOSE 0.93 OF 343 NOT INCLUDED IN JOHN W. M. WHITING'S STUDY OF SOCIALIZATION PROCESS AND PERSONALITY (353)	23 24 34 319 XSQ= 49.27 PHI= 0.351 XP = 0.
522	TEND TO BE THOSE 0.70 OF 57 INCLUDED IN MARJCRIE GRANT WHITING'S STUDY OF DIET (82)	522	TEND TO BE THOSE 0.88 OF 343 NOT INCLUDED IN MARJORIE GRANT WHITING'S STUDY OF DIET (318)	40 42 17 301 XSQ= 97.12 PHI= 0.493 XP = 0.
523	TEND TC BE THOSE 0.54 OF 57 INCLUDED IN WHITING AND CHILD'S STUDY OF CHILD TRAINING AND PERSCNALITY (61)	523	TEND TO BE THOSE 0.91 OF 343 NOT INCLUDED IN WHITING AND CHILD'S STUDY OF CHILD TRAINING AND PERSONALITY (339)	31 30 26 313 XSQ= 75.28 PHI= 0.434 XP = 0.
524	TEND TO BE THOSE 0.60 OF 57 INCLUDED IN WHITING, KLUCKHCHN, ANC ANTHONY'S STUDY OF MALE INITIATICN CEREMONIES (44)	524	TEND TO BE THOSE 0.97 OF 343 NOT INCLUDED IN WHITING, KLUCKHOHN, AND ANTHONY'S STUDY OF MALE INITIATION CEREMONIES (356)	34 10 23 333 XSQ= 154.95 PHI= 0.622 XP = 0.

503 CULTURES
INCLUDED IN JOHN M. HICKMAN'S
STUDY OF THE FOLK-URBAN CONTINUUM (54)

503 CULTURES
NOT INCLUDED IN JOHN M. HICKMAN'S
STUDY OF THE FOLK-URBAN CONTINUUM (346)

SUBJECT ONLY, F.C. 1-480 AND 527-536
BOTH SUBJECT AND PREDICATE, F.C. 481-526

BACKGROUND ON PAGE 180

54 IN LEFT COLUMN

ANDAMANESE	ARANDA	ARAUCANIANS	AZANDE	AZTEC	BEMBA	BULGARIANS	BURMESE	BURUSHO	CAMBODIANS
CAYAPA	CHAGGA	CHUKCHEE	COPR ESKIMO	CREEK	CROW	CUNA	DARD	GILYAK	IBAN
JIVARO	KAREN	KASKA	KHASI	KOREANS	KORYAK	KURTATCHI	LOLO	MANDAN	MARSHALLESE
MBUNDU	MIAO	NAMA	NAVAHO	NUER	OJIBWA	PUKAPUKA	RWALA	SAMOANS	SAMOYED
SIRIONO	TALLENSI	TEHUELCHE	THONGA	TIKOPIA	TIMBIRA	TIV	TODA	TROBRIAND	TUPINAMBA
VIETNAMESE	WOLEAIANS	YAKUT	YUROK						

346 IN RIGHT COLUMN

	Included (54)			Not included (346)		
4	DRIFT MORE TOWARD BEING THOSE LOCATED OUTSIDE OF THE CIRCUM-MEDITERRANEAN (355)	0.96 OF 54	4	DRIFT LESS TOWARD BEING THOSE LOCATED OUTSIDE OF THE CIRCUM-MEDITERRANEAN (355)	0.88 OF 346	2 43 52 303 XSQ= 2.74 PHI= -0.083 XP = 0.0978
5	LEAN LESS TOWARD BEING THOSE LOCATED OUTSIDE OF EAST EURASIA (330)	0.69 OF 54	5	LEAN MORE TOWARD BEING THOSE LOCATED OUTSIDE OF EAST EURASIA (330)	0.85 OF 346	17 53 37 293 XSQ= 7.37 PHI= 0.136 XP = 0.0066
11	DRIFT LESS TOWARD BEING THOSE WHERE THE LATITUDE IS LESS THAN SIXTY DEGREES (385)	0.91 OF 54	11	DRIFT MORE TOWARD BEING THOSE WHERE THE LATITUDE IS LESS THAN SIXTY DEGREES (385)	0.97 OF 346	5 10 49 336 XSQ= 3.63 PHI= 0.095 XP = 0.0566
62	TILT MORE TOWARD BEING THOSE WHERE HUSBANDRY OF SOME KIND IS PRESENT (228)	0.72 OF 54	62	TILT LESS TOWARD BEING THOSE WHERE HUSBANDRY OF SOME KIND IS PRESENT (228)	0.55 OF 346	39 189 15 157 XSQ= 5.21 PHI= 0.114 XP = 0.0225
91	DRIFT TOWARD BEING THOSE WHERE SOCIETAL COMPLEXITY IS LOW (22) F-W	0.70 OF 23	91	DRIFT TOWARD BEING THOSE WHERE SOCIETAL COMPLEXITY IS HIGH (18) F-W	0.65 OF 17	7 11 16 6 XSQ= 3.36 PHI= -0.290 EP = 0.0534

130	TILT TOWARD BEING THOSE WHERE LEATHER WORKING IS MAINLY DONE BY FEMALES (45)	0.78 OF 18	130	TILT TOWARD BEING THOSE WHERE LEATHER WORKING IS MAINLY DONE BY MALES (39)	0.53 OF 66	4 35 14 31 XSQ= 4.23 PHI= -0.224 XP = 0.0397
190	DRIFT LESS TOWARD BEING THOSE WHERE THE KIN GROUP IS PATRILINEAL OR DOUBLE-DESCENT, RATHER THAN MATRILINEAL (186)	0.61 OF 36	190	DRIFT MORE TOWARD BEING THOSE WHERE THE KIN GROUP IS PATRILINEAL OR DOUBLE-DESCENT, RATHER THAN MATRILINEAL (186)	0.78 OF 211	22 164 14 47 XSQ= 3.71 PHI= -0.123 XP = 0.0539
210	DRIFT LESS TOWARD BEING THOSE WHERE MARITAL RESIDENCE IS PATRILOCAL, RATHER THAN MATRILOCAL (169)	0.71 OF 28	210	DRIFT MORE TOWARD BEING THOSE WHERE MARITAL RESIDENCE IS PATRILOCAL, RATHER THAN MATRILOCAL (169)	0.87 OF 172	20 149 8 23 XSQ= 3.17 PHI= -0.126 XP = 0.0752
285	DRIFT TOWARD BEING THOSE WHERE THE SEX TABOO DURING PREGNANCY IS ABSENT OR INFERRED ABSENT (17) BCA	0.82 OF 11	285	DRIFT TOWARD BEING THOSE WHERE THE SEX TABOO DURING PREGNANCY IS PRESENT (14) BCA	0.60 OF 20	2 12 9 8 XSQ= 3.46 PHI= -0.334 EP = 0.0570
341	DRIFT TOWARD BEING THOSE WHERE THE CHILD'S INFERRED ANXIETY OVER NON-PERFORMANCE OF NURTURANT BEHAVIOR IS LOW (16) B-B-C	0.56 OF 16	341	DRIFT TOWARD BEING THOSE WHERE THE CHILD'S INFERRED ANXIETY OVER NON-PERFORMANCE OF NURTURANT BEHAVIOR IS HIGH (30) B-B-C	0.77 OF 30	7 23 9 7 XSQ= 3.64 PHI= -0.281 XP = 0.0565
395	DRIFT TOWARD BEING THOSE WHERE BELIEF IN THE UNCLEANNESS OF WOMEN IS UNIMPORTANT OR ABSENT (15) LWS	0.63 OF 16	395	DRIFT TOWARD BEING THOSE WHERE BELIEF IN THE UNCLEANNESS OF WOMEN IS PRESENT (18) LWS	0.71 OF 17	6 12 10 5 XSQ= 2.43 PHI= -0.271 EP = 0.0844
428	TILT TOWARD BEING THOSE WHERE A HIGH GOD, IF PRESENT AND ACTIVE, DOES NOT SUPPORT HUMAN MORALITY, RATHER THAN SUPPORTING IT (26) GES,EA	0.62 OF 13	428	TILT TOWARD BEING THOSE WHERE A HIGH GOD, IF PRESENT AND ACTIVE, SUPPORTS HUMAN MORALITY, RATHER THAN NOT SUPPORTING IT (61) GES,EA	0.76 OF 74	5 56 8 18 XSQ= 5.64 PHI= -0.255 XP = 0.0176
432	DRIFT MORE TOWARD BEING THOSE WHERE AN ATTRACTIVE AFTERLIFE IS BELIEVED IN (27) LWS	0.88 OF 16	432	DRIFT LESS TOWARD BEING THOSE WHERE AN ATTRACTIVE AFTERLIFE IS BELIEVED IN (27) LWS	0.59 OF 22	14 13 2 9 XSQ= 2.38 PHI= 0.251 EP = 0.0776
449	TILT LESS TOWARD BEING THOSE WHERE THE OBSERVATION OF FOOD TABOOS IS MEDIUM OR LOW, RATHER THAN HIGH (61) JRL	0.60 OF 42	449	TILT MORE TOWARD BEING THOSE WHERE THE OBSERVATION OF FOOD TABOOS IS MEDIUM OR LOW, RATHER THAN HIGH (61) JRL	0.82 OF 44	17 8 25 36 XSQ= 4.16 PHI= 0.220 XP = 0.0415

475	DRIFT TOWARD BEING THOSE WHERE EXHIBITIONISTIC DANCING IS STRONGLY OR MODERATELY EMPHASIZED (48) PES	0.69 OF 35	475	DRIFT TOWARD BEING THOSE WHERE EXHIBITIONISTIC DANCING IS NEGLIGIBLY EMPHASIZED (38) PES	0.53 OF 51	24 24 11 27 XSQ= 3.07 PHI= 0.189 XP = 0.0797
489	TEND LESS TO BE THOSE NOT INCLUDED IN CHARLES ACKERMAN'S STUDY OF DIVORCE (343)	0.61 OF 54	489	TEND MORE TO BE THOSE NOT INCLUDED IN CHARLES ACKERMAN'S STUDY OF DIVORCE (343)	0.90 OF 346	21 36 33 310 XSQ= 28.73 PHI= 0.268 XP = 0.0000
490	TEND LESS TO BE THOSE NOT INCLUDED IN ALBERT S. ANTHONY'S SAMPLE ON MALE INITIATION RITES (287)	0.52 OF 54	490	TEND MORE TO BE THOSE NOT INCLUDED IN ALBERT S. ANTHONY'S SAMPLE ON MALE INITIATION RITES (287)	0.75 OF 346	26 87 28 259 XSQ= 11.09 PHI= 0.166 XP = 0.0009
491	LEAN LESS TOWARD BEING THOSE NOT INCLUDED IN DORRIAN APPLE'S STUDY OF GRANDPARENTHOOD (352)	0.74 OF 54	491	LEAN MORE TOWARD BEING THOSE NOT INCLUDED IN DORRIAN APPLE'S STUDY OF GRANDPARENTHOOD (352)	0.90 OF 346	14 34 40 312 XSQ= 9.99 PHI= 0.158 XP = 0.0016
492	TEND LESS TO BE THOSE NOT INCLUDED IN BARBARA CHARTIER AYRES' STUDY OF FEMALE INITIATION RITES (361)	0.76 OF 54	492	TEND MORE TO BE THOSE NOT INCLUDED IN BARBARA CHARTIER AYRES' STUDY OF FEMALE INITIATION RITES (361)	0.92 OF 346	13 26 41 320 XSQ= 12.74 PHI= 0.178 XP = 0.0004
493	TEND TO BE THOSE INCLUDED IN BACON, BARRY, AND CHILD'S STUDY OF CHILD REARING (78)	0.54 OF 54	493	TEND TO BE THOSE NOT INCLUDED IN BACON, BARRY, AND CHILD'S STUDY OF CHILD REARING (322)	0.86 OF 346	29 49 25 297 XSQ= 44.04 PHI= 0.332 XP = 0.
495	TEND TO BE THOSE INCLUDED IN JUDITH K. BROWN'S STUDY OF FEMALE INITIATION RITES (65)	0.52 OF 54	495	TEND TO BE THOSE NOT INCLUDED IN JUDITH K. BROWN'S STUDY OF FEMALE INITIATION RITES (335)	0.89 OF 346	28 37 26 309 XSQ= 55.16 PHI= 0.371 XP = 0.
496	TEND LESS TO BE THOSE NOT INCLUDED IN ROY G. D'ANDRADE'S STUDY OF DREAMS (345)	0.52 OF 54	496	TEND MORE TO BE THOSE NOT INCLUDED IN ROY G. D'ANDRADE'S STUDY OF DREAMS (345)	0.92 OF 346	26 29 28 317 XSQ= 58.98 PHI= 0.384 XP = 0.
497	TEND LESS TO BE THOSE NOT INCLUDED IN WILLIAM M. EVAN'S STUDY OF LAW (339)	0.59 OF 54	497	TEND MORE TO BE THOSE NOT INCLUDED IN WILLIAM M. EVAN'S STUDY OF LAW (339)	0.89 OF 346	22 39 32 307 XSQ= 29.15 PHI= 0.270 XP = 0.0000

No.		Proportion	No.		Proportion	Statistics
498	TEND LESS TO BE THOSE NOT INCLUDED IN C. S. FORD'S STUDY OF SEX (349)	0.59 OF 54	498	TEND MORE TO BE THOSE NOT INCLUDED IN C. S. FORD'S STUDY OF SEX (349)	0.92 OF 346	22 29 32 317 XSQ= 41.11 PHI= 0.321 XP = 0.
499	TEND LESS TO BE THOSE NOT INCLUDED IN FORD AND BEACH'S SAMPLE ON SEXUAL EXPRESSION BY THE YOUNG (314)	0.52 OF 54	499	TEND MORE TO BE THOSE NOT INCLUDED IN FORD AND BEACH'S SAMPLE ON SEXUAL EXPRESSION BY THE YOUNG (314)	0.83 OF 346	26 60 28 286 XSQ= 24.47 PHI= 0.247 XP = 0.0000
500	TEND LESS TO BE THOSE NOT INCLUDED IN FREEMAN AND WINCH'S STUDY OF SOCIETAL COMPLEXITY (360)	0.57 OF 54	500	TEND MORE TO BE THOSE NOT INCLUDED IN FREEMAN AND WINCH'S STUDY OF SOCIETAL COMPLEXITY (360)	0.95 OF 346	23 17 31 329 XSQ= 69.56 PHI= 0.417 XP = 0.
501	TEND LESS TO BE THOSE NOT INCLUDED IN JOAN FRIENDLY GOODMAN'S STUDY OF ASCETIC MOURNING BEHAVIOR (333)	0.61 OF 54	501	TEND MORE TO BE THOSE NOT INCLUDED IN JOAN FRIENDLY GOODMAN'S STUDY OF ASCETIC MOURNING BEHAVIOR (333)	0.87 OF 346	21 46 33 300 XSQ= 20.15 PHI= 0.224 XP = 0.0000
502	TEND LESS TO BE THOSE NOT INCLUDED IN JOHN K. HARLEY'S STUDY OF ADOLESCENT PEER GROUPS (343)	0.69 OF 54	502	TEND MORE TO BE THOSE NOT INCLUDED IN JOHN K. HARLEY'S STUDY OF ADOLESCENT PEER GROUPS (343)	0.88 OF 346	17 40 37 306 XSQ= 13.58 PHI= 0.184 XP = 0.0002
504	TEND LESS TO BE THOSE NOT INCLUDED IN DONALD HORTON'S STUDY OF ALCHOLISM (351)	0.69 OF 54	504	TEND MORE TO BE THOSE NOT INCLUDED IN DONALD HORTON'S STUDY OF ALCHOLISM (351)	0.91 OF 346	17 32 37 314 XSQ= 19.46 PHI= 0.221 XP = 0.0000
505	TEND LESS TO BE THOSE NOT INCLUDED IN MERRILL JACKSON'S STUDY OF CRIMINAL LAW AND MEDICINE (380)	0.81 OF 54	505	TEND MORE TO BE THOSE NOT INCLUDED IN MERRILL JACKSON'S STUDY OF CRIMINAL LAW AND MEDICINE (380)	0.97 OF 346	10 10 44 336 XSQ= 20.84 PHI= 0.228 XP = 0.0000
506	TEND LESS TO BE THOSE NOT INCLUDED IN LAMBERT, TRIANDIS, AND WOLF'S STUDY OF SUPERNATURAL BEINGS (364)	0.78 OF 54	506	TEND MORE TO BE THOSE NOT INCLUDED IN LAMBERT, TRIANDIS, AND WOLF'S STUDY OF SUPERNATURAL BEINGS (364)	0.93 OF 346	12 24 42 322 XSQ= 11.53 PHI= 0.170 XP = 0.0007
507	TEND TO BE THOSE INCLUDED IN JAMES R. LEARY'S STUDY OF FOOD TABOOS (86)	0.78 OF 54	507	TEND TO BE THOSE NOT INCLUDED IN JAMES R. LEARY'S STUDY OF FOOD TABOOS (314)	0.87 OF 346	42 44 12 302 XSQ= 113.33 PHI= 0.532 XP = 0.

```
508  TEND LESS TO BE THOSE            0.69 OF  54    508  TEND MORE TO BE THOSE            0.93 OF 346          17   23
     NOT INCLUDED IN DAVID C. MCCLELLAND'S                NOT INCLUDED IN DAVID C. MCCLELLAND'S                   37  323
     STUDY OF ACHIEVEMENT MOTIVATION  (360)               STUDY OF ACHIEVEMENT MOTIVATION  (360)          XSQ=   29.31
                                                                                                          PHI=   0.271
                                                                                                          XP =  0.0000

509  TILT LESS TOWARD BEING THOSE     0.85 OF  54    509  TILT MORE TOWARD BEING THOSE     0.95 OF 346           8   17
     NOT INCLUDED IN MONI NAG'S                           NOT INCLUDED IN MONI NAG'S                              46  329
     STUDY OF FERTILITY  (375)                            STUDY OF FERTILITY  (375)                       XSQ=    6.22
                                                                                                          PHI=   0.125
                                                                                                          XP =  0.0127

510  TEND LESS TO BE THOSE            0.83 OF  54    510  TEND MORE TO BE THOSE            0.97 OF 346           9   11
     NOT INCLUDED IN RAOUL NARROLL'S                      NOT INCLUDED IN RAOUL NARROLL'S                         45  335
     STUDY OF SOCIETAL COMPLEXITY  (380)                  STUDY OF SOCIETAL COMPLEXITY  (380)             XSQ=   15.16
                                                                                                          PHI=   0.195
                                                                                                          XP =  0.0001

511  TEND TO BE THOSE                 0.78 OF  54    511  TEND TO BE THOSE                 0.58 OF 346          42  147
     INCLUDED IN ROBERTS, ARTH AND BUSH'S                 NOT INCLUDED IN ROBERTS, ARTH AND BUSH'S                12  199
     SAMPLE ON GAMES, AS MODIFIED                         SAMPLE ON GAMES, AS MODIFIED                    XSQ=   21.95
     BY THE ETHNOGRAPHIC ATLAS  (189)                     BY THE ETHNOGRAPHIC ATLAS  (211)                PHI=   0.234
                                                                                                          XP =  0.0000

512  TEND LESS TO BE THOSE            0.76 OF  54    512  TEND MORE TO BE THOSE            0.94 OF 346          13   20
     NOT INCLUDED IN SHIRLEY AND ROMNEY'S                 NOT INCLUDED IN SHIRLEY AND ROMNEY'S                    41  326
     STUDY OF LOVE MAGIC  (367)                           STUDY OF LOVE MAGIC  (367)                      XSQ=   18.31
                                                                                                          PHI=   0.214
                                                                                                          XP =  0.0000

513  TEND LESS TO BE THOSE            0.70 OF  54    513  TEND MORE TO BE THOSE            0.92 OF 346          16   27
     NOT INCLUDED IN LEO W. SIMMONS'                      NOT INCLUDED IN LEO W. SIMMONS'                         38  319
     STUDY OF THE TREATMENT OF THE AGED  (357)            STUDY OF THE TREATMENT OF THE AGED  (357)       XSQ=   20.97
                                                                                                          PHI=   0.229
                                                                                                          XP =  0.0000

514  TEND TO BE THOSE                 0.67 OF  54    514  TEND TO BE THOSE                 0.84 OF 346          36   54
     INCLUDED IN PHILIP E. SLATER'S                       NOT INCLUDED IN PHILIP E. SLATER'S                      18  292
     STUDY OF NARCISSISM  (90)                            STUDY OF NARCISSISM  (310)                      XSQ=   66.94
                                                                                                          PHI=   0.409
                                                                                                          XP =  0.

515  TEND LESS TO BE THOSE            0.63 OF  54    515  TEND MORE TO BE THOSE            0.91 OF 346          20   32
     NOT INCLUDED IN WILLIAM N. STEPHENS'                 NOT INCLUDED IN WILLIAM N. STEPHENS'                    34  314
     SAMPLE ON AVOIDANCE RELATIONSHIPS  (348)             SAMPLE ON AVOIDANCE RELATIONSHIPS  (348)        XSQ=   29.48
                                                                                                          PHI=   0.271
                                                                                                          XP =  0.0000

516  LEAN MORE TOWARD BEING THOSE     0.96 OF  54    516  LEAN LESS TOWARD BEING THOSE     0.81 OF 346          52  279
     INCLUDED IN GUY E. SWANSON'S                         INCLUDED IN GUY E. SWANSON'S                             2   67
     SAMPLE ON LOCAL JURISDICTION, AS MODIFIED            SAMPLE ON LOCAL JURISDICTION, AS MODIFIED       XSQ=    6.97
     BY THE ETHNOGRAPHIC ATLAS  (331)                     BY THE ETHNOGRAPHIC ATLAS  (331)                PHI=   0.132
                                                                                                          XP =  0.0083
```

517	TEND MORE TO BE THCSE INCLUDED IN GUY E. SWANSON'S SAMPLE ON HIGH GODS, AS MODIFIED BY THE ETHNOGRAPHIC ATLAS (260)	0.87 OF 54	517	TEND LESS TO BE THOSE INCLUDED IN GUY E. SWANSON'S SAMPLE ON HIGH GODS, AS MODIFIED BY THE ETHNOGRAPHIC ATLAS (260)	0.62 OF 346	47 213 7 133 XSQ= 12.23 PHI= 0.175 XP = 0.0005
518	TEND TO BE THCSE INCLUDED IN STANLEY H. UDY, JR.'S STUDY OF WCRK ORGANIZATION (105)	0.70 OF 54	518	TEND TO BE THOSE NOT INCLUDED IN STANLEY H. UDY, JR.'S STUDY OF WORK ORGANIZATION (295)	0.81 OF 346	38 67 16 279 XSQ= 60.16 PHI= 0.388 XP = 0.
519	TEND LESS TO BE THCSE NOT INCLUDED IN JOSEPH VEROFF'S STUDY OF ACHIEVEMENT MOTIVATION AS REVEALED IN FCLKTALES (364)	0.69 OF 54	519	TEND MORE TO BE THOSE NOT INCLUDED IN JOSEPH VEROFF'S STUDY OF ACHIEVEMENT MOTIVATION AS REVEALED IN FOLKTALES (364)	0.95 OF 346	17 19 37 327 XSQ= 35.42 PHI= 0.298 XP = 0.
520	TEND LESS TO BE THCSE NOT INCLUDED IN BEATRICE BLYTH WHITING'S STUDY OF SCRCERY (360)	0.74 OF 54	520	TEND MORE TO BE THOSE NOT INCLUDED IN BEATRICE BLYTH WHITING'S STUDY OF SORCERY (360)	0.92 OF 346	14 26 40 320 XSQ= 15.61 PHI= 0.198 XP = 0.0001
521	TEND LESS TO BE THCSE NOT INCLUDED IN JOHN W. M. WHITING'S STUDY OF SCCIALIZATION PROCESS AND PERSCNALITY (353)	0.67 OF 54	521	TEND MORE TO BE THOSE NOT INCLUDED IN JOHN W. M. WHITING'S STUDY OF SOCIALIZATION PROCESS AND PERSONALITY (353)	0.92 OF 346	18 29 36 317 XSQ= 25.69 PHI= 0.253 XP = 0.0000
522	TEND LESS TO BE THCSE NOT INCLUDED IN MARJORIE GRANT WHITING'S STUDY OF DIET (318)	0.54 OF 54	522	TEND MORE TO BE THOSE NOT INCLUDED IN MARJORIE GRANT WHITING'S STUDY OF DIET (318)	0.84 OF 346	25 57 29 289 XSQ= 23.69 PHI= 0.243 XP = 0.0000
523	TEND LESS TO BE THCSE NOT INCLUDED IN WHITING AND CHILD'S STUDY OF CHILD TRAINING AND PERSONALITY (339)	0.69 OF 54	523	TEND MORE TO BE THOSE NOT INCLUDED IN WHITING AND CHILD'S STUDY OF CHILD TRAINING AND PERSONALITY (339)	0.87 OF 346	17 44 37 302 XSQ= 11.32 PHI= 0.168 XP = 0.0008
524	TEND LESS TO BE THCSE NCT INCLUDED IN WHITING, KLUCKHCHN, AND ANTHONY'S STUDY OF MALE INITIATICN CEREMONIES (356)	0.70 OF 54	524	TEND MORE TO BE THOSE NOT INCLUDED IN WHITING, KLUCKHOHN, AND ANTHONY'S STUDY OF MALE INITIATION CEREMONIES (356)	0.92 OF 346	16 28 38 318 XSQ= 19.99 PHI= 0.224 XP = 0.0000

504 CULTURES INCLUDED IN DONALD HORTON'S STUDY OF ALCOHOLISM (49)

504 CULTURES NOT INCLUDED IN DONALD HORTON'S STUDY OF ALCHOLISM (351)

SUBJECT ONLY, F.C. 1-480 AND 527-536
BOTH SUBJECT AND PREDICATE, F.C. 481-526

BACKGROUND ON PAGE 180

49 IN LEFT COLUMN

ABIPON	AINU	ANDAMANESE	APINAYE	ASHANTI	AZANDE	BALINESE	CARIB	CAYAPA	CHAGGA
CHOROTI	CHUKCHEE	CREEK	CUNA	DUSUN	GOAJIRO	GOND	HANO	HUICHOL	IFUGAO
JIVARO	KAZAK	KHALKA	KHASI	LAKHER	LAMBA	LANGO	LEPCHA	MACRI	MARICOPA
MASAI	MBUNDU	MURNGIN	NAMA	NASKAPI	OMAHA	PAPAGO	SAMOYED	TANALA	TARAHUMARA
TEHUELCHE	THONGA	TIV	TODA	TUPINAMBA	VENDA	WOLOF	YOKUTS	ZUNI	

351 IN RIGHT COLUMN

4	DRIFT MORE TOWARD BEING THOSE 0.98 OF 49 LOCATED OUTSIDE OF THE CIRCUM-MEDITERRANEAN (355)	4	DRIFT LESS TOWARD BEING THOSE 0.87 OF 351 LOCATED OUTSIDE OF THE CIRCUM-MEDITERRANEAN (355)	1 44 48 307 XSQ= 3.75 PHI= -0.097 XP = 0.0528
33	TILT LESS TOWARD BEING THOSE 0.73 OF 49 WHERE THE NATURAL ENVIRONMENT IS OTHER THAN 'VERY HARSH,' I.E., DESERT, DESERT GRASSES AND SHRUBS, TUNDRA, OR HIGH PLATEAU STEPPE (341) FWM	33	TILT MORE TOWARD BEING THOSE 0.87 OF 351 WHERE THE NATURAL ENVIRONMENT IS OTHER THAN 'VERY HARSH,' I.E., DESERT, DESERT GRASSES AND SHRUBS, TUNDRA, OR HIGH PLATEAU STEPPE (341) FWM	13 46 36 305 XSQ= 5.14 PHI= 0.113 XP = 0.0234
36	TEND LESS TO BE THOSE 0.51 OF 49 WHERE THE NATURAL ENVIRONMENT IS OTHER THAN 'VERY HARSH,' OR SUB-TROPICAL BUSH, OR TEMPERATE GRASSLAND (292) FWM	36	TEND MORE TO BE THOSE 0.76 OF 351 WHERE THE NATURAL ENVIRONMENT IS OTHER THAN 'VERY HARSH,' OR SUB-TROPICAL BUSH, OR TEMPERATE GRASSLAND (292) FWM	24 84 25 267 XSQ= 12.45 PHI= 0.176 XP = 0.0004
42	DRIFT MORE TOWARD BEING THOSE 0.73 OF 49 WHERE THE NATURAL ENVIRONMENT IS OTHER THAN TROPICAL OR SUB-TROPICAL RAIN FOREST, OR MONSOON FOREST (244) FWM	42	DRIFT LESS TOWARD BEING THOSE 0.59 OF 351 WHERE THE NATURAL ENVIRONMENT IS OTHER THAN TROPICAL OR SUB-TROPICAL RAIN FOREST, OR MONSOON FOREST (244) FWM	13 143 36 208 XSQ= 3.08 PHI= -0.088 XP = 0.0794
73	TILT TOWARD BEING THOSE 0.65 OF 40 WHERE WEAVING IS PRESENT (118)	73	TILT TOWARD BEING THOSE 0.56 OF 208 WHERE WEAVING IS ABSENT (130)	26 92 14 116 XSQ= 5.00 PHI= 0.142 XP = 0.0254

77	TILT MORE TOWARD BEING THOSE 0.94 OF 17 WHERE THE WRITING SYSTEM IS MNEMONIC CR ABSENT, RATHER THAN BEING ALPHABETIC-OR-PHCNETIC (39) JMH	77	TILT LESS TOWARD BEING THOSE 0.62 OF 37 WHERE THE WRITING SYSTEM IS MNEMONIC OR ABSENT, RATHER THAN BEING ALPHABETIC-OR-PHONETIC (39) JMH	1 14 16 23 XSQ= 4.44 PHI= -0.287 XP = 0.0350
79	IN ALL CASES ARE THOSE 1.00 OF 37 WHERE NC CITY IS PRESENT (201)	79	DRIFT LESS TOWARD BEING THCSE 0.88 OF 187 WHERE NO CITY IS PRESENT (201)	0 23 37 164 XSQ= 3.82 PHI= -0.131 XP = 0.0505
80	TILT MORE TOWARD BEING THCSE 0.97 OF 37 WHERE NO CITY OR TCWN IS PRESENT (185)	80	TILT LESS TOWARD BEING THOSE 0.80 OF 187 WHERE NO CITY OR TOWN IS PRESENT (185)	1 38 36 149 XSQ= 5.50 PHI= -0.157 XP = 0.0190
107	DRIFT MORE TCWARD BEING THOSE 0.93 OF 29 WHERE CLASS STRATIFICATION, IF PRESENT, IS BASED CN SCMETHING CTHER THAN OCCUPATIONAL STATUS (160)	107	DRIFT LESS TOWARD BEING THCSE 0.76 OF 174 WHERE CLASS STRATIFICATION, IF PRESENT, IS BASED ON SOMETHING OTHER THAN OCCUPATIONAL STATUS (160)	2 41 27 133 XSQ= 3.20 PHI= -0.126 XP = 0.0737
137	TILT TOWARD BEING THOSE 0.76 OF 29 WHERE INVIDIOUS DISPLAY OF WEALTH IS MODERATELY, LITTLE, CR NEGATIVELY EMPHASIZED (52) PES	137	TILT TOWARD BEING THOSE 0.50 OF 60 WHERE INVIDIOUS DISPLAY OF WEALTH IS STRONGLY EMPHASIZED (37) PES	7 30 22 30 XSQ= 4.37 PHI= -0.222 XP = 0.0365
256	TILT TOWARD BEING THOSE 0.57 OF 7 WHERE GRANDPARENT AND GRANDCHILD ARE NCT FRIENDLY EQUALS (8) DA	256	TILT TOWARD BEING THOSE 0.85 OF 26 WHERE GRANDPARENT AND GRANDCHILD ARE FRIENDLY EQUALS (25) DA	3 22 4 4 XSQ= 3.21 PHI= -0.312 EP = 0.0418
282	LEAN TOWARD BEING THOSE 0.68 OF 19 WHERE THE STRENGTH OF DESIRE FOR CHILDREN IS HIGH (16) BCA	282	LEAN TOWARD BEING THOSE 0.82 OF 17 WHERE THE STRENGTH OF DESIRE FOR CHILDREN IS LOW OR ABSENT (20) BCA	13 3 6 14 XSQ= 7.42 PHI= 0.454 EP = 0.0031
301	DRIFT LESS TCWARD BEING THOSE 0.61 OF 23 WHERE THE POST-PARTUM SEX TABOO LASTS LONGER THAN CNE MONTH (96)	301	DRIFT MORE TOWARD BEING THOSE 0.81 OF 101 WHERE THE POST-PARTUM SEX TABOO LASTS LONGER THAN ONE MONTH (96)	14 82 9 19 XSQ= 3.34 PHI= -0.164 XP = 0.0677
304	DRIFT TOWARD BEING THOSE 0.77 OF 13 WHERE THE EARLY ANAL SATISFACTION POTENTIAL IS LOW (22) W-C	304	DRIFT TOWARD BEING THOSE 0.57 OF 28 WHERE THE EARLY ANAL SATISFACTION POTENTIAL IS HIGH (19) W-C	3 16 10 12 XSQ= 2.89 PHI= -0.265 XP = 0.0893

338	DRIFT MORE TOWARD BEING THOSE 0.78 OF 23 WHERE THE CHILD'S INFERRED ANXIETY OVER PERFORMANCE OF RESPONSIBLE BEHAVIOR IS HIGH (44) B-B-C	338	DRIFT LESS TOWARD BEING THOSE 0.52 OF 50 WHERE THE CHILD'S INFERRED ANXIETY OVER PERFORMANCE OF RESPONSIBLE BEHAVIOR IS HIGH (44) B-B-C	18 26 5 24 XSQ= 3.51 PHI= 0.219 XP = 0.0611
391	TILT TOWARD BEING THOSE 0.71 OF 31 WHERE PREMARITAL SEX RELATIONS ARE PUNISHED ONLY IF PREGNANCY RESULTS, OR FREELY PERMITTED (90) JTW,EA	391	TILT TOWARD BEING THOSE 0.54 OF 148 WHERE PREMARITAL SEX RELATIONS ARE STRONGLY PUNISHED AND IN FACT RARE, OR WEAKLY PUNISHED AND IN FACT NOT RARE (89) JTW,EA	9 80 22 68 XSQ= 5.46 PHI= -0.175 XP = 0.0195
398	DRIFT TOWARD BEING THOSE 0.67 OF 15 WHERE THE INTENSITY OF SEX ANXIETY IS LOW (16) WNS	398	DRIFT TOWARD BEING THOSE 0.65 OF 17 WHERE THE INTENSITY OF SEX ANXIETY IS HIGH (16) WNS	5 11 10 6 XSQ= 2.01 PHI= -0.250 EP = 0.0938
428	TILT TOWARD BEING THOSE 0.57 OF 14 WHERE A HIGH GOD, IF PRESENT AND ACTIVE, DOES NOT SUPPORT HUMAN MORALITY, RATHER THAN SUPPORTING IT (26) GES,EA	428	TILT TOWARD BEING THOSE 0.75 OF 73 WHERE A HIGH GOD, IF PRESENT AND ACTIVE, SUPPORTS HUMAN MORALITY, RATHER THAN NOT SUPPORTING IT (61) GES,EA	6 55 8 18 XSQ= 4.47 PHI= -0.227 XP = 0.0345
432	DRIFT MORE TOWARD BEING THOSE 0.92 OF 12 WHERE AN ATTRACTIVE AFTERLIFE IS BELIEVED IN (27) LWS	432	DRIFT LESS TOWARD BEING THOSE 0.62 OF 26 WHERE AN ATTRACTIVE AFTERLIFE IS BELIEVED IN (27) LWS	11 16 1 10 XSQ= 2.31 PHI= 0.246 EP = 0.0704
456	TILT TOWARD BEING THOSE 0.75 OF 12 WHERE THE INTERNALIZATION OF THE INDIVIDUAL'S CONTACT WITH THE DIVINE IS NOT CONDUCIVE TO THE DEVELOPMENT OF THE INDIVIDUAL'S NEED TO ACHIEVE (17) DCM	456	TILT TOWARD BEING THOSE 0.67 OF 24 WHERE THE INTERNALIZATION OF THE INDIVIDUAL'S CONTACT WITH THE DIVINE IS CONDUCIVE TO THE DEVELOPMENT OF THE INDIVIDUAL'S NEED TO ACHIEVE (19) DCM	3 16 9 8 XSQ= 4.03 PHI= -0.334 EP = 0.0328
458	TILT LESS TOWARD BEING THOSE 0.53 OF 34 WHERE GAMES, IF PRESENT, DO NOT INCLUDE GAMES OF STRATEGY (119) R-A-B,EA	458	TILT MORE TOWARD BEING THOSE 0.74 OF 137 WHERE GAMES, IF PRESENT, DO NOT INCLUDE GAMES OF STRATEGY (119) R-A-B,EA	16 36 18 101 XSQ= 4.62 PHI= 0.164 XP = 0.0316
488	TILT MORE TOWARD BEING THOSE 0.91 OF 34 ABOUT WHICH THE PRINCIPAL ETHNOGRAPHIES WERE PUBLISHED BEFORE 1950 (185)	488	TILT LESS TOWARD BEING THOSE 0.69 OF 223 ABOUT WHICH THE PRINCIPAL ETHNOGRAPHIES WERE PUBLISHED BEFORE 1950 (185)	31 154 3 69 XSQ= 6.10 PHI= 0.154 XP = 0.0135
489	TEND LESS TO BE THOSE 0.65 OF 49 NOT INCLUDED IN CHARLES ACKERMAN'S STUDY OF DIVORCE (343)	489	TEND MORE TO BE THOSE 0.89 OF 351 NOT INCLUDED IN CHARLES ACKERMAN'S STUDY OF DIVORCE (343)	17 40 32 311 XSQ= 17.24 PHI= 0.208 XP = 0.0000

No.		Proportion	No.		Proportion	Statistics
490	TEND TO BE THOSE INCLUDED IN ALBERT S. ANTHONY'S SAMPLE ON MALE INITIATION RITES (113)	0.57 OF 49	490	TEND TO BE THOSE NOT INCLUDED IN ALBERT S. ANTHONY'S SAMPLE ON MALE INITIATION RITES (287)	0.76 OF 351	28 85 21 266 XSQ= 21.40 PHI= 0.231 XP = 0.0000
491	TILT LESS TOWARD BEING THOSE NOT INCLUDED IN DORRIAN APPLE'S STUDY OF GRANDPARENTHOOD (352)	0.78 OF 49	491	TILT MORE TOWARD BEING THOSE NOT INCLUDED IN DORRIAN APPLE'S STUDY OF GRANDPARENTHOOD (352)	0.89 OF 351	11 37 38 314 XSQ= 4.70 PHI= 0.108 XP = 0.0301
492	TEND LESS TO BE THOSE NOT INCLUDED IN BARBARA CHARTIER AYRES' STUDY OF FEMALE INITIATION RITES (361)	0.59 OF 49	492	TEND MORE TO BE THOSE NOT INCLUDED IN BARBARA CHARTIER AYRES' STUDY OF FEMALE INITIATION RITES (361)	0.95 OF 351	20 19 29 332 XSQ= 57.29 PHI= 0.378 XP = 0.
493	TEND TO BE THOSE INCLUDED IN BACON, BARRY, AND CHILD'S STUDY OF CHILD REARING (78)	0.53 OF 49	493	TEND TO BE THOSE NOT INCLUDED IN BACON, BARRY, AND CHILD'S STUDY OF CHILD REARING (322)	0.85 OF 351	26 52 23 299 XSQ= 37.67 PHI= 0.307 XP = 0.
494	TEND LESS TO BE THOSE NOT INCLUDED IN HERBERT M. BARRY III'S STUDY OF ART (371)	0.73 OF 49	494	TEND MORE TO BE THOSE NOT INCLUDED IN HERBERT M. BARRY III'S STUDY OF ART (371)	0.95 OF 351	13 16 36 335 XSQ= 27.69 PHI= 0.263 XP = 0.0000
495	TEND LESS TO BE THOSE NOT INCLUDED IN JUDITH K. BROWN'S STUDY OF FEMALE INITIATION RITES (335)	0.53 OF 49	495	TEND MORE TO BE THOSE NOT INCLUDED IN JUDITH K. BROWN'S STUDY OF FEMALE INITIATION RITES (335)	0.88 OF 351	23 42 26 309 XSQ= 36.12 PHI= 0.300 XP = 0.
496	TEND LESS TO BE THOSE NOT INCLUDED IN ROY G. D'ANDRADE'S STUDY OF DREAMS (345)	0.67 OF 49	496	TEND MORE TO BE THOSE NOT INCLUDED IN ROY G. D'ANDRADE'S STUDY OF DREAMS (345)	0.89 OF 351	16 39 33 312 XSQ= 15.06 PHI= 0.194 XP = 0.0001
497	TEND LESS TO BE THOSE NOT INCLUDED IN WILLIAM M. EVAN'S STUDY OF LAW (339)	0.59 OF 49	497	TEND MORE TO BE THOSE NOT INCLUDED IN WILLIAM M. EVAN'S STUDY OF LAW (339)	0.88 OF 351	20 41 29 310 XSQ= 26.03 PHI= 0.255 XP = 0.0000
498	TEND TO BE THOSE INCLUDED IN C. S. FORD'S STUDY OF SEX (51)	0.67 OF 49	498	TEND TO BE THOSE NOT INCLUDED IN C. S. FORD'S STUDY OF SEX (349)	0.95 OF 351	33 18 16 333 XSQ= 144.09 PHI= 0.600 XP = 0.

499	TEND TO BE THOSE INCLUDED IN FORD AND BEACH'S SAMPLE ON SEXUAL EXPRESSION BY THE YOUNG (86)	0.73 OF 49	499	TEND TO BE THOSE NOT INCLUDED IN FORD AND BEACH'S SAMPLE ON SEXUAL EXPRESSION BY THE YOUNG (314)	0.86 OF 351	36 50 / 13 301 / XSQ= 85.88 / PHI= 0.463 / XP = 0.
500	TEND LESS TO BE THOSE NOT INCLUDED IN FREEMAN AND WINCH'S STUDY OF SOCIETAL COMPLEXITY (360)	0.57 OF 49	500	TEND MORE TO BE THOSE NOT INCLUDED IN FREEMAN AND WINCH'S STUDY OF SOCIETAL COMPLEXITY (360)	0.95 OF 351	21 19 / 28 332 / XSQ= 62.89 / PHI= 0.397 / XP = 0.
501	TEND TO BE THOSE INCLUDED IN JOAN FRIENDLY GOODMAN'S STUDY OF ASCETIC MOURNING BEHAVIOR (67)	0.67 OF 49	501	TEND TO BE THOSE NOT INCLUDED IN JOAN FRIENDLY GOODMAN'S STUDY OF ASCETIC MOURNING BEHAVIOR (333)	0.90 OF 351	33 34 / 16 317 / XSQ= 98.42 / PHI= 0.496 / XP = 0.
502	TEND LESS TO BE THOSE NOT INCLUDED IN JOHN K. HARLEY'S STUDY OF ADOLESCENT PEER GROUPS (343)	0.57 OF 49	502	TEND MORE TO BE THOSE NOT INCLUDED IN JOHN K. HARLEY'S STUDY OF ADOLESCENT PEER GROUPS (343)	0.90 OF 351	21 36 / 28 315 / XSQ= 34.78 / PHI= 0.295 / XP = 0.
503	TEND LESS TO BE THOSE NOT INCLUDED IN JOHN M. HICKMAN'S STUDY OF THE FOLK-URBAN CONTINUUM (346)	0.65 OF 49	503	TEND MORE TO BE THOSE NOT INCLUDED IN JOHN M. HICKMAN'S STUDY OF THE FOLK-URBAN CONTINUUM (346)	0.89 OF 351	17 37 / 32 314 / XSQ= 19.46 / PHI= 0.221 / XP = 0.0000
506	LEAN LESS TOWARD BEING THOSE NOT INCLUDED IN LAMBERT, TRIANDIS, AND WOLF'S STUDY OF SUPERNATURAL BEINGS (364)	0.78 OF 49	506	LEAN MORE TOWARD BEING THOSE NOT INCLUDED IN LAMBERT, TRIANDIS, AND WOLF'S STUDY OF SUPERNATURAL BEINGS (364)	0.93 OF 351	11 25 / 38 326 / XSQ= 10.53 / PHI= 0.162 / XP = 0.0012
507	TEND TO BE THOSE INCLUDED IN JAMES R. LEARY'S STUDY OF FOOD TABOOS (86)	0.51 OF 49	507	TEND TO BE THOSE NOT INCLUDED IN JAMES R. LEARY'S STUDY OF FOOD TABOOS (314)	0.83 OF 351	25 61 / 24 290 / XSQ= 26.87 / PHI= 0.259 / XP = 0.0000
508	TEND LESS TO BE THOSE NOT INCLUDED IN DAVID C. MCCLELLAND'S STUDY OF ACHIEVEMENT MOTIVATION (360)	0.71 OF 49	508	TEND MORE TO BE THOSE NOT INCLUDED IN DAVID C. MCCLELLAND'S STUDY OF ACHIEVEMENT MOTIVATION (360)	0.93 OF 351	14 26 / 35 325 / XSQ= 19.11 / PHI= 0.219 / XP = 0.0000
510	TILT LESS TOWARD BEING THOSE NOT INCLUDED IN RAOUL NARROLL'S STUDY OF SOCIETAL COMPLEXITY (380)	0.88 OF 49	510	TILT MORE TOWARD BEING THOSE NOT INCLUDED IN RAOUL NARROLL'S STUDY OF SOCIETAL COMPLEXITY (380)	0.96 OF 351	6 14 / 43 337 / XSQ= 4.55 / PHI= 0.107 / XP = 0.0328

No.		No.		
511	TEND TO BE THOSE 0.82 OF 49 INCLUDED IN ROBERTS, ARTH AND BUSH'S SAMPLE ON GAMES, AS MODIFIED BY THE ETHNOGRAPHIC ATLAS (189)	511	TEND TO BE THOSE 0.58 OF 351 NOT INCLUDED IN ROBERTS, ARTH AND BUSH'S SAMPLE ON GAMES, AS MODIFIED BY THE ETHNOGRAPHIC ATLAS (211)	40 149 9 202 XSQ= 24.94 PHI= 0.250 XP = 0.0000
512	TEND LESS TO BE THOSE 0.71 OF 49 NOT INCLUDED IN SHIRLEY AND ROMNEY'S STUDY OF LOVE MAGIC (367)	512	TEND MORE TO BE THOSE 0.95 OF 351 NOT INCLUDED IN SHIRLEY AND ROMNEY'S STUDY OF LOVE MAGIC (367)	14 19 35 332 XSQ= 27.48 PHI= 0.262 XP = 0.0000
513	TEND LESS TO BE THOSE 0.71 OF 49 NOT INCLUDED IN LEO W. SIMMONS' STUDY OF THE TREATMENT OF THE AGED (357)	513	TEND MORE TO BE THOSE 0.92 OF 351 NOT INCLUDED IN LEO W. SIMMONS' STUDY OF THE TREATMENT OF THE AGED (357)	14 29 35 322 XSQ= 16.43 PHI= 0.203 XP = 0.0001
514	TEND TO BE THOSE 0.61 OF 49 INCLUDED IN PHILIP E. SLATER'S STUDY OF NARCISSISM (90)	514	TEND TO BE THOSE 0.83 OF 351 NOT INCLUDED IN PHILIP E. SLATER'S STUDY OF NARCISSISM (310)	30 60 19 291 XSQ= 45.52 PHI= 0.337 XP = 0.
515	LEAN LESS TOWARD BEING THOSE 0.71 OF 49 NOT INCLUDED IN WILLIAM N. STEPHENS' SAMPLE ON AVOIDANCE RELATIONSHIPS (348)	515	LEAN MORE TOWARD BEING THOSE 0.89 OF 351 NOT INCLUDED IN WILLIAM N. STEPHENS' SAMPLE ON AVOIDANCE RELATIONSHIPS (348)	14 38 35 313 XSQ= 10.45 PHI= 0.162 XP = 0.0012
516	TILT MORE TOWARD BEING THOSE 0.94 OF 49 INCLUDED IN GUY E. SWANSON'S SAMPLE ON LOCAL JURISDICTION, AS MODIFIED BY THE ETHNOGRAPHIC ATLAS (331)	516	TILT LESS TOWARD BEING THOSE 0.81 OF 351 INCLUDED IN GUY E. SWANSON'S SAMPLE ON LOCAL JURISDICTION, AS MODIFIED BY THE ETHNOGRAPHIC ATLAS (331)	46 285 3 66 XSQ= 4.00 PHI= 0.100 XP = 0.0456
517	LEAN MORE TOWARD BEING THOSE 0.86 OF 49 INCLUDED IN GUY E. SWANSON'S SAMPLE ON HIGH GODS, AS MODIFIED BY THE ETHNOGRAPHIC ATLAS (260)	517	LEAN LESS TOWARD BEING THOSE 0.62 OF 351 INCLUDED IN GUY E. SWANSON'S SAMPLE ON HIGH GODS, AS MODIFIED BY THE ETHNOGRAPHIC ATLAS (260)	42 218 7 133 XSQ= 9.52 PHI= 0.154 XP = 0.0020
518	TEND TO BE THOSE 0.57 OF 49 INCLUDED IN STANLEY H. UDY, JR.'S STUDY OF WORK ORGANIZATION (105)	518	TEND TO BE THOSE 0.78 OF 351 NOT INCLUDED IN STANLEY H. UDY, JR.'S STUDY OF WORK ORGANIZATION (295)	28 77 21 274 XSQ= 25.74 PHI= 0.254 XP = 0.0000
519	TEND LESS TO BE THOSE 0.76 OF 49 NOT INCLUDED IN JOSEPH VEROFF'S STUDY OF ACHIEVEMENT MOTIVATION AS REVEALED IN FOLKTALES (364)	519	TEND MORE TO BE THOSE 0.93 OF 351 NOT INCLUDED IN JOSEPH VEROFF'S STUDY OF ACHIEVEMENT MOTIVATION AS REVEALED IN FOLKTALES (364)	12 24 37 327 XSQ= 14.27 PHI= 0.189 XP = 0.0002

520	TEND LESS TO BE THCSE NOT INCLUDED IN BEATRICE BLYTH WHITING'S STUDY OF SORCERY (360)	0.57 OF 49	TEND MORE TO BE THOSE NOT INCLUDED IN BEATRICE BLYTH WHITING'S STUDY OF SORCERY (360)	0.95 OF 351	21 19 28 332 XSQ= 62.89 PHI= 0.397 XP = 0.
521	TEND LESS TO BE THCSE NOT INCLUDED IN JOHN W. M. WHITING'S STUDY OF SCCIALIZATION PROCESS AND PERSCNALITY (353)	0.55 OF 49	TEND MORE TO BE THOSE NOT INCLUDED IN JOHN W. M. WHITING'S STUDY OF SOCIALIZATION PROCESS AND PERSONALITY (353)	0.93 OF 351	22 25 27 326 XSQ= 55.58 PHI= 0.373 XP = 0.
522	TEND LESS TO BE THCSE NCT INCLUDED IN MARJCRIE GRANT WHITING'S STUDY OF DIET (318)	0.51 OF 49	TEND MORE TO BE THOSE NOT INCLUDED IN MARJORIE GRANT WHITING'S STUDY OF DIET (318)	0.83 OF 351	24 58 25 293 XSQ= 25.83 PHI= 0.254 XP = 0.0000
523	TEND LESS TO BE THCSE NOT INCLUDED IN WHITING AND CHILD'S STUDY OF CHILD TRAINING AND PERSCNALITY (339)	0.51 OF 49	TEND MORE TO BE THOSE NOT INCLUDED IN WHITING AND CHILD'S STUDY OF CHILD TRAINING AND PERSONALITY (339)	0.89 OF 351	24 37 25 314 XSQ= 46.23 PHI= 0.340 XP = 0.
524	TEND LESS TO BE THCSE NOT INCLUDED IN WHITING, KLUCKHCHN, ANC ANTHONY'S STUDY OF MALE INITIATICN CEREMONIES (356)	0.71 OF 49	TEND MORE TO BE THOSE NOT INCLUDED IN WHITING, KLUCKHOHN, AND ANTHONY'S STUDY OF MALE INITIATION CEREMONIES (356)	0.91 OF 351	14 30 35 321 XSQ= 15.62 PHI= 0.198 XP = 0.0001

505 CULTURES INCLUDED IN MERRILL JACKSON'S STUDY OF CRIMINAL LAW AND MEDICINE (20)

505 CULTURES NOT INCLUDED IN MERRILL JACKSON'S STUDY OF CRIMINAL LAW AND MEDICINE (380)

BACKGROUND ON PAGE 180

SUBJECT ONLY, F.C. 1-480 AND 527-536
BOTH SUBJECT AND PREDICATE, F.C. 481-526

20 IN LEFT COLUMN

ANDAMANESE BEMBA BURMESE COMANCHE COPR ESKIMO JAVANESE JIVARO KIKUYU KUNG LAMBA MUNDURUCU MURNGIN NAMA NAVAHO NUPE SAMOANS SIUAI THAI TROBRIAND VIETNAMESE

380 IN RIGHT COLUMN

107	DRIFT LESS TOWARD BEING THOSE WHERE CLASS STRATIFICATION, IF PRESENT, IS BASED ON SOMETHING OTHER THAN OCCUPATIONAL STATUS (160)	0.55 OF 11	107	DRIFT MORE TOWARD BEING THOSE WHERE CLASS STRATIFICATION, IF PRESENT, IS BASED ON SOMETHING OTHER THAN OCCUPATIONAL STATUS (160)	0.80 OF 192	5 38 6 154 XSQ= 2.71 PHI= 0.116 XP = 0.0997
144	IN ALL CASES ARE THOSE WHERE THE RATIO OF RESTITUTIVE TO REPRESSIVE SANCTIONS IS LOW (25) WME	1.00 OF 5	144	TILT TOWARD BEING THOSE WHERE THE RATIO OF RESTITUTIVE TO REPRESSIVE SANCTIONS IS HIGH OR MEDIUM (27) WME	0.57 OF 47	0 27 5 20 XSQ= 3.89 PHI= -0.274 XP = 0.0484
197	TILT LESS TOWARD BEING THOSE WHERE RULES FOR THE INHERITANCE OF REAL PROPERTY, IF PRESENT, FAVOR EITHER THE MALE HEIR OR LINE, OR THE FEMALE HEIR OR LINE (165)	0.56 OF 9	197	TILT MORE TOWARD BEING THOSE WHERE RULES FOR THE INHERITANCE OF REAL PROPERTY, IF PRESENT, FAVOR EITHER THE MALE HEIR OR LINE, OR THE FEMALE HEIR OR LINE (165)	0.86 OF 185	5 160 4 25 XSQ= 4.25 PHI= -0.148 XP = 0.0391
198	TILT TOWARD BEING THOSE WHERE RULES FOR THE INHERITANCE OF REAL PROPERTY, IF PRESENT, FAVOR THE FEMALE HEIR OR LINE, RATHER THAN THE MALE (21)	0.60 OF 5	198	TILT TOWARD BEING THOSE WHERE RULES FOR THE INHERITANCE OF REAL PROPERTY, IF PRESENT, FAVOR THE MALE HEIR OR LINE, RATHER THAN THE FEMALE (144)	0.89 OF 160	2 142 3 18 XSQ= 6.45 PHI= -0.198 XP = 0.0111
201	TILT LESS TOWARD BEING THOSE WHERE MARITAL RESIDENCE IS NON-OPTIONAL, RATHER THAN AMBILOCAL OR NEOLOCAL (334)	0.65 OF 20	201	TILT MORE TOWARD BEING THOSE WHERE MARITAL RESIDENCE IS NON-OPTIONAL, RATHER THAN AMBILOCAL OR NEOLOCAL (334)	0.85 OF 378	13 321 7 57 XSQ= 4.21 PHI= -0.103 XP = 0.0403
204	TILT LESS TOWARD BEING THOSE WHERE MARITAL RESIDENCE IS PATRILOCAL, VIRILOCAL, OR AVUNCULOCAL, RATHER THAN AMBILOCAL OR NEOLOCAL (270)	0.53 OF 15	204	TILT MORE TOWARD BEING THOSE WHERE MARITAL RESIDENCE IS PATRILOCAL, VIRILOCAL, OR AVUNCULOCAL, RATHER THAN AMBILOCAL OR NEOLOCAL (270)	0.82 OF 319	8 262 7 57 XSQ= 5.92 PHI= -0.133 XP = 0.0149

277	IN ALL CASES ARE THOSE 1.00 OF 7 WHERE THE STATUS OF WOMEN IS NOT STRONGLY INFERIOR OR SUBJECTED (22) LWS	277	TILT LESS TOWARD BEING THOSE 0.52 OF 29 WHERE THE STATUS OF WOMEN IS NOT STRONGLY INFERIOR OR SUBJECTED (22) LWS	0 14 7 15 XSQ= 3.68 PHI= -0.320 EP = 0.0288
335	DRIFT TOWARD BEING THOSE 0.86 OF 7 WHERE INITIAL INDULGENCE OF DEPENDENCY IS HIGH (20) WNS	335	DRIFT TOWARD BEING THOSE 0.55 OF 31 WHERE INITIAL INDULGENCE OF DEPENDENCY IS LOW (18) WNS	6 14 1 17 XSQ= 2.32 PHI= 0.247 EP = 0.0934
382	DRIFT MORE TOWARD BEING THOSE 0.90 OF 10 WHERE FEMALE INITIATION RITES ARE PRESENT (38) JKB	382	DRIFT LESS TOWARD BEING THOSE 0.53 OF 55 WHERE FEMALE INITIATION RITES ARE PRESENT (38) JKB	9 29 1 26 XSQ= 3.43 PHI= 0.230 XP = 0.0641
435	DRIFT TOWARD BEING THOSE 0.71 OF 7 WHERE ABANDONMENT OF THE HOUSE OF THE DEAD IS PRACTICED (12) LWS	435	DRIFT TOWARD BEING THOSE 0.71 OF 24 WHERE ABANDONMENT OF THE HOUSE OF THE DEAD IS NOT PRACTICED (19) LWS	5 7 2 17 XSQ= 2.49 PHI= 0.284 EP = 0.0776
489	TEND LESS TO BE THOSE 0.55 OF 20 NOT INCLUDED IN CHARLES ACKERMAN'S STUDY OF DIVORCE (343)	489	TEND MORE TO BE THOSE 0.87 OF 380 NOT INCLUDED IN CHARLES ACKERMAN'S STUDY OF DIVORCE (343)	9 48 11 332 XSQ= 13.75 PHI= 0.185 XP = 0.0002
492	TILT LESS TOWARD BEING THOSE 0.75 OF 20 NOT INCLUDED IN BARBARA CHARTIER AYRES' STUDY OF FEMALE INITIATION RITES (361)	492	TILT MORE TOWARD BEING THOSE 0.91 OF 380 NOT INCLUDED IN BARBARA CHARTIER AYRES' STUDY OF FEMALE INITIATION RITES (361)	5 34 15 346 XSQ= 3.89 PHI= 0.099 XP = 0.0486
493	LEAN LESS TOWARD BEING THOSE 0.55 OF 20 NOT INCLUDED IN BACON, BARRY, AND CHILD'S STUDY OF CHILD REARING (322)	493	LEAN MORE TOWARD BEING THOSE 0.82 OF 380 NOT INCLUDED IN BACON, BARRY, AND CHILD'S STUDY OF CHILD REARING (322)	9 69 11 311 XSQ= 7.09 PHI= 0.133 XP = 0.0077
494	TEND LESS TO BE THOSE 0.70 OF 20 NOT INCLUDED IN HERBERT M. BARRY III'S STUDY OF ART (371)	494	TEND MORE TO BE THOSE 0.94 OF 380 NOT INCLUDED IN HERBERT M. BARRY III'S STUDY OF ART (371)	6 23 14 357 XSQ= 12.84 PHI= 0.179 XP = 0.0003
495	TEND TO BE THOSE 0.50 OF 20 INCLUDED IN JUDITH K. BROWN'S STUDY OF FEMALE INITIATION RITES (65)	495	TEND TO BE THOSE 0.86 OF 380 NOT INCLUDED IN JUDITH K. BROWN'S STUDY OF FEMALE INITIATION RITES (335)	10 55 10 325 XSQ= 15.11 PHI= 0.194 XP = 0.0001

No.		No.		
496	TEND TO BE THOSE 0.55 OF 20 INCLUDED IN ROY G. D'ANDRADE'S STUDY OF DREAMS (55)	496	TEND TO BE THOSE 0.88 OF 380 NOT INCLUDED IN ROY G. D'ANDRADE'S STUDY OF DREAMS (345)	11 44 9 336 XSQ= 26.66 PHI= 0.258 XP = 0.0000
498	TILT LESS TOWARD BEING THOSE 0.70 OF 20 NOT INCLUDED IN C. S. FORD'S STUDY OF SEX (349)	498	TILT MORE TOWARD BEING THOSE 0.88 OF 380 NOT INCLUDED IN C. S. FORD'S STUDY OF SEX (349)	6 45 14 335 XSQ= 4.12 PHI= 0.101 XP = 0.0424
500	LEAN LESS TOWARD BEING THOSE 0.70 OF 20 NOT INCLUDED IN FREEMAN AND WINCH'S STUDY OF SOCIETAL COMPLEXITY (360)	500	LEAN MORE TOWARD BEING THOSE 0.91 OF 380 NOT INCLUDED IN FREEMAN AND WINCH'S STUDY OF SOCIETAL COMPLEXITY (360)	6 34 14 346 XSQ= 7.16 PHI= 0.134 XP = 0.0074
502	TILT LESS TOWARD BEING THOSE 0.65 OF 20 NOT INCLUDED IN JOHN K. HARLEY'S STUDY OF ADOLESCENT PEER GROUPS (343)	502	TILT MORE TOWARD BEING THOSE 0.87 OF 380 NOT INCLUDED IN JOHN K. HARLEY'S STUDY OF ADOLESCENT PEER GROUPS (343)	7 50 13 330 XSQ= 5.74 PHI= 0.120 XP = 0.0166
503	TEND TO BE THOSE 0.50 OF 20 INCLUDED IN JOHN M. HICKMAN'S STUDY OF THE FOLK-URBAN CONTINUUM (54)	503	TEND TO BE THOSE 0.88 OF 380 NOT INCLUDED IN JOHN M. HICKMAN'S STUDY OF THE FOLK-URBAN CONTINUUM (346)	10 44 10 336 XSQ= 20.84 PHI= 0.228 XP = 0.0000
507	TEND TO BE THOSE 0.65 OF 20 INCLUDED IN JAMES R. LEARY'S STUDY OF FOOD TABOOS (86)	507	TEND TO BE THOSE 0.81 OF 380 NOT INCLUDED IN JAMES R. LEARY'S STUDY OF FOOD TABOOS (314)	13 73 7 307 XSQ= 20.97 PHI= 0.229 XP = 0.0000
512	TEND LESS TO BE THOSE 0.65 OF 20 NOT INCLUDED IN SHIRLEY AND ROMNEY'S STUDY OF LOVE MAGIC (367)	512	TEND MORE TO BE THOSE 0.93 OF 380 NOT INCLUDED IN SHIRLEY AND ROMNEY'S STUDY OF LOVE MAGIC (367)	7 26 13 354 XSQ= 16.36 PHI= 0.202 XP = 0.0001
513	LEAN LESS TOWARD BEING THOSE 0.65 OF 20 NOT INCLUDED IN LEO W. SIMMONS' STUDY OF THE TREATMENT OF THE AGED (357)	513	LEAN MORE TOWARD BEING THOSE 0.91 OF 380 NOT INCLUDED IN LEO W. SIMMONS' STUDY OF THE TREATMENT OF THE AGED (357)	7 36 13 344 XSQ= 10.38 PHI= 0.161 XP = 0.0013
514	TEND TO BE THOSE 0.55 OF 20 INCLUDED IN PHILIP E. SLATER'S STUDY OF NARCISSISM (90)	514	TEND TO BE THOSE 0.79 OF 380 NOT INCLUDED IN PHILIP E. SLATER'S STUDY OF NARCISSISM (310)	11 79 9 301 XSQ= 10.87 PHI= 0.165 XP = 0.0010

No.		No.		
515	TEND LESS TO BE THOSE 0.60 OF 20 NOT INCLUDED IN WILLIAM N. STEPHENS' SAMPLE ON AVOIDANCE RELATIONSHIPS (348)	515	TEND MORE TO BE THOSE 0.88 OF 380 NOT INCLUDED IN WILLIAM N. STEPHENS' SAMPLE ON AVOIDANCE RELATIONSHIPS (348)	8 44 12 336 XSQ= 11.17 PHI= 0.167 XP = 0.0008
517	DRIFT MORE TOWARD BEING THOSE 0.85 OF 20 INCLUDED IN GUY E. SWANSON'S SAMPLE ON HIGH GODS, AS MODIFIED BY THE ETHNOGRAPHIC ATLAS (260)	517	DRIFT LESS TOWARD BEING THOSE 0.64 OF 380 INCLUDED IN GUY E. SWANSON'S SAMPLE ON HIGH GODS, AS MODIFIED BY THE ETHNOGRAPHIC ATLAS (260)	17 243 3 137 XSQ= 2.83 PHI= 0.084 XP = 0.0923
518	TEND TO BE THOSE 0.65 OF 20 INCLUDED IN STANLEY H. UDY, JR.'S STUDY OF WORK ORGANIZATION (105)	518	TEND TO BE THOSE 0.76 OF 380 NOT INCLUDED IN STANLEY H. UDY, JR.'S STUDY OF WORK ORGANIZATION (295)	13 92 7 288 XSQ= 14.29 PHI= 0.189 XP = 0.0002
520	LEAN LESS TOWARD BEING THOSE 0.70 OF 20 NOT INCLUDED IN BEATRICE BLYTH WHITING'S STUDY OF SORCERY (360)	520	LEAN MORE TOWARD BEING THOSE 0.91 OF 380 NOT INCLUDED IN BEATRICE BLYTH WHITING'S STUDY OF SORCERY (360)	6 34 14 346 XSQ= 7.16 PHI= 0.134 XP = 0.0074
522	DRIFT LESS TOWARD BEING THOSE 0.60 OF 20 NOT INCLUDED IN MARJORIE GRANT WHITING'S STUDY OF DIET (318)	522	DRIFT MORE TOWARD BEING THOSE 0.81 OF 380 NOT INCLUDED IN MARJORIE GRANT WHITING'S STUDY OF DIET (318)	8 74 12 306 XSQ= 3.73 PHI= 0.097 XP = 0.0533
523	TEND LESS TO BE THOSE 0.55 OF 20 NOT INCLUDED IN WHITING AND CHILD'S STUDY OF CHILD TRAINING AND PERSONALITY (339)	523	TEND MORE TO BE THOSE 0.86 OF 380 NOT INCLUDED IN WHITING AND CHILD'S STUDY OF CHILD TRAINING AND PERSONALITY (339)	9 52 11 328 XSQ= 12.10 PHI= 0.174 XP = 0.0005
524	TILT LESS TOWARD BEING THOSE 0.70 OF 20 NOT INCLUDED IN WHITING, KLUCKHOHN, AND ANTHONY'S STUDY OF MALE INITIATION CEREMONIES (356)	524	TILT MORE TOWARD BEING THOSE 0.90 OF 380 NOT INCLUDED IN WHITING, KLUCKHOHN, AND ANTHONY'S STUDY OF MALE INITIATION CEREMONIES (356)	6 38 14 342 XSQ= 5.85 PHI= 0.121 XP = 0.0155

```
506  CULTURES                                              506  CULTURES
     INCLUDED IN                                                NOT INCLUDED IN
     LAMBERT, TRIANDIS, AND WOLF'S                              LAMBERT, TRIANDIS, AND WOLF'S
     STUDY OF SUPERNATURAL BEINGS  (36)                         STUDY OF SUPERNATURAL BEINGS  (364)

                                                              SUBJECT ONLY, F.C. 1-480 AND 527-536
BACKGROUND ON PAGE 180                                   BOTH SUBJECT AND PREDICATE, F.C. 481-526

       36  IN LEFT COLUMN

ALORESE    ANDAMANESE   ARAPESH    ASHANTI    AYMARA    CHAGGA    CHENCHU   CHEYENNE    CHIR-APACHE COMANCHE
FON        HANC         KURTATCHI  KWAKIUTL   LEPCHA    LESU      MANUS     MAORI       MBUNDU      NAVAHO
OJIBWA     ONTONG-JAVA  PAPAGO     PUKAPUKA   SAMOANS   SIRIONO   TALLENSI  TENETEHARA  TETON       THONGA
TIKOPIA    VENDA        WINNEBAGO  WOGEO      YAGUA     ZUNI

      364  IN RIGHT COLUMN

-----------------------------------------------------------------------------------------------------------
  4  IN ALL CASES ARE THOSE         1.00 OF  36      4  TILT LESS TOWARD BEING THOSE   0.88 OF 364       0   45
     LOCATED OUTSIDE OF                                 LOCATED OUTSIDE OF                              36  319
     THE CIRCUM-MEDITERRANEAN  (355)                    THE CIRCUM-MEDITERRANEAN  (355)          XSQ=     3.85
                                                                                                 PHI=   -0.098
                                                                                                 XP =   0.0497

  6  DRIFT LESS TOWARD BEING THOSE  0.69 OF  36      6  DRIFT MORE TOWARD BEING THOSE  0.84 OF 364      11   59
     LOCATED OUTSIDE OF                                 LOCATED OUTSIDE OF                              25  305
     THE INSULAR PACIFIC  (330)                         THE INSULAR PACIFIC  (330)               XSQ=     3.73
                                                                                                 PHI=    0.097
                                                                                                 XP =   0.0535

  8  DRIFT LESS TOWARD BEING THOSE  0.69 OF  36      8  DRIFT MORE TOWARD BEING THOSE  0.84 OF 364      11   59
     LOCATED OUTSIDE OF                                 LOCATED OUTSIDE OF                              25  305
     NORTH AMERICA  (330)                               NORTH AMERICA  (330)                     XSQ=     3.73
                                                                                                 PHI=    0.097
                                                                                                 XP =   0.0535

 63  TILT TOWARD BEING THOSE        0.54 OF  24     63  TILT TOWARD BEING THOSE        0.70 OF 202      11  141
     WHERE HUSBANDRY, IF PRESENT,                       WHERE HUSBANDRY, IF PRESENT,                    13   61
     IS PRINCIPALLY IN THE FORM OF                      IS PRINCIPALLY IN THE FORM OF            XSQ=     4.56
     PIGS, SHEEP, OR GOATS, RATHER THAN                 BOVINE, EQUINE, CAMEL-LIKE, OR DEER-LIKE PHI=   -0.142
     BOVINE, EQUINE, CAMEL-LIKE, OR DEER-LIKE           ANIMALS, RATHER THAN                     XP =   0.0327
     ANIMALS  (74)                                      PIGS, SHEEP, OR GOATS  (152)

 86  DRIFT TOWARD BEING THOSE       0.69 OF  29     86  DRIFT TOWARD BEING THOSE       0.51 OF 275       9  139
     WHERE THE LEVEL OF POLITICAL INTEGRATION           WHERE THE LEVEL OF POLITICAL INTEGRATION        20  136
     IS THE AUTONOMOUS COMMUNITY, OR                    IS THE LARGE STATE, THE LITTLE STATE,    XSQ=     3.25
     THE FAMILY  (156) GPM                              OR THE MINIMAL STATE  (148) GPM          PHI=   -0.103
                                                                                                 XP =   0.0712
```

91	DRIFT TOWARD BEING THOSE WHERE SOCIETAL COMPLEXITY IS HIGH (18) F-W	0.67 OF 12	91	DRIFT TOWARD BEING THOSE WHERE SOCIETAL COMPLEXITY IS LOW (22) F-W	0.64 OF 28	8 10 4 18 XSQ= 2.12 PHI= 0.230 EP = 0.0927
98	DRIFT MORE TOWARD BEING THOSE WHERE THE HIERARCHY OF LOCAL JURISDICTION HAS FOUR OR THREE LEVELS (238) GES,EA	0.88 OF 33	98	DRIFT LESS TOWARD BEING THOSE WHERE THE HIERARCHY OF LOCAL JURISDICTION HAS FOUR OR THREE LEVELS (238) GES,EA	0.70 OF 298	29 209 4 89 XSQ= 3.79 PHI= 0.107 XP = 0.0514
99	DRIFT MORE TOWARD BEING THOSE WHERE, WITH NATIONAL HIERARCHY ABSENT, THE HIERARCHY OF LOCAL JURISDICTION HAS FOUR OR THREE LEVELS (93) GES,EA	0.83 OF 18	99	DRIFT LESS TOWARD BEING THOSE WHERE, WITH NATIONAL HIERARCHY ABSENT, THE HIERARCHY OF LOCAL JURISDICTION HAS FOUR OR THREE LEVELS (93) GES,EA	0.57 OF 138	15 78 3 60 XSQ= 3.71 PHI= 0.154 XP = 0.0542
107	IN ALL CASES ARE THOSE WHERE CLASS STRATIFICATION, IF PRESENT, IS BASED ON SOMETHING OTHER THAN OCCUPATIONAL STATUS (160)	1.00 OF 17	107	DRIFT LESS TOWARD BEING THOSE WHERE CLASS STRATIFICATION, IF PRESENT, IS BASED ON SOMETHING OTHER THAN OCCUPATIONAL STATUS (160)	0.77 OF 186	0 43 17 143 XSQ= 3.70 PHI= -0.135 XP = 0.0545
108	TILT TOWARD BEING THOSE WHERE CLASS STRATIFICATION, IF PRESENT, IS BASED ON A HEREDITARY ARISTOCRACY (74)	0.65 OF 17	108	TILT TOWARD BEING THOSE WHERE CLASS STRATIFICATION, IF PRESENT, IS BASED ON SOMETHING OTHER THAN A HEREDITARY ARISTOCRACY (129)	0.66 OF 186	11 63 6 123 XSQ= 5.13 PHI= 0.159 XP = 0.0235
109	IN ALL CASES ARE THOSE WHERE CASTES ARE ABSENT (317)	1.00 OF 35	109	TILT LESS TOWARD BEING THOSE WHERE CASTES ARE ABSENT (317)	0.85 OF 333	0 51 35 282 XSQ= 5.01 PHI= -0.117 XP = 0.0253
128	TILT TOWARD BEING THOSE WHERE, IF SUBSISTENCE IS PRIMARILY BY AGRICULTURE, THE WORK IS MAINLY DONE BY FEMALES (37)	0.88 OF 8	128	TILT TOWARD BEING THOSE WHERE, IF SUBSISTENCE IS PRIMARILY BY AGRICULTURE, THE WORK IS MAINLY DONE BY MALES (40)	0.57 OF 69	1 39 7 30 XSQ= 3.94 PHI= -0.226 XP = 0.0471
213	LEAN MORE TOWARD BEING THOSE WHERE FIRST COUSIN MARRIAGE IS NOT PERMITTED (198)	0.78 OF 36	213	LEAN LESS TOWARD BEING THOSE WHERE FIRST COUSIN MARRIAGE IS NOT PERMITTED (198)	0.51 OF 334	8 164 28 170 XSQ= 8.39 PHI= -0.151 XP = 0.0038
259	DRIFT TOWARD BEING THOSE WHERE THE SEVERITY OF MOTHER-IN-LAW AVOIDANCE IS LOW (20) WNS	0.60 OF 20	259	DRIFT TOWARD BEING THOSE WHERE THE SEVERITY OF MOTHER-IN-LAW AVOIDANCE IS HIGH (26) WNS	0.69 OF 26	8 18 12 8 XSQ= 2.83 PHI= -0.248 XP = 0.0925

280	DRIFT TOWARD BEING THOSE WHERE THE COMPOSITE FERTILITY LEVEL IS HIGH (13) MN	0.78 OF 9	DRIFT TOWARD BEING THOSE WHERE THE COMPOSITE FERTILITY LEVEL IS LOW (12) MN	0.63 OF 16	7 6 2 10 XSQ= 2.30 PHI= 0.304 EP = 0.0968
312	DRIFT TOWARD BEING THOSE WHERE DEPENDENCE SOCIALIZATION ANXIETY IS LOW (23) W-C	0.61 OF 28	DRIFT TOWARD BEING THOSE WHERE DEPENDENCE SOCIALIZATION ANXIETY IS HIGH (24) W-C	0.68 OF 19	11 13 17 6 XSQ= 2.77 PHI= -0.243 XP = 0.0962
343	TILT TOWARD BEING THOSE WHERE THE CHILD'S INFERRED CONFLICT REGARDING NURTURANT BEHAVIOR IS LOW (18) B-B-C	0.52 OF 29	TILT TOWARD BEING THOSE WHERE THE CHILD'S INFERRED CONFLICT REGARDING NURTURANT BEHAVIOR IS HIGH (29) B-B-C	0.83 OF 18	14 15 15 3 XSQ= 4.39 PHI= -0.306 XP = 0.0362
347	TILT TOWARD BEING THOSE WHERE THE CHILD'S INFERRED CONFLICT REGARDING SELF-RELIANT BEHAVIOR IS LOW (39) B-B-C	0.66 OF 35	TILT TOWARD BEING THOSE WHERE THE CHILD'S INFERRED CONFLICT REGARDING SELF-RELIANT BEHAVIOR IS HIGH (37) B-B-C	0.61 OF 41	12 25 23 16 XSQ= 4.37 PHI= -0.240 XP = 0.0366
368	DRIFT TOWARD BEING THOSE WHERE DISSOCIATION OF THE SEXES AT ADOLESCENCE IS HIGH OR MEDIUM (16) JKH	0.67 OF 12	DRIFT TOWARD BEING THOSE WHERE DISSOCIATION OF THE SEXES AT ADOLESCENCE IS LOW (21) JKH	0.68 OF 25	8 8 4 17 XSQ= 2.68 PHI= 0.269 EP = 0.0768
398	DRIFT TOWARD BEING THOSE WHERE THE INTENSITY OF SEX ANXIETY IS HIGH (16) WNS	0.67 OF 18	DRIFT TOWARD BEING THOSE WHERE THE INTENSITY OF SEX ANXIETY IS LOW (16) WNS	0.71 OF 14	12 4 6 10 XSQ= 3.17 PHI= 0.315 EP = 0.0732
404	DRIFT LESS TOWARD BEING THOSE WHERE EXPLANATIONS OF ILLNESS OF A SEXUAL NATURE ARE ABSENT (42) W-C	0.55 OF 29	DRIFT MORE TOWARD BEING THOSE WHERE EXPLANATIONS OF ILLNESS OF A SEXUAL NATURE ARE ABSENT (42) W-C	0.81 OF 32	13 6 16 26 XSQ= 3.68 PHI= 0.246 XP = 0.0549
405	DRIFT TOWARD BEING THOSE WHERE EXPLANATIONS OF ILLNESS OF A DEPENDENCE NATURE ARE ABSENT (27) W-C	0.59 OF 29	DRIFT TOWARD BEING THOSE WHERE EXPLANATIONS OF ILLNESS OF A DEPENDENCE NATURE ARE PRESENT (34) W-C	0.69 OF 32	12 22 17 10 XSQ= 3.58 PHI= -0.242 XP = 0.0586
420	TILT TOWARD BEING THOSE WHERE BELLICOSITY IS MODERATE OR NEGLIGIBLE (46) PES	0.71 OF 28	TILT TOWARD BEING THOSE WHERE BELLICOSITY IS EXTREME (41) PES	0.56 OF 59	8 33 20 26 XSQ= 4.66 PHI= -0.231 XP = 0.0309

426	TILT TOWARD BEING THOSE WHERE A HIGH GOD IS ABSENT (104) GES,EA	0.60 OF 30	426	TILT TOWARD BEING THOSE WHERE A HIGH GOD IS PRESENT (156) GES,EA	0.63 OF 230	12 144 18 86 XSQ= 4.75 PHI= -0.135 XP = 0.0293
439	DRIFT TOWARD BEING THOSE WHERE FEAR OF GHOSTS IS HIGH (30) W-C	0.62 OF 29	439	DRIFT TOWARD BEING THOSE WHERE FEAR OF GHOSTS IS LOW (31) W-C	0.63 OF 32	18 12 11 20 XSQ= 2.76 PHI= 0.213 XP = 0.0968
443	TILT TOWARD BEING THOSE WHERE OVERALL FEAR OF OTHERS IS LOW (30) W-C	0.66 OF 29	443	TILT TOWARD BEING THOSE WHERE OVERALL FEAR OF OTHERS IS HIGH (31) W-C	0.66 OF 32	10 21 19 11 XSQ= 4.72 PHI= -0.278 XP = 0.0298
449	TILT TOWARD BEING THOSE WHERE THE OBSERVATION OF FOOD TABOOS IS HIGH, RATHER THAN MEDIUM OR LOW (25) JRL	0.56 OF 16	449	TILT TOWARD BEING THOSE WHERE THE OBSERVATION OF FOOD TABOOS IS MEDIUM OR LOW, RATHER THAN HIGH (61) JRL	0.77 OF 70	9 16 7 54 XSQ= 5.52 PHI= 0.253 XP = 0.0188
476	DRIFT TOWARD BEING THOSE WHERE THE DEGREE OF INSOBRIETY IS MODERATE OR SLIGHT (18) DH	0.64 OF 11	476	DRIFT TOWARD BEING THOSE WHERE THE DEGREE OF INSOBRIETY IS STRONG (31) DH	0.71 OF 38	4 27 7 11 XSQ= 3.05 PHI= -0.250 XP = 0.0807
479	DRIFT TOWARD BEING THOSE WHERE THE NEED TO ACHIEVE, AS INFERRED FROM FOLKTALES, IS LOW (18) JV	0.67 OF 18	479	DRIFT TOWARD BEING THOSE WHERE THE NEED TO ACHIEVE, AS INFERRED FROM FOLKTALES, IS HIGH (18) JV	0.67 OF 18	6 12 12 6 XSQ= 2.78 PHI= -0.278 EP = 0.0564
482	DRIFT LESS TOWARD BEING THOSE WHERE THE PRINCIPAL ETHNOGRAPHERS HAVE BEEN OTHER THAN BRITISH (336)	0.75 OF 36	482	DRIFT MORE TOWARD BEING THOSE WHERE THE PRINCIPAL ETHNOGRAPHERS HAVE BEEN OTHER THAN BRITISH (336)	0.88 OF 352	9 43 27 309 XSQ= 3.56 PHI= 0.096 XP = 0.0591
488	DRIFT MORE TOWARD BEING THOSE ABOUT WHICH THE PRINCIPAL ETHNOGRAPHIES WERE PUBLISHED BEFORE 1950 (185)	0.89 OF 28	488	DRIFT LESS TOWARD BEING THOSE ABOUT WHICH THE PRINCIPAL ETHNOGRAPHIES WERE PUBLISHED BEFORE 1950 (185)	0.70 OF 229	25 160 3 69 XSQ= 3.75 PHI= 0.121 XP = 0.0528
489	LEAN LESS TOWARD BEING THOSE NOT INCLUDED IN CHARLES ACKERMAN'S STUDY OF DIVORCE (343)	0.69 OF 36	489	LEAN MORE TOWARD BEING THOSE NOT INCLUDED IN CHARLES ACKERMAN'S STUDY OF DIVORCE (343)	0.87 OF 364	11 46 25 318 XSQ= 7.20 PHI= 0.134 XP = 0.0073

490	TEND TO BE THOSE 0.92 OF 36 INCLUDED IN ALBERT S. ANTHCNY'S SAMPLE ON MALE INITIATICN RITES (113)	490	TEND TO BE THOSE 0.78 OF 364 NOT INCLUDED IN ALBERT S. ANTHCNY'S SAMPLE ON MALE INITIATICN RITES (287)	33 80 3 284 XSQ= 75.09 PHI= 0.433 XP = 0.
491	TEND TO BE THCSE 0.50 OF 36 INCLUDED IN DORRIAN APPLE'S STUDY OF GRANDPARENTHCOD (48)	491	TEND TO BE THOSE 0.92 OF 364 NOT INCLUDED IN DORRIAN APPLE'S STUDY OF GRANDPARENTHOOD (352)	18 30 18 334 XSQ= 50.21 PHI= 0.354 XP = 0.
492	TEND TO BE THOSE 0.64 OF 36 INCLUDED IN BARBARA CHARTIER AYRES' STUDY OF FEMALE INITIATION RITES (39)	492	TEND TO BE THOSE 0.96 OF 364 NOT INCLUDED IN BARBARA CHARTIER AYRES' STUDY OF FEMALE INITIATICN RITES (361)	23 16 13 348 XSQ= 125.10 PHI= 0.559 XP = 0.
493	IN ALL CASES ARE THCSE 1.00 OF 36 INCLUDED IN BACCN, BARRY, AND CHILC'S STUDY OF CHILD REARING (78)	493	TEND TO BE THOSE 0.88 OF 364 NOT INCLUDED IN BACON, BARRY, AND CHILD'S STUDY OF CHILD REARING (322)	36 42 0 322 XSQ= 157.73 PHI= 0.628 XP = 0.
494	TEND TO BE THOSE 0.50 OF 36 INCLUDED IN HERBERT M. BARRY III'S STUDY OF ART (29)	494	TEND TO BE THOSE 0.97 OF 364 NOT INCLUDED IN HERBERT M. BARRY III'S STUDY OF ART (371)	18 11 18 353 XSQ= 100.65 PHI= 0.502 XP = 0.
495	TEND LESS TO BE THCSE 0.56 OF 36 NOT INCLUDED IN JUCITH K. BROWN'S STUDY OF FEMALE INITIATION RITES (335)	495	TEND MORE TO BE THOSE 0.87 OF 364 NOT INCLUDED IN JUDITH K. BROWN'S STUDY OF FEMALE INITIATICN RITES (335)	16 49 20 315 XSQ= 20.89 PHI= 0.229 XP = 0.0000
496	TEND LESS TO BE THCSE 0.67 OF 36 NOT INCLUDED IN ROY G. D'ANDRADE'S STUDY CF DREAMS (345)	496	TEND MORE TO BE THOSE 0.88 OF 364 NOT INCLUDED IN ROY G. D'ANDRADE'S STUDY OF DREAMS (345)	12 43 24 321 XSQ= 11.04 PHI= 0.166 XP = 0.0009
497	LEAN LESS TOWARD BEING THCSE 0.67 OF 36 NOT INCLUDED IN WILLIAM M. EVAN'S STUDY OF LAW (339)	497	LEAN MORE TOWARD BEING THOSE 0.87 CF 364 NOT INCLUDED IN WILLIAM M. EVAN'S STUDY OF LAW (339)	12 49 24 315 XSQ= 8.53 PHI= 0.146 XP = 0.0035
498	TEND LESS TO BE THCSE 0.64 OF 36 NOT INCLUDED IN C. S. FORC'S STUDY CF SEX (349)	498	TEND MORE TO BE THOSE 0.90 OF 364 NOT INCLUDED IN C. S. FORD'S STUDY OF SEX (349)	13 38 23 326 XSQ= 17.17 PHI= 0.207 XP = 0.0000

499	TEND TO BE THOSE INCLUDED IN FORD AND BEACH'S SAMPLE ON SEXUAL EXPRESSION BY THE YOUNG (86)	0.69 OF 36	499	TEND TO BE THOSE NOT INCLUDED IN FORD AND BEACH'S SAMPLE ON SEXUAL EXPRESSION BY THE YOUNG (314)	0.83 OF 364	25 61 11 303 XSQ= 50.80 PHI= 0.356 XP = 0.
500	TEND LESS TO BE THOSE NOT INCLUDED IN FREEMAN AND WINCH'S STUDY OF SOCIETAL COMPLEXITY (360)	0.67 OF 36	500	TEND MORE TO BE THOSE NOT INCLUDED IN FREEMAN AND WINCH'S STUDY OF SOCIETAL COMPLEXITY (360)	0.92 OF 364	12 28 24 336 XSQ= 21.17 PHI= 0.230 XP = 0.0000
501	TEND TO BE THOSE INCLUDED IN JOAN FRIENDLY GOODMAN'S STUDY OF ASCETIC MOURNING BEHAVIOR (67)	0.67 OF 36	501	TEND TO BE THOSE NOT INCLUDED IN JOAN FRIENDLY GOODMAN'S STUDY OF ASCETIC MOURNING BEHAVIOR (333)	0.88 OF 364	24 43 12 321 XSQ= 66.81 PHI= 0.409 XP = 0.
502	TEND TO BE THOSE INCLUDED IN JOHN K. HARLEY'S STUDY OF ADOLESCENT PEER GROUPS (57)	0.50 OF 36	502	TEND TO BE THOSE NOT INCLUDED IN JOHN K. HARLEY'S STUDY OF ADOLESCENT PEER GROUPS (343)	0.89 OF 364	18 39 18 325 XSQ= 38.22 PHI= 0.309 XP = 0.
503	TEND LESS TO BE THOSE NOT INCLUDED IN JOHN M. HICKMAN'S STUDY OF THE FOLK-URBAN CONTINUUM (346)	0.67 OF 36	503	TEND MORE TO BE THOSE NOT INCLUDED IN JOHN M. HICKMAN'S STUDY OF THE FOLK-URBAN CONTINUUM (346)	0.88 OF 364	12 42 24 322 XSQ= 11.53 PHI= 0.170 XP = 0.0007
504	LEAN LESS TOWARD BEING THOSE NOT INCLUDED IN DONALD HORTON'S STUDY OF ALCHOLISM (351)	0.69 OF 36	504	LEAN MORE TOWARD BEING THOSE NOT INCLUDED IN DONALD HORTON'S STUDY OF ALCHOLISM (351)	0.90 OF 364	11 38 25 326 XSQ= 10.53 PHI= 0.162 XP = 0.0012
507	TEND LESS TO BE THOSE NOT INCLUDED IN JAMES R. LEARY'S STUDY OF FOOD TABOOS (314)	0.56 OF 36	507	TEND MORE TO BE THOSE NOT INCLUDED IN JAMES R. LEARY'S STUDY OF FOOD TABOOS (314)	0.81 OF 364	16 70 20 294 XSQ= 10.89 PHI= 0.165 XP = 0.0010
508	TEND TO BE THOSE INCLUDED IN DAVID C. MCCLELLAND'S STUDY OF ACHIEVEMENT MOTIVATION (40)	0.61 OF 36	508	TEND TO BE THOSE NOT INCLUDED IN DAVID C. MCCLELLAND'S STUDY OF ACHIEVEMENT MOTIVATION (360)	0.95 OF 364	22 18 14 346 XSQ= 108.67 PHI= 0.521 XP = 0.
509	TEND LESS TO BE THOSE NOT INCLUDED IN MONI NAG'S STUDY OF FERTILITY (375)	0.75 OF 36	509	TEND MORE TO BE THOSE NOT INCLUDED IN MONI NAG'S STUDY OF FERTILITY (375)	0.96 OF 364	9 16 27 348 XSQ= 20.35 PHI= 0.226 XP = 0.0000

510	TEND LESS TO BE THCSE NOT INCLUDED IN RACUL NARRCLL'S STUDY OF SCCIETAL COMPLEXITY (380)	0.81 OF 36	510	TEND MORE TO BE THOSE NOT INCLUDED IN RAOUL NARRCLL'S STUDY OF SOCIETAL COMPLEXITY (380)	0.96 OF 364	7 13 29 351 XSQ= 14.20 PHI= 0.188 XP = 0.0002
511	TEND TO BE THCSE INCLUDED IN ROBERTS, ARTH AND BUSH'S SAMPLE ON GAMES, AS MCDIFIED BY THE ETHNOGRAPHIC ATLAS (189)	0.78 OF 36	511	TEND TO BE THOSE NOT INCLUDED IN ROBERTS, ARTH AND BUSH'S SAMPLE ON GAMES, AS MODIFIED BY THE ETHNOGRAPHIC ATLAS (211)	0.56 OF 364	28 161 8 203 XSQ= 13.48 PHI= 0.184 XP = 0.0002
512	TEND TC BE THOSE INCLUDED IN SHIRLEY ANC RCMNEY'S STUDY OF LCVE MAGIC (33)	0.50 OF 36	512	TEND TO BE THOSE NOT INCLUDED IN SHIRLEY AND ROMNEY'S STUDY OF LOVE MAGIC (367)	0.96 OF 364	18 15 18 349 XSQ= 85.14 PHI= 0.461 XP = 0.
513	TILT LESS TOWARD BEING THCSE NOT INCLUDED IN LEC W. SIMMONS' STUDY OF THE TREATMENT OF THE AGEC (357)	0.78 OF 36	513	TILT MORE TOWARD BEING THOSE NOT INCLUDED IN LEO W. SIMMONS' STUDY OF THE TREATMENT OF THE AGED (357)	0.90 OF 364	8 35 28 329 XSQ= 4.19 PHI= 0.102 XP = 0.0406
514	TEND TC BE THOSE INCLUDED IN PHILIP E. SLATER'S STUDY OF NARCISSISM (90)	0.86 OF 36	514	TEND TO BE THOSE NOT INCLUDED IN PHILIP E. SLATER'S STUDY OF NARCISSISM (310)	0.84 OF 364	31 59 5 305 XSQ= 87.84 PHI= 0.469 XP = 0.
515	TEND TO BE THOSE INCLUDED IN WILLIAM N. STEPHENS' SAMPLE ON AVOIDANCE RELATIONSHIPS (52)	0.67 OF 36	515	TEND TO BE THOSE NOT INCLUDED IN WILLIAM N. STEPHENS' SAMPLE ON AVOIDANCE RELATIONSHIPS (348)	0.92 OF 364	24 28 12 336 XSQ= 95.59 PHI= 0.489 XP = 0.
517	TILT MORE TOWARD BEING THOSE INCLUDED IN GUY E. SWANSON'S SAMPLE ON HIGH GODS, AS MODIFIED BY THE ETHNOGRAPHIC ATLAS (260)	0.83 OF 36	517	TILT LESS TOWARD BEING THOSE INCLUDED IN GUY E. SWANSON'S SAMPLE ON HIGH GODS, AS MODIFIED BY THE ETHNOGRAPHIC ATLAS (260)	0.63 OF 364	30 230 6 134 XSQ= 4.99 PHI= 0.112 XP = 0.0255
518	TEND TO BE THOSE INCLUDED IN STANLEY H. UDY, JR.'S STUDY OF WCRK ORGANIZATION (105)	0.67 OF 36	518	TEND TO BE THOSE NOT INCLUDED IN STANLEY H. UDY, JR.'S STUDY OF WORK ORGANIZATION (295)	0.78 OF 364	24 81 12 283 XSQ= 31.13 PHI= 0.279 XP = 0.
519	TEND TO BE THOSE INCLUDED IN JOSEPH VEROFF'S STUDY OF ACHIEVEMENT MCTIVATICN AS REVEALED IN FOLKTALES (36)	0.50 OF 36	519	TEND TO BE THOSE NOT INCLUDED IN JOSEPH VEROFF'S STUDY OF ACHIEVEMENT MOTIVATION AS REVEALED IN FOLKTALES (364)	0.95 OF 364	18 18 18 346 XSQ= 75.79 PHI= 0.435 XP = 0.

```
520  TEND LESS TO BE THCSE            0.64 OF  36     520  TEND MORE TO BE THOSE             0.93 OF 364        13   27
     NOT INCLUDED IN                                       NOT INCLUDED IN                                        23  337
     BEATRICE BLYTH WHITING'S                              BEATRICE BLYTH WHITING'S                         XSQ=   26.87
     STUDY OF SCRCERY  (360)                               STUDY OF SORCERY  (360)                          PHI=   0.259
                                                                                                            XP =  0.0000

521  TEND TO BE THOSE                 0.83 OF  36     521  TEND TO BE THOSE                  0.95 OF 364        30   17
     INCLUDED IN JOHN W. M. WHITING'S                      NOT INCLUDED IN JOHN W. M. WHITING'S                    6  347
     STUDY OF SCCIALIZATION                                STUDY OF SOCIALIZATION                           XSQ=  187.98
     PRCCESS AND PERSCNALITY  (47)                         PROCESS AND PERSONALITY  (353)                   PHI=   0.686
                                                                                                            XP =  0.

522  TEND TO BE THOSE                 0.89 OF  36     522  TEND TO BE THOSE                  0.86 OF 364        32   50
     INCLUDED IN                                           NOT INCLUDED IN                                         4  314
     MARJORIE GRANT WHITING'S                              MARJORIE GRANT WHITING'S                         XSQ=  108.97
     STUDY OF DIET  (82)                                   STUDY OF DIET  (318)                             PHI=   0.522
                                                                                                            XP =  0.

523  TEND TO BE THOSE                 0.81 OF  36     523  TEND TO BE THOSE                  0.91 OF 364        29   32
     INCLUDED IN WHITING ANC CHILC'S                       NOT INCLUDED IN WHITING AND CHILD'S                     7  332
     STUDY OF CHILD TRAINING                               STUDY OF CHILD TRAINING                          XSQ=  125.05
     AND PERSONALITY  (61)                                 AND PERSONALITY  (339)                           PHI=   0.559
                                                                                                            XP =  0.

524  TEND TC BE THOSE                 0.56 OF  36     524  TEND TO BE THOSE                  0.93 OF 364        20   24
     INCLUDED IN                                           NOT INCLUDED IN                                        16  340
     WHITING, KLUCKHCHN, AND ANTHONY'S                     WHITING, KLUCKHOHN, AND ANTHONY'S                XSQ=   75.30
     STUDY OF MALE INITIATICN CEREMONIES  (44)             STUDY OF MALE INITIATION CEREMONIES  (356)       PHI=   0.434
                                                                                                            XP =  0.
```

507 CULTURES INCLUDED IN JAMES R. LEARY'S STUDY OF FOOD TABOOS (86)

507 CULTURES NOT INCLUDED IN JAMES R. LEARY'S STUDY OF FOOD TABOOS (314)

BACKGROUND ON PAGE 180

SUBJECT ONLY, F.C. 1-480 AND 527-536
BOTH SUBJECT AND PREDICATE, F.C. 481-526

86 IN LEFT COLUMN

ANDAMANESE	ARANDA	ARAUCANIANS	AWEIKOMA	AYMARA	AZANDE	AZTEC	BAMBARA	BEMBA	BHIL
BURUSHO	CALLINAGO	CARIB	CAYAPA	CHUKCHEE	COMANCHE	COPR ESKIMO	CREEK	CROW	CUNA
CZECHS	DARD	FANG	GOND	IBAN	IFUGAO	IRISH	JIVARO	KAPAUKU	KASKA
KAZAK	KHASI	KIKUYU	KOREANS	KURTATCHI	LAU	LEPCHA	LOLO	LUO	MACASSARESE
MALAYS	MANDAN	MARQUESANS	MATACO	MBUNDU	MENDE	MIAO	MISKITO	MONGO	MOSSI
MUNDURUCU	NAMA	NAMBICUARA	NASKAPI	NAVAHO	NUER	NUPE	OJIBWA	OMAHA	PAPAGO
PUKAPUKA	RIFFIANS	RUNDI	RWALA	SAMOANS	SANPOIL	SEMANG	SIRIONO	SOMALI	TALLENSI
TANALA	TEHUELCHE	THAI	THONGA	TIBETANS	TIKOPIA	TIMBIRA	TIV	TODA	TROBRIAND
TUBATULABAL	TUPINAMBA	WOGEO	WOLEAIANS	WOLOF	YORUBA				

314 IN RIGHT COLUMN

	Included (86)			Not included (314)		
62	TEND MORE TO BE THOSE WHERE HUSBANDRY OF SOME KIND IS PRESENT (228)	0.73 OF 86	62	TEND LESS TO BE THOSE WHERE HUSBANDRY OF SOME KIND IS PRESENT (228)	0.53 OF 314	63 165 23 149 XSQ= 10.98 PHI= 0.166 XP = 0.0009
71	TILT TOWARD BEING THOSE WHERE METAL WORKING IS PRESENT (98)	0.51 OF 81	71	TILT TOWARD BEING THOSE WHERE METAL WORKING IS ABSENT (153)	0.66 OF 170	41 57 40 113 XSQ= 6.03 PHI= 0.155 XP = 0.0140
77	TILT TOWARD BEING THOSE WHERE THE WRITING SYSTEM IS MNEMONIC OR ABSENT, RATHER THAN BEING ALPHABETIC-OR-PHONETIC (39) JMH	0.81 OF 42	77	TILT TOWARD BEING THOSE WHERE THE WRITING SYSTEM IS ALPHABETIC-OR-PHONETIC, RATHER THAN BEING MNEMONIC OR ABSENT (15) JMH	0.58 OF 12	8 7 34 5 XSQ= 5.36 PHI= -0.315 XP = 0.0207
91	DRIFT TOWARD BEING THOSE WHERE SOCIETAL COMPLEXITY IS LOW (22) F-W	0.68 OF 25	91	DRIFT TOWARD BEING THOSE WHERE SOCIETAL COMPLEXITY IS HIGH (18) F-W	0.67 OF 15	8 10 17 5 XSQ= 3.26 PHI= -0.285 EP = 0.0504

96	DRIFT TCWARD BEING THCSE 0.62 OF 82 WHERE THE HIERARCHY OF NATICNAL JURISDICTICN HAS FCUR, THREE, TWC OR CNE LEVEL (174) GES,EA	96	DRIFT TOWARD BEING THOSE 0.50 OF 248 WHERE THE HIERARCHY OF NATIONAL JURISDICTION HAS NO LEVELS (156) GES,EA	51 123 31 125 XSQ= 3.43 PHI= 0.102 XP = 0.0638
98	TILT MORE TOWARC BEING THCSE 0.82 OF 83 WHERE THE HIERARCHY OF LCCAL JURISDICTICN HAS FCUR CR THREE LEVELS (238) GES,EA	98	TILT LESS TOWARD BEING THOSE 0.69 OF 248 WHERE THE HIERARCHY OF LOCAL JURISDICTICN HAS FOUR OR THREE LEVELS (238) GES,EA	68 170 15 78 XSQ= 4.87 PHI= 0.121 XP = 0.0274
100	TILT MORE TOWARD BEING THOSE 0.89 OF 82 WHERE HIERARCHIES ARE MORE COMPLEX THAN THE 'SIMPLEST,' I. E., MORE COMPLEX THAN TWC LCCAL LEVELS WITH NC NATICNAL LEVELS (267) GES,EA	100	TILT LESS TOWARD BEING THOSE 0.78 OF 248 WHERE HIERARCHIES ARE MORE COMPLEX THAN THE 'SIMPLEST,' I. E., MORE COMPLEX THAN TWO LOCAL LEVELS WITH NO NATIONAL LEVELS (267) GES,EA	73 194 9 54 XSQ= 3.98 PHI= 0.110 XP = 0.0461
107	DRIFT LESS TOWARD BEING THOSE 0.69 OF 49 WHERE CLASS STRATIFICATICN, IF PRESENT, IS BASED CN SOMETHING CTHER THAN CCCUPATIONAL STATUS (160)	107	DRIFT MORE TOWARD BEING THOSE 0.82 OF 154 WHERE CLASS STRATIFICATION, IF PRESENT, IS BASED ON SOMETHING OTHER THAN OCCUPATIONAL STATUS (160)	15 28 34 126 XSQ= 2.74 PHI= 0.116 XP = 0.0981
236	TILT TOWARD BEING THOSE 0.66 OF 86 WHERE THE FAMILY IS OF AN EXTENDED TYPE, RATHER THAN AN INDEPENDENT TYPE (213)	236	TILT TOWARD BEING THOSE 0.50 OF 312 WHERE THE FAMILY IS OF AN INDEPENDENT TYPE, RATHER THAN AN EXTENDED TYPE (185)	57 156 29 156 XSQ= 6.54 PHI= 0.128 XP = 0.0105
243	TILT TOWARD BEING THOSE 0.53 OF 34 WHERE POLYGYNY, IF PRESENT, HAS A HIGH INCIDENCE (24) W-C,S	243	TILT TOWARD BEING THOSE 0.77 OF 26 WHERE POLYGYNY, IF PRESENT, HAS A LOW INCIDENCE (36) W-D,S	18 6 16 20 XSQ= 4.30 PHI= 0.268 XP = 0.0381
296	TILT TOWARD BEING THOSE 0.65 OF 17 WHERE INFANTICIDE IS ABSENT CR INFERRED ABSENT (15) BCA	296	TILT TOWARD BEING THOSE 0.75 OF 16 WHERE INFANTICIDE IS PRESENT (18) BCA	6 12 11 4 XSQ= 3.76 PHI= -0.338 EP = 0.0366
303	DRIFT TOWARD BEING THOSE 0.73 OF 22 WHERE THE EARLY ORAL SATISFACTION POTENTIAL IS HIGH (32) W-C	303	DRIFT TOWARD BEING THOSE 0.54 OF 35 WHERE THE EARLY ORAL SATISFACTION POTENTIAL IS LOW (25) W-C	16 16 6 19 XSQ= 2.98 PHI= 0.229 XP = 0.0842
390	TILT MCRE TOWARD BEING THOSE 0.85 OF 61 WHERE PREMARITAL SEX RELATIONS ARE WEAKLY PUNISHED ANC IN FACT NOT RARE OR PUNISHED CNLY IF PREGNANCY RESULTS, OR FREELY PERMITTEC (132) JTW,EA	390	TILT LESS TOWARD BEING THOSE 0.68 OF 118 WHERE PREMARITAL SEX RELATIONS ARE WEAKLY PUNISHED AND IN FACT NOT RARE OR PUNISHED ONLY IF PREGNANCY RESULTS, OR FREELY PERMITTED (132) JTW,EA	9 38 52 80 XSQ= 5.45 PHI= -0.175 XP = 0.0195

```
395  TILT TOWARD BEING THOSE          0.67 OF  18     395  TILT TOWARD BEING THOSE          0.80 OF  15          6   12
     WHERE BELIEF IN                                      WHERE BELIEF IN                                         12    3
     THE UNCLEANNESS CF WOMEN IS                          THE UNCLEANNESS OF WOMEN IS                        XSQ=    5.43
     UNIMPCRTANT OR ABSENT  (15) LWS                      PRESENT  (18) LWS                                  PHI=  -0.406
                                                                                                             EP =  0.0135

432  LEAN TOWARD BEING THOSE          0.94 OF  18     432  LEAN TOWARD BEING THOSE          0.50 OF  20         17   10
     WHERE AN ATTRACTIVE AFTERLIFE IS                     WHERE AN ATTRACTIVE AFTERLIFE IS                         1   10
     BELIEVED IN  (27) LWS                                NOT BELIEVED IN  (11) LWS                          XSQ=    7.07
                                                                                                             PHI=   0.431
                                                                                                             EP =  0.0037

489  TEND LESS TO BE THCSE            0.55 OF  86     489  TEND MORE TO BE THOSE            0.94 OF 314         39   18
     NCT INCLUDED IN CHARLES ACKERMAN'S                   NOT INCLUDED IN CHARLES ACKERMAN'S                      47  296
     STUDY OF DIVORCE  (343)                              STUDY OF DIVORCE  (343)                            XSQ=   83.50
                                                                                                             PHI=   0.457
                                                                                                             XP =  0.

490  TEND TC BE THOSE                 0.50 OF  86     490  TEND TO BE THOSE                 0.78 OF 314         43   70
     INCLUDED IN ALBERT S. ANTHCNY'S                      NOT INCLUDED IN ALBERT S. ANTHONY'S                     43  244
     SAMPLE CN MALE INITIATION RITES  (113)               SAMPLE ON MALE INITIATICN RITES  (287)             XSQ=   24.22
                                                                                                             PHI=   0.246
                                                                                                             XP =  0.0000

491  DRIFT LESS TOWARD BEING THOSE 0.81 OF  86        491  DRIFT MORE TOWARD BEING THOSE 0.90 OF 314            16   32
     NOT INCLUDED IN DORRIAN APPLE'S                      NOT INCLUDED IN DORRIAN APPLE'S                         70  282
     STUDY OF GRANDPARENTHCCD  (352)                      STUDY OF GRANDPARENTHOOD  (352)                    XSQ=    3.76
                                                                                                             PHI=   0.097
                                                                                                             XP =  0.0524

492  TEND LESS TO BE THCSE            0.78 OF  86     492  TEND MORE TO BE THOSE            0.94 OF 314         19   20
     NOT INCLUDED IN BARBARA CHARTIER AYRES'              NOT INCLUDED IN BARBARA CHARTIER AYRES'                 67  294
     STUDY OF FEMALE INITIATION RITES  (361)              STUDY OF FEMALE INITIATION RITES  (361)            XSQ=   17.22
                                                                                                             PHI=   0.208
                                                                                                             XP =  0.0000

493  TEND LESS TO BE THCSE            0.56 OF  86     493  TEND MORE TO BE THOSE            0.87 OF 314         38   40
     NOT INCLUDED IN                                      NOT INCLUDED IN                                         48  274
     BACCN, BARRY, AND CHILC'S                            BACON, BARRY, AND CHILD'S                          XSQ=   40.55
     STUDY OF CHILD REARING  (322)                        STUDY OF CHILD REARING  (322)                      PHI=   0.318
                                                                                                             XP =  0.

495  TEND LESS TO BE THCSE            0.53 OF  86     495  TEND MORE TO BE THOSE            0.92 OF 314         40   25
     NOT INCLUDED IN JUCITH K. BROWN'S                    NOT INCLUDED IN JUDITH K. BROWN'S                       46  289
     STUDY OF FEMALE INITIATICN RITES  (335)              STUDY OF FEMALE INITIATICN RITES  (335)            XSQ=   70.91
                                                                                                             PHI=   0.421
                                                                                                             XP =  0.

496  TEND TO BE THOSE                 0.53 OF  86     496  TEND TO BE THOSE                 0.97 OF 314         46    9
     INCLUDED IN ROY G. D'ANCRADE'S                       NOT INCLUDED IN ROY G. D'ANDRADE'S                      40  305
     STUDY OF DREAMS  (55)                                STUDY OF DREAMS  (345)                             XSQ=  141.64
                                                                                                             PHI=   0.595
                                                                                                             XP =  0.
```

```
497  TEND LESS TO BE THCSE              0.58 OF  86     497  TEND MORE TO BE THOSE              0.92 OF 314        36   25
     NOT INCLUDED IN WILLIAM M. EVAN'S                       NOT INCLUDED IN WILLIAM M. EVAN'S                      50  289
     STUDY OF LAW  (339)                                     STUDY OF LAW  (339)                               XSQ=   57.43
                                                                                                               PHI=   0.379
                                                                                                               XP =  0.

498  TEND LESS TO BE THCSE              0.66 OF  86     498  TEND MORE TO BE THOSE              0.93 OF 314        29   22
     NOT INCLUDED IN C. S. FORC'S                            NOT INCLUDED IN C. S. FORD'S                           57  292
     STUDY OF SEX  (349)                                     STUDY OF SEX  (349)                               XSQ=   40.94
                                                                                                               PHI=   0.320
                                                                                                               XP =  0.

499  TEND LESS TO BE THCSE              0.59 OF  86     499  TEND MORE TO BE THOSE              0.84 OF 314        35   51
     NOT INCLUDED IN FORD ANC BEACH'S                        NOT INCLUDED IN FORD AND BEACH'S                       51  263
     SAMPLE ON SEXUAL EXPRESSION                             SAMPLE ON SEXUAL EXPRESSION                       XSQ=   22.50
     BY THE YOUNG  (314)                                     BY THE YOUNG  (314)                               PHI=   0.237
                                                                                                               XP =  0.0000

500  TEND LESS TO BE THCSE              0.71 OF  86     500  TEND MORE TO BE THOSE              0.95 OF 314        25   15
     NOT INCLUDED IN FREEMAN ANC WINCH'S                     NOT INCLUDED IN FREEMAN AND WINCH'S                    61  299
     STUDY OF SCCIETAL CCMPLEXITY  (360)                     STUDY OF SOCIETAL COMPLEXITY  (360)               XSQ=   41.61
                                                                                                               PHI=   0.323
                                                                                                               XP =  0.

501  TEND LESS TO BE THCSE              0.63 OF  86     501  TEND MORE TO BE THOSE              0.89 OF 314        32   35
     NOT INCLUDED IN JOAN FRIENCLY GOODMAN'S                 NOT INCLUDED IN JOAN FRIENDLY GOODMAN'S                54  279
     STUDY OF                                                STUDY OF                                          XSQ=   31.04
     ASCETIC MCURNING BEHAVIOR  (333)                        ASCETIC MOURNING BEHAVIOR  (333)                  PHI=   0.279
                                                                                                               XP =  0.

502  TEND LESS TO BE THCSE              0.67 OF  86     502  TEND MORE TO BE THOSE              0.91 OF 314        28   29
     NOT INCLUDED IN JOHN K. HARLEY'S                        NOT INCLUDED IN JOHN K. HARLEY'S                       58  285
     STUDY OF ADOLESCENT PEER GROUPS  (343)                  STUDY OF ADOLESCENT PEER GRCUPS  (343)            XSQ=   28.17
                                                                                                               PHI=   0.265
                                                                                                               XP =  0.0000

503  TEND LESS TO BE THCSE              0.51 OF  86     503  TEND MORE TO BE THOSE              0.96 OF 314        42   12
     NOT INCLUDED IN JOHN M. HICKMAN'S                       NOT INCLUDED IN JOHN M. HICKMAN'S                      44  302
     STUDY OF THE FOLK-URBAN CCNTINUUM  (346)                STUDY OF THE FOLK-URBAN CONTINUUM  (346)          XSQ=  113.33
                                                                                                               PHI=   0.532
                                                                                                               XP =  0.

504  TEND LESS TO BE THCSE              0.71 OF  86     504  TEND MORE TO BE THOSE              0.92 OF 314        25   24
     NOT INCLUDED IN DONALC HORTON'S                         NOT INCLUDED IN DONALD HORTON'S                        61  290
     STUDY OF ALCHOLISM  (351)                               STUDY OF ALCHOLISM  (351)                         XSQ=   26.87
                                                                                                               PHI=   0.259
                                                                                                               XP =  0.0000

505  TEND LESS TO BE THCSE              0.85 OF  86     505  TEND MORE TO BE THOSE              0.98 OF 314        13    7
     NOT INCLUDED IN MERRILL JACKSON'S                       NOT INCLUDED IN MERRILL JACKSON'S                      73  307
     STUDY OF                                                STUDY OF                                          XSQ=   20.97
     CRIMINAL LAW ANC MEDICINE  (380)                        CRIMINAL LAW AND MEDICINE  (380)                  PHI=   0.229
                                                                                                               XP =  0.0000
```

507/

506	TEND LESS TO BE THOSE NOT INCLUDED IN LAMBERT, TRIANDIS, AND WOLF'S STUDY OF SUPERNATURAL BEINGS (364)	0.81 OF 86	506	TEND MORE TO BE THOSE NOT INCLUDED IN LAMBERT, TRIANDIS, AND WOLF'S STUDY OF SUPERNATURAL BEINGS (364)	0.94 OF 314	16 20 70 294 XSQ= 10.89 PHI= 0.165 XP = 0.0010
508	TEND LESS TO BE THOSE NOT INCLUDED IN DAVID C. MCCLELLAND'S STUDY OF ACHIEVEMENT MOTIVATION (360)	0.76 OF 86	508	TEND MORE TO BE THOSE NOT INCLUDED IN DAVID C. MCCLELLAND'S STUDY OF ACHIEVEMENT MOTIVATION (360)	0.94 OF 314	21 19 65 295 XSQ= 23.31 PHI= 0.241 XP = 0.0000
509	LEAN LESS TOWARD BEING THOSE NOT INCLUDED IN MONI NAG'S STUDY OF FERTILITY (375)	0.86 OF 86	509	LEAN MORE TOWARD BEING THOSE NOT INCLUDED IN MONI NAG'S STUDY OF FERTILITY (375)	0.96 OF 314	12 13 74 301 XSQ= 9.48 PHI= 0.154 XP = 0.0021
510	TEND LESS TO BE THOSE NOT INCLUDED IN RAOUL NARROLL'S STUDY OF SOCIETAL COMPLEXITY (380)	0.87 OF 86	510	TEND MORE TO BE THOSE NOT INCLUDED IN RAOUL NARROLL'S STUDY OF SOCIETAL COMPLEXITY (380)	0.97 OF 314	11 9 75 305 XSQ= 11.99 PHI= 0.173 XP = 0.0005
511	TEND TO BE THOSE INCLUDED IN ROBERTS, ARTH AND BUSH'S SAMPLE ON GAMES, AS MODIFIED BY THE ETHNOGRAPHIC ATLAS (189)	0.73 OF 86	511	TEND TO BE THOSE NOT INCLUDED IN ROBERTS, ARTH AND BUSH'S SAMPLE ON GAMES, AS MODIFIED BY THE ETHNOGRAPHIC ATLAS (211)	0.60 OF 314	63 126 23 188 XSQ= 28.41 PHI= 0.267 XP = 0.0000
512	TEND LESS TO BE THOSE NOT INCLUDED IN SHIRLEY AND ROMNEY'S STUDY OF LOVE MAGIC (367)	0.80 OF 86	512	TEND MORE TO BE THOSE NOT INCLUDED IN SHIRLEY AND ROMNEY'S STUDY OF LOVE MAGIC (367)	0.95 OF 314	17 16 69 298 XSQ= 17.31 PHI= 0.208 XP = 0.0000
513	TEND LESS TO BE THOSE NOT INCLUDED IN LEO W. SIMMONS' STUDY OF THE TREATMENT OF THE AGED (357)	0.78 OF 86	513	TEND MORE TO BE THOSE NOT INCLUDED IN LEO W. SIMMONS' STUDY OF THE TREATMENT OF THE AGED (357)	0.92 OF 314	19 24 67 290 XSQ= 13.22 PHI= 0.182 XP = 0.0003
514	TEND TO BE THOSE INCLUDED IN PHILIP E. SLATER'S STUDY OF NARCISSISM (90)	0.57 OF 86	514	TEND TO BE THOSE NOT INCLUDED IN PHILIP E. SLATER'S STUDY OF NARCISSISM (310)	0.87 OF 314	49 41 37 273 XSQ= 72.18 PHI= 0.425 XP = 0.
515	TEND LESS TO BE THOSE NOT INCLUDED IN WILLIAM N. STEPHENS' SAMPLE ON AVOIDANCE RELATIONSHIPS (348)	0.67 OF 86	515	TEND MORE TO BE THOSE NOT INCLUDED IN WILLIAM N. STEPHENS' SAMPLE ON AVOIDANCE RELATIONSHIPS (348)	0.92 OF 314	28 24 58 290 XSQ= 34.88 PHI= 0.295 XP = 0.

516	TEND MORE TO BE THCSE 0.97 OF 86 INCLUDED IN GUY E. SWANSON'S SAMPLE ON LOCAL JURISCICTICN, AS MODIFIED BY THE ETHNOGRAPHIC ATLAS (331)	516	TEND LESS TO BE THOSE 0.79 OF 314 INCLUDED IN GUY E. SWANSCN'S SAMPLE ON LOCAL JURISDICTICN, AS MODIFIED BY THE ETHNOGRAPHIC ATLAS (331)	83 248 3 66 XSQ= 13.33 PHI= 0.183 XP = 0.0003
517	TEND MORE TO BE THCSE 0.93 OF 86 INCLUDED IN GUY E. SWANSON'S SAMPLE ON HIGH GODS, AS MOCIFIED BY THE ETHNOGRAPHIC ATLAS (260)	517	TEND LESS TO BE THOSE 0.57 OF 314 INCLUDED IN GUY E. SWANSON'S SAMPLE ON HIGH GODS, AS MODIFIED BY THE ETHNOGRAPHIC ATLAS (260)	80 180 6 134 XSQ= 36.26 PHI= 0.301 XP = 0.
518	TEND TO BE THOSE 0.63 OF 86 INCLUDED IN STANLEY H. UDY, JR.'S STUDY OF WCRK ORGANIZATION (105)	518	TEND TO BE THOSE 0.84 OF 314 NOT INCLUDED IN STANLEY H. UDY, JR.'S STUDY OF WORK ORGANIZATICN (295)	54 51 32 263 XSQ= 73.17 PHI= 0.428 XP = 0.
519	TEND LESS TO BE THCSE 0.76 OF 86 NOT INCLUDED IN JOSEPH VEROFF'S STUDY OF ACHIEVEMENT MOTIVATION AS REVEALED IN FCLKTALES (364)	519	TEND MORE TO BE THOSE 0.95 OF 314 NOT INCLUDED IN JOSEPH VEROFF'S STUDY OF ACHIEVEMENT MOTIVATION AS REVEALED IN FOLKTALES (364)	21 15 65 299 XSQ= 29.45 PHI= 0.271 XP = 0.0000
520	TEND LESS TO BE THCSE 0.77 OF 86 NOT INCLUDED IN BEATRICE BLYTH WHITING'S STUDY OF SCRCERY (360)	520	TEND MORE TO BE THOSE 0.94 OF 314 NOT INCLUDED IN BEATRICE BLYTH WHITING'S STUDY OF SORCERY (360)	20 20 66 294 XSQ= 19.55 PHI= 0.221 XP = 0.0000
521	TEND LESS TO BE THCSE 0.71 OF 86 NOT INCLUDED IN JOHN W. M. WHITING'S STUDY OF SOCIALIZATION PROCESS AND PERSCNALITY (353)	521	TEND MORE TO BE THOSE 0.93 OF 314 NOT INCLUDED IN JOHN W. M. WHITING'S STUDY OF SOCIALIZATION PROCESS AND PERSONALITY (353)	25 22 61 292 XSQ= 29.60 PHI= 0.272 XP = 0.0000
522	TEND LESS TO BE THCSE 0.59 OF 86 NOT INCLUDED IN MARJCRIE GRANT WHITING'S STUDY OF DIET (318)	522	TEND MORE TO BE THOSE 0.85 OF 314 NOT INCLUDED IN MARJORIE GRANT WHITING'S STUDY OF DIET (318)	35 47 51 267 XSQ= 25.87 PHI= 0.254 XP = 0.0000
523	TEND LESS TO BE THCSE 0.72 OF 86 NOT INCLUDED IN WHITING AND CHILD'S STUDY OF CHILD TRAINING AND PERSCNALITY (339)	523	TEND MORE TO BE THOSE 0.88 OF 314 NOT INCLUDED IN WHITING AND CHILD'S STUDY OF CHILD TRAINING AND PERSONALITY (339)	24 37 62 277 XSQ= 12.36 PHI= 0.176 XP = 0.0004
524	LEAN LESS TOWARD BEING THOSE 0.80 OF 86 NOT INCLUDED IN WHITING, KLUCKHCHN, ANC ANTHONY'S STUDY OF MALE INITIATICN CEREMONIES (356)	524	LEAN MORE TOWARD BEING THOSE 0.91 OF 314 NOT INCLUDED IN WHITING, KLUCKHOHN, AND ANTHCNY'S STUDY OF MALE INITIATION CEREMONIES (356)	17 27 69 287 XSQ= 7.50 PHI= 0.137 XP = 0.0062

508 CULTURES INCLUDED IN DAVID C. MCCLELLAND'S STUDY OF ACHIEVEMENT MOTIVATION (40)

508 CULTURES NOT INCLUDED IN DAVID C. MCCLELLAND'S STUDY OF ACHIEVEMENT MOTIVATION (360)

BACKGROUND ON PAGE 180

SUBJECT ONLY, F.C. 1-480 AND 527-536
BOTH SUBJECT AND PREDICATE, F.C. 481-526

40 IN LEFT COLUMN

AINU	ARANDA	ARAPESH	ARAUCANIANS	ASHANTI	AZANDE	CHAGGA	CHENCHU	CHEYENNE	CHIR-APACHE
CHUKCHEE	COMANCHE	CROW	CUNA	HANO	KASKA	KIKUYU	KORYAK	KURTATCHI	KWAKIUTL
LEPCHA	MANDAN	MARQUESANS	MASAI	MBUNDU	NAVAHO	OJIBWA	PAPAGO	PUKAPUKA	SOTHO
TENETEHARA	TETON	THONGA	TUCUNA	VENDA	WICHITA	WINNEBAGO	WOLEAIANS	YORUBA	ZUNI

360 IN RIGHT COLUMN

	Included (40)			Not included (360)		Statistics
4	IN ALL CASES ARE THOSE LOCATED OUTSIDE OF THE CIRCUM-MEDITERRANEAN (355)	1.00 OF 40	4	TILT LESS TOWARD BEING THOSE LOCATED OUTSIDE OF THE CIRCUM-MEDITERRANEAN (355)	0.88 OF 360	0 45 40 315 XSQ= 4.45 PHI= -0.105 XP = 0.0349
8	LEAN LESS TOWARD BEING THOSE LOCATED OUTSIDE OF NORTH AMERICA (330)	0.63 OF 40	8	LEAN MORE TOWARD BEING THOSE LOCATED OUTSIDE OF NORTH AMERICA (330)	0.85 OF 360	15 55 25 305 XSQ= 10.82 PHI= 0.164 XP = 0.0010
15	DRIFT TOWARD BEING THOSE WHERE THE LATITUDE IS TWENTY DEGREES OR GREATER (183)	0.60 OF 40	15	DRIFT TOWARD BEING THOSE WHERE THE LATITUDE IS LESS THAN TWENTY DEGREES (217)	0.56 OF 360	24 159 16 201 XSQ= 3.03 PHI= 0.087 XP = 0.0819
36	LEAN LESS TOWARD BEING THOSE WHERE THE NATURAL ENVIRONMENT IS OTHER THAN 'VERY HARSH,' OR SUB-TROPICAL BUSH, OR TEMPERATE GRASSLAND (292) FWM	0.52 OF 40	36	LEAN MORE TOWARD BEING THOSE WHERE THE NATURAL ENVIRONMENT IS OTHER THAN 'VERY HARSH,' OR SUB-TROPICAL BUSH, OR TEMPERATE GRASSLAND (292) FWM	0.75 OF 360	19 89 21 271 XSQ= 8.36 PHI= 0.145 XP = 0.0038
42	TILT MORE TOWARD BEING THOSE WHERE THE NATURAL ENVIRONMENT IS OTHER THAN TROPICAL OR SUB-TROPICAL RAIN FOREST, OR MONSOON FOREST (244) FWM	0.77 OF 40	42	TILT LESS TOWARD BEING THOSE WHERE THE NATURAL ENVIRONMENT IS OTHER THAN TROPICAL OR SUB-TROPICAL RAIN FOREST, OR MONSOON FOREST (244) FWM	0.59 OF 360	9 147 31 213 XSQ= 4.34 PHI= -0.104 XP = 0.0371

62	DRIFT MORE TOWARD BEING THOSE 0.72 OF 40 WHERE HUSBANDRY OF SOME KIND IS PRESENT (228)	62	DRIFT LESS TOWARD BEING THOSE 0.55 OF 360 WHERE HUSBANDRY OF SOME KIND IS PRESENT (228)	29 199 11 161 XSQ= 3.68 PHI= 0.096 XP = 0.0550
108	DRIFT TOWARD BEING THOSE 0.59 OF 17 WHERE CLASS STRATIFICATION, IF PRESENT, IS BASED ON A HEREDITARY ARISTOCRACY (74)	108	DRIFT TOWARD BEING THOSE 0.66 OF 186 WHERE CLASS STRATIFICATION, IF PRESENT, IS BASED ON SOMETHING OTHER THAN A HEREDITARY ARISTOCRACY (129)	10 64 7 122 XSQ= 3.02 PHI= 0.122 XP = 0.0821
109	DRIFT MORE TOWARD BEING THOSE 0.97 OF 39 WHERE CASTES ARE ABSENT (317)	109	DRIFT LESS TOWARD BEING THOSE 0.85 OF 329 WHERE CASTES ARE ABSENT (317)	1 50 38 279 XSQ= 3.66 PHI= -0.100 XP = 0.0556
334	TILT TOWARD BEING THOSE 0.63 OF 40 WHERE THE INDULGENCE OF THE CHILD IS LOW (38) B-B-C	334	TILT TOWARD BEING THOSE 0.66 OF 38 WHERE THE INDULGENCE OF THE CHILD IS HIGH (40) B-B-C	15 25 25 13 XSQ= 5.16 PHI= -0.257 XP = 0.0231
349	TILT TOWARD BEING THOSE 0.71 OF 34 WHERE THE CHILD'S INFERRED ANXIETY OVER NON-PERFORMANCE OF ACHIEVEMENT BEHAVIOR IS HIGH (34) B-B-C	349	TILT TOWARD BEING THOSE 0.64 OF 28 WHERE THE CHILD'S INFERRED ANXIETY OVER NON-PERFORMANCE OF ACHIEVEMENT BEHAVIOR IS LOW (28) B-B-C	24 10 10 18 XSQ= 6.20 PHI= 0.316 XP = 0.0128
350	LEAN TOWARD BEING THOSE 0.74 OF 34 WHERE THE CHILD'S INFERRED ANXIETY OVER PERFORMANCE OF ACHIEVEMENT BEHAVIOR IS HIGH (34) B-B-C	350	LEAN TOWARD BEING THOSE 0.65 OF 26 WHERE THE CHILD'S INFERRED ANXIETY OVER PERFORMANCE OF ACHIEVEMENT BEHAVIOR IS LOW (26) B-B-C	25 9 9 17 XSQ= 7.57 PHI= 0.355 XP = 0.0059
421	DRIFT TOWARD BEING THOSE 0.59 OF 29 WHERE KILLING, TORTURING, OR MUTILATING OF THE ENEMY IS STRONGLY OR MODERATELY EMPHASIZED (37) PES	421	DRIFT TOWARD BEING THOSE 0.64 OF 55 WHERE KILLING, TORTURING, OR MUTILATING OF THE ENEMY IS NEGLIGIBLY EMPHASIZED (47) PES	17 20 12 35 XSQ= 2.97 PHI= 0.188 XP = 0.0850
428	LEAN TOWARD BEING THOSE 0.78 OF 9 WHERE A HIGH GOD, IF PRESENT AND ACTIVE, DOES NOT SUPPORT HUMAN MORALITY, RATHER THAN SUPPORTING IT (26) GES,EA	428	LEAN TOWARD BEING THOSE 0.76 OF 78 WHERE A HIGH GOD, IF PRESENT AND ACTIVE, SUPPORTS HUMAN MORALITY, RATHER THAN NOT SUPPORTING IT (61) GES,EA	2 59 7 19 XSQ= 8.59 PHI= -0.314 XP = 0.0034
432	IN ALL CASES ARE THOSE 1.00 OF 8 WHERE AN ATTRACTIVE AFTERLIFE IS BELIEVED IN (27) LWS	432	DRIFT LESS TOWARD BEING THOSE 0.63 OF 30 WHERE AN ATTRACTIVE AFTERLIFE IS BELIEVED IN (27) LWS	8 19 0 11 XSQ= 2.54 PHI= 0.258 EP = 0.0765

433	DRIFT TOWARD BEING THOSE WHERE BELIEF IN REINCARNATION IS PRESENT (10) GES	0.50 OF 10	433	DRIFT TOWARD BEING THOSE WHERE BELIEF IN REINCARNATION IS ABSENT (28) GES	0.82 OF 28	5 5 5 23 XSQ= 2.44 PHI= 0.254 EP = 0.0901
447	DRIFT TOWARD BEING THOSE WHERE LOVE MAGIC IS PRESENT (20) S-R	0.79 OF 14	447	DRIFT TOWARD BEING THOSE WHERE LOVE MAGIC IS ABSENT (13) S-R	0.53 OF 19	11 9 3 10 XSQ= 2.11 PHI= 0.253 EP = 0.0873
450	LEAN MORE TOWARD BEING THOSE WHERE THE OBSERVATION OF FOOD TABOOS IS HIGH OR MEDIUM, RATHER THAN LOW (60) JRL	0.95 OF 21	450	LEAN LESS TOWARD BEING THOSE WHERE THE OBSERVATION OF FOOD TABOOS IS HIGH OR MEDIUM, RATHER THAN LOW (60) JRL	0.62 OF 65	20 40 1 25 XSQ= 7.02 PHI= 0.286 XP = 0.0080
469	IN ALL CASES ARE THOSE WHERE CONTACT WITH OTHER CULTURES IS FREQUENT OR REGULAR, RATHER THAN IRREGULAR (43) JMH	1.00 OF 17	469	TILT LESS TOWARD BEING THOSE WHERE CONTACT WITH OTHER CULTURES IS FREQUENT OR REGULAR, RATHER THAN IRREGULAR (43) JMH	0.70 OF 37	17 26 0 11 XSQ= 4.65 PHI= 0.293 XP = 0.0311
489	TEND LESS TO BE THOSE NOT INCLUDED IN CHARLES ACKERMAN'S STUDY OF DIVORCE (343)	0.65 OF 40	489	TEND MORE TO BE THOSE NOT INCLUDED IN CHARLES ACKERMAN'S STUDY OF DIVORCE (343)	0.88 OF 360	14 43 26 317 XSQ= 13.83 PHI= 0.186 XP = 0.0002
490	TEND TO BE THOSE INCLUDED IN ALBERT S. ANTHONY'S SAMPLE ON MALE INITIATION RITES (113)	0.67 OF 40	490	TEND TO BE THOSE NOT INCLUDED IN ALBERT S. ANTHONY'S SAMPLE ON MALE INITIATION RITES (287)	0.76 OF 360	27 86 13 274 XSQ= 31.66 PHI= 0.281 XP = 0.
491	TEND LESS TO BE THOSE NOT INCLUDED IN DORRIAN APPLE'S STUDY OF GRANDPARENTHOOD (352)	0.63 OF 40	491	TEND MORE TO BE THOSE NOT INCLUDED IN DORRIAN APPLE'S STUDY OF GRANDPARENTHOOD (352)	0.91 OF 360	15 33 25 327 XSQ= 24.75 PHI= 0.249 XP = 0.0000
492	TEND LESS TO BE THOSE NOT INCLUDED IN BARBARA CHARTIER AYRES' STUDY OF FEMALE INITIATION RITES (361)	0.57 OF 40	492	TEND MORE TO BE THOSE NOT INCLUDED IN BARBARA CHARTIER AYRES' STUDY OF FEMALE INITIATION RITES (361)	0.94 OF 360	17 22 23 338 XSQ= 50.12 PHI= 0.354 XP = 0.
493	IN ALL CASES ARE THOSE INCLUDED IN BACON, BARRY, AND CHILD'S STUDY OF CHILD REARING (78)	1.00 OF 40	493	TEND TO BE THOSE NOT INCLUDED IN BACON, BARRY, AND CHILD'S STUDY OF CHILD REARING (322)	0.89 OF 360	40 38 0 322 XSQ= 177.82 PHI= 0.667 XP = 0.

494	TEND LESS TO BE THOSE 0.63 OF 40 NOT INCLUDED IN HERBERT M. BARRY III'S STUDY OF ART (371)	494	TEND MORE TO BE THOSE 0.96 OF 360 NOT INCLUDED IN HERBERT M. BARRY III'S STUDY OF ART (371)	15 14 25 346 XSQ= 55.59 PHI= 0.373 XP = 0.
495	TEND LESS TO BE THOSE 0.63 OF 40 NOT INCLUDED IN JUDITH K. BROWN'S STUDY OF FEMALE INITIATION RITES (335)	495	TEND MORE TO BE THOSE 0.86 OF 360 NOT INCLUDED IN JUDITH K. BROWN'S STUDY OF FEMALE INITIATION RITES (335)	15 50 25 310 XSQ= 13.06 PHI= 0.181 XP = 0.0003
496	TEND LESS TO BE THOSE 0.60 OF 40 NOT INCLUDED IN ROY G. D'ANDRADE'S STUDY OF DREAMS (345)	496	TEND MORE TO BE THOSE 0.89 OF 360 NOT INCLUDED IN ROY G. D'ANDRADE'S STUDY OF DREAMS (345)	16 39 24 321 XSQ= 23.42 PHI= 0.242 XP = 0.0000
498	TEND LESS TO BE THOSE 0.60 OF 40 NOT INCLUDED IN C. S. FORD'S STUDY OF SEX (349)	498	TEND MORE TO BE THOSE 0.90 OF 360 NOT INCLUDED IN C. S. FORD'S STUDY OF SEX (349)	16 35 24 325 XSQ= 27.01 PHI= 0.260 XP = 0.0000
499	TEND TO BE THOSE 0.55 OF 40 INCLUDED IN FORD AND BEACH'S SAMPLE ON SEXUAL EXPRESSION BY THE YOUNG (86)	499	TEND TO BE THOSE 0.82 OF 360 NOT INCLUDED IN FORD AND BEACH'S SAMPLE ON SEXUAL EXPRESSION BY THE YOUNG (314)	22 64 18 296 XSQ= 27.39 PHI= 0.262 XP = 0.0000
500	TEND LESS TO BE THOSE 0.63 OF 40 NOT INCLUDED IN FREEMAN AND WINCH'S STUDY OF SOCIETAL COMPLEXITY (360)	500	TEND MORE TO BE THOSE 0.93 OF 360 NOT INCLUDED IN FREEMAN AND WINCH'S STUDY OF SOCIETAL COMPLEXITY (360)	15 25 25 335 XSQ= 34.03 PHI= 0.292 XP = 0.
501	TEND TO BE THOSE 0.63 OF 40 INCLUDED IN JOAN FRIENDLY GOODMAN'S STUDY OF ASCETIC MOURNING BEHAVIOR (67)	501	TEND TO BE THOSE 0.88 OF 360 NOT INCLUDED IN JOAN FRIENDLY GOODMAN'S STUDY OF ASCETIC MOURNING BEHAVIOR (333)	25 42 15 318 XSQ= 63.12 PHI= 0.397 XP = 0.
502	LEAN LESS TOWARD BEING THOSE 0.70 OF 40 NOT INCLUDED IN JOHN K. HARLEY'S STUDY OF ADOLESCENT PEER GROUPS (343)	502	LEAN MORE TOWARD BEING THOSE 0.88 OF 360 NOT INCLUDED IN JOHN K. HARLEY'S STUDY OF ADOLESCENT PEER GROUPS (343)	12 45 28 315 XSQ= 7.65 PHI= 0.138 XP = 0.0057
503	TEND LESS TO BE THOSE 0.57 OF 40 NOT INCLUDED IN JOHN M. HICKMAN'S STUDY OF THE FOLK-URBAN CONTINUUM (346)	503	TEND MORE TO BE THOSE 0.90 OF 360 NOT INCLUDED IN JOHN M. HICKMAN'S STUDY OF THE FOLK-URBAN CONTINUUM (346)	17 37 23 323 XSQ= 29.31 PHI= 0.271 XP = 0.0000

No.	Subset (40)	No.	Remainder (360)	Statistics
504	TEND LESS TO BE THOSE 0.65 OF 40 NOT INCLUDED IN DONALD HORTON'S STUDY OF ALCHOLISM (351)	504	TEND MORE TO BE THOSE 0.90 OF 360 NOT INCLUDED IN DONALD HORTON'S STUDY OF ALCHOLISM (351)	14 35 26 325 XSQ= 19.11 PHI= 0.219 XP = 0.0000
506	TEND TO BE THOSE 0.55 OF 40 INCLUDED IN LAMBERT, TRIANDIS, AND WOLF'S STUDY OF SUPERNATURAL BEINGS (36)	506	TEND TO BE THOSE 0.96 OF 360 NOT INCLUDED IN LAMBERT, TRIANDIS, AND WOLF'S STUDY OF SUPERNATURAL BEINGS (364)	22 14 18 346 XSQ= 108.67 PHI= 0.521 XP = 0.
507	TEND TO BE THOSE 0.52 OF 40 INCLUDED IN JAMES R. LEARY'S STUDY OF FOOD TABOOS (86)	507	TEND TO BE THOSE 0.82 OF 360 NOT INCLUDED IN JAMES R. LEARY'S STUDY OF FOOD TABOOS (314)	21 65 19 295 XSQ= 23.31 PHI= 0.241 XP = 0.0000
509	TILT LESS TOWARD BEING THOSE 0.85 OF 40 NOT INCLUDED IN MONI NAG'S STUDY OF FERTILITY (375)	509	TILT MORE TOWARD BEING THOSE 0.95 OF 360 NOT INCLUDED IN MONI NAG'S STUDY OF FERTILITY (375)	6 19 34 341 XSQ= 4.27 PHI= 0.103 XP = 0.0389
510	DRIFT LESS TOWARD BEING THOSE 0.88 OF 40 NOT INCLUDED IN RAOUL NARROLL'S STUDY OF SOCIETAL COMPLEXITY (380)	510	DRIFT MORE TOWARD BEING THOSE 0.96 OF 360 NOT INCLUDED IN RAOUL NARROLL'S STUDY OF SOCIETAL COMPLEXITY (380)	5 15 35 345 XSQ= 3.65 PHI= 0.096 XP = 0.0559
511	TEND TO BE THOSE 0.75 OF 40 INCLUDED IN ROBERTS, ARTH AND BUSH'S SAMPLE ON GAMES, AS MODIFIED BY THE ETHNOGRAPHIC ATLAS (189)	511	TEND TO BE THOSE 0.56 OF 360 NOT INCLUDED IN ROBERTS, ARTH AND BUSH'S SAMPLE ON GAMES, AS MODIFIED BY THE ETHNOGRAPHIC ATLAS (211)	30 159 10 201 XSQ= 12.52 PHI= 0.177 XP = 0.0004
512	TEND LESS TO BE THOSE 0.65 OF 40 NOT INCLUDED IN SHIRLEY AND ROMNEY'S STUDY OF LOVE MAGIC (367)	512	TEND MORE TO BE THOSE 0.95 OF 360 NOT INCLUDED IN SHIRLEY AND ROMNEY'S STUDY OF LOVE MAGIC (367)	14 19 26 341 XSQ= 38.18 PHI= 0.309 XP = 0.
513	TILT LESS TOWARD BEING THOSE 0.77 OF 40 NOT INCLUDED IN LEO W. SIMMONS' STUDY OF THE TREATMENT OF THE AGED (357)	513	TILT MORE TOWARD BEING THOSE 0.91 OF 360 NOT INCLUDED IN LEO W. SIMMONS' STUDY OF THE TREATMENT OF THE AGED (357)	9 34 31 326 XSQ= 5.11 PHI= 0.113 XP = 0.0238
514	TEND TO BE THOSE 0.72 OF 40 INCLUDED IN PHILIP E. SLATER'S STUDY OF NARCISSISM (90)	514	TEND TO BE THOSE 0.83 OF 360 NOT INCLUDED IN PHILIP E. SLATER'S STUDY OF NARCISSISM (310)	29 61 11 299 XSQ= 60.57 PHI= 0.389 XP = 0.

515	TEND LESS TO BE THOSE NOT INCLUDED IN WILLIAM N. STEPHENS' SAMPLE ON AVOIDANCE RELATIONSHIPS (348)	0.55 OF 40	515	TEND MORE TO BE THOSE NOT INCLUDED IN WILLIAM N. STEPHENS' SAMPLE ON AVOIDANCE RELATIONSHIPS (348)	0.91 OF 360	18 34 22 326 XSQ= 37.16 PHI= 0.305 XP = 0.
518	TEND TO BE THOSE INCLUDED IN STANLEY H. UDY, JR.'S STUDY OF WORK ORGANIZATION (105)	0.55 OF 40	518	TEND TO BE THOSE NOT INCLUDED IN STANLEY H. UDY, JR.'S STUDY OF WORK ORGANIZATION (295)	0.77 OF 360	22 83 18 277 XSQ= 17.36 PHI= 0.208 XP = 0.0000
519	TEND TO BE THOSE INCLUDED IN JOSEPH VEROFF'S STUDY OF ACHIEVEMENT MOTIVATION AS REVEALED IN FOLKTALES (36)	0.90 OF 40	519	IN ALL CASES ARE THOSE NOT INCLUDED IN JOSEPH VEROFF'S STUDY OF ACHIEVEMENT MOTIVATION AS REVEALED IN FOLKTALES (364)	1.00 OF 360	36 0 4 360 XSQ= 345.14 PHI= 0.929 XP = 0.
520	TEND LESS TO BE THOSE NOT INCLUDED IN BEATRICE BLYTH WHITING'S STUDY OF SORCERY (360)	0.67 OF 40	520	TEND MORE TO BE THOSE NOT INCLUDED IN BEATRICE BLYTH WHITING'S STUDY OF SORCERY (360)	0.92 OF 360	13 27 27 333 XSQ= 22.30 PHI= 0.236 XP = 0.0000
521	TEND TO BE THOSE INCLUDED IN JOHN W. M. WHITING'S STUDY OF SOCIALIZATION PROCESS AND PERSONALITY (47)	0.75 OF 40	521	TEND TO BE THOSE NOT INCLUDED IN JOHN W. M. WHITING'S STUDY OF SOCIALIZATION PROCESS AND PERSONALITY (353)	0.95 OF 360	30 17 10 343 XSQ= 164.76 PHI= 0.642 XP = 0.
522	TEND TO BE THOSE INCLUDED IN MARJORIE GRANT WHITING'S STUDY OF DIET (82)	0.72 OF 40	522	TEND TO BE THOSE NOT INCLUDED IN MARJORIE GRANT WHITING'S STUDY OF DIET (318)	0.85 OF 360	29 53 11 307 XSQ= 70.24 PHI= 0.419 XP = 0.
523	TEND TO BE THOSE INCLUDED IN WHITING AND CHILD'S STUDY OF CHILD TRAINING AND PERSONALITY (61)	0.52 OF 40	523	TEND TO BE THOSE NOT INCLUDED IN WHITING AND CHILD'S STUDY OF CHILD TRAINING AND PERSONALITY (339)	0.89 OF 360	21 40 19 320 XSQ= 44.57 PHI= 0.334 XP = 0.
524	TEND LESS TO BE THOSE NOT INCLUDED IN WHITING, KLUCKHOHN, AND ANTHONY'S STUDY OF MALE INITIATION CEREMONIES (356)	0.65 OF 40	524	TEND MORE TO BE THOSE NOT INCLUDED IN WHITING, KLUCKHOHN, AND ANTHONY'S STUDY OF MALE INITIATION CEREMONIES (356)	0.92 OF 360	14 30 26 330 XSQ= 23.50 PHI= 0.242 XP = 0.0000

509 CULTURES INCLUDED IN MONI NAG'S STUDY OF FERTILITY (25)

509 CULTURES NOT INCLUDED IN MONI NAG'S STUDY OF FERTILITY (375)

BACKGROUND ON PAGE 180

SUBJECT ONLY, F.C. 1-480 AND 527-536
BOTH SUBJECT AND PREDICATE, F.C. 481-526

25 IN LEFT COLUMN

ALORESE	ASHANTI	DUSUN	GANDA	HAVASUPAI	KAPAUKU	KOREANS	LESU	MASAI	MBUNDU
MENDE	MONGO	NAVAHO	NGONI	NUPE	OJIBWA	PURARI	SINHALESE	TALLENSI	THONGA
TIKOPIA	TODA	YAKO	YAO	YAPESE					

375 IN RIGHT COLUMN

	Included (25)			Not included (375)		
3	TEND LESS TO BE THOSE LOCATED OUTSIDE OF AFRICA (320)	0.52 OF 25	3	TEND MORE TO BE THOSE LOCATED OUTSIDE OF AFRICA (320)	0.82 OF 375	12 68 13 307 XSQ= 11.27 PHI= 0.168 XP = 0.0008
9	IN ALL CASES ARE THOSE LOCATED OUTSIDE OF SOUTH AMERICA (335)	1.00 OF 25	9	TILT LESS TOWARD BEING THOSE LOCATED OUTSIDE OF SOUTH AMERICA (335)	0.83 OF 375	0 65 25 310 XSQ= 3.98 PHI= -0.100 XP = 0.0461
16	LEAN TOWARD BEING THOSE WHERE THE LATITUDE IS LESS THAN TEN DEGREES (123)	0.56 OF 25	16	LEAN TOWARD BEING THOSE WHERE THE LATITUDE IS TEN DEGREES OR GREATER (277)	0.71 OF 375	11 266 14 109 XSQ= 6.77 PHI= -0.130 XP = 0.0093
62	DRIFT MORE TOWARD BEING THOSE WHERE HUSBANDRY OF SOME KIND IS PRESENT (228)	0.76 OF 25	62	DRIFT LESS TOWARD BEING THOSE WHERE HUSBANDRY OF SOME KIND IS PRESENT (228)	0.56 OF 375	19 209 6 166 XSQ= 3.14 PHI= 0.089 XP = 0.0762
63	DRIFT TOWARD BEING THOSE WHERE HUSBANDRY, IF PRESENT, IS PRINCIPALLY IN THE FORM OF PIGS, SHEEP, OR GOATS, RATHER THAN BOVINE, EQUINE, CAMEL-LIKE, OR DEER-LIKE ANIMALS (74)	0.53 OF 19	63	DRIFT TOWARD BEING THOSE WHERE HUSBANDRY, IF PRESENT, IS PRINCIPALLY IN THE FORM OF BOVINE, EQUINE, CAMEL-LIKE, OR DEER-LIKE ANIMALS, RATHER THAN PIGS, SHEEP, OR GOATS (152)	0.69 OF 207	9 143 10 64 XSQ= 2.81 PHI= -0.111 XP = 0.0940

71	TILT TOWARD BEING THOSE 0.63 OF 19 WHERE METAL WORKING IS PRESENT (98)	71	TILT TOWARD BEING THOSE 0.63 OF 232 WHERE METAL WORKING IS ABSENT (153)	12 86 7 146 XSQ= 3.99 PHI= 0.126 XP = 0.0459
81	TILT TOWARD BEING THOSE 0.65 OF 20 WHERE A CITY OR TOWN IS PRESENT, OR THE AVERAGE COMMUNITY SIZE IS 200 OR GREATER (89)	81	TILT TOWARD BEING THOSE 0.63 OF 204 WHERE NO CITY OR TOWN IS PRESENT, AND THE AVERAGE COMMUNITY SIZE IS SMALLER THAN 200 (135)	13 76 7 128 XSQ= 4.75 PHI= 0.146 XP = 0.0292
83	TILT TOWARD BEING THOSE 0.53 OF 15 WHERE, WITH NO CITY AND NO TOWN PRESENT, THE AVERAGE COMMUNITY SIZE IS BETWEEN 200 AND 999, RATHER THAN SMALLER THAN 200 (45)	83	TILT TOWARD BEING THOSE 0.78 OF 165 WHERE, WITH NO CITY AND NO TOWN PRESENT, THE AVERAGE COMMUNITY SIZE IS SMALLER THAN 200, RATHER THAN BETWEEN 200 AND 999 (135)	8 37 7 128 XSQ= 5.45 PHI= 0.174 XP = 0.0195
89	DRIFT TOWARD BEING THOSE 0.70 OF 10 WHERE, IF A NON-HEREDITARY HEADMANSHIP IS PRESENT, SUCCESSION IS BY MEANS OTHER THAN CONSENSUS (43)	89	DRIFT TOWARD BEING THOSE 0.63 OF 96 WHERE, IF A NON-HEREDITARY HEADMANSHIP IS PRESENT, SUCCESSION IS BY CONSENSUS (63)	3 60 7 36 XSQ= 2.73 PHI= -0.161 XP = 0.0982
95	TILT LESS TOWARD BEING THOSE 0.57 OF 23 WHERE THE HIERARCHY OF NATIONAL JURISDICTION HAS ONE OR NO LEVELS (254) GES,EA	95	TILT MORE TOWARD BEING THOSE 0.79 OF 307 WHERE THE HIERARCHY OF NATIONAL JURISDICTION HAS ONE OR NO LEVELS (254) GES,EA	10 66 13 241 XSQ= 4.66 PHI= 0.119 XP = 0.0309
96	DRIFT MORE TOWARD BEING THOSE 0.74 OF 23 WHERE THE HIERARCHY OF NATIONAL JURISDICTION HAS FOUR, THREE, TWO OR ONE LEVEL (174) GES,EA	96	DRIFT LESS TOWARD BEING THOSE 0.51 OF 307 WHERE THE HIERARCHY OF NATIONAL JURISDICTION HAS FOUR, THREE, TWO OR ONE LEVEL (174) GES,EA	17 157 6 150 XSQ= 3.59 PHI= 0.104 XP = 0.0583
98	DRIFT MORE TOWARD BEING THOSE 0.91 OF 23 WHERE THE HIERARCHY OF LOCAL JURISDICTION HAS FOUR OR THREE LEVELS (238) GES,EA	98	DRIFT LESS TOWARD BEING THOSE 0.70 OF 308 WHERE THE HIERARCHY OF LOCAL JURISDICTION HAS FOUR OR THREE LEVELS (238) GES,EA	21 217 2 91 XSQ= 3.63 PHI= 0.105 XP = 0.0567
100	IN ALL CASES ARE THOSE 1.00 OF 23 WHERE HIERARCHIES ARE MORE COMPLEX THAN THE 'SIMPLEST,' I. E., MORE COMPLEX THAN TWO LOCAL LEVELS WITH NO NATIONAL LEVELS (267) GES,EA	100	TILT LESS TOWARD BEING THOSE 0.79 OF 307 WHERE HIERARCHIES ARE MORE COMPLEX THAN THE 'SIMPLEST,' I. E., MORE COMPLEX THAN TWO LOCAL LEVELS WITH NO NATIONAL LEVELS (267) GES,EA	23 244 0 63 XSQ= 4.58 PHI= 0.118 XP = 0.0323
136	IN ALL CASES ARE THOSE 1.00 OF 6 WHERE FULL-TIME ENTREPRENEURS ARE PRESENT (18) JV	136	TILT TOWARD BEING THOSE 0.54 OF 26 WHERE FULL-TIME ENTREPRENEURS ARE ABSENT (14) JV	6 12 0 14 XSQ= 3.76 PHI= 0.343 EP = 0.0238

149	DRIFT TOWARD BEING THOSE WHERE THE INCIDENCE OF THEFT IS HIGH (18) B-B-C	0.83 OF 6	149	DRIFT TOWARD BEING THOSE WHERE THE INCIDENCE OF THEFT IS LOW (19) B-B-C	0.58 OF 31	5 13 1 18 XSQ= 1.99 PHI= 0.232 EP = 0.0897
188	TILT MORE TOWARD BEING THOSE WHERE THE KIN GROUP IS OTHER THAN EXCLUSIVELY COGNATIC (252)	0.84 OF 25	188	TILT LESS TOWARD BEING THOSE WHERE THE KIN GROUP IS OTHER THAN EXCLUSIVELY COGNATIC (252)	0.62 OF 375	4 144 21 231 XSQ= 4.13 PHI= -0.102 XP = 0.0421
192	TILT MORE TOWARD BEING THOSE OTHER THAN WHERE THE ONLY KIN GROUP PRESENT IS A KINDRED OR ELSE BILATERAL DESCENT IS INFERRED (289)	0.96 OF 25	192	TILT LESS TOWARD BEING THOSE OTHER THAN WHERE THE ONLY KIN GROUP PRESENT IS A KINDRED OR ELSE BILATERAL DESCENT IS INFERRED (289)	0.71 OF 375	1 110 24 265 XSQ= 6.29 PHI= -0.125 XP = 0.0121
201	IN ALL CASES ARE THOSE WHERE MARITAL RESIDENCE IS NON-OPTIONAL, RATHER THAN AMBILOCAL OR NEOLOCAL (334)	1.00 OF 25	201	TILT LESS TOWARD BEING THOSE WHERE MARITAL RESIDENCE IS NON-OPTIONAL, RATHER THAN AMBILOCAL OR NEOLOCAL (334)	0.83 OF 373	25 309 0 64 XSQ= 3.92 PHI= 0.099 XP = 0.0477
204	IN ALL CASES ARE THOSE WHERE MARITAL RESIDENCE IS PATRILOCAL, VIRILOCAL, OR AVUNCULOCAL, RATHER THAN AMBILOCAL OR NEOLOCAL (270)	1.00 OF 22	204	TILT LESS TOWARD BEING THOSE WHERE MARITAL RESIDENCE IS PATRILOCAL, VIRILOCAL, OR AVUNCULOCAL, RATHER THAN AMBILOCAL OR NEOLOCAL (270)	0.79 OF 312	22 248 0 64 XSQ= 4.34 PHI= 0.114 XP = 0.0373
234	DRIFT TOWARD BEING THOSE WHERE THE COUSIN TERMINOLOGY IS OF CROW, OMAHA, OR IROQUOIS TYPE, RATHER THAN ESKIMO OR HAWAIIAN TYPE (152)	0.67 OF 24	234	DRIFT TOWARD BEING THOSE WHERE THE COUSIN TERMINOLOGY IS OF ESKIMO OR HAWAIIAN TYPE, RATHER THAN CROW, OMAHA, OR IROQUOIS TYPE (170)	0.54 OF 298	16 136 8 162 XSQ= 3.14 PHI= 0.099 XP = 0.0763
255	DRIFT TOWARD BEING THOSE WHERE GRANDPARENTAL AUTHORITY OVER PARENTS IS PRESENT (7) CA	0.50 OF 6	255	DRIFT TOWARD BEING THOSE WHERE GRANDPARENTAL AUTHORITY OVER PARENTS IS ABSENT (26) DA	0.85 OF 27	3 4 3 23 XSQ= 1.84 PHI= 0.236 EP = 0.0929
309	DRIFT TOWARD BEING THOSE WHERE ORAL SOCIALIZATION ANXIETY IS HIGH (26) W-C	0.86 OF 7	309	DRIFT TOWARD BEING THOSE WHERE ORAL SOCIALIZATION ANXIETY IS LOW (27) W-C	0.57 OF 46	6 20 1 26 XSQ= 2.81 PHI= 0.230 XP = 0.0936
314	TILT TOWARD BEING THOSE WHERE THE INCIDENCE OF MOTHER-CHILD HOUSEHOLDS IS HIGH (19) W-D,S	0.60 OF 10	314	TILT TOWARD BEING THOSE WHERE THE INCIDENCE OF MOTHER-CHILD HOUSEHOLDS IS LOW (61) W-D,S	0.81 OF 70	6 13 4 57 XSQ= 6.16 PHI= 0.278 XP = 0.0130

317	DRIFT TOWARD BEING THOSE 0.73 OF 11 WHERE DISPLAY OF AFFECTION TOWARD THE INFANT IS LOW (29) B-B-C	317	DRIFT TOWARD BEING THOSE 0.63 OF 57 WHERE DISPLAY OF AFFECTION TOWARD THE INFANT IS HIGH (39) B-B-C	3 36 8 21 XSQ= 3.50 PHI= -0.227 XP = 0.0614
318	TILT TOWARD BEING THOSE 0.82 OF 11 WHERE THE OVERALL INDULGENCE OF THE INFANT IS LOW (31) B-B-C	318	TILT TOWARD BEING THOSE 0.63 OF 60 WHERE THE OVERALL INDULGENCE OF THE INFANT IS HIGH (40) B-B-C	2 38 9 22 XSQ= 5.98 PHI= -0.290 XP = 0.0145
321	TILT TOWARD BEING THOSE 0.80 OF 10 WHERE THE IMMEDIACY OF REDUCTION OF THE INFANT'S DRIVES IS LOW (25) B-B-C	321	TILT TOWARD BEING THOSE 0.66 OF 50 WHERE THE IMMEDIACY OF REDUCTION OF THE INFANT'S DRIVES IS HIGH (35) B-B-C	2 33 8 17 XSQ= 5.49 PHI= -0.302 XP = 0.0192
322	TILT TOWARD BEING THOSE 0.90 OF 10 WHERE THE CONSISTENCY OF REDUCTION OF THE INFANT'S DRIVES IS LOW (32) B-B-C	322	TILT TOWARD BEING THOSE 0.53 OF 49 WHERE THE CONSISTENCY OF REDUCTION OF THE INFANT'S DRIVES IS HIGH (27) B-B-C	1 26 9 23 XSQ= 4.59 PHI= -0.279 XP = 0.0321
326	DRIFT TOWARD BEING THOSE 0.80 OF 10 WHERE THE INFERRED TRANSITION ANXIETY BETWEEN INFANCY AND CHILDHOOD IS HIGH (32) B-B-C	326	DRIFT TOWARD BEING THOSE 0.58 OF 57 WHERE THE INFERRED TRANSITION ANXIETY BETWEEN INFANCY AND CHILDHOOD IS LOW (35) B-B-C	8 24 2 33 XSQ= 3.50 PHI= 0.228 XP = 0.0615
337	DRIFT TOWARD BEING THOSE 0.82 OF 11 WHERE THE CHILD'S INFERRED ANXIETY OVER NON-PERFORMANCE OF RESPONSIBLE BEHAVIOR IS HIGH (38) B-B-C	337	DRIFT TOWARD BEING THOSE 0.53 OF 62 WHERE THE CHILD'S INFERRED ANXIETY OVER NON-PERFORMANCE OF RESPONSIBLE BEHAVIOR IS LOW (35) B-B-C	9 29 2 33 XSQ= 3.30 PHI= 0.213 XP = 0.0693
339	DRIFT TOWARD BEING THOSE 0.73 OF 11 WHERE THE CHILD'S INFERRED CONFLICT REGARDING RESPONSIBLE BEHAVIOR IS HIGH (31) B-B-C	339	DRIFT TOWARD BEING THOSE 0.63 OF 62 WHERE THE CHILD'S INFERRED CONFLICT REGARDING RESPONSIBLE BEHAVIOR IS LOW (42) B-B-C	8 23 3 39 XSQ= 3.51 PHI= 0.219 XP = 0.0612
353	TILT MORE TOWARD BEING THOSE 0.91 OF 11 WHERE THE CHILD'S INFERRED ANXIETY OVER NON-PERFORMANCE OF OBEDIENT BEHAVIOR IS HIGH (42) B-B-C	353	TILT LESS TOWARD BEING THOSE 0.51 OF 63 WHERE THE CHILD'S INFERRED ANXIETY OVER NON-PERFORMANCE OF OBEDIENT BEHAVIOR IS HIGH (42) B-B-C	10 32 1 31 XSQ= 4.61 PHI= 0.250 XP = 0.0317
366	TEND TO BE THOSE 0.88 OF 8 WHERE DISSOCIATION OF THE SEXES AT ADOLESCENCE IS HIGH (16) JKH	366	TEND TO BE THOSE 0.82 OF 49 WHERE DISSOCIATION OF THE SEXES AT ADOLESCENCE IS MEDIUM OR LOW (41) JKH	7 9 1 40 XSQ= 13.03 PHI= 0.478 XP = 0.0003

```
370  DRIFT TOWARD BEING THOSE        0.60 OF  20     370  DRIFT TOWARD BEING THOSE        0.63 OF 223         12   83
     WHERE THE SEGREGATION OF ADOLESCENT BOYS             WHERE THE SEGREGATION OF ADOLESCENT BOYS             8  140
     IS COMPLETE OR PARTIAL  (95)                         IS ABSENT  (148)                              XSQ=     3.10
                                                                                                        PHI=    0.113
                                                                                                        XP =   0.0783

427  TILT TOWARD BEING THOSE         0.89 OF   9     427  TILT TOWARD BEING THOSE         0.59 OF 147          1   86
     WHERE A HIGH GOD, IF PRESENT, IS                     WHERE A HIGH GOD, IF PRESENT, IS                     8   61
     INACTIVE, RATHER THAN                                ACTIVE, RATHER THAN                           XSQ=     5.92
     ACTIVE  (69) GES,EA                                  INACTIVE  (87) GES,EA                         PHI=   -0.195
                                                                                                        XP =   0.0150

441  DRIFT TOWARD BEING THOSE        0.88 OF   8     441  DRIFT TOWARD BEING THOSE        0.53 OF  53          1   28
     WHERE FEAR OF HUMAN BEINGS                           WHERE FEAR OF HUMAN BEINGS                           7   25
     IS LOW  (32) W-C                                     IS HIGH  (29) W-C                             XSQ=     3.06
                                                                                                        PHI=   -0.224
                                                                                                        XP =   0.0802

443  DRIFT TOWARD BEING THOSE        0.88 OF   8     443  DRIFT TOWARD BEING THOSE        0.57 OF  53          1   30
     WHERE OVERALL FEAR OF OTHERS                         WHERE OVERALL FEAR OF OTHERS                         7   23
     IS LOW  (30) W-C                                     IS HIGH  (31) W-C                             XSQ=     3.79
                                                                                                        PHI=   -0.249
                                                                                                        XP =   0.0516

458  TILT TOWARD BEING THOSE         0.62 OF  13     458  TILT TOWARD BEING THOSE         0.72 OF 158          8   44
     WHERE GAMES, IF PRESENT,                             WHERE GAMES, IF PRESENT,                             5  114
     INCLUDE GAMES OF STRATEGY  (52) R-A-B,EA             DO NOT INCLUDE                                XSQ=     4.95
                                                          GAMES OF STRATEGY  (119) R-A-B,EA             PHI=    0.170
                                                                                                        XP =   0.0261

482  TILT LESS TOWARD BEING THOSE    0.68 OF  25     482  TILT MORE TOWARD BEING THOSE    0.88 OF 363          8   44
     WHERE THE PRINCIPAL ETHNOGRAPHERS                    WHERE THE PRINCIPAL ETHNOGRAPHERS                   17  319
     HAVE BEEN OTHER THAN BRITISH  (336)                  HAVE BEEN OTHER THAN BRITISH  (336)           XSQ=     6.34
                                                                                                        PHI=    0.128
                                                                                                        XP =   0.0118

483  TILT TOWARD BEING THOSE         0.67 OF  12     483  TILT TOWARD BEING THOSE         0.71 OF 153          4  109
     WHERE THE PRINCIPAL ETHNOGRAPHERS                    WHERE THE PRINCIPAL ETHNOGRAPHERS                    8   44
     HAVE BEEN BRITISH,                                   HAVE BEEN AMERICAN,                           XSQ=     5.76
     RATHER THAN AMERICAN  (52)                           RATHER THAN BRITISH  (113)                    PHI=   -0.187
                                                                                                        XP =   0.0164

490  LEAN TOWARD BEING THOSE         0.56 OF  25     490  LEAN TOWARD BEING THOSE         0.74 OF 375         14   99
     INCLUDED IN ALBERT S. ANTHONY'S                      NOT INCLUDED IN ALBERT S. ANTHONY'S                 11  276
     SAMPLE ON MALE INITIATION RITES  (113)               SAMPLE ON MALE INITIATION RITES  (287)        XSQ=     8.72
                                                                                                        PHI=    0.148
                                                                                                        XP =   0.0031

491  LEAN LESS TOWARD BEING THOSE    0.68 OF  25     491  LEAN MORE TOWARD BEING THOSE    0.89 OF 375          8   40
     NOT INCLUDED IN DORRIAN APPLE'S                      NOT INCLUDED IN DORRIAN APPLE'S                     17  335
     STUDY OF GRANDPARENTHOOD  (352)                      STUDY OF GRANDPARENTHOOD  (352)               XSQ=     8.18
                                                                                                        PHI=    0.143
                                                                                                        XP =   0.0042
```

492	TEND LESS TO BE THCSE 0.68 OF 25 NOT INCLUDED IN BARBARA CHARTIER AYRES' STUDY OF FEMALE INITIATION RITES (361)	492	TEND MORE TO BE THOSE 0.92 OF 375 NOT INCLUDED IN BARBARA.CHARTIER AYRES' STUDY OF FEMALE INITIATICN RITES (361)	8 31 17 344 XSQ= 12.43 PHI= 0.176 XP = 0.0004
493	LEAN LESS TOWARC BEING THCSE 0.56 OF 25 NCT INCLUDED IN BACON, BARRY, AND CHILC'S STUDY OF CHILD REARING (322)	493	LEAN MORE TOWARD BEING THOSE 0.82 OF 375 NOT INCLUDED IN BACON, BARRY, AND CHILD'S STUDY OF CHILD REARING (322)	11 67 14 308 XSQ= 8.60 PHI= 0.147 XP = 0.0034
494	TILT LESS TOWARC BEING THOSE 0.80 OF 25 NOT INCLUDED IN HERBERT M. BARRY III'S STUDY OF ART (371)	494	TILT MORE TOWARD BEING THOSE 0.94 OF 375 NOT INCLUDED IN HERBERT M. BARRY III'S STUDY OF ART (371)	5 24 20 351 XSQ= 4.58 PHI= 0.107 XP = 0.0323
495	TILT LESS TOWARC BEING THOSE 0.64 OF 25 NOT INCLUDED IN JUDITH K. BROWN'S STUDY OF FEMALE INITIATICN RITES (335)	495	TILT MORE TOWARD BEING THOSE 0.85 OF 375 NOT INCLUDED IN JUDITH K. BROWN'S STUDY OF FEMALE INITIATION RITES (335)	9 56 16 319 XSQ= 6.17 PHI= 0.124 XP = 0.0130
497	TEND LESS TO BE THCSE 0.52 OF 25 NOT INCLUDED IN WILLIAM M. EVAN'S STUDY OF LAW (339)	497	TEND MORE TO BE THOSE 0.87 OF 375 NOT INCLUDED IN WILLIAM M. EVAN'S STUDY OF LAW (339)	12 49 13 326 XSQ= 19.51 PHI= 0.221 XP = 0.0000
498	TILT LESS TOWARC BEING THCSE 0.72 OF 25 NOT INCLUDED IN C. S. FCRC'S STUDY OF SEX (349)	498	TILT MORE TOWARD BEING THOSE 0.88 OF 375 NOT INCLUDED IN C. S. FORD'S STUDY OF SEX (349)	7 44 18 331 XSQ= 4.21 PHI= 0.103 XP = 0.0402
499	TEND TO BE THOSE 0.56 OF 25 INCLUDED IN FCRC AND BEACH'S SAMPLE ON SEXUAL EXPRESSION BY THE YOUNG (86)	499	TEND TO BE THOSE 0.81 OF 375 NOT INCLUDED IN FORD AND BEACH'S SAMPLE ON SEXUAL EXPRESSION BY THE YOUNG (314)	14 72 11 303 XSQ= 16.69 PHI= 0.204 XP = 0.0000
501	DRIFT LESS TOWARD BEING THOSE 0.68 OF 25 NOT INCLUDED IN JOAN FRIENDLY GOODMAN'S STUDY OF ASCETIC MOURNING BEHAVIOR (333)	501	DRIFT MORE TOWARD BEING THOSE 0.84 OF 375 NOT INCLUDED IN JOAN FRIENDLY GOODMAN'S STUDY OF ASCETIC MOURNING BEHAVIOR (333)	8 59 17 316 XSQ= 3.36 PHI= 0.092 XP = 0.0669
502	TILT LESS TOWARC BEING THOSE 0.68 OF 25 NOT INCLUDED IN JOHN K. HARLEY'S STUDY OF ADOLESCENT PEER GROUPS (343)	502	TILT MORE TOWARD BEING THOSE 0.87 OF 375 NOT INCLUDED IN JOHN K. HARLEY'S STUDY OF ADOLESCENT PEER GROUPS (343)	8 49 17 326 XSQ= 5.41 PHI= 0.116 XP = 0.0200

503	TILT LESS TOWARD BEING THOSE 0.68 OF 25 NOT INCLUDED IN JOHN M. HICKMAN'S STUDY OF THE FOLK-URBAN CONTINUUM (346)	503	TILT MORE TOWARD BEING THOSE 0.88 OF 375 NOT INCLUDED IN JOHN M. HICKMAN'S STUDY OF THE FOLK-URBAN CONTINUUM (346)	8 46 17 329 XSQ= 6.22 PHI= 0.125 XP = 0.0127
506	TEND LESS TO BE THOSE 0.64 OF 25 NOT INCLUDED IN LAMBERT, TRIANDIS, AND WOLF'S STUDY OF SUPERNATURAL BEINGS (364)	506	TEND MORE TO BE THOSE 0.93 OF 375 NOT INCLUDED IN LAMBERT, TRIANDIS, AND WOLF'S STUDY OF SUPERNATURAL BEINGS (364)	9 27 16 348 XSQ= 20.35 PHI= 0.226 XP = 0.0000
507	LEAN LESS TOWARD BEING THOSE 0.52 OF 25 NOT INCLUDED IN JAMES R. LEARY'S STUDY OF FOOD TABOOS (314)	507	LEAN MORE TOWARD BEING THOSE 0.80 OF 375 NOT INCLUDED IN JAMES R. LEARY'S STUDY OF FOOD TABOOS (314)	12 74 13 301 XSQ= 9.48 PHI= 0.154 XP = 0.0021
508	TILT LESS TOWARD BEING THOSE 0.76 OF 25 NOT INCLUDED IN DAVID C. MCCLELLAND'S STUDY OF ACHIEVEMENT MOTIVATION (360)	508	TILT MORE TOWARD BEING THOSE 0.91 OF 375 NOT INCLUDED IN DAVID C. MCCLELLAND'S STUDY OF ACHIEVEMENT MOTIVATION (360)	6 34 19 341 XSQ= 4.27 PHI= 0.103 XP = 0.0389
510	TILT LESS TOWARD BEING THOSE 0.84 OF 25 NOT INCLUDED IN RAOUL NAROLL'S STUDY OF SOCIETAL COMPLEXITY (380)	510	TILT MORE TOWARD BEING THOSE 0.96 OF 375 NOT INCLUDED IN RAOUL NAROLL'S STUDY OF SOCIETAL COMPLEXITY (380)	4 16 21 359 XSQ= 4.55 PHI= 0.107 XP = 0.0330
512	DRIFT LESS TOWARD BEING THOSE 0.80 OF 25 NOT INCLUDED IN SHIRLEY AND ROMNEY'S STUDY OF LOVE MAGIC (367)	512	DRIFT MORE TOWARD BEING THOSE 0.93 OF 375 NOT INCLUDED IN SHIRLEY AND ROMNEY'S STUDY OF LOVE MAGIC (367)	5 28 20 347 XSQ= 3.35 PHI= 0.092 XP = 0.0672
514	LEAN LESS TOWARD BEING THOSE 0.52 OF 25 NOT INCLUDED IN PHILIP E. SLATER'S STUDY OF NARCISSISM (310)	514	LEAN MORE TOWARD BEING THOSE 0.79 OF 375 NOT INCLUDED IN PHILIP E. SLATER'S STUDY OF NARCISSISM (310)	12 78 13 297 XSQ= 8.45 PHI= 0.145 XP = 0.0037
515	LEAN LESS TOWARD BEING THOSE 0.64 OF 25 NOT INCLUDED IN WILLIAM N. STEPHENS' SAMPLE ON AVOIDANCE RELATIONSHIPS (348)	515	LEAN MORE TOWARD BEING THOSE 0.89 OF 375 NOT INCLUDED IN WILLIAM N. STEPHENS' SAMPLE ON AVOIDANCE RELATIONSHIPS (348)	9 43 16 332 XSQ= 10.40 PHI= 0.161 XP = 0.0013
519	TILT LESS TOWARD BEING THOSE 0.76 OF 25 NOT INCLUDED IN JOSEPH VEROFF'S STUDY OF ACHIEVEMENT MOTIVATION AS REVEALED IN FOLKTALES (364)	519	TILT MORE TOWARD BEING THOSE 0.92 OF 375 NOT INCLUDED IN JOSEPH VEROFF'S STUDY OF ACHIEVEMENT MOTIVATION AS REVEALED IN FOLKTALES (364)	6 30 19 345 XSQ= 5.50 PHI= 0.117 XP = 0.0190

521	TEND LESS TO BE THCSE NOT INCLUDED IN JOHN W. M. WHITING'S STUDY OF SOCIALIZATION PROCESS AND PERSCNALITY (353)	0.64 OF 25	521	TEND MORE TO BE THOSE NOT INCLUDED IN JOHN W. M. WHITING'S STUDY OF SOCIALIZATION PROCESS AND PERSONALITY (353)	0.90 OF 375	9 38 16 337 XSQ= 12.73 PHI= 0.178 XP = 0.0004
522	TEND TO BE THOSE INCLUDED IN MARJORIE GRANT WHITING'S STUDY OF DIET (82)	0.52 OF 25	522	TEND TO BE THOSE NOT INCLUDED IN MARJORIE GRANT WHITING'S STUDY OF DIET (318)	0.82 OF 375	13 69 12 306 XSQ= 14.24 PHI= 0.189 XP = 0.0002
523	TILT LESS TOWARD BEING THCSE NOT INCLUDED IN WHITING ANC CHILD'S STUDY OF CHILD TRAINING AND PERSCNALITY (339)	0.68 OF 25	523	TILT MORE TOWARD BEING THOSE NOT INCLUDED IN WHITING AND CHILD'S STUDY OF CHILD TRAINING AND PERSONALITY (339)	0.86 OF 375	8 53 17 322 XSQ= 4.49 PHI= 0.106 XP = 0.0341
524	TEND LESS TO BE THCSE NOT INCLUDED IN WHITING, KLUCKHCHN, ANC ANTHONY'S STUDY OF MALE INITIATICN CEREMONIES (356)	0.64 OF 25	524	TEND MORE TO BE THOSE NOT INCLUDED IN WHITING, KLUCKHOHN, AND ANTHONY'S STUDY OF MALE INITIATION CEREMONIES (356)	0.91 OF 375	9 35 16 340 XSQ= 14.41 PHI= 0.190 XP = 0.0001

510 CULTURES
INCLUDED IN RAOUL NARROLL'S
STUDY OF SOCIETAL COMPLEXITY (20)

510 CULTURES
NOT INCLUDED IN RAOUL NARROLL'S
STUDY OF SOCIETAL COMPLEXITY (380)

BACKGROUND ON PAGE 180

SUBJECT ONLY, F.C. 1-480 AND 527-536
BOTH SUBJECT AND PREDICATE, F.C. 481-526

20 IN LEFT COLUMN

AINU NUER, AZTEC NUPE, CROW CNA, CUNA SAMOANS, FON SELUNG, HANO TIKOPIA, INCA TIMBIRA, LEPCHA TODA, LESU YAGUA, NAMA YAHGAN

380 IN RIGHT COLUMN

	Left column (20)			Right column (380)		
74	DRIFT TOWARD BEING THOSE WHERE POTTERY IS ABSENT (93)	0.61 OF 18	74	DRIFT TOWARD BEING THOSE WHERE POTTERY IS PRESENT (145)	0.63 OF 220	7 138 11 82 XSQ= 3.03 PHI= -0.113 XP = 0.0816
139	DRIFT TOWARD BEING THOSE WHERE SUPERORDINATE PUNISHMENT IS PRESENT (15) BBW	0.80 OF 5	139	DRIFT TOWARD BEING THOSE WHERE SUPERORDINATE PUNISHMENT IS ABSENT (25) BBW	0.69 OF 35	4 11 1 24 XSQ= 2.58 PHI= 0.254 EP = 0.0564
182	TILT MORE TOWARD BEING THOSE OTHER THAN WHERE THE COMMUNITY IS STRUCTURED ON A NON-CLAN BASIS AND AGAMOUS (256)	0.90 OF 20	182	TILT LESS TOWARD BEING THOSE OTHER THAN WHERE THE COMMUNITY IS STRUCTURED ON A NON-CLAN BASIS AND AGAMOUS (256)	0.66 OF 362	2 124 18 238 XSQ= 4.01 PHI= -0.102 XP = 0.0453
220	DRIFT MORE TOWARD BEING THOSE WHERE FIRST COUSIN MARRIAGE IN SOME FORM OR OTHER IS NOT PRESCRIBED OR PREFERRED (273)	0.95 OF 19	220	DRIFT LESS TOWARD BEING THOSE WHERE FIRST COUSIN MARRIAGE IN SOME FORM OR OTHER IS NOT PRESCRIBED OR PREFERRED (273)	0.73 OF 351	1 96 18 255 XSQ= 3.48 PHI= -0.097 XP = 0.0623
303	TILT TOWARD BEING THOSE WHERE THE EARLY ORAL SATISFACTION POTENTIAL IS LOW (25) W-C	0.88 OF 8	303	TILT TOWARD BEING THOSE WHERE THE EARLY ORAL SATISFACTION POTENTIAL IS HIGH (32) W-C	0.63 OF 49	1 31 7 18 XSQ= 5.28 PHI= -0.304 XP = 0.0215
334	TILT TOWARD BEING THOSE WHERE THE INDULGENCE OF THE CHILD IS HIGH (40) B-B-C	0.79 OF 14	334	TILT TOWARD BEING THOSE WHERE THE INDULGENCE OF THE CHILD IS LOW (38) B-B-C	0.55 OF 64	11 29 3 35 XSQ= 3.84 PHI= 0.222 XP = 0.0500

338	DRIFT TOWARD BEING THOSE 0.64 OF 14 WHERE THE CHILD'S INFERRED ANXIETY OVER PERFORMANCE OF RESPONSIBLE BEHAVIOR IS LOW (29) B-B-C	338	DRIFT TOWARD BEING THOSE 0.66 OF 59 WHERE THE CHILD'S INFERRED ANXIETY OVER PERFORMANCE OF RESPONSIBLE BEHAVIOR IS HIGH (44) B-B-C	5 39 9 20 XSQ= 3.19 PHI= -0.209 XP = 0.0742
344	DRIFT TOWARD BEING THOSE 0.79 OF 14 WHERE THE TOTAL POSITIVE PRESSURE TOWARD DEVELOPING SELF-RELIANT BEHAVIOR IN THE CHILD IS LOW (40) B-B-C	344	DRIFT TOWARD BEING THOSE 0.53 OF 62 WHERE THE TOTAL POSITIVE PRESSURE TOWARD DEVELOPING SELF-RELIANT BEHAVIOR IN THE CHILD IS HIGH (36) B-B-C	3 33 11 29 XSQ= 3.44 PHI= -0.213 XP = 0.0635
345	TILT TOWARD BEING THOSE 0.79 OF 14 WHERE THE CHILD'S INFERRED ANXIETY OVER NON-PERFORMANCE OF SELF-RELIANT BEHAVIOR IS LOW (39) B-B-C	345	TILT TOWARD BEING THOSE 0.55 OF 62 WHERE THE CHILD'S INFERRED ANXIETY OVER NON-PERFORMANCE OF SELF-RELIANT BEHAVIOR IS HIGH (37) B-B-C	3 34 11 28 XSQ= 3.85 PHI= -0.225 XP = 0.0496
347	TILT TOWARD BEING THOSE 0.79 OF 14 WHERE THE CHILD'S INFERRED CONFLICT REGARDING SELF-RELIANT BEHAVIOR IS LOW (39) B-B-C	347	TILT TOWARD BEING THOSE 0.55 OF 62 WHERE THE CHILD'S INFERRED CONFLICT REGARDING SELF-RELIANT BEHAVIOR IS HIGH (37) B-B-C	3 34 11 28 XSQ= 3.85 PHI= -0.225 XP = 0.0496
349	DRIFT TOWARD BEING THOSE 0.69 OF 13 WHERE THE CHILD'S INFERRED ANXIETY OVER NON-PERFORMANCE OF ACHIEVEMENT BEHAVIOR IS LOW (28) B-B-C	349	DRIFT TOWARD BEING THOSE 0.61 OF 49 WHERE THE CHILD'S INFERRED ANXIETY OVER NON-PERFORMANCE OF ACHIEVEMENT BEHAVIOR IS HIGH (34) B-B-C	4 30 9 19 XSQ= 2.72 PHI= -0.209 XP = 0.0993
350	TILT TOWARD BEING THOSE 0.77 OF 13 WHERE THE CHILD'S INFERRED ANXIETY OVER PERFORMANCE OF ACHIEVEMENT BEHAVIOR IS LOW (26) B-B-C	350	TILT TOWARD BEING THOSE 0.66 OF 47 WHERE THE CHILD'S INFERRED ANXIETY OVER PERFORMANCE OF ACHIEVEMENT BEHAVIOR IS HIGH (34) B-B-C	3 31 10 16 XSQ= 5.98 PHI= -0.316 XP = 0.0145
372	DRIFT TOWARD BEING THOSE 0.69 OF 13 WHERE MALE INITIATION RITES ARE PRESENT (48) ASA	372	DRIFT TOWARD BEING THOSE 0.60 OF 98 WHERE MALE INITIATION RITES ARE ABSENT (63) ASA	9 39 4 59 XSQ= 2.94 PHI= 0.163 XP = 0.0864
373	DRIFT TOWARD BEING THOSE 0.75 OF 8 WHERE MALE INITIATION CEREMONIES AT PUBERTY ARE PRESENT (17) W-K-A	373	DRIFT TOWARD BEING THOSE 0.69 OF 36 WHERE MALE INITIATION CEREMONIES AT PUBERTY ARE ABSENT (27) W-K-A	6 11 2 25 XSQ= 3.74 PHI= 0.292 XP = 0.0531
489	TILT LESS TOWARD BEING THOSE 0.65 OF 20 NOT INCLUDED IN CHARLES ACKERMAN'S STUDY OF DIVORCE (343)	489	TILT MORE TOWARD BEING THOSE 0.87 OF 380 NOT INCLUDED IN CHARLES ACKERMAN'S STUDY OF DIVORCE (343)	7 50 13 330 XSQ= 5.74 PHI= 0.120 XP = 0.0166

490	TEND TO BE THOSE INCLUDED IN ALBERT S. ANTHONY'S SAMPLE ON MALE INITIATION RITES (113)	0.65 OF 20	490	TEND TO BE THOSE NOT INCLUDED IN ALBERT S. ANTHONY'S SAMPLE ON MALE INITIATION RITES (287)	0.74 OF 380	13 100 7 280 XSQ= 12.18 PHI= 0.175 XP = 0.0005
491	TILT LESS TOWARD BEING THOSE NOT INCLUDED IN DORRIAN APPLE'S STUDY OF GRANDPARENTHOOD (352)	0.70 OF 20	491	TILT MORE TOWARD BEING THOSE NOT INCLUDED IN DORRIAN APPLE'S STUDY OF GRANDPARENTHOOD (352)	0.89 OF 380	6 42 14 338 XSQ= 4.79 PHI= 0.109 XP = 0.0286
492	TEND LESS TO BE THOSE NOT INCLUDED IN BARBARA CHARTIER AYRES' STUDY OF FEMALE INITIATION RITES (361)	0.65 OF 20	492	TEND MORE TO BE THOSE NOT INCLUDED IN BARBARA CHARTIER AYRES' STUDY OF FEMALE INITIATION RITES (361)	0.92 OF 380	7 32 13 348 XSQ= 12.38 PHI= 0.176 XP = 0.0004
493	TEND TO BE THOSE INCLUDED IN BACON, BARRY, AND CHILD'S STUDY OF CHILD REARING (78)	0.70 OF 20	493	TEND TO BE THOSE NOT INCLUDED IN BACON, BARRY, AND CHILD'S STUDY OF CHILD REARING (322)	0.83 OF 380	14 64 6 316 XSQ= 30.90 PHI= 0.278 XP = 0.
494	LEAN LESS TOWARD BEING THOSE NOT INCLUDED IN HERBERT M. BARRY III'S STUDY OF ART (371)	0.75 OF 20	494	LEAN MORE TOWARD BEING THOSE NOT INCLUDED IN HERBERT M. BARRY III'S STUDY OF ART (371)	0.94 OF 380	5 24 15 356 XSQ= 7.28 PHI= 0.135 XP = 0.0070
495	TEND TO BE THOSE INCLUDED IN JUDITH K. BROWN'S STUDY OF FEMALE INITIATION RITES (65)	0.50 OF 20	495	TEND TO BE THOSE NOT INCLUDED IN JUDITH K. BROWN'S STUDY OF FEMALE INITIATION RITES (335)	0.86 OF 380	10 55 10 325 XSQ= 15.11 PHI= 0.194 XP = 0.0001
497	TEND LESS TO BE THOSE NOT INCLUDED IN WILLIAM M. EVAN'S STUDY OF LAW (339)	0.55 OF 20	497	TEND MORE TO BE THOSE NOT INCLUDED IN WILLIAM M. EVAN'S STUDY OF LAW (339)	0.86 OF 380	9 52 11 328 XSQ= 12.10 PHI= 0.174 XP = 0.0005
498	TEND LESS TO BE THOSE NOT INCLUDED IN C. S. FORD'S STUDY OF SEX (349)	0.55 OF 20	498	TEND MORE TO BE THOSE NOT INCLUDED IN C. S. FORD'S STUDY OF SEX (349)	0.89 OF 380	9 42 11 338 XSQ= 16.75 PHI= 0.205 XP = 0.0000
499	TEND TO BE THOSE INCLUDED IN FORD AND BEACH'S SAMPLE ON SEXUAL EXPRESSION BY THE YOUNG (86)	0.65 OF 20	499	TEND TO BE THOSE NOT INCLUDED IN FORD AND BEACH'S SAMPLE ON SEXUAL EXPRESSION BY THE YOUNG (314)	0.81 OF 380	13 73 7 307 XSQ= 20.97 PHI= 0.229 XP = 0.0000

500	DRIFT LESS TOWARD BEING THOSE 0.75 OF 20 NOT INCLUDED IN FREEMAN AND WINCH'S STUDY OF SOCIETAL COMPLEXITY (360)	500	DRIFT MORE TOWARD BEING THOSE 0.91 OF 380 NOT INCLUDED IN FREEMAN AND WINCH'S STUDY OF SOCIETAL COMPLEXITY (360)	5 35 15 345 XSQ= 3.65 PHI= 0.096 XP = 0.0559
501	TEND TO BE THOSE 0.50 OF 20 INCLUDED IN JOAN FRIENDLY GOODMAN'S STUDY OF ASCETIC MOURNING BEHAVIOR (67)	501	TEND TO BE THOSE 0.85 OF 380 NOT INCLUDED IN JOAN FRIENDLY GOODMAN'S STUDY OF ASCETIC MOURNING BEHAVIOR (333)	10 57 10 323 XSQ= 14.28 PHI= 0.189 XP = 0.0002
502	DRIFT LESS TOWARD BEING THOSE 0.70 OF 20 NOT INCLUDED IN JOHN K. HARLEY'S STUDY OF ADOLESCENT PEER GROUPS (343)	502	DRIFT MORE TOWARD BEING THOSE 0.87 OF 380 NOT INCLUDED IN JOHN K. HARLEY'S STUDY OF ADOLESCENT PEER GROUPS (343)	6 51 14 329 XSQ= 3.02 PHI= 0.087 XP = 0.0820
503	TEND LESS TO BE THOSE 0.55 OF 20 NOT INCLUDED IN JOHN M. HICKMAN'S STUDY OF THE FOLK-URBAN CONTINUUM (346)	503	TEND MORE TO BE THOSE 0.88 OF 380 NOT INCLUDED IN JOHN M. HICKMAN'S STUDY OF THE FOLK-URBAN CONTINUUM (346)	9 45 11 335 XSQ= 15.16 PHI= 0.195 XP = 0.0001
504	TILT LESS TOWARD BEING THOSE 0.70 OF 20 NOT INCLUDED IN DONALD HORTON'S STUDY OF ALCHOLISM (351)	504	TILT MORE TOWARD BEING THOSE 0.89 OF 380 NOT INCLUDED IN DONALD HORTON'S STUDY OF ALCHOLISM (351)	6 43 14 337 XSQ= 4.55 PHI= 0.107 XP = 0.0328
506	TEND LESS TO BE THOSE 0.65 OF 20 NOT INCLUDED IN LAMBERT, TRIANDIS, AND WOLF'S STUDY OF SUPERNATURAL BEINGS (364)	506	TEND MORE TO BE THOSE 0.92 OF 380 NOT INCLUDED IN LAMBERT, TRIANDIS, AND WOLF'S STUDY OF SUPERNATURAL BEINGS (364)	7 29 13 351 XSQ= 14.20 PHI= 0.188 XP = 0.0002
507	TEND TO BE THOSE 0.55 OF 20 INCLUDED IN JAMES R. LEARY'S STUDY OF FOOD TABOOS (86)	507	TEND TO BE THOSE 0.80 OF 380 NOT INCLUDED IN JAMES R. LEARY'S STUDY OF FOOD TABOOS (314)	11 75 9 305 XSQ= 11.99 PHI= 0.173 XP = 0.0005
508	DRIFT LESS TOWARD BEING THOSE 0.75 OF 20 NOT INCLUDED IN DAVID C. MCCLELLAND'S STUDY OF ACHIEVEMENT MOTIVATION (360)	508	DRIFT MORE TOWARD BEING THOSE 0.91 OF 380 NOT INCLUDED IN DAVID C. MCCLELLAND'S STUDY OF ACHIEVEMENT MOTIVATION (360)	5 35 15 345 XSQ= 3.65 PHI= 0.096 XP = 0.0559
509	TILT LESS TOWARD BEING THOSE 0.80 OF 20 NOT INCLUDED IN MONI NAG'S STUDY OF FERTILITY (375)	509	TILT MORE TOWARD BEING THOSE 0.94 OF 380 NOT INCLUDED IN MONI NAG'S STUDY OF FERTILITY (375)	4 21 16 359 XSQ= 4.55 PHI= 0.107 XP = 0.0330

511	LEAN TOWARD BEING THOSE 0.80 OF 20 INCLUDED IN ROBERTS, ARTH AND BUSH'S SAMPLE ON GAMES, AS MODIFIED BY THE ETHNOGRAPHIC ATLAS (189)	511	LEAN TOWARD BEING THOSE 0.54 OF 380 NOT INCLUDED IN ROBERTS, ARTH AND BUSH'S SAMPLE ON GAMES, AS MODIFIED BY THE ETHNOGRAPHIC ATLAS (211)	16 173 4 207 XSQ= 7.73 PHI= 0.139 XP = 0.0054
513	TEND TO BE THOSE 0.50 OF 20 INCLUDED IN LEO W. SIMMONS' STUDY OF THE TREATMENT OF THE AGED (43)	513	TEND TO BE THOSE 0.91 OF 380 NOT INCLUDED IN LEO W. SIMMONS' STUDY OF THE TREATMENT OF THE AGED (357)	10 33 10 347 XSQ= 29.63 PHI= 0.272 XP = 0.0000
514	TEND TO BE THOSE 0.85 OF 20 INCLUDED IN PHILIP E. SLATER'S STUDY OF NARCISSISM (90)	514	TEND TO BE THOSE 0.81 OF 380 NOT INCLUDED IN PHILIP E. SLATER'S STUDY OF NARCISSISM (310)	17 73 3 307 XSQ= 43.46 PHI= 0.330 XP = 0.
515	TEND TO BE THOSE 0.50 OF 20 INCLUDED IN WILLIAM N. STEPHENS' SAMPLE ON AVOIDANCE RELATIONSHIPS (52)	515	TEND TO BE THOSE 0.89 OF 380 NOT INCLUDED IN WILLIAM N. STEPHENS' SAMPLE ON AVOIDANCE RELATIONSHIPS (348)	10 42 10 338 XSQ= 22.16 PHI= 0.235 XP = 0.0000
516	IN ALL CASES ARE THOSE 1.00 OF 20 INCLUDED IN GUY E. SWANSON'S SAMPLE ON LOCAL JURISDICTION, AS MODIFIED BY THE ETHNOGRAPHIC ATLAS (331)	516	DRIFT LESS TOWARD BEING THOSE 0.82 OF 380 INCLUDED IN GUY E. SWANSON'S SAMPLE ON LOCAL JURISDICTION, AS MODIFIED BY THE ETHNOGRAPHIC ATLAS (331)	20 311 0 69 XSQ= 3.21 PHI= 0.090 XP = 0.0732
517	TILT MORE TOWARD BEING THOSE 0.90 OF 20 INCLUDED IN GUY E. SWANSON'S SAMPLE ON HIGH GODS, AS MODIFIED BY THE ETHNOGRAPHIC ATLAS (260)	517	TILT LESS TOWARD BEING THOSE 0.64 OF 380 INCLUDED IN GUY E. SWANSON'S SAMPLE ON HIGH GODS, AS MODIFIED BY THE ETHNOGRAPHIC ATLAS (260)	18 242 2 138 XSQ= 4.68 PHI= 0.108 XP = 0.0304
518	LEAN TOWARD BEING THOSE 0.60 OF 20 INCLUDED IN STANLEY H. UDY, JR.'S STUDY OF WORK ORGANIZATION (105)	518	LEAN TOWARD BEING THOSE 0.76 OF 380 NOT INCLUDED IN STANLEY H. UDY, JR.'S STUDY OF WORK ORGANIZATION (295)	12 93 8 287 XSQ= 10.62 PHI= 0.163 XP = 0.0011
520	DRIFT LESS TOWARD BEING THOSE 0.75 OF 20 NOT INCLUDED IN BEATRICE BLYTH WHITING'S STUDY OF SORCERY (360)	520	DRIFT MORE TOWARD BEING THOSE 0.91 OF 380 NOT INCLUDED IN BEATRICE BLYTH WHITING'S STUDY OF SORCERY (360)	5 35 15 345 XSQ= 3.65 PHI= 0.096 XP = 0.0559
521	TEND LESS TO BE THOSE 0.55 OF 20 NOT INCLUDED IN JOHN W. M. WHITING'S STUDY OF SOCIALIZATION PROCESS AND PERSONALITY (353)	521	TEND MORE TO BE THOSE 0.90 OF 380 NOT INCLUDED IN JOHN W. M. WHITING'S STUDY OF SOCIALIZATION PROCESS AND PERSONALITY (353)	9 38 11 342 XSQ= 19.20 PHI= 0.219 XP = 0.0000

522	TEND TO BE THOSE INCLUDED IN MARJORIE GRANT WHITING'S STUDY OF DIET (82)	0.55 OF 20	522	TEND TO BE THOSE NOT INCLUDED IN MARJORIE GRANT WHITING'S STUDY OF DIET (318)	0.81 OF 380	11 71 9 309 XSQ= 13.23 PHI= 0.182 XP = 0.0003
523	LEAN LESS TOWARD BEING THOSE NOT INCLUDED IN WHITING AND CHILD'S STUDY OF CHILD TRAINING AND PERSONALITY (339)	0.60 OF 20	523	LEAN MORE TOWARD BEING THOSE NOT INCLUDED IN WHITING AND CHILD'S STUDY OF CHILD TRAINING AND PERSONALITY (339)	0.86 OF 380	8 53 12 327 XSQ= 8.06 PHI= 0.142 XP = 0.0045
524	TEND LESS TO BE THOSE NOT INCLUDED IN WHITING, KLUCKHOHN, AND ANTHONY'S STUDY OF MALE INITIATION CEREMONIES (356)	0.60 OF 20	524	TEND MORE TO BE THOSE NOT INCLUDED IN WHITING, KLUCKHOHN, AND ANTHONY'S STUDY OF MALE INITIATION CEREMONIES (356)	0.91 OF 380	8 36 12 344 XSQ= 15.10 PHI= 0.194 XP = 0.0001

511 CULTURES
INCLUDED IN ROBERTS, ARTH AND BUSH'S
SAMPLE ON GAMES, AS MODIFIED
BY THE ETHNOGRAPHIC ATLAS (189)

511 CULTURES
NOT INCLUDED IN ROBERTS, ARTH AND BUSH'S
SAMPLE ON GAMES, AS MODIFIED
BY THE ETHNOGRAPHIC ATLAS (211)

BACKGROUND ON PAGE 180

SUBJECT ONLY, F.C. 1-480 AND 527-536
BOTH SUBJECT AND PREDICATE, F.C. 481-526

189 IN LEFT COLUMN

ABIPON	ABOR	AINU	ALACALUF	ALBANIANS	AMERICANS	ANDAMANESE	APINAYE	ARANDA	ARAUCANIANS
ASHANTI	ATSUGEWI	AYMARA	AZANDE	AZTEC	BACAIRI	BASSERI	BHIL	BHUIYA	BORORO
BUNLAP	BURUSHO	CACUVEC	CAGABA	CAMAYURA	CARIB	CAYAPA	CHAGGA	CHENCHU	CHEROKEE
CHEYENNE	CHIR-APACHE	CHIRIGUANO	CHOROTI	CHORTI	CHUKCHEE	COORG	COPR ESKIMO	CREE	CREEK
CROW	CUNA	CZECHS	DARC	DIEGUENO	DIERI	EGYPTIANS	ELLICE	EYAK	FANG
FON	GANDA	GARO	GOAJIRO	GROS VENTRE	HAIDA	HASINAI	HAWAIIANS	HUICHOL	HUKUNDIKA
HURON	HUTSUL	IBAN	ILA	INCA	INGALIK	IRISH	JAPANESE	JEMEZ	JIVARO
JUKUN	KASKA	KATAB	KAZAK	KERAKI	KHASI	KIKUYU	KOREANS	KORYAK	KUBA
KUNG	KURTATCHI	KUTENAI	KWAKIUTL	LAKHER	LAMBA	LAPPS	LAU	LEPCHA	LESU
LHOTA NAGA	LUC	MACASSARESE	MANGAIANS	MANIHIKI	MANUS	MAORI	MARICOPA	MARQUESANS	MARSHALLESE
MASAI	MATACO	MAYA	MBUNDU	MENDE	MIAMI	MIN CHINESE	MISKITO	MIWCK	MOSSI
MOTA	MURNGIN	NABESNA	NAMA	NATCHEZ	NAVAHO	NICOBARESE	NOMLAKI	NUNIVAK	NYAKYUSA
NYORO	OKINAWANS	OMAHA	ONA	PAEZ	PAIWAN	PALAUANS	PAPAGO	PUKAPUKA	RUNDI
RWALA	SAGADA	SAMOANS	SANPOIL	SEMANG	SENIANG	SERBS	SHERENTE	SIRIONO	SIWANS
SOMALI	SYRIANS	TALAMANCA	TALLENSI	TANALA	TAOS	TAPIRAPE	TARAHUMARA	TAREUMIUT	TEHUELCHE
TENETEHARA	TENINO	THAI	THONGA	TIKOPIA	TIMBIRA	TIV	TIWI	TODA	TOLOWA
TROBRIAND	TRUKESE	TRUMAI	TUCANO	TUCUNA	TUPINAMBA	TWANA	ULAWANS	UTE	VEDDA
VENDA	VIETNAMESE	WANTOAT	WAPISHANA	WARRAU	WASHO	WITOTO	WOGEO	WOLEAIANS	WOLOF
YAGUA	YAHGAN	YAKUT	YAO	YARURO	YOKUTS	YUKI	YUROK	ZUNI	

211 IN RIGHT COLUMN

3	LEAN MORE TOWARD BEING THOSE LOCATED OUTSIDE OF AFRICA (320) 0.86 OF 189	3	LEAN LESS TOWARD BEING THOSE LOCATED OUTSIDE OF AFRICA (320) 0.75 OF 211	27 53 162 158	XSQ= 6.65 PHI= -0.129 XP = 0.0099
4	TILT MORE TOWARD BEING THOSE LOCATED OUTSIDE OF THE CIRCUM-MEDITERRANEAN (355) 0.93 OF 189	4	TILT LESS TOWARD BEING THOSE LOCATED OUTSIDE OF THE CIRCUM-MEDITERRANEAN (355) 0.85 OF 211	13 32 176 179	XSQ= 6.05 PHI= -0.123 XP = 0.0139
8	LEAN LESS TOWARD BEING THOSE LOCATED OUTSIDE OF NORTH AMERICA (330) 0.76 OF 189	8	LEAN MORE TOWARD BEING THOSE LOCATED OUTSIDE OF NORTH AMERICA (330) 0.88 OF 211	45 25 144 186	XSQ= 9.07 PHI= 0.151 XP = 0.0026

No.			Statistics
9	LEAN LESS TOWARD BEING THOSE 0.78 OF 189 LOCATED OUTSIDE OF SOUTH AMERICA (335)	LEAN MORE TOWARD BEING THOSE 0.89 OF 211 LOCATED OUTSIDE OF SOUTH AMERICA (335)	41 24 148 187 XSQ= 7.06 PHI= 0.133 XP = 0.0079
15	DRIFT TOWARD BEING THOSE 0.51 OF 189 WHERE THE LATITUDE IS TWENTY DEGREES OR GREATER (183)	DRIFT TOWARD BEING THOSE 0.59 OF 211 WHERE THE LATITUDE IS LESS THAN TWENTY DEGREES (217)	96 87 93 124 XSQ= 3.30 PHI= 0.091 XP = 0.0694
33	DRIFT LESS TOWARD BEING THOSE 0.81 OF 189 WHERE THE NATURAL ENVIRONMENT IS OTHER THAN 'VERY HARSH,' I.E., DESERT, DESERT GRASSES AND SHRUBS, TUNDRA, OR HIGH PLATEAU STEPPE (341) FWM	DRIFT MORE TOWARD BEING THOSE 0.89 OF 211 WHERE THE NATURAL ENVIRONMENT IS OTHER THAN 'VERY HARSH,' I.E., DESERT, DESERT GRASSES AND SHRUBS, TUNDRA, OR HIGH PLATEAU STEPPE (341) FWM	35 24 154 187 XSQ= 3.50 PHI= 0.094 XP = 0.0614
51	TEND LESS TO BE THOSE 0.52 OF 189 WHERE SUBSISTENCE IS PRIMARILY BY FOOD PRODUCTION -- I. E., AGRICULTURE OR HUSBANDRY -- RATHER THAN BY GATHERING (253)	TEND MORE TO BE THOSE 0.73 OF 211 WHERE SUBSISTENCE IS PRIMARILY BY FOOD PRODUCTION -- I. E., AGRICULTURE OR HUSBANDRY -- RATHER THAN BY GATHERING (253)	99 154 90 57 XSQ= 17.33 PHI= -0.208 XP = 0.0000
62	TILT MORE TOWARD BEING THOSE 0.62 OF 189 WHERE HUSBANDRY OF SOME KIND IS PRESENT (228)	TILT LESS TOWARD BEING THOSE 0.52 OF 211 WHERE HUSBANDRY OF SOME KIND IS PRESENT (228)	118 110 71 101 XSQ= 3.91 PHI= 0.099 XP = 0.0481
63	TILT LESS TOWARD BEING THOSE 0.60 OF 118 WHERE HUSBANDRY, IF PRESENT, IS PRINCIPALLY IN THE FORM OF BOVINE, EQUINE, CAMEL-LIKE, OR DEER-LIKE ANIMALS, RATHER THAN PIGS, SHEEP, OR GOATS (152)	TILT MORE TOWARD BEING THOSE 0.75 OF 108 WHERE HUSBANDRY, IF PRESENT, IS PRINCIPALLY IN THE FORM OF BOVINE, EQUINE, CAMEL-LIKE, OR DEER-LIKE ANIMALS, RATHER THAN PIGS, SHEEP, OR GOATS (152)	71 81 47 27 XSQ= 4.98 PHI= -0.148 XP = 0.0257
91	DRIFT TOWARD BEING THOSE 0.62 OF 34 WHERE SOCIETAL COMPLEXITY IS LOW (22) F-W	DRIFT TOWARD BEING THOSE 0.83 OF 6 WHERE SOCIETAL COMPLEXITY IS HIGH (18) F-W	13 5 21 1 XSQ= 2.57 PHI= -0.253 EP = 0.0734
97	TILT MORE TOWARD BEING THOSE 0.87 OF 188 WHERE THE HIERARCHY OF LOCAL JURISDICTION HAS THREE OR TWO LEVELS (273) GES,EA	TILT LESS TOWARD BEING THOSE 0.76 OF 143 WHERE THE HIERARCHY OF LOCAL JURISDICTION HAS THREE OR TWO LEVELS (273) GES,EA	24 34 164 109 XSQ= 6.07 PHI= -0.135 XP = 0.0137
106	DRIFT LESS TOWARD BEING THOSE 0.56 OF 102 WHERE CLASS STRATIFICATION, IF PRESENT, IS BASED ON SOMETHING OTHER THAN WEALTH (126)	DRIFT MORE TOWARD BEING THOSE 0.68 OF 101 WHERE CLASS STRATIFICATION, IF PRESENT, IS BASED ON SOMETHING OTHER THAN WEALTH (126)	45 32 57 69 XSQ= 2.83 PHI= 0.118 XP = 0.0928

109	TILT MORE TOWARD BEING THOSE 0.91 OF 181 WHERE CASTES ARE ABSENT (317)	109	TILT LESS TOWARD BEING THOSE 0.82 OF 187 WHERE CASTES ARE ABSENT (317)	17 34 164 153 XSQ= 5.24 PHI= -0.119 XP = 0.0221
110	LEAN MORE TOWARD BEING THOSE 0.65 OF 184 WHERE SLAVERY IS ABSENT (218)	110	LEAN LESS TOWARD BEING THOSE 0.50 OF 197 WHERE SLAVERY IS ABSENT (218)	65 98 119 99 XSQ= 7.50 PHI= -0.140 XP = 0.0062
118	TILT TOWARD BEING THOSE 0.59 OF 39 WHERE THE PERCENTAGE OF OCCUPATIONS THAT ARE SPECIALIZED IS HIGH OR MEDIUM (24) WME	118	TILT TOWARD BEING THOSE 0.90 OF 10 WHERE THE PERCENTAGE OF OCCUPATIONS THAT ARE SPECIALIZED IS LOW (25) WME	23 1 16 9 XSQ= 5.81 PHI= 0.344 XP = 0.0160
120	TILT TOWARD BEING THOSE 0.78 OF 41 WHERE THE CRAFT SPECIALIZATION SCORE IS HIGH OR MEDIUM (36) WME	120	TILT TOWARD BEING THOSE 0.67 OF 12 WHERE THE CRAFT SPECIALIZATION SCORE IS LOW (17) WME	32 4 9 8 XSQ= 6.59 PHI= 0.353 XP = 0.0103
129	DRIFT MORE TOWARD BEING THOSE 0.76 OF 75 WHERE WEAVING IS MAINLY DONE BY FEMALES (73)	129	DRIFT LESS TOWARD BEING THOSE 0.55 OF 29 WHERE WEAVING IS MAINLY DONE BY FEMALES (73)	18 13 57 16 XSQ= 3.40 PHI= -0.181 XP = 0.0653
135	TILT TOWARD BEING THOSE 0.52 OF 25 WHERE INDIVIDUAL OWNERSHIP OF ECONOMICALLY SIGNIFICANT PROPERTY IS NEGLIGIBLE OR ABSENT (14) GES	135	TILT TOWARD BEING THOSE 0.92 OF 13 WHERE INDIVIDUAL OWNERSHIP OF ECONOMICALLY SIGNIFICANT PROPERTY IS PRESENT (24) GES	12 12 13 1 XSQ= 5.44 PHI= -0.378 EP = 0.0118
179	TILT LESS TOWARD BEING THOSE 0.85 OF 184 WHERE THE COMMUNITY IS OTHER THAN STRUCTURED ON A NON-CLAN BASIS AND COMMONLY EXOGAMOUS (340)	179	TILT MORE TOWARD BEING THOSE 0.92 OF 198 WHERE THE COMMUNITY IS OTHER THAN STRUCTURED ON A NON-CLAN BASIS AND COMMONLY EXOGAMOUS (340)	27 15 157 183 XSQ= 4.21 PHI= 0.105 XP = 0.0401
183	LEAN LESS TOWARD BEING THOSE 0.78 OF 110 WHERE THE LARGEST NON-COGNATIC KIN GROUP IS SMALLER THAN A MOEITY, I. E., A PHRATRY OR SIB OR LINEAGE (218)	183	LEAN MORE TOWARD BEING THOSE 0.93 OF 142 WHERE THE LARGEST NON-COGNATIC KIN GROUP IS SMALLER THAN A MOEITY, I. E., A PHRATRY OR SIB OR LINEAGE (218)	24 10 86 132 XSQ= 10.36 PHI= 0.203 XP = 0.0013
184	TILT LESS TOWARD BEING THOSE 0.62 OF 110 WHERE THE LARGEST NON-COGNATIC KIN GROUP IS SMALLER THAN A PHRATRY, I. E. A SIB OR LINEAGE (175)	184	TILT MORE TOWARD BEING THOSE 0.75 OF 142 WHERE THE LARGEST NON-COGNATIC KIN GROUP IS SMALLER THAN A PHRATRY, I. E. A SIB OR LINEAGE (175)	42 35 68 107 XSQ= 4.73 PHI= 0.137 XP = 0.0296

185 DRIFT MORE TOWARD BEING THOSE 0.83 OF 110 WHERE THE LARGEST NON-COGNATIC KIN GROUP IS THE MOEITY OR PHRATRY OR SIB (194)	185 DRIFT LESS TOWARD BEING THOSE 0.73 OF 142 WHERE THE LARGEST NON-COGNATIC KIN GROUP IS THE MOEITY OR PHRATRY OR SIB (194)	91 103 19 39 XSQ= 3.08 PHI= 0.111 XP = 0.0792
186 LEAN MORE TOWARD BEING THOSE 0.70 OF 189 WHERE THE KIN GROUP IS OTHER THAN EXCLUSIVELY PATRILINEAL (250)	186 LEAN LESS TOWARD BEING THOSE 0.56 OF 211 WHERE THE KIN GROUP IS OTHER THAN EXCLUSIVELY PATRILINEAL (250)	57 93 132 118 XSQ= 7.66 PHI= -0.138 XP = 0.0057
188 DRIFT LESS TOWARD BEING THOSE 0.58 OF 189 WHERE THE KIN GROUP IS OTHER THAN EXCLUSIVELY COGNATIC (252)	188 DRIFT MORE TOWARD BEING THOSE 0.67 OF 211 WHERE THE KIN GROUP IS OTHER THAN EXCLUSIVELY COGNATIC (252)	79 69 110 142 XSQ= 3.16 PHI= 0.089 XP = 0.0754
190 DRIFT LESS TOWARD BEING THOSE 0.69 OF 106 WHERE THE KIN GROUP IS PATRILINEAL OR DOUBLE-DESCENT, RATHER THAN MATRILINEAL (186)	190 DRIFT MORE TOWARD BEING THOSE 0.80 OF 141 WHERE THE KIN GROUP IS PATRILINEAL OR DOUBLE-DESCENT, RATHER THAN MATRILINEAL (186)	73 113 33 28 XSQ= 3.55 PHI= -0.120 XP = 0.0595
196 TEND LESS TO BE THOSE 0.57 OF 138 WHERE INDIVIDUAL RIGHTS IN REAL PROPERTY, AND RULES FOR INHERITANCE, ARE PRESENT (194)	196 TEND MORE TO BE THOSE 0.81 OF 143 WHERE INDIVIDUAL RIGHTS IN REAL PROPERTY, AND RULES FOR INHERITANCE, ARE PRESENT (194)	78 116 60 27 XSQ= 18.74 PHI= -0.258 XP = 0.0000
213 DRIFT TOWARD BEING THOSE 0.59 OF 184 WHERE FIRST COUSIN MARRIAGE IS NOT PERMITTED (198)	213 DRIFT TOWARD BEING THOSE 0.52 OF 186 WHERE FIRST COUSIN MARRIAGE IS PERMITTED (172)	76 96 108 90 XSQ= 3.55 PHI= -0.098 XP = 0.0596
263 LEAN LESS TOWARD BEING THOSE 0.50 OF 189 WHERE WIVES ARE OBTAINED BY RELATIVELY DIFFICULT MEANS, NAMELY BY BRIDE-PRICE, BRIDE-SERVICE, OR EXCHANGING A FEMALE RELATIVE (233)	263 LEAN MORE TOWARD BEING THOSE 0.67 OF 206 WHERE WIVES ARE OBTAINED BY RELATIVELY DIFFICULT MEANS, NAMELY BY BRIDE-PRICE, BRIDE-SERVICE, OR EXCHANGING A FEMALE RELATIVE (233)	95 138 94 68 XSQ= 10.72 PHI= -0.165 XP = 0.0011
309 DRIFT TOWARD BEING THOSE 0.56 OF 43 WHERE ORAL SOCIALIZATION ANXIETY IS HIGH (26) W-C	309 DRIFT TOWARD BEING THOSE 0.80 OF 10 WHERE ORAL SOCIALIZATION ANXIETY IS LOW (27) W-C	24 2 19 8 XSQ= 2.85 PHI= 0.232 XP = 0.0911
360 DRIFT TOWARD BEING THOSE 0.70 OF 30 WHERE ADOLESCENT PEER GROUPS ARE PRESENT ONLY IN A SETTING OF LEISURE, OR ELSE ARE ABSENT (23) JKH	360 DRIFT TOWARD BEING THOSE 0.71 OF 7 WHERE ADOLESCENT PEER GROUPS ARE PRESENT IN A SETTING OF WORK AND PUBLIC GATHERINGS AND LEISURE, OR AT LEAST OF PUBLIC GATHERINGS AND LEISURE (14) JKH	9 5 21 2 XSQ= 2.57 PHI= -0.263 EP = 0.0801

377	TEND MORE TO BE THOSE WHERE MALE GENITAL MUTILATION IS ABSENT (242)	0.82 OF 186	377	TEND LESS TO BE THOSE WHERE MALE GENITAL MUTILATION IS ABSENT (242)	0.65 OF 139	34 49 152 90 XSQ= 11.17 PHI= -0.185 XP = 0.0008
385	DRIFT LESS TOWARD BEING THOSE WHERE SEXUAL EXPRESSION BY THE YOUNG IS SEMI-RESTRICTED OR PERMITTED (64) F-B	0.68 OF 63	385	DRIFT MORE TOWARD BEING THOSE WHERE SEXUAL EXPRESSION BY THE YOUNG IS SEMI-RESTRICTED OR PERMITTED (64) F-B	0.91 OF 23	20 2 43 21 XSQ= 3.57 PHI= 0.204 XP = 0.0588
426	LEAN LESS TOWARD BEING THOSE WHERE A HIGH GOD IS PRESENT (156) GES,EA	0.53 OF 169	426	LEAN MORE TOWARD BEING THOSE WHERE A HIGH GOD IS PRESENT (156) GES,EA	0.74 OF 91	89 67 80 24 XSQ= 9.98 PHI= -0.196 XP = 0.0016
440	TILT TOWARD BEING THOSE WHERE FEAR OF SPIRITS IS LOW (29) W-C	0.55 OF 49	440	TILT TOWARD BEING THOSE WHERE FEAR OF SPIRITS IS HIGH (32) W-C	0.83 OF 12	22 10 27 2 XSQ= 4.27 PHI= -0.265 XP = 0.0387
446	DRIFT LESS TOWARD BEING THOSE WHERE WITCHCRAFT IS MODERATELY PRESENT OR ABSENT (24) GES	0.52 OF 25	446	DRIFT MORE TOWARD BEING THOSE WHERE WITCHCRAFT IS MODERATELY PRESENT OR ABSENT (24) GES	0.85 OF 13	12 2 13 11 XSQ= 2.63 PHI= 0.263 EP = 0.0773
455	DRIFT TOWARD BEING THOSE WHERE THE MODE OF THE INDIVIDUAL'S CONTACT WITH THE DIVINE IS NOT CONDUCIVE TO THE DEVELOPMENT OF THE INDIVIDUAL'S NEED TO ACHIEVE (19) DCM	0.63 OF 27	455	DRIFT TOWARD BEING THOSE WHERE THE MODE OF THE INDIVIDUAL'S CONTACT WITH THE DIVINE IS CONDUCIVE TO THE DEVELOPMENT OF THE INDIVIDUAL'S NEED TO ACHIEVE (17) DCM	0.78 OF 9	10 7 17 2 XSQ= 3.01 PHI= -0.289 EP = 0.0551
481	TILT LESS TOWARD BEING THOSE WHERE THE PRINCIPAL ETHNOGRAPHERS HAVE BEEN OTHER THAN AMERICAN (275)	0.65 OF 187	481	TILT MORE TOWARD BEING THOSE WHERE THE PRINCIPAL ETHNOGRAPHERS HAVE BEEN OTHER THAN AMERICAN (275)	0.77 OF 201	66 47 121 154 XSQ= 6.09 PHI= 0.125 XP = 0.0136
488	LEAN MORE TOWARD BEING THOSE ABOUT WHICH THE PRINCIPAL ETHNOGRAPHIES WERE PUBLISHED BEFORE 1950 (185)	0.81 OF 125	488	LEAN LESS TOWARD BEING THOSE ABOUT WHICH THE PRINCIPAL ETHNOGRAPHIES WERE PUBLISHED BEFORE 1950 (185)	0.64 OF 132	101 84 24 48 XSQ= 8.55 PHI= 0.182 XP = 0.0035
489	LEAN LESS TOWARD BEING THOSE NOT INCLUDED IN CHARLES ACKERMAN'S STUDY OF DIVORCE (343)	0.80 OF 189	489	LEAN MORE TOWARD BEING THOSE NOT INCLUDED IN CHARLES ACKERMAN'S STUDY OF DIVORCE (343)	0.91 OF 211	38 19 151 192 XSQ= 9.17 PHI= 0.151 XP = 0.0025

490	TEND LESS TO BE THCSE 0.58 OF 189 NOT INCLUDED IN ALBERT S. ANTHONY'S SAMPLE CN MALE INITIATION RITES (287)	490	TEND MORE TO BE THOSE 0.84 OF 211 NOT INCLUDED IN ALBERT S. ANTHONY'S SAMPLE ON MALE INITIATICN RITES (287)	80 33 109 178 XSQ= 33.73 PHI= 0.290 XP = 0.
491	LEAN LESS TOWARC BEING THCSE 0.83 OF 189 NOT INCLUDED IN DORRIAN APPLE'S STUDY OF GRANDPARENTHCOC (352)	491	LEAN MORE TOWARD BEING THOSE 0.93 OF 211 NOT INCLUDED IN DORRIAN APPLE'S STUDY OF GRANDPARENTHOOD (352)	33 15 156 196 XSQ= 9.16 PHI= 0.151 XP = 0.0025
492	TEND LESS TO BE THCSE 0.84 OF 189 NOT INCLUDED IN BARBARA CHARTIER AYRES' STUDY OF FEMALE INITIATICN RITES (361)	492	TEND MORE TO BE THOSE 0.96 OF 211 NOT INCLUDED IN BARBARA CHARTIER AYRES' STUDY OF FEMALE INITIATICN RITES (361)	31 8 158 203 XSQ= 16.61 PHI= 0.204 XP = 0.0000
493	TEND LESS TO BE THCSE 0.68 OF 189 NOT INCLUDED IN BACCN, BARRY, AND CHILC'S STUDY OF CHILD REARING (322)	493	TEND MORE TO BE THOSE 0.92 OF 211 NOT INCLUDED IN BACON, BARRY, AND CHILD'S STUDY OF CHILD REARING (322)	61 17 128 194 XSQ= 35.72 PHI= 0.299 XP = 0.
494	LEAN LESS TOWARC BEING THCSE 0.88 OF 189 NOT INCLUDED IN HERBERT M. BARRY III'S STUDY OF ART (371)	494	LEAN MORE TOWARD BEING THOSE 0.97 OF 211 NOT INCLUDED IN HERBERT M. BARRY III'S STUDY OF ART (371)	22 7 167 204 XSQ= 9.07 PHI= 0.151 XP = 0.0026
495	TEND LESS TO BE THCSE 0.74 OF 189 NOT INCLUDED IN JUCITH K. BROWN'S STUDY OF FEMALE INITIATION RITES (335)	495	TEND MORE TO BE THOSE 0.92 OF 211 NOT INCLUDED IN JUDITH K. BROWN'S STUDY OF FEMALE INITIATION RITES (335)	49 16 140 195 XSQ= 23.32 PHI= 0.241 XP = 0.0000
496	TEND LESS TO BE THCSE 0.78 OF 189 NOT INCLUDED IN ROY G. C'ANDRADE'S STUDY OF DREAMS (345)	496	TEND MORE TO BE THOSE 0.93 OF 211 NOT INCLUDED IN ROY G. D'ANDRADE'S STUDY OF DREAMS (345)	41 14 148 197 XSQ= 17.81 PHI= 0.211 XP = 0.0000
497	TEND LESS TO BE THCSE 0.75 OF 189 NOT INCLUDED IN WILLIAM M. EVAN'S STUDY OF LAW (339)	497	TEND MORE TO BE THOSE 0.94 OF 211 NOT INCLUDED IN WILLIAM M. EVAN'S STUDY OF LAW (339)	48 13 141 198 XSQ= 27.07 PHI= 0.260 XP = 0.0000
498	TEND LESS TO BE THCSE 0.78 OF 189 NCT INCLUDED IN C. S. FORC'S STUDY OF SEX (349)	498	TEND MORE TO BE THOSE 0.96 OF 211 NOT INCLUDED IN C. S. FORD'S STUDY OF SEX (349)	42 9 147 202 XSQ= 27.31 PHI= 0.261 XP = 0.0000

499	TEND LESS TO BE THCSE 0.67 OF 189 NOT INCLUDED IN FORD ANC BEACH'S SAMPLE CN SEXUAL EXPRESSION BY THE YOUNG (314)	499	TEND MORE TO BE THOSE 0.89 OF 211 NOT INCLUDED IN FORD AND BEACH'S SAMPLE ON SEXUAL EXPRESSION BY THE YOUNG (314)	63 23 126 188 XSQ= 28.41 PHI= 0.267 XP = 0.0000
500	TEND LESS TO BE THCSE 0.82 OF 189 NCT INCLUDED IN FREEMAN ANC WINCH'S STUDY OF SCCIETAL CCMPLEXITY (360)	500	TEND MORE TO BE THOSE 0.97 OF 211 NOT INCLUDED IN FREEMAN AND WINCH'S STUDY OF SOCIETAL COMPLEXITY (360)	34 6 155 205 XSQ= 23.76 PHI= 0.244 XP = 0.0000
501	TEND LESS TO BE THCSE 0.69 OF 189 NCT INCLUDED IN JOAN FRIENCLY GOOCMAN'S STUDY CF ASCETIC MCURNING BEHAVIOR (333)	501	TEND MORE TO BE THOSE 0.96 OF 211 NOT INCLUDED IN JOAN FRIENDLY GCCDMAN'S STUDY OF ASCETIC MOURNING BEHAVIOR (333)	59 8 130 203 XSQ= 51.83 PHI= 0.360 XP = 0.
502	TEND LESS TO BE THCSE 0.76 OF 189 NCT INCLUDED IN JOHN K. HARLEY'S STUDY OF ADOLESCENT PEER GROUPS (343)	502	TEND MORE TO BE THOSE 0.95 OF 211 NOT INCLUDED IN JOHN K. HARLEY'S STUDY OF ADOLESCENT PEER GROUPS (343)	46 11 143 200 XSQ= 28.30 PHI= 0.266 XP = 0.0000
503	TEND LESS TO BE THCSE 0.78 OF 189 NOT INCLUDED IN JOHN M. HICKMAN'S STUDY OF THE FOLK-URBAN CONTINUUM (346)	503	TEND MORE TO BE THOSE 0.94 OF 211 NOT INCLUDED IN JOHN M. HICKMAN'S STUDY OF THE FOLK-URBAN CONTINUUM (346)	42 12 147 199 XSQ= 21.95 PHI= 0.234 XP = 0.0000
504	TEND LESS TC BE THCSE 0.79 OF 189 NOT INCLUDED IN DONALC HORTON'S STUDY OF ALCHOLISM (351)	504	TEND MORE TO BE THOSE 0.96 OF 211 NOT INCLUDED IN DONALD HORTON'S STUDY OF ALCHOLISM (351)	40 9 149 202 XSQ= 24.94 PHI= 0.250 XP = 0.0000
506	TEND LESS TO BE THCSE 0.85 OF 189 NOT INCLUDED IN LAMBERT, TRIANDIS, ANC WOLF'S STUDY OF SUPERNATURAL BEINGS (364)	506	TEND MORE TO BE THOSE 0.96 OF 211 NOT INCLUDED IN LAMBERT, TRIANDIS, AND WOLF'S STUDY OF SUPERNATURAL BEINGS (364)	28 8 161 203 XSQ= 13.48 PHI= 0.184 XP = 0.0002
507	TEND LESS TO BE THCSE 0.67 OF 189 NCT INCLUDED IN JAMES R. LEARY'S STUDY OF FCOC TABCCS (314)	507	TEND MORE TO BE THOSE 0.89 OF 211 NOT INCLUDED IN JAMES R. LEARY'S STUDY OF FOOD TABOOS (314)	63 23 126 188 XSQ= 28.41 PHI= 0.267 XP = 0.0000
508	TEND LESS TO BE THCSE 0.84 OF 189 NCT INCLUDED IN CAVID C. MCCLELLANC'S STUDY OF ACHIEVEMENT MCTIVATICN (360)	508	TEND MORE TO BE THOSE 0.95 OF 211 NOT INCLUDED IN DAVID C. MCCLELLAND'S STUDY OF ACHIEVEMENT MOTIVATION (360)	30 10 159 201 XSQ= 12.52 PHI= 0.177 XP = 0.0004

510	LEAN LESS TOWARC BEING THCSE 0.92 OF 189 NOT INCLUDED IN RACUL NARRCLL'S STUDY OF SCCIETAL COMPLEXITY (380)	510	LEAN MORE TOWARD BEING THOSE 0.98 OF 211 NOT INCLUDED IN RAOUL NARROLL'S STUDY OF SOCIETAL COMPLEXITY (380)	16 4 173 207 XSQ= 7.73 PHI= 0.139 XP = 0.0054
512	TEND LESS TO BE THCSE 0.86 OF 189 NCT INCLUDED IN SHIRLEY ANC ROMNEY'S STUDY OF LCVE MAGIC (367)	512	TEND MORE TO BE THOSE 0.97 OF 211 NOT INCLUDED IN SHIRLEY AND ROMNEY'S STUDY OF LOVE MAGIC (367)	26 7 163 204 XSQ= 13.01 PHI= 0.180 XP = 0.0003
513	TEND LESS TO BE THCSE 0.80 OF 189 NOT INCLUDED IN LEC W. SIMMONS' STUDY OF THE TREATMENT CF THE AGEC (357)	513	TEND MORE TO BE THOSE 0.97 OF 211 NOT INCLUDED IN LEO W. SIMMONS' STUDY OF THE TREATMENT OF THE AGED (357)	37 6 152 205 XSQ= 27.38 PHI= 0.262 XP = 0.0000
514	TEND LESS TO BE THCSE 0.60 OF 189 NOT INCLUDED IN PHILIP E. SLATER'S STUDY OF NARCISSISM (310)	514	TEND MORE TO BE THOSE 0.93 OF 211 NOT INCLUDED IN PHILIP E. SLATER'S STUDY OF NARCISSISM (310)	76 14 113 197 XSQ= 62.55 PHI= 0.395 XP = 0.
515	TEND LESS TO BE THCSE 0.79 OF 189 NCT INCLUDED IN WILLIAM N. STEPHENS' SAMPLE CN AVCIDANCE RELATICNSHIPS (348)	515	TEND MORE TO BE THOSE 0.94 OF 211 NOT INCLUDED IN WILLIAM N. STEPHENS' SAMPLE ON AVOIDANCE RELATICNSHIPS (348)	39 13 150 198 XSQ= 17.21 PHI= 0.207 XP = 0.0000
516	TEND MORE TO BE THCSE 0.99 OF 189 INCLUDED IN GUY E. SWANSON'S SAMPLE ON LOCAL JURISCICTION, AS MODIFIED BY THE ETHNOGRAPHIC ATLAS (331)	516	TEND LESS TO BE THOSE 0.68 OF 211 INCLUDED IN GUY E. SWANSON'S SAMPLE ON LOCAL JURISDICTION, AS MODIFIED BY THE ETHNOGRAPHIC ATLAS (331)	188 143 1 68 XSQ= 67.98 PHI= 0.412 XP = 0.
517	TEND TO BE THCSE 0.89 OF 189 INCLUDED IN GUY E. SWANSON'S SAMPLE CN HIGH GODS, AS MODIFIED BY THE ETHNOGRAPHIC ATLAS (260)	517	TEND TO BE THOSE 0.57 OF 211 NOT INCLUDED IN GUY E. SWANSON'S SAMPLE ON HIGH GODS, AS MODIFIED BY THE ETHNOGRAPHIC ATLAS (140)	169 91 20 120 XSQ= 91.88 PHI= 0.479 XP = 0.
518	TEND LESS TO BE THCSE 0.62 OF 189 NCT INCLUDED IN STANLEY H. UDY, JR.'S STUDY OF WCRK ORGANIZATICN (295)	518	TEND MORE TO BE THOSE 0.84 OF 211 NOT INCLUDED IN STANLEY H. UDY, JR.'S STUDY OF WORK ORGANIZATION (295)	71 34 118 177 XSQ= 22.60 PHI= 0.238 XP = 0.0000
519	TEND LESS TO BE THCSE 0.86 OF 189 NOT INCLUDED IN JOSEPH VERCFF'S STUDY OF ACHIEVEMENT MCTIVATION AS REVEALED IN FCLKTALES (364)	519	TEND MORE TO BE THOSE 0.96 OF 211 NOT INCLUDED IN JOSEPH VEROFF'S STUDY OF ACHIEVEMENT MOTIVATION AS REVEALED IN FOLKTALES (364)	27 9 162 202 XSQ= 11.03 PHI= 0.166 XP = 0.0009

520	TEND LESS TO BE THCSE NOT INCLUDED IN BEATRICE BLYTH WHITING'S STUDY OF SCRCERY (360)	0.83 OF 189	520	TEND MORE TO BE THOSE NOT INCLUDED IN BEATRICE BLYTH WHITING'S STUDY OF SORCERY (360)	0.96 OF 211	32 8 157 203 XSQ= 17.69 PHI= 0.210 XP = 0.0000
521	TEND LESS TO BE THCSE NOT INCLUDED IN JOHN W. M. WHITING'S STUDY OF SCCIALIZATION PROCESS AND PERSCNALITY (353)	0.80 OF 189	521	TEND MORE TO BE THOSE NOT INCLUDED IN JOHN W. M. WHITING'S STUDY OF SOCIALIZATION PROCESS AND PERSONALITY (353)	0.96 OF 211	38 9 151 202 XSQ= 22.62 PHI= 0.238 XP = 0.0000
522	TEND LESS TO BE THCSE NOT INCLUDED IN MARJCRIE GRANT WHITING'S STUDY OF DIET (318)	0.67 OF 189	522	TEND MORE TO BE THOSE NOT INCLUDED IN MARJORIE GRANT WHITING'S STUDY OF DIET (318)	0.91 OF 211	63 19 126 192 XSQ= 34.73 PHI= 0.295 XP = 0.
523	TEND LESS TO BE THCSE NOT INCLUDED IN WHITING ANC CHILD'S STUDY OF CHILD TRAINING AND PERSONALITY (339)	0.74 OF 189	523	TEND MORE TO BE THOSE NOT INCLUDED IN WHITING AND CHILD'S STUDY OF CHILD TRAINING AND PERSONALITY (339)	0.94 OF 211	49 12 140 199 XSQ= 30.05 PHI= 0.274 XP = 0.0000
524	TEND LESS TO BE THCSE NOT INCLUDED IN WHITING, KLUCKHCHN, ANC ANTHONY'S STUDY OF MALE INITIATICN CEREMONIES (356)	0.80 OF 189	524	TEND MORE TO BE THOSE NOT INCLUDED IN WHITING, KLUCKHOHN, AND ANTHONY'S STUDY OF MALE INITIATION CEREMONIES (356)	0.97 OF 211	37 7 152 204 XSQ= 25.29 PHI= 0.251 XP = 0.0000

512 CULTURES
INCLUDED IN SHIRLEY AND ROMNEY'S
STUDY OF LOVE MAGIC (33)

512 CULTURES
NOT INCLUDED IN SHIRLEY AND ROMNEY'S
STUDY OF LOVE MAGIC (367)

BACKGROUND ON PAGE 180

SUBJECT ONLY, F.C. 1-480 AND 527-536
BOTH SUBJECT AND PREDICATE, F.C. 481-526

33 IN LEFT COLUMN

AINU	ALORESE	ANDAMANESE	ARAPESH	AZANDE	BALINESE	CHAGGA	CHENCHU	COMANCHE	DOBUANS
IFUGAO	KURTATCHI	KWAKIUTL	LAKHER	LAMBA	LESU	MAORI	MARQUESANS	MURNGIN	NAVAHO
PAPAGO	PUKAPUKA	RIFFIANS	SAMOANS	SANPOIL	SIRIONO	THONGA	TIKOPIA	TIV	TROBRIAND
VENDA	WITOTO	YAKUT							

367 IN RIGHT COLUMN

	Included (33)			Not included (367)			
6	TEND LESS TO BE THOSE LOCATED OUTSIDE OF THE INSULAR PACIFIC (330)	0.58 OF 33	6	TEND MORE TO BE THOSE LOCATED OUTSIDE OF THE INSULAR PACIFIC (330)	0.85 OF 367	14 56 19 311 XSQ= 13.65 PHI= 0.185 XP = 0.0002
53	DRIFT MORE TOWARD BEING THOSE WHERE FOOD PRODUCTION IS BY SIMPLE AGRICULTURE OR INCIPIENT FOOD PRODUCTION, RATHER THAN BY INTENSIVE AGRICULTURE (147)	0.82 OF 22	53	DRIFT LESS TOWARD BEING THOSE WHERE FOOD PRODUCTION IS BY SIMPLE AGRICULTURE OR INCIPIENT FOOD PRODUCTION, RATHER THAN BY INTENSIVE AGRICULTURE (147)	0.60 OF 216	4 87 18 129 XSQ= 3.25 PHI= -0.117 XP = 0.0716
63	TILT TOWARD BEING THOSE WHERE HUSBANDRY, IF PRESENT, IS PRINCIPALLY IN THE FORM OF PIGS, SHEEP, OR GOATS, RATHER THAN BOVINE, EQUINE, CAMEL-LIKE, OR DEER-LIKE ANIMALS (74)	0.61 OF 18	63	TILT TOWARD BEING THOSE WHERE HUSBANDRY, IF PRESENT, IS PRINCIPALLY IN THE FORM OF BOVINE, EQUINE, CAMEL-LIKE, OR DEER-LIKE ANIMALS, RATHER THAN PIGS, SHEEP, OR GOATS (152)	0.70 OF 208	7 145 11 63 XSQ= 5.82 PHI= -0.160 XP = 0.0159
107	IN ALL CASES ARE THOSE WHERE CLASS STRATIFICATION, IF PRESENT, IS BASED ON SOMETHING OTHER THAN OCCUPATIONAL STATUS (160)	1.00 OF 17	107	DRIFT LESS TOWARD BEING THOSE WHERE CLASS STRATIFICATION, IF PRESENT, IS BASED ON SOMETHING OTHER THAN OCCUPATIONAL STATUS (160)	0.77 OF 186	0 43 17 143 XSQ= 3.70 PHI= -0.135 XP = 0.0545
108	TEND TO BE THOSE WHERE CLASS STRATIFICATION, IF PRESENT, IS BASED ON A HEREDITARY ARISTOCRACY (74)	0.76 OF 17	108	TEND TO BE THOSE WHERE CLASS STRATIFICATION, IF PRESENT, IS BASED ON SOMETHING OTHER THAN A HEREDITARY ARISTOCRACY (129)	0.67 OF 186	13 61 4 125 XSQ= 11.01 PHI= 0.233 XP = 0.0009

133	IN ALL CASES ARE THOSE WHERE CONTRACTEC DEBTS ARE SIGNIFICANTLY PRESENT (17) GES	1.00 OF 6	133	TILT TOWARD BEING THOSE WHERE CONTRACTED DEBTS ARE MODERATELY PRESENT OR ABSENT (17) GES	0.61 OF 28	6 11 0 17 XSQ= 5.06 PHI= 0.386 EP = 0.0184
279	IN ALL CASES ARE THCSE WHERE WIFE-LENDING AND WIFE EXCHANGE ARE UNIMPCRTANT CR ABSENT (19) LWS	1.00 OF 6	279	DRIFT LESS TOWARD BEING THCSE WHERE WIFE-LENDING AND WIFE EXCHANGE ARE UNIMPORTANT OR ABSENT (19) LWS	0.57 OF 23	0 10 6 13 XSQ= 2.29 PHI= -0.281 EP = 0.0676
305	LEAN TOWARD BEING THOSE WHERE THE EARLY SEXUAL SATISFACTION POTENTIAL IS HIGH (27) W-C	0.69 OF 32	305	LEAN TOWARD BEING THOSE WHERE THE EARLY SEXUAL SATISFACTION POTENTIAL IS LOW (24) W-C	0.74 OF 19	22 5 10 14 XSQ= 7.00 PHI= 0.370 XP = 0.0082
311	TILT TCWARD BEING THCSE WHERE SEXUAL SOCIALIZATION ANXIETY IS LCW (23) W-C	0.58 OF 33	311	TILT TOWARD BEING THOSE WHERE SEXUAL SOCIALIZATION ANXIETY IS HIGH (28) W-C	0.78 OF 18	14 14 19 4 XSQ= 4.54 PHI= -0.298 XP = 0.0331
323	TILT MORE TOWARD BEING THCSE WHERE THE CONSTANCY OF PRESENCE OF THE INFANT'S NURTURANT AGENT IS LCW (45) B-B-C	0.78 OF 27	323	TILT LESS TOWARD BEING THOSE WHERE THE CONSTANCY OF PRESENCE OF THE INFANT'S NURTURANT AGENT IS LOW (45) B-B-C	0.51 OF 47	6 23 21 24 XSQ= 4.08 PHI= -0.235 XP = 0.0435
342	TILT TOWARD BEING THOSE WHERE THE CHILD'S INFERREC ANXIETY OVER PERFCRMANCE CF NURTURANT BEHAVIOR IS HIGH (18) B-B-C	0.65 OF 17	342	TILT TOWARD BEING THOSE WHERE THE CHILD'S INFERRED ANXIETY OVER PERFORMANCE OF NURTURANT BEHAVIOR IS LOW (28) B-B-C	0.76 OF 29	11 7 6 22 XSQ= 5.80 PHI= 0.355 XP = 0.0160
368	DRIFT TOWARD BEING THCSE WHERE DISSCCIATICN OF THE SEXES AT ADCLESCENCE IS HIGH OR MEDIUM (16) JKH	0.67 OF 12	368	DRIFT TOWARD BEING THOSE WHERE DISSOCIATION OF THE SEXES AT ADOLESCENCE IS LOW (21) JKH	0.68 OF 25	8 8 4 17 XSQ= 2.68 PHI= 0.269 EP = 0.0768
391	TILT TCWARD BEING THCSE WHERE PREMARITAL SEX RELATIONS ARE PUNISHED CNLY IF PREGNANCY RESULTS, OR FREELY PERMITTEC (90) JTW,EA	0.73 OF 26	391	TILT TOWARD BEING THOSE WHERE PREMARITAL SEX RELATICNS ARE STRONGLY PUNISHED AND IN FACT RARE, OR WEAKLY PUNISHED AND IN FACT NOT RARE (89) JTW,EA	0.54 OF 153	7 82 19 71 XSQ= 5.30 PHI= -0.172 XP = 0.0213
402	TILT TCWARD BEING THOSE WHERE EXPLANATICNS CF ILLNESS OF AN ORAL NATURE ARE PRESENT (31) W-C	0.67 OF 33	402	TILT TOWARD BEING THOSE WHERE EXPLANATIONS OF ILLNESS OF AN ORAL NATURE ARE ABSENT (30) W-C	0.68 OF 28	22 9 11 19 XSQ= 5.91 PHI= 0.311 XP = 0.0151

438	TILT TOWARD BEING THOSE 0.77 OF 26 WHERE OTHER-WORLDLY FEARS OF GHOSTS OR SPIRITS ARE GREATER THAN THIS-WORLDLY FEARS OF HUMANS OR ANIMALS (27) W-C,JFG	438	TILT TOWARD BEING THOSE 0.61 OF 18 WHERE THIS-WORLDLY FEARS OF HUMANS OR ANIMALS ARE GREATER THAN OTHER-WORLDLY FEARS OF GHOSTS OR SPIRITS (17) W-C,JFG	20 7 6 11 XSQ= 4.98 PHI= 0.337 XP = 0.0256
442	TILT TOWARD BEING THOSE 0.61 OF 33 WHERE FEAR OF ANIMAL SPIRITS IS HIGH (28) W-C	442	TILT TOWARD BEING THOSE 0.71 OF 28 WHERE FEAR OF ANIMAL SPIRITS IS LOW (33) W-C	20 8 13 20 XSQ= 5.04 PHI= 0.287 XP = 0.0248
449	TEND TO BE THOSE 0.71 OF 17 WHERE THE OBSERVATION OF FOOD TABOOS IS HIGH, RATHER THAN MEDIUM OR LOW (25) JRL	449	TEND TO BE THOSE 0.81 OF 69 WHERE THE OBSERVATION OF FOOD TABOOS IS MEDIUM OR LOW, RATHER THAN HIGH (61) JRL	12 13 5 56 XSQ= 15.29 PHI= 0.422 XP = 0.0001
450	IN ALL CASES ARE THOSE 1.00 OF 17 WHERE THE OBSERVATION OF FOOD TABOOS IS HIGH OR MEDIUM, RATHER THAN LOW (60) JRL	450	LEAN LESS TOWARD BEING THOSE 0.62 OF 69 WHERE THE OBSERVATION OF FOOD TABOOS IS HIGH OR MEDIUM, RATHER THAN LOW (60) JRL	17 43 0 26 XSQ= 7.48 PHI= 0.295 XP = 0.0062
452	DRIFT TOWARD BEING THOSE 0.69 OF 13 WHERE TOTEMISM WITH FOOD TABOOS IS PRESENT (19) WNS	452	DRIFT TOWARD BEING THOSE 0.67 OF 30 WHERE TOTEMISM WITH FOOD TABOOS IS ABSENT (24) WNS	9 10 4 20 XSQ= 3.40 PHI= 0.281 XP = 0.0654
456	TILT TOWARD BEING THOSE 0.75 OF 12 WHERE THE INTERNALIZATION OF THE INDIVIDUAL'S CONTACT WITH THE DIVINE IS NOT CONDUCIVE TO THE DEVELOPMENT OF THE INDIVIDUAL'S NEED TO ACHIEVE (17) DCM	456	TILT TOWARD BEING THOSE 0.67 OF 24 WHERE THE INTERNALIZATION OF THE INDIVIDUAL'S CONTACT WITH THE DIVINE IS CONDUCIVE TO THE DEVELOPMENT OF THE INDIVIDUAL'S NEED TO ACHIEVE (19) DCM	3 16 9 8 XSQ= 4.03 PHI= -0.334 EP = 0.0328
488	TILT MORE TOWARD BEING THOSE 0.96 OF 23 ABOUT WHICH THE PRINCIPAL ETHNOGRAPHIES WERE PUBLISHED BEFORE 1950 (185)	488	TILT LESS TOWARD BEING THOSE 0.70 OF 234 ABOUT WHICH THE PRINCIPAL ETHNOGRAPHIES WERE PUBLISHED BEFORE 1950 (185)	22 163 1 71 XSQ= 5.79 PHI= 0.150 XP = 0.0161
489	TILT LESS TOWARD BEING THOSE 0.70 OF 33 NOT INCLUDED IN CHARLES ACKERMAN'S STUDY OF DIVORCE (343)	489	TILT MORE TOWARD BEING THOSE 0.87 OF 367 NOT INCLUDED IN CHARLES ACKERMAN'S STUDY OF DIVORCE (343)	10 47 23 320 XSQ= 6.22 PHI= 0.125 XP = 0.0126
490	TEND TO BE THOSE 0.82 OF 33 INCLUDED IN ALBERT S. ANTHONY'S SAMPLE ON MALE INITIATION RITES (113)	490	TEND TO BE THOSE 0.77 OF 367 NOT INCLUDED IN ALBERT S. ANTHONY'S SAMPLE ON MALE INITIATION RITES (287)	27 86 6 281 XSQ= 48.08 PHI= 0.347 XP = 0.

491	TEND LESS TO BE THOSE NOT INCLUDED IN DORRIAN APPLE'S STUDY OF GRANDPARENTHOOD (352)	0.61 OF 33	491	TEND MORE TO BE THOSE NOT INCLUDED IN DORRIAN APPLE'S STUDY OF GRANDPARENTHOOD (352)	0.90 OF 367	13 35 20 332 XSQ= 22.81 PHI= 0.239 XP = 0.0000
492	TEND TO BE THOSE INCLUDED IN BARBARA CHARTIER AYRES' STUDY OF FEMALE INITIATION RITES (39)	0.76 OF 33	492	TEND TO BE THOSE NOT INCLUDED IN BARBARA CHARTIER AYRES' STUDY OF FEMALE INITIATION RITES (361)	0.96 OF 367	25 14 8 353 XSQ= 170.01 PHI= 0.652 XP = 0.
493	TEND TO BE THOSE INCLUDED IN BACON, BARRY, AND CHILD'S STUDY OF CHILD REARING (78)	0.88 OF 33	493	TEND TO BE THOSE NOT INCLUDED IN BACON, BARRY, AND CHILD'S STUDY OF CHILD REARING (322)	0.87 OF 367	29 49 4 318 XSQ= 102.44 PHI= 0.506 XP = 0.
494	TEND TO BE THOSE INCLUDED IN HERBERT M. BARRY III'S STUDY OF ART (29)	0.55 OF 33	494	TEND TO BE THOSE NOT INCLUDED IN HERBERT M. BARRY III'S STUDY OF ART (371)	0.97 OF 367	18 11 15 356 XSQ= 112.10 PHI= 0.529 XP = 0.
495	TEND LESS TO BE THOSE NOT INCLUDED IN JUDITH K. BROWN'S STUDY OF FEMALE INITIATION RITES (335)	0.61 OF 33	495	TEND MORE TO BE THOSE NOT INCLUDED IN JUDITH K. BROWN'S STUDY OF FEMALE INITIATION RITES (335)	0.86 OF 367	13 52 20 315 XSQ= 12.36 PHI= 0.176 XP = 0.0004
496	TEND LESS TO BE THOSE NOT INCLUDED IN ROY G. D'ANDRADE'S STUDY OF DREAMS (345)	0.58 OF 33	496	TEND MORE TO BE THOSE NOT INCLUDED IN ROY G. D'ANDRADE'S STUDY OF DREAMS (345)	0.89 OF 367	14 41 19 326 XSQ= 22.37 PHI= 0.236 XP = 0.0000
497	LEAN LESS TOWARD BEING THOSE NOT INCLUDED IN WILLIAM M. EVAN'S STUDY OF LAW (339)	0.64 OF 33	497	LEAN MORE TOWARD BEING THOSE NOT INCLUDED IN WILLIAM M. EVAN'S STUDY OF LAW (339)	0.87 OF 367	12 49 21 318 XSQ= 10.69 PHI= 0.163 XP = 0.0011
498	TEND TO BE THOSE INCLUDED IN C. S. FORD'S STUDY OF SEX (51)	0.64 OF 33	498	TEND TO BE THOSE NOT INCLUDED IN C. S. FORD'S STUDY OF SEX (349)	0.92 OF 367	21 30 12 337 XSQ= 78.81 PHI= 0.444 XP = 0.
499	TEND TO BE THOSE INCLUDED IN FORD AND BEACH'S SAMPLE ON SEXUAL EXPRESSION BY THE YOUNG (86)	0.73 OF 33	499	TEND TO BE THOSE NOT INCLUDED IN FORD AND BEACH'S SAMPLE ON SEXUAL EXPRESSION BY THE YOUNG (314)	0.83 OF 367	24 62 9 305 XSQ= 52.67 PHI= 0.363 XP = 0.

```
500  TEND LESS TO BE THOSE            0.55 OF  33    500  TEND MORE TO BE THOSE            0.93 OF 367        15   25
     NOT INCLUDED IN FREEMAN AND WINCH'S                   NOT INCLUDED IN FREEMAN AND WINCH'S                   18  342
     STUDY OF SOCIETAL COMPLEXITY  (360)                   STUDY OF SOCIETAL COMPLEXITY  (360)              XSQ=   46.03
                                                                                                            PHI=   0.339
                                                                                                            XP =  0.

501  TEND TO BE THOSE                 0.79 OF  33    501  TEND TO BE THOSE                 0.89 OF 367        26   41
     INCLUDED IN JOAN FRIENDLY GOODMAN'S                   NOT INCLUDED IN JOAN FRIENDLY GOODMAN'S                7  326
     STUDY OF ASCETIC MOURNING BEHAVIOR  (67)              STUDY OF                                         XSQ=   94.48
                                                           ASCETIC MOURNING BEHAVIOR  (333)                 PHI=   0.486
                                                                                                            XP =  0.

502  TEND TO BE THOSE                 0.64 OF  33    502  TEND TO BE THOSE                 0.90 OF 367        21   36
     INCLUDED IN JOHN K. HARLEY'S                          NOT INCLUDED IN JOHN K. HARLEY'S                      12  331
     STUDY OF ADOLESCENT PEER GROUPS  (57)                 STUDY OF ADOLESCENT PEER GROUPS  (343)           XSQ=   67.45
                                                                                                            PHI=   0.411
                                                                                                            XP =  0.

503  TEND LESS TO BE THOSE            0.61 OF  33    503  TEND MORE TO BE THOSE            0.89 OF 367        13   41
     NOT INCLUDED IN JOHN M. HICKMAN'S                     NOT INCLUDED IN JOHN M. HICKMAN'S                     20  326
     STUDY OF THE FOLK-URBAN CONTINUUM  (346)              STUDY OF THE FOLK-URBAN CONTINUUM  (346)         XSQ=   18.31
                                                                                                            PHI=   0.214
                                                                                                            XP =  0.0000

504  TEND LESS TO BE THOSE            0.58 OF  33    504  TEND MORE TO BE THOSE            0.90 OF 367        14   35
     NOT INCLUDED IN DONALD HORTON'S                       NOT INCLUDED IN DONALD HORTON'S                       19  332
     STUDY OF ALCHOLISM  (351)                             STUDY OF ALCHOLISM  (351)                        XSQ=   27.48
                                                                                                            PHI=   0.262
                                                                                                            XP =  0.0000

505  TEND LESS TO BE THOSE            0.79 OF  33    505  TEND MORE TO BE THOSE            0.96 OF 367         7   13
     NOT INCLUDED IN MERRILL JACKSON'S                     NOT INCLUDED IN MERRILL JACKSON'S                     26  354
     STUDY OF                                              STUDY OF                                         XSQ=   16.36
     CRIMINAL LAW AND MEDICINE  (380)                      CRIMINAL LAW AND MEDICINE  (380)                 PHI=   0.202
                                                                                                            XP =  0.0001

506  TEND TO BE THOSE                 0.55 OF  33    506  TEND TO BE THOSE                 0.95 OF 367        18   18
     INCLUDED IN                                           NOT INCLUDED IN                                       15  349
     LAMBERT, TRIANDIS, AND WOLF'S                         LAMBERT, TRIANDIS, AND WOLF'S                    XSQ=   85.14
     STUDY OF SUPERNATURAL BEINGS  (36)                    STUDY OF SUPERNATURAL BEINGS  (364)              PHI=   0.461
                                                                                                            XP =  0.

507  TEND TO BE THOSE                 0.52 OF  33    507  TEND TO BE THOSE                 0.81 OF 367        17   69
     INCLUDED IN JAMES R. LEARY'S                          NOT INCLUDED IN JAMES R. LEARY'S                      16  298
     STUDY OF FOOD TABOOS  (86)                            STUDY OF FOOD TABOOS  (314)                      XSQ=   17.31
                                                                                                            PHI=   0.208
                                                                                                            XP =  0.0000

508  TEND LESS TO BE THOSE            0.58 OF  33    508  TEND MORE TO BE THOSE            0.93 OF 367        14   26
     NOT INCLUDED IN DAVID C. MCCLELLAND'S                 NOT INCLUDED IN DAVID C. MCCLELLAND'S                 19  341
     STUDY OF ACHIEVEMENT MOTIVATION  (360)                STUDY OF ACHIEVEMENT MOTIVATION  (360)           XSQ=   38.18
                                                                                                            PHI=   0.309
                                                                                                            XP =  0.
```

509	DRIFT LESS TOWARD BEING THOSE 0.85 OF 33 NOT INCLUDED IN MONI NAG'S STUDY OF FERTILITY (375)	509	DRIFT MORE TOWARD BEING THOSE 0.95 OF 367 NOT INCLUDED IN MONI NAG'S STUDY OF FERTILITY (375)	5 20 28 347 XSQ= 3.35 PHI= 0.092 XP = 0.0672
511	TEND TO BE THOSE 0.79 OF 33 INCLUDED IN ROBERTS, ARTH AND BUSH'S SAMPLE ON GAMES, AS MODIFIED BY THE ETHNOGRAPHIC ATLAS (189)	511	TEND TO BE THOSE 0.56 OF 367 NOT INCLUDED IN ROBERTS, ARTH AND BUSH'S SAMPLE ON GAMES, AS MODIFIED BY THE ETHNOGRAPHIC ATLAS (211)	26 163 7 204 XSQ= 13.01 PHI= 0.180 XP = 0.0003
513	LEAN LESS TOWARD BEING THOSE 0.73 OF 33 NOT INCLUDED IN LEO W. SIMMONS' STUDY OF THE TREATMENT OF THE AGED (357)	513	LEAN MORE TOWARD BEING THOSE 0.91 OF 367 NOT INCLUDED IN LEO W. SIMMONS' STUDY OF THE TREATMENT OF THE AGED (357)	9 34 24 333 XSQ= 8.44 PHI= 0.145 XP = 0.0037
514	TEND TO BE THOSE 0.97 OF 33 INCLUDED IN PHILIP E. SLATER'S STUDY OF NARCISSISM (90)	514	TEND TO BE THOSE 0.84 OF 367 NOT INCLUDED IN PHILIP E. SLATER'S STUDY OF NARCISSISM (310)	32 58 1 309 XSQ= 109.78 PHI= 0.524 XP = 0.
515	TEND TO BE THOSE 0.64 OF 33 INCLUDED IN WILLIAM N. STEPHENS' SAMPLE ON AVOIDANCE RELATIONSHIPS (52)	515	TEND TO BE THOSE 0.92 OF 367 NOT INCLUDED IN WILLIAM N. STEPHENS' SAMPLE ON AVOIDANCE RELATIONSHIPS (348)	21 31 12 336 XSQ= 76.73 PHI= 0.438 XP = 0.
517	LEAN MORE TOWARD BEING THOSE 0.88 OF 33 INCLUDED IN GUY E. SWANSON'S SAMPLE ON HIGH GODS, AS MODIFIED BY THE ETHNOGRAPHIC ATLAS (260)	517	LEAN LESS TOWARD BEING THOSE 0.63 OF 367 INCLUDED IN GUY E. SWANSON'S SAMPLE ON HIGH GODS, AS MODIFIED BY THE ETHNOGRAPHIC ATLAS (260)	29 231 4 136 XSQ= 7.22 PHI= 0.134 XP = 0.0072
518	TEND TO BE THOSE 0.58 OF 33 INCLUDED IN STANLEY H. UDY, JR.'S STUDY OF WORK ORGANIZATION (105)	518	TEND TO BE THOSE 0.77 OF 367 NOT INCLUDED IN STANLEY H. UDY, JR.'S STUDY OF WORK ORGANIZATION (295)	19 86 14 281 XSQ= 16.51 PHI= 0.203 XP = 0.0000
519	TEND LESS TO BE THOSE 0.61 OF 33 NOT INCLUDED IN JOSEPH VEROFF'S STUDY OF ACHIEVEMENT MOTIVATION AS REVEALED IN FOLKTALES (364)	519	TEND MORE TO BE THOSE 0.94 OF 367 NOT INCLUDED IN JOSEPH VEROFF'S STUDY OF ACHIEVEMENT MOTIVATION AS REVEALED IN FOLKTALES (364)	13 23 20 344 XSQ= 36.63 PHI= 0.303 XP = 0.
520	TEND TO BE THOSE 0.58 OF 33 INCLUDED IN BEATRICE BLYTH WHITING'S STUDY OF SORCERY (40)	520	TEND TO BE THOSE 0.94 OF 367 NOT INCLUDED IN BEATRICE BLYTH WHITING'S STUDY OF SORCERY (360)	19 21 14 346 XSQ= 84.79 PHI= 0.460 XP = 0.

```
521  TEND TO BE THOSE                0.58 OF  33      521  TEND TO BE THOSE                0.92 OF 367           19   28
     INCLUDED IN JOHN W. M. WHITING'S                      NOT INCLUDED IN JOHN W. M. WHITING'S                  14  339
     STUDY OF SOCIALIZATION                                STUDY OF SOCIALIZATION                          XSQ=   68.10
     PROCESS AND PERSONALITY  (47)                         PROCESS AND PERSONALITY  (353)                  PHI=   0.413
                                                                                                           XP =  0.

522  TEND TO BE THOSE                0.67 OF  33      522  TEND TO BE THOSE                0.84 OF 367           22   60
     INCLUDED IN                                           NOT INCLUDED IN                                       11  307
     MARJORIE GRANT WHITING'S                              MARJORIE GRANT WHITING'S                        XSQ=   44.00
     STUDY OF DIET  (82)                                   STUDY OF DIET  (318)                            PHI=   0.332
                                                                                                           XP =  0.

523  IN ALL CASES ARE THOSE          1.00 OF  33      523  TEND TO BE THOSE                0.92 OF 367           33   28
     INCLUDED IN WHITING AND CHILD'S                       NOT INCLUDED IN WHITING AND CHILD'S                    0  339
     STUDY OF CHILD TRAINING                               STUDY OF CHILD TRAINING                         XSQ=  192.80
     AND PERSONALITY  (61)                                 AND PERSONALITY  (339)                          PHI=   0.694
                                                                                                           XP =  0.

524  TEND LESS TO BE THOSE           0.52 OF  33      524  TEND MORE TO BE THOSE           0.92 OF 367           16   28
     NOT INCLUDED IN                                       NOT INCLUDED IN                                       17  339
     WHITING, KLUCKHOHN, AND ANTHONY'S                     WHITING, KLUCKHOHN, AND ANTHONY'S               XSQ=   47.53
     STUDY OF MALE INITIATION CEREMONIES  (356)            STUDY OF MALE INITIATION CEREMONIES  (356)      PHI=   0.345
                                                                                                           XP =  0.
```

513 CULTURES
INCLUDED IN LEO W. SIMMONS'
STUDY OF THE TREATMENT OF THE AGED (43)

513 CULTURES
NOT INCLUDED IN LEO W. SIMMONS'
STUDY OF THE TREATMENT OF THE AGED (357)

BACKGROUND ON PAGE 180

SUBJECT ONLY, F.C. 1-480 AND 527-536
BOTH SUBJECT AND PREDICATE, F.C. 481-526

43 IN LEFT COLUMN

ABIPON	AINU	ALBANIANS	ANDAMANESE	ARANDA	ARAUCANIANS	ASHANTI	AZTEC	CHUKCHEE	CREEK
CROW	DIERI	FANG	FON	HAIDA	HANO	HEBREWS	IBAN	INCA	JIVARO
KAZAK	KUNG	KUTENAI	KWAKIUTL	LANGO	LAPPS	MAORI	MOTA	NAMA	NAVAHO
OMAHA	RWALA	SAMOANS	SEMANG	SERI	SHILLUK	TODA	TROBRIAND	VEDDA	WITOTO
YAHGAN	YAKUT	YUKAGHIR							

357 IN RIGHT COLUMN

	Left column (43)		Right column (357)	Statistics
15	DRIFT TOWARD BEING THOSE 0.60 OF 43 WHERE THE LATITUDE IS TWENTY DEGREES OR GREATER (183)	15	DRIFT TOWARD BEING THOSE 0.56 OF 357 WHERE THE LATITUDE IS LESS THAN TWENTY DEGREES (217)	26 157 17 200 XSQ= 3.57 PHI= 0.094 XP = 0.0590
33	LEAN LESS TOWARD BEING THOSE 0.67 OF 43 WHERE THE NATURAL ENVIRONMENT IS OTHER THAN 'VERY HARSH,' I.E., DESERT, DESERT GRASSES AND SHRUBS, TUNDRA, OR HIGH PLATEAU STEPPE (341) FWM	33	LEAN MORE TOWARD BEING THOSE 0.87 OF 357 WHERE THE NATURAL ENVIRONMENT IS OTHER THAN 'VERY HARSH,' I.E., DESERT, DESERT GRASSES AND SHRUBS, TUNDRA, OR HIGH PLATEAU STEPPE (341) FWM	14 45 29 312 XSQ= 10.62 PHI= 0.163 XP = 0.0011
36	LEAN LESS TOWARD BEING THOSE 0.53 OF 43 WHERE THE NATURAL ENVIRONMENT IS OTHER THAN 'VERY HARSH,' OR SUB-TROPICAL BUSH, OR TEMPERATE GRASSLAND (292) FWM	36	LEAN MORE TOWARD BEING THOSE 0.75 OF 357 WHERE THE NATURAL ENVIRONMENT IS OTHER THAN 'VERY HARSH,' OR SUB-TROPICAL BUSH, OR TEMPERATE GRASSLAND (292) FWM	20 88 23 269 XSQ= 8.23 PHI= 0.143 XP = 0.0041
42	DRIFT MORE TOWARD BEING THOSE 0.74 OF 43 WHERE THE NATURAL ENVIRONMENT IS OTHER THAN TROPICAL OR SUB-TROPICAL RAIN FOREST, OR MONSOON FOREST (244) FWM	42	DRIFT LESS TOWARD BEING THOSE 0.59 OF 357 WHERE THE NATURAL ENVIRONMENT IS OTHER THAN TROPICAL OR SUB-TROPICAL RAIN FOREST, OR MONSOON FOREST (244) FWM	11 145 32 212 XSQ= 3.04 PHI= -0.087 XP = 0.0811
44	DRIFT LESS TOWARD BEING THOSE 0.52 OF 42 WHERE SETTLEMENTS ARE FIXED (222)	44	DRIFT MORE TOWARD BEING THOSE 0.69 OF 290 WHERE SETTLEMENTS ARE FIXED (222)	22 200 20 90 XSQ= 3.84 PHI= -0.108 XP = 0.0501

46	LEAN LESS TOWARD BEING THOSE 0.60 OF 42 OTHER THAN WHERE SETTLEMENTS ARE NON-FIXED AND MOVEMENT IS NOMADIC (260)	46	LEAN MORE TOWARD BEING THOSE 0.81 OF 290 OTHER THAN WHERE SETTLEMENTS ARE NON-FIXED AND MOVEMENT IS NOMADIC (260)	17 55 25 235 XSQ= 8.77 PHI= 0.163 XP = 0.0031
47	DRIFT MORE TOWARD BEING THOSE 0.85 OF 20 WHERE, IF SETTLEMENTS ARE NON-FIXED, MOVEMENT IS NOMADIC, RATHER THAN NON-NOMADIC (72)	47	DRIFT LESS TOWARD BEING THOSE 0.61 OF 90 WHERE, IF SETTLEMENTS ARE NON-FIXED, MOVEMENT IS NOMADIC, RATHER THAN NON-NOMADIC (72)	17 55 3 35 XSQ= 3.14 PHI= 0.169 XP = 0.0763
51	TILT TOWARD BEING THOSE 0.53 OF 43 WHERE SUBSISTENCE IS PRIMARILY BY FOOD GATHERING -- I. E., HUNTING, FISHING, OR COLLECTING -- RATHER THAN FOOD PRODUCTION (147)	51	TILT TOWARD BEING THOSE 0.65 OF 357 WHERE SUBSISTENCE IS PRIMARILY BY FOOD PRODUCTION -- I. E., AGRICULTURE OR HUSBANDRY -- RATHER THAN BY GATHERING (253)	20 233 23 124 XSQ= 5.03 PHI= -0.112 XP = 0.0249
82	TILT LESS TOWARD BEING THOSE 0.63 OF 30 WHERE A CITY OR TOWN IS PRESENT, OR THE AVERAGE COMMUNITY SIZE IS FIFTY OR GREATER (178)	82	TILT MORE TOWARD BEING THOSE 0.82 OF 194 WHERE A CITY OR TOWN IS PRESENT, OR THE AVERAGE COMMUNITY SIZE IS FIFTY OR GREATER (178)	19 159 11 35 XSQ= 4.44 PHI= -0.141 XP = 0.0351
131	TILT LESS TOWARD BEING THOSE 0.68 OF 22 WHERE THE CONSTRUCTION OF PERMANENT HOUSES OR THE ERECTION OF TEMPORARY DWELLINGS IS MAINLY DONE BY MALES (136)	131	TILT MORE TOWARD BEING THOSE 0.90 OF 135 WHERE THE CONSTRUCTION OF PERMANENT HOUSES OR THE ERECTION OF TEMPORARY DWELLINGS IS MAINLY DONE BY MALES (136)	15 121 7 14 XSQ= 5.77 PHI= -0.192 XP = 0.0163
179	TILT LESS TOWARD BEING THOSE 0.79 OF 42 WHERE THE COMMUNITY IS OTHER THAN STRUCTURED ON A NON-CLAN BASIS AND COMMONLY EXOGAMOUS (340)	179	TILT MORE TOWARD BEING THOSE 0.90 OF 340 WHERE THE COMMUNITY IS OTHER THAN STRUCTURED ON A NON-CLAN BASIS AND COMMONLY EXOGAMOUS (340)	9 33 33 307 XSQ= 4.12 PHI= 0.104 XP = 0.0424
180	DRIFT LESS TOWARD BEING THOSE 0.55 OF 42 WHERE THE COMMUNITY IS COMMONLY NON-EXOGAMOUS, RATHER THAN EXOGAMOUS (258)	180	DRIFT MORE TOWARD BEING THOSE 0.69 OF 340 WHERE THE COMMUNITY IS COMMONLY NON-EXOGAMOUS, RATHER THAN EXOGAMOUS (258)	19 105 23 235 XSQ= 2.89 PHI= 0.087 XP = 0.0891
184	TILT TOWARD BEING THOSE 0.54 OF 26 WHERE THE LARGEST NON-COGNATIC KIN GROUP IS THE MOEITY OR PHRATRY (77)	184	TILT TOWARD BEING THOSE 0.72 OF 226 WHERE THE LARGEST NON-COGNATIC KIN GROUP IS SMALLER THAN A PHRATRY, I. E. A SIB OR LINEAGE (175)	14 63 12 163 XSQ= 6.24 PHI= 0.157 XP = 0.0125
196	TILT TOWARD BEING THOSE 0.50 OF 34 WHERE INDIVIDUAL RIGHTS IN REAL PROPERTY, OR RULES FOR INHERITANCE, ARE ABSENT (87)	196	TILT TOWARD BEING THOSE 0.72 OF 247 WHERE INDIVIDUAL RIGHTS IN REAL PROPERTY, AND RULES FOR INHERITANCE, ARE PRESENT (194)	17 177 17 70 XSQ= 5.59 PHI= -0.141 XP = 0.0181

198	TILT LESS TOWARD BEING THOSE 0.67 OF 15 WHERE RULES FOR THE INHERITANCE OF REAL PROPERTY, IF PRESENT, FAVOR THE MALE HEIR OR LINE, RATHER THAN THE FEMALE (144)	198	TILT MORE TOWARD BEING THOSE 0.89 OF 150 WHERE RULES FOR THE INHERITANCE OF REAL PROPERTY, IF PRESENT, FAVOR THE MALE HEIR OR LINE, RATHER THAN THE FEMALE (144)	10 134 5 16 XSQ= 4.43 PHI= -0.164 XP = 0.0353
256	IN ALL CASES ARE THOSE 1.00 OF 3 WHERE GRANDPARENT AND GRANDCHILD ARE NOT FRIENDLY EQUALS (8) DA	256	TILT TOWARD BEING THOSE 0.83 OF 30 WHERE GRANDPARENT AND GRANDCHILD ARE FRIENDLY EQUALS (25) DA	0 25 3 5 XSQ= 6.27 PHI= -0.436 EP = 0.0103
302	TILT TOWARD BEING THOSE 0.75 OF 12 WHERE THE AVERAGE EARLY SATISFACTION POTENTIAL IS LOW (17) W-C	302	TILT TOWARD BEING THOSE 0.71 OF 28 WHERE THE AVERAGE EARLY SATISFACTION POTENTIAL IS HIGH (23) W-C	3 20 9 8 XSQ= 5.63 PHI= -0.375 EP = 0.0130
305	TILT TOWARD BEING THOSE 0.73 OF 15 WHERE THE EARLY SEXUAL SATISFACTION POTENTIAL IS LOW (24) W-C	305	TILT TOWARD BEING THOSE 0.64 OF 36 WHERE THE EARLY SEXUAL SATISFACTION POTENTIAL IS HIGH (27) W-C	4 23 11 13 XSQ= 4.49 PHI= -0.297 XP = 0.0341
307	TILT TOWARD BEING THOSE 0.67 OF 15 WHERE THE EARLY AGGRESSION SATISFACTION POTENTIAL IS LOW (19) W-C	307	TILT TOWARD BEING THOSE 0.76 OF 37 WHERE THE EARLY AGGRESSION SATISFACTION POTENTIAL IS HIGH (33) W-C	5 28 10 9 XSQ= 6.53 PHI= -0.354 XP = 0.0106
313	TILT TOWARD BEING THOSE 0.75 OF 16 WHERE AGGRESSION SOCIALIZATION ANXIETY IS HIGH (26) W-C	313	TILT TOWARD BEING THOSE 0.63 OF 38 WHERE AGGRESSION SOCIALIZATION ANXIETY IS LOW (28) W-C	12 14 4 24 XSQ= 5.13 PHI= 0.308 XP = 0.0236
338	DRIFT MORE TOWARD BEING THOSE 0.82 OF 17 WHERE THE CHILD'S INFERRED ANXIETY OVER PERFORMANCE OF RESPONSIBLE BEHAVIOR IS HIGH (44) B-B-C	338	DRIFT LESS TOWARD BEING THOSE 0.54 OF 56 WHERE THE CHILD'S INFERRED ANXIETY OVER PERFORMANCE OF RESPONSIBLE BEHAVIOR IS HIGH (44) B-B-C	14 30 3 26 XSQ= 3.39 PHI= 0.215 XP = 0.0656
348	TILT TOWARD BEING THOSE 0.80 OF 15 WHERE THE TOTAL POSITIVE PRESSURE TOWARD DEVELOPING ACHIEVEMENT BEHAVIOR IN THE CHILD IS HIGH (32) B-B-C	348	TILT TOWARD BEING THOSE 0.58 OF 48 WHERE THE TOTAL POSITIVE PRESSURE TOWARD DEVELOPING ACHIEVEMENT BEHAVIOR IN THE CHILD IS LOW (31) B-B-C	12 20 3 28 XSQ= 5.27 PHI= 0.289 XP = 0.0217
349	TILT TOWARD BEING THOSE 0.87 OF 15 WHERE THE CHILD'S INFERRED ANXIETY OVER NON-PERFORMANCE OF ACHIEVEMENT BEHAVIOR IS HIGH (34) B-B-C	349	TILT TOWARD BEING THOSE 0.55 OF 47 WHERE THE CHILD'S INFERRED ANXIETY OVER NON-PERFORMANCE OF ACHIEVEMENT BEHAVIOR IS LOW (28) B-B-C	13 21 2 26 XSQ= 6.49 PHI= 0.323 XP = 0.0109

393	DRIFT TOWARD BEING THOSE WHERE EXTRAMARITAL COITUS IS PUNISHED, RATHER THAN PERMITTED (43) F-B	0.70 OF 23	393	DRIFT TOWARD BEING THOSE WHERE EXTRAMARITAL COITUS IS PERMITTED, RATHER THAN PUNISHED (41) F-B	0.56 OF 61	16 27 7 34 XSQ= 3.33 PHI= 0.199 XP = 0.0681
419	TILT MORE TOWARD BEING THOSE WHERE MILITARY GLORY IS STRONGLY OR MODERATELY EMPHASIZED (55) PES	0.81 OF 31	419	TILT LESS TOWARD BEING THOSE WHERE MILITARY GLORY IS STRONGLY OR MODERATELY EMPHASIZED (55) PES	0.55 OF 55	25 30 6 25 XSQ= 4.78 PHI= 0.236 XP = 0.0288
420	TILT TOWARD BEING THOSE WHERE BELLICOSITY IS EXTREME (41) PES	0.66 OF 32	420	TILT TOWARD BEING THOSE WHERE BELLICOSITY IS MODERATE OR NEGLIGIBLE (46) PES	0.64 OF 55	21 20 11 35 XSQ= 5.83 PHI= 0.259 XP = 0.0158
421	DRIFT TOWARD BEING THOSE WHERE KILLING, TORTURING, OR MUTILATING OF THE ENEMY IS STRONGLY OR MODERATELY EMPHASIZED (37) PES	0.59 OF 29	421	DRIFT TOWARD BEING THOSE WHERE KILLING, TORTURING, OR MUTILATING OF THE ENEMY IS NEGLIGIBLY EMPHASIZED (47) PES	0.64 OF 55	17 20 12 35 XSQ= 2.97 PHI= 0.188 XP = 0.0850
428	DRIFT TOWARD BEING THOSE WHERE A HIGH GOD, IF PRESENT AND ACTIVE, DOES NOT SUPPORT HUMAN MORALITY, RATHER THAN SUPPORTING IT (26) GES,EA	0.54 OF 13	428	DRIFT TOWARD BEING THOSE WHERE A HIGH GOD, IF PRESENT AND ACTIVE, SUPPORTS HUMAN MORALITY, RATHER THAN NOT SUPPORTING IT (61) GES,EA	0.74 OF 74	6 55 7 19 XSQ= 2.95 PHI= -0.184 XP = 0.0858
444	TILT TOWARD BEING THOSE WHERE THE USE OF DREAMS TO SEEK AND CONTROL SUPERNATURAL POWERS IS HIGH (28) RGD	0.75 OF 16	444	TILT TOWARD BEING THOSE WHERE THE USE OF DREAMS TO SEEK AND CONTROL SUPERNATURAL POWERS IS LOW (27) RGD	0.59 OF 39	12 16 4 23 XSQ= 3.97 PHI= 0.269 XP = 0.0464
475	DRIFT TOWARD BEING THOSE WHERE EXHIBITIONISTIC DANCING IS NEGLIGIBLY EMPHASIZED (38) PES	0.59 OF 29	475	DRIFT TOWARD BEING THOSE WHERE EXHIBITIONISTIC DANCING IS STRONGLY OR MODERATELY EMPHASIZED (48) PES	0.63 OF 57	12 36 17 21 XSQ= 2.87 PHI= -0.183 XP = 0.0905
487	LEAN LESS TOWARD BEING THOSE ABOUT WHICH THE PRINCIPAL ETHNOGRAPHIES WERE PUBLISHED IN 1930 OR AFTER (227)	0.63 OF 19	487	LEAN MORE TOWARD BEING THOSE ABOUT WHICH THE PRINCIPAL ETHNOGRAPHIES WERE PUBLISHED IN 1930 OR AFTER (227)	0.90 OF 240	7 25 12 215 XSQ= 9.04 PHI= 0.187 XP = 0.0026
488	LEAN MORE TOWARD BEING THOSE ABOUT WHICH THE PRINCIPAL ETHNOGRAPHIES WERE PUBLISHED BEFORE 1950 (185)	0.96 OF 27	488	LEAN LESS TOWARD BEING THOSE ABOUT WHICH THE PRINCIPAL ETHNOGRAPHIES WERE PUBLISHED BEFORE 1950 (185)	0.69 OF 230	26 159 1 71 XSQ= 7.55 PHI= 0.171 XP = 0.0060

489	LEAN LESS TOWARC BEING THCSE NOT INCLUDED IN CHARLES ACKERMAN'S STUDY OF DIVCRCE (343)	0.70 OF 43	489	LEAN MORE TOWARD BEING THOSE NOT INCLUDED IN CHARLES ACKERMAN'S STUDY OF DIVORCE (343)	0.88 OF 357	13 44 30 313 XSQ= 8.66 PHI= 0.147 XP = 0.0033
490	TEND TO BE THOSE INCLUDED IN ALBERT S. ANTFONY'S SAMPLE ON MALE INITIATICN RITES (113)	0.51 OF 43	490	TEND TO BE THOSE NOT INCLUDED IN ALBERT S. ANTHONY'S SAMPLE ON MALE INITIATICN RITES (287)	0.75 OF 357	22 91 21 266 XSQ= 11.24 PHI= 0.168 XP = 0.0008
492	TEND LESS TO BE THCSE NCT INCLUDED IN BARBARA CFARTIER AYRES' STUDY OF FEMALE INITIATION RITES (361)	0.72 OF 43	492	TEND MORE TO BE THOSE NOT INCLUDED IN BARBARA CHARTIER AYRES' STUDY OF FEMALE INITIATICN RITES (361)	0.92 OF 357	12 27 31 330 XSQ= 15.81 PHI= 0.199 XP = 0.0001
493	TEND LESS TO BE THCSE NOT INCLUDED IN BACCN, BARRY, AND CHILC'S STUDY OF CHILD REARING (322)	0.58 OF 43	493	TEND MORE TO BE THOSE NOT INCLUDED IN BACON, BARRY, AND CHILD'S STUDY OF CHILD REARING (322)	0.83 OF 357	18 60 25 297 XSQ= 13.79 PHI= 0.186 XP = 0.0002
494	TEND LESS TO BE THCSE NOT INCLUDED IN HERBERT M. BARRY III'S STUDY OF ART (371)	0.72 OF 43	494	TEND MORE TO BE THOSE NOT INCLUDED IN HERBERT M. BARRY III'S STUDY OF ART (371)	0.95 OF 357	12 17 31 340 XSQ= 27.23 PHI= 0.261 XP = 0.0000
495	TILT LESS TOWARC BEING THOSE NOT INCLUDED IN JUCITH K. BROWN'S STUDY OF FEMALE INITIATION RITES (335)	0.72 OF 43	495	TILT MORE TOWARD BEING THOSE NOT INCLUDED IN JUDITH K. BROWN'S STUDY OF FEMALE INITIATION RITES (335)	0.85 OF 357	12 53 31 304 XSQ= 3.90 PHI= 0.099 XP = 0.0483
496	TEND LESS TO BE THCSE NOT INCLUDED IN ROY G. C'ANDRADE'S STUDY OF DREAMS (345)	0.63 OF 43	496	TEND MORE TO BE THOSE NOT INCLUDED IN ROY G. D'ANDRADE'S STUDY OF DREAMS (345)	0.89 OF 357	16 39 27 318 XSQ= 20.20 PHI= 0.225 XP = 0.0000
497	TEND LESS TO BE THCSE NOT INCLUDED IN WILLIAM M. EVAN'S STUDY OF LAW (339)	0.60 OF 43	497	TEND MORE TO BE THOSE NOT INCLUDED IN WILLIAM M. EVAN'S STUDY OF LAW (339)	0.88 OF 357	17 44 26 313 XSQ= 19.93 PHI= 0.223 XP = 0.0000
498	TEND LESS TO BE THCSE NOT INCLUDED IN C. S. FORC'S STUDY OF SEX (349)	0.53 OF 43	498	TEND MORE TO BE THOSE NOT INCLUDED IN C. S. FORD'S STUDY OF SEX (349)	0.91 OF 357	20 31 23 326 XSQ= 46.02 PHI= 0.339 XP = 0.

499	TEND TO BE THOSE 0.51 OF 43 INCLUDED IN FORD AND BEACH'S SAMPLE ON SEXUAL EXPRESSION BY THE YOUNG (86)	499	TEND TO BE THOSE 0.82 OF 357 NOT INCLUDED IN FORD AND BEACH'S SAMPLE ON SEXUAL EXPRESSION BY THE YOUNG (314)	22 64 21 293 XSQ= 23.19 PHI= 0.241 XP = 0.0000
500	TEND LESS TO BE THOSE 0.65 OF 43 NOT INCLUDED IN FREEMAN AND WINCH'S STUDY OF SOCIETAL COMPLEXITY (360)	500	TEND MORE TO BE THOSE 0.93 OF 357 NOT INCLUDED IN FREEMAN AND WINCH'S STUDY OF SOCIETAL COMPLEXITY (360)	15 25 28 332 XSQ= 30.12 PHI= 0.274 XP = 0.0000
501	TEND LESS TO BE THOSE 0.53 OF 43 NOT INCLUDED IN JOAN FRIENDLY GOODMAN'S STUDY OF ASCETIC MOURNING BEHAVIOR (333)	501	TEND MORE TO BE THOSE 0.87 OF 357 NOT INCLUDED IN JOAN FRIENDLY GOODMAN'S STUDY OF ASCETIC MOURNING BEHAVIOR (333)	20 47 23 310 XSQ= 28.26 PHI= 0.266 XP = 0.0000
502	LEAN LESS TOWARD BEING THOSE 0.70 OF 43 NOT INCLUDED IN JOHN K. HARLEY'S STUDY OF ADOLESCENT PEER GROUPS (343)	502	LEAN MORE TOWARD BEING THOSE 0.88 OF 357 NOT INCLUDED IN JOHN K. HARLEY'S STUDY OF ADOLESCENT PEER GROUPS (343)	13 44 30 313 XSQ= 8.66 PHI= 0.147 XP = 0.0033
503	TEND LESS TO BE THOSE 0.63 OF 43 NOT INCLUDED IN JOHN M. HICKMAN'S STUDY OF THE FOLK-URBAN CONTINUUM (346)	503	TEND MORE TO BE THOSE 0.89 OF 357 NOT INCLUDED IN JOHN M. HICKMAN'S STUDY OF THE FOLK-URBAN CONTINUUM (346)	16 38 27 319 XSQ= 20.97 PHI= 0.229 XP = 0.0000
504	TEND LESS TO BE THOSE 0.67 OF 43 NOT INCLUDED IN DONALD HORTON'S STUDY OF ALCHOLISM (351)	504	TEND MORE TO BE THOSE 0.90 OF 357 NOT INCLUDED IN DONALD HORTON'S STUDY OF ALCHOLISM (351)	14 35 29 322 XSQ= 16.43 PHI= 0.203 XP = 0.0001
505	LEAN LESS TOWARD BEING THOSE 0.84 OF 43 NOT INCLUDED IN MERRILL JACKSON'S STUDY OF CRIMINAL LAW AND MEDICINE (380)	505	LEAN MORE TOWARD BEING THOSE 0.96 OF 357 NOT INCLUDED IN MERRILL JACKSON'S STUDY OF CRIMINAL LAW AND MEDICINE (380)	7 13 36 344 XSQ= 10.38 PHI= 0.161 XP = 0.0013
506	TILT LESS TOWARD BEING THOSE 0.81 OF 43 NOT INCLUDED IN LAMBERT, TRIANDIS, AND WOLF'S STUDY OF SUPERNATURAL BEINGS (364)	506	TILT MORE TOWARD BEING THOSE 0.92 OF 357 NOT INCLUDED IN LAMBERT, TRIANDIS, AND WOLF'S STUDY OF SUPERNATURAL BEINGS (364)	8 28 35 329 XSQ= 4.19 PHI= 0.102 XP = 0.0406
507	TEND LESS TO BE THOSE 0.56 OF 43 NOT INCLUDED IN JAMES R. LEARY'S STUDY OF FOOD TABOOS (314)	507	TEND MORE TO BE THOSE 0.81 OF 357 NOT INCLUDED IN JAMES R. LEARY'S STUDY OF FOOD TABOOS (314)	19 67 24 290 XSQ= 13.22 PHI= 0.182 XP = 0.0003

508	TILT LESS TOWARC BEING THOSE 0.79 OF 43 NOT INCLUDED IN DAVID C. MCCLELLAND'S STUDY OF ACHIEVEMENT MOTIVATION (360)	508	TILT MORE TOWARD BEING THOSE 0.91 OF 357 NOT INCLUDED IN DAVID C. MCCLELLAND'S STUDY OF ACHIEVEMENT MOTIVATION (360)	9 31 34 326 XSQ= 5.11 PHI= 0.113 XP = 0.0238
510	TEND LESS TO BE THCSE 0.77 OF 43 NOT INCLUDED IN RACUL NARRCLL'S STUDY OF SOCIETAL COMPLEXITY (380)	510	TEND MORE TO BE THOSE 0.97 OF 357 NOT INCLUDED IN RAOUL NARRCLL'S STUDY OF SOCIETAL COMPLEXITY (380)	10 10 33 347 XSQ= 29.63 PHI= 0.272 XP = 0.0000
511	TEND TO BE THCSE 0.86 OF 43 INCLUDED IN ROBERTS, ARTH AND BUSH'S SAMPLE ON GAMES, AS MCDIFIED BY THE ETHNOGRAPHIC ATLAS (189)	511	TEND TO BE THOSE 0.57 OF 357 NOT INCLUDED IN ROBERTS, ARTH AND BUSH'S SAMPLE ON GAMES, AS MODIFIED BY THE ETHNOGRAPHIC ATLAS (211)	37 152 6 205 XSQ= 27.38 PHI= 0.262 XP = 0.0000
512	LEAN LESS TOWARD BEING THCSE 0.79 OF 43 NCT INCLUDED IN SHIRLEY ANC ROMNEY'S STUDY OF LCVE MAGIC (367)	512	LEAN MORE TOWARD BEING THOSE 0.93 OF 357 NOT INCLUDED IN SHIRLEY AND ROMNEY'S STUDY OF LOVE MAGIC (367)	9 24 34 333 XSQ= 8.44 PHI= 0.145 XP = 0.0037
514	TEND TO BE THOSE 0.74 OF 43 INCLUDED IN PHILIP E. SLATER'S STUDY OF NARCISSISM (90)	514	TEND TO BE THOSE 0.84 OF 357 NOT INCLUDED IN PHILIP E. SLATER'S STUDY OF NARCISSISM (310)	32 58 11 299 XSQ= 71.18 PHI= 0.422 XP = 0.
515	TEND LESS TO BE THCSE 0.70 OF 43 NOT INCLUDED IN WILLIAM N. STEPHENS' SAMPLE ON AVOIDANCE RELATICNSHIPS (348)	515	TEND MORE TO BE THOSE 0.89 OF 357 NOT INCLUDED IN WILLIAM N. STEPHENS' SAMPLE ON AVOIDANCE RELATIONSHIPS (348)	13 39 30 318 XSQ= 11.00 PHI= 0.166 XP = 0.0009
516	TILT MORE TOWARD BEING THCSE 0.98 OF 43 INCLUDED IN GUY E. SWANSON'S SAMPLE ON LOCAL JURISDICTICN, AS MODIFIED BY THE ETHNOGRAPHIC ATLAS (331)	516	TILT LESS TOWARD BEING THOSE 0.81 OF 357 INCLUDED IN GUY E. SWANSON'S SAMPLE ON LOCAL JURISDICTION, AS MODIFIED BY THE ETHNOGRAPHIC ATLAS (331)	42 289 1 68 XSQ= 6.39 PHI= 0.126 XP = 0.0115
517	TEND MORE TO BE THCSE 0.91 OF 43 INCLUDED IN GUY E. SWANSON'S SAMPLE ON HIGH GODS, AS MODIFIED BY THE ETHNOGRAPHIC ATLAS (260)	517	TEND LESS TO BE THOSE 0.62 OF 357 INCLUDED IN GUY E. SWANSON'S SAMPLE ON HIGH GODS, AS MODIFIED BY THE ETHNOGRAPHIC ATLAS (260)	39 221 4 136 XSQ= 12.75 PHI= 0.179 XP = 0.0004
518	TEND TO BE THOSE 0.51 OF 43 INCLUDED IN STANLEY H. UDY, JR.'S STUDY OF WCRK ORGANIZATION (105)	518	TEND TO BE THOSE 0.77 OF 357 NOT INCLUDED IN STANLEY H. UDY, JR.'S STUDY OF WORK ORGANIZATION (295)	22 83 21 274 XSQ= 14.04 PHI= 0.187 XP = 0.0002

520	TEND LESS TO BE THCSE NOT INCLUDED IN BEATRICE BLYTH WHITING'S STUDY OF SCRCERY (360)	0.70 OF 43	520	TEND MORE TO BE THOSE NOT INCLUDED IN BEATRICE BLYTH WHITING'S STUDY OF SORCERY (360)	0.92 OF 357	13 27 30 330 XSQ= 19.47 PHI= 0.221 XP = 0.0000
521	TEND LESS TO BE THCSE NOT INCLUDED IN JOHN W. M. WHITING'S STUDY OF SOCIALIZATION PROCESS AND PERSCNALITY (353)	0.70 OF 43	521	TEND MORE TO BE THOSE NOT INCLUDED IN JOHN W. M. WHITING'S STUDY OF SOCIALIZATION PROCESS AND PERSONALITY (353)	0.90 OF 357	13 34 30 323 XSQ= 13.94 PHI= 0.187 XP = 0.0002
522	TEND LESS TO BE THCSE NOT INCLUDED IN MARJORIE GRANT WHITING'S STUDY OF DIET (318)	0.58 OF 43	522	TEND MORE TO BE THOSE NOT INCLUDED IN MARJORIE GRANT WHITING'S STUDY OF DIET (318)	0.82 OF 357	18 64 25 293 XSQ= 12.06 PHI= 0.174 XP = 0.0005
523	TEND LESS TO BE THCSE NOT INCLUDED IN WHITING AND CHILD'S STUDY OF CHILD TRAINING AND PERSONALITY (339)	0.56 OF 43	523	TEND MORE TO BE THOSE NOT INCLUDED IN WHITING AND CHILD'S STUDY OF CHILD TRAINING AND PERSONALITY (339)	0.88 OF 357	19 42 24 315 XSQ= 28.75 PHI= 0.268 XP = 0.0000
524	LEAN LESS TOWARD BEING THCSE NOT INCLUDED IN WHITING, KLUCKHCHN, AND ANTHONY'S STUDY OF MALE INITIATION CEREMONIES (356)	0.74 OF 43	524	LEAN MORE TOWARD BEING THOSE NOT INCLUDED IN WHITING, KLUCKHOHN, AND ANTHONY'S STUDY OF MALE INITIATION CEREMONIES (356)	0.91 OF 357	11 33 32 324 XSQ= 8.86 PHI= 0.149 XP = 0.0029

514 CULTURES INCLUDED IN PHILIP E. SLATER'S STUDY OF NARCISSISM (90)

514 CULTURES NOT INCLUDED IN PHILIP E. SLATER'S STUDY OF NARCISSISM (310)

BACKGROUND ON PAGE 180

SUBJECT ONLY, F.C. 1-480 AND 527-536
BOTH SUBJECT AND PREDICATE, F.C. 481-526

90 IN LEFT COLUMN

ABIPON	AINU	ALBANIANS	ALORESE	AMERICANS	ANDAMANESE	ARANDA	ARAPESH	ARAUCANIANS	ASHANTI
AYMARA	AZANDE	AZTEC	BALINESE	BEMBA	BHIL	CHAGGA	CHENCHU	CHEYENNE	CHIR-APACHE
CHUKCHEE	COMANCHE	COPR ESKIMO	CREEK	CROW	CUNA	CZECHS	DOBUANS	FON	GANDA
GOND	HAIDA	HANO	HEBREWS	IBAN	IFUGAO	INCA	JIVARO	KASKA	KAZAK
KOREANS	KURTATCHI	KWAKIUTL	LAKHER	LANGO	LAPPS	LAU	LEPCHA	LESU	MANUS
MAORI	MARQUESANS	MASAI	MURNGIN	NAMA	NAVAHO	NUER	NYAKYUSA	OJIBWA	PAPAGO
PUKAPUKA	RIFFIANS	RWALA	SAMOANS	SANPOIL	SIRIONO	SIWANS	SOMALI	TALLENSI	TANALA
TAPIRAPE	THONGA	TIKOPIA	TIMBIRA	TIV	TODA	TROBRIAND	TRUMAI	VENDA	VIETNAMESE
WARRAU	WITOTO	WOGEO	WOLEAIANS	WOLOF	YAGUA	YAHGAN	YAKUT	YUROK	ZUNI

310 IN RIGHT COLUMN

	Included (90)		Not included (310)	
62	LEAN MORE TOWARD BEING THOSE WHERE HUSBANDRY OF SOME KIND IS PRESENT (228) — 0.70 OF 90	62	LEAN LESS TOWARD BEING THOSE WHERE HUSBANDRY OF SOME KIND IS PRESENT (228) — 0.53 OF 310	63 165 27 145 XSQ= 7.34 PHI= 0.135 XP = 0.0068
87	DRIFT LESS TOWARD BEING THOSE WHERE THE LEVEL OF POLITICAL INTEGRATION IS THE LARGE STATE, THE LITTLE STATE, THE MINIMAL STATE, OR THE AUTONOMOUS COMMUNITY (281) GPM — 0.87 OF 78	87	DRIFT MORE TOWARD BEING THOSE WHERE THE LEVEL OF POLITICAL INTEGRATION IS THE LARGE STATE, THE LITTLE STATE, THE MINIMAL STATE, OR THE AUTONOMOUS COMMUNITY (281) GPM — 0.94 OF 226	68 213 10 13 XSQ= 3.19 PHI= -0.102 XP = 0.0739
120	TILT TOWARD BEING THOSE WHERE THE CRAFT SPECIALIZATION SCORE IS HIGH OR MEDIUM (36) WME — 0.77 OF 39	120	TILT TOWARD BEING THOSE WHERE THE CRAFT SPECIALIZATION SCORE IS LOW (17) WME — 0.57 OF 14	30 6 9 8 XSQ= 4.04 PHI= 0.276 XP = 0.0446
163	DRIFT TOWARD BEING THOSE WHERE THE EMPHASIS ON INDIVIDUAL VOLITION AS THE CAUSE OF CRIME IS LOW (10) MJ — 0.80 OF 10	163	DRIFT TOWARD BEING THOSE WHERE THE EMPHASIS ON INDIVIDUAL VOLITION AS THE CAUSE OF CRIME IS HIGH (7) MJ — 0.71 OF 7	2 5 8 2 XSQ= 2.62 PHI= -0.393 EP = 0.0584

179	DRIFT LESS TOWARD BEING THOSE 0.83 OF 89 WHERE THE COMMUNITY IS OTHER THAN STRUCTURED ON A NON-CLAN BASIS AND COMMONLY EXOGAMOUS (340)	179	DRIFT MORE TOWARD BEING THOSE 0.91 OF 293 WHERE THE COMMUNITY IS OTHER THAN STRUCTURED ON A NON-CLAN BASIS AND COMMONLY EXOGAMOUS (340)	15 27 74 266 XSQ= 3.33 PHI= 0.093 XP = 0.0681
180	TILT LESS TOWARD BEING THOSE 0.57 OF 89 WHERE THE COMMUNITY IS COMMONLY NON-EXOGAMOUS, RATHER THAN EXOGAMOUS (258)	180	TILT MORE TOWARD BEING THOSE 0.71 OF 293 WHERE THE COMMUNITY IS COMMONLY NON-EXOGAMOUS, RATHER THAN EXOGAMOUS (258)	38 86 51 207 XSQ= 4.95 PHI= 0.114 XP = 0.0260
182	DRIFT MORE TOWARD BEING THOSE 0.75 OF 89 OTHER THAN WHERE THE COMMUNITY IS STRUCTURED ON A NON-CLAN BASIS AND AGAMOUS (256)	182	DRIFT LESS TOWARD BEING THOSE 0.65 OF 293 OTHER THAN WHERE THE COMMUNITY IS STRUCTURED ON A NON-CLAN BASIS AND AGAMOUS (256)	22 104 67 189 XSQ= 3.12 PHI= -0.090 XP = 0.0776
213	DRIFT MORE TOWARD BEING THOSE 0.62 OF 89 WHERE FIRST COUSIN MARRIAGE IS NOT PERMITTED (198)	213	DRIFT LESS TOWARD BEING THOSE 0.51 OF 281 WHERE FIRST COUSIN MARRIAGE IS NOT PERMITTED (198)	34 138 55 143 XSQ= 2.81 PHI= -0.087 XP = 0.0937
243	TILT TOWARD BEING THOSE 0.50 OF 42 WHERE POLYGYNY, IF PRESENT, HAS A HIGH INCIDENCE (24) W-C,S	243	TILT TOWARD BEING THOSE 0.83 OF 18 WHERE POLYGYNY, IF PRESENT, HAS A LOW INCIDENCE (36) W-D,S	21 3 21 15 XSQ= 4.53 PHI= 0.275 XP = 0.0334
278	DRIFT TOWARD BEING THOSE 0.50 OF 16 WHERE PROPERTY RIGHTS IN WOMEN ARE PRESENT (8) LWS	278	IN ALL CASES ARE THOSE 1.00 OF 6 WHERE PROPERTY RIGHTS IN WOMEN ARE UNIMPORTANT OR ABSENT (14) LWS	8 0 8 6 XSQ= 2.80 PHI= 0.357 EP = 0.0511
280	TILT TOWARD BEING THOSE 0.75 OF 12 WHERE THE COMPOSITE FERTILITY LEVEL IS HIGH (13) MN	280	TILT TOWARD BEING THOSE 0.69 OF 13 WHERE THE COMPOSITE FERTILITY LEVEL IS LOW (12) MN	9 4 3 9 XSQ= 3.28 PHI= 0.362 EP = 0.0472
325	DRIFT TOWARD BEING THOSE 0.64 OF 55 WHERE THE DEGREE OF DIFFUSION AMONG THE INFANT'S NURTURANT AGENTS IS HIGH (42) B-B-C	325	DRIFT TOWARD BEING THOSE 0.63 OF 19 WHERE THE DEGREE OF DIFFUSION AMONG THE INFANT'S NURTURANT AGENTS IS LOW (32) B-B-C	35 7 20 12 XSQ= 3.11 PHI= 0.205 XP = 0.0778
390	DRIFT MORE TOWARD BEING THOSE 0.81 OF 70 WHERE PREMARITAL SEX RELATIONS ARE WEAKLY PUNISHED AND IN FACT NOT RARE OR PUNISHED ONLY IF PREGNANCY RESULTS, OR FREELY PERMITTED (132) JTW,EA	390	DRIFT LESS TOWARD BEING THOSE 0.69 OF 109 WHERE PREMARITAL SEX RELATIONS ARE WEAKLY PUNISHED AND IN FACT NOT RARE OR PUNISHED ONLY IF PREGNANCY RESULTS, OR FREELY PERMITTED (132) JTW,EA	13 34 57 75 XSQ= 2.89 PHI= -0.127 XP = 0.0894

442	DRIFT TOWARD BEING THOSE WHERE FEAR OF ANIMAL SPIRITS IS HIGH (28) W-C	0.53 OF 49	442	DRIFT TOWARD BEING THOSE WHERE FEAR OF ANIMAL SPIRITS IS LOW (33) W-C	0.83 OF 12	26 2 / 23 10 / XSQ= 3.78 / PHI= 0.249 / XP = 0.0519
445	DRIFT TOWARD BEING THOSE WHERE SORCERY IS IMPORTANT (26) BBW,DH	0.65 OF 31	445	DRIFT TOWARD BEING THOSE WHERE SORCERY IS UNIMPORTANT (23) BBW,DH	0.67 OF 18	20 6 / 11 12 / XSQ= 3.28 / PHI= 0.259 / XP = 0.0700
449	LEAN LESS TOWARD BEING THOSE WHERE THE OBSERVATION OF FOOD TABOOS IS MEDIUM OR LOW, RATHER THAN HIGH (61) JRL	0.57 OF 49	449	LEAN MORE TOWARD BEING THOSE WHERE THE OBSERVATION OF FOOD TABOOS IS MEDIUM OR LOW, RATHER THAN HIGH (61) JRL	0.89 OF 37	21 4 / 28 33 / XSQ= 9.00 / PHI= 0.324 / XP = 0.0027
450	LEAN MORE TOWARD BEING THOSE WHERE THE OBSERVATION OF FOOD TABOOS IS HIGH OR MEDIUM, RATHER THAN LOW (60) JRL	0.84 OF 49	450	LEAN LESS TOWARD BEING THOSE WHERE THE OBSERVATION OF FOOD TABOOS IS HIGH OR MEDIUM, RATHER THAN LOW (60) JRL	0.51 OF 37	41 19 / 8 18 / XSQ= 8.97 / PHI= 0.323 / XP = 0.0028
456	TILT TOWARD BEING THOSE WHERE THE INTERNALIZATION OF THE INDIVIDUAL'S CONTACT WITH THE DIVINE IS NOT CONDUCIVE TO THE DEVELOPMENT OF THE INDIVIDUAL'S NEED TO ACHIEVE (17) DCM	0.60 OF 25	456	TILT TOWARD BEING THOSE WHERE THE INTERNALIZATION OF THE INDIVIDUAL'S CONTACT WITH THE DIVINE IS CONDUCIVE TO THE DEVELOPMENT OF THE INDIVIDUAL'S NEED TO ACHIEVE (19) DCM	0.82 OF 11	10 9 / 15 2 / XSQ= 3.81 / PHI= -0.325 / EP = 0.0312
468	TILT TOWARD BEING THOSE WHERE CONTACT WITH OTHER CULTURES IS REGULAR OR IRREGULAR, RATHER THAN FREQUENT (37) JMH	0.81 OF 36	468	TILT TOWARD BEING THOSE WHERE CONTACT WITH OTHER CULTURES IS FREQUENT, RATHER THAN REGULAR OR IRREGULAR (17) JMH	0.56 OF 18	7 10 / 29 8 / XSQ= 5.68 / PHI= -0.324 / XP = 0.0172
476	DRIFT LESS TOWARD BEING THOSE WHERE THE DEGREE OF INSOBRIETY IS STRONG (31) DH	0.52 OF 31	476	DRIFT MORE TOWARD BEING THOSE WHERE THE DEGREE OF INSOBRIETY IS STRONG (31) DH	0.83 OF 18	16 15 / 15 3 / XSQ= 3.66 / PHI= -0.273 / XP = 0.0557
488	TILT MORE TOWARD BEING THOSE ABOUT WHICH THE PRINCIPAL ETHNOGRAPHIES WERE PUBLISHED BEFORE 1950 (185)	0.85 OF 61	488	TILT LESS TOWARD BEING THOSE ABOUT WHICH THE PRINCIPAL ETHNOGRAPHIES WERE PUBLISHED BEFORE 1950 (185)	0.68 OF 196	52 133 / 9 63 / XSQ= 6.14 / PHI= 0.155 / XP = 0.0132
489	TEND LESS TO BE THOSE NOT INCLUDED IN CHARLES ACKERMAN'S STUDY OF DIVORCE (343)	0.67 OF 90	489	TEND MORE TO BE THOSE NOT INCLUDED IN CHARLES ACKERMAN'S STUDY OF DIVORCE (343)	0.91 OF 310	30 27 / 60 283 / XSQ= 32.62 / PHI= 0.286 / XP = 0.

No.			No.			
490	TEND TC BE THCSE INCLUDED IN ALBERT S. ANTHONY'S SAMPLE ON MALE INITIATION RITES (113)	0.64 OF 90	490	TEND TO BE THOSE NOT INCLUDED IN ALBERT S. ANTHONY'S SAMPLE ON MALE INITIATION RITES (287)	0.82 OF 310	58 55 32 255 XSQ= 72.77 PHI= 0.427 XP = 0.
491	TEND LESS TO BE THCSE NOT INCLUDED IN DORRIAN APPLE'S STUDY OF GRANDPARENTHCCD (352)	0.68 OF 90	491	TEND MORE TO BE THOSE NOT INCLUDED IN DORRIAN APPLE'S STUDY OF GRANDPARENTHOOD (352)	0.94 OF 310	29 19 61 291 XSQ= 42.53 PHI= 0.326 XP = 0.
492	TEND LESS TO BE THCSE NOT INCLUDED IN BARBARA CHARTIER AYRES' STUDY OF FEMALE INITIATION RITES (361)	0.61 OF 90	492	TEND MORE TO BE THOSE NOT INCLUDED IN BARBARA CHARTIER AYRES' STUDY OF FEMALE INITIATION RITES (361)	0.99 OF 310	35 4 55 306 XSQ= 107.82 PHI= 0.519 XP = 0.
493	TEND TO BE THOSE INCLUDED IN BACCN, BARRY, AND CHILD'S STUDY OF CHILD REARING (78)	0.63 OF 90	493	TEND TO BE THOSE NOT INCLUDED IN BACON, BARRY, AND CHILD'S STUDY OF CHILD REARING (322)	0.93 OF 310	57 21 33 289 XSQ= 138.56 PHI= 0.589 XP = 0.
494	TEND LESS TO BE THCSE NOT INCLUDED IN HERBERT M. BARRY III'S STUDY OF ART (371)	0.72 OF 90	494	TEND MORE TO BE THOSE NOT INCLUDED IN HERBERT M. BARRY III'S STUDY OF ART (371)	0.99 OF 310	25 4 65 306 XSQ= 68.89 PHI= 0.415 XP = 0.
495	TEND LESS TO BE THCSE NOT INCLUDED IN JUCITH K. BROWN'S STUDY OF FEMALE INITIATION RITES (335)	0.56 OF 90	495	TEND MORE TO BE THOSE NOT INCLUDED IN JUDITH K. BROWN'S STUDY OF FEMALE INITIATION RITES (335)	0.92 OF 310	40 25 50 285 XSQ= 65.18 PHI= 0.404 XP = 0.
496	TEND LESS TO BE THCSE NOT INCLUDED IN ROY G. D'ANDRADE'S STUDY OF DREAMS (345)	0.58 OF 90	496	TEND MORE TO BE THOSE NOT INCLUDED IN ROY G. D'ANDRADE'S STUDY OF DREAMS (345)	0.95 OF 310	38 17 52 293 XSQ= 76.31 PHI= 0.437 XP = 0.
497	TEND LESS TO BE THCSE NOT INCLUDED IN WILLIAM M. EVAN'S STUDY OF LAW (339)	0.51 OF 90	497	TEND MORE TO BE THOSE NOT INCLUDED IN WILLIAM M. EVAN'S STUDY OF LAW (339)	0.95 OF 310	44 17 46 293 XSQ= 98.34 PHI= 0.496 XP = 0.
498	TEND LESS TO BE THCSE NOT INCLUDED IN C. S. FORC'S STUDY OF SEX (349)	0.57 OF 90	498	TEND MORE TO BE THOSE NOT INCLUDED IN C. S. FORD'S STUDY OF SEX (349)	0.96 OF 310	39 12 51 298 XSQ= 94.13 PHI= 0.485 XP = 0.

No.			No.			
499	TEND TO BE THCSE INCLUDED IN FORD ANC BEACH'S SAMPLE ON SEXUAL EXPRESSICN BY THE YOUNG (86)	0.54 OF 90	499	TEND TO BE THOSE NOT INCLUDED IN FORD AND BEACH'S SAMPLE ON SEXUAL EXPRESSION BY THE YOUNG (314)	0.88 OF 310	49 37 41 273 XSQ= 72.18 PHI= 0.425 XP = 0.
500	TEND LESS TO BE THCSE NOT INCLUDED IN FREEMAN ANC WINCH'S STUDY OF SCCIETAL CCMPLEXITY (360)	0.61 OF 90	500	TEND MORE TO BE THOSE NOT INCLUDED IN FREEMAN AND WINCH'S STUDY OF SOCIETAL COMPLEXITY (360)	0.98 OF 310	35 5 55 305 XSQ= 103.58 PHI= 0.509 XP = 0.
501	TEND TO BE THCSE INCLUDED IN JOAN FRIENDLY GOODMAN'S STUDY OF ASCETIC MCURNING BEHAVIOR (67)	0.57 OF 90	501	TEND TO BE THOSE NOT INCLUDED IN JOAN FRIENDLY GOODMAN'S STUDY OF ASCETIC MOURNING BEHAVIOR (333)	0.95 OF 310	51 16 39 294 XSQ= 129.03 PHI= 0.568 XP = 0.
502	TEND LESS TO BE THCSE NOT INCLUDED IN JOHN K. HARLEY'S STUDY OF ADOLESCENT PEER GROUPS (343)	0.54 OF 90	502	TEND MORE TO BE THOSE NOT INCLUDED IN JOHN K. HARLEY'S STUDY OF ADOLESCENT PEER GROUPS (343)	0.95 OF 310	41 16 49 294 XSQ= 89.86 PHI= 0.474 XP = 0.
503	TEND LESS TO BE THCSE NOT INCLUDED IN JOHN M. HICKMAN'S STUDY OF THE FOLK-URBAN CCNTINUUM (346)	0.60 OF 90	503	TEND MORE TO BE THOSE NOT INCLUDED IN JOHN M. HICKMAN'S STUDY OF THE FOLK-URBAN CONTINUUM (346)	0.94 OF 310	36 18 54 292 XSQ= 66.94 PHI= 0.409 XP = 0.
504	TEND LESS TO BE THCSE NOT INCLUDED IN DONALC HORTON'S STUDY OF ALCHOLISM (351)	0.67 OF 90	504	TEND MORE TO BE THOSE NOT INCLUDED IN DONALD HORTON'S STUDY OF ALCHOLISM (351)	0.94 OF 310	30 19 60 291 XSQ= 45.52 PHI= 0.337 XP = 0.
505	TEND LESS TO BE THCSE NOT INCLUDED IN MERRILL JACKSON'S STUDY OF CRIMINAL LAW ANC MEDICINE (380)	0.88 OF 90	505	TEND MORE TO BE THOSE NOT INCLUDED IN MERRILL JACKSON'S STUDY OF CRIMINAL LAW AND MEDICINE (380)	0.97 OF 310	11 9 79 301 XSQ= 10.87 PHI= 0.165 XP = 0.0010
506	TEND LESS TO BE THCSE NOT INCLUDED IN LAMBERT, TRIANDIS, AND WOLF'S STUDY OF SUPERNATURAL BEINGS (364)	0.66 OF 90	506	TEND MORE TO BE THOSE NOT INCLUDED IN LAMBERT, TRIANDIS, AND WOLF'S STUDY OF SUPERNATURAL BEINGS (364)	0.98 OF 310	31 5 59 305 XSQ= 87.84 PHI= 0.469 XP = 0.
507	TEND TC BE THOSE INCLUDED IN JAMES R. LEARY'S STUDY OF FCOD TABOCS (86)	0.54 OF 90	507	TEND TO BE THOSE NOT INCLUDED IN JAMES R. LEARY'S STUDY OF FOOD TABOOS (314)	0.88 OF 310	49 37 41 273 XSQ= 72.18 PHI= 0.425 XP = 0.

508	TEND LESS TO BE THOSE 0.68 OF 90 NOT INCLUDED IN DAVID C. MCCLELLAND'S STUDY OF ACHIEVEMENT MOTIVATION (360)	508	TEND MORE TO BE THOSE 0.96 OF 310 NOT INCLUDED IN DAVID C. MCCLELLAND'S STUDY OF ACHIEVEMENT MOTIVATION (360)	29 11 61 299 XSQ= 60.57 PHI= 0.389 XP = 0.
509	LEAN LESS TOWARD BEING THOSE 0.87 OF 90 NOT INCLUDED IN MONI NAG'S STUDY OF FERTILITY (375)	509	LEAN MORE TOWARD BEING THOSE 0.96 OF 310 NOT INCLUDED IN MONI NAG'S STUDY OF FERTILITY (375)	12 13 78 297 XSQ= 8.45 PHI= 0.145 XP = 0.0037
510	TEND LESS TO BE THOSE 0.81 OF 90 NOT INCLUDED IN RAOUL NARROLL'S STUDY OF SOCIETAL COMPLEXITY (380)	510	TEND MORE TO BE THOSE 0.99 OF 310 NOT INCLUDED IN RAOUL NARROLL'S STUDY OF SOCIETAL COMPLEXITY (380)	17 3 73 307 XSQ= 43.46 PHI= 0.330 XP = 0.
511	TEND TO BE THOSE 0.84 OF 90 INCLUDED IN ROBERTS, ARTH AND BUSH'S SAMPLE ON GAMES, AS MODIFIED BY THE ETHNOGRAPHIC ATLAS (189)	511	TEND TO BE THOSE 0.64 OF 310 NOT INCLUDED IN ROBERTS, ARTH AND BUSH'S SAMPLE ON GAMES, AS MODIFIED BY THE ETHNOGRAPHIC ATLAS (211)	76 113 14 197 XSQ= 62.55 PHI= 0.395 XP = 0.
512	TEND LESS TO BE THOSE 0.64 OF 90 NOT INCLUDED IN SHIRLEY AND ROMNEY'S STUDY OF LOVE MAGIC (367)	512	TEND MORE TO BE THOSE 1.00 OF 310 NOT INCLUDED IN SHIRLEY AND ROMNEY'S STUDY OF LOVE MAGIC (367)	32 1 58 309 XSQ= 109.78 PHI= 0.524 XP = 0.
513	TEND LESS TO BE THOSE 0.64 OF 90 NOT INCLUDED IN LEO W. SIMMONS' STUDY OF THE TREATMENT OF THE AGED (357)	513	TEND MORE TO BE THOSE 0.96 OF 310 NOT INCLUDED IN LEO W. SIMMONS' STUDY OF THE TREATMENT OF THE AGED (357)	32 11 58 299 XSQ= 71.18 PHI= 0.422 XP = 0.
515	TEND LESS TO BE THOSE 0.54 OF 90 NOT INCLUDED IN WILLIAM N. STEPHENS' SAMPLE ON AVOIDANCE RELATIONSHIPS (348)	515	TEND MORE TO BE THOSE 0.96 OF 310 NOT INCLUDED IN WILLIAM N. STEPHENS' SAMPLE ON AVOIDANCE RELATIONSHIPS (348)	41 11 49 299 XSQ= 105.14 PHI= 0.513 XP = 0.
516	TEND MORE TO BE THOSE 0.97 OF 90 INCLUDED IN GUY E. SWANSON'S SAMPLE ON LOCAL JURISDICTION, AS MODIFIED BY THE ETHNOGRAPHIC ATLAS (331)	516	TEND LESS TO BE THOSE 0.79 OF 310 INCLUDED IN GUY E. SWANSON'S SAMPLE ON LOCAL JURISDICTION, AS MODIFIED BY THE ETHNOGRAPHIC ATLAS (331)	87 244 3 66 XSQ= 14.52 PHI= 0.191 XP = 0.0001
517	TEND MORE TO BE THOSE 0.91 OF 90 INCLUDED IN GUY E. SWANSON'S SAMPLE ON HIGH GODS, AS MODIFIED BY THE ETHNOGRAPHIC ATLAS (260)	517	TEND LESS TO BE THOSE 0.57 OF 310 INCLUDED IN GUY E. SWANSON'S SAMPLE ON HIGH GODS, AS MODIFIED BY THE ETHNOGRAPHIC ATLAS (260)	82 178 8 132 XSQ= 33.34 PHI= 0.289 XP = 0.

No.			No.			
518	TEND TO BE THOSE INCLUDED IN STANLEY H. UDY, JR.'S STUDY OF WORK ORGANIZATION (105)	0.56 OF 90	518	TEND TO BE THOSE NOT INCLUDED IN STANLEY H. UDY, JR.'S STUDY OF WORK ORGANIZATION (295)	0.82 OF 310	50 55 40 255 XSQ= 49.58 PHI= 0.352 XP = 0.
519	TEND LESS TO BE THOSE NOT INCLUDED IN JOSEPH VEROFF'S STUDY OF ACHIEVEMENT MOTIVATION AS REVEALED IN FOLKTALES (364)	0.72 OF 90	519	TEND MORE TO BE THOSE NOT INCLUDED IN JOSEPH VEROFF'S STUDY OF ACHIEVEMENT MOTIVATION AS REVEALED IN FOLKTALES (364)	0.96 OF 310	25 11 65 299 XSQ= 47.08 PHI= 0.343 XP = 0.
520	TEND LESS TO BE THOSE NOT INCLUDED IN BEATRICE BLYTH WHITING'S STUDY OF SORCERY (360)	0.63 OF 90	520	TEND MORE TO BE THOSE NOT INCLUDED IN BEATRICE BLYTH WHITING'S STUDY OF SORCERY (360)	0.98 OF 310	33 7 57 303 XSQ= 87.97 PHI= 0.469 XP = 0.
521	TEND LESS TO BE THOSE NOT INCLUDED IN JOHN W. M. WHITING'S STUDY OF SOCIALIZATION PROCESS AND PERSONALITY (353)	0.57 OF 90	521	TEND MORE TO BE THOSE NOT INCLUDED IN JOHN W. M. WHITING'S STUDY OF SOCIALIZATION PROCESS AND PERSONALITY (353)	0.97 OF 310	39 8 51 302 XSQ= 107.82 PHI= 0.519 XP = 0.
522	TEND TO BE THOSE INCLUDED IN MARJORIE GRANT WHITING'S STUDY OF DIET (82)	0.57 OF 90	522	TEND TO BE THOSE NOT INCLUDED IN MARJORIE GRANT WHITING'S STUDY OF DIET (318)	0.90 OF 310	51 31 39 279 XSQ= 90.36 PHI= 0.475 XP = 0.
523	TEND TO BE THOSE INCLUDED IN WHITING AND CHILD'S STUDY OF CHILD TRAINING AND PERSONALITY (61)	0.54 OF 90	523	TEND TO BE THOSE NOT INCLUDED IN WHITING AND CHILD'S STUDY OF CHILD TRAINING AND PERSONALITY (339)	0.96 OF 310	49 12 41 298 XSQ= 134.15 PHI= 0.579 XP = 0.
524	TEND LESS TO BE THOSE NOT INCLUDED IN WHITING, KLUCKHOHN, AND ANTHONY'S STUDY OF MALE INITIATION CEREMONIES (356)	0.62 OF 90	524	TEND MORE TO BE THOSE NOT INCLUDED IN WHITING, KLUCKHOHN, AND ANTHONY'S STUDY OF MALE INITIATION CEREMONIES (356)	0.97 OF 310	34 10 56 300 XSQ= 81.56 PHI= 0.452 XP = 0.

515 CULTURES
INCLUDED IN WILLIAM N. STEPHENS'
SAMPLE ON AVOIDANCE RELATIONSHIPS (52)

515 CULTURES
NOT INCLUDED IN WILLIAM N. STEPHENS'
SAMPLE ON AVOIDANCE RELATIONSHIPS (348)

BACKGROUND ON PAGE 180

SUBJECT ONLY, F.C. 1-480 AND 527-536
BOTH SUBJECT AND PREDICATE, F.C. 481-526

52 IN LEFT COLUMN

ALORESE	ARAPESH	ARAUCANIANS	ASHANTI	BEMBA	CALLINAGO	CHAGGA	CHENCHU	CHEYENNE	CHIR-APACHE
COMANCHE	CROW	FON	GANDA	GISU	GROS VENTRE	HANO	IBAN	IFUGAO	KURTATCHI
LAMBA	LANGO	LAU	LEPCHA	LESU	MANUS	MARQUESANS	MARSHALLESE	MURNGIN	NAMA
NAVAHO	NUER	NYAKYUSA	OJIBWA	OMAHA	ONTONG-JAVA	PAPAGO	PUKAPUKA	SAMOANS	SANPOIL
SEMANG	SIRIONO	SUBANUN	TALLENSI	TARAHUMARA	THONGA	TIKOPIA	TIMBIRA	TIV	TROBRIAND
TRUKESE	WARRAU								

348 IN RIGHT COLUMN

4	IN ALL CASES ARE THOSE LOCATED OUTSIDE OF THE CIRCUM-MEDITERRANEAN (355)	1.00 OF 52	4	TILT LESS TOWARD BEING THOSE LOCATED OUTSIDE OF THE CIRCUM-MEDITERRANEAN (355)	0.87 OF 348	0 45 52 303 XSQ= 6.34 PHI= -0.126 XP = 0.0118
5	TILT MORE TOWARD BEING THOSE LOCATED OUTSIDE OF EAST EURASIA (330)	0.94 OF 52	5	TILT LESS TOWARD BEING THOSE LOCATED OUTSIDE OF EAST EURASIA (330)	0.81 OF 348	3 67 49 281 XSQ= 4.80 PHI= -0.110 XP = 0.0284
6	LEAN LESS TOWARD BEING THOSE LOCATED OUTSIDE OF THE INSULAR PACIFIC (330)	0.65 OF 52	6	LEAN MORE TOWARD BEING THOSE LOCATED OUTSIDE OF THE INSULAR PACIFIC (330)	0.85 OF 348	18 52 34 296 XSQ= 10.80 PHI= 0.164 XP = 0.0010
15	TILT MORE TOWARD BEING THOSE WHERE THE LATITUDE IS LESS THAN TWENTY DEGREES (217)	0.69 OF 52	15	TILT LESS TOWARD BEING THOSE WHERE THE LATITUDE IS LESS THAN TWENTY DEGREES (217)	0.52 OF 348	16 167 36 181 XSQ= 4.73 PHI= -0.109 XP = 0.0296
16	TILT LESS TOWARD BEING THOSE WHERE THE LATITUDE IS TEN DEGREES OR GREATER (277)	0.54 OF 52	16	TILT MORE TOWARD BEING THOSE WHERE THE LATITUDE IS TEN DEGREES OR GREATER (277)	0.72 OF 348	28 249 24 99 XSQ= 5.85 PHI= -0.121 XP = 0.0155

45	TILT TOWARD BEING THOSE 0.52 OF 33 WHERE SETTLEMENTS, IF FIXED, ARE NON-COMPACT, RATHER THAN COMPACT (73)	45	TILT TOWARD BEING THOSE 0.70 OF 189 WHERE SETTLEMENTS, IF FIXED, ARE COMPACT, RATHER THAN NON-COMPACT (149)	16 133 17 56 XSQ= 5.15 PHI= -0.152 XP = 0.0233
48	DRIFT TOWARD BEING THOSE 0.64 OF 36 WHERE THE FOOD SUPPLY IS NOT SECURE, AND FOOD SHORTAGES ARE FREQUENT OR ANNUAL (41) MGW	48	DRIFT TOWARD BEING THOSE 0.58 OF 43 WHERE THE FOOD SUPPLY IS SECURE, AND FOOD SHORTAGES ARE RARE OR OCCASIONAL (38) MGW	13 25 23 18 XSQ= 2.98 PHI= -0.194 XP = 0.0844
62	LEAN MORE TOWARD BEING THOSE 0.77 OF 52 WHERE HUSBANDRY OF SOME KIND IS PRESENT (228)	62	LEAN LESS TOWARD BEING THOSE 0.54 OF 348 WHERE HUSBANDRY OF SOME KIND IS PRESENT (228)	40 188 12 160 XSQ= 8.77 PHI= 0.148 XP = 0.0031
63	LEAN TOWARD BEING THOSE 0.55 OF 40 WHERE HUSBANDRY, IF PRESENT, IS PRINCIPALLY IN THE FORM OF PIGS, SHEEP, OR GOATS, RATHER THAN BOVINE, EQUINE, CAMEL-LIKE, OR DEER-LIKE ANIMALS (74)	63	LEAN TOWARD BEING THOSE 0.72 OF 186 WHERE HUSBANDRY, IF PRESENT, IS PRINCIPALLY IN THE FORM OF BOVINE, EQUINE, CAMEL-LIKE, OR DEER-LIKE ANIMALS, RATHER THAN PIGS, SHEEP, OR GOATS (152)	18 134 22 52 XSQ= 9.74 PHI= -0.208 XP = 0.0018
73	DRIFT TOWARD BEING THOSE 0.65 OF 43 WHERE WEAVING IS ABSENT (130)	73	DRIFT TOWARD BEING THOSE 0.50 OF 205 WHERE WEAVING IS PRESENT (118)	15 103 28 102 XSQ= 2.77 PHI= -0.106 XP = 0.0958
79	IN ALL CASES ARE THOSE 1.00 OF 37 WHERE NO CITY IS PRESENT (201)	79	DRIFT LESS TOWARD BEING THOSE 0.88 OF 187 WHERE NO CITY IS PRESENT (201)	0 23 37 164 XSQ= 3.82 PHI= -0.131 XP = 0.0505
85	DRIFT MORE TOWARD BEING THOSE 0.89 OF 45 WHERE THE LEVEL OF POLITICAL INTEGRATION IS THE MINIMAL STATE, THE AUTONOMOUS COMMUNITY, OR THE FAMILY (234) GPM	85	DRIFT LESS TOWARD BEING THOSE 0.75 OF 259 WHERE THE LEVEL OF POLITICAL INTEGRATION IS THE MINIMAL STATE, THE AUTONOMOUS COMMUNITY, OR THE FAMILY (234) GPM	5 65 40 194 XSQ= 3.48 PHI= -0.107 XP = 0.0622
99	TILT MORE TOWARD BEING THOSE 0.81 OF 27 WHERE, WITH NATIONAL HIERARCHY ABSENT, THE HIERARCHY OF LOCAL JURISDICTION HAS FOUR OR THREE LEVELS (93) GES,EA	99	TILT LESS TOWARD BEING THOSE 0.55 OF 129 WHERE, WITH NATIONAL HIERARCHY ABSENT, THE HIERARCHY OF LOCAL JURISDICTION HAS FOUR OR THREE LEVELS (93) GES,EA	22 71 5 58 XSQ= 5.43 PHI= 0.187 XP = 0.0198
107	IN ALL CASES ARE THOSE 1.00 OF 24 WHERE CLASS STRATIFICATION, IF PRESENT, IS BASED ON SOMETHING OTHER THAN OCCUPATIONAL STATUS (160)	107	TILT LESS TOWARD BEING THOSE 0.76 OF 179 WHERE CLASS STRATIFICATION, IF PRESENT, IS BASED ON SOMETHING OTHER THAN OCCUPATIONAL STATUS (160)	0 43 24 136 XSQ= 5.95 PHI= -0.171 XP = 0.0147

109	TILT MORE TOWARD BEING THOSE 0.98 OF 51 WHERE CASTES ARE ABSENT (317)	109	TILT LESS TOWARD BEING THOSE 0.84 OF 317 WHERE CASTES ARE ABSENT (317)	1 50 50 267 XSQ= 5.91 PHI= -0.127 XP = 0.0150
179	DRIFT LESS TOWARD BEING THOSE 0.81 OF 52 WHERE THE COMMUNITY IS OTHER THAN STRUCTURED ON A NON-CLAN BASIS AND COMMONLY EXOGAMOUS (340)	179	DRIFT MORE TOWARD BEING THOSE 0.90 OF 330 WHERE THE COMMUNITY IS OTHER THAN STRUCTURED ON A NON-CLAN BASIS AND COMMONLY EXOGAMOUS (340)	10 32 42 298 XSQ= 3.26 PHI= 0.092 XP = 0.0712
201	DRIFT LESS TOWARD BEING THOSE 0.75 OF 52 WHERE MARITAL RESIDENCE IS NON-OPTIONAL, RATHER THAN AMBILOCAL OR NEOLOCAL (334)	201	DRIFT MORE TOWARD BEING THOSE 0.85 OF 346 WHERE MARITAL RESIDENCE IS NON-OPTIONAL, RATHER THAN AMBILOCAL OR NEOLOCAL (334)	39 295 13 51 XSQ= 2.81 PHI= -0.084 XP = 0.0938
204	TILT LESS TOWARD BEING THOSE 0.68 OF 41 WHERE MARITAL RESIDENCE IS PATRILOCAL, VIRILOCAL, OR AVUNCULOCAL, RATHER THAN AMBILOCAL OR NEOLOCAL (270)	204	TILT MORE TOWARD BEING THOSE 0.83 OF 293 WHERE MARITAL RESIDENCE IS PATRILOCAL, VIRILOCAL, OR AVUNCULOCAL, RATHER THAN AMBILOCAL OR NEOLOCAL (270)	28 242 13 51 XSQ= 3.87 PHI= -0.108 XP = 0.0491
210	DRIFT LESS TOWARD BEING THOSE 0.68 OF 22 WHERE MARITAL RESIDENCE IS PATRILOCAL, RATHER THAN MATRILOCAL (169)	210	DRIFT MORE TOWARD BEING THOSE 0.87 OF 178 WHERE MARITAL RESIDENCE IS PATRILOCAL, RATHER THAN MATRILOCAL (169)	15 154 7 24 XSQ= 3.72 PHI= -0.136 XP = 0.0537
213	TILT MORE TOWARD BEING THOSE 0.69 OF 51 WHERE FIRST COUSIN MARRIAGE IS NOT PERMITTED (198)	213	TILT LESS TOWARD BEING THOSE 0.51 OF 319 WHERE FIRST COUSIN MARRIAGE IS NOT PERMITTED (198)	16 156 35 163 XSQ= 4.75 PHI= -0.113 XP = 0.0293
277	TILT TOWARD BEING THOSE 0.91 OF 11 WHERE THE STATUS OF WOMEN IS NOT STRONGLY INFERIOR OR SUBJECTED (22) LWS	277	TILT TOWARD BEING THOSE 0.52 OF 25 WHERE THE STATUS OF WOMEN IS INFERIOR OR SUBJECTED (14) LWS	1 13 10 12 XSQ= 4.25 PHI= -0.344 EP = 0.0247
280	DRIFT TOWARD BEING THOSE 0.78 OF 9 WHERE THE COMPOSITE FERTILITY LEVEL IS HIGH (13) MN	280	DRIFT TOWARD BEING THOSE 0.63 OF 16 WHERE THE COMPOSITE FERTILITY LEVEL IS LOW (12) MN	7 6 2 10 XSQ= 2.30 PHI= 0.304 EP = 0.0968
296	TILT TOWARD BEING THOSE 0.63 OF 19 WHERE INFANTICIDE IS ABSENT OR INFERRED ABSENT (15) BCA	296	TILT TOWARD BEING THOSE 0.79 OF 14 WHERE INFANTICIDE IS PRESENT (18) BCA	7 11 12 3 XSQ= 4.10 PHI= -0.353 EP = 0.0329

305	DRIFT TOWARD BEING THOSE WHERE THE EARLY SEXUAL SATISFACTION POTENTIAL IS HIGH (27) W-C	0.66 OF 29	305	DRIFT TOWARD BEING THOSE WHERE THE EARLY SEXUAL SATISFACTION POTENTIAL IS LOW (24) W-C	0.64 OF 22	19 8 10 14 XSQ= 3.18 PHI= 0.250 XP = 0.0746
323	DRIFT TOWARD BEING THOSE WHERE THE CONSTANCY OF PRESENCE OF THE INFANT'S NURTURANT AGENT IS LOW (45) B-B-C	0.73 OF 37	323	DRIFT TOWARD BEING THOSE WHERE THE CONSTANCY OF PRESENCE OF THE INFANT'S NURTURANT AGENT IS HIGH (29) B-B-C	0.51 OF 37	10 19 27 18 XSQ= 3.63 PHI= -0.221 XP = 0.0568
325	LEAN TOWARD BEING THOSE WHERE THE DEGREE OF DIFFUSION AMONG THE INFANT'S NURTURANT AGENTS IS HIGH (42) B-B-C	0.74 OF 38	325	LEAN TOWARD BEING THOSE WHERE THE DEGREE OF DIFFUSION AMONG THE INFANT'S NURTURANT AGENTS IS LOW (32) B-B-C	0.61 OF 36	28 14 10 22 XSQ= 7.76 PHI= 0.324 XP = 0.0054
348	TILT TOWARD BEING THOSE WHERE THE TOTAL POSITIVE PRESSURE TOWARD DEVELOPING ACHIEVEMENT BEHAVIOR IN THE CHILD IS HIGH (32) B-B-C	0.67 OF 30	348	TILT TOWARD BEING THOSE WHERE THE TOTAL POSITIVE PRESSURE TOWARD DEVELOPING ACHIEVEMENT BEHAVIOR IN THE CHILD IS LOW (31) B-B-C	0.64 OF 33	20 12 10 21 XSQ= 4.62 PHI= 0.271 XP = 0.0315
349	TILT TOWARD BEING THOSE WHERE THE CHILD'S INFERRED ANXIETY OVER NON-PERFORMANCE OF ACHIEVEMENT BEHAVIOR IS HIGH (34) B-B-C	0.70 OF 30	349	TILT TOWARD BEING THOSE WHERE THE CHILD'S INFERRED ANXIETY OVER NON-PERFORMANCE OF ACHIEVEMENT BEHAVIOR IS LOW (28) B-B-C	0.59 OF 32	21 13 9 19 XSQ= 4.27 PHI= 0.263 XP = 0.0387
390	DRIFT MORE TOWARD BEING THOSE WHERE PREMARITAL SEX RELATIONS ARE WEAKLY PUNISHED AND IN FACT NOT RARE OR PUNISHED ONLY IF PREGNANCY RESULTS, OR FREELY PERMITTED (132) JTW,EA	0.86 OF 36	390	DRIFT LESS TOWARD BEING THOSE WHERE PREMARITAL SEX RELATIONS ARE WEAKLY PUNISHED AND IN FACT NOT RARE OR PUNISHED ONLY IF PREGNANCY RESULTS, OR FREELY PERMITTED (132) JTW,EA	0.71 OF 143	5 42 31 101 XSQ= 2.81 PHI= -0.125 XP = 0.0939
395	DRIFT TOWARD BEING THOSE WHERE BELIEF IN THE UNCLEANNESS OF WOMEN IS UNIMPORTANT OR ABSENT (15) LWS	0.67 OF 12	395	DRIFT TOWARD BEING THOSE WHERE BELIEF IN THE UNCLEANNESS OF WOMEN IS PRESENT (18) LWS	0.67 OF 21	4 14 8 7 XSQ= 2.21 PHI= -0.259 EP = 0.0827
397	DRIFT LESS TOWARD BEING THOSE WHERE SEX DISABILITY IS ABSENT (42) JKH	0.62 OF 26	397	DRIFT MORE TOWARD BEING THOSE WHERE SEX DISABILITY IS ABSENT (42) JKH	0.87 OF 30	10 4 16 26 XSQ= 3.45 PHI= 0.248 XP = 0.0634
400	TILT TOWARD BEING THOSE WHERE HOMOSEXUAL ACTIVITY IS PROHIBITED (22) F-B	0.56 OF 25	400	TILT TOWARD BEING THOSE WHERE HOMOSEXUAL ACTIVITY IS PERMITTED (36) F-B	0.76 OF 33	14 8 11 25 XSQ= 4.82 PHI= 0.288 XP = 0.0281

426	DRIFT TOWARD BEING THOSE WHERE A HIGH GOD IS ABSENT (104) GES,EA	0.52 OF 48	426	DRIFT TOWARD BEING THOSE WHERE A HIGH GOD IS PRESENT (156) GES,EA	0.63 OF 212	23 133 25 79 XSQ= 2.99 PHI= -0.107 XP = 0.0838
438	DRIFT TOWARD BEING THOSE WHERE OTHER-WORLDLY FEARS OF GHOSTS OR SPIRITS ARE GREATER THAN THIS-WORLDLY FEARS OF HUMANS OR ANIMALS (27) W-C,JFG	0.75 OF 24	438	DRIFT TOWARD BEING THOSE WHERE THIS-WORLDLY FEARS OF HUMANS OR ANIMALS ARE GREATER THAN OTHER-WORLDLY FEARS OF GHOSTS OR SPIRITS (17) W-C,JFG	0.55 OF 20	18 9 6 11 XSQ= 2.97 PHI= 0.260 XP = 0.0847
439	DRIFT TOWARD BEING THOSE WHERE FEAR OF GHOSTS IS HIGH (30) W-C	0.61 OF 31	439	DRIFT TOWARD BEING THOSE WHERE FEAR OF GHOSTS IS LOW (31) W-C	0.63 OF 30	19 11 12 19 XSQ= 2.78 PHI= 0.213 XP = 0.0955
445	DRIFT TOWARD BEING THOSE WHERE SORCERY IS IMPORTANT (26) EBW,DH	0.79 OF 14	445	DRIFT TOWARD BEING THOSE WHERE SORCERY IS UNIMPORTANT (23) BBW,DH	0.57 OF 35	11 15 3 20 XSQ= 3.79 PHI= 0.278 XP = 0.0516
449	TEND TO BE THOSE WHERE THE OBSERVATION OF FOOD TABOOS IS HIGH, RATHER THAN MEDIUM OR LOW (25) JRL	0.57 OF 28	449	TEND TO BE THOSE WHERE THE OBSERVATION OF FOOD TABOOS IS MEDIUM OR LOW, RATHER THAN HIGH (61) JRL	0.84 OF 58	16 9 12 49 XSQ= 13.91 PHI= 0.402 XP = 0.0002
454	DRIFT TOWARD BEING THOSE WHERE THE OBJECTIVE OF THE INDIVIDUAL'S CONTACT WITH THE DIVINE IS NOT CONDUCIVE TO THE DEVELOPMENT OF THE INDIVIDUAL'S NEED TO ACHIEVE (18) DCM	0.69 OF 16	454	DRIFT TOWARD BEING THOSE WHERE THE OBJECTIVE OF THE INDIVIDUAL'S CONTACT WITH THE DIVINE IS CONDUCIVE TO THE DEVELOPMENT OF THE INDIVIDUAL'S NEED TO ACHIEVE (18) DCM	0.65 OF 20	5 13 11 7 XSQ= 2.81 PHI= -0.280 EP = 0.0922
468	TILT MORE TOWARD BEING THOSE WHERE CONTACT WITH OTHER CULTURES IS REGULAR OR IRREGULAR, RATHER THAN FREQUENT (37) JMH	0.90 OF 20	468	TILT LESS TOWARD BEING THOSE WHERE CONTACT WITH OTHER CULTURES IS REGULAR OR IRREGULAR, RATHER THAN FREQUENT (37) JMH	0.56 OF 34	2 15 18 19 XSQ= 5.31 PHI= -0.313 XP = 0.0213
475	TILT TOWARD BEING THOSE WHERE EXHIBITIONISTIC DANCING IS STRONGLY OR MODERATELY EMPHASIZED (48) PES	0.71 OF 41	475	TILT TOWARD BEING THOSE WHERE EXHIBITIONISTIC DANCING IS NEGLIGIBLY EMPHASIZED (38) PES	0.58 OF 45	29 19 12 26 XSQ= 5.96 PHI= 0.263 XP = 0.0146
479	DRIFT TOWARD BEING THOSE WHERE THE NEED TO ACHIEVE, AS INFERRED FROM FOLKTALES, IS LOW (18) JV	0.69 OF 16	479	DRIFT TOWARD BEING THOSE WHERE THE NEED TO ACHIEVE, AS INFERRED FROM FOLKTALES, IS HIGH (18) JV	0.65 OF 20	5 13 11 7 XSQ= 2.81 PHI= -0.280 EP = 0.0922

482	TILT LESS TOWARD BEING THOSE 0.75 OF 52 WHERE THE PRINCIPAL ETHNOGRAPHERS HAVE BEEN OTHER THAN BRITISH (336)	482	TILT MORE TOWARD BEING THOSE 0.88 OF 336 WHERE THE PRINCIPAL ETHNOGRAPHERS HAVE BEEN OTHER THAN BRITISH (336)	13 39 39 297 XSQ= 5.85 PHI= 0.123 XP = 0.0155
488	DRIFT MORE TOWARD BEING THOSE 0.86 OF 35 ABOUT WHICH THE PRINCIPAL ETHNOGRAPHIES WERE PUBLISHED BEFORE 1950 (185)	488	DRIFT LESS TOWARD BEING THOSE 0.70 OF 222 ABOUT WHICH THE PRINCIPAL ETHNOGRAPHIES WERE PUBLISHED BEFORE 1950 (185)	30 155 5 67 XSQ= 3.04 PHI= 0.109 XP = 0.0812
489	TEND LESS TO BE THOSE 0.65 OF 52 NOT INCLUDED IN CHARLES ACKERMAN'S STUDY OF DIVORCE (343)	489	TEND MORE TO BE THOSE 0.89 OF 348 NOT INCLUDED IN CHARLES ACKERMAN'S STUDY OF DIVORCE (343)	18 39 34 309 XSQ= 18.42 PHI= 0.215 XP = 0.0000
490	TEND TO BE THOSE 0.75 OF 52 INCLUDED IN ALBERT S. ANTHONY'S SAMPLE ON MALE INITIATION RITES (113)	490	TEND TO BE THOSE 0.79 OF 348 NOT INCLUDED IN ALBERT S. ANTHONY'S SAMPLE ON MALE INITIATION RITES (287)	39 74 13 274 XSQ= 61.82 PHI= 0.393 XP = 0.
491	TEND LESS TO BE THOSE 0.52 OF 52 NOT INCLUDED IN DORRIAN APPLE'S STUDY OF GRANDPARENTHOOD (352)	491	TEND MORE TO BE THOSE 0.93 OF 348 NOT INCLUDED IN DORRIAN APPLE'S STUDY OF GRANDPARENTHOOD (352)	25 23 27 325 XSQ= 69.79 PHI= 0.418 XP = 0.
492	TEND LESS TO BE THOSE 0.56 OF 52 NOT INCLUDED IN BARBARA CHARTIER AYRES' STUDY OF FEMALE INITIATION RITES (361)	492	TEND MORE TO BE THOSE 0.95 OF 348 NOT INCLUDED IN BARBARA CHARTIER AYRES' STUDY OF FEMALE INITIATION RITES (361)	23 16 29 332 XSQ= 76.32 PHI= 0.437 XP = 0.
493	TEND TO BE THOSE 0.75 OF 52 INCLUDED IN BACON, BARRY, AND CHILD'S STUDY OF CHILD REARING (78)	493	TEND TO BE THOSE 0.89 OF 348 NOT INCLUDED IN BACON, BARRY, AND CHILD'S STUDY OF CHILD REARING (322)	39 39 13 309 XSQ= 113.26 PHI= 0.532 XP = 0.
494	TEND LESS TO BE THOSE 0.65 OF 52 NOT INCLUDED IN HERBERT M. BARRY III'S STUDY OF ART (371)	494	TEND MORE TO BE THOSE 0.97 OF 348 NOT INCLUDED IN HERBERT M. BARRY III'S STUDY OF ART (371)	18 11 34 337 XSQ= 61.97 PHI= 0.394 XP = 0.
495	TEND LESS TO BE THOSE 0.60 OF 52 NOT INCLUDED IN JUDITH K. BROWN'S STUDY OF FEMALE INITIATION RITES (335)	495	TEND MORE TO BE THOSE 0.87 OF 348 NOT INCLUDED IN JUDITH K. BROWN'S STUDY OF FEMALE INITIATION RITES (335)	21 44 31 304 XSQ= 23.58 PHI= 0.243 XP = 0.0000

No.		Proportion	No.		Proportion	Statistics
496	TEND LESS TO BE THCSE NCT INCLUDED IN ROY G. C'ANDRADE'S STUDY OF DREAMS (345)	0.54 OF 52	496	TEND MORE TO BE THOSE NOT INCLUDED IN ROY G. D'ANDRADE'S STUDY OF DREAMS (345)	0.91 OF 348	24 31 28 317 XSQ= 49.83 PHI= 0.353 XP = 0.
497	TEND LESS TO BE THCSE NOT INCLUDED IN WILLIAM M. EVAN'S STUDY OF LAW (339)	0.58 OF 52	497	TEND MORE TO BE THOSE NOT INCLUDED IN WILLIAM M. EVAN'S STUDY OF LAW (339)	0.89 OF 348	22 39 30 309 XSQ= 31.49 PHI= 0.281 XP = 0.
498	TEND LESS TO BE THCSE NOT INCLUDED IN C. S. FORC'S STUDY OF SEX (349)	0.65 OF 52	498	TEND MORE TO BE THOSE NOT INCLUDED IN C. S. FORD'S STUDY OF SEX (349)	0.91 OF 348	18 33 34 315 XSQ= 23.48 PHI= 0.242 XP = 0.0000
499	TEND TO BE THOSE INCLUDED IN FORC AND BEACH'S SAMPLE ON SEXUAL EXPRESSICN BY THE YCUNG (86)	0.60 OF 52	499	TEND TO BE THOSE NOT INCLUDED IN FORD AND BEACH'S SAMPLE ON SEXUAL EXPRESSION BY THE YOUNG (314)	0.84 OF 348	31 55 21 293 XSQ= 48.89 PHI= 0.350 XP = 0.
500	LEAN LESS TOWARC BEING THCSE NOT INCLUDED IN FREEMAN ANC WINCH'S STUDY OF SCCIETAL CCMPLEXITY (360)	0.77 OF 52	500	LEAN MORE TOWARD BEING THOSE NOT INCLUDED IN FREEMAN AND WINCH'S STUDY OF SOCIETAL COMPLEXITY (360)	0.92 OF 348	12 28 40 320 XSQ= 9.75 PHI= 0.156 XP = 0.0018
501	TEND TO BE THOSE INCLUDED IN JOAN FRIENDLY GOODMAN'S STUDY OF ASCETIC MCURNING BEHAVIOR (67)	0.60 OF 52	501	TEND TO BE THOSE NOT INCLUDED IN JOAN FRIENDLY GOODMAN'S STUDY OF ASCETIC MOURNING BEHAVIOR (333)	0.90 OF 348	31 36 21 312 XSQ= 75.26 PHI= 0.434 XP = 0.
502	TEND TO BE THOSE INCLUDED IN JOHN K. HARLEY'S STUDY OF ADOLESCENT PEER GROUPS (57)	0.50 OF 52	502	TEND TO BE THOSE NOT INCLUDED IN JOHN K. HARLEY'S STUDY OF ADOLESCENT PEER GROUPS (343)	0.91 OF 348	26 31 26 317 XSQ= 59.20 PHI= 0.385 XP = 0.
503	TEND LESS TO BE THCSE NOT INCLUDED IN JOHN M. HICKMAN'S STUDY OF THE FOLK-URBAN CCNTINUUM (346)	0.62 OF 52	503	TEND MORE TO BE THOSE NOT INCLUDED IN JOHN M. HICKMAN'S STUDY OF THE FOLK-URBAN CONTINUUM (346)	0.90 OF 348	20 34 32 314 XSQ= 29.48 PHI= 0.271 XP = 0.0000
504	LEAN LESS TOWARC BEING THCSE NOT INCLUDED IN DONALC HORTON'S STUDY OF ALCHOLISM (351)	0.73 OF 52	504	LEAN MORE TOWARD BEING THOSE NOT INCLUDED IN DONALD HORTON'S STUDY OF ALCHOLISM (351)	0.90 OF 348	14 35 38 313 XSQ= 10.45 PHI= 0.162 XP = 0.0012

No.		No.		
505	TEND LESS TO BE THOSE 0.85 OF 52 NOT INCLUDED IN MERRILL JACKSON'S STUDY OF CRIMINAL LAW AND MEDICINE (380)	505	TEND MORE TO BE THOSE 0.97 OF 348 NOT INCLUDED IN MERRILL JACKSON'S STUDY OF CRIMINAL LAW AND MEDICINE (380)	8 12 44 336 XSQ= 11.17 PHI= 0.167 XP = 0.0008
506	TEND LESS TO BE THOSE 0.54 OF 52 NOT INCLUDED IN LAMBERT, TRIANDIS, AND WOLF'S STUDY OF SUPERNATURAL BEINGS (364)	506	TEND MORE TO BE THOSE 0.97 OF 348 NOT INCLUDED IN LAMBERT, TRIANDIS, AND WOLF'S STUDY OF SUPERNATURAL BEINGS (364)	24 12 28 336 XSQ= 95.59 PHI= 0.489 XP = 0.
507	TEND TO BE THOSE 0.54 OF 52 INCLUDED IN JAMES R. LEARY'S STUDY OF FOOD TABOOS (86)	507	TEND TO BE THOSE 0.83 OF 348 NOT INCLUDED IN JAMES R. LEARY'S STUDY OF FOOD TABOOS (314)	28 58 24 290 XSQ= 34.88 PHI= 0.295 XP = 0.
508	TEND LESS TO BE THOSE 0.65 OF 52 NOT INCLUDED IN DAVID C. MCCLELLAND'S STUDY OF ACHIEVEMENT MOTIVATION (360)	508	TEND MORE TO BE THOSE 0.94 OF 348 NOT INCLUDED IN DAVID C. MCCLELLAND'S STUDY OF ACHIEVEMENT MOTIVATION (360)	18 22 34 326 XSQ= 37.16 PHI= 0.305 XP = 0.
509	LEAN LESS TOWARD BEING THOSE 0.83 OF 52 NOT INCLUDED IN MONI NAG'S STUDY OF FERTILITY (375)	509	LEAN MORE TOWARD BEING THOSE 0.95 OF 348 NOT INCLUDED IN MONI NAG'S STUDY OF FERTILITY (375)	9 16 43 332 XSQ= 10.40 PHI= 0.161 XP = 0.0013
510	TEND LESS TO BE THOSE 0.81 OF 52 NOT INCLUDED IN RAOUL NARROLL'S STUDY OF SOCIETAL COMPLEXITY (380)	510	TEND MORE TO BE THOSE 0.97 OF 348 NOT INCLUDED IN RAOUL NARROLL'S STUDY OF SOCIETAL COMPLEXITY (380)	10 10 42 338 XSQ= 22.16 PHI= 0.235 XP = 0.0000
511	TEND TO BE THOSE 0.75 OF 52 INCLUDED IN ROBERTS, ARTH AND BUSH'S SAMPLE ON GAMES, AS MODIFIED BY THE ETHNOGRAPHIC ATLAS (189)	511	TEND TO BE THOSE 0.57 OF 348 NOT INCLUDED IN ROBERTS, ARTH AND BUSH'S SAMPLE ON GAMES, AS MODIFIED BY THE ETHNOGRAPHIC ATLAS (211)	39 150 13 198 XSQ= 17.21 PHI= 0.207 XP = 0.0000
512	TEND LESS TO BE THOSE 0.60 OF 52 NOT INCLUDED IN SHIRLEY AND ROMNEY'S STUDY OF LOVE MAGIC (367)	512	TEND MORE TO BE THOSE 0.97 OF 348 NOT INCLUDED IN SHIRLEY AND ROMNEY'S STUDY OF LOVE MAGIC (367)	21 12 31 336 XSQ= 76.73 PHI= 0.438 XP = 0.
513	TEND LESS TO BE THOSE 0.75 OF 52 NOT INCLUDED IN LEO W. SIMMONS' STUDY OF THE TREATMENT OF THE AGED (357)	513	TEND MORE TO BE THOSE 0.91 OF 348 NOT INCLUDED IN LEO W. SIMMONS' STUDY OF THE TREATMENT OF THE AGED (357)	13 30 39 318 XSQ= 11.00 PHI= 0.166 XP = 0.0009

No.		Proportion	No.		Proportion	Statistics
514	TEND TO BE THOSE INCLUDED IN PHILIP E. SLATER'S STUDY OF NARCISSISM (90)	0.79 OF 52	514	TEND TO BE THOSE NOT INCLUDED IN PHILIP E. SLATER'S STUDY OF NARCISSISM (310)	0.86 OF 348	41 49 / 11 299 / XSQ= 105.14 / PHI= 0.513 / XP = 0.
516	LEAN MORE TOWARD BEING THOSE INCLUDED IN GUY E. SWANSON'S SAMPLE ON LOCAL JURISDICTION, AS MODIFIED BY THE ETHNOGRAPHIC ATLAS (331)	0.98 OF 52	516	LEAN LESS TOWARD BEING THOSE INCLUDED IN GUY E. SWANSON'S SAMPLE ON LOCAL JURISDICTION, AS MODIFIED BY THE ETHNOGRAPHIC ATLAS (331)	0.80 OF 348	51 280 / 1 68 / XSQ= 8.64 / PHI= 0.147 / XP = 0.0033
517	TEND MORE TO BE THOSE INCLUDED IN GUY E. SWANSON'S SAMPLE ON HIGH GODS, AS MODIFIED BY THE ETHNOGRAPHIC ATLAS (260)	0.92 OF 52	517	TEND LESS TO BE THOSE INCLUDED IN GUY E. SWANSON'S SAMPLE ON HIGH GODS, AS MODIFIED BY THE ETHNOGRAPHIC ATLAS (260)	0.61 OF 348	48 212 / 4 136 / XSQ= 18.24 / PHI= 0.214 / XP = 0.0000
518	TEND TO BE THOSE INCLUDED IN STANLEY H. UDY, JR.'S STUDY OF WORK ORGANIZATION (105)	0.56 OF 52	518	TEND TO BE THOSE NOT INCLUDED IN STANLEY H. UDY, JR.'S STUDY OF WORK ORGANIZATION (295)	0.78 OF 348	29 76 / 23 272 / XSQ= 25.18 / PHI= 0.251 / XP = 0.0000
519	TEND LESS TO BE THOSE NOT INCLUDED IN JOSEPH VEROFF'S STUDY OF ACHIEVEMENT MOTIVATION AS REVEALED IN FOLKTALES (364)	0.69 OF 52	519	TEND MORE TO BE THOSE NOT INCLUDED IN JOSEPH VEROFF'S STUDY OF ACHIEVEMENT MOTIVATION AS REVEALED IN FOLKTALES (364)	0.94 OF 348	16 20 / 36 328 / XSQ= 31.60 / PHI= 0.281 / XP = 0.
520	TEND LESS TO BE THOSE NOT INCLUDED IN BEATRICE BLYTH WHITING'S STUDY OF SORCERY (360)	0.67 OF 52	520	TEND MORE TO BE THOSE NOT INCLUDED IN BEATRICE BLYTH WHITING'S STUDY OF SORCERY (360)	0.93 OF 348	17 23 / 35 325 / XSQ= 31.36 / PHI= 0.280 / XP = 0.
521	TEND TO BE THOSE INCLUDED IN JOHN W. M. WHITING'S STUDY OF SOCIALIZATION PROCESS AND PERSONALITY (47)	0.52 OF 52	521	TEND TO BE THOSE NOT INCLUDED IN JOHN W. M. WHITING'S STUDY OF SOCIALIZATION PROCESS AND PERSONALITY (353)	0.94 OF 348	27 20 / 25 328 / XSQ= 88.63 / PHI= 0.471 / XP = 0.
522	TEND TO BE THOSE INCLUDED IN MARJORIE GRANT WHITING'S STUDY OF DIET (82)	0.71 OF 52	522	TEND TO BE THOSE NOT INCLUDED IN MARJORIE GRANT WHITING'S STUDY OF DIET (318)	0.87 OF 348	37 45 / 15 303 / XSQ= 90.56 / PHI= 0.476 / XP = 0.
523	TEND TO BE THOSE INCLUDED IN WHITING AND CHILD'S STUDY OF CHILD TRAINING AND PERSONALITY (61)	0.60 OF 52	523	TEND TO BE THOSE NOT INCLUDED IN WHITING AND CHILD'S STUDY OF CHILD TRAINING AND PERSONALITY (339)	0.91 OF 348	31 30 / 21 318 / XSQ= 87.12 / PHI= 0.467 / XP = 0.

515/

```
524  TEND TO BE THOSE               0.50 OF  52     524  TEND TO BE THOSE               0.95 OF 348         26   18
     INCLUDED IN                                         NOT INCLUDED IN                                    26  330
     WHITING, KLUCKHOHN, AND ANTHONY'S                   WHITING, KLUCKHOHN, AND ANTHONY'S            XSQ=   88.34
     STUDY OF MALE INITIATION CEREMONIES  (44)           STUDY OF MALE INITIATION CEREMONIES  (356)   PHI=   0.470
                                                                                                      XP =  0.
```

****

516 CULTURES INCLUDED IN GUY E. SWANSON'S SAMPLE ON LOCAL JURISDICTION, AS MODIFIED BY THE ETHNOGRAPHIC ATLAS (331)	516 CULTURES NOT INCLUDED IN GUY E. SWANSON'S SAMPLE ON LOCAL JURISDICTION, AS MODIFIED BY THE ETHNOGRAPHIC ATLAS (69)

BACKGROUND ON PAGE 180

SUBJECT ONLY, F.C. 1-480 AND 527-536
BOTH SUBJECT AND PREDICATE, F.C. 481-526

....

331 IN LEFT COLUMN

ABIPON	ABOR	AINU	AKHA	ALACALUF	ALBANIANS	ALORESE	AMBA	AMERICANS	ANDAMANESE
APINAYE	ARANDA	ARAPESH	ARAUCANIANS	ASHANTI	ATAYAL	ATSUGEWI	AWEIKOMA	AYMARA	AZANDE
AZTEC	BABWA	BACAIRI	BAMBARA	BAMILEKE	BANDA	BARABRA	BARI	BASSERI	BAYA
BEJA	BEMBA	BHIL	BHUIYA	BIRIFOR	BLACK CARIB	BOERS	BORORO	BOTOCUDO	BOZO
BRAZILIANS	BULGARIANS	BUNLAP	BURUSHO	CADUVEO	CAGABA	CALLINAGO	CAMAYURA	CAMBODIANS	CARIB
CAYAPA	CHAGGA	CHAMACOCO	CHENCHU	CHERKESS	CHEROKEE	CHEYENNE	CHIBCHA	CHIR-APACHE	CHIRIGUANO
CHOCO	CHOROTI	CHORTI	CHUKCHEE	COCHITI	COORG	COPR ESKIMO	CREE	CREEK	CROW
CUNA	CZECHS	DAGUR	DARD	DELAWARE	DIEGUENO	DIERI	DILLING	DOGON	DOROBO
DUTCH	EGYPTIANS	ELLICE	ENGA	EYAK	FANG	FON	FOX	FUTAJALONKE	GANDA
GARO	GILYAK	GISU	GOAJIRO	GOND	GROS VENTRE	GUAHIBO	GUATO	GURE	HAIDA
HANO	HANUNOO	HASINAI	HAVASUPAI	HAWAIIANS	HAZARA	HEBREWS	HERERO	HUICHOL	HUKUNDIKA
HURON	IBAN	IFUGAO	ILA	INCA	INGALIK	INGASSANA	IRAQW	IRISH	JAPANESE
JAVANESE	JEMEZ	JIVARO	JUKUN	KABYLE	KACHIN	KAPAUKU	KARIERA	KASKA	KATAB
KAZAK	KERAKI	KERALA	KHALKA	KHASI	KIKUYU	KISSI	KCHISTANI	KOL	KOREANS
KORYAK	KPE	KUBA	KUNG	KURTATCHI	KUTENAI	KWAKIUTL	LAKHER	LAMBA	LAMET
LANGO	LAPPS	LAU	LEPCHA	LESU	LHOTA NAGA	LOLO	LOZI	LUO	MACASSARESE
MALAYS	MAN	MAMBILA	MAMVU	MANDAN	MANGAIANS	MANIHIKI	MANUS	MAORI	MARGI
MARICOPA	MARQUESANS	MARSHALLESE	MASAI	MATACO	MATAKAM	MAYA	MBUNDU	MBUTI	MENDE
MERINA	MIAMI	MIAO	MIN CHINESE	MINCHIA	MISKITO	MIWOK	MNONG GAR	MONGO	MONGUOR
MOSSI	MOTA	MOTILON	MUNDURUCU	MURINBATA	MURNGIN	MZAB	NABESNA	NAMA	NAMBICUARA
NANDI	NATCHEZ	NAVAHO	NDEMBU	NICOBARESE	NOMLAKI	NUER	NUNIVAK	NUPE	NURI
NYAKYUSA	NYORO	OJIBWA	OKINAWANS	OMAHA	ONA	ONTONG-JAVA	ORAON	PAEZ	PAIWAN
PALAUANS	PAPAGO	PARAUJANO	PATHAN	PAWNEE	PONAPEANS	PUKAPUKA	PURARI	PURUM	REGEIBAT
RIFFIANS	RUNDI	RWALA	SAGADA	SAMOANS	SAMOYED	SANDAWE	SANPOIL	SANTAL	SARSI
SELUNG	SEMANG	SENIANG	SERBS	SHERENTE	SHILLUK	SHLUH	SINHALESE	SIRIONO	SIUAI
SIWANS	SOMALI	SONGHAI	SOTHO	SUBANUN	SWAZI	SYRIANS	TAGBANUA	TALAMANCA	TALLENSI
TANALA	TAOS	TAPIRAPE	TARAHUMARA	TAREUMIUT	TEDA	TEHUELCHE	TENDA	TENETEHARA	TENINO
TERA	TERENA	TESO	THAI	THONGA	TIGRINYA	TIKOPIA	TIMBIRA	TIMUCUA	TIV
TIWI	TODA	TOKELAU	TOLOWA	TORAJA	TOTONAC	TRISTAN	TROBRIAND	TRUKESE	TRUMAI
TSHIMSHIAN	TUBATULABAL	TUCANO	TUCUNA	TUNEBO	TUPINAMBA	TURKANA	TURKMEN	TWANA	ULAWANS
UTE	VEDDA	VENDA	VIETNAMESE	WAICA	WALLOONS	WANTOAT	WAPISHANA	WARRAU	WASHO
WICHITA	WIKMUNKAN	WITOTO	WOGEO	WOLEAIANS	WOLOF	YABARANA	YAGUA	YAHGAN	YAKO
YAKUT	YAO	YAPESE	YARURO	YOKUTS	YOMBE	YORUBA	YUKAGHIR	YUKI	YUROK
ZUNI									

69 IN RIGHT COLUMN

4	TILT MORE TOWARD BEING THOSE 0.90 OF 331 LOCATED OUTSIDE OF THE CIRCUM-MEDITERRANEAN (355)	4	TILT LESS TOWARD BEING THOSE 0.81 OF 69 LOCATED OUTSIDE OF THE CIRCUM-MEDITERRANEAN (355)	32 13 299 56 XSQ= 3.94 PHI= -0.099 XP = 0.0472
9	DRIFT LESS TOWARD BEING THOSE 0.82 OF 331 LOCATED OUTSIDE OF SOUTH AMERICA (335)	9	DRIFT MORE TOWARD BEING THOSE 0.91 OF 69 LOCATED OUTSIDE OF SOUTH AMERICA (335)	59 6 272 63 XSQ= 2.86 PHI= 0.085 XP = 0.0909
54	TEND TO BE THOSE 0.83 OF 229 WHERE FOOD PRODUCTION IS BY INTENSIVE OR SIMPLE AGRICULTURE, RATHER THAN BY INCIPIENT FOOD PRODUCTION (192)	54	TEND TO BE THOSE 0.78 OF 9 WHERE FOOD PRODUCTION IS BY INCIPIENT FOOD PRODUCTION, RATHER THAN BY INTENSIVE OR SIMPLE AGRICULTURE (46)	190 2 39 7 XSQ= 16.78 PHI= 0.266 XP = 0.0000
56	TEND TO BE THOSE 0.72 OF 140 WHERE FOOD PRODUCTION IS BY SIMPLE AGRICULTURE, RATHER THAN BY INCIPIENT FOOD PRODUCTION (101)	56	IN ALL CASES ARE THOSE 1.00 OF 7 WHERE FOOD PRODUCTION IS BY INCIPIENT FOOD PRODUCTION, RATHER THAN BY SIMPLE AGRICULTURE (46)	101 0 39 7 XSQ= 12.96 PHI= 0.297 XP = 0.0003
62	TEND TO BE THOSE 0.68 OF 331 WHERE HUSBANDRY OF SOME KIND IS PRESENT (228)	62	TEND TO BE THOSE 0.94 OF 69 WHERE HUSBANDRY OF ANY KIND IS ABSENT (172)	224 4 107 65 XSQ= 86.69 PHI= 0.466 XP = 0.
74	DRIFT TOWARD BEING THOSE 0.62 OF 230 WHERE POTTERY IS PRESENT (145)	74	DRIFT TOWARD BEING THOSE 0.75 OF 8 WHERE POTTERY IS ABSENT (93)	143 2 87 6 XSQ= 3.06 PHI= 0.113 XP = 0.0801
80	TILT TOWARD BEING THOSE 0.83 OF 222 WHERE NO CITY OR TOWN IS PRESENT (185)	80	IN ALL CASES ARE THOSE 1.00 OF 2 WHERE A CITY OR TOWN IS PRESENT (39)	37 2 185 0 XSQ= 4.65 PHI= -0.144 XP = 0.0310
242	TILT MORE TOWARD BEING THOSE 0.82 OF 328 WHERE MARRIAGE IS COMMONLY OR OCCASIONALLY POLYGYNOUS, RATHER THAN MONOGAMOUS (314)	242	TILT LESS TOWARD BEING THOSE 0.69 OF 67 WHERE MARRIAGE IS COMMONLY OR OCCASIONALLY POLYGYNOUS, RATHER THAN MONOGAMOUS (314)	268 46 60 21 XSQ= 5.04 PHI= 0.113 XP = 0.0248
353	DRIFT TOWARD BEING THOSE 0.60 OF 70 WHERE THE CHILD'S INFERRED ANXIETY OVER NON-PERFORMANCE OF OBEDIENT BEHAVIOR IS HIGH (42) B-B-C	353	IN ALL CASES ARE THOSE 1.00 OF 4 WHERE THE CHILD-S INFERRED ANXIETY OVER NON-PERFORMANCE OF OBEDIENT BEHAVIOR IS LOW (32) B-B-C	42 0 28 4 XSQ= 3.37 PHI= 0.214 XP = 0.0662

380	TILT TOWARD BEING THOSE 0.69 OF 51 WHERE SEGREGATICN CF GIRLS AT MENARCHE IS PRESENT (35) F-B	380	IN ALL CASES ARE THOSE 1.00 OF 4 WHERE SEGREGATION OF GIRLS AT MENARCHE IS ABSENT (20) F-B	35 0 16 4 XSQ= 4.87 PHI= 0.298 XP = 0.0273
406	DRIFT TOWARD BEING THCSE 0.50 OF 56 WHERE EXPLANATICNS CF ILLNESS OF AN AGGRESSICN NATURE ARE PRESENT (28) W-C	406	IN ALL CASES ARE THOSE 1.00 OF 5 WHERE EXPLANATIONS OF ILLNESS OF AN AGGRESSION NATURE ARE ABSENT (33) W-C	28 0 28 5 XSQ= 2.83 PHI= 0.215 XP = 0.0927
425	DRIFT TOWARD BEING THCSE 0.61 OF 33 WHERE SUPERNATURALS ARE MAINLY AGGRESSIVE, RATHER THAN BENEVCLENT (20) L-T-W	425	IN ALL CASES ARE THOSE 1.00 OF 3 WHERE SUPERNATURALS ARE MAINLY BENEVOLENT, RATHER THAN AGGRESSIVE (16) L-T-W	13 3 20 0 XSQ= 2.00 PHI= -0.236 EP = 0.0784
455	DRIFT TOWARD BEING THCSE 0.58 OF 33 WHERE THE MODE CF THE INDIVIDUAL'S CONTACT WITH THE DIVINE IS NOT CONDUCIVE TC THE DEVELOPMENT OF THE INDIVIDUAL'S NEED TC ACHIEVE (19) DCM	455	IN ALL CASES ARE THOSE 1.00 OF 3 WHERE THE MODE OF THE INDIVIDUAL'S CONTACT WITH THE DIVINE IS CONDUCIVE TO THE DEVELOPMENT OF THE INDIVIDUAL'S NEED TO ACHIEVE (17) DCM	14 3 19 0 XSQ= 1.71 PHI= -0.218 EP = 0.0952
482	DRIFT LESS TOWARC BEING THOSE 0.85 OF 323 WHERE THE PRINCIPAL ETHNOGRAPHERS HAVE BEEN CTHER THAN BRITISH (336)	482	DRIFT MORE TOWARD BEING THCSE 0.94 OF 65 WHERE THE PRINCIPAL ETHNOGRAPHERS HAVE BEEN OTHER THAN BRITISH (336)	48 4 275 61 XSQ= 2.82 PHI= 0.085 XP = 0.0929
489	TILT LESS TOWARD BEING THCSE 0.84 OF 331 NOT INCLUDED IN CHARLES ACKERMAN'S STUDY OF DIVCRCE (343)	489	TILT MORE TOWARD BEING THOSE 0.96 OF 69 NOT INCLUDED IN CHARLES ACKERMAN'S STUDY OF DIVORCE (343)	54 3 277 66 XSQ= 5.75 PHI= 0.120 XP = 0.0165
490	LEAN LESS TOWARC BEING THOSE 0.68 OF 331 NOT INCLUDED IN ALBERT S. ANTHONY'S SAMPLE ON MALE INITIATION RITES (287)	490	LEAN MORE TOWARD BEING THOSE 0.88 OF 69 NOT INCLUDED IN ALBERT S. ANTHONY'S SAMPLE ON MALE INITIATICN RITES (287)	105 8 226 61 XSQ= 10.44 PHI= 0.162 XP = 0.0012
493	LEAN LESS TOWARC BEING THCSE 0.78 OF 331 NOT INCLUDED IN BACCN, BARRY, AND CHILC'S STUDY OF CHILD REARING (322)	493	LEAN MORE TOWARD BEING THOSE 0.94 OF 69 NOT INCLUDED IN BACON, BARRY, AND CHILD'S STUDY OF CHILD REARING (322)	74 4 257 65 XSQ= 8.95 PHI= 0.150 XP = 0.0028
495	TILT LESS TOWARC BEING THCSE 0.82 OF 331 NOT INCLUDED IN JUCITH K. BROWN'S STUDY OF FEMALE INITIATION RITES (335)	495	TILT MORE TOWARD BEING THOSE 0.94 OF 69 NOT INCLUDED IN JUDITH K. BROWN'S STUDY OF FEMALE INITIATICN RITES (335)	61 4 270 65 XSQ= 5.80 PHI= 0.120 XP = 0.0160

496	DRIFT LESS TOWARD BEING THOSE 0.85 OF 331 NOT INCLUDED IN ROY G. D'ANDRADE'S STUDY OF DREAMS (345)	DRIFT MORE TOWARD BEING THOSE 0.94 OF 69 NOT INCLUDED IN ROY G. D'ANDRADE'S STUDY OF DREAMS (345)	51 4 280 65 XSQ= 3.67 PHI= 0.096 XP = 0.0553
497	TEND LESS TO BE THOSE 0.82 OF 331 NOT INCLUDED IN WILLIAM M. EVAN'S STUDY OF LAW (339)	TEND MORE TO BE THOSE 0.99 OF 69 NOT INCLUDED IN WILLIAM M. EVAN'S STUDY OF LAW (339)	60 1 271 68 XSQ= 11.03 PHI= 0.166 XP = 0.0009
498	LEAN LESS TOWARD BEING THOSE 0.85 OF 331 NOT INCLUDED IN C. S. FORD'S STUDY OF SEX (349)	LEAN MORE TOWARD BEING THOSE 0.99 OF 69 NOT INCLUDED IN C. S. FORD'S STUDY OF SEX (349)	50 1 281 68 XSQ= 8.38 PHI= 0.145 XP = 0.0038
499	TILT LESS TOWARD BEING THOSE 0.76 OF 331 NOT INCLUDED IN FORD AND BEACH'S SAMPLE ON SEXUAL EXPRESSION BY THE YOUNG (314)	TILT MORE TOWARD BEING THOSE 0.90 OF 69 NOT INCLUDED IN FORD AND BEACH'S SAMPLE ON SEXUAL EXPRESSION BY THE YOUNG (314)	79 7 252 62 XSQ= 5.58 PHI= 0.118 XP = 0.0181
500	DRIFT LESS TOWARD BEING THOSE 0.89 OF 331 NOT INCLUDED IN FREEMAN AND WINCH'S STUDY OF SOCIETAL COMPLEXITY (360)	DRIFT MORE TOWARD BEING THOSE 0.97 OF 69 NOT INCLUDED IN FREEMAN AND WINCH'S STUDY OF SOCIETAL COMPLEXITY (360)	38 2 293 67 XSQ= 3.77 PHI= 0.097 XP = 0.0523
501	LEAN LESS TOWARD BEING THOSE 0.80 OF 331 NOT INCLUDED IN JOAN FRIENDLY GOODMAN'S STUDY OF ASCETIC MOURNING BEHAVIOR (333)	LEAN MORE TOWARD BEING THOSE 0.97 OF 69 NOT INCLUDED IN JOAN FRIENDLY GOODMAN'S STUDY OF ASCETIC MOURNING BEHAVIOR (333)	65 2 266 67 XSQ= 10.30 PHI= 0.160 XP = 0.0013
502	LEAN LESS TOWARD BEING THOSE 0.83 OF 331 NOT INCLUDED IN JOHN K. HARLEY'S STUDY OF ADOLESCENT PEER GROUPS (343)	LEAN MORE TOWARD BEING THOSE 0.99 OF 69 NOT INCLUDED IN JOHN K. HARLEY'S STUDY OF ADOLESCENT PEER GROUPS (343)	56 1 275 68 XSQ= 9.95 PHI= 0.158 XP = 0.0016
503	LEAN LESS TOWARD BEING THOSE 0.84 OF 331 NOT INCLUDED IN JOHN M. HICKMAN'S STUDY OF THE FOLK-URBAN CONTINUUM (346)	LEAN MORE TOWARD BEING THOSE 0.97 OF 69 NOT INCLUDED IN JOHN M. HICKMAN'S STUDY OF THE FOLK-URBAN CONTINUUM (346)	52 2 279 67 XSQ= 6.97 PHI= 0.132 XP = 0.0083
504	TILT LESS TOWARD BEING THOSE 0.86 OF 331 NOT INCLUDED IN DONALD HORTON'S STUDY OF ALCHOLISM (351)	TILT MORE TOWARD BEING THOSE 0.96 OF 69 NOT INCLUDED IN DONALD HORTON'S STUDY OF ALCHOLISM (351)	46 3 285 66 XSQ= 4.00 PHI= 0.100 XP = 0.0456

507	TEND LESS TO BE THOSE 0.75 OF 331 NOT INCLUDED IN JAMES R. LEARY'S STUDY OF FOOD TABOOS (314)	507	TEND MORE TO BE THOSE 0.96 OF 69 NOT INCLUDED IN JAMES R. LEARY'S STUDY OF FOOD TABOOS (314)	83 3 248 66 XSQ= 13.33 PHI= 0.183 XP = 0.0003
510	DRIFT LESS TOWARD BEING THOSE 0.94 OF 331 NOT INCLUDED IN RAOUL NARROLL'S STUDY OF SOCIETAL COMPLEXITY (380)	510	IN ALL CASES ARE THOSE 1.00 OF 69 NOT INCLUDED IN RAOUL NARROLL'S STUDY OF SOCIETAL COMPLEXITY (380)	20 0 311 69 XSQ= 3.21 PHI= 0.090 XP = 0.0732
511	TEND TO BE THOSE 0.57 OF 331 INCLUDED IN ROBERTS, ARTH AND BUSH'S SAMPLE ON GAMES, AS MODIFIED BY THE ETHNOGRAPHIC ATLAS (189)	511	TEND TO BE THOSE 0.99 OF 69 NOT INCLUDED IN ROBERTS, ARTH AND BUSH'S SAMPLE ON GAMES, AS MODIFIED BY THE ETHNOGRAPHIC ATLAS (211)	188 1 143 68 XSQ= 67.98 PHI= C.412 XP = 0.
513	TILT LESS TOWARD BEING THOSE 0.87 OF 331 NOT INCLUDED IN LEO W. SIMMONS' STUDY OF THE TREATMENT OF THE AGED (357)	513	TILT MORE TOWARD BEING THOSE 0.99 OF 69 NOT INCLUDED IN LEO W. SIMMONS' STUDY OF THE TREATMENT OF THE AGED (357)	42 1 289 68 XSQ= 6.39 PHI= 0.126 XP = 0.0115
514	TEND LESS TO BE THOSE 0.74 OF 331 NOT INCLUDED IN PHILIP E. SLATER'S STUDY OF NARCISSISM (310)	514	TEND MORE TO BE THOSE 0.96 OF 69 NOT INCLUDED IN PHILIP E. SLATER'S STUDY OF NARCISSISM (310)	87 3 244 66 XSQ= 14.52 PHI= 0.191 XP = 0.0001
515	LEAN LESS TOWARD BEING THOSE 0.85 OF 331 NOT INCLUDED IN WILLIAM N. STEPHENS' SAMPLE ON AVOIDANCE RELATIONSHIPS (348)	515	LEAN MORE TOWARD BEING THOSE 0.99 OF 69 NOT INCLUDED IN WILLIAM N. STEPHENS' SAMPLE ON AVOIDANCE RELATIONSHIPS (348)	51 1 280 68 XSQ= 8.64 PHI= 0.147 XP = 0.0033
517	TEND TO BE THOSE 0.78 OF 331 INCLUDED IN GUY E. SWANSON'S SAMPLE ON HIGH GODS, AS MODIFIED BY THE ETHNOGRAPHIC ATLAS (260)	517	TEND TO BE THOSE 0.97 OF 69 NOT INCLUDED IN GUY E. SWANSON'S SAMPLE ON HIGH GODS, AS MODIFIED BY THE ETHNOGRAPHIC ATLAS (140)	258 2 73 67 XSQ= 138.07 PHI= 0.588 XP = 0.
518	LEAN LESS TOWARD BEING THOSE 0.71 OF 331 NOT INCLUDED IN STANLEY H. UDY, JR.'S STUDY OF WORK ORGANIZATION (295)	518	LEAN MORE TOWARD BEING THOSE 0.87 OF 69 NOT INCLUDED IN STANLEY H. UDY, JR.'S STUDY OF WORK ORGANIZATION (295)	96 9 235 60 XSQ= 6.71 PHI= 0.130 XP = 0.0096
520	DRIFT LESS TOWARD BEING THOSE 0.89 OF 331 NOT INCLUDED IN BEATRICE BLYTH WHITING'S STUDY OF SORCERY (360)	520	DRIFT MORE TOWARD BEING THOSE 0.97 OF 69 NOT INCLUDED IN BEATRICE BLYTH WHITING'S STUDY OF SORCERY (360)	38 2 293 67 XSQ= 3.77 PHI= 0.097 XP = 0.0523

522	LEAN LESS TOWARD BEING THOSE 0.76 OF 331 NOT INCLUDED IN MARJORIE GRANT WHITING'S STUDY OF DIET (318)	522	LEAN MORE TOWARD BEING THOSE 0.94 OF 69 NOT INCLUDED IN MARJORIE GRANT WHITING'S STUDY OF DIET (318)	78 4 253 65 XSQ= 10.00 PHI= 0.158 XP = 0.0016
523	DRIFT LESS TOWARD BEING THOSE 0.83 OF 331 NOT INCLUDED IN WHITING AND CHILD'S STUDY OF CHILD TRAINING AND PERSONALITY (339)	523	DRIFT MORE TOWARD BEING THOSE 0.93 OF 69 NOT INCLUDED IN WHITING AND CHILD'S STUDY OF CHILD TRAINING AND PERSONALITY (339)	56 5 275 64 XSQ= 3.42 PHI= 0.092 XP = 0.0645
524	LEAN LESS TOWARD BEING THOSE 0.87 OF 331 NOT INCLUDED IN WHITING, KLUCKHCHN, AND ANTHONY'S STUDY OF MALE INITIATION CEREMONIES (356)	524	LEAN MORE TOWARD BEING THOSE 0.99 OF 69 NOT INCLUDED IN WHITING, KLUCKHOHN, AND ANTHONY'S STUDY OF MALE INITIATION CEREMONIES (356)	43 1 288 68 XSQ= 6.63 PHI= 0.129 XP = 0.0100

517 CULTURES INCLUDED IN GUY E. SWANSON'S SAMPLE ON HIGH GODS, AS MODIFIED BY THE ETHNOGRAPHIC ATLAS (260)

517 CULTURES NOT INCLUDED IN GUY E. SWANSON'S SAMPLE ON HIGH GODS, AS MODIFIED BY THE ETHNOGRAPHIC ATLAS (140)

BACKGROUND ON PAGE 180

SUBJECT ONLY, F.C. 1-480 AND 527-536
BOTH SUBJECT AND PREDICATE, F.C. 481-526

260 IN LEFT COLUMN

ABIPON	ABOR	AINU	ALACALUF	ALBANIANS	ALORESE	AMBA	AMERICANS	ANDAMANESE	APINAYE
ARANDA	ARAPESH	ARAUCANIANS	ASHANTI	ATAYAL	ATSUGEWI	AWEIKOMA	AYMARA	AZANDE	AZTEC
BACAIRI	BAMBARA	BAMILEKE	BARABRA	BARI	BASSERI	BEJA	BEMBA	BHIL	BHUIYA
BIRIFOR	BLACK CARIB	BOERS	BORORO	BOZO	BRAZILIANS	BULGARIANS	BUNLAP	BURUSHO	CAGABA
CALLINAGO	CAMAYURA	CARIB	CAYAPA	CHAGGA	CHAMACOCO	CHENCHU	CHERKESS	CHEYENNE	CHIR-APACHE
CHOCO	CHOROTI	CHORTI	CHUKCHEE	COCHITI	COORG	COPR ESKIMO	CREE	CREEK	CROW
CUNA	CZECHS	DAGUR	DARD	DELAWARE	DIEGUENO	DIERI	DOROBO	DUTCH	EGYPTIANS
EYAK	FANG	FON	FOX	FUTAJALONKE	GANDA	GARO	GILYAK	GISU	GOAJIRO
GOND	GROS VENTRE	GURE	HAIDA	HASINAI	HAWAIIANS	HAZARA	HEBREWS	HUKUNDIKA	HURON
HUTSUL	IBAN	IFUGAO	ILA	INCA	INGALIK	IRISH	JAVANESE	JIVARO	KABYLE
KACHIN	KAPAUKU	KASKA	KATAB	KAZAK	KERAKI	KHASI	KIKUYU	KOHISTANI	KOREANS
KORYAK	KPE	KUBA	KUNG	KURTATCHI	KUTENAI	LAKHER	LAMBA	LANGO	LAPPS
LAU	LEPCHA	LESU	LHOTA NAGA	LOLO	LOZI	LUO	MACASSARESE	MALAYS	MAM
MAMVU	MANGAIANS	MANIHIKI	MANUS	MAORI	MARICOPA	MARQUESANS	MARSHALLESE	MATACO	MATAKAM
MBUNDU	MBUTI	MENDE	MIAMI	MISKITO	MNONG GAR	MONGO	MOSSI	MOTA	MUNDURUCU
MURINBATA	MURNGIN	MZAB	NABESNA	NAMA	NAMBICUARA	NANDI	NATCHEZ	NAVAHO	NOMLAKI
NUER	NUNIVAK	NUPE	NYAKYUSA	NYORO	OKINAWANS	OMAHA	ONA	ONTONG-JAVA	PAIWAN
PALAUANS	PAPAGO	PARAUJANO	PATHAN	PONAPEANS	PUKAPUKA	PURUM	REGEIBAT	RIFFIANS	ROMANS
RUNDI	RWALA	SAGADA	SAMOANS	SAMOYED	SANDAWE	SANPOIL	SANTAL	SEMANG	SERBS
SHERENTE	SHILLUK	SHLUH	SIRIONO	SIUAI	SIWANS	SOMALI	SONGHAI	SOTHO	SWAZI
SYRIANS	TALAMANCA	TALLENSI	TANALA	TAPIRAPE	TARAHUMARA	TAREUMIUT	TEDA	TEHUELCHE	TENDA
TENETEHARA	TENINO	TERENA	TESO	THAI	THONGA	TIGRINYA	TIKOPIA	TIMBIRA	TIMUCUA
TIV	TIWI	TOCA	TOLOWA	TRISTAN	TROBRIAND	TRUKESE	TRUMAI	TSHIMSHIAN	TUBATULABAL
TUCANO	TUCUNA	TUNEBO	TUPINAMBA	TURKANA	TURKMEN	TWANA	ULAWANS	UTE	VEDDA
VENDA	WALLOONS	WANTOAT	WARRAU	WASHO	WITOTO	WOGEO	WOLEAIANS	WOLOF	YABARANA
YAGUA	YAHGAN	YAKO	YAKUT	YAO	YOKUTS	YORUBA	YUKI	YUROK	ZUNI

140 IN RIGHT COLUMN

51	TILT LESS TOWARD BEING THOSE WHERE SUBSISTENCE IS PRIMARILY BY FOOD PRODUCTION -- I. E., AGRICULTURE OR HUSBANDRY -- RATHER THAN BY GATHERING (253)	0.59 OF 260	51	TILT MORE TOWARD BEING THOSE WHERE SUBSISTENCE IS PRIMARILY BY FOOD PRODUCTION -- I. E., AGRICULTURE OR HUSBANDRY -- RATHER THAN BY GATHERING (253)	0.71 OF 140	154 99 106 41 XSQ= 4.68 PHI= -0.108 XP = 0.0305
62	TEND TO BE THOSE WHERE HUSBANDRY OF SOME KIND IS PRESENT (228)	0.67 OF 260	62	TEND TO BE THOSE WHERE HUSBANDRY OF ANY KIND IS ABSENT (172)	0.61 OF 140	174 54 86 86 XSQ= 28.70 PHI= 0.268 XP = 0.0000

74	DRIFT TOWARD BEING THOSE 0.64 OF 206 WHERE POTTERY IS PRESENT (145)	74	DRIFT TOWARD BEING THOSE 0.56 OF 32 WHERE POTTERY IS ABSENT (93)	131 14 75 18 XSQ= 3.79 PHI= 0.126 XP = 0.0517
81	TILT TOWARD BEING THOSE 0.64 OF 182 WHERE NO CITY OR TOWN IS PRESENT, AND THE AVERAGE COMMUNITY SIZE IS SMALLER THAN 200 (135)	81	TILT TOWARD BEING THOSE 0.55 OF 42 WHERE A CITY OR TOWN IS PRESENT, OR THE AVERAGE COMMUNITY SIZE IS 200 OR GREATER (89)	66 23 116 19 XSQ= 4.13 PHI= -0.136 XP = 0.0420
83	TILT MORE TOWARD BEING THOSE 0.78 OF 148 WHERE, WITH NO CITY AND NO TOWN PRESENT, THE AVERAGE COMMUNITY SIZE IS SMALLER THAN 200, RATHER THAN BETWEEN 200 AND 999 (135)	83	TILT LESS TOWARD BEING THOSE 0.59 OF 32 WHERE, WITH NO CITY AND NO TOWN PRESENT, THE AVERAGE COMMUNITY SIZE IS SMALLER THAN 200, RATHER THAN BETWEEN 200 AND 999 (135)	32 13 116 19 XSQ= 4.10 PHI= -0.151 XP = 0.0428
106	DRIFT LESS TOWARD BEING THOSE 0.58 OF 144 WHERE CLASS STRATIFICATION, IF PRESENT, IS BASED ON SOMETHING OTHER THAN WEALTH (126)	106	DRIFT MORE TOWARD BEING THOSE 0.73 OF 59 WHERE CLASS STRATIFICATION, IF PRESENT, IS BASED ON SOMETHING OTHER THAN WEALTH (126)	61 16 83 43 XSQ= 3.51 PHI= 0.131 XP = 0.0611
181	DRIFT MORE TOWARD BEING THOSE 0.91 OF 254 WHERE THE COMMUNITY IS OTHER THAN A DEME (337)	181	DRIFT LESS TOWARD BEING THOSE 0.84 OF 128 WHERE THE COMMUNITY IS OTHER THAN A DEME (337)	24 21 230 107 XSQ= 3.32 PHI= -0.093 XP = 0.0683
185	TILT MORE TOWARD BEING THOSE 0.81 OF 171 WHERE THE LARGEST NON-COGNATIC KIN GROUP IS THE MOEITY OR PHRATRY OR SIB (194)	185	TILT LESS TOWARD BEING THOSE 0.68 OF 81 WHERE THE LARGEST NON-COGNATIC KIN GROUP IS THE MOEITY OR PHRATRY OR SIB (194)	139 55 32 26 XSQ= 4.83 PHI= 0.138 XP = 0.0280
196	DRIFT LESS TOWARD BEING THOSE 0.65 OF 191 WHERE INDIVIDUAL RIGHTS IN REAL PROPERTY, AND RULES FOR INHERITANCE, ARE PRESENT (194)	196	DRIFT MORE TOWARD BEING THOSE 0.77 OF 90 WHERE INDIVIDUAL RIGHTS IN REAL PROPERTY, AND RULES FOR INHERITANCE, ARE PRESENT (194)	125 69 66 21 XSQ= 3.10 PHI= -0.105 XP = 0.0784
319	TILT TOWARD BEING THOSE 0.53 OF 55 WHERE PROTECTION OF THE INFANT FROM ENVIRONMENTAL DISCOMFORTS IS LOW (30) B-B-C	319	TILT TOWARD BEING THOSE 0.90 OF 10 WHERE PROTECTION OF THE INFANT FROM ENVIRONMENTAL DISCOMFORTS IS HIGH (35) B-B-C	26 9 29 1 XSQ= 4.62 PHI= -0.266 XP = 0.0317
335	DRIFT TOWARD BEING THOSE 0.59 OF 32 WHERE INITIAL INDULGENCE OF DEPENDENCY IS HIGH (20) WNS	335	DRIFT TOWARD BEING THOSE 0.83 OF 6 WHERE INITIAL INDULGENCE OF DEPENDENCY IS LOW (18) WNS	19 1 13 5 XSQ= 2.18 PHI= 0.240 EP = 0.0828

349	TILT TOWARD BEING THOSE 0.52 OF 52 WHERE THE CHILD'S INFERRED ANXIETY OVER NON-PERFORMANCE OF ACHIEVEMENT BEHAVIOR IS LOW (28) B-B-C	349	TILT TOWARD BEING THOSE 0.90 OF 10 WHERE THE CHILD'S INFERRED ANXIETY OVER NON-PERFORMANCE OF ACHIEVEMENT BEHAVIOR IS HIGH (34) B-B-C	25 9 27 1 XSQ= 4.38 PHI= -0.266 XP = 0.0364
360	LEAN TOWARD BEING THOSE 0.74 OF 31 WHERE ADOLESCENT PEER GROUPS ARE PRESENT ONLY IN A SETTING OF LEISURE, OR ELSE ARE ABSENT (23) JKH	360	IN ALL CASES ARE THOSE 1.00 OF 6 WHERE ADOLESCENT PEER GROUPS ARE PRESENT IN A SETTING OF WORK AND PUBLIC GATHERINGS AND LEISURE, OR AT LEAST OF PUBLIC GATHERINGS AND LEISURE (14) JKH	8 6 23 0 XSQ= 8.82 PHI= -0.488 EP = 0.0013
392	DRIFT TOWARD BEING THOSE 0.66 OF 149 WHERE PREMARITAL SEX RELATIONS ARE STRONGLY PUNISHED AND IN FACT RARE, OR WEAKLY PUNISHED AND IN FACT NOT RARE, OR PUNISHED ONLY IF PREGNANCY RESULTS (112) JTW,EA	392	DRIFT TOWARD BEING THOSE 0.53 OF 30 WHERE PREMARITAL SEX RELATIONS ARE FREELY PERMITTED (67) JTW,EA	98 14 51 16 XSQ= 3.12 PHI= 0.132 XP = 0.0774
431	DRIFT TOWARD BEING THOSE 0.77 OF 31 WHERE SUPERNATURAL SANCTIONS FOR MORALITY, HAVING AN EFFECT ON AN INDIVIDUAL'S AFTERLIFE, ARE ABSENT OR UNREPORTED (25) GES	431	DRIFT TOWARD BEING THOSE 0.75 OF 4 WHERE SUPERNATURAL SANCTIONS FOR MORALITY, HAVING AN EFFECT ON AN INDIVIDUAL'S AFTER LIFE, ARE PRESENT (10) GES	7 3 24 1 XSQ= 2.55 PHI= -0.270 EP = 0.0613
433	TILT TOWARD BEING THOSE 0.79 OF 34 WHERE BELIEF IN REINCARNATION IS ABSENT (28) GES	433	TILT TOWARD BEING THOSE 0.75 OF 4 WHERE BELIEF IN REINCARNATION IS PRESENT (10) GES	7 3 27 1 XSQ= 3.02 PHI= -0.282 EP = 0.0484
453	LEAN TOWARD BEING THOSE 0.76 OF 29 WHERE THE ROLE OF RELIGIOUS EXPERTS IS NOT CONDUCIVE TO THE DEVELOPMENT OF THE INDIVIDUAL'S NEED TO ACHIEVE (23) DCM	453	LEAN TOWARD BEING THOSE 0.86 OF 7 WHERE THE ROLE OF RELIGIOUS EXPERTS IS CONDUCIVE TO THE DEVELOPMENT OF THE INDIVIDUAL'S NEED TO ACHIEVE (13) DCM	7 6 22 1 XSQ= 6.79 PHI= -0.434 EP = 0.0049
487	DRIFT MORE TOWARD BEING THOSE 0.90 OF 168 ABOUT WHICH THE PRINCIPAL ETHNOGRAPHIES WERE PUBLISHED IN 1930 OR AFTER (227)	487	DRIFT LESS TOWARD BEING THOSE 0.82 OF 91 ABOUT WHICH THE PRINCIPAL ETHNOGRAPHIES WERE PUBLISHED IN 1930 OR AFTER (227)	16 16 152 75 XSQ= 2.83 PHI= -0.105 XP = 0.0922
489	TEND LESS TO BE THOSE 0.81 OF 260 NOT INCLUDED IN CHARLES ACKERMAN'S STUDY OF DIVORCE (343)	489	TEND MORE TO BE THOSE 0.95 OF 140 NOT INCLUDED IN CHARLES ACKERMAN'S STUDY OF DIVORCE (343)	50 7 210 133 XSQ= 13.94 PHI= 0.187 XP = 0.0002
490	TEND LESS TO BE THOSE 0.65 OF 260 NOT INCLUDED IN ALBERT S. ANTHONY'S SAMPLE ON MALE INITIATION RITES (287)	490	TEND MORE TO BE THOSE 0.84 OF 140 NOT INCLUDED IN ALBERT S. ANTHONY'S SAMPLE ON MALE INITIATION RITES (287)	90 23 170 117 XSQ= 13.97 PHI= 0.187 XP = 0.0002

491	DRIFT LESS TCWARC BEING TFOSE 0.86 OF 260 NOT INCLUDED IN DORRIAN APPLE'S STUDY OF GRANDPARENTHCOD (352)	491	DRIFT MORE TOWARD BEING THCSE 0.92 CF 140 NOT INCLUDED IN DORRIAN APPLE'S STUDY OF GRANDPARENTHOOD (352)	37 11 223 129 XSQ= 2.92 PHI= 0.085 XP = 0.0873
492	TILT LESS TOWARC BEING THCSE 0.88 OF 260 NOT INCLUDED IN BARBARA CFARTIER AYRES' STUDY OF FEMALE INITIATION RITES (361)	492	TILT MORE TOWARD REING THOSE 0.95 OF 140 NOT INCLUDED IN BARBARA CHARTIER AYRES' STUDY OF FEMALE INITIATICN RITES (361)	32 7 228 133 XSQ= 4.72 PHI= 0.109 XP = 0.0298
493	TEND LESS TO BE THCSE 0.74 OF 260 NOT INCLUDED IN BACON, BARRY, AND CHILC'S STUDY OF CHILD REARING (322)	493	TEND MORE TO BE THOSE 0.93 OF 140 NOT INCLUDED IN BACON, BARRY, AND CHILD'S STUDY OF CHILD REARING (322)	68 10 192 130 XSQ= 19.76 PHI= 0.222 XP = 0.0000
495	TEND LESS TO BE THCSE 0.78 OF 260 NOT INCLUDED IN JUCITH K. BROWN'S STUDY OF FEMALE INITIATION RITES (335)	495	TEND MORE TO BE THOSE 0.95 OF 140 NOT INCLUDED IN JUDITH K. BROWN'S STUDY OF FEMALE INITIATICN RITES (335)	58 7 202 133 XSQ= 18.78 PHI= 0.217 XP = 0.0000
496	TEND LESS TO BE THCSE 0.82 OF 260 NOT INCLUDED IN ROY G. D'ANDRADE'S STUDY OF DREAMS (345)	496	TEND MORE TO BE THOSE 0.95 OF 140 NOT INCLUDED IN ROY G. D'ANDRADE'S STUDY OF DREAMS (345)	48 7 212 133 XSQ= 12.79 PHI= 0.179 XP = 0.0003
497	TEND LESS TO BE THCSE 0.79 OF 260 NOT INCLUDED IN WILLIAM M. EVAN'S STUDY OF LAW (339)	497	TEND MORE TO BE THOSE 0.96 OF 140 NOT INCLUDED IN WILLIAM M. EVAN'S STUDY OF LAW (339)	55 6 205 134 XSQ= 18.75 PHI= 0.217 XP = 0.0000
498	TEND LESS TO BE THCSE 0.83 OF 260 NOT INCLUDED IN C. S. FORC'S STUDY OF SEX (349)	498	TEND MORE TO BE THOSE 0.96 OF 140 NOT INCLUDED IN C. S. FORD'S STUDY OF SEX (349)	45 6 215 134 XSQ= 12.73 PHI= 0.178 XP = 0.0004
499	DRIFT LESS TCWARD BEING THCSE 0.75 OF 260 NOT INCLUDED IN FORD AND BEACH'S SAMPLE ON SEXUAL EXPRESSICN BY THE YOUNG (314)	499	DRIFT MORE TOWARD BEING THCSE 0.84 OF 140 NOT INCLUDED IN FORD AND BEACH'S SAMPLE ON SEXUAL EXPRESSION BY THE YOUNG (314)	64 22 196 118 XSQ= 3.76 PHI= 0.097 XP = 0.0525
500	TEND LESS TO BE THCSE 0.86 OF 260 NOT INCLUDED IN FREEMAN ANC WINCH'S STUDY OF SCCIETAL CCMPLEXITY (360)	500	TEND MORE TO BE THOSE 0.97 CF 140 NOT INCLUDED IN FREEMAN AND WINCH'S STUDY OF SOCIFTAL COMPLEXITY (360)	36 4 224 136 XSQ= 11.02 PHI= 0.166 XP = 0.0009

501	TEND LESS TO BE THCSE 0.78 OF 260 NOT INCLUDED IN JOAN FRIENCLY GOOCMAN'S STUDY OF ASCETIC MCURNING BEHAVIOR (333)	501	TEND MORE TO BE THOSE 0.94 OF 140 NOT INCLUDED IN JOAN FRIENDLY GOODMAN'S STUDY OF ASCETIC MOURNING BEHAVIOR (333)	58 9 202 131 XSQ= 15.34 PHI= 0.196 XP = 0.0001
502	TEND LESS TO BE THCSE 0.81 OF 260 NOT INCLUDED IN JOHN K. HARLEY'S STUDY CF ADOLESCENT PEER GROUPS (343)	502	TEND MORE TO BE THOSE 0.94 OF 140 NOT INCLUDED IN JOHN K. HARLEY'S STUDY OF ADOLESCENT PEER GROUPS (343)	49 8 211 132 XSQ= 11.79 PHI= 0.172 XP = 0.0006
503	TEND LESS TO BE THCSE 0.82 OF 260 NOT INCLUDED IN JOHN M. HICKMAN'S STUDY OF THE FOLK-URBAN CONTINUUM (346)	503	TEND MORE TO BE THOSE 0.95 OF 140 NOT INCLUDED IN JOHN M. HICKMAN'S STUDY OF THE FOLK-URBAN CONTINUUM (346)	47 7 213 133 XSQ= 12.23 PHI= 0.175 XP = 0.0005
504	LEAN LESS TOWARC BEING THCSE 0.84 OF 260 NOT INCLUDED IN DONALC HORTON'S STUDY OF ALCHCLISM (351)	504	LEAN MORE TOWARD BEING THOSE 0.95 OF 140 NOT INCLUDED IN DONALD HORTCN'S STUDY OF ALCHOLISM (351)	42 7 218 133 XSQ= 9.52 PHI= 0.154 XP = 0.0020
505	DRIFT LESS TOWARC BEING THOSE 0.93 OF 260 NOT INCLUDED IN MERRILL JACKSON'S STUDY OF CRIMINAL LAW ANC MEDICINE (380)	505	DRIFT MORE TOWARD BEING THCSE 0.98 OF 140 NOT INCLUDED IN MERRILL JACKSON'S STUDY OF CRIMINAL LAW AND MEDICINE (380)	17 3 243 137 XSQ= 2.83 PHI= 0.084 XP = 0.0923
506	TILT LESS TOWARD BEING THOSE 0.88 OF 260 NOT INCLUDED IN LAMBERT, TRIANDIS, ANC WOLF'S STUDY OF SUPERNATURAL BEINGS (364)	506	TILT MORE TOWARD BEING THCSE 0.96 OF 140 NOT INCLUDED IN LAMBERT, TRIANDIS, AND WOLF'S STUDY OF SUPERNATURAL BEINGS (364)	30 6 230 134 XSQ= 4.99 PHI= 0.112 XP = 0.0255
507	TEND LESS TO BE THCSE 0.69 OF 260 NOT INCLUDED IN JAMES R. LEARY'S STUDY OF FCOD TABOCS (314)	507	TEND MORE TO BE THOSE 0.96 OF 140 NOT INCLUDED IN JAMES R. LEARY'S STUDY OF FOOD TABOOS (314)	80 6 180 134 XSQ= 36.26 PHI= 0.301 XP = 0.
510	TILT LESS TOWARD BEING THOSE 0.93 OF 260 NOT INCLUDED IN RACUL NARRCLL'S STUDY OF SCCIETAL CCMPLEXITY (380)	510	TILT MORE TOWARD BEING THOSE 0.99 OF 140 NOT INCLUDED IN RAOUL NARRCLL'S STUDY OF SOCIETAL COMPLEXITY (380)	18 2 242 138 XSQ= 4.68 PHI= 0.108 XP = 0.0304
511	TEND TO BE THOSE 0.65 OF 260 INCLUDED IN ROBERTS, ARTH AND BUSH'S SAMPLE CN GAMES, AS MCDIFIED BY THE ETHNOGRAPHIC ATLAS (189)	511	TEND TO BE THOSE 0.86 OF 140 NOT INCLUDED IN ROBERTS, ARTH AND BUSH'S SAMPLE ON GAMES, AS MODIFIED BY THE ETHNOGRAPHIC ATLAS (211)	169 20 91 120 XSQ= 91.88 PHI= 0.479 XP = 0.

512	LEAN LESS TOWARD BEING THOSE 0.89 OF 260 NOT INCLUDED IN SHIRLEY AND ROMNEY'S STUDY OF LOVE MAGIC (367)	512	LEAN MORE TOWARD BEING THOSE 0.97 OF 140 NOT INCLUDED IN SHIRLEY AND ROMNEY'S STUDY OF LOVE MAGIC (367)	29 4 231 136 XSQ= 7.22 PHI= 0.134 XP = 0.0072
513	TEND LESS TO BE THOSE 0.85 OF 260 NOT INCLUDED IN LEO W. SIMMONS' STUDY OF THE TREATMENT OF THE AGED (357)	513	TEND MORE TO BE THOSE 0.97 OF 140 NOT INCLUDED IN LEO W. SIMMONS' STUDY OF THE TREATMENT OF THE AGED (357)	39 4 221 136 XSQ= 12.75 PHI= 0.179 XP = 0.0004
514	TEND LESS TO BE THOSE 0.68 OF 260 NOT INCLUDED IN PHILIP E. SLATER'S STUDY OF NARCISSISM (310)	514	TEND MORE TO BE THOSE 0.94 OF 140 NOT INCLUDED IN PHILIP E. SLATER'S STUDY OF NARCISSISM (310)	82 8 178 132 XSQ= 33.34 PHI= 0.289 XP = 0.
515	TEND LESS TO BE THOSE 0.82 OF 260 NOT INCLUDED IN WILLIAM N. STEPHENS' SAMPLE ON AVOIDANCE RELATIONSHIPS (348)	515	TEND MORE TO BE THOSE 0.97 OF 140 NOT INCLUDED IN WILLIAM N. STEPHENS' SAMPLE ON AVOIDANCE RELATIONSHIPS (348)	48 4 212 136 XSQ= 18.24 PHI= 0.214 XP = 0.0000
516	TEND MORE TO BE THOSE 0.99 OF 260 INCLUDED IN GUY E. SWANSON'S SAMPLE ON LOCAL JURISDICTION, AS MODIFIED BY THE ETHNOGRAPHIC ATLAS (331)	516	TEND LESS TO BE THOSE 0.52 OF 140 INCLUDED IN GUY E. SWANSON'S SAMPLE ON LOCAL JURISDICTION, AS MODIFIED BY THE ETHNOGRAPHIC ATLAS (331)	258 73 2 67 XSQ= 138.07 PHI= 0.588 XP = 0.
518	TEND LESS TO BE THOSE 0.67 OF 260 NOT INCLUDED IN STANLEY H. UDY, JR.'S STUDY OF WORK ORGANIZATION (295)	518	TEND MORE TO BE THOSE 0.87 OF 140 NOT INCLUDED IN STANLEY H. UDY, JR.'S STUDY OF WORK ORGANIZATION (295)	87 18 173 122 XSQ= 18.91 PHI= 0.217 XP = 0.0000
519	DRIFT LESS TOWARD BEING THOSE 0.89 OF 260 NOT INCLUDED IN JOSEPH VEROFF'S STUDY OF ACHIEVEMENT MOTIVATION AS REVEALED IN FOLKTALES (364)	519	DRIFT MORE TOWARD BEING THOSE 0.95 OF 140 NOT INCLUDED IN JOSEPH VEROFF'S STUDY OF ACHIEVEMENT MOTIVATION AS REVEALED IN FOLKTALES (364)	29 7 231 133 XSQ= 3.49 PHI= 0.093 XP = 0.0617
520	LEAN LESS TOWARD BEING THOSE 0.87 OF 260 NOT INCLUDED IN BEATRICE BLYTH WHITING'S STUDY OF SORCERY (360)	520	LEAN MORE TOWARD BEING THOSE 0.96 OF 140 NOT INCLUDED IN BEATRICE BLYTH WHITING'S STUDY OF SORCERY (360)	35 5 225 135 XSQ= 8.82 PHI= 0.149 XP = 0.0030
521	LEAN LESS TOWARD BEING THOSE 0.85 OF 260 NOT INCLUDED IN JOHN W. M. WHITING'S STUDY OF SOCIALIZATION PROCESS AND PERSONALITY (353)	521	LEAN MORE TOWARD BEING THOSE 0.95 OF 140 NOT INCLUDED IN JOHN W. M. WHITING'S STUDY OF SOCIALIZATION PROCESS AND PERSONALITY (353)	40 7 220 133 XSQ= 8.49 PHI= 0.146 XP = 0.0036

522	TEND LESS TO BE THOSE NOT INCLUDED IN MARJORIE GRANT WHITING'S STUDY OF DIET (318)	0.74 OF 260	522	TEND MORE TO BE THOSE NOT INCLUDED IN MARJORIE GRANT WHITING'S STUDY OF DIET (318)	0.90 OF 140	68 14 192 126 XSQ= 13.60 PHI= 0.184 XP = 0.0002
523	LEAN LESS TOWARD BEING THOSE NOT INCLUDED IN WHITING AND CHILD'S STUDY OF CHILD TRAINING AND PERSONALITY (339)	0.81 OF 260	523	LEAN MORE TOWARD BEING THOSE NOT INCLUDED IN WHITING AND CHILD'S STUDY OF CHILD TRAINING AND PERSONALITY (339)	0.91 OF 140	49 12 211 128 XSQ= 6.66 PHI= 0.129 XP = 0.0099
524	LEAN LESS TOWARD BEING THOSE NOT INCLUDED IN WHITING, KLUCKHOHN, AND ANTHONY'S STUDY OF MALE INITIATION CEREMONIES (356)	0.85 OF 260	524	LEAN MORE TOWARD BEING THOSE NOT INCLUDED IN WHITING, KLUCKHOHN, AND ANTHONY'S STUDY OF MALE INITIATION CEREMONIES (356)	0.96 OF 140	38 6 222 134 XSQ= 8.89 PHI= 0.149 XP = 0.0029

518 CULTURES
INCLUDED IN STANLEY H. UDY, JR.'S
STUDY OF WORK ORGANIZATION (105)

518 CULTURES
NOT INCLUDED IN STANLEY H. UDY, JR.'S
STUDY OF WORK ORGANIZATION (295)

BACKGROUND ON PAGE 180

SUBJECT ONLY, F.C. 1-480 AND 527-536
BOTH SUBJECT AND PREDICATE, F.C. 481-526

105 IN LEFT COLUMN

ABIPON	ANDAMANESE	ARANDA	ASHANTI	ATAYAL	AWEIKOMA	AYMARA	AZANDE	BELU	BEMBA
BURMESE	BURUSHO	CAGABA	CAMAYURA	CAMBODIANS	CARIB	CAYAPA	CHAGGA	CHUKCHEE	COPR ESKIMO
CROW	CUNA	DARD	DOGON	FANG	FON	GILYAK	GOND	HAIDA	HANO
HAVASUPAI	HAZARA	HUTSUL	IBAN	IFUGAO	ILA	JIVARO	JUKUN	KABYLE	KAREN
KAZAK	KIKUYU	KURTATCHI	KWAKIUTL	LAPPS	LAU	MACASSARESE	MALAYS	MAM	MANGAIANS
MAORI	MARICOPA	MARSHALLESE	MBUNDU	MIN CHINESE	MURNGIN	MZAB	NAMA	NAMBICUARA	NAVAHO
NUER	NUPE	NYORO	OJIBWA	ONA	PAPAGO	PENOBSCOT	POPOLUCA	PUKAPUKA	RIFFIANS
ROMANS	RWALA	SAMOANS	SAMOYED	SANPOIL	SEMANG	SENIANG	SIRIONO	SOMALI	SONGHAI
SOTHO	TALLENSI	TAOS	TARAHUMARA	TENETEHARA	TERENA	THAI	THONGA	TIBETANS	TIKOPIA
TIMBIRA	TIV	TROBRIAND	TRUMAI	TUBATULABAL	TUPINAMBA	TURKANA	WAPISHANA	WINNEBAGO	WOGEO
WOLEAIANS	WOLOF	YAGUA	YOKUTS	ZUNI					

295 IN RIGHT COLUMN

---

33 TILT LESS TOWARD BEING THOSE 0.77 OF 105
WHERE THE NATURAL ENVIRONMENT IS
OTHER THAN 'VERY HARSH,' I.E., DESERT,
DESERT GRASSES AND SHRUBS, TUNDRA, OR
HIGH PLATEAU STEPPE (341) FWM

33 TILT MORE TOWARD BEING THOSE 0.88 OF 295
WHERE THE NATURAL ENVIRONMENT IS
OTHER THAN 'VERY HARSH,' I.E., DESERT,
DESERT GRASSES AND SHRUBS, TUNDRA, OR
HIGH PLATEAU STEPPE (341) FWM

24 35
81 260
XSQ= 6.59
PHI= 0.128
XP = 0.0102

62 TILT MORE TOWARD BEING THOSE 0.66 OF 105
WHERE HUSBANDRY OF SOME KIND
IS PRESENT (228)

62 TILT LESS TOWARD BEING THOSE 0.54 OF 295
WHERE HUSBANDRY OF SOME KIND
IS PRESENT (228)

69 159
36 136
XSQ= 3.94
PHI= 0.099
XP = 0.0471

63 DRIFT LESS TOWARD BEING THOSE 0.58 OF 69
WHERE HUSBANDRY, IF PRESENT,
IS PRINCIPALLY IN THE FORM OF
BOVINE, EQUINE, CAMEL-LIKE, OR DEER-LIKE
ANIMALS, RATHER THAN
PIGS, SHEEP, OR GOATS (152)

63 DRIFT MORE TOWARD BEING THOSE 0.71 OF 157
WHERE HUSBANDRY, IF PRESENT,
IS PRINCIPALLY IN THE FORM OF
BOVINE, EQUINE, CAMEL-LIKE, OR DEER-LIKE
ANIMALS, RATHER THAN
PIGS, SHEEP, OR GOATS (152)

40 112
29 45
XSQ= 3.31
PHI= -0.121
XP = 0.0690

77 TILT TOWARD BEING THOSE 0.82 OF 38
WHERE THE WRITING SYSTEM IS
MNEMONIC OR ABSENT, RATHER THAN BEING
ALPHABETIC-OR-PHONETIC (39) JMH

77 TILT TOWARD BEING THOSE 0.50 OF 16
WHERE THE WRITING SYSTEM IS
ALPHABETIC-OR-PHONETIC, RATHER THAN BEING
MNEMONIC OR ABSENT (15) JMH

7 8
31 8
XSQ= 4.13
PHI= -0.277
XP = 0.0420

129	TILT LESS TOWARD BEING THOSE WHERE WEAVING IS MAINLY DONE BY FEMALES (73)	0.56 OF 36	129	TILT MORE TOWARD BEING THOSE WHERE WEAVING IS MAINLY DONE BY FEMALES (73)	0.78 OF 68	16 15 20 53 XSQ= 4.62 PHI= 0.211 XP = 0.0316
136	TILT TOWARD BEING THOSE WHERE FULL-TIME ENTREPRENEURS ARE PRESENT (18) JV	0.78 OF 18	136	TILT TOWARD BEING THOSE WHERE FULL-TIME ENTREPRENEURS ARE ABSENT (14) JV	0.71 OF 14	14 4 4 10 XSQ= 5.88 PHI= 0.429 EP = 0.0110
149	DRIFT TOWARD BEING THOSE WHERE THE INCIDENCE OF THEFT IS HIGH (18) B-B-C	0.60 OF 25	149	DRIFT TOWARD BEING THOSE WHERE THE INCIDENCE OF THEFT IS LOW (19) B-B-C	0.75 OF 12	15 3 10 9 XSQ= 2.70 PHI= 0.270 EP = 0.0789
280	DRIFT TOWARD BEING THOSE WHERE THE COMPOSITE FERTILITY LEVEL IS HIGH (13) MN	0.78 OF 9	280	DRIFT TOWARD BEING THOSE WHERE THE COMPOSITE FERTILITY LEVEL IS LOW (12) MN	0.63 OF 16	7 6 2 10 XSQ= 2.30 PHI= 0.304 EP = 0.0968
285	TILT TOWARD BEING THOSE WHERE THE SEX TABOO DURING PREGNANCY IS ABSENT OR INFERRED ABSENT (17) BCA	0.70 OF 20	285	TILT TOWARD BEING THOSE WHERE THE SEX TABOO DURING PREGNANCY IS PRESENT (14) BCA	0.73 OF 11	6 8 14 3 XSQ= 3.65 PHI= -0.343 EP = 0.0309
320	LEAN TOWARD BEING THOSE WHERE THE DEGREE OF REDUCTION OF THE INFANT'S DRIVES IS HIGH (45) B-B-C	0.79 OF 39	320	LEAN TOWARD BEING THOSE WHERE THE DEGREE OF REDUCTION OF THE INFANT'S DRIVES IS LOW (24) B-B-C	0.53 OF 30	31 14 8 16 XSQ= 6.67 PHI= 0.311 XP = 0.0098
335	DRIFT TOWARD BEING THOSE WHERE INITIAL INDULGENCE OF DEPENDENCY IS HIGH (20) WNS	0.65 OF 23	335	DRIFT TOWARD BEING THOSE WHERE INITIAL INDULGENCE OF DEPENDENCY IS LOW (18) WNS	0.67 OF 15	15 5 8 10 XSQ= 2.53 PHI= 0.258 EP = 0.0960
365	DRIFT LESS TOWARD BEING THOSE WHERE THE TIME SPENT IN ADOLESCENT PEER GROUP ACTIVITY IS HIGH OR HIGH-MEDIUM (30) JKH	0.52 OF 23	365	DRIFT MORE TOWARD BEING THOSE WHERE THE TIME SPENT IN ADOLESCENT PEER GROUP ACTIVITY IS HIGH OR HIGH-MEDIUM (30) JKH	0.82 OF 22	12 18 11 4 XSQ= 3.21 PHI= -0.267 XP = 0.0731
368	TILT TOWARD BEING THOSE WHERE DISSOCIATION OF THE SEXES AT ADOLESCENCE IS HIGH OR MEDIUM (16) JKH	0.61 OF 18	368	TILT TOWARD BEING THOSE WHERE DISSOCIATION OF THE SEXES AT ADOLESCENCE IS LOW (21) JKH	0.74 OF 19	11 5 7 14 XSQ= 3.25 PHI= 0.296 EP = 0.0489

369	TILT MORE TOWARD BEING THOSE WHERE DISSOCIATION OF THE SEXES AT ADOLESCENCE, OR CUSTOMS OF INITIATION AT ADOLESCENCE, ARE PRESENT (42) JKH	0.87 OF 30	369	TILT LESS TOWARD BEING THOSE WHERE DISSOCIATION OF THE SEXES AT ADOLESCENCE, OR CUSTOMS OF INITIATION AT ADOLESCENCE, ARE PRESENT (42) JKH	0.59 OF 27	26 16 4 11 XSQ= 4.18 PHI= 0.271 XP = 0.0408
373	LEAN TOWARD BEING THOSE WHERE MALE INITIATION CEREMONIES AT PUBERTY ARE PRESENT (17) W-K-A	0.58 OF 24	373	LEAN TOWARD BEING THOSE WHERE MALE INITIATION CEREMONIES AT PUBERTY ARE ABSENT (27) W-K-A	0.85 OF 20	14 3 10 17 XSQ= 6.91 PHI= 0.396 XP = 0.0086
395	DRIFT TOWARD BEING THOSE WHERE BELIEF IN THE UNCLEANNESS OF WOMEN IS UNIMPORTANT OR ABSENT (15) LWS	0.61 OF 18	395	DRIFT TOWARD BEING THOSE WHERE BELIEF IN THE UNCLEANNESS OF WOMEN IS PRESENT (18) LWS	0.73 OF 15	7 11 11 4 XSQ= 2.65 PHI= -0.283 EP = 0.0801
406	TILT TOWARD BEING THOSE WHERE EXPLANATIONS OF ILLNESS OF AN AGGRESSION NATURE ARE PRESENT (28) W-C	0.59 OF 34	406	TILT TOWARD BEING THOSE WHERE EXPLANATIONS OF ILLNESS OF AN AGGRESSION NATURE ARE ABSENT (33) W-C	0.70 OF 27	20 8 14 19 XSQ= 4.06 PHI= 0.258 XP = 0.0440
441	TILT TOWARD BEING THOSE WHERE FEAR OF HUMAN BEINGS IS HIGH (29) W-C	0.62 OF 34	441	TILT TOWARD BEING THOSE WHERE FEAR OF HUMAN BEINGS IS LOW (32) W-C	0.70 OF 27	21 8 13 19 XSQ= 5.01 PHI= 0.287 XP = 0.0252
445	TILT TOWARD BEING THOSE WHERE SORCERY IS IMPORTANT (26) BBW,DH	0.70 OF 27	445	TILT TOWARD BEING THOSE WHERE SORCERY IS UNIMPORTANT (23) BBW,DH	0.68 OF 22	19 7 8 15 XSQ= 5.77 PHI= 0.343 XP = 0.0163
488	LEAN MORE TOWARD BEING THOSE ABOUT WHICH THE PRINCIPAL ETHNOGRAPHIES WERE PUBLISHED BEFORE 1950 (185)	0.87 OF 70	488	LEAN LESS TOWARD BEING THOSE ABOUT WHICH THE PRINCIPAL ETHNOGRAPHIES WERE PUBLISHED BEFORE 1950 (185)	0.66 OF 187	61 124 9 63 XSQ= 9.95 PHI= 0.197 XP = 0.0016
489	TEND LESS TO BE THOSE NOT INCLUDED IN CHARLES ACKERMAN'S STUDY OF DIVORCE (343)	0.70 OF 105	489	TEND MORE TO BE THOSE NOT INCLUDED IN CHARLES ACKERMAN'S STUDY OF DIVORCE (343)	0.92 OF 295	32 25 73 270 XSQ= 28.90 PHI= 0.269 XP = 0.0000
490	TEND LESS TO BE THOSE NOT INCLUDED IN ALBERT S. ANTHONY'S SAMPLE ON MALE INITIATION RITES (287)	0.50 OF 105	490	TEND MORE TO BE THOSE NOT INCLUDED IN ALBERT S. ANTHONY'S SAMPLE ON MALE INITIATION RITES (287)	0.79 OF 295	52 61 53 234 XSQ= 30.38 PHI= 0.276 XP = 0.

491	LEAN LESS TOWARD BEING THCSE 0.80 OF 105 NOT INCLUDED IN CORRIAN APPLE'S STUDY OF GRANDPARENTHCCD (352)	491	LEAN MORE TOWARD BEING THOSE 0.91 OF 295 NOT INCLUDED IN DORRIAN APPLE'S STUDY OF GRANDPARENTHOOD (352)	21 27 84 268 XSQ= 7.63 PHI= 0.138 XP = 0.0057
492	TEND LESS TO BE THCSE 0.78 OF 105 NOT INCLUDED IN BARBARA CHARTIER AYRES' STUDY OF FEMALE INITIATION RITES (361)	492	TEND MORE TO BE THOSE 0.95 OF 295 NOT INCLUDED IN BARBARA CHARTIER AYRES' STUDY OF FEMALE INITIATION RITES (361)	23 16 82 279 XSQ= 22.07 PHI= 0.235 XP = 0.0000
493	TEND LESS TO BE THCSE 0.58 OF 105 NOT INCLUDED IN BACCN, BARRY, AND CHILD'S STUDY OF CHILD REARING (322)	493	TEND MORE TO BE THOSE 0.88 OF 295 NOT INCLUDED IN BACON, BARRY, AND CHILD'S STUDY OF CHILD REARING (322)	44 34 61 261 XSQ= 43.61 PHI= 0.330 XP = 0.
494	TEND LESS TO BE THCSE 0.85 OF 105 NOT INCLUDED IN HERBERT M. BARRY III'S STUDY OF ART (371)	494	TEND MORE TO BE THOSE 0.96 OF 295 NOT INCLUDED IN HERBERT M. BARRY III'S STUDY OF ART (371)	16 13 89 282 XSQ= 11.95 PHI= 0.173 XP = 0.0005
495	TEND LESS TO BE THCSE 0.67 OF 105 NCT INCLUDED IN JUCITH K. BROWN'S STUDY OF FEMALE INITIATION RITES (335)	495	TEND MORE TO BE THOSE 0.90 OF 295 NOT INCLUDED IN JUDITH K. BROWN'S STUDY OF FEMALE INITIATION RITES (335)	35 30 70 265 XSQ= 28.85 PHI= 0.269 XP = 0.0000
496	TEND LESS TO BE THCSE 0.67 OF 105 NOT INCLUDED IN ROY G. C'ANDRADE'S STUDY OF DREAMS (345)	496	TEND MORE TO BE THOSE 0.93 OF 295 NOT INCLUDED IN ROY G. D'ANDRADE'S STUDY OF DREAMS (345)	35 20 70 275 XSQ= 43.83 PHI= 0.331 XP = 0.
497	TEND LESS TO BE THCSE 0.68 OF 105 NOT INCLUDED IN WILLIAM M. EVAN'S STUDY OF LAW (339)	497	TEND MORE TO BE THOSE 0.91 OF 295 NOT INCLUDED IN WILLIAM M. EVAN'S STUDY OF LAW (339)	34 27 71 268 XSQ= 30.56 PHI= 0.276 XP = 0.
498	TEND LESS TO BE THCSE 0.69 OF 105 NOT INCLUDED IN C. S. FORC'S STUDY OF SEX (349)	498	TEND MORE TO BE THOSE 0.94 OF 295 NOT INCLUDED IN C. S. FORD'S STUDY OF SEX (349)	33 18 72 277 XSQ= 42.40 PHI= 0.326 XP = 0.
499	TEND LESS TO BE THCSE 0.57 OF 105 NOT INCLUDED IN FORD ANC BEACH'S SAMPLE ON SEXUAL EXPRESSICN BY THE YCUNG (314)	499	TEND MORE TO BE THOSE 0.86 OF 295 NOT INCLUDED IN FORD AND BEACH'S SAMPLE ON SEXUAL EXPRESSION BY THE YOUNG (314)	45 41 60 254 XSQ= 36.78 PHI= 0.303 XP = 0.

500	TEND LESS TO BE THCSE 0.74 OF 105 NOT INCLUDED IN FREEMAN ANC WINCH'S STUDY OF SCCIETAL CCMPLEXITY (360)	500	TEND MORE TO BE THOSE 0.96 OF 295 NOT INCLUDED IN FREEMAN AND WINCH'S STUDY OF SOCIETAL COMPLEXITY (360)	27 13 78 282 XSQ= 36.73 PHI= 0.303 XP = 0.
501	TEND LESS TO BE THCSE 0.62 OF 105 NOT INCLUDED IN JOAN FRIENCLY GOOCMAN'S STUDY CF ASCETIC MCURNING BEHAVICR (333)	501	TEND MORE TO BE THOSE 0.91 OF 295 NOT INCLUDED IN JOAN FRIENDLY GCODMAN'S STUDY OF ASCETIC MOURNING BEHAVIOR (333)	40 27 65 268 XSQ= 44.47 PHI= 0.333 XP = 0.
502	TEND LESS TO BE THCSE 0.71 OF 105 NOT INCLUDED IN JOHN K. HARLEY'S STUDY OF ADOLESCENT PEER CROUPS (343)	502	TEND MORE TO BE THOSE 0.91 OF 295 NOT INCLUDED IN JOHN K. HARLEY'S STUDY OF ADOLESCENT PEER GRCUPS (343)	30 27 75 268 XSQ= 22.33 PHI= 0.236 XP = 0.0000
503	TEND LESS TO BE THCSE 0.64 OF 105 NOT INCLUDED IN JCHN M. HICKMAN'S STUDY CF THE FOLK-URBAN CCNTINUUM (346)	503	TEND MORE TO BE THOSE 0.95 OF 295 NOT INCLUDED IN JOHN M. HICKMAN'S STUDY OF THE FOLK-URBAN CONTINUUM (346)	38 16 67 279 XSQ= 60.16 PHI= 0.388 XP = 0.
504	TEND LESS TO BE THCSE 0.73 OF 105 NOT INCLUDED IN DONALD HORTON'S STUDY OF ALCHCLISM (351)	504	TEND MORE TO BE THOSE 0.93 OF 295 NOT INCLUDED IN DONALD HORTON'S STUDY OF ALCHOLISM (351)	28 21 77 274 XSQ= 25.74 PHI= 0.254 XP = 0.0000
505	TEND LESS TO BE THCSE 0.88 OF 105 NOT INCLUDED IN MERRILL JACKSON'S STUDY OF CRIMINAL LAW ANC MEDICINE (380)	505	TEND MORE TO BE THOSE 0.98 OF 295 NOT INCLUDED IN MERRILL JACKSON'S STUDY OF CRIMINAL LAW AND MEDICINE (380)	13 7 92 288 XSQ= 14.29 PHI= 0.189 XP = 0.0002
506	TEND LESS TO BE THCSE 0.77 OF 105 NOT INCLUDED IN LAMBERT, TRIANDIS, ANC WOLF'S STUDY OF SUPERNATURAL BEINCS (364)	506	TEND MORE TO BE THOSE 0.96 OF 295 NOT INCLUDED IN LAMBERT, TRIANDIS, AND WOLF'S STUDY OF SUPERNATURAL BEINGS (364)	24 12 81 283 XSQ= 31.13 PHI= 0.279 XP = 0.
507	TEND TO BE THCSE 0.51 OF 105 INCLUDED IN JAMES R. LEARY'S STUDY OF FCOD TABOCS (86)	507	TEND TO BE THOSE 0.89 OF 295 NOT INCLUDED IN JAMES R. LEARY'S STUDY OF FOOD TABOOS (314)	54 32 51 263 XSQ= 73.17 PHI= 0.428 XP = 0.
508	TEND LESS TO BE THCSE 0.79 OF 105 NOT INCLUDED IN DAVID C. MCCLELLAND'S STUDY OF ACHIEVEMENT MOTIVATION (360)	508	TEND MORE TO BE THOSE 0.94 OF 295 NOT INCLUDED IN DAVID C. MCCLELLAND'S STUDY OF ACHIEVEMENT MOTIVATION (360)	22 18 83 277 XSQ= 17.36 PHI= 0.208 XP = 0.0000

510	LEAN LESS TOWARD BEING THOSE 0.89 OF 105 NOT INCLUDED IN RAOUL NARROLL'S STUDY OF SOCIETAL COMPLEXITY (380)	510	LEAN MORE TOWARD BEING THOSE 0.97 OF 295 NOT INCLUDED IN RAOUL NARROLL'S STUDY OF SOCIETAL COMPLEXITY (380)	12 8 93 287 XSQ= 10.62 PHI= 0.163 XP = 0.0011
511	TEND TO BE THOSE 0.68 OF 105 INCLUDED IN ROBERTS, ARTH AND BUSH'S SAMPLE ON GAMES, AS MODIFIED BY THE ETHNOGRAPHIC ATLAS (189)	511	TEND TO BE THOSE 0.60 OF 295 NOT INCLUDED IN ROBERTS, ARTH AND BUSH'S SAMPLE ON GAMES, AS MODIFIED BY THE ETHNOGRAPHIC ATLAS (211)	71 118 34 177 XSQ= 22.60 PHI= 0.238 XP = 0.0000
512	TEND LESS TO BE THOSE 0.82 OF 105 NOT INCLUDED IN SHIRLEY AND ROMNEY'S STUDY OF LOVE MAGIC (367)	512	TEND MORE TO BE THOSE 0.95 OF 295 NOT INCLUDED IN SHIRLEY AND ROMNEY'S STUDY OF LOVE MAGIC (367)	19 14 86 281 XSQ= 16.51 PHI= 0.203 XP = 0.0000
513	TEND LESS TO BE THOSE 0.79 OF 105 NOT INCLUDED IN LEO W. SIMMONS' STUDY OF THE TREATMENT OF THE AGED (357)	513	TEND MORE TO BE THOSE 0.93 OF 295 NOT INCLUDED IN LEO W. SIMMONS' STUDY OF THE TREATMENT OF THE AGED (357)	22 21 83 274 XSQ= 14.04 PHI= 0.187 XP = 0.0002
514	TEND LESS TO BE THOSE 0.52 OF 105 NOT INCLUDED IN PHILIP E. SLATER'S STUDY OF NARCISSISM (310)	514	TEND MORE TO BE THOSE 0.86 OF 295 NOT INCLUDED IN PHILIP E. SLATER'S STUDY OF NARCISSISM (310)	50 40 55 255 XSQ= 49.58 PHI= 0.352 XP = 0.
515	TEND LESS TO BE THOSE 0.72 OF 105 NOT INCLUDED IN WILLIAM N. STEPHENS' SAMPLE ON AVOIDANCE RELATIONSHIPS (348)	515	TEND MORE TO BE THOSE 0.92 OF 295 NOT INCLUDED IN WILLIAM N. STEPHENS' SAMPLE ON AVOIDANCE RELATIONSHIPS (348)	29 23 76 272 XSQ= 25.18 PHI= 0.251 XP = 0.0000
516	LEAN MORE TOWARD BEING THOSE 0.91 OF 105 INCLUDED IN GUY E. SWANSON'S SAMPLE ON LOCAL JURISDICTION, AS MODIFIED BY THE ETHNOGRAPHIC ATLAS (331)	516	LEAN LESS TOWARD BEING THOSE 0.80 OF 295 INCLUDED IN GUY E. SWANSON'S SAMPLE ON LOCAL JURISDICTION, AS MODIFIED BY THE ETHNOGRAPHIC ATLAS (331)	96 235 9 60 XSQ= 6.71 PHI= 0.130 XP = 0.0096
517	TEND MORE TO BE THOSE 0.83 OF 105 INCLUDED IN GUY E. SWANSON'S SAMPLE ON HIGH GODS, AS MODIFIED BY THE ETHNOGRAPHIC ATLAS (260)	517	TEND LESS TO BE THOSE 0.59 OF 295 INCLUDED IN GUY E. SWANSON'S SAMPLE ON HIGH GODS, AS MODIFIED BY THE ETHNOGRAPHIC ATLAS (260)	87 173 18 122 XSQ= 18.91 PHI= 0.217 XP = 0.0000
519	TEND LESS TO BE THOSE 0.82 OF 105 NOT INCLUDED IN JOSEPH VEROFF'S STUDY OF ACHIEVEMENT MOTIVATION AS REVEALED IN FOLKTALES (364)	519	TEND MORE TO BE THOSE 0.94 OF 295 NOT INCLUDED IN JOSEPH VEROFF'S STUDY OF ACHIEVEMENT MOTIVATION AS REVEALED IN FOLKTALES (364)	19 17 86 278 XSQ= 12.91 PHI= 0.180 XP = 0.0003

	Tend less			Tend more		
520	TEND LESS TO BE THCSE NOT INCLUDED IN BEATRICE BLYTH WHITING'S STUDY OF SCRCERY (360)	0.77 OF 105	520	TEND MORE TO BE THOSE NOT INCLUDED IN BEATRICE BLYTH WHITING'S STUDY OF SORCERY (360)	0.95 OF 295	24 16 81 279 XSQ= 24.25 PHI= 0.246 XP = 0.0000
521	TEND LESS TO BE THCSE NOT INCLUDED IN JOHN W. M. WHITING'S STUDY CF SCCIALIZATION PROCESS AND PERSCNALITY (353)	0.74 OF 105	521	TEND MORE TO BE THOSE NOT INCLUDED IN JOHN W. M. WHITING'S STUDY OF SOCIALIZATION PROCESS AND PERSONALITY (353)	0.93 OF 295	27 20 78 275 XSQ= 24.98 PHI= 0.250 XP = 0.0000
522	TEND LESS TO BE THCSE NOT INCLUDED IN MARJCRIE GRANT WHITING'S STUDY OF DIET (318)	0.56 OF 105	522	TEND MORE TO BE THOSE NOT INCLUDED IN MARJORIE GRANT WHITING'S STUDY OF DIET (318)	0.88 OF 295	46 36 59 259 XSQ= 45.55 PHI= 0.337 XP = 0.
523	TEND LESS TO BE THCSE NOT INCLUDED IN WHITING AND CHILD'S STUDY OF CHILD TRAINING AND PERSCNALITY (339)	0.68 OF 105	523	TEND MORE TO BE THOSE NOT INCLUDED IN WHITING AND CHILD'S STUDY OF CHILD TRAINING AND PERSONALITY (339)	0.91 OF 295	34 27 71 268 XSQ= 30.56 PHI= 0.276 XP = 0.
524	TEND LESS TO BE THCSE NOT INCLUDED IN WHITING, KLUCKHCHN, ANC ANTHONY'S STUDY OF MALE INITIATION CEREMONIES (356)	0.77 OF 105	524	TEND MORE TO BE THOSE NOT INCLUDED IN WHITING, KLUCKHOHN, AND ANTHONY'S STUDY OF MALE INITIATION CEREMONIES (356)	0.93 OF 295	24 20 81 275 XSQ= 18.84 PHI= 0.217 XP = 0.0000

519 CULTURES
INCLUDED IN JOSEPH VEROFF'S
STUDY OF ACHIEVEMENT MOTIVATION AS
REVEALED IN FOLKTALES (36)

519 CULTURES
NOT INCLUDED IN JOSEPH VEROFF'S
STUDY OF ACHIEVEMENT MOTIVATION AS
REVEALED IN FOLKTALES (364)

BACKGROUND ON PAGE 180

SUBJECT ONLY, F.C. 1-480 AND 527-536
BOTH SUBJECT AND PREDICATE, F.C. 481-526

36 IN LEFT COLUMN

AINU	ARANDA	ARAPESH	ARAUCANIANS	ASHANTI	AZANDE	CHAGGA	CHENCHU	CHIR-APACHE	CHUKCHEE
COMANCHE	CROW	CUNA	KASKA	KIKUYU	KORYAK	KURTATCHI	LEPCHA	MANDAN	MARQUESANS
MASAI	MBUNDU	NAVAHO	OJIBWA	PAPAGO	PUKAPUKA	SOTHO	TENETEHARA	TETON	THONGA
TUCUNA	VENDA	WICHITA	WINNEBAGO	WOLEAIANS	YORUBA				

364 IN RIGHT COLUMN

4	IN ALL CASES ARE THOSE LOCATED OUTSIDE OF THE CIRCUM-MEDITERRANEAN (355)	1.00 OF 36	4	TILT LESS TOWARD BEING THOSE LOCATED OUTSIDE OF THE CIRCUM-MEDITERRANEAN (355)	0.88 OF 364		0 45 36 319 XSQ= 3.85 PHI= -0.098 XP = 0.0497
8	DRIFT LESS TOWARD BEING THOSE LOCATED OUTSIDE OF NORTH AMERICA (330)	0.69 OF 36	8	DRIFT MORE TOWARD BEING THOSE LOCATED OUTSIDE OF NORTH AMERICA (330)	0.84 OF 364		11 59 25 305 XSQ= 3.73 PHI= 0.097 XP = 0.0535
36	TILT LESS TOWARD BEING THOSE WHERE THE NATURAL ENVIRONMENT IS OTHER THAN 'VERY HARSH,' OR SUB-TROPICAL BUSH, OR TEMPERATE GRASSLAND (292) FWM	0.56 OF 36	36	TILT MORE TOWARD BEING THOSE WHERE THE NATURAL ENVIRONMENT IS OTHER THAN 'VERY HARSH,' OR SUB-TROPICAL BUSH, OR TEMPERATE GRASSLAND (292) FWM	0.75 OF 364		16 92 20 272 XSQ= 5.17 PHI= 0.114 XP = 0.0229
62	DRIFT MORE TOWARD BEING THOSE WHERE HUSBANDRY OF SOME KIND IS PRESENT (228)	0.72 OF 36	62	DRIFT LESS TOWARD BEING THOSE WHERE HUSBANDRY OF SOME KIND IS PRESENT (228)	0.55 OF 364		26 202 10 162 XSQ= 3.09 PHI= 0.088 XP = 0.0788
109	DRIFT MORE TOWARD BEING THOSE WHERE CASTES ARE ABSENT (317)	0.97 OF 35	109	DRIFT LESS TOWARD BEING THOSE WHERE CASTES ARE ABSENT (317)	0.85 OF 333		1 50 34 283 XSQ= 2.97 PHI= -0.090 XP = 0.0849

334	TILT TOWARD BEING THOSE 0.64 OF 36 WHERE THE INDULGENCE OF THE CHILD IS LOW (38) B-B-C	334	TILT TOWARD BEING THOSE 0.64 OF 42 WHERE THE INDULGENCE OF THE CHILD IS HIGH (40) B-B-C	13 27 23 15 XSQ= 5.08 PHI= -0.255 XP = 0.0242
349	TILT TOWARD BEING THOSE 0.70 OF 30 WHERE THE CHILD'S INFERRED ANXIETY OVER NON-PERFORMANCE OF ACHIEVEMENT BEHAVIOR IS HIGH (34) B-B-C	349	TILT TOWARD BEING THOSE 0.59 OF 32 WHERE THE CHILD'S INFERRED ANXIETY OVER NON-PERFORMANCE OF ACHIEVEMENT BEHAVIOR IS LOW (28) B-B-C	21 13 9 19 XSQ= 4.27 PHI= 0.263 XP = 0.0387
350	DRIFT TOWARD BEING THOSE 0.70 OF 30 WHERE THE CHILD'S INFERRED ANXIETY OVER PERFORMANCE OF ACHIEVEMENT BEHAVIOR IS HIGH (34) B-B-C	350	DRIFT TOWARD BEING THOSE 0.57 OF 30 WHERE THE CHILD'S INFERRED ANXIETY OVER PERFORMANCE OF ACHIEVEMENT BEHAVIOR IS LOW (26) B-B-C	21 13 9 17 XSQ= 3.33 PHI= 0.235 XP = 0.0682
386	DRIFT TOWARD BEING THOSE 0.75 OF 20 WHERE SEXUAL EXPRESSION BY THE YOUNG IS RESTRICTED OR SEMI-RESTRICTED (46) F-B	386	DRIFT TOWARD BEING THOSE 0.53 OF 66 WHERE SEXUAL EXPRESSION BY THE YOUNG IS PERMITTED (40) F-B	15 31 5 35 XSQ= 3.79 PHI= 0.210 XP = 0.0517
421	DRIFT TOWARD BEING THOSE 0.60 OF 25 WHERE KILLING, TORTURING, OR MUTILATING OF THE ENEMY IS STRONGLY OR MODERATELY EMPHASIZED (37) PES	421	DRIFT TOWARD BEING THOSE 0.63 OF 59 WHERE KILLING, TORTURING, OR MUTILATING OF THE ENEMY IS NEGLIGIBLY EMPHASIZED (47) PES	15 22 10 37 XSQ= 2.81 PHI= 0.183 XP = 0.0936
428	LEAN TOWARD BEING THOSE 0.78 OF 9 WHERE A HIGH GOD, IF PRESENT AND ACTIVE, DOES NOT SUPPORT HUMAN MORALITY, RATHER THAN SUPPORTING IT (26) GES,EA	428	LEAN TOWARD BEING THOSE 0.76 OF 78 WHERE A HIGH GOD, IF PRESENT AND ACTIVE, SUPPORTS HUMAN MORALITY, RATHER THAN NOT SUPPORTING IT (61) GES,EA	2 59 7 19 XSQ= 8.59 PHI= -0.314 XP = 0.0034
432	IN ALL CASES ARE THOSE 1.00 OF 7 WHERE AN ATTRACTIVE AFTERLIFE IS BELIEVED IN (27) LWS	432	DRIFT LESS TOWARD BEING THOSE 0.65 OF 31 WHERE AN ATTRACTIVE AFTERLIFE IS BELIEVED IN (27) LWS	7 20 0 11 XSQ= 1.98 PHI= 0.228 EP = 0.0842
433	TILT TOWARD BEING THOSE 0.56 OF 9 WHERE BELIEF IN REINCARNATION IS PRESENT (10) GES	433	TILT TOWARD BEING THOSE 0.83 OF 29 WHERE BELIEF IN REINCARNATION IS ABSENT (28) GES	5 5 4 24 XSQ= 3.41 PHI= 0.300 EP = 0.0362
450	LEAN MORE TOWARD BEING THOSE 0.95 OF 21 WHERE THE OBSERVATION OF FOOD TABOOS IS HIGH OR MEDIUM, RATHER THAN LOW (60) JRL	450	LEAN LESS TOWARD BEING THOSE 0.62 OF 65 WHERE THE OBSERVATION OF FOOD TABOOS IS HIGH OR MEDIUM, RATHER THAN LOW (60) JRL	20 40 1 25 XSQ= 7.02 PHI= 0.286 XP = 0.0080

```
469  IN ALL CASES ARE THOSE           1.00 OF  17     469  TILT LESS TOWARD BEING THOSE   0.70 OF  37          17   26
     WHERE CONTACT WITH CTHER CULTURES                     WHERE CONTACT WITH OTHER CULTURES                     0   11
     IS FREQUENT OR REGULAR, RATHER THAN                   IS FREQUENT OR REGULAR, RATHER THAN            XSQ=    4.65
     IRREGULAR  (43) JMH                                   IRREGULAR  (43) JMH                            PHI=   0.293
                                                                                                          XP =  0.0311

480  DRIFT TOWARD BEING THCSE         0.75 OF  12     480  DRIFT TOWARD BEING THOSE       0.65 OF  17           3   11
     WHERE COMPLEXITY OF ARTISTIC DESIGN                   WHERE COMPLEXITY OF ARTISTIC DESIGN                   9    6
     IS LCW  (15) HB                                       IS HIGH  (14) HB                               XSQ=    2.99
                                                                                                          PHI=  -0.321
                                                                                                          EP =  0.0604

489  TEND LESS TO BE THCSE            0.64 OF  36     489  TEND MORE TO BE THOSE          0.88 OF 364          13   44
     NOT INCLUDED IN CHARLES ACKERMAN'S                    NOT INCLUDED IN CHARLES ACKERMAN'S                   23  320
     STUDY OF DIVORCE  (343)                               STUDY OF DIVORCE  (343)                        XSQ=   13.57
                                                                                                          PHI=   0.184
                                                                                                          XP =  0.0002

490  TEND TO BE THOSE                 0.67 OF  36     490  TEND TO BE THOSE               0.76 OF 364          24   89
     INCLUDED IN ALBERT S. ANTHONY'S                       NOT INCLUDED IN ALBERT S. ANTHONY'S                  12  275
     SAMPLE ON MALE INITIATION RITES  (113)                SAMPLE ON MALE INITIATION RITES  (287)         XSQ=   26.76
                                                                                                          PHI=   0.259
                                                                                                          XP =  0.0000

491  TEND LESS TO BE THCSE            0.64 OF  36     491  TEND MORE TO BE THOSE          0.90 OF 364          13   35
     NOT INCLUDED IN DORRIAN APPLE'S                       NOT INCLUDED IN DORRIAN APPLE'S                      23  329
     STUDY OF GRANDPARENTHCOD  (352)                       STUDY OF GRANDPARENTHOOD  (352)                XSQ=   19.34
                                                                                                          PHI=   0.220
                                                                                                          XP =  0.0000

492  TEND LESS TO BE THCSE            0.58 OF  36     492  TEND MORE TO BE THOSE          0.93 OF 364          15   24
     NOT INCLUDED IN BARBARA CHARTIER AYRES'               NOT INCLUDED IN BARBARA CHARTIER AYRES'              21  340
     STUDY OF FEMALE INITIATION RITES  (361)               STUDY OF FEMALE INITIATION RITES  (361)        XSQ=   41.90
                                                                                                          PHI=   0.324
                                                                                                          XP =  0.

493  IN ALL CASES ARE THOSE           1.00 OF  36     493  TEND TO BE THOSE               0.88 OF 364          36   42
     INCLUDED IN                                           NOT INCLUDED IN                                       0  322
     BACCN, BARRY, AND CHILD'S                             BACON, BARRY, AND CHILD'S                      XSQ=  157.73
     STUDY OF CHILD REARING  (78)                          STUDY OF CHILD REARING  (322)                  PHI=   0.628
                                                                                                          XP =  0.

494  TEND LESS TO BE THCSE            0.67 OF  36     494  TEND MORE TO BE THOSE          0.95 OF 364          12   17
     NOT INCLUDED IN HERBERT M. BARRY III'S                NOT INCLUDED IN HERBERT M. BARRY III'S               24  347
     STUDY OF ART  (371)                                   STUDY OF ART  (371)                            XSQ=   35.88
                                                                                                          PHI=   0.299
                                                                                                          XP =  0.

495  TEND LESS TO BE THCSE            0.61 OF  36     495  TEND MORE TO BE THOSE          0.86 OF 364          14   51
     NOT INCLUDED IN JUDITH K. BROWN'S                     NOT INCLUDED IN JUDITH K. BROWN'S                    22  313
     STUDY OF FEMALE INITIATION RITES  (335)               STUDY OF FEMALE INITIATION RITES  (335)        XSQ=   13.13
                                                                                                          PHI=   0.181
                                                                                                          XP =  0.0003
```

```
496  TEND LESS TO BE THCSE           0.56 OF  36     496  TEND MORE TO BE THOSE           0.89 OF 364          16   39
     NOT INCLUDED IN ROY G. D'ANDRADE'S                   NOT INCLUDED IN ROY G. D'ANDRADE'S                   20  325
     STUDY CF DREAMS  (345)                               STUDY OF DREAMS  (345)                         XSQ=    28.65
                                                                                                         PHI=    0.268
                                                                                                         XP =   0.0000

498  TEND LESS TO BE THCSE           0.61 OF  36     498  TEND MORE TO BE THOSE           0.90 OF 364          14   37
     NOT INCLUDED IN C. S. FORC'S                         NOT INCLUDED IN C. S. FORD'S                         22  327
     STUDY OF SEX  (349)                                  STUDY OF SEX  (349)                            XSQ=    21.78
                                                                                                         PHI=    0.233
                                                                                                         XP =   0.0000

499  TEND TO BE THOSE                0.56 OF  36     499  TEND TO BE THOSE                0.82 OF 364          20   66
     INCLUDED IN FCRC ANC BEACF'S                         NOT INCLUDED IN FORD AND BEACH'S                     16  298
     SAMPLE CN SEXUAL EXPRESSICN                          SAMPLE ON SEXUAL EXPRESSION                    XSQ=    25.01
     BY THE YOUNG  (86)                                   BY THE YOUNG  (314)                            PHI=    0.250
                                                                                                         XP =   0.0000

500  TEND LESS TO BE THCSE           0.61 OF  36     500  TEND MORE TO BE THOSE           0.93 OF 364          14   26
     NOT INCLUDED IN FREEMAN ANC WINCH'S                  NOT INCLUDED IN FREEMAN AND WINCH'S                  22  338
     STUDY OF SCCIETAL COMPLEXITY  (360)                  STUDY OF SOCIETAL COMPLEXITY  (360)            XSQ=    33.24
                                                                                                         PHI=    0.288
                                                                                                         XP =   0.

501  TEND TO BE THCSE                0.58 OF  36     501  TEND TO BE THOSE                0.87 OF 364          21   46
     INCLUDED IN JOAN FRIENCLY GOOCMAN'S                  NOT INCLUDED IN JOAN FRIENDLY GOODMAN'S              15  318
     STUDY OF ASCETIC MCURNING BEHAVIOR  (67)             STUDY OF                                       XSQ=    45.83
                                                          ASCETIC MOURNING BEHAVIOR  (333)               PHI=    0.339
                                                                                                         XP =   0.

502  TILT LESS TOWARD BEING THOSE    0.72 OF  36     502  TILT MORE TOWARD BEING THOSE    0.87 OF 364          10   47
     NOT INCLUDED IN JOHN K. HARLEY'S                     NOT INCLUDED IN JOHN K. HARLEY'S                     26  317
     STUDY OF ADOLESCENT. PEER GROUPS  (343)              STUDY OF ADOLESCENT PEER GROUPS  (343)         XSQ=     4.77
                                                                                                         PHI=    0.109
                                                                                                         XP =   0.0290

503  TEND LESS TO BE THCSE           0.53 OF  36     503  TEND MORE TO BE THOSE           0.90 OF 364          17   37
     NOT INCLUDED IN JOHN M. HICKMAN'S                    NOT INCLUDED IN JOHN M. HICKMAN'S                    19  327
     STUDY OF THE FOLK-URBAN CONTINUUM  (346)             STUDY OF THE FOLK-URBAN CONTINUUM  (346)       XSQ=    35.42
                                                                                                         PHI=    0.298
                                                                                                         XP =   0.

504  TEND LESS TO BE THCSE           0.67 OF  36     504  TEND MORE TO BE THOSE           0.90 OF 364          12   37
     NOT INCLUDED IN DONALC HORTON'S                      NOT INCLUDED IN DONALD HORTON'S                      24  327
     STUDY OF ALCHCLISM  (351)                            STUDY OF ALCHOLISM  (351)                      XSQ=    14.27
                                                                                                         PHI=    0.189
                                                                                                         XP =   0.0002

506  TEND TC BE THOSE                0.50 OF  36     506  TEND TO BE THOSE                0.95 OF 364          18   18
     INCLUDED IN                                          NOT INCLUDED IN                                      18  346
     LAMBERT, TRIANDIS, AND WOLF'S                        LAMBERT, TRIANDIS, AND WOLF'S                  XSQ=    75.79
     STUDY OF SUPERNATURAL BEINGS  (36)                   STUDY OF SUPERNATURAL BEINGS  (364)            PHI=    0.435
                                                                                                         XP =   0.
```

507	TEND TO BE THOSE INCLUDED IN JAMES R. LEARY'S STUDY OF FOOD TABOOS (86)	0.58 OF 36	507	TEND TO BE THOSE NOT INCLUDED IN JAMES R. LEARY'S STUDY OF FOOD TABOOS (314)	0.82 OF 364	21 65 15 299 XSQ= 29.45 PHI= 0.271 XP = 0.0000
508	IN ALL CASES ARE THOSE INCLUDED IN DAVID C. MCCLELLAND'S STUDY OF ACHIEVEMENT MOTIVATION (40)	1.00 OF 36	508	TEND TO BE THOSE NOT INCLUDED IN DAVID C. MCCLELLAND'S STUDY OF ACHIEVEMENT MOTIVATION (360)	0.99 OF 364	36 4 0 360 XSQ= 345.14 PHI= 0.929 XP = 0.
509	TILT LESS TOWARD BEING THOSE NOT INCLUDED IN MONI NAG'S STUDY OF FERTILITY (375)	0.83 OF 36	509	TILT MORE TOWARD BEING THOSE NOT INCLUDED IN MONI NAG'S STUDY OF FERTILITY (375)	0.95 OF 364	6 19 30 345 XSQ= 5.50 PHI= 0.117 XP = 0.0190
511	TEND TO BE THOSE INCLUDED IN ROBERTS, ARTH AND BUSH'S SAMPLE ON GAMES, AS MODIFIED BY THE ETHNOGRAPHIC ATLAS (189)	0.75 OF 36	511	TEND TO BE THOSE NOT INCLUDED IN ROBERTS, ARTH AND BUSH'S SAMPLE ON GAMES, AS MODIFIED BY THE ETHNOGRAPHIC ATLAS (211)	0.55 OF 364	27 162 9 202 XSQ= 11.03 PHI= 0.166 XP = 0.0009
512	TEND LESS TO BE THOSE NOT INCLUDED IN SHIRLEY AND ROMNEY'S STUDY OF LOVE MAGIC (367)	0.64 OF 36	512	TEND MORE TO BE THOSE NOT INCLUDED IN SHIRLEY AND ROMNEY'S STUDY OF LOVE MAGIC (367)	0.95 OF 364	13 20 23 344 XSQ= 36.63 PHI= 0.303 XP = 0.
514	TEND TO BE THOSE INCLUDED IN PHILIP E. SLATER'S STUDY OF NARCISSISM (90)	0.69 OF 36	514	TEND TO BE THOSE NOT INCLUDED IN PHILIP E. SLATER'S STUDY OF NARCISSISM (310)	0.82 OF 364	25 65 11 299 XSQ= 47.08 PHI= 0.343 XP = 0.
515	TEND LESS TO BE THOSE NOT INCLUDED IN WILLIAM N. STEPHENS' SAMPLE ON AVOIDANCE RELATIONSHIPS (348)	0.56 OF 36	515	TEND MORE TO BE THOSE NOT INCLUDED IN WILLIAM N. STEPHENS' SAMPLE ON AVOIDANCE RELATIONSHIPS (348)	0.90 OF 364	16 36 20 328 XSQ= 31.60 PHI= 0.281 XP = 0.
517	DRIFT MORE TOWARD BEING THOSE INCLUDED IN GUY E. SWANSON'S SAMPLE ON HIGH GODS, AS MODIFIED BY THE ETHNOGRAPHIC ATLAS (260)	0.81 OF 36	517	DRIFT LESS TOWARD BEING THOSE INCLUDED IN GUY E. SWANSON'S SAMPLE ON HIGH GODS, AS MODIFIED BY THE ETHNOGRAPHIC ATLAS (260)	0.63 OF 364	29 231 7 133 XSQ= 3.49 PHI= 0.093 XP = 0.0617
518	TEND TO BE THOSE INCLUDED IN STANLEY H. UDY, JR.'S STUDY OF WORK ORGANIZATION (105)	0.53 OF 36	518	TEND TO BE THOSE NOT INCLUDED IN STANLEY H. UDY, JR.'S STUDY OF WORK ORGANIZATION (295)	0.76 OF 364	19 86 17 278 XSQ= 12.91 PHI= 0.180 XP = 0.0003

519/

```
520  TEND LESS TO BE THOSE               0.72 OF  36     520  TEND MORE TO BE THOSE            0.92 OF 364        10   30
     NOT INCLUDED IN                                          NOT INCLUDED IN                                      26  334
     BEATRICE BLYTH WHITING'S                                 BEATRICE BLYTH WHITING'S                       XSQ=   11.81
     STUDY OF SORCERY  (360)                                  STUDY OF SORCERY  (360)                        PHI=   0.172
                                                                                                             XP =  0.0006

521  TEND TO BE THOSE                    0.75 OF  36     521  TEND TO BE THOSE                 0.95 OF 364        27   20
     INCLUDED IN JOHN W. M. WHITING'S                         NOT INCLUDED IN JOHN W. M. WHITING'S                  9  344
     STUDY OF SOCIALIZATION                                   STUDY OF SOCIALIZATION                         XSQ=  146.00
     PROCESS AND PERSONALITY  (47)                            PROCESS AND PERSONALITY  (353)                 PHI=   0.604
                                                                                                             XP =  0.

522  TEND TO BE THOSE                    0.72 OF  36     522  TEND TO BE THOSE                 0.85 OF 364        26   56
     INCLUDED IN                                              NOT INCLUDED IN                                      10  308
     MARJORIE GRANT WHITING'S                                 MARJORIE GRANT WHITING'S                       XSQ=   61.50
     STUDY OF DIET  (82)                                      STUDY OF DIET  (318)                           PHI=   0.392
                                                                                                             XP =  0.

523  TEND TO BE THOSE                    0.50 OF  36     523  TEND TO BE THOSE                 0.88 OF 364        18   43
     INCLUDED IN WHITING AND CHILD'S                          NOT INCLUDED IN WHITING AND CHILD'S                  18  321
     STUDY OF CHILD TRAINING                                  STUDY OF CHILD TRAINING                        XSQ=   34.07
     AND PERSONALITY  (61)                                    AND PERSONALITY  (339)                         PHI=   0.292
                                                                                                             XP =  0.

524  TEND LESS TO BE THOSE               0.69 OF  36     524  TEND MORE TO BE THOSE            0.91 OF 364        11   33
     NOT INCLUDED IN                                          NOT INCLUDED IN                                      25  331
     WHITING, KLUCKHOHN, AND ANTHONY'S                        WHITING, KLUCKHOHN, AND ANTHONY'S              XSQ=   13.34
     STUDY OF MALE INITIATION CEREMONIES  (356)               STUDY OF MALE INITIATION CEREMONIES  (356)     PHI=   0.183
                                                                                                             XP =  0.0003
```

520 CULTURES INCLUDED IN BEATRICE BLYTH WHITING'S STUDY OF SORCERY (40)

520 CULTURES NOT INCLUDED IN BEATRICE BLYTH WHITING'S STUDY OF SORCERY (360)

BACKGROUND ON PAGE 180

SUBJECT ONLY, F.C. 1-480 AND 527-536
BOTH SUBJECT AND PREDICATE, F.C. 481-526

40 IN LEFT COLUMN

ARANDA	ASHANTI	AZANDE	BALINESE	CARIB	CAYAPA	CHAGGA	CHEYENNE	CHUKCHEE	COPR ESKIMO
CROW	DELAWARE	DIERI	DOBUANS	GOND	IFUGAO	JAPANESE	JIVARO	KAZAK	KURTATCHI
KWAKIUTL	LAMBA	LANGO	LEPCHA	LESU	MAORI	MASAI	MURNGIN	ONTONG-JAVA	RIFFIANS
SAMOANS	SANPOIL	TANALA	TIKOPIA	TIV	TROBRIAND	VENDA	WITOTO	YUROK	ZUNI

360 IN RIGHT COLUMN

6	TILT LESS TOWARD BEING THOSE LOCATED OUTSIDE OF THE INSULAR PACIFIC (330)	0.67 OF 40	6	TILT MORE TOWARD BEING THOSE LOCATED OUTSIDE OF THE INSULAR PACIFIC (330)	0.84 OF 360		13 57 27 303 XSQ= 5.82 PHI= 0.121 XP = 0.0158
77	IN ALL CASES ARE THOSE WHERE THE WRITING SYSTEM IS MNEMONIC OR ABSENT, RATHER THAN BEING ALPHABETIC-OR-PHONETIC (39) JMH	1.00 OF 14	77	TILT LESS TOWARD BEING THOSE WHERE THE WRITING SYSTEM IS MNEMONIC OR ABSENT, RATHER THAN BEING ALPHABETIC-OR-PHONETIC (39) JMH	0.63 OF 40		0 15 14 25 XSQ= 5.52 PHI= -0.320 XP = 0.0188
107	DRIFT MORE TOWARD BEING THOSE WHERE CLASS STRATIFICATION, IF PRESENT, IS BASED ON SOMETHING OTHER THAN OCCUPATIONAL STATUS (160)	0.95 OF 22	107	DRIFT LESS TOWARD BEING THOSE WHERE CLASS STRATIFICATION, IF PRESENT, IS BASED ON SOMETHING OTHER THAN OCCUPATIONAL STATUS (160)	0.77 OF 181		1 42 21 139 XSQ= 3.05 PHI= -0.123 XP = 0.0808
108	TILT TOWARD BEING THOSE WHERE CLASS STRATIFICATION, IF PRESENT, IS BASED ON A HEREDITARY ARISTOCRACY (74)	0.59 OF 22	108	TILT TOWARD BEING THOSE WHERE CLASS STRATIFICATION, IF PRESENT, IS BASED ON SOMETHING OTHER THAN A HEREDITARY ARISTOCRACY (129)	0.66 OF 181		13 61 9 120 XSQ= 4.42 PHI= 0.148 XP = 0.0356
148	TILT TOWARD BEING THOSE WHERE THE INCIDENCE OF PERSONAL CRIME IS HIGH (12) B-B-C	0.60 OF 15	148	TILT TOWARD BEING THOSE WHERE THE INCIDENCE OF PERSONAL CRIME IS LOW (21) B-B-C	0.83 OF 18		9 3 6 15 XSQ= 4.90 PHI= 0.385 EP = 0.0143

185	TILT MORE TOWARD BEING THOSE 0.96 OF 25 WHERE THE LARGEST NON-COGNATIC KIN GROUP IS THE MOEITY OR PHRATRY OR SIB (194)	185	TILT LESS TOWARD BEING THOSE 0.75 OF 227 WHERE THE LARGEST NON-COGNATIC KIN GROUP IS THE MOEITY OR PHRATRY OR SIB (194)	24 170 1 57 XSQ= 4.54 PHI= 0.134 XP = 0.0332
198	TILT LESS TOWARD BEING THOSE 0.67 OF 15 WHERE RULES FOR THE INHERITANCE OF REAL PROPERTY, IF PRESENT, FAVOR THE MALE HEIR OR LINE, RATHER THAN THE FEMALE (144)	198	TILT MORE TOWARD BEING THOSE 0.89 OF 150 WHERE RULES FOR THE INHERITANCE OF REAL PROPERTY, IF PRESENT, FAVOR THE MALE HEIR OR LINE, RATHER THAN THE FEMALE (144)	10 134 5 16 XSQ= 4.43 PHI= -0.164 XP = 0.0353
262	DRIFT MORE TOWARD BEING THOSE 0.90 OF 40 WHERE WIVES ARE OBTAINED BY MEANS INVOLVING THE PRESENCE OF SOME CONSIDERATION (305)	262	DRIFT LESS TOWARD BEING THOSE 0.76 OF 355 WHERE WIVES ARE OBTAINED BY MEANS INVOLVING THE PRESENCE OF SOME CONSIDERATION (305)	36 269 4 86 XSQ= 3.37 PHI= 0.092 XP = 0.0666
301	TILT LESS TOWARD BEING THOSE 0.57 OF 23 WHERE THE POST-PARTUM SEX TABOO LASTS LONGER THAN ONE MONTH (96)	301	TILT MORE TOWARD BEING THOSE 0.82 OF 101 WHERE THE POST-PARTUM SEX TABOO LASTS LONGER THAN ONE MONTH (96)	13 83 10 18 XSQ= 5.66 PHI= -0.214 XP = 0.0173
304	TILT TOWARD BEING THOSE 0.76 OF 17 WHERE THE EARLY ANAL SATISFACTION POTENTIAL IS LOW (22) W-C	304	TILT TOWARD BEING THOSE 0.63 OF 24 WHERE THE EARLY ANAL SATISFACTION POTENTIAL IS HIGH (19) W-C	4 15 13 9 XSQ= 4.61 PHI= -0.335 XP = 0.0318
323	DRIFT MORE TOWARD BEING THOSE 0.76 OF 25 WHERE THE CONSTANCY OF PRESENCE OF THE INFANT'S NURTURANT AGENT IS LOW (45) B-B-C	323	DRIFT LESS TOWARD BEING THOSE 0.53 OF 49 WHERE THE CONSTANCY OF PRESENCE OF THE INFANT'S NURTURANT AGENT IS LOW (45) B-B-C	6 23 19 26 XSQ= 2.76 PHI= -0.193 XP = 0.0969
333	IN ALL CASES ARE THOSE 1.00 OF 7 WHERE THE AGE AT BEGINNING OF TRAINING IN HETEROSEXUAL PLAY INHIBITION IS EIGHT YEARS OR HIGHER (8) W-C	333	LEAN TOWARD BEING THOSE 0.89 OF 9 WHERE THE AGE AT BEGINNING OF TRAINING IN HETEROSEXUAL PLAY INHIBITION IS LOWER THAN EIGHT YEARS (8) W-C	7 1 0 8 XSQ= 9.14 PHI= 0.756 EP = 0.0014
342	TILT TOWARD BEING THOSE 0.64 OF 14 WHERE THE CHILD'S INFERRED ANXIETY OVER PERFORMANCE OF NURTURANT BEHAVIOR IS HIGH (18) B-B-C	342	TILT TOWARD BEING THOSE 0.72 OF 32 WHERE THE CHILD'S INFERRED ANXIETY OVER PERFORMANCE OF NURTURANT BEHAVIOR IS LOW (28) B-B-C	9 9 5 23 XSQ= 3.94 PHI= 0.293 XP = 0.0473
350	DRIFT TOWARD BEING THOSE 0.75 OF 20 WHERE THE CHILD'S INFERRED ANXIETY OVER PERFORMANCE OF ACHIEVEMENT BEHAVIOR IS HIGH (34) B-B-C	350	DRIFT TOWARD BEING THOSE 0.52 OF 40 WHERE THE CHILD'S INFERRED ANXIETY OVER PERFORMANCE OF ACHIEVEMENT BEHAVIOR IS LOW (26) B-B-C	15 19 5 21 XSQ= 3.06 PHI= 0.226 XP = 0.0801

```
403  DRIFT TOWARD BEING THOSE        0.52 OF  27     403  DRIFT TOWARD BEING THOSE        0.74 OF  34           14    9
     WHERE EXPLANATICNS OF ILLNESS                         WHERE EXPLANATIONS OF ILLNESS                           13   25
     OF AN ANAL NATURE                                     OF AN ANAL NATURE                               XSQ=     3.12
     ARE PRESENT  (23) W-C                                 ARE ABSENT  (38) W-C                            PHI=    0.226
                                                                                                           XP =   0.0774

419  DRIFT MCRE TCWARD BEING THOSE  0.77 OF  31     419  DRIFT LESS TOWARD BEING THOSE  0.56 OF  55           24   31
     WHERE MILITARY GLORY                                  WHERE MILITARY GLORY                                     7   24
     IS STRONGLY OR                                        IS STRONGLY OR                                  XSQ=     2.95
     MODERATELY EMPHASIZED  (55) PES                       MODERATELY EMPHASIZED  (55) PES                 PHI=    0.185
                                                                                                           XP =   0.0857

428  TEND TO BE THOSE                0.80 OF  10     428  TEND TO BE THOSE                0.77 OF  77            2   59
     WHERE A HIGH GCD, IF PRESENT AND ACTIVE,              WHERE A HIGH GOD, IF PRESENT AND ACTIVE,                 8   18
     DOES NOT SUPPORT HUMAN MORALITY,                      SUPPORTS HUMAN MORALITY, RATHER THAN            XSQ=    10.98
     RATHER THAN SUPPORTING IT  (26) GES,EA                NOT SUPPORTING IT  (61) GES,EA                  PHI=   -0.355
                                                                                                           XP =   0.0009

441  DRIFT TOWARD BEING THCSE        0.63 OF  27     441  DRIFT TOWARD BEING THOSE        0.65 OF  34           17   12
     WHERE FEAR OF HUMAN BEINGS                            WHERE FEAR OF HUMAN BEINGS                              10   22
     IS HIGH  (29) W-C                                     IS LOW  (32) W-C                                XSQ=     3.58
                                                                                                           PHI=    0.242
                                                                                                           XP =   0.0586

446  TILT TOWARD BEING THOSE         0.70 OF  10     446  TILT TOWARD BEING THOSE         0.75 OF  28            7    7
     WHERE WITCHCRAFT                                      WHERE WITCHCRAFT                                         3   21
     IS SIGNIFICANTLY PRESENT  (14) GES                    IS MODERATELY PRESENT OR                        XSQ=     4.62
                                                           ABSENT  (24) GES                                PHI=    0.349
                                                                                                           EP =   0.0207

452  DRIFT TCWARD BEING THCSE        0.65 OF  17     452  DRIFT TOWARD BEING THOSE        0.69 OF  26           11    8
     WHERE TOTEMISM WITH FCCD TABOOS                       WHERE TOTEMISM WITH FOOD TABOOS                          6   18
     IS PRESENT  (19) WNS                                  IS ABSENT  (24) WNS                             XSQ=     3.52
                                                                                                           PHI=    0.286
                                                                                                           XP =   0.0605

456  TILT TOWARD BEING THOSE         0.82 OF  11     456  TILT TOWARD BEING THOSE         0.68 OF  25            2   17
     WHERE THE INTERNALIZATION OF THE                      WHERE THE INTERNALIZATION OF THE                         9    8
     INDIVIDUAL'S CONTACT WITH THE DIVINE                  INDIVIDUAL'S CONTACT WITH THE DIVINE            XSQ=     5.74
     IS NOT CONDUCIVE TC THE DEVELOPMENT OF                IS CONDUCIVE TO THE DEVELOPMENT OF              PHI=   -0.399
     THE INDIVIDUAL'S NEED TO ACHIEVE  (17) DCM            THE INDIVIDUAL'S NEED TO ACHIEVE  (19) DCM      EP =   0.0103

468  DRIFT MCRE TOWARD BEING THOSE  0.93 OF  14     468  DRIFT LESS TOWARD BEING THOSE  0.60 OF  40            1   16
     WHERE CONTACT WITH CTHER CULTURES                     WHERE CONTACT WITH OTHER CULTURES                       13   24
     IS REGULAR OR IRREGULAR, RATHER THAN                  IS REGULAR OR IRREGULAR, RATHER THAN            XSQ=     3.78
     FREQUENT  (37) JMH                                    FREQUENT  (37) JMH                              PHI=   -0.265
                                                                                                           XP =   0.0519

470  DRIFT MORE TOWARD BEING THOSE  0.86 OF  14     470  DRIFT LESS TOWARD BEING THOSE  0.52 OF  40            2   19
     WHERE INNCVATIONS ARE                                 WHERE INNOVATIONS ARE                                   12   21
     ACCEPTED CNLY SELECTIVELY  (33) JMH                   ACCEPTED ONLY SELECTIVELY  (33) JMH             XSQ=     3.52
                                                                                                           PHI=   -0.255
                                                                                                           XP =   0.0607
```

476	LEAN TOWARD BEING THOSE WHERE THE DEGREE OF INSOBRIETY IS MODERATE OR SLIGHT (18) DH	0.62 OF 21	476	LEAN TOWARD BEING THOSE WHERE THE DEGREE OF INSOBRIETY IS STRONG (31) DH	0.82 OF 28	8 23 13 5 XSQ= 8.21 PHI= -0.409 XP = 0.0042
482	TILT LESS TOWARD BEING THOSE WHERE THE PRINCIPAL ETHNOGRAPHERS HAVE BEEN OTHER THAN BRITISH (336)	0.72 OF 40	482	TILT MORE TOWARD BEING THOSE WHERE THE PRINCIPAL ETHNOGRAPHERS HAVE BEEN OTHER THAN BRITISH (336)	0.88 OF 348	11 41 29 307 XSQ= 6.34 PHI= 0.128 XP = 0.0118
483	DRIFT TOWARD BEING THOSE WHERE THE PRINCIPAL ETHNOGRAPHERS HAVE BEEN BRITISH, RATHER THAN AMERICAN (52)	0.50 OF 22	483	DRIFT TOWARD BEING THOSE WHERE THE PRINCIPAL ETHNOGRAPHERS HAVE BEEN AMERICAN, RATHER THAN BRITISH (113)	0.71 OF 143	11 102 11 41 XSQ= 3.09 PHI= -0.137 XP = 0.0787
488	IN ALL CASES ARE THOSE ABOUT WHICH THE PRINCIPAL ETHNOGRAPHIES WERE PUBLISHED BEFORE 1950 (185)	1.00 OF 25	488	LEAN LESS TOWARD BEING THOSE ABOUT WHICH THE PRINCIPAL ETHNOGRAPHIES WERE PUBLISHED BEFORE 1950 (185)	0.69 OF 232	25 160 0 72 XSQ= 9.29 PHI= 0.190 XP = 0.0023
489	TILT LESS TOWARD BEING THOSE NOT INCLUDED IN CHARLES ACKERMAN'S STUDY OF DIVORCE (343)	0.72 OF 40	489	TILT MORE TOWARD BEING THOSE NOT INCLUDED IN CHARLES ACKERMAN'S STUDY OF DIVORCE (343)	0.87 OF 360	11 46 29 314 XSQ= 5.24 PHI= 0.114 XP = 0.0221
490	TEND TO BE THOSE INCLUDED IN ALBERT S. ANTHONY'S SAMPLE ON MALE INITIATION RITES (113)	0.75 OF 40	490	TEND TO BE THOSE NOT INCLUDED IN ALBERT S. ANTHONY'S SAMPLE ON MALE INITIATION RITES (287)	0.77 OF 360	30 83 10 277 XSQ= 45.39 PHI= 0.337 XP = 0.
491	LEAN LESS TOWARD BEING THOSE NOT INCLUDED IN DORRIAN APPLE'S STUDY OF GRANDPARENTHOOD (352)	0.72 OF 40	491	LEAN MORE TOWARD BEING THOSE NOT INCLUDED IN DORRIAN APPLE'S STUDY OF GRANDPARENTHOOD (352)	0.90 OF 360	11 37 29 323 XSQ= 8.55 PHI= 0.146 XP = 0.0035
492	TEND LESS TO BE THOSE NOT INCLUDED IN BARBARA CHARTIER AYRES' STUDY OF FEMALE INITIATION RITES (361)	0.52 OF 40	492	TEND MORE TO BE THOSE NOT INCLUDED IN BARBARA CHARTIER AYRES' STUDY OF FEMALE INITIATION RITES (361)	0.94 OF 360	19 20 21 340 XSQ= 67.29 PHI= 0.410 XP = 0.
493	TEND TO BE THOSE INCLUDED IN BACON, BARRY, AND CHILD'S STUDY OF CHILD REARING (78)	0.65 OF 40	493	TEND TO BE THOSE NOT INCLUDED IN BACON, BARRY, AND CHILD'S STUDY OF CHILD REARING (322)	0.86 OF 360	26 52 14 308 XSQ= 55.44 PHI= 0.372 XP = 0.

494	TEND LESS TO BE THOSE NOT INCLUDED IN HERBERT M. BARRY III'S STUDY OF ART (371)	0.72 OF 40	494	TEND MORE TO BE THOSE NOT INCLUDED IN HERBERT M. BARRY III'S STUDY OF ART (371)	0.95 OF 360	11 18 29 342 XSQ= 23.86 PHI= 0.244 XP = 0.0000
495	TEND LESS TO BE THOSE NOT INCLUDED IN JUDITH K. BROWN'S STUDY OF FEMALE INITIATION RITES (335)	0.57 OF 40	495	TEND MORE TO BE THOSE NOT INCLUDED IN JUDITH K. BROWN'S STUDY OF FEMALE INITIATION RITES (335)	0.87 OF 360	17 48 23 312 XSQ= 20.41 PHI= 0.226 XP = 0.0000
496	TEND LESS TO BE THOSE NOT INCLUDED IN ROY G. D'ANDRADE'S STUDY OF DREAMS (345)	0.65 OF 40	496	TEND MORE TO BE THOSE NOT INCLUDED IN ROY G. D'ANDRADE'S STUDY OF DREAMS (345)	0.89 OF 360	14 41 26 319 XSQ= 14.99 PHI= 0.194 XP = 0.0001
497	TEND LESS TO BE THOSE NOT INCLUDED IN WILLIAM M. EVAN'S STUDY OF LAW (339)	0.52 OF 40	497	TEND MORE TO BE THOSE NOT INCLUDED IN WILLIAM M. EVAN'S STUDY OF LAW (339)	0.88 OF 360	19 42 21 318 XSQ= 33.05 PHI= 0.287 XP = 0.
498	TEND TO BE THOSE INCLUDED IN C. S. FORD'S STUDY OF SEX (51)	0.72 OF 40	498	TEND TO BE THOSE NOT INCLUDED IN C. S. FORD'S STUDY OF SEX (349)	0.94 OF 360	29 22 11 338 XSQ= 136.73 PHI= 0.585 XP = 0.
499	TEND TO BE THOSE INCLUDED IN FORD AND BEACH'S SAMPLE ON SEXUAL EXPRESSION BY THE YOUNG (86)	0.65 OF 40	499	TEND TO BE THOSE NOT INCLUDED IN FORD AND BEACH'S SAMPLE ON SEXUAL EXPRESSION BY THE YOUNG (314)	0.83 OF 360	26 60 14 300 XSQ= 47.01 PHI= 0.343 XP = 0.
500	TEND LESS TO BE THOSE NOT INCLUDED IN FREEMAN AND WINCH'S STUDY OF SOCIETAL COMPLEXITY (360)	0.52 OF 40	500	TEND MORE TO BE THOSE NOT INCLUDED IN FREEMAN AND WINCH'S STUDY OF SOCIETAL COMPLEXITY (360)	0.94 OF 360	19 21 21 339 XSQ= 64.89 PHI= 0.403 XP = 0.
501	TEND TO BE THOSE INCLUDED IN JOAN FRIENDLY GOODMAN'S STUDY OF ASCETIC MOURNING BEHAVIOR (67)	0.67 OF 40	501	TEND TO BE THOSE NOT INCLUDED IN JOAN FRIENDLY GOODMAN'S STUDY OF ASCETIC MOURNING BEHAVIOR (333)	0.89 OF 360	27 40 13 320 XSQ= 78.10 PHI= 0.442 XP = 0.
502	TEND TO BE THOSE INCLUDED IN JOHN K. HARLEY'S STUDY OF ADOLESCENT PEER GROUPS (57)	0.67 OF 40	502	TEND TO BE THOSE NOT INCLUDED IN JOHN K. HARLEY'S STUDY OF ADOLESCENT PEER GROUPS (343)	0.92 OF 360	27 30 13 330 XSQ= 98.35 PHI= 0.496 XP = 0.

No.			No.			
503	TEND LESS TO BE THOSE NOT INCLUDED IN JOHN M. HICKMAN'S STUDY OF THE FOLK-URBAN CONTINUUM (346)	0.65 OF 40	503	TEND MORE TO BE THOSE NOT INCLUDED IN JOHN M. HICKMAN'S STUDY OF THE FOLK-URBAN CONTINUUM (346)	0.89 OF 360	14 40 26 320 XSQ= 15.61 PHI= 0.198 XP = 0.0001
504	TEND TO BE THOSE INCLUDED IN DONALD HORTON'S STUDY OF ALCOHOLISM (49)	0.52 OF 40	504	TEND TO BE THOSE NOT INCLUDED IN DONALD HORTON'S STUDY OF ALCHOLISM (351)	0.92 OF 360	21 28 19 332 XSQ= 62.89 PHI= 0.397 XP = 0.
505	LEAN LESS TOWARD BEING THOSE NOT INCLUDED IN MERRILL JACKSON'S STUDY OF CRIMINAL LAW AND MEDICINE (380)	0.85 OF 40	505	LEAN MORE TOWARD BEING THOSE NOT INCLUDED IN MERRILL JACKSON'S STUDY OF CRIMINAL LAW AND MEDICINE (380)	0.96 OF 360	6 14 34 346 XSQ= 7.16 PHI= 0.134 XP = 0.0074
506	TEND LESS TO BE THOSE NOT INCLUDED IN LAMBERT, TRIANDIS, AND WOLF'S STUDY OF SUPERNATURAL BEINGS (364)	0.67 OF 40	506	TEND MORE TO BE THOSE NOT INCLUDED IN LAMBERT, TRIANDIS, AND WOLF'S STUDY OF SUPERNATURAL BEINGS (364)	0.94 OF 360	13 23 27 337 XSQ= 26.87 PHI= 0.259 XP = 0.0000
507	TEND TO BE THOSE INCLUDED IN JAMES R. LEARY'S STUDY OF FOOD TABOOS (86)	0.50 OF 40	507	TEND TO BE THOSE NOT INCLUDED IN JAMES R. LEARY'S STUDY OF FOOD TABOOS (314)	0.82 OF 360	20 66 20 294 XSQ= 19.55 PHI= 0.221 XP = 0.0000
508	TEND LESS TO BE THOSE NOT INCLUDED IN DAVID C. MCCLELLAND'S STUDY OF ACHIEVEMENT MOTIVATION (360)	0.67 OF 40	508	TEND MORE TO BE THOSE NOT INCLUDED IN DAVID C. MCCLELLAND'S STUDY OF ACHIEVEMENT MOTIVATION (360)	0.92 OF 360	13 27 27 333 XSQ= 22.30 PHI= 0.236 XP = 0.0000
510	DRIFT LESS TOWARD BEING THOSE NOT INCLUDED IN RAOUL NARRCLL'S STUDY OF SOCIETAL COMPLEXITY (380)	0.88 OF 40	510	DRIFT MORE TOWARD BEING THOSE NOT INCLUDED IN RAOUL NARRCLL'S STUDY OF SOCIETAL COMPLEXITY (380)	0.96 OF 360	5 15 35 345 XSQ= 3.65 PHI= 0.096 XP = 0.0559
511	TEND TO BE THOSE INCLUDED IN ROBERTS, ARTH AND BUSH'S SAMPLE ON GAMES, AS MODIFIED BY THE ETHNOGRAPHIC ATLAS (189)	0.80 OF 40	511	TEND TO BE THOSE NOT INCLUDED IN ROBERTS, ARTH AND BUSH'S SAMPLE ON GAMES, AS MODIFIED BY THE ETHNOGRAPHIC ATLAS (211)	0.56 OF 360	32 157 8 203 XSQ= 17.69 PHI= 0.210 XP = 0.0000
512	TEND LESS TO BE THOSE NOT INCLUDED IN SHIRLEY AND ROMNEY'S STUDY OF LOVE MAGIC (367)	0.52 OF 40	512	TEND MORE TO BE THOSE NOT INCLUDED IN SHIRLEY AND ROMNEY'S STUDY OF LOVE MAGIC (367)	0.96 OF 360	19 14 21 346 XSQ= 84.79 PHI= 0.460 XP = 0.

513	TEND LESS TO BE THCSE 0.67 OF 40 NOT INCLUDED IN LEC W. SIMMONS' STUDY OF THE TREATMENT OF THE AGEC (357)	TEND MORE TO BE THOSE 0.92 OF 360 NOT INCLUDED IN LEO W. SIMMONS' STUDY OF THE TREATMENT OF THE AGED (357)	13 30 27 330 XSQ= 19.47 PHI= 0.221 XP = 0.0000
514	TEND TO BE THOSE 0.82 OF 40 INCLUDED IN PHILIP E. SLATER'S STUDY OF NARCISSISM (90)	TEND TO BE THOSE 0.84 OF 360 NOT INCLUDED IN PHILIP E. SLATER'S STUDY OF NARCISSISM (310)	33 57 7 303 XSQ= 87.97 PHI= 0.469 XP = 0.
515	TEND LESS TO BE THCSE 0.57 OF 40 NOT INCLUDED IN WILLIAM N. STEPHENS' SAMPLE ON AVOIDANCE RELATICNSHIPS (348)	TEND MORE TO BE THOSE 0.90 OF 360 NOT INCLUDED IN WILLIAM N. STEPHENS' SAMPLE ON AVOIDANCE RELATIONSHIPS (348)	17 35 23 325 XSQ= 31.36 PHI= 0.280 XP = 0.
516	DRIFT MORE TOWARD BEING THCSE 0.95 OF 40 INCLUDED IN GUY E. SWANSON'S SAMPLE CN LOCAL JURISCICTION, AS MODIFIED BY THE ETHNOGRAPHIC ATLAS (331)	DRIFT LESS TOWARD BEING THOSE 0.81 OF 360 INCLUDED IN GUY E. SWANSON'S SAMPLE ON LOCAL JURISDICTION, AS MODIFIED BY THE ETHNOGRAPHIC ATLAS (331)	38 293 2 67 XSQ= 3.77 PHI= 0.097 XP = 0.0523
517	LEAN MORE TOWARC BEING THCSE 0.88 OF 40 INCLUDED IN GUY E. SWANSON'S SAMPLE ON HIGH GODS, AS MCDIFIED BY THE ETHNOGRAPHIC ATLAS (260)	LEAN LESS TOWARD BEING THOSE 0.63 OF 360 INCLUDED IN GUY E. SWANSON'S SAMPLE ON HIGH GODS, AS MODIFIED BY THE ETHNOGRAPHIC ATLAS (260)	35 225 5 135 XSQ= 8.82 PHI= 0.149 XP = 0.0030
518	TEND TO BE THOSE 0.60 OF 40 INCLUDED IN STANLEY H. UDY, JR.'S STUDY OF WCRK ORGANIZATION (105)	TEND TO BE THOSE 0.77 OF 360 NOT INCLUDED IN STANLEY H. UDY, JR.'S STUDY OF WORK ORGANIZATION (295)	24 81 16 279 XSQ= 24.25 PHI= 0.246 XP = 0.0000
519	TEND LESS TO BE THCSE 0.75 OF 40 NOT INCLUDED IN JCSEPH VEROFF'S STUDY OF ACHIEVEMENT MOTIVATION AS REVEALED IN FCLKTALES (364)	TEND MORE TO BE THOSE 0.93 OF 360 NOT INCLUDED IN JOSEPH VEROFF'S STUDY OF ACHIEVEMENT MOTIVATION AS REVEALED IN FOLKTALES (364)	10 26 30 334 XSQ= 11.81 PHI= 0.172 XP = 0.0006
521	TEND TO BE THCSE 0.55 OF 40 INCLUDED IN JCHN W. M. WHITING'S STUDY CF SCCIALIZATION PROCESS AND PERSCNALITY (47)	TEND TO BE THOSE 0.93 OF 360 NOT INCLUDED IN JOHN W. M. WHITING'S STUDY OF SOCIALIZATION PROCESS AND PERSONALITY (353)	22 25 18 335 XSQ= 75.61 PHI= 0.435 XP = 0.
522	TEND TC BE THOSE 0.57 OF 40 INCLUDED IN MARJCRIE GRANT WHITING'S STUDY CF DIET (82)	TEND TO BE THOSE 0.84 OF 360 NOT INCLUDED IN MARJORIE GRANT WHITING'S STUDY OF DIET (318)	23 59 17 301 XSQ= 34.85 PHI= 0.295 XP = 0.

```
523  TEND TO BE THOSE                 0.67 OF  40     523  TEND TO BE THOSE                 0.91 OF 360          27   34
     INCLUDED IN WHITING AND CHILD'S                       NOT INCLUDED IN WHITING AND CHILD'S                   13  326
     STUDY OF CHILD TRAINING                               STUDY OF CHILD TRAINING                         XSQ=   89.44
     AND PERSONALITY  (61)                                 AND PERSONALITY  (339)                          PHI=   0.473
                                                                                                           XP =  0.

524  TEND LESS TO BE THOSE            0.55 OF  40     524  TEND MORE TO BE THOSE            0.93 OF 360          18   26
     NOT INCLUDED IN                                       NOT INCLUDED IN                                       22  334
     WHITING, KLUCKHOHN, AND ANTHONY'S                     WHITING, KLUCKHOHN, AND ANTHONY'S               XSQ=   48.69
     STUDY OF MALE INITIATION CEREMONIES  (356)            STUDY OF MALE INITIATION CEREMONIES  (356)      PHI=   0.349
                                                                                                           XP =  0.
```

522 CULTURES INCLUDED IN MARJORIE GRANT WHITING'S STUDY OF DIET (82)

522 CULTURES NOT INCLUDED IN MARJORIE GRANT WHITING'S STUDY OF DIET (318)

BACKGROUND ON PAGE 180

SUBJECT ONLY, F.C. 1-480 AND 527-536
BOTH SUBJECT AND PREDICATE, F.C. 481-526

82 IN LEFT COLUMN

ALORESE	ANDAMANESE	ARANDA	ARAPESH	ARAUCANIANS	ASHANTI	AYMARA	AZANDE	BALINESE	CAGABA
CAMAYURA	CHAGGA	CHENCHU	CHEYENNE	CHIR-APACHE	COPR ESKIMO	CUNA	EGYPTIANS	FON	GANDA
GROS VENTRE	HANO	JIVARO	KASKA	KAZAK	KORYAK	KURTATCHI	KWAKIUTL	LAKHER	LAMBA
LANGO	LAPPS	LAU	LEPCHA	LESU	MAGUZAWA	MAORI	MASAI	MBUNDU	MENDE
MINCHIA	NAMA	NAMBICUARA	NAVAHO	NUER	NYAKYUSA	OJIBWA	OMAHA	ONA	ONTONG-JAVA
PAPAGO	PUKAPUKA	SAMOANS	SANPOIL	SENIANG	SHERENTE	SIRIONO	TALLENSI	TANALA	TARAHUMARA
TENETEHARA	TENINO	TERENA	TETON	THONGA	TIMBIRA	TOKELAU	TROBRIAND	TRUKESE	TUPINAMBA
TURKANA	VENDA	WAPISHANA	WARRAU	WINNEBAGO	WOGEO	WOLEAIANS	YAGUA	YAO	YAPESE
YORUBA	YUKAGHIR								

318 IN RIGHT COLUMN

	Included (82)	Not included (318)	
4	TILT MORE TOWARD BEING THOSE 0.96 OF 82 LOCATED OUTSIDE OF THE CIRCUM-MEDITERRANEAN (355)	TILT LESS TOWARD BEING THOSE 0.87 OF 318 LOCATED OUTSIDE OF THE CIRCUM-MEDITERRANEAN (355)	3 42 79 276 XSQ= 5.04 PHI= -0.112 XP = 0.0248
16	DRIFT LESS TOWARD BEING THOSE 0.60 OF 82 WHERE THE LATITUDE IS TEN DEGREES OR GREATER (277)	DRIFT MORE TOWARD BEING THOSE 0.72 OF 318 WHERE THE LATITUDE IS TEN DEGREES OR GREATER (277)	49 228 33 90 XSQ= 3.82 PHI= -0.098 XP = 0.0506
53	TILT MORE TOWARD BEING THOSE 0.75 OF 52 WHERE FOOD PRODUCTION IS BY SIMPLE AGRICULTURE OR INCIPIENT FOOD PRODUCTION, RATHER THAN BY INTENSIVE AGRICULTURE (147)	TILT LESS TOWARD BEING THOSE 0.58 OF 186 WHERE FOOD PRODUCTION IS BY SIMPLE AGRICULTURE OR INCIPIENT FOOD PRODUCTION, RATHER THAN BY INTENSIVE AGRICULTURE (147)	13 78 39 108 XSQ= 4.24 PHI= -0.134 XP = 0.0394
55	DRIFT TOWARD BEING THOSE 0.67 OF 39 WHERE FOOD PRODUCTION IS BY SIMPLE AGRICULTURE, RATHER THAN BY INTENSIVE AGRICULTURE (101)	DRIFT TOWARD BEING THOSE 0.51 OF 153 WHERE FOOD PRODUCTION IS BY INTENSIVE AGRICULTURE, RATHER THAN BY SIMPLE AGRICULTURE (91)	13 78 26 75 XSQ= 3.21 PHI= -0.129 XP = 0.0734

No.			No.			
63	TILT LESS TOWARD BEING THOSE WHERE HUSBANDRY, IF PRESENT, IS PRINCIPALLY IN THE FORM OF BOVINE, EQUINE, CAMEL-LIKE, OR DEER-LIKE ANIMALS, RATHER THAN PIGS, SHEEP, OR GOATS (152)	0.53 OF 53	63	TILT MORE TOWARD BEING THOSE WHERE HUSBANDRY, IF PRESENT, IS PRINCIPALLY IN THE FORM OF BOVINE, EQUINE, CAMEL-LIKE, OR DEER-LIKE ANIMALS, RATHER THAN PIGS, SHEEP, OR GOATS (152)	0.72 OF 173	28 124 25 49 XSQ= 5.72 PHI= -0.159 XP = 0.0168
79	DRIFT MORE TOWARD BEING THOSE WHERE NO CITY IS PRESENT (201)	0.96 OF 56	79	DRIFT LESS TOWARD BEING THOSE WHERE NO CITY IS PRESENT (201)	0.88 OF 168	2 21 54 147 XSQ= 2.73 PHI= -0.110 XP = 0.0985
80	DRIFT MORE TOWARD BEING THOSE WHERE NO CITY OR TOWN IS PRESENT (185)	0.91 OF 56	80	DRIFT LESS TOWARD BEING THOSE WHERE NO CITY OR TOWN IS PRESENT (185)	0.80 OF 168	5 34 51 134 XSQ= 2.99 PHI= -0.116 XP = 0.0837
107	TILT MORE TOWARD BEING THOSE WHERE CLASS STRATIFICATION, IF PRESENT, IS BASED ON SOMETHING OTHER THAN OCCUPATIONAL STATUS (160)	0.93 OF 41	107	TILT LESS TOWARD BEING THOSE WHERE CLASS STRATIFICATION, IF PRESENT, IS BASED ON SOMETHING OTHER THAN OCCUPATIONAL STATUS (160)	0.75 OF 162	3 40 38 122 XSQ= 4.92 PHI= -0.156 XP = 0.0265
108	DRIFT LESS TOWARD BEING THOSE WHERE CLASS STRATIFICATION, IF PRESENT, IS BASED ON SOMETHING OTHER THAN A HEREDITARY ARISTOCRACY (129)	0.51 OF 41	108	DRIFT MORE TOWARD BEING THOSE WHERE CLASS STRATIFICATION, IF PRESENT, IS BASED ON SOMETHING OTHER THAN A HEREDITARY ARISTOCRACY (129)	0.67 OF 162	20 54 21 108 XSQ= 2.74 PHI= 0.116 XP = 0.0981
109	TILT MORE TOWARD BEING THOSE WHERE CASTES ARE ABSENT (317)	0.94 OF 80	109	TILT LESS TOWARD BEING THOSE WHERE CASTES ARE ABSENT (317)	0.84 OF 288	5 46 75 242 XSQ= 4.18 PHI= -0.107 XP = 0.0410
116	TILT TOWARD BEING THOSE WHERE OCCUPATIONAL SPECIALIZATION IS PART-TIME ONLY (34) JMH	0.80 OF 25	116	TILT TOWARD BEING THOSE WHERE OCCUPATIONAL SPECIALIZATION IS FULL-TIME, WHETHER OR NOT FOR SURPLUS PRODUCTION (20) JMH	0.52 OF 29	5 15 20 14 XSQ= 4.51 PHI= -0.289 XP = 0.0336
127	DRIFT TOWARD BEING THOSE WHERE THE FEMALES' CONTRIBUTION TO SUBSISTENCE IS HIGH (33) JKB	0.62 OF 39	127	DRIFT TOWARD BEING THOSE WHERE THE FEMALES' CONTRIBUTION TO SUBSISTENCE IS LOW (32) JKB	0.65 OF 26	24 9 15 17 XSQ= 3.51 PHI= 0.232 XP = 0.0610
148	TILT TOWARD BEING THOSE WHERE THE INCIDENCE OF PERSONAL CRIME IS LOW (21) B-B-C	0.71 OF 28	148	TILT TOWARD BEING THOSE WHERE THE INCIDENCE OF PERSONAL CRIME IS HIGH (12) B-B-C	0.80 OF 5	8 4 20 1 XSQ= 2.88 PHI= -0.295 EP = 0.0471

179	LEAN LESS TOWARD BEING THOSE 0.80 OF 82 WHERE THE COMMUNITY IS OTHER THAN STRUCTURED ON A NON-CLAN BASIS AND COMMONLY EXOGAMOUS (340)	179	LEAN MORE TOWARD BEING THOSE 0.91 OF 300 WHERE THE COMMUNITY IS OTHER THAN STRUCTURED ON A NON-CLAN BASIS AND COMMONLY EXOGAMOUS (340)	16 26 66 274 XSQ= 6.67 PHI= 0.132 XP = 0.0098
182	TILT MORE TOWARD BEING THOSE 0.78 OF 82 OTHER THAN WHERE THE COMMUNITY IS STRUCTURED ON A NON-CLAN BASIS AND AGAMOUS (256)	182	TILT LESS TOWARD BEING THOSE 0.64 OF 300 OTHER THAN WHERE THE COMMUNITY IS STRUCTURED ON A NON-CLAN BASIS AND AGAMOUS (256)	18 108 64 192 XSQ= 5.13 PHI= -0.116 XP = 0.0235
197	TILT MORE TOWARD BEING THOSE 0.97 OF 36 WHERE RULES FOR THE INHERITANCE OF REAL PROPERTY, IF PRESENT, FAVOR EITHER THE MALE HEIR OR LINE, OR THE FEMALE HEIR OR LINE (165)	197	TILT LESS TOWARD BEING THOSE 0.82 OF 158 WHERE RULES FOR THE INHERITANCE OF REAL PROPERTY, IF PRESENT, FAVOR EITHER THE MALE HEIR OR LINE, OR THE FEMALE HEIR OR LINE (165)	35 130 1 28 XSQ= 4.04 PHI= 0.144 XP = 0.0444
213	TILT MORE TOWARD BEING THOSE 0.65 OF 81 WHERE FIRST COUSIN MARRIAGE IS NOT PERMITTED (198)	213	TILT LESS TOWARD BEING THOSE 0.50 OF 289 WHERE FIRST COUSIN MARRIAGE IS NOT PERMITTED (198)	28 144 53 145 XSQ= 5.32 PHI= -0.120 XP = 0.0210
234	DRIFT TOWARD BEING THOSE 0.57 OF 72 WHERE THE COUSIN TERMINOLOGY IS OF CROW, OMAHA, OR IROQUOIS TYPE, RATHER THAN ESKIMO OR HAWAIIAN TYPE (152)	234	DRIFT TOWARD BEING THOSE 0.56 OF 250 WHERE THE COUSIN TERMINOLOGY IS OF ESKIMO OR HAWAIIAN TYPE, RATHER THAN CROW, OMAHA, OR IROQUOIS TYPE (170)	41 111 31 139 XSQ= 3.04 PHI= 0.097 XP = 0.0810
277	TILT TOWARD BEING THOSE 0.81 OF 16 WHERE THE STATUS OF WOMEN IS NOT STRONGLY INFERIOR OR SUBJECTED (22) LWS	277	TILT TOWARD BEING THOSE 0.55 OF 20 WHERE THE STATUS OF WOMEN IS INFERIOR OR SUBJECTED (14) LWS	3 11 13 9 XSQ= 3.51 PHI= -0.312 EP = 0.0407
295	TILT TOWARD BEING THOSE 0.61 OF 18 WHERE THE SEVERITY OF PUNISHMENT FOR ABORTION IS HIGH (11) BCA	295	IN ALL CASES ARE THOSE 1.00 OF 5 WHERE THE SEVERITY OF PUNISHMENT FOR ABORTION IS LOW OR ABSENT (12) BCA	11 0 7 5 XSQ= 3.66 PHI= 0.399 EP = 0.0373
300	DRIFT TOWARD BEING THOSE 0.52 OF 44 WHERE THE POST-PARTUM SEX TABOO LASTS LONGER THAN SIX MONTHS (51)	300	DRIFT TOWARD BEING THOSE 0.65 OF 80 WHERE THE POST-PARTUM SEX TABOO LASTS SIX MONTHS OR LESS (73)	23 28 21 52 XSQ= 2.82 PHI= 0.151 XP = 0.0931
302	TILT TOWARD BEING THOSE 0.68 OF 31 WHERE THE AVERAGE EARLY SATISFACTION POTENTIAL IS HIGH (23) W-C	302	TILT TOWARD BEING THOSE 0.78 OF 9 WHERE THE AVERAGE EARLY SATISFACTION POTENTIAL IS LOW (17) W-C	21 2 10 7 XSQ= 4.20 PHI= 0.324 EP = 0.0231

304	DRIFT TOWARD BEING THOSE 0.63 OF 32 WHERE THE EARLY ANAL SATISFACTION POTENTIAL IS LOW (22) W-C	304	DRIFT TOWARD BEING THOSE 0.78 OF 9 WHERE THE EARLY ANAL SATISFACTION POTENTIAL IS HIGH (19) W-C	12 7 20 2 XSQ= 3.11 PHI= -0.275 XP = 0.0780
306	LEAN TCWARD BEING THCSE 0.69 OF 36 WHERE THE EARLY DEPENDENCE SATISFACTION POTENTIAL IS HIGH (28) W-C	306	LEAN TOWARD BEING THOSE 0.81 OF 16 WHERE THE EARLY DEPENDENCE SATISFACTION POTENTIAL IS LOW (24) W-C	25 3 11 13 XSQ= 9.51 PHI= 0.428 XP = 0.0020
322	DRIFT TOWARD BEING THOSE 0.53 OF 47 WHERE THE CONSISTENCY CF REDUCTION OF THE INFANT'S DRIVES IS HIGH (27) B-B-C	322	DRIFT TOWARD BEING THOSE 0.83 OF 12 WHERE THE CONSISTENCY OF REDUCTION OF THE INFANT'S DRIVES IS LOW (32) B-B-C	25 2 22 10 XSQ= 3.77 PHI= 0.253 XP = 0.0521
335	TILT TOWARD BEING THOSE 0.64 OF 28 WHERE INITIAL INDULGENCE CF DEPENCENCY IS HIGH (20) WNS	335	TILT TOWARD BEING THOSE 0.80 OF 10 WHERE INITIAL INDULGENCE OF DEPENDENCY IS LOW (18) WNS	18 2 10 8 XSQ= 4.16 PHI= 0.331 EP = 0.0265
356	DRIFT TCWARD BEING THCSE 0.53 OF 36 WHERE NEITHER ADCLESCENT PEER GROUPS NCR PAIRS ARE PRESENT IN A SETTING CF COURTSHIP (22) JKH	356	DRIFT TOWARD BEING THOSE 0.80 CF 15 WHERE ADOLESCENT PEER GROUPS OR PAIRS ARE PRESENT IN A SETTING OF COURTSHIP (29) JKH	17 12 19 3 XSQ= 3.40 PHI= -0.258 XP = 0.0653
391	TILT TOWARD BEING THOSE 0.64 OF 55 WHERE PREMARITAL SEX RELATIONS ARE PUNISHED CNLY IF PREGNANCY RESULTS, OR FREELY PERMITTED (90) JTW,EA	391	TILT TOWARD BEING THOSE 0.56 OF 124 WHERE PREMARITAL SEX RELATICNS ARE STRONGLY PUNISHED AND IN FACT RARE, OR WEAKLY PUNISHED AND IN FACT NOT RARE (89) JTW,EA	20 69 35 55 XSQ= 4.92 PHI= -0.166 XP = 0.0265
419	DRIFT LESS TCWARC BEING THOSE 0.55 OF 49 WHERE MILITARY GLORY IS STRONGLY CR MODERATELY EMPHASIZED (55) PES	419	DRIFT MORE TOWARD BEING THCSE 0.76 OF 37 WHERE MILITARY GLORY IS STRONGLY OR MODERATELY EMPHASIZED (55) PES	27 28 22 9 XSQ= 3.03 PHI= -0.188 XP = 0.0818
424	DRIFT TCWARD BEING THOSE 0.76 OF 25 WHERE RELIGICUS SPECIALISTS ARE PART-TIME, RATHER THAN FULL-TIME (33) JMH	424	DRIFT TOWARD BEING THOSE 0.52 OF 29 WHERE RELIGIOUS SPECIALISTS ARE FULL-TIME, RATHER THAN PART-TIME (21) JMH	6 15 19 14 XSQ= 3.25 PHI= -0.245 XP = 0.0712
449	TILT LESS TOWARD BEING THOSE 0.54 OF 35 WHERE THE CBSERVATION CF FCOD TABOOS IS MEDIUM CR LOW, RATHER THAN HIGH (61) JRL	449	TILT MORE TOWARD BEING THOSE 0.82 OF 51 WHERE THE OBSERVATION OF FCOD TABCOS IS MEDIUM OR LOW, RATHER THAN HIGH (61) JRL	16 9 19 42 XSQ= 6.63 PHI= 0.278 XP = 0.0100

450	LEAN MORE TOWARD BEING THOSE 0.89 OF 35 WHERE THE OBSERVATION OF FOOD TABOOS IS HIGH OR MEDIUM, RATHER THAN LOW (60) JRL	LEAN LESS TOWARD BEING THOSE 0.57 OF 51 WHERE THE OBSERVATION OF FOOD TABOOS IS HIGH OR MEDIUM, RATHER THAN LOW (60) JRL	31 29 4 22 XSQ= 8.45 PHI= 0.313 XP = 0.0037
468	TILT MORE TOWARD BEING THOSE 0.88 OF 25 WHERE CONTACT WITH OTHER CULTURES IS REGULAR OR IRREGULAR, RATHER THAN FREQUENT (37) JMH	TILT LESS TOWARD BEING THOSE 0.52 OF 29 WHERE CONTACT WITH OTHER CULTURES IS REGULAR OR IRREGULAR, RATHER THAN FREQUENT (37) JMH	3 14 22 15 XSQ= 6.60 PHI= -0.349 XP = 0.0102
470	DRIFT TOWARD BEING THOSE 0.76 OF 25 WHERE INNOVATIONS ARE ACCEPTED ONLY SELECTIVELY (33) JMH	DRIFT TOWARD BEING THOSE 0.52 OF 29 WHERE INNOVATIONS ARE GENERALLY ACCEPTED (21) JMH	6 15 19 14 XSQ= 3.25 PHI= -0.245 XP = 0.0712
477	DRIFT TOWARD BEING THOSE 0.73 OF 15 WHERE ALCOHOLIC AGGRESSION IS MODERATE OR SLIGHT (19) DH	DRIFT TOWARD BEING THOSE 0.58 OF 19 WHERE ALCOHOLIC AGGRESSION IS STRONG (15) DH	4 11 11 8 XSQ= 2.17 PHI= -0.253 EP = 0.0915
482	TILT LESS TOWARD BEING THOSE 0.79 OF 80 WHERE THE PRINCIPAL ETHNOGRAPHERS HAVE BEEN OTHER THAN BRITISH (336)	TILT MORE TOWARD BEING THOSE 0.89 OF 308 WHERE THE PRINCIPAL ETHNOGRAPHERS HAVE BEEN OTHER THAN BRITISH (336)	17 35 63 273 XSQ= 4.53 PHI= 0.108 XP = 0.0333
488	TILT MORE TOWARD BEING THOSE 0.85 OF 55 ABOUT WHICH THE PRINCIPAL ETHNOGRAPHIES WERE PUBLISHED BEFORE 1950 (185)	TILT LESS TOWARD BEING THOSE 0.68 OF 202 ABOUT WHICH THE PRINCIPAL ETHNOGRAPHIES WERE PUBLISHED BEFORE 1950 (185)	47 138 8 64 XSQ= 5.47 PHI= 0.146 XP = 0.0193
489	LEAN LESS TOWARD BEING THOSE 0.76 OF 82 NOT INCLUDED IN CHARLES ACKERMAN'S STUDY OF DIVORCE (343)	LEAN MORE TOWARD BEING THOSE 0.88 OF 318 NOT INCLUDED IN CHARLES ACKERMAN'S STUDY OF DIVORCE (343)	20 37 62 281 XSQ= 7.67 PHI= 0.138 XP = 0.0056
490	TEND TO BE THOSE 0.70 OF 82 INCLUDED IN ALBERT S. ANTHONY'S SAMPLE ON MALE INITIATION RITES (113)	TEND TO BE THOSE 0.82 OF 318 NOT INCLUDED IN ALBERT S. ANTHONY'S SAMPLE ON MALE INITIATION RITES (287)	57 56 25 262 XSQ= 84.10 PHI= 0.459 XP = 0.
491	TEND LESS TO BE THOSE 0.68 OF 82 NOT INCLUDED IN DORRIAN APPLE'S STUDY OF GRANDPARENTHOOD (352)	TEND MORE TO BE THOSE 0.93 OF 318 NOT INCLUDED IN DORRIAN APPLE'S STUDY OF GRANDPARENTHOOD (352)	26 22 56 296 XSQ= 35.62 PHI= 0.298 XP = 0.

492	TEND LESS TO BE THCSE 0.63 OF 82 NOT INCLUDED IN BARBARA CHARTIER AYRES' STUDY OF FEMALE INITIATION RITES (361)	492	TEND MORE TO BE THOSE 0.97 OF 318 NOT INCLUDED IN BARBARA CHARTIER AYRES' STUDY OF FEMALE INITIATION RITES (361)	30 9 52 309 XSQ= 80.62 PHI= 0.449 XP = 0.
493	TEND TO BE THCSE 0.72 OF 82 INCLUDED IN BACCN, BARRY, AND CHILC'S STUDY OF CHILD REARING (78)	493	TEND TO BE THOSE 0.94 OF 318 NOT INCLUDED IN BACON, BARRY, AND CHILD'S STUDY OF CHILD REARING (322)	59 19 23 299 XSQ= 176.59 PHI= 0.664 XP = 0.
494	TEND LESS TO BE THCSE 0.76 OF 82 NOT INCLUDED IN HERBERT M. BARRY III'S STUDY OF ART (371)	494	TEND MORE TO BE THOSE 0.97 OF 318 NOT INCLUDED IN HERBERT M. BARRY III'S STUDY OF ART (371)	20 9 62 309 XSQ= 41.91 PHI= 0.324 XP = 0.
495	TEND LESS TO BE THCSE 0.52 OF 82 NOT INCLUDED IN JUCITH K. BROWN'S STUDY OF FEMALE INITIATION RITES (335)	495	TEND MORE TO BE THOSE 0.92 OF 318 NOT INCLUDED IN JUDITH K. BROWN'S STUDY OF FEMALE INITIATICN RITES (335)	39 26 43 292 XSQ= 71.44 PHI= 0.423 XP = 0.
496	TEND LESS TO BE THCSE 0.66 OF 82 NOT INCLUDED IN ROY G. C'ANDRADE'S STUDY OF DREAMS (345)	496	TEND MORE TO BE THOSE 0.92 OF 318 NOT INCLUDED IN ROY G. D'ANDRADE'S STUDY OF DREAMS (345)	28 27 54 291 XSQ= 34.05 PHI= 0.292 XP = 0.
497	TEND LESS TO BE THCSE 0.65 OF 82 NOT INCLUDED IN WILLIAM M. EVAN'S STUDY OF LAW (339)	497	TEND MORE TO BE THOSE 0.90 OF 318 NOT INCLUDED IN WILLIAM M. EVAN'S STUDY OF LAW (339)	29 32 53 286 XSQ= 30.37 PHI= 0.276 XP = 0.
498	TEND LESS TO BE THCSE 0.63 OF 82 NCT INCLUDED IN C. S. FORC'S STUDY OF SEX (349)	498	TEND MORE TO BE THOSE 0.93 CF 318 NOT INCLUDED IN C. S. FORD'S STUDY OF SEX (349)	30 21 52 297 XSQ= 50.02 PHI= 0.354 XP = 0.
499	TEND TO BE THOSE 0.55 OF 82 INCLUDED IN FCRC ANC BEACH'S SAMPLE ON SEXUAL EXPRESSICN BY THE YCUNG (86)	499	TEND TO BE THOSE 0.87 OF 318 NOT INCLUDED IN FORD AND BEACH'S SAMPLE ON SEXUAL EXPRESSION BY THE YOUNG (314)	45 41 37 277 XSQ= 65.62 PHI= 0.405 XP = 0.
500	TEND LESS TO BE THCSE 0.70 OF 82 NOT INCLUDED IN FREEMAN ANC WINCH'S STUDY OF SOCIETAL COMPLEXITY (360)	500	TEND MORE TO BE THOSE 0.95 OF 318 NOT INCLUDED IN FREEMAN AND WINCH'S STUDY OF SOCIETAL COMPLEXITY (360)	25 15 57 303 XSQ= 45.28 PHI= 0.336 XP = 0.

501	TEND TO BE THOSE 0.56 OF 82 INCLUDED IN JOAN FRIENDLY GOODMAN'S STUDY OF ASCETIC MOURNING BEHAVIOR (67)	501	TEND TO BE THOSE 0.93 OF 318 NOT INCLUDED IN JOAN FRIENDLY GOODMAN'S STUDY OF ASCETIC MOURNING BEHAVIOR (333)	46 21 36 297 XSQ= 111.00 PHI= 0.527 XP = 0.
502	TEND LESS TO BE THOSE 0.51 OF 82 NOT INCLUDED IN JOHN K. HARLEY'S STUDY OF ADOLESCENT PEER GROUPS (343)	502	TEND MORE TO BE THOSE 0.95 OF 318 NOT INCLUDED IN JOHN K. HARLEY'S STUDY OF ADOLESCENT PEER GROUPS (343)	40 17 42 301 XSQ= 97.12 PHI= 0.493 XP = 0.
503	TEND LESS TO BE THOSE 0.70 OF 82 NOT INCLUDED IN JOHN M. HICKMAN'S STUDY OF THE FOLK-URBAN CONTINUUM (346)	503	TEND MORE TO BE THOSE 0.91 OF 318 NOT INCLUDED IN JOHN M. HICKMAN'S STUDY OF THE FOLK-URBAN CONTINUUM (346)	25 29 57 289 XSQ= 23.69 PHI= 0.243 XP = 0.0000
504	TEND LESS TO BE THOSE 0.71 OF 82 NOT INCLUDED IN DONALD HORTON'S STUDY OF ALCHOLISM (351)	504	TEND MORE TO BE THOSE 0.92 OF 318 NOT INCLUDED IN DONALD HORTON'S STUDY OF ALCHOLISM (351)	24 25 58 293 XSQ= 25.83 PHI= 0.254 XP = 0.0000
505	DRIFT LESS TOWARD BEING THOSE 0.90 OF 82 NOT INCLUDED IN MERRILL JACKSON'S STUDY OF CRIMINAL LAW AND MEDICINE (380)	505	DRIFT MORE TOWARD BEING THOSE 0.96 OF 318 NOT INCLUDED IN MERRILL JACKSON'S STUDY OF CRIMINAL LAW AND MEDICINE (380)	8 12 74 306 XSQ= 3.73 PHI= 0.097 XP = 0.0533
506	TEND LESS TO BE THOSE 0.61 OF 82 NOT INCLUDED IN LAMBERT, TRIANDIS, AND WOLF'S STUDY OF SUPERNATURAL BEINGS (364)	506	TEND MORE TO BE THOSE 0.99 OF 318 NOT INCLUDED IN LAMBERT, TRIANDIS, AND WOLF'S STUDY OF SUPERNATURAL BEINGS (364)	32 4 50 314 XSQ= 108.97 PHI= 0.522 XP = 0.
507	TEND LESS TO BE THOSE 0.57 OF 82 NOT INCLUDED IN JAMES R. LEARY'S STUDY OF FOOD TABOOS (314)	507	TEND MORE TO BE THOSE 0.84 OF 318 NOT INCLUDED IN JAMES R. LEARY'S STUDY OF FOOD TABOOS (314)	35 51 47 267 XSQ= 25.87 PHI= 0.254 XP = 0.0000
508	TEND LESS TO BE THOSE 0.65 OF 82 NOT INCLUDED IN DAVID C. MCCLELLAND'S STUDY OF ACHIEVEMENT MOTIVATION (360)	508	TEND MORE TO BE THOSE 0.97 OF 318 NOT INCLUDED IN DAVID C. MCCLELLAND'S STUDY OF ACHIEVEMENT MOTIVATION (360)	29 11 53 307 XSQ= 70.24 PHI= 0.419 XP = 0.
509	TEND LESS TO BE THOSE 0.84 OF 82 NOT INCLUDED IN MONI NAG'S STUDY OF FERTILITY (375)	509	TEND MORE TO BE THOSE 0.96 OF 318 NOT INCLUDED IN MONI NAG'S STUDY OF FERTILITY (375)	13 12 69 306 XSQ= 14.24 PHI= 0.189 XP = 0.0002

510	TEND LESS TO BE THCSE 0.87 OF 82 NOT INCLUDED IN RACUL NARRCLL'S STUDY OF SCCIETAL COMPLEXITY (380)	510	TEND MORE TO BE THOSE 0.97 OF 318 NOT INCLUDED IN RAOUL NARRCLL'S STUDY OF SOCIETAL COMPLEXITY (380)	11 9 71 309 XSQ= 13.23 PHI= 0.182 XP = 0.0003
511	TEND TO BE THCSE 0.77 OF 82 INCLUDED IN RCBERTS, ARTH AND BUSH'S SAMPLE ON GAMES, AS MCDIFIED BY THE ETHNOGRAPHIC ATLAS (189)	511	TEND TO BE THOSE 0.60 OF 318 NOT INCLUDED IN ROBERTS, ARTH AND BUSH'S SAMPLE ON GAMES, AS MODIFIED BY THE ETHNOGRAPHIC ATLAS (211)	63 126 19 192 XSQ= 34.73 PHI= 0.295 XP = 0.
512	TEND LESS TO BE THCSE 0.73 OF 82 NOT INCLUDED IN SHIRLEY AND ROMNEY'S STUDY OF LCVE MAGIC (367)	512	TEND MORE TO BE THOSE 0.97 OF 318 NOT INCLUDED IN SHIRLEY AND ROMNEY'S STUDY OF LOVE MAGIC (367)	22 11 60 307 XSQ= 44.00 PHI= 0.332 XP = 0.
513	TEND LESS TO BE THCSE 0.78 OF 82 NCT INCLUDED IN LEC W. SIMMONS' STUDY OF THE TREATMENT OF THE AGEC (357)	513	TEND MORE TO BE THOSE 0.92 OF 318 NOT INCLUDED IN LEO W. SIMMONS' STUDY OF THE TREATMENT OF THE AGED (357)	18 25 64 293 XSQ= 12.06 PHI= 0.174 XP = 0.0005
514	TEND TO BE THOSE 0.62 OF 82 INCLUDED IN PHILIP E. SLATER'S STUDY OF NARCISSISM (90)	514	TEND TO BE THOSE 0.88 OF 318 NOT INCLUDED IN PHILIP E. SLATER'S STUDY OF NARCISSISM (310)	51 39 31 279 XSQ= 90.36 PHI= 0.475 XP = 0.
515	TEND LESS TO BE THCSE 0.55 OF 82 NOT INCLUDED IN WILLIAM N. STEPHENS' SAMPLE CN AVOIDANCE RELATICNSHIPS (348)	515	TEND MORE TO BE THOSE 0.95 OF 318 NOT INCLUDED IN WILLIAM N. STEPHENS' SAMPLE ON AVOIDANCE RELATICNSHIPS (348)	37 15 45 303 XSQ= 90.56 PHI= 0.476 XP = 0.
516	LEAN MCRE TOWARC BEING THCSE 0.95 OF 82 INCLUDED IN GUY E. SWANSCN'S SAMPLE ON LOCAL JURISCICTION, AS MODIFIED BY THE ETHNOGRAPHIC ATLAS (331)	516	LEAN LESS TOWARD BEING THOSE 0.80 OF 318 INCLUDED IN GUY E. SWANSCN'S SAMPLE ON LOCAL JURISDICTION, AS MODIFIED BY THE ETHNOGRAPHIC ATLAS (331)	78 253 4 65 XSQ= 10.00 PHI= 0.158 XP = 0.0016
517	TEND MORE TO BE THCSE 0.83 OF 82 INCLUDED IN GUY E. SWANSON'S SAMPLE CN HIGH GODS, AS MCDIFIED BY THE ETHNOGRAPHIC ATLAS (260)	517	TEND LESS TO BE THOSE 0.60 OF 318 INCLUDED IN GUY E. SWANSCN'S SAMPLE ON HIGH GODS, AS MODIFIED BY THE ETHNOGRAPHIC ATLAS (260)	68 192 14 126 XSQ= 13.60 PHI= 0.184 XP = 0.0002
518	TEND TO BE THOSE 0.56 OF 82 INCLUDED IN STANLEY H. UDY, JR.'S STUDY OF WCRK ORGANIZATION (105)	518	TEND TO BE THOSE 0.81 OF 318 NOT INCLUDED IN STANLEY H. UDY, JR.'S STUDY OF WORK ORGANIZATION (295)	46 59 36 259 XSQ= 45.55 PHI= 0.337 XP = 0.

```
519  TEND LESS TO BE THCSE            0.68 OF  82     519  TEND MORE TO BE THOSE            0.97 OF 318          26   10
     NOT INCLUDED IN JOSEPH VEROFF'S                       NOT INCLUDED IN JOSEPH VEROFF'S                      56  308
     STUDY OF ACHIEVEMENT MOTIVATION AS                    STUDY OF ACHIEVEMENT MOTIVATION AS            XSQ=   61.50
     REVEALED IN FCLKTALES  (364)                          REVEALED IN FOLKTALES  (364)                  PHI=   0.392
                                                                                                         XP =  0.

520  TEND LESS TO BE THCSE            0.72 OF  82     520  TEND MORE TO BE THOSE            0.95 OF 318          23   17
     NOT INCLUDED IN                                       NOT INCLUDED IN                                      59  301
     BEATRICE BLYTH WHITING'S                              BEATRICE BLYTH WHITING'S                      XSQ=   34.85
     STUDY OF SCRCERY  (360)                               STUDY OF SORCERY  (360)                       PHI=   0.295
                                                                                                         XP =  0.

523  TEND TO BE THOSE                 0.51 OF  82     523  TEND TO BE THOSE                 0.94 OF 318          42   19
     INCLUDED IN WHITING AND CHILD'S                       NOT INCLUDED IN WHITING AND CHILD'S                  40  299
     STUDY OF CHILD TRAINING                               STUDY OF CHILD TRAINING                       XSQ=   99.78
     AND PERSONALITY  (61)                                 AND PERSONALITY  (339)                        PHI=   0.499
                                                                                                         XP =  0.

524  TEND LESS TO BE THCSE            0.51 OF  82     524  TEND MORE TO BE THOSE            0.99 OF 318          40    4
     NOT INCLUDED IN                                       NOT INCLUDED IN                                      42  314
     WHITING, KLUCKHCHN, AND ANTHONY'S                     WHITING, KLUCKHOHN, AND ANTHONY'S             XSQ=  145.57
     STUDY OF MALE INITIATION CEREMONIES  (356)            STUDY OF MALE INITIATION CEREMONIES  (356)    PHI=   0.603
                                                                                                         XP =  0.
```

523 CULTURES INCLUDED IN WHITING AND CHILD'S STUDY OF CHILD TRAINING AND PERSONALITY (61)

523 CULTURES NOT INCLUDED IN WHITING AND CHILD'S STUDY OF CHILD TRAINING AND PERSONALITY (339)

BACKGROUND ON PAGE 180

SUBJECT ONLY, F.C. 1-480 AND 527-536
BOTH SUBJECT AND PREDICATE, F.C. 481-526

61 IN LEFT COLUMN

ABIPON	AINU	ALORESE	ANDAMANESE	ARAPESH	ASHANTI	AZANDE	BALINESE	CHAGGA	CHENCHU
CHIR-APACHE	COMANCHE	COPR ESKIMO	DOBUANS	DUSUN	FON	HANO	IFUGAO	JIVARO	KURTATCHI
KUTENAI	KWAKIUTL	LAKHER	LAMBA	LAPPS	LEPCHA	LESU	MANUS	MAORI	MARQUESANS
MARSHALLESE	MASAI	MURNGIN	NAVAHO	OMAHA	ONTONG-JAVA	PAPAGO	PUKAPUKA	RIFFIANS	RWALA
SAMOANS	SANPOIL	SENIANG	SIRIONO	TANALA	TAOS	TENINO	TETON	THONGA	TIKOPIA
TIV	TROBRIAND	VENDA	WAPISHANA	WARRAU	WITOTO	WOGEO	YAGUA	YAKUT	YUKAGHIR
ZUNI									

339 IN RIGHT COLUMN

6	LEAN LESS TOWARD BEING THOSE LOCATED OUTSIDE OF THE INSULAR PACIFIC (330)	0.67 OF 61	6	LEAN MORE TOWARD BEING THOSE LOCATED OUTSIDE OF THE INSULAR PACIFIC (330)	0.85 OF 339	20 50 41 289 XSQ= 10.43 PHI= 0.162 XP = 0.0012
63	TILT TOWARD BEING THOSE WHERE HUSBANDRY, IF PRESENT, IS PRINCIPALLY IN THE FORM OF PIGS, SHEEP, OR GOATS, RATHER THAN BOVINE, EQUINE, CAMEL-LIKE, OR DEER-LIKE ANIMALS (74)	0.51 OF 37	63	TILT TOWARD BEING THOSE WHERE HUSBANDRY, IF PRESENT, IS PRINCIPALLY IN THE FORM OF BOVINE, EQUINE, CAMEL-LIKE, OR DEER-LIKE ANIMALS, RATHER THAN PIGS, SHEEP, OR GOATS (152)	0.71 OF 189	18 134 19 55 XSQ= 5.98 PHI= -0.163 XP = 0.0144
79	IN ALL CASES ARE THOSE WHERE NO CITY IS PRESENT (201)	1.00 OF 40	79	TILT LESS TOWARD BEING THOSE WHERE NO CITY IS PRESENT (201)	0.88 OF 184	0 23 40 161 XSQ= 4.30 PHI= -0.139 XP = 0.0382
94	TILT MORE TOWARD BEING THOSE WHERE THE HIERARCHY OF NATIONAL JURISDICTION HAS TWO, ONE, OR NO LEVELS (296) GES,EA	0.98 OF 56	94	TILT LESS TOWARD BEING THOSE WHERE THE HIERARCHY OF NATIONAL JURISDICTION HAS TWO, ONE, OR NO LEVELS (296) GES,EA	0.88 OF 274	1 33 55 241 XSQ= 4.24 PHI= -0.113 XP = 0.0394
107	IN ALL CASES ARE THOSE WHERE CLASS STRATIFICATION, IF PRESENT, IS BASED ON SOMETHING OTHER THAN OCCUPATIONAL STATUS (160)	1.00 OF 30	107	LEAN LESS TOWARD BEING THOSE WHERE CLASS STRATIFICATION, IF PRESENT, IS BASED ON SOMETHING OTHER THAN OCCUPATIONAL STATUS (160)	0.75 OF 173	0 43 30 130 XSQ= 8.03 PHI= -0.199 XP = 0.0046

108	LEAN TOWARD BEING THOSE 0.60 OF 30 WHERE CLASS STRATIFICATION, IF PRESENT, IS BASED CN A HEREDITARY ARISTCCRACY (74)	108	LEAN TOWARD BEING THOSE 0.68 OF 173 WHERE CLASS STRATIFICATION, IF PRESENT, IS BASED ON SOMETHING OTHER THAN A HEREDITARY ARISTOCRACY (129)	18 56 12 117 XSQ= 7.28 PHI= 0.189 XP = 0.0070
186	DRIFT MORE TCWARC BEING THOSE 0.74 OF 61 WHERE THE KIN GRCUP IS OTHER THAN EXCLUSIVELY PATRILINEAL (250)	186	DRIFT LESS TOWARD BEING THOSE 0.60 OF 339 WHERE THE KIN GROUP IS OTHER THAN EXCLUSIVELY PATRILINEAL (250)	16 134 45 205 XSQ= 3.35 PHI= -0.092 XP = 0.0670
201	DRIFT LESS TOWARD BEING THOSE 0.75 OF 61 WHERE MARITAL RESIDENCE IS NCN-CPTICNAL, RATHER THAN AMBILCCAL CR NECLOCAL (334)	201	DRIFT MORE TOWARD BEING THCSE 0.85 OF 337 WHERE MARITAL RESIDENCE IS NON-OPTIONAL, RATHER THAN AMBILOCAL OR NEOLOCAL (334)	46 288 15 49 XSQ= 3.16 PHI= -0.089 XP = 0.0756
204	DRIFT LESS TCWARD BEING THOSE 0.71 OF 52 WHERE MARITAL RESIDENCE IS PATRILOCAL, VIRILOCAL, CR AVUNCULOCAL, RATHER THAN AMBILCCAL CR NECLOCAL (270)	204	DRIFT MORE TOWARD BEING THOSE 0.83 OF 282 WHERE MARITAL RESIDENCE IS PATRILOCAL, VIRILOCAL, OR AVUNCULOCAL, RATHER THAN AMBILOCAL OR NEOLOCAL (270)	37 233 15 49 XSQ= 3.03 PHI= -0.095 XP = 0.0820
213	TILT MORE TOWARC BEING THCSE 0.67 OF 60 WHERE FIRST CCUSIN MARRIAGE IS NCT PERMITTED (198)	213	TILT LESS TOWARD BEING THOSE 0.51 OF 310 WHERE FIRST COUSIN MARRIAGE IS NOT PERMITTED (198)	20 152 40 158 XSQ= 4.37 PHI= -0.109 XP = 0.0366
259	TILT TOWARD BEING THOSE 0.59 OF 27 WHERE THE SEVERITY OF MOTHER-IN-LAW AVOIDANCE IS LOW (20) WNS	259	TILT TOWARD BEING THOSE 0.79 OF 19 WHERE THE SEVERITY OF MOTHER-IN-LAW AVOIDANCE IS HIGH (26) WNS	11 15 16 4 XSQ= 5.16 PHI= -0.335 XP = 0.0231
328	TILT TCWARD BEING THOSE 0.65 OF 23 WHERE THE AGE OF THE INFANT AT THE ONSET OF SERIOUS SOCIALIZATION, CTHER THAN WEANING, IS TWC YEARS CR LOWER (20) B-B-C	328	TILT TOWARD BEING THOSE 0.72 OF 18 WHERE THE AGE OF THE INFANT AT THE ONSET OF SERIOUS SOCIALIZATICN, OTHER THAN WEANING, IS HIGHER THAN TWO YEARS (21) B-B-C	8 13 15 5 XSQ= 4.27 PHI= -0.323 XP = 0.0389
342	DRIFT TOWARD BEING THOSE 0.52 OF 25 WHERE THE CHILD'S INFERREC ANXIETY OVER PERFORMANCE OF NURTURANT BEHAVIOR IS HIGH (18) B-B-C	342	DRIFT TOWARD BEING THOSE 0.76 OF 21 WHERE THE CHILD'S INFERRED ANXIETY OVER PERFORMANCE OF NURTURANT BEHAVIOR IS LOW (28) B-B-C	13 5 12 16 XSQ= 2.72 PHI= 0.243 XP = 0.0993
347	DRIFT TOWARD BEING THCSE 0.62 OF 42 WHERE THE CHILD'S INFERREC CONFLICT REGARDING SELF-RELIANT BEHAVIOR IS LCW (39) B-B-C	347	DRIFT TOWARD BEING THOSE 0.62 OF 34 WHERE THE CHILD'S INFERRED CONFLICT REGARDING SELF-RELIANT BEHAVIOR IS HIGH (37) B-B-C	16 21 26 13 XSQ= 3.32 PHI= -0.209 XP = 0.0685

360	TILT TOWARD BEING THOSE 0.79 OF 19 WHERE ADOLESCENT PEER GROUPS ARE PRESENT ONLY IN A SETTING OF LEISURE, OR ELSE ARE ABSENT (23) JKH	360	TILT TOWARD BEING THOSE 0.56 OF 18 WHERE ADOLESCENT PEER GROUPS ARE PRESENT IN A SETTING OF WORK AND PUBLIC GATHERINGS AND LEISURE, OR AT LEAST OF PUBLIC GATHERINGS AND LEISURE (14) JKH	4 10 15 8 XSQ= 3.33 PHI= -0.300 EP = 0.0448
365	DRIFT LESS TOWARD BEING THOSE 0.52 OF 23 WHERE THE TIME SPENT IN ADOLESCENT PEER GROUP ACTIVITY IS HIGH OR HIGH-MEDIUM (30) JKH	365	DRIFT MORE TOWARD BEING THOSE 0.82 OF 22 WHERE THE TIME SPENT IN ADOLESCENT PEER GROUP ACTIVITY IS HIGH OR HIGH-MEDIUM (30) JKH	12 18 11 4 XSQ= 3.21 PHI= -0.267 XP = 0.0731
391	TILT TOWARD BEING THOSE 0.64 OF 45 WHERE PREMARITAL SEX RELATIONS ARE PUNISHED ONLY IF PREGNANCY RESULTS, OR FREELY PERMITTED (90) JTW,EA	391	TILT TOWARD BEING THOSE 0.54 OF 134 WHERE PREMARITAL SEX RELATIONS ARE STRONGLY PUNISHED AND IN FACT RARE, OR WEAKLY PUNISHED AND IN FACT NOT RARE (89) JTW,EA	16 73 29 61 XSQ= 4.10 PHI= -0.151 XP = 0.0429
400	DRIFT TOWARD BEING THOSE 0.52 OF 29 WHERE HOMOSEXUAL ACTIVITY IS PROHIBITED (22) F-B	400	DRIFT TOWARD BEING THOSE 0.76 OF 29 WHERE HOMOSEXUAL ACTIVITY IS PERMITTED (36) F-B	15 7 14 22 XSQ= 3.59 PHI= 0.249 XP = 0.0582
449	LEAN TOWARD BEING THOSE 0.54 OF 24 WHERE THE OBSERVATION OF FOOD TABOOS IS HIGH, RATHER THAN MEDIUM OR LOW (25) JRL	449	LEAN TOWARD BEING THOSE 0.81 OF 62 WHERE THE OBSERVATION OF FOOD TABOOS IS MEDIUM OR LOW, RATHER THAN HIGH (61) JRL	13 12 11 50 XSQ= 8.55 PHI= 0.315 XP = 0.0035
456	LEAN TOWARD BEING THOSE 0.76 OF 17 WHERE THE INTERNALIZATION OF THE INDIVIDUAL'S CONTACT WITH THE DIVINE IS NOT CONDUCIVE TO THE DEVELOPMENT OF THE INDIVIDUAL'S NEED TO ACHIEVE (17) DCM	456	LEAN TOWARD BEING THOSE 0.79 OF 19 WHERE THE INTERNALIZATION OF THE INDIVIDUAL'S CONTACT WITH THE DIVINE IS CONDUCIVE TO THE DEVELOPMENT OF THE INDIVIDUAL'S NEED TO ACHIEVE (19) DCM	4 15 13 4 XSQ= 8.94 PHI= -0.498 EP = 0.0021
468	DRIFT MORE TOWARD BEING THOSE 0.88 OF 17 WHERE CONTACT WITH OTHER CULTURES IS REGULAR OR IRREGULAR, RATHER THAN FREQUENT (37) JMH	468	DRIFT LESS TOWARD BEING THOSE 0.59 OF 37 WHERE CONTACT WITH OTHER CULTURES IS REGULAR OR IRREGULAR, RATHER THAN FREQUENT (37) JMH	2 15 15 22 XSQ= 3.24 PHI= -0.245 XP = 0.0720
479	DRIFT TOWARD BEING THOSE 0.67 OF 18 WHERE THE NEED TO ACHIEVE, AS INFERRED FROM FOLKTALES, IS LOW (18) JV	479	DRIFT TOWARD BEING THOSE 0.67 OF 18 WHERE THE NEED TO ACHIEVE, AS INFERRED FROM FOLKTALES, IS HIGH (18) JV	6 12 12 6 XSQ= 2.78 PHI= -0.278 EP = 0.0564
488	TEND MORE TO BE THOSE 0.96 OF 45 ABOUT WHICH THE PRINCIPAL ETHNOGRAPHIES WERE PUBLISHED BEFORE 1950 (185)	488	TEND LESS TO BE THOSE 0.67 OF 212 ABOUT WHICH THE PRINCIPAL ETHNOGRAPHIES WERE PUBLISHED BEFORE 1950 (185)	43 142 2 70 XSQ= 13.65 PHI= 0.230 XP = 0.0002

489	DRIFT LESS TOWARD BEING THOSE 0.77 OF 61 NOT INCLUDED IN CHARLES ACKERMAN'S STUDY OF DIVORCE (343)	489	DRIFT MORE TOWARD BEING THOSE 0.87 OF 339 NOT INCLUDED IN CHARLES ACKERMAN'S STUDY OF DIVORCE (343)	14 43 47 296 XSQ= 3.66 PHI= 0.096 XP = 0.0558
490	TEND TO BE THOSE 0.77 OF 61 INCLUDED IN ALBERT S. ANTHONY'S SAMPLE ON MALE INITIATION RITES (113)	490	TEND TO BE THOSE 0.81 OF 339 NOT INCLUDED IN ALBERT S. ANTHONY'S SAMPLE ON MALE INITIATION RITES (287)	47 66 14 273 XSQ= 81.75 PHI= 0.452 XP = 0.
491	TEND LESS TO BE THOSE 0.66 OF 61 NOT INCLUDED IN DORRIAN APPLE'S STUDY OF GRANDPARENTHOOD (352)	491	TEND MORE TO BE THOSE 0.92 OF 339 NOT INCLUDED IN DORRIAN APPLE'S STUDY OF GRANDPARENTHOOD (352)	21 27 40 312 XSQ= 31.82 PHI= 0.282 XP = 0.
492	TEND TO BE THOSE 0.64 OF 61 INCLUDED IN BARBARA CHARTIER AYRES' STUDY OF FEMALE INITIATION RITES (39)	492	IN ALL CASES ARE THOSE 1.00 OF 339 NOT INCLUDED IN BARBARA CHARTIER AYRES' STUDY OF FEMALE INITIATION RITES (361)	39 0 22 339 XSQ= 232.94 PHI= 0.763 XP = 0.
493	TEND TO BE THOSE 0.72 OF 61 INCLUDED IN BACON, BARRY, AND CHILD'S STUDY OF CHILD REARING (78)	493	TEND TO BE THOSE 0.90 OF 339 NOT INCLUDED IN BACON, BARRY, AND CHILD'S STUDY OF CHILD REARING (322)	44 34 17 305 XSQ= 123.09 PHI= 0.555 XP = 0.
494	TEND LESS TO BE THOSE 0.54 OF 61 NOT INCLUDED IN HERBERT M. BARRY III'S STUDY OF ART (371)	494	TEND MORE TO BE THOSE 1.00 OF 339 NOT INCLUDED IN HERBERT M. BARRY III'S STUDY OF ART (371)	28 1 33 338 XSQ= 153.20 PHI= 0.619 XP = 0.
495	TEND LESS TO BE THOSE 0.64 OF 61 NOT INCLUDED IN JUDITH K. BROWN'S STUDY OF FEMALE INITIATION RITES (335)	495	TEND MORE TO BE THOSE 0.87 OF 339 NOT INCLUDED IN JUDITH K. BROWN'S STUDY OF FEMALE INITIATION RITES (335)	22 43 39 296 XSQ= 19.08 PHI= 0.218 XP = 0.0000
496	TEND LESS TO BE THOSE 0.64 OF 61 NOT INCLUDED IN ROY G. D'ANDRADE'S STUDY OF DREAMS (345)	496	TEND MORE TO BE THOSE 0.90 OF 339 NOT INCLUDED IN ROY G. D'ANDRADE'S STUDY OF DREAMS (345)	22 33 39 306 XSQ= 28.04 PHI= 0.265 XP = 0.0000
497	TEND LESS TO BE THOSE 0.66 OF 61 NOT INCLUDED IN WILLIAM M. EVAN'S STUDY OF LAW (339)	497	TEND MORE TO BE THOSE 0.88 OF 339 NOT INCLUDED IN WILLIAM M. EVAN'S STUDY OF LAW (339)	21 40 40 299 XSQ= 18.77 PHI= 0.217 XP = 0.0000

No.	Left	Proportion	No.	Right	Proportion	Statistics
498	TEND TO BE THOSE INCLUDED IN C. S. FORD'S STUDY OF SEX (51)	0.51 OF 61	498	TEND TO BE THOSE NOT INCLUDED IN C. S. FORD'S STUDY OF SEX (349)	0.94 OF 339	31 20 / 30 319 / XSQ= 89.78 / PHI= 0.474 / XP = 0.
499	TEND TO BE THOSE INCLUDED IN FORD AND BEACH'S SAMPLE ON SEXUAL EXPRESSION BY THE YOUNG (86)	0.69 OF 61	499	TEND TO BE THOSE NOT INCLUDED IN FORD AND BEACH'S SAMPLE ON SEXUAL EXPRESSION BY THE YOUNG (314)	0.87 OF 339	42 44 / 19 295 / XSQ= 92.34 / PHI= 0.480 / XP = 0.
500	TEND LESS TO BE THOSE NOT INCLUDED IN FREEMAN AND WINCH'S STUDY OF SOCIETAL COMPLEXITY (360)	0.66 OF 61	500	TEND MORE TO BE THOSE NOT INCLUDED IN FREEMAN AND WINCH'S STUDY OF SOCIETAL COMPLEXITY (360)	0.94 OF 339	21 19 / 40 320 / XSQ= 44.57 / PHI= 0.334 / XP = 0.
501	TEND TO BE THOSE INCLUDED IN JOAN FRIENDLY GOODMAN'S STUDY OF ASCETIC MOURNING BEHAVIOR (67)	0.69 OF 61	501	TEND TO BE THOSE NOT INCLUDED IN JOAN FRIENDLY GOODMAN'S STUDY OF ASCETIC MOURNING BEHAVIOR (333)	0.93 OF 339	42 25 / 19 314 / XSQ= 135.75 / PHI= 0.583 / XP = 0.
502	TEND TO BE THOSE INCLUDED IN JOHN K. HARLEY'S STUDY OF ADOLESCENT PEER GROUPS (57)	0.51 OF 61	502	TEND TO BE THOSE NOT INCLUDED IN JOHN K. HARLEY'S STUDY OF ADOLESCENT PEER GROUPS (343)	0.92 OF 339	31 26 / 30 313 / XSQ= 75.28 / PHI= 0.434 / XP = 0.
503	TEND LESS TO BE THOSE NOT INCLUDED IN JOHN M. HICKMAN'S STUDY OF THE FOLK-URBAN CONTINUUM (346)	0.72 OF 61	503	TEND MORE TO BE THOSE NOT INCLUDED IN JOHN M. HICKMAN'S STUDY OF THE FOLK-URBAN CONTINUUM (346)	0.89 OF 339	17 37 / 44 302 / XSQ= 11.32 / PHI= 0.168 / XP = 0.0008
504	TEND LESS TO BE THOSE NOT INCLUDED IN DONALD HORTON'S STUDY OF ALCHOLISM (351)	0.61 OF 61	504	TEND MORE TO BE THOSE NOT INCLUDED IN DONALD HORTON'S STUDY OF ALCHOLISM (351)	0.93 OF 339	24 25 / 37 314 / XSQ= 46.23 / PHI= 0.340 / XP = 0.
505	TEND LESS TO BE THOSE NOT INCLUDED IN MERRILL JACKSON'S STUDY OF CRIMINAL LAW AND MEDICINE (380)	0.85 OF 61	505	TEND MORE TO BE THOSE NOT INCLUDED IN MERRILL JACKSON'S STUDY OF CRIMINAL LAW AND MEDICINE (380)	0.97 OF 339	9 11 / 52 328 / XSQ= 12.10 / PHI= 0.174 / XP = 0.0005
506	TEND LESS TO BE THOSE NOT INCLUDED IN LAMBERT, TRIANDIS, AND WOLF'S STUDY OF SUPERNATURAL BEINGS (364)	0.52 OF 61	506	TEND MORE TO BE THOSE NOT INCLUDED IN LAMBERT, TRIANDIS, AND WOLF'S STUDY OF SUPERNATURAL BEINGS (364)	0.98 OF 339	29 7 / 32 332 / XSQ= 125.05 / PHI= 0.559 / XP = 0.

507	TEND LESS TO BE THCSE 0.61 OF 61 NOT INCLUDED IN JAMES R. LEARY'S STUDY OF FCOD TABOCS (314)	507	TEND MORE TO BE THOSE 0.82 OF 339 NOT INCLUDED IN JAMES R. LEARY'S STUDY OF FOOD TABOOS (314)	24 62 37 277 XSQ= 12.36 PHI= 0.176 XP = 0.0004
508	TEND LESS TO BE THCSE 0.66 OF 61 NOT INCLUDED IN DAVID C. MCCLELLAND'S STUDY OF ACHIEVEMENT MOTIVATION (360)	508	TEND MORE TO BE THOSE 0.94 OF 339 NOT INCLUDED IN DAVID C. MCCLELLAND'S STUDY OF ACHIEVEMENT MOTIVATION (360)	21 19 40 320 XSQ= 44.57 PHI= 0.334 XP = 0.
509	TILT LESS TOWARD BEING THOSE 0.87 OF 61 NOT INCLUDED IN MONI NAG'S STUDY OF FERTILITY (375)	509	TILT MORE TOWARD BEING THOSE 0.95 OF 339 NOT INCLUDED IN MONI NAG'S STUDY OF FERTILITY (375)	8 17 53 322 XSQ= 4.49 PHI= 0.106 XP = 0.0341
510	LEAN LESS TOWARD BEING THCSE 0.87 OF 61 NOT INCLUDED IN RAOUL NARROLL'S STUDY OF SOCIETAL COMPLEXITY (380)	510	LEAN MORE TOWARD BEING THOSE 0.96 OF 339 NOT INCLUDED IN RAOUL NARROLL'S STUDY OF SOCIETAL COMPLEXITY (380)	8 12 53 327 XSQ= 8.06 PHI= 0.142 XP = 0.0045
511	TEND TO BE THOSE 0.80 OF 61 INCLUDED IN ROBERTS, ARTH AND BUSH'S SAMPLE ON GAMES, AS MODIFIED BY THE ETHNOGRAPHIC ATLAS (189)	511	TEND TO BE THOSE 0.59 OF 339 NOT INCLUDED IN ROBERTS, ARTH AND BUSH'S SAMPLE ON GAMES, AS MODIFIED BY THE ETHNOGRAPHIC ATLAS (211)	49 140 12 199 XSQ= 30.05 PHI= 0.274 XP = 0.0000
512	TEND TO BE THOSE 0.54 OF 61 INCLUDED IN SHIRLEY AND ROMNEY'S STUDY OF LOVE MAGIC (33)	512	IN ALL CASES ARE THOSE 1.00 OF 339 NOT INCLUDED IN SHIRLEY AND ROMNEY'S STUDY OF LOVE MAGIC (367)	33 0 28 339 XSQ= 192.80 PHI= 0.694 XP = 0.
513	TEND LESS TO BE THCSE 0.69 OF 61 NOT INCLUDED IN LEO W. SIMMONS' STUDY OF THE TREATMENT OF THE AGED (357)	513	TEND MORE TO BE THOSE 0.93 OF 339 NOT INCLUDED IN LEO W. SIMMONS' STUDY OF THE TREATMENT OF THE AGED (357)	19 24 42 315 XSQ= 28.75 PHI= 0.268 XP = 0.0000
514	TEND TO BE THOSE 0.80 OF 61 INCLUDED IN PHILIP E. SLATER'S STUDY OF NARCISSISM (90)	514	TEND TO BE THOSE 0.88 OF 339 NOT INCLUDED IN PHILIP E. SLATER'S STUDY OF NARCISSISM (310)	49 41 12 298 XSQ= 134.15 PHI= 0.579 XP = 0.
515	TEND TO BE THOSE 0.51 OF 61 INCLUDED IN WILLIAM N. STEPHENS' SAMPLE ON AVOIDANCE RELATIONSHIPS (52)	515	TEND TO BE THOSE 0.94 OF 339 NOT INCLUDED IN WILLIAM N. STEPHENS' SAMPLE ON AVOIDANCE RELATIONSHIPS (348)	31 21 30 318 XSQ= 87.12 PHI= 0.467 XP = 0.

516	DRIFT MORE TOWARD BEING THOSE 0.92 OF 61 INCLUDED IN GUY E. SWANSON'S SAMPLE ON LOCAL JURISDICTION, AS MODIFIED BY THE ETHNOGRAPHIC ATLAS (331)	516	DRIFT LESS TOWARD BEING THOSE 0.81 OF 339 INCLUDED IN GUY E. SWANSON'S SAMPLE ON LOCAL JURISDICTION, AS MODIFIED BY THE ETHNOGRAPHIC ATLAS (331)	56 275 5 64 XSQ= 3.42 PHI= 0.092 XP = 0.0645
517	LEAN MORE TOWARD BEING THOSE 0.80 OF 61 INCLUDED IN GUY E. SWANSON'S SAMPLE ON HIGH GODS, AS MODIFIED BY THE ETHNOGRAPHIC ATLAS (260)	517	LEAN LESS TOWARD BEING THOSE 0.62 OF 339 INCLUDED IN GUY E. SWANSON'S SAMPLE ON HIGH GODS, AS MODIFIED BY THE ETHNOGRAPHIC ATLAS (260)	49 211 12 128 XSQ= 6.66 PHI= 0.129 XP = 0.0099
518	TEND TO BE THOSE 0.56 OF 61 INCLUDED IN STANLEY H. UDY, JR.'S STUDY OF WORK ORGANIZATION (105)	518	TEND TO BE THOSE 0.79 OF 339 NOT INCLUDED IN STANLEY H. UDY, JR.'S STUDY OF WORK ORGANIZATION (295)	34 71 27 268 XSQ= 30.56 PHI= 0.276 XP = 0.
519	TEND LESS TO BE THOSE 0.70 OF 61 NOT INCLUDED IN JOSEPH VEROFF'S STUDY OF ACHIEVEMENT MOTIVATION AS REVEALED IN FOLKTALES (364)	519	TEND MORE TO BE THOSE 0.95 OF 339 NOT INCLUDED IN JOSEPH VEROFF'S STUDY OF ACHIEVEMENT MOTIVATION AS REVEALED IN FOLKTALES (364)	18 18 43 321 XSQ= 34.07 PHI= 0.292 XP = 0.
520	TEND LESS TO BE THOSE 0.56 OF 61 NOT INCLUDED IN BEATRICE BLYTH WHITING'S STUDY OF SORCERY (360)	520	TEND MORE TO BE THOSE 0.96 OF 339 NOT INCLUDED IN BEATRICE BLYTH WHITING'S STUDY OF SORCERY (360)	27 13 34 326 XSQ= 89.44 PHI= 0.473 XP = 0.
522	TEND TO BE THOSE 0.69 OF 61 INCLUDED IN MARJORIE GRANT WHITING'S STUDY OF DIET (82)	522	TEND TO BE THOSE 0.88 OF 339 NOT INCLUDED IN MARJORIE GRANT WHITING'S STUDY OF DIET (318)	42 40 19 299 XSQ= 99.78 PHI= 0.499 XP = 0.
524	TEND LESS TO BE THOSE 0.56 OF 61 NOT INCLUDED IN WHITING, KLUCKHOHN, AND ANTHONY'S STUDY OF MALE INITIATION CEREMONIES (356)	524	TEND MORE TO BE THOSE 0.95 OF 339 NOT INCLUDED IN WHITING, KLUCKHOHN, AND ANTHONY'S STUDY OF MALE INITIATION CEREMONIES (356)	27 17 34 322 XSQ= 77.38 PHI= 0.440 XP = 0.

524 CULTURES INCLUDED IN WHITING, KLUCKHOHN, AND ANTHONY'S STUDY OF MALE INITIATION CEREMONIES (44)

524 CULTURES NOT INCLUDED IN WHITING, KLUCKHOHN, AND ANTHONY'S STUDY OF MALE INITIATION CEREMONIES (356)

BACKGROUND ON PAGE 180

SUBJECT ONLY, F.C. 1-480 AND 527-536
BOTH SUBJECT AND PREDICATE, F.C. 481-526

44 IN LEFT COLUMN

ALORESE	AMERICANS	ARAUCANIANS	ASHANTI	AZANDE	BALINESE	CAGABA	CAMAYURA	CHAGGA	CHEYENNE
CHIR-APACHE	COPR ESKIMO	EGYPTIANS	FON	GANDA	HANO	JAPANESE	JIVARO	KORYAK	KWAKIUTL
LAKHER	LAMBA	LAPPS	LEPCHA	LESU	MAORI	NAVAHO	NUER	NYAKYUSA	OJIBWA
ONTONG-JAVA	PAPAGO	SAMOANS	SERBS	SIRIONO	TALLENSI	TANALA	THONGA	TIMBIRA	TIV
TROBRIAND	TRUKESE	YAGUA	YAPESE						

356 IN RIGHT COLUMN

	Left column			Right column			
62	TILT MORE TOWARD BEING THOSE WHERE HUSBANDRY OF SOME KIND IS PRESENT (228)	0.73 OF 44	62	TILT LESS TOWARD BEING THOSE WHERE HUSBANDRY OF SOME KIND IS PRESENT (228)	0.55 OF 356	32 196 12 160 XSQ= 4.29 PHI= 0.104 XP = 0.0382
73	DRIFT TOWARD BEING THOSE WHERE WEAVING IS PRESENT (118)	0.62 OF 39	73	DRIFT TOWARD BEING THOSE WHERE WEAVING IS ABSENT (130)	0.55 OF 209	24 94 15 115 XSQ= 2.98 PHI= 0.110 XP = 0.0842
99	DRIFT MORE TOWARD BEING THOSE WHERE, WITH NATIONAL HIERARCHY ABSENT, THE HIERARCHY OF LOCAL JURISDICTION HAS FOUR OR THREE LEVELS (93) GES,EA	0.80 OF 20	99	DRIFT LESS TOWARD BEING THOSE WHERE, WITH NATIONAL HIERARCHY ABSENT, THE HIERARCHY OF LOCAL JURISDICTION HAS FOUR OR THREE LEVELS (93) GES,EA	0.57 OF 136	16 77 4 59 XSQ= 3.05 PHI= 0.140 XP = 0.0808
138	DRIFT TOWARD BEING THOSE WHERE SUPERORDINATE JUSTICE IS PRESENT (22) BBW	0.72 OF 18	138	DRIFT TOWARD BEING THOSE WHERE SUPERORDINATE JUSTICE IS ABSENT (18) BBW	0.59 OF 22	13 9 5 13 XSQ= 2.76 PHI= 0.263 EP = 0.0620
210	DRIFT LESS TOWARD BEING THOSE WHERE MARITAL RESIDENCE IS PATRILOCAL, RATHER THAN MATRILOCAL (169)	0.67 OF 18	210	DRIFT MORE TOWARD BEING THOSE WHERE MARITAL RESIDENCE IS PATRILOCAL, RATHER THAN MATRILOCAL (169)	0.86 OF 182	12 157 6 25 XSQ= 3.42 PHI= -0.131 XP = 0.0643

260	TILT LESS TOWARD BEING THOSE 0.58 OF 33 WHERE THE AGE OF MALES AT MARRIAGE IS LESS THAN TWENTY (38) JKH	260	TILT MORE TOWARD BEING THOSE 0.86 OF 22 WHERE THE AGE OF MALES AT MARRIAGE IS LESS THAN TWENTY (38) JKH	19 19 14 3 XSQ= 3.86 PHI= -0.265 XP = 0.0494
300	DRIFT TOWARD BEING THOSE 0.57 OF 28 WHERE THE POST-PARTUM SEX TABOO LASTS LONGER THAN SIX MONTHS (51)	300	DRIFT TOWARD BEING THOSE 0.64 OF 96 WHERE THE POST-PARTUM SEX TABOO LASTS SIX MONTHS OR LESS (73)	16 35 12 61 XSQ= 3.02 PHI= 0.156 XP = 0.0821
327	DRIFT TOWARD BEING THOSE 0.64 OF 28 WHERE THE AGE OF THE INFANT AT TIME OF REDUCED CONTACT WITH MOTHER IS HIGHER THAN TWO YEARS (28) B-B-C	327	DRIFT TOWARD BEING THOSE 0.63 OF 27 WHERE THE AGE OF THE INFANT AT TIME OF REDUCED CONTACT WITH MOTHER IS TWO YEARS OR LOWER (27) B-B-C	18 10 10 17 XSQ= 3.07 PHI= 0.236 XP = 0.0799
400	DRIFT TOWARD BEING THOSE 0.55 OF 20 WHERE HOMOSEXUAL ACTIVITY IS PROHIBITED (22) F-B	400	DRIFT TOWARD BEING THOSE 0.71 OF 38 WHERE HOMOSEXUAL ACTIVITY IS PERMITTED (36) F-B	11 11 9 27 XSQ= 2.75 PHI= 0.218 XP = 0.0971
406	TILT TOWARD BEING THOSE 0.63 OF 27 WHERE EXPLANATIONS OF ILLNESS OF AN AGGRESSION NATURE ARE PRESENT (28) W-C	406	TILT TOWARD BEING THOSE 0.68 OF 34 WHERE EXPLANATIONS OF ILLNESS OF AN AGGRESSION NATURE ARE ABSENT (33) W-C	17 11 10 23 XSQ= 4.51 PHI= 0.272 XP = 0.0336
424	DRIFT MORE TOWARD BEING THOSE 0.81 OF 16 WHERE RELIGIOUS SPECIALISTS ARE PART-TIME, RATHER THAN FULL-TIME (33) JMH	424	DRIFT LESS TOWARD BEING THOSE 0.53 OF 38 WHERE RELIGIOUS SPECIALISTS ARE PART-TIME, RATHER THAN FULL-TIME (33) JMH	3 18 13 20 XSQ= 2.77 PHI= -0.226 XP = 0.0961
430	TILT TOWARD BEING THOSE 0.73 OF 11 WHERE SUPERNATURAL SANCTIONS FOR MORALITY, HAVING AN EFFECT ON AN INDIVIDUAL'S HEALTH, ARE PRESENT (16) GES	430	TILT TOWARD BEING THOSE 0.70 OF 27 WHERE SUPERNATURAL SANCTIONS FOR MORALITY, HAVING AN EFFECT ON AN INDIVIDUAL'S HEALTH, ARE ABSENT OR UNREPORTED (22) GES	8 8 3 19 XSQ= 4.32 PHI= 0.337 EP = 0.0280
449	TEND TO BE THOSE 0.71 OF 17 WHERE THE OBSERVATION OF FOOD TABOOS IS HIGH, RATHER THAN MEDIUM OR LOW (25) JRL	449	TEND TO BE THOSE 0.81 OF 69 WHERE THE OBSERVATION OF FOOD TABOOS IS MEDIUM OR LOW, RATHER THAN HIGH (61) JRL	12 13 5 56 XSQ= 15.29 PHI= 0.422 XP = 0.0001
450	IN ALL CASES ARE THOSE 1.00 OF 17 WHERE THE OBSERVATION OF FOOD TABOOS IS HIGH OR MEDIUM, RATHER THAN LOW (60) JRL	450	LEAN LESS TOWARD BEING THOSE 0.62 OF 69 WHERE THE OBSERVATION OF FOOD TABOOS IS HIGH OR MEDIUM, RATHER THAN LOW (60) JRL	17 43 0 26 XSQ= 7.48 PHI= 0.295 XP = 0.0062

475	TILT TOWARD BEING THOSE WHERE EXHIBITIONISTIC DANCING IS STRONGLY OR MODERATELY EMPHASIZED (48) PES	0.73 OF 33	475	TILT TOWARD BEING THOSE WHERE EXHIBITIONISTIC DANCING IS NEGLIGIBLY EMPHASIZED (38) PES	0.55 OF 53	24 24 9 29 XSQ= 5.15 PHI= 0.245 XP = 0.0233
476	TILT TOWARD BEING THOSE WHERE THE DEGREE OF INSOBRIETY IS MODERATE OR SLIGHT (18) DH	0.64 OF 14	476	TILT TOWARD BEING THOSE WHERE THE DEGREE OF INSOBRIETY IS STRONG (31) DH	0.74 OF 35	5 26 9 9 XSQ= 4.85 PHI= -0.315 XP = 0.0277
490	TEND TO BE THOSE INCLUDED IN ALBERT S. ANTHONY'S SAMPLE ON MALE INITIATION RITES (113)	0.68 OF 44	490	TEND TO BE THOSE NOT INCLUDED IN ALBERT S. ANTHONY'S SAMPLE ON MALE INITIATION RITES (287)	0.77 OF 356	30 83 14 273 XSQ= 36.71 PHI= 0.303 XP = 0.
491	TEND LESS TO BE THOSE NOT INCLUDED IN DORRIAN APPLE'S STUDY OF GRANDPARENTHOOD (352)	0.59 OF 44	491	TEND MORE TO BE THOSE NOT INCLUDED IN DORRIAN APPLE'S STUDY OF GRANDPARENTHOOD (352)	0.92 OF 356	18 30 26 326 XSQ= 36.11 PHI= 0.300 XP = 0.
492	TEND TO BE THOSE INCLUDED IN BARBARA CHARTIER AYRES' STUDY OF FEMALE INITIATION RITES (39)	0.50 OF 44	492	TEND TO BE THOSE NOT INCLUDED IN BARBARA CHARTIER AYRES' STUDY OF FEMALE INITIATION RITES (361)	0.95 OF 356	22 17 22 339 XSQ= 85.95 PHI= 0.464 XP = 0.
493	TEND TO BE THOSE INCLUDED IN BACON, BARRY, AND CHILD'S STUDY OF CHILD REARING (78)	0.82 OF 44	493	TEND TO BE THOSE NOT INCLUDED IN BACON, BARRY, AND CHILD'S STUDY OF CHILD REARING (322)	0.88 OF 356	36 42 8 314 XSQ= 117.89 PHI= 0.543 XP = 0.
494	TEND LESS TO BE THOSE NOT INCLUDED IN HERBERT M. BARRY III'S STUDY OF ART (371)	0.66 OF 44	494	TEND MORE TO BE THOSE NOT INCLUDED IN HERBERT M. BARRY III'S STUDY OF ART (371)	0.96 OF 356	15 14 29 342 XSQ= 48.58 PHI= 0.348 XP = 0.
495	TEND TO BE THOSE INCLUDED IN JUDITH K. BROWN'S STUDY OF FEMALE INITIATION RITES (65)	0.61 OF 44	495	TEND TO BE THOSE NOT INCLUDED IN JUDITH K. BROWN'S STUDY OF FEMALE INITIATION RITES (335)	0.89 OF 356	27 38 17 318 XSQ= 70.26 PHI= 0.419 XP = 0.
496	TEND LESS TO BE THOSE NOT INCLUDED IN ROY G. D'ANDRADE'S STUDY OF DREAMS (345)	0.61 OF 44	496	TEND MORE TO BE THOSE NOT INCLUDED IN ROY G. D'ANDRADE'S STUDY OF DREAMS (345)	0.89 OF 356	17 38 27 318 XSQ= 23.51 PHI= 0.242 XP = 0.0000

No.	Statement	Proportion	No.	Statement	Proportion	Statistics
497	TEND TO BE THOSE INCLUDED IN WILLIAM M. EVAN'S STUDY OF LAW (61)	0.52 OF 44	497	TEND TO BE THOSE NOT INCLUDED IN WILLIAM M. EVAN'S STUDY OF LAW (339)	0.89 OF 356	23 38 21 318 XSQ= 49.26 PHI= 0.351 XP = 0.
498	TEND LESS TO BE THOSE NOT INCLUDED IN C. S. FORD'S STUDY OF SEX (349)	0.68 OF 44	498	TEND MORE TO BE THOSE NOT INCLUDED IN C. S. FORD'S STUDY OF SEX (349)	0.90 OF 356	14 37 30 319 XSQ= 14.29 PHI= 0.189 XP = 0.0002
499	TEND TO BE THOSE INCLUDED IN FORD AND BEACH'S SAMPLE ON SEXUAL EXPRESSION BY THE YOUNG (86)	0.59 OF 44	499	TEND TO BE THOSE NOT INCLUDED IN FORD AND BEACH'S SAMPLE ON SEXUAL EXPRESSION BY THE YOUNG (314)	0.83 OF 356	26 60 18 296 XSQ= 38.93 PHI= 0.312 XP = 0.
500	TEND LESS TO BE THOSE NOT INCLUDED IN FREEMAN AND WINCH'S STUDY OF SOCIETAL COMPLEXITY (360)	0.68 OF 44	500	TEND MORE TO BE THOSE NOT INCLUDED IN FREEMAN AND WINCH'S STUDY OF SOCIETAL COMPLEXITY (360)	0.93 OF 356	14 26 30 330 XSQ= 23.50 PHI= 0.242 XP = 0.0000
501	TEND TO BE THOSE INCLUDED IN JOAN FRIENDLY GOODMAN'S STUDY OF ASCETIC MOURNING BEHAVIOR (67)	0.61 OF 44	501	TEND TO BE THOSE NOT INCLUDED IN JOAN FRIENDLY GOODMAN'S STUDY OF ASCETIC MOURNING BEHAVIOR (333)	0.89 OF 356	27 40 17 316 XSQ= 67.02 PHI= 0.409 XP = 0.
502	TEND TO BE THOSE INCLUDED IN JOHN K. HARLEY'S STUDY OF ADOLESCENT PEER GROUPS (57)	0.77 OF 44	502	TEND TO BE THOSE NOT INCLUDED IN JOHN K. HARLEY'S STUDY OF ADOLESCENT PEER GROUPS (343)	0.94 OF 356	34 23 10 333 XSQ= 154.95 PHI= 0.622 XP = 0.
503	TEND LESS TO BE THOSE NOT INCLUDED IN JOHN M. HICKMAN'S STUDY OF THE FOLK-URBAN CONTINUUM (346)	0.64 OF 44	503	TEND MORE TO BE THOSE NOT INCLUDED IN JOHN M. HICKMAN'S STUDY OF THE FOLK-URBAN CONTINUUM (346)	0.89 OF 356	16 38 28 318 XSQ= 19.99 PHI= 0.224 XP = 0.0000
504	TEND LESS TO BE THOSE NOT INCLUDED IN DONALD HORTON'S STUDY OF ALCHOLISM (351)	0.68 OF 44	504	TEND MORE TO BE THOSE NOT INCLUDED IN DONALD HORTON'S STUDY OF ALCHOLISM (351)	0.90 OF 356	14 35 30 321 XSQ= 15.62 PHI= 0.198 XP = 0.0001
505	TILT LESS TOWARD BEING THOSE NOT INCLUDED IN MERRILL JACKSON'S STUDY OF CRIMINAL LAW AND MEDICINE (380)	0.86 OF 44	505	TILT MORE TOWARD BEING THOSE NOT INCLUDED IN MERRILL JACKSON'S STUDY OF CRIMINAL LAW AND MEDICINE (380)	0.96 OF 356	6 14 38 342 XSQ= 5.85 PHI= 0.121 XP = 0.0155

No.	Left	No.	Right	Statistics
506	TEND LESS TO BE THCSE 0.55 OF 44 NCT INCLUDED IN LAMBERT, TRIANDIS, ANC WOLF'S STUDY CF SUPERNATURAL BEINGS (364)	506	TEND MORE TO BE THOSE 0.96 OF 356 NOT INCLUDED IN LAMBERT, TRIANDIS, AND WOLF'S STUDY OF SUPERNATURAL BEINGS (364)	20 16 24 340 XSQ= 75.30 PHI= 0.434 XP = 0.
507	LEAN LESS TOWARC BEING THCSE 0.61 OF 44 NOT INCLUDED IN JAMES R. LEARY'S STUDY OF FCOD TABOCS (314)	507	LEAN MORE TOWARD BEING THOSE 0.81 OF 356 NOT INCLUDED IN JAMES R. LEARY'S STUDY OF FOOD TABOOS (314)	17 69 27 287 XSQ= 7.50 PHI= 0.137 XP = 0.0062
508	TEND LESS TO BE THCSE 0.68 OF 44 NOT INCLUDED IN CAVID C. MCCLELLAND'S STUDY OF ACHIEVEMENT MOTIVATION (360)	508	TEND MORE TO BE THOSE 0.93 OF 356 NOT INCLUDED IN DAVID C. MCCLELLAND'S STUDY OF ACHIEVEMENT MOTIVATION (360)	14 26 30 330 XSQ= 23.50 PHI= 0.242 XP = 0.0000
509	TEND LESS TO BE THCSE 0.80 OF 44 NOT INCLUDED IN MONI NAG'S STUDY OF FERTILITY (375)	509	TEND MORE TO BE THOSE 0.96 OF 356 NOT INCLUDED IN MONI NAG'S STUDY OF FERTILITY (375)	9 16 35 340 XSQ= 14.41 PHI= 0.190 XP = 0.0001
510	TEND LESS TO BE THCSE 0.82 OF 44 NOT INCLUDED IN RACUL NARRCLL'S STUDY OF SCCIETAL COMPLEXITY (380)	510	TEND MORE TO BE THOSE 0.97 OF 356 NOT INCLUDED IN RAOUL NARRCLL'S STUDY OF SOCIETAL COMPLEXITY (380)	8 12 36 344 XSQ= 15.10 PHI= 0.194 XP = 0.0001
511	TEND TO BE THOSE 0.84 OF 44 INCLUDED IN ROBERTS, ARTH AND BUSH'S SAMPLE ON GAMES, AS MODIFIED BY THE ETHNOGRAPHIC ATLAS (189)	511	TEND TO BE THOSE 0.57 OF 356 NOT INCLUDED IN ROBERTS, ARTH AND BUSH'S SAMPLE ON GAMES, AS MODIFIED BY THE ETHNOGRAPHIC ATLAS (211)	37 152 7 204 XSQ= 25.29 PHI= 0.251 XP = 0.0000
512	TEND LESS TO BE THCSE 0.64 OF 44 NOT INCLUDED IN SHIRLEY ANC ROMNEY'S STUDY OF LCVE MAGIC (367)	512	TEND MORE TO BE THOSE 0.95 OF 356 NOT INCLUDED IN SHIRLEY AND ROMNEY'S STUDY OF LOVE MAGIC (367)	16 17 28 339 XSQ= 47.53 PHI= 0.345 XP = 0.
513	LEAN LESS TOWARC BEING THCSE 0.75 OF 44 NCT INCLUDED IN LEC W. SIMMONS' STUDY OF THE TREATMENT OF THE AGEC (357)	513	LEAN MORE TOWARD BEING THOSE 0.91 OF 356 NOT INCLUDED IN LEO W. SIMMONS' STUDY OF THE TREATMENT OF THE AGED (357)	11 32 33 324 XSQ= 8.86 PHI= 0.149 XP = 0.0029
514	TEND TC BE THCSE 0.77 OF 44 INCLUDED IN PHILIP E. SLATER'S STUDY OF NARCISSISM (90)	514	TEND TO BE THOSE 0.84 OF 356 NOT INCLUDED IN PHILIP E. SLATER'S STUDY OF NARCISSISM (310)	34 56 10 300 XSQ= 81.56 PHI= 0.452 XP = 0.

515	TEND TO BE THOSE INCLUDED IN WILLIAM N. STEPHENS' SAMPLE ON AVOIDANCE RELATIONSHIPS (52)	0.59 OF 44	515	TEND TO BE THOSE NOT INCLUDED IN WILLIAM N. STEPHENS' SAMPLE ON AVOIDANCE RELATIONSHIPS (348)	0.93 OF 356	26 26 18 330 XSQ= 88.34 PHI= 0.470 XP = 0.
516	LEAN MORE TOWARD BEING THOSE INCLUDED IN GUY E. SWANSON'S SAMPLE ON LOCAL JURISDICTION, AS MODIFIED BY THE ETHNOGRAPHIC ATLAS (331)	0.98 OF 44	516	LEAN LESS TOWARD BEING THOSE INCLUDED IN GUY E. SWANSON'S SAMPLE ON LOCAL JURISDICTION, AS MODIFIED BY THE ETHNOGRAPHIC ATLAS (331)	0.81 OF 356	43 288 1 68 XSQ= 6.63 PHI= 0.129 XP = 0.0100
517	LEAN MORE TOWARD BEING THOSE INCLUDED IN GUY E. SWANSON'S SAMPLE ON HIGH GODS, AS MODIFIED BY THE ETHNOGRAPHIC ATLAS (260)	0.86 OF 44	517	LEAN LESS TOWARD BEING THOSE INCLUDED IN GUY E. SWANSON'S SAMPLE ON HIGH GODS, AS MODIFIED BY THE ETHNOGRAPHIC ATLAS (260)	0.62 OF 356	38 222 6 134 XSQ= 8.89 PHI= 0.149 XP = 0.0029
518	TEND TO BE THOSE INCLUDED IN STANLEY H. UDY, JR.'S STUDY OF WORK ORGANIZATION (105)	0.55 OF 44	518	TEND TO BE THOSE NOT INCLUDED IN STANLEY H. UDY, JR.'S STUDY OF WORK ORGANIZATION (295)	0.77 OF 356	24 81 20 275 XSQ= 18.84 PHI= 0.217 XP = 0.0000
519	TEND LESS TO BE THOSE NOT INCLUDED IN JOSEPH VEROFF'S STUDY OF ACHIEVEMENT MOTIVATION AS REVEALED IN FOLKTALES (364)	0.75 OF 44	519	TEND MORE TO BE THOSE NOT INCLUDED IN JOSEPH VEROFF'S STUDY OF ACHIEVEMENT MOTIVATION AS REVEALED IN FOLKTALES (364)	0.93 OF 356	11 25 33 331 XSQ= 13.34 PHI= 0.183 XP = 0.0003
520	TEND LESS TO BE THOSE NOT INCLUDED IN BEATRICE BLYTH WHITING'S STUDY OF SORCERY (360)	0.59 OF 44	520	TEND MORE TO BE THOSE NOT INCLUDED IN BEATRICE BLYTH WHITING'S STUDY OF SORCERY (360)	0.94 OF 356	18 22 26 334 XSQ= 48.69 PHI= 0.349 XP = 0.
522	TEND TO BE THOSE INCLUDED IN MARJORIE GRANT WHITING'S STUDY OF DIET (82)	0.91 OF 44	522	TEND TO BE THOSE NOT INCLUDED IN MARJORIE GRANT WHITING'S STUDY OF DIET (318)	0.88 OF 356	40 42 4 314 XSQ= 145.57 PHI= 0.603 XP = 0.
523	TEND TO BE THOSE INCLUDED IN WHITING AND CHILD'S STUDY OF CHILD TRAINING AND PERSONALITY (61)	0.61 OF 44	523	TEND TO BE THOSE NOT INCLUDED IN WHITING AND CHILD'S STUDY OF CHILD TRAINING AND PERSONALITY (339)	0.90 OF 356	27 34 17 322 XSQ= 77.38 PHI= 0.440 XP = 0.

525 CULTURES
INCLUDED IN AT LEAST ONE
CONTRIBUTOR'S SAMPLE
(DISREGARDING SAMPLES EXPANDED BY THE
ETHNOGRAPHIC ATLAS) (245)

525 CULTURES
NOT INCLUDED IN ANY
CONTRIBUTOR'S SAMPLE
(DISREGARDING SAMPLES EXPANDED BY THE
ETHNOGRAPHIC ATLAS) (155)

BACKGROUND ON PAGE 180

SUBJECT ONLY

245 IN LEFT COLUMN

ABIPON	AINU	ALBANIANS	ALORESE	AMERICANS	ANDAMANESE	APINAYE	ARANDA	ARAPESH	ARAUCANIANS
ASHANTI	ATAYAL	ATSUGEWI	AWEIKOMA	AYMARA	AZANDE	AZTEC	BALINESE	BAMBARA	BARI
BATAK	BELU	BEMBA	BHIL	BHUIYA	BULGARIANS	BUNLAP	BURMESE	BURUSHO	CAGABA
CALLINAGO	CAMAYURA	CAMBODIANS	CARIB	CAYAPA	CHAGGA	CHAMACOCO	CHENCHU	CHEROKEE	CHEYENNE
CHIR-APACHE	CHOROTI	CHUKCHEE	COCHITI	COMANCHE	COORG	COPR ESKIMO	CREE	CREEK	CROW
CUNA	CZECHS	DARD	DELAWARE	DIERI	DILLING	DOBUANS	DOGON	DOROBO	DUSUN
EGYPTIANS	EYAK	FANG	FON	FOX	GANDA	GILYAK	GISU	GOAJIRO	GOND
GROS VENTRE	HAIDA	HANO	HAVASUPAI	HAZARA	HEBREWS	HEHE	HO	HUICHOL	HUTSUL
IBAN	IFUGAO	ILA	INCA	INGASSANA	IRISH	JAPANESE	JAVANESE	JIVARO	JUKUN
KABYLE	KACHIN	KAPAUKU	KAREN	KARIERA	KASKA	KATAB	KAZAK	KERAKI	KERALA
KHALKA	KHASI	KIKUYU	KIOW-APACHE	KOREANS	KORYAK	KUNG	KURTATCHI	KUTENAI	KWAKIUTL
LAKHER	LAMBA	LANGO	LAPPS	LAU	LEPCHA	LESU	LHOTA NAGA	LOLO	LOZI
LUO	MACASSARESE	MAGUZAWA	MALAYS	MAM	MANDAN	MANGAIANS	MANUS	MAORI	MARGI
MARICOPA	MARQUESANS	MARSHALLESE	MASAI	MATACO	MBUNDU	MENDE	MIAO	MIN CHINESE	MINCHIA
MISKITO	MONGO	MOSSI	MOTA	MUNDURUCU	MURNGIN	MZAB	NAMA	NAMBICUARA	NANDI
NASKAPI	NATCHEZ	NAVAHO	NGONI	NUER	NUPE	NYAKYUSA	NYORO	OJIBWA	OMAHA
ONA	ONTONG-JAVA	ORAON	PALAUANS	PAPAGO	PAWNEE	PENOBSCOT	PONAPEANS	POPOLUCA	PUKAPUKA
PURARI	RIFFIANS	ROMANS	RUNDI	RWALA	SAMOANS	SAMOYED	SANPOIL	SARAMACCA	SELUNG
SEMANG	SEMINOLE	SENIANG	SERBS	SERI	SHERENTE	SHILLUK	SINHALESE	SIRIONO	SIUAI
SIWANS	SOMALI	SONGHAI	SOTHO	SUBANUN	SWAZI	TALLENSI	TANALA	TAOS	TAPIRAPE
TARAHUMARA	TEDA	TEHUELCHE	TENETEHARA	TENINO	TERENA	TETON	THAI	THONGA	TIBETANS
TIKOPIA	TIMBIRA	TIV	TODA	TOKELAU	TROBRIAND	TRUKESE	TRUMAI	TUBATULABAL	TUCUNA
TUPINAMBA	TURKANA	VEDDA	VENDA	VIETNAMESE	WAPISHANA	WARRAU	WICHITA	WINNEBAGO	WITOTO
WOGEO	WOLEAIANS	WOLOF	YAGUA	YAHGAN	YAKO	YAKUT	YAO	YAPESE	YARURO
YOKUTS	YORUBA	YUKAGHIR	YUROK	ZUNI					

155 IN RIGHT COLUMN

ABOR	AJIE	AKHA	ALACALUF	AMBA	ARYANS	BABWA	BACAIRI	BAJUN	BAMILEKE
BANDA	BARABRA	BASQUES	BASSERI	BAYA	BEJA	BENGALI	BERGDAMA	BETE	BIRIFOR
BLACK CARIB	BOERS	BORORO	BOTOCUDO	BOZO	BRAZILIANS	BUDUMA	BURYAT	CADUVEO	CAMBA
CARAJA	CARINYA	CHEREMIS	CHERKESS	CHIBCHA	CHINANTEC	CHIRIGUANO	CHOCO	CHORTI	DAGUR
DIEGUENO	DUTCH	ELLICE	ENGA	FUTAJALONKE	GARO	GILBERTESE	GUAHIBO	GUATO	GURE
HANUNOO	HASANIA	HASINAI	HAWAIIANS	HERERO	HUKUNDIKA	HURON	ICELANDERS	INGALIK	IRAQW
JEMEZ	KALMYK	KET	KHEVSUR	KISSI	KOHISTANI	KOL	KONSO	KPE	KUBA
KUMYK	LAKALAI	LAMET	LIFU	LUBA	MAMBILA	MAMVU	MANCHU	MANIHIKI	MATAKAM
MAYA	MAZATECO	MBUGWE	MBUTI	MENTAWEI	MERINA	MIAMI	MINANGKABAU	MIWOK	MNONG GAR
MONGUOR	MOTILON	MURINBATA	NABESNA	NDEMBU	NICOBARESE	NOMLAKI	NUNIVAK	NURI	NYANEKA
NYARO	OKINAWANS	PAEZ	PAIWAN	PALIKUR	PARAUJANO	PATHAN	PENDE	PORTUGUESE	PURUM

RAROIANS	REGEIBAT	ROTINESE	ROTUMANS	SAGADA	SANDAWE	SANTAL	SARSI	SHLUH	SIMBOESE
SINDHI	SYRIANS	TAGBANUA	TALAMANCA	TAMIL	TANIMBARESE	TAREUMIUT	TENDA	TERA	TESO
TIGRINYA	TIMUCUA	TIWI	TOLOWA	TORAJA	TOTONAC	TRISTAN	TSHIMSHIAN	TUCANO	TUNEBO
TURKMEN	TWANA	TZELTAL	ULAWANS	UTE	WAICA	WALLOONS	WANTOAT	WAROPEN	WASHO
WIKMUNKAN	WUTE	YABARANA	YOMBE	YUKI					

No.	Left	Proportion	No.	Right	Proportion	Statistics
4	TILT MORE TOWARD BEING THOSE LOCATED OUTSIDE OF THE CIRCUM-MEDITERRANEAN (355)	0.91 OF 245	4	TILT LESS TOWARD BEING THOSE LOCATED OUTSIDE OF THE CIRCUM-MEDITERRANEAN (355)	0.85 OF 155	21 24 224 131 XSQ= 3.88 PHI= -0.098 XP = 0.0489
62	TEND TO BE THOSE WHERE HUSBANDRY OF SOME KIND IS PRESENT (228)	0.65 OF 245	62	TEND TO BE THOSE WHERE HUSBANDRY OF ANY KIND IS ABSENT (172)	0.55 OF 155	159 69 86 86 XSQ= 15.27 PHI= 0.195 XP = 0.0001
71	DRIFT LESS TOWARD BEING THOSE WHERE METAL WORKING IS ABSENT (153)	0.57 OF 175	71	DRIFT MORE TOWARD BEING THOSE WHERE METAL WORKING IS ABSENT (153)	0.70 OF 76	75 23 100 53 XSQ= 3.02 PHI= 0.110 XP = 0.0821
84	LEAN LESS TOWARD BEING THOSE WHERE THE LEVEL OF POLITICAL INTEGRATION IS THE LITTLE STATE, THE MINIMAL STATE, THE AUTONOMOUS COMMUNITY, OR THE FAMILY (262) GPM	0.82 OF 208	84	LEAN MORE TOWARD BEING THOSE WHERE THE LEVEL OF POLITICAL INTEGRATION IS THE LITTLE STATE, THE MINIMAL STATE, THE AUTONOMOUS COMMUNITY, OR THE FAMILY (262) GPM	0.95 OF 96	37 5 171 91 XSQ= 7.71 PHI= 0.159 XP = 0.0055
85	TILT LESS TOWARD BEING THOSE WHERE THE LEVEL OF POLITICAL INTEGRATION IS THE MINIMAL STATE, THE AUTONOMOUS COMMUNITY, OR THE FAMILY (234) GPM	0.73 OF 208	85	TILT MORE TOWARD BEING THOSE WHERE THE LEVEL OF POLITICAL INTEGRATION IS THE MINIMAL STATE, THE AUTONOMOUS COMMUNITY, OR THE FAMILY (234) GPM	0.85 OF 96	56 14 152 82 XSQ= 4.97 PHI= 0.128 XP = 0.0258
99	TILT TOWARD BEING THOSE WHERE, WITH NATIONAL HIERARCHY ABSENT, THE HIERARCHY OF LOCAL JURISDICTION HAS FOUR OR THREE LEVELS (93) GES,EA	0.66 OF 101	99	TILT TOWARD BEING THOSE WHERE, WITH NATIONAL HIERARCHY ABSENT, THE HIERARCHY OF LOCAL JURISDICTION HAS TWO LEVELS (63) GES,EA	0.53 OF 55	67 26 34 29 XSQ= 4.61 PHI= 0.172 XP = 0.0317
100	TILT MORE TOWARD BEING THOSE WHERE HIERARCHIES ARE MORE COMPLEX THAN THE 'SIMPLEST,' I. E., MORE COMPLEX THAN TWO LOCAL LEVELS WITH NO NATIONAL LEVELS (267) GES,EA	0.85 OF 220	100	TILT LESS TOWARD BEING THOSE WHERE HIERARCHIES ARE MORE COMPLEX THAN THE 'SIMPLEST,' I. E., MORE COMPLEX THAN TWO LOCAL LEVELS WITH NO NATIONAL LEVELS (267) GES,EA	0.74 OF 110	186 81 34 29 XSQ= 4.97 PHI= 0.123 XP = 0.0259
179	TILT LESS TOWARD BEING THOSE WHERE THE COMMUNITY IS OTHER THAN STRUCTURED ON A NON-CLAN BASIS AND COMMONLY EXOGAMOUS (340)	0.86 OF 242	179	TILT MORE TOWARD BEING THOSE WHERE THE COMMUNITY IS OTHER THAN STRUCTURED ON A NON-CLAN BASIS AND COMMONLY EXOGAMOUS (340)	0.94 OF 140	33 9 209 131 XSQ= 4.00 PHI= 0.102 XP = 0.0455

185	TILT MORE TOWARD BEING THOSE 0.82 OF 156 WHERE THE LARGEST NON-COGNATIC KIN GROUP IS THE MOEITY OR PHRATRY OR SIB (194)	185	TILT LESS TOWARD BEING THOSE 0.69 OF 96 WHERE THE LARGEST NON-COGNATIC KIN GROUP IS THE MOEITY OR PHRATRY OR SIB (194)	128 66 28 30 XSQ= 5.21 PHI= 0.144 XP = 0.0225
236	DRIFT TOWARD BEING THOSE 0.57 OF 245 WHERE THE FAMILY IS OF AN EXTENDED TYPE, RATHER THAN AN INDEPENDENT TYPE (213)	236	DRIFT TOWARD BEING THOSE 0.52 OF 153 WHERE THE FAMILY IS OF AN INDEPENDENT TYPE, RATHER THAN AN EXTENDED TYPE (185)	140 73 105 80 XSQ= 3.00 PHI= 0.087 XP = 0.0833
428	TILT LESS TOWARD BEING THOSE 0.62 OF 63 WHERE A HIGH GOD, IF PRESENT AND ACTIVE, SUPPORTS HUMAN MORALITY, RATHER THAN NOT SUPPORTING IT (61) GES,EA	428	TILT MORE TOWARD BEING THOSE 0.92 OF 24 WHERE A HIGH GOD, IF PRESENT AND ACTIVE, SUPPORTS HUMAN MORALITY, RATHER THAN NOT SUPPORTING IT (61) GES,EA	39 22 24 2 XSQ= 5.99 PHI= -0.263 XP = 0.0143
458	TILT LESS TOWARD BEING THOSE 0.65 OF 135 WHERE GAMES, IF PRESENT, DO NOT INCLUDE GAMES OF STRATEGY (119) R-A-B,EA	458	TILT MORE TOWARD BEING THOSE 0.86 OF 36 WHERE GAMES, IF PRESENT, DO NOT INCLUDE GAMES OF STRATEGY (119) R-A-B,EA	47 5 88 31 XSQ= 4.93 PHI= 0.170 XP = 0.0263
459	TILT TOWARD BEING THOSE 0.56 OF 135 WHERE GAMES, IF PRESENT, DO NOT INCLUDE GAMES OF CHANCE (89) R-A-B,EA	459	TILT TOWARD BEING THOSE 0.64 OF 36 WHERE GAMES, IF PRESENT, INCLUDE GAMES OF CHANCE (82) R-A-B,EA	59 23 76 13 XSQ= 3.87 PHI= -0.150 XP = 0.0493

526 CULTURES
INCLUDED IN BETWEEN SIX AND TWENTY-SEVEN
CONTRIBUTORS' SAMPLES
(DISREGARDING SAMPLES EXPANDED BY THE
ETHNOGRAPHIC ATLAS) (108)

526 CULTURES
INCLUDED IN BETWEEN ONE AND FIVE
CONTRIBUTORS' SAMPLES
(DISREGARDING SAMPLES EXPANDED BY THE
ETHNOGRAPHIC ATLAS) (137)

BACKGROUND ON PAGE 180 SUBJECT ONLY

108 IN LEFT COLUMN

ABIPCN	AINU	ALCRESE	ANDAMANESE	ARANDA	ARAPESH	ARAUCANIANS	ASHANTI	AYMARA	AZANDE
AZTEC	BALINESE	BEMBA	BHIL	BURMESE	CARIB	CAYAPA	CHAGGA	CHENCHU	CHEYENNE
CHIR-APACHE	CHUKCHEE	COMANCHE	COPR ESKIMO	CREEK	CROW	CUNA	DOBUANS	FON	GANDA
GOND	HANC	IBAN	IFUGAO	INCA	JIVARO	JUKUN	KASKA	KAZAK	KIKUYU
KOREANS	KORYAK	KURTATCHI	KUTENAI	KWAKIUTL	LAKHER	LAMBA	LANGO	LAPPS	LAU
LEPCHA	LESU	MANDAN	MANUS	MAORI	MARQUESANS	MARSHALLESE	MASAI	MATACO	MBUNDU
MUNDURUCU	MURNGIN	NAMA	NAMBICUARA	NAVAHO	NUER	NYAKYUSA	OJIBWA	OMAHA	ONTONG-JAVA
PAPAGO	PUKAPUKA	RIFFIANS	RWALA	SAMOANS	SANPOIL	SEMANG	SENIANG	SIRIONO	SOMALI
TALLENSI	TANALA	TARAHUMARA	TENETEHARA	TETON	THAI	THONGA	TIKOPIA	TIMBIRA	TIV
TODA	TROBRIAND	TRUKESE	TUBATULABAL	TUPINAMBA	VENDA	VIETNAMESE	WARRAU	WINNEBAGO	WITOTO
WOGEO	WOLEAIANS	WOLOF	YAGUA	YAKUT	YORUBA	YUROK	ZUNI		

137 IN RIGHT COLUMN

ALBANIANS	AMERICANS	APINAYE	ATAYAL	ATSUGEWI	AWEIKOMA	BAMBARA	BARI	BATAK	BELU
BHUIYA	BULGARIANS	BUNLAP	BURUSHO	CAGABA	CALLINAGO	CAMAYURA	CAMBODIANS	CHAMACOCO	CHEROKEE
CHOROTI	COCHITI	COORG	CREE	CZECHS	DARD	DELAWARE	DIERI	DILLING	DOGON
DOROBO	DUSUN	EGYPTIANS	EYAK	FANG	FOX	GILYAK	GISU	GOAJIRO	GROS VENTRE
HAIDA	HAVASUPAI	HAZARA	HEBREWS	HEHE	HO	HUICHOL	HUTSUL	ILA	INGASSANA
IRISH	JAPANESE	JAVANESE	KABYLE	KACHIN	KAPAUKU	KAREN	KARIERA	KATAB	KERAKI
KERALA	KHALKA	KHASI	KIOW-APACHE	KUNG	LHOTA NAGA	LOLO	LOZI	LUC	MACASSARESE
MAGUZAWA	MALAYS	MAM	MANGAIANS	MARGI	MARICOPA	MENDE	MIAO	MIN CHINESE	MINCHIA
MISKITO	MONGO	MOSSI	MOTA	MZAB	NANDI	NASKAPI	NATCHEZ	NGONI	NUPE
NYORO	ONA	ORACN	PALAUANS	PAWNEE	PENOBSCOT	PONAPEANS	POPOLUCA	PURARI	ROMANS
RUNDI	SAMOYED	SARAMACCA	SELUNG	SEMINOLE	SERBS	SERI	SHERENTE	SHILLUK	SINHALESE
SIUAI	SIWANS	SONGHAI	SOTHO	SUBANUN	SWAZI	TAOS	TAPIRAPE	TEDA	TEHUELCHE
TENINO	TERENA	TIBETANS	TOKELAU	TRUMAI	TUCUNA	TURKANA	VEDDA	WAPISHANA	WICHITA
YAHGAN	YAKC	YAO	YAPESE	YARURO	YOKUTS	YUKAGHIR			

155 EXCLUDED BECAUSE IRRELEVANT

4 DRIFT MORE TOWARD BEING THOSE 0.95 OF 108
LOCATED OUTSIDE OF
THE CIRCUM-MEDITERRANEAN (355)

4 DRIFT LESS TOWARD BEING THOSE 0.88 OF 137
LOCATED OUTSIDE OF
THE CIRCUM-MEDITERRANEAN (355)

5	16
103	121
XSQ=	2.98
PHI=	-0.110
XP =	0.0842

53	TILT MORE TOWARD BEING THOSE 0.69 OF 67 WHERE FOOD PRODUCTION IS BY SIMPLE AGRICULTURE OR INCIPIENT FOOD PRODUCTION, RATHER THAN BY INTENSIVE AGRICULTURE (147)	53	TILT LESS TOWARD BEING THOSE 0.52 OF 93 WHERE FOOD PRODUCTION IS BY SIMPLE AGRICULTURE OR INCIPIENT FOOD PRODUCTION, RATHER THAN BY INTENSIVE AGRICULTURE (147)	21 45 46 48 XSQ= 3.99 PHI= -0.158 XP = 0.0457
55	DRIFT TOWARD BEING THOSE 0.60 OF 52 WHERE FOOD PRODUCTION IS BY SIMPLE AGRICULTURE, RATHER THAN BY INTENSIVE AGRICULTURE (101)	55	DRIFT TOWARD BEING THOSE 0.59 OF 76 WHERE FOOD PRODUCTION IS BY INTENSIVE AGRICULTURE, RATHER THAN BY SIMPLE AGRICULTURE (91)	21 45 31 31 XSQ= 3.66 PHI= -0.169 XP = 0.0557
63	LEAN LESS TOWARD BEING THOSE 0.54 OF 74 WHERE HUSBANDRY, IF PRESENT, IS PRINCIPALLY IN THE FORM OF BOVINE, EQUINE, CAMEL-LIKE, OR DEER-LIKE ANIMALS, RATHER THAN PIGS, SHEEP, OR GOATS (152)	63	LEAN MORE TOWARD BEING THOSE 0.78 OF 85 WHERE HUSBANDRY, IF PRESENT, IS PRINCIPALLY IN THE FORM OF BOVINE, EQUINE, CAMEL-LIKE, OR DEER-LIKE ANIMALS, RATHER THAN PIGS, SHEEP, OR GOATS (152)	40 66 34 19 XSQ= 8.88 PHI= -0.236 XP = 0.0029
81	TILT MORE TOWARD BEING THOSE 0.68 OF 79 WHERE NO CITY OR TOWN IS PRESENT, AND THE AVERAGE COMMUNITY SIZE IS SMALLER THAN 200 (135)	81	TILT LESS TOWARD BEING THOSE 0.51 OF 86 WHERE NO CITY OR TOWN IS PRESENT, AND THE AVERAGE COMMUNITY SIZE IS SMALLER THAN 200 (135)	25 42 54 44 XSQ= 4.36 PHI= -0.163 XP = 0.0368
94	DRIFT MORE TOWARD BEING THOSE 0.93 OF 101 WHERE THE HIERARCHY OF NATIONAL JURISDICTION HAS TWO, ONE, OR NO LEVELS (296) GES,EA	94	DRIFT LESS TOWARD BEING THOSE 0.84 OF 119 WHERE THE HIERARCHY OF NATIONAL JURISDICTION HAS TWO, ONE, OR NO LEVELS (296) GES,EA	7 19 94 100 XSQ= 3.46 PHI= -0.125 XP = 0.0630
107	DRIFT MORE TOWARD BEING THOSE 0.84 OF 57 WHERE CLASS STRATIFICATION, IF PRESENT, IS BASED ON SOMETHING OTHER THAN OCCUPATIONAL STATUS (160)	107	DRIFT LESS TOWARD BEING THOSE 0.69 OF 74 WHERE CLASS STRATIFICATION, IF PRESENT, IS BASED ON SOMETHING OTHER THAN OCCUPATIONAL STATUS (160)	9 23 48 51 XSQ= 3.29 PHI= -0.159 XP = 0.0696
109	DRIFT MORE TOWARD BEING THOSE 0.91 OF 105 WHERE CASTES ARE ABSENT (317)	109	DRIFT LESS TOWARD BEING THOSE 0.82 OF 123 WHERE CASTES ARE ABSENT (317)	9 22 96 101 XSQ= 3.43 PHI= -0.123 XP = 0.0641
196	TILT LESS TOWARD BEING THOSE 0.61 OF 79 WHERE INDIVIDUAL RIGHTS IN REAL PROPERTY, AND RULES FOR INHERITANCE, ARE PRESENT (194)	196	TILT MORE TOWARD BEING THOSE 0.76 OF 99 WHERE INDIVIDUAL RIGHTS IN REAL PROPERTY, AND RULES FOR INHERITANCE, ARE PRESENT (194)	48 75 31 24 XSQ= 3.95 PHI= -0.149 XP = 0.0468
201	DRIFT LESS TOWARD BEING THOSE 0.81 OF 108 WHERE MARITAL RESIDENCE IS NON-OPTIONAL, RATHER THAN AMBILOCAL OR NEOLOCAL (334)	201	DRIFT MORE TOWARD BEING THOSE 0.89 OF 137 WHERE MARITAL RESIDENCE IS NON-OPTIONAL, RATHER THAN AMBILOCAL OR NEOLOCAL (334)	87 122 21 15 XSQ= 2.83 PHI= -0.108 XP = 0.0924

No.		No.		
204	DRIFT LESS TOWARD BEING THOSE 0.76 OF 87 WHERE MARITAL RESIDENCE IS PATRILOCAL, VIRILOCAL, OR AVUNCULOCAL, RATHER THAN AMBILOCAL OR NEOLOCAL (270)	204	DRIFT MORE TOWARD BEING THOSE 0.87 OF 113 WHERE MARITAL RESIDENCE IS PATRILOCAL, VIRILOCAL, OR AVUNCULOCAL, RATHER THAN AMBILOCAL OR NEOLOCAL (270)	66 98 21 15 XSQ= 3.23 PHI= -0.127 XP = 0.0724
213	TILT TOWARD BEING THOSE 0.64 OF 107 WHERE FIRST COUSIN MARRIAGE IS NOT PERMITTED (198)	213	TILT TOWARD BEING THOSE 0.53 OF 129 WHERE FIRST COUSIN MARRIAGE IS PERMITTED (172)	39 68 68 61 XSQ= 5.60 PHI= -0.154 XP = 0.0179
348	DRIFT TOWARD BEING THOSE 0.56 OF 55 WHERE THE TOTAL POSITIVE PRESSURE TOWARD DEVELOPING ACHIEVEMENT BEHAVIOR IN THE CHILD IS HIGH (32) B-B-C	348	DRIFT TOWARD BEING THOSE 0.88 OF 8 WHERE THE TOTAL POSITIVE PRESSURE TOWARD DEVELOPING ACHIEVEMENT BEHAVIOR IN THE CHILD IS LOW (31) B-B-C	31 1 24 7 XSQ= 3.76 PHI= 0.244 XP = 0.0523
391	DRIFT TOWARD BEING THOSE 0.56 OF 78 WHERE PREMARITAL SEX RELATIONS ARE PUNISHED ONLY IF PREGNANCY RESULTS, OR FREELY PERMITTED (90) JTW,EA	391	DRIFT TOWARD BEING THOSE 0.59 OF 59 WHERE PREMARITAL SEX RELATIONS ARE STRONGLY PUNISHED AND IN FACT RARE, OR WEAKLY PUNISHED AND IN FACT NOT RARE (89) JTW,EA	34 35 44 24 XSQ= 2.73 PHI= -0.141 XP = 0.0987
393	DRIFT TOWARD BEING THOSE 0.58 OF 57 WHERE EXTRAMARITAL COITUS IS PUNISHED, RATHER THAN PERMITTED (43) F-B	393	DRIFT TOWARD BEING THOSE 0.67 OF 24 WHERE EXTRAMARITAL COITUS IS PERMITTED, RATHER THAN PUNISHED (41) F-B	33 8 24 16 XSQ= 3.15 PHI= 0.197 XP = 0.0758
426	DRIFT LESS TOWARD BEING THOSE 0.51 OF 94 WHERE A HIGH GOD IS PRESENT (156) GES,EA	426	DRIFT MORE TOWARD BEING THOSE 0.65 OF 93 WHERE A HIGH GOD IS PRESENT (156) GES,EA	48 60 46 33 XSQ= 2.94 PHI= -0.125 XP = 0.0865
428	TILT TOWARD BEING THOSE 0.54 OF 28 WHERE A HIGH GOD, IF PRESENT AND ACTIVE, DOES NOT SUPPORT HUMAN MORALITY, RATHER THAN SUPPORTING IT (26) GES,EA	428	TILT TOWARD BEING THOSE 0.74 OF 35 WHERE A HIGH GOD, IF PRESENT AND ACTIVE, SUPPORTS HUMAN MORALITY, RATHER THAN NOT SUPPORTING IT (61) GES,EA	13 26 15 9 XSQ= 4.01 PHI= -0.252 XP = 0.0453
432	LEAN TOWARD BEING THOSE 0.86 OF 28 WHERE AN ATTRACTIVE AFTERLIFE IS BELIEVED IN (27) LWS	432	LEAN TOWARD BEING THOSE 0.70 OF 10 WHERE AN ATTRACTIVE AFTERLIFE IS NOT BELIEVED IN (11) LWS	24 3 4 7 XSQ= 8.58 PHI= 0.475 EP = 0.0022
438	DRIFT TOWARD BEING THOSE 0.66 OF 41 WHERE OTHER-WORLDLY FEARS OF GHOSTS OR SPIRITS ARE GREATER THAN THIS-WORLDLY FEARS OF HUMANS OR ANIMALS (27) W-C,JFG	438	IN ALL CASES ARE THOSE 1.00 OF 3 WHERE THIS-WORLDLY FEARS OF HUMANS OR ANIMALS ARE GREATER THAN OTHER-WORLDLY FEARS OF GHOSTS OR SPIRITS (17) W-C,JFG	27 0 14 3 XSQ= 2.71 PHI= 0.248 XP = 0.0995

No.		No.		
450	LEAN TCWARD BEING THOSE 0.81 OF 62 WHERE THE CBSERVATION CF FCOC TABOOS IS HIGH CR MEDIUM, RATHER THAN LOW (60) JRL	450	LEAN TOWARD BEING THOSE 0.58 OF 24 WHERE THE OBSERVATION OF FOOD TABCOS IS LOW, RATHER THAN HIGH OR MEDIUM (26) JRL	50 10 12 14 XSQ= 10.68 PHI= 0.352 XP = 0.0011
468	LEAN TCWARD BEING THOSE 0.79 OF 43 WHERE CONTACT WITH OTHER CULTURES IS REGULAR OR IRREGULAR, RATHER THAN FREQUENT (37) JMH	468	LEAN TOWARD BEING THOSE 0.73 OF 11 WHERE CONTACT WITH OTHER CULTURES IS FREQUENT, RATHER THAN REGULAR OR IRREGULAR (17) JMH	9 8 34 3 XSQ= 8.63 PHI= -0.400 XP = 0.0033
476	DRIFT LESS TOWARD BEING THOSE 0.55 OF 38 WHERE THE DEGREE OF INSOBRIETY IS STRONG (31) DH	476	DRIFT MORE TOWARD BEING THOSE 0.91 OF 11 WHERE THE DEGREE OF INSOBRIETY IS STRONG (31) DH	21 10 17 1 XSQ= 3.26 PHI= -0.258 XP = 0.0711
488	TILT MORE TOWARD BEING THOSE 0.89 OF 73 ABOUT WHICH THE PRINCIPAL ETHNOGRAPHIES WERE PUBLISHED BEFCRE 1950 (185)	488	TILT LESS TOWARD BEING THOSE 0.72 OF 83 ABOUT WHICH THE PRINCIPAL ETHNOGRAPHIES WERE PUBLISHED BEFORE 1950 (185)	65 60 8 23 XSQ= 5.83 PHI= 0.193 XP = 0.0157
489	TEND LESS TO BE THCSE 0.60 OF 108 NOT INCLUDED IN CHARLES ACKERMAN'S STUDY OF DIVORCE (343)	489	TEND MORE TO BE THOSE 0.90 OF 137 NOT INCLUDED IN CHARLES ACKERMAN'S STUDY OF DIVORCE (343)	43 14 65 123 XSQ= 28.00 PHI= 0.338 XP = 0.0000
490	TEND TO BE THOSE 0.66 OF 108 INCLUDED IN ALBERT S. ANTHONY'S SAMPLE ON MALE INITIATICN RITES (113)	490	TEND TO BE THOSE 0.69 OF 137 NOT INCLUDED IN ALBERT S. ANTHONY'S SAMPLE ON MALE INITIATION RITES (287)	71 42 37 95 XSQ= 28.52 PHI= 0.341 XP = 0.0000
491	TEND LESS TO BE THCSE 0.69 OF 108 NOT INCLUDED IN DORRIAN APPLE'S STUDY OF GRANDPARENTHCCD (352)	491	TEND MORE TO BE THOSE 0.90 OF 137 NOT INCLUDED IN DORRIAN APPLE'S STUDY OF GRANDPARENTHOOD (352)	34 14 74 123 XSQ= 16.01 PHI= 0.256 XP = 0.0001
492	TEND LESS TO BE THCSE 0.65 OF 108 NOT INCLUDED IN BARBARA CHARTIER AYRES' STUDY OF FEMALE INITIATION RITES (361)	492	TEND MORE TO BE THOSE 0.99 OF 137 NOT INCLUDED IN BARBARA CHARTIER AYRES' STUDY OF FEMALE INITIATION RITES (361)	38 1 70 136 XSQ= 51.02 PHI= 0.456 XP = 0.
493	TEND TO BE THOSE 0.64 OF 108 INCLUDED IN BACCN, BARRY, AND CHILD'S STUDY OF CHILD REARING (78)	493	TEND TO BE THOSE 0.93 OF 137 NOT INCLUDED IN BACON, BARRY, AND CHILD'S STUDY OF CHILD REARING (322)	69 9 39 128 XSQ= 88.81 PHI= 0.602 XP = 0.

```
523  TEND TO BE THOSE                 0.52 OF 108      523  TEND TO BE THOSE                 0.96 OF 137          56    5
     INCLUDED IN WHITING ANC CHILD'S                         NOT INCLUDED IN WHITING AND CHILD'S                   52  132
     STUDY OF CHILD TRAINING                                 STUDY OF CHILD TRAINING                         XSQ=   72.49
     AND PERSONALITY  (61)                                   AND PERSONALITY  (339)                          PHI=   0.544
                                                                                                             XP =  0.

524  TEND LESS TO BE THCSE            0.66 OF 108      524  TEND MORE TO BE THOSE            0.95 OF 137          37    7
     NCT INCLUDED IN                                         NOT INCLUDED IN                                       71  130
     WHITING, KLUCKHCHN, ANC ANTHONY'S                       WHITING, KLUCKHOHN, AND ANTHONY'S               XSQ=   32.88
     STUDY OF MALE INITIATICN CEREMONIES  (356)              STUDY OF MALE INITIATICN CEREMCNIES  (356)      PHI=   0.366
                                                                                                             XP =  0.
```

513	TEND LESS TO BE THOSE NOT INCLUDED IN LEO W. SIMMONS' STUDY OF THE TREATMENT OF THE AGED (357)	0.71 OF 108	513	TEND MORE TO BE THOSE NOT INCLUDED IN LEO W. SIMMONS' STUDY OF THE TREATMENT OF THE AGED (357)	0.91 OF 137	31 12 77 125 XSQ= 15.25 PHI= 0.250 XP = 0.0001
514	TEND TO BE THOSE INCLUDED IN PHILIP E. SLATER'S STUDY OF NARCISSISM (90)	0.75 OF 108	514	TEND TO BE THOSE NOT INCLUDED IN PHILIP E. SLATER'S STUDY OF NARCISSISM (310)	0.93 OF 137	81 9 27 128 XSQ= 118.76 PHI= 0.696 XP = 0.
515	TEND LESS TO BE THOSE NOT INCLUDED IN WILLIAM N. STEPHENS' SAMPLE ON AVOIDANCE RELATIONSHIPS (348)	0.56 OF 108	515	TEND MORE TO BE THOSE NOT INCLUDED IN WILLIAM N. STEPHENS' SAMPLE ON AVOIDANCE RELATIONSHIPS (348)	0.97 OF 137	48 4 60 133 XSQ= 59.82 PHI= 0.494 XP = 0.
516	DRIFT MORE TOWARD BEING THOSE INCLUDED IN GUY E. SWANSON'S SAMPLE ON LOCAL JURISDICTION, AS MODIFIED BY THE ETHNOGRAPHIC ATLAS (331)	0.94 OF 108	516	DRIFT LESS TOWARD BEING THOSE INCLUDED IN GUY E. SWANSON'S SAMPLE ON LOCAL JURISDICTION, AS MODIFIED BY THE ETHNOGRAPHIC ATLAS (331)	0.87 OF 137	102 119 6 18 XSQ= 3.12 PHI= 0.113 XP = 0.0774
517	TEND MORE TO BE THOSE INCLUDED IN GUY E. SWANSON'S SAMPLE ON HIGH GODS, AS MODIFIED BY THE ETHNOGRAPHIC ATLAS (260)	0.87 OF 108	517	TEND LESS TO BE THOSE INCLUDED IN GUY E. SWANSON'S SAMPLE ON HIGH GODS, AS MODIFIED BY THE ETHNOGRAPHIC ATLAS (260)	0.68 OF 137	94 93 14 44 XSQ= 11.22 PHI= 0.214 XP = 0.0008
518	TEND TO BE THOSE INCLUDED IN STANLEY H. UDY, JR.'S STUDY OF WORK ORGANIZATION (105)	0.59 OF 108	518	TEND TO BE THOSE NOT INCLUDED IN STANLEY H. UDY, JR.'S STUDY OF WORK ORGANIZATION (295)	0.70 OF 137	64 41 44 96 XSQ= 20.04 PHI= 0.286 XP = 0.0000
519	TEND LESS TO BE THOSE NOT INCLUDED IN JOSEPH VEROFF'S STUDY OF ACHIEVEMENT MOTIVATION AS REVEALED IN FOLKTALES (364)	0.69 OF 108	519	TEND MORE TO BE THOSE NOT INCLUDED IN JOSEPH VEROFF'S STUDY OF ACHIEVEMENT MOTIVATION AS REVEALED IN FOLKTALES (364)	0.98 OF 137	33 3 75 134 XSQ= 36.54 PHI= 0.386 XP = 0.
520	TEND LESS TO BE THOSE NOT INCLUDED IN BEATRICE BLYTH WHITING'S STUDY OF SORCERY (360)	0.66 OF 108	520	TEND MORE TO BE THOSE NOT INCLUDED IN BEATRICE BLYTH WHITING'S STUDY OF SORCERY (360)	0.98 OF 137	37 3 71 134 XSQ= 43.15 PHI= 0.420 XP = 0.
522	TEND TO BE THOSE INCLUDED IN MARJORIE GRANT WHITING'S STUDY OF DIET (82)	0.60 OF 108	522	TEND TO BE THOSE NOT INCLUDED IN MARJORIE GRANT WHITING'S STUDY OF DIET (318)	0.88 OF 137	65 17 43 120 XSQ= 59.78 PHI= 0.494 XP = 0.

No.			No.			
503	TEND LESS TO BE THCSE NOT INCLUDED IN JOHN M. HICKMAN'S STUDY OF THE FOLK-URBAN CONTINUUM (346)	0.60 OF 108	503	TEND MORE TO BE THOSE NOT INCLUDED IN JOHN M. HICKMAN'S STUDY OF THE FOLK-URBAN CONTINUUM (346)	0.92 OF 137	43 11 65 126 XSQ= 33.68 PHI= 0.371 XP = 0.
504	TEND LESS TO BE THCSE NCT INCLUDED IN DONALD HORTON'S STUDY OF ALCHOLISM (351)	0.66 OF 108	504	TEND MORE TO BE THOSE NOT INCLUDED IN DONALD HORTON'S STUDY OF ALCHOLISM (351)	0.91 OF 137	37 12 71 125 XSQ= 22.98 PHI= 0.306 XP = 0.0000
505	LEAN LESS TOWARD BEING THCSE NOT INCLUDED IN MERRILL JACKSON'S STUDY OF CRIMINAL LAW AND MEDICINE (380)	0.85 OF 108	505	LEAN MORE TOWARD BEING THOSE NOT INCLUDED IN MERRILL JACKSON'S STUDY OF CRIMINAL LAW AND MEDICINE (380)	0.97 OF 137	16 4 92 133 XSQ= 9.87 PHI= 0.201 XP = 0.0017
506	TEND LESS TO BE THCSE NOT INCLUDED IN LAMBERT, TRIANDIS, AND WOLF'S STUDY OF SUPERNATURAL BEINGS (364)	0.67 OF 108	506	IN ALL CASES ARE THOSE NOT INCLUDED IN LAMBERT, TRIANDIS, AND WOLF'S STUDY OF SUPERNATURAL BEINGS (364)	1.00 OF 137	36 0 72 137 XSQ= 50.91 PHI= 0.456 XP = 0.
507	TEND TO BE THOSE INCLUDED IN JAMES R. LEARY'S STUDY OF FCOD TABOCS (86)	0.57 OF 108	507	TEND TO BE THOSE NOT INCLUDED IN JAMES R. LEARY'S STUDY OF FOOD TABOOS (314)	0.82 OF 137	62 24 46 113 XSQ= 40.45 PHI= 0.406 XP = 0.
508	TEND LESS TO BE THCSE NOT INCLUDED IN DAVID C. MCCLELLAND'S STUDY OF ACHIEVEMENT MOTIVATION (360)	0.66 OF 108	508	TEND MORE TO BE THOSE NOT INCLUDED IN DAVID C. MCCLELLAND'S STUDY OF ACHIEVEMENT MOTIVATION (360)	0.98 OF 137	37 3 71 134 XSQ= 43.15 PHI= 0.420 XP = 0.
510	LEAN LESS TOWARD BEING THCSE NOT INCLUDED IN RAOUL NARRCLL'S STUDY OF SOCIETAL COMPLEXITY (380)	0.85 OF 108	510	LEAN MORE TOWARD BEING THOSE NOT INCLUDED IN RAOUL NARRCLL'S STUDY OF SOCIETAL COMPLEXITY (380)	0.97 OF 137	16 4 92 133 XSQ= 9.87 PHI= 0.201 XP = 0.0017
511	TEND TO BE THOSE INCLUDED IN ROBERTS, ARTH AND BUSH'S SAMPLE ON GAMES, AS MODIFIED BY THE ETHNOGRAPHIC ATLAS (189)	0.80 OF 108	511	TEND TO BE THOSE NOT INCLUDED IN ROBERTS, ARTH AND BUSH'S SAMPLE ON GAMES, AS MODIFIED BY THE ETHNOGRAPHIC ATLAS (211)	0.55 OF 137	86 61 22 76 XSQ= 29.56 PHI= 0.347 XP = 0.0000
512	TEND LESS TO BE THCSE NOT INCLUDED IN SHIRLEY AND ROMNEY'S STUDY OF LOVE MAGIC (367)	0.69 OF 108	512	IN ALL CASES ARE THOSE NOT INCLUDED IN SHIRLEY AND ROMNEY'S STUDY OF LOVE MAGIC (367)	1.00 OF 137	33 0 75 137 XSQ= 45.79 PHI= 0.432 XP = 0.

494	TEND LESS TO BE THCSE 0.74 OF 108 NOT INCLUDED IN HERBERT M. BARRY III'S STUDY OF ART (371)	494	TEND MORE TO BE THOSE 0.99 OF 137 NOT INCLUDED IN HERBERT M. BARRY III'S STUDY OF ART (371)	28 1 80 136 XSQ= 34.36 PHI= 0.375 XP = 0.
495	TEND LESS TO BE THCSE 0.56 OF 108 NOT INCLUDED IN JUDITH K. BROWN'S STUDY OF FEMALE INITIATION RITES (335)	495	TEND MORE TO BE THOSE 0.88 OF 137 NOT INCLUDED IN JUDITH K. BROWN'S STUDY OF FEMALE INITIATION RITES (335)	48 17 60 120 XSQ= 30.18 PHI= 0.351 XP = 0.0000
496	TEND LESS TO BE THCSE 0.56 OF 108 NOT INCLUDED IN ROY G. D'ANDRADE'S STUDY OF DREAMS (345)	496	TEND MORE TO BE THOSE 0.94 OF 137 NOT INCLUDED IN ROY G. D'ANDRADE'S STUDY OF DREAMS (345)	47 8 61 129 XSQ= 47.11 PHI= 0.438 XP = 0.
497	TEND LESS TO BE THCSE 0.56 OF 108 NOT INCLUDED IN WILLIAM M. EVAN'S STUDY OF LAW (339)	497	TEND MORE TO BE THOSE 0.90 OF 137 NOT INCLUDED IN WILLIAM M. EVAN'S STUDY OF LAW (339)	47 14 61 123 XSQ= 34.05 PHI= 0.373 XP = 0.
498	TEND LESS TO BE THCSE 0.57 OF 108 NOT INCLUDED IN C. S. FORC'S STUDY OF SEX (349)	498	TEND MORE TO BE THOSE 0.96 OF 137 NOT INCLUDED IN C. S. FORD'S STUDY OF SEX (349)	46 5 62 132 XSQ= 53.23 PHI= 0.466 XP = 0.
499	TEND TO BE THOSE 0.57 OF 108 INCLUDED IN FORD AND BEACH'S SAMPLE ON SEXUAL EXPRESSICN BY THE YOUNG (86)	499	TEND TO BE THOSE 0.82 OF 137 NOT INCLUDED IN FORD AND BEACH'S SAMPLE ON SEXUAL EXPRESSION BY THE YOUNG (314)	62 24 46 113 XSQ= 40.45 PHI= 0.406 XP = 0.
500	TEND LESS TO BE THCSE 0.68 OF 108 NOT INCLUDED IN FREEMAN ANC WINCH'S STUDY CF SCCIETAL CCMPLEXITY (360)	500	TEND MORE TO BE THOSE 0.96 OF 137 NOT INCLUDED IN FREEMAN AND WINCH'S STUDY OF SOCIETAL COMPLEXITY (360)	35 5 73 132 XSQ= 34.49 PHI= 0.375 XP = 0.
501	TEND TC BE THOSE 0.55 OF 108 INCLUDED IN JCAN FRIENCLY GOODMAN'S STUDY OF ASCETIC MOURNING BEHAVIOR (67)	501	TEND TO BE THOSE 0.94 OF 137 NOT INCLUDED IN JOAN FRIENDLY GOODMAN'S STUDY OF ASCETIC MOURNING BEHAVICR (333)	59 8 49 129 XSQ= 69.92 PHI= 0.534 XP = 0.
502	TEND LESS TO BE THCSE 0.58 OF 108 NOT INCLUDED IN JOHN K. HARLEY'S STUDY OF ADOLESCENT PEER GROUPS (343)	502	TEND MORE TO BE THOSE 0.91 OF 137 NOT INCLUDED IN JOHN K. HARLEY'S STUDY OF ADOLESCENT PEER GROUPS (343)	45 12 63 125 XSQ= 34.81 PHI= 0.377 XP = 0.

527 CULTURES
THAT BELONG TO THE FIFTY PERCENT
THAT HAVE PURPLE WHISKERS (200)

527 CULTURES
THAT BELONG TO THE FIFTY PERCENT
THAT DO NOT HAVE PURPLE WHISKERS (200)

SUBJECT ONLY

BACKGROUND ON PAGE 184

200 IN LEFT COLUMN

AKHA	ALORESE	AMBA	ANDAMANESE	APINAYE	ARAPESH	ARAUCANIANS	ARYANS	ASHANTI	AZTEC
BALINESE	BARI	BASQUES	BASSERI	BATAK	BAYA	BHIL	BHUIYA	BOERS	BOTOCUDO
BRAZILIANS	BURMESE	BURUSHC	CAGABA	CAMBA	CAMBODIANS	CARAJA	CARIB	CHENCHU	CHEYENNE
CHIBCHA	CHIR-APACHE	CHIRIGUANO	CHOCO	CHORTI	COCHITI	COMANCHE	COORG	COPR ESKIMO	CREE
CREEK	CRCW	CUNA	DAGUR	DARD	DIERI	DILLING	DOBUANS	DOROBO	DUSUN
DUTCH	EGYPTIANS	EYAK	FANG	FOX	FUTAJALONKE	GILBERTESE	GILYAK	GONC	GROS VENTRE
GUATO	GURE	HANUNCC	HASANIA	HAZARA	HEBREWS	HEHE	HUICHOL	HURCN	HUTSUL
IFUGAO	INCA	INGALIK	INGASSANA	IRAQW	IRISH	JAPANESE	JAVANESE	JEMEZ	JIVARO
JUKUN	KABYLE	KACHIN	KALMYK	KAREN	KARIERA	KAZAK	KERALA	KONSO	KOREANS
KPE	KUMYK	KUNG	KURTATCHI	KWAKIUTL	LAKALAI	LAKHER	LAMBA	LEPCHA	LIFU
MALAYS	MAM	MANCHU	MANDAN	MANIHIKI	MANUS	MARGI	MARSHALLESE	MASAI	MATAKAM
MBUGWE	MBUTI	MENTAWEI	MIAMI	MIAO	MIN CHINESE	MINANGKABAU	MIWOK	MONGUOR	MOSSI
MUNDURUCU	MURINBATA	MURNGIN	MZAB	NASKAPI	NATCHEZ	NAVAHO	NGCNI	NICOBARESE	NOMLAKI
NUER	NYAKYUSA	OJIBWA	ONTONG-JAVA	ORAON	PAEZ	PAIWAN	PALAUANS	PAPAGO	PARAUJANO
POPOLUCA	PORTUGUESE	PURARI	RAROIANS	RIFFIANS	ROMANS	ROTINESE	ROTUMANS	RUNDI	SARSI
SEMANG	SERBS	SERI	SHERENTE	SHILLUK	SIMBOESE	SINDHI	SIUAI	SOMALI	SOTHO
SUBANUN	SWAZI	TAMIL	TANALA	TAPIRAPE	TARAHUMARA	TEDA	TEHUELCHE	TENCA	TENINO
TERA	TESC	TIGRINYA	TIMBIRA	TIV	TIWI	TODA	TOKELAU	TSHIMSHIAN	TUCUNA
TUPINAMBA	TURKANA	TWANA	ULAWANS	VENDA	WAICA	WAPISHANA	WARRAU	WICHITA	WIKMUNKAN
WINNEBAGO	WITCTO	WOLEAIANS	WUTE	YAKO	YAPESE	YARURO	YOKUTS	YORUBA	YUROK

200 IN RIGHT COLUMN

---

11 TILT MORE TOWARD BEING THOSE 0.98 OF 200
WHERE THE LATITUDE IS
LESS THAN SIXTY DEGREES (385)

11 TILT LESS TOWARD BEING THOSE 0.94 OF 200
WHERE THE LATITUDE IS
LESS THAN SIXTY DEGREES (385)

3 12
197 188
XSQ= 4.43
PHI= -0.105
XP = 0.0353

89 DRIFT TOWARD BEING THOSE 0.68 OF 57
WHERE, IF A NON-HEREDITARY HEADMANSHIP
IS PRESENT, SUCCESSION IS
BY CONSENSUS (63)

89 DRIFT TOWARD BEING THOSE 0.51 OF 49
WHERE, IF A NON-HEREDITARY HEADMANSHIP
IS PRESENT, SUCCESSION IS BY MEANS
OTHER THAN CONSENSUS (43)

39 24
18 25
XSQ= 3.36
PHI= 0.178
XP = 0.0666

107 DRIFT LESS TOWARD BEING THOSE 0.73 OF 100
WHERE CLASS STRATIFICATION, IF PRESENT,
IS BASED ON SOMETHING OTHER THAN
OCCUPATIONAL STATUS (160)

107 DRIFT MORE TOWARD BEING THOSE 0.84 OF 103
WHERE CLASS STRATIFICATION, IF PRESENT,
IS BASED ON SOMETHING OTHER THAN
OCCUPATIONAL STATUS (160)

27 16
73 87
XSQ= 3.34
PHI= 0.128
XP = 0.0677

108	TILT MORE TOWARD BEING THOSE 0.72 OF 100 WHERE CLASS STRATIFICATION, IF PRESENT, IS BASED ON SOMETHING OTHER THAN A HEREDITARY ARISTOCRACY (129)	108	TILT LESS TOWARD BEING THOSE 0.55 OF 103 WHERE CLASS STRATIFICATION, IF PRESENT, IS BASED ON SOMETHING OTHER THAN A HEREDITARY ARISTOCRACY (129)	28 46 72 57 XSQ= 5.38 PHI= -0.163 XP = 0.0203
109	TILT LESS TOWARD BEING THOSE 0.82 OF 186 WHERE CASTES ARE ABSENT (317)	109	TILT MORE TOWARD BEING THOSE 0.90 OF 182 WHERE CASTES ARE ABSENT (317)	33 18 153 164 XSQ= 4.12 PHI= 0.106 XP = 0.0425
135	DRIFT TOWARD BEING THOSE 0.76 OF 21 WHERE INDIVIDUAL OWNERSHIP OF ECONOMICALLY SIGNIFICANT PROPERTY IS PRESENT (24) GES	135	DRIFT TOWARD BEING THOSE 0.53 OF 17 WHERE INDIVIDUAL OWNERSHIP OF ECONOMICALLY SIGNIFICANT PROPERTY IS NEGLIGIBLE OR ABSENT (14) GES	16 8 5 9 XSQ= 2.29 PHI= 0.245 EP = 0.0943
149	TILT TOWARD BEING THOSE 0.71 OF 17 WHERE THE INCIDENCE OF THEFT IS LOW (19) B-B-C	149	TILT TOWARD BEING THOSE 0.65 OF 20 WHERE THE INCIDENCE OF THEFT IS HIGH (18) B-B-C	5 13 12 7 XSQ= 3.34 PHI= -0.301 EP = 0.0489
185	DRIFT MORE TOWARD BEING THOSE 0.82 OF 122 WHERE THE LARGEST NON-COGNATIC KIN GROUP IS THE MOEITY OR PHRATRY OR SIB (194)	185	DRIFT LESS TOWARD BEING THOSE 0.72 OF 130 WHERE THE LARGEST NON-COGNATIC KIN GROUP IS THE MOEITY OR PHRATRY OR SIB (194)	100 94 22 36 XSQ= 2.79 PHI= 0.105 XP = 0.0948
210	TILT MORE TOWARD BEING THOSE 0.90 OF 94 WHERE MARITAL RESIDENCE IS PATRILOCAL, RATHER THAN MATRILOCAL (169)	210	TILT LESS TOWARD BEING THOSE 0.79 OF 106 WHERE MARITAL RESIDENCE IS PATRILOCAL, RATHER THAN MATRILOCAL (169)	85 84 9 22 XSQ= 3.94 PHI= 0.140 XP = 0.0472
224	TILT MORE TOWARD BEING THOSE 0.70 OF 84 WHERE COUSIN MARRIAGE IS PREFERENTIALLY OR PERMISSIVELY SYMMETRICAL, RATHER THAN EITHER PATRI- OR MATRILATERAL (106)	224	TILT LESS TOWARD BEING THOSE 0.53 OF 88 WHERE COUSIN MARRIAGE IS PREFERENTIALLY OR PERMISSIVELY SYMMETRICAL, RATHER THAN EITHER PATRI- OR MATRILATERAL (106)	25 41 59 47 XSQ= 4.46 PHI= -0.161 XP = 0.0347
309	TILT TOWARD BEING THOSE 0.67 OF 27 WHERE ORAL SOCIALIZATION ANXIETY IS LOW (27) W-C	309	TILT TOWARD BEING THOSE 0.65 OF 26 WHERE ORAL SOCIALIZATION ANXIETY IS HIGH (26) W-C	9 17 18 9 XSQ= 4.24 PHI= -0.283 XP = 0.0395
315	DRIFT MORE TOWARD BEING THOSE 0.83 OF 30 WHERE MOTHER AND NURSING CHILD CUSTOMARILY SLEEP IN THE SAME BED (37) W-C,S	315	DRIFT LESS TOWARD BEING THOSE 0.57 OF 21 WHERE MOTHER AND NURSING CHILD CUSTOMARILY SLEEP IN THE SAME BED (37) W-D,S	25 12 5 9 XSQ= 3.04 PHI= 0.244 XP = 0.0812

```
344  DRIFT TOWARD BEING THOSE         0.59 OF  41     344  DRIFT TOWARD BEING THOSE          0.66 OF  35          24    12
     WHERE THE TOTAL POSITIVE PRESSURE TOWARD              WHERE THE TOTAL POSITIVE PRESSURE TOWARD             17    23
     DEVELOPING SELF-RELIANT BEHAVIOR                      DEVELOPING SELF-RELIANT BEHAVIOR                XSQ=     3.53
     IN THE CHILD                                          IN THE CHILD                                    PHI=    0.216
     IS HIGH  (36) B-B-C                                   IS LOW  (40) B-B-C                              XP =   0.0601

368  TILT TOWARD BEING THOSE          0.68 OF  28     368  TILT TOWARD BEING THOSE           0.78 OF   9           9     7
     WHERE DISSOCIATION OF THE SEXES                       WHERE DISSOCIATION OF THE SEXES                      19     2
     AT ADOLESCENCE                                        AT ADOLESCENCE                                  XSQ=     4.07
     IS LOW  (21) JKH                                      IS HIGH OR MEDIUM  (16) JKH                     PHI=   -0.332
                                                                                                           EP =   0.0239

400  DRIFT TOWARD BEING THOSE         0.52 OF  27     400  DRIFT TOWARD BEING THOSE          0.74 OF  31          14     8
     WHERE HOMOSEXUAL ACTIVITY                             WHERE HOMOSEXUAL ACTIVITY                            13    23
     IS PROHIBITED  (22) F-B                               IS PERMITTED  (36) F-B                          XSQ=     3.13
                                                                                                           PHI=    0.232
                                                                                                           XP =   0.0771

453  TILT TOWARD BEING THOSE          0.50 OF  22     453  TILT TOWARD BEING THOSE           0.86 OF  14          11     2
     WHERE THE ROLE OF RELIGIOUS EXPERTS                   WHERE THE ROLE OF RELIGIOUS EXPERTS                  11    12
     IS CONDUCIVE TO THE DEVELOPMENT OF THE                IS NOT CONDUCIVE TO THE DEVELOPMENT OF THE      XSQ=     3.31
     INDIVIDUAL'S NEED TO ACHIEVE  (13) DCM                INDIVIDUAL'S NEED TO ACHIEVE  (23) DCM          PHI=    0.303
                                                                                                           EP =   0.0390

454  DRIFT TOWARD BEING THOSE         0.64 OF  22     454  DRIFT TOWARD BEING THOSE          0.71 OF  14           8    10
     WHERE THE OBJECTIVE OF THE INDIVIDUAL'S               WHERE THE OBJECTIVE OF THE INDIVIDUAL'S              14     4
     CONTACT WITH THE DIVINE                               CONTACT WITH THE DIVINE                         XSQ=     2.92
     IS NOT CONDUCIVE TO THE DEVELOPMENT OF THE            IS CONDUCIVE TO THE DEVELOPMENT OF THE          PHI=   -0.285
     INDIVIDUAL'S NEED TO ACHIEVE  (18) DCM                INDIVIDUAL'S NEED TO ACHIEVE  (18) DCM          EP =   0.0858

480  DRIFT TOWARD BEING THOSE         0.69 OF  16     480  DRIFT TOWARD BEING THOSE          0.69 OF  13           5     9
     WHERE COMPLEXITY OF ARTISTIC DESIGN                   WHERE COMPLEXITY OF ARTISTIC DESIGN                  11     4
     IS LOW  (15) HB                                       IS HIGH  (14) HB                                XSQ=     2.76
                                                                                                           PHI=   -0.309
                                                                                                           EP =   0.0656
```

528 CULTURES
THAT BELONG TO THE FIFTY PERCENT
THAT HAVE PURPLE WHISKERS
(WHERE N EQUALS 200 AND THERE IS
A RESIDUE OF 200) (100)

528 CULTURES
THAT BELONG TO THE FIFTY PERCENT
THAT DO NOT HAVE PURPLE WHISKERS
(WHERE N EQUALS 200 AND THERE IS
A RESIDUE OF 200) (100)

BACKGROUND ON PAGE 184

SUBJECT ONLY

100 IN LEFT COLUMN

AKHA	AMBA	APINAYE	ARAUCANIANS	ASHANTI	BALINESE	BASQUES	BATAK	BHIL	BOERS
BRAZILIANS	BURUSHO	CAMBA	CARAJA	CHENCHU	CHIBCHA	CHIRIGUANO	CHORTI	COMANCHE	COPR ESKIMO
CREEK	CUNA	DARD	DILLING	DOROBO	DUTCH	EYAK	FOX	GILBERTESE	GOND
GUATO	HANUNOO	HAZARA	HEHE	HURON	IFUGAO	INGALIK	IRAQW	JAPANESE	JEMEZ
JUKUN	KACHIN	KAREN	KAZAK	KONSO	KPE	KUNG	KWAKIUTL	LAKHER	LEPCHA
MALAYS	MANCHU	MANIHIKI	MARGI	MASAI	MBUGWE	MENTAWEI	MIAO	MINANGKABAU	MONGUOR
MUNDURUCU	MURNGIN	NASKAPI	NAVAHO	NICOBARESE	NUER	OJIBWA	ORAON	PAIWAN	PAPAGO
POPOLUCA	PURARI	RIFFIANS	ROTINESE	RUNDI	SEMANG	SERI	SHILLUK	SINDHI	SOMALI
SUBANUN	TAMIL	TAPIRAPE	TECA	TENDA	TERA	TIGRINYA	TIV	TODA	TSHIMSHIAN
TUPINAMBA	TWANA	VENDA	WAPISHANA	WICHITA	WINNEBAGO	WOLEAIANS	YAKO	YARURO	YORUBA

100 IN RIGHT COLUMN

200 EXCLUDED BECAUSE IRRELEVANT

	Left column			Right column		Statistics
5	DRIFT LESS TOWARD BEING THOSE LOCATED OUTSIDE OF EAST EURASIA (330)	0.77 OF 100	5	DRIFT MORE TOWARD BEING THOSE LOCATED OUTSIDE OF EAST EURASIA (330)	0.87 OF 100	23 13 77 87 XSQ= 2.74 PHI= 0.117 XP = 0.0976
109	TILT LESS TOWARD BEING THOSE WHERE CASTES ARE ABSENT (317)	0.78 OF 93	109	TILT MORE TOWARD BEING THOSE WHERE CASTES ARE ABSENT (317)	0.91 OF 92	20 8 73 84 XSQ= 4.95 PHI= 0.164 XP = 0.0260
176	DRIFT TOWARD BEING THOSE WHERE THE COMMUNITY IS OTHER THAN A CLAN-COMMUNITY OR A COMMUNITY STRUCTURED OR SEGMENTED ON A CLAN BASIS (213)	0.64 OF 94	176	DRIFT TOWARD BEING THOSE WHERE THE COMMUNITY IS A CLAN-COMMUNITY OR A COMMUNITY STRUCTURED OR SEGMENTED ON A CLAN BASIS (169)	0.50 OF 94	34 47 60 47 XSQ= 3.12 PHI= -0.129 XP = 0.0772
236	TILT TOWARD BEING THOSE WHERE THE FAMILY IS OF AN EXTENDED TYPE, RATHER THAN AN INDEPENDENT TYPE (213)	0.65 OF 100	236	TILT TOWARD BEING THOSE WHERE THE FAMILY IS OF AN INDEPENDENT TYPE, RATHER THAN AN EXTENDED TYPE (185)	0.53 OF 99	65 47 35 52 XSQ= 5.52 PHI= 0.167 XP = 0.0188

343	TILT TOWARD BEING THOSE 0.71 OF 14 WHERE THE CHILD'S INFERRED CONFLICT REGARDING NURTURANT BEHAVIOR IS HIGH (29) B-B-C	343	TILT TOWARD BEING THOSE 0.82 OF 11 WHERE THE CHILD'S INFERRED CONFLICT REGARDING NURTURANT BEHAVIOR IS LOW (18) B-B-C		10 2 4 9 XSQ= 5.03 PHI= 0.448 EP = 0.0154
368	TILT TOWARD BEING THOSE 0.77 OF 13 WHERE DISSOCIATION OF THE SEXES AT ADOLESCENCE IS LOW (21) JKH	368	TILT TOWARD BEING THOSE 0.86 OF 7 WHERE DISSOCIATION OF THE SEXES AT ADOLESCENCE IS HIGH OR MEDIUM (16) JKH		3 6 10 1 XSQ= 4.90 PHI= -0.495 EP = 0.0166
421	TILT LESS TOWARD BEING THOSE 0.54 OF 26 WHERE KILLING, TORTURING, OR MUTILATING OF THE ENEMY IS NEGLIGIBLY EMPHASIZED (47) PES	421	TILT MORE TOWARD BEING THOSE 0.86 OF 21 WHERE KILLING, TORTURING, OR MUTILATING OF THE ENEMY IS NEGLIGIBLY EMPHASIZED (47) PES		12 3 14 18 XSQ= 4.06 PHI= 0.294 XP = 0.0439
477	DRIFT TOWARD BEING THOSE 0.83 OF 12 WHERE ALCOHOLIC AGGRESSION IS MODERATE OR SLIGHT (19) DH	477	DRIFT TOWARD BEING THOSE 0.60 OF 10 WHERE ALCOHOLIC AGGRESSION IS STRONG (15) DH		2 6 10 4 XSQ= 2.75 PHI= -0.354 EP = 0.0743
479	TILT TOWARD BEING THOSE 0.73 OF 15 WHERE THE NEED TO ACHIEVE, AS INFERRED FROM FOLKTALES, IS HIGH (18) JV	479	TILT TOWARD BEING THOSE 0.75 OF 8 WHERE THE NEED TO ACHIEVE, AS INFERRED FROM FOLKTALES, IS LOW (18) JV		11 2 4 6 XSQ= 3.19 PHI= 0.372 EP = 0.0393

Left column		Right column	Statistics
529 CULTURES THAT BELONG TO THE FIFTY PERCENT THAT HAVE PURPLE WHISKERS (WHERE N EQUALS 100 AND THERE IS A RESIDUE OF 300) (50)		529 CULTURES THAT BELONG TO THE FIFTY PERCENT THAT DO NOT HAVE PURPLE WHISKERS (WHERE N EQUALS 100 AND THERE IS A RESIDUE OF 300) (50)	

BACKGROUND ON PAGE 184

SUBJECT ONLY

50 IN LEFT COLUMN

AKHA	APINAYE	ASHANTI	BASQUES	BHIL	BRAZILIANS	CAMBA	CHENCHU	CHIRIGUANO	COMANCHE
CREEK	DARD	DOROBO	EYAK	GILBERTESE	GUATO	HAZARA	HURON	INGALIK	JAPANESE
JUKUN	KAREN	KONSO	KUNG	LAKHER	MALAYS	MANIHIKI	MASAI	MENTAWEI	MINANGKABAU
MUNDURUCU	NASKAPI	NICOBARESE	OJIBWA	PAIWAN	POPOLUCA	RIFFIANS	RUNDI	SERI	SINDHI
SUBANUN	TAPIRAPE	TENDA	TIGRINYA	TODA	TUPINAMBA	VENDA	WICHITA	WOLEAIANS	YARURO

50 IN RIGHT COLUMN

300 EXCLUDED BECAUSE IRRELEVANT

No.	Left column		No.	Right column		Statistics
108	TILT TOWARD BEING THOSE WHERE CLASS STRATIFICATION, IF PRESENT, IS BASED ON SOMETHING OTHER THAN A HEREDITARY ARISTOCRACY (129)	0.72 OF 25	108	TILT TOWARD BEING THOSE WHERE CLASS STRATIFICATION, IF PRESENT, IS BASED ON A HEREDITARY ARISTOCRACY (74)	0.65 OF 23	7 15 18 8 XSQ= 5.27 PHI= -0.331 XP = 0.0217
109	TILT LESS TOWARD BEING THOSE WHERE CASTES ARE ABSENT (317)	0.79 OF 47	109	TILT MORE TOWARD BEING THOSE WHERE CASTES ARE ABSENT (317)	0.96 OF 45	10 2 37 43 XSQ= 4.35 PHI= 0.218 XP = 0.0369
110	TILT TOWARD BEING THOSE WHERE SLAVERY IS ABSENT (218)	0.69 OF 48	110	TILT TOWARD BEING THOSE WHERE SLAVERY IS PRESENT (163)	0.53 OF 49	15 26 33 23 XSQ= 3.88 PHI= -0.200 XP = 0.0490
137	TILT LESS TOWARD BEING THOSE WHERE INVIDIOUS DISPLAY OF WEALTH IS MODERATELY, LITTLE, OR NEGATIVELY EMPHASIZED (52) PES	0.62 OF 13	137	IN ALL CASES ARE THOSE WHERE INVIDIOUS DISPLAY OF WEALTH IS MODERATELY, LITTLE, OR NEGATIVELY EMPHASIZED (52) PES	1.00 OF 11	5 0 8 11 XSQ= 3.27 PHI= 0.369 EP = 0.0411
176	TILT TOWARD BEING THOSE WHERE THE COMMUNITY IS OTHER THAN A CLAN-COMMUNITY OR A COMMUNITY STRUCTURED OR SEGMENTED ON A CLAN BASIS (213)	0.72 OF 47	176	TILT TOWARD BEING THOSE WHERE THE COMMUNITY IS A CLAN-COMMUNITY OR A COMMUNITY STRUCTURED OR SEGMENTED ON A CLAN BASIS (169)	0.50 OF 48	13 24 34 24 XSQ= 4.09 PHI= -0.207 XP = 0.0432

182	TILT TOWARD BEING THOSE WHERE THE COMMUNITY IS STRUCTURED ON A NON-CLAN BASIS AND AGAMOUS (126)	0.53 OF 47	182	TILT TOWARD BEING THOSE OTHER THAN WHERE THE COMMUNITY IS STRUCTURED ON A NON-CLAN BASIS AND AGAMOUS (256)	0.71 OF 48	25 14 22 34 XSQ= 4.71 PHI= 0.223 XP = 0.0299
322	TILT TOWARD BEING THOSE WHERE THE CONSISTENCY OF REDUCTION OF THE INFANT'S DRIVES IS LOW (32) B-B-C	0.86 OF 7	322	TILT TOWARD BEING THOSE WHERE THE CONSISTENCY OF REDUCTION OF THE INFANT'S DRIVES IS HIGH (27) B-B-C	0.75 OF 8	1 6 6 2 XSQ= 3.36 PHI= -0.473 EP = 0.0406
349	IN ALL CASES ARE THOSE WHERE THE CHILD'S INFERRED ANXIETY OVER NON-PERFORMANCE OF ACHIEVEMENT BEHAVIOR IS HIGH (34) B-B-C	1.00 OF 6	349	DRIFT TOWARD BEING THOSE WHERE THE CHILD'S INFERRED ANXIETY OVER NON-PERFORMANCE OF ACHIEVEMENT BEHAVIOR IS LOW (28) B-B-C	0.50 OF 8	6 4 0 4 XSQ= 2.11 PHI= 0.388 EP = 0.0849
356	TILT TOWARD BEING THOSE WHERE ADOLESCENT PEER GROUPS OR PAIRS ARE PRESENT IN A SETTING OF COURTSHIP (29) JKH	0.80 OF 5	356	IN ALL CASES ARE THOSE WHERE NEITHER ADOLESCENT PEER GROUPS NOR PAIRS ARE PRESENT IN A SETTING OF COURTSHIP (22) JKH	1.00 OF 5	4 0 1 5 XSQ= 3.75 PHI= 0.612 EP = 0.0476
419	TILT TOWARD BEING THOSE WHERE MILITARY GLORY IS STRONGLY OR MODERATELY EMPHASIZED (55) PES	0.77 OF 13	419	TILT TOWARD BEING THOSE WHERE MILITARY GLORY IS NEGLIGIBLY EMPHASIZED (31) PES	0.73 OF 11	10 3 3 8 XSQ= 4.09 PHI= 0.413 EP = 0.0377
420	DRIFT TOWARD BEING THOSE WHERE BELLICOSITY IS EXTREME (41) PES	0.58 OF 12	420	DRIFT TOWARD BEING THOSE WHERE BELLICOSITY IS MODERATE OR NEGLIGIBLE (46) PES	0.82 OF 11	7 2 5 9 XSQ= 2.38 PHI= 0.322 EP = 0.0894
421	DRIFT TOWARD BEING THOSE WHERE KILLING, TORTURING, OR MUTILATING OF THE ENEMY IS STRONGLY OR MODERATELY EMPHASIZED (37) PES	0.64 OF 11	421	DRIFT TOWARD BEING THOSE WHERE KILLING, TORTURING, OR MUTILATING OF THE ENEMY IS NEGLIGIBLY EMPHASIZED (47) PES	0.82 OF 11	7 2 4 9 XSQ= 3.01 PHI= 0.370 EP = 0.0805
477	IN ALL CASES ARE THOSE WHERE ALCOHOLIC AGGRESSION IS MODERATE OR SLIGHT (19) CH	1.00 OF 6	477	DRIFT TOWARD BEING THOSE WHERE ALCOHOLIC AGGRESSION IS STRONG (15) DH	0.67 OF 3	0 2 6 1 XSQ= 2.01 PHI= -0.472 EP = 0.0833

	530 CULTURES THAT BELONG TO THE FIFTY PERCENT THAT HAVE PURPLE WHISKERS (WHERE N EQUALS 50 AND THERE IS A RESIDUE OF 350) (25)		530 CULTURES THAT BELONG TO THE FIFTY PERCENT THAT DO NOT HAVE PURPLE WHISKERS (WHERE N EQUALS 50 AND THERE IS A RESIDUE OF 350) (25)		

BACKGROUND ON PAGE 184 — SUBJECT ONLY

25 IN LEFT COLUMN

ALORESE, KAREN, SOMALI, ARYANS, KARIERA, TENINO, ASHANTI, KAZAK, TUCUNA, BOTOCUDO, MALAYS, ULAWANS, CARAJA, MAM, WOLEAIANS, CHIBCHA, NOMLAKI, EYAK, ORAON, FOX, PAIWAN, HUICHOL, PORTUGUESE, INGALIK, ROTINESE

25 IN RIGHT COLUMN

350 EXCLUDED BECAUSE IRRELEVANT

	Left column			Right column			Statistics
85	TILT LESS TOWARD BEING THOSE WHERE THE LEVEL OF POLITICAL INTEGRATION IS THE MINIMAL STATE, THE AUTONOMOUS COMMUNITY, OR THE FAMILY (234) GPM	0.67 OF 18	85	IN ALL CASES ARE THOSE WHERE THE LEVEL OF POLITICAL INTEGRATION IS THE MINIMAL STATE, THE AUTONOMOUS COMMUNITY, OR THE FAMILY (234) GPM	1.00 OF 17		6 0 12 17 XSQ= 4.69 PHI= 0.366 EP = 0.0191
102	TILT TOWARD BEING THOSE WHERE CLASS STRATIFICATION IS PRESENT (203)	0.70 OF 23	102	TILT TOWARD BEING THOSE WHERE CLASS STRATIFICATION IS ABSENT (180)	0.70 OF 23		16 7 7 16 XSQ= 5.57 PHI= 0.348 XP = 0.0183
224	IN ALL CASES ARE THOSE WHERE COUSIN MARRIAGE IS PREFERENTIALLY OR PERMISSIVELY SYMMETRICAL, RATHER THAN EITHER PATRI- OR MATRILATERAL (106)	1.00 OF 10	224	TEND TO BE THOSE WHERE COUSIN MARRIAGE IS PREFERENTIALLY OR PERMISSIVELY EITHER PATRI- OR MATRILATERAL, RATHER THAN SYMMETRICAL (66)	0.78 OF 9		0 7 10 2 XSQ= 9.20 PHI= -0.696 EP = 0.0007
300	TILT TOWARD BEING THOSE WHERE THE POST-PARTUM SEX TABOO LASTS LONGER THAN SIX MONTHS (51)	0.60 OF 5	300	IN ALL CASES ARE THOSE WHERE THE POST-PARTUM SEX TABOO LASTS SIX MONTHS OR LESS (73)	1.00 OF 8		3 0 2 8 XSQ= 3.32 PHI= 0.505 EP = 0.0350
337	IN ALL CASES ARE THOSE WHERE THE CHILD'S INFERRED ANXIETY OVER NON-PERFORMANCE OF RESPONSIBLE BEHAVIOR IS HIGH (38) B-B-C	1.00 OF 4	337	TILT TOWARD BEING THOSE WHERE THE CHILD'S INFERRED ANXIETY OVER NON-PERFORMANCE OF RESPONSIBLE BEHAVIOR IS LOW (35) B-B-C	0.80 OF 5		4 1 0 4 XSQ= 2.98 PHI= 0.575 EP = 0.0476

```
444  IN ALL CASES ARE THCSE           1.00 OF    4        444  IN ALL CASES ARE THOSE            1.00 OF    3            0     3
     WHERE THE USE CF DREAMS                                   WHERE THE USE OF DREAMS                                    4     0
     TO SEEK AND CCNTROL SUPERNATURAL POWERS                   TO SEEK AND CONTROL SUPERNATURAL PCWERS          XSQ=     3.51
     IS LCW  (27) RGC                                          IS HIGH  (28) RGD                                PHI=   -0.708
                                                                                                                EP =   0.0286

450  TILT TOWARD BEING THOSE          0.75 OF    4        450  IN ALL CASES ARE THOSE            1.00 OF    5            1     5
     WHERE THE CBSERVATICN CF FCOC TABOOS                      WHERE THE OBSERVATION OF FCCD TABCOS                       3     0
     IS LCW, RATHER THAN                                       IS HIGH OR MEDIUM, RATHER THAN                   XSQ=     2.76
     HIGH CR MEDIUM  (26) JRL                                  LOW  (60) JRL                                    PHI=   -0.553
                                                                                                                EP =   0.0476
```

```
******************************************************************************************************************

531  CULTURES                                             531  CULTURES
     THAT BELONG TO THE FIFTY PERCENT                          THAT BELONG TO THE FIFTY PERCENT
     THAT HAVE PURPLE WHISKERS                                 THAT DO NOT HAVE PURPLE WHISKERS
     (WHERE N EQUALS 25 AND THERE IS                           (WHERE N EQUALS 25 AND THERE IS
     A RESIDUE OF 375)   (13)                                  A RESIDUE OF 375)   (12)

BACKGROUND ON PAGE 184
                                                                                                  SUBJECT ONLY
..................................................................................................................

      13   IN LEFT COLUMN

AKHA          ARAPESH     DILLING      HANUNOO     HEHE       MALAYS      MIAMI       ROTUMANS    SHILLUK     SINDHI
TIMBIRA       TODA        ULAWANS

      12   IN RIGHT COLUMN

     375   EXCLUDED BECAUSE IRRELEVANT

------------------------------------------------------------------------------------------------------------------
 51  TILT TOWARD BEING THOSE        0.85 OF  13       51  TILT TOWARD BEING THOSE        0.58 OF  12           11     5
     WHERE SUBSISTENCE IS PRIMARILY BY                    WHERE SUBSISTENCE IS PRIMARILY BY                      2     7
     FOOD PRODUCTION -- I. E., AGRICULTURE                FOOD GATHERING -- I. E., HUNTING,               XSQ=     3.31
     OR HUSBANDRY -- RATHER THAN BY                       FISHING, OR COLLECTING -- RATHER THAN           PHI=    0.364
     GATHERING   (253)                                    FOOD PRODUCTION   (147)                         EP  =  0.0414

176  DRIFT TOWARD BEING THOSE       0.67 OF  12      176  DRIFT TOWARD BEING THOSE       0.75 OF  12            8     3
     WHERE THE COMMUNITY IS                               WHERE THE COMMUNITY IS OTHER THAN                      4     9
     A CLAN-COMMUNITY OR A COMMUNITY                      A CLAN-COMMUNITY OR A COMMUNITY                 XSQ=     2.69
     STRUCTURED OR SEGMENTED                              STRUCTURED OR SEGMENTED                         PHI=    0.334
     ON A CLAN BASIS   (169)                              ON A CLAN BASIS   (213)                         EP  =  0.0995

186  DRIFT TOWARD BEING THOSE       0.54 OF  13      186  DRIFT TOWARD BEING THOSE       0.83 OF  12            7     2
     WHERE THE KIN GROUP IS                               WHERE THE KIN GROUP IS                                 6    10
     EXCLUSIVELY PATRILINEAL   (150)                      OTHER THAN                                      XSQ=     2.30
                                                          EXCLUSIVELY PATRILINEAL   (250)                 PHI=    0.304
                                                                                                          EP  =  0.0968

188  TILT TOWARD BEING THOSE        0.77 OF  13      188  TILT TOWARD BEING THOSE        0.67 OF  12            3     8
     WHERE THE KIN GROUP IS                               WHERE THE KIN GROUP IS                                10     4
     OTHER THAN                                           EXCLUSIVELY COGNATIC   (148)                    XSQ=     3.21
     EXCLUSIVELY COGNATIC   (252)                                                                         PHI=   -0.358
                                                                                                          EP  =  0.0472

201  IN ALL CASES ARE THOSE         1.00 OF  13      201  TILT LESS TOWARD BEING THOSE   0.67 OF  12           13     8
     WHERE MARITAL RESIDENCE IS                           WHERE MARITAL RESIDENCE IS                             0     4
     NON-OPTIONAL, RATHER THAN                            NON-OPTIONAL, RATHER THAN                       XSQ=     2.98
     AMBILOCAL OR NEOLOCAL   (334)                        AMBILOCAL OR NEOLOCAL   (334)                   PHI=    0.345
                                                                                                          EP  =  0.0391
```

531/

204 IN ALL CASES ARE THOSE 1.00 OF 10
WHERE MARITAL RESIDENCE IS
PATRILOCAL, VIRILOCAL, OR AVUNCULOCAL,
RATHER THAN
AMBILCCAL OR NECLOCAL (270)

204 TILT LESS TOWARD BEING THOSE 0.56 OF 9
WHERE MARITAL RESIDENCE IS
PATRILOCAL, VIRILOCAL, OR AVUNCULOCAL,
RATHER THAN
AMBILOCAL OR NEOLOCAL (270)

	10	5
	0	4
XSQ=	3.27	
PHI=	0.415	
EP =	0.0325	

532 CULTURES
THAT BELONG TO THE FORTY PERCENT
THAT HAVE BLUE WHISKERS (160)

532 CULTURES
THAT BELONG TO THE SIXTY PERCENT
THAT DO NOT HAVE BLUE WHISKERS (240)

BACKGROUND ON PAGE 184

SUBJECT ONLY

160 IN LEFT COLUMN

ABOR	AINU	AJIE	ALACALUF	ALBANIANS	ALORESE	AMBA	AMERICANS	ANDAMANESE	ARAPESH
ASHANTI	ATSUGEWI	AYMARA	AZANDE	BACAIRI	BAJUN	BARI	BASQUES	BASSERI	BEJA
BELU	BENGALI	BERGDAMA	BHIL	BHUIYA	BOERS	BUNLAP	CALLINAGO	CAMBA	CAMBODIANS
CARIB	CAYAPA	CHERKESS	CHINANTEC	CHIRIGUANO	CREE	CUNA	DAGUR	DARD	DIEGUENO
DIERI	DOROBO	DUSUN	EGYPTIANS	ELLICE	EYAK	FUTAJALONKE	GANDA	GILBERTESE	GOAJIRO
GUATO	GURE	HAIDA	HANO	HANUNOO	HASANIA	HASINAI	HAVASUPAI	HAWAIIANS	HAZARA
HEBREWS	HEHE	HUICHOL	IBAN	ICELANDERS	ILA	INGALIK	JAPANESE	JAVANESE	JIVARO
KARIERA	KASKA	KERALA	KET	KHALKA	KIKUYU	KISSI	KOREANS	KPE	KUMYK
KWAKIUTL	LAKHER	LAMBA	LAPPS	LESU	LOLO	LUO	MACASSARESE	MANIHIKI	MANUS
MARQUESANS	MATACO	MBUGWE	MERINA	MINANGKABAU	MINCHIA	MISKITO	MIWOK	MNONG GAR	MOTA
MUNDURUCU	MURINBATA	MZAB	NAMBICUARA	NATCHEZ	NAVAHO	NDEMBU	NGONI	NOMLAKI	NUER
NYARO	NYORO	OKINAWANS	ONA	ONTONG-JAVA	PALIKUR	PARAUJANO	PAWNEE	PORTUGUESE	RUNDI
RWALA	SAMOANS	SAMOYED	SANPOIL	SARAMACCA	SELUNG	SEMANG	SONGHAI	SUBANUN	SYRIANS
TALAMANCA	TANIMBARESE	TAOS	TERENA	THAI	TIGRINYA	TIWI	TOLOWA	TRISTAN	TROBRIAND
TRUKESE	TUCANO	TUCUNA	ULAWANS	UTE	VEDDA	VENDA	VIETNAMESE	WAICA	WALLOONS
WICHITA	WIKMUNKAN	WITOTO	WOGEO	WUTE	YAKUT	YAPESE	YARURO	YOMBE	YORUBA

240 IN RIGHT COLUMN

77 TILT LESS TOWARD BEING THOSE 0.53 OF 19
WHERE THE WRITING SYSTEM IS
MNEMONIC OR ABSENT, RATHER THAN BEING
ALPHABETIC-OR-PHONETIC (39) JMH

77 TILT MORE TOWARD BEING THOSE 0.83 OF 35
WHERE THE WRITING SYSTEM IS
MNEMONIC OR ABSENT, RATHER THAN BEING
ALPHABETIC-OR-PHONETIC (39) JMH

9 6
10 29
XSQ= 4.20
PHI= 0.279
XP = 0.0404

78 DRIFT MORE TOWARD BEING THOSE 0.84 OF 19
WHERE THE WRITING SYSTEM IS
ALPHABETIC-OR-PHONETIC, OR MNEMONIC,
RATHER THAN BEING ABSENT (36) JMH

78 DRIFT LESS TOWARD BEING THOSE 0.57 OF 35
WHERE THE WRITING SYSTEM IS
ALPHABETIC-OR-PHONETIC, OR MNEMONIC,
RATHER THAN BEING ABSENT (36) JMH

16 20
3 15
XSQ= 2.93
PHI= 0.233
XP = 0.0868

89 LEAN TOWARD BEING THOSE 0.79 OF 38
WHERE, IF A NON-HEREDITARY HEADMANSHIP
IS PRESENT, SUCCESSION IS
BY CONSENSUS (63)

89 LEAN TOWARD BEING THOSE 0.51 OF 68
WHERE, IF A NON-HEREDITARY HEADMANSHIP
IS PRESENT, SUCCESSION IS BY MEANS
OTHER THAN CONSENSUS (43)

30 33
8 35
XSQ= 8.14
PHI= 0.277
XP = 0.0043

97	LEAN MORE TOWARD BEING THOSE 0.90 OF 136 WHERE THE HIERARCHY OF LOCAL JURISDICTION HAS THREE OR TWO LEVELS (273) GES,EA	97	LEAN LESS TOWARD BEING THOSE 0.77 OF 195 WHERE THE HIERARCHY OF LOCAL JURISDICTION HAS THREE OR TWO LEVELS (273) GES,EA	14 44 122 151 XSQ= 7.52 PHI= -0.151 XP = 0.0061
98	TILT LESS TOWARD BEING THOSE 0.65 OF 136 WHERE THE HIERARCHY OF LOCAL JURISDICTION HAS FOUR OR THREE LEVELS (238) GES,EA	98	TILT MORE TOWARD BEING THOSE 0.77 OF 195 WHERE THE HIERARCHY OF LOCAL JURISDICTION HAS FOUR OR THREE LEVELS (238) GES,EA	88 150 48 45 XSQ= 5.33 PHI= -0.127 XP = 0.0210
99	TILT TOWARD BEING THOSE 0.51 OF 70 WHERE, WITH NATIONAL HIERARCHY ABSENT, THE HIERARCHY OF LOCAL JURISDICTION HAS TWO LEVELS (63) GES,EA	99	TILT TOWARD BEING THOSE 0.69 OF 86 WHERE, WITH NATIONAL HIERARCHY ABSENT, THE HIERARCHY OF LOCAL JURISDICTION HAS FOUR OR THREE LEVELS (93) GES,EA	34 59 36 27 XSQ= 5.63 PHI= -0.190 XP = 0.0177
100	LEAN LESS TOWARD BEING THOSE 0.73 OF 135 WHERE HIERARCHIES ARE MORE COMPLEX THAN THE 'SIMPLEST,' I. E., MORE COMPLEX THAN TWO LOCAL LEVELS WITH NO NATIONAL LEVELS (267) GES,EA	100	LEAN MORE TOWARD BEING THOSE 0.86 OF 195 WHERE HIERARCHIES ARE MORE COMPLEX THAN THE 'SIMPLEST,' I. E., MORE COMPLEX THAN TWO LOCAL LEVELS WITH NO NATIONAL LEVELS (267) GES,EA	99 168 36 27 XSQ= 7.68 PHI= -0.153 XP = 0.0056
133	TILT TOWARD BEING THOSE 0.89 OF 9 WHERE CONTRACTED DEBTS ARE SIGNIFICANTLY PRESENT (17) GES	133	TILT TOWARD BEING THOSE 0.64 OF 25 WHERE CONTRACTED DEBTS ARE MODERATELY PRESENT OR ABSENT (17) GES	8 9 1 16 XSQ= 5.44 PHI= 0.400 EP = 0.0167
137	DRIFT TOWARD BEING THOSE 0.54 OF 35 WHERE INVIDIOUS DISPLAY OF WEALTH IS STRONGLY EMPHASIZED (37) PES	137	DRIFT TOWARD BEING THOSE 0.67 OF 54 WHERE INVIDIOUS DISPLAY OF WEALTH IS MODERATELY, LITTLE, OR NEGATIVELY EMPHASIZED (52) PES	19 18 16 36 XSQ= 3.02 PHI= 0.184 XP = 0.0820
141	TILT TOWARD BEING THOSE 0.74 OF 19 WHERE THE LEVEL OF SOCIAL SANCTION IS PUBLIC CORPOREAL SANCTION, RATHER THAN PUBLIC PROPERTY SANCTION OR PRIVATE SETTLEMENT (28) JMH	141	TILT TOWARD BEING THOSE 0.60 OF 35 WHERE THE LEVEL OF SOCIAL SANCTION IS PUBLIC PROPERTY SANCTION OR PRIVATE SETTLEMENT, RATHER THAN PUBLIC CORPOREAL SANCTION (26) JMH	14 14 5 21 XSQ= 4.33 PHI= 0.283 XP = 0.0375
254	TILT TOWARD BEING THOSE 0.71 OF 7 WHERE HOUSEHOLD AUTHORITY IS ON THE MOTHER'S SIDE, RATHER THAN THE FATHER'S (6) CA	254	TILT TOWARD BEING THOSE 0.88 OF 8 WHERE HOUSEHOLD AUTHORITY IS ON THE FATHER'S SIDE, RATHER THAN THE MOTHER'S (9) DA	2 7 5 1 XSQ= 3.23 PHI= -0.464 EP = 0.0406
320	DRIFT LESS TOWARD BEING THOSE 0.52 OF 29 WHERE THE DEGREE OF REDUCTION OF THE INFANT'S DRIVES IS HIGH (45) B-B-C	320	DRIFT MORE TOWARD BEING THOSE 0.75 OF 40 WHERE THE DEGREE OF REDUCTION OF THE INFANT'S DRIVES IS HIGH (45) B-B-C	15 30 14 10 XSQ= 3.05 PHI= -0.210 XP = 0.0805

328	DRIFT TOWARD BEING THOSE 0.65 OF 20 WHERE THE AGE OF THE INFANT AT THE ONSET OF SERIOUS SOCIALIZATION, OTHER THAN WEANING, IS TWO YEARS OR LOWER (20) B-B-C	328	DRIFT TOWARD BEING THOSE 0.67 OF 21 WHERE THE AGE OF THE INFANT AT THE ONSET OF SERIOUS SOCIALIZATION, OTHER THAN WEANING, IS HIGHER THAN TWO YEARS (21) B-B-C	7 14 13 7 XSQ= 2.94 PHI= -0.268 XP = 0.0863
348	DRIFT TOWARD BEING THOSE 0.65 OF 23 WHERE THE TOTAL POSITIVE PRESSURE TOWARD DEVELOPING ACHIEVEMENT BEHAVIOR IN THE CHILD IS LOW (31) B-B-C	348	DRIFT TOWARD BEING THOSE 0.60 OF 40 WHERE THE TOTAL POSITIVE PRESSURE TOWARD DEVELOPING ACHIEVEMENT BEHAVIOR IN THE CHILD IS HIGH (32) B-B-C	8 24 15 16 XSQ= 2.78 PHI= -0.210 XP = 0.0957
353	DRIFT TOWARD BEING THOSE 0.70 OF 30 WHERE THE CHILD'S INFERRED ANXIETY OVER NON-PERFORMANCE OF OBEDIENT BEHAVIOR IS HIGH (42) B-B-C	353	DRIFT TOWARD BEING THOSE 0.52 OF 44 WHERE THE CHILD-S INFERRED ANXIETY OVER NON-PERFORMANCE OF OBEDIENT BEHAVIOR IS LOW (32) B-B-C	21 21 9 23 XSQ= 2.76 PHI= 0.193 XP = 0.0969
358	DRIFT MORE TOWARD BEING THOSE 0.95 OF 19 WHERE ADOLESCENT PEER GROUPS ARE PRESENT IN A SETTING OF WORK AND PUBLIC GATHERINGS AND LEISURE, OR OF PUBLIC GATHERINGS AND LEISURE, OR OF LEISURE ONLY (41) JKH	358	DRIFT LESS TOWARD BEING THOSE 0.70 OF 33 WHERE ADOLESCENT PEER GROUPS ARE PRESENT IN A SETTING OF WORK AND PUBLIC GATHERINGS AND LEISURE, OR OF PUBLIC GATHERINGS AND LEISURE, OR OF LEISURE ONLY (41) JKH	18 23 1 10 XSQ= 3.16 PHI= 0.246 XP = 0.0757
380	DRIFT MORE TOWARD BEING THOSE 0.79 OF 24 WHERE SEGREGATION OF GIRLS AT MENARCHE IS PRESENT (35) F-B	380	DRIFT LESS TOWARD BEING THOSE 0.52 OF 31 WHERE SEGREGATION OF GIRLS AT MENARCHE IS PRESENT (35) F-B	19 16 5 15 XSQ= 3.33 PHI= 0.246 XP = 0.0681
391	DRIFT TOWARD BEING THOSE 0.58 OF 81 WHERE PREMARITAL SEX RELATIONS ARE STRONGLY PUNISHED AND IN FACT RARE, OR WEAKLY PUNISHED AND IN FACT NOT RARE (89) JTW,EA	391	DRIFT TOWARD BEING THOSE 0.57 OF 98 WHERE PREMARITAL SEX RELATIONS ARE PUNISHED ONLY IF PREGNANCY RESULTS, OR FREELY PERMITTED (90) JTW,EA	47 42 34 56 XSQ= 3.50 PHI= 0.140 XP = 0.0615
429	IN ALL CASES ARE THOSE 1.00 OF 11 WHERE SUPERNATURAL SANCTIONS FOR MORALITY ARE PRESENT (28) GES	429	TILT LESS TOWARD BEING THOSE 0.65 OF 26 WHERE SUPERNATURAL SANCTIONS FOR MORALITY ARE PRESENT (28) GES	11 17 0 9 XSQ= 3.33 PHI= 0.300 EP = 0.0357
470	DRIFT TOWARD BEING THOSE 0.58 OF 19 WHERE INNOVATIONS ARE GENERALLY ACCEPTED (21) JMH	470	DRIFT TOWARD BEING THOSE 0.71 OF 35 WHERE INNOVATIONS ARE ACCEPTED ONLY SELECTIVELY (33) JMH	11 10 8 25 XSQ= 3.31 PHI= 0.247 XP = 0.0690
480	LEAN TOWARD BEING THOSE 0.77 OF 13 WHERE COMPLEXITY OF ARTISTIC DESIGN IS HIGH (14) HB	480	LEAN TOWARD BEING THOSE 0.75 OF 16 WHERE COMPLEXITY OF ARTISTIC DESIGN IS LOW (15) HB	10 4 3 12 XSQ= 5.80 PHI= 0.447 EP = 0.0092

533 CULTURES
THAT BELONG TO THE THIRTY PERCENT
THAT HAVE GREEN WHISKERS (120)

533 CULTURES
THAT BELONG TO THE SEVENTY PERCENT
THAT DO NOT HAVE GREEN WHISKERS (280)

BACKGROUND ON PAGE 184

SUBJECT ONLY

120 IN LEFT COLUMN

AINU	ARAPESH	AWEIKOMA	AZANDE	AZTEC	BAMBARA	BAMILEKE	BASSERI	BATAK	BEJA
BHUIYA	BIRIFOR	BOZO	BULGARIANS	BUNLAP	CAGABA	CARINYA	CHAGGA	CHENCHU	CHEREMIS
CHEROKEE	CHINANTEC	CHIR-APACHE	CHOCO	CHOROTI	CHORTI	CREEK	CROW	CZECHS	DAGUR
DARD	DUTCH	EGYPTIANS	GUAHIBO	GUATO	HASANIA	HEHE	HERERO	ICELANDERS	ILA
INGASSANA	JAPANESE	JAVANESE	JIVARO	JUKUN	KABYLE	KACHIN	KAREN	KARIERA	KAZAK
KERAKI	KERALA	KOHISTANI	KONSO	KORYAK	LAKHER	LAMET	LHOTA NAGA	LOLO	MALAYS
MAM	MANVU	MANCHU	MARICOPA	MARQUESANS	MATAKAM	MBUGWE	MBUTI	MERINA	MISKITO
MIWOK	MOTA	MOTILON	MURNGIN	NAVAHO	NUER	NYAKYUSA	NYARO	NYORO	OKINAWANS
OMAHA	ONA	PALIKUR	PENDE	ROTINESE	SAMOYED	SANPOIL	SANTAL	SARSI	SEMANG
SERBS	SERI	SHERENTE	SHLUH	SIMBOESE	SYRIANS	TALAMANCA	TANALA	TANIMBARESE	TAREUMIUT
TENETEHARA	TENINO	TESO	TIV	TRUKESE	TRUMAI	TSHIMSHIAN	TUCANO	TUNEBO	TURKMEN
VEDDA	WAROPEN	WICHITA	WIKMUNKAN	WINNEBAGO	WOLOF	YAGUA	YAKO	YAO	YUROK

280 IN RIGHT COLUMN

	Left column (120)			Right column (280)		
47	DRIFT LESS TOWARD BEING THOSE WHERE, IF SETTLEMENTS ARE NON-FIXED, MOVEMENT IS NOMADIC, RATHER THAN NON-NOMADIC (72)	0.53 OF 38	47	DRIFT MORE TOWARD BEING THOSE WHERE, IF SETTLEMENTS ARE NON-FIXED, MOVEMENT IS NOMADIC, RATHER THAN NON-NOMADIC (72)	0.72 OF 72	20 52 18 20 XSQ= 3.40 PHI= -0.176 XP = 0.0652
73	TILT TOWARD BEING THOSE WHERE WEAVING IS PRESENT (118)	0.58 OF 74	73	TILT TOWARD BEING THOSE WHERE WEAVING IS ABSENT (130)	0.57 OF 174	43 75 31 99 XSQ= 4.10 PHI= 0.129 XP = 0.0428
79	DRIFT LESS TOWARD BEING THOSE WHERE NO CITY IS PRESENT (201)	0.83 OF 65	79	DRIFT MORE TOWARD BEING THOSE WHERE NO CITY IS PRESENT (201)	0.92 OF 159	11 12 54 147 XSQ= 3.44 PHI= 0.124 XP = 0.0635
102	DRIFT TOWARD BEING THOSE WHERE CLASS STRATIFICATION IS ABSENT (180)	0.54 OF 115	102	DRIFT TOWARD BEING THOSE WHERE CLASS STRATIFICATION IS PRESENT (203)	0.56 OF 268	53 150 62 118 XSQ= 2.77 PHI= -0.085 XP = 0.0960

143	DRIFT TOWARD BEING THOSE 0.60 OF 15 WHERE THE RATIO OF RESTITUTIVE TC REPRESSIVE SANCTIONS IS HIGH (20) WME	143	DRIFT TOWARD BEING THOSE 0.70 OF 37 WHERE THE RATIO OF RESTITUTIVE TO REPRESSIVE SANCTIONS IS MEDIUM OR LOW (32) WME	9 11 6 26 XSQ= 2.95 PHI= 0.238 XP = 0.0858
184	TILT LESS TOWARD BEING THOSE 0.60 OF 82 WHERE THE LARGEST NON-COGNATIC KIN GROUP IS SMALLER THAN A PHRATRY, I. E. A SIB OR LINEAGE (175)	184	TILT MORE TOWARD BEING THOSE 0.74 OF 170 WHERE THE LARGEST NON-COGNATIC KIN GROUP IS SMALLER THAN A PHRATRY, I. E. A SIB OR LINEAGE (175)	33 44 49 126 XSQ= 4.72 PHI= 0.137 XP = 0.0298
186	DRIFT LESS TOWARD BEING THOSE 0.55 OF 120 WHERE THE KIN GRCUP IS OTHER THAN EXCLUSIVELY PATRILINEAL (250)	186	DRIFT MORE TOWARD BEING THOSE 0.66 OF 280 WHERE THE KIN GROUP IS OTHER THAN EXCLUSIVELY PATRILINEAL (250)	54 96 66 184 XSQ= 3.67 PHI= 0.096 XP = 0.0554
220	LEAN LESS TOWARC BEING THOSE 0.64 OF 111 WHERE FIRST COUSIN MARRIAGE IN SOME FCRM OR CTHER IS NCT PRESCRIBEC CR PREFERREC (273)	220	LEAN MORE TOWARD BEING THOSE 0.78 OF 259 WHERE FIRST COUSIN MARRIAGE IN SOME FORM OR OTHER IS NOT PRESCRIBED OR PREFERRED (273)	40 57 71 202 XSQ= 7.20 PHI= 0.139 XP = 0.0073
221	TILT LESS TOWARD BEING THCSE 0.85 OF 111 WHERE MATRILATERAL CRCSS-COUSIN MARRIAGE IS NCT PRESCRIBED CR PREFERREC (335)	221	TILT MORE TOWARD BEING THOSE 0.93 OF 259 WHERE MATRILATERAL CROSS-CCUSIN MARRIAGE IS NOT PRESCRIBED OR PREFERRED (335)	17 18 94 241 XSQ= 5.41 PHI= 0.121 XP = 0.0200
224	LEAN TOWARD BEING THOSE 0.54 OF 56 WHERE COUSIN MARRIAGE IS PREFERENTIALLY CR PERMISSIVELY EITHER PATRI- OR MATRILATERAL, RATHER THAN SYMMETRICAL (66)	224	LEAN TOWARD BEING THOSE 0.69 OF 116 WHERE COUSIN MARRIAGE IS PREFERENTIALLY OR PERMISSIVELY SYMMETRICAL, RATHER THAN EITHER PATRI- OR MATRILATERAL (106)	30 36 26 80 XSQ= 7.19 PHI= 0.204 XP = 0.0073
331	DRIFT TOWARD BEING THOSE 0.70 OF 10 WHERE THE AGE AT BEGINNING OF INDEPENDENCE TRAINING IS 3.8 YEARS OR HIGHER (16) W-C	331	DRIFT TOWARD BEING THOSE 0.67 OF 27 WHERE THE AGE AT BEGINNING OF INDEPENDENCE TRAINING IS LOWER THAN 3.8 YEARS (21) W-C	7 9 3 18 XSQ= 2.64 PHI= 0.267 EP = 0.0667
343	DRIFT MORE TOWARD BEING THOSE 0.85 OF 13 WHERE THE CHILD'S INFERREC CONFLICT REGARDING NURTURANT BEHAVICR IS HIGH (29) B-B-C	343	DRIFT LESS TOWARD BEING THOSE 0.53 OF 34 WHERE THE CHILD'S INFERRED CONFLICT REGARDING NURTURANT BEHAVICR IS HIGH (29) B-B-C	11 18 2 16 XSQ= 2.76 PHI= 0.243 XP = 0.0964
370	DRIFT MCRE TOWARD BEING THCSE 0.70 OF 73 WHERE THE SEGREGATION CF ACOLESCENT BOYS IS ABSENT (148)	370	DRIFT LESS TOWARD BEING THOSE 0.57 OF 170 WHERE THE SEGREGATION OF ADOLESCENT BOYS IS ABSENT (148)	22 73 51 97 XSQ= 3.00 PHI= -0.111 XP = 0.0833

```
437  DRIFT TOWARD BEING THOSE          0.69 OF  16     437  DRIFT TOWARD BEING THOSE          0.64 OF  28          11    10
     WHERE FEAR OF GHOSTS, SPIRITS,                         WHERE FEAR OF GHOSTS, SPIRITS,                          5    18
     HUMANS OR ANIMALS                                      HUMANS OR ANIMALS                                XSQ=     3.23
     IS HIGH   (21) W-C,JFG                                 IS LOW   (23) W-C,JFG                            PHI=    0.271
                                                                                                             XP  =  0.0724

443  LEAN TOWARD BEING THOSE           0.82 OF \17     443  LEAN TOWARD BEING THOSE           0.61 OF  44          14    17
     WHERE OVERALL FEAR OF OTHERS                           WHERE OVERALL FEAR OF OTHERS                            3    27
     IS HIGH   (31) W-C                                     IS LOW   (30) W-C                                XSQ=     7.71
                                                                                                             PHI=    0.355
                                                                                                             XP  =  0.0055

458  TILT LESS TOWARD BEING THOSE      0.57 OF  49     458  TILT MORE TOWARD BEING THOSE      0.75 OF 122          21    31
     WHERE GAMES, IF PRESENT,                               WHERE GAMES, IF PRESENT,                               28    91
     DO NOT INCLUDE                                         DO NOT INCLUDE                                   XSQ=     4.24
     GAMES OF STRATEGY   (119) R-A-B,EA                     GAMES OF STRATEGY   (119) R-A-B,EA               PHI=    0.157
                                                                                                             XP  =  0.0395
```

534 CULTURES THAT BELONG TO THE TWENTY PERCENT THAT HAVE PINK WHISKERS (80)

534 CULTURES THAT BELONG TO THE EIGHTY PERCENT THAT DO NOT HAVE PINK WHISKERS (320)

BACKGROUND ON PAGE 184

SUBJECT ONLY

80 IN LEFT COLUMN

ABOR	AJIE	AZANDE	BARABRA	BEJA	BELU	BENGALI	BIRIFOR	BORORO	BOZO
BRAZILIANS	BULGARIANS	BURYAT	CAMBODIANS	CHEREMIS	CHINANTEC	COORG	COPR ESKIMO	DUSUN	FON
GILYAK	GISU	GURE	HAVASUPAI	HEHE	HERERO	INGASSANA	KONSO	KURTATCHI	KWAKIUTL
LEPCHA	LIFU	LOZI	LUO	MACASSARESE	MAMBILA	MANDAN	MATACO	MBUNDU	MERINA
MIAO	MINANGKABAU	MISKITO	MOSSI	NANDI	NASKAPI	NAVAHO	NGONI	NICOBARESE	NOMLAKI
NUER	NUNIVAK	NURI	NYARO	ORAON	PENOBSCOT	ROMANS	SEMINOLE	SHILLUK	SHLUH
SIUAI	TAMIL	TANIMBARESE	TARAHUMARA	TEDA	TEHUELCHE	TENETEHARA	TESO	TIGRINYA	TIMBIRA
TORAJA	TROBRIAND	TRUKESE	TRUMAI	TSHIMSHIAN	YABARANA	YAO	YOKUTS	YOMBE	ZUNI

320 IN RIGHT COLUMN

	Left column (80)		Right column (320)		Statistics
3	DRIFT LESS TOWARD BEING THOSE LOCATED OUTSIDE OF AFRICA (320)	0.72 OF 80	DRIFT MORE TOWARD BEING THOSE LOCATED OUTSIDE OF AFRICA (320)	0.82 OF 320	22 58 58 262 XSQ= 2.95 PHI= 0.086 XP = 0.0857
45	TILT LESS TOWARD BEING THOSE WHERE SETTLEMENTS, IF FIXED, ARE COMPACT, RATHER THAN NON-COMPACT (149)	0.51 OF 45	TILT MORE TOWARD BEING THOSE WHERE SETTLEMENTS, IF FIXED, ARE COMPACT, RATHER THAN NON-COMPACT (149)	0.71 OF 177	23 126 22 51 XSQ= 5.67 PHI= -0.160 XP = 0.0172
51	DRIFT MORE TOWARD BEING THOSE WHERE SUBSISTENCE IS PRIMARILY BY FOOD PRODUCTION -- I. E., AGRICULTURE OR HUSBANDRY -- RATHER THAN BY GATHERING (253)	0.72 OF 80	DRIFT LESS TOWARD BEING THOSE WHERE SUBSISTENCE IS PRIMARILY BY FOOD PRODUCTION -- I. E., AGRICULTURE OR HUSBANDRY -- RATHER THAN BY GATHERING (253)	0.61 OF 320	58 195 22 125 XSQ= 3.20 PHI= 0.089 XP = 0.0736
53	DRIFT TOWARD BEING THOSE WHERE FOOD PRODUCTION IS BY INTENSIVE AGRICULTURE, RATHER THAN BY SIMPLE AGRICULTURE OR INCIPIENT FOOD PRODUCTION (91)	0.50 OF 46	DRIFT TOWARD BEING THOSE WHERE FOOD PRODUCTION IS BY SIMPLE AGRICULTURE OR INCIPIENT FOOD PRODUCTION, RATHER THAN BY INTENSIVE AGRICULTURE (147)	0.65 OF 192	23 68 23 124 XSQ= 2.75 PHI= 0.108 XP = 0.0971
71	TILT TOWARD BEING THOSE WHERE METAL WORKING IS PRESENT (98)	0.56 OF 39	TILT TOWARD BEING THOSE WHERE METAL WORKING IS ABSENT (153)	0.64 OF 212	22 76 17 136 XSQ= 5.02 PHI= 0.141 XP = 0.0251

74	DRIFT MORE TCWARD BEING THOSE WHERE PCTTERY IS PRESENT (145)	0.76 OF 37	74	DRIFT LESS TOWARD BEING THCSE WHERE POTTERY IS PRESENT (145)	0.58 OF 201	28 117 9 84 XSQ= 3.30 PHI= 0.118 XP = 0.0691
78	DRIFT TOWARD BEING THOSE WHERE A WRITING SYSTEM IS ABSENT, RATHER THAN BEING PRESENT IN EITHER ALPHABETIC-CR-PHONETIC FORM OR MNEMCNIC FORM (18) JMH	0.57 OF 14	78	DRIFT TOWARD BEING THOSE WHERE THE WRITING SYSTEM IS ALPHABETIC-OR-PHONETIC, OR MNEMONIC, RATHER THAN BEING ABSENT (36) JMH	0.75 OF 40	6 30 8 10 XSQ= 3.48 PHI= -0.254 XP = 0.0620
82	DRIFT MORE TOWARD BEING THOSE WHERE A CITY OR TOWN IS PRESENT, OR THE AVERAGE COMMUNITY SIZE IS FIFTY OR GREATER (178)	0.92 OF 38	82	DRIFT LESS TOWARD BEING THOSE WHERE A CITY OR TOWN IS PRESENT, OR THE AVERAGE COMMUNITY SIZE IS FIFTY OR GREATER (178)	0.77 OF 186	35 143 3 43 XSQ= 3.60 PHI= 0.127 XP = 0.0579
98	DRIFT MORE TOWARD BEING THOSE WHERE THE HIERARCHY OF LCCAL JURISDICTICN HAS FOUR CR THREE LEVELS (238) GES,EA	0.82 OF 61	98	DRIFT LESS TOWARD BEING THOSE WHERE THE HIERARCHY OF LOCAL JURISDICTION HAS FOUR OR THREE LEVELS (238) GES,EA	0.70 OF 270	50 188 11 82 XSQ= 3.16 PHI= 0.098 XP = 0.0753
99	TILT MORE TOWARD BEING THCSE WHERE, WITH NATICNAL HIERARCHY ABSENT, THE HIERARCHY OF LCCAL JURISDICTION HAS FOUR CR THREE LEVELS (93) GES,EA	0.79 OF 28	99	TILT LESS TOWARD BEING THOSE WHERE, WITH NATIONAL HIERARCHY ABSENT, THE HIERARCHY OF LOCAL JURISDICTION HAS FOUR OR THREE LEVELS (93) GES,EA	0.55 OF 128	22 71 6 57 XSQ= 4.18 PHI= 0.164 XP = 0.0409
100	DRIFT MORE TOWARD BEING THOSE WHERE HIERARCHIES ARE MORE COMPLEX THAN THE 'SIMPLEST,' I. E., MORE COMPLEX THAN TWO LCCAL LEVELS WITH NO NATIONAL LEVELS (267) GES,EA	0.90 OF 61	100	DRIFT LESS TOWARD BEING THOSE WHERE HIERARCHIES ARE MORE COMPLEX THAN THE 'SIMPLEST,' I. E., MORE COMPLEX THAN TWO LOCAL LEVELS WITH NO NATIONAL LEVELS (267) GES,EA	0.79 OF 269	55 212 6 57 XSQ= 3.45 PHI= 0.102 XP = 0.0634
135	DRIFT TOWARD BEING THCSE WHERE INDIVIDUAL OWNERSHIP OF ECONOMICALLY SIGNIFICANT PROPERTY IS NEGLIGIBLE OR ABSENT (14) GES	0.58 OF 12	135	DRIFT TOWARD BEING THOSE WHERE INDIVIDUAL OWNERSHIP OF ECONOMICALLY SIGNIFICANT PROPERTY IS PRESENT (24) GES	0.73 OF 26	5 19 7 7 XSQ= 2.26 PHI= -0.244 EP = 0.0812
149	DRIFT TOWARD BEING THOSE WHERE THE INCIDENCE OF THEFT IS HIGH (18) B-B-C	0.78 OF 9	149	DRIFT TOWARD BEING THOSE WHERE THE INCIDENCE OF THEFT IS LOW (19) B-B-C	0.61 OF 28	7 11 2 17 XSQ= 2.65 PHI= 0.267 EP = 0.0625
333	IN ALL CASES ARE THOSE WHERE THE AGE AT BEGINNING OF TRAINING IN HETERCSEXUAL PLAY INHIBITION IS EIGHT YEARS CR HIGHER (8) W-C	1.00 OF 4	333	DRIFT TOWARD BEING THOSE WHERE THE AGE AT BEGINNING OF TRAINING IN HETEROSEXUAL PLAY INHIBITICN IS LOWER THAN EIGHT YEARS (8) W-C	0.67 OF 12	4 4 0 8 XSQ= 3.00 PHI= 0.433 EP = 0.0769

```
366  IN ALL CASES ARE THOSE          1.00 OF  11      366  DRIFT LESS TOWARD BEING THCSE  0.65 OF  46          0    16
     WHERE DISSCCIATION OF THE SEXES                       WHERE DISSOCIATION OF THE SEXES                    11    30
     AT ADCLESCENCE                                        AT ADOLESCENCE                              XSQ=     3.74
     IS MEDIUM CR LOW   (41) JKH                           IS MEDIUM OR LOW   (41) JKH                 PHI=   -0.256
                                                                                                       XP =   0.0533

393  DRIFT TOWARD BEING THCSE        0.71 OF  17      393  DRIFT TOWARD BEING THOSE       0.57 OF  67          5    38
     WHERE EXTRAMARITAL COITUS IS                          WHERE EXTRAMARITAL COITUS                          12    29
     PERMITTED, RATHER THAN                                IS PUNISHED, RATHER THAN                    XSQ=     3.03
     PUNISHED   (41) F-B                                   PERMITTED   (43) F-B                        PHI=   -0.190
                                                                                                       XP =   0.0819

447  IN ALL CASES ARE THOSE          1.00 OF   5      447  DRIFT LESS TOWARD BEING THCSE  0.54 OF  28          5    15
     WHERE LOVE MAGIC IS                                   WHERE LOVE MAGIC IS                                 0    13
     PRESENT   (20) S-R                                    PRESENT   (20) S-R                          XSQ=     2.13
                                                                                                       PHI=    0.254
                                                                                                       EP =   0.0707
```

535 CULTURES THAT BELONG TO THE TEN PERCENT THAT HAVE YELLOW WHISKERS (40)	535 CULTURES THAT BELONG TO THE NINETY PERCENT THAT DO NOT HAVE YELLOW WHISKERS (360)

BACKGROUND ON PAGE 184 — SUBJECT ONLY

40 IN LEFT COLUMN

ABOR	ARAUCANIANS	BABWA	BANCA	BARABRA	BLACK CARIB	BOTOCUDO	BUNLAP	CAMBA	CAMBODIANS
CHEREMIS	CHERKESS	CHEROKEE	CROW	HAWAIIANS	KALMYK	KAREN	KASKA	KHEVSUR	KUBA
LHOTA NAGA	MAMBILA	MANUS	MISKITO	NOMLAKI	NUER	NUPE	NYANEKA	NYCRO	ORAON
PARAUJANO	SANTAL	SIMBOESE	TALLENSI	TURKMEN	ULAWANS	VIETNAMESE	WAROPEN	WASHO	YAKO

360 IN RIGHT COLUMN

	Left column (40)			Right column (360)		
176	DRIFT TOWARD BEING THOSE WHERE THE COMMUNITY IS A CLAN-COMMUNITY OR A COMMUNITY STRUCTURED OR SEGMENTED ON A CLAN BASIS (169)	0.59 OF 39	176	DRIFT TOWARD BEING THOSE WHERE THE COMMUNITY IS OTHER THAN A CLAN-COMMUNITY OR A COMMUNITY STRUCTURED OR SEGMENTED ON A CLAN BASIS (213)	0.57 OF 343	23 146 16 197 XSQ= 3.19 PHI= 0.091 XP = 0.0743
178	TILT LESS TOWARD BEING THOSE WHERE THE COMMUNITY IS OTHER THAN SEGMENTED ON A CLAN BASIS AND NON-EXOGAMOUS (295)	0.62 OF 39	178	TILT MORE TOWARD BEING THOSE WHERE THE COMMUNITY IS OTHER THAN SEGMENTED ON A CLAN BASIS AND NON-EXOGAMOUS (295)	0.79 OF 343	15 72 24 271 XSQ= 5.12 PHI= 0.116 XP = 0.0236
214	DRIFT LESS TOWARD BEING THOSE WHERE FIRST COUSIN MARRIAGE, IF PERMITTED, IS OTHER THAN UNILATERAL (144)	0.64 OF 14	214	DRIFT MORE TOWARD BEING THOSE WHERE FIRST COUSIN MARRIAGE, IF PERMITTED, IS OTHER THAN UNILATERAL (144)	0.85 OF 158	5 23 9 135 XSQ= 2.81 PHI= 0.128 XP = 0.0934
390	DRIFT TOWARD BEING THOSE WHERE PREMARITAL SEX RELATIONS ARE STRONGLY PUNISHED AND IN FACT RARE (47) JTW,EA	0.50 OF 14	390	DRIFT TOWARD BEING THOSE WHERE PREMARITAL SEX RELATIONS ARE WEAKLY PUNISHED AND IN FACT NOT RARE OR PUNISHED ONLY IF PREGNANCY RESULTS, OR FREELY PERMITTED (132) JTW,EA	0.76 OF 165	7 40 7 125 XSQ= 3.19 PHI= 0.134 XP = 0.0740

536 CULTURES
THAT BELONG TO THE FIVE PERCENT
THAT HAVE WHITE WHISKERS (20)

536 CULTURES
THAT BELONG TO THE NINETY-FIVE PERCENT
THAT DO NOT HAVE WHITE WHISKERS (380)

BACKGROUND ON PAGE 184

SUBJECT ONLY

20 IN LEFT COLUMN

ARANDA	ASHANTI	AYMARA	BALINESE	BEMBA	CHOCO	COPR ESKIMO	DORCBO	HASANIA	KARIERA
NAMA	NDEMBU	OJIBWA	SANCAWE	THAI	TIMUCUA	TRUMAI	UTE	WAROPEN	WOLEAIANS

380 IN RIGHT COLUMN

	Five percent (20)				Ninety-five percent (380)			
33	TILT LESS TOWARD BEING THOSE WHERE THE NATURAL ENVIRONMENT IS OTHER THAN 'VERY HARSH,' I.E., DESERT, DESERT GRASSES AND SHRUBS, TUNDRA, OR HIGH PLATEAU STEPPE (341) FWM	0.65 OF	20	33	TILT MORE TOWARD BEING THOSE WHERE THE NATURAL ENVIRONMENT IS OTHER THAN 'VERY HARSH,' I.E., DESERT, DESERT GRASSES AND SHRUBS, TUNDRA, OR HIGH PLATEAU STEPPE (341) FWM	0.86 OF 380	7 52 13 328 XSQ= 5.27 PHI= 0.115 XP = 0.0216
44	TILT TOWARD BEING THOSE WHERE SETTLEMENTS ARE NON-FIXED (110)	0.59 OF	17	44	TILT TOWARD BEING THOSE WHERE SETTLEMENTS ARE FIXED (222)	0.68 OF 315	7 215 10 100 XSQ= 4.19 PHI= -0.112 XP = 0.0408
46	DRIFT LESS TOWARD BEING THOSE OTHER THAN WHERE SETTLEMENTS ARE NON-FIXED AND MOVEMENT IS NOMADIC (260)	0.59 OF	17	46	DRIFT MORE TOWARD BEING THOSE OTHER THAN WHERE SETTLEMENTS ARE NON-FIXED AND MOVEMENT IS NOMADIC (260)	0.79 OF 315	7 65 10 250 XSQ= 2.89 PHI= 0.093 XP = 0.0892
82	TILT TOWARD BEING THOSE WHERE NO CITY OR TOWN IS PRESENT, AND THE AVERAGE COMMUNITY SIZE IS SMALLER THAN FIFTY (46)	0.50 OF	14	82	TILT TOWARD BEING THOSE WHERE A CITY OR TOWN IS PRESENT, OR THE AVERAGE COMMUNITY SIZE IS FIFTY OR GREATER (178)	0.81 OF 210	7 171 7 39 XSQ= 6.14 PHI= -0.165 XP = 0.0133
98	TILT TOWARD BEING THOSE WHERE THE HIERARCHY OF LOCAL JURISDICTION HAS TWO LEVELS (93) GES,EA	0.53 OF	17	98	TILT TOWARD BEING THOSE WHERE THE HIERARCHY OF LOCAL JURISDICTION HAS FOUR OR THREE LEVELS (238) GES,EA	0.73 OF 314	8 230 9 84 XSQ= 4.26 PHI= -0.113 XP = 0.0391
99	TILT TOWARD BEING THOSE WHERE, WITH NATIONAL HIERARCHY ABSENT, THE HIERARCHY OF LOCAL JURISDICTION HAS TWO LEVELS (63) GES,EA	0.86 OF	7	99	TILT TOWARD BEING THOSE WHERE, WITH NATIONAL HIERARCHY ABSENT, THE HIERARCHY OF LOCAL JURISDICTION HAS FOUR OR THREE LEVELS (93) GES,EA	0.62 OF 149	1 92 6 57 XSQ= 4.44 PHI= -0.169 XP = 0.0351

133	IN ALL CASES ARE THOSE 1.00 OF 5 WHERE CONTRACTED DEBTS ARE MODERATELY PRESENT OR ABSENT (17) GES	133	TILT TOWARD BEING THOSE 0.59 OF 29 WHERE CONTRACTED DEBTS ARE SIGNIFICANTLY PRESENT (17) GES	0 17 5 12 XSQ= 3.75 PHI= -0.332 EP = 0.0445
144	IN ALL CASES ARE THOSE 1.00 OF 5 WHERE THE RATIO OF RESTITUTIVE TO REPRESSIVE SANCTIONS IS LOW (25) WME	144	TILT TOWARD BEING THOSE 0.57 OF 47 WHERE THE RATIO OF RESTITUTIVE TO REPRESSIVE SANCTIONS IS HIGH OR MEDIUM (27) WME	0 27 5 20 XSQ= 3.89 PHI= -0.274 XP = 0.0484
175	TILT TOWARD BEING THOSE 0.55 OF 20 WHERE THE COMMUNITY IS 'KIN-HOMOGENEOUS,' I. E. A CLAN COMMUNITY OR A DEME (122)	175	TILT TOWARD BEING THOSE 0.69 OF 362 WHERE THE COMMUNITY IS 'KIN-HETEROGENEOUS,' I. E. OTHER THAN A CLAN COMMUNITY OR A DEME (260)	11 111 9 251 XSQ= 4.11 PHI= 0.104 XP = 0.0427
220	DRIFT LESS TOWARD BEING THOSE 0.53 OF 19 WHERE FIRST COUSIN MARRIAGE IN SOME FORM OR OTHER IS NOT PRESCRIBED OR PREFERRED (273)	220	DRIFT MORE TOWARD BEING THOSE 0.75 OF 351 WHERE FIRST COUSIN MARRIAGE IN SOME FORM OR OTHER IS NOT PRESCRIBED OR PREFERRED (273)	9 88 10 263 XSQ= 3.55 PHI= 0.098 XP = 0.0595
345	IN ALL CASES ARE THOSE 1.00 OF 6 WHERE THE CHILD'S INFERRED ANXIETY OVER NON-PERFORMANCE OF SELF-RELIANT BEHAVIOR IS HIGH (37) B-B-C	345	TILT TOWARD BEING THOSE 0.56 OF 70 WHERE THE CHILD'S INFERRED ANXIETY OVER NON-PERFORMANCE OF SELF-RELIANT BEHAVIOR IS LOW (39) B-B-C	6 31 0 39 XSQ= 4.82 PHI= 0.252 XP = 0.0282
354	IN ALL CASES ARE THOSE 1.00 OF 6 WHERE THE CHILD'S INFERRED ANXIETY OVER PERFORMANCE OF OBEDIENT BEHAVIOR IS HIGH (36) B-B-C	354	TILT TOWARD BEING THOSE 0.55 OF 67 WHERE THE CHILD'S INFERRED ANXIETY OVER PERFORMANCE OF OBEDIENT BEHAVIOR IS LOW (37) B-B-C	6 30 0 37 XSQ= 4.69 PHI= 0.254 XP = 0.0303
396	DRIFT TOWARD BEING THOSE 0.71 OF 7 WHERE THE STRENGTH OF MENSTRUAL TABOOS IS HIGH (18) WNS	396	DRIFT TOWARD BEING THOSE 0.72 OF 46 WHERE THE STRENGTH OF MENSTRUAL TABOOS IS LOW (35) WNS	5 13 2 33 XSQ= 3.31 PHI= 0.250 XP = 0.0690
429	TILT TOWARD BEING THOSE 0.57 OF 7 WHERE SUPERNATURAL SANCTIONS FOR MORALITY ARE ABSENT OR UNREPORTED (9) GES	429	TILT TOWARD BEING THOSE 0.83 OF 30 WHERE SUPERNATURAL SANCTIONS FOR MORALITY ARE PRESENT (28) GES	3 25 4 5 XSQ= 3.09 PHI= -0.289 EP = 0.0450
431	IN ALL CASES ARE THOSE 1.00 OF 7 WHERE SUPERNATURAL SANCTIONS FOR MORALITY, HAVING AN EFFECT ON AN INDIVIDUAL'S AFTERLIFE, ARE ABSENT OR UNREPORTED (25) GES	431	DRIFT LESS TOWARD BEING THOSE 0.64 OF 28 WHERE SUPERNATURAL SANCTIONS FOR MORALITY, HAVING AN EFFECT ON AN INDIVIDUAL'S AFTERLIFE, ARE ABSENT OR UNREPORTED (25) GES	0 10 7 18 XSQ= 1.97 PHI= -0.237 EP = 0.0835